THE OXFORD BIBLE COMMENTARY

EDITORS

John Barton, *Oriel and Laing Professor of the Interpretation of Holy Scripture, University of Oxford*
John Muddiman, *Fellow of Mansfield College, Oxford*

ASSOCIATE EDITORS

Loveday Alexander, *University Lecturer in New Testament Studies, University of Sheffield*
Martin Goodman, *Professor of Jewish Studies and Fellow of Wolfson College, Oxford*
Rex Mason, *Emeritus Fellow of Regent's Park College, Oxford*
Henry Wansbrough OSB, *Master of St Benet's Hall, Oxford*

THE OXFORD
BIBLE
COMMENTARY

EDITED BY

JOHN BARTON AND JOHN MUDDIMAN

OXFORD
UNIVERSITY PRESS

OXFORD
UNIVERSITY PRESS

Great Clarendon Street, Oxford ox2 6DP

Oxford University Press is a department of the University of Oxford.
It furthers the University's objective of excellence in research, scholarship,
and education by publishing worldwide in

Oxford New York

Athens Auckland Bangkok Bogotá Buenos Aires Cape Town
Chennai Dar es Salaam Delhi Florence Hong Kong Istanbul Karachi
Kolkata Kuala Lumpur Madrid Melbourne Mexico City Mumbai Nairobi
Paris São Paulo Singapore Taipei Tokyo Toronto Warsaw

with associated companies in Berlin Ibadan

Oxford is a registered trade mark of Oxford University Press
in the UK and certain other countries

Published in the United States
by Oxford University Press Inc., New York

British Library Cataloguing in Publication Data

Data available

Library of Congress Cataloging-in-Publication Data
Oxford Bible Commentary / edited by John Barton and John Muddiman.
p. cm.
Includes bibliographical references and indexes.
1. Bible—Commentaries. I. Barton, John, 1948- II. Muddiman, John.
BS491.3 .094 2001   220.7—dc21   2001021139
ISBN 0-19-875500-7

1 3 5 7 9 10 8 6 4 2

Typeset in FontFont Scala by
Kolam Information Services Pvt. Ltd, Pondicherry, India
Printed in Italy by Giunti

Acknowledgements

We gratefully and fully acknowledge the assistance we have received from our co-editors, Dr Rex Mason (for the Old Testament), Professor Martin Goodman (for the Apocrypha), Dr Loveday Alexander and Dom Henry Wansbrough, OSB (for the New Testament). Our thanks are also due to the contributors of the individual articles, and to the expert management and editing team of the Oxford University Press, in particular Hilary O'Shea, the commissioning editor, and Sylvia Jaffrey, to whom we are indebted for her expert copy-editing of such a huge work.

J. B.
J. M.

OXFORD
July 2000

List of Contents

List of Maps

between pages 1346 and 1347

List of Contributors

Dr K. T. Aitken
University of Aberdeen

Dr Loveday Alexander
University of Sheffield

Professor Philip Alexander
University of Manchester

Professor Dale C. Allison Jr
Pittsburgh Theological Seminary

Professor Harold W. Attridge
Yale Divinity School

Professor John Barclay
University of Glasgow

Professor Richard Bauckham
University of St Andrews

Dr Athalya Brenner
University of Amsterdam

Professor George J. Brooke
University of Manchester

Dr Christoph Bultmann
University of Göttingen

R. Coggins
King's College London

Professor John J. Collins
Yale Divinity School

Professor James L. Crenshaw
Duke University, Durham, North Carolina

Professor P. R. Davies
University of Sheffield

Dr G. I. Davies
University of Cambridge

Dr John Day
University of Oxford

Professor Walter Dietrich
University of Bern

Dr Jennifer M. Dines csa
University of London

Dr Terence L. Donaldson
Wycliffe College, Toronto

Professor R. Doran
Amherst College, Massachusetts

Clare Drury
University of Cambridge

Dr Jeremy Duff
University of Oxford

Professor J. D. G. Dunn
University of Durham

David J. Elliott
Wycliffe College, Stonehouse

Professor J. K. Elliott
University of Leeds

Dr Grace I. Emmerson
Worcester

Professor Philip F. Esler
University of St Andrews

Dr Eric Eve
University of Oxford

Professor Joseph A. Fitzmyer sj
Catholic University of America, Washington DC

Eric Franklin
St Stephen's House, Oxford

Professor Terence E. Fretheim
Luther Seminary, St Paul, Minnesota

Professor J. Galambush
College of William and Mary, Williamsburg

Professor Martin Goodman
University of Oxford

Professor Donald E. Gowan
Pittsburgh Theological Seminary

Professor Lester L. Grabbe
University of Hull

Dr Peter Hayman
University of Edinburgh

Dr Craig C. Hill
Wesley Theological Seminary, Washington DC

Professor William Horbury
University of Cambridge

Professor Leslie Houlden
King's College, London

Dr Walter Houston
Mansfield College, Oxford

Professor Sara Japhet
Hebrew University of Jerusalem

Professor Gwilym H. Jones
University of Wales, Bangor

Dr P. M. Joyce
University of Oxford

Professor Carl-A. Keller
University of Lausanne

Professor René Kieffer
University of Uppsala

Dr Katrina J. A. Larkin
King's College London

Professor Amy-Jill Levine
Vanderbilt Divinity School, Nashville

Professor Judith Lieu
King's College London

Professor Margaret MacDonald
St Francis Xavier University, Nova Scotia

Dr Rex Mason
University of Oxford

Professor H. P. Mathys
University of Basel

Dr Gordon McConville
Cheltenham & Gloucester College of Higher Education

Professor Carol Meyers
Duke University, Durham, North Carolina

Professor Jerome Murphy-O'Connor OP
École Biblique et Archéologique Française, Jerusalem

Dr Robert Murray SJ
University of London

Professor George W. E. Nickelsburg
University of Iowa

Professor Susan Niditch
Amherst College, Massachusetts

Professor Julia M. O'Brien
Lancaster Theological Seminary, Pennsylvania

Professor Kathleen M. O'Connor
Columbia Theological Seminary, Decatur, Georgia

Dr Sarah Pearce
University of Southampton

Professor D. L. Petersen
Iliff School of Theology, Denver

Professor Uriel Rappaport
University of Haifa

Dr Adele Reinhartz
McMaster University, Hamilton, Ontario

Dr Rainer Riesner
Dusslingen

Dr C. S. Rodd
Emsworth, Hampshire

Professor J. Rogerson
University of Sheffield

Professor C. Rowland
University of Oxford

Dr Alison Salvesen
University of Oxford

Professor Daniel L. Smith-Christopher
Loyola-Marymount University, Los Angeles

Peter J. M. Southwell
University of Oxford

Professor G. N. Stanton
University of Cambridge

Professor C. M. Tuckett
University of Oxford

Dom Henry Wansbrough OSB
University of Oxford

Dr Craig S. Wansink
Virginia Wesleyan College, Norfolk, Virginia

Dr Stuart Weeks
University of Durham

†Professor R. N. Whybray
formerly University of Hull

Professor H. G. M. Williamson
University of Oxford

Abbreviations

AASF	Annales academiae scientiarum fennicae
AASOR	Annual of the American Schools of Oriental Research
ÄAT	Ägypten und Altes Testament
AB	Anchor Bible
ABD	D. N. Freedman (ed.), *Anchor Bible Dictionary* (6 vols.; New York: Doubleday, 1992)
AfO	*Archiv für Orientforschung*
AGJU	Arbeiten zur Geschichte das antiken Judentums und des Urchristentums
AJS Review	*Review of Association for Jewish Studies*
AnBib	Analecta biblica
ANET	James B. Pritchard (ed.), *Ancient Near Eastern Texts Relating to the Old Testament* (Princeton: Princeton University Press, 3rd. edn. 1969)
ANRW	*Aufstieg und Niedergang der römischen Welt*
AOAT	Alter Orient und Altes Testament
AP	Aramaic Papyrus, -ri
APOT	R. H. Charles (ed.), *Apocrypha and Pseudepigrapha of the Old Testament* (2 vols.; Oxford: Clarendon, 1912)
Aram.	Aramaic
ARN	Aboth de-Rabbi Nathan *see 'Abot R. Nat. below*
ARW	*Archiv für Religionswissenschaft*
ASOR	American Schools of Oriental Research
ATANT	Abhandlungen zur Theologie des Alten und Neuen Testaments
ATAT	Arbeiten zu Text und Sprache im Alten Testament
ATD	Das Alte Testament Deutsch
ATDan	Acta theologica danica
b.	Babylonian Talmud
B	4th-cent. MS of part of NT, in the Vatican Library
BA	*Biblical Archaeologist*
BAGD	W. Bauer, W. F. Arndt, F. W. Gingrich, and F. W. Danker, *Greek–English Lexicon of the NT and other Early Christian Literature* (Chicago: Univ of Chicago Press, 1979 rev. edn.)
BAR	*Biblical Archaeologist Reader*
BASOR	*Bulletin of the American Schools of Oriental Research*
BBB	Bonner biblische Beiträge
BBET	Beiträge zur biblischen Exegese und Theologie
BBR	*Bulletin for Biblical Research*
BCE	Before Common Era
BDF	F. Blass, A. Debrunner, and R. W. Funk, *A Greek Grammar of the New Testament* (Chicago: Univ of Chicago Press, 1961)
BEATAJ	Beiträge zur Erforschung des Alten Testaments und des antiken Judentums
BETL	Bibliotheca ephemeridum theologicarum lovaniensium
BEvT	Beiträge zur evangelischen Theologie
BHS	*Biblia hebraica stuttgartensia*

Bib.	*Biblica*
BJ	Bonner Jahrbücher
BJRL	*Bulletin of the John Rylands Library*
BKAT	Biblischer Kommentar: Altes Testament
BN	*Beiträge zur Namenforschung*
BNTC	Black's New Testament Commentaries
BR	*Biblical Research*
Br. Arch. Rep.	British Archaeological Reports
BSac	*Bibliotheca Sacra*
BSO(A)S	*Bulletin of the School of Oriental (and African) Studies*
BWANT	Beiträge zur Wissenschaft vom Alten und Neuen Testament
BWAT	Beiträge zur Wissenschaft vom Alten Testament
BZAW	Beihefte zur *ZAW*
BZNW	Beihefte zur *ZNW*
CAT	Commentaire de l'Ancien Testament
CBC	Cambridge Bible Commentary
CBQ	*Catholic Biblical Quarterly*
CBQMS	Catholic Biblical Quarterly—Monograph Series
CChr.SL	Corpus Christianorum Series Latina
CD	Cairo Geniza, Damascus Document
CE	Common Era
CGTC	Cambridge Greek Testament Commentaries
CII	*Corpus inscriptionum iudaicarum*
ConBOT	Coniectanea biblica, Old Testament
CP	*Classical Philology*
CQ	*Church Quarterly*
CRINT	Compendia rerum iudaicarum ad novum testamentum
CSCO	Corpus scriptorum christianorum orientalium
CTA	A. Herdner, *Corpus des tablettes en cunéiforme alphabétiques*
ctr.	contrast
CurTM	*Currents in Theology and Mission*
D	Deuteronomist source in the Pentateuch
DCH	*Dictionary of Classical Hebrew* (Sheffield: Sheffield Academic Press, 1993)
Dittenberg. *SIG*	W. Dittenberger, *Sylloge Inscriptionum Graecarum*, 3rd edn., Leipzig, 1915–24
DJD	Discoveries in the Judaean Desert
DOTT	D. W. Thomas (ed.), *Documents from Old Testament Times* (London: Harper and Row, 1958)
E	Elohist source in the Pentateuch
EB	Echter Bibel
Ebib	Études bibliques
ECL	Early Christian Literature (Extracanonical)
EDNT	H. Balz and G. Schneider (eds.), *Exegetical Dictionary of the New Testament* (3 vols.; Grand Rapids: Eerdmans, 1990)
EI	*Eretz-Israel*
EKKNT	Evangelisch-katholischer Kommentar zum Neuen Testament
ErFor	Erträge der Forschung

ES	Seleucid Era
ET	English Translation
ETL	*Ephemerides theologicae lovanienses*
ETR	*Études théologiques et religieuses*
EvT	*Evangelische Theologie*
FAT	Forschungen zum Alten Testament
FB	Forschung zur Bibel
FBBS	Facet Books, Biblical Series
FCB	Feminist Companion to the Bible
FGrH	F. Jacoby, *Die Fragmente der griechischen Historiker* (Berlin: Weidmann, 1923–58)
fn.	footnote
Fr.	French
frag.	fragment
FRLANT	Forschungen zur Religion und Literatur des Alten und Neuen Testaments
FS	*Festschrift für*
GCS	Greichische christliche Schriftsteller
Gk.	Greek
GNB	Good News Bible
GNS	Good News Series
GTA	Göttinger theologische Arbeiten
H	Holiness Code
HALOT	*Hebrew and Aramaic Lexicon of the Old Testament* (L. Köhler and W. Baumgartner, *Hebräisches und aramäisches Lexikon das Alten Testaments*, Leiden: Brill 1994–2000, tr. by M. E. J. Richardson)
HAT	Handbuch zum Alten Testament
HB	Hebrew Bible
HBC	J. L. Mays *et al.* (eds.), *Harper's Bible Commentary* (San Francisco: Harper & Row, 1988)
HDR	Harvard Dissertations in Religion
Heb.	Hebrew
HKAT	Handkommentar zum Alten Testament
HNT	Handbuch zum Neuen Testament
HSCP	Harvard Studies in Classical Philology
HSM	Harvard Semitic Monographs
HTR	*Harvard Theological Review*
HUCA	*Hebrew Union College Annual*
IA	Introduction to Apocrypha
IB	*Interpreter's Bible*
ICC	International Critical Commentary
IDB	G. A. Buttrick (ed.), *Interpreter's Dictionary of the Bible* (Nashville: Abingdon Press, 1976)
IDBSup	Supplementary volume to *IDB*
IEJ	*Israel Exploration Journal*
INJ	*Israel Numismatic Journal*
INT	Introduction to New Testament
IOT	Introduction to Old Testament
IP	Introduction to Pentateuch
IPC	Introduction to Pauline Corpus

J	Yahwist source in the Pentateuch
JAAR	*Journal of the American Academy of Religion*
JANESCU	*Journal of the Ancient Near Eastern Society of Columbia University*
JBL	*Journal of Biblical Literature*
JBR	*Journal of Bible and Religion*
JCS	*Journal of Cuneiform Studies*
JETS	*Journal of the Evangelical Theological Society*
JJGL	*Jahrbuch für jüdische Geschichte und Literatur*
JJS	*Journal of Jewish Studies*
JNES	*Journal of Near Eastern Studies*
JQR	*Jewish Quarterly Review*
JSHRZ	Jüdische Schriften aus hellenistisch-römischer Zeit
JSJ	*Journal for the Study of Judaism in the Persian, Hellenistic and Roman Period*
JSNT	*Journal for the Study of the New Testament*
JSNTSup	Journal for the Study of the New Testament—Supplement Series
JSOT	*Journal for the Study of the Old Testament*
JSOTSup	Journal for the Study of the Old Testament—Supplement Series
JSP	*Journal for the Study of the Pseudepigrapha*
JSS	*Journal of Semitic Studies*
JTS	*Journal of Theological Studies*
KAT	Kommentar zum Alten Testament
KHCAT	Kurzer Handcommentar zum Alten Testament
Lat.	Latin
LCL	Loeb Classical Library
LXX	Septuagint
m.	*Mishnah*
marg.	margin
MeyerK	H. A. W. Meyer, Kritisch-exegetischer Kommentar über das Neue Testament
Midr.	*Midrash*
MLB	Modern Language Bible
MNTC	Moffatt New Testament Commentary
MS	Monograph Series; manuscript
MSU	Mitteilungen des Septuginta-Unternehmens
Mt.	Mount
MT	Masoretic Text
NAB	New American Bible
NCB	New Century Bible
NHS	Nag Hammadi Studies
NIBC	New International Bible Commentary
NICNT	New International Commentary on the New Testament
NICOT	New International Commentary on the Old Testament
NIGTC	New International Greek Testament Commentary
NIV	New International Version
NJB	H. Wansbrough (ed.), *New Jerusalem Bible*
NJBC	R. E. Brown, J. A. Fitzmyer, and R. E. Murphy (eds.), *The New Jerome Biblical Commentary* (London: Geoffrey Chapman, 1989)

NJPS	New Jewish Publication Society Translation
NovT	*Novum Testamentum*
NovTSup	Novum Testamentum, Supplements
NTS	*New Testament Studies*
NTT	*Norsk Teologisk Tidsskrift*
OBL	Orientalia et biblica lovaniensis
OBO	Orbis biblicus et orientalis
OBT	Overtures to Biblical Theology
OCB	*Oxford Companion to the Bible*
ODCC	*Oxford Dictionary of the Christian Church*
OG	Old Greek
OL	Old Latin
OTG	Old Testament Guides
OTL	Old Testament Library
OTP	J. H. Charlesworth (ed.), *The Old Testament Pseudepigrapha* (2 vols.; Garden City, NY: Doubleday, 1983–5)
OTS	*Oudtestamentische Studiën*
P	Priestly Work source in the Pentateuch
p^{66}	Papyrus of parts of the Gospel of John, *c.*200 CE, Bodmer Library, Cologny-Geneva, and Chester-Beatty Library, Dublin
p^{74}	Papyrus of parts of Acts and Catholic epistles, 7th cent., Bodmer Library, Cologny-Geneva
p^{75}	Papyrus of parts of the Gospels of Luke and John, 3rd cent., Bodmer Library, Cologny-Geneva
PAAJR	*Proceedings of the American Academy of Jewish Research*
par.	parallel(s)
PBJL	Post-Biblical Jewish Literature
PG	J. Migne, *Patrologia graeca*
PJ	*Palästina-Jahrbuch*
pl.	plural
P.Oxy.	Oxyrhynchus Papyri
P.Ryl.	Rylands Papyrus
PSBA	*Proceedings of the Society of Biblical Archaelogy*
QD	Quaestiones disputatae
RAC	*Reallexikon für Antike und Christentum*
RB	*Revue biblique*
REJ	*Revue des études juives*
RHPR	*Revue d'histoire et de philosophie religieuses*
RSN [=SNR]	*Revue Suisse de Numismatique = Schweizerische Numismatische Rundschau*
RSO	*Rivista degli studi orientali*
RSR	*Recherches de science religieuse*
RTR	*Reformed Theological Review*
SAA	State Articles of Assyria
SANT	Studien zum Alten und Neuen Testament
SB	Sources bibliques

SBAB	Stuttgarter biblischer Aufsatzbände
SBL	Society of Biblical Literature
SBLDS	SBL Dissertation Series
SBLEJL	SBL Early Judaism and its Literature
SBLMS	SBL Monograph Series
SBLRBS	SBL Resources for Biblical Study
SBLSBS	SBL Sources for Biblical Study
SBLTT	SBL Texts and Translations
SBS	Stuttgarter Bibelstudien
SBT	Studies in Biblical Theology
SC	Sources chrétiennes
ScEs	*Science et esprit*
SCI	*Scripte Classica Israelica*
SCM	Student Christian Movement
SEG	*Supplementum Epigraphicum Graecum*
Sem.	*Semitica*
SESJ	Suomen Eksegeettisen Seuran julkaisuja
SHAW	Sitzungsberichte der Heidelberger Akademie der Wissenschaften
SJLA	Studies in Judaism in Late Antiquity
SJT	*Scottish Journal of Theology*
SJOT	*Scandinavian Journal of the Old Testament*
SNR	See *RSN*
SNTSMS	Society for New Testament Study Monograph Series
SNTW	Studies of the New Testament and its World
SOTS	Society for Old Testament Study
SOTSMS	Society for Old Testament Study Monograph Series
SP	Sacra Pagina
SPCK	Society for Promoting Christian Knowledge
SR	*Studies in Religion*
SSN	Studia semitica neerlandica
ST	*Studia theologica*
Str-B	[H. Strack and] P. Billerbeck, *Kommentar zum Neuen Testament aus Talmud und Midrasch* (6 vols.; Munich: C. K. Beck, 1926–61)
SUNT	Studien zur Umwelt des Neuen Testaments
S.V.	Sub vide
SVTP	Studia in Veteris Testamenti pseudepigrapha
t.	Tosefta
TBü	Theologische Bücherei
T. Dan.	Testament of Dan
TDNT	G. W. Bromiley (ed. and trans.), *Theological Dictionary of the New Testament* (10 vols.; Grand Rapids: Eerdmans, 1964–78).
TDOT	*Theological Dictionary of the Old Testament* (G. J. Botterweck, H. Ringgren, and H-J Fabry, Theologisches Wörterbuch zum Alten Testament tr. J. T. Willis, Grand Rapids: Eerdmans 1974–)
TOB	Traduction œcuménique de la bible
TT	*Teologisk Tidsskrift*
tr(s).	translation(s), translated (by)
TU	Texte und Untersuchungen

TWAT	G. J. Botterweck and H. Ringgren (eds.), *Theologisches Wörterbuch zum Alten Testament* (Stuttgart: Kohlhammer, 1970–)
TZ	*Theologische Zeitschrift*
v.	versus
Vg	Vulgate
VL	Vetus Latina
VT	*Vetus Testamentum*
VTSup	Vetus Testamentum, Supplements
WBC	Word Biblical Commentary
WMANT	Wissenschaftliche Monographien zum Alten und Neuen Testament
WTJ	*Westminster Theological Journal*
WUNT	Wissenschaftliche Untersuchungen zum Neuen Testament
y.	Jerusalem Talmud
YNER	Yale Near Eastern Researches
ZAR	*Zeitschrift für Altorientalische und Biblische Rechtsgeschichte*
ZAW	*Zeitschrift für die alttestamentliche Wissenschaft*
ZB	Zürcher Bibelkommentare
ZDPV	*Zeitschrift des deutschen Palästina-Vereins*
ZNW	*Zeitschrift für die neutestamentliche Wissenschaft*
ZPE	*Zeitschrift für Papyrologie und Epigraphik*
ZTK	*Zeitschrift für Theologie und Kirche*

CLASSICAL

'Abot R. Nat.	*'Abot de Rabbi Nathan*
Aesch.	Aeschylus
Ag.	*Agamemnon*
Pers.	*Persae*
Ap.	Apuleius
Met.	*Metamorphoses*
Ap. John	*Apocryphon of John*
Ap. Con.	*Apostolic Constitutions*
Apoc. Abr.	*Apocalypse of Abraham*
2–3 Apoc. Bar.	*Apocalypse of Baruch*
Apoc. Sed.	*Apocalypse of Sedrach*
Arist.	Aristotle
Eth. Nic.	*Ethica Nicomachea*
Arr.	Arrian
Anab.	*Anabasis*
As. Mos.	*Assumption of Moses*
Athenagorus	
Apol.	*Apologia*
Leg. pro Christ.	*Legatio pro Christianis*
Aug.	Augustine
Conf.	*Confessions*

De civ. dei	*De civitate dei*
De Gen. c. Manich.	*De Genesi contra Manichaeos*
En.	*Enarrationes in Psalmos*
Barn.	*Epistle of Barnabas*
B. Bat.	*Baba Batra*
Ber.	*Berakot*
B. Qam.	*Baba Qamma*
B. Mes.	*Baba Mesi'a*
Calvin	
Inst.	*Institutes*
Cic.	Cicero
Nat. D.	*De Natura Deorum*
Tusc.	*Tusculanae Disputationes*
Clem. Al.	Clement of Alexandria
Ped.	*Pedagogus*
Strom.	*Stromateis*
Coptic Apoc. Zeph.	*Coptic Apocalypse of Zephaniah*
Cyp.	Cyprian
Test.	*Testimoniorum libri tres*
Dem.	*Demai*
Did.	*Didache*
Dio Chrystostom	
Or.	*Orationes*
Diod. Sic.	Diodorus Siculus
Diog. Laert.	Diogenes Laertius
Eccles. Rab.	*Ecclesiastes Rabbah*
Ep. Arist.	*Epistle of Aristeas*
Ep. Diogn.	*Epistle to Diognetus*
Ep. Heraclit.	*Epistle of Heraclitus*
Epict.	Epictetus
Diss.	*Dissertationes*
Epicurus	
Ep. Men.	*Epistula ad Menoeceum*
Epiph.	Epiphanius
Pan.	*Panarion*
Eur.	Euripides
Bacch.	*Bacchae*
Or.	*Orestes*
Phoen.	*Phoenissae*
Eusebius	
Hist. eccl.	*Historia Ecclesiastica*
Praep. evang.	*Praeparatio evangelica*
Flacc.	Flaccus
Frg. Tg.	*Fragmentary Targum*

Gen. Rab.	Genesis Rabbah
Giṭ	*Giṭṭim*
Mor.	*Moralia* Gregory the Great, *Moralia in Job*
Gos. Pet.	*Gospel of Peter*
Gos. Thom.	*Gospel of Thomas*
Ḥag.	*Ḥagiga*
Hdt.	Herodotus
Herc. Furens	*Hercules Furens*
Herc. Oetaeus	*Hercules Oetaeus*
Herm. Sim.	*Hermas, Similitudes*
Herm. Vis.	*Hermas, Visions*
Hes.	Hesiod
Op.	*Opera et Dies*
Theog.	*Theogonia*
Hippol.	Hippolytus
Haer.	*Refutatio Omnium Haeresium*
Ḥul.	*Ḥullin*
Ign.	Ignatius
Eph.	*Ephesians*
Rom.	*Letter to the Romans*
Magn.	*Letter to the Magnesians*
Smyrn.	*Letter to the Smyrnaeans*
Trall.	*Letter to the Trallians*
Irenaeus	
Adv. haer.	*Adversus haereses*
Isoc.	Isocrates
Con. Dem.	*Contra Demosthenem*
Jer.	Jerome
Comm. in Ezek.	*Commentariorum in Ezekielem*
Comm. in Isa.	*Commentariorum in Isaiam Prophetam*
De vir. ill.	*De viris illustribus*
Jos.	Josephus
Ag. Ap.	*Against Apion*
Ant.	*Antiquities of the Jews*
J.W.	*Jewish War*
Jos. Asen.	*Joseph and Asenath*
Jub.	*Jubilees*
Just.	Justin Martyr
Dial.	*Dialogus*
Apol.	*Apologia*
1 Kgdms	1 Kingdoms
Lev. Rab.	*Leviticus Rabbah*
Lucr.	Lucretius

Mak.	Makkot
Marc. Aur.	Marcus Aurelius
Medit.	Meditationes
Mart. Isa.	Martyrdom of Isaiah
Mart. Pol.	Martyrdom of Polycarp
Meg.	Megilla
Mek.	Mekilta
Ned.	Nedarim
Origen	
C. Cels.	Contra Celsum
De princ.	De principiis
Pal. Tg.	Palestinian Targum
Paus.	Pausanius
Pesiq. R.	Pesiqta Rabbati
Pesiq. Rab Kah	Pesiqta de Rabbi Kahana
Phil.	Polycarp, Letter to the Philippians
Philo	Philo Judaeus
Abr.	De Abrahamo
Agr.	De agricultura
Cher.	De Cherubim
Conf. Ling.	De confusione linguarum
Dec.	De Decalogo
Det.	Quod deterius potiori insidiari soleat
Deus Imm.	Quod Deus sit immutabilis
Ebr.	De ebrietate
Flacc.	In Flaccum
Fug.	De fuga et inventione
Gig.	De gigantibus
Leg. ad Gaium	Legatio ad Gaium
Leg. All.	Legum allegoriae
Migr. Abr.	De migratione Abrahami
Mutat.	De mutatione nominum
Opif.	De opificio mundi
Praem.	De Praemiis et Poenis
Quaes. Ex.	Quaestiones in Exodum
Quis heres	Quis rerum divinarum heres sit
Sacr.	De sacrificiis Abelis et Caini
Somn.	De somniis
Spec. Leg.	De specialibus legibus
Virt.	De virtutibus
Vit. Cont.	De vita contemplativa
Vit. Mos.	De vita Mosis
Pind.	Pindar
Ol.	Olympian Odes
Plato	
Ap.	Apologia

Cra.	*Cratylus*
Epin.	*Epinomis*
Phd.	*Phaedo*
Phdr.	*Phaedrus*
Resp.	*Respublica*
Symp.	*Symposium*
Tim.	*Timaeus*
Pliny	
Ep.	*Epistulae*
Nat. Hist.	*Natural History*
Plut.	Plutarch
Art.	*Artaxerxes*
Cic.	*Cicero*
Cleom.	*Cleomenes*
De fac.	*De facie in orbe lunae*
De Is. et Os.	*De Iside et Osiride*
De tranq. anim.	*De tranquillitate animi*
Luc.	*Lucullus*
Mor.	*Moralia*
Nic.	*Nicias*
Thes.	*Theseus*
Polyb.	Polybius
Polycarp	
Phil.	*Letter to the Philippians*
Ps. Heracl.	Pseudo-Heraclitus
Ep.	*Epistle*
Ps.-Philo	Pseudo-Philo
Bib. Ant.	*Biblical Antiquities*
LAB	*Liber Antiquitatum Biblicarum*
Ps.-Phoc.	Pseudo-Phocylides
Pss. Sol.	*Psalms of Solomon*
Odes Sol.	*Odes of Solomon*
1QapGen 20	Qumran Cave 1, *Genesis Apocryphon*
1QDeut[b]	Qumran Cave 1, frags. of Deuteronomy, 2nd copy
1QH	Qumran Cave 1, *Hôdayôt (Thanksgiving Hymns)*
1QM	Qumran Cave 1, *War Scroll*
1QpHab	Qumran Cave 1, *Pesher on Habakkuk*
1QS	Qumran Cave 1, *Serek hayyahad (Rule of the Community, Manual of Discipline)* [2h dot]
1QSa	Appendix A (*Rule of the Congregation*) to 1QS
2Q18	Qumran Cave 2, frags. of Sirach
2Q Jer	Qumran Cave 2, fragment of Jeremiah
3Q15	Qumran Cave 3, Copper Scroll
4Q174	Qumran Cave 4, collection of verses on the last days
4Q175	Qumran Cave 4, collection of messianic testimonia
4Q270	Qumran Cave 4, Zadokite fragments
4Q186	Qumran Cave 4, Horoscope
4Q491	Qumran Cave 4, War Scroll

4Q521	Qumran Cave 4, Messianic Apocalypse
4Q560	Qumran Cave 4, fragments of *Book of Mysteries*
4Qxii[a]	Qumran Cave 4, fragment of Zechariah
4Qxii[c]	Qumran Cave 4, fragment of Zechariah
4Qxii[e]	Qumran Cave 4, fragment of Zechariah
4QCant[a, b, c]	Qumran Cave 4, Song of Solomon, 1st–3rd copies
4QDeut[j]	Qumran Cave 4, frags. of Deuteronomy, 10th copy
4QDeut[q]	Qumran Cave 4, frags. of Deuteronomy, 17th copy
4QDibHam	Qumran Cave 4, Words of the Luminaries
4QFlor	Qumran Cave 4, *Florilegium*
4QJer[a, b, c]	Qumran Cave 4, frags. of Jeremiah
4QMelch	Qumran, Cave 4, *Melchizedek* text
4QMMT	Qumran Cave 4, *Miqsat Ma'aseh Torah* (*Halakic Letter*)
4QpIsa[a]	Qumran Cave 4, frag. of *Pesher on Isaiah*
4QpJer	Qumran Cave 4, *Pesher on Jeremiah*
4QpNah	Qumran Cave 4, *Pesher on Nahum*
4QPrNab	Qumran Cave 4, *Prayer of Nabonidus*
4QSam[a, b, c]	Qumran Cave 4, Samuel, 1st, 2nd, 3rd copies
4QSapA	Qumran Cave 4, Sapiential Work A
4QLam[a]	Qumran Cave 4, Lamentations, 1st copy
6QCant	Qumran Cave 6, Song of Solomon
7Q486	Qumran Cave 6, frag. of Letter of Jeremiah
11QMelch	Qumran Cave 11, *Melchizedek* text
11QPss	Qumran Cave 11, *Psalms Scroll*
11QTemple	Qumran Cave 11, *Temple Scroll*
Rab.	*Rabbah*
Šabb.	*Šabbat*
Sanh.	*Sanhedrin*
Ṣem.	*Ṣemaḥot*
Sen.	Seneca
Ben.	*De beneficiis*
Ep.	*Epistulae*
Sib. Or.	*Sibylline Oracles*
Soph.	Sophocles
El.	*Electra*
Oed. Rex	*Oedipus Rex*
Strabo	
Geog.	*Geographical Sketches*
Suetonius	
Dom.	*Domitian*
Vesp.	*Vespasianus*
Sukk.	*Sukka*
T. 12 Patr.	*Testaments of the Twelve Patriarchs*
Tac.	Tacitus
Ann.	*Annales*
Hist.	*Historia*

T. Abr.	*Testament of Abraham*
Tert.	Tertullian
Adv. Marc.	*Adversus Marcionem*
An.	*De anima*
Apol.	*Apologeticus*
Scorp.	*Scorpiace*
T. Gad	*Testament of Gad*
Tg. Ps.-J.	*Targum Pseudo-Jonathan*
T. Iss.	*Testament of Issachar*
T. Job	*Testament of Job*
T. Judah	*Testament of Judah*
T. Levi	*Testament of Levi*
T. Naph.	*Testament of Naphtali*
tr(s).	translation(s), translated (by)
v.	versus
Vg	Vulgate
VL	Vetus Latina
Xen. *An.*	Xenophon, *Anabasis*
Xen. *Mem*	Xenophon, *Memorabilia*
y.	Jerusalem Talmud
Yad.	*Yadayim*
Yebam.	*Yebamot*

1. General Introduction

A. Studying the Bible. 1. People's reasons for studying the Bible—and therefore for using a biblical commentary—are many and various. The great majority of Bible readers have a religious motivation. They believe that the Bible contains the 'words of life', and that to study it is a means of deepening their understanding of the ways of God. They turn to the Bible to inform them about how God desires human beings to live, and about what God has done for the human race. They expect to be both challenged and helped by what they read, and to gain clearer guidance for living as religious believers. Such people will use a commentary to help them understand the small print of what has been disclosed about the nature and purposes of God. The editors' hope is that those who turn to the Bible for such religious reasons will find that the biblical text is here explained in ways that make it easier to understand its content and meaning. We envisage that the Commentary will be used by pastors preparing sermons, by groups of people reading the Bible together in study or discussion groups, and by anyone who seeks a clearer perspective on a text that they hold in reverence as religiously inspiring. Jews, Catholics, Protestants, and Orthodox Christians have different expectations of the Bible, but we hope that all will find the Commentary useful in elucidating the text.

2. A somewhat smaller group of readers studies the Bible as a monument to important movements of religious thought in the past, whether or not they themselves have any personal commitment to the religious systems it represents. One of the most striking developments of recent decades has been the growth of interest in the Bible by those who have no religious commitment to it, but for whom it is a highly significant document from the ancient world. Students who take university or college courses in theology or religious or biblical studies will often wish to understand the origins and meaning of the biblical text so as to gain a clearer insight into the beginnings of two major world religions, Judaism and Christianity, and into the classic texts that these religions regard as central to their life. We hope that such people will find here the kinds of information they need in order to understand this complex and many-faceted work. The one-volume format makes it possible to obtain an overview of the whole Bible before going on to use more advanced individual commentaries on particular biblical books.

3. Finally, there are many Bible readers who are committed neither to a religious quest of their own nor to the study of religion, but who are drawn by the literary quality of much of the Bible to want to know more about it. For them it is a major classic of Western—indeed, of world—literature, whose influence on other literature, ancient and modern, requires that it should be taken seriously and studied in depth. A generation ago 'the Bible as literature' was regarded by many students of the Bible, especially those with a religious commitment to it, as a somewhat dilettante interest, insufficiently alert to the Bible's spiritual challenge. Nowadays, however, a great deal of serious scholarly work is being done on literary aspects of the Bible, and many commentaries are written with the needs of a literary, rather than a religious, readership in mind. We think that those who approach the Bible in such a way will find much in this Commentary to stimulate their interest further.

B. Biblical Criticism. 1. The individual authors of commentaries have been free to treat the biblical books as they see fit, and there has been no imposition of a common editorial perspective. They are, however, united by an approach that we have called 'chastened historical criticism'. This is what is traditionally known as a *critical* commentary, but the authors are aware of recent challenges to what is generally called biblical criticism and have sought (to a greater or lesser extent) to take account of these in their work. Some explanation of these terms is necessary if the reader is to understand what this book seeks to offer.

2. Biblical criticism, sometimes known as historical criticism of the Bible or as the historical-critical method, is the attempt to understand the Bible by setting it in the context of its time of writing, and by asking how it came into existence and what were the purposes of its authors. The term 'historical' is not used because such criticism is necessarily interested in reconstructing history, though sometimes it may be, but because biblical books are being studied as anchored in their own time, not as freely floating texts which we can read as though they were contemporary with us. It starts with the acknowledgement that the Bible is an ancient text. However much the questions with which it deals may be of perennial interest to human beings (and perhaps no one would study it so seriously if they were not), they arose within a particular historical (and geographical) setting. Biblical criticism uses all available means of access to information about the text and its context, in order to discover what it may have meant when it or its component parts were written.

3. One precondition for a critical understanding of any text is a knowledge of the language in which it is written, and accordingly of what individual words and expressions were capable of meaning at the time of the text's composition. The critical reader is always on guard against the danger of anachronism, of reading later meanings of words into their use in an earlier period. Frequently, therefore, commentators draw attention to problems in understanding particular words and phrases, and cite evidence for how such words are used elsewhere in contemporary texts. A second prerequisite is that the text itself shall be an accurate version of what the author actually wrote. In the case of any ancient text this is an extremely difficult thing to ensure, because of the vagaries of the transmission of manuscripts down the centuries. Copying by hand always introduces errors into texts, even though biblical texts were often copied with special care because of their perceived sacred status. In all the individual commentaries here there are discussions of how accurately the original text is available to us, and what contribution is made to our knowledge of this by various manuscripts or ancient translations. The art of textual criticism seeks to explain the evolution of texts, to understand how they become corrupted (through miscopying), and how their original form can be rediscovered.

4. In reading any piece of text, ancient or modern, one needs to be aware of the possibility that it may not be a unity. Some documents in our own day come into existence through the work of several different authors, which someone else then edits into a reasonably unified whole: such is the case, for example, with documents produced by committees. In the ancient world it was not uncommon for books to be produced by joining together, and sometimes even interweaving, several already existing shorter texts, which are then referred to as the 'sources' of the resulting single document. In the case of some books in the Bible it is suspected by scholars that such a process of production has resulted in the texts as we now have them. Such hypotheses have been particularly prevalent in the case of the Pentateuch (Genesis–Deuteronomy) and of the Synoptic Gospels (Matthew, Mark, and Luke). The attempt to discover the underlying sources is nowadays usually called 'source criticism', though older books sometimes call it 'literary criticism' (from German *Literarkritik*, but confusing in that 'literary criticism' usually means something else in modern English), or 'higher criticism'—by contrast with 'lower', that is, textual criticism. It is important to see that biblical critics are not committed to believing that this or that biblical book is in fact the result of the interweaving of sources (R. N. Whybray's commentary on Genesis in this volume argues against such a hypothesis), but only to being open to the possibility.

5. A further hypothesis that has had a long and fruitful history in the study of both Testaments is that our present written texts may rest on materials that were originally transmitted orally. Before the biblical books were written, the stories or other units of which they are composed may have had an independent life, circulating orally and being handed on from parent to child, or in circles where stories were told and retold, such as a 'camp-fire' or a liturgical context. The attempt to isolate and study such underlying oral units is known as form criticism, and it has been much practised in the case of the gospels, the stories in the Pentateuch and in the early historical books of the Old Testament, and the prophetic books. Again, by no means all critics think that these books do in fact rest on oral tradition, but all regard the question whether or not they do so as important because it is relevant to understanding their original context.

6. Where texts are composite, that is, the result of weaving together earlier written or oral sources, it makes sense to investigate the techniques and intentions of those who carried out the weaving. We should now call such people 'editors', but in biblical studies the technical term 'redactor' tends to be preferred, and this branch of biblical criticism is thus known as 'redaction criticism'. Once we know what were a biblical redactor's raw materials—which source and form criticism may be able to disclose to us—we can go on to ask about the aims the redactor must have had. Thus we can enquire into the intentions (and hence the thought or the 'theology') of Matthew or Luke, or of the editor of the book of Isaiah. Redaction criticism has been a particular interest in modern German-speaking biblical study, but it is also still widely practised in the English-speaking world. It is always open to the critic to argue that a given book is not composite in any case and therefore never had a redactor, only an author. Most scholars probably think this is true of some of the shorter tales of the Old Testament, such as Jonah or Ruth, or of many of Paul's epistles. Here too what makes study critical is not a commitment to a particular outcome, but a willingness to engage in the investigation. It is always possible that there is simply not enough evidence to resolve the matter, as R. Coggins argues in the case of Isaiah. This conclusion does not make such a commentary 'non-critical', but is arrived at by carefully sifting the various critical hypotheses that have been presented by previous scholars. An uncritical commentary would be one that was unaware of such issues, or unwilling to engage with them.

7. Form and redaction criticism inevitably lead to questions about the social setting of the underlying units that make up biblical books and of the redactors who put them into their finished form. In recent years historical criticism has expanded to include a considerable interest in the contribution the social sciences can make to understanding the Bible's provenance. The backgrounds of the gospels and of Paul's letters have been studied with a view to discovering more about the social context of early Christianity: see, for example, the commentary here on 1 Thessalonians by Philip Esler. In the study of the Old Testament also much attention has been directed to questions of social context, and this interest can be seen especially in D. L. Smith-Christopher's commentary on Ezra–Nehemiah.

C. Post-Critical Movements. 1. In the last few decades biblical studies has developed in many and varied directions, and has thrown up a number of movements that regard themselves as 'post-critical'. Some take critical study of the Bible as a given, but then seek to move on to ask further questions not part of the traditional historical-critical enterprise. Others are frankly hostile to historical criticism, regarding it as misguided or as outdated. Though the general tone of this commentary continues to be critical, most of its contributors believe that these newer movements have raised important issues, and have contributed materially to the work of biblical study. Hence our adoption of a critical stance is 'chastened' by an awareness that new questions are in the air, and that biblical criticism itself is now subject to critical questioning.

2. One important style of newer approaches to the Bible challenges the assumption that critical work should (or can) proceed from a position of neutrality. Those who write from feminist and liberationist perspectives often argue that the older critical style of study presented itself as studiedly uncommitted to any particular programme: it was simply concerned, so its practitioners held, to understand the biblical text in its original setting. In fact (so it is now argued) there was often a deeply conservative agenda at work in biblical criticism. By distancing the text as the product of an ancient culture, critics managed to evade its challenges to themselves, and they signally failed to see how subversive of established attitudes much of the Bible really was. What is needed, it is said, is a more engaged style of biblical study in which the agenda is set by the need for human liberation from oppressive political forces, whether these constrain the poor or some other particular group such as women. The text must be read not only in its reconstructed 'original' context but also as relevant to modern concerns: only then will justice be done to the fact that it exercises an existential claim upon its readers, and it will cease to be seen as the preserve of the scholar in his (*sic*) study.

3. Such a critique of traditional biblical criticism calls attention to some of the unspoken assumptions with which scholars have sometimes worked, and can have the effect of deconstructing conventional commentaries by uncovering their unconscious bias. Many of the commentators in this volume are aware of such dangers in biblical criticism, and seek to redress the balance by asking about the contribution of the books on which they comment to contemporary concerns. They are also more willing than critics have often been to 'criticize' the text in the ordinary sense of that word, that is, to question its assumptions and commitments. This can be seen, for example, in J. Galambush's commentary on Ezekiel, where misogynist tendencies are identified in the text.

4. A second recent development has been an interest in literary aspects of the biblical texts. Where much biblical criticism has been concerned with underlying strata and their combination to make the finished books we now have, some students of the Bible have come to think that such 'excavative' work (to use a phrase of Robert Alter's) is at best only preparatory to a reading of the texts as finished wholes, at worst a distraction from a proper appreciation of them as great literature just as they stand. The narrative books in particular (the Pentateuch and 'historical' books of the Old Testament, the gospels and Acts in the New) have come to be interpreted by means of a 'narrative criticism', akin to much close reading of modern novels and other narrative texts, which is alert to complex literary structure and to such elements as plot, characterization, and closure. It is argued that at the very least readers of the Bible ought to be aware of such issues as well as those of the genesis and formation of the text, and many would contend, indeed, that they are actually of considerably *more* importance for a fruitful appropriation of biblical texts than is the classic agenda of critical study. Many of the commentaries in this volume (such as those on Matthew and Philippians) show an awareness of such aesthetic issues in reading the Bible, and claim that the books they study are literary texts to be read alongside other great works of world literature. This interest in things literary is related to the growing interest in the Bible by people who do not go to it for religious illumination so much as for its character as classic literature, and it is a trend that seems likely to continue.

5. Thirdly, there is now a large body of work in biblical studies arguing that traditional biblical criticism paid insufficient attention not only to literary but also to theological features of the text. Here the interest in establishing the text's original context and meaning is felt to be essentially an antiquarian interest, which gives a position of privilege to 'what the text meant' over 'what the text means'. One important representative of this point of view is the 'canonical approach', sometimes also known as 'canonical criticism', in which biblical interpreters ask not about the origins of biblical books but about their integration into Scripture taken as a finished whole. This is part of an attempt to reclaim the Bible for religious believers, on the hypothesis that traditional histor-

ical criticism has alienated it from them and located it in the study rather than in the pulpit or in the devotional context of individual Bible-reading. While this volume assumes the continuing validity of historical-critical study, many contributors are alive to this issue, and are anxious not to make imperialistic claims for historical criticism. Such criticism began, after all, in a conviction that the Bible was open to investigation by everyone, and was not the preserve of ecclesiastical authorities: it appealed to evidence in the text rather than to external sources of validation. It is important that this insight is not lost by starting to treat the Bible as the possession of a different set of authorities, namely historical-critical scholars! Canonical approaches emphasize that religious believers are entitled to put their own questions to the text, and this must be correct, though it would be a disaster if such a conviction were to result in the outlawing of historical-critical method in its turn. Contributors to this volume, however, are certainly not interested only in the genesis of the biblical books but are also concerned to delineate their overall religious content, and to show how one book relates to others within the canon of Scripture.

6. Thus the historical-critical approach may be chastened by an awareness that its sphere of operations, though vital, is not exhaustive, and that other questions too may reasonably be on the agenda of students of the Bible. In particular, a concern for the finished form of biblical books, however that came into existence, unites both literary and canonical approaches. Few scholars nowadays believe that they have finished their work when they have given an account of how a given book came into being: the total effect (literary and theological) made by the final form is also an important question. The contributors to this volume seek to engage with it.

D. The Biblical Canon. 1. Among the various religious groups that recognize the Bible as authoritative there are some differences of opinion about precisely which books it should contain. In the case of the New Testament all Christians share a common list, though in the centuries of the Christian era a few other books were sometimes included (notably The Shepherd of Hermas, which appears in some major New Testament manuscripts), and some of those now in the canon were at times regarded as of doubtful status (e.g. Hebrews, Revelation, 2 and 3 John, 2 Peter, and Jude). The extent of the Old Testament varies much more seriously. Protestants and Jews alike accept only the books now extant in Hebrew as fully authoritative, but Catholics and Orthodox Christians recognize a longer canon: on this, see the Introduction to the Old Testament. The Ethiopic and Coptic churches accept also *Enoch* and *Jubilees*, as well as having minor variations in the other books of the Old Testament.

2. In this Commentary we have included all the books that appear in the NRSV—that is, all the books recognized as canonical in any of the Western churches (both Catholic and Protestant) and in the Greek and Russian Orthodox churches and those in communion with them. We have not included the books found only in the Ethiopic or Coptic canons, though some extracts appear in the article Essay with Commentary on Post-Biblical Jewish Literature.

3. It is important to see that it is only at the periphery that the biblical canon is blurred. There is a great core of central books whose status has never been seriously in doubt: the

Pentateuch and Prophets in the Old Testament, the gospels and major Pauline epistles in the New. Few of the deutero-canonical books of the Old Testament have ever been of major importance to Christians—a possible exception is the Wisdom of Solomon, so well respected that it was occasionally regarded by early Christians as a New Testament book. There is nowadays comparatively little discussion among different kinds of Christian about the correct extent of the biblical canon (which at the Reformation was a major area of disagreement), and our intention has been to cover most of the books regarded as canonical in major churches without expressing any opinion about whether or not they should have canonical status.

E. How to Use this Commentary. 1. A commentary is an aid towards informed reading of a text, and not a substitute for it. The contributors to this volume have written on the assumption that the Bible is open before the reader all the while, whether in hard copy or electronic form. The NRSV is the normal or 'default' version. When other versions or the commentator's own renderings are preferred this is indicated; often this is because some nuance in the original has been lost in the NRSV (no translation can do full justice to all the possible meanings of a text in another language) or because some ambiguity (and these abound in the text of the Bible) has been resolved in a way that differs from the judgement of the commentator.

2. The NRSV is the latest in a long line of translations that go back to the version authorized by King James I of England in 1611. It is increasingly recognized as the most suitable for the purposes of serious study, because it is based on the best available critical editions of the original texts, because it has no particular confessional allegiance, and because it holds the balance between accuracy and intelligibility, avoiding paraphrase on the one hand and literalism on the other. But comparison between different English translations, particularly for the reader who does not know Hebrew or Greek, is often instructive and serves as a reminder that any translation is itself already an interpretation.

3. *The Oxford Annotated Bible*, based on the NRSV, is particularly useful for those who wish to gain a quick overview of the larger context before consulting this Commentary on a particular passage of special interest. It is useful in another way too: its introductions and notes represent a moderate consensus in contemporary biblical scholarship with which the often more innovative views of the contributors to this Commentary may be measured.

4. When a commentator wishes to draw attention to a passage or parallel in the Bible, the standard NRSV abbreviations apply. But when the reference is to a fuller discussion to be found in the Commentary itself, small capitals are used. Thus (cf. Gen 1:1) signifies the biblical text, while GEN 1:1 refers to the commentary on it. In the same way GEN A etc. refers to the introductory paragraphs of the article on Genesis. The conventions for transliteration of the biblical languages into the English alphabet are the same as those used by *The Oxford Companion to the Bible* (ed. B. M. Metzger and M. Coogan, Oxford: Oxford University Press, 1994).

5. The traditional kind of verse-by-verse commentary has in recent times come under attack as a 'disintegrating' approach that diverts the attention of the reader from the natural flow of the text. The paragraph or longer section, so it is argued, is the real unit of thought, not the verse. However, certain commentators commenting on certain texts would still defend the traditional approach, since they claim that readers chiefly need to be provided with background information necessary to the proper historical interpretation of the text, rather than a more discursive exposition which they could work out for themselves. Examples of both the older and newer methods are to be found in the commentaries below. But even when a particular commentator offers observations on individual verses, we would recommend readers to read the whole paragraph or section and not just the comment on the verse that interests them, so as to gain a more rounded picture. And to encourage this we have not peppered the page with indications of new verses in capitals (V.1) or bold type (**v.1**), but mark the start of a new comment less obtrusively in lower case (v.1,).

6. The one-volume Bible commentary, as this genre developed through the twentieth century, aimed to put into the hands of readers everything they needed for the study of the biblical text. Alongside commentaries on the individual books, it often included a host of general articles ranging from 'Biblical Weights and Measures' to 'The Doctrine of the Person of Christ'. In effect, it tried to be a Commentary, Bible Dictionary, Introduction (in the technical sense, i.e. an analysis of evidence for date, authorship, sources, etc.) and Biblical Theology all rolled into one. But it is no longer possible, given the sheer bulk and variety of modern scholarship, even to attempt this multipurpose approach: nor indeed is it desirable since it distracts attention from the proper task of a commentary which is the elucidation of the text itself. Readers who need more background information on a particular issue are recommended to consult *The Oxford Companion to the Bible* or the six volumes of *The Anchor Bible Dictionary* (ed. D. N. Freedman, New York: Doubleday, 1992), though older bible dictionaries may be used instead: the basic factual information they contain remains largely reliable and relatively stable over time.

7. Each article concludes with a bibliography of works cited. But in addition at the end of the volume there is an aggregated bibliography that points the reader towards the most important specialist works in English on the separate books of the Bible, and also major reference works, introductions, theologies, and so forth.

8. The contributors to *The Oxford Bible Commentary*—and this will probably apply to its users as well—belong to different faith traditions or none. They have brought to their task a variety of methods and perspectives, and this lends richness and depth to the work as a whole. But it also creates problems in coming to an agreed common terminology. As we have noted already, the definition of what is to be included in the Bible, the extent of the canon, is disputed. Further, should we refer to the Old and New Testaments, or to the scriptures of Israel and of early Christianity; to the Apocrypha or the deutero-canonical literature? How should dates be indicated, with BC and AD in the traditional manner or with BCE and CE in reference to the *Common Era*? The usages we have actually adopted should be understood as simple conventions, without prejudice to the serious issues that underlie these differences. A particular problem of a similar kind was whether or not to offer some assistance with a welter of texts, dating from the late biblical period up to 200 CE, which, while not biblical on any definition, are nevertheless relevant to the serious study of the Bible: these are the Dead Sea scrolls, the Old Testament pseudepigrapha, and the apocryphal New Testament. The compromise solution we have reached is to offer not exactly commentary, but two more summarizing articles on this literature (chs. 55 and 82) which, however, still focus on the texts themselves in a way consistent with the commentary format. Some readers may wish to distinguish sharply between the status of this material and that in the Bible; others will see it as merging into the latter.

9. In addition to the overall introductions to the three main subdivisions of the commentary, there are other articles that attempt to approach certain texts not individually but as sets. The Pentateuch or Five Books of Moses functions not only doctrinally but also in terms of its literary history as one five-part work. Similarly, the letters of Paul were once a distinct corpus of writings before they were expanded and added to the growing canon of the New Testament. The four gospels may properly be studied separately, but, both as historical and theological documents, may also be read profitably 'in synopsis'. No attempt has been made by the editors to make these additional articles that group certain texts together entirely consistent with the individual commentaries on them, for the differences are entirely legitimate. The index of subjects at the end of the volume relates only to this introductory material and not to the commentaries themselves. To locate discussions of biblical characters, places, ideas etc. the reader is recommended to consult a concordance first and then to look up the commentary on the passages where the key words occur.

The Bible is a vast treasury of prose and poetry, of history and folklore, of spirituality and ethics; it has inspired great art and architecture, literature and music down the centuries. It invites the reader into its own ancient and mysterious world, and yet at the same time can often surprise us by its contemporary relevance. It deserves and repays all the efforts of critical and attentive reading which the *Oxford Bible Commentary* is designed to assist.

2. Introduction to the Old Testament   JOHN BARTON

A. The Old Testament Canon. 1. 'The Old Testament' is the term traditionally used by Christians and others to refer to the Holy Scriptures of Judaism, which the Church inherited as part of its Jewish origins and eventually came to see as a portion of its own composite Bible, whose other main section is the New Testament. The early Church recognized as Old Testament Scripture both those books which now form the Hebrew Scriptures accepted as authoritative by Jews, and a number of other books, some of them originally written in Hebrew but now (with a few exceptions) found only in Greek and other, later, translations. Since the Reformation, the Hebrew Scriptures alone are recognized as part of the Bible by Protestants, but Catholic and Orthodox Christians continue to acknowledge also these 'Greek' books—sometimes called the 'deuterocanonical' books—which are referred to as 'The Apocrypha' in Protestantism. In this commentary all the books recognized by any Christian church have been included, just as they are in the NRSV, but (again as in the NRSV) we have followed the Protestant and Jewish custom of separating the Apocrypha from the Hebrew Scriptures.

2. The official list of books accepted as part of Scripture is known as the 'canon', and there are thus at least two different canons of the OT: the Hebrew Scriptures (for which Jews do not use the title 'Old Testament'), and the OT of the early church, which contained all the Hebrew Scriptures together with the deuterocanonical/apocryphal books. This second canon has in turn been received in a slightly different form in the Catholic and Orthodox churches, so that there are a few books in the Orthodox canon which do not appear in the Catholic Bible (e.g. 3 Maccabees, Ps 151) and one book (2 Esdras) which is often found in Catholic Bibles but is not extant in Greek and therefore not canonical in the Orthodox churches. The Protestant Apocrypha has traditionally included the deuterocanonical books of the Catholic rather than of the Orthodox church. For a comparison of the Hebrew and Greek canons, see the chart at 1.

3. How did this situation arise? There are many theories about the origins of the various canons, but one which is widely accepted is as follows. By the beginning of the Common Era, most if not all of the books now in the HB were already regarded as sacred Scripture by most Jews. Many, however, especially in Greek-speaking areas such as Egypt, also had a high regard for other books, including what are now the deuterocanonical or apocryphal books, along with others which are no longer in any Bible. The early Christian church, which was predominantly Greek-speaking, tended to accept this wider canon of books. In due course, mainstream Judaism decided to canonize only the books extant in Hebrew, but the Christian churches continued to operate with a wider canon. Certain Church Fathers, notably Melito of Sardis (died *c*.190 CE) and Jerome (*c*.345–420) proposed that the church should exclude the deuterocanonical books, but this proposal was not accepted. It was only at the Reformation in the sixteenth century that Jerome's suggestion was reconsidered, and Protestants opted for the shorter, Jewish canon of the Hebrew Scriptures as their OT. The Catholic Church continued to use the longer canon, and the Orthodox churches were unaffected by the Reformation in any case. Some Protestants, notably Lutherans and Anglicans, treated what they now called the Apocrypha as having a sub-scriptural status, but Calvinists and other Protestants rejected it entirely. (See Sundberg 1964; 1968; Anderson 1970; Barton 1986; 1997a; 1997b; Beckwith 1985; Davies 1998.)

4. Since we have included a separate Introduction to the Apocrypha in this Commentary, little more will be said about these deuterocanonical books here. But it is important to grasp that the term 'Old Testament' does not identify a corpus of books so simply as does the corresponding 'New

Testament', since different Christians include different books within it. 'Hebrew Bible' or 'Hebrew Scriptures' is unambiguous and is nowadays often preferred to 'Old Testament', but it cannot be used to refer to the longer OT of the ancient church.

B. Collecting the Hebrew Scriptures. 1. If the Hebrew Scriptures were complete by the beginning of the Common Era, that does not mean that the collection was new at that time. Many of the OT books were recognized as authoritative long before the first century BCE. The Pentateuch, or five books of Moses (Genesis, Exodus, Leviticus, Numbers, and Deuteronomy), probably existed in something like its present form by the fourth century BCE, and the historical and prophetic books (Joshua, Judges, Samuel, Kings, Isaiah, Jeremiah, Ezekiel, and the twelve Minor—i.e. shorter—prophets) may well have been compiled no later than the third century BCE. The Jewish arrangement of the Hebrew Scriptures recognizes these two collections, which it calls respectively 'the Torah' and 'the Prophets', as having a certain special prestige above that of 'the Writings', which is the Hebrew title for the third collection in the canon, consisting of other miscellaneous works (Psalms, Proverbs, Job, Daniel, Chronicles, Ezra, Nehemiah, and the five scrolls read at festivals, Esther, Ruth, Song of Songs, Lamentations, and Ecclesiastes). This may well be because the Writings were formed rather later, perhaps not until the first century BCE—indeed, some of the books contained in them, notably Daniel, are themselves much later than most of the books in the Torah and Prophets, and so did not exist to be collected until that later time.

2. In the Greek Bible, followed by the traditional, pre-Reformation Christian canon, this division into three collections is not followed, but a roughly thematic arrangement is preferred, with all the 'historical' books at the beginning, the 'wisdom' or teaching books such as Proverbs in the middle, and the prophetic books (including Daniel) at the end. This produces what looks like a more rational arrangement, but it may obscure the process of canonization to which the Hebrew arrangement is a more effective witness. This commentary follows the traditional Protestant arrangement, which adopts the order of books in the Greek Bible but extracts the deutero-canonical books and groups them into the separate Apocrypha. The different arrangements can be seen in the chart at 1.

3. The collection of scriptural texts was probably undertaken by learned scribes, the forerunners of the people described as 'scribes' in the NT. But it should not be thought of as a conscious process of selection. On the whole the HB probably contains most of what had survived of the writings of ancient Israel, together with more recent books which had commended themselves widely. Growth, rather than selection, was the operative factor. Specific Jewish communities, such as that which produced the Dead Sea scrolls, may have worked with a larger corpus of texts, but there too the texts we now know as biblical had pride of place. There is no evidence of disputes about the contents of the Bible until some time into the Common Era: in earlier times, it seems, old books were venerated and not questioned. Even where one book was clearly incompatible with another, as is the case with Kings and Chronicles, both were allowed to stand unreconciled within the one canon.

C. Writing the Hebrew Scriptures. 1. People often think of the books of the Bible as each having an author. This was normal in ancient times, too: Jews and Christians thought that the 'books of Moses' were written by Moses, the 'books of Samuel' by Samuel, the Psalms by David, the Proverbs by Solomon, and each of the prophetic books by the prophet whose name the book bears. This raises obvious historical problems—for example, Moses and Samuel then have to be seen as having recorded the details of their own deaths! But modern study has made it clear that many of the books of the OT are the product not of a single author but of several generations of writers, each reworking the text produced by his predecessors. Furthermore, some material in the biblical books may not have originated in written form at all, but may derive from oral tradition. In their finished form most of the books are the product of redactors—editors who (more or less successfully) smoothed out the texts that had reached them to make the books as we now have them.

2. Modern scholarship recognizes important collections of material in the OT that are not coterminous with the books in their present form. In the Pentateuch, for example, it is widely believed that earlier sources can be distinguished. These sources ran in parallel throughout what are now the five books, in particular an early (pre-exilic) strand called 'J' which is to be found throughout Genesis–Numbers, and 'P', a product of priestly writers after the Exile, which is now interwoven with J to form the present form of these books (see INTROD. PENT.). Scholarship has also pointed to the existence of originally longer works which have been broken up to make the books as they now stand. An example is the so-called Deuteronomistic History, supposed by many to have been compiled during the Exile and to have comprised what are now the books of Deuteronomy, Joshua, Judges, Samuel, and Kings, with points of division falling elsewhere than at the present limits of the books. The Psalter has clear evidence of the existence of earlier, shorter collections, such as the Psalms of Asaph and the Psalms of the sons of Korah, which were partly broken up to make the book of Psalms as we now have it. The book of Isaiah seems likely to have consisted originally of at least three lengthy blocks of material, chs. 1–39, 40–55, and 56–66, which have been brought together under the name of the great prophet.

3. Underlying these longer works there were legends, tales, prophetic oracles, wise sayings, and other traditions which may once have existed without any larger context, and circulated orally in particular areas of Israel. The stories of the patriarchs in Genesis, for instance, may go back to individual hero-tales which originally had only a local importance, but which later writers have incorporated into cycles of stories purporting to give information about the ancestors of the whole Israelite people. Individual proverbs may have originated in the life of this or that Israelite village, only much later collected together to form the book of Proverbs. Prophets taught small groups of disciples about matters of immediate concern, but later their words were grouped together by theme and applied to the history of the whole nation and its future.

4. Thus the process which gave us the OT is almost infinitely complicated. Recently, however, literary critics have begun to argue that alongside much anonymous, reworked material, there are also books and sections of books which do betray the presence of genuinely creative writers: the popular idea of biblical 'authors', that is, is not always wide of the mark. The story of David's court in 2 Samuel and 1 Kings, for example, is now widely regarded as the work of a literary genius, and similar claims have been made for other narrative parts of the OT, including segments of the Pentateuch. This Commentary tries to maintain a balance between continuing to hold that most OT books came about as the result of a process stretching over several generations, and a willingness to recognize literary artistry and skilful writing where it can be found. The general trend in OT study at present is towards a greater interest in the present form of the text and away from an exclusive concentration on the raw materials from which it may have been assembled. This present form is often more coherent than an older generation of critics was willing to accept, even though evidence of reworked older material often remains apparent. (See Rendtorff 1985; Smend 1981.)

D. Language. 1. The original language of the OT is predominantly Hebrew, though there are a few sections in Aramaic (Ezra 4:8–6:18, 7:12–26; Dan 2:4–7:28). Aramaic and Hebrew are related, but not mutually comprehensible, languages belonging to the Semitic family, which also includes Arabic, Ethiopic, and the ancient language Akkadian. Aramaic was more important historically, since it was the lingua franca of the Assyrian, Babylonian, and Persian empires, whereas Hebrew is simply the language of Palestine, closely related to the tongues of Israel's neighbours, Moab, Edom, and Ammon.

2. Hebrew and Aramaic, like some other Semitic languages, were originally written without vowels. In any language written with an alphabet more information is provided in the writing-system than is actually needed to make sense of most words: for example, if we wrote 'Th Hbrw lngg' no-one would have any difficulty in understanding this as 'the Hebrew language', especially if they were helped by the context. So long as Hebrew was a living language, this caused few problems. Although some words might be ambiguous, the context would usually determine which was meant. Modern Hebrew is usually written without vowels, too, and this seldom causes difficulties for readers. Once biblical Hebrew became a 'learned' language and passed out of daily use, however, systems of vowel points—dots and dashes above and below the consonant letters—were devised to help the reader, and the system now used in printed Bibles is the work of the Masoretes (see E.2). The unpointed text continues in use today in the scrolls of the Torah read in synagogue worship.

3. Most scholars think that two phases in the development of Hebrew can be found in the pages of the OT: a classical Hebrew which prevailed until some time after the Exile, and a later Hebrew, first attested in Ezekiel and P, which develops through Ecclesiastes and Chronicles in the direction of later Mishnaic Hebrew—the learned language of Jews from about the first century CE onwards, by which time Aramaic had become the everyday tongue. However, this is disputed, and anyone who acquires classical Hebrew can read any biblical book without difficulty. As in many languages, there are wide differences between the Hebrew of prose narrative and that used in verse, where there is often a special vocabulary and many grammatical variations. In some cases these may be due to the use of dialect forms, though this is not certain. Some scholars believe that the oldest parts of the OT, such as the Song of Deborah in Judg 5, preserve an archaic form of the language. (See Saenz-Badillos 1993.)

E. The Text. 1. Until the discovery of the Dead Sea scrolls, which include at least portions of every biblical book except Esther, scholars were dependent on Hebrew MSS no earlier than the ninth century CE. The three most important are the Cairo Codex (of the Prophets only), written in 896 CE; the Aleppo Codex (c.930 CE), unfortunately damaged by fire in 1947; and the Leningrad Codex, dated 1009 CE. The latter is a complete text of the whole HB, and has become the standard text which modern printed Bibles take as their basis.

2. In general terms the Dead Sea discoveries have confirmed the accuracy with which the Leningrad Codex has transmitted the Hebrew text. Although there are innumerable differences in detail, the Dead Sea MSS, though one thousand years older, do not show major deviations from the text as we know it. The HB was transmitted from the beginning of the Common Era by schools of scribes, the most important of whom are the Masoretes, who worked from 500 to 1000 CE; and their claims to have transmitted the Hebrew text with great faithfulness is on the whole confirmed by the evidence from the Dead Sea. One of their tasks was to record the traditional pronunciation of biblical Hebrew, by then a dead language, by adding pointing, that is, signs indicating vowels, to the basic Hebrew text (see D. 2). The Masoretes set themselves the task, almost impossible to imagine in an age before computers, of recording every detail of the text: they compiled lists of unusual spellings, the frequency with which particular words or combinations of words occurred, and even obvious errors in the text. Their work can be seen in the margins and at the top and bottom of the text in a printed HB, in the form of many tiny comments, written in unpointed Aramaic. Their object was not to improve or emend the text they had received, but to preserve it accurately in every detail, and they succeeded to an astonishing extent. The student of the Bible can have confidence that the text translated by modern versions such as the NRSV rests on a faithful tradition going back to NT times.

3. This of course is not to say that that the text was preserved with equal faithfulness between NT times and the times of the original authors. The work of the Masoretes, together with the evidence of the Dead Sea scrolls, ensures that we can feel confident of knowing in general terms what text of Isaiah was current in the time of Jesus. That does not mean that we can know what version of Isaiah was current in the days of the prophet Isaiah himself. Here we are dependent on conjecture, and the reconstruction of the *original* text, in the literal sense of 'original', is beyond our powers. What we can say is that the HB we possess today is the HB that was known to Jews and Christians in the first centuries of our era, carefully preserved even where it does not make sense (which is occasionally the case)! (See Weingreen 1982; Würthwein 1979; Talmon 1970.)

F. Ancient Translations of the Old Testament. 1. By the end of the Second Temple period (4th–2nd cents. BCE) there were substantial communities of Jews who no longer had Hebrew as their first language, certainly outside the land of Palestine and perhaps even inside it. For many, Aramaic had become the everyday tongue, and all around the Mediterranean Greek became the lingua franca in the aftermath of the conquests of Alexander the Great (d. 323 BCE). Aramaic paraphrases of the HB began to be compiled, for use in the liturgy, where readings in Hebrew would be followed by an Aramaic translation, or Targum. Initially Targums were apparently improvised, and there was a dislike of writing them down for fear they might come to seem like Holy Scripture themselves. But later they were collected in writing, and a number have survived to this day.

2. Various Greek versions of the Bible were also made. A legend says that the initiator of Greek translations was Ptolemy Philadelphus of Egypt (285–247 BCE), who ordered that a translation of the Torah should be made so that he could know under what laws his Jewish subjects lived. According to the legend, seventy-two scholars worked on the project for seventy-two days: hence their work came to be known as the Septuagint (meaning 'seventy', traditionally abbreviated LXX). The truth is probably more prosaic, but the third century remains the period when Greek translations of the Torah began to be made, followed by versions of other books too. Later translators set about correcting the LXX versions, among them Aquila, Symmachus, and Theodotion (see Salvesen 1991). About six different translators can be detected in the LXX itself. The version is in general faithful to the Hebrew, and far less of a paraphrase than the Aramaic Targums. Quite often the LXX seems to be a translation of a different Hebrew original from the one that has come down to us, and in some books, notably Jeremiah, it is obvious that the translators were dealing with a quite different (in this case, shorter) version of the book. Any quest for an 'original' text of Jeremiah underlying the MT therefore has to treat the evidence of the LXX very seriously.

3. In the early church Greek was at first the commonest language, and the LXX has come down to us largely because it was preserved in Christian hands. Its divergent ordering of the books, as well as its inclusion of more books than the Hebrew Scriptures, came to be regarded as distinctively Christian features, even though in origin it is plainly a Jewish work. Once Latin displaced Greek as the language of the Western church the need was felt for a further translation into Latin, and various Old Latin MSS have survived, alongside the evidence of biblical quotations in Christian writers who used Latin. The Old Latin versions are translations from the Greek and thus stand at two removes from the Hebrew text. In the fifth century CE Jerome made a complete Latin version of the whole Bible from the original languages. This translation, which came to be known as the Vulgate, became the official Bible of the Western church until the Reformation, and continues to enjoy a high prestige in the Catholic church. Naturally both the Greek and Latin Bibles, like the Hebrew, have come down to us in a range of different MSS, and the quest for 'the original LXX' is no easier than that for the original HB. (See Roberts 1951.)

G. Contents of the Old Testament. 1. The OT contains a huge variety of material, much wider than the contents of the NT, embracing every aspect of the social and political life of ancient Israel and post-exilic Judaism. The variety can be suggested by looking briefly at some of the genres of literature to be found there.

2. **Narrative.** More than half the OT consists of narrative, that is, the consecutive description of events set in the past. It is hard to distinguish between what we might call history, legend, saga, myth, folktale, or fiction. There are passages in the books of Kings which seem to be excerpts from official documents and thus approach close to something we might recognize as history. At the other end of the spectrum there are at least three stories—Jonah, Ruth, and Esther—which from our perspective are probably fiction, since they rest on no historically true data at all. Then there are a lot of stories that seem to lie between these two extremes: the stories about the creation, the first human beings, and the ancestors of the Israelites in Genesis, the early history of Israel from Exodus through into the books of Samuel, tales about early prophets such as Elijah and Elisha, an account of the court of David which is almost novelistic, and the retellings of older stories in the books of Chronicles, as well as a very small amount of first-person narration in Ezra and Nehemiah. But the OT itself shows no awareness of any differences or gradations within this range of material, but records it all in the same steady and neutral style as if it were all much on a level. Sometimes God or an angel makes regular appearances in the narrative, as in Genesis and Judges, sometimes events are recorded without overt reference to divine causation, as in 2 Samuel; but the OT itself does not draw attention to the difference, and we cannot assume that the writers saw any distinction between 'sacred' and 'secular' history. (See Barr 1980.)

3. **Law.** Within the narrative framework of the Pentateuch we find several collections of laws, such as the so-called Book of the Covenant (Ex 21–4), the Holiness Code (Lev 17–26), and the Deuteronomic legislation (Deut 12–26). In fact the whole of Leviticus and large parts of Exodus and Numbers contain legal material, and from the perspective of the redactors of the Pentateuch the giving of the law is the main purpose of Israel's sojourn at Sinai. At the heart of the law lie the Ten Commandments (Ex 20, Deut 5), and the rest of the legislation is presented as a detailed exposition of the principles the Commandments enshrine.

4. From a historical point of view the laws in the Pentateuch have much in common with the laws of other nations in the ancient Near East, such as the famous Code of Hammurabi. But they also differ from them in striking ways—e.g. in a higher valuation of human life, much more interest in regulations concerning worship, and a greater tendency to lay down general principles. As presented in the Pentateuch, however, the laws are understood as the foundation of the highly distinctive relationship of Israel with its god, YHWH. They are the terms of the solemn agreement, or 'covenant', made between YHWH and the people through the mediation of Moses. The idea of a legislative framework which regulates the relation between a god and his people was unusual in the ancient world. It led in post-biblical times to the idea of Torah, a complete ethical code covering all aspects of life as lived before God, which would become the foundation-stone of later Judaism. This tendency can already be discerned in Deuteronomy, where the laws are not just to be enacted and observed jurisprudentially but are also to be a subject for constant meditation and delight. (See Noth 1966.)

5. Hymns and Psalms. The Psalms have sometimes been described as the hymnbook of the temple, though since they are hard to date there is no agreement as to whether they are best seen as the hymnbook of Solomon's Temple or of the Second Temple, built after the Exile. We do not know which psalms were intended for public liturgical and which for private prayer—indeed, that distinction may be a false one in ancient Israel. There have been many theories about the use of the Psalms in worship, but all are highly speculative. What can be said is that Israel clearly had a tradition of writing sophisticated religious poems, and that this continued over a long period: Ps 29, for example, seems to be modelled on a Canaanite psalm and must therefore have originated in early pre-exilic times, while Ps 119 reflects a piety based on meditation on the Torah, and is generally dated in the late post-exilic period. Psalms can also be found outside the Psalter itself, for example in Ex 15, 1 Sam 2, and Jon 2. (See Gillingham 1994.)

6. Wisdom. There are at least three kinds of wisdom literature in the OT. The book of Proverbs preserves many sayings and aphorisms which draw moral and practical conclusions from aspects of daily life. These may in some cases have originated in the life of the Israelite village, in others in the royal court, but all have been gathered together to form the great collection of sayings that runs from Prov 10 to 30. A second kind of wisdom is more speculative in character, concerned with theological and cosmological questions, as seen e.g. in Prov 8:22–36. Frequently in such passages Wisdom is itself personified as a kind of goddess, and the writer speculates on the involvement of this being in the creation of the world and on its/her relationship to YHWH. Thirdly, we find what is sometimes called mantic wisdom, which draws on ancient Near-Eastern traditions about the interpretation of dreams and portents to gain insight into the future, and this is manifested by Joseph in Genesis, and in the book of Daniel. Two books, Job and Ecclesiastes, seem to reflect on deficiencies within the traditions of wisdom, and argue for a generally sceptical and non-committal attitude towards the mysteries of life. They are part of a general tendency towards greater pessimism about human capabilities of reason and understanding, characteristic of post-exilic Jewish thought. (See Crenshaw 1981.)

7. Prophecy. 'Prophecy', like 'wisdom', is something of a catch-all term covering a wide diversity of material. Its basic form is the oracle: a (usually) short, pithy saying in which the prophet either denounces some current evil, or predicts what YHWH will do in the immediate future as a response to human conduct. One of the difficulties of studying the prophetic books is that these oracles are often arranged in an order which reflects the interests of the editors, rather than registering the chronological sequence of what the prophet himself said. The matter is complicated further by the insertion of many non-authentic oracles, representing perhaps what later writers thought the prophet might or would have said in later historical situations, had he still been alive and able to do so. It is probably in the prophetic books that the concept of authorship breaks down most completely. Many prophetic books also contain brief narratives and biographical details about the prophet whose name they bear. Sometimes these are indistinguishable in style and approach from narratives in the 'historical' books—e.g. Jeremiah contains many

stories about the prophet that would not be out of place in Kings, and perhaps comes from the same school of writers.

8. Sometimes the prophets relate visions and their divine interpretations, and towards the end of the OT period this became the normal way of conveying divine revelation, in the form usually called 'apocalyptic'. Daniel is the only book in the HB generally called apocalyptic, but later portions of the prophetic books show developments in this direction and are sometimes referred to as proto-apocalyptic. Prime candidates for this description are Isa 24–7, Joel, and Zech 9–14. (See Blenkinsopp 1984.)

H. Themes of the Old Testament. 1. Despite its variety, the OT is a document from a religious tradition that retained, over time, certain characteristic features. These can be introduced here only in the most sketchy outline, but it may be helpful to the reader to be aware of four interlocking themes.

2. Creation and Monotheism. YHWH is consistently presented throughout the OT as the God who created the world, and as the only God with whom Israel is to be concerned. Older strands of thought do not yet treat him as the only God there is (strict monotheism), a development generally thought to have taken place around the time of the Exile. But it is never envisaged that any other god is a proper object of worship for Israelites. There are occasional survivals of a polytheistic system—e.g. in Ps 82—but no extended text in the OT speaks of the actions of gods other than YHWH as real or other than purported. The OT presents much of the life of the pre-exilic period as one of warfare between YHWH and the gods of Canaan for Israel's allegiance. We know that as a matter of historical fact many people were far from being monotheistic in their religious practice in this period. But all our texts imply or affirm that for Israel there can in the end be only YHWH.

3. Alongside the majestic account of creation in Gen 1, where God creates by mere diktat, the OT is familiar with older creation stories in which creation was accomplished when the chief god killed a dragon and made the world out of its body (see Ps 74, Job 3)—a pattern of thought widespread in the ancient Near East. However, this theme seems to be used in a literary way, rather than reflecting a genuine belief of the authors—much as English poets in the past might conventionally invoke the Muses though they did not believe these beings actually existed. Jews and Christians alike have seen the Hebrew Scriptures as important, among other reasons, because they affirm the oneness of God and his absolute power over the creation, and in this they have correctly captured a theme which is of central importance in the Bible itself. It finds its most eloquent expression in the oracles of Deutero-Isaiah, as the author of Isa 40–55 is known: see especially Isa 40:12–26. (See Theissen 1984; Whybray 1983.)

4. Covenant and Redemption. It is a central point in many OT texts that the creator God YHWH is also in some sense Israel's special god, who at some point in history entered into a relationship with his people that had something of the nature of a contract. Classically this contract or covenant was entered into at Sinai, and Moses was its mediator. As we saw above, the laws in the Pentateuch are presented as the terms of the contract between YHWH and his people. Acting in accordance with his special commitment to Israel, YHWH is thought to have guided their history, in particular bringing them out of Egypt and giving them the promised land as a perpetual possession. Later prophets hoped for a restoration to this land after the Jews had lost political control of it to a succession of great powers: Assyria, Babylonia, and Persia.

5. In the prophetic version of the covenant theory, the contractual nature of the arrangement is stressed in such a way as to imply the possibility of the destruction of Israel if the nation is disobedient. It is not too much to say that the main preoccupation of most of the prophets was with how YHWH would 'manage' this strict interpretation of the covenant, punishing his people and yet somehow preserving the special relationship with them which the covenant implied. In other strands of OT thought, however, the emphasis falls more heavily on YHWH's commitment to his people and the idea of a bargain is less apparent. Thus the covenant with Abraham, and that with David and his descendants, tend to be presented as almost unconditional. Either the obedience required from the human partner is seen as minimal, or else disobedience (though it will be punished) does not have the power to lead to a complete breakdown in the relationship with YHWH. After the Exile the covenant between YHWH and Israel was often seen as unbreakable on the national scale, but individuals had a duty to remain *within* the covenant community by faithful adherence to Torah.

6. The God who makes a covenant with Israel is a God of redemption as well as of creation. He saves his people from Egypt, and then constantly intervenes in their history to deliver them from their enemies, even though he can also use these enemies as agents of his just punishment. In every national crisis Israel can call on YHWH for help, and though his mercy must not be presumed on, he is a reliable source of support in the long term. (See Nicholson 1986; Spriggs 1974.)

7. **Ethics.** In some OT traditions, such as that of the law, ethical obligation is tightly bound up with Israel's contractual obligations to YHWH, whereas in others (notably wisdom) there is more appeal to universally applicable standards of justice and uprightness. Everywhere in the OT, however, it is taken as given that God makes moral demands on both Israel and all human beings. These demands characteristically include two aspects which to modern, non-Jewish readers do not seem to belong naturally together: a strong commitment to social justice, and a deep concern for ritual purity. Ritual and ethical punctiliousness are seen as points on a single spectrum, so that some texts can speak of gross moral outrages such as murder as polluting the sanctuary of YHWH just as do ritual infringements (see Ezek 18). Pagan writers in the ancient world often drew attention to the high moral standards of Jews, while simultaneously being puzzled that they were so concerned about matters of diet and ritual purity. At the same time there are prophetic books, such as Amos and Hosea, which seem to distinguish the two types of ethical concern, and which argue that YHWH requires social justice more than ritual purity, and perhaps that he does not care about ritual purity at all: this latter possibility is also envisaged in some wisdom texts.

8. The OT's moral code is remarkably consistent throughout the period covered by the literature. It stresses justice, both in the sense of fairness to everyone, rich and poor alike, and in the sense of intervention on behalf of those who cannot help themselves. It forbids murder, theft, bribery and corruption,

deceitful trading standards (e.g. false weights and measures), and many sexual misdemeanours, including adultery, incest, bestiality, and homosexual acts. It insists on the duty of those in power to administer justice equitably, and forbids exploitation of the poor and helpless, especially widows and orphans. All moral obligation is traced back to an origin in God, either by way of 'positive' law—YHWH's explicit commands—or else through the way the divine character is expressed in the orders of nature. Some moral obligations at least are assumed to be known outside Israel (as was of course the case), and especially in the wisdom literature appeal is made to the consensus of right-minded people and not only to the declared will of YHWH. (See Wright 1983; Barton 1998; Otto 1994.)

9. **Theodicy.** In a polytheistic system it is easy to explain the disasters that overtake human societies: they result from disagreements among the gods, in which human beings get caught in the crossfire, or from the malevolence of particular gods towards humankind. This kind of explanation is not available in a monotheistic culture, and consequently the kind of problem which philosophers deal with under the title 'theodicy'—how to show that God is just in the face of the sufferings of the world—bulk large in the writings of the OT.

10. On the corporate level, the Exile seems to have been the crisis that first focused the minds of Israel's thinkers on the problem of how to make sense of apparently unjust sufferings. Lamentations is an extended expression of grief at the rough treatment that YHWH has apparently handed out to the people he had chosen himself; Jeremiah also reflects on the problem. Ezekiel tries to show that God is utterly just, and that those who complain of his injustice are in fact themselves to blame for what has befallen them. Second Isaiah combines a conviction that God has been just to punish Israel with an assurance that destruction is not his last word, and that he will remain true to his ancient promises to Abraham, Isaac, and Jacob. Through reflection on the disaster that has befallen Israel all these thinkers come to an affirmation of the superior justice of God—greater, not less, than that of any human power.

11. At the level of the individual the problems of theodicy are discussed in Job and, to some extent, in Ecclesiastes. Here explanations in terms of human guilt are for the most part rejected, since we are told at the outset that Job is a righteous man, who manifestly does not deserve to suffer as he does. The book concludes that God cannot be held to account, and that his ways are imponderable, though perhaps also that there are forms of fellowship with him in which understanding why one suffers is not a first priority. For Ecclesiastes, the world manifests no moral order such that the righteous can expect to be rewarded and the wicked punished, but 'time and chance happen to all'.

12. Convictions about the justice of God are crucial to the way the story of Israel is told in the historical books: Kings and Chronicles in particular are concerned to show that God is always just in his dealings with his people. Kings sees this as manifested in the fact that sin is always avenged, even if it takes many generations for God's justice to be implemented; while Chronicles believes instead in immediate retribution. The Psalms, too, contain many reflections on the respective fate of righteous and wicked, and contain some profound insights on this theme—see especially Ps 37, 49, and 73.

There are, in fact, few books in the OT where the theme of theodicy is absent. (See Crenshaw 1983.)

I. Arrangement of Books in Hebrew and Greek Bibles

The Hebrew Bible	The Greek Bible
Torah:	*Historical Books*:
Genesis	Genesis
Exodus	Exodus
Leviticus	Leviticus
Numbers	Numbers
Deuteronomy	Deuteronomy
Prophets:	
Joshua	Joshua
Judges	Judges
Samuel	Ruth
Kings	1 Samuel
Isaiah	2 Samuel
Jeremiah	1 Kings
Ezekiel	2 Kings
The Twelve:	1 Chronicles
Hosea	2 Chronicles
Joel	1 Esdras
Amos	Ezra
Obadiah	Nehemiah
Jonah	Esther (*with additions*)
Micah	*Judith*
Nahum	*Tobit*
Habakkuk	*1 Maccabees*
Zephaniah	*2 Maccabees*
Haggai	*3 Maccabees*
Zechariah	*4 Maccabees*
Malachi	
Writings:	*Didactic Books*:
Psalms	Psalms
Job	Proverbs
Proverbs	Ecclesiastes
Ruth	Song of Songs
Song of Songs	Job
Ecclesiastes	*Wisdom of Solomon*
Lamentations	*Ecclesiasticus*
Esther	
Daniel	
Ezra-Nehemiah	*Prophetic Books*:
Chronicles	Twelve Minor Prophets:
	Hosea
	Amos
	Micah
	Joel
	Obadiah
	Jonah
	Nahum
	Habakkuk
	Zephaniah
	Haggai
	Zechariah
	Malachi
	Isaiah

The Hebrew Bible	The Greek Bible
	Jeremiah
	Baruch 1–5
	Lamentations
	Letter of Jeremiah (=Baruch 6)
	Ezekiel
	Susanna (=Daniel 13)
	Daniel 1–12 (with additions *Song of Azariah* and *Song of the Three Jews*)
	Bel and the Dragon (=Daniel 14)

Notes: Books additional to the HB are in italics

Books are given the names familiar to English readers: Samuel and Kings are in Greek the 'Four Books of Kingdoms', and Ezra-Nehemiah is '2 Esdras'.

REFERENCES

Anderson, G. W. (1970), 'Canonical and Non-canonical', *Cambridge History of the Bible* (Cambridge: Cambridge University Press), i. 113–59.

Barr, J. (1980), *The Scope and Authority of the Bible*, Explorations in Theology, 7 (London: SCM).

Barton, J. (1986), *Oracles of God: Perceptions of Ancient Prophecy in Israel after the Exile* (London: Darton, Longman & Todd).

—— (1991), *What is the Bible?* (London: SPCK).

—— (1997a), *Making the Christian Bible* (London: Darton, Longman & Todd).

—— (1997b), *The Spirit and the Letter: Studies in the Biblical Canon* (London: SPCK).

—— (1998), *Ethics and the Old Testament* (London: SCM).

Beckwith, R. T. (1985), *The Old Testament Canon of the New Testament Church and its Background in Early Judaism* (London: SPCK).

Blenkinsopp, J. (1984), *A History of Prophecy in Israel from the Settlement in the Land to the Hellenistic Period* (London: SPCK).

Crenshaw, J. L. (1981), *Old Testament Wisdom: An Introduction* (Atlanta: John Knox).

—— (1983) (ed.), *Theodicy in the Old Testament* (Philadelphia: Fortress).

Davies, P. R. (1998), *Scribes and Schools: The Canonization of the Hebrew Scriptures* (Louisville, Ky.: Westminster/John Knox).

Gillingham, S. E. (1994), *The Poems and Psalms of the Hebrew Bible* (Oxford: Oxford University Press).

Nicholson, E. W. (1986), *God and his People: Covenant and Theology in the Old Testament* (Oxford: Clarendon).

Noth, M. (1966), 'The Laws in the Pentateuch: Their Assumptions and Meaning', in his *The Laws in the Pentateuch and Other Essays* (Edinburgh: T. & T. Clark), 1–107.

Otto, E. (1994), *Theologische Ethik des Alten Testaments* (Stuttgart: Kohlhammer).

Rendtorff, R. (1985), *The Old Testament: An Introduction* (London: SCM).

Roberts, B. J. (1951), *The Old Testament Text and Versions: The Hebrew Text in Transmission and the History of the Ancient Versions* (Cardiff: University of Wales Press).

Saenz-Badillos, A. (1993), *A History of the Hebrew Language* (Cambridge: Cambridge University Press).

Salvesen, A. (1991), *Symmachus in the Pentateuch* (Manchester: University of Manchester Press).

Smend, R. (1981), *Die Entstehung des Alten Testaments* (Stuttgart: Kohl-hammer).

Spriggs, D. S. (1974), *Two Old Testament Theologies* (London: SCM).

Sundberg, A. C. (1964), *The Old Testament of the Early Church* (Cambridge, Mass.: Yale University Press).

——(1968), 'The "Old Testament": A Christian Canon', *CBO* 30: 143–55.

Talmon, S. (1970), 'The Old Testament Text', *Cambridge History of the Bible* (Cambridge: Cambridge University Press), i. 159–98.

Theissen, G. (1984), *Biblical Faith: An Evolutionary Perspective* (London: SCM).

Weingreen, J. (1982), *Introduction to the Critical Study of the Text of the Hebrew Bible* (Oxford: Oxford University Press).

Whybray, R. N. (1983), *The Second Isaiah*, Old Testament Guides (Sheffield: Academic Press).

Wright, C. J. H. (1983), *Living as the People of God* (Leicester: Inter-varsity Press).

Würthwein, E. (1979), *The Text of the Old Testament: An Introduction to the Biblia Hebraica* (Grand Rapids: Eerdmans).

3. Introduction to the Pentateuch   G. I. DAVIES

A. What is the Pentateuch? 1. The name 'Pentateuch' means literally 'the work comprising five scrolls', from Greek *pente* and *teukhos*, which can mean 'scroll'. It has been used since at least early Christian times for the first five books of the OT, Genesis to Deuteronomy. The Jewish name for these books was usually and still is 'the law': Hebrew *tôrâ*, Greek *nomos* or *nomothesia* (the latter is literally 'legislation'), and it is this name which appears in the NT: e.g. Lk 24:11, 'What is written in the *law*, the prophets and the psalms', where we meet the threefold subdivision of the Hebrew canon that continues to be used, with the substitution of 'writings' for 'psalms' as the third section. Cf. also the Greek Prologue to Sirach (*c*.132 BCE).

2. But there is a much deeper way of asking, and answering, the question, 'What is the Pentateuch?', one which goes beyond merely defining its external limits to enquire into its nature. In other words, what sort of a thing is this section of the Bible? This question can only really be answered after a full examination of the text, and one justification for the kind of detailed critical analysis which has been popular in modern OT scholarship is that it enables us to give a well-judged (if complicated!) answer to that question. It is a question of considerable theological importance, as can be seen from an introductory look at a few answers that have been given to it, some of which will be examined more fully later on.

2.1. Four of the five books in the Pentateuch deal with the time of Moses, and one recent suggestion has been that we should think of the Pentateuch as *a biography of Moses* with an introduction, that is, Genesis. This attempts to answer the question in terms of the literary genre of the Pentateuch.

2.2. Its main weakness, however, is that it puts Moses as an individual too much in the centre of the picture, important as he undoubtedly is as the leader of his people Israel. We might do better to call the Pentateuch the *story of Israel in the time of Moses*, with an introduction (Genesis) which sets it in the light of universal creation and history.

2.3. To many, however, this would not be theological enough to do justice to the strongly religious element that pervades the story from beginning to end. Gerhard von Rad suggested that the Pentateuch (or to be more precise, the Hexateuch, that is the Pentateuch plus the sixth book of the Bible, Joshua—see below) was an amplified creed, more specifically *an amplified historical creed*, as will be seen in more detail later. The implication is then that the Pentateuch is a product and an expression of faith—it is preceded as it were by an implicit 'I believe in God who...', it is a confessional document, as one might put it. Of course the adjective 'histor-ical' before 'creed' raises some problems, for example whether the story which the Pentateuch as a whole tells is real history, a question whose answer has important theological implications which critics of von Rad were quick to point out. But there are also problems of a simpler kind which relate specifically to its accuracy as a description of Genesis 1–11. Von Rad was, for much of his scholarly career, fascinated by the historical focus of so much of Israel's faith, and he tended to overlook or play down its teaching about God the Creator. This may well have been due to an understandable wish on his part not to allow a foothold in the OT for crude Nazi ideas about racial supremacy grounded in the order of creation which were current at the time he wrote his earliest works on the Hexateuch. It is, nevertheless, necessary to emphasize that the beginning of Genesis is not about history in the ordinary sense of that word, or indeed in any sense, and the idea that the Pentateuch is a 'historical' creed is in danger of losing sight of the important theological statements about creation in those chapters.

2.4. A different way of representing the theological character of the Pentateuch is of course the traditional Jewish expression: *the law*. This is as characteristic of Judaism as von Rad's emphasis on faith is characteristic of his Lutheranism. If it seems at first sight to focus too much on the second half of the Pentateuch, where the laws are concentrated, and to give insufficient attention to the 'story' character of the earlier books, it is worth saying that this problem has not escaped the notice of Jewish commentators, and a very early one, Philo of Alexandria, in the first century CE, had what he thought was a perfectly satisfactory answer to it. It is that while written law is indeed mainly found in the later books of the Pentateuch, the personalities who appear in Genesis, for example, constitute a kind of 'living law', since through their example, and in some less obvious ways, it was God's intention to regulate human behaviour, just as he does later by the written law. Another way of making the description 'law' more widely applicable involves going back to the Hebrew term *tôrâ*. Although commonly translated 'law', its original meaning is something like 'instruction', and it could be used of other kinds of instruction as well as law in the strict sense. For example, the word *tôrâ* is found in Proverbs, where the context shows that the reference is to the kind of teaching contained there, not to the law as such. If we use *tôrâ* as a description for the Pentateuch in this more general sense of 'teaching' or 'instruction', it can easily embrace the non-legal parts of these books as well as the legal ones. On the other hand, while *tôrâ* understood in this wider way does preserve an important truth about the Pentateuch (especially if it is thought of as 'The Teaching', with a capital T), it is in danger of being too vague a description to identify its distinctive character within the OT.

2.5. Another theological definition, which has the merit of combining the advantages of the last two, is to call the Pentateuch a *covenant book*, a document which presents the terms of God's relationship to his people, in the form of his promises to them and the laws which he requires them to obey. The support of the apostle Paul can probably be claimed for this description, for when he speaks of 'the old covenant' in 2 Cor 3:14 it is very likely that he means specifically the Pentateuch. He is clearly thinking of a written document, because when he refers to the 'reading' of the old covenant, and the substitution of the expression 'whenever Moses is read' in the following verse points firmly to the Pentateuch (for 'Moses' as shorthand for 'the books of Moses' see Lk 24:27). A somewhat earlier Jewish reference to the Pentateuch as 'the book of the covenant' occurs in 1 Macc 1:57. Despite the antiquity and authority of this description, it scarcely does justice to the narrative element in the Pentateuch, especially in Genesis.

2.6. A description which combines the literary and the theological aspects has been proposed by David Clines: he regards the Pentateuch as *the story of the partial fulfilment of the promise to the patriarchs*. This has the great advantage of highlighting the important theological theme of promise in Genesis, and of showing how Genesis is linked to the later books theologically, and not just by the continuation of the story. But of course it says nothing about Gen 1–11, and one may wonder whether it takes enough account of the vast amount of legislative material in Leviticus and Deuteronomy especially.

2.7. One might legitimately wonder whether there can be any brief answer to the question which is not open to some objection or another! If nothing else these quite different descriptions, and the comments on them, should have shown that the Pentateuch is a many-sided piece of literature and one which has features which appeal to a variety of religious and other points of view. The final description that I will mention is that the Pentateuch is an incomplete work, a *torso*, because the story which it tells only reaches its climax in the book of Joshua, with the Israelites' entry into the land of Canaan. For von Rad, as we saw, the real literary unit is the 'Hexateuch', 'the six books', and he had many predecessors who also took this view. It was especially popular among the source-critics of the late nineteenth and early twentieth centuries, who believed (as some still do) that the sources out of which the Pentateuch was composed were also used by the editor or editors who composed Joshua. It is less popular today, because Joshua is generally treated as part of the long historical work which extends to the end of 2 Kings, the Deuteronomistic History. In fact since Deuteronomy formed the introduction to that work and, even when taken alone, its connection with the first four books of the Bible can seem very weak, some scholars therefore speak of 'the Tetrateuch', that is the four books from Genesis to Numbers, as the primary literary unit at the beginning of the Bible. From this point of view the Pentateuch would be not so much a torso as a hybrid, the combination of one literary work with the first section of another. If nothing else this view serves to underline the differences in character, concerns, and origin of Deuteronomy, as compared with the earlier books. Yet those differences should not be exaggerated, and it can be argued that Deuteronomy belongs as much with the Tetrateuch as with the books that follow it, and when we come to look at the theology of the Pentateuch in more detail that will become clearer.

B. The Documentary Hypothesis. 1. To make further progress with our question, 'What is the Pentateuch?', we need to dig deeper and consider more closely how it came to exist and what kinds of material it is made up of. A useful way into such study is to review, critically where necessary, the main directions which Pentateuchal scholarship has taken over the past century and a half (see also Clements 1997: ch. 2).

2. The year 1862 was auspicious for the development of Pentateuchal study in England and Germany. It was in that year that Julius Wellhausen went, at the age of 18, as a new student to the German university of Göttingen to study theology. That same year a young British student, T. K. Cheyne, was also in Göttingen, and he was to play an important part in bringing Wellhausen's later ideas to prominence in Britain— he became a professor at Oxford. The year 1862 was also when a series of books by John Colenso, a Cambridge mathematician, began to be published, and so brought critical OT scholarship very much into the public eye in Britain only shortly after the publication of Charles Darwin's *Origins of Species* and the collection called *Essays and Reviews*. And yet by 1862 the critical study of the Pentateuch was already some 150 years old.

3. There is no need to amplify this statement here—the details are in most Introductions to the OT—except to say that particularly since about 1800 strenuous efforts had been made, chiefly in Germany, to discover the process by which the Pentateuch had reached its present form, and that at the beginning of the 1860s the leading scholars held to what was known as the Supplementary Hypothesis (*Ergänzungshypothese*). According to this, the original core of the Pentateuch was a document known as the Book of Origins (*Das Buch der Ursprünge*), which was put together by a priest or Levite in about the time of King Solomon. A distinguishing mark of this book was that in Genesis and the beginning of Exodus (up to ch. 6) it avoided using the name YHWH for God, and employed other words, especially *'ĕlōhîm*, which means 'God', instead. This core, it was held, was expanded in the eighth century BCE, the time of the first great classical prophets, by the addition of stories and other matter in which the name YHWH was freely used from the very beginning. Later still, in the time of Jeremiah (7th cent.), the work was further supplemented by the addition of the major part of Deuteronomy and shorter sections with a similar spirit elsewhere, and so the Pentateuch reached its present form, before the Babylonian Exile. Wellhausen's teacher at Göttingen, Heinrich Ewald, had played an important part in the development of this theory and still held to it in its essential points in 1862, though not with the rigidity of some of its other adherents.

4. But changes were in the air. An important challenge to this theory had already been made by the publication in 1853 of a book by Hermann Hupfeld. Its main theses were: (1) that the so-called 'original core' contained some passages which were of later origin than the rest and represented a first stage of expansion of the core; and (2) that both these later passages and the passages which the Supplementary Hypothesis itself had distinguished from the core were not fragments picked up from all over the place but had been parts of large pre-existing narrative compositions which the compilers of the Pentateuch had drawn on as sources.

5. Hupfeld thus did two things. He refined the analysis of the Pentateuch into its component parts, which were now seen to be not three but four in number, and he replaced the idea of the expansion of an original core with a truly documentary theory of Pentateuchal origins. His four originally independent source-documents correspond closely in extent to those of later theories, three parallel narrative sources and the law-code of Deuteronomy (with some other passages related to it). His oldest narrative corresponds closely to what is now called the Priestly Work (P), the remainder of the Book of Origins is the later Elohist (E), and the source which uses the name YHWH is the Yahwist (J). Hupfeld did not depart from the dominant view at the time about the relative ages of the materials in these sources, and his position can be represented in terms of the modern symbols for them as P-E-J-D (for a fuller account of the sources as later understood see sections c.7 and G).

Hupfeld's new ideas did not succeed in displacing the dominant Supplementary Hypothesis, at any rate not immediately. But some time before 1860 Ewald had recognized the existence of a second Elohist and the character of J and E as continuous sources—which places him very close to Hupfeld. A. Knobel, though less well-known, had reached similar conclusions independently of Hupfeld about the same time, and over a larger range of texts. His work is ignored in most modern accounts of the history of Pentateuchal criticism (though not by Wellhausen) and deserves greater recognition. These scholars brought the *analysis* of the Pentateuch to a state which received only relatively minor modification at the hands of those such as Wellhausen, whose work was to become the classical account of Pentateuchal origins and indeed remained so until very recently. Hupfeld's contribution at least was fully recognized: Wellhausen, for example, wrote in his own work on the composition of the Hexateuch: 'I make Hupfeld in every respect my starting-point.' Where he and subsequent scholarship departed from Hupfeld was in the chronological *order* in which the sources were to be placed.

6. Two changes were in fact made. One, the placing of the YHWH-source—what we now call J—before the second Elohim-source—what we now call E—did not make a fundamental difference to the time at which either source was thought to have been written, and we shall not spend long on it. Once Hupfeld had made the separation between E and P it was really inevitable, as it was the supposed antiquity of the P texts which had led to the idea that the Book of Origins was the earliest source. When E was detached from this, it could easily be seen that in certain respects it had a more sophisticated approach to religion than the rather primitive J, and so it was natural to date it a little later.

7. The second change in order was much more decisive, in fact it was quite revolutionary. According to both the Supplementary Hypothesis and Hupfeld's theory, the oldest part of the Pentateuch was a Book of Origins that began with the account of creation in Gen 1 and included most of the priestly laws in Exodus, Leviticus, and Numbers. Doubts about the antiquity of these texts had already been expressed in the 1830s, but detailed critical arguments only began to appear in the early 1860s. One can see this in the work of the Dutch scholar Abraham Kuenen (1828–91), whose *Introduction to the OT* began to be published in 1861. Kuenen, who accepted Hupfeld's division of the Book of Origins into earlier and later layers, also held that the priestly laws in the supposedly earlier layer were not in fact all ancient but had developed over a long period of time, some of them being later in date than Deuteronomy. An even more radical conclusion had been reached by a German schoolteacher, Karl Heinrich Graf, who on 7 October 1862 wrote to his former OT professor, one Eduard Reuss, 'I am completely convinced of the fact that the whole middle part of the Pentateuch [apparently Exodus 25 to the end of Numbers] is post-exilic in origin,' i.e. it all belongs to the final, not the first, stage of the growth of the Pentateuch, after the writing of Deuteronomy. Wellhausen himself, looking back on his early student days, also in the early 1860s, wrote that he had been puzzled at the lack of reference to the allegedly very old priestly laws in the early historical books such as Samuel and Kings and in the prophets, though he had no idea at the time why this was. It was not until 1865 that these very new ideas came out into the open, when Graf published his views in book form. But while he maintained that all the legal parts of the Book of Origins were post-exilic in origin, he still held to the traditional early date for its narratives. In response to the appearance of Graf's book Kuenen now argued that the Book of Origins could not be divided up in this way, because the narratives were intimately related to the laws; so, if (as Graf had so powerfully demonstrated) the laws were late in origin, the narratives associated with them in the 'earlier' part of the Book of Origins must be late too. Graf's letter to Kuenen accepting the validity of this point survives—it is dated 12 Nov. 1866—and subsequently Graf put this change of mind into print in an article in which he responded to various criticisms of his book, though the article only came out in 1869 after Graf's death. In this way the order (as represented by the modern symbols) P-E-J-D of Hupfeld was transformed into the J-E-D-P that became standard.

8. It is clear that Abraham Kuenen played a very important part in the development of this revised theory, although it (like Knobel's contribution) is often overlooked. What is interesting is that Kuenen gave a great deal of the credit for the contribution which he himself was able to make to John Colenso's series of volumes entitled *The Pentateuch and The Book of Joshua Critically Examined*. These books were one reason why an attempt was made to depose Colenso from the see of Natal, which he held, an attempt which was only the beginning of a long wrangle in the Anglican Church in South Africa. Much of what Colenso wrote merely echoed what was already being done in Germany, but in the first volume of the study he presented what seemed to him to be a devastating attack on the genuineness of the narratives of the Book of Origins and particularly the large numbers which they give for the participants in the Exodus (e.g. Ex 12:37), the very thing which had seemed to others a guarantee of the accuracy and

antiquity of the source; on the contrary, argued Colenso, it was quite impossible that the numbers could represent real historical facts: they must be fictional. This argument so impressed Kuenen that he found no difficulty at all in regarding those narratives, as well as the priestly laws which Graf had examined, as a late and artificial composition.

9. It is evident from all this that the classical documentary theory of Pentateuchal origins owes little or nothing, as far as its origin is concerned, to Wellhausen: this was mainly the work of Hupfeld, Graf, and Kuenen, themselves of course building on much earlier work. To call it 'the Wellhausen theory', as is often done, is a misnomer, though a revealing one. What the new theory still needed, and what Wellhausen was to provide, was a presentation of it which would convince the many scholars who still held either to the Supplementary Hypothesis or to Hupfeld's version of the documentary theory. The work in which Wellhausen did this so successfully was originally called *History of Israel. Volume I (Geschichte Israels I)*—when no further volumes appeared this was changed to *Prolegomena to the History of Israel (Prolegomena zur Geschichte Israels)*—and it was published in 1878. It is still worth reading and its thorough attention to detail, its treatment of evidence from all parts of the OT, and the force and vigour of its arguments still make a strong impression on the reader.

10. Two criticisms are often made of it. The first is that it embodies a Hegelian view of history which has been imposed upon the data of the OT (so e.g. W. F. Albright and R. K. Harrison). This is not justified as a criticism of Wellhausen's method of working, whatever similarities may be traced between some of his conclusions and those of Hegel-inspired history-writing. It is a complicated issue but essentially it seems that what Wellhausen did was to approach the Pentateuch as a secular ancient historian would approach his primary sources in an effort to discover their character and closeness to the events described: his presuppositions and methods are those of a historian rather than those of a philosopher, and not significantly different from those with which more recent historians have worked. Where he does refer to Hegel once it seems to be an implied criticism. The other criticism is that Wellhausen presented his theory in isolation from knowledge of the ancient Near East, which makes it of no more than antiquarian interest: so Harrison again and especially K. A. Kitchen. Wellhausen did not of course have the benefit of knowing many of the archaeological discoveries of subsequent years, and what he did know he did not regard as of primary importance for interpreting the OT (unlike Gunkel: see below). But the main structure of his source-critical arguments has seemed to most subsequent scholars to be unaffected by these discoveries, rightly in my opinion. Where they have departed from them it has been because they sensed weaknesses in his treatment of the OT evidence, and not because of fresh evidence from the ancient Near East.

11. This brief historical introduction to the origins of the so-called Graf–Wellhausen theory about the sources of the Pentateuch should have removed some misconceptions about it, and in particular it has shown that far from being the product of one man's mind it was arrived at through a process of research and discussion which lasted over several decades

and involved a number of different scholars in several countries. But it also begins to open up a topic of quite central importance at the present time when some very searching questions are once again being asked about the validity of what, for brevity, we may continue to call Wellhausen's theory.

C. The Logic of Source-Criticism. It is in fact possible to distinguish, logically at least and to some extent chronologically as well, four stages in the argument which led to the formulation of Wellhausen's account of the origins of the Pentateuch, and if we define them appropriately we shall find that they are quite generally applicable to all attempts to analyse the Pentateuch into its constituent parts, and indeed to all attempts at discovering what sources were used in biblical and other writings.

1. The first step was the acceptance that an enquiry into the sources of the Pentateuch was permissible at all, i.e. that it was *not ruled out by the tradition* which regarded Moses as the author of the whole Pentateuch. This tradition goes back to the NT and contemporary writings, though it is probably not implied by anything in the OT text itself. Clearly if this tradition is not open to question, there is little room for Pentateuchal criticism of any kind: one could only enquire into the sources that Moses may have used for the writing of Genesis, which is exactly what one early work of criticism, published in 1753, purported to uncover (Jean Astruc's *Conjectures sur les mémoires originaux dont il paroit que Moyse s'est servi pour composer le livre de la Genèse*). The reasons for questioning the tradition of Mosaic authorship of the Pentateuch are broadly of two kinds: (1) the relatively late date of the first appearance of this tradition (not at any rate before the Babylonian exile); (2) various data in the Pentateuch itself which seem to be inconsistent with it: an obvious one is the account of Moses' death (Deut 34).

2. The second step was the *analysis* of the text, the demonstration of its lack of unity in detail. In the eighteenth century, well before the formulation of the Wellhausen theory, theories had been developed to account for what seemed to be signs of composite authorship, or the use of sources. Some passages, such as the Flood Story, appeared to arise from the combination of two originally separate accounts of the same event. In other cases it seemed unlikely or even impossible that two separate passages could have belonged to the same continuous account, the two creation stories for example. In the history of Pentateuchal criticism the distinction between this, analytical, stage of the enterprise and the next stage, synthesis or the attribution of passages or parts of passages to a particular source or layer of the Pentateuch, has not always been carefully observed. Indeed a clear distinction is perhaps not to be found before the handbook of Wolfgang Richter (*Exegese als Literaturwissenschaft*, 1971). But the two operations can and should be regarded as separate. To put it in a quite general formula: if ABCD represents a section of the Pentateuch, the assertion that A is of separate origin from B and that C is of separate origin from D is one thing; but the question of whether A belongs to the same source as C or D or neither, for example, is another question, and different answers to it will produce different theories about the larger sources of the Pentateuch.

So on what basis is it argued that the Pentateuch is of composite origin? Four main kinds of *criteria* have commonly been used:

1. repeated accounts of the same action or story.
2. the occurrence of statements (or commands) that are incompatible or inconsistent with each other.
3. vocabulary and style—the use of different words for the same thing, including e.g. different names for God; and variations of style.
4. the appearance of different viewpoints on matters of religion in particular, but also on other matters.

Two observations on these criteria should be made at this stage: their use will be clarified by an example later on.

1. The argument for disunity is strongest when several of these criteria occur together—so for example in the analysis of Gen 1–3.
2. In recent years it has been generally realized that criteria 3 and 4 are of far less value for analysis, at least when they occur alone, than 1 and 2. Variations in relation to 3 and 4 may perfectly well occur within a single account (so Noth 1972 and Westermann 1984). In fact it is much more at the next, constructive, stage that such factors enter in, by suggesting which of the various fragments into which the Pentateuch has been analysed have a common origin, i.e. belong to the same source or layer.

3. The third step is the development of hypotheses about *the major constituent parts* of the Pentateuch and their interrelation. Various *models* are possible, of which the idea that a number of independent source-documents have been combined is only the best-known because it is the pattern exemplified by the classical Documentary Hypothesis of Graf, Kuenen, and Wellhausen. Other 'models' are possible, however, and indeed have been tried, such as that the Pentateuch is simply a conglomeration of small units put together by an editor (the Fragmentary Hypothesis) or that an original core was amplified by the addition of fresh material, either material that had previously existed independently as small units or new material that was composed for the first time for the purpose of modifying the existing core (a Supplementary Hypothesis such as that which was dominant in the middle of the 19th cent.). It is also possible, and in fact common today, to have a combined theory which exhibits features of all three models.

With all of these models (except the Fragmentary theory) there is the problem of *attribution*, deciding what material belongs to the same source or stage of supplementation. Sometimes this can be determined by what we may call narrative continuity: i.e. an episode in the story presupposes that an earlier part of the story has been told in a particular way. For example, Gen 9:6, 'Whoever sheds the blood of a human, by a human shall that person's blood be shed; for in his own image God made humankind,' clearly presupposes the account of the creation of human beings in Gen 1:26–7 (note the reference to 'in his own image'), rather than that in Gen 2:7, and so they presumably belong to the same source or layer. Fortunately the character of the Pentateuch is such that this kind of argument can quite often be used. Where it cannot, one must have recourse to such factors as agreement

over criteria such as 3 and 4 at c.2 above to argue that sections of the Pentateuch have a common source.

4. The fourth step is that of arranging the sources (or supplements) in *chronological order* and dating them. It is in this area that Graf, Kuenen, and Wellhausen made a real innovation. In relation to c. 1, 2, and 3 they did little more than refine the results of their predecessors, especially Hupfeld: but on this point they made a radical change from him, in arguing that the Book of Origins/First Elohist (P) was the latest, not the earliest of the four sources, and in dating it to the post-exilic period. How are such conclusions reached, in general terms? Along two main lines, which must still be taken into consideration in any discussion of the matter:

4.1. The *relative age* of the sources can be considered in various ways: Does one source or layer take for granted the prior existence of another one? Is one source obviously more primitive in its way of presenting events, or its legal requirements, than another? Numerous examples of both these kinds of arguments can be found in Wellhausen's *Prolegomena* (1885). They can be cogent, but it must be pointed out that the argument from primitiveness to antiquity and from sophistication to lateness is a dangerous one, because it too quickly assumes that the religion of Israel developed in a single line with no setbacks or decline throughout its history or divergent patterns of religion coexisting at the same time. In practice the classical theory has relied much more heavily on arguments of a second kind.

4.2. The actual or *absolute dates* of the sources can be fixed by reference to evidence outside the Pentateuch. Such arguments can themselves be subdivided according to whether reference is being made to fixed points in the events of Israel's political and religious history (such as the Babylonian exile) as we know them from the historical books of the OT, or to doctrines (such as the demand for the centralization of worship in Jerusalem) whose first formulation we can date by reference to these same historical books and the writings of the prophets, for example. Even here it is fair to say that the strength of the arguments used varies, and where a link can be established with something like the Exile, it can still be difficult to deduce a very precise date for the source in question. But for all that, it has seemed possible to define in broad terms the time when the various source-documents were put into their definitive form. I emphasize that last phrase because when scholars assign a date to a source they are not saying that this is when it was suddenly created out of nothing. They recognize that much of the material in the sources is older than the sources themselves, it comes from earlier tradition. What they are looking for when they date a source is the latest element within it, because that will show when it reached its definitive form.

D. An Example of a Source-Critical Argument: The Analysis of the Flood Story (Gen 6–9) into its sources. 1. Now we shall move back from theory to practice, and look at some of the detailed claims made by the classical theory associated with Wellhausen and the arguments that were used to support them. Historically, Pentateuchal source-criticism seems to have begun with the observation that Genesis opens with not one but two different *accounts of creation* (so already H. B. Witter in 1711): 1:1–2:3 (or 2:4*a*) and 2:4 (or 2:4*b*)–25). The second repeats a number of events already described in the first, but not in exactly the same order, and with some notable differences in presentation. The difference that was to be put to most productive use in subsequent scholarship was, of course, the difference over the divine names: the fact that whereas the first account refers to God only by the word 'God' (*'ĕlōhîm*); the second used the compound phrase 'the Lord God' = YHWH *'ĕlōhîm*, combining with the word 'God' the proper name by which Israel knew her God, YHWH.

2. According to the word used to refer to God, the second account of creation was referred to as 'Yahwistic' and given the symbol J. J was used (after the German form, *jahwistisch*) because the abbreviations were worked out in Germany and the 'y' sound is represented by 'j' in German. The first account could be and was for a time called Elohistic (E), although this description of it was given up after Hupfeld's discovery that there were two major source-documents which avoided the name YHWH in Genesis. This source is known today as the Priestly Code, or Priestly Work (abbreviated as P), because of the prominent place given to priesthood and ritual in its later parts, particularly in the books from Exodus to Numbers. *The early history of mankind*, prior to the Flood, is also described twice, once in the form of a series of stories (chs. 3–4, 6:1–4), and once in the form of a genealogy (ch. 5). The first of these connects directly with ch. 3, while the second has various similarities to ch. 1, so they were attributed to J and P respectively.

3. In *the Flood story* (6:5–9:17) things are not so tidy. Does it belong to J or P? Uses of the name YHWH do occur, but only in restricted parts of the story (6:5–8; 7:1–5, 16; 8:20–2): elsewhere the word 'God' (*'ĕlōhîm*) is employed. Thus the story is hardly typical of P, which avoids YHWH, but yet it is not typical of J either, which uses YHWH much more consistently. What is one to make of this situation? Should one attribute the Flood story to a third source occupying an intermediate position with regard to the divine names between P and J? Or has either J or P changed its practice at this point?

4. Careful attention to the details of the story suggests that neither of these solutions is correct. We may note that there are a surprising number of repetitions or overlaps of details in it. Thus (1) vv. 5–7 describe how YHWH saw the evil which men did on the earth and declared that he would therefore destroy the human race. When, after three verses referring specifically to Noah, we come to vv. 11–13 we find another reference, this time to God seeing the corruption of 'all flesh' and saying that he will therefore destroy it. (2) The paragraph then continues with instructions to Noah about how the ark is to be built (vv. 14–16), how Noah and his family are to enter it (vv. 17–18) and how he is to take a pair of every kind of living creature with him (vv. 19–21). And this, we are told, is exactly what Noah did, 'he did all that God commanded him' (v. 22). It therefore comes as something of a surprise when, in 7:1–4, we find YHWH telling Noah again to enter the ark with his family and the animals, and it again being said (v. 5) that Noah did as he was told. (3) By the time we get to the actual entry into the ark we are more prepared for repetitions, and we are not disappointed: 7:7–9 make explicit that Noah, his family, and the animals entered the ark, apparently with plenty of time to spare, as it was another 7 days before the flood started (v. 10). Then the rain began (vv. 11–12), and then we are told again that

Noah, his family, and the animals all went into the ark, cutting it a bit fine this time we may suppose! It is a strange way to tell a story, and there are further curiosities to follow which we must forgo because of shortage of space, as we must do also with some details of the explanation which seems to be required to do justice to them.

5. But let us consider again the first two cases of repetition, in a slightly different way. We have in the paragraph 6:11–22 a speech of God to Noah with introduction and conclusion, a passage which makes perfectly coherent sense. But before it are two verses which parallel vv. 11–13, and after it are five verses which parallel vv. 17–22. And the striking thing is that whereas 6:11–22 use the word God (vv. 11, 12, 13, 22), the parallel passages placed before and after it use YHWH (6:5, 6, 7; 7:1, 5). That is, we seem to have here two versions of a part of the Flood story, one of them, like the creation account in Gen 2, using the name YHWH, the other, like the creation account in Gen 1, avoiding it and using *'ĕlōhîm* instead. But instead of being placed one after the other, as with the creation accounts, the two versions of the Flood story have been interwoven, with sections from one alternating with sections of the other. This interpretation of the situation is strengthened by two additional factors:

1. tensions or contradictions within the story which seem likely to be due to the combination of two different versions of it; e.g. the number of pairs of animals taken into the ark (one pair according to 6:19–20; seven pairs of clean animals, i.e. those that could be eaten, and of birds, but only one pair of the unclean animals according to 7:2–3).
2. the fact that when the whole story is analysed, one is left with two substantially complete accounts of the Flood, one showing affinities (including the name YHWH) with the second creation account and the other showing affinities with the first.

One or two details remain unclear but the majority of scholars are agreed on something very like the following analysis: (*a*) 6:5–8; 7:1–5, 7–10, 12, 16b–17, 22–3; 8:2b–3a, 6–12, 13b, 20–2 (= J); (*b*) 6:9–22; 7:6, 11, 13–16a, 18–21, 24; 8:1–2a, 3b–5, 13a, 14–19; 9:1–17 (= P). A more detailed presentation of the argument can be found in the commentaries on Genesis by S. R. Driver (1904: 85–6) and J. Skinner (1910: 147–50); cf. Habel (1971: 14–15).

6. This brief but important example will give an idea of how the analysis of the Pentateuch proceeds in the classical documentary hypothesis. It is work of this kind which lies behind the lists of passages belonging to J, E, D, and P in the standard introductions to the OT. There are, it should be said, some passages where scholars have not been unanimous about the recognition of the sources, and here caution is necessary. The following sketch will give a general idea of what has been thought to belong to each of the four sources:

Genesis: Chs. 1–11 are formed from J (2:4b–4:26; 6:1–4; part of the Flood Story (see above); 9:18–27; parts of 10; 11:1–9) and P (1:1–2:4a; most of 5; the rest of the Flood Story; 9:28–9; the rest of 10; most of 11:10–32); most of chs. 12–50 come from J (including 12–13; 18; most of 19 and 24), E (including most of 20–2 and 40–2), and P (17; 23; 28:1–9; 35:9–13; and most of the genealogies).

Exodus: Chs. 1–24 are again made up of extracts from J, E, and P. The only passages of any length which are clearly from E are 1:15–21 and 3:9–15. P is the source of 6:2–7:13; 12:1–20, 40–51, and various shorter passages. Traditionally the Decalogue (20:1–17) and the Book of the Covenant (20:22–23:33) were ascribed to E, but it is now widely doubted if they appeared in any of the main sources. Chs. 32–4 are usually thought to have been based on J and E (32 E; 34 J; 33 parts from both), but they may be all J except for some late editorial additions. Chs. 25–31 and 35–40 are all from P.

Leviticus: The whole book, together with Num 1:1–10:28, is from P, though it is clear that already existing collections of laws have been incorporated in Lev 1–7 and Lev 17–26 (the latter section being known as the Holiness Code = H).

Numbers: The rest of the book, from 10:29, is again a mixture of J, E, and P. E is most clearly present in the story of Balaam (ch. 23 and some verses in 22). P provided the sections of chs. 16–18 that deal with the revolt of Korah and the vindication of the Aaronite priesthood, most of 25:6–36:13, and some other passages; again older documents (including the wilderness itinerary in ch. 33) have been worked in.

Deuteronomy: from the D source, with the exception of a few passages, mostly at the end. But an original core in 4:45–29:1 from pre-exilic times can be distinguished from a framework placed around it in the Babylonian Exile (so esp. chs. 4 and 29–30).

7. Fuller details can be found, (1) in commentaries, among which special mention should be made of the 'Polychrome Bible', published from 1893 onwards, in which the sections drawn from the various sources were marked in different colours, a custom which has been widely followed by theological students in their own copies of the Bible as an *aide-mémoire* (The proper title of the series was The Sacred Books of the OT, gen. ed. P. Haupt. A less colourful way of achieving the same end is by using different typefaces, as in von Rad's commentary on Genesis and Noth's on Exodus in the Old Testament Library series, where the P sections are printed in italics and the rest in ordinary type); and (2) in a synopsis of the Pentateuch, like those which are produced to show the relationships between the Synoptic Gospels, though they are hard to come by in English (but see Carpenter and Harford-Battersby (1900), ii; Campbell and O'Brien (1993) gives the texts of the sources separately, but not in parallel columns).

E. A Second Example: The Dating of the Priestly Source (P). 1.
The second example of source criticism to be given here concerns the dating of the sources (step c.4), and in particular *the claim that P is the latest* of the four. Wellhausen used two kinds of argument to establish this view. First he noted the almost unbroken silence of the older historical books, Samuel and Kings, with regard to the distinctive institutions of the cult prescribed by P (the tabernacle, detailed laws about sacrifice, the Day of Atonement, the limitation of full priesthood to the descendants of Aaron, and the development of tithing as a means of support for the priests). In view of the fact that these books have plenty to say about ritual, this must imply that these institutions were not yet known in the pre-exilic period. It follows that P could not yet have been written. The specific reference to 'the older historical books' is deliberate, so as to exclude the books of Chronicles. The force of this argument

could only be felt when a true appreciation of the late date and largely fictional character of Chronicles had been gained, and the dating of P is closely connected with the study of Chronicles. Graf's epoch-making essay of 1865 on the Pentateuch was published along with a study of the books of Chronicles, while Wellhausen devoted more than 50 pages of the *Prolegomena* to them. Chronicles does relate the existence of institutions characteristic of P in the pre-exilic period, and it was only when it had been shown that these elements of the Chronicler's account were fictional that a clear view of the nature of pre-exilic religion could be obtained, and so the necessity of a late date for P established.

2. The second kind of argument was based on the relationship of the laws and narratives of P to the laws in Deuteronomy and the final chapters of Ezekiel. The origin of Deuteronomy in the eighth or seventh century BCE was generally regarded in the mid-nineteenth century as having been established beyond doubt by the critical arguments of W. M. L. de Wette and others, and Ezekiel was of course a prophet of the early sixth century. In a number of ways it was argued that the Priestly texts must be later than those in Deuteronomy and Ezekiel. This is not just a simple evolutionary argument, saying that the practices referred to by P must by their very character lie at the end of a long process of development. The argument is rather that in some cases Deuteronomy and Ezekiel make no reference to features of P which one might have expected them to mention if it were indeed a document of pre-exilic origin; while elsewhere what Deuteronomy and Ezekiel prescribe would make no sense if P already existed.

3. As an example we will look at Wellhausen's argument in the case of admission to the priesthood (1885: 121–51). The crucial points in the argument are set out in the first few pages of the chapter (pp. 121–7), but Wellhausen believed that they received some confirmation from the more thorough account of the history of the priesthood which follows. He begins by summarizing the regulations about priesthood in the P sections of Exodus–Numbers. He points out that there are two important distinctions made in them: the first between the Levites and the twelve secular tribes, which is vividly reflected in the arrangement of the camp in Num 2; and the second between the Levites and the sons, or descendants, of Aaron, which receives, to quote Wellhausen, 'incomparably greater emphasis'. He continues: 'Aaron and his sons alone are priests, qualified for sacrificing and burning incense; the Levites are *hieroduli* [temple servants], bestowed on the Aaronidae for the discharge of the inferior services.' The unique privilege of the descendants of Aaron is underlined in the story of the Korahite rebellion in Num 16–18. The setting apart of the two priestly groups is the result of two separate acts of a quite different character. First Aaron is chosen by YHWH to be a priest (Ex 28:1–5), and then later the Levites are given their role, by being offered at YHWH's bidding by the people as a substitute for their firstborn who, according to the law, belonged to YHWH (Num 3:40–4:49; cf. also ch. 18).

4. This picture of the demarcation of the Aaronide and Levite groups is located by P at Mount Sinai in the time of Moses—but how ancient is it really? Wellhausen believed that the answer was to be found in Ezek 44:6–16, a passage from the early years of the Babylonian exile (40:1 refers to the year 573), which both refers to pre-exilic practices on admission to

the priesthood and prescribes what practices shall be followed in this matter in the future. According to this account, in the pre-exilic temple in Jerusalem ('my sanctuary') the menial tasks had been performed by foreigners (44:8), a practice of which Ezekiel very strongly disapproved. And in the future, he says, these tasks are to be performed by Levites (vv. 9–14). Not however in accordance with a role assigned to them by the people in ancient times—of this explanation (the one given by P) Ezekiel says not a word—but as a punishment for their sins in the pre-exilic period. 'They shall bear their punishment', it says in vv. 10 and 12 (cf. v. 13b). This only makes sense as a degradation from a previously higher position, which was no doubt that of full priesthood, which the Levites had enjoyed previously to this (cf. v. 13a). That Levites were full priests in pre-exilic times is implied also by Deuteronomy (cf. ch. 18). To what is their punishment due? It is because they 'went astray from me after their idols when Israel went astray' (v. 10—cf. v. 12). This evidently refers to service at the high places or bāmôt outside Jerusalem: because those who had been priests at the Jerusalem temple, 'my sanctuary' (vv. 15–16), are explicitly excluded from blame and are to retain an exclusive right to full priesthood in the future: they are called 'the sons of Zadok' after Zadok the priest under David and Solomon. The antithesis between the Jerusalem temple, the one place of legitimate worship, and all other shrines had of course been at the heart of the reform programme of King Josiah (640–609) half a century earlier which, as described in 2 Kings 23, was inspired by the somewhat earlier prescriptions of Deuteronomy (cf. esp. Deut 12:1–14). Ezek 44 is fully at one with Josiah and the Deuteronomists on this point though he differs from Deuteronomy on the extent of the priesthood for the future. He agrees with P that most Levites are to have an inferior role, but he gives a completely different reason for it and he has a different view about what they were originally meant to do.

5. The relationship between what Ezekiel says and the regulations of P is most forcibly expressed in two quotations, one from Wellhausen himself and the other from Kuenen. First Wellhausen:

What he [Ezekiel] regards as the original right of the Levites, the performance of priestly services, is treated in the latter document [P] as an unfounded and highly wicked pretension which once in the olden times brought destruction upon Korah and his company [Wellhausen is referring to the (P) story of the rebellion of Korah in Num 16–17]; what he [Ezekiel] considers to be a subsequent withdrawal of their right, as a degradation in consequence of a fault, the other [P] holds to have been their hereditary and natural destination. The distinction between priest and Levite which Ezekiel introduces and justifies as an innovation, according to the Priestly Code has always existed; what in the former appears as a beginning, in the latter has been in force ever since Moses—an original datum, not a thing that has become or been made. That the prophet [Ezekiel] should know nothing about a priestly law with whose tendencies he is in thorough sympathy admits of only one explanation—that it did not then exist.   (1885: 124)

The quotation from Kuenen uses an analogy which is particularly comprehensible in Britain: 'If by reason of their birth it was already impossible for the Levites to become priests [as P lays down], then it would be more than strange to deprive them of the priesthood on account of their faults—much as if one were to threaten the commons with the punishment of

being disqualified from sitting or voting in the House of Lords' (ibid.). This was written before the introduction of life peerages! One may put the essential argument as follows: if P had been in existence in 573, Ezekiel surely would have developed his argument in a different way.

6. For these reasons, then, Wellhausen concluded that the regulations about the priesthood, which are absolutely central to P, could not have originated before Ezekiel, but only afterwards. Arguments of similar kinds were brought forward to justify a late date for other aspects of the ritual system prescribed by P. But how much later than Ezekiel was P to be dated? Quite a lot later, according to Wellhausen (ibid. 404–10). He took as his point of departure the statement in Ezra 7:14 that when Ezra came from Babylon to Jerusalem in 458 BCE he had the law of God in his hand. This Wellhausen understood to be a new law book, which consisted of the completed Pentateuch, incorporating not only the older sources J, E, and D but the Priestly Code, which had quite recently been compiled. He seems to have believed that the completed Pentateuch (and the new Priestly Code) must owe its authority to some act of authorization, and only Ezra's mission seemed to be available to meet this requirement. According to Wellhausen, Neh 8–10 describes Ezra's publication and the people's acceptance of the new (or rather partly new) law code, and these events are dated not earlier than 444 BCE (compare Neh 1:1 with 8:2). This, Wellhausen held, gave the approximate date when the Priestly Code was written up and combined with the older Pentateuchal sources. A different kind of argument which lends some support to this position was used by Kuenen: early post-exilic literature, such as the books of the prophets Haggai and Zechariah, shows no awareness of the P legislation. The book of Malachi, probably from the early fifth century BCE, is especially significant, as it says quite a lot about priests, but calls them Levites, not sons of Aaron. By contrast the Chronicler, writing some time after 400 BCE is clearly familiar with P's regulations. So a date within the fifth century becomes likely on this argument too.

7. In the last quarter of the nineteenth century a majority of scholars gradually came to accept the conclusions of the Newer Documentary Hypothesis, as the viewpoint propounded by Graf, Kuenen, and Wellhausen came to be known. In essence they held that the Pentateuch had been composed from four documents or sources, whose dates and places of origin were as follows:

J   9th cent., Judah
E   8th cent., northern kingdom of Israel
D   7th cent., Judah
P   5th cent., Babylon

8. There have, however, from the beginning been those who repudiated this position vociferously. In Britain and the United States today the best-known opponents of the theory are among conservative evangelical Christians. In an earlier generation scholars such as J. Orr and A. H. Finn, later E. J. Young and G. C. Aalders, and most recently K. A. Kitchen and R. K. Harrison, sought to minimize the force of such arguments as those which we have been considering. But opposition came from other quarters too. In the Roman Catholic church the theory became a matter of controversy in the first decade of the twentieth century and the Pontifical Biblical Commission

decreed in 1906 that the Mosaic authorship of the Pentateuch was not a subject that was open to discussion. This ban lasted until the 1940s. Some Jewish scholars too have been resolutely opposed to the documentary theory, e.g. U. Cassuto and M. H. Segal of Jerusalem, but others have disagreed only at one particular point, the rejection of the idea that P is the latest of the documents (see below). Among Protestant Christian scholars there has been a further group consisting mainly of Scandinavian scholars, who, for a distinctive reason, have rejected many of the conclusions of the documentary theory. The leader of this group was I. Engnell of Uppsala, who wrote mainly in Swedish. Engnell proposed to replace the dominant theories by the use of what he called 'the traditio-historical method', which as far as the Pentateuch was concerned meant that its origin lay not in the combination of written sources for the most part but in developments that took place while the stories etc. were being transmitted orally, by word of mouth, a process which, according to Engnell, only ended at the time of the Babylonian exile or even later. The enthusiasm which Engnell's approach generated seems now to have waned, and it belongs for the most part to the history of Pentateuchal study rather than to its present concerns.

9. There have also been several modifications proposed to the classical theory. Some scholars have taken up a suspicion already expressed by Wellhausen himself that the J material in Gen 1–11 is not an original unity, and have gone on to argue that the whole of J is the result of the combination of two originally separate sources or the enlargement of the original J by additions. This is only a minority view, but it has obtained wide publicity through its presentation in two *Introductions* that were at one time popular, those of Otto Eissfeldt and Georg Fohrer. Eissfeldt called the extra source L ('Lay Source', because of the absence of cultic material) and Fohrer called it N ('Nomadic Source', because it seemed opposed to settled life), but both attribute much the same passages to it: e.g. in Gen 1–11 Fohrer ascribed a few verses in chs 2–3 to N, as well as 4:17–24 and 11:1–9, all it is said expressing the frustration of man's attempts to develop. Similar subdivisions have been proposed of the other sources, with more justification in the cases of D and P, but hardly so in the case of E.

10. In fact it has been repeatedly suspected that E is not a true source at all, that is that the passages attributed to it do not belong to a single continuous account of Israel's early history (partial rejection of step c.3 in the systematic presentation). Two German scholars, P. Volz and W. Rudolph, pressed the case for this view between the First and Second World Wars, and Noth was influenced by it to some extent, although he never gave up a belief in E altogether. The problem was that what were supposed to be the remnants of E seemed to show neither the completeness nor the theological unity that appears in J. However, important defences of the existence of E as an independent source have been put forward (Brueggemann and Wolff 1975: 67–82; Jenks 1977).

11. A further kind of modification, or rather extension, of the theory has been the claim that the Pentateuchal sources extend into the following books of the OT, the historical books. This is quite widely held for Joshua, but it was also maintained by some scholars for Judges, Samuel, and even parts of Kings (so Eissfeldt, C. A. Simpson). There are certainly some signs of duplicate or parallel narratives in these books, especially in

1 Samuel, but few scholars today accept this explanation of them.

12. Despite all these modifications and even rejections of the theory, the great majority of OT scholars were prepared, after the early years of debate, to accept it substantially as it left Wellhausen's hands. This was true, in recent times, of the major figures in Britain (e.g. Rowley, G. W. Anderson), Germany (von Rad, Noth, Weiser) and America (Albright, Bright). For close on a century the view that the Pentateuch was composed from the four documents J, E, D, and P, which originated in that order, belonged to what used to be called the assured results of Old Testament criticism. This was an unfortunate phrase, and it would have been better to speak of the dominant or most satisfactory theory: neither a proven fact nor mere speculation, but a plausible account of the phenomena of the text. It needs to be emphasized that Mosaic authorship is also a theory: all that we *know* is that the Pentateuch existed by about the fourth century BCE. And Mosaic authorship is a theory which seems to account less well for the phenomena than critical theories; so at least the majority of scholars have believed. And since this theory seemed a solid foundation to them, their fresh thinking about the Pentateuch was until recently generally not about source criticism but proceeded along two rather different lines of enquiry: (1) the study of the traditions, both narrative and law, in the *preliterary stage* of their history, before they were incorporated into the Pentateuchal source-documents; (2) the definition of the particular *theological content* of the different source-documents.

F. The Preliterary Origins of the Pentateuch. 1. By 1900 the source-critical theory was in need of a corrective of a much more fundamental kind than any of those mentioned so far, for both historical and literary reasons. On the one hand there had opened up a significant gap between the dates attributed to even the earliest sources of the Pentateuch (9th–8th cents. BCE) and the period which they purported to describe, which ended about 1200 BCE or even earlier. How much, if any, real historical information had survived this passage of time? Was it necessary to conclude, as Wellhausen (1885: 318–19) tended to imply, that the sources could inform us only about conditions in the time when they were written? On the other hand, the investigations of the source-critics had isolated the Pentateuch from the life of the people of ancient Israel, and left the text as a product of writers and redactors who were to some extent created in the image of the scholars who studied them—an intellectual *élite* far removed from ordinary people. Was it really from such circles that the Pentateuch had ultimately originated? These are in fact very topical issues for biblical scholarship at the present time, when interest has reverted to the discussion of sources and especially the work of redactors or editors. Although there are some more positive aspects of the situation now, this preoccupation with the later, literary stages of composition poses exactly the same threat today to a historical and living appreciation of the Pentateuch as it did around 1900. Then the way forward was marked out by Hermann Gunkel, who was in fact much more of a pioneering, original thinker than Wellhausen. His correctives are as much needed today as they ever were.

2. In 1901 Gunkel (1862–1932) published a commentary on the book of Genesis, with a long introduction which was separately published and also translated into English under the title *The Legends of Genesis*. The change of perspective can very quickly and easily be seen if we compare the contents of this introduction with the introductions to other commentaries on Genesis which appeared in the years immediately before 1901, such as that of H. Holzinger of 1898. (In English Driver (1904) still shows the pre-Gunkel approach.) Holzinger's introduction of some 18 pages included the following subsections: Content of the Hexateuch and of Genesis; Tradition about the Author; History of Criticism [i.e. source criticism]; the source J; the source E; the source P; the Combination of the Sources. This clearly reflects, almost exclusively, the preoccupations of the source critics. Although Holzinger was aware that the material in J and E was ultimately derived from popular oral tradition, as indeed Wellhausen had been before him, he was not apparently interested in, or perhaps capable of, exploring the character of this 'popular oral tradition'.

3. The contrast with Gunkel's introduction could hardly be greater. Its first subsection has a polemical title which sums up the whole thesis: 'Genesis is a collection of legends (German *Sagen*)'—the English translation waters this down to 'The Significance and Scope of the Legends'. Then follow sections on 'The Varieties of the Legends'; 'The Artistic Form of the Legends'; 'History of the Transmission of the Legends in Oral Tradition'. These four sections, all of them dealing with the stages of tradition prior to the written sources, comprise about 80 pages, that is over three-quarters of a much enlarged introduction. Only after this does Gunkel bring in two more traditional-sounding sections: one on 'Yahwist, Elohist, the Older Collections' (but note how what were 'sources' are now 'collections', reflecting the change of perspective); the other on 'The Priestly Code and Final Redaction'. An English commentary which shows the influence of Gunkel's work was J. Skinner's International Critical Commentary, published in 1910: sections 2–5 of the introduction are taken over almost directly from Gunkel.

4. There were in fact two basic changes of approach with Gunkel: (1) *chronologically*, he dug deeper, there is the concentration on the preliterary form of the tradition, instead of the written sources of Genesis themselves, as we have seen; and changes in the tradition at the earlier stage are regarded as a possible and indeed necessary subject for study; (2) but there is also, *analytically*, a transfer of attention away from long connected narratives to individual sections or episodes, each of which turns out to comprise a more or less self-contained story, which Gunkel believed had once existed independently of the larger narrative context. These two new departures are interconnected, but it may be said with good reason that the first of them led to *tradition criticism*, as particularly practised later by von Rad and Noth, while the second gave rise to *form criticism*, which is where Gunkel himself made his main contribution. In fact both of these methods were designed by Gunkel to reach a higher goal, a more adequate account of the history of Hebrew literature, and his work is most accurately described as literary history: he could see that source criticism alone would never do justice to the art of the Hebrew writers.

5. The general principles of Gunkel's form-critical work on Genesis are the same as those used by him elsewhere, for example on the Psalms. Briefly we may distinguish: (1) determination of the literary genre; (2) classification of the material; and (3) the reconstruction of its social setting (*Sitz im Leben*).

6. Gunkel begins by making the general point that history-writing as we know it, and as it is represented in the later historical books of the OT, is not 'an innate endowment of the human mind'. 'Only at a certain stage of civilization has objectivity so grown and the interest in transmitting national experiences to posterity so increased that the writing of history becomes possible. Such history has for its subjects great public events, the deeds of popular leaders and kings, and especially wars.' Apart from such political organization, the past is remembered and cherished in the form of popular tradition, for which Gunkel used the genre-description *Sage* (pl. *Sagen*); 'legend' is a better English equivalent for this than saga, and perhaps 'tale' is best of all. The preservation of some historical memories in *Sage* is not ruled out—Gunkel speaks of 'the senseless confusion of legend with lying' in discussion of this issue—but at the same time strong emphasis is laid on the creativity of the story-tellers and it is significant that Gunkel followed up his remark that 'Legends are not lies' with 'on the contrary they are a particular form of poetry': this is perhaps a pointer to the kind of truth which he believed them to contain, it is more the truth of poetry, i.e. general truths about the (or a) human situation, than the truth of history. His argument that the stories in Genesis are to be classed as *Sagen* is quite a simple one. The basic difference, he says, between history-writing as a literary genre and *Sage* is that history-writing is a written composition, whereas *Sage*, as its derivation from the German word 'to say' shows, is a genre of oral tradition. The stories in Genesis, at least most of them, bear the marks of having been originally composed orally—he gives more detail later, but here mentions especially the existence of variant versions of essentially the same story (e.g. the patriarch who passed his wife off as his sister (Gen 12; 20; 26))—and therefore they are *Sagen*. In addition, the general lack of interest in political events, the long period between the events reported and their being put in written form, and the inclusion of numerous details that are, from a modern point of view, fantastic (such as Lot's wife turning into a pillar of salt: Gen 19:26), serve to confirm the general description as *Sagen*. This description of the stories as *Sagen* has important consequences for Gunkel's understanding of them which he illustrates by reference to the sacrifice of Isaac in Gen 22: 'The important matter [sc. for the narrator] is not to establish certain historical facts, but to impart to the hearer the heart-rending grief of the father who is commanded to sacrifice his child with his own hand, and then his boundless gratitude and joy when God's mercy releases him from this grievous trial.' The positive implications of using such language about the Genesis stories were to be developed further by Karl Barth (*Church Dogmatics*, iii. 1) as well as by Gerhard von Rad (in the introduction to his commentary on Genesis).

7. Gunkel went on to subdivide the *Sagen* of Genesis into various types, first of all making a sharp distinction between those of Gen 1–11, which tell of the ancestors of the human race as a whole, and Gen 12–50, which tell of the ancestors of particular peoples, especially Israel. Nowadays it seems

appropriate to use the terms 'myth' and 'legend' to distinguish these two types of story, but they were not often so used by Gunkel. Gen 12–50 was further subdivided into *Sagen* of different types: the two main ones being tribal legends and aetiological legends. The former (1) can be either (*a*) historical, if they represent events in the history of tribes, such as the treaty between Abraham or Isaac and Abimelech king of Gerar (21:22–34; 26) or the migrations of the various patriarchs from one place to another; or (*b*) ethnographic if they represent tribal relations, as in the stories of Jacob and Esau. Aetiological legends (2) are those whose purpose is to explain the origin of some aspect of contemporary experience, and they subdivide into (*a*) ethnological legends, which explain why different peoples live where they do, e.g. Gen 19; (*b*) etymological legends, which explain the meaning of names, e.g. Beersheba in Gen 21:31; (*c*) cultic legends, which explain why a place is holy, or a particular ritual act carried out (32:32); (*d*) geological legends, explaining features of the landscape (19:26). These categories are not mutually exclusive, a particular legend may exhibit the characteristics of two or more of them, e.g. Gen 22. This is the analysis worked out by Gunkel for the first edition of his commentary in 1901: an important consequence of it was that, while the aetiological legends were of little or no use for the historian, the tribal legends could (if read correctly) provide information about the history of the various tribes. In the course of his preoccupation with Genesis over the next few years Gunkel changed his mind over certain topics, and in particular he gave up the 'tribal' interpretation of groups (1)(*a*) and (1)(*b*) above and supposed instead that they too were based on folklore motifs and had no historical kernel at all.

8. Gunkel's account of the social setting of such stories is given in a chapter in which he attempts to formulate their literary character more clearly. 'The common situation which we have to suppose is this: In the leisure of a winter evening the family sits about the hearth; the grown people, but more especially the children, listen intently to the beautiful old stories of the dawn of the world, which they have heard so often yet never tire of hearing repeated.' It is to be noted, because of the contrast with von Rad and Noth, that it is a domestic scene that Gunkel reconstructed, not one of a cultic festival. He lived before the time when all (or nearly all) the OT was thought to be related to the setting of worship. In the remaining chapters he reconstructed the processes by which the originally separate stories were collected together, so as eventually to form the source-documents J and E—this is really tradition-history—and, as we have seen, went on to deal with the sources themselves and their combination together by the editors of the Pentateuch. Gunkel's views about the origins of Genesis have been enormously influential and have shaped subsequent research just as much as the documentary source-theory. They are not however satisfactory in every respect, as we shall see.

9. Form-critical study of the Pentateuch was extended to the stories involving Moses by Hugo Gressmann in 1913 and to the Pentateuchal laws by Albrecht Alt in 1934 (Alt 1966: 87–132: see further below), and many others followed them. But at the same time the study of the preliterary history of the Pentateuch began to be carried forward in a different way, which considered not isolated individual stories or laws but the overall structure of the Pentateuch, with its sequence of creation, patriarchs, Exodus, revelation at Sinai, wilderness wandering and conquest of Transjordan. Was this order of events, which already appeared in the J source, simply derived from the historical sequence of events; or was it to be explained as the result of some process or processes of development in the tradition which had oversimplified an originally more complicated story? We come with this to the traditio-historical work of von Rad and Noth (see on this especially Nicholson 1973).

10. Von Rad's very influential views on this subject are set out in a long essay published in 1938 and entitled 'The Form-Critical Problem of the Hexateuch' (von Rad 1966: 1–78). The reference to form criticism in the title is at first surprising but is justified by the use, at the beginning of the essay, of the basic principles of that discipline, the difference being that von Rad suggested applying them to the Hexateuch as a whole (like others before and since he believed that the book of Joshua was intimately linked with the Pentateuch) instead of only to the short episodes or pericopae from which it was made up. So he asks first about the literary genre of the Hexateuch in its final form, and answers that it is essentially a statement of faith, a creed: not just popular tradition, or history, but a historical creed. Then he proposed the question of other and especially earlier examples of this genre, the historical creed, in Israel, and coupled with it the question of its social setting or *Sitz im Leben*. He found the answers to these questions given above all in the prayer prescribed in Deut 26:5–9 to be said at the presentation of the first fruits of the harvest, in which the following 'confession of faith' bears a striking resemblance to the outline of the narrative of the Hexateuch:

A wandering Aramaean was my ancestor; he went down into Egypt and lived there as an alien, few in number; and there he became a great nation, mighty and populous. When the Egyptians treated us harshly and afflicted us, by imposing hard labour on us, we cried to the Lord, the God of our ancestors; the Lord heard our voice and saw our affliction, our toil and our oppression. The Lord brought us out of Egypt with a mighty hand and an outstretched arm, with a terrifying display of power, and with signs and wonders; and he brought us into this place and gave us this land, a land flowing with milk and honey.

11. This 'short historical creed', as it has come to be called, was taken by von Rad to be a very ancient formula embedded in the Deuteronomic law book and one which had originally been composed for just the purpose which Deuteronomy gives it, namely to accompany a ritual action in the cult. This passage represented, according to von Rad, the first stage in the history of the genre 'historical creed', at the end of which stood the composition of the Hexateuch in its final form, and it indicated an originally cultic setting for the genre. This implied for von Rad that the origin of the Hexateuch too was bound up with the history of the Israelite cult, a subject which had already before 1938 come to interest OT scholars considerably, particularly through the work of Sigmund Mowinckel on the Psalms, and von Rad was in fact only developing suggestions made previously by other scholars about particular sections of the Hexateuch (Mowinckel on the Sinai pericope (1927), Alt on a covenant-festival as a setting for apodictic

law (1934), and Pedersen on the link between Exodus and Passover (1934)).

12. At this point we move out of the strictly form-critical sphere into that of tradition criticism or tradition history. Von Rad noticed that the creed in Deut 26:5–9 does not mention the meeting with God at Mount Sinai among the events which it enumerates, and that the same is true of various other 'credal' passages in the OT, especially Deut 6:20–4 and Josh 24:2–13. On the other hand, the final form of the Hexateuch does give considerable space to events at Mount Sinai, and thus represents a departure from the original form of the creed. Even within the Hexateuchal narrative itself, von Rad believed, there were signs that the Sinai narrative had been artificially fitted into an original sequence, running from the Exodus to the Conquest, in which it did not appear. This sequence on the one hand and the Sinai narrative on the other at one time therefore existed quite independently of one another. As we have seen, von Rad had come to the conclusion from his study of the genre 'creed' that the origins of the Hexateuch were bound up with the history of the cult, and he proceeded in the next stage of his essay to develop this view by a detailed argument that these two blocks of tradition had been the theme-material of two different festivals celebrated in the period of the Judges at two different sanctuaries. The patriarchs–Exodus–Conquest sequence (which von Rad usually refers to as the 'settlement-tradition' from its concluding item, the possession of the promised land) belonged to the festival of Weeks or First-Fruits, celebrated at the sanctuary of Gilgal near Jericho, while the Sinai narrative belonged to a festival of the Renewal of the Covenant, referred to in the OT as Tabernacles or Booths, which took place at Shechem in the central highlands of Israel.

13. If that is so, the question arises as to when and by whom the two blocks of tradition were combined together. Von Rad's answer is that it was the author of the J source in the Hexateuch, whom he dates to the tenth century BCE, for in it, as traditionally reconstructed, the canonical sequence already appears. It is also to the Yahwist that the prefacing of Gen 1(2)–11, the primeval history, to the pattern dictated by the creed is attributed, so that this writer takes on immense stature as the originator of the canonical form of the narrative, and indeed in other ways too, which von Rad also spelt out at the end of his essay.

14. Noth's work on the Pentateuch (he did not believe that Joshua was so closely connected) is to be found above all in his book published in 1948 and later translated into English under the title *A History of Pentateuchal Traditions* (1972). It sets out to be a comprehensive and systematic treatise, which builds on von Rad's work, but also introduces fresh ideas and draws in elements of Gunkel's work on particular passages. Beginning from the conclusions of source criticism, Noth observed that the canonical pattern of narrative from the patriarchs to the settlement appeared not only in J but also in E, and since it seemed unlikely to him that E simply imitated J (since sometimes one seems more primitive and sometimes the other), he proposed that both were drawing on a common source in which the canonical pattern already appeared. He seems to have been unsure whether to postulate a written source or just common oral tradition, but he proposed the symbol G (for *Grundlage*, 'foundation') to represent

it. This is already an important departure from von Rad's view, since it implied that J inherited the canonical pattern from earlier tradition and was not himself the first to combine the Sinai narrative with the others, as von Rad had thought.

15. But in general Noth regarded von Rad's account of the preliterary history of the tradition as sound. He accepted the idea that the Sinai narrative had once been separate from the rest, and the early Israelite cult as the locus of preservation and transmission of the traditions. Von Rad was only at fault in that he did not take the process of analysis far enough for Noth. In Noth's view there were not just two originally separate blocks of tradition but five, which he generally refers to as 'themes'. These were the promise to the patriarchs, the deliverance from Egypt (Exodus), the leading through the wilderness, the revelation at Sinai, and the settlement in the land of Canaan.

16. To understand what Noth has to say about the origin of these themes it is necessary to remind ourselves of his views about the earliest history of Israel. For him there can be no question of a history of Israel before the settlement in Canaan, because prior to the settlement various groups of semi-nomads existed quite separately and they only became 'Israel' when they combined together in a sacred tribal league or 'amphictyony' on the soil of Canaan. Whatever came before was not, could not be, the history or story of the 'children of Israel', but could only be the history or story of parts of what later became Israel. The arrangement of Noth's own book on the history of Israel is the logical consequence of this view: its first main chapter deals with the arrival in Canaan of those groups which were eventually to become Israel, and only in the third chapter are the traditions about the Exodus, the patriarchs, and Mount Sinai dealt with, under the heading 'The Traditions of the Sacral Confederation of the Twelve Tribes'. In Noth's picture these traditions could only have originated as the traditions of one of the constituent parts of Israel in each case: that is, the implication of the Pentateuchal texts themselves that they are talking about the origin of 'all Israel' is historically false. Further there is no reason to think that the same constituent part of Israel was involved in the events of all the five themes, and it is quite possible that each theme derived originally from a different group, so that there was no original historical continuity at all between them.

17. Apart from these general considerations about the history of the tradition, Noth continued with the examination of the individual stories that had been begun by Gunkel and Gressmann, emphasizing their typical and legendary features. He seems to have held that the tradition began with five raw statements of faith corresponding to the five themes, of the form 'YHWH brought us out of the land of Egypt', to which only the slightest historical recollections were attached. These statements of faith then became the inspiration for a process of amplification by the creativity of story-tellers or bards, who developed the various episodes with which we are familiar.

18. One result of Noth's theory was his reluctance to regard any element of the tradition which represented continuity between the different themes as an early component of the story. The most celebrated example of this is his treatment of Moses, who of course appears throughout the central section of the Pentateuch, in the Exodus, wilderness, and Sinai themes. In all of this, Noth argued, Moses is dispensable and therefore a secondary element. He originally belonged in fact to the story of the settlement in Canaan, because his grave was located in land claimed by the Israelite tribes (cf. Deut 34:1–6 with Josh 13:15–23), and those elements of the stories about him that are not likely to have been invented (his foreign wife, criticism of his leadership) therefore originally belong here.

19. While the views of von Rad and Noth have been very influential, they have also come in for criticism from many scholars. Among the counter-arguments the following may be mentioned:

1. von Rad's reliance on Deut 26:5–9 may have too readily assumed that it is an ancient piece of traditional liturgy: its style is strongly Deuteronomic, and perhaps it was composed by the authors of Deuteronomy in the eighth or seventh century BCE.
2. whether that is so or not, von Rad's reconstruction of the history of the genre 'creed' too readily assumes that shorter forms are earlier than longer ones, a common misconception of form critics; or to put it another way, that development invariably proceeds by supplementation and never by selection or subtraction. It is not necessarily the case that the 'canonical pattern' of the creed with Sinai included is later than the shorter form.
3. Even if Noth's historical views about the settlement are true, they do not in fact rule out the possibility that all the themes represent experiences of the *same* group of 'ancestors of Israel', so that there might be an element of historical continuity between them.
4. Noth too quickly disposed of Moses, who is very firmly linked with the Exodus, Sinai, and wilderness traditions and scarcely as 'dispensable' as Noth believed. But if he is allowed to remain in them, this is an indication of an original historical continuity between Exodus, Sinai, wilderness, and settlement.

20. In addition to these objections, which are widely current, it should be observed that many of Noth's arguments are only possible if it is assumed that the tradition possessed the degree of creativity ascribed to it by Gunkel and Gressmann: and it is not at all certain that it did, particularly as far as the tradition about the Exodus and subsequent events is concerned. In fact, a number of questions have been raised in recent years about the validity of some of Gunkel's inferences. Two questions in particular need to be asked: (1) Is Gunkel's overall description of the stories as 'legend' (*Sage*) adequate? (2) Was his growing conviction that Genesis lacked any historical basis justified? These are clearly related questions, for the historical reliability of the stories is bound to be affected by the type of stories that we suppose them to be.

21. The description 'legend' was arrived at by Gunkel by a deceptively simple process of reasoning: the stories originated before the Israelites organized themselves politically into a state, therefore they are oral compositions, therefore they are legends (*Sagen*), and their purpose is to convey experiences of human existence which are not to be equated with particular historical events. The attraction of this line of reasoning is that at its end there is something that certainly needs to be said if we are to do justice to the literary art of the Genesis narratives.

But it is not a cast-iron argument, and cogent objections can be raised to it at virtually every point. To take only one point, is it really true that oral literature knows only the genre of *Sagen* as defined by Gunkel? Comparisons over a wider range than he undertook have suggested that oral literature is a much more varied phenomenon, with several different functions. Detailed studies of the text of Genesis itself also suggested weaknesses in Gunkel's description. He seems to have lost sight of the essential difference in character between the myths of Gen 1–11, which are pure imagination as far as the events they describe are concerned, and the stories of the patriarchs, where imagination is constrained by a particular historical situation.

The most comprehensive attempt to develop a new form criticism of the patriarchal stories has been made by C. Westermann, in the introduction to the second volume of his commentary on Genesis. Westermann's main assertion about the patriarchal narratives is that they are above all *family narratives*, not only in the sense that they are about family life but also because they are told and handed on by people who are the descendants (or think they are the descendants) of the chief characters in the story. In his commentary he makes a comparison between them and Galsworthy's 'family novels', *The Forsyte Saga*. Plato in the *Hippias Major* said that people in his day liked hearing stories of the foundation of cities; other classical parallels can be found in stories of the founding of colonies and in Virgil's *Aeneid*. According to Westermann, it is also possible to show that the aetiological stories and motifs, which are where creativity is at its greatest, belong to a comparatively late stage of the process of growth of the patriarchal stories. In the rest of the tradition, there is no reason why memories of quite ancient situations should not have been preserved, indeed this is to be expected. This is not to say that we can read Genesis as if it were a series of biographies: for the sequence of stories is less to be relied on than some of the stories themselves, and in addition there are some individual stories which owe a lot to later narrators with a particular theological point to make.

22. In looking at Westermann's fresh description of the patriarchal stories we thus encounter some pointers to a somewhat more positive historical evaluation of them than Gunkel allowed. To these archaeological evidence lends some support, though this must not be exaggerated. The claim that such evidence can prove the substantial reliability of the stories has rightly been criticized by T. L. Thompson and J. Van Seters. There are no direct references to Abraham, Isaac, or anyone else in Genesis in contemporary Near-Eastern texts. But in a variety of ways certain details of the stories (though not others) can be shown to fit in with our knowledge from external sources of how life was lived in the second millennium BCE. That is, the stories of the patriarchs did transmit to ancient Israel and do transmit to us some authentic information about conditions of life, both external and internal, social and spiritual, in the time before the Exodus. Creative development there may indeed be, but it is not creation in this case out of nothing: it is an enlarging and deepening of the story of a family, or families, who came to be regarded as the ancestors of all Israel and the recipients of a divine promise whose fulfilment was believed to have been worked out in the life of Israel as a historical people.

23. Despite the various criticisms we have looked at, it needs to be remembered that, even if the answers have weaknesses, the questions posed by von Rad, Noth, and Gunkel about the preliterary stage of the tradition are still with us and are ultimately unavoidable. I have already mentioned Westermann's more fruitful treatment of the patriarchal stories from this point of view. There is nothing quite comparable yet for the Exodus and subsequent episodes—T. L. Thompson's work suffers from the same defect as Gunkel's—but B. S. Childs's commentary contains some useful material and G. W. Coats recently brought out an excellent study, based on a series of articles written over a period of some twenty years, which, in direct contrast to Noth's position, takes Moses as its central theme (Coats 1988).

G. The Theology of the Pentateuchal Sources. 1. General considerations. Twentieth-century scholars have been occupied by another development in Pentateuchal study, going beyond the analysis into sources: that is, the theology—or rather theologies, for they differ considerably—of the sources. In fact the realization of the differences is one of the main benefits of source-analysis. One may draw an analogy with what has happened in NT study of the Gospels—there too a source-critical phase and a form-critical phase have been followed by a phase that focuses on the theologies of the different evangelists. The theological study of the sources of the Pentateuch seems to date from von Rad's 'Hexateuch' essay (1938), in which he identified the author of the J source as a creative theological writer. The modifications which von Rad thought J had made to the tradition (combination of Sinai and settlement; addition of primeval history) were clearly an advance in theology and not just innovations on the literary level. It is now widely recognized that the interpretation of a particular Pentateuchal passage must take account of its setting within the context of the source-document to which it belongs and ask, 'How is the inclusion of this passage related to the author's overall purpose and plan?' Von Rad again is a good illustration of this at many places in his Genesis commentary, though he concentrates mainly on the J source. Further studies of this kind can be found in Brueggemann and Wolff (1975). Before looking briefly at each source in turn I want to make some general, and rather polemical, points about our method and aim.

2. First, the method must be addressed: how are we to determine the theology of a document which is essentially in narrative form? There are various possibilities:

2.1. The best-known studies of this topic have tended to concentrate either on *specific passages* that make clearly theological statements or on *expressions* which recur in a number of passages. For example, Gen 12:1–3 has been regarded as almost the motto of the J writer (so by von Rad, Wolff, and others), with special emphasis being laid on Abraham as the means of blessing for all the peoples of the earth. Other passages have also been thought to shed particular light on the theology of this writer: thus, in Gen 1–11; 6:5; 8:21, and later on 18:22b–33. Again, Wolff's brilliant study of the theology of E is largely concerned with the recurring expressions 'the fear of God' (20:11, etc.) and God 'testing' or 'proving' someone (Gen 22:1; Ex 20:20). In the case of Deuteronomy

the key terms 'covenant' and 'law' have often been picked out, or the demand for the centralization of the cult (Deut 12:1–14). Finally, in his essay on the theology of P, Brueggemann sees the declaration of blessing in Gen 1:28 as 'the central message in the faith of the priestly circle', which is recapitulated in later passages such as Gen 9:7; 17:20; 28:1–4; 35:11; Ex 1:7. There is no doubt that this is a natural and useful approach to take, but if it is used alone as it sometimes is, it is in danger of producing an account of the theology of the sources that is both one-sided and oversimplified. For that reason it is very important to look also at two other aspects of the texts.

2.2. One of these is the *range of contents* of a particular source, that is, particularly, where it begins and ends. Again the study of the Gospels is an illuminating comparison, for they all begin and end at different points, at least if it is kept in mind that Luke's Gospel is only the first part of a 2-volume work. The different beginnings were already noticed by Irenaeus in the second century CE. The Pentateuchal sources also all begin at different points, but unfortunately the question of their endings is not so simple, and it is much argued whether J, E, and P did or did not go on to describe the conquest of Canaan under Joshua, while Deuteronomy can be said to 'end' at two very different places. Still, the different beginnings are clear enough, and they have important implications for the theology of the sources.

2.3. Also important is what I would call the *form* of presentation and the *arrangement* of the contents of the source, and in fact von Rad makes these factors fundamental for his exploration of the theology of the Yahwist. What I have in mind is first the general shape of the source—is it essentially a narrative or a collection of speeches? And what kind of narrative or speeches?—and then the more detailed structure of the contents.

3. Secondly, the aim must be decided: what is it that we are trying to do? I would see this as being to state the religious assertions that are made by *the document as a whole*, or at least in so far as it has been preserved. I say this over against the approach which seeks out only what is distinctive or what is new in a particular source. This has sometimes been the way of putting the question—it is in these terms that von Rad puts it in relation to the Yahwist—but (1) we then presuppose that we can make a clear distinction between the contribution of an author himself and what he inherited from his predecessors. This may sometimes be possible but frankly we are often not in a position to do that with any certainty when dealing with the Pentateuchal sources, and that is an important part of the reason why scholars have found it difficult sometimes to agree in this area. (2) In any case the theology of an author is shaped and expressed as much by what he reproduces from earlier tradition as by the fresh insights (if any) which he brings to it himself.

4. One further point: the authors produced their work in particular *historical situations* and addressed themselves to those situations. It must therefore be part of our aim to discover what those situations were, i.e. to date the work, and to relate what it says to the events of its time. But since most of the evidence for dating comes from the theological themes that are prominent in the sources, this part of our task can only be approached after we have reached an understanding of its theology by the methods described above.

5. Two important features are common to all four sources of the Pentateuch: (1) they all alike seek to define the character of the relationship between YHWH and Israel; (2) they do this by reference to certain ancient events, among which the sequence patriarchs–Exodus–Sinai–occupation of the land is present in all of them. Nevertheless in their handling of these common features they differ considerably.

6. The Theology of J. J, in overall shape, is clearly a narrative. But what kind of a narrative? Some of the important events described would clearly justify von Rad's term, used of the Hexateuch as a whole, 'creed', but others, such as the stories of Abraham's or Jacob's exploits, do not fit this description very well. One might say then that there is a credal framework filled out with what might be called illustrative material. An alternative approach is to begin at the other end with the genre-description 'epic', and then qualify this by a term such as 'religious' or 'theological'. Somewhere at the convergence of these two approaches an accurate description is to be found. The narrative shape of J has led to the view that his theology, like that of other OT writers, is a theology of history, i.e. a witness to and interpretation of the acts of God in history. The question does of course arise as to how far the 'history' in J's account is real history, especially in Gen 1–11, and the recently coined term 'narrative theology' is more widely applicable. Either way, the difference between J's theology and a timeless, philosophical theology needs to be noted.

7. J begins with creation: but it is worth amplifying this to 'the creation of human beings', because in Gen 2:4–5 the references to the creation of the natural world are in a subordinate clause, and not part of the actual story, which begins only in v. 7: 'Then the Lord God formed man . . .'. J's story is thus human history from its beginning to—wherever J ended! That we do not know for sure, but the occupation of the land of Canaan by Israel seems the most likely ending, whether, as some still think, that ending is preserved in the book of Joshua or not.

8. The contents of J can be subdivided into two parts: Gen 2–11, 'The Early History of Mankind in General'; and Gen 12 onwards, 'The Early History of Israel and their Ancestors'. An account of J's theology must address both parts of the document and, which is very important, the fact that they have been brought together. In Gen 2–11 we have a number of stories about the earliest ages of human history, which now have an interesting parallel in the Babylonian *Epic of Atrahasis*, which covers a similar span of early history. They do not pretend to present a complete history of these times, but only certain episodes with a particular importance for later generations. These episodes are presented either as the cause of a present state of affairs (human mortality, the need to work for a living, the existence of many languages, for example) or as paradigms of situations that may occur at any time (the rivalry of brothers, the attempt to break through the limits imposed on man by God), or as both. Westermann points out how the family is often in view. Of course in all cases the context is theological, and the sequence of sin–punishment–mercy appears several times, both as the cause of the present state of the world and as typical of God's government of the world at all times.

9. J's presentation of the early history of Israel is shot through with the idea of election, that Israel is YHWH's own people, which he brought into being, protected, and settled in her land, to fulfil the promises which he had made to her distant ancestors Abraham, Isaac, and Jacob. That history too illustrates the themes of sin–punishment–grace (especially in the wilderness), but more especially that of YHWH as a powerful deliverer and provider of his people's needs: corresponding to this, faith in God is the primary virtue (Gen 15:6, cf. Ex 4:30–1; 14:13, 31). There are some passages, chiefly poetic, in this section which seem to relate to events of J's own time and are the basis for attempts to date him to the tenth century BCE: according to them Israel is destined to be a great nation, who will rule her neighbours and have a king from the tribe of Judah (Gen 24:60; 27:27–9; 49:8–12; Num 24:15–19). Interestingly none of these passages is exactly in the form of a divine promise and perhaps this means that J did not regard political power as of the very essence of Israel's relationship to YHWH.

10. What is the significance of the combination of the two parts together? There has of late been a tendency to focus on the gloomy side of Gen 1–11, which ends, as von Rad points out, with the story of the scattering of the nations. Unlike earlier acts of judgement, this one is not mitigated by any word of grace and mercy. The word of mercy to the nations comes, according to this view, in a quite new form, in 12:1–3, where YHWH promises his blessing of Abraham's descendants, i.e. of Israel, and that 'in you [or: your seed] all the families of the earth shall be blessed' (12:3—cf. 26:4; 28:14), i.e. that Abraham/Israel is destined to mediate YHWH's blessing to other nations. J's theology is thus universalistic: it looks beyond Israel to God's work in the wider world. There is however a snag with this interpretation (see the note on this verse), and that is that the crucial words in Gen 12:3 could be translated in a different way: 'by you all the families of the earth shall bless themselves', that is, Abraham would be the standard to which all others would want to rise, without it being implied that this was in fact YHWH's intention for them (cf. Ps 72:17; and for the idea Zech 8:13). Then J is only speaking directly about YHWH's purpose for Israel. However that may be, we must certainly not make the mistake of thinking that Gen 1–11 serves in its present context only to indicate what the world needs to be saved from. In other respects, as we saw, it specifies the unchanging conditions under which human life has to be lived, as much in Israel as anywhere else, and shows YHWH's dominion as creator over the whole world. This is also a kind of universal theology and ethics, but it differs from the salvation-history kind that has been found in 12:3 etc. and is not dependent upon it. Other signs of a universal interest are the Table of Nations (ch. 10) and the use of Mesopotamian materials in the Flood story, as well as the Tower of Babel story in ch. 11, which seems implicitly to challenge the pretensions of the great world-empires of the ancient Near East, and especially those of Babylon. The approach is reminiscent of the wisdom literature in a number of ways. In this respect Gen 2–11 is not the antithesis to the kerygma of 12:1–3, law to gospel as it were, but displays God's wider work in creation and providence as the basis for his work in his own people's history.

11. The Theology of E. The E source survives to a much smaller extent than J. In *shape* or general character E seems to have been very similar to J, and what was said earlier about this in relation to J applies broadly to E. On the other hand the *range* covered seems to be less, for there is no evidence that E had any account of creation or the early history of the human race as a whole: it began its account with the patriarchs, specifically with Abraham. Most of Gen 20–2 is attributed to E, and it has commonly been thought that part of Gen 15, which describes the making of a covenant between God and Abraham, is also from E and indeed its beginning. It is certainly an appropriate place to begin the story of Israel's origins.

12. From Abraham on the contents of E apparently corresponded closely to those of J, with even greater uncertainty about whether it originally included an account of the occupation of Canaan or not. This means that the theological affirmations of E about the actions and character of YHWH are to a large extent the same as J's, and to save repetition it is possible to note just some important differences:

12.1. The most obvious difference is the lack of the universal perspective (in whatever sense) provided in J by the primeval history (Gen 1–11) and perhaps by Gen 12:3. For E God's purposes are in the main limited to his people Israel. Individual foreigners are, however, shown to have recognized the authority of Israel's God (cf. Abimelech in Gen 20 and Jethro in Ex 18). This is reminiscent of the widow of Zarephath in 1 Kings 17 and Naaman in 2 Kings 5, in prophetic stories from the northern kingdom, which is often seen as the environment in which E was composed.

12.2. It is apparently the view of E that the special name for God, YHWH, was not known to the patriarchs, but was first revealed to Moses (Ex 3:14–15: the same view is also held by P (Ex 6:2–3)). This has two effects: it links the beginning of Israel's religion particularly strongly with the Exodus and the mountain of God in the wilderness, and it makes a distinction between patriarchal religion and Israelite religion which, while not absolute, remains important. The character of God as conveyed in his name is given a rare, though elusive, exposition by E in 3:14: 'I am who I am', or 'I will be what I will be' (see the commentary).

12.3. On the subject of political power, E also includes passages which speak of Israel's great destiny (cf. Gen 46:1–4; Num 23:18–24), but it is noticeable that they do not give any special place to Judah, but rather celebrate the supremacy of the northern tribes Ephraim and Manasseh (cf. Deut 33:13–17; also Gen 48:15–16). This is one reason for thinking that E originated in the northern kingdom (cf. Jenks 1977).

13. Each of these three features in which E differs from J is probably due to E's having retained the attitudes and presentation of the story which were current in earlier times, while J represents a new approach in each. Two other differences are more likely to be due to E's own contribution.

13.1. H. W. Wolff (1975) has noted the concern of E for 'the fear of God', as an all-embracing religious attitude (in addition to Gen 20:11 cf. 22:12; 42:18: Ex 1:17, 21; 18:21; 20:20).

13.2. E's narratives reflect a greater preoccupation than the corresponding passages in J with ethical standards of behaviour as the condition of God's blessing of his people. This is particularly clear if one compares the parallel stories in Gen

12:10–20J and 20:1–18E, where the latter passage includes Abimelech's protestation of his innocence and the implication that Abraham's behaviour is reprehensible. It would be even clearer if it were certain that the Decalogue and the Book of the Covenant were included in E, as used to be thought, but this has been questioned in recent years, perhaps rightly.

14. The Theology of Deuteronomy (D). Deuteronomy/D stands in great contrast to J and E in both its *shape* and its *range*, not to speak of its structure, whether one considers its original nucleus (4:44–29:1) or its amplified form. As regards its shape it consists not of narrative, but of a series of *speeches*, which can most adequately be described as preaching: they speak directly to the people in the second person and urge them to do certain things for reasons that are also stated. Events of the early history are generally referred to in passing and are not the main subject of what is being said. This leads on to the range of the contents: in the nucleus there is no attempt at a connected description of early history as found in J and E, but rather the portrayal of a single event in great detail, namely Moses' parting speeches to the Israelites as they are encamped on the banks of the river Jordan. The structure is consequently also quite different and has been a topic of major interest to scholars, who have related it to the liturgy of a festival for the renewal of the covenant (von Rad) or to the pattern of ancient Near-Eastern treaties (Weinfeld), or indeed to both. The amplified form (i.e. chs. 1–34 as a whole), on the other hand, is most probably the first section of a long *historical work* with a quite different range from J and E, extending through the books of Joshua, Judges, Samuel, and Kings, commonly referred to as the Deuteronomistic History. So in neither form is D at all similar externally to J and E.

15. There is more common ground with the other sources, not surprisingly, when we come to look at its actual teaching, though here too there are new features. In the speeches of Deuteronomy the themes of the promise to the patriarchs, YHWH's deliverance and protection of his people, and his gift to them of the land of Canaan as a land full of every good thing, repeatedly appear. Thus far there is a real continuity with the older sources. The creation story, however, is ignored (though cf. 4:32), and the book is dominated by the theme of the covenant based on God's laws and obedience to them. This central concern is reflected in the title of the original core of Deuteronomy (4:45): 'These are the decrees and the statutes and ordinances, that Moses spoke to the Israelites…' (cf. Moses' opening words: 'Hear, O Israel, the statutes and the ordinances that I am addressing to you today' (5:1)). The picture of Moses himself is changed: instead of being the inspired leader of his people in all kinds of circumstances, he has become above all what we might call a 'prophetic legislator'. The laws too in chs 12–26 go far beyond the most that can be ascribed to J and E and allude to many aspects of life, both private and national—in the latter sphere it is notable that they make provision for the offices of priest, judge, prophet, and king, and imply that public worship is to be concentrated at a single sanctuary, which is referred to as 'the place that the LORD your God will choose as a dwelling for his name' (e.g. 12:11). National prosperity, indeed survival in the land which YHWH has given, now depends upon observance of these commands (cf. ch. 28). It is not the connection of sin and punishment which is new in Deuteronomy but the explicit definition, in the form of a code of laws, of what counts as sin in the sight of YHWH and the dire threats ('curses') held out in the case of disobedience.

16. The amplified form of D incorporates one additional theme of great significance to the community in exile, which is evidence of its origin in the sixth century BCE: this is the call to return to YHWH (cf. 4:27–31; 30:1–6). If sinful Israel, now under the judgment of YHWH, will once more be obedient to YHWH's law, then he will bring them back to Canaan and will even transform them inwardly so that they do not fail again (30:6), a thought that is closely related to Jeremiah's teaching of a new covenant and Ezekiel's of a new heart.

17. The Theology of P. As regards its *shape*, P stands somewhere between J and E on the one hand and D on the other. It does have a narrative structure, with its story extending from creation (this time explicitly including the natural world) to at least the eve of the Israelites' entry into Canaan. But in Genesis one can scarcely speak of a real story, as hardly any episodes are described in detail and the P material is mostly genealogies and chronological notes. And throughout this source long *speeches* (as in D) are very much in evidence, but this time in the form of divine revelations (or rather promises and commands) communicated to such figures as Noah, Abraham, and Moses. Not infrequently it is clear that a narrative episode is only there to reinforce what has been said in one of the divine speeches. So despite some superficial resemblance to J and E we are clearly in a quite different world. It is difficult to specify the genre of P as a whole. An anthropologist once suggested that because of his interest in myth, kinship, and ritual P could rank as the world's first social anthropologist! But anthropologists are only observers, while for P (which was probably produced by priests for priests) these things clearly have existential importance. Perhaps a report of a Liturgical Commission is a closer modern analogy!

18. While the theology of P is without doubt very largely a theology of ritual (especially priesthood and sacrifice), it does have a broader base. God/YHWH is the creator of the whole world (Gen 1), which he declared to be good and on which he bestowed his blessing. Humanity as such, male and female, is made 'in his image', a difficult phrase which should probably be translated 'as his image', implying that they are God's representatives on earth, to whom dominion over the earth is therefore naturally given (1:26). Gen 9:1–17, which incorporates the covenant with Noah and all living creatures (v. 10), amplifies this definition of the place of mankind in the world. Alongside these universal statements P also reaffirms the tradition of the election of Israel in her ancestor Abraham (Gen 17) and tells in his own way the story of the Exodus, the meeting with God at Mount Sinai, and the wilderness wanderings.

19. But already in Genesis P's interest in ritual can be seen: God himself, by his own example, inaugurates the sabbath (2:2–3); the instructions to Noah include the ban on eating meat with the blood, a basic element of Jewish food laws (9:4); and Abraham receives and obeys the command to be circumcised (17:9–14, 22–7). It is interesting that the three rituals given such great antiquity by P are all private, domestic rituals, which did not need a temple and could therefore be practised in the diaspora, in exile. There is some sign that P thought of four great epochs of revelation, beginning at creation (where God is called Elohim), Noah (again Elohim), Abraham (El Shaddai), and Moses (YHWH), and it used to be customary to speak of P as the Book of the Four Covenants, leading to the use (for example in Wellhausen's early work) of the symbol Q (for *quattuor*, Latin for 'four'). But in only two of the cases (Noah and Abraham) does P actually speak of the making of a 'covenant' (*bĕrît*), and other common features, such as the presence of a 'sign', are also hard to trace all through the series.

20. Be that as it may, the weight of P's emphasis certainly falls on the making, according to a detailed, divinely revealed plan, of the tabernacle, or desert shrine, at Mount Sinai (Ex 25–31; 35–40). This, or rather the altar outside it, was of course a place of sacrifice, and P has a lot to say, both practical and theological, about the ritual of sacrifice and the priests who were needed to carry it out. But this was not all. The name 'tabernacle' (*miškān*) means 'dwelling-place' (sc. for the divine glory) and it was also known as the 'tent of meeting' (i.e. for meeting with God). That is, what made the tabernacle a holy place, and an appropriate place to offer sacrifice, was that YHWH was in a special sense there, in the midst of his people. And that was its purpose. According to Ex 25:8 YHWH said to Moses: 'And have them [the Israelites] make me a sanctuary, that I may dwell among them.' And after the work was finished (40:34), 'Then the cloud covered the tent of meeting, and the glory of the LORD filled the tabernacle.' P's account of the relationship of YHWH to Israel, therefore, while it does not bypass other categories, is above all a theology of the divine presence in the midst of the people, which necessitates the construction of a sanctuary. For P God's presence is inconceivable without a sanctuary and its associated personnel and rituals. The people need also to know about what is holy and profane, what is clean and unclean, and it is a major part of the priests' task to instruct them in such matters: they are 'to distinguish between the holy and the common, and between the unclean and the clean' (Lev 10:10). This emphasis on the necessity of a sanctuary makes the most natural time for the composition of P the period between the destruction of the First Temple in 587/6 BCE and the completion of the Second Temple in 516, and not later, as Wellhausen and Kuenen thought.

H. Law. 1. What is law? The most familiar, and most general Hebrew word for 'law', *tôrâ*, is not necessarily the best place to begin an answer to this question. The very fact that it has the wider meaning 'instruction, teaching' led to its use for the teaching given by parents (Prov 1:8; 4:2), by the wise (Prov 13:14), or by prophets (Isa 1:10; 8:16, 20), as well as for what is commonly meant by law. This is an important insight, but it does not help with the definition of law as distinct from these other kinds of instruction. For that a more general (though possibly anachronistic) account is needed, which would recognize that what holds together the different types of law (constitutional, civil, criminal, cultic) is their prescriptive character, the regulation of specific kinds of recurrent (interpersonal) behaviour between members of a community, their enactment (and modification) by a recognized authority, political or ecclesiastical, and the existence of sanctions or penalties and procedures for their determination.

2. Most biblical law is found in the Pentateuch (some cultic law is included in 1 Chr 23–7). The *main collections of laws* in the Pentateuch are (1) the Decalogue or Ten Commandments (Ex 20:1–17; Deut 5:6–21); (2) the Book of the Covenant (Ex 20:22–23:23: for the title cf. 24:7); (3) the cultic commandments in Ex 34:10–27; (4) the Priestly laws about sacrifice, priesthood, and related matters, including land tenure (Ex 25–31 *passim*; Lev 1–7; 11–16; 27; Num 5–6; 8:1–10:10; 15; 18–19; 27:1–11; 28–30; 33:50–34:15; 35–6), among which (5) the Holiness Code (Lev 17–26) forms a distinct section; and (6) the law of Deuteronomy 4:1–30:20). All these collections are presented as having been revealed by God to Moses (and sometimes Aaron) for proclamation to the people at Mount Sinai/Horeb (or, in certain cases, most notably (6), elsewhere). There are, however, numerous instances where the same topic is dealt with more than once, often in different and even contradictory ways (cf. e.g. Ex 21:7 with Deut 15:17). From this, and from comparison with other biblical texts, scholars have concluded that the legal collections derive from very diverse times and situations, and that most probably none goes back to Moses himself. There is also reason to think that several of the collections at least have been revised since their original promulgation. In several cases the collections have an introductory or concluding exhortation or both, and much of the legal collection in Deuteronomy is interleaved with exhortations and 'motive' clauses' (cf. G. von Rad's description 'preached law': on biblical law in general see further Patrick (1986) and art. 'Law' in *ABD*).

3. Within these collections it is possible to distinguish different styles or *types of law*. In an essay first published in 1934, A. Alt initiated a new phase in the study of biblical law. He began from the important axiom that 'The making of law is basically not a literary process at all, but part of the life of a community' (Alt 1966: 86). Using the form-critical method, mainly on the Book of the Covenant (as being the oldest collection), he distinguished two major types of law. One, which he called 'casuistic', was conditional and (originally) expressed in the third person: 'If a man . . . then . . . '. This type was represented by most of Ex 21:2–22:17, and was similar to the form of law found among other ancient Near-Eastern peoples (see below). Alt concluded that such laws provided the norms for the village courts 'at the gate' in early Israel and that they had probably been taken over from the Canaanite inhabitants of the land. By contrast there was another type of law which Alt called 'apodictic'. Some examples of it express the same kind of case-law in a different way (e.g. Ex 21:13–14, 23–5; 21:12, 15–17; 22:19–20): most of these laws require the death penalty, and they are formulated in a simpler, more direct style than the laws referred to above. But generally laws of this type contain no explicit penalty at all: they are in many cases direct commands or prohibitions, like the Decalogue (cf. also Ex 22:18, 21–2, 28; 23:1–3, 6–9; and the 'table of affinity' in Lev 18:7–18), but they also appear as curses (Deut 27:15–26). Alt argued that these laws were of a distinctive Israelite form and origin, and that they originated not in the local courts but in a religious context, specifically in a festival for the renewal of the covenant celebrated at Shechem in the Judges period (cf. Deut 27; 31:10–13; Josh 24). Indeed the major impulse for such a formulation of law might well go back into the pre-settlement period, when the worship of YHWH began.

4. The key difference between apodictic and casuistic law as defined by Alt is that the former prescribes before the event what ought or ought not to be done, while the latter declares to a situation after the event what the appropriate penalty is. Thus the former belongs to a context of teaching or instruction, while the latter belongs to a judicial context. This distinction can be extended to cover the laws about worship to which Alt gave very little attention. Some of these lay down in the apodictic style what forms worship is or is not to take (e.g. the largely parallel series in Ex 23:10–19 and 34:11–26, and the later Priestly ordinances of Ex 25–31 and Lev 23); others provide, in the casuistic style, guidance for the remedy for particular circumstances that may arise (e.g. Lev 4–5, 12–15). In the context of worship and ritual the apodictic laws may well have been intended for occasions of public instruction or modelled on them, but the casuistic cultic laws were presumably not administered by judges, but by the priests at the temples.

5. Some of Alt's conclusions, especially about apodictic law, have been rejected by more recent scholars. The 'festival for the renewal of the covenant' is no longer widely accepted as an ancient feature of the religion of Israel. It can be questioned whether all the subtypes of apodictic law have the same origin. Even Alt's more general claims that the apodictic laws are distinctively Israelite and come from a liturgical context have been challenged on the basis of parallels in non-Israelite, non-legal texts. Direct commands and prohibitions have been found in Egyptian wisdom literature, in Hittite and Assyrian treaties, and even occasionally in Mesopotamian law-codes. There is a growing consensus that much if not all apodictic law originated in a family or clan setting and that it originally had nothing to do with the cult or the covenant (Gerstenberger 1965, summarized in Stamm and Andrew 1967; Otto 1994). It is striking that the cases where such a view is most difficult to accept are those where laws about worship are involved: the opening of the Decalogue and the cultic commandments in Ex 34 (cf. 23:10–19). It may be that initially it was only laws such as these which formed part of a cultic ceremony. On the other hand, if that much is accepted, one ought not perhaps to rule out the possibility that other commandments dealing with everyday life also had a place in such a ceremony. The fact that commands and prohibitions are found in a school or family or treaty context elsewhere does not mean that they may not have had a cultic context in Israel. Those who deny this have to see the literary formulation of the law-codes as commandments of God as a relatively late innovation. The alternative view is, with Alt, to see the literary formulation of all law as continuing what had been the basis for some law since its beginning.

6. Since the archaeological discoveries of the late nineteenth century it has become clear that Pentateuchal law has an important relationship with other *ancient Near-Eastern law* (cf. Boecker (1980) and, for specific parallels, *IDBSup* 533). Whether that relationship is one of dependence or just similarity is not the main issue here. Several collections of laws are now known from ancient Mesopotamia. The best known is the Code of Hammurabi of Babylon, from the eighteenth century BCE. The most fully preserved copy was taken in antiquity from Babylon to Susa in Elam, where it was found during excavations in 1901–2. It is now in the Louvre. Other copies of parts of the text are also known. The Code consisted of 282 laws and a prologue and epilogue (see *ANET* 164–80 for ET). The laws deal with such matters as the administration of justice, state and temple property, service to the king, private property, borrowing, family relationships, bodily injury, and agriculture. Earlier and later legal collections from Mesopotamia are also known: the Code of Ur-Nammu (21st cent.), the Code of Lipit-Ishtar (19th cent.), the Code of Eshnunna (18th cent.), the Middle Assyrian Laws (13th cent.), and the Neo-Babylonian Laws (?7th cent.). Another important collection is the Hittite Laws (14th cent.: the surviving parts of all these collections are translated in *ANET* 160–3, 180–8, 523–5). These collections are all apparently state law and they are predominantly in the 'casuistic' form, with a penalty or remedy specified for each particular set of circumstances. At present no comparable documents are known from ancient Egypt or Canaan.

7. The *history of law* in the OT, in the sense of the study of how and why the prescriptions about particular matters arose and developed through the OT period, is not straightforward. It requires that the relative ages of the different legal collections be determined and that, where appropriate, the inner growth of each individual collection be examined. Wellhausen's conclusions about the ages of the major Pentateuchal sources J, E, D, and P were largely based on such a history of law, specifically of the laws about worship. The source-critical approach held that the cultic laws in Ex 34 belonged to the J source and the Decalogue and the Book of the Covenant to E. Both sources were dated to the early monarchy period and it was thought that the legal collections might be earlier still. Deuteronomy came from the seventh century and P (including the Holiness Code) from the fifth century. In the latter two cases a specific link could be made with official ratifications of law, by Josiah (2 Kgs 22–3) and Ezra (Neh 8–10), which gave the biblical laws a similar official status to that enjoyed by the Mesopotamian legal collections. It was not so clear what gave authority to the earlier legal collections, especially the Book of the Covenant. M. Noth made the important observation that both the content of these collections and the linking of their promulgation with Moses asserted their validity for 'all Israel', which he took to be based on the memory of the 'amphictyony' (sacred tribal league) of the Judges period. But the existence of such a union of the tribes is widely doubted today. Recently Albertz has suggested that the Book of the Covenant was in its original form the basis for reforms introduced by Hezekiah *c.*700 BCE, thus giving it too a royal stamp of approval. But there is little solid evidence for such an association with Hezekiah. Recent scholarship, much influenced by redaction criticism, has tended to doubt whether J or E originally contained any of the legal collections.

8. The *distinctiveness of biblical law* can be seen in its form, its ethics, and its theology. Attention has already been drawn to the hortatory element which is frequently present in the OT legal collections, and a specific feature of this is the numerous 'motive clauses', which ground the laws in the divine will, a historical event, or a promise of future well-being (Sonsino 1980). Close comparisons between the contents of biblical and non-biblical laws have shown that, despite many similarities, there are differences here too. The laws apply equally to all free-born Israelites, whereas in Mesopotamia the penalty imposed may vary according to the social status of the other party. Biblical law goes further in its provision for the disadvantaged in society, including the 'resident alien' (*gēr*) as well as widows and orphans. More generally, a higher value tends to be set on human life as opposed to property, as can be seen in the respective laws about the 'goring ox' (Ex 21:28–32) and theft (Ex 22:1–4). Finally, the mingling of laws on sacred and secular matters, found in the Decalogue, the Book of the Covenant, Deuteronomy, and the Holiness Code, reflects a sense of the unity of life and especially of the claim made by the religion of Israel on the secular as well as the sacred. This latter point is closely associated with the theological, and specifically covenantal, context in which all the laws now stand, as well as the motive clauses already mentioned. The historical fiction whereby the lawgiving of Moses occurs at the behest of YHWH in the period between the creative event of the Exodus from Egypt and the entry into the land of Canaan promised to Israel anchors the law in the fundamental structure of OT faith. This is explicitly brought out in such passages as Ex 20:1 and Deut 6:20–5. Particularly in the later collections, Deuteronomy and the Holiness Code, the observance of the law is presented as a communal responsibility and failure to keep it as the cause of a national catastrophe, ultimately exile from the land. In several places this theology is specifically summed up by a reference to the establishment of a covenant between YHWH and his people (Ex 24:7–8; 34:10, 27; Lev 26:42, 44, 45; Deut 5:2–3, 29:1).

I. Recent Questioning of the Classical Documentary Theory. 1. The work on oral tradition and theological interpretation that we reviewed earlier was based on the assumption that the classical (Wellhausen) theory of Pentateuchal origins is correct. It would need at least considerable revision if that theory proved to be wrong, though no doubt some of the insights would survive. When a theory has come to support such a superstructure of further speculation, it is clearly important that its own foundations should be examined from time to time and possible alternatives to it should be considered. Perhaps this is one reason why recent years have seen a return of interest to the source-critical questions which the classical theory sought to answer. At the present time the study of the Pentateuch is a matter of discussion and controversy such as it has scarcely been since the time of Wellhausen and Kuenen. A variety of fresh approaches is being tried, and discarded ones revived, to seek a well-founded way forward in this most basic of all Pentateuchal studies. Much of what will be described in the following sections is still very much a matter for discussion.

2. The fresh approaches have taken two main forms:

2.1. New attempts to formulate the principles according to which study of the Pentateuch and other parts of the Bible must proceed, i.e. a concern with methodology; which has arisen partly from the need to define more closely the relationship between source criticism and other methods such as tradition criticism and form criticism, and also partly from the impact on biblical studies of 'structural analysis' and other modern literary methods for the exegesis of texts (see esp. Barton 1984).

2.2. The development of particular alternative theories about the origins of the Pentateuch, involving a partial or total abandonment of the classical theory.

We have, then, two lines of research, reflection on method and the formation of new theories, which have sometimes reinforced one another but sometimes proceeded quite separately. For some evaluation of them in print see the *Introductions* of Soggin and Childs, and Whybray (1987). It is possible to distinguish six 'new directions in research' in this area.

3. An earlier date for P. First we have the view that P is not the latest of the four sources, from the exilic or post-exilic period, but is earlier in origin than D or at least contemporary with it. This view has recently been argued for at some length (Haran 1979). But it in fact originated with the Israeli scholar Y. Kaufmann as long ago as 1930 and it has been accepted widely among Israeli scholars, though hardly at all elsewhere. In the form that Haran presents it, this view holds that the composition of P is to be dated to the reign of Hezekiah, *c.*700 BCE, and that P was in fact the stimulus for Hezekiah's re-forms of national religion reported in 2 Kings 18:3–5. As with Wellhausen, we find that the dating of P by Haran is based on the place which P's regulations seem to occupy in the history of Israel's religion, and Haran argues that, contrary to what Graf and Wellhausen had said, all the P regulations make sense, and some of them only make sense, if P was composed before the exile.

4. A 'sounding' can be made by considering what Haran says about the issue considered earlier in connection with Wellhausen's dating of P, namely admission to the priest-hood. In order to show that P's regulations reflect pre-exilic conditions, Haran draws attention to the list of Levitical cities in Josh 21, in which the descendants of Aaron appear as a distinct group, and are assigned cities in the tribal areas of Judah and the related Benjamin and Simeon, that is the southernmost tribes, while the other Levites are given cities in the other tribal areas. A number of scholars have argued, on grounds of historical geography, that this list is pre-exilic in origin, which would, if taken seriously, imply that the Aaro-nides were a recognizable group before the exile, and that they already then had an exclusive right to full priesthood (cf. v. 19) and not only afterwards. Nevertheless, while the list may have a pre-exilic basis, its present context is in a historical work of the exilic period (the Deuteronomistic History), so that it is not clear evidence of pre-exilic practices. Haran also claims support from references to Aaron in the older Pentateuchal sources J and E; but they do not present Aaron and his descendants as having the sole right to the priesthood, as P does. Nor is there any greater force in the passages cited to show the existence of Levites in subservient positions before the exile, as prescribed by P: 2 Kings 11:18 and 1 Sam 2:31–3. In the former case there are subordinate cultic officials but there is no indication that they are Levites, while in the latter case it is not actually said whether Eli's descendants were to be given any role at all, even an inferior one, in the future temple service.

5. An argument against Wellhausen's view which is per-haps more telling arises from statistics. P appears to envisage a large number of Levites compared with priests (cf. the tithe-law), whereas the lists in Ezra and Nehemiah suggest that there were actually relatively few Levites in post-exilic times. This makes it difficult to believe that P originated in the time to which these lists refer. Even the force of this argument, however, is reduced if P is dated to the years of exile itself in the sixth century, as this would leave time for conditions to have changed before Ezra and Nehemiah, and more Levites than had at first been anticipated may have been able to lay claim to full priestly status by finding a genealogical link with Aaron, thus reducing the number of ordinary Levites. The nub of Wellhausen's argument was Ezek 44, and Haran does attempt a different interpretation of this which would leave room for an older distinction within the priesthood. But it does not convince.

6. In general, many of Haran's arguments seem to turn out on examination to be less conclusive than they at first appear. Moreover, it is surely revealing that Haran has after all to concede that 'it was only in the days of Ezra . . . that P's pres-ence became perceptible in historical reality and began to exercise its influence on the formation of Judaism' (1979: p. v). To attribute a document nearly three centuries of existence before it became perceptible is rather unsatisfactory when set against the very explicit arguments of Wellhausen.

7. Other Israeli scholars have used different arguments to support similar views. Weinfeld has argued that D presup-poses P at various points so that P must be earlier: but these turn out either to be in passages which are for other reasons not thought to be an original part of D, or else to concern regulations which there is every reason to think existed on their own before their inclusion in P, so that D may have known them without knowing P as a whole. Again, Hurvitz has examined the language of P and shown that the vocabu-lary includes many words characteristic of pre-exilic rather than post-exilic Hebrew. This need not mean that P is pre-exilic: it could be due to the use of traditional vocabulary in priestly circles—a not unheard of phenomenon—and in fact there are several cases where P's vocabulary seems closest to Ezekiel, an argument again perhaps for a sixth-century date. Further, Hurvitz's study of vocabulary must be viewed in the light of R. Polzin's work on syntax, which shows that in this respect P's language differs from that of pre-exilic writings and represents a transitional stage in the development to Late Biblical Hebrew, as represented by the books of Chronicles—just what would be expected from a sixth-century work.

8. It has not been established that this earlier dating of P should be adopted. Discussion of it has, however, been useful for two reasons: (1) it has emphasized that the P document did not emerge out of thin air, but in some passages is a compila-tion of older traditions, particularly laws; (2) it has brought to light one or two reasons for preferring a sixth-century date for the composition of P to the fifth-century one advocated by earlier critics.

9. Renewed emphasis on the final form of the text. A second feature of recent Pentateuchal scholarship has been the ten-dency of certain scholars to direct attention to what they sometimes refer to as 'the final form of the text', that is the form in which the Pentateuch actually appears in the OT, as distinct from the sources and traditions which lie behind, or beneath the surface of, the biblical text itself. Those who have advocated this approach are agreed that the style of scholar-ship which has been dominant in academic circles for a century and more has been too preoccupied with questions of origin and sources, and has neglected the interpretation of the text in the form that became standard for synagogue and church for twenty centuries. In their view it is not so much a revision of particular theories that is needed but a completely new approach to the study of the Pentateuch. Indeed it is not only the Pentateuch that needs a new approach, but the whole OT (and perhaps the NT as well). Within this group of scholars it is possible, and perhaps useful, to distinguish two different kinds of concern for the final form of the text.

10. On the one hand there are those who emphasize the need to treat the Pentateuch as a work of literature in its own right, which means seeking to understand its present form, purpose, and meaning, just as one would with, say, a play by Shakespeare or a novel by D. H. Lawrence. A good example of this literary approach is David Clines's *The Theme of the Pentateuch* (1978): he is quite explicit (cf. ch. 2) about his debt to the general study of literature. Another kind of literary approach is represented by structuralist studies of parts of the Pentateuch which appear from time to time, and sometimes claim to be the sole representatives of a general literary approach to the biblical text, an impression that is far from being a true one. A good indication of the rich possibilities of such a literary approach to the Pentateuch can be gained from Robert Alter's *The Art of Biblical Narrative* (1981), which has been very well received.

11. To be distinguished from this literary approach there are those, above all Brevard Childs, who have urged afresh the need for exegesis to read the OT as the Scripture of synagogue and church, and who speak of a 'canonical approach' to the OT. Here too the exegete is thought of as having much to learn from an unfamiliar direction, and in view of the emphasis on the term 'Scripture' it is not surprising to find that it is the history of biblical interpretation, among both Jews and Christians, that is meant: the great (and not so great) commentaries and other works which grappled with the meaning of Scripture long before the modern historical approach was thought of. One can see Childs's high respect for the commentaries of the past in his own on Exodus, in which one section of the treatment of each passage is reserved for a consideration of them (see also Childs 1979: chs. 3, 5).

12. Clearly both varieties of this development have a real attraction, which is due partly to the fact that they recognize important dimensions of the texts which are commonly overlooked in other OT scholarship, and partly to the fact that what they say seems so much simpler and more familiar than talk of sources and stages of tradition does. At the same time it is important to recognize their limitations, which mean that they cannot and should not take the place of traditional historical scholarship. Clines and Childs are both clear that their methods leave room for historical study of the origins of the Pentateuch, but they do not stress this point sufficiently. One can see the limitations as well as the advantages of their methods if one remembers the descriptions of the Pentateuch which lie at their foundation: on the one hand, a unified work of literature, on the other, Scripture. It is only questions arising out of these descriptions which the methods proposed are capable of answering: that is the questions of students of literature and of preachers and systematic theologians. For the answering of historical questions they are of little or no use: such questions are ones that can and should be asked, and they will be answered by the use of other, more appropriate methods. I think it is also necessary to go a stage further and ask whether Childs's canonical approach is really adequate, by itself, even for the answering of theological questions about the Pentateuch. Does it not involve turning one's back on matters of enormous theological importace, such as the original message of the Pentateuchal sources taken one by one, and the relation of this to the historical situation which they addressed? For Childs the only historical situation which seems ultimately to matter is that addressed by the text in its canonical form, sometime in the post-exilic or even intertestamental period, and the only theological viewpoint which ultimately matters is that of the final redactor of the text. Is not a theological exegesis based on such principles going to be impoverished compared with what historically based exegesis has to offer?

13. This is also an appropriate place for a brief comment on R. N. Whybray's recent book, *The Making of the Pentateuch* (1987). It contains a review of recent (and not so recent) work on the Pentateuch, and as such it has many useful things to say. The conclusion is, however, rather different from that which will be proposed here: Whybray supports the more far-reaching criticisms of the Documentary Theory, and he takes the view that the final author of the Pentateuch, sometime in the post-exilic period, employed such a 'high degree of imagination and [such] great freedom in the treatment of sources' that source criticism of the traditional kind is not possible and one must limit oneself to the study of the final form of the text, but on critical rather than literary or canonical grounds. This view has found very little support among critical scholars, whose continued discussion of the composition of the Pentateuch from earlier material shows that they do not consider that the situation is as desperate as Whybray proposes. In particular it is remarkable that Whybray does not even seem to recognize the possibility of distinguishing Deuteronomy and the Priestly material from the remainder.

14. Redaction criticism. Back in the world of traditional biblical criticism, it is necessary to consider the growing emphasis on redaction criticism. This can be defined as the study of the way in which *editorial processes* have shaped the Pentateuch. In early biblical criticism the redactor was chiefly thought of as a scribe who combined together older sources into a composite narrative, without contributing much if anything out of his own head by way of interpretation or additional material. He was what has sometimes been called a scissors-and-paste man. He was thought to have taken extracts from existing documents and joined them together, often in a rather careless way. The symbol R^{JE}, for example, was used to denote the redactor who combined the J source with the E source of the Pentateuch. Over the years the emphasis has changed, and when scholars speak of a redactor today they are thinking more often of a figure who may only have had in front of him a single document or account, and amplified it by the addition of words or sentences which would alter its overall meaning to present more clearly the teachings which he himself believed to be most important for his day. This development can be seen with particular clarity in recent study of the prophetic and historical books of the OT, but it has also considerably modified the way in which some scholars have seen the composition of the Pentateuch as taking place. It of course brings attention firmly back to the written stage of the tradition and sometimes there is an explicit polemic against the oral tradition approach. Some scholars in Germany have applied this approach to the detection of layers within the sources recognized by earlier scholarship (e.g. E. Zenger; P. Weimar). But, perhaps because of the importance of Deuteronomic/Deuteronomistic editing in other parts of the OT, this approach often asserts that redactional work by the same 'school' of writers can be traced in the Pentateuch, or rather the Tetrateuch. This is particularly true of L. Perlitt's book, *Bundestheologie im Alten Testament*, 'Covenant Theology in the OT', which made a big impression through the acceptance of some of its theses by influential scholars (cf. Nicholson 1973). For our purposes what is most important is that Perlitt reckons with an extensive Deuteronomic reworking of the chapters in Exodus which deal with events at Mount Sinai. According to Perlitt, all passages in these chapters which imply the making of a covenant between YHWH and Israel at Sinai belong to this redactional level, which he calls Deuteronomic, because he believes that covenant theology is peculiarly the creation of the authors of Deuteronomy, and was imposed by them and their disciples on the other parts of the OT. Much of Perlitt's detailed work on the Sinai narrative is directed at showing that verses normally attributed to J or E do not belong to them, but are part of this later redactional layer, the result of which is to argue that covenant was not an original component of the Sinai tradition. There is something of a vicious circle in this argument. The references to a covenant in Exodus are said to be due to a late Deuteronomic redactor—because the covenant idea is no older than Deuteronomy—but this can only be sustained by assuming that the verses in Exodus are due to a Deuteronomic redactor. Little attention seems to be given to the possibility that the covenantal texts in Exodus are the seeds from which the Deuteronomic theology grew. There is also a failure to notice important differences between the way that the Sinai covenant is presented in Exodus and the Deuteronomic literature (cf. the critique of Perlitt in Nicholson 1986: ch. 8).

15. However redactional explanations have been brought forward for other sections of the Pentateuch as well. Auld has argued that the passages at the end of Numbers which speak about plans for the conquest of Canaan and its division among the tribes are dependent on the passages in Joshua which describe these episodes, and did not form part of any of the main Pentateuchal sources (Auld 1980). It has also been suggested that many of the notes of movement from place to place in Exodus and Numbers, which form a framework to the wilderness narrative as we now have it, were added in an 'itinerary-redaction', which made use of a full account of the wilderness journey preserved in Num 33:1–49. On a more theological level it has been argued that the promises to the patriarchs in Genesis were greatly multiplied and enlarged by redactors working at a time when one of the themes of these promises, the possession of the land of Canaan, was threatened in the late monarchy or even the exilic period by the appearance of the great imperial powers of Assyria and Babylon. Nicholson, again, has argued that the Decalogue in Ex 20 did not originally appear there but was inserted by a redactor who took it more or less as it stood from its other occurrence in Deut 5. Each of the theories has of course to be judged on its merits.

16. It is appropriate to refer briefly here to C. Westermann's massive commentary on Genesis. Westermann does not accept that there is any trace of an E source in Genesis. The passages usually said to have been derived from E, such as most of chs. 20–2, he takes to be stories that had circulated separately before being added to the J narrative, which was already in a connected form. They are, in effect, supplements to J, and with Westermann here we are right back in the world of the supplementary theory of Pentateuchal origins. It is for that reason that he is included here, even though the additional matter is too extensive and too self-contained for the process of its inclusion really to be referred to as a redaction. In coming to this view, Westermann is taking up the approach advocated by W. Rudolph many years ago, and also followed by S. Mowinckel. It is not clear that he has made that approach any the more likely, but it remains an option that must be carefully examined. Wolff's essay on the theology of E, of course, noted some important recurring features in the E material which suggest that it did come from a connected narrative or source.

17. With redactional explanations covering so much of the Pentateuch, it is not a big step to suggest that comprehensive redactional activity has sought to remould the whole Pentateuch into a new form. This is the direction in which William Johnstone has moved. He argues that the Pentateuch is the result of a Priestly revision of an original Deuteronomic version of the story, which was based on Deuteronomy (he does not say on what else), so that a close parallel exists with the composition of the historical books, where the 'priestly' Chronicles is seen by most scholars as a revision of the Deuteronomic historical books of Samuel and Kings (Johnstone 1998). This leads straight into a wider questioning about the nature of P.

18. P as a Supplement, not a Source. Questions have been raised not only about the date, but about the nature of the Priestly Source. F. M. Cross and others have argued that P is not a separate source which once existed independently of J etc., perhaps as a rival version of the story of Israel's origins, but a series of supplements overlaid on the older narrative. According to this view, P was thus reworking the older narrative by expanding it with material of a new, generally cult-centred character, so as to shift the balance of the story in this direction. Like the elimination of E as a separate source, this is in fact an old view revived which can be traced back to P. Volz in the years between the two World Wars. It is also the view that was held by the Scandinavian scholar Ivan Engnell, whose views on oral tradition were mentioned briefly earlier. The important difference it makes is that the purpose of the P writer must now be investigated on the assumption that he reproduced the older traditions, e.g. about legislation at Sinai, as well as incorporating material reflecting his own special interests. It is, for example, then no longer possible to say, as some have done, that P knows nothing of a covenant at Sinai but only the founding of a pattern of ritual. P incorporated the older covenant-making story and had no need to add one of his own. One of the attractions of this view, and indeed of the other 'supplementary' theories, is that it appears to spare us the allegedly unreal picture of redactors sitting at their desks with scissors and paste, selecting half a verse from here and half a verse from there in the four sources to make the completed Pentateuch. There are also some passages, especially in the patriarchal stories, where the P material is so meagre that it seems at first sight unlikely that it ever existed alone, and unjustified to claim that it represents extracts from a fuller, now lost, parallel account of the events, and it might better be explained as amplification of an existing narrative.

19. And yet there are a number of passages which seem to defy explanation in these terms, and to require a hypothesis of the traditional kind, which allows for the existence of an independent P source (see especially Emerton 1988; Davies 1996). These are passages where it is possible by analysis to identify both a relatively complete P version of the story and a relatively complete version from one of the older sources. The Flood story is a prime example, but there are others. A redactor would not compose duplicates such as we observed in the Flood story: whether it seems 'natural' or 'likely' to us or not, the only explanation which makes sense of the situation there is that he had two complete narratives of the Flood and combined them. Another point arises from the P passage Ex 6:2–3, according to which God did not make himself known to the patriarchs by the name YHWH but only as El Shaddai/ God Almighty. This corresponds well to the beginnings of speeches in P such as Gen 17:1 and 35:11, but it conflicts directly with passages where the patriarchs show familiarity with the name YHWH, which are quite frequent in J (12:8 etc.). It is hardly conceivable that P would have left such passages unamended if he had included them in his overall presentation. This implies that there is a continuing need to reckon with the independent existence of P prior to its combination with the other sources. But it also seems that there has been some minor editing of the completed Pentateuch by a Priestly writer at a very late stage which has introduced the vocabulary of P into older material (e.g. Ex 16:1, 17:1, the phrase 'the congregation of the people of Israel'), and this could help to explain the isolated 'P' verses in the patriarchal stories that were mentioned.

20. A Late Date for J. A further recent development concerns the dating of J. The first scholar to mention here is H. H. Schmid who argued in his book *Der sogenannte Jahwist* (1976) ('The So-Called Yahwist') that the composition of the whole of J took place after the rise of classical prophecy and is contemporary with the rise of the Deuteronomic movement. In his own words: 'The historical work designated in research by the word "Yahwist", with its comprehensive theological redaction and interpretation of the Pentateuchal material cannot derive from the time of Solomon, but already presupposes pre-exilic prophecy and belongs close to the deuteronomic-deuteronomistic shaping of the tradition and literary activity.' He declines to give an absolute date but this view would put the composition of J in the 7th or 6th century BCE. How, briefly, does Schmid arrive at this conclusion? By two main kinds of argument: (1) he points to features in the J narrative which, according to him, are prophetic in character and are not found in literature before the classical prophets in the eighth century and later. For example, the 'call of Moses' in Ex 3 resembles the call-narratives found in the books of the prophets Isaiah, Jeremiah, and Ezekiel, but finds no earlier analogues. (2) He

points to traditions in J which are noticeably absent from pre-exilic literature outside the Pentateuch: the meeting with God at Mount Sinai, Moses (with one exception), the patriarchs (with one or two exceptions), the unity of all Israel in her early history. The 'silence' of the other texts is strange if J (and E) had existed since the early monarchy, but is readily explicable if J did not originate until the late pre-exilic period.

21. The consequences of such a view for the history of Israelite religion are considerable. It implies that there was no connected written account of the early history of Israel until the seventh century BCE, and also conversely that the seventh and sixth century BCE made an even greater contribution to the shaping of OT tradition than has been recognized in the past, even more than Perlitt thinks. If one asks, 'What then was the nature of Israelite religion before this?', Schmid's books on wisdom and the cult provide an answer: YHWH was seen above all as the creator of an order in the world, which wisdom sought to understand and the cult sought to maintain, very much like the gods of Israel's neighbours. Israel's specific faith in a God of history was the result of the insights of the prophets and the Deuteronomic school. But is Schmid's late date for J correct? It is clearly as valid or invalid as the arguments on which it stands. They need careful examination. Let us look at the two main types:

21.1. The similarity between the call of Moses and, say, the call of Isaiah is undeniable, but it should not be exaggerated. Moses in J is not called to be a prophet in the later sense, but to lead his people out of Egypt, in a manner similar to that by which Gideon in Judg 6 and Saul in 1 Sam 9 were called, older narratives without doubt. In so far as there are real prophetic motifs, these can be attributed either to the old Moses-tradition itself or to the influence of the early prophetic movement, which we know to have been active already in the tenth or ninth century. There is no need to come any later.

21.2. The 'silence' about certain Pentateuchal themes in other pre-exilic literature is remarkable but it really proves too much, for if taken with full seriousness it would imply not just that J was a late composition but that these themes were only invented in the late pre-exilic period, an extremely radical position which Schmid clearly does not wish to take up. And yet if he is ready to conceive that the prophetic and other texts might have failed to mention a tradition which nevertheless existed in oral form, surely it is not appreciably more difficult to conceive of their failing to mention what was written down, in J? Moreover, the silence is not, as Schmid has to recognize, total, at least in some of the cases. The prophet Hosea, for example, clearly refers to a number of events in Israel's early history.

Many of Schmid's arguments are open to criticism along one of these lines, and he has given no compelling reason why J should not have originated in the early monarchy or why it should be dated to the late monarchy or the exilic period. J is after all notably lacking in references to the great powers or the possibility of exile (contrast Deuteronomy).

22. Another scholar who dates the Yahwist very late, in the exilic period, is John Van Seters. In his first book-length study on the subject, *Abraham in History and Tradition* (1975), he did not date all of J so late. In fact he suggested that the Pentateuch had 'grown' through a series of expansions of an original core, and that core consisted of part of the J source. To this was

added first E, then D, then the rest of J (the larger part of it in fact) and finally P. Even then, however, he was saying that the J material as a whole only came into being in the exile, shortly before P. In Van Seters' more recent work it is on this stage of composition that he has concentrated. Already in *Abraham* Van Seters was developing a series of arguments for a late date for the Yahwist: they include historical anachronisms, the use of formulae from prophecy and the royal cult, and particularly the prominence given to Abraham as the source of Israel's election. This, he argued, corresponds closely to the view of Deutero-Isaiah (see Isa 41:8 and 51:2), but it is a theme which is not yet emphasized in the late pre-exilic writings of Deuteronomy, Jeremiah, and Ezekiel. It does, of course, reappear in P, which is also exilic.

23. In his more recent books Van Seters has widened the textual base of his studies by looking at the rest of the Pentateuch, at least its non-Priestly sections. An important new stage in his work was *In Search of History* (1983). This actually has very little to say about the Pentateuch—it is mostly about the Deuteronomistic History. But in it Van Seters draws numerous comparisons between Old Testament history-writing and comparable literature from other cultures, and he particularly emphasizes the similarity with ancient Greek historians such as Herodotus, who lived in the fifth century BCE. From these comparisons Van Seters argued for a greater appreciation that the Deuteronomistic History was a literary work whose author was ready to write creatively where his sources did not provide what he needed, and in fact was the beginning, as far as Israel was concerned, of such historical literature. These findings have worked their way into his more recent work on the Pentateuch and strengthened his opinion that in J we are dealing with a highly literate, but also quite late, author. Actual Greek parallels to passages in the Pentateuch have also come to play a more important part in his work, though Near-Eastern ones are still cited.

24. A good example of this work is Van Seters' study of Gen 1–11 (1993; see also *The Life of Moses* (1994)). He notes some parallels of form and substance between the Yahwist's primeval history and Hesiod's *Catalogue of Women*, which is thought to have been written about 550 BCE. He sees this as representative of a 'Western genealogies tradition', which influenced the J author in Genesis about the same time. Some of the parallels are probably not very significant: it is difficult to see, for example, how similarities of form are likely to have been transmitted independently of content; and different communities could easily have brought their traditions together independently in similar ways. The most impressive parallel concerns Gen 6:1–4: the *Catalogue* is very largely about such divine–human liaisons which produced the 'heroes' or demi-gods of primeval times, and one passage suggests that a natural disaster may have been sent by Zeus to get rid of them (cf. the Flood). Van Seters sees several of the 'origins of civilisation' stories in Gen 2–11 as linked to 6:1–4 and modelled on the 'Western tradition'. In most cases it is possible to say that similar stories may have originated independently. But in the case of Gen 6:1–4 Van Seters may be right: this story is very much the odd one out among the stories in Gen 1–11 and perhaps it does have a distant origin. However, it may not be necessary to look as far as Greece for this: the Ugaritic myths include at least one description of a god having

sexual intercourse with human women (Shachar and Shalim, *CTA* 23). A different kind of argument is used by Van Seters to place the composition of Gen 2–3 (J) in the exilic period. He sees these chapters as the end of a development which begins with a Babylonian myth about the creation of a king, dated to the seventh or sixth century: this, he argues, was the basis for Ezekiel's oracle against Tyre, which speaks of a mythical king who was once in the Garden of Eden but was expelled from it (Ezek 28), and Gen 2–3 in turn was a transformation of this oracle to describe the creation and fall of mankind generally. Hence Gen 2–3, and therefore J, would be later than Ezekiel. It remains possible, however, that the relationship between these three texts is a different one: Ezekiel may have combined motifs from a myth about the origins of kingship and Gen 2–3 or something like it. In that case Gen 2–3, and J, would be, as generally thought, earlier than Ezekiel.

25. The New Tradition-Criticism. But—and this brings us to the final issue that has been raised in the recent debate— was there a J at all? This is the question that has been asked— and answered in the negative—in a book published in 1977 (cf. Rendtorff 1990). In certain respects Rendtorff's arguments and conclusions are similar to those of the redaction critics and of Schmid, and in subsequent discussion they have been able to find quite a lot of common ground with him. For example, Rendtorff also believes that P never existed as a separate document, but should rather be described as a redactional layer or rather a series of redactional layers belonging to a late stage of the Pentateuch's composition. But Rendtorff has arrived at his views by a quite different route and maintains some theses which go far beyond the views of the other scholars.

26. The key to Rendtorff's approach is the high value which he places on tradition criticism. The origins of this method, which seeks to trace the history of the Pentateuchal traditions from their beginning to the stage of the completed Pentateuch, can be found in Gunkel's introduction to his Genesis commentary and it was taken further by von Rad and Noth in their famous works. Now all these scholars regarded tradition criticism as a method which was complementary to and needing to be combined with source criticism, the JEDP analysis or something like it. And in this, according to Rendtorff, they made a serious error: to quote some words of his from an earlier paper, 'It must be said that adherence to the Documentary Hypothesis is an anachronism from the point of view of tradition-criticism.' That is, the two methods are not complementary, they are incompatible with each other. We may note, in passing, that this had been said before, by Ivan Engnell, the Scandinavian scholar, and his closest followers. In Rendtorff's polarization of source and tradition criticism the theses of Engnell have received, in part, a new lease of life.

27. Why does Rendtorff polarize the two methods? Because according to him, they represent the use of diametrically opposed starting-points in the analysis of the text. Source criticism begins from 'the final form of the text' and examines the question of its unity, and seeks to explain its apparent diversity in terms of the combination of parallel 'sources' (such as J, E, and P). Tradition criticism, on the other hand, starts from the smallest originally independent unit, say an individual episode in the story or a law, and seeks to explain how it was combined with other similar units to make a series to make a yet larger whole, and how editorial processes or redaction shaped the units until they reached their present form. So it is not a matter of doing source criticism first and then tradition criticism: you have to choose your starting-point and follow through the analysis until you reach the other end. As it stands this is not a very strong point: tradition criticism too has to start with the present text. The contrast of approaches could be put better by saying that traditional source criticism has been ready to believe that a sequence of narratives was a unity unless it was proved otherwise; whereas Rendtorff wants to say that prior to the present text narratives were not united unless that can be positively proved. This is not specifically a traditio-critical view: it is noticeable above all in fact in some of the newer revisions of source criticism, specifically in those emanating from the pupils of W. Richter.

28. Quite apart from this methodological point, Rendtorff is in little doubt that source criticism is a bankrupt business. In a chapter of his book entitled 'Criticism of Pentateuchal Criticism' he exposes at length the disagreements of source critics both about individual passages and about the number and nature of the sources they find. There is no consensus, he repeatedly affirms; there is no 'classical documentary theory', but several competing theories, none of which has been able to drive the others from the field. In particular the status of the J document, which according to von Rad gave the Pentateuch its canonical shape, is very doubtful. Is it one document or two (cf. its subdivision by Eissfeldt and Fohrer)? And more generally, what evidence is there of its unity? Here Rendtorff points to the method of elimination which lies so often behind the identification of J passages. First the easily recognizable P sections are eliminated from the existing Pentateuch, to reveal the older sources; then likewise the book of Deuteronomy (D) is removed; then E, marked by its use of Elohim in Genesis; and then what is left is called J. But how do we know that what is left is a unity? To give an analogy: how do we know that the Pentateuch is not like a basket containing many kinds of fruit, from which the apples, bananas, and oranges are removed, to leave—just pears? No, surely a mixture of these with peaches, grapes, strawberries, and so on.

29. It is not of potential disunity in a source-critical sense (i.e. two parallel Yahwist (J) strands, as with Eissfeldt and Fohrer) that Rendtorff is primarily thinking, but rather in a traditio-historical sense: what reason have we for thinking that the residue was a single continuous narrative describing everything from creation to the conquest of the land, rather than a series of smaller-scale stories, one about the patriarchs, one about the Exodus, etc.? In fact Rendtorff believes that it is possible to show that the J material is in this sense definitely not a unity. This he endeavours to do by an examination of the various sections of the Pentateuchal narrative taken one by one: the sections bear a notable resemblance to Noth's themes—patriarchs, Exodus, Sinai, wilderness, and settlement. The primeval history seems to be passed over, but the same approach could be applied to it. Rendtorff's point is that the theological perspective of the editing is not consistent throughout but varies from one section to the next. Comprehensive theological evaluations of the whole history are surprisingly rare, and tend to be concentrated in what look like late passages. In his book Rendtorff did not spell his argument out in full detail for all the sections, but he indicated his method of applying tradition criticism in a very detailed study

of the patriarchal narratives. He begins with the observation (which is not new) that the theological texts of the patriarchal stories are chiefly concentrated in the 'promises': passages, that is, where YHWH makes a promise or several promises to Abraham, Isaac, or Jacob. The interrelation of the contents of these promise-passages to one another is extremely complex, and Rendtorff attributes it to a succession of stages of editing of the patriarchal traditions. At any rate it is clear that the promises are the major theological theme of the patriarchal narratives. Now von Rad had seen this and attributed the main body of the promises to the Yahwist, who he supposed inserted them to impress on the Pentateuchal material his theological understanding of Israel's early history: it was a history worked out under the shadow of YHWH's promise. But against this Rendtorff is able to show that this theme virtually vanishes at the end of Genesis, and is missing from JE passages such as Ex 3, which mention the land to which YHWH now says he will lead the Israelites without any hint that this had been promised long ago to their forefathers, time and time again! The conclusion he draws is that the development of the promise theme in Genesis is not the work of a J author who composed or compiled a document extending the whole length of the Pentateuch, but rather the theological enrichment of a story which did not extend beyond the limits of the patriarchal period itself. Only at the time of the Priestly redaction and a further stage of editing related to the Deuteronomic school is there any sign of the various sections of the Pentateuch being co-ordinated together into a continuous narrative. Prior to this there existed only shorter compositions which circulated separately and were edited separately—Rendtorff seems not to have any suggestion to offer about the social context in which this took place or the purpose that such compositions might have served, but clearly there are in some cases at least possibilities of an association with cultic festivals.

30. It is not clear whether Rendtorff's particular proposals will be able to withstand detailed criticism. The denial of a unity in J will have to contend not only with von Rad but with the more wide-ranging studies of G. Hölscher and H. Schulte. There are in fact various ways in which scholars might respond to the dilemmas with which Rendtorff has faced us, apart from accepting in full his own reading of the situation. But he has, whatever we may decide, exposed some tensions at the heart of modern critical method which need to be resolved. I do not myself think that tradition criticism is a very secure base from which to attack the literary-critical enterprise. It is a bit like trying to move a piano while standing on a tea-trolley!

31. Since it was first put forward in 1977 this view has been rather neglected. Rendtorff himself quite quickly lost interest in it: he was persuaded by Childs's arguments that attention ought to be focused on the final canonical form of the text—a dramatic change for him—and he became particularly interested in the coherence of the book of Isaiah as a whole. His Introduction to the Old Testament (ET 1985) reflects this change of perspective, though it also shows that he retains some interest in older traditions and redaction criticism. A student of Rendtorff's, Erhard Blum, has continued some of his ideas in two large books on the Pentateuch (1984, 1990), but it is noticeable that he too increasingly concentrates not on the earliest stages of the tradition, when the stories of

the primeval history, the patriarchs, the Exodus, etc. may have been told separately from one another, but on the stages at which they were already combined together: he investigates what he calls the Deuteronomistic Composition (KD)—which does not include the J portions of Gen 1–11—and the Priestly Composition (KP), which successively amplified the traditions from their particular points of view (cf. Johnstone 1990).

J. Review and Assessment. 1. In reviewing these recent developments it should be noted that by different routes quite a lot of scholars are coming to support more or less the same alternative to the older source-critical view. The developments outlined in the last four sections are increasingly merging into what is in effect the same understanding of the origin of the Pentateuch. This holds that:

1. The first major comprehensive Pentateuchal narrative was composed either late in pre-exilic times or in the Babylonian exile (7th or 6th cent. BCE), rather than in the early monarchy. Some prefer to speak of a 'late Yahwist' (Schmid, Van Seters), some of a Deuteronomistic narrative (Johnstone, Blum), but they are largely talking about the same thing and using the same arguments.
2. The Priestly Work never existed as a separate source, but involved the insertion into the older narrative of the specifically Priestly narratives and laws, so as to produce a work very like our present Pentateuch.

In each case the model or overall approach is a 'supplementary' one, that is, the old idea of redactors interweaving extracts from distinct sources, a verse from here and a verse from there, is abandoned and we go right back to the approach that was followed in the first half of the nineteenth century and think of a core which in successive stages was amplified until the present Pentateuch was produced: the major difference being—and it is a very significant one—that then what we call P was (part of) the original core, while now it represents the final stage of the process. An important theological consequence of the new approach is the increased prominence which it gives to the sections of the Pentateuch which contain or are associated with law, namely the Deuteronomistic and Priestly passages. It should be noted that theses 1 and 2 are in fact logically independent. It is possible to accept one of them and not the other, and some scholars have done and still do this, following the Wellhausen approach or something like it on the other issue. Thus Cross accepts 2 but not 1; and Schmid and Blenkinsopp hold 1 but not 2.

2. The supporters of the new views are not having things all their own way. Some difficulties with them have already been mentioned, and some further criticisms of thesis 1 have been made by E. W. Nicholson in a recent paper (see also Nicholson 1998). This thesis also fails, in its strongest form, to do justice to the evidence of Deuteronomy itself. The very setting of Deuteronomy on the eve of the conquest of the promised land presupposes a tradition about Israel's origins; likewise there are many passing allusions to features of that tradition in the text of Deuteronomy which would only have made sense if the hearers of the Deuteronomic preaching had been familiar with a quite detailed account of the Exodus and so on. As for thesis 2, we have seen that some passages,

such as the Flood story, are very difficult for it to accommodate.

3. So what are we to think? Which view will prevail? As far as 1 is concerned, I think we are at a stage when all the emphasis is on late elements of the Pentateuch, and some scholars write as though that is all there is. The arguments for lateness are of varying strength. For myself I am more convinced that the Decalogue is a late addition to the Sinai narrative in Exodus than that the idea of a covenant is a latecomer in Exodus, for example. But more important, I think we shall before long find more work being done again on what we may call for now the 'pre-Deuteronomic Pentateuchal narratives and laws'—their contents, their theology, and their origins. Then the Deuteronomic or late J layer (which may turn out to be 'thinner' than currently thought!) will be seen as more clearly that, rather than seeming to comprise the whole of the non-P part of the Pentateuch. On 2 an interesting mediating position has been put forward by R. E. Friedman (1981). He thinks that at a first stage there were independent P versions of certain parts of the Pentateuch, such as the Flood story; but the major composition of P as a whole took place at a second stage in very much the way Cross proposed, i.e. by supplementation of the older narrative. Where P texts from the first stage had to be worked into the older narrative, they were sometimes interwoven with the older version, as in the case of the Flood story. Blum, working in detail on certain passages, ends up with a partly similar view to this. Maybe it will be necessary to hold some such view to accommodate all the evidence—the case for supplementation has been argued to be particularly strong in relation to the Table of Nations and the plague-story by Van Seters—or maybe it will be better, in view of the coherence of so much of the P material, to retain the idea of an original, once-separate source, and explain the most intractable counter-indications by a further, still later layer of redaction.

4. But there are problems within the literary-critical method itself, arising from the fact that we now feel compelled to treat each unit separately for analysis. While it is quite clear that the Pentateuch is not a literary unity and that analysis can separate out parallel strands at numerous points, it is not so obvious that a rigorous approach to the assembly of the 'bits' leads automatically to the division of the Pentateuch into four or five major sources, such as traditional source criticism proposes. In other words the model for synthesis (step c.3) need not be a wholly documentary one. About the coherence and original independence of the bulk at least of the P material, it seems to me, there is little doubt, and equally about the separate character and development of Deuteronomy. However it is more difficult to be sure how the residue of the books Genesis–Numbers is to be thought of and Rendtorff's thesis of shorter works may well have a part to play, and equally processes of redaction which did not extend the whole length of the Pentateuch, but concerned only a particular range of the narrative.

5. We may conclude by returning, very briefly, to the question with which we began, 'What is the Pentateuch?', in the light of the modern study of the text which we have just reviewed. Whichever of the approaches that have recently been advocated prevails, or even if things eventually stay very much as they were, we must build into our view of the

Pentateuch the fact that it is the product of a long process of tradition. In other words we must recognize that its teaching, while organized into some sort of unity by the various redactors, derives from various periods in the history of Israel within which certain individuals or schools have contributed an especially creative shaping and rethinking of the traditions which they inherited. In varying degrees these individuals or schools deserve the name 'theologians'. To some extent the difficulty of finding a fully satisfactory description for the Pentateuch as a whole is due to the differing emphases of these writers. In a real sense, then, the Pentateuch bears witness to the whole history and life of Israel, and not just to the period which it purports to describe. As a comprehensive description I would suggest the following, which I think can apply to all stages of the composition of the Pentateuch:

'The charter of YHWH's people Israel, which lays down the founding principles of their life in creation, history and law, under the guidance of his word of promise and command.'

REFERENCES

Alt, A. (1966), 'The Origins of Israelite Law', in *Essays on Old Testament History and Religion*, ET (Oxford: Blackwell), 87–132; 1st edn. 1934.

Alter, R. (1981), *The Art of Biblical Narrative* (London: George Allen & Unwin).

Auld, A. G. (1980), *Joshua, Moses and the Land* (Edinburgh: T. & T. Clark).

Barton, J. (1984), *Reading the Old Testament* (London: Darton, Longman & Todd).

Boecker, H.-J. (1980), *Law and the Administration of Justice in the OT and the Ancient Near East*, ET (London: SPCK).

Brueggemann, W., and Wolff, H. W. (1975), *The Vitality of OT Traditions* (Atlanta: John Knox).

Campbell, A. F., and O'Brien, M. A. (1993), *Sources of the Pentateuch: Texts, Introductions, Annotations* (Minneapolis: Fortress).

Carpenter, J. E., and Harford-Battersby, G. (1900), *The Hexateuch According to the Revised Version* (2 vols. (London: Longmans, Green and Co.); vol. ii is a synopsis).

Childs, B. S. (1979), *Introduction to the OT as Scripture* (London: SCM).

Clements, R. E. (1997), *A Century of Old Testament Study* (Guildford: Butterworth).

Clines, D. J. A. (1978), *The Theme of the Pentateuch* (Sheffield: JSOT).

Coats, G. W. (1988), *Moses: Heroic Man, Man of God* (Sheffield: JSOT).

Davies, G. I. (1996), 'The Composition of the Book of Exodus: Reflections on the Theses of E. Blum', in M. Fox *et al.* (eds.), *Texts, Temples and Tradition: A Tribute to Menahem Haran* (Winona Lake, Ind.: Eisenbrauns), 71–85.

Driver, S. R. (1904), *The Book of Genesis*, Westminster Commentaries (London: Methuen).

Emerton, J. A. (1988), 'The Priestly Writer in Genesis', *JTS* NS 39: 381–400.

Friedman, R. E. (1981), *The Exile and Biblical Narrative* (Chico, Calif.: Scholars Press).

Gerstenberger, E. (1965), *Wesen und Herkunft des 'apodiktischen Rechts'*, WMANT 20 (Neukirchen-Vluyn: Neukirchener Verlag).

Habel, N. C. (1971), *Literary Criticism of the OT* (Philadelphia: Fortress).

Haran, M. (1979), *Temples and Temple-Service in Ancient Israel* (Oxford: Oxford University Press).

Jenks, A. W. (1977), *The Elohist and North Israelite Traditions* (Chico, Calif.: Scholars Press).

Johnstone, W. (1998), *Chronicles and Exodus: An Analogy and its Application* (Sheffield: JSOT).

Nicholson, E. W. (1973), *Exodus and Sinai in History and Tradition* (Oxford: Blackwell).

—— (1986), *God and his People* (Oxford: Oxford University Press).

—— (1998), *The Pentateuch in the Twentieth Century: The Legacy of Julius Wellhausen* (Oxford: Clarendon Press).

Noth, M. (1972), *A History of Pentateuchal Traditions*, ET (Englewood Cliffs, NJ: Prentice-Hall), from Germ. orig., *Überlieferungsgeschichte des Pentateuch* (1948).

Otto, E. (1994), *Theologische Ethik des Alten Testament* (Stuttgart: Kohlhammer).

Patrick, D. (1986), *Old Testament Law* (London: SCM).

Rad, G. von (1966), 'The Form-Critical Problem of the Hexateuch' (1938), in his *The Problem of the Hexateuch and Other Essays* (Edinburgh: Oliver & Boyd), 1–78.

Rendtorff, R. (1990), *The Problem of the Process of Transmission in the Pentateuch*, ET (Sheffield: JSOT), from German original, *Das überlieferungsgeschichtliche Problem des Pentateuch*, BZAW 147 (1977).

Skinner, J. (1910), *A Critical and Exegetical Commentary on Genesis*, International Critical Commentary (Edinburgh: T. & T. Clark).

Soggin, J. A. (1989), *Introduction to the Old Testament*, 3rd edn. (London: SCM).

Sonsino, R. (1980), *Motive Clauses in Biblical Law*, SBLDS 45 (Chico, Calif.: Scholars Press).

Stamm, J. J., and Andrew, M. E. (1967), *The Ten Commandments in Recent Research*, SBT 2/2 (London: SCM).

Van Seters, J. (1992), *Prologue to History* (Louisville, Ky.: Westminster/John Knox).

—— (1994), *The Life of Moses: The Yahwist as Historian in Exodus–Numbers* (Louisville, Ky.: Westminster/John Knox).

Wellhausen, J. (1885), *Prolegomena to the History of Israel*, ET (Edinburgh: A. & C. Black); from German original, *Geschichte Israels I* (1878).

Westermann, C. (1984), 'The Formation and Theological Meaning of the Primeval Story', in *Genesis 1–11: A Commentary* (Minneapolis: Augsburg), 567–606; German original *Genesis I–II* (Neukirchen-Vluyn: Neukirchener Verlag, 1974–6).

Wolff, H. W. (1975), 'The Elohistic Fragments in the Pentateuch', in Brueggemann and Wolff (1975), 67–82.

Whybray, R. N. (1987), *The Making of the Pentateuch* (Sheffield: JSOT).

4. Genesis   R. N. WHYBRAY

INTRODUCTION

A. Genesis and the Pentateuch. Genesis forms part of a series of 'historical' books that begin with the creation of the world and end with the destruction of the tiny kingdom of Judah in the sixth century BCE (the final chs. of 2 Kings). The events narrated are all arranged in a single chronological sequence into which the non-narrative material, mainly poems and

laws, has been fitted. But this great history was not originally conceived as a single work. It is generally agreed that it consists of two complexes, but the point at which the first ends and the second begins has long been a disputed question. According to ancient tradition the first complex comprises the first five books, ending with Deuteronomy. This is known to the Jews by the name of Torah (or 'the law'), and is the first and most sacred part of the canon of the Hebrew Scriptures. Modern scholars know it as the Pentateuch, a Greek word meaning '(of) five books'. However, its integrity was challenged in the nineteenth century CE, when many scholars held that it is incomplete without Joshua: it is only in Josh that God's promise, made in Genesis, of possession of the land of Canaan is fulfilled (hence the term Hexateuch, *six* books). This hypothesis has few supporters today. In 1948 Martin Noth (ET 1972) also rejected the traditional view but in a contrary sense: the first *four* books constituted a complete work (the Tetrateuch). Deuteronomy, though later joined with these to form the Pentateuch, belonged to a second and distinct work, the Deuteronomistic History, comprising Deuteronomy, Joshua, Judges, Samuel, and Kings. Noth's theory has been widely accepted. It may perhaps seem that these questions are irrelevant to a study of Genesis; but this is not so. Genesis, although it has its own distinctive character—it is the only book in the Pentateuch that is not dominated by the figure of Moses—is intimately linked with the books that follow, and can only be fully understood as part of a more extended history. It is essentially a book of promise, a preface to all that follows in the history of Israel, having specific links to many events narrated in those books. It establishes the identity of the nation of Israel and of its God. In particular, it is a necessary prelude to the great events associated with the Exodus from Egypt, which is the foundation of Jewish history and faith. At the same time it presents the reader with the God who is creator of the world but also a God who cares for his human creatures and reveals his nature especially in his protection and guidance of those whom he chose to be his special people.

B. Literary Genre. It is important for an understanding of Genesis (and of the Pentateuch as a whole) to see it as a literary work and to attempt to define its literary genre. This involves an appreciation of the nature of ancient, pre-scientific, historiography, of which the most notable examples are to be found in the work of certain early Greek historians of the sixth century BCE. The aim of these historians was to write accounts of the origins, genealogical descent, and history of the notable families of their own day, tracing them back to a remote, heroic age: see Van Seters (1983: 8–54; 1992: 24–38). In their accounts of past ages they did not distinguish between myth, legend, and what we now call 'historical facts'. It was not their primary purpose to establish the exact truth of the events that they described, but rather to raise in their readers a consciousness of their own identity and a feeling that they were citizens of a great and noble city or race. These historians made full use of extant traditions about the past, but they were also *creators* of tradition: where extant traditions were lacking or scanty, they did not hesitate to fill them out with details, and even entire stories, supplied from their own imaginations. This kind of imaginative writing has analogies with that of the Israelite historians; but the purposes of the latter were somewhat different. They were certainly concerned to create—or, perhaps, to restore—a sense of national identity in their readers; but their intention was far from triumphalist: the principal human characters were not heroes in the fullest sense. For them it is always God who has the principal role; the human characters are represented as foolish and fre-

quently sinful creatures who time and time again frustrate God's good intentions towards them.

C. Types of Material. The character and intention of Genesis as a completed book cannot be deduced from the wide miscellany of materials which constitute its sources. Gunkel (1901) (see Gunkel 1964 for ET of the Introduction to his commentary) identified many of the sources and demonstrated their nature. Particularly in chs. 12–36 he identified many *Sagen*—that is, brief, originally independent, folktales—which had been strung together only at a relatively late stage, eventually taking shape as accounts of the lives of Abraham, Isaac, and Jacob. The somewhat different characters of chs. 1–11, which narrate cosmic and universal events (often classified as 'myths'—an ambiguous term) and of the story of Joseph in chs. 37–50, a single, homogeneous narrative not formed by the combination of *Sagen*, has long been recognized. All this material has been pieced together and provided with a continuous narrative thread and a chronological sequence by a skilful editor and compiler, who by his selection and arrangement of material and his own original contributions converted it into an expression of his own view of history and theology. With regard to the *Sagen* used by this compiler, Gunkel held that much of this material had previously been transmitted in oral form over many generations and so may be seen as preserving, even though in garbled form, genuine reminiscences of the persons and events described, but this has recently been questioned: see Whybray (1987: 133–219).

D. Composition. About the process or processes by which the diverse material was combined to form a single literary work there is at present no consensus of opinion. The Documentary Hypothesis (see INTROD.PENT B), which was the dominant theory for about a century, envisaged an interweaving of comprehensive 'horizontal' written sources (in Genesis, J, E, and P); but this view has met strong opposition during the last twenty years; and none of the alternative theories that have been proposed has yet found general acceptance. One thorough investigation of the composition of the patriarchal stories (Blum 1984), which envisages a gradual process of composition in which the traditions about each of the patriarchs were gradually and independently built up before their combination into larger complexes, has considerable plausibility; on the other hand, the notion of a fragment hypothesis according to which there was no lengthy process of growth but a single act of composition in which a mass of material was collated by a single author, as in the case of the early Greek historians cited above, has undergone something of a revival: see Whybray (1987: 221–42). In this commentary the Documentary Hypothesis is referred to only occasionally. Obvious differences of point of view implied in the material employed have been noted; but no attempt has been made to define or to date these. References to the 'author', 'editor' etc., are to those responsible for the final shaping of the book.

E. The Date of Genesis. Nothing in the book directly indicates the time when it reached its final shape. However, many passages reflect episodes and situations of post-patriarchal times: the tradition of a nation comprising twelve tribes (49:16, 28); the Exodus from Egypt (15:13–14); the future possession of Canaan and the areas occupied by the various tribes (15:17–20; 17:8; 28:4); the predominance of the tribe of Judah (49:10) and of the Joseph tribes (especially Ephraim (48:17–20)); and the Davidic monarchy (49:10). There are also anachronisms such as the references to the 'land of the Philistines' (21:32, 34), whose arrival in Canaan was roughly contemporary with that of the Israelites, and to the Chaldeans (11:28, 31; 15:7), a people of southern Mesopotamia whose names do not appear in historical records before the time of the neo-Assyrian empire (from the 8th cent. BCE) and who were otherwise unknown to the OT before the sixth century BCE. Other features of the book—for example the constantly reiterated theme of the promise of possession of the land of Canaan—are perhaps best understood as particularly relevant to a time when the nation had been dispossessed from the land—that is, either the Babylonian exile during the sixth century BCE or the ensuing period when the Jewish community living in and around Jerusalem were once more, like the patriarchs of Genesis, aliens in the land, needing encouragement to hope that God would enable them to throw off the yoke of Persian domination and would restore to them the fullness of his blessing as the rightful owners of the land which he had promised long ago to them.

F. Themes. **1.** The primeval history (Gen 1–11) heralds some of the main themes of the book. It defines Israel's place in the world of nations and links the human figures of the remote past with Abraham and his descendants by a series of genealogies. It also functions as a universal history of beginnings. It afforded the author the opportunity to state his belief that there is only one, supreme God and that he created the world with all its inhabitants. It is concerned with the nature of this God and with the nature of his human creatures. This universal history taught the Israelite readers a moral lesson as well as a theology: human beings are both foolish and prone to sinful rebellion against God, arrogant and ambitious, seeking to achieve divine status for themselves and capable of murderous intentions towards one another. It warned about the consequences of such behaviour: God, who at the beginning had approved his created world as good, determined to obliterate the human race when it became corrupted; but he mercifully refrained from carrying out this intention: he punished, but did not destroy. So the first man and woman were banished from the garden but allowed to live outside it; the first murderer also was banished, but his life was preserved; the human race, despite its total corruption, was given a second chance in the persons of Noah and his family; the builders of the Tower of Babel were scattered and divided, but survived and peopled the world. The picture of humanity painted in these chapters is dark but realistic; however, it is lightened by the corresponding theme of divine forbearance which, in the context of the book as a whole, foreshadows a more hopeful destiny for a human race that will be blessed in Abraham.

2. The two main themes of chs. 12–36 are God's choice of Abraham and his descendants out of the entire human race and the promises that he made to them. The particularity of this choice is striking: it is seen not only in the initial selection of Abraham but also in a series of subsequent choices: not Ishmael but Isaac, not Esau but Jacob are chosen. (The theme is pursued further in the succeeding Joseph story: Joseph, Jacob's eleventh son, is chosen to be the saviour of his family,

and even in the next generation Ephraim is preferred before Manasseh.) The promises in their fullest form comprise divine blessing, guidance and protection, wealth and political power, and the possession of the land of Canaan as a permanent home. But there is also an important counter-theme: that of the perils into which the recipients of the promises (and their wives) constantly fall, sometimes through their own fault and sometimes at God's instigation (Gen 22). It is this counter-theme that gives liveliness and excitement to the narratives; indeed, without it there would be no story to tell. The failure of the promise of the land to materialize within the timespan of the book gives these narratives a forward-looking character: the possession of the land is clearly the goal to which they aspire. There are, of course, a number of subsidiary themes, corresponding to the variety of the material. There is throughout a strong emphasis on the inscrutability of God's purposes.

3. The story of Joseph (chs. 37–50) continues that of the previous section, but has its own independent character and its own themes. Except at the very end of the book the divine promises are not specifically mentioned in these chapters, though the theme of the endangered heirs continues to be prominent: at different times both Joseph and his family are placed in peril. The Egyptian setting is a major feature of the Joseph story and is described in some detail, partly to give it a plausible local colour but mainly in order to enhance the impression of Joseph's eminent position in Egypt. Joseph's character is portrayed with consummate skill. This final part of the book leaves the readers with hopes of a splendid future. The final verses specifically foretell the Exodus from Egypt which will lead at last to the possession of the promised land.

COMMENTARY

A History of Origins (chs. 1–11)

These chapters may be regarded as a prologue to Genesis, and indeed to the whole Pentateuch. Beginning as they do with the activity of God even before the universe came into existence (Gen 1:1–2), they clearly cannot be based on any record of what actually occurred; and the fact that in them a number of persons are reported as having lived preternaturally long lives is sufficient to show that the world depicted here is different even from that of the later chapters of the book. These stories do not constitute a connected sequence; they have been linked together only in a very artificial way by a series of genealogies (Gen 4:17–22; 5:1–32; 10:1–32; 11:10–32). They are universal stories, depicting not human beings as we know them but giants or heroes in something like the fairytale sense of those words. What is being conveyed is how the authors or collectors of the stories imagined that it might all have begun. However, as we shall see, these stories were intended to convey a much more profound meaning than that.

Many peoples have at an early stage of their development possessed a fund of stories about the origin of the world and the earliest history of the human race; and many of the stories in Gen 1–11 have a family likeness to origin-stories current in the Near-Eastern milieu to which ancient Israel belonged (cf. *ANET* 3–155). These Israelite versions, however, are unique in that they are monotheistic: all the divine actions that they depict are attributed to a single deity, and there is no mention of other gods. The term 'myth' is often applied to them; but since there is no agreement about the meaning of that term it is probably best avoided.

It is possible that the final author or compiler of these chapters has left an indication of their structure by his use of the word *tôlĕdôt*, especially in the phrase 'These are the *tôlĕdôt* of...' (2:4; 6:9; 10:1; 11:10, 27; cf. also 5:1). However, this phrase, which also occurs at intervals in the later chapters of the book, can hardly be adequate as a structural marker since it is used with different meanings, e.g. genealogy or list of descendants (6:9; 10:1) and story or history (2:4; 37:1). One way of viewing the purpose and structure of chs. 1–11 is to see them as presenting a picture of the growing power of sin in the world, together with a parallel picture of a 'hidden growth of grace' (von Rad 1966a: 64–5). This view has some plausibility as regards chs. 3–9. If this is so, however, the story of the Tower of Babel (11:1–9) surely stands outside the pattern. There, as also in ch. 3, it appears to be God's concern for his own status rather than his grace that is to the fore. It may be best to regard this story as an appendix to chs. 1–9, or as a negative foil to the story of Abraham that begins at the end of ch. 11.

Why does the Pentateuch preface its history of Israel's ancestors with these universal stories? It is of interest to note that the origin-stories of other nations (see Van Seters 1983) show a similar pattern: many of them also begin with mythical tales and then proceed gradually to the more historical. The aim of such works, apart from a wish to satisfy the readers' natural curiosity about 'how it all began', was to create or strengthen their sense of national or ethnic identity, especially at critical times when for specific reasons this was threatened. In order to foster such a sense it was thought necessary to account for the nation's place in the world; and, since the human race was thought to have had a single origin, to explain how the various peoples had come into existence. In Gen 1–11 these aims come to the fore in ch. 10, which was clearly intended to be a 'map' of all the peoples of the world, and in 11:1–9, which accounts for their failure to remain united. At this point the history of Israel's ancestors could begin.

But beyond these motives Gen 1–11 was designed to reflect certain distinctive Israelite (Yahwistic) articles of faith. Not the least of these was monotheism. Despite the inclusion of the phrases 'Let *us* make man in our own image' (1:26) and 'like one of *us*' (3:22), on which see below, this monotheistic stance is quite striking and sometimes even polemical—that is, anti-polytheistic—especially in ch. 1. The conflict-tradition of Mesopotamia, according to which the creator-god had had to fight and kill a hostile monster before he could create the world, although traces of it are to be found elsewhere in the OT (e.g. Ps 74:13–14; Isa 51:9), is entirely absent here: the 'great sea monsters' (*tannînîm*, 1:21) are simply listed together with God's other creatures. Similarly the sun, moon, and other heavenly bodies, which in the Near-Eastern religious systems are powerful deities coexisting with the creator-god, are here a part of God's creation and are entirely subservient to him, being assigned by him their proper functions (1:14–18). Equally distinctive of Israelite religion is the setting aside by God of the seventh day, the day on which he rested from his work of creation, to be observed as a day of rest—presumably by the whole created world—in the institution of the Sabbath (2:1–3).

Some scholars have interpreted these chapters as reflecting the experiences of the Babylonian exile or the early post-exilic period. Thus the themes of punishment for sin, especially banishment from God's presence and/or dispersal or destruction (3:23–4; 4:12, 16; 6–8; 11:4, 9), have been taken as symbolic of Israel's richly deserved banishment from the land of Canaan, while the signs of divine grace and forgiveness, especially God's acceptance of Noah's sacrifice and the covenant which he made with him (8:20–9:17) would suggest to the exilic or post-exilic reader that God had even now not cast off his people but was a God of infinite patience and forgiveness who would rescue Israel from its folly and its guilt as he had done for humanity in ancient times.

Some of these stories also betray an interest in aetiology: that is, in seeking the origin of various phenomena of universal human experience which appear to defy rational explanation. These aetiologies are of many kinds. One of the most important ones concerns the reason for human mortality, a common theme in both Near-Eastern and classical literature that sometimes took the form of narratives in which human beings attempted to wrest immortality from the gods but failed; this is alluded to in Gen 3:22—which appears to imply that mortality is inherent in mankind's status as creature—and in the mysterious incident of 6:1–3. The nature of the relationship between man and woman is discussed in 2:18, which explains why both sexes are necessary to a complete humanity, and in 2:23–4, which explains the attraction between the sexes and the forming of permanent relationships between them as due to God's providence. In ch. 3, however, the less ideal realities of the relationship are attributed to disobedience to God's command, in which both partners are implicated.

There is also an aetiology of work here. Work in itself is not regarded as a punishment: rather, it is a natural (male) activity (2:15); but—it is implied—it is an agreeable one. The cursing of the ground and the consequent harshness of agricultural labour (3:17–19) are the result of disobedience. The final line of 3:19 ('You are dust, and to dust you shall return'), possibly a common saying, does not imply that human mortality is the result of disobedience.

Another matter that evidently called for explanation was the wearing of clothing. The feeling of shame at appearing naked before others (cf. 9:20–7) and the universal custom of wearing clothes are explained as a consequence of the eating of the forbidden fruit (3:7–12, 21): previously (2:25), nakeness had not been shameful. Other aetiologies in these chapters include the reason for the human dislike of snakes and for the ability of snakes to move without legs (3:14–15), the reason for the rainbow (9:12–17), and the origin of the sabbath.

It is generally agreed that the stories in Gen 1–11 are not a pure invention of the final compiler: however much he may have adapted them for his own purpose, he was using material current in his own time. On the nature and date of this material, however, there is at present no agreement. Arguments have recently been advanced which suggest that, at least in their present form, these chapters cannot be older than the sixth century BCE. For example, the Chaldeans, referred to in 11:28, a verse assigned by the followers of the Documentary

Hypothesis to the oldest source J, did not become significant on the international scene until about that time, while the garden of Eden is nowhere mentioned in OT texts before the time of the exilic Isaiah (Deutero-Isaiah, Isa 51:3) and Ezekiel (Ezek 28:13; 36:35). Similarly Abraham (Abram 11:26–30) appears to have been unknown in the pre-exilic period: he is never mentioned by the pre-exilic prophets, and his name occurs only in two OT passages which may be pre-exilic but are probably not (1 Kings 18:36; Ps 47:9). This fact is, of course, significant also for the dating of the story of Abraham in chs. 12–25. Finally it is remarkable that there is no extant ancient Near-Eastern text that in any way covers the same ground as Gen 1–11, and no evidence that any other people compiled a comparable narrative before the Graeco-Roman period.

(1:1–2:4a) The Creation of the World This creation story is only one of many current in the ancient Near East; there are, for example, several extant Egyptian ones in which the creation of the world is attributed to different gods, and the creator-god is not necessarily the principal god. This multiplicity is due to the existence of different local traditions. In the OT also, where there is only one God, we find several quite distinct creation traditions. In addition to Gen 1 there is a different account in Gen 2, and another version is reflected especially in Ps 74:13–14 and Isa 51:9, in which the creation of the world appears to have followed a conflict in which YHWH defeated and killed a sea monster or monsters. Other somewhat different versions are found in Prov 8:22–31, in parts of the book of Job, and elsewhere.

The creation story in Gen 1:1–2:4 has long been thought to have particular affinities with the Babylonian *Enuma Elish* (*ANET* 60–72); but a glance at the latter shows that the relationship is at most a very remote one. Apart from the fact that the Genesis story is monotheistic, the most crucial difference between the two accounts is that *Enuma Elish* belongs to the category of the conflict tradition, which is entirely absent from Gen 1. In the former, the god Marduk first summons the other deities and, after killing the sea monster Tiamat, creates heaven and earth by splitting Tiamat's body into two. (The commonly repeated notion that the word 'the deep'—*tĕhôm*, in 1:2—is a pale reminiscence of Tiamat cannot be sustained.) There is no trace of a conflict here: God is alone, and he is supreme.

This account contains no explicit statement about God's *purpose* in creating the world; but this purpose is clearly implied in the great emphasis that is placed on the position of mankind in God's plan: the creation of mankind, the last of God's creative acts, is evidently the climax of the whole account, and receives the greatest attention (1:26–30). The creatures created on the previous days—light, day and night, dry land, heavenly bodies, plants and animals—are all by implication provided for mankind's use and convenience; human beings are given the plants for food, and power over the animals. Above all they are created in God's image and likeness (1:26–7). Whatever may be the precise meaning of that phrase—this question has been endlessly debated (see below)—it sets human beings apart from all the other creatures and puts them in a unique relationship with God himself.

A further clue to God's intention when he created the world is to be found in the successive statements made at the conclusion of each act of creation, that 'God saw that it was good' (1:4, 10, 12, 18, 21, 25), culminating in the final comprehensive statement that he 'saw everything that he had made, and indeed, it was very good' (1:31). This is the craftsman's assessment of his own work; and it says something about his intention as well as about his artistry. A competently crafted artefact implies a good intention. The word 'good' (*tôb*) here, however, refers more directly to the *usefulness* of the world—presumably its usefulness to mankind. It does not necessarily have an ethical connotation: it is not mankind that is said to be 'good', but God's work as craftsman. The author was well aware of the subsequent catastrophic introduction of evil into the world.

In its cosmology—that is, its understanding of the structure and different parts of the universe—this account of the creation conforms to that generally current in the ancient Near East. (In some OT passages this cosmology is described in more detail.) The pre-existent watery waste (1:1–2) was divided into two by the creation of a solid dome or vault (the sky, 1:6–8), so that there was water both above and below it. The lower mass of water was then confined to a limited area, the sea, revealing the dry land, which God called 'the earth' (1:9–10). (According to Gen 7:11 the sky had 'windows' which when opened allowed the rain to fall.) The heavenly bodies, sun, moon, and stars, moved across the vault of the sky, giving light and following a prescribed programme (1:14–18).

A characteristic feature of this account of creation is its precise and meticulous style. It frequently repeats the same phraseology, listing the various acts of creation with the dryness of a catalogue, and possesses nothing of the imaginative or dramatic skill characteristic of chs. 2–3. Yet, as has long been recognized, there remain a number of variations or inconsistencies of detail, which suggests that two or more accounts have been combined. In particular, the creative acts are introduced in different ways. While in some cases God creates simply by speaking ('And God said . . . '), in others we are told that he performed certain actions: he made, separated, named, blessed, placed. A second anomalous feature is that although the entire work of creation was carried out in six days (presumably to conform to the concept of six days of creation concluding with a Sabbath rest on the seventh day), there are in fact eight creative acts: on the third day and again on the sixth (1:9–13, 24–31), *two* acts of creation are performed. It is not possible, however, to reconstruct the earlier accounts whose existence is thus implied.

The sentence with which ch. 1 begins (1:1–2) has been translated in several ways (see NRSV marg.). The older English versions have 'In the beginning God created . . .'. Some other features of these verses call for comment. The use of the word 'God' (*'ĕlōhîm*) rather than YHWH (2:4b–3:24 mainly uses 'the LORD God'—*YHWH 'ĕlōhîm*) is found elsewhere in Genesis and has been taken to indicate the use of different sources. The word rendered by 'created' (*bārā'*) is a rare and probably late term confined almost entirely in the OT to Gen 1–6, where it occurs 9 times, and Isa 40–66; it is used exclusively of the creative activity of God. Elsewhere in the OT that activity is denoted by words meaning 'to form' or 'to make', which are also used of human activity.

1:2 refers to the situation before God's creative action began. There is no question here of a *creatio ex nihilo*, a 'creation out of nothing'. The earth (*hā'āreṣ*) already existed, but it was a 'formless void' (*tōhû wābōhû*)—not a kind of non-existence but something empty and formless, without light and covered by the water of the deep (*tĕhôm*). There are echoes here of the Near-Eastern cosmologies. The word *rûaḥ*, rendered by 'wind' in NRSV, can also mean 'spirit' (see NRSV marg.). Whichever is the correct interpretation, NRSV's 'swept' is a participle, denoting a continuous action; it should perhaps be rendered 'was hovering'.

In 1:3 as in some later verses God creates by means of a command. His words are presumably addressed to the 'formless void' of 1:2. The creation of light before that of the sun and moon (1:14–18) has led to the suggestion that this feature of the account is derived from an earlier, somewhat different tradition. God's separation of light from darkness and his naming them (1:4–5), like his other acts of separating and naming (1:6, 8, 10, 14, 18), are the acts of a sovereign who determines the destinies of his subordinates.

In 1:11, 12, 21, 24, 25 the phrase 'of every kind' might be better rendered by '(each) according to its species'. The reference to signs and seasons and days and years in the description of the heavenly bodies in 1:14 suggests the establishment of the calendar with particular reference to the determination of the dates of the sacred festivals. When the account moves on to the creation of the animal kingdom, first the water animals and birds (1:20–3) and then the land animals (1:24–5), these are distinguished from all that had been previously created as being 'living creatures' (*nepeš [ha] ḥayyâ*, 1:20, 21, 24, 30)—clearly a higher status than that of the plants. They receive God's blessing (1:22, 28). Unlike the plants which are to serve as food for both human beings and animals (1:29, 30) it is significantly not said of them that they may be killed and eaten. This is a vegetarian regime.

The meaning of the statement that mankind was created in God's image (*ṣelem*) and likeness (*dĕmût*) (1:26, 27) has always been a matter of discussion, as also has been the use of the plural form ('Let *us* make', 'in *our* image', 1:26, although in 1:27 the singular form 'in *his* image' is used). The most probable explanation of the second point is that the plural is used to denote the court of heavenly beings who exist to do God's bidding. The terms 'image' and 'likeness' are probably not to be differentiated: the double phrase is simply for emphasis. It clearly defines human beings as resembling God in a way that is not the case with the animals (cf. 1:28 and Ps 8:3–8). The nature of this resemblance is not apparent, however, and hypotheses abound. Since God is often represented elsewhere in the OT as having bodily organs—hands, feet, eyes, etc.— and the word *ṣelem* is elsewhere used of images of gods, it has been supposed that the passage refers to a resemblance to God's external form. It is more probable, however, that some less material resemblance is intended: that human beings, in distinction from the animals, possess the unique capacity to communicate meaningfully with God, or—particularly with reference to the animals—are God's representatives or vice-gerents on earth.

The ordinance that mankind is to rule over the animal kingdom (1:26, 28), like the statement that the sun and moon are to rule over the day and the night (1:16), determines mankind's function in the world. It does not imply exploitation, for food or for any other purpose; rather, it is a conse-quence of the gift to mankind of the image of God. Mankind is, as it were, a manager or supervisor of the world of living creatures. The blessing, accompanied by the command to 'be fruitful and multiply' (1:28) is, as with the animals (1:22), a guarantee that life is to continue.

God's rest (*šābat*, 2:2) on the seventh day implies the sabbath (*šabbāt*—the word itself does not occur here—which is thereby 'hallowed' or made holy (2:3; cf. Ex 20:8). The same reason for the observance of the sabbath is given in the Decalogue (Ex 20:11).

(**2:4b–3:24**) This narrative, which could stand by itself as an independent story, has taken up themes and motifs quite different from those employed in 1:1–2:4a. It was once gen-erally believed to be older and more primitive in its theology than the preceding chapter (J as contrasted with P); but more recently this view has been challenged. Blenkinsopp (1992: 63, 65), for example, suggests that it may have been 'generated by reflection on the creation account in Genesis 1' and may be seen as 'standing in a wisdom tradition which indulged in "philosophizing by means of myth"'. Undoubtedly some of the motifs employed are considerably older than the author's own time; but the telling of tales for edifying or didactic purposes is more a characteristic of a late stage of civilization than an early one. There is evidence, too, that some elements of the vocabulary employed here are late rather than early.

This is a story about two people, a man and a woman, and what happened to them. Although in the context they are necessarily pictured as the *first* man and woman, they are symbols as well as ancestors of the human race: behind his statements that 'This is what happened' the author is saying 'This is how human beings behave, and these are the conse-quences that follow.' The eating of the fruit is not a single event of the remote past, but something that is repeated again and again in human history. The traditional view that it was the first sin that caused all later generations to be born in 'original sin' is not borne out by this story, although it has the aetiological purpose of explaining the present conditions of human existence. It teaches that God's intention for human beings is wholly good, but that they can be led astray by subtle temptations; and that, while disobedience to God, which is self-assertion, may bring greater self-knowledge, it leads to disaster: the intimate relationship with God is broken. Life then becomes harsh and unpleasant; however, God does not entirely abandon his creatures but makes special provisions for their preservation. An Israel that had suffered devastation and exile from its land could hardly fail to get the message.

It is hardly correct to call ch. 2 a second and alternative creation story. The reference to the creation of the world only occupies 2:4b–6, and is expressed in a subordinate clause: 'In the day when . . .'. It is introduced in order to provide a setting for the main story. It belongs to a different tradition from that of ch. 1 with its Mesopotamian perspective—that of Palestine, where *rain* (2:5) is vitally important for the existence of plant and animal life. But other motifs may have Mesopotamian or other origins. In 2:7 the author chose to depict the creation of the first (male) human in terms of formation from the soil (perhaps rather, clay). This is a tradition also found among modern preliterate peoples (Westermann 1984: 204). In Egyptian mythology the god Khnum fashioned living creatures on a potter's wheel (*ANET* 368, 431, 441), while in the Babylonian tradition the wild man Enkidu was fashioned from clay (*ANET* 74).

Eden (2:8—the word means 'delight') as the garden of God occurs again in Ezek 28:13; 31:9; Joel 2:3, and Eden by itself in a few passages in Ezekiel and in Isaiah (51:3), always as a place of ideal fertility and beauty. (It also occurs in Gen 4:16 as a place-name.) In Ezek 28:13–16 there is an allusion to a myth of an expulsion from the garden, but this differs markedly from Gen 2–3.

The two named trees in the garden—the tree of the knowledge of good and evil (2:9, 17, and also, it must be presumed, the 'tree that is in the middle of the garden', 3:3; cf. 3:11, 12) and the tree of life (2:9; 3:22) constitute a puzzle in that the latter does not appear in the main story but only in the two verses mentioned above. The problem is usually, and probably rightly, solved by supposing that the author combined two variant traditions in order to introduce the theme of life and death, and was not concerned with consistency of detail. Both trees have connections with wisdom themes. In the book of Proverbs knowledge is a synonymous with wisdom; and in Prov 3:18 it is stated that wisdom is 'a tree of life to those who lay hold of her'. This might lead one to suppose that the two trees are the same, but it is clear from 2:9 and 3:22 that this is not so. So knowledge and (eternal) life are *not* synonymous in this story.

2:15 resumes the main narrative after what appears to be a digression. The identity of the first two of the four rivers of 2:10–14 is not known. 2:16–17 contain the first instance of a divine prohibition, on which the plot of ch. 3 depends. The naming of the animals by the man in 2:19–20 establishes their distinct characteristics and confirms the man's rule over them. The creation of woman from the man's rib is a detail that no doubt derives from an older tradition. In 2:23 the word 'woman' (*'iššâ*) is stated—erroneously—to be derived from 'man' (*'îš*). 2:24*a* is an aetiology explaining the origin of the relation between the sexes; it appears, however, to run counter to actual practice. 2:25*b* probably expresses a view that was generally held about primitive man. It also points ahead to 3:8–11: shame is one of the consequences of sin.

The serpent (3:1) is neither a supernatural enemy threatening God's creation from outside nor some kind of inner voice within the woman urging her to disobedience. It is specifically stated that it was one of God's creatures, but that it was craftier (*'ārûm*) than all the others. (There is a play on words here: *'ārôm* (2:25) means 'naked'.) *'ārûm* is an ambiguous word: it can also denote 'wisdom' in a positive sense. But here it is the wrong kind of wisdom possessed by the serpent that initiates mankind's fall into disaster. Snakes played a significant part in the mythologies and religious practices of the ancient Near East, as objects both of fear and worship. The question of the origin of the serpent's wickedness is not raised here. The phenomenon of the speaking snake (cf. Balaam's ass, Num 22:28–30) is a folkloric one.

In its conversation with the woman (3:1*b*–5) the serpent asserts that God's threat of immediate death for eating the fruit of the tree of knowledge (2:17) is a false one. The acquisition of the knowledge of good and evil (that is, of wisdom) will lead rather to the human pair becoming 'like God'. There is truth in what the serpent says: eating the fruit does not result

in immediate death, and although the man and woman do not become wholly like God since they still lack immortality, God fears that if they also eat the fruit of the tree of life they will obtain full divine status (3:22). But the serpent fails to say what will be their actual fate.

The various punishments imposed by God on the guilty (3:14–19) all have aetiological bases: serpents have no legs and are thought to 'eat dust', and bite human beings but are killed by them; women are attached to their husbands, suffer pain in childbirth, and also suffer from their husbands' domination (contrast 'helper' and 'partner' in 2:18). The final clause of 3:19, probably a common saying, adds point to the first half of that verse, which refers back to 2:7. The derivation of the name Eve (*ḥawwâ*, 3:20) which occurs in the OT only here and in 4:1, is unknown. There is a play on words here: *ḥawwâ* echoes *ḥay*, 'living (person)'. This verse seems to have no connection with the previous verses, though it is separated from the notice of Eve's becoming a mother (4:1) by only a few verses.

The somewhat ludicrous picture in 3:21 of God's acting as seamstress for the man and his wife is an indication of his continuing concern for mankind now that he has abandoned his original intention to impose the death sentence (2:17) on them. 3:22–4 is not to be regarded as the imposition of an additional punishment: God has already made it clear that mankind's way of life must now change radically and for the worse. The reason for the expulsion from the garden is specifically stated in 3:22: it is to prevent mankind from eating the fruit of the tree of life and so obtaining eternal life. The theme echoes Mesopotamian myths about mankind's failure to attain immortality (see *ANET* 89–96, 101–3). There is no implication here or anywhere else in chs. 2–3 that mankind was originally intended to be immortal.

In 3:24 God takes elaborate precautions to ensure that the man and woman do not re-enter the garden. The cherubim (cf. Ezek 10; Ps 18:10) are supernatural beings closely associated with God who carry out his commands, here as guardians; the flaming and turning sword reflects a Mesopotamian tradition.

(4:1–16) In its present context this story is a continuation of the previous chapter, as is shown by the mention of the name Eve. However, the use of a different source is indicated by the fact that God is now called not by the appellation 'the LORD God' (*YHWH 'ĕlōhîm*) but by the single name YHWH. In v. 1 there is a play on words: Eve called her firstborn Cain (*qayin*) because she had 'acquired' (*qānâ*) him from YHWH.

This is a story about Cain: his brother Abel's role is entirely passive. The account of Cain's murder of his brother Abel follows the pattern of ch. 3. This motif of fratricide is found in other ancient myths, for example in the Egyptian story of the murder of Osiris by his brother Seth and, in Roman mythology, that of Romulus's murder of Remus. The similarity of motif, however, does not help to elucidate the *point* of Gen 4:1–16. Some scholars have seen this in the difference between the brothers' occupations (v. 2) and in YHWH's acceptance of Abel's meat offering while he rejected Cain's fruit offering (vv. 3–5), which was the cause of Cain's anger. But no explanation is given in the text of God's preference, and it is not probable that the story, at any rate in its present form, reflects an age-old rivalry between pastoralists and farmers.

The story is of course significant in that this is the earliest instance in Genesis of death and also of violence committed by one human being against another. Although there is no suggestion in the text that the sin of disobedience committed by the first human pair is here seen as the *cause* of the universal corruption of human nature, the fact that the first murder immediately follows it can hardly be without significance. There is in these chapters a progression in evil which culminates in the statements in 6:5, 11 that mankind has become wholly corrupt.

In his reply to God's questioning (v. 9) Cain intensifies his sin by a lie: he pretends that he does not know where Abel is. He also declines responsibility for his brother—a denial of family solidarity that would be anathema to Israelite readers. The blood of Abel is understood as crying out from the ground (v. 10), demanding vengeance. God's answer to this cry is a curse (vv. 11, 12). Cain is condemned to have no permanent place to dwell: he will henceforth be a wanderer or fugitive on the earth (v. 14), subject to the vengeance of anyone who may meet him (v. 13). (The implication that there are other human beings on the earth shows that the story is not in fact a continuation of ch. 2–3; cf. the statement in 4:17 that Cain later married a wife.) But in v. 15 God mitigates his punishment, cursing in turn Cain's potential murderers, and puts him under his protection. The nature of the mark (*'ôt*) that God placed on him as a sign that he was not to be killed is not explained in the text, and the various explanations that have been offered by scholars are purely speculative. The 'land of Nod (*nôd*)' to which Cain took himself (v. 16) should not be understood as a geographical location: the word probably means 'aimless wandering'.

(4:17–26) The genealogy in vv. 17–22 is in two parts: vv. 17–18 list six generations (making seven in all if Adam, v. 1, is included), while vv. 19–22 are of a different, collateral, type, listing the children of Lamech by his two wives. The latter passage has something of the character of an aetiology of the origin of various aspects of civilized life; the origin of cities is interestingly placed very early (v. 17). This propensity to satisfy a demand for historical information about origins by naming the inventors of existing aspects of life is not peculiar to Israel: we may compare the Sumerian 'seven sages' who taught mankind the pursuits of civilization, and the Greek myth of Prometheus, who gave mankind the gift of fire.

The song of Lamech (vv. 23–4) is an elaboration of the preceding genealogy. It may originally have been a boasting song; but in its present context its prediction of dramatically increased violence marks a new stage in the progress of human wickedness. vv. 25–6 appear to be a fragment of a separate genealogy (of Seth) from that of Cain; it is given in a more complete form in ch. 5. v. 25 refers back to 4:1. The name Seth is connected by the author with the verb *šît*, 'to put, procure' (NRSV 'appointed'). The statement at the end of v. 26 that mankind (*'ĕnôš*—the word is identical with the name Enosh) began 'at that time' to invoke the name of YHWH appears to contradict Ex 6:2–3, where it is stated that the worship of YHWH began with Moses (cf. also Ex 3:13–15). The attempt to reconcile v. 26 with the Exodus passages by arguing that the former only refers to divine worship in general is hardly convincing. That there is a discrepancy here should be admitted. The proponents of the Documentary Hypothesis regarded the discrepancy as providing strong evidence of their source theory.

(5:1–32) The genealogy of Seth of which this chapter consists, which traces the history of mankind from the beginning to the birth of Noah, is linked to ch. 1 by the résumé in vv. 1–2. This is a somewhat different tradition from that of the genealogy of Cain in ch. 4, though it has some of the names in common. In this chapter Lamech becomes the father of Noah (v. 29). Enoch appears in both lists, but in v. 22 there is an additional note about his character and fate. He 'walked with God', as is also said of Noah in 6:9; and, presumably on account of this exceptional piety, he was mysteriously taken away by God and disappeared from the earth. (Cf. the similar translation of Elijah, 2 Kings 2:10–11.) (The late Jewish books of Enoch used this information to develop elaborate speculations about Enoch's adventures after his translation.)

There is a partial parallel between this list and the Mesopotamian King Lists, especially the old Babylonian (Sumerian) King List (*ANET* 265–6) which ascribes even more fantastically long reigns to kings who lived both before and after the Flood. However, these lists differ in important respects from Gen 5, and there is no reason to suppose that the latter was modelled on the former. But they do share a common notion of a succession of distant forebears; and they also have in common the idea that these human beings of the unimaginably remote past were of a quite different order of vitality and durability from the puny men and women of the present age.

v. 29 refers back to 3:17. The name Noah (*nōaḥ*) is improbably associated in the Hebrew text with the root *n-ḥ-m*, 'to comfort' (NRSV 'bring us relief'); the Greek translation seems to presuppose a form of the root *n-w-ḥ*, which would be closer to 'Noah' and would mean 'give rest'. This verse is evidently intended to introduce the story of the Flood, though this summary of Noah's achievements, whichever version is accepted, is not particularly appropriate.

(6:1–4) It must be admitted that the meaning and purpose of this story remain uncertain after a long history of attempts to interpret it. Every verse presents difficulties. v. 1 speaks of a great increase of human population—a motif of Mesopotamian origin-stories, where this constituted a threat to the gods; but as far as one can see this is not central to the biblical story. Especially problematic is the interpretation of the phrase 'the sons of God' (*bĕnê-hā'ĕlōhîm*), which can also be rendered by 'the sons of the gods', in v. 2. These are mentioned again in Job 1:6; 2:1 and—with slightly different wording (*bĕnê 'ĕlîm*)—in Ps 29:1; 89:6. In those passages they are heavenly beings subordinate to YHWH and members of his council. In the texts from Ras Shamra (Ugarit) the sons of the gods are themselves gods and members of the pantheon of which the high god El is the head. The traditional view of the sons of God here in v. 2 is that they are angels; but the implication of vv. 1–4 as a whole is that their activities do not meet with YHWH's approval. There are other ancient myths describing marriages between gods and human women, and also well-known myths about a rebellion in heaven. The story here may have been derived from an otherwise unknown Canaanite myth.

In v. 3 YHWH is represented as speaking to himself, expressing his determination to limit the span of human life to

120 years. Here we have once more the motif of a divine prohibition of human immortality, which might have resulted from the union of divine beings with human women. God's spirit (*rûaḥ*) here is probably equivalent to the 'breath of life' of 2:7. v. 4 appears to be a series of comments on the story, identifying the nature of the children born of the divine–human union. They were the Nephilim, interpreted in Num 13:33 as giants. In the second half of the verse they are identified with the famous 'heroes (*gibbōrîm*) of old'. The reason why the author chose to include this strange story with its polytheistic overtones may be that it served as a further mark of the corruption of human nature and thus as an appropriate prelude to the story of the Flood in chs. 6–9.

(6:5–8:22) The Story of the Flood Stories of a great flood sent in primeval times to destroy mankind are so common to many peoples in different parts of the world between whom no kind of historical contact seems possible that the theme seems almost to be a universal feature of the human imagination. The flood story of Genesis is a clear example of a type that was characteristic of the Mesopotamian world. The two extant literary accounts that most closely resemble it are *Atrahasis* (ET in Lambert and Millard 1969) and Tablet XI of the *Epic of Gilgamesh* (*ANET* 93–5). The Babylonian text translated in *ANET* was, according to Lambert and Millard, largely derived from *Atrahasis*, although the latter in its fragmentary state lacks some of the details preserved in the former such as the sending out of birds to discover whether the waters had receded. But unlike *Gilgamesh*, *Atrahasis* resembles Genesis in that it contains an account of the creation of mankind from clay before proceeding to the story of the Flood.

As was pointed out long ago, there are a number of details in the Genesis story such as the chronology and the numbers of animals taken into the ark that are mutually contradictory. Attempts to reconcile these, however ingenious, can hardly be convincing. It is clear that more than one version of the story have been combined. But the text as it stands can no longer be separated into two complete versions: there is, for example, only *one* account of God's detailed instructions to Noah about the construction and dimensions of the ark (6:14–16), without which there could be no story. The author, who may have known several versions from which he could choose, has spliced two of them together without concerning himself about total consistency—a method already noted above with regard to chs. 2–3.

The story of the Flood in Genesis is the climax of a sequence that begins with the creation of the world and ends, after almost total disaster for mankind, with the renewal of mankind through Noah and his descendants. Despite similarities in some of the details of the account of the Flood itself, no such sequence is to be found in either *Gilgamesh* or *Atrahasis*. In the former, the Flood is only an episode recounted by the 'Babylonian Noah', one Utnapishtim; no information is given about the future of the survivors. In *Atrahasis* as in Genesis the Flood is part of a connected story, but a quite different one which involves a quarrel among the gods, while the fate of the survivors is barely sketched in the fragmented manuscripts that have been preserved. The Genesis story on the other hand has in the hands of the author acquired a purposeful theological meaning in the context of the book's presentation of

human nature and of the *one* God's treatment of it which combines mercy and grace with severity.

vv. 5–12 give the reason for the bringing of the Flood: human wickedness has now become total and universal (Noah being the sole exception, 6:9); and God, faced with this apparently complete failure of his hopes, now regrets his decision to create human beings (6:6) and determines on their destruction together with all other living creatures (6:7). This striking anthropomorphism (i.e. the representation of God as fallible and reacting to a situation as with human weakness) is reminiscent of 3:22. Such a view of God runs counter to the belief expressed elsewhere in the OT (e.g. Num 23:19; 1 Sam 15:29), but is not unparalleled (cf. e.g. Ex 32:14; Am 7:3, 6), though in those instances God's 'repentance' is favourable rather than unfavourable to those concerned. More analogous to the present passage is God's threat in Ex 32:10 to destroy his rebellious people and to start again with Moses.

The statement that humanity had become totally corrupt is repeated in 6:11–12. Since there is a change in the appellation of God here—from YHWH to *'ĕlōhîm*—this verse has been thought to come from a different source (P as opposed to J); but in the present context the repetition is appropriate since it immediately follows the statement about the uniquely righteous Noah in 6:8–9. In 6:12, 13 'all flesh' evidently includes the animals, though some of these were to be preserved by being taken into the ark together with Noah and his family. The word 'ark' (*tēbâ*, 6:14) occurs in the OT only here and in the story of the infant Moses (Ex 2:3, 5). It is probably derived from an Egyptian word meaning a chest or box. The usual word for 'ship' has been avoided. The use of the word *tēbâ* may point to an earlier version of the story. The identity of the word rendered by 'cypress' (*gōper*, older English versions 'gopher') is uncertain. The impression given of the ark is that of a flat-bottomed box-like construction about 450 ft. long, 75 ft. broad and 45 ft. deep (6:15) with three decks, a roof or window (the meaning of *ṣōhar* is uncertain), and a door (6:16; 'finish it to a cubit above' is incomprehensible).

At 6:18 is the first mention of a covenant (*bĕrît*) in the book. This promise to Noah is reaffirmed in 9:11–17. Since Noah and his family were to be the only human survivors, it is by implication a covenant made by God with the whole future human race; it points forward also, however, to the specific covenant to be made later with the people of Israel. It is an obligation that God imposes on himself; its contents are unspecified, but it clearly implies divine protection and blessing, conditional only on Noah's complete obedience to God's instructions in 6:18–21, which he carried out (6:22).

In its specification of the numbers of each species of animal to be taken into the ark 6:19–20 differs from that of 7:2–3, which is clearly from a different source. In 7:2–3 a distinction is made between clean and unclean animals. This refers to the lists of clean and unclean animals in Lev 11:3–31 and Deut 14:4–20: it is an example of a tendency to carry back the origin of fundamental institutions (in this case, Mosaic laws) to primeval times. The main reason for the command to take seven rather than two pairs of the clean species into the ark was that some of the clean animals were to be reserved to be used, for the first time, as animal sacrifices (8:20).

The discrepancies in the statements about the duration of the Flood in 7:4–8:14, which are due to the combination of different sources, are difficult to disentangle, although the main outline of the narrative is clear. The immediate cause of the Flood is a dual one: the bursting forth of the 'fountains (i.e. springs) of the great deep (*tĕhôm rabbâ*)' below the earth (cf. 1:2) and the opening of the 'windows of the heavens' (7:11; cf. Isa 24:18; Mal 3:10) to let the torrential rain fall unremittingly for forty days and nights (7:12). This signalled the undoing of his creation by God's command: chaos had come again.

Ararat (8:4) is mentioned again in 2 Kings 19:37; Isa 37:38; Jer 51:27. It was known to the Assyrians as Urartu, and was an independent kingdom in the early first millennium BCE until its destruction in the sixth century BCE. The area corresponds roughly to that of modern Armenia. The *Epic of Gilgamesh* also records the landing of the ark on a mountain. The sending out of a raven and a dove to test the subsidence of the waters (8:6–12) also corresponds to a similar incident in *Gilgamesh*. The first animal sacrifice on the first altar (8:20) is an act of thanksgiving, not an attempt to propitiate God, who had already (6:8, 18) shown his acceptance of Noah. But this sacrifice inaugurates a new era in which the slaughter of animals was permitted (9:3–4). The anthropomorphical statement that God 'smelled the pleasing odour', unique in the OT, is no doubt a reminiscence of an earlier version of the story: it is a way of saying that he approved of the sacrifice. In *Gilgamesh* at this point in the story the gods 'smelled the savour' and 'crowded like flies about the sacrificer'. In determining never again to destroy mankind God now appears to accept that the evil tendency of the human heart is innate and ineradicable. The negative decision of 8:21 is then matched by a positive one: the orderly alternations of day and night and of the seasons will now resume and will not again be interrupted. 'As long as the earth endures' makes it clear, however, that it will not continue for ever but will have an end.

(9:1–17) In vv. 1–7 God, addressing Noah and his sons, inaugurates the new era and the renewed humanity. There are strong indications here that this is regarded as a new creation. The passage begins and ends with a blessing (cf. 1:28) and there is a repetition of the command to be fruitful and multiply and fill the earth and to rule over the animal world; but there are significant differences from ch. 1. The animals are now to *fear* their rulers (v. 2), and may be killed for food: things are not after all as idyllic as at the beginning. v. 4 prescribes the manner of their slaughter, once more carrying back the institution of a Mosaic law to the primeval period (cf. 7:2–3); this is the kosher law prohibiting the consumption of an animal's blood (cf. Lev 7:26–7 and other passages). vv. 5–6 forbid homicide: mankind, in contrast to the animals, was created in the image of God. The story of the Flood concludes in vv. 8–17 on a hopeful note with God's reaffirmation of the covenant that he had made with Noah (6:18), which now includes all living creatures as well as Noah's descendants. He reveals his previous decision (cf. 8:21–2) never again to destroy the earth, and makes the rainbow—literally a 'bow in the clouds'—a 'sign' of the covenant, a reminder both to himself and to mankind—another example of aetiology.

(9:18–29) The story of Noah's drunkenness can hardly be seen as related to that of the Flood. It appears to be a resumption of the history of human generations in chs. 4 and 5 with its theme of human sin and corruption. vv. 18–19, however, have a connection with the Flood story in their reference to the departure of Noah's sons from the ark. The notice in v. 18 that Ham was the father of Canaan is a link with vv. 20–7; an attempt to account for the curse on Canaan in vv. 25–7.

The statement in v. 20 that Noah was the inventor of viticulture is an aetiology comparable with 4:20–2, but with a story attached to it. The point of the story in vv. 20–7 is not that Noah committed a sin in becoming drunk, but that Ham sinned in seeing his father when he was naked, an act which called forth a curse on Canaan, Ham's son. There is nothing in the text to support the view advanced by some scholars that Ham's sin was in fact either an act of homosexuality or the incestuous rape of his mother (Lev 18:6–19, which speaks of 'uncovering' nakedness, is not speaking of the same thing). Nakedness was shameful (3:7–11), and Ham humiliated his father by not decently covering him. In vv. 25–7 it is already presupposed that Noah's sons are to become the ancestors of different nations. The incongruity that it is Canaan and not his father who is cursed (vv. 25, 27) is connected with Israel's traditional hatred of the Canaanites, who are seen as destined to become slaves; but attempts to identify the circumstances in which these verses were written have not been successful. The name Japheth is here aetiologically associated with a rare Hebrew verb meaning 'to enlarge'.

(10:1–32) This chapter, often known as the 'table of the nations', is an attempt, on the basis of the presupposition that all humanity is descended from Noah's three sons, to name all the nations of the world and to state from which genealogical branch they are derived. It appears to be quite unique: no comparable ancient texts exist. Certain stylistic variations and inconsistencies in the lists of names have led the source critics to postulate a combination of the sources J and P, despite the fact that there is only one reference to God, where he is referred to by his name YHWH (v. 9). Many but by no means all the names are readily identifiable. The descendants of Japhet, for example, include the Medes (Madai), the Ionian Greeks (Javan), possibly the Cypriots (Kittim), and Rhodians (if the emendation of Rodanim from the Dodanim of the Hebrew text is correct). The list of Ham's descendants, which begins with Nubia (Cush), Egypt, and possibly Lybia (Put), also contains Canaan, a country which would in modern terminology be ranked as Semite (i.e. Shemite). This is true also of Babylon (Babel) and Assyria. The descendants of Shem, who is called 'the father of all the sons of Eber', that is, Hebrews, are listed last as more immediately relevant to the readers. There is some inconsistency here: Assyria, listed under Ham in v. 11, is given as a descendant of Shem in v. 22. Other well-attested peoples listed as descendants of Shem include Elam and Aram (the Arameans); but most of the remaining names in these verses are unknown or not certainly identifiable, as also is the territory mentioned in v. 30. By thus peopling the world the author has prepared for Abraham's world, which was already divided into nations. The cause of these divisions is given in 11:1–9.

(11:1–9) This is a compact and self-contained narrative. It contains an aetiological element in that it purports to explain why the human population, which had originally shared the same language, came to be divided by the development of many languages which prevented their mutual comprehension and so hindered co-operation; and also how they came to be dispersed throughout the world (though this is already implied in the command to 'fill the earth', 9:1, and its fulfilment in 9:19). But aetiology is not the main point of the story, which is another account (cf. ch. 3) of human ambition to rise above the human condition, the threat that this posed to God's supremacy, and the action taken by God to frustrate this. The story is located in the land of Shinar, that is, Mesopotamia (cf. 10:10); the city which they began to build, perhaps including the tower (v. 4) is identified in v. 9 with Babylon. There is nothing specifically in the text to indicate that the story was inspired by one of the Mesopotamian ziggurats: it is true that the Esagil in Babylon was supposed to link heaven and earth; but it was a completed building, not one left unfinished as was the city in v. 8. There is no extant Mesopotamian story comparable with this, though some of its motifs are found in a Sumerian epic. The anonymous builders ('they') are represented as the whole human population ('the whole earth', v. 1). This means that 'make a name for ourselves' implies a universal ambition to attain to a greatness superior to their present status, which must mean an infringement of God's absolute supremacy. God's decision to come down from heaven to see what his puny creatures are trying to do ('Let us go down', v. 7) is expressed in the same plural terms as are 1:26 and 3:22. In v. 9 the word 'Babel' is seen as related to the verb *bālal*, 'to mix, confuse'.

(11:10–32) This genealogy spans the generations from Shem to Abram (Abraham). It concentrates on succession from father to son, and deals with individuals: thus it is intended to be seen as the family history of a single individual, Abraham. It forms a link between the primeval world and that of the patriarchs, Abraham, Isaac, and Jacob, the 'fathers' of Israel. vv. 27–32, the genealogy of Terah, Abraham's father, in fact function as the beginning of the story of Abraham, and introduce principal characters in that story: Abraham, his wife Sarai (Sarah), and his brother Lot. It briefly refers to Sarai's barrenness and a migration of the family from Ur of the Chaldeans, probably in southern Mesopotamia (but 'Chaldeans' is an anachronism), with the intention of settling in Canaan but instead getting no further than Haran, a city of northern Mesopotamia.

Abraham and his Family (chs. 12–36)

The world of Israel's ancestors, Abraham, Isaac, and Jacob, and their families, is different from that of chs. 1–11: here we are dealing with 'real' individuals and their life stories. Yet it is still not *our* world. Frequent attempts have been made to find historical situations into which these patriarchs can be fitted, but they have all failed to convince (see Thompson 1974). Gunkel, in his famous commentary on Genesis (1901), put forward a view which was long accepted: that most of these stories were independent short folk-tales (*Sagen*) which circulated by word of mouth for a very long time before they were combined into longer complexes and eventually set down in writing. That they have an oral origin and are not to be seen as accounts of the lives of historical personages remains a common opinion; but that they had a long history before their incorporation into the present work is regarded by some recent scholars as by no means certain (see Whybray 1987). The possibility that these stories may not be much older than the time of the final redactor of the Pentateuch is supported by the fact that the pre-exilic parts of the OT with one possible exception (Hos 12:3–4, 12) show no knowledge of Abraham, Isaac, and Jacob *as individuals* or of events connected with them.

The true purpose of this part of Genesis was theological rather than historical in the modern sense of the latter term. Like some other parts of the OT which must be regarded as historical fiction (e.g. Job, Ruth, Jonah, Esther, and Dan 1–6), its purpose is to teach a religious lesson. It is generally admitted that the three patriarchs were originally unrelated to one another and that their stories have been combined in order to create a family story whose main theme is set out at the very start (Gen 12:1–3), where Abraham is commanded by God to leave the country where he has been residing and to migrate to another country whose identity will later be revealed to him, where he will become the ancestor of a great nation, especially blessed and in turn conferring his blessing on other peoples. This theme of God's promise dominates these chapters: the promise is repeated on several more occasions to Abraham himself (15:4–7, 18–21; 17:4–8; 22:17–18) and then to Isaac (26:2–5, 24) and Jacob (35:11–12). The promise of future blessing implies material success; and it is made clear that God will guide the fortunes of the family. But the continuity of that family depends on the production of an heir in each succeeding generation; and the difficulties and dangers attending this provide the dramatic content of many incidents in the story.

The promise of the possession of the land, which proved to be the land of Canaan, was not in fact fulfilled in the course of the book of Genesis; but by the end of the book there had been a positive development. The twelve sons of Jacob, who were to be the ancestors of the twelve tribes of Israel, had been born, and had received their blessings (ch. 49). So the nation of Israel now existed in embryo. Their migration to Egypt during a famine, in the final section of the book, may be considered on the one hand as one of the many causes of delay of the fulfilment of the promise; but it is also to be seen as the springboard for the miracle at the Sea in the book of Exodus and for the subsequent series of events related in the rest of the Pentateuch which led eventually to the possession of the land. The readers were thus presented in these chapters with a picture of a God who was totally in control of events and who had marvellously created their nation and preserved it from the beginning, one whose promises they knew to have been ultimately fulfilled; but they were also made aware, through the account of the wanderings and vicissitudes of their ancestors, of the precariousness of the life of faith.

Basically these chapters fall into three sections, each concerned with the life of one of the three patriarchs, Abraham, Isaac, and Jacob. However, since in their present form they are a combination of separate parts to form the history of a single family, the three stories have been made to interlock so as to produce a continuous family saga. Thus Abraham's death is recorded in 25:8, but the birth of his heir Isaac had taken place long before (21:2); similarly the birth of Isaac's son Jacob is noted in 25:25–6, but Isaac's death only in 35:29. Jacob's own death (noted in 49:33) did not occur until the completion of his son Joseph's extraordinary success story (Joseph's birth is recorded in 30:23). (On the story of the life of Joseph, chs. 37–50, which belongs to a different literary genre from the previous stories, see below.) Meanwhile the births of all Jacob's twelve sons had taken place, recorded at intervals between 29:32 and 35:18. Recently attempts have been made to reconstruct the stages of the process by which the patriarchal stories have been composed (especially Blum 1984), but these remain hypothetical.

The Story of Abraham (chs. 12–25)

(12:1–3) The story begins with a divine command and a dual promise. First, God promises to make Abraham into a great nation; this of course implies that Abraham himself will have a male heir and that the succeeding generations will all have numerous progeny, and also that the future nation will enjoy great political power (the word *gôy*, 'nation', suggests a fully organized group, and the 'great name' in this context implies international pre-eminence or superiority). The second promise is really implied by the first: it is a promise of divine blessing, which will ultimately be extended to all peoples. There is no specific promise of possession of the land here; this appears for the first time in 12:7 as a promise not to Abraham personally but to his descendants. A number of recent scholars, regarding 12:1–3 as representing the earliest stage of the Abraham story, have maintained that the promise of the land belongs to a later stage of redaction. This may be so; but the initial command to Abraham in v. 1 to travel to a land later to be identified cannot be without significance, especially to the original readers, who would naturally identify that land with the land of Canaan, which they knew had in fact come into the possession of Abraham's descendants. The fact that God had arbitrarily uprooted Abraham and exiled him from his original country would, however, remind them of the precariousness of their own residential status. In Gen 23:4 Abraham himself spoke of his being 'a stranger and an alien' in the land. In 12:1–3, then, the basic promises to the patriarchs are all already presented.

(12:4–9) takes Abraham on his journey south from Haran to Canaan, which God now identifies (v. 7) as the land to which he was to go (v. 1). His unquestioning obedience to God's command is seen by NT writers (Heb 11:8–10; cf. Rom 4; Gal 3) as an outstanding act of faith to be imitated. The reference in v. 4 to Lot (cf. 11:27, 31) as Abraham's travelling companion sets the stage for the story in 13:5–13. The oak of Moreh near Shechem (v. 6) is represented as an already sacred tree at which oracles were given (*môreh* means 'one who teaches'); but it was God's appearance to Abraham that led him to build an altar there and—presumably—to offer sacrifice (cf. Noah's sacrifice, 8:20). On the invocation of the name of YHWH at the second altar that he built near Bethel (v. 8) see at 4:26 above. In travelling to the Negeb (the semi-desert area to the south of Judah) he reached the southern border of Canaan, having traversed the land completely from north to south. It is significant that it is not stated that he entered any of the ancient cities of Canaan; instead, he lived in tents as a travelling stranger.

(12:10–20) is one of a group of three stories in Genesis with the same theme. In 20:1–18, as here, Abraham passes Sarah off as his sister during a temporary residence in Gerar, with similar consequences, and again in 26:6–11 Isaac, driven by famine (26:1), as was Abraham in ch. 12, seeks refuge, again, in Gerar. It is generally recognized that these are three variants of one and the same story, which was defined by Gunkel as a folk-tale; but there is no agreement today about their relationship to one another or the reasons why despite their basic similarities they differ substantially in details. Attempts to discover which of the variants is the oldest have resulted in different conclusions.

Migrations of groups of people at various times across the eastern frontier of Egypt to seek more favourable conditions of life are well attested historically (see e.g. *ANET* 251). In the OT the migration of Jacob and his sons to Egypt (Gen 47) is another example of this. 12:10–20 is the first instance of many in which the fulfilment of the promise to Abraham is endangered. Not only is the departure from Canaan a move away from the promised land; even more serious is the threat to the marriage of Abraham and Sarah which is still childless, and so to the promise of progeny. Faced with a choice between death from starvation and the potential danger entailed in migrating to an alien and unknown country, Abraham chooses the latter course; but, fearful for his own safety, he sacrifices his wife to a life in Pharaoh's harem, which would also make the promise null and void. In contrast to his shabby conduct, which also involves telling a lie, the behaviour of Pharaoh, whose unsuspecting action is rewarded by God with 'great plagues' (presumably soon cured; a lacuna in the story has been suspected between vv. 17 and 18) is exemplary and even generous (v. 20). Abraham is left speechless before Pharaoh's justified reproach. The story is told without the making of an overt moral judgement; but the contrast between the obedient Abraham of 12:1–9 and the Abraham of this story is unmistakable. The story considered by itself is clearly not favourable to Abraham; but in its present context it has become an illustration of the theme of the promise constantly endangered but never annulled. Paradoxically, Abraham emerges from this incident not only unscathed but rewarded with great wealth (vv. 16, 20). It is important to note that it is not said of Abraham as it is of Noah (6:9) that he was morally perfect. The point of the story in its present context is not his moral character but that he is the bearer of God's promise to him and his descendants. The threefold repetition of what is basically the same story cannot be adequately accounted for in terms of a dovetailing of written continuous strands that were originally independent of one another. The reason for it is of a literary nature. Repetition to create particular effects is a common literary device in narrative; and this is eminently the case in Genesis (see Alter (1981), especially on type-scenes, 47–62). Here each version of the story marks a crucial point in the total narrative. 12:10–20 stands at its head, immediately following the initial promise to Abraham of numerous descendants (12:2–3), and shows how God safeguards that promise, keeping both the prospective parents from harm in a dangerous situation. 20:1–18 occurs immediately before the crucial account of the birth of Isaac (21:1–2) which marks the first stage in the fulfilment of that promise. 26:6–11 is similarly closely connected with the birth of Isaac's son Jacob, the next heir (25:21–4) and is immediately preceded in 26:3–5 by a further reiteration of that promise. These repeated stories thus help to provide a structure for the patriarchal stories.

(13:1–18) This chapter and ch. 14, which are mainly concerned with relations between Lot and Abraham, are a kind of interlude or digression: Lot is not a leading character in the main patriarchal story; after the events of ch. 19 he disappears from it, though at the end of that chapter it is noted that he became the ancestor of the Moabites and Ammonites whose later dealings with Israel have a part to play in other OT books (19:37–8). Continuity with the main plot is, however, maintained in the incident which determines Abraham's future area of residence well away from the corruption and temptations of Sodom and Gomorrah, whose evil inhabitants (v. 13) were later to suffer destruction at the hands of YHWH (v. 10). The final verses of ch. 13 revert to the principal theme of the promise.

In v. 2 Abraham's wealth is again stressed, though he continued to live an itinerant life. The quarrel between Abraham's and Lot's herdsmen (vv. 5–7) is to be understood as due to inadequate living space for the herds in a land which was occupied by other, settled, peoples. (The identity of the Perizzites, v. 7, who are mentioned fairly frequently in Genesis, is uncertain.) Abraham's offer to settle the dispute, which was not of his making or of Lot's, by giving Lot the choice of territory is explained as due to a desire to preserve amicable relations with his kinsman (lit. brother), while Lot's disastrous choice is determined by the attraction of the fertility of the Jordan plain, which is compared to that of Egypt and of the garden of Eden. The passage ends with a more detailed reaffirmation of the promise to Abraham of numerous descendants and of the *whole* land, with the additional assurance that it will remain in their possession for ever (v. 15).

(14:1–24) This chapter is an unusual one in several respects. It is self-contained and appears to be unrelated to the surrounding chapters except for the names of Abraham and Lot and of Sodom and Gomorrah. The documentary critics with some exceptions were unable to connect it with any of their main sources (J, E, and P), and concluded that it is a quite independent episode. It is the only passage in which the otherwise entirely peaceable Abraham is represented as taking part in military activity. It begins in the style of a historical narrative; yet none of the nine kings mentioned (vv. 1–2) has been identified, nor is any war such as is described here known to have occurred. It puts Abraham in a very good light both as an outstanding warrior who comes to the aid of members of his family, and as forgoing the spoils of war. Its purpose thus seems to have been to glorify Abraham as a great and powerful hero of international stature. It has been argued that it is not a single unitary composition; the Melchizedek episode (vv. 18–20) has been thought by some scholars to be a later addition to the original story. There is no agreement about its date: while some believe that it is a reworking of old traditions, its heroic character and also perhaps its style may point to a post-exilic origin.

The peoples named in vv. 5–6 are legendary groups who inhabited the Transjordan; the Valley of Siddim is unknown. The reference in v. 13 to Abraham as 'the Hebrew' conveys the impression that he has not been previously introduced to the reader. The word 'Hebrew' is used in the OT only by foreigners speaking about the Israelites and not by Israelites about themselves (see Jon 1:9). In Genesis it occurs elsewhere only in the story of Joseph when he is spoken of by Egyptians or addresses Egyptians. The tiny size of Abraham's military force, which consists entirely of members of his own household (v. 14) enhances his heroic stature.

Melchizedek, in v. 18, provides a royal banquet to welcome Abraham on his return after his victory. It is strange that he should suddenly appear in the story, having taken no part in the preceding events. He is a mysterious and enigmatic figure. His name probably means '(The god) Melek is righteousness' and closely resembles that of a pre-Israelite king of Jerusalem, Adoni-zedek ('The Lord is righteousness'), who was defeated and killed by Joshua (Josh 10). It is not clear whether Salem is intended to be identified with Jerusalem, as Jerusalem is never so-called in any of the non-biblical texts that refer to (pre-Israelite) Jerusalem. In the OT, only in Ps 76:2 is Salem equated with Zion, God's dwelling-place. In Gen 14:18 Melchizedek is described as a priest-king serving El Elyon (*'ēl elyôn*, 'God Most High') who is stated to be the creator of heaven and earth. In Ps 110:4, the only other OT passage where his name occurs, Melchizedek is taken to be a precursor of the later priest-kings of Israel. The author of Gen 14 clearly intended the reader to identify El Elyon with YHWH as is the case with the titles El Olam (*'ēl 'ôlām*, 'the Everlasting God', 21:33), El Shaddai 'God Almighty', (*'ēl šadday*, 17:1), etc. But in fact El was the high god of the Canaanite pantheon, who is not infrequently identified with YHWH in the OT, and Elyon sometimes occurs in the texts from Ugarit as an epithet of El. The phrase 'maker of heaven and earth' is virtually identical with what is said of El in those texts. In v. 22 El Elyon is specifically identified with YHWH in the solemn oath that Abraham swears to forgo his share of the spoils of victory.

(15:1–21) There has been much scholarly discussion about the composition of this chapter. It has proved resistant to a division into sources along the lines of the Documentary Hypothesis, and attempts to demonstrate that a relatively short piece has been massively supplemented by a late hand have also failed to be entirely convincing. Some recent scholars have reverted to something like the pre-critical position that it is mainly or wholly the work of a single author. But all agree that it is in two parts: vv. 1–6 and 7–21. Both contain further divine revelations to Abraham reiterating the earlier promises, but they differ considerably in the mode of revelation.

vv. 1–6 are introduced in the same way as a prophetical oracle, but take the form of a vision—the word 'vision' (*maḥăzeh*) is very rare and probably indicates a late date. The call not to be afraid is characteristic of Deutero-Isaiah (Isa 40–55). This is what is often called an 'oracle of salvation', and it sounds the note of encouragement. But it becomes clear that Abraham has begun to doubt whether God will carry out his promise to give him an heir of his body: he has been obliged to appoint his own servant Eleazar as his heir. YHWH reiterates his original promise and shows him the stars as a demonstration of how numerous his descendants will be. This direct vision of God convinces him: he believes, that is, trusts, God's word. The author's statement that YHWH 'reckoned it to him as righteousness', which forms the climax of the episode, has rightly been seen as one of the most significant in the whole of Scripture (see Gal 3:7–9; Jas 2:23; cf. Heb 11:8–10) and has been taken, together with other instances of Abraham's faith, particularly his readiness to leave Haran and his willingness to sacrifice his son Isaac (ch. 22) as the foundation of the doctrine of justification by faith, even though its precise meaning has been disputed. That it is an expression of Abraham's readiness to trust God's promise cannot be doubted.

vv. 7–21, like 1–6, are probably a creation of the author with no older tradition behind it. They are also concerned with the promise, but now specifically with the promise of the land rather than with the question of progeny. Like vv. 1–6, they present Abraham as hesitant to believe the promise and demanding to know how it is to be fulfilled. YHWH satisfies him by means of a solemn but curious ritual which Abraham is commanded to carry out. This ritual does not conform precisely with anything known from elsewhere, although the cutting of the animals into two is reminiscent of some covenant rituals. The animals specified are those used in sacrifice in the laws of the OT; but the purpose of the ritual is indicated by the solemn oath-like statement to Abraham by YHWH in vv. 13–16 and his making of a covenant with him (vv. 18–21). Its awesome accompaniments—the 'deep sleep' (tardēmâ, a rare word also used of Adam when Eve was created) and the terrifying darkness—add to the solemnity of the event. The smoking fire pot and the flaming torch (v. 17) represent YHWH's passing between the rows of animals to symbolize his binding himself to keep the covenant. vv. 13–16 are a 'prophecy after the event' foretelling the captivity in Egypt and the Exodus; its purpose is to account for the long gap between promise and fulfilment. The 400 years of v. 13 and the 'fourth generation' of v. 16 can hardly be reconciled; it has been suggested that v. 16, which foreshadows the Israelites' conquest of the Amorites (Canaanites), is a later revision of the prophecy. The Amorites are said not to be sufficiently wicked as yet to deserve this fate. The promise of vv. 18–21, which contains a comprehensive list of the peoples believed to have preceded Israel in the land, describes the boundaries of the land in very grand terms—from the borders of Egypt to the Euphrates. In fact the borders of the state of Israel were probably never as extensive (1 Kings 4:21 is hardly a sober historical statement). The covenant with Abraham (v. 18), who here represents the future nation of Israel, is a free, unconditional promise, unlike the covenant of Sinai.

(16:1–16) Like the stories in chs. 12, 20, and 26 (see above on 12:10–20), the story of Hagar in this chapter has a counterpart (21:9–21). These are clearly variants of an older folk-tale; and once again their placement in the ongoing story of Abraham is significant. Both are further examples of the threat to the fulfilment of the promise that Abraham will have a legitimate heir by his wife Sarah and of the setting aside of that threat (cf. 15:2–4). Ch. 16 immediately precedes the repetition of the promise guaranteeing Abraham's progeny and their destiny (17:1–8); 21:9–21 immediately follows the birth of Isaac (21:1–8) and confirms that it is he who is to be the heir. But the motif of God's protection of the rejected Ishmael which is common

to both versions of the story is an indication that before the story was inserted into the Abraham narrative and placed in its two respective positions it was the figure of Hagar who was the centre of interest and the principal character. There is a somewhat similar story of acrimonious relations between a barren wife and her rival in 1 Sam 1:2–8.

The practice alluded to in vv. 2–3 was a common and accepted one in the ancient Near East; it is consequently not possible to fix the date of the story by reference to any particular extant Near-Eastern law or legal contract as has been proposed by some scholars. The words of the 'angel' (mal'āk) of YHWH who speaks to Hagar in 16:7 are identified with the words of YHWH himself in 16:13. Westermann's comment (1985: 244) is apt: 'God is present not in the messenger, but in the message.' The promise that YHWH makes to Hagar in v. 10, which is curiously like that made elsewhere about Isaac, identifies Ishmael as the ancestor of the Ishmaelites, whose supposed characteristics are described in v. 12. There are two aetiologies in the later part of the narrative, but they are subordinate to the main theme of the story. First, the name Ishmael, who is to be preserved by YHWH's intervention (v. 11), means 'God hears'. In the second aetiology the name El-rei ('ēl rō'î) (v. 13, probably 'God who sees me'), is stated in v. 14 to be the origin of the name of the—now unidentifiable—well where the angel spoke to Hagar. The aetiology, like others in Genesis, is not exact, as it is Hagar who 'sees' God, and not vice versa.

(17:1–27) This chapter is primarily concerned with the covenant (bĕrît) which God undertakes to make with Abraham—the word bĕrît occurs 13 times in the chapter. It reiterates the promises of progeny, of future greatness for Abraham's descendants, and of the gift of the land; but it contains several new and significant features. In v. 1 YHWH introduces himself as El Shaddai ('God Almighty'): the author supposes that at this time Abraham did not know YHWH by name. The name Shaddai, the meaning of which is uncertain (it may mean 'the one of the mountain' or 'the one of the field') was probably used as a divine epithet from an early period. This incident is regarded as opening a new stage in the life of Abraham: this is why he now receives a new name (v. 5). (So also with Sarah, v. 15.) Abraham is to be the father of not one but many nations, including that of the Ishmaelites; but the covenant is clearly for Israel alone, and will be for ever. It is to Israel that the land of Canaan is to be given 'for a perpetual holding' (v. 8) and YHWH will be their God. But the covenant is now to be two-sided: Abraham and his descendants must keep it by obeying God's command to practise circumcision, a rite not practised by the peoples of Mesopotamia from which Abraham has come. There is now for the first time in the Abraham story a warning against the breach of the covenant, which will entail exclusion from its privileges and from the new special relationship with God; this could be a warning to Jews of the immediate post-exilic community who were tempted to abandon their Jewish identity. The concept of the crucial importance of circumcision was a particular characteristic of the post-exilic period.

Two further additional features of the chapter are the personal promise to Sarah (vv. 15–19) with the precise announcement of the time when her son will be born (v. 21) and the blessing of Ishmael (v. 20). Abraham's sceptical laughter at the announcement that Sarah will give birth combined with his deep obeisance (cf. Sarah's laughter on a parallel occasion, 18:12) is strange; but there is here a play on the name Isaac (*yiṣḥāq*, that is, 'he laughs', possibly an abbreviated form of *yiṣḥāq-ʾēl*, 'God laughs'). Abraham's wish that Ishmael should be preserved under God's protection (v. 18) shows that he still places his hopes in Ishmael. God grants his wish, conferring a special blessing on Ishmael, but excludes him from the covenant that is for Isaac and his descendants. The chapter concludes with a notice that Abraham duly carried out God's commands about circumcision, which was performed on all Abraham's household (including Ishmael) as prescribed in later legislation (Ex 12:48).

(18:1–16) The motif of the appearance to human beings of gods in human disguise is a common mythological theme of the ancient world. A Greek myth, preserved by the Roman poet Ovid, tells of such a visit in which a miraculous birth is announced; there is a similar story in Judg 6:11–24. Gen 18:1, 13 make it clear that, although Abraham and Sarah are unaware of this, the three mysterious visitors (or one of them?) are in fact YHWH himself. This passage is thus another version of ch. 17, but expressed in a quite different, more circumstantial style, with a precise note of time and place. Abraham's treatment of the strangers is an example of the traditional customs of hospitality observed by tent-dwellers. The laughter of Sarah, like that of Abraham in 17:17, involves a play on words and is an expression of unbelief about the news that the visitors have brought. Sarah is firmly reminded that God has unlimited power and can bring about the impossible. Her denial that she laughed (v. 15) is caused by fear: she now dimly recognizes the identity of the speaker. The reference to Sodom in v. 16 introduces the theme that follows in the second half of the chapter and ch. 19. The passage is an admirable example of the high quality of Hebrew narrative art at its best.

(18:17–33) This passage is not based on an older folk-tale but is a discussion of a theological question of the utmost importance, that the author has himself composed in the form of a dialogue. The question, which is about God's justice (v. 25), was not, for the readers, a purely theoretical one, but one of immense *practical* importance, especially for those who had suffered, and were still suffering, the effects of the devastation of the Babylonian conquest of Judah in 587 BCE. It is raised in various forms in other OT books of a relatively late period, e.g. in Job, and Ezek 14:12–23. The fate of Sodom is here a paradigm of this much wider question.

The passage is remarkable in more than one respect. It begins (vv. 17–21) with the author's notion of YHWH's private thoughts: YHWH comes to a decision to inform Abraham of his intention—if the inhabitants of Sodom and Gomorrah prove to be as wicked as they have been reported to be—to destroy them, so that Abraham, whom he has chosen, may not imitate their wickedness and so prove unworthy of the promise (cf. 17:1–2, where Abraham's righteousness appears to have been made a condition of the making of the covenant with him). A second outstanding feature of the passage is Abraham's boldness in rebuking YHWH: although he frequently shows awareness of his temerity (vv. 27, 30, 31, 32), he dares to remind YHWH of his duty, as universal judge, to deal justly (v. 25)! His rebuke is reminiscent of the passionate speeches of Job. Equally remarkable is YHWH's readiness to listen to the rebuke and even to modify his intention. The precise accusation which Abraham makes is that in proposing to destroy the whole population of Sodom and Gomorrah YHWH intends to treat the righteous in the same way as the wicked (v. 25). He extracts from YHWH a promise that he will not do so (v. 26). The point appears to be not that YHWH fell short of his true nature but rather that he is shown to be a just God after all! There is no particular significance in the diminishing numbers of righteous persons for whose sake he will not destroy Sodom (vv. 28–32). The principle of justice towards individuals as against indiscriminate collective punishment has been established.

(19:1–29) This story is an episode in the life of Lot, who had chosen to live in the plain of Jordan, whose principal cities (unknown to archaeology) were Sodom and Gomorrah in the vicinity of the Dead Sea (13:10–13). But it is now also connected with ch. 18: the 'men' who visited Abraham (18:2) departed towards Sodom with the exception of YHWH himself, who remained to talk to Abraham (18:22). In v. 1 the other two, now called 'angels' or 'messengers' (*malʾākîm*), who are clearly supernatural beings (v. 11), arrive in Sodom, presumably to investigate the reported wickedness of the inhabitants (it appears to be assumed that there are *no* righteous persons among them), where they find Lot sitting in the city gate. It is to be noted that there is no mention at all of Abraham in the main story: he appears only after the event (v. 27) and looks down on the catastrophe in the valley below. His absence may suggest that this was originally a story about an unnamed man (now identified with Abraham's nephew Lot) and the destruction of a city, which the author has incorporated into the story of Abraham. The reason for its inclusion is not obvious; however, it illustrates the consequences of grave sin against which Abraham has been warned. It should further be noted that the main story recounts only the fate of Sodom: Gomorrah is not mentioned until v. 24. But the two cities are regularly mentioned together in a number of passages elsewhere in the OT as examples of exemplary sin and consequent annihilation (e.g. Deut 29:22–4; 32:32; Isa 1:9–10; Jer 23:14).

It is strongly stressed in 19:4 that every male individual was involved in the homosexual attack intended against the two angels. This is no doubt to be seen as a justification of the subsequent annihilation of the whole populace; but the omission of any reference to the women of the city (or to the children) reflects at least a residuary notion of communal rather than of individual guilt. Lot's offer of his daughters (v. 8) also reflects a moral code, repulsive to the modern reader, which put the duty of hospitality above other ethical concerns. vv. 24, 28 attempt to describe the nature of the catastrophe that overwhelmed Sodom. That it was an earthquake that caused the release of combustible gases is a plausible guess; but—apart from the fact that no historical basis can be found for the story—it is not possible to be sure what the author had in mind. The city of Zoar (*ṣôʿār*) to which Lot was allowed to flee (vv. 18–23) actually existed in OT times (Isa 15:5; Jer 48:34). Like Sodom and Gomorrah, it lay in the valley, but was counted as belonging to Moab. Its name is here stated to be derived from a verb *ṣāʿar* meaning to be small or insignificant;

Lot calls it 'a little one' (miṣ'ār). The point of this conclusion to the story is to emphasize that it is Lot who is the central character and to present God's merciful nature towards those of whom he approves (19:29) as well as his punitive side. The incident of the fate of Lot's disobedient wife (v. 26) may be an aetiology based on a rock formation that existed in later times.

(19:30–8) These verses mark the conclusion of the story of Lot, who now disappears from Genesis. This is a story of double incest involving father and daughters; but no moral judgement is made or implied. The information that the children born of the incestuous union became the ancestors of the Moabite and Ammonite peoples is probably a secondary feature of the story rather than its main point. It is presupposed (v. 31) that the male population of the region has entirely perished in the catastrophe which befell Sodom; the observation that Lot is old cannot, in the context, mean that he is too old to father children; it probably means that he will not marry again and so have legitimate children. This is a situation in which the need to perpetuate the race is paramount, and sanctions desperate remedies. Like Noah (9:21), Lot is unaware, in his drunkenness, of what is happening.

(20:1–18) This story is a variant of 12:10–20 and 26:1–11 (see at 12:10–20 above). Its position immediately before the notice of the conception and birth of Isaac, which at last fulfilled YHWH's promise, is an example of dramatic irony: the reader is made to feel the danger of the situation. The relationship between the three variants is disputed. This version is fuller than 12:10–20, and there are a number of differences of detail. The scene is set not in Egypt but in Gerar, near Gaza (already mentioned in 10:19), and the king is Abimelech—a Canaanite name. Abraham's residence in Gerar is not due to a famine. The main variant detail is Abimelech's dream in which God speaks to him. God exonerates Abimelech as he has acted in ignorance of Sarah's status as Abraham's wife. An additional detail is Abraham's excuse, made on the specious grounds that Sarah is his half-sister as well as his wife (not previously mentioned!), together with his claim to know that the most basic moral standards are not observed in Gerar (vv. 11–12). Also, instead of the plagues inflicted on Pharaoh (12:17) we are told that YHWH had made Abimelech's wives unable to bear children during Sarah's residence in his harem; and we are explicitly told that Abimelech did not have sexual relations with her. Like Pharaoh in 12:16, Abimelech behaves with great generosity to Abraham, while Abraham, though he is said by God to be a 'prophet' (v. 7) and bidden to pray for Abimelech, is portrayed as a guilty man. Nevertheless (21:1) God does not abrogate his promise.

(21:1–21) This story, although it begins with the birth of Isaac, is really about Abraham's two sons, Isaac and Ishmael. vv. 8–21 are a variant of the earlier story of the banishment of Hagar and Ishmael because of Sarah's jealousy (ch. 16). While it is emphasized that it is Isaac who is Abraham's promised heir, the author stresses God's concern for Ishmael, contrasting it with the harsh attitude and action of Sarah. According to the chronology given in 16:16 and v. 5, Ishmael would have been about 14 years old when Isaac was born, yet the story used here by the narrator assumes that he was a small child whom his mother put on her shoulder and carried away (v. 14). In v. 6 there is yet another explanation of the name Isaac (see on 17:17

and 18:12). The circumcision of Isaac (v. 4) is in accordance with the command in 17:12. Abraham's reactions to Sarah's demand (vv. 10–11) are more forthright than in 16:5–6, but he gives way when God intervenes. Hagar's distress in vv. 15–16 is depicted with psychological sensitivity. God's reaction to her distress illustrates his compassion (vv. 17–20). Finally when he grows up under God's protection Ishmael goes to live in the wilderness of Paran near the border of Egypt where he becomes the ancestor of the Ishmaelites.

(21:22–34) These verses presuppose ch. 20, but are not closely related to it. They are concerned to enhance Abraham's status: although he remains an alien (v. 34) he is recognized by Abimelech as especially protected and favoured by God; he is thus treated by a king, who commands an army, as an equal. In vv. 22–4 Abimelech thinks it important to safeguard himself by obtaining from him an oath that he will remain his ally (the phrase is 'āśâ ḥesed) and that this alliance will continue in future generations. The second incident is quite different: Abraham becomes involved in a dispute with Abimelech over the possession of a well (vv. 25–32). The dispute is settled in Abraham's favour with the offering of seven lambs and the making of a treaty of friendship (bĕrît, v. 32). There are two different aetiologies of the name Beersheba here: it is the place of the well (bĕ'ēr) of the oath (šĕbū'â) but also of seven (šeba'). The tree planted by Abraham marked the spot where the covenant was made. The 'Everlasting God' ('ēl 'ôlām) worshipped by Abraham here, and implicitly identified with YHWH, was probably originally a local deity associated with Beersheba. The 'land of the Philistines' is an anachronism: the Philistines in fact arrived in Canaan and established their cities there near the Mediterranean coast during the twelfth century BCE and cannot have been known to Abraham. Abimelech has a Semitic name, and so was evidently a local Canaanite ruler, not a Philistine.

(22:1–19) This story is one of the most brilliantly told narratives in the book. It has generated an immense quantity of interpretative comment beginning in early times with Heb 11:17 and Jas 2:21 and continuing up to the present, and many works of art. It is widely agreed that no one interpretation is entirely adequate (see von Rad 1972: 243–5). Its psychological sensitivity and stylistic skill in portraying the distress of Abraham when commanded by God to kill his beloved son and heir are unequalled. It may be that somewhere in its background lies a story about human sacrifice, specifically the sacrifice of the firstborn; but there is no indication at all that that practice, which was not only forbidden but regarded with horror in Israel, was in the mind of the author of the present story. The statement in the opening verse that God's purpose in demanding Isaac's death was to test Abraham's obedience—to see whether he 'feared God' (v. 12)—is an accurate summary of the plot. Abraham was forced to choose between obedience to an incomprehensible and abhorrent command and his love for his child (v. 2). There is a terrible dramatic irony here: God did not intend that his command should be carried out; but Abraham had no means of knowing that. He passed the test. On a different level, this is yet another example of the theme of the endangerment of God's promise: with Isaac's birth the promise of an heir has apparently been miraculously fulfilled; but now the very life of that heir is—

as far as the reader knows—to be prematurely brought to an end.

The location of the 'land of Moriah' is unknown. A later tradition identified Moriah with the mountain on which Solomon later built the Jerusalem temple (2 Chr 3:1); but there is no indication in the text of Gen 22 that this is what the author had in mind. Every particular of the journey and of the preparations for the sacrifice (vv. 3–9) is meticulously recorded in order to retard the pace of the action and so increase the tension to an almost unbearable degree; it reaches its greatest intensity with 22:10 and is then suddenly released in v. 11. Abraham's reply to Isaac's question (vv. 7, 8) is understandably evasive, but he speaks more than he knows. The angel of YHWH is here clearly identified with YHWH himself. The name given to the place by Abraham (*YHWH yir'eh*, 'Yahweh provides'—lit. sees, or looks out) echoes his reply to Isaac in 22:8; it expresses his joy that YHWH has now done so in a miraculous way. The note in v. 14*b* is a later addition to the story, perhaps linking the place with Jerusalem. vv. 15–18 are also probably an addition to the story: by its repetition of the promise of blessing this makes explicit its place in the wider context of Abraham's life—by his obedience Abraham has confirmed that he is worthy of the blessing.

(22:20–4) This genealogy defines Abraham's kinship with the Arameans (Aram) and points forward to Isaac's marriage with Rebekah (ch. 24).

(23:1–20) Full possession of the land of Canaan was a crucial matter for a people that had lost it with the Babylonian conquest in the sixth century BCE and were, even under the milder policy of the Persian empire, like Abraham, only 'strangers and aliens' (v. 4) in it, subject to foreign rule. Abraham's legal purchase from the 'Hittite'—that is, Canaanite—owner of a single field containing the cave where he could bury Sarah (vv. 17, 20) was a hopeful sign to these readers, even though it was no more than symbolic—the first fruits, as it were, of the promise that Abraham's descendants would possess the whole land.

The name Kiriath-arba, here identified with Hebron (v. 2), means 'city of four'—probably referring to its consisting of four districts or 'quarters' or to its position at the intersection of four roads. The name 'Hittite' here and elsewhere in the Pentateuch does not designate the great Hittite empire of Asia Minor, long extinct when this chapter was written, but is used as a general designation of the Canaanites. Abraham, having no settled home, is obliged to seek a place of burial for Sarah from the local inhabitants. The cave in question belongs to one Ephron (v. 8); but the decision to convey it to Abraham's use evidently rests with the people of Hebron as a whole—the 'people of the land' (vv. 10–13). The negotiation is carried on with great courtesy; it is a legal transaction, and the terminology resembles that used in extant neo-Babylonian legal contracts. Abraham, who is regarded by the Hebronites as a 'mighty prince' (v. 6), is first offered a choice of burial places, but not legal ownership. He insists that the latter is what he seeks; and he finally succeeds in buying the entire field, though at what is known to have been a very high price (v. 15).

(24:1–67) This is by far the longest story in this part of the book, and has with some justification been called a novella, or short story (in the modern sense of that term). It is divided into distinct scenes, and is told with great sensitivity and with acute psychological insight. An unusual feature is the extent to which dialogue is used to portray character and to move the action along: more than half the verses consist of or contain reported speech. Apart from its intrinsic interest as literature, the story marks a new and positive stage in the theme of the promise: Abraham's heir has not only survived; he is now provided with an eminently suitable wife, who is destined in turn to produce an heir, the inheritor of the promise in the third generation. The narrative speaks of the continued guidance of God at every stage.

Abraham, who is evidently too old to undertake a long journey (but note his second marriage in 25:1!), sends his trusted and confidential servant or steward, whom he has entrusted with all his possessions, to seek a wife for Isaac from among those of his kindred who have remained in Mesopotamia (Aram-naharaim, lit. Aram of the two rivers): marriage with an alien Canaanite is ruled out as unthinkable, and it is equally out of the question that Isaac should return to fetch his bride from the country from which his father had departed at God's command. If the girl chosen should refuse the match, the messenger is to return alone to Abraham.

The rite of touching the genitals of the other party while swearing an oath, mentioned in the OT only here (vv. 2, 9) and Gen 47:29, is attested in a Babylonian document and is also known from Arabic usage (*TWAT* 7, 984). Its significance is not clear; but it may be related to the more common practice of swearing by a person's life. The messenger sets out with an impressive retinue and carries valuable gifts appropriate to his master's great wealth and high status (v. 10). On arrival at his destination he takes no action but kneels down at a well that he knows will be frequented by the young girls of the town when they come to draw water, and prays that YHWH will signify his choice of a bride for Isaac in a particular way (vv. 13–14); he is miraculously rewarded when the first girl who comes to draw water proves to be not only beautiful, a virgin, and of a kindly disposition but also Abraham's own niece, so confirming that YHWH has made his mission unexpectedly and completely successful (vv. 15–27; cf. 11:29; 22:22, 23). The reason why it is Rebekah's brother Laban rather than her father who plays the principal role in the remainder of the story (from v. 29) is not clear, though he is to be a principal character in later chapters (29–31). The reference to Rebekah's mother's house rather than that of her father (v. 28) might lead the reader to suppose that her father Bethuel was dead; but he appears in a minor role in v. 50.

Although it is not specifically stated that Rebekah's consent to the marriage was sought, this seems to be implied in her acceptance of the valuable jewellery and the ring (v. 22) and by her running home to tell the news (v. 28). It is also strongly implied by the fact that, when consulted, she agreed to leave her family immediately and accompany the servant home to meet her designated husband (v. 58). There is some difficulty about the Hebrew text of v. 62 and about Isaac's place of residence. According to 25:20 Isaac was 40 years old when he married, and had a separate establishment. The absence of any reference to Abraham in the last part of the story is strange: one would have expected that the servant would have first conducted Rebekah to Abraham and have made his report to him. The story concludes with the rare statement that Isaac loved his wife, paralleled in Genesis only by the love of Jacob for Rachel (29:18) and of Shechem the Hivite for Dinah (34:3).

(25:1–18) With these verses the story of Abraham comes to an end. They are a somewhat miscellaneous collection consisting mainly of genealogies but including a brief statement of Abraham's death and burial (vv. 7–10). They contain no real continuous narrative. The point of the genealogies is to continue the theme of Abraham as the 'father of many nations' (cf. 17:5, 20; 21:13). These lists contain the names of several nations and tribes known from elsewhere, notably Midian (v. 1) and the Ishmaelites (vv. 12–16). The note about Abraham's life in v. 8 reflects the Israelite attitude towards both life and death. Death was not regarded as tragic if it closed a long and fulfilled, honourable life. The statement that Abraham was 'gathered to his people' (v. 8) obviously does not mean that his body was placed in an ancestral tomb, since only Sarah had yet been buried in the cave of Machpelah (v. 10): it was a conventional expression testifying a strong sense of family solidarity.

The Story of Jacob (25:19–37:2)

Of the three 'patriarchs' Abraham, Isaac, and Jacob only Isaac lacks a really independent story. Although as Abraham's heir and Jacob's father he obviously holds an essential place in the family history and is in his turn the recipient of the promise of blessing and of numerous descendants 'for Abraham's sake' (26:3–5, 23–5), he is the principal character in only one chapter (26). It must be presumed that the author or editor of the book did not possess a wealth of narrative material about Isaac as he did about Abraham and Jacob. A large part of the story of Jacob is concerned with the relations between Jacob and his elder brother Esau. God's choice of Jacob rather than Esau as the heir and recipient of the promise recounted in these chapters introduces a new major theme: God in his sovereignty is not bound by the 'natural' or legal principle of inheritance by primogeniture but inscrutably singles out younger sons to carry out his purpose (cf. the choice of David as king of Israel, 1 Sam 16:1–13). So not Ishmael but Isaac is chosen, and not Esau but Jacob; and, of Jacob's twelve sons, it is his eleventh son Joseph who is chosen to rule over his brothers (Gen 37:5–11) and to preserve the lives of the embryo people of Israel (Gen 45:5; 50:20). Similarly Ephraim is given precedence over his elder brother Manasseh (Gen 48:8–20).

(25:19–34) In vv. 19–20, which introduce the stories about Isaac's children, the author has inserted a short notice which repeats what the reader already knows, adding the information that Isaac was 40 years old when he married. But the chronology in this chapter is somewhat confused. If Isaac was 60 when Rebekah bore his first children (v. 26), Abraham, who was 175 when he died (25:7), would still have fifteen years to live, since he was 100 when Isaac was born (21:5)! The two stories about the birth of Esau and Jacob (vv. 21–6) and the birthright (25:27–34) both point forward to the later antagonism between the two and to the precedence of Jacob over his brother. The former story, which begins with YHWH's decree that the elder is to serve the younger, contains a pun on the name Jacob (*ya'ăqōb*) who grasped the heel (*'āqēb*) in the

womb (v. 26) and another on Esau, the ancestor of the Edomites (v. 30; 36:1) who 'came out red' (*'admônî*) from the womb. There is yet another pun on the name Edom in the second story, where Esau calls the dish that Jacob has prepared 'that red stuff' (*'ādōm*, v. 30). The two brothers are also caricatured as two contrasting types: the ruddy, hairy hunter (vv. 25, 27) who is an easy prey to the cunning 'quiet man' who stays at home (v. 27; Jacob is later to become a shepherd, ch. 29). vv. 27–34 especially have been seen as based on an earlier civilization story which reflected problems that arose when the sedentary way of life began to supersede the hunting stage (see Westermann 1985: 414–15). The motif is of crucial importance later in ch. 27; but the point of the present story is to show that Esau already forfeited the privileges of the elder son.

(26:1–35) This chapter is given a unity by the theme of Isaac's relations with Abimelech the 'Philistine' (i.e. Canaanite) king of Gerar. vv. 6–11 are a variant of 12:10–20 and 20:1–18 (on which see the commentary above), the main difference from both the other stories being that it concerns Isaac and Rebekah, not Abraham and Sarah. It contains motifs from both the other versions; and it is commonly held that its author was familiar with, and intended to make certain changes with regard to, both. In particular, the lie told by Isaac (v. 7) is the same as that told by Abraham in the other two versions, but the consequences are less critical, since Rebekah is not taken into the royal harem. vv. 1–5 introduce the story by accounting for Isaac's move to Gerar. It includes an appearance to Isaac by YHWH in which he repeats the promise of the land and of numerous progeny but couples it with an injunction not to depart from Canaan as Abraham had done in similar circumstances (12:10).

In vv. 12–33 the motif of the dispute with the Canaanites of Gerar over the ownership of the wells that were essential to life and livelihood (21:25–34) recurs. But Isaac, who was the first of the patriarchal family to grow crops (v. 12) as well as owning flocks and herds (v. 14) and who had become wealthy even beyond the wealth accumulated by his father, had aroused the envy of the 'Philistines' (vv. 12–14) who were making life difficult for him. However, this series of incidents ends with the making of a treaty of peace between Isaac and Abimelech, in which Isaac is credited with taking the initiative (vv. 26–31). The aetiologies of the names of the wells (v. Ezek 20, 'contention'; Sitnah, v. 21, 'quarrel, accusation'; Rehoboth, v. 22, 'broad space') probably come from ancient local traditions. The naming of Shibah (v. 33) is attributed, as is Beersheba in 21:31, to an oath, this time between Isaac and Abimelech (v. 31).

The Adventures of Jacob (chs. 27–33)

At one level this is a story of withdrawal and return, a familiar folk-tale motif. It is also a story of hatred between brothers followed by eventual reconciliation; but in the context of the book as a whole it is a continuation of the history of the promise made to the patriarchs. Although Esau has his reward in the end in terms of material wealth (33:9–11), it is made clear that he was deprived not only of his birthright but also of the blessing (27:36). He is to be the ancestor of the Edomites and not of Israel, and accordingly establishes his residence in the region of Seir, later to be part of Edom (32:3; 33:14, 16; cf. 36:9). Later events are clearly reflected here.

Isaac's blessing of Jacob (27:27–9) and his lesser 'blessing' of Esau (27:39–40) reflect the history of the later relations between the state of Israel and Edom: Israel will rule over Edom, but eventually Edom will 'break his yoke' and achieve its independence (cf. 2 Sam 8:14; 1 Kings 11:14; 2 Chr 21:8–10). This account of Jacob's adventures is not made of whole cloth: it has incorporated many elements which the final author/ editor has combined. In particular, one major section, ch. 29–31, which describes Jacob's extended residence in the house of his uncle Laban, originally belonged to a quite distinct tradition about the relations between two peoples: Israel and the Arameans.

(27:1–46) This chapter is another example of narrative skill. It is structured in a number of distinct scenes, in each of which, as in folk-tales, only two characters appear: Isaac and Esau in vv. 1–4, Jacob and Rebekah in vv. 5–17, Jacob and Isaac in vv. 18–29, Esau and Isaac in vv. 30–40, Esau alone in v. 41, Rebekah and Jacob in vv. 42–5, Rebekah and Isaac, v. 46. The theme is Jacob's trickery by which he obtains the paternal blessing that would normally be given to the elder son and the consequent implacable hatred of Esau for his brother which makes it necessary for Jacob to leave home and set out on his travels. One of the most remarkable features of the story is the portrayal of Rebekah, who plays a crucial role in the story and whose personality is thus displayed in marked contrast to the passivity of Sarah in the previous chapters (but we may compare the enterprising action of Rachel in 31:34–5). Despite Jacob's disgraceful behaviour in deceiving his aged and blind father, the story is presented in a way that arouses the reader's sympathy for such a rogue, though the depiction of Esau's distress (vv. 34–8) is intended to elicit some sympathy for him as well. There is also a humorous quality in the tale that should not be missed. The predominance of dialogue helps to give the narrative a particularly lively character. The fact that the action takes place entirely on the human plane, with no mention of God (except for his invocation in Isaac's blessing, v. 28, and Jacob's lying assertion in v. 20) sets the chapter, together with 25:27–34, apart from the surrounding chapters in which the hand of God is prominent.

It is noteworthy that it is Rebekah, who evidently loves her 'smooth' son Jacob more than the uncouth, hairy Esau (v. 11) and is even prepared to risk her husband's curse, who proposes the deception; but Jacob, in agreeing to her proposal, is equally guilty. The story turns on the belief that blessings and curses possess objective power and cannot be taken back (v. 33). In v. 36 Jacob's name is once more (cf. 25:26) associated with the root ʿ-q-b, here in a verbal form and interpreted as 'supplant'. It is again Rebekah who takes the initiative, overhearing Esau's intention to kill Jacob and warning him to flee to Haran to his uncle Laban (vv. 43–5). The chapter ends with her fear that Jacob may marry a 'Hittite' (cf. 26:34–5)—an echo of the theme of 24:3–4.

(28:1–9) A different account of the circumstances of Jacob's departure to Laban is given in vv. 1–5 from that given in ch. 27. Here his father sends him off so that he may marry a girl from his own family as Isaac himself had done, and Isaac prays that he will inherit the promise once given to Abraham. Laban's home is now given as Paddan-aram, which may mean 'country of Aram' (so also in 25:20). This region of north Mesopo-

tamia is called Aram-naharaim in 24:10. vv. 6–9 relate how Esau also conformed to Isaac's wish in that he now married a relation in addition to his previous Canaanite wives.

(28:10–22) On his way to Laban, whose home is now specified (as in 27:43) as the city of Haran, Jacob rests for the night at an unnamed place (v. 11) and takes a large stone there as a pillow. He has a dream in which he sees a ladder (probably rather a ramp) stretching from earth to heaven on which God's angels—that is, heavenly messengers—are passing up and down to perform tasks assigned to them by God. He recognizes the ladder as 'the gate of heaven' (v. 17), that is, as the means of communication between God in his dwelling in heaven and his manifestations to human beings on earth; and so concludes with awe that the place where he is resting must therefore be 'the house of God', that is, a place where God manifests himself on earth. The imagery of the dream corresponds to Babylonian religious beliefs as expressed in their structures known as ziggurats. In the dream Jacob becomes aware that God is indeed communicating with him: God repeats to him the promise of the land of Canaan, in which he is now resting, and of numerous progeny, and adds a further promise that he will guide and protect him on his journey and wherever he may go (vv. 13–15).

It is generally agreed that this passage has undergone several accretions, but there is no consensus about the details. Jacob names the place Bethel (lit., 'house of God'), thus naming a place which was later to be one of Israel's most important sanctuaries. The story is thus to be seen as the origin story of the sanctuary of Bethel and will have been used from ancient times by the worshippers at that sanctuary. Its importance to later generations accounts for the fact that it later came to be embellished in various ways (for a recent study of its redactional history which understands it without ascribing it to an interweaving of two major written sources see Rendtorff 1982: 511–23). The stone used by Jacob as a pillow (v. 11), which he erected as a pillar and consecrated with oil (v. 18), marked the site as a holy place where God had revealed himself and so might be expected to do so again—that is, as a sanctuary. Such a pillar (maṣṣēbâ) might be no more than a memorial stone or marker, e.g. of a frontier (31:51); but it was often a feature of sanctuaries both Canaanite and Israelite, though later condemned in Israel (e.g. Lev 26:1). In his concluding vow (vv. 20–2) Jacob acutely translates God's promise of guidance into concrete, down-to-earth terms, and in turn promises to worship YHWH as his God. He also undertakes to pay a tithe of future produce, in anticipation of the cult that will be established at Bethel. He is clearly speaking as a representative of a future Israel and as the founder of the Bethel sanctuary.

(29:1–30) This chapter begins the story of Jacob and Laban which continues to the end of ch. 31. It is set in foreign territory, outside Canaan. As yet another story about an encounter at a well that ends with marriage of the heir to the promise to a member (here two members!) of his Aramean kindred, it has many affinities with ch. 24; but there are significant differences. There is again the apparently fortuitous meeting with the Aramean kindred; but, unlike Isaac, who was forbidden to leave Canaan to seek his wife, Jacob makes precisely that journey. He travels to 'the land of the people of the east' (a rather vague term denoting the land to the east of Canaan, but here including the more northern territory in the vicinity of Haran); but he does not go specifically to seek a wife, and does not at first realize where he is. Further, in contrast to the religious atmosphere of 28:10–22 and with the pious mission of Abraham's servant in ch. 24, this is a purely secular story in which God does not appear, although no doubt he is invisibly present in the background in the mind of the final editor.

vv. 1–14 are an idyllic tale that gives no hint of troubles to come. Jacob is presented as the mighty hero who is able alone to move the stone, which normally required several men to move it, from the mouth of the well to enable the flocks to be watered (cf. 28:18, where also he moves a massive stone); and he does this on perceiving the arrival of Rachel. The kiss which he gives her is no doubt a cousinly kiss (v. 11; cf. v. 13); but his weeping (for joy) surely speaks of love at first sight. The continuation of the story in vv. 15–30, however, already introduces the reader to the calculating character of Laban, who succeeds in employing Jacob for fourteen years without wages and in tricking him into marrying the unwanted Leah. There are two further motifs in this story: Jacob's marriages are a further example of the younger being preferred to the elder; and, in view of Jacob's earlier behaviour (25:27–34; 27), vv. 21–30 may be seen as an example of the motif of the deceiver deceived. Jacob's love for Rachel is again emphasized in vv. 20 and 30. In vv. 24 and 29 Laban's assignment of the two maids Zilpah and Bilhah respectively to serve Leah and Rachel prepares the reader for the accounts of the birth of Jacob's twelve sons, who are to be the ancestors of the twelve tribes of Israel.

(29:31–30:24) This section consists mainly of a miscellaneous collection of notices of the births of Jacob's first eleven sons (and one daughter, Dinah), whose names are those of later Israelite tribes. The reasons given for their names, which all refer to the circumstances of the mothers (unlike the tribal blessings in ch. 49) are quite fanciful and hardly genuine popular etymologies. The words attributed to the mothers in naming their sons have been made to fit the names; but they do not fit very well. In some cases they involve the use of very rare words. The name Reuben (*rĕʾûbēn*) would naturally be taken to mean 'Behold a son' (29:32), but has been connected with *ʿônî*, 'affliction'. Simeon (29:33) is more reasonably connected with *šāmaʿ*, 'to hear'. Levi (29:34) is supposedly derived from *lāwâ*, 'to join'. Judah (29:35) has been associated with the mother's exclamation *ʾôdeh*, 'I will praise'; Dan (30:6) with the verb *dîn*, 'to give judgement'; Naphtali (30:8) with a rare verb *pātal*, possibly meaning 'to twist', here interpreted as 'wrestle'. Gad (30:11) is the name of a god of good fortune; Asher (30:13) is explained as related to *ʾiššēr*, 'to pronounce happy'; Issachar (30:18) as connected with *śākār*, 'hire, wages'. In two cases (and possibly a third, Reuben) two alternative explanations are given: the name Zebulon (30:20) is associated with a verb that occurs nowhere else in the OT but which may refer to exaltation, hence honour, but also with *zēbed*, 'gift', while Joseph (30:24) is related both to *ʾāsap*, 'gather, remove, take away', and to *yāsap*, 'add, increase'. It was not deemed necessary to offer an explanation of the name of the daughter, Dinah.

Only scraps of narrative and dialogue are attached to these birth notices. The motif of the two wives, one of whom is unable to bear children (29:31–2), is found also in the story of the birth of Samuel (1 Sam 1), but with significant differences. In both cases the childless wife is enabled to bear a son through divine intervention; but here this happens to the 'hated' wife (i.e. the one who is unwanted by her husband) whereas in 1 Sam 1 it happens to the one who is especially beloved; here too God takes the initiative rather than acting in response to prayer as in the case of Hannah. There are other OT parallels to God's initiative in such cases: not only in the case of Sarah but also in the story of the birth of Samson (Judg 13). All these stories differ considerably in detail; but behind them lies the conviction that God alone bestows or withholds life. 30:1–7 is another example of the custom of surrogate birth earlier practised by Sarah (so also 30:9–11). The 'birth on the knees' of Rachel (30:3) is a rite which ensures that the child born is to be regarded as Rachel's own. 30:14–18 reflects an ancient belief that the fruit of the mandrake plant has aphrodisiac properties, although the birth of Issachar is attributed to divine operation.

(30:25–43) The details of this story are not clear, and have puzzled the commentators. There are strange contradictions, no doubt due to glossators who themselves did not fully grasp what was happening but attempted to set matters right. The thrust of the story, however, is sufficiently plain. This is a battle of wits between Jacob and Laban from which Jacob emerges victorious. Jacob, who has suffered before from Laban's trickery, repays it in kind. The story begins with an abrupt request by Jacob to Laban for his release from his servitude which puts Laban in an embarrassing situation. Jacob points out that Laban has greatly benefited from his service, but now requests to be allowed to return to his homeland accompanied by his wives and children, who are of course Laban's own daughters and grandchildren (v. 26). This request may not have been within Jacob's rights: Ex 21:2–4 does not permit a freed slave to take his family with him; but Jacob's status is not clear (cf. Laban's action in ch. 31). Laban recognizes the value of Jacob's service to him, and adopts a conciliatory tone. He admits that his prosperity is due to Jacob, perhaps claiming that he has learned by divination (the meaning of this word is uncertain) that this is due to YHWH's having blessed Jacob (v. 27), but complains that the loss of Jacob may damage his own economic status. He makes an offer to reward Jacob, who replies that he is not asking for a reward, but then inconsistently requests to be allowed to keep some of Laban's flocks. He proposes (v. 32) that he should be given those animals that are particoloured (a rarity among sheep and goats) and promises to carry out this operation honestly. Laban pretends to agree, but then himself deceitfully separates the particoloured animals from the rest, and sends them away with his sons to be kept at a distance (vv. 35–6).

The account of Jacob's retaliatory action (vv. 37–42) is again somewhat muddled and repetitive, but here again its general import is clear. To gain an advantage over Laban Jacob had recourse to a trick based on a superstitious, farmers' belief (taken seriously by the author) that newborn animals (and also human babies) can derive certain characteristics from the visual impressions experienced by their mothers at the moment of conception. Taking advantage of Laban's absence,

Jacob arranged that the ewes, which mated while they were drinking, should do so while standing facing some rods which he had taken from appropriate trees that he had partly peeled and set before the drinking troughs, so producing particoloured young. (v. 40 is unfortunately obscure.) In addition (vv. 41–2) he selected for this purpose only the more robust animals. As a result he became the owner, following his previous arrangement with Laban, of the choice animals because they were particoloured, while Laban was left only with the feebler ones. By this device he increased his wealth, though the final verse of the chapter (v. 43) about the extraordinary wealth which he acquired in this way seems entirely disproportionate to the preceding account and is probably a later addition made to enhance the impression that the patriarchs, although landless, were nevertheless persons of substance in the world. This is another secular story in which (apart from Laban's remark in v. 27) God does not appear.

(31:1–55) This chapter concludes the Jacob–Laban stories. It is a continuation of ch. 30, but it also marks a return to the theme of the promise. The question of Jacob's departure broached in ch. 30 has remained unresolved. Now he has determined to leave, with his family, without Laban's permission, partly because relations with Laban and his sons have deteriorated, but above all because YHWH has commanded him to do so and has promised to continue to guide and protect him (vv. 2–3). Jacob meets his wives secretly and speaks to them of his reasons for departure: Laban's animosity towards him, restrained only by God's protection, and God's command, here represented as mediated by an angel in a dream (vv. 11–13). There are inconsistencies again here, e.g. Jacob's claim that Laban has changed his wages ten times does not accord with what has been said in the previous two chapters. In his account of his dream (v. 13) he cites God's command, but with an additional reference to ch. 28. Jacob's proposal to his wives, which involved for them the abandonment of their family and their community, is accepted without demur: they too have a grudge against their father, who has used for himself their bridal price and has thus 'sold' them and in fact treated them as foreigners (vv. 14–16). These verses involve legal questions of marriage and inheritance customs which are not completely clear to the modern reader; but what the wives are saying is that owing to their father's actions they no longer belong to their community, and are prepared to put their trust in what Jacob has told them of God's call to him. So the heir of the promise effects his escape from the alien territory of Paddan-aram and returns to the land of promise.

The second scene (vv. 19–42) opens with Laban, accompanied by his kinsmen, pursuing Jacob, and overtaking him when he has reached the hill country of Gilead, east of the Jordan. Once more Laban receives a divine message warning him not to interfere with Jacob (v. 24); and in fact when they meet Laban exercises restraint. His final complaint against him is that he has stolen his 'household gods' (těrāphîm), though in fact it was Rachel who had stolen them without Jacob's knowledge (vv. 19, 32). The incident of the search for the teraphim (vv. 33–5) is recounted with crude humour. Teraphim, which are mentioned in several other OT texts, appear to have been fairly small hominiform images of gods whose use was not confined to Israel. There is a reference to

their manufacture in Judg 17:5, and Hos 3:4 implies that they were in common use in Israel during the period of the monarchy. Later, however, they were condemned as idolatrous (Zech 10:2) together with the practice of divination with which they appear to have been associated (Ezek 21:21). They were obviously very important to Laban, who may have used them for divination. In recent times it was widely supposed, on the basis of purportedly similar practices known from second-millennium BCE texts discovered at the Mesopotamian city of Nuzi, that possession of such objects could be used to substantiate legal claims to the inheritance of property; but it has now been shown that this view is not tenable, at least as far as this passage in Genesis is concerned (see Thompson 1974: 272–80). There is nothing in the Genesis text that indicates why Laban's teraphim were so important to him.

Jacob in his defence of his conduct (vv. 36–42) attributes his present material success to the ancestral God, whom he here refers as 'The Fear of Isaac' (or possibly 'Kinsman of Isaac', probably an ancient name of a god who was later identified with YHWH). Laban (vv. 43–4) still maintains his legal right to all Jacob's possessions, but is forced to admit defeat. The treaty or covenant now made between the two is a non-aggression pact (vv. 48–50); but in a different version of the event (v. 52) it also defines a territorial boundary which each partner swears to observe. This is really an agreement not simply between two individuals but between representatives of two nations, as is indicated by the double naming of the boundary cairn that they have set up in two distinct languages: both Jegar-sahadutha (Aramaic) and Galeed (Hebrew galʿēd) mean 'cairn of witness'. Behind this incident there undoubtedly lies an ancient tradition of an agreement once made between Israel and the Arameans, who were, however, later to be involved in territorial wars (cf. especially 2 Sam 8; 10; 1 Kings 11; 20; 22; 2 Kings 7–16).

(32:1–21) After reporting the peaceful solution of Jacob's dispute with Laban (31:54–5) the story resumes the account of his relations with his brother Esau, from whose hostile intentions he had fled (ch. 27). First, however, there is a short notice of a (presumably) favourable appearance of a group of divine messengers or angels (cf. 28:12) during his journey, which he perceives as 'God's camp' (maḥănēh ʾělōhîm) and so names the place Mahanaim. This incident is no doubt based on a local foundation legend about the city of Mahanaim in Gilead east of the Jordan, later to become an important Israelite city. Now, aware that he is close to the land of Edom, Esau's home, and fearful for his life and the lives of his family, he sends an embassy to Esau. Learning that Esau is advancing towards him with a strong military force (v. 6), he prays to God that he will protect him, and then makes preparations for the encounter, sending a further conciliatory message to Esau together with valuable presents which he sends by instalments, himself remaining behind with his family in the hope of protecting them in case of attack. Here again the reader finds the heir to the promise and his family in danger of their lives; and once again the narrative is slowed down to increase the dramatic tension.

(32:22–32) This incident, which interrupts the account of Jacob's concluding encounter with Esau, is of central importance in the story of Jacob, even more significant than Jacob's experience at Bethel (28:10–22). Here once more the heir to the promise is placed in danger of his life. But the incident remains essentially mysterious, and several of its features are difficult to interpret. This is at least partly due to the fact that it is evidently a pre-Israelite story that has been reworked, probably more than once. The original version strongly resembles pagan, even animistic, tales of spirits or demons guarding particular places such as streams, who attack travellers who are endeavouring to pass on their way, but who are powerful only at night; here we are told that the sun rose only when the incident was over (v. 31). The place in question here is a ford over the stream Jabbok, which rises in the mountains east of the Jordan and descends precipitately to flow into the Jordan—a place where it is difficult to cross on foot. The supposed connection between its name and the rare Hebrew verb 'ābaq, 'wrestle' (v. 24) may have given rise to the story in its original version. The man ('îš) who attacked Jacob and struggled with him all night remains unidentified until v. 30, but is clearly possessed of supernatural power as well as of great physical strength (30:25), and is recognized by Jacob as one who is able to confer a blessing on him. He subsequently reveals himself as divine ('ĕlōhîm, v. 28); but the statements that Jacob overmatched him and forced him to bless him (vv. 26, 29) remain mysterious in the face of Jacob's final realization that he has been locked in a struggle with God, and has seen him face to face (pĕnî'ēl means 'face of God'). At this point of the story, as in others, features of the original tale are still present. The central and crucial point of the story in its present form is that Jacob not only received the divine blessing (despite the refusal of the 'man' to declare his own name), but that his name is changed to 'Israel' (this name is here associated with the rare verb śārâ, 'struggle', used in v. 28). The passage thus declares Jacob to be not only a towering, heroic figure who has close dealings with God himself, but also the founder of the nation of Israel. Despite its evidently somewhat composite nature, attempts to analyse its sources have been controversial; but the final verse is certainly a separate comment on the incident as being the origin of an otherwise unknown food taboo.

(33:1–20) The reconciliation between Jacob and his wronged brother resolves the tension built up in 32:1–21. The chapter is a riot of deferential bowings and honorific expressions ('my lord', 'your servant') in oriental fashion on the part of Jacob and his household and magnanimity and solicitous concern on the part of Esau. Esau's emotional welcome of Jacob signifies his complete forgiveness, after so many years, of a grievous offence which is never mentioned, but of which Jacob still remains painfully aware. Until the moment of greeting he appears still to be apprehensive of Esau's intention; and even subsequently he is still reluctant to travel in his company, pretending that they will meet again in Seir, Esau's home territory (vv. 12–15), whereas in fact he makes for Succoth ('booths'), where he builds a house for himself and settles down. Another version (vv. 18–20), however, takes him across the Jordan, still living in tents, to the 'city of Shechem'. This phrase must, on grounds of Hebrew syntax, refer to a person of that name (cf. v. 19) who was the owner or founder of the city (see Westermann 1985: 528). The further reference to the man Shechem and to the sons of Hamor in v. 19 links this

chapter to the events of ch. 34. Jacob's naming of the altar that he erects on the plot of land that he has bought ('God, the God of Israel') might be a reference to Jacob's new personal name Israel, but the reader would understand it as a proclamation that Jacob's God was to be the God of the *people* Israel.

(34:1–31) This brutal and—to the modern reader—repulsive story, which may be based on a reminiscence of some actual event in the early history of the Israelite tribes, is widely supposed to have existed in two versions, which have been combined and used by a later writer to make the point that Israelites should abstain from intermarriage with the Canaanites. The massacre which it describes is in conformity with the teaching of the Deuteronomists, who represent Moses as having demanded their extermination (Deut 7:1–3). The protagonists are Simeon and Levi, who first ensure by a trick that the victims will be in a weakened condition (vv. 25–6). Their brothers, however, all participate in the subsequent plundering of the city. That Jacob may not have figured in the original story is suggested by the fact that he plays only a marginal and passive role. Jacob's fear that the neighbouring Canaanites will take their revenge on his family and destroy it in turn (v. 30) qualifies the story as yet another example of the endangerment of the lives of the heirs to the promise, a situation that leads to Jacob's removal with his family to Bethel and is only relieved by the mysterious 'terror' that falls on the surrounding cities (35:5, which appears to be intended as the sequel to this story).

The Shechemites are here (v. 2) specified as Hivites, one of the tribes supposed to have constituted the Canaanite people (cf. e.g. Gen 10:15–18; Deut 7:1). After forcing Dinah into illicit intercourse with him, Shechem falls in love with her and wishes to marry her at all costs. The inhabitants of the city, with Hamor as spokesman, attempt to negotiate the marriage in all innocence, but are rebuffed (vv. 8–14). The imposing of circumcision on all the Shechemite men as a condition of the marriage is a trick with sinister and ironical overtones, a mere excuse for the real cause of the massacre, the desire for revenge for the initial rape (v. 31). In the Blessing of Jacob (49:2–27) in which Jacob foretells what will be the future destiny of each of his sons (now openly called the twelve tribes of Israel, 49:28), Simeon and Levi are not blessed but cursed (49:5–7) for their violent behaviour, with an apparent reference to the incident of ch. 34.

(35:1–15) Jacob's departure from Shechem to Bethel is here attributed to a positive command by God. The preparations for the journey (vv. 2–4) and the use of the technical term 'to go up' ('ālâ) suggest that this was no ordinary journey but a pilgrimage. Alt (1959: 79–88), followed by others including von Rad (1972: 336), maintained that these verses reflect an actual annual pilgrimage made by the Israelites at later times. Bethel was the place where Jacob had already encountered God and set up a sacred pillar (28:10–22) during his flight to Laban, and which he had vowed to visit again on his return home 'in peace' (28:21). The connection between the two episodes is specifically made in vv. 1, 3, 7. The change of clothes (v. 2) was an act of purification necessary before an encounter with God (cf. Ex 19:10–14). More important is the putting away and burial of 'foreign gods' (vv. 2, 4). The fact that a similar rite, also performed at Shechem, is recorded in

Josh 24:23 suggested to Alt (1959) that something of the kind constituted an esential feature of a regular pilgrimage from Shechem to Bethel, marking an annual demonstration of exclusive loyalty to YHWH. (On v. 5 see above on ch. 34.) The name given to the place where Jacob set up an altar (v. 7) is the same as in 33:20. In vv. 9–15 there occurs a further repetition of the promise of numerous descendants and of the land, followed by a further account of the setting up of a pillar and its consecration with oil.

(35:16–22) is concerned with events in Jacob's family. The birth of his twelfth and last son Benjamin is recorded. Jacob does not accept the name given to him by his dying mother, which means 'son of my sorrow', but gives him a name which may mean either 'son of the right hand' or 'son of the south' but perhaps, more appropriately and hopefully, 'son of good fortune' (Soggin 1961: 432–40). The incest committed by Reuben is condemned when Jacob blesses his sons (49:4). vv. 23–9 conclude the story of Jacob's adventures with his return home at last in time to be with his father Isaac before he dies. Jacob lived many more years after this (his death is recorded in 49:33, at the end of the story of his son Joseph's brilliant career), but he no longer plays an active role in the book.

(36:1–43) After the lengthy story of Jacob the author turns his attention to Esau, the ancestor of the Edomites, and his descendants—an indication that although Israel and Edom were often hostile to one another Israel still considered them to be 'brothers'. These genealogical lists are derived from different sources and contain not a few repetitions and inconsistencies. The extent to which they contain genuine information about a people about whom little is otherwise known is disputed. In vv. 20–30 the clan of the Horites appears to be reckoned as related to Esau, but in Deut 2:12, 22 the Horites are said to have been one of the former peoples whom the Edomites dispossessed. The lists distinguish between three types of socio-political organization, referring to heads of families (vv. 1–8, 20–8), tribal leaders (vv. 15–19, 29–30, 40–3), and kings (vv. 31–9). The kings of Edom are said to have reigned 'before any king reigned over the Israelites' (v. 31). This list, which obviously cannot be very early, may contain some genuine historical information (so Westermann 1985). The Edomites are known from the evidence of archaeology to have settled in their territory before the arrival of Israel in Canaan, and that they had acquired the status of a monarchy before Israel had done so is plausible (Num 20:14 mentions a 'king of Edom' in the time of Moses). That their monarchy was at first non-hereditary as stated in Gen vv. 31–9 is of interest in the light of recent studies of the early history of Israel.

The Story of Joseph (chs. 37–50)

These chapters are of a different kind from the rest of Genesis. Instead of a catena of brief incidents and notices about family and tribal affairs we have here—interrupted only by some obviously interpolated material, notably chs. 38 and parts of 48–50—a single, well-constructed, continuous narrative comprising some 300 verses in our Bibles and skilfully arranged in a series of distinct consecutive scenes, about the career of one man, Jacob's eleventh son, who rose to an undreamed-of eminence in Egypt as ruler of that whole land second only to Pharaoh himself (41:40–4) and so became, under God's guid-ance, the saviour of his father Jacob and all his family (45:7–8; 50:19–21). This story raises for the reader a number of questions which have been the subject of much discussion, e.g.: What is its relationship to the rest of the patriarchal stories? What is its literary genre? Is it the work of a single author? Does it contain reliable information about ancient Egypt, and if so, of what period? What is its purpose?

The function of the story in the context of the foregoing patriarchal stories and of the following book of Exodus is that it bridges a gap in the chronological scheme of the Pentateuch. The material available to the compiler of Genesis about Abraham, Isaac, and Jacob appears to have come to an end. The story of Joseph, whose connection with that material is tenuous though real (his birth and his genealogy are recorded in Gen 30:22–4; 35:22–6) serves the purpose of accounting for the migration of Jacob and his family to Egypt, from which country the Exodus tradition recounts the subsequent departure of the Israelites (the sons of Jacob), so ensuring the continuity of the larger narrative tradition. At the same time, it constitutes yet another example of the theme of danger to the heirs of the promise—again as a result of famine—and their miraculous deliverance. But neither of these functions required or could account for such an elaborate narrative as this. Von Rad (1966b), who found parallels between the story and Egyptian short stories, saw it as narrative wisdom literature depicting Joseph as an ideal wise man. But others have questioned this assessment of the character of Joseph as here portrayed.

It is this quality that has led to a questioning of the conventional view that the story is the result of a combination of two separate versions, attributed respectively to J and E. Von Rad's attempt to combine the latter view with an appreciation of its literary quality was shown to be inconsistent by Whybray (1968), followed independently by Donner (1976). The possibility that it is the work of a single author, first proposed by Volz and Rudolph in 1933, who threw doubt on the existence of an E strand, is now seriously, though not universally, accepted. Whether the story betrays accurate knowledge of Egyptian life and customs of any period has been disputed by Egyptologists. Some (e.g. Vergote 1959) took a positive view of this, arguing that it fits well into the Ramesside period which was believed by some to be a plausible time for the career of a historical Joseph, but others (e.g. Redford 1970) were sceptical about the authenticity of the Egyptian allusions. Redford maintained that if the author did in fact have genuine knowledge of Egypt the work cannot be dated earlier than the seventh century BCE.

(37:1–34) The minor inconsistencies and duplications in this chapter (e.g. the apparent confusion between Ishmaelites and Midianites in v. 28; the duplication of Joseph's dreams in vv. 6–7 and 9; the similarity of the compassionate actions of Reuben and Judah in vv. 21–2 and 26–7) are not sufficient to show that two complete versions of the story have been interwoven; at most they may suggest that the author made use at some points of earlier oral material. The story itself is quite straightforward: it recounts the first of a series of incidents which once again put in danger of his life the person who is destined to hold in his hands the survival of the heirs of the promise. This destiny is foreshadowed here by Joseph's dreams; but the dramatic suspense is to continue concerning his fate for several more chapters. Another motif, that of hatred between brothers, is reminiscent of the hostility between Jacob and Esau; once again the issue is solved by the end of the story with the indication that it is not the elder brother who has been chosen by God to assure the continuation of the chosen race. vv. 1–2 are an introduction to the whole Joseph story, providing the necessary link between the earlier patriarchal stories and the present one. In v. 3 the precise nature of the 'long coat with sleeves' (kĕtōnet passîm) is not certain. Outside this chapter this garment is referred to in the OT only in 2 Sam 13:18, 19, where it is the apparel of a princess. Here it is a token of Jacob's especial affection for Joseph and a mark of esteem which incites the brothers' hatred. The description of Jacob's grief at the supposed death of his son (vv. 33–5) closes this first part of the story of Joseph, after which (in ch. 39) the scene changes to Egypt.

(38:1–30) This chapter, in which Joseph does not appear at all, is an interpolation that interrupts the Joseph story, which resumes in 39:1 at the point at which it is broken off at the end of ch. 37. Attempts to interpret it as in some way relevant to the events narrated in the surrounding chapters have hardly been convincing, although on the other hand no convincing explanation has been found for its interpolation. Probably, as a story about a member of Jacob's family it was thought to deserve a place in the total narrative, but no satisfactory placement for it could be found. It is wholly concerned with events in the life of Judah, Jacob's fourth son. But he can hardly be called the hero of the story: it is his daughter-in-law Tamar who fills that role. The story is a complicated one and involves a number of customs that call for elucidation. These can only be briefly sketched here. vv. 1–11 are introductory to the main story. Judah's decision to settle apart from his brothers probably reflects the fact that the tribe of Judah was located in historical times in the south, away from the other tribes, and had a separate existence until politically united with them by David (Adullam and Timnah were both Judaean cities in later times). The story also reflects fraternization and intermarriage between Israelites and Canaanites. Tamar's second marriage, to Onan, conforms to the custom of levirate marriage (see Deut 25:5–6). With the death of her first two husbands Tamar evidently expected to be married to the third brother, Shelah; but, afraid that he too might die prematurely, Jacob made an excuse to avoid this; and Tamar, according to custom, returned to the unenviable state of living with her parents. In desperation she then tried to force Judah's hand. She arranged to have sexual relations with her father-in-law in the guise of a prostitute without his being aware of her identity, and retained proof of the relationship by keeping his cylinder seal with its cord and his staff as pledge for her fee (v. 18). It is not clear on what grounds she was condemned to death by Judah in his capacity as undisputed head of the family with powers of life and death (v. 24); it is perhaps assumed that she was betrothed to Shelah, though not actually married to him (cf. Deut 22:23–4). After Judah's recognition that her action was justified (!) the story ends with her giving birth to twin boys, Judah's children, whose names (Perez and Zerah) are interpreted as meaning 'breaking out' and (perhaps) 'bright, shining' respectively.

(39:1–41:57) This account of Joseph's humiliation and subsequent exaltation has some of the characteristics of the folktale, but is an integral part of the story of Joseph as a whole. It is full of dramatic tension: Joseph is again placed in great danger; but the tension is finally resolved in an equally dramatic fashion. It is several times (39:3, 5, 21, 23; 41:51–2) specifically emphasized that both his preservation in danger and his later success are due not to his own abilities but to the unseen operation of God. Although there is no evidence in extant Egyptian texts of any comparable elevation of a person of humble status to a position of great power, the theme of the elevation of exiled Jews by foreign potentates was evidently a favourite one in post-exilic times, and is found also in Dan 1–6 and Esther. 39:1, which repeats information given at the end of ch. 37, is deliberately resumptive following the interpolation of ch. 38. It specifies that it was Ishmaelites rather than Midianites who sold Joseph into slavery in Egypt (as in 37:28b). The Egyptian name Potiphar means 'the one whom Re gives'. The initial success of the good-looking Joseph (39:6) as Potiphar's trusted servant (39:2–6) is brought to a sudden end and his life once more endangered by the lie told by Potiphar's wife when he twice virtuously refuses her sexual advances (39:14–18). (On the use of the term 'Hebrew', 39:14, which occurs several times in the story of Joseph, see above on 14:13.) But the punishment which Potiphar imposes on Joseph is surprisingly mild for the crime of adultery, and suggests that Potiphar was not entirely convinced of his guilt. The chapter ends on a more positive note: Joseph's attractive personality (as well as God's protection) once more leads to success, when he obtains the favour of the jailer.

The chief cupbearer and chief baker, whom Joseph waited upon in prison (40:1–4) were high officials imprisoned for some undisclosed offences by the dictatorial king of Egypt. Unlike Joseph's own dreams in ch. 37, whose meaning needed no explanation, their dreams, as also those of Pharaoh in ch. 41, were dreams whose meaning was not obvious and which required an interpreter with special powers. The interpretation of such dreams was, both in Egypt and in Mesopotamia, the speciality and occult art of the professional diviner. Like Daniel, who was required not only to interpret Nebuchadnezzar's dream but also to remind the king of its contents (Dan 2:31–45), Joseph possessed the power to interpret dreams, but attributed this power to special divine revelation rather than to his own ability (40:8)—although in 44:15 he speaks of his ability to practise divination (niḥēš). The difference between the cupbearer's and the baker's dreams—the fact that in the latter's dream the birds were eating from the basket of food which he was carrying to Pharaoh, whereas the cupbearer dreamed that he had resumed his former function—determined Joseph's interpretations, in which Joseph played—gruesomely—on two meanings of the phrase 'to lift up the head', whose normal meaning was to restore to favour, but in the case of the baker referred to decapitation or hanging. Both interpretations proved to be correct. The last verse of the chapter reintroduces the tension into the story: although the cupbearer had promised to intercede for Joseph when he was restored to favour with Pharaoh, he forgot him, leaving him in prison with no apparent hope, and possibly again in danger of his life should judgement be given against him.

Pharaoh's dreams (41:1–7) are of the same symbolic kind as those of the cupbearer and baker, and required expert decipherment. Like Nebuchadnezzar in similar circumstances (Dan 2:4) Pharaoh sent for his experts (ḥarṭummîm, 'magicians', is a form of an Egyptian word meaning 'soothsayer-priest'), who proved to be incapable of the task. On the suggestion of the cupbearer, who at last remembered Joseph's talents, Joseph was sent for from his prison cell and, having shaved and put on clean clothes—matters of great importance to the Egyptians—appeared before Pharaoh. His preparations are symbolic of a great change in his life; from this moment he never looked back. But it was his successful interpretation of the dreams that—under God, 41:39—was the cause of his sudden elevation to greatness, together with his eminently practical advice about the measures to be taken in the face of an otherwise certain disaster. In a manner typical of the folktale, Pharaoh put his entire faith in this one demonstration of Joseph's ability (41:39–40) and lost no time in appointing him Grand Vizier of Egypt, endowing him with all the symbols and the reality of that office, which are attested in Egyptian art and tomb furniture. The meaning of the word 'abrēk ('Bow the knee!', 41:43) may be related to the Semitic root b-r-k, 'kneel', or may be related to an Egyptian word meaning 'Watch out!' In receiving a new and Egyptian name (Zaphenath-paneah means 'God speaks and lives'), Joseph was received into the ranks of the Egyptian nobility; and this was confirmed by his being given the daughter of the high priest of Heliopolis ('On') as his bride. He is presented (41:34–6, 47–57) as a foresighted administrator. The establishment of large granaries against times of low grain production was a well-known Egyptian economic measure. The final verse of the chapter (57) prepares for the events of the following chapters by emphasizing the world-wide nature of the food shortage against which Joseph successfully prepared Egypt.

(42:1–45:28) With ch. 42 the scene switches back to Canaan and to Jacob and his other sons. Egypt was the granary of the ancient world; and journeys from such countries as Canaan to try to buy food in times of famine are recorded in extant Egyptian texts (see ANET 250–1) and depicted in Egyptian graphic art. The main problem of the interpretation of these chapters is to understand the reason for Joseph's harsh treatment of his brothers before he reveals his identity in ch. 45. One of his motives was certainly to force them to bring his youngest brother Benjamin to see him. But there can be little doubt that a main motive was connected with his brothers' treatment of him many years before (ch. 37). In his present position of unlimited power he was in a position to punish them, and he did so; but in the end brotherly love and family feelings proved stronger than his desire for revenge (ch. 45). The story is replete with dramatic tension and also with dramatic irony (the brothers do not know who he is, but the readers do) and is told with psychological subtlety. By pretending to believe that the brothers are spies (42:9), Joseph extracts the information that they have left their youngest brother behind with his father, and demands that he should be brought to him. Imprisoned for three days, they suppose that they are being punished for their earlier crime, even though they do not recognize Joseph (42:21). In releasing them all except Simeon, however, Joseph is deeply affected,

and supplies them with corn and provisions; but the return of their money increases their fears (42:28, 35), and their misery is increased when on their return home Jacob, in a mood of self-pity, refuses to let Benjamin return with them to Egypt.

When a further supply of corn became an absolute necessity to Jacob and his family a second visit to Egypt was mooted, and Jacob was persuaded against his will to let Benjamin go with his brothers, with Judah as a guarantor of his safety (43:1–11). This time, fearful of their reception, they take with them tribute in the form of choice products of Canaan and double the previous sum of money, to prove their honesty (43:11–12). Joseph, however, was to continue to play his tricks on them (ch. 44). The scene with Joseph's steward (43:16–25) is intended to allay the brothers' fears: they are at first suspicious and naïvely afraid of a trap (in such a setting!), but are reassured. They have been naturally astonished and awed by the luxury of Joseph's house and by the invitation to dinner; but when Joseph arrives he shows his concern for his aged father, and is overjoyed, and again deeply affected, on seeing Benjamin (43:30). There is again astonishment at Benjamin's treatment as guest of honour, and probably at Joseph's dining at a separate table in accordance with Egyptian rules of purity; but in the relaxed atmosphere they forget their fears and even drink to excess ('were merry') in Joseph's company, unaware of further trouble to come.

(44:1–34) By the repetition of the earlier incident of 42:35 with the planting in the brother's luggage of Joseph's cup (the reference to the money here is probably a later addition), the pursuit and apprehension of the brothers and the accusation of theft (vv. 1–13) the tension is still further increased. It seems to them that Joseph has now trapped them as they had feared all along, and that it is all up with them. The cup is particularly important to Joseph because he uses it to practise lecanomancy (v. 5), a form of divination in which oil was poured into a cup or bowl to give psychic insight (see Cryer 1994: 145–7, 285)—a practice somewhat resembling modern foretelling of the future by tea-leaves. Joseph's purpose in so tricking the brothers was to test them to see whether they had changed their nature, and whether they genuinely cared for their father and for Benjamin. They protest their innocence, but recognize that if found guilty they merit condign punishment (v. 9), though both the steward and Joseph himself are inclined to mercy except towards the thief, who must be enslaved (vv. 10, 17). Joseph adds to their dismay by claiming that he has the gift of divination even without the use of the cup, and knows what has occurred (v. 15). But Judah's lengthy speech in which he heartrendingly depicts the inevitable fate of Jacob if he is bereft of yet another son and offers himself as a scapegoat in Benjamin's place is a masterpiece of rhetoric which Joseph finds too hard to endure (45:1).

(45:1–28) This chapter probably marks the end of the Joseph story proper. With it all the tension is released and the problems solved; there is a reconciliation and a happy ending. From the literary point of view the story is complete, and the chapters that complete the book have rather the character of an appendix or series of appendices designed to provide an answer to the question, 'And how did it all end?' (46:1–5 already reverts to the style and concerns of the earlier patriarchal stories, with an appearance of God in the night to Jacob, reiterating the promise of making a great nation of him, but this time in Egypt rather than Canaan. The remaining chapters lack the high literary quality of the Joseph story proper, and are rather piecemeal in contents.) vv. 1–15 describe a touching scene in which, apart from the emotions that are expressed between Joseph and his brothers, the author is concerned to emphasize Joseph's forgiveness of his brothers and the hidden hand of God in preserving the lives of Jacob's family through Joseph's agency. In vv. 10–15, however, a new theme is announced: Jacob and his family are to migrate to Egypt to share in Joseph's good fortune. (His question in v. 3 is strange: the brothers have already told him that his father is still alive.) The rest of the chapter is concerned with the arrangements for the move. Joseph proposes it on his own initiative (vv. 9–11), and Pharaoh himself confirms this, offering the family the best land in Egypt for their residence. In vv. 21–8 Joseph's lavish provisions for the journey and Jacob/Israel's astonishment, incredulity, and final acceptance of the news of Joseph and of his offer are described.

(46:1–34) Jacob was last heard of as living in Hebron (37:14). Now he passes through Beersheba on his way to Egypt, and it is there that he has his reassuring message from God. The list of names of those who went with him (vv. 8–27) is supposedly a roll-call of the persons mentioned in vv. 6–7; but it clearly comes from a different source and interrupts the narrative. Among the total of sixty-six persons alleged to have made the journey (v. 26), expanded to seventy by (presumably) including Jacob himself and also Joseph and his two sons Ephraim and Manasseh, who are counted twice, though not named the second time (v. 27) there are some who are expressly stated not to have been among them: Er and Onan (v. 12) were already dead (38:7, 10), and Manasseh and Ephraim had been born in Egypt. Joseph, of course, was still in Egypt. Moreover, the statement that Benjamin had ten sons who accompanied him on the journey (v. 21) does not accord with what had previously been said about his youth. Probably this list was originally intended as a list of all Jacob's descendants through three generations and had no original connection with this narrative. vv. 28–34 are concerned with Jacob's projected meeting with Pharaoh and with the place of residence designated for the immigrants. Goshen (vv. 28, 34, already mentioned in 45:10) was an area on the eastern edge of the Nile delta, where the Egyptians, who were suspicious of foreign immigrants, commonly settled them. There is a strong hint to the reader in v. 34 about the future in the statement that shepherds are abhorrent to the Egyptians, and in Joseph's advice to his father to be open in his interview with Pharaoh about his profession. However, Pharaoh is represented in 47:5–6 as being prepared to welcome Jacob for Joseph's sake on condition that he lived in Goshen, as he had already promised (45:17–20).

(47:1–26) The narrative of vv. 1–12 follows immediately on ch. 46, and is continued in v. 27. vv. 13–26 are an account of Joseph's economic policy as Grand Vizier, and has no connection, except for the motif of the famine, with the story of Jacob and his family in Egypt. The audience with Pharaoh (vv. 1–12) is in two parts: first Joseph presents five of his brothers to Pharaoh (vv. 2–6) and then, separately, his father (vv. 7–12). It is probable that two distinct versions have been used here; this

is suggested by the fact that in v. 11 the land assigned to the immigrants is called (only here) the land of Rameses (cf. Ex 1:11) rather than of Goshen. The location, however, is probably the same. The point of the audience with the brothers seems to be that the brothers do not, as they might have done, try to use their kinship with Joseph to enhance their social status: they do not ask for permanent residence in Egypt, which would have been tantamount to Egyptian citizenship, and they wish to continue their hereditary profession, although Pharaoh suggests that some of them may be capable of positions of some responsibility (v. 6). The point of the second audience is to present Jacob as a dignified old man who is not overawed by Pharaoh but dares to bless him (vv. 7, 10). vv. 13–26 are designed to demonstrate Joseph's superior wisdom in using his control over the corn supply to make slaves of the whole Egyptian nation—a triumph which, whatever the modern reader may think of its morality, perhaps—although this is a secular story—foreshadows the later triumph of the Israelites over Pharaoh himself (Ex 6–15).

(47:27–48:22) The story of Jacob and his family is now resumed; but the narrative is not all of one piece. It contains a number of inconsistencies and incongruities, and is the result of the combination of several different kinds of material. 47:27–8 notes the family's successful life in the land of Goshen and the period of their residence there together with a note of the length of Jacob's life—though his death is not recorded until 49:33. 47:29–31, however, begins the account of his last years and death. His request to be taken back to Canaan for burial reintroduces—though indirectly—the theme of the promise of the land: life in Egypt is not to be the permanent destiny of the nation of Israel. In his deathbed speech in 48:1–4 Jacob first repeats the story of his blessing and the promise made to him at Bethel (35:6–12; Luz = Bethel; 28:19; 35:6) and then informs Joseph that he is adopting his (Joseph's) sons Ephraim and Manasseh as his own sons. This action, which points beyond the brothers as individuals to their future character as Israelite tribes, would mean that the traditional number of twelve tribes (implied, for example, in 35:23–6) is augmented to thirteen (if Ephraim and Manasseh are to be counted instead of their father). In fact the traditional number of twelve is a fiction; they are listed in several different ways in various places in the OT, and their numbers vary between ten and thirteen.

The scene of Jacob's blessing of Ephraim and Manasseh (48:8–20), in which Jacob is called by his other name Israel, appears not to presuppose the previous passage but to be from a different source. Since it is implied here that Joseph's sons are not yet adult and Jacob appears to be encountering them for the first time, the scene is evidently supposed to have taken place soon after Jacob's arrival in Egypt rather than just before his death (cf. 47:28). This is another example of the younger son being given precedence over the elder (cf. ch. 27). The right hand is assumed to confer the greater blessing. Jacob deliberately crosses his hands despite Joseph's protest, in order to give Ephraim, the younger, the greater blessing. 48:15–16 is somewhat confused, and interrupts the main narrative. It is stated here that it is Joseph who is blessed (48:15a), but in fact it is his sons who are blessed (48:16), and no difference is made between them. 48:20 also is a somewhat confusing addition to the story: it purports to be an alternative blessing of Ephraim and Manasseh ('them'), but in fact it is a wish rather than a blessing, and it is addressed to one person ('you' is singular). It is noteworthy that 'Israel' here (and perhaps also in 47:27) refers to the *nation* of Israel, not to the individual Jacob/Israel. The last sentence in the verse reverts to the main story, summing it up: Ephraim was preferred before Manasseh. There is a clear allusion in this story to the later predominance of the tribe of Ephraim (cf. e.g. Deut 33:17).

The significance of 48:22 is not clear. 'Joseph' here does not refer simply to the individual but to the 'house of Joseph', which comprised the tribes of Ephraim and Manasseh, and was to be the most powerful of the northern group of Israelite tribes. Jacob confers on 'Joseph' one 'portion' (*šěkem*), here unidentified, more than he gives to the others. The word *šěkem* is also the name of the city of Shechem, but as a common noun means 'shoulder'. Here it plainly means a shoulder of land or a mountain ridge. The military exploit of Jacob referred to here is unknown; certainly he did not capture the city of Shechem from the Amorites (= Canaanites; cf. ch. 34).

(49:1–33) The sayings about the twelve tribes of Israel preserved here in the guise of a deathbed address by Jacob to his twelve sons (vv. 3–27) are generally known as the Blessing of Jacob, partly on the basis of the statement in v. 28. v. 1, however, describes their character somewhat more accurately: in their present form the sayings are, to a large extent, *predictions* of 'what will happen' to the various tribes in the future. They vary considerably in their contents, and their assessments are by no means all favourable. They cannot be said to constitute a single poem, but differ greatly in form and length as well as in contents. They are in fact a collection of originally quite separate sayings or slogans each characterizing an individual tribe (in the case of Simeon and Levi, vv. 5–7, two are treated together), some of them alluding to particular incidents in which they were involved that are now wholly or partly obscure. Some have been greatly augmented; in those cases it is often possible to identify the original, usually pointed, saying. The intention of the author/collector was to provide a complete survey of all the twelve tribes of Israel (Joseph, vv. 22–6 being treated as a single tribe—see above); however, the persistent tradition that Israel was composed of exactly twelve tribes is not derived from this chapter. This is not the only passage of this kind in the OT: Deut 33, known as the Blessing of Moses, is a parallel instance, and Judg 5, the Song of Deborah, also assesses the characters of almost all the tribes (Judg 5:14–18). The latter, however, is a unitary poem which comments on a single incident, and praises or blames the various tribes according to their co-operation or otherwise. Here in Gen 49 it is significant that Judah (vv. 8–12) and Joseph (vv. 22–6)—that is, the tribes which were later to become the most powerful and important tribes—are treated much more fully than the others.

The Blessing of Jacob is here presented as a scene that took place at Jacob's bedside just before his death in the presence of all his sons, and thus as a farewell discourse (a frequent feature in the accounts of the deaths of great men in the OT—cf. e.g. the Blessing of Moses, Deut 33; Josh 24; David's farewell speech, 1 Kings 2:1–9). However, it is clearly an independent piece that has been inserted at an appropriate point into the story of Jacob's death. In its present expanded form it cannot be earlier than the time of David, as it speaks of Judah as the ruler of the other tribes and of other peoples (v. 10). The full and favourable assessment of Joseph—that is, of the central tribes—as numerous and powerful (vv. 22–6) expresses a different picture of leadership; but it also clearly reflects a later period and has a different orientation from that of Judah. The chapter appears to have been subject to more than one process of redaction. The function of the individual sayings in their original brief state is not obvious and has been frequently debated. They were presumably comments by tribes about other tribes made at an early period; but the circumstances in which they were made remain obscure.

v. 2 is a formal poetical introduction to the collection of sayings, which are also in poetical form. Reuben (vv. 3–4) is addressed directly and accused of incest—probably referring to 35:22. Little is known of Reuben either as an individual or as a tribe. It played no prominent part in subsequent history; Deut 33:6 suggests that it died out as a distinct tribe at a fairly early period despite its initial prominence reflected in Reuben's being the eldest son of Jacob. Simeon and Levi (vv. 5–7) are not blessed but cursed. The crime of which they are accused in v. 6 is almost certainly their treacherous murder of the Shechemites in ch. 34, though no mention is made there of their hamstringing oxen. In historical times Levi was a priestly tribe which, unlike the others, had no inheritance in the land: it thus ceased to be counted among the ordinary tribes, though the connection between the Levi of this saying and the later priestly tribe is uncertain. According to Judg 1:3, 17 Simeon was associated with Judah in its invasion of Canaanite territory, and was probably absorbed into the more powerful tribe of Judah, so being 'scattered in Israel'. The use in v. 6 of the first person singular can hardly be supposed to be that of Jacob, and this is also true of 'are brothers' in v. 5. The statement at the end of v. 7 reads like a divine pronouncement of judgement similar to those found in the prophetical books.

Judah (vv. 8–12) was David's tribe, pre-eminent in the time of the united kingdom; it was the name of the southern kingdom after the dissolution of the union until its destruction in the sixth century BCE. This passage has incorporated more than one shorter saying. The reference to Judah as a lion (v. 8) is the first of several examples in the chapter of the association of a tribe with a particular animal. The lion later became the traditional symbol of the tribe of Judah (cf. Rev 5:5). 'shall praise you' (*yôdûkā*) is a play on the word 'Judah'. 'Until tribute comes to him' (v. 10) is only one among many alternative renderings of the Hebrew phrase '*ad kî-yābō' šîlōh*, the meaning of which is one of the unsolved problems of OT interpretation. Its literal translation could be either 'Until Shiloh comes' or 'Until he comes to Shiloh'; but no plausible connection between Judah (or David) and the Ephraimite city and sanctuary of Shiloh can be found. The Hebrew text may be corrupt, or the word 'Shiloh' may have some hitherto undiscovered meaning; but attempts to correct it or to find some other explanation based on comparative philology have achieved no consensus. 'Until' suggests that some event will put an end to Judah's domination; but the traditional notion that this is a prophecy of the coming of the Messiah to bring to an end temporal earthly rule lacks support in the text. That it should be a prophecy of the accession to rule of David is also improbable, as he can hardly be said to have put an end to the rule of Judah! Westermann (1986: 231) comments: 'It is no praiseworthy page in the history of O.T. exegesis that so many studies have been preoccupied with this one word [Shiloh]'. vv. 11–12 appear to be a somewhat fanciful prediction of great fertility and prosperity which will follow the accession of the future ruler, when wine will flow in abundance, and of the ruler's outstanding beauty. There is an analogous prediction of a future king in Num 24:5–9; the last two lines of v. 9 are repeated almost word for word in Num 24:9a.

The saying about Zebulon (v. 13) makes no comment on the character of this tribe, but only—somewhat vaguely—on its territorial location. These statements do not correspond very closely with the description of its location in Josh 19:10–16, which places it in Galilee to the east of the Sea of Tiberias, but at least ten miles from the Mediterranean at its nearest point. It is not known at what period it expanded its territory so far west. Ancient Israel was not, of course, a maritime people. The saying may have been intended to emphasize Zebulon's isolation from the other tribes, though in Judg 5:14 it is commended for its participation with other tribes in the battle against Jabin and Sisera in the nearby valley of Jezreel. Issachar's name and character (vv. 14–15) are probably associated here, as in 30:18, with śākār, 'hire, wages'. Although the tribe, like Zebulon, is praised in Judg 5:15, it is here portrayed as submitting itself to the harshest form of slavery—that is, under the neighbouring Canaanite cities. Dan's name (v. 16) is understood here, as in 30:6, to be derived from the verb dîn, 'to judge'; but whereas in 30:6 it is God who is the subject of the verb, here it is Dan who is the subject: he will be the judge of his people. In v. 17, however, Dan is described as a snake that attacks horsemen by biting the horses' heels. The analogy may be a reference to the small size of the tribe, that cannot attack enemies openly. This verse is probably intended as praise rather than condemnation, referring to attacks against the enemy Canaanites. v. 18 is probably a pious exclamation of a general kind, not specifically connected with the tribe of Dan.

The name of Gad (v. 19) is here derived from the Hebrew root g-d-d, 'to band together', which occurs in various forms four times in the verse. It is an appropriate name in that this tribe, which was located east of the Jordan bordering on the desert, would be subject to attacks by marauding raiders. The saying comments that it is known for its ability to give a good account of itself in such encounters. Asher (v. 20), whose name means 'happiness, good fortune' (cf. 30:13), settled in the fertile coastal strip between Carmel and the Phoenician border (Josh 19:24–31). But according to Judg 1:31–2 it was unable to drive out the local Canaanites and so lived among them. The 'royal delicacies' referred to here may refer to a period when Asher was renowned for its provision of delicacies for royal courts—either for those of Jerusalem or Samaria or for Canaanite or Phoenician royal courts. The saying about Naphtali (49:21) is obscure: the text may be corrupt. A different spelling of 'doe' ('ayyālâ) would yield 'terebinth' ('êlâ); 'fawns' could also mean 'words'. But if the text is correct and 'fawns' is a correct interpretation, this is another animal analogy: Naphtali is called a female deer 'let loose', that is, free to roam at will in the mountains of Galilee.

The section on Joseph (vv. 22–6) is, like that on Judah, made up of a number of originally separate elements, not all of which are tribal sayings. It is divided into two main parts, a characterization of the 'tribe' of Joseph with an allusion to Joseph's behaviour when attacked (vv. 22–5a) and a series of blessings (vv. 25b–6). Unfortunately much in these verses is difficult to understand: there are rare and obscure words, and the syntax is sometimes unusual and difficult. There are probably textual corruptions, and the rendering of NRSV—and of all other translations—is based to some extent on conjectural interpretation. v. 22 is a metaphorical reference to Joseph as a strong and flourishing plant well supplied with water; 'fruitful' (pōrāt) plays on the word 'Ephraim', the predominant member of the 'house of Joseph'. vv. 23–4 describe an incident, now unidentifiable, in which 'Joseph' was attacked by enemies but overcame them with God's help. v. 24b introduces a series of divine blessings, and prayers for blessings to be conferred on Joseph. In vv. 24–5 God is invoked with an amazing, and unique, concatenation of divine names, all found elsewhere in the OT, but together betraying a fairly late date of composition. 'Mighty One of Jacob' occurs in Isa 49:26; 60:16; Ps 132:2, 5. God is referred to as a shepherd a number of times, e.g. Ps 23:1 and 80:1. 'Rock ('eben) of Israel' occurs only here, but there are fairly frequent references in the Psalms to him as 'Rock' (ṣûr), and in that form 'Rock of Israel' occurs in Isa 30:29. 'God of your father' most obviously refers to Abraham or Jacob, and similar epithets are found throughout Genesis. 'Almighty' (šadday) elsewhere in Genesis occurs in the phrase 'El Shaddai', but is found frequently by itself in Job and elsewhere. v. 26 is probably a very ancient form of blessing. In vv. 25 and 26a Joseph is addressed in the second person, but not in the previous verses or in v. 26b. v. 26b refers primarily to Joseph's separation from his brothers while in Egypt, but is also intended to emphasize his pre-eminence over the other tribes. The description of Benjamin (v. 27) refers to the tribe rather than to the individual: it has nothing in common with the Benjamin of the preceding narratives. This is a fierce tribal saying of great antiquity, unaugmented by later comment. Benjamin is here presented, and apparently commended, as a ruthless brigand-like fighter. Jacob's charge, now to all his sons, to bury him with his ancestors in the cave of Machpelah (vv. 29–32) essentially repeats his charge to Joseph alone in 47:29–31. The repetition was intended by the final redactor of the book to form a framework for the whole section about Jacob's arrangements in anticipation of his death that stretches from 47:29 to 49:32.

(50:1–26) This chapter forms an appropriate conclusion to the patriarchal stories that began in ch. 12. Like the deaths of Moses at the end of Deut (34:5–12) and of Joshua at the end of Josh (24:29–31), that of Joseph marks the end of an epoch. The chapter satisfactorily ties up several of the themes of the book, at the same time hinting that it marks no more than a temporary stopping-place in the history of the nation: the final words of the book, 'in Egypt', make this clear. The reconciliation of the brothers with Joseph is completed and their crime forgiven; God's promise of protection and guidance is once more affirmed and demonstrated; the promise of the land is renewed; and the future of the heirs of the promise is assured. Joseph's love for his father, already noted in his enquiry about him in Gen 45:3, is poignantly brought out in v. 1. The elaborate treatment of Jacob's corpse (vv. 2–3) and of his burial (vv. 4–14) reflects the almost royal position of Joseph in Egypt. Joseph's application for permission to bury Jacob in Canaan through the court officials rather than personally to Pharaoh (vv. 4–6), the granting of which was presumably a foregone conclusion, though his promise to return to Egypt afterwards (v. 5) may have some significance, is strange; it may mean that as a recent mourner he refrained from appearing at court. The great detail with which the ceremonies of the burial are described (vv. 7–13) certainly reflects his immense prestige among the Egyptians and so was a matter of great pride to the Israelite reader. The curious route taken by the funeral procession with a first stopping-place east of the Jordan before the actual burial in Machpelah (i.e. Hebron) on the western side (vv. 10–13) is also strange; it has been suggested that an alternative tradition about Jacob's burial place has been incorporated into the narrative (see von Rad 1972: 431). The place-name Abel-mizraim (v. 11) is interpreted here as meaning 'the mourning of Egypt'; its true meaning, however, may be 'brook of Egypt'.

(50:15–21) Joseph had given the brothers no cause to believe that he was only waiting for their father's death to take his revenge on them; but their consciousness of their guilt still remained, and they were afraid. Whether the author means the readers to understand that they invented the story—otherwise unattested—that Jacob had asked that Joseph should forgive them (v. 17) cannot be determined; to tell such a lie would be an indication of their panic. On the other hand, there is nothing in the text to suggest that they acted in bad faith. Joseph's weeping when they spoke in this way was a sign of deep emotion, but gives no hint of his thoughts. In their fear the brothers fell at his feet in supplication and acknowledged that their fate was in his hands, so unconsciously—though this was certainly in the mind of the author—fulfilling Joseph's former dreams that he would eventually rule over them (37:6–10). But his reply (vv. 19–21) reassures them completely. He first points out that it is not for human beings, however exalted, to take revenge, which is a prerogative of God, and then, as he had already done on a previous occasion (45:5–8), he attributes all that had happened to the hidden hand of God, whose purpose had been to preserve their lives so that they would become a 'numerous people' (the word 'am, 'people', can denote a group or family, but here has also overtones of 'nation'). This speech, which expresses a high theology and also sums up a major theme of the book, is the climax of the whole.

(50:22–6) constitutes the epilogue to the book. v. 23 hints at the fulfilment of the promise of numerous progeny, reported in Ex 1:7 as having already been realized in Egypt. In v. 24 Joseph on his deathbed at the end of a long life affirmed the promise of the land—not a feature of the Joseph story proper; and in v. 25 he charged 'the Israelites' (lit., 'the sons of Israel'), to rebury him after they left Egypt and returned to Canaan. That they did so is recorded in Josh 24:32, after the land had been conquered and its territory distributed among the tribes.

Meanwhile Joseph died in Egypt and was duly buried according to Egyptian custom, as befitted the man who had been the effective ruler of Egypt. Ex 1:6–7 takes up the story. So, the author tells us, Israel became a nation.

REFERENCES

Alt, A. (1959), 'Die Wallfahrt von Sichem nach Bethel', Kleine Schriften zur Geschichte des Volkes Israel I (Munich: Beck), 79–88.

Alter, R. (1981), The Art of Biblical Narrative (London: Allen & Unwin).

Blenkinsopp, J. (1992), The Pentateuch. An Introduction to the First Five Books of the Bible (London: SCM).

Blum, E. (1984), Die Komposition der Vätergeschichte (WMANT 57; Neukirchen-Vluyn: Neukirchener Verlag).

Cryer, F. H. (1994), Divination in Ancient Israel and its Near Eastern Environment. A Socio-Historical Investigation, JSOTSup 142 (Sheffield: JSOT).

Donner, H. (1976), Die literarische Gestalt der alttestamentlichen Josephsgeschichte (SHAW; Heidelberg: Carl Winter).

Driver, S. R. (1909), An Introduction to the Literature of the Old Testament (8th ed.; Edinburgh: T. & T. Clark).

Gunkel, H. (1964), Genesis übersetzt und erklärt (HK 1/1; Göttingen: Vandenhoeck & Ruprecht, 1901; 6th ed.).

—— (1901), The Legends of Genesis (New York: Schocken, 1964; German original).

Lambert, W. G., and Millard, A. R. (1969), Atra-hasīs. The Babylonian Story of the Flood (Oxford: Clarendon Press).

von Rad, G. (1966), 'The Form-Critical Problem of the Hexateuch', The Problem of the Hexateuch and Other Essays (Edinburgh and London: Oliver & Boyd) 1–78 (German original, Munich: Kaiser, 1958) 9–86.

—— (1966), 'The Joseph Narrative and Ancient Wisdom', The Problem of the Hexateuch and Other Essays (Edinburgh and London: Oliver & Boyd) 292–300 (German original, VT supplement, Leiden: Brill, 1953) 120–7.

—— (1972), Genesis (OTL; 2nd ed.; London: SCM) (German original, Göttingen: Vandenhoeck & Ruprecht).

Redford, D. B., (1970), A Study of the Biblical Story of Joseph (Genesis 37–50) (VT Supplement 20; Leiden: Brill).

Rendtorff, R. (1982), 'Jakob in Bethel. Beobachtungen zum Aufbau und zur Quellenfrage in Gen 28, 10–22', ZAW 94, 511–23.

Soggin, J. A. (1961), 'Die Geburt Benjamins, Genesis xxxv 16–20 (21)', VT 11, 432–40.

Van Seters, J. (1983), In Search of History (New Haven and London: Yale University Press).

—— (1992), Prologue to History. The Yahwist as Historian in Genesis (Louisville, Kentucky: Westminster/John Knox).

de Vaux, R. (1978), The Early History of Israel I, (London: Darton, Longman & Todd; French original, Paris: Gabalda, 1971).

Vergote, J. (1959), Joseph en Egypte. Genèse chap. 37–50 à la lumière des études égyptologiques récentes (OBL 3; Louvain: Publications Universitaires).

Volz, P., and Rudolph, W. (1933), Der Elohist als Erzähler ein Irrweg der Pentateuchkritik? (BZAW 63; Giessen: Töpelmann).

Westermann, C. (1985), Genesis 12–36 (London: SPCK; German original, Neukirchen-Vluyn: Neukirchener Verlag, 1981).

Whybray, R. N. (1968), 'The Joseph Story and Pentateuchal Criticism', VT 18, 522–8.

—— (1987), The Making of the Pentateuch. A Methodological Study, JSOTSup 53 (Sheffield: JSOT).

5. Exodus

WALTER HOUSTON

INTRODUCTION

A. What Kind of Book is Exodus? 1. The second book of the Pentateuch is in many ways its centrepiece. Genesis is about Israel's ancestors, Exodus tells how they became a nation through the action of their God. It is Israel's foundation story, their identity document, telling them where they have come from and showing them their place in the world under God's sovereignty.

2. Is Exodus a work of history? That is, could it be appropriately put on the history shelves in a library? If we define a historical work as one whose 'chief purpose is to trace the network of causation between events at a mundane level' (Johnstone 1990: 31), then Exodus is not one. It portrays the entire sweep of events as the direct result of the purpose and intervention of God. Although people have sometimes tried to understand parts of the story as heightened accounts of natural sequences of events (see EX 7:6–11:10, EX 16, or EX 19), this flies in the face of the basic intention of the text, which is to relate the glorious works of God. Not only does God intervene directly in an astonishing series of powerful acts, but he himself appears on the scene several times in more or less plainly visible forms (see EX 3:1–6). The writers draw freely on imagination or legend to create the scenes which we read. The historical setting is only very hazily sketched in. In brief, Exodus is not the kind of history recognized by the Greeks or by modern historians.

3. Yet several points show that its intention is to relate, however imaginatively, a story of the actual past, not a simple fiction. The story focuses on a people of history and is part of a continuous narrative (Genesis to 2 Kings) which takes their story down to the fall of Jerusalem to the Babylonians in 587 BCE; and there are links with earlier and later parts of this narrative. Often the story serves to explain known facts, such as the name of Israel's God (see 3:13–15). Occasionally, chronological information is given, as in 12:40. If the writing of history can be defined as imaginatively re-creating a people's past so that they may understand themselves in the present, then Exodus *is* a work of history. As such, it has literary, historical, and theological aspects, which we shall briefly look at in turn in this introduction.

B. Exodus as Literature. 1. Exodus falls into the category of narrative, literature which tells a story. Even the large parts of the text which present law or instructions are cast into the form of speeches by God at appropriate points in the story. The story has two main themes. The first theme is the deliverance of the Israelites from oppression in Egypt by their God, usually referred to by his name YHWH (see EX 3:7–12). This theme is completed in the first fifteen chapters, which are set mainly in Egypt or on its borders. The second theme is how YHWH establishes his presence among the Israelites and brings them into obedience to himself. This is told mainly in the second half of the book, from 15:22 onwards, which is set in the wilderness to the east of Egypt, but it is fore-shadowed in the earlier part of the book. The two themes are united in that both events are ways in which YHWH makes himself known and fulfils his promises to Israel's ancestors.

2. YHWH is the dominant character. The text underlines his sovereignty even at the expense of the interest of the story in places. Although the Israelites are essential to the story, they rarely act independently. Between the two stands Moses. He can be described as the hero of the story. He is hardly ever off-stage from the moment of his birth; the story alternates constantly between scenes between Moses and YHWH and scenes between Moses and the Israelites or Pharaoh. Yet even he, throughout the greater part of the story, acts simply as YHWH's agent, and it is only in places that he asserts his independence (Ex 32 is a notable example). The main foil to YHWH in the first part of the book is the Pharaoh of the plagues. Yet, as I will show in EX 7:6–11:10, YHWH increasingly constrains him to act in the way he does, and ultimately he seems to be little more than a puppet whom YHWH manipulates to demonstrate his own power (Gunn 1982).

3. The development of the plot has, then, decided limitations. Through much of the story the characters do not have sufficient independence to oppose YHWH's purposes. Nevertheless there is a plot. There is a struggle between YHWH and Pharaoh; its end is inevitable and clearly foreseen, but it is a struggle. Israel's acceptance that YHWH must be obeyed is not as automatic as it seems to be at first sight (in 19:8); they do rebel in Ex 32. Their rebellion is of course doomed from the start; the interest of this part of the story lies in whether Moses will persuade YHWH to restore the people to his favour; and here the end is by no means a foregone conclusion. The rebellion sets up a tension in YHWH himself, which Moses exploits. To destroy them and to restore them to favour are in different ways humiliating for YHWH. He resolves the tension by declaring himself a God of mercy, whose glory it is to forgive as much as to punish affronts to his honour.

4. But in general the story proceeds on lines that are not only expected but explicitly forecast (3:12, 16–20; 4:21–3), and its sympathies are unambiguous. In Ex 1–15 we are constrained to be against the oppressors, and on the side of the innocent sufferers and their deliverers. As D. Robertson (1977: 16–32) points out, there is no irony in the moral structure of the story. It is all black and white, there are no shades of grey. Of course, moral simplicity is to be expected in a nation's foundation story. The reader, however, may not find it so simple: could a righteous god destroy so many innocent lives for his own glory?

C. Exodus and History. 1. On the assumption that the book is intended as history, it is natural to ask how it has come by what it knows or claims to know about the early history of Israel. The first step is to ask about the history of the book itself; but as it is only a part of the Pentateuch we can refer to PENT for discussion of the various proposals. The view taken in this commentary (broadly that of Van Seters 1994) can only be stated here, that the work consists of two main strands with different styles and interests, which I refer to as J and P. J was created from a variety of source material by an author writing probably in the seventh or sixth century BCE. Some J material is earlier than Deuteronomy, some of it later and clearly dependent on that book; see e.g. EX 23:10–19 contrasted with 13:3–10. P was written by a priestly author in the later sixth or fifth century. It seems to me likely that P was not an independent work later combined with J, but was written from the beginning as an expansion of J.

2. Exodus, then, was developing during a time when the nation's continuing existence as a distinct community was in prolonged doubt. It was written to strengthen national feeling and support national identity. The two main traditions or ideas which J uses to achieve this are those of Israel's origin from a group of exploited aliens in Egypt, and of YHWH's covenant with them at Mt. Sinai. They were, according to this writer, a nation specially claimed by the God of all the earth as his own (19:5). His claim, his care and protection, and in return their exclusive attachment to him and faithful obedience to his moral direction would preserve them as a nation. The main ideas added by P were that of YHWH's covenant of promise to Israel's ancestors and that of his presence among his people in a sanctuary specially built at his direction, and this has obvious relevance to the time of restoration. Note that 'covenant' has various shades of meaning in the OT (see Mendenhall 1992a, Nicholson 1986).

3. Despite the great attention given by scholars in this century to what they have called 'tradition history' (I again refer to PENT for a brief survey), I do not believe it is possible to write a history of the way in which these traditions developed. The evidence is simply insufficient. Nor is there much to go on to distinguish traditional material from the authors' own contributions. However, the central narrative assertion, that YHWH delivered Israel's ancestors from slavery in Egypt, is certainly traditional: it is central to the prophecy of Hosea in the eighth century BCE, as well as to the book of Deuteronomy in the late seventh. It is much more doubtful that the claim that YHWH made a covenant with Israel at Sinai can be described as traditional (Nicholson 1986). It is important in Deuteronomy and writings influenced by it; but it plays no significant role in any prophetic book before Jeremiah, itself influenced by Deuteronomy. Still less securely rooted in tradition is the concept of the mobile sanctuary; although it depends on the ancient tradition of temple-building in the Near East (see EX 25–31), it appears practically only in the P strand in Exodus, Leviticus, and Numbers.

4. With the exception of the Exodus from Egypt itself, the major ideas of the book are not popular traditions but ideas of an intellectual élite striving to preserve or excite national feeling in a time of crisis, and to reshape the national spirit through an exclusive monotheistic ideal which they saw as the only way to preserve the nation at all.

5. What then is the likelihood that the traditions of Exodus reach right back, as the book claims, to the origin of Israel? (See, among others, S. Herrmann 1973; de Vaux 1978: i. 321–472; Ramsey 1981: 45–63; Houtman 1993: 171–90.) If one abstracts the many miraculous elements, the story in itself is not implausible, and indeed similar events appear in Egyptian records (S. Herrmann 1973: 23–9, de Vaux 1978: i.374). The names Moses and Aaron are best explained as of Egyptian origin (Houtman 1993: 75, 83). It is generally assumed that before the traditions were committed to writing they were carried by oral tradition, maybe in connection with the feast of Passover which celebrates the Exodus, and possibly in poetry (Cross 1973: 124 n. 38), which is less subject to loss and distortion than a prose tale. The date of the event is most often put at the end of the Bronze Age, in the thirteenth century BCE. But some (e.g. Bimson 1978) maintain the fifteenth-century date suggested by the Bible's own chronology.

6. However, recent research into traditions about historical events in modern non-literate societies shows that it would be difficult for reliable historical knowledge to survive the hundreds of years separating any possible date for the events related and any likely date for the writing, even if that was much earlier than I have suggested (Kirkpatrick 1988). Moreover, the hard archaeological evidence that would show that the nation of Israel came from outside Canaan is lacking. The material culture of early Iron Age Israel is like that of Late Bronze Age Canaan, only poorer (Finkelstein 1988, Dever 1992). At most there could have been a small group which escaped from Egypt and passed on its traditions to related groups in Canaan (so Gottwald 1980: 36, etc.). And the Passover did not become a national festival until the end of the seventh century (2 Kings 23:22); could the rustic family celebration from which it arose have been the bearer of a national tradition?

7. It therefore remains unclear to what extent Exodus presents authentic historical events. It should in any case be clear from the way in which it speaks of history (see c.2) that we cannot use the book as a historical source. Its aim is not to present an objective record, but to celebrate the glory of YHWH.

D. Exodus as Theology. 1. Exodus is based on a thoroughly monotheistic world-view. Even though YHWH is known by a name distinguishing him from other gods, he is the only God who counts as such: the others are mere idols. He is the creator (4:11), and to him the whole earth belongs (9:29; 19:5). Yet he has committed himself to one people, the people of Israel, long in advance (6:3), and in return asks for their exclusive commitment to him (20:3). Although his presence and power is made known to the Egyptians (7:5) and to the whole earth (9:16), it is permanently promised to Israel (29:45–6) in a specially beneficent form: he will 'dwell among them'.

2. This is not simply the theology *found* in Exodus: the story which it tells is intended as the foundation and legitimation of this theology. YHWH demonstrates that he is the God of all the earth in his victory over Pharaoh. No other god even enters the contest. He demonstrates his commitment to Israel in his calling of Moses, his revelation of his name, his deliverance of Israel from slavery in Egypt, and his appearance to them at Sinai. The covenant which he offers the Israelites embodies the basic demand that they should be committed to him alone, and governs the entire story of the nation from this point onwards. The instructions he gives to Moses in 25–31 are intended to govern the way in which his presence with his people is to be safeguarded for all time.

3. Obviously in the above two paragraphs I have combined points from the two or more main writers of the book. P's particular contributions are the recollection of the promise to the ancestors, the definition of the name YHWH as a new revelation, and the instructions for the building of the sanctuary for his presence.

4. Exodus raises questions about the character and motives of YHWH, which can be followed through the commentary. Miranda (1973: 89) asserts that (in J) YHWH acts to deliver the Israelites from slavery simply because he is the God of justice who delivers the oppressed, and not because they are his people or because of any prior commitment. In the text as it stands the prior commitment is clearly stated (2:24 (P)). Even in J the prior connection between YHWH and the ancestors is emphasized. That is not to say that YHWH does not act because of his justice; 'justice' in the HB is a term of relationship, and denotes, among other things, acting in accordance with the commitments one has to other particular people. YHWH's self-proclamation in 34:6–7 lays great stress on the virtues of relationship, and his compassion, also emphasized there, has to be seen in that context.

5. There is, however, an increasing emphasis as one moves into the plagues narrative and beyond on YHWH's action for his own sake: 'that the Egyptians shall know that I am the LORD [YHWH]' (7:5). YHWH's need to achieve a resounding victory over Pharaoh leads him to manipulate him into fruitless opposition (see EX 7:6–11:10). His motive appears to be not so much compassion for or commitment to Israel as the need to have his own Godhead recognized (Durham 1987: 99; Gunn 1982: 84). This is a particular emphasis of the P material, though it is not absent from J. However, the ancient reader would have seen it differently. Human patrons' generous treatment of their clients redounded to their honour; likewise there was no contradiction between the divine patron's commitment to his people and to his own glory. Moreover, the good order of the world demanded that its ruler should be recognized.

E. Exodus and the Reader. 1. As with any great work of literature, what Exodus means is in the end up to the reader. Creative readings of the book depend not merely on the readers' needs and perspectives, but upon their propensity to read themselves into the book. Thus, although Miranda's reading of YHWH's motives in Ex 3 (see above, D.4) may seem distorted, we understand it when we realize that he speaks for the Latin-American base communities, conscious of their own oppression, who identify themselves with oppressed Israel and claim God's just deliverance for themselves. Thus Exodus, despite its emphasis on God's self-regarding motives and destructive activity, has taken a central place in liberation perspectives on the Bible (cf. also Gutiérrez 1988; Croatto 1981).

2. The book's original purpose was to create or strengthen the identity of the community of Israel, and that is certainly the way in which it has been read by Jews ever since. The book forms the warrant for the festival of Passover. In traditional Christian exegesis, on the other hand, Christians have seen themselves as the Israelites brought through the Red Sea by the hand of God, and the experience of the Sea has been identified with the Resurrection, as in John of Damascus's Easter hymns (e.g. 'Come ye faithful, raise the strain') or with baptism (1 Cor 10:1–5; Origen, *Homily on Exodus*, 5.5).

3. More recently, some readers have read Exodus 'against the grain' of the text, identifying themselves with groups who are marginal to it, such as women (Exum 1993, 1994; Fewell and Gunn 1993), or simply reading as moderns sceptical of the values maintained by the book (Clines 1995a and b), and pointing to their socially relative character. This procedure, of course, makes it more difficult to embrace the witness of the book; but that does not make these any less legitimate readings. On the contrary, they should be welcomed as powerful tests of the validity of the far-reaching claims that the book makes.

COMMENTARY

(1:1–2:22) The first two chapters of the book set out the problem to which God responds and introduce the person through whom he will act; they are the exposition of the plot. God is hardly mentioned; it is implied that he is active behind the scenes, but he does not appear on stage until he hears the cry of his people (2:24). At first sight Pharaoh's command to kill the baby boys (1:16, 22) does not fit in with the main story in which the Israelites are subjected to forced labour, especially as it is not mentioned again after ch. 2. It was clearly intended as context for the traditional story in 2:1–10. However, there is no contradiction. In Pharaoh's speech Israel is presented not as a convenient source of labour but as a danger. The two measures have the same object: to crush and weaken the Israelites (Houtman 1993: 245). To destroy only boys is not a very efficient way of wiping out a nation: the object could rather be to deprive it of its leadership.

Most of 1:1–2:22 belongs to J, but P is responsible for 1:1–5, 7, 13–14.

(1:1–7) These verses form a link between Genesis and Exodus. They refer back to Gen 46:5–27 and 50:26, and set the scene for the story of the oppression and deliverance of Israel in Ex 1–15. We are reminded in v. 7 of the promise to the patriarchs that they would have a multitude of descendants (e.g. Gen 15:5), but at the same time it begins the exposition of the plot of Exodus. We are reminded of it twice in the following verses (12, 20); whatever the Egyptians may do, the Israelites continue to increase, so God is perhaps secretly at work. v. 1, the Jewish name for Exodus, *šĕmôt*, 'Names', comes from the first words. v. 5, seventy names are listed in Gen 46.

(1:8–14) This section relates the beginning of the oppression of Israel. The new king 'did not know Joseph'. 'Know' in Hebrew often has an overtone of relationship. The relation of friendship and service set up between Joseph and the earlier king is forgotten. In the king's speech (vv. 9–10) the writer uses irony to undermine the king's credibility. He grossly exaggerates the numbers of the Israelites, but in doing so confirms the divine promise to the patriarchs. He says 'let us deal shrewdly with them', but the story shows that his plan is anything but shrewd; and he ends by posing the danger that the Israelites may escape—which was exactly what happened! The Israelites have to perform conscript labour for the state. Often the OT writers describe them as slaves. Strictly speaking this is not the same thing: a conscript labourer is not the property of his master. But understandably the writers tend to ignore the distinction. Forced labour was a practice of Israelite kings also, but the biblical tradition has a moral repugnance to it (1 Kings 12:18; Jer 22:13). v. 11, the names of the supply cities (see *ABD* for each, and Redford 1963; they are in the east of the Nile Delta) have often been taken as a clue to the historical setting of the Exodus. Rameses is probably the capital of Rameses II, abandoned after his death in 1212 BCE. On the other hand, the form of the name Rameses in Hebrew suggests that it was borrowed no earlier than 700 BCE (Redford 1963: 411–13). A writer at a later time could have used the names to give his story colour without having an old tradition.

(1:15–22) Pharaoh's attempt to deprive the Israelites of male leadership is first of all frustrated by the courage of two women, and three more frustrate the second stage of his plan. For feminist reflections on this irony, see Exum (1993, 1994). v. 15, 'the Hebrew midwives'. This is the first appearance of the word 'Hebrew' in the book. It is used to refer to the Israelites from the point of view of the Egyptians (or, later, of other foreigners). For the origin of the word see 'Hebrew', and 'Habiru, Hapiru' in *ABD* iii. v. 19. The midwives' lie is not disapproved of—the OT reflects the moral sense of ordinary people, not moral philosophers!

(2:1–10) The birth story of Moses appears to be based on a very old folk-tale, which we first find as the birth story of King Sargon of Akkad (about 2300 BCE; *ANET* 119). Moses is destined to die; the human compassion of Pharaoh's daughter impels her to disobey her father and rescue him. v. 1, 'a Levite woman': the Hebrew text actually says 'the daughter of Levi', but may be influenced by 6:20 (Schmidt 1988: 50). v. 9, Moses is brought up as a Hebrew, even though adopted as an Egyptian. This ironic twist serves to explain his later role. v. 10, the name 'Moses' is probably derived from an Egyptian word often found in personal names such as that of the Pharaoh Thutmosis. But here, as so often in the OT, it is given a fanciful Hebrew derivation: 'Moses' is *Moshe* (*mōšeh*), which means 'one who draws out'.

(2:11–15a) Can it be right for the oppressed to take justice into their own hands? The story neither approves nor disapproves. It shows us that Moses is a man who is passionate for justice (so is God's choice of him so odd?), but also imprudent. For without the divine authorization which he later receives, there is no possibility that his action could succeed. As far as the plot is concerned, the episode gets Moses from Egypt to Midian, where he is to meet God.

(2:15b–22) Moses in Midian. The resemblance of this story to that of Jacob in Gen 29, and more distantly to Gen 24, has often been noted. It may be a literary convention, in stories of the hero's finding a wife in distant parts (Alter 1981: 47–62), or a deliberate imitation (Van Seters 1994: 32).

'Midian' was an Arab people occupying an area to the east of the Gulf of Aqaba; but it is possible that their shepherds came as far west as the Sinai peninsula (Mendenhall 1992b), where Mt. Sinai/Horeb (3:1, 12) has traditionally been located. In v. 17 the word translated 'came to their defence' is the word which the OT regularly uses of God's 'saving' people. Here is another sign marking Moses out as one who is ready to save people who are suffering injustice. v. 18, Moses' future father-in-law is called Reuel here and probably in Num 10:29, Jethro in 3:1

and 18:1–12, Jether in 4:18, and Hobab in Judg 4:11 and perhaps Num 10:29. He is a Midianite in Exodus and Numbers and a Kenite in Judges. Probably he originally had no name in the tradition (Schmidt 1988: 85–7), and the writers, or the traditions they draw on, have filled in the blank in various ways. In Exodus this may point to different source material. v. 22, there may be a hidden meaning in Moses' words. Which is the 'foreign land', Midian or Egypt?

(2:23–5:21) God's intervention: Act I In this section the Israelites call for help, and the God of Israel responds by appointing Moses as his agent, and promises him he will deliver the Israelites; but Moses' first attempts to ask Pharaoh to let them go meet with failure. This creates a crisis which can only be overcome by a further and more powerful divine intervention.

The God of Israel is usually given his name YHWH, but in places he is referred to by the more general *'ĕlōhîm*, 'God'. 2:23–5 (and probably not much else here) belongs to P, who avoids using 'YHWH' before YHWH himself reveals the name. 3:9–15 is often ascribed to a distinct source, E; but the writer (J) may simply find it appropriate to use *'ĕlōhîm* in describing the dialogue with Moses, who does not yet know the name. See Moberly (1992: 5–35). 2:23, the statement about the death of the king expresses the passage of time, and prepares for 4:19. But this makes no difference to the oppression. 2:23–5 adds a theologically important link between the Israelites' oppression and God's action. God's action is a response not only to what he sees, but also to what he hears, the cry of a suffering people. His action is then determined by his prior commitment to Israel's ancestors (see Gen 17; 35:11–13; 6:2–8). 'Covenant' here refers to a solemn promise made by God to the patriarchs. In Israelite society it was the responsibility of the nearest relative to redeem a person from the grip of the creditor and the slaveholder (Lev 25:25, 47–9). P expresses YHWH's responsibility to Israel, which was not based on physical kinship, in the concept of this 'covenant' with the ancestors. See further EX 6:2–8.

(3:1–4:17) The Call of Moses This passage follows basically the same pattern as some other accounts of God's call of individuals to special tasks, e.g. Gideon in Judg 6:11–24, Jeremiah in Jer 1:4–10. In all of them, five things happen. There is a *meeting* between God and the chosen one; God gives him a *commission*; he *objects* that he is unfit; God *reassures* him; God gives him a *sign* (Habel 1965). Here, however, the pattern is expanded. It is complete by 3:12; but Moses keeps finding new objections, which God responds to seriously; the elements of commission and assurance are thus taken up again in various ways, and a whole section (4:1–9) is devoted to signs. It is often suggested that Moses is here cast in the role of a prophet. It is true that much of the material is typical of prophecy (e.g. Moses is to speak to a king in the name of God); but some is more typical of a military leader, for example the assurance 'I will be with you' (3:12; see Gowan 1994: 56–61). Moses is both. This simple storytelling device of repeated objections enables the passage to be much richer than a simple call to service. It is in the first place God's promise that he himself will act to deliver Israel. Moses' work takes its place within the divine plan, and is impossible without God's action. God's words dominate the passage, and they refer backwards and forwards; the whole of the Pentateuchal story is set out here. The story of Exodus is a plot with few surprises, because the chief character promises beforehand everything that is to happen. It is essential to this that God should here reveal his name YHWH (3:13–15), backing his promise with it, as we might sign our name to a contract.

The passage pictures the interplay of divine sovereignty and human freedom. It ends, of course, with total victory for YHWH. Moses, for all his show of independence, is forced to submit, and for many chapters will play the role of a mere agent. Yet he has not been deprived of his humanity, and will later (14:13–14 and esp. 32–3) show that he can take the initiative (Gunn 1982: 84–7).

(3:1–6) Moses' meeting with God is the experience of a mysterious and awe-inspiring, but attractive presence, an example of the experience of the holy, as defined by Rudolf Otto (Gowan 1994: 25–53). It cannot be described literally, but only pictured, as in e.g. Judg 5:4–5; Ps 18:7–15; 50:1–6; Hab 3. When God is described in such passages as coming in visible ways to judge and save, scholars call it a 'theophany'. Fire is the most regular accompaniment of theophanies. Therefore, although people have tried to explain what the burning bush was in natural terms, this misses the point. But who is it who appears to Moses? The narrator calls him first 'the angel' (lit. messenger) of YHWH ('the LORD') (v. 2), and then in one verse (4) both YHWH ('the LORD') and 'ĕlōhîm ('God'). It is common in theophanies for the one who appears to be called 'the angel of YHWH/'ĕlōhîm' (as in Judg 6:11–24); but it normally becomes clear (as in Judg 6:14) that it is YHWH himself who is speaking. In this way the narrator makes it clear that the event is a real visitation of God, but avoids saying that YHWH himself became visible. v. 6 finally makes it clear that the mysterious apparition is none other than the God who is spoken of in Genesis, and was known to Israel's ancestors and Moses' own father. v. 1, for Jethro see EX 2:18. Horeb and 'the mountain of God' are alternative names, particularly in Deuteronomy, for the mountain called Sinai in Ex 19 where God reveals himself to Israel. v. 5, similarly Josh 5:15. The practice of removing footwear in holy places is regular in Judaism, Islam, and Buddhism, but its meaning is disputed: see Houtman (1993: 351–2).

(3:7–12) The divine promise and commission, Moses' initial objection and God's fundamental reassurance. Because v. 9 seems to repeat the substance of v. 7, it has often been thought that vv. 9–12 come from a different source (E) from vv. 7–8. But it is important that God's promise to 'bring up' the Israelites out of Egypt stands alongside his commission to Moses to 'bring them out'. Neither the divine initiative nor the human agency can be dispensed with. The phrases in v. 8 are conventional. The list of former inhabitants occurs in many places with slight variations; it is impossible to give a precise meaning to the names, except for the Jebusites, who were the people of Jerusalem before David captured the city (2 Sam 5). Moses' objection in v. 11 is a standard expression to avoid commitment. See Judg 6:15, Jer 1:6, which get the same answer; 1 Sam 18:23. The 'sign' in v. 12 has caused problems, since it is not something that Moses can see and be convinced by now (contrast 4:1–9). Gowan (1994: 55–6) rightly says that 'I will be with you' is sufficient in itself as an assurance; if Moses

hangs on to that, he will *eventually* see the confirmation of his mission in the meeting of all the people (the last 'you' is plural) with their God.

(3:13–15) Here the god in the bush, so far nameless to Moses, reveals his name. Why does Moses ask this question (v. 13)? The call is to be a messenger, and a messenger needs a name to authenticate his credentials. Moses, however, does not know the name of his 'father's god'; but he cannot be sure that the Israelites do not know it either. The story at this point does not commit itself on whether the Israelites know YHWH's name already; it focuses on *Moses'* ignorance, not Israel's. But while this is Moses' reason for raising the question, the author has a deeper motive for highlighting it. A strong tradition held that the bond between Israel and YHWH went back to the time of the Exodus from Egypt (see Hos 2:15; 11:1; 13:4; Jer 2:2–8). Therefore it is appropriate that it is at this point, when he announces his intention to save, that YHWH becomes known to Israel. But here the episode is part of a larger story in which Israel's ancestors have already encountered this God, so the story must be told in a way which allows for this. 6:2–8 (P) clears up the ambiguity of this passage.

God answers Moses' question in v. 15. But first he tantalizes him with a play on words. The Hebrew for 'I am' or 'I will be' is *ehyeh*. Changed into the third person this would be *yihyeh* or in an older form *yahweh*, which was probably the pronunciation of YHWH. Many meanings have been seen in 'I AM WHO I AM' or 'I WILL BE WHO I WILL BE'; probably the simplest is 'I will be whoever I will be', that is, while I will graciously reveal my name to you, I will not be bound or defined by it (Gowan 1994: 84). But as a wordplay the meaning is not as important as the sound! The actual origin of the name YHWH is quite uncertain (see de Vaux 1978: i. 338–57).

(3:16–22) YHWH follows up his revelation of his name by telling Moses how he is to use it, and so goes into his *commission* in detail, along with the *assurance* that he will unleash his own power to compel the king to let the Israelites go. Thus the whole story up to Ex 12 is given here in outline.

'The elders of Israel' do not in fact accompany Moses to the king (v. 18, cf. 5:1). Is this an inconsistency in the story, or a mistake on Moses' part? The request they are to make of the king (v. 18) is of course a ruse, which ought not to worry anyone's conscience when dealing with tyrants (see EX 1:19). But it also picks up 3:12.

(3:21–2) The puzzling instruction is carried out in Ex 12:35–6. Daube (1947: 49–50) offers a plausible explanation. There was a custom (Deut 15:14) that a released slave should get a generous endowment. The Israelites are to deceive the Egyptians—if it is deception—into giving them their rightful due!

(4:1–9) Moses may well mean that *he* does not know whether to believe YHWH. YHWH's answer is to demonstrate his power by means of 'signs' that he enables Moses to perform. These signs achieve what that in 3:12 could not, in immediately convincing a wavering Moses. Such signs, however external and artificial they may appear to us, are common in OT narrative (compare Judg 6:17–22, 36–40). In the story that follows they are used not only to convince the Israelites (4:30), but, with variations, to impress the Egyptians (7:8–24; foreshadowed in 4:21).

(4:10–17) Moses offers his final excuse (v. 10). YHWH's answer (vv. 11–12) shows that the author takes for granted that YHWH is the Creator. Moses has now run out of excuses and simply turns the job down (v. 13). And YHWH runs out of patience, but his answer harks back to Moses' pretext in v. 10. Moses *must* go, but his brother may do the speaking for him. However, in the event, this does not happen in any consistent way (explicitly only in 4:30); and Aaron sometimes performs the signs (as in 4:30; 7:10, etc.) rather than, or as well as, speaking. It is probable that Moses' pretext is simply, for the author, a device to bring Aaron into the story, for the sake of a group in Jewish society that was attached to him, presumably the priests who claimed descent from him. It is not clear why Aaron is called 'the Levite' (v. 14) when Moses was one himself according to 2:1. It probably refers to his task rather than his descent. 'You shall serve as God for him', Moses is told in v. 16. That is, the relation between Moses and Aaron is like that between God and his prophet.

(4:18–26) Moses' return to Egypt is told in a rather disjointed narrative which probably shows the effect of the piecing together of different sources or traditions. v. 19 refers back to 2:23, but seems to ignore all that has happened in between, since Moses already has his marching orders and has even said goodbye. vv. 21–3 develop Moses' instructions in a new direction as compared with 3:20. Pharaoh will refuse to let Israel go *because YHWH so wills*. This important theme is taken up again at 7:3. The mention of the 'firstborn son' anticipates another major theme of the story (Ex 11–13).

   In the obscure vv. 24–6 the biggest puzzle is: why should YHWH try to kill the messenger whom he has only just commissioned? There are other questions. Why does Zipporah do what she does and how does it work? What is the meaning of her words? Many scholars have regarded the piece as an old legend in which the attacker was a demon, possibly intended to explain the origin of the practice of the circumcision of infants. Maybe, but this does not really explain what it means in this context. The first question is not really answerable, but at least two other episodes are in some way similar: the command to Abraham to sacrifice Isaac (Gen 22) and Jacob's wrestling with God at the Jabbok (Gen 32). The God of the Bible has a dark side. Zipporah circumcises her son and touches Moses' own penis ('feet' is a euphemism) with the severed foreskin. Along with her words, this suggests a symbol legitimizing this marriage between the leader of Israel and a foreign woman, which may have been a scandal to some of the first readers of Exodus in the Second Temple period (Römer 1994—only one of many proposals). For circumcision, see GEN 17 and 'Circumcision' in *ABD* i.

(4:27–5:21) describes Moses and Aaron's first attempt to carry out YHWH's commission. It fails, and Pharaoh's oppression of Israel is simply intensified; a common experience for many who have challenged tyranny. Significant for the future development of the story is Pharaoh's dismissal of their request in 5:2: 'I do not know the LORD'. The long series of 'plagues' in chs. 7–12, according to YHWH's own statement in 7:3, has just one aim: that the Egyptians *should* know YHWH. See EX 7:8–11:10. For 5:1 see EX 3:18. For 'the Hebrews' in 5:3 see EX 1:16. In 5:16 ' "You are unjust to your own people" ' is odd, since the Israelites are not Pharaoh's

people. The text is uncertain, and a better reading may be 'The fault is with you.'

(5:21–13:16) The Intervention of God: Act II This is the key act of the story, in which YHWH's powerful action enables the Israelites to leave Egypt, though not yet to escape finally from Pharaoh's reach. It has much the same structure as the previous act: the appeal to God, his response of promise and commission, Moses and Aaron's request to Pharaoh. The vital differences are God's supporting action (the plagues) on the one hand and his delaying action (hardening Pharaoh's heart) on the other.

(5:21–7:7) In response to Moses' despairing complaint, God again reveals his name, confirms his promise to deliver the Israelites from slavery, and repeats his commission to go to Pharaoh. 6:1 advances the story and points forward to the plagues. Eventually, in 7:3–5, we return to this point. But from 6:2 to 7:2 (except for 6:14–25) the episode appears to go over the same ground as 3:1–4:17, but with new language. In the context this is quite appropriate, since Moses has been brought to the point where only fresh encouragement and a fresh mandate from God can restore his confidence. But it is also the sign of a fresh hand at work. The whole passage from 6:2 is the work of P, probably working on the basis of the existing story. (6:14–25 may be a still later expansion.)

   The formal speech of God in 6:2–8 has an elegant structure (see Auffret 1983 for details). The pronouncement 'I am the LORD [YHWH]' occurs in key places and is clearly the key to the entire speech (see also Zimmerli 1982). It is more than a bare statement of authority: it is the self-giving of a person, whose personality and character are summed up in his name, but who can be fully known for who he is only in his gracious act of salvation (6:7).

   The ambiguity in 3:13–15 is cleared up in 6:3. How could Israel's ancestors have known the God whose name is now newly revealed? Answer: they knew him under another name. Therefore Moses can be sure that the promise to them is still valid. 'God Almighty' (NRSV, etc.) is a conventional translation of 'ēl šadday. 'ēl means 'God'; the meaning of šadday is unknown. See Gen 17:1; 35:11; 28:3. For 'covenant' in 6:4 see EX 2:23–5. 6:5 takes up the wording of Ex 2:24.

   Something new is introduced at 6:7a. YHWH's rescue of Israel from Egypt is the beginning of a permanent relationship between them. This promise will be fulfilled at Sinai in Ex 19–40, with the establishment of institutions by which God and people are related. In 6:8 the speech returns to its beginning, by promising the imminent fulfilment of what God swore to Israel's ancestors.

   For 6:12 see 4:10. The genealogical material in 6:14–25 is to our mind quite out of place in the middle of a story. But the author had different ideas of literary appropriateness. His object is expressed in 6:26–7: to locate the heroes of the tale within the Israelite social structure and so validate them as historical according to his ideas of history (Childs 1974: 116), and probably to claim them as members of his own social group. Social and political status depended mainly on kinship, and genealogies, real or fictitious, were essential to validate it (Wilson 1977). As in many genealogies in the Bible, many of the names are those of kinship groups who trace their descent from a supposed ancestor with the same name. Moses and Aaron, then, belong to the Kohathite Levites, and Aaron is the ancestor of the Jerusalem priests. Aaron's wife (6:23) is a Judahite (see Num 1:7), which signifies the close connection between the priests of Jerusalem and the people of Judah. Korah (6:21), the sons of Aaron (6:23), and his grandson Phinehas (6:25) will all play parts in the story which follows (Num 16; Ex 24 and Lev 8–10; Num 25). 6:28–30 takes up the story again by summarizing 6:2–13.

(7:1–5) completes Moses' recommissioning, and like 3:20 and 4:21–3 points forwards very clearly, and in more detail, to the plague story, which follows straight away. 7:1–2 takes up the theme of 4:14–16. In 7:3–5 several points are made which define the meaning of the following episodes. I will discuss most of them at greater length in the next section, EX 7:8–11:10. YHWH will 'harden Pharaoh's heart'. The 'heart' in Hebrew refers to the understanding and the will. What YHWH will do is to make Pharaoh uncomprehending and obstinate. The effect is that he will 'not listen to you' (7:4), and it will trigger YHWH's move to 'multiply my signs and wonders', 'lay my hand on Egypt', and bring the Israelites out 'by great acts of judgement'. A sign is anything that shows God's power; a wonder is a remarkable event of any kind; 'hand' usually means power at work; and a judgement is not necessarily a punishment, but an act of force undertaken to effect the decision of a judge or ruler. So in several different ways YHWH makes it clear that by making Pharaoh obstinate he will be enabled to display his power as ruler of the world on the Egyptians. And the result is that they 'shall know that I am YHWH'. Israel will know YHWH in his gracious act of deliverance (6:7), Egypt in a very different way. 7:7, the apparently excessive ages of Moses and Aaron fit the widespread belief that age brings wisdom.

(7:8–11:10) The Narrative of the Plagues (a traditional rendering of the Hebrew word in 9:14, which would be better translated 'blows', with which YHWH *strikes* Egypt). Here general remarks will be made on the passage as a whole, not on the separate plagues, followed only by notes on individual verses.

There are ten plagues, starting with the turning of water to blood in 7:14–24 and finishing with the death of the firstborn in 11–12. But as the book has been edited, the section is introduced by 7:8–13, though it does not describe a 'plague' but only a sign, and closed by an obvious summary in 11:9–10; the last plague has been announced, but its execution is tied up with the Passover narrative. In this part of the story the narrative, usually so concise, spreads itself at length. Attempts to explain the series of plagues historically as the effect of natural causes (Hort 1957–8) surely miss the point of the story, that they are the direct work of God for his purposes. From a literary point of view, they can be seen as intended to create tension. Since we already know the final result (3:20; 6:6; 7:4–5), we know *that* YHWH will achieve his purpose but we can still be intrigued as to *how* he will. To some extent the number of the plagues and the length of the narrative may be accounted for by the likelihood that different authors have had a hand in it. But the division of sources is very much disputed. The simplest theory (Van Seters 1994: 80) is that the original narrative (J) had seven plagues, and the Priestly editor added three more, as well as extra material in the others.

TABLE 1. *Patterns in plague narratives*

Pattern 1: 'Go to Pharaoh in the morning'	Pattern 1: 'Go to Pharaoh'	Pattern 2: not to go to Pharaoh, but simply to bring the plague
1. blood, 7:14–24	2. frogs, 7:25–8:15	3. gnats, 8:16–19
4. flies, 8:20–32	5. cattle plague, 9:1–7	6. boils, 9:8–12
7. hail, 9:13–35	8. locusts, 10:1–20	9. darkness, 10:21–9

Patterns in the plague narratives. The story is composed by taking a couple of basic patterns and repeating them with variations (see Table 1). In the first pattern YHWH tells Moses to go to Pharaoh and require him to let YHWH's people go, and to threaten him with a plague if he does not. Moses' delivery of this message is not described, but taken for granted. (This is varied in plagues 8 and 10.) Pharaoh's response is not given either; YHWH's first speech is immediately followed (except in plagues 4 and 5) by another telling Moses (and often Aaron) to bring the plague. Except in plagues 1 and 5 Pharaoh then summons Moses and Aaron and attempts to negotiate, and asks Moses to pray to YHWH for the plague to be removed, which he does, and it is.

In the second pattern, there is no message to Pharaoh, but YHWH simply tells Moses to bring the plague. There are negotiations in plague 9, but in this pattern Pharaoh does not ask for the removal of the plague. In both patterns, and all the episodes except the last, the conclusion is the same, though expressed in different ways: Pharaoh's 'heart was hardened' (see above, EX 7:1–7, for the meaning of this), and he refuses to let them go. This enables another round to begin. It is P who has added the three plagues in the second pattern, each after two plagues in the first pattern. This helps to create a larger recurring pattern: three groups of three, according to the start of YHWH's speech to Moses, followed by the final plague.

We would expect the plagues to get steadily worse, and this is broadly true. Other climactic effects include the contest with the magicians. They can duplicate the staff-into-snake sign, and the first two plagues, but they stick on the third, and the boils, finally, make it impossible for them even to appear in Moses' presence (9:11). Then there is the series of negotiations between Moses and Pharaoh. Much of the interest of the section lies in them, for these are the only parts of the whole story where Pharaoh is allowed some human personality. Broadly speaking, Pharaoh's concessions (always withdrawn once the plague has gone) are progressively more generous (8:8; 8:25, 28; 9:28; 10:8–10; 10:24). True, if he realizes that the Israelites do not intend to come back, they are nicely calculated to be always unacceptable to Moses. So even before the removal of each plague Pharaoh seems not to understand the real situation, that he cannot win.

Other variations include the gradual downgrading of Aaron, who in spite of 4:14–16 and 7:1–2 never actually speaks, but uses his staff in the initial sign and the first three plagues, but never after that; and whether the protection of the Israelites is mentioned (8:22–3; 9:4, 6–7; 9:26; 10:23; 11:7—five out of nine).

'That they may know that I am YHWH'. More serious issues arise when we ask why YHWH brings the plagues. YHWH

himself says that it is so that Pharaoh and his people (and Israel, 10:2) may know him: 7:5, 17; 9:14; 10:2; cf. also 8:10, 22; 9:29; 11:7. Pharaoh had said in 5:2 that he did not know YHWH. He will now—to his cost. From each new round of the struggle he will find that YHWH, not he, emerges with the real power in his own land, and indeed throughout the world. 9:14–16 is especially clear. If it had just been a question of liberating Israel, one stroke would have been enough. This long-drawn torture has a different goal: 'that you may know that there is none like me in all the world'.

The hardening of Pharaoh's heart. We may well wonder why YHWH's demonstrations of his power must be so violent and destructive. And why do they have to be repeated so often, with increasing destructiveness? The answer is there at the end of every single episode. Pharaoh fails to draw the right conclusion from his experience, so it needs to be repeated. Other people get the point (9:20; 10:7), but not Pharaoh.

Now if we had not already had the clues in 4:21 and 7:3, we might at first think that Pharaoh was responsible for his own incomprehension and obstinacy, especially as in three places we are told that 'Pharaoh hardened' his own heart (8:15, 32; 9:34). It is after all quite natural in the first three episodes (7:13; 7:22; 8:15), when his own magicians can produce the same effects, so that there is no clear demonstration of YHWH's superiority; though even here we are reminded that YHWH had foretold it, and that only he can remove the effects (8:10). Pharaoh's obstinacy in 8:15 seems to be a response to the respite from the frogs, but as plague succeeds plague this gradually ceases to be a convincing explanation. The magicians themselves point out the truth after the third plague (8:19), and his continuing blindness at 8:32 and 9:7 becomes increasingly puzzling. From 9:12, after the sixth plague, it becomes increasingly plain that it is YHWH who is hardening Pharaoh's heart, for his own purposes; so in 10:1, 20, 27, and in the summary at 11:10. This is something which Pharaoh himself and his officials do not know, hence the officials' despairing protest at 10:7. Even if Pharaoh appears to act independently, he is in fact a puppet in the hands of YHWH. Taken as a whole the narrative gives little support to the common preacher's idea that Pharaoh falls victim to a paralysis of the will set up originally by his own free decision. (This paragraph summarizes the fine analysis of Gunn 1982.)

It is possible (Childs 1974: 172) that an older version of the story was much simpler: YHWH's sole purpose was to force Pharaoh to release the Israelites, and the successive plagues were simply a response to Pharaoh's own refusal to act sensibly. But that is not the case in the story as we have it. Here YHWH *prevents* Pharaoh from acting sensibly in order to have an excuse for bringing the plagues on him. Gowan's comment (1994: 138) is to the point: 'If freeing the Hebrews from slavery had been God's main intention ... then for God to harden Pharaoh's heart so as to extend the agonies of the process would be indefensible on any grounds.' But if his purpose is as stated in 7:5, 17, etc., to make Pharaoh know that he is God, it is strange that he acts every time to frustrate his own purpose. For that is the effect of the 'hardening', to prevent Pharaoh from understanding the truth. However often and destructively YHWH displays his power, it will have no effect on Pharaoh until YHWH wants it to. As Gowan sees (1994: 138), the truth must be that the object is not to

enlighten Pharaoh but to triumph over him, to 'gain glory over him' (14:4). He will truly 'know that I am YHWH' only at the very end of the process (14:18), when it will do him no good at all: this must be ironical. Durham (1987: 96) and Gunn (1982: 84) may well be right in suggesting that the true audience for the demonstration is Israel, certainly from the point of view of the authors. The account is shaped by a theology interested above all in maintaining the absolute sovereignty of the God they serve.

Believing readers will need to reflect on the question whether a God so anxious to display his power and triumph over his enemies is the God that they believe in. See Gunn 1982: 84 and, by contrast, Croatto 1981: 29. But Brueggemann (1995: 47) suggests that the struggle between YHWH and Pharaoh is not a matter of personalities; they are embodiments of opposed social policies; so that the victory of YHWH is the victory of a no-slavery policy.

Notes on individual verses. 7:8–13 develops 4:2–5. The motif of the contest between courtiers is a popular one (see Gen 41; Dan 2; 4; 5; 1 Esd 3–4), and it serves here as a comic counterpoint to the tragic struggle between YHWH and Pharaoh. Not that the magicians are clowns. They have real power, but it is soon shown not to compare with YHWH's (Durham 1987: 92). The turning of water into blood takes up 4:9, but is much more extensive and drastic. There is a seasonal reddening of the Nile waters at the time of the inundation (Hort 1957–8: 87–95), but it cannot be taken seriously as the origin of an account of water being actually turned into blood (Durham 1987: 97). For 'Hebrews' in 7:16 see EX 1:15, and for the request to Pharaoh, obviously a blind, see EX 3:18. In 8:10, the lesson about YHWH's power is derived by Moses from the exact fulfilment of *Pharaoh's* definition of the time. 8:16, 'gnats' (NRSV), or lice: biting insects at all events. 8:21, 'swarms of flies': the Hebrew simply says 'mixed swarms', without specifying the insects. 8:22: the land of Goshen, see Gen 45:10, has never been satisfactorily identified. There is no particular reason known why any animal the Israelites sacrificed would be 'offensive' (8:26; same word as in Deut 14:3) to the Egyptians; presumably it is meant to be the invention of the wily negotiator. It is odd that after all the Egyptians' livestock have died in the cattle pestilence (9:1–7), there are still some alive to be affected by the boils (9:10) and the hail (9:19–25). OT authors or editors are not concerned for narrative coherence in the way we might be.

In 9:13–35, the seventh and longest of all the plague episodes, except the last, things are moving towards a climax, and this is signalled by YHWH's especially detailed explanation of why he is acting as he is (9:14–16). 9:31–2 is a note added, not in the right place, perhaps to explain how the locusts had anything to destroy in the next plague. Pharaoh's remark in 10:10 is ironical, actually a curse. Of course he understands very well what Moses really wants; he imposes a similar unacceptable condition in 10:24.

Ch. 11 is awkward; Moses appears to be leaving in 10:29, but at 11:8 it turns out he has been speaking to Pharaoh since 11:4. No doubt there has been some rearrangement of the text, in order to accommodate the detailed ritual instructions which are given in 12:1–28 before the final blow is actually struck. But the chapter does impressively introduce this final act. 11:2–3 repeats the instructions of 3:21–2 (see EX 3:21–2). 11:9–10 sums up the section, so that it is tied up before launching into the Passover instructions, which will be followed by the final blow and then immediately by the leaving of Egypt.

(12:1–13:16) The Passover and the Exodus from Egypt Once more the style of the narrative changes abruptly. The climax of the account of YHWH's blows against Egypt does not come until 12:29–39, and this brief narrative is surrounded with detailed ritual instructions. Some of them concern not what the people are to do immediately, but how they are to repeat the rite in time to come, which to us seems inappropriate in the context. Once again we need to understand the motivation of the writers. They are not simply writing about the past; they are offering to their people an account of events which made them a people, events which are to be celebrated and relived. The little dialogues between child and parent in 12:25–7 and 13:14–15 show how by celebration a people can keep memory alive and recreate the saving and founding act of their God. As this passage is the climax of the story of deliverance, it is natural that the theme of observance should be concentrated here.

Three ritual observances are presented in this text as memorials of the Exodus, but the first two are held at the same time and virtually merged: Passover (*pesaḥ*), the Festival of Unleavened Bread (*maṣṣôt*), and the consecration of the first-born. The first two celebrate the Exodus in other texts: Unleavened Bread in Ex 23:15, and Passover (and Unleavened Bread) in Deut 16:1–8; but the consecration of the firstborn is related to the Exodus only here (compare Deut 15:19–20). All three are widely believed to be very old rites of various origins which at some stage have been given an interpretation related to the Exodus. (For details see Childs 1974: 186–9; de Vaux 1961: 484–93; *ABD* vi. 755–65; Van Seters: 1994: 113–27 dissents.)

A widespread opinion (following Rost 1943; disputed by Van Seters 1994: 114, following Wambacq 1976: 206–24) is that Passover was originally a rite carried out by nomad shepherds when moving to new pastures in the spring, while Unleavened Bread was an agricultural rite, marking the beginning of the barley harvest (which takes place in spring in the Near East) by getting rid of all the remains of bread from the last year's harvest and starting afresh. However, if that is so the distinctive features of the rites are given quite different interpretations, relating them to the last night in Egypt.

The very name *pesaḥ* is interpreted in this way. The verb in 12:13, 27 translated 'pass over' is *pāsaḥ*—a wordplay characteristic of Hebrew narrative. The verb is rather uncertain in meaning: a more precise translation might be 'leap over'. This is connected with the use of the blood to protect each family. Though this may be an ancient rite, and may have been thought of as a kind of magic, forcing evil spirits to swerve away, the text avoids this idea: the blood is a 'sign' (v. 13), YHWH sees it and of his own goodwill 'passes'—or leaps—'over'. Then there is the continuing importance of Passover as a mark of identity. All Israelites must celebrate it, and no one who does not belong to the community may share in it (12:43, 47–8). But it is not only a question of national identity. The eating of the passover lamb is a family activity, must take place within the house, and cannot be shared with those who are not members of the household: 12:44–6. So the Passover serves to

strengthen and celebrate ritually both the identity of the nation *and* its social structure of patriarchal extended families. Unleavened Bread is not explained in 12:14–20, simply commanded; but in 12:34, 39 it is explained in story terms. Probably the story was invented to explain it, and Moses' subsequent commands in 13:3–10 do not refer to it, simply emphasizing the feast's commemorative function.

The relation between the consecration of the firstborn, also probably a very ancient practice, and the events described in the story is obvious, and is explained in 13:15. It is not just that the firstborn males of cattle are consecrated to YHWH in sacrifice, but that human firstborn are redeemed (by payment or substitution), just as they were in Egypt. There may have been a time in Israel when firstborn sons were sacrificed—see Ezek 20:26; Jer 7:31. Therefore it is appropriate that the 'horrifying' edict, as Ezekiel calls it, should be presented as revoked as a symbol of the deliverance of the whole people from slavery.

Instructions for Passover and Unleavened Bread are also given at Deut 16:1–8; there are striking differences. Jewish interpreters have traditionally distinguished between 'the Passover of Egypt' and 'the Passover of the [subsequent] generations'. Critical scholars have tended instead to see the history of the rite in the differences: the usual view is that Passover began as a family observance, and was transferred to the temple in the time of Josiah as part of the centralization required by Deuteronomy, and that during the Exile P kept the festival alive by reviving its family character.

YHWH gives instructions for each rite to Moses before Moses passes them on to the people; but the speeches are interwoven in a curious way which points to the editorial history of the text (see Table 2).

TABLE 2. *Speeches of Moses and YHWH*

	YHWH	Moses
Passover	12:1–13 (14) + 43–9	12:21–7
Unleavened Bread	12:14–20	13:3–10
Firstborn	13:1–2	13:11–16

In each case YHWH's speech is the work of the P writer; but scholars have disagreed about the attribution of Moses' speeches. The simplest solution is that in J Moses gave instructions for the Passover before the Exodus and for the other two observances after it; and that P added the speeches of YHWH, taking Passover and Unleavened Bread together because they belonged together in the liturgical calendar. However, many scholars take 12:21–7 as P work (see Van Seters 1994: 114–19).

The first speech falls into two parts. 12:1–13 gives immediate instructions, while 14–20 looks forward to the future. This part is generally thought of as referring exclusively to Unleavened Bread; but the natural order of the speech shows that it is closely bound up with Passover. 12:2, 3, 6, 18: the month of Passover is called Abib in Ex 23:15; Deut 16:1. This is the old name for the first month of spring. P, writing after the Exile, always uses numbers instead of names, and begins the year in the spring as the Babylonian calendar did. It is likely that under the monarchy the new year began in the autumn, as it does for Jews today, and possible that 12:1 is to be interpreted as a call for a new calendar. See 'Calendar' in *ABD* i. The Hebrew word translated 'lamb' in 12:3, etc. by NRSV is wider than our word 'lamb', as you can see from 12:5. The requirement for a yearling male is quite practical—these were the most expendable members of the flock. The 'bitter herbs' in 12:8 are today taken as a symbol of the bitterness of oppression: the interpretation of the rite is an ongoing process. The requirement for the animal to be roasted whole (12:9, 46) differentiates it from a public sacrifice, which was boiled (as in Deut 16:7), and also perhaps symbolizes the integrity of the family and the nation. The identification of the lamb as the passover is held back to the climax of YHWH's speech in 12:11.

Moses passes on the instructions in 12:21–7. '*The* passover lamb' may be intended to refer back to 12:11. In 12:23, 'the destroyer' has been taken as a relic of an ancient belief in demons as the object of the blood-smearing; but it can just as well be interpreted as YHWH's own angel. 12:29 resumes the thread of the story broken off at 11:8. At 12:32 is a reference back to Pharaoh's last negotiations with Moses in 10:24–6, and at 12:35–6 to 11:2. 'Succoth' in 12:37 may be identified with Tell el-Maskutah on the east border of Egypt, close to the present Suez Canal (*ABD* s.v. Succoth).

The 600,000 in 12:37 is obviously historically impossible, but it is the standard biblical figure, repeated in the censuses in Num 1 and 26. The origin of the figure is disputed. But it was habitual for ancient scribes to exaggerate numbers. The writer produced a number which seemed fitting to him as a representation of the might of YHWH's people marching out in freedom.

The P editor, or a later one, adds his own reflections in 12:40–2. The figure of 430 years is fitted to his scheme of chronology. The Exodus happens 2,666 years after creation—two-thirds of 4,000 years (Blenkinsopp 1992: 48; but see Hughes 1990: 5–54). 12:41, 51 again liken the Exodus to the marching out of a military force.

In 12:43–9 some further provisions for Passover are added. They underline the close connection of the feast with the integrity of the nation, symbolized by circumcision, and of the family. The translation 'bound servant' in 12:45 NRSV is very dubious, and the word is more usually thought to refer to a lodger or temporary visitor. A very brief speech by YHWH in 13:1–2 ensures that the theme of the consecration of the first-born is given divine authority; but Moses has first to introduce the Israelites to the festival of Unleavened Bread in 13:3–10. This speech has strong Deuteronomic overtones (see EX C.1); many of the phrases can be found in Deuteronomy (e.g. the sign on the hand and the emblem on the forehead is in Deut 6:8), and the device of the dialogue with the child is used in Deut 6:20–5. But there is also a reference back to Ex 3:8 in 13:5. Moses goes on to instruct the people about the consecration of the firstborn. The first offspring of every female, if it is male, whether human or of domestic animals, belongs in principle to YHWH. However, only cattle, sheep, and goats can be sacrificed. The donkey is an 'unclean' animal which cannot (Lev 11:3—it has undivided hoofs), so a sheep must be sacrificed instead, or the donkey simply killed (13:13). A substitute sacrifice must be offered in place of human firstborn.

(13:17–15:21) The Intervention of God: Final Act The Israelites have left Egypt, but they are not yet out of the reach of Pharaoh. His attempt to recapture them is rewarded with the total destruction of himself and his army. With the end of Israel's oppressors the story of their deliverance reaches a conclusion. It has been argued that the story of the deliverance at the sea is the original basic story of the Exodus (Noth 1962: 114–15). But we have already seen that the commemoration of the Exodus is concentrated on the last night in Egypt. It is better to see this as the last twist in the tale, the final example of the pattern where a crisis evokes a desperate cry from the people, to which YHWH graciously responds, as in 2:23–5 and 5:22–6:1. From another point of view this is the beginning of the Israelites' 'wanderings in the wilderness'. We are introduced to the way in which YHWH will lead them in the wilderness, and the story is the first of several in which the people complain to Moses and YHWH graciously provides for them.

(13:17–22) The Israelites are, in fact, not 'wandering' in the wilderness, even if it looks like it. Their movements are determined by the purposes of God. 13:17 tells us *why* God does not lead them by the obvious route; vv. 18, 20 trace the route on the map, first in general terms, then by mentioning the staging posts; and vv. 21–2 tell us *how* God leads them.

The quickest route to Canaan was along the Mediterranean coast. The author appears to suggest they would meet the Philistines there—an anachronism if the Exodus took place in the late thirteenth century BCE. But this is imaginative history which cannot be fixed in time (EX C.3). Instead, they went inland 'by way of the wilderness toward the Red Sea'. In other places (23:31; Num 21:4; 1 Kings 9:26) 'the Red Sea' (Heb. 'sea of reeds', weeds') refers to the Gulf of Aqaba. It is often thought that the Gulf of Suez is meant here, or one of the lakes north of it, because 15:4, 22 and other texts (but not 14) fix it as the place where the great deliverance took place, and the Gulf of Aqaba is too far away (see 14:2). For Succoth (v. 20) see EX 12:1–13:16; Etham is unknown. For all topographical details from this point on, see Davies (1979). v. 19 refers back to Gen 50:25, and forward to Josh 24:32. In vv. 21–2 God's leadership is represented in a literal, visible manner. Cloud and fire are two of the commonest accompaniments of God's presence in theophanies (see EX 3:1–6). In the pillar of cloud and fire God's presence becomes permanent and mobile. This visible presence continues with them presumably to the borders of the promised land.

(14:1–31) It is clear that the action of this chapter is presented from two different points of view; but these do not clash, because they are focused on different characters. vv. 1–4, 15–18 are words of YHWH showing us the events from his point of view as the climax of his struggle with Pharaoh in the plagues narrative. (For a full discussion of this, see EX 7:8–11:10.) YHWH deliberately entices him out to recapture the Israelites, so that he may 'gain glory' for himself (vv. 4, 17). One last time, with deepest irony, he announces 'the Egyptians shall know that I am the LORD' (v. 18): as they sink to their deaths, they will know that YHWH is the true ruler of the world.

But in vv. 10–14, 30–1 we see things from the Israelites' point of view. They are in panic, but Moses tells them to trust in YHWH's deliverance: 'Do not be afraid . . . you have only to keep still' (vv. 13, 14). Moses uses a form of assurance that recurs again and again in the accounts of Israel's wars, where prophets urge the king or commander not to be afraid, but to trust in YHWH. Cf. particularly Isa 7:4; 28:16; 30:15. However, in the end faith comes *as a result* of seeing YHWH's act of salvation (v. 31). This pattern of events is repeated several times in the story of Israel in the wilderness: three times in the next three chapters, so that the lesson is rubbed in.

Although these points of view do not clash on the theological level, there are obvious unevennesses in the story. v. 4 seems at first to be fulfilled in v. 5, but actually looks forward to v. 8. YHWH's order in v. 16 is carried out only in v. 21 and has effect only next morning! According to a widely accepted source division, in J (vv. 5–7, 10–14, 19–20, 21*b*, 24–5, 27*b*, 30–1) Pharaoh changes his own mind, and the sea is driven back by the wind and then returns to overwhelm the Egyptians. This is the account which concentrates on the Israelites and Moses' call for faith. In P (vv. 1–4, 8–9, 15–18, 21*a*, 21*c*, 22–3, 26–7*a* (to 'over the sea'), 28–9) YHWH 'hardens Pharaoh's heart', and the sea is split into two walls when Moses stretches out his hand, which fall in when he stretches out his hand again.

On one central point the text is at one. The Israelites are delivered and the Egyptians destroyed by God's power. Whether he uses the natural elements or the hand of Moses, he triumphs in person over the enemies of Israel, who are his own enemies.

YHWH's opening instructions to Moses (v. 2) are to *turn back*. This is intended as deliberate deception: it is to make Pharaoh think the Israelites are lost, and tempt him to follow them (v. 3). The place-names in v. 2 cannot be located exactly, but they are on the borders of Egypt, and by 'the sea' (see EX 13:17–22). In v. 5 Pharaoh's motive is different. He receives an intelligence report that the Israelites have 'fled'. Since he knew they were going, this must mean that they have not returned as implied in the negotiations (7:16, etc.). In vv. 9, 18, 23, 26, 28 the NRSV has 'chariot drivers' where other versions have 'horsemen' or 'cavalry'. The Hebrew word normally means 'horseman'. NRSV is probably based on the fact that armies are known not to have had mounted cavalry before the first millennium BCE. But the author of Exodus would not have known that, and almost certainly meant 'horsemen'. A different word *is* translated 'rider' in 15:1, 21.

What the Israelites claim to have told Moses in Egypt (v. 12) they have not said anywhere in the text of Exodus; but this kind of allusion is very common in Hebrew narrative. In v. 15 YHWH asks Moses why he is crying out to him ('you' is singular), but the narrator has not told us he has. Moses may be assumed to have relayed the *Israelites'* cry in v. 10 to YHWH. In v. 19 as elsewhere (see EX 3:1–6) 'the angel of God' may be a substitute for YHWH himself (cf. 13:21). But the statement is repeated with reference to the pillar of cloud; so it is often held that in v. 19 there are two parallel sources. v. 29 is not a simple repetition of v. 22. It tells us that the Israelites had passed through in safety while the Egyptians were destroyed behind them.

(15:1–21) Pieces of poetry occasionally break the flow of prose in the Pentateuch, often at significant points. This one is particularly suitable here: it is fitting that Israel should praise YHWH when they are finally delivered from their oppressors. This is a victory song, but the victor is God, so it is also a hymn of praise and thanksgiving. It has parallels in the Psalms, which are pointed out in the notes, but it does not rigidly follow any one model of psalm. Psalms of praise often begin with a call to the people to praise, such as Ps 118:1–4. The song sung by Miriam in v. 21 is such a call and could be intended as the opening to which the men's song in 1–18 is the response (Janzen 1992). The song does not describe the previous state of distress or the cry to God for help, unlike many thanksgiving psalms (Ps 18; 30; 118). Everything is concentrated on YHWH and his victory. The song achieves its effect by repeating the account of the victory in several different vivid and allusive ways, punctuated with words of praise.

There is a dispute about the age of the song. One school (see Cross 1973), argues that the grammar and poetic style mark it out as very old, perhaps from the eleventh or twelfth century BCE, so a very ancient and important witness to the event of the Exodus. Others (recently Brenner 1991) say that the song relies on Ex 14 as it now stands, so that it must be quite late (fifth century?), and composed to occupy its present place; the author has deliberately created a song which looks old enough to be sung by Moses. But it is possible (Houston 1997) that v. 8 was the source from which the P author in Ex 14 took his account by interpreting its imaginative picture literally. This would make the song older than P, but not necessarily older than J. Of course, now that the song is part of the Ex text we inevitably read it in line with the account in ch. 14. The song looks forward to the completion of YHWH's work in the settling of Israel in his own land. All the promises in 3:7–12 and 6:2–8 are seen as fulfilled, really or virtually, in the miracle at the sea.

The song can be divided into: an introduction, vv. 1–3; a main section praising YHWH for the victory, 4–12; and a coda looking forward to the entry into the promised land, 13–18. For 'rider' in vv. 1, 21 see the note on 14:9, etc. in EX 14:1–31. But the word here *could* mean 'charioteer'. v. 2 is closely similar to Ps 118:14, 28. The word for 'heap' in v. 8 is used in the account of the Jordan crossing in Josh 3:13, 16. As the text stands, this verse has to be taken as describing the 'walls' of water in 14:22, 29; but if the poem is older, it could have been a poetic description of a wave rearing up and about to break; the breaking is described in 10 (Houston 1997).

For the question 'who is like YHWH' (v. 11) cf. Ps 89:6–8. 'Your holy abode' in v. 13 could be Sinai or the temple at Jerusalem, but v. 17 makes the latter more likely. The song praises YHWH not just for the settlement in Canaan but for the establishment of his dwelling among them at Zion. The final verse is another psalm-type motif: see Ps 93:1; 95:3; 96:10; etc. v. 19 recalls the essence of the story after the look into the future in vv. 13–18.

There was a custom, when men came back victorious from a battle, for women to come out from the towns to meet them (hence 'went out' in v. 20) with victory songs and dances (see 1 Sam 18:6–7). Since this victory has been won by YHWH, not by the men, the men have celebrated it, but the women's role is not forgotten, and may well be intended to be prior to the men's (see above, and Janzen 1992; against Trible 1994: 169–73). Miriam is called a prophet probably because of this song, which is seen as inspired.

(15:22–18:27) Israel in the Wilderness The two main accounts in Exodus are of YHWH's deliverance of Israel from Egypt and of his gracious provision for their future life with him at Sinai. But Israel have first to reach Sinai through the wilderness. What is meant by 'wilderness' in the Bible is not totally barren sand-desert, but steppe with low rainfall and sparse vegetation, suitable as pasture for sheep and goats but not much else. So there is a linking section describing this journey, but it is more than a simple link. The episodes are based on the well-known conditions of life in the wilderness, but these are used as an opportunity to develop the characterization of the Israelites and the relationship between them, Moses, and YHWH. The first three episodes in particular go very closely together. Two short stories about water frame the much longer one about the manna. In each the people raise a complaint against Moses, to which YHWH responds with gracious provision for their needs. In each Moses acts as the intermediary between YHWH and the people, both ruling them and interceding for them. The word used for 'complain' implies bad-tempered grumbling; in 16:3 and 17:3 they even suggest they would have been better off back in Egypt—thus rejecting YHWH's act of salvation. In spite of this YHWH is patient and gracious. Yet there is a harder note to the relationship, for another word which occurs in each story is 'test'. YHWH tests Israel (15:25; 16:4) to see whether they will be faithful and obedient; Israel tests or provokes YHWH (17:2, 7) by their grumbling. The theological point is very clear: life for Israel depends on trust in God's provision and obedience to his requirements. This is a lesson that reaches far beyond their temporary life in the wilderness; the best commentary is Deut 8. The main outlines of the relationship that will be literally cast in stone at Sinai begin to emerge; hence we should not be surprised that most of these stories anticipate points that are eventually grounded formally in the law given there: the 'statute and ordinance' at Marah (15:25); the sabbath provision in the manna story (16:5; 22–30); the legal system established on Jethro's advice (18:13–27). There is a similar group of stories in Num 11; 12; 14; 16; 20:2–13, but in most of these the people's grumbling arouses YHWH's anger and his punishment. This arrangement is surely deliberate. Once the people have received the law and accepted the covenant, there is no excuse for them.

It is impossible to say to what extent these stories are based on a tradition in Israel (see EX C.2). The references to the wilderness time in Old Testament literature are very varied: in some it is a time of happiness and obedience in contrast to the apostasy of the time in Canaan (e.g. Hos 2:14; Jer 2:2–3), in some a time of disobedience (e.g. Deut 9:7; Ps 95). Deut 8 comes closest to Exodus in seeing it as a time of testing.

By putting in place-names, the authors must have intended to give a precise idea of the Israelites' route, but this no longer works for us because we do not know where the places are. The people are now on their way to Sinai. If Sinai was, as traditionally supposed, in the south of the Sinai peninsula (see Davies 1979: 63–9), the places mentioned in 15:22, 27; 16:1; 17:1 are likely to be strung out along the west side of the peninsula. But there are other theories about the location of Sinai, and they would change the location of these places.

(15:22–7) For general comments and comments on the location of the place-names, see the previous section. Nothing is said about how or why the 'tree' or 'piece of wood' (15:25) made the water sweet. It seems like magic, but to the author it is simply the way in which YHWH chooses to act. And it is YHWH who 'tests' them. They have known YHWH as a 'healer' in his 'healing' of the water; they should beware lest he act in the opposite way (as he does in Numbers).

(16:1–36) For general comments and comments on the location of the place-names, see EX 15:22–18:27. This story seems to have originally been based on the fact that the tamarisk tree of the Sinai peninsula in May and June exudes drops of a sweet substance which is gathered and eaten by the local people, who still call it *man*. But the amounts are small, and obviously the story goes far beyond that natural fact. It speaks of a miracle which provides enough food every day, all the year round, to sustain a whole people on the march. And to that miracle of provision are added two further miracles which test the obedience and faith of the people. There is the miracle of precise quantity (vv. 17–18). God's providing is always enough for the day, it cannot be stored (v. 20). And there is the miracle of the sabbath exception to this miracle (vv. 22–30). The meaning of these miracles is found first in the saying in v. 5 which has echoed in one form or another through the narrative since 6:7. Here it is a rebuke to the Israelites who have spoken of *Moses and Aaron* as having brought them out of Egypt (v. 3). They need to understand that it is YHWH alone who can and will provide for them. The second lesson is that the generosity of YHWH is only of value to them if they on their part obey his commands. The full meaning of the sabbath will not be revealed until 20:11; but for the moment they need to understand simply that it is possible to rest for a day and still live, by YHWH's grace.

This chapter has been through a process of editing. It is mainly P, but there is probably an older narrative behind it. It is a somewhat awkward effect of the editing that when YHWH appears he simply repeats what Moses and Aaron have said already; and another awkward feature is the half-hearted way in which the quails are introduced into the narrative from Num 11, where they play a greater part. It is only the manna that the people eat for their whole time in the wilderness. v. 1, 'the second month'. The reckoning is inclusive: it is exactly a month since they left Egypt. In v. 7 'the glory of the LORD' is probably another way of referring to the way YHWH makes himself known in his miraculous provision; but in 10 it is the usual way in P of describing the appearance of YHWH in brightness wrapped in a cloud. In v. 15 the word translated 'what?' is *man*, which is not the normal word for 'what?' (*mah*), but near enough for a Hebrew pun: it is the word for 'manna' (v. 31). Aaron kept the preserved manna 'before the covenant' or 'testimony' (v. 34), that is before or in the ark, which is made in ch. 37. Since they 'ate manna forty years' (v. 35), Moses' order could have been given at any time: there is no anachronism.

(17:1–7) For general comments and comments on the location of the place-names, see EX 15:22–18:27. The episode closely follows the general pattern of the two previous episodes; its distinctive feature is the people's 'testing' or 'provoking' of YHWH, which gives its name to the place (vv. 2, 7).

Once again Moses directs their attention away from himself, whom the Israelites blame, to YHWH who is able to provide. 'Horeb' in v. 6 is the name in Deuteronomy, but not in Exodus (except 3:1), of the mountain of revelation. It may be identified with Sinai here, which cannot be far away. It is confusing that the place is given two names, not only Massah, 'testing', but Meribah, 'quarrelling', and that the latter is given to another place where a similar thing happens in Num 20:13. The poetic references at Deut 33:8 and Ps 95:8 use the two names. Possibly the author has taken both names from one of the poems and assumed they referred to the same place.

(17:8–16) Amalek was a nomadic people dwelling in the wilderness to the south of Canaan. All references to them in the HB are fiercely hostile: see especially Deut 25:17–19 and 1 Sam 15. There seems to be a long-standing feud: Deut 25 offers a reason for this, but it is not reflected in this story. The strangest feature of the story is the connection between the position of Moses' arms and the fortunes of the battle. Older commentators presume that his arms were raised in prayer; but if so why does the narrative not say he was praying? As Van Seters (1994: 203) points out, Josh 8:18–26 is similar. In both cases the automatic connection suggests magic; it is only implicit that God was in action. It is only the end of the story (17:14–16) that makes it clear that Israel's battle is, as always, YHWH's—to the death in this case. The Hebrew text in v. 16 is unclear. The NRSV's 'A hand upon the banner of the LORD' is the best suggestion, since it explains the name Moses has just given to his altar.

(18:1–12) This episode links up with the early part of the story (chs. 2–4). Cf. in particular v. 5 with 3:12. There are difficulties in the placement of the story. The Israelites have not at this point actually reached the mountain of God. Moses' father-in-law appears to be still with them in Num 10:29; and the measures of 18:13–27 are placed after leaving Horeb in Deut 1:9–18. For all these reasons it is often believed that the story originally belonged *after* the Sinai narrative; but the reason why it was moved is unclear (see Childs 1974: 322; Durham 1987: 242; Van Seters 1994: 209 n. 3). Zipporah and her family also create a problem. In 2:22 we are only told of one son of Moses (but see 4:20); and we last heard of Zipporah and her son on the way to Egypt, not left behind with her father (4:24–6). The best explanation may be that 4:24–6 is a late addition to the narrative. 'After Moses had sent her away' would then be an addition in v. 2 to harmonize the narrative with 4:20–6. 'Took her back' in v. 2 (NRSV) is not a correct translation of the Hebrew, which refers to what Jethro did *after* hearing about Moses: he 'took her and her two sons . . . and came' (v. 5).

The author has a tolerant acceptance of foreign peoples, and sees no sharp distinction between their religion and Israel's. Jethro, a foreign priest, gladly acknowledges the supremacy of YHWH (v. 11); but he makes this acknowledgement from within his own religious tradition, not as an act of conversion. Probably for this reason (unless one accepts the existence of a special E source (see PENT)) the chapter tends to use 'ĕlōhîm rather than YHWH except in vv. 8–11. For the multiple names of Moses' father-in-law, see EX 2:15b–22.

(18:13–27) The theme of this section is also addressed in Num 11:11–17; Deut 1:9–18. It is not clear why the advice to Moses to

share the burden is given by his father-in-law. Moses here is a judge deciding civil disputes, and a lawgiver mediating God's 'statutes and instructions'; and people come to him 'to inquire of God' (v. 15), that is, to seek directions in particular situations. There is no sharp line drawn between these functions in the Bible: so in Deut 17:8–13 the priest is associated with the judges in the decision of difficult cases, because the direction of God must be sought. The legal system which is established is actually based on a military organization (v. 21). Practice in the ancient Near East tended to give military and judicial functions to the same officers. The organization is artificial, it does not arise out of the existing social structure. Moses here acts like ancient kings, who tended to impose their systems on society. Possibly the story is intended to account for the later judicial system of the Israelite/Judean monarchy.

The interesting theological point is seen by Childs: that hard-headed, practical advice is seen as the 'command of God' (v. 23). There is no distinction between divine revelation and practical wisdom: the latter is as much the will of God as the former.

(19:1–40:38) The Establishment of Israel's Relationship with YHWH The people of Israel are no longer slaves. They have been saved from the land of oppression. But they are not yet a nation. The authors of Exodus believed that their being as a nation depended on the presence of their God with them, and that in turn depended on certain conditions. The second half of the book of Exodus is mainly concerned to set these out. The chapters contain two main kinds of answer to the question: on what conditions can Israel be YHWH's people and YHWH their God? The first answer is: on condition of obeying his commandments, which can be summed up as to worship him alone, and to behave with justice towards one another. These are set out in chs. 20–3, and the people's formal acceptance of them is narrated in ch. 24. This solemn imposition of requirements and undertaking of obedience is what this part of the book means by 'covenant' (19:5; 24:7, 8; 31:18; for covenant see EX C.1; and for law and commandments, Patrick 1986). The book then goes on, in chs. 32–4, to deal with the question: what happens if the people break the covenant? They then depend essentially on the mercy of God (33:19). But interleaved with this account is another way of dealing with the question. It is not contradictory to the first, but its presuppositions are different. YHWH safeguards his presence among his people by locating it in a physical site which moves as they move, and is hedged about with restrictions so that they receive blessing rather than harm from the presence of the holy God among them (29:43–6). YHWH gives Moses directions for the establishment of this 'tent of meeting' or 'tabernacle' in 25–31, and it is set up in accordance with his directions in 35–40.

The first answer sees the relationship as above all a moral one—not a matter of morals in a narrow sense, but based on how God and people behave towards one another. It is deeply marked by the influence of the prophets and the Deuteronomic writers, and is the work of the author I call J (see EX C.1). The second answer sees the main issue as being that of holiness. From God radiates a power that is the source of life and blessing, but is destructive to anyone who approaches too close or does not take precautions. This answer is the contribution of P.

(19:1–20:21) Before any of this can happen, the coming of YHWH to his people must be described. Mount Sinai becomes the symbol, not of the permanent presence of YHWH, which goes with them, but of his coming in unimaginable power and glory. This is the work of an imaginative writer, not a record from history. But it describes, symbolically, the experience of the presence of the holy and righteous God. The account proves difficult to follow, at least with our ideas of narrative logic. 19:3–8 appears to anticipate the whole process which culminates in ch. 24, and vv. 20–5 seem inconsequential. YHWH's speech to the people in ch. 20 begins abruptly: 19:25 breaks off with: 'and Moses said to them' which ought to be followed by what he said (NRSV 'and told them' smooths over the difficulty). After YHWH's speech, in 20:18–21, the people react in a way that suggests they have not heard what he has said. Two main types of solution are on offer. The first is that the difficulty arises from a complex literary history (see, for different analyses, Childs 1974: 344–51; Van Seters 1994: 248–52; Albertz 1994: 55). It is possible, for example, that the Ten Commandments are a late addition to this context, from Deut 5, although they are fundamental to the covenant in the text as it stands. The alternative is that a literary technique is being used which we tend not to understand. For example, Sprinkle (1994: 18–27) suggests that ch. 19 gives us an overview of events to come, which are described in greater detail later: possibly 20:1 picks up 19:19 and 20:21 picks up 19:20; YHWH's command to Moses in 19:24 is taken up again in 24:1–2. Patrick (1994) suggests that 19:3–8 makes clear at the outset the nature of the transaction. YHWH does not give commandments until the Israelites have formally declared themselves ready to accept them.

The description of YHWH's coming is created from traditional materials. So far as the site of the theophany (see EX 3:1–6) is concerned, there was a very ancient literary tradition describing the coming of YHWH in power from the deep southern wilderness, and one of the geographical names used was Sinai (Judg 5:5; Ps 68:8). The idea that the gods live on a high mountain was a very widespread one. But here the idea is more refined: YHWH does not actually live on the mountain, but comes down on it (19:11, 18; cf. 3:8). The theophany (19:16–20) is described in terms drawn from thunderstorms, earthquakes, and volcanic eruptions, the greatest displays of natural power that can be observed; and such descriptions are found in Hebrew literature of all periods—see e.g. Ps 18:7–15. They are ways of describing the indescribable, and certainly should not be taken to mean that what the Israelites actually saw was a thunderstorm or earthquake, or that Mt. Sinai was a volcano. The one unusual feature in the theophany is the sound of the trumpet (19:13, 16, 19; more precisely the ram's horn). This was used in temple services. YHWH comes so that the Israelites may come to him in worship. They have to make preparations to meet a holy God (19:10–15), preparations which are similar to those undertaken before entering a temple for sacrifice, and the mountain is fenced off in the same way as the most holy parts of a shrine are fenced off. 'On the third new moon', 19:1; more likely 'in the third month', reckoning inclusively. This would bring

them in the Priestly calendar to the feast of Pentecost, when the Jews to this day celebrate the giving of the Law.

'A priestly kingdom and a holy nation' (19:6): each of the two phrases expresses both sides of Israel's future existence. They will be a nation, with a social and political structure; they will at the same time and *through* their nationhood and state structures be dedicated to YHWH as priests are dedicated to the God they serve. The covenant to be announced will explain how this will be possible. A further purpose of YHWH's coming is explained in v. 9: it is to confirm the position of Moses as the confidant of YHWH in the eyes of the people, so that they trust him (cf. 14:31). The severe rules for anyone touching the mountain in 19:12–13 arise from the idea that holiness is a physical infection which can be 'caught' and is dangerous for people in an ordinary state. The command 'do not go near a woman' (v. 15)—a euphemism for sex; the 'people' who receive the command are the men—again arises because of the conception that certain bodily states create a danger in the face of holiness (see Lev 15, esp. 31; 1 Sam 21:4). The mention of priests in 19:22, 24 is difficult, since at this point Israel has no priests. Presumably it means those who will become priests later (Lev 8–9).

(20:1–17) The Ten Commandments The central place which this passage has had in the religious and moral teaching of Judaism and Christianity is a fair reflection of the centrality which it is given here in Exodus and in Deut 5. The Ten Commandments are, in this story, the prime expression of the covenant demands. They stand first in the account of the covenant-making. It is unclear whether they are spoken directly to the people; they certainly are in Deuteronomy. But the centrality also emerges from the very form and content of the text. In the first place it begins with YHWH's self-introduction (cf. 6:2 and see Zimmerli 1982), and asserts his right to authority, by recalling to the Israelites his goodness to them. And the first and much the greater part of the text is concerned with the requirements of his honour. Secondly, it is obviously designed to include all the most basic religious and moral requirements over a wide sphere of life. Thirdly, every command is expressed in the broadest possible way, sometimes by detailed elaboration (vv. 8–11), sometimes by avoiding any details which might narrow down the application (vv. 13–15). In a word, it is the most basic statement possible of the conditions on which Israel may be in relationship with YHWH. It combines in one text the specific demand for Israel to worship YHWH alone with those few moral requirements which are essential in one form or another for any human society.

But it is not a legal text. What laws in ancient Israel looked like we see in chs. 21–2. It is instruction addressed personally to Israel, or to the individual Israelite (the 'you' is singular and masculine, but that does not necessarily mean that women are not addressed; see below on vv. 8–11). It does not suggest how it is to be implemented or say what is to happen if the commands are ignored, but simply asks for obedience. (But Phillips 1970 regards it as Israel's fundamental law, and many scholars connect it with the form of ancient treaties: see Mendenhall 1992a.) If the setting in life of this type of text is not legal, what is it? Material of this kind, with its brief memorable clauses, could be designed as an aid to religious instruction in the home (Albertz 1994: 214–16). But this text goes beyond that function. With YHWH's self-announcement and personal demand for exclusive loyalty, vv. 2–6 belong nowhere else but in this present setting of covenant-making. Afterwards, in vv. 7–12, he is referred to in the third person, which is more suitable for a catechism. Perhaps catechetical material has been adapted to its place in the narrative.

This is the fundamental text of the covenant, but that does not mean that it is necessarily historically the earliest of the OT 'legal' texts, although many scholars firmly believe that it is, at least in an older form (see Durham 1987: 282). Reflection on all God's commands and requirements may have led to a more profound grasp of their basic meaning, which has then been expressed in this text. In fact vv. 2–12 are written very much in the style of Deuteronomy, except for v. 11, which is Priestly, so they are unlikely to be earlier than the late seventh century. Although this passage has always been called (literally) the Ten Words (Ex 34:28; Deut 4:13; 10:4), it is not obvious how the roughly twenty sentences of the text are to be grouped into ten. Different religious traditions have come to different conclusions. Jews call v. 2 the first Word and vv. 3–6 the second. Roman Catholics and Lutherans group vv. 2–6 as the first commandment and divide v. 17 into two to make up the tally of ten; other Christians separate v. 3 as the first commandment and treat vv. 4–6 as the second. (See further EX 20:2–6.) This commentary will simply use verse numbers. (For detailed discussion of the Commandments see Childs 1974: 385–439; Weinfeld 1991: 242–319.)

(20:2–6) The first section of the Commandments is quite different from the rest, being spoken in the first person and expressing what is most distinctive of the religion of the OT: the requirement to worship YHWH alone, and the prohibition of using images in worship. Two basic demands: can the Catholic tradition be right in treating it as one 'commandment'? Many scholars (e.g. Durham 1987: 286; B. B. Schmidt 1995) would see v. 4 as prohibiting images of YHWH in particular, after v. 3 has dealt with worshipping other gods. However, there is no sharp break anywhere in these verses: they treat throughout of YHWH's exclusive claim. The 'them' in v. 5 must refer to the 'other gods' in v. 3, because all the nouns in v. 4 are singular (Zimmerli 1968). This means that the command not to make an idol is part of a context forbidding the worship of any god but YHWH. That *YHWH* might be worshipped by means of an idol is simply inconceivable for this text. If you are using an idol, you must be worshipping another god. In those OT passages where people appear to be worshipping YHWH with idols (Ex 32:4; Judg 17; 1 Kings 12:28), the context implies that they are not genuinely worshipping YHWH. In the Syria–Canaan area generally, the central worship symbol in official sanctuaries tended not to be an image, but images of subordinate gods and especially goddesses were freely used (Mettinger 1995). But in the pure monotheism demanded here YHWH brooked no such rivals.

Modern preachers interpret this command in a moralistic way: anything which absorbs a person's devotion is his/her god (cf. Luther). But this is not what it means in the OT context. It was not self-evident to people in OT times that there was only one God; the demand to worship only one

God had to struggle against a polytheism which to many people seemed more natural, reflecting the complexity and unpredictability of the world. Even the Bible has to recognize the existence of other powers; the uniqueness of its demand is that even so only one of them is worthy of Israel's worship, the one 'who brought you . . . out of the house of slavery'; who is 'a jealous God'—better, perhaps, 'passionate', 'watchful of my rights'. The issue is one of YHWH's honour as the protector and saviour of his people. The harshness of the threat in 5b–6 (see also 34:7) has to be evaluated in the light of a far stronger community feeling than is normal with us. The worship of a god could not be an individual matter: the whole extended family shared in the sin—and therefore in the punishment. But contrast Ezek 18.

(20:7) It is uncertain what this command was intended to refer to: suggestions include deceitful oaths (as in Lev 19:12), unwarranted use of formal curses (Brichto 1963: 59–68), the use of God's name in magic spells, or all of these and other things (Childs 1974: 410–12). But it is quite clear that the improper use of the name YHWH is prohibited. The command is closely related to 20:2–6. It is YHWH's honour that is at stake. To wrest his name to one's own private and deceitful purposes is to dishonour the one who bears it.

(20:8–11) The sabbath likewise is an institution for the honour of YHWH; it is a sabbath 'to YHWH your God', and must be 'kept holy'. The day is dedicated to YHWH by abstaining from work, that is, from anything that is intended for one's own benefit, or human purposes generally. In order to ensure that the entire community keeps it, the householder is required to ensure that everyone in the house, which is also the work unit in peasant society, abstains from work on the seventh day. The list of persons does not include 'your wife'. The best explanation is that the lady of the house is not mentioned because she is addressed along with her husband (as in e.g. Deut 16:11; Smith 1918: 169; Weinfeld 1991: 307–8; contrast Clines 1995a). v. 11 gives a motivation for observing the commandment. The primary emphasis is on the special character of the day, determined by YHWH in the beginning, rather than on the need for people to rest (contrast Deut 5:15). The verse is obviously P, referring back to Gen 2:1–3 (so also Ex 31:14). The sabbath commandment is the only positive ritual requirement among the Ten Commandments. The main reason is likely to be that it had to be observed by every individual in the community without exception (the dietary laws, for example, did not have to be observed by aliens).

(20:12) Ancient Israel was a hierarchical society in which respect for superiors, parents in the first place, was fundamental. Care for their honour therefore comes next in the series after the honour of God (similarly Lev 19:3–4). This commandment is formulated positively, so its effect is broader than the law against insulting parents in Ex 21:17, etc. It will include care and comfort in old age (Mk 7:9–13). The commandments are addressed to adults, not children, and the need for this commandment may arise from tension between older men at the head of extended families and their sons with their own families.

The remaining commandments define serious transgressions against the rights of members of the community (generally of male householders).

(20:13) 'Murder' is the correct translation, i.e. the unlawful killing of a member of the community. The commandment does not cover capital punishment, killing in war, or the killing of animals for food; which is not to say that the OT is unconcerned with the ethical problems posed by these things.

(20:14) Adultery in the Bible is definable as intercourse between a married (or betrothed) woman and a man not her husband. The commandment is concerned with a man's rights over his wife. As in all traditional patriarchal cultures, the men of the family need to be assured of the faithfulness of their wives to be sure that their children are theirs. No similar restrictions apply to a husband in OT morality. It is the only sexual offence in the Ten Commandments, since others do not infringe the rights of a third party in a serious way.

(20:15) This commandment would include kidnapping as well as the theft of movable property. The word translated 'steal' does not cover the violent or dishonest alienation of land and houses: that is probably covered by 20:17.

(20:16) This is concerned with testimony in the courts. In Israelite courts the witness was in effect a prosecutor, as there was no state prosecution system. False accusation could put one's life, not merely one's reputation, in danger (see 1 Kings 21; Deut 19:15–21).

(20:17) The dominant interpretation of this commandment is that it is concerned simply with the *desire* to possess what is not one's own as a sin in itself (Rom 7:7–8; Calvin 1953: i. 354–6). However, there is also an interpretation which sees it as concerned with overt action to dispossess one's neighbour (Mk 10:19; Luther; J. Herrmann 1927). Even if the Hebrew word refers primarily to desire (Moran 1967), the concern is for the danger to one's neighbour posed by one's covetousness; and in particular the kind of covetousness described in Mic 2:1–2. As Luther saw, the machinations of the powerful to dispossess the weak are not covered elsewhere in the Ten Commandments.

(20:18–21) Moses' point is that they should not be terrified at the divine appearance because it is for their good: 'fear' in v. 20 is not the panic terror that is now seizing them, but reverence and awe which should lead to the right conduct that God asks of them. Once again (cf. 15:25) they are being 'tested' or 'challenged' to make the right response.

(20:22–23:33) The 'Book of the Covenant' The very long speech that YHWH now delivers to Moses to pass on to the Israelites includes a much wider range of religious, moral, and legal instruction than the Ten Commandments. The Ten Commandments make absolute demands; this speech shows how the demands of God for fairness and justice and for the proper honouring of himself work out in practice in a particular society. That is why much of it is at first sight of little interest to people who live in a different society under different conditions. It has been given the name Book of the Covenant by modern scholars, from 24:7. The name suggests that the speech existed as a single document simply slotted into the text. (There continues to be discussion among scholars about its date (see Albertz 1994: 182–3).) But it is unlikely ever to have been a single document. Most of the material has been taken from earlier sources, but it has been

shaped to fit its narrative context (see 20:22; 22:21; 23:15 (13:6–7); 23:20–33), and as it stands is likely to have been put together by J.

The main areas covered are religious observance; civil law, specifically the law of bondage for debt, personal injury, and property torts; social justice; and judicial integrity. The arrangement of material sometimes seems capricious to us, but there is logic behind it, as Sprinkle (1994) shows. There is a general heading in 21:1, which suggests that 20:22–6 could be described as a prologue; and 23:20–33 is concerned with the immediate situation rather than with permanent rules, so it might be described as an epilogue. The material between is arranged as follows:

21:2–11	Release of slaves
21:12–32	Personal injury
21:33–22:17	Property damage (these two bridged by the case of the goring ox)
22:18–20	Offences against covenant holiness
22:21–7	Treatment of dependants
22:28–30	Treatment of superiors
22:31	Covenant holiness (bracketing with 22:18–20)
23:1–9	Judicial integrity
23:10–19	Sabbaths and festivals

The speech contains material of very different types. Most of the material between 21:2 and 22:17 is in an impersonal legal style which contrasts sharply with the personal address of most of the rest, in which YHWH speaks of himself in the first person and addresses Israel as 'you' (usually in the singular, sometimes the plural). For detail on these different types of law see Patrick (1986: 13–33). The impersonal style sets out a legal case, giving the situation 'when such-and-such happens', and laying down what should then be done. This is the style used in the Mesopotamian legal codes such as the Code of Hammurabi (see *ANET* 159–98), and it is technically referred to as 'casuistic' law. There is also a good deal of overlap in content between this section and the Mesopotamian codes (summarized by Childs 1974: 462–3). This does not mean that the laws have been borrowed from a foreign source, simply that legal style and stock examples were similar all over the ancient Near East. Laws of this type were probably not used as the basis of judicial decisions (see Jackson 1989: 186). The skill of judges lay not in the interpretation of a body of written law, but in being able to perceive how a dispute could best be resolved and where justice lay in a particular case. Laws such as these would help in educating them in this skill, but they did not have to rely on them in reaching a verdict. That is why the laws here do not have the detail and precision one would expect in a modern body of law. They are probably borrowed from an old legal text to illustrate the kind of justice required by YHWH in the resolution of disputes.

The other main style is that of personal admonition. This is the kind of style in which a tribal elder might give moral instruction (cf. Jer 35:6–7; Gerstenberger 1965: 110–17), but in this text it is clear that God is the speaker. It is therefore unlikely to have been borrowed from a specific social setting; the suggestion of a ritual of covenant renewal (see Childs 1974: 455–6) is pure speculation. So although the content of the instruction would have been derived from Israel's moral and religious tradition, its form has been designed to fit its present literary setting.

In each case the style is appropriate to the subject-matter: casuistic for the settlement of disputes, personal address for religious instruction and for teaching about justice as a personal responsibility.

(20:22–6) Prologue: YHWH's Presence YHWH begins his address to Moses by speaking of his own person and presence in worship. The first point, as in the Ten Commandments, is his intolerance of idols, that is, other gods, alongside him: see EX 20:2–6, and Sprinkle (1994: 37–8) for a different view. He goes on to speak positively of how he should be worshipped. The altar must be of natural materials (E. Robertson 1948; for the different kinds of sacrifices, see LEV 1–7). The key religious point, however, is in v. 25. YHWH's presence and blessing depends not on the humanly organized cult, but on his own decision: 'where *I* proclaim my name'. This has generally been understood as permitting many altars for sacrifice, while Deut 12 permits only one, so that it would belong to an earlier stage in religious history than Deuteronomy. But it could be saying that while one altar is allowed, YHWH's blessing may be received quite apart from altars and sacrifice (Van Seters 1994: 281).

(21:2–11) The 'ordinances' begin with the demands of justice in relation to the use of people as slaves, no doubt because the people addressed have just been released from slavery themselves. For detail on the laws of slavery, see Chirichigno (1993); also 'Slavery' in *ABD* vi. The law is concerned with 'Hebrew' bondservants, not with foreign slaves who might be owned outright (ibid. 200–18; another view of the meaning of 'Hebrew' in e.g. Childs 1974: 468). It is an attempt to deal with social distress caused by debt among peasants (see Lang 1983 for background). A creditor could seize a defaulting debtor or a member of his family (2 Kings 4:1) and either sell or use him/her as a slave; or a man could sell a member of his family into bondage to pay off his debts (Neh 5:1–5). The law limits the period of such bondage to six years. Permanent bondage could only be at the bondsman's own choice; but often he may have had no genuine choice. 21:7–11 is concerned with a girl who is sold as a concubine or slave-wife. A woman who had been sexually used and might be the mother of her master's children could not normally be released after six years; but the law lists situations in which justice would demand that she should be. In effect she is given the privileges of a legal wife.

(21:12–17) Four capital cases are listed in descending order of severity. All are worthy of death; this indicates how seriously the requirement to honour parents (20:12) was taken. In v. 17 'dishonour' or 'reject' might be a better translation than 'curse'. It was customary for the relatives of the victim to take vengeance. v. 13 limits this by protecting someone who is accidentally responsible for a person's death (Deut 19:1–13 elaborates); traditionally the altar provided sanctuary (1 Kings 2:28). Frequently the victim or relatives would accept monetary compensation (see 21:30), though in the case of murder Num 35:31 forbids this.

(21:18–27) The general principle of justice exemplified here is that of fair compensation for injury. The principle is stated in general terms in the famous vv. 23–5. Later this was interpreted as requiring reasonable monetary compensation (Daube 1947: 106–9; Childs 1974: 472), but at some earlier stage its literal application prevented excessive vengeance and would have ensured the rich were not at an advantage. In the case of slaves, the compensation for serious injury or unintended killing (v. 21) is that the owner loses his property. If he murders his slave he must face punishment (v. 20). It is important that as against Mesopotamian codes the slave is treated as a legal person.

(21:28–36) The case of the goring ox is a topic also in Mesopotamian codes. It serves as a standard example of the way to treat cases of negligence, and of how to distinguish between accident (vv. 28, 35) and culpable negligence. The one feature that would not be found in contemporary or modern laws is that the ox itself, if it has killed a person, is treated as a criminal and stoned rather than slaughtered in the normal way (vv. 28, 29, 32). Here religious factors enter in. The ox has transgressed boundaries between human and animal and between wild and tame animals (see Houston 1993: 182–200), so is treated as ritually detestable and not simply dangerous; see Gen 9:5.

(22:1–15) The principle adopted in the property section of the laws is that equal compensation is acceptable for negligence (vv. 5, 6, 12, 14), but is enhanced as a deterrent to deliberate theft or fraud (vv. 1, 4, 7, 9); while no compensation is payable in the case of accident or *force majeure* (vv. 11, 13).

Theft and sale of livestock (v. 1) is treated more severely than theft of money or articles (v. 7), perhaps because they represented the farmer's livelihood; oxen are compensated on a higher scale than sheep perhaps because of their working capacity (Daube 1947: 133). vv. 2–3a draw a line between justified killing in self-defence and unnecessary killing, which is murder. The time of day is simply an example of the factors that could be taken into account. The other issue raised in this section is that of evidence. Where the matter could not be settled by witnesses, the only recourse was religious. 'Before God' (8, 9) probably means at a sanctuary; but how was the decision made? In 11 it is clearly by oath; this may be true in 8 and 9 as well (Sprinkle 1993: 146–7); other suggestions include ordeal and divination by the priest.

(22:16–17) Seduction is treated on the one hand as a matter of responsibility on the part of the seducer: he does not have the right to decide not to marry the girl. On the other, it is a matter of the father's rights. Normally a father had the right to dispose of his daughter, and to receive 'bride-price' for her. If he chooses to exercise his right, he is compensated for the difficulty he will have in giving her away. The girl has no say in the matter.

(22:18–20) gives a series of three practices which the advocates of exclusive loyalty to YHWH saw as fundamentally threatening to it, and therefore deserving of death. We do not know precisely what is meant by sorcery, but it probably involved treating with spiritual powers other than YHWH. Bestiality transgressed fundamental ritual boundaries (cf. 21:28 and see Lev 18:23). Here it is the community which must inflict punishment on YHWH's behalf.

(22:21–7) Earlier sections have treated disputes in the community as resolvable by applying norms of justice. But there were great disparities in wealth and power in Israelite society, as in ours. Some people were in a dependent situation either temporarily or permanently. It was easy to take advantage of them and prevent them from obtaining legal redress. So those who hold power over them must be both reminded of what is just and warned of the possible consequences when they have to deal with a just God. The 'resident alien' meant an incomer from another area without a property stake in the local community. Widows and orphans were vulnerable because they had no adult male protector in the immediate family. A 'poor' person means primarily a peasant who cannot maintain his family until the next harvest, and so needs a charitable loan.

(22:28–30) As the independent Israelite has duties to his dependants, he also has duties to those above him, especially God (see also 13:11–16).

(22:31) In an economy of scarcity, people would be inclined to make use of any source of food, however suspect. But being dedicated to YHWH means using a diet fitted to his dignity. Mangled meat is fit only for the universal scavenger. This theme is developed in much more detail in Lev 11; Deut 14; see Houston (1993: 241–4, 248–53).

(23:1–9) It is all very well to have norms of justice. But unless the courts can be relied on to enforce them fairly and impartially, they are of no use. vv. 4, 5, which do not seem to fit this theme, underline the requirement of total impartiality. You may have a long-standing dispute with another family: but you should be fair to them in daily life, and, just the same, you should show no partiality against them in court. v. 9 ties up the section on social justice by repeating the warning not to oppress the alien which begins it in 22:21.

(23:10–19) A people dedicated to YHWH, who are called by him to act with justice, honour him particularly in ways which serve the cause of justice. Two institutions particularly characteristic of Israel's religious culture are the sabbath year (vv. 10–11) and the sabbath day (v. 12). Neither of them is called that here, possibly because the name was attached to a different holy day in the pre-exilic period when these verses may have originated (Robinson 1988). The original function of the sabbath year (cf. Lev 25:1–7) is unclear, but here it is given a charitable purpose; likewise the sabbath day is commended for its beneficial effects on dependants, as in Deut 5:15, not as in 20:11 (P!) for its sacral character in itself. v. 13 looks like a concluding verse, so what follows may be an addendum. vv. 14, 17 bracket the brief instruction about the major pilgrimage festivals of the agricultural year. Passover is not mentioned, possibly because it was not yet a pilgrimage festival at the time of writing. The Israelites are reminded that they have already been told (13:3–10) of Unleavened Bread. The other two festivals are described in exclusively agricultural terms, and are given different names from those customary later. 'Harvest' is Weeks or Pentecost, Deut 16:9–12; Lev 23:15–21; 'Ingathering', when all produce is taken in before the autumn rains begin, is Booths or Tabernacles, Deut 16:13–15; Lev 23:33–6.

The instructions in vv. 18–19 are connected with festival worship. The taboos in v. 18 possibly arise because the ideas of fermentation and corruption are opposed to the purity of the sacrifice. The 'kid in mother's milk' prohibition is an old conundrum. See the full discussion in Milgrom (1991: 737–41).

(23:20–33) Epilogue: Entering the Land As the whole of the speech has looked forward to Israel's settled life in the land, it is appropriate that it should be concluded with a word of promise, along with some admonition, about their journey to and entering of it. The promise of an 'angel' or messenger does not really revoke YHWH's personal presence with them (13:21–2)—see EX 3:1–6; especially in view of YHWH's statement that 'my name is in him'. vv. 23–33 look back to the promises in 3:7–10 and expand them. Here, as in Deuteronomy (see Deut 7 especially), the native nations stand for the constant threat of the worship of the gods of the land (seen as idols, as in the opening of the speech at v. 24): 'you shall . . . demolish *them*') to the exclusive loyalty demanded by YHWH. He will do all the fighting for them (as in ch. 14!); their sole responsibility is to be faithful to him. v. 31 very much exaggerates the territory that Israel ever held at any time in her history; but as in vv. 25–6 the implication may well be that they never received the fullness of the promise because they were *not* faithful.

(24:1–8) The Conclusion of the Covenant Ch. 24 is the climax of the Sinai narrative, but it contains a number of themes rather roughly pieced together. There has never been any consensus among critics about the sources or editing of the chapter. vv. 1–2 take us back to the end of ch. 19. v. 1a is most accurately translated in the Jerusalem Bible: 'To Moses he *had* said', i.e. in 19:24. YHWH's invitation here includes more people, but variation is common when speeches are repeated. Though we are reminded of the invitation here, it is only taken up at v. 9. vv. 3–8 are the account of the ceremonial sealing of the covenant on the basis of the words which YHWH has given to Moses, that is the Ten Commandments and the Book of the Covenant. The meaning of the covenant has already been explained in 19:4–6. There (19:8) we heard of the people's response in advance, and it is repeated twice here (vv. 3, 7): first Moses secures their acceptance of YHWH's terms, then he formally seals their covenant with YHWH by writing the terms down, reading them to them, and hearing their acceptance again; then he consecrates them as YHWH's holy people (19:6) in a sacrificial ritual. Nicholson (1986: 171–2) has shown that although there is no ritual precisely like this in the OT we can understand its meaning by comparing rituals which have some similarity, such as the ordination of priests in 29:20. The blood of the holy offering makes them holy to YHWH. This is an imaginative way of expressing in narrative form the bond of will and obedience between YHWH and Israel.

(24:9–18) Vision of God on the Mountain The invitation of 24:1 (19:24) is now taken up. Representatives of the people, and of the future priests (Aaron and his sons), ascend the mountain and receive a vision of God himself. As with other similar visions (Isa 6; Ezek 1), the Bible avoids describing the appearance of God, but simply gives one vivid glimpse of the glory that surrounded him. 'Sapphire' (NRSV) should probably be 'lapis lazuli', a common material in the decoration of temples. The eating and drinking of the people's representatives in the presence of YHWH himself is an appropriate conclusion to the story of how they became his holy people. The promise of 19:13b is at last fulfilled. (See Nicholson 1986: 121–33, 173–4.) vv. 12–14 prepare for YHWH's giving of the tablets of stone to Moses, and it also makes a bridge to ch. 32. What exactly is written on the tablets is not made clear here: it is only at 34:28 (and Deut 5:22) that it emerges it is the Ten Commandments. It is also unclear how the tablets relate to the book that Moses has written. The tablets are to be placed in the Ark when it is made (25:16; 40:20; Deut 10:2–5); as Cassuto (1967: 331) notes, this is similar to the provisions in ancient treaties for copies to be placed in the sanctuaries of the contracting parties. Perhaps, then, the tablets are meant to be the official original of the covenant, while copies on papyrus may be made for practical purposes. vv. 15–18 are a P paragraph preparing for the giving of the instructions about the tabernacle which now follow.

(25:1–31:17) The Prescriptions for the Sanctuary This third long speech by YHWH from Sinai is an entirely Priestly passage. He gives instructions here for the building of a portable structure which has two functions. It enables the living presence of YHWH, which the Israelites have met at Sinai, to go with them on their journey and continue to bless them (40:34–8); and it enables Moses to continue to receive instructions from YHWH after the people have left Sinai (see 25:22; 29:42; Lev 1:1).

This double function is reflected in the names 'tabernacle' and 'tent of meeting'. In part, these names refer to different parts of the structure (see ch. 26, especially v. 7): the tabernacle is the arrangement of frames or boards over which curtains of fine material are stretched, and the tent is the curtains of goat's hair which cover the tabernacle. But theologically the name 'tent of *meeting*' implies (as in 33:7–11) the place where God meets with Moses as the prophetic representative of Israel; while 'tabernacle' (*miškān*, lit. 'dwelling') implies the place where God dwells among his people. Both these understandings are expressed in the conclusion to the main body of instructions in 29:43–6.

But though the name 'tent of meeting' is rather the commoner of the two, the physical image is that of a temple, differing from other temples only in being portable; and a temple was primarily thought of as a god's permanent dwelling-place on earth. (For thorough discussion of the priestly picture of the tabernacle and its service see Haran 1985: 149–259.)

The main body of instructions, chs. 25–9, moves outwards from the centre which represents the divine presence. First (25:10–40) the sacred furniture is prescribed, beginning with the ark and its cover which stand in the innermost sanctum; then (ch. 26) the tabernacle-tent structure which screens these sacred objects from public view; then (ch. 27) the altar outside and the hangings which surround the court where it stands. A consecrated priesthood is required to serve in this holy place, so the instructions proceed by prescribing their vestments (ch. 28) and the rite of their ordination (ch. 29) which qualifies them to serve. Chs. 28–9 on the priesthood are framed by two passages which prescribe the permanent daily service which is to be carried on, and so explain why a priesthood is necessary: 27:20–1 on the tending of the lamp in the tabernacle; and 29:38–42 on the daily burnt offerings.

The instructions are rounded off (29:43–6) with a statement by YHWH of how he will use the sanctuary, as the place of meeting and of presence. However, some additional prescriptions follow in ch. 30; the first (vv. 1–10) is part of the main speech, the others, like those in ch. 31, are added as separate short speeches. As a conclusion has already been given to the instructions, and the incense altar and basin have not been mentioned in their logical places, these prescriptions are generally taken as later additions.

The whole passage is framed by the call for contributions in 25:2–9 and the provisions for design and manufacture in 31:1–11. Why this is followed by the repetition of the sabbath commandment in 31:12–17 is discussed below.

The general outline of the sanctuary is similar to that of Solomon's temple described in 1 Kings 6, and to that of many of the shrines in Palestine and its surrounding area found in archaeological excavations. It clearly reflects very ancient ideas of the deity's dwelling in the temple and having his needs attended to there by his priestly servants. A covered rectangular structure stands in an open court, and is divided by a crosswise partition into two rooms (for a slightly different picture see Friedman 1992). The inner, smaller room contains the principal symbol of the presence of the deity. The two cherubim originally represented a throne for the invisible YHWH (see 1 Sam 4:4). In the outer room stands furniture required for the personal service of the deity: the lampstand for light, the table for the 'bread of the Presence', and the incense altar for pleasant scent. Outside in the court stands the 'altar of burnt offering', where offerings are burnt, wholly or partially, as a 'pleasing odour' to YHWH (29:18, etc.).

Taken literally, this mode of service would imply a very crude conception of God. But the ritual goes back to time immemorial, and the text does not imply such a literal conception. It avoids implying that YHWH was enthroned over the ark (Mettinger 1982: 88), and gives no indication beyond the use of traditional clichés that YHWH was literally benefited by his service. In fact no one had ever believed that gods literally lived in their temples, in the sense that they were bounded by them. God's true temple is in heaven, where he sits enthroned in glory (see Isa 6); the temple on earth is a copy of this (Ex 25:9; Cassuto 1967: 322), and there he makes himself present to his people in a particular way.

The presence of God in the centre is believed to generate an intense holiness which is like a physical influence, radiating outwards in declining degree. This is marked by the materials used and by the persons allowed to enter. The materials decrease in value as one moves outwards (Haran 1985: 158–65). No one may enter the inner sanctum except the high priest once a year (Lev 16:2, 29); no one but priests may enter the outer hall or ascend the altar. The high priest (Aaron) and the priests (the sons of Aaron) are specially consecrated (29) and must preserve a special degree of ritual purity (Lev 21) so that they can venture into these holy areas. Any Israelite who is ritually clean for the time being (see Lev 11–16) may enter the court, but the hangings mark out the area beyond which the unclean may not proceed. (For further details see Haran 1985: 158–88.)

Clearly this whole arrangement is symbolic. At the centre of the people's life stands the Presence of God, and order, life, and blessing flow out from there. But there are also powers of disorder and death that have to be kept at bay. Contact between these would be deadly: hence the carefully ordered gradation of boundaries, material, and personnel. (See also Jenson

1992: 56–88.) At the same time the system would have served to guarantee the power of the priests who controlled it.

The system is more obviously appropriate for a settled people, despite the great care with which it is adapted to life on the move. No doubt it represents what the priests believed about the temple. The question arises whether the picture of the mobile tabernacle is imaginary or derived from a real sanctuary. Portable shrines existed, but the one described is far too elaborate to have been produced in the wilderness. Critical scholars have tended to argue that it is an imaginary projection of the Jerusalem temple into the period of the wilderness. Some (e.g. Friedman 1992), however, have suggested that there was a real portable shrine, not as elaborate as is here described, referred to in Ex 33:7–11 and in Num 11 and 12, which was preserved at Shiloh and perhaps later at Jerusalem, and that this is what the writer is describing.

But if P is dependent on the earlier sources, it is likely that it has taken the idea of a tent-shrine and the name 'tent of meeting' from 33:7, and with it the function of the shrine as a place of meeting between God and his prophet, and has combined that with the temple image (similarly Childs 1974). But there are details that do not accord with the Jerusalem temple either before or after the Exile.

(25:1–9) The Israelites are to make a 'holy place' (v. 8; NRSV 'sanctuary'), a place marked out for and by YHWH's presence. The verse is echoed by 29:43 at the end of the main body of instructions. In v. 9, YHWH does not merely tell Moses what to make: he shows him a 'pattern' (very necessary in view of the obscurity and ambiguity of some of the prescriptions!). Perhaps the writer believed that the tabernacle was a copy of a heavenly temple (as Heb 8:5 deduces). Other ancient Near-Eastern priestly writers claimed this for their temples.

(25:10–22) The word translated 'covenant' (vv. 16, 25) in the NRSV and 'testimony' in many other versions is not the same as the word for 'covenant' earlier; it is P's regular term for the written record of YHWH's commandments on the stone tablets. P follows the conception in Deut 10:2–5, so that the ark becomes not only the place of YHWH's meeting with Moses (v. 22), but also the sign of the obligations he lays upon Israel. v. 18, 'cherubim' were probably imaginary winged four-footed creatures such as are found constantly in ancient Near-Eastern art. YHWH is depicted as 'riding' or 'seated' on cherubim in e.g. Ps 18:10; 80:1.

(25:23–40) The table is used both for the bread of the Presence (v. 24; see Lev 24:5–9) and for vessels for drink-offerings; however, these were not offered inside the tabernacle. The prescriptions for the lampstand are hard to follow, but the well-known relief of the lampstand from Herod's temple on the Arch of Titus in Rome probably gives a fair idea of what the writer had in mind; see also Meyers (*ABD* iv. 142; cf. Meyers 1976). Solomon's temple had ten lampstands (1 Kings 7:49), but it is not said that these were branched. The branched lampstand appears to be a later innovation, thrown back into the time of the wilderness.

(26:1–37) The description is ambiguous, and various reconstructions have been made. The main structure is the 'frames', or boards, described in vv. 15–25. These are set up on end, so that the height of the tabernacle is 10 cubits (a cubit was about 50 cm. or 1ft. 8 in.); but disagreement arises over whether they are set side by side, giving the tabernacle a length of 30 cubits, or overlapping (Friedman 1992), giving a length of (perhaps) 20 cubits. The breadth is very uncertain, because of the difficulty of vv. 23–4. The tabernacle curtains are meant to be stretched over the top of the structure, forming its roof and hanging down the sides; they are joined together lengthwise to make an area 28 × 40 cubits, with the long side running the length of the tabernacle and hanging down the back; similarly with the tent curtains which are stretched over the top of the tabernacle curtains and cover the parts these cannot reach.

The key ritual element here is the 'curtain' (not the same word as in v. 1, etc.) in vv. 31–5, which marks off the 'most holy place' (Heb. 'holy of holies'). Within the curtain is the ark, outside it the other furniture. Most scholars envisage the curtain as dividing the tabernacle crosswise in the same way as the solid wall dividing the main hall from the inner sanctum of permanent temples, with the pillars side by side; Friedman however sees it as a canopy hanging down from four pillars set in a square.

(27:1–8) This description is once again very ambiguous. The altar is a hollow box of wooden boards overlaid with bronze: so much is clear. But as it is doubtful whether such a structure could stand a fire, it is argued by Cassuto (1967: 362) that it has no top and in use would be filled with stones or earth (cf. 20:24–6), so that the fire would be laid on the stones. Even more unclear is the placing and function of the 'grating'. The horns (v. 2) at least are a regular feature of altars in that cultural area. Their origin is uncertain, but their use in Israelite ritual appears in 29:12.

(27:9–19) The dimensions and function of the enclosure which surrounds the altar and tabernacle are clear, even though details of the spacing of the pillars on which the hangings are hung are not, and the placing of the altar and tabernacle within the court is not specified.

(27:20–1) It is not immediately clear why this passage is placed here (it is repeated almost word for word in Lev 24:2–4); for my suggestion see above, EX 25:1–31:17. Why it speaks of only one light is also unclear; it is likely that it is a fragment of a different tradition from that which calls for seven, which has become dominant in the text.

(28:1–43) This chapter now introduces the priesthood to serve in the holy place, and details the vestments they are to wear for that purpose. Aaron is to be the high priest, his sons the priests. Obviously what is said of Aaron will apply to each high priest after him. Most of the chapter (vv. 2–39) is concerned with Aaron's vestments, which are designed for officiating within the tabernacle (Haran 1985: 210–13). v. 40 lists the garments of Aaron's sons, for service at the altar, and v. 41 points forward to their vesting and ordination prescribed in detail in the next chapter. The undergarments or drawers prescribed in vv. 42–3 may be a later development, but as their function is a negative one (cf. 20:26) they might in any case not be mentioned along with the garments which are designed for 'glorious adornment' (vv. 2, 40). These are made of the same costly materials (v. 5) as the tabernacle itself. The ephod (vv. 6–14) appears to be a sort of apron with shoulder-straps; it is the most visible and impressive of the vestments. The 'breastpiece of judgement' (vv. 15–30) is so called because it holds the Urim and Thummim (v. 30), which are objects used for divination (Num 27:21). The robe (vv. 31–5) is worn under the ephod, and is of simpler workmanship, except for the hem. The bells protect Aaron (v. 35) perhaps by preventing him making an unannounced approach before the throne (Cassuto 1967: 383). Like the other elements of ritual in the tabernacle, they go back to a more primitive conception of deity. The tunic goes under the robe, but it may have sleeves, unlike the other vestments.

The balance and structure of the account emphasize those elements in Aaron's attire which express his representative function: the stones on which he bears the names of the sons of Israel 'before the LORD'—that is, in the tabernacle; Urim and Thummim in which he would 'bear the judgement of the Israelites'; the rosette with its inscription, which reminds YHWH that the whole people (not just Aaron) is 'holy to YHWH', so that any unintentional failures may be overlooked. During the monarchy, it was the king who was the representative of the people before God; it is likely that it was in the post-exilic period that the high priests took over this function, and perhaps much of the array ascribed here to Aaron was originally the king's.

(29:1–37) This chapter prescribes a ritual which is carried out in Lev 8, where it is again described in detail; Lev 9 goes on to describe the ritual of the eighth day, when Aaron enters fully on his priesthood. Fuller comment will therefore be found at LEV 8–9; for the details of the different sacrifices LEV 1–4; and for the 'elevation offering' (vv. 24, 26) Lev 7:28–38. Briefly, the elements of the ordination ritual are as follows: investiture in the sacred vestments (vv. 5–6, 8–9); anointing, a symbol of appointment (v. 7; only for Aaron, though 28:41 mentions anointing for them all); and ordination proper (vv. 10–35), which is a seven-day rite of passage (v. 35) consisting of particular sacrifices. The defining moment is the ritual in vv. 19–21, in which some of the blood of the 'ram of ordination' is smeared on representative extremities of the ordinands and the rest dashed on the sides of the altar. Cf. 24:6–8: the smearing or sprinkling of a token portion of the blood of a sacrifice which is at the same time made holy by its offering to God makes the person holy to God. The altar (vv. 36–7) also requires purification from any uncleanness it may have contracted, and consecration. 'Sin offering' and 'atonement' (NRSV) are clearly unsatisfactory translations in reference to an inanimate object: 'purification offering' and 'purification' (Milgrom 1991: 253–4) are better. Its consecration is not simply dedication: it becomes actively holy so as to engulf in its holiness anything that touches it: this is a warning, for it is certain death for anyone who is not already consecrated.

(29:38–42) Mention of the altar leads into instruction for its one regular daily use; but as I have suggested it also serves, with 27:20–1, to frame the instructions for the priesthood with a representative reminder of the daily need for a priesthood: Aaron to enter the tabernacle to dress the lamps, and his sons to serve at the altar. The prime reason for the existence of a public sanctuary is to offer public offerings paid for out of public resources (see 30:11–16) as a formal expression of the community's homage to its God. The Jerusalem temple under the monarchy would have had such a regular offering paid for

by the king: P needs to emphasize the importance of continuing it by placing its beginning in the wilderness.

(29:43–6) The speech comes to a fitting climax in which YHWH defines the purpose of all the elaborate provisions which he has been reciting, and makes it clear that they are the fulfilment of the promise he had made while the people were slaves in Egypt, that 'I will take you as my people, and I will be your God' (6:7). What he had not said there was that he would *meet* with them and *dwell* among them. It is the tent of meeting that makes this possible. And even though he has been giving directions for *Moses* to consecrate the tent, the altar, and the priests, he makes it clear that it is he himself, YHWH, who will really consecrate them, and he will do this by his presence, which is summed up in the symbol of his 'glory', which for P is a literal dazzling radiance. 'And they shall know…' (v. 46): of all the acts by which Israel comes to know their God, this, for P, is the supreme one, that he dwells among them and speaks with them.

(30:1–10) This may reflect an addition to the furniture of the Second Temple. Incense was at all times in the ancient Near East a common element of ritual; its sweet smell was held to attract the favour of the deity and appease the deity's wrath. But we more commonly hear of its being offered in censers carried in the hand. Although it is an addition to the ritual, it is fully integrated into the complex of acts of 'service' which Aaron performs in the tabernacle (vv. 7–8) (Haran 1985: 230–45). For v. 10, see Lev 16.

(30:11–16) During the monarchy the regular offering would have been the king's responsibility; in Neh 10:32–3 we find the community as a whole taking the responsibility on themselves through a poll-tax; the census ransom is P's version of this. It was an ancient belief that carrying out a census was a dangerous act which might arouse the envy of the deity: see 2 Sam 24. The token offering averts this, as well as providing for the offering.

(30:17–21) The concern here is not for ordinary dirt, but for ritual uncleanness (Lev 11–15), which to the priests, who are constantly in the holy place and handling holy things, is a constant threat. Washing the body is the normal way of removing low-grade uncleanness.

(30:22–38) These two sections each provide for the compounding of distinctive substances which are to be used exclusively in the service of the tabernacle. They are 'holy' (vv. 25, 36) both in this sense and as far as the oil is concerned in the sense that it is a sign which conveys holiness to the objects and persons which are anointed with it.

(31:1–11) Bezalel's qualifications come to him by a twofold action of YHWH, who both calls him and fills him with divine spirit. Although these graces are most frequently referred to as bestowing gifts of leadership and of prophecy, they are clearly not confined to those connections. P has laid stress throughout on the importance of the materials and design of the tabernacle and its furniture; they help to give them their holy character. It is therefore natural that the skill which is needed to create them should be seen as a divine gift.

(31:12–17) It is appropriate that the sabbath command should be repeated here, with its grounding in the creation account in Gen 1:1–2:3. The tabernacle represents God's heavenly dwelling-place, where he rested after his exertions in creation, and the sabbath represents his heavenly rest (cf. Levenson 1988: 79–99). The passage bears a number of marks of the style and concerns of the editor of the Holiness Code (Lev 17–26), who may have been the final editor of the Priestly material (Knohl 1994). The sabbath is not only holy itself, but is a way God has given of expressing the holiness of the people (v. 13). For the first time a penalty is given for breaking it (vv. 14–15): as with other offences against Israel's holiness to YHWH, it is death (cf. Lev 20).

(Chs. 32–4) Covenant Breaking and Renewal (For a thorough treatment of 32–4, see Moberley 1983; also Van Seters 1994: 290–360.) The story here takes a turn which is of great importance for the theological message of the book. After the people have solemnly accepted YHWH's covenant on the basis of his commandments, the first thing they do is to break the most fundamental of them; they desert the worship of YHWH for an idol. This is a 'test' (see 17:2) of the covenant, and of YHWH's commitment to his people, of the most radical sort. He would have every justification in destroying them and starting afresh, and says so in 32:10. But this does not happen; why not?

The story makes Moses responsible for reconciling YHWH to the people. Moses struggles with YHWH from 32:11 to 34:9, first to avert the threatened destruction, and then to ensure the full restoration of his presence with them and graciousness to them. And this he achieves. The people do nothing towards this, and make no renewed promises. They express no repentance for their apostasy; Moberly (1983: 60–1) shows that their mourning in 33:4 is not repentance. Moses here comes into his own as a heroic figure (see EX A). For months he has simply obeyed orders; now he not only acts on his own initiative, but, with deference but determination, sets himself against YHWH's expressed intention and fights on behalf of the people whom YHWH himself has made his responsibility, ignoring inducements (32:10), and putting his own life on the line for their sake (32:32). Aaron makes a pitiful contrast: 'Aaron was too weak to restrain the people; Moses was strong enough to restrain even God' (Childs 1974: 570). But if Moses acquires new stature in this episode, so too does YHWH. What Moses appeals to is YHWH's own promise and character. He cannot persuade him to do something that he does not want to do. And when YHWH at the climax of the story proclaims his own characteristics, what comes first is his mercy, steadfast love, and forgiveness (34:6–7). He proves himself a God able in the end to bear with a people who not only have sinned but are likely to go on sinning, as Moses confesses (34:9). The legalistic interpretation of the covenant, that breaking the commandment means death, suggested in 20:5, 23:21, and 32:10, is set aside without being formally repudiated (34:7b). It is on this basis that YHWH's presence is able to go with the people, as he has already promised in 33:17; and so the elaborate provisions that he has made for this are able to go forward.

We may treat this passage as a literary unity, though many would see 32:9–14 and 25–9 as later expansions (see Moberly 1983: 157–86 and Van Seters 1994: 290–5). Interesting questions arise when we compare the story, particularly 32:1–6, with the story of Jeroboam and his calves in 1 Kings 12. In both cases the cultic object is described as a golden calf, and the cry in 32:4 is identical to Jeroboam's announcement in 1 Kings 12:28. There can be no doubt that one or other of the writers has deliberately described the event in terms drawn from the other account. It is likely that Kings is the source. The bull was a common symbol of deity in Canaanite culture; it fits with this that the kingdom of Israel should have had bulls as its official cult symbols, and the story in 1 Kings 12 is a slanted and polemical account of how they were introduced. Calling the bulls 'calves' is deliberate disparagement, probably begun by Hosea (Hos 8:5, 6; 10:5). J follows his usual practice of tracing back key themes in Israel's later history into the wilderness period. (For another view, see Moberly 1983: 161–71.)

(32:1–6) The calf which Aaron makes is in the first place a subsitute for Moses, who represented God's guidance in a concrete way. Without him, the people feel the need for a visible expression of divine guidance. The course they urge on Aaron is described in terms which suggest that they are behaving exactly like pagans. Gods are something that can be made. Why 'gods', when there is only one image? Because to speak of 'gods' in the plural is typical of pagans (see 1 Sam 4:7–8; 1 Kings 20:23); the sentence is probably taken from 1 Kings 12:28, but not unthinkingly—the fact that there are two calves does not make it more appropriate there (see Moberly 1983: 163). Is the calf intended as an image of YHWH? It is hailed as having 'brought you up out of the land of Egypt', and the feast which Aaron announces is a festival for YHWH. But the author leaves no doubt that they are not really worshipping YHWH. See EX 20:2–6. Therefore the people have indeed broken the first commandment.

(32:7–14) This passage has caused difficulty. Why should Moses react so violently in v. 19 if YHWH had already told him on the mountain? How can the long process of intercession in 32:30–34:9 be understood if Moses has already secured YHWH's forgiveness in v. 14? It is a matter of literary technique. The key issues are set out here, right after the account of Israel's sin, and they govern the whole story. There is, in any case, no real difficulty in understanding Moses' reaction on actually seeing the worship of the golden calf; and it is often overlooked that Moses is not himself told of YHWH's change of heart. v. 14 is a narrative comment which gives the reader the advantage over Moses; as far as he knows, there is everything still to play for; and YHWH, as befits the seriousness of the sin, will not immediately reveal his forgiveness. 'Stiff-necked' (v. 9) is one of the motifs of the story, repeated in 33:3, 5; 34:9. In YHWH's demand 'Now let me alone', 'he pays such deference to [Moses'] prayers as to say they are a hindrance to him' (Calvin 1854: iii. 341); and he then indirectly reminds Moses of the right basis for such prayers. 'Of you I will make a great nation' recalls his promise to Abraham, Gen 12:2. Moses in his reply picks this up, as well as reminding YHWH of the danger to his reputation, which had been one of the main themes of the struggle with Pharaoh.

(32:15–24) The tablets are the focus in vv. 15–19. Moses' breaking of them appears to signify that the covenant is at an end, and this is confirmed in ch. 34, where a new covenant is made on conditions inscribed on new tablets. Could a calf made of gold be burnt and ground to powder? It is possible that the description has simply been taken over from Deut 9:21 (Van Seters 1994: 303–7); Deuteronomy does not say what the calf was made of. vv. 21–4 recall Gen 3. Aaron contrives to throw all the blame on the people and minimizes his own part, in contrast with Moses, who identifies himself with the people in his struggles with God.

(32:25–9) is another passage that has caused difficulty, partly because Moses inflicts a fearful punishment on the people, whereas elsewhere he pleads for forgiveness, partly because the punishment seems quite random. It should be noted that what Moses pleads against is the total destruction of the people, and then YHWH's withdrawal of his presence from Israel's midst; this does not rule out an exemplary punishment. v. 35 expresses the same idea, though it has been interpreted as the much later fulfilment of the threat in v. 34. The passage serves to account for the special position of the Levites in Israelite society.

(32:30–33:6) In this episode of intercession, Moses clearly does not achieve his object, though it is not easy to follow the conversations between Moses and YHWH because of their polite and allusive language. 32:33 rejects Moses' offer, and v. 34 warns that a time of punishment is yet to come. YHWH is not yet reconciled. For v. 35, see above on vv. 25–9. In 33:1–3 YHWH sends the people off to Canaan, but without his presence among them. The 'angel', as in 23:20, may represent YHWH and even be a form of his presence. But what he refuses to give them is his presence *among* them. Moberly (1983: 62–3) suggests that this presence would be experienced through the medium of a sanctuary; and the following section supports this.

(33:7–11) This section is a digression from the main thread of the narrative, but not an irrelevant digression. It describes not what Moses did next, but what he regularly did; the period over which he did it is not specified, but see Num 11 and Deut 31:14–15. It is mentioned to make clear how Moses was still able to communicate with YHWH although he had refused his presence in their midst. He does it through the medium of a tent shrine; but unlike the one provided for in chs. 25–6 it is pitched way outside the camp, a clear enough sign of the danger of YHWH's coming any closer. v. 11 underlines the special privilege of Moses in speaking with YHWH 'face to face', and this leads in appropriately to the next passage of intercession.

Although P takes over the name 'tent of meeting', there are many differences between this tent and his, besides its location. It is a place not of priestly service and sacrifice but of prophetic revelation, and YHWH appears not in its innermost recesses but at its entrance. It has been conjectured that this tent of meeting was an ancient prophetic institution in Israel. But Van Seters (1994: 341–4) suggests that it is J's imaginative reconstruction.

(33:12–23) The story of Moses' intercession with YHWH is taken up again at the point where it was left in 33:4. Moses' object is to gain YHWH's personal presence among the people. In v. 14 the translation 'I will go with you' (NRSV and others) makes nonsense of the conversation. Only in v. 17 does YHWH finally grant Moses what he has been asking for, his presence *with* the people. At v. 14 all he says is 'My presence will go', without the vital word 'with'. Moses' success

is remarkable: a holy God has agreed to be present with a people who are still sinful and show no serious sign of repentance. Moses' further request in v. 18 seems at first sight to be purely selfish. But it becomes clear when YHWH grants it (in his own way) in 34:5–7 that the vision of his 'goodness' which he has promised Moses has everything to do with the people's need of mercy and forgiveness. Moses has achieved much, but he has still not gained the main point, absolute forgiveness. The answer he got to the direct request in 32:32 was not encouraging, so he tries an indirect one, and this time receives definite, though still indirect, encouragement (v. 20). YHWH is merciful, though he reserves to himself absolute discretion in deciding whom to be merciful to.

(34:1–9) The episode moves to its climax. YHWH's order to Moses in v. 1 leaves no doubt now that he intends to restore the covenant shattered with the tablets in 32:19. Moses alone goes up the mountain. The people's rebellion leaves them no role but humbly to accept their Lord's good pleasure. YHWH's proclamation of his own name and qualities in vv. 6–7 is another version of the descriptions in 20:5–6 and Deut 7:9–10, and is itself repeatedly quoted elsewhere (e.g. Ps 103:8). It lays stress on his forgiveness, and avoids saying that he is gracious 'to those that love me and keep my commandments'. The centre is his 'steadfast love' (Heb. *ḥesed*; other translations 'faithfulness', 'mercy'). This is the gracious favour which a patron shows to those who have come under his protection (or the loyalty which they show to him); it is gracious and yet at the same time required of him by the relationship, an idea difficult for us to grasp in a society which has separated institutional obligation and personal motivation (cf. Kippenberg 1982: 32). There remains a paradox in the proclamation: YHWH forgives iniquity, and yet he also punishes it, even to the fourth generation. As we have already seen, punishment is not excluded even where he has resolved to forgive. The essential thing is that the relationship is restored and maintained in perpetuity, however much Israel's sinfulness may test it.

(34:10–28) And this is what YHWH promises in his proclamation 'I hereby make a covenant'. A covenant, because what he now does is new. The precise reference of the rest of v. 10 is unclear; even whether 'you' is Moses or Israel; but it is clear that the covenant is primarily YHWH's promise to Moses to forgive Israel. There are conditions; they are not new, but almost entirely a selection of the commandments from the Book of the Covenant (see EX 20:22–23:33) with particular emphasis on the exclusive worship of YHWH. vv. 11–16 are a rewriting of 23:23–4, 32–3; v. 17 is a version of 20:23; and vv. 18–26 are 23:15–19 with some expansion, mostly from 13:12–13 (cf. 22:29–30). The implication is that, as YHWH has already said in 34:1, the covenant terms are still in force, but it is not necessary for the author to repeat the entire code, as only certain things need to be emphasized. Moses is commanded to write the words, as he had done in 24:4. The text in 28 seems to say that Moses wrote on the tablets. But YHWH has already said (34:1) that he himself would write the words on them. So probably the subject of the last sentence in v. 28 is YHWH, and Moses is thought of as writing a separate copy. But what did YHWH write? Up to this point the implication has been that it would be the words in vv. 11–26, yet the text

adds that it was 'the ten commandments'. This can only mean
20:2–17. The likely explanation is that someone has added the
words 'the ten commandments', remembering that in Deut 5
it is these which are written on the tablets and trying to make
Exodus and Deuteronomy agree.

(34:29–35) The shining of Moses' face as a sign of intense
spiritual experience is not unparalleled: one might think of
Jesus' transfiguration (Mk 9:2–8) or the experience reported
of St Seraphim of Sarov. It is not clear why Moses puts a veil
over his face when he has finished reporting YHWH's commands, unless perhaps simply to avoid standing out unnecessarily when not performing his religious and leadership
functions.

(Chs. 35–40) The Building of the Sanctuary With the covenant relationship restored, the instructions given by YHWH
to create a sanctuary for him can now be carried out. This
account obviously depends very closely on chs. 25–31; in the
parts which describe the actual construction the instructions
are reproduced word for word with the appropriate changes.
As the incense altar and laver are described in their proper
places, the account was obviously written from the start in
dependence on the whole passage chs. 25–31 including its
afterthoughts. Every paragraph concludes 'as YHWH had
commanded Moses' to underline the authority behind the
construction. As the instructions had concluded with the
repetition of the sabbath command, Moses' commands to
the Israelites begin with it. A detailed account of the offering
follows in 35:4–36:7, together with the calling of Bezalel and
Oholiab. The construction of the various items occupies 36:8–
39:43. The account begins with the tabernacle itself before
moving on to the furniture which is placed in it. It is broken
only by the account of the contributed metals in 38:24–31. This
does not reproduce any single passage in 25–31, but is deduced
from its data; as far as the silver is concerned the figure in
38:25 is derived from the census figure in Num 1:46 on the
assumption that the ransom commanded in 30:11–16 was
intended for the construction.

(38:8) No one can really explain this odd note. 1 Sam 2:22 is
no help.

When all is complete, YHWH gives the order to set the
tabernacle up and consecrate it and ordain its priesthood
(40:1–15). For the fulfilment of much of this we must wait
till Lev 8; but here we are told of the setting up of the tabernacle (40:16–33), and this is followed immediately by the
climax of the whole account, the entry of the glory of YHWH
into his dwelling-place. The glory is described as cloud and
fire, as it appeared on Sinai in 24:16–17. The object of all the
work has been achieved: the presence of YHWH, as it had
been on Sinai, is with his people for ever, and guides them on
their journeys.

REFERENCES

Albertz, R. (1994), *A History of Israelite Religion in the Old Testament Period* (2 vols.; London: SCM).

Alter, R. (1981), *The Art of Biblical Narrative* (London: Allen & Unwin).

Auffret, P. (1983), 'The Literary Structure of Ex. 6.2–8', *JSOT* 27: 46–54.

Bimson, J. J. (1978), *Redating the Exodus and Conquest*, JSOTSup 5 (Sheffield: JSOT).

Blenkinsopp, J. (1992), *The Pentateuch: An Introduction to the First Five Books of the Bible* (London: SCM).

Brenner, M. L. (1991), *The Song of the Sea: Ex. 15, 1–21*, BZAW 195 (Berlin: de Gruyter).

Brichto, H. C. (1963), *The Problem of 'Curse' in the Hebrew Bible*, JBL Monograph Ser. 13 (Philadelphia: Society for Biblical Literature and Exegesis).

Brueggemann, W. (1995), 'Pharaoh as Vassal: A Study of a Political Metaphor', *CBQ* 57: 27–51.

Calvin, J. (1854), *Commentary on the Four Last Books of Moses, arranged in the Form of a Harmony*, tr. C. W. Bingham (4 vols.; Edinburgh: Calvin Translation Society).

—— (1953), *Institutes of the Christian Religion*, tr. H. Beveridge (2 vols.; London: James Clarke).

Cassuto, U. (1967), *A Commentary on Exodus* (Jerusalem: Magnes).

Childs, B. S. (1974), *Exodus: A Commentary* (London: SCM).

Chirichigno, G. C. (1993), *Debt-Slavery in Israel and the Ancient Near East*, JSOTSup 141 (Sheffield: JSOT).

Clines, D. (1995a), 'The Ten Commandments, Reading from Left to Right', in *Interested Parties: The Ideology of Writers and Readers of the Hebrew Bible* (Sheffield: Sheffield Academic Press), 26–45.

—— (1995b), 'God in the Pentateuch; Reading against the Grain', ibid. 187–211.

Croatto, J. S. (1981), *Exodus: A Hermeneutics of Freedom* (Maryknoll, NY: Orbis Books).

Cross, F. M. (1973), 'The Song of the Sea and Canaanite Myth', in *Canaanite Myth and Hebrew Epic* (Cambridge, Mass.: Harvard University Press), 112–44.

Daube, D. (1947), *Studies in Biblical Law* (Cambridge: Cambridge University Press).

Davies, G. I. (1979), *The Way of the Wilderness: A Geographical Study of the Wilderness Itineraries in the Old Testament*, SOTSMS 5 (Cambridge: Cambridge University Press).

Dever, W. G. (1992), 'Israel, History of (Archaeology and the "Conquest")', *ABD* iii. 545–58.

Durham, J. I. (1987), *Exodus*, WBC (Waco, Tex.: Word Books).

Exum, J. C. (1993), '"You Shall Let Every Daughter Live": A Study of Exodus 1.8–2.10', *Semeia*, 28: 53–82, repr. in Athalya Brenner (ed.), *A Feminist Companion to Exodus to Deuteronomy* (Sheffield: Sheffield Academic Press, 1994), 37–61.

—— (1994), 'Second Thoughts about Secondary Characters: Women in Exodus 1.8–2.10', ibid. 75–87.

Fewell, D. N. and Gunn, D. M. (1993), *Gender, Power and Promise: The Subject of the Bible's First Story* (Nashville: Abingdon).

Finkelstein, I. (1988), *The Archaeology of the Israelite Settlement* (Jerusalem: Israel Exploration Society).

Friedman, R. E. (1992), 'Tabernacle' in *ABD* vi. 292–300.

Gerstenberger, E. (1965), *Wesen und Herkunft des 'apodiktischen Rechts'*, WMANT 20 (Neukirchen-Vluyn: Neukirchener Verlag).

Gottwald, N. K. (1980), *The Tribes of Yahweh: A Sociology of Liberated Israel, 1250–1050 B.C.E.* (London, SCM).

Gowan, D. E. (1994), *Theology in Exodus: Biblical Theology in the Form of a Commentary* (Louisville, Ky.: Westminster/John Knox).

Gunn, D. M. (1982), 'The Hardening of Pharaoh's Heart', in David J. A. Clines, David M. Gunn, and Alan J. Hauser (eds.), *Art and Meaning: Rhetoric in Biblical Literature*, JSOTSup 19 (Sheffield: JSOT), 72–96.

Gutiérrez, G. (1988), *A Theology of Liberation*, rev. edn. (London: SCM).

Habel, N. (1965), 'The Form and Significance of the Call Narratives', *ZAW* 77: 297–323.

Haran, M. (1985), *Temples and Temple Service in Ancient Israel*, 2nd edn. (Winona Lake, Ind.: Eisenbrauns).

Herrmann, J. (1927), 'Das zehnte Gebot', in A. Jirku (ed.), *Sellin-Festschrift* (Leipzig: A. Deichert), 69–82.

Herrmann, S. (1973), *Israel in Egypt*, CSBT 2nd ser. 27 (London: SCM).

Hort, G. (1957–8), 'The Plagues of Egypt', *ZAW* 69: 84–103; 70: 48–59.

Houston, W. (1993), *Purity and Monotheism: Clean and Unclean Animals in Biblical Law*, JSOTSup 140 (Sheffield: JSOT).

—— (1997), 'Misunderstanding or Midrash?', *ZAW* 109: 342–55.

Houtman, C. (1993), *Exodus*, Historical Commentary on the Old Testament (3 vols.; vols. i, ii (1996) Kampen: Kok, vol. iii Leuven: Peeters, 2000), i.

Hughes, J. (1990), *Secrets of the Times: Myth and History in Biblical Chronology*, JSOTSup 66 (Sheffield: JSOT).

Jackson, B. S. (1989), 'Ideas of Law and Legal Administration', in R. E. Clements (ed.), *The World of Ancient Israel* (Cambridge: Cambridge University Press), 185–202.

Janzen, J. G. (1992), 'Song of Moses, Song of Miriam: Who is Seconding Whom?', *CBQ* 54: 211–20, repr. in Athalya Brenner (ed.), *A Feminist Companion to Exodus to Deuteronomy* (Sheffield: Sheffield Academic Press, 1994), 187–99.

Jenson, P. P. (1992), *Graded Holiness*, JSOTS 106 (Sheffield: Sheffield Academic Press).

Johnstone, W. (1990), *Exodus*, Old Testament Guides (Sheffield: JSOT).

Kippenberg, H. G. (1982), *Religion und Klassenbildung im antiken Judäa: Eine religionssoziologische Studie zum Verhältnis von Tradition und gesellschaftlicher Entwicklung* (SUNT 14), 2nd edn. (Göttingen: Vandenhoeck & Ruprecht).

Kirkpatrick, P. (1988), *The Old Testament and Folklore Study*, JSOTSup 62 (Sheffield: Sheffield Academic Press).

Knohl, I. (1994), *The Sanctuary of Silence: The Priestly Torah and the Holiness School* (Minneapolis: Fortress).

Lang, B. (1983), 'The Social Organization of Peasant Poverty in Biblical Israel', in *Monotheism and the Prophetic Minority* (Sheffield: Almond), 114–27, repr. in Lang, Bernhard (ed.), *Anthropological Approaches to the Old Testament* (London: SPCK, 1985), 83–99.

Levenson, J. D. (1988), *Creation and the Persistence of Evil* (San Francisco: Harper & Row).

Luther, M. (1896), 'The Larger Catechism', in Wace and Buchheim (eds.), *Luther's Primary Works*, ii.

Mendenhall, G. E. (1992a), 'Covenant' in *ABD*, i. 1179–1202.

—— (1992b), 'Midian' in *ABD*, iv. 815–18.

Mettinger, T. N. D. (1982), *The Dethronement of Sabaoth: Studies in the Shem and Kabod Theologies*, ConBOT 18 (Lund: Gleerup).

—— (1995), *No Graven Image? Israelite Aniconism in its Ancient Near Eastern Context*, ConBoT (Stockholm: Almqvist & Wiksell Int.).

Meyers, C. (1976), *The Tabernacle Menorah* (Missoula, Mont.: Scholars Press).

Milgrom, J. (1991), *Leviticus 1–16*, AB 3 (New York: Doubleday).

Miranda, J. P. (1973), *Marx and the Bible* (London, SCM).

Moberly, R. W. L. (1983), *At the Mountain of God: Story and Theology in Exodus 32–34*, JSOTSup 22 (Sheffield: JSOT).

—— (1992), *The Old Testament of the Old Testament: Patriarchal Narratives and Mosaic Yahwism* (Minneapolis: Fortress).

Moran, W. L. (1967), 'The Conclusion of the Decalogue (Ex. 20, 17 = Dt. 5, 21)', *CBQ* 29, 543–4.

Nicholson, E. W. (1986), *God and his People: Covenant and Theology in the Old Testament* (Oxford: Clarendon).

Noth, M. (1962), *Exodus: A Commentary* (London: SCM).

Patrick, D. (1986), *Old Testament Law* (London: SCM).

—— (1994), 'Is the Truth of the First Commandment Known by Reason?', *CBQ* 56: 423–41.

Phillips, A. C. J. (1970), *Ancient Israel's Criminal Law: A New Approach to the Decalogue* (Oxford: Blackwell).

Ramsey, G. W. (1981), *The Quest for the Historical Israel* (London: SCM).

Redford, D. B. (1963), 'Exodus 1, 11', *VT* 13: 401–18.

Robertson, D. (1977), *The Old Testament and the Literary Critic* (Philadelphia: Fortress).

Robertson, E. (1948), 'The Altar of Earth (Exodus xx, 24–26)', *JJS* 1: 12–21.

Robinson, G. (1988), *The Origin and Development of the Old Testament Sabbath*, BBET 21 (Bern: Peter Lang).

Römer, T. (1994), 'De l'archaïque au subversif: le cas d'Exode 4/24–26', *ETR* 69: 1–12.

Rost, L. (1943), 'Weidewechsel und altisraelitischer Festkalendar', *ZDPV* 66: 205–16.

Schmidt, B. B. (1995), 'The Aniconic Tradition: On Reading Images and Viewing Texts', in Diana V. Edelman (ed.), *The Triumph of Elohim* (Kampen: Kok Pharos), 75–105.

Schmidt, W. H. (1988), *Exodus 1. Teilband: Exodus 1–6*, BKAT (Neukirchen-Vluyn: Neukirchener Verlag).

Smith, G. A. (1918), *The Book of Deuteronomy*, Cambridge Bible for Schools and Colleges (Cambridge: Cambridge University Press).

Sprinkle, J. M. (1994), *'The Book of the Covenant', a Literary Approach*, JSOTSup 174 (Sheffield: JSOT).

Trible, P. (1994), 'Bringing Miriam out of the Shadows', in Athalya Brenner (ed.), *A Feminist Companion to Exodus to Deuteronomy* (Sheffield: Sheffield Academic Press), 166–86; repr. from *Bible Review* 5/1 (1989), 170–90.

Van Seters, J. (1994), *The Life of Moses: The Yahwist as Historian in Exodus–Numbers* (Kampen: Kok Pharos).

Vaux, R. de (1978), *The Early History of Israel* (2 vols.; London: Darton, Longman & Todd).

—— (1961), *Ancient Israel, its Life and Institutions* (London: Darton, Longman & Todd).

Wambacq, B. N. (1976), 'Les Origines de la *Pesah* israelite', *Biblica*, 57: 206–24, 301–26.

Weinfeld, M. (1991), *Deuteronomy 1–11* AB 5 (New York: Doubleday).

Wilson, R. R. (1977), *Genealogy and History in the Biblical World*, YNER 7 (New Haven: Yale University Press).

Zimmerli, W. (1968), 'Das zweite Gebot', in *Gottes Offenbarung* (Munich: Kaiser), 234–48.

—— (1982), 'I am Yahweh', in *I am Yahweh* (Atlanta: John Knox), 1–28.

6. Leviticus

LESTER L. GRABBE

INTRODUCTION

A. Structure and Contents. 1. The structure and content of Leviticus as a whole can be briefly outlined as follows:

Sacrificial system (chs. 1–7)
  Introduction (1:1–2)
  Whole burnt offering (1:3–17)
  Cereal offering (ch. 2)
  Well-being offering (ch. 3)
  Sin offering (chs. 4–5)
    Normal sin offering (ch. 4)
    Graduated sin offering (5:1–13)

2. At various points in this commentary, the form critical structure of passages will be discussed. For further detailed information on the structure and contents of Leviticus, one should consult the Leviticus volume of the Abingdon series, the Forms of Old Testament Literature, when it appears. In the meantime, the commentary by Hartley (1992) is very valuable for its extensive discussion of the form criticism of each section of the book.

B. History of the Tradition. 1. We can say with some confidence that the book of Leviticus has had a long period of growth, with numerous additions and editings. Scholarship is practically unanimous on this point. We can also state that much of the material within it seems to derive from priestly circles. Thus, Leviticus is a 'Priestly' document as it now stands, whether or not there was a P source as envisaged by the Documentary Hypothesis. More controversial are the precise stages of this growth. In recent years many monographs, as well as commentaries, have attempted to tease out the different layers (in addition to the writers cited below, see Reventlow 1961; Kilian 1963; Rendtorff 1963; Koch 1959).

2. The Documentary Hypothesis has dominated study of the Pentateuch for the past century (see INTROD. PENT B). According to that theory, most of Leviticus belongs to the Priestly source (P), though the P writers may have used a

diversity of material in composing it. For example, many would see chs. 17–26 (usually referred to as H, for the Holiness Code) as originally a separate block of material which was taken over by P. Since Wellhausen's time, this dating to the sixth century—whether the exilic or the early post-exilic period—has remained fairly constant among critics. An exception was Vink who put it in the fourth century, though few have followed him. All agree that this is only the date of the final form of the work, though, since the editor/author drew on various priestly traditions, some of them of substantial antiquity.

3. In recent years, however, there have been two challenges to this consensus: (1) some ask whether P may not date from before the Exile (see below), and (2) others have questioned whether the traditional alleged sources exist at all (Whybray 1987). Although biblical fundamentalists have continually rejected the Documentary Hypothesis for dogmatic reasons, it should not be assumed that recent challenges fall into the same category. While some of the arguments may have been around a long time, those who oppose the old consensus do so for critical reasons which have nothing to do with a desire to 'defend' the biblical text.

4. The question of P is discussed at length above (INTROD. PENT B.5) and need not be repeated here. I shall only point out that the composition and dating of the book of Leviticus is very much tied up with the question of when P is to be dated—assuming that it exists. One school of thought, currently a minority but with a growing number of adherents and a strong voice in the debate, now favours a pre-exilic dating (Haran 1978; Milgrom 1991; Hurvitz 1982, 1988; Zevit 1982). Indeed, Milgrom even suggests that P was originally composed for the pre-monarchic territory centring on the temple at Shiloh. On the other hand, Gerstenberger (1993) continually discusses how the book fits into the situation in the post-exilic community, and Blenkinsopp (1996) has recently challenged the linguistic arguments of Hurvitz and others for a pre-exilic dating. A further factor to consider is the current debate on the history of Israel in which a number of scholars are arguing that the present text of the HB is no earlier than the Persian period and perhaps even later (see e.g. Lemche 1993). This debate has taken on a new impetus with the launch of the European Seminar on Historical Methodology (see Grabbe 1997).

5. The question is rightly being vigorously debated on several fronts, and I believe it is premature to anticipate the outcome. Yet we should not forget that there is some agreement on several issues. One is that the present form of the book was not reached until the Persian period; another is that the text as it now stands incorporates some material of considerable antiquity. Finally, the book probably says a good deal about the temple cult in the Second Temple period, but one should be cautious in assuming it is an actual description of what went on at that time. For this last point, see further below ('Leviticus and the Actual Temple Cult').

6. Throughout the rest of this commentary on Leviticus, I shall often refer to P, by which the material normally identified as part of the P document is being referred to. However, in each case one should always understand the qualifying phrase, 'if it exists' or 'as normally identified'. I have no intention of begging the question of whether P exists or, if so, what it consisted of.

7. The Holiness Code. Lev 17–26 is commonly divided off from the rest as the so-called Holiness Code (H), with ch. 27 as an appendix to the book. Not all would accept this delineation, but most would agree that within 17–26 is another document which has been incorporated into the present book but is not necessarily fully integrated with 1–16. That is, both 1–16 and 17–26 are collections with their own stages of growth, but each has a relative unity which marks it off from the other. There are tensions between the two parts, with some major differences of outlook on certain issues. There is also the difficult problem of trying to give the relative dates of the two collections. In the past it was customary to consider H earlier than most of the material in 1–16. Nevertheless, a number of prominent scholars had not accepted the existence of H as such. For example, Elliger had proposed several independent legal corpora which had been brought together, with several redactional hands. A. Cholewski took a similar view. I. Knohl (1995; cf. 1987), although accepting the existence of H, has come to the conclusion that it was later than Lev 1–16. He argues the question mainly on the basis of Lev 23 which he thinks is constructed on Num 28–9. Knohl concludes that there were two priestly schools, one that produced the earlier P document and the other that not only wrote H (the later document) but also did the final editing of the Pentateuch. Similarly, Milgrom (1991) has taken the position that most of H is later than most of 1–16, and in his opinion H was one of the editors of the book.

8. Methods and Approaches to Interpretation. Having now seen a general consensus that the book grew up over a long period of time, the reader might ask, 'What level of the book do we interpret?' There is more than one legitimate answer to the question. In recent years, many interpreters have argued for the final form of the text as the primary object of study, whatever the stages of growth of the book or its dating. This has led to a number of new disciplines under the general rubric of the 'literary approach' to the biblical text, including 'close reading', structuralism, deconstruction, and rhetorical criticism. So far, few seem to have applied these to Leviticus specifically (but see Damrosch (1987) and Schwarz (1991) for examples). From a different perspective, those interested in the 'canonical' form of the text for theological purposes are also concerned mainly with the final form of the text (see esp. Childs 1979). Douglas (1993: 8–12) has recently argued that the book can be properly understood only if one recognizes a basic ring structure of the text in its present form.

9. This does not mean that the final form of the text has been ignored even by some of the traditional disciplines. For decades, many form critics have practised a structural analysis of the text as we have it before asking questions of growth or even questions of genre and the like. The results of this approach can be seen in the series Forms of Old Testament Literature edited by R. P. Knierim and G. Tucker. Knierim's recent book (1992) on exegesis combines traditional form criticism with broader concerns, including theological and sociological ones. Some exegetes, while not abandoning traditional source criticism, have severely demoted it in their concerns. For example, although Rendtorff (1982–95: 4) does not reject 'reconstruction' of earlier phases of the tradition, he thinks these should be seen primarily as an aid to understanding the present text.

10. This by no means suggests that older methods of source criticism and the like can be forgotten. On the contrary, they are often presupposed in the new methods. This means that traditio-historical analysis is very important for two further legitimate stages to be interpreted. The second level of interpretation is that of the book as a part of the P document (see below). A third object of interpretation would be the various levels in the growth of the book as determined by form and redaction criticism. This is the most hypothetical and is less favoured today for that very reason (cf. Rendtorff 1982–95: 4), yet most commentators give some attention to the internal growth of the book, and many see it as their primary concern.

C. Importance of the Cult to Ancient Israel. 1. It is easy for modern Christians to dismiss the Levitical and other passages dealing with the sacrificial cult as outdated or irrelevant. For that reason, the cult is often slighted or even ignored when Israel's religion is discussed. But it must not be forgotten that many Jews still observe the regulations concerning ritual purity, in some form or other, even though the sacrificial regulations can no longer be applied in the absence of a functioning temple. Any description of Israelite religion has to take stock of its complexities, but one cannot get away from the fact that the sacrificial cult, especially blood sacrifice, lay at the heart of worship in Israel. On the other hand, the Israelite cult, like all religious ritual—and all religions have their ritual—was extremely meaningful to the participants even if we do not always understand it from our time and culture millennia later. A number of recent studies have focused on the symbolism of the cult and attempted to decipher the priestly world-view that lay behind it. For example, Gorman (1990) argues that a complex creation theology is presupposed and represented by the cult, and Jenson (1992) has made similar points. The priestly view had a cosmological and sociological dimension, as well as a cultic. In order to express this, it made distinctions between holy and profane, clean and unclean, life and death, order and chaos.

2. The idea of sacrifice seems to be ubiquitous among human societies the world over. Even those which have abandoned it in their contemporary form, especially in the developed countries, have sacrifice as a part of their past. Since the concept goes so far back in human history that its origins are no longer traceable, we are left only with hypothesis and speculation as to how sacrifice came to be a part of the religious culture of most peoples. (For further information, see the account of the debate in Grabbe 1993: 43–7.) But the inescapable conclusion seems to be that central to most sacrifices are the notions of expiation, cleansing, and re-establishment of cosmic—or at least microcosmic—harmony. If evil cannot be removed, sin wiped away, pollution purified, and harmony restored, there would be little point in sacrifice. Therefore, regardless of the precise terms in which sacrifices are conceived (substitution, ritual detergent, etc.), the desired outcome is clear. The scapegoat sort of ceremony is perhaps not strictly a sacrifice, in that the animal is not killed (though according to later Jewish tradition, the scapegoat was pushed over a cliff: *m. Yoma* 6:6; cf. Grabbe 1987), but the concept seems to be very much the same as that of sacrifice. In this case, the sins are heaped onto the head of the victim which is then separated from the community. In other cases, the victim is in some way identified with the offerer even if precise identification is not required. The laying of the hands on the victim by the offerer in Israelite sacrifice may have a function along these lines. But regardless of the rite, the desire is to cause the sins, pollutions, illness, or troubles to vanish.

3. Perhaps one of the most misunderstood concepts is that of ritual purity. It has little or nothing to do with hygiene or with the clean/dirty distinction in a physical sense. For example, in the Israelite system, excrement was not usually included in the category of unclean, even though ancient Israelites had much the same view towards it that we do today. One of the important discoveries of anthropology in the past half-century is that purity and pollution systems are not arcane, primitive superstition. The precise form of the rituals may well be arbitrary, at least to some extent, but recent study suggests that broader concerns are at the heart of the purity system. The insights offered by social and cultural anthropology have gone a long way towards explaining the deeper meaning and foundation of these laws which may seem primitive to many today. Purity and pollution form an important mirror of the society itself, especially its social relations and attitudes. They map the ideological cosmos of the people who hold these views. These regulations can be seen as a language, in the broad sense of the term, communicating to those within the society the 'correct' attitudes towards relations between the sexes, marriage, kinship, and intercourse with outsiders. Ritual cleanliness tells the people how to classify the entities—human and animal—which inhabit the world around them and communicates to the society how to fit in new forms which enter its world. The animal world and how it is treated is also a map of human society, and the human community is represented by the body of the individual.

4. One of the major attempts to work out the meaning of the biblical system in detail was by Mary Douglas in her seminal book *Purity and Danger* (1966; for an account of this book and criticisms of it, see Grabbe 1993: 56–9). Despite some criticisms against Douglas, some of her points about the meaning of the system in Israelite society have not been affected and still seem valid, especially the notion that the system of permitted and forbidden animals was a microcosm of the world according to the Israelite view. The many forbidden animals represented the surrounding nations; the few clean animals, the Israelites; and the sacrificial animals, the priests. Just as Israelites were not to eat certain animals, they were not to mix with other nations. The dietary regulations had both a practical and a symbolic function; symbolically they stood for the fact that Israel was to keep itself free from intercourse with non-Israelites; practically, inability to eat certain animals meant that Jews could not socialize with those who ate these animals. The rules of pollution and purity also drew strict boundaries around the altar and sanctuary. No pollution and no polluted persons were allowed to penetrate into the sacred area. This clear and rigid boundary drawing suggests a concern with political boundaries as well as social ones. Just as the Israelites were concerned about mixing with the surrounding peoples, so their political boundaries may have been threatened by others who claimed the territory for themselves. If so, the message of the rules which, on the surface, might seem arcane ritual turn out to be a rich symbolic system with significant meaning for understanding the concerns of ancient Israel.

D. Women and the Cult. 1. The place of women in society and literature has become a much-discussed subject in the past couple of decades (see e.g. Newsom and Ringe 1992; Schüssler Fiorenza 1994*a* and *b*). Some have seen the treatment of women as very negative. It is not my purpose to enter into this debate, but Wegner (1992) gives a mainly positive assessment of Leviticus on women, recognizing its general context in the ancient world. Women are mentioned specifically in only two sections of Leviticus: one concerns childbirth, which made a woman impure for ritual purposes (Lev 12). In order to be allowed to re-enter the temple, she had to undergo a period of cleansing which culminated in sacrifices in the temple. The implication is that the woman herself is envisaged as participating in the sacrificial cult. Although the directions relating to sacrifice are addressed in the masculine form of the verb (whether singular or plural), this could be thought to include women under normal circumstances. Women are not specifically excluded in the P legislation. If women were not allowed to enter the altar area, as was the case in the time of the Second Temple, this is nowhere stated.

2. The other occasion of impurity with women was menstruation (15:19–24). The regulations about bodily issues in Lev 12–15 do not make a particular point about menstruation; on the contrary, it is only one of a number of issues of blood or fluid which are polluting. Nevertheless, most of the other regulations concern unusual occurrences, whereas the rules about menstruation would regularly affect all women between puberty and menopause, as well as their families more indirectly. It is clear that these purity regulations were extremely important to all Israelites of both sexes. However, it should be noted that menstruation, like the impurity contracted from normal sexual intercourse, did not require a sacrifice for cleansing. These were in a different category from 'abnormal' discharges.

3. Anthropological studies have suggested that regulations about menstruation often mirror the relationship between the sexes and the place of either sex within the society. Societies in which women have considerable freedom of choice and independence from men will usually have this reflected in various customs about ritual purity, including menstruation. Those societies in which women are restricted to a particular place and function and are discouraged from entering the province of men will usually have constrictive regulations about menstruation.

4. It seems clear that in Israelite society, women had a particular sphere and place in which they were confined. They were not generally allowed to participate in activities which were associated with the male Israelite. These customs were not necessarily absolute since the OT tradition has stories of exceptional women who broke through the traditional boundaries. But any woman who carefully observed the rules about menstrual pollution would have found her activities severely restricted in certain ways. A similar purpose seems to be associated with the rules surrounding childbirth. The longer purification time after bearing a daughter could be a symbol that women had an appropriate place in society which was different from that of men. On the other hand, any evaluation of these regulations would do well to take account of the fact that many Jews still observe these or similar regulations today and give them a positive value (cf. Wegner 1992).

E. Leviticus and the Actual Temple Cult. 1. Does Leviticus (or it and the rest of P) describe the rites in the temple, or is it merely a theoretical document, a programme, or even a mere fantasy? We can say with some confidence that Leviticus does not describe the cult in a tabernacle built by the Israelites under Moses during 40 years in the wilderness. The whole story as described in the biblical text (from Exodus to the end of Deuteronomy) is now generally rejected by biblical scholars. A generation ago, many would have given greater credence to the story, or at least certain parts of it. New archaeological information and further study has convinced most that Israel did not enter the land as a unified group out of the wilderness after escaping from Egypt. Rather, even if some had been in Egypt, they would have been a small group. The bulk of those who came to make up Israel were probably indigenous people in some sense, though there may also have been immigrants from outside the area. Those who coalesced to produce Israel no doubt had their shrines, permanent or portable, but the description of building the tabernacle in Exodus is fiction as it stands. For example, the altar described in Exodus is made of wood and bronze. This sort of construction would hardly stand the heat of the fire necessary to consume the sacrificial portions, and any actual altar was probably made of stone and earth (Gerstenberger 1993: 29). Nevertheless, some reality may have lain behind it. What might that have been?

2. It is possible that the description in P is purely hypothetical or utopian. Priests who had a vision of an idealized cult could write it up and present it as if that was what happened long ago under Moses. There is no doubt that we find a certain amount of idealization in the description of the tabernacle and the setting up of its cult. However, most scholars would see some relationship to what went on in an actual temple or shrine. Those who date P to the post-exilic period consider the Priestly material to reflect generally the situation in the Second Temple which was built in the early Persian period. If P is dated to the exilic period, one would expect that it is presenting a programme for a renewed cult in Jerusalem (which was expected imminently), with the hope of influencing the structure of the new cult.

3. Cross (1947) advanced the thesis that the tent of David, which housed the ark before and after its removal to Jerusalem but before the temple was built, was the basis of the tabernacle tradition. The proposal of Haran (1962), followed by Milgrom (1991), makes the core of Leviticus relate to the temple at Shiloh in the early period of the monarchy. Part of Milgrom's argument concerns later editings which attempted to bring the material up to date, with some of these even as late as the post-exilic period. Therefore, despite possible earlier origins the cult and regulations in the present text of Leviticus in most cases can be related to the practice in the First Temple.

4. What most would accept is that Leviticus represents to a large extent actual cultic practice, despite some tensions and contradictions. No doubt there have been editings, perhaps in part because of changes and developments in actual practice.

But it is also likely that many cultic procedures remained essentially unchanged over long periods of time (Rendtorff 1985–92: 5; Grabbe 1995: 207). The many differences in detail between Leviticus and other passages in the OT do not suggest major differences in the overall shape of the cult. Those who see Leviticus as by and large a description of cultic observance in the Second Temple period are probably correct since, even if much of it goes back to the First Temple, the same practices were probably continued when the temple was rebuilt.

COMMENTARY

Chs. 1–7 describe the sacrificial system. Contrary to popular opinion, there is more to the book of Leviticus than just a description of various sacrifices. Nevertheless, the cult was central to Israelite worship, and it is important to understand the sacrifices if one wishes to understand Israelite religion (see C.1–2 above). It was through the sacrificial cult that sins were forgiven and evil was removed from the land. And an important question is what was thought to happen when an animal was slain at the altar. Milgrom (1976) has dismissed the idea of the sacrificial victim being a substitute for the sinner. He does acknowledge, though, that on the 'day of *kippûrîm*' (Day of Atonement) the sins were placed metaphorically on the head of the goat for Azazel. In this case, there is no sense of 'wiping off' but of the transfer of sins from the people to the animal (see further at LEV 1:4 and 16). That this is really a type of substitute or surrogate for the sinner, however, is a point well made by Kiuchi (1987). Kiuchi argues that the sin offering is envisaged as a substitute for the sinner; in other words, it purges the sin of the individual and not just, as Milgrom asserts, the effects of these sins on the sanctuary. (The transfer of sins in the Day of Atonement ceremony may be somewhat different from this, since the victim is sent away and not slain. Nevertheless, he argues that the scapegoat ceremony is a form of sin offering.) This transfer of sins might be indicated when the offerer lays hands on the animal's head. Kiuchi (1987: 112–19) notes that there are a number of interpretations of this act. Although he favours the interpretation that it represents substitution, he recognizes that the evidence is scanty. Knierim (1992: 34–40) opposes the idea of substitution and considers the gesture (which he translates as 'firm pressing down of the hand') a means of denoting transfer of ownership, i.e. from the offerer to God. If so, this aspect of the discussion does not help resolve the main problem of the elimination of sin.

Perhaps part of the problem is being too literal in interpretation. The sacrificial system was a symbolic system, filled with metaphor, allegory, and analogy. It would be a mistake to assume that only one symbol or metaphor was used for removing sin (e.g. ritual detergent). In the same way, the cultic terminology may have a more general meaning and should not be defined in terms of the specific metaphor used. The individual's sins were removed, whatever the precise symbolic conceptualization used.

Chs. 1–5 tend to address the whole people, lay as well as priest, in contrast to 6–7 which seem aimed primarily at the priests. The main term for offering is *qorbān*, a generic term which refers to a variety of different types (cf. the reference to the term in its Greek transliteration *korban* 'gift' in Mk 7:11).

The instructions about how to prepare the sacrifice are often stereotyped, so that similar instructions are given about those which are parallel; however, it is interesting to notice that small differences in wording are often found, even when the same instructions seem to be in mind. The sacrificial pattern for animals generally goes according to the following schema:

1. The sacrificer laid hands on the head of the animal.
2. It was killed at the entrance to the tabernacle, north of the altar, and cut up. The most natural interpretation of the Hebrew wording is that the slaughtering was done by the one making the offering rather than by the priest. If so, it contradicts Ezek 44:11, where it is done by the Levites, and 2 Chr 29:22, 24 where done by the priests.
3. Blood was sprinkled or dashed or poured, usually on the sides and/or base of the altar.
4. The parts burned for cattle included the entrails with their fat, the kidneys and suet, and the caul of the liver; the same was true with sheep or goats, except that the fat tail was also added.
5. Except for the whole burnt offering, the breast of the animal went to the priests as a body, while the right thigh went to the presiding priest specifically.

(1:1–2) is an introduction to the entire section of chs. 1–7 and forms an *inclusio* with 7:37–8, to mark off chs. 1–7 as a unit.

(1:3–17) describes the whole burnt offering (*'ôlâ*). Sometimes referred to as the 'holocaust', this whole burnt offering was the complete sacrifice, for none of it went to the sacrificing priest (except for the hide, 7:8) or to the one bringing the offering. The entire animal was 'turned into smoke', to use the Hebrew expression (*hiqtîr*). The offering could be from the herd or flock, a male animal in either case, or from the birds (turtle-doves or pigeons). Although the animal was cut up, all the pieces (not just the fat, kidneys, etc.) were placed on the altar. The legs and entrails were washed but placed on the altar as well. The burnt offering had expiatory function, as indicated by 1:4, 9:7, 14:20, and 16:24 (cf. also Ezek 45:15, 17). But it also seems to have been used for a wide range of functions, according to other passages, including entreaty (1 Sam 13:12) and appeasement of God's wrath (1 Sam 7:9; 2 Sam 24:21–5). It could also be used as an occasion for rejoicing (Lev 22:17–19; Num 15:3). It has been proposed that because of its ubiquity in early texts, it and the well-being offering (Lev 3) were the only sacrifices in the earliest period, with the sin and guilt offerings being added later when the temple was established. Gerstenberger (1993: 31) also suggests that the sin offering was a later replacement for the whole burnt offering.

(1:4) says that the purpose of the sacrifice is for 'atonement' for the one making the offering. The Hebrew word is *kipper* and is used in a number of contexts to describe the removal of sin or ritual impurity. Although often translated as 'atone' or 'cover up', the precise connotation has been much debated. The denominative verb can mean 'serve as a ransom, expiation gift'. Levine (1974: 56–77) has argued that it means 'remove, wipe off' impurity, not 'cover up'. In the cult, the word was used primarily in functional terms to mean 'perform rites of expiation' rather than 'to clean'. Milgrom (1991: 1079–84) sees a development in the word from a basic meaning 'purge'. It also carried the idea of 'rub, wipe', so that the

meanings 'cover' ('wipe on') and 'wipe off' are complementary rather than contradictory. In ritual texts, the idea of 'wipe off' predominated in that the blood was thought of as wiping off impurity, acting as a sort of cultic detergent. With certain rituals, such as those on the Day of Atonement or involving the red cow (Num 19:1–10), the idea of 'ransom' or 'substitute' was the main connotation. This finally led to the meaning 'atone, expiate' in some passages, especially with regard to all sacrifices where blood was not daubed on the horns of the altar.

Central to the cult was the shedding of blood. There is a major disagreement about the function of the blood between Milgrom and Levine, however. Levine argues that it has two functions: (1) an apotropaic function for the deity; that is, the blood was placed on the altar to protect God from the malignancy of impurity which was regarded as an external force; (2) purificatory or expiatory, in which the blood served as a ransom substituting for the life owed by the offerer. According to Milgrom, the idea of demonic or malignant forces which might harm the deity had no place in the thought of the P tradition. Impurities did compromise the holiness of the sanctuary and altar, so the purpose of the offering was to remove these. As noted above, Milgrom's opinion is that the blood acted as a ritual detergent, washing off the impurities which had attached themselves to the sacred things. For further comments on the blood, see at LEV 17:10–14.

(1:14–17) gives instructions for a whole burnt offering of birds. There are differences from those of other animals. For birds the neck was wrung off but, rather than being cut up, the body was torn open by the wings without severing it. The crop and excrement were placed on the ash pile. The whole of the offering was done by the priests, perhaps because only the poorest, such as slaves, used birds and were perhaps not as observant of the cult (Gerstenberger 1993: 27–8). On fowls for the sin offering, see at LEV 5:14–6:7.

(2:1–16) describes the cereal or meal offering (*minḥāh*). The word *minḥāh* means 'gift' and is used with such a general meaning in some texts (e.g. in reference to animals in Gen 4:3–4 and 1 Sam 2:17). It could even have the meaning of 'tribute' (Judg 3:15; 2 Sam 8:2). In Leviticus and priestly tradition in general, it refers exclusively to the offering of grain or meal. The cereal offering was the only non-blood sacrifice. It had two functions: (1) it was often an accompanying offering to one of the others, in particular the burnt and thanksgiving offerings; (2) it could be offered in its own right as an independent sacrifice. The meal offering follows this basic pattern:

1. Choice flour was to be used, with oil mixed in before cooking or added afterwards; anything cooked was always unleavened; frankincense accompanied the offering.
2. The frankincense and a token portion of the flour or cake were burnt on the altar.
3. The rest of the offering went to the priest.

It could be raw flour (mixed with oil) or it could be baked in an oven, cooked on a griddle, or fried in a pan. It was always unleavened since no leaven was to be burnt on the altar (v. 11), and was to be salted (v. 13) as a sign of the covenant. Other vegetable offerings could be brought: first fruits (v. 12: *rēʾšît*, no details given) and a cereal offering of first fruits (*bikkûrîm*) which was to consist of roasted grain with the usual oil and frankincense (vv. 14–16).

In his recent study Marx (1994) argues that the vegetable offering plays a central role in the system of P (including Ezek 40–8 and Chr), and is an accompaniment not only of the whole burnt offering but also of the well-being offering, the sin offering, and the guilt offering. (P represents a utopian ideal which views vegetarianism as the original state of mankind.) As noted above, the cereal offering can also stand alone and be offered independently of other offerings. By contrast, the J source (followed by Deut, Hos, and Ezek 1–39) limits its horizon to the blood offering, according to Marx.

(3:1–17) describes the *šĕlāmîm* offering. There is no agreed translation for this term. It was long connected with *šālôm* 'peace' and called the 'peace offering', a translation still found in the RSV. More recent translations have often derived the name from *šālēm* 'well-being', the translation used in the New Jewish Publication Society translation and the NRSV (the NEB and REB have 'shared-offering'). Levine himself suggests the meaning 'gift', based on the Akkadian *šulmānu* which means 'gift of greeting'. These are all only educated guesses, and exactly how one renders the term is to some extent arbitrary. The actual terminology used for the well-being offering is *zebaḥ šĕlāmîm* 'sacrifice of well-being'. The term *zebaḥ* is often translated by the general term 'sacrifice'; however, it seems to be limited to those sacrifices which were eaten by the offerer and would not be applied to the burnt offering or the sin offering since these were burnt whole or eaten only by the priests. The question is why the double terminology is used. Rendtorff has suggested that two originally separate offerings must have been combined, since such double terminology is unparalleled in cultic language. Also, *zebaḥ šĕlāmîm* is limited to Leviticus and Numbers; *zebaḥ* often occurs by itself outside these two books, but *šĕlāmîm* is never alone and often in the context of the burnt offering. Milgrom (1991), on the other hand, argues that *zebaḥ šĕlāmîm* is merely a synonym for *šĕlāmîm*. This passage does not discuss the various sorts of well-being offerings, and one must see the later treatment at 7:11–18 for a breakdown of the types of usage for this offering.

v. 11: A number of offerings are said to be *'iššeh*, which is often translated as 'offerings by fire'. This depends on the presumed origin of the word from *'ēš* 'fire', which is also reflected in later translations. This presents two difficulties: some offerings are referred to as *'iššeh* even when they are not burned (e.g. the wine offering: Num 15:10), whereas some offerings burned on the altar (e.g. the sin offering) are not called *'iššeh*. Milgrom has related the zword to Ugaritic *itt* 'gift' and perhaps Arabic *'aâu* 'possession of every kind'. He suggests the translation 'food gift', perhaps a shortened term from *leḥem 'iššeh* 'food gift' (Lev 3:11, 16). In his opinion, the word may have become obsolete by exilic times since it is absent from later OT collections.

(4:1–6:7) (HB 4:1–5:26) treats the sin and guilt offerings. There is considerable difficulty in separating these. The guilt offering especially has been a notorious problem since antiquity. Early Jewish commentators already had difficulties in interpreting it (cf. Philo, *Spec. leg.* 1.226–38; Josephus, *Ant.*

3.9.3 §§ 230–2). The same quandary has afflicted modern commentators, with various solutions proposed. For example Kellermann (1977) suggested that the guilt offering developed from the sin offering, to provide a form of sacrifice between the sin and burnt offerings, as the atonement sacrifice for all cases of gross negligence. In Lev 5:15, however, it is probably equivalent to the sin offering. Levine (1974) believes that it was not originally an altar sacrifice but a cultic offering presented to the deity in the form of silver or an object of value in expiation for certain offences. A necessary precondition is that the sin be done inadvertently, although Lev 5:20–6 may seem to go against this, because a false oath cannot be given inadvertently, Levine explains this as a separate category of crime. Milgrom (1976) opposes Levine with the view that the guilt offering must be a blood sacrifice. Any mention of silver has reference to buying an animal to sacrifice. Milgrom thinks he has found a solution in the meaning of the name, which he takes to mean 'feel guilt' when there is no verbal object. The notion common to all offences which call for it is that they are all cases of sacrilege against God, i.e. either an actual infringement of holy things or a trespass against the name of God.

(4:1–35) The term *ḥaṭṭā't* is traditionally translated 'sin offering' because the word also means 'sin'. The difficulty with this translation is that the sacrifice is required in certain cases where no sin is involved (e.g. Lev 12:6). Therefore, Milgrom argues for the translation 'purificatory offering'. His point is well taken; however, it seems a cumbersome title and one which may not be readily apparent to those more used to 'sin offering'. For this reason, 'sin offering' is still used here despite being somewhat problematic. The sin offering is to be offered when one has committed a sin unwittingly. The instructions vary according to the rank of the person offering it, and the pattern differs in certain details from that given at the head of this section on LEV 1–5. It is clear that two sorts of sin offering are in mind here. There is the one which is offered because of the sin of the priests or the congregation as a whole and is burnt entirely. The other, offered on behalf of the ordinary Israelite (including the tribal chieftain), was eaten by the priests after the normal parts were burned on the altar. vv. 3–12, if the anointed priest (high priest?) is atoning for his own sin, he is to offer a bull. The blood is sprinkled inside the tabernacle itself, before the curtain covering the Holy of Holies, and some of it put on the horns of the incense altar. The normal portions are burnt on the altar, but the rest of the animal is taken outside the camp and burned where the ashes from the altar are dumped. vv. 13–21, if the whole community has sinned, the ceremony is the same as for the priest, except that the elders take the part of the offerer. vv. 22–6, if a tribal chieftain (*nāśî'*) has sinned, a male goat is offered, with blood put on the horns of the altar of burnt offerings. In this case only the normal portions are burned, while the rest goes to the priest to be eaten. vv. 27–31, if an ordinary person (*'am hā'āreṣ*) has sinned, a female goat or sheep is offered, with the other details being the same as for the chieftain.

(5:1–13) is generally interpreted as describing the graduated sin offering. That is, there are two sorts of sin offering: the normal sin offering (4:1–35) and the graduated sin offering. Confusion is caused by the fact that the term *'āšām* is used here (vv. 6–7) as in 5:14–6:7 (HB 5:14–26), suggesting that the offerings of ch. 5 are separate from ch. 4. However, it is usually argued that *'āšām* means 'atonement for guilt' in vv. 6–7 rather than 'guilt offering', especially since reference is specifically made to the 'sin offering' in vv. 6, 7, 11. The breaches for which this is offered do not form a clear pattern: not acting as a witness, uttering a rash oath, or touching the corpse of an unclean animal or some other unclean thing without realizing it. The person must first confess the sin, then bring an offering of a female goat or sheep. If he does not have enough wealth for sheep or goat, he can bring two turtle-doves or two pigeons, one for a burnt offering and one for a sin offering. Since there are no instructions about fowls for a sin offering, some details are given: the neck is wrung but the head not severed from the body, and part of the blood is sprinkled on the side of the altar while the rest is poured out at the base. What happens then is not stated. The flesh of the guilt offering normally went to the priest, after the fat etc. were burned on the altar, but we do not have precise instructions about birds. The other bird is treated as a burnt offering. If the person does not have enough for birds, a tenth of an ephah of fine flour (without oil or frankincense) is offered. A token portion is burnt, and the rest goes to the priest, as is normal in cereal offerings. This is the only case where a cereal offering can serve for a transgression (though cf. Num 5:15).

(5:14–6:7) (HB 5:14–26) describes the guilt offering. The precise meaning of *'āšām* is not clear. The verb can mean 'commit an offence' and 'become guilty' (by committing an offence); hence, the traditional translation 'guilt offering'. Milgrom (1976) opposes this, arguing that when confined to cultic usage it has four meanings: (1) reparation, (2) reparation offering, (3) incur liability to someone, (4) feel guilt. It is especially this last which he emphasizes. The translation 'realize guilt' or 'become conscious of guilt', as found in a number of translations, he thinks is wrong. Rather, the clue to the sacrifice lies in the fact that the person becomes conscience-stricken, afraid that he has committed an offence. For the offering itself, he uses the translation 'reparation offering'.

5:14–16: the first transgression relating to the guilt offering involves unwitting violation of the 'holy things' of God (*qodšê yhwh*). The type of violation is not described, but the later ceremony suggests that the person has used something belonging to God for his own purposes, for restitution has to be made with another 20 per cent (fifth part) added to it (v. 16). A ram is also brought (v. 15; cf. 6:6 (HB 5:25)). A debate has arisen concerning the expression 'convertible into silver' (v. 15). Does this mean that only the value of the ram in money was brought rather than the animal itself (Noth 1977: 47)? Hartley (1992: 81–2) disagrees. However, Levine (1974: 98–100) thinks this was the earlier practice which later developed into the use of a ram of a minimal value, while Milgrom (1991: 326–7) argues that the value of the ram could be assessed and the equivalent value paid. vv. 17–19 follow the instructions about the transgression with regard to holy things by a general statement that a ram is to be brought for any transgressions of YHWH's commands which at first escape the person's notice. 6:1–7 (HB 5:20–6) expands the the concept of 5:17–19 further to include defrauding one's neighbour by illicitly appropriating a pledge or not returning a lost object. Again, restitution

has to be made, with 20 per cent added, and a ram or its equivalent value is brought for a guilt offering.

(6:8–7:38) (HB 6:1–7:38) gives the laws (*tôrôt*) of the offerings. The term *tôrâ* in these texts often refers to a priestly ruling. The sacrifices enumerated in chs. 1–5 are covered once more, but this time the instructions relate to the responsibilities of the priests rather than focusing on the offerings from the point of view of the lay person. It also emphasizes the priestly dues to be given over from each sacrifice. 6:8–13 (HB 6:1–6) gives the law of the burnt offering; cf. 1:3–17. 6:14–18 (HB 6:7–11) gives the law of the cereal offering; cf. Lev 2. 6:19–23 (HB 6:12–16) discusses the offering at Aaron's anointing. This section seems out of place because of its subject, though it was probably put here because a cereal offering is being described. It seems to be referring to a type of *tāmîd* or daily meal offering. It consisted of a tenth of an ephah of fine flour (about 2 litres), mixed with oil, and cooked on a griddle. Half is offered in the morning and half in the evening. This is burned entirely on the altar, with no portion eaten by the priests. We know that there was a daily or *tāmîd* offering made on the altar, and it seems to have included a cereal offering as well as a burnt offering in the morning. The daily offering was extremely important in antiquity because it was the chief sign that the temple was functioning and God accessible to the people. The times when the daily sacrifice was stopped were times of dire consequences, as when the temple was destroyed by Nebuchadnezzer or the Romans, or when the sacrifice was stopped by force in the time of the Maccabees. Surprisingly, though, what constituted the daily offering is not clear. Leviticus mentions only the cereal offering of the high priest, made in the morning and in the evening. Other priestly passages mention a daily burnt offering of two lambs, one in the morning and one in the evening (Ex 29:38–42; Num 28:3–8). Was this separate from the cereal offering or was the cereal offering thought of only as a companion offering? If the cereal offering accompanied it, why is this not mentioned in Leviticus, and why is the required drink offering also ignored? Other passages are different yet again. Dating from the time of the Maccabees, the practice of sacrificing the *tāmîd* twice a day is attested in Dan 8:11–14, while 9:21 mentions an evening cereal offering. 2 Kings 16:15 refers to a morning whole burnt offering and an evening cereal offering. Ezek 46:13–15 differs from Exodus, Leviticus, and Numbers by describing a daily sacrifice of one lamb (not two), accompanied by one-sixth of an ephah of flour (instead of one-tenth). The question is, What is the offering of 6:19–23? Is it identical with the cereal offering of the *tāmîd*? Most likely, it is a separate offering but one offered daily by the high priest (Milgrom 1991).

6:24–30 (HB 6:17–23) gives the law of the sin offering; cf. 4:1–5:13. 7:1–10 gives the law of the guilt offering; cf. 5:14–6:7. 7:11–21 gives the law of the well-being offering. 3:1–16 gives the details of the ritual, but it is only here that the basic rationale is given, i.e. the various sorts of well-being offering. Three types seem to be included under the well-being offering:

1. The freewill offering (*nĕdābâ*), given voluntarily on the part of the offerer, without any special motivation.
2. The votive offering (*nēder*). Whenever a vow was made, it was completed by an offering.

3. The thanksgiving offering (*tôdâ*), given as an expression of thanks for deliverance in time of trouble. There are several problems with understanding this offering.

Is it the same as the freewill offering? Some scholars have thought so. Others (e.g. Milgrom 1976) think the two are always clearly distinguished in the OT and should be kept separate. There are certain anomalies about the *tôdâ* offering when compared with the other well-being offering, suggesting that it was once considered separate. The main distinction from the other similar offerings is that it is accompanied by a cereal offering and must be eaten the same day it is offered. The freewill and votive offerings do not have the accompanying cereal offering and can be eaten both on the day of the offering and the next day. Indeed, in other passages the thanksgiving does seem to be an independent offering alongside the well-being (Lev 22:21, 29; Jer 17:26; 2 Chr 29:31–3; 33:16) and only in the supposed P source is it made a subdivision of the well-being offering.

7:22–38 has a set of miscellaneous instructions. Formally, it consists of two speeches of YHWH to Moses, and it seems to form a sort of appendix or supplement to instructions on the various sacrifices: vv. 22–7 prohibit the eating of any fat or blood, under pain of the penalty of being 'cut off' (*nikrat*; also in 7:21). This expression of being 'cut off' has been much debated but without a clear resolution (e.g. Levine 1989: 241–2; Milgrom 1991: 457–60). In some passages it refers to an early death, perhaps because of judicial punishment (Lev 20:2–3). Others have argued that passages with the expression generally imply divine punishment, not human. Some passages envisage that one's line of descendants would be cut off, not necessarily involving human action (1 Sam 2:30–4; Ps 109:13; Mal 2:12; Ruth 4:10). vv. 28–36 talk specifically of the well-being offering, but the main theme concerns those portions of the animal which are due to the priests: the breast and the right thigh. In Leviticus the maintenance of the priesthood is alluded to only in chs. 6–7, plus a brief discussion of tithing of animals (see at LEV 27:26–7). But the priesthood could not have been supported on portions of sacrifices alone, and other P passages speak of tithes and other support; see the discussion in Grabbe (1993: 70–2). vv. 37–8 are a concluding summary for the entire section on sacrifices, i.e. chs. 1–7; cf. 1:1–2.

(Chs. 8–10) describe the initiation of Aaron and sons into the priesthood and an unfortunate episode relating to priestly service in the sanctuary. Chs. 8–9 concern the ceremony in which Aaron and his sons were anointed and consecrated to their offices. There is general agreement that this is a priestly fiction; that is, these chapters do not describe an actual event involving a literal Aaron and Moses in the wilderness of Sinai. On the other hand, these chapters may tell us something about priestly belief or practice. Leviticus seems to envisage the anointing of Aaron and his sons as a once-only event, setting apart their descendants to the priesthood forever, as apparently does Exodus (29:9; 40:15). But each new high priest was customarily designated by anointing (Lev 6:22 (HB 6:15)). The lengthy ritual described in Lev 8–9 has many characteristics of what is often referred to as a 'rite of passage' (Gennep 1960). This is an anthropological term for rites which take place as a person passes from one stage to

another, such as from boyhood to manhood or girlhood to womanhood. There is first a rite of separation, next a transitional rite during which the person is in a 'liminal' state (on the doorstep between one phase and another). There may be dangers while in this liminal state, and various rituals have to be carefully performed to protect the one undergoing the transition. In the case of Aaron and sons, they were undergoing the passage from 'common' to 'sacred'. Various purification and burnt offerings and washings were performed, a special ordination offering carried out (8:22–9), and the anointing done. Those involved were then required to remain a week segregated in the Tent of Meeting (transitional rite). The final act was a ritual of incorporation, in this case sacrifices and ceremonies on the eighth day (Lev 9). Thus, the ceremony of consecration in Lev 8–9 is very much parallel to rites of passage known both from preliterate modern societies and from many examples in modern Western culture. Ch. 10 seems to be an inset chapter relating the incident of Nadab and Abihu (sons of Aaron) and its consequences, though the chapter follows naturally on the anointing ritual of Aaron and his sons.

(10:1–20) vv. 1–7 describe the death of Nadab and Abihu as a result of offering 'alien fire' (*'ēš zārâ*) on the altar. The episode is very puzzling since the 'sin' of the two sons is never clearly indicated, with the result that the passage generated many explanations in later Judaism (Hecht 1979–80; Kirschner 1982–3). Thus, as with the Golden Calf episode, one must ask what lies behind the story. Those who date this part of Leviticus late usually look for some event in the exilic or postexilic period. For example, Noth (1977) thought he saw internal disputes between different priestly groups. However, others are willing to ascribe the background to one or other event during the time of the monarchy. Milgrom (1976) suggests that it is a polemic against private offerings of incense. There are textual and archaeological indications that it was common for Israelites to offer incense to God in their homes and elsewhere outside the Jerusalem temple. Those who believed in cult centralization would have disapproved of this practice. Thus, a graphic story like that in Lev 10 would serve as a salutary reminder that private incense offerings were fraught with danger. vv. 6–7 command Aaron and his other sons not to mourn for Nadab and Abihu. This is parallel to the passage in 21:10–12 which forbids the high priest to mourn for his near kin. vv. 8–11 give a general instruction about not drinking alcohol when on duty in the sanctuary, another possible occasion for divine punishment for a serving priest. vv. 12–20 use the the death of Aaron's sons related in the previous verses to discuss a particular situation—the question of consuming the offerings in a time of mourning.

(Chs. 11–15) form an important section on ritual purity and pollution. An explanation now almost universally rejected is that the various laws in this section have hygiene as their basis. Although some of the laws of ritual purity roughly correspond to modern ideas of physical cleanliness, many of them have little to do with hygiene. For example, there is no evidence that the 'unclean' animals are intrinsically bad to eat or to be avoided in a Mediterranean climate, as is sometimes asserted. For a further discussion, see LEV C.3–4.

(11:1–47) describes the clean and unclean animals. Eating was very much involved with purity. Certain things were not to be eaten. The Israelite was especially to be concerned about the types of animal considered fit for consumption and how they were to be prepared. Lev 11 (paralleled by Deut 14) lists the various animals available for food and those to be avoided. There are some difficulties here because it is not always clear which animals were being referred to. The standard treatment of this chapter is now the study by Houston (1993). He argues that the animals allowed or forbidden under Israelite law were generally those similarly permitted or prohibited in the surrounding cultures. The laws of the Pentateuch thus reflect and systematize the general habits not only of the Israelites but also of their north-west Semitic neighbours. Thus, the animals permitted or forbidden seem to have come first, and the criteria for distinguishing them were worked out only subsequently. The presentation in this chapter is an intellectual exercise, a learned attempt to systematize and provide formal criteria and probably had little practical significance (Houston 1993: 231).

In vv. 2–12 the mammals and sea life are fairly easy to identify. For mammals (vv. 2–8) two questions are asked: 'Does it chew the cud?' 'Does it have cloven hooves?' If 'yes' is the response to both these, the animal can be eaten; if 'no' to either or both, it is off limits. A few borderline cases are mentioned to clarify the situation: the pig has cloven hooves but does not chew the cud; the camel chews the cud but does not have cloven hooves; the hare might be thought to chew the cud, because of the movements of its jaws, but it has no hooves. In scientific terminology, mammal food is limited to the ruminating bi-hooved ungulates. The practical implications were that edible mammals were limited to those offered on the altar and to their wild counterparts. Although pigs are attested in many areas of Palestine (Hübner 1989), the number seems to have declined fairly rapidly during the Iron Age. There is almost no evidence for their being used for sacrifice (even where they were eaten), with the possible exception of some special rites to underworld gods. However, it should be noted that pigs were included in these particular sacrifices *because* they were unclean, rather than that they were declared unclean because of being used in cults, as so often asserted (Houston 1993: 253). So the Israelite avoidance of pork fits with the general practice in the west Semitic area.

Consumption of sea creatures is restricted to those that have fins and scales (vv. 9–12). No animals are named, but it is clear that some fish (those without scales), all crustaceans, and most other fresh and saltwater animals are forbidden. The birds are hard to categorize because not all can be positively identified (vv. 13–19). Nevertheless, the majority of those which can be recognized are carnivorous or scavengers. Other flying things are also discussed here, including the bat (unclean) and some insects. A few insects could be eaten, mainly of the locust, cricket, or grasshopper type (vv. 20–3). This concession of some insects seems to be because of common dietary habits among the people, since insects seem to have been forbidden in the parallel passage in Deut 14:29 (Houston 1993: 236). vv. 24–40 seem to repeat earlier instructions, with quadrupeds again (vv. 24–8), followed by a long section on 'swarming things' (vv. 29–45). However, some sort of structure does emerge with a closer look, since vv. 24–40 are primarily about the carcasses of unclean animals, not the animals themselves. Then, vv. 41–5 are about the swarming things which had not really been discussed in vv. 1–23. Despite a somewhat coherent structure, though, most critics have seen evidence of growth and supplementation here. Further evidence of this is found in vv. 43–5 which use language reminiscent of H: 'be holy as I am holy'. vv. 41–5 discuss the 'swarming things', which seem to be a miscellaneous collection of small animals regarded as abhorrent by the Israelites. vv. 46–7 are a summary of the chapter.

(Ch. 12) gives directions about the purity procedure which follows childbirth. The first form of impurity for women listed in Leviticus is that of childbirth. If a woman bore a boy, she was unclean for 7 days, until the circumcision of the boy on the eighth day. For another 33 days she was not unclean as such (i.e. passing on uncleanness to others who had contact with her) but was not allowed to come into the sanctuary or touch any holy thing.

These periods were doubled for the birth of a girl: 14 days and 66 days. The allotted period was completed and purity restored with a lamb for a burnt offering and a pigeon or dove for a sin offering. A poor person could substitute two pigeons or doves, one for the burnt offering and one for the sin offering.

(Chs. 13–14) discuss a variety of skin diseases under the general Hebrew term of ṣāraʿat. Although this is often presented in older English translations as 'leprosy', the modern condition of leprosy is limited to Hanson's disease; by contrast, it is not clear that modern leprosy is even covered by the ancient disease; in fact, there is some question as to whether Hanson's disease was known in the Mediterranean world before the Hellenistic period. Also, some objects can be infected with 'leprosy'.

(13:1–59) Various skin afflictions are listed in vv. 1–46, along with the priestly response to them. The main function of the priest was to examine any affliction or inflammation brought to him, isolate the individual if it looked like the real disease, check again after seven days, and finally pronounce the afflicted person whole or leprous. Despite the length of the regulations, they are fairly repetitive, with slightly different criteria for scaly patches, burns, boils, and so on. As with Lev 11, the text is not dealing with medical treatment or hygiene but rather with ritual. What is being discussed is not how to treat the various diseases under the rubric ṣāraʿat but only how to recognize them and how to view them from the point of view of cultic purity. The medical question was no doubt of concern in Israel but it is not within the scope of the discussion here. The job of the priest was to pronounce on ritual purity and impurity, and the text gives some guidance on how to decide whether the person is clean or not, but he was not treating the disease as such. Even the isolation was not a quarantine for purposes of preventing the spread of the disease but only a way of allowing it time to develop or recede so an authoritative pronouncement could be made about it. In vv. 47–59 the infected object is a piece of cloth or leather. This is an additional complication to the identification of the disease(s) falling under the generic term ṣāraʿat. This section appears to deal with mould or fungus infections. From a medical point of view, there is no connection between these and the skin diseases otherwise dealt with. This reinforces the view that something other than pathological conditions is in the mind of the writer.

(14:1–53) In vv. 1–32 a good deal of space is devoted to the question of re-entry into the cultic community once the disease is cured. A major feature was a ritual in which two birds were taken, one killed but the other released into the open country. As is obvious, this ritual has certain features in common with the scapegoat ritual, especially the use of two creatures, one of which is slain and the other released (see further at LEV 16). The cured person then had to wash himself and his clothes, shave off his hair, and remain outside his tent (though within the camp) for a further 7 days. He then presented three lambs (one for a guilt offering, one for a sin offering, and one for a burnt offering), a cereal offering, and a quantity of oil. Some of the blood of the guilt offering and some of the oil was put on different parts of the former sufferer's anatomy. A poor person need bring only one lamb (for the guilt offering), two turtle-doves or pigeons (for the sin and burnt offerings), the cereal offering, and the oil. The range of offerings required in this case is paralleled only by those required for the nazirites to finish their vow (Num 6:13–20). vv. 33–53 envisage that a house could get ṣāraʿat, in the same way as a piece of cloth or leather. Again, it seems to be some sort of fungus which the writer has in mind. As with a person, the cleansing would be completed with the ceremony of the two birds.

(15:1–30) deals with a variety of genital discharges, normal and abnormal, for both men and women. vv. 2–24: a number of discharges were regarded as more or less normal, because they were a part of everyday life, and the person becoming polluted by them would be purified by washing and the passage of time. There was no requirement to offer a sacrifice. First to be treated, in vv. 1–16, are men. If there is an abnormal emission of semen or other penile discharge, the man (*zab*) becomes impure. The pollution is passed on to anyone touching him or anything on which he sits, as it is also if he spits on anyone or touches anyone without first washing his hands. The person so polluted was required to bathe in spring water, wash his clothes, and would become clean with the going down of the sun. A normal discharge of semen in marital intercourse (vv. 16–18) was also polluting, though less contagious than an abnormal discharge. The man and woman both were to wash themselves and remain unclean until evening. Any cloth or leather object on which semen fell was also to be washed and remain unclean until evening.

With regard to women (vv. 19–24), the flow of blood caused by childbirth was already dealt with in 12:1–8. The most basic and regular genital discharge was the monthly menstrual period. The time of impurity lasted 7 days even if the actual flow of blood finished sooner. During this time the woman transmitted impurity by direct contact or indirectly via anything on which she sat or lay. The person who touched her or that on which she lay or sat would need to wash himself or herself and his or her clothes and be unclean until evening. A man who had sexual relations with her would be unclean for 7 days. Any other prolonged discharge of blood for a woman also brought on uncleanness on the same order as menstruation (vv. 25–30). If the flow stopped, the woman would become

clean after 7 days. In this case, though, there was a significant difference, for she had to make a sacrifice. On the eighth day she was to bring two pigeons or doves, one for a burnt offering and one for a sin offering.

(16:1–34) describes the atonement for sanctuary and people popularly known as the 'scapegoat ritual'. The central core of the ritual was the ceremony with the two goats. One goat was for God and one was for 'Azazel' (on this word, see at v. 8), the choice being determined by lot. This ceremony differs from most of the cultic rituals in having the sins of the people placed on a live animal rather than sacrificing one and putting its blood on the altar. Part of the peculiarities of this chapter may arise from its origins. A variety of possibilities have been suggested, the most recent seeing parallels—and perhaps even the origin—of the rite in southern Anatolia and northern Syria (Janowski and Wilhelm 1993). Expiation rituals in the Hittite and Hurrian texts have some striking points in common with the scapegoat ritual (ibid. 134–57; Wright 1987: 31–60).

v. 1 connects the chapter back to the regulations about the priests in chs. 8–10, linking it with the one proper occasion when a priest (limited to the high priest) could appear before God in the Holy of Holies. That is, whereas Adab and Abihu had acted improperly (though their sin is never specified) and had been punished by death, the right ceremony at the right time could allow the right priest to come into God's actual presence. vv. 2–14, before the high priest could come into God's presence, he first had to offer a bull as a sin offering for himself and his household. Then he went inside the veil and placed incense on the coals of his censer to make a cloud of smoke and hide the ark, thus protecting himself from God who was seated on top of the ark, and sprinkled the blood of the bull on the ark. This was all to atone for his own sins. Before this was done, however, two goats were chosen to perform separate roles by lot (vv. 7–10). One goat was for YHWH, the other for 'Azazel' (v. 8). What was this Azazel? Unfortunately, it remains an enigma. No explanation is found in the text of Lev 16, and the word does not occur elsewhere in the OT or early inscriptions. Various etymologies have been proposed, but none is clearly compelling. Later Jewish tradition identified Azazel with the leader of the fallen angels (Grabbe 1987). Although this identification may itself be the result of exegesis, scholars have often proposed that Azazel represents some sort of demonic figure. This is suggested by the context as well as later Jewish interpretation. While accepting this interpretation as the one which developed in Judaism, Janowski and Wilhelm (1993: 161–2) argue that the original meaning of the word was 'for (the elimination of) God's wrath'. vv. 15–19, after the priest had sacrificed for himself and his family, he next sacrificed the goat on whom the lot for God had fallen. This goat became a sin offering and was sacrificed and the blood sprinkled on the ark, which atoned for the holy place (polluted because of the sins of the people). The altar was atoned for by sprinkling on it the blood from both the bull and goat. vv. 20–8, in the rituals earlier in the chapter the various sacrifices had been used to atone for the sins of the high priest himself and then to cleanse the sanctuary of impurities because of the sins of the people. Now a unique ceremony takes place in which the sins of the people are removed by the treatment of the goat 'for Azazel'. It was not slain. Rather, the high priest laid hands on it and confessed the sins of the congregation, thus transferring them to its head. The goat was then taken away and sent into the wilderness, bearing away all the sins of Israel on its head. As noted above, the different conceptualization of removing sins in this ritual may be due to its origins.

vv. 29–34 summarize the ceremony and associate it with the tenth day of the seventh month. The detailed ceremony of ch. 16 is only at this point connected with the Day of Atonement listed as one of the festivals of Israel (Lev 23). It also specifies that the day should be one of fasting by the people. This suggests that the ritual of ch. 16 may have been only secondarily connected with the Day of Atonement in the list of festivals (Noth 1977). Before this it was likely to have been a ceremony evoked by the high priest whenever it was needed (Milgrom 1991: 1061–5).

Chs. 17–26 form the Holiness Code according to a long-term consensus in scholarship; nevertheless, there have been significant voices raised against this identification. See LEV B. 7 above.

(17:1–16) Ch. 17 does not provide a formal introduction to the Holiness Code (assuming one accepts the idea of H). Indeed, Gerstenberger sees chs. 16–26 as a unit separate from chs. 1–15, and puts ch. 17 in with ch. 16 as a thematic unit on 'the prime festival and the prime rule of the offerings' (1993: 17). The subject of ch. 17 is proper sacrifice; under this heading come the matters of handling blood and of eating meat. The reason for these is that eating of meat is intimately associated with cultic sacrifice in the mind of the writer.

vv. 3–7 cover the law regarding slaughter, requiring that domestic animals be killed at the altar. The reason is that the blood can be disposed of at the altar, and people will not sacrifice to goat demons (vv. 6–7). It is generally assumed that this chapter envisages all slaughter as being done at the altar so that the blood can be dashed against the altar and the fat burned on it. The exception to this rule was the case of clean wild animals or birds which could be hunted, killed, and eaten apart from the shrine as long as the blood was drained out onto the earth. If so, all slaughter of domestic animals for food would have to take place in a sacrificial context. How could this be carried out from a practical point of view, if no butchering or eating of meat could be done apart from the shrine? The difficulty is highlighted by Deut 12:20–5 which seems to be changing just such a regulation when it states that profane slaughter is now allowed, as long as the blood is drained out of the animal. This means that Lev 17 must either be an idealized system divorced from reality or have in mind a society small enough in numbers and territory to allow a trip to the altar and back within a day or so. The post-exilic community had just such a size, and the majority of scholars apply this to the post-exilic community (cf. Gerstenberger 1993: 216–17). Milgrom, however, argues that the original setting was the pre-monarchic community, which was also quite small and allowed such laws to operate. Another interpretation argues that only the sacrifice of well-being offerings is in mind and that profane slaughter for food was permitted outside the temple (cf. Hartley 1992), though this seems to go against the most obvious meaning of the passage.

vv. 8–9 are a separate law and seem to repeat vv. 3–7. They may have had a separate existence at one time and thus came to be included in the collection despite some duplication. The penalty of being 'cut off' is characteristic of Leviticus (see at LEV 7:22–7). vv. 10–14 focus on the question of blood which is a central element in this chapter. The life of both humans and animals is in the blood (vv. 11, 14). For that reason, blood should not be eaten but dashed on the altar or poured on the ground and covered with dust. Blood functions as a potent symbol within the sacrificial cult and must be given due weight in any theological discussion of the meaning of the cult (see at LEV 1:4). Schwartz (1991: 55–61) argues that *kipper* in 17:11 has the meaning of 'ransom' and is the only biblical passage where sacrificial blood is said to be a ranson for human life. Elsewhere blood has the quality of purifying or cleansing, so v. 11 is a unique verse. Because of the characteristic of blood to serve as a ransom for life, its consumption is prohibited.

(17:15–16) deals with eating that which dies of itself or is killed by animals. One of the reasons is no doubt that the blood is still in the animal and has not been drained away as required (vv. 6, 11, 13–14). Surprisingly, though, such eating is not prohibited but only requires the eater to bathe, wash clothes, and be unclean until sunset. No sacrifice is necessary. Priests were specifically prohibited from eating meat not properly slaughtered in Lev 22:8, while Ex 22:31 (HB 22:30) and Deut 14:21 are even more stringent, and prohibit Israelites from eating such meat at all.

(18:1–30) discusses primarily forbidden sexual relations, in two sets of laws (vv. 7–18 and 19–23). Much of this chapter covers what is usually referred to as incest, that is, sexual relations forbidden because of the closeness of kinship of the person involved; however, some other sorts of sexual acts are also mentioned. Sexual relations sit at the heart of social practice within any community. Each society has strict views about which sort are allowed and which are not; these views may change over time and—human nature and passions being what they are—such rules are often breached, but they are still there even in what might seem the most promiscuous of societies. Indeed, promiscuity in one area of a society may be matched by great rigidity in another. Social anthropologists have found that laws about permitted and forbidden sexual relationships are an important clue to attitudes towards relatives and outsiders (cf. LEV C.3–4). In many preliterate societies elaborate codes govern marriage. Often these force exogamy, even if the only source of wives or husbands might be an enemy tribe. Israel's rules here are very lenient (despite the claim that 'the Canaanites' allowed sex with close of kin), allowing even first cousins to marry. Israel was thus an endogamous society. This fits their emphasis on rigid barriers to non-Israelites. Easy marriage between groups internally would, of course, help to prevent any feeling of need for marriage to outsiders.

vv. 1–5: the prohibited relations are framed in two sets of admonitions or paranaetic material (vv. 1–5, 24–30). The sections justify the laws by an appeal to the 'abominations' of the Egyptians and Canaanites (vv. 3, 24–8). In fact, there is no evidence that these peoples were less moral than the Israelites, nor that their sexual practices were necessarily that different. There may have been some differences in definition of what constituted incest among these peoples compared with Israel, as is to be expected, but they had their own strict society codes. (The 'abominations of the Egyptians and Canaanites' is a fiction which still dominates some discussions, especially with regard to Canaanite religion.) On the theological construction of the Canaanites in the biblical text, see Lemche (1991).

The following sexual relations are considered off limits for the Israelite male (vv. 7–23): first are those 'with his own flesh' (i.e. near of kin): mother or step-mother (vv. 6–7); sister, half-sister, stepsister, or sister-in-law (vv. 9, 11, 16); daughter-in-law (v. 10, 15); aunt (vv. 12–14); a woman and her daughter or granddaughter (v. 17). Other regulations seem to have to do more with what is deemed appropriate: not to take a wife's sister as rival wife (v. 18); not to have sex during the menstrual period (v. 19) or with the neighbour's wife (v. 20), with another male (v. 22), or with animals (v. 23). One should not offer one's children to Molech (v. 21—on this, see further at LEV 20:1–6). Omitted is prohibition of relations with a daughter or a sister. The reason may be that the laws are phrased to forbid violation of one's father and one's mother (Rattray 1987). Also omitted is any prohibition against homosexual acts between women, though the framers of the laws may not have envisaged that such even existed.

vv. 24–30 put blame for exile from the land on the sins of the inhabitants. The Israelite is the object of the command but, as noted above in the general comments on ch. 18, the attribution of such abominable sins to the original inhabitants of the land is not based on any objective criteria. Sexual mores were fairly uniform throughout the ancient Near East. For example, adultery was universally condemned (cf. Codex Hammurabi 129–32). Sex with animals seems otherwise unattested in the Near East at this time (Gerstenberger 1993: 232).

(Chs. 19–20) list a set of miscellaneous laws on being holy. The term 'miscellaneous' is used from a modern perspective; no doubt the ancient authors/compilers had their own view and may have arranged the material according to a perfectly logical pattern from their standpoint. The contents of this section have a number of parallels with the Covenant Code (Ex 21:1–23:33) and Deut 12–24, as well as with laws known elsewhere in the ancient Near East (on Israelite law in the context of ancient Near-Eastern law, see Grabbe (1993: 23–8) and the bibliography cited there).

(Ch. 19) has a series of laws preceded by an introduction (vv. 1–2) and with a concluding verse (v. 37): revere parents (v. 3); unusually, the mother is mentioned first; keep the sabbaths (v. 3); avoid idols (v. 4); law of well-being sacrifice (vv. 5–8); leave some of harvest for the poor (vv. 9–10); do not steal (v. 11); do not lie or deceive (v. 11); do not swear falsely (v. 12); do not exploit others: friend, hired person, deaf, blind (vv. 13–14); judge justly (v. 15); do not be a slanderer (v. 16); do not hate your fellows but love them (vv. 17–18); avoid mixtures (v. 19); if a man has sex with a betrothed slave woman (vv. 20–2); the first fruits of a fruit tree (vv. 23–5); do not eat blood (v. 26); do not practice divination (v. 26); do not disfigure yourself for the dead (vv. 27–8); do not make your daughter a prostitute (v. 29); keep the sabbaths and honour the sanctuary (v. 30); do not seek to contact spirits of the dead (v. 31); show respect for the elderly (v. 32); love the resident alien (vv. 33–4); have honest scales and measures (vv. 35–6).

Many of these are what we might call civil law, but here they are given a religious sanction and thus brought under cultic law. The motive clause, '(for) I am YHWH', occurs frequently. The laws proper (vv. 3–36) are not of a piece because there is some overlap between the various ones. For example, the sabbath is mentioned twice (vv. 3, 30). It has been noted that vv. 11–18 have a common vocabulary in 'friend' (rēaʿ), 'associate' (ʿāmît), and 'people' (ʿam) (Wenham 1979: 267). Scholars have noted connections between the Decalogue (Ex 20; Deut 5) and this chapter (Morgenstern 1955). Some have thought they could even find two decalogues (Kilian 1963: 58–9) or a dodecalogue and a decalogue (Elliger 1966: 254), though a good deal of textual rearrangement is required and the precise construction is not agreed on. It is true that the contents of much of the Ten Commandments are echoed here: graven images (19:4 || Ex 20:3); using God's name in vain (19:12 || Ex 20:7); the sabbath (19:3, 30 || Ex 20:8–12); honouring parents (19:3 || Ex 20:12); murder (19:16 || Ex 20:13); adultery (19:29 || Ex 20:14); stealing (19:11, 13 || Ex 20:15). Lev 19 also has a command against lying (v. 11) which might be taken as somewhat parallel to bearing false witness (Ex 20:16). Nevertheless, the wording and even the precise concept is often different, and the order of presentation has nothing in common, and there is much here not in the Ten Commandments. Thus, there is no obvious relationship between this chapter and the Decalogue. Comparison of the OT and the legal material elsewhere in the ancient Near East suggests a large amount of traditional exhortative material widespread in the area. The coincidences between the traditional Decalogue and this chapter are most likely due to this fact.

(20:1–8) is a section prohibiting seeking after false sources of supernatural aid. It primarily concerns dedicating children to Molech (vv. 2–5) but also forbids necromancy (v. 6). The prohibitions about Molech raise two questions: what does it refer to, and why should it be in this collection? There has been much discussion about the first question (cf. Day 1989; Heider 1985). Who or what is Molech? Some have argued that the term refers to a type of sacrifice; others assert that Molech is a deity of some sort. Although recent writings have favoured the latter hypothesis, it cannot be said that the matter is settled. Similarly, the expression 'pass (a child) over to Molech' has been taken to mean only 'to dedicate to' Molech or, more drastically, 'to sacrifice (the child) to' Molech. Again, recent writings have tended to support the latter viewpoint. The same prohibition occurs in a similar series in 18:19–23, but there the writer/editor must have seen a connection between the sexual acts and offering children to Molech. Its presence is more easily explained here in ch. 20. But why is the law included in a series having to do with sexual relations? Perhaps both were seen as threatening to family solidarity (Hartley 1992: 289–90). As its position here indicates, worship of Molech may be a form of seeking the deities of the underworld. Necromancy was another means of gaining help from the dead and the forces associated with death and the netherworld. The precise development of the cult of the dead and its significance is debated (cf. the summary in Grabbe 1995: 141–5), some thinking it was early in Israel's history (Bloch-Smith

1992) while others think it developed only fairly late (Schmidt 1994). What is clear is that in Leviticus, as in other passages (e.g. Deut 18:9–14), the practice of necromancy was known and forbidden, suggesting that it was practised at the time of writing, whenever that was.

(20:9–27) has parallels to Lev 19 and, especially, Lev 18. vv. 10–21 primarily concern the question of sexual relations between relatives and others, though it is introduced by a prohibition against cursing one's parents (v. 9). These are similar to Lev 18:6–23. vv. 22–6 give the rationale for these laws (the previous inhabitants did these things and the land vomited them out) in a manner parallel to 18:24–30. The section finally ends in a prohibition against necromancy (v. 27). This probably forms an *inclusio* with 20:1–6 (i.e. the chapter begins and ends with the same subject), suggesting that ch. 20 was composed as an independent unit. This implies that the repetition between chs. 18 and 20 is probably due to their being originally separate collections. If so, the final editor included both, despite the parallel material, rather than choosing between them or attempting the difficult task of editing them together. Gerstenberger (1993: 262–6), however, argues that one of the chapters must be dependent on the other, most likely the editor of ch. 20 was dependent on ch. 18; the intention of this revision is to give new perspectives relating to the community.

(21:1–23) The concentration in chs. 17–20 has been the community and people; now the text turns to laws relating primarily to the priests. Formally, the passage is divided into two parts by two speeches by YHWH to Moses. The first speech (vv. 1–15) is addressed to all the priests, whereas the second (vv. 16–23) is specifically to Aaron. The reason the second speech is addressed to Aaron may be because he (and subsequent high priests) were the ones to decide whom to allow near the holy food (Hartley 1992: 346). Otherwise, all the regulations relate to all the priests, since they were all thought of as descendants of Aaron.

vv. 1–9: the presumption is that all Israel is to be holy, but the priests had to be even more rigorous. They were not allowed to defile themselves by contact with a corpse by participating in funerals other than of close blood relatives: only for a mother, father, son, daughter, brother, or an unmarried sister (vv. 1–4). They were not to carry out mourning rites by disfiguring their hair, beards, or flesh by cutting it (vv. 5–6). They were not allowed to marry a harlot or divorcee, and the priest's daughter who became a harlot was to be burned (vv. 7–9). However, v. 8 makes the holiness of the priests a responsibility of the whole community. vv. 10–15, the OT as a whole does not say much about a high priest, though we know that the high priest became very important in Second Temple times (Grabbe 1992: 73–83). Leviticus does envisage a high priest, however, as this and other passages (e.g. Lev 16) show. The special nature of his office is shown by special restrictions which were even more stringent than in 21:1–9: he was not to participate in a funeral, even for a close relative, or engage in mourning rites of any kind; he was to marry only a virgin of his own people. vv. 16–23, the regulations about the physical condition of those who could preside at the altar were also rigorous. Just as animals to be sacrificed were to be without physical defect, so the officiating priests were to be with-

out physical blemish. A number of these defects are described, though they may be only representative. Nevertheless, even priests whose physical deformity or disease prevented them from carrying out their priestly duties were still allowed to eat of the priestly gifts.

(22:1–33) carries on the theme at the end of ch. 21 by giving laws on holy offerings and who may eat of them. Certain portions of the sacrificial animal and other offerings were to go to the priests, as noted in chs. 5–7. These were sacred and to be eaten only by those qualified and only under certain conditions. vv. 3–16, the priests and their families who were in a state of purity, and they alone, were to partake of these offerings. The various sorts of uncleanness are specified, but these do not differ from those already known. The basic rule was that only members of the priest's household could eat, including slaves but not hired servants, and unmarried daughters but not married ones. Any unqualified person who ate of holy things had to restore it plus 20 per cent; cf. at 5:14–16.

vv. 17–25 link again the bodily perfection of both sacrificial animals and the presiding priests. The first part of ch. 22 covers the priest; this section now specifies that all offerings were to be whole, normal animals without major physical defects. Anything which was blind, injured, maimed, or had certain sorts of disease was rejected. Neither was a castrated animal to be accepted. (The implication is that Israelites did not castrate their animals, contrary to the normal practice of those around them.) An animal with a limb extraordinarily short or long could be accepted for a free-will offering but not for a vow. This was the only explicit concession made about blemishes, though how the rules might be interpreted in practice we do not know. v. 21 mentions only the votive (*nēder*) and the free-will (*nĕdābâ*) offerings as falling under the well-being offering; this seems to differ from the description given at 7:11–18 which also seems to include the thanksgiving offering (*tôdâ*), though even this is a moot point. See the discussion at LEV 7:11–18. vv. 26–30 list another set of miscellaneous laws. A newborn animal was not to be sacrificed until it had been with its mother 7 days (v. 26), nor were it and its mother to be sacrificed on the same day (v. 27). Any thanksgiving offering had to be eaten on the day it was offered, and anything left over after that time had to be burnt (vv. 29–30). This agrees with 7:15. vv. 31–3 provide a concluding admonition to the chapter.

(Ch. 23) is one of several lists itemizing the major religious festivals (cf. Ex 23:14–17; 34:18–26; Deut 16:1–17), but it tends to be the most detailed and, in the opinion of many, one of the latest. There is also a late list of festivals in Ezek 45:18–25; however, this one is a bit difficult to correlate with the others because it focuses on the duties of the 'prince' and perhaps was not meant to be comprehensive in other respects. The list to be most closely compared to Lev 23 is Num 28–9, however. The conventional view of scholarship has been that Num 28–9 (a part of the P document) is secondary to Lev 23 (a mixture of P and H). This view has now been stood on its head by Knohl (1995; cf. 1987) who argues that H is secondary to P. Specifically, he thinks Lev 23 is an adaptation of Num 28–9 and thus represents the later list. Form-critically, ch. 23 is divided into five commands to Moses for him to speak to Israel: 23:1–8, 9–22, 23–5, 26–32, 33–44. This serves to give each festival an independent treatment, but it also highlights the fact that the weekly sabbath does not fit easily in the list and draws attention to what seem to be additions made to the original list, especially vv. 39–43 (Feast of Booths). For further information on a number of the festivals, see Grabbe (1993: ch. 6).

(23:3) the word 'sabbath' is from the Hebrew root š-b-t which means 'rest, cessation'. The basic characteristic of the sabbath was that no work (mělā'kâ) of any kind was to be done. What exactly made up that prohibited work is not stated in this passage and is nowhere else spelled out as such. Outside Leviticus one passage notes that work is also prohibited on the holy days except 'that which each person must eat' (Ex 12:16), suggesting that the preparation of food was allowed on these annual sabbaths but not on the weekly sabbath. The sabbath seems to have a long history in Israel and was hardly invented by the Priestly writers, but it is difficult to say how far back the development of sabbath observance can be pushed. It was once common to regard the sabbath as primarily a post-exilic innovation. Sabbath observance is emphasized mainly in exilic and post-exilic texts (e.g. Isa 56; Neh 13:15–22). There is also the question of the sabbath passage here, since from a form-critical point of view, v. 3 appears to be a later insertion and not part of the original list. Yet some texts generally acknowledged to be pre-exilic seem to presuppose sabbath observance (Hos 2:11; Am 8:5; Isa 1:13), indicating that it was known and followed in some circles as early as the eighth century BCE. Some have even argued for an earlier observance based on such passages as Ex 23:12 and 34:21 (cf. 2 Kings 4:23). Although it does not seem to be clearly attested as early as some of the annual festivals, certain scholars have argued that the weekly sabbath goes far back in Israel's history and is not a late development (see Andreasen 1972; Shafer 1976).

(23:5) briefly mentions the Passover, but Leviticus is otherwise silent about this important celebration. This may not be significant if there is a P document since other passages normally labelled P include a lengthy description of the observance, especially Ex 12:1–20. The important point about Leviticus is that Passover is presupposed but intimately tied up with the Festival of Unleavened Bread (23:6–8). This was the 7-day period when only unleavened bread (maṣṣôt) was eaten and no leavening or leavened products were allowed in the land. The festival was inaugurated by the Passover meal, at which unleavened bread was eaten, on the evening between 14 and 15 Nisan. The first full day (15th) was a holy day, as was the last day (1st). A major question is when the Passover became associated with the Feast of Unleavened Bread. It is now generally admitted that some early traditions do mention the Passover (e.g. Ex 23:18; 34:25). Haran (1962: 317–48) has argued that the Passover was associated with Unleavened Bread from an early time and is already so linked in all the biblical sources. However, his argument that the Passover goes back to a 'nomadic' way of life, with Unleavened Bread arising in settled conditions, is problematic in the light of recent discussion about nomadism and the Israelite settlement (cf. Lemche 1985: esp. 84–163). Haran also makes the point that the Passover in Ex 12 and elsewhere is actually envisaged as a temple sacrifice.

(23:9–14) An important day within the festival of unleavened bread was the Wave Sheaf ('ōmer) Day. On this day a symbolic sheaf of grain was cut as the first fruits of the harvest and presented before God. In addition, certain specific offerings are enjoined: a male lamb as a burnt offering, a cereal offering of two ephahs of flour mixed with oil, and a quarter hin of wine as a drink offering. This ceremony marked the start of the grain harvest. No bread or grain from the new crop was to be eaten until the first sheaf had been brought. The ceremony took place on the Sunday ('the day after the sabbath') during the days of unleavened bread. In later centuries, the various sects disagreed over whether the 'day after the sabbath' meant the day after the first annual sabbath (the holy day on 15 Nisan) or after the weekly sabbath, but the most natural reading of the Hebrew text was that which interpreted it as the weekly sabbath (cf. Grabbe 2000: 141). This date also affected the date of Pentecost.

(23:15–21) The spring grain harvest began on the Wave Sheaf Day and continued for 7 weeks until the Feast of Weeks. For some reason, though, no specific term ('Feast of Weeks' or otherwise) occurs for this festival in Leviticus. The Feast of Weeks did not fall on a specific day of the month but was counted from the Wave Sheaf Day, reckoning 7 sabbaths. The Feast of Weeks (ḥag šābu'ôt: Ex 34:22) was on the day after the seventh sabbath, called the fiftieth day when counting inclusively (i.e. including both the starting and finishing day in the total). Hence, in later times the day was given the Greek name of Pentēkostē 'fiftieth (day)', from which the English Pentecost comes. From later Jewish sources, we know that there was disagreement among the various sects about the day of this festival. The dispute concerned whether one counted 7 weeks from a floating annual sabbath on 15 Nisan or 7 sabbaths from the first day of the week, to arrive at another first day of the week. (As noted above, the debate mainly concerned the exact time of the Wave Sheaf Day.) Some translations and lexicons render the Hebrew phrase šeba' šabbātôt as 'seven weeks', but this would be the only place where šabbāt means week in the OT; more likely is that the word means 'sabbath' here as elsewhere. It was only in Second Temple times that the meaning 'week' developed and allowed some sects to try to count from a fixed day of the month. Hebrew usage and later priestly practice indicate that Shavuot was always celebrated on a Sunday as long as the temple stood and only later became fixed on 6 Sivan as it is among most Jews today (Grabbe 1992: 486). Shavuot also had its own specific offerings. Two loaves of bread were baked from flour made from the new grain and presented before God. Unusually, they were to be baked with leaven; this seems the only exception to the requirement that cereal offerings were to be unleavened, though nothing is said about their being burnt on the altar.

(23:23–5) the first day of the seventh month (Tishri) was a holy day celebrated by the blowing of trumpets. The type of trumpet used is not specified. Another passage usually associated with P mentions a set of silver trumpets to be used for ceremonial occasions and war (Num 10:1–10). One might therefore think of these, but the symbolic blowing may not have been confined to them. The ram's horn (šôpār) associated with the festival in modern times may have been a later development or interpretation, but we have no way of knowing. Other than the blowing of trumpets and the command to do no work, nothing further is stated about this day here. Num

29:1–5 lists sacrifices to be offered, though why they should be omitted here is a problem.

(23:26–32) The tenth day of the seventh month was the Day of Atonement (*yôm hakkippûrîm*). This passage states that the day is a time of no work, fasting ('you shall afflict your souls'), a holy convocation, with an 'offering of fire' (see at 3:11) to be carried out. No further data are given. Yet we know that the ceremony of the two goats was also associated with this day, as Lev 16 describes in detail. Was the ceremony of Lev 16 once an independent observance which only later became associated with 10 Tishri? Most of the chapter gives no indication of when the ceremony was to take place. It is only towards the end of the chapter (16:29–34) that the ritual is connected with the Day of Atonement known from Lev 23.

(23:33–6, 39–43) The Feast of Booths or Tabernacles (*sukkôt*) was the final festival of the year, celebrated after the autumn harvest (23:33–6, 39–43) on 15–22 Tishri. It probably arose from the practice of farmers who would build a temporary shelter (booth) in the field to sleep in to protect the harvest and maximize the daylight until it was gathered. The people were to take fruit, palm leaves, tree branches, and willows and make booths as a part of the celebration. The first day was a holy day on which no work was to be done, as was the eighth day. As with the Day of Trumpets, no sacrifices are listed for Sukkot in Leviticus. At Num 29:12–39, however, we find that an elaborate series of sacrifices was to take place, with each of the eight days having its own particular ceremony. They followed a diminishing series, beginning with 13 bulls on the first day, 12 bulls on the second, and so on down to 7 bulls on the seventh day. The eighth day had its own separate ceremony.

(24:1–9) describes the lamps and the bread of the presence in the foyer of the temple. Why this section and the next (24:10–23) go here is not immediately apparent, but both 24:2–4 and 24:5–9 relate to the area inside the Holy Place, in front of the curtain separating it from the Holy of Holies. A very pure olive oil was to be provided to keep the lampstand burning on a regular basis (vv. 2–4). (The concept of a perpetual lamp occurs in 1 Sam 3:3.) There was also to be a table on which 12 loaves (along with frankincense) were to be placed each sabbath. The frankincense was burned at the end of the week, and the priests were allowed to eat the loaves. This was known as the 'bread of presence' or 'show bread'. It is these loaves or something similar which David and his men ate in 1 Sam 21:1–6. This bread is referred to in passing at Ex 39:36, but it is a puzzle why an actual description is delayed until this point in Leviticus.

(24:10–23) discusses the question of blasphemy. Here and there within Leviticus narrative replaces direct commands. In such cases, the episode seems meant to explain what should be done by example rather than just instruction. It is similar to Lev 8–10 which is also a narrative section and, especially, to Num 15:32–6 where a sinner is likewise imprisoned until God decides the punishment for the crime (in this case, the sin is sabbath-breaking). The passage is made of up two sections: a narrative about the blasphemer and his ultimate fate (vv. 10–12, 23), and the command of YHWH not only about blasphemy but also other sins (vv. 13–22). The narrative tells how a man with an Israelite mother but an Egyptian father used God's name in a blasphemous way. He was put in custody until God could be consulted. God's judgement was that he be stoned to death by the entire community. Anyone in the future blaspheming with God's name was likewise to be executed by stoning. The commands of YHWH (vv. 13–22) concern not only blasphemy but also causing death to a man (which brings the death penalty) or a beast (compensation has to be paid), and they apply not only to Israelites but also to the resident alien. Within this section is an inset paragraph about life and reciprocation of punishment, otherwise known as the *lex talionis*.

(24:17–22) makes the point of the importance of life, especially human life. The one who kills a person is to be executed. Anyone who kills an animal must make restitution. There is also the principle that injuries were to be compensated by having a reciprocal injury done to the perpetrator, the famous 'eye for an eye and a tooth for a tooth'. This law has often been misunderstood as if it were a primitive barbaric practice which embarrassed legislators later did their best to soften. In fact, the earlier principle was that a person injuring another was to pay compensation. For example, the earliest Mesopotamian law codes (Eshnuna 42–7; Ur-Nammu 15–19 = A324–325? || B§§13–24) have monetary compensation. In the case of an extended family or community, that was the simplest way of handling it. The injured party received some benefit, or at least his family did. On the other hand, the later law codes (Hammurabi 195–223) evoke the *lex talionis* for those of equal status (though monetary compensation applies to injury of someone of lower status). The *lex talionis* was an important advance in jurisprudence for two reasons: first, it made all equal before the law. The rich man could not get away with his crime of injuring another by monetary payment. The 'eye for an eye' principle was a great leveller. Secondly, it marks the stage at which the tribe or state takes over the function of justice from the local community.

(Chs. 25–6) seem to be envisaged as a unit by the author or editor, because they consist of one speech by YHWH to Moses and because they are marked off by an *inclusio* (the phrase 'on Mount Sinai') in the first verse (25:1) and the last verse (26:46). Each of the two chapters has different subject-matter and can be treated separately, but they are also connected in that the punishments of ch. 26 are in part the result of not observing the sabbatical year commanded in ch. 25.

(Ch. 25) describes two year-long observances: the seventh or sabbatical year (year of release: *šĕmiṭṭâ*) in vv. 2–7, and the jubilee (*yôbēl*) year in vv. 8–55. Comparison has been made with the Mesopotamian *mîšarum* and the *andurāru* (Lewy 1958) which go back to the Old Babylonian and Old Assyrian periods (early second millennium BCE). Among the points to note are the following: Babylonian *andurāru* is cognate with the Hebrew *dĕrôr* release. A king would declare a *mîšarum* which was a general declaration of justice. He might also declare an *andurāru* 'release', which could include a remission of certain taxes, a release of debts, reversion of property to its original owners, or manumission of slaves. It was common for a king to declare such in his first year of reign. The Israelite innovation was to declare a jubilee at regular intervals rather than in the first year of a king as in Mesopotamia. The Akkadian evidence for the *mîšarum* and *andurāru* is generally accepted (cf. Finkelstein 1961), but its interpretation in relation to the Israelite institution is not necessarily simple. In solidly argued studies of both the biblical and the Mesopotamian evidence, N. P. Lemche (1976; 1979) found a lot of sloppy comparison in earlier studies. For example, OT material was used to interpret the Old Babylonian which was then used to interpret the Israelite, with clear dangers of circular reasoning. The existence of the practice of a king's granting a release in his first year in the Old Babylonian period proves nothing about the antiquity of the jubilee in Israel which is, after all, somewhat different. Lemche admits some evidence for the antiquity of a seventh fallow year in agriculture, but the development of a sabbatical year with all its social accoutrements seems late.

(25:2–7) envisages a basic cycle of 7-year periods or sabbatical years. The last year of this cycle was a year when the land had to be left fallow. No crops were to be sown. That which grew up by itself (volunteer growth) was allowed, and the people could eat it for food on a day-to-day basis, but no harvesting as such was permitted. Of course, by a divine miracle there would be no hardship since the land would produce enough in the sixth year to tide the inhabitants over to the harvest of the crops sown in the new cycle (vv. 19–22). In Leviticus the seventh year seems to be primarily an agricultural observance (cf. also Ex 23:10–11). According to some passages, however, loans and the enslavement of Israelites were also cancelled in the seventh year (Deut 15:1–3, 12–15; Jer 34:8–16). If so, the seventh year would have been an integral part of the nation's life, with widespread implications for the economy. On the other hand, there seems to be a contradiction between Leviticus, which sees the year of release as the jubilee, and those other passages which ascribe release to the sabbatical year (see below). This suggests that we find two separate systems, one in which the year of release is the seventh year, and the other in which the year of release is the fiftieth. Those texts which view the seventh year as the year of release do not seem to envisage a jubilee year at all.

The existence of a sabbatical year is attested in historical sources of the Second Temple period (Grabbe 1991: 60–3). This included a rest from growing crops, at least from the time of the Maccabees (1 Macc 6:49, 53; Josephus, *Ant.* 13.7.4–8.1 §§228–35; 14.16.2 §475). We also know from actual documents found in the Judean Desert that the cancellation of debts and return of property in the seventh year was a known institution (*Murabbaʿat* 18; 24). There is no mention of the jubilee year, however, except in literature such as the *Book of Jubilees*. The indication is, therefore, that the sabbatical year but not the jubilee was observed in Second Temple times. It is also reasonable to conclude that the seventh year was in some way observed in early post-exilic times, though how much further back it can be projected is a question. Whether the jubilee was ever observed is a matter of speculation.

The tithing cycle is not mentioned in Leviticus (or other P passages) but, if a sabbatical year existed, the tithes of Deut 14–15 would work only if operated on a 7-year cycle. That is, the tithe of the third year (Deut 14:28–9) would have to be co-ordinated with the seventh year, or it would sometimes fall on the sabbatical year when there was no produce on which to pay tithes. Thus, the tithe of the third year would have been paid on the third and sixth year out of the cycle rather than forming an independent 3-year cycle. On the matter of tithing in general, see Grabbe (1993: 66–72).

(25:8–55) describes the jubilee which took place after seven sabbatical-year cycles. The text is somewhat ambiguous. On the one hand, the jubilee might be thought to coincide with the last year of the seventh cycle (Lev 25:8); on the other hand, it is explicitly said to be the fiftieth year (Lev 25:10–11). If it was indeed the fiftieth year, it would mean two fallow years in a row, yet nothing is said about the effects of such a situation or how to cope with it. The later Jewish *Book of Jubilees* definitely counts a jubilee cycle of 49 years, showing that the 'fiftieth year' might be counted inclusively (i.e. including both the starting and finishing years in the calculation). It may be that this is what the author of Lev 25 has in mind, but the point is never clarified.

vv. 13–28, the jubilee was also a fallow year but, according to Leviticus, it was more than this; it was a year of release (also Lev 27:16–24; Num 36:4). Land was to return to its original family. Agrarian land was considered an inalienable heritage granted by God and to be kept in the family in perpetuity. Therefore, the land could not be sold permanently. Any sale was viewed really as a long-term lease which reverted back to the family in the jubilee year. The sale price was determined according to the length of time to the next jubilee, so that the purchaser was really paying for the number of crops obtained before it reverted to the original owners; the less time until the jubilee, the less was paid for the property. vv. 29–34 note that town property was treated differently and could be transferred without right of repossession, after a probation year in which the seller could change his mind and redeem it. On the other hand, Levitical property was treated like agrarian land in that it would revert to the original owner at the jubilee. vv. 35–55 deal with the question of helping the poor and needy among the Israelites by necessary loans, without charging interest. It moves on to the question of debt slavery. Slavery was accepted as an institution (as, indeed, it was in the NT). Foreign slaves could be bought and sold as chattels (vv. 44–6), though there were laws which regulated how they were treated (e.g. Deut 21:15–17). But Israelites were not to be treated as slaves. If someone sold himself or his family because of debts or poverty, the person was to be treated as a hired servant. He may also redeem himself or be redeemed by a relative, the redemption price being calculated according to the number of years until the jubilee. If he is not redeemed, he and his family were allowed to go free in the jubilee year. On the question of the release of slaves and cancellation of loans, there is some contradiction between Leviticus and other passages, as already noted above. Lev 25 and Lev 27 are the only descriptions of the jubilee year.

(26:1–46) is mainly composed of a list of blessings for obedience and curses for disobedience, and makes a fitting end to the book. An appropriate literary closure of a book such as this is a section which demonstrates the consequences of heeding or not heeding the commands contained in it. A similar conclusion is found in Deut 28. Such blessings and curses are well known from other ancient Near-Eastern literature. International treaties usually ended with a list of blessings and, especially, curses for disobedience (cf. McCarthy 1978:

172–87). The so-called 'law codes' often include a similar section. For example, the epilogue to the Code of Hammurabi spells out how the gods will punish the king in various ways for not heeding the marvellous laws which had just been listed (*ANET* 163–5). Probably the clearest example of an international treaty is that of Esarhaddon (Wiseman 1958; *ANET* 534–41). As with the list in Lev 26, the curses tend to dominate, with the blessings listed only briefly.

vv. 1–2 at first sight seem out of place in the context of chs. 25–6. However, they may form a connecting section between the two chapters. vv. 3–13 list the blessings for obedience which come first. There seem to be four of these, based on the formal structure (Hartley 1992): rain in due season (vv. 4–5), peace (vv. 6–8), fertility (vv. 9–10), and God's presence (vv. 11–13), though victory over enemies could be said to be a fifth (vv. 7–8), judging from the content (Porter 1976). vv. 14–38 give a much longer and more clearly structured section on the curses for disobedience. Five sections are marked off with the phrase, 'If you (still) disobey, I will punish you sevenfold' or similar words. The desire seems to be to create a crescendo effect, so that the longer the Israelites refuse to obey, the stronger becomes the punishment, multiplying sevenfold each time. This does not seem to be carried through consistently, though there is a sort of climax in the exile from the land. In fact, the individual curses seem to be listed by subject rather than according to any sense of increasing malignancy: defeat in battle (vv. 14–17), drought (vv. 18–20), wild animals (vv. 21–2), war, pestilence, famine (vv. 23–6), dire conditions and exile (vv. 27–39). Finally, hope is expressed for repentence and a return from captivity (vv. 39–45).

vv. 31–45 end the chapter with reference to an exile and return, which led many scholars to claim that this shows knowledge of the Exile of the Jews in 587/586 BCE and their return in 538. This may be a correct interpretation, but it is interesting to note that one of the traditional punishments is to have the people of the land taken captive (e.g. Codex Hammurabi, xxvi. 73–80; xxviii. 19–23). If the actual Exile is presupposed, the writer is surprisingly vague about the details; alternatively, the account of the Exile known to him was rather different from that described elsewhere in the OT. This suggests that the punishment of exile was a traditional one in such curses and not necessarily to be related to the historical situation. v. 46 forms a concluding piece. Is it the conclusion of ch. 26 only or is it a conclusion to a larger section? Its reference to 'statutes' (*ḥuqqîm*), 'judgements' (*mišpāṭîm*), and 'laws/teachings' (*tôrôt*) suggest that something larger than a chapter or even a couple of chapters is intended. Thus, this seems to be a concluding formula for the entire book (Hartley 1992: 414).

(Ch. 27) describes vows and tithe of livestock. It is also an important chapter about support for the priesthood. The chapter is usually seen as an appendix to the book and not part of the Holiness Code proper. The reason is that ch. 26 makes an appropriate ending with its general blessings and curses and, as noted above, 26:46 fits well as a concluding statement for the entire book. On the other hand, in the present structure of the book ch. 27 is parallel with chs. 1–7 in giving specific halakic instructions. Also, just as Deuteronomy does not end with the blessings and curses of ch. 28, so the final editors of Leviticus may have been reluctant to end with ch. 26. Therefore, Lev 27 may indeed be a later addition but one which the final editors regarded as appropriate and even essential.

(27:1–29) Much of this chapter is devoted to the question of vows and consecration of objects and property to God. It was possible to dedicate human beings, animals, houses, and land to God. vv. 2–8: if the dedicated object was a person, then he or she had to be redeemed by money. The valuation of the redemption money was according to age and sex and seems to be primarily economic; that is, it is according to how much the person is likely to earn by physical labour. This means that males were worth more than females of a similar age, and adults in their prime were worth more than children, youths, or the elderly. vv. 9–13, if an animal suitable for offering had been vowed, it had to be sacrificed, with no substitution being allowed. Any attempt at substitution meant that both the original vow and the substitute became dedicated to God. However, in the case of an unclean animal no sacrifice was possible. Therefore, it had to be redeemed by its valuation plus 20 per cent. vv. 14–15, if a house was dedicated, it could also be redeemed by paying its value plus 20 per cent. vv. 16–24: land was valued in relation to the jubilee year. In other words, the number of harvests remaining until the jubilee was calculated and the value set according to that number. Inherited land could then be redeemed for its valuation plus 20 per cent. If the owner did not redeem the land and it was sold, however, it was no longer in his power to redeem. Instead it became priestly property. According to Deut 18:1–21, Levites (including priests) were not to own land as individuals. Apparently, though, the temple and priesthood could own land jointly. (We know that such was the case in the Second Temple period.) Land which had been purchased (as opposed to inherited) did not belong perpetually to the purchaser but reverted to the original owner in the jubilee. Thus, if such land was consecrated, it would still go back to the owner in the jubilee, so its valuation without any addition was given to the priests.

vv. 26–7, firstling animals belonged automatically to God. This brief mention is all that Leviticus has on the subject. Other passages of priestly instruction fill this out (Ex 13:11–15; 34:19–20; Num 18:15–18): all clean animals were to be offered at the altar, with the appropriate portions burned, but the rest of the meat went entirely to the priests. Unclean animals were more complicated since there seems to be more than one set of instructions. It is clear that they were normally to be redeemed, though Ex 34:20 says this was to be with a lamb, whereas Lev 27:27 states that it is by their monetary value plus 20 per cent. Similarly, if not redeemed, 27:27 says they were to be sold for their assessed value, with the money going to the temple personnel, but Ex 34:20 says the animal's neck was to be broken.

vv. 28–9 devoted things (*ḥērem*) belonged solely to God and were not to be made use of by man. They could not be sold or redeemed. A devoted human being was to be put to death. This last statement is puzzling because normally the human beings which belonged to God were to be redeemed. For example, the first-born were to be redeemed for money because their place was taken by the Levites (Num 3:5–13; 18:15).

It seems unlikely that an Israelite would be allowed to devote another Israelite to God in this way. Therefore, it is unclear who the devoted person might be who would be put to death; however, there are several examples of prisoners-of-war being slain at God's orders, suggesting that this might be what was in mind (cf. Josh 10:24–7; 1 Sam 15).

(27:30–3) speaks of the tithe of livestock. The tithe of animals is nowhere else referred to in the Pentateuch. They were to be tithed apparently by running them past and cutting out every tenth animal, regardless of whether it was good or bad. If the owner tried to substitute an animal, not only was the original tithe animal still considered as belonging to YHWH but also the substitute. The point was that no substitution was to be made. Nothing is said about how the tithe was to be used. By inference from other passages (2 Chr 31:6), it was to go to the priests as a part of their income. A number of questions arise. Why is not the tithe of animals referred to elsewhere in the OT (apart from 2 Chr 31:6)? How was the tithing to be carried out? If the entire herd or flock was run by each year, the breeding stock would gradually become decimated (literally). Would it just have been the new crop of calves, kids, and lambs each time? This makes sense, but no discussion is given. Why? Is it because this was only a theoretical law which was never put into practice? Giving the first-born of each breeding animal would equal roughly 10 per cent, so how did the tithe relate to the command about the first-born? The question of how these instructions of Leviticus related to the actual situation in Israel is brought forcefully to our attention in these verses. For a further comment on the situation, see LEV E.4 above.

REFERENCES

Andreasen, N.-E. A. (1972), *The Old Testament Sabbath*, SBL Dissertation 7 (Missoula, Mont: Scholars Press).

Blenkinsopp, J. (1996), 'An Assessment of the Alleged Pre-Exilic Date of the Priestly Material in the Pentateuch', *ZAW* 108: 495–518.

Bloch-Smith, E. (1992), *Judahite Burial Practices and Beliefs about the Dead*, JSOTSup 123; JSOT/ASOR MS. 7 (Sheffield: JSOT)

Childs, B. S. (1979), *Introduction to the Old Testament as Scripture* (Philadelphia: Fortress).

Cross, F. M. (1947), 'The Priestly Tabernacle', *BA* 10: 45–68 (=*BAR* 1: 201–28).

Damrosch, D. (1987), 'Leviticus', in R. Alter and F. Kermode (eds.), *The Literary Guide to the Bible* (London: Collins), 66–77.

Day, J. (1989), *Molech: A God of Human Sacrifice in the Old Testament*, University of Cambridge Oriental Publications, 41 (Cambridge University Press).

Douglas, M. (1966), *Purity and Danger: An Analysis of the Concepts of Pollution and Taboo* (London: Routledge & Kegan Paul).

—— (1993), 'The Forbidden Animals in Leviticus', *JSOT* 59: 3–23.

Elliger, K. (1966), *Leviticus*, HAT 4 (Tübingen: Mohr [Siebeck]).

Finkelstein, J. J. (1961), 'Amisaduqa's Edict and the Babylonian "Law Codes"', *JCS* 15: 91–104.

Gennep, A. van (1960), *The Rites of Passage* (London: Routledge & Kegan Paul).

Gerstenberger, E. S. (1993), *Das dritte Buch Mose: Leviticus*, ATD 6 (Göttingen: Vandenhoeck & Ruprecht); ET *Leviticus: A Commentary*, OTL, tr. Douglas W. Stott (London: SCM; Louisville, Ky.: Westminster/John Knox, 1996).

Gorman, F. H., Jr. (1990), *The Ideology of Ritual: Space, Time and Status in the Priestly Theology*, JSOTSup 91 (Sheffield: Sheffield Academic Press).

Grabbe, L. L. (1987), 'The Scapegoat Ritual: A Study in Early Jewish Interpretation', *JSJ* 18: 152–67.

—— (1991), 'Maccabean Chronology: 167–164 or 168–165 BCE?' *JBL* 110: 59–74.

—— (1992), *Judaism from Cyrus to Hadrian*, i. *Persian and Greek Periods*; ii. *Roman Period* (Minneapolis: Fortress); British edn. in one vol. (London: SCM, 1994).

—— (1993), *Leviticus*, SOTS, Old Testament Guides (Sheffield: JSOT).

—— (1995), *Priests, Prophets, Diviners, Sages: A Socio-Historical Study of Religious Specialists in Ancient Israel* (Valley Forge, Pa.: Trinity Int.).

—— (ed.) (1997), *Can a History of Israel Be Written?* JSOTSup 245 = European Seminar in Historical Methodology, 1 (Sheffield: Sheffield Academic Press).

—— (2000), *Judaic Religion in the Second Temple Period: Belief and Practice from the Exile to Yavneh* (London: Routledge).

Haran, M. (1962), 'Shilo and Jerusalem: The Origin of the Priestly Tradition in the Pentateuch', *JBL* 81: 14–24.

—— (1978), *Temples and Temple-Service in Ancient Israel* (Oxford: Clarendon).

Hartley, J. E. (1992), *Leviticus*, WBC 4 (Dallas: Word Books).

Hecht, R. (1979–80), 'Patterns of Exegesis in Philo's Interpretation of Leviticus', *Studia Philonica*, 6: 77–155.

Heider, G. C. (1985), *The Cult of Molek: A Reassessment*, JSOTSup 43 (Sheffield: JSOT).

Houston, W. (1993), *Purity and Monotheism: Clean and Unclean Animals in Biblical Law*, JSOTSup 140 (Sheffield: Sheffield Academic Press).

Hübner, U. (1989), 'Schweine, Schweineknochen und ein Speiseverbot im Alten Israel', *VT* 39: 225–36.

Hurvitz, A. (1982), *A Linguistic Study of the Relationship between the Priestly Source and the Book of Ezekiel: A New Approach to an Old Problem*, Cahiers de la Revue Biblique, 20 (Paris: Gabalda).

—— (1988), 'Dating the Priestly Source in Light of the Historical Study of Biblical Hebrew: A Century after Wellhausen', *ZAW* 100 Suppl., 88–100.

Janowski, B. and Wilhelm, G. (1993), 'Der Bock, der die Sünden hinausträgt: Zur Religionsgeschichte des Azazel-Ritus Lev 16,10.21f', in Bernd Janowski, Klaus Koch, and Gernot Wilhelm (eds.), *Religionsgeschichtliche Beziehungen zwischen Kleinasien, Nordsyrien und dem Alten Testament: Internationales Symposion Hamburg 17.–21. März 1990*, OBO 129 (Fribourg: Universitätsverlag; Göttingen: Vandenhoeck 69.

Jenson, P. P. (1992), *Graded Holiness: A Key to the Priestly Conception of the World*, JSOTSup 106 (Sheffield: Sheffield Academic Press).

Kellermann, D. (1977), "*āshām*', *TDOT* (Grand Rapids, Mich.: Eerdmans), i. 429–37.

Kilian, R. (1963), *Literarkritische und formgeschichtliche Untersuchung des Heiligkeitsgesetzes*, BBB 19 (Bonn: Peter Hanstein).

Kirschner, R. (1982–3), 'Rabbinic and Philonic Exegesis of the Nadab and Abihu Incident (Lev. 10:1–6)', *JQR* 73: 375–93.

Kiuchi, N. (1987), *The Purification Offering in the Priestly Literature: Its Meaning and Function*, JSOTSup 56 (Sheffield: JSOT).

Knierim, R. P. (1992), *Text and Concept in Leviticus 1:1–9: A Case in Exegetical Method*, FAT 2 (Tübingen: Mohr [Siebeck]).

Knohl, I. (1987), 'The Priestly Torah Versus the Holiness School: Sabbath and the Festivals', *HUCA* 58: 65–117.

—— (1995), *The Sanctuary of Silence: The Priestly Torah and the Holiness School* (Minneapolis: Fortress).

Koch, K. (1959), *Die Priesterschrift von Exodus 25 bis Leviticus 16: Eine überlieferungsgeschichtliche und literarische Untersuchung*, FRLANT 71 (Göttingen: Vandenhoeck & Ruprecht).

Lemche, N. P. (1976), 'The Manumission of Slaves—the Fallow Year—the Sabbatical Year—the Jobel Year', *VT* 26: 38–59.

Lemche, N. P. (1979), 'Andurārum and Mīšarum: Comments on the Problem of Social Edicts and their Application in the Ancient Near East', *JNES* 38: 11–22.

—— (1985), *Early Israel: Anthropological and Historical Studies on the Israelite Society before the Monarchy*, VTSup 37 (Leiden: Brill).

—— (1991), *The Canaanites and Their Land: The Tradition of the Canaanites*, JSOTSup 110 (Sheffield: Sheffield Academic Press).

—— (1993), 'The Old Testament—a Hellenistic Book', *SJOT* 7: 163–93.

Levine, B. A. (1974), *In the Presence of the Lord: A Study of Cult and Some Cultic Terms in Ancient Israel*, SJLA 5 (Leiden: Brill).

Lewy, H. (1958), 'The Biblical Institution of D^{e}rôr in the Light of Akkadian Documents', *EI* 5: 21*–31*.

McCarthy, D. J. (1978), *Treaty and Covenant*, 2nd edn., AnBib 21A (Rome: Biblical Institute).

Marx, A. (1989), 'Sacrifice pour les péchés ou rites de passage? Quelques réflexions sur la fonction du, *ḥaṭṭā'ṭ'*, *RB* 96: 27–48.

—— (1994), *Les Offrandes végétales dans l'Ancien Testament: Du tribut d'hommage au repas eschatologique*, VTSup 57 (Leiden: Brill).

Milgrom, J. (1976), *Cult and Conscience: The ASHAM and the Priestly Doctrine of Repentance* (Leiden: Brill).

—— (1991), *Leviticus 1–16*, AB 3 (Garden City, NY: Doubleday).

—— (1992), 'Priestly ("P") Source', *ABD* v. 454–61.

Morgenstern, J. (1955), 'The Decalogue of the Holiness Code', *HUCA* 26: 1–27.

Newsom, C. A., and Ringe, S. H. (eds.) (1992), *The Women's Bible Commentary* (Louisville, Ky.: Westminster/John Knox; London: SPCK).

Noth, M. (1977), *Leviticus: A Commentary*, OTL, rev. trans. (London: SCM).

Porter, J. R. (1976), *Leviticus*, Cambridge Bible Commentary on the New English Bible (Cambridge: Cambridge University Press).

Rattray, S. (1987), 'Marriage Rules, Kinship Terms and Family Structure in the Bible', *Society of Biblical Literature Abstracts and Seminar Papers*, 26, ed. K. Richards (Atlanta: Scholars Press), 537–44.

Rendtorff, R. (1963), *Die Gesetze in der Priesterschrift: Eine gattungsgeschichtliche Untersuchung*, 2nd edn. (Göttingen: Vandenhoeck & Ruprecht).

—— (1982–95), *Leviticus*, BKAT 3 (Neukirchen-Vluyn: Neukirchener Verlag).

Reventlow, H. G. (1961), *Das Heiligkeitsgesetz formgeschichtlich untersucht*, WMANT (Neukirchen-Vluyn: Neukirchener Verlag).

Schüssler Fiorenza, E. (ed.) (1994a), with the assistance of S. Matthews, *Searching the Scriptures*, i. *A Feminist Introduction* (London: SCM).

—— (1994b), with the assistance of A. Brock and S. Matthews, *Searching the Scriptures* ii. *A Feminist Commentary* (London: SCM).

Schmidt, B. B. (1994), *Israel's Beneficent Dead: Ancestor Cult and Necromancy in Ancient Israelite Religion and Tradition*, FAT 11 (Tübingen: Mohr[Siebeck]).

Schwartz, B. J. (1991), 'The Prohibitions Concerning the "Eating" of Blood in Leviticus 17', in G. A. Anderson and S. M. Olyan (eds.), *Priesthood and Cult in Ancient Israel*, JSOTSup 125 (Sheffield: Sheffield Academic Press), 34–66.

Shafer, B. E. (1976), 'Sabbath', *IDBSup* 760–2.

Wegner, J. R. (1992), 'Leviticus', in C. A. Newsom and S. H. Ringe (eds.), *The Women's Bible Commentary* (Louisville, Ky.: Westminster/John Knox; London: SPCK), 36–44.

Wenham, G. J. (1979), *The Book of Leviticus*, NICOT (Grand Rapids, Mich.: Eerdmans).

Whybray, R. N. (1987), *The Making of the Pentateuch: A Methodological Study*, JSOTSup 53 (Sheffield: JSOT).

Wiseman, D. J. (1958), 'The Vassal-Treaties of Esarhaddon', *Iraq* 20, Part 1.

Wright, D. P. (1987), *The Disposal of Impurity: Elimination Rites in the Bible and in Hittite and Mesopotamian Literature*, SBL Dissertation, 101 (Atlanta: Scholars Press).

Zevit, Z. (1982), 'Converging Lines of Evidence Bearing on the Date of P', *ZAW* 94: 481–511.

7. Numbers

TERENCE E. FRETHEIM

INTRODUCTION

A. Character. 1. The book of Numbers, named for its census lists, is the most complex of the books of the Pentateuch. This can be seen in the variety of types of literature represented, e.g. lists, itineraries, various statutes, ritual and priestly prescriptions, poetic oracles, songs, wilderness stories, and even a well-known benediction (6:22–7). The interweaving of law and narrative characteristic of Exodus and Deuteronomy is most evident in Numbers; specific statutes again and again emerge from specific life situations, revealing a dynamic relationship of law and life.

2. Moreover, some of these texts border on the bizarre, with talking donkeys, curses from a non-Israelite diviner turned into blessings that have messianic implications, the earth swallowing up people, copper snakes that have healing powers, an almond-producing rod, an execution for picking up sticks on the sabbath, Miriam turning leprous, and repulsive instructions for discerning a wife's faithfulness. One is tempted to claim that these strange goings-on were constructed to match the incredible character of Israel's response to its God. To complicate these matters, God is often depicted in ways that challenge traditional understandings; at times it seems that God's identity is in the process of being shaped too.

B. Source and Tradition. 1. The origin of Numbers is also complex. Most scholars consider the book to be a composite of sources (both oral and written) from various historical periods. The book itself speaks of sources, the Book of the Wars of the Lord (21:14) and popular songs (21:17–18, 27–30). The tradition most identifiable is the Priestly writing (in several redactions), with its interest in matters of worship and priesthood; it is most attested in chs. 1–10; 26–36, and provides continuity with Ex 25–40 and Leviticus. Other sources, such as J and E (esp. in chs. 11–25), are more difficult to distinguish; it is common to speak simply of an older epic tradition. The association of blocks of texts with three primary locales (Sinai, 1:1–10:10; Kadesh, chs. 13–20; Moab, chs. 22–36) could reflect a way in which traditions were gathered over time. Beyond this, editorial activity seems unusually common (for detail, see Milgrom 1990: pp. xvii–xxi).

2. Also of scholarly import has been the study of individual traditions and their development, e.g. the Balaam cycle, the murmuring stories, the censuses, the wilderness encampment, the Transjordan conquest, the cities of refuge, land apportionment, and the priesthood. It is clear from such work that various Israelite interests from different times and places inform the present redaction. These traditions have in time (perhaps during and after the Exile) been brought to-gether to form a unified composition, but the character of that unity has been difficult to discern.

C. Structure. 1. The structure of Numbers, often thought to be non-existent, is best seen from two angles, those of the census lists and the geography of a journey.

2. The Census Lists (for detail, see Olson 1985). The over-arching structure of the book is laid out in terms of its two census lists (chs. 1; 26). The first registers the generation that experienced the Exodus and the giving of the law at Sinai, which is prepared to move towards the land of promise. When faced with dangers, however, the people do not trust the promise; they experience God's judgement (14:32–3) and fi-nally, in the wake of apostasy, die off in a plague (25:9). Even Moses and Aaron mistrust God and are prohibited from en-tering the land (20:12); only the faithful scouts, Caleb and Joshua, and the young (14:29) are allowed to do so. The oracles of Balaam (chs. 22–4) provide a hopeful sign of things to come, as God blesses the insiders through this outsider.

3. The second census (ch. 26) lists the members of the new generation (though no births are reported in Numbers). They are a sign of God's continuing faithfulness to ancestral prom-ises and will enter the land. The following texts (chs. 27–36) raise issues focused on the future in the land. No deaths, no murmurings, and no rebellions against the leadership are in view, while various hopeful signs are presented. This new generation is the audience for Deuteronomy.

4. Generally speaking, the censuses include representatives from each of the twelve tribes. This inclusiveness may have functioned in the wake of various devastating events in Israel's history as an assurance that all tribes were included among the chosen (see Douglas 1993).

5. The Geography of a Journey. The movement through Numbers can also be tracked in terms of three stages of a journey toward the fulfilment of the land promise, with all the problems encountered along the way in spite of careful pre-parations. The itinerary of 33:2–49 emphasizes the import-ance of the journey as such, apart from specific occasions. Laws are integrated into the story, providing for an ongoing ordering of the community as it encounters new situations. The positive opening and closing sections enclose a sharply negative picture.

(*a*) Numbers begins with the people still situated at Sinai, preparing to leave (1:1–10:10). That includes the organization of the camp and various statutes, especially regarding the sanctuary and its leadership. A somewhat idealistic picture emerges: a community ordered in all ways appropriate to God's dwelling in the centre of the camp, and the precise obedience to every divine command (e.g. 1:17–19, 54). The reader may wonder how anything could go wrong.

(*b*) In episodic fashion, Israel moves through the wilder-ness from Sinai to Transjordan (10:11–25:18). The disjunction with the opening (and closing) chapters is remarkable: obedi-ence to God's command turns to rebellion; trust becomes mistrust; the holy is profaned; order becomes disorder; the future of the people of God is threatened. Continuities with the wilderness journey story in Ex 15:22–19:1 are seen in the gifts of quail and manna, the ongoing complaints, and mili-tary victory; but discontinuities are also sharply presented,

evident especially in the conflict among leaders, sin, and divine judgement. Integrated with these journey reports are miscellaneous statutes (chs. 15; 18; 19), focused on purifica-tion and leadership support, the need for which grows out of these experiences.

(*c*) The journey concludes in the plains of Moab (26:1–36:13). This is an entirely positive stage. Conflicts are resolved through negotiation and compromise and land begins to be settled. Various statutes anticipate the future in the land; the community is to so order its life that this new dwelling-place of both God and people will not be polluted.

6. These three stages may also be characterized in terms of Israel's changing relationship with God, moving from fidelity to unfaithfulness and back to fidelity. But, through all these developments, God remains faithful and does not turn back from the ancestral promises to Israel (articulated most clearly by Balaam). Though Israel's journey involves judgement, that judgement is finally in the service of God's objectives of bles-sing and salvation.

7. Such a portrayal mirrors the situation of the implied (exilic) readers of the Pentateuch (for details, see the proposal in Fretheim 1996: 40–65). Israel's apostasy and experience of divine judgement lie in their recent past; signs of a hopeful future are articulated in both law and promise. The paradigm of old generation and new generation would be especially pertinent during the years of exile in a situation which could be seen to have parallels with that of the Israelites in the wilderness.

D. Leading Themes. 1. Certain themes provide compass points for negotiating the journey through Numbers: the wilderness book, the ancestral promises, the divine presence and guidance, divine revelation and human leadership, and holy people and holy priests.

2. A Wilderness Book. The entire book is set in the wil-derness. Appropriately, 'In the Wilderness' is the Hebrew title for Numbers. This setting presents problems and possibilities for shaping a community identity for the newly redeemed people of God. As a long-oppressed community, Israel has a deeply ingrained identity as 'slave'. It does not have the re-sources to move quickly to a 'slaves no more' (Lev 26:13) mentality; God must be at work to enable them to 'walk erect' once again. The period of wandering is a necessary buffer between liberation and landedness for the sake of forming such an identity. Such a process does not unfold easily for Israel or for God; even the most meticulous preparations for the journey are not able to make things go right. It is possible to take the people out of Egypt, but it proves difficult to take Egypt out of the people. The familiar orderliness of Egypt seems preferable to the insecurities of life lived from one oasis to the next. In other words, the problem is not so much the law as an inability to rely on the God who has brought freedom and keeps promises.

3. Israel's time in the wilderness is finally shaped by God's extraordinary patience and mercy, and the divine will to stay with Israel in this time of adolescence. No divine flick of the wrist is capable of straightening them out without comprom-ising their freedom. If God wants a mature child, the possi-bility of defiance must be risked. But it soon becomes clear that the process of maturation will take longer than a single generation. God will not compromise in holding Israel to high standards.

4. Ancestral Promises. God is committed to the ancestral promises, especially of land. As Israel moves out from Sinai, the goal is the land God is 'giving' (10:29 and often). Conditions regarding the land promise are expressed (14:8), which affect the future of individuals—even an entire generation—but not finally Israel as such. Beyond that, the promises are spoken almost exclusively by Balaam. His oracles ironically gather the clearest references to the promises in Numbers; no Israelite, including Moses, has standing enough left to bring them to expression.

5. The middle section (chs. 11–25) problematizes the movement toward fulfilment; the wilderness is a time of endangered promises. Again and again the people trust the deceptive securities of the past more than God's promised future (11:5; 21:5). Hence, they experience disasters of various kinds that threaten progress towards the goal, including plagues (11:33; 16:49), an abortive conquest (chs. 13–14), and snake infestation (21:6).

6. The final section (chs. 26–36), with the new generation in place, bespeaks confidence in the promises with the apportionment of lands (26:53–6) and the specification of boundaries (34:1–15). Initial settlements in Transjordan function as a 'down-payment' on the fulfilment of the promise (chs. 31–2). Moreover, various laws dealing with emerging issues constitute a hopeful sign in the midst of much failure and grief; a community will exist to obey them. In some sense, the ongoing promulgation of *law* is a witness that the *promise* of land will indeed be fulfilled.

7. Divine Presence and Guidance. God, not Moses, has given birth to this people (11:12) and has chosen to stay with the family and to dwell in the heart of their camp (5:3). From this womb-like centre blessings flow out into the encircled community. This intense kind of presence is promised for Israel's future in the land as well (35:34). Even Balaam testifies to the presence of such a God among this people (23:21–2).

8. Because of the intense presence of God in Israel's midst, and the recognition of God's holiness, the tabernacle was to be protected from casual contact. This concern is sharpened in view of the golden calf apostasy and the near annihilation of Israel (Ex 32:9–10). Precautions must be taken to prevent a recurrence for the sake of the integrity of the divine–human relationship. The tribe of Levi was consecrated for service at the tabernacle and made responsible for guarding this holy place (1:50–3). Sharp warnings about intrusion are issued (1:51–3; 3:10, 38); even Levites could die if furnishings were mishandled (4:17–20). Strikingly, encroachment is not a serious problem in the subsequent narratives, except as related to conflict over leadership (ch. 16). The more problematic issue is mistrust and rebellion with respect to God and God's chosen leaders. These forms of sinfulness in particular pervade chs. 11–25 and deeply affect the character of the journey and the shape of Israel's future. On God's wrath and judgement, see especially at NUM 1:53 and ch. 14.

9. Israel's God not only dwells in the midst of Israel, but also goes before them. The accompanying presence of God is associated with the pillar of cloud/fire; 9:15–23 speaks of it in such a way that the itinerary is not predictable or routinized. This symbol is linked to the ark of the covenant, which represents the presence of God (10:35–6). God's ongoing presence is the decisive factor in Israel's journey, but various texts witness also to the importance of human leadership; for example, the passage regarding Hobab's skills (10:29–32) is placed immediately before the ark text (10:33–6). God works in and through what is available, even characters such as Balaam, to move towards the divine objectives.

10. Divine Revelation and Human Leadership. Revelation is not confined to Sinai; it occurs throughout Israel's journey. Statutes and other divine words newly enjoin Israel all along the way. This was the case with Israel's wanderings *before* Sinai as well (15:26; 18:23). God's word is not delivered in a once-and-for-all fashion; it is a dynamic reality, intersecting with life and all its contingencies. This is demonstrated in the very form of this material in the interweaving of law and narrative (for detail, see Fretheim 1991: 201–7).

11. God's word is usually mediated through Moses, but not uniquely so. This becomes an issue during the journey. Challenges to Moses' (and Aaron's) leadership that began in the pre-Sinai wanderings are intensified in Numbers, and other leaders take up the argument. Related issues and disputes are pursued in various chapters (11; 12; 16; 17).

12. The issue is voiced most sharply by Miriam and Aaron: has God spoken only through Moses (12:2)? The response is negative. God is not confined to only one way to speak to this community; indeed, if need be, God will go around the chosen ones to get a word through. God's spirit even rests upon the outsider Balaam who mediates remarkably clear words of God (24:2–4, 15–16). Nevertheless, Moses does have a special relationship with God and challenges to his role are not countenanced.

13. God communicates to and through Moses often in Numbers; indeed, 7:89 speaks of Moses' contact with God in an almost routinized way. In 12:8 God himself claims for Moses a unique face-to-face encounter. Moses actually 'beholds the form of the LORD' and lives to tell about it. One facet of this relationship is especially remarkable: the genuine interaction between them as they engage issues confronting the wandering community. Characteristic of their relationship in Exodus (chs. 3–6; 32–4, cf. GEN 18:22–33), it intensifies in Numbers (chs. 11; 12; 14; 16; 21; cf. Ps 106:23).

14. This says something about both Moses and God. Moses' leadership credentials are considerable, including a capacity to tolerate threats to his authority (11:29) and to persevere with God (chs. 11; 14; 16), calling forth the strong statement regarding his unique devotion (12:3). God also is remarkably open to such discourse, treats the relationship with integrity, and honours the insights that Moses offers. Indeed, God may shape a different future in view of the encounter (14:13–20; 16:20–2). But such divine openness to change will always be in the service of God's unchanging goals for Israel and the creation (Balaam's point in 23:19).

15. Some of the disputes are focused on Aaron (and his sons) and their priestly leadership (chs. 16; 17). Actual tests are carried out which substantiate their unique role with respect to the sanctuary in the eyes of God. Members of this family also take actions that have an intercessory function; they stand 'between the dead and the living' and a plague is averted (16:47–50; cf. 25:7–13). This correlates with their mediating role in various rituals (chs. 5; 15).

16. Interest in the proper succession of leaders (Eleazar, 20:22–9; Joshua 27:12–23) demonstrates the crucial importance of good leaders for the stability of the community. Rebellion against God-chosen leaders is deeply subversive of God's intentions for the community and risks death short of the goal. But the leaders themselves are not exempt from strict standards (20:10–12). They may be held to a higher standard, because the impact of their mistakes has such a deep and pervasive effect on the community.

17. Holy People and Holy Priests. The call in Leviticus for the people to be holy (i.e. to live a life that exemplifies the holy people they are) is continued here (15:40). What constitutes a holy life, or that which is inimical to it, is continuous with the provisions of Leviticus in some ways. Various uncleannesses—whether moral or ritual in nature—are incompatible with holiness (chs. 5; 6). Yet, for Numbers, Israel's sins are focused on matters relating to leadership, mistrust of God and failure to believe in promises, and finally idolatry (ch. 25).

18. A case for more democratic forms of priestly leadership is pursued by Korah on the basis of the holiness of all the people (16:3). Moses' reply assumes gradations of holiness; even if all are holy, God chooses from among them certain persons to exercise priestly leadership, and this chosen status constitutes a holiness that sets them apart from other holy ones. The disaster experienced by Korah and his company (16:23–35) demonstrates their special status (16:40), as does the test with staffs (ch. 17).

19. Gradations of holiness are also evident within the members of the tribe of Levi. The Levites are set aside to care for the tabernacle, symbolized by their encampment between the tabernacle and the people. Among the Levites the family of Aaron is especially set aside for priestly duties (16:40; 17; 18:7–11, 19). Indeed, a 'covenant of perpetual priesthood' is made with this family because of the mediatorial actions of Phinehas (25:10–13).

20. The NT works with several themes from Numbers. It cites God's providing for Israel in the wilderness and lifts up Israel's infidelity as a warning for the people of God. These themes are carefully interwoven in 1 Cor 10:1–13, where many texts from Num 11–25 are referenced; it is carefully noted that these passages were 'written down to instruct us' (cf. Jn 3:14; Heb 3:7–4:11; 2 Pet 2:15–16; Jude 5–11; Rev 2:14–17).

E. Outline

COMMENTARY

Israel Prepares to Leave Sinai (1:1–10:10)

This entire section comes from the Priestly tradition. The chronological report (1:1) situates the census one month after the completion of the tabernacle (Ex 40:17) and nineteen days before the departure from Sinai (10:11), where Israel had been for almost a year (Ex 19:1). The tabernacle stands in the centre of the camp. Encamped around it are members of the tribe of Levi. Encircling them are the various tribes of Israel, three in each direction. The tabernacle situated in the centre of the camp expresses a divine centring for the community generally. At the same time, while God dwells among the people and guides them through the wilderness (9:17), the nature of that guidance is divinely limited. Hence, while God leads them from one oasis to the next, the divine guidance is not all-controlling and human leadership is crucial (10:29–32). The divine presence does not issue in a situation where the people have no option but to obey; disobedience is a lively possibility. Indeed, warning signs punctuate the narrative (e.g. 1:53); they alert Israel to the care needed by the community with respect to the near presence of God in their midst and the importance this has for the shape of the journey.

(1:1–54) The First Census The early mention of the 'tent of meeting' (v. 1) signals its importance for what precedes as well as what follows; it is synonymous with the tabernacle. How it is to be related to the tent of the epic tradition (Ex 33:7–11) is uncertain; the tabernacle may have assumed the role of the tent (see 7:89). The rare phrase, 'tabernacle of the covenant' (1:50, 53; 10:11; Ex 38:21) extends the designation for its major sacred object, the 'ark of the covenant'; the language focuses on the God–Israel relationship and the divine speaking associated with that.

This census list plays an important structural role in Numbers (see NUM C.2). God commands the census and also names one male from each tribe to assist (except Levi; two Joseph tribes keep the number at twelve, see Gen 48), 'the leaders of their ancestral tribes' (v. 16; cf. 2:3–31; 7:12–83; 10:14–28). To appear on this list was a continuing sign assuring each tribal group of their present identity and future place among God's chosen.

The census is to include the males of the old generation, 20 years and older. The purpose is conscription, to determine 'everyone able to go to war' (cf. 2 Sam 24:9); battles are expected (though there will be few to fight, see 21:1–3). Israel has good reason to be confident with these numbers (but they are not, 14:1–4). The results of the census (perhaps the same census as in Ex 38:26; cf. 12:37): 603,550 males; the second census yields 601,730 (26:51), though the tribal distribution changes somewhat. When women, children, and Levites are added, the total must have been about 2 million. The unrealistic number has not been resolved (for a survey, see Ashley 1993: 60–6); probably it was thought, if mistakenly, to be actually this large. Whether literal or symbolic, the number testifies to God's blessing and preserving this people, and keeping the divine promises. This generation will be unfaithful and, by divine decree (14:22–30), will die off in the wilderness. At the time of the new census, 'not one of them was left', except Joshua and Caleb (26:65).

The Levites, who do not bear arms and are not registered here (see 3:14), are given duties with respect to the tabernacle and its furnishings (detailed in NUM 4). They are charged to encamp around it, protect it from casual contact, maintain it, carry it during the journey, and pitch it at each stop. The 'outsider' (v. 51) refers to all who are not Levites, whether Israelite or alien (16:40). The sense of 'come near' is 'encroach' (see Milgrom 1990: 342–3). Violation of the tabernacle precincts means death, not as a court verdict, but as a penalty delivered on the spot by the levitical guards (see 18:7).

This drastic action is in the interests of the community as a whole, so that it will not experience the wrath of God (v. 53). God's wrath in Numbers is impersonal in its basic sense; it 'goes forth' or 'comes upon' (16:46; 18:5). Wrath is not a legal penalty, or a divine decision, but inevitably issues from the deed as a matter of the moral order; it is an effect intrinsically related to, growing out of, the violation of the place of God's presence or the divine–human relationship (see NUM 14). God is not conceived in deistic ways, however, and sees to the movement from deed to consequence, in sometimes sharp language (11:33). The effect may be death, often in Numbers because of plague (16:46–50; 31:16). It can be overcome by various means, from sacrificial ritual (8:19) to priestly intercession (16:47–50; 25:11).

Looming large over the exacting concern for the tabernacle are Israel's past infidelities, especially the golden calf *débâcle*, where Israel violated its relationship with God and jeopardized its future (Ex 32:9–10). God graciously chose to dwell among them; but, given the people's propensity to apostasy, safeguards had to be instituted. These strict measures are not to protect God from the people or the people from God (though violation could mean violence, v. 53), but to preserve a proper *relationship* between God and people. Israel has been honoured by this incredible divine condescension, but God remains God and this divine move is not to be presumed upon without the endangerment of life.

In v. 54 and throughout chs. 1–9, the Israelites are reported to have done exactly as God commanded. One wonders how anything could go wrong. Later failures cannot be blamed on faulty preparations.

(2:1–34) The Encampment With the tabernacle centred in the camp, and the Levites camped immediately around it (see NUM 3), God commands that the tribes be precisely ordered around the perimeter. They are to be ordered as companies ('hosts' or 'armies'), specifying military readiness. Three tribes are to be positioned at each side of the tabernacle, under their distinctive banners; each triad is named for the dominant tribe of the three (seen from the perspective of Israel's later history; cf. Gen 49), which is flanked by the other two tribes in each case—the camp of Judah (the most dominant) to the east, the side where the tabernacle opening was located, and Moses and the Aaronides were camped; Reuben to the south; Ephraim to the west; Dan to the north (the leaders of the tribes as in 1:5–15). This order of the tribes is the order for the march, beginning with Judah. The tabernacle, set in the midst of the Levites (v. 17), is to move between the camps of Reuben and Ephraim. God's commands are again followed. This camp may have been modelled after an Egyptian pattern (see Milgrom 1990: 340).

(3:1–4:49) The Levites This section describes two censuses of the tribe of Levi, its organization, and its responsibilities for transporting and guarding the tabernacle and its furnishings. The genealogical formula (3:1) links the generation of Moses and Aaron with those in Genesis (the last is 37:2; cf. Ex 6:14–25).

(3:1–13) occurs 'at the time when God spoke with Moses on Mount Sinai' (v. 1). Since that time Aaron's sons, Nadab and Abihu, have died childless (Lev 10:1–2); this reference alerts the reader to dangers associated with handling holy things, and the tasks of the Kohathites in particular (4:15–20). Aaron's other sons, Eleazar and Ithamar, were ordained as priests by Moses (the 'he' of v. 3; cf. Lev 8:30) and served with their father throughout his lifetime.

A distinction is made within the tribe of Levi between the descendants of Aaron, who attend to priestly duties, and other Levites, who assist the priests, with responsibilities for 'service at the tabernacle' (cf. 1:50–3 for an earlier summary). vv. 11–13 (restated in 8:16–18) recall the killing of the Egyptian firstborn and the sparing of the Israelite firstborn (see Ex 13:1–2, 11–15), in remembrance of (or repayment for) which God had consecrated the latter to a life of religious service; the Levites serve as substitutes for them (and their livestock for Israel's firstborn livestock). While the Levites are responsible to the sons of Aaron, it is as representatives of all Israel. It may be that God himself takes the census of the Levites and reports the results to Moses (3:12, 15–16).

(3:14–39) continues in narrative time and space from 2:34 and describes God's command of a census of the non-Aaronide Levites (total: 22,000), their encampment positions, and their specific responsibilities. The census of Levites was prohibited in 1:47–9 because they were non-military, served the tabernacle, included all from one month and older, and represented all Israel's firstborn (cf. 3:40–1). The levitical camp is ordered in terms of Levi's sons (Gershon, Kohath, and Merari); their clans encamp on three sides of the tabernacle and have varying duties with respect to its transit. The Kohathites (from whom Moses and Aaron are descended) are responsible for the most sacred objects (4:4; e.g. the ark), the Gershonites for the fabrics, and the Merarites for the supporting structures (responsibilities are detailed in 4:1–33). Aaron and his sons encamp on the pre-eminent, entrance (eastern) side of the tabernacle (v. 38). Aaron's son, Eleazar, is in charge of the leaders of the three clans (v. 32) and has general oversight of the tabernacle and certain special details (4:16); his brother Ithamar has oversight over the work of the Gershonites and the Merarites (4:28, 33). Again, God's commands are followed (3:16, 39, 42, 51).

(3:40–51) The firstborn system is detailed more fully here, where the firstborn of all Israel are numbered (22,273); each of the 273 persons over and above the 22,000 Levites is redeemed by five shekels apiece (paid apparently by the firstborn, v. 50, and given to the priests; cf. Lev 27:6). The figure of 22,273 seems too low in view of the census numbers in 2:32 (even assuming an equal number of female to male firstborn, this would entail an average of fourteen male children per family); no satisfactory explanation has been given. The redemption of the firstborn keeps the exodus action of God explicitly before the people as a reminder of their redeemed status. The recurring phrase 'I am the LORD' (common in Leviticus) is shorthand for the divine origin of the commands.

(4:1–33) delineates God's commands regarding the second levitical census, taken to determine the number of those (ages 30–50) who are to perform the actual duties; these ages differ somewhat from 8:24–6 and from other OT texts (e.g. Ezra 3:8), perhaps reflecting expanding community needs. Aaron and his sons are responsible for packing and unpacking the most holy things, with differently coloured cloths marking gradations of holiness (vv. 5–15); only they are allowed to see and touch them. The responsibilities of the three levitical groups for certain sanctuary items, as noted above, are also divinely commanded in detail, so that each item is exactly accounted for (Kohathites, vv. 1–20; Gershonites, vv. 21–8; Merarites, vv. 29–33). A special emphasis is given regarding the work of the Kohathites (4:17–20), not because their status is higher, but because they handle the 'most holy things'. God graciously takes their greater risk into account and specifies precautionary procedures for their handling of these objects. To die for improper contact with the most holy objects (vv. 15, 19–20) seems to have reference to direct, though mediated action by God (see NUM 1:53; Lev 10:1–2). This concern may be rooted in the golden calf apostasy, where the holiness of God was compromised.

(4:34–49) describes the implementation of God's commands; once again, they are obeyed to the letter (vv. 46–8 summarizes the results). The encampment is now fully prepared for the journey through the wilderness.

(5:1–6:21) Purification of the Camp This section, probably added late in the redactional process, deals with matters needing attention for the journey. Why these particular issues are collected at this point and ordered in this way is uncertain; some links are evident (e.g. 'be unfaithful' in 5:6, 12; guilt offerings) and they deal both with matters of ritual purity and moral living among the laity (male and female), and the priests have responsibilities relating to both spheres. More generally, matters of purity are important in recognition of God's dwelling in the camp (5:3), but so also are matters of moral wrongdoing, which 'break faith with the Lord' (5:6). Several cases extend or modify statutes in Leviticus.

(5:1–4) Persons who are ritually (and communicably) unclean for various reasons are to be put outside the camp to live in tents or caves, without access to worship, so as not to contaminate the community or defile the tabernacle. This statute reinforces or extends those in Leviticus (see Lev 13:45–6; 15:31–3; 21:1–3, 11).

(5:5–10) extends Lev 6:1–7; the new focus is on wrongdoing (including a false oath) where the injured party dies without next of kin, in which case priests receive the appropriate restitution. The public confession of this deliberate sin against the neighbour (see Lev 5:5) is also newly integral to the ritual; note that the sin against the neighbour 'breaks faith with God'. vv. 9–10 note that priests are to receive their rightful dues.

(5:11–31) has a complex history given the literary difficulties; yet at least some features (e.g. repetition) serve a purpose in the present redaction (for detail, Milgrom 1990: 350–4). Though often called a trial by ordeal, the coalescence of verdict and sanction, effected by God not the community, suggests rather an oath that is dramatized. The focus of this case-law is a wife, possibly pregnant, whose husband suspects ('is jealous of') her of adultery but has no evidence, whether she has actually committed adultery (vv. 12–14a) or is only suspected of doing so (14b). In the former case, this text softens the penalty prescribed for an adulteress in Lev 20:10, probably because there was no evidence. In the latter case, a woman unjustly accused could be vindicated; so the jealous husband (or the community) could not arbitrarily decide her fate.

In either case, the man brings his wife (who is 'under [his] authority', vv. 19, 29) to the priest with a grain offering, though without the usual oil and frankincense (Lev 2:1–10), as was the case with sin offerings (Lev 5:11). Such offerings bring 'the [potential] iniquity to remembrance' before God. The procedure: the priest prepares a mixture of holy water (see Ex 30:17–21) and dust from the tabernacle floor, probably thought to have potency because of its contact with holy things, in an earthen vessel (which could be broken after use, Lev 11:33). The priest is then to bring the woman 'before the LORD' (the altar), loosen her hair—a sign of (potential) uncleanness, Lev 13:45—and put the grain offering in her hands. The priest has her take an oath regarding the suspicions registered (vv. 19–22): if she has been faithful, she will be immune from the water; if unfaithful, the water will cause her sexual organs to be affected adversely in some way (the effect is correlated with the crime) and she will be ostracized among the people (see Job 30:9) and precluded from having children (v. 28). If the woman is pregnant, the effect may be a miscarriage. The nature of the effect of the water upon the woman is considered a sign as to whether the woman has told the truth. The repeated 'Amen. Amen' ('so be it'), expresses her willingness to accept either result of the ritual (see Deut 27:15–26). Unlike her husband, she is given no other voice in the ritual.

In 5:23–8 (v. 24 anticipates 26b, as v. 16a does 18a), the priest writes the curses on a surface from which the ink could be washed off into the water the woman is to drink; the imbibed water is thought to contain the power of the curses (cf. Ex 32:20; Ezek 3:1–3). The priest takes the grain offering from her and burns a portion of it on the altar, after which she drinks the water (vv. 25–6). If the woman has been unfaithful, she will experience distress (no time frame is specified), hence the phrase, 'waters of bitterness'. The potion actually has no bitter taste nor brings pain in itself, but this would be the effect if God adjudged the woman guilty (v. 21; cf. Zech 5:1–4; Jer 8:14; 9:15).

(5:29–31) summarizes the essence of the two types of case for which this ordeal would be applied. The husband is freed from any responsibility for a false accusation (the need to express this is striking, and it opens the way to frivolous expressions of jealousy). If the woman is guilty, she bears the consequences (by divine agency).

One might claim that the ritual could not accurately determine the truth; but, as in the sacrificial system, it is God, before whom the woman is brought, who knows the truth of the situation and is believed to act in the ritual and to effect the proper result. Yet, one wonders if this procedure ever verified suspicions; perhaps the threat was sufficient to elicit confessions. It was only women who lived under such threat, and the ritual is degrading; that no comparable law existed for the male, or no concern is expressed that undisclosed male infidelity might contaminate the camp, is revealing of the patriarchy involved. The language of jealousy is also used in the marriage analogy for Israel's relationship with God, her husband (who is jealous, e.g. Ex 20:5; 34:14), and may have informed prophetic rhetoric (e.g. Isa 3:16–17; Ezek 23:31–4). Jesus' attitude towards women (Lk 7:36–50; Jn 4:1–30; 8:1–11) breaks open the one-sidedness of the Numbers ritual (see Olson 1996: 38–9).

(6:1–21) provides for a temporary, voluntary nazirite vow (from nāzîr, meaning 'set apart'; the unpruned vine was also called a nāzîr, perhaps a symbol of Israel as consecrated to the Lord; the word for uncut hair is nezer). As with the other statutes in this section, the laity are the focus of concern; yet these statutes highlight priestly obligations relating thereto (and may suggest priestly control over their activity). The text does not institute the nazirite vocation, but regulates a consecrated life in certain ways. Vows, always individual acts, were common in ancient Israel (see 30:1–16) and this vow was 'special' (v. 2).

Yet, the precise purpose for becoming a nazirite remains elusive. Generally, nazirites were male or female individuals who took a vow of consecration for a special vocation. Am 2:11–12 states that God raised up nazirites; the parallel with the prophets means they had a high calling (as does their parallel with the priests). That they generated opposition among the people, who made them drink wine and thereby prevented them from fulfilling their calling, suggests their importance. The stories of Samson and probably Samuel, lifelong nazirites (dedicated by their parents from the womb, cf. Jer 1:5), suggest that God called such persons to specific tasks (cf. Judg 5:2; Gen 49:26). Wenham (1981: 85) calls them 'the monks and nuns of ancient Israel', but we do not know if this was considered an 'office', whether many took the vow, or how long a term was.

The nazirite vow entailed separation from products of the vineyard (and other intoxicants), haircuts, and corpses; their return to secular life was signified by cutting the hair. As such, these persons were highly visible members of the community, signs to all of total dedication to God. They bore similarities to the Rechabites (2 Kings 10:15; Jer 35), conservative proponents of ancient Israelite traditions who rejected Canaanite culture, including viticulture and building houses.

Like the high priests, nazirites were not to come into contact with (even within sight of) a corpse, but unlike them, accidental contact required rites of purification (vv. 6–12; cf. 5:2–3; 19:11–12, 19). Upon being purified, they were to 'sanctify the head [hair]', i.e. be reconsecrated (vv. 11c–12). vv. 13–20 describe the ritual at the completion of their consecration; the range of offerings (cf. Lev 8) suggests the high status of the nazirite; returning to secular life was a major step. The ritual includes the shaving of the head and the burning of the hair (because it is considered holy). v. 21 summarizes the force of the previous verses. On possible links to Jesus, John the Baptist, and the early church, see Mt 2:23; Lk 1:15; Acts 18:18; 21:23–4; on nazirites in Second-Temple Judaism, see Milgrom (1990: 355–8).

(6:22–7) **The Aaronic Benediction** The placement of this benediction seems unusual; it may be another item that prepares the people for the journey through the wilderness. This is the blessing for the time of departure, and daily throughout their journey. Each line, with God as subject, is progressively longer (three, five, seven Hebrew words); besides the name YHWH, twelve Hebrew words signify the twelve tribes.

This benediction in some form was widely used in ancient Israel, especially at the conclusion of worship (see Lev 9:22; Deut 21:5; 2 Chr 30:27; Ps 67:1; 121:7–8; see its ironic use in Mal 1:8–10). Putting the name of God on the people may have been understood literally, given the inscription on two cigarette-sized silver plaques found near Jerusalem, dating from the seventh–sixth centuries BCE (for such parallels, see Milgrom 1990: 360–2). The blessing has been commonly used in post-biblical Jewish and Christian communities.

One probably should not see a climactic arrangement in the clauses; so, for example, blessing would include peace. Perhaps the second verb in each case defines the first more specifically, but together the six verbs cover God's benevolent activity from various angles and state God's gracious will for the people.

Blessing has a wide-ranging meaning, touching every sphere of life. It testifies most basically to the work of God the Creator, both within the community of faith and without. No conditions are attached. It signifies any divine gift that serves the life, health, and well-being of individuals and communities. Keeping is a specific blessing to those with concerns for safety, focusing on God's protection from all forms of evil (Ps 121:7–8), pertinent for wilderness wandering.

God's face/countenance (the same Hebrew word) is a common anthropomorphism (esp. in Psalms; see Balentine 1983). The shining face of God (contrast the hiding face) signifies God's benevolent disposition towards the other, here in gracious action, for which Israel can make no claims

(Ps 67:1). The lifting up of the Lord's countenance signifies a favourable movement towards the other in the granting of peace, that is, wholeness and fullness of life. Putting God's name on the people (supremely by means of the word) emphasizes the divine source of all blessings.

(7:1–8:26) **Final Preparations for Tabernacle Worship** The chronological note at 7:1 indicates that what follows is a flashback (it continues through 10:10); it is one month earlier than the time of 1:1 and coincides with Ex 40 and the day Moses set up the tabernacle; yet it assumes Num 3–4 and the provisions made for carrying the tabernacle. This literary technique suspends the forward movement of the narrative and returns the reader to the occasion of the divine descent to dwell among the people and their grateful response.

(7:1–88) describes the consecration of the tabernacle in connection with which offerings were made by the leaders of the twelve tribes. vv. 1–9 describe one gift: six wagons and twelve oxen to carry the tabernacle and its furnishings. The Merarites received two-thirds of the wagons and oxen because they carry the supporting structure; the Kohathites carry the most holy things by hand. 7:10 refers to the offerings presented in both vv. 1–9 and 12–88. vv. 11–83 specify other gifts: necessities for the public altar sacrifices and the priesthood—silver and gold vessels, animals, and flour mixed with oil and incense—to be offered at the altar whenever needed (not at one dedication occasion). The tribal leaders, in the order given in 2:3–31, each give the same offerings on the successive days of the celebration; they are listed out twelve times, and vv. 84–8 provide a total. This striking repetition underlines the unity and equality of the tribal groups and the generosity of their support for the tabernacle.

(7:89) seems out of place, but it emphasizes that God's ongoing commitment to Israel (not only to dwell among them, but to speak to Moses) matches the people's obedient response regarding God's dwelling-place. The mercy seat is the cover of the ark of the covenant, upon which were fixed two cherubim, sphinx-like creatures, shaped to form a throne for the invisible God (1 Sam 4:4; 2 Sam 6:2); in effect, the ark was God's footstool (2 Kings 19:15; 1 Chr 28:2; for description, see Ex 25:17–21). From this place, God will speak to Moses on a regular basis when he enters the tabernacle; this fulfils God's promise in Ex 25:22 and is reported in the narrative that follows (Num 11:16–30).

(8:1–4) specifies lighting directions for the seven tabernacle lamps (commanded by God in Ex 25:37, but not reported in Ex 37:17–24), with a reminder of how the lamps were constructed. Their seven branches and flowery design may have symbolized the tree of life (see 1 Kings 7:49 for the temple lampstands; cf. also Zech 4:1–14; Rev 11:4); the branched lampstand or menorah remains an important symbol of light in Judaism.

(8:5–26) (the setting is still as Ex 40; cf. Num 3:11–13); the Levites are consecrated 'to do service at the tent of meeting' (v. 15; cf. Lev 8; the priests are sanctified, while the Levites are purified). vv. 5–19 state the divine command and rationale for the ceremony and vv. 20–2 stress that it was obeyed. This entails participation in a purification rite (vv. 5–7; cf. 6:9;

19:1–22; Lev 14:8–9) so they can perform this service without endangering themselves or the community. The Levites are then presented 'before the LORD' (v. 10) and before 'Aaron and his sons' (v. 13) in the presence of the people. The people lay their hands on them, symbolizing that the Levites have become their sacrifice, a 'living sacrifice' dedicated to the service of God in their stead (vv. 10–11; cf. 3:40–51). The Levites in turn lay their hands on the head of the bulls, which are sacrificed to cleanse the sanctuary (the whole burnt offering, v. 8a) and to atone for sins they had committed (v. 12b). God claims that the choice of the Levites is rooted in the Exodus events (3:5–13), and that they are 'mine...unreservedly given to me from among the Israelites' (vv. 14–16); God in turn gives them to the Aaronides for service at the tabernacle (see 3:9). This constitutes an act of atonement for the Israelites (for whom the Levites undertake the work) to prevent any plague resulting from too close a contact with the holy things. The section concludes with the typical reference to obedience and a summary of the Levites' cleansing (vv. 20–2), followed by a reference to age requirements (vv. 23–6; cf. 4:47) and a clarification that they are not priests, but assist the Aaronides in their responsibilities.

(9:1–14) **The Passover at Sinai** This section continues the flashback begun at 7:1. vv. 1–5 report a second celebration of the Passover in fulfilment of the 'perpetual ordinance' of Ex 12:24. This celebration also precedes the wilderness journey, and enhances this moment of departure in Israel's life.

A question is presented to Moses (and Aaron) as to whether those who had become unclean through touching a corpse (see 5:1–4; 19:11–20) could celebrate Passover. Upon consulting the Lord (see 7:89), Moses is told that such unclean persons (and possible descendants) should not be denied Passover and are to keep it one month later, i.e. the fourteenth day of the *second* month. In view of v. 6 ('could not keep') this represents an adjustment in the law (see NUM D.10). The (later?) addition of another case of persons away from the camp (v. 9) assumes the land settlement and is a still further adjustment of passover law. For stipulations regarding celebration, see Ex 12:10, 46. For reference to not breaking the bones of the passover lamb (9:12), see Jn 19:36.

Supplemental instructions also adapt older regulations for those who are clean and at home (v. 13). Such a strict ordinance at this point reflects a concern that others might delay celebration until the second month. A permissive rubric in v. 14 is given for the aliens, non-Israelites who are residing permanently in the land (cf. Ex 12:19, 48–9). Being 'cut off from the people' is explained as bearing (the effects of) one's own sin, which is either banishment or execution, either judicially or at God's own hand. As in 5:31, the last seems likely (see Milgrom 1990: 405–8).

(9:15–23) **Divine Guidance in the Wilderness** This section begins (v. 15) with a flashback to Ex 40:34 and supplements Ex 40:36–8 regarding the relation between the cloud/fire and the stages of Israel's journey. It describes in advance an ongoing feature of that journey; the actual departure is not reported until 10:11. vv. 17–23 anticipate the march, stressing Israel's obedience to the divine leading at every stage.

In Israel's pre-tabernacle journeying, God 'in' (not 'as') the pillar of cloud and fire led them through the wilderness (Ex

13:21–2). Divine leading follows this Passover as it did the first. This was a single pillar, with the fire within the cloud (Ex 14:24; 40:38); references to the 'glory' of the Lord in the cloud (Ex 16:10) refer to the fire (Ex 24:17). Here this 'glory-cloud' is linked to the tabernacle (and the ark, 10:33–6); its rising and setting schedule the stages of Israel's journey. It is likely that the cloud would rest on the tabernacle and, while the tabernacle remained in the middle of the marching people, the cloud would proceed to the front of the procession (see v. 17; 14:14). The various timings of this cloud activity (v. 22) emphasize obedience and the need to follow a schedule ('charge') set by God, however irregular. At the same time, divine activity does not function apart from human agency (see 10:1–10, 29–32).

(10:1–10) The Two Silver Trumpets God commands Moses to make two trumpets of hammered silver (about 1 ft. long with a wide bell). They are to be blown by priests on various occasions: summoning the congregation or its leaders (vv. 3–4), breaking camp (vv. 5–6, presumably all four sides according to the order in Num 2, so the LXX), engaging in battle (v. 9; see 31:6), and on days of rejoicing (see 2 Kings 11:14; Ezra 3:10), appointed festivals (see chs. 28–9), and monthly offerings (v. 10; see 28:11–15). In vv. 9–10, the language anticipates the land settlement. A distinction is made (v. 7) between an 'alarm', perhaps a series of short blasts, and a 'blow', one long blast.

A rationale for the blowing of trumpets is given in vv. 9–10: to bring Israel's situation before God, who is thereby called to act on their behalf, either in battle (salvation from enemies) or in and through the offerings (forgiveness and well-being). The call of the trumpet is picked up in eschatological contexts (Zech 9:14; 1 Cor 15:51–2), exemplifying continuity across all generations of God's people. The blowing of the trumpets by the sons of Aaron complements the rising and the setting of the cloud. With the role of Hobab in 10:29–32, it becomes apparent that clear-sighted human leadership is integral to effective divine guidance.

The Wilderness Journey (10:11–25:18)

This middle section of Numbers describes Israel's journey from Sinai to the plains of Moab. The emphasis upon Israel's obedience to this point stands in sharp contrast to what follows. The beginnings of the march (10:11–36) signal no problems, but with 11:1 the carefully woven fabric comes apart at the seams. In spite of precise preparations, disloyalty now fills the scene and severely complicates the move towards the land. Warnings of divine judgement have been given (1:53; 3:4, 10; 4:15, 18–20; 8:19), but they go unheeded, with disastrous results.

Many of these narratives (a mixture of the traditional sources) are ordered in a comparable way (see at 11:1–3) and mirror the wilderness stories of Ex 15:22–18:27. Once again we hear of manna, rocks producing water, battles with desert tribes, and non-stop complaints. But Numbers is different. The complaints in Exodus are tolerated, as if a long-oppressed people is entitled to some grumbling. In Numbers, however, in view of the giving of the law and the golden calf débâcle, the themes of sin, repentance, and judgement are introduced. The people are sharply identified as rebellious, against both God and Moses/Aaron, and the judgement of God is invited into the picture again and again.

(10:11–28) Departure from Sinai The date in v. 11 is nineteen days after the census (1:1), which was eleven months after arrival at Sinai (Ex 19:1). The time of departure is set by divine command, signalled by the cloud (see 9:15–23). In vv. 14–28 the marching order of the tribal units according to a three-tribe standard (or regiment) follows the arrangement in Num 2. The positioning of the Levites, those who carry the tabernacle items (vv. 17, 21), is not precisely symmetrical (see chs. 3–4). For the leaders see 1:5–15; 2:3–31; 7:12–83. The end of the first stage of the journey is anticipated in the reference to the settling of the cloud in the wilderness of Paran (v. 12; see 12:16), the setting up of the tabernacle framework (v. 21), and the reference to three days' journey (10:33).

(10:29–36) Human and Divine Guidance These verses formed part of the older epic tradition. Both v. 29 and the tradition are ambiguous as to whether Hobab or Reuel is Moses' father-in-law; in Ex 2:18 Reuel is, but in Judg 4:11 Hobab is so identified (and Jethro in Ex 3:1; 18:1). Perhaps 'father-in-law' refers to any relative by marriage. The Midianites are often mentioned positively (contrast chs. 25; 31); being a desert tribe, they would know the wilderness. Moses' invitation shows that the guidance of the cloud is not deemed sufficient. The marching community is in need of the 'eyes' of a human guide, even from outsiders such as Hobab (cf. also Balaam; Jethro in Ex 18). Both divine and human activity are necessary for the people to find their way (so also the spies in ch. 13). Moses promises that Hobab's people will obtain the goodness the Israelites receive from God (see Judg 4:11).

The ark in association with the cloud (see 9:15–23) precedes the community here (v. 33). The second 'three days' journey' is probably a dittograph. Moses' directives to the Lord (vv. 35–6), at the departure and arrival of the ark, are old poetic pieces. They portray the march as a liturgical procession. God was believed to be intensely present wherever the ark was (7:89; see Ps 68:1; 132:7–8). God, the Lord of Hosts ('the ten thousand thousands of Israel'), leads Israel in battle against its enemies (14:44; 1 Sam 4:1–7:2). That Moses would invite the Lord to become active on behalf of Israel demonstrates again the integration of human activity and divine.

(11:1–3) A Paradigm of Rebellion These verses provide a pattern in both form and content for several episodes that follow: murmuring; judgement; cry (of repentance); intercession; deliverance (on Exodus parallels, see above; for content see NUM 13:1–14:45). Place-names are at times etymologized for convenient recall of the story.

The peoples' complaints of unidentified misfortunes are not specifically directed to God, but God hears them. The divine anger is provoked and 'the fire of the LORD', perhaps lightning (see Ex 9:23–4; 2 Kings 1:9), consumes outlying areas of the camp (a threat to its integrity). The people direct their response to Moses, who intercedes on their behalf, and the storm stops. The place was called Taberah ('Burning'), referring to both divine anger and its effects.

(11:4–35) Rebellion and Leadership The coherence of this passage is difficult, perhaps reflecting different traditions; yet good sense can be made of the awkwardness. On the 'miraculous' provision of food in the wilderness see NUM 20:1–13.

This murmuring immediately follows the first; complaining has become a pattern of life. The complaints of the rabble (non-Israelites, Ex 12:38), intensified by Israelites, despise God's gifts of food (vv. 6, 18) and deliverance (v. 20). Nostalgically recalling the (mostly vegetable!) diet typical for Egyptians, they cry out for fish (cf. v. 5). God's gift of manna (see EX 16), which the narrator notes was tasty and choice, was not thought to provide the strength they needed. This amounts to a rejection of God and a request for the Exodus to be reversed (v. 20)!

God's anger is revealed to Moses, who joins the people in complaint about a related matter (vv. 10–15). In language typical of lament psalms, Moses complains that, given what the people have become, God has mistreated him, placed too heavy a leadership burden on him (see Ex 18:18), and provided insufficient resources. Feeling caught in the middle, he asks for either relief or death. The maternal imagery Moses uses is striking; God has conceived and birthed this people (see Deut 32:18), and hence God should assume the responsibilities of a wet-nurse and see to their nourishment. Moses should not have to carry this burden 'alone', implying that God is somehow negligent.

A lively exchange between God and Moses follows (vv. 16–23). God replies to Moses in two respects: he will share the spirit given to Moses with others, who will help bear the burden (see vv. 24–30); God will provide the meat for which the people have asked (see vv. 31–2). Regarding the latter, however, God's anger at the people remains. Repeating their complaints, God declares that they are to prepare for an encounter with him; they will indeed get meat, a month's worth, but so much that it will become loathsome. Moses responds by wondering how meat can be found for so many people (only soldiers are counted, 1:46). God responds with a rhetorical question: in effect, God's hand is not too short (NRSV fn.; no general statement is made about divine power; cf. Isa 50:2; 59:1) to provide this amount of food. God will show that his word is good.

As for burden-sharing (vv. 16–17, 24–30), Moses obeys God and gathers seventy elders around the tent (probably in the centre of the camp in spite of vv. 26, 30, which may speak of movement within the camp). God shares Moses' spirit (*rûaḥ*, not quantitatively understood), which had its source in God, with the elders, who prophesy. Such a charisma was given to various leaders (see 24:2, 27:18, 1 Sam 10:5–10) and was transferable (see 2 Kings 2:9; on prophecy and ecstasy, see Milgrom 1990: 380–4). While they prophesy only once (unlike Moses), 16:25 suggests they assume some ongoing burdens. Even two elders who remained in the camp (Eldad and Medad) receive a share of *God's* spirit. In the face of efforts by Joshua to stop them, Moses refuses any protection of his authority or restriction of the divine word to established channels (see 12:1–16; Balaam); indeed, he wishes that all God's people could receive this charisma.

The gift of meat (vv. 18–20, 31–5) comes in the form of quails (see Ex 16:13; Ps 78:26–31), carried into the camp on a wind (*rûaḥ*) provided by God. They cover the ground for miles to a depth of two cubits (about 3 ft.); the least that anyone gathered was ten homers (probably 60 bushels). But before they had finished eating (the entire amount; cf. vv. 19–20), God's anger was provoked and a plague (related to the food?) swept the camp.

The place was called Kibroth-hattaavah ('Graves of craving'), recalling the people's complaint (v. 4) and the effects of the plague.

(12:1–16) Familial Challenge to Moses' Leadership This text concerns the authority of the Mosaic tradition in view of rival claims regarding divine revelation; it may reflect later power struggles among priestly groups (cf. NUM 16).

Challenges to Moses as a unique spokesman for God are brought by his sister and brother (though God alone hears them, v. 2?). The stated basis for the challenge is that Moses had married a Cushite woman. Cush usually refers to Ethiopia (if so, this would be Moses' second wife; so the LXX), but here it probably refers to a Cush in northern Arabia (see Hab 3:7). If so, she would be Zipporah, a Midianite (10:29; Ex 2:15–22).

Why this issue is raised remains uncertain. If v. 1 is integral to the reason given in v. 2, the issue centres on intrafamilial conflict regarding authority in view of Zipporah's (growing?) leadership role and/or influence with Moses (see Ex 4:24–6; 18:2). Miriam and Aaron assume that God has spoken through them (cf. Mic 6:4), confirmed by God in v. 5, for Miriam is a prophet (Ex 15:20) and Aaron speaks for God (Ex 4:15). 11:4–35 has shown that God does not speak only through Moses; moreover, God's spirit will rest upon Joshua (27:18) and even on Balaam (24:2–4, 15–16). God is not restricted to a single way into this community.

Yet, challenges to Moses' status with God are not countenanced. The narrator bases this point on Moses' unique relationship with God, stated generally (v. 3, devout, humble before God) and, in an act of conflict resolution, God's own words to Aaron and Miriam in Moses' presence. God customarily speaks to prophets in visions and dreams, but Moses is different for two reasons: he is uniquely entrusted with the house of Israel (see Ex 40:38) and God speaks to him directly (lit. mouth to mouth) and he sees the form of YHWH, a human form that God assumes (cf. 14:14; Ex 24:9–11; Deut 34:10; in Deut 4:15, the *people* see no form). The issue pertains both to what is heard (that is, clarity) and what is seen (God). Unlike with dreams and visions, Moses' entire person, with all senses functioning, is engaged in the experience (for detail, see Fretheim 1984: 79–106). God assumes (v. 8c) that Miriam and Aaron were aware of this uniqueness, and his response is anger (see 11:33).

When Miriam becomes leprous (an unidentified skin disease), Aaron interprets it as a consequence of *their* foolish sin and pleads ironically to 'my lord' Moses that he (not God!) spare both Miriam and himself. The Hebrew 'do not lay sin upon us' (NRSV fn.) should not be translated 'punish'; rather, the effect is intrinsic to the deed. The whiteness of Miriam's skin (a reversal of the dark skin of Moses' wife?) occasions the stillborn analogy, in effect: do not let her waste away to death. Aaron may not suffer the same effects because of his confession and plea or perhaps because he is high priest (see Lev 22:4), revealing a clerical (and male) bias.

Moses prays to God on Miriam's behalf, but God responds that she is to be barred from the camp for seven days. The levitical regulations speak of a fourteen day process for leprosy (Lev 13:4; 14:8), so the banishment is probably an external sign of shame (like a parent spitting in a child's face, Deut 25:9). Miriam bears her shame, and the people honour her by not resuming the march until she returns (apparently healed). v. 16 probably means they remain in the wilderness of Paran (see 10:12).

(13:1–14:45) The Spy Mission The setting for chs. 13–20 is Kadesh-barnea (13:26), about 50 miles south of Beersheba in the wilderness of Paran (or Zin, 20:1). On historiographic considerations, see Levine (1993: 372–5). This passage interweaves at least two traditions; the epic story has Caleb as hero and the Priestly tradition adds Joshua. This rebellion proves to be the decisive one for the future of Israel.

Twelve scouts, one from each tribe, are sent to spy out the land of Canaan at God's command (cf. 32:6–13; Deut 1:22–45). Moses gives instructions regarding destination (the Negeb and the hill country) and observations to be made regarding military readiness and the character of the land (13:17–20). According to 13:21 they scout the entire length of the country, from the wilderness of Zin in the south to Rehob in the north; 13:22–4 (from the epic tradition) reports only on the Negeb and Judah, from which they bring back fruit; especially noted is a cluster of grapes (hence the name Eshcol), the season for which is July/August. After some forty days the scouts bring back a mixed report. The initial report (13:28–9) is realistic; the land is bountiful but filled with strong people and fortified cities. The identity and placement of indigenous peoples is not always clear (cf. 13:29 with 14:25, 45), reflecting different traditions. The Amalekites are a perennial enemy of Israel (see EX 17:8–16). The Anakites (13:22, 29, 33) are a people remembered as giant in stature and associated with the Nephilim (see GEN 6:1–4); they are later defeated (Josh 15:14). For the other peoples, see GEN 15:19–21.

Unrest among the people at the report (13:30) occasions a division among the spies. Caleb responds by expressing confidence in Israel's ability to overcome all obstacles. The other scouts (Joshua is not separated out until 14:6–9, 30) give 'an unfavourable report of the land' (13:32), voicing alarm at the size and strength of its inhabitants and their cities and expressing a belief that Israel would be defeated (so 'devours' in 13:32). This report is exaggerated for effect; it succeeds. The people are seduced by the negative report (14:36), despise God's promise of land (14:31), and complain against Moses and Aaron out of fear for their lives and the fate of their dependants (cf. 31:13–18). They plot to choose a new leader and reverse the Exodus (14:4)! They persist in spite of the leaders' urgent pleas ('fell on their faces'; 16:4, 22), expressions of distress ('tore their clothes'; Gen 37:34), and assurances that the indigenous peoples are 'bread' (that is, we will 'devour' them, not they us, contrary to 13:32; cf. Ps 14:4) and their gods will provide no protection (lit. 'shadow'; cf. Ps 91:1), for 'the LORD is with us'. Rather than rejoice in the report of 'an exceedingly good land' and trust that God will see to the promise, the people 'rebel against the LORD' and threaten to stone Joshua and Caleb to death.

To these developments God responds (on 'glory' see 9:15–23). This response has several dimensions. If this kind of detail were present in the other sin and judgement stories, a comparable understanding would no doubt be evident.

1. God voices a lament (14:11), echoing those of the people and Moses (11:11–14), using language familiar to the psalms (cf. Ps 13:1–2). God does not remain coolly unaffected in the face of these developments. But the judgement that follows is spoken, not with the icy indifference of a judge, but with the mixed sorrow and anger of a suitor who has been rejected. That God's lament is repeated in 14:26, interrupting the announcement of judgement, reinforces this understanding (see Fretheim 1984: 107–26). The phrase 'you shall know my displeasure' (14:34) may refer to this divine frustration.

2. God announces a disastrous judgement (14:12), comparable to that visited upon Egypt (Ex. 9:15). God will disown Israel and start over with Moses. Given what follows, this is a preliminary announcement, a point for debate with Moses (cf. 16:20–1; Ex 32:9–14). Yet, such a judgement would be deserved.

3. God engages Moses in conversation (14:13–35). Moses argues (cf. EX 32:11–14; Deut 32:26–7) that God's reputation among the nations (the Egyptians and, remarkably, the Canaanites) is at stake; they will conclude that God failed in his promise to give them the land. Their opinion should count with God; God agrees that it does, for God's goal is that his glory fill the earth (14:21). Moses also appeals to God's promise from that previous interaction (see EX 34:6–7), pleading for God to act according to his steadfast love: to forgive the people as he had done 'ten times' (frequently, Gen 31:7). Such intercession is reported elsewhere as prayer (11:2; 21:7) or action that 'turned back my wrath' (25:11) and diminished the effects of a plague (16:46–50).

4. God responds favourably to Moses and forgives Israel (14:20); but forgiveness, while it ameliorates the effects of sin (Israel is not annihilated), does not cut off all consequences. This is true for all acts of forgiveness; the consequences of sin, which can catch up the innocent (as here), need ongoing salvific attention (e.g. abuse in its various forms). In this case, the build-up of the effects of sin means that the old generation will die in the wilderness and their children suffer the fall-out of the adults' infidelity (14:33; 26:64–5; 32:10–12). Those who brought the bad report die off early (14:37). Yet, the consequences are not total: the children, ages 1–19 (14:29, 31; cf. 1:3), and the *clans* (see Josh 14:6–14) of Caleb (14:14) and Joshua (14:30) will enter the land. So, finally, God does not disinherit this people, and a new generation will possess the land. But the entire community is now to turn away and continue their wandering for a generation (14:25, 34).

5. God announces the judgement (14:21–35), this time as a solemn oath, made as certain as God's own life (14:21, 28), and details that judgement in moral order terms, i.e. what goes around comes around (14:28–35). They have sinned, they will bear (the effects of) their sin (14:34). A key verse is 14:28, 'I will do to you the very things I heard you say'. In effect: your will be done, not mine. Their desire for death in the wilderness (14:2) is granted (14:32–3); their rejection of the land (14:3) is agreed to (14:30); their desire for a return to Egypt (14:3–4) is brought close to hand (14:25); their claim that the children would become booty (14:3) causes the children to suffer that fate at their own hands (14:33) rather than in the land (14:31); they want different leaders (14:4), they will get them (14:30). They

do not believe that God is with them (14:8–9); they discover he is not (14:43–4). The forty days of scouting become forty years of wandering (14:34). Judgement is intrinsic to the deed ('you shall bear your iniquity', 14:34; cf. 32:23); God does not introduce it into the situation. God is not arbitrary, but facilitates a consequence that correlates with the deed. One might speak of a wearing down of the divine patience in view of 14:22; the other side of the coin is that persistent negative human conduct will in time take its toll, and God will see to the proper functioning of the moral order.

Having heard these words of judgement, the people mourn at what has been lost, confess their sin, and seek to make things right by taking the land on their own (14:39–45; cf. Deut 1:41–5). Moses sees that it is too late. God has now issued a new command (14:25) and they will be defeated, for God will not be with them (cf. 14:9). The die has been cast, and God's word about their future is certain. Moses' word proves to be correct; God (the ark) does not go with them and they are defeated. God's presence, not human strength, is what finally will count in Israel's life.

(15:1–41) Statutes for Life in the Land The wilderness narrative is interrupted by a series of statutes—probably late Priestly additions—pertaining to the time 'when you come into the land' (vv. 2, 18) 'throughout your generations' (vv. 15, 21, 23, 37). For the coherence of this chapter in its context, see Olson (1996: 90–101). Such laws, following upon rebellion and judgement, function to assure the community in a concrete way that God still intends a future for them; hence, law essentially functions as promise, at least for the new generation. For the old generation, however, the laws would function only as threat, for they would not live to obey them. Such an interweaving of law and narrative is common in the Pentateuch, and is revealing of the dynamic relationship of law and changing life circumstances.

One such matter pertains to the non-Israelites in the camp. The statutes in vv. 1–31 apply equally to outsiders (vv. 14–16, 26, 29, 30; cf. 9:14). They are given equal status before God: 'you and the alien shall be alike before the LORD' (v. 15; cf. Lev 19:33–4, 'you shall love the alien as yourself'). Other changes are evident.

(15:1–16) prescribes that a grain offering (flour mixed with oil) and a drink offering (wine)—agricultural products—are to accompany each animal (vv. 11–12) presented for the 'offerings by fire' listed in v. 3 (for detail, see LEV 1–7). What was previously required only for the offering of first fruits and the festival of Weeks (Lev 23:12–18) and for the nazirite consecration (6:14–17) now applies to all offerings. The amount of these offerings increases with the size of the animal (lamb, vv. 4–5; ram, vv. 6–7; bull, vv. 8–10). The repeated reference to 'a pleasing odour to the LORD' (vv. 3, 7, 10, 13, 14, 24) is a vivid way of speaking of that which brings pleasure to God (see GEN 8:21–2) because it signifies a healthy relationship.

(15:17–21) prescribes, on the occasion of baking bread (in the land), a donation of one loaf from the first batch of dough. A donation is any gift for the service of the sanctuary, given to acknowledge that all such gifts come from God. In this case the bread would be food for the priests. This statute broadens earlier statutes regarding first fruits to include that produced by humans (see Ex 23:19; Lev 23:9–14; cf. 18:13–18).

(15:22–36) Various sacrifices for atonement for unintentional sins (cf. LEV 4:13–21; for detail see Milgrom 1990: 402–5), for the 'whole people' (vv. 22–6) and for the individual (vv. 27–9), and penalties for individuals who commit 'high-handed' sins, i.e. who are defiant and unrepentant (vv. 30–1; see Milgrom 1990: 122–5). In 5:5–8 (cf. LEV 6:7) even intentional sins can be atoned for, apparently because the persons are repentant (though see 16:46). The priests are those who make atonement for both congregation and individual (vv. 25, 28). This is the means God has established in and through which to effect both corporate and individual forgiveness.

Those who sin defiantly (the old generation of chs. 11–14 is in view) will be 'cut off' from the people (see 9:13). The following incident of intentional sabbath-breaking (vv. 32–6) illustrates such defiance. The sabbath-breaker's labour did carry the death penalty (see EX 31:14–15; 35:2–3); yet it was not clear what to do with him (15:34). Though much disputed (see Milgrom 1990: 408–10), this may mean (cf. LEV 24:12) that, though the death penalty was clear, the community awaited a word from God either regarding the means of execution or before proceeding to such a severe punishment (gang stoning).

(15:37–41) (cf. Deut 22:12) pertains to clothing. Tassels are to be attached to each corner of the garments of *all* Israelites, with a blue(-purple) cord on each (still worn on prayer shawls by Orthodox Jewish men). This cord was a public sign of Israel's status as a holy people and a reminder of what that entailed. The call to be holy (v. 40; see EX 19:6; LEV 19:2) is a call to exemplify that holiness in daily life, to be true to the relationship in which they already stand. The fundamental way in which the people do justice to this relationship is by obedience to the commandments. Israel's holiness is not simply an internal disposition; it is to be expressed in every sphere of life. The fundamental grounding for this is the fact that God is YHWH, the Lord who brought them out of Egypt.

(16:1–50) The Rebellions of Korah and Others Num 16–18 focuses on issues relating to the value and legitimacy of leadership within Israel, especially priestly leadership as it relates to service at the tabernacle.

This passage in its present form portrays two major rebellions, one by Korah, Dathan, Abiram, and 250 lay leaders (vv. 1–40) and, in response to their deaths, a second rebellion by 'the whole congregation' (vv. 41–50). The role of Korah, one of the Levites (about whom the narratives have been silent heretofore), draws the entire community into a rebellious stance. The conflict between the Levites and the Aaronides may reflect later controversies between rival priestly groups (cf. 12:1–16; 17:1–13).

Issues of coherence make it likely that at least two major traditions have been interwoven. The epic tradition centred on a revolt led by the Reubenites (Dathan and Abiram, vv. 12–15); it has been overlaid by a Priestly tradition, wherein Korah leads the rebellion (vv. 3–11, 16–24, 35). Other expansions may be evident, e.g. the role of the 250 lay leaders, but it is possible to read the whole as an (awkwardly ordered) unity.

Korah, a son of Kohath, belonged to the Levite clan responsible for the tabernacle's 'most holy things' (4:4), but they were not to touch or see them (4:15, 20). Korah is the eponymous ancestor of a later group of temple singers (1 Chr 6:31–48;

his name occurs in eleven Psalm superscriptions, e.g., 44–9). Dathan and Abiram (and On, not mentioned again) were members of the tribe of Reuben, the firstborn son of Jacob (the demotion of the tribe may be due to this rebellion, 26:9–11). These persons (probably with different agendas) make common cause against Moses and Aaron. They are joined by 250 lay leaders and confront Moses and Aaron with the charge that they 'have gone too far' in 'exalting' themselves above other members of the community (vv. 3, 13). While this charge may have been sparked by their prominence in 15:1–41, it may also be related to their harsh words about the old generation (14:26–35), among whom the rebels would be numbered.

The claim (v. 3) that 'everyone' in the camp is holy is not incorrect (as just noted in 15:40, and perhaps prompted by it); the problem is the implication drawn, namely, that Aaron and Moses have no special prerogatives for leadership. The claim for the holiness of everyone is not simply related to a move to gain priestly prerogatives for all Levites (as Moses interprets it, v. 10), though this is primary. The presence of Reubenites and 250 laymen reveals another interest, namely, extending 'secular' leadership prerogatives beyond Moses to representatives from all twelve tribes, especially firstborn Reuben (so vv. 12–15).

Moses responds in deed and word to this confrontation (vv. 4–17). After 'falling on his face' (see 14:5), Moses proposes a test. The antagonists are to bring censers (metal trays that hold hot coals on which incense is burned, cf. LEV 10:1–2) to the tabernacle and prepare them for offering incense. If God accepts their offerings, their priestly status would be recognized. The phrase 'and who is holy' (v. 5) assumes gradations of holiness; even if all are holy, God chooses the priest and this status entails a holiness that sets him apart from other holy ones (cf. 6:8). So *God*, not Moses, will decide the identity of 'the holy one' who is to approach the altar. But Moses makes his opinions clear. *They* (and here Levites, whom Korah represents, become the focus), not we (v. 3), have gone too far (v. 7)!

The reply in vv. 8–11 addresses the Levites' challenge to Aaron's leadership (v. 11). Their displeasure with the duties they have been assigned by God (1:48–54), and their desire for higher status, is a move 'against the LORD' (v. 11). They have elevated privilege above service. Next Moses speaks to challenges to his own leadership (vv. 12–15), sending for Dathan and Abiram. They twice refuse to come, believing themselves to be deceived (to 'put out the eyes'). In their complaint about Moses' authoritarianism (after all, Reuben was the firstborn son), they give Moses' own words in v. 9 an ironic twist (v. 13), and even call *Egypt* the land of milk and honey! Moses tells God (spitefully?) to ignore their offerings, i.e. not act through them on their behalf, for he has taken nothing (cf. 1 Sam 12:3) from them or harmed them. Finally, Moses repeats his instructions to Korah, adding that Aaron is also to appear (vv. 16–17).

The time for the divine decision arrives (vv. 18–35). Each of the men stands before the Lord at the tent with his censer prepared. In addition, Korah assembles the entire congregation, apparently in sympathy with him, to watch the proceedings. The glory of the Lord appears (see 9:15–16) and God tells Moses and Aaron to move away for God is going to destroy the assembled congregation (in essence, the old generation; cf. v. 45) immediately. But Moses and Aaron intercede on behalf of the congregation (v. 22), for not all should bear the consequences for the 'one person' (an exaggeration for Korah is representative of the rebellious group; cf. GEN 18:22–33). The 'God of the spirits of all flesh' (cf. 27:16) is an appeal to God as Creator, who gives breath (i.e. spirit) to all.

God responds positively to the intercession and separates the congregation from the 'dwelling' (sing. here and v. 27; since sing. is used only for God's dwelling, does it refer to their 'tents', v. 26, ironically?) of the rebels and their families. Dathan and Abiram had refused to leave their homes (16:14) and Korah had apparently joined them. The 250 men remain at the tent to offer incense, and are later consumed by fire (v. 35; cf. 3:4; 11:1; LEV 10:1–2). The inclusion of the families and the command not even to touch (v. 26) suggests their sins have polluted all that is theirs (on corporate guilt, see JOSH 7:24–6).

When the separation occurs, Moses sets up a test to demonstrate that this is God's decision not his own. If these people die a natural death, then he is wrong; if God 'creates something new' (a creation for this moment) and the ground opens up and swallows them, and they descend prematurely to Sheol (the abode of all the dead; cf. the image in Isa 5:14), then they have despised the Lord (note: not Moses). The latter happens immediately to 'everyone who belonged to Korah and all their goods' (v. 32). Korah, Dathan, and Abiram are not specifically mentioned (they are in 26:9–10; cf. Deut 11:6; Ps 106:17). The people panic, perhaps because of complicity; it quickly turns to accusation, v. 41.

In the wake of the killing of the 250 men because of their presumption, special attention is given to their censers (vv. 36–40), which became holy because of the use to which they were put, even by unqualified persons ('at the cost of their lives'). They are gathered from the fire by Eleazar and not Aaron (see Lev 21:11) and, at God's command, hammered into an altar covering (perhaps a supplement; cf. Ex 38:2) to serve as a reminder that only Aaron's sons can approach the Lord to offer incense.

The congregation, however, remembers only the killings, blames Moses and Aaron, and threatens them (16:41). Again the glory of the Lord appears, this time to Moses and Aaron, and God again threatens to annihilate this people (cf. vv. 19–21). Once again Moses and Aaron intercede by falling on their faces, presumably pleading with God (cf. v. 22). In the absence of God's response, they take the initiative and act to make atonement for the (intentional! cf. 15:22–31) sins of the people through the use of incense (unprecedented, but appropriate for this story). They do so with haste, and at some risk (he 'stood between the dead and the living'—a job description for a priest!), because a plague had already broken out (on divine judgement, see NUM 13–14; note that wrath is impersonally described, see NUM 1:53). The act of atonement had the effect of stopping the plague, but not before many died (14,700).

The disaster experienced by Korah and his company proves the special status of both Moses (vv. 28–9) and Aaron (v. 40). It is not that such leaders never fail (12:1–16; 20:12) or that other persons are never channels God might use to reveal his will (11:24–30; Balaam), but these persons are chosen and are deserving of respect. Implicit is that the way to adjudicate differences with leaders in the community is not through envy or personal attack (common in Numbers), but

through a careful discernment of God's will for the flourishing of the community. God goes to enormous lengths to
protect the place of good leaders (on the divine wrath, see
NUM 1:53).

(17:1–13) Aaron's Blossoming Rod Whereas 16:1–40 was concerned about the status of both Aaron and Moses, and Aaron
among other Levites, this passage focuses on Aaron 'the man'
(v. 5) among other tribal leaders. In view of the renewed
rebellions of the people *and* Aaron's risking his life on their
behalf (16:41–50), God makes another effort to demonstrate
Aaron's priestly status. Whereas 16:40 showed that through
an ordeal that led to death, this passage makes the same point
through an ordeal that symbolizes life (the budding staff),
emblematic of Aaron's life-saving actions in 16:46–50. Both
the bronze covering for the altar (16:38) and Aaron's staff serve
as ongoing visual signs for the community of God's choice of
Aaron's priestly leadership. This story, best designated a legend (with parallels in many cultures), may reflect later struggles between rival priestly groups. Yet, unlike 16:3–11, rivalry
with the Levites is not evident.

God's effort on behalf of Aaron's priestly status is settled by
means of a unique ordeal. At God's command, Moses places
twelve staffs (a symbol of authority; 'staff' and 'tribe' translate
the same Hebrew word) from the leaders (cf. 16:2) of the
tribes, each inscribed with a leader's name, before the Lord,
i.e. the ark (see 10:35–6), in which the 'covenant', the Decalogue, was placed (Ex 25:16, 21). Aaron's staff, the powers of
which had already been demonstrated (EX 7:8–12, 19; 8:16–
17), was added to them (the Levites are the thirteenth tribe in
Numbers). God set the terms: the staff that sprouts would
indicate which leader God had chosen for priestly prerogatives. Upon Moses' inspection the following morning, only
the staff of Aaron had sprouted; moreover, it flowered and
bore *ripe* almonds (symbolic of the life-enhancing, fruit-bear-
ing capacity of priests for the community). Moses shows the
evidence to all the people. At God's command Moses put
Aaron's staff before the ark, to be kept as a warning (Hebrew
'sign') to the rebels. For usage of this image in messianic texts,
see ISA 11:1–2.

God had performed such a sign 'to put a stop to the complaints' against 'you' (pl.; Moses and Aaron) and 'me' (vv. 5,
10); it soon becomes clear that God did not succeed in his
objective (see 21:5).

The concluding verses (12–13) lead into the next chapter.
The people, apparently convinced, express their dismay and
worry about dying. Yet the focus is not on what they have done,
but on the possibility of encroaching upon the tabernacle
precincts. The next chapter provides protections against
such a possibility.

**(18:1–32) Rights and Responsibilities of Priests and Levi-
tes** The Priestly material of chs. 18–19 constitutes a second
break in the narrative flow (cf. 15:1–14). On law and narrative,
see NUM 15.

Given the establishment of Aaron's status with the people
and other Levites (chs. 16–17), and the concern of the people
about encroachment on the tabernacle (17:12–13), a redefinition of the responsibilities of the tribe of Levi is now given
along with their means of support (though the people are not
said to hear this). vv. 1, 8, 20 contain the only cases (except Lev

10:8), of God's speaking to Aaron alone, indicating its importance for Aaronides.

vv. 1–7 gather previous material (see 1:50–3; 3:5–10, 14–39;
4:1–33; 8:14–19) and delineate the relationship among the
various groups regarding their duties at the tent of meeting
('covenant', 17:7). The protection of the community as a whole
('outsider') from 'wrath' (v. 5, see NUM 1:53) is a prime concern
(vv. 1a, 4–5, 7, 22; 'outsider' in v. 7 would also include Levites).
Aaronides and Levites alone (not laity) 'bear responsibility for
offences', that is, suffer the consequences for violations (their
own and that of the laity) relative to the sanctuary (vv. 1a, 23).
In addition, priests are responsible for other priests (v. 1b) and
priests and Levites for Levites (v. 3, 'they and you'). God
stresses to the Aaronides that priesthood is a gift from God
as is the service of their 'brother Levites' (vv. 6–7; cf. v. 19); they
cannot presume upon their office in relationship to their
brothers or all Israel.

vv. 8–32, a gathering of materials from Lev 6–7; v. 27 primarily reviews the God-commanded portion due to the Aaronides
from the people (vv. 8–20) and the Levites (vv. 25–32, a new
provision) and that due to the Levites (vv. 21–4), in perpetuity
(vv. 8, 11, 19, 23), in spite of their failures.

In vv. 8–20 the 'portion' consists of those 'holy gifts' the
people give to the Lord, which in turn God 'gives' to the priests
and Levites and their 'sons and daughters' for the sake of their
support and for that of the sanctuary. vv. 9–10 specify the
'most holy' gifts, reserved for the priests: 'every offering
of theirs' (those parts not burned, 'reserved from the fire').
vv. 11–18 specify the 'holy' gifts (v. 19), 'elevation offerings'
(*tĕnûpâ*) or gifts dedicated to God, to be eaten by any clean
member of the priests' families. They include first fruits
('choice produce'); anything 'devoted' to the Lord's service, proscribed under the provisions of the ban (see LEV 27:21, 28); and
firstborn human and unclean animals, for which the priests
receive the redemption price (v. 15 is detailed in 16–18). On the
redemption of the firstborn, see NUM 3:11–13, 40–51.

These holy gifts of God to the priests are called 'a covenant
of salt forever before the LORD' (v. 19). Salt is presented with all
offerings (Lev 2:13); as a preservative it becomes a symbol for
an everlasting covenant (see 2 Chr 13:5). This provision is
God's commitment to the priests in perpetuity, for the Aaronides have no property. God alone is their share and possession, that is, they are dependent for life and health upon the
gifts of God, albeit gifts mediated through human beings,
rather than on land.

The Levites' portion for their work is the Israelites' tithe of
agricultural produce (vv. 21–4). The tithe belongs to YHWH
(v. 24) and is given to the Levites (on the title see Milgrom
1990: 432–6). They also have no tribal territory, but are given
forty-eight cities with pasture land (see 35:1–8). On vv. 22–3,
see vv. 1–7.

Finally, in a speech to Moses, God commands the Levites to
give a tithe of the tithe they have received (the 'best of it') to the
Aaronides (vv. 25–32). The other nine-tenths of the offering
shall be no longer holy and become in effect their own produce, 'as payment for your service'. But if they do not give their
tithe, that will 'profane' the holy gifts, and they shall die.

(19:1–22) Ritual of the Red Heifer 5:1–4 stipulated a measure
to be taken in cases of 'contact with a corpse'. Such unclean

persons were to be placed 'outside the camp' so as not to defile the community. This passage expands upon that statute, providing for rituals of purification for such persons in perpetuity (mostly laypersons, Israelite and alien), especially in view of all who had died (e.g. 16:32–5, 49) and would die (14:32–5). Caring for the dead is a necessary (and dangerous) task, so this impurity is not linked to sin. On purity issues, see Nelson (1993: 17–38). The origin of this ritual is unknown, but it probably can be traced to ancient Near Eastern rites developed to deal with the same issue. These statutes are to be conveyed to the Israelites (v. 2; contrast 18).

The choice of a (brownish-)red heifer (actually, cow) perhaps symbolized blood/life (red animals were so used in the ancient Near East); it was to be unblemished (see Lev 21:16–24; 22:20) and never used for work (Deut 21:3–4). The burning of the entire animal (including its blood/life, v. 5, uniquely here) may have been thought to concentrate life in the ashes which, when mixed with water and applied to the unclean person or thing, would counteract (literally thought to absorb?) the contagious impurity of death and the diminishment of life in the community. This happened, not in some magical way, but because God had decreed it so. The placement of cedar wood and hyssop (cleansing agents), and crimson material (symbolizing blood?), during the burning intensified the purifying quality (literal and symbolic) of the resultant ashes. The sprinkling of the blood/life seven times *towards* the entrance of the tabernacle (that is, towards God; cf. Lev 4:6) shows the importance of the ritual for maintaining the integrity of the community in relationship to God (19:4, 13, 20).

vv. 1–10 specify the procedure by which the life-giving and cleansing agent was prepared under the supervision of the priest (the absence of reference to death may mean an earlier, more general application). Eleazar is charged with this duty (Aaron dies in 20:28); he and those who assist him must be clean, but they become unclean in the process (because of contact with the holy) and short-term 'decontamination' rituals are prescribed for each.

vv. 11–13, detailed in 14–22, specify the use to which the ashes and fresh ('running') water are put for persons and things (vv. 14–16) that have had contact with death. As in other cases (see Lev 12:2) they are unclean for seven days; during this time, if they are to become clean, they must twice be sprinkled with this mixture by a clean person (vv. 17–19; outside the camp? cf. v. 9 and 5:3–4). Otherwise they 'defile the tabernacle' where God dwells (5:3) and shall be 'cut off from Israel' (19:13, 20; see NUM 9:13) for the sake of the community's wholeness.

(20:1–29) The Disobedience of Moses and Aaron The text returns to a narrative mode, explaining why Israel's key leaders did not enter Canaan. It is enclosed by the deaths of Miriam and Aaron and marked especially by the 'rebellion' of Moses and Aaron. It may be a reworking of the story in EX 17:1–7, which also took place at a place called Meribah ('Quarrelled'). Priestly materials surround a report from the epic tradition in 20:14–21.

v. 1 is difficult given the reference to Kadesh in 13:26. Perhaps God's command in 14:25 to wander back towards Egypt was in fact carried out (contrast 33:36–7), and so they arrive again in Kadesh (they set out again in v. 22). Probably the forty years in the wilderness has been completed, as v. 12 and the time of Aaron's death (v. 28 with 33:38) suggests. The 'first month' in v. 1 would thus be in the fortieth year. On the problems of redaction in chs. 20–1 see Milgrom (1990: 463–7).

The people again complain to Moses and Aaron about wilderness conditions, but this time the narrator agrees that 'there was no water' (vv. 2, 5). They return to the basic questions they had in 14:2–4; events have apparently not changed this people. They even express the wish that they had died with Korah, Dathan, and Abiram (16:32–5, 49)! Again, Moses and Aaron fall on their faces and turn towards God (14:5; 16:4); again the glory of the Lord appears (see 9:15–16).

The reader expects to hear about God's judgement; but God has a different response this time, recognizing that the people's need for water is real. God commands Moses to take 'the staff' (from v. 9 this is Aaron's staff that had been placed in the tent, 17:10–11; 'his' staff refers to the one he was using, v. 11) and '*command* [speak to] the rock before their eyes to yield its water' (my itals.). The reference to 'the rock' (v. 8) suggests a prominent rock in the area. This was the way in which Moses was 'to bring water out of the rock for them'.

Moses takes the staff as God had commanded him. The reference to Moses' obedience usually concludes his actions; here it breaks into the sequence, suggesting that his following actions are less than what God commanded. Having gathered the people, Moses calls them rebels (as does God, 17:10), and asks them:'shall *we* bring water for you out of the rock?' (my itals.). He proceeds to *strike* the rock twice with Aaron's staff, and water flows. God's response is negative: Moses and Aaron did not trust God to 'show my holiness' before the people, and hence they will not lead the people into the land. The place name Meribah is linked to the *people's* quarrelling with God (as in EX 17:7, without judgement) and to God's showing his holiness, perhaps because of the gift of water (but apparently less so than if Moses and Aaron had trusted, v. 12).

A much debated question: what did Moses and Aaron (Aaron stays in the background) do to deserve this divine response (for the history of interpretation, see Milgrom 1990: 448–56)? The charge in v. 12—they did not 'trust' in God (used of the people in 14:11, with the same result) 'to show my holiness' before Israel; in v. 24—they 'rebelled against my command'; in 27:14—they 'rebelled against my word . . . and did not show my holiness' before Israel; in Deut 32:51—they 'broke faith . . . by failing to maintain my holiness among the Israelites'; in Deuteronomy elsewhere (1:37; 3:26; 4:21)—God was angry towards Moses because of the *people*, as if Moses suffered vicariously; in Ps 106:32–3—the people make Moses' spirit bitter and his words rash (v. 10?), qualifying Moses' fault.

It is difficult to bring coherence to this variety; it may be purposely ambiguous. The 'we' of v. 10 could suggest that this was their work not God's, hence reducing the witness to God. But the focus in v. 24 and 27:14 is 'rebelling against' God's command (a major issue in Numbers), ironically using Moses' own word regarding the people (v. 10). This could entail a lack of trust or breaking faith. Neither the questioning of the people nor the striking of the rock (rather than speaking to it) followed God's command. The former, with its negative address, does not recognize the real needs of the people (as God did *twice* in v. 8), and the latter would be less a witness to God's power. Thus God's compassion and power, both analytic of God's holiness, are compromised 'in the eyes of' the people.

The point is sharply made that the end result (here, water to drink) is not only what counts as a witness to God, but also the means by which that result is achieved. The most trusted of God's leaders fall into the trap of thinking that the end justifies any means. The reader should beware of both 'rationalization' and supernaturalism in interpreting stories such as this (as with the manna and quail, 11:7–9, 31). The provision of food and water is not to be divorced from a recognition of nature's God-given potential. Even in the wilderness God's world is not without resources. In ways not unlike the gifts of manna and quail, water courses through rock formations. God is not creating out of nothing here; water does not materialize out of thin air. God works in and through the natural to provide for his people. The rock itself plays a significant role in this.

(20:14–21) Before reporting the death of Aaron, an interlude recounts developments in Israel's journeying. They are 'on the edge' of Edom (v. 16) and request permission from the Edomites to use the King's Highway (the major north–south route through Transjordan) to pass through and, presumably, enter Canaan from the east (cf. the failure from the south in 14:39–45). Edom's refusal to allow Israel to pass creates an external difficulty that matches the internal difficulties in the chapter. Together they raise questions about endangered promises. The text gives no reason for the reader to think this request of Edom was unfaithful because God was not consulted.

The Edomites are the first people Israel encounters since Sinai (cf. GEN 25:19–36:43 on Jacob/Esau). Moses initiates the contact by sending messengers to the 'king of Edom' (no evidence exists that Edom was a kingdom at this time; cf. the chieftains of GEN 36). Moses' letter, typical in that world, uses the word 'brother' for Edom, a dual reference assuming a relationship of both ally and actual brother (see Gen 33:9).

Moses briefly recounts Israel's history from the descent into Egypt through the Exodus to the present time. Notable is the confessional character of this account: they cried to YHWH, who heard and sent an angel, God in human form (see NUM 9:15–23; EX 14:19; 23:20–3), to bring them out. It is assumed that the king of Edom knows who YHWH is (cf. Ex 15:15)! Given the last reference to an Edom–Israel encounter, which ends on an ambivalent note (33:4–17), it is not surprising that Edom refuses (Judg 11:17). Edom refuses even though Israel promises not to trouble them and, after negotiation, even promises to pay for water (vv. 19–20). Edom's show of military force convinces Israel to go 'around' Edom (so 21:4; Judg 11:18; Deut 2:4–8 has access to a memory that the Israelites passed through Edom without incident).

(20:22–9) returns to internal issues, with the installation of Eleazar as successor to his father as high priest and the death of Aaron. The people continue their journey along the border of Edom and come to Mount Hor (site unknown). In view of Aaron's imminent death, and at God's command and as a reminder of their rebellion ('you' is pl.), Moses, Aaron, and Eleazar climb to the top of the mountain (cf. Moses' death in

DEUT 32:50; 34). Aaron's vestments are transferred to Eleazar before 'the whole congregation', an assuring sight signifying continuity into the future. Aaron dies (is 'gathered to his people', cf. Gen 25:8) and is mourned by Israel for thirty days (as with Moses, Deut 34:8), rather than the usual seven.

The next five chapters are transitional. The new generation seems to be essentially, if not entirely in place (20:12). And so the texts portray a mix of the old and the new.

(21:1–35) Victory, Complaint, and Healing The narrative from 11:1 to this point has been predominantly negative. The promulgation of laws for life in the land (chs. 15; 18; 19) and the installation of Eleazar have given signs of hope. As the narrative moves towards the census of the new generation (ch. 26), these signs become more frequent. Indeed, from this time on Israel will be successful in all its battles. Yet negative realities still abound. In this passage military victories enclose a negative report about further complaint and judgement.

Victory over Arad (vv. 1–3): this text functions paradigmatically for other holy war texts in a way that 11:1–3 did for the complaint passages; it summarizes the essence of what is at stake. For the geographical and chronological problems associated with Canaanite contact at Arad and Hormah (a region in the Negeb), given the references to Edom in 20:21 and 21:4, see Milgrom (1990: 456–8).

The Canaanites of Arad fought with some success against Israel; this prompts 'Israel' to make a vow to wage holy war against them if God would give them victory (cf. Jephthah's vow, Judg 11:30–1). Israel's victory reverses the earlier failure at Hormah (14:45).

Israel then fulfils the vow, utterly destroying the people and their towns. Such texts (see also ch. 31) are virtually genocidal in their ferocity towards others. These understandings are grounded in a concern about infidelity and extreme danger to Israel's future (Deut 20:16–18) and unfaithful Israel experiences similar destruction (see Deut 28:15–68). Such practices are followed only in this era of land settlement (and hence are not paradigmatic, even for Israel). Yet they rightly remain incomprehensible to modern sensibilities. That Israel understands their God to want such destruction makes this practice even more difficult to fathom. The canon as a whole subverts such understandings (see Isa 2:1–4).

(21:4–9) returns for a final time to the complaining mode (for form, NUM 11; for content, NUM 14), qualifying the victories that enclose it. The seriousness of the complaint is evident in that it is directed for the first time against both God and Moses (though see 14:2–3), yet for the first time the people sincerely (cf. 14:40) confess their sin, and the segment ends on a healing note. This occurs as the people turn towards the Red Sea, that is, the Gulf of Aqaba, and begin their journey around Edom. The complaint focuses on the lack of (palatable) food and water, and God is charged with intending death in the Exodus. The God-facilitated effect of their complaining is an infestation of poisonous (lit. fiery, because of the burning) snakes that results in many deaths (not unheard of in this area). The people confess their sin to Moses and request his intercession to have the snakes taken away. Though the people repent (and presumably are forgiven), the snakes are not removed nor kept from biting. In other words, as is typical, the effects of sin continue beyond forgiveness. But God works on those effects by commanding a means (a homeopathic Egyptian technique to ward off snakes and heal snakebite), with which the promise of God is associated, through which to heal those who are bitten (cf. Wis 16:7; the combination of prayer and medicine in 2 Kings 20:1–7). Moses makes a copper image of a snake and sets it upon a pole for all to see; God is true to promises made, healing those who look to it and trust the means God has provided. The copper snake ends up in the temple, but its meaning is distorted and Hezekiah has it destroyed (2 Kings 18:4). On snakes as symbols of both death and life in the ancient Near East and the discovery of copper snakes in that area, including a copper snake 5 in. long near Timnah in a copper-smelting region, see Joines (1974); Milgrom (1990: 459–60) (for NT usage, see JN 3:14–15).

(21:10–20) Travel in Transjordan: the tempo of the journey picks up as Israel moves through various places on its way to Canaan. The character of the journey changes as well; water is provided at the *divine* initiative at Beer (v. 16, meaning 'well', the first positive etymology in Numbers) and the people sing songs of appreciation (vv. 17–18, 27–30, from unknown sources).

Though several sites cannot be identified (and do not fully correspond to the itinerary in 33:41–9), the route takes Israel around Edom and Moab. The Wadi Zered is the boundary between Moab and Edom and the Wadi Arnon the northern boundary of Moab. The Arnon prompts the narrator to insert a portion from the otherwise unknown Book of the Wars of the Lord (apparently an early collection of poems about Israel's conquests). This poetic piece (though not spoken by Israel) and the songs in vv. 17–18 and 27–30 contribute to the increasingly anticipatory character of the march. Finally, they arrive at Mount Pisgah 'across the Jordan from Jericho' (22:1).

(21:21–35) Victories over the Amorites: these reports probably precede 21:10–20 chronologically. For greater detail, cf. Deut 2:24–3:7. With Israel situated on the 'boundary of the Amorites' (21:13), Moses sends a message (similar to 20:17) to King Sihon requesting safe passage. Moses receives the same reply as he got from Edom, but Sihon also pursues Israel in battle. In response, Israel defeats his armies, kills him, and takes possession of his lands, to the border of the Ammonites in the east (at the Wadi Jabbok), including the capital Heshbon, perhaps a short distance east of Jericho. These lands include former Moabite lands, and the song in 21:27–30 (cf. Jer 48:45–6) praises the victory of the *Amorites* over the Moabites and their god Chemosh (21:29) and the capture of their lands, now belonging to Israel. Notable is Israel's integration of a non-Israelite story into their own story of these events. Because Sihon defeated Moab and Israel defeated Sihon this enhances Israel's strength. Israel's 'settling' in the land of the Amorites sets up a later controversy (see NUM 32).

The victory over the aggressor Og, another Amorite king (vv. 33–5), mirrors that of the victory over Arad in 21:1–3 (cf. Josh 10:8), with its stress upon holy war, and this in express response to a word from God. The total destruction is like what was done to Sihon (v. 34).

Israel is now situated at the boundary of the promised land and is given a foretaste of victories and settlements to come. Those promises are now raised in the story of Balaam.

(22:1–24:25) The Story of Balaam This text has been deemed intrusive in its context, and its central figure Balaam thought less than worthy of God's purposes for Israel. He is a travelling professional seer, and a non-Israelite at that, who seems all too ready to pronounce curses if the price is right. But the story with its oracles has in fact been cleverly woven into the larger fabric of Numbers and God uses Balaam in remarkable ways to bring blessing to Israel.

Source-critical attempts to divide this story into J and E (only 22:1 is P) have not been successful. Coherence difficulties and the various divine names may reflect a long history of transmission and editing of both narrative and poetry, the earliest forms of which may date from before the monarchy. An Aramaic inscription from the eighth century BCE has been found at Tell Deir 'Alla in Jordan, the contents of which are ascribed to a 'seer of the gods' named 'Balaam, son of Beor'. He reports a vision of a meeting of the gods who are planning disaster for the earth (for text and details, see Milgrom 1990: 473–6). Scholars agree that this text and Num 22–4 both have roots in Transjordan traditions about this legendary figure. A few biblical traditions have a negative assessment of Balaam, perhaps having access to still other traditions (cf. Num 31:8, 18; Josh 13:22; Rev 2:14).

The text combines a narrative and four poetic oracles, the basic content of which is blessing. Literary studies have noted the repetition of key words such as '(not)seeing' and the number three, including a probable tripartite structure: (a) Balaam's three encounters with God (22:1–40); (b) Balak's three attempts to curse Israel thwarted by Balaam's three blessings (22:41–24:13); (c) A climactic fourth blessing (24:14–25).

The function of this material at this juncture in Numbers has been delineated by Olson (1985: 156–64) especially. With its focus on the blessing of Israel and its remarkable reiteration of divine promises, the story envisages a marvellous future for Israel at a key transition between old generation and new. The material also functions ironically; a non-Israelite with less than sterling credentials voices God's promises in a way that no Israelite in Numbers does, not even Moses. God finds a way to get the word through in spite of the rebellions of Israel and its leaders (and Balaam's own failings, 22:22–35; 31:8, 16). The disastrous activities in 25:1–18 make the words of Balaam stand out all the more brightly. That the people do not actually hear these words is testimony that, contrary to appearances, God continues to be at work in fulfilling these promises. Indeed, God turns even the worst of situations (the potential curses of Balaam) into blessing.

(22:1–40) Balak, king of Moab, is fearful that Israel, given their numbers and victories over the Amorites, will next turn on what is left of his kingdom (which includes Midianites, 22:4, 7; 31:7–9) and overcome his armies with ease. And so, as kings were wont to do in that world (cf. 1 Kings 22), he turns to a mercenary diviner from Syria (the exact location is uncertain), famous for his effective blessings and cursings (v. 6, an ironic statement, given later developments!). Messengers, prepared to pay for his services, inform Balaam of Balak's request to have him curse Israel so that he can defeat them (in v. 11 the compliment of v. 6 is omitted). Note that the curses were not thought to be finally effective apart from Balak's subsequent actions. Divination (usually condemned in Israel, Deut 18:9–14) was a widely practised 'art' whereby the meaning and course of events was sought through interpretation of various natural phenomena.

Asking for a delay in order to consult YHWH(!), Balaam has the first of three encounters with God. That YHWH's name is placed in the mouth of Balaam, that he is called 'my God', converses with him, and is accepted as a matter of course by the visitors, is remarkable. Such a usage expresses, not a historical judgement, but the narrator's conviction that the god with whom Balaam had to do is none other than YHWH (cf. Ex 15:15; Gen 26:28). The divine enquiry into the visitors' identity (v. 9) is designed to elicit the response Balaam gives; how he responds—absolute divine foreknowledge is not assumed—will shape the nature of God's response. God prohibits Balaam from going to Moab to curse Israel, for they are blessed (see 6:22–7). Balaam obeys God and recounts the divine refusal to the visitors (both acts relate to Balaam's faithfulness to God), who report back to Balak but without any reference to God (v. 14).

Readers would expect such a reply from God and think this is the end of the matter, but not Balak: he sends a larger and more distinguished delegation, who make a more attractive offer—promising honour and writing a blank cheque (v. 17). Even with such a tempting offer, Balaam again demonstrates his faithfulness by consulting with 'YHWH my God' and telling the visitors that he is subject *exactly* (not 'less or more', v. 18) to the divine command. In view of Balaam's demonstrated and promised faithfulness, God changes the strategy and *commands* him to go and do 'only what I tell you to do' (v. 20), a word which the reader is led to think God can now speak with more confidence. Balaam goes, but the reader is left to wonder what God might tell him to do.

What follows is surprising (v. 22), probably to both ancient and modern readers (in view of various disjunctions most regard vv. 22–35 as a later interpolation). The reader (but not Balaam) is told of God's anger because he departed (for the translation, 'as he was going', see Ashley 1993: 454–5); indeed, God has become Balaam's 'adversary'. To create curiosity about the reason, the narrator delays informing the reader until v. 32, where it is clear that God still has questions about Balaam's faithfulness, remarkable in view of his responses in vv. 13–21. This strange encounter thus amounts to a 'blind' test. The reader will remember Jacob in GEN 32:22–32 and Moses in EX 4:24–6, both of whom encounter a God who creates trials as they embark upon a new venture relative to God's call. The language is also similar to Joshua's experience (JOSH 5:13–15). At the end of this test (v. 35), God's command to Balaam remains the same as it was in v. 20—to speak only what God tells him.

But to get to that goal, the narrator makes use of fable motifs with a talking donkey (cf. GEN 3:1–6; JUDG 9:7–15) to portray the test. God here uses irony and humour to get through to Balaam. The donkey becomes his teacher (!), one who sees the things of God (including potential disaster) more clearly than Balaam sees and subverts Balaam's supposed powers. Balaam's treatment of the donkey during the journey is a sign of his unfaithfulness; he does not see the God who stands before him in increasingly inescapable ways and respond appropriately (cf. Joshua in JOSH 5:13–15). The donkey is

a vehicle through which God works to show Balaam's dependence upon God for his insight and words and to sharpen his faithfulness.

With sword drawn, the angel of YHWH (God in human form, see 9:15–23) confronts Balaam and donkey three times in increasingly restrictive circumstances. The donkey alone sees the figure in the road; twice it is able to avoid a confrontation, but the third time it proves impossible and so it lies down under Balaam. Each time Balaam strikes the donkey, becoming angry (like God in v. 22) the third time. God opens the donkey's mouth and it questions Balaam about its mistreatment. Balaam thinks that he has been made to look the fool; if he had had a sword, he would have killed the animal. When the donkey queries him about their long history together, Balaam admits that the donkey has not acted this way before.

At this point God opens Balaam's eyes so that he can see as the donkey sees. When he sees the angel with drawn sword he falls on his face, presumably pleading for his life. It was not the donkey who was against him but God. The angel gives the reason for the confrontation, noting that if it had not been for the donkey's manœuverings, he would have killed Balaam. Balaam responds that, though he did not know that God opposed him, he has sinned; he offers to return home if God remains displeased. But God renews the commission (v. 35) and Balaam proceeds.

The three episodes of Balaam with his donkey are mirrored in the first three oracles of 22:41–24:13. These oracles show that the experiences of Balaam with his donkey parallel the experiences of Balak with Balaam. The donkey's experience becomes Balaam's experience. Just as the donkey is caught between God's threatening presence and Balaam's increasing anger so Balaam is caught between God's insistence on blessing and Balak's increasing anger about the curse. From another angle, Balaam's difficulties with the donkey are like God's experience with Balaam. It is a conflict of wills. Balaam has to be brought more certainly to the point where he will allow God to use him as God sees fit (see v. 38). God will open Balaam's mouth just as God opened the donkey's mouth (v. 28). From still another angle, the donkey becomes a God figure(!), speaking for God and reflecting *God's* relationship to Balaam (vv. 28–30). God has been mistreated by Balaam along the journey because Balaam thinks this trip is making him look the fool. The donkey reminds Balaam of their long life together and his faithfulness to him.

Having arrived at the boundary of Moab (v. 36), Balaam is greeted by Balak, who chides him for his initial refusal. Balaam responds by saying, rhetorically, that he does not have the power 'to say just anything' (v. 38). What God puts in his mouth, as with the prophets (see Jer 1:9; 15:16; Ezek 2:8–3:3), this is what he must say (cf. Jer 20:7–9).

(22:41–24:13) Balaam's first three oracles. The first two oracles are integral to the surrounding narrative; the third (as with the fourth) is less so but still has close links. Each situation contains seven similar elements; the third time around breaks the pattern in key ways (cf. Olson 1996: 145–7):

1. Balak brings Balaam to a high point overlooking the Israelite camp (22:41; 23:13–14, 27–8), a people so vast he cannot see them all (23:13). The place changes each time and

Balak hopes that the venue (and the sight of a smaller portion of the people) might change the word spoken; in the third instance Balak uses (will of) God language (23:27). But the place makes no difference, and he finally sees all the people (24:2).

2. Balak builds seven altars and sacrifices a bull and a ram on each (23:1–2, 14, 29–30), the first and the last at Balaam's request. Sacrifices were a typical part of the diviner's art, perhaps to appease the deity and to look for omens in the entrails. Balaam's purpose may be to show Balak that he is proceeding in a proper manner. But, in fact, divination is seen to be bankrupt as a means of revelation (23:23; 24:1).

3. Balaam twice turns aside from the offerings to consult with YHWH, but the third time he does not 'look for omens' (24:1; diviner's language is used for consulting with YHWH). In the first case, he is uncertain that YHWH will meet him and informs God about the offerings (23:3–4); the second time he is certain and says nothing about offerings (23:15).

4. God twice meets Balaam and puts a word in his mouth and commands him to return and speak that word (23:5, 16). God's insistence on what he must say recognizes that Balaam does have options. It becomes increasingly clear, even to Balak (23:17), that God reveals through the word, not divination. In the third instance, the spirit of God comes upon him (see 11:17, 25–6) without consultation after he 'sets his face' and 'sees' Israel's situation (24:2).

5. Balaam speaks God's blessings on Israel rather than curses. The blessings become less descriptive, more future oriented, and more properly blessings as one moves through the four oracles. Even more, those who curse Israel will themselves be cursed, while those who bless will be blessed (24:9). Prominent throughout is the language of seeing; the one who did not see the purposes of God (22:22–30) now does see them (23:9, 21, 23–4; 24:3–4, 15–17). Indeed, the clarity of his seeing increases over the course of the oracles; the most expansive claims are the 'knowledge' of 24:16 and the seeing into the future of 24:17. Falling down but alert (24:4, 16) may refer to a qualified ecstatic reception of God's word.

Balaam 'sees' Israel's history and God's promises, moving from the past through the present to a more and more specific future: election from among the nations (23:9); promise (and fulfilment) of many descendants, like the dust of the earth (23:10; see Gen 13:16, 28:14), and blessing (24:9, cf. GEN 12:3); exodus (23:22; 24:8); God's presence among them and his care in the wilderness (23:21; cf. 24:5–6). He anticipates a successful conquest, as both Israel and God are imaged as lions (22:23–4; 24:7–9), the rise of the monarchy and specific conquests relating thereto (24:7, 17–19). The overall scene for Balaam is a blessed people: numerous, confident, flourishing, powerful, and its king is God. In Balaam's words (23:10):'let my end be like his!'

Balaam 'sees' some of Israel's basic convictions about God. God is not a human being, is not deceptive, blesses Israel, reveals his word to people such as Balaam, and makes promises and keeps them (23:19–20). The claim that God has spoken and will not change his mind (23:19) refers to these promises for Israel and is not a general statement about divine immutability (see Gen 6:5–6; Ex 32:14) or a general claim about prophecy (see Jer 18:7–10). This God chooses to dwell among this people and is acclaimed as their king (23:21), is a

strong deliverer, imaged as strong animals (23:22; 24:8–9), and will defeat Israel's enemies (24:8–9).

6. Balak's reactions to Balaam's oracles are increasingly negative, issuing finally in anger and dismissal (23:11, 25–6; 24:10–11). But Balak comes to recognize that Balaam's God is the one with whom he has to do (23:17, 27) and finally blames YHWH for the fact that Balaam will not be paid for his services (24:11).

7. Balaam's response to Balak in each case is a testimony to the word of God (23:12, 26; 24:12–13). That he must 'take care' to say what God has put in his mouth again indicates that he does have other options. But he knows he must speak in view of the source of the words.

(24:14–25) Balaam's fourth oracle stands outside the form delineated above and comes directly from Balaam, with no reference to the spirit of the Lord (as in 24:2), but with a claim that he himself 'knows the knowledge of the Most High' (24:16). This oracle is suddenly introduced as Balaam's word to Balak upon his departure, a word that ironically makes clear that Balak and Moab are expressly in Israel's future. Israel will bring Moab (24:17, and perhaps Ir in 24:19; cf. 22:36), Edom, and the other peoples in the region (the Shethites) under the aegis of Israel and its God and will be exalted among the nations.

The means by which this will be accomplished is anticipated in the kingdom language of 24:7; God will raise up a star and sceptre (the future 'him') of 24:17a; from the tribe of Judah, for whom lion imagery is also used (see Gen 49:9–10), and Israel will be established among the nations (24:17–20). These royal images are usually associated with the Davidic dynasty and its victories over Moab and Edom (2 Sam 8:2, 12–14) and have been messianically interpreted.

The obscure (and possibly added) brief oracles against the nations (24:20–4) name the Amalekites (cf. its king Agag, 24:7, and 1 SAM 15; 30); the Kenites (Kain), a subgroup of the Midianites; Assyria (or an obscure tribal group, Gen 25:3); Eber (perhaps another tribal group in the area); and the Philistines or other sea people (Kittim). The oracles announce their ultimate demise. In all of these events Israel's God will be the chief actor (24:23).

But the Moabites come back to haunt Israel almost immediately. The Israelites remain at the boundary of Moab across from Jericho.

(25:1–18) The Final Rebellion Scholars agree that this chapter combines two separate stories about Israelite men and foreign women (often assigned to JE and P), with a conclusion that assumes both stories. The second story may have been added to illustrate the first and to raise up the stature of the Aaronic line (at the expense of Moses?). The chapter is highly condensed and the reader must fill in many gaps. The focus is violation of the first commandment, the first notice of idolatry since Ex 32 (for parallels, see Olson 1996: 153–4), anomalous given God's blessings in chs. 22–4. In these events the old generation seems finally to die off (14:26–35; 26:64–5). The decks are cleared for the new generation (whose census follows in ch. 26).

The first story (vv. 1–5; cf. Deut 4:3–4) involves Moabite women who, through acts of prostitution, invite Israelite males into idolatrous practices associated with the god (sing.) Baal, the Canaanite god of Peor (on Balaam's advice, 31:16). God tells Moses to impale the chiefs of Israel so that the anger of God is turned away from Israel; no notice is given of obedience (unusual in Numbers; a failure of Moses?). Moses issues a different command, namely to kill only the idolaters (also not executed). vv. 8–9 speak of a severe plague, which v. 18 and 31:16 associate with the idolatry of Peor, and must have begun in 25:3 (cf. weeping in 25:7). Because the wrath of God was not turned away by following God's command to execute a few, a more devastating plague occurred, a working out of the consequences of the deed (see NUM 1:53; 14).

The second story (vv. 6–15) involves a relationship between a Midianite woman and a Simeonite; the detail given in vv. 14–15 testifies to their status (and may link the man with v. 4). The phrase 'into his family' (v. 6) suggests marriage, but the Hebrew is 'to his brothers'; the tabernacle setting suggests something more sinister, as does the word 'trickery' in v. 18 (see 31:16). He did this 'in the sight of Moses' and *all* Israelites as they voiced their lament to God at the tabernacle. The wrong committed is uncertain, but the combination of marriage to a Midianite (paired with idolatrous Moabites, v. 18) and the defiance exhibited in parading themselves before the lamenting people suggests idolatrous practice.

Perhaps Moses had difficulty acting because he himself had married a Midianite. In any case, the blatant act exhibited in his sight was serious enough to call for a decisive response. Moses' failure entails two instances of disobedience in quick succession. But Phinehas, grandson of Aaron, does not hesitate. He enters their tent (perhaps a nearby shrine?—the Hebrew word occurs only here) and pierces them through. The single act suggests they were having intercourse and the tabernacle vicinity suggests an act of cultic prostitution, which would link back to v. 1. The effect of his action (in effect a 'sacrifice') was to 'make atonement for the Israelites' (v. 13; cf. 16:46–8) and stop the plague, which God's command to Moses in v. 4 had called for, and Phinehas now fulfils at least in part. God interprets this action as a zeal exercised on behalf of the divine jealousy (the related Hebrew words show that God's zeal became Phinehas's), which links the action to idolatry (see Ex 34:14–16; Hos 9:10). So, this is a zeal for the first commandment (and the first reference to Baal, which may account for the god's later infamy, e.g. Ps 106:28).

This action of Phinehas becomes the basis for God's establishing with the Aaronides an everlasting covenant of peace, which is interpreted to mean a covenant of perpetual priesthood ('my' means that its fulfilment is solely dependent on God). What is new, given earlier divine commitments to Aaron (Ex 29:9; 40:15; cf. Mal 2:4–5)? Covenant (of peace) language is new (see Isa 54:10; Ezek 34:25), suggesting a formalization of a prior commitment.

This text may reflect later priestly rivalries. The status of Phinehas is raised up over Aaron's other son Ithamar (whose descendants were banished by Solomon, 1 Kings 2:26–7) and God's commitment to Phinehas, whose descendants were Zadokites (1 Chr 6:4–10; Ezek 44:15), is eternal.

The conclusion (vv. 16–18) combines elements from both stories (known to Num 31:8–16 and Ps 106:28–31). The divine word to 'harass [be an enemy to] the Midianites' is directly correspondent to their harassment of Israel; see NUM 31, where Israel goes to war against the Midianites and Balaam

is killed for his participation in Israel's apostasy. The condemnation of a Simeonite, when combined with the actions of Levites and Reubenites in ch. 16, means that the curse on these three tribes in Jacob's last testament (Gen 49:1–7) is brought to completion (see Douglas 1993: 194–5).

The New Generation on the Plains of Moab (26:1–36:13)

The balance of Numbers (all Priestly material) contains little narrative in the usual sense, though enough to keep the law and narrative rhythm alive (see chs. 31; 32). Various statutes and lists are presented that prepare Israel for its life in the land.

This census marks the beginning of the new generation without the presence of the old (see NUM C.2). Given the obedient preparations for the journey in chs. 1–10, the reader may wonder whether anything external can be developed to prevent the rebellions of a new generation. The oracles of Balaam, however, have made it clear that God will be true to promises made, and those promises have been focused on this new generation by God himself (14:24, 31). From the assumptions of land ownership and allocation in chs. 27–36, this new generation will inherit the land, regardless of what it does. Hence, these chapters have a promissory force (see NUM 15).

Yet this does not lessen the call to be faithful (Caleb and Joshua stand as examples) and so chs. 27–36 (and Deuteronomy, also addressed to the new generation) seek to assist Israel in its faithfulness through new orderings of a community confronted with many of the same issues. Many signs of hope will surface, not least the complete absence of death notices. But this picture dare not contribute to undue optimism. Deut 28–31 will make it clear that this new generation will be no more faithful than the old and will experience many of the same failures and consequences (see Deut 29:22–8; 31:20–9). On parallels between Num 1–25 and 26–36, see Olson (1996: 158–9).

Characteristic of chs. 27–36 is the recognition that older law may need to change in view of new life situations. The heart of the matter is community justice and stability; for that reason God becomes engaged in social and economic change. Such ongoing divine involvement witnesses to a dynamic understanding of law, in which the tradition is reinterpreted for the sake of life in a new situation. Instead of an immutable, timeless law, Israel insists on a developing process in which experience in every sphere of life is drawn into the orbit of law, but always in the service of life and the flourishing of community.

(26:1–65) The Census of the New Generation The second census begins as did the first (cf. v. 2 with 1:2–3), with military service in mind, Eleazar replacing his father Aaron, and land allotment issues paramount. The reference to all these persons having come out of Egypt seems strange; perhaps this is how they identify themselves as a *community*. See GEN 46:8–24, whose list of seventy individuals have here—basically—become seventy clans (cf. also 1 Chr 2–8). Even with the failures of certain tribal groups and the diminishment of numbers, the twelve-tribe reality remains intact here (only Manasseh and Ephraim are inverted). The listing focuses on clans rather than individuals (for land allotment); the totals are given for each *tribe* and the total for all: 601,730 compared to 603,550 in 1:46. Even with all the deaths in chs. 11–25, the numbers remain essentially the same. God's blessings have been at work behind the scenes.

Several events of previous chapters are recalled, the rebellion of Korah and the Reubenites (vv. 9–11; cf. also v. 19), the deaths of Er and Onan (v. 19; cf. Gen 38:3–10), the deaths of Nadab and Abihu (v. 61; cf. Lev 10:1–2), and a reference to Jochebed, the mother of Moses (v. 59). Another reference to women anticipates events yet to occur (v. 33), and is the reason for the lengthier generation list of Manasseh. A new reason for the census is given in vv. 52–6, i.e. land apportionment is to be based on tribal size after the conquest is complete (though the location of land will be based on lot, a means of eliminating human bias). Such a method sought to ensure a fair distribution of the land to the various families.

The Levites are also newly enrolled (cf. 3:14–39, with an increase of 1,000), separately as before (1:48–9), with reference to the absence of tribal allotment (18:23–4). As God had said (14:20–35), no member of the old generation is still alive except Caleb and Joshua and, for a time, Moses.

(27:1–11) The Daughters of Zelophehad Because ancestral lands are to be kept within the tribe (see Lev 25; 1 Kings 21:1–4), a way to pass on the inheritance must be found if a man has no sons. In such cases daughters may inherit; that possibility is here given Moses' blessing (it occurs in Josh 17:3–6). A restriction is added in 36:1–2, providing an *inclusio* for Num 27–36 (for less restrictive practices in that world, see Milgrom 1990: 482–4).

The daughters of Zelophehad take the initiative with Moses in pursuing inheritance rights inasmuch as their father had no sons (see the census, 26:33). The allusion to their father not being with Korah may refer to the 250 laymen of 16:2; 'his own sins' may refer to the old generation (26:64–5). They note that their father's name would still be associated with this land (27:4); apparently their sons would pass on the name (see 36:1–12; Ezra 2:61). Moses consults with God, who agrees with the daughters. In addition, God decrees other ways in which the inheritance is to be passed on in the absence of sons, with preference given to direct lineage (see Sakenfeld 1995). Levirate marriage (Deut 25:5–10) was probably not applicable here, either because the mother was dead or no longer of child-bearing age.

Israel's patrilineal system sought to ensure the endurance of the family name (see 27:4; Deut 25:5–6), a questionable issue from a modern perspective; yet, such a concern sought to safeguard a just distribution of land among the tribes (see 36:1–12). These women challenge the practice that only males inherit land; yet their appeal remains fundamentally oriented in terms of their father's name (vv. 3–4), perhaps practising politics as the art of the possible. So they commendably challenge current practice, and take an important step toward greater gender equality, but they do not finally (seek to) overturn the patrilineal system. (See Fishbane 1985: 98–105.)

(27:12–23) From Moses to Joshua This segment describes the transfer of authority from Moses to Joshua. A good case can be made, especially given the reference to the death of Moses (v. 13), that the report of Moses' death (now in Deut 34; note also the similarity between Num 27:12–14 and Deut 32:48–52)

originally stood here (or after 36:13) and concluded an earlier version of the 'Pentateuch'.

The need for a successor to Moses on the eve of the entry into the land is made clear by his (and Aaron's) earlier rebellion (v. 14; see 20:12). It is striking that Moses is the one who initiates the issue of succession (v. 15), appealing to God as Creator, the one who gives breath (spirit) to all people (see 16:22), in an apparent reference to God as the one who has given Joshua the spirit, a specific charisma for leadership (27:18; cf. 11:17, 26; Deut 34:9). Joshua has been an 'assistant' to Moses since the Exodus (11:28; Ex 24:13; 33:11). Here his responsibilities are especially associated with leading the Israelites in battle (see Ex 17:8–14), the basic meaning of 'go out before them and come in before them' (27:17, 21; Josh 14:11). Yet the image of sheep and shepherd suggests a more comprehensive leadership role, even royal in its basic sense (see 2 Sam 5:2).

In response to Moses, God commands him to take Joshua and commission him by laying his hand upon him, a symbolic act signifying the transfer of authority through which God was active (so v. 20; cf. 8:10–11; Deut 34:9). The investiture is public, before 'all the congregation', so that it is clear that he is the one whom the people are to obey (v. 20). The act is also to take place before Eleazar the high priest (see 20:22–9), to whom Joshua is responsible with respect to the discernment of the will of God (esp. regarding battle) through the use of Urim and Thummim (see EX 28:29–30). The latter explains why only 'some' of Moses' authority was given to Joshua (v. 20; cf. Moses' role in 12:6–8; Deut 34:10; Josh 1:7–8). Moses did as God had commanded him.

(28:1–29:40) Offerings for Life in the Land In chs. 28–9 offerings are instituted for various regular and festival occasions (the number seven is prominent throughout) for Israel's life in the land. They assume all previous texts in the Pentateuch regarding these matters (e.g. LEV 23; NUM 7; 15; DEUT 16:1–17) and may be a late addition. Whereas the opening chapters of Numbers centre on the spatial ordering of the community, these ordinances focus on its temporal ordering, in anticipation of a more settled life in the land. By marking out these times Israel placed itself in tune with God's temporal ordering in creation, a rhythm and regularity essential for the life God intends for all (for links to Gen 1, see Olson 1996: 170–3). At these times through the year Israel is to be attentive to offerings given by God in and through which God acted for the sake of the life and well-being of the community (indeed, the cosmos). For a convenient summary of the significance of offerings, see Nelson (1993).

(28:1–2) introduces all the offerings (brought by the people) that belong wholly to YHWH (whole burnt offerings; purification or 'sin' offerings; each with meal and drink offerings, cf. NUM 15) for the various times. This totals thirty days of the year (252 total male animals—lambs (140), rams (20), bulls (79), and goats (13) for the purification offerings), besides the daily and sabbath offerings (two lambs in each case). 29:39–40 concludes the list, with a list of private offerings not covered here. On 'pleasing odour' (28:2, 24) see NUM 15:3.

The first three offerings (28:3–15) mark the basic temporal frame of days, weeks, and months. The remainder mark out the festival year, set primarily in terms of the beginning of the two halves of the year, the first month (Passover and Unleavened Bread) and the seventh month (Rosh Hashanah, Day of Atonement, and Booths), with Weeks between these major seasons. These three festival periods are closely timed to Israel's three harvest times, and in time become associated with three events of Israel's early history (Exodus; giving of the law; wilderness wanderings).

(28:3–8) Daily (continual) Offerings (*tāmîd*), offered every day (even on special days) at dawn and dusk, the points of transition between night and day. See EX 29:38–42.

(28:9–10) Sabbath Offerings, which help focus on that hallowed seventh day of creation, separated from all other days. No purification offering is presented on the sabbath because of the theme of joyfulness.

(28:11–15) Monthly (New Moon) Offerings. Cf. NUM 10:10.

(28:16–25) Passover and Unleavened Bread, celebrated in the first month. v. 16 assumes the provisions for Passover (see 9:1–14; Ex 12:1–27; Deut 16:1–8). Unleavened bread (vv. 17–25; see Ex 13:3–10) was celebrated on the seven days following Passover; it was begun and concluded with a 'holy convocation', on which days there was to be no occupational work.

(28:26–31) Festival of First Fruits (Weeks; Harvest; Pentecost), one day with no occupational work. Celebrated fifty days (a sabbath plus seven times seven days) after Unleavened Bread at the start of the wheat harvest (June). See LEV 23:15–21; DEUT 16:9–12.

(29:1–6) The first day of the seventh month is the traditional New Year's Day (this time in the autumn is thought to be the first month in an older agricultural year calendar, cf. Ex 23:16; 34:22). This is an occasion for a holy convocation, with no occupational work. The shofar is blown (v. 1); on blowing the trumpets at the appointed festivals, see NUM 10:10.

(29:7–11) Day of Atonement (Yom Kippur), celebrated on the tenth day of the seventh month, with a holy convocation, fasting, and no work at all (as on sabbath). See LEV 16:29–34; 23:26–32.

(29:12–38) Tabernacles (Booths; Sukkot; Ingathering) is the autumn harvest festival. Celebrated from the fifteenth day (when there was no occupational work) of the month for seven days, offerings are specified for each day, with many more animals than at other festivals. Fewer offerings are ordered for an eighth day, a day of 'solemn assembly' (the seventh one for the year) with no occupational work, which ends the celebration. See LEV 23:33–6, DEUT 16:13–15.

The large number of animals and amounts of produce anticipate settlement in a land of abundance. These statutes will help the wilderness community face into the future.

(30:1–16) Vows and their Limits The mention of votive offerings in 29:39 perhaps provides the link to this material (see LEV 7:16–18; 22:17–25; 27; NUM 15:1–10). These statutes in casuistic style (cf. DEUT 23:21–3) concern vows or pledges (*nēder*) made by men (v. 2), who are bound by their word, and by women who are as well (vv. 3–15). But women are usually (v. 9) bound to their vows within limits placed by the actions of a father or husband. These are (sworn) promises to God ('oath' is used with human beings) related to service (nazirite, 6:2) or in exchange for the (potential) fulfilment of

a request, often in crisis (see 21:2; Jacob in GEN 28:20–2; Jephthah in JUDG 11:30–1; Hannah in 1 SAM 1:11).

Three categories of women whose vows are conditional are presented: those who are still in their father's house and under his authority (vv. 3–5); women who are under vows (even rash ones, see Lev 5:4) at the time they are married, vows not annulled by the father (vv. 6–8); women who are married and under their husband's authority (vv. 10–15). Widows and divorcees are excluded because they are under no man's authority (v. 9).

In the cases presented essentially the same principles are operative. If a father or husband disapproves of a vow, he must speak up at the time he hears (of) the vow (not least a vow to fast, v. 13) or the vow stands. If the father or husband disapproves, the vow is annulled, the woman is forgiven by God and is to suffer no consequences. The fourth case is expanded (3:14–15): if a husband annuls his wife's vow after some time has passed, then he (not she) will be guilty of breaking the vow and will have to suffer the (unspecified) consequences (see Deut 23:21).

These statutes assume dependence of the woman upon the man rather than a culture of reciprocity. They protect both men (from having the responsibility to fulfil a vow a woman has made) and, to a lesser extent, women (whose vows remain intact unless there is immediate male response). Lines of responsibility are thus clearly drawn. The overarching concern is that voiced in v. 2—individuals are to keep their word. Failed promises adversely affect one's relationship to God and disrupt the stability of a community.

(31:1–54) War Against the Midianites This narrative (with 32:1–42) focuses on traditions associated with Israel's conquests and settlement in the Transjordan. It is often called a Midrash, with its frequent reference to prior texts in Numbers and its exaggerations (e.g. the amount of spoil and that no Israelite warrior was lost in battle, v. 49). Certainly the entire narrative is idealized, probably in the interests of the portrayal of the new generation, though a nucleus seems rooted in some event.

vv. 1–2 pick up the story line from 25:17–18. God had commanded Israel to attack the Midianites in response to their corresponding attacks on Israel. v. 16 interprets this harassment in terms of Moabite/Midianite—merged here—women, at the instigation of Balaam, seducing Israelite men into idolatrous practices. Israel's obedient response to God's command is military in character and is interpreted as 'avenging' (*n-q-m*) Israel and God (vv. 2–3). But the language of 'vengeance' for *n-q-m* is problematic; preferred is the sense of vindication, to seek redress for past wrongs. Israel is God's instrument of judgement against the Midianites, which would vindicate the honour of both God and the Israelites.

This narrative is also linked to two earlier successful battles against Canaanites and Amorites (21:1–3, 21–35), each waged according to holy war principles in which their entire populations were destroyed (cf. Josh 6:20–1; 10:28–42). This battle takes a somewhat different turn. It has the earmarks of a Holy War, with the presence of the priest as 'chaplain' (see Deut 20:2–4; Phinehas rather than Eleazar because of Lev 21:11) and the sanctuary vessels (v. 6, presumably including the ark,

14:44) and the sounding of alarm (10:9). Only 1,000 men from each tribe are engaged, a small percentage of those available (26:51; cf. Judg 7:2–8; 21:10–12). The battle itself is only briefly described (vv. 7–8) and every male (including Balaam) is killed and their towns destroyed (v. 10; cf. Josh 13:21–2). The presence of Midianites in Judg 6–8 would seem to question this, but there were other Midianite clans (see Hobab in 10:29–32). Then (unlike Num 21) the women and children (and animals) are not killed but taken captive (with other booty) brought before Moses, Eleazar, and the congregation (v. 12). This action represents a variation in the practice of Holy War as outlined in Deut 20:13–18 (and 21:10–14), where a distinction is made between the peoples of Canaan (including Amorite areas where some tribes settled, 32:33) and others more distant. Apparently the Midianites are considered among the latter, though qualified in view of Israel's prior history with them (ch. 25).

Moses expresses anger that captives have been taken, or at least that 'all the women' have (vv. 14–15). He isolates 'these women here', because they were involved in the Peor apostasy. But he commands not only that they be killed, but all women who are not virgins (because all are suspect?) and all male children (certainly a genocidal move), while female virgins can be preserved alive 'for yourselves', as wives or slaves (vv. 16–18). No word from the Lord is given regarding this matter (common in Numbers), and there is no arbitration, so the reader might ask how legitimate it is. One cannot help but wonder if the unmarried women were checked one by one! The text informs the reader only indirectly that these commands of Moses were carried out (see v. 35).

The commands regarding purification for persons (soldiers and captives) and organic materials which have come into contact with the dead are begun by Moses (vv. 19–20; in terms of NUM 19, as is v. 24) and extended by Eleazar (vv. 21–3, in terms of a word of God to Moses not previously reported) with respect to distinctions between flammable and non-flammable (metallic) items.

vv. 25–47 focus on the distribution of the spoil. God speaks for the first time since v. 2 (vv. 25–30) with commands regarding the disposition of captives and booty. They are to be divided evenly between the warriors and the rest of the congregation (cf. 1 Sam 30:24). One in 500 of the warriors' items are to be given to the priests as an offering to the Lord; one in fifty of the congregation's items (more because of less risk) are to be given to the Levites (see NUM 18:8–32 for other such portions; cf. also NUM 7). This command is carried out (v. 31) and vv. 32–47 detail the disposition and quantity of the spoil; the total—just of the officers!—is immense: 808,000 animals, 32,000 young women, and (from v. 52) 16,750 shekels of gold. vv. 48–54 deal with non-living booty. The officers approach Moses with information that no Israelite was killed and announce their gift to YHWH of the precious metals each soldier (v. 53 includes everyone) had taken. These valuables are brought to Moses to make atonement for themselves and as a memorial before God—through tabernacle furnishings made from the metals—regarding this event (vv. 50, 54). The need for atonement is usually linked to EX 30:11–16 and the taking of a military census, but this seems strained; it might have to do with the taking of human life, not fully commanded by God in this case (see above).

On the offensiveness of these holy war practices, see NUM 21:1–3. This victory is the first of the new generation and bodes well for the future.

(32:1–42) Early Land Settlement Issues This chapter reports a crisis among members of the new generation regarding land settlement to the east of the Jordan (outside the usual definition of Canaan, but present in some texts, GEN 15:16–21, Exod 23:31). Its resolution by means of compromise stands in sharp contrast to earlier experiences (see 32:6–13) and witnesses to a change in this Israelite generation.

The focus is on tribes who settled in the highlands of Gilead east of the Jordan river—Reuben, Gad, and the half-tribe of Manasseh (see also Deut 3:12–20; Josh 13:8–32; 22:1–34). These tribes receive a somewhat mixed evaluation here and elsewhere in the tradition (see 16:1; Gen 49:3–4; Josh 22:10–34; Judg 5:15–17; 11:29–40; 1 Chr 5:23–6).

In 21:21–35 the Israelites had defeated the Amorite kings Sihon and Og and obliterated their communities; this happened at God's command (21:34). This theological point is correctly made by Reuben and Gad (32:4) in their request for this territory as their possession (32:1–5). These areas with their fertile pasture lands were now 'vacant', and their availability attracted the attention of these cattle-rich tribes (later joined by the half-tribe of Manasseh, 32:33–42).

Their final words, 'do not make us cross the Jordan', trigger Moses' memories of past disasters associated with reluctance to enter the land (32:8–15; see NUM 13–14), 'land' here understood to mean Canaan. Moses questions whether they are trying to avoid upcoming battles; indeed, he considers them 'a brood of sinners' (v. 14) who repeat the unfaithfulness exhibited by the spies, the effects of which he rehearses, and which could now recur with even more disastrous consequences—the destruction of Israel.

But, unlike Israel in chs. 13–14, these tribes propose a compromise (vv. 16–19). They will settle in the Transjordan and leave their families and animals behind. And they will fight, indeed serve in the vanguard of the Israelites as they move across the Jordan. They will not return to their homes until 'all the Israelites' are secure and they will not inherit any of those lands (vv. 16–19).

Moses responds positively, if cautiously, and mention of God is especially prominent. Picking up on the 'vanguard' of v. 16, they are to go 'before the LORD' (vv. 20–2), that is, before the ark (see JOSH 4:12–13; 6:7–13). If they follow through on their agreement they have fulfilled their obligation. If they do not, they can be sure that their sin will find them out (vv. 20–4). The effects of sin are here understood to have an intrinsic relationship to the deed and such effects will in time reveal what they have done (see NUM 14).

Gad and Reuben, using deferential language ('your servants', 'my lord'), agree with those terms (vv. 25–7). And so Moses commands Eleazar, Joshua, and tribal heads to witness and honour (he will soon be dead) this agreement and these tribes formally and publicly agree (vv. 28–32). If these tribes fail, they will have to take lands west of the Jordan (v. 30). The words, 'As the LORD has spoken' (v. 31) are striking because the text does not report God having so spoken; Moses' word seems to be as good as God's. When the agreement has been made, Moses gives the lands to these tribes, who rebuild Amorite cities and rename them (vv. 33–8; see JOSH 13:8–32 for land allotments).

The integration of the half-tribe of Manasseh (vv. 33, 39–42) into the tribes settling in Transjordan comes as something of a surprise; it may be an old tradition added later (see 26:29–34; Josh 13:29–32). They oust more Amorites for their lands, and hence their situation is different from that of Gad and Reuben who possess already conquered lands. The land for two and one-half tribes is thus already in place before the Jordan is crossed.

(33:1–49) The Wilderness Journey Remembered This passage is a recollection of the forty-two stages of Israel's journey through the wilderness, from Egypt (vv. 3–5) to their present situation across the Jordan (v. 49). Its placement may recognize the end of the journey narrative and the beginning of the land settlement. The itinerary is represented as something Moses wrote at God's command (v. 2); it probably has its origin in one or more ancient itineraries that circulated in Israel through the generations (see Milgrom 1990: 497–9). Many sites are not mentioned elsewhere (vv. 13, 18–29); most are not geographically identifiable. The itinerary is a surprisingly 'secular' document; divine activity is mentioned only at the beginning (v. 4) and at the death of Aaron (v. 38). This omission emphasizes the importance of human activity on this journey.

The reader can recognize two uneven segments, up to and following the death of Aaron (vv. 38–9), perhaps betraying priestly interests, and the reference to the king of Arad (v. 40), perhaps because this is the first contact with Canaanites. Only v. 8 speaks of the travel time involved.

The first segment is vv. 3–37 (see Ex 12:37–19:1; Num 10:11–20:29). Noteworthy is the detail regarding the Passover, and the note about it as a battle among the gods (see v. 52; cf. Ex 12:12; 15:11). Strikingly, Sinai is simply another stop along the way (vv. 15–16), with no mention of the giving of the law, and the sea crossing is mentioned only in passing. The presence and absence of water is raised (vv. 9, 14), perhaps because of its import for the journey. This levelling of the journey to its bare bones highlights the journey itself rather than the events along the way.

The second segment (vv. 41–9; see Num 21:1–22:1) moves quickly to the present situation (with a passing reference to Mt. Nebo, the site of Moses' death and burial).

(33:50–6) Directions for Conquest of Canaan This segment constitutes hortatory instructions from God to Moses regarding the nature of the attack on Canaan, which God has given for Israel to possess (v. 53). In possessing the land, they are to drive out (not exterminate; cf. Ex 23:23; Deut 7:1–6) all the present inhabitants, destroy their images and sanctuaries, and apportion the land by lot according to the size of the clans (v. 54, essentially a repetition of 26:54–5, perhaps because of the events of NUM 32). If they do not drive out the inhabitants (which is what actually happens; cf. JUDG 1:1–2:5; 1 Kings 9:21), those left shall 'be as barbs in your eyes and thorns in your sides' (v. 55), which is what they prove to be over the years (see Judg 2:11–3:6). The reader will recognize these themes from EX 23:23–33 and 34:11–16; they anticipate such texts as Deut 12:2–4. The final verse (v. 56) anticipates the destructions of Samaria and Jerusalem and the exiling of Israel, a warning that will be more fully developed in Deuteronomy (see esp. chs. 28–31).

(34:1–29) The Apportionment of the Land This chapter delineates the boundaries of the promised land (vv. 1–15) and the leaders who are to apportion that land among the tribes (vv. 16–29). Both are chosen by God. The content suggests that the land will soon be in Israel's hands.

The boundaries of the land of Canaan are idealized; they do not correspond to the boundaries known from any time during Israel's history. On the other hand, the boundaries correspond well to the Canaan known from Egyptian sources prior to the Israelite settlement and a few other texts (see Josh 13–19; Ezek 47:13–20). Several sites are not known and so the boundaries cannot be determined with precision (see Milgrom 1990: 501–2).

The southern border (vv. 2–5) moves from the southern end of the Dead Sea south and west across the wilderness of Zin to south of Kadesh to the Wadi of Egypt to the Mediterranean (the western boundary, v. 6). The northern border (vv. 7–9) is less clear, extending from the Mediterranean to Mount Hor (not the southern mountain, 20:22–9) into southern Syria (Lebo-hamath). The boundary to the east moves from a line north of the eastern slope of the Sea of Chinnereth (Galilee) down the Jordan river to the Dead Sea (vv. 10–12). Hence, the boundaries given here do not include Transjordan where two and one-half tribes had settled (v. 32), confirmed by Moses' statement (vv. 13–15). From the perspective of v. 2 (cf. 32:17; 33:51), Israel has not yet entered the land of its inheritance. Yet God had commanded the destruction of the Amorites (21:34) and cities of refuge are assigned in the Transjordan (35:14). Deut 2:24–5 includes the area west of the Jordan.

Ten tribal leaders (not from Reuben and Gad) are appointed to apportion the land, generally listed from south to north (vv. 16–29). Eleazar and Joshua (v. 17) are to supervise the work.

(35:1–34) Special Cities and Refinements in the Law These stipulations are given by God to Moses for the enhancement of life for various persons in the new land. The taking of human life puts the land in special danger. vv. 1–8 allocate cities for the Levites (for lists see Josh 21:1–42; 1 Chr 6:54–81). Stipulations for land distribution in Num 34 are here continued, with provision for the Levites, who have no territorial rights (see 18:21–4; 26:62). Inasmuch as they will be active throughout the land (with unspecified functions more extensive than care for the tabernacle, such as teaching), they are to be allotted forty-eight cities (six of which are cities of refuge, vv. 9–15). These cities provide for their housing and for grazing lands for their livestock, though not as permanent possessions (and others would live in them). 1,000 cubits (450 m.) in each direction from the town wall issues in a square of 2,000 cubits per side (see Milgrom 1990: 502–4). The various tribes will contribute cities according to their size.

(35:9–15) institutes cities of refuge (cf. Ex 21:12–14; Deut 4:41–3; 19:1–3, 9; for a list see Josh 20:1–9). When established in the land, the people were to choose three cities of refuge on each side of the Jordan (well distributed north to south). These cities were set aside as a place of asylum for persons (Israelite or alien) who killed someone without intent, until their case could be properly tried. Their purpose was to ensure that justice was done and to prevent blood feuds. As long as such persons remained within one of these cities they were secure from the avenger. The avenger of blood (or redeemer, *gōʾēl*; cf. Lev 25:25, 47–9) was the relative of the deceased charged to ensure proper retribution for the sake of the land (see 35:33). These cities were probably functioning during the monarchial period.

(35:16–34) Distinctions are made in the homicide laws between murder (including death through negligence) and unpremeditated killing (on the intentional/unintentional distinction, see 15:22–31; Ex 21:13–14). The burden of proof is on the slayer. Those who murder another with intent, regardless of the means or motivation (six examples are given, vv. 16–21), are to be put to death by the avenger (vv. 19, 21), though not without trial (v. 24 covers both cases, see below) and, according to the supplement (vv. 30–4), evidence of more than one witness (v. 30; cf. Deut 19:15–21), and no monetary ransom ('loophole') is possible (v. 31). Murder pollutes the land and its wholeness, not least because God dwells there (v. 34); only the blood of the killer can expiate the land, that is, remove the impurity that the murder has let loose (vv. 33–4). The avenger's action is necessary for the sake of the future of the land and its inhabitants.

On the other hand, killing without intent and hostility issues in a different response (vv. 22–3). A trial is to be held (v. 24, outside the city of refuge, with national judges representing the congregation, cf. Deut 19:12; Josh 20:4–6) to decide whether the killing was truly unintentional. If so decided, the slayer was returned to the city where he originally took refuge (cf. Josh 20:6), where he remained until the high priest died.

The cities of refuge were a kind of exile, a home away from home for those who killed unintentionally, so this was a penalty. Because the city of refuge only masked the polluting effects of the murder, expiation was still necessary. This was accomplished through the death of the high priest, which had expiatory significance, issuing in a kind of general amnesty. Only then was release possible. If the slayer left the city before this happened (and no ransom was possible, v. 32), he was not protected from the avenger, whose actions would not incur guilt.

(36:1–13) Once Again: The Daughters of Zelophehad This chapter picks up the issues raised by the daughters of Zelophehad; they provide an *inclusio* for Num 26–36. In 27:1–11 they had requested Moses that they inherit their father's property inasmuch as he had no sons. They based their case on the continuance of their father's name and his property in their clan (27:4). Now members of their tribe (Manasseh) come to Moses, recall the previous arrangement (v. 2), and ask for an interpretation in view of the fact that upon marriage any property held by the wife became that of her husband. Hence, if a daughter were to marry outside her tribe, the property would transfer to that tribe and Manasseh (in this case) would lose its full original allotment. Even the jubilee

year property transfer would not return it to the family, because the property would have been inherited rather than sold (v. 4; see Lev 25:13–33). Moses agrees with this reasoning and apparently receives a word form the Lord on the matter (it may be his interpretation of the 'word of the Lord' more generally, cf. Ex 18:23). The daughters may marry whom they wish, but it must be from within their own tribe (common in patrilineal systems) so that the tribal allotment of every tribe remains as originally determined. The daughters of Zelophehad—Mahlah, Tirzah, Hoglah, Milcah, and Noah—actually marry within their *clan*, sons of their father's brothers.

The final verse in Numbers speaks of God's commandments given through Moses since 22:1, when Israel arrived by the Jordan at Jericho. These commandments have been essentially forward-looking, anticipating Israel's future life in the land. Inasmuch as Deuteronomy takes place over the course of a single day, at the end of Numbers Israel's entrance into the promised land is just hours away.

REFERENCES

Ashley, T. R. (1993), *The Book of Numbers*, NICOT (Grand Rapids: Eerdmans).

Balentine, S. E. (1983), *The Hiding of the Face of God* (Oxford: Oxford University Press).

Douglas, M. (1993), *In the Wilderness: The Doctrine of Defilement in the Book of Numbers* (Sheffield: Sheffield Academic Press).

Fishbane, M. (1985), *Biblical Interpretation in Ancient Israel* (Oxford: Oxford University Press).

Fretheim, T. E. (1984), *The Suffering of God: An Old Testament Perspective*, Overtures to Biblical Theology, (Philadelphia: Fortress).

——(1991), *Exodus*, Interpretation: A Bible Commentary for Teaching and Preaching (Louisville, Ky.: John Knox).

——(1996), *The Pentateuch*, Interpreting Biblical Texts (Nashville: Abingdon).

Joines, K. R. (1974), *Serpent Symbolism in the Old Testament: A Linguistic, Archaeological, and Literary Study* (Haddonfield, NJ: Haddonfield House).

Levine, B. (1993), *Numbers 1–20: A New Translation with Introduction and Commentary*, Anchor Bible (New York: Doubleday).

Milgrom, J. (1990), *Numbers*, JPS Torah Commentary (Philadelphia: Jewish Publication Society of America).

Nelson, R. D. (1993), *Raising Up a Faithful Priest: Community and Priesthood in Biblical Theology* (Louisville, Ky.: Westminster/John Knox).

Olson, D. (1985), *The Death of the Old and the Birth of the New: The Framework of the Book of Numbers and the Pentateuch*, Brown Judaic Studies, 71 (Chico, Calif.: Scholars Press).

—— *Numbers*, Interpretation: A Bible Commentary for Teaching and Preaching (Louisville, Ky.: John Knox).

Sakenfeld, K. D. (1995), *Journeying with God: A Commentary on the Book of Numbers*, International Theological Commentary on the Old Testament (Grand Rapids: Eerdmans).

Wenham, G. J. (1981), *Numbers: An Introduction and Commentary*, Tyndale Old Testament Commentary (Downer's Grove, Ill.: Inter-Varsity).

8. Deuteronomy

CHRISTOPH BULTMANN

INTRODUCTION

A. Character. Deuteronomy represents a major strand of Judean theology of the seventh to fifth centuries BCE. Its anonymous authors develop pivotal ideas such as the uniqueness of YHWH, the human 'love' and 'fear' of God (6:4–5, 24), and the excellence and accessibility of Israel's law (4:5–8; 30:11–14). The book contains a version of the Decalogue and relates all other laws to these basic commandments (ch. 5). It gives expression to the ideas of a 'covenant' between YHWH and Israel and of Israel's 'election' through YHWH (5:2; 7:6; 26:16–19). Deuteronomy focuses narrowly on Israel's land, while at the same time viewing it from a perspective of expectation (6:10–12, 17–18; 30:20). Its concern for the exclusiveness and purity of the worship of YHWH results in drastic admonitions about the conquest of the land (7:1–2; 12:1–4, 29–31) and harsh regulations concerning apostasy (13:1–18; 17:2–7). Originally the document of a religious movement, the oldest parts of the book functioned as a law to enforce the centralization of the sacrificial cult at the temple in Jerusalem (ch. 12) and as a law to promote social solidarity in Judah (ch. 15). The spirit of Deuteronomy in regard to cultic matters may be grasped from the law on religious vows in 23:21–3 (MT 22–4), and in regard to ethical matters from the law on just measures in 25:13–16. Deuteronomy reflects a tendency towards rationalization within the Israelite religious tradition. However, as the book developed over a long period, there are many tensions within it.

B. Name. The name 'Deuteronomy' is derived from the LXX where it is called *deuteronomion*, the 'second law'. This goes back to a misinterpretation of 17:18 by the LXX translators, where the expression *mišneh hattôrâ* means a 'copy of (this) law'. In the Jewish tradition, the name of the book is *děbārîm* (words), which is a name taken from the opening verse of the book.

C. Place within the Canon. 1. Deuteronomy is the fifth book of the Pentateuch. Its last chapter reports the death of Moses and thus, on the plane of narrative, concludes the story of the Exodus which began with the oppression of the Israelites and the call of Moses in Exodus. With its numerous references to the patriarchs it also relates to the patriarchal stories in Genesis. Above all, Deuteronomy indicates the end of the era of divine legislation for Israel. All of the laws which Moses delivers to the people were revealed to him at Mount Horeb (which is called Mount Sinai in Exodus and Numbers). According to Deuteronomy, however, they were only promulgated by Moses towards the end of his life in the 'land of Moab' (except for the Decalogue). This concept allowed later redactors of the Pentateuch to co-ordinate competing laws which claimed Mosaic authority by making Deuteronomy a sequel to the so-called Priestly Document.

2. Deuteronomy is the first book of a historical work which consists of Deuteronomy plus the Former Prophets (Joshua, Judges, Samuel, Kings). Thus, it is the opening of what is known as the Deuteronomistic History and leads directly on to the book of Joshua (Noth 1991; McKenzie 1994). In many instances, Deuteronomic laws function as criteria for the representation of Israel's history in the land during the period from the crossing of the river Jordan to the fall of Jerusalem. The process of the formation of the Pentateuch loosened the literary link between Deuteronomy and its continuation.

D. Literary Genre and Structure. 1. A clue to the problem of genre lies in 1:5 which says that Moses set out 'to expound this law' (*bě'ēr 'et hattôrâ hazzō't*). From 1:6 to 30:20, Deuteronomy is a great oration with a didactic purpose. However, the speaker is presented to the readers of Deuteronomy by a narrator, who framed the oration with short narrative sections in 1:1–5 and 34:1–12, thus making the oration the valedictory address of Moses before his death in the land east of the Jordan. This concept is also reflected in a few more instances where the voice of a narrator is heard in Deuteronomy (e.g. 4:41–3, 44–9; 5:1; 27:1; 29:1, 2 (MT 28:69; 29:1); 31:1, 2, 7, 9–10, and see Polzin 1993).

2. Deuteronomy is a multifaceted oration. 'To expound *tôrâ*' means more than just the transmission of a law code. The speaker relates the laws to the land as the area of their future application as well as to the Decalogue as the essential compilation of commandments for Israel. He instructs his audience about the theological significance of the Torah and calls for faithful obedience. This gives Deuteronomy its unrivalled paraenetic tone. The speaker also predicts the consequences of violating the law and even hints at the prospects beyond. The resulting structure of the oration is very complex indeed. Historical reviews in 1:6–3:29; 5:1–33; 9:7–10:11 and paraenetic sections in 4:1–40; 6:4–9:6; 10:12–11:25 form a prologue to the laws in 12:1–26:15, a large collection of blessings and curses in 28:1–68 and a further paraenetic section in 29:2–30:20 forms an epilogue to them. In addition, the speaker gives instructions for a future ritual commitment to the law after the crossing of the Jordan in 11:26–32 and 27:1–26. At the climax in 26:16–19, the speaker himself enacts a declaration of covenantal relationship between Israel (his audience) and YHWH. The overall form of an oration thus combines a number of distinct materials.

3. Many attempts have been made to describe the literary unity of Deuteronomy in more precise terms than that of an oration. A basic structural pattern of four elements consisting of a historical and paraenetic prologue—laws—covenant (26:16–19)—blessings and curses, was regarded as reflecting the pattern of a cultic ceremony (von Rad 1966). A similar basic pattern of four main elements, namely a historical prologue—a fundamental statement of allegiance (6:4–7)—detailed stipulations—blessings and curses, was regarded as reflecting a pattern of ancient Near-Eastern political treaties (McCarthy 1978; Weinfeld 1992: 65–9). However, a simple basic pattern of laws, introduced by a prologue and concluded by an epilogue with curses, may already be found in the Code of Hammurabi of the eighteenth century BCE (where the curses threaten any future king who might abolish or alter the laws: *ANET* 163–80). Deuteronomy cannot be reduced to a literary structure which directly corresponds to any typical pattern because its erudite authors freely employ several elements from a common Near-Eastern cultural background.

E. History of Research. From patristic times onwards there was always a tradition that Deuteronomy was somehow related to the 'book of the law' (*sēper hattôrâ*) which, according to 2 Kings 22:1–23:25, was found in the Jerusalem temple during the reign of Josiah in the late seventh century BCE (e.g. Jerome, CChr.SL 75. 5). T. Hobbes, in his *Leviathan* (1651, chs. 33, 42), explicitly identified that law code with Deut 12–26 and emphasized that, in his opinion, it had been written by Moses. One hundred and fifty years later (1805–6), W. M. L. de Wette at the University of Jena came to the conclusion that Deuteronomy was not only the book which was found in the temple but had also been written not long before Josiah's times (see Rogerson 1992: 19–63). Whereas for de Wette this hypothesis meant that Deuteronomy was a late part of the Pentateuch, later research into the history of the Israelite religion, conducted by A. Kuenen and J. Wellhausen around 1870, established the view that most parts of the Pentateuch were even later than the Josianic Deuteronomy (for a convenient presentation of this view see W. Robertson Smith 1892: 309–430). The valuable commentary by S. R. Driver (1895) rests on this seminal model of the history of Israel's religious traditions. Subsequent scholarship tried to identify several editions of Deuteronomy which had been conflated into the extant book or to discover distinct redactional layers within it (see Mayes 1979; for a retrospective discussion see Nielsen 1995; for the current state of debate see Veijola (forthcoming)). Meanwhile it has become clear that the age of Josiah only stands for the beginnings of the literary development of Deuteronomy which reaches well into the Second Temple period.

F. Historical Background. 1. The age of Josiah, king of Judah 639–609 BCE (2 Kings 22–3), was characterized by the decline of the Neo-Assyrian empire. As very little is known about the impact of Assyrian politics and religion upon Judah, which since the second half of the eighth century had to some extent been a vassal state of Assyria, it is hard to decide what liberation from Assyrian domination would have meant to the Judeans (see McKay 1973; Spieckermann 1982; Halpern 1991). However, even in a very critical reading of Kings, scholars accept the historicity of the information given in 2 Kings 23:11–12, according to which Josiah removed Assyrian religious symbols from the temple in his capital Jerusalem (Würthwein 1984: 459; cf. Uehlinger 1995). It is less certain whether he also carried out the centralization of sacrificial worship which is attributed to him in 2 Kings 23:8–9, and whether this was instigated by the Deuteronomic law or conversely inspired the composition of a corresponding law code (see Lohfink 1985; Clements 1996). Even more disputed is the historical reliability of the information about Josiah's encroachment on the territory of the former Assyrian provinces north of Judah (2 Kings 23: 15–20). Any general conclusions

concerning the spirit of the Josianic age are severely restricted by the nature of the historical sources informing us about his times (cf. also P. R. Davies 1992: 40–1). Nevertheless, even if most of 2 Kings 22–3 is only legendary, the historical background of the representation in these chapters of Josiah's religious reform in 622 BCE may be sought in the activity of a movement which promoted the exclusiveness and purity of the Judean religion and gave literary expression to these ideas in a law code which later became the core of Deuteronomy. It is therefore not amiss to attribute the origin of Deuteronomy to a 'YHWH alone movement' in the seventh century BCE (M. Smith 1987: 11–42) and even to a distinct class of scribes who were educated in a Judean wisdom tradition (Weinfeld 1992: 158–78, 244–319).

2. An important factor in the development of the Deuteronomic movement is the language of political treaties in the ancient Near East (McCarthy 1978; Weinfeld 1992). Although the dependence of Deuteronomy upon such documents has often been overstated (see the critique by Nicholson 1986: 56–82), there are clear parallels in terminology and in the compositional function of a curse section. The relevant texts for comparison may be found in Parpola and Watanabe (1988) and *ANET* 531–41, also 201–6. The succession treaty of the Assyrian king Esar-haddon in favour of his son Assurbanipal, which dates from 672 BCE, is of particular interest here. Copies of this treaty were discovered during an excavation in Nimrud on the upper Tigris in 1955. They represent versions of the treaty as it was concluded with vassal states in the eastern periphery of Assyria and one can assume that the same treaty was also concluded with vassal states in the west, including Judah. The treaty must have been known to the scribe who wrote Deut 28:20–44 (Steymans 1995) and may also be alluded to in Deut 13. However, the question of under what political circumstances a Judean scribe would have borrowed those motifs from ancient Near-Eastern traditions remains open to conjecture.

3. The literary history of Deuteronomy developed further after the Babylonian conquest of Jerusalem in 587 BCE. According to Noth's theory of a Deuteronomistic History (see DEUT C.2), the author who wrote the history of Israel in her land must be seen against the background of this exilic age (see, however, Cross 1973). That author opened his narrative with Deut 1–3; 4; 31; 34 (apart from some later additions) and placed the book of the law which had been passed on to him into this narrative framework. Furthermore, not only do such passages as 4:25–31 and 29:22–30:10 refer to Israel in exile; the entire concept which dominates the paraenetic sections, namely that Israel finds herself outside the promised land and has to regain it, looks like a response to the end of monarchic Judah.

4. More refined analyses of the distinct redactional layers within the Deuteronomistic History led many scholars to the conclusion that the work of the Deuteronomistic scribal school extended far beyond the middle of the sixth century BCE and right into the Persian period. Passages which secondarily add theological reflections on the relevance of the Torah to preceding narrative or paraenetic texts (such as Josh 1:7–8; Deut 6:17–18) are seen as an expression of a specific 'nomistic' or 'covenant-related' stage in the Deuteronomistic tradition (Smend 1971; 1983; Veijola 1996a). Modifications in anti-syncretistic paraenetic passages which seem to reflect later historical experience of the Second Temple period (e.g. Deut 7:22; 7:3–4; cf. Neh 13:23–7; Ezra 9:1–2) are another point in question. An important formal criterion for these analyses is the recurrent shift of address in Deuteronomy between second person singular and second person plural (cf. DEUT 12:1–32) for which, however, an explanation in purely stylistical terms has also been suggested.

G. Sources. 1. The legal core in chs. 12–26 incorporates many older materials. A direct comparison is possible between Deuteronomy and the so-called Book of the Covenant in Ex 20:22–23:33. This shows parallels between Ex 20:24–5 ‖ Deut 12:13–14, Ex 21:2–11 ‖ Deut 15:12–18, Ex 21:12–14 ‖ Deut 19:1–13, Ex 22:25–7 (MT 24–6) ‖ 23:19–20 (MT 20–1); 24:10–13, Ex 23:4–5 ‖ Deut 22:1–4, Ex 23:10–11 ‖ Deut 15:1–11, Ex 23:14–18 ‖ Deut 16:1–17. These as well as some less obvious parallels make it clear that the Deuteronomic law represents a later stage in the history of Israelite law (Otto 1996a; Levinson 1997; contrast Van Seters 1996), although the Book of the Covenant may itself contain post-Deuteronomic as well as pre- and proto-Deuteronomic materials. At least two more collections of laws were taken up by the authors of the law code, namely a collection of family and sex laws (21:15–21; 22:13–29; 24:1–4; 25:5–12) and a collection of laws on warfare (20:10–14, 19–20; 21:10–14; 23:10–15) (Seitz 1971; Rofé 1987; 1985b). Further laws may have been taken up from oral tradition, possibly with some paraenetic elements attached to them urging and motivating obedience, such as, e.g. 22:6–7. The series of curses in 27:16–25 belongs to the apodictic law in Israelite tradition which commands an unconditional condemnation of or punishment for certain offences.

2. The large section of blessings and curses in ch. 28 contains a traditional series of blessings in vv. 3–6 (which are reversed in vv. 16–19). vv. 20–44 closely follow a sequence of curses in Esar-haddon's succession treaty (see DEUT F.2).

3. Ch. 5 contains the Decalogue (vv. 6–21) which found its place also in Exodus (20:2–17). However, instead of being a source of Deuteronomy, it is a composition which originated inside the Deuteronomic movement (Hossfeld 1982).

4. On the plane of the history of ideas, Deuteronomy is often seen as belonging to a Hoseanic prophetic tradition. The basic command of Deut 6:4–5 which centres on the notion of 'love' of God is regarded as a consequence of the theological concern and the metaphorical language of Hosea. As a second instance of Hoseanic influence the law concerning the king over YHWH's people (Deut 17:14–20) is appealed to. However, the available evidence does not sufficiently support the conclusion that Deuteronomy originated in the monarchy of northern Israel and was taken to Judah by refugees after the defeat of Israel in 722 BCE (Alt 1953).

5. The historical reviews in 1:6–3:29; 5:1–33; 9:7–10:11 show a relationship with narrative traditions in Exodus and Numbers and presuppose the Yahwistic work in the Pentateuch. Whether 11:26–32 and 27:1–14, together with Josh 8:30–5, reflect an ancient tradition (Nielsen 1995; Weinfeld 1991) remains doubtful.

6. Two independent documents have been added to Deuteronomy, in ch. 32 the Song of Moses, and in ch. 33 the Blessing of Moses. Whereas the collection of sayings about the tribes in ch. 33 mostly predates the seventh century, the poem of ch. 32 has its origin in the context of later reflections about the relationship between YHWH and Israel amongst the nations.

H. Literary History. 1. Deuteronomy developed from a law code to an oration of Moses within a narrative frame. The original law code aimed at a cultic reform in Judah and addressed its lay audience in the second person singular. It consisted of laws which were relevant to the centralization of sacrificial worship (12:13–19; 14:22–9; 15:19–23; 16:1–17; 18:1–8) and probably also of laws concerning social and judicial matters (15:1–18; 16:18–19; 17:8–13; 19:1–21; 21:1–9; cf. Morrow 1995), family and sex laws (see DEUT G.1), laws promoting equity in response to poverty (mainly in 23:15–25:16), and some ritualistic materials (e.g. 21:22–3; 22:9–10; 23:17–18), cf. Crüsemann 1996. 6:4–9 may have been the prologue to this law code. However, any detailed reconstruction of the original law code remains highly hypothetical. Whether or not it was presented as a law of Moses depends on the evaluation of 4:44–5 as its superscription.

2. The incorporation of Deuteronomy into the Deuteronomistic History was a distinct stage in its literary history (see DEUT C.2 and F.3), which created an explicit interrelation between the law and the issue of Israel's land as well as the differentiation between the law code and the Decalogue in ch. 5. In this process, the historians added laws to the code which look towards the subsequent history of Israel, such as the law on the king (17:14–20) and the law on the conquest (20:10–18, and further laws on warfare, see DEUT G.1).

3. The literary development of the paraenetic sections in 4:1–40; 6:4–11:25; 29:2–30:20 as well as of the laws which are primarily concerned with the problem of syncretism or religious assimilation such as 12:1–7, 29–31; 13:1–18; 18:9–20 is a special problem (see DEUT F.4). Many suggestions have been made for attributing the respective texts to only a few successive editions or redactional layers. However, it seems more appropriate to think in terms of a prolonged literary process which led to what ideally may be called the canonical shape of Deuteronomy no earlier than the 4th century.

I. Outline

Review of the Conquest of the Land East of the Jordan ((1:1–5) 1:6–3:29)
Discourse on the Excellence of the Law (4:1–40 (41–3, 44–9))
Review of the Covenant at Horeb and the Decalogue (5:1–33 (6:1–3))
Discourse on Faithful Obedience to the Law (6:4–11:25 (26–32))
Promulgation of the Laws (12:1–25:19 (26:1–15))
Declaration of Mutual Commitments between YHWH and Israel (26:16–19)
Instructions for a Ceremony West of the Jordan (27:1–26)
The Consequences of Obedience and Disobedience through Blessings and Curses (28:1–68)
Discourse on the Significance of the Law ((29:1) 29:2–30:20)
Report of Moses' Parting from Israel, Including his Poem and his Blessings (31:1–34:12)

COMMENTARY

Review of the Conquest of the Land East of the Jordan ((1:1–5) 1:6–3:29)

(1:1–5) Moses as Orator The superscription to Deuteronomy introduces the book as the words of *Moses* to *all Israel* at a location east of the river Jordan. As Moses is never to cross the Jordan (3:23–8), the following oration will be his valedictory address. This, however, is only explicitly indicated in 31:1–2 (cf. 4:22). The basic form of the superscription, 'These are the words that Moses spoke to all Israel beyond the Jordan as follows', has been considerably expanded. v. 5, which may be part of a specific compositional scheme (cf. 4:44; 29:1 (MT 28:69)), emphasizes the qualification of Moses' oration as law (*tôrâ*). 'Of all the terms for God's instructions, none better characterizes Deuteronomy, since it connotes both law and an instruction that must be taught, studied, and pondered, and it is expected to shape the character, attitudes, and conduct of those who do so' (Tigay 1996: 3). For v. 4 see further on 2:24–3:11. v. 2 can best be explained as a misplaced gloss on 1:19, while v. 1b, which adds some topographical information, remains elusive. v. 3 reflects an interest in chronology that is typical of Priestly texts in the Pentateuch, cf. e.g. Ex 40:17; Num 10:11.

(1:6–3:29) The Conquest of Israel's Land Moses gives an account of the partly unsuccessful and partly paradigmatic beginning of Israel's taking possession of the promised land. The section gives expression to a deliberate concept of the land as YHWH's gift to Israel which Israel entered from outside at a certain moment in history. The Deuteronomistic History (see DEUT C.2) thus starts with an idealized image of the conquest of the land, and ends with a somewhat stylized image of the loss of the land, cf. 2 Kings 15:29; 17:6, 23; 25:21, 26. It thus shapes a coherent overall view of one extended period of Israel's history. Although the Deuteronomistic authors of the sixth and fifth centuries BCE include several historical traditions in their composition, their work cannot be called historiographical in a strict sense.

(1:6–8) YHWH's Command Moses' retrospective does not start from the Exodus but with a reference to Mount Horeb. Thus it alludes to all the events which this name implies (cf. 5:2; 9:8). The land which Israel is to conquer is called 'the hill country of the Amorites' (*har hā 'ĕmōrî*) by a designation based on the name for the area in Neo-Assyrian inscriptions. An alternative general designation is 'the land of the Canaanites' (*'ereṣ hakkĕna'ănî*), and elsewhere in Deuteronomy a list of peoples is used for describing the population of the land (cf. 7:1; 20:17). Whereas chs. 2–3 carefully define Israel's territorial claims east of the Jordan (cf. 3:8), the vision of Israel's land as extending to the north as far as the river Euphrates (v. 7; cf. Josh 1:4) is alien to the concept of a conquest as well as to Israel's historical traditions. It may be either an echo of imperial rhetoric (Weinfeld 1991: 133–4) or a reflection of political experience in the late seventh century when victory in a battle at Carchemish on the Euphrates in 605 BCE made the Neo-Babylonians the political overlords of Palestine (cf. Jer 46:2; 2 Kings 24:7). v. 8 emphasizes that Israel's hope for the land is founded on an oath which YHWH swore to her ancestors, cf. Gen 15:18. The verse forms an *inclusio* with 30:20.

(1:9–18) Officers in Israel This insertion, which separates vv. 6–8 from its continuation in v. 19, authorizes an organization of the people modelled on 16:18–19 and 17:8–11. The passage is remarkable in that it grounds the position of 'leaders' on the consent of the people (v. 14) and specifies their qualification as 'wise, discerning, and reputable' persons (v. 13)—a profile which one may read as a self-portrait of the Deuteronomistic school. The designation of these leaders (*rā'šîm*) in military terms (*śārîm, šōṭĕrîm*, v. 15) corresponds with the literary context of the conquest narrative. Their designation as 'judges' (*sōpĕṭîm*) may reflect their actual function in the society of the author's time. A similar concern with the institution of leaders is expressed in Ex 18:13–27; 2 Chr 19:5–10; Num 11:14–17, 24–5, whereas no details about the appointment of officials during the time of the Judean monarchy (cf. e.g. Jer 36:12; 2 Kings 24:15) are known. vv. 16–17, integrity of the judges is essential to the idea of justice, and just claims of the poor merit protection (cf. 24:14–15; Am 5:10–12).

(1:19–2:1) The Failed Conquest In an artistic retrospective account, Moses indicates the reason why, after the Exodus, the Israelites did not conquer the promised land west of the Jordan from its southern border (cf. also the time-scale implied in 1:2). Disobedience (1:26; cf. 1:7–8) and lack of faith (1:32, RSV; contrast Ex 14:31) led to divine punishment of the Exodus generation (1:34–5; cf. 2:14–15). Kadesh-barnea has been identified with an oasis about 80 km. to the south-west of Beersheba, the town which normally marks the southern border of Judah (1 Kings 4:25 (Mt 5:5); 2 Kings 23:8; cf. however Josh 15:2–4). Instead of being the starting-point for the conquest, it becomes the starting-point for a journey of nearly forty years south-eastwards to the Red Sea and back northwards on the eastern side of Mount Seir until the successful conquest begins with the crossing of the Wadi Arnon (2:24), a wadi which runs towards the Dead Sea from the east opposite En-gedi. The narrative has been constructed upon the basis of a tradition about the Calebites who had expelled 'the three sons of Anak' from the fertile Hebron area (cf. Josh 15:14 and some fragments in Num 13–14).

(2:2–23) The Neighbouring Nations The second episode in Moses' account opens with a phrase similar to 1:6–7. The approach to the Wadi Arnon offers an opportunity to define Israel's territorial claims against the Edomites, the Moabites, and the Ammonites (see *ABD*, ad loc.). The section has been expanded by several successive scribes. One basic feature is the idea that YHWH, and not the respective national deities, assigned these three peoples their territories (vv. 5, 9, 19; contrast Judg 11:12–28, esp. v. 24). A second basic feature is the analogy between Israel's conquest of her land and the way in which these and other peoples took possession of their respective territories 'just as Israel did in the land they were to possess, which the LORD had given to them' (v. 12, NJPS). According to this view, the history of the historical nations follows on a mythological age in which 'Rephaim' (giants) inhabited the land. They may be called 'Emim', or 'Zamzummim', or 'Anakim' (vv. 10–11, 20–1), and are comparable with 'Horim' and 'Avvim' in other regions (vv. 12, 22–3; cf. also Am 9:7). As far as the Rephaim are concerned, a mythological tradition has been identified through a Ugaritic text (*c.*14–12th cents. BCE) which also establishes a link between Rephaim and the place-names Ashtaroth and Edrei (cf. 1:4; 3:11; see Margulis 1970). All these glosses amount to a striking reinterpretation of the conquest imagery which finds expression also in 9:2. vv. 14–15, pointing back to 1:34–5, these verses mark a transition between two periods of Israel's history after the Exodus.

(2:24–3:11) The Model Conquest YHWH's command also stands at the beginning of the third episode in Moses' account. 2:32–6, the first act of the conquest draws on an ancient tradition about a Transjordanian city ruler which has been preserved in the parallel narrative in Num 21:21–31. The account follows a highly stylized pattern: YHWH gives the enemy over, and the Israelites' army then 'strikes him down—captures his towns—utterly destroys all human beings in them—keeps the livestock and plunder as spoil' (2:33–5 and again in 3:3–7). This pattern agrees with the Deuteronomistic law on warfare in 20:10–18 and especially the injunction to 'utterly destroy' (*ḥ-r-m* hifil) all former inhabitants of the land (20:16–17; see DEUT 7:1–2). Moses is thus represented as conducting an exemplary war against the Amorites east of the Jordan, cf. 3:21; 31:4. 2:25–30, the basic structure of the account has been supplemented by several additions which focus on divine providence: YHWH puts 'the dread and fear' of Israel upon the peoples (2:25), YHWH 'hardens the spirit' of the Amorite king (2:30). Moses acts in accordance with the law of 20:10 although neither this law nor the analogy with Israel's passing through the land of the neighbouring nations applies to the case of the Amorite territory (2:26–9). 3:1–7, the second Amorite king is seen not as a city ruler but as king of a vast region; see, however, 1:4 and DEUT 2:10–11, 20–1. His name has been adopted from an etiological tradition which links this mythological figure to Rabbah of the Ammonites (3:11, however, the Ammonite territory itself is exempted from the land which the Israelites claim, 2:19, 37). The description of the conquered towns probably depends on 1 Kings 4:13. 3:8 states the result of Moses' ideal conquest which a scribe, probably in the sixth century BCE, created from very remote memories of some early history of Israelite tribes in the land east of the Jordan.

(3:12–20) Tribal Territories On the distribution of the land see Josh 13:8–32. vv. 18–20, the 'rest' (*n-w-ḥ* hifil I.) which YHWH has given to these tribes is an ideal for all Israel. Therefore, these tribes are summoned to support the conquest of the land west of the Jordan, cf. Josh 1:12–15; 22:1–4 (for the notion of 'rest' cf. also Deut 12:9; Josh 23:1; 2 Sam 7:1; 1 Kings 8:56). The notion of a rest in which the towns may be left without any defence (v. 19) conveys a peaceful vision in strong contrast with the military ideology of 2:34.

(3:21–9) The End of Moses' Leadership vv. 21–2, Moses' and Joshua's leadership in the conquest are seen in close parallel, cf. Josh 1:5. v. 28 is resumed in 31:7; Josh 1:6. The scene of Moses' rejected prayer is not continued by the narrator until 34:1–3. Moses wants to 'cross over' into the land and 'see' it (v. 25), but he may only 'see' it, whereas Joshua is to 'cross over' into it (v. 27–8). Moses thus becomes the symbol for an unfulfilled hope to live in the promised land. The reason for this is that YHWH makes him bear the consequences of the people's lack of faith—which Moses deplored in 1:32 (v. 26; the same thought has been added in 1:37–8). Not unlike 9:13–

14, 25–9, the scene thus includes reflections on the relationship between Moses and the people. The opening of the prayer proclaims YHWH's uniqueness (as in 1 Kings 8:23); one might compare the hymnic praise of the sun god in an Akkadian hymn (Lambert 1960: 129 ll. 45–6; ANET 388): 'Among all the Igigi (gods) there is none who toils but you, | None who is supreme like you in the whole pantheon of gods.'

Discourse on the Excellence of the Law (4:1–40)

This great discourse has been inserted between the historical retrospective and the superscription to the law in 4:44. Although it combines several components and although the form of address changes between second person plural and second person singular (see DEUT F.4 and Begg 1980), it eventually forms a unit framed by vv. 1–2 and 40. The discourse gives an interpretation of the Exile after the destruction of Jerusalem in 587 BCE as a time of 'serving' gods who are nothing but 'wood and stone' (v. 28; cf. 28:64) and addresses the issue of Israel's 'return' to YHWH (v. 30; cf. 30:1–2). It presupposes the prohibition of idols in the Decalogue (vv. 12–13, 16; cf. 5:8) and contains an explicit monotheistic confession (vv. 35, 39). Both these fundamental theological doctrines are being derived from the visual scene of YHWH's revelation at Mount Horeb and presented as an epitome of the Torah.

(4:1–8) Israel's Wisdom Obedience to the 'statutes and ordinances' brings with it the promise of life (v. 1; cf. 30:15–16) and is also seen as a condition for the conquest of the promised land (v. 1; cf. 6:17–18). At the same time, the 'statutes and ordinances' are defined as rules for life in the land (v. 5; cf. 12:1). The substance and the extent of the law must be protected from any changes (v. 2). This principle lies on the way to the formation of a canon. In vv. 6–8, a scribe gives expression to the ideal of Israel as a 'wise and discerning people' (*'am ḥākām wĕnābôn*). Israel will be recognized as such a people from YHWH's protection (v. 7) as well as from her divine law (v. 8, cf. DEUT 1:5). Obedience to this incomparable law would counteract the 'foolishness' of the people which is attacked in Jer 4:22. The designation of Israel as a 'great nation' echoes Gen 12:2, cf. Deut 1:10. In the final shape of Deuteronomy, the admiration of the nations in 4:6–8 corresponds with their puzzlement in 29:24–8 (MT 23–7). vv. 3–4, the warning against apostasy may be a gloss based on Num 25:1–5, cf. also Hos 9:10.

(4:9–14) YHWH's Voice at Mount Horeb The praise of the Torah is complemented by a graphic representation of the revelation of the Decalogue. The Israelites are to keep that day in their memory and their heart and pass the tradition on to all future generations (v. 9). YHWH revealed the Ten Commandments directly to the people so that they could hear 'the sound of words' (v. 12; cf. 4:33; 5:24), and he thus established his 'covenant' (*bĕrît*) with them. The poetic imagery underlines the priority of the Decalogue over the several statutes and ordinances (vv. 12–14). The account is based on 5:1–6:3 which, in turn, depends on fragments of older traditions in Ex 19–34. It makes the special point that Israel did not see any 'form' (*tĕmûnâ*; 'shape' NJPS, 'similitude' KJV) in the theophany (v. 12).

(4:15–20) Prohibition of Idols and Astral Cults Like 5:8, Moses' warning excludes all sculptured images in wood or stone (*pesel*) from Israel's cult. No image of the deity can signify religious truth, because the fundamental tradition of YHWH's theophany at Mount Horeb knows of no anthropo- morphic or zoomorphic shape, cf. also the imagery of 1:33; Ex 13:21–2, contrast Ex 32:4. The strongly anthropomorphic lan- guage of the HB should be considered in the light of this critical thought. The section takes the law of 16:21–2 one step further and reflects a development which is also indicated by Isa 40:18–20, 25–6; Jer 10:14–16 (on religious iconography in Israel in antiquity see Keel and Uehlinger 1998). Astral cult, which is also an issue in the law code itself (17:2–7), seems to have been a major threat to Judean religious identity in the late monarchic period, cf. 2 Kings 23:11–12; Zeph 1:4–6; Jer 8:1–3, and see the quotations from an Assyrian treaty at DEUT 28:1–68. This type of religion is interpreted in vv. 19–20 on a line with 32:8–9, according to which YHWH as the God most high assigns celestial beings as deities to the nations, whereas Israel is his own people (*'am naḥălâ*, cf. 1 Kings 8:51–3 and the term *'âm sĕgullâ* in 26:18). However, the polemics in v. 28 and the confession in v. 35 seem to invalidate this inter- pretation of polytheism.

(4:21–31) Moses' Prophetic Warning A scribe here gives Moses a prophetic role on his parting from Israel (cf. 31:14–30). Moses foresees YHWH's wrath and YHWH's mercy in Israel's future history which centres on the Exile after the defeat of Jerusalem in 587 BCE. He confronts Israel's faith with two conflicting views of God: 'the LORD your God is a jealous God', and 'the LORD your God is a merciful God' (vv. 24, 31; cf. 5:9–10; Ex 34:6–7). The tension between these two statements should not be superficially resolved, as both perceptions of God claim their place in religious experience and stimulate as much as restrict theological reflection. In the present context, the experience of divine punishment is seen as a consequence of violating the prohibition of idols (v. 23), not of the service of 'other gods' as e.g. in 29:24–5 (MT 25–6); cf. also Rom 1:22–3. On the other hand, the expectation to 'find' YHWH 'if you search after him with all your heart and soul' (v. 29; cf. Jer 29:13–14; Am 5:4) is founded on YHWH's covenant with the ancestors (cf. 29:13 (MT 12)) which, unlike the covenant at Mount Horeb (4:13, 23) does not depend on obedience to the law (cf. Gen 15:6). v. 31, therefore, shows a greater kerygmatic depth than a passage like 28:58–68.

(4:32–40) A Confession of Monotheism vv. 32–5, this unique statement in Deuteronomy must be seen on one level with Isa 45:5–6, 12, 18, 21–2; 46:9–10, although it may reflect a later liturgical adaptation of these sayings from the sixth century BCE. In a perspective of a theology of creation, the unit leads to a climax in a monotheistic creed, cf. 32:39. In a universal horizon, YHWH's revelation at Mount Horeb in a voice 'out of the midst of the fire' (RSV, cf. vv. 12–13) and his prodigious actions in the Exodus (cf. 5:15; 34:11–12) are considered a proof of his exclusive divinity. The knowledge of God (v. 35) which Israel will arrive at through an understanding of her traditions is finally to become the knowledge of 'all the people of the earth': 1 Kings 8:60; cf. Isa 49:6. vv. 36 (cf. 8:5) and 37–9 read like homiletic amplifications of the preceding sections. In liturgical diction, v. 38 refers to the completed conquest of the land. vv. 39–40 echo v. 35 and vv. 1–2 respectively and form a finale to the discourse.

(4:41–3) Cities of Refuge Based on 19:1–13, a narrative inser- tion identifies three towns in the allotted territory east of the Jordan (3:12–17) as places of refuge. This is repeated in Josh 20:1–9.

(4:44–9) A Superscription v. 44 marks the transition from Moses' historical review in 1:6–3:29 to the publication of the *tôrâ* in a more limited sense than that implied by 1:5. Still, the notion of *tôrâ* includes paraenesis as well as the laws. Together with the subscription in 29:1 (MT 28:69), the superscription in v. 44 forms a frame around the extended law code as the document of a covenant, and 31:9 may refer to this unit. A parallel superscription in v. 45, which is taken up in 6:20–5, is terminologically interesting, cf. 5:31. The term 'decrees' (*'ēdōt*) may designate the Decalogue, cf. 2 Kings 17:15 and the singu- lar noun in such priestly texts as Ex 25:16; 31:18. As neither of these superscriptions can be shown to have been the original superscription to the law code which Hilkiah is said to have sent to Josiah (2 Kings 22:3–10), it remains an open question whether that document had already been attributed to Moses then. vv. 46–9, these later additions are based on chs. 1–3. Instead of 'the land of Moab' as in 1:5, they speak more correctly of 'the land of . . . Sihon'.

Review of the Covenant at Horeb and the Decalogue (5:1–33 (6:1–3))

(5:1–5) The Covenant at Mount Horeb The superscription which announces the Torah (4:44) is not directly followed by a code of laws, but instead by an explanation of the relation between the laws of Deuteronomy and the Decalogue (5:1–31) as well as by a series of discourses on faithful commitment to YHWH (chs. 6–11). Chs. 5–11 may altogether be attributed to Deuteronomistic scribes of the sixth and fifth centuries BCE; cf. DEUT F.3, H.3. The Decalogue is the foundation of YHWH's covenant with Israel (v. 2) which is linked to the place name 'Horeb' (as 'Sinai' in Exodus) and the imagery of God's speak- ing to the Israelites directly from 'out of the fire' (v. 4). Two further considerations have been added to this original con- cept: v. 3 emphasizes the continuous relevance of the covenant to all generations of Israel. The weight of this issue becomes clear in contrast to Jer 31:32 where the original covenant refers to the 'ancestors' and, after a history of unfaithfulness, needs eschatological renewal. v. 5 emphasizes the role of Moses as mediator between YHWH and Israel. A similar concern guides the narrators in Ex 19–24; 32–4. For a circumspect analysis of Deut 5 see Hossfeld (1982).

(5:6–21) The Decalogue A proper biblical perspective on the Decalogue can be gained through 5:24 (cf. 4:33): 'Today we have seen that God may speak to someone and the person may still live.' The Decalogue is fundamental not only to the cov- enant relationship between YHWH and Israel, but through Israel as God's revelation to humankind. Within the Christian tradition, it remains a valid exposition of the commandment to love God and one's neighbour (Mk 12:28–34; Rom 13:8–10). The Decalogue is a literary composition of the Deuteron- omists and may be more original in its context in Deut 5 than in Ex 20. It could, however, always function as a self-contained sequence of basic commandments and probably originated independently of its literary setting. The Decalogue integrates several distinct elements; see also Schmidt (1993). Its three main sections are the self-presentation of YHWH and the prohibition of other gods (vv. 6–10), the sabbath commandment (vv. 12–15) and the series of six prohibitions in vv. 17–21.

vv. 6–10, in a first person singular address of YHWH, two basic features of Israel's faith are being expressed: the God who demands obedience to his commandments is the God who delivered his people from oppression in Egypt, and this God is a 'jealous God' (ʾēl qannāʾ) and therefore demands exclusive worship. God's punishment for 'iniquity' (ʿāwôn) extends to an entire family, i.e. to the four generations which may at most be living at any one time. Ezek 18 revises this doctrine of 5:9–10 and Ex 34:7 in an extensive theological discussion, cf. especially 18:19–20 and also Deut 7:10; 29:18–21 (MT 17–20). The first section of the Decalogue is framed by a witness to the gracious God who is known to those who love God through the Exodus and through a promise to show 'steadfast love' (ḥesed). The human being's response is to love God (v. 10; cf. 6:5), and this implies acknowledging God's uniqueness (v. 7) and keeping God's commandments (v. 10). v. 8, which separates v. 7 from its continuation in v. 9, is an addition which anchors the concern of 4:15–18 in the Decalogue. The prohibition effects a sharp distinction between visual representations of God and metaphorical representations of God in human language. v. 11, invoking the name of a deity is part of an oath (cf. 6:13; Jer 5:2; Ps 24:4). The prohibition reflects the strong concern with judicial matters typical of Deuteronomy (cf. 16:19; 19:15–19).

vv. 12–15, the Decalogue includes only one distinctive religious custom, namely keeping the sabbath as a weekly day of rest from work. The commandment continues an older tradition (cf. Ex 23:12; 34:21) and at the same time probably transforms the day called šabbāt from a celebration of full moon (cf. e.g. 2 Kings 4:23; Hos 2:11 (MT 13)) into a weekly day of rest. vv. 14–15 particularly emphasize the social significance of a periodical day of rest and call for generous treatment of all dependent persons, whether they be formally linked to a family as slaves or live as 'resident alien[s] in your towns'. Obeying this commandment is a way of remembering God's liberation of Israel from oppression in Egypt (cf. 15:15; 26:6–8). In Ex 20:11, this motivation has been substituted with the concept of a cosmic dimension of a seven-day week, cf. Gen 1:1–2:3. Notwithstanding this notion of its universal character, the sabbath must also be protected as a 'sign' of the unique relationship between YHWH and Israel, cf. Ex 31:12–17.

v. 16, except for v. 12, this commandment of the Decalogue is the only one which is expressed in a positive form. It has a traditional background in the legal sentences in Ex 21:15, 17; cf. also Deut 21:18–21. It aims at protecting solidarity within a family and securing support for parents in their old age by their sons and daughters. The first part of the motive clause (cf. 22:7) reflects the idea that honourable behaviour will repay the person who exercises it. The second part refers to life in Israel's land, and this shows that the Decalogue was given preeminence over the 'statutes and ordinances' for observance in the land (5:31; 12:1) only through the literary construction of 5:1–5, 22–31.

vv. 17–19, these three prohibitions are probably based on Hos 4:2 and are alluded to in Jer 7:9. Fundamental ethical criteria for accusations in prophetic speech are being reformulated as positive law here. The life of the community is to be guided by three essential principles: the protection of human life, of marriage, and of property. Natural indignation at any offences against these rules is a powerful demonstration of their universal validity. The death penalty within a society (cf. 19:11–13) and war between hostile societies (cf. 20:10–14) are not addressed by the commandment at v. 17, cf. also Gen 9:6. However, as the commandment expresses great respect for human life, it should strengthen a commitment to peace and protection of life in all fields. vv. 20–1, the three concluding prohibitions can be related to the three preceding ones. Bearing false witness may be used as a strategy for causing another person's death, cf. 19:15–21; 1 Kings 21:8–14. Coveting a married woman may lead to adultery, and desiring another person's property may end in its misappropriation. The authors of the Decalogue have thus reduplicated the three basic rules of vv. 17–19 in order to warn against the psychological origin of obvious violations of basic ethical norms, cf. Job 31:5–12. The same line of interpretation is pursued further in Jesus' teaching in Mt 5:21–2, 27–8. As much as the social world of ancient Judah can be recognized behind 5:12–21, and as strongly as the conflict between the God of the Exodus and 'other gods' in Israel's religious history characterizes 5:6–11, the Decalogue still remains the most comprehensive compilation of life-enhancing religious and ethical insights within the OT.

(5:22–31) Moses as Mediator The idea which was only secondarily added in 5:5, that Moses is the unique mediator of YHWH's revelation of the law (cf. 34:10), is fundamental to this section of Moses' review of the events at Mount Horeb. YHWH invites Moses, 'stand here by me' (v. 31), after approving of what the people demanded of Moses (vv. 28, 30). Following the people's pledge to listen and do whatever YHWH would tell Moses (v. 27, cf. Ex 19:7–8), YHWH begins to tell Moses the whole instruction (kol-hammiṣwâ), and 'the statutes and ordinances' which Moses in turn shall teach the people (v. 31). All the laws are thus referred back to a revelation at Mount Horeb although, prior to entering the land, the Decalogue is the only law known to the people. In correspondence with this differentiation between the Decalogue and all other laws, the idea that YHWH wrote the Ten Commandments on two stone tablets further underlines their significance (v. 22; cf. 9:8–10; 10:1–5; Ex 24:12; 31:18). Scribal comments (vv. 24b, 26) on the notion of the divine voice from 'out of the fire' reflect on the uniqueness of God's revelation (cf. 4:32–3) as well as the frailty of the human being beside God (cf. Isa 40:6–7; Jer 17:5–8). v. 29, which has a close parallel in Jer 32:39–40, is a further comment on Israel's pledge to obey the laws: the ideal of 'fear of God' as the true disposition for obedience to the law was realized in an exemplary situation during the foundational theophany. This 'fear' is 'not terror but inner religious feeling' (Weinfeld 1991: 325).

(5:32–6:3) Exhortations 5:32–3 may be a reflection of liturgical practice, cf. 6:17–18; 7:11. In general terms, a scribe here relates obedience to God's will to the rewards which an obedient person will gain from it. Within the OT, such a liturgical and doctrinal tradition, which is characteristic of Deuteronomistic writing (cf. also 8:1; Josh 1:7; Jer 7:23), is questioned by the book of Job which gives expression to a different religious experience. 6:1 marks the beginning of Moses' teaching Israel the 'instruction' (*miṣwâ*) which YHWH commanded him (5:31). A further superscription in 12:1 introduces the 'statutes and ordinances', cf. already 4:44, 45. 6:2–3 may again reflect liturgical practice. A strong endeavour to keep the religious tradition alive throughout the generations also motivates 6:20–5.

Discourse on Faithful Obedience to the Law (6:4–11:25 (26–32))

(6:4–9) The Central Confession The opening vocative in v. 4 gives this section its name, Shema, and vv. 4–9 together with 11:13–21 and Num 15:37–41 form a liturgical text of highest importance in Jewish worship. The translation of the second half of v. 4 (*YHWH ʾĕlōhênû YHWH ʾeḥād*) is much debated and remains ambivalent. Stylistically, the words may form one prose sentence or, alternatively, two parallel hymnic exclamations. Thematically, the words may be a statement about YHWH or, alternatively, a statement about YHWH's relationship with Israel. The translation adopted by NRSV and NJPS, 'The LORD is our God, the LORD alone', is probably the best, cf. however LXX and Mk 12:29. The audience is being admonished and confesses that Israel stands in an exclusive relationship with YHWH. This excludes the worship of any other deities (cf. 5:7; 17:2–7) as well as a consort of YHWH (cf. DEUT 16:21). Josh 24 reflects a similar concern regarding Israel's exclusive allegiance to YHWH. At a later stage in the history of Israel's religious thought, this fundamental confession could be accommodated to a monotheistic creed like 4:35, 39; 32:39; and in this sense Zech 14:9 unfolds the universal dimension of v. 4; cf. also 1 Cor 8:4. v. 5, cf. Mk 12:30. What human sentiment can correspond to the confession of v. 4? A scribe here designates the true faith commitment as 'love of God'. This notion has been further developed in 30:16–20, and it equals the notion of 'fear of God' as in 5:29, see DEUT A.1. The fact that v. 5 is an injunction need not surprise. First, it may have been modelled after a demand of undivided loyalty in the political sphere (cf. Parpola and Watanabe 1988: 39 (ll. 266–8); ANET 537). Secondly, as faith is a human response to divine revelation (cf. 5:6, 24), it can be given guidance, and the notion of love here functions as the fundamental guiding idea; cf. also Mic 6:6–8. The scribe circumscribes the totality of the human being with three terms in order to emphasize the seriousness of a faith commitment, cf. the idealized characterization of Josiah in 2 Kings 23:25 and also 1 Kings 8:46–50; contrast Jer 12:2. vv. 6–9, all Israelites are asked to memorize, to teach, and to publicly confess the dogma of v. 4. As the intrusive relative clause 'that I am commanding you today' (cf. 7:11) shows, this later came to be understood of the entire law; see Veijola (1992a, b) and on the customs mentioned in vv. 8–9, Keel (1981).

(6:10–19) Against Forgetting YHWH The paraenetic discourses in chs. 6–11 are styled so as to correspond to the imagined situation of Moses' audience east of the Jordan (1:1–5; 3:29; 4:46). Taking possession of the promised land (cf. 1:8) is seen by the Deuteronomists as the one great threat to Israel's belief in the God of the Exodus (5:6). Looking back to the defeat of Jerusalem in 587 BCE, these scribes understand the catastrophe as caused by the 'anger' (*ʾap̄*) of YHWH who,

as a 'jealous God' (cf. 5:9), punishes apostasy (v. 15; cf. 29:25–8 (MT 24–7)). The extraordinary thought that YHWH might 'destroy' Israel (v. 15) is made the subject of reflection in 9:7–10:11, especially 9:13–14; cf. also Am 9:8 and Deut 28:63. 'Forgetting YHWH' while devoting oneself to the worship of local, autochthonous deities is a recurring reason for accusations in Hosea (2:13 (MT 15); 8:14; 13:6) and Jeremiah (2:32; 13:25; 18:15; 23:27), cf. 8:7–20. v. 14 reflects a situation of Israel as a community not yet consolidated after the destruction of the central royal sanctuary. Like ch. 13, the verse indicates the Deuteronomists' anti-assimilationist concerns. v. 16 points back to Ex 17:1–7: YHWH's presence in Israel must not be 'put to the test'. For vv. 17–18 cf. DEUT 5:32–3. v. 19 reflects the same situation as v. 14, cf. Josh 23:5 and see on 7:1–6.

(6:20–5) Basic Religious Instruction The section emphasizes that the Exodus creed is the foundation of the law, as the internal structure of the Decalogue also makes clear. The introduction shows the catechetical purpose of a unit such as vv. 21–4, cf. Ex 13:14–15. The graphic elaboration in v. 22 may be secondary, cf. García López (1978). v. 25 formulates a fundamental theology of the law: observing the law (*kol-ham-miṣwâ*) will be 'righteousness (*ṣĕdāqâ*) for us' (RSV), 'to our merit before the LORD our God' (NJPS), cf. 24:13. LXX offers a remarkable translation: 'mercy (*eleēmosynē*) will be for us, if . . .' In the NT, Paul in Phil 3:9 expresses his acceptance and his rejection of this theological thought, cf. also Gal 2:16–17, 21.

(7:1–11) The Election of Israel v. 1 takes 6:10 as a model, and v. 4 depends on 6:15. However, the perspective in which the land is seen is totally different from the one adopted in 6:10–15 and 8:7–18 or such texts as Hos 2:2–13 (MT 4–15); Jer 2:5–7 where the wealth and fertility of the land are considered a threat to Israel's allegiance to YHWH. According to vv. 1–5, the land is a territory where the religious habits of many ancient 'nations' prevail and where, because of this, Israel's identity is in danger. This idea is being expressed through the imagery of a military conquest. v. 2 represents the same concept which underlies 2:32–5; here as in 20:16–17 it is shaped as a command to 'utterly destroy' (*ḥ-r-m* hifil) the nations of the land. (On the antiquarian list of names see the entries for the respective names in ABD.) The concept of 'ritual destruction' of entire communities can be traced back to at least the ninth century BCE as it is also found on the Mesha stone, a Moabite royal inscription from about 830 BCE, which includes this episode:

And Chemosh said to me, 'Go, take Nebo [a town east of the Jordan] from Israel!' So I went by night and fought against it from the break of dawn until noon, taking it and slaying all, seven thousand [men and women], for I had devoted them to destruction [*ḥrm*] for (the god) Ashtar-Chemosh. And I took from there the [vessels] of Yahweh, dragging them before Chemosh. (ll.14–18 (abbreviated): cf. ANET 320)

However, v. 2 does not intend to document ancient military practice, but rather to construe an ideal of Israel's conquest of the land. This ideal does not tell anything about Israel's early history, but mainly has two functions: it serves as a basis for explaining the defeat of Jerusalem in 587 BCE in terms of Israel's apostasy which is seen to have been induced by her assimilation to the nations of the land in defiance of a Mosaic command (cf. 20:18; 29:25–8 (MT 24–7); Josh 23:1 to Judg 3:6), and it serves as a warning against assimilation for the community of those who are faithful to the law, probably at some time in the Second Temple period. v. 3 may be directly related to the policy of Nehemiah in the fifth century BCE, cf. Neh 13:23–7 and also Gen 24:3; 28:1. v. 5 proscribes all cultic sites besides the temple, cf. 12:3; Ex 34:13. In vv. 1–2, Israel's claim to the land and fear of apostasy resulted in an ideal which induces doubt about God's relation to humankind and frightens the human being away from God. Even within Deuteronomy itself, this voice finds a theologically more promising context, cf. 4:19–20, 32–5 (however, also 36–8); 9:1–6. v. 6 can justify a separation from people who worship 'other gods' (v. 4; 20:18), but not the ideal of vv. 1–2. On the exegetical problem of vv. 1–2 see Barr (1993: 207–20).

v. 6 (cf. 26:16–19) puts the exclusive relationship between YHWH and Israel (cf. 6:4) into a universal horizon in relating it to the entire created world (cf. Ex 19:5; Am 3:2), thus going far beyond an orientation towards Israel's land. The connection between mythological primeval history and YHWH's call of Abraham in Gen 9:18–12:3 gives a narrative representation of this creed. Its climax in Gen 12:3 (cf. Jer 4:1–2) must be considered an aspect of the canonical context of Deut 7:6. vv. 7–8, Israel's election is founded solely on YHWH's love, cf. Hos 11:1, which also manifests itself in YHWH's promise to the ancestors, cf. Gen 22:16–18. A scribe here confronts the triumphant conception of vv. 1–2 with a deliberate antithesis which sees Israel as 'the fewest of all peoples'. vv. 9–10 quote 5:9–10 but restrict YHWH's punishment to any individually responsible person.

(7:12–26) Hope and Israel's History This section presents further Deuteronomistic elaborations of some of the subjects addressed in 6:10–7:11. YHWH's oath to Israel's ancestors (7:8) will only motivate YHWH to keep the 'gracious covenant' if Israel observes the commandments; v. 12, together with 8:19–20, thus relate the theology of 7:7–8 to the doctrine of YHWH as a 'jealous God' (5:9–10; 6:15; 7:9–10). God's love unfolds in blessings in the spheres of daily life (vv. 13–15; cf. Ex 23:25–6; Deut 28:1–14). v. 16 forms a transition to scribal reflections on the impossible vision of 7:1–2 in the light of the historical experience of a small community living amongst different peoples (cf. 6:14). Although hope remains that taking possession of the land will eventually be as successful as the Exodus from Egypt (vv. 18–19; cf. 1:30; Ex 13:17–14:31), YHWH will 'clear away' (NRSV; dislodge: NJPS: *nāšal*, v. 22 as in 7:1) the peoples only 'little by little', cf. Ex 23:28–33; Josh 23:6–13. This concept prepares for the biblical picture of Israel's early history as much as for an understanding of the post-exilic period in the light of YHWH's exuberant promises. In the realm of history, what is essential is not to allow the religions of these peoples to become a 'snare' (v. 16) for the people of YHWH. Cf. also the liturgical use of the warning example of the earlier generations in Ps 106:34–41.

(8:1–20) Knowledge of God and Praise Characterized by its poetic beauty and a rich diversity of paraenetic verbs, ch. 8 returns to the subject of 6:10–15: the wealth of the land as a possible threat to Israel's faithful adherence to the God of the Exodus. For a critical analysis see Veijola (1995 a). vv. 7–10 ('When the LORD your God brings you into a good land …

then you shall bless the LORD your God …'; cf. Weinfeld 1991: 391) is an exhortation to praise God for all the good which the community enjoys. In v. 11, the notion of 'forgetting YHWH' is explained in terms of disobedience to the law. vv. 12–18 enlarge on the preceding texts, notably in hymnic praise of YHWH's mighty deeds. A scribe here warns against impious arrogance (cf. Hos 13:4–6), as Israel's wealth is owed to God's blessing (7:13; cf. Hos 2:8 (MT 10)). vv. 19–20 add a reinterpretation of vv. 7–18 on the lines of 7:1–5, turning the concept of annihilation into a conditional threat against Israel, cf. 6:15. vv. 1 and 6 (cf. 6:1) frame the first unit of ch. 8 which demonstrates how the imagery of Israel's forty years wandering in the wilderness (cf. 1:3; 2:14; Am 2:10; Ex 15:22–17:7; Num 10:33–12:16; 20:1–21:20) should lead towards a knowledge of God. To the several interpretations of this period (cf. 1:31; 32:10–11; Hos 2:14–15 (MT 16–17); Jer 2:2), v. 2 adds the aspect of God's 'testing' (*n-s-h* piel) Israel's faithfulness (cf. Judg 3:4). This thought may even prepare the ground for the discussion of the problem of theodicy in the book of Job. In v. 5, this interpretation is modified by the concept of God's 'disciplining' (*y-s-r* piel) Israel, cf. Zeph 3:2; Jer 2:30; 30:11, 14; 31:18. v. 3 is a keystone of theology within the OT. A scribe here develops an understanding of religious faith and, at the same time, claims that this faith must have its foundation in God's words of promise and command; cf. 5:24; 30:15–16; also Mt 4:4.

(9:1–6) Righteousness and the Conquest of the Land Rhetorically, this section has been carefully adapted to the fictitious situation indicated by 1:1–5; 3:28; cf. also 31:3–6. It is probably an insertion, and borrows a number of motifs from its literary context. Moses 'encourages and strengthens' Israel in such a way that his words even create a contradiction between v. 3 and 7:22. However, the specific subject of vv. 1–6 is the question of why YHWH would destroy the nations of the land, cf. 7:1–2; 8:19–20. Israel is being warned not to ascribe YHWH's great deeds to her own 'righteousness' (*ṣĕdāqâ*; contrast 6:25; 8:1). Instead, the nations of the land are being qualified by a 'wickedness' (*rišʿâ*) which provokes divine punishment, cf. Ezek 18:20 and also Gen 15:16; Lev 18:24–30. There is no way of determining what the 'wickedness' of these nations who could not have offended against the laws from Mount Horeb is seen to have been, although one might refer to the 'abhorrent things' (*tôʿēḇôt*) according to 12:31; 18:9–12; 20:18. This problem may have motivated the scribe who, by adding v. 2, altogether transforms the imagery of conquest. Building on elements adopted from 1:28 and 7:24, this scribe imagines the entire land as populated not by ancient nations, but rather by 'the offspring of the Anakim' (see DEUT 1:28), i.e. mythological creatures, cf. Am 2:9; Josh 11:21–2; Bar 3:24–8. Mythological imagination thus counterbalances the rhetoric of annihilation.

(9:7–10:11) YHWH's Wrath at Mount Horeb This section reads like a homily on the doctrine of YHWH as a 'jealous God' in 6:15. Looking back to Mount Horeb as the place of a 'covenant' ceremony (9:9, based on 5:2, 22), a scribe here reflects on the threat that YHWH might 'destroy' (*š-m-d* hifil, 6:15; 9:8, 13–14) Israel. In his representation of Israel's foundational period under Moses' leadership, he shows how, in a paradigmatic way, this threat had been averted through Moses' intercession for the people. Thus, Israel's future is grounded in the Mosaic age (as well as in the promise to the ancestors, 9:27; cf. 7:7–8), although the catastrophe of 587 BCE could not be averted, cf. Jer 5:18–19; 30:11, the interdiction of intercession theme in Jer 7:16; 11:14; also 15:1. The basic narrative, which may have included 9:7–18, 26–9; 10:10b–11, is based on an earlier version of the story of the Golden Calf in Ex 32–4; see Driver (1895 (1901)) and especially Aurelius (1988). Several additions have been joined to it, notably referring to Aaron (9:20; 10:6–7), the Levites (10:8–9), and the ark (10:1–5; cf. 1 Kings 8:9). The section starts from a striking reinterpretation of the period in the wilderness (9:7; cf. Jer 7:24–6, and see DEUT 8:2), and this has been enlarged by more instances of Israel's rebellious character as a 'stubborn people' (ʿam qĕšê-ʿōrep, 9:13) in 9:22–4 (for which cf. 1:19–46; Ex 17:1–7; Num 11:1–34; Ps 106:19–33).

(10:12–11:32) Nomistic Paraenesis The exhortation 'So now, O Israel' opens a sequence of loosely connected paraenetic addresses which borrow many elements from the preceding chapters. Although the section may include some vague reminiscences of a treaty form (cf. Mayes 1979: 30–4, 207–9), it has no overall coherence. Regarding the conquest of the land west of the Jordan, 11:22–32 returns as it were to the point where Moses' historical review had left the reader in 3:29.

The first unit, 10:12–11:1, builds upon 6:2, 5 and emphasizes that 'fear of God' and 'love of God' denote a belief in God which is the basis for all faithful obedience to the divine commandments. vv. 14–15 refer to Israel's election in a universal horizon (cf. 7:6–8; 4:32–5), and vv. 17–18 establish a connection between election and behaviour (cf. 4:5–8; Ps 146:6–9). v. 19 gives an example of how hymnic praise of a just and benevolent God must entail practical ethical consequences for the life within a community. For the command itself cf. Lev 19:18b, 33–4. The 'sojourner' (RSV; NRSV translates 'stranger' in 10:19, but 'resident alien' in 5:14; 24:17, etc.) is a typical needy person because he holds no property in land and does not belong to a landowner's household either. In dense metaphorical language, v. 16 gives a paraenetic response to 9:13 (cf. also Jer 4:4; 6:10); however, in 30:6 a scribe arrives at an even more radical understanding of human opposition to the divine word and of God's will to overcome this opposition, cf. Jer 31:33–4; Ezek 18:31; 36:26. For v. 22 cf. Gen 46:27. The second unit, 11:2–9, gives an enumeration of the mighty deeds of God (cf. esp. Ex 14; Num 16) that will contribute to an understanding of God's 'greatness', cf. 3:24. As v. 2 is an anacoluthon, it is not clear in what sense a scribe here addresses the problem of the succession of generations in Israel, cf. 29:14–15 (MT 13–14); Josh 24:31; Judg 2:7, 10. The liturgical fragment does not take the situation of Moses' oration into account, cf. 1:34–5, 39; 2:16. For vv. 8–9 cf. 8:1. vv. 10–12, cf. 8:7–10: the praise of the land also implies a rejection of idolatrous fertility cults, cf. Hos 2:2–13 (MT 4–15). vv. 13–15 cf. 7:12–15, a scribe here turns the praise into a conditional promise, cf. Jer 5:23–5. vv. 16–17 are based on 6:15 and echo the curse of 28:23. For vv. 18–21 see DEUT 6:6–9. vv. 22–5 (cf. 7:16–24; 9:1; Josh 1:1–9): this unit leads on to the conquest narratives of the book of Joshua. For the ideal delineation of Israel's territory cf. 1:7 and Josh 1:4. For the motif of the nations' dread of Israel cf. 2:25; Josh 2:9–11, 24.

11:26–32 (cf. 27:11–13; 30:15–20). Crossing the Jordan and entering into the land marks the situation for a decision between faithful adherence to YHWH, the God of the Exodus, and apostasy: obedience or disobedience, blessing or curse are being presented as straightforward alternatives. A similar ceremony at Shechem, i.e. between Mount Gerizim to the south and Mount Ebal to the north, is narrated in Josh 24, cf. especially vv. 14–15. A puzzling gloss in v. 30 transfers the ceremony of v. 29 to a location directly in the valley of the Jordan, cf. Josh 4:20; 5:10. Here as elsewhere in chs. 4–11, the great paraenetic alternative is as much a reflection of liturgical practice as it is part of the Deuteronomistic literary invention of Moses' oration.

Promulgation of the Laws (12:1–25:19 (26:1–15))

(12:1–32 (MT 12:1–13:1)) The Law of Centralization of Sacrificial Worship Ch. 12 contains the law which defines the place of Deuteronomy in the history of Israelite cult. It is based on an opposition between a multiplicity of cultic sites ('any place you happen to see') and 'the place that the LORD will choose' as the one legitimate place for performing acts of sacrificial cult (vv. 13–14). On the one hand, the law contradicts that of Ex 20:22–6 which gives permission to erect 'an altar of earth' or 'an altar of stone' in many places, for that law includes the divine promise that 'in every place where I [YHWH] cause my name to be remembered I will come to you and bless you'. On the other hand, the law is presupposed by the Priestly Document. In that code, the one single 'place' of sacrificial worship is imagined as a sanctuary the design of which was revealed to Moses on Mount Sinai, and this unique sanctuary was to allow YHWH 'to dwell among the Israelites' (wĕšākantî bĕtôkām, Ex 25:8–9 MT). The law of Deut 12 in its hypothetical original form is often regarded as the law which caused the Judean king Josiah 'to defile the high places . . . from Geba to Beersheba', i.e. throughout his kingdom, and to leave only 'the altar of the LORD in Jerusalem' (2 Kings 23:8–9; see DEUT F.1), and this historical connection remains a plausible assumption. The law does not name Jerusalem directly but, instead, speaks of 'the place that the LORD will choose'. This may be due to the fact that, according to Israel's historical tradition, it was David who first conquered Jerusalem and made it an Israelite city in the tenth century BCE (2 Sam 5:6–10). The temple at Jerusalem, therefore, was not a sanctuary of YHWH from time immemorial (cf. also 2 Sam 6–7; 1 Kings 5–9). However, there is no reason to suppose that the formula 'the place that the LORD will choose' should be interpreted in a distributive sense as 'at all the respective places that YHWH will choose', even if, according to Jer 7:12–15, Shiloh had at some time been a sanctuary of the same legitimacy as Jerusalem. Deut 12 clearly has Jerusalem in view.

The law of Deut 12 is addressed to a laity which must be seen as living outside the capital in a rural milieu (v. 17). It has several repetitions and employs the second person singular as well as plural. There is a broad scholarly consensus which says that the sections in the plural (or mixed forms of address) are later than those in the singular, and that the singular sections may have been part of the original Deuteronomic law code. As far as cultic matters are concerned, 12:13–19; 14:22–9; 15:19–23; 16:1–17 represent the core of the Deuteronomic legislation.

A correspondence has often been noted between these laws on cultic centralization and the concept of YHWH's unity and uniqueness as expressed in 6:4. For an extensive discussion of Deut 12 see Reuter (1993), Levinson (1997).

(12:1–7) Centralization and Anti-Syncretism v. 1 is a superscription to the law which closely follows 5:31; cf. 6:1. It introduces a second-person plural section (however, in the MT the formula relating to the land and its conquest is in the singular). vv. 2–3 echo 7:5 and introduce into the Deuteronomic law a criterion for the judgement of Israel's history of the monarchic period which is pronounced in Deuteronomistic historiography (cf. 1 Kings 14:23–4; 2 Kings 17:7–12). The stereotypical description of the high places may be based on Hos 4:13; Jer 2:20. Their interpretation as the remains of the cult of an earlier non-Israelite population represents a distinct development within Deuteronomistic thought, which results from the concept of the legitimacy of one single sanctuary of YHWH only. In 1 Sam 9:11–14, for example, the fact that a country town (*ʿîr*) has its shrine on a hilltop (*bāmâ*) does not worry the narrator. The list of cult-related objects in v. 3 also represents a late stage of religious polemics when compared to 16:21–2; 5:8.

(12:8–12) Centralization and the Periodization of Israel's History vv. 8–12 are another second-person plural section. Like Jer 7:21–2, the text builds upon the idea that Israel did not receive laws concerning cultic matters prior to entering the land. However, according to this Deuteronomistic scribe, the period of cultic tolerance lasted not only until the age of Joshua (cf. Josh 21:43–5; 23:1) but until that of Solomon, during which the temple in Jerusalem was built. Like 1 Kings 8:16, Deut 12:8–12 identifies the moment at which YHWH 'chose' the place of the only sanctuary with the inauguration of the temple in Jerusalem, cf. 1 Kings 5:3–5 (MT 5:17–19); 2 Sam 7:1 for the notion of 'rest'. It is clear from these links between the law and the narrative that vv. 8–12 are an addition to the Deuteronomic law after it had become part of the Deuteronomistic History.

(12:13–19) Centralization and Sacrifices vv. 13–19 are a second-person singular section and are the most original and the most radical part of the legislation of the Deuteronomic reform movement in the late-monarchic era (see DEUT F.1). The first and the last sentences of this section open with the imperative 'take care that you do not . . .' and it may be debated whether this is an appropriate beginning for a law (cf. 8:11; however, in 6:10–12; 12:29–31 the imperative follows a temporal clause). However, no alternative beginning suggests itself. In vv. 13–14, the lawgiver commands the restriction of sacrifices to the one single place 'that the LORD will choose' and thus puts an end to all other cultic sites which used to exist in Judah. A connection between the concept of a single sanctuary and the concept of tribal territories is made only here (and, depending on this verse, in 12:5), and the Deuteronomistic authors are not agreed on whether Jerusalem could be claimed by Judah (Josh 15:63) or by Benjamin (Judg 1:21).

The formula concerning the chosen place of sacrificial worship in v. 14 lacks a complement as in 14:23; 16:2, 6, 11; 26:2 which qualifies the chosen place as a place which YHWH chooses 'to make his name dwell there' (*lĕšakkēn šĕmô šām*; also in a second-person plural text in 12:11; a later variation

reads 'to put his name there' as in 12:5 etc.). The concept of the sanctuary as dwelling-place not of the deity, but of the divine 'name' reflects a critique of a concept of holiness which is founded upon too anthropomorphic a notion of the deity (see Weinfeld 1992: 191–209; Mettinger 1982: 38–79). It counterbalances a theological understanding of the temple which may have been prevalent in the monarchic era and again in the Second Temple period (cf. Ps 46:5). According to 26:15, the 'heaven' is YHWH's 'holy habitation', and this idea also underlies Solomon's prayer in 1 Kings 8:22–53. The LXX translators may have had this prayer in mind when they translated the phrase 'to make his name dwell there' as 'for his name to be invoked there', cf. also Isa 56:7 and Mk 11:17.

vv. 13–14 speak of one type of sacrifice only, the 'burnt offering' (*ʿôlâ*), when the entire animal is presented to the deity. It gives permission to slaughter (*zābaḥ*) animals for food 'within any of your towns' (v. 15) and thus makes slaughter a secular matter which does not have to be performed at an altar any more (see Maag 1956). In consequence, no ritual purity is demanded of those who eat the meat. v. 16 adds a detailed instruction concerning the blood which was formerly put on an altar. vv. 17–18 deal with cultic offerings which can no longer be brought to a local shrine but are not entirely divested of their ritual quality either. On the tithe see the additional law in 14:22–9, on the firstlings the law in 15:19–23, on pilgrimages to the sanctuary the laws in 16:1–17. The LXX has the second half of v. 17 in the second person plural which might suggest that the references to 'votive gifts' (*nĕdārîm*, cf. 23:21–3 (MT 22–4)), 'freewill offerings', and 'donations' are a later addition. The law envisages cultic celebrations of the entire family and makes 'rejoicing' the main characteristic of a religious festival. In the LXX, the list of participants does not include the Levite but rather the 'resident alien', as in 5:14. v. 19 commands permanent support of the Levite who used to be the priest at a local shrine and was to lose his cultic functions through the centralization of sacrificial worship (see, however, 18:6–8).

(12:20–8) Restrictions on Profane Slaughter The section gives a restrictive interpretation of v. 15. Permission is given to 'eat' meat 'whenever you have the desire', but an animal may be 'slaughtered' (*zābaḥ*) 'within your towns' only if, after the expansion of the territory, the sanctuary is 'too far from you' (v. 21; the structuring of the verse in the NRSV is not convincing). vv. 23–5 show the great concern this scribe has about the blood taboo (cf. Gen 9:4; Lev 17:10–12). v. 27 restores the *zebaḥ* type of sacrifice as a consequence of the restrictions on the law of v. 15, and this is presupposed in the enumeration of offerings in vv. 6, 11. At an even later stage, the law of Lev 17:1–7 abrogates Deut 12:15 (Cholewiński 1976: 149–78; see, however, Rofé, quoted in Fishbane 1985: 228, who suggests that vv. 20–8 should be understood as a late scribal harmonization of Deut 12:13–19 and Lev 17:1–7).

(12:29–32) Anti-Syncretistic Paraenesis In a second-person singular section, the same concept as in vv. 2–7 is being repeated, namely that even after the extinction of the nations in the land west of the Jordan, a temptation will remain for Israel to imitate religious rites which the divine ceremonial law does not permit. For paraenetic purposes, all 'abhorrent' rites are equated with a syncretistic corruption of Israel's religion (and vice versa). The end of v. 31 addresses a ritual practice which is severely criticized in such Deuteronomistic texts as e.g. Jer 7:30–4; 2 Kings 21:6. This type of child-sacrifice may betray Phoenician influence in Judah in the period after the fall of Jerusalem in 587 BCE (see Müller 1997). v. 32 (MT 13:1) concludes the law of centralization with a general exhortation and a formula which serves to protect the text from any changes and thus leads towards its canonical status (cf. 4:2). The law of Deut 12 was not only of enormous importance in the religious history of ancient Israel, but it retains its theological significance as a reflection on God's presence in worship in relation to God's supreme freedom.

(13:1–18 (MT 13:2–19)) Incitement to Apostasy The law deals with incitement to apostasy or idolatry in three paragraphs and in each case commands the death penalty (vv. 5, 10, 15) as in 17:2–7. The laws echo some motifs which are also found in Esar-haddon's succession treaty (see DEUT F.2), and thus apply instructions concerning disloyalty in the political sphere to apostasy in the religious sphere. Whether this betrays a revolutionary atmosphere in late seventh century Judah (Weinfeld 1992: 91–100; Dion 1991; Otto 1996b) or whether a later learned scribe employed the language of political treaties for paraenetic variations on the commandment of 5:7 (Veijola 1995b) remains open to debate. It may be useful to quote some lines from the Assyrian treaty for comparison here:

If you hear any evil, improper, ugly word which is not seemly nor good to Assurbanipal . . . either from the mouth of his ally, or from the mouth of his brothers . . . or from the mouth of your brothers, your sons, your daughters, or from the mouth of a prophet, an ecstatic, an inquirer of oracles, or from the mouth of any human being at all, you shall not conceal it but come and report it to Assurbanipal . . . If anyone should speak to you of rebellion and insurrection . . . or if you should hear it from the mouth of anyone, you shall seize the perpetrators of insurrection, and bring them before Assurbanipal . . . If you are able to seize them and put them to death, then you shall destroy their name and their seed from the land . . . (ll. 108–46: Parpola and Watanabe 1988: 33–4; *ANET* 535–6; an Aramaic treaty of the 8th cent. even includes the instruction to destroy a treasonous town: Sfire stela, 3. 12–13; *ANET* 661).

(13:1–5) Prophets The possibility of magic acts in the name of other gods than YHWH is also a motif in the Exodus narrative (cf. Ex 7:8–13). However, in the light of Jer 23:9–32, especially vv. 25–32, it is doubtful whether prophetic incitement to apostasy was ever an issue in late-monarchic Judah. The problem of untrue oracles in the name of YHWH is addressed in Deut 18:9–22. The author of vv. 1–2 interprets the criterion of fulfilment of an oracle as referring to thaumaturgic competence and decidedly subordinates it to the first commandment of the Decalogue (5:6–10). The law exhibits a concern for the exclusiveness of the worship of Israel's God, probably against a background of strong tendencies towards assimilation to foreign cults after the fall of Jerusalem (cf. 12:29–31). The second half of v. 3 which is based on 6:5 aims at a theological understanding of any conceivable enticement to a new religious allegiance.

(13:6–11) Family The second law concentrates on an instigator's confidentiality with the tempted believer and is therefore supported by an explicit order to suppress any feelings of sympathy. In comparison to the careful legal proceeding spelled out in 17:2–7 ('. . . and you make a thorough inquiry, and the charge is proved true'), the instructions for punishing the offender in vv. 8–9 look awkward. A double textual tradition for the beginning of v. 9 reads 'you shall surely kill him' (MT) or, alternatively, 'you shall surely report him' (LXX). However, it is clear that the formal legal verdict 'and he shall die' (*wāmēt*, cf. 19:12 contrast 19:4 'and he shall live', *wāḥāy*, and cf. 24:7 etc.) is only pronounced in v. 10 (MT 11; cf. also Tigay 1996: 132). The law represents a specific conception of 'Israel' in whose midst (MT vv. 2, 6, 12, 14) any attempt to incite apostasy must be punished. At a later literary stage within Deuteronomy, this is restricted to a threat of divine punishment (29:16–21 (MT 15–20)). v. 7 (28:64) may reflect an awareness of the religious world of antiquity in which Israel struggled to retain her faith.

(13:12–18) An Insurrectionary Town The model idea of ritual destruction of the nations in the promised land (7:1–2) is applied to an Israelite town in the case of its turning to the worship of foreign gods. The detailed instructions about the 'ban' (*ḥērem*) are reminiscent of Josh 6–7, cf. also Deut 7:25–6. vv. 17b–18 prove the author to have lived some time after the fall of Jerusalem, which was explained by the Deuteronomists as the consequence of YHWH's 'fierce anger' (*ḥărôn'ap*, cf. 2 Kings 23:26). The community lives in the expectation of YHWH's 'compassion' (*raḥămîm*), and faithful obedience to the law is understood as a condition for future restoration.

(14:1–2) Rites of Mourning This law, a late insertion into the law code, forbids two rites still considered to be habitual rites in Judah in Jer 16:6. The Israelites must neither gash their skin nor 'make baldness between the eyes', i.e. on the forehead. The kerygmatic introductory statement employs parent–child imagery in a way reminiscent of Isa 63:8–9, 16. Its metaphorical aspects are more evident in 8:5; Isa 1:2–3; Jer 3:19. In the monarchic period, the title of a 'son' of YHWH could be given to the king in royal ideology (cf. Ps 2:7; 2 Sam 7:14), and also the entire people could be called YHWH's 'son' (Hos 11:1). v. 2 is a repetition of 7:6.

(14:3–21) Dietary Laws The law opens with the general instruction not to eat 'any abhorrent thing' (*kol-tô'ēḇâ*) This is explained by detailed lists which have a more extended parallel in Lev 11. The section may be a secondary addition induced by the question of profane slaughter (12:15). A theological reason for these distinctions is given in Lev 20:22–6; for an interpretation of these rules see Douglas (1966: 41–57). v. 21, animals which have died of natural causes are a taboo for the people to which the law code is addressed but may be given as a charitable support to members of the non-landowning class, cf. 24:19–22, and may even be sold to foreigners. Later laws in Lev 11:39–40 and 17:15–16 only demand rites of purification after eating such meat. The prohibition at the end of v. 21 may reflect religious awe in regard to an animal and its mother as at 22:6–7, cf. Ex 23:18–19.

(14:22–9) Tithes A detailed law on tithes further clarifies 12:17–19. The tithe (or a less clearly defined offering: Ex 23:19) seems to have been a conventional contribution which peasants gave for ceremonies at local shrines, cf. Am 4:4–5. Any suggestion to link it to royal taxation remains speculative (Crüsemann 1996: 215–19). The tithe is made the subject of a formal command in Deuteronomy in an attempt to abolish the traditional rites and to link the offering to the central sanctuary. A tendency towards desacralization of the tithe is reflected by the permission to turn it into money and to reserve the money for a pilgrimage. A later scribe restricted this permission by adding a conditional clause like that at 12:21 ('if/because the place . . . is too far from you', v. 24). In legislation of the Second Temple period, the tithe is formally declared a source of income for the Levites, cf. Num 18:20–32; Neh 13:10–14. vv. 28–9 (cf. 26:12–15), twice within a seven-year cycle (15:1), the tithe must be put to charitable support of the poor in the country towns. The attached promise makes it clear that divine blessing does not depend on any fertility rites.

(15:1–11) Remission of Debts and God's Blessing Within the sequence of cultic laws, the law indicates that the divine blessing on which economic success of farming depends (v. 10, cf. v. 18) may be won through humanitarian behaviour. vv. 1–3 revise the traditional institution of a fallow year (cf. Ex 23:10–11) and either complement or even replace it by a command to remit any debts which a fellow farmer might have incurred. It is clear from the context that the law concerns a loan which helped the 'neighbour' or 'brother' (RSV) to survive until the next harvest. The law does not include 'foreigners', because they did not belong to the community of those who had to observe the 'release' (*šĕmiṭṭâ*) that was proclaimed in YHWH's honour. A lucid philosophical understanding of this controversial differentiation (cf. again in 23:19–20 (MT 20–1)) has been suggested by H. Grotius who says that the Israelites owed the foreigners only whatever was demanded by 'natural law' because of the unity of humankind, but not what would have been motivated by an extraordinary benevolence ('Talibus incolis debebantur ob humani generis cognationem ea quae sunt iuris naturalis: non etiam ea quae maioris sunt bonitatis,' *Annotata ad Vetus Testamentum*, 1644).

The instruction of vv. 7–10 implies rich observations on the human heart and comes close to the commandment of Lev 19:18 to love one's neighbour (cf. Deut 10:17–19; Mk 12:31). In vv. 4–5, a later scribe expresses a vision of the fullness of God's blessing in response to the people's faithful obedience (cf. Isa 58:6–9) and v. 11 reconciles this expansion with the original intention of the law. v. 6 may be a late gloss on vv. 4–5 which is partly based on 28:12 and possibly reflects a political hope of the community in the Persian empire.

(15:12–18) Debt Servitude The law commands that any Hebrew slave is to be set free (*ḥopší*) after six years of service. This seven-year period is not directly related to the year of release of vv. 1–11. The law is based on Ex 21:2–6. However, it does not take up the second law of Ex 21:7–11 (which is more a family law), but instead extends the force of the first law to apply equally to male and female slaves. The term 'Hebrew' (*'ibrî*) is known from narratives which confront the Israelites with the Egyptians or the Philistines (e.g. Ex 1; 1 Sam 4). It remains doubtful whether it was originally related to the term *ḥab/piru* which, in Egyptian and Near-Eastern texts of the second millennium BCE, designates a certain stratum of society (see *ABD* iii. 6–10, 95). The subject of the law has a parallel in the Code of Hammurabi (18th cent. BCE) which

decrees: 'If an obligation came due against a seignior and he sold (the services of) his wife, his son, or his daughter . . . they shall work (in) the house of their purchaser . . . for three years, with their freedom reestablished in the fourth year' (§ 117, *ANET* 170–1). The version in Deuteronomy puts special emphasis on the obligation to provide the slave generously with some goods on leaving, 'in proportion to YHWH's blessing' which the master had enjoyed (v. 14, following the LXX reading). However, it does not become clear on what economic basis former slaves would sustain themselves, and instead of becoming landless poor, it might be more advantageous for them to stay with their masters (vv. 16–17). In the circumspect social vision of Lev 25, the release of slaves is connected to the restitution of landed property in the jubilee year; cf. also Neh 5:1–13. v. 15 adduces the fundamental article of Israel's faith according to Deuteronomy in order to encourage unrestrained obedience. 'Remembering' (*zākar*) is a vital act of faith. Additionally, a rational argument in v. 18 says that a slave gives his master 'double the service of a hired man' (NJPS; NRSV's translation is based on a contentious interpretation of *mišneh* as 'equivalent').

(15:19–23) Firstlings Instructions for annual offerings in 14:22–7 and here form a framework for the humanitarian laws in 14:28–15:18 which refer to three-year and seven-year cycles or periods respectively. On firstlings see Ex 13:1–2; 34:19–20.

(16:1–8) *Pesaḥ* and the Feast of Unleavened Bread The law conflates *pesaḥ* and the *maṣṣôt* feast into one festival in the month of Abib (March/April; a later name is Nisan; see also Lev 23:5). The *pesaḥ* is thus integrated into the traditional cycle of three agricultural festivals (Ex 23:14–19). For a critical analysis of vv. 1–8 see Veijola (1996b); Gertz (1996). Read in conjunction with 12:13–19, it appears that the *pesaḥ* is the main *zebaḥ* type offering in the original law code. It may only be offered at the central sanctuary (vv. 2, 5–6). The ancient prohibition of eating leavened bread with a *zebaḥ* (Ex 23:18) forms a transition to the instructions concerning the Feast of Unleavened Bread. This is to last for seven days and radiates into the entire territory (vv. 3–4). At a later stage, v. 8 introduces a cultic assembly at the close of the festival week. In the history of the *pesaḥ*, this law is unique in that it does not allow the slaughtering of the passover lamb in the individual homes, cf. Ex 12. For the Deuteronomic movement, this festival in spring is of foremost religious significance because it causes the participants to remember the Exodus as the foundational intervention of God in Israel's history; cf. also 2 Kings 23:21–3.

(16:9–12) The Feast of Weeks In Ex 23:16a, the *šābu'ôt* festival is called 'the feast of harvest'. The date of this feast depends on the beginning of the grain harvest which would normally fall in April. Its main characteristic is the liberal consumption of portions of the new yield, and therefore it is supposed to include all the people within the rural community. The appeal to generosity is underlined by v. 12 in a way similar to 15:15. According to the Deuteronomic law, 'rejoicing' in YHWH's presence is the primary *raison d'être* of the harvest festivals (vv. 11, 14–15; cf. 12:18, see Braulik 1970), which, in pre-Deuteronomic times, may have had numerous and confusing mythological aspects, cf. Hos 2:2–15 (MT 4–17).

(16:13–15) The Feast of Booths In Ex 23:16*b*, the *sukkôt* festival is called 'the festival of ingathering'. It is the autumn festival which follows the grape harvest. Before the beginning of the calendar year in ancient Israel was moved to spring in the late seventh or early sixth century, the festival must have coincided with the New Year and many suggestions have been made concerning its ritual aspects, notably as a celebration of YHWH's enthronement as a 'king' and 'creator god' (Mowinckel 1962: i. 118–30; Mettinger 1982: 67–77).

(16:16–17) The Rule of Pilgrimages The law summarizes the festival calendar with a revised version of the rule of Ex 23:17. It is clear from vv. 11, 14; 12:18; 14:26 that 'all your males' includes entire 'households', if not entire villages. 31:10–13 gives a more extensive list of participants in a religious festival.

(16:18–20) Judges Possibly as one aspect of royal administration and judicature, the law institutes judges (*šōpĕṭîm*) in the Judean country towns. These are coupled with 'officials' (*šōṭĕrîm*), i.e. a certain type of scribe, to which the specification 'according to your tribes' (RSV) may relate, possibly a secondary addition (as in 1:15) which alludes to a tribal and military model, cf. 20:5–9. The city gate was the normal place for trials, cf. 21:19; Am 5:10. One layer of laws in Deuteronomy, esp. the collection of family laws (see DEUT G.1), is built upon the judicial authority of the 'elders' (*zĕqēnîm*) of a town who may have been a more traditional body. v. 19 is a concise expression of the juridical ethos which, in 10:17–18, is even related to God as example. Taking a bribe (cf. Ex 23:8) is condemned as a threat to justice in all currents of Israel's religious thought, cf. e.g. Am 5:12; Isa 5:23; Ps 15:5; Prov 17:23; cf. also Lambert (1960: 133). v. 20 is a later addition which makes taking possession of the land depend on obedience to the law as in 6:17–18. The subject of legal procedures is further pursued in 17:8–13; 19:1–21; 21:1–9.

(16:21–2) Cultic Sites This pair of instructions concerning the features of a sanctuary is puzzling in its literary context. The reference to 'the altar that you make for the LORD your God' is reminiscent of Ex 20:24–5 rather than Deut 12:13–14. The temple at Jerusalem does not seem to be an obvious place for an 'ăšērâ, a sacred tree or a wooden object, nor a maṣṣēbâ, a standing stone (cf., however, 2 Kings 23:6). In Deuteronomistic literature, these objects are normally connected with cultic sites in the open country (1 Kings 14:23) and are ascribed to the pre-Israelite population (Deut 7:5; 12:2–3). Following recent archaeological discoveries, it is strongly debated whether an asherah might originally have been devoted to the goddess Asherah as a divine consort of YHWH, see Wiggins (1993); Frevel (1995).

(17:1) A Sacrificial Rule The mention of an altar entails a rule like that of 15:21 concerning sacrifices, cf. further Lev 22:17–25.

(17:2–7) Apostasy as a Legal Case This law may be more original in Deuteronomy than 13:1–18 from which laws it is distinguished by the prescription of a careful legal procedure. Apostasy is explicitly called a breach of the covenant (*bĕrît*) between YHWH and Israel. This points back to the interpretation of the Decalogue (esp. 5:6–10) as the main stipulation of a 'covenant' in 5:2, cf. also 4:12–13. Whether or not this idea of a covenant can be ascribed to the Josianic age depends on the critical understanding of Hos 8:1 and 2 Kings 23:1–3; see Nicholson (1986).

(17:8–13) The Authority of a High Court As the abolition of local sanctuaries eliminates the possibility of seeking an ordeal (cf. Ex 22:7–8), the law establishes the judicial authority of the priests at the central sanctuary (cf. 12:13–14). Later additions in vv. 9, 12 seem to anchor the office of a judge in this text which is presupposed in the book of Judges. The death penalty for 'presumptuously' (*bĕzādôn*) disregarding divine authority is commanded in a second case in 18:20–2.

(17:14–20) The Israelite King The law deals with the legitimacy of the Israelite, i.e. Judean monarchy, as does the Deuteronomistic discourse in 1 Sam 8. It is often regarded as the core of a supposed Deuteronomic constitutional law in 16:18–18:22. As such, it could be directed against revolutionary tendencies as known from the history of the northern kingdom (cf. 1 Kings 15:27–8; 16:9–10, 16; 2 Kings 9:14; 15:10, 14, 25, 30; Hos 8:4) or it could be a utopian model for the political role of a future Israelite king after the destruction of the Judean monarchy in 587 BCE (cf. Lohfink 1971*a*). However, a more plausible interpretation sees the law related to the diverse reflections within the Deuteronomistic representation of Israel's history (see DEUT C.2 and F.3) about the responsibility of the kings for the national disasters under the Assyrians and Babylonians (2 Kings 15:17–25:21). In any case it is worth noting that the law does not mention any royal officers (cf. 1 Kings 4:1–6).

According to vv. 14–15, instituting a monarchy was fundamentally legitimate although not without ambivalence, as it meant that Israel would become similar to 'all the nations that are around', thus verging on apostasy. The prohibition against appointing a foreigner (v. 15) as well as the reference to the king and his descendants (v. 20) intend to protect the Davidic dynasty, cf. 2 Sam 7. However, the restrictions imposed on the king in vv. 16–17, 20 are an indirect critique of Solomon, cf. 1 Kings 9:10–11:13. They correspond to the more general paraenesis of 8:11–14 and can even be traced back to prophetic criticism in Isa 31:1. The reference to a divine oracle in v. 16*b* (and again in 28:68) may reflect controversies which also lie behind Jer 41:16–43:7. At a later stage, the law was supplemented by vv. 18–19 which emphasize the pre-eminence of the Torah in Israel. The king shall have his own copy of the law which may lead him like any Israelite to fear God (6:24) and keep God's commandments (5:31–2). Deuteronomy ideally subjects the supreme representative of political power to the same religious and ethical obligations of the highest possible moral standard (4:8) which are valid for the entire community. It is this concern which invites comparison of this law with Paul's reflections on political power under the conditions of the Roman empire (Rom 13:1–7).

(18:1–8) Priests The law, which may originally have followed on 17:13, only addresses two issues which concern the typical audience of the law code in the Judean country towns. In a legislative form similar to 15:1–2, it defines the claims of the priests at the central sanctuary (cf. Ex 23:19). The priests, who are not entitled to landed property, are regarded as levitical priests, and vv. 6–8 state that all Levites have a right to perform priestly duties, even if, due to the centralization of the cult, they lose their functions outside Jerusalem. The relation between this law and Josiah's actions as reported in 2 Kings 23:8–9 is a controversial issue (see DEUT F.1). In additions to the law in vv. 1, 2, 5, a scribe underlines YHWH's 'electing' the entire 'tribe of Levi'. However, in later legal developments the priesthood is restricted to the descendants of Aaron (Num 3:9–10).

(18:9–22) Prophets As sacrificial cult does not exhaust all religious energies, a section on divination and magic has been added to the law code. Like 17:14, vv. 9–12 reflect the Deuteronomistic narrative framework of Deuteronomy. As in 12:2–4, 29–31, what is 'abominable' to Israel's God is equated with the religious practices of the former inhabitants of the land, cf. also Lev 20:1–8, 22–7. Besides child sacrifice (see DEUT 12:31), seven forms of superstition make a contrast to the one exclusive form of communication between God and his people through a prophet (nābî'). vv. 16–18, the author establishes the notion of a succession of prophets by the same interpretation of the events at Mount Horeb which is employed to define the relation between the Decalogue and the law code in ch. 5. The idea of a prophet in v. 18 and the law concerning a 'presumptuous' prophet in vv. 20–2 are closely related to the book of Jeremiah (Jer 1:7–9; 23:9–32). Israel's prophetic traditions are thus anchored in the Torah. However, 34:10 makes a distinction between Moses and all later prophets. On theories concerning the end of the prophetic age sometime during the Persian period see Barton (1986: 105–16).

(19:1–13) Cities of Refuge The law continues the section on judicial matters which began in 16:18. However, it does not mention any judges but only the 'elders' of a city (v. 12). The introductory v. 1 appears to be an addition made after 17:14–20 and 18:9–22 had been inserted into the law code. The institution of three cities of refuge in Judah compensates for the abolition of local sanctuaries where, prior to the reform, an asylum-seeker could have found protection (Ex 21:13–14; cf. 1 Kings 1:49–53). vv. 8–9 are an addition which provides for three cities of refuge east of the Jordan, cf. 4:41–3; Num 35; Josh 20. The central concern of the law finds expression in v. 10 and is the same as in 21:1–9.

(19:14) Boundaries Laws such as this (cf. 27:17); 23:24–5 (MT 25–6); 24:19–22, and also 15:7–11 address likely causes of conflict in a rural community and may be compared with the laws on agriculture in Plato's *Laws*, 842e–846c (Driver (1895) 1901: 234). The issue is also dealt with in wisdom literature: Prov 23:10–11; the Egyptian *Instruction of Amen-em-ope* (12th cent. BCE: *ANET* 422, 'Do not carry off the landmark at the boundaries of the arable land, | Nor disturb the position of the measuring-cord; | Be not greedy after a cubit of land, | Nor encroach upon the boundaries of a widow' (7.12–13)), the Akkadian series of incantations, *Shurpu* (copies from the 7th cent. BCE: Reiner 1958: 14, 'He set up an untrue boundary, (but) did not set up the [tr]ue bound[ary], | He removed mark, frontier and boundary' [the sun god is asked to release this person] (2, 45)).

(19:15–21) Legal Witnesses v. 15 is of great consequence for setting up standards for legal proceedings. vv. 16–21 nevertheless discuss the problem of false testimony by a single witness and threaten him with a penalty based on the *lex*

talionis. This rule, which applies to manslaughter and bodily harm, intends to keep punishment and revenge within strict limits (cf. Ex 21:23–5). Taken out of its original legal context, it is rejected in Mt 5:38–42, whereas within that context a line of interpretation within Judaism leads towards monetary fines (Tigay 1996: 185).

(20:1–21:14) Laws on Warfare Except for 21:1–9, these laws form a sequence of four laws on the army, on conquest, and on booty. Their background in antiquity is well illustrated by 2 Sam 8:2; 12:26–31, and 2 Kings 15:16; and especially in view of 20:10–14 it is worth comparing Thucydides, *Peloponnesian War*, 5: 84–116. The first two laws have been heavily supplemented. In 20:1–9, a priest has been given a role beside the officials (šōṭĕrîm) in vv. 2–4, and the officials' enquiry has been reinterpreted in v. 8, cf. Judg 7:1–7. In 20:10–18, the original law of vv. 10–14 has been given an opposite meaning in accordance with the idea of a military conquest of the promised land in vv. 15–18 (cf. Rofé 1985b). Whereas the original sequence of laws aimed at restricting destructive energies in case of war, the eventual result of its reworking provides another affirmation of the concept of annihilation of the peoples in the land, see DEUT 7:2. The anti-assimilationist motive for this fictitious historiographical concept is emphasized in v. 18, cf. 18:9–13. However, the authors of 1 Kings 14:24; 2 Kings 21:2 point towards the futility even of this concept.

(21:1–9) Expiation for Unresolved Murder Thematically contiguous to 19:1–13, the rite allows the elders of an Israelite town to make atonement for a murder in a case where the murderer cannot be identified and punished. v. 5 is a later attempt to see this unique ceremony directed by priests, cf. Lev 4:20.

(21:15–23) Family Laws vv. 15–17, the rule that the firstborn son shall inherit twice as much of his father's estate as any other heirs must not be violated (cf. E. W. Davies 1986). vv. 18–21, conversely, parents must be able to rely on that son for support in their old age, cf. 5:16; Ex 21:15, 17. The elders of a town play a remarkable role in traditional family law in Deuteronomy, cf. 22:15; 25:7. The law imposes a death penalty and stresses its function as a deterrent. By association, it is followed by a regulation which limits public exhibition of an executed offender.

(22:1–4) Fairness and Co-operation Like Ex 23:4–5, the law looks at disturbed social relations in a rural community and forbids 'ignoring' (hit'allēm) obvious cases for mutual help. Although it also draws a distinction between lost property and theft, its main characteristic is the strong paraenetic tone which aims at overcoming indifference and irresponsibility.

(22:5–12) Ordinances Protecting Life and Manners This section, notably vv. 5, 9–12, must be seen against the background of the notion that certain practices would be 'abominable' to YHWH. Of special interest is the restriction on human greed and power over animal life in vv. 6–7. It concludes with a motive clause similar to the one in 5:16, and from this one may infer that respect for the parent–child relationship stands behind the law, cf. also 14:21b.

(22:13–30 (MT 23:1)) Family and Sex Laws Part of a more extended collection (see DEUT G.1 and Otto 1993), the laws address issues of dishonesty and violence in sexual relations. They are arranged according to the marital status of a woman. The death penalty is imposed in most cases, although vv. 23–7 reflect a development towards restricting this through careful considerations. In one case only (v. 19) a fine is imposed, even if this seems to contradict the principle expressed in 19:19. A complementary law to vv. 28–9 can be found in Ex 22:16–17 (MT 15–16). v. 30, if a man was married polygamously, his son must not marry any of his father's former wives; cf. 27:20; Lev 18:8.

(23:1–8 (MT 23:2–9)) The Assembly of the Lord The law probably concerned local assemblies in monarchic Judah (cf. Mic 2:5), however, it does not indicate what functions such an assembly (*qĕhal YHWH*) would have had. Edomites and Egyptians are to be admitted under certain conditions, whereas Ammonites and Moabites are not (see *ABD*). vv. 1–2 may allude to cultic perversions, however, this is not entirely conclusive, and the designation 'born of an illicit union' (NRSV) follows the LXX interpretation of the unknown Hebrew word *mamzēr*. The law originally seems to think of Jacob as Israel's ancestor (v. 7; cf. Gen 25:21–6) and, in v. 3, to express the same spirit of contempt as Gen 19:30–8. The list of peoples does not exhaustively reflect the political situation of Judah (cf. e.g. 2 Kings 23:13; Jer 27:3; Zeph 2:4–9) but concentrates on those three Transjordanian neighbours with whom 2:2–23 is also concerned. vv. 4–6 are obvious secondary additions based on reinterpretations of 2:8–25 and Num 22–4. 1 Kings 11:2; Ezra 9:12; Neh 13:1–3 refer to this law in combination with 7:3–4. It has been suggested that Isa 56:3–7 abrogates this law (Donner 1985).

(23:9–14) The Military Camp Possibly by association a transition is made from the assembly (*qāhāl*) to the camp (*maḥăneh*). YHWH is not seen to appear in an epiphany during a campaign (cf. Judg 5:4–5; 2 Sam 22:8–16), instead, the law is intended to protect the deity's continuous presence in the camp (cf. 20:2–4).

(23:15–16) A Fugitive Slave The law may originally have followed on v. 8 since it deals with slaves who presumably have fled from a foreign country: they are given permission to settle 'in any one of your towns'. If a political dimension should be implied here, the law overturns provisions such as are known from an Aramaic treaty of the eighth century BCE which specifies that a fugitive must be returned (Sfire stela, 3, 4–6; *ANET* 660). If, however, the law must be understood within a domestic horizon only, it is worth comparing contrary regulations in the Code of Hammurabi (§16, *ANET* 167).

(23:17–18) Laws against Prostitution As in 23:1–2, it is not clear what kind of cultic rites, if any, lie behind these laws (cf. *ABD* v. 505–13). Even Hos 4:13–14 and 2 Kings 23:7 hardly offer a firm basis for historical explanation.

(23:19–25:12) Religious, Economic, and Civil Laws 23:19–20, like 15:1–3, the law is intended to facilitate a fellow Israelite's economic survival. 23:21–3, the law is typical of the conflation of religious and sapiential thought in Deuteronomy (Weinfeld 1992: 270–2). On the one hand it fully recognizes and teaches the religious implications of a vow, on the other hand it asserts that this custom is dispensable, thus putting into effect the liberating power of reflection. A further development of this line of thought can be found in Mic 6:6–8. If someone made a vow, whatever had been dedicated to the deity would have to be taken to the central sanctuary (12:17–18). 23:24–5, a number of rules, such as this, in the final section of the law code (also 24:6, 10–13, 14–15, 17–18, 19–22) anticipate conflicts in a rural community. Most of them express the same spirit as 22:1–4 or 15:7–11. They refer to the relationship between economically independent 'neighbours' (*rēa'*) as well as between such peasants and the landless poor who are employed as 'labourers' (*śākîr*) or are not attached to any household at all (*gēr*, also needy orphans and widows). The rules are based on an ethos of fairness and generosity, and this is an obvious moral consequence of a faith which centres on the Exodus creed (24:22; cf. 5:6–21, esp. 14–15). 24:1–4, a man had the right to divorce his wife (cases such as 22:13–19, 28–9 excepted), and he could get married to more than one woman (cf. 21:15). By implication, a woman had the right to get married more than once. However, a man did not have the right to call back his divorced wife once she had been married to and thus 'defiled' by (*ṭāmē'*) another man. As generally in Deuteronomy, the law does not take the perspective of the woman, whose fate may be deplorable. For discussions about this law in early Christianity cf. Mk 10:2–12; Mt 19:9; 5:31–2. 24:5, cf. 20:5–7. 24:7, the death penalty is imposed on anybody who kidnaps a person, cf. Ex 21:16. In the Code of Hammurabi a similar law reads: 'If a seignior has stolen the young son of another seignior, he shall be put to death' (§ 14, *ANET* 166). 24:8–9, a later addition to the collection, asserts the authority of the levitical priests in cases of an infectious disease which LXX identifies as leprosy. Lev 13 14 offers detailed instructions for dealing with such diseases. The concluding exhortation points to Num 12. 24:16, capital punishment (cf. e.g. 24:7) must be executed only on the person of the offender. Thematically, this belongs to a group of laws on the administration of justice (21:22–3; 25:1–3). Although in its immediate context the term for 'crime' (*ḥēṭ'*) is also being used for 'guilt' in a religious sense (24:15), the principle of individual responsibility here does not engage with the teaching of 5:9 which states that YHWH will punish 'iniquity' (*'āwôn*) through four generations. 25:1–3, a further law on practical legal matters. The notion of 'degradation' within the community also underlies the two following laws. 25:4, proverbial from its reinterpretation in 1 Cor 9:9–11, may have been linked with 24:19–22. In four Hebrew words it says a lot about treatment of animals and its original sense merits pondering. Prov 12:10 may be a help. 25:5–10, if a man dies without leaving a son, his name is 'blotted out of Israel', and this is seen as a great misfortune (the same view may be implied in 24:5). Where circumstances allow, securing the continuity of a deceased man's family through levirate marriage has first priority. Fear of disgrace is to motivate a reluctant brother-in-law. 25:11–12, except for the *lex talionis* (19:21), this is the only instance of mutilation as punishment in the law code.

(25:13–16) Fairness and Honesty The concluding paragraph of the law code is permeated by the sapiential spirit of humanism typical of many sections of Deuteronomy. The law on just weights and measures has parallels in Israelite as well as ancient Near-Eastern wisdom texts (Prov 11:1; 20:10, 23; *Shurpu*, 8. 64–7 (Reiner 1958: 42–3); cf. Code of Hammurabi,

§94 (*ANET* 169)). It appeals to a common sense of what is just in order to keep the human being from doing 'unrighteousness' ('*āwel*); cf. also Lev 19:35–4; Ezek 18:5–9. Moral behaviour guided by such self-evidently just principles is related to the blessing of a long life, whereas its opposite is considered an 'abomination' (*tô'ēbâ*) for God. However, in such laws as 15:1–11 and 23:19–20 (MT 20–1), Deuteronomy goes beyond the limits of this moral order: fairness is not enough in the service of Israel's God.

(25:17–19) **War against Amalek** A historical reminiscence of relations between Israelites and Amalekites may have been preserved in 1 Sam 30, whereas the traditio-historical background behind the three texts in Ex 17:8–16; Deut 25:17–19; 1 Sam 15:1–35 remains obscure; cf. Foresti (1984). The peculiar episode in Ex 17:8–16 is taken up here (in a secondary addition to the law code in the 2nd person pl., like 23:4a (MT 5a); 24:9) and reinterpreted in terms of a lack of 'fear of God' (cf. Gen 20), in order to account for the command to exterminate the Amalekites. Looking forward to a time when Israel will enjoy 'rest from all her enemies' (cf. 12:9–10) prepares the ground for the story of 1 Sam 15 (although this is not coherent with 2 Sam 7:1). Cf. also the motif of just retribution in Jer 2:3; 30:16.

(26:1–11) **A Form for Liturgical Recitation** On a redactional level similar to 17:14–20, a Deuteronomistic scribe makes the traditional custom of taking the first fruits to a YHWH sanctuary (Ex 23:19a; Deut 18:4) the occasion for a pilgrimage which seems not to coincide with one of the three main festivals (16:1–17). The core of the instruction is an artistic composition in vv. 5–10. In twentieth-century scholarship, it has often been considered an ancient confessional formula on which the oldest literary source of the Pentateuch was modelled (von Rad 1966). However, it is more likely that the confession did not originate in Israelite cult in pre-monarchic times, but instead within the Deuteronomistic School (cf. Richter 1967; Lohfink 1971b). The confession starts from a reminiscence of an ancestor who was 'a perishing Aramean' (NRSV reads 'a wandering'; see, however, Janzen 1994). As this must refer to Jacob, the scribe here integrates the Jacob tradition into the Exodus tradition and thereby to a certain degree invalidates the former which was closely linked to the sanctuary at Bethel (Gen 28; 35; cf. 2 Kings 23:15). The confession then unfolds four times in three sentences with a characteristic pause at the end of each section (cf. RSV). It is built on numerous allusions to the Exodus narrative, notably Ex 1:9–14; 3:7–10, 15 (in v. 8, 'signs and wonders' may be secondary as is 6:22). v. 10 leads up to the actual ceremony which is followed by a celebration. A scribe here designs a concise picture of Israel's salvation history and thus gives profound witness to God's mercy in a perspective of Judean theology. The basic structure of the composition reflects the conviction of biblical faith that God helps the oppressed who cry out to him (cf. Judg 3:9; Ex 22:20–3), even if his ways are inscrutable (cf. Ex 34:10; Isa 55:6–9). vv. 3–4, as v. 10 instructs the farmer himself to set down his basket 'before YHWH', the reference to a priest must have been introduced at a later stage, perhaps sometime during the Second Temple period (cf. Neh 10:35–7 (MT 36–8)).

(26:12–15) **A Declaration of Obedience** A declaration at the sanctuary corresponds to the law of 14:28–9 and also responds to an exhortation such as 6:17–18. It includes a list of three forbidden abuses of the third year's tithe, which presumably are related to some form of death-cult, possibly a problem in the Second Temple period. For the designation of heaven as YHWH's dwelling place cf. 1 Kings 8:27–30 and also Zech 2:17; Isa 63:15; 2 Chr 30:27.

Declaration of Mutual Commitments between YHWH and Israel (26:16–19)

In its present literary context, the passage represents the covenant ceremony which is presupposed in 29:1 (MT 28:69). It has been suggested that it originated in a cultic event and that this might even be identified with the covenant ceremony under King Josiah which is narrated in 2 Kings 23:1–3 (Smend 1963). After its introduction (v. 16a; cf. 6:1; 12:1), the declaration revolves around the solemn statements: 'You have affirmed this day that the LORD is your God', and 'And the LORD has affirmed this day that you are [...] His treasured people' (NJPS). In the unique form of a mutual declaration, this corresponds to 6:4. The covenant relationship between YHWH and Israel has an ethical dimension, and the Deuteronomists are strongly concerned with the ensuing idea of a divine law. This accounts for the first explication concerning Israel's obligation 'to walk in his ways, and to keep his statutes [...] and his ordinances, and to obey his voice'. Equally, the covenant relationship has a universal dimension. This is expressed in the second explication concerning YHWH's promise to Israel 'to set you high above all nations that he has made, in praise and in fame and in honour' (cf. RSV; there are some further additions to the text which partly may depend on 7:6). God the creator of all humankind sets his people 'high above' ('*elyôn*) all nations 'that he has made'. A similar thought is expressed in Ex 19:5–6, where the clause 'for all the earth is mine' also implies a theology of creation which in its hymnic form may have been a constituent motif in the cult of the Jerusalem temple even in the monarchic period (cf. Ps 24:1). Deut 7:6, too, refers to 'all the peoples that are on the face of the earth'. All these reflections (cf. also 32:8–9) should be understood in a dialectical relation to Gen 12:3 or Isa 49:6 which speak of the blessing that comes to all humankind through Israel.

Instructions for a Ceremony West of the Jordan (27:1–26)

In vv. 1, 9, 11, as well as in 29:1–2 (MT 28:69; 29:1), the narrator interrupts Moses' speech, which comes to an end only in 31:1. Concurring conceptions of cultic ceremonies on entering the land have been combined here just as in the book of Joshua. v. 2–3, the scribe who commands the erection of stelae with the law code written on them may be responding to the accusation that Israel spoiled her land as soon as she entered it (cf. Jer 2:7). Josh 4:20 mentions twelve memorial stones in Gilgal near the river Jordan (on the place-names see *ABD*). vv. 5–7, a second scribe thinks of sacrifices and consequently of the need for an altar, built in accordance with Ex 20:24–5, but not with Deut 12:13–14. The location of this altar, which Joshua is said to have built (Josh 8:30–1), is near Shechem, to where v. 4 also transfers the stelae. vv. 11–13, the valley between Mount Gerizim and Mount Ebal is defined as the place for a third ritual (cf. 11:29–30). vv. 14–26, this in turn has been expanded by a liturgy (cf. Neh 8:1–8). The series of curses, framed by vv. 15 and 26, has its focus mainly on clandestine evil deeds which threaten human dignity and a peaceful society.

The Consequences of Obedience and Disobedience through Blessings and Curses (28:1–68)

As part of his address to Israel, Moses gives conditional promises of divine blessings (vv. 1–14) and curses (vv. 15–68) respectively. The parallel introductory clauses to these two sections (vv. 1–2, 15) presuppose the shaping of the law code as an oration of Moses (cf. Mayes 1979: 348–51). They refer back to the declaration in 26:16–19, and this connection to the idea of a covenant scene is further underlined by the subscription in 29:1 (MT 28:69). However, it is disputable whether 28:1–68 originated as part of a covenant pattern or as a homiletic elaboration based on a pattern of a good and a bad alternative, cf. the Deuteronomistic passages in 1 Kings 9:4–7 and Jer 22:3–5. The latter suggestion would account for the promise of blessings which cannot be traced back to treaty rhetoric.

There is strong evidence that the section of curses, notably vv. 20–35, incorporates material adopted from Esar-haddon's succession treaty of 672 BCE (see DEUT F.2 and on Deut 13; Weinfeld 1992: 116–29; Steymans 1995). In this treaty an extended series of curses invoking the gods of the Assyrian pantheon is pronounced against anyone who should breach the oath imposed by the Assyrian king:

37 May Aššur, king of the gods, who decrees [the fates], decree an evil and unpleasant fate for you. May he not gra[nt yo]u long-lasting old age and the attainment of extreme old age. 38 May Mullissu, his beloved wife, make the utterance of his mouth evil, may she not intercede for you. 38A May Anu, king of the gods, let disease, exhaustion, malaria, sleeplessness, worries and ill health rain upon all your houses (cf. 28:22). 39 May Sin, the brightness of heaven and earth, clothe you with leprosy and forbid your entering into the presence of the gods or king. Roam the desert like the wild ass and the gazelle (cf. 28:27). 40 May Šamaš, the light of heaven and earth, not judge you justly. May he remove your eyesight. Walk about in darkness! (cf. 28:28–9). 41 May Ninurta, the foremost among the gods, fell you with his fierce arrow; may he fill the plain with your blood and feed your flesh to the eagle and the vulture (cf. 28:25–6). 42 May Venus, the brightest of the stars, before your eyes make your wives lie in the lap of your enemy; may your sons not take possession of your house, but a strange enemy divide your goods (cf. 28:30). .... 63 May all the gods that are [mentioned by name] in th[is] treaty tablet make the ground as narrow as a brick for you. May they make your ground like iron (so that) nothing can sprout from it. 64 Just as rain does not fall from a brazen heaven so may rain and dew not come upon your fields and your meadows; instead of dew may burning coals rain on your land (cf. 28:23–4). .... 69 Just as [thi]s ewe has been cut open and the flesh of [her] young has been placed in her mouth, may they make you eat in your hunger the flesh of your brothers, your sons and your daughters (cf. 28:53). (Parpola and Watanabe 1988: 45–52; ANET 538)

In addition to this Assyrian treaty, an Aramaic treaty of the eighth century BCE has been adduced as a possible source for motifs in 28:38–42 (Sfire stela, 1A. 27–8; ANET 659–60).

The curses of Deut 28, notably vv. 20–42, must be seen against this ancient Near-Eastern background, and it seems most likely that they were contrived once the disaster which Judah and Jerusalem suffered in 587 BCE had come to be

interpreted as the experience of a divine curse (cf. 29:24–7 (MT 23–6); 1 Kings 9:8–9). In this process, YHWH became the subject of all those curses on an almost monotheistic level, cf. Isa 45:6–7. Referring back to the curses and 'afflictions' pronounced in vv. 20–35, a scribe in vv. 58–9 calls them a 'stupendous' doing of YHWH (p-l-' hifil).

(28:1–14) Moses promises God's blessing for obedience to the law. vv. 3–6 may be a traditional formula of blessing which originated in a cultic setting, cf. 1 Sam 2:20; Ps 24:5; 118:26; 121:8. vv. 7–14 can best be described as an attempt by later scribes to counterbalance the curses in vv. 20–44 (see Seitz 1971: 273–6). The blessing of Israel functions as a witness to YHWH's divinity (v. 10; cf. 1 Kings 8:43).

(28:15–68) vv. 15–19, the curse section opens in close correspondence with vv. 1–6. vv. 20–9, the second section adopts a rhetoric from the political sphere, see above. vv. 30–3, the third section, marked off by the repetition of expressions from v. 29 in v. 33, refers to a typical military defeat, cf. 20:5–7, 10–14. vv. 34–5, the fourth section, partly an inverted repetition of vv. 27–8, lays an elaborate curse upon the mental and bodily state of an individual. vv. 36–7, the fifth section goes beyond the motifs of vv. 30–3 and refers to the entire nation's exile, cf. v. 64 and 4:27–8. The scribe looks back to the Babylonian conquest of Jerusalem in 587 BCE, cf. 1 Kings 9:7; Jer 24:9. vv. 38–44, the sixth section to a certain degree runs parallel to vv. 30–3; it includes a series of so-called futility curses (vv. 38–42) which again reflect the rhetoric of political documents, see above. The elaborate curse in 43–4 envisages a total subversion of the social order in which 'aliens' were the landless poor, cf. 14:28–9. vv. 45–8, the seventh section is a transitional passage which forms a conclusion to vv. 15–44 and an introduction to vv. 49–57. The curses in vv. 20–44 are called 'a sign and a wonder' (RSV), which expression may even allude to the Egyptian plagues (cf. 6:22) and thereby draw a parallel between these two sets of images of punitive disasters. The following reflections on the Exile and the fall of Jerusalem (as well as some additions in vv. 20, 25) betray connections to the book of Jeremiah. For vv. 47–8 cf. Jer 5:18–19 and 28:13–14. vv. 49–53, the eighth section gives a stylized representation of the Babylonian attack on Jerusalem. Cf. Jer 5:15–17; 6:11; 19:9; 48:40. v. 51 reverses the blessing of 7:13. Whether v. 53 refers to historical experience during the siege of Jerusalem or only alludes to a recurring motif in treaty curses (see above, and Weinfeld 1992: 126–8) is not conclusive (cf. also Lev 26:26, 29). vv. 54–7, the ninth section elaborates the scenes of horror during a siege, cf. also 2 Kings 6:24–9. vv. 58–68, the concluding section adds several scribal reflections on what is written in the 'book of this law (tôrâ)'. vv. 58–61 focus on the issue of diseases (vv. 21–2, 27, 35) and reverse the blessing of 7:15. The line of interpretation of the curses as 'a sign and a portent' in v. 46 seems to be continued here. v. 62 points back to 26:5 on the one hand, and to 1:10 on the other. The verse implies a total reversal of Israel's salvation history, even if it might still hint at a vague possibility of a new beginning. This in turn is excluded by v. 68 which refers back to Ex 14:13 (Reimer 1990) and leaves no room even for the expectation of a miserable life in Egyptian slavery. vv. 64–7, the threat concerning life in the Diaspora cuts Israel off from any relationship with YHWH, the protection of which is the central concern of Deuteronomy, cf. 13:6–11 (MT 7–12). The frightful picture of the conditions of that life enlarges v. 34 in a different age. v. 68 sets a seal on the nullification of the relationship between YHWH and Israel (cf. 5:6) in case of disobedience to the Torah.

A most extraordinary interpretation of the curse section and, by implication, of the destruction of Jerusalem, is given in v. 63a. The verse is an artistic expression of the climax of negativity. While its structure may depend on such oracles as Zech 8:14–15; Jer 31:28; 32:42, the verb employed (śîś) may have been adopted from other promises of salvation (cf. Deut 30:9; Zeph 3:17; Jer 32:41 MT; Isa 65:18–19). This peculiar statement finds a wider context in reflections on YHWH's compassion (r-ḥ-m piel, n-ḥ-m nifal; cf. e.g. Jer 4:28; 13:13–14; 18:7–10; Deut 4:31; 30:3).

Discourse on the Significance of the Law
((29:1) 29:2–30:20)

(29:1 (MT and LXX 28:69)) The Covenant in the Land of Moab Whether this verse is a subscription to the preceding law or a superscription to the following speech of Moses is subject to debate. As it cannot be demonstrated that a traditional ancient Near-Eastern covenant pattern underlies 29:2b–30:20 (see, however, Weinfeld 1992: 100–16; Rofé 1985a), it is more likely that v. 1 is a concluding statement and that 4:44–28:68 are subsumed under the expression 'these are the words of the covenant'. Thus, the verse is part of an editorial framework around the law, and it also connects to 1:1–5 and to 5:1–5. Just as a 'covenant at Horeb' defines the theological dimension of the Decalogue, so a 'covenant in the land of Moab' defines that of the Deuteronomic law. However, the unique concept of two covenants which supplement each other does not blur the distinction between the Decalogue and the Deuteronomic law which is developed in ch. 5.

(29:2 (MT 29:1)) A Concluding Address The narrator introduces a speech which reaches as far as 30:20 and mainly consists of three thematically distinct units. 29:3–21 focuses on the religious obligation of every single Israelite and on the limitation of divine punishment for apostasy to an individual. 29:22–30:10 gives an interpretation of the fall of Jerusalem in 587 BCE and turns towards a prediction of future salvation. 30:11–20 is a general reflection concerning the law delivered by Moses and functions as a magnificent coda to it.

(29:2–9) Exhortations The notion of 'covenant' in 29:1 triggers off a paraenetic discourse which seems to be looking at the conquest of the land (cf. the verb 'to succeed', ś-k-l hifil, in v. 9 (MT 8) and in Josh 1:7–8). vv. 2–3 highlight the mighty deeds of YHWH in the Exodus, cf. 6:22. vv. 7–8 remind the reader of the paradigmatic conquest of the land under Moses' leadership as narrated in 2:24–3:17. v. 4, which may depend on Isa 6:9–10, is a gloss on vv. 2–3: unless God himself directs the human heart, even his mighty deeds which are represented through the kerygmatic narrative tradition will not lead to faith. vv. 5–6 quote from Deut 8 in direct speech by YHWH (MT; LXX reads the 3rd person). The final clause of 8:3 is substituted by a formula which mostly occurs in Ezekiel and in the Priestly Document in the Pentateuch (e.g. Ezek 20:20; 28:26; Ex 6:7), and this demonstrates a combining of diverse theological traditions.

(29:10–15) Covenant and Oath This section sets forth a liturgical scene comparable to the one narrated in Neh 10. The term 'covenant' (bĕrît) is doubled by the term 'oath' or 'curse' ('ālâ, v. 12; cf. Neh 10:29 (MT 30)). The idea of a covenant ceremony finds a less direct expression than in 26:16–19. The reference to the ancestors (cf. Gen 17:7) sees the patriarchal age as the foundation of Israel's existence as the people of God in an even more fundamental sense than that of the concept of a divine promise of the land (1:8; 30:20). According to vv. 14–15, the covenant also includes people who are not present at the assembly, although this is not coherent with the fictional setting of Moses' speech. The addition may be by a scribe having in mind the Jewish Diaspora in the Persian empire (cf. 30:3–4).

(29:16–21) A Warning against Apostasy The view of the 'nations' in this homiletic passage is informed by 1 Kings 11:1–8 and 2 Kings 23:13 rather than Deut 2:1–23. The polemics against foreign gods and their visual representations echo such passages as Ezek 20:1–44; Isa 44:9–20; Jer 10:1–16. Historically, it betrays a strong tendency towards a separation from rival groups within the land, cf. Neh 10:28 (MT 29). The metaphors of v. 18 (cf. also Am 6:12), as well as the term 'stubbornness of heart' (šĕrirût lēb), link the passage with Jer 9:12–16 (MT 11–15). The threat of divine punishment is restricted to an individual and left entirely to YHWH. A scribe thus revises 5:9–10; 17:2–7, and also gives the curses of ch. 28 a new application.

(29:22–8) The Devastated Land The passage looks back to the destruction of Judah in 587 BCE. The rhetorical form of vv. 24–8 has close parallels in 1 Kings 9:8–9 and Jer 22:8–9 and is also known from an Assyrian source from the seventh century where a report of a punitive campaign reads: 'Whenever the inhabitants of Arabia asked each other: "On account of what have these calamities befallen Arabia?" (they answered themselves:) "Because we did not keep the solemn oaths (sworn by) Ashur, because we offended the friendliness of Ashurbanipal, the king, beloved by Enlil!"' (ANET 300). v. 25 is founded on the first commandment of the Decalogue as the central stipulation of the covenant at Horeb (5:1–10, cf. also 4:20; Judg 2:11–15). vv. 22 (cf. 1 Kings 8:41–3) and 23 (cf. Jer 49:18; Gen 19) may be later additions.

(29:29) Secret and Revealed Things Taken in its literary context, this verse may refer to the human inability to fully understand the past (29:25–8) or the future (30:1–10). It may also refer to a concealed background of the Torah which would be irrelevant to obedience (30:11–14), or an interpretation in the light of Ps 19:12 (MT 19:13), which speaks of 'secret faults', might also be a possibility. NJPS reads: 'Concealed acts concern the LORD our God; but with overt acts, it is for us and our children ever to apply all the provisions of this Teaching.'

(30:1–10) Hope for Future Restoration From the image of the land devastated by a curse, the speech turns towards predictions of salvation. These have close parallels in the book of Jeremiah (e.g. Jer 29:10–14; 32:36–41). As in Deut 4:25–31, Israel is envisaged as returning to YHWH who will show his mercy to the people (rāḥam: 4:31; 30:3). However, whereas according to vv. 1–2 returning to YHWH is a precondition for better fortunes, a scribe in v. 6 (contrast 10:16) makes Moses pronounce an unconditional promise, cf. Jer 31:33–4.

Within this horizon of expectation, v. 7 gives a new interpretation of the curses in ch. 28. vv. 8–10 are based on motifs adopted from 28:11, 63.

(30:11–14) The Accessibility of the Law Here as in 6:1, 25, 'commandment' (*miṣwâ*) designates the entire law which Moses delivers in his speech. In terms of composition, the declaration may be seen as an equivalent to 4:5–8. Whereas the expression 'in your mouth' refers to the regular repetition of the received law (cf. 6:7; Josh 1:8), the expression 'in your heart' takes the internalization of the law even further than 6:6 does, cf. also Jer 31:33–4. The scribe demonstrates the essential conformity of the divine law to the human being with the help of impressive poetic imagery. In Rom 7, especially vv. 7–13, Paul opposes this anthropological concept of Deuteronomistic theology in the light of his understanding of sin, and therefore, in Rom 10:5–8, applies the figures of Deut 30:11–14 to 'the word of faith which we proclaim'.

(30:15–20) Choice between Good and Evil This solemn finale to Moses' speech reflects an aspect of the wisdom tradition, cf. Prov 11:19; Am 5:14–15. The invitation to 'choose' (*bāḥar*) in v. 19*b* recalls the scene in Josh 24, especially vv. 14–15. v. 20, the revealed law is the source of life (cf. Lev 18:5 and Rom 10:5), and true obedience to its commandments is based on the love of God (cf. Mk 12:28–34). Faith is a possible decision in the face of death and 'evil' (RSV). The beginning of the secondary vv. 16–19*a* has been lost in the MT but can be restored following the LXX, cf. 7:12–13; 8:19–20.

Report of Moses' Parting from Israel, Including his Poem and his Blessings (31:1–34:12)

(31:1–8) The Appointment of Joshua NRSV rightly restores the beginning of this section following the LXX and the fragmentary MS 1Q Deut[b] from Qumran (DJD 1. 59). The narrator resumes 3:28–9 and prepares the transition to the book of Joshua, cf. Josh 1:1–9. Additions in vv. 3, 4–6 take up material from 7:17–23; 9:3; 29:7–8 (MT 6–7). What is presented in 2:33–4 and 3:3, 6 as actions of the Israelites, is interpreted directly as a divine action in v. 4, cf. 3:21–2.

(31:9–30) Codification of the Law and Announcement of Moses' Poem Two themes overlap in this section: a description of the Torah as a book, and, in vv. 16–22, the designation of a Mosaic poem as a 'witness' against Israel. vv. 9–11, the written Torah is handed over to the levitical priests and significantly also to representatives of the laity. Its public reading gives the festival of the tabernacles (*ḥag hassukkôt*) in every seventh year (following 15:1–3) a theological significance as great as that of the Passover which is designed to remember the Exodus (16:1–8). In a later addition in vv. 24–7, the book of the Torah is brought into connection with the ark in which, according to 10:1–8, the tablets of the Decalogue are being kept. The same scribe possibly also depicted the levitical priests in v. 9 (cf. 17:18) as those 'who carried the ark of the covenant'. vv. 14–15 make the tent of meeting (*'ōhel mô'ēd*) the place where YHWH speaks to Moses, cf. Ex 27:21; 33:7–11, etc. vv. 16–22 are motivated by the problem of what will happen to Israel once her incomparable first leader has died and the foundational period of her history has come to a close, cf. the analogous problem in Josh 3:11 to Judg 23:1. The author introduces an independent poem in 32:1–43 which he wants

to hand down as a song of Moses. He makes YHWH address Moses in a prophetic speech which characterizes Israel by her breach of the covenant on entering the land, cf. 5:2, 7; Jer 31:32; Hos 13:4–6. The notion of YHWH concealing himself (v. 18) which is predicted in the poem (32:20; cf. Jer 18:17; 33:5; also Isa 8:17 and Ps 44:24 (MT 25); 80:3 (MT 4) *et al.*) is a remarkable interpretation of the motif of YHWH's anger which elsewhere dominates in the Deuteronomistic literature (e.g. 29:27 (MT 26); Judg 2:14–15; 2 Kings 23:26). The secondary vv. 20–1 borrow from 6:10–12, and, with the notion of 'inclination' (*yēṣer*), possibly even allude to the framing verses of the Flood story in Gen 6:5; 8:21. vv. 24–9 imitate the introduction to the Song of Moses and make the entire Torah a 'witness' against Israel. This thought is further underlined in 32:45–7 with material taken from 30:15–20.

(32:1–43) Moses' Poem The Song of Moses adds a new facet to the Mosaic oration and thus to the picture of the Mosaic age in Deuteronomy. Attributed to Moses as it is, the poem has a prophetic purpose (cf. 31:16–22), although its main characteristic is that of wisdom poetry. It has its climax in a monotheistic creed in v. 39, and this is prepared by a theodicy (vv. 4–5), a reference to mythological primeval history (vv. 8–9), a résumée of the earliest salvation history (vv. 11–12), an explication of YHWH's concealing of himself (v. 20), and a critique of a polytheistic misinterpretation of Israel's apparent abandonment by her God (vv. 30–1). S. R. Driver was right when he wrote: 'The Song shows great originality of form, being a presentation of prophetical thoughts in a poetical dress, on a scale which is without parallel in the OT' (1895 (1901): 345). A notable feature of the poem is its wealth of metaphors and images (e.g. in vv. 6, 10, 11, 13, 15, 18–19) as well as mythological motifs (vv. 8–9, 22, 23–4). Stylistically, it is characterized by the typical parallelism of two sentences or expressions which together form a poetic line; cf. Alter (1990, notably 24–5 on vv. 10, 13).

The poem's basic structure is built upon Deuteronomistic motifs. Israel first became guilty before YHWH when she prospered in her land and forgot her God (vv. 15–18; cf. 6:10–12; 8:7–18). In consequence, YHWH's anger was aroused (vv. 21–2; cf. 6:15; 29:24–8 (MT 23–7)). However, when the poet speaks of YHWH's mercy (v. 36), he does not see Israel's return to YHWH as a condition for it, in contrast to the Deuteronomistic vision of Israel's future restoration in 4:29–31; 30:1–3. The concept of YHWH taking revenge on his enemies and destroying them (vv. 34–5, 40–1) leads beyond Deuteronomistic expectations. Instead, it has parallels in oracles in Nahum; Jer 46–51; Isa 63:1–6, etc.

The poem is anthological in character and obviously presupposes the development of monotheistic thought as reflected in Deutero-Isaiah (Isa 45:5–7). Despite the attempt by Sanders (1996), in his authoritative study of Deut 32, to demonstrate a pre-exilic origin of the poem, it is more plausibly considered a composition from the Second Temple period.

(32:1–6) The poet and wisdom teacher stresses the perfection and justice of God in sharp contrast to the foolishness of the people. Upon the doctrinal foundation which is established by this antithesis, any historical experience of disaster will be reflected in a straight scheme of theodicy. It is worth noting how the poet places himself within a horizon of hymnic praise of YHWH (v. 3) and thus responds to the superior importance of the concept of 'fear of the LORD' in the wisdom tradition (Prov 9:10). There is a striking similarity between the opening of Moses' poem and the introduction to Isaiah (Isa 1:2–3).

(32:7–9) An insight into right behaviour as well as a knowledge of God's actions in a mythical primeval age are preserved in the wisdom of former generations (v. 7; cf. Job 8:8–10; Jer 6:16–17; Isa 45:20–1; 46:8–11). Therefore, the poet grounds the Deuteronomistic notion of Israel's election (7:6) on a mythological concept of the primeval age and adduces a polytheistic concept of the order of the nations corresponding with the number of celestial beings. It has been suggested that this may be traced back to Ugaritic mythology which, in the epic *The Palace of Ba'al* of the fourteenth century BCE, has the 'seventy sons of Athirat', cf. the seventy nations in Gen 10 (see Lipiński 1998: 300–1; Gibson 1978: 63; *ANET* 134). v. 8 thus is a poetic echo of polytheistic mythology as e.g. Ps 82:6–7; 89:5–14 (MT 6–15); Job 38:7. Whereas the LXX reads 'according to the number of the angels of God' (one MS reads 'of the sons of God'; cf. 4Q Deutʲ (DJD 14. 90), and see Sir 17:17), the Hebrew text testifies to a revision which reads 'according to the number of the sons of Israel' (for which cf. Gen 46:27; Deut 10:22). The designation of God as 'the Most High' ('elyôn) in v. 8 refers to Israel's God as much as does the divine name 'the LORD' (YHWH) in v. 9; cf. the use of 'elyôn in Ps 18:13 (MT 14); 83:18 (MT 19); 97:9, etc. and see the discussion in Sanders (1996: 362–74).

(32:10–14) For the poetic images of the eerie desert and the prodigious land, cf. 8:1–18. The poet mentions neither the theme of the Exodus nor that of the conquest of the land, cf. also Jer 2:2. The fascinating imagery of v. 10b is unique in the OT, that of v. 11 has a parallel in Ex 19:3–4. Against the background of the splendour of Israel's early salvation history, v. 12 prepares the ground for the monotheistic creed in v. 39. In contrast to the obvious uniqueness of YHWH in this early period, the foreign gods to which vv. 15–18 refer are called 'new ones recently arrived' (v. 17).

(32:15–18) The representation of Israel's sin stands in the tradition of prophetic accusations (Hos 11:1–3; 13:4–6). The poet compares Israel to a rebellious animal that 'kicks out' (LXX *apolaktizein*), cf. Hos 4:16. 'Jeshurun' as a name for Israel has only three other references in the OT, namely in the poems which frame the Blessing of Moses in 33:2–5, 26–9, and in Isa 44:1–5. The name is a nominal form of the root *y-š-r* 'to be straight/right', perhaps in a play on the name '*Jacob*' which, in Hos 12:3 (MT 4), is derived from the root '*-q-b* possibly meaning 'to deceive'. LXX translates the name as 'the beloved' (*ho ēgapēmenos*).

(32:19–25) The poet attributes to the hiddenness and to the anger of YHWH all disastrous events which strike Israel. In vv. 21 and 25 he refers to military catastrophes, in v. 22 he represents YHWH's anger in a cosmological dimension (cf. Job 9:5–6). vv. 23–4 portray mythical powers of destruction as 'arrows' which YHWH will shoot at his people (cf. Ezek 5:16; Job 6:4).

(32:26–7) YHWH who is the God Most High, is also the originator of Israel's disaster (cf. Isa 45:6–7). However, the

nations do not understand his work, because they attribute their triumph over Israel to their own strength (cf. Isa 10:5–15). Therefore, the relationship between YHWH and Israel which existed ever since the mythological origin of history (vv. 8–9) does not permit YHWH to destroy Israel totally, because then his name could not be known and honoured any more, cf. Isa 48:9–11.

(32:28–33) Israel's enemies are portrayed as being foolish (some commentators, however, suggest that vv. 28–30 refer rather to Israel). In v. 31, the poet points to the impotence of the enemies' gods who, following v. 8, can at most be subordinate divine beings.

(32:34–5) The future destiny of Israel's enemies has been decided by YHWH long ago, and the time of its arrival is conceived of as imminent. The nations will be hit by YHWH's 'vengeance'. This is a recurring motif in oracles of doom against the nations in the prophetic books (Jer 50:15; Isa 34:8; see Peels 1995). At the beginning of v. 35, the reading of the Samaritan Pentateuch and the LXX, 'for the day of vengeance and recompense' may be more original than the MT which, however, is clearly presupposed in Rom 12:19, where Paul combines Deut 32:35 and Lev 19:18 in a paraenetic call. In the *Targum Onqelos*, the phrase 'for the time when their foot shall slip' is rendered as 'for the time when they go into exile', because the entire passage, vv. 28–35, is seen as referring to Israel.

(32:36–8) The central idea is that of YHWH, the gracious God, who has 'compassion' on his people, cf. 4:31. Looking back to vv. 15–18, the poet derides Israel's aberration from her faith in YHWH, the only true God.

(32:39) The climax of Moses' poem. Even the most contradictory experiences which Israel may suffer must be referred to YHWH. The uniqueness of God has been given expression in 6:4 and it is now emphasized in a monotheistic creed. As a prayer of an individual, the Song of Hannah in 1 Sam 2:1–10 has close parallels to this verse, which may be considered the culmination of such passages as Hos 6:1–3 and Isa 45:5–7, cf. also Rom 4:17.

(32:40–2) The image of YHWH's hand raised for an oath (cf. Ezek 20) introduces an amplification of the expectation of vv. 34–5. The poet portrays YHWH as a warrior. Arrows and a sword as YHWH's weapons are mentioned in many oracles of doom, cf. e.g. Nah 3; Hab 3. The poet envisages the total extinction of the enemy. Within the OT as a whole, this image of vengeance finds its counterpart in the vision of universal peace as in Isa 2:2–4. That vision breaks up the dualism of 'compassion' and 'vengeance' which underlies any apocalyptic concept of 'salvation' and 'doom'.

(32:43) As in v. 8, MT has been revised in order to avoid all possible reminiscences of polytheism. Where MT reads 'praise, O nations, his people', a MS from Qumran reads 'praise, O heavens, his people, | worship him, all you gods' (4QDeutᑫ, see DJD 14. 141; this is followed by NRSV; cf. also Ps 97:9 and see Rofé (2000)), which partly corresponds to the double reading in LXX 'rejoice, O heavens, with him, | and let all the sons of God worship him; | rejoice, O nations, with his people, | and let all the angels of God confirm for him'. The last colon of v. 43 goes beyond the thrust of the poem and addresses the question of impurity and atonement (*kipper*), which according to the LXX and 4QDeut^q refers to Israel's land, but according to MT refers to the people as well as the land; on this theological issue cf. Ezek 36.

(32:48–52) Moses on Mount Nebo Harmonizing between different sources of the Pentateuch, a late redactor makes an instruction by YHWH precede the report of Moses' death in 34:1–8. He does not refer to 3:26–7, where no sin of Moses is thought of, but rather adopts motifs from Num 20:1–13, 22–4; 27:12–14. Deut 10:6 represents a different tradition about Aaron's death.

(33:1–29) The Blessing of Moses It has been suggested that the framing verses in vv. 2–5 and vv. 26–9 (together with v. 21*b*) originally formed an independent psalm from the earliest period of Israel's history (Seeligmann 1964; Jeremias 1987: 82–92). However, the text and its numerous mythological allusions pose many virtually unanswerable philological and traditio-historical questions. It opens with a hymnic description of a theophany of YHWH, surrounded by celestial beings (vv. 2–3, cf. Steiner 1996; Müller 1992: 30) and ends with praise of the incomparability of Israel's God (vv. 26–9). If v. 5*a* has YHWH as subject and is more original than v. 4, the poem may originally have celebrated the kingship of YHWH in 'Jeshurun' (see DEUT 32:15, and cf. e.g. Ps 93). Parallels to consider would have to include Judg 5:4–5 and Hab 3:3–6, also 1 Kings 8:23, 56 and Num 23:9.

(33:6–25) The Blessings On the individual tribes see *ABD*. Here, as in Gen 49, the tribes are mostly characterized by metaphors. In general, the sayings date from before the Assyrian expansion to the west in the eighth century BCE. The order of the tribes does not follow an established system like e.g. that of Jacob's sons according to Gen 29:31–30:24; 35:16–20. v. 6, Reuben, a tribe mostly paired with Gad in the land east of the Jordan, is seen as nearing extinction. v. 7, the saying about Judah is a blessing for success in a military campaign. The expression 'bring him to his people' has often been interpreted as commenting on the division of Solomon's reign (1 Kings 12) from a northern Israelite perspective. However, it refers rather to a return from battle. vv. 8–11, Levi is a tribe which does not have its own territory (10:8–9; 18:1). It is characterized as a priestly tribe by the Urim and Thummim, technical means for giving oracles, cf. Ex 28:30. The reference to a trial of Levi at 'Massah' and 'Meribah' gives a surprising interpretation of the story of Ex 17:1–7 (cf. Deut 6:16); Num 20:1–13, which may allude to Ex 32:25–9. An addition in vv. 9*b*–10 makes the Levites the true teachers of the Torah, cf. 31:9. vv. 12–17, Benjamin, Ephraim, and Manasseh are tribes in the hill country north of Jerusalem. vv. 18–19, the saying about Zebulun and Issachar may refer to a former border sanctuary. vv. 20–1, Gad has its territory east of the Jordan. It is also mentioned there as a tribe in the Mesha stone of the ninth century BCE (see *ANET* 320–1). vv. 23–5, Dan, Naphtali, and Asher are tribes in the north of Israel's territory.

(34:1–12) Moses' Death and Praise of Moses The scene resumes the command in 3:27. The exact location of 'the top of Pisgah' (cf. Num 23:14) is unknown and its identification with Mount Nebo conflates two different traditions (cf. 32:48–52). v. 6 is based on 3:29; however, the important point is that no

veneration for the site of Moses' burial may arise as it is said to be unknown. Moses' survey of the land from Gilead in the north-east to the Negeb in the south-west is reminiscent of Gen 13:14–15, and YHWH thus confirms his promise to Israel's ancestors (v. 4, cf. 1:8; 30:20). v. 5, like 29:1 (MT 28:69), refers back to the concept of 1:5: the era of Moses, who delivered the Torah to Israel, comes to a close in the land east of the Jordan. v. 7, Moses died at the highest age that, according to Gen 6:3, a human being could possibly reach; see, however, Num 33:39 and cf. Josh 24:29. v. 10, in a paradoxical way, stresses the primary importance which prophecy has for the Deuteronomistic school. On the one hand the verse classifies Moses as a prophet, on the other, it underlines his incomparable status (contrast 18:18) and thus subordinates all later prophets to the Torah; see Blenkinsopp 1977: 80–95. The expression 'face to face' may refer to the scene at Horeb as represented by 5:5, 31; the motif has been elaborated further in Ex 33:8–11, cf. also Num 12:1–8. v. 9 again addresses the problem of succession and continuity after Moses' death and portrays Joshua according to an ideal of wisdom. vv. 9–10 thus relate the Torah, prophecy, and wisdom to each other. vv. 1*a*, 7–9 are often considered fragments of the Priestly Document, see, however, Perlitt (1988). Finally, vv. 11–12 follow the same tendency of magnifying the miraculous which can be observed in 6:22. The verses stimulate the poetic imagination of the readers with a reference to the miracles that Moses wrought in Egypt and thus emphasize God's intervention when Israel's history started with the Exodus.

REFERENCES

Alt, A. (1953), 'Die Heimat des Deuteronomiums', in id., *Kleine Schriften zur Geschichte des Volkes Israel* (Munich: Beck), ii. 250–75.

Alter, R. (1990), *The Art of Biblical Poetry* (Edinburgh: T. & T. Clark); first pub. 1985.

Aurelius, E. (1988), *Der Fürbitter Israels: Eine Studie zum Mosebild des Alten Testaments*, ConBOT 27 (Stockholm: Almqvist & Wiksell).

Barr, J. (1993), *Biblical Faith and Natural Theology* (Oxford: Clarendon).

Barton, J. (1986), *Oracles of God: Perceptions of Ancient Prophecy in Israel after the Exile* (London: Darton, Longman & Todd).

Begg, C. T. (1980), 'The Literary Criticism of Deut 4, 1–40', EThL 56: 10–55.

Blenkinsopp, J. (1977), *Prophecy and Canon* (Notre Dame, Ind.: University of Notre Dame Press).

Braulik, G. (1970), 'Die Freude des Festes: Das Kultverständnis des Deuteronomium—die älteste biblische Festtheorie', (1988) in id., *Studien zur Theologie des Deuteronomiums*, SBAB 2 (Stuttgart: Katholisches Bibelwerk; ET in id., *The Theology of Deuteronomy* (N. Richland Hills, Tx.: BIBAL Press, 1994), 27–65.

Cholewiński, A. (1976), *Heiligkeitsgesetz und Deuteronomium*, AnBib 66 (Rome: Biblical Institute).

Christensen, D. L. (1993) (ed.), *A Song of Power and the Power of Song*, Sources for Biblical and Theological Studies, 3 (Winona Lake, Ind.: Eisenbrauns).

Clements, R. E. (1996), 'The Deuteronomic Law of Centralization and the Catastrophe of 587 B.C.', in J. Barton and D. J. Reimer (eds.), *After the Exile* (Macon, Ga.: Mercer University Press), 5–25.

Cross, F. M. (1973), 'The Themes of the Book of Kings and the Structure of the Deuteronomistic History', in id., *Canaanite Myth and Hebrew Epic* (Cambridge, Mass.: Harvard University Press), 274–89.

Crüsemann, F. (1996), *The Torah: Theology and Social History of Old Testament Law* (Edinburgh: T. & T. Clark); first pub. in German 1992.

Davies, E. W. (1986), 'The Meaning of pî šĕnayim in Deuteronomy XXI 17', *VT* 36: 341–7.

Davies, P. R. (1992), *In Search of 'Ancient Israel'*, JSOTSup 148 (Sheffield: JSOT).

Dion, P. E. (1991) 'Deuteronomy 13: The Suppression of Alien Religious Propaganda in Israel during the Late Monarchical Era', in B. Halpern and D. W. Hobson (eds.), *Law and Ideology in Monarchic Israel*, JSOTSup 124 (Sheffield: JSOT), 147–216.

Donner, H. (1985), 'Jesaja LVI 1–7: Ein Abrogationsfall innerhalb des Kanons—Implikationen und Konsequenzen', *VTSup* 36: 81–95.

Douglas, M. (1966), *Purity and Danger: An Analysis of Concepts of Pollution and Taboo* (London: Routledge & Kegan Paul).

Driver, S. R. (1895), *Deuteronomy*, ICC; 3rd edn. 1901; repr. (Edinburgh: T. & T. Clark).

Fishbane, M. (1985), *Biblical Interpretation in Ancient Israel* (Oxford: Clarendon).

Foresti, F. (1984), *The Rejection of Saul in the Perspective of the Deuteronomistic School* (Rome: Edizioni del Teresianum).

Frevel, C. (1995), *Aschera und der Ausschließlichkeitsanspruch YHWHs*, BBB 94 (2 vols.; Weinheim: Beltz Athenäum).

García López, F. (1978), 'Deut. VI et la tradition-rédaction du Deutéronome', *RB* 85: 161–200.

Gertz, J. (1996), 'Die Passa-Massot-Ordnung im deuteronomischen Festkalender', in T. Veijola (ed.), *Das Deuteronomium und seine Querbeziehungen* (Göttingen: Vandenhoeck & Ruprecht), 56–80.

Gibson, J. C. L. (1978), *Canaanite Myths and Legends* (Edinburgh: T. & T. Clark).

Halpern, B. (1991), 'Jerusalem and the Lineages in the Seventh Century BCE: Kinship and the Rise of Individual Moral Liability', in B. Halpern and D. W. Hobson (eds.), *Law and Ideology in Monarchic Israel*, JSOTSup 124 (Sheffield: JSOT), 11–107.

Hossfeld, F.-L. (1982), *Der Dekalog*, OBO 45 (Göttingen: Vandenhoeck & Ruprecht).

Janzen, J. G. (1994), 'The "Wandering Aramean" Reconsidered', *VT* 44: 359–75.

Jeremias, J. (1987), *Das Königtum Gottes in den Psalmen*, FRLANT 141 (Göttingen: Vandenhoeck & Ruprecht).

Keel, O. (1981), 'Zeichen der Verbundenheit: Zur Vorgeschichte und Bedeutung der Forderungen von Dt 6,8f. und par.', in P. Casetti, O. Keel and A. Schenker (eds.), *Mélanges Dominique Barthélemy*, OBO 38 (Göttingen: Vandenhoeck & Ruprecht), 160–240.

Keel, O., and Uehlinger, C. (1998), *Gods, Goddesses, and Images of God in Ancient Israel* (Edinburgh: T. & T. Clark); first pub. in German 1992.

Lambert, W. G. (1960), *Babylonian Wisdom Literature* (Oxford: Clarendon).

Levinson, B. M. (1997), *Deuteronomy and the Hermeneutics of Legal Innovation* (Oxford: Oxford University Press).

Lipiński, E. (1998), 'naḥal', in TDOT 9 (Grand Rapids, Mich.: Eerdmans), 319–35.

Lohfink, N. (1993), *Das Hauptgebot: Eine Untersuchung literarischer Einleitungsfragen zu Dtn 5–11*, AnBib 20 (Rome: Pontificium Institutum Biblicum).

—— (1971a), 'Die Sicherung der Wirksamkeit des Gotteswortes durch das Prinzip der Gewaltenteilung nach den Ämtergesetzen des Buches Deuteronomium (Dt 16,18–18,22)', in id., *Studien zum Deuteronomium und zur deuteronomistischen Literatur*, SBAB 8 (Stuttgart: Katholisches Bibelwerk, 1990), i. 305–23; ET in Christensen (1993), 336–52.

—— (1971b), 'Zum "kleinen geschichtlichen Credo" Dtn 26,5–9', in id., *Studien zum Deuteronomium und zur deuteronomistischen Literatur* (as above), i. 263–90.

—— (1985), 'Zur neueren Diskussion über 2Kön 22–23', in id. (ed.), *Das Deuteronomium: Entstehung, Gestalt und Botschaft*, BETL 68 (Leuven: Leuven University Press), 24–48; ET in Christensen (1993), 36–61.

Maag, V. (1956), 'Erwägungen zur deuteronomischen Kultzentralisation', in id., *Kultur, Kulturkontakt und Religion* (Göttingen: Vandenhoeck & Ruprecht, 1980), 90–8.

McCarthy, D. J. (1978), *Treaty and Covenant: A Study in Form in the Ancient Oriental Documents and in the Old Testament*, rev. edn., AnBib 21A (Rome: Biblical Institute Press); first pub. 1963.

McKay, J. W. (1973), *Religion in Judah under the Assyrians*, SBT 26 (London: SCM).

McKenzie, S. L. et al. (eds.) (1994), *The History of Israel's Traditions: The Heritage of Martin Noth*, JSOTSup 182 (Sheffield: Sheffield Academic Press).

Margulis, B. (1970), 'A Ugaritic Psalm (RS 24.252)', *JBL* 89: 292–304.

Mayes, A. D. H. (1979), *Deuteronomy*, NCB (Grand Rapids, Mich.: Eerdmans); repr. 1991.

Mettinger, T. N. D. (1982), *The Dethronement of Sabaoth*, ConBOT 18 (Lund: Gleerup).

Miller, P. D. (1990), *Deuteronomy*, Interpretation (Louisville, Ky.: John Knox).

Morrow, W. S. (1995), *Scribing the Center*, SBLMS 49 (Atlanta, Ga.: Scholars Press).

Mowinckel, S. (1962), *The Psalms in Israel's Worship* (2 vols.; Oxford: Blackwell).

Müller, H.-P. (1997), 'molæk', in TDOT 8 (Grand Rapids, Mich.: Eerdmans), 375–88.

—— (1992), 'Kolloquialsprache und Volksreligion in den Inschriften von Kuntillet 'Ajrud und Ḥirbet el-Qōm', *Zeitschrift für Althebraistik*, 5: 15–51.

Nicholson, E. W. (1986), *God and His People: Covenant and Theology in the Old Testament* (Oxford: Clarendon).

Nielsen, E. (1995), *Deuteronomium*, HAT 1/6 (Tübingen: Mohr[Siebeck]).

Noth, M. (1991), *The Deuteronomistic History*, JSOTSup 15, 2nd ed. (Sheffield: Sheffield Academic Press); first pub. in German 1943.

Otto, E. (1993), 'Das Eherecht im Mittelassyrischen Kodex und im Deuteronomium', in id., *Kontinuum und Proprium*, Orientalia Biblica et Christiana, 8 (Wiesbaden: Harrassowitz, 1996), 172–91.

—— (1996a), 'The Pre-exilic Deuteronomy as a Revision of the Covenant Code', in id., *Kontinuum und Proprium* (as above), 112–22.

—— (1996b), 'Treueid und Gesetz', *Zeitschrift für Altorientalische und Biblische Rechtsgeschichte*, 2: 1–52.

Parpola, S., and Watanabe, K. (1988), *Neo-Assyrian Treaties and Loyalty Oaths*, SAA 2 (Helsinki: Helsinki University Press).

Peels, H. G. L. (1995), *The Vengeance of God*, OTS 31 (Leiden: Brill).

Perlitt, L. (1988), 'Priesterschrift im Deuteronomium?', in id., *Deuteronomium-Studien* (Tübingen: Mohr[Siebeck], 1994), 123–43.

Polzin, R. (1993), *Moses and the Deuteronomist* (Bloomington, Ind.: Indiana University Press); first pub. 1980.

Rad, G. von (1966), 'The Problem of the Hexateuch', in id., *The Problem of the Hexateuch and other Essays* (Edinburgh and London: Oliver & Boyd), 1–78; first pub. in German 1938.

Reimer, D. (1990), 'Concerning Return to Egypt: Deuteronomy XVII 16 and XXVIII 68 Reconsidered', in J. A. Emerton (ed.), *Studies in the Pentateuch*, VTSup 41 (Leiden: Brill), 217–29.

Reiner, E. (1958), *Šurpu: A Collection of Sumerian and Akkadian Incantations*, AfO 11 (Graz: Selbstverlag des Herausgebers (Ernst Weidner)).

Reuter, E. (1993), *Kultzentralisation*, BBB 87 (Frankfurt am Main: Anton Hain).

Richter, W. (1967), 'Beobachtungen zur theologischen Systembildung in der alttestamentlichen Literatur anhand des "kleinen geschichtlichen Credo"', in L. Scheffczyk et al. (eds.), *Wahrheit und Verkündigung* (Paderborn: Ferdinand Schöningh), i. 176–212.

Rofé, A. (1985a), 'The Covenant in the Land of Moab (Deuteronomy 28:69–30:20)', in Lohfink (ed.), *Das Deuteronomium* (1985), 310–20; repr. in Christensen (1993), 269–80.

—— (1985b), 'The Laws of Warfare in the Book of Deuteronomy', *JSOT* 32: 23–44.

—— (1987), 'Family and Sex Laws in Deuteronomy and the Book of Covenant', *Henoch*, 9: 131–59.

—— (2000), 'The End of the Song of Moses (Deuteronomy 32:43)', in R. G. Kratz et al. (eds.), *Liebe und Gebot*, FRLANT 190 (Göttingen: Vandenhoeck & Ruprecht), 164–72.

Rogerson, J. W. (1992), *W. M. L. de Wette: Founder of Modern Biblical Criticism*, JSOTSup 126 (Sheffield: JSOT).

Sanders, P. (1996), *The Provenance of Deuteronomy 32*, OTS 37 (Leiden: Brill).

Schmidt, W. H. (1993), *Die Zehn Gebote im Rahmen Alttestamentlicher Ethik*, ErFor 281 (Darmstadt: Wissenschaftliche Buchgesellschaft).

Seeligmann, I. L. (1964), 'A Psalm from Pre-Regal Times', *VT* 14: 75–92.

Seitz, G. (1971), *Redaktionsgeschichtliche Studien zum Deuteronomium*, BWANT 93 (Stuttgart: Kohlhammer).

Smend, R. (1963), 'Die Bundesformel', in id., *Die Mitte des Alten Testaments*, BEvT 99 (Munich: Kaiser, 1986), 11–39.

—— (1971), 'Das Gesetz und die Völker', in id., *Die Mitte des Alten Testaments* (as above), 124–37.

—— (1983), 'Das uneroberte Land', in id., *Zur ältesten Geschichte Israels*, BEvT 100 (Munich: Kaiser, 1987), 217–28.

Smith, M. (1987), *Palestinian Parties and Politics that Shaped the Old Testament* (London: SCM); first pub. 1971.

Smith, W. Robertson (1892), *The Old Testament in the Jewish Church*, 2nd edn. (London: A. & C. Black).

Spieckermann, H. (1982), *Juda unter Assur in der Sargonidenzeit*, FRLANT 129 (Göttingen: Vandenhoeck & Ruprecht).

Steiner, R. C. (1996), '"dat" and "'en"', *JBL* 115: 693–8.

Steymans, H. U. (1995), *Deuteronomium 28 und die 'adê' zur Thronfolgeregelung Asarhaddons*, OBO 145 (Göttingen: Vandenhoeck & Ruprecht).

Tigay, J. H. (1996), *Deuteronomy*, JPS Torah Commentary (Jerusalem: Jewish Publication Society).

Uehlinger, C. (1995), 'Gab es eine joschijanische Kultreform?', in W. Groß (ed.), *Jeremia und die 'deuteronomistische Bewegung'*, BBB 98 (Weinheim: Beltz Athenäum), 57–89.

Van Seters, J. (1996), 'Cultic Laws in the Covenant Code (Exodus 20:22–23:33) and their Relationship to Deuteronomy and the Holiness Code', in M. Vervenne (ed.), *Studies in the Book of Exodus*, BETL 126 (Leuven: Leuven University Press), 319–45.

Veijola, T. (1992a), 'Das Bekenntnis Israels: Beobachtungen zur Geschichte und Theologie von Dtn 6, 4–9', *TZ* 48: 369–81.

—— (1992b), 'Höre Israel! Der Sinn und Hintergrund von Deuteronomium VI 4–9', *VT* 42: 528–41.

—— (1995a), '"Der Mensch lebt nicht vom Brot allein": Zur literarischen Schichtung und theologischen Aussage von Deuteronomium 8', in G. Braulik (ed.), *Bundesdokument und Gesetz: Studien zum Deuteronomium*, Herders Biblische Studien, 4 (Freiburg: Herder), 143–58.

—— (1995b), 'Wahrheit und Intoleranz nach Deuteronomium 13', *ZTK* 92: 287–314.

—— (1996a), 'Bundestheologische Redaktion im Deuteronomium', in id. (ed.), *Das Deuteronomium und seine Querbeziehungen* (Göttingen: Vandenhoeck & Ruprecht), 242–76.

—— (1996b), 'The History of the Passover in the Light of Dtn 16, 1–8', *ZAR* 2: 53–75.

—— (forthcoming), *Deuteronomium*, ATD (Göttingen: Vandenhoeck & Ruprecht).

Weinfeld, M. (1991), *Deuteronomy 1–11*, AB 5 (New York: Doubleday).

—— (1992), *Deuteronomy and the Deuteronomic School* (Winona Lake, Ind.: Eisenbrauns); first pub. 1972.

Wevers, J. W. (1995), *Notes on the Greek Text of Deuteronomy*, Septuagint and Cognate Studies Series, 39 (Atlanta, Ga.: Scholars Press).

Wiggins, S. A. (1993), *A Reassessment of 'Asherah'*, AOAT 235 (Kevelaer: Butzon & Bercker).

Würthwein, E. (1984), *Die Bücher der Könige*, ATD 11–2 (Göttingen: Vandenhoeck & Ruprecht).

9. Joshua

GORDON MCCONVILLE

INTRODUCTION

A. Text and Language. The text on which the commentary is based is the Masoretic Text (MT) in the edition Biblia Hebraica Stuttgartensia. It is well preserved and probably represents the oldest text form. The Greek version (LXX) of Joshua differs in numerous details from MT. While the differences are frequently attributable to the theological interpretation by the translators, LXX sometimes witnesses to better readings than MT. However, it does not represent an older or better text form. Fragments of Joshua have been recovered from Qumran Cave 4, and may testify to an independent text form.

B. Subject Matter and Literary Genre. 1. Joshua stands at a mid-point in the narrative of Israel's origins that spans Genesis–Kings. It continues the basic story-line of Exodus–Numbers, with its elements of promise of land (Ex 3:8); spying it out and first failing (Num 13–14); conquest of Transjordan (Num 21); the theme of guidance and the ark (Num 10:33–6); Moses and Joshua, his second-in-command (Ex 17:8–13); Joshua and Caleb, the faithful spies (Num 14:6–10); Joshua and Eleazar to divide the land (Num 34:17); cities of refuge, and cities for the Levites (Num 35). The correspondence of Joshua with the expectations created by Numbers has led to

the idea of a 'Hexateuch' (Genesis–Joshua), where Joshua is the culmination of the story of promise that begins in Genesis (12:1–3; Tengström 1976).

2. Yet Joshua also points forward. In its themes of Torah- and covenant-keeping, it looks to Israel's ongoing life in the land. Its reflections on the role of the leader, where Joshua inherits the responsibilities of Moses, also point forward to a crucial issue in Judges–Kings. Its covenant-renewal ceremonies at Shechem (8:30–5; 24:1–28) have solemn exhortations to faithfulness, and there are other important notes of warning. Joshua thus heralds both the possession of land and the possibility of exile. In these respects it has significant links with Deuteronomy, and also with Judges–Kings.

3. The book falls into four sections: entry to the land (1:1–5:12); its conquest (5:13–12:24); dividing it among the tribes (13:1–21:45), and serving YHWH in it (22:1–24:33). The narrative of conquest is at the centre of this. The other parts belong intimately to that concept, however (see c below).

4. The genre of Joshua may be seen as a conquest narrative, similar in many respects to ancient Near-Eastern conquest accounts, as perpetrated by kings who claimed a religious mandate for their campaigns (Younger 1990). Joshua is the account of YHWH's war-campaign in Palestine, providing Israel's entitlement to the land.

C. The Religious Teaching. 1. Joshua plays its part in the OT's insistence on the worship of YHWH alone, as taught supremely by Deuteronomy. It also takes forward that book's theology of a single people of YHWH, worshipping him in the land he has given them, and subject to their covenant with him. Joshua makes its own contribution to the notion of a unified people, recognizing the particularity of the tribes and their lands, yet insisting on their oneness both in the responsibility for the conquest (Josh 1:12–15) and in their loyalty to the single sanctuary (Josh 22). Deuteronomy's requirement of a single place of worship is met here above all in Shiloh (Josh 18; cf. Deut 12:1–5).

2. Closely connected with worship and land is the Holy War theology, of which Joshua is the OT's classic example. Put in place in several Pentateuchal texts (Ex 14; Num 22–4; Deut 2–3), it is here embodied in Israel's foundational narrative of land possession. The various victories manifest the central concept of the Holy War, namely the *ḥērem*, or sentence of total destruction on the enemy population. This sentence of destruction on a population, civilian and non-aggressor, and expressly commanded by YHWH, presents the greatest moral difficulty in the book for modern readers.

3. In its own context, the *ḥērem* has an intelligible theology, involving YHWH's sovereignty over all nations, his ownership of the land, his right to grant it to whomever he wishes, his agency in the military victory, his judgement on the sin of the victims, and the need to remove from Israel any risk of religious contamination. (There is further comment along these lines in JOSH 5:13–6:27). This theology is idealized in our accounts, however. The actual Israelite entry to the land was not swift and tidy, as even a careful reading of Joshua itself makes clear. The contrast between the real and the ideal may be illustrated by a text in Deuteronomy (Deut 7:2–3), in which an uncompromising requirement is followed immediately by one that implies that Israelites and Canaanites do and will live alongside each other in Canaan. Of course, even the idea that these commands and accounts are an idealization may only compound the modern reader's problem, rather than alleviate it! It *may* help, however, to recall that Joshua is a conventional conquest-narrative (as we noticed above). In Old Testament times, kings went to war and wrote up their victories, attributing their success to their gods. Joshua is YHWH's victory account, an indispensable part of the narrative of the demonstration of his ownership of the land, and not necessarily realistic. Understood in that way, it may be seen as belonging to its time, and as superseded by other biblical perspectives on God (OT and NT), which present him as seeking the salvation of the whole world. Yet the ideas of divine gift, dependence on God, and even judgement, find echoes in the NT.

4. The book of Joshua's theology of land has another unique feature (within Joshua–Kings) in the close connection it makes between the Exodus from Egypt and the conquest of Canaan. This is expressed especially in Josh 3–4, where the crossing of the Jordan deliberately evokes the older crossing of the Reed Sea (Ex 14). The whole drama from deliverance from slavery in Egypt to possession of land in Canaan is thus unified here.

5. These twin elements, Exodus and possession, give to Joshua its essential dynamic. The possession is always in the shadow of the first deliverance. To these is added the call to serve YHWH and obey his word, with severe warnings against compromise and failure to keep covenant. When interpretation of Joshua understands and maintains this tripod—liberation, possession, service—it can avoid the characteristic danger of the book, namely an appropriation of the divine authority given to Joshua for self-devised ends in modern conflicts.

D. Joshua and History. The classic view of Joshua is that it narrates the 'conquest' of Canaan by the Israelites. Where this is accepted as a broadly historical picture, the event is normally dated to the thirteenth century BCE. Early excavators of Jericho thought they had discovered evidence that verified the story of its capture by Joshua, but subsequent investigations have produced at best a mixed picture (contrast Jericho and Hazor below; 5:13–6:27 and 11:1–23). In modern scholarship, a form of the 'conquest' model is favoured principally by the so-called Albright school, who think that the destruction patterns at a number of sites is best explained by an Israelite invasion about the time of Joshua (Bright 1981). Others have suggested a gradual process of peaceful settlement (Noth 1960), or the emergence of 'Israel' within the population of Canaan (Gottwald 1979). Some even question whether Israel as a separate entity can be discerned at all in the Late Bronze–Early Iron Age archaeological levels (Thompson 1992; Whitelam 1996). The issues in this kind of study are complex, and there are no unambiguous data. The view taken in the present commentary is that the the book preserves real memories of Israel's early days in Canaan. The principal general reason is the prominence in the narrative of places that play little part in the periods of the late monarchy, the Exile, and after (Gilgal, Shechem, Shiloh). Furthermore, a close reading of Joshua itself shows that it is not offering a simple conquest model, but rather a mixed picture of success and failure, sudden victory and slow, compromising progress.

E. Date and Place of Composition. 1. Theories of the composition of Joshua are closely connected with those concerning the history of Israel. Scholars who are sceptical about the historical picture given in the book suppose a late (exilic or after), theologically contrived composition, with few ancient sources if any. Others have postulated ancient sources behind the present form of the book, as a means of connecting it to the events that it purports to relate. Formerly, such sources were sought in the four documents of Pentateuchal source-analysis. The prevailing view in modern scholarship thinks rather in terms of a variety of sources available to a Deuteronomic, or Deuteronomistic, author or authors, who composed the whole history from Joshua to Kings, prefaced by Deuteronomy, in the time of Josiah, or the Exile, or both (Noth 1981; Cross 1973).

2. The Deuteronomic theory has always encountered problems in Joshua. This is because of its strong continuities with story-lines in Exodus–Numbers (as noted in B above). Furthermore, commentators have often felt unable to attribute large parts of the book to the Deuteronomist(s), and find various degrees of Priestly reworking, for example, in the strong Priestly elements in Josh 3–4. There are signs of a modern

trend towards a different view of the composition of the historical books, that postulates the various books' independent growth and editing (Westermann 1993). The present commentary takes such a view. It allows for the preservation of ancient material within a 'Joshua' tradition that maintains its special themes and concerns. This explains, for example, the prominence of the ark of the covenant and the centrality of Shiloh, topics which, incidentally, put the book closer to 1 Samuel than to other historical books. It also enables Joshua to be read on its own terms, and not principally typologically, as sometimes happens in the Deuteronomic theory, where Joshua himself becomes a kind of cipher for Josiah. The mediators of the Joshua tradition may well have been the priests at Shiloh. The book of Joshua, in its present form, however, has been carefully shaped theologically. The narrative of the taking of Jericho, for example, is a stylized liturgical composition (see on Josh 5:13–6:27).

3. It is impossible, in my view, to trace the growth of the book into its present shape in any detail. For example, a key Deuteronomic text such as Josh 24 is capable of widely varying dates, and language that can be thought Deuteronomic may be much earlier (Koopmans 1990). However, the book was utimately edited together with the other historical books (Judges–Kings) to form a continuous narrative from the occupation of the land to the Exile. The perception of the unity of the whole story may be seen in the tacit designation of Shiloh as the 'chosen place' (Josh 9:27), in terms recalling Deut 12:5, and pointing forward to the identification of this 'place' with Jerusalem in 1 Kings 8:29; 2 Kings 21:4. This final stage of the composition probably took place during the Exile in Babylon.

F. Outline

COMMENTARY

The Entry to the Land (1:1–5:12)

(1:1–9) Commissioning of Joshua The overture to the book of Joshua forms a transition from the narratives of the wilderness wanderings of Israel into that of the settlement in Canaan. The underlying theology is the ancient promise that YHWH would give his people a land (vv. 3–4; cf. Gen 15:17–21; Ex 3:17; Deut 1:7–8). The commissioning of Joshua in succession to Moses is at the centre of this transitional narrative, and the reference to the latter's death makes an express link with the closing words of Deuteronomy.

The life of Moses had spanned Israel's Exodus from Egypt and its time in the wilderness. He was not to enter the promised land; rather, Joshua would do that. The tradition of a relationship between Moses and Joshua is found in Ex 17:8–16; Num 27:12–23, and pursued in Deuteronomy (1:37–8; 3:21–8; 31:1–23; 34:9). Now the first command to Joshua is to cross the Jordan (v. 2), in order to enable the people to possess their land (v. 6).

If Joshua is second to Moses (he is Moses' 'assistant', v. 1), his present commissioning virtually puts him in Moses' place. The phrase 'servant of YHWH', marking both relationship and responsibility, is elsewhere used of Moses (v. 1; cf. Ex 14:31; Deut 34:5), and of King David (2 Sam 7:5). The present passage (vv. 6–9) strongly suggests a transfer of the privileges and role of Moses to Joshua, perhaps in a special ceremony (Lohfink 1962). The elements in this transfer are (1) the encouragement of Joshua (vv. 6, 7, 9); (2) the giving of a task, namely putting the people in possession of the land (v. 6), implying the distribution of its parts to the tribes, the subject of Josh 13–19, and (3) the assurance of God's presence with him (v. 9). The theory of a ceremony should not be pressed to argue that Joshua is thus a 'royal' figure (by analogy with the passing of an office from David to Solomon, Gerbrandt 1986). But the three elements identified do characterize the role of Joshua as it emerges here.

Joshua's special position appears in the fact that YHWH addresses him several times in the singular in this passage. The promise that he will be with him is peculiarly his (v. 9). But Joshua is also to place himself under the authority of the word of God already given to Moses (v. 7). The terms of the responsibility recall the law of the king (Deut 17:14–20), but are valid for all who would lead in Israel, thus marking out such leadership from all other, in the sense that it is received and held only by way of God's gift, not by personal power (McCarthy 1971).

(1:10–18) The Transjordanian Tribes Joshua's first command emphasizes the military nature of the coming campaign, and follows Deuteronomy in thought and language (Deut 11:31). 'Officers' over the people are presupposed in Ex 5:10–19, and there are narratives of commissioning in Num 1:16, Deut 1:15. The latter makes them tribal officials. Their role here and in Deuteronomy is administrative; Numbers knows of a spiritual responsibility. The fine balance here between careful preparation and the recognition that the land is God's gift is a feature of Joshua.

If the crossing of the Jordan is the mark of land-occupation, a problem is posed by the settling of some Israelites east of the river (cf. Num 32; Deut 3:12–21). The topic is returned to in Josh 22, thus virtually framing the book. Common to these narratives is the requirement that the tribes of Reuben, Gad, and the half-tribe of Manasseh should participate in the conquest of the land of Canaan, thus expressing their belonging in Israel, before settling finally in their own land. The region does not seem to be formally part of the promised land (Num 32 distinguishes it from the land of Canaan, vv. 29–30; for Deuteronomy, however, the war of conquest begins there).

The key theological idea here is 'rest' (vv. 12, 15; cf. Deut 12:9). Rest is a goal of the occupation narratives, entailing the complete possession of the land and the subduing of enemies (Josh 11:23). Its definitive enjoyment, however, is elusive (cf. again 2 Sam 7:1). Finally, the response of Israel is important here (vv. 16–18; see Barth 1971). Specifically, it could be either the officers accepting the command of v. 11, or the Transjordanian tribes agreeing the terms of vv. 13–15. More important is the pattern of command and response, essential to covenantal arrangements (cf. Ex 19:8; 24:3, 7), and the words are as from Israel as a whole. Israel shows its willingness to submit to Joshua as successor of Moses, and thus to YHWH and his word.

(2:1–24) Rahab and the Spies The mission of the spies recalls the first such mission, which had resulted in failure to take the promised inheritance because of fear (Num 13–14). The present enterprise focuses on Jericho. Some therefore see the story originally as an aetiological tale, explaining the continuing presence in Israel of a family or group associated with Rahab (Josh 6:25; Wagner 1964; cf. Long 1968). However, the reference to 'the land' alongside 'Jericho', v. 1, puts this story in the context of the larger narrative of conquest; there is also an echo of the first mission, recalling that such efforts can fail. The outcome this time is successful, however, in so far as the spies return to encourage the people (v. 24; contrast Num 13:31–3).

Yet this is an odd beginning to the conquest (vv. 1–3). Joshua has no command from God to send spies (contrast Num 13:1–3). The secrecy of the project (v. 1) seems inconsistent with a victorious march into the land, and in any case is not sustained (vv. 2–3). And the involvement of the Canaanite prostitute Rahab in Israel's advance seems to compromise its integrity.

The involvement of the 'king of Jericho' (v. 2) reminds us of the real issues at stake, namely Israel's challenge to the city-states of Canaan, the more profound because Israel's only king is YHWH. The king is well aware (as Balak, king of Moab, had been, Num 22:2–4) of the threat posed by Israel to the whole land (v. 3).

These great issues sit oddly with the setting of the action in a prostitute's bedroom. The next scene (vv. 4–7) has an element of farce, the secret police being easily dispatched in the wrong direction. The city-gate closes to keep enemies out, but they are already inside, and settling down for the night.

Rahab's words (vv. 8–11) borrow the language of Israel's confessions of faith. Her admission of the city's fear at Israel's progress corresponds to God's promise (cf. Ex 23:27; Num 22:3). And she sees the victories in Transjordan as evidence that they will carry the day in Canaan (Deut 3:21–2). The confession of YHWH's universal rule in heaven and on earth

(v. 11) has Deuteronomic overtones (Deut 4:39). This may be intelligible as a matter of strategy (cf. the Gibeonites' tactics, Josh 9). Yet the author may wish to show ironically the superior faith of the enemy in YHWH's power.

Rahab demands the life of herself and her family, borrowing a significant Hebrew term, ḥesed, 'deal kindly' (v. 12), denoting the loyalty expected in a covenant relationship (cf. 1 Sam 20:8). The spies agree, in spite of the Holy War theology which underlies their presence there (Deut 2:32–7; 7:1–5; 20:16–18). The men swear on their own lives that they will guarantee those of Rahab and family (vv. 14, 19), provided she does not 'tell this business of ours' (vv. 14, 20). It is hard to know what is left to tell that the Jericho authorities do not know! But the reader feels that the Israelites have somehow entrusted the success of their cause to a Canaanite. Polzin has rightly detected the irony of the whole episode, and its suggestion that Israel, already, has failed to adhere to the terms of the ḥērem (Polzin 1980).

In the event the present adventure would play no part in the entry to Canaan or the fall of the city—except perhaps to warn the inhabitants that it is coming (6:1)!—since YHWH's power is irresistible.

(3:1–5:1) Crossing the Jordan There now comes the account of the entry of the whole people to the land (3:1–5:12). This great culmination of promise makes express connections with the Exodus story. The crossing of the Jordan by a miraculous parting of the waters (Josh 3:16) recalls the crossing of the Reed Sea (Ex 14:21–2); the first Passover kept in the new land (Josh 5:10–12) corresponds to the first of all, in Egypt (Ex 12–13); the centrality of the ark here symbolizes the guidance of YHWH on the way to the land (Mann 1977), and prepares for the Holy War ahead (Num 10:33–6).

The narrative in 3:1–5:1 has resisted alignment with the traditional Pentateuchal sources. While a number of elements in it occur twice (e.g. the selection of men to carry the stones, 3:12; 4:2; the setting up of the stones, 4:8–9, 20) the central incident, the passage of the ark through the river, is told only once (4:11). It has been widely seen as an aetiological liturgical narrative from the sanctuary at Gilgal, near Jericho on the banks of the Jordan (possibly Khirbet-Mafjar). This was an important cultic centre in the monarchic period (1 Sam 11:14–15), and perhaps earlier. The festival would have celebrated the memory of exodus together with the triumphant entry to the land (Kraus 1951), perhaps in the context of the Feast of Unleavened Bread, or maṣṣôt (cf. 5:10–12; Otto 1975; otherwise Halbe 1975: 329–44). The crossing of the Jordan would have echoed that of the Reed Sea (cf. Ps 114:3, 5; Mic 6:4–5). This type of explanation may account better for the prominence of ark and priests in the narrative than the 'literary' solution of Noth and others (Noth 1953; Fritz 1994), which postulates 'post-Priestly' additions to a Deuteronomic narrative.

The account of the crossing is connected to that of the spies (ch. 2) by the further mention of Shittim (3:1). The first verse sets the theme when it brings Joshua, together with 'all the Israelites', to the verge of Jordan for the crossing (cf. v. 17). The tribal officials play their part, and the due timing is observed (vv. 2–3; cf. 1:10–11). The theme of the ark as a guide on the journey (v. 4a) is connected (as in Num 10:33–6) with that of

Holy War (v. 10), anticipating the sack of Jericho. The crossing respects the requirements of holiness, the ark being attended by the properly authorized personnel (vv. 3, 6; cf. Num 3:5–10, 31), and the people keeping due distance. In this respect the story recalls the encounter with YHWH at Sinai (cf. Ex 19:10–12).

Preparations for the crossing are now joined with a reaffirmation of Joshua's leadership, and of YHWH's special promise to accompany him (3:7; cf. 1:5). YHWH's fundamental promise to Israel (Ex 3:12) is thus applied to Joshua himself. The themes of his leadership, YHWH's law (words), his powerful presence and his promise to dispossess the enemy (cf. Ex 3:17) are all closely combined here (vv. 10–11). The phrase 'the LORD, the Lord of all the earth' (v. 13; cf. Mic 4:13; Ps 97:5) is a claim to absolute universal dominion, similar to claims made by other ancient Near-Eastern deities. Baal, for example, was known at Ugarit as *zbl b'l arṣ* ('the prince, lord of the earth'; see Fritz 1994: 51–2).

Following the scene-setting there is an initial, succinct report of the crossing (vv. 14–17), with only a note to make the point that it was truly miraculous, the river being in its spring flood (v. 15). This passage has a complex relationship with the following (ch. 4), both anticipating that fuller account of the crossing, and participating in it (only here is the entry into the water by the priests narrated).

There now follows (4:1–5:1) an extended account of the crossing, though it has been briefly narrated just before. Parallel and anticipatory accounts of events are known elsewhere in the OT (cf. 2 Kings 18:13–16; 18:17–19:37). v. 1, which refers to the crossing as if complete, yet introduces instructions about actions to be performed before or during it, may be intelligible as a link with ch. 3, and a kind of announcement that what follows tells how the crossing was accomplished. This intersection of temporal points of view, both here and at the conclusion of ch. 3, may be a function of the liturgical character of the text.

The twelve tribal representatives (3:12; 4:2) are now appointed to carry stones from the midst of the Jordan to the far side. The stones present a difficulty. Did Joshua set up twelve stones in the Jordan besides those which the people carried across, as suggested by NRSV's parenthesis (v. 9)? A better solution is to see v. 9a as explaining how it came about that twelve suitable stones were found in the middle of the Jordan (cf. v. 3). Thus v. 9b ('and they are there to this day') should fall outside the parenthesis, and be seen as a continuation of v. 8b (with Ehrlich 1968: 16).

The liturgical function of the actions performed is clear. That is, the narrative is not merely relating events, but also instituting an act of worship for all future generations (vv. 6–7, 21–2). In this it resembles the narrative of the first Passover (cf. Ex 12:24–7).

The importance of Joshua's performance of the commands given to Moses is now re-emphasized, together with his comparable standing in Israel (vv. 10–14). In heralding the accomplishment of the crossing this passage echoes the signal given of Joshua's importance at its beginning (3:7–8). The two passages mark out the key players in the whole action, namely Joshua (the bearer of God's commands), the priests (guardians of his holiness), and the people, constituted as an army (4:13). The numbers of warriors here are small by comparison with those given in the tribal lists in Num 1. In that place they may simply be exaggerated (see NUM 1). It is also possible that the word translated 'thousand' really means 'platoon' in such cases, and therefore implies smaller and indeterminate numbers.

Finally, the priests, who have been in the water with the ark during the crossing of the people and the ceremonies with the stones (4:10), emerge last from it, and when they do the river resumes its normal course (4:15–18).

The date of the people's emergence from the river is significant, the tenth day of the 'first month' being part of the Passover celebration, when the lamb was prepared for the feast (Ex 12:2–3). (On calendars in Israel and the date of the Passover see Clines 1976.) Thus, the crossing of the river is expressly connected with that of the Reed Sea. The two events frame the larger narrative of exodus and conquest, as archetypal acts of salvation. The stones taken from the river are set up in Gilgal (v. 20), and the link between exodus and entry is established.

Finally, in the perspective of the larger narrative, the purpose of the demonstration of God's power in this event is that all the peoples of the earth might know it. The narrative thus points towards the triumphs of YHWH that lie ahead. The effect of the Israelites' approach on the inhabitants of the land is devastating (5:1). Their designation 'Amorites' and 'Canaanites' follows Deut 1–3, e.g. Deut 1:7. That passage recorded how it was the Israelites whose hearts 'melted' (1:28), and how they then rashly took on the enemy unprepared (1:41–5). Now it is the turn of the Amorites; the misadventure of Moab is in the past, and the land trembles before the approach of Israel and YHWH.

(5:2–15) Circumcision and Passover Before the march of Jericho, three things occur. The first is a circumcision of Israel, designed to ensure that the nation is properly constituted ritually. Circumcision was widespread among ancient Semites. In Israel, however, it marked the convenantal relationship with God. Its institution is traced in the Old Testament back to Abraham, and is told in a text which states that no uncircumcised male can be regarded as an Israelite (Gen 17:9–14). The institution of the Passover reiterates the requirement, allowing resident aliens in Israel to be included on condition that they are circumcised (Ex 12:43–9).

The connection between circumcision and Passover is important; Israel must be ritually pure to celebrate its central memorial feast. That connection is re-established here, at a place not otherwise known, Gibeath-haaraloth, or 'the Hill of the Foreskins'. The name of the place is presumably connected aetiologically with the action. How it relates to Gilgal, which is also named as a result of this action (v. 9), is unclear. Perhaps there was a special site in the locality for the ceremony (Soggin 1972: 70).

According to MT, the circumcision was necessary because the wilderness generation had not been circumcised (vv. 4–7), though it is not clear why this was so. (Against MT, LXX adds that some Israelites who came out of Egypt had not been circumcised; but this is unlikely to be a better tradition.) God's decree banning the Sinai generation from seeing the land of Canaan is prominent here (vv. 4, 6; cf. Num 14:22–3; Deut 1:34–40). The point is that as that generation had been unfit to go into the land, this generation will be fit. The circumcision of adult males would therefore have been a necessary precaution. The term 'a second time' shows, however, that Joshua did not initiate the practice in Israel.

The first section of the passage ends with an aetiology of the name of Gilgal. In the phrase 'I have rolled away from you the disgrace of Egypt' the verb closely resembles the name Gilgal. The explanation is of a sort that is frequent in the OT, not a scientific etymology, but rather a paronomasia designed to bring out a connection between word and event (cf. the re-naming of Jacob 'Israel', Gen 32:27–8). Gilgal thus becomes a necessary stage, theologically speaking, in the progress to the land, the place where the people were made fit to possess their inheritance. The 'disgrace' of Egypt cannot refer to the mere fact of uncircumcision (though Gen 34:14 might suggest so), for the people were circumcised there (v. 5). The reference is probably to the social disgrace of servitude; the entry to the land will mean freedom, and a realization of who Israel properly is.

Gilgal then becomes the place of the first Passover held in the land (vv. 10–12)—the second event preparatory to taking possession. The allusion to Jericho (v. 10) has ominous overtones for the Canaanite population. While the correct date is given for the Passover, the cultic rituals are not spelt out in detail (there is no account of the Feast of Unleavened Bread that followed Passover for seven days, Lev 23:5–6; and the language, especially the combination 'unleavened cakes and parched grain', does not suggest the P source). Rather, the Passover is here associated with the ceasing of the manna (cf. Ex 16) and the eating of the produce of land. Yet the 'unleavened cakes' also recall the 'unleavened bread' which had been the food of hasty flight from Egypt (Ex 12:15–20; Deut 16:3). The eating of it now, along with 'parched grain', is consistent with a people not yet settled; nevertheless, they have already begun to enjoy what they themselves had not planted or laboured over—a sign of the beginning of legitimate possession (Deut 6:10–11). With circumcision and Passover, the cessation of manna and the bounty of the land, a full circle has been turned since the departure from Egypt.

The Taking of the Land (5:13–12:24)

(5:13–6:27) The Fall of Jericho Joshua's encounter with the 'commander of the army of the LORD' close to Jericho proclaims the beginning of the war of conquest. The figure seems to be the same as the 'angel (or messenger) of the LORD', who represents the presence of YHWH himself (cf. Judg 6:14; 13:20–2). The angel's function is sometimes military (Num 22:23; 2 Sam 24:16–17; 2 Kings 19:35); at other times there is a commissioning, as with Gideon (Judg 6:11–12). Both elements are present here. The closest echo of our passage is the appearance of the angel to Moses early in his ministry (Ex 3:2), also clearly a manifestation of God (Ex 3:4–6). The words of the 'commander' here recall God's words on that occasion (v. 5). Joshua evidently knows the angel's military role (v. 13), and also recognizes him as God when he worships him. The idea of Holy War was universal in the ancient Near East, where kings typically believed they were mandated by their gods to undertake campaigns of conquest (Younger 1990:

65–7; Kang 1989: 38–40). When armies went to war, it was a war of the god against the god(s) of the enemy.

Against this background, YHWH asserts that the battle against the Canaanites is his. (His unexpected 'No!', v. 14—not 'Neither', NRSV—presumably denies only that he is on the side of the enemies.) But the incident also serves to grant to Joshua a direct experience of God, like that of Moses, at the beginning of the real test of his leadership.

The story of the attack on Jericho raises a tricky historical question. Early excavators discovered a section of collapsed wall, which they thought was evidence for our narrative (Garstang 1931). Later work revealed, however, that the wall was earlier, from the Early Bronze Age (late third millennium; Kenyon 1979). The town was briefly reoccupied in the Middle Bronze Age. Thereafter the evidence for settlement is slight, apparently because of erosion of the mud-brick defences. There is, therefore, no clear evidence of the Israelite attack (mid-thirteenth century).

The commissioning scene (5:13–15) passes directly to the attack. There is a pregnant pause (v. 1), which recalls the fear in the city (2:24). The note that the city was 'shut up inside and out' presents a challenge, though it may also recall ironically the easy entry and egress achieved by the spies, and that even now there is a fifth column within.

The preparations for the attack (vv. 2–7) continue the religious note struck in the crossing of the Jordan. The armed men precede the priests, who blow trumpets as they in turn precede the ark. The ark itself symbolizes Israel's Holy War (cf. 1 Sam 4:1–3), and is therefore likely to be original to the narrative (against Noth 1953: 41–2; Fritz 1994: 75–6, who assign ark and priests to secondary Deuteronomistic additions). A 'rearguard' (v. 13), not otherwise specified, completes the procession that marches round the city. The marching round the city is not a military manoeuvre in the proper sense, though one of the verbs used is reminiscent of the encircling of a city in a siege (Soggin 1972: 86–7). The encirclement actually reported is stylized; the procession of priests and ark, the blowing of trumpets, and finally the great shout of all the people (v. 5), show that the whole procedure is an act of religious obedience and devotion. The lack of military realism, despite the involvement of the 'men of war', stresses that in this primary account of Israel's Holy War the victory is YHWH's. The language of v. 2 ('I have given into your hand Jericho, with its king and mighty men of valour') is reminiscent of Deuteronomy's theology of the gift of the land (and of ancient Near-Eastern Holy War language; Kang 1989: 130–2). Early victories in the Holy War were recorded there with the triumphs in Transjordan (Deut 2:26–3:11, esp. 2:31). Yet there is a new significance and solemnity about the taking of Jericho, as a 'first fruits' of the conquest of the land proper.

The repetitiveness of the account of the action itself (vv. 8–21) may be liturgical; the taking of Jericho could have been rehearsed on great religious occasions. Equally, it may simply be a feature of ancient narrative's manner of building towards a climax. The prominence of the number seven is noticeable (seven trumpets, v. 8; days, circuits on the final day, vv. 14–15; cf. v. 4). The use of seven (and multiples) in religious texts is a feature not only of the OT (Gen 1:1–2:4; 4:24), but also of the ancient world. In the literature of Ugarit epic events often occur in seven-day cycles, with the climax on the seventh day

(*IDB* iii. 564). The literary and theological character of the account means that no firm answer can be given to the question as to what actually happened. Yet it is by no means impossible that an actual event, remarkable in some way, might have come to be memorialized in this particular way.

The theology of the *ḥērem*, or 'ban', is at the centre of the narrative, and of the Holy War. (The notion was known also outside Israel; King Mesha of Moab boasts of having laid Israelites under the *ḥērem*, on the mid-ninth century Moabite Stone; see Kang 1989: 80–4). The implications of it are spelt out in vv. 17, 21 (cf. Deut 20:16–18 for the law). All living creatures are to be put to death, and all the city's wealth is to be devoted to God by being placed in the 'treasury of the LORD' (that is, in any sanctuary of YHWH). The rationale derives from 'holiness' ideas; in animal sacrifice, the animal is regarded as having become 'holy' in a technical sense. Similarly, the slaughter of a city's population in Holy War is a kind of sacrifice to God. Further, since it is seen in this way, it is not optional but an absolute obligation. Transgression in this area could rebound on the transgressor, and indeed the whole people (v. 18).

The OT's justification of the *ḥērem* is in terms, first, of God's judgement on the sin of the peoples thus condemned (Deut 9:5), and second, as a measure for preserving the purity of Israel (Deut 20:18). This is subordinate, in the wider biblical picture, to the project of bringing salvation to the nations (Ex 19:5–6). For modern readers the positive theology in such ideas is hard to discern. Perhaps it may be attempted in terms of God's holiness, consistency, and loyalty.

Modern sensitivities aside, there are further strictly theological problems. First, the picture given here represents the extreme of the tendency to exclusivism in the OT. The OT ultimately keeps in view the purpose of salvation for all the nations (Isa 40:5; 42:6; Jonah), and even sees the election of Israel as a means to that end (Gen 12:1–3; Ex 19:5–6). Election as an end in itself becomes monstrous. Our present text is part of an inner biblical dialogue in which the salvation of all nations is balanced by a concern for the preservation and purity of the chosen people. Second, the idea of the *ḥērem* can lead to the prevailing of the 'holy' over the ethical, a dilemma which the OT seeks to avoid by entering a justification in terms of God's judgement on evil (Deut 9:5).

The story concludes with the notes about the sparing of Rahab and her family (vv. 22–5), according to the commitment made in ch. 2. It is laid to rest in Joshua's curse of the city (v. 26, grimly echoed in 1 Kings 16:34), with its hint that, in the story's own terms, the command to destroy has been somewhat compromised. That suggestion will be taken up again in the narrative.

(7:1–26) Achan's Sin Against the 'Devoted Things' After Jericho, Joshua now turns his attention to Ai (literally 'the heap') a city near Bethel in the central mountain ridge, giving an important foothold in the heartland, yet at this stage avoiding one of the toughest strongholds, Jerusalem. The reference to Beth-aven (v. 2) is obscure. Lacking in LXX, it is a contemptuous corruption (lit. house of iniquity). It is elsewhere used of Bethel (Hos 4:15; 5:8), but not in Joshua (cf. Josh 18:12). Some see it as referring here to Ai itself (with apparent support from a minority Gk text). But it may be a third site in the vicinity.

The narrative of Josh 7–8 combines the story of Achan's offence against the 'devoted things', and the battle report concerning Ai. The two themes are connected. Israel's approach to the heartland will proceed via the Valley of Achor, an important route from the Jordan valley into the central ridge, and later part of the northern boundary of Judah (Josh 15:7). Progress is temporarily halted, however, by Achan's sin. The name 'Achor' is explained by association with 'Achan' (7:26). The name Achan is sometimes remembered as 'Achar' (1 Chr 2:7, and regularly in LXX), the letters 'r' and 'n' being easily confused in Hebrew.

The immediate sequel to the triumphant demolition of Jericho is a reverse (7:1). It now emerges that the Israelites' respect for the ban on Jericho was not complete. The word 'break faith' indicates rebellion against God, meriting severe punishment (cf. 1 Chr 10:13–14). And the whole people is affected by the sin of one person.

Joshua now sends spies into the interior (7:2–9), recalling both the first intelligence mission that he had authorized (2:1), and the still earlier one sent by Moses (Num 13–14; Deut 1). The message of these spies contrasts starkly with that of Moses' fearful spies (Deut 1:28). In that case, initial fear gave way to a false confidence which resulted in ignominious defeat (Deut 1:41–5); here there is false confidence (as it transpires) in the first place, with similar results. In both cases the people's hearts 'melt' (Deut 1:28; Josh 7:5) at the apparent invincibility of the enemy. And there as here Israel's advance is halted as YHWH withdraws his presence from them (Deut 1:42; Josh 7:12). Ironically, Israel's fear here also directly reverses the fear (once again the 'melting hearts') already felt by the Amorites before their own advance (5:1).

The numbers involved in the first attack (2,000–3,000) are much less than in the second (8:3). Ai is no mean city (the number of its citizens who fall in the final battle are 12,000; 8:25). Israel has to learn again not to take this enemy for granted; God must be among them or they cannot succeed. When that is in place numbers are not the main factor.

Joshua now assumes the Mosaic role of intercessor (vv. 6–9). When he prays together with the 'elders of Israel', it is Israel as a whole that cries to YHWH in this crisis. Joshua's wish that they had remained on the far side of the Jordan seems to run counter to God's declared intent (Ex 17:3). Yet the prayer finishes with an appeal to God to glorify his 'name', that is to establish his reputation, by finishing the task he had begun.

YHWH's reply to Joshua (7:10–15) is the theological centre of the passage. The problem, known to the reader since vv. 1–2, but not yet to Joshua, is now revealed. Israel, having been unfaithful in respect of the ban, has become subject to the ban itself. The sin against the ban is a breach of the covenant (v. 11). As at previous times, the very continuance of the life of Israel with God is at stake. The call to 'sanctify' the people means to make them ritually ready for a solemn encounter with God (cf. Ex 19:10). God now prescribes the harsh penalty for infringement of the ban (vv. 13–15). The theology of the ban implies a division within all of reality between the holy and the profane (meaning common, or normal). The holy sphere may be described as that which belongs entirely to God. The distinction is symbolized in the geography of temple and tabernacle, which portrays a stepped progression from the profane sphere (outside the sanctuary) to the holy of holies itself. Rituals from the consecration of priests to the act of sacrifice are conceived as a transfer from the profane sphere to the holy. The sin of Achan consists not merely in having stolen the goods, but in having illegitimately transferred them from the holy realm to the profane. This is not only a kind of robbery of God, but also a contamination (in a technical sense) of the profane realm. This is what makes the offence so serious; the penalty for the infringement of holiness conventions or regulations was death (cf. Num 16). And the culprit must be found because otherwise the guilt of the offence would fall on all Israel.

The method of discovering the guilty party is important. The division of Israel into tribes, clans, households gives a glimpse of its pre-monarchical constitution (see Wright 1992). The identification of the culprit was probably made by sacred lot (cf. 1 Sam 10:20–1). Its use here may function to preserve unity among the tribes in a judicial action which must lay the blame at the door of one (Wilson 1983), as well as to establish that the procedure is God's.

The remaining narrative (7:16–26) tells how the divine command was carried out. The execution of Achan's family along with him is one of the most shocking incidents in the book. The narrative may suppose that they were actually implicated in the sin, but it must be admitted that there is no hint of that. The logic of the judgement may be, not that they were deemed guilty by association, but that they had had contact with the holy things. It is thus comprehensible within the world-view that is represented in the text, though alien and even outrageous within a modern world-view.

The whole action takes place at God's initiative and 'before' him (v. 23). The narrative illuminates some of the central concepts of the account of the conquest. The war on Canaan is a Holy War, conducted by YHWH himself; the people, in covenant with him, are holy, in the sense of belonging specially to him; this is the root of the solidarity of Israel that plays a role here. Overcoming God's enemies means uncompromising loyalty to him. The call to probity before God, and the solemnity of commitment, is echoed in the NT too (Acts 5:1–11).

(8:1–29) The Fall of Ai The action in this chapter follows both from Josh 6, the taking of Jericho, and Josh 7, in which the defeat of Ai was delayed. Now that the problem reported in ch. 7 has been resolved, God is with his people again in their conquest of the land. Ai is thus next after Jericho, and like it, will fall to the Israelites (v. 2). The narrative is a battle account, told with unusual military and topographical detail.

The history and geography of this incident are complicated. In the narrative, Ai is located by reference to Bethel (cf. above, 7:2). Bethel is almost universally identified with modern Beitin, a few miles north of Jerusalem in the central ridge. That being so, the site of Ai must be a place called Et-Tell (meaning, like Ai, 'heap' or 'ruin'), the ruined remains of a once substantial city. Et-Tell, however, shows no sign of having been occupied between the late third millennium and the eleventh century, when there is evidence of Israelite occupation. In other words Et-Tell seems not to have been a living city at the time of the conquest.

One proposed solution is that Ai, though uninhabited, was a military outpost of Bethel. This is supported by the mention

of Bethel along with Ai in v. 17. The narrative really relates the defeat of the more important Bethel. This theory has to assume that Ai has been virtually substituted for Bethel throughout, to explain how this mere outpost could have a 'king' (8:1). A more radical suggestion, based on the topographical data of vv. 9–11, is that Et-Tell is not Ai, an option which entails an alternative siting of Bethel too (Livingston 1970; but against this, Rainey 1971).

YHWH now commissions the taking of Ai (8:1–2), in contrast to ch. 7, where Joshua acted on his own initiative. The words of encouragement, 'Do not fear or be dismayed', recall Deut 1:21, where they also preface a new phase in the story of the conquest. The ban is reiterated for Ai, as for Jericho, except that the people may on this occasion take plunder.

The strategem of pretended flight was well-known to the ancient world (see Fritz 1994: 90 for examples and cf. Judg 20:36–8). Here, the mimicry of the first defeat is an added narrative factor (v. 6, cf. 7:4–5). The garrison having been tricked into leaving the city, a second unit set in ambush would come in from the west and destroy it. Though the initiative is God's (vv. 1–2), Joshua's resourceful leadership also comes into play. Numbers are now commensurate with the task (v. 3). (On the numbers themselves, see on 4:13.)

The forces move into place (vv. 10–17). The Israelites take up a position to the north of the city (v. 13). Their general direction of approach, however, is from the east, the 'Arabah' (v. 14), or Jordan valley, with Gilgal and Jericho. The ambush to the west is thus from the opposite direction. Bethel lies a little further west again. The possible exposure of the ambush to Bethel gives some support to the view that the peoples of Ai and Bethel are in reality one here, as does the remark in v. 17.

God's command to stretch out the sword towards Ai (v. 18) recalls the staff that Moses held out, also at God's command, at the crossing of the Reed Sea (Ex 14:16, 21). Joshua holds out the sword until the battle is won (v. 26). The relative strength of the two armies is not an issue. For when the forces of Bethel and Ai see their city in flames they have no more power even to flee (v. 20; 'power' is literally 'hands', in contrast to the 'hand' of Joshua, mentioned four times in vv. 18–19).

As in Jericho, the population of the city is not spared. The stipulations of the ban in this case are carried out, and the livestock and wealth taken as plunder. Two memorials of the victory are left behind: the pile of rubble that was the city; and a second heap of stones, where the body of the king of Ai was thrown at its entrance (vv. 28–9). As at Jericho, it is not only an army but a king who is defeated.

(8:30–5) Ceremony at Mt. Gerizim The taking of Ai, and the implied defeat of Bethel as well, marks an important point in the conquest, as the ceremony that is now described makes clear. Deuteronomy had provided that, 'on the day that you cross over the Jordan', the people should set up large stones on Mt. Ebal, cover them with plaster, and write 'all the words of this law' on them (for the erection of stones in solemn rituals, see Koopmans 1990: 404–5). In addition they were to erect an altar for sacrifice (Deut 27:2–8), and solemnly accept the terms of the covenant (Deut 27:11–26).

There are some differences between that passage and this. While Deuteronomy requires two separate kinds of construction (stone stelae for writing and an altar for sacrifice), Joshua makes no such distinction. Here, the ceremony involves a reading of the law, with its blessings and curses; Deuteronomy had recorded only a proclamation of curses. Even so, our narrative sees itself as the fulfilment of that one (vv. 30–1).

The 'words of the law' are probably the Deuteronomic law, the basis of the ceremony on Mts. Ebal and Gerizim, near ancient Shechem. If the 'book of the law' was first made the rule for Joshua himself as he led Israel into the land (1:7–8), it now becomes so for the whole people, in anticipation of the fuller covenant renewal ceremony at Shechem reported at the end of the book (Josh 24).

This narrative does not sit naturally, chronologically or geographically, within the account of the conquest. Shechem lies well to the north of Bethel and Ai, and the subjugation of the whole land has not yet been related. Furthermore, a report of the covenant renewal at Shechem comes appropriately at the end of the book (Josh 24). The present passage has been put here, however, for a theological purpose. Following the setback at Ai, it shows first, that the people are now committed to proceeding in obedience to God; and second, that a decisive point has been reached; there will be no stopping till the land has been taken.

One further point is important, namely the inclusion of the 'aliens' among the Israelites as full members of the community (v. 33). Deuteronomy provided liberally for non-Israelites who lived among the people (Deut 14:28–9), and the religious community was in principle open to them (Deut 23:7–8). This picture is consistent with that.

(9:1–27) Covenant with Gibeon The first two verses prepare for the battles ahead. An alliance by some of the Canaanite kings begins to form. The geographical limits and the names of the peoples are familiar from Deuteronomic description (Deut 1:7; 7:1; Josh 3:10—see on that passage; the Girgashites are missing here). What the kings 'hear' is presumably a report of the successes of Israel at Jericho and Bethel/Ai.

First, however, there is an extraordinary incident, and a fresh setback. Gibeon lay to the south of Bethel and Ai, a little to the north of Jerusalem. The Israelite camp is still at Gilgal (v. 6), near Jericho. (This reinforces the chronological point made above; the Israelites have not yet marched north.) The Gibeonites were Hivites, one of the native peoples (Deut 7:1; see 'Hivites', *ABD* ii. 234). They too 'hear' what Israel has done (9:3), fear for their lives, and decide to pretend that they are not indigenous to the land, but foreign travellers. They approach Joshua and 'a man of Israel' (a way of referring to the Israelite army, Judg 7:23). In asking for a treaty (v. 6) they are aware that Israel's Holy War rules out such a treaty with the local population. (For treaties, see Mendenhall and Herion, 'Covenant', *ABD* i, 1179–202.)

The prohibition of treaty-making with the population of Canaan is the theological rationale of the episode, spelt out in Deut 7:1–5, and echoed by Joshua here (v. 7; Mayes 1985). Treaties, or covenants (the word is *bĕrît*, the same that is used for God's covenant with Israel, Ex 24:7) were a universal means of establishing relationships among peoples in the ancient Near East (see JOSH 24). The Gibeonites here seek an inferior, vassal status as the price of survival. Their knowledge of Israel's successes extends back to Egypt, and includes the victories in Transjordan (vv. 9–10). In this

sense they are like the king of Moab, Balak, who had tried to employ magic against Israel on its approach to the land (Num 22).

The theological heart of the present passage is in vv. 14–15. The 'leaders' (v. 14), or 'leaders of the congregation' (v. 18) are presumably the elders and judges who represent Israel, as the people of YHWH, in an official way. They conclude the treaty, eating the Gibeonites' bread. Joshua then makes peace with them (the narrative excludes him from the treaty-making, perhaps to show that he was not implicated in the duping of Israel). In the narrator's view, the treaty was not according to the will of YHWH, and Israel was tricked because they did not consult him. Once again, Israel's fortunes decline rapidly after a triumph.

When the truth is out, the issue is whether Israel should go ahead and implement the ban (vv. 16–21), or stand rather by the oath. The answer is that the oath must stand, in accordance with treaty practice. However, the Gibeonites are consigned to servitude, to mark their deceit.

The final paragraph (vv. 22–7) expands the sentence reported in v. 21, with a dialogue between Joshua and the Gibeonites, in which he pronounces them 'cursed', and they accept his right to decide their fate. The curse properly belongs to a situation in which a treaty has been violated, and is therefore unexpected here. The thought is probably that the deceit used by the Gibeonites is itself a violation of trust.

The servitude imposed on the Gibeonites is now specified as service of the 'place that he [YHWH] should choose', that is, the main worship sanctuary of Israel. The term occurs in Deuteronomy in a number of forms (Deut 12:5, 14, and frequently in Deut 12–26; see DEUT 12:1–5). It is often taken in the critical literature to refer cryptically to Jerusalem, a device to maintain the Mosaic guise (Clements 1989: 28). However, the phrase is connected with Shiloh in Jer 7:12, a central sanctuary for Israel before Jerusalem (1 Sam 1–3). And here it could refer to Gibeon itself, the great 'high place' at which Solomon would worship before building the temple (1 Kings 3:4; Chronicles goes further and locates the tent of meeting there at the time; 2 Chr 1:3).

The story of the treaty with the Gibeonites echoes an actual early encounter of Israel in Canaan. When the Gibeonite covenant reappears in the OT, in the traditions about Saul, it is as a fact already well established. Saul, it seems, broke the covenant with the Gibeonites, perhaps to extend his territory in Benjamin, and suffered the consequences of a famine in Israel (2 Sam 21). The 'curse' of Joshua's covenant thus rebounded on Israel for its failure to keep its terms.

(10:1–43) Defeat of the Southern Alliance The submission of Gibeon has a devastating effect on the region (vv. 1–15). It now transpires that Gibeon is a relatively powerful city, 'like one of the royal cities' (v. 2). This means that it was a significant city-state, though it may imply that it did not have a king. (Strikingly, no king is mentioned in Josh 9, in a narrative which otherwise regularly focuses on the non-Israelite kings.) The power of Gibeon here seems at odds with its weakness in Josh 9 (Soggin 1972: 121). Yet Josh 9 need only imply that Gibeon perceived Israel to be very strong. And the war that is now declared on Gibeon by neighbouring states may in any case suggest uneasy relations between them, which might have contributed to Gibeon's seeking alliance with Israel. Under that alliance, Gibeon can now turn to Israel for help (v. 6).

The chain effect of Joshua's conquest continues when, in the style of preceding accounts, the king of Jerusalem 'heard' about both Ai and Gibeon (v. 1). Suddenly Joshua is playing for control of the whole southern region of Canaan. The king of Jerusalem, Adoni-zedek, is called Adoni-bezek by LXX, as in Judg 1:5–7 (the confusion has led some to suppose the tradition about both is unhistorical (Auld 1975: 268–9)). He initiates an alliance of city-states against Gibeon, to maintain control of the region. The cities involved are located across the southern highlands (cf. 12:10–13). Jerusalem occupies an important position on the central ridge, between south and north. The other cities were further south, in the heart of what would be Judah. Lachish was a major city-state in Joshua's time (now illuminated by the reliefs of Sennacherib's siege in the British Museum). Hebron, south-east of Lachish, was known to the patriarchs as Kiriath-arba. We are less well informed about the others; there is nevertheless an authenticity about the kind of political response narrated here.

Joshua marches again from Gilgal. The battle report stresses the hand of God in the defeat of these powerful enemies, the hailstones from heaven proving more devastating than the Israelite forces. The famous staying of the sun and moon (meaning simply that the day was lengthened) showed that it was YHWH, not Joshua, who defeated the kings; and he controlled not only Israel but even the heavenly bodies. The latter miracle poses a bigger problem to the imagination, perhaps, than the hailstones, though neither can be conceived in a strictly literal way. The two belong in the same category. The day was remembered in Israel as especially remarkable, the victory having been attended by strange natural phenomena, which are attributed to YHWH's power.

The first general account of the battle had reported that Israel pursued the fleeing armies of the alliance into their territory, 'as far as Azekah and Makkedah' (v. 10). Azekah lies on the route from Jerusalem to Lachish; Makkedah has not been identified. There is now a further report (vv. 16–27), that tells how Joshua captured the five kings and held them until their armies were thoroughly defeated and only a number of survivors had regained their cities (v. 20). (The passage has been thought originally to be independent of vv. 1–15, an aetiology based on five trees, and a separate story about the caves (Noth 1971: i. 282–3). It is now, in any case, well integrated with the preceding.) The five kings are made subject to a demonstration of Joshua's victory (v. 24), and executed and exposed, recalling the fate of the king of Ai (8:29). Memorial stones are again erected to mark the triumph. Joshua's words of encouragement to the troops (v. 25) recall God's words to Joshua at the beginning of the campaign (1:6).

The last stage in the campaign (vv. 28–43) is the destruction of the cities from which the alliance had come, now defended only by the stragglers from the battlefield. The passage thus records the completeness of the victory. The towns taken here do not correspond exactly to the towns that formed the original alliance. Jerusalem is omitted, in keeping with the picture given in Joshua and Judges that it was not subjugated by Joshua (Josh 15:63). Jarmuth is omitted too. Libnah, Gezer, and Debir are the new entrants. Gezer was an important city

overlooking the coastal plain west of Jerusalem, and not finally taken until the time of Solomon (1 Kings 9:16; cf. Josh 16:10). Debir lay south of Hebron. Its name, incidentally, was attributed to the king of Eglon at first (vv. 3), and may bespeak a transference in the course of the narrative's transmission.

The unity of Joshua's victories in the land to date has been conveyed by various rhetorical and literary means, for example, by the catchword of 'hearing' (10:1), and by making Jericho and Ai paradigms of subsequent victories. In this section there is a reappearance of the ḥērem, or ban (vv. 28, 35, 37, 40). The narrative ends with a summary statement of Joshua's control of the entire southern part of the land. Kadesh-barnea is important because it recalls the starting-point of the journey of conquest (Deut 1:2; 2:14). Gaza takes in the coastal area of the Philistines, even though there is no report of victories there. Goshen is probably an area in the southern reaches of the Negeb (not the Goshen of Joseph's Egypt (Gen 45:10)). The geographical perspective here is the ideal one that pictures a total conquest of the land in a series of swift campaigns by Joshua himself.

(11:1–23) Defeat of the Northern Alliance There is no account of a march north by Joshua and Israel, and no specific military or strategic plan is explained. It is simply assumed that Joshua's task is the conquest of the whole land of Palestine, the 'promised land' of Pentateuchal narrative. The narrative of the northern campaign begins with the familiar formula, 'when x heard'—here Jabin, king of Hazor. Here again, an alliance forms around a leading power, and the campaign runs a similar course.

The centre of the new threat is Hazor (vv. 1–9). The partly excavated tell shows that Hazor was by far the largest city of Joshua's day, perhaps ten times larger than Jerusalem, with as many as 40,000 inhabitants. Known from the Amarna letters and other texts, it is a historically plausible leader of an alliance against an incomer that threatened its interests in the area. Furthermore, archaeology shows that this great city was destroyed in the thirteenth century BCE, not to be rebuilt as a fortified city till the days of Solomon (1 Kings 9:15), though there was some settlement in the interim.

The other cities of the alliance may be identified with various sites in the region between the Sea of Galilee (Chinneroth) and the Mediterranean. The size of the region depends on identifications. The 'Arabah south of Chinneroth' (v. 2) may mean the Jordan valley south of the Sea of Galilee, which would imply a very large area for the alliance, but the phrase has also been taken to denote some more restricted area east or west of the Sea. The peoples involved are mixed (v. 3), but the names are familiar from the formulaic designation of the Canaanites in Deuteronomy 7:1 and elsewhere. The Jebusites are normally associated with Jerusalem.

The name of Jabin is associated with a defeat of Hazor also in Judg 4–5, where it is sometimes considered secondary (Soggin 1972: 136). Alternatively the name is dynastic. In the latter case, some revival in Hazor's fortunes in the period after Joshua is implied.

Battle is joined at Merom (v. 7). This may be identical with the Madon of v. 1 (both are 'Marron' in LXX), and is probably near Hazor. LXX also adds 'from the mountain' in v. 7, giving a

picture of an ambush by a people that would become natur-
alized in the hills, while the Canaanites would hold to the
plains. The rout extends to the Mediterranean far to the north
at Sidon, and returns south-eastwards past Lake Huleh (now a
fertile plain) towards Hazor itself. It is a mighty sweep as far as
'Lebanon and . . . to the Western Sea', to borrow part of Deuteronomy's classical description of the extent of the land.
Victory is complete.

The hamstringing of the Canaanites' horses and the burning of their chariots incapacitates them at the point of their
natural advantage over the Israelites (v. 9). This is done in
fulfilment of YHWH's command, a vital element in the narrative of Joshua's success. Command and fulfilment are closely related here (vv. 6, 9).

Hazor itself is now put to the ban (vv. 10–15); its king is
executed, and the city burned. The other towns are also
destroyed, but not burned, an authentic note in an account
that otherwise stresses the total extirpation of the enemy. As
at Ai the booty is excepted from the ban (v. 14), a further
exception to the law of Deut 20:16, though the terms of that
law are borrowed here (as elsewhere in our account) in the
phrase 'all who breathed'. Here as in the case of Jericho the
report of the total destruction of human life reflects the 'ideal'
perspective of a pure Israel in the land (see JOSH C.1–3). Even
so, it is hard to avoid the implication that Hazor was thoroughly razed.

The present paragraph also ends on the note of command-
fulfilment (v. 15). The chain of command extends from
YHWH through Moses to Joshua. The line from YHWH to
Moses appears twice, framing the sentence, the name of
Joshua occurring twice in the centre. By this rhetorical means,
the author portrays Joshua as the one who acts according to
God's word, and who therefore successfully leads Israel into
its inheritance.

The summary paragraph (vv. 16–20) records the full extent
of the land now under Israelite control, from south to north.
Mt. Halak is on the borderland of Edom (Seir) in the far south-
east; Baal-gad is in the shadow of Mt. Hermon. The defeat of
all the kings of the land is stressed by means of a repetition
(vv. 17–18). The exception of Gibeon is recalled, perhaps as a
blemish on the record. And the rationale is given: God 'hardened their hearts' against Israel, so that they might be utterly
destroyed (the term refers again to the ban). The language is
similar to that which is used of Pharaoh in the great confrontation between that king and Moses (Ex 7:13; and esp. 10:20,
where, as here, it is YHWH who does the hardening). The
phraseology does not mean that the enemies were helpless
puppets; rather, it is designed to show their determination to
oppose the will of God. The parallel between Pharaoh and the
kings of Canaan is no doubt purposefully drawn. God took
Israel from one situation to the other, overcoming powerful
opposition, both political and moral.

The Anakim (vv. 21–3) had inspired fear in Israel at the
first, and deterred timid Israel from proceeding to inherit
their land (Num 13:28; Deut 1:28). The ease of this victory
comments on the misplaced fear there, and fulfils the promise of Deut 9:1–3.

The allocation of land according to tribes, though it belongs
properly to the next major section of the book, is intimated
here, to reinforce the message that the mission of Joshua is

essentially complete. The phrase 'the land had rest from war'
is the ideal perspective on events that dominates this part of
the book. It recalls Deut 12:10, which anticipates the blessed
life of Israel in the land after all wars are won.

(12:1–24) The Subduing of the Whole Land In closing the
account of the conquest, this chapter reverts again (vv. 1–6) to
the victories in Transjordan, already recalled in Josh 1:12–15
(cf. Num 21; Deut 2–3). This accords with the Deuteronomic
view that the promised land includes territory in Transjordan
and Cisjordan, the ban having been applied there first (Deut
2:34; 3:6). The promised land began, therefore, at the river
Arnon, running from the east into the Dead Sea, and forming
the northern boundary of Moab; and it extended on the east
side of Jordan as far north as Mt. Hermon.

The two principal adversaries in Transjordan were Sihon of
Heshbon and Og of Bashan. Sihon's kingdom extended from
the Arnon to the next major tributary of Jordan to the north,
the Jabbok (where Jacob had wrestled with God; Gen 32:22–
32), and eastwards to the Ammonites' borderland. Chinneroth is the Sea of Galilee; this implies that Sihon controlled a
stretch of the Arabah well to the north of the Jabbok. Og's
territory lay to the north and east. His major cities, Ashtaroth
and Edrei, lay well to the east of the Sea of Galilee, but his land
extended south to the Jabbok. The biblical author's point,
however, is that Moses took all the Transjordan from the
Arnon to Hermon. He also distributed these kings' lands to
the tribes of Reuben and Gad, and half the tribe of Manasseh
(cf. Num 32: Deut 2–3).

The next section (vv. 7–24) portrays Joshua's conquests as
the continuation of the land possession and promise fulfilment that had begun under Moses. Baal-gad and Mt. Halak
are the northern and southern extremes of the land, as in
11:17. The parts of the land, and the peoples in it, are recorded
here as on other occasions (Deut 1:7; 7:1; Josh 11:16–17), and
the theme of land distribution is continued.

The list of cities (vv. 9–24) roughly follows the progress of
the conquest as reported in Joshua: Jericho and Ai come first,
then the southern alliance under Jerusalem, and the northern, under Hazor. Some of the names mentioned here are
new: Geder, Hormah, Arad, Adullam, Tappuah, Hepher,
Aphek, Lasharon, Taanach, Megiddo, Kedesh, Jokneam,
Tirzah. This suggests that the list was originally independent
of Josh 1–11. It is doubtful if these towns were all occupied at
any one time (Fritz 1994: 136–7). Some of the locations are
well-known (e.g. Arad, on the southern borders of Judah, with
its temple to YHWH; Megiddo, an important fortress on
the north–south route, commanding the entrance to the
plain of Esdraelon). Others are less certain. Bethel is unexpected in v. 16, because of its mention in v. 9; it is omitted
in LXX, and may not be original here. (Judges records the
fall of Bethel to the 'house of Joseph', Judg 1:22–5; this was
'after the death of Joshua', Judg 1:1.) Shechem is a striking
omission.

The list represents a spread from north to south, and epitomizes the completeness of Joshua's success. The recurrence
of the 'kings' is significant. Again, it is not only geography that
interests our writer, but the character of the enemy. YHWH
empowers Joshua, who is not a king, to overcome the kings of
Canaan.

Dividing the Land (13:1–21:45)

(13:1–7) The Command to Allot the Land Following the conquest narrative, the next major section concerns the allocation of territory to the tribes. Noth thought that this section derived from a second Deuteronomistic author, citing 13:1 as a secondary anticipation of 23:1 (Noth 1953: 10), designed to introduce the long insertion (13:1–21:42). Both conquest and land division belong within the Deuteronomic concept, however, and the appeal to a second source is not necessary (Wenham 1971).

The command to Joshua (v. 1) is at first surprising, in view of the summary statements of complete conquest that we have just read (11:23). The same tension, between the conquest as accomplished and as not yet accomplished, is found in vv. 6–7. But there is a counterpoint of real and ideal in Joshua. Its author, like that of Deuteronomy, knows that possessing and not possessing are always twin possibilities. These commands to Joshua resemble other challenges to Israel in the book, which promise and warn at the same time (23:16; 24).

The centre of vv. 1–7 outlines land not yet won. It covers three areas: the Philistine lands from the border with Egypt (the Shihor is probably a branch of the Nile's eastern delta) to the five Philistine cities in the coastal plain above it (v. 3); the Phoenician coast (v. 4), and the mountains of Lebanon (vv. 5–6). The exact limits are not clear (e.g. Aphek could be a location close to the Philistine lands, or another in Galilee). Nor is it obvious how these areas relate to the conquests already described (cf. 11:8), or to the total area of Joshua's activity, which apparently does not include Lebanon. They are, however, part of Deuteronomy's ideal extent of the land (Deut 1:7), and as such, unfinished business. Joshua's task is to divide the land in Cisjordan (v. 7), the Transjordanian land having already been distributed.

Theologically, this passage establishes that it is YHWH who will now divide the land. Joshua may die, but YHWH will still give the land.

(13:8–33) The Settling of Transjordan Transjordan now also prefaces the section about the distribution of land. The lists of cities have a more abbreviated parallel in Num 32:34–8. But the extended narrative here draws more widely on other material (e.g. with 13:21–2; cf. Num 31:8). And the explanation of the Levites' non-inheritance of territory (vv. 14, 33) is based on Deut 18:1.

It was Moses who had conquered in Transjordan (vv. 12, 21), and could therefore 'give' it; the expression 'Moses gave' occurs here several times, in connection with the land as 'inheritance' (vv. 8, 14–15, 24, 29, 33). Moses continues to 'give' in ch. 14 (vv. 3–4, 9, 12), but there it is finally Joshua who 'gives for an inheritance' (v. 13). The narrative concerning Transjordan therefore affirms the unity of Moses' and Joshua's work.

It also stresses the unity of all Israel. The twelve tribes have a stake in the land, and inherit in it. The concern to show this explains the repeated assertion that the tribe of Levi did not receive land of its own (vv. 14, 33). Their compensation for this is elaborated in Josh 21. The immediate point is clarified, however, in 14:3–4, where it is connected with the division of the large tribe of Joseph into two, Ephraim and Manasseh, thus maintaining the twelvefold character of Israel.

The possibility of non-possession is hinted at afresh, in the notice about Israel's failure to drive out the inhabitants of Geshur and Maacath (v. 13), an area in the far north, below Hermon. This will become a kind of motif in chapters to come, and will present the other side of the picture of conquest, namely of failure to conquer entirely (see Mitchell 1993).

Finally, though Moses and Joshua distribute the land, it remains an 'inheritance', and its ultimate giver is God. While Joshua succeeds Moses, neither figure acts like a dynastic king (against Nelson 1981; see Schäfer-Lichtenberger 1995: 219–24). Joshua has no successor. In this respect Israel is unlike the kings of the ancient Near East, whose prerogative was the land grant.

(14:1–15) Caleb's Inheritance The allocation of the land in Cisjordan by Joshua together with Eleazar the priest and tribal chiefs (vv. 1–5) continues directly from Num 26, where Moses and Eleazar had taken a census of the people precisely for this distribution (Num 26:1–4, 52–6; cf. Num 32:28). The use of the sacred lot was commanded in Num 26:55. The explanation of Levi's exclusion from land inheritance, and the dividing of Joseph, supplies the lack of such an explanation in Num 26.

The grant of land to Caleb (vv. 6–15) is a special case. Caleb had dissented from the first spies' timid report (Num 13:30–3), as had Joshua, according to another text (Num 32:12). For his faithfulness he was promised a possession of his own (Num 14:24; Deut 1:36), and this is now fulfilled in the area of Hebron, which Caleb requests (v. 12). Hebron is in the south of the territory shortly to be allocated to Caleb's tribe of Judah. Caleb's speech emphasizes his vigour into old age, like Moses (Deut 34:7). This also is part of the promise to him (Num 26:65). In his trust in YHWH, he is not even dismayed by the Anakim, the giants who had terrified Israel at first (v. 12; cf. Num 13:22, 28, 32–3). And the next chapter records his conquest of the city (15:13–14).

Hebron plays a distinctive role from the beginnings of Israel until long after the conquest. Sarah died and and was buried there (Gen 23:1–7); its ancient name Kiriath-arba (lit. city of four) has been interpreted variously (four cities? clans?). In our passage (v. 15) Arba is the name of one of the Anakim. A story about David's time also links Caleb to the area, albeit in a crisis (1 Sam 30, note v. 14). David will rule at first from there (2 Sam 5:3–5). The city will thus have a strategic importance for Israel as a whole, and Judah in particular.

Hebron becomes the first place in Cisjordan to be allocated, and this is Joshua's first such act, in which he assumes completely the mantle of Moses.

(15:1–63) The Territory of Judah The description of Judah's tribal land, the first and longest of such descriptions, consists principally of a definition of its boundaries (vv. 1–12), and a list of its cities (vv. 20–63), with a further passage on the inheritance of Caleb (vv. 13–19). (For treatments of Judah's boundaries, see Alt 1953; and for the boundaries in general, Na'aman 1986.)

The boundary description (15:1–12) proceeds in the order south, east, north, west. The southern boundary runs from the southern tip of the Dead Sea to the Mediterranean, taking in the old sanctuary of Kadesh-barnea in the Sinai border-land, and extending to the 'Wadi [or brook] of Egypt', that is the Wadi el-Arish (different from the Shihor, 13:3), which flows into the Mediterranean between Gaza and the Nile Delta. The east is bounded by the Dead Sea. The northern border is the most detailed, representing, no doubt, hard political realities. It is constructed carefully round the southern extremities of the city of Jerusalem (v. 8), pointedly excluding it from Judah. And the western limit is the Mediterranean.

Although Jerusalem is not counted to Judah here, its presence is felt. The last verse of the chapter (v. 63) notes that Judah could not take it. It is elsewhere assigned to Benjamin (18:28), whose southern border corresponds closely to the northern limit of Judah outlined here (Josh 18:15–19). Alongside this neat picture, however, must be laid Judg 1:8, which records that Judah did indeed take the city! Yet the same chapter notes that the Benjaminites could not drive out the Jebusites, who thus remained alongside them in the land (Judg 1:21). This complex picture suggests that Jerusalem was indeed fought for, perhaps by both tribes, the final outcome being failure. There may in addition have been contention over it between Judah and Benjamin. (Judg 1:8 then either recalls some short-lived triumph there, or belongs to the idealizing perspective found in passages such as Josh 11:23.) In the biblical history, it would be left to David to oust the Jebusites, and then to make a virtue of the city's disputed status by making it his capital over all Israel (2 Sam 5:6–10, cf. v. 5).

Caleb, having been granted Hebron, now has to take it in war (vv. 13–19). This action of his may be regarded as part of Joshua's, reported in 10:36–7. Caleb becomes a 'distributor' in turn, granting land to his 'brother' (or close relative) Othniel, as well as his daughter Achsah, because of his role in the conquest. Her request for water reflects the realities of life in the drier areas of the land, such as the Negeb, Judah's southern desert. (Othniel later becomes the first 'judge-deliverer' of Israel: Judg 3:8–11.)

The list of cities can be divided into twelve groups (by the repeated phrase 'with their villages'), possibly reflecting a monarchical administrative system (Soggin 1972: 176–80). The cities also fall into four geographical groups: the Negeb (or 'extreme south', v. 21), the lowlands (the Shephela), between the higher hills and the Mediterranean, v. 33, the hill country, that is the high hills of the central ridge (v. 48), and the wilderness, east of the central ridge towards the Dead Sea (v. 61). This division has been thought to be military.

The long list shows how extensive and varied Judah was, incorporating both the rich plain and the dry wilderness. The blessing of Jacob associates Judah with viticulture, at home in the terraced slopes of the hill country and lowlands (Gen 49: 11–12). The lands bordering the drier area were more suitable for sheep-rearing than agriculture. Carmel and Maon (v. 55) feature in the story of Nabal, a sheep-farmer who crossed David (2 Sam 25:2).

The final verse (v. 63) belongs to the pattern that indicates Israel's partial failure to take the land, and thus to obey God's command, predicated as it is on faith. The note of failure is an important counterpoint to the claims of sweeping victory that we have met in Josh 1–12, especially 11–12.

(16:1–17:18) The Territory of Joseph The tribe of Joseph ranks elsewhere too as next after Judah (cf. the relative space devoted to each in Jacob's blessing, Gen 49:8–12, 22–6). As we have seen, Joseph was subdivided into Ephraim and Manasseh (14:4). Together they receive a huge swathe of land between the Jordan and the Mediterranean from just north of the Dead Sea to Mt. Carmel in the north-west (as well as the lands held by the other half of Manasseh in Transjordan). (For the border descriptions that follow see Seebass 1984.)

The southern border (vv. 1–3) runs from Jericho (converging there with both Judah and Benjamin) up towards Bethel, along the route followed by Joshua from Jericho to Ai. It borders Benjamin to the south (16:2–3 is paralleled by 18:12–13), and goes past the important military outpost of Gezer, guarding the entry to the hill country from the plain. Bethel and Luz are remembered as separate places here, whereas they are elsewhere regarded as one (18:13; Judg 1:23).

The boundary of Ephraim (vv. 5–10) is most carefully defined in relation to Manasseh on its northern and eastern side (6b–7). It seems from v. 9 that the relations between them at the borders were complex; perhaps there were disputes between them. The theological comment on Ephraim concerns its failure to take Gezer (v. 10), which was taken at last—and then as a gift of Pharaoh—only by Solomon (1 Kings 9:16).

The description of Manasseh's land in Cisjordan is prefaced by a passage about the tribe as a whole (17:1–6). The genealogical information, unusual in the narratives of land distribution, is closely related to Num 26:29–34. It may be required because the allocation of land to Manasseh was peculiarly complicated, as indeed the inter-clan relationships may have been. Machir and Gilead appear as the names of tribes in Judg 5 (vv. 14, 17). There Machir appears to be west of the Jordan, while Gilead is east. Personal names are hardening into names of geographical regions in that text (see Lemaire 1981).

The six clans named are said in Numbers to descend directly from Gilead, Manasseh's grandson, while our passage traces them simply to Manasseh himself. (NRSV's 'tribe of Manasseh', v. 2, is literally 'sons of Manasseh', which need not mean the following generation.) The story of Zelophehad's daughters resumes a line of narrative from Num 27, 36, in which Moses established the right of inheritance for female descendants, in the absence of male ones, to protect family property. Num 36 specified in consequence that the daughters should marry within the tribe. The story is now concluded, to show that Moses' provisions were respected, and also to explain the division of territory in Manasseh. The five daughters of Zelophehad, son of Hepher, receive shares along with the five Gileadite clans (in place of Hepher), making 'ten portions' (v. 5). Of the eleven names (six sons of Gilead and five daughters of Zelophehad) six appear on ostraca (potsherds) found at Samaria, as geographical locations.

Manasseh stretches from Asher (the tribal land to the north of it) to Michmethath, on the border with Ephraim to the south (v. 7, cf. 16:6). Again the description (vv. 7–13) shows that borders were not absolute lines, with Ephraimite towns belonging within Manassite land, and Manasseh having towns within the territories of Asher and Issachar. The picture is further complicated by the continuing presence, here too, of Canaanite enclaves (vv. 11–12, cf. Judg 1:27–8). The comment about forced labour (v. 13) suggests Israelite ascendancy, yet failure in terms of the underlying programme of expulsion.

The request of Joseph (vv. 14–18) relates oddly to the distribution already described. It may be out of chronological sequence, in which case the demand for more than one portion may actually have been met in the separate allocation to Manasseh and Ephraim, though this is not said. Joshua accepts the basis of the tribe of Joseph's claim, namely great numbers. His answer—that they should clear the hill country of trees and make it habitable—corresponds to a reality in the history of the hill country, namely agricultural deforestation. And the Joseph tribes may be assumed to have taken him at his word.

Yet there is another undercurrent. Joseph's sense of constriction is related to their inability to confront the Canaanites of the plain, with their iron chariots, the tanks of the day. But Joshua ends on a note of challenge: Joseph must drive them out in spite of their strength. The point thus chimes in with the developing theme of Israel's limited grasp on the land that they have 'conquered'.

(18:1–19:51) Shiloh, and the Remaining Tribal Territories The allocations for the remaining tribes are now suddenly located at Shiloh, where, we are told, the tent of meeting is set up (18:1). There is other OT evidence that Shiloh was once an important sanctuary for all Israel at some time before the pre-eminence of Jerusalem. It appears as such in 1 Sam 1–2 (where it has a 'house of the LORD', 1:24, and the 'tent of meeting', 2:22, as in our text); and it is named as the place of God's choice, following Deut 12, in Jer 7:12. It also features as the central sanctuary for Israel in Josh 22.

Yet hitherto Gilgal and Shechem have been the important centres for Israel. For this reason, Noth and others saw the 'Shiloh' material here as secondary (Noth 1953: 107–8; Fritz 1994: 179–80; but contrast Milgrom 1976). However, there is logic in its positioning here. First, it fits with the flow of the narrative, which has just recorded the allocation of land to the Joseph tribes, in which Shiloh lies. Second, Shiloh is projected here as the central sanctuary for all Israel in a way that Gilgal and Shechem were not. Principally this is because the tent of meeting is set up there. This has been conspicuously absent in the narrative so far (despite a reference to the 'altar of the LORD' and 'the place that he would choose' in Josh 9:27). Yet the introduction of Shiloh at this point is not just incidental. Its centrality is indicated in an artistic way by its placing between the allocations of land to Judah and Joseph on the one hand, and the remaining tribes on the other. This patterning of the narrative extends further: the distribution to Judah and Joseph is preceded by the settling of land on Caleb (14:6–15), while the remaining distribution is followed by an account of an inheritance for Joshua (19:49–50). The accounts of rewards for the two faithful spies are woven carefully into the whole story of the distribution, which is thus seen to be constructed according to an elaborate pattern. The notice about Shiloh is at the centre of this pattern, suggesting that the erecting of the tent of meeting there is important in the concept of the narrative as a whole. It fulfils the promise-command that God would be among Israel in the land he was giving them (Lev 26:11–12: 'I will place my dwelling [tent, tabernacle] in your midst': Deut 12:5). Shiloh's role in the

distribution is reiterated in vv. 2–9; and it reappears in 19:51, rounding off this section on land allocation, which is thus bound up carefully with Israel's religious life (Koorevaar 1990: 217–34; 289–91).

Allocations have now been made to five tribes: Judah, Ephraim, Manasseh, Reuben, and Gad. The division of Joseph into Ephraim and Manasseh compensates for the fact that Levi has no territorial inheritance (18:7; the arithmetic is not affected by the fact that Manasseh falls into two parts, on either side of the Jordan). Seven tribes remain, therefore, to receive land (v. 2).

The characteristic paradox of Joshua reappears in vv. 1, 3: the land is 'subdued', yet the people have still to take it. The last stage of the allocation is prefaced by a survey (lit. writing, v. 4), a new feature in the story (and unexpected, but the account need not be supposed to follow a strict chronological order). Joshua continues to control events from Shiloh (v. 4), and provides for the allocation to take place by means of the sacred lot, 'here before the LORD our God' (v. 6, cf. vv. 8, 10). This recalls the general requirement in 14:1; only now is the casting of the lot located in Shiloh, however.

Benjamin (vv. 11–28) lies between Judah and Ephraim. The description of its northern border (18:12–14) is as for Ephraim's southern one (16:1–3), but less detailed. Its southern boundary, as we have seen, follows closely that of Judah's northern one (18:15–19; cf. 15:8–11). The list of its towns (vv. 21–8) simply includes Jebus (Jerusalem), though it is elsewhere made clear that the city did not fall to Joshua (15:63). It also embraces Gibeon and its satellites (cf. 9:17), making no mention of their special status (Josh 9) or Israel's defence of them against the Jerusalemite alliance (Josh 10). The present concern is description, not conquest, and represents an ideal.

The territory of Simeon (19:1–9) lay in the semi-arid Negeb, in the far south. Its description consists of a number of towns, some of which also appear in Judah's list (15:21–32). The narrative here locates Simeon within the territory of Judah, without a boundary description. It also provides a rationale for this arrangement (v. 9). In fact the identity of Simeon was lost early in Israel's life, as is clear already in Jacob's blessing (Gen 49:7), where it is paired with Levi, and condemned to be scattered in Israel. It is missing too in the Blessing of Moses (Deut 33) and the Song of Deborah, again perhaps because of its early failure to settle. The Judah list in Josh 15 seems to reflect this, while here in Josh 19 Simeon's separate identity is retained in accordance with the twelve-tribe ideal.

The lots now follow for Zebulun, Issachar, Asher, and Naphtali (19:10–38), which form a cluster between the Sea of Galilee and the Mediterranean. Proceeding from east to west, Issachar, Zebulun, and Asher have southern borders with Manasseh along the line of the Carmel range and the plain of Esdraelon. Naphtali is to the north of Issachar and Zebulun.

The data for these tribes consist of a mixture of town lists and border descriptions. The name of Mt. Tabor occurs in connection with three of the tribes (vv. 12, 22, 34, twice in place-names), distinguishing it as a reference-point in this area. The other important landmark is the Mediterranean. Asher (vv. 24–31) lies along the sea-coast from Carmel (at modern Haifa) as far north as Tyre and Sidon, cities of Phoenicia. Kabul is known as the place where Solomon made an agreement with King Hiram of Tyre (1 Kings 9:10–14).

(Bethlehem, v. 15, is obviously a place in Galilee, not the 'city of David' south of Jerusalem. 'Judah on the east of the Jordan' (v. 34)—lit. 'Judah of the Jordan'—can have nothing to do with the tribal territory far to the south.)

The description of Dan (19:40–8) stands apart from the preceding group. Although it settled finally in the extreme north (hence perhaps its inclusion here along with the Galilee tribes), its original territory was farther south, and that first inheritance is described here. It consists of land to the west of Judah, running down to the Mediterranean at Joppa (Tel-Aviv), and including certain Philistine territory (Ekron). It is debatable land between Judah and the Philistines, and some of the names here are known from the stories of Samson, who clashed with the Philistines on the edges of the Shephelah (low hills) and their coastal areas (cf. Judg 13:2, 25; 14:1). Ir-shemesh is Beth-shemesh in the same region.

The Danites may never have had a strong foothold in this region. It was only David who subdued the Philistines. Aijalon and Shaalbim are mentioned in Judg 1:35 as places where Canaanites (Amorites) continued to live, under pressure, admittedly, from 'the house of Joseph'—but not from Dan. Dan's failure is admitted in the narrative, which also reports its migration north, to the outer edges of the territory. Its 'conquest' of Leshem is not celebrated as part of Joshua's conquest. It is told more fully in Judg 18, where the slaughter of Leshem (Laish) is implicitly criticized (18:27). The final note in the description of the tribal inheritances, therefore, is decidedly downbeat. The summary in 19:48 appears to refer to the places that have been enumerated in the original territory (since there is nothing in v. 47 that could correspond to 'these towns with their villages'). Dan's 'inheritance', therefore, was not inherited, and the 'complete' conquest is in the end incomplete.

Joshua's personal inheritance (19:49–50) corresponds, as we saw, to that of Caleb the other courageous spy (see JOSH 14:6–15). Unlike the case of Caleb, there is no special preparation for such an allocation. Yet, as we saw (18:1), the two accounts balance each other within the structure of the larger narrative of the division of the land. There is an equilibrium too in the fact that Caleb inherits in (southern) Judah, while Joshua does so in (northern) Ephraim.

The conclusion (19:51) returns to Shiloh and the tent of meeting. It thus emphasizes again that that is the spiritual centre of the land, symbolizing the hand of God in the division of it, as in the giving. Joshua and Eleazar are named once more as jointly responsible for the execution of it (cf. 14:1; cf. Num 26:1–4; 52–6).

(20:1–21:43) Cities of Refuge and Levitical Cities The next two chapters complete the picture of land occupation by designating 'cities of refuge' (20:1–9), and levitical cities (21:1–41). These show how two classes of people, who are in some sense dispossessed, are granted the right to life and a place among the people. The concluding summarizing statement of God's victory over all Israel's enemies (21:43–5) shows that these provisions belong within the theme of land possession.

The instructions regarding cities of refuge (20:1–9) in Num 35:9–28 and Deut 4:41–3; 19:1–10 are now appealed to (v. 2), and what was commanded there is reiterated and put into practice. The requirement is essentially the same in all the texts. The accidental homicide was subject, by virtue of the homicide itself, to a form of justice deriving from familial relations in a tribal context. The 'avenger of blood' was appointed by the familial group to exact blood for blood in cases of homicide. The word translated 'avenger' is elsewhere 'redeemer' (Ruth 2:20). The connection is in terms of responsibility for the protection of the family group. The blood vengeance system had no mechanism in itself to cope with accidental homicides, as exemplified in Num 35:22–3 and Deut 19:5. The present text, and parallels, permit the killer to escape to designated cities for asylum.

One criterion for deciding intentionality emerges from three of the texts, namely whether there had been previous enmity between the parties (v. 5b, cf. Deut 19:4b, Num 35:23b). The means of determining guilt or innocence is never clearly spelt out, however. The procedure at the gates of the city of refuge may be no more than formal request for sanctuary (v. 4). It is followed by a trial before the '$ēdâ$, or 'congregation', that is, the whole people constituted as a religious assembly (v. 6; cf. Num 35:12). It may have been represented by judges in the city of refuge, or indeed Levites (as all the cities of refuge are also levitical cities; see below). Deuteronomy reserves the right of the elders of the killer's city, where they believe him guilty, to demand extradition (Deut 19:11–12). It is not clear how these various procedures relate to each other.

Sanctuary is a common concept in the ancient world, often associated with places of worship ('sanctuaries' in that sense). A law of Exodus also connects the principle of asylum with an altar (Ex 21:12–14). Our text and its parallels are unique in providing for asylum cities. These may actually have had sanctuaries, yet it is not likely that the refugee was intended to remain strictly within them. The rationale may be deduced from the implied analogy with the Levites. It is to be afforded a place in the land where life and sustenance are possible. We may surmise that a refugee might be joined there by his immediate family and resume a normal life.

The provision that the refugee must stay until the death of the high priest (v. 6b) may be intended to set a time-limit on the stalemate produced by a verdict of innocent, a verdict which nevertheless cannot revoke the right of blood vengeance in principle (Num 35:27c). The asylum laws are often dated to the post-exilic period on the grounds that the office of high priest is thought to date from that time. The laws themselves, however, make best sense in the context of an attempt to impose a unified administration on a diversified justice system, perhaps in the early monarchy. And the office of high priest is apparently known in the administrations of David and Solomon, with Zadok (1 Kings 1:38–40). (The Priestly sections of the Old Testament trace the beginnings of the office to the desert period, with Aaron, but there is no special evidence to confirm the historicity of this.) It is difficult, moreover, to make sense of the prominence of the Transjordanian cities in the laws on the assumption of a post-exilic setting, or indeed of the residual familial law. A compromise is to think of the high priest clause as a post-exilic addition. (For other views see Auld 1978; Gertz 1994: 117–57.)

Instead of tribal territory (13:14; 14:3–4) Levi would receive towns and their pasturelands throughout Israel (21:1–3), according to the Pentateuchal rationale that YHWH himself is the Levites' 'inheritance' (Num 18:20; Deut 18:1–2, cf. Deut 10:9). This meant in practice that they received shares of the Israelites' sacrifices and offerings (Num 18:9–24). In addition, Num 35 provides for forty-eight Levitical cities, including the six cities of refuge (Num 35:6–7—all noted in Josh 21; vv. 11, 21, 27, 32, 36, 38; the number forty-eight, vv. 4–7, 41, is significant perhaps as a multiple of twelve, the number of the tribes). The Levites now come to Joshua and Eleazar at Shiloh (vv. 1–2) to claim their part in the land; the allocation of their cities is thus included in the general apportionment of territory. The function of levitical cities has often been supposed to lie in their possessing sanctuaries, in line with the provision that Levites should have their living from sacrifices. However, there is no evidence of the existence of a sanctuary in most of the towns in this chapter. They may have served merely as residences, and places where Levites could enjoy some personal wealth and status, while performing their priestly duties elsewhere (Deut 18:6–8 can be read in this sense; McConville 1984: 144–7).

The tribe of Levi was associated with priesthood from early in Israel's history (Judg 18:3–6). According to Priestly Pentateuchal texts (Num 3–4), it was divided into two groups: priests proper and Levites, or assistants to the priests. The priests were traced to the line of Aaron, and through him to Kohath, one of the sons of Levi. Kohathites who were not of the Aaronite line, together with descendants of Levi's other sons Gershom and Merari, were 'Levites'. These texts are widely regarded as exilic or post-exilic, because the distinctions they make are not evident generally in the historical books of the OT, nor clearly in Deuteronomy. The system is presupposed here, however (vv. 4–7). The territorial order adopted roughly follows that of the allocation to the tribes (Judah, Joseph, the rest). Judah's primacy here is not only chronological, but also consists in receiving the sons of Aaron (v. 4). To an audience in the late Judahite monarchy, or in the exilic period, the association of Judah with Aaron would seem natural, for by then the Aaronide priesthood was well established in Jerusalem. Yet there is no express allusion to Jerusalem here, and Shiloh retains its prominence in the context. The account of Aaron's geographical foothold in the south, therefore, seems to be independent of late-monarchic/exilic theologizing.

In the list of towns in Judah and Simeon (vv. 9–12), these two are simply amalgamated (v. 9; see JOSH 19:1–9). Surprisingly, Hebron is assigned to the priests, having previously been granted to Caleb (14:14–15), a fact that is acknowledged here, and explained (v. 12). Debir too (v. 15) had fallen to Caleb (15:15–17). The list may be dated to the early monarchy (with Albright 1945). Some of these towns were not taken till then, and after the division of the monarchy, with Jeroboam's anti-levitical measures (1 Kings 12:31), Levites will scarcely have been able to hold them.

The summarizing conclusion (21:43–5) is in line with 11:23, emphasizing promise fulfilment and rest from enemies. There are echoes of Deuteronomy in the language, especially v. 43a.

Serving YHWH in the Land (22:1–24:33)

(22:1–34) The Altar by the Jordan Joshua now (vv. 1–9) takes up the charge addressed to the Transjordanian tribes at the outset of the conquest (1:12–18), which in turn looked back to Deut 3:18–20 (hence the reference here to Moses' command, v. 2). Though they had settled in their lands before their fellow-Israelites had crossed the Jordan, they were obliged to participate with them in the war for the land. They are permitted to return home, with a strongly Deuteronomic exhortation (vv. 2–5; cf. Deut 10:12–13). Joshua's 'blessing' of them (v. 6) belongs to the language of peaceful farewell. Shiloh is the place of this parting, which may have had a ceremonial aspect.

The unity of the people is now called into question (vv. 10–34) when the two and a half tribes, on their return, erect an altar by the Jordan, on the Israelite side of the border between the two lands (vv. 10–11). This is interpreted by the Israelites as an act of war, because it is held to challenge the claims of the sanctuary of Shiloh, so closely bound up with the theology of land possession (v. 12).

The case against the two and a half tribes is outlined (vv. 13–20) in terms of holiness requirements—hence the role of Phinehas (son of Eleazar) in the accusation, rather than Joshua. The sin is compared with two other sins in the religious realm (vv. 17, 20): the idolatry at Peor in the days of the wilderness wanderings (Num 25), and Achan's transgression of the ban on Jericho (Josh 7). It is all Israel, as a religious assembly or congregation, that pursues the errant tribes (vv. 12, 16). The issue, furthermore, is framed in religious terms by raising the question whether the land across the Jordan might be ritually 'unclean', and therefore itself unfit for worship (v. 19).

The Transjordanians, in reply (22:21–9), recognize the unique claims of both YHWH and his altar. The phrase 'The LORD, God of gods' ('ēl 'ĕlōhîm YHWH) is a strong affirmation of YHWH's supremacy. To a Canaanite it might literally have meant the supreme god among a number of gods; in the OT it merely means that he is unrivalled. The Transjordanians' argument is that this altar is not itself for sacrifice, but rather, as a copy of the true altar, it symbolizes their participation in the worship that takes place there (v. 27a). As such it is a 'witness' (vv. 28, 34). This last idea strikes two important Deuteronomic notes, namely the unity of Israel and the preservation of the true faith for future generations (vv. 24–8; cf. Deut 6:2, 7).

The events recorded here probably testify to complicated relationships in Israel's early years between the peoples east and west of the Jordan. The focus on Shiloh again suggests a memory from pre-monarchic times (cf. JOSH 18:1). The potential relevance of the narrative to post-exilic times should also be noticed, however, because of the questions that arose then about the status of Jews who chose to live in the Diaspora, away from their restored temple at Jerusalem. For this reason the chapter is often held to have an ancient core, but to have been revised by both Deuteronomic and Priestly writers (Noth 1953: 133–5; Kloppenborg 1981).

(23:1–16) Joshua's Farewell Address The book of Joshua comes to a close with two distinct ceremonies, each seeming in itself to be a finale. The first, in Josh 23, is a farewell address of Joshua to the gathered tribes in an unnamed place (the logic of the narrative would suggest Shiloh); the second, Josh 24, is a covenant renewal ceremony at Shechem. These are sometimes seen as a duplication, Josh 23 being later than Josh 24, and in certain respects modelled on it. There are, however, important differences between the two chapters.

Joshua's farewell address is linked expressly to the narrative of conquest. It connects (v. 1) with the resumptive statements in 11:23 and 21:43–5, and their themes of fulfilment of promise, complete conquest, and rest from war. The opening verse (1b) also repeats verbatim a phrase from 13:1, referring to Joshua's advanced age (see JOSH 13:1). The fact that there is no reference here to the allocation of land (chs. 13–21) and that it is assumed that land remains to be taken, has been thought to argue for the secondariness of Josh 13–21. However, 13:1 also introduced a catalogue of places not yet subdued. Both passages, therefore, simply express the tension between land possession as a fact and as a project that still awaits accomplishment. When chs. 23 and 24 are read together, the distribution of land may simply be assumed here, and the two ceremonies culminate in 24:28: 'Joshua sent the people away to their inheritances' (itself an echo of 22:1–6).

Following Deuteronomic requirements, the people are to hold fast to the law of Moses (v. 6; cf. Josh 1:7), and indeed 'love' YHWH himself (v. 11, cf. Deut 6:5—the term denotes covenant loyalty). They must not adopt the worship practices of the peoples that still remain among them (vv. 7, 16), nor intermarry with them (v. 12; cf. Deut 7:1–5). If they do, YHWH will cease to drive out the nations, and Israel itself will be driven off its newly acquired land (vv. 15, 16; cf. Deut 30: 17–18).

The tension between the ideal and the real is theologized in the speech as a reproach to Israel for imperfect obedience to the command to take the land (Judg 2:2–3). Joshua here expresses the twin possibilities of the covenant: faithfulness and possession, or unfaithfulness and loss. This choice, with its consequences, is most fully spelt out in Deut 28. Joshua goes even further, appearing to imply that the 'curses' of the covenant will certainly come (v. 15b), in a passage reminiscent of Deut 4:25–31; 30:1–5. This might suggest that our passage has the Babylonian exile in view, and must therefore date to a time after it. Unlike Deut 4:30, however, there is no mention here of repentance and return to the land. It is therefore not dependent on them in any simple way, and the allusion to the Babylonian exile is not certain.

(24:1–28) The Covenant at Shechem Unlike the speech in Josh 23, the ceremony in Josh 24 is clearly located in Shechem (v. 1). The shift of location from Shiloh is unheralded (hence LXX's reading 'Shiloh', which must be regarded as a late harmonization). Shechem, however, has important roots in the broader narrative of exodus and conquest (Deut 11:29; 27; Josh 8:30–5), which bespeak its strong association with covenant. Other narratives about Shechem support this. In a story from Judges there is reference to a temple of 'Baal-berith' (also 'El-berith'), that is, the lord, or god, 'of the covenant' (Judg 9:4, 46). Gen 34 tells of an ancient agreement (covenant?), albeit quickly broken. These texts suggest obliquely that Shechem was known as a place of covenant from early times.

Formal parallels have been observed between ancient Near-Eastern treaties of both the second and first millennium (but

especially second millennium Hittite vassal-treaties) and some OT covenants, notably Deuteronomy more or less in its entirety (Baltzer 1971). Josh 24 exhibits the characteristic features: a preamble (v. 1), a rehearsal of the historical relationship between the parties (vv. 2–13), stipulations and the requirement of loyalty (vv. 14–15, 25), formal witnesses (vv. 22, 27), depositing a document (vv. 26–7), and a statement of consequences (v. 20—here only the bad consequences of disloyalty are recorded, in contrast to Deut 28). YHWH is thus depicted as the suzerain, who requires loyalty from his partner in the context of his commitment to protect them in the land which he grants them. Properly, the present narrative merely resembles the ancient treaty form, being itself a literary construction. However, the use of the form has real significance, in that it records the actual commitment of the people to YHWH rather than to other gods, and their acceptance of this as the basis of their lives.

The historical context of the narrative is differently estimated. Some scholars, on the basis of Deuteronomic language and themes (e.g. vv. 16–18, 25, 26a), conclude that the whole passage comes from Assyrian (Perlitt 1969: 239–84) or exilic (Nicholson 1986) times. This is not necessary, however. Much of the material draws on themes that belong to Israel's traditions broadly understood: the origins of Israel's ancestors in Mesopotamia and the patriarchal line (vv. 2–4, cf. Gen 11:27–12:9), the Exodus from Egypt and the wilderness wanderings (vv. 5–9), the conflicts in Transjordan and the Balaam tradition (vv. 9–10, cf. Num 22–4), and the conquest itself. While there are Deuteronomic elements here (v. 11, the seven nations, cf. Deut 7:1; v. 13, cf. Deut 8:10–11), other features are more individual. An example is the statement that Abraham and his family worshipped other gods 'beyond the River' (v. 2). And the references to the stone as witness and particularly to the oak in the 'sanctuary of the LORD' (vv. 26–7) contrast with Deuteronomic prescriptions (Deut 16:21–2), and are signs of antiquity. Deuteronomic language, furthermore, is equivocal as a means of dating texts, since many of its terms are found in ancient treaties (Koopmans 1990: 407; Sperling 1987). Archaeology has found structures both at ancient Shechem and on Mt. Ebal. These have been linked both with this ceremony and with the one described in Josh 8:30–5, though such links cannot be made conclusively.

Josh 24 obliges the Israelites to enter into a solemn covenant, or better, a covenant renewal (if the Deuteronomic Horeb and Moab covenants are presupposed). The 'historical prologue' recalls YHWH's faithfulness in bringing Israel to their land, and reaffirms his agency in the Holy War. The 'Amorites' (v. 8) are the kings Sihon and Og, who were defeated in the Transjordanian campaign (Num 21:21–35; Deut 2:26–3:17). They are bracketed here with Balak, king of Moab, who hired Balaam the magician to curse Israel, in a vain attempt to stall their progress (Num 22–4; cf. Josh 13:21–2). Here YHWH says that he would not listen to Balaam (v. 10); in Numbers, Balaam knows from the outset that God was determined to bless the people (Num 22:12). The translation 'hornet' (NRSV, v. 12) is based on LXX and early versions, but is obscure, and sometimes rendered 'terror', picking up an important theme in the exodus tradition (cf. Ex 15:14–16; Num 22:3). The whole argument stresses both God's irresistibility, and his commitment to Israel.

The appeal to Israel is a call to exclusive loyalty (vv. 14–15). The phrase 'You cannot serve the LORD' is a surprisingly strong assertion that Israel will be unfaithful. It may be taken as a forceful warning not to enter this covenant lightly, or to think that loyalty to YHWH will be easy. As such it fits with Deuteronomy's view that Israel cannot keep covenant (Deut 9:4–7). The warning may be compared with v. 23, in which failure to worship YHWH alone is pictured as a present reality. This also is in line with the general picture of the early generations of Israel, ready to resort to other gods from the beginning (Ex 32; Num 25). Deuteronomy too, at its climax, portrays Israel as unfaithful (Deut 32). The effect here may be rhetorical. Elsewhere the Joshua generation is pictured as faithful (Judg 2:7, 10). The outcome in any case is the conclusion of the covenant, and the people go at last to their appointed homes (v. 28).

(24:29–33) Endings Four short units complete the narrative of the book, and in a sense of the Hexateuch (Genesis–Joshua). Joshua and Eleazar were co-responsible for the division of the land. Their deaths are now told, in the outer framing sections of these four units, signalling the end of the era of conquest and settlement, as Moses' death had signalled the end of the period of exodus (Deut 34). Like Moses, Joshua is given the title 'servant of the LORD'. He is buried in the territory that had been given him as a personal inheritance (Josh 19:49–50; cf. Judg 2:8–9).

The note concerning Israel records that they were faithful during Joshua's lifetime, agreeing with Judg 2:7, but stopping short of the ominous sequel (Judg 2:10). It brings to completion the aspiration in Joshua of a people dwelling peacefully and obediently in a land given in fulfilment of God's promise. The emphasis is on 'service', or worship, of YHWH, echoing the commitment undertaken in the covenant dialogue (vv. 14–22).

The record of Joseph's burial connects expressly with Gen 50:24–6. It puts the story of Joshua in a broader context, suggesting that the 'ending' achieved in it relates to the story that began long before with the promises to the patriarchs, the great theme of Genesis. He is buried in Shechem, in the territory of his son Manasseh. This also connects the report with the immediate context.

REFERENCES

Albright, W. F. (1945), 'The List of Levitical Cities', Louis Ginzberg Memorial, 1 (New York: American Academy for Jewish Research).

Alt, A. (1925), 'Judas Gaue unter Josia', PJ 21: 100–16; repr. in Kleine Schriften zur Geschichte des Volkes Israel (Munich: C. H. Beck, 1953), ii. 276–88.

Auld, A. G. (1975), 'Judges 1 and History: A Reconsideration', VT 25: 261–85.

—— (1978), 'Cities of Refuge in Israelite Tradition', JSOT 10: 26–40.

Baltzer, K. (1971), The Covenant Formulary in Old Testament, Jewish and Early Christian Writings (Oxford: Blackwell). German original, Das Bundesformular: Sein Ursprung und seine Verwendung im Alten Testament, WMANT 4 (Neukirchen: Neukirchener Verlag, 1960).

Barth, C. (1971), 'Die Antwort Israels', in H. W. Wolff (ed.), Probleme biblischer Theologie (Munich: Chr. Kaiser), 44–56.

Bright, J. (1981), A History of Israel, 3rd edn. (London: SCM).

Clements, R. E. (1989), Deuteronomy (Sheffield: JSOT).

Clines, D. J. A. (1976), 'New Year', IDBSup 625–9.

Cross, F. M. (1973), Canaanite Myth and Hebrew Epic (Cambridge Mass.: Harvard University Press).

Ehrlich, A. B. (1968), Randglossen zur Hebräischen Bibel, iii. Josua, Richter, I. u. II. Samuelis (Hildesheim: Georg Olms).

Fritz, V. (1994), Das Buch Josua, HAT 1/7 (Tübingen: Mohr).

Garstang, J. (1931), The Foundations of Biblical History: Joshua, Judges (London: Constable).

Gerbrandt, G. E. (1986), Kingship According to the Deuteronomistic History, SBLDS 87 Atlanta: (Scholars Press).

Gertz, J. (1994), Die Gerichtsorganisation Israels im deuteronomischen Gesetz (Göttingen: Vandenhoeck & Ruprecht).

Gottwald, N. K. (1979) The Tribes of Yahweh: A Sociology of the Religion of Liberated Israel, 1250–1050 BCE (London: SCM).

Halbe, J. (1975), 'Erwägungen zum Ursprung und Wesen des Massotfestes', ZAW 87: 324–45.

Kang, S.-M. (1989), Divine War in the Old Testament, BZAW 177 (Berlin: Mouton, de Gruyter).

Kenyon, K. (1979), Archaeology in the Holy Land, 4th edn. (London: Ernest Benn).

Kloppenborg, J. S. (1981), 'Joshua 22: The Priestly Editing of an Ancient Tradition', Biblica, 62: 347–71.

Koopmans, W. T. (1990), Joshua 24 as Poetic Narrative, JSOTSup 93 (Sheffield: JSOT).

Koorevaar, H. J. (1990), De Opbouw van het Boek Jozua (Heverlee: Centrum voor Bijbelse Vorming, België VZW).

Kraus, H.-J. (1951), 'Gilgal: ein Beitrag zur Kultusgeschichte Israels', VT 1: 181–99.

Lemaire, A. (1981), 'Galaad et Makîr', VT 31: 39–61.

Livingston, D. (1970), 'Location of Biblical Bethel and Ai Reconsidered', WTJ 33: 20–44.

Lohfink, N. (1962), 'Die deuteronomistische Darstellung des Übergangs der Führung Israels von Mose auf Josua', Scholastik, 37: 32–44.

Long, B. O. (1968), The Problem of Etiological Narrative in the Old Testament, BZAW 108 (Berlin: A. Töpelmann).

McCarthy, D. J. (1971), 'The Theology of Leadership in Joshua 1–9', Biblica, 52: 165–75.

McConville, J. G. (1984), Law and Theology in Deuteronomy, JSOTSup 33 (Sheffield: JSOT).

Mann, T. W. (1977), Divine Presence and Guidance in Israelite Traditions: The Typology of Exaltation (Baltimore: Johns Hopkins University Press).

Mayes, A. D. H. (1985), 'Deuteronomy 29, Joshua 9, and the Place of the Gibeonites in Israel', in N. Lohfink (ed.), Das Deuteronomium: Entstehung, Gestalt und Botschaft (Leuven: Leuven University Press), 321–5.

Milgrom, J. (1976), 'Priestly Terminology and Social Structure of Pre-Monarchic Israel', JQR 69: 66–76.

Mitchell, G. (1993), Together in the Land, JSOTSup 134 (Sheffield: JSOT).

Na'aman, N. (1986), Borders and Districts in Biblical Historiography (Jerusalem: Simor).

Nelson, R. D. (1981), 'Josiah in the Book of Joshua', JBL 100: 531–40.

Nicholson, E. W. (1986), God and his People: Covenant and Theology in the Old Testament (Oxford: Clarendon).

Noth, M. (1953), Das Buch Josua, HAT 1/7 2nd edn. (Tübingen: Mohr).

—— (1960), The History of Israel (London: A. and C. Black).

—— (1971), 'Die fünf Könige in der Höhle von Makkeda', in H. W. Wolff (ed.), Aufsätze zur biblischen Landes- und Altertumskunde (2 vols.; Neukirchen: Neukirchener Verlag), i. 281–93. German original, PJ 33 (1937), 22–36.

—— (1981), The Deuteronomistic History, JSOTSup (Sheffield: JSOT); German original Überlieferungsgeschichtliche Studien: Die sammelnden und bearbeitenden Geschichtswerke im Alten Testament (Halle, 1943; 2nd edn. Tübingen, 1957).

Otto, E. (1975), Das Mazzotfest in Gilgal, BWANT 107 (Stuttgart: Kohlhammer).

Perlitt, L. (1969), *Bundestheologie im Alten Testament*, WMANT 36 (Neukirchen: Neukirchener Verlag).

Polzin, R. (1980), *Moses and the Deuteronomist* (New York: Seabury).

Rainey, A. F. (1971), 'Bethel is Still Beitin', *WTJ* 33: 175–8.

Schäfer-Lichtenberger, C. (1995), *Josua und Salomo: Eine Studie zur Autorität und Legitimität des Nachfolgers im Alten Testament*, VTSup 58 (Leiden: Brill).

Seebass, H. (1984), 'Zur Exegese der Grenzbeschreibungen von Josua 16, 1–17, 13', *ZDPV* 100: 70–93.

Soggin, J. A. (1972), *Joshua*, OTL (London, SCM).

Sperling, S. D. (1987), 'Joshua 24 Re-examined', *HUCA* 58: 119–36.

Tengström, E. (1976), *Die Hexateucherzählung*, CBOTS 7 (Lund: C. W. K. Gleerup).

Thompson, T. L. (1992), *The Early History of the Israelite People: From the Written and Archaeological Sources* (Leiden: Brill).

Wagner, S. (1964), 'Die Kundschaftergeschichten im Alten Testament', *ZAW* 76: 255–69.

Westermann, C. (1994), *Die Geschichtsbücher des Alten Testaments: Gab es ein deuteronomistisches Geschichtswerk?* (Gütersloh: Chr. Kaiser).

Wenham, G. J. (1971), 'The Deuteronomic Theology of the Book of Joshua', *JBL* 90: 40–8.

Whitelam, K. (1996), *The Invention of Ancient Israel: The Silencing of Palestinian History* (London: Routledge).

Wilson, R. R. (1983), 'Enforcing the Covenant: The Mechanics of Judicial Authority in Early Israel', in H. B. Huffmon, F. A. Spina, and A. R. W. Green (eds.), *The Quest for the Kingdom of God: Studies in Honor of George E. Mendenhall* (Winona Lake, Ind.: Eisenbrauns), 59–75.

Wright, C. J. H. (1992), 'Family', *ABD* ii. 761–9.

Younger, L. (1990) *Ancient Conquest Accounts: A Study in Ancient Near Eastern and Biblical History Writing*, JSOTSup 98 (Sheffield: JSOT).

10. Judges

SUSAN NIDITCH

INTRODUCTION

A. The Biblical Timeframe. 1. Within the Bible's chronology, that is within the pan-Israelite portrayal of the history of the people, Judges is set in a time before kings ruled in Israel and before ritual actions and spaces were regularized and centralized. Leaders are swashbuckling bandits whose influence lasts only during their lifetimes, and Israelite groups unite to fight enemies as members of a loosely organized confederation. Two important heroes are women, an unusual gender for such roles in the androcentric Israelite tradition preserved in the HB.

2. Judges presents the period of the 'conquest' when Israelites wrest control of portions of the land from various non-Israelite overlords, defeating and dispossessing rival inhabitants. In contrast, however, to portions of the book of Joshua which portray the conquest as linear, unstoppable, and totalistic, Judges presents the events of a take-over much more haltingly as Israel, a poorly armed resistance force, wins some battles and loses others, has periods of relative success and some significant setbacks, never completely gaining control of the promised land. Indeed Israelite encounters with the enemy seem less like the warfare of conquest than the activities of subversive insurgents, guerrillas. Leaders are often at odds with the people while Israel itself is presented as composed of rather fragmentary groups and individuals that are sometimes at war with one another.

B. The Story. The narrative frame of the book as it now stands largely parallels its theological message. Israel is unable to defeat its foes because of lack of faithfulness to YHWH, patron deity who rescued Israel from the oppression of slavery in Egypt. At intervals, however, YHWH raises up leaders who inspire Israel to renewed faith in him, assuring their capacity to succeed in battle. The tales of Israel's insurgency feature various heroes including Ehud the left-handed man; Deborah, the prophet, and her aide Barak; Jael the female assassin of the Canaanite general Sisera; Gideon, destroyer of the altar of the deity Baal, competing god of the Canaanite enemy; Jephthah whose only daughter becomes a war-vowed sacrifice to YHWH; and Samson the superhero of ancient Israelite tradition. Additional tales include the story of Abimelech, a would-be Israelite king, a Danite founding myth, and a fascinating tale of civil war that describes the ways in which the ideal of pan-Israelite unity conflicts with strong local tribal or clan-related loyalties. Interwoven with the unifying theme concerning Israel's relationship to God are a host of other fascinating issues in Israelite world-view dealing with attitudes to gender, to centralized authority—in particular in the form of monarchy—attitudes to war, and other essential aspects of Israelite self-definition.

C. Relation to Actual History of Israel. 1. Do the stories of Judges reflect the actual events of early Israelite history of the pre-monarchic, pre-tenth-century BCE era, or at least in general capture the flavour and tone of the times? Who are these leaders called 'judges' who rarely serve in a juridical context and act more as military and political liberators (see Judg 4:5 for one exception)? Does the politically decentralized confederation presented in or implied as lying behind many of the narratives reflect the realities of a pre-monarchic form of Israelite self-governance? As is the case with epic traditions of other cultures, it is extremely difficult to match specific events and persons in Judges with detailed facts of Israelite history. It is certainly possible that some elements are rooted in actual experience, now stylized and formulated in the contours of the literary tradition. (For a full discussion of such issues see Boling (1975).) To pose such questions is to enter the vexing problem concerning Israelite origins in the land of Israel. Four major theories have been proposed: the conquest model; the infiltration model; the liberation model; and the pioneer settlement model.

2. The conquest model is closely wedded to the version of Israel's arrival in the land found in the biblical book of Joshua. Archaeological finds of the twentieth century seemed to evidence strafing and burning in various locations mentioned in the Bible, destruction that took place in the second half of the second millennium BCE, the period appropriate to the biblical chronology, and thus encouraged many American scholars to find in the Scriptures the outline of actual historical events. They thought it possible to prove in essentials that land-hungry Israelites making a transition from nomadic life to a more settled pattern of existence violently supplanted the inhabitants of the land (see Albright 1939; Bright 1981). In this model, the confederation or league served to organize and rally the conquering army.

3. Theories about Israelite nomadism have been strongly challenged in recent years and confidence in the conquest model has waned as the matches between biblical accounts of conquest and archaeological evidence have proven far less than perfect (see Hayes and Miller 1977). More suited to the stories in Judges is the infiltration model that suggests that Israelites gradually moved into the land and that battles with the natives were largely defensive (Alt 1967; Noth 1960). The confederation was a means of unifying various elements of the group that would become Israel for purposes of defensive war. This model too, however, rests upon outmoded notions of Israelite nomadism (Gottwald 1979). Scholars have also become increasingly suspicious about the existence of a formal Israelite league, especially about the existence of a single confederation that consisted of twelve tribes (Mayes 1974).

4. The liberation model allows that some of those who would come to constitute the group called Israel came from outside the land of Canaan but that their take-over of the land was aided by large segments of the native population. Marxian in orientation, this view of Israelite formation suggests that a group of immigrants, perhaps people who have escaped from Egyptian slavery, becomes the spearhead of an ideologically based revolution of have-nots against haves. The have-nots consist of the immigrants and the native population of Canaan living in a repressive feudal system common among the many petty tyrannies of the ancient Near East. The newcomers and those who share their political goals are united by their belief in YHWH and eventually defeat their better armed, urban rivals (Mendenhall 1973; Gottwald 1979).

5. The pioneer settlement model does not look beyond the land for origins, but regards Israelites as native to the land of Canaan, elements that leave the more settled and urban lowland areas to deforest and tame the wilds of the highlands. This movement of pioneers is economically motivated by the collapse of trade in the difficult times of the Late Bronze era. The pioneer settlements grow and prosper and their population eventually takes over the lowlands as well (Coote and Whitelam 1987). In contrast to the other models, the pioneer model does not rely on biblical traditions at all in an attempt to reconstruct Israelite history. Rather, scholars employ archaeological data and pertinent ethnographic models from other cultures to build their portrait of the origins of ancient Israel.

6. The world-views and the sorts of situation portrayed in Judges suit the liberation model remarkably well—indeed, better than any other portion of the Israelite literary tradition. Whereas the various enemies are ruled by kings, their armed force equipped with chariots, their deity housed in a temple, and their women awaiting them in fine houses with latticework windows, the Israelites are the underdogs, their leaders charismatic figures many of whom are marginal in some sense even within their own culture. Jephthah, for example, is an illegitimate son born to a prostitute, Deborah is a woman, an unusual qualification for Israelite military and political leadership, while Samson is a wild man caught between the realms of nature and culture and regarded as somewhat dangerous by his own people even while they admire him. Israelite warriors fight in the name of YHWH by means of

subterfuge and ambush, practitioners of the military ideology of trickerism (Niditch 1987; 1993: 106–22). One thinks e.g. of the hero Ehud's assassination of the Moabite king Eglon, who is described literally as a fat calf whose ample girth folds over the assassin's knife, or of the heroine Jael who poses as a friend of the Canaanite general Sisera, luring him to her tent with offers of succour, only to kill him by driving a tent peg through his head as he sleeps. Of course, the portrayal of battles between haves and have-nots could also reflect the sort of world described by Coote and Whitelam (1987), as highland pioneers feel themselves threatened by those in control of the lowlands and by various rivals to the territories they have settled.

7. In Judges, Israelite political motives are completely intertwined with religious motives. The hero Gideon's revolt begins with a night-time act of subversion as he overturns the statue of Baal. Samson's exploits are a means by which YHWH shows his power. Deborah is after all a prophet and Samson a nazirite, one consecrated to God at birth. The national agenda and the Yahwistic agenda are one.

D. Judges as Part of a Larger Whole. 1. If these traditional narratives do reflect the social world of Israel's pre-state origins as a people, in its current form the book also serves as an important segment of essential pan-Israelite myth. The process by which a host of traditions about the judges came together as a distinct corpus is difficult to reconstruct, involving a complex interplay between the oral and the written, individuals and the group, the ancient and the more recent. Along the way, what were once disparate traditions came to be an expression of the larger group's sense of history and identity. This is not to suggest that the process was superorganic without reference to specific composers set in time and place, but to admit uncertainty about the whos and wherefores. Scholars generally consider the book of Judges in its current form to be a part of the Deuteronomistic History, a corpus spanning Deuteronomy–2 Kings, whose collection and setting down is attributed to nationalistic and devotedly Yahwistic writers during the time of the reforming seventh century BCE Judean king Josiah (see INTROD.OT).

2. Such writers combine the radical monotheism, aniconism, and condemnation of fertility rituals, divination, and child sacrifice found in Deuteronomy with a strongly pro-Davidic, pro-southern emphasis on centralization of worship in the temple in Jerusalem. The Deuteronomistic History is considered to have undergone revision by ideological offspring of these seventh century reformers, exilic writers responding to the crisis of Babylonian conquest. The theme of YHWH's control of history and the book's strongly nationalistic pride in Israel's military successes appear to suit well the interests of such writers, monarchic and exilic. The varieties of religious expression revealed in the tales and their implicit distrust of kings and political authority, however, seem to point in other directions. Either Judges is not appropriately Deuteronomistic, or one must adjust suggestions about the Deuteronomistic corpus as pro-Josianic propaganda and come to appreciate the various threads in world-view preserved in this book as indeed in other material from Deuteronomy to 2 Kings. It has been suggested that the refrain, 'In those days there was no king in Israel; all the people did what

was right in their own eyes' (Judg 17:6; 18:1; 19:1; 21:25), allows pro-monarchic, southern writers to present received traditions as a reflection of olden times, romantic and appealing in some senses, but chaotic and better left in the past. Nevertheless, the subversive and anti-establishment qualities of Judges shine through and together with the lively traditional style of the narratives help to explain the continuing appeal of tales of the judges.

E. Ethics and the Book of Judges. As with virtually every biblical book, Judges confronts the modern reader with much that seems offensive or repugnant: the bloodthirsty violence of heroes such as Ehud; the sacrifice of a daughter to God by Jepththah; the rape, condoned by her husband, of the woman in Judg 19, her murder, and subsequent dismemberment. How does one engage such texts? One might disassociate oneself from Scripture and conclude that ancient Israelite culture is not our culture, their world-view not ours. A person who does consider himself within a more continuous line of biblical tradition for cultural or religious reasons might attempt to appropriate selectively, appreciating Jephthah's appeal to criteria of just war (11:12–27), the Israelites' condemnation of the evildoing at Gibeah, their heroism in confronting better-armed enemies. In this commentary we attempt to stand at some critical distance from the ancient representations in Judges, nevertheless empathizing with their authors and audiences. We have to imagine a world in which human sacrifice is not unthinkable even while we, like the voices of Deuteronomy and Leviticus, condemn it. We must also consider the possibility that the ancient Israelites were self-critical and unsure: their frequent enquiries of God portrayed in Judges, and their need for, but distrust of, leadership being evidence of inner tensions and self-doubt concerning the nature of human action and the moral underpinnings of received literary traditions.

COMMENTARY

(1:1–36) Bridging the era of Joshua and the period of the judges, this chapter is a chronicle describing Israel's military progress and lack of progress in the land. The author draws brief sketches of military encounters in economic strokes and includes a few vignettes that may have been described at greater length in the non-preserved tradition. Notice the range of terms used in the first half of the chapter that describe going to war and conquering. The author varies the traditional language producing a certain texture in these verses, but, in describing defeats and inability to conquer, monotonously and repeatedly employs the same phrase, 'did not drive out', creating an aura of dejected resignation. Scholars frequently point to the south to north geographic orientation of the chapter. For a detailed discussion and identification of the particular sites named in the chapter see Boling (1975). Many suggest that Judg 1 preserves a more accurate view of the period preceding the establishment of the monarchy than Joshua (e.g. Boling), while one scholar eschews questions of historicity, pointing rather to the way in which different literary genres make for different varieties of historiography (Younger 1994). The prominent role played by Judah in this introductory chapter has led one scholar to view the chronicle

as a piece of pro-Judahite propaganda (Brettler 1989). In its current form, the chronicle accommodates and begins to explain the clear differences between views of Israel's early history that were inherited in the tradition.

v. 1, the opening words of the book betoken a time of transition; Moses' successor Joshua has died and new leadership is necessary. The Israelites, here treated as a whole, request an oracle from God concerning the individual or group that will lead the conquest as a vanguard. Such pre-battle requests for divine guidance are usual not only in Israelite war texts but throughout comparable material in the wider ancient Near East (see e.g. 2 Sam 5:19; 1 Sam 23:2; 1 Kings 12:22). In such views of war the deity or deities are ultimately involved in the battles of men while war itself is framed and characterized by ritual action (see Kang 1989: 56–72, 98–107, 215–22). 'Canaanite' and 'Amorite' are traditional designations for the purported natives of the land. For more detailed discussion of terms for people of the land see Boling (1975). vv. 2–4, Judah and Simeon are treated as individuals by the singular verbs and pronouns of the language, lending the brief mention of their victories the quality of hero accounts, comparable to tales of the judges. vv. 5–7, the story of Judah and Simeon's victories focuses on one cameo scene as is frequent in the war tales of Judges. A conquered king is captured and rendered less than human with the loss of his ability to grip and his capacity to balance easily on two feet. Like the blinding of King Zedekiah by his Babylonian conquerors, such treatment of the enemy indicates how symbols of one's power are as important as the power itself. The enemy leader becomes the spoils of war, a doglike creature confirming the impotence of this and other enemies. He expects no better treatment (v. 7); his words point to the reversal of his own fortunes as a practitioner of this crude war code and are filled with irony and pathos. God has paid Adoni-bezek back. v. 8, this is one of the few uses in Judges of formulaic language implying imposition of the ban, a war ideology that involves the killing of all enemies, frequently by the sword, and often burning of the enemy city or town. Compare conflicting comments concerning the taking of Jerusalem at 1:21 and Josh 15:63. Notice also in the latter the use of the plural, 'people of Judah' (cf. vv. 2–4). vv. 12–15, this little piece of the tradition preserved also in Josh 15:15–19 presents a common folk theme concerning an elder rewarding a younger hero with a patrilineal culture's most valuable commodity, a nubile woman, his very own daughter. Heroes are frequently offered such rewards in 'dragon-slaying' and other combat contexts; the battle itself is sometimes presented as the difficult task posed by a powerful future father-in-law to test the mettle of the hero or to eliminate him. So Saul tests David (1 Sam 18:17). The interactions between Caleb, lone surviving leader of the generation of the Exodus, Othniel the hero, who also is Caleb's younger brother, and Achsah, Caleb's daughter, portray the young woman as resourceful and capable. She urges her husband to ask for land along with her, a piece of fertile earth being an appropriate extension of the gift of a woman. She herself demands water rights as her father allows and seems to expect. The theme of a hero's reward thus becomes a comment on a daughter's rights as Achsah is the first of a group of powerful women in Judges. Notice also the closely endogamous nature of the marriage.

1:17, a direct reference to the imposition of the ban (see v. 8). The folk etymology for the name given to the conquered city plays on the term meaning 'devote to destruction' (cf. Num 21:3). v. 19, the first of several 'excuses' offered in Judges to explain defeat and the implicit incompleteness of the portrayal of the conquest found in Joshua. With some historical verisimilitude it suggested that Israelite groups control the hill country, but not the lowlands. Actual chariots of the period would have been made of wood and leather with some iron fittings, but the image of iron chariots expresses well the author's view of his people as underdogs confronting better-armed, professional military forces. vv. 22–6, as is frequent in biblical war portrayals and in actual warring situations, reconnaissance troops are sent to assess the situation before battle (e.g. Num 13; Josh 3). As in the tale of Rahab (Josh 3), a local person is recruited with promises that he and his family will be rewarded or spared if he provides useful information to the Israelites (see also 1 Sam 30:11–15). The man in this case is treated in the style of ancient genealogies as a city founder (see Gen 4:17).

(2:1–6) This brief theophany functions as a connecting link between what precedes and what follows. It is a continuing response to the Israelites' request for divine guidance at 1:1 and an introduction to themes concerning the link between military failure and apostasy developed in more detail in ch. 2 and following. v. 1, God's covenantal promise to give Israel the land reaches back to the era of the patriarchs, while his own covenant faithfulness is witnessed by the rescue from Egypt. vv. 2–3, the covenant is conditional, however, upon Israel's fealty to YHWH alone. The tone and the concerns of the Deuteronomistic writer emerge strongly. Has Israel failed to drive out the enemy because of military weakness (1:19) or have they chosen to live among the forbidden, idolatrous Other? The writer here seems to understand failures described at 1:28–36 as evidence of the latter. Subsequent political and military problems are punishment for Israel's weaknesses as a covenant partner. vv. 4–5, the people's reaction to these dire predictions provide the folk etymology for the place where the angel has appeared.

(2:6–23) A theologically grounded view of history is laid out: Israel's military and political fortunes depend upon covenantal faithfulness which in turns appears to depend upon strong leadership. vv. 6–10, a brief recapitulation of land-allotting events described in Joshua, an indication that indeed Joshua was the sort of leader who kept the people faithful to God, and notice of his demise and burial, and the death of the generation of the Exodus. Note the ominous comment that another generation replaces them who did not know YHWH or the work he had done for Israel. Such allusions to new young men in power generally signal trouble for Israel in biblical texts (cf. Ex 1:8; 1 Kings 12:8). vv. 11–23, in formulaic language typical of the Deuteronomistic writers, the pattern of Israel's history under the judges is outlined: apostasy; punishment by military defeat and subjugation; the people's distress; the raising of a hero, the judge, who inspires Israel and delivers her; the death of the leader; relapse into apostasy; defeat. Compare the theology and the language in Deut 4:21–31; 6:10–15; 9:4–7; 12:29–32; 28:25, and notice how the framework set out in this chapter unifies Judges as a whole (see e.g. the language and

content at 3:7–10, 12, 15; 4:1; 6:1–10; 10:6–16; 13:1), making sense not only of this period in the biblical chronology but of the subsequent monarchic periods as well. Israel's fortunes depend not upon pragmatic matters such as economic strength, political unity, or military preparedness but rather upon the health of the covenantal relationship with God. Notice the language of interpersonal relationship through which covenant is expressed. Israel 'abandons' YHWH (vv. 12–13) to follow other gods, especially the Canaanite Baal and his consort. YHWH in turn becomes 'angry' and 'incensed' with them (vv. 12, 14, 20), while they 'lust after' these foreign gods (v. 17). This passage ends with an additional twist on the theme of Israel's incomplete conquest: enemies have been left in the land to test Israel's faithfulness.

(3:1–31) The activities of the first judges, Othniel, Ehud, and Shamgar. vv. 1–4, this introductory section lists by name and place Israel's competitors in the land. See Boling (1975), for a discussion of terms and sites. v. 3 provides an additional explanation for the continued presence of such groups in the land promised by YHWH to Israel. The newcomers to the land require some enemies in order to sharpen their agonistic skills. This together with the repeated suggestion that the idolatrous enemy tests Israel's capacity to resist idols (v. 4; 2:22), the indication that the enemy has better armaments (1:19), and the overriding theme that apostasy guarantees failure, reveal an author attempting to make sense of traditions about Israel's incomplete conquest that challenge the more triumphalist ideology of Joshua. vv. 5–6, typically Deuteronomic in outlook, suggest that living in close proximity to those not of one's own people, the uncivilized Other, leads to foreign marriages and cultural contamination (cf. Deut 7:1–6). It is the world-view of a group strongly defining 'us' as 'not them'. vv. 7–11, the report concerning Othniel (see JUDG 1:11–15), the younger brother and son-in-law of Caleb, traces the conventionalized pattern (see 2:11–31) in language that is largely formulaic.

vv. 12–30, within the recurring narrative frame of apostasy, the people's cry to God, the raising of a judge-rescuer, the successful battle against the enemy, and the lengthy respite from war, comes the beautifully crafted tale of the trickster-hero Ehud. The trickster succeeds through deception and disguise, a marginal person who uses his wits to alter his status at the expense of those holding power over him (see Niditch 1987). v. 15, in this case, the rescuer's ruse is made possible by his left-handedness. In the Hebrew, the term for left-handed is literally 'bound' or 'impaired with regard to the right hand'. To be left-handed is thus to be unusual or marginal, the right being the preferred side in other biblical contexts (see Ex 29:20, 22; Lev 7:32; 8:23, 25; Eccl 10:2). Benjaminites, Ehud's fellow-tribesmen, are described in the tradition as predisposed to left-handedness (see 20:16). This trait makes them especially effective warriors. The effectiveness comes not only from the lefties' capacity to surprise the enemy or to make a defensive posture more difficult. Left-handedness suggests also the power of a wild man, the ecstatic, and the socially uncontrolled. Notice the play in this verse and below upon terms for and images of ritual sacrifice. Eglon's name plays on the term for 'calf' while the 'tribute' to be offered to the king of Moab is also the term for sacrificial offering (Anderson 1987: 74). It is however the 'fatted calf' himself who will be slaughtered. v. 16, the typical right-handed man would be expected to wear his sword on the left in order to draw with the right hand. Thus Ehud hides his weapon. vv. 19–20, these verses contain language of intimacy. On 'in secret' see Jer 40:15; 37:17; and 38:16; with nuances of enticement see Deut 13:6 and Job 31:27; and with eroticism see 2 Sam 12:12. 'Coming to' may also have erotically intimate connotations (see Ruth 3:4). v. 21, the 'thrust' term also used in Judg 4:21 combined with the short sword that had been worn on the thigh, a male erogenous zone in the HB, and its destination the belly, a term also employed for 'womb' completes the womanization of the enemy whose defeat by an Israelite hero is enriched narratively by a metaphoric mixing of images of sex and slaughter, a trait of epic battle scenes elsewhere in the world (see Vermeule (1979: 101–2, 145–58, 171–3) on classical Greek material and Shulman (1986) on Tamil material). v. 24, what did Eglon's servants assume he was doing in his quarters? The phrase translated 'relieving himself' in NRSV literally reads 'pouring out' or 'covering his feet', the feet being a biblical euphemism for the male member. The phrase thus may mean that he was urinating or defecating. In any event, the language suggests intimate activity involving private parts again pointing to Eglon's vulnerability and unmanning. In this context compare the encounter between David and Saul in the cave (1 Sam 24:1–7).

v. 31 has a brief reference to another of the Israelite liberating heroes, one that lacks the usual conventional frame in content and language. While some suggest the appellation Anath refers to a place, others suggest that the warrior's name includes that of the Canaanite goddess Anath, herself a warrior and patroness of warriors (see Boling 1975: 89). The latter points to the varieties of Israelite religious identity preserved however briefly in the epic traditions of Judges. Shamgar, like Samson, performs superhuman feats, able to conquer hundreds of the enemy with a mere ox-goad, a symbol of the agrarian roots that typify many of the heroes of Judges. Indeed an agrarian thread in Israelite identity dominates the book. Has an editor purposefully omitted much of Shamgar's story because the tradition associates this hero with things Canaanite? Has material simply been lost or forgotten? Or, for an ancient Israelite audience, perhaps the mere mention of Shamgar, the ox-goad, and the Philistines metonymically suggested a wide range of relevant and familiar stories, cited here only in brief, but more fully rendered in other contexts not preserved for us, as perhaps also is the case for the briefly described Othniel (vv. 9–11).

(4:1–24) This chapter introduces Deborah the prophet, Barak the Israelite warrior hero, and Jael, a woman warrior who exemplifies the traditional character motif, 'the iron fist in the velvet glove'. v. 1, notice that the conventional narrative pattern resumes without reference to Shamgar. v. 3, as at 1:19 the enemy is described as having iron chariots, a well-armed oppressive force. Israel does not have the use of iron weaponry until the beginning of the monarchy. v. 4, Deborah, who is introduced at the saviour point in the pattern, after the formulaic cry to God for relief from oppression, is described as a prophet who judges Israel at this time. Other female prophets are alluded to in the HB, such as Huldah who provides an

important oracle concerning the need for reform in the time of Josiah (2 Kings 22:14–20); Noadiah mentioned in Neh 6:14; and the wife of Isaiah (8:3). Were women prophets in fact common in ancient Israel, having been deleted or not preserved in the biblical corpus, or were prophetesses rare? One suspects the former given how workaday and mundane are the references to Huldah, Noadiah, and Isaiah's wife, but the current biblical context makes Deborah leap off the page as special and unusual in her mediating and leadership roles. This is how she is understood by the compiler of the traditions in Judges. (See JUDG 4:9.)

The phrase usually translated 'wife of Lappidoth' may be translated 'woman of fire', or 'woman of torches/lightning flashes', in a parallel to Barak whose name means 'lightning'. The latter conveys a more charismatic image than the identification by husband's name. Much has been written on Deborah's role as judge. Key terms in v. 5 portray her as an oracle, critical to Israel's military success because of her capacity to mediate between God and Israel. Such holy men and women are often called upon in traditional cultures to mediate between humans as well and to provide advice in a wide range of areas.

v. 5, Deborah 'sitting' under a tree named for her, and the verb 'go up' that elsewhere in the HB describes those who seek divinely inspired counsel, suggest oracular and prophetic processes involved in rendering various sorts of judgement. See relevant terminology and content in 1 Sam 9:13, 14, 18; 2 Kings 19:14 || Isa 37:14; 2 Kings 22:14; Jer 26:10–11. vv. 6–7, Deborah delivers to Barak, the apparent leader of Israelite forces, military instructions received directly from God concerning a confrontation with the army of Jabin, led by Sisera his general. YHWH is the ultimate military commander in the holy wars fought by his people. The promise of victory by divine communication (v. 7) is essential to waging war throughout the ancient Near East (see JUDG 1:1). v. 8, Barak's desire to have Deborah attend the battle certainly highlights her status as a leader, but it is not at all unusual to have the holy person present in a military setting. Indeed, Samuel incorporates roles of priest, prophet, and general, while Elisha refers to Elijah as 'the chariots of Israel and its horsemen' (2 Kings 2:12). v. 9, the 'woman' is Jael whose tale follows. v. 11, the Kenites are another of the intriguing but difficult to identify pre-Israelite groups inhabiting the land. Moses' father-in-law Jethro, a priest of Midian according to traditions in Exodus and Numbers, is called a Kenite in Judg 1:16 and the present text, leading some to attribute sacral dimensions to Jael's tent (Cross 1973: 200). The point here is that Heber has disassociated himself from those Israelite connections and has become a military and political ally of the Canaanite king Jabin. His wife Jael, whose name means 'YHWH is God', has different loyalties from her husband, allowing for the deception in vv. 17–22. vv. 12–16, the pattern reversing Israel's fortunes is completed with the underdogs' victory as predicted by the prophetess. Only the general Sisera is said to survive, underscoring the epic proportions of YHWH's victory for his people and allowing the bardic author to focus on one dramatic scene involving Sisera and Jael, a cameo that encapsulates central themes and employs favourite recurring literary topoi in Judges. vv. 17–22, like Ehud, Jael deceives the enemy into thinking that she can be of service. Sisera needs a place to hide from Israelite pursuers. Like Eglon, Sisera is rendered vulnerable and impotent, and in this case the assassin is not only one of the underdogs but a woman as well. Jael poses as Sisera's saviour and his seductress, urging him twice to turn aside to her, covering him with a rug (v. 18). He asks for water, but mother-like she gives him milk to drink, setting him at his ease with the wiles of women. He, like the child, drops off to sleep comforted that Jael will protect him from the Israelites (v. 20) whereupon, warrior-like, she strikes him dead. The phrase, 'Comes to him quietly' imports the language of lovers (Ruth 3:7) into an aggressive and agonistic scene. The tent-peg and hammer, accoutrements of settled domesticity, become weapons of the assassin. These exquisite juxtapositions—lover/killer, mother/assassin, tent-dweller/warrior—are drawn with greater detail and nuance in the ancient poem of Judg 5. v. 22, the fulfilment of Deborah's prediction (v. 9). vv. 23–4, a reminder that the battle is YHWH's, as the conventionalized pattern is again completed with relief from Israel's oppressors. Now Israel herself bears down upon and destroys her enemies, at least for the time being.

(5:1–31) The victory song attributed to Deborah is one of the oldest extant Israelite literary compositions dating perhaps to the twelfth century BCE, a time roughly contemporaneous with the era it depicts. Like the earlier works of the Canaanites discovered at Ugarit, the composition is characterized by a parallelistic variety of repetition whereby imagery unfolds in a beautifully layered or impressionistic style (Cross 1974), so that the parallel line adds colour, nuance, or contrast to its neighbouring description. The lines in such bicola or tricola are in general roughly parallel in length, while language selected by the composer to create content and the content itself draw upon traditional Israelite media of expression, also employed by others whose work is preserved in the biblical tradition. The song contains three major narrative thrusts: an introduction to the Divine Warrior and an overview of the historical setting for the poem (vv. 1–11); a catalogue of the participants and their successes or failures (vv. 12–23); a telling of the tale of Jael that includes a poignant cameo scene of women in the enemy camp (vv. 24–31).

v. 1, the victory song is attributed to Deborah and Barak, recalling perhaps the attribution of victory songs to Moses and Miriam in the Exodus story (Ex 15). The victory song is a genre frequently associated with women composers in the Israelite tradition. v. 2, while the translation in NRSV appears to refer to the Samson-like hairstyle of the warriors, others translate the first line of v. 2, 'When they cast off restraint in Israel' (Boling, 1975: 107; see also Soggin: 1981: 84 for alternatives). v. 3, notice the parallel terms and syntax in the call to hear this song, the formulaic introduction 'hear/give ear' (cf. Deut 32:1; Isa 1:2). YHWH, both muse and victor, is the ultimate source and receiver of the song. vv. 4–5, God as Divine Warrior (cf. Ex 15:3) is described in his march to battle. Like Marduk, Baal, and Zeus he is a storm god whose rousing disrupts the natural realm. The epithet 'One of Sinai' invokes a wide range of traditional lore concerning God's place of habitation and the dramatic encounter with Israel. Imagery of earthquake also dominates the scene at Sinai (Ex 19:16–24).

v. 7, the term translated 'peasantry' in NRSV has also been interpreted to mean 'warriors' (Boling 1975: 102) and 'leading

class' (Soggin 1981: 82) while the verb 'grew fat' also means 'ceased'. A translation that allows that villagers cease to prosper better suits the pattern of the song's plot depicting Deborah as rescuer, and better supports the cessation of trade described in v. 6 where the same term for 'cease' is found. The author describes a period of subjugation and disruption until Deborah, an archetypal mother in Israel, goddess-like and powerful, arises. v. 8, the variously interpreted first bicolon may be a proverb that links times of political change or revolution with the exchange of power between deities. Events in the divine realm parallel the changing course of human events: 'When new gods are chosen, war is at the gates.' The second bicolon points to the poorly armed Israelite forces who rely less on the sort of weapons utilized by their feudal enemies than on the power of the Lord, an image well suited to Gottwald's theory about Israelite wars of liberation in the late second millennium BCE (see JUDG c.4). vv. 10–11, these verses are among the few in extant Israelite literature that may point to the bardic process behind the composition of some biblical works. v. 12, like the Divine Warrior himself, Deborah and Barak are formulaically encouraged into battle (cf. Isa 51:9; 52:1).

vv. 13–15, in the procession motif of the mythological pattern that describes the battle with and victory over the forces of chaos, the composer describes the members of an Israelite confederation. Scholars suggest that in the absence of a centralized government, various Israelite tribes or clans would come together for purposes of defence. vv. 15–18, this section is usually translated and interpreted to mean that some Israelite groups did not willingly join in battle with their compatriots. Yet the section sits apart from v. 23 in which Meroz is cursed for its lack of support. Providing examples from cognate languages, one scholar suggests that the term translated 'why' in vv. 16 and 17 is an emphatic particle that might be translated 'verily' (Cross 1973: 235 n.). In this case, vv. 15–18 continue the catalogue of warrior groups with references to their geographic origins and ways of life (cf. Iliad 2:485–759). For example, Reuben dwells among the sheepfolds (v. 16), Gilead tents beyond the Jordan (v. 17). The translations 'tarry' and 'stayed' (NRSV et al.) for terms that ordinarily mean 'to dwell' are forced. vv. 20–1, the battle takes on cosmic and supramundane nuances as even the hosts of heaven, YHWH's army, join the fray and as the onrushing torrent, evocative of the sea in Ex 14–15, sweeps the enemy away. v. 23, Meroz, whose identity is uncertain, was one of those local groups expected to be committed to the Israelite cause. As in all ancient Near-Eastern treaty relationships, the punishment for shirking one's responsibility is a curse, understood to have real and physical power.

vv. 24–7, another version of the tale of Jael presented in wonderfully economic style. Notice the way the author builds to the assassin's deception. Sisera asks for water, she gives him milk, or no, is it not cream in a lordly bowl? And then with repetition that underscores the violent turn in the action she is described as one who strikes, crushes, shatters, and pierces. v. 27, the description of Sisera's death is rich in double entendres that play upon themes of eroticism and death. Sisera kneels, a defeated warrior or a would-be lover (cf. Ps 20:9 and Job 31:10)? Is he at her feet (so NRSV) or more literally between her legs, 'feet' being a euphemism for genitals (see Isa 7:20; Deut 28:57;

Ezek 16:25 AV)? The same ambivalences in meaning apply to the terms translated 'lay' and 'dead' in NRSV (cf. 1 Kings 1:21; 2 Kings 14:22; Ezek 32:29; and Gen 19:32, 34, 35; 35:22). The last term of v. 27 variously translated 'dead', 'laid waste', 'destroyed', might also be translated 'despoiled', cf. Isa 15:1; 23:1; and Jer 4:30 (see Niditch 1989: 47–51). The repetitive cadences of the verse, moreover, have the quality of a ritual dance of death. The enemy is at the same time seduced and slaughtered, the one serving as metaphor for the other. vv. 28–30, the author powerfully juxtaposes the scene of Sisera's death at the hands of a woman with a glimpse of another female figure, the hero's mother who anxiously awaits his victorious return from battle. This gifted composer is able to picture the enemy camp with pathos and empathy much as Homer depicts the Trojan women. In contrast to Jael, the tent-dwelling woman, the mother of Sisera is an aristocrat peering from a house with lattice-work windows (see 2 Kings 10:30), accompanied by ladies-in-waiting. They assure her in poetic parallelism that her son is late because he and his men are busy dividing up the spoil. Among the spoil are women booty, a term derived from the root literally meaning 'womb' (v. 30). We know, whereas his mother does not, that no Israelite women are to be raped. Ironically in the sexually charged language of v. 27 it is Sisera himself who has been despoiled at the hands of a warrior woman practising the art of tricksterism.

Tales of Gideon (6:1–8:35)

Chs. 6, 7, and 8 contain stories of Gideon who rescues Israel from the Midianites, and draw upon traditional Israelite topoi such as the theophany and the miracle account while suggesting a more international bardic tradition concerning the exploits of hero warriors.

(6:1–40) vv. 1–10, the introduction to Gideon's history outlines the conventionalized pattern of the judge (see JUDG 2:11–23; 3:12–30) enriched with a detailed description of Israel's oppression as an agriculturally based community (see vv. 3–5). YHWH's response is through a prophet who explains Israel's woes in Deuteronomic terms; Israel has worshipped gods other than YHWH. YHWH is formulaically identified as the rescuer of the Exodus (cf. Ex 20:2) and, with the call to Gideon, does send help. v. 11, like Saul and many other Israelite heroes, Gideon's roots are in the farming community beset by enemies round about. v. 12, the divine presence—as in tales of Abraham, Jacob, Manoah's wife, and others—involves an intermediary messenger who appears at first to be a human being. v. 13, Gideon responds to the visitor's encouraging formulaic greeting with a complaint typical of Israelite national laments (cf. Ps 74; 77:7–20). God is capable of wonders known from the great myths that mark the foundation of the world and the people Israel. Where is he now? See also Abraham's response to divine promises (Gen 15:2). vv. 14–15, the charge to or commissioning of the hero (cf. Moses: Ex 3:10; Jeremiah: Jer 1:4–5; and Saul: 1 Sam 9:20) and the hero's humble attempt to refuse (cf. Ex 3:11; Jer 1:6; 1 Sam 9:21). v. 16, cf. Ex 3:12. v. 17, as is typical in the pattern of the theophany, the hero requests a sign, assurance that the commission comes from God or that the words spoken are true (Gen 15:8; Ex 4:1; also 3:12–13). vv. 19–23, evidence that the message to Gideon is backed by divine favour is provided by the fiery

consummation of Gideon's offering. YHWH's power is frequently revealed in the fire (see Gen 15:17; Ex 3:1–6; cf. Judg 13:20). Gideon's fearful response is typical of biblical theophanies, and the subsequent building of an altar and folk etymology commemorating the dramatic experience of God place Gideon in a line of Israelite ancestor heroes (see Gen 29:17–18; 32:30). v. 23, having experienced the power of God through an intermediary, Gideon now receives messages directly from the Lord. vv. 25–35, God's charge to Gideon is to commit a bold act of subversion, to cut down the sacred pole or asherah, a symbol of the Canaanite deity Baal's indwelling presence, and to overthrow his altar, replacing it with an altar to YHWH. The wood of the pole is to provide the fire while the offering is a bull of his father's. Under cover of darkness Gideon and his men thus challenge both the ruling Canaanite establishment and his own people. Will they defend his actions and YHWH or will they submit to the rule of Canaanite culture? Joash, Gideon's father, comes to his support, as a folk etymology for Gideon's new name, 'Let Baal contend against him', completes Gideon's transformation from farmer's son to warrior hero. Now Gideon is filled with the spirit of God (v. 34), such possession being the mark of charismatic leaders such as Samson, Jephthah, and Saul. War is not the purview of cold military professionals, but the very will of YHWH himself whose power infuses and energizes those who fight his battles. vv. 36–40, Gideon requests and receives again a sign of YHWH's support. The symbol chosen, a fleece of wool, is drawn from the agricultural world that defines the Israelite community for many of the traditions in Judges, while the evidence of God's presence and power involves the deity's capacity to control and alter the normal course of nature. The hero's repeated request for a sign recalls Moses (see JUDG 6:17) and more generally is a favourite biblical motif of the hesitant or insecure hero. Indeed YHWH favours those who are aware of their own weaknesses (see ch. 7).

(7:1–25) vv. 1–8 war, in this case against the Midianites, is not for the glory of Israel but for the glory of God. As in Deut 20:5–7, the Lord orders the Israelites to limit the size of their fighting force by allowing the fearful to return home (v. 2). Even so, the fighting men are too numerous, for the battle, like the Exodus itself, is to be not proof of Israelite prowess but a miracle account in which success is guaranteed by God the warrior. Thus God devises a method, the test of the mode of drinking, to reduce the force to a mere 300 men (v. 8). Only the 'lappers' are allowed to fight. (Cf. 2 Chr 25:7–8 and the humbled stance of Israelite kings in the face of war at 2 Chr 14:9–15; 12:6; 20:12; 16:8.) vv. 9–11, reconnaissance before the battle is a common biblical war motif (Num 13; Josh 2). Here the descent into the enemy camp is suggested by YHWH as a means of offering the always humble and hesitant hero Gideon a positive sign before the battle. v. 12, notice the description of the enemy in the parallel style of Israelite poets. Each repetition serves to emphasize the enemy's massive strength over against the two Israelite observers and their skeleton army. v. 13, dreams have divinatory significance (cf. Joseph's dreams and his dream interpretations in Gen 37:5–7; 40:8–22; 41:1–36). The interpretation, moreover, like a curse or a blessing has the capacity to bring about that which is predicted. Hence the rabbinic saying, 'All dreams follow the mouth'. The overheard conversation functions as a particular sort of omen akin to the Greek *klēdōn*. vv. 15–23, the instructions before the battle and the mentioned instruments of war are reminiscent of the battle of Jericho (Josh 6). The shouting, the trumpets, the torches, and the breaking jars lead to the enemy's rout. v. 23, as judge, Gideon calls up members of the Israelite confederation to pursue the Midianites (cf. Judg 5:14–18). vv. 24–5, in a final mop-up operation, Gideon calls up the tribe of Ephraim, whose heroes capture and behead the Midianite captains Oreb and Zeeb.

(8:1–35) vv. 1–3, one of the benefits of making war in this traditional culture is access to booty and to a manly sort of honour. The Ephraimites are interested in their part of the glory and the spoils, and accuse Gideon of leaving them only the dregs (v. 1). Gideon responds in a proverb designed to reduce tension and win over one's opponent without violence. In the form of a rhetorical question he states that Ephraim's 'gleaning', that is, what is left after the harvest, is preferable to his (Gideon the Abiezrite's) grape harvest. He thus suggests not only that they have received much in the battle, but also—diplomatically and self-effacingly—that their worth or honour is greater than his own. vv. 4–9, Gideon's interactions with the people of Succoth and Penuel are similar to David's encounters with Nabal, husband of Abigail (1 Sam 25), and Ahimelech, priest of Nob (1 Sam 21). A popular hero who might also be considered 'a Robin Hood type of social bandit' (Hobsbawm 1969) asks for support in the form of food for his fighting men. As in the Nabal episode, the request is denied and threats ensue. The officials of Succoth in fact taunt Gideon (v. 6), implying that his prowess as a fighter is more in tales than in deeds. vv. 10–17, Gideon does succeed militarily, captures the Midianite kings Zebah and Zalmunna and makes good his threat to punish those who would doubt him. It is unwise to tangle with a bandit, especially one supported by God, as Nabal finds out.

vv. 13–14, these verses are often cited as proof of Israelite literacy at an early period or as an indication that a later writer portrayed an ordinary young man who happen to pass by as literate. In fact the term translated 'young man' may be used as technical language for a particular variety of government bureaucrat, one who would have access not only to writing but also to the sort of detailed political information that Gideon is pictured to request. Such bureaucrats would have been associated with centralized monarchic governments rather than with the more fluid political situation that Judges claims to portray, but such anachronisms are in fact typical of traditional literatures. vv. 18–21, this scene poignantly portrays a particular bardic ideology of war. The foreign kings respect their enemies suggesting they looked like princes (v. 18). Gideon for his part executes the Midianites because of his kinship bonds to those they had killed. Warriors are to face their equals in battle (hence Goliath's disdain for the lad David in 1 Sam 17:42–3; see also 2 Sam 2:20–3), and the inexperienced son of Gideon is not up to the task. The kings, quoting a proverb, request that the hero leader himself kill them, for such is the appropriate death of a king. vv. 22–3 Gideon rejects hereditary kingship though the people press it upon him (cf. 1 Sam 8). The attitude behind this scene and the tale of Abimelech that follows is strongly anti-monarchic, glorifying

the days when Israel's only king was YHWH and when her leaders recognized their limitations as tools of YHWH. vv. 24–7, the story of Gideon's ephod as here included transforms what may have been an etiology for a local cultic object into a mini golden calf episode. The leader responds to the people's lack of faith as in Ex 32 by requesting they give him gold, out of which he fashions a sacred object. In Ex 28 and 39 the ephod is described as a golden and woven vestment worn by the priest Aaron, one of the various items that allow for mediation between heaven and earth. Here the ephod appears to be more self-standing and iconic and is treated as an idol by the Deuteronomistic writer of v. 28 who interrupts the positive assessment of Gideon with this episode. v. 31, a brief introduction to Abimelech's humble origins (see JUDG 9:1). vv. 33–5, the conventionalized pattern of the judges resumes. With the death of the faithful leader, Israel suffers a moral relapse, worshipping Canaanite deities, forgetting YHWH, and abandoning loyalty to the house of Gideon, the hero.

(9:1–57) The story of the rise and fall of one of Gideon's sons, Abimelech, a would-be king, told from the perspective of an anti-monarchic writer. v. 1, Abimelech is the son of a concubine, a secondary wife (see 8:31) whose origins are in Schechem. Such humble roots are not unusual for the judge as social bandit (cf. Jephthah, 11:1–3); Abimelech, however, is not a patriot for God, but a self-server. vv. 2–3, Abimelech appeals to his mother's kin for support in his murderous plans for a take-over of political power. The phrase 'he is our brother' not only refers to kinship bonds but also to related political or covenantal ties (cf. 1 Kings 20:32). vv. 4–6, the mercenaries that Abimelech hires with his kinsmen's financial backing are described with derision as literally 'empty' and 'wanton' (cf. Gen 49:4). The simple narration of heinous crimes, unadorned by editorial comment, condemns a system of selecting leadership that was common in the petty tyrannies of the ancient Near East. If any doubt remains about the narrator's view of kingship one need only read the parable that follows. vv. 7–21, one son of Gideon survives the slaughter of his brothers and is said to go to the top of Mount Gerizim, appropriately, one of the peaks involved in the ancient ceremony of blessings and curses described in Deut 27–8. There he delivers a *māšal*, an ancient Israelite genre that creates a message by means of implicit comparison, an analogy drawn between a saying, story, or other form and the situation of the listeners. In this *māšal*, the choosing of a human king, Abimelech, is likened to a search for a leader among the trees. Notice the recurring frame language that unifies the *māšal* and builds to the answer as to who will reign. The debate among objects of a particular group or among the members of one body concerning who is the most important or who is to lead is a common folk motif (see Thompson 1955–8: J242; J461). In this case, however, the useful trees decline rulership as beneath them. Only the useless and prickly bramble agrees to reign. One might expect the *māšal* to end with v. 11 and thereby serve as a comment on those who overtly desire power. The author contextualizes this potentially universal *māšal* in terms of the story of Abimelech. That such contextualization was typical of *māšal* use even in oral contexts is possible (cf. e.g. Ezek 17; 2 Sam 12). The message in context appears to suggest that kingship is a reasonable if not desirable form of leadership, but that the system will work well only if there is trust between the leader and the led. As Jotham states in a gloss upon the *māšāl*, the situation in Shechem involves an evil coup, actions undertaken without 'good faith' and doomed to failure (vv. 16–20). Those who are disloyal to Gideon (vv. 17–18) will not be capable of loyalty to Abimelech who himself has been proven prone to self-serving violence. Jotham's parable serves as an ominous prediction. As the righteous complaint of a wronged person, this speech act also helps to bring about vengeance through divine intervention.

vv. 22–49, the story of Abimelech's decline is framed in terms of God's control. It is YHWH who 'sent an evil spirit' between Abimelech and the Shechemites. (For YHWH's control of persons through such means see 1 Sam 16:14.) The wresting of political power through violence that is not divinely sanctioned is condemned. vv. 25–7, the Shechemite chieftains attempt to undermine the stability of Abimelech's fledgling state through acts of banditry, and soon transfer their affections to a new strongman. They are pictured as drunken louts taunting the status and credentials of Abimelech and loyalists such as Zebul. vv. 34–41, Zebul informs Abimelech of Gaal's would-be coup and taunts the challenger to face the king (v. 38). He does and is defeated by Abimelech and Zebul. vv. 42–9, Abimelech takes further vengeance on the people of Shechem, a practitioner of the ideology of total 'pacification'. Such acts of killing, burning, and strafing without attention to the military status, age, or gender of those destroyed are sometimes portrayed to be business as usual among the monarchs of the ancient Near East. Even David, the ideal king in some threads in the tradition, engages in brutal, terror-inspiring acts of warfare (see 2 Sam 5:7–8). In the tale of Abimelech is implicit criticism, for the king's violent victory and deadly excesses only foreshadow his own ignominious defeat. vv. 50–7, Abimelech continues his tour of vengeance at Thebez, another fortress city. Here as in Shechem the people flock to the tower for protection, and, as at Shechem, Abimelech plans to burn it down (vv. 48–9). This time, however, a woman of unknown name or origins throws down an upper millstone, a symbol of the woman's domestic realm, and crushes the skull of this would-be hero. He in fact begs his armour-bearer to kill him quickly lest it be said that a woman slew the hero Abimelech (cf. 2 Sam 11:21). She, like Jael, does render the hero impotent, while the millstone itself is an evocative symbol not only of domesticity but of woman's sexuality as well (cf. Isa 47:2; Job 31:10). vv. 56–7, the writer sets the story in context as an example of just deserts, condemning Abimelech's style of assuming political authority and emphasizing both the power of curses and YHWH's control over the affairs of humans.

(10:1–18) vv. 1–3, brief notes about the judges Tola and Jair. The larger traditions about these men may have been lost, or an author has purposefully decided to abbreviate, knowing that his audience is aware of the fuller tradition (see JUDG 3:7–11 on Othniel and 73:31 on Shamgar). vv. 6–17, the conventionalized pattern—death of judge, backsliding, cry for help—resumes, as the passage reviews Israel's major enemies. vv. 10–16 is a dialogue between the Israelites and YHWH in which Israel confesses her sins of idolatry, YHWH describes

his saving actions and Israel's unfaithfulness in terms familiar from prophetic oracles of the lawsuit form (cf. Hos 7:11–16), and Israel repents (cf. similar pattern of motifs in Ezra 9, Neh 9, and 2 Chr 20). Finally, as in Ex 2:23–5, YHWH has pity upon Israel and will send a rescuer. Indeed God's pity is invoked by displays of humility and contrition on the part of the people and its leaders (see 2 Chr 20:12; 16:8; 12:6–7). v. 17, the phrase 'called to arms' (NRSV), lit. 'were called', is technical language used elsewhere in Judges to suggest military muster of an essentially non-professional fighting force (cf. 4:10; 6:35; 7:23–4). v. 18, the scene is set for the re-entry of the unlikely hero who, as in traditional narrative patterns, is precisely the one who will succeed.

The Story of Jephthah (11:1–12:7)

Jephthah is another of the bandit chiefs who rises to power because of military prowess in the raiding sort of warfare described in Judges. Whereas other 'judges' initially display their anti-establishment orientation in opposition to kings and generals who oppress the Israelites (e.g. Ehud, Gideon), Jephthah's marginality is kin-based as well. He is the son of a prostitute denied rights of inheritance by his father's legitimate children. Such a background, of course, is typical of a host of folk heroes. The tales of Jephthah's exploits provide fascinating insight into aspects of Israelite views of war.

(11:1–40) vv. 1–3, the term 'mighty warrior' is applied to Gideon (Judg 6:12), David (1 Sam 16:18), and a host of other heroes in the biblical bardic tradition. Like David in retreat from King Saul who has declared him an enemy of the state, Jephthah becomes a 'social bandit'. Surrounded by other uprooted fighting men, such bandits can cause much mischief for the establishment or provide sorely needed protection for their sympathizers. vv. 4–11, now faced with the Ammonite threat the leaders of Gilead seek to woo back the hero. They offer him the position of commander, but when he balks they have to increase their offer to the position of chieftain, literally 'head'. The agreement between Jephthah and the elders is sealed with an appeal to YHWH as witness as is appropriate in a covenantal form (v. 10). Interweaving a traditional story about the success of the once marginalized hero is an account about the workings of the political process in non-dynastic societies with fluid patterns of leadership. vv. 12–28, this exchange between Jephthah and the king of the Ammonites provides insight into certain Israelite concepts of just war. Employing juridical language (cf. formula in 2 Chr 35:21; 2 Kings 3:13; 1 Kings 17:18), Jephthah and the king are portrayed as arguing by messenger about land rights and in effect about the direction of a thread in Israel's founding myth. vv. 12–13, Jephthah demands to know what cause justifies the Ammonites' military posture against Israel, and the Ammonite king responds that it is a matter of territory. He provides a version of events related in Num 21:21–31 (see an additional version in Deut 2:26–35), but portrays Israel as an unjust aggressor. vv. 14–27, in a lengthy response, Jephthah provides a pro-Israelite version of the taking of the disputed border territory. The argument has three components: (1) Israel took the land in a defensive war. Had Sihon, king of Heshbon, allowed Israel to pass peacefully through his territory during the Exodus from Egypt, there would have been no need for war or the accompanying conquest of the disputed area (vv. 15–22); (2) YHWH, God of the Israelites, has conquered this land for his people, and peoples are allowed the lands their deities are able to procure for their benefit. Note the reference to Balak (v. 25) who according to tradition seems to accept grudgingly that YHWH has granted Israel certain lands (see Num 22–4, esp. 24:25; also Num 21:10–20 (vv. 23–5); (3) Israel has been in possession of the disputed territory for some 300 years, so that the statute of limitations on land claims appears to be over (vv. 26–8).

That the Israelite author feels called upon to portray his hero as appealing to just cause is in itself interesting. The arbiter of the dispute is YHWH whose judgement will be made apparent in the outcome of the battle (11:27). War, as in many traditional cultures and accounts, makes manifest divine judgement.

(11:29–40) The Sacrifice of Jephthah's Daughter Some scholars describe Jephthah's vow as rash, evidence perhaps of the warrior's madness that manifests the spirit of YHWH within him. Although shocking to modern readers, the sacrificial vow is a feature of an Israelite ideology of war, reflected also in other ancient Near-Eastern cultures. The warriors promise the deity something of value in return for his assistance in war. This particular belief in the efficacy of sacrifice underlies the ideology of the ban, whereby conquered persons are regarded as devoted to the deity; the transfer of these valuable commodities is accomplished by wholesale destruction (see Num 21:2–3; the terminology at Deut 13:16; and Niditch 1993: 28–55). v. 31, in Hebrew the term translated 'whoever' in NRSV could also be understood as 'whatever'. Surely the Israelite audience knew of the pathos to follow. In fact, the tale of a war vow gone awry becomes the foundation myth for a woman's rite of maturation. v. 34, on women and victory songs see Ex 15:20–1; 1 Sam 18:6–7; Judg 5:28–30. vv. 34–40, implicit in the story of Jephthah's daughter is an analogy drawn between a father's offering his daughter in sacrifice to a male deity and the nubile woman's passage from virginity in her father's household to adult responsibilities of marriage and childbearing in the home of a husband. Each woman is a sacrifice mediating the relationship between the males who control her life and sexuality. Notice the emphasis on the daughter's stage in life (vv. 37, 39) and upon that of her companions who form a support group of people undergoing a similar experience. Together they model a rite marking the bittersweet transition to adulthood experienced by all Israelite women (v. 40; see Day 1989).

(12:1–7) As in 8:1–3, the Ephraimites complain that they have not been asked to join in the battle and thereby to enjoy the spoils. The events referred to in vv. 2–3 are not part of the recorded tradition, but tales well-known to an Israelite audience may lie behind Jephthah's words. In contrast to the dispute with Gideon, this one ends in inner Israelite war, a battle which the Gileadites win. Notice the reference to regional dialects in vv. 5–6. This passage points not only to causes of conflict when decentralized military forces compete for glory and spoils, but also to some of the regional flavours and tensions in ancient Israel, differences sometimes

flattened out or covered up by the pan-Israelite myth that dominates the HB.

(12:7–13) The notice of Jephthah's demise is followed by a listing of three judges identified by the details that for an Israelite audience may have been metonymic markers of other stories. The reference to the marriages of the thirty (v. 9) and to the sons and donkeys (v. 14) are intriguing hints of tales that have been lost. Several times in Judges, such brief catalogues of leaders serve as a transition from the exploits of a leader whose story is told in detail to an indication of Israel's return to apostasy, to be followed by another substantial slice of the tradition (see 10:1–5; 3:31).

The Epic of Samson (13:1–16:31)

(13:2–24) The Birth of a Hero v. 2, in Israelite tradition, the barrenness of the mother is a virtual guarantee that what follows is the birth story of a hero. So with Sarah, Rebekah, Rachel, and Hannah. vv. 3–23, the annunciation, a special theophany of which women are the primary recipients. Traditional motifs of this form include the appearance of the deity or his emissary, and the announcement of the birth (v. 3); special instructions or information for the mother and son (vv. 4–6); expression of fear or awe (v. 22). Cf. Rebekah (Gen 25:22–3); Hagar (Gen 16:11–12); Sarah and Abraham (Gen 18). Note how the language used in the annunciation concerning Samson is economical, as similar language is used to express similar content, unifying the story and emphasizing key themes, in particular the nazirite identity of Samson (vv. 4–6; 7; 14). vv. 4–6, as described in the Priestly text at Num 6:1–21, nazirite status (lit. consecration, dedication, separation) is a self-imposed and temporary state of holiness that an adult takes upon himself or herself by a vow. The symbolization of nazirite holiness is rich in contrasts between nature and culture. For example, the nazir is not to drink wine and beer that are fermented and transformed from grapes and grain into culture-affirming products of human invention (cf. the extension in Num 6:3); he or she is not to cut the hair which must grow in a natural state unaltered by man-made instruments. Samson is to be a nazir by divine direction, even *in utero*. The nature/culture dichotomy implicit in nazirite status and the specific motif of hair are central to his characterization and to the story cycle. v. 5, a critical feature of the divine message: Samson is to be a saviour. vv. 8–24, interesting dimensions involving gender and status emerge in the annunciation scene. The woman is unnamed but she is the one whom the man of God seeks out. She alone receives the important message about the hair (v. 5), and appears to have a down-to-earth good sense that contrasts with her named husband's fretful and repeated enquiries. Unsure and fearful, he believes that the divine being will harm them, but she realizes that he comes in blessing. Cf. vv. 8, 12, 16, and 21 with 6–7, 10, 23. In a confirmation of her status in these annunciation events, she is the one who names the boy, 'man of the sun' or 'Sunny' (Samson in Hebrew is *šimšôn*, sun is *šemeš*). Indeed, naming the child is usually the purview of the mother (so Hannah (1 Sam 1:20); so Eve (Gen 4:1); so the matriarchs), as are other matters concerning the birth and career of her children. v. 18, cf. Gen 33:29. vv. 19–21, on God's power revealed in fire see JUDG 6:19–22, Gideon's theophanic experience. v. 25, the term translated 'stir' in NRSV has a more pressing nuance: compel or thrust (on this term repeated in the tales of Samson see Alter 1990). The warrior, a sort of holy man in his own right, is one possessed by the divine spirit. This war frenzy allows him to burst forth in massive destruction (see also 14:6, 19 and cf. 16:20).

Samson and the Philistines: Episode One (14:1–15:8)

The first of several stories in which relations with a woman lead to a power struggle between Samson and the Philistines. Themes of 'us' versus 'them', and symbols of the wild and untamed versus the socialized and cultural emerge in a tale of trickery and counter-trickery as God uses the life of this Israelite culture hero to challenge and defeat the Philistines who 'rule over Israel at this time' (14:4).

(14:1–20) vv. 1–4, the issues of Israelite status and the otherness of the Philistines emerge in the parents' disapproving words to Samson concerning his chosen match (14:3; cf. Gen 34:14–15) and in the unequivocally ethnic way in which Samson describes her. Samson is not a son who is swayed by parental wishes; they defer to the strongman, a folk hero in the style of Hercules, one not bound by social convention. v. 5, the killing of the lion with bare hands, an act kept secret (see also v. 9), prepares for the hidden answer to the riddle that follows (v. 14) as the story of ethnic rivalry among exogamous groups continues. The tearing apart of the lion with bare hands also helps to portray Samson as a superhero with power over the forces of the natural world. A pattern is established whereby Samson's overtures to the settled, social world of the Philistines is followed by a superhuman feat emphasizing his qualities as wild man (cf. 15:1, 4; 16:1, 3; 16:4, 9, 12, 14). v. 8, the honey in the lion's carcass has the serendipitous quality of spontaneous generation, a source of nourishment appropriate to one who often comports himself in a manner that is beyond the boundaries of cultural convention. On honey and warriors see 1 Sam 14:27–9.

vv. 10–18, the wedding between Samson and the Timnite woman becomes an occasion for trickery, as a would-be union between groups instead leads to resentment and destruction—ultimately God's plan for the Philistines, oppressors of Israel. The wedding story is framed by a traditional narrative pattern seen in tales of Ehud and Jael whereby the person of marginal or outsider status gains power over those in power through deception. In this setting, Samson is clearly the outsider surrounded by Philistines, and the riddling contest with its wager provides him with a clever means of increasing his status at Philistine expense. Samson hopes not only to win the bet but to show himself more clever than the oppressors of Israel.

Riddling contests, in fact, are frequent at the wedding ceremonies of many traditional cultures, providing a safe means of acting out the animosities that may exist between the members of exogamous groups. In this case, however, neither side plays fair (in epic literatures they rarely do). Whereas the usual or expected answer to the riddle, given the wedding context, is 'love' or 'sex' (see Camp and Fontaine 1990: 140–2), Samson's experience with the lion and the honey provides him with a response that could be known to him alone. In turn, the Philistines coerce Samson's fiancée to

extricate the solution to the riddle from her man, threatening to kill her and her family by burning. Indeed fire is a recurring motif in the Samson narrative, a means of expressing the boiling rage of the hero and his enemies.

Notice the poetic parallelism of the riddle and the solution as formulated. In the Hebrew the words play on 'm' sounds. The answer, moreover, has the same double range of responses as the riddle itself (see Camp and Fontaine 1990), for the solution could be read as another riddle whose answer is 'love' or 'sex'. In turn Samson reacts with a proverb that has a sexual innuendo (ibid.). Ploughing with another man's heifer, in Israelite culture as in others, refers to cuckolding. The Philistines have had their way with Samson's woman by obtaining his secret from her. Knowledge, deception, sexuality, and power intertwine in this story about competition for status, a juxtaposition of motifs that recurs in the Samson cycle. vv. 19–20, Samson pays his riddling debt by killing thirty men of Ashkelon and giving the spoils to his riddle opponents. He then withdraws to his own people, but his father-in-law gives Samson's bride to another man, thereby preparing the way for a counter-match in trickery and violence. Indeed tension escalates as the fissure between Philistine and Israelite is shown to be unbridgeable.

(15:1–8) v. 1, the desire for his woman coincides with the harvest season, a time of fertility—a pairing of themes common in traditional literatures (e.g. Ruth). Samson bears a peace offering, but approaches as if all is forgiven, further revealing his obliviousness to social convention. v. 2, the father controls his daughters' sexuality, a commodity his to exchange. He offers Samson another deal (cf. Saul, 1 Sam 17:25; 18:17–22), the younger sister. v. 4, Samson's vengeance is described in the fantastic hyperbole appropriate to tales of superheroes, the use of torches somehow attached to the tails of 300 foxes to spread fire among the standing grain, vineyards, and olive groves of the Philistines (on fire, see JUDG 14:10–18). Samson bends nature to destroy what Philistine labour has carved out of nature. In a pattern that recurs in the story cycle, Samson's flirtation with the social world of the Philistines is followed by a violent outburst frequently directed at aspects of Philistine culture (see JUDG 16:3 on city gate and 16:29–30 on the house of Dagon). vv. 6–8, violence escalates as the Philistines take vengeance upon Samson's Philistine in-laws (on fire and vengeance see JUDG 14:10–18), and he exacts massive vengeance upon the Philistines, then withdraws to a cave in a beautiful symbolization of his status as wild man. The Philistines' cruel treatment of members of their own group serves to paint them as barbarians; the Israelite author provides a more generous portrait of the Judahites who seek to capture Samson (15:12–13).

Samson and the Philistines: Episode Two (15:9–20)

(15:9–17) A saviour such as Samson is a mixed blessing, although to be sure Israelites are elsewhere portrayed as preferring collaboration with tyranny to revolt (see Ex 2:14; 5:21). The men of Judah, responding to a Philistine counter-raid, wish to hand over the man whom the Philistines seek (for a scene that raises comparable issues in political ethics see 2 Sam 20:14–22). Gingerly, 3,000 Judahites come to Samson with a formulaic accusation of wrongdoing ('What . . . have you done to us?') and convince Samson to allow himself to be given over to the enemy. Samson the trickster goes quietly, but merely bides his time, bursting forth upon the Philistines with a power fuelled by the divine frenzy. Notice the wonderful imagery used to describe the impotence of the ropes that bind him (v. 14), and again the fire motif. As he kills the lion with bare hands and uses foxes to destroy Philistine property, he uses the jawbone of a donkey, a weapon pulled serendipitously from nature, to kill a thousand men. v. 16, Samson the propounder of riddles and the speaker of proverbs here declares his victory in a war-taunt that plays upon the repetition of sounds and words and two meanings of the root *ḥ-m-r*, 'donkey' and 'pile up'. In synchronic parallelism the many slain Philistines are called 'heaps and heaps'. v. 17, the narrative ends with a folk etymology. The place is called 'Jawbone Height'.

(15:18–20) The great victory over the Philistines concludes with an amusing little vignette that emphasizes both Samson's swaggering ways and his position as a favourite of God. Thirsty after the battle, he speaks in the hyperbole one expects of Samson to YHWH, his protector, asking essentially if God intends to reward the hero of Israel with death by thirst (v. 18). Notice again the epithet 'uncircumcised' applied to the Philistine Other (cf. JUDG 14:3). God responds by splitting open a spring from a rocky hollow (lit. mortar-like place) so that Samson drinks and is revived. In doing so he takes his place with Elijah and Moses, other biblical heroes for whom God opens sources of fertility and nourishment. The story is completed with another place etiology, 'Spring of the Caller'.

v. 20, this verse is taken by some to mark the end of an earlier version of the Samson epic, to be followed by supplemental tales (Boling 1975: 240–1). The verse might be seen to function as a transition to the story of Samson's fall. He judges for twenty years and then comes Delilah.

Samson and the Philistines: Episode Three (16:1–31)

(16:1–3) This brief episode foreshadows the longer Delilah narrative in structure and content, and echoes patterns established earlier. Once again Samson approaches the uncircumcised Other through one of their women, a prostitute, and the encounter ends in his violent departure. The trickster pattern is also found, as the enemy seeks surreptitiously to capture the strongman (v. 2) and as he feigns lack of knowledge of them only to escape in the night by lifting off the very gates of the city in another Herculean display (v. 3). Coming before the encounter with Delilah that brings Samson down, this scene might be seen as contributing to the hubris of the hero and to our own expectations about his invincibility, an attribute that turns out to be false. The appeal of Philistine women might be seen as Samson's tragic flaw (so implicitly Alter 1990). It does seem clear that the Samson tradition as preserved emphasizes a favourite biblical theme, the danger of foreign (and loose) women (Deut 7:3–4; Prov 5:3–6; 7:10–23). This theme would have appealed to nationalist Israelite writers throughout the tradition and certainly to Deuteronomistic writers usually credited with the preservation of the material.

(16:4–22) The story of Samson's downfall that ends with a hint of his last hurrah (v. 22) traces a pattern now familiar from the cycle: encounter with a Philistine woman; attempted

entrapment or trickery; counter-trickery or escape. The plot follows this path three times, in the style of traditional folk narration, but in the fourth instance Samson is caught. The victorious and superhuman outburst that follows this tale of deception (see JUDG 15:4) must await the next episode (16:23–30).

v. 4, the name of Samson's final lover, Delilah (Heb. *dĕlîlâ*), is of uncertain etymology possibly having to do with 'loose hair' or 'flirtatiousness', but the word plays on the term for 'night' (*layĕlâ*) as Samson's name derives from the term for 'sun' (*šemeš*). v. 5, the Philistine lords or, better, 'tyrants' offer Delilah a fortune in silver if she is able to uncover and divulge to them the source of Samson's strength. The narrative revolves around a folk motif, the secret source of power (Thompson 1955–8: D1830; D1840). Some heroes' strength or their very life-force resides in their sword or an amulet; the source of Samson's power is integral to his status as nazir, declared even before his birth. The traditional folk motif thus intertwines with particular theological concerns having to do with Samson's relationship to YHWH.

vv. 6–17, Delilah's question to Samson is repeated four times with nuances, as the formulaic request is elaborated, exerting more and more pressure upon the hero and building to the climax of his revelation (vv. 6, 10, 13, 15). Also repeated is Delilah's test to Samson: 'The Philistines are upon you' (vv. 9, 12, 14, 20). While some suggest that Samson is a foolish buffoon to reveal his secret and others that Samson so loved Delilah that he never truly believed she would betray him, the theological interests of this traditional story suggest that Samson is guilty of hubris. He has come to believe that his strength is not contingent upon the symbol of his holy otherness, his consecration to YHWH. The repetition, 'The Philistines are upon you', at v. 20 produces a special pathos, for in contrast to the other times when Samson breaks free, this time, shorn of his hair, he does not realize that YHWH has left him and that he has become vulnerable like other men.

The passage is unified by the repetition with nuances described above and by the progression of false revelations that lead finally to the truth. These counter-deceptions by Samson each play on the dichotomy between nature and culture so important in the cycle of stories as a whole. Samson first declares that raw bowstrings would hold him (v. 8), these being minimally treated natural materials. Then he claims that new ropes would bind him, ropes being a more processed material (v. 12). Then comes the reference to the quintessential art of women's culture, weaving, as an image of safely tying or taming the locks of Samson's hair intermingles with an evocation of the dangerous and seductive woman, a weaver of webs and plots. Samson's bold mention of the hair in the third deception is followed by the truth: a razor that cuts off the natural wildness of Samson's hair will tame Samson. The hair on one level is a symbol of Samson's particular manliness. His power resides on the border of the cultural and the natural, for Samson the riddler is able to kill lions with bare hands, Samson the trickster withdraws to a cave, darting in and out of the social world of Philistine dominance. It is the hair that binds him to the God whose power is revealed in nature, the God who often prefers the wilderness to the city.

v. 21, powerless and now blind, Samson is made to grind at a mill in the prison. He thus does the work of a fettered beast or the work of women. The 'grind' term, however, has additional sexual connotations in the HB (see Job 31:10; Isa 47:2–3), as euphemism for intercourse. Samson, like Job's wife, now 'grinds for another'. The mighty hero has been feminized, playing Sisera to a Philistine Jael (see on JUDG 4, 5).

(16:23–31) Samson's rehabilitation and his final victory are set appropriately during a Philistine festival in which the adherents of the god Dagon rejoice, thanking their god for helping them to defeat Samson, their enemy. The Philistines' victory prayer is a rhythmic ditty built upon rhyme and poetic parallelism (v. 24). They have Samson brought out that 'he might sport' (my tr.) before them. Humiliation is implied, but the term 'sport' may also have sexual connotations. Feigning weakness, Samson asks the lad who leads him to allow him to support himself by leaning against the pillars of the great house that is filled to the rafters and beyond with Philistines. With a final prayer to God, Samson pulls down the house, killing himself and his enemies. The narrative ends with a declaration of admiration for Samson's final deed (v. 30). In contrast to other threads in the HB, traditions of the judges do not reveal concern with innocent enemies that are killed or the like, but are informed by jingoistic national pride, defining 'us' in terms of 'not them'. Samson is buried and commemorated with full honour.

The Founding of Dan (17:1–18:31)

These chapters offer a fascinating Danite founding myth that provides insight into Israelite notions of their ancestors' religious lives, and perhaps also a glimpse of aspects of Israelite popular religion that continue to hold meaning throughout biblical times. Also of interest is the ideology of war that serves as background to the establishment of Dan.

(17:1–6) The tale opens with the confession of a guilty son named Micah. He has stolen his mother's money, but now returns it to her. Like the father of the prodigal son, she harbours no resentment, but praises God for her son's rehabilitation and asks him to dedicate the money to YHWH by making a *pesel*, a term translated 'idol' in NRSV, but better understood as a carved statue of iconographic significance, and a *massēkâ*, a cast metal icon. Such icons were symbols of the deity's indwelling presence and closely identified with the deity (hence Micah's statement to the Danites at 18:24). The son, still a bit of a con artist, uses only a small portion of the endowment (cf. vv. 3 and 4), but commissions the statuary. Since only the smelter is mentioned, some suggest that the phrase, 'carved statue and cast statue', refers only to the metal icon (so NRSV translates). Without making a negative value judgement, the narrator describes how Micah completes his home shrine with a divinatory ephod (see JUDG 8:27) and teraphim, movable statuary that several scholars have associated with cults of ancestors (cf. Gen 31:30, 34–5), installing his own son to serve as priest. v. 6, some read this verse and other echoes of it (18:1; 19:1; 21:25) as a pro-Josianic or pro-Davidic writer's comment on the need for strong centralized leadership in the form of monarchy. The statement reflects an author's effort to separate himself in chronology and world-view from what he portrays to be olden times, but is not clearly readable as a negative assessment when compared, for example, with the commentary on Gideon's ephod at 8:27.

(17:7–13) It is likely that early in Israel's history not all priests were Levites. Even the venerable Samuel who trained under the priest Eli of the shrine at Shiloh is given an Ephraimite genealogy in some threads of the tradition (see 1 Sam 1:1 and cf. 1 Chr 6:26). These verses suggest, however, that the levitical priest lends special status to a shrine, granting its owner prestige and divine blessing. This passage nicely captures the quality of itineracy attached to Levites in the biblical tradition. Notice the designation 'father' that Micah attaches to the holy man (v. 10) and cf. 2 Kings 6:21; 8:9; 13:14; and Judg 5:7.

(18:1–13) v. 1, from Levitical itineracy, the narrator turns to Danite wanderings in search of a homeland, as the tales of Micah, the young Levite, and the Danites weave together in a founding myth. vv. 2–10, the reconnaissance mission is a frequent motif in Israelite war accounts (cf. Num 13; Josh 2; and JUDG 6:10–14). While spying out the land in the north, the Danites receive hospitality in Micah's household. v. 3, do the Danites know the Levite from elsewhere (Soggin 1981: 272)? The text may mean that they recognize the priest's southern accent or dialect (Boling 1975: 263). vv. 5–6, the request for a sign or an oracle before battle is also a frequent feature of traditional Israelite war accounts and points to the belief in divine control of the wars of humans (see JUDG 4:5, 8; 6:13 on Deborah and Gideon). vv. 7–10, the neutrality of the author concerning the Danites' cheerful response to the Laishians' military vulnerability is troubling, but reflects an ideology of expedience in which the use of war to achieve political goals is a given. In contrast to other biblical war texts, the battle is not justified by appeal to a righteous cause, e.g. the sinfulness of the enemy, but like all war succeeds only with divine sanction. v. 12, an etiology for the name of a location in Judah, 'The Camp of Dan'.

(18:14–26) This passage contributes to the aura of banditry that permeates not only the stories of the judges but also the tales of David's early career. Like David in his encounters with the priest at Nob (1 Sam 21:1–9) and with the household of Nabal (1 Sam 25:2–38), the Danites propose to help themselves to what they need or desire, and only a brazen fool would attempt to deny them their requests. Armed and dangerous, the Danites, like David, make their intentions seem inevitable and logical, managing in their rather convincing speeches to make it seem as if the robbed party is in the wrong if he protests their actions or attempts to deny them his possessions (see vv. 19, 23–5). Notice the wonderfully disingenuous if not self-righteous response of the Danites to Micah, lit. 'What's it to you?' or 'What troubles you that you call up [a force against us]?' (v. 22). The Levite is convinced to join the Danites, while Micah, himself a Laban-like character not above cheating his own mother, knows when he has been bested. v. 18, compare to 17:4, 5, and 18:14 in the HB and see JUDG 17:5 concerning the number of icons commissioned by Micah.

(18:27–31) The conquest of Laish by the Danites. While the language of putting to the sword and burning is reminiscent of biblical ban texts in Deuteronomy and Joshua, the ideology behind the conquest is quite different (see on JUDG 18:7–10 and Niditch 1993: 127–8). vv. 30–1, variant manuscript traditions read not Manasseh, as in the Hebrew, but Moses (so NRSV). In this way, the hereditary priesthood of Dan is said to belong to the line of Moses rather than the line of Aaron (v. 30). The translation of *pesel*, 'idol', in vv. 30–1 as in 17:3, 4; 18:14, gives the impression that the narrator strongly disapproves of Micah, the Danites, and the shrine itself, but the language could not be more matter of fact. While special status is accorded implicitly to the rival sanctuary at Shiloh by describing it as the place where 'God's house' was located in pre-monarchic times, the founding of Dan is treated with good humour and respect.

Civil War (19:1–21:25)

This gripping story of an ancient Israelite civil war contains three major parts: the rape that leads to the war; the war itself; and the process of reconciliation. Motifs of hospitality and kinship run throughout the whole, as the tales pose essential questions about the nature of group unity and the causes of dissensions and fissure. Women play key roles in the narratives but in contrast to Deborah, Jael, and other strong women of Judges, they are silent characters who join or separate the men who control them in a strongly androcentric and agonistic work. In Judg 19–21, women are doorways leading into and out of war, sources of contention and reconciliation. These chapters serve as an important transition to the early history of the monarchy in 1 Samuel, for they point to the inevitable tension between kinship or clan loyalties and loyalties to the larger Israelite group, understood as a nation and a whole.

(19:1–31) v. 1, like chs. 17–18, this account points to a certain interest in the travels and experiences of Levites who are often those most in need of local support and hospitality, having no patrilineal holdings of their own. The concubine is a second wife, having less status than the first wife, but some rights nevertheless. v. 2, the Hebrew text reads that 'she played the harlot towards him', i.e. was disloyal but not necessarily adulterous. Other MS traditions followed by NRSV read 'she became angry with him'. A misogynistic tradition could more easily understand her leaving the man to return home in terms of the adultery idiom. Whatever the cause for the rupture, this brief allusion to tensions in one couple's relationship foreshadows the more serious disruptions in the larger social family that are to follow. v. 3, after four months the Levite goes after her, hoping to win her back (cf. situation and language in Gen 34:3).

vv. 3–10, at the home of his father-in-law the Levite receives full hospitality as is proper in traditional cultures, especially between affines. The grand dimensions of the in-law's generosity is emphasized by traditional style repetition at vv. 4, 6, 8 and 5, 7, 8, 9. Each time the Levite rises to leave, the host urges him to stay, he accedes, and they feast. Finally, at v. 10 comes the break with the repetition in action and language that signals an important shift in the action and mood (see on Samson and Delilah at JUDG 16:20–1).

vv. 11–15, in his journey north from Bethlehem, the Levite ironically refuses his servant's advice to stop in Jebus, a non-Israelite town, instead suggesting they stay at a town 'of the people Israel'. It is in this town, Gibeah of Benjamin, that the outrage takes place. vv. 16–21, instead of meeting with the expected hospitality, the party finds itself ignored in the open square, an ominous adumbration of the troubles to come

(v. 15). One elderly gentleman, however, greets them, and after a brief conversation welcomes them to his home. Notice the formulaic reference to feasting, 'they ate and they drank' (cf. 19:4, 6). vv. 22–6, this account is a variant of the tale about Lot in Gen 19. In both, visitors find hospitality in the house of an Israelite, but 'base fellows', miscreants (in Gen 19 it is 'the men of Sodom' who become synonymous in Western tradition with miscreants) surround the house and demand that the stranger/s be sent out to them that they might rape them, lit. 'know them', a biblical euphemism for sexual intercourse. v. 22, for ancient Israelites homosexual rape is as quintessential an expression of anti-social behaviour as cannibalism is in the Greek tradition. Strangers in need of succour in the *Odyssey* find themselves being eaten, whereas Israelite strangers are threatened with rape. A number of threads in the Israelite tradition indicate special disapproval of homosexuality as a form of relationship that blurs neat categories of creation as the Israelites understood them (see e.g. Lev 18:22; 20:13, and Deut 22:5 in context). This negative attitude even to consensual relations between men blends in Gen 19 and Judg 19 with the frequently found theme of the womanization of the enemy Other, as discussed at JUDG 16:19, 21 (Samson) and 4:27 (Sisera). Thus their threat of homosexual rape marks the evildoers as consummately aggressive, prepared to act out in a literal way the metaphor of conquest in war. In Gen 19 the aggressors are Sodomites, but the tale in Judg 19 shocks its audience even more because the enemy is within, Israelites in the Israelite town of Gibeah. vv. 23–4, in both versions of the tale, the host attempts to appease the wild men outside by offering them women instead, prized virgin daughters (as also in Gen 19:8) and the man's concubine as well. To modern readers, the offer is as shocking as the threat, if not more so, and seems to suggest a world in which women are valuable, but expendable commodities. The crafter of the tale here, however, is critical of the husband who throws his wife to the vicious mob (v. 25; see discussion at JUDG 19:28; 20:6). vv. 25–8, whereas in Gen 19:11 danger is averted by the miraculous intervention of the threatened men who are actually a manifestation of God, here the concubine is cast out to the crowd. The language conveys extreme violence and force not only in describing the actions of the abusive men outside the house, but also in describing the husband's giving his wife over to them. The term translated 'seize' in NRSV is rooted in the term 'strong'. The husband strong-arms the woman; the abuse begins inside the house. With the break of day, the evildoers let the woman go, such anti-social outbursts being the work of night. The narrator juxtaposes the collapse of the victimized woman at the doorway with the husband's crass and brusque orders to her (v. 28), a command requiring only two words in the Hebrew. The wife cannot answer, for she is dead. The portrait of the husband is singularly unsympathetic, as the composer of the story deftly juxtaposes the Levite's criminal disregard for the well-being of his spouse, a member of his own family, with questions about Israelite unity and mutual responsibility.

vv. 29–30, the Levite's grisly actions upon returning home echo in visceral fashion the ritual calling up to military action of members of the Israelite confederacy or league (see 1 Sam 11:5–8). Whereas the leader would divide a sacrificial animal into pieces and send them to the tribes, the Levite cuts up the human victim in a powerful and troubling symbolization of the soon to be clear fissures in Israel's body politic.

(20:1–48) From the gathering of Israelite fighting forces to the defeat finally of Benjamin, the tribe of Gibeah, this chapter describes the wrenching process of a civil war that pits the ideal of pan-Israelite unity against tribal and kinship-based unity. The war and subsequent events in ch. 20 test the ideology of the ban. Will Israel root out the evil in its own midst as required in Deut 13:12–18 (see the use of the term 'base fellows' in Deut 13:13)? vv. 1–2, the narrator presents an orderly idealization of the way in which an Israelite confederation may have worked (see discussion of notions of a 'league' at JUDG 5 and JUDG c.3). vv. 3–7, as required in Deut 13:14, an investigation is undertaken before war is declared against alleged miscreants. Note the way in which the composer has the Levite cover up his cowardly sacrifice of his wife. vv. 8–11, the emphasis here, as in the opening verses, is upon the unity of the group and their single-mindedness in rooting out the evil in their midst. And yet the apparent unity belies the fact that Benjaminite representatives are not among them (see v. 3: Benjamin has heard about the gathering but has not gathered with the other tribes). Moreover, while the Hebrew is difficult at v. 10, it appears to suggest that vengeance is to be meted out to the entire city of Gibeah, because of the evildoers in their midst. Such an action would be consistent with the ban in which evil is understood to be like a contagious humour that spreads beyond the breakers of covenant to their families and townsmen (see Deut 13:15–16; Josh 7:24–5). Nevertheless in contrast to an invocation of the ban against foreigners, an inner Israelite enactment risks destroying the covenant community itself. One could well expect Benjaminites to balk at giving up all of Gibeah. v. 12, a variation on a formulaic expression that makes accusation of wrongdoing (see Gen 3:13; 12:18; 29:25). v. 13, this sentence may mean, 'Hand over the specific people in Gibeah who have done wrong,' or 'Hand over those Gibean scoundrels,' i.e. all people of Gibeah are scoundrels (see JUDG 20:8–11). v. 16, the Benjaminites have a reputation as especially fine warriors, aided by a tendency to left-handedness. Saul is of Benjamin as is Ehud, the left-handed judge.

vv. 18, 23, 27–8, on the importance of receiving divine guidance before battle see JUDG 1:1. Notice the frequent emphasis on the presumed kinship bonds between all Israelites (vv. 28, 23, 13). The repetitions in content and language betoken a traditional style of narration that beautifully captures and creates the rhythms of the forward and backward progress of the battles. vv. 32–4, the break with repetition signals a change in the action, as the Benjaminites who met with initial success finally succumb to the Israelite forces (cf. 17:20). vv. 35–48, with a comment in v. 36 on the Benjaminites' realization that they are defeated, the battle accounts appear to end, but vv. 36–47 provide a more detailed encore of the account of the war's denouement. Noting that vv. 31–2 parallel v. 39, that v. 41 repeats the content if not the language of v. 36, and that vv. 36–7 appear to be an explanatory commentary on or continuation of vv. 33–4, many scholars have suggested that ch. 20 concludes with a conflation of two variant accounts of the end of the war. This is certainly a possibility, although confusion and expansiveness also characterize some works composed in oral-traditional style, as the narrator warms to his tale, loses his place a bit, and in the very process manages to reflect the chaos of battle. v. 40, the image of the whole city burning is reminiscent of impositions of the ban (see JUDG 1:8). In this case, however, some Benjaminites survive (v. 47). vv. 44, 46, here, as at 20:16, respect is expressed for the warriors of Benjamin. In such bardic accounts, the narrator and the characters of the tales themselves frequently honour those on both sides of the battle (see e.g. JUDG 6:19, 21 above). This stance is not uniform throughout Judges in which the majority of accounts treat the enemies of Israel as the unredeemable Other. See especially attitudes to the Philistines expressed in tales of Samson. Of course, one might expect a more generous depiction of fellow Israelites. v. 48, the language and imagery of the ban is very strong in this verse (see JUDG 20:40), but because some 600 Benjaminites escape, the finale of the battle is not technically a full imposition of the ban. The most consistent feature of the ban ideology as described in Deuteronomy and Joshua is the killing of all human enemies.

(21:1–25) This passage describes the way in which the Benjaminites are reintegrated into the pan-Israelite community. Paradoxically, the process requires renewed violence against fellow Israelites and the irregular and antisocial stealing of women, men helping themselves to sources of procreation without appeal to proper social mores. As violence against a woman leads into conflict, violence against women leads out of war to a rebuilding of the community. The story-teller appears to justify this renewed violence by appeal to the Benjaminite emergency. Literarily, the final episodes of the story of the civil war do provide an *inclusio* with the beginning, emphasizing again the androcentric bent of the material. One wonders, however, if the narrator is so approving or accepting of the world-views and war views implicit in chs. 19–21.

v. 1, no mention of a prohibition against marriage with Benjaminites is found in the gathering at Mizpah (20:1–11), in the decision to go to war, or in the battle itself. v. 2, weeping to YHWH is a frequent motif in Judges (2:4; 20:23, 26) implying an appeal for advice or assistance in times of great stress. vv. 3–4, the juxtaposition of weeping and questioning YHWH, and the offering of sacrifices (cf. 20:26–8) strongly suggests the formal request for an oracle. vv. 5–7, does v. 5 suggest that YHWH has offered a way out of the people's dilemma? The absence of a rubric implying divine response may well mean, to the contrary, that Israel falls back upon its own devices, employing an unorthodox version of the ideology of the ban as a means of procuring women for Benjamin. If not answering the call of the confederation is to be considered an act worthy of total destruction (such an act warrants a curse in Judg 5:23, but no call for total destruction), then all associated with the miscreants, including young women, are to be destroyed, guilty by contagion (see JUDG 20:8–11). The notion of wreaking near total destruction upon the one 'of all the tribes' who did not heed the call against Benjamin appears more an excuse to obtain women than a means of imposing divine justice. It is upon this issue that the composer has his characters dwell (see vv. 1, 5–7). Indeed if not answering the call against miscreants were the issue then the

191 JUDGES

600 remaining Benjaminite men would be worthy of death. It is not by chance that no divine command or sanction appears in this account, an indication of a narrator's critical point of view. vv. 8–9, a search indicates that the inhabitants of Jabesh-gilead did not join the Israelites at Mizpah. Given that the Benjaminite who becomes first king of Israel, Saul, is described as rushing to the rescue of the inhabitants of this town in northern Gilead when they are threatened by the Ammonites (1 Sam 11) and that they in turn show undying loyalty to him and his sons (1 Sam 31:8–13; 2 Sam 2:5–7), one wonders if some ancient tie is believed to bond Jabesh-gilead to the tribe of Benjamin.

vv. 10–12, this partial imposition of the ban suggests parallels with Num 31, a priestly war account. In both narratives, all males are killed but women who have not known a man sexually are spared. The contexts of and world-views behind the war episodes differ. Num 31 reveals a view suggesting that the virgin girl is an unmarked slate differing in identity from sexually active women who have been marked by men, and from men of all ages who carry in their persons the identity of the group. The woman who has not had intercourse is treated as a sort of fresh, fertile ground available for a man's seed. In Num 31, virgin girls are not tainted with Moabite contagion and can become the bearers of Israelite offspring. In Judg 20, a passage not concerned per se with priestly issues of purity, virgins provide the requisite assurance that Benjaminite children will be the offspring of their legal fathers, an issue of vital importance to a culture grounded in traceable patrilineages. The men of Jabesh-gilead are eliminated to make the virgin girls vulnerable to capture and easily available. In the process of procuring the young women, issues of justice under the ban seem muted, a rationale at best. vv. 13–25, the daughters of Jabesh-gilead being inadequate in number to provide women for the surviving Benjaminites, another plan is hatched. Fearing the curse they have placed upon any of their number who willingly help Benjamin as a tribe to survive (v. 18), the Israelites find for the Benjaminites an opportunity to engage in wife-stealing.

vv. 19–24, like the story of Jephthah's daughter, this tale may well reflect or be the myth used to explain the origins of an ancient Israelite festival involving young women of marriageable age. The association between vineyards, dancing nubile women, festival at an important cultic centre, and wife-stealing may suggest some sort of yearly occasion for betrothals and the reinforcing of aspects of a patrilineal, endogamous culture. As a literary form, the tale shares much with traditional narratives such as the rape of the Sabine women. In the larger Israelite tradition and in the specific war story that the wife-stealing brings to a close, the tale emphasizes that women's sexuality has to do with relations between men (v. 22). In this case as in Gen 34, the normal and proper channels for exchanging women have been disregarded. Ultimately, the tale is a founding myth marking the renewal of the tribe of Benjamin. Such stories of beginnings are often characterized by departures from the workaday norm if only to reinforce them or to grant, in a return to beginnings, a brief chance of participation in an institutionalized form of revolt. v. 25, while some suggest that this formula indicates disapproval, it seems more likely a composer's way of lending the tales an ancient, early, and otherly quality.

REFERENCES

Albright, W. F. (1939), 'The Israelite Conquest of the Land in the Light of Archaeology', *BASOR* 74: 11–23.

Alt, A. (1967), *Essays on Old Testament History and Religion* (Garden City, NY: Doubleday), 173–221; German original, *Die Landnahme der Israeliten in Palästina* (Leipzig: Reformationsprogramm der Universität, 1925).

Alter, R. (1990), 'Samson Without Folklore', in Niditch (ed.) (1990), 47–56.

Anderson, G. A. (1987), *Sacrifices and Offerings in Ancient Israel: Studies in their Social and Political Importance* (Englewood Cliffs, NJ: Prentice Hall).

Boling, R. G. (1975), *Judges: Introduction, Translation, and Commentary*, AB 6A.

Brettler, M. (1989), 'The Book of Judges: Literature as Politics', *JBL* 103: 395–418.

Bright, J. (1981), *A History of Israel*, 3rd edn. (Philadelphia: Westminster).

Camp, C. V., and Fontaine, C. R. (1990), 'The Words of the Wise and their Riddles', in Niditch (ed.) (1990), 127–51.

Coote, R., and Whitelam, K. W. (1987), *The Emergence of Early Israel in Historical Perspective* (Sheffield: Almond).

Cross, F. M. (1973), *Canaanite Myth and Hebrew Epic* (Cambridge, Mass.: Harvard University Press).

—— (1974), 'Prose and Poetry in the Mythic and Epic Texts from Ugarit', *HTR*: 1–15.

Day, P. L. (1989), 'From the Child Is Born the Woman: The Story of Jephthah's Daughter', in Day (ed.), *Gender and Difference in Ancient Israel* (Minneapolis: Fortress), 58–74.

Gottwald, N. K. (1979), *The Tribes of Yahweh: A Sociology of the Religion of Liberated Israel 1250–1050 B.C.* (Maryknoll, NY: Orbis).

Hayes, J. H., and Miller, J. M. (eds.) (1977), *Israelite and Judean History* (Philadelphia: Westminster).

Hobsbawm, E. (1969), *Bandits* (New York: Delacorte).

Kang, S.-M. (1989), *Divine War in the Old Testament and in the Ancient Near East* (Berlin: de Gruyter).

Mayes, A. D. H. (1974), *Israel in the Period of the Judges*, SBT 2/29 (Naperville, Ill.: Allenson).

Mendenhall, G. E. (1973), *The Tenth Generation* (Baltimore: Johns Hopkins University Press).

Niditch, S. (1987), *Underdogs and Tricksters: A Prelude to Biblical Folklore* (San Francisco: Harper & Row).

—— (1989), 'Eroticism and Death in the Tale of Jael', in Day (1989), 43–57.

—— (ed.) (1990), *Text and Tradition: The Hebrew Bible and Folklore* (Atlanta: Scholars Press).

—— (1993), *War in the Hebrew Bible: A Study in the Ethics of Violence* (New York: Oxford University Press).

Noth, M. (1960), *The History of Israel*, tr. P. R. Ackroyd, rev. edn. (New York: Harper & Row); German original, *Geschichte Israels*, 2nd edn. (Gottingen: Vandenhoeck & Ruprecht, 1954).

Shulman, D. D. (1986), 'Battle as a Metaphor in Tamil Folk and Classical Traditions,' in Stuart H. Blackburn and A. K. Ramanujan (eds.), *Another Harmony: New Essays on the Folklore of India* (Berkeley and Los Angeles: University of California Press), 105–30.

Soggin, A. J. (1981), *Judges: A Commentary* (Philadelphia: Westminster).

Thompson, S. (1955–8), *The Motif-Index of Folk Literature* (Bloomington, Ind.: Indiana University Press).

Vermeule, E. (1979), *Aspects of Death in Early Greek Art and Poetry* (Berkeley and Los Angeles: University of California Press).

Younger, K. L., Jr. (1994), 'Judges 1 in Its Near Eastern Context', in A. R. Millard, James K. Hoffmeier, and David W. Baker (eds.), *Faith, Tradition, and History: Old Testament Historiography in Its Near Eastern Context* (Winona Lake, Ind.: Eisenbrauns), 207–27.

11. Ruth

INTRODUCTION

A. Description, Date, and Purpose. 1. At first sight Ruth is a delightfully simple tale of domestic life. It moves from sorrow to joy, from emptiness to fullness, largely through the initiative and resourcefulness of two women. This description, however, masks many intractable questions not only of date and purpose but of relationship to OT law and practice. In the prominence it gives to women, and its unconventional attitude to society, it resembles Esther, although contrasting with this in its overtly religious dimension. Although YHWH's active intervention in human life is acknowledged only twice (1:6; 4:13), the frequent invocation of the Name in blessing affirms that he is in ultimate control. Yet this aspect is deliberately muted; at times God seems not even 'in the shadows' (Campbell 1975), and twice significant events are attributed to chance (2:3; 3:18). Throughout it is a story of faithfulness (ḥesed) human and divine. Each of the blessings invoked is fulfilled ultimately through human agency.

2. The questions of date and purpose are interrelated. Uncertainty as to the one compounds the problems concerning the other. Arguments can be adduced for both a pre-exilic and a post-exilic date. In neither case are they conclusive and the matter remains unresolved. From a general consensus on linguistic grounds that it belongs to the post-exilic period and, despite its non-polemical tone, may have been a protest against the exclusivism of Ezra and Nehemiah, preference has moved now to a pre-exilic date on the grounds that the alleged Aramaisms are, with few exceptions, open to other explanations. Neither the fact that it is included among the měgillôt (the five scrolls) in the third section of the Hebrew canon, nor comparison with the attitude to foreigners in the book of Jonah, justifies assigning it to a late date. The setting of the story in the period of the Judges, which accounts for its position in the Christian canon, is, however, clearly remote from the author's own time (1:1; 4:7). If the concluding references to David are original they provide a *terminus a quo* for its written form and open the possibility that it may have had a political purpose in supporting David's claim to the throne, whether in his or in Solomon's time (Hubbard 1988). The acceptance of Moab as an appropriate refuge for a Judahite family, and of Ruth as the wife of a prominent Israelite, suggests a time prior to the growth of the intense hostility represented by Deut 23:3–6. Whatever its original purpose, its position in the Christian canon introduces a note of hope after the negative anarchical tone of the end of Judges and restores woman, and the male–female relationship, to an honourable position after the sordid, misogynist events of Judg 19–21.

3. In the HB the position of the book of Ruth varies. When it immediately follows Proverbs Ruth herself is to be seen as an example of the 'capable wife' (*'ēšet ḥayil*) of Prov 31. In Judaism the book of Ruth is associated with the harvest celebration of Pentecost, the biblical Feast of Weeks, and the giving of the law.

B. Literary Structure. Of all the OT books Ruth has the highest ratio of dialogue to narrative, hence the immediacy of its appeal. Best described as a short story (novella), it is a skilfully structured interweaving of darkness and light. It begins with death and ends with birth, the transforming of emptiness into fullness. The central chapters 2 and 3 are parallel in structure; beginning and ending with scenes in which only Ruth and Naomi participate, their main focus is on Ruth's encounters with Boaz which bring for her blessings both material and spiritual. Their settings, however, are strongly contrasted; the former takes place in public in the countryside by daylight, the latter in the intimate privacy of a threshing floor by night.

C. Feminist readings. Although written from a female perspective and illustrative of the courage and resourcefulness of a woman, it is merely speculative to suggest that a woman was its author. Feminist commentators are divided in their appraisal of Ruth's character. For some she is an example of strength and independence, for others she merely subserves a male agenda, for in the end it is a man who makes the decisions and a male child over whom the women rejoice and with whom the future lies.

D. Text. Fragments of four Hebrew MSS of the book of Ruth dating from the last century BCE and the first CE, found in caves 2 and 4 at Qumran, attest only slight variations from the MT.

COMMENTARY

(1:1–5) The references to time and place (v. 1) have a significance beyond the simply chronological and geographical. They point to a time of anarchy (Judg 21:25) from which Ruth's descendant, David, will deliver Israel, and to a foreign land outside the covenant, yet within which God works out his purpose. The contrast between Ruth, this Moabite heroine through whom Israel's future is secured, and the Moabite women who led Israel into idolatry on their journey into the promised land (Num 25:1–3), cannot have escaped either the author or the readers of this narrative. The intimate relationship of Ruth and Boaz, with its promise of a glorious future for Israel under David, redeems the apostasy and degradation of the earlier incident.

From conventional beginnings with its focus on Elimelech and his sons, the narrative quickly becomes a woman's story. Through bereavement and barrenness (v. 5) it appears as a story without a future. But the death of sons at the story's beginning is counterbalanced at the end by a son whose birth holds promise of a future, not only for the family concerned but for the nation (4:14–17).

(1:6–13) Naomi's initiative marks a new beginning. But the real initiative is YHWH's in showing his care for his people by 'giving them food' (v. 6, in Hebrew an alliterative phrase, *lātēt lāhem lāhem*). This is the first of only two references in the whole narrative to YHWH's direct intervention in human life. In both instances he acts to secure the future, first by the provision of food, and second by the conception of a child (see 4:13). The sixfold repetition in this section of the verb 'return, turn back' (*šûb*) indicates a keynote of these verses. With v. 8 the dialogue begins. Naomi's command to her daughters-in-law, 'Go back', is repeated in vv. 11–12 in a more peremptory way. The expression 'mother's house' is to be noted. It occurs elsewhere in contexts of love and marriage (cf. Gen 24:28; Song 3:4; 8:2). In general, however, a widow returned to her father's house (Gen 38:11; Lev 22:13), but the death of Ruth's father is not implied (cf. 2:11). Naomi's horizons are restricted to the idea that 'security' (v. 9) is to be found only in marriage, a thought which continues through vv. 11–13. It is debatable whether or not the idea of levirate marriage (Lat. *levir*, 'brother-in-law'; see Deut 25:5–6) is present here. In a strict sense this was the responsibility of a dead man's brother within a tightly knit family unit. Future sons of Naomi's would be but half-brothers to the dead. Her words are better understood as an outburst of hopeless despair and possibly self-pity. The ambivalence of Naomi's character already becomes apparent. Does her instruction to her daughters-in-law arise from genuine concern for their future, or is it a cynical rejection of them in despair? The alternatives turn on the meaning of the ambiguous v. 13*b*, whether it expresses self-pity, 'it has been far more bitter for me than for you' (NRSV, taking the Hebrew preposition *min* to indicate comparison), or altruistic concern, 'it is exceedingly bitter to me for your sake' (RSV). YHWH is regarded as the source both of blessing as reward for meritorious action (v. 8), and of catastrophe which, however, is not necessarily regarded as punishment (v. 20).

(1:14–18) portrays the depth of Ruth's commitment to Naomi and to YHWH. The terminology of v. 16 is reminiscent of marriage vows (cf. Gen 2:24) and of covenant making (Ex 6:7; Lev 26:12). Ruth's action demands comparison with that of Abraham who left his homeland with promise of a future; Ruth at this moment has no promise and no future. Naomi's silence is significant. Nowhere does she respond to Ruth's devotion. Ruth's allegiance to YHWH is signified by the form of her oath (v. 17). Her use of the name YHWH here, and here only, implies renunciation of Chemosh, god of Moab, and the aligning of herself with Israel.

(1:19–22) The deficiencies of Naomi's character are exposed. She defines 'full' and 'empty' (v. 21) simply in terms of male relatives. In fact, she left for Moab not 'full' but famine stricken; she returned to Israel not empty but with Ruth's remarkable devotion.

The narrative in this chapter is skilfully structured and powerful in its simplicity. From famine (v. 1) it moves to harvest (v. 22), from Moab to Bethlehem. It began with Elimelech; it ends with Naomi's story. There is both pathos and irony. Despite Ruth's extraordinary avowal of loyalty to Naomi and her God, choosing a future without promise or hope, she is ignored by Naomi and the townswomen in Bethlehem. She is still designated a foreigner (v. 22) even though it is with her that the future lies.

(2:1–7) The sequence of events is interrupted by a circumstantial clause (v. 1) which supplies details germane to the story as it unfolds. Boaz is better described here as 'friend' rather than 'kinsman', for *môda'* (a rare word) is not strictly a kinship term but refers to acquaintance or familiarity (cf. Prov 7:4, 'intimate friend'). The vocalized Hebrew text differs here from the consonantal text which indicates a more common word of comparable meaning (*měyudda'*; cf. 2 Kings 10:11; Ps 55:14). Boaz is bound to Naomi by friendship with Elimelech, as well as by ties of kinship as members of the same clan (*mišpāḥâ*), an intermediate grouping between the smaller family unit ('father's house') and the larger tribe. The phrase translated 'a prominent rich man' (*gibbōr ḥayil*) signifies, in some instances, a man of military prowess (Judg 6:12; 1 Sam 16:18) as well as wealth (2 Kings 15:20). An element of physical prowess is not to be excluded too readily from this portrayal of Boaz (cf. LXX, 'powerful in strength').

Ruth had for 10 years been the wife of an Israelite (1:4) yet still she is reckoned an outsider and designated as 'the Moabite' (vv. 2, 6). The situation at the beginning of ch. 1 is reversed. It is Ruth now, not Naomi, who is a widow without family in a foreign country. Thus she claims the right of the poor, enshrined in law, to glean at harvest (Lev 19:9–10). Ruth's arrival on Boaz's land (v. 3; the picture is of unfenced strips of land with various owners) is attributed to chance (*miqreh*). There is no overt intervention here by YHWH in the course of events (contrast 1:6), yet the frequent invocation of his name in blessing throughout the narrative (2:4; cf. 2:12, 20; 3:10; 4:14) affirms his ultimate responsibility in human affairs. The greeting of v. 4 is a traditional one (see Ps 129:8). The nature of Boaz's question, 'To whom does this young woman belong?' (v. 5), reflects the assumptions of the patriarchal society of the time. The answer identifies Ruth impersonally, not by name but by her foreign origins and her relationship to Naomi.

(2:7) presents two difficulties, in v. 7*a* an apparent disjunction with the following narrative in v. 15; in v. 7*b* an exegetical problem arising from the ambiguity of the Hebrew. As regards the latter, NRSV 'without resting even for a moment' (following the LXX) is to be compared with REB 'she has hardly had a moment's rest in the shelter' (a more literal rendering of the Heb.; cf. NIV). Either way Ruth's unstinting activity is emphasized. The former relates to her request to glean 'among the sheaves' (v. 7*a*, an advance on v. 2) which fits awkwardly with v. 15 where this is clearly an outstanding privilege accorded to her by Boaz, not a matter of right. Sasson (1989) attempts to resolve this difficulty by understanding v. 7*b*, 'she has been on her feet from early this morning until now', to refer not to Ruth's untiring gleaning but to her patient waiting for her request to be granted, a privilege outside the competence of the overseer and finally granted by Boaz himself only in v. 15. Two considerations, however, militate against this view: (1) it is unrealistic to assume that a woman in Ruth's needy circumstances would refrain from gleaning in the customary way while requesting permission for an uncertain privilege; (2) it disregards the explicit statement that she 'gleaned in the field behind the reapers' (v. 3). A possible solution consists in emending *bā'ŏmārîm* ('sheaves') in v. 7 to *bā'ămîrîm* ('swathes'; cf. NEB), thus creating a clear distinction from v. 15. Some prefer to omit v. 7*a* following the Vulgate and Syriac.

(2:8–16) This section is dominated by the first encounter between Ruth and Boaz, the main characters in the narrative. Ruth's status above that of a servant is acknowledged by Boaz in relieving her of the menial task of drawing water (v. 9; the vessels would be either large clay pots or goatskins). Boaz's protection of Ruth (v. 9), 'I have ordered the young men not to touch you', contains echoes of the divine protection afforded to Sarah (Gen 20:6) and Rebekah (26:11). Ruth's response plays on the verb 'acknowledge' (root *n-k-r*) and the noun 'foreigner' (*nokrî*), a category of persons distinct from the 'resident alien' (*gēr*) who had legal rights of protection within the community.

Boaz alone, in contrast to Naomi, appreciates the cost of Ruth's loyalty to her mother-in-law (v. 11). The motif of reward (v. 12) has occurred already in 1:8. The figure of YHWH's protective wings (*kānāp*) derives either from bird imagery (Deut 32:11; Isa 31:5), a figurative description of deities found elsewhere in the ancient Near East, or from the cherubim in the sanctuary, symbolizing YHWH's presence, which provided a place of refuge in times of need (Ps 36:7; 57:1). The combining of YHWH's blessing and Boaz's favour in vv. 12–13 is significant. Only YHWH can pay her 'wages in full' (*maśkurtēk šēlēmâ*; NRSV 'full reward'), but Boaz himself is to be the agent of this blessing for under his 'skirts' (*kānāp*) Ruth will eventually find security (3:9). Behind Ruth's bland words 'you have . . . spoken kindly' (literally 'to speak to the heart', v. 13) lies a more ambivalent meaning; in some contexts this expression signifies the tender wooing of a lover (Hos 2:14). The narrative is rich in such ambiguities which foreshadow the outcome of the story. The overwhelming generosity and superabundance of Boaz's provision for Ruth (vv. 14–16) is reminiscent of YHWH's unstinting provision for his people (Ps 81:10; cf. also 1:6).

(2:17–23) The picture in v. 17 is of grain beaten out with a stick (cf. Judg 6:11). The weight of an ephah is unknown. Although a surprisingly large quantity to result from gleaning, it was not more than Ruth could carry home—possibly, but by no means certainly, about 25 kilos.

The most significant aspect of Boaz's relationship to Naomi and Ruth is now disclosed (v. 20). He is a 'kinsman redeemer' (*gō'ēl*; Lev 25:25, 47–9). v. 21 has a playful, humorous touch. Boaz's instruction, 'keep close to my young women' (v. 8), becomes on Ruth's lips, 'keep close to my young men'. Naomi responds with an appropriate warning!

The chapter's close marks the end of harvest (June) and the start of a new uncertain future. Where will provision be found? Once again the initiative is Naomi's (cf. 1:6).

(ch. 3) Unlike chs. 1 and 2, ch. 3 has no public aspect. It begins and ends with private conversation between Ruth and Naomi, and pivots on the intimate scene between Ruth and Boaz at the threshing floor.

(3:1–5) Naomi continues her efforts to secure Ruth's, and with it her own, future by the only means she understands, namely marriage (cf. 1:9). To this end she plans an extraordinary and entirely unconventional scheme, although whether from genuine concern for Ruth or from self-interest is unclear. Certainly its outcome is to her own advantage (4:15). The ambivalence of Naomi's character remains unresolved. The instruction to Ruth to wash, perfume herself, and put on her 'best clothes' (an interpretative rendering of 'cloak', *simlâ*) may suggest deliberate preparation as a bride (v. 3). There is a hint of unconscious irony in Naomi's words, '[Boaz] will tell you what to do' (v. 4). In the event it is Ruth who tells Boaz what to do (v. 9). In Naomi's eyes Ruth is merely passive and unquestioningly obedient; in her dealings with Boaz she proves herself independent and resourceful (cf. 2:11).

(3:6–14) This dramatic scene is couched in tantalizingly obscure language, perhaps deliberately so. It is unclear whether the expression 'uncover his feet' (vv. 4, 8) implies sexual intercourse. That a threshing floor with its piles of grain afforded considerable privacy is evident from its use as a haunt of prostitutes (Hos 9:1). Moreover the word 'feet' (*raglaim*) occurs in some instances as a euphemism for 'genitals' (cf. Isa 6:2). Yet the word used here signifies rather 'the place of his feet' (*margĕlôt*; see v. 14), hence the REB rendering, 'the covering at his feet', is to be preferred to the NRSV. Nevertheless, sexual overtones are undoubtedly present both in the repeated use of the verb 'lie' (*šākab*, vv. 4, 7, 8, 13, 14) and in Ruth's request, 'spread your skirt [literally "wings"; cf. 2:12] over your servant', a highly unconventional proposal of marriage (cf. Deut 22:30; 27:20; Ezek 16:8). Far from finding this morally offensive, Boaz gives Ruth his blessing and reaffirms the public regard for her as 'a worthy woman' (v. 11, *'ēšet hayil*; cf. Prov 31:10). Yet the unconventional nature of her behaviour is implied by the secrecy which Boaz urges (v. 14). There is no suggestion that Ruth is a woman of loose morals. Her action is motivated by the fact that Boaz is 'next-of-kin' (*gō'ēl*, v. 9).

This, however, raises acutely the question of the relationship of the book of Ruth to OT law, for nowhere else in the OT are the obligations of a *gō'ēl* said to include marriage. His duties were the restoration of property to his impoverished kin and the redemption of their persons from slavery (Lev 25:25, 47–9). The *gō'ēl's* responsibility in the matter of Elimelech's property is not made specific until 4:3–4. The focus here appears to be solely on Ruth's marriage. Yet for the story to have credibility Ruth's request must have appeared reasonable. Indeed Boaz does not question it. It may be that, in different areas, local practice varied and that the laws of Leviticus were formulated in order to regulate the matter, or the term *gō'ēl* is used here in a less technical sense. What is involved here is not to be confused with levirate marriage, an obligation imposed only upon the brother of a dead man and then only in the case of brothers living together in a closely knit family unit (Deut 25:5). Whereas the refusal to undertake the obligation of levirate marriage was regarded as a grave dereliction of duty (cf. Gen 38:14, 26; Deut 25: 7–10), this was not so in Ruth's case. Marriage to her was clearly a voluntary undertaking (v. 13).

The meaning of Boaz's statement in v. 10 is not entirely clear. The 'first instance' of Ruth's loyalty was her selfless devotion in leaving homeland and family for Naomi's sake (2:11). 'The last instance', v. 10*b* implies, relates to her single-minded commitment to build up Naomi's family by avoiding other relationships. On these grounds Boaz pledges himself to fulfil Ruth's request (v. 11). With v. 12 (where there is a slight dislocation of the Heb.) an element is introduced into the story of which neither Naomi nor Ruth appear to have been aware, the existence of a yet closer relative.

(3:15–18) The themes of emptiness and fullness, prominent in Naomi's lament in 1:21, recur in these last verses. Naomi's physical emptiness is relieved, but this is but the prelude to the satisfying of her deeper need. Naomi had the first word in this chapter. Now she has the last word. Boaz's mention of the closer relative has introduced an element of uncertainty into her carefully conceived plan. Once again the element of chance is taken into account as she bids Ruth wait to see 'how the matter will fall' (v. 18). There is no overt reference here to Yahweh's intervention or direction, implicit though it has been in the several references to his name in blessing. The emphasis throughout falls on the human obligation to act according to loyalty (ḥesed).

(4:1–6) Action moves now from the private to the public arena and hence to exclusively male participants and the arrival of the unnamed next-of-kin, known only as 'so-and-so' (pĕlōnî 'almōnî), a deliberately shadowy figure. The area inside the city gate, the traditional place for executing business, is the scene of a double legal transaction, the redemption of Elimelech's land and the marriage of Ruth. The exact nature of the relationship between these two issues is unclear, and this uncertainty may perhaps account both for a slight dislocation in the Hebrew of v. 5 and, more significantly, for the disjunction between the consonantal text and its vocalized form. The consonantal text is represented by the NRSV, 'The day you acquire the field from the hand of Naomi, you are also acquiring Ruth the Moabite'; in contrast the vocalic text, represented by the REB, reads, 'On the day you take over the field from Naomi, I take over the widow, Ruth the Moabite.' Either way, the mention of this young woman of child-bearing age complicates the situation. Up to this point mention had been made only of Naomi (v. 3). Ruth's prospective child, however, would inherit the land and thus disadvantage the family of the unnamed kinsman. It is this new factor in the situation that accounts for his sudden change of mind from unqualified agreement (v. 4) to instant refusal (v. 6).

A number of unanswered questions remain: why did Ruth glean as one of the landless poor if the family was already in possession of land, and why was the kinsman not aware of the existence of property (cf. 2 Kings 8:3–6)? These are not the narrator's concern.

(4:7–12) Although the marriage in question does not accord with the regulations of a strictly levirate marriage, its purpose, 'to maintain the dead man's name on his inheritance' (vv. 5, 10), is expressed in identical terms (lĕhāqîm šēm; cf. Deut 25:7). Nevertheless there are striking differences between the transaction described here and the procedures set out in Deut 25:5–10. There the removal of the sandal by the rejected widow, accompanied by spitting in the reluctant brother-in-law's face, was a potent sign of his disgrace; here the bestowal of the sandal by its wearer is the solemn confirmation of a transaction.

The amount of space proportionate to the whole narrative which is devoted to this legal transaction emphasizes its importance in the story. The agreement concerning both the property and the marriage is ratified by a properly constituted group of elders (v. 2) and by the people (v. 11). Ruth's relations with Boaz which began furtively and unconventionally are publicly acknowledged. Theirs is no illicit liaison, and Ruth is no longer an outsider, the Moabite. Significantly the blessing (v. 11) compares her to Rachel and Leah, the mothers of the twelve tribes of Israel. v. 12 further associates her with Tamar, like Ruth a foreigner who, by unconventional means, secured the future of a line threatened with extinction (Gen 38). The clan named after her son Perez rose eventually to a degree of prominence (Neh 11:4–6; 1 Chr 27:3). Is there a hint here that the speakers knew of Ruth's unconventional behaviour at the threshing floor? Thus Ruth was not the first foreign woman with a place in the genealogy of the royal Davidic line.

(4:13–22) Now, for only the second time in the narrative, YHWH intervenes, this time in enabling Ruth to conceive (cf. 1:6). Yet, from v. 14 to the end of the book, Ruth is relegated to the shadows, regarded as little more than a surrogate mother for Naomi's child. Although no longer termed 'the Moabite' she is still an outsider. The story ends as it began with Naomi, empty through bereavement of husband and sons, filled now by the birth 'to her' of a male child (v. 17). The identity of the gō'ēl (v. 14) is ambiguous, referring perhaps to Boaz through whom Naomi's future has been secured, or more probably, in view of v. 15, to the newborn child. A woman still needs a male gō'ēl. Yet the response of the women (v. 15) puts the importance of sons in perspective; Ruth's love for Naomi is of more value than seven sons (cf. 1 Sam 1:8). But thereafter the focus is on Naomi and the child. Ruth is ignored. The concluding genealogy is entirely male. Yet the remarkable fact is that the title of the book bears Ruth's name.

Although the book of Ruth is often termed a love story, the only reference to 'love' occurs in v. 15, not between Ruth and Boaz but between Ruth and Naomi, unreciprocated though it was on the older woman's part. The women who shared Naomi's distress (1:19–21) share her joy, and, in the only instance of its kind in the OT, name the child (v. 17). Elsewhere this is a function of the parents alone.

Whether vv. 17b and 18–22 are an original part of the narrative is open to question. It is, however, arguable on literary grounds that the names of the genealogy form a counterpart to the tragic names of ch. 1. From a tale of death and bereavement they point to a glorious future. In the canonical context their importance lies in giving the story a wider significance than the purely domestic, and in introducing the promise of hope after the despair with which the book of Judges ends.

REFERENCES

Campbell, E. F. (1975) Ruth (New York: Doubleday).

Hubbard Jr., R. L. (1988), The Book of Ruth, NICOT (Grand Rapids, Mich.: Eerdmans).

Sasson, J. M. (1989), Ruth: A New Translation with a Philological Commentary and a Formalist-Folklorist Interpretation, The Biblical Seminar, 2nd edn. (Sheffield: JSOT).

12. 1 and 2 Samuel

GWILYM H. JONES

INTRODUCTION

A. Title. 1. In the Hebrew canon the books of Samuel were read as one continuous work, with only a very brief space between the final words of the first and the beginning of the second. Their appearance as one work in Hebrew MSS was known to Eusebius (*Hist. Eccles.* 6. 25), Jerome (*Prologus galeatus*), and Origen (quoted by Eusebius). This is the position reflected too in the Masoretic note at the end of 2 Samuel, which gives the sum total of verses as 1,506 and the middle verse as 1 Sam 28:24. The simple title is 'Samuel'; if the title refers to content, it is only appropriate to the first half of the first book, for David takes centre stage from then on; it is equally inappropriate if it is an indication of authorship, as suggested by the Talmud (*B. Bat.* 14b), for it reports Samuel's death at 1 Sam 25:1.

2. The division into two books was made by the LXX, which gives them and the books of Kings the title *basileiōn* ('kingdoms'), with the books of Samuel designated as I and II and the two books of Kings as III and IV. It may be that the conventional size scrolls used by Greek writers demanded such a division, and a fitting conclusion to the first half was found in the report of the death of Saul in 1 Sam 31. The Latin accepted this division, but modified 'Kingdoms' to 'Kings' (*Regum*). The division was first introduced into the Hebrew text with the publication of Daniel Bomberg's first edition of the Hebrew Bible (Venice 1516–17).

3. 'Samuel' belonged with Joshua, Judges, and Kings to the section of the HB known as 'former prophets' (*nĕbî'îm rišōnîm*), a terminology used by the Bible itself (cf. Zech 1:4; 7:7). It is only to a limited extent that this section of the Bible is concerned with prophets, but it was assumed in antiquity that Samuel was the author of Judges and Samuel, and that further material was added by Nathan and Gad (1 Chr 29:29). Likewise, the books of Kings were attributed to Jeremiah (*B. Bat.* 14b–15a). But the tradition of 'prophetic' authorship is no longer tenable.

B. Text. 1. The Hebrew text of the books of Samuel (MT) is in a poor state, evident mainly in the number and extent of its haplographies, i.e. scribal omissions from the text caused by the use of identical consonants at the end of words or sentences (known as *homoioteleuton*). For examples, reference can be made to: 1 Sam 4:1b, where the Greek text contains the additional words, 'And Eli grew very old, and his sons continued to act more and more wickedly in the presence of the Lord'; 1 Sam 11, at the beginning of which 4QSam² has a few lines of additional text; 1 Sam 17–18, where, in the account of David's contest with Goliath, the Greek text is shorter and more consistent. Nevertheless, reference to the Greek text raises as many problems as it solves, for it has to be admitted that some of the divergences between the MT and the LXX are not due to the Greek's preservation of the original, but may have been caused by the tendency of the Greek to paraphrase the Hebrew. A different evaluation of the Greek text has led to various approaches to the books of Samuel by textual critics (for a summary see McCarter 1980).

2. A positive approach to the LXX can lead to an extensive use of it to reconstruct what was the original Hebrew text before its emergence in the shorter version preserved in the MT. This was the approach initiated by Julius Wellhausen in 1871 and built upon by a succession of commentators. It was a method of study that was not thrown off course when it was realized that a number of recensions of the Greek were in existence, each of different value and reliability. There was confidence that from the surviving recensions an original Greek translation could be reconstructed; cases where this reconstructed Greek text was superior to the Hebrew could be distinguished from those where the Greek was merely paraphrasing the original.

3. Taking a more negative attitude towards the LXX, it was claimed that the divergent readings of the LXX could not confidently be used to reconstruct the Hebrew original. Other reasons can be suggested for such divergences; most may be attributed to the wish of the Greek translators to correct the Hebrew or else to their practice of paraphrasing the Hebrew rather than translating it. Nor could it be assumed that it was possible to recover the original Greek translation from the various recensions available. Consequently a more wary attitude towards the Greek was adopted, and serious questions were raised concerning its value for reconstructing the text of the books of Samuel. As an example of this approach McCarter refers to P. de Boer's studies in 1938 and 1949.

4. However, the position had to be reassessed with the discovery of Hebrew MSS of the books of Samuel in Cave 4 at Qumran and in view of the work done on these fragments since 1952. The three relevant MSS are: 4QSam², containing fragments of most of 1 and 2 Samuel and dating from 50–25 BCE; 4QSamᵇ, fragments of a small part of 1 Samuel and dated in the third century BCE; 4QSamᶜ, small fragments of 1 Sam 25 and 2 Sam 14–15 and dated in the first century BCE. The significance of these fragments is that the Hebrew text preserved in them is generally at variance with the MT, but close to the LXX (cf. Cross 1953a; 1955), and thus they give some confirmation to the more positive attitude towards the Greek text. Detailed comparisons have enabled textual critics to be more precise in their reconstruction of the text of Samuel. In many instances the Qumran fragments are closer to the Lucianic MSS of the LXX (LXXᴸ) than to the Codex Vaticanus (LXXᴮ)—not that the evidence of LXXᴮ is to be ignored, for it is fuller than the MT and in many ways superior to it. Nevertheless, like the MT, it does suffer from extensive haplographies. The evidence of LXXᴸ is especially valuable for recovering the Hebrew text of Samuel, particularly when it is in agreement with the ancient Qumran fragments and is supported, as is frequently the case, by other ancient witnesses, such as the third century CE's Old Latin and Josephus's *Jewish Antiquities* (see further Ulrich 1978; Tov 1979).

C. Composition. 1. On first appearance the books of Samuel may give the impression of a well-organized composition dealing with three main characters, Samuel, Saul, and David. But on a closer reading of the narrative, a number of discrepancies, contradictions, and duplications become evident. Although Samuel seems to be the main character in the first block of narratives, he disappears completely from 1 Sam 4–6 only to be reintroduced again in 1 Sam 7. Two different interpretations of the movement to secure a king are evident in 1 Sam 8–11; in some sections YHWH disapproves of the development and it was contrary to his will that a king was chosen, but in others the kingship, and Saul its first incumbent, gain divine approval. There are a number of duplicates in both the Saul and David cycle of narratives. In the case of Saul, there are two accounts of his rejection by YHWH (1 Sam 13 and 15) and two again of David's introduction to his court (1 Sam 16 and 17). The Davidic cycle has double reports of his betrothal to Saul's daughter (1 Sam 18), his defection to the king of Gath (1 Sam 21 and 27) and his unwillingness to grasp the chance to kill Saul (1 Sam 24 and 26). These features demand a consideration of the composition of the books.

2. Continuous Strands. An approach that found favour among scholars of an earlier generation was to find in 1 and 2 Samuel evidence of continuous strata of material. It was an approach that was developed under the influence of Pentateuchal criticism and its apparent success in identifying the main narrative strands combined to form the Pentateuch. Examples of duplicate narratives, with their repetitions and deviations, naturally led to a search for strands or sources similar to the ones which had proved so successful in Pentateuchal source criticism. The traditions in 1 Sam 8–11 about the founding of a monarchy provided a good starting-point for such an investigation. In the older strand in 1 Sam 9:1–10:16; 11; 13–14 is found an account which takes a favourable attitude towards the monarchy and is thought to be historically reliable. A later account in 1 Sam 8:1–22; 10:17–27; 12; 15 is critical of the monarchy and is thought to reflect the theocratic view of the post-exilic period to such extent as to make it of little historical value. Moving from these parallel strands to other duplicate narratives, attempts have been made to identify one strand as a continuation of the Pentateuchal J and the other as a continuation of E; others found in the antimonarchial strand traces of Deuteronomistic thinking. A fairly late example of this line of thought is found in Otto Eissfeldt's Introduction (1965), where it is argued that in at least 1 Samuel there is an E sequence almost without gaps. Because this sequence was by nature a reshaping of an earlier secular presentation, it follows by implication that there was an original continuous strand which betrayed the marks of the Pentateuchal J stratum. Although Eissfeldt's work appeared in its third German edition in 1964, he was by then out of step with the general trend of OT literary criticism, which had abandoned the idea that continuous strata could be traced in the books of Samuel, and with that the possibility of identifying them as a continuation of Pentateuchal strands.

3. Independent Units. A different and more acceptable approach is to posit that the books attained their present form after the combination of a number of independent narrative units, some long and some short. Many of the narratives had a previous existence as independent pieces before becoming attached to a narrative complex. The most influential study in this area was Rost's examination of the succession narrative in 2 Sam 9–10; 1 Kings 1–2 (1982). Following the success of his approach other studies concentrated on complexes such as the ark narrative (Campbell 1975; Miller and Roberts 1977) and the story of David's rise (Grønbaek 1971), and others again on shorter units.

4. The Ark Narrative. Narratives about the ark in 1 Sam 4:1b–7:1 are taken as one unit because of their concentration on the fate of the ark during a particular period, their total exclusion of Samuel, who is the key figure in the surrounding chapters, and their distinctive vocabulary. Some have also included 2 Sam 6, recording the transportation of the ark to Jerusalem, as a climax to the complex; there is, however, no general agreement on this, mainly because of the difficulties caused by variations in nomenclature between 1 Sam 7:1 and 2 Sam 6:2–4.

5. The historical setting suggests an early date for the ark narrative. The tenth century BCE has been proposed as a possibility, with the pilgrims coming up to festivals in Jerusalem as the intended audience. Its purpose was to give them an outline of the ark's previous history. Others, whilst accepting a tenth-century date, find in the narrative an underlying theological theme, namely YHWH's activity in the history of Israel (Campbell 1975) and by implication his power and invincibility (Gordon 1986).

6. An earlier date, taking the narrative back to the time of Saul and David, has also been proposed (Miller and Roberts 1977). The main argument given in support is that an account of the previous misfortunes of the ark would be unnecessary and irrelevant once David was on his way to be king in Jerusalem. A date between the defeat at Ebenezer and the bringing of the ark to Jerusalem has therefore been suggested. This issue has been made more complex by Miller and Roberts' proposal to connect other passages with the ark narrative, more especially the passages in ch. 2 which are critical of Eli and his sons and therefore provide a reason for the defeat at Ebenezer.

7. An early date seems more appropriate for the ark narrative than the later date proposed by some investigators. To date some parts of it after the fall of Samaria in 722 BCE and others in the reign of Hezekiah in the late eighth or early seventh centuries, and to interpret it as a narrative intended to combat the tide of Assyrian religious beliefs and practices (Schicklberger 1973), divorces it entirely from the historical setting to which it belongs. So too does the emphasis on its timelessness and therefore its possible relevance to those in the Babylonian exile (Timm 1966). On the contrary, it is best understood as an ancient independent unit which eventually found its way into the books of Samuel (cf. also Gordon 1986).

8. The Founding of the Monarchy. As noted above, the presence of duplicate accounts of the founding of the monarchy in 1 Sam 8–11 was one of the main reasons for finding in Samuel a continuation of Pentateuchal sources. With the abandonment of that approach an alternative method of dealing with these chapters had to be sought. The contrast between pro-monarchial and antimonarchial attitudes cannot be missed; it must also be observed that they have been set side by side and allowed to intertwine; however, the placing of an antimonarchial section at the beginning of the complex

(8:1–22) and another at its end (12:1–25) is a clear indication of the sentiment of the final editor.

9. These features have been given a different interpretation in recent studies. First, instead of searching for evidence in support of Pentateuchal sources there is a tendency to find the origin of individual narratives at different centres. Some, such as 8:1–22, originated at Ramah, others, such as 10:17–27, at Mizpah; some again, such as 11:1–25, obviously preserve ancient semi-historical material (see Weiser 1962). Secondly, there has been a shift of opinion regarding the priority of the two different attitudes towards the monarchy. Instead of taking the pro-monarchial strand as older and more reliable than the antimonarchial, which was later and reflects a post-exilic view of the institution, it is now claimed that the antimonarchial stance was a natural immediate reaction towards such an innovation (cf. Ishida 1977; Crüsemann 1978). Thirdly, the nature of the opposition to the monarchy in these chapters has been reassessed. One contention is that the antimonarchial sections were not absolutely opposed to the monarchy but to particular forms of monarchy, especially those encroaching upon the sovereignty of YHWH (Boecker 1969; cf. Birch 1976).

10. It does not concern us at this point to decide how the monarchy was founded, nor to attempt a description of the historical circumstances leading to the election and anointing of Israel's first king. But, as far as the composition of the books of Samuel is concerned, what is envisaged is that a number of traditions about the early beginnings were available at different key centres, each reflecting the interests of its particular centre. When they were brought together into this complex, they were set side by side without any apparent awareness of the contradiction involved.

11. The History of David's Rise. The extensive collection of narratives in 1 Sam 16–31 has been designated as 'The History of David's Rise', whose theme is the advance of David under the guidance of YHWH, a theme supported by its counterpart, namely that Saul had lost divine favour and was no longer competent to rule (cf. Grønbaek 1971). Although Saul is present throughout these chapters, interest focuses on David, and the story of his rise to power, from his initial anointing at Bethlehem by Samuel until his acceptance as king over Israel in Jerusalem, is traced step by step.

12. There are some uncertainties about this History. Its natural starting-point is with Samuel's commission to find a successor for Saul (1 Sam 16:1); but alternative starting-points have been proposed. Some have argued against the inclusion of the report of David's anointing in 16:1–13, mainly because no other reference to his anointing is found in the History, and furthermore because it is Saul that is consistently called 'God's anointed'. Others have taken the starting-point back to 15:1. Likewise there is disagreement about the History's conclusion. A suitable climax is provided by the account in 2 Sam 5:1–10 of David's occupation of Jerusalem. But arguments have been presented for including other sections within the History, most notably the account of David's victories over the Philistines in 2 Sam 5:17–25 in fulfilment of the promise in 2 Sam 3:18, and also 2 Sam 6:1–23 because of linguistic similarities to 5:17–25. Also included by some is Nathan's oracle in 2 Sam 7, which seems to be presupposed by 2 Sam 3:9–10 and 5:2. However, the fact that such a variety of opening and concluding sections have been proposed is not in itself a sufficient reason for doubting the existence of the History.

13. Unquestionably the impression gained is that an author has brought together material relating to David's advance to the throne and has worked it around a dominant theme. Its obvious aim was to demonstrate that David was the legitimate successor of Saul as king of all Israel and that he gained the throne lawfully by respecting 'the LORD's anointed' and not taking any of the many chances given to him to usurp the throne. This latter point is made clear in the two accounts of David's refusal to take Saul's life (1 Sam 24 and 26); the same point is brought out again in the emphasis on David's non-complicity in the deaths of Saul (1 Sam 29:1–11), Abner (2 Sam 3:28–39), and Ishbaal (2 Sam 4:9–12), as it is in Abigail's specific statement to this effect in 1 Sam 25:30–1. David behaved honourably on all these occasions, and it is impossible to support the view that he was an opportunist engaged in guerrilla warfare against Saul and joining with bands of malcontents to usurp the throne (as argued by Ishida 1977; cf. Gordon 1984 for a refutation of this argument).

14. A tenth-century date for this History has been suggested; a justification of David's conduct as he was moving towards the throne was perhaps necessary in the reign of Solomon, when a Saulide faction was in danger of threatening the unity of the kingdom. It has been suggested that a member of Solomon's court prepared the history and deliberately took a positive attitude towards the Saulides. Not quite as convincing is the proposal to date it in the early years of the divided kingdom, soon after Solomon's death, and to give it the specific aim of supporting Davidic and Jerusalemite claims to supremacy over 'all Israel'.

15. The comparison made recently between the History and the thirteenth-century BCE 'Apology of Ḥattushilish' throws an interesting light on the history of the genre (McCarter 1980). Ḥattushilish, a Hittite king, after absolute allegiance to his predecessor, finally usurped the throne when his life was in danger. In his revolt he was assisted by the goddess Ishtar who had promised him the throne. Similarly David had been faithful to Saul until he was finally compelled to leave court; he too came to the throne because YHWH had promised it to him. In both versions it was divine will that finally decided the issue of succession.

16. The Succession Narrative. L. Rost's (1926) study of the succession narrative identified 2 Sam 9–20; 1 Kings 1–2 as a separate unit that was mainly concerned with the issue of succession to David's throne. It is an issue that is given full expression in 1 Kings 1:20, and the narrative as a whole is concluded with the statement in 1 Kings 2:46 that 'the kingdom was established in the hand of Solomon'. Other possible candidates for the throne have been dismissed one by one until the final scene portrays the contest between the two last candidates, Adonijah and Solomon.

17. There are no real grounds for disagreement about the conclusion of the succession narrative, despite the attempts to take 1 Kings 1–2 with the Solomonic corpus which follows rather than the Davidic section which precedes. Another view that has been taken is that the original corpus was a Court History of Davidic times, upon which was superimposed the theme of succession when 1 Kings 1–2 was added to it (Flanagan 1972). There is more room for disagreement about the specific point at which the narrative begins. It can be argued that the promise to David in 2 Sam 7 is an appropriate introduction to a section concerned about the succession (Jones 1990). Links have been noted too with the bulk of 2 Sam 2–4 (Gunn 1976), possibly with 5:1–3 and also with 6:16, 20–3; but the case for connecting these sections with the corpus is not as convincing as is the one for connecting 2 Sam 7. Strict adherence to the theme of succession helps to eliminate some of these sections.

18. Giving it the title Court History raises the question of the character of this complex of narratives. A court history must be envisaged as a document giving an account of events which keeps as faithfully as possible to their course, and would depend possibly on some records, and definitely on recollections of eyewitnesses. Eyewitness accounts would have been possible here if the History is dated in the period of the Solomonic Enlightenment which came soon after the events described. Consequently it has won acclamation as 'the oldest specimen of ancient Israelite historical writing' and as 'genuine historical writing' (von Rad 1966). Nevertheless, the validity of the term 'history' has been doubted. Reports of private scenes and conversations suggest that some of its contents are more akin to court gossip than to reliable history. Its interest in personalities rather than in the political implication of events, its lack of reference to the international scene, and the absence of citation of sources and of chronology have led to the judgement that, whilst using historical facts and possessing a historical theme, it cannot be classified as historical writing (Whybray 1968). Although the author displays remarkable narrative skill, his work is more a historical novel. Admittedly all the characteristics of a good novel are present: a theme, division into scenes, artistic structure, use of dialogue, portrayal of characters, and mastery of style. But to consider it as a novel, or a 'work of art and entertainment' (Gunn 1978), fails to do justice to its aim and purpose. There are good reasons for placing it in the category of political propaganda.

19. The aim and purpose of the complex thus becomes an issue. As noted, its aim has been described as seeking to demonstrate the legitimacy of Solomon's accession to the throne and to justify the elimination of his opponents. The narrative's aim is to make a point. Works disseminating political propaganda were known in the days of Solomon; Egyptian precedents also sought to legitimize claims to the throne, such as the claims of Amenemhet in the Prophecy of Neferty and the claims of Sesostris in the Instruction of Amenemhet (Whybray 1968; Mettinger 1976). Doubts have been raised, however, regarding its designation as 'succession narrative' and also the definition of its aim as legitimizing Solomon. Against the former it has been pointed out that succession is not the dominant issue in most of these chapters, especially in 2 Sam 13–20 (Conroy 1978; Gunn 1978); against the latter a case has been made for seeing an anti-Solomonic tendency in 1 Kings 1–2 and anti-Davidic elements in 2 Sam 10–12. Many of the discussions of purpose are combined with complex analyses of the Deuteronomistic History into editions by successive redactors, with the various editions modifying the view taken of David and Solomon. For such reasons some have been inclined to abandon altogether the concept of 'succession narrative'. Carlson (1964), for instance, claims that

this corpus of material is too closely integrated with the remainder of the narrative in Samuel–Kings to be separated and treated as an entity. He finds in the narrative 'recollections' of previous sections as well as thematic and verbal similarities to other parts of Samuel–Kings. Rejecting the term 'succession narrative', he finds the schema 'David under the blessing' (2 Sam 2–5) and 'David under the curse' (2 Sam 9–24) adequate to deal with the Davidic corpus of tradition.

20. Whatever difficulties may arise in connection with such terms as 'court history' and 'succession narrative', it is clear that a block of tradition reaches its climax with the statement in 1 Kings 2:46, which causes a break between it and what follows. Although the succession of Solomon to the throne gives a general indication of the theme of that section, the concept of 'succession narrative', as originally defined, may well have to be modified. But it is conceivable that during the early years of Solomon the events leading to his accession to the throne were recorded. It may be that the unease caused by the executions of 1 Kings 2:39 prompted the writing of a political tract to show that Solomon was the legitimate heir. Its contents suggest that it emerged from court circles.

D. The Deuteronomistic History. 1. The final compilation of the books of Samuel, like that of Joshua, Judges, and Kings, with which they formed a corpus, is generally attributed to a Deuteronomistic author or authors. The complex, covering the period from the death of Moses (Deut 34) to the account of Jehoiachin's favourable treatment in exile in 561 BCE; (2 Kings 25:27–30), is generally known as the Deuteronomistic History (see Noth 1943). Without surveying the long and complex debate about the Deuteronomistic History, the position can be generally stated as follows: in Joshua–2 Kings is found a presentation of history according to a single line of interpretation; there are links of language and thought between these books and the Deuteronomic law and its accompanying speeches in the book of Deuteronomy (see Weinfeld 1972); despite its influence on subsequent studies, Noth's concept of a single Deuteronomistic historian (Noth 1943) presented too simple a view of the history; similarly the idea of a double redaction, one working before the Exile, soon after 621 BCE, and the other in the Exile, after 561 BCE (see Nelson 1981), also presents too simplistic a picture of compilation; a more prolonged and complex development, reflecting continuing activity by a Deuteronomic school or circle, has found support because it attempts to do justice to both the unity and diversity found in the Deuteronomistic History (see Jones 1984).

2. It must be recognized, however, that the contribution of the Deuteronomists to the final form of the books of Samuel is less pronounced than their part in fashioning Judges and Kings. The exploits of the 'judges' were presented within the Deuteronomists' own rigid formula; likewise they imposed their own structure on their presentation of the kings of Israel and of Judah, sometimes including very little material within their standard formulae. Evidence of such a domineering structuring is absent from the books of Samuel. A possible reason is that the blocks of tradition mentioned above were complete narratives in themselves, and because they more or less subscribed to the Deuteronomistic viewpoint there was very little need for editorial activity. A full list of verses which can be regarded as Deuteronomistic annotations is given by

McCarter (1980; (1 Sam); 1984 (2 Sam)). In some places in 1 Samuel relatively lengthy additions have been made to the text, such as the polemic against a non-Jerusalemite priesthood in 1 Sam 2:27–36; 3:11–14, or the interpolation to Abigail's speech at 1 Sam 25:28–31 with its anticipation of some sections in Nathan's oracle. 1 Sam 12 is certainly Deuteronomistic, for Samuel's speech is reckoned to be one of the orations included by the Deuteronomist to mark one of the important milestones in Israelite history. A review of Israel's past history, when God performed some of his mighty acts on behalf of his people, serves to emphasize that the monarchy was an unwelcome development. Other annotations are very brief and have been inserted in order to incorporate material into the Deuteronomistic History, such as YHWH's reply in 1 Sam 8:8 or notices about Saul's kingship at 1 Sam 13:1–2; 14:47–51. Similarly in 2 Samuel, some interpolations are more significant than others, such as the ones in the report of Nathan's prophecy (2 Sam 7:12b–13a, 22–4), which make the prohibition of a temple only temporary and typically occur on an important historical occasion. Less significant ones are in the form of formulaic introductions to the reigns of kings, such as 2 Sam 2:10a, 11; 5:4–5.

3. Deuteronomistic editing, although only slight, served to give expression to some theological themes which were important in the eyes of the Deuteronomists. Among these are the primacy of the Jerusalem temple and the Davidic covenant, which stands out in contrast to the earlier period of disobedience to God's will and the later period which similarly deserved an unfavourable judgement. The Deuteronomists had a very positive view of the dynastic promise to David; on its basis they held out a hope for the restoration and renewal of the Davidic dynasty in the future. Connected with this hope was their emphasis on repentance; a return to God would save them from Philistine oppression (2 Sam 7:3), and the real basis for future security was a confession of wrong and the continuation of their relationship with YHWH (1 Sam 12:19–24). The presence of these themes in 1–2 Samuel is sufficient evidence of some Deuteronomistic editing.

E. A Prophetic History. 1. It cannot be denied that the history given in 1–2 Samuel, especially in the sections relating to the foundation of the monarchy, is prophetic in perspective and therefore very critical of the monarchy. In these sections the figure of Samuel dominates. He appears in 1 Sam 1–7 as an ideal prophetic leader, and for that reason the move towards a kingship is presented as an act of folly and of unfaithfulness to God. Even after the founding of the monarchy, the prophet still had a role; Samuel remained as an intercessor between God and people and had the task of condemning Saul's kingship because of his disobedience. As the narrative proceeds, David is presented as the man chosen by YHWH. This is established as the ideal of Israelite kingship—the king was YHWH's chosen, but he was subject to prophetic authority, for the prophet had a hand in choosing, anointing, and instructing the king. This prophetic perspective cannot be ignored.

2. One approach to this question is to argue that at a pre-Deuteronomistic stage of the tradition the narratives were placed together to form a 'prophetic history'. Noth's (1981) idea of a Deuteronomistic editor, who for the first time

brought all this material together by means of redactional links and editorial expansions, and gave the material an anti-monarchial slant, has been challenged. Weiser (1962) saw in this antimonarchial stratum an earlier, pre-Deuteronomistic, prophetic layer. Although Weiser refused to think of this layer as a literary unit, others have seen in it evidence of a complete pre-Deuteronomistic edition of Samuel which had originated in prophetic circles (cf. Birch 1976). McCarter (1980) has accepted that there was a pre-Deuteronomistic structure belonging to a middle or penultimate stage of tradition and having its own characteristics or slant. It is further claimed that it was this prophetic history that gave the first edition of Samuel its basic shape; beyond the negative portrayal of kingship as a concession, it sought to set out the essential elements of the new institution from a prophetic perspective. Its point of view was distinctly northern. McCarter accepted too that the origin of Deuteronomic law and theology was to be found in northern prophetic circles (cf. Nicholson 1967) and that the intermediate prophetic stratum can therefore quite easily be called 'proto-Deuteronomic'.

3. Another approach associates the prophetic viewpoint with a later rather than earlier stage in the history of tradition. The view taken by Dietrich (1972) and Veijola (1975; 1977) is that three layers of Deuteronomistic tradition succeeded one another in the following order. First of all came a basic historical work (DtrH), whose intention was to present one great history of God's dealings with his people. It was composed soon after 587 BCE, possibly at Mizpah, and probably knew nothing of the fate of king Zedekiah after his transportation to Babylon. Secondly came a redaction which included prophetical texts (DtrP) and sought to emphasize the importance of the prophetic role and the function of the divine word in history. It has been dated between 580 and 560 BCE and connected with Judah, probably Jerusalem. Finally came a nomistic redaction (DtrN) containing law-oriented additions which brought out more clearly the place of the law. It has been ascribed to the period immediately after the rehabilitation of Jehoiachin in 561 BCE. Admittedly, the views of Dietrich and Veijola have not been generally or enthusiastically received, and they have been accused of classifying texts according to subject-matter rather than producing firm evidence of redactional activity. Nevertheless, it is an interpretation that has the advantage of being able to hold together two different emphases: on the one hand it gives full recognition to the unified theological outlook of the history, and on the other it allows for the various emphases being brought out in different redactions. The idea of continuous activity by a 'Deuteronomic school' gives room for unity and diversity.

4. Whichever of these approaches finds favour, it is accepted without question that at some stage or other prophetical interests and emphases found expression in the Deuteronomistic History. The work cannot be read without observation of a very pronounced prophetic slant in many of its narratives.

F. Outline

Succession to David's Throne (2 Sam 9–20)
Appendices (2 Sam 21–4)

COMMENTARY

1 Samuel

Samuel (1:1–4:1a)

(1:1–2:10) Samuel's Birth and Dedication Samuel, the last of
the judges and the maker of Israel's first two kings, is presented as a significant person in this account of the extraordinary circumstances surrounding his conception and birth.
Although his father came from an old, prestigious stock in
Ramah (v. 1) in the land of Zuph (see 9:5–6), Elkanah's first
wife was childless and he had decided to take a second wife (cf.
Gen 16:1–4). There was inevitable tension and rivalry between
the two women, with Hannah being constantly provoked and
distressed; this provided a perfect scene for a miraculous
intervention and the subsequent contrast between her humiliation and ultimate triumph. These events are connected
with Shiloh, where Elkanah and his family attended annually
for a feast (Judg 21:19–24), and where Hannah, whose plight
was made more obvious when she received only one portion
of the sacrifice (v. 5), came into contact with Eli the high priest.
Worship at Shiloh, one of the most important sanctuaries and
the home of the ark (3:3), was regulated by Eli and his two
unworthy sons. The second main contrast introduced in the
narrative is that between the corrupt priesthood of Shiloh and
the ideal prophet Samuel. Although the narrator emphasizes
the themes suggested by these two contrasts, his account
contains obvious legendary elements (as in the accounts of
the births of Isaac and Samson).

Another element introduced into the narrative is Hannah's
vow to dedicate the son requested as a nazirite (v. 11). The MT
refers to only one feature of the nazirite vow, leaving the hair
uncut, but the longer text of the LXX, to some extent supported by 4QSam^a, includes an undertaking to abstain from
strong drink (Num 6:1–21; Judg 13:5, 7). The actual dedication
is reported in vv. 21–8. On his annual visit to Shiloh Elkanah
paid his vow, which may have been related to Samuel's birth,
but Hannah delayed her visit until the child had been weaned
and then took him to Shiloh to 'abide there forever'. 4QSam^a
makes it quite clear that she was dedicating him as a nazirite.
Votive offerings were brought, a 'three-year old bull' (with
4QSam^a and LXX in preference to the MT's 'three bulls')
accompanied by flour and wine (Num 15:8–10). See Willis
(1972).

There is a repeated wordplay on š-ʾ-l—(to ask, request)—
'what you have asked of him' (v. 17 REB), 'I have asked him'
(v. 20), 'what I asked' (v. 27 REB), 'he is given' (v. 28). Although
such wordplays appear in birth narratives, it is obvious that
what occurs here is more appropriate to Saul (cf. šāʾûl, v. 28)
than to Samuel, which is taken to suggest that the story about
the birth and dedication of a nazirite belonged originally to
Saul but was secondarily applied to Samuel. Saul is closer
than Samuel to another nazirite, Samson (Judg 16). See more
fully Dus (1968), and for an opposite view Gordon (1984: 23–
4). The account of Samuel's birth is thus a combination of the
Shiloh/Eli traditions with the nazirite/Saul traditions.

Embedded in these traditions is Hannah's song (2:1–10),
which, like other Hebrew psalms, celebrates a victory granted
by God. As noted from NRSV's footnotes, the MT is not
satisfactory and the LXX and 4QSam^a must be consulted to
obtain a better version. The theme is clear: the singer has been
exalted by God and exults in this good fortune. To emphasize
God's work comes a series of contrasts: the mighty and the
feeble (v. 4), the full and the hungry (v. 5), the barren and
the mother of children (v. 6), the faithful and the wicked (v. 9).
God's absolute power is celebrated (vv. 6–8, 10). It is appropriate in its context, for the reference to the barren bearing
children in v. 5 connects it with Hannah, and the reference to
'king' and 'anointed' in v. 10 links it with its wider context in
which the rise of Samuel was to lead to the anointing of
Israel's first king.

The reference to 'king' in v. 10 raises the question of date.
The song itself betrays a number of affinities with early pre-
monarchial Hebrew psalmody (Deut 32; Ex 15; Judg 5; 2 Sam
22; and Ps 113). See Albright (1968), Willis (1973), and Wright
(1962). Possible ways of dealing with this reference are: to
find here an allusion to early rulers, such as Abimelech; to
date the song to the late years of Samuel when Israel had a
king; to regard v. 10b as a later addition. Whichever solution is
accepted, a reference to 'king' suits a narrative depicting the
decline of Shiloh and the rise of the Samuel–Saul–David regime. Like 2 Sam 22, it truly represents Israel's royal ideology.

(2:11–36) The Depravity of the House of Eli After describing
the total depravity of Hophni and Phinehas (vv. 11–26), this
section describes the visit of a man of God to Eli to deliver an
oracle of doom (vv. 27–36). Like other levitical priests, Eli's
sons bore Egyptian names. But the main interest is in depicting their evil ways, which stand in contrast to Samuel's exemplary behaviour. Several short statements about Samuel
are introduced (vv. 11, 18, 19, 26); he is ministering before
YHWH and gaining in maturity and favour. But the sons of Eli
are unfaithful ministers. This is a further development of the
theme introduced in ch. 1, the contrast between the corrupt
priesthood of Shiloh and the ideal prophet Samuel.

The malpractices at Shiloh are noted in vv. 13–17. The
priests took more than their share of the offering. Although
receiving only what was forked from the pot suggests trust in
providence, it is clear that they took more than their due. A
reconstructed text based on 4QSam^a suggests that they took
meat in addition to 'the breast for wave-offering and the right
thigh', which belonged to them by right (Lev 7:31, 32). Another
malpractice was their insistence, on taking by force if necessary, a piece of meat before the fat was burnt off, for the fat
belonged to the Lord (Lev 7:22–5).

Whereas his sons were corrupt, Eli himself was old and
unable to check them. They were guilty of prostitution with
female sanctuary assistants, and were possibly resorting to a
Canaanite practice of cultic prostitution (Num 25:6–15). It is
interesting that the reference to prostitution is absent from the
LXX and 4QSam^a, which may suggest that it was a later addition. They did not respond to the pleading of their aged father,
who accepted that they were beyond human intercession.

Samuel in contrast was gaining in favour and maturity, for
his ministry was acceptable to God (vv. 11, 18). According to
priestly custom he wore a linen ephod (1 Sam 22:18), and his

mother used to make him an outer garment. Hannah was rewarded for her faithfulness with a family of five children. Although the narrative brings out clearly the contrast between the Elides and Samuel, it may not have been originally intended to describe Samuel's rise. Possibly it was an introduction to the ark narrative and showed why YHWH rejected Shiloh and departed from Israel (Willis 1971).

An oracle against the house of Eli was spoken by 'a man of God' (vv. 27–36), an anonymous figure (1 Kings 13:1–13), who took the role of a prophet and pronounced words of doom. It may be that the introduction of an anonymous spokesman was a literary device whereby the Deuteronomistic historian gave his own judgement. The Aaronide house of Eli is about to fall, despite the self-revelation of God in Egypt to his family (Moses) and the election of this house to perform all priestly duties, such as offering incense, wearing the ephod, and accepting gift-offerings. It is rejected on the basis of the charges brought in vv. 15–16; the choicest parts of the sacrifices, belonging to the Lord, had been taken and Eli had shown himself unable to prevent this. God's promise of a perpetual priesthood to the house of Eli is now rescinded because the conditions had not been met. Although Eli himself will be spared the ultimate downfall, the death of his two sons will give him a sure sign of what is coming (v. 34). Allusions to the fate of the priesthood are seen in vv. 33–5: the slaughter of the house of Eli refers to the massacre of the priests of Nob; the one spared was Abiathar (1 Sam 22:20); the faithful priest given a sure house is Zadok (1 Kings 2:35); the impoverished priests were the non-Zadokites living outside Jerusalem and playing only a minor role after the Josianic reform (2 Kings 23:9). See McCarter (1980).

Although the narrative in 1 Sam 1–2 presents a contrast between Samuel and the house of Eli, the oracle in vv. 27–36 introduces another major theme belonging to the Deuteronomistic History, namely that the true priesthood was the Zadokite one of Jerusalem.

(3:1–4:1a) Samuel is Called Samuel is now set within the tradition of the great prophets, for this narrative, despite some formal variations, belongs to the genre of prophetic-call narratives (Isa 6; Jer 1:4–10; Ezek 1:1–3:16). Samuel will now be acting as God's mouthpiece (see Newman 1962). Dream theophanies were not uncommon in the ancient Near East, and elements from that genre have been preserved here (Gnuse 1982).

However, the narrative in its present context elaborates the contrast between Samuel and the house of Eli and brings it to a climax. It was in a period when divine oracles were infrequent and visions out of the ordinary that Samuel received his call-vision. Thus is introduced the theme of the whole chapter, namely the difference between the old regime and the new (Fishbane 1982). Under the former, Samuel was a boy assistant in the temple, where he lived night and day in order to perform his duties; he was under Eli's supervision, for despite his failing physical condition he was still in charge. But these respective positions were changed dramatically with the call-vision, which shifted the seat of power. Even then Eli was presiding for a limited period, for Samuel 'did not yet know the Lord' and mistook his voice for that of Eli. It was Eli who instructed Samuel and gave him the right words of response

(vv. 9–10). But once God had spoken and given Samuel the oracle of vv. 11–14, Samuel became more powerful than Eli and spoke the oracle of doom over his house. It is an oracle that confirms the words of the man of God in 2:27–36: the house of Eli will fall because of the iniquity of his sons and his own inability to check them. Eli accepted God's verdict (v. 18). Samuel was no longer a boy, but a powerful person whose words were fulfilled and whose position as a prophet was acclaimed. For a time Samuel was associated with Shiloh, but before long that centre was to be stripped of its pre-eminence.

The Ark Narrative (4:1b–7:1)

The narrative now focuses on the ark; Samuel disappears from the scene, Eli and his sons are mentioned only briefly (4:4b, 12–22) and there is little interest in Shiloh. It is generally accepted that the ark narrative (4:1b–7:1; 2 Sam 6) is a self-contained literary entity recording the fortunes of the ark until its installation in Jerusalem (Rost 1926); there is no need to attach to it sections about the sons of Eli from chs. 1–3 (as by Willis 1979 and Miller and Roberts 1977). The main theme of this theological narrative is the power of YHWH as it was invested in 'the ark of the covenant of God'; this point is missed if it is interpreted only as a cult myth showing how the Shilonite cultic object was transferred to Jerusalem (Rost), or as a polemic against the Assyrian plague-god Nergal-Resheph (Schicklberger 1973), or a reflection on the end of an epoch in Israel's history (Campbell 1975). As noted above (C.4–7), there is reason to date the narrative soon after the events described, sometime in the tenth century BCE. For a fuller discussion see Gordon (1984: 30–9).

(4:1b–22) The Capture of the Ark The Philistines appear on the scene without introduction (see OCB). According to the longer Greek text they were responsible for engaging Israel in battle, and the position of the two camps at Ebenezer and Aphek in the southern end of the plain of Sharon indicates that they were intent on gaining land further north, which was also of interest to the Israelites in their movement westwards. This reflects a recurring position until their ultimate defeat by David. Israel was conquered twice; on the first occasion the enemy's success was due to God's decision 'to put us to rout today' (v. 3), and on the second occasion it occurred despite God's presence in battle (v. 7). The ark is also introduced into the narrative without explanation (see OCB), but it is known from such passages as Num 10:35–6 and 2 Sam 11:11 that it was given an important place in Israel's battles. It was the visible sign of God's presence and designated his covenant with his people and his enthronement in majesty on the cherubim. Although it was brought out to secure victory and was greeted with a battle-cry (v. 5), Israel was defeated. No explanation is given for such calamity, but v. 11 (recalling 2:34) attributes it to the degenerate priesthood of Shiloh.

Two speeches are included in the narrative, both acknowledging the power of YHWH. After the first defeat the elders of Israel advised the people to bring the ark 'that he may come among us and save us' (v. 3). When the ark came the Philistines felt helpless against 'the power of these mighty gods' (vv. 7–9). Although the Philistines, according to this account, regarded the Israelites as worshippers of several gods, they were aware of the Exodus tradition.

News of Israel's defeat was brought to Eli (vv. 12–23), who was more concerned about the ark than anything else (v. 13). It was the fate of the ark, mentioned as a climax to a triad of calamities, that killed him (vv. 17–18). News about the ark (v. 19) also made Phinehas's wife give premature birth leading to her untimely death. The name of her son, Ichabod ('where is glory?' or 'alas (for) glory'), and her death-cry both allude to the loss of the ark.

(5:1–12) The Ark among the Philistines The clash between Israelites and Philistines moves to another plane; the struggle for possession of territory became a contest between the gods of the two peoples. As was customary in the ancient Near East, idols of the gods of those who had been vanquished (in this case 'the ark of God') were carried to the temple of the victors and placed beside the idols of their gods as an indication of the latter's supremacy over the former. Thus the ark was taken to the temple of Dagon, a Semitic deity identified in Ugaritic texts as the father of Baal and possibly a vegetation deity (cf. Heb. *dāgān*, 'grain'). The Philistines on their arrival in Canaan probably adopted such deities.

The narrative's main theme is the power of YHWH, which is illustrated in the contest with other deities (vv. 2–5) and in the plagues which he brought upon his foes (vv. 6–12). Dagon was twice humiliated in his own temple in Ashdod; on the first occasion he was thrown down in front of the ark, and on the second his head and hands were cut off and were lying on the threshold. Thus an aetiological motif is introduced into the narrative to explain the sacred character of the threshold which was not trodden by the Ashdodites. In displaying his power against the Philistines God humiliated them in three of their five cities, Ashdod, Gath, and Ekron. The plagues sent by God are referred to as 'tumours', which some, on the basis of the reading 'mice' in the LXX, have identified as bubonic plague, and which others have taken to be an attack of dysentery (cf. Josephus, *Ant.* 6§3).

It may be that the aetiological narrative in vv. 2–3 and the report of the plague in vv. 6–12 were not connected with real events. However, there are several significant features in their emphasis on the power of YHWH: 'the hand of YHWH' is given prominence (vv. 6, 7, 9, 11); striking the Philistines with tumours is reminiscent of the Exodus tradition (Ex 9:15–16); the supremacy of YHWH over other gods is a recurring theme in the OT; overcoming humiliation is not only a reminder of 2:1–10, but also forms a bridge between the conquest of the ark (ch. 4) and its return (ch. 6).

(6:1–7:1) The Return of the Ark Having realized that the ark had to be returned (v. 2, cf. 5:11), the Philistines took consultation on the manner of its return to avoid further humiliation (vv. 1–9). Priests and diviners were consulted, but it is not known if they were Philistines or outsiders hired for the purpose. Attention focuses on the double issue raised in v. 3 (Campbell 1975). The first matter of concern was the appropriate offering to accompany the ark. It was recognized that gifts had to be sent (cf. the Exodus tradition, Ex 3:21); they were chosen on the basis of value ('gold'), correspondence with the victims ('five' for the five lords of the Philistines), and representation of the plagues suffered ('tumours' and 'mice').

Although they are called 'guilt offering' (*'āšām*), they had a double function: as sacrifice they would ensure that YHWH would 'lighten his hand', and as gifts they were regarded as a compensatory tribute to YHWH. The Exodus tradition teaches the people not to be obstinate and prevent the return of the ark (v. 6).

The second concern belonged to the realm of divination (vv. 7–9), and they sought confirmation that it was YHWH who had humiliated them. They were to select untrained cows, separated from their calves and therefore inclined to return home, and not to give them guidance which way to take. If the cows went in the direction of Beth-shemesh, the Philistines would know that it was YHWH who had harmed them. The cows had a second function. Because they were to be sacrificed in order to remove contamination, they and the cart had to be new, unused, and therefore ritually clean (cf. Num 19:2). The rituals described in vv. 3–9 are found elsewhere among the Israelites and more generally in the ancient Near East (McCarter 1980).

The narrative proceeds in vv. 10–18 to record the outcome. The direction taken by the cows confirmed that YHWH had been responsible for the plagues, and it is evident that the gifts sent by the Philistines were acceptable (vv. 16–18). The Israelites celebrated the return of the ark by sacrificing the cows on a 'large stone' in the field of an unknown Joshua. A secondary, later addition in v. 15 introduces the Levites to be responsible for sacrifices and changes the function of the stone by making it a resting place for the ark.

The ark was equally dangerous for Israelites if they did not pay it due respect, either by not celebrating its return (LXX), or by looking into it (MT). Possibly a plague had spread from Philistine territory to Beth-shemesh, and in seeking to give a reason for it this narrative again connected it with the ark. Consequently the ark was moved to Kiriath-jearim ('city of the forests'), which had probably been connected previously with Baal-worship (cf. 'city of Baal', Josh 18:14 and 'Baalah', Josh 15:9, 10); its custodian was Eleazar, son of Abinadab, both bearing names that appear frequently in levitical lists.

Moving towards a Monarchy (7:2–15:35)

1 Sam 7–15 reports the rise of the monarchy and gives an account of the first years of King Saul. As already noted (c.9), it is probable that many of the sections included in these chapters originated independently at different centres, such as Ramah and Mizpah. It is a complex section, and, as is commonly recognized, contains two accounts that betray strikingly different attitudes towards the monarchy. A pro-monarchial strand (A) is intertwined with an antimonarchial one (B): 8:1–22 (B), 9:1–10:16 (A), 10:17–27 (B), 11:1–15 (A), 12:2–25 (B). The main features noted are: the accounts are placed together without any attempt to suppress or to harmonize; an arrangement which opens and closes with antimonarchial sections gives a dominant antimonarchial emphasis to the whole; the antimonarchial stance is now thought to be early rather than late, and may reflect the same opposition to this innovation as was present in the time of David and Solomon (Crüsemann 1978); the message of the A strand, that God himself was involved in the establishment of the monarchy, is preserved (see Childs 1979).

(7:2–17) Samuel's Victory at Mizpah Although this chapter is not directly concerned with the establishment of the monarchy, it is not to be separated from the events of chs. 8–12. First, it portrays the background against which the monarchy arose, namely the threat to Israel from the Philistines (cf. 9:16) and other peoples (11:1–15). Secondly, it subscribes to the view that a monarchy became a necessity when Israel was unfaithful to God; theocracy, based on Israel's faithfulness to the covenant, brought success against enemies.

The Philistines, despite being forced to return the ark, were still a threat, and Samuel decided to give the people a lead. His assembly at Mizpah (v. 5) is preceded by an address in v. 3, which must be regarded as an intrusion (McCarter 1980); it contains Deuteronomistic phrases, such as 'returning to the LORD with all your heart', and many expressions taken over from the editorial framework of the book of Judges (cf. Judg 10:6–16 for 'remove foreign gods', 'serve him only', 'the Baals and Astartes'). For Baals and Astartes see *OCB*. Mizpah, identified as Tell en-Naṣbeh a few miles north of Jerusalem, was important as a tribal centre and the scene of much prophetical activity. Prayer was on this occasion accompanied by two rites. The significance of the first, drawing and pouring water, is not clear; since water is the source of life, it may have been connected with a fertility rite, but more probably, in view of its association with the Feast of Tabernacles and the Day of Atonement, it was a purification rite. Fasting was a sign of penitence (see *OCB*).

Consequently, when the Philistines attacked Israel, they suffered a decisive defeat. The account in vv. 7–11 bears the marks of the holy war tradition: an enemy assault causing panic among the Israelites; petition by Samuel, accompanied by sacrifice; YHWH himself enters into battle and by a thunderstorm causes utter confusion among the Philistines; the Israelites pursue the disarrayed Philistines as far as Beth-car (probably to the west of Jerusalem in the direction of Philistine territory). These elements, found also in war reports such as Josh 10, emphasize the basic claim of the holy war tradition: victory belongs to YHWH alone (von Rad 1951). To conclude the section it is claimed, again using a formula well-known from the book of Judges (cf. Judg 4:23–4), that the Philistines were completely subjugated with Israel repossessing towns and territories formerly lost to the Philistines. The position as it was before an earlier battle at Ebenezer (ch. 4) was now restored; a 'Stone of Help' reminded Israel that 'thus far the LORD has helped us'.

Samuel the prophet ruled Israel in the style of the preceding charismatic leaders known as judges, who saved the people from their enemies (Judg 2:18); he also fulfilled the narrower judicial role of a judge (vv. 15–17). Thus the effectiveness of a charismatic, non-royal leadership is affirmed, and the inappropriateness of Israel's wish to have a king is established.

(8:1–22) Israel Requests a King This section, with its negative attitude towards the monarchy, contains the elders of Israel's request for a king and reports their persistence despite Samuel's warning about the oppressive ways of kings. There were two reasons for the quest for a king, one implicit and the other explicitly stated. According to vv. 1–3, Samuel's position was similar to that of Eli before him, for his sons were unfit to succeed him (v. 5). Perverting justice in Beersheba, which was more southerly than Samuel's normal circuit, gave sufficient grounds for supporters of the monarchy to press for a different succession. Their more explicit reason was that they wished to be governed 'like other nations' (cf. Deut 17:14), which had military advantages (v. 20). Thus the elders requested a king rather than a new line of judges.

The antimonarchial stance of the chapter is brought out in three different sections. First, in vv. 6–9, where the proposal displeased Samuel (v. 6) and was regarded by YHWH as a rejection of himself and of Samuel. It is a rejection that in a truly Deuteronomistic statement is placed in the context of Israel's propensity towards idolatry from the time of the Exodus. Secondly, in vv. 10–17, which give Samuel's view of 'the ways of the king', it is shown that a monarchy will have to be supported by the conscription of personnel for military duties (vv. 11–12a) and to provide labour (vv. 12b–13), submitting to the confiscation of property and provisions for maintaining a court (vv. 14–15), and even accepting slavery and the confiscation of stock (v. 16, reading 'cattle' with LXX in preference to 'young men' in the MT). The origin of this list of a monarch's oppressive measures is debatable. On the one hand it is claimed that it reflects the common practices of Canaanite kings as known to Samuel and his contemporaries. Akkadian texts from Ras Shamra testify to many of the practices listed in vv. 11–17 (so Mendelsohn 1956 and Crüsemann 1978). On the other hand, the similarity of the list to the practices of Solomon as described in 1 Kings 10–11 suggests that it must have its origin there; it is claimed that the Deuteronomistic historian's criticisms of Solomon were transferred to 1 Sam 8 in order to censure Saul and to show that the monarchy from its very foundation was corrupt (cf. Clements 1974). Other kings followed the same practices, and it is more likely that this passage recalls some bitter experiences of the abuse of royal power by Israelite monarchs. The concluding verse of the passage (v. 18) echoes the language of Judges: under oppression the people cried to YHWH, but on this occasion he would not deliver. Thirdly, in vv. 19–21, it is stated that the kingship was reluctantly permitted because of Israel's determination; it was tolerated rather than approved (cf. v. 7). In this way the narrative successfully combines two opposing views: on the one hand, the monarchy was an undesirable development and was not approved by YHWH, and on the other, YHWH himself was responsible for selecting the first kings of Israel.

(9:1–10:16) Saul Becomes King This narrative, which is strikingly different in character from the preceding chapter, has some features of the popular folk-tale: a young man setting out to find lost asses returns as designated king. Originally it may have related how Saul visited an unnamed seer, and may well have the same function as the birth legends associated with other notable characters (Ishida 1977). The original folkloric material has been incorporated in this biblical narrative which subscribes to the view that Saul was chosen by God. However, several inconsistencies show that it does not fit smoothly into its present context (cf. Birch 1971). According to 9:6–10 Saul was persuaded to visit a nameless seer who was unknown to them (cf. 9:18); but as the narrative proceeds we learn that Samuel was well-known 'from Dan to Beersheba' (so 3:20), and 10:14 suggests that they chose him deliberately.

The seer is described as a popular diviner; but Samuel was the designated successor of Eli.

God's direct participation in the events is emphasized by their providential character. Saul, a mere youth belonging to the smallest of the tribes and the humblest of families (9:21), is endowed with extraordinary characteristics (9:1–2); it was a journey looking for stray donkeys that brought them to the land of Zuph; on the advice of a boy assistant the seer was consulted (9:6); by chance the boy had a quarter shekel to pay the seer for consultation (9:8); after a chance meeting with a group of girls they met the seer, who had just arrived in town and was on his way to a sacrifice (9:11–12); Samuel had been told beforehand by YHWH that the one chosen to be king would visit him (9:16); the three signs given by Samuel to Saul were fulfilled (10:2–7).

Although the issue of kingship is settled (8:22), this chapter makes an important contribution to the definition of 'kingship' according to prophetic ideology. Saul was anointed to the office of *nāgîd* (prince, leader) and not *melek* (king); to define the task of 'ruling' the verb used is *'āṣar* (to restrain) not *mālak* (to reign) (Gordon 1984). The emphasis is on YHWH's choice of ruler; blood succession was not to be practised. That Saul was YHWH's chosen ruler is confirmed elsewhere in the narrative: his anointing (10:1), which was a private matter not disclosed to others (10:1b); his participation in sacrificial meals reserved normally for priests (9:24); his direct experience of inspiration (10:10–13).

(**10:17–27a**) **Choosing a King at Mizpah** The narrative of 8:1–22 is continued, and the dismissed assembly is now reconvened to appoint a king. Although it belongs to the antimonarchial strand, this section recognizes that Saul was an elected ruler (see Gordon 1984).

The words spoken by Samuel (vv. 17–19) present this development in an unfavourable light. Preceding the command to assemble for an election (v. 19b) are words in the form of a judgement oracle (cf. Birch 1975). Despite God's protection of his people and his ability to deliver them, they have chosen to reject him and elect a king. Set in this context, the election was under judgement. Furthermore, Saul's election by lot must be considered in conjunction with the use of lottery elsewhere in the OT to find a hidden offender (Josh 7; 1 Sam 14:38–44); this casts some doubt over Saul's election (McCarter 1980). Nevertheless, Saul was God's choice, whether taken by lot (vv. 17–21b) or acclaimed because of his stature (vv. 21b–27). Possibly two traditions about Saul's election have been preserved here, a later one followed by an older tradition about his stature (cf. 9:2). Both traditions allow for God's freedom of choice: the lot confirms that he was God's choice, and what was known in secret now becomes public; his choice on account of stature confirms what is already known from the lost asses narrative. YHWH's displeasure with the people's resolve to have a king does not make Saul's kingship invalid.

Public acclamation (v. 24), an important element in a king's installation (cf. 1 Kings 1:25, 34, 39; 2 Kings 11:12), is followed by Samuel's proclamation of the rights and duties of the kingship, which may have been similar to 8:11–18 or to the law-book in Deut 17:18–20, but not identical with either. What is clearly established here is the subjugation of the monarchy to prophetic authority.

(**10:27b–11:15**) **A Saviour for Jabesh-gilead** The inhuman treatment of the inhabitants of Jabesh by Nahash the Ammonite gave Saul an opportunity to prove himself leader. The description of Nahash's oppression in Transjordan (10:27b) is absent from the MT but provided by 4QSamᵃ; it was also in the Greek text known to Josephus (*Ant*. 6 §§ 68–71). His action against Jabesh on the east bank to the south of the Sea of Galilee occurred 'about a month later' (following 4QSamᵃ and the LXX), which was after Saul's return to Gibeah.

Saul is presented as a deliverer in the style of the ancient judges, which may well be a true historical representation of the emergence of the monarchy. The last of the judges became the first king. The conditions of pre-monarchial times are reflected in vv. 3–4, when the tribes in their separation lacked central authority and a united front in battle. It is not clear if the messengers came to Gibeah specifically to consult Saul and so test the new king (Edelman 1991); however, his leadership is unmistakable and his action decisive. Like the judges, Saul was seized by the spirit (v. 6, cf. Samson in Judg 14:6, 19; 15:14) and this brought him success in battle. This specific charismatic gift is different from his previous endowment of the gift of prophecy and may also be different from the charismatic leadership of later monarchs. Divine choice and inspiration constitute an ideal of kingship that existed in Israel before the introduction of dynastic succession by David, and it persisted for some time in the northern kingdom (Alt 1968).

Saul's technique for calling assistance is not without parallel; dismembering animals occurred in covenant ceremonies and was accompanied by making an oath (cf. Judg 19:29–30, and Wallis 1952 for an extra-biblical parallel). A curse was invoked on the oxen and possibly on the people who refused to respond; their fate would be like that of the oxen. Saul's victory was also similar to that of former judges. By dividing the forces (cf. Judg 7) the camp was surrounded and an early morning attack was made. His unmistakable victory over the enemies was attributed to YHWH (v. 12). Saul was deemed worthy of the kingship contrary to the words of his opponents (10:26), but they were spared according to Saul's own wish (the name 'Samuel' is unnecessarily introduced in v. 12). Saul was acclaimed king at Gilgal; but the word 'renew' suggests that v. 14 was an attempt to harmonize this account with the preceding Mizpah narrative.

(**12:1–25**) **Samuel's Farewell Speech** This chapter closes the period of the judges, and, like other Deuteronomistic orations placed at junctures in the Deuteronomistic History, marks the end of an epoch. The cycle of alternative pro- and antimonarchial strands is concluded, as it began, with an antimonarchial stance and a repetition of the negative words spoken in 8:1–22. However, in the introductory vv. 1–5 Samuel's words introduce a new element, a contrast between the old prophetic regime and the new royal one. After suggesting that kingship was a concession in response to popular demand (v. 1) and was a departure from the kind of leadership exercised by himself, Samuel poses a number of questions with the aim of justifying his own rule. The key is provided by the verb 'take'; in his just leadership the prophet had 'taken' nothing from the people. But according to 'the ways of the king' in 8:11–18, a number of things will be 'taken' from the people by the king. In pressing for a king the people had taken a step backwards.

The résumé of history in vv. 6–15 shows that it was an unnecessary step, for God 'in all his saving deeds' had given saviours or judges who had achieved great successes in the period prior to the call for a king. Set in the context of calling Moses and Aaron to deliver the people from Egypt (vv. 6, 8), three oppressors from the period of the judges are mentioned: Sisera (Judg 4–5), the Philistines (Judg 13–16), and the Moabites (Judg 3). Within a skeletal pattern of apostasy–oppression–repentance–deliverance, the saviours named (with assistance from the LXX) are Jerubbaal (Gideon), Barak, Jephthah, and Samson. The newly appointed king belongs to the same tradition.

Although the demand for a king was a wicked act (v. 17), there is a way forward: people and king must show faithfulness to YHWH. Covenantal language is used here, and also a historical summary as was usual in covenant ceremonies. vv. 14–15 announce the blessing and curse of the covenant: it will be well if people and king remain faithful, but if not, people and 'king' (following the LXX in preference to 'ancestors' in the MT) will be wiped away (cf. v. 25). Parallels between this passage and the covenantal passage in Josh 24 have been noted (McCarter 1980): introduction, antecedent history, transition to the present, requirements, blessings, and curses. A covenant between God, people, and king holds the key to the future, for it is not God's wish to abandon his people (v. 22, cf. Muilenburg 1959). Nor will Samuel abandon the people, for he has a prophetic role in the period of the monarchy. Samuel's sons are not expected to follow him because they were among the people (v. 2); in any case judges did not have a line of descent. Although old, Samuel still possessed supernatural powers (v. 17); bringing thunder and rain was a sign of God's displeasure, but it also confirmed that Samuel was true to the prophetic office and acted according to God's will. He will continue to serve the people as intercessor and instructor (v. 23), which was the norm for the prophetic office under this new regime (Gordon 1986).

(13:1–23) Saul's Disobedience A skeletal introduction to a king's reign in v. 1 (absent from the LXX) lacks Saul's age when he began to reign and gives an incorrect figure of 'two' as the length of his reign. Some Greek MSS give 30 as his age, and in both Josephus (*Ant.* 10 § 8) and Acts 13:21 the length of his reign is 40 years.

Saul had been appointed to save his people 'from the hand of their enemies' (10:1), more specifically the Philistines (9:16). A Philistine campaign to weaken Israel and restrict its expansion into the plains (Mayes 1977) led to the activities described here. First, they had a strong presence in the central hill country. The territory of Saul's own tribe, Benjamin, had to be freed, for Geba and Michmash were in Benjaminite territory to the south of Bethel (referred to as Beth-aven, 'house of wickedness', v. 5). Both Saul's capital, Gibeah of Benjamin (Tell el-Ful), and Geba of Benjamin are mentioned (vv. 2, 3, 15 with a different reading in the LXX, v. 16), and it has been suggested that two accounts have been fused, a victory by Saul at Gibeah and another by Jonathan at Geba (Mayes 1977). Secondly, the Philistines were able to send out bands of raiders to the north (Ophrah), west (Beth-horon), and south (valley of Zeboim) (vv. 17–18), undermining Israelite confidence and causing fear. Thirdly, the Philistines, by forbidding the manufacture of weapons, disarmed the Israelites. By securing a monopoly in servicing Israelite agricultural implements they exacted revenue from them (vv. 19–22).

One outcome of Philistine presence was that Saul could no longer depend on a militia, but had to establish a standing army (v. 2). He and Jonathan achieved successes against Philistine garrisons, although the Philistines had a better-equipped and numerically stronger force. To man 'three thousand chariots' (following the LXX in preference to the MT's 'thirty thousand') they had 'six thousand horsemen', two for each chariot, and their infantry for action in the hills was numerous (v. 5). Israel panicked, some fleeing eastwards to hide in the hills and some as far afield as Transjordan (vv. 6–7). Lack of action led to further depletion of the Israelite army (v. 8). Thus the scene is set for the battle of Michmash, where a Philistine garrison had been placed (v. 23).

An intrusion in vv. 7b–15a introduces a new perspective; the description of deteriorating Israelite–Philistine relations becomes a narrative explaining Saul's disapproval by YHWH. The emphasis is on disobedience. Saul's action could be justified: Samuel had not kept his appointment, and Saul did not infringe upon priestly prerogatives, since kings did offer sacrifices (2 Sam 6:17–18; 24:25; 1 Kings 3:3–4). But the issue is obedience, upon which the future of Saul's kingship depended (v. 13, cf. 12:14). Because he failed a Saulide dynasty was not established, and God chose another king to follow him. This represents a prophetic viewpoint: kings must obey prophets and kings are charismatic persons chosen by YHWH.

(14:1–52) The Battle of Michmash This narrative betrays a mixed attitude towards Saul, oscillating between a sympathetic, favourable view and a negative, unfavourable verdict. It may well be that an original positive source has been overlaid with other material to reinforce the conviction that Saul was not a man after God's heart. (On the chapter see Blenkinsopp 1964.)

The Philistines' camp at Michmash was to the north of the deep ravine, Wadi es-Ṣuwēnīṭ, and that of the Israelites in Geba to the south of it. Jonathan and his armour-bearer succeeded in the first encounter (vv. 1–15) by clambering up from the ravine through rock formations that were difficult to negotiate, as indicated by their names, Bozez ('slippery one') and Seneh ('thorny one'). The enterprise and bravery of Jonathan brought success against a superior Philistine force. There is a contrast between Jonathan the hero and the reckless Saul, who acted foolishly on one occasion (13:13), interrupted a consultation to rush to battle on another (14:19), and finally endangered the life of his son (14:44) (Gordon 1984). After Jonathan had defeated the garrison and caused panic (v. 15), Saul and his troops later engaged in battle (v. 20). It is also emphasized that Jonathan was but an instrument in God's hand: he set out on the assumption 'it may be that the LORD will act for us' (v. 6), depended on God's approval of his action (vv. 8–12), and it is concluded that it was God's victory (v. 23, cf. v. 45). Jonathan, possessing the characteristics of a charismatic leader, stood in the tradition of those who waged God's battles (Jobling 1976). To ensure success Saul had placed an oath on his troops, a rash act (as noted in v. 24, following the LXX in preference to the MT), which became a threat to

Jonathan's life (vv. 24–6). Taking the oath seriously, the troops refrained from eating of the plentiful honey available; Jonathan, unaware of the oath, ate and was refreshed ('his eyes brightened'). A clash between Jonathan and Saul is hinted at by the son's reference to his father as one who 'has troubled the land' and who had prevented a total wiping out of the Philistines (v. 30).

A separate tradition, which does not involve Jonathan, interrupts the narrative at vv. 31–5. By observing the oath the troops were famished by evening when the oath was expiring. They seized animals from the spoil, but were not careful enough to drain blood from the meat; they slaughtered on the ground, not on a stone from which the blood could flow away (vv. 33–4). 'Eating with blood' (as in NRSV against Hertzberg 1964) was contrary to regulation (Deut 12:23–7; Lev 19:26). Following the intrusion, the narrative proceeds to Saul's determination to wipe out the Philistines (vv. 36–46); it was thwarted by lack of divine support. Upon investigation, by means of a sacred lot, fault was found with the king's family and more specifically with Jonathan. The NRSV reads the longer text of the LXX, which refers to Urim and Thummim, probably the black and white stones used for casting lots (see OCB). Although Jonathan, and to his credit Saul, were willing to accept the verdict, the warriors resisted and saved Jonathan's life (v. 44). Saul, condescending to the better judgement of the people, does not appear in a favourable light. There is, however, no proof that Saul and the priest manipulated the oracle in order to be rid of Jonathan his rival (Long 1989). The chapter closes on a more positive note depicting Saul as a successful warrior (vv. 47–8) and the head of a household (vv. 49–51).

(15:1–35) The Rejection of Saul This conclusion to the section on relations between Saul and Samuel has two prominent themes, the relationship between prophet and king and the necessity for obedience. Samuel plays a central role. His command in response to a divine message led to war against the Amalekites, as punishment for their opposition to the Israelites on their way from Egypt (vv. 1–3, cf. Ex 17:8–16; Deut 25:17–19). A holy war to fulfil a divine sentence was instigated by a prophetic figure. Again God's views of Saul's kingship were transmitted to Samuel (v. 10), and the prophet spoke an oracle of judgement to Saul (vv. 17–31). The same prophetic attitude is expressed here as in 8:1–22 and 13:8–15; the people had been warned against a monarchy, and it became obvious from the Gilgal episode that Saul's kingship was doomed. Here the rejection of Saul is final and absolute (vv. 28–9) and it is parabolically confirmed by the accidental tearing of Samuel's robe when Saul made his last desperate supplication (Brauner 1974). The rejection is set out in rhythmic form in vv. 22–3, taking up Saul's reference to sacrifice (v. 21) and in true prophetic spirit contrasting sacrifice and obedience (cf. Isa 1:11–15; Hos 6:6; Am 5:21–4; Mic 6:6–8) and declaring finally that he who rejected God's word has been rejected.

The issue of obedience is as prominent in Saul's final rejection as it was in the preliminary warning in 13:13 (cf. 12:14). The ban was operative in this Holy War, and so every living thing captured had to be exterminated (cf. Deut 20:10–18; Gordon 1986), but Saul in his selective application of it

disobeyed the divine command. His kindness to the Kenites is not an issue (v. 6). Reasons could be given for his other actions; it may be that he believed in sparing the life of a king, as was done on other occasions (cf. 1 Kings 20:30–4, 42), and he attempted to justify sparing the best animals for sacrifice and not for personal gain (v. 14). Whatever his reasons, they were not acceptable. He was guilty of gross disobedience, as is seen from the selection of words chosen to describe his action: disobedience (v. 19), doing evil (v. 19), rebellion (v. 23), stubborness (v. 23), rejection of God's word (v. 23). Saul had to admit that it was a sin and transgression (v. 24). Disobedience was the reason for his rejection and for God to regret that he had made him king (vv. 10, 35). To complete the narrative, Samuel himself fulfilled the terms of the ban (vv. 32–3), which was a criticism of Saul. Relations between them were then broken off (vv. 34–5).

The cycle of Samuel–Saul narratives is now completed and the next section consists of a Saul–David cycle. The basic question of this cycle, 'Is Saul a man after God's heart?', has been finally answered in the negative. He has been rejected because he rejected God's word (13:13; 15:23, 26), but it must be remembered that he was only reluctantly made king and that his kingship was under a cloud from the beginning (cf. Gunn 1980).

Saul and David (1 Sam 16:1–2 Sam 1:27)

The block of narrative in 1 Sam 16–2 Sam 5 has become known as the History of David's Rise (see Grønbaek 1971), with David identified as the central character. Good reasons can be given for taking 1 Sam 16:1–2 Sam 1:27 as an independent unit with its own central theme, the decline of Saul and the rise of David (see c.11–15). Although the section emphasizes that David is God's chosen (1 Sam 16:1–13), the rejected Saul was still king and David was careful not to seize the kingdom from God's anointed (1 Sam 24:6; 26:9). The recognition of David's stature is balanced by the decline of Saul's authority; whilst David was under blessing, Saul was under curse. Saul and his son Jonathan knew that David was the chosen successor, and the narrative stresses that he did not come to power by shedding Saulide blood. Jonathan even assisted him by his own virtual abdication (Jobling 1976). Saul's position was made even more pitiful by his intense jealousy. Gordon (1984) rightly refutes an alternative reading of the narrative (as by Ishida 1977), which makes Saul a popular king who was forced to oppress David, the usurper engaged in guerrilla warfare against the king.

As noted above, various dates have been proposed for the composition of the History of David's Rise. The most likely are either the Solomonic period, when the kingdom was undivided and an effort was made to justify David's succession to the throne, or the period of David himself, when an attempt was made to refute charges brought against David by demonstrating that 'the LORD was with him' (1 Sam 16:18; 18:14).

(16:1–23) David's Anointing and Introduction to Court Saul's rejection (v. 1), Samuel's fear of Saul's reprisal (v. 2), and Samuel's pretence of going to Bethlehem to offer sacrifice (v. 2), provide the background for David's election and anointing. The narrative bears similarities and dissimilarities to Saul's own election to the kingship. A similarity of fundamental importance is the concept that YHWH alone chooses a king, both accounts using the verb *bāḥar* (choose) (10:24; 16:8, 9, 10) and thus emphasizing that David, like Saul before him, did not come to the throne by chance or force. A miraculous and unexpected feature belongs to the actual choice; as Saul belonged to the smallest clan of the smallest tribe, David was the youngest of seven or eight sons, which may be a folkloric motif (McCarter 1980). It is also possible that the actual process of election was similar; Saul was chosen by elimination by means of lots (10:17–27*a*), and it is possible that the elimination of all Jesse's sons, from Eliab the eldest and a man of stature through to David, the youngest and the chosen, occurred through a similar procedure. David, who was not present for examination, had to be brought from the fields, exactly as Saul had to be brought from among the baggage. Such obvious similarities are taken as indications that the Davidic narrative deliberately reflects the previous one about Saul. Nevertheless, there is a clear intention to bring out the dissimilarity between David and Saul. Although David was handsome (v. 12), it is emphasized that God does not 'look on the outward appearance'; it was precisely for that reason that Eliab was rejected. There is perhaps some justification for the comment that this is a veiled attack on Saul's personal appearance and stature (9:2; 10:23); the rejection of Eliab, a kind of second Saul, confirms Saul's rejection (Mettinger 1976). Whatever the similarities, the major difference introduced by this narrative is that Saul was rejected but David chosen. That difference is made explicit in v. 13 with the transfer of YHWH's spirit from Saul to David and the abandonment of Saul to a malevolent spirit.

The next section (vv. 14–23) introduces an ironic element into the narrative. Immediately after David's anointing and his endowment with YHWH's spirit, Saul becomes troubled and unwell, which provides an opportunity for his servants to introduce David to court. By this strange turn of events, Saul gives David the court experience and training that will enable David to replace him. Although David was chosen because of his skill in playing (v. 18), he had many other attributes and pride of place goes to his military prowess. This made him even more attractive to Saul, whose policy was to enlist all men capable of assisting him in his fight against the Philistines (14:52); thus David became his armour-bearer. In addition David possessed good judgement and intellect, and was a man of presence (v. 18). To crown the list of qualifications it is stated that 'YHWH is with him', which superficially means that David's personal attributes are proof of God's blessing, but at a deeper level indicates that he had a special endowment. v. 21 states that 'Saul loved him'; reading 'Saul' with the LXX removes the possible suggestion of the MT that 'David' was the subject, thus leading to the interpretation of it as a covenant relationship (Thompson 1974). However, a key to the Saul–David narrative is the love–hate relationship between the two (Gunn 1980). Another key is provided in v. 23: Saul was entirely in David's hands, and the narrative shows how David responded to that responsibility.

(17:1–58) David and Goliath The place of this narrative in the History of David's Rise is unclear. In view of vv. 12–16, which so glaringly contradict what has gone before in 16:14–23, it is generally assumed that it is an alternative account of David's

introduction to Saul, possibly derived from a different source. Others interpret it, not as an alternative, but as providing the next step in David's progression to the throne by testing his suitability. In contrast to the testing of Jonathan at Michmash (vv. 13–14) David proves himself a worthy successor to the throne.

To avoid the difficulty caused by the statement in 2 Sam 21:19 that another Bethlehemite, called Elhanan, killed Goliath, several proposals have been made. Chronicles obviously attempted to harmonize the text by claiming that 'Elhanan the son of Jair slew Lahmi the brother of Goliath' (1 Chr 20:5). A suggestion that has found some support is that Elhanan was the original name of the Bethlehemite who killed Goliath, David his throne name (Honeyman 1948). Other more acceptable solutions are: either that elements from a popular tradition about Elhanan became attached later to David (McCarter 1980), or else that in the course of time the name Goliath was given to an anonymous challenger (Hertzberg 1964).

A shorter account of the narrative is given in the Vaticanus MS of the LXX (known as LXX[B]); it is thought that this is the result of a shortening of the text, probably for harmonizing purposes. It is not a satisfactory explanation; the shorter text does not harmonize with preceding or succeeding sections. Furthermore, the parts omitted in the shorter version form more or less a complete narrative on their own. A primary short narrative received an interpolation of a full alternative account (Stoebe 1973). The shorter version, consisting of vv. 1–11, 32–40, 42–8*a*, 49, 51–4, reports how David, who was with Saul as his armour-bearer, volunteered to meet the challenge of the Philistine Goliath. Although the NRSV calls him 'champion', the Hebrew *bênayim* denotes 'one who steps out to fight between the two battle lines', which was later interpreted in the Qumran *War Scroll* as 'infantryman' (McCarter 1980). According to the MT, preferred by the NRSV, he was over 'six cubits' tall (approximately 9 ft. 6 in.), but 4QSam[a] and the LXX have 'four cubits' (6ft. 6 in.). His armour, described in detail in vv. 5–7, made him a formidable opponent; he was far superior to David, who refused to take the armour offered him (vv. 38–9) and relied entirely on his shepherd's sling (v. 40). However, his forehead had not been covered, an omission that was to prove fatal. The inequality in size, experience (v. 33), and armour, and the fact that David went to meet him without assistance, set the stage for presenting the theological theme of the narrative, namely that God was with David (vv. 37, 45–7). David stood the test, and proved that he belonged to the tradition of Israel's great saviours. Like Saul he triumphed against the Philistines, and was now poised to succeed him.

Additional verses included in the MT version are: 12–31, 41, 48*b*, 50, 55–8. Originally this had been an independent narrative, but has now been revised to fit into its present context. David was not in Saul's service (vv. 17–18) and was unknown to the king (v. 55), but an editorial note in vv. 14–15 attempts to harmonize the two versions. Again the editorial v. 31 seeks to harmonize the additional narrative, which does not contain conversation between David and Saul, with the shorter narrative to which the conversation in vv. 32–7 belonged. The aim of this account is to portray David as a mere shepherd boy, not a king's armour-bearer, and how he successfully joined battle with the Philistine. The conversation of vv. 26–32 emphasizes that David did not enter into battle because of arrogance or a spirit of adventure, but because he was destined for this part in God's plan. This account has all the characteristics of popular legendary material about David. Although it was not added to the text of the original narrative until the fourth century BCE (after the divergence of the MT from the ancient Greek tradition), it may nevertheless consist of an ancient tradition about David (so McCarter 1980). Other biblical texts show that the shepherd motif attached to David in this narrative had 'royal' connotations (cf. Ps. 78:70–2 and the prophecies of Jeremiah, Ezekiel, and Zechariah); this was also the case throughout the ancient Near East.

(18:1–30) David, Jonathan, and Michal vv. 1–5 are a fitting conclusion to the narrative in ch. 17. David became permanently attached to the court (v. 2), probably as a reward for his success and to ensure military assistance in the future (v. 5); another possible reason is that he could be kept under observation to avoid any revolt (Edelman 1991). David was attractive and popular, and was retained (v. 2) and elevated (v. 5) by Saul; he also won general acclaim by the populace and the courtiers. Especially important is Jonathan's attachment to David, which is described in terms of 'covenant' and 'love'. The word 'love' here denotes more than personal attachment; as with 'bound to' (v. 1) it signifies some kind of political liaison (see Thompson 1974; Ackroyd 1975). The word 'covenant' too signifies more than a bond of friendship; they were sealing a pact which had political implications; this is confirmed by Jonathan's act of handing over his clothes and armour to David (v. 4), by which he was symbolically transferring the right of succession and making him heir-apparent (Mettinger 1976). Saul's jealousy was aroused, and his relationship with David developed into one of respect and hatred, recognition and desire to kill. The couplet in v. 7, which made him equal to Saul, not superior to him (McCarter 1980), gave the unmistakable message that he would become king and led to more suspicion and caution. The mixed and complicated attitude of Saul appears throughout this chapter. On the one hand, there is fear (vv. 12, 29) and awe (v. 15) and a recognition that God was with David (v. 12). Saul was willing to give him his daughter Merab as wife, although for an unexplained reason he gave her to another. He was pleased to give him Michal, who became his wife. On the other hand, Saul hated him and sought to kill him (vv. 10–12); he placed him in stations where he was likely to fall to the Philistines, such as sending him to battle as commander (v. 13), encouraging him to fight so that the Philistines could deal with him (v. 17), and making a demand upon him that would certainly deliver him to the Philistines (v. 25).

Another prominent theme is that, whereas Saul was thwarted in all his plans, David was successful in all his undertakings. It was 'an evil spirit' from God that troubled Saul, but God was with David and gave him outstanding successes (vv. 14, 30). Every attempt to hinder David was a failure and turned out to be a further opportunity for his triumph.

(19:1–24) David Escapes Death The loyalty of Saul's own family, Jonathan and Michal, saved David from Saul's further attempts to kill him. No reason is given for Saul's renewed plans, which were now brought into the open (v. 1), but Jonathan, after warning David of the danger, became a successful conciliator. His plea for David is based simply on David's service to Saul when he secured victory for Israel by defeating 'the Philistine' (Goliath), a victory in which Saul himself had rejoiced. Moreover, Saul is reminded that it was YHWH's victory, with perhaps a hidden suggestion that he should not kill a person so clearly endowed with divine power. Saul listened, and, after a promise under divine oath not to kill David, relations were restored. Saul's anger was aroused again (vv. 8–10), and after an unsuccessful attempt to kill David with his spear he set guard over him (v. 11). Michal warned her husband of the danger (v. 11), helped him to escape (v. 12), and to give him time used a household idol with goats' hair (as a net or a wig) to confirm the impression that he was sick in bed (vv. 13–17). The point is made, however, that he was to save his own life that night (v. 11) and that Michal in protecting her husband was only acting in obedience to him (v. 17). Michal, so as not to dissatisfy her father, did not plan the escape, but in obedience to David only assisted him in executing it; she was thus loyal to both sides (Edelman 1991).

An independent tradition, possibly originating from Ramah (Hertzberg 1964), records David's escape to Samuel and their journey together to Naioth. This was a prophetic centre, exactly as Nob was a priestly centre. After three different groups of messengers were seized by prophetic frenzy, Saul himself decided to go to Naioth, and he was similarly possessed; his nakedness may be a symbolic indication that he had lost his authority as king. A different explanation to the one found in 10:5–12 is given to the saying 'Is Saul also among the prophets?', and that may have been the narrative's original intention. In its present context the incident demonstrates how YHWH used Saul's possession by the spirit to protect David; the spirit has thus become a sign of disfavour and a means of protecting God's chosen one.

(20:1–42) David and Jonathan After escaping from Saul's wrath, David once again sought Jonathan, and tried to obtain some indication of Saul's intentions. They agreed on a plan whereby Jonathan, after establishing Saul's attitude, would, unknown to anyone else, give David a coded answer. A major theme in this narrative is a continuation from the previous chapter, namely that Saul's family sided with David against Saul. Jonathan, who had previously proved an effective conciliator between them, has now been forced to take sides. At the beginning he stands by his father, and refuses to believe that in view of the oath in 19:6 he will harm David without consulting him. But after David's assurance that he feels close to death he agrees to find out Saul's will. After a confirmation of their 'love' (or 'pact'), it is agreed to sound him on the Feast of the New Moon, which according to this section lasted for three days (see also Num 28:11–15), and then to inform David according to their agreed method. Jonathan, after providing an excuse for David's absence, came out in his defence using words (v. 32) which echo David's own words in v. 1. Jonathan has now moved from being conciliator between David and his father to the position of David's friend under threat from his father (vv. 30–3). Saul's use of strong words to insult his own son demonstrates the extent of the rift between Saul and his family. His enmity towards David had isolated him from his own kin.

In emphasizing the fierceness of Saul's actions this narrative shows that David had little choice but to leave court and escape. Saul's intention becomes clear in v. 31, 'bring him to me, for he shall surely die', and Jonathan was now convinced of his intention (v. 33). As noted by McCarter (1980), this confirms one of the main emphases of the History of David's Rise, namely that he did not leave Saul's court out of disloyalty or in order to further his own cause. He was forced to leave because of events which were beyond his control; he was the legitimate successor who did not act in any way to usurp the throne. A significant comment is made by Saul in vv. 30–1. Previous hints have been given of his fear of David (18:12, 15, 29) and of his recognition that he would ultimately take the kingdom (18:8). Saul now makes explicit to Jonathan that David stands between him and the kingship. Saul's intention to establish a dynasty by making Jonathan his successor could not be realized as long as David was alive. This sets the scene for those narratives describing Saul's tireless pursuit of David, for he was seen as an enemy who threatened the proposed dynasty.

Insertions into the narrative have been identified in vv. 11–17, 23, 40–2 (McCarter 1980). A promise is made by David to extend his pact with Jonathan to include his 'house' (v. 15) and his 'descendants' (v. 42). These verses anticipate David's kindness to Jonathan's son Mephibosheth (2 Sam 9) and attribute the survival of the house of Saul to this pact between David and Jonathan. It is suggested that this strand in the narrative is an addition made by a Josianic historian. Thus the narrative serves as an introduction to David's period of flight before Saul and also to later relations between David and the house of Saul.

(21:1–15) David in Nob and Gath David's visit to Nob is the first scene in a plot continued in 22:6–23, but which is at present interrupted by the incidents recorded in 21:11–22:5 (McCarter 1980 following Grønbaek 1971). Taken as a whole the unit shows that David secured the support of the priesthood; however, it was obtained through deception, not willingly like that of Michal and Jonathan, and it was accompanied by tragic events. The high-priest of Nob, a little to the north of Jerusalem, was Ahimelech the grandson of Eli. His suspicion of David's visit was allayed by a concocted story about a secret mission, and he was persuaded to give provision to David and his young men from 'holy bread' or 'bread of Presence' reserved for priests (Lev 24:9). David obtained this favour after giving assurances that the young men were ceremonially clean through abstention from sex and that their 'vessels' (euphemism for genitals, Hertzberg 1964) were clean.

The passing reference to Doeg in v. 7 becomes meaningful in the next scene of the plot (22:9–10, 18). The presence of an Edomite spells trouble in view of the long-standing animosity between Israel and Edom (Gen 25:25, 30; Num 20:1–21; Judg 3:7–11). His 'detention' in the sanctuary was probably connected with an act of penance (Hertzberg 1964) rather than a mere holiday (McCarter 1980). The reference to him as 'chief of Saul's shepherds' need not refer in any way to the office of king (as has been suggested by Edelman 1991). By another probable act of deception David obtained from Nob Goliath's sword, which was 'wrapped in cloth behind the

ephod' (v. 9). A cloth other than the ephod suggests that the word 'ephod' does not here signify a garment worn by priests, as is usually the case, but that it was some kind of image (cf. Judg 8:27; *OCB*). Obtaining Goliath's sword was significant, since it was proof of David's success in battle and an omen of future successes; it may also signify that the object of power has been transferred from the sanctuary and entrusted to God's chosen king (Edelman 1991). Another act of deception, a feigned madness, was devised by David in Gath. The recognition of David by the courtiers of Gath, who used the words specifically connected with his successes against the Philistines, was made much easier by the fact that he was carrying Goliath's sword. His fear of Achish is significant; he was now outside YHWH's territory and within reach of the Philistines, and was perhaps more vulnerable because he had not consulted YHWH before fleeing to Gath (Edelman 1991). David acted quickly to feign madness; 'he scratched marks on the doors', which is preferred to the LXX's 'he drummed the doors', and he also 'let his spittle run down his beard'. Achish was deceived and was eager to get rid of him; madmen were thought to be under divine protection, and so Achish could not touch David.

The series of deceptions associated with David in this chapter caused no moral problems for the narrator. David was in flight, had to depend on his presence of mind, and by whatever means was under divine protection.

(22:1–23) The Priesthood of Nob Before presenting the consequences of David's previous actions in Nob (vv. 6–23), his sojourn in Adullam (vv. 1–2) and Mizpah of Moab (vv. 3–5) are briefly recorded. At Adullam (in 'the cave' according to MT, so NRSV, but 'the stronghold' according to LXX, so McCarter 1980), which is to the south-west of Jerusalem in the Shephelah, David was joined by his family and all those who were deprived and embittered. This marks a new development in the History of David's Rise; he was now an outlaw (cf. chs. 23–6) and a leader of a group of malcontents. Although forced to this position by Saul's own actions, this development may have given Saul some grounds for suspecting a conspiracy (vv. 8, 13). Travelling to Mizpah of Moab, a place not known or mentioned elsewhere, David, because of the uncertainty of his position as outlaw, sought asylum for his parents in Moab. Reasons for his approach to Moab were: his family connections with Moab (Ruth 4:17–22), and the likely support for an enemy of Saul, who had defeated Moab in battle (14:47). After a further stay in Adullam ('the stronghold'), David returned to Judah on the advice of Gad, who later became a court prophet (2 Sam 24:11–19). Receiving divine communication through a prophet gave David strength and respectability.

The sequel to David's visit to Nob is introduced by Saul's pitiful appeal to those servants not involved in a conspiracy against him. Saul, sitting in council at Gibeah (cf. 14:2), began accusing the members of his own tribe ('you Benjaminites') of conspiracy and so immediately isolated himself from them. His point in v. 7 is that his rival can in no way offer them the benefits they had received from him, possibly suggesting that they would be directed towards his own clan. He further isolates himself from his servants by accusing them of not disclosing to him the pact between David and Jonathan (v. 8). Doeg the Edomite, chief of the shepherds (21:7), appears now to be 'in charge of Saul's servants' (Edelman 1991), in preference to 'standing against'. His initial contribution was to report Ahimelech's assistance to David by giving him sustenance and Goliath's sword. Naturally Ahimelech protested his innocence by claiming that he only treated David, as in the past, as Saul's obedient servant and honoured son-in-law and that he was not aware of a change in his position. When his other servants refused to obey Saul's command, Doeg killed the entire priesthood of Nob and executed blood revenge on the whole city (v. 19). One priest, Abiathar, escaped and attached himself to David. Not only did his escape fulfil the prophecy of 2:27–36, but it also secured for David the service of a priest. The main point of the narrative is to contrast Saul, whose demented act of reprisal had lost for him the service of a priesthood, and David, who had access to YHWH through the only priest left; Saul destroyed the priesthood, David preserved the only contact with it that was available. Although David acknowledged his own culpability (v. 22, reading 'responsible' with the LXX), he emerges triumphantly, with divine counsel available to him through prophet (Gad) and priest (Abiathar). The priest Abiathar remained with him as high priest until he was eventually banished by Solomon (1 Kings 2:26–7).

(23:1–29) The Liberation of Keilah In the account of the liberation of Keilah David is shown to have access to YHWH through the oracle and is also assisted by Abiathar and the ephod. Keilah, although designated as a city of Judah (Josh 15:44), was presumably in Philistine territory ('in the recesses of the Philistines', v. 3, according to McCarter 1980, on the basis of the LXX instead of 'against the armies of the Philistines,' NRSV); thus it was of interest to Israelites and Philistines. After inquiring of YHWH twice, once on his own initiative and a second time in response to his men's uncertainty, David is given a positive response and an assurance of divine participation (v. 5). David's next consultation with YHWH was by means of Abiathar and the ephod; v. 6 suggests that it was after the liberation of the city that the priest joined David. Saul saw that David could be captured easily in a closed-in town such as Keilah, and believed that God had 'given him' into his hand (so NRSV, following the Greek and Targum, in preference to the MT's 'made a stranger of him'). In his consultation David asked two questions: Will Saul come to Keilah? Will the inhabitants of Keilah betray him? These questions (vv. 11–12) are set out clearly in the NRSV, following 4QSam[b] in preference to the MT. After an affirmative answer to both, David and his men depart and Saul's plan is thwarted. David obviously had advantage over Saul in that he had access to YHWH through the priest.

On his visit to David in Ziph, which was on the edge of the wilderness of Judah, Jonathan sought to encourage him. The pact between them was reaffirmed after Jonathan assured David that Saul would not find him and that he himself was content with being second to David. With the priesthood and the house of Saul behind him, David was in a strong position. However, as vv. 19–23 show, he was still in danger. For some reason or other, the Ziphites were willing to deliver David into Saul's hand. Although the places mentioned in v. 19 have not been identified, it is obvious from the reference to 'the wilderness of Maon' (v. 24) that David was now moving to the

wilderness southwards of Hebron. Saul obviously treated David as an enemy and sought an opportunity to kill him; the Ziphites were willing to provide him with the necessary information. After double-checking to make sure that he did not fall into the hands of the 'cunning' David, Saul went in pursuit into the wilderness of Maon. It is clear that David was in real danger (v. 26); as he was moving away along one side of the mountain, Saul and his troops were 'closing in' on him from both sides. But David was saved at a critical moment because Saul had to meet a Philistine attack; thus the place was called Rock of Escape (NRSV) or Rock of Parting (possibly denoting that Saul and David parted company). Whatever the significance of the name, it is correct to regard this chapter as an aetiological narrative. It may have existed on its own originally, but has by now been included into the history of David.

(24:1–22) A Cave in Engedi The scene for this narrative is set in 23:29 (24:1 in the HB), which reports David's move to Engedi in the hilly area around the Dead Sea. Saul, enjoying a respite from Philistine threat, was free to pursue David.

Another account of sparing Saul's life is found in 26:1–25, and because of the marked similarities between the two the relationship between them has been widely discussed. One interpretation regards the version in ch. 26 as the older, with the present one in ch. 24 containing expansions and revisions, especially in the speeches which portray David as an exemplary figure and Saul in a most unfavourable light. This view is favoured by McCarter (1980). Another interpretation takes them as different versions developed from a common source, one coming from Engedi and the other from Ziph. It is possible that this account too contains some core of older material; this can probably be traced in vv. 2–5a, 7–11, 17–20, 23b. David is portrayed in a very favourable light, for from his hiding place in the inner recesses of the cave he resisted the encouragement of his men to kill Saul when he came to the open part of the cave to relieve himself. His men's words of encouragement are oracular in form (v. 4), probably reflecting some previous divine saying rather than being a complete fabrication (as suggested by Gordon 1984). There is some confusion in vv. 4–5. 'Then David went' (v. 4) suggests that he was listening to his men's words, but the statement that 'he was stricken' (v. 5) seems to indicate a change of heart. The section emphasizes two points: first, that David was in a position to kill Saul and seize the kingship; the possession of part of his skirt was proof; secondly, that he resisted the temptation to kill 'the LORD's anointed' and prevented his men from bringing him to harm (v. 7). These points are elaborated in David's speech (vv. 8–15): David could easily have taken vengeance on Saul for pursuing him and treating him like an insignificant dog or flea; David, duly acknowledging Saul's position as king (v. 8), did not take matters in his own hand, but entrusted vengeance to God (v. 12). The narrative thus repeats a recurring theme in the History of David's Rise; David was no usurper of the throne, for he did not take action against Saul, who was still God's anointed, but left such matters as vengeance and succession to the throne entirely in God's hands. Saul's speech (vv. 16–21) truly reflects his weak position. First, he has to concede that his actions have been evil and that David is more 'righteous' than he (v. 17). Secondly, in words reminiscent of Jonathan's words at

Horesh (23:17), he acknowledges that David will become king. Thirdly, again echoing David's agreement with Jonathan concerning the house of Saul (20:14–15), he pleads with David to preserve his name and not to cut off his descendants.

In its present form, therefore, this narrative subscribes to the general theme of David's uprightness in submitting to the will of God and not taking matters into his own hands. He stands in contrast to the pitiful figure of Saul.

(25:1–44) David, Nabal, and Abigail A note recording Samuel's death stands in v. 1; it may be appropriate at this juncture since Saul has acknowledged that the issue of succession is settled (24:20) and that the one anointed by Samuel will come to the throne (so Edelman 1991). Following this David returned to 'the wilderness of Maon' (following the LXX, in preference to 'Paran' in the MT), and a man and wife from Maon now take centre stage.

Nabal's refusal of David's request for provision occupies the first part of the narrative (vv. 2–12). Nabal ('fool') is described as 'surly and mean', but his wife Abigail as 'clever and beautiful'; such descriptions do not necessarily suggest that he was a surrogate Saul and she a surrogate David (as in Edelman 1991), or that they are personifications of the fool and the virtuous wife in wisdom literature (Levenson 1978). To treat the designation 'Calebite' as an intentional pun on 'dog' (*keleb*, so LXX, cf. 24:14) is also unnecessary. Nabal's foolishness on this occasion was to refuse the request of a king-designate, which may suggest a struggle for power. David's request in vv. 5–8 is very carefully structured; first comes the offer of peace and friendship to Nabal and his house; secondly, there is a reminder that Nabal's shepherds were not harmed when they were with David's men, a fact that could be easily verified; thirdly, there is a request for supplies, possibly in payment for the protection provided by David to Nabal's shepherds. Nabal's reply was negative and arrogant (especially if 'he behaved arrogantly' is read at the end of v. 9 for 'and they waited'; there is some basis for this in the LXX and 4QSam[b]). With his two questions in v. 10 he dismisses David as a nonentity; he also hints that he knows of his breach with Saul and was not willing to hand over supplies to 'men who come from I do not know where', casting doubt perhaps on the honesty of the young men and on their ties with David (Edelman 1991). The reference to Nabal as *ben bĕlîya'al* in v. 17 may link him with those who despised Saul when he was king-elect (10:27) and suggests that he too was rejecting a king-elect and not paying him tribute. In his response, which was a call to arms, David proved that he was ready for confrontation in order to force Nabal to produce what had been requested.

David was in danger of taking matters in his own hand and not relying on YHWH. But he was saved from taking violent action through the interference of Abigail. She was prompted to action by one of Nabal's assistants, who was well-disposed towards David and critical of his own master; he reported that David's men gave them kindness and protection and that he saw danger in Nabal's rash response (vv. 14–18). By her swift action Abigail intercepted David as he was about to annihilate the house of Nabal (v. 22). She did not consult her husband, and obviously counted him a fool (v. 25). Abigail's words (vv. 26–31) and David's response (vv. 32–4) are concerned with

blood-guiltiness. Without Abigail's intervention David would have become guilty of 'blood-guilt' and would have 'taken vengeance' with his own hand instead of restraining himself and trusting God. Whereas David was saved from Saul in chs. 24 and 26, he is in this chapter saved from himself by Abigail (McCarter 1980). Abigail's words have been elaborated to include phrases like 'sure house', 'fighting the battles', and 'prince over Israel', all implying David's future kingship. She also asks David to remember her when all is well with him.

The next section reports that David did remember Abigail. When her husband died (v. 30), he decided to take Abigail as his wife. He was no doubt impressed by her beauty and cleverness (v. 4), and by the good turn that she had done him (v. 33); but he was also making a wise political move. Nabal was a prominent member of the Calebite clan, possibly its leader, and had control over Hebron. By marrying his widow, David was probably taking over that particular territory, as he may have done elsewhere by marrying Ahinoam of Jezreel. This gave him the power he needed after the loss of Michal. It is also significant that later he became king at Hebron (2 Sam 2:1–4).

(26:1–25) Sparing Saul's Life As noted under 24:1–22, this chapter contains an older version of how David spared Saul's life. As in 23:19, the Ziphites betrayed David's whereabouts to Saul, but there are differences between the two narratives. Whereas the other account describes David cutting off a piece of Saul's cloak, in this report he takes away Saul's spear and water jug as he lies asleep in the camp. At Engedi there was a chance meeting between the two men in a cave, but in this chapter David seems to be taking the initiative by secretly entering Israel's camp. Other important differences are due to the more elaborate revisions in ch. 24, especially in David's speech and in Saul's blessing and plea for mercy upon his descendants. In this account again David had an opportunity to kill Saul. After using spies to establish the position of Saul's camp, David himself was able to find where Saul slept, although it was within the encampment and beside his commander Abner (vv. 4–5). On seeking company it was only Abishai who volunteered to accompany him, and they went into the camp. Saul's spear was stuck in the ground, possibly to indicate the leader's tent (Blenkinsopp 1969b). As before, David was encouraged to kill Saul, but on this occasion Abishai declared his willingness to do the killing with a single thrust of Saul's own spear; a single stroke possibly introduces a deliberate contrast with Saul's twofold attempt to kill David (18:11). To prove that Saul had been in David's hands, his spear and water jug were confiscated (v. 11) and later produced as evidence (v. 16). The spear was a symbol of his royal office and the water jug his life; at this moment both were in David's hands. According to Abishai (v. 8), confirmed by a reference to 'deep sleep from the LORD' (v. 11), it was God who had given Saul into David's hands.

This narrative again emphasizes that Saul was spared because of David's unwillingness to harm 'the LORD's anointed'. Even when he had a chance to avoid being personally responsible for killing him, he restrained Abishai from action. David confirms that he was not willing to permit the elimination of Saul; all had to be left to YHWH, who could strike him, as he had done with Nabal, or bring him to natural death, or hand him over to an enemy (v. 10). It was not for Abishai or David to kill him. In his words to Abner, David accuses him of failing to protect the king, thereby putting the king's life in danger. Abner not only failed in his duty to Saul, but also failed to recognize the king-elect (v. 14). However, Saul did recognize him, and this version of their conversation differs from that of ch. 24. After protesting his own innocence (v. 18), David challenges Saul by suggesting that in his action he did not have the support of YHWH or his fellow-men (v. 19). In view of his decision to leave Israelite territory, David pleads with Saul not to let his blood fall to the earth in exile; it would be disastrous for Israel if this were to happen to its king-elect (v. 20). Saul's personal vengeance is likened to a partridge hunt, partridge (*qōrē'*) being possibly a pun on Abner's question in v. 14, 'Who are you that calls (*qārā'tā*)?' Saul's reply on this occasion makes no reference to David's future destiny, but simply acknowledges that he has been at fault and calls on David to return. But the die is cast, and before leaving the king-elect receives a blessing from the king.

(27:1–12) David with Achish at Gath David's sojourn for a year and four months in Gath raises some difficult problems. Although it is clear that he was crossing over to Philistine territory to escape from Saul (v. 1), and that his aim was immediately achieved (v. 4), his relationship with YHWH becomes a problem. As he himself stated, YHWH would deal with Saul (26:10); but the question raised by this chapter is YHWH's protection of the king-elect. Instead of relying on YHWH to defend him, David now seems to be taking matters into his own hands to avoid confrontation with Saul (Edelman 1991). Another difficulty is that David has become a vassal of Achish of Gath. For a brief period he and his retinue lived 'in the royal city' with Achish, but soon, in response to his own request, he was given Ziklag. It was presumably given to him in return for military service, and from this time it remained in the hands of Judean kings as crown property. There is no agreement about the location of Ziklag, some identifying it with Tell el-Khuweilfeh, north of Beersheba, others with Tell esh-Sheri'ah, south-east of Gaza. Wherever it was located, the full implication of these events cannot be missed. David had defected and was granted property for assisting the Philistines.

This narrative has an apologetic note, and in vv. 8–12 offers some justification for David's action. From his base in Ziklag he attacked Israel's enemies, the Geshurites, the Girzites, and the Amalekites, who were on the route from Telam (with the LXX in preference to the MT) to Egypt. He gave Achish the impression that he was attacking enemies of the Philistines, but such was the extent of their annihilation that no contrary evidence was available. By conquering these prospective enemies and amassing booty, David was making preparations for his kingship. That seems to have been accepted by the narrator as justification for his actions; the moral problem of David's gross dishonesty is bypassed.

(28:1–25) Saul's Consultation at Endor The story of David's time among the Philistines continues in vv. 1–2, and is taken up again in chs. 29–30. Saul's consultation with a medium at Endor (vv. 3–25), although in some ways an interruption, belongs to this complex of narratives. As he was in camp at Gilboa, facing the Philistines at Shunem, Saul was in utter

desperation; it is in this context that he took this extraordinary step. Some background information is provided by vv. 3–6. First, the reader is reminded that Samuel is dead and buried; Saul is therefore without access to YHWH through a prophetic figure. Secondly, it is stated that Saul had removed 'mediums and wizards' from the land, as was required by law (Lev 19:31; 20:6, 27; Deut 18:11). Thirdly, Saul was not answered when he sought YHWH's guidance through normal channels, namely dreams, sacred lots (Urim) and prophets (cf. Jer 18:18; Ezek 7:26). This is what caused Saul such panic as he came face-to-face with the Philistine army; in desperation he turned to prohibited means of getting to know the divine will.

When he turned to the medium at Endor, showing disloyalty to his own laws, Saul obviously wanted to consult the ancestral spirit of Samuel (v. 3). It is debatable, however, if he had set out to visit the medium incognito; possibly his disguise was a necessity so that he could pass through the Philistine camp to Endor, which was north-east of Shunem (Gordon 1986). The discarding of royal clothes may have been symbolic, and marks the end of Saul's kingship (Edelman 1991). At first he was not recognized by the medium and so made his request. The narrative as it proceeds after Saul's request is not without difficulties (McCarter 1980). The medium's recognition of Saul immediately after Samuel's appearance is not explained. The references in vv. 17–18 to Samuel's previous oracle and to Saul's battle with the Amalekites are superfluous. It has therefore been suggested that originally the woman recognized Saul from his tone in v. 10, and that vv. 11–12a, referring to the appearance of Samuel, are secondary; then the ghost's words are confined to vv. 16 and 19, which answer Saul's request about the battle. In other words the original account has been revised, and Samuel has been introduced to prove that Saul failed and died because of his disobedience to the prophet Samuel. Even if the narrative has been revised along these lines, its main point cannot be mistaken. It portrays Saul as one totally cut off from YHWH having to resort to illegal divination. His failure as a king will now become finally evident when Israel will be defeated and he himself and his heirs will die at the hands of the Philistines.

(29:1–11) The Philistines Reject David Preparations were now proceeding for the battle between Saul and the Philistines. Saul may have taken the initiative and set up camp in the plain of Jezreel to await the Philistine response to his challenge; they were mustering their forces at Aphek (v. 1, cf. Edelman 1991). This chapter postpones giving a full account of the battle in order to describe David's predicament; he was with the Philistine forces and would soon be engaged in battle against Saul and his own people. By partaking in bringing about Saul's downfall he would at a stroke reverse a policy which he had hitherto consistently pursued. David's problem was resolved for him by the Philistine commanders, who objected to having 'Hebrews' in their ranks. They were easily recognized from their clothing (so Edelman 1991) rather than from any racial characteristics (as suggested by Hertzberg 1964). The commanders were adamant, and probably remembered how 'Hebrews' had defected at Michmash (1 Sam 13–14). To support their suspicion of David they quote the victory song which ascribed to him the death of 'tens of thousands' of Philistines. Because they did not trust David (v. 4), and were afraid that he would turn against them in battle (cf. 14:21), they could not approve of his presence in their ranks (v. 6), and Achish was compelled to send him back to Ziklag. Achish had never personally doubted David's loyalty, as he emphasizes in his reply to the commanders (v. 3) and again in his word to David himself (vv. 6–7, 9–10); he had found him faultless, honest, blameless 'as an angel of God'. In declaring his innocence to Achish, and confirming that he had gone out 'to fight the enemies of my lord the king', David ironically uses words which allude to his dishonest methods.

This narrative again makes a contribution to the theme that YHWH was protecting David; in this case he was saved from the undesirable situation of being a member of the Philistine army fighting against Saul.

(30:1–31) David against the Amalekites A report on the battle between Saul and the Philistines is delayed yet again to give an account of David's return to Ziklag, which had by now been burned by the Amalekites and its inhabitants carried away. David was prepared for immediate revenge. The Amalekite attack was probably in retaliation for David's raid on them (27:8, 10); although lives had not been taken, David and his men had lost their wives and families, which was a cause for great lamentation (v. 4) and placed David in personal danger (v. 6).

One feature that stands out in the narrative is David's ability to consult YHWH. The contrast between his access to YHWH and Saul's dependence on illegal consultation at Endor cannot be missed. David 'strengthened himself in the LORD' (cf. 23:16), and through Abiathar the priest he was able to contact YHWH. The answer he received was positive (vv. 7–8) and so he was encouraged to set out in pursuit of the attackers. Thus the narrative again subscribes to the theme that YHWH was with David, although that is not specifically stated. A chance meeting with an exhausted Egyptian, probably recognized from his clothing, brought David and his men instantly to the raiders. After reviving the Egyptian and questioning him carefully, it becomes obvious that he had been engaged in enemy operations against Ziklag; however, he secured an undertaking from David that he would not take revenge upon him nor deliver him to his previous master, and in return he took them down to the Amalekite camp. By another coincidence David and his troops arrived as the Amalekites were celebrating their victory, and with feasting and revelry were enjoying the booty that they had taken from Ziklag. The Hebrew root *h-g-g*, translated 'dancing' in the NRSV, can be translated 'behaving as at a festival' (*hag*, S. Driver 1913), which has given rise to the suggestion that the Amalekites had timed their raid to secure booty to offer as sacrifice at an annual festival (Edelman 1991). The point is that David was able to take advantage of their condition, and only 400 camel riders were able to escape; the families captured were saved and the booty returned.

Through the events described in this narrative David is prepared for the throne, and is by now more or less there. He had avenged not only Ziklag but also the areas mentioned in v. 14—the Negeb of the Cherethites, i.e. the Cretan Negeb in the southern area controlled by the Philistines, the Negeb of Caleb, i.e. around Hebron, as well as Judean areas (McCarter

1980). This narrative, therefore, is a preparation for 2 Sam 2:1–4, where David becomes king of Judah, for it gives an explanation of the special bond between David and the people of Judah. His success enabled him to hand over gifts to the people of Judah (vv. 26–31); in this, as in his ruling on the suggestion made by 'worthless fellows' (vv. 22–5), he is already assuming the role of king.

(31:1–13) The Death of Saul and his Sons At about the same time ('now' of the NRSV is translated 'meanwhile' by Hertzberg 1964) as David's defeat of the Amalekites, Saul came at last face to face with the Philistines and their troops. The linking of events also serves to bring out the contrast between the two; whereas David succeeded in saving the lives of his own family and others, Saul and his family, with many others, fell in battle. David, as suggested by events described in the previous chapter, was favoured with divine guidance and protection; but Saul, as emphasized in this chapter, is a rejected and pitiful person. In the course of the battle on Mount Gilboa his three sons, Jonathan, Abinadab, and Malchishua were killed and Saul himself was wounded. His death was now inescapable, and, after an unheeded request to his trustworthy personal armour-bearer to kill him before the Philistines derived pleasure from doing so, Saul fell on his sword and committed suicide. The armour-bearer's unwillingness and terror at Saul's request was due to his respect for the sacrosanct person of Saul as YHWH's anointed; he showed the same restraint as David had exercised on several occasions. Saul thus came to a dishonourable end (against Edelman 1991).

Saul's failure brought total defeat to his troops, as is emphasized in v. 6. 'All his men' in this case were not only his bodyguard, but 'the men of Israel' of v. 1; it was a disastrous outcome for all Israel. Even those who were not engaged in battle (suggesting that Saul did not have all Israel behind him) fled from the surrounding areas to the north of Jezreel and even from as far as Transjordan, and left their towns and villages for the Philistines to occupy. The final ignominy was the disrespectful fate of Saul's body. After beheading him, spreading the news of his death throughout the land, and taking his armour into the temple of Astarte, the chief goddess of Beth-shan, his body was fastened to the wall of Beth-shan. Hanging the body for public display was a declaration of victory; it is not stated whether his head was taken with his body (cf. 1 Chr 10:10) or was placed in the temple with the armour (cf. 17:54). However, this horrific scene is not the final one before the curtain is drawn; the men of Jabesh-gilead, remembering Saul's action on their behalf (11:1–13), came to take the body for cremation and burial. Although it is not clear if cremation was acceptable among the Semites, it appears in this instance to be preferable and more honourable than the treatment given by the Philistines to the bodies of Saul and his sons.

2 Samuel

(2 Sam 1:1–27) David's Mourning for Saul and Jonathan Before proceeding to events concerned with the succession to Saul's throne, there is an account of how his death was reported to David, and then his reaction to the loss of Saul and Jonathan. This chapter is a fitting conclusion to the narrative about Saul and David; it is more appropriate to take it with that section than to treat it as the opening chapter of the following section on David's rule in Judah.

The problem here is that vv. 1–16 give an entirely different account of Saul's death to the one read in 1 Sam 31:3–5. The Amalekite who brought the news to David claims that he killed Saul, and as proof presents the king's crown and armlet to David. There is no suggestion that Saul committed suicide; his 'leaning on his spear' (v. 6) was no more than an attempt to support himself. Moreover, Saul was overtaken by 'chariots and horsemen' (v. 6), not 'archers' as in 31:3; there is no mention of an armour-bearer in this account, and it mentions only Jonathan of the three sons killed. Of the various solutions offered the most likely explanation of the discrepancy is that the Amalekite was lying in order to gain favour with David. This is preferable to the suggestion that this chapter continues the narrative in 1 Sam 31, but is the result of the combination of literary strands (Grønbaek 1971), and also to the view that it is an alternative account emphasizing that Saul's death was the result of divine judgement (Ackroyd 1977). If it is accepted that the Amalekite was lying, several features of the narrative fall into place. The Amalekites, as old enemies of Israel, were not trusted; once the messenger is identified as an Amalekite (v. 8), only treachery can be expected. He came showing signs of grief, his 'clothes torn and dirt on his head', but they may well have been contrived in an attempt to give authenticity to his account. Although he claims to have killed Saul, it is more probable that he went to Mount Gilboa in search of plunder and chanced on Saul's body; he immediately stripped him of his crown and armlet, and then realized that these insignia of kingship would be valuable to David. He saw in this an opportunity to curry the favour of the king-elect (McCarter 1984). The messenger describes himself as 'a resident alien' (gēr); an Amalekite who was resident was bound by the laws of his adopted community (Lev 24:22), and therefore his disregard for the sanctity of 'the LORD's anointed' could not go unpunished and he was sentenced to death. Not only does this narrative confirm once again David's respect for YHWH's anointed, but may also have been intended to exonerate David entirely of the events that led to his succession. It also has an apologetic aim, for it explains how David came quite innocently to be in possession of Saul's crown and armlet (McCarter 1984).

David's lament in vv. 17–20, with its very personal expression of his grief over the loss of Jonathan, can be attributed to David himself (cf. Hertzberg 1964; McCarter 1984). The introduction in v. 17 contains a difficult phrase, 'and he said to teach the sons of Judah a bow', which the NRSV has taken to refer to the lament's title, 'The Song of the Bow'. Another possibility, having some support in the LXX, is to omit 'bow' as an intrusion. The poem was preserved in an anthology known as the Book of Jashar (cf. Josh 10:12–13; 1 Kings 8:12–13), and although it is called a lament it does not adhere strictly to the qînâ metre. A kind of refrain, 'How the mighty have fallen', occurs in three places (vv. 19, 25, 27). After stating that Israel's 'glory' has fallen (a reference to Saul, according to McCarter 1984, to its 'young men' according to Hertzberg 1964), the poet expresses his wish that the news be kept from the cities of the Philistines to prevent their exultation over Judah (v. 20). He then curses Mt. Gilboa (v. 21), the scene of defeat, and condemns it to barrenness; it is the place where

Saul's shield is left to rust. In turning to Saul and Jonathan (vv. 22–4), David extols them as heroes who, although now slain, persevered in battle and had slain the enemy (v. 22), for they were strong and swift in battle (v. 23). Father and son were joined in death (v. 23). Then the women of Israel are called upon to mourn Saul, who had brought them prosperity and luxury (v. 24). Before the final refrain in v. 27, David gives vent to his personal grief for Jonathan (vv. 25b–26), and the word 'love' echoes once again the covenant of friendship between the two.

The Kingship of David (2 Sam 2–8)

Not one of the proposed divisions of material in 2 Sam 2–20 is entirely satisfactory. Superficially chs. 2–8 appear to be dealing with the period when David set up his kingdom, or, as is often claimed, his empire, and chs. 9–20, concerned as they are with intrigue and rivalries, address the issue of succession to his throne, with a final solution being found in 1 Kings 1–2. However, the place of ch. 7 is unclear; on the one hand, it has appropriately been described as a climax to the period when the Davidic empire was being established, but on the other, it can be regarded as an introduction to the section on succession to his throne. It can also be argued that other parts of this complex would fit more naturally elsewhere (see c.16). The clash between Michal and David (6:20–3), for instance, is really concerned with the succession; again the account of his Philistine wars (5:17–25), as well as the list of his successes (8:1–14), could be placed within the History of David's Rise. It could also be legitimately claimed that a climax is reached in ch. 5 when David became king at Hebron and made a covenant with the people. Nevertheless, because of the possibility of identifying a complex in 2 Sam 9–20, 1 Kings 1–2 dealing specifically with the succession narrative, a natural break occurs at the end of ch. 8.

(2 Sam 2:1–32) David Becomes King at Hebron David's move to Hebron is presented as an act of obedience to God's instructions after an enquiry from David, and is, therefore, part of God's plan to bring his king-elect to the throne. Although that is the interpretation of events given in the biblical account, there is evidence that David himself had taken several shrewd steps aimed at strengthening his position in readiness for taking the throne. By marrying Abigail he had already obtained a power-base in Hebron (1 Sam 25:3), and he had also sent gifts to its inhabitants after his defeat of the Amalekites (1 Sam 30:31). Hebron was certainly the most powerful town in the region, and it was there that David was 'anointed king over Judah' (v. 4). Although he had been anointed previously by Samuel (1 Sam 16:13), the action taken on this occasion by 'the people of Judah', as later by 'the elders of Israel' (5:3), was a significant step in his recognition as king.

David had also attempted to secure support in northern areas. Two of the marriages he contracted, to Ahinoam of Jezreel and also to Maacah, daughter of Talmai of Geshur, are probably to be considered as marriage alliances through which he established contacts and gained support in those particular areas. His overtures to the men of Jabesh-gilead, who had been loyal to Saul (vv. 4b–7), were again aimed at establishing a relationship with that area. With the death of Saul their relationship with him had come to an end, and now they were being offered a renewed relationship with David (McCarter 1984). David was obviously making moves which were a direct challenge to the house of Saul, which was enjoying special ties with Gilead, Jezreel, and Geshur, together with several other northern territories. Consequently civil war broke out between north and south. Ishbaal (reading with the Greek, for the Hebrew Ishbosheth, 'man of shame'), Saul's son, had Abner, Saul's cousin, as his military commander, and David was assisted by Joab, son of Zeruiah. Both armies set out for Gibeon, the Saulide contingent travelling from Mahanaim in Transjordan, and when they met Abner suggested a contest between the young men, twelve on each side. A serious contest between trained warriors to settle an issue was widely practised in the ancient world, cf. ordeals by battle among the Hittites (Fensham 1970). A combat ordeal was settled by the will of the deity. To gain the advantage the contestant grasped the head of his opponent and with the other hand thrust a sword into his side. All the contestants were killed (v. 16), which made the contest inconclusive, but the more general battle that ensued was to David's advantage (v. 17). The slaughter of the contestants occurred at Helkath-hazzurim, usually translated Field of Flints or Field of Sword-edges (NRSV marg.), which is preferred to the Greek, Field of Sides, referring to the nature of the contest. This, it is claimed (McCarter 1984), was a secondary addition, which means that the verses originally constituted an aetiological narrative explaining a place-name.

The pursuit of Abner by Asahel was significant, and throws light on some events which were to follow. Three sons of Zeruiah, David's sister (1 Chr 2:16), are mentioned here, and they have been described as rash, cold-blooded, and violent (McCarter 1984). One of them, Abishai, had accompanied David to Saul's camp (1 Sam 26:6-22) and later became joint military leader with Joab. On this occasion Asahel (the youngest of the three) relentlessly pursued Abner, and because he ignored his warning Abner had no choice but to kill him (vv. 18-23a). Joab and Abishai took up the pursuit, which was halted when Abner reminded them of their bond of kinship (v. 26). Although these hostilities, which had obviously been to David's advantage (v. 31), ceased, and the armies returned to their bases, this was not the end of the feud between north and south. Joab was determined to avenge Asahel's death (3:17); when the opportunity arose for him to do this, it is emphasized that he was not acting officially, rather it was a personal feud. As events developed we learn that David felt unable to restrain the violence of the sons of Zeruiah (3:39).

(2 Sam 3:1-39) The Death of Abner Hostilities were only temporarily suspended (2:28), for the struggle between the houses of David and Saul was a long one, and, continuing the theme of 2:30-1, was generally in David's favour and added to his strength (v. 1). This provides the setting for the narrative continuing from v. 6. A list of sons born to David at Hebron (vv. 2-5) interrupts the flow of the narrative, but may have been occasioned by the reference in v. 1 to the increasing strength of David.

Ishbaal's quarrel with Abner, whose stature in court was increasing, was occasioned by his relationship with one of Saul's concubines and the mother of two of his sons (21:8). There is ground for suggesting that Abner's behaviour was an

open bid for Ishbaal's throne, cf. 1 Kings 2:13-25, where Adonijah made a similar bid for Solomon's throne and 2 Sam 16:20-3, where Absalom openly visited David's harem (McCarter 1984, following Tsevat 1958). It was probably Abner's growing power in Ishbaal's court that gave him confidence to make public his interest in the crown. When challenged by Ishbaal, however, he replied angrily and defiantly, although the meaning of the phrase 'dog's head' in his reply is not clear; it may denote insignificance or else is a euphemism for his sexual drive (see further Thomas 1960). Abner does not admit that he is in the wrong, but dismisses the affair as insignificant in comparison with the loyalty he has shown to the house of Saul (v. 8). It has been suggested that the remainder of his reply (vv. 9-10) is a Deuteronomistic interpolation; it shows acquaintance with the Deuteronomistic presentation of Saul and David, i.e. a condemnation of Saul, a promise to give his kingdom to another, and the identification of David as the chosen king (Ackroyd 1977; McCarter 1984). In his message to David at Hebron (following the LXX in preference to an unclear MT) Abner sought a pact (a 'covenant') with him on the understanding that Israelite territories, i.e. Ishbaal's kingdom, would be transferred to David. His question, 'To whom does the land belong?' suggests that power was in his own hand (cf. v. 6) and that he could negotiate as he wished with Ishbaal's land. David set his own conditions: the return to him of Michal, Saul's daughter. The significance of his request has escaped the narrator, who probably understood it simply as proof of Abner's good faith (cf. Gen 43:4, 5). There were political implications to this move, and David was now staking a legal claim to Saul's throne. Despite the prohibition of remarriage in Deut 24:1-4, it is known that there were special provisions for husbands forced to give up their wives (McCarter 1984, following Ben-Barak 1979). The legality of the case was one reason why Ishbaal complied with David's request (vv. 15-16); Abner's power in court was another reason. Doubt has been cast on the historicity of David's marriage to Michal (1 Sam 18-19; Noth 1960), and therefore on vv. 14-15 in this chapter. However, it is a tradition that serves a purpose in this context; it confirms that David had legitimate rights to Saul's estate.

Abner successfully negotiated with both sides. His approach to the senior leaders of Israel was based on their desire to have David as king; he knew of their dissatisfaction with Ishbaal and their realization that he could not withstand the Philistines as David had done in the past. The support of Saul's tribe and his own, the Benjaminites, was secured, as is emphasized in the narrative. When he reported his success to David, he and his men were feasted, which probably on this occasion denotes covenant-making. Joab's recapture of Abner (vv. 22-7) may have been due to a combination of reasons. The one given immediately, that Abner was planning to deceive David (v. 25), is not repeated in the narrative and does not play any part in it. Another obvious reason is that Joab did not wish to face competition from such a powerful commander and leader as Abner. However, the narrator more than once emphasizes that it was blood-revenge for the death of Asahel (vv. 27, 30); this suited the narrator's aim, for he wished to make clear that David had no part in Abner's death. This point is confirmed by the references to Abner departing in peace from David (vv. 21, 22, 24), by the statement that David did not know of Joab's plan (v. 26), by including David's claim that he was guiltless as well as his curse upon the guilty Joab (vv. 28–9), which is very Deuteronomistic in tone (cf. Veijola 1975), by describing David's public display of grief (vv. 31–2), by citing David's tribute to Abner (vv. 33–4), and by noting that David was unable to resist the violence of the family of Zeruiah (v. 39).

By implication this narrative subscribes to the theme that David was God's chosen; first, he had a rightful claim to Saul's throne, and secondly he was not involved in any of the violent actions that brought him nearer the throne.

(2 Sam 4:1–12) The Death of Ishbaal Because Abner was so strong that he virtually ruled Israel (cf. 2:8–9; 3:6), his death threw the country and its reigning monarch into confusion and uncertainty. Two officers in Ishbaal's army decided to take the initiative and make a bid for David's favour. The lineage of Baanah and Rechab is given in detail, although some of the information in vv. 2–3 stands in parenthesis and may have been a later insertion. Although the two captains were from Beeroth, they were Benjaminites, for, despite uncertainty about its exact location, Beeroth 'was considered to belong to Benjamin' (v. 2, cf. Josh 18:25); it was definitely not in Benjaminite territory, but apparently had Benjaminite inhabitants (Hertzberg 1964). The original inhabitants had at some time or other fled to Gittaim, which may have been in Philistine territory.

The interpolation in vv. 2–3 is followed by yet another unnecessary insertion in v. 4, which refers to Jonathan's son, Mephibosheth (or Meribaal, cf. 1 Chr 8:34; 9:40). It would be more appropriate at 9:1–13. The note may have been included here to make the point that after the death of Ishbaal there would be no serious contender for the throne from the house of Saul; Mephibosheth was only a minor ('five years old') and a cripple.

The two assassins gained access into Ishbaal's house at noon, when he was taking a siesta. The NRSV simply states that they entered the house on the pretext of taking wheat; because they appeared to have business in the house they were allowed to enter. Other translators (cf. REB) and commentators (Hertzberg 1964; McCarter 1984) have, on the basis of the LXX, seen a reference here to a porteress, who had been cleaning wheat and had fallen asleep. Once they had entered they swiftly accomplished their gruesome task (v. 7). In seeking David's favour they claimed to have avenged him on Saul, who is described as an 'enemy' because he had sought his life (v. 8). David immediately distances himself from their action, for, as he had so consistently demonstrated, he respected a reigning monarch and did not wish to seize the throne. The narrator does not entertain any thought of the sons of Rimmon being agents working for David, any more than he thought of Joab killing Abner with David's foreknowledge. David, YHWH's elect, was to advance naturally to the throne, and and did not have to stoop to intrigue and violence. His attitude is made explicit in vv. 9–11. He had commanded than the Amalekite, who claimed to have killed Saul, be put to death. The sin of these assassins was worse; they had 'killed a righteous man on his bed in his own house' (v. 11), and they are to suffer the same fate (v. 12). Although these men had by their action participated in David's advance to the throne, this narrative, like the account of Abner's death, shows that David was totally innocent of such assassinations.

(2 Sam 5:1–25) Kingship at Hebron and the Capture of Jerusalem With Ishbaal's death David was at last free to take the throne of Israel. Because of his connection with the house of Saul, his proven leadership against the Philistines and the promises made to him by God, there was no rival or opposition (vv. 1–2). Words to this effect were spoken to David by the 'tribes of Israel' (translated 'staff-bearers' by McCarter 1984), but their words are frequently considered to be a secondary addition to the older brief statement in v. 3 (see Veijola 1975). His installation by the 'elders of Israel' (cf. 'elders of Judah' in 2:4) at Hebron consisted of making 'a covenant . . . before the Lord', which must have contained some reference to the obligations undertaken by both sides, an anointing and his designation as 'king'. The chronological note about the reigns of David and Ishbaal in vv. 4–5 is also an addition; it is the kind of Deuteronomistic notice that usually appears on the accession of a monarch and was probably absent from 4QSam[a], Old Greek, and 1 Chron 11. Nevertheless, it underlines the historical significance of the occasion.

The next important step was the capture of Jerusalem (vv. 6–9). The name of Jerusalem (see *OCB*) is found in Egyptian Execration texts of the nineteenth and eighteenth centuries BCE and in the Amarna texts of the fourteenth century BCE. Its pre-Israelite inhabitants were known as 'Jebusites' (*OCB*), who were of Canaanite origin (Gen 10:16). The Israelites did not drive them out when they conquered Canaan (Josh 15:63; Judg 1:21); the city preserved its independence until the time of David, and was a foreign enclave. Such a strong fortress, away from the main north–south routes, was as advantageous to David as it had been to its previous inhabitants. Because it had been in Jebusite hands, and was independent of both northern and southern factions, and was situated more or less on the border between Israel and Judah, it was a wise choice as capital. A survey of the different interpretations proposed for the difficult account of its capture in vv. 6–9 is available in major commentaries; special studies of the passage are discussed by McCarter (1984). A reasonable understanding of it is found in the rendering of the NRSV. The Jebusites were confident that their city could not be taken by David; it was such a strong fortress that even handicapped persons, 'the blind and the lame', would be able to defend it (v. 6). David later picked up the phrase and used it to refer to the defenders of Jerusalem, who were to be defeated, as 'the lame and the blind' (v. 8); the third reference to them in v. 8b has probably been added by an annotator who was probably using a proverbial expression. The city was taken by those who went 'up the water shaft' to the city (v. 8); they made use of the vertical shaft from the city to the Spring of Gihon, either by stopping its flow and climbing up to the city (NRSV), or by forcing the city into submission by stopping its water supply (see McCarter 1984). On entering the city David occupied the fortress on the hill in the south-eastern corner, also called Ophel, and renamed it 'the city of David'. The 'Millo' was an earth-fill to form a rampart or a platform, and has been identified as Solomonic terracing on the eastern slope (Kenyon 1974). David also added to the fortification. This account of the capture of the city has a fitting conclusion in v. 10, which may well have been intended as the closing verse of the History of David's Rise. Two brief notes are included in vv. 11–16. The first (vv. 11–12) reports on negotiations with Hiram of Tyre, who had building materials and craftsmen for David's building projects. It is a chronologically misplaced note and probably refers to a later period in David's reign. Hiram also gave invaluable assistance with Solomon's building projects. At this juncture it makes the point that David was an internationally known figure and that his kingdom had status. The second (vv. 13–16), a list of sons born to David in Jerusalem, is a continuation of the list in 3:2–5.

Two of David's victories over the Philistines (vv. 17–25) are placed after his capture of Jerusalem; these are also chronologically misplaced and are probably to be connected with an earlier point when he was 'anointed king over Israel' (v. 17). 'The stronghold' was not necessarily Jerusalem, but more probably Adullam (McCarter 1984). On both occasions David consulted the oracle, receiving a positive reply on the first occasion and a negative one, supplemented by further advice, on the second. The Philistines came up to Rephaim, a plain to the south-west of Jerusalem, and David defeated them at Baal-perazim ('Lord of Bursting Forth'); there is here an aetiological play on the sanctuary's name. The second battle was likewise connected with Rephaim, although it is uncertain if the second account is authentic or is a variant of the first one. David was advised to take a different route and attack from the flank in the vicinity of 'balsam trees', bushy growths characteristic of a hilly region. This time David secured a decisive victory, and they were struck 'from Geba' (probably to be read with the LXX as 'from Gibeon', six miles north-west of Jerusalem) back to their border at Gezer.

(2 Sam 6:1–23) Taking the Ark to Jerusalem The ark had presumably remained in Kiriath-jearim since it was taken there after its return from the Philistines (1 Sam 7:1), but now David was determined to bring it to Jerusalem. A continuation of the ark narrative in 1 Sam 4:1–7:1 is to be found here in vv. 1–19 (Campbell 1975). Whether they were originally one piece of writing composed at the same time is another matter. Recent studies have on several grounds (such as the difference between Kiriath-jearim and Baalah, between Eleazar and Uzza, between a narrative written before a decisive battle and one written after it, and between the character of the two narratives) argued against reading the chapters together as one continuous piece (so MacCarter 1984, following Miller and Roberts 1977). Whatever its original context, this narrative continues the story of the ark and fits extremely well into this particular setting. Thematically it is part of the Deuteronomistic concern with the choice of David and Jerusalem. Chronologically it was only after a decisive victory over the Philistines (such as the one described in 5:17–25) that David would have been in a position to bring the ark to Jerusalem (cf. Hertzberg 1964). Undoubtedly the narrative has been given a suitable context.

The ark's journey from Kiriath-jearim, known in this passage as Baale-judah (on the basis of 4QSamᵃ for 'Baalah'), was a mixed event. Reference to the ark as 'the ark of God [YHWH]', and to YHWH as 'enthroned on the cherubim' shows similarity to 1 Sam 4:4, and again 'new cart' echoes 1

Sam 6:7. 'The house of Abinadab' is also known from 1 Sam 7:1, but his sons 'Uzzah and Ahio' appear here instead of 'Eleazar', who was in charge of the ark. It was an occasion for joy and celebration, with David and his people dancing vigorously ('with all his strength' in v. 14 and 1 Chr 13:8, for the Heb. 'with instruments of might') accompanied with 'songs' (following 4QSamᵃ, the LXX and 1 Chr 13:8 for the MT's 'fir-trees'). But a cultic aberration brought disaster. Although the striking of Uzzah is sub-Christian, the narrative emphasizes once again the power and the danger that ancient Israel associated with the most holy object; it is this same ark that brought plagues upon the Philistines (1 Sam 5) and devastation to the town of Beth-shemesh (1 Sam 6:19). Uzzah's assistance had not been offered with the care and precaution necessary for performing a sacred rite, and according to ancient Israelite tradition he was justifiably punished. David was also unwilling to take the risk, and the ark was left for three months with Obed-edom the Gittite. Obed-edom was one of David's loyal servants since his time in Ziklag; he was a non-Israelite and the worshipper of a strange god, and was willing to house the ark.

Despite some bitter experience with the ark, it was undoubtedly accompanied by blessing (v. 12), which prompted David to bring it to Jerusalem, again with much celebration and sacrifice. Offering sacrifice after those carrying the ark 'had gone six paces' does not mean one sacrifice after the first six steps (as by Hertzberg 1964), but must refer to repeated sacrifice every six steps, as was practised elsewhere (Miller and Roberts 1977). David was wearing 'a linen ephod', a priestly garment, which only covered the body and loins, and was inappropriate for the vigorous circular dance that he was performing. With blasts on the trumpet, the *šôpār* or ram's horn, the people were assembled for this joyous event. When the ark was brought into Jerusalem, it was housed in a tent made for it by David (v. 17); this was not the same as the wilderness 'tabernacle', but was probably a special construction with some features that were later adopted when constructing a permanent abode for the ark. The whole ceremony was concluded with sacrifices, blessings, and gifts; it was indeed a great festive occasion.

Connections between 2 Sam 6 and Ps 132, and again with cultic processions, have been widely discussed (see more fully McCarter 1984). It can be cautiously stated that Ps 132 is based on the story of the transfer of the ark to Jerusalem; it is similar to 2 Sam 6 and does not rest on a divergent version (as argued by Cross 1973). Several ceremonial parallels connected with introducing a god to a new capital have been found, and it has been suggested that there was an annual procession of the ark to the Jerusalem temple. It may well be that the celebrations described in this chapter gave rise to annually repeated celebrations.

Michal, Saul's daughter, was not pleased with David's behaviour, as is reported in a section that did not belong originally to the present context (vv. 16, 19–23), but may have been part of the succession narrative (Rost 1982). She found David's dancing most vulgar, for the scantily clothed king in a mere linen ephod had exposed himself to 'his servants' maids'. Michal's words referring to the king 'honouring himself' are full of irony; David's vow to make himself 'more contemptible than this' has a veiled reference to his piety.

There is no need to see in this episode a reference to a sacral marriage rite to accompany the ritual of the previous section (against Porter 1954), nor is it to be taken as criticism of David's affairs with women (Crüsemann 1980). The key to understanding the section is the statement in v. 23 that Michal had no child. It offers an explanation of her childlessness, and in some ways is significant when surveying David's relations with the house of Saul and with his own descendants.

(2 Sam 7:1–29) Oracle and Prayer This chapter, dealing with two key issues, building a temple and succession to David's throne, is one of the most important in the OT, and has been subject to intense research (see Jones 1990). Although the succession narrative has been identified as 2 Sam 9–10; 1 Kings 1–2, this chapter provides a fitting introduction to the succession issue. The appearance of unity in vv. 1–17 is only superficial, for two separate oracles concerning two different issues have been combined, each originating from a particular occasion.

The appropriateness of constructing a temple is the subject of the first oracle in vv. 1–7. Extra-biblical parallels, especially the Egyptian *Königsnovelle*, show that it was usual to seek divine approval for building a temple (cf. Hermann 1953–4). David thus consulted Nathan, a court-prophet at hand to advise the king, and possibly affiliated to the pre-Israelite Jebusite cult of Jerusalem. Whatever other reasons are given in the OT why David was prohibited from building a temple (1 Chr 22:8; 28:3; 1 Kings 5:17), it is stated here that he was prohibited by Nathan, who was speaking for YHWH ('Thus says the LORD'). Why he was forbidden is not clear. One possible ground for rejection is that David himself had taken the initiative ('are *you* the one to build *me* . . . ?', v. 5, emphases added); another is that there was opposition from Israel's 'tent' or 'nomadic' tradition (v. 6); another is that there was a subtle theological difference between the concepts of 'dwelling' (*yā-šab*) and 'staying' (*šakan*) as suggested by v. 2. It is not unreasonable to suggest that the original oracle was later modified to accommodate a different and more theological interpretation. v. 6 becomes suspect, and its omission leads to a concentration on the reason given in v. 7; a temple was contrary to the past traditions of the tribes, for God had not indicated to the Hebrew tribes that he desired one particular sanctuary to be designated as his dwelling-place. If that is identified as Nathan's reason, before it acquired later theological interpretations, it must be asked if he had hidden motives. Why would Nathan be interested in Israel's tribal traditions? It is significant that, although he resisted a Davidic temple, Nathan was in the pro-Solomonic camp (1 Kings 1–2) and did not object to a Solomonic temple. A possible interpretation of these events is that Nathan objected to a Davidic temple because it was intended to replace the old Jebusite one, but did not object to a Solomonic temple because the Jebusites were in the Solomonic camp and could therefore influence him. Whatever Nathan's motives and the stages through which the oracle passed between its original form and the present version, the point of the rhetorical question in vv. 5 and 7 is that David was prohibited from building a temple for YHWH in Jerusalem.

The second oracle (vv. 8–16) addresses a different issue, succession to David's throne; the two issues have been linked by giving the second oracle the same historical setting as the first (vv. 1–3) and by employing the word *bayit* (house) in two different ways. David had not been allowed to build God a 'house' (*bayit*, vv. 5, 6, 13), but YHWH was going to found for David a 'dynasty' (*bayit*, vv. 11, 16). Adaptations were necessary in joining the two oracles, among them a promise that Solomon would build a temple. The core message of the second oracle can be identified as follows: David had been called by God (v. 9), had been protected by him against his enemies and made into a great name (v. 10); God would raise up his son to follow him and would establish his kingdom (v. 12) and he would enjoy the status of God's adopted son (v. 14). It is an oracle that refers to David's choice, his protection, and the promise of a successor. Several new elements have been introduced by extending the oracle: God's interest in the people of Israel (vv. 10–11), the eternity of David's kingdom (vv. 13, 16) and the contrast between David and Saul (vv. 14b–15). The similarity between this oracle and other texts, such as Ps 89, points to a development in Jerusalem of the combined theme of David's greatness and the certainty of succession. It is possible that Nathan, the court prophet, spoke an oracle along these lines either on David's initial enthronement as king in Jerusalem or on a subsequent celebration of it. His words were later accompanied by more elaborate Israelite royal ideology, which became the basis for Israel's messianic expectations. When this oracle was combined with the first one, links were forged by referring to Solomon as builder of the temple (v. 13) and by using 'house' with a double meaning. Thus both oracles have the appearance of being concerned with the dynasty.

The second half of the chapter (vv. 18–29) contains David's prayer, and is to be separated from the first half because: Nathan has disappeared from the scene, no allusion is made to the temple theme, and David requests God's blessing on his house, a blessing which has already been granted. The prayer shows affinity with the work of the Deuteronomists, and it may either be entirely their own composition or their thorough revision of an earlier form. A core may have been originally connected with bringing the ark to Jerusalem (6:1–19) rather than with the dynastic oracle in 7:1–7. It is known that in ceremonies for introducing gods into capital cities, there was an opportunity for invoking their blessing on king and people; David had invoked blessing on the people (6:18), but not on his own house, and the core of this prayer may well have belonged to that part of the ceremony (McCarter 1984). When that prayer was modified for its present context, a number of additions were made, especially the allusion to God's promise and its 'eternal' nature (vv. 22, 28–9), God's redemption of his people from Egypt (vv. 23–4), and several Deuteronomistic clichés (vv. 22b–26).

(2 Sam 8:1–18) David's Empire and Court The list of David's conquests in vv. 1–14 provides valuable historical insight into the extent of his power and kingdom. David's military leadership brought him phenomenal successes leading to the establishment of what was virtually an 'empire' (Malamat 1958; Mazar 1962). These verses, like other passages (cf. 5:17–25), give a catalogue of victories, probably compiled from ancient fragments, and are arranged thematically rather than chronologically. David's supremacy over the Philistines, although placed 'some time afterwards', was gained through a number of military victories (cf. ch. 5). The exact meaning of the word translated in the NRSV as a proper name, Metheg-ammah, is unclear; among other possibilities are 'from Gath to Ammah' (cf. 1 Chr 18:1) or 'took the leading reins out of the hands of the Philistines' (Hertzberg 1964). Whatever the translation, what is implied is that David seized control of the land from the Philistines and restricted their movement to coastal areas. He also defeated Moab (v. 2), and despite previous good relations with the Moabites (1 Sam 22:3–5), he selected two out of every three prisoners of war for execution.

David had to face competition from Aram Zobah in the north; under Hadadezer it was expanding its territory (Malamat 1958) and was the leading state in the area before the rise of Damascus. Hadadezer seems to have been the leader of a strong coalition (vv. 5, 10; Malamat 1963), and he and David were competing for ascendancy over the same area. When Hadadezer (not David, as suggested by McCarter 1984) had gone to reinforce his power by the Euphrates (which is the meaning of 'restore his monument'), he was attacked by David, who took prisoners, mutilated horses, and defeated their helpers from Damascus. According to 2 Sam 10:1–19 and this passage, three successive battles were fought against the Arameans. As a result of this success, Toi of Hamath (which was on the Orontes to the north of Zobah) sent his son to make an alliance with David, and brought him expensive gifts, which indicates that David was the stronger partner in the alliance. He also conquered Edom and placed garrisons there (v. 14). As a result of his campaigns David had wrested control over what is now Palestine from the Philistines, had garrisons in Moab, Edom, and Ammon (which corresponds to modern Jordan), and had conquered Aramean states (corresponding to modern Syria and eastern Lebanon) (cf. Soggin 1977). The Deuteronomistic historian attributes all David's victories to YHWH (vv. 6, 14).

The list of David's court officials in vv. 15–18 is not exactly identical with another version in 2 Sam 20:23–6, which has a different order and additional names, Ira the Jairite and Adoram. Lists were available in archives, and these two are probably variants (Ackroyd 1977; McCarter 1984). Joab had been some time with David and had command of the army (see 2 Sam 2); Jehoshaphat was still in office in the time of Solomon (1 Kings 4:3). Zadok and Abiathar shared the priesthood until David's death (1 Kings 2:26). The Cherethites and Pelethites were the royal bodyguard, and their captain (reading 'was over' with the English versions and 1 Chr 18:17) was Benaiah. The statement that 'David's sons were priests', although difficult and therefore revised to 'stewards' in 1 Chr 18:17, probably means that they were able to act as priests within the royal household.

Succession to David's Throne (2 Sam 9–20)

2 Sam 9–20 and 1 Kings 1–2 are thought to have originally formed an unbroken unit (Rost 1926), whose theme is clearly enunciated in its climax, 'so the kingdom was established in the hand of Solomon' (1 Kings 2:46). Among the reasons given for considering these chapters as a self-contained unit are: a common theme, common subsidiary themes, stylistic affinities, a consistent treatment of characters. By describing the elimination over the years of all candidates for David's throne, Absalom, Amnon, and Adonijah, it is demonstrated that Solomon was the sole legitimate successor. Reference has already been made (c.16–20) to the key issues relating to the succession narrative: the boundaries of the complex, stages in its growth, historical value, date, genre, and motive. Whatever the difficulties that have arisen regarding the appropriateness of the term 'succession narrative', it can be retained as an indication of the most prominent theme in the complex and the one that binds the various narratives together. Although the narrative does not emphasize the involvement of God in the elimination of candidates for the throne, from the few references made to his activity (2 Sam 11:27; 12:24; 17:14) it becomes clear that Solomon was God's choice as David's successor. The scarcity of such references, together with a lack of interest in cultic matters, has given rise to the suggestion that it is a secular narrative. This has been taken by some as proof of mastery of narrative art, by which a point is made through action and dialogue rather than by making explicit theological assertions (Conroy 1978; Gordon 1984).

(2 Sam 9:1–13) Kindness to Mephibosheth David's promise to Jonathan not to cut off his faithful love from his house (1 Sam 20:15–16) is fulfilled with respect to his last remaining son, Mephibosheth. This chapter does not stand alone, but is connected with the story of the Gibeonites' revenge in 2 Sam 21:1–14 and with events concerning the house of Saul and the death of Ishbaal in 2 Sam 2–4. The link with 2 Sam 21:1–14 is the strongest. Chronologically the revenge of the Gibeonites preceded the accommodation of Mephibosheth at David's table. The slaughter of seven Saulide descendants gave occasion for David's enquiry in v. 3 (taking v. 1 as a superfluous editorial link, so Veijola 1975); they could not have been alive at this time. The original continuous narrative of 21:1–14; 9:1–13 was later separated by an editor, who probably saw in the presence of a Saulide held in honour in David's household some contribution to the theme of succession. Whatever the original motive of David's kindness to Mephibosheth, the present narrative emphasizes that David was dealing honourably with Jonathan's son; the word 'kindness' (ḥesed) occurs in vv. 1, 3, 7. There is no suggestion of imprisonment or of keeping guard over him; David was granting him special patronage (v. 7). Despite Mephibosheth's assertion that he was insignificant ('a dead dog', v. 8), he was granted special privileges at royal expense (v. 11), had his grandfather's property restored to him (v. 7) and arrangements were made for Ziba to act as estate manager to provide for the family (v. 10). Thus Saul's household was enjoying privileges at David's hand, and it is obvious that Mephibosheth, brought to court from Transjordanian Lo-debar, and his son Mica, were under his protection. Undoubtedly it was advantageous for David to have the only survivor of Saul's household under his roof. But there was no real threat from Mephibosheth, for a man who was 'lame in both his feet' would hardly have made a serious contender for the throne.

(2 Sam 10:1–19) Ammonite and Aramean Wars Problems arise here in connection with the history of the wars with Ammon and Aram, their connection with the David–Bathsheba affair and the reason for including 2 Sam 10–12 in the succession narrative. The chapter begins with an insult to David by Hanun the king of the Ammonites after the death of Nahash, who was an enemy of Saul (1 Sam 11) but a supporter of David. After the Ammonites had summoned help from the Arameans (v. 6), who were Israel's rivals in the conflict of interest between the two powers, attention seems to focus on the Arameans. Four states were called to the assistance of Hanun: Zobah and Beth-rehob to the south, Maacah (Aram Maacah in 1 Chr 19:6) north of Manasseh in Transjordan, and Tob, further south. By connecting this narrative with 8:3–5 it is possible to reconstruct the course of the Aramean conflict as follows: a first battle outside the gate of Rabbah (10:6–15); a second battle in the region of Helem in northern Gilead (10:15–19); a final and decisive battle in which Hadadezer's coalition was conquered (8:3–8) (following the reconstruction of McCarter 1984). In planning his action on two fronts (v. 9) David encouraged his own troops to be brave for the sake of 'our people and for the cities of our God' (v. 12). The reference to 'cities' is textually sound and must be retained; it is probably a reference to cities in south Transjordan, which had associations with YHWH, and David is thus attempting to arouse religious fervour (Giveon 1964). After a successful battle in Rabbah, Joab, having fought on two fronts, was not in a position to take advantage of his conquest and returned to Jerusalem (v. 14). When the next battle was fought under the leadership of David himself (vv. 15–19), matters were different, and after this defeat Hadadezer's vassals transferred their allegiance to David. The war account in ch. 10 and the David–Bathsheba narrative in ch. 11 are obviously different in character and style. The former betrays the flavour of archival records, the latter the style of a narrator. Rather than accepting the suggestion that the narrative is an intrusion that interrupts the sequence of the war report, it is more reasonable to accept that the narrator borrowed material from an archival source to provide the David–Bathsheba narrative with a framework. Because David's affair with Bathsheba was associated with the siege of Rabbah the choice was obvious. Thus we are given the historical setting (10:1–11:1), the affair and its outcome (11:2–12:25), and in conclusion the continuation of the war with the Ammonites (12:26–31).

Points of contact between chs. 10–12 and their setting in the succession narrative can be established. David's affair with Bathsheba was to reach its fulfilment in the birth of Solomon (12:24), which binds it firmly to the main thrust of 2 Sam 9–12; 1 Kings 1–2, which show how Solomon became David's legitimate successor. Contacts have also been found between this section and the story of Absalom's rebellion in the following chapters, especially with the events at Mahanaim in 17:24–9 with a specific reference being made to 17:24–7 in 10:2. It has been claimed that theologically this reference provides a preface to the account of Absalom's revolt.

(2 Sam 11:1–27a) David and Bathsheba When the time for military activity came round again (i.e. in the spring, after the end of the winter rains), and the Israelite troops under Joab had laid siege to Rabbah, David had not joined the forces, a decision that was by no means exceptional (cf. 10:7–14). This was the setting for his downfall; it provided him with an opportunity to see Bathsheba bathing and then to commit adultery with her. Bathsheba is identified as the daughter of Eliam, who, according to 2 Sam 23:34, was the son of Ahithophel, and as the wife of Uriah, one of David's corps of 'Thirty'

élite warriors. He is referred to in 4QSam[a] as Joab's armour-bearer and was also known as 'the Hittite', which may denote the family origin of one that was born in Israel, as the 'yah' element in his name suggests. Another bit of information produced about Bathsheba is that she was purifying herself after menstruation; after the passing of the seven days of ritual impurity (Lev 15:19) she was in the best possible period for conception.

David's misbehaviour is not glossed over, nor is there any attempt to explain his action. Although attempts have been made to excuse his behaviour, especially by the rabbis (see McCarter 1984), no mitigation is offered in the biblical narrative. No explanation is given of his motivation, whether he acted because of love, or lust, or because he wanted to reassert his flagging manhood (Cohen 1965). However, this story which is so openly and honestly related in 2 Samuel is totally ignored in 1 Chronicles.

David's attempt to cast paternity on Uriah, and when that failed, his desperate plan to secure his death in battle, add to the enormity of his misbehaviour. He realized his guilt in the eyes of the law (Deut 22:22), and under the pretext of wishing to gain news of the military situation called Uriah from the battleground; he then tried to persuade him to go home and have intercourse with his wife ('wash your feet' being a euphemism for sexual intercourse). Uriah, although on leave, maintained the ritual purity expected during battle (cf. Deut 23:9–14; Josh 3:5); with words full of irony he claims that it is wrong to enjoy comforts when the ark was 'in booths' (or preferably 'at Sukkot') and the army encamped. He resisted the king's persuasive words and his efforts to put him in a relaxed mood through food and wine. Uriah eventually carried the letter assigning him to the front line and to certain death. It is assumed that Uriah was unable to read the message (Ackroyd 1977). Joab took matters in his own hands and unnecessarily endangered life by placing his men under the city wall, an action which had proved fatal in the case of Abimelech (Judg 9:23); on this occasion it saw the death of Uriah, and, according to the LXX[L], eighteen other soldiers. A messenger from Joab to David did not carry the message in the form that it was given, and in order to achieve consistency the LXX has a longer version of v. 22. Nevertheless the vital information about Uriah's death was transferred, and David sent back to Joab a hidden message of acceptance and encouragement. After the customary period of mourning, seven days (1 Sam 31:13; Gen 50:10), Bathsheba was taken into the king's household and in the course of time gave birth to a son.

(2 Sam 11:27b–12:25) Nathan's Parable David's actions were not explained or condemned in the previous narrative, but in 11:27b it becomes clear that his behaviour was unacceptable to God. Nathan's parable follows in 12:1–7a, which may at first have existed independently of the high moral tone in 11:27b and 12:9. Nevertheless, the implication of the parable itself is that David was guilty and deserved the punishment which he himself had pronounced on the rich man. Although vv. 1–7a are usually described as a parable it has to be noted that parallels need not be sought for each of its constituent parts, but that the unit intended to emphasize one particular point. Even if the search for an exact parallelism between all elements in the narrative and the parable is abandoned, it is not easy to decide on the main point of comparison between them. A parallelism between the theft of a ewe lamb and the theft of Uriah's wife is possible, but not likely. It may be that the story was told with the sole purpose of eliciting words of condemnation from David, and then to throw them back at him with the simple application 'You are the man' (v. 7a). The pronouncement of the king's verdict and its one-sentence application then becomes the focal point of the section. Interference by Nathan, the court prophet and counsellor, may have been prompted by political rather than religious motives; the kingship was a young institution, and he saw that it was in great danger if the holder began to take advantage of his status and exploit his subjects.

The terse application of v. 7a was obviously not considered adequate. Two complete units, which follow in vv. 7b–10 and 11–12, each with its own beginning and a prophetic-messenger formula, concentrate on different aspects of David's crime and consequent judgement. The first unit (vv. 7b–10) is more concerned with the murder of Uriah than with the taking of Bathsheba. After a rehearsal of YHWH's mighty works on behalf of David (vv. 7b–8), a list that is concluded with the statement that God would be able to add more, the main accusation was that he had 'struck down Uriah the Hittite with the sword'. By such an act he had despised God (v. 9), and his punishment will fit his crime, 'the sword shall never depart from your house'. The second unit (vv. 11–12) does not mention David's crime, but introduces a punishment that fits the crime of adultery: a member of his household will take possession of his harem, and that public act of humiliation will stand out in contrast to what he did secretly. David's response to Nathan was a brief admission of guilt (v. 13); by implication he had deserved death. But Nathan's immediate reply gave a revised sentence; his repentance had been accepted, his sin forgiven, and the sentence of death on him personally commuted. Nevertheless, the child born from his adultery with Bathsheba was not to escape, but had to die (v. 14). The theme of repentance and forgiveness in vv. 13–14, like the interpretation of Nathan's parable in vv. 7b–12, probably arose from later reflections on the course of David's kingship and the fate of his dynasty. David's house, including the son born to Bathsheba, suffered death; there was rebellion against David which included the ravishing of his harem (vv. 11–12). But the house of David remarkably survived because he himself had been forgiven (v. 13). Omitting these later reflections, the natural conclusion to Nathan's parable is found in v. 15a.

The prophecy in v. 14 is fulfilled in vv. 15b–23; the child's death was followed by David's unconventional behaviour. His fast and vigil, the traditional signs of mourning, occurred before the child's death (v. 16), but were abandoned instantly after the child had died (v. 20). It was a strange behaviour that perplexed his courtiers. However, understood in conjunction with the theme of sin and forgiveness in vv. 13–14, David's behaviour was reasonable (cf. Gerleman 1977). Through his actions before the child's death, he was pleading 'with God for the child' (v. 16); that was the only reasonable course to take (cf. v. 22). But once he knew, upon the child's death, that his plea had not been accepted, it was reasonable to abandon his actions (v. 23). David resigned to these events with serenity; they proved that God was fulfilling his word, and by implica-

tion he had received forgiveness. A brief notice of Solomon's birth in vv. 24–5 is beset with difficulties. A possible understanding of the events is that, if the Nathan parable and the secondary vv. 15b–24a are ignored, v. 24b follows on 11:27a, thus giving 'and bore him a son and she called his name Solomon'. The whole section relating to the death of the firstborn and the birth of 'his replacement' (šĕlômôh) was inserted to avoid the identification of Solomon as David's illegitimate son (Veijola 1979). However, such an interpretation is not necessary; it can be accepted that a second son was born after the death of the first, but not necessarily within the short time suggested by placing both in the period of the Rabbah campaign, that he was named Solomon because he was a replacement of the first and that Nathan gave him another name, Jedidiah, meaning 'Beloved of the LORD'.

In vv. 26–31 we return to the siege of Rabbah, last mentioned in 11:1. Joab captured the fortified area of Rabbah known as 'the royal citadel'; this meant that he was in control of its water supply (v. 27). David was then invited to take personal charge of the army for the final siege so that the city could be reckoned as his conquest. Among the treasures taken by David, before he dismantled the city's fortifications, was the crown of its national god, Milcom (a reading preferred to the MT's malkām, 'their king').

(2 Sam 13:1–39) Amnon and Tamar Amnon's love for Tamar, his rape of his half-sister, and the vengeance of Absalom for this wrong are incidents which have direct bearing on the succession issue. The outcome of these events was the death of Solomon's older brothers, Amnon and eventually Absalom. The latter, after his temporary exclusion from court, was briefly reconciled with David, but his dissatisfaction led to a revolt (chs. 15–19) and finally his death. The private affairs of chs. 13–14, like the more public events of chs. 15–19, are really concerned with Absalom (cf. 13:1, 23, 38; 14:28; see Conroy 1978). Those later events arose from the clash of personalities evident in chs. 13–14 (see McCarter 1984). It was inevitable that Absalom, vindictive (14:33) and determined (14:28–32), was on a collision course with the compliant (13:7), indecisive (14:1), and lenient (13:21) David. Joab was always ready to step in and force a quick solution.

The narrative has been skilfully written; the historical significance of the events for the kingdom of David has not been elaborated, nor has the theological theme that God's will to place Solomon on David's throne was being fulfilled, nor again has the parallel between Amnon's desire for Tamar and David's desire for Bathsheba. The position, as straightforwardly described in vv. 1–2, was that Amnon, son of David and Ahinoam, fell in love with Tamar, full sister of Absalom, both children of David and Maacah. His desire for Tamar was so intense that it made him ill, and he had to resort to a trickery proposed by his cousin Jonadab (vv. 3–5). Apparently virgins were under close guard, and Amnon did not have access to Tamar (v. 3), but a request to David, when he visited the ill crown-prince, brought Tamar to him and he raped her. He did not heed her pleading, in which she indicated the consequences for both of them; marriage between them was possible at this time (cf. Gen 20:12), although later such a marriage was prohibited by law (Lev 18:9, 11; 20:17; Deut 27:22). Amnon was obviously driven by lust not love, and his action was followed by an intense loathing of Tamar. Despite Tamar's expectation that Amnon would marry her (v. 16, cf. Ex 22:16; Deut 22:8), she was put away with contempt (vv. 15, 17–18) and immediately went into mourning. Tearing the long gown, which she was wearing as a virgin princess, was a sign of grief rather than lost virginity, as was putting ashes on the head and placing a hand on the head (cf. Jer 2:37). David, according to v. 21, was angry when he heard, but, following the LXX and 4QSam[a], the NRSV adds 'but he would not punish his son Amnon, because he loved him, for he was his firstborn'. David's leniency probably incurred Absalom's resentment, but he restrained himself for the time being (v. 22).

Absalom's revenge had been planned for some time, and was timed to coincide with sheep-shearing at Baal-hazor near Ephraim, which cannot be identified with certainty, but was probably a few miles from Jerusalem. Sheep-shearing was a time for festivities, and it was perfectly normal for Absalom to invite the king and his servants to the celebrations. No reason has been given for David's reluctance, nor for the fact that Absalom had to press the king for his permission (vv. 25, 27). It has been suggested that David was suspicious of Absalom, and that by inviting the king specifically (v. 24) he had his eyes on the throne. If so, it is not easy to understand why he gave permission for Amnon to go to the festival; perhaps he did not realize the extent of Absalom's hatred until he was briefed by Jonadab (cf. v. 32). Once permission had been granted 'Absalom made a feast like a king's feast' (following the LXX and 4QSam[a]). Nothing is known of the murderers (v. 29) nor of their fate afterwards; but it is obvious that Absalom was taking the lead, for it was he who gave the orders and encouraged them. An initial report that all the king's sons had been killed had to be corrected by Jonadab; in asserting that it was only Amnon who had died, Jonadab made David aware of the reason for Absalom's action (v. 32). Jonadab's report was confirmed when the king's sons returned along the 'Horonaim road' (with some support from the LXX for the MT 'the road behind him'). A period of bitter court mourning for Amnon followed (vv. 36–7). Absalom took refuge with Talmai, king of Geshur, his grandfather on his mother's side, and was three years in exile (vv. 37–8). Giving a time-scale in these verses, as well as noting a change in David, prepares the way for Absalom's return, and these verses are frequently read with ch. 14. David's change of heart (following the LXX and 4QSam[a]) has been attributed to his affection for his sons and his realization that Absalom was second in line for succession (Gordon 1984); but the fact that Joab had to resort to a ploy to persuade the king suggests that his change of heart was merely an abating of open hostility towards Absalom and that he could be persuaded step by step to allow him to return.

(2 Sam 14:1–33) Absalom's Return Reading signs that David was ready for Absalom's return, Joab took matters in hand. The text gives no hint of his motives. He probably considered it necessary for Absalom, a possible heir to the throne, to be in Jerusalem; he was therefore acting in the kingdom's best interest (Gunn 1978). The special gift of the wise woman from Tekoa, called to his assistance and closely briefed by him, was either the gift of speech, in which she had been trained, or more probably a gift for feigning or acting lamentation. The incident does not provide sufficient evidence for

contending that Tekoa had a distinctive wisdom tradition (against Wolff 1964). Possible connections between this incident and other biblical texts have been suggested. First, it is the same in style as Nathan's parable; there a king condemns himself in his response to the situation described, and here the king in his judgement convicts himself (v. 13). Secondly, the tale about two brothers fighting and one killing the other is reminiscent of Cain and Abel in Gen 4 (Blenkinsopp 1966), and especially the protection given to the murderer, in one case by divine promise (Gen 4:15) and in the other by royal oath (v. 11). Thirdly, there are several links with the account of Joab's interview with the wise woman of Abel of Beth-maacah (2 Sam 20, cf. Conroy 1978).

Whatever the parallels proposed, the interview reported in this chapter has its own problems. The woman's dilemma is succinctly presented: she was a widow and the murderer was her only heir; she was thus torn between her duty to avenge the other son's death and her duty to her husband to preserve his name by protecting the son still alive (v. 7). Her community rightly insisted on blood revenge, but her appeal for special consideration so that her last ember would not be quenched touched David's heart, and he promised a ruling (v. 8). The woman persisted until that very general promise became an oath that no one would touch her son. The meaning of v. 9 in this particular context is difficult to ascertain (see Hoftijzer 1970), but it is not to be regarded as an isolated text that disrupts the sequence (McCarter 1984). It is assumed that, if David responded to the woman's plea and suspended blood-revenge, he would be guilty; the woman, realizing that he would be responding to pressure from her, was willing to accept guilt. The exact meaning of the woman's words in v. 13 is not clear. Examples from the several interpretations offered are that the king had devised something against the people by banning the heir from their midst, or that he himself was in jeopardy because he had condemned himself for his treatment of Absalom. Her argument in v. 14 is easier to follow: all die, and the fact of Amnon's death cannot be changed by keeping Absalom in exile.

Another problem is posed by the placement of vv. 15–17, which do not have any knowledge of vv. 12–14, where the woman has related the meaning of the king's ruling to the banishment of Absalom. On the contrary vv. 15–17 seem to constitute part of the woman's request in vv. 5–7, and are read between vv. 7 and 8 by many commentators (cf. McCarter 1984, but not so Hertzberg 1964). In her final plea the woman stated that the king was 'like the angel of God', which may be no more than flattery spoken by one trying to ingratiate herself with the king (so Hoftijzer 1970). After establishing that the woman's action was Joab's doing, David acceded to the request that Absalom be allowed to return; but he was not granted full privileges (v. 24). The section which follows (vv. 25–7) gives a description of Absalom's person, noting his beauty and drawing attention in particular to the weight of his hair. The statement that he had three sons is contradicted by 18:18, where he says that he had no son. This section is a secondary addition, probably intended to show the popularity of Absalom despite his absence from court for two more years (Hoftijzer 1970). Finally Absalom was accepted by David; the king's kiss (v. 33) is to be taken as a sign of reconciliation. It was only after one desperate action against Joab that Absalom gained recognition; Joab was compelled to go to David and bring Absalom to the king.

(2 Sam 15:1–37) Absalom's Rebellion Absalom, the prince in exile, soon became a contender for the throne. His intention was made known when he acquired a royal retinue, 'chariot and horses', and a personal bodyguard, 'men to run ahead of him' (cf. 1 Kings 1:5). He also set out to win popular support among those coming to the seat of justice ('the gate') for litigation. Although the king was responsible for justice, Absalom was determined to capitalize on discontent because of David's failure to act efficiently and sympathetically. By making himself accessible and friendly Absalom gained popularity (v. 6).

Reference to the tribes of Israel in v. 2, if taken literally, may suggest that Absalom was taking advantage of discontent among northern tribes and was thus fanning the jealousy between north and south (as suggested by Alt 1968). There are, however, overwhelming reasons for accepting that Absalom's support was widespread and included Judahite as well as Israelite elements (see fully McCarter 1984). Absalom himself was a Hebronite, and the choice of Hebron as the seat of kingship (v. 10) would be unacceptable if he was supported exclusively by northern tribes. But Judahites, Ahithophel and Amasa, were among the leaders of his revolt, and it is significant that David did not seek refuge in Judah. It seems that Absalom had gathered support from Dan to Beersheba (cf. 17:11). The revolt was caused by deficiencies in the administration of justice under David; this is the implication of vv. 2–6, although it has not been explicitly stated in this pro-Davidic writing. The whole thrust of the biblical narrative is to attribute these events to Absalom's desire for revenge on Amnon and his own ambition to take the throne. But such causes would not have attracted the measure of support enjoyed by Absalom (McCarter 1984). Consequently several other reasons have been proposed, such as dissatisfaction with David's expansionist policy, or with his ruthless military campaigns, or with the loss of personal freedom as state bureaucracy developed. Absalom probably gained a following because of 'a mass of indefinable grievances' (Bright 1972, followed by McCarter 1984). After a wait of four years (following the Greek and Syriac for the MT's 'forty'), Absalom planned his revolt without arousing any suspicion. His request for permission to fulfil a vow in Hebron was readily granted. It had to be fulfilled in Hebron because it was made to YHWH as he manifested himself there; parallels to 'YHWH-in-Hebron' are found elsewhere, such as 'Dagon-in-Ashdod' (1 Sam 5:5) and 'YHWH of Samaria' and 'YHWH of Teman' in ancient inscriptions. Absalom swelled the ranks of his supporters by bringing to Hebron innocent and unsuspecting guests (v. 11), and his revolt was assisted by the presence of Ahithophel, David's counsellor and grandfather of Bathsheba.

David's flight from Jerusalem to the Jordan was evidently a wise move, although the text offers no explanation. Absalom's presence in Hebron, discontent among the Israelites and the enmity of the Philistines left him with no other real alternative. On the outskirts of Jerusalem, probably in the Kidron valley before the ascent to the Mount of Olives, his supporters marched past David; they included the Jerusalem garrison ('his servants'), loyal troops ('the people'), his personal bodyguard ('Cherethites and Pelethites', cf. 2 Sam 8:18) and a detachment of 600 Philistines from Gath (vv. 17–18). During David's flight from the city there were five meetings or conversations (15:19–16:13), bearing some symmetrical correspondence to the three encounters on his homeward journey (19:16–40) (see Conroy 1978). In his meeting with Ittai (vv. 19–23), the leader of the Gittites, David tried to persuade him to stay with Absalom ('the king') and avoid the uncertainty that would not be pleasing to him as a foreigner and exile. But for Ittai there was no king other than David, and he was determined to stay with him. David was presumably testing his loyalty. Other motives become apparent in David's conversation with the two priests, Abiathar and Zadok (vv. 24–9). The mention of Levites carrying the ark is usually regarded as a later addition. In his conversation with them David gives them two reasons for returning to Jerusalem. The first is theological; it presents David in a favourable light as one who resigns to the will of YHWH knowing that it is he who decides the outcome. This is to be attributed to the pro-Davidic editors. The second is practical; David is obviously planning to make a comeback and is planting the priests in Jerusalem in order to gain information (v. 28).

David's advance up the Mount of Olives (vv. 30–1), which breaks the sequence of the five conversations, has been described as a pilgrimage or an act of penance. It was a march undertaken in sorrow and humility, which is mixed with a prayer that Ahithophel's counsel be confounded.

A third conversation occurred between David and Hushai of the Archite clan of Benjamin (vv. 32–7); it has been suggested that his appearance 'where God was worshipped' was a direct reply to David's prayer in v. 31, for he is commissioned as an informer in order to defeat Ahithophel's counsel. He, with the two priests and their sons, were to penetrate Absalom's inner circle and report back to David.

(2 Sam 16:1–23) David in Flight and Absalom in Jerusalem David's first three meetings with supporters are followed by two other meetings, but this time with two persons connected with the family of Saul. It is doubtful if the reports of these two particular meetings came from the same source as the other three; some derive them from an independent source which had no connection with the present revolt. His first encounter, with Ziba, the servant of Mephibosheth (vv. 1–4), is rather confusing. Ziba brought provisions to sustain David on his way and reported that Mephibosheth had stayed in Jerusalem, confident that Saul's kingdom was to be returned to him. Ziba was clearly an opportunist, who probably calculated that David would eventually suppress the revolt, and sought to be in favour with him at the expense of Mephibosheth. If Mephibosheth's words in 19:27–9, accusing Ziba of slander, are trustworthy, he is exonerated; nevertheless, it has been claimed that Mephibosheth was as guilty as Ziba (Conroy 1978). If that is the case, he had grossly misjudged his position, for the revolt was focused on Absalom. David, against his better judgement, accepted Ziba's report and granted him Saul's estates.

As David was coming to Bahurim on the edge of the wilderness, he was met by another Saulide called Shimei

(vv. 5–14), who was cursing David and calling him 'Murderer'; he was interpreting Absalom's take-over of the kingdom as God's revenge for what David had done to the house of Saul. It is not clear what is meant by 'the blood of the house of Saul' (v. 8) as there are many possibilities: the execution of seven Saulides at Gibeon (21:1–14), the death of Abner and Ishbaal, for which David may have been held responsible, or the deaths of Saul and Jonathan at Mount Gilboa, David perhaps being implicated by some factions because he had gone over to the Philistines. David's reply to Abishai and his unwillingness to take action against Shimei are significant. He was accepting the possibility that Shimei was cursing because YHWH had ordered him to do so (v. 10) and he resigned to God's will without protest (cf. also 1 Sam 26:9–11). In view of his circumstances at the time, having been forced into exile by his own son, David could only accept that he was under a curse. Action against Shimei would not change the situation. David's response has been interpreted as penitential, but according to v. 12 he was hopeful that God would improve his situation at a future date; it has been suggested, however, that vv. 11–12 are secondary.

Hushai, now known as David's friend, came to Absalom in Jerusalem, and with the standard acclamation, 'Long live the king', recognized his authority as king and declared his allegiance to him (v. 16). Absalom instinctively rejected Hushai's signs of disloyalty to David. But he was persuaded to accept Hushai, when he was assured by him that he considered Absalom to be God's elect and king by public acclamation and promised him the same loyalty as he had shown his father. During his brief period in Jerusalem, Absalom unwisely accepted Ahithophel's advice, which, according to v. 23, was always esteemed and regarded as divine guidance. But, by going to his father's harem, Absalom was publicly declaring his claim to the throne, which he had already taken (cf. Tsevat 1958). Other instances of this practice are found in 2 Sam 12:8; 1 Kings 2:22–3. Ahithophel saw in such action a decisive breaking of relations between son and father and therefore an opportunity to consolidate support from the anti-Davidic camp.

(2 Sam 17:1–29) Hushai and Ahithophel Hushai's task, as set by David, was to 'defeat . . . the counsel of Ahithophel' (15:34), and, despite the respect shown to Ahithophel and his counsel (16:23), Hushai succeeded in defeating him. The account of the contest between them (vv. 1–14) has been rightly seen as pivotal in the story of Absalom (McCarter 1984). David's earlier conversations with the two priests, Zadok and Abiathar, and with Hushai (15:24–9, 32–7), as well as previous introductions to Ahithophel (15:12; 16:20–3), have prepared for the contest between Hushai and Ahithophel. Ahithophel advised Absalom to take action quickly; if he were given the troops he would make a sudden night attack on David's weary companions. As was often the case with this frequently used military strategy, they would be thrown into panic. The advantages of Ahithophel's plan were that action would be swift and successful and the loss of life minimal; his aim was to kill David alone and return all other fugitives to Jerusalem, as a young wife returns to her husband after a brief quarrel (reading v. 3a with the LXX rather than the MT). This was sound advice, and had it been accepted, as seemed likely from the initial response of Absalom and his elders, it would no doubt have proved successful.

For an unspecified reason Absalom wished to consult Hushai. He played for time, so that David and his men could regain their strength and muster the troops. In a long and colourful speech, Hushai made full use of his persuasive powers (vv. 8–13). First, he sought to discourage Absalom from precipitate action by reminding him of David's military prowess; he and his men were brave professionals, and a night attack would be futile, for an old warrior like him would not be sleeping in camp with his men and he would throw Absalom's army into panic. Secondly, by suggesting that Absalom muster 'all Israel . . . from Dan to Beersheba' to battle, he was appealing to any illusions of grandeur that he may have held; he could envisage a pan-Israelite army supporting him and totally annihilating the enemy. Thirdly, his suggestion that Absalom himself go to battle in person was a direct appeal to his vanity. Hushai's eloquence and reasoning impressed Absalom and his advisers; nevertheless, as is emphasized in v. 14, the narrator found YHWH's will to be the decisive factor. Hushai had left the council before a decision had been taken. Although he had given his own counsel, his advice to David to cross the Jordan immediately (v. 16) took into account the possibility of a sudden attack as recommended by Ahithophel. The arrangement for passing information to David through the sons of Abiathar and Zadok and a girl informant was in danger of failing when they were spotted by Absalom's servants. However, after the message was successfully transferred, David and his followers safely crossed the Jordan.

Three other pieces of information are included in vv. 23–9. First, the spurned Ahithophel committed suicide (v. 23); although the narrative suggests that he took this decision because of wounded pride, it has been suggested that it was more from fear of cruel death at the hands of David (Hertzberg 1964). Secondly, Joab had been replaced at the head of the Israelite army by Amasa, an Ishmaelite (with the LXX and 1 Chr 2:17 in preference to 'Israelite' of the MT) related to Joab through the two mothers. Thirdly, David had powerful friends in Transjordan, Shobi, the Ammonite, Machir, who had previously assisted Mephibosheth of the house of Saul, and Barzillai from Gilead (see 19:31–9). It was important from the narrator's point of view to show that David had the support of past followers from the house of Saul. They gave David practical assistance by providing for him.

(2 Sam 18:1–33) The Death of Absalom The delay in Absalom's attack, which had been secured through Hushai's counsel, gave David an opportunity to gather and arrange his troops. By the time he was ready for battle he had an army that he could divide into three groups, which was the traditional division of an army (Judg 7:16; 1 Sam 11:11; Conroy 1978). The army passed out in front of David, who had himself been prevented by the men from marching out with them (v. 3); no such caution was taken by the opposing camp, and Absalom fell. The narrator was anxious to emphasize that David was not with the army and could not be implicated in Absalom's death. The point is made more forcibly in his specific instructions to his three commanders to 'deal gently' with Absalom, and it is deliberately noted that all the people heard him giving that order. Little information is given about the battle. 'The men of Israel', a corps of conscripted men, was defeated by 'the servants of David', presumably a more professional force. The latter were better placed to take advantage of the dangerous terrain in which the battle was fought. 'The forest of Ephraim' was probably wooded hill-country in Transjordan settled by some Ephraimites (Hertzberg 1964). It was rough country made treacherous by the large pits found there (v. 17), and took more casualties than the actual fighting, a hint perhaps that other forces were fighting for David. Absalom became victim to the forest, for as his mule made its way under the branches 'he was left hanging' (as understood by the English versions) in mid-air. Probably his neck became lodged between two branches (G. Driver 1962), which is more likely than the suggestion that he was caught by his phenomenal crop of hair (see 14:26; cf. Josephus, *Ant.* 7 § 239). Ignoring David's command regarding Absalom, Joab himself thrust a spear through Absalom's heart and left his young men to finish the work (v. 15). A man, who was likely to receive a reward for killing Absalom, had three good reasons for not accepting the task: his unwillingness to kill a king's son, his obedience to David's known wish, and his realization that Joab would not protect him from David's wrath (vv. 12–13).

Joab suspended hostilities, realizing that it was not a war between the people but was focused on an individual (Hertzberg 1964). Absalom was thrown into a pit by the troops and they heaped stones over him; it was not a respectable burial (cf. Josh 7:26; 8:29). But Absalom had during his lifetime erected a memorial for himself in the Jerusalem area, although there is no certainty that it can be identified with the tomb of Absalom in the Kidron valley. He could have erected a memorial in the year when he was prince in Jerusalem; his period there as king was very short. The contradiction between v. 18 and 14:27 can be resolved by accepting that the sons he had died at an early age. The drama in connection with announcing the outcome of the battle to David can be explained as follows (following McCarter 1984). As suggested by vv. 28–9, Ahimaaz was unaware of Absalom's death. Joab tried to dissuade him from carrying news of the battle to David; he would have to be informed of Absalom's death, and he could not rely on Ahimaaz to make that report as positively as he would wish. Another messenger was appointed, and the Cushite, like Joab, wanted to give the impression that it was good news despite Absalom's death. When Ahimaaz arrived, amid expectations of good tidings because he was a good man, he reported that 'all was well', but was unable to answer the king's question about Absalom. The Cushite too brought good news, but, in reply to the king's question about Absalom, gave him the news with a positive slant (v. 32). David began a period of mourning for Absalom (v. 33), and this continues into the next chapter.

(2 Sam 19:1–43) David Returns to Jerusalem David's prolonged mourning for Absalom became an embarrassment for his troops and supporters. The king had allowed his personal grief to eclipse his responsibility towards the men who had fought against Absalom, their enemy. Joab took matters in hand and spoke to the king some hard words which probably exaggerated the situation. David's behaviour had brought shame on those who saved him, and had given the impression that he loved those who hated him and hated those who loved

him. By threatening another possible rebellion (v. 7), Joab managed to raise the king from his depression and to see him sitting on his throne with the troops marching past. 'Bringing the king back' to his residence in the capital obviously gave prestige and privileges to those involved; they would be the king's guards and his closest supporters. The people of Israel, former supporters of Absalom, had to reconsider their position; although they had not been satisfied with David's management of internal affairs, they had reaped benefits from his campaigns against the Philistines. Now that Absalom was dead the Israelites were ready to forget the past and transfer their allegiance again to David. But David saw danger in accepting these Israelite overtures at the expense of his supporters in Judah. No reason is given for Judah's tardiness in declaring its support; it may have been connected with the fact that Absalom's rebellion had centred on Hebron (15:10). David's approach to the elders of Judah, made through his representatives in Jerusalem, Zadok and Abiathar (cf. 15:24–9), was in two parts: a reminder of his Judahite descent, and a notice of his intention to appoint Amasa to replace Joab as commander of his army. The response was as David had wished, and the Judahites went to Gilgal to protect his crossing of the Jordan.

On David's return journey to Jerusalem there were three meetings or conversations to correspond to those on his departure from the city (15:9–16:13). His first encounter was with Shimei, a Benjaminite from the house of Saul. The two Saulides, Ziba and Shimei, had rushed down to the Jordan in order to bring back the king; the group with Ziba assisted the king's household to cross. Shimei, because of his guiltiness for previously cursing David (2 Sam 16:5–13), pleaded with the king to forget his past actions. He had made a special effort to be the first northerner ('house of Joseph') to meet him. David, as customary on coronation day, showed magnanimity; he could not accept the advice of the vengeful sons of Zeruiah (cf. 16:9), and dismissed Abishai as an 'adversary' (*sātān*). Although he kept his oath to Shimei, he did not forget or forgive his insulting behaviour (see 1 Kings 2:8–9).

Although the conversation with Mephibosheth follows next (vv. 24–30), there is some doubt concerning its correct historical placing. It obviously took place after David's conversation with Barzillai in Transjordan, for Mephibosheth did not cross over. Despite the reference in v. 30, he had gone out to Jerusalem to meet David (v. 25). When he arrived he was unkempt, probably intentionally to demonstrate his grief for David's departure. He pleaded innocence, claiming that he had been deceived by Ziba (cf. 16:1–4), and relied on the king's mercy. In his attempt to get a favourable decision he referred to him as an 'angel of God' (cf. 14:17, 20) and reminded him of previous favour granted to him. David's reply, curt and to the point, was a compromise, and he divided Saul's territories between Ziba and Mephibosheth. Barzillai had made provision for the king and his troops (17:27), and David wished to recompense him by giving him a place in the court (vv. 31–40). Because of his old age Barzillai could no longer enjoy the pleasures of the court; he only wants his home and the family grave. He handed over Chimham to accompany David; according to MSS of the LXX he was his 'son'. Not forgetting Barzillai's kindness, David blessed him (vv. 38b–39), and later commended him to Solomon (1 Kings 2:26).

Conflict between north and south had not ceased (vv. 41–3). These verses are in one sense a continuation of vv. 8–13, where the Israelites considered their position and vacillated, leading David to appeal to Judah. When they saw the Judahites leading the king to Jerusalem, they felt excluded. In the ensuing quarrel Judah claimed priority because David was a kinsman, and Israel because the northern tribes formed the larger part of his kingdom ('ten shares' to two) and were the first to mention bringing back the king. These verses prepare for the revolt of ch. 20 and the ultimate division of the kingdom in 1 Kings 12.

(2 Sam 20:1–25) A Rebellion under Sheba A leader for discontented elements was found in Sheba, 'the son of Bichri, a Benjaminite', and a representative of the Saulide camp (cf. Bechorath in 1 Sam 9:1). The nature of his uprising has to be defined. Although v. 2 suggests that 'all Israel' left David and followed Sheba, it is clear from v. 14 that he had only the limited following of all the Bichrites. The use of such terms as 'revolt' and 'uprising' has been questioned; it was the dissension of a small group (McCarter 1984). The significance of this group must not be overlooked, however. The narrative reaffirms the presence of a northern, Saulide element which was not satisfied with being part of a united kingdom under David. According to David's perception in v. 6 this dissent was potentially more harmful than Absalom's rebellion. In that particular case, a contender was rising against a monarch, but Sheba's dissension showed that the structure of the kingdom was in danger. The allegiance of the northern tribes could no longer be relied upon, and it is significant that Sheba's rallying cry (v. 1) was repeated when the kingdom was divided after the death of Solomon (1 Kings 12:16).

Once he had settled in Jerusalem and made arrangements for his concubines (v. 3), David attended to the dissension. Amasa, the newly appointed commander (19:13), was given three days to rally a force, but failed to act as requested. No reason is given, but v. 11 may suggest that he was disloyal to David (Gordon 1984). Abishai was immediately put in charge of the army, for David saw trouble ahead if Sheba and his followers had time to establish themselves in fortified cities. Joab, reluctant to accept demotion, still had 'men' under his command (v. 7) and took the lead in the pursuit of Sheba. When they met Amasa at Gibeon, Joab operated his preconceived plan to murder him. Grasping Amasa by the beard to kiss him was not a suspicious act; but hidden in his girdle he had a short sword, which 'fell out' (into his hand, not onto the ground, according to Hertzberg 1964), and with which he killed Amasa. His body was thrown into a field. Joab was now unquestionably the leader of the army; his brother Abishai is not mentioned after v. 10. Hostilities centred on Abel of Beth-maacah in the north, near Dan, where Sheba had established himself. When Joab and his forces were attacking the besieged city a 'wise woman' spoke from the rampart. There are obvious links between her appearance and that of the wise woman of Tekoa in ch. 14; Joab was involved on both occasions, and the 'heritage of the LORD' became an issue in both (v. 19; cf. 14:16; see Conroy 1978). She had a plan to save Abel, a city which had a reputation for wisdom (v. 18) and which was a 'mother city' in Israel (v. 19); by saving it the integrity of Israel as 'the heritage of the LORD' would be safe-

guarded (v. 19). The proposal was to behead an individual to save the city (v. 21).

The chapter is concluded with another list of David's officials (cf. 8:15–18). Joab is the established commander of the army, and Benaiah in charge of the Cherethites and Pelethites. Adoram (Adoniram in 1 Kings 4:6), not mentioned in the previous list, was in charge of forced labour, which may have been introduced in the latter part of David's reign. All the other names are identical with those in the previous list, except Ira, who replaces David's sons at 8:18. He is called 'the Jairite', probably because he came from the village of Jair (Num 32:41; Deut 3:14). The present list has been variously interpreted as later than the one in 8:15–18 (Noth 1960), a duplication of it (Kapelrud 1955), or a more primitive form of it (McCarter 1984).

Appendices (2 Sam 21–4)

This miscellaneous collection of narratives, lists, and poems is usually referred to as 'appendices'. However, it is not a haphazard collection of material, for commentators usually find here a concentric arrangement of the various pieces. At the centre are two poems, the Psalm of David in 22:2–51, reviewing the mighty acts of God, and the oracle in 23:1–7 giving assurances that the Davidic dynasty was to endure. Each side of the central poems are the warrior exploits recorded in 21:15–22 and again in 23:8–39, where they are accompanied by a warrior list. Moving to the outer circle we find a famine story (21:1–14) and a plague story (24:11–25) (cf. Gordon 1984, with reference to Budde's commentary of 1902). Sections of these appendices are closely linked with both preceding and succeeding parts of the Deuteronomistic History. The episode relating to the Gibeonites in 21:1–14 continues one of the main themes of the preceding chapters, namely the relationship between David and the house of Saul. The final section, the plague story in ch. 24, prepares the way for the building of Solomon's temple, and is therefore appropriately placed immediately before 1 Kings. The structure of these chapters is usually attributed to a final compiler (Hertzberg 1964).

(2 Sam 21:1–22) A Famine and the Gibeonites A prolonged famine caused by drought led David, accepting that it was a sign of divine displeasure, to enquire of YHWH. The reason given is that the house of Saul had incurred blood-guilt by putting the Gibeonites to death (v. 1). It is known from Josh 9 that the Gibeonites had an irrevocable treaty with the Israelites (vv. 19–20), and as is evident from biblical and extra-biblical material breaching a treaty led to national calamities (Malamat 1955). The position of the Gibeonites is explained in v. 2; they were 'Amorites', i.e. inhabitants of the land before the Israelite occupation, but were protected by an Israelite oath. The fact that they were settled in Benjaminite territory irritated Saul; he was further aggravated because he had designs on Gibeon as his capital (Blenkinsopp 1974). Although there is no biblical account of Saul's slaughter of the Gibeonites, his dealings with the priests of Nob (1 Sam 22:6–23) makes the statement in v. 1 credible.

David's wish to expiate for the sin of Saul has been widely discussed. One suggestion is that David was acting for the sake of fertility, and his action was therefore a royal sacrifice (Kapelrud 1955), an action that is paralleled elsewhere in times of great emergency (see 2 Kings 3:26–7). In such a context, the note in v. 9 that the sacrifice was made 'at the beginning of barley harvest' acquires significance. Other interpretations of the passage concentrate on the issue of causality, which ascribes present disaster to past sin. Parallels show that a succeeding king made expiation for the sins of the past, more expressly for the breach of an oath (Malamat 1955), which required the death of the guilty (Fensham 1964). Another issue is the involvement of David in the deaths of the Saulides for political reasons. It would unquestionably be to David's advantage to be rid of groups which had shown steadfast loyalty to the house of Saul, and his motives have been under suspicion. The intention of this narrative, together with its sequel in 9:1–13, is to show that David was not acting solely to gain political advantage. Although he was ultimately responsible for the deaths (v. 6), he was acting out of concern for the welfare of the land and in obedience to YHWH's will. His actions were also tempered by his kindness to Mephibosheth (see 9:1–13). Nevertheless, it has to be admitted that, whatever the primary considerations in David's mind, he did gain significant political advantages. David also secured an honourable burial for Saul and Jonathan, as well as for those executed on this occasion. Whatever criticisms can be made of David's treatment of the family of Saul, he showed respect to the dead. Rizpah's vigil on a sackcloth until the coming of rain (probably an unseasonal shower rather than the November rains, Hertzberg 1964) was not simply intended as protection for the corpses, but was also in expectation of rainfall as a sign of God's favour. The bones of Saul and Jonathan were brought from Jabesh-gilead (but according to 1 Sam 31:12–13 the corpses had been burnt), and laid in a family grave at Zela (a place-name according to the NRSV, but a 'chamber' in a grave possibly at Gibeah according to Hertzberg 1964). The LXX adds that the bones of the executed sons of Saul were buried with them.

A stereotyped section in vv. 15–22, probably derived from archival sources, gives an outline of clashes during the Philistine wars with persons of extraordinary size called 'descendants of the giants' (so NRSV, which is preferred to 'votaries of Rapha', a cultic association of warriors, following l'Heureux 1976). According to the NRSV the first giant was Ishbi-benob, whose hefty armour is reminiscent of Goliath (1 Sam 17:7); he was killed by Abishai. No details are given of the second giant, Saph; he was killed by Sibbecai the Hushathite, who was one of David's élite 'Thirty' (23:27 where the LXX is read for the MT Mebunnai). Goliath, the Gittite, was the third opponent (cf. 1 Sam 17), and he was killed by Elhanan, a Bethlehemite; this is probably an older tradition than the one which names David as the victor. There is no reason for claiming that David was the throne name of the person whose real name was Elhanan (Honeyman 1948). No name is given to the fourth giant, who possessed some abnormal physical characteristics; he was killed by Jonathan, David's nephew, who is not named elsewhere.

(2 Sam 22:1–51) David's Song of Thanksgiving This song celebrating David's achievements due to God's marvellous works corresponds to Ps 18. The differences between them are minor ones which can be attributed to scribal errors or to the process of transmission. The song contains some ancient poetry, which may well go back to the tenth century BCE. In its present form, however, the song contains a linking section in vv. 21–8, which reflects Deuteronomistic language and theology. But there is general recognition that the language of the psalm itself is archaic; earlier attempts to date it in the Maccabean period have been abandoned in favour of the tenth century (Cross 1953b). Although some commentators refer to a long association between the psalm and David, and admit the possibility of Davidic authorship, there is no internal evidence to support the contention. For a discussion of the song's structure, type and provenance see under PS 18. The analysis which finds in the song two ancient poems (vv. 2–20 and vv. 29–31, 35–51) belonging to the monarchial period has much to commend it (McCarter 1984). The two poems were later combined by a Deuteronomistic editor who added vv. 21–8 and v. 1 (and also according to some v. 51a). The completed song celebrates two aspects of David's life: his deliverance from his enemies and his military conquests.

The song, according to the title, relates generally to the protection of David from Saul and his enemies, and does not concentrate on one particular event. Rescue from enemies is the prominent theme of vv. 2–20. Using images of a place of refuge on a rock, God, it is claimed, is the speaker's refuge and thus when he calls he is saved from his enemies (vv. 2–4). The image changes in vv. 5–6, where the speaker's distress, presumably at the hands of his enemies although they are not mentioned, is compared to being encompassed by the waters of Sheol. God's response to his cry for help (v. 7) is described as a theophany (vv. 8–20); for the language and imagery cf. other OT theophany passages (Ex 19; Judg 5:4–5; 1 Kings 19; Ps 68:8; Hab 3). A number of features stand out in these verses: references to God's appearance are distinctly anthropomorphic ('nostrils', 'mouth', 'came down', 'rode'); storm imagery dominates the whole section, with fire, earthquake, clouds, lightning, and thunder accompanying God's presence; in its present context this description of God emphasizes his presence with his distressed servant, for his voice reaches to the caller at the bottom of the sea (v. 5).

Prominent traces of Deuteronomistic language are evident in the transitional vv. 21–8 (McCarter 1984, following Veijola 1975). Claiming that he is innocent, righteous, and blameless, the speaker considers God's salvation as a reward and recompense (vv. 21–5). Among the most obvious Deuteronomistic clichés are: 'the ways of the LORD' (cf. Deut 8:6; 10:11, etc.), 'judgements and statutes' (Deut 4:5; 5:1, etc.). The theme of YHWH's help to the blameless and pure is asserted again in the fourfold statement of vv. 26–7, which have been described as an ancient quatrain (Cross 1953a). The final section (vv. 29–51) is more concerned with David's victories over his enemies, and has been called a 'royal victory song'. After an acknowledgement of YHWH as the speaker's 'light' and 'shield', the sphere of God's assistance is made specific (v. 30); he is given help to conquer an army and 'leap over a wall' (NRSV, preferred to the many other translations suggested). A break in the sequence of thought occurs with the introduction of v. 32; it is a monotheistic outburst in the same vein as Deutero-Isaiah (cf. Isa 43:11; 44:6, 8; 45:21) and must be regarded as a later expansion. The theme of vv. 30–1 is continued in vv. 33–43, which are mainly concerned with victory in warfare. The king has received strength (vv. 33a, 40), facility of access

(vv. 33b, 34, 37), and outstanding victory (vv. 38–9, 41–3). In these verses again his success is attributed to God's help; it is he who has given him strength and guidance. His victories have brought peoples (v. 44, following the LXX) to him, and it is obvious from vv. 45–6 that the reference is to foreign nations. The song reaches its climax with praise of God. David and his descendants are named only in the last phrase of the song, a feature paralleled in other victory songs (Hertzberg 1964); it is therefore to be regarded as original (cf. McCarter 1984) rather than a later addition (Veijola 1975).

(2 Sam 23:1–39) David's Last Words and a List of Warriors The poem in vv. 1–7 containing David's last words stands deliberately after the song of ch. 22, exactly as the blessing of Moses follows the song of Moses in Deut 32–3 (cf. Hertzberg 1964). It is not a blessing in the strict sense of the word, but concentrates on the covenant with the house of David and its continued prosperity. The opening words, identifying David as the speaker and his words as an oracle, are similar in structure to other OT opening formulae (cf. Num 24:3, 15; Prov 30:1). He is raised on high by God (following 4QSam^a) and is his 'favourite' (in preference to 'the sweet Psalmist of Israel', RSV, see Richardson 1971). A wisdom-saying with its own introduction (vv. 2–4) attributes to David a prophetic role because God's spirit speaks through him; it is a glorification of a just king. In vv. 3b–4 it is claimed that a just king is like the sun on a cloudless morning; its rays gleam through the rain and cause grass to sprout from the earth; his reign is as beneficial to his subjects as the morning sun. The metaphor of the sun is common in ancient Near-Eastern royal ideology, as for example in Egypt, where the solar god-king is the source of growth (cf. Mal 4:1–2a; McCarter 1984). In applying the metaphor to the house of David (vv. 5–7) it is asserted that he is this kind of ruler, as is testified by the everlasting covenant God made with him. The 'everlasting covenant' (bĕrît ʿōlām) was the promise of a dynasty made to David through Nathan (2 Sam 7) and designates a relationship that was to last for ever (cf. also Ps 89:28; 132:12, etc.). Those disloyal to David ('the godless') are compared to worthless thorns which are cast away and burnt on a fire. A contrast is drawn between the loyal subjects of the just king, who enjoy the benefits of his rule as the grass benefits from the sun, and his disloyal subjects, who are no better than uprooted thorns cast on a fire.

It is difficult to date David's last words; some favour a monarchical date, even the Davidic period (Richardson 1971; Cross 1973), but others argue for the period of Hezekiah or Josiah. On the whole it can be said that there are no compelling reasons for rejecting an early monarchical dating for it.

The list of David's warriors in vv. 8–39 is not without its difficulties, and the various sections of it must be separated. It begins with the exploits of 'the Three' (so the LXX and Vulgate), whose names are given (vv. 8b–12, possibly concluded in v. 17b). Josheb-basshebeth was the chief of the three, and he, like the other two, had probably been victorious against the Philistines (cf. 1 Chr 11:11). The second, Eleazar, had also distinguished himself in battle against the Philistines (vv. 9–10), for, when the Israelites were driven back, he stood his ground and won a great victory. The third, Shammah, likewise repelled a Philistine attack during the harvest of

lentils (vv. 11–12). The Three did not belong to the Thirty, but are named as a special group. The 'three of the thirty' in vv. 13–17a are not to be identified with the previous three. The episode associated with them is probably linked with the advance of the Philistines to Rephaim mentioned in 2 Sam 5:17–21. Their exploit was to break through the Philistine ranks to obtain water for David from the well of Bethlehem. Realizing his mistake in causing them to risk their lives, David poured the water on the ground and called it 'blood' (cf. Lev 17:10–13; Deut 12:23–4). The status of Abishai and Benaiah is not clear, the former being called 'chief of the Thirty' and the 'most renowned' of them, and the latter was among the Thirty but did not attain to the status of the Three (vv. 18–23). Their membership of the Thirty is uncertain, caused possibly by the fluidity of the list with the course of time and by casualties. The status of these two seems to be somewhere between the Three and the Thirty.

Asahel is the first name on the list of Thirty beginning in v. 24. If Abishai and Benaiah are included, the list has a total of thirty-three names, and it is debatable if 'thirty' was more than a round number, and again if 'thirty' was a particularly significant number because of a 'host of thirty' in Pharaoh's court. It is also debatable if the list in vv. 24–39 is arranged geographically, with the places listed in vv. 24–35 being close to Bethlehem, and those in vv. 36–9 being non-Israelite.

(2 Sam 24:1–25) A Census and a Plague The plague story at the end of the collection balances the famine story at its beginning; in both cases the catastrophe is caused by divine anger in response to a transgression by the king.

The pestilence troubling Israel was a punishment for the census (v. 15), which was regarded as a sin (v. 10). But v. 1 suggests that God had invited David to count the people. A possible solution of this difficulty is that David was incited by God so that he could punish Israel for a sin committed previously. The difficulty is avoided by the Chronicler, who states that it was Satan who incited David to count the people (1 Chr 21:1). Whatever the solution, it is obvious that the census was the reason for the plague. Several reasons for this have been suggested. One is that it was an introduction to a fiscal organization or military conscription (Bright 1972), and therefore a sign that David was moving towards self-sufficiency; possibly Joab sensed the danger of this move from a charismatic levy to a human organization (v. 3; Hertzberg 1964). Another reason is that there was a religious taboo on counting heads (cf. Ex 30:11–16), or more probably on recording names, some connecting this with regulations governing ritual purification (Speiser 1958). The reference in v. 9 to those 'able to draw the sword' (cf. Num 1:2–3) indicates that it was an enrolment for military service, and that possibly rules of purity had been neglected (cf. Josh 3:5; Deut 23:9–14). The choice given to David through the prophet Gad (vv. 11–14) raises questions about the composition of the narrative. He had to choose between three possible punishments, varying from three years to three days, but on a reverse scale of intensity. David left it to Gad to choose (v. 15), although the LXX attributes the choice of pestilence to David himself. It has been suggested that the plague story in vv. 11b–17 was an independent folk-tale; its motif was the choice of three punishments and theophany (Schmid 1970). Others have presented a more complicated picture of the narrative's growth from a very simple original account of a census (vv. 2, 4b, 8–9), followed by a plague (v. 15c), and then David's repentance leading to a commission to build an altar (vv. 17–19) (cf. Fuss 1962).

David's purchase of Araunah's threshing-floor (vv. 18–25) constitutes the third section, and has been called an aetiological narrative explaining the presence of an altar which became the site of Solomon's temple, cf. also the pillar at Bethel (Gen 28:11–22) and the altar at Ophrah (Judg 6:11–24). Araunah, a Jebusite, was one of the original inhabitants of Jerusalem before its conquest by David (see OCB), and the non-Semitic form of his name given in the MT is possibly older than Ornan in Chronicles and Orna in the LXX. The text does not claim that Araunah's threshing-floor was originally a Jebusite sanctuary, although traditionally a threshing-floor was a site of theophany (Judg 6:37) and a place for receiving divine messages (2 Kings 22:10); this was also the case at Ugarit (see McCarter 1984). But it was the appearance of an angel (v. 16) and the erection of an altar (vv. 18, 25) that made it a sanctuary. David's conversation with Araunah is reminiscent of Abraham's negotiations with the Hittites for the purchase of the cave of Machpelah (Gen 23). In both cases the offer of a gift was rejected and a formal purchase made; 1 Chr 21:24 makes it explicit that a gift from a non-Israelite could not be accepted, for it was to become the site of the Jerusalem temple. David's action was acceptable and the plague was averted (v. 25).

The placing of this chapter at the end of the appendices and of 2 Samuel is no accident. It may have belonged originally to earlier sections of the book, possibly to the account of the conquest of Jerusalem in 5:6–10 or to the arrival of the ark in Jerusalem (ch. 6). On the one hand it confirms the critical stance taken elsewhere towards David; on two occasions he declares himself a sinner (vv. 10, 17), and therefore punishment was inevitable (v. 13). On the other hand, David responds to God's invitation, made known to him through the prophet Gad, and this leads to the erection of an altar offering pleasing sacrifice to God. It is a forward-looking narrative, for the erection of a holocaust altar on Araunah's threshing-floor was in preparation for the building of Solomon's temple.

REFERENCES

Ackroyd, P. R. (1971), *The First Book of Samuel*, CBC (Cambridge: Cambridge University Press).

——(1977), *The Second Book of Samuel*, CBC (Cambridge: Cambridge University Press).

——(1975), 'The Verb Love—'*āhēb* in the David-Jonathan Narratives—a Footnote', *VT* 25: 213–14.

Albright, W. F. (1968), *Yahweh and the Gods of Canaan* (Garden City, NY: Doubleday).

Alt, A. (1968), *Essays on Old Testament History and Religion*, tr. R. A. Wilson (Garden City, NY: Doubleday).

Ben-Barak, Z. (1979), 'The Legal Background to the Restoration of Michal to David', in J. A. Emerton (ed.), *Studies in the Historical Books of the Old Testament*, VTSup 30: 15–29.

Birch, B. C. (1971), 'The Development of the Tradition on the Anointing of Saul in 1 Sam 9:1–10:16', *JBL* 90: 55–68.

——(1975), 'The Choosing of Saul at Mizpah', *CBQ* 37: 447–57.

——(1976), *The Rise of the Israelite Monarchy: The Growth and Development of 1 Samuel 7–15*, SBLDS 27 (Missoula: Scholars Press).

Blenkinsopp, J. (1964), 'Jonathan's Sacrilege, 1 Sam 14, 1–46: A Study in Literary History', *CBQ* 26: 423–49.

——(1966), 'Theme and Motif in the Succession History (2 Sam xi 2 ff.) and the Yahwist Corpus', *Volume du Congrès, Genève 1965*, VTSup 44–57.

——(1969a), 'Kiriath-jearim and the Ark', *JBL* 88: 143–56.

——(1969b), '1 and 2 Samuel', in R. C. Fuller (ed.), *A New Catholic Commentary on Holy Scripture* (London: Nelson), 305–27.

——(1974), 'Did Saul Make Gibeon his Capital?', *VT* 24: 1–7.

Boecker, H. J. (1969), *Die Beurteilung der Anfänge des Königtums in den deuteronomistischen Abschnitten des ersten Samuelisbuches*, WMANT 31 (Neukirchen-Vluyn: Neukirchener Verlag).

Boer, P. A. H. de (1938), *Research into the Text of 1 Samuel i–xvi* (Amsterdam: H. J. Paris).

——(1949), 'Research into the Text of 1 Samuel xviii–xxxi', *OTS* 6: 1–100.

Brauner, R. A. (1974), '"To Grasp the Hem" and 1 Samuel 15:27', *JANESCU* 6: 35–8.

Bright, J. (1972), *A History of Israel*, 2nd edn., OTL (London: SCM).

Campbell, A. F. (1975), *The Ark Narrative (1 Sam 4–6, 2 Sam 6): Form-Critical and Traditio-Historical Study*, SBLDS 16 (Missoula: Scholars Press).

Carlson, R. A. (1964), *David, the Chosen King: A Traditio-Historical Approach to the Second Book of Samuel* (Stockholm: Almqvist & Wiksell).

Childs, B. S. (1979), *Introduction to the Old Testament as Scripture* (London: SCM).

Clements, R. E. (1974), 'The Deuteronomistic Interpretation of the Founding of the Monarchy in 1 Sam VIII', *VT* 24: 398–410.

Cohen, H. H. (1965), 'David and Bathsheba', *JBR* 33: 142–8.

Conroy, C. C. (1978), *Absalom Absalom! Narrative and Language in 2 Sam 13–20*, AnBib 81 (Rome: Pontifical Biblical Institute).

Cross, F. M. (1953a), 'A New Qumran Biblical Fragment Related to the Original Hebrew Underlying the Septuagint', *BASOR* 132: 15–26.

——(1953b), 'A Royal Song of Thanksgiving: 2 Sam 22 = Psalm 18', *JBL* 72: 15–34.

——(1955), 'The Oldest Manuscripts from Qumran', *JBL* 74: 147–72.

——(1973), *Canaanite Myth and Hebrew Epic: Essays in the History of the Religion of Israel* (Cambridge, Mass.: Harvard University Press).

Crüsemann, F. (1978), *Der Widerstand gegen das Königtum: Die antiköniglichen Texte des Alten Testaments und der Kampf um den frühen israelitischen Staat*, WMANT 49 (Neukirchen-Vluyn: Neukirchener Verlag).

——(1980), 'Zwei alttestamentliche Witze: 1 Sam 21:11–15 und 2 Sam 6:16, 20–23', *ZAW* 92: 215–27.

Dietrich, W. (1972), *Prophetie und Geschichte: Eine redaktionsgeschichtliche Untersuchung zum deuteronomistischen Geschichtswerk*, FRLANT 108 (Göttingen: Vandenhoeck & Ruprecht).

Driver, G. R. (1962), 'Plurima Mortis Imago', in M. Ben-Horin et al. (eds.), *Studies and Essays in Honor of Abraham A. Neuman* (Leiden: Brill).

Driver, S. R. (1913), *Notes on the Hebrew Text of the Books of Samuel*, 2nd rev. edn. (Oxford: Clarendon).

Dus, J. (1968), 'Die Geburtslegende Samuels, 1 Sam 1 (Eine traditionsgeschichtliche Untersuchung zu 1 Sam 1–3)', *RSO* 43: 163–94.

Edelman, D. V. (1991), *King Saul in the Historiography of Judah*, JSOTSup 121 (Sheffield: Academic Press).

Eissfeldt, O. (1965), *The Old Testament: An Introduction*, tr. P. R. Ackroyd (Oxford: Blackwell).

Fensham, F. C. (1964), 'The Treaty between Israel and the Gibeonites', *BA* 27: 96–100.

——(1970), 'The Battle between the Men of Joab and Abner as a Possible Ordeal by Battle?', *VT* 20: 356–7.

Fishbane, M. (1982), '1 Samuel 3: Historical Narrative and Narrative Politics', in K. R. R. Gros Louis (ed.), *Literary Interpretations of Biblical Narratives*, ii (Nashville: Abingdon).

Flanagan, J. W. (1972), 'Court History or Succession Document? A Study of 2 Samuel 9–20 and 1 Kings 1–2', *JBL* 91: 172–81.

Fuss, W. (1962), '2 Samuel 24', *ZAW* 74: 145–64.

Gerleman, G. (1977), 'Schuld und Sühne: Erwägungen zu 2 Sam 12', in H. Donner *et al.* (eds.), Beiträge zur *alttestamentliche Theologie, Festschrift für Walther Zimmerli* (Göttingen: Vandenhoeck & Ruprecht), 132–9.

Giveon, R. (1964), ' "The Cities of Our God" (2 Sam 10:12)', *JBL* 83: 415–16.

Gnuse, R. (1982), 'A Reconsideration of the Form-Critical Structure in 1 Samuel 3: An Ancient Near Eastern Dream Theophany', *ZAW* 94: 379–90.

Gordon, R. P. (1984), *1 & 2 Samuel*, Old Testament Guides (Sheffield: JSOT).

——(1986), *I & II Samuel: A Commentary*, Library of Biblical Interpretation (Grand Rapids, Mich.: Zondervan).

Grønbaek, J. H. (1971), *Die Geschichte vom Aufstieg Davids (1 Sam 15–2 Sam 5): Tradition und Komposition*, ATDan 10 (Copenhagen: Munksgaard).

Gunn, D. M. (1976), 'Traditional Composition in the "Succession Narrative" ', *VT* 26: 214–19.

——'Narrative Patterns and Oral Tradition in Judges and Samuel', *VT* 24: 286–317.

——(1978), *The Story of King David: Genre and Interpretation*, JSOTSup 6 (Sheffield: JSOT).

——(1980), *The Fate of King Saul*, JSOTSup 14 (Sheffield: JSOT).

Hermann, S. (1953–4), 'Die Königsnovelle in Ägypten und in Israel', *Wissenschaftliche Zeitschrift der Karl-Marx-Universität, Leipzig*, 3: 51–62.

Hertzberg, H. W. (1964), *1 and 2 Samuel: A Commentary*, tr. J. S. Bowden, OTL (London: SCM).

Hoftijzer, J. (1970), 'David and the Tekoite Woman', *VT* 20: 419–44.

Honeyman, A. M. (1948), 'The Evidence for Regnal Names among the Hebrews', *JBL* 67: 13–25.

Ishida, T. (1977), *The Royal Dynasties in Ancient Israel: A Study on the Formation and Development of Royal Dynastic Ideology*, BZAW 142 (Berlin: de Gruyter).

Jobling, D. (1976), 'Saul's Fall and Jonathan's Rise: Tradition and Redaction in 1 Samuel 14: 1–46', *JBL* 95: 367–76.

Jones, G. H. (1984), *1 and 2 Kings*, NCB Commentary, 2 vols. (Grand Rapids, Mich.: Eerdmans).

——(1990), *The Nathan Narratives*, JSOTSup 80 (Sheffield: JSOT).

Kapelrud, A. S. (1955), 'King and Fertility: A Discussion of 2 Sam 21: 1–14', *NTT* 56: 113–22.

Kenyon, K. M. (1974), *Digging Up Jerusalem* (London: Benn).

Levenson, J. D. (1978), '1 Samuel 25 as Literature and History', *CBQ* 40: 11–28.

l'Heureux, C. (1976), 'The *yᵉlîdê hārāpā*—A Cultic association of Warriors', *BASOR* 221: 83–5.

Long, V. P. (1989), *The Reign and Rejection of King Saul: A Case for Literary and Theological Coherence*, SBLDS 118 (Atlanta: Scholars Press).

McCarter, P. K. (1980), *1 Samuel*, AB 8 (Garden City, NY: Doubleday).

——(1984), *2 Samuel*, AB 9 (Garden City, NY: Doubleday).

Malamat, A. (1955), 'Doctrines of Causality in Biblical and Hittite Historiography: A Parallel', *VT* 5: 1–12.

——(1958), 'The Kingdom of David and Solomon in its Contact with Egypt and Aram Naharaim', *BA* 21: 96–102.

——(1963), 'Aspects of the Foreign Policies of David and Solomon', *JNES* 22: 1–17.

Mayes, A. D. H. (1977), 'The Reign of Saul', in J. H. Hayes and J. M. Miller (eds.), *Israelite and Judaean History*, OTL (London: SCM), 322–31.

Mazar, B. (1962), 'The Aramaean Empire and Its Relations with Israel', *BA* 25: 98–120.

Mendelsohn, I. (1956), 'Samuel's Denunciation of Kingship in the Light of the Akkadian Documents from Egypt', *BASOR* 143: 17–22.

Mettinger, T. N. D. (1976), *King and Messiah: The Civil and Sacral Legitimation of the Israelite Kings*, ConBOT 8 (Lund: Gleerup).

Miller, P. D., and Roberts, J. M. M. (1977), *The Hand of the Lord: A Reassessment of the 'Ark Narrative' of 1 Samuel* (Baltimore: Johns Hopkins University Press).

Muilenburg, J. (1959), 'The Form and Structure of Covenant Formulations', *VT* 9: 347–65.

Nelson, R. D. (1981), *The Double Redaction of the Deuteronomistic History*, JSOTSup 18 (Sheffield: JSOT).

Newman, M. (1962), 'The Prophetic Call of Samuel', in B. W. Anderson and W. Harrelson (eds.), *Israel's Prophetic Heritage* (London: SCM).

Nicholson, E. W. (1967), *Deuteronomy and Tradition* (Oxford: Blackwell).

Noth, M. (1960), *The History of Israel*, tr. P. R. Ackroyd (London: A. & C. Black).

——(1981), *The Deuteronomistic History*, JSOTSup 15 (Sheffield: JSOT). German original, *Überlieferungsgeschichtliche Studien*, I (Tübingen: Max Niemeyer, 1943).

Porter, J. R. (1954), 'The Interpretation of 2 Samuel vi and Psalm cxxxii', *JTS* 5: 161–73.

Richardson, H. N. (1971), 'The Last Words of David: Some Notes on 2 Sam 23:1–7', *JBL* 90, 257–66.

Rost, L. (1982), *The Succession to the Throne of David* (Sheffield: Almond). German original, *Die Überlieferung von der Thronnachfolge Davids*, BWANT 3/6 (Stuttgart: Kohlhammer, 1926).

Schicklberger, F. (1973), *Die Ladeerzählungen des ersten Samuel-Buches: Eine literaturwissenschaftliche und theologiegeschichtliche Untersuchung*, FB 7 (Würzburg: Echter).

Schmid, H. (1970), 'Der Tempelbau Salomos in religionsgeschichtlicher Sicht', in A. Kuschke and E. Kutsch (eds.), *Archäologie und Altes Testament: Festschrift für Kurt Galling* (Tübingen: Mohr), 241–50.

Soggin, J. A. (1977), 'The Davidic-Solomonic Kingdom', in J. H. Hayes and J. M. Miller (eds.), *Israelite and Judaean History*, OTL (London: SCM), 332–80.

Speiser, E. A. (1958), 'Census and Ritual Expiation in Mari and Israel', *BASOR* 149: 171–6.

Stoebe, H. J. (1973), *Das erste Buch Samuelis*, KAT 8/1 (Gütersloh: Gütersloher Verlagshaus).

Thomas, D. W. (1960), 'KELEBH "Dog": Its Origin and Some Usages of it in the Old Testament', *VT* 10: 410–27.

Thompson, J. A. (1974), 'The Significance of the Verb "Love" in the David–Jonathan Narratives in 1 Samuel', *VT* 24: 334–8.

Timm, H. (1966), 'Die Ladeerzählung (1 Sam 4–6; 2 Sam 6) und das Kerygma des deuteronomistischen Geschichtswerks', *EvT* 26: 509–26.

Tov, E. (1979), 'The Textual Affiliations of 4QSamᵃ', *JSOT* 14: 37–53.

Tsevat, M. (1958), 'Marriage and Monarchical Legitimacy in Ugarit and Israel', *JSS* 3: 237–43.

Ulrich, E. C. (1978), *The Qumran Text of Samuel and Josephus*, HSM (Missoula: Scholars Press).

Veijola, T. (1975), *Die ewige Dynastie: David und die Entstehung seiner Dynastie nach der deuteronomistischen Darstellung*, Annales Academiae Scientiarum Fennicae B 193 (Helsinki: Suomalainen Tiedeakatemia).

——(1977), *Das Königtum in der Beurteilung der deuteronomistischen Historiographie: Eine redaktionsgeschichtliche Untersuchung*, Annales Academiae Scientiarum Fennicae, B 198 (Helsinki: Suomalainen Tiedeakatemia).

——(1979), 'Salomo—der Erstgeborene Bathsebas', in J. A. Emerton (ed.), *Studies in the Historical Books of the Old Testament*, VTSup 30 (Leiden: Brill), 230–50.

von Rad, G. (1951), *Der heilige Krieg in alten Israel*, ATANT 20 (Zurich: Zwingli).

——(1966), 'The Beginnings of Historical Writing in Ancient Israel', *The Problem of the Hexateuch and Other Essays* (Edinburgh: Oliver & Boyd), 166–204.

Wallis, G. (1952), 'Eine Parallele zu Richter 19:29 ff und 1 Sam 11:5 ff aus dem Briefarchiv von Mari', *ZAW* 64: 57–61.

Weinfeld, M. (1972), *Deuteronomy and the Deuteronomic School* (Oxford: Clarendon).

Weiser, A. (1962), *Samuel: Seine geschichtliche Aufgabe und religiöse Bedeutung: Traditionsgeschichtliche Untersuchungen zu 1 Samuel 7–12*, FRLANT 81 (Göttingen: Vandenhoeck & Ruprecht).

Wellhausen, J. (1871), *Der Text der Bücher Samuelis untersucht* (Göttingen: Vandenhoeck & Ruprecht).

Whybray, R. N. (1968), *The Succession Narrative: A Study of 2 Sam 9–20 and 1 Kings 1 and 2*, SBT 9 (London: SCM).

Willis, J. T. (1971), 'An Anti-Elide Narrative Tradition from a Prophetic Circle at the Ramah Sanctuary', *JBL* 90: 288–308.

—— (1972), 'Cultic Elements in the Story of Samuel's Birth and Dedication', *ST* 26: 33–61.

—— (1973), 'The Song of Hannah and Psalm 113', *CBQ* 35: 139–54.

—— (1979), 'Samuel Versus Eli, 1 Sam 1–7', *TZ* 35: 201–12.

Wolff, H. W. (1964), *Amos' geistige Heimat*, WMANT 18 (Neukirchen-Vluyn: Neukirchener Verlag).

Wright, G. E. (1962), 'The Lawsuit of God: A Form-Critical Study of Deuteronomy 32', in B. W. Anderson and W. Harrelson (eds.), *Israel's Prophetic Heritage* (London: SCM), 26-67.

13. 1 and 2 Kings

WALTER DIETRICH

INTRODUCTION

A. Literary and Religious Character. 1. The books of Kings contain the history of Israel and Judah from the time of King Solomon to the period of exile, i.e. from the middle of the tenth to the middle of the sixth century BCE. They cover the entire duration of the state of Israel apart from the reigns of its first two kings, Saul and David, who feature in the books of Samuel. Israel existed before and after this period without being a state. According to the Bible, it was present as the people of the God YHWH long before it became politically organized—indeed, even before it had its own land—and remained so during its period as a state; it continued even after the two states founded on that land had been destroyed by great oriental powers and a large number of their citizens dispersed abroad. Monarchical constitution was more or less merely an experiment in the history of the people of God: one that partly succeeded impressively, but which finally failed. The biblical history of the four long and eventful centuries is described in such a way that light and darkness are in constant alternation—where, however, light predominates at the beginning and darkness overwhelms at the end. The impression is given of an unstoppable, increasing decline terminating in exile.

2. Several eras can be distinguished during this period of history: the era of the united kingdom under Solomon in the tenth century (1 Kings 1–11), the era of the two kingdoms of Israel and Judah from 926 to 722 BCE (1 Kings 12–2 Kings 17) and the era of the remaining kingdom of Judah between 722 and 587 or 562 BCE (2 Kings 18–25). The history of the two great Israelite dynasties of Omri (1 Kings 16–2 Kings 8) and Jehu (2 Kings 9–15) emerges from the lengthy middle era. There is a stylistic variation between passages which are narrated in an attractive and detailed manner (1 Kings 1–3; 10–12; 17–22; 2 Kings 1–11; 18–20) and those in which information is passed on in a sober and curtailed form (1 Kings 4–9; 13–16; 2 Kings 12–17; 21–5). In the narrative, the prophets gradually replace the kings as protagonists. Indeed the history of Israel seems to be as much the story of its prophets as the story of its kings.

3. The colourful diversity of the narrative and historical information is all held together by a structure which repeatedly reorientates the reader within a sequence of time. As a rule, each king is introduced at the time of his accession to the throne with an introductory formula and taken leave of with a concluding formula on his death. This so-called king-frame almost always includes the same formulae with slight standard variations between the northern and southern kingdoms (apart from exceptional cases showing larger variations).

The King-Frame

Introductory formula:

- synchronized date reference ('X/Israel became king in the year of Y/Judah')
- age at accession (only with kings of Judah)
- length of reign (including the year of accession and co-reign, if applicable)
- name of the queen mother (only with kings of Judah)
- religious judgement (using the first commandment as a guideline)

Concluding formula:

- source reference (often including special events and accomplishments)
- acknowledgement of death
- statement on funeral 'with the fathers' (only with kings of Judah)
- naming and accession of the successor

The introductory formula almost always includes a verdict on the relevant king. Grades ranging from the extremes, 'He did what was evil in the sight of the LORD' and 'He did what was right in the sight of the LORD', were handed out. For this verdict, kings were not assessed on their political accomplishments, but on their attitude towards the commandment requiring the exclusive worship of YHWH. Right from the beginning, the northern kings bear the heavy burden of maintaining state sanctuaries in Bethel and Dan, in the south and north of the country, and later even in the capital Samaria, which, according to the authors of the Bible, had heathen influences or were in fact heathen. It was only possible to worship YHWH properly in the temple of Jerusalem, which was naturally accessible only to the kings of Judah. Inevitably, many Judean kings described in the Bible did not confine themselves to this one holy site, but also maintained or tolerated 'high places', holy places in Judah. Some are said to have paganized even the temple in Jerusalem.

4. Thus the religious line of the books of Kings is that the temple of Jerusalem is the only legitimate place to worship YHWH, evidenced by the number of reports on the building, its decoration and maintenance, its occasional plundering, and the final destruction of this house of God. All points clearly to a specific period in the religious history of Israel: in 621 BCE, King Josiah carried out cultic reforms the core of which centralized the cult at Jerusalem (cf. 2 Kings 22–3). Such reforms relate to the corresponding order of law in Deut 12. Their object was to ensure that the entire people of Judah serve YHWH alone and no other god. The first commandment, 'I am the LORD your God . . . you shall have no other gods before me' (Deut 5:6–7) was given prominence. The authors of Kings in effect reviewed the history of Israel and evaluated each king on the grounds of his adherence to the first commandment, ordering exclusive worship of YHWH. Josiah receives an especially good rating (2 Kings 22:2; 23:25); in fact all his predecessors and his few successors are compared to him and his actions. In this way the fall of the state of Judah in 587 BCE is seen (like the fall of the kingdom of Israel in 722 BCE) as the result of countless breaches of the first commandment.

B. Authorship and Sources. 1. Since the verdict on the kings was rigidly integrated into the king-frames which form the skeletal structure of Kings, the latter cannot have been written before the time of Josiah. Whilst researchers agree on this basic point, variations have been discussed. Was there in fact one single author who described the history of the kings (and beyond this a greater work about the history of Israel from the time of Moses) during the period of exile under the influence of the catastrophe in 587 BCE (as in Noth 1991; Hoffmann 1980)? Or did an underlying text with an optimistic tendency already exist at the time of Josiah which was reworked during the period of exile, giving it a basic tone of pessimism (as in Cross 1973; Nelson 1981)? Or was an underlying text mainly confined to historiographical aims reworked at the end of and after the period of exile, from the perspective of prophecy and the Torah (as in Smend 1989; Veijola 1982; Dietrich 1972)?

2. In each case, the authors of the entire text of 1 and 2 Kings are Deuteronomists in so far as they are marked by Deuteronomy and Deuteronomic thought, especially by the basic Deuteronomic creed that 'The LORD is our God, the LORD alone' (Deut 6:4). Their way of thinking and working, their comments, and their written texts can therefore be called Deuteronomistic. They wrote the history of Israel with the intention of making it transparent and understandable to themselves and their contemporaries and to declare it meaningful and guided by God. The internal motivation driving all external events is Israel and Judah's relationship to their God who chose his people, leading them strictly and lovingly through the ages and demanding to be their one single God, worthy of all respect and love. In this Commentary the Deuteronomistic theologians of history, to whom we owe the books of Kings, are often simply referred to as 'the editors' for the sake of brevity.

3. The Deuteronomists used specific sources, by no means merely writing Kings as they felt appropriate, let alone freely inventing it. In this way they were true historians whose work is not an original essay or fiction, but a work of tradition (Noth 1991). The authors took older, historically orientated extant sources, checked them, noted excerpts, sorted them, commented on and added to them, and thus created a running chronology of events from the tenth century BCE (or the thirteenth, if one includes Deuteronomy, Joshua, Judges, and Samuel) up to the sixth century BCE, i.e. from the beginning of the state (from the occupation of the land) to its collapse (or to the loss of the land).

4. One especially important source was the 'Books of the Annals of the Kings of Israel/Judah', which were referred to in the concluding formula of almost every king. The historical information for the framing formula is taken from these books. These Annals seem to have been kept in both royal courts (by the end, naturally, only in Judah), and contained the names and dates of each king as well as short reports of important events occurring during the time of his reign. The authors of Kings chose sections of the Annals which seemed to them to be of especial importance. Such reports remained partly in the concluding formulae of a frame, were also placed into the corresponding narrative about that king, or were enhanced with other, primarily prophetic sources. It is possible that the Judean Annals also included reports from the temple at Jerusalem, which after all stood on the palace grounds, though perhaps temple registers were used as a separate source. These known sources seem to have been written in a rather sober style and are likely to be historically reliable—individual mistakes, a certain pro-palace slant, or an occasional erroneous transcript by the Deuteronomists excepted.

5. Another much more clearly biased source is the obviously pro-Solomon 'Book of the Acts of Solomon', named in 1 Kings 11:41. A large number of the reports in 1 Kings 3–11 seem to have stemmed from it. Besides pure information (e.g. about the districts of government in 1 Kings 4:7–20), it also included elaborate and colourful narrative (e.g. Solomon's dream revelation and wise verdict in 1 Kings 3). It should perhaps be placed in the eighth century (Wälchli 1996), although older material was also used. The report of Solomon's accession to power (1 Kings 1–2) seems to have been taken from another source which was already used in Samuel: a longer narrative of the transition of power from Saul to David and then from David to Solomon. This narrative is outstanding literature, but paints a much less glowing picture of the kingdom than the story of Solomon that followed it.

6. The Deuteronomists could also draw from a wealth of prophetic tradition. There were first the stories of Elijah (1 Kings 17–19) and Elisha (2 Kings 2–8), which were probably bound together with other stories of prophets (1 Kings 20; 22), and the story of the *coup d'état* of Jehu (2 Kings 9–10) in a larger narrative about the struggle of the prophets of Israel and Judah against Baal (1 Kings 17–2 Kings 10, cf. Dietrich 1998). This may have been produced in the seventh century, although the collected stories within it partly go back as far as the eighth and even ninth centuries. Beyond this there was a collection of legends concerning the prophet Isaiah and King Hezekiah during the Assyrian crisis around 701 BCE (2 Kings 18:17–20:19). This collection, which was entirely transcribed from Kings into Isa 36–9, was probably written in stages and not integrated into the Deuteronomistic History text at a single point in time (Camp 1990). Its oldest part is the underlying story, 2 Kings 18:17–19:9, 36–7, which, according to a plausible theory, was produced during the period of crisis shortly before 587 BCE (Hardmeier 1990). Beyond this is a series of individual prophetic stories scattered across the entire Deuteronomistic work which repeatedly contain conflicts between prophets and kings (e.g. 1 Kings 14; 21; 2 Kings 1). These may have been taken from a collection of prophet stories which were quite critical of the kings and were written in the late pre-exilic period (Dietrich 1992) in order to serve as a less pro-monarchical reworking of the historical text. A number of speeches by the prophets (e.g. 1 Kings 16:1–4; 2 Kings 9:7–10a; 21:10–15) were probably written in a prophetic-Deuteronomistic style with this in mind.

7. All the prophetic material is without exception written in a narrative style. Collections of words and speeches attributed to individual prophets did not find their way into the Deuteronomistic History, but were put together into books of their own. Thus the absence of Amos, Hosea, Micah, and Jeremiah in the Deuteronomistic narrative is not surprising and does not point to a tendency against prophecies of woe (as suggested by Albertz 1992). What the prophets said and experienced had been documented elsewhere. This did not need to be duplicated in a historical work and would in any case have been too extensive to do so. The tone of the Deuteronomistic History (as well as Deuteronomy itself) is deeply influenced by prophecy, as can be seen throughout the historical narrative. On the other hand there are dates quoted from the Deuteronomistic History and there is a Deuteronomistic slant noticeable in the subsequent editing of many books of prophets, and indeed the entire prophet-canon.

C. Historical Nature. 1. This theological perspective, which one could call Deuteronomic-prophetic, does not distort the Deuteronomists' view of historic events and processes. One can see how poetic, symbolic, and kerygmatic the pure prophetic historical perspective is by studying Am 4:6–12, Isa 2:6–22; 22:1–14; Ezek 16. By contrast the Deuteronomists are true historians: administrators of historical facts which are kept and passed on simply because they had been transmitted. They are naturally far from a modern historian's ideal. They do not pretend to report things objectively as they truly happened. This idea is in any case impossible and smacks of ideology. The Deuteronomists do not hide the fact that they *interpret* history from a certain standpoint, but they also *document* it! The strictly chronological structure of the work in itself bears witness to its truly historical nature. The closely bound narrative block about Elijah and Elisha (1 Kings 17–19 + 2 Kings 2–8, 13:14–21) is broken up so that it can be sorted into the king-frames in smaller parts. Even kings who reigned for only a few months and about whom little can be reported apart from their short existence, are listed carefully so that the succession of kings, as found in the sources, remained complete. Furthermore, unpleasant and embarrassing events were not concealed: for instance Solomon's sale of Israelite villages and cities to the Phoenicians (1 Kings 9:11), the political folly leading to the partition of the kingdom (1 Kings 12), Elijah's lack of courage (1 Kings 19:3–4), poor recognition of the prophets (2 Kings 9:11), the peaceful death of evil kings and the violent death of good ones (1 Kings 22:40; 2 Kings 21:18; 23:29), the reign of the non-queen Athaliah (2 Kings 11) and the placing of heathen cult symbols in the temple of Jerusalem (2 Kings 21:3–5). It is true that the Deuteronomists tried to give such reports meaning in terms of their view of history, but the great effort exerted to do this does them credit.

2. The Deuteronomists only had a limited amount of source material at their disposal and used it only selectively. They were neither pedants nor accountants and had neither access to an inexhaustible archive, nor the will or the means to get over-involved in underlying research. They have in the past been accused of documenting history in an all too biased and incomplete way. Leaving aside the fact that it is unfair and irrelevant to judge an ancient work by modern standards, the fact remains: had the Deuteronomistic History not existed, we would not know countless details and many greater connections in the history of Israel and Judah. Even if it is currently fashionable (as it has occasionally been in the past) to place the historical reliability of the Bible as low as possible, the Deuteronomistic books of Kings especially are not only *stories*, but also *history*. This is due to the fact that the Deuteronomists quoted their sources in large parts of their narrative rather than writing something original themselves. Although the historical value of each case must be carefully and critically checked—a miracle story about Elisha cannot be given the same historical value as the list of Solomon's ministers or synchronized date references—they still deliver a lot of essential historical information.

3. The books of Kings offer us information which other (archaeological or non-biblical) sources say nothing about or perhaps only hint at: for example, that the Judean kingdom united two separate state structures, namely the land of Judah and the city-state of Jerusalem; or that the monarchies in Israel and in Judah had very different qualities—one being more or less legitimized by God, leading to an unshakeable ruling dynasty, and the other having a more democratic or tribal view of government, leading to a more frequent change of dynasties; or that critical prophecy, which became so important to the religious history of Israel in general and specifically for the exclusive worship of the God YHWH by Israel, initially emerged from northern Israel. It is of fundamental and inestimable value that the Deuteronomists created an unbroken chain of dated events from the establishment of the state (and even had the intention of spanning the time from the claiming of land) up to the time of the Exile. This allowed all those who followed them, beginning with the chroniclers and the editors of the books of prophets, moving on to Jewish and Christian interpreters right up to the present day, to place information (biblical and non-biblical text documents, archaeological finds, etc.) from the pre-exile period into a historical context and thereby fulfil a fundamental requirement of Israelite existence and Judeo-Christian religion, namely a historical basis. God's relationship to man is, according to biblical belief, not merely a spiritual and psychological process, but one that gains concrete form in space and time. This is evidenced for the first time in the history of this small and ancient oriental people of Israel. Thus the forty-seven chapters of 1 and 2 Kings form a fundamental episode in the humanization of God.

COMMENTARY

1 Kings

The first major section of the two books, 1 Kings 1:1–11:41, documents Solomon's reign over Judah and Israel.

Solomon's Accession to Power (1:1–2:46)

(1:1–4) David's Weakness and Old Age The opening scene of Kings shows King David as an old and impotent man, shivering with cold. Such a depiction of a highly respected king is probably unique in ancient historiography. No man is deified by the Bible, not even David. Even the beautiful young Abishag cannot arouse him, though she later turns the wheel of history significantly without us ever learning of one word or feeling from her (2:17, 22).

(1:5–10) The Parties in the Struggle for Succession to the Throne The time for David's succession seems to have arrived. Adonijah, who is the oldest of David's sons following the death of his brothers Amnon and Absalom (2 Sam 13; 18; cf. 2 Sam 3:2–5) announces his ambitions. Unfortunately he does it in precisely the same manner as Absalom had once done and failed (2 Sam 15:1). The narrator qualifies this behaviour negatively ('exalted himself'). David, whose motives are unclear, makes no comment on the activity. Is he simply too old? Adonijah seems to have understood the paternal silence as implied approval. He finds support with the leading personalities and classes in the land of Judah: with Joab, commander of the militia (cf. 2 Sam 20:23; 24:1–9), with Abiathar, a country priest and trusted old companion of David (cf. 1 Sam 22:20–3; 2 Sam 15:24–9), with Judean court civil servants and members of the royal family. Solomon, however, has ambitions of his own. Although he is only the tenth in the line of David's sons (cf. 2 Sam 3:2–5; 5:14–16) he has the political and military heavyweights of the city of Jerusalem on his side: the mercenary general Benaiah, with his élite troops stationed on the premises (2 Sam 20:23; 23:8–39), the high priest Zadok (2 Sam 15:24–9) and the prophet Nathan (2 Sam 7; 12). The situation is tense, particularly because Adonijah—as Absalom had once done (2 Sam 13:23–9; 15:7–12)—invites members of his party to a great feast at a well, probably in the valley of Kidron. We do not discover what he has in mind.

(1:11–37) David's Decision in Favour of Solomon The story unfolds within the confines of the palace walls. The narrator reports as if he were there at the time. Two people are constantly in dialogue as the drama of the ensuing events escalates: Nathan talks to Bathsheba (Solomon's mother, cf. 2 Sam 11–12), Bathsheba talks to David, David to Nathan, David to Bathsheba; finally David gives a firm order to Zadok, Nathan, and Benaiah: Solomon should be anointed king. Two questions remain open until the end: whether Adonijah actually allows himself to be proclaimed king, and whether David had really sworn an oath in favour of Solomon in the past. One thing, however, is finally certain. David abdicates to make way for Solomon. Again his motives are unclear. Has he been manipulated? Is he bound to his word? Has he more affection for Solomon than for Adonijah? Is he in favour of centralized state government, more likely under Solomon and his Jerusalem party than under Adonijah and his Judeans?

(1:38–53) Solomon's Accession to Power The anointing of Solomon takes place at the well of Gihon, just below the palace grounds. The Cherethites and Pelethites are present: David's powerful and readily available mercenary troop (see 2 Sam 15:18). The holy oil is brought from the tent in which the ark of the covenant stands (2 Sam 6:17). Solomon's accession thus has heavenly blessing. The people (are only soldiers present or are these the people of Jerusalem?) cheer in celebration. The noise strikes fear into the festive society of Adonijah. A trusted messenger, Jonathan ben Abiathar (cf. 2 Sam 17:17–21) brings the shocking news of Solomon's accession to the throne. Adonijah capitulates before the turn of events. He flees to the altar, certainly standing in the tent: the holiness of the latter will offer him amnesty (cf. Ex 21:13–14). Solomon promises him protection, though only on probation.

(2:1–12) David's Bequest to Solomon It is the first and last time that David and Solomon speak to each other, or more precisely that David speaks to Solomon. He first gives him a spiritual warning. He must keep the laws of YHWH. In Israel everyone, even the king, falls under God and his laws. The question whether the Davidic covenant in 2 Sam 7:11–16 is fulfilled depends on the king's loyalty to the Torah. The expression 'law of Moses' hints probably at Deuteronomy. vv. 1–4 are unmistakably Deuteronomistic (cf. Deut 6:1–3; Josh 1:1–9). Then the tone changes: David complains to the 'wise' Solomon about his enemies Joab and Shimei (cf. 2 Sam 3:27; 20:9–10; 16:5–14—but also 19:24) and incites him to murder. The ensuing wave of purges is thus clearly legitimized. Encouragement to reward the old Barzillai (v. 7, cf. 2 Sam 17:26–9; 19:32–9), can hardly brighten the bleak picture. David can now die in peace. He is buried in the 'city of David', i.e. the necropolis of the descendants of David on the Ophel Hill in Jerusalem, which is said to be visible still today in the form of some caves. David is reported to have reigned for forty years—a conspicuously round number. The seven years in Hebron (cf. 2 Sam 2–5) could be historically correct. The rest is probably an estimate.

(2:13–25) The Elimination of Adonijah Having remained quiet for some time, Adonijah begins to dig his own grave. He lusts after the beautiful Abishag of Shunam. This is dangerous, since she has, after all, lain in his father's bed. Proud and submissive at the same time, he first tells Bathsheba about his frustrated ambitions for the throne: now, all he wants is Abishag. Adonijah has correctly recognized the power and influence of the queen mother (as the ceremonial in v. 19 shows), but he fails to understand her intentions and character. She seems to champion Adonijah's cause, but by slipping in the phrase 'your brother', she rouses Solomon's guilty conscience and awakens his fears. The latter immediately orders Adonijah's execution and lets the unscrupulous Benaiah carry it out. To our consternation, Solomon refers to the Davidic covenant as justification: was it meant to be invoked in this way?

(2:26–7) The Elimination of Abiathar Solomon does not dare to harm David's trusted priest and successful minister. He does, however, relieve him of all his duties and send him into exile in Anathoth, a small country town about 5km north of Jerusalem. Jeremiah, who also originates from here (Jer 1:1; 32), could be his descendant. It is interesting that David mentions neither Abiathar nor Adonijah in his will. Their fate depends solely on Solomon.

(2:28–35) The Elimination of Joab Alarmed by the escalating purge, Joab flees to the holy tent. Even Benaiah is incapable of killing him at the altar. Joab cleverly refuses to leave the holy place. In irony, Solomon interprets the pathetic statement 'I will die here' literally. Benaiah murders Joab at the altar, following Solomon's explicit orders. This is a serious crime against Israel's religion and law. Even Solomon's justifying speech in vv. 31*b*–33 (which is attributable to the same author as 2:5–9, 24) cannot hide this fact. As a reward for his loyal service Benaiah takes over Joab's post as army chief, whilst Zadok (cf. 1:8, 10, 34, 39) becomes Abiathar's successor.

(2:36–46) The Elimination of Shimei Solomon plays a cruel game with Shimei, probably a former officer in the private guard who has switched sides from Solomon to Adonijah (cf. 1:8, 10), but who is linked here with the Benjaminite leader of 2 Sam 16:5–14 and 19:17–24. He places him under house-arrest only to sentence him to death when he is forced to leave his house. The author of vv. 44–5, the pro-Solomon, pro-dynastic thinker already known to us, gives Solomon's cynical condemnation (vv. 42–3) a religious justification. Once again Benaiah is the willing accomplice. The reader cannot feel pleased about the outcome that the kingdom is now firmly in Solomon's hands.

Solomon's Initial Acts as King (3:1–4:34)

(3:1) Marriage to the Pharaoh's daughter Remarkably, Solomon's first act as ruler is this obviously diplomatic marriage. Is such intermarriage a positive symbol of Solomon's importance? The Egyptian lady plays a surprisingly large role in the story of Solomon (cf. 7:8; 9:16; 11:1). However, an Ammonite will become the mother of his heir, not an Egyptian (14:21).

(3:2–3) A Religious Assessment of Solomon In this passage, we have the first beginnings of a king's assessment which the editors make of almost every following ruler. On the whole, Solomon receives a good rating. He 'loved' YHWH (just as YHWH loved him, 2 Sam 12:24). Solomon has, like many of his successors, weaknesses: there were in Judah 'high places', small sacrificial sites in or near individual towns, although, according to the Torah of Moses (Deut 12), only one place of worship was permitted, Jerusalem. But Solomon had not yet built his temple there.

(3:4–15) The Dream-Revelation in Gibeon Gibeon (today el-Jib, 8 km. north-west of Jerusalem) is traditionally seen by Israel as a heathen city (cf. Josh 9; 2 Sam 21:2). An important sanctuary was there dedicated to YHWH or perhaps to the sun-god Shemesh (cf. Josh 10:12–13). Solomon arranges a great sacrifice and remains overnight in the high place, perhaps with the intention of instigating a divine revelation. God does indeed appear to him and grants him a free wish—an age-old theme in fairy-tales and legends. Solomon shows modesty and insight. He requires great wisdom to rule, and wisdom is, according to the OT (e.g. Prov 2:6), a gift of God. God promises Solomon wisdom as well as everything else he did not wish for, but which the narrative describes him as having. This passage paints an extraordinarily positive picture of Solomon. The hand of the author of the Book of the Acts of Solomon (11:41) is especially noticeable in its praise of Solomon (vv. 12*b*, 13*b*) and Israel (vv. 8, 9*b*). In the passages regarding the Davidic covenant and loyalty to the Torah (vv. 6, 14), the editors are particularly tangible (Wälchli 1996). The original story shows a high regard for the importance of the dream. The beginning of v. 15 expresses no disappointment; quite the opposite, dreams are a legitimate method of discovering God's will (cf. Gen 28; 37; 1 Sam 28:6, 15; Joel 3:1; Dan 2; Mt 2:13). Such means are, of course, also open to abuse (cf. Jer 23:25–7; Zech 10:2, also Ps 73:20; in general Ehrlich 1953).

(3:16–28) Solomon's Judgement The wisdom granted Solomon in his dream is immediately put to effect in making an unusually clever court judgement. The king is confronted with an insoluble problem: claim against counter-claim without witnesses or evidence. Maternal love, however, in itself not a legally relevant factor, provides the key to truth and justice. Yet our admiration for Solomon's wisdom should not distract us from the fact that this is a repeated theme found in various cultures and used to make the sagacity of numerous judges famous (Gressmann 1907) right up to the character of Azdak in Bertolt Brecht's *Caucasian Chalk Circle*. What is unique about Solomon's version is that the argument about the child is not between two wives of one man (who would have had a decisive influence on the outcome), but between two prostitutes. Such *personae miserae* (who also include widows) are given special care by the community and above all by the king (cf. 2 Sam 14:4–10; 2 Kings 8:1–6). Solomon's praise in v. 28 again stems from the author of the story of Solomon.

(4:1–6) Solomon's Ministers A comparison with David's ministerial lists (2 Sam 8:16–18; 20:23–6) shows both the young monarchy's continuity and its development. The cabinet posts of 'forced labour' (Ado[ni]ram) and State Department (Jehoshaphat, his title literally meaning 'reminder') remain unchanged. Joab and Abiathar have been removed. Benaiah, who had moved up from the fifth to the second rank of importance under David, is the only military officer, although he is now ranked fourth. Zadok's son Azariah is solely in charge of religious policy and is first on the list. (v. 4*b* in which Zadok and Abiathar are listed as they used to be, beside each other, is probably a gloss.) David's 'secretary', administrator of the royal offices and archives, is replaced by two new officers. The number of ministers has generally increased as the administration has obviously become more complicated. Beyond the existing departments, the posts of 'chief of officials', the provincial governors (see 4:7–19), 'the king's friend' (probably the king's chief adviser and representative), and 'chief of the palace' (head administrator of the royal estate and its buildings) are created. It seems that Solomon has rewarded his party followers with high rank: not only for Benaiah, but also Zadok, Nathan, and their sons (assuming that the prophet Nathan is meant in v. 5). This kind of text is likely to have stemmed from the palace archive in Jerusalem and is therefore of great historical value.

(4:7–19) Israel's Provinces under Solomon This list describes the twelve regions of northern Israel: the most influential part of the Davidic-Solomonic kingdom. The city-state of Jerusalem and the land of Judah are not included, nor are foreign possessions. It is not entirely clear what purpose Israel's division into districts had: was it simply to mark out spheres of influence, in which Solomon ensured loyalty through trusted representatives (see Niemann 1993)? Or were they provinces with strict borders that were expected to pay fixed duties at regular intervals to the royal court (see 4:8, 27) as well as provide forced labour (cf. 9:23)? According to Alt's (1964*a*) analysis, the list reveals interesting geographical organization. It begins with the central mountain country of Ephraim, then describes the surrounding area, moves on from here to the north (Naphtali, Asher, and Issachar) and concludes with the south and south-east (Benjamin and Gad, to be read with LXX for Gilead in v. 19). It is striking that traditionally Israelite territories are separated from those which had been Canaanite city-states in the past. Solomon seems to have separated these two great populations due to their differing histories, lifestyles, and self-perceptions, but united them in serving him. As provincial governors he appointed loyal court officials (the names Ahilud, Ahimaaz, and Hushai are well known from the David–Solomon narrative) and trusted administrators from the Canaanite regions (Alt 1959).

(4:20–8) The Wealth and Security of Solomon's Time Other parts of the kingdom than Israel are presented in this passage. The narrator states that the land of Judah prospered as much as Israel, since the latter did not have to support Solomon's court alone, but could share the burden with neighbouring states from the Euphrates to Egypt (this is surely a gross exaggeration!). Next comes an assessment of how much the king costs his people—the author really means how much the people let this king cost them. Conversion rates for 1 cor shift between 220 and 450 litres. This amounts to tens of thousands of kilos of flour per day and the same number of cattle annually. Whether these numbers refer to the residence in Jerusalem or also to the provincial administration is unclear. Added to this were fodder and straw for thousands of chariot-horses. Even if these figures are exaggerated, one can assume that costs were relatively high. Israel and Judah were beginning to have large courts to feed. State administration had become increasingly centralized and voluminous from the time of Saul.

(4:29–34) Solomon's Wisdom This passage opens with praise for the king typical of the book of the history of Solomon. Here his wisdom is given prominence. We have come full circle since the opening passage in 3:1–15. This time Solomon's wisdom is not that of a king or a judge, but of an academic. It is said that he simply knew a very great deal, much more than any other person. The geographical horizon opens unexpectedly: science was international even then. Indeed texts of wisdom from the whole of the ancient Near East do exist. They generally contain accumulated general knowledge, tested rules for success in life. The classic example in the OT is the older part of Proverbs (Prov 10–31). It is no coincidence that Solomon is named as its author (Prov 10:1; 25:1; hence also 1:1). A different kind of wisdom is implied in this text, namely that of natural order (v. 33); it has to do with the ability to enumerate creation, as declared in Job 38–9, Ps 104, and Gen 1. This form of early science also helped one to succeed in life.

The Temple of Solomon (5:1–9:9)

According to Hurowitz (1992) the entire account of temple-building is shaped in a way that is reminiscent of analogous Assyrian descriptions. It may have belonged to the Book of the Acts of Solomon which seems to originate in the Assyrian epoch, but apparently used older documents. Later on it was reworked by the editors.

(5:1–12) The Contract with Hiram of Tyre By now Solomon has gathered enough wealth and wisdom to undertake larger building projects. Nevertheless, he requires foreign help for this since Israel is a lowly developed agrarian country. The Phoenicians are suitable partners due to their world-wide trading connections and high cultural standards, and above all, their large timber stocks in the mountains of Lebanon. Hiram (whose Phoenician name is ʾaḥiram), king of the important city of Tyre, is said to have collaborated with David (2 Sam 5:11) and is the first to take up relations with Solomon. Yet it is Solomon who makes a request. It is possible to discern an older textual layer (according to Wälchli 1996: vv. 15a, 16, 20, 22–5, 26b) containing very dry contract agreements: Solomon orders timber shipments and offers compensation not only for the materials but also for labour. He also suggests dispatching his own workforce. Hiram ignores this suggestion, but promises to fell the necessary trees and deliver them as rafts to the coast of Israel. His price for this is delivery of a large quantity of wheat and oil (to be produced, of course, by Israelite farmers). The editors also let the two kings discuss the importance of the Davidic covenant and clarify why it is Solomon rather than David before him who is building a temple: waging war and supporting religion seem to be mutually exclusive achievements in the Bible!

(5:13–18) Forced Labour in Israel The massive availability of forced labour from 'all Israel' seems to be reported with pride (the tone of 9:20–3 will be different). The core of the reports is surely correct, given that (unpaid!) forced labour is later the cause of the kingdom's partition (1 Kings 12). The figures mentioned here are probably grossly exaggerated. The Israelites do unexpectedly appear in Lebanon. Did Hiram actually allow this or did the biblical narrators insist upon their inclusion? Stone, as opposed to timber, is abundant in the hills surrounding Jerusalem. Gebalites, i.e. people from Byblos (in today's northern Lebanon) were also used as masons: this is not surprising given the context.

(6:1–10) Construction of the Temple Walls It is important to ask what motives lie behind the detailed descriptions in 1 Kings 6–7. Is this a construction order, a description of building procedure, or the memory of a destroyed building? The text is full of technical terms whose meaning is no longer wholly intelligible. The contours of the building are nevertheless imaginable. The foundation stone is said to have been laid in the 480th year since the Exodus, placing construction of the temple in a chronological line with this holy date in Israel's history. It is possible to count the years in the Deuteronomistic History from Deut 1:3 onwards and actually arrive at the sum of roughly 480. None the less, this is also a round number heavy with significance: not only can it be divided in many ways, but it also encompasses twelve forty-year generations. It is symbolic that construction should have begun in that year. The ground-plan of the temple shows it to have been long and narrow, as was commonly found in the region of Israel. The passages surrounding the building were striking, the temple walls against which they were built being stepped to create rebates for the gallery floor beams, so that they were thicker at the bottom, and the gallery passages correspondingly narrowed. Opposite the holy place was the low-ceilinged *debir*, most holy place of all. The ceiling beams were made of especially precious cedar wood. The building was not particularly large: about 30×10×15 metres. But it was not for accommodating the worshippers—they gathered in the courtyard—and God was intangible anyway. According to Isa 6:1, the train of his robe alone filled the temple.

(6:11–13) A Word from God to Solomon The Deuteronomists took pains to show that God was not bound to the confines of the temple building. In the background lies faith in Zion as the place of God's permanent presence and therefore eternal security, as expressed, for example, in Ps 46 and 2 Kings 19:32–4. This text clarifies that the presence of God is contingent upon his commandments being kept. The prophets say the same, in e.g. Jer 7; 26:1–6; Mic 3:9–12; Mk 11:15–19; 13:1–2.

(6:14–36) The Interior Decoration of the Temple: Wood-Carvings All the walls of the holy site were clad with wooden panels and carvings made of costly materials. The ornamentation described is emphatically non-figural: plant—and at most animal—decoration rather than human (let alone divine) figures. The aniconic trait is characteristic of the YHWH-religion from early times. Yet the plants and animals mentioned are full of religious connotation, representing power, happiness, and blessing, as other ancient oriental temples (Bloch-Smith 1994) and Palestinian iconography (Keel and Uehlinger 1992: 189–96) show. Cherubim (vv. 23–7; there was originally *one*, according to Hentschel 1984–5) are the clearest concession to the figurative perceptions of Canaanite-Phoenician religion. Such creatures were partly animal, human, and angelic (cf. their description in Isa 6:2, though, here they are called 'seraphim'). They were built into ancient oriental thrones and apparently symbolized metaphysical powers carrying the monarch on his throne. In this way, the cherubim can be seen as carrying the invisible king, YHWH, upon his throne above them (see Keel 1977: 15–36). The doors, constructed in a technically and artistically complicated way, are the subject of special description (vv. 31–5). It is probably the author's vivid imagination rather than Solomon's wealth that makes the entire temple and all its interior shine with gold.

(7:1–12) Construction of the Palace Almost by chance, we learn that the temple is integrated into a larger complex of government buildings. Going by the construction period and its measurements, the temple can hardly have been more than a palace chapel. Other buildings are of course not described in such a detailed and concrete manner as the temple (although cf. efforts, especially by Busink 1970: 334–6). The 'House of the Forest of the Lebanon' seems to have been especially monumental, named for its richly crafted and precious Lebanese timber. It was roughly 50×25 metres large, making it an enormous hall of great splendour. Forty-five pillars carried the ceiling and partly an upper floor which perhaps served as the royal bodyguard's armoury and quarters (cf. 10:17 and Isa 22:8). Beyond this were a separate throne-hall and various accommodation and administration buildings. The palace and the temple seem to have been similar in architectural style and material, giving the entire complex an impressive appearance.

(7:13–51) The Interior Decoration of the Temple: Metalworks The Bible records the name of the Phoenician crafts-man responsible for the large and wonderful bronze structures in the temple of Solomon. Like his king, he was called Hiram or Ahiram. First of all, two pillars built by him which stood at the entrance to the temple are described (vv. 15–22). Their names have been preserved (yet are hardly translatable), their appearance can be pictured (9 m. high with capitals of lotus-leaf wreaths: Keel and Uehlinger 1992: 194), but their function is a mystery. They probably did not represent goddesses, as has been suggested in the past (Görg 1991), but were enormous, stylized depictions of God-given, creative life, decorated with lotus-plants interwoven with pomegranates. The circular bronze sea (vv. 23–6) had a diameter of 5m. and was 2.5 m. high. It probably depicted the primeval sea, a theme connected with Creation across the ancient Near East and in the OT (cf. Gen 1:1–10; Isa 51:9–10; Ps 24:2; 89:10–11; and Kaiser 1962). The oxen are a remarkable feature, generally symbolizing gods such as Baal or Hadad to whom fighting strength and virile fertility were attributed. The ten identical mobile basins (vv. 27–39) each had a capacity of over 900 l. of water. Is this an image of heaven's or God's generous gift of water (cf. H. Weippert 1992) or do they have a more practical purpose (cf. 2 Chr 4:6)? Closer observation of the temple's interior reveals the dominance of an inclusive rather than exclusive monotheism: YHWH had taken up and integrated qualities from all manner of other gods and thereby become *the* universal, all-encompassing God. In vv. 40–7 everything mentioned is recapitulated. It is added that Solomon established his own ore-refinery in the Jordan valley to produce the necessary copper. An appendor felt the necessity to include the as yet unmentioned holy instruments and royal blessing-gifts, richly covering everything with gold (vv. 48–51).

(8:1–21) The Dedication of the Temple For the temple dedication, all the oldest and most honourable people (vv. 1, 3; not all men, v. 2) in Israel (and certainly Judah) are invited to the capital city. The festivities begin with a procession. The ark is carried out of the tent in the city of David where it has stood so far (cf. 2 Sam 6) and taken up to the temple grounds. The ark was originally a transportable war palladium which was carried into battle in the conviction that YHWH was enthroned upon it and would lead his people to victory (cf. 1 Sam 4; 2 Sam 11:11 and Smend 1970). We do not know what the wooden chest (this being the meaning of the Hebrew word for 'ark') contained, if anything. It was the editors who placed the tablets of the Ten Commandments into it (cf. v. 9 and Ex 25:21). The ark's place was the most holy place in the temple, beneath the spread wings of the cherubim. Should they be carriers of the throne, the ark is king YHWH's pedestal. He himself is not depicted, only the equipment with which he rules. The ark retains the signs of mobility, its carrying staves. These symbolize that YHWH is not bound to one place. In fact he does bind himself to this place. He resides in the impenetrable darkness of the most holy place, is therefore doubly invisible, yet is close enough to touch. The festive dedication speech correlates the secretive nature of this God with the light of the sun, which was worshipped as a divine power elsewhere in the orient and possibly also in pre-Davidic Jerusalem (cf. Keel and Uehlinger 1994). Here, the sun is used as a symbol of YHWH's ruling power (vv. 12–13 in the LXX version; it should be noted that the speech is passed on from an ancient Israelite book of songs, probably the Book of the Righteous, cf. Josh 10:13; 2 Sam 1:18). The next point of ceremony is the blessing of the assembly. Here the king assumes the duties of a priest (v. 14), whereupon the editors have Solomon give a short sermon (vv. 15–21): since the Exodus from Egypt (cf. 6:1!), God had intended to reside in Jerusalem. David's successes and Solomon's succession find their goal in the temple in Zion. One can infer what the building meant to later generations, especially to those standing before its ruins.

(8:22–53) Solomon's Dedicational Prayer at the Temple The introductory prayer reflects in great theological depth the relationship between God's promise to David and the people's loyalty to the Torah (vv. 23–6), and between the inestimable size of God and his residence in Zion (vv. 27–30). A sentence such as v. 27 rejects any temple (or church) ideology. God is too great to be caught up by anyone or anything, yet he can be found in the place he has designated, making himself tangible to his chosen people. In the main prayer Solomon bids God to hear all future prayers made to heaven in this temple: in particular in the event of difficult trials (vv. 31–2), wartime hardship (vv. 33–4), drought (vv. 35–6), and any other misfortune (vv. 37–40). To close, Solomon clearly foresees the state of affairs following exile: He prays for the proselytes who will come to Jerusalem (vv. 41–3) and for the Israelites or Jews who will dwell in other countries (vv. 44–5, 46–51). Zion should give every member of YHWH's chosen people a common identity (vv. 52–3). The passage does not seem to be a single unit. The interests of different periods and people are probably collected in it. Talstra (1993) claims to have discerned the different textual layers: one pre-Deuteronomist (vv. 31–2, 37–40, 41–3), a first Deuteronomist from the time of Josiah (vv. 14 20, 22–5, 28–9), a second from the period of exile (vv. 44–5, 46–51), and one post-Deuteronomist (vv. 33–6, 52–3, as well as 57–61). This dating seems on the whole to be too early. Veijola (1982) distinguishes between three Deuteronomistic layers from during and after the period of exile: (1) vv. 14, 15a, 17–21, 62–3, 65–6; (2) vv. 16, 22–6, 54a, 55–8, 61, 66a; (3) vv. 29–30, 31–51a, 52–3, 59–60.

(8:54–61) Blessing and Warning Solomon again blesses the gathering, cf. v. 14—or were all of the sermon and prayer passages between them later additions? The Deuteronomistic author lets Solomon movingly confirm the fulfilment of all the promises of Moses, i.e. complete ownership of all the land, assured existence for all God's people and the enduring presence of YHWH in this country with them. The hopes and dreams of the (post-)exile period can be inferred in the significant word 'rest', cf. Josh 21:43–5; 2 Sam 7:1, 11. The plea for God not to cast his people out but to instil in their hearts a willingness to abide by the commandments, expresses their awe of God's judgement and acceptance of their own insufficiencies. Israel knows that it owes its existence to God's mercy. And it knows that its existence is not an end in itself, but serves the purpose of manifesting God to all the peoples of the world. v. 60 is reminiscent of Deutero-Isaiah and is an outstanding statement of monotheism (cf. Isa 43:10–12; 45:4–6).

(8:62–6) The Feast of the Temple Dedication The festivities take the form of a seven-day feast. Solomon makes a huge number of sacrifices, naturally many more than in Gibeon

(3:4) and far too many for the usual altar to suffice (v. 64 is an explicatory addendum). The numbers go beyond all realistic measure. The narrator wishes to show that Solomon is, as always, generous in making every effort to satisfy God and God's people.

(9:1–9) God's Appearance This entire passage is late-Deuteronomistic. The author explicitly refers to the episode in Gibeon (v. 2). God need no longer appear to Solomon in such an inappropriate place, but can do so in the temple designed for this purpose! He assures him of his approval of the dynasty and the temple, though they are made on the condition that his laws are kept. Should king and countrymen not abide by the commandments, especially the first, by worshipping other gods, they risk the severest of punishments: the loss of their country and the destruction of the newly dedicated temple. The events of 587 BCE are unmistakably predicted here. We are given a reading guide for the ensuing description of history. Israel and Judah began with such greatness under David and Solomon, only to end so sadly. The temple collapses in ruins, David's dynasty is forced from power, Judah and Israel's land is stolen. What remains is God's love for his people, as well as the possibility that his people will learn to be true to him. Thus this section is two things at once: an explanation for woe and an offer of salvation.

Continuation of Solomon's Governmental Activity, his Fall and Death (9:10–11:43)

1 Kings 9–10 overlaps several times with 3:1–4:34. The construction of the temple stands at its centre. It is not easy to answer the question whether 1 Kings 3–10 depicts a golden age which is framed by 1 Kings 1 and 11 (see Frisch 1991), or whether Solomon's decline already begins in 1 Kings 9 (see Parker 1988). The latest editor perhaps intended the latter.

(9:10–14) The Tribute to Tyre Having read in 5:25, that Solomon paid for the Hiram of Tyre's help with agricultural products: we are surprised to learn that he had to cede entire villages (probably not the whole of Galilee, but the strip of land at the Bay of Akko—see Knauf 1991). The embarrassing situation is only slightly alleviated by the comment that Hiram was not satisfied with this payment. The Israelites living there will not have taken much comfort from this. In 2 Chr 8:2 the problem is solved by the assertion that Hiram made Solomon a present of the towns.

(9:15–23) Construction of Towns and Forced Labour This section seems to try to correct the news of 5:13–18 in favour of Solomon. It is probably a late Deuteronomistic addition (see Dietrich 1986). The narrator assures us that it was not Israelites who were driven to forced labour, but 'only' Canaanites. This statement is palliative, but the list of cities the editor uses to underline it is highly interesting. Thus we learn that Solomon built not only the palace court of Jerusalem, but also the storage and defence structures of various cities in the land. The list, whose authenticity can hardly be doubted, has repeatedly been used by archaeologists for dating purposes. This is legitimate in itself, though it could easily lead to hasty conclusions. At the centre of disputes about biblical texts and archaeological facts lie the cities of Gezer, Megiddo, and Hazor (cf. Dever 1982; 1990). To an objective observer, building works attributable to Solomon seem rather modest.

(9:24–7) Individual Acts of Government Following her mention in 9:16, the elusive daughter of the Pharaoh reappears. As in 9:15, the 'Millo' is referred to in connection with the house built for her (alone?). This term is probably related to the Hebrew word for 'to fill'. It is probably a substructure designed to secure the sloping terrain of the palace grounds (cf. 2 Sam 5:9; 1 Kings 11:27; 2 Kings 12:20). A single note speaks of Solomon's triannual sacrificial feasts at the temple. This is followed by a report on Solomon's shipping on the Red Sea (here dubiously connected to the Reed Sea of Ex 14). One can assume that the Tyrians, who were far more experienced in this field, actually carried out the trade. The destination port of Ophir may have been near Aden or on the Horn of Africa.

(10:14–29) The Queen of Sheba This story had great spiritual and even political after-effects all the way to Ethiopia (Pritchard 1974). It essentially praises Solomon's wisdom and cleverness by making a noble and wise ruler so deeply impressed by him. The story now appears decorated with exclusive gifts, much gold, and a sermon showing that the well-travelled lady has understood several of the underlying ideas of Deuteronomistic thought: since God loves Israel, he put Solomon on its throne. Today Sheba is no longer sought amongst the Sabians of Saudi Arabia, but in a north Arabian principality mentioned in an eighth-century Assyrian text (cf. Särkiö 1994: 186–91). This undercuts, though not significantly, the effect a meeting between a fabulous king and a fairy-tale queen has on one's imagination.

(10:14–29) Solomon's Wealth Here everything around Solomon is literally dipped in gold. King Midas does not seem a far cry. Silver 'was not considered as anything in the days of Solomon' (v. 21). The warning in the law of Deut 17:17, that too much silver and gold should not be hoarded by a king, is hereby clearly unheeded. From this point, Solomon's splendour is somewhat dimmed (cf. Dietrich 1996b). Not all that glittered, however, was of solid gold. The man-size shields (v. 16) were each coated with 600 shekels (about 7 kg.) of gold or gold alloy. Nor, of course, was the throne entirely made of ivory. The Phoenicians were famous for their ivory marquetry and carvings. The material for this must have come from Africa, either via the Nile or the Red Sea from East Africa, or via Tarshish (probably Tartessos), i.e. the Mediterranean, from West Africa, as v. 22 may suggest. The lion and bull decorations symbolize power, almost superhuman power (cf. 7:29). Notes in vv. 26–9 on armament and arms trade are historically interesting. David lamed captured horses, not knowing what else to do with them (2 Sam 8:4). Solomon had a large chariot fleet (which is, however, not as large here as in 5:6). He also profited from serving as an agent for the export of arms from Egypt to Syria and Asia Minor: a practice which was as common and questionable as it is today (cf. also Deut 17:16).

(11:1–8) Solomon's Wives and their Idolatry It was not unlikely, nor would many have considered it unethical at the time, that Solomon maintained a harem including, for diplomatic reasons, foreign women. The reputed thousand women is surely an exaggeration and would again, in view of the Torah (cf. Deut 17:17), have been intolerable. The text concentrates on religious rather than moral arguments. In a tone similar to other post-exilic texts (Ezra 10; Neh 10), women, especially foreign ones, are regarded as a temptation threatening loyalty to the God of Israel. On the one hand this is patriarchal slander, but on the other, it is simply realistic: women tend not to be so susceptible to rigid ideology as men. In today's terms, Solomon gave his wives something similar to minority rights and religious freedom. According to the biblical author, he hereby committed a grave sin leading to dire political consequences.

(11:9–13) A Divine Manifestation The late-Deuteronomistic theologian and author of this section defines the nature of Solomon's crime: he has broken the first commandment. As a consequence he will lose power—though naturally, in recognition of David's merits, not all power and not immediately. Such reflections come to the firm conclusion that people's actions, in private and in public life, are connected to their future well-being. God himself ensures that wrong deeds have unpleasant consequences and good deeds have pleasant ones. The biblical authors differentiate between good and evil according to the Torah. This guideline helps them to explain catastrophes such as the division of the state or exile. (The Book of Job shows, however, what happens if such guidelines are applied systematically: the crime–punishment formula does not always add up. Excessive and unimaginable suffering cannot be subsumed under such a world-view.)

(11:14–28) Signs of Decline in the Kingdom of Solomon Now that Solomon is disloyal to God, the first 'adversary' (Heb. *sāṭān*) of several events emerges. The editor stresses that God is the initiator of these events (vv. 14, 23, then also 29–33). The story of Hadad, the Edomite prince who was cast out of the country by David, his hardship, and his recapture of power whilst in exile in Egypt is told with marked sympathy (cf. M. Weippert 1971: 295–305; Bartlett 1976 claims that Hadad was in reality a political lightweight). The text reveals that he returned home shortly after David and Joab's deaths (v. 21). The editors shifted his return into the age of Solomon, for purely religious reasons. The same is also possible, though not as clear, for Rezin of Damascus. Both stories suggest that the young monarchy's temporary subjugation of neighbouring countries was not just a figment of the author's imagination. Their rediscovered independence would otherwise not require any explanation. It is unclear whether Edom and Aram were already territorial kingdoms at the time of David. Perhaps they were tribal chiefdoms, only assuming the structures of a state in their resistance to Israel, as it may itself have done whilst opposing the Philistines. Solomon's third enemy arises from within northern Israel, tellingly from amongst the forced labourers which the provinces, specifically Ephraim, had to provide. As is often the case with revolutionaries, Jeroboam stems from the élite of a repressed people (v. 28). The causes of the revolt he leads, also forcing him into Egyptian exile (v. 40), are replaced here by a prophet-story (11:29–39).

(11:29–40) Ahijah of Shiloh and Jeroboam ben Nebat The story is multilayered and probably completely Deuteronomistic (cf. Dietrich 1972: 15–20; as opposed to H. Weippert 1983 who sees an old core in vv. 29–31, 37, 38, 40 and beyond that several pre-exilic additions). It is designed to show that it was not Jeroboam's revolutionary drive, nor Solomon's repressive regime that brought Jeroboam to power, but the will of God as revealed by the prophets. The editors knew Ahijah of Shiloh from the story in 14:1–18. Whereas there he is Jeroboam's enemy, they make him his supporter here. The symbolically torn coat probably stems from 1 Sam 15:27–8. The editors explain (vv. 31–9) Jeroboam's rise in advance as a consequence of Solomon's decline. The delay in Solomon's punishment is, as in 11:9–13, due to God's affection for David. Furthermore, the powers of Judah, Jerusalem, and the dynasty of David are permanently bound together, a triple gift of mercy alleviating the pain of the loss of the northern kingdom (vv. 35–6). The prophet (i.e. the editor) does not miss the opportunity to measure Jeroboam by the same guidelines of the commandments. His covenant is immediately made subject to conditions much stricter than those attached to David's in 2 Sam 7. Every reader of the time knew that northern Israel failed miserably in keeping these laws and was therefore destroyed much more brutally than Judah and long before it.

(11:41–3) **Solomon's Death** Here we find the first (almost) regular concluding formula for a king. The editors admit that they have not told everything they know about Solomon. The rest can be read in the Book of the Acts of Solomon. Some over-sceptical critics believe this reference to be fictive. Unfortunately, only the excerpts quoted in 1 Kings 3–10 exist today. In its basic tone it was probably highly celebratory. Solomon's reign is reported to have lasted for the round sum of forty years. Death unites him with his 'ancestors', explicitly, of course, with David. As with all family graves, the deceased's body was probably laid upon a stone bench in the royal tomb, whilst the bones of his dead relatives were collected in an ossuary. The transition from a state of earth-life to the diminished state in Sheol, the realm of death, takes place between lying on the bench and being taken to the ossuary. Resurrection is still a distant thought, but its foundations have been laid.

The next major section, 1 Kings 12:1–16:14, documents the consolidation of the two kingdoms Israel and Judah.

Division of the realm (12:1–24)

(12:1–20) **The Scandal in Shechem** Whilst Rehoboam could take his father Solomon's place in Judah apparently without opposition, he required confirmation from the northern kingdom. Reports of contractual agreements between northern tribes and the relevant kings go back as far as the earliest beginnings of the kingdom (cf. 1 Sam 10:24–5; 2 Sam 5:3; 19:10–11, 42–4). After Solomon's death, Israel forced negotiations which took place in Shechem, known today as Nablus, in the central mountain country of Ephraim. (It is incorrect to say that Jeroboam ben Nebat already had a role to play in events, as v. 2 states. Although he had returned from exile in Egypt by then, he was called upon only after the failure of negotiations with the south, cf. v. 20 and McKenzie 1987.) The northern tribes demanded that Rehoboam reduce the state burdens which Solomon had imposed upon them—a clear indication of how at least northern Israel had previously regarded the regime. Rehoboam seeks advice from 'the older men who had attended his father Solomon' and with 'the young men who had grown up with him and now attended him' (vv. 6, 8). These do not form two separate advising bodies (so Malamat 1965), but represent a political conflict between two generations (so Evans 1966). The king's experienced advisers encourage him to make a moderate contract, whilst

younger hotheads demand clear, authoritarian conditions and do so in an extremely vulgar manner, 'loins' being a euphemism for 'phallus'. The narrator tries to explain the Davidic dynasty's surprising loss of most of the kingdom by using this stylized old–young opposition. Actually, the cause is the way Solomon squeezed Israel dry, and the trigger was the undiplomatic arrogance of Rehoboam's men. Perhaps Solomon had already lost the north. A language of separation almost identical to v. 16 can be found in 2 Sam 20:1. In other words, by the time of Absalom's failed revolt, if not before, the northern tribes had privately distanced themselves from Davidic rule. Although they no longer lived in tents (except in times of war, see 2 Sam 11:11) the expression reveals something of the semi-nomadic lifestyle of at least some of the northern Israelites in the past. This trait must have influenced their critical stance towards their rulers. The author of this passage is unmistakably a Judean who admits that Rehoboam played a part in the partition, but who regards it as a perverse rebellion (v. 19) against the legitimate reign of the descendants of David. A later editor, inspired by the spirit of the prophets, adds that things come to pass exactly as the prophet Ahijah of Shiloh had forecast (v. 15, cf. 11:29–32).

(12:21–4) **A War between Brothers Averted** The Judean scribes found it hard to come to terms with Israel's partition. Before catastrophe struck in 11:29–39, the prophet Ahijah had appeared to announce a harsh, but as yet limited, divine judgement upon the ruling house of Jerusalem. After its occurrence, another prophet, Shemaiah, confirms God's irreversible decision. This is an attempt to explain that however understandable their anger and laudable their courage, Rehoboam and the Judeans cannot prevail by taking up arms against the will of God, especially when it means fighting against their 'kindred'. Although the entire story is a mental construct which contradicts 14:30, it is still impressive that the usual way of thinking in terms of power politics and military categories is subordinate to strictly theological and ethical criteria.

(12:24a–z LXX) **A Special Greek Version of the Story of Jeroboam** The Greek version has an addition after 12:24 which is not present in the Hebrew, referred to with small letters (from a to z). In this version, the story of Jeroboam often concurs literally with the Hebrew text in 1 Kings 11–14, yet occasionally differs from it decisively. Thus we discover, for instance, that Jeroboam was the commander of a chariot unit, that he laid claim to the entire kingdom during Solomon's lifetime (b), leading to his expulsion. Following his return from exile, he expanded his home town Zereda and waited there. Even then his wife Anot had told Ahijah's woeful prophecy about her son (g–n, cf. 14:1–18 in the Heb. text). He is promised ten of the twelve tribes (o) in Shechem by the prophet Shemaiah (not by Ahijah near Jerusalem, as in 11:29–31 of the Heb. text). Following the failure of negotiations with Rehoboam (p–s; more detailed in the Heb. text, 12:3–14) and the threat of civil war (cf. 12:21–4), the compromise settlement gave Jeroboam ten tribes and Rehoboam two (t–z). We probably have a midrashic rewriting of the Hebrew text here (Gordon 1975) rather than the core of an old and historically valuable northern Israelite version (as in Seebass 1967; Gray 1977: 310–11).

Jeroboam I of Israel (12:25–14:24)

(12:25–33) State Worship in Bethel and Dan King Jeroboam I, founder and quasi-democratically legitimized ruler of northern Israel (12:20), initiated a number of building projects, like Solomon before him: he built castles in the central towns of his realm (v. 5)—in the cis-Jordanian Shechem and in trans-Jordanian Penuel (as the central city of the original Israelite region of Gilead, cf. 1 Sam 11). Much more important for the Bible, however, is the fact that he established state holy sites in the far north and deep in the south of his kingdom. This too likens him to Solomon. Everywhere in the East, rulers who wished to be recognized or who tried to introduce a new era in history became active in founding new cult sites. A state requires a state religion or ideology. Jeroboam knew this and became active in religious politics. It was probably the Judean author's wishful thinking that made Jeroboam worry whether his subjects were too fond of the Davidic–Judean state religion (vv. 26–7). Jeroboam could have confined himself to Bethel had this been the case. The temples in Bethel and Dan had long existed and were influential beyond their regions (cf. Judg 17–18; Gen 28; 35). Canaanite deities must originally have resided there (as was almost certainly the case with Jerusalem's previous temple!), but the Israelite YHWH had in the meantime (also?) begun to be worshipped. Thus the temples were well suited as a place of intellectual and spiritual integration for the most important population groups of the country. The intention to link 'Canaan' with 'Israel' can be seen in the central cult figures used and the way they are inaugurated. Jeroboam did not make 'calves', but (young) bulls, the animal symbolizing Canaan's main gods El and Baal. But the Israelite YHWH 'who brought you up out of the land of Egypt', is claimed to be worshipped by Israelites in Bethel and Dan (v. 28; today the words 'calves' and 'gods' correspond with each other, a feature arising from Judean polemics). The combination of Israelite faith in the liberating power of the God of the Exodus and Canaanite faith in the power to bless of their national gods stands in opposition to the Judean belief that God resides in Zion. This is an impressive, yet dubious functionalization of religion. The Judean scribes recognized this correctly, regardless of their biased perspective, and severely criticized Jeroboam's policy, even interpreting it as the seed of the fall of his dynasty and indeed the kingdom he founded (cf. 12:29; 13:33–4 and the references in dealing with all northern kings to 'the sins of Jeroboam'). Various cultic alterations for which Jeroboam is seen to have been responsible are criticized in this light: the creation of holy high places (cf. v. 31 with Lev 26:30; Deut 12; 2 Kings 17:9–10), the appointment of non-Levite priests (cf. v. 31 with Deut 18:1–8), and the unauthorized introduction of a religious feast (cf. v. 32 with Lev 23:34). This is a heavy burden for the northern kingdom to bear right from its very beginnings!

(13:1–32) The Judean Man of God and the Prophet in Bethel Mention of this illegitimate feast invites the authors to make Jeroboam plan illegitimate cult activities at the illegitimate holy site of Bethel and be caught red-handed by a prophet loyal to YHWH. An editor has inserted a detailed prophet story (between 12:32 and 13:33) which is marked by Jeroboam's cult-sacrilege, but which also illustrates the function of the office of prophet and its historical significance for the history of

Israel (cf. Klopfenstein 1996). The story is probably based on two narratives (cf. Würthwein 1994): one concerning the conflict between Jeroboam and a man of God from Judah at the holy site of Bethel (vv. 1–10), the other telling of the meeting between an Israelite and a Judean prophet (vv. 11–32). The first legend demonstrates how superior a prophet is even to a king. An earthly ruler is powerless when faced with the miraculous might of God and his power to give events a favourable or detrimental turn as he wishes. The books of Kings vary the prophet–king conflict several times, each time leaving the prophet the upper hand, although historical reality often proved to be different (cf. Jer 26:20–4; 36). Here, Jeroboam's conflict in Bethel led to the theory that this is a folklore version of the appearance of the prophet Amos in Bethel (cf. Am 7:10–17). The second narrative deals with the relationship between two prophets, often a tense and sensitive affair. Who can decide who is right when two prophets speak, claiming God's authority, yet contradict each other? (cf. 1 Kings 22 and Jer 27–8 on this problem; Walsh claims that 1 Kings 13 demonstrates that only prophets who kept YHWH's commandments are to be trusted). In our story, the 'true' prophet allows himself to be deceived by the 'false' prophet and pays for it with his life. His death does convince his opponent of the truth of the 'true' prophet's relationship to God—and makes him want to join him in death. Not only is this bizarre, but it is also related to the old theme of God's mighty actions compared to the insufficiencies of his human instruments. The two stories focus on the holy site in Bethel and its altar, both of which are contaminated by 'Jeroboam's sin' and will sooner or later feel the power of the true God: the prophet's word immediately destroys the altar (vv. 3, 5) and the holy site is abolished 300 years later by King Josiah (2 Kings 23:15–18), although the common grave of both prophets is preserved. Thus prophetic words are proved to contain the power of God. He directs history in such a way as to fulfil the prophecies so that truth may prevail.

(14:1–20) A Breach between Ahijah of Shiloh and Jeroboam Jeroboam feels the might of the prophetic word from a further prophet: Ahijah of Shiloh. In vv. 1–6, 12, 13a, 17–18, an older prophet story concerning the king's failed oracular seance with Ahijah can be discerned. (There are thematically similar scenes in 1 Sam 9:1–10:16; 2 Kings 1.) It demonstrates how it is impossible to cheat a prophet, even if he is old and blind and one has the perfect disguise (contrast Gen 27). Ahijah mercilessly reveals to the queen that her child will die. The reason for this is unclear in the text, although the context of 1 Kings 13–14 provides an explanation. In addition, the editors turn the oracle of vv. 7–11, 13b–16 into an extensive statement against Jeroboam and a comprehensive declaration against his dynasty. Even the entire history of the northern kingdom is observed here (Holder 1988). The same prophet who announced Jeroboam's rise to power (11:29–39) now forecasts that his sins will lead to the fall of Jeroboam's dynasty. Later, a coup sweeping Jeroboam's son Nadab aside provides confirmation of the prophecy's truth (15:29–30). This pattern of prophecy and fulfilment can be plotted across the books of Kings (cf. already 1 Kings 11:29–31 + 12:15 and then 16:1–4 + 16:11–12; 21:21–3 + 22:38 + 2 Kings 9:36–7; 2 Kings 9:7–10 + 10:17; 21:10–15 + 24:2; 22:16–17 + 25:1–7). In all evidence of the dates and facts we should not forget that the history of Israel, in the eyes of the author, is dictated not by internal connections of causality, but by its relationship to God (cf. von Rad 1961 and Dietrich 1972).

Rehoboam, Abijah, and Asa of Judah (14:25–15:24)

(14:21–31) Rehoboam Although we have come to know Rehoboam from the story of the kingdom's division, the introductory formula is only now inserted. This is an editorial principle in Kings: up to this point the Israelite Jeroboam stood at the centre of affairs, whilst the Judean Rehoboam was only a minor character. Now our eyes turn to the south and Rehoboam becomes the protagonist. Little good can be reported of him: he was 41 when he came to power, somewhat too old to follow the foolish advice of his young counsellors. His mother was an Ammonite, a twice-mentioned fact (14:21, 31) which can be compared to that of Solomon's foreign wives and their idol-worship (11:1–8). By now all kinds of heathen rituals are said to have found their way into Judah (and not confined to Jerusalem, as with Solomon before him). 'Pillars', tall standing stones, perhaps represented deified ancestors. 'Sacred poles' are probably stylized trees symbolizing either the old goddess Asherah or her power to bless which had become integrated into YHWH. The editors use standard sentences (vv. 22–4) which are often repeated later. They hammer out how breaches of the first commandment formed the underlying evil which led to Judah's (and even earlier, Israel's) downfall. As with almost all kings, the editors report the most important—and in this case unpleasant—events of Rehoboam's reign. On the one hand there is the constantly rekindling war with Jeroboam, a plausible account (v. 30, probably taken from the Book of the Annals of the Kings of Judah) and on the other a short report of a confrontation with Egypt which had grave consequences for the temple at Jerusalem (vv. 25–30, perhaps taken from the temple's own registers). Pharaoh Shishak, known in Egypt as Shoshenk (about 945–924 BCE, founder of the 22nd 'Libyan' dynasty) undertook a campaign to Palestine and Syria. He later ordered it to be recorded in the temple at Karnak. All the cities he claims to have conquered are listed there—they do not include Jerusalem (cf. Noth 1971). In our text, Jerusalem is made the sole object of the campaign. It is possible that the city had to pay a high price for freedom, a first sign of warning for 'the city that the LORD had chosen out of all the tribes of Israel, to put his name there' (v. 21).

(15:1–8) Abijam This is the first king who is given synchronized dating, i.e. correlation to the line of kings in the sister state. Such references remind us of their common heritage despite their separate development. Israel and Judah *together* form the people of YHWH. The names of the Judean queen mothers are always included. This has specific political reasons. Since David's dynasty reigned exclusively in Judah and there were several different parties and interest-groups (cf. 1 Kings 1 alone), rival parties always had to present a Davidide as pretender, though his rank was decisive. In this the queen mother was an overriding factor: the kinship and party represented by her decided who took up the reins of government (Dietrich 1979). In Judah, as in other parts of the ancient Near East, such as amongst the Hittites, the queen mother held a specific rank of 'mistress' (in Heb. synonymous with the word for queen mother), giving her power especially in the case of her son's death. Abijam's mother was Maacah, daughter of Abishalom. Going by his name, this could have been David's son, who died during the rebellion and would naturally have had clear political influence. One would have, however, to interpret 'daughter' as 'granddaughter', making Maacah's mother Tamar, the daughter of Absalom mentioned in 2 Sam 14:27. All this is hypothesis and rather unlikely, especially since Maacah's father is named as Uriel of Gibeah in 2 Chr 13:2. Thus names cannot tell us much about this queen mother (but see 15:10). Her son did not rule for long (about two full years, cf. v. 1 with 15:9; the number 'three' in 15:2 can be explained since the years of accession and death were not complete calendar years). There were conflicts with the northern state at this time (v. 7b, probably a note from the diaries of the Judean kings). The editors give Abijam a poor rating, probably because he did not reverse the (alleged) atrocities introduced by Rehoboam. Later theologians have pondered why YHWH continued to reside in Jerusalem despite such unworthy rulers. The answer is that David's merits were so great—even considering the Bathsheba–Uriah scandal—that his sinful successors could still profit from them. Would this store of good deeds be exhausted one day? The question is not yet relevant, due to the existence of other rulers, more faithful than Abijam.

(15:9–24) Asa King Asa reigned for an unusually long time. We learn that he was 'diseased in his feet' in old age: this is perhaps an indication of paralysis and possibly of his son Jehoshaphat's regency during Asa's lifetime. Asa is given a good assessment by the editors. He can even be compared to David, though he did not abolish the high places outside Jerusalem. That was left to Josiah (2 Kings 23:8). Otherwise, Asa was exemplary: he made pious donations to the temple, chased the cult-prostitutes out of the country (cf. 14:24), and dismissed the queen mother 'because she had made an abominable image for Asherah'. It is striking that the queen mother has the same name here as in 15:2. She is certainly the same person. Maacah was, of course, the mother of Abijam, not Asa, but kept her position as queen mother following Abijam's early death until Asa relieved her of the post (cf. Noth 1968: 335–6). The note on this must have been taken from the Annals of the Kings and is therefore historically reliable, especially since such actions were very unusual in a country so loyal to its dynasty. Perhaps it shows a new political direction: away from the present dominance of the Jerusalem aristocracy and towards the Judeans of the country. This would explain Asa's steps against syncretistic tendencies in the state cult of Jerusalem. Ackerman (1993) argues that the queen mother was regarded as Asherah's representative, making her son the offspring of a goddess as well as the adopted son of YHWH (cf. Ps 2:7). Did Asa oppose such religious and ideological perceptions? It is certain that he successfully fended off northern Israel's activities in the border area of Benjamin, even if his methods were questionable. His reaction to northern Israel's provocative expansion of the Benjaminite town of Ramah into a border fortress (cf. Josh 18:25) was to incite the Aramean king in Damascus to carry out a

TABLE 13.1 *Dates of the reigns of the first kings of Israel and Judah*

Israel	Dates	Judah	Dates
Jeroboam	926–906	Rehoboam	926–909
Nadab	906–905	Abijam	909–907
Baasha	905–882	Asa	907–867
Elah	882–881		
Zimri	881		

Source: Gunneweg 1972.

military attack on northern Israel. Galilee was devastated, and as the Israelite king turned his back on the south to concentrate on the enemy in the north, Asa took the chance to build his own border fortress in Ramah, using the materials already present.

Baasha of Israel and his successors (15:25–16:14)

(15:25–32) Baasha's *coup d'état* The narrative now turns its eyes on the kingdom of northern Israel. Here Nadab, son of Jeroboam I, attempted to found a dynasty in the manner of the Davidides in the south. He failed after only a short time (which does not keep him from receiving a poor rating from the editors—it is enough that he was Jeroboam's successor). Nevertheless we see Nadab waging war against the Philistines, indeed upon Philistine territory. He apparently resumed the war which Saul had begun (1 Sam 13–14; 31). We find out nothing about his motives or those of Baasha, his overthrower. The entire royal family is liquidated in the coup, partly due to collective thinking, partly in fear of blood-revenge. The Bible is not interested in this, however, only stating that everything came to pass as it had to: Jeroboam was sinful, his 'house' had to disappear. The prophet Ahijah had announced as much and Baasha carried it out. Is this a licence for political murder? Not at all: we are told in 16:7 that Baasha and his son will pay for the bloodbath he brought upon the house of Jeroboam. Even if God uses humans as instruments of his judgement, he does not condone their crimes.

(15:33–16:7) Baasha's Reign We already know a significant amount about the second (if you include Saul, the third) founder of a dynasty: where he came from, when and how he came to power (15:27–8), and how he became involved in a war on two fronts against Judah and Syria (15:17–22). Now all we learn is that he reigned for twenty-four years in Tirzah, a Manassite city which Jeroboam had already used as a residence (14:17) and which is generally identified as el-Far'ah (about 10 km. north of Nablus). Despite his bloody slaughter of the previous dynasty, the editors regard Baasha as 'walking in the way of Jeroboam'. The criteria for judgement are not political but religious. Baasha may have destroyed a sinful dynasty, but left its sin, the bull cult of Bethel (and Dan), untouched. Thus a prophet confronts him, as with Jeroboam, and gives him a warning and a scolding (vv. 2–4) very similar to that of Ahijah of Shiloh (14:7–11). Both the Deuteronomistic authorship and a conscious effort to draw parallels between the two dynasties are unmistakable. Their fates, as we shall see, are indeed strikingly similar. One can assume that only the name of the prophet, Jehu ben Hanani, and the fact of his appearance at the time of Baasha were known to

the editors. This may be implied by the separate note 16:7, the core of which stems from the Annals, according to some critics.

(16:8–14) Zimri's reign As was the case with Jeroboam, woe does not befall the founder of the dynasty, but his son, very soon after his accession. This time it is not war that gives the usurper his chance to strike, but a drinking bout. The rebel Zimri is a high-ranking officer, commander of half the chariot troop, a military form used in Israel since Solomon's times (1 Kings 5:6, 10:26). Again one can draw parallels, this time with the later putsch organized by another officer of a chariot troop, namely Jehu (2 Kings 9). The army often seems to have a hand in overthrowing regimes in northern Israel. The ideas of charismatic leadership and democracy do not seem to have been important factors in their view of monarchy (see Alt, 1951 = 1964). The underlying instability in northern Israel could, however, be attributed to its tribal origins: attempts to centralize power conflict with the centrifugal force of the regions. The editors are not interested in such assumptions. They are only convinced that YHWH steered the history of Israel with justice and purpose. Those who ignore his will cannot expect a stable mutual co-existence.

The period of Omri's dynasty (1 Kings 16:15–18:29)

The dynasty founded in northern Israel by King Omri is of great significance to the political development of the country, which may only have become a true state at this time. Archaeological studies of Palestine have shown that a great amount of building took place during the ninth century across the entire land: city walls and fortifications, administration centres etc. Non-biblical sources from Assyria, Aram, and Moab show reluctant respect for the far-reaching power and influence of Israel at the time of Omri's dynasty. The biblical authors, however, are not interested in the kingdom's fame, describing it as thoroughly godless. Thus the prophets are increasingly brought to the fore, especially Elijah and Elisha. Always loyal to YHWH, they become necessary counterparts to and sometimes comrades of the kings. They set the standards of what is important and right in Israel.

Omri and Ahab of Israel (1 Kings 16:15–34)

(16:15–28) Omri's Seizure of Power The rebel Zimri (cf. 16:9) sweeps to power in the place of Baasha's son Elah whom he has murdered. He only survives for one week, however (which does not hinder the editors from bestowing him with the standard judgement given to all Israelite kings: they did nothing to undo 'Jeroboam's sin' of maintaining holy sites in Bethel and Dan, v. 19). Embroiled in war with the Philistines, the army is not pleased with the coup in its capital. Being a chariot officer, Zimri probably represented the urban, Canaanite elements of the state too strongly for the army to tolerate, it being dominated by more Israelite, tribal forces. In any case, the army chief Omri is spontaneously hailed by the 'people' (i.e. the soldiers) as their leader and immediately marches with them to the royal residence in Tirzah. The city is quickly taken, Zimri loses the citadel after apparently setting it alight himself, and is then killed. Not only Zimri, however, yearns for power, but also a certain Tibni: either a loyal follower of Zimri or precisely the opposite, someone particularly faithful to tribal Israel. Four years later Tibni dies (cf. the dates in 16:15 and 16:23), probably not of natural causes. The victor's name, Omri, is not Israelite, but might be Arabian. Perhaps he worked his way from army general to head of state due to his unusually charismatic personality. He certainly created Israel's first long-living dynasty and achieved political stability. By founding a new capital city belonging to the crown, as David had done before him (cf. 2 Sam 5), Omri took a first step towards such stability. Samaria (later Sebaste) was geopolitically and strategically well situated and could be built without taking larger, existing structures into account. Omri equipped it with a generous acropolis (about 180 × 90 m., from Ahab's time about 200 × 100m.), and created an opulent city in all respects (cf. Isa 28:1), which served as the royal residence of the Israelites until the destruction of the state. The editors report that the Israelite rulers' religious failings were even worse than those of their predecessors, though they do not explain why.

(16:29–34) Ahab and Jezebel Omri's son and successor, Ahab, sinks some degrees lower in the editors' rating system by marrying the Phoenician princess Jezebel, building a temple for Baal in Samaria, and erecting a cult symbol in honour of the goddess Asherah. Baal is the classic Canaanite god of fertility, responsible for nature's rebirth. Asherah is the mother goddess of the Canaanite pantheon and stands at El's, Baal's, or even YHWH's side, presumably symbolized by some wooden object such as a stylized tree. Perhaps these really are signs of Phoenician influence (cf. Jezebel's father's name: Ethbaal). Ahab, however, must have been driven by the need to appease the religious influence of Israel's urban Canaanite population, since Bethel and Dan were mainly Israelite YHWH-worshipping sites (cf. 1 Kings 12:25–30). The note in v. 34 could stem from the 'Annals'. It is unclear what had been constructed in Jericho by that time, although according to archaeological studies it is unlikely that the entire city had already been built. Two sons of Hiel, who was responsible for the construction of Jericho, died during the building of it (they were not ritually killed, cf. Kaiser 1984)—an event interpreted by the editors as an example of God's unambiguous word: Joshua's curse upon Jericho (Josh 6:26) was a prophetic statement.

Elijah and Ahab (1 Kings 17:1–19:21)

(17:1–6) Elijah's Conflict with Ahab and his Flight The description of Ahab's mistake is followed immediately by the prophet Elijah's sudden appearance. His name alone is telling: 'My God is YHWH!' Such exclusive worship must have been unusual at that time. Elijah confronts the king with YHWH's word against Ahab's policy of ensuring harmony by syncretizing the worship of YHWH and Baal: the land will suffer drought and hunger. This is a declaration of war against Baal, god of fertility and rain. It will finally be YHWH, not Baal, who brings rain. From here onwards, a tense conflict begins between the two deities which is resolved only in 18:41–5. The prophet of YHWH withdraws to a small east-Jordanian river valley as soon as he has made his declaration. The narrative lays great store by ensuring that each change of scene is directed by a divine order. It is said that Elijah is a man led by God and obedient to him. Miraculously it is ravens,

usually greedy (ravenous) birds, that feed the hermit Elijah. Who can harm such a man?

(17:6–16) Elijah and the Widow in Zarephath But Elijah suffers the same fate as his people: his water runs dry. So God sends him on to the Sidon region, home of Queen Jezebel, the lion's den. He expects to find a widow to feed him there. Men of God are often poor, needing the help of others, especially of women. Elijah does not know that the one God has chosen for him this time is terribly impoverished herself. He learns this only after having randomly asked a woman at the gates of Zarephath for water and then for bread. She claims, 'as the LORD your God lives', that she and her son are starving themselves. Elijah repeats his wish, but adding the soothing words, 'Do not be afraid', and continues by prophesying an endless supply of food. The editors explicitly remark that it comes to pass as Elijah had predicted. The power and truth of a prophet's word is proved repeatedly, it being a hallmark of the Deuteronomistic view of prophets.

(17:17–24) Elijah Awakens the Dead This story was probably an unconnected piece, attached to the previous episode by the editors. Both stories contain the same three people and deal with the question of whether it is worthwhile to support itinerant men of God. vv. 7–16 show clearly that those who share their food with them end up eating more rather than less. In this passage we learn that their presence does not bring only death (by seeing guilt and bestowing punishment, v. 18), but also life. This story is closely related to that in 2 Kings 4:18–37, and perhaps even stems from it. The prophet plays the role of a magician reviving a dead soul by a ritual action. It is of course God making all this possible—the prophet calls upon and pleads with him twice. Finally death withdraws, though not permanently. The entire OT accepts death, while showing us how to use God's guidance in shaping life. Passages such as this stress that death is not an independent supernatural power, contrary to other oriental beliefs which feared and revered death as a deity. Thus this story is central to the main theme of the Elijah cycle: the true God versus false gods.

(18:1–20) Elijah and Obadiah The theme of drought and rain is now resumed in the narrative. The land of Israel thirsts and even the king suffers under the drought. YHWH sends for Elijah in order to bring about the crisis and then the solution to the unfolding conflict. The meeting between the prophet and the (godless) king is preceded by one with a (God-fearing) minister. His name is also telling: Obadiah, 'servant of YHWH'. He is said to have come to the aid of YHWH's servants during a purge of prophets. On unexpectedly seeing Elijah standing before him, he falls to the ground in fear and respect. Elijah can obviously be everywhere and nowhere: a repeating theme for which Elijah was famous. We also learn that Ahab organized a search for Elijah and that Jezebel pursued prophets of YHWH in general. Thus we begin to understand why Elijah's journey took him across the lonely river of Kerith into the foreign territory of Phoenicia.

(18:21–40) Elijah and the Competition Between the Gods on Mount Carmel The king asks Elijah, as soon as he meets him, the same question as his minister had (18: 7, 17), only he does not call the prophet 'my lord', but 'troubler of Israel'. Elijah immediately throws the accusation back at him (which is followed by a longer explanation, probably added by the editors). Ahab organizes a gathering of the people on Mount Carmel, after which he has no further role in the story. This is another unconnected story which is probably only placed in its present context out of necessity (cf. for instance the wastage of water in v. 34–5, although there is a drought everywhere). It has been suggested that this story reflects a real political and religious conflict at the time of Ahab regarding a holy place on Mount Carmel near to the Phoenician border (Alt 1964b: 135–49). It is more probable that it is a theologically planned anticipation of Jehu's bloody deeds against Baal followers (2 Kings 10:18–27, see Smend 1987). In this sense the horrifying ending in v. 40 is both necessary and highly unsettling. But before this point, a bitter struggle concerning the true god and the right religion flares up. Elijah stands against the people. They do not seem to understand the choice Elijah offers at all: 'YHWH *or* Baal', since the idea of YHWH monotheism was not yet sufficiently established in Israel. Elijah then turns to the Baal prophets and suggests a competition between them. They do not answer, but the people do, on their behalf. A miracle must bring truth to light. Those who have read 1 Kings 17 know that YHWH can perform miracles. It is quickly revealed that Baal is incapable of doing this. Here the cultic and ritual activities of Baalistic religion are reliably reported: their prayer, rhythmic movements, and self-mortification building up to ecstasy (vv. 26–9). But Baal remains inactive. By contrast, YHWH-religion concentrates on the spoken word (prayer) and can immediately work miracles. The people to whom this is demonstrated turn to YHWH's side at once. This call of faith, 'The LORD indeed is God', unmistakably reminds us of Elijah's name ('my God is YHWH'). Elijah's belief has become that of the people.

(18:41–6) Elijah Brings Rain The return of the rains is another triumph for Elijah. The theme of drought reappears along with king Ahab. King and prophet are no longer enemies, but in agreement. The fact that the king can eat again is perhaps a sign that he was once depicted as a remorseful and therefore God-fearing king (Würthwein 1984). Elijah acts like a magician who uses his superhuman powers—as symbolized by the gesture in v. 42—to call for rain seven times. At the climax, he slips into ecstasy, similar to the Baal prophets' trance earlier. He differs from them decisively, however: the 'hand of the LORD' grasps him and he storms ahead of the royal chariots for more than 20 km. from Carmel (some see Samaria as the starting-point) to Jezreel. This archaic-sounding anecdote again shows how YHWH breaks the boundaries of what is humanly possible. The opening conflict of 16:32–3 and 17:1 is thus solved as YHWH proves himself to be the only effective God (although not necessarily the only one that exists).

(19:1–8) Elijah's Flight to Horeb Even Elijah is human, as Jezebel proves. According to the LXX, she opens her warning of revenge—sworn by 'the gods'—with the proud statement, 'If you are Elijah, I am Jezebel!' The fact that this woman repeatedly plays the role of Elijah's (and YHWH's) strongest antagonist in his stories may have to do with the real history or be a further version of the text written shortly after Ahab's death, which made Jezebel rather than Ahab the main villain (see Steck 1968). Both interpretations could depend too heav-

ily on the story's historical precision and not set enough store by the theological freedom of the narrator—who after all wrote at a much later time. The struggle for the exclusive worship of YHWH and against Baalism was much more long-term and less triumphant than 1 Kings 18 suggests—a fact reflected in Elijah's sudden need to flee. His destination is Horeb, the name used by Deuteronomy and the editors for Sinai. Mention of Beer-sheba and Elijah's loss, in the desert, of all will to live remind us of Hagar and Ishmael's fate in Gen 21. Here too God's messenger brings salvation in the form of food and water. He must, however, encourage the dispirited man of God twice before he is willing to make his way to the mountain of God, inspired by miraculous powers (cf. 18:46).

(19:9–18) Elijah's Meeting with God on Horeb As Moses had done before him (Ex 24; 33) Elijah hopes to meet God on Mount Horeb. He does *not* appear: at least, not in impressive natural phenomena (which one would have connected with the weather god Baal) and not in demonstrations of violent power (as were sometimes cherished in religious arguments, e.g. in 18:40 and in countless other examples up to the present day). Elijah encounters a completely different God on Mount Horeb. The description of his approach is extremely powerful and quietly beautiful. The image of God suggested here is in clear contrast to that of 1 Kings 18 and especially 2 Kings 10. Hosea's criticism of Jehu's bloody wrath (Hos 1:4) is probably the background to this scene. Although it is difficult to see the figure of Elijah as an ironic reflection of Moses in general (see Hauser and Gregory 1990), this story does show ironic traits. The prophet is twice asked the reason for his presence, and twice the same frustration breaks out in him, as if God had not appeared to him in the meantime. In speaking of the 7,000 Israelites who do not kneel before Baal in the ensuing battle, God redresses the balance of Elijah's complaint about his complete solitude. At the same time Elijah is charged with enlisting three warriors for YHWH's cause of whom at least two draw a line of blood through history: the insurgents Hazael of Aram and Jehu of Israel. The third in the group is the prophet Elisha who doubtless belongs historically more with the other two than Elijah does (see 2 Kings 8:7–15; 9:1–10). The latter's enormous influence seems to have attracted various traditions and not least the figure of Elisha.

(19:19–21) Elijah Charges Elisha The first of Elijah's three required appointments in 19:15–16 is that of Elisha. In fact it will be the only one, since Elisha immediately takes over Elijah's staff—or his mantle!—and carries it further. Elijah's mantle was apparently his hallmark (cf. 2 Kings 2:8, 14; in 1:8 a different Heb. word is used). By enveloping Elisha with it, Elijah passes on to him his spirit and his mission. Elisha appears as a rich farmer, Elijah as a restlessly wandering prophet. Acceptance of this duty requires Elisha's relinquishment of his property and family. He seems to be prepared to do this on certain conditions. Elijah's answer can be interpreted in two ways: as scoldingly rejective ('Go back again; for what have I done to you?') or as understandingly warning ('Go, but [remember] what I have done to you', Gray 1977: 413). It is also unclear whether Elisha bids farewell to his parents, but he determinedly takes leave of his property and gives it to the people. From now on he is Elijah's servant and 'follows him', cf. Mt 4:19; 8:18–22. The two men were historically not so closely tied as it appears here. They stand for different styles of prophecy, being representative of single and group prophets (Schmitt 1972: 183–4). Our text may mark the beginnings of the idea of prophetic succession.

Ahab and YHWH's Prophets (1 Kings 20:1–22:40)

(1 Kings 20:1–34) Ahab's Victory over the Arameans Following a Prophetic Oracle In 1 Kings 20 and 22 we are told of a series of wars between an Aramean king, Benhadad, and King Ahab of Israel. This does not fit the fact proved by Assyrian sources that Ahab and the Aramean king, Adad-idri (Aram. Hadadezer), were closely allied to each other (*ANET* 276–7). It is probable that the Omri dynasty was at peace with Aram, and that this relationship deteriorated only under Hazael (cf. 2 Kings 8:12–13, 28–9; 13:3, and elsewhere). Thus, should our stories reflect historical fact, they belong to the time following Jehu's coup. At this point, however, they wish to describe the confrontation between King Ahab and the prophets of his time. It has been suggested that scenes containing the prophets were added to the text at a later point, and that originally the stories dealt with profane scenes of war. This is possible, though not certain. In ch. 20, the Israelite king repeatedly defeats an aggressive and arrogant enemy with the help of prophetic oracles of war. Interestingly, the Arameans considered YHWH to be a mountain god who had no power on the plains (v. 23), a belief that stemmed from underlying religious and social history. YHWH's home was originally the mountains of southern Sinai and Edom (Ex 3; Judg 5:4) and Israel itself initially developed into an ethnic and political power on the mountains of Palestine (Judg 1:27–35; 1 Sam 13–14; 2 Sam 2:9). Now, however, so the story tells us, the entire country belongs to YHWH (and his Israelite people)! Ahab even manages to force Ben-hadad to agree to an Israelite trading office in Damascus (v. 34).

(20:35–43) A Prophetic Warning to Ahab The initially positive outcome of the war against Aram is tarnished by the following scene, as Ahab transforms from being a victor to a sinner: he should not have made business contracts with Benhadad, but should have 'devoted him to destruction', i.e. killed him. Devoting to destruction, or 'banning', passing spoils of war and their previous owners on to God, later became an underlying principle of Deuteronomistic theory and historical writing (Deut 13:12–18; 20:16–18; Josh 6–7; 11:10–15, and elsewhere). It was probably practised in the early times of the kings in Israel as in Moab—although not in every war, but only out of extreme necessity (cf. Dietrich 1996a). As gruesome as this ritual is, it is equally clear that war is being waged without prospect of material gain. Once a 'banning war' had been declared, it seems that especially prophetic, i.e. strictly YHWH-following circles, insisted upon its compliance (cf. also 1 Sam 15). In this case, the prophet's ingenious scheming forces the king to catch himself out and bring judgement upon himself—as Nathan had once done to David (2 Sam 12).

(21:1–16) Ahab's and Jezebel's Judicial Murder of Naboth This story is a paradigm for the conflict between the demands of the state and the rights of the people. The farmer Naboth has the right and indeed the duty to bequeath his land to his family and not to outsiders. The ruling ideal in ancient Israel was that each farming family—over 90 per cent of the population—was given a secure economic existence and thus firm citizen's rights by the allocation of sufficient land. This is shown by the attempt to legally protect landownership for everyone (Lev 25; Deut 5:21). Initially, King Ahab was forced to capitulate to this (probably still unwritten) right of his subjects: an idea which paints a positive picture of the monarchy. Nevertheless, this story shows how unscrupulously the king's power over the civilian rights could still be used and how compliant the lay assessors' court was to his wishes. The queen is the driving force behind this, since she comes from abroad and does not respect Israelite ethics, or perhaps does not know them. In any case, nobody attempts to stop her, so that evil can poison society from the top down—not merely a modern experience. If the scandal of Naboth is still an individual case for which the royal court is responsible, the theft of land by the ruling class 100 years later becomes an economic principle (Isa 5:8; Am 2:6; Mic 2:1–2).

(21:17–29) Elijah's Judgement against Ahab and his Court The loss of the farming population's rights in Israel did not occur without resistance. This can be seen in the bitterly outraged tone of the Naboth narrative, though it lacks further elaboration or explanation of this point (*contra* Würthwein 1984, who sees vv. 1–16 as a closed short story in its own right). Someone is required to confront the king and under such circumstances this is normally a prophet. A parallel rendering of this story in 2 Kings 9:25–6 shows that although a prophet apparently did protest against the judicial murder of Naboth (and his family) it can hardly have been Elijah. The latter's appearance in these verses has obviously been reworked several times. Originally, there was probably only a brief scene: suddenly, Elijah stands before the king in the vineyards of Naboth. He listens to Ahab's surprised question (v. 20: 'Have you found me, O my enemy?'), briefly and firmly throws his accusation at him (v. 19: 'Have you killed, and also taken possession?'), and immediately announces his judgement (v. 19: 'In the place where dogs licked the blood of Naboth, dogs will also lick up your blood'). This prophecy does not come true to the letter. Editors ensured that God gives Elijah detailed instructions regarding his task (vv. 17–19, in which the slight discrepancy of the setting between Samaria and Jezreel is glossed over). Elijah must scold and warn Ahab in a lengthy speech (vv. 20b–22, 24, closely related to the speeches in 1 Kings 14:7–11 and 2 Kings 9:7–10) in which the king's religious failings are repeated (vv. 25–6). Ahab's transformation into a repentant sinner postpones his judgement to the next generation (vv. 27–9). v. 23 does not (as suggested by Steck 1968) belong to a particularly anti-Jezebel authorial layer dating from the time following Ahab's death. The reference in 2 Kings 9:36–7 ascertaining the fulfilment of the prophecy proves that this section must clearly be Deuteronomistic. The text describes Elijah angrily breaking his staff over Omri's dynasty, preparing the reader for terrible deeds in the future.

(22:1–40) Micaiah ben Imlah's Prophecy and Ahab's Death Although great punishment only befalls his sons (the OT thought collectively right up to the period of exile), Ahab is not left unreprimanded. Despite his dying of natural causes according to the Annals of the Kings (22:40), the editors emend this. They insert an account of the Israelite king's mortal wounding during a war with Aram. The story is the-matically linked with 1 Kings 20, although here Judah and Israel are allies. The sister states were closely tied at the time of Omri's dynasty and remained so until after the uprisings of Jehu and Joash (2 Kings 9–11). So the editors entered the appropriate names, Ahab and Jehoshaphat. Ahab is given the role of the villainous hero. He causes war, gains Judah's support in arms (vv. 1–4), but does not hesitate to sacrifice his ally to the enemy in order to save his own skin (vv. 29–30). The outcome, however, is different (vv. 31–6). The Judean remains unhurt whilst a stray arrow hits the Israelite. He remains courageous during battle (making it unclear whether he died on the battlefield, which weakens the discrepancy of 22:40), but succumbs to his injuries in the evening. v. 38 relates these events back to Elijah's prophecy (21:19). The story of Micaiah ben Imlah is inserted within this narrative frame (vv. 5–28). It continues the theme of the relationship between the kings of Judah and Israel, but concentrates on the conflict between optimistic court prophets and independent prophets of woe. The Judean king is apparently willing to listen to prophecy even when it is critical—a sign that this passage has been reworked by Judeans. By contrast, the Israelite king only wishes to hear what he wants from the prophets. When one prophet finally says something else, the king and his court prophets take action against the troublemaker. Nevertheless, the latter is proved right, whilst all others, despite also seeing themselves as messengers of God and using impressive sym-bols to prove this, are wrong. A fundamental problem regard-ing the prophets is the unaccountability of their own attitude towards God's messages. Here (as in Jer 28 and Mic 3:5–8) the basic rule seems to be that a prophet is less convincing the more clearly he confirms wishes and expectations. Micaiah ben Imlah declares that his opponents are possessed by an evil spirit with whose help they wish to drive the king to death. His knowledge of this stems from witnessing (in a vision, cf. Isa 6) discussions at a heavenly council. In passing on his secret knowledge to the mortally endangered king, Micaiah gives him a final chance to change course. The lying spirit, however, prevails over the spirit of truth. Micaiah's warnings to the king have the same effect as those of Isaiah to the people (Isa 6:9–10): they serve to entrench opinions rather than change them. True prophets seem to experience this repeatedly.

Jehoshaphat of Judah and Ahaziah of Israel (1 Kings 22:41–2 Kings 1:18)

(22:41–54) Jehoshaphat and Ahaziah's Governments Only now is Jehoshaphat officially introduced, although he has already been closely linked to Ahab. This agrees well with the statement in the Annals that there was no war with Israel at that time, no doubt a consequence of the Omri dynasty's

TABLE 13.2 *Dates of reigns during the Omri dynasty*

Israel	Dates	Judah	Dates	Aram-Damascus	Dates
Omri	881–870	Asa	907–867		
Ahab	870–851	Jehoshaphat	867–850	Hadadezer	about 853
Ahaziah	851–850			Ben-hadad II (?)	up to 845(?)
Jehoram	850–845	Jehoram	850–845	Hazael	from 845

dominance. Whenever the sister states were at harmony with each other, their Transjordanian neighbours suffered hard-ship. Judah controlled Edom and therefore had access to the Red Sea. They probably lacked the nautical skill, however, to undertake trade projects. Nevertheless they refused such help from Israel, perhaps out of age-old defensiveness towards the more powerful northern kingdom. This may be a reason for the good religious rating given to Jehoshaphat by the editors. Ahaziah, Ahab's son and successor, had no chance of mild judgement, especially since punishment of the Omri dynasty had only been postponed. Besides this, the editors knew in what light the following story would show the king and his short reign.

2 Kings

(1:1–18) Elijah and the Death of Ahaziah Having fallen through a lattice—it is unclear whether this is a window or a grid on the roof protecting an upper chamber—and suffered permanent injury, the king calls for an oracle (cf. 1 Kings 14), though from Baal rather than YHWH. Two qualities of this Syro-Palestinian god are described: he is the patron-god of the Philistine city Ekron (similarly Ashdod's patron seems to have been Dagon, cf. 1 Sam 5) and he has a second name, Zebub, meaning 'fly'. Fly-Baal: is this a title of honour revealing that his oracles were carried out to the sound of humming, or is it a (Jewish) term of abuse, derived from *zĕbûl* (prince)? In any case, this deity seems to have been particularly appropriate for a case such as Ahaziah's. An oracular consultation does not take place due to Elijah's interference in the name of YHWH. According to the present text, he does so following the explicit order of an 'angel of the LORD' (vv. 3–4) and three (fifty-strong) army divisions are unable to stop him (vv. 9–16). These are additions designed to underline the almost transcendental position of the prophet who cannot be ordered about and must be treated with utmost reverence! (Many biblical stories show that this advice was highly necessary: prophets had no protection, carried no weapons apart from their word, and were often faced with evil and even deadly enemies.) The original version of this story (vv. 2, 5–7, 17) is rather short. Ahaziah asks the wrong god, Elijah gives him a reply devoid of hope in the name of the right one. This is thematically similar to 1 Kings 18: Elijah's action to promote the exclusive worship of YHWH in Israel. Clearly his name ('My God is YHWH!') was closely linked to this mission. The king does not yet know the name of the seer of woe. Description of his appearance, however—an ascetic hermit—immediately puts him in the picture. Aside from his mantle (cf. 2 Kings 2:13), another recognizable feature of Elijah seems to be that he suddenly appears precisely when he is not expected or wanted, fear-lessly saying what was to be said in the name of his God (cf. 1 Kings 18:7; 21:17–20). It is almost unnecessary to say that king Ahaziah soon died.

The Acts of Elisha (2 Kings 2:1–8:15)

(2:1–18) Elisha's Appointment and Elijah's Ascension Elijah's life was coming to an end. In general, people in the time of the OT did not regard death as their enemy, but as a natural conclusion to life. YHWH is a God of life—what happens beyond the boundary of death remains out of his reach. Elijah's ascension is one of the very few breaches of the wall of death made by the OT, from which the faith in resurrection develops later. It is no coincidence that of all people, Elijah was expected to return at the time of the NT (Mk 6:15; 8:28). Since he only departed rather than died, he did not even need to be resurrected, but merely return from his heavenly journey to announce the Messiah's arrival. According to the present text (vv. 2–6), Elijah, Elisha, and many prophet disciples were aware of the impending departure. Elijah wishes to be alone when the time comes: miracles tended to occur at times of silence. Elisha, however, is required and wants to accompany him: as a witness to the miracle and an heir to the master. He does indeed inherit his 'spirit' (not completely, though still the double portion due the eldest son, v. 9, cf. Deut 21:17). The spirit is that which is closest to the sphere of God, cf. Judg 3:10; 14:6; 1 Sam 10:10; 11:6; Isa 11:2, and elsewhere. Elisha also inherits Elijah's mantle, which was not only his hallmark (1 Kings 19:13, 19; cf. 2 Kings 1:8), but also proved to possess magic powers. Both Elijah and Elisha could divide the river Jordan with it, reminding us of Moses' division of the Reed Sea (Ex 14:21). It is strange that Elijah is given a military title of honour: 'chariot of Israel and its horsemen [better: horses]' (v. 12). Originally it seems to have belonged to Elisha (2 Kings 13:14), having then been transferred to his predecessor: by contrast to Elijah, Elisha does seem to have been awarded this kind of merit: an entire cluster of stories (which was, according to Schmitt 1972, at one time an independent collection, and can be found especially in 2 Kings 3; 6–7) tells of wartime successes achieved by the Israelite kingdom with the aid of Elisha.

(2:19–25) Elisha Brings Life and Death First, however, we are shown that Elisha has the same power to perform miracles as Elijah before him. To this day, one can see the spring named after Elisha at the oasis in Jericho, its wonderfully fresh and abundant water in the heat of the region being attributed to a miracle by the prophet. By stark contrast, another miracle uses incredibly destructive power against teasing children. Apparently Elisha, like his adherents, wore a tonsure which was often the subject of mockery. History tells us that ridiculing prophets can be costly (cf. 2 Kings 1:9–14), but so costly? Another forty-two deaths are mentioned in 2 Kings 10:12–14, where Jehu orders the massacre of Judean princes. Is this later crime prepared for in order to legitimize its methods in the same way as Jehu's massacre of Baal-worshippers in 2 Kings 10:17–27 is preceded in 1 Kings 18:40 by Elijah's murder of prophets of Baal?

(3:1–3) King Jehoram of Israel The last ruler of the Omri dynasty—not a son, but a (presumably younger) brother of his predecessor Ahaziah—received, like all northern kings, a negative, yet nevertheless more favourable, rating than his parents Ahab and Jezebel. He is said to have abolished the 'pillar of Baal', a cult-stone set up by his father. In 1 Kings 16:32 this is not mentioned; perhaps because it was a minor sacrilege, or confused with the 'altar of Baal'. Perhaps it is even a Deuteronomistic invention, designed to shed a positive light on Jehoram compared to his father. The usurper Jehu's arrow still struck him from behind (2 Kings 9:24), not because he personally deserved it, but because the woe which had long hung over his dynasty now befell him. The last king of Israel, Hoshea, suffered a similar fate: his concluding judgement is

particularly mild (2 Kings 17:2)—not because he was a relatively God-fearing ruler, but in order to avoid the misunderstanding that he alone was the cause of the northern kingdom's demise. The Deuteronomistic theologians teach us that God is forbearing, allowing guilt to pile up over a long period of time before demanding atonement. The reader is then asked to apply this perspective to the fall of Judah: its cause is not its last king (Zedekiah), nor even the last kings (including Josiah!). Here too guilt has accumulated over a long period of time, up to the point when, in God's eyes, the mark was overstepped.

(3:4–27) Elisha's Contribution to the Campaign against Moab Israel under the Omri dynasty was consistently a regional superpower—especially at the time of this story. The kingdoms of Judah and Edom were compliant (vv. 7–8), the kingdom of Moab was a vassal liable to pay tribute (v. 4), and refusal to do so resulted in military reprisals. One such campaign, however, threatens to fail as water supplies ran out in the desert of Edom. The Judean king has the idea of calling for a prophet of YHWH, and Elisha—an Israelite!—wishes only to deal with the king of Judah (vv. 11–14). This must be a remnant of Judean reworking of the text (cf. already 1 Kings 22). The older Israelite version of the story reports that Elisha ensured the success of the Israelite king's campaign. He placed himself in a state of trance using music (not only a modern phenomenon!) in which he could simultaneously serve as oracle and adviser. It is pointless to dig holes arbitrarily in an arid country, unless one is ordered to do so by a prophet: miraculously, the holes were filled with water (shall we think that there was an impermeable layer just below the surface?). It is still more unbelievable that the enemy believed this water to be blood (either due to its colouring or because of light reflection), leading them to throw caution to the winds, leave the protection of their defences, and be easily defeated. All this was due to Elisha. It is possible that the oldest version of this tale was a relatively sober report: the advance of the allied army against Moab was initially successful (vv. 4–9a, 24b–26)—so far as one can describe the devastation of an entire region as successful—until the Moabite king, out of desperation, made a terrible sacrifice, struck Israel with 'great wrath', and forced the invaders to retreat (v. 27). The source of this 'great wrath', be it YHWH, the Moabites, or their god, remains unclear. At this point one should take note of an unusual piece of extra-biblical evidence. King Mesha of Moab (mentioned in 3:4) erected a victory stele which was discovered in the Moabite town of Diban in 1863. On it he boasts of his triumphs against Israel (text in *ANET*, analysis and interpretation in Dearman 1989). His description is in some points similar to 2 Kings 3: during the years before his reign Israel dominated Moab until he turned his trust to the god Chemosh and subsequently forced Israel out of the country. Mesha does not report that Israel, Judah, and Edom made a great campaign against Moab. Nevertheless such action fits well with the time of Omri's dynasty, which tended to have a policy of broad alliances (e.g. against Assyria) and which could always drag Judah in its wake. The sinister, final scene in 2 Kings 3:27 reflects something of the Moabites' religious faith, though nothing of this kind is mentioned in Mesha's report. Chemosh was in no way a lover of child sacrifices, as it may appear here. The crown-prince's sacrifice was rather a desperate attempt to force the god into action, as we have already seen with Jephthah during his war against the Ammonites (Judg 11:30–1). We also discover from the Mesha stele that Chemosh exacted a far higher sacrifice from Israel: several Israelite villages were 'banned', i.e. given to the god and completely eradicated (cf. the Israelite analogy, 1 Kings 20:35–43). The war rituals hinted at here are archaically gruesome, though one must not be deceived by them: they were sporadic rather than widespread. Mass armies, the destruction of entire countries, religious wars dominated by fanaticism, extensive genocide, weapons of mass destruction: none of these phenomena were contrived or practised by the small states of the ancient Near East, but are the invention of our own time.

(4:1–7) Elisha Helps a Poor Widow 2 Kings 4 gives us a view of the way of life of the groups of prophets such as the one gathered around Elisha. They led an eremitic existence in deserted areas, but had followers in the cities from where they received visitors. Occasionally they made preaching journeys to the cities themselves. Apparently, their faith filled their entire lives, so that their needs were extremely modest. The widow of a prophet-disciple is the principal figure in the first anecdote. Her husband had probably given up his material goods when he joined Elisha. He died, leaving a family in debt. The wife was unable to pay these debts and the creditor wanted her sons to work them off. This arrangement existed not only in Israel, but also throughout the ancient Near East (cf. Ex 21:2–4; Deut 15:12). In itself, the idea of forcing insolvent debtors to work for their creditors for a limited period of time is not reprehensible, since it ensures the creditor his rights and prevents the debtor from losing his land or long-term freedom. In the eighth century, though, as the prophets complain, this method was used systematically in order to rob farmers of their land (Isa 5:8; Am 2:6; Mic 2:2). The present story shows how hard debt-slavery can hit a socially weak family. In the eyes of the law a widow has lost the protection of her husband; if she then loses the support of her sons, she runs the risk of ruin. The fact that she turns to Elisha shows that he was regarded not only as the spiritual leader of the prophet-fraternity, but also as a kind of clan-chief carrying social responsibility for its members. Unfortunately, he does not have the material or legal means to help her. He can, however, perform miracles. Elisha uses one to increase what little she has beyond all measure, though not without asking for her active help. In carrying out his apparently senseless request, the widow proves her faith in him (cf. the strikingly similar structure in 1 Kings 17:7–16 and Mk 6:35–44; 8:1–10). The result is several full oil-jars, obviously a fortune enough to relieve poor people of their plight. The story teaches us that those who have faith in the prophet (and his God) will not be let down.

(4:8–37) Elisha Helps a Childless Woman to Bear a Son Elisha is described as a frequent traveller. He is regularly taken in by a rich lady in Shunem on the northern border of Jezreel (a common situation amongst wandering prophets). The guest room set up on the roof by the husband upon his wife's request shows wealth and generosity: it has firm walls and is equipped with luxurious furniture (v. 10). Wishing to show his host

appreciation, Elisha offers support from the highest offices in the state (he is obviously a very influential man). The lady proudly refuses this, referring to her own (equally influential) clan. Elisha's servant Gehazi—who was perhaps added to the Elisha stories at a later date—guesses what the lady might secretly desire: she is childless and will, according to all accounts, remain so. Elisha immediately promises her a son: a repeated theme in the Bible, usually announcing the coming of a great Israelite (cf. e.g. Gen 18:10; Judg 13:3; 1 Sam 1:17; Lk 1:13), but used here simply to demonstrate the power of prophetic miracles. Initially, the lady hardly dares to take Elisha at his word. She is not disrespectful in v. 16, only afraid of possible failure—an all too understandable fear, as we shall see. Although the announced birth takes place promptly and punctually (v. 17), the child is snatched away at a tender age, by sunstroke, it seems (vv. 18–20). He becomes sick in the morning and dies at midday (v. 20). The desperate mother immediately knows that only Elisha can help her now. She carries the dead child's body to his chamber and locks it in there, as if to stop the spirit from going too far from the body. A dramatic race against time begins, incredible for the reader, since the child has already died. Without explaining much to her husband (his short retort still tells us that one usually only sought out prophets on holy days), the mother swiftly rides for about 20 km. to the nearby Carmel mountains and finds Elisha there. Gehazi cannot hold her back or send her away before, 'in bitter distress', she reports to the prophet what has happened (v. 28). Nor is she satisfied with the suggestion that Gehazi should rush to Shunem with the prophet's staff (v. 29). Her wish prevails, namely that Elisha should accompany her personally (v. 30). She hopes for nothing less than an awakening of the dead and seems to realize that the prophet must be personally present for this. Gehazi can indeed achieve nothing (v. 31) and Elisha himself steps in. First of all he prays (v. 33): probably a concession to the piety of a later time. Then he undertakes a magical task in two steps (vv. 34–5): by laying his entire body exactly next to the corpse he transfers his own life-energy to the child. Initially his warmed body, then a hefty sneeze, show a return to life. The story finishes abruptly (vv. 36–7): Elisha places the child in its mother's arms for the second time. Presumably the drama ends on the same day as it had begun. As with other miracles, natural explanations for this phenomena, such as mouth-to-mouth resuscitation, are unnecessary. Something metaphysical has happened, achieved through the miracle-working power of a prophet and the decisive action and faith of a mother.

(4:38–44) Elisha Allows his Disciples to Eat their Fill It is pleasing that a biblical story has daily domestic chores as its theme—and even makes the men do the work. In the barren landscape of the lower Jordan valley, the group of prophets must literally scrape together a living. An obviously inexperienced man finds a vegetable he does not recognize. It is the wild pumpkin (*Citrullus colocynthis*), which grows on flat tendrils in arid places and is used as a medicine, but if consumed in great quantities it has a toxic effect (Zohary 1983: 185). It is cut and thrown into the large cooking-pot. During the meal a woeful cry is heard. 'There is death in the pot' reveals the terror of men who often enough had too little in the pot to meet their needs. Elisha comes to their aid. A little flour makes their meal palatable. In the past, the search for a natural explanation for this has distracted from the intention of the story. This is a further example of Elisha's miracle-working power and how it helps those who trust in it. The same applies to the following short episode in vv. 42–4, which is surely a type of the stories of the multiplication of food in the NT. Out of little comes a great deal, so much that all who are hungry can eat their fill and still not finish the food. These are symbolic stories against hunger, encouraging solidarity amongst people, and also showing God's care for his creatures.

(5:1–27) Elisha Heals the Aramean General Naaman This story brings astonishing news: that Elisha healed neighbouring Aram's highest-ranking military officer of a stubborn illness. Unlike the kings of the time, his name has been remembered. Perhaps he was connected with unhappy memories in Israel. An Aramean campaign through Israel is mentioned (v. 2) and it is said that Aram could give Israel orders (vv. 6–7). We are placed in a period of widespread Aramean hegemony over Israel, perhaps the time of Hazael and Jehu or Joash (cf. 2 Kings 8:11–12; 10:32–3; 13:22). In helping the Aramean general, Elisha simultaneously helps the Israelite king. His reputation as a miracle-worker initially crosses the border by chance, through a young Israelite prisoner-of-war (v. 3). By mentioning Elisha, the girl does great service not only to her master, but also to her people and finally her God. Typically of men, however, it initially results in misunderstandings and threats rather than healing and freedom. The Aramean king orders his colleague/vassal in Samaria to produce the necessary miracle immediately, something he is naturally unable to do (vv. 6–7). Naaman expects respectful behaviour and conventional miracle-healing from Elisha and threatens to leave when he does not receive this. The consequences are imaginable (vv. 11–12). The general of course refuses to descend from his chariot to see the prophet who in turn sends his servant to the door instead of meeting the (enemy!) commander in person (vv. 9–10). Nevertheless he is willing to help, but only according to his rules and with the active participation of the patient (v. 10). Naaman promptly finds Elisha's demand to ritually bathe in the Jordan unreasonable: as if the rivers in and around Damascus were unsuitable! As soon as Naaman complies with Elisha's instructions, following encouragement from his subjects— these are often more sensible than their rulers, v. 13!—he is immediately cured (presumably he did not suffer from leprosy, but psoriasis). Some critics have suggested that the story originally ended here, though there is no need for this hypothesis, nor is it probable, let alone the eight narrative layers suggested by Hentschel (1985: 158–60). Naaman understandably returns to his benefactor. He wishes to ensure the future proximity of the God who helped him so tangibly. Since this God resides only in Israel, he wishes to take two mule-loads of Israelite earth to Damascus in order to be able to sacrifice to YHWH there (vv. 15a, 17): a splendid earthbound understanding of God, still far removed from the theoretical monotheism of, for instance, Deutero-Isaiah (e.g. Isa 45:5–6). Elisha understands the request and grants it immediately, parting from Naaman in peace (v. 19; discussion of the problems of the proselytes, as mentioned clearly in v. 18, is

probably a later addition). Appended to this main story, designed to hail the glory of God and Elisha, a secondary narrative deals with the teaching of disciples: what can a prophet accept as recompense for such services and at what point is he selling his soul? The episode has its precursor in vv. 5b, 15b, 16, where Elisha serves as a good example: in a case like this, a prophet accepts *nothing*. It must be clear that great power and wealth cannot force or buy the support of prophets and God. Nor must prophets let themselves be used as tools for any interest groups (cf. also Mic 3:5). Gehazi, Elisha's servant named in other stories (and probably also included at a later date, 4:27–37; 8:4–5) serves as a complementary negative example: he cunningly accepts the presents brought by Naaman for himself, but is strongly condemned by his master for this and is afflicted by the same sickness as the recently healed Aramean. *Exempla docent*, or: disciples of the prophet, be warned!

(6:1–7) Elisha also Helps his Disciples The following short story is deliberately inserted to show what can really help the disciples of the prophet. When they are confronted by the need for craftsmanship, someone's axe-blade falls into the water. This seemingly trivial matter was a serious problem to Elisha's followers, since they did not themselves own such valuable tools. They were borrowed and had, of course, to be returned. Called by his student, the master is willing to help. He does not, however, conjure up a new axe, but hurries to the place where the blade sank, asks to know the exact spot, and uses a kind of analogical magic before letting the disciple fish the piece of metal out of the water. The apparently banal episode is symbolically touching: God and his prophet can, in exceptional cases, defy the laws of gravity if God's people require them to do so.

(6:8–23) Elisha Captures Arameans and Subsequently Ensures their Release The scene moves back from the smaller-scale group of disciples to the larger political world, where Aramean troops can move across Israelite territory unhindered. The only thing the Israelite king can do is to avoid falling into their hands. Indeed he survives ambushes against him several times. The Aramean king (possibly Hazael, should this story have historical roots) can only presume he has been betrayed (v. 11). But on discovering that the Israelite king (v. 12—it could be Joash) is guided by the hand of a clairvoyant prophet, he sends an army regiment with horses and chariots to Dothan (about 15 km. north of Samaria) to arrest Elisha. The city is quickly surrounded and there is no escape for Elisha. The reader sees through the eyes of the despairing servant what nobody else but Elisha can see: a heavenly host stands by Elisha, who also have horses and chariots, but theirs are made of fire (v. 17). Perhaps this is an early interpretation of Elisha's archaic title: 'chariots of Israel and its horsemen [better: horses]' (2 Kings 13:14). But it does not come to a battle with the Arameans. God 'struck them with blindness' (v. 18), so that Elisha can mock them: the one they seek—himself!—is not here. He will lead them to him. Thus he lures them into his trap, right into the middle of the strongly fortified royal city of Samaria, from which—the tide has turned—they themselves have no escape (vv. 19–20). Does the core of the story form a cunning wartime tactic by Elisha? Or was the prophet always considered to be in league with God? He hinders the king, however, whom he respect-fully calls 'father' (cf., however, 13:14), from simply killing the enemy that has fallen into his hands. Prisoners, he teaches, are not to be killed, but to be fed and released (vv. 21–2). Such humane principles helped reduce tensions and enmities even back in such times (v. 23); but they are not universally kept to the present day.

(6:24–7:20) Elisha Brings Hope in Great Wartime Hardship

Despite the kind gesture of 6:23, the Aramean threat to Israel becomes critical. The enemy no longer makes plundering raids through the country, but now stands before the capital, Samaria. It was common practice to besiege cities for months, even years, in order literally to starve them out (cf. 2 Kings 17:5; 25:1–2). The narrative stresses the increasingly desperate situation: even poor-quality food and fuel is extremely expen-sive (v. 25), ravenous hunger drives people to cannibalism (vv. 26–9, cf. also Lam 2:20; 4:10), the king is completely powerless and deeply dejected (vv. 27, 30). At last Elisha comes on the scene—not as a possible helper, but as his opponent who must fear for his life (vv. 31–2). It seems he encouraged resistance to the enemy and trust in YHWH, though now the king's patience has come to an end (v. 33). Elisha sees attack as the best form of defence: God has told him that good-quality food will be available at normal prices within one day (7:1). A more astute and practical prophecy of salvation is hardly imaginable under the circumstances. When the king's adviser shows doubts, Elisha even risks a woeful prophecy against him (7:2). The king's silence seems to suggest that he is prepared to give Elisha one final chance. The story reaches its dramatic climax—and then surprisingly digresses to a few lepers standing at the city gates, rejected and avoided by other citizens. They are the first to witness the Arameans' sudden retreat, take personal advantage of the situation, and subse-quently announce the news to state officials (vv. 3–11). This is a wonderful precursor to Jesus' recognition that God loves mak-ing the last first (Mk 10:31 par.). Meanwhile the reader also learns what the lepers do not know: that God brought hallu-cinations to the Arameans, leading them to believe in the advance of great Egyptian and Hittite armies, and forcing them to break off the siege immediately (vv. 6–7). Even if there were a small number of Hittites in the area (and Egyptians further away), they would never have had the power or the will to free Samaria. This, however, is not an indication of the narrator's ignorance, but of the Arameans' confusion. Not believing in God, the Israelite king is not convinced by such a story, and suspects a trick (v. 12; cf. a very similar scene in 3:23–4). Finally, however, they dare carefully to investigate the situation—and find the Arameans' eastward retreat route to the Jordan littered with weapons and goods discarded in panic. Only now do they dare to enter the camp before the city and take possession of their provisions. Lo and behold, food prices do indeed sink to the level forecast by Elisha (vv. 13–16). The story cannot end without showing the doubting adviser meeting the fate he deserves (v. 17; vv. 18–20 were probably added later as further clarification and explanation). The narrative themes are war and victory, though neither is glorified. War brings terrible suffering to mankind, especially to civilians and above all to women and children (6:28!). Furthermore, Israel is not victorious due to its own means, but is granted victory when almost all hope has disappeared. Only the prophet believes that God can help even when one's own resources have been exhausted.

(8:1–6) Elisha Helps a Refugee

The episode refers back to the story in 4:8–37, but concentrates only on the woman and her property. Her son and husband play no further part—prob-ably a sign that the story was handed down separately. Elisha foresees famine, warns the woman, and recommends her to emigrate in advance (cf. the motive named in the stories of Ruth and Joseph and countless reports of so-called economic refugees today). In this way she does indeed survive the famine, but finds that her property belongs to someone else when she returns. It probably fell into the crown's hands since it had no owner. Had neighbours taken it over, an argument within the clan would have had to be solved. The woman appeals to the king who returns her the land on hearing of her connections with Elisha. Once again we see what influ-ence the prophet has with the king and how much he uses it to support his followers, especially those who are in social need (cf. also 4:1–7)! Referring back to 1 Kings 4, this story seems to add a new aspect in vv. 4–5. Here, Elisha's servant Gehazi announces all his master's great deeds to the king who is highly impressed with the prophet's miracle-working power. A recently published ostracon (inscribed potsherd) contains the plea of a widow to an official asking for transference to her of her late husband's land (see Bordreuil, Israel, and Pardee 1998). Whether or not she was successful remains unclear; she did not have a prophet as her ally.

(8:7–15) Elisha Supports a Change of Power in Damascus

An eminently political story is placed at the end of the Elisha cycle (though cf. also 2 Kings 13:14–21). It is highly surprising that a prophet can move about in the capital city of his most dangerous enemy and even influence the highest polit-ical circles there. The Aramean king, named here as Ben-hadad, becomes seriously ill and sends his general Hazael to Elisha—the prophet of YHWH and not of Hadad or Baal!—in order to request an oracle. Elisha's reply is ambiguous: Hazael should tell the king he will recover although he will also die (v. 10). The riddle is solved a little later: the king would have survived his illness (v. 14), but cannot survive Hazael's assassination attempt (v. 15). Hazael probably did not wish to wait for his predecessor's natural death, as Elisha foresaw. At the same time, a vision shows the prophet how brutally the new ruler will attack Israel (vv. 11–13; cf. 1 Kings 19:17; 2 Kings 8:28; 10:32–3; 12:17–18; 13:3; Am 1:3). It seems that Elisha, even if only after an inner struggle, actually en-courages Hazael to carry out the coup and to murder. If one remembers that the relationship between Israel and Aram at the time of the Omri dynasty was relaxed, and that the change of power in Damascus dramatically worsened it, Elisha seems to be shown in an unnervingly lurid light. The war which Hazael declares shortly after his accession leads to the Omride Joram's wounding and his murder by general Jehu (who hated Arameans). All this was suggested by Elisha (2 Kings 9–10). Was this his intention in going to Damascus? Did he take the suffering and death of many people into account in his efforts to bring about political change in Israel? Or is this story not to be understood historically, but as an

TABLE 13.3 *The liaison between Israel and Judah during the Omri dynasty*

Relationships		Mutual undertakings	
Israel	Judah		
Omri	Asa		
Ahab m.	Jehoshaphat	[Together against Aram?]	1 Kings 22:1–40]
Jezebel		Almost a common fleet	1 Kings 22:49
		Together against Moab	2 Kings 3
Ahaziah			
Athaliah m.	Joram		
Joram	Ahaziah	Together against Aram	2 Kings 9
70 princes	*42 princes*	Die together	2 Kings 10:1–14

Note: Italic indicates the increasing influence of Israel upon Judah.

attempt to explain the kings' murders and the Arameans' strikes against Israel as events in accordance with God's purposes?

The Kings Joram and Ahaziah of Judah (8:16–29)

(8:16–24) Joram of Judah This descendant of David receives the harshest possible verdict from the editors: religiously, he is placed on the same level as the kings of Israel, and especially 'the house of Ahab'. This means he sold out Judah's religious policy (amongst others!) to northern Israel. According to the authors of Kings, evidence of this can be seen in Joram's marriage to the Omride princess Athaliah. She was not merely one wife among others, but became the queen mother when her son Ahaziah came to the throne (cf. vv. 18 and 26; it is unclear from these verses whether Athaliah is Omri's daughter or Ahab's, i.e. Omri's granddaughter; the former is probably correct). The relationship between Judah and Israel, having often been extremely tense and belligerent after their separation (cf. eg. 1 Kings 14:30; 15:16), clearly changed at the time of the powerful rulers of the Omri dynasty to northern supremacy over the south.

A late editor claims that this link between Judah and the sinful kingdom of Israel could also have brought the former down, but God, true to the Davidic covenant (2 Sam 7:11–16), mercifully spared them (v. 19). Nevertheless a major political crisis broke out as the Edomites, previously vassals of Judah (1 Kings 22:48; 2 Kings 3:8–9), heavily defeated Joram's troops and achieved independence. This report must originate from the Judean annals, in which unpleasant news was also documented.

(8:25–9) Ahaziah of Judah Ahaziah is seen in the same light as his father Joram (and his mother, the Omride Athaliah). He did not really have much time to prove this, since he reigned for (at the most) one year. The northern kingdom was currently involved in a war with Aram. Fighting centred upon Ramoth, a town on the border between Israelite Gilead and Aram's sphere of influence to the north. Hazael was evidently on the attack, forcing Israel into a defensive position. This can be seen in the phrase, 'Israel had been on guard at Ramoth-gilead against King Hazael' in 9:14. The repeated reports of 8:28–9 in 9:14, 15a and then again in 9:16 are remarkable.

Such notes could stem from three different sources: the Judean and the Israelite annals and the Jehu novella. The Judean annals claim that their king took part in the war against Aram and that he followed his wounded cousin Joram from Ramoth to Jezreel (8:28f). According to the Israelite annals, Joram alone waged war against Aram, his wounding giving Jehu the opportunity to carry out a putsch. This coup is referred to very sparingly in both annals, as opposed to in the Jehu novella (cf. 9:14a with 1 Kgs 15:27; 16:9, 15b–17). The author of the Books of Kings placed excerpts from both annals in their correct position, having to accept their interruption of the novella's narrative flow (9:15b is a continuation of the novella's narrative flow (9:15b is a continuation of 9:13) and the duplication of the brief report in 9:16. He wished to make very clear that Jehu was a schemer, that he was not the first in Israel, and that it is astonishing how carelessly Joram and Ahaziah fell into his trap. After all, the threat of coups was known to be particularly high during wartime. But the fate of these two pagan kings was predestined and therefore took its inevitable course.

The fourth major section, 2 Kings 9:1–15:12, covers the period of Jehu's dynasty.

Jehu's coup d'état (9:1–10:36)

(9:1–13) The Anointing Prophets have political influence! In 8:7–15 we heard that Elisha played a part in Hazael's coup against Ben-hadad in Damascus; now we hear that he supports Jehu's ousting of the Omri dynasty. Both were announced beforehand in 1 Kings 19:15–17 and both are connected: nationalist trends with corresponding religious overtones were gaining the upper hand in Israel and probably in Aram. Internal and external confrontation rather than cooperation seem to be the dominant tone from now on. Elisha uses a military crisis to his advantage, the Arameans' attack on Israel and King Joram's wounding. Elisha's disciple is given exact instructions (vv. 1–3): to seek the officer Jehu in the military camp (Elisha seems to know him and thinks he is capable of doing what must be done). There the disciple is to talk to him privately (witnesses would only restrict Jehu's choice of action), anoint him king (in northern Israel, prophets obviously performed this rite, cf. 1 Sam 10:1; 1 Kings 11:31; 19:16, whilst priests did this in Judah, cf. 1 Kings 1:39; 2 Kings 11:12) before withdrawing quickly (any discussion would be unwanted or even dangerous). The young prophet fulfils his task exactly (vv. 4–6, 10b), but also makes an impassioned speech against the house of Omri: Jehu should eradicate it completely for worshipping idols and Jezebel especially should meet her deserved fate (vv. 7–10a). This is a Deuteronomistic addition announcing that the end of the Omri dynasty is, as with the houses of Jeroboam and Baasha before it (v. 9), God's decision. Its intention is to show that no important change in the history of Israel happened without God's will or without its proclamation by his messengers. What applies to dynasties later applies to the kingdoms of Israel and Judah. Their demise is not due to chance, nor the result of political power-struggles, and most certainly not a failing by YHWH, but is punishment for past faithlessness. In this way, those who knew God and the Torah could give meaning to history. Jehu himself hesitates for a moment from taking on the role of instrument of God. He does not disclose what the prophet, 'that madman', has told him (v. 11), perhaps to protect himself from being considered a 'madman'. Finally he divulges his secret and receives spontaneous support (vv. 12–13). When he realizes he has the army behind him, he becomes unstoppable. Radical literary critics have claimed that the entire prophetic opening to the story of Jehu is secondary. They see the coup as a profane political event which is also reported profanely by the narrator, whose personal attitude towards it is distanced (see Würthwein 1984, *contra* almost all others, including Minokami 1989 in this case). Politics and political reports had, however, religious implications at the time (as they can have today). Jehu conspires with both military and religious circles (see 10:15–16). His actions have both political and religious motives and release religious emotions.

(9:14–37) The Kings and the Queen Mother are Murdered
Before rumours have time to spread Jehu arrives in Jezreel (on the southern border of the plain of the same name) where King Joram is recovering from injury. We are told besides that his colleague (and cousin!) Ahaziah of Judah is also residing with him (v. 16). In an impressive scene from the sentinel's viewpoint (Gk. *teichoskopia*), the narrator depicts the way in which Jehu steers his chariot, a usurper's irresistible charge ('like a maniac') in vv. 17–20. Jehu and the reader know what drives him, although Joram is still ignorant. Since he can learn nothing from his messengers, he investigates the matter himself (v. 21), an action which leads to his downfall. He harmlessly asks if Jehu himself and his army have peace (*šālôm*). Jehu's reply mimics the question and continues with sharp criticism of the Omrides' religious policy, especially the Phoenician queen mother Jezebel (v. 22; here too the religious dimension cannot have been added secondarily, *contra* Würthwein 1984, Minokami 1989). Joram now recognizes Jehu's aggressive intentions, but it is too late to flee, there only being time to warn Ahaziah. Jehu's arrow strikes him from behind between his shoulders. The narrator lets the traitor give a reason for his deed: Joram had to suffer for a sin committed by his father Ahab (vv. 25, 26*a*). Unlike in 1 Kings 21, not only Naboth's murder, but that of his entire family is mentioned here, whilst the threatened judgement is not connected with Elijah. Precisely these discrepancies suggest the originality of the passage in the context (*contra* Würthwein 1984; Minokami 1989; Timm 1982). v. 26*b* is, however, a Deuteronomistic addition. The Judean Ahaziah can initially flee to the south, but is overtaken after about 10 km. on his ascent to the mountains and shot down. Severely wounded, he manages to get as far as Megiddo, but dies there and is taken to Jerusalem by his followers. Jehu can now turn his attention to Jezebel, who is still in Jezreel. He obviously encounters no resistance on entering the city—other than from Jezebel who defends herself in her own way: lavishly decorated, she appears at the window from which royalty show themselves to the people. Thus she demonstratively and symbolically takes over the business of government following the king's death. She addresses the approaching Jehu as Zimri, thereby bringing to mind another usurper who murdered his royal master, only to be overcome himself—by Omri! (see 1 Kings 16:8–20). The affront is cutting and not without nobility. Jehu reacts impatiently and orders the lady to be thrown out of the win-

dow. Apparently, no one dares to disobey him. He impertubably goes in to eat, a man without emotions. As an afterthought, he remembers that one must give people of good birth a decent burial, but there is not enough left of Jezebel to bury (v. 30–5). Not for the first time, the narrator is extremely reserved in his commentary on the situation. The attempt at legitimizing events by referring back to the judgement made in 1 Kings 21:23 in vv. 36–7 must be by the hand of editors.

(10:1–14) The Eradication of the Dynasties In the ancient Near East it was common to eradicate not only the ruling king, but also the entire ruling house after a coup. This minimized the threat of blood-revenge and claims to the throne. The royal house of Omri resided in Samaria (1 Kings 16:24). Jehu addresses the Samarians and with seeming fairness, but implicitly threatening them, lets them choose between loyalty to the previous dynasty and defection to him, the murderer of their king (vv. 1–5). Letters regarding the fate of the Omrides strongly remind us of Ahab and Jezebel's correspondence with the nobles of Jezreel concerning Naboth's fate (1 Kings 21:8–10)—and the Samarians show no more character than the Jezreelites. Jehu's order was ambiguous: 'Take the heads of your master's sons and come to me,' could mean he wanted them to deliver the leading figures of the royal family into his hands. But they bring the heads of the decapitated Omrides to Jezreel, apparently seventy in number (vv. 6–7). Jehu reacts cold-bloodedly. He takes responsibility for murdering the king, but not for the slaughter of the royal family. The prophet Hosea does not accept this. Roughly 100 years later, he is convinced that God 'will punish the house of Jehu for the blood of Jezreel' (Hos 1:4). A Deuteronomistic reworker of the story of Jehu feels obliged to add a pious explanation legitimating his deeds (v. 10). The Jehu narrator himself again withholds judgement, moving swiftly on to the next remarkable event instead. Forty-two male members of the Judean royal family—at that time closely tied and related to the Israelite royal house (cf. 2 Kings 3:7; 8:26, 29)—fall into his hands near Betheked (an unlocatable village, presumably between Jezreel and Samaria). The unfortunate men are obviously ignorant of the latest developments, announce their allegiance to the Omrides, and thereby condemn themselves to death (vv. 13–14).

(10:15–27) The Massacre of Baal-Worshippers An indication of the contents of the drama's last act is given when Jehu meets Jehonadab ben Rechab and they become allies. Jehonadab is presumably the leader of a nomadic YHWH-worshipping religious order which had strictly detached itself from the culture and religion of the country (cf. Jer 35; Levin 1994 is most probably wrong in stating that Jehonadab is merely a chariot officer). In their common 'zeal for the LORD', they ride to Samaria. The news that further Omrides have been killed there (v. 17) is due to Deuteronomistic thoroughness, wishing to see the announcement made in 2 Kings 9:8–9 carried out to the end. Jehu (and Jehonadab) now turn their attention from the house of Omri to the house of Baal. Since the time of Ahab, there had been a temple of Baal in Samaria (1 Kings 16:32) which perhaps played a similar role for the Omrides as the temple in Jerusalem did for the Davidides. As in Jerusalem, the religious leaders were close to the political powers;

throne and altar had always been closely linked. In this sense the ensuing attack upon the servants of Baal is clearly in line with Jehu's revolution (and not merely later theology, as suggested by Würthwein 1984, Minokami 1989). The text in vv. 19b–23 was certainly filled out at a later date. (v. 19b is a weighted reading aid—'cunning'!—which would be too ignominious for the Jehu narrator. v. 20 strengthens the motif of Jehu's deception. According to v. 21, all servants of Baal throughout Israel should be eradicated: wishful thinking which would breach the narrative's time-frame as well as the confines of the temple. Now the next problem arises, which is solved in v. 22b: individual YHWH-worshippers must be selected from the mass of Baal-worshippers, cf. the same problem in the later text Gen 18:17–33. Finally v. 26 is a doublet of v. 27.) Ignoring these verses, a logical chain of events is discernible: Jehu gathers all the prophets and priests in the temple using lures and threats (vv. 18–19). His intentions with the religious functionaries are clear (the 'worshippers' in v. 19 do not appear in some MSS and were probably added secondarily). Jehu's announcement, 'I have a great sacrifice to offer to Baal' (v. 19) is cruelly ambiguous. He initially performs the sacrificial rites as a devout king would do (v. 24), only to order the ensuing human sacrifice. The soldiers present for the task carry out the order thoroughly, penetrate the cella ('the citadel of the temple'), destroy it and the mazzeba within it and transform the holy site into a latrine, to remain so 'unto this day' (vv. 25, 27). In this way, the Jehu story has come full circle. The appearance of a prophet of YHWH at the beginning anticipates what is revealed at the end: Jehu's battle is both for the throne and its religion. Nobody knows to what extent religious motives really played a part and how much was pretence. Not even the narrator speculates on this. In any case, the coup carried out by military powers was supported by YHWH-worshipping circles. Together they must have formed the front line of an opposition which had its roots in the provincial small-farming population of the Israelite tribes who were suspicious of the Omrides and hated their urban, syncretist pattern of state. Their victory led to a decisive turn in the political and religious history of Israel.

(10:28–36) Jehu's Reign In the final passage concerning Jehu the editors make an explicit statement, building upon some annal notes. Jehu (supposedly) eradicated Baal, but the holy sites still stood in Bethel and Dan. Thus even Jehu cannot expect the highest rating. Even so, his dynasty lasted four generations: no more than the Omrides, but they only reigned for thirty-six years whilst Jehu's house was in power for 100 years, its founder himself ruling for an impressive twenty-eight years. v. 32 immediately shows that this was not a particularly happy time for Israel. The Arameans, allies turned enemies, put Israel under pressure. An inscription which has in recent years been the source of much furore (see Biran and Naveh 1993; 1995; Dietrich 1997) can be dated from this time. In Tel Dan on the northern border of Israel fragments of a stele were found, on which an Aramean ruler—most probably Hazael—boasts of comprehensive victories over Israel and Judah, also naming, according to plausible textual additions, the names of the kings Joram of Israel and Ahaziah of Judah. Did the Aramean make himself

responsible for their deaths and not Jehu? Was Jehu Hazael's willing or unwilling accomplice? Soon the Aramean pressure upon Israel was so strong that Jehu submitted to Assyrian dominance. The Black Obelisk of Shalmaneser III depicts him or one of his ambassadors paying tribute at the feet of the Assyrian king (about 825 BCE, found in Nimrud, now in the British Museum; for Nimrud, see Oxford Encyclopedia of Archaeology (1997), iv. 140–4).

Athaliah's Reign and Death (11:1–20)

(11:1–3) Athaliah's Accession to Power and Joash's Rescue The queen mother in Jerusalem was Omri's daughter (8:26). She entered the Judean royal family by marrying the Davidide Joram and was the mother of his son and successor Ahaziah (8:18). At a stroke, Jehu's coup left her with no male relatives in either Samaria or Jerusalem. Her reaction to this brutal attack is as powerful and even more successful than that of her sister-in-law Jezebel. She becomes—despite being a woman and an Omride!—formally ruler of Judah. She personifies the Omridic politics in Judah, so violently cut away from Israel, for a further six years. Despite this, or perhaps because of this, the editors do not grant her the introductory and concluding formulae usually given to kings. The statement in v. 1 that she became a mass murderer of David's house, which had already been eradicated by Jehu according to 10:12–14, is not commented on. Are we to interpret the doublet, either tolerated or deliberately included by the editors, as Athaliah completing the work of Jehu? In fact we probably have a second text, the parallel Judean version of the same events. This requires a saviour of Prince Joash: his aunt Jehosheba. According to the other version, Joash would have survived simply because he was a baby at the time of the bloodbath. In either case, Athaliah came to power because her ruling son Ahaziah and all members of David's house who were capable of ruling had been killed.

(11:4–20) Joash's Enthronement and Athaliah's Liquidation The priest Jehoiada plays a significant role in deposing Athaliah. He apparently kept Joash hidden for six years before bringing the 7-year-old (12:1) to the throne. Was his reason for taking the queen mother's power merely to hold the reins of power himself (Levin 1982)? Jehoiada builds up a subversive organization in the temple (and in the palace?) with a good infrastructure, sufficient weaponry, and above all a close relationship with the 'people of the land' (vv. 14, 18, 20). The final sentence of v. 20, contrasting the land (Judah) and the city (Jerusalem), sheds particular light on the political constellation: Athaliah, like all Omrides, enjoyed the support of all members of the urban and aristocratic circles of the capital city. The opposition, such as Jehu, drew their power from the provincial farming population. The question is whether religious factors played a role in the overthrow in Judah as they had done in Israel. Jehoiada is a priest of the temple of Jerusalem. Since the time of Solomon, there had been syncretistic, but also strictly YHWH-worshipping tendencies there (cf. e.g. 1 Kings 15:13; 2 Kings 18:4, 22). Both are probable: the Omride influence strengthened the former, this in turn strengthening the opposition by reaction. In this sense, the news in v. 18a of an outbreak of anti-Baal sentiment is plausible. Levin (1982) attributes this passage to a late-Deuteronomistic reworking of the text, beyond which he also discerns the influence of early chroniclers (especially in v. 10) and a priest's reworking (especially in vv. 7, 9, 15), leaving a sober and purely secular report of Athaliah's fall stemming from the annals (vv. 1–6a, 8a, 11–14, 16, 17, 19–20). In its present form, 2 Kings 11 looks like a counterpart to 2 Kings 9–10 (cf. Barré 1988, who even claims that Jehoiada's deeds were meant to be seen as exemplary compared to those of Jehu). Both perish together, the queen and her favoured god. Baal naturally had many lives, whilst Athaliah's only one was mercilessly extinguished. Piety was reserved for the temple alone, so that the execution took place in the nearby palace grounds. In this way, the political change forced by Jehu in Israel took effect six years later in Judah. The biblical authors are convinced that this was right and necessary in order to prevent God's people from losing their souls to Baal, the 'possessor' (this is the meaning of his name!) and god of possessors.

Joash of Judah (12:1–21)

(12:1–16) The Temple Renovation Fund Created by Joash Joash is given a relatively positive rating by the editors. This is first because he succeeds the irregular reign of queen Athaliah, even being helped by the priest Jehoiada, and secondly due to his care of the temple of YHWH. The editors found a note on this in the annals or in a temple-source. According to these notes, temple renovation was no longer solely directed by the priests, but was decreed by the palace. Donations for this project were placed in a collection box, counted communally at intervals, and then paid out to a kind of building administration (vv. 6–12, 15). Across the whole of the Near East, kings were responsible for maintaining state holy sites. This was an expensive task. The temple of Jerusalem seems to have had a building administration merely to accomplish construction projects (vv. 11–12). It is plausible to assume that financial provision came from pious donations rather than the state coffers. Such donors brought gifts and duties to the holy site. Animal and vegetable sacrifices were reserved for God and his priests (as is expressed in v. 17, probably a later addition). Some gifts, however, such as those honouring a vow or those exempting people from sacrifices that would otherwise have been demanded, could be made by paying in silver. (Though minted coins only existed from Persian times onwards, so that the term 'money' as used in the NRSV is misleading.) The somewhat lower caste of 'priests who guarded the threshold' received the donated silver, deposited it in the designated chest and guarded its contents. (This honourable duty was no longer theirs by the time of exile: according to 2 Chr 24:10, the believers threw

their money into the collection box themselves.) These priests were also in a position of trust, since no accounts were demanded from them (v. 15). 2 Kings 22:3–7 is closely related to this section: Josiah acts according to the order introduced by Joash with extremely far-reaching consequences. It is debatable whether 2 Kings 22 is the model for 2 Kings 12 (as suggested by Levin 1990) or vice versa (see Dietrich 1977). If the latter is true, later analytical additions would have to be conceded, such as the introductory vv. 4–5 which attempts to describe the situation before Joash's reforms, or the detailed descriptions in vv. 13–14 and 16. In general, the passage gives the impression that Joash loyally attended to the house of God to avoid its gradual decay and to honour God (and naturally the king and priests).

(12:17–21) Joash's Reign Judging by the order of the following texts, Joash was not rewarded for doing 'what was right in the sight of the LORD'. The books of Kings are not influenced by clumsy rules of causality, by which good people are granted happiness. Hazael, the ruler in Damascus (cf. 1 Kings 19:15–17; 2 Kings 8:7–15), placed both the northern kingdom of Jehu (cf. 2 Kings 10:32–3) and the kingdom of Judah under severe pressure. The way in which he is paid to keep away from Jerusalem is lamentable. Various predecessors of Joash are credited with pious bequests made to the temple, no matter whether they are positively or negatively judged by the Bible. Similarly, Joash's murder (v. 20) cannot be ascribed to simple cause and effect. The biblical authors speculate neither on political nor on religious grounds for his death. Or is Hazael's humiliation of Joash such a reason? We can no longer verify the scene of the murder. Concerning Millo, see 1 KINGS 9:24–7. 'Silla' appears only here and could be based on a textual error. The names of the king's murderers are noted exactly: probably an attempt to maintain their disgrace throughout history. It is also notable that Joash's career began and ended under the same circumstances: a plot against the king and his murder.

The Last Kings of the Jehu Era (13:1–15:12)

(13:1–9) Jehoahaz of Israel During Joash's long reign, Jehu's son Jehoahaz comes to the throne in Israel. This is the beginning of a relatively long dynasty, though internal stability contrasted starkly with problems from abroad. After the great power change in 845, Aram-Damascus increasingly dominated Syria-Palestine as its regional superpower, bringing bitter consequences for Israel. The power relationship described in v. 7 speaks for itself. The original author of the Deuteronomistic books of Kings regarded Israel's humiliation as similar to the oppression under the judges: the superiority

TABLE 13.4 *Dates of the reigns of the kings during the Jehu dynasty, 845–742 BCE*

Judah		Israel		Aram		Assyria	
Ahaziah	845	Jehu	845–817	Hazael	845–800	Shalmaneser III	859–824
Athaliah	845–839					Shamshi-added V	824–810
Joash	839–800	Jehoahaz	817–801			Adadnirari III	810–782
Amaziah	800–786	Jehoash	801–786	Ben-hadad	800–?		
Azariah (Uzziah)	786–736	Jeroboam II	786–746				
Jotham	756–742	Zechariah	746				

of Hazael and his son Ben-hadad (who probably came to power only after the time of Jehoahaz) is a consequence of God's anger, Israel's faithlessness, and more specifically, 'the sins of Jeroboam' (cf. vv. 2–3 with Judg 2:13–14; 3:7–8, 11–12; 4:1–2, etc.). A later editor expands the parallel in vv. 4–6: like Israel at the time of the judges, Jehoahaz appeals to God for help which arrives in the form of a 'saviour'. The editor does not know who this saviour is. God's patience runs out, however, when Israel continues to adhere to 'the sins of Jeroboam' and even worships Asherah in Samaria. This note probably has two thoughts behind it: first that the glory of Jehu's struggle against Baal should also benefit his son and successor; secondly, that God's anger should not appear quite so inexorable and uncompromising.

(13:10–25) Jehoash of Israel and Elisha's Death The passage regarding Jehoash of Israel (his name is spelt 'Joash' in v. 12, 'Joahaz' in 2 Kings 14:1) is unusually structured. v. 10 contains the introductory formula, v. 11 gives his rating, and v. 12 is an early concluding formula. The following passage still concerns Jehoash and the concluding formula is repeated in 14:15–16. This distortion could be the result of the secondary insertion of two Elisha legends in vv. 14–19 and 20–1, which were grafted onto the narrative context by means of vv. 12–13 and 22–5. The second short legend tells the story of an incredible occurrence caused by an attack by the Moabites. It seems that the northern kingdom was weakened to such an extent after Jehu's coup that not only the Arameans, but other neighbours also took advantage of the situation. The hasty burial of a body in Elisha's grave (a burial cave?) results in a resurrection. There is no need to research the secret. Speculation, for example that the body only seemed dead, is entirely incorrect. The story glorifies Elisha's miraculous powers which could defy death even beyond his own grave, as it had done during his lifetime (2 Kings 4:18–37). The other legend contains Elisha's meeting with the king of Israel (the editors identify him as Jehoash) shortly before the prophet's death. Once more, Elisha acts as military support against the Arameans (as at 2 Kings 6–7). His honorary title, 'chariots of Israel and its horsemen', first used for Elijah in 2 Kings 2:12, originates from here. Elisha performs two magical deeds, or rather lets the king do so, due to his own weakness. The king does not know what he is doing, and is only enlightened by an explanation after the deed. The arrow shot to the east is an indication of future victory against Aram. It is significant that this shot is not to the north, showing us how far south the Arameans had advanced (cf. 2 Kings 10:32–3) and the point from where they are to be driven back. Striking upon the ground symbolizes the successful strikes against Aram. Unfortunately the king does not strike the ground often enough (perhaps a limitation of the first symbol's comprehensive claim). Here we learn that prophecy is not only a verbal phenomenon, but also has a material quality. Prophecies anticipate the future in words and deeds. Thus they do not only speak, but also use obscure sign language (cf. e.g. Isa 8:1–4; 20; Jer 27–8; Ezek 4–5; 12, amongst others). In vv. 22–5, the editor discloses the reason for attributing the legend to Jehoash: It would not fit Jehoahaz, since he, according to 13:3, was under lifelong pressure from Hazael and Ben-hadad. The passage concerning Jehoash (13:10–12; 14:15–16) does not,

however, mention Aramean pressure. The ailing Elisha's legend offered an explanation for this. Jehoash, as v. 25 explicitly states, is exactly as successful as Elisha had announced. God gave such aid to Israel despite its faithlessness because he still wished to honour his covenants with Abraham, Isaac, and Jacob (v. 23). If Israel still falls, it is not the fault of God!

(14:1–22) Amaziah of Judah and Joash of Israel We learn a number of remarkable things about the Judean king Amaziah which, apart from the framing information, no doubt stem exclusively from the Judean annals. He took revenge for his father's murder (v. 5, cf. 2 Kings 12:20–1; vv. 6–7 are an educated scribe's addition according to Deut 24:16, cf. also Ezek 18) only to fall victim to murder himself (vv. 19–20). The background to such uncharacteristic unrest in Jerusalem's royal house is no longer discernible. Amaziah also defeated the Edomites in the Arabah (v. 7, cf. also v. 22). There seems to have been a bitter struggle between Edom and Judah at the time, cf. 1 Kings 22:48; 2 Kings 16:6. Finally, the most detail is reserved for the way in which Amaziah waged a war with Israel which he ultimately lost (vv. 8–14). The cause of their enmity is unclear. According to tradition, it began with a challenging message from the Judean; the Israelite reply is flowery in style and proudly threatening in content. The military sparring takes place on Judean territory. Did Judah finally wish to free itself from subservience to Israel? Was it encouraged by the pressure exerted by Assyria upon Syria and Israel? Adadnirari III claims a successful westward campaign in 806, in which he defeated, amongst others, 'Omri-Land' (as Israel was ironically still called in Assyria) and also Edom (*ANET* 281–2). Perhaps this explains Amaziah's success against Edom and his boldness regarding Israel. He completely miscalculates, however. His army is defeated, he himself is captured, his palace and temple are plundered and a 200 m. breach in the particularly sensitive northern wall of Jerusalem is struck, allowing the Israelites virtually unhindered access to the city. Surprisingly, Amaziah actually outlives this devastating defeat by at least fifteen years. Nevertheless, his violent death probably relates back to these events. Before this is reported, however, the chronology of events is kept by the insertion of the concluding information about Joash of Israel and the accession of Jeroboam II (vv. 15–16). The choice of Amaziah's successor is made by 'the people of Judah' (v. 21), probably meaning 'the people of the land', the united free citizens of the Judean provinces who had played an increasingly influential role in Judean politics since Athaliah's displacement.

(14:23–9) Jeroboam II of Israel Although Joash achieved impressive success in a number of ways, Jeroboam's reign outshines him as the northern kingdom enjoys a glorious period. The blood and tears that flowed during the great political swing seem finally to have been rewarded. Aram-Damascus was ensnared between Israel and Assyria (cf. the comment on the war with Damascus in v. 28). Apparently, Jeroboam finally controlled the territories (on the Bekaa plain?) northwards to Hamath on the Orontes, and also to the east and south as far as the Dead Sea (v. 25). This would imply that he had a firm grip on Judah, or at least the Jordan valley and the regions east of the Jordan, Gilead and Gad. Amos's prophecy granted further highlights to Israel's momentary political success:

they were proud of the land they gained (Am 6:13), the higher classes at least enjoyed the incoming wealth (Am 6:4–6), the people believed they were God's favourites (Am 6:1). Amos prophesied that this happiness would not last long. The original author of the Deuteronomistic books of Kings passes over Jeroboam almost as quickly as he does over other, far less successful predecessors and successors. Later Deuteronomists see Israel's temporary prosperity as an opportunity to reflect (vv. 25–7): they obviously know of the prophet Jonah ben Amittai who was active in Israel at the time and had forecast Jeroboam's successes. Thus these were not coincidental, but God's will, occurring, like so many previous political events, 'according to the word of the LORD, which he spoke by the hand of . . .' (cf. the underlying rule in Deut 18:21–2 and the examples in 1 Kings 15:29; 16:12; 22:38; 2 Kings 10:17). But why did God want Israel to prosper at this time? Because it had suffered so much in the past, thereby arousing God's pity! This thought is closely connected to 13:5–6, 23–5. Such suggestions show how much the fate of the sister-state to the north still meant to the Judean historiographers. Jonah ben Amittai's brief appearance here also serves to lend the much later author of Jonah a historical basis for his claim that God's pity extended not only to Israel, but also to other peoples, even including Assyria.

(15:1–12) Azariah/Uzziah of Judah and Zechariah of Israel Azariah, also called Uzziah in Isa 6:1 and 2 Kings 15:13, was brought to the throne as a youth by the 'people of Judah', (14:21, cf. the analogous case in 2 Kings 11). When he later became incapable of ruling, the crown prince Jotham not only led the palace, but also explicitly 'govern[ed] the people of the land' (v. 5), indicating that this political group remained dominant. It is unclear how long the co-regency lasted. God is explicitly named as the source of Azariah's disease—further proof that direct causality did not apply, since the king had just received a positive judgement on his reign (vv. 3–4). Zechariah, the last ruler of the Jehu dynasty, is granted only half a year's reign before being killed in a coup (v. 8), in spite of his strong and successful father. Even so, the Deuteronomistic author knows that Zechariah 'did what was evil in the sight of the LORD'. The continuing presence of the state holy sites in Bethel and Dan suffices for such an assessment. Above all, it is important that the Jehu dynasty's fall is not seen as a coincidental event in history, but as the result of divine guidance. Lacking an appropriate prophet for the statement, the editor known to us from 13:5–6, 23–5; 14:25–7 lets God himself make the relevant announcement to the founder of the dynasty (2 Kings 10:30) and confirms it in v. 12. Here the editor implies that nothing, either good or bad, occurs or has occurred in the history of the people of God against his will. History cannot be understood on the basis of internal causality or powerful rulers, but only by concentrating on God's will.

In the next major section, 2 Kings 15:13–20:21, Israel falls and Judah is spared.

The Last Kings of Israel and Jotham of Judah (15:13–38)

(15:13–31) The Last Kings of Israel The northern kingdom's downfall is preceded by a spate of insurrections. The king's murderer, Shallum, who brought an end to the Jehu dynasty (15:10), can only enjoy his success for a month before himself

TABLE 13.5 *Dates of the reigns of the kings until the downfall of Israel*

Judah		Israel		Assyria	
Azariah (Uzziah)	786–736[?]	Menahem	746–736	Tiglath-pileser III	745–727
Jotham	756–742				
Ahaz	742–725	Pekahiah	736–734		
		Pekah	734–732	Shalmaneser V	727–722
		Hoshea	732–723	Sargon II	722–705
Hezekiah	725–696			Sennacherib	705–681

being slain by Menahem. The latter reigns for ten years before being succeeded by his son Pekahiah, but the young dynasty is again broken by another royal murder. The usurper Pekah is himself killed by Hoshea two years later (not twenty, as erroneously stated in 15:27). The Deuteronomistic historiographers report on the bloody events with laconic brevity. Presumably they interpret them as the cruelties of civil war (v. 16) and the Assyrian invasions (vv. 19–20, 29) as the destructive consequences of the 'sins of Jeroboam' burdening the state of Israel from the beginning. The political climate was, of course, especially unstable at the time. The Assyrian empire constantly pushed further into Syria-Palestine, whilst Egypt also tried to retain a share of influence there. The great powers naturally wished to take advantage of the tensions and rivalries with Israel. This is why the prophet Hosea, who lived through these events, criticized not only the many coups (Hos 8:4), but also the constantly switching alliances with Assyria and Egypt (Hos 7:11). Long-term political tendencies underlay these alliances. The Omrides joined the Arameans against Assyria, whilst Jehu and his entire dynasty did the opposite. Shallum's coup was probably an attempt—perhaps using Egyptian aid—to turn the tide back the other way (the editors are particularly interested in the fact that this fulfils a divine promise, cf. v. 12 with 2 Kings 10:30). The next ruler, Menahem, secured the throne by paying the Assyrians a large amount of silver (15:19). He does indeed appear on Tiglath-pileser's tribute list as an Assyrian vassal (*ANET* 283); 15:20 states that he collected the tribute 'from all the wealthy'—presumably to the relief and applause of poorer people. Perhaps the coup against his son was the consequence. Thus social contrasts which Amos criticized so sharply (eg. Am 2:6–7; 5:10–12), and which were greatly increased by pressure exerted by the great powers, become visible. As expected, Pekah's foreign policy was, like that of the Omrides, anti-Assyrian and pro-Aramean (cf. 15:29, 37; 16:5). But the power balance had meanwhile shifted. Lost territories are listed in 15:29, following the Syro-Ephraimite war (see 2 KINGS 16:6–9), leaving Israel as a rump state upon the mountains of Ephraim. This bitter defeat led to a plot by the (pro-Assyrian) opposition. Pekahiah was overthrown, whilst Tiglath-pileser claims to have personally installed his successor Hoshea (*ANET* 284). Though the Bible states that he came to power by his own actions (15:30), this need not be a contradiction.

(15:32–8) Jotham of Judah Like his father Azariah before him (15:3), Jotham is given a surprisingly good assessment by the editors—notwithstanding that both failed to abolish the 'high places' (this was done only by Hezekiah and Josiah, 18:4; 23:8), both had to endure adversity (15:5, 37) which could easily be ascribed to God's anger, nor is either king reported to have performed great political deeds. The short note, 'He built the upper gate of the house of the LORD' (v. 35) hardly merits the judgement, 'He did what was right in the sight of the LORD' (v. 34). Here we see that the Deuteronomistic theologians advocated a kind of collective, rather than individual causality (unlike the later Chroniclers). All Judean kings were doubly lucky: they were David's heirs and therefore heirs to the Davidic covenant (2 Sam 7:11–16), and they resided in Jerusalem, in the immediate vicinity of the house of YHWH. In most cases, this suffices to secure YHWH's favour. But it is important to remember that this double blessing is a gift and not a reward. After all, the Deuteronomists thought in terms of God's grace and mercy rather than of implacable demands.

Ahaz of Judah (16:1–20)

(16:1–9) Ahaz and the Syro-Ephraimite War Ahaz—a king who enjoyed the support of the prophet Isaiah (Isa 7)—is sharply criticized by the editors. In contrast to positive judgements given, this seems to require extensive explanation. In other words, God's favour may often be unmerited, but his anger is always deserved. The statement that Ahaz 'walked in the way of the kings of Israel' (v. 3) is not meant politically (where the opposite is the case, see below), but religiously: Ahaz has the same pagan tendencies as the kings of Israel. Not only does he allow the people to worship at the 'high places' outside Jerusalem (as Azariah and Jotham had also done, 15:4, 35), but himself makes sacrifices there (v. 4). The phrase 'on the hills and under every green tree' implies that these were Canaanite fertility rites (cf. 1 Kings 14:23–4; Jer 3:6, 13). Sacrifices of children are particularly foreign to YHWH-worship (cf. Deut 18:10 with v. 3 and 2 Kings 17:17; 21:6; 23:10). It is highly unlikely that the Deuteronomistic author could refer back to sources for all these allegations. He did, however, have information concerning Ahaz's construction of a non-YHWH altar in the temple of YHWH (see 2 KINGS 16:10–20 below). The rest of the claims are added from the standard Deuteronomic/Deuteronomistic repertoire, thus characterizing Ahaz as a quasi-heathen king sitting upon David's throne. The author is more interested in his type than his deeds. It is simply convenient that the 'Annals' offered a number of unfavourable political developments during this king's reign. In taking Elath from Judah, the Edomites took their Judean opponent's access to the Red Sea and thereby their control of the King's Highway through east Jordan to northern Arabia and Syria (v. 6). For the time being the shifting struggle between these two nations ends here, with Judah finally drawing the shorter straw (cf. 1 Sam 14:47; 2 Sam 8, 3; 1 Kings 11:14–22, 25b; 22:48; 2 Kings 3:8; 8:20–2). Later, during the time of exile, when the Deuteronomistic History is written, Judah will suffer greatly under Edom (Ob 8–15). Even more severe are the consequences of the Syro-Ephraimite war (vv. 5, 7–9). Around 734, Aram-Damascus and northern Israel form a powerful alliance with the background support of the Phoenician and Philistine city-states and Egypt in order to resist the advance of the Assyrians. Ahaz apparently refused to join this alliance and was therefore to be replaced by a

certain ben Tabeel, a man with an Aramean or Phoenician name (cf. Isa 7:6). Ahaz does not know what to do other than to appeal (against the advice of Isaiah, cf. Isa 7:3–9) to the Assyrian king for help, to become his vassal ('I am your servant and your son'), but first of all to pay him a heavy tribute (v. 8; he accordingly appears in the list of Tiglath-pileser's tributes in 733, ANET 282). The 'Annals' seem to consider Ahaz's move to be decisive in bringing about war (v. 9). In fact (and according to Isa 8:1–4) the Assyrians would probably have attacked such a dangerous alliance in any case. The kingdom of Aram was already defeated by 732, its capital Damascus conquered and destroyed, whilst Israel was heavily punished and decimated (2 Kings 15:29). Judah, having voluntarily placed itself in Assyrian hands, was now in danger of being crushed by them.

(16:10–20) Ahaz Paganizes the Temple Ahaz wishes or is forced to give his oath of allegiance to his master personally, in Damascus, where Tiglath-pileser has set up headquarters. Here he sees an altar which he uses as a model for a new altar in the temple at Jerusalem. He himself later consecrates it and orders the required sacrificial rite (vv. 12–15a). This was not sacrilegious in itself—the altar was dedicated to YHWH and the offerings were quite regular (cf. Num 29:39). The problem was the bronze altar which had previously stood at its place and had been commissioned (or perhaps taken over, 1 Kings 8:64) by Solomon. The mere fact that it had to make way for a stone altar would have been sacrilegious to conservatives. Worse still, Ahaz orders that the revered old altar 'shall be for me to inquire by' (v. 15b), i.e. it should subsequently serve the purpose of divining omens from the inspection of entrails and liver, as was common practice in Assyrian religion. Thus sacrifice was made to YHWH at the new altar in front of the temple whilst Assyrian rites were performed at the old YHWH-altar behind the temple. In this way Ahaz tried to balance out the expectations of his new master with the sensitivities of his own population (cf. Spieckermann 1982: 368). The note in v. 17f. shows what little regard the Assyrians took for the religious feelings of their vassals. The heavy bronze instruments once installed by Solomon in the temple court (cf. 1 Kings 7:27–39) were probably dismantled as part of the tribute demanded, along with other structural changes to the temple, made 'because of the king of Assyria'.

Israel's Downfall (17:1–41)

(17:1–6) The Military Collapse Assyrian pressure hit Judah's sister-state far harder. It existed only as a rump state from 732, its northern, western, and eastern territories having been placed directly under Assyrian administration (15:29). Despite, or perhaps because of, this, anti-Assyrian resistance, naturally instigated by Egypt, soon arose (v. 4). The Assyrians struck back mercilessly: after resisting bitterly, the capital Samaria was conquered and part of the population (not all of Israel, v. 6, probably the upper class) was deported. They were not displaced en bloc, as the Jews were later to Babylon, but were shifted decentrally to north-east Syria. This method of destroying races resulted in the exiled northern Israelite people leaving few traces in history and tradition, unlike the Jews. The last Israelite king, Hoshea, is given a relatively mild judgement by the Deuteronomists (v. 2), though not out of compassion, but to stress that the catastrophe had deeper roots than the unfortunate or mistaken policy of a single king.

(17:7–23) Theological Causes of the Catastrophe The Deuteronomistic theologians make explicit statements at decisive moments in history: in Josh 1: 23–4; Judg 1–2; 1 Sam 7–8; 12; 2 Sam 7; 1 Kings 8, and also at this point. We must clearly understand the meaning of events. It seems that several hands were responsible for this reflection. vv. 21–3 certainly differ from the previous verses, recapitulating the kingdom's division, 'the sin of Jeroboam' tainting northern Israel's subsequent history and the woeful announcements of the prophets. The conclusion is that it had to end this way. The state cult in Bethel steered the state onto a collision course which no northern dynasty turned away from. Thus all the prophets could do was to predict the fall of every house (1 Kings 14:7–11; 16:1–4; 21:21–4; 2 Kings 9:7–10). By contrast to this stereotypical Deuteronomistic view of woeful prophecy, v. 13 shows another of the prophets' roles, namely to state the Torah. The entire passage (vv. 12–19) expresses an underlying tone of strict laws: YHWH forbade a number of things, but Israel did them anyway (vv. 12, 15). He also ordered a number of things which Israel did not do (vv. 13, 15). Israel is accused of all manner of syncretism and paganism (vv. 9–10, 15–17), interestingly including actions which are only attributed to Judah in the Deuteronomistic History (cf. vv. 9–10 with 1 Kings 14:23–4, vv. 16–17 with 2 Kings 16:3; 21:3–6, as well as Judah's explicit mention in v. 19). This implies that Judah will experience the same fate for the same reasons as Israel some time in the future. There is perhaps a further (and older) textual layer in vv. 7–8, 20, in which Israel is accused of being influenced by other cultures although YHWH expelled all foreign peoples from Israel before its land was taken—a perspective also found in the original edition of the Deuteronomistic book of Joshua. Whatever the case, the Deuteronomists all agree that the state of Israel was condemned to fall for breaking the first commandment. One should not consider this too narrow-mindedly religious. The first commandment underlies all the other commandments. Those who disregard God also disregard his laws and therefore the rights of their fellows and of all mankind. Recent history is full of examples of this.

(17:24–41) The Immigrants from the East and their Cults True to their principle of destroying races in newly conquered territories, the Assyrians not only displaced Israelites eastwards, but also—probably over a longer period of time—deported people from other areas of the empire to Israel. The cities listed in vv. 24, 29–31 are partly in Mesopotamia and partly in Syria. Ethnic mixing was carried out in order to avoid the development of cores of resistance, and to paralyse the regions using the tension between peoples. The Deuteronomistic historiographers are primarily interested in the religious consequences of this policy: inevitably, religion in the province of Samaria became mixed. The gods and ritual traditions of various peoples are listed academically. The authors observed with a certain amazement how such religions established themselves so close to Judah. But they were also surprised by the fact that the religion of YHWH by no means disap-

peared, but united with others syncretistically (vv. 32–4, 41). The episode reported in vv. 25–8 offers an explanation for this phenomenon. It is unrealistic not only because of the plague of lions caused by religious problems. It also states that the foreigners had been imported without any prior instruction in how to worship YHWH. Another orthodox addition rigidly asserts that this colourful mixture of religions amongst the Samarians goes against the Torah (vv. 35–40). This is the beginning of the Jewish–Samaritan split. The line of theology and history leading up to the HB does indeed run via Judah and no longer via Israel. But the influence of Israelite tradition and faith had long been absorbed and would continue to be. The originally northern Israelite traditions of, for instance, Jacob, Joseph, the Exodus, the conquest of the land of Benjamin, the deliverers, Saul, Elijah and Elisha, Jehu, Hosea, and many others eventually found their way into the Bible through southward-fleeing refugees of the time or by other means. Also, conversely, the Judeans and Jews never forgot their Israelite brothers and sisters. This can be seen not only in surviving Israelite tradition, but also in Judean reflections such as Jer 30–1 and 1 Chr 7.

Hezekiah of Judah and the Prophet Isaiah (18:1–20:21)

(18:1–12) Hezekiah's Reign This king receives exceptional praise: he and Josiah (2 Kings 22:2) alone are comparable to David. There are various reasons for this: during Hezekiah's reign, Jerusalem was in mortal danger from the Assyrians, but, unlike Samaria, it did not fall. The prophet Isaiah is said to have supported him during this crisis, giving rise to a number of detailed stories. Furthermore, Hezekiah, like his successor Josiah, is said to have carried out religious reform. Reports of this (v. 4), however, are extremely brief and cannot be regarded as undoubted historical fact. Only the destruction of the Nehushtan, a snake-shaped cultic image traced back to none other than Moses (cf. Num 21:9), can really be attributed to Hezekiah, though details can no longer be discerned. Besides his piety (vv. 6–7), Hezekiah's foreign political activity is highlighted: he frees the land from Assyrian subservience and conducts successful campaigns against the Philistines (vv. 7–8). We know from an Assyrian source that Hezekiah was indeed the leader of an anti-Assyrian coalition from 705 BCE onwards, arresting the pro-Assyrian king of Ekron in this capacity. The editors—perhaps on a late textual level—repeat the description of the northern sister-state's defeat at the hands of the Assyrians (cf. vv. 9–11 with 2 Kings 17:3–6), not without naming the entire population's lack of loyalty to the Torah as its cause (v. 12). How will Judah fare by comparison?

(18:13–16) The Assyrians Attack and Force Tribute Payment The Assyrians also stormed Judah. Soon the entire country was occupied and Jerusalem besieged. King Sennacherib depicted his victory over the strong fortress Lachish in a stone relief in his palace at Nineveh (now in the British Museum) and showed Hezekiah's desperate situation on a victory monument: 'As to Hezekiah, the Jew, he did not submit to my yoke, I laid siege to 46 of his strong cities . . . Himself I made a prisoner in Jerusalem, his royal residence, like a bird in a cage. I surrounded him with earthwork in order to molest those who were leaving his city's gate' (*ANET* 288).

The Bible text admits that Hezekiah could only free himself from Assyrian pressure by conceding defeat and paying a heavy tribute. This also conforms with Sennacherib's report: 'Hezekiah . . . did send me, later, to Nineveh, my lordly city, together with 30 talents of gold, 800 talents of silver, precious stones . . . [and] all kinds of valuable treasures, his [own] concubines, male and female musicians' (ibid.). This happened in 701 BCE. There is hardly a doubt that the biblical text, presumably stemming from Judean annals, reports on the same incidents. Thus it is all the more surprising that we are told of further Assyrian pressure *after* these events. So from 18:17 onwards another source seems to have been used, i.e. the legends of Isaiah which are inserted here by the editors. They give the impression that the Assyrians break their word after receiving the tribute and put further pressure on Jerusalem (cf. the equivalent chain of events in 1 Kings 20:1–7). They are given a clear response!

(18:17–37) Rabshakeh's Speeches The Assyrian king sends a delegation of leaders from his camp in Lachish under the leadership of Rabshakeh (which means 'chief cup-bearer') with the intention of forcing Jerusalem to capitulate. The Assyrians did indeed use such psychological warfare. The envoy delivers two speeches: one to King Hezekiah and his negotiators (vv. 19–25) and one to the (warring) people on the city walls (vv. 27–35). His arguments are well thought out: Hezekiah cannot expect help from anywhere, not from Egypt (v. 21), nor from his own army (vv. 23–4), nor even from YHWH (vv. 25 and 22—this is probably an editorial cross-reference to 18:4). The people should not rely on false promises made by their king (vv. 29–30), nor on the help of YHWH (vv. 33–5), but should accept the Assyrian king's peace proposals and surrender (vv. 31–2). The Assyrian's speech, written by a Jewish narrator, is full of bitter sarcasm: exile seen as temptation (vv. 31–2), YHWH placed on the same level as any other city god (vv. 34–5), Rabshakeh in the role of a prophet of woe (v. 25). The key to placing this text historically may lie here. The deceptive language of the Assyrian ambassador is similar to that of Jeremiah, who advised capitulation when the Babylonians besieged Jerusalem in 589–587 (cf. Jer 37–8). It is possible that the core of the Isaiah legends was conceived to support the last Jewish king Zedekiah shortly before Judah's fall (Hardmeier 1990, exactly dating the event at 588). In any case the caricature of the imperial demagogue underlines a faith in YHWH's allegiance to his people and his holy city. Those who take no account of this miscalculate.

(19:1–8) Isaiah's First Oracle Rabshakeh's arguments do not go unnoticed. Hezekiah is aware of his serious predicament and sends a delegation to the prophet Isaiah for advice and encouragement. His answer is clear: 'Do not be afraid', a classic opening to a positive oracle. YHWH will send a 'spirit' to the Assyrian king (cf. 1 Kings 22:21–2) who will retreat to Assyria in panic after merely hearing a rumour. On returning home, he will be murdered. Each part of this oracle is mentioned as fulfilled in 19:8, 9a, 36–7. According to the text, an Egyptian army appears and forces Sennacherib to retreat. The Assyrian king also mentions the advance of an Egyptian army in his inscription, though he claims to have defeated them at Eltekeh (*ANET* 287, near the Philistine border, cf. Josh 19:44).

Perhaps this was indeed true, or perhaps exaggerated, or maybe he received news of an insurrection in the Baylonian heartlands, or merely retreated after accepting Hezekiah's surrender and payment of the tribute.

(19:9–19) Sennacherib's Letter and Hezekiah's Prayer All this, however, has still to happen. The Assyrians were still in Syria-Palestine. According to the text, Sennacherib tried to intimidate Hezekiah a second time. There is strong evidence that this is a second, more recent version of the story of Jerusalem's miraculous rescue, inserted by later Deuteronomistic historians (Camp 1990, whereby editorial emendments to assimilate v. 13 with 18:34 and v. 11 with 18:30 seem to have been carried out). In his letter, Sennacherib is even bolder than Rabshakeh in his comparison of YHWH with the useless gods of other defeated nations. Hezekiah also appears even more pious than in 19:1–4. His prayer has the unmistakable tone of YHWH-monotheism as expressed by Deutero-Isaiah. Hezekiah and the reader understand that YHWH, as opposed to all other gods, can help since he is the only one that exists!

(19:20–37) Isaiah's Second Oracle and Jerusalem's Liberation Isaiah's second response is much more detailed than the first. A separate song of scorn is inserted in vv. 21–8, probably composed later for this specific context. YHWH himself throws down the gauntlet to the king of Assyria (and Babylon and Persia): you boast about your power (vv. 22–4—cf. already Isa 10:7–10)—although it was I who granted it to you (vv. 25–7). Now I shall take it away from you (v. 28—the metaphor of a world leader being led away like an ox with a hook in his nose is defiantly comical!). The very late addition in vv. 29–31 draws attention to the blessed activity in the Jewish exiled community. The oracle actually continues in vv. 32–3 (v. 34 is a late-Deuteronomistic inclusion, cf. 1 Kings 11:12–13). The speech has an ABCBA structure. After the introductory and before the concluding formula ('thus says the LORD—says the LORD') is the double assurance that the enemy 'shall not come into this city' surrounding the central statement: the enemy's weapons cannot harm Jerusalem and he shall retreat in failure. This prophecy immediately takes effect: a plague-bringing angel kills scores of soldiers in the Assyrian camp (v. 35), upon which Sennacherib retreats (v. 36a). Attempts to make such a miracle historically plausible—by stating that Herodotus once mentioned a plague of mice in the Assyrian army and that mice are known to be carriers of disease—misunderstand the story's actual intention. It is a call to acknowledge the unlimited power of God and the strictly limited power of man.

(20:1–11) Hezekiah's Illness is Cured by Isaiah The following passage contains two individual episodes from Hezekiah's life. The first tells how Hezekiah received Isaiah's help during a severe illness. It is probable that the story originally depicted the prophet as a miracle healer: he goes to the king (v. 1a), promises him a further fifteen years of life (v. 6a) and orders a fig paste to be spread on the diseased part of his body, 'so that he may recover' (v. 7—according to the original version in Isa 38:21). The king asks for a sign that he really will get better (v. 8a), upon which the prophet uses his miraculous powers to reverse the movement of the shadow on the sundial put up by Hezekiah's father, Ahaz: a symbol that Hezekiah's life-clock has also been turned back (vv. 9–11). The recovery itself is not reported on further, though it must have occurred. A late editor picked up this story and converted it into a didactic narrative regarding an exemplary king: Isaiah initially makes a prophecy of woe (v. 1*b*, cf. 2 Kings 1:16), upon which Hezekiah complains to God, referring to his piety (vv. 2–3). God mercifully sends Isaiah back to the king with a positive prophecy: he will recover—significantly in order soon to return to the temple (vv. 4–5). During his remaining lifetime, he witnesses Jerusalem's liberation from the Assyrians (v. 6*b*, close parallel to 19:34). The way this story is inserted leads to a strange chronology of events: Hezekiah did not reign a further 15 years after 701 (up to 686). This leads to the suggestion that the number 15 belonged to the core of the formerly independent story and also that the story should be placed chronologically *before* 2 Kings 18–19 (see Ruprecht 1990).

(20:12–21) The Babylonian Envoys and Isaiah's Attitude towards them This episode, containing Hezekiah's negotiations with envoys sent by the Babylonian leader Merodach-Baladan, would also be more plausible if it took place before 701: the anti-Assyrian coalition would have thus extended beyond Egypt to Syria. Marduk-apla-iddina (as he was correctly called) was chief of the Aramean tribe Bit Jakini and troubled both Sargon and Sennacherib with his claim to the Babylonian throne in the late eighth century. It seems that Hezekiah wanted to win him over as an ally and thus tried to impress his envoys by putting his military might and his war-funds on display (he might have even passed some of this on to Babylon). According to the narrative, this caused the prophet Isaiah to turn against him. This conforms with the 'real' Isaiah's strong criticism of Hezekiah's alliance policy in Isa 30–1. It is unlikely that Isaiah explicitly forecast the catastrophe of 587 (see vv. 17–18). By placing this episode at the end of the Isaiah–Hezekiah narrative, the late editor could refer forwards to Jerusalem's fate despite its miraculous rescue in 701. Hezekiah's flirtation with Judah's later deadly enemy and his feather-headed reaction to Isaiah's warning (v. 19) do not show the king in a good light. Perhaps the editor of this passage was particularly critical of the kings (Camp 1990). The concluding comments on Hezekiah (v. 20*f.*) stress the king's energy and stem from the original author of Kings. Here he quotes from the Annals of the Kings of Judah, which also mention the construction of the conduit to Siloam which carried water from Gihon, Jerusalem's main well, under the city of David to the Pool of Siloam and was a technical masterpiece of its time. So that the new source of water was not outside the city walls, namely to the west instead of the east of the old city of David, one wall had to be built, stretching far further westwards. Remains of such fortifications have indeed been found. The newly created city district seems primarily to have been inhabited by refugees from the fallen kingdom of Israel.

The final major section, 2 *Kings 21:1–25:30*, documents the last kings of Judah and the downfall of the kingdom.

Manasseh and Amon (2 Kings 21:1–26)

Manasseh's 55-year reign is the longest of all the kings of Judah—and in the eyes of the author of Kings, he is the worst. He is the Judean image of the Israelite arch-rogue Ahab. Like Ahab in Samaria, Manasseh introduces the worship of Baal and Asherah to Jerusalem (cf. vv. 3, 7 with 1 Kings 16:32–3). He too sheds innocent blood, in fact excessively (cf. v. 16 with 1 Kings 18:4; 19:10; 21). Just as Ahab's enemy was Elijah, so is Manasseh strongly opposed by prophets (vv. 10–15). Manasseh is also a sinister reflection of the glorious king Josiah, who must abolish all the deities reintroduced by his predecessor (cf. 2 Kings 23). In brief: the extensive list of sins in vv. 2–9 must rather be the editors' nightmare than a record of reality. There are, however, elements that fit exactly into the time and situation. Manasseh was Assyria's vassal, one could even say servant. Assyrian sources mention him as a bringer of tribute and as a military follower. There is not the slightest indication that he resisted his masters. This is precisely the reason for the length of his reign. Manasseh represented and reproduced Assyrian violence (v. 16). If he knew how to adapt to the political power, why not do the same in the field of religion (see Spieckermann 1982 and van Keulen 1996, *contra* McKay 1973)? vv. 3 and 5 mention the worship of the 'host of heaven', astral deities of Mesopotamian origin. Baal and Asherah (v. 3) could be the conventional names for the highest god and goddess in the Assyrian pantheon, Asshur and Ishtar. Prophetic resistance to Manasseh's policy is indeed probable and is made tangible for us through figures such as Nahum and Habakkuk (Dietrich 1994). The summarizing prophetic speech in vv. 10–15 was composed by Deuteronomistic authors, however, looking specifically forward to Jerusalem's first siege and defeat (a reference back to this speech is made in the passage concerning the siege in 2 Kings 24:2, see Dietrich, 1972). The editors worsen Manasseh's historically bad reputation in other ways also (especially in vv. 3*a*, 4, 6–9). The entire section concerning

TABLE 13.6 *Dates of the reigns of the last kings of Judah and Assyria, and kings of Babylon*

Judah		Assyria		Babylon	
Manasseh	696–641	Sennacherib	705–681		
		Esar-haddon	681–669		
Amon	641–639	Assurbanipal	669–631		
Josiah	639–609			Nabopolassar	626–604
Jehoahaz	608	Assur-uballit	611–606		
Jehoiakim	608–598			Nebuchadnezzar	604–562
Jehoiachin	598[–562]				
Zedekiah	598–587			Evil-Merodach	562–560

his reign, encompassing more than half a century of Judean history, does not contain a single positive word for him. One feels the apprehension that Judah is heading swiftly towards an abyss. This impression is strengthened when one learns that Amon, Manasseh's son and successor, 'walked in the way which his father walked' (v. 21). Unlike his father, he soon meets his fate. But then something surprisingly hopeful happens: 'The people of the land'—the same political group who brought about the downfall of the 'evil' queen Athaliah, enabling the 'good' king Joash to come to power (2 Kings 11:18, 20)—intervene to punish the king's murderers and place a certain Josiah on the throne. The struggle between loyalty and disloyalty to YHWH, and thus between the existence and destruction of the kingdom of Judah, has taken an unexpected turn.

Josiah (2 Kings 22:1–23:30)

(22:1–20) The Book of the Law is Discovered Josiah comes to the throne as a child. 'The people of the land' guide and support him. Even the great reforms introduced eighteen years later accord with their views. In 621, Assyria's fortune is in deep decline. In 612 Nineveh was to be defeated by Babylon, having achieved independence under Nabopolassar in 625. It is high time to leave the sinking ship of Assyria. Judean reformers held in opposition by Manasseh urged internal change, including religious reforms. Whether they smuggled the ominous 'book of the law' into the temple and ensured that the high priest 'found' it during routine renovations (cf. 2 Kings 12), or whether the book had indeed been there for a longer time, will always remain a secret. A recently published ostracon (see Bordreuil, Israel, and Pardee 1998) seems to strengthen the evidence for a temple renovation just during the reign of Josiah. Critical research is united in believing that the discovered book was Deuteronomy or its core (Deut 6ab–28). It takes the form of a speech made by Moses shortly before taking the land of Israel and could thus have been considered to be very old. It does include older material, but cannot have been compiled before the seventh century. Apart from the closing admonitions (Deut 28), it is the strict demand for the exclusive worship of YHWH (Deut 6:5!) and the cultic veneration of YHWH alone in the central holy site of Jerusalem (Deut 12) which seem to impress Josiah especially. One can be certain that other rules such as the social laws of Deuteronomy (e.g. Deut 15; 24) became state law under Josiah (cf. Crüsemann 1992; Albertz 1992; Kessler 1992). All of this represents a pro-YHWH reform movement with allies in the highest circles of the court and the temple as well as the king himself. The prophetess Huldah, to whom Josiah appeals for an oracle, also supports the reforms. She encourages the king to make a great new beginning—even if the original wording of her prophecy was later overwritten by Deuteronomistic phrases pointing out the continued inevitability of the end of the kingdom of Judah (Dietrich 1972). What is being stated clearly is that Josiah and his reforms are not to blame for Judah's fate!

(23:1–24) Implementation of Religious Reforms First of all, in an almost democratic manner, Josiah makes sure he has a broad basis of support for his reform plans: 'All the people joined in the covenant' (v. 4); the terms 'people' and 'coven-

ant' play a significant role in Deuteronomy. The ensuing reforms cover three areas. The temple of Jerusalem which was to be cleansed of non-YHWH influences was given the designated central role (vv. 4–7, 11–12). The cult sites in the Judean provinces which were regarded as paganized (vv. 8–10, 13–14) and cult sites on the land of the former northern kingdom, above all the altar of Bethel upon which lay 'the sin of Jeroboam' (vv. 12–20), were to be eradicated. The third area introduced the communal passover feast in accordance with the newly introduced covenant (vv. 21–3, cf. Deut 16:5–6). The historical question of whether Josiah actually took all the measures listed here is not easily answered. It depends on the perspective of the text's source: are the reform measures of 'good' kings (as well as the cultic deviations of 'bad' kings) simply part of an inner-Deuteronomistic reference system, and therefore theological rather than historical phenomena (Hoffmann 1980; Würthwein 1984)? Or do the reports in 2 Kings 22–3 stem from a relatively extensive, older source which was close to the events (Dietrich 1977; Spieckermann 1982)? Similarly to the list of Manasseh's sins (21:3–9), there are passages in the report on Josiah's reforms which fit exactly with the state of affairs in the last years of the Assyrian empire: he sets aside astral worship (23:5), horses and chariots of the sun (v. 11), roof-top altars (for sacrifices to the astral gods, v. 12), perhaps also the worship of Asshur and Ishtar in the form of Baal and Asherah (vv. 4, 6–7—here, the hardly inventable reference to chosen women weaving robes for 'Asherah'; cf. also the extremely exact naming and placing of cult sites in v. 8b). There are also notes which stem from Deuteronomistic ideology, however (e.g. vv. 10, 13–14, 19–20, 24). The Bethel-scene's core (vv. 15–18) could be historically correct—Bethel lies 20 km. north of Jerusalem—but has clear political references to 1 Kings 13. Closing down cultic sites outside Jerusalem accords with Deuteronomic thought (Deut 12), whilst displacing and degrading the resident priests to the rank of *clerus minor* is definitely not demanded there (cf. the role of the Levites, for instance, in Deut 14:27–9). Thus both policies seem plausible. On the whole, one could say that Josiah's reforms significantly changed conditions within his sphere of influence. Judah was beginning to free itself from the cultural and political influence of its neighbours in order to concentrate on its essential qualities: faith in YHWH and a corresponding religious and social lifestyle.

(23:25–30) Josiah's End and Judgement The editors give Josiah the highest praise for his religious reforms (v. 25). Jeremiah also describes him as a popular ruler who was modest and socially just (Jer 22:15–16). Thus it is all the more painful and inexplicable that God should surrender his chosen people and the holy city to their enemies. The phrases used in vv. 26–7 show how threatening the demise of the state of Judah was to the Jewish people and the religion of YHWH. Nor does Josiah's personal fall encourage faith. He confronts Pharaoh Necho (609–593) who was on a campaign northwards to protect the ailing Assyrians from the Babylonians. This action displays Josiah's principally anti-Assyrian attitude, whilst his presence in Megiddo shows that he was free to move about on Israelite territory. But the Pharaoh 'met him' and 'killed him' (v. 29), which makes it sound as if victory was easily accomplished. Were the Judeans simply too weak or did Josiah perhaps lack the support of the entire army? 'The people of the land' were at any rate loyal to him even beyond his death, ensuring a decent funeral and making his son Jehoahaz his successor. It was obviously a conscious choice, since Jehoahaz had an elder brother, as the comparison between 23:31 and 36 shows. This fact shortly proved to be disastrous.

Jehoahaz, Jehoiakim, Jehoiachin, and Jerusalem's First Capture (2 Kings 23:31–24:17)

Jehoahaz presumably follows Josiah's policies (even if the editors give him a negative assessment—perhaps due to a lack of detailed information and in order to explain his sorry end). Jeremiah at least uses no words of anger concerning him, only grief (Jer 22:10–12). Yet only a few months after his accession, Necho, returning from his northern campaign, orders Jehoahaz to Syria, takes him prisoner, and deports him to Egypt where he dies. Necho places his older brother Eliakim upon the throne, giving him the throne-name Jehoiakim and thereby underlining his subservience. Tribute is also collected. Is this recompense for the Egyptian's intervention in favour of Eliakim? It is no coincidence that the tribute is collected from 'the people of the land' (23:35). The reform party who had the upper hand under Josiah is thus powerless—with the consequence that Judah, having just been freed of Assyrian influence, is now firmly in Egyptian hands. When Babylon's new and powerful ruler Nebuchadnezzar II defeats Egypt in 604 BCE at Carchemish on the Euphrates, however, Jehoiakim slips into the role of Babylonian vassal, only to return under Egypt's wing a little later (24:1). Jehoiakim is cunning and mean as well as antisocial and brutal (Jer 22:13–19; 36). The editors are relatively mild in their judgement (23:37), referring back to the sins of Manasseh and the ensuing prophecies to explain Nebuchadnezzar's measures against Judah's resistance (24:2–4). Jehoiakim dies of natural causes—just before Nebuchadnezzar arrives in Jerusalem with a large army (24:6). His poor son Jehoiachin has to pay for his father's deeds. Nebuchadnezzar besieges Jerusalem, completely unhindered by Judah's protector, Egypt (24:7). Jehoiachin capitulates to the superior enemy without resistance (24:12). According to Jer 13:18–19, the southern parts of the kingdom of Judah were partitioned and placed under foreign administration. What led Jehoiachin to accept all these measures? Was it wisdom or fear, or even inadequate support from his own people? Or was it perhaps relatively generous conditions granted by Nebuchadnezzar on receiving Jerusalem? Hard as the tributes and deportations were, they were not fatal, not even to those hit hardest, the élite 'ten thousand', and certainly not to the simple farmers, 'the poorest people of the land' (24:14). The latter were perhaps even glad to see the back of Jehoiachin's upper class, whilst the Babylonians cleverly took advantage of such internal tensions (Dietrich 1997c). On the other hand, the exiles could expect a relatively bearable lifestyle in Babylonia and maintain the hope of soon returning home (cf. Jer 29). This hope was soon to be dashed as the first deportation was quickly followed by a second. Death had knocked on Judah's door.

Zedekiah and the Final Conquest of Jerusalem (2 Kings 24:18–25:21)

Judah's last king is a real brother of Jehoahaz (cf. 24:21 with 23:31) and therefore an uncle of the previously deported Jehoiachin (24:17), though he is in fact not much older. Thus Nebuchadnezzar reverts back to the old line of Josiah in placing Mattaniah upon the throne and giving him the throne-name Zedekiah. From him one could expect a policy which would be acceptable to both 'the people of the land' and Babylon. Thus Jeremiah is shown to have been his confidant (Jer 37:17–21; 38:14–28). Zedekiah, however, goes against the prophet's advice in choosing to turn his back on Babylon (cf. 2 Kings 24:20 and Ezek 17). Exiled opposition spreading nationalistic propaganda obviously manages to win him over (Jer 27–8). The editors do not concern themselves too much with such political matters and are satisfied with a brief and negative statement regarding Zedekiah (24:19). Greater attention is given to Jerusalem's defeat. The siege lasts nineteen months (25:1, 8). 'The people of the land' seem to resist bitterly before being overcome by hunger (v. 3, Lam 2:11–12; 4:4–5, 9–10). When the besiegers manage to breach the city walls, Zedekiah undertakes a sortie, is captured and horrifically punished (vv. 4–7). What follows is a detailed and brutally sober description of the horrors which accompany defeat: destruction, burning, plundering, deportation, executions (vv. 8–21a). Not only the people's woe, but also the fate of the temple—after all the place of which YHWH said 'My name shall be there' (23:27)—is the subject of the narrator's pity (25:13–17). The concluding statement in 25:21b, 'So Judah went into exile out of its land' is clearly too general. As 25:12 indicates (though also too hesitantly!) the second wave of deportations still left the majority of the population in the country. Are we here dealing with an exile-oriented perspective of the events?

The Jews under Babylonian Rule (2 Kings 25:22–30)

(25:22–6) Gedaliah's Governorship The books of Kings and the Deuteronomistic History do not close with the horrific news of Jerusalem's defeat, but with reports of tentative new beginnings following the end. The first of these, however, ends in disaster despite commencing so promisingly: the Babylonians try to consolidate their position in the country, placing the more or less pro-Babylonian agrarian population under a Judean governor. The choice of Gedaliah shows intimate knowledge of Judean internal politics, since he stemmed from the famous Shaphan family who had always supported the political aims of Josiah's line (cf. 2 Kings 22:8–12; Jer 36:10). It is not coincidental that Jeremiah decides to remain amongst the people of the land, rather than joining the upper class in Babylon (Jer 40). Gedaliah significantly resides in Mizpah, a rural town 10 km. north-west of Jerusalem. The old royal residence has served its time (and in any case lies in ruins). Soon, however—perhaps only a few weeks later, as v. 25 seems to suggest if compared to v. 8, perhaps after a number of years—hope of a fresh start under Babylonian rule is rudely crushed. Ishmael, probably a representative of the Manasseh–Jehoiakim line within the royal family, carries out a terrorist attack against Gedaliah and his closest supporters. A large number of refugees flee to Egypt (expecting reprisals from Babylon), a land enjoying the sympathy of important political circles in Judah and already the residence of a large Jewish community in exile. This text passage is probably an excerpt from the more detailed description in Jer 40–1.

(25:27–30) Jehoiachin's Pardon The author of Kings shifts his view from the land of Judah and from the community in Egypt to that in Babylonia. Here, King Jehoiachin has been kept prisoner since his capture in 598 BCE. Clay tablets from 592 report on regular provisions from his Babylonian administrators. He himself becomes a symbol of the exiles' enduring hope for freedom, a return to the homeland, and the restoration of the Davidic kingdom. The prophecies of Ezekiel, who was also in exile, are dated according to Jehoiachin's 'years of rule' (e.g. Ezek 29:17; 31:1). He has sons and grandchildren (1 Chr 3:17–19), one of whom, Zerubbabel, would become a hopeful political figure following Babylon's decline (Ezra 2:2; Hag 2:20–3). The final report of Jehoiachin's pardon and even special honour is especially revealing: the author of the Deuteronomistic History must have composed his work shortly after this event. He correctly wished to stress that the history of Judean royalty did not end with the fate of Zedekiah and his sons (25:7). Above all, however, he wished to end the book with a sign of hope. Even if YHWH has repeatedly to punish his people (most severely at the end), he still regards them with steadfast love.

REFERENCES

Ackerman, S. (1993), 'The Queen Mother and the Cult in Ancient Israel', *JBL* 112: 385–401.

Albertz, R. (1992), *Religionsgeschichte Israels in alttestamentlicher Zeit* (2 vols.; Göttingen: Vandenhoeck & Ruprecht).

—— (1997), 'Wer waren die Deuteronomisten? Das historische Rätsel einer literarischen Hypothese', *EvT* 57: 319–38.

Alt, A. (1959), 'Menschen ohne Namen', in id., *Kleine Schriften zur Geschichte des Volkes Israel* (Munich: Beck), iii. 198–213.

—— (1964a), 'Israels Gaue unter Salomo', in id., *Kleine Schriften zur Geschichte des Volkes Israel* (Munich: Beck), ii. 76–89.

—— (1964b), 'Das Gottesurteil auf dem Karmel', in id., *Kleine Schriften zur Geschichte des Volkes Israel* (Munich: Beck), ii. 135–49.

Bartlett, J. R. (1976), 'An Adversary against Solomon, Hadad the Edomite', *ZAW* 88: 205–26.

Barré, L. M. (1988), *The Rhetoric of Political Persuasion: The Narrative Artistry and Political Intentions of II Kings 9–11*, CBQMS 20 (Washington, DC: Catholic Biblical Association of America).

Biran, A., and Naveh, J. (1993), 'An Aramaic Stele Fragment from Tel Dan', *IEJ* 43: 81–98.

—— (1995), 'The Tel Dan Inscription: A New Fragment', *IEJ* 45: 1–18.

Bloch-Smith, E. M. (1994), ' "Who is the King of Glory": Solomon's Temple and its Symbolism', in *Scripture and Other Artefacts: FS P. J. King* (Louisville, Ky.: Westminster/John Knox), 18–31.

Bordreuil, P., Israel, F., and Pardee, D. (1998), 'King's Command and Widow's Plea: Two New Hebrew Ostraca of the Biblical Period', *Near Eastern Archaeology* (formerly *BA*), 61: 2–13.

Busink, T. A. (1970), *Der Tempel von Jerusalem von Salomo bis Herodes I* (Leiden: Brill), i.

Camp, L. (1990), *Hiskija und Hiskijabild: Analyse und Interpretation von 2 Kön 18–20* (Altenberge: Telos Verlag).

Cross, F. M. (1973), 'The Themes of the Book of Kings and the Structure of the Deuteronomistic History', in id., *Canaanite Myth and Hebrew Epic* (Cambridge, Mass.: Harvard University Press), 274–89.

Crüsemann, F. (1992), *Die Tora: Theologie und Sozialgeschichte des alttestamentlichen Gesetzes* (Munich: Kaiser).

Dearman, J. A. (1989) (ed.), *Studies in the Mesha Inscription and Moab*, Archaeology and Biblical Studies 2 (Atlanta: Scholars Press).

Dever, W. G. (1982), 'Monumental Architecture in Ancient Israel in the Period of the United Monarchy', in T. Ishida (ed.), *Studies in the Period of David and Solomon and Other Essays* (Winona Lake: Eisenbrauns), 269–306.

—— (1990), *Recent Archeological Discoveries and Biblical Research* (Seattle: University of Washington Press), 85–117.

Dietrich, W. (1972), *Prophetie und Geschichte: Eine redaktionsgeschichtliche Untersuchung zum deuteronomistischen Geschichtswerk*, FRLANT 108 (Göttingen: Vandenhoeck & Ruprecht).

—— (1977), 'Josia und das Gesetzbuch (2 Reg XXII)', *VT* 27: 13–35.

—— (1979), *Israel und Kanaan: Vom Ringen zweier Gesellschaftssysteme*, SBS 94 (Stuttgart: Katholisches Bibelwerk).

—— (1986), 'Das harte Joch (1. Kön 12, 4): Fronarbeit in der Salomo-Überlieferung', *BN* 34: 7–16.

—— (1992), *David, Saul und die Propheten: Das Verhältnis von Religion und Politik nach den prophetischen Überlieferungen vom frühesten Königtum in Israel*, 2nd edn., BWANT 122 (Stuttgart: Kohlhammer).

—— (1994), 'Der Eine Gott als Symbol politischen Widerstands: Religion und Politik im Juda des 7. Jahrhunderts', in W. Dietrich and M. A. Klopfenstein, *Ein Gott allein?*, OBO 139 (Fribourg: Universitäts-Verlag Göttingen: Vandenhoeck and Ruprecht), 463–90.

—— (1996a), 'The "Ban" in the Age of the Early Kings', in V. Fritz and P. R. Davies (eds.), *The Origins of the Ancient Israelite States*, JSOTSup 228 (Sheffield: Academic Press), 196–210.

—— (1996b), 'Histoire et Loi: Historiographie deutéronomiste et Loi deutéronomique à l'exemple du passage de l'époque des Juges à l'époque royale', in A. de Pury, T. Römer, and J.-D. Macchi (eds.), *Israël construit son histoire* (Geneva: Labor et Fides), 297–323.

—— (1997), 'Wem das Land gehört: Ein Beitrag zur Sozialgeschichte Israels im 6. Jahrhundert v. Chr', *Ihr Völker alle, klatscht in die Hände*, FS E. S. Gerstenberger (Münster: Lit), 350–76.

—— (1998), 'Samuel und Königsbücher', *TRE* 30:

Ehrlich, E. L. (1953), *Der Traum im Alten Testament*, BZAW 73 (Berlin: de Gruyter).

Evans, D. G. (1966), 'Rehoboam's Advisors at Shechem, and Political Institutions in Israel and Sumer', *JNES* 25: 273–9.

Frisch, A. (1991), 'Structure and its Significance: The Narrative of Solomon's Reign', *JSOT* 51: 3–14.

Gordon, R. P. (1975), 'The Second Septuagint Account of Jeroboam: History or Midrash?', *VT* 25: 368–93.

Görg, M. (1991), 'Jachin und Boas: Namen und Funktion der beiden Tempelsäulen', in id., *Aegyptiaca-Biblica: Notizen und Beiträge zu den Beziehungen zwischen Ägypten und Israel*, Ägypten und Altes Testament 11 (Wiesbaden: O. Harrassowitz), 79–98.

Gray, J. (1977), *I & II Kings*, OTL, 3rd edn. (Philadelphia: Westminster).

Gressmann, H. (1907), 'Das Salomonische Urteil', *Deutsche Rundschau*, 130: 212–28.

Gunneweg, A. H. J. (1972), *Geschichte Israels bis Bar Kochba* (Stuttgart: Katholisches Bibelwerk).

Hardmeier, C. (1990), 'Umrisse eines vordeuteronomistischen Annalenwerkes in der Zidkijazeit', *VT* 40: 165–84.

Hauser, A. J., and Gregory, R. (1990), *From Carmel to Horeb: Elijah in Crisis*, JSOTSup 85 (Sheffield: JSOT).

Hentschel, G. (1984–5), *1 Könige, 2 Könige*, EB (Würzburg: Echter).

Hoffmann, H.-D. (1980), *Reform und Reformen*, ATANT 66 (Zurich: Theologischer Verlag).

Holder, J. (1988), 'The Presuppositions, Accusations, and Threats of 1 Kings 14: 1–18', *JBL* 107: 27–38.

Hurowitz, V. (1992), *I Have Built You an Exalted House: Temple Building in the Bible in Light of Mesopotamian and Northwest Semitic Writings*, JSOTSup 115 (Sheffield: JSOT).

Kaiser, O. (1962), *Die mythische Bedeutung des Meeres in Ägypten, Ugarit und Israel*, 2nd edn. BZAW 78 (Berlin: de Gruyter).

—— (1984), 'Den Erstgeborenen deiner Söhne sollst du mir geben', in id., *Von der Gegenwartsbedeutung des Alten Testaments* (Göttingen: Vandenhoeck and Ruprecht), 142–66.

Keel, O. (1977), *Jahwe-Visionen und Siegelkunst: Eine neue Deutung der Majestätsschilderungen in Jes 6, Ez 1 und 10 und Sach 4*, SBS 84/85 (Stuttgart: Katholisches Bibelwerk).

—— and Uehlinger, C. (1992), *Göttinnen, Götter und Gottessymbole: Neue Erkenntnisse zur Religionsgeschichte Kanaans und Israels aufgrund bislang unerschlossener Quellen*, QD 134 (Fribourg: Herder).

—— —— (1994), 'Jahwe und die Sonnengottheit von Jerusalem', in W. Dietrich and M. A. Klopfenstein, *Ein Gott allein?*, OBO 139 (Fribourg: Universitäte Verlag; Göttingen: Vandenhoeck and Ruprecht).

Kessler, R. (1992), *Staat und Gesellschaft im vorexilischen Juda: Vom 8. Jahrhundert bis zum Exil*, VTSup 47 (Leiden: Brill).

Keulen, P. S. F. van (1996), *Manasseh through the Eyes of the Deuteronomists: The Manasseh Account (2 Kings 21:1–18) and the Final Chapters of the Deuteronomistic History*, OTS 38 (Leiden: Brill).

Klopfenstein, M. A. (1996), '1 Könige 13', in id., *Leben aus dem Wort: Beiträge zum Alten Testament*, Beiträge zur Erforschung des Alten Testaments und des antiken Judentums 40 (Frankfurt am Main: Lang), 75–116.

Knauf, E. A. (1991), 'King Solomon's Copper Supply', in E. Lipinski (ed.), *Phoenicia and the Bible* (Leuven: Peeters), 167–86.

Levin, C. (1982), *Der Sturz der Königin Atalja: Ein Kapitel zur Geschichte Judas im 9. Jahrhundert v. Chr.*, SBS 105 (Stuttgart: Katholisches Bibelwerk).

—— (1994), *Die Entstehung der Rechabiter: FS O. Kaiser* (Göttingen: Vandenhoeck & Ruprecht), 301–17.

McKay, J. W. (1973), *Religion in Judah under the Assyrians 732–609 B.C.*, Studies in Biblical Theology, second series 26 (London: SCM Press).

McKenzie, S. L. (1987), 'The Source for Jeroboam's Role at Shechem (1 Kgs 11:43–12:3, 12, 20)', *JBL* 106: 297–300.

Malamat, A. (1965), 'Organs of Statecraft in the Israelite Monarchy', *BA* 28/2:34–65.

Minokami, Y. (1989), *Die Revolution des Jehu*, GTA 38 (Göttingen: Vandenhoeck & Ruprecht).

Mulder, M. J. (1998), *1 Kings, i. 1 Kings 1–11*, Historical Commentary on the Old Testament (Leuven: Peeters).

Nelson, R. (1981), *The Double Redaction of the Deuteronomistic History*, JSOTSup 18 (Sheffield: Academic Press).

Niemann, H. M. (1993), *Herrschaft, Königtum und Staat: Skizzen zur soziokulturellen Entwicklung im monarchischen Israel*, FAT 6 (Tübingen: Mohr).

Noth, M. (1968), *Könige I. Teilband*, BKAT 9/1 (Neukirchen-Vluyn: Neukirchener Verlag).

—— (1971), 'Die Wege der Pharaonenheere in Palästina und Syrien', in id., *Aufsätze zur biblischen Landes- und Al/tertumskunde* (Neukirchen-Venyn: Neukirchener Verlag), ii. 3–118.

—— (1991), *The Deuteronomistic History*, JSOTSup 15 (Sheffield: Academic Press). German original, 1943.

Parker, K. I. (1988), 'Repetition as a Structuring Device in 1 Kings 1–11', *JSOT* 42: 19–27.

Pritchard, J. (1974) (ed.), *Solomon & Sheba* (London: Phaidon).

Rad, G. von (1961), 'Die deuteronomistische Geschichtstheologie in den Königsbüchern', in id., *Gesammelte Studien zum Alten Testament*, TBü 8 (Munich: Kaiser), 189–204.

Ruprecht, E. (1990), 'Die ursprüngliche Komposition der Hiskia-Jesaja-Erzählungen und ihre Umstrukturierung durch den Verfasser des deuteronomistischen Geschichtswerkes', *ZTK* 87: 33–66.

Särkiö, P. (1994), *Die Weisheit und Macht Salomos in der israelitischen Historiographie: Eine traditions- und redaktionskritische Untersuchung über 1.Kön. 3–5 und 9–11*, Schriffen der finnischen exegetischen Gesellschaft 60 (Helsinki: Finnische exegetische Gesellschaft; Göttingen: Vandenhoeck and Ruprecht).

Schmitt, H.-C. (1972), *Elisa: Traditionsgeschichtliche Untersuchungen zur vorklassischen nordisraelitischen Prophetie* (Gütersloh: Gerd Mohn).

Seebass, H. (1967), 'Zur Königserhebung Jeroboams I', *VT* 17: 325–33.

Smend, R. (1970), *Jahweh War and Tribal Confederation: Reflections on Israel's Earliest History* (Nashville: Westminster/John Knox).

—— (1987), 'Der biblische und der historische Elia', in id., *Zur ältesten Geschichte Israels*, BEvT 100 (Munich: Kaiser), 229–43.

—— (1989), *Die Entstehung des Alten Testaments*, 4th edn. (Stuttgart: Kohlhammer).

Spieckermann, H. (1982), *Juda unter Assur in der Sargonidenzeit*, FRLANT 129 (Göttingen: Vandenhoeck & Ruprecht).

Steck, O. H. (1968), *Überlieferung und Zeitgeschichte in den Elia-Erzählungen*, WMANT 26 (Neukirchen-Vluyn: Neukirchener Verlag).

Talstra, E. (1993), *Solomon's Prayer: Synchrony and Diachrony in the Composition of 1 Kings 8, 14–61* (Kampen: KokPharos).

Timm, S. (1982), *Die Dynastie Omri: Quellen und Untersuchungen zur Geschichte Israels im 9. Jahrhundert vor Christus*, FRLANT 124 (Göttingen: Vandenhoeck & Ruprecht).

Veijola, T. (1982), *Verheissung in der Krise: Studien zur Literatur und Theologie der Exilszeit anhand des 89. Psalms*, Suomalaisen Tiedakatemian toimituksia ser. B 220 (Helsinki: Suomalainen Tiedeakatemia).

Wälchli, S. (1999), *Der weise König Salomo: Eine Studie zu den Erzällungen von der Weisheit Salomos in ihrem alt-testamentlichen und altoricutalischen Kontext*, BWANT 141 (Stuttgart: Kohlhammer).

Weippert, H. (1983), 'Die Ätiologie des Nordreiches und seines Königshauses (I Reg. 11,29–40)', *ZAW* 95: 344–75.

—— (1992), 'Die Kesselwagen Salomos', *ZDPV* 108: 8–41.

Weippert, M. (1971), *Edom: Studien und Materialien zur Geschichte der Edomiter auf Grund schriftlicher und archäologischer Quellen*, Diss. ev. theol., Berne.

Würthwein, E. (1984), *Die Bücher die Könige*, ATD 11/1–2 (Göttingen: Vandenhoeck & Ruprecht).

—— (1994), 'Naboth-Novelle und Elia-Wort', in id., *Studien zum deuteronomistischen Geschichtswerk*, BZAW 227 (Berlin: de Gruyter), 155–77.

Zohary, N. (1983), *Pflanzen der Bibel* (Stuttgart: Kohlhammer).

14. 1 and 2 Chronicles

H. P. MATHYS (tr. BENJAMIN LIEBELT)

INTRODUCTION

Name. 1. The Latin Father St Jerome (347/8–420 CE) gave the text the name of Chronicles (Chronicon totius divinae histor-iae, Chronicle of the Whole of Sacred History), whilst it was still known as Paraleipomena (the things omitted from earlier historical texts) in the Septuagint. In the Vulgate and HB editions, it has almost identical titles (Verba dierum and *dibrê hayyāmîm*). Chronicles contains a new version of events from Genesis to 2 Kings and continues its story up to Cyrus's edict, which it takes from Ezra 1:1–3.

2. According to a long-standing but now contested theory, the similarity between 2 Chr 36:22–3 and Ezra 1:1–3 indicates that the books of Chronicles, Ezra, and Nehemiah originally all had the same author or were two works by the same person, and were separated only on their inclusion in the canon. But even in the sections where the texts concur, their language and content differ significantly. The Chronicler was interested in all Israel (rather than merely in Judah) and did not object to mixed marriage with foreigners. The books of Ezra and Nehemiah contain contrary opinions, however, showing little interest in the house of David, prophets, or the dogma of retribution, whilst displaying an anti-Samaritan perspective. Such differences cannot simply be explained by the varying subject matter of 1 and 2 Chronicles and Ezra/Nehemiah. The latter two books were probably written as a sequel to the unsatisfactory ending to the books of Kings (Knauf 1995: 16–17).

3. Chronicles contains the entire history of the Davidic monarchy within the context of the genealogical development of the history of mankind and continues up to Cyrus's edict. At the turn of the 4th and 3rd centuries BCE, the Ptolomaic and Seleucid historiographers Manetho, Hekataios, and Berossos claimed that the origins of civilization lay in Egypt and Babylon respectively—i.e. the places where they themselves wrote. Civilization subsequently spread from those areas. The Chronicler countered this with the theological argument that God's actions began with all mankind, before focusing his narrative on Israel (1 Chr. 2–9), the reign of David (1 Chr 10–29) and the history of the Judean monarchy (2 Chr 1–36), and concluding with (the almost unmentioned exile and) Cyrus's edict (2 Chr 36:22–3). LXX's division of Chronicles into two books is logical since David's reign was one of the greatest events in his people's history, even if it is closely linked with Solomon's rule.

4. Another factor, which was just as important in Chronicles as the rule of God through the Davidic kings, was the temple and its music, both introduced and controlled by David. This has prompted many to suggest that the Chronicler was a Levite, especially in view of his distanced attitude towards the priests. The unusually high degree of scriptural learning in his text suggests that it could have been conceived by a well-read author for an educated readership.

Unity. As far as the text's unity is concerned, Galling (1954: 10–17) suggests two Chroniclers with close theological ties who wrote around 300 and 200 BCE respectively, the second author being especially responsible for the material in Chronicles which is unique in the OT. This and similar theories have had little support. The majority of researchers presume one underlying text which was added to at length (large parts of 1 Chr 1–9, 23–7, as well as other passages relevant to the Levites) or emended slightly to underline certain interests (such as the cult or priesthood).

Date. Chronicles is authorial rather than traditional litera-ture. It possibly stems from the late Persian period or more probably early Ptolemaic times. Cross's (1975) extremely early dating of a first edition (520 BCE) is unlikely since this pre-sumes a very brief period between the sources used and the text itself. Placing it in the Maccabean period is difficult because of a probable reference by the Greek historian Eupolemos to the LXX edition of Chronicles. 'Paralcipomena' contains no dating criteria. The daric coin mentioned in 1 Chr 29:7 was not introduced before 515 BCE and remained in use until Hellenistic times. The list of David's descendants (1 Chr 3:19–24)—the number of generations it contains is unclear—leads roughly up to 460 or 320 BCE; it is not of much help.

Theology. 1. The underlying presumption of this commen-tary is that Chronicles can be seen as a counter to Manetho, Hekataios, and Berossos, whilst providing an alternative to the predominant Hellenistic values of the time. It ascribes well-received Hellenistic improvements (in agriculture, fort-ress construction, army organization, and warfare technol-ogy) to Israel, but virtually ignores or implicitly combats Greek culture and theology.

This thesis has been partially anticipated by Welten (1973). According to him the war reports which are unique material in Chronicles reflect the constant threat to which Judah was exposed during the 3rd century through the conflicts of the Seleucids (in Babylonia) and the Ptolemeans (in Egypt). The unique material in Chronicles, in addition to war reports, encompasses information on the army's composition, build-ing activities of the kings, speeches, prayers, and cultic mater-ial. It seldom contains valuable source material which was overlooked by the books of Kings.

2. Despite attempting to be historical literature, Chronicles is surprisingly unhistorical in its portrayal. Once the Davidic monarchy has been installed, the temple constructed, and the cult accommodated, nothing more of fundamental import-ance occurs. The Chronicler only briefly refers to such im-portant events in Israelite history as the Exodus, the taking of the Land, and the judges period. As an author he viewed the history of Israel up to Cyrus's edict in its entirety. One example of this can be seen in his anticipation of the deportation of Transjordanian tribes to Assyria in 1 Chr 5:6.

3. It is of special significance that the Chronicler almost entirely ignored the Exodus. Those who see Chronicles as part of an anti-Samaritan historical text can easily explain this: Chronicles only deals with controversial subjects, whilst the Exodus had already been documented in the Pentateuch, a text common to Samaritans and Jews. Japhet (1997) argues that the Chronicler's relative silence regarding the Exodus expresses Israel's conviction of being native in the land since the beginning of time. This may at least be partly true, since Israel's exile in Babylon is also treated with extreme brevity. Beyond this the Chronicler regarded the temple and not the Exodus as the way to salvation and, after all, was mainly concerned with the history of the Davidic monarchy.

4. The text's major sources are Genesis to 2 Kings and Ezra 1:1–3, whilst a large number of other OT texts are incorporated. One can regard Chronicles (though not quite as exclusively as Willi (1972) suggests) as textual interpretation, particularly in passages where the Chronicler interprets events using the Pentateuch and other parts of the canon as his source, instead of the more frequently used books of Samuel and Kings (the wording of 2 Chr 7:18, e.g., contains elements taken from 1 Kings 9:5 and Mic 5:1 (ruler over Israel)). The Chronicler's reworking of sources can more or less be described as a midrash, Targum, or 'the rewritten Bible'. Exegetic techniques systematically developed and applied more strictly by the rabbis, among others, stem from Chronicles. The text has often been criticized for its lack of care and its poor language, although (with a few exceptions) it actually reveals thoughtful conception and an awareness of style and form.

5. The Chronicler omitted much from the source materials he used, such as the story of David and Bathsheba. This is not an attempt to show David in a better light, since the author presumed that the reader already knew the source text. The Chronicler was interested merely in the public side of David's reign.

6. The Chronicler's theology is impressive in its encompassing, strict, and even rational nature. God, who is never mentioned using his old names or any reference to place, is distant, but still keeps in touch with mankind. Intermediary bodies play no part in Paraleipomena. All the kings' actions derived directly from YHWH. YHWH imposed *his* monarchy, the kings sat upon *his* throne. This does not mean that the kings were simply puppets; the Chronicler depicted good kings as active and dynamic.

7. There was only one legitimate monarchy, namely the Davidides in Jerusalem. The kings of the northern kingdom were regarded as usurpers. Similarly, there was only one people, to whom the inhabitants of the north belonged if they acknowledged Jerusalem's exclusive rights of representation and accepted the cult performed there as uniquely legitimate. (This claim is underlined by the southern kingdom's right to use the name Israel.) Since the northern kingdom was illegitimate, its history is not described by the Chronicler. Nevertheless he often mentions the northern kingdom when it comes into contact with the south. Chronicles contains hardly any anti-Samaritan arguments, distinguishing it from Ezra/Nehemiah.

8. One of the most important and prevalent characteristics of Chronicles is the dogma of retribution applied to individuals: those who act correctly are rewarded, whilst crimes against YHWH are punished. In other words, a long and wealthy reign is proof of good behaviour, although a fall from grace is possible at any time. This dogma, which strongly distinguishes Chronicles from its (Deuteronomist) source in the books of Kings, forces the author to rewrite Israel's history, as the example of Manasseh clearly shows: his fifty-five-year reign shows him to be a God-fearing king, though reports from source texts suggest the opposite. The Chronicler elegantly solves this problem: as punishment for his godlessness, Manasseh is deported to Babylon by the Assyrians, where he repents. This allows him to return to Jerusalem and reign for a further 30 years. This strict dogma of retribution, which Albertz (1992: 622) cautiously interprets as a reaction to Greek Moira (or rather Tyche as I think) faith, can be seen as a plea by the Chronicler for responsible conduct. According to this Greek conception man is not the master of his own destiny.

It is recommended that two Bibles be used by readers of this commentary, the second for comparison of the relevant Chronicles chapter with parallel texts. Parallels are noted in good (academic) editions of the Bible.

COMMENTARY

1 Chronicles

The 'Genealogical Forecourt' (1 Chr 1:1–9:44)
Genealogies have different functions: legal (e.g. inheritance), political (e.g. legitimizing rule), sociological (necessary preconditions for positions of rank and profession), and psychological (personal identity and self-justification). Some of these aspects are relevant to Chronicles' genealogies and can perhaps be proved by interpreting individual cases in chs. 1–9. Another factor relevant to these nine chapters as a whole is that genealogies form an important part of historical literature. Ephoros of Kyme (4th cent. BCE), the first universal historian, used them, along with geographical data, when relating early history. The Chronicler used a similar method for his period, but writing a national history, focused upon Israel from 1 Chr 2 onwards. The people of Israel formed the core of the world's population, whilst Jerusalem (and its temple) formed its geographical centre. Within this people, Judah, Benjamin, and Levi stand at its heart. The Davidic genealogies extend beyond their exile, revealing a continued interest in them. In contrast with Ezra and Nehemiah (Ezra 2:59–63; Neh 7:61–5), narrow individual interests do not appear. The Chronicler's reluctance to extend the genealogies to his own period might have been a method of concealing his own situation. As well as genealogies, chs. 1–9 also contain a number of references to areas where groups settled, struggles between groups and professions, etc. Where the author did not use biblical source material, he mainly used contemporary knowledge and attitudes. His documentation forms an important source of the history of his time, although the inclusion of invented material is also possible.

Strictly theological matters also unfold in the 'genealogical forecourt'.

From Adam to Israel (1 Chr 1–2:2)

Taking material exclusively from Genesis and reducing it to a skeletal framework, the Chronicler portrayed the regularly changing family trees and genealogical lists of human history. He omitted only a few names, those of people whose lines ended with their deaths, such as Cain and the brothers of Abraham. A comparison of names with the source (Genesis) shows that some were incorrectly copied.

The structure of this section is: vv. 1–4: Adam to Noah; Noah's three sons Shem, Ham, and Japheth; vv. 5–7: Japhethites; vv. 8–23: Hamites; vv. 24–7: Semites; vv. 28–34a: the sons of Abraham; 34b–2:2 the sons of Isaac and Israel. The descendants of Noah's three sons were listed in inverse order so that the (major) line of Israel could be continued directly. This system of recording the major line last was repeated in subsequent passages.

Apparent contradictions and imbalances, which have often been used as evidence for certain critical approaches, can be readily explained by the Chronicler's intentions. The chapter primarily portrays the human world (areas of settlement are not mentioned), thus inviting the reader to read horizontally. Historical elements, however (see v. 43), are not entirely lacking. The chapter underlines the unity of mankind, whilst Genesis emphasizes individual differences. According to Tarn (1941: 74), the idea of universal humanity was only possible after the reign of Alexander the Great. Did the Chronicler apply such Hellenistic ideas to his text, influenced by the mood of the time, or did he develop them himself? Such a question can hardly be answered. Similarly, is the unquestionable universalism of ch. 1 an autonomous idea or does it serve as a background against which Israel's central position can be highlighted? The list comprises seventy-one names and almost exactly forms a world of seventy peoples (if we omit Nimrod).

v. 4, the reader can know that Shem, Ham, and Japhet are sons of Noah, and not successive generations only if he has read Gen 5. Chronicles frequently assumes knowledge of the reworked source models and is incomprehensible without it. vv. 32–4a, believed by many to be secondary since the source model seems to have been more extensively reworked than usual and given a different order. Going by the source, these verses belong to v. 28. vv. 43–54, Edom and Judah were neighbours and had the closest ties through the best and worst of times. This explains the disproportionately extensive reworking of the source material in Gen 36. 2:1, the third founding father in Chronicles is exclusively called Israel (not Jacob), except for the citation of Ps 105 at 1 Chr 16:17. He was the father of the people of Israel, which was still significant (if physically changed) during the Chronicler's lifetime.

Israel (1 Chr 2:3–9:44)

(2:2–55) Judah Chs. 2–9 describe Israel's identity using the genealogy of individual tribes, geographical information regarding settlements, and historical notes. The Chronicler mentions every tribe with the exception of Zebulun and Dan, whose omission cannot be explained. The three dominant tribes throughout Chronicles also dominate the 'genealogical fore-court', because of both the greater proportion of text given to them and their position at the beginning (Judah), the middle (Levi), and the end (Benjamin) of the relevant passage. It is not entirely clear by what criteria the Chronicler ordered his material as a whole. He takes both geographical and historical perspectives into account, as well as following the guidelines in Num 26.

The chapters (2–4) concerning Judah are split into three parts: chs. 2 and 4 deal with the tribes of Judah and Judah/Simeon respectively, whilst ch. 3 lists the sons of David.

vv. 3–5, the sources for this information are chiefly Gen 38, and also Gen 46:12 and Num 26:19–22 (for v. 5, cf. also Ruth 4:18). Only a small part of the narrative in Gen 38 was used. v. 3, it is not clear why the Chronicler mentioned the death of Er but ignored Onan's demise. A certain loss due to incomplete texts should be taken into account. God's name, YHWH, is first mentioned here. v. 7, Achar, the troubler of Israel: a reference to the story reported in Josh 7:25. The Chronicler renamed the man called Achan in Joshua, thereby continuing the play on words in the original story, in which he brings trouble (*achar*) upon Israel. He has to be called Achar: *nomen est omen*. vv. 10–12 contain the line from Ram to Jesse, whose seven sons are listed in vv. 13–17. The last of these is David, creating the climax of the chapter. The source for these verses (as well as v. 9) is, amongst others, Ruth 4:19–22 (see also 1 Sam 16:6–10; 17:13). (It is less likely that Chronicles served as a source for Ruth.) v. 15, David as the seventh son: 1 Sam 16:10–11; 17:12 assumes eight sons of Jesse. Nethaneel, Raddai, and Ozem do not exist in other texts. vv. 16–17, the fact that David's sisters are mentioned (cf. 2 Sam 17:25) shows that despite the great respect he commanded as a king, David was still no more than a human being. vv. 34–5, the Chronicler's attitude towards foreigners is particularly clear here: since Sheshan had no sons, his line could continue through his daughters and an Egyptian servant.

(3:1–24) The Davidides This chapter contains the (almost purely) genealogical profile of David's line from his own time right up to the post-exilic period. At the extreme, this could mean that the Davidic line remained unbroken during the exile period, making the reinstatement of the Davidic monarchy in Jerusalem with its rightful heir a possibility, should circumstances allow. In this sense, the chapter would be almost messianic and eschatological. Depending on whether v. 21 contains six sons of one generation or six successive generations, the list of Davidides (calculating 25 years for each generation) lasts until 460 or 320 BCE. This would present us with a date for Chronicles' conception. The chapter, however, can also be regarded as a secondary addition (strengthening the messianic tone of the passage), since its original position should have been after 2:17. Rudolf (1955: 11, 26) suggests that there is evidence for this in chs. 3–4, since parts of ch. 14:4–7 are repeated, some kings have different names from the rest of Chronicles (e.g. Azariah instead of Uzziah), and Zerubbabel's father is called Pedaiah, and not Shealtiel, as in Ezra 3:2, 8. None of these arguments is conclusive. The chapter is divided into three parts: (1) the sons of David (born in Hebron, vv. 1–4; born in Jerusalem, vv. 5–9); (2) those who ruled as kings in Jerusalem (apart from the usurper Queen Athaliah, vv. 10–16); (3) the Davidides during and after the exile period, vv. 17–24. (1) is based on exactly copied or heavily reworked material from 2 Sam: vv. 1–4a = 2 Sam

3:2–5; v. 4*b* = 2 Sam 5:5 (reworked); vv. 5–8 (2 Sam 5:14–16 = 1 Chr 14:4–7), v. 9 = 2 Sam 5:13; 13:1, are a selection. (2) is probably the Chronicler's own collection (and does not stem from any reworked lists). (3) contains few names which are also documented in other OT texts.

vv. 1–4*a*, sons born in Hebron: this list is copied almost word for word from 2 Sam 3:2–5. v. 4, according to 1 Chr 11: 3–4, David moved to Jerusalem with all Israel shortly after his crowning in Hebron. In contrast with the source material and 1 Chr 3:4, there is no (explicit) mention of an initial seven-year reign in Hebron, cf., however, 1 Chr 29:27 too. Despite this contradiction, there is no reason to presume a different source, since Chronicles is not free from discrepancies. Furthermore, the Chronicler also concealed the source material's note that David ruled Judah alone from Hebron, taking power in Israel only on his move to Jerusalem.

vv. 5–9, sons born in Jerusalem: v. 5, the Chronicler ignored the note in 2 Sam 5:13 that David took even more concubines and wives in Jerusalem, making Bathsheba the mother of David's first four children—though Solomon was the eldest according to the source model. This indirectly frees Solomon from the stigma of being an illegitimate child, as the books of Kings suggest. Bathsheba is called Bathshua in Chronicles. Shua is the name of the first (Canaanite) wife of Judah (Gen 38:2), David's own ancestor. Does this similarity of names express the idea that the Davidic monarchy began in the same way as the history of the tribe of Judah, namely with a mixed marriage? vv. 6–8, in addition to the four oldest sons, source material names a further seven born to David, whilst the Chronicler mentions nine. Since he mentions the number explicitly, it is likely that he found one source stating this number. Nogah and the first Eliphelet are occasionally deleted as secondary.

vv. 10–16, a list of the kings of Judah up to the period of exile. Up to Josiah, it monotonously names kings according to the formula: his son was X. The situation becomes more complicated after Josiah, since sons did not always succeed their fathers, leading the Chronicler to change his listing method. vv. 15–16, the number and names of kings (and their sons) in Chronicles differ from the source, as do their periods of rule. The two perspectives can be seen in Japhet 1993: 98.

The source model representation is more reliable than Chronicles. The Chronicler tried to organize seemingly incongruous information from 2 Kings 22–4 and Jeremiah (where the alternative name of Joahaz is Shallum, Jer 22:11) so that the two versions should conform better with each other.

vv. 17–24 give David's descendants during the Exile and post-exilic periods. The authenticity of this list is unquestioned. v. 18, it is unclear whether Shenazar is identical to Sheshbazzar in Ezra 1:8, 11; 5:14, 16. v. 19, Zerubbabel, in Ezra, Nehemiah, and Haggai, is known as 'son of Shealtiel'. He is the son of Pedaiah in Chronicles. Attempts to harmonize the two names (such as the idea of a levirate marriage) are not convincing. Shelomith: other women mentioned in these lists are well-known figures. Thus, Shelomith must have been prominent in post-exilic times, though not necessarily identical to the woman on a seal from the same period (Avigad 1976: 11). This might represent a relative end to the list, since women's names do sometimes appear in this position.

(4:1–43) The Southern Tribes The first part of this chapter deals with the sons of Judah (vv. 1–23), whilst the second concentrates on Simeon (vv. 24–43), a tribe which had constant close ties with Judah (cf. for instance Josh 19:1, 9; Judg 1:3–4: historically Simeon was quickly engulfed by Judah). The second part has a clear structure, whereas the first shows no obvious pattern. vv. 1–23 fragment into many small, seemingly unrelated pieces. Lack of textual clarity also makes it difficult to interpret. The chapter is potentially a valuable historical source, although one cannot say for which period: the time of its conception, the period described, or an even earlier era. The following notes discuss only clear or especially important aspects of the text. The lists partly refer back to ch. 2. vv. 9–10, this is a passage typical of the Chronicler in several ways: it highlights the Chronicler's respect for wealth and property as well as his belief in the effectiveness of prayer; there is another example of the Chronicler's frequent use of meaningful names: Jabez was thus named because his mother bore him *with sorrow* (*bĕʾōzeb*). He himself prays that no *sorrow* (*ʾozbî*) fall upon him.

vv. 24–43, Simeon's genealogy (vv. 24–7) is followed by a list of the tribe's settlement territories (vv. 28–33), then a list of the Simeonite leaders (vv. 34–8) plus two episodes in their history (vv. 39–43). v. 31, 'until David became king': the Chronicler hereby stresses that the tribe of Simeon was engulfed by Judah during David's reign (if not before).

(5:1–26) The Transjordanian Tribes Genealogical aspects are not so prominent in the description of the Transjordanian tribes. Gad and Manasseh are not presented in the same way as other tribes. The two and a half tribes are shown as one entity, bound together by similar living conditions and a common history. The structure of the passage is confusing: descriptions of Reuben (vv. 1–10) and Gad (vv. 11–17) are followed by an account of the war against the Hagrites. Only then is the half-tribe of Manasseh introduced (vv. 23–4). Finally, the passage explains why the Transjordanian tribes were driven into exile (vv. 25–6). Although this is clearly an anticipation of later events, the Exile belongs here since the history of the northern kingdom is not discussed elsewhere in the text. It is typical for the chapter that it also refers to other, later historical events.

Whereas ch. 4 closes with the southernmost west-Jordanian tribe, ch. 5 begins with the southernmost Transjordanian tribe, whilst Gad and the half tribe of Manasseh are also ordered geographically.

vv. 1–3, Reuben's genealogy (cf. Gen 46:8*b*–9; Ex 6:14; Num 26:5–9). In v. 1 the Chronicler begins to present it, going on then to explain, in a kind of midrash, why Reuben did not receive the rights of a firstborn son. His four sons are only named in v. 4. Reuben lost his rights as firstborn son for sleeping with Bilhah, his father's concubine (Gen 35:22; cf. 49:3–4). His rights were passed on to the sons of Joseph (the ancestors of the later state of Israel). The strength of Judah underlined in v. 2 is reflected in the lists of tribes themselves. The fact that one prince of Judah need not be named due to the context points to his importance—he is, of course, David.

v. 6, Tilgath-pilneser: Chronicles always uses this spelling of Tiglath-pileser, who was active further north. v. 10 speaks of wars against the Hagrites (descendants of Hagar) under Saul; cf. also vv. 19–20; and Ps 83:7 (where they are mentioned along with Edom, Ishmael, and Moab). The struggle was over pastureland (possibly mirroring conflicts during the Chronicler's lifetime; cf. vv. 18–22). The war depicted in vv. 18–22 gives the impression of being an elaboration of the conflict mentioned here. v. 16 'Sharon', is not the identically named plain south of Carmel, but a Transjordanian region (mentioned on the inscription of Mesha, king of Moab (line 13) which can be dated around 830–810 BCE). Its precise position is unsure. vv. 18–22 again mention war against the Hagrites and their allies. This multilayered account is typical of Chronicles' many war reports, mixing spiritual with military and economic factors. Here, local conflicts (in the Transjordanian north) during the Chronicler's own lifetime seem to have been greatly exaggerated, interpreted theologically, and projected back into the past. v. 20 is again typical of the Chronicler's war theology: those who trust in God and call upon him will be heard and receive help. v. 22, although God's active participation in the war is self-evident to the Chronicler, he still mentions it.

vv. 25–6, the deportation of the Transjordanian tribes: the Chronicler turns the two phases of the northern kingdom's deportation (2 Kings 15:29 and 2 Kings 17:6; 18:11) into a single period by copying only the information he finds useful (taking the name of the king from the first, whilst using the deportation place-names of the second). In historical terms, the Chronicler thereby ignores the fact that Tiglath-pileser conquered only Gilead in the east. The language of this passage is typical for Chronicles (transgression against God, 'prostitution', stress on 'the God of their ancestors', stirring up the spirits of aggressors). In 2 Kings 15:19, 29, the Assyrian king is called Pul (as in late-Babylonian sources) and Tiglath-pileser (see I CHR 5:6 for the form of name). It is difficult to see how he thinks the two names are related.

Having described the Transjordanian tribes' exile, the Chronicler then makes no mention of the same fate awaiting the rest of the northern kingdom. He may have had contemporary motives for this. Did such a diplomatic silence leave the door open for the Samaritans' conversion? This was impossible for the Transjordanians, since they were still in exile.

(6:1–81) Levi The Chronicler's special love for the Levites (the tribe of Levi) can mainly be seen in the great scope of relevant material he inserted (this is also true for Judah and Benjamin). The list in this chapter differs from others in its striking uniformity. The tribe's priestly nature, giving little occasion for historical comment, partly explains this characteristic. About half the material stems from other parts of the OT, the rest is unique material. Whether the chapter as it stands today is the work of the Chronicler or the product of successive accretions is still a subject of debate. The structure is clear, however: the line of the high priests (vv. 1–15); the three lines of the families Gershom, Kohath, and Merari (vv. 16–30); the lines of the singers (vv. 31–47); duties of Levites and priests (vv. 48–9); list of high priests (vv. 50–3); the Aaronites' and Levites' settlements (vv. 54–81). The Chronicler reveals his particular affinity towards the musicians and the settlements (i.e. towards historical geography) in this passage.

vv. 1–15, the line of the high priests. The list first names Levi, then his three sons, and subsequently three generations of the Kohathites, always continuing with only the branches leading to the Aaronite high priests. Miriam's name stands out in this list, which has parallels in the OT (cf. for instance Ex 6:16–25). The Chronicler mentioned this woman (!) because of her importance for the people's history. A number of names we know from other passages (even Jehoiada, cf. 2 Chr 22:11–24:17) are omitted from this list, which also contains errors. It is obviously not a historical document, but a construct and thus comparable with Mt 1: it contains twelve high priests (slight doubts regarding their counting cannot be discussed here) from their beginnings up to the temple's construction, and eleven up to Jehozadak, under whom Judah was deported. Going by this historical time-scale, the period from Aaron to the construction of Solomon's temple is just as long as the time until its destruction. The list plays a legitimizing role: the high priests in office at the Chronicler's time could genealogically refer back to Zadok and even further to Aaron. This claim is historically unfounded, nor is the idea that the Zadokites were the descendants of Aaron universally accepted in the OT. v. 15, most explicit mention of Judah's exile (cf. 1 Chr 9:1; 2 Chr 36 only refers to Jerusalem). The Chronicler regards the Exile—like many other events—as caused by YHWH (due to human sin—not mentioned here, but self-evident).

vv. 16–30 set out the Levites' genealogy (source: Num 3:17–35; cf. Ex 6:16–25). vv. 16–19 contain a complete genealogy of the sons of Levi (up to his grandchildren), while vv. 20–30 present the lines of his sons Gershom, Kohath, and Merari, starting with their eldest sons and continuing vertically for seven generations. This principle is interrupted by Kohath. Japhet (1993: 154) shows how vv. 16–30 can be correctly understood.

6:31–47 sets out the genealogy of the temple singers Heman, Asaph, and Ethan. As explained extensively in 1 Chr 15–16, the bearers of the ark were given an additional role once it had been transferred to Jerusalem: that of singers. Until the construction of the temple, they performed their duty before the tent of meeting. David appoints them (v. 31)—there was no relevant law of Moses—and from Solomon's time onwards they sang in their definitive workplace, the temple. Consecutive mention of David and Solomon (vv. 31, 32) is not coincidental.

vv. 48–53, the activities of the Levites are briefly described in general (v. 48). The Chronicler is more elaborate and detailed in his description of the priests' tasks. It includes the interesting and (for this passage) surprising statement that sacrifices fulfil the role of atoning for Israel. (This is not their only function, but in later times the most important one.) Just as the singers are said to have been appointed by David, v. 49 points out that the priests held their office according to Moses' instructions.

6:54–81 sets out living and grazing areas for the Levites. This list corresponds to that in Josh 21:9–42, though with some differences in the arrangement of its elements. Each list has a different purpose in its present context: Josh 21 designates the areas the Levites are to settle in, this one the areas in which they already live.

(7:1–40) The Northern Tribes This chapter consists of a number of diversely structured lists with information concerning the remaining tribes. The principles behind their order and form is unclear. The tribe of Naphtali is dealt with entirely within one verse (v. 13). Dan and Zebulon are omitted completely, whilst Benjamin appears here as well as in ch. 8 (if viewed from a somewhat different perspective). The reasons for such irregularities can only be speculated upon. Occasionally, loss of textual material could have been a factor. The missing or scarcely described tribes were all in the north and therefore played no important role after their deportation by Tiglath-pileser. The tribes of Issachar, Benjamin, and Asher are all treated differently from the sons of Joseph (a story is even told about the Ephraimites in vv. 21–3).

v. 5, the term 'reckoned' is used for the first time here. The fact that this word appears only in Ezra, Nehemiah, and Chronicles suggests that the list in its present form is relatively late. vv. 6–12 (11), Benjamin: his genealogy has been passed down in many, strongly varying versions in Chronicles and the entire OT, representing different developments (or programmes and claims). The only uniting element is that Bela is the firstborn son (cf. Gen 46:21; Num 26:38; 1 Chr 8:1). The present list has a regular structure: Bela and Becher are followed for a further generation and Jediael for another two.

vv. 14–19, Manasseh: this section is difficult to understand, since the text is probably corrupt in places. It differs in a number of respects from its source (Num 26:29–34).

vv. 20–7, Ephraim's passage comprises three parts: a list of his descendants, a story, and Joshua's genealogy, which is often regarded as a direct continuation of v. 21a. v. 22, this verse reminds us of the opening of the story of Job (Job 2:11) and it is quite possible that the Chronicler wished to draw a parallel between the two figures. vv. 25–7, Joshua's genealogy here resembles that of David (2:10–15) and somewhat artificially reworks information from the Pentateuch. The Chronicler is scarcely interested in Joshua elsewhere, contributing to the suspicion that he wished to portray Joshua as a resident, rather than as a man who conquered the land.

vv. 30–40, Asher: the first verse (with Asher's sons) goes back to Gen 46:17 (cf. also Num. 26:44–7). There is no other source in the OT for the rest of this very complicated list, which contains far more non-Hebrew names than most such texts.

(8:1–40) Benjamin and Jerusalem In Chronicles, Benjamin and Judah distinguish themselves from the other ten tribes of the Israelite kingdom in forming the 'true Israel'. Thus Benjamin has a central place in the tribes' presentation. This is underlined by the fact that the entire description of tribes begins with Judah and returns to its centre at the end, giving Benjamin (along with Judah and Levi) the most extensive presentation in the 'genealogical forecourt' (cf. 7:6–12). This chapter, which has often been regarded as a later addition to the Chronicler's original (although there are some common interests), shows no compelling structure. It documents family trees of individual Benjaminite families (without giving a complete genealogy of the tribe), their dwelling-places and historical notes. vv. 33–40 contain a family tree of the Saulites. The first part falls into four sections which are not divided by any strict method, as can be seen by their abrupt endings (vv. 7, 12, 28, marking the end of the first three sections; cf. Rudolph 1955: 75, 77). The emphasis of each section always lies upon the last generation of each family. Although dated to the time of Josiah by some, the chapter's

individual parts are sometimes more logical if placed at the time of Nehemiah.

v. 28, from this point the passage runs parallel to 9:35–44. Jerusalem lay on the border between Judah and Benjamin and could be attributed to both tribes, cf. for instance Josh 15:63 with Judg 1:21. It is more than likely that this particular passage regarded the city as part of Judah, thus supposing an expansion and/or a resettlement of Benjaminite elements. vv. 29–40, Saul's family: it is generally presumed that the entire section deals with Saul's family. Rudolph (1955: 80–1) amongst others disputes this, pointing out how late vv. 29–32 were conceived: the names Kish and Ner remind him of the family of the first king of Israel. It is for their sake that his genealogy begins only with these names and not earlier. Rudolph also claims that the Saulite folk dwelt in Gibea, rather than Gibeon. Other exegetes disagree, pointing out that vv. 29–40 alternate between horizontal and vertical elements in their portrayal of the family. v. 33, Eshbaal (Man of Baal): the original name of this son of Saul was probably corrected and disfigured in 2 Sam 2:8 (etc.) into Ishbosheth (Man of Shame) in order to conceal the baal component (which can be interpreted as the name of the god Baal). Since the books of Samuel were more frequently used, they were 'cleansed' more thoroughly than Chronicles. In 1 Sam 14:49, he is known as Ishvi.

(9:1–44) Jerusalem and its Inhabitants, Saul's Family Following the lineage of Benjamin (cf. v. 1a) is a list of Jerusalem's residents in the post-exilic period (vv. 1b–34). The chapters close with an almost literal repetition of the list of Gibeonites of 8:29–38 (vv. 35–44). Such an arrangement of the chapter has a dual purpose: it underlines the fact that the post-exilic period in Judah/Jerusalem immediately followed the pre-exilic period. The list of Gibeonites, to whom Saul also belonged, leads us suitably to his downfall. The list need not be secondary to chs. 8 or 9. The Chronicler could easily have used it twice for different ends. vv. 2–17 are also copied (and adapted), probably from Neh 11:3–19. It is very likely that the Chronicler found this list, which he simplified at certain points, in that book and nowhere else. The list of Jerusalem's residents follows the order of Judeans, Benjaminites, priests, and Levites. The clear distinction between laymen and clerics is typical of the books of Ezra and Nehemiah, but not of Chronicles. These historically important lists paint an especially representative picture of Israel and Judah.

v. 1, 'Book of the Kings of Israel' reoccurs at 2 Chr 20:34 (cf. 33:18). 2 Chr 27:7 and 36:8 use the expression 'Book of the Kings of Israel and Judah'. These expressions are factually identical.

'And Judah was taken into exile in Babylon because of their unfaithfulness': the Chronicler takes less than a verse to discuss Judah's (or rather Jerusalem's) exile in 2 Chr 36:20 before moving straight on to the Persian rule and Cyrus's permission to return. The Exile is dealt with with equal brevity here. There is no reason to regard this passage as a post-Chronicles addition. The Chronicler is simply as brief with the Exile as he can be. In doing so, he underlines that the residents of Jerusalem mentioned in v. 3–34 belong to the post-exilic period. 'Because of their unfaithfulness': typical of the Chronicler, this phrase is also used to characterize Saul's crimes (a king who prefigured the Exile) in the following chapter (10:13).

v. 2, the source for this is Neh 11:3. The Chronicler deletes 'the province' from this source, probably because the phrase recalled too strongly that Judah had long been a province of the Achaemenide empire. Generally (cf. v. 1's ending), 'the first' should be understood as referring to after the return from exile. Other translations are also possible: 'the main, most important residents', 'the first inhabitants from old'. The latter translation is plausible if one (such as Japhet 1993: 206) considers the reference to the Exile in v. 1b to be perhaps a gloss, especially since nothing else in this text refers to a return. The phrase in the source, Neh 11:3, 'And the descendants of Solomon's servants', is omitted by the Chronicler.

v. 3, 'some of the people of . . . Ephraim, and Manasseh' is an addition by the Chronicler that goes beyond the source model. Residents of the northern kingdom who were loyal to YHWH are repeatedly called upon to find asylum in Judah/Jerusalem on religious grounds; this passage indirectly implies that these calls were also repeatedly heeded. vv. 17–26, the Chronicler goes to great lengths lovingly to portray the gatekeepers. Whilst they are not yet Levites in Neh 11:19, this is precisely what is stated in this paragraph. vv. 18–19 'gatekeepers' ('porters', AV), 'thresholds of the tent': according to the Chronicler, the gatekeepers' duty, which was above all to guard entrances, had its roots in the desert-dwelling period and had not been changed since that time. This is what lent it such special dignity and distinguished it from that of the singers, who had only held their office since their job as bearers of the ark became unnecessary (cf. 6:13).

vv. 35–44, the section 1:1–9:34 leads from Adam up to the temple community of the post-exilic period; the chapters are a kind of population assessment. These verses, the end of the first review, provide an ideal lead into the second review, comprising the period from David until the restoration after the Exile. This period and the events portrayed within it are regarded as the history of the kingdom of YHWH, as manifested by the Davidides. The verses differ only in detail from their source model.

David's Rule (1 Chr 10:1–29:30)

Saul's Downfall and Rejection (1 Chr 10:1–14)

In this chapter Chronicles changes its form from a list-based presentation to a more narrative portrayal (in which lists are inserted). From now on, the Chronicler bases his work on the books of Samuel and of Kings, using their information on the sole legitimate Davidic kingdom, whilst also adding his own material. He begins with Saul's downfall. This chapter is not merely a necessary introduction to David's reign, making it more legitimate and comprehensible. Nor is it simply an evil backdrop to make David's rule shine all the brighter. It is there in its own right, portraying the monarchy in its negative form. The Chronicler makes slight, but theologically significant changes to his sources, linking Saul's defeat with the Babylonian Exile. The source models portray Saul's defeat as a purely earthly event, depicting Saul almost as a tragic figure—elements which are entirely absent from Chronicles. The author adds to his source materials in vv. 13–14 by including a theological interpretation of events, strongly highlighting Saul's culpable behaviour.

v. 6, the Chronicler replaces the words, 'his armour-bearer and all his men' in the source (1 Sam 31:6) with 'and all his house'. This underlines the fact that the Saulites were wiped out. The episode containing Ishbaal's brief rule in 2 Sam 2–4 is irrelevant to the Chronicler, though this does not deter him from occasionally mentioning Saul's descendants (8:33–40; 9:39–40). v. 7, the source's 'men of Israel' becomes 'all the men of Israel' in Chronicles. The precise positioning, 'on the other side of the valley [Jezreel] and . . . beyond the Jordan' is also changed into the vaguer 'in the valley'. This turns a specifically located defeat into a general, comprehensive, 'primeval' failure, providing us with a first reference to the analogous situation of the Babylonian Exile.

vv. 9–10, the source model (1 Sam 31:9) reports that the Philistines decapitated Saul, while the Chronicler omits this fact. He does, however, note that Saul's armour was placed in the temple of their gods and that his head was fixed in the temple of Dagon. According to the source model Saul's armour was placed in the temple of Astarte and his body fastened to the walls of Beth-shan. These discrepanices are easily explained: Saul's descration cannot take place in Israel (Bethshan). Naming 'the temple of Dagon' reminds readers knowledgeable of the Bible that the same deity lost his head and hands at that very place after the Philistines carried YHWH's ark there (1 Sam 5:4). This is Dagon's moment of power. Here references to the Exile in Babylon cannot be missed: Israel's (dead) king is in a foreign land, in exile. Saul's fate also reminds us of Goliath. v. 10, as elsewhere (with the exception of 2 Chr 15:16), the Chronicler deletes any mention of a goddess, replacing 'Astarte' with 'their god'. It is impossible to fight her since she cannot even be named.

vv. 13–14, the Chronicler gives no less than four reasons for Saul's rejection, which is explicitly ascribed to the Lord. (1) His transgression (NRSV, 'unfaithfulness'): using this typical term, which does not appear in the source model, the Chronicler describes religious crimes as the way to defeat and exile. (2) For not keeping the word of God. This is a general judgement of Saul's behaviour (as declared in Deuteronomy and Ps 119, for instance). It may also refer to crimes committed by Saul as reported in 1 Sam 13 and 15. He takes the term 'kept' from the first chapter (1 Sam 13:13–14) and '[YHWH's] word' (NRSV, 'commandment') from the second (1 Sam 15, passim). In using this construction, the Chronicler underlines his own knowledge of the Scriptures and makes clear what he expects from the reader. (3) For consulting a medium. This accusation, which contains a pun (Saul and 'enquire' (NRSV, 'consulted') are made up of the same consonants in Hebrew), refers to his visit to the witch of Endor (1 Sam 28). (4) Because he did not seek the Lord: this phrase emphasizes the Chronicler's positive (and internalized) attitude towards God in as general a way as possible.

David's Rule until the Preparations for the Temple's Construction (1 Chr 11:1–22:1)

(11:1–47) The Installation of David as King, Conquest of Jerusalem, David's Heroes ch. 11 begins the most extensive part of Chronicles and deals with David. Beyond the material he took from his sources (chs. 11–21), the Chronicler includes unique material in chs. 22–9. This structure is also mirrored in chs. 11–12, which contain David's installation as King of all Israel. The reports concerning David's crowning in Hebron, the conquest of Jerusalem, and David's heroes can all be found in the books of Samuel, though in a different order. The subsequent list of people (soldiers) (ch. 12; unique material in Chronicles) who joined David underlines the fact that all Israel supported David, whilst at the same time recapping the omitted story of David's past (together with Saul). The two chapters are artfully structured, as short key statements show (cf. e.g. 12:18).

vv. 4–9, the conquest of Jerusalem. The source's report of this event (2 Sam 5:6–10) is rather obscure and may have seemed unclear to the Chronicler. He uses the narrative framework, but fills it out by making Joab the main protagonist of Jerusalem's capture (and repairer of some of the buildings). It is possible that the source model's unclear term ṣinnor (2 Sam 5:8; NRSV: water shaft, left out by the Chronicler) reminded him of Joab's mother Ṣeruiah and incited him to mention her name in his version. v. 4, it is historically likely that David captured Jerusalem with his private army (if it was not handed over peacefully). The Chronicler cannot allow this for theological reasons, making the conquest a pan-Israelite issue. v. 9, this sentence is an almost identical copy of the source (2 Sam 5:10), but strongly supports the Chronicler's theology (the LORD . . . was with him). This is also true of the seldom-used phrase 'the LORD of hosts', where the source has 'the LORD, the God of hosts'.

vv. 10–47 list David's men. Apart from vv. 42–7, which are the Chronicler's own material, the passage conforms with 2 Sam 23:8–39. Since the original list is torn from its historical context, it is difficult to know whether it refers to the period before or after David's accession to the throne. In the source, it is made up of three parts: (1) The three men (whom nobody could match); one act of heroism is mentioned in respect of each of them. (2) Two other heroes, again with their acts of heroism. (3) The thirty heroes. The Chronicler keeps this structure, which is not totally consistent, deleting the name of the third hero, Shammah, as well as the act of heroism ascribed to Eleazar, the second hero, who consequently inherits Shammah's deed. v. 10, the Chronicler strongly diverges from the source material here, in order to domesticate David's heroes and their actions, i.e. to insert them into David's (and YHWH's) kingdom. Pushed linguistically, the Chronicler underlines that this is David's kingdom, pertaining to and encompassing all Israel, whilst referring back to YHWH's word (and pledge) to Israel—though this promise is never directly described. vv. 11–41 (47), many details of the list differ from the source material, including the names of heroes. In many cases it is difficult to distinguish whether this is due to scribal errors or the Chronicler's own perspective. The source already contains many textual problems. v. 23, 'five cubits tall . . . like a weaver's beam': these two details, which are not from the source model, draw parallels with the story of David and Goliath, though what exactly the Chronicler is referring to is difficult to judge.

(12:1–40) David's Supporters This chapter divides into two parts: vv. 1–22 contain a list of people who joined David before his coronation, whilst vv. 23–40 name those who came to him

in Hebron. Both parts stem from detailed information from various sources and are not rigidly structured. Both contain few, yet significant, theological statements. One subject binds the whole chapter together (using catchwords amongst other methods), namely help for David from his supporters and God. The Chronicler does not discuss Saul's kingdom, especially ignoring his conflict with David. That period is presented only covertly here. Since the information in this chapter is concerned with aspects regarded as untypical for the Chronicler (aside from certain high numbers), it is often seen as in part old and dependable, and in part consisting of newer additions from a later period than the Chronicler's own. On the other hand, one can regard this passage as largely stemming from the Chronicler, who refers strongly back to biblical source material (especially 1 Samuel) and expresses his admiration for strength and power in a literary manner. The first part divides into four sections: vv. 1–8, the Benjaminites come to David in Ziklag; vv. 9–16, the Gadites come to David's mountain stronghold; vv. 17–19, the same occurs to Benjamin and Judah; vv. 20–2, the people of Manasseh come to David in Ziklag. The section, which clearly shows a structure despite large individual differences, concludes with a summary in v. 22: David received much support. Only four tribes are mentioned, perhaps because they play a particularly important role in the Chronicler's sources.

vv. 23–40 cover David's coronation in Hebron. vv. 23, 38–40 only briefly describe the accession itself, whilst portraying the subsequent feast at much greater length. In the middle of the passage, a kind of military census is inserted. v. 23, the kingdom of Saul is passed on to David in Hebron (cf. 10:14–11:3)—peacefully. v. 38, David is accepted as king by everyone and with all their hearts. Unanimity and acts of conviction enjoy the Chronicler's highest regard, as the entire text shows. vv. 39–40, after David's crowning, a great secular feast takes place that is unrivalled in the OT—the Chronicler cannot be challenged on this point. The joy of feasts also characterizes his work (cf. e.g. 29:22; 2 Chr 30:21–6).

(13:1–14) An Unsuccessful Attempt to Bring Back the Ark of the Covenant Once David has been anointed king in Hebron, Jerusalem has been conquered, and his followers have been named, Chronicles' David immediately thinks of bringing the ark of the covenant to Jerusalem, rather than making war against the Philistines. The Chronicler changes the order of events given in the source material, driven by the theological idea of the cult's primacy. He regards the ark as the origin and the centre of Jerusalem's holy site. The source model hardly concerns itself with the first, unsuccessful attempt to transport the ark. Chronicles, however, portrays it as motivating David to wage a war against the Philistines, to behave in a God-fearing manner (and later to take precautionary measures), thereby fulfilling the preconditions for the success of the second transportation attempt. The source model depicts the first attempt as a personal task primarily carried out by David, whilst Chronicles makes it an issue for all Israel. This underlines the Chronicler's consistently held opinion that important events (especially of cultic nature) were carried out not merely by the monarch. He begins with an original passage concerning plans for the project; then follows a report which he draws from his source (2 Sam 6:1–11), having to omit v. 12.

vv. 1–4 detail preparations for the project. Consistent with the previous chapters, David initially consults his military leaders (i.e. he makes a suggestion), though this rapidly transforms into a (cultic) congregation (v. 2). It is a classic example of the Chronicler's three-way division of society between the king, the notables, and the people/congregation. v. 2, there are two conditions for the project's execution: the willingness of those present and God's acceptance of the plan. As is revealed later on, the second condition has not yet been fulfilled. This verse also emphasizes that the plan is impossible without the collaboration of the priests and Levites. Some regard 'who remain in all the land(s) of Israel' as a neutral phrase, referring to the different regions of the land (cf. also 12:39b). Others see it as a reflection of Israel's diaspora situation. '[L]et us send abroad' is a double-worded phrase in Hebrew. Its first component (to break out, perez) is not only repeated in this chapter (Perez-uzzah), but also plays a central role elsewhere in 1 Chronicles (13:11; 14:11; 15:13). v. 3, the ark suddenly appears and represents Israel's fate. 'Because Saul neglected it' (i.e. did not look for it—a favourite phrase of the Chronicler) makes an indirect, though transparent, allusion to 10:14. At that time the people experienced hardship. So pay heed!

vv. 5–14, the Chronicler followed his source more closely from this point onwards. v. 5, Chronicles goes beyond the source in naming the borders of Israel. Instead of the usual boundaries, from Beersheba to Dan, the Shihor river in Egypt (probably the Nile) and Lebo-hamath are used to increase the size of Israel, which achieved such proportions only after David's spectacular victories (cf. Josh 13:3, 5 as source; Joshua was not able to conquer these regions). v. 6, the Chronicler makes the source model more 'Israelite' by explicitly mentioning that the people who were with him stemmed from 'all Israel'. The identification of Baalah as Kiriath-jearim is a logical deduction from Josh 15:9; the source (1 Sam 7:1–2) only mentions Kiriath-jearim.

v. 9, the owner of the threshing-floor is called Nachon rather than Chidon, in the source model. 'Uzzah reached out his hand to the ark of God and took hold of it' (2 Sam 6:6); here, 'Uzzah put out his hand to hold the ark'. Does the Chronicler's emendation imply that the mere attempt to touch the ark, not just the deed, was sacrilegious? Or perhaps the Chronicler is expressing the same idea as his source model using more contemporary Hebrew. v. 13, Obed-edom the Gittite: he is a Philistine. In 15:25 the Chronicler deletes the word 'Gittite'. v. 14, the Chronicler will use the three months of the ark's stay with Obed-edom to insert David's victories over the Philistines (ch. 14). In the source model, David is so overjoyed about the blessing of the ark's presence in Obed-edom's home that he arranges for its onward transportation (2 Sam 6:12).

(14:1–17) David Increases in Power; Victories over the Philistines The three months during which the ark remains with Obed-edom facilitate the insertion of 2 Sam 5:11–25 at this point, but they do not explain it, especially since the two wars against the Philistines would have been better placed in the context of chs. 18–20. The Chronicler chooses this position for their insertion in order to underline the blessing bestowed upon David. His efforts to transport the ark pay off and are rewarded. The (initial) failure of the project is due to clumsy technical measures. Just as YHWH 'burst out against Uzzah' (13:11), he 'has burst out against' the place where the Philistines will be conquered (14:11). This chapter has close parallels with ch. 10, as the interreferential language underlines. David succeeds where Saul failed. The Chronicler makes small but significant changes to the source model, in both style and content.

vv. 1–2, in the source, these statements follow the conquest of Jerusalem rather than the successful transportation of the ark. It is the ark that gives David's reign its greatness for the sake of Israel, as the Chronicler emphasizes more strongly than the source model. vv. 8–16, the Chronicler copies two similarly structured battle reports from the source (the advance of the Philistines, an enquiry to God with a positive response and the Philistines' defeat). He changes the geography, however, along with the place-names (vv. 8, 11, 16), since he saw the battles from the perspective of Isa 28:21, where the Gibeon valley as well as Mount Perazim are mentioned (resulting in the replacement of Geba with Gibeon in v. 16). v. 16, Isa 28:21 refers to battles described in Josh 10 and 2 Sam 5 to illustrate the strange acts God is about to perform. In its Chronicles form ch. 14 is itself interpreted using the interpretation of 2 Sam 5 in Isaiah. Thus the source of the comparison becomes its target. v. 17, David's geographically limited military successes have an astonishing effect: his fame (name) spreads world-wide and he is feared everywhere. This sentence stems from the Chronicler's own material and can only be correctly understood in view of Jerusalem's status at the time it was written. David drove fear into the hearts of people round the world, so Jerusalem, a small temple state within an enormous empire, need not be meek.

(15:1–29) Taking the Ark to Jerusalem; Cultic Regulations This chapter can be regarded as an artfully conceived unity or as one which has had its relatively small original element more than doubled using the insertion of two extensive lists (vv. 4–10 and vv. 16–24) and other methods. Whether these lists belong to the basic element is matter for debate, as is also their age, i.e. the cultic organization they reflect. The lists are either not entirely uniform or cannot be reconciled with others, leaving the question of their interpretation open: it is precisely these elements that reflect shifts within the cult and power structure, especially amongst the Levites, as will briefly be discussed below. In assessing the literary unity of this chapter, one question is dominant: was only such material included originally as was directly relevant to the transportation of the ark and the introduction of cultic music, or did the chapter already contain at least elements of everything pertaining to the cult in its original form? If the first case is true, some later additions were made. If the second is true, one can regard the chapter as relatively unified. The second theory is preferable, based on the assumption that the Chronicler found it easier to accept contradictions in his text than to ignore material.

vv. 1–3, preparations are made for the ark's transportation. In keeping with his habitual tendency, the Chronicler portrays the project as one which involves all Israel (v. 3). He takes advantage of the opportunity to highlight the role of the Levites. Only they have the right to carry the ark. v. 2, since David has been bestowed with blessing, as ch. 14 shows, the failure of the first attempt to transport the ark can only be due to its irregular execution. It is hoped that this error can be corrected by allowing only the Levites to bear the ark, as the Law prescribes (Deut 10:8; 31:25). The Chronicler is referring to these passages here. It is not possible to discern whether the Chronicler's primary concern is that David fulfilled these requirements or that the laws of Moses have been adhered to. vv. 4–10, this absolutely even list has often been regarded as a later addition that parallels and expands v. 11. It is more probable that the Chronicler inserted a list known to him here, forcing him to make v. 11 similar to v. 4 (resumptive repetition). As well as the three traditional priest families, Gershom, Kohath, and Merari, listed in a different order here, the list contains also Hebron and Uzziel, Kohath's sons according to Ex 6:18, and Elizaphan. vv. 11–15, in a speech typical of Chronicles, David announces his intentions, calling upon the priests and Levites to sanctify themselves, referring back to the failed first attempt. They immediately follow these instructions and take up the ark. v. 12, what exactly is meant by sanctification can be deduced from Ex 19:14–15: washing their clothes and sexual abstinence. vv. 16–24 expand upon the Levitical duties. This complicated passage, which cannot be entirely understood in all its points and which probably contains information from different periods, interrupts the contextual flow. This does not necessarily mean that it is a secondary addition. It seems important to the Chronicler that the relevant instructions were carried out and put into practice immediately after the ark's arrival. If taken to its furthest degree, it can be claimed that the introduction of cultic music in this passage is indirectly based upon 2 Sam 6:12–15.

vv. 25–9, the transportation of the ark. v. 25, unlike in the source model, David is not informed that the house of Obed-edom is blessed because of the presence of the ark. His reasons for transporting the ark are therefore less egoistic. In Chronicles the project is more democratic since it is carried out by David together with the elders of Israel and the captains over thousands. v. 26, the Chronicler replaces the neutral word 'bearers' with 'the Levites', who are, as he emphasizes, helped by God. The number of sacrifices, which differs from the source model, corresponds with later practice (see e.g. Num 23:1; Ezek 45:23; Job 42:8). v. 27, 'David danced' (2 Sam 6:14): the Chronicler changes two consonants in his source so that 'danced' becomes 'wore' (NRSV, 'was clothed with'). This is typical of the Chronicler's emendments. He then digresses from his source model by adding that David's gown was of fine linen—as were those of all the cult personnel who were present, before returning to the source model ('and David was girded with a linen ephod'). Due to this change and the mention of several Levites, David, in a way, appears as a member of the 'normal' cult personnel. v. 28, 'all Israel': this democratizes the source material ('David and all the house of Israel'). The ark's transportation is also accompanied by more music in Chronicles. v. 29, Michal, who is never declared as David's wife in Chronicles, (indirectly) shows contempt for the ark, thereby taking on the same attitude as the Saulides (13:3), whose last remaining member she represents. According to the source model David is leaping and dancing before the Lord; in the Chronicler's version he only dances, but not before the Lord, though it is unclear why.

(16:1–43) The Festive Psalm of David, the Religious Ceremonies in Jerusalem and Gibeon The source (2 Sam 6:17–19; the Chronicler omits the dispute with Michal in vv. 20–3) describes the last act of transporting the ark to Jerusalem and the dismissal of the people. In Chronicles, this act is part of a great religious festival, in which the sacrifices play only a part. David takes the opportunity to determine the musical service for all time (vv. 4–6, 37) and also to carry it out for the first time (v. 7). He lays down the rules for the service at the tabernacle of Gibeon here. The Chronicler's own material (vv. 4–42) is situated at the centre of the chapter. The psalm sung by the Levites (vv. 8–36) is occasionally attributed to later editors, though its close adherence to the Chronicler's own theology contradicts this.

vv. 1–3, the wording of these verses closely resembles the source, but fulfils a different purpose: they are not the conclusion, but the beginning of the final act. It would have been difficult for the Chronicler to imagine that God was not praised and thanked (cf. for instance 2 Chr 20:26, 28; 29:30; 30:21, 27). v. 6, trumpets are the instruments reserved for the priests (but cf. v. 42). The Shofar (horn) was used in earlier times. There must be *two* trumpet-playing priests, since according to Num 10:2, YHWH ordered Moses to produce *two* silver trumpets. v. 7, David has Asaph and his brothers deliver a psalm for the first time (as emphasized, more are to follow). vv. 8–36, David's festive psalm is made up of three smaller psalms: Ps 105:1–15; 96; 106:1, 47–8. The Chronicler slightly changes their form and greatly alters some of their content, adapting them to the context and his own theology. His reworking of the psalms is similar to his reworking of other sources. The Chronicler could not have expressed his concerns better than by the psalms he chooses. In order to remain convincing, he had to choose well-known psalms that were used by the cult, rather than produce his own psalms. Nor could he portray them in any other order: his composition initially looks back at the history of events up to that point (Ps 105:1–15)—interrupting them in line with his consistent tendency to ignore the Exodus and the conquest of the land—before praising YHWH (Ps 96), and finally asking him for deliverance from enemies (Ps 106:1, 47–8). The Chronicler's composite psalm contains a hidden political message: in its first section Ps 105 speaks of Israel as 'few in number'—as was the case at the time of the Chronicler. Of the nine passages mentioning foreign peoples in the sources, the Chronicler copies seven (vv. 8, 20, 24, 26, 28, 31, 35, cf. also 'all the earth', v. 30). The foreign nations are above all shown the greatness of YHWH (in contrast to the gods). They are obliged to recognize him. Finally, a prayer is made for independence from the power of other nations. The two sections of Ps 96 which could be interpreted as YHWH's mighty acts towards other nations (vv. 10, 13), are ignored by the Chronicler. The small and (religiously) self-confident nation of Israel, hoping for political independence, is identical to the Israel at the time of the Chronicler! The theological profile of the psalm also conforms to his own religious priorities: the composite psalm is filled with calls to praise and thank God: a central theme of Chronicles, as are the greatness and awesomeness of God. Such ideas are highlighted by the psalms.

v. 22, 'anointed ones' (especially kings) and 'prophets' are central figures in Chronicles. This title fits the patriarchs in the source model, however, as it does in Chronicles. The patriarchs have therefore been robed in the prophet's mantle and given the king's sceptre in this passage. v. 35, 'Save us . . . and gather and rescue us from among the nations' (Ps 106:47: 'Save us, O LORD our God, and gather us from among the nations'). The plea in the source refers to the Exile. The Chronicler erases this reference. He does so in a way to comment on the situation of his own time: some Jews were dispersed about (but no longer in exile), whilst the temple state of Jerusalem is not politically independent (against this background the request 'deliver us from the heathen' can be read as a sort of political manifesto).

vv. 39–42 describe procedures for the ceremony at God's residence in Gibeon. No other OT book mentions a regular (sacrificial) cult in Gibeon. Its historical authenticity is sometimes supported by the argument that 1 Kings 3:3 confirms its existence and speaks out against it. It is more likely, however, that these four verses were conceived by the Chronicler (although this passage has even occasionally been ascribed to later priestly writers). The Chronicler is at pains to portray an uninterrupted and legitimate (sacrificial) cult spanning the entire period from the desert era (with its tabernacle), including the Lord's residence at Gibeon, right up to Solomon's establishment of the temple in Jerusalem. Aside from the presence of the tabernacle, Gibeon's importance is underlined by its priests, musicians, and gatekeepers.

(17:1–27) Nathan's Covenant and David's Prayer The Chronicler stays close to his source model in 2 Sam 7 for this passage. Striking variations are made only in v. 1 (to suit the context and ch. 18), v. 13 (partial omission), and v. 17 (divergent version of an unclear source). He also makes a number of theologically motivated corrections to the source material.

v. 1, 'and the Lord had given him rest from all his enemies around him' (2 Sam 7:1) is omitted by the Chronicler, since David's wars have yet to take place (chs. 18–20). It is important to the Chronicler that David first thinks of finding a residence for the ark. v. 13, the Chronicler deletes the following sentence from 2 Sam 7:14: 'when he commits iniquity, I will punish him with a rod such as mortals use, with blows inflicted by human beings'. This deletion has been explained in various ways: (1) The Chronicler portrays Solomon as free of guilt. (2) Unlike the source model, in which the entire dynasty is included, this oracle refers only to the combined reign of David and Solomon, making the comment irrelevant. (3) The promise made to David is irrespective of his son's behaviour. '[A]s I took it from him who was before you': the source mentions Saul by his name. In remaining unnamed, his status as persona non grata is emphasized.

v. 14, the Chronicler makes two changes of emphasis which strengthen his theological perspective, especially his idea of the king's role, and are of central significance. The promise is directed at Solomon and not at (the house of) David. He also underlines a subsequently repeated theme: the Davidides including Solomon are not rulers of their own kingdom, but of YHWH's (cf. e.g. 28:5; 29:11, 23; 2 Chr 9:8; 13:8). This divine rule (over/in Israel) extends beyond the Davidic dynasty. vv. 16–27, David's prayer forms a reply to the promise given by means of Nathan. Prayers and speeches play a considerable role in interpreting past or future events in the

Deuteronomistic History. Indeed this increases in Chronicles. This second section is less theologically deviant from its source model, apart from the name used for God.

(18:1–17) David's Wars against Neighbouring Peoples: A List of David's Executive The Chronicler uses almost all the reports of David's wars from his source model (2 Sam 8:1–18), although he summarizes them. This creates a single section with a unified content. Only 18:15–17 (the list of his officers), which also follows the war reports in the source, falls out of this mould. This underlines the Chronicler's interest in war, politics, and economy, especially since he deletes the disorder regarding David's successor from the chapters he used. (He ignores it because he is not interested in the private affairs of individuals and because he regards Solomon as the only possible successor. After all, the unpleasant affair was well known to readers of Samuel and Kings.) By concentrating David's three wars within one chapter, the Chronicler gives the reader the impression that David is a warrior, which is precisely the desired effect: David is a warrior and thus denied the task of building the temple, since this requires peace (cf. e.g. Deut 12). This idea is highlighted by the deliberate sandwiching of chs. 18–20 between two passages concerning the temple's construction. The Chronicler did not need to create this effect artificially, since it can be found in his source model (2 Sam 7: Nathan's prophesy; 2 Sam 8: war reports). An interpretation of the war reports belongs in a commentary on Samuel. Only the significant changes made by Chronicles are discussed here.

v. 4, Chronicles has: 1,000 chariots, 7,000 horsemen, 20,000 foot-soldiers; the source has: 1,700 horsemen, 20,000 foot-soldiers. The original source probably read as follows: 1,000 chariots, 700 horsemen. The number was probably multiplied by ten by the Chronicler (cf. 19:18). vv. 15–17, the list of David's highest officers is appropriately placed after David's wars, since military ranks play a central role in it. v. 17, the Chronicler allows David and Solomon to perform priest's tasks, although in general Chronicles distinguishes itself from earlier texts in its tendency to put greater distance between the roles of the king and the priests. This leads to David's sons becoming 'chief officials in the service of the king', rather than priests, a vague term allowing several different interpretations.

(19:1–20:3) War against the Ammonites (and Arameans) This passage corresponds with 2 Sam 10:1–11:1; 12:26–31. It is a relatively close representation of the text, with the exceptions of the omitted Bathsheba episode and 2 Sam 12:27–9. The Chronicler only slightly reworks the source model's theology and content. Details, however, do differ in almost every verse. This could be due to both the complicated history of the text and stylistic improvements made by the Chronicler. 19:6–8 and its source model have a parallel in the Qumran text (4QSamᵃ), which stands between them and demonstrates that the relationship between Samuel and Chronicles was not one of unilateral or unambiguous independence. 19:6, the Chronicler omits Tob from the source model's list of kingdoms, also replacing Aram Beth-rehob with Aram-naharaim (Mesopotamia). Perhaps Beth-rehob no longer existed at the Chronicler's time. In any case the scale of the war is increased by the change. The extremely high price paid by the Ammonites (1,000 talents of silver, cf. 2 Chr 25:6) is mentioned only by the Chronicler who is highly interested in monetary matters. 19:18, Chronicles and its source model again vary in the stated weaponry and the size of the army David defeats. The Chronicler multiplies the number of chariots by ten (cf. 18:4). Whatever the original text stated, 40,000 foot-soldiers (Chronicles), even if grossly exaggerated, are more convincing than 40,000 horsemen (source).

20:1, which corresponds to 2 Sam 11:1 and contradicts it to some extent, implies that Joab devastated the Ammonites' land and besieged Rabbah without any foreign help. This version of events, which has often been regarded as historically correct, contradicts the Chronicler's ideology since he is keen to increase David's role and to allow all Israel to participate in the conflict. King David is suddenly in Rabbah in v. 2, leading some to believe that the verses in 2 Sam 12:27–9 were deliberately omitted here. This interpretation is possible, though it is also feasible that the Chronicler presumed knowledge of the relevant passage.

(20:4–8) The Wars Fought by David's Heroes The source (2 Sam 21:15–22) reports four battles (against the Philistines) involving David's heroes. In the first, Ishbi-benob attempts to slay David. But Abishai, the son of Zeruiah, hurries to his aid and slays Ishbi-benob. From this point, David is no longer permitted to enter into battle alongside his men: the light of Israel must not be quenched. This first battle episode is omitted by the Chronicler, probably because the idea that a Philistine could even endanger David was unpleasant to him. He consequently deletes the number 'four' from his source model in v. 8. By slightly changing a consonant in the source, the Chronicler turns Rapha's descendants into Rephaites, i.e. legendary giants also mentioned in Deut 2:11, 20–1; 3:11–13. This increases the significance of the battles noted here. This allusion does not appear as such in the English translation. v. 5, according to 2 Sam 21:19, Elhanan, the son of Jaare-oregim of Bethlehem, slew Goliath. This report is transferred to David and greatly extended (1 Sam 17). The Chronicler presumes this story to be well known, thus omitting it. He resolves the contradiction by slightly changing the Hebrew text in 2 Sam 21:19 to make Elhanan slay Goliath's brother Lahmi. Thus, according to Chronicles, David slew Goliath, whilst Elhanan killed his brother Lahmi.

(21:1–22:1) David's Census and Purchase of a Site for the Temple The Chronicler reports less extensively on the census than his source model, concentrating more on events at Ornan's threshing-floor. It is here that the temple will be built, the unspoken central theme of the chapter: the rest of 1 Chronicles concerns preparations for its construction. Certain passages resemble the Qumran version of 2 Sam 24, 4QSam[a] more closely than the canonized Hebrew text. Thus the Chronicler must have had a different source from the version of 2 Sam 24 printed in Hebrew Bibles today; one which would explain the numerous discrepancies between ch. 21 and 2 Sam 24.

21:1–16, it is not God's newly rekindled anger that leads David to carry out a census (as in the source model), but Satan. Japhet (1997: 145–8) presumes this to be an anonymous human persuader. It is more likely, however, that this is the same

figure mentioned in Job 1 and Zech 3. The Chronicler reinterprets unacceptable elements of the source model, taking the perspective of Job 1. Nothing explicit in the text explains the sinful nature of a census. Joab resists David's plan more strongly here than in the source model, actually using the word 'trespass' (v. 3; NRSV, 'guilt') and thereby increasing David's responsibility. The Chronicler omits the individual stages of the census (due to its insignificance or incomprehensibility), merely documenting the result: 1,100,000 men of the united kingdom of Israel and Judah, of whom 470,000 are Judeans (source model: 500,000; have 30,000 Benjaminites been omitted? cf. 2 Sam 24:9). This is 200,000 fewer than in the source. Levi and Benjamin have not been counted, as the Chronicler states in v. 6 (unique material). According to Num 1:49, it is forbidden to carry out a military census in Levi, whilst Benjamin was probably omitted since the tabernacle resided upon its territory. v. 6 thus contains a key to understanding this chapter.

21:7, since Satan persuaded David, YHWH's disapproval, rather than David's remorse, is portrayed here (unlike 2 Sam 24). '[A]nd he struck Israel': this summary forecasts the events reported in v. 14. 21:16, the Chronicler describes the angel hanging in the air more extensively than his source model (cf. Qumran); cf. also the descriptions in Num 22:31 and Josh 5:13–15 upon which the verses are probably based (cf. also v. 18); furthermore cf. Dan 8:15; 12:6. 21:18, in the source, the order to erect an altar upon the threshing-floor of Ornan (the later name for Araunah) is made solely by Gad, who in Chronicles is sent by an angel. Does this angel play the same mediating role as in Zechariah, or is it more comparable to Num 22:35? 21:21–5, the purchase of Ornan's threshing-floor is modelled on Abraham's purchase of Machpelah's cave (Gen 23), even repeating specific details, the most important of which is David's insistence on paying the full price (an expression used only in Gen 23:9 and vv. 22, 24). The 600 silver shekels David pays is more than Abraham's 400 silver shekels for Machpelah's cave. The site of the temple is more valuable than Sarah's burial site (600 is also a multiple of 12, an important number in various ways within Chronicles).

21:28–30, the grammar and content of 22:1 would be more suitable as a continuation of v. 28, hence some have suggested that vv. 29–30 are a later gloss. They can, however, also be regarded as a parenthesis. They explain why David made sacrifices upon Ornan's threshing-floor, rather than at the high place at Gibeon (because an angel obstructed his way). This underscores the idea that only one place can be legitimately used at any time as a site for sacrifice made by the cult of God's people.

22:1, in the section's climax, the site is gloriously announced as the future site of YHWH's temple and place for sacrifices. It becomes 'synonymous' with the desert tabernacle, the high place at Gibeon (and Ornan's threshing-place); all legitimate cultic sites and buildings that play an important part in Israel's history, have now been enumerated. The language of this verse is very similar to Gen 28:17, which concerns the construction of the holy site at Bethel. This is occasionally interpreted to imply that neither Bethel nor any other Samaritan holy place is a legitimate sacrificial site for YHWH.

Preparations for the Temple's Construction (1 Chr 22:2–29:30)

(22:2–19) Material and Spiritual Preparations This chapter introduces the long section stretching up to ch. 29 which has no parallel in 2 Samuel. The whole of its contents—including the lists!—serve the sole purpose of the following eight chapters: the construction of the temple, David and Solomon's joint project, one conceiving it and the other executing it. The reigns of David and Solomon appear almost to form a single entity, especially in this chapter. Many commentaries have regarded chs. 23–7 as a supplementary gloss to the Chronicler's work. If this were true, the Chronicler would have accentuated the theme of a Davidic-Solomonic joint kingship even more strongly. The chapter, which contains much speech and little narrative, divides into three parts: vv. 2–5, David's (own) preparations for the temple's construction; vv. 6–16, his speech to Solomon; vv. 17–19, a speech to Israel's rulers.

v. 4, mention of the Sidonians and Tyrians, who bring cedar wood, is reminiscent of King Hiram (14:1). The Chronicler probably took literary guidance from Ezra 3:7, where Sidonians and Tyrians are also responsible for providing timber (cedar wood) for the second temple. v. 5, David introduces his son Solomon in a similar manner to his self-introduction whilst in prayer at Gibeon (1 Kings 3:7). Solomon's youth and inexperience, a literary theme and not a pointer to his actual age, is made with reference not to his ability to rule the country, but to his ability to build the temple. David takes responsible measures in the light of Solomon's inexperience and the size of the task at hand.

vv. 6–16, the Chronicler uses David's final decrees as portrayed in 1 Kings 2 for David's speech to Solomon in his own work. Ignoring the confusion surrounding the accession, however, he copies only David's call to abide by the law and act courageously (1 Kings 2:2–3). The relationship between David and Solomon in Chronicles is similar to that of Moses and Joshua (cf. also vv. 11–13). v. 6, the direct order to build the temple comes from David. v. 8, Nathan's prophecy (2 Sam 7) contains no explanation as to why David cannot construct the temple. One is included at 1 Kings 5:17: because of the wars forced upon David, he is impeded from carrying out the plan. The Chronicler takes this theme up, transforming it, however, into a greater principle: because David is a warrior who has shed much blood, he is forbidden to build the temple. This is neither pacifist nor does it refer to individual actions such as Uriah's murder: it simply and objectively excludes the blemish of bloodshed from the temple's construction. v. 9, through the use of a pun, Solomon is depicted as a man of peace and the calm atmosphere is strengthened. According to Deut 12, sacrificial cult can take place from the moment when Israel has peace from its enemies. This precondition is hereby fulfilled. vv. 11–13, David encourages Solomon, refers to the forthcoming work, forecasts his success (if he follows God) and confirms God's presence. All these elements can also be found in Josh 1 (Joshua's succession to Moses). The Chronicler is drawing deliberate parallels in this chapter, at the same time using terms which are very important to him: 'the LORD be with you', 'success'.

(23:1–32) The Departments and Duties of the Levites Once the preparations for the temple's construction have been completed (ch. 22), one would expect a building order to follow (ch. 28). Yet between these two chapters lies a large section (chs. 23–7) dealing with the Levites and priests as well as with David's secular officials. Many exegetes regard these chapters as secondary—and partly unified. According to one argument, their strongly cultic theme (cf. also chs. 15–16) does not correspond with the Chronicler's main interests and even contradicts his views on certain points. It is also stated that 28:1 refers back to 23:2 in an example of resumptive repetition. None of these arguments has remained undisputed. For instance, it has also been pointed out that the Chronicler shows great interest in the Levites (whilst dealing more briefly with the priests), that his specific theological profile can still be discerned in this section, and that contradictions should not be overestimated, in view of the large amount of (not always mutually compatible) material he reworked. The parallels between 23:2 and 28:1 are clear, though their differences are also apparent. Furthermore, 13:5 and 15:3 demonstrate that repetitions need not always be 'resumptive', nor necessarily lead to the presumption that the text between them is secondary. Williamson (1987: 157–8) suggests an original compromise solution: 23:3–6a contains the plan for what follows: everything pertaining to it stems from the Chronicler's hand (23:6b–13a, 15–24; 25:1–6; 26:1–3, 9–11, 19; 26:20–32), whilst the rest is part of a pro-priestly reworking of the text which can also be recognized in chs. 15–16. Wide-reaching personnel restructuring measures were carried out in the temple between the conception of the two editions, possibly as a result of notable Jerusalem figures moving over to Samaritan society during the late post-exilic period. Whatever the case, the chapters in their present form declare that David set all the significant religious and secular institutions in place. For readers of Chronicles, this means that David's introduction of these institutions and their officers demands their respect.

vv. 3–5, the Levites' census is not a contradiction of 21:6, since it is not a general population census and merely deals with dividing up the duties ascribed to them. The high numbers of Levites (cf. Num 4:48: 8,580) is evidence of the Chronicler's esteem for them. The size of the numbers concerning individual groups reflects the relative significance attributed to them. The Levites are not recorded according to their family trees here, but according to their functions: officers and judges, gatekeepers, musicians. They are listed in inverse order in 25–6. A further list, ch. 24, is inserted between chs. 23 and 25, including, amongst others, names of Aaronite priests. v. 3, the minimum age for holding office varies: 30 in Num 4:3, 23, 30, as here; 25 in Num 8:24; 20 in Ezra 3:8; 1 Chr 23:24–7; 2 Chr 31:17. Perhaps the age was reduced at times when there were fewer Levites.

vv. 6–24, genealogical registers of the three great Levite clans: depending on the counting method used, 24 (Japhet (1993): 43): Gershon 10, Kohath 9, Merari 5) or 22 (Rudolph (1955): 155): Gershon 9, Kohath 9, Merari 4) families existed. These lists reflect the shifts in the relative size and power of the clans (cf. e.g. vv. 11, 17). vv. 25–32 cover the Levites' duties (partly repeating those mentioned in ch. 9). vv. 25–6, 28–32, YHWH grants his people peace (cf. Deut 12:8–12; by contrast 1 Chr 22:9), forcing changes to be made to the cult. In other words, since the Levites no longer need to carry the tabernacle, they are free to perform other cultic duties which are not stipulated in the Pentateuch, as described in vv. 28–32: they must assist the priests. The descriptions in vv. 28 and 32 are held together by the phrase 'work for the service of the house of the LORD'. v. 32, duties at the tabernacle and the sanctuary: this describes both the Levites' duties in the desert and their tasks in the (future) temple of Jerusalem, thus closely binding the two sites and their sacred buildings. v. 27 is a gloss interrupting the clear continuity of vv. 26 and 28. It is probably a crude attempt to explain the contradiction between vv. 3 and 24: David made an earlier and a later order regarding the Levites' minimum age in office.

(24:1–31) The Classes of Priests This chapter divides into three parts: the first (vv. 1–19) deals with the priests, their organization, and their departments. The second contains a list of non-priestly Levites (vv. 20–31). Since they are already listed in the previous chapter, and because v. 31 follows on well from 20b, Japhet (1993: 423) and other researchers have suggested this list to be a secondary insertion. They claim that the original text contained only vv. 20a and 31, which by analogy apply the priests' method of drawing lots to the Levites. The inserted list (which omits some names at its beginning) is seen as an attempt to correct and add to the previous list in 23:6–23.

vv. 1–19, the priests' organization as portrayed here is more advanced and systematic than anywhere else in the OT and is rigidly adhered to in the sequel. It is perhaps a result of the surplus of priests during post-exilic times. The system of departments allowed job-sharing and is applied to Levites and gatekeepers (of whom there were initially only a few, as one can see in Ezra and Nehemiah) by later writers. Despite their undisputed place at the top of the cultic hierarchy, the priests, a branch of the Levites, are dealt with only briefly in Chronicles. vv. 2–3, all priests were descendants of Aaron's two sons, Eleazar and Ithamar. Eleazar is often mentioned in the Pentateuch and elsewhere. According to this passage, he is the ancestor of Zadok, the priest active during David and Solomon's time. This is merely a theoretical proposition, as is the much less frequently mentioned relationship between Ithamar and Ahimelech: if Zadok is Eleazar's descendant, Ahimelech must stem from Ithamar! David is assisted by Zadok and Ahimelech in organizing the priests. vv. 4–5, no doubt there were power struggles between the unevenly matched groups of priests. Rudolph (1955: 159, 161) even assumes that the (stronger) descendants of Eleazar claimed both (honorary) titles of 'holy princes' and 'princes of God', whose meanings remain unclear. The Chronicler stresses the equal treatment of the two groups in the passage (cf. 24:31; 26:13). Naturally the larger faction is represented by a relatively larger number of priests in the departments. v. 5, the procedure of drawing lots, in 1 Chronicles (24:31; 25:8; 26:13) as elsewhere (see e.g. Neh 10:35), emphasizes God's hand in the distribution of the priests, though the practical reasons for such distribution are not known. It is also unclear whether lots were drawn alternately (i.e. one to Eleazar, one to Ithamar), thus leaving the last eight lots to Eleazar, or whether they were drawn in rotation in a two (Eleazar) to one (Ithamar) ratio. v. 7, since Mattathias is a descendant of Jehoiarib's clan

(1 Macc 2:1) and is the first to be named in ch. 24, it has occasionally been suggested that the list (at least in its present form) stems from Maccabean times. This theory is based on two disputed assumptions: (1) The list in ch. 24 names the priest clans in order of their importance. (2) Mattahias's clan was the most important of his time.

vv. 20–30, the list of Levites is certainly incomplete—the most important Gershonites should have been included. The text has also been damaged here. Although it is very similar to the list in ch. 23, it differs in significant points, reflecting the shifts in power between individual groups, which thus shrink or expand accordingly. New groups appear and existing ones disappear. The list is a kind of update on its equivalent in ch. 23. Some branches include an extra generation compared to ch. 23. v. 31, the Levites use the same system of drawing lots as the priests, using almost the same witnesses. This makes clear that the Levites are (almost) as important as the priests.

(25:1–31) The Musicians and their Duties The list of temple musicians logically follows on from that of the Levites, to whom they strictly belong (23:30–1; cf. 15:16–24; 16:4–6). The chapter divides into two parts: the first names the three musician families (Asaph, Jeduthun, and Heman), whilst the second deals with the drawing of lots to allocate individual members' duties. Whether the Chronicler is the author of all or any of the chapter, and whether the two parts were even written by the same hand, is a matter of debate. Whatever the case may be regarding the first question, it is clear that the lists are entirely artificial, written to create the impression that sacrifice and music are closely intertwined (cf. 23:29–30): since the 24 different temple duties have been individually assigned to the priests, the musicians are also allocated 24 different duties, which are not, however, specified as such. The lists' artificiality is underlined by the fact that none of those named in them are proved to have existed in other texts. Whilst the first and second parts of the chapter are basically in harmony, they differ in some details. Williamson (1987: 165–6) suggests that this is evidence of their literary independence from each other. The musicians' families (Chronicler) have been transformed into types of duties (post-Chronicles), without entirely losing their significance.

The organization of the musicians greatly changed with time, whilst individual family influences grew and diminished respectively. Interpretations differ as to whether these developments can be retraced in this passage, or whether it is used to harmonize contradictions within the text. Occasionally all musicians are regarded as descendants of Asaph (Ezra 2:41; 3:10; Neh 7:44). Neh 11:17 and 1 Chr 9:15–16 mention both Asaph and Jeduthun. A third tradition speaks of three musicians' guilds, referring back to Asaph, Heman, and Ethan (see 1 CHR 6:44; 15:17, 19 for Ethan). The identification of Jeduthun and Ethan has been facilitated by the similar way in which the names are written. It is difficult to reconstruct a history of the temple musicians from the diverse material in the OT, which is only briefly summarized here. The order of the three families is Asaph, Jeduthun, Heman. This probably reflects the earlier hierarchy. In fact the tone of the passage lets Heman's family emerge as the largest ('according to the promise of God to exalt him', v. 5).

vv. 1–7 show a clear attempt to legitimize the musicians. They are introduced only with their duties (in the case of the singers) and instruments. One of their duties is also prophecy (vv. 1–3; a marginal interpretation even regards them as prophets). It is unlikely, however, that this duty makes them the heirs to (great) classical prophecy. Moreover they probably do not form part of the continuum of traditional pre-exilic cult prophets. Their singing/playing—and thus the content of their music, the psalms they conceived—can be seen as a kind of prophecy, particularly in view of the fact that 1 Sam 10:5 and 2 Kings 3:15 emphasize the close relationship between music and prophecy. The Chronicler may even have been thinking of these two passages (especially the first) in connecting prophecy with the musicians. 2 Chr 29:25 refers to the order given by David and supported by two prophets (Gad and Nathan) confirming the Levites' (permanent!) office as temple musicians. v. 1, 'the officers of the army' does not actually refer to the army. The Hebrew word 'army' upon which this is based is an expression for the Levites' rank—as in Num 4, e.g. The Chronicler adopted the term from that chapter; 15:16 uses the term 'chiefs of the Levites', who select the musicians for their office. The term 'set apart' often differentiates the holy from the profane and is used here to denote appointment for a special duty. The 'list' is an appropriate translation for a term usually meaning 'number'. Some commentaries see this word as evidence that vv. 2–6 are an insertion, since one would expect the word to be followed by a number, which does not appear until v. 7, after a list of names. v. 5, Heman is the (king's) seer. Asaph (2 Chr 29:30) and Jeduthun (2 Chr 35:15; perhaps together with Asaph and Heman here) are also given this title. This stresses their dependence upon the king and their prophetic role.

The last nine sons of Heman have artificial names which form the following (rather awkward) Psalm if read one after the other: 'Be gracious to me YHWH, be gracious to me, my God art thou; I have magnified, and I will exalt my helper (thy help); sitting in adversity I said, "Clear signs give plentifully"'. This is probably another example of the Chronicler's love of meaningful names. Alternatively, musician families of the period may have been given names corresponding to incipits of individual psalms, although this theory cannot explain why these names form an entire psalm.

v. 7, each of the twenty-four musical families has twelve members (24 × 12 = 288). The Chronicler explicitly mentions their skilful ability, since he greatly valued hard work. vv. 8–31, lots are drawn to assign offices.

(26:1–32) The Gatekeepers; Further Duties of the Levites The unifying factor in this chapter is that it deals only with Levites: gatekeepers in vv. 1–19, the temple treasurers in vv. 20–8, and the Levite officials in vv. 29–32. This structure is logical since gatekeepers tend to be linked to the musicians, whilst ch. 27 deals with civil administration. There are strongly differing arguments regarding the text's unity and sources.

vv. 1–12 contain a list of gatekeepers, whereas vv. 13–19 describe the work ascribed to them by lot, with vv. 12–13 perhaps serving as a transition passage between the two sections. The gatekeepers in Ezra 2:42–3 (i.e. during the period of return from exile) were not of levitical rank but gradually achieved this status in the course of time. In the list in vv. 1–11,

the verses concerning Obed-edom (vv. 4–8) are almost universally regarded as a gloss: they interrupt the connection between vv. 3 and 9. Japhet (1993: 451), however, contests this. Although the gatekeepers' duties are not based on David's orders, the following passage is an attempt to legitimize their existence. v. 15, in monarchical times, the southern gate did not require guards since the south wall formed part of the royal palace. This is the clearest, though not the sole, indication that the Chronicler envisaged the second, post-exilic temple, which he knew from his own experience, when writing this passage.

vv. 20–8, this list of treasury officers is linked to vv. 29–31 in as far as the Izharites and the Hebronites (v. 23) are mentioned in both passages. It has occasionally been presumed that vv. 20–32 were once an independent document containing levitical ranks and their officers. A number of those listed here are also mentioned in 23:6–23. The section distinguishes between the treasuries of the house of God (vv. 20, 22) and the treasuries for the dedicated things (vv. 20, 26). Shebuel of Amram's clan, whose Kohathite origin is not explicitly mentioned (and who also appears in 23:16; 24:20), seems to carry general responsibility for both treasuries. He is mentioned only in v. 24. Gershonites are responsible for the treasuries of the house of God, whilst the Kohathite family administers the treasuries for the dedicated things. vv. 26–8, the treasuries of the dedicated things, which are described in detail (unlike those of the house of God), include spoils of war provided by different important persons in a 'democratic' manner typical of Chronicles. The Chronicler probably used Num 31:48, 52, 54 as a literary source for this 'democratic' behaviour. According to Chronicles, these wars had always served the purpose of building a temple. The wars fought by David and Saul are well known. Samuel's wars probably refer to 1 Sam 7:7–14, whilst Abner and Joab's conflicts probably stem from 2 Sam 2–4.

At this point, part of the story is implicitly incorporated without being explicitly described by the Chronicler. The reader must know the texts at which the Chronicler is hinting. Mention of Saul, despite receiving a negative judgement by the Chronicler, is not a reflection of popular tradition, nor does it suffice to prove that the Chronicler was not the author of this passage.

vv. 29–32, in pre-exilic times, the Levites can hardly have performed the administrative tasks ascribed to them in addition to their religious roles here (cf. also 23:4 and 2 Chr 19:11). These must have developed in post-exilic times, though it is naturally impossible to ascertain to what extent. They seem to have been especially important during the Maccabean period. The structure described here resembles an ideal draft: the Levites are responsible both for the business of the Lord and for the service of the king (a duplication typical of Chronicles). Their office incorporated both west-Jordan and Transjordanian territory (the latter being stressed by the style of its presentation). This order is based on David's plans. It was partly carried out in post-exilic times (and not during Josiah's reign, as often presumed). It reflects a time in which spiritual and secular elements were closely intertwined and the religious and political claim to Transjordanian territories had not been relinquished. It was important for the Chronicler that it encompassed the entire region (cf. 2 Chr 19; similar phenomenon).

(27:1–34) The Organization and Administration of the Kingdom This chapter comprises five parts, of which four deal with the secular organization of David's kingdom and the fifth contains a comment on his census. vv. 1–15: the military divisions and their commanders; vv. 16–22: the leaders of the tribes; vv. 23–4: a comment on the census; vv. 25–31: David's civil officers; vv. 32–4: David's advisers. Some commentaries regard this chapter to be secondary. Whilst Williamson (1987: 174) also believes this passage to be post-Chronicles, his evidence is its *incompatibility* with the list of contents in 23:3–6a. Others claim its authenticity by pointing to some elements which are typical of the Chronicler (cf. esp. 1 CHR 27:25–31). Whatever the case, the question whether the passage uses older, historically reliable sources regarding David's (or a later king's) reign must also be answered. It follows on well from ch. 26, which is concerned with the Levites' secular tasks. Seen in their entirety, the previous and present chapters give us an impression of perfect administration and organization—and this is, no doubt, intentional.

vv. 1–15, the commanders of the divisions: according to this representation, the military forces consist of 12 divisions of 24,000 men, each subdivided into thousands and hundreds. Each division serves for one month a year. The divisions' commanders are all mentioned in the list of David's heroes (11:10–47), though they are not the first twelve names stated. The total army is enormous (288,000 men) and is only deployed as a militia in times of war. Its organization somewhat resembles the ranks of officers amongst the priests and Levites, whilst the one-month spell of duty reminds one of Solomon's system of twelve royal officers in charge of supplying the royal court (1 Kings 4:7). Although this army cannot have existed in this form, some incongruities with ch. 11 as well as certain other details (such as two commanders of some departments) suggest that this passage is based on real circumstances. The question is, what circumstances? In this context, one should note that by contrast to ch. 11, the army commanders' origins are named here: they all come from the centre of David's kingdom.

vv. 16–22 (24). The list of army leaders (and their departments) is followed by the (political) leaders of the tribes, though their role is not revealed. Presuming vv. 23–4 are an integral part of the passage, it is easy to suspect that they were involved in carrying out the census reported in v. 23.

The twelve tribes are not listed according to a consistent system in the OT, nor does it always use the same names. Different lists reflect different historical realities. This list is most similar to its equivalent in Num 1 (which also involves a census), though the two are not identical. The omission of Gad and Asher and the claim that the Aaronites were an independent tribe apart from Levi are particularly notable in the present list. Why is the latter, if named at all, not named first? The names of some tribal chiefs can only be found in Chronicles. vv. 23–4 are an extremely artistic attempt at twisting the story of the census (ch. 21) to grant David forgiveness for his deed. According to this chapter David forces Joab to carry out the census. Joab, however, fearing the Lord's word, does not include Benjamin and Levi. This passage contains no explicit incrimination of Joab, but (implicitly) exonerates David by making him follow the rules laid down for censuses in Num 1 (vv. 2–4). He counts only those men who were older

than 20. The Chronicler's justification for this way of proceeding 'for the LORD had promised to make Israel as numerous as the stars of heaven' (cf. e.g. Gen 15:5), is nevertheless inappropriate here. If this were true, the significance of those over 20 would be lost. The passage, to a certain extent, remains a mystery.

vv. 25–31, David's treasurers: this section contains detailed information about David's fortune, the geographical dispersal of his estates, and his highest-ranking administrative officers. The list is often regarded as a reliable historical document that correctly reflects David's treasury. Its historical authenticity is supported by a number of impressive arguments: the administration is even simpler than during Solomon's reign and nothing contradicts the list's authenticity. The use of foreigners (Bedouin) as David's administrators would have been concealed in post-Davidic times. These were chosen for their skill at keeping camels and smaller livestock. The round number of twelve senior administrators, which has often been seen as a coincidence, is unsettling. So is the extensive discussion of agriculture, which seems to correspond with the economically obsessed *Zeitgeist* of the Chronicler (see Uzziah's love of agriculture in 2 Chr 26:10).

vv. 32–4, David's closest officials: his kitchen cabinet. These verses are not a parallel to 18:15–17, in which David's state officials are listed. The historical information is given as an aside, showing that they do not form an official list.

(28:1–21) The Order to Build the Temple Together with ch. 29, this chapter follows on from ch. 23:1–2. David (who in contrast to his portrayal in 1 Kings 1–2 is still in full possession of his powers) addresses all the officials of Israel at an important assembly (vv. 2–8). He then turns to Solomon (vv. 9–10, 20–1), handing him plans for the temple's construction. The central themes of this chapter are (David and) Solomon's rule and their keeping of the law, in which the people and the construction of the temple also play an important part. The Chronicler repeats certain points which he has already introduced, varying them significantly, whilst other material is entirely new.

vv. 1–2, David addresses all of his people in v. 2, but his first comments in v. 1 are addressed to the leading ranks of his state, which are listed here more comprehensively than anywhere else in the OT. Thus the Chronicler manages to emphasize both the special responsibility laid upon his officers and the presence of the entire population in a way that would not have been possible if David had addressed both at the same time. vv. 2–8 report David's speech to his people. The Chronicler repeats Nathan's promise (2 Chr 17), varying it in a familiarly individual way. vv. 4–5, the choice of David and Solomon here is in a sense compared to the system of drawing lots. The resulting impression is stronger than in the source model: YHWH is the active force in creating a kingdom which (as the Chronicler stresses) will be eternal (cf. vv. 7–8). Solomon does not accede to the throne after terrible human turmoil. The Chronicler merely refers to such events with the seemingly innocuous words 'And of all my sons, for the Lord has given me many...'. vv. 9–10, having given a lengthy sermon to all the officials of Israel, containing many references to YHWH, David addresses Solomon more briefly. In the slightly (but significantly) adapted tone of a Deuteronomistic theologoumenon, David calls upon his son to serve YHWH with an undivided mind and a willing heart (a phrase characteristic of the Chronicler). The relationship between this statement and the subsequent explanation that YHWH can search all the hearts of men and understand all men's thoughts is not wholly clear. It is certainly motivating, perhaps stirring up a deeper obedience to the law.

vv. 11–19, David now gives his orders for the temple's construction, its contents, and all matters pertaining to it. They are based upon God's plans, which David possesses in writing and declares to Solomon. This is probably the best way to understand v. 19. According to Ex 25–31, YHWH first instructed Moses to build a tabernacle before this was carried out. Great weight is given to the fact that it occurred following divine orders. This is also true (though in a different way) of the new temple's construction, which Ezekiel sees in a vision (Ezek 40–4). The Chronicler uses these texts, thus clearly diverging from 1 Kings, where Solomon builds the temple without referring back to divine instructions. This also emphasizes how closely the tabernacle and the temple are connected in Chronicles: the temple is a kind of completion of the preceding tabernacle. Perhaps this passage is an accurate impression of the second temple's actual condition, or at least gives an idea of its ideal form. One peculiarity here is the lack of concrete instructions. The Chronicler only states that they have been given. In a general way they cover all aspects of the cult, including the buildings, their rooms, personnel, (cultic) services, equipment, and the temple's treasury. v. 18 contains three objects: the incense altar made of particularly valuable gold, the golden chariot, and the cherubim which spread their wings to protect the Lord's ark of the covenant.

vv. 29–31, David calls upon Solomon to be strong and courageous and to be persistent until all the work has been completed. He encourages his son, reminding him of God's presence (a common phrase (theologoumenon) in Chronicles) and the willing support of the priests, the Levites, and the entire population, providing him with the ideal conditions for the project's implementation.

(29:1–30) Donations for Construction of Temple, David's Prayer, Solomon's Accession to the Throne, Conclusion of Story of David This chapter, which concludes the story of David, divides into four parts: vv. 1–9: the voluntary gifts; vv. 10–20: David's prayer and the people's reply; vv. 21–5: Solomon's accession to the throne; vv. 26–30: concluding praise of David's rule.

vv. 1–9 concern the voluntary gifts. The youth and inexperience of Solomon, David's chosen successor (according to the story of succession), leads the outgoing king to draw the necessary conclusions and take some prudent measures. There are clear parallels here with reports concerning the tabernacle. Moses' call upon the Israelites for voluntary gifts was in fact rather imperative; David prefers to promote his cause. This principle of freedom shows David contributing to the costs of the temple's construction both as a king (as in 1 Kings) and as an ordinary believer. His people's leading classes respond to his call and the people rejoice at the 'willing' (a key word in this chapter) nature of their deeds. Freedom and joy are closely connected. The people give far more than David's private donation. The passage concerning the

construction materials they used refers back to many other biblical texts.

vv. 10–29, like other prayers in Chronicles, this one serves to emphasize central theological thoughts close to the author's heart at an important turning-point in the narrative. This technique, which is also significant in the Deuteronomistic History becomes increasingly important in Chronicles and intertestamental scriptures. The prayer begins with a doxology which does not directly refer to the context, continues with an interpretation of the voluntary donations and concludes with a double wish, referring backwards and forwards in the text— one calling for these thoughts never to be forgotten by the people, the other addressing the future rule of King Solomon.

vv. 10–20, the form of this praise of God is unusual, being in the second rather than the third person. Everything belongs to God (the tenfold repetition of the key word 'thine' cannot be a coincidence). In his hand is power and might. The Chronicler develops these thoughts more elaborately than anywhere else. The same idea is contained in the Chronicler's repeated claim that Israel's kingdom belongs to and is granted by YHWH. In an extension of these general ideas, the Chronicler continues by claiming that the voluntary gifts made by the people ultimately stem from the hand of God. The people own nothing but the sincere convictions with which they make the donations (v. 17). There is a combination of absolute humility and profound pride here. An indirectly motivated passage concerning the fragile human condition, which the Chronicler has taken from a variety of source material, is inserted into this second part of the chapter.

vv. 26–30, summaries of the rule of individual kings are standard practice in the books of Kings. David's rule differs greatly from the usual pattern and is integrated more smoothly into the narrative context (1 Kings 2:10–12). Chronicles' version is closer to the other kings' concluding formulae in the books of Kings, though it differs in significant ways. Like its source model, Chronicles distinguishes between David's reign in Hebron and in Jerusalem. Unlike Kings and their Deuteronomistic prototype, Chronicles does not mention David's funeral. This is not due to lost text, since the positive judgement that can accompany a burial note is present in the indirect comparison with Abraham (Gen 25:8), (Isaac 35:29), Gideon (Judg 8:32), and Job (Job 42:17), all of whom died in old age. The Chronicler bestows more riches and honour upon David than upon any of these men.

In stating his sources, the Chronicler refers back to the three prophets (with their differing titles) who appeared in his text during David's reign. At this point, David's rule is indirectly portrayed as having influence across the entire known world (beyond merely the neighbouring countries). This is clearly an allusion to the Persian empire (and Alexander's realm).

2 Chronicles

Solomon's Rule over the United Kingdom (2 Chr 1:1–9:31)

The Beginnings of Solomon's Reign (2 Chr 1:1–17)

The Chronicler ignores the confusion surrounding David's successor, beginning this chapter, after an introductory note in v. 1, with the sacrifice made by Solomon and God's appearance to him at Gibeon. He simultaneously extends and shortens his source model material. As is his habit, he organizes the procession to Gibeon democratically. At the same time he creates a close link between the tabernacle and the temple in Jerusalem, which does not exist in 1 Kings 3. The extended scene at Gibeon in this chapter is a shortened version of the source model which has then been enriched with the Chronicler's own theology. vv. 3–13 contain a 'theology of the sanctuary' in a nutshell.

In the source model, God's appearance at Gibeon is followed by the story of Solomon's judgement. It allows Solomon to display the wisdom that has just been bestowed upon him. As with all pieces in the source concerning Solomon's wisdom, the Chronicler omits this episode. While some exegetes claim that the passage taken from 1 Kings 10:26–9 describing Solomon's wealth (vv. 14–17) is used to stress Solomon's wisdom, others argue that this insertion serves the purpose of proving that Solomon had the necessary wealth to construct the temple. (David had, however, already supplied the necessary materials.) The passage is repeated in an only slightly altered form in 9:25–8, at the end of Solomon's rule. This repetition underlines the importance the Chronicler attached to wealth (and thus power) as signs of God's blessing.

(1:1–13) Solomon's Sacrifice and Prayer at Gibeon vv. 3–5, the Chronicler attempts to unite all legitimate cultic sites and the most important cultic objects. Solomon begins his reign by concerning himself with the cult once he has secured his accession—just as David did. The priestly theology of the Pentateuch concentrates on the tabernacle bearing the ark at its centre, whilst the historical texts focus entirely on the ark. The Chronicler combines both perspectives, underlining the presence of the tabernacle as the temple's precursor. It is stressed that Moses created the tabernacle in the desert. The tabernacle which is mentioned earlier in 1 Chr 16:39; 21:29 must be distinguished from the tent for the ark that David erects in Jerusalem. v. 9, the Chronicler no doubt deliberately turns 'a great people, so numerous they cannot be numbered or counted' (1 Kings 3:8) into 'a people as numerous as the dust of the earth': the same address is made to Jacob (i.e. Israel), the most important founding father in Chronicles (Gen 28:14). Despite shortening his source material, the Chronicler adds a new element here, namely the reference to a promise of an eternal dynasty made to his father ('let your promise to my father David now be fulfilled'; cf. 1 Chr 17:11–12). This reflection back to David can also be found in v. 1, where Solomon is pointedly introduced as David's son.

(1:14–17) Solomon's Wealth vv. 14–17, Solomon's riches here are almost identical with the source model (1 Kings 10:26–9).

Construction of the Temple (2 Chr 1:18–7:22)

(1:18–2:17) Solomon's Contract with Hiram of Tyre Solomon eagerly engages in his father's (and not the Phoenician king's) construction project. Unlike the author of his source material, the Chronicler takes every step to diminish the Tyrian's contribution to the temple's construction. Above all he states that Solomon is stronger and more important than Hiram. The temple he erects is both a sacrificial site and God's residence. This explains the strong emendations the Chronicler makes

to his source model. Narrative elements almost entirely give way to speech and letters. vv. 2–9, in Solomon's message to Hiram he makes the initial move and keeps the initiative. This skilfully structured passage actually contains temple and temple-cult theology. The temple clearly appears to be the second tabernacle. v. 3, Solomon names everything pertaining to the temple cult here, ordered on the basis of the Pentateuch: see amongst others Ex 30:1–8; Lev 24:5–9; Num 28–9. vv. 4–5, the Chronicler uses an adapted argument from the dedicatory prayer in 6:18. He is less concerned with God's transcendence than with his own subjective inability to build a house for God. He must do this, however, in order to make sacrifices to God. v. 6, the man sent by Hiram should—unlike in the source material—not only be skilled in carpentry, but also understand other crafts and be able to work with various materials (note e.g. the curtain in 3:14 which does not appear in the source). He is the equivalent of Bezalel and his assistant Oholiab, who constructed the tabernacle (cf. Ex 31:1–8). The Chronicler creates another parallel with David here: just as he worked together with the Phoenicians (1 Chr 22:4) so does his son Solomon here. It is, however, made clear that foreign craftsmen do not build the temple alone. They work under the auspices of masters stemming from Judah and Jerusalem (the two names are often employed for the post-exilic temple community). vv. 10–15, letters as part of historic works are known from Greek (and Roman) historiography. The Chronicler is perhaps orientating his text by them. v. 14, 'my lord': this statement completely endorses Solomon's supremacy over Hiram. v. 15, Joppa is an important post-exilic Israelite port (if not the most important, Jon 1:3; Ezra 3:7). Ezra 3:7, which also concerns trading relations with the Phoenicians (Sidon and Tyre), is probably the source for this passage. Above all it explicitly mentions Lebanese wood being transported across the sea to Joppa. v. 16, the possible interpretation of 1 Kings 9:22 (cf. 5:29), by which no Israelites were employed as forced labourers, becomes a certainty here. In keeping with the general tendency of Chronicles, the foreigners are no longer regarded as such, since they have such a close relationship with the people of Israel. Again the Chronicler stresses that Solomon acts like his father (1 Chr 22:2).

(3:1–17) Construction of the Temple: Measurements, Holy of Holies, Interior Decoration However much the Chronicler wished to legitimize the temple as a place of worship, he comments much more briefly on its construction and interior decoration than his source text, though keeping its structure. The report in 1 Kings 6 was greatly reworked, resulting in a rather poor piece of literature. This may have been one reason for the Chronicler's alterations. Another reason could be his lack of interest in God's dwelling as a building. It is impossible to say by what criteria he shortens this passage. He occasionally concentrates on the central theme, whilst noting details (which he perhaps knew from the second temple) elsewhere. The Chronicler often draws parallels between the temple and the desert tabernacle. This chapter even links it with Abraham. Many parts of this text are unclear or even spoilt, especially concerning the measurements. This commentary only touches upon such a technically complicated subject.

vv. 1–2, the author of the books of Kings calculates dates not only from the year of Solomon's accession, but also by the

Exodus, which is important to Deuteronomistic historiographers. This emphasis is greatly reduced in Chronicles. The Chronicler is not as interested in the exact date of the temple's construction (omitting the month Ziv as recorded in 1 Kings 6:1), as in its exact position and its authentication: YHWH appeared to David on Mount Moriah, and the king fixed its place which was confirmed by YHWH who sent fire from heaven on the altar of burnt offering. The name of Mount Moriah appears elsewhere only in the story of Isaac's sacrifice (Gen 22:2), which clearly contains hidden references to the temple of Jerusalem. Moriah can be interpreted in folk etymology as 'appearance of the Lord'. Since YHWH has already appeared to David, the Chronicler can use this element to develop a motif which has its roots in Gen 22. (The Samaritans identify their holy Mount Gerizim as the mountain upon which Isaac was to be sacrificed, although only much later; however, v. 3 does not contain any polemic content directed against the Samaritans.)

vv. 6–7, perhaps there was a mosaic made with precious stones on the floor (cf. 1 Chr 29:2).

From v. 8 onwards, the parallels between the temple and the tabernacle become stronger, as the repeated phrase 'he made', which characterizes the report in Exodus, emphasizes. v. 9, 'nails . . . of gold': fifty shekels of gold is far too much for one nail and too little for all of them. This is probably a symbolic number (cf. 2 Sam 24:24). The fact that such small objects as nails are mentioned at all could suggest that a relatively small amount of gold was used for the second temple. These golden nails have certain parallels with the (differently named) golden nails in Ex 26:32, 37. v. 10, unlike his source, the Chronicler does not mention the height of the cherubim, instead stressing the art with which they were constructed and the gold used to cover them. He values quality above all. vv. 11–13, again, unlike the source, this text gives a more exact impression of the cherubims' position. This addition may have been due to the Chronicler's desire to be precise. v. 14, the source does not mention a curtain in Solomon's temple. Was it originally mentioned in 1 Kings 6:21b and later lost? According to Josephus (*J.W.* 5.5.5) a curtain certainly existed in the second temple. In any case the curtain reminds us strongly of the tabernacle (Ex 26:31).

(4:1–5:1) Further Interior Decoration By contrast to his reworking of previous passages, the Chronicler followed his source model in 1 Kings 7:39–50 closely to produce 4:10–22, which has led some commentators to suggest that this passage is a later insertion intended to bring Chronicles closer to Kings and to add omitted material. This is supported by several contradictions to ch. 3 in this section (cf. e.g. 3:16 with 4:12). (The Chronicler's description of the temple's construction omits references to gates (1 Kings 6:31–5), probably because the curtain replaced them; they reappear in 4:22 (1 Kings 7:50).) The theory is flawed for two reasons, however: such an insertion or gloss would also have been necessary elsewhere and there is no specific reason for changing this section alone. Japhet (1993: 562) takes a different line, pointing out that the Chronicler adhered strictly to his source model for orientation—even using its order of events—whilst omitting some parts and making other additions: 1 Kings 7:23–6 corresponds to 2 Chr 4:2–5; 1 Kings 7:27–37 is omitted

from 2 Chronicles; 1 Kings 7:38 corresponds to 2 Chr 4:6; 1 Kings 7:38–9a is reworked at 2 Chr 4:6aa, but vv. 6ab–9 have no origin in Kings, and 1 Kings 7:39b–51 corresponds to 2 Chr 4:10–5:1.

This gives the literary action in ch. 4 a clear unity. The attempt at a solution cannot, however, explain why the Chronicler was prepared to take so many contradictions into account (though this is also the case elsewhere). It is notable that the Chronicler omits the (lengthy) passage concerning the stands for the basins, though they reappear in v. 14. Perhaps the figures upon them seemed too heathen for the Chronicler! His insertion of vv. 7–10 disturbs the more convincing order of his source text. He seems keen to add some golden implements at this point of the text.

v. 1, the bronze altar appears only later in the source model (1 Kings 8:64; 2 Kings 16:14–15). The style of the description here (including mention of measures) is more typical of 1 Kings. This leads to the suggestion that this section was lost from 1 Kings 7 over the course of time. The altar, probably made of wood and covered with bronze, was an impressive size. The measures mentioned probably refer to the base. v. 6, the basins' original function is unclear: they seem to have been related to cosmological symbolism and were thus heathen in the eyes of the Chronicler. He claims them to be Israelite in order to allow him to refer back to Ex 30:17–21, where a copper basin is used for ceremonial washing, thus integrating them into the sacrificial cult.

vv. 7–9, the Chronicler uses the list of golden materials in 1 Kings 7:48–50 (cf. vv. 19–22) earlier than his source model, presenting them in the order of his own (original) list in 1 Chr 28:15–18. v. 7, the tabernacle was equipped with only one lampstand (Ex 25:31), an interesting similarity to 13:11. v. 8, in both the tabernacle (Ex 25:23–30) and Solomon's temple (1 Kings 7:48) the number of tables was not ten, but one. By contrast to the one table (Ex 25; 1 Kings 7) and the Chronicler's shewbread tables (1 Chr 28:16), these are not explicitly characterized as covered in gold—a surprise, given the Chronicler's love of the material. v. 9, 1 Kings 6:36 mentions the inner courtyard only briefly. In keeping with the values of the time, the Chronicler distinguishes clearly between the priests' court and the precinct for laymen.

(5:2–6:2) The Ark's Installation The Chronicler made extensive cuts to his report on the temple's construction, as a comparison with his source model shows. Apart from 1 Kings 8:53–61, he does, however, use everything in Kings relating to its consecration, even adding his own material. Whilst 1 Kings 8–9 consists almost entirely of speeches, there are more narrative elements in its equivalent passage in Chronicles. Ch. 5 follows its source in Kings quite closely, though it includes a festive ceremony celebrating the ark's placement in the temple. YHWH then takes (provisional) possession of the temple and his magnificence is hailed.

5:4, the Chronicler replaces the ark-bearing priests with Levites, thereby conforming with Moses' instructions in Deut 10:8; 31:25 and David's orders in 1 Chr 15:2 (leaving the priests with the more important sacrificial duties). As v. 7 and 29:16 show, Levites are forbidden to enter the most holy place. 5:11–13, the Chronicler cannot imagine that the final act of placing the ark in the most holy place was not accompanied by a ceremony. He therefore creates one himself. It lacks nothing that he values and is uplifting. All participants are sanctified (cf. 1 Chr 15:14) and all three musician families are present, singing and playing. Their cries, 'For he is good, for his steadfast love endures for ever' (cf. 1 Chr 16:41), are especially close to the Chronicler's heart. Everything occurs unanimously (resembling the support for David in 1 Chr 12:39). 5:13, only once music has begun does a cloud fill the house— one which must have reminded the Chronicler of the cloud which came down on the tent of meeting in the desert (e.g. Num 12:5). 6:1, the Chronicler simplifies the scarcely comprehensible text in his source model, keeping only the idea that God wished to dwell in darkness. The Hebrew expression for this links it with God's manifestation on Mt. Sinai (Ex 20:21; Deut 4:11; 5:22), which must have suited the Chronicler. God now appears at his eternal cultic residence.

(6:3–42) Consecration of the Temple; King's Speech; Dedicatory Prayer After a doxology, the first part of this chapter deals with the choice of Jerusalem and David and the temple's construction. The promises given by YHWH regarding them have been fulfilled. The second part of the chapter contains a lengthy prayer, or rather a prayer-formula (and a prayer-theory) that refers particularly to the perilous situation of the individual and the people (vv. 32–3 are concerned with foreigners). Only the chapter's conclusion and its final plea differ greatly from its source model. The Chronicler follows 1 Kings 8 so closely because the subject-matter is also central to his own theological perspective (David's dynasty and the temple). Furthermore, the perilous situations described in the prayer-formula are both timeless and also may have been a contemporary problem (to some extent) for the Chronicler.

vv. 24–39, According to Williamson (1987: 219) vv. 24–5, 34–5, 36–9 could be a reference to the revolution against the Persians led by Tennes the Sidonian, which resulted in deportation to Hyrcania, Babylon, and elsewhere. vv. 32–3, in the time between the conception of Kings and the Chronicler's own lifetime, the significance of foreigners to the people of Israel had increased; this led to a changed theological perspective on God's attitude towards them. They are clearly given the opportunity of turning to God here. vv. 34–9, the theme of imprisonment plays a central role in this passage. The author of the source model in 1 Kings 8 had the (Babylonian) Exile in mind, which had developed into a diaspora (in Babylon and Egypt) by the Chronicler's time. This changed situation is reflected in the unspecific nature of the Chronicler's call to help those still living abroad. 1 Kings 8:50 ('and grant them compassion in the sight of their captors, so that they may have compassion on them') can be seen as a call for them to return to the holy land. Such a return is not appropriate for the diaspora of the Chronicler's time. He also omits mention of the Exodus here and in Solomon's concluding plea. Interestingly, however, 1 Kings 8:50 is taken up again in the letter written by Hezekiah to the rest of the northern kingdom (30:9). v. 40, the Chronicler keeps only a bare skeleton of the source model's plea, deleting the reference to the Exodus and therefore to Moses.

vv. 41–2, by contrast to the source model, Solomon's prayer ends positively. Here, the Chronicler takes Ps 132:8–10 and greatly changes it to enhance the central themes of his own theology by highlighting the importance of the ark and the anointed. Peace and calm under Solomon's reign are the prerequisites for the temple's construction. Only Solomon (not David) can supply them. Once the temple has been constructed God can be at rest. The psalm passage also refers to the priests who play a central role in the (Chronicler's) temple cult. It includes the terms 'salvation' (source model: 'righteousness'), rejoice (source model: 'shout for joy'), goodness, all of which are central themes for the Chronicler, though he only touches on them here.

(7:1–22) Conclusion of the Ceremony and God's Covenant for the Temple By a series of omissions and additions, the Chronicler changes his source material (1 Kings 8–9) to give the narrative a more flowing and logical structure. He deletes 1 Kings 8:54–61, much of which is a paraenetic warning conforming with the Chronicler's own principles. In v. 55, Solomon blesses his people, a privilege reserved for priests in post-exilic society. The main reason for the omission of this relatively long passage lies in the Chronicler's wish to report on God's positive response to the plea expressed in 6:41, most importantly his acceptance of the temple as his own. He thus describes God's descent upon the temple in the Chronicler's own material in vv. 1–3. The Chronicler subsequently returns to his source model for orientation, though he cannot resist mentioning the musical duties of the Levites in connection with the sacrifices performed (v. 6). vv. 13–15 form a third substantial addition to the source text, in which YHWH does not summarize his response (as in Kings), but actually uses some of the dedicatory prayer's language in his reply.

vv. 1–3 legitimize the sacrifices, the altar, and the temple. This section applies Lev 9:(22)23–4 to the temple. (The people's blessing as performed by Moses and Aaron in v. 23 is omitted, however.) The tabernacle and the temple are two forms of the same holy place. YHWH's glory took provisional possession of the temple in 5:13–14 and was described in similar terms. Here, there is the added element of an endorsing fire which falls from the heavens. These events are witnessed not only by the religious élite, but also by all the Israelites, since God's glory does not only fill the temple, but is also above it (cf. also Ex 40:34 for v. 2). Williamson (1987: 222) goes against the general consensus by claiming that this report does refer back to 5:13–14, and that v. 2 ought to be translated as an adverbial sentence in English: 'and during all this time the glory of YHWH still filled the temple'.

vv. 8–10, in 1 Kings 8:66, the celebration surrounding the temple's dedication and the Feast of Tabernacles, lasting seven days, seem to be simultaneous. This impression is corrected at the end of the previous verse ('seven days and seven days, even fourteen days'—there were two separate feasts) and the Chronicler removes any remaining doubt on this. According to his version the temple dedication and the Feast of Tabernacles cannot possibly take place simultaneously: the temple dedication takes place from the 8th to the 14th of the seventh month, whilst the Feast of Tabernacles lasts from the 15th until the 21st of the same month. The concluding feast (as in Lev 23:36, 39) is on the 22nd, so that Solomon can dismiss the festive community on the 23rd, as stated in v. 10. The Chronicler's Solomon adheres strictly to the festal calendar according to the Pentateuch, Moses' law. v. 11 grandly concludes the section in Chronicles, whilst the parallel text in its source model opens the following section. It is an opportunity to deliver one of the Chronicler's favourite messages: since Solomon behaves in an exemplary manner, his every undertaking succeeds.

v. 14, there are four ways in which the Israelites could move YHWH to action: humility, prayer, seeking his face, and turning from wicked ways. These become repeated themes in the following chapters. vv. 17–22, a form of theodicy: it explains the Davidic monarchy's collapse and the temple's destruction. v. 18. In an important alteration from the source model, the Chronicler turns 'a successor on the throne of Israel' (1 Kings 9:5) into 'a successor to rule over Israel'. Should this phrase (which is taken from Mic 5:1) imply messianic undertones? if it does, could it be that the Chronicler did not necessarily require the Messiah to be a king? This would mean that an exemplary high priest could have taken this position at the time of the Chronicler. v. 18 contradicts this theory, since the Chronicler deletes the phrase 'over Israel for ever' from his source. In v. 19, he omits the phrase 'or your children', thereby invoking the responsibilities of the present generation.

Various Reports on Solomon (2 Chr 8:1–18)

The source text of this passage (1 Kings 9:10–28) is not homogeneous in its content; however, the Chronicler regards the events described in it as a unity. They are placed in the period of the temple's foundation up to the project's conclusion. The successful expedition to Ezion-geber takes place at the same time (cf. vv. 16, 17). As Williamson (1987: 233) has nicely demonstrated, it represents a reward for the temple's construction. The Chronicler employs his usual methods in reworking his source material in this passage: he deletes (1 Kings 9:14–17a), he inserts (3, 4b–5, 11b, 13–16a), and he emends (v. 2).

vv. 1–6, according to Willi (1972: 76), the source model the Chronicler used was damaged, which would explain many of the discrepancies between the two texts. It is difficult to regard the Chronicler's usual editing methods as the cause of some of these. vv. 1–2, in the source text, Solomon is forced to cede twenty cities to Hiram, king of Tyre, the quality of which Hiram complains about. The Chronicler probably inverts this unwelcome information and drastically reduces its length. Another theory suggests that both versions could be applicable: Hiram and Solomon cede cities to each other (in an exchange?). Willi shows how easily the manuscript (see, amongst others, LXX) could be misinterpreted as to who gave what to whom. The source model's text does not presume that Hiram had to pay for the cities. The 120 talents of gold mentioned there do not appear in Chronicles and are more probably a gift or tribute, both of which are historically more unlikely than the cession of cities to Hiram. The idea that Solomon sent Israelites to settle there is unique and strange (cf. the Assyrian policy towards the defeated northern kingdom in 2 Kings 17:24–8).

vv. 7–10, the remaining population of other peoples were brought up as slave workers by Solomon. Israelites, who acted as guards, were exempted. v. 11, Solomon, proud at having the Pharaoh's daughter as his bride, builds her a house. This motif is unknown to the Chronicler (if he had taken it over, he would have asserted that the Pharaoh was proud to be able

to marry his daughter to Solomon). He rewrites the information given in the source. Solomon's wife is not to come into close contact with holy matters, not because she is a foreigner, but because she is a woman. Thus a house is built out of necessity, rather than in a gesture of high regard.

vv. 12–16, the cult: the source model reports that Solomon made burnt-offerings and peace-offerings including incense three times a year (i.e. at pilgrim festivals) at the altar. The Chronicler greatly extends this passage. v. 13, the order of sacrifice is derived from Moses' instructions and conforms with the Pentateuch (cf. however, v. 14). The three annual festivals are named here, along with the daily sacrifices, which are sorely missed by the Chronicler in his source model. The sabbath and the new moons are also mentioned here. This systematized description aims at being complete. v. 14, the regulations regarding the temple personnel cannot be as easily derived from Moses as the Pentateuch's sacrifices, leading the Chronicler to refer them back to David. Does this signify a lesser dignity ascribed to them than the sacrificial rules?

The Queen of Sheba, Solomon's Wealth, and his Death (2 Chr 9:1–31)

(9:1–12) The Queen of Sheba's Visit The story of the Queen of Sheba's visit to Jerusalem, along with other reports regarding Solomon's wisdom, are probably among the latest pieces in the books of Kings. The Chronicler makes an almost identical copy of this story, since it fits extremely well in his political and theological plan, particularly in his striving for international recognition of Judah's rulers (cf. e.g. 1 Chr 14:17). The Chronicler makes a few stylistic changes to his source model (1 Kings 10:1–13) as well as two important theological alterations in v. 8, whilst strengthening Solomon's position in his relationship with the Queen of Sheba at certain points.

v. 8, the monarchy and the throne belong to God, as the Chronicler never tires of declaring. Thus he replaces 'set you on the throne of Israel' with 'set you on his [i.e. God's] throne'. Going beyond his source model, the Chronicler also emphasizes that God established Israel forever—a logical statement since the kingdom belongs to God.

(9:13–28) Solomon's Wealth The section contains substantial information regarding Solomon's splendour and power, following on well from the story of the Queen of Sheba's visit. Its content partly overlaps with the descriptions in 1:14–17. Solomon's power and wealth frame the description of Solomon's reign; in v. 26 the Chronicler includes 1 Kings 5:1. This insertion and other alterations distinguish the episode in Chronicles from its source model in 1 Kings 10.

v. 18, the Hebrew source model (wrongly) vocalizes 'round head' instead of 'bull head'. The Chronicler reads 'bull head', seeing it as a reference to heathen deities, unacceptable to him. Thus he replaces the phrase with 'a footstool of gold', adding more gold to the already richly decorated passage. v. 21, the expression 'ships of Tarshish' (1 Kings 10:22) roughly means 'large, seaworthy vessels'. The Chronicler misunderstands the phrase and lets the ships sail to Spain (Tarshish). Solomon and Hiram undertake a combined expedition in the source model. The Chronicler does not accept this, sending the king's ship to sea with no more than Hiram's *men*.

vv. 25–8, in this passage v. 25*a* corresponds with 1 Kings 5:6 (though the source model contains 40,000, instead of 4,000—a transcription error?), v. 25*b* with 1 Kings 10:26*b*, and vv. 27–8 with 1 Kings 10:27–8. Some of the omitted parts of 1 Kings 10 can be found in 1:14–17. It is difficult to discover the individual reasons for this complicated reorganization of the text.

(9:29–31) Solomon's Death v. 29, the Chronicler makes three changes to the source text's concluding acknowledgment of Solomon: 'from first to last' replaces 'all that he did' (1 Kings 11:41), a common correction made by the Chronicler. He also deletes Solomon's wisdom from the source model. The king is wise also in Chronicles, but this is not his most significant quality. For the same reason, the Chronicler deletes other passages referring to his wisdom. '[I]n the Book of the Acts of Solomon' (source model) is replaced by 'in the history of the prophet Nathan, and in the prophecy of Ahijah the Shilonite, and in the visions of the seer Iddo concerning Jeroboam son of Nebat'. Like David (1 Chr 29:29), Solomon is given three prophetic sources which the Chronicler claims to have reworked (they are of course none other than 1 Kings 1–11): Nathan was active at the beginning of Solomon's reign (1 Kings 1), whilst Ahijah appears at its end (1 Kings 11:29). Iddo is mentioned again as a source for the books of Kings in 12:15 (Rehoboam) and 13:22 (Abijah). He is not mentioned at all in 1 Kings, though the Chronicler may have recognized Iddo in the anonymous prophet of 1 Kings 13:1–10.

The History of Judah from the Division of the United Kingdom to its Collapse, and to Cyrus's Edict (2 Chr 10:1–36:23)

The Loss of the Ten Northern Tribes (2 Chr 10:1–19)

The kingdom's division presents the Chronicler with a difficult problem. According to Deuteronomistic literature, it is caused above all by Solomon's falling away from God. It is YHWH's will that the northern tribes should be ruled by Jeroboam, as his prophet Ahijah the Shilonite proclaims (1 Kings 11). The Chronicler ignores Solomon's falling away and sin, regarding the northern kingdom as illegitimate. Whilst he cannot even out all the contradictions resulting from this clash between the source model and his own ideology, the Chronicler attempts to conceal some of them: the omission of 1 Kings 11 increases Rehoboam's responsibility, even if this is immediately revoked by the reference to his tender age and the cowardly men around him at 13:7. Jeroboam appears in the same chapter, not as the upright man of 1 Kings 11, but as a rebel against Solomon rising up against the legitimate monarchy. The Chronicler's reinterpretation of 1 Kings 12 is a central theme in ch. 13 but only a side issue in ch. 10. Clearly, the Chronicler conforms with the source model's interpretation that the kingdom's division was God's will, thereby implying a reference to Ahijah's prophecy (omitted by the Chronicler) and thus to Solomon's guilt. The Chronicler's omission of Jeroboam's accession to the throne is self-explanatory.

v. 7, the Chronicler weakens the source model, by which Rehoboam should be a servant to his people, listen to them... only a friendly attitude towards the people, kindness, and good words are expected of him in Chronicles. Despite his democratic inclinations, the Chronicler cannot compromise the high position of the king.

Rehoboam (2 Chr 11:1–12:16)

(11:1–23) The Beginning of Rehoboam's Reign Rehoboam's reign clearly falls into two phases: he is rewarded for his adherence to the way of God by constructing fortresses, increasing the number of priests, Levites, and laymen from the north, and bringing up a large family. His increased power makes him arrogant, however, leading to his godless phase.

From now on, the Chronicler ignores everything that exclusively concerns the northern kingdom, concentrating on Judah (and its relations with the northern kingdom!). The Chronicler compensates for the loss of the report on Jeroboam by dealing with all important matters within the report inversely: building (1 Kings 12:25: Jeroboam's motives in building a fortress are to reunify the kingdom of Israel), religious life (1 Kings 12:26–33: the king makes two golden calves and sets them up in Bethel and Dan, and he appoints new priests; these measures are judged negatively), the family (1 Kings 14:1–18: Jeroboam loses a son). Conclusion: wherever Jeroboam acts wrongly or is unlucky, Rehoboam behaves correctly and is fortunate.

vv. 1–4, Rehoboam refrains from waging war against Jeroboam due to prophetic intervention. This is an example of the obedience for which he is rewarded. Here the Chronicler keeps closely to the source text (although he naturally omits the report on Jeroboam's coronation, since this affects the northern kingdom alone). vv. 5–12, God-fearing kings may build, and especially may erect fortresses. This is part of the Chronicler's dogma of retribution for which the enormous buildings of Alexander and the Diadochian kingdoms during the Chronicler's time must have served as an impressive example. vv. 6–10 are a list of the cities that were transformed into fortresses. Apart from Adoraim, all cities are mentioned elsewhere in the OT. They lie east, south, and west of Judah, but are not listed in any strict order, although the first four lie to the east. It is especially surprising that Arad is omitted and Hebron is mentioned last. The north is not protected by fortresses, inferring that Rehoboam did not wish to endanger the reunification they hoped for.

vv. 13–17 describe the consequences in Judah of Jeroboam's cult 'reforms'. According to the source model, Jeroboam placed two golden calves in Bethel and Dan and recruited new non-Levite priests who pledged allegiance to him. The Chronicler combines these two reports in one and adds to them (v. 15). He then states the essential consequences this had upon Judah. v. 14, 'they left their common lands and their holdings': a remark typical of the Chronicler, who was interested in possessions above all. The remark is not essential to the present context. 'Jeroboam and his sons': this expression makes a cryptic reference to the religious nature of future conflicts between the northern and southern kingdoms. v. 16, the reaction: laymen from the northern kingdom come to Jerusalem in an attempt to take part in the only legitimate sacrificial rite. Whether they are merely pilgrims or wish to settle in Judah is not entirely clear. Precisely what Jeroboam wished to avoid with his religious policy actually takes place: people pour out of the northern kingdom into Jerusalem.

vv. 18–21, according to the Chronicler, as is evident in the 'genealogical forecourt', a large family and numerous children are an indication of God's blessing. The Chronicler does not report on Solomon's large family, perhaps because it is combined with the idea of idolatry. His work contains numerous other references to large families (which do not appear in his sources—see e.g. 1 Chr 3:1–9). vv. 18–20, the statements concerning Rehoboam's two wives cannot be made compatible with others mentioned elsewhere (or only by using extremely audacious constructions). What appears important is that (at least) the reader notices that Mahalath and Maachah are both closely related to David's family.

(12:1–16) Rehoboam's Established Rule and his Falling away from God The Chronicler typically reworks 1 Kings 14:21–31, using deletions and insertions, amongst other editing methods. The source text begins with a general description of Rehoboam's rule, portraying the Judahites as terrible sinners, before continuing with Shishak's military campaign and ending with the concluding judgement passed upon all kings in the books of Kings. In Chronicles, Rehoboam has already been active as king (11:5–23). Thus the text contains merely a programmatic reference to his kingdom's increase in power and the king's violation of the law, before leading directly on to Shishak's campaign. As elsewhere in Chronicles, a prophet (Shemaiah) intervenes with words of reprimand. These have the desired effect, as Rehoboam becomes more God-fearing and therefore more powerful. From this point on, the Chronicler follows his source model more closely, with the paradoxical result of having to let Rehoboam sin once more to conform with it. The passage closes with references to the sources and a note on the king's burial. Thus the Chronicler transforms a three-part structure in his source model (Rehoboam's rule, Shishak's campaign, Rehoboam's rule) into two parts: Shishak's campaign, Rehoboam's rule.

The chapter is closely related to the story of the siege of Jerusalem by the Assyrian Sennacherib (ch. 32), i.e. the Chronicler creates this parallel by his restructuring of the text. In both cases a foreign ruler captures almost all of Judah, leaving Jerusalem untouched, having been saved by the correct actions of the relevant ruler (Rehoboam and Hezekiah respectively). Why is this story so important to the Chronicler that he should tell it twice, once with Rehoboam and once with Hezekiah? Because both ch. 12 and ch. 32 also shed light upon post-exilic Jewish life: Israel is punished, realizes what it is like to be ruled by a foreign kingdom (v. 8), but is not entirely destroyed (v. 12). Its life is restricted to Jerusalem, as was actually the case in post-exilic Jerusalem. These references are not immediately recognizable today, but would have been clear to the Chronicler's contemporary reader.

vv. 1–2, at the moment of Rehoboam's height of power— 'establishment' becomes a central keyword in his reign—he (and his people alike) forsake God. Uzziah behaves similarly in 26:16. The decline is described in rather colourless terms that are typical of the Chronicler—as in v. 2, where his favourite phrase, 'transgressed against the LORD', appears. The source model is more explicit in its description of Rehoboam's crime. The Chronicler wishes to portray Rehoboam in a more positive light since he does not fail and receives an honourable burial. v. 3, going beyond the source model, the Chronicler

describes the composition of the army according to the soldiers' place of origin and weaponry. Lybians and Ethiopians: also in Nah 3:9; Dan 11:43 (perhaps taken from here); 2 Chr 16:8. The Sukkites appear only here. Does this structure perhaps indirectly mirror the Chronicler's contemporary situation? The army is rather large, but not enormous in comparison to other armies against which Judah must fight. Those who regard this as documentation of a historic source readily assume that the 60,000 horsemen were actually 6,000.

v. 4, according to the inscription upon which Shishak describes his campaign, he seems mainly to have conquered (unfortified) settlements in the Negeb. Aijalon is the only city fortified by Rehoboam that is mentioned on the inscription. The Chronicler cannot allow the Pharaoh to conquer these cities without giving theological reasons. Thus, Rehoboam must be punished where he is strongest and where it hurts most. vv. 5–8, the prophet Shemaiah's intervention is an example of regular interventions made by prophets at times when the king and his kingdom are in danger (cf. e.g. ch. 20). Shemaiah addresses the king and the princes of Judah. Judah is a political term while Israel is meant religiously, implying Judah's claim to be the sole legitimate monarchy instituted by YHWH. Shemaiah's speech is filled with theologoumena which are typical for the Chronicler, their order and the inclusion of elements found only here giving the text its unmistakable character. v. 5, 'You abandoned me, so I have abandoned you': the Chronicler uses such repetitions of the same (Heb.) words in his constructions. This also linguistically emphasizes the dogma of retribution expressed here.

vv. 6–8, the kings and princes act immediately and correctly as a consequence of this criticism. They humble themselves, which leads, also immediately, to God's leniency in response: Jerusalem is not conquered, but its people must experience being ruled by foreign powers instead of the Lord. The Hebrew root of 'servant/service' is highlighted here and used three times. v. 12, things also went well in Judah: this either means that Judah itself behaved correctly, or that it did not suffer too much. For the Chronicler, these two sentences go together like two sides of a coin. Thus the uncertainty surrounding its correct translation is not important. vv. 13–14 describe a further phase of Rehoboam's rule. As soon as he has recovered, Rehoboam immediately apostasizes again (cf. v. 1). Once more he is criticized only in general terms: 'He did not set his heart to seek the LORD' (typical terminology).

vv. 15–16, concluding remarks: by contrast to the source model text, the Chronicler clearly distinguishes between the earlier and later acts of Rehoboam. Which periods he separates thus is not, however, entirely clear. It is also unclear whether the records of Shemaiah and Iddo are a single text or two separate sources (cf. e.g. 1 Chr 29:29; 2 Chr 9:29). Cf. also 11:2 (1 Kings 12:22) (different spelling) regarding Shemaiah, and 13:22 regarding Iddo (probably identical with the one named here).

Abijah (2 Chr 13:1–23)

Both 1 Kings 15 and ch. 13 deviate from their usual descriptive practices when they turn to reporting on King Abijah. The source text contains only one piece of historical information that goes beyond the biographical notice (v. 7: 'And there was war between Abijah and Jeroboam'). It also includes a negative judgement on Abijah's religious behaviour. Indeed, interestingly, it contains more information about David than about Abijah. The Chronicler does not use all of this information for his work; most surprisingly he deletes the negative judgement even though it was almost predetermined given that the king ruled Judah for only three years (short periods of rule were interpreted as an expression of a lack of divine blessing and thus insufficient God-fearing qualities). He offers no judgement on Abijah at all—treatment which is otherwise given only to Jehoahaz (36:1–4)! This is probably because the Chronicler did not wish to contradict his source model in Kings. There may be justification for his implied positive judgement in his reference to the state of war between the northern and southern kingdoms: the Chronicler understands the only information taken from the source text to mean that Abijah (only) once defeated Jeroboam in battle. He regards Abijah (rather than Rehoboam) as Solomon's worthy successor, as can be seen in some of his allusions. His war report is also an addition to his source material, the battle being preceded by a sermon on the mount which forms the core of the chapter, once again portraying the basic relationship between the northern and southern kingdoms.

vv. 3–20, this passage is composed of preparations for war, a lengthy speech, and the description of an actual battle. vv. 3–4, Abijah makes the initial impetus for war. His large army (400,000 men) is still only half the size of Jeroboam's (800,000—a figure originating from 2 Sam 24:9 and referring to David's census). Abijah's 'valiant warriors . . . picked men', are faced by Jeroboam's 'picked mighty warriors'. Both these differences suggest that on human terms, Jeroboam/ Israel should be victorious. vv. 5–12, Abijah's stylistically and rhetorically artistic speech concerns the legitimate rule of the Davidides (YHWH's rule), the legitimate office of priesthood in Jerusalem, and the legitimate (and pure) performance of ritual cult in the temple of Jerusalem. The northern kingdom has broken faith with all these principles. But Abijah's speech does not attempt to prove this fact, instead calling upon the people of the northern kingdom to return (to the Davidides and therefore to God). Mention of the legitimate priesthood (and the correct performance of rites) here clearly points to post-exilic times, perhaps even indicating a conflict with the Samaritans. vv. 6–7, 'Jeroboam, son of Nebat, a servant of Solomon son of David': naming the fathers of Jeroboam and Solomon serves to prove the illegitimacy of Jeroboam's claim to the throne. An explicit judgement on Jeroboam's errancy appears only here in Chronicles: he rose up and rebelled against Solomon; Rehoboam is partly excused by his youth and inexperience (though he was 41 years old when he acceded to the throne: 12:13). The judgement has a theological nature. Who exactly the vain men that gathered around Jeroboam were remains unclear—possibly mercenaries, though more probably the young men who advised Rehoboam poorly (10:10).

v. 9, it is important for the Chronicler that the priesthood comprises the sons of Aaron (actual priests) and the Levites. The accusation made here refers to 2 Chr 11:14. The northern kingdom appoints its own men as priests, bringing forward a young bullock and seven rams (two were prescribed by the law for the anointing of priests—this may be an exaggeration rather than an alternative interpretation of the law). Does this imply that the northern priesthood could be bribed? For the phrase, 'no gods', cf. Hos 8:6. v. 11, here the people of the northern kingdom are also indirectly accused of failing to perform the cultic rites correctly (though, of course, by definition there can be no legitimate cult in the north). The correct temple service is described at some points (cf. e.g. 8:12–15). Whilst 1 Kings 7:49 (cf. 2 Chr. 4:7) describes Solomon ordering ten lampstands, there is only one here. It may be that there was only one lampstand in the post-exilic temple, or that the Chronicler was inspired by Ex 25:31, which describes the tabernacle with only one golden lampstand.

v. 12, 'the LORD, the God of your ancestors', YHWH cannot be taken from the Israelites! God, the priests, the war trumpets and the battle sound (in that order) form the Judeans' 'arsenal' for holy war. This indeed subsequently takes place, its elements naturally appearing in a spiritual form. vv. 13–15, the battle and the way it is carried out show a mixture of elements of holy warfare—especially on the Judean side— and tactics, as pursued by the Israelites, who prepare àn ambush which proves unsuccessful. Judah itself must take the initiative and cry to the Lord, who alone brings Jeroboam and all of Israel to its knees. vv. 16–17, only once YHWH has triumphed can the Judeans become active in (pursuing and) defeating the Israelites, destroying more than half its army. The Chronicler emphasizes with a note of regret that these were chosen men. v. 18, he who is God-fearing and seeks the Lord will be heard and supported—this is a central declaration of the Chronicler's theology. v. 19, the precise references (along with the place-name in v. 4) have been interpreted by some exegetes as evidence underlining the plausibility of the reported battle. More probably, however, this reflects post-exilic Judean territorial claims.

v. 20, the phrasing suggests that Rehoboam died an unnatural death (cf. 21:18; 1 Sam 25:38), though no mention of this is made elsewhere in the tradition. Contrary to the Chronicler's statement (which is perhaps meant only theologically), Jeroboam outlives Abijah by several years. It is also possible that the Chronicler inverted information he possessed to create this version of events (cf. 2 CHR 8:2). v. 21, as is so often the case, Abijah's blessing consists of increased power and a large number of wives and children. v. 22, in this passage the Chronicler mentions a different source, that is, the midrash ('story') of the prophet Iddo, from those of his own source model. 'Midrash' must be understood in the ancient sense (the term is repeated only once in the entire OT, at 24:27), rather than in the technical sense of 'interpretation'. Both 9:29 and 12:15 refer to the prophet Iddo. v. 23 (cf. 14:1), the Chronicler emends his model slightly, adding (amongst other changes) that the land had rest for ten years. This suggests that the king behaved in a God-fearing manner (cf. next section).

Asa (2 Chr 14:1–16:14)

(14:1–7) Asa's Rule until the War against the Cushites This section deals with three themes: (1) Asa's cultic reforms (vv. 1–5); (2) his building projects (vv. 6–7); and (3) his reinforcement of the army (v. 8).

v. 1, 'In his days the land had rest for ten years': this sentence has often been seen as a reference to the reign of Asa's predecessor Abijah (especially due to its position). Here the

Chronicler probably uses it to highlight Asa's religious reforms. vv. 2–4, in view of such ideal rule, these reforms seem unnecessary, at least for the period reported. But the Chronicler respects his source model which reported the measures, and such reforms often characterized kings judged positively in Chronicles. He also makes some changes to his source material, which, for instance, mentions abolition of the hierodules (male prostitutes) and all edifices (1 Kings 15:12–13). The situation Asa is confronted with at the beginning of his reign in Chronicles is not as serious as in the source model, though bad enough for the Chronicler. v. 3, the abolition of the high places contradicts 1 Kings 15:14. v. 4 is a description of desired positive action using key terminology ('seek the LORD') and Deuteronomistic ideas of the law and the commandments. vv. 6–7, the information regarding Asa's building projects (which also characterize kings who are judged positively) can hardly be based upon non-biblical sources, since it is too general.

v. 8, one of the most controversial debates on Chronicles concerns its possible use of non-biblical sources to report on the structure of the Jewish (and Benjaminite) army. Junge (1937) suggests references to such sources using the argument that the information given is precise and free from any religious bias or a Chronicles-based perspective. It is based on the army levy, though the figures given portray the situation at the time of Josiah rather than Asa. Welten (1973: 100–7) also points out the probability that the difference between the heavily armed Judeans and the lightly armed Benjaminites stems from the existing Hellenistic armies at the time of the Chronicler. The same influence also results in the Chronicler's evident interest in economics, power, and the military: he is a child of his own time.

(14:9–15) Asa's War against Zerah the Ethiopian The Chronicler takes the opportunity of the newly established army to prove its—and therefore YHWH's—effectiveness. He describes a (holy) war in which human strength is nothing in comparison to divine intervention. Such portrayals are common in Chronicles, the most prominent of which can be found in ch. 20. The Chronicler probably expands both these local conflicts into all-out wars which leave Judah victorious and richly rewarded, having called upon the help of God. The report is unlikely to portray a conflict during Asa's rule, but should be regarded as a reflection of contemporary Jewish conflicts with their neighbours rather than as mere fiction.

v. 9, neither the Pharaoh Osorkon I nor Egyptian mercenaries from a settlement in Gerar can be meant by the Cushite (NRSV, Ethiopian) here. They are probably Edomite-Arab nomads (and contemporaries of the Chronicler) searching for slaves and booty. Zerah is an Edomite name in the OT, whilst Cush is connected with Midian in Hab 3:7 and does not refer exclusively to Egypt/Ethiopia. Mareshah, one of the cities that Rehoboam is said to have fortified, was a centre for Edomite (Idumean) slave trade according to the Zenon papyri (261–252 BCE). Cf. also 1 Chr 4:39–43; 5:10. vv. 11–12, are a carefully structured theological interpretation of the battle events. Asa calls upon YHWH, the only hope for the greatly outnumbered Judeans against the advancing enemy. The Lord acts, leaving the Israelites as onlookers. vv. 13–15, once the battle has ended successfully, the Judean army is

permitted to go into action. The booty plundered from the enemy is a rich reward. The Chronicler emphasizes these aspects by his detailed description. v. 14, 'the fear of the LORD was on them': elements of a holy war which seem incongruous with the contextual descriptions of pillage but which suit the Chronicler's theology well. v. 14, 'the cities around Gerar': in the 9th century this area was under the influence of the Philistines. v. 15, 'tents…sheep…goats… camels': this clearly confirms that the defeated enemy was an Arab-Edomite tribe.

(15:1–19) Prophetic Words and the Renewal of the Covenant The contents of this passage do not seem to fit into the present context, since there is no reason for a warning after a war had been won because of dependence on God, and it has therefore occasionally been attributed to a different author. According to G. von Rad (1958: 261–2), the passage is a Levite address, while other OT commentaries see its source in postexilic synagogue ceremonies. Such theories overlook the fact that Azariah's speech forms a carefully crafted theological commentary whilst simultaneously looking to the future with a particular call not to sit around doing nothing. The Chronicler does not restrict himself to commenting on individual events in his speeches and prayers, often at least hinting at theological principles and sometimes discussing them extensively. This particularly applies to v. 2. Azariah's speech, which has a strongly anthological style, can be divided into three parts following its introduction: (1) principles; (2) a historical retrospect (without concrete historical information); (3) consequences for the future.

v. 1, Azariah is a common name in the OT, though a prophet Azariah is unknown elsewhere. Like so many other figures, he is probably the Chronicler's own invention. 'The spirit of God came upon…': as Japhet (1993: 717) demonstrates, this phrase is used in Chronicles in connection with prophets who are lesser known elsewhere in the OT. Their endowment with the Spirit is also their initiation: cf. 1 Chr 12:18; 2 Chr 20:14; 24:20. v. 2, the speech's introduction addresses a notably broad audience: Asa, Judah, and Benjamin (the Israelites from the northern kingdom cannot be mentioned here). The Chronicler states his general case three times using some of his favourite vocabulary, in keeping with his dogma of retribution: God's attitude towards his people corresponds with their attitude towards him. Only part of the vocabulary of the previous passage is used here.

vv. 3–6, his historical perspective clearly refers to the judges period (cf. e.g. Judg 2:11–14; 17:6). It is interesting as a time of political and religious unrest during which the highest priority corresponded with the Chronicler's attitude towards his own time, namely the need for (religious) order and security. v. 3 is a midrash-like reworking of Hos 3:4. But whilst the source model uses three pairs of political and cultic images to illustrate the anarchy at this stage, the Chronicler limits himself to religious/theological aspects. He probably used Hosea here due to his affinity for pithy expressions. v. 6, whilst vv. 4–5 can be understood in the context of the judges period, this cannot be applied to v. 6. Is this a reflection of the problems facing the Chronicler's own time, which he wishes to portray as solvable by inserting hidden references to the judges period into other verses? v. 7, typically for Chronicles,

Azariah's speech ends with a call for courageous deeds. Here the Chronicler explicitly claims what he elsewhere indirectly hints at, clearly using Jer 31:16 as a model: 'For your work shall be rewarded'. The idea of reward was important to the contemporary period since the Jews' actual room for manœuvre was very limited. If they did not make full use of it they might disappear. But for them it was worthwhile to use all their strength only when they were sure that their work would be rewarded.

Asa reacts immediately to Azariah's sermon, carries out cultic reforms, and subsequently initiates a great assembly (modelled on 2 Kings 23), during which the people enter into a covenant. The sacrificial ceremony is characterized by great joy and enthusiasm, two emotions close to the Chronicler's heart. The passage closes with events also described in the source model (Maacah the queen mother is removed, the high places remain, dedicated silver and gold is handed over to the temple). There are close linguistic parallels with Azariah's sermon here (especially as regards the vocabulary).

v. 8, the reform and the festival are not only characterized by generalizations, but also by concrete reform measures which are not described elsewhere. '[A]bominable idols' is an expression found only here in Chronicles, although the author came across the term several times in his source text. '[A]nd from the towns that he had taken in the hill country of Ephraim': is the Chronicler referring to Geba and Mizpah here—cities Asa built (!) after his war with Baasha? These are only roughly in the vicinity of the mountains of Ephraim (16:6). Perhaps he is referring to his father Abijah's conquest (13:19), since the reigns of both kings are regarded almost in unison. The statement could also stem from the Chronicler's assumption that the northern kingdom repeatedly lost land to Judean kings after the kingdom's division right up to the time of Josiah. '[R]epair the altar of the LORD': this seems to be a normal measure (cf. Ezra 3:2–3) which perhaps marks the resumption of ordered cultic life.

v. 9, besides Judah and Benjamin, the general assembly includes people from the northern kingdom who are understandably regarded as 'strangers' from the Chronicler's perspective. Not only do they come from Ephraim and Manasseh, but also from Simeon (cf. 34:6). This (southern!) tribe had historically disappeared much earlier. The Chronicler was perhaps thinking biblically, referring to the Simeon who settled near Shechem (Gen 34:25). It is important for the author that there were always reasonable northern people seeking reunion with the only legitimate cult and the legitimate Davidic monarchy. v. 10, 'fifteenth year': probably a round number. The war with the northern kingdom must have taken place during that year. 'Third month': the date of the Sinai theophany and the Feast of Weeks. The connection between the Sinai theophany—including the law—and the Feast of Weeks stems from an idea from the Christian era (2nd cent. CE) and probably was not thought of by him or at his time. He was probably thinking only of the Feast of Weeks, though he does not mention it specifically. v. 11, this feast, probably more ideal than real, begins rather than ends, unusually, with sacrifices. '[S]even hundred . . . and seven thousand' are rounded, ideal numbers with seven as their root, linking them with the term for the Feast of Weeks.

v. 12, are God and the people or the king and the people partners of this one-sided covenant aimed at seeking God with heart and soul? Azariah's sermon (including the Chronicler's important theologoumenon, 'If you seek him . . .') is successful (cf. v. 13). v. 13, punishment for breaking the covenant is draconian. The death penalty is used only for serious religious crimes (cf. e.g. Deut 13). It underlines that seeking YHWH is not regarded as a casual duty. The text explicitly emphasizes that this applies not only to grown men, but also to the young and the old, and to men and women. vv. 14–15, the surprising oath made during this festival has a simple reason: in Hebrew the term for 'swear' has the same consonants as 'week' and 'seven'. The Chronicler uses an almost plethoric vocabulary in describing the joy, enthusiasm, and commitment felt by the people. vv. 16–18 detail cultic (and political) measures also described in 1 Kings 15:13–15. v. 16, Asa destroys and burns his mother's idol in the Kings source. The Chronicler adds to this a third action, 'crushed it', which draws parallels between Asa and Josiah, who is shown to have acted likewise towards Asherah in 2 Kings 23:6. v. 17 contradicts 14:2, so it has occasionally been suggested that the author meant only the high places in the northern kingdom of Israel. (This placename is not found in the source model.) Other commentaries assume that the Chronicler originally omitted the verse in the source model, but later transcripts accidentally included it.

v. 19 leads into the next, negative phase of Asa's reign.

(16:1–14) Asa's Dark Period and Death In the second brief phase of Asa's reign (the 1st–36th years were positive; up to the 41st year was negative) the king behaves badly and is accordingly punished. Whilst he proves himself in battle in the first period, he fails in war in the second. Once, he listens to Azariah, later he ignores Hanani's sermon. But since his reign is judged positively when viewed in its entirety, Asa is given an honourable, indeed exceptional, burial. Besides the seer Hanani, three other (unnamed) prophets dominate the chapter: Isaiah's proclamation (v. 7), the words of Zechariah (v. 9), and Jeremiah's suffering (v. 10).

v. 1, in his report on Baasha's war with Asa, the Chronicler keeps to his source model (1 Kings 15:16–22) aside from a few stylistic, geographical, and theological alterations. Seen in its entirety, the Chronicler shows little interest in the course of events. v. 2, this is illustrated by his omission here of Benhadad's more detailed presentation as the 'son of Tabrimmon son of Hezion'. vv. 7–9, Hanani's speech is short and strongly prophetic. v. 7, the Chronicler knew Hanani the prophet (from 1 Kings 16:1, 7) as the father of another seer, Jehu. Since he needed a 'contemporary' prophet/seer, he uses him here, cf. also 19:2. The Chronicler makes a central statement in Isaiah's message his own. In dangerous military circumstances, it is important to trust in the Lord rather than a coalition with a foreign army; cf. Isa 7:9; 10:20; 31:1. v. 8 is a reference to the first, God-fearing period of Asa's reign and his successful application of faith in battle. Chariots and horsemen do not win the war, but God does, a truth enshrined in many classic statements of the OT, cf. Isa 31:1. v. 9, the wording of 'you have done foolishly' is a reference to 1 Sam 13:13 (Saul's first rejection). The first part is a clear parallel to Zech 4:10. 'The eyes of the LORD viewing all the lands' underlines his omnipresence and his ability to help Asa should he wish to do so. '[F]rom now on you will have wars': since Asa took Azariah's sermon to heart during the positive period of his reign, the Lord granted him 'rest all around' (15:15). There is, however, no further mention of war, so does this refer to Jehoshaphat, despite its contradiction of the Chronicler's theology (cf. 2 CHR 16:11–14)? v. 10, Hanani suffers a similar fate as Jeremiah (Jer 20:2–3) at the hands of an angry Asa. The people Asa is said to have repressed are perhaps followers of Hanani.

vv. 11–14, the concluding acknowledgement of Asa's reign is much more extensive than the source model. The unusual placing of words of appreciation before the description of his burial is perhaps due to the fact that his son Jehoshaphat had already taken on the business of government since Asa's illness rendered him unable to rule. v. 12, Asa becomes ill due to his shameful behaviour towards the seer Hanani. The Chronicler may have chosen sickness as punishment since the king's name can be interpreted as 'YHWH heals'. An alternative theory is suggested in the comment on v. 14. It is impossible to say whether Asa died of gout, dropsy, gangrene, venereal disease ('feet' being a euphemism for sexual organs), or another disease. v. 14, the extensive and positive description of Asa's burial clearly shows that on the whole he was judged favourably (though the king had already prepared for his own burial). There is hardly any reliable historical evidence on this matter. The Chronicler takes the reference to the funeral pyre from Jer 34:5 (cf. also 2 Chr 21:19), whilst the incense and the delicate spices probably accord with contemporary practices. Asa's name is occasionally interpreted as stemming from the Aramaic word for 'myrrh'. The Chronicler consequently allowed Asa to be buried in a way that accorded with his name (see comment on v. 12 for an alternative interpretation).

Jehoshaphat (2 Chr 17:1–20:37)

This reign is reported with relative brevity in 1 Kings 22:41–51, though everything portrayed is positive with the exception of the still-remaining high places, where sacrifices and incense offerings continue to take place. v. 46 refers to successes and wars fought by the king as documented in the 'Book of the Annals of the Kings of Judah'. The Chronicler frames his description of events with this material (vv. 41, 42–51) adding to them his description of the war against Aram which was fought together with Ahab (1 Kings 22:1–38). He also inserts a large amount of information: a general description of the king's reign (ch. 17), a report on judicial reform (ch. 19), and finally the story of his successful military campaign against a coalition of Transjordanian peoples (ch. 20). The Chronicler probably did not find this original material in any sources, but inferred it from 1 Kings 22:46 and the king's unusually long period of reign, as well as the positive judgement on him. There is a simple reason why the source model does not praise the king so extensively. Ahab is the dominant figure in the text and is particularly interesting due to his confrontations with prophets faithful to YHWH.

(17:1–18:1) Jehoshaphat's Peaceful Period This chapter divides into three parts: two general judgements on Jehoshaphat's rule (17:1–6, 10–19), the first concerning itself more with domestic politics and religion, the second dealing with foreign and military policy. The third part reports on teaching the law to the people (17:7–9).

17:1–7, the language and subject of these verses are typical of Chronicles. v. 1, 'strengthened himself over Israel' (i.e. the southern kingdom) is a more probable translation than 'strengthened himself against Israel' (i.e. the northern kingdom), in view of the content and context of 1:1. At the time of Jehoshaphat/Ahab there were no conflicts between the two kingdoms. The Chronicler perhaps phrased this sentence in a manner similar to 1:1 in order to draw a parallel between Jehoshaphat and Solomon. v. 5, Judah gives presents to Jehoshaphat, i.e. pays tribute to him—something which was usually reserved for those who have forced subservience upon others (but cf. 1 Sam 10:27): such is the reward for God-fearing behaviour, making Jehoshaphat a very wealthy man. The term usually translated as 'honour' should here be translated as 'wealth'. v. 6, despite his wealth, Jehoshaphat remains humble and behaves in a God-fearing manner: he removes the high places and Asherah poles from Judah—though this contradicts 20:33.

17:7–9, all Judah is informed by the royal officers, Levites, and priests (in that order!) on the book of the law of the Lord (probably the five books of Moses). This is surprisingly undertaken on the king's initiative (Japhet (1993: 749) suggests that this relates to normal practice during the Persian period: Ezra 7:25). In pre-exilic times, this was the task of the priests. According to the OT, it was only in post-exilic times that Levites were also included. The Deuteronomistic demand that the people should know the law is put into practice here in a democratic manner appropriate for the Chronicler: the ruling classes play the role of educators to the advantage of the entire population. To what extent post-exilic custom (cf. Ezra's reading of the law in Jerusalem) has been revised to conform with pre-exilic practices is difficult to discern.

17:10–19 is a second summarizing description of Jehoshaphat's reign. v. 10, the Chronicler clearly emphasizes that all the lands around Judah (and therefore Judah itself by implication) were struck by fear of the Lord. This thought must have been a consolation to members of the tiny temple state in the middle of an almighty Alexandrian or Ptolemaic kingdom. v. 11 documents the tribute paid by other peoples. See also 27:5. Mention of the Arabians makes it unlikely that the Chronicler used a (historically reliable) independent source here. vv. 14–19, these statements on the army's composition are closely linked with those concerning the construction of forts. Their language shows that they are later additions, since expressions such as 'the muster of them according to ancestral houses' clearly point to exilic and post-exilic times. If the Chronicler had copied a list here, it would have been more rigidly structured (Welten 1973: 84). As elsewhere, he differentiates between army divisions from Judah and Benjamin, also mentioning the Benjaminites' (light) armour, that is, bows and shields. The numbers of individual army divisions are strongly exaggerated (going beyond all contemporary estimates of Judah's population), especially since these figures do not include the soldiers already deployed in the forts. The Chronicler does at least respect the fact that Judah is larger than Benjamin. v. 16, voluntary service is one of the Chronicler's favourite attitudes.

(18:1–19:3) Jehoshaphat's Support of Ahab's Campaign Focusing more on prophecy than on the campaign against Ramoth-gilead, the Chronicler uses 1 Kings 22 as material for this chapter, whilst giving it a different introduction and conclusion. The motivation behind following this source might be to show that true YHWH-prophecy also existed in the northern kingdom, or perhaps to underline that Jehoshaphat is somewhat better than Ahab, for it is on his initiative that the four hundred prophets are consulted, followed by Micaiah. But these are at best secondary issues. Japhet (1997: 311) refers to the most important reason: although the Chronicler ignores the history of the northern kingdom, he follows parts of the books of Kings in which Israel and Judah interact with each other.

The Chronicler makes only few changes to his source model. Nevertheless, the story's two versions carry different weights: in 1 Kings 22, it forms part of the conflicts between the northern kingdom and Aram. It concentrates particularly on how Ahab dies (which is greatly shortened in Chronicles). The later version neglects the historical background, turning a story about Ahab into one about Jehoshaphat (nor is the Israelite king's death interpreted as fulfilment of prophecy).

18:1–3 does not follow the source model closely. v. 1, referring back to 17:5, the Chronicler points out that Jehoshaphat is a wealthy man, whilst his comment that Jehoshaphat's son Joram married one of Ahab's daughters stems from 2 Kings 8:18, 27. This marriage was probably driven by mutual political interests. Mentioning Jehoshaphat's wealth underlines that it was not necessary for his family to marry into Ahab's house, since he was regarded as an apostate. The statement could also imply that Jehoshaphat's wealth made him immune to blackmail. From v. 4, the text follows 1 Kings 22 closely.

19:1–3, unlike Ahab, Jehoshaphat returns home peacefully, thereby literally fulfilling Micaiah's demands (18:16), though not complying with the spirit of his plea. v. 2, Jehu, Hanani's son (see 16:7), confronts Jehoshaphat. 'Love' and 'hate' are not emotional terms here, but are used as part of a political vocabulary. Here, 'to love' means virtually to form a coalition. God's anger at Jehoshaphat does not materialize, unless the attack made by the Transjordanian alliance described in ch. 20 is seen in this light. v. 3, without going back on the accusations made in v. 2, the Chronicler places them in relation to the good things/deeds (singular expression) Jehoshaphat did. He removed the Asherahs from the land and, going beyond this concrete action, showed a positive attitude towards the Lord by setting his heart to seek God (one of the Chronicler's favourite expressions).

(19:4–11) Jehoshaphat's Legal Reforms The Chronicler's report can be divided into two parallel sections: vv. 5–7: judges in the fortress cities, and vv. 8–11: judges in Jerusalem, each consisting of their appointment (vv. 5, 8), and Jehoshaphat's speeches (vv. 6–7, 9–11).

The historical reliability of the legal reforms, which scholars have occasionally ascribed to Josiah, is the subject of strong debate. Whilst there is consensus regarding the tone of the sermon, which is heavily influenced by the Chronicler's opinions, the question of whether reliable historical information lies behind the speech is unclear. Evidence for such a possibility has been shown in a large number of general and specific arguments, of which only some can be mentioned here: Japhet (1993: 772–4) points out that such reforms would have been necessary following the division of the Davidic/Solomonite double monarchy, and that Jehoshaphat's skilful handling of domestic and foreign politics indicates that he was capable of reforming his system of government. Certain details do not correspond with Deuteronomic specifications. Ordering the Levites before the priests (v. 8) is not regarded as the Chronicler's work, whilst the rank of 'governor of the house of Judah' (nāgîd, v. 11) was only necessary during the monarchical period. According to Wellhausen (1886: 96–7) and many commentaries following him, the report is a complete fabrication by the Chronicler, who developed a 'midrash' from Jehoshaphat's name (which means 'YHWH judges'); vv. 5–11 reflect the legal system during the Chronicler's lifetime. We accept this theory, whilst suggesting that the Chronicler also inserted some ideas on an ideal legal system.

v. 5, the appointment of judges in the fortress cities, city by city. The Chronicler was particularly interested in the fortress cities, taking pains to deal with each equally and fairly (city by city, cf. e.g. 17:7–9). For this reason he digresses from his source model, Deut 16:18, where judges are appointed in all cities and all tribes. v. 6, two significant factors emerge in the first of the Chronicler's two sermons: he values the deeds of those addressed, therefore often using the verb 'to do', as he does here. Furthermore it is important that everything occurs in the service of YHWH and in his name.

'[H]e is with you': a theologoumenon typical of the Chronicler, which he probably drew from Ex 18:19, a passage also dealing with legal reforms. The Chronicler is probably attempting to draw parallels between Moses and Jehoshaphat here. v. 7, attributes of YHWH here are directly demanded from the judges in Deut 16:19 (though cf. Deut 10:17). The judges must behave as the Lord does. This, though indirectly expressed, is a more weighty responsibility than the demands made in Deut 16:19. v. 11, the many names and functions give the impression of concrete, historical reliability and are especially representative of the Chronicler. The names Amariah and Zebadiah appear only in Chronicles. On the Levites' description as officers cf. 1 Chr 26:29 (23:4) and 2 Chr 34:13. The term is probably used here because it appears in the source model, Deut 16:18.

It is difficult to determine what exactly is meant by the 'matters of the LORD' and the 'king's matters'. Because he makes this distinction, the Chronicler must name a 'governor of the house of Judah', who is responsible for the matters of the king, to stand by the high priest, who obviously deals with religious matters. The Hebrew term for him (nāgîd) is rather neutral, but the Chronicler did not have a better word at his disposal.

(20:1–21:1) Jehoshaphat's War against a Transjordanian Coalition and other Reports This lengthy battle report is unique to the Chronicler and serves as a replacement for 2 Kings 3. The action on the field is kept to a minimum, since the battle is exclusively YHWH's affair (v. 15) and the enemies destroy themselves. Israel only gains the spoils of war and, more importantly, speaks, prays, sings, and plays music (in unison), thereby giving the battle an entirely spiritualized atmosphere.

The exact place-names, not all of which can be identified (the region of En-gedi, the Dead Sea, Judean desert, Tekoa, Bethlehem, Jerusalem), point to a limited area and therefore to local skirmishes rather than a great battle. It is unlikely that Jehoshaphat's conflict with his Transjordanian neighbours forms the core of this report. It probably reflects hostilities between the temple state and groups of its eastern neighbours during or shortly before the Chronicler's lifetime. The Chronicler shifts these minor conflicts into the past and inflates them to almost cosmic proportions. So long as God is at its side, even a small community need not be afraid. This is the consoling message the Chronicler is attempting to pass on to the reader.

v. 1, the Transjordanian armies advance to face Jehoshaphat in battle: they comprise Moabites, Ammonites, and Meunites (as named in the Septuagint, replacing the already mentioned Ammonites). Noth (1944–5: 58–60) believes them to be Nabateans, whilst Welten (1973: 142–5) and others regard them as Idumeans. vv. 2–4, Jehoshaphat is informed about the opposition and vast size of the enemy army. 'Edom' instead of 'Aram' would be more geographically fitting here. Jehoshaphat is afraid, not because he is timid by nature, but because the enemy army is huge. He seeks YHWH (one of the Chronicler's favourite phrases) and proclaims a fast (as was particularly popular in post-exilic times) in reaction to the crisis. The ensuing success is great and their efforts are impressive.

vv. 6–12, Jehoshaphat's prayer, which has often been called a 'national lament', refers to their present crisis, but also contains an element of dogmatism. YHWH is addressed here with one of the Chronicler's favoured expressions, namely, 'O LORD, God of our ancestors'. He is described as the ruler of all peoples who gave the Israelites their land, thus being simultaneously the God of the whole world and the God of a specific people. He can aid his people against all the enemies in the world. The recapitulation of salvation history by the Chronicler is limited to vague references to the Conquest. Its beginning is linked with the name of Abraham. v. 9 is a traditional list of possible calamities and can also be found in ch. 6 (and elsewhere). (The specific situations in which one can call upon God are not restricted to moments of crisis in this chapter.) vv. 10–12, YHWH's might and his gift of land strongly contrast with the Transjordanian military power-structures which are swiftly shown to be no match. Israel had refrained from attacking their Transjordanian neighbours on YHWH's orders (Deut 2). Now, however, Jehoshaphat draws attention to their threat by appealing to YHWH's own interests: they must be expelled from *his* land. Jehoshaphat closes his prayer with a plea for help, using the language of psalms in his emphasis upon human weakness.

v. 13, in another example of the Chronicler's democratic tendencies, this verse stresses that all Judah—even women and children—assembled in such a time of need. vv. 14–16, a characteristic, salvatory oracle takes centre-stage in the portrayal of YHWH's war. God's spirit does not fall upon a prophet, but (appropriately for the temple setting) a Levite whose long lineage links him with Asaph, the original temple musician at the time of David. Jahaziel, who addresses Judah, Jerusalem, and the king (in that order!), calls upon them twice not to be afraid and repeats two of the Chronicler's most important theologoumena: the war is YHWH's; he is with

the Judeans. Jahaziel speaks in v. 17 as Moses does in Ex 14:13–14. Geographical points have also been inserted in v. 16. The religious speech dominates the section, insisting that it represents an answer to the concrete Transjordanian threat. vv. 18–19, Jehoshaphat, all Judeans and the citizens of Jerusalem worship YHWH in joyful reaction to the oracle's promise of salvation. They are followed by the Levites, who also praise God even before he has saved them.

vv. 20–8, following Jehoshaphat's orders, the Israelites behave in battle as if they were holding a religious service. Jehoshaphat makes a further speech, calling upon his people to have faith in God and his prophets (a reference to Isaiah's 'If you do not stand firm in faith, you shall not stand at all', Isa 7:9. Cf. also the same logic in sentences such as Ex 14:31). If they take these thoughts to heart, success is assured. After these brief words of encouragement, the king consults the people to develop a liturgical battle order. In keeping with Chronicles' continuous theme, 'His steadfast love endures for ever' (cf. e.g. 5:13; 7:3, 6), Israel draws its enemy nearer so that YHWH can act at the moment of greatest faith. He sets (either heavenly or worldly) ambushes amongst the three advancing armies so that they destroy each other. Both motifs (ambush and self-destruction) exist elsewhere in the OT and are therefore part of a tradition. The entire action in v. 20 takes place early in the morning, i.e. the time at which God usually acted.

vv. 24–5, the spiritual battle is interrupted. The Chronicler uses all his skill to portray the size of the spoils, the largest in the entire OT: the list of booty is long, many objects are qualified by adjectives, the spoils take three days to be collected and can hardly be carried. This enormous prize and the fact that not a single member of the enemy armies survives, underline the momentous nature of the victory. In holy wars, the spoils must be left to YHWH. The Chronicler, however, has good reason to break with this tradition. King and country are to be rewarded for their exemplary behaviour. The dogma of retribution is a little stronger than the rules of YHWH's wars. vv. 26–8, the war ends where it began, in Jerusalem, in the temple, and (typically for Chronicles) with music. vv. 29–30, cf. 17:10. By contrast to that passage, fear of YHWH spreads not only across all Judah's neighbouring kingdoms, but beyond this, to all the kingdoms in the region. Only now is Judah safe from all its enemies—a reward for the country's exemplary behaviour.

v. 33, 'yet the high places remained': this contradicts 17:6 and, like other incongruencies in Chronicles, cannot be explained. 'The people had not yet set their hearts on the God of their ancestors' represents the Chronicler's characteristic interpretation of his source model. He gives the *reason* for the *acts* mentioned in the source model. He is interested in the basic attitude underlying them. ('The people still sacrificed and offered incense', 1 Kings 22:43.) Chronicles asserts the same basic attitude towards Jehoshaphat as expressed in its source model. v. 34, as so often, the Chronicler names a prophetic source for his portrayal of Jehoshaphat's reign; one, however, which was also used in the book of the Kings of Israel. For Jehu, see 19:2. vv. 35–7, in Kings, Jehoshaphat acts alone in building up the fleet that is destroyed at Ezion-geber, before declining Ahaziah's offer of support. Chronicles, however, portrays both kings acting together and consequently failing together. Failure implies a sin in the Chronicler's eyes. In this case, it is the result of the otherwise good King Jehoshaphat's alliance with the northern king. The Chronicler justifies such a reinterpretation of the story by interpreting 'Then said Ahaziah' (1 Kings 22: 49) as 'Ahaziah had said'. So Ahaziah's offer referred not only to the journey but also to the building of the fleet. Jehoshaphat accepted this offer.

v. 37, as customary for Chronicles, a warning is made by means of a prophet. Jehoshaphat is given the opportunity to cancel his godless plans; he does not take this chance and is therefore condemned to failure. His concluding judgement, however, is not particularly affected by his final act of godlessness.

Jehoram (2 Chr 21:2–20)

Asa and Jehoshaphat, two kings with relatively positive judgements, are followed by Jehoram, who receives very poor verdicts in Kings and (consequently) in Chronicles. Since 2 Kings 8 does not report much about him, the Chronicler is forced to expand substantially on his model, thereby omitting one source reference (v. 23). He reports extensively on the king's brothers—something which occurs nowhere else in Kings or Chronicles with the exception of David. Ch. 21 is thus unique. It is also special since not a single prophet appears in flesh and blood, since Elijah only sends a letter containing a threat of punishment (rather than a warning). Jehoram is not granted an opportunity to convert—another unusual factor in Chronicles. The passage following the letter contains a description of the punishments threatened by Elijah.

The relationship between the source model and its interpretation is one of doubling: the source model describes one sin and one punishment, whilst Chronicles portrays several sins and consequently double punishment. The chapter is dominated by the ubiquitous theme of the Davidic dynasty, influencing events even beyond the source model.

vv. 2–4 concern Jehoram and his brothers. One would expect v. 5 (describing Jehoram's reign) to be placed before this passage. The Chronicler, however, refrains from using this sensible order so that he can insert the text from the source material in a single block. Jehoram's brothers, who are twice notably described as the sons of Jehoshaphat, are given tasks in the fortified cities. Although this passage contains no concrete references other than names, commentaries are surprisingly unanimous in regarding this assertion as historically reliable. v. 2, Jehoshaphat is called 'King of Israel' (though this has erroneously been corrected to read 'King of Judah' in certain Bible translations, including NRSV). 'Israel' must be regarded here as the ideal Israel, comprising both the southern kingdom of Judah and the northern kingdom of Israel, a title the Chronicler consistently clung to. v. 4, both good and bad deeds often occur in Chronicles immediately after the relevant king's accession to the throne. Thus Jehoram has hardly come to power before he brutally murders all his brothers and several notables. No reason is given for these murders (perhaps because they were known to the reader). He was probably driven by a lust for power or the fear of losing it.

vv. 8–11, it is unclear in the source whether Jehoram actually defeated the Edomites. It may be that they defeated him, forcing the king to escape through enemy lines. The Chronicler subtly changes the text (or perhaps used a different source), thereby clarifying events. He does not mention the people's flight into their tents and writes 'and his chariot commanders' instead of 'to Zair' (two phrases which sound similar in Hebrew). Is this a reading or writing error, or the version considered most appropriate by the Chronicler? vv. 10–11, Jehoram ought to have understood the loss of Edom and Libnah as a warning, but instead he continues to commit sin. At this point, the Chronicler's unique material begins. The high places are cultic sites respected above all others by the people. A king's continuing tolerance of such places is not regarded as a particular crime. Jehoram, however, is accused here of the grave crime of establishing (rather than tolerating) them as well as encouraging Jerusalem and Judah to worship idols.

vv. 12–15 document Elijah's letter. It is impossible to establish from biblical accounts whether Elijah, who is largely ignored in Chronicles since he was active in the northern kingdom, could have lived during Jehoram's reign (cf. e.g. 2 Kings 1:17). In any case the Chronicler was not particularly interested in questions of chronology. The idea that a prophet could make a written declaration probably stems from a (postexilic) time in which the transcription of oral prophecy enjoyed increased importance. vv. 12–13, in the first part of the letter, Elijah accuses Jehoram of the crimes already described, keeping close to the text of the previous verses. Jehoram is directly and indirectly compared with various other kings: David, Jehoshaphat, Asa, and Ahab. The theme of the Davidic dynasty strongly influences this chapter. vv. 14–15 list Elijah's threats of punishment, all of which are fulfilled (vv. 16–19). vv. 14–15, 16–19, use very similar language. Jehoram must be punished, along with his people, his family, his property, and (representing the only details mentioned by Elijah) his body.

vv. 16–19, maybe these verses reflect contemporary events, i.e. skirmishes of the temple state with its south-western neighbours. '[T]he Arabs who are near the Ethiopians': cf. 2 CHR 14:9. Keeping the focus of his attention on the Davidic dynasty, the Chronicler only briefly describes the plague which strikes the people (cf. v. 14), whilst portraying the deportation of the king's property, wives, and sons in greater detail. Only the youngest son survives. Jehoram's crimes lead almost to the disappearance of the Davidic monarchy. vv. 18–19, the Chronicler describes Jehoram's final punishment most extensively, namely his painful, incurable, yet indefinable sickness. Suggestions include diarrhoea or a stomach ulcer leading to a chronic rectal prolapse.

v. 20 is a continuation of the statement on Jehoram in v. 5. As a consequence of his godless life, Jehoram does not receive an honourable funeral. Nobody mourns for him (unsure translation). The Chronicler knew from his study of the Elijah tradition that idol-worshipping led to the destruction of Ahab's dynasty and applied this logic to the (almost eradicated) Davidic line.

Ahaziah's Year-Long Reign (2 Chr 22:1–9)

The source model for this chapter portrays events during the king's reign in the context of the revolutionary crisis developing in the politically more significant northern kingdom. Ahaziah's death is integrated into the story of Jehu's revolution and plays only a minor role. In Chronicles, however, events in the northern kingdom are mentioned only if they are required to explain Athaliah's fate. The following sources are used: vv. 1–6 correspond with 2 Kings 8:24b–9 (although the Chronicler made some changes and, above all, additions). vv. 7–9 are the Chronicler's extremely brief summary of 2 Kings 9:1–28 and 10:12–14. Only here does he use such a literary technique. The main message of his reworking summary of these verses in Kings is that religious and political co-operation with the breakaway, godless northern kingdom must lead to downfall.

v. 1, in an emendment to his source model, the Chronicler stresses that the people of Jerusalem made Ahaziah king. There is no parallel with this in the entire OT: reports concerning the co-operation of larger classes at the royal installation refer to the 'people of the land'. The verse refers back to 21:17 and clarifies why of all Jehoram's sons, the youngest should become king. v. 2, 'forty-two years old': cannot be correct, since it would mean that on the day of Ahaziah's accession to the throne he was older than his father. (The source states twenty-two years, whilst LXX states twenty.)

vv. 7–9, from this point, the Chronicler writes quite independently. The passage is framed by two sentences in which the authorial voice is particularly clear. This digression from the source model's narrative flow can be explained by the Chronicler's theologically motivated interest in placing Ahaziah in the centre of his account. He does not use an old source for this. v. 8, according to Chronicles, it is the sons of Ahaziah's brothers that are murdered, and not his own brothers, as in 2 Kings 10:12–14. There is a simple explanation for this: Ahaziah's brothers have been deported (and perhaps murdered, 2 Chr 21:17). The two texts should not be assimilated by interpreting 'brothers' in terms of 'relatives'. Chronicles also describes the murder of several princes. Are these a replacement for the Israelite notables murdered by Jehu in 2 Kings 10:11? v. 9, the source model describes events differently: Ahaziah is wounded while fleeing near Ibleam, but gets as far as Megiddo, where he dies. He is subsequently transported to Jerusalem and buried alongside his fathers. The Chronicler omits many of these details, perhaps because he presumed knowledge of these events, leaving Ahaziah to die in Samaria, the evil capital. The Chronicler does not explicitly confirm that he is also buried there. Ahaziah receives a burial here only because of his ancestor, Jehoshaphat, who is regarded as having been God-fearing his whole life. This somewhat undermines the dogma of retribution. 'And the house of Ahaziah had no one able to rule the kingdom': the Hebrew term for 'be able' is one of the Chronicler's favourite expressions, since he admired strength and power and repeatedly wrote about such values.

Athaliah the Usurper Queen and the Enthronement of Joash (2 Chr 22:10–23:21)

Once Ahaziah and the Judean princes have been murdered, the kingdom finds itself in a similar situation to that at the end of Saul's career (as portrayed in 1 Chr 10), giving meaning to the reference to David (see e.g. 23:3). Indeed the Chronicler's description of the early phase of Joash's reign shows similarities with that king (especially the theme of concern for the

temple and the cult). King Joash is saved by a secret plot and later placed upon the throne. The Chronicler characteristically turns this plot into a popular enterprise. The fact that, had the people been involved, Athaliah would have discovered the plan and crushed it does not concern the author. He turns a political act in the source text into one of religious politics, in which the priests and Levites play the leading roles. The high priest Jehoiada, somehow the guardian of the young king (24:3), is more prominent in the Chronicler's version than in the source model. What is his exact position? Some commentaries see him as unifying in some way the offices of king and high priest, as was practised during the Chronicler's lifetime. Williamson (1987: 113–14) and some others, however, think that the portrayal of Jehoiada by the Chronicler contains implicit criticism of the lust of contemporary high priests for political power; Jehoida is just not striving for it. The king's daughter Jehoshabeath is also given a more conspicuous role in Chronicles (v. 11). A large number of commentaries regard the statement that she is the high priest's wife to be historically reliable despite the lack of evidence to support this from elsewhere. It would at least explain why she had such easy access to the temple grounds (cf., however, 8:11). It is more likely that the Chronicler joined them together on the logical basis that since both played key roles in the same project, they must be husband and wife.

(23:1–21) vv. 1–3 are analogous with 2 Kings 11:4. The Chronicler turns Jehoiada's secret plot, involving only the captains of the royal guard, into a major campaign including the Levites and the entire community. v. 1, going beyond the source model, the Chronicler characterizes and judges Jehoiada's actions: he 'took courage'. All those involved in the plot are named, lending it a degree of tangibility. With the exception of Elishaphat, all the names appear in the lists of priests and Levites in Ezra, Nehemiah, and Chronicles. vv. 4–5a, neither these orders nor those in the source are entirely clear, since routine tasks that the author of Kings (and presumably the reader) knew well enough are not reported. The Chronicler follows certain guidelines laid down by Kings, describing the guards and the division of forces into three parts. The rest of the content is completely altered, so that the royal guards, whose duty it is to protect the king, are replaced by priests, Levites, and the people. Here, they serve the added purpose of keeping others from entering the temple. It is difficult to interpret the significance of the different localities mentioned. v. 7, the royal guard can only be composed of Levites since they alone have the right to enter the temple precinct. '[A]nd whoever enters the house' is a religious adaptation of the more militarily orientated 'whoever approaches the ranks' in the source (2 Kings 11:8). The Levites are also required to prevent the king from entering the temple.

v. 8, 'for the priest Jehoiada did not dismiss the divisions': the way the Chronicler conceives the temple personnel's organization (see also 1 Chr 23–6) clearly serves as a background for this reference. v. 13, 'standing by his pillar at the entrance' should perhaps be corrected to read, 'at his place at the entrance'. The source reads: 'standing by the pillar, as was the custom'. The Chronicler clearly wishes to emphasize that even the king could not enter the temple. Unlike the source, Chronicles does not have just trumpets announcing the joyful occasion, but adds various other musical instruments. This also strengthens the religious atmosphere of the celebrations.

vv. 16–21, the source reports on two covenants: (1) Between the king, the people, and God. (2) Between the king and the people. Since the Chronicler has already introduced the second in v. 3, he limits his description to the first (according to the Hebrew text) between Jehoiada, the people, and the king (although the people are mentioned first, unlike the source). God is not a reciprocal partner in the covenant; the human partner alone has obligations—towards God (cf. 15:12). vv. 18–19 describe positive cultic reforms. In Chronicles, these occur at times when the legitimate temple service has entirely collapsed. Jehoiada organizes the offices (priests and Levites) and their cultic duties (sacrifices and music), referring back to the law of Moses and David's orders (since Moses made no law concerning cultic music).

Joash's Reign (2 Chr 24:1–27)

As with Asa, this description is divided into two phases, namely a God-fearing and an apostate period. The second phase hangs not on a rather implausible criticism of 2 Kings 12:3, but on the king's violent death indicating previous failings. This leads to a radical reinterpretation of the source model, and especially to striking additions such as the lengthy passage concerning the appearance of prophets and Zechariah, the son of the priest Jehoiada (vv. 17–22). The Chronicler can hardly have used his own independent sources for this section (cf. 2 CHR 24:26, however).

(24:1–3) The Chronicle v. 2, 'all the days of the priest Jehoiada' (source: 'all his days, because the priest Jehoiada instructed him'): this slight emendment makes it easier for the Chronicler, who is unique in describing Jehoiada's death (v. 15), to divide Joash's reign into two periods. The source model judges the king positively, since 2 Kings 12:3 is only a minor comment. The result is that the Deuteronomist generally judges the king positively (v. 3, which deals with sacrifices and incense-burning by the people at the high places, had to be omitted by the Chronicler since it occurred during Joash's positive period).

(24:4–16) The Restoration of the Temple and Collection of Money This passage sticks as closely to its source model in some ways as it diverges from it in others. Only the main variations are mentioned here. According to the source, priests can claim a certain amount of money for the temple, but have the responsibility of using such money to restore the temple. Since they have neglected this duty for a long time the king relieves them of it, and with it the right to oversee the temple contributions. These are collected in a chest and passed on to craftsmen as payment for their work in good faith. This becomes a long-term system. The Chronicler converts it into a single payment (though to be repeated, v. 5) which primarily involves the Levites (Levite priests), deletes the source's criticism of the priests (vv. 4–8), and interprets the laymen's contributions as a form of taxation, similar to the tax collected in the desert in connection with the tabernacle. Furthermore, in another divergence from the source, he allows the unspent contributions to be used to buy cultic material.

v. 6, this is a relatively awkward definition of the tax imposed upon the Israelites by Moses to pay for the tabernacle

(Ex 30:13; 38:26). In a certain way it replaces the still more difficult expression in 2 Kings 12:5. Since the tax should be equally high for everyone, the laymen's generosity cannot be mentioned here. The joy with which they make their contributions is emphasized instead (v. 10). v. 8, by changing the source model, the Chronicler secures the chest's position in a place to which laymen have access. v. 13, in characteristic fashion, the Chronicler underlines the craftsmen's good work, pointing out that the temple will look as it did at the time of its original construction. Thus continuity is guaranteed. v. 14, unlike the source model, the unused money is used to produce cultic objects so that proper sacrificial burnt-offerings can be carried out. This occurs as long as Jehoiada is alive. vv. 15–16, only Jehoiada, who lives longer than Aaron (Num 33:39) and dies as an aged man 'full of days' (like patriarchs and others), is buried 'among the kings'. This is the clearest expression of his standing as a truly regal priest.

(24:17–22) Joash's Falling Away v. 18, the Chronicler uses typical vocabulary to describe Joash's fall: e.g. 'abandoned the house of the LORD', 'sacred poles', and 'idols'. To clarify the connection between his deeds and his fate, the Chronicler already mentions the result of his religious crimes, although the idea is only brought to its conclusion in vv. 23–5, after the theological/historical exposition in v. 19 and Zechariah's appearance in v. 20. v. 19, the Chronicler expresses one of his most important theological statements here: the Lord gives sinners the opportunity to return to his way by sending prophets to them. These occasionally manage to convert their addressees. Unfortunately this is not the case here. v. 20, the principle is followed by its application. The prophet Zechariah, who is not mentioned elsewhere, wishes to convert the people. He does not use this term, however, merely pointing out that God-fearing behaviour leads to success (one of the Chronicler's favourite themes). 'Because you have forsaken the LORD, he has also forsaken you': a precise expression of the dogma of retribution. v. 21, the reaction to this mild, well-intended call to repent is shocking: the king orders Zechariah to be stoned to death, in the forecourt of the temple. (A legal stoning must take place in a public place, cf. Deut 17:2–7.) v. 22, showing no gratitude to Jehoiada, the king kills his son Zechariah. His dying words are slightly emended lines from Ex 5:21, expressing the king's inability to escape his fate.

(24:23–7) The Syrians' Victory and Joash's Death The Chronicler uses no source of his own here, radically rewriting 2 Kings 12:17–18 to emphasize his theological priorities: the source text describes Joash being spared by the invading King Hazael upon payment of an enormous tribute from the temple and palace treasuries. In Chronicles, the Arameans take action (though their king does not appear). Although they are greatly outnumbered by the Judeans, they defeat them. Thus the Chronicler's favoured theme of a small Judean force defeating powerful armies with the help of God is reintroduced and inverted. vv. 25–6, although the king's burial takes place in the city of David (due to his earlier good behaviour) he is not buried amongst the kings (as a result of his sins). v. 26, the Chronicler changes the names of the conspirators (there is probably no damage to the text). This gives them similar names (since they carry out their plan together), turns their fathers into mothers, perhaps because Shimeath's '-ath' ending was mistakenly interpreted as female, and declares them to be foreigners, for which there is no evidence in the source model. Does this imply that nothing better can be expected from sons of foreigners? The Chronicler's positive attitude towards mixed marriage would contradict this. His attitude towards the plot itself is also unclear. v. 27, 'Story' is the right rendering of 'midrash' here: cf. 2 CHR 13:22, which is the only other passage in the OT containing the word.

Amaziah (2 Chr 25:1–28)

The Chronicler takes all his material concerning Amaziah from 2 Kings 14, reworking it according to his narrative and theological principles. He greatly extends 2 Kings 14:7, which describes the victorious battle against Edom, by portraying the troops' selection, the appearance of a man of God before the battle, and of a prophet after its conclusion. vv. 7–10 are often regarded as having stemmed from an independent source available to the Chronicler, since they do not conform with his theology. In the source model, King Amaziah is judged positively except for one small criticism. Since he falls victim to a conspiracy, the Chronicler's logic dictates that he must somehow have offended God: he is thus accused of worshipping Edomite gods, although this seems to contradict his honourable burial (cf. 2 CHR 25:28, however).

vv. 1–4, apart from minor, yet characteristic emendments, the Chronicler keeps close to his source model. v. 2, he repeats the source's positive judgement on Amaziah, though radically shortening the criticism it contains, adding one of his favourite phrases as replacement: 'yet not with a true heart'. This serves as a precursor to his later fall whilst at the same time being relatively mild. vv. 5–6 describe the selection of troops and the recruitment of mercenaries. The notes regarding this army differ from comparable passages connected with military campaigns (and are not used to assess the king). Despite the traditional mention of both Judah and Benjamin, only Judah's weaponry is listed, leading Welten (1973: 92) to suggest that the inclusion of Benjamin is a secondary gloss. Recruiting Israelites is not only a godless act (v. 7), but is also unnecessary given the size of the Judean army (cf. 14:7; 17:14–19, however).

vv. 7–10, a man of God appears. Like the prophet in vv. 15–16, but contrary to the Chronicler's more common practice, he remains unnamed. This, however, need not indicate a source which the Chronicler did not dare to emend, since the passage contains the Chronicler's usual theology: a battle is not decided by armies (and their strength), but by YHWH alone. v. 7, 'the LORD is not with Israel': this is not a principle, but is due to their faithless attitude. v. 8, the Hebrew text may be damaged here and may require correction to clarify the point that the king is mistaken if he believes he can achieve victory by strengthening his forces with mercenaries, and will fall.

vv. 11–13, the Chronicler takes the report of a victorious battle against the Edomites in 2 Kings 14:7 and develops it further to create a midrash. Although he does not mention the name of the battleground (Sela is Joktheel), he uses the meanings of these two names. He probably understood Sela to be the contemporary Petra (i.e. 'rock', selaᶜ in Heb.). This name and Joktheel (God destroys) probably gave him the idea of the Edomites' cruel treatment. It also allows him to omit the conquest of the city of Sela. vv. 14–16, the king behaves both foolishly and godlessly. The great powers of the Near East often took the gods of defeated nations back home with them in order to win their new subjects' favour. This does not occur here. To worship the gods of defeated powers is seen as particularly futile. In keeping with the Chronicler's habit, the king is warned about this matter by another anonymous prophet. Yet the king dismisses the prophet and even threatens to execute him. The passage is cleverly interwoven with several keywords: according to v. 10, the mercenaries' anger is kindled against Judah, whilst the Lord's wrath is kindled against Amaziah in v. 15. The king accuses the prophet of being an unwanted counsellor, whilst the latter reminds him of God's own forgotten counsel (v. 16). The same Hebrew root—meaning 'take counsel' also occurs in v. 17.

vv. 17–24, having reworked and extended his source model up to this point, the Chronicler has created the conditions to use the source's subsequent description of Amaziah's defeat without significant changes. The king must fail since he sought the Edomite deities (vv. 15, 20). His foolish behaviour is contrasted with that of his sensible Israelite counterpart. This is another example of the Chronicler's subtly diversified attitude towards the northern kingdom. v. 20, 'it was God's doing' is the most important addition made by the Chronicler in this section, since it explains Judah's subsequent defeat: they sought the Edomite gods. The vocabulary here is typical for the Chronicler: cf. 10:15; 22:7.

v. 28, 'in the city of Judah' (Heb. text): the source writes: 'in Jerusalem ... in the city of David' (probably 'in Jerusalem' because he died in Lachish). Perhaps the text should be corrected to conform with the source. Perhaps the Chronicler changed it, however, so that this not-so-glorious king did not receive too splendid a funeral.

Uzziah (2 Chr 26:1–23)

Uzziah's fifty-two year reign is surpassed in length only by that of Manasseh. Beyond the customary information, the books of Kings (2 Kings 14:21–2; 15:1–7) report only on the fortification and conquest of Elath and the king's illness. The Chronicler adopts this meagre frame, deletes its mention of the people's continued sacrifices carried out at the high places, and inserts details concerning wars, construction projects, agriculture, military organization, and the army's weaponry (vv. 6–15). In keeping with the Chronicler's dogma, Uzziah's long reign and successes are regarded as a result of seeking God. The same logic dictates that Uzziah's illness was caused by a previous failing as described in vv. 16–21. Thus, like some kings before him, Uzziah's reign falls into two periods: one positive and one negative.

v. 5, Uzziah's positive attitude towards YHWH is expressed by the favoured term, 'to seek God', which is coupled with the resulting, 'God made him prosper'. Zechariah, who is given no title here, teaches the king to seek God (maybe the Heb. text should be emended—as in NRSV: 'in the fear of God'). He appears at this point because Uzziah is named in the book of Zechariah (Zech 14:5; unless this is a reference to the Zechariah mentioned in Isa 8:2). As long as Zechariah lives, Uzziah behaves well, thus linking him with Joash, who falls away only after the death of the priest Jehoiada.

vv. 6–15, the historical reliability of these statements is the subject of debate. Some exegetes regard its precise, informative style and the exact place-names as evidence of its plausibility, and even as archaeological fact. This is contradicted by the existence of nearly all the Chronicler's most valued themes and the possibility that the details described could reflect events that occurred shortly before or during the Chronicler's own lifetime. If sources were used here, they were radically reworked. v. 7, the existence of Arabs in the Judean sphere of influence is anachronistic. Exegetes view them as Bedouin, and consequently regard v. 7 as being based on contemporary sources. See comment on 2 CHR 20:1 regarding Meunites. v. 8, the Chronicler always describes 'Ammonites' (in Heb.), as 'sons of Ammon' elsewhere. This may be another spelling mistake for Meunites (v. 7). v. 10, the description of Uzziah's building projects in the south is supported by archaeological evidence that could, however, stem from the time of Jehoshaphat or another king! It is written in the tone of Ptolomaic times, emphasizing economic factors which had already gained importance during the Persian period and were further developed by the Ptolemeans. The claim that Uzziah loved agricultural matters should be regarded in this light. v. 15, the artfully designed machines are probably catapults which were invented around 400 BCE in Syracuse, according to Didorus Siculus' literary documentation. Jews must first have encountered catapults (and similar hurling implements) during the siege of Tyre in 332 BCE. The Chronicler transforms them into defensive weapons, accrediting their invention to a Judean king. Other interpretations of these machines are too artificial.

vv. 16–23, at the zenith of his power, Uzziah grows proud and commits a sin. His fall, which is described using typical terminology, is caused by his entrance into the temple. This would have been permitted in pre-exilic times, but post-exilic values forbid such an action. His attempts to burn incense are, however, entirely unacceptable. The priests warn the king, thus serving the same purpose as prophets: according to the Chronicler's logic, every sinner is given the opportunity to turn away from his godless behaviour and be reassured of YHWH's good intentions. Uzziah becomes angry, opposes the priests, and is immediately smitten with leprosy. From this moment on, he must live in a separate house, euphemistically described as the house of freedom. His son rules as regent. This episode, which contrasts with the Chronicler's usually calm and schematic style, shows signs of OT sources which inspire his own imaginative narration: one such source may have been 1 Kings 13, in which the fallen King Jeroboam burns incense at the altar in Bethel.

Jotham (2 Chr 27:1–9)

The Chronicler is unlimited in his praise for Jotham. This explains the changes he makes to his source model. Rezin and Pekah cannot threaten Judah as early as Jotham's reign since he commits no sin. The positive judgement on Uzziah (25:2), which is repeated in the chapter on Jotham (v. 2), is weakened by the Chronicler, using a positive statement on the latter: 'only he did not invade the temple of the LORD'. The statement is linguistically linked to the source model's, 'Nevertheless the high places were not removed' (2 Kings 15:35), which it replaces. Jotham receives threefold reward for the exemplary behaviour described in the Chronicler's unique material in vv. 3–6: (1) He builds more than in the source model, namely various kinds of fortresses on Judean territory, as well as the upper gate of the house of the Lord and on the wall of Ophel. (2) He defeats the Ammonites, who do not have a common border with Judah at the time of Jotham's reign. This note is made slightly more historically plausible (though by no means convincing) by suggestions that he is referring to the Meunites here. (3) Jotham receives an extremely high tribute from the Ammonites for the period of three years. The Chronicler probably had contemporary circumstances in mind when writing these three statements.

Ahaz (2 Chr 28:1–27)

From a historical perspective, Ahaz's reign is dominated by the Syro-Ephraimite war, during which the kingdoms of Israel and Judah were in conflict with each other. The Chronicler, who takes every opportunity to expand on the errant nature of the northern kingdom, does just that here. He wishes to emphasize that reunification is almost possible at this point in time. But whereas Israel was responsible for the original partition of the kingdom, it is Judah that prevents a reunion here. Ahaz is godless and does not regard punishment as an opportunity to convert, indeed even worsening his behaviour following each form of punishment. After its victory over Judah, Israel is humane towards the vanquished, heeding YHWH's word. This chapter is a mirror image of ch. 13, in which Judah and Israel have exchanged their roles. This main goal explains almost all of the (sometimes surprising) changes the Chronicler makes to his source model, including those statements whose meanings he inverts.

v. 3, whilst the source model reports that Ahaz let his 'son pass through fire', the Chronicler has his 'sons'. He thus turns a unique act into a cultic rite known to have been performed more than once by Ahaz. He even specifies the site of the ritual (cf. amongst others Jer 7:31–2), simultaneously using it as the place at which Ahaz carries out his (obviously illegitimate) sacrifices. These elements do not exist in the source model. vv. 5–8 concern the war against Syria and the Ephraimites. Whereas the source model describes Israel and Aram's campaign against Judah as a minor success and draws no causal links with the southern kingdom's apostasy, the Chronicler transforms this into a series of painful blows to Judah under Ahaz. He does not use an unknown report on the Syrian-Ephraimite war or any other conflict as a source here. He also separates previously coherent factors in order to allow for his description of the lengthy conflict between Israel and Judah (vv. 5b–15), whilst the war against Aram takes up merely half a verse (5a). vv. 5b–8, in a battle which is not clearly described, Israel crushes Judah, the number of victims perhaps being an implicit comment on the kingdom's original unity (120,000 = 12 tribes). The Chronicler's explanation for this defeat is stereotypical—because they had forsaken 'the LORD, the God of their ancestors'.

vv. 9–15: the Good Samaritans. The following report is, as its title suggests, the main source used by Luke for his well-known story (Lk 10:25–37), as a number of identical details underline. It was conceived exclusively by the Chronicler. Suggestions that this is not the Chronicler's own narrative, due to its pro-Israelite tone, are not plausible. The Chronicler has nothing against the (all too rare!) YHWH-faithful Israelites, even rejoicing at their existence. Furthermore, his praise for their exemplary behaviour is facilitated by the absence of the king's name, as if the northern kingdom had already been destroyed by the Syrians. (The entire chapter makes allusions to the Babylonian Exile: cf. e.g. vv. 5, 8.) vv. 9–11, Oded's sermon is typical for Chronicles, declaring to his people that YHWH's wrath, rather than they themselves, was responsible for the defeat of the Judeans. Should they continue to live in such an godless fashion, YHWH's wrath would also befall them. Using a keyword for this chapter, Oded describes them as 'brothers' (NRSV, kindred) thereby using the strongest term to describe the political and religious connection between the Israelites and the Judeans. vv. 14–15, the prisoners receive clothes, food, water, and medical attention—evidence of their humane treatment. The Chronicler may have been inspired by the description of the Israelites' exemplary behaviour in 2 Kings 6:22 and applied it to Oded's sermon. v. 15, the parallels with Lk 10 are strongest here. Why are the prisoners taken to Jericho of all places? Is it merely because Jericho lies on the border between Judah and Israel?

vv. 16–21, the source model describes how Ahaz is forced to seek Tiglath-pileser's support and thus pay him a tribute from the temple and the palace. Tiglath-pileser accepts the offer, defeats Damascus and deports its citizens, and kills king Rezin. The Chronicler changes the chronology of events, by placing the statement that Rezin had returned Elath to Edomite hands, forcing the Judeans out of the city, before Tiglath-pileser's campaign. He also radically rewrites the passage: he describes the Edomites waging war against Judah (deporting further captives—an allusion to the Exile, v. 17), also allows the Philistines to attack Judah (v. 18), all because of Ahaz's godless behaviour (v. 19). This is the reason for Ahaz's appeal to the Assyrian king (v. 16). vv. 20–1, contrary to the source model's description (and historical fact), Tiglath-pileser does not come to his aid, he even attacks him. The Chronicler's logic dictates such circumstances, since those who are in difficulties should not appeal to foreign powers, but to the Lord. Ahaz calls upon the Assyrian king for *help* (v. 16), but is not *helped* by him (v. 20; another verb in Heb.), nor does it *help* to offer him a tribute (v. 21). The play on 'help' is obvious. Unlike the source model, the tribute does not stem only from the temple and the palace, but is also financed by the princes—a further, somewhat curious example of the Chronicler's democratic tendencies.

vv. 22–5 document the cultic sins of the king. According to the source model, Ahaz orders the construction of a copy of the altar he saw in Damascus, giving the priest Uriah comprehensive instructions concerning it. The Chronicler transforms the altar into a place of worship for the gods of Damascus, thereby increasing Ahaz's sin.

Hezekiah (2 Chr 29:1–32:33)

(29:1–36) Cultic Reform and the Temple's Consecration The Chronicler wrote more extensively about Hezekiah than any other king who ruled Judah alone. He used 2 Kings 18:9–12 as a source model, greatly reworking its middle sections and adding material on the cult. Hezekiah the politician in Kings (only 2 Kings 18:4 concerns the cult) is thereby transformed into Hezekiah the reformer of cult in Chronicles.

vv. 3–11 report the king's speech. vv. 3–4, immediately after his accession, i.e. without delay, the king opens the doors of the temple: this act, which takes place on the eighth day of his

reign according to v. 17, symbolizes his resolute attempt to restore order. Since the temple is still unclean, Hezekiah is forced to hold the meeting with his priests and Levites elsewhere, at the square on the east. vv. 5–11, the frame of the speech (vv. 5, 11) calls upon the Levites (and priests) to become active. The middle section (vv. 6–10) concerns sins (vv. 6–7), their effects (vv. 8–9), and the consequences the king draws from them. The vocabulary used to describe Judah's situation warns of the forthcoming exile, clearly drawing parallels with the terminology used in Jeremiah.

vv. 12–19 describe the cleansing of the temple. vv. 12–14, the Levites immediately begin their work. Two sons of each of the seven families are named. The number seven is a keyword in this chapter (cf. e.g. vv. 17, 21) and can be regarded as an aesthetic concept. The last three sons named (Asaph, Heman, and Jeduthun) are the singers ascribed to the Levites. Cf. 1 Chr 15:5–7 regarding the first three names. The Kohathites are probably priests (who are required for the temple's cleansing, since they alone are permitted to enter). Elizaphan is mentioned elsewhere only in 1 Chr 15:8; maybe he serves to make up the number. vv. 15–17, having sanctified themselves (an act that is not described further), the Levites and priests go straight to work. The king's order is in accordance with YHWH's law as applied by Hezekiah. The tasks are divided in the only way possible: the priests remove unholy material from the temple whilst the Levites carry it from the forecourt into the Kidron valley. v. 17, the chronological statements here do not conform with the information in v. 3. It is, however, an important point that sanctification of the temple was completed on the sixteenth day, forcing a delay in the Passover feast. This could be regarded as early muted criticism of the priests as a precursor to a more overt reproach later on (30:3). vv. 18–19, the report to Hezekiah indirectly underlines his leading role in the project. For the first time in this chapter, Ahaz is explicitly mentioned. It is no doubt deliberate that the temple equipment is the centre of attention here. The utensils guaranteed continuity with Solomon's temple in post-exilic times for the construction of the second temple; they were returned by the Persians to those who resettled Jerusalem.

vv. 20–36, a great cultic feast, without parallel in the OT, takes place once the consecration of the temple has been completed. It probably represents a mixture of cultic rituals during the Chronicler's lifetime and sacrificial laws laid down in the OT. Besides Leviticus, Ezek 43–5, the procedure for sanctifying altars (Num 7:88), and the report concerning the consecration of the second temple (Ezra 6:17; 8:35) all play an important role. These similarities mainly apply to the sacrificial animals. The feast has three parts: preparations, sacrifices made by the princes (and carried out to purify the temple and free it from sin, along with great musical accompaniment), and the sacrifices made by the people, which are made voluntarily and joyfully. v. 24, it is perhaps a measure of the festive occasion that the priests themselves and not the laymen perform the slaughter. The verse is a further indication of the king's initiative. vv. 25–6, the Chronicler emphasizes how Hezekiah reorders the cult (making him almost comparable to David). This new order is secured as rigidly as possible: it refers back not only to David, but also to Gad and Nathan, who lived during his reign. The order of music, however, is from the Lord through his prophets. vv. 31–5, once the temple has been made worthy for ordinary worship by sacrifices, the second part of the feast takes place. Hezekiah then calls upon the congregation to make further burnt offerings, to which it responds positively. The Chronicler first mentions the people's voluntary offerings here—they are not mentioned elsewhere in his book.

(30:1–27) The Passover The measures described in the previous chapter are closely linked to the Passover feast. It is important for the Chronicler that Hezekiah should carry out all the significant measures in the first year of his reign. His accession comes at a time when the northern kingdom may already have fallen. The Chronicler cannot imagine that there would be anything Hezekiah would not have undertaken to achieve reunification. Since this is impossible by political means, due to the Assyrian threat, he portrays the king making a final attempt to restore the unity of the cult. This description is often considered to contain historically reliable elements, especially since negative aspects are also reported on. But these are limited and probably reflect contemporary problems.

Ch. 30 contains the first description of a complete pilgrimage in the OT, perhaps mirroring one as it took place during the Chronicler's time. The first part of the chapter (vv. 1–13) describes preparations for the Passover feast, whilst the second, slightly longer section deals with its celebration. It surprisingly coincides with the festival of Unleavened Bread, as does the subsequent festivity.

vv. 1–7, in keeping with the Chronicler's democratic convictions, the king, the princes and the people decide to celebrate Passover. Due to the lack of preparation for such a feast (v. 3), they decide to delay it until the second month. This strictly speaking grave aberration from the cultic calendar is not criticized by the Chronicler since he values the basic change in attitudes here and also tacitly refers to a previous occasion when this occurred (Num 9:6–13). According to Deuteronomistic teachings, the Passover was a family celebration until King Josiah centralized it in Jerusalem. This is of no interest to the Chronicler, who refers directly to the duties laid down by the law, describing them comprehensively, though rather unconventionally. Following this successful, indeed unanimous assembly, the king sends messengers all around the country and particularly to the northern kingdom. v. 1, in an example of his narrative skill, the Chronicler begins the chapter with calling his readers' attention to this point before mentioning the assembly.

vv. 6–9, the messengers spread across the country and recite a sermon to the audience. Its central message is expressed using a play on words: return to YHWH, he will return to you. The largely unreported demise of the northern kingdom has led to difficult circumstances for those who remain on the land and those who have been deported. If the Israelites turn back to the Lord and express this through a pilgrimage, perhaps even those who have been deported may find the Lord's mercy. Repentance is always possible. v. 6, does such use of messengers and letters to inform the people of royal decisions mirror similar practices in Persia? vv. 10–13, reactions to the invitation are varied. Most inhabitants of the northern kingdom react with derision and scorn, though some accept the offer by humbling themselves (typical

vocabulary). This reaction conforms with the usual pattern in Chronicles; only the Judeans react in an exemplary manner, acting with 'one heart' (v. 12—also typical terminology). v. 12, as much as the Chronicler emphasizes the importance of individual responsibility, he does occasionally point out that correct behaviour ultimately stems from God's actions (cf. 1 CHR 29). He does not regard this double causality as a contradiction. v. 13, it is surprising that the 'very large assembly' (one of the Chronicler's favourite phrases) gather to celebrate the festival of Unleavened Bread. Passover and Unleavened Bread were originally two independent festivals that grew together in the course of time, as this verse demonstrates more clearly than any other OT text. v. 14, once the temple has been cleansed (ch. 29), the city is also freed from all foreign influence: only thus can legitimate rituals take place.

vv. 15–20 report the celebration of Passover. A number of aspects are unclear. As may have been the case during the Chronicler's lifetime, many pilgrims have not prepared themselves for the Passover since they have not cleansed themselves as stipulated by the law. But good religious intentions make up for the lack of cultic correctness. Hezekiah calls upon YHWH to pardon the people who have not cleansed themselves and is heard. The Chronicler may deliberately have created a precedent to follow in the future here. The cult officials, the priests and the Levites, also fall short of the usual standards. But they are trying hard to show their change of heart, and that is what seems most important to the Chronicler. v. 17, according to the law, the person making the sacrifice, i.e. a layman, is responsible for its slaughter. But since the people have not been cleansed properly, the Levites assume this role.

vv. 21–2, this summary again refers to the festival of Unleavened Bread rather than the Passover. It is a typically unanimous and joyful festival (involving priests, Levites, and laymen), a very important factor for a feast in Chronicles. vv. 23–7, voluntary action is another important theme in Chronicles. It is underlined here by the fact that the whole assembly remains for a further seven days in celebration. A great sense of unity, joy, and generosity is prevalent amongst the king and the notables, and many animals are sacrificed. v. 26, the Chronicler's statement that such scenes had not been seen since the days of Solomon refers to the manner of the celebration alone and is a logical reference: after Solomon, the kingdom fell apart, but the present festivities give the impression that reunification may be possible. Such scenes are repeated only during Josiah's reign. Thus, the Chronicler mentions the kings with whom Hezekiah is to be compared: Solomon and Josiah. v. 27, at this point it is clear that the Chronicler wrote in post-exilic times: during the monarchical period it was the privilege of the kings, rather than the priests to bless the people, though the Chronicler does not entirely remove this element from his source (cf. 2 Sam 6:18; 1 Kings 8:14, 54–6; 2 Chr 6:3). The Levite priests bless the people, a concept the Chronicler derived from Josh 8:33 amongst others.

(31:1–21) Cultic Reform and the Reorganization of the Temple Service The Chronicler uses 2 Kings 18:4, 5–7 as a source model for this chapter, including the single-versed summary of Hezekiah's reforming measures (v. 4) and the assessment of their effectiveness (vv. 5–7). Both of these elements are strongly emended by the Chronicler to suit his purposes.

Within this frame, he inserts detailed descriptions of the temple tithes and their distribution (vv. 2–19).

v. 1 details the destruction of the cultic images. The brief mention of Hezekiah's reforming measures in the source model becomes a small part of the Chronicler's report on Hezekiah's reorganization here. Furthermore, the snake Nehushtan is ignored in Chronicles, perhaps because the idea that it derived from Moses was unpleasant to the Chronicler. Otherwise, the source model is greatly extended upon. The destruction of local cults by the entire population is unique in the OT and extends into the territory of the fallen northern kingdom, though this may be a reflection of events during the Chronicler's lifetime.

vv. 2–10, once the king has reinstalled the temple service, in which priests and Levites are mentioned in connection with their main duties (cf. 8:14; 23:18–19), he prepares orders regarding the tithes. These partly conform with the regulations found in the Pentateuch, though they no doubt reflect contemporary practice (or the Chronicler's ideal conception). The king is responsible for the sacrifices, whilst laymen undertake to support the priests and Levites financially. It is impossible to determine to what extent this really was the case during the monarchical period. The king after all carried the main responsibility for maintaining the cult. Reports from Persian times, which might have inspired the Chronicler, contradict each other. Whilst Darius states that the cult is financed by the state coffers, the book of Nehemiah (10:32–3) mentions a temple tithe for this purpose which is paid by everyone. The Chronicler spreads responsibility amongst the king and his people, thereby conforming with his own ideals. vv. 5–6, the king's word spreads with extreme speed and the first tithes are paid in abundance, i.e. correctly. This is another example of what the Chronicler might regard as lacking in his own society and what he expected from it. v. 7, the third month is the month of the grain harvest and at the same time the month of the harvest festival (Feast of weeks) whereas the Feast of Ingathering is celebrated in the seventh month which is the period of vine and fruit harvesting. vv. 9–10, the generosity also causes problems: the king approaches the priests and Levites and asks them to explain the great piles of donations (though the wording is vague). They repeat the message of v. 8 using different terms: generosity is rewarded by wealth and the Lord's blessing. Azariah: the chief priest under Solomon is also called Azariah. This may be the reason why the present chief priest has this name. Although David (and Solomon) are not explicitly mentioned in this chapter, it is clear that Hezekiah is portrayed in a similar light to them.

vv. 11–19, the tithes are stored and duties allocated. vv. 11–13, the king orders chambers either to be built or renovated in order to store the tithes. It is difficult to determine which of these two options is the case. Two Levites administer the tithes, offerings, and dedicated things (terms stemming from priestly literature and used slightly differently by the Chronicler here). They command ten men, leading to the round sum of twelve (which may be an organizational formula). vv. 14–19 describe the distribution of the offerings amongst the priests and Levites. Priests and Levites have the right to financial support, as carried out here. Several points in this text are difficult to comprehend, but the basic guidelines are clear: from the age of 3, all priests have the right to

support. They are registered according to their lineage and must have a purely priestly 'pedigree'. Distribution is made on the basis of the number of priests. Payment of Levites is made on the basis of the size of the family, whereby the eligible age is 30 years (see 1 CHR 23:3). (Levites rather than the priests are referred to in v. 18.) Distribution occurs both in Jerusalem and in the other cities. The main gatekeeper at the eastern gate and his six subordinates are responsible for it. v. 18, 'they were faithful in keeping themselves holy': one of the many statements praising the Levites which characterize Chronicles.

vv. 20–1, the verdict on Hezekiah: the source model upon which the Chronicler partly bases this chapter has more praise for Hezekiah than for any other king. The Chronicler's version seems weak by comparison, even though his praise is also great. This is, however, made good by his extensive description of Hezekiah's reign and the implicit praise within it. '[g]ood and right and faithful before the LORD': Hezekiah alone is given this threefold praise, and he alone is described as someone who was faithful.

(32:1–33) Jerusalem Saved from Sennacherib; Testing of Hezekiah What is true in many parts of Chronicles is particularly true in ch. 32: this chapter cannot be understood without knowledge of its source model (and of Isaiah's statements on Judah's behaviour whilst under threat from Sennacherib). The Chronicler uses his source texts as a framework for all important components of the story, but rewrites them to a great extent. He also makes severe cuts, especially regarding concrete information such as figures. According to the Chronicler, Sennacherib does not conquer the towns of Judah, nor does he besiege Jerusalem, but remains in Lachish. Moreover, Hezekiah, who, unlike the source model, has no fear, does not have to pay a tribute to the Assyrian king. The Chronicler even converts the two advances made by Rabshakeh and Sennacherib into a single event. It is notable that Hezekiah's prayer, in which the king underlines YHWH's exclusive existence, is also omitted. Beyond this, the Chronicler shortens the text further by almost entirely ignoring Isaiah, the protagonist of the source model and of the book named after him. He merely portrays Isaiah praying with Hezekiah and cites him in his list of sources at the end of the chapter.

Whilst the source model portrays a political Hezekiah, the Chronicler's king is a religious figure. In this sense it is surprising that he diverges from the source model to add extensive details concerning the defensive measures taken in vv. 2–6, 30 (though he does give military details elsewhere). He may have reinterpreted information given in Isa 22:8–11 in a curious way to come up with this information, though the critical consensus believes that he used his own sources to do so. vv. 23, 27–9 (especially concerning the economy), vv. 7–8 (a speech by Hezekiah), and vv. 25–6, 31b (theological comments), are the Chronicler's original material.

v. 1 is transitional. 'After these things and these acts of faithfulness': owing to his exemplary behaviour in connection with the cultic reforms, Hezekiah must immediately be rewarded—in the form of deliverance from Sennacherib—and not have to wait until the fourteenth year of his reign, as in the source model. Unlike in the earlier text, Sennacherib does not manage to conquer the fenced cities in Judah, but only intends to do so. vv. 2–6, defensive measures are taken. Since

Hezekiah has proved his God-fearing behaviour through his cultic reforms, he does not need to pray to YHWH, as would have normally been the case under such threatening circumstances. Instead he can concentrate his efforts on military defence measures. The Chronicler knew from his sources roughly what kind of measures these were (see 2 Kings 20:20 and particularly Isa 22:8–11). This is not contradicted by the fact that he describes and interprets them differently, especially by comparison with Isaiah (v. 11: 'But you did not look to him who did it'). Hezekiah concentrates on the water supply, carries out the necessary building works, acquires the weaponry required, and organizes his army. The general nature of his statements also suggests the absence of additional sources. vv. 6b–8, Hezekiah's encouraging speech is a patchwork of biblical expressions and statements, even using Isaiah to contradict Isaiah. v. 9, unlike the source model, Jerusalem is not besieged. This statement is an extreme and hardly justifiable interpretation of 2 Kings 19:32: 'He shall not come into this city'.

vv. 10–17, this speech by Sennacherib's servants summarizes the speeches made by Rabshakeh and the Assyrian king in the source model, whilst emphasizing different aspects. v. 10, unlike 2 Kings 18:21, the Assyrians are not even permitted to claim that Judah is reliant upon Egypt. It is almost as if they had heard Hezekiah's speech and respected it. Ironically, they phrase the most important question correctly: 'On what are you relying . . . ?' v. 12, 'Before one altar': a clarification and strengthening of the source model ('before this altar'). Just as there can be only one God, there can also be only one altar. If God wants to help, king Hezekiah has destroyed his altars! This is the logic used by Rabshakeh in 2 Kings 18:22. By making a slight change in the text, the Chronicler changes its emphasis: Can Hezekiah be trusted?

v. 18, even Rabshakeh's speech threatening Hezekiah and his people is alluded to: cf. 2 Kings 18:28, 27 (in that order). v. 19, this verse curiously breaks with the source model, following a very complicated line of interpretation. Unlike the source text, the conflict is based on nothing other than theological principles. The Assyrians speak of the God of Jerusalem as they do of all foreign deities (since they assume that Jerusalem will be conquered in a similar manner). They do not realize, however, that the deities of the peoples of the world are merely human creations. The Assyrians' speech and the Chronicler's comments on it are also summarized here. v. 20, unlike the account in the book of Isaiah, the prophet and King Hezekiah are not opponents here, but pray together side by side. This must be so since Hezekiah is a God-fearing man and therefore (like all prophets) on the right side. v. 21, cf. 2 Kings 19:35–7. 'And the LORD sent an angel': the source model makes the angel the active party, but this is not possible in the eyes of the Chronicler. He also omits the number of men killed and shortens the report on the unrest within the Babylonian royal family, mentioning no names. vv. 22–3, the Chronicler uses these two verses to interpret events, naturally emphasizing that Hezekiah's and Jerusalem's (aid and) salvation is due to YHWH.

vv. 24–6, according to the Chronicler, Hezekiah's illness must have been caused by a previous failing on his part. This sin may be his boastful behaviour during the Babylonian delegation's visit (2 Kings 20:12–15). The Chronicler, however, only mentions this visit in v. 31, without describing Hezekiah's behaviour. Despite knowing of Hezekiah's illness, the Chronicler knew of no sin he had committed. Is this the reason for describing his failing (arrogance and ingratitude) so briefly and vaguely? Hezekiah also behaves correctly by praying to his Lord and humbling himself. Such explanations can only be vague speculation. See comment on v. 31 regarding his miraculous recovery. vv. 27–9, God-fearing kings are wealthy and economically active, as the Chronicler confirms once more here. Such unspecific descriptions cannot stem from any non-biblical sources, but are his own invention.

v. 31, 2 Kings 20:12 specifically reports that the Babylonian delegation came to Jerusalem because they had heard of Hezekiah's illness. The Chronicler probably assumes knowledge of this fact. 'The sign that had been done in the land': does he mean the reverse movement of the sundial (2 Kings 20:8–11) or the king's recovery? Perhaps the two events should not be separated too strictly. Since the Babylonians were famous for their astrology, the reader at least initially would have thought of the sundial's reversal. The nature of Hezekiah's temptation is stated explicitly ('God left him to himself; in order to . . . know all that was in his heart') and is taken from Deut 8:2. Is Hezekiah's humility (v. 26) being tested here? The verse does not state the outcome, though it is obvious.

vv. 32–3 are the concluding verdict on the king. v. 32, instead of 'all his power' (source text) that Hezekiah is reported to have obtained, the Chronicler describes his 'good deeds', a term used elsewhere only to describe Josiah (35:26). According to the Hebrew text (and unlike some translations), the History of the Prophet Isaiah forms part of the Book of the Kings of Judah and Israel. The author is therefore the most important prophet of that period. It is impossible to determine whether the Hebrew text is meant to refer to Hezekiah's burial-site (Galling: 1954: 166: the upper level of a double-layered royal burial site situated on a hill to the south-west) or whether it serves to emphasize the special honour his funeral received. Whatever is the case, Hezekiah receives one of the most impressive burials given to kings in Chronicles.

Manasseh and Amon (2 Chr 33:1–25)

(33:1–20) Manasseh Manasseh, who is historically regarded as having been an exceptionally skilful ruler, remained on David's throne longer than any other king, for 55 years. The books of Kings portray him as the most godless king of all and describe at great length his disgraceful behaviour which leads to the downfall of Judah (2 Kings 21:1–18). The Chronicler changes none of the account's factual content, but rewrites Manasseh's biography to conform with his implicit principle that a long reign is a result of God-fearing behaviour. He therefore causes Manasseh to repent during his deportation to Babylon. On his return to Jerusalem, he removes all foreign images and carries out the usual construction measures. The story of Manasseh is a spectacular indication of the strict dogma of retribution applied in Chronicles, combined with the constant opportunity to repent. It serves as an image with which to comment on the forthcoming theme of exile and return, stressing that the Judeans will always have the chance to return to their homeland. The chapter also contains a hidden reference to the Babylonian Exile. This theory is supported by the fact that Manasseh is deported to Babylon, instead of the historically more plausible Assyrian capital.

The historical reliability of Manasseh's deportation to Babylon has occasionally been claimed on the basis of the following points: Manasseh was encouraged by the unrest led by Ashurbanipal's brother Shamash-shum-ukin in 652–648 and became unruly himself. He was thereupon deported to Babylon before being allowed to return as ruler. Some commentaries have referred to the Egyptian pharaoh Neco, who was deported by Ashurbanipal and later returned to his homeland. This assumption is contradicted by the fact that the Assyrian annals describe Manasseh as a consistently loyal vassal, and that his journey to Babylon would certainly have been mentioned in Kings if it had any historical basis. However convincing the story seems, it is therefore more probably an invention inspired by the Babylonian Exile and biblical material.

vv. 1–9, the Chronicler closely follows his source model here, with a few minor changes. v. 10, at this point in the source model (2 Kings 21:10–15) there is a lengthy prophetic speech to Manasseh predicting Judah's downfall. It is followed by a comment that Manasseh shed innocent blood in abundance. The Chronicler omits the last comment completely and replaces the speech (which he cannot include due to its content) with a comment that Manasseh and the people did not heed God's warning.

vv. 11–13, the advancing Assyrians' treatment of Manasseh is based on the similar treatment of Jehoiachin (Ezek 19:9; 2 Chr 36:10). The Chronicler probably also used 2 Kings 19:28 as a literary source: the Assyrian king is called upon to wear a ring through his nose so that he could be dragged back up the road down which he was advancing. vv. 12–13, Manasseh does exactly what is expected of a sinful king. He humbles himself and prays to God, as instructed by the temple-consecration prayer (cf. 6:36–9; 7:14). The reaction is swift: the Lord (and not the Assyrian king!) allows the king to return to Jerusalem.

vv. 14–17 relate Manasseh's actions after his return to the throne. Like many God-fearing kings, Manasseh is shown God's blessing by being allowed to carry out construction projects and build fortresses in Jerusalem and Judah. It is unlikely that this report is based on historically reliable sources, although it would not be surprising if he strengthened his fortification following Sennacherib's campaigns in Judah.

(33:21–5) Amon The description of Amon's rule is also brief in the source model. The Chronicler makes slight changes to make it conform with his depiction of Manasseh, as a godless king.

Josiah (2 Chr 34:1–35:27)

(34:1–33) Renewal of the Cult; Reinstatement of the Law; Confirmation of the Covenant 2 Kings 22–3 describes how in the eighteenth year of his reign, Josiah coincidentally discovers a book (which can easily be identified as Deuteronomy), upon which he undertakes a comprehensive reform of the cult, combined with its centralization in Jerusalem. The Chronicler could not use this version without changing it, for several reasons. Josiah, who is judged positively, cannot begin his reforms as late as his eighteenth year of reign, since the

delay would constitute a sin. His reforms must also be different from those in the source model, since in Chronicles, Manasseh had already taken similar measures and his son Amon had not resumed all of Manasseh's old, godless rituals. Since the Chronicler did not wish to change the date at which the book is found (it is the entire Pentateuch, rather than simply Deuteronomy here), he weakens the significance of the discovery by making Josiah's reforms pre-empt it. It is thus not a case of coincidence, but the king's God-fearing will that brings improvement. This explains the changes to the source text undertaken by the Chronicler. Many points are summarized descriptions of the source model, in which details are omitted, whilst other areas are expanded to accommodate some of his favourite theologoumena and opinions, i.e. the Levites, the inclusion of the north, etc. At first sight, his somewhat weaker praise for Josiah may be surprising, since he is one of his favourite kings. But Josiah died on the battlefield and therefore must have committed some previous sin. The Chronicler's description of the process of reforms is more historically reliable than his source. All alterations are dictated by the Chronicler's own specific profile.

vv. 3–7 detail cultic reforms. Since Manasseh had already cleansed the temple (33:15) and Amon had hardly changed this, the present king must concentrate on cleansing the country, first Judah and Jerusalem (vv. 3–5), and later also the north (vv. 6–7). Unlike the source model, Chronicles merely summarizes this report. v. 3, although still young (16 years old), Josiah already begins to seek God (one of the Chronicler's favourite phrases). Since he is not yet of age, he does not undertake any public measures. These are carried out in the twelfth year of his reign, i.e. in adulthood. vv. 6–7, the inclusion of the north in his reform of the legitimate kingdom plays a central role in Chronicles here (cf. vv. 9, 21, 33) and later in 35:17–18. v. 7, 'he returned to Jerusalem': with this statement, which relates to 2 Kings 23:20, the Chronicler underlines that the king is personally responsible for the named undertaking.

vv. 8–13 describe donations for the temple's improvement. The Chronicler extends a relatively brief order to collect money to pay for the necessary improvements to the temple, transforming it into an extensive report. v. 9, in his description of the collection of tithes (from the entire population)— cf. 24:5–9 and David's approach in connection with the temple's construction (1 Chr 29), the Chronicler emphasizes the co-operation of all the people more strongly than does the source text, listing those involved (including people from the north). vv. 12–13, the workmen *work* honestly (source model: *deal* honestly). The Chronicler highly esteems good work. Going beyond his source model, the Chronicler names those responsible. They are naturally Levites who have similar duties to those in 1 Chr 26, though they perform these tasks for Josiah only in Chronicles. One would expect from 29:12 that Gershonites were among them. Perhaps the singers mentioned here dictated the rhythm of their work with their music.

vv. 14–33, document the discovery of the book of the law, its study, and the renewal of the covenant. Apart from some minor details, the Chronicler follows his source text here. v. 14, first the money for the temple, then the book: this amendment to the source model once again underlines the

Chronicler's outlook. The book is found because Josiah and his people behave in an exemplary manner. It is not clear where the book of the law, which was written by Moses (though only in the Chronicles version), was discovered. Since not only Deuteronomy, but the entire Pentateuch is discovered in Chronicles, it is not surprising that Shaphan reads 'from' it (in Heb. text; source model: read it) rather than all of it, before the king (cf. v. 18). v. 24 has 'all the curses that are written in the book', instead of the source model's 'all the words of the book'. Perhaps the Chronicler was thinking of Lev 26; Deut 27–9 here. v. 30, 'the Levites' (source model: 'the prophets'): this slight change displays the Chronicler's conviction that the Levites have 'replaced' the prophets to some extent by his own lifetime and fulfil their role of announcing God's word. This replacement does not, however, represent a demotion of the prophets, who still have their place of honour in Chronicles. v. 33 is an extremely shortened summary of 2 Kings 23:4–20 and seems to contradict vv. 3–7, which already mention the cult's cleansing. The two passages use different terms, however, so it is possible that the Chronicler is describing two different forms of cleansing.

(35:1–27) The Passover and Josiah's Death This chapter can be divided into three parts: the extensive description of the Passover feast, which Josiah feels obliged to celebrate after his reforms, the report on Josiah's death, and the concluding verdict upon him. The Chronicler uses his source model for all three parts of the chapter, but greatly changes and extends the material in the first two parts in order to apply his cultic and theological priorities to the king he loved so much. It is unlikely that these additions (regarding the Passover feast) and alterations (in connection with Josiah's death) are based on older sources not present in the OT.

vv. 1–19, the special features of the Passover feast carried out by Josiah can be explained almost entirely by the following factors: (1) The OT contains contradictory instructions regarding the Passover. Whilst it is a feast celebrated within the family in Ex 12, during which sacrificial animals are roasted, Deut 16 describes it as a ritual performed in the central holy place (in Jerusalem) at which the sacrificial animals are boiled. (2) The main difference between the Passover feasts of Hezekiah and Josiah is that Josiah's is not celebrated with such great haste. Its liturgy is also described more extensively. To a certain extent, Josiah represents a solid, legal version of what Hezekiah put into place. This is emphasized by the Chronicler's lengthy explanation of the 'legal' basis of the feast (Moses, David/Solomon, Josiah). This order is probably both the Chronicler's concept of an ideal procedure and common practice during his lifetime, though it is difficult to determine which factor is decisive. (3) The Chronicler firmly places his beloved Levites (and musicians) into the Passover procedures. (4) He links well-being offerings with the Passover procedures in an obscure way. (5) As so often, he uses speeches to express his own theological convictions.

vv. 1–9 (10) detail the preparations. v. 1, as implicitly suggested in Deut 16, the feast takes place in Jerusalem on the appointed day. v. 3. 'Put the holy ark in the house . . .': does this appeal suggest that the ark had been removed from the temple, perhaps during Manasseh's reign, or is it a literary technique to mark the renewal of the cult? It could even be the

result of textual damage. vv. 4, 6, cf. comments on David (1 Chr 23–7) and Solomon (2 Chr 8:14) concerning the ancestral houses and their order. Moses did not lay down a law regarding this aspect, unlike the Passover procedure itself, to which the last verse exclusively refers (cf. v. 13). vv. 7–9, as with the temple construction and King Hezekiah's Passover feast, King Josiah and his officials (in this case the princes and the notable Levites—but not priests) are characterized by their generosity. One of the Chronicler's keywords, 'willingly', is repeated here.

vv. 10–15, once the king's instructions have been carried out, the actual sacrifice takes place. Here the priests are limited to their central role of performing the blood ritual and offering the sacrifice, whilst the Levites make all the necessary preparations (a role reserved for laymen according to Leviticus). This included slaughtering the animals, skinning them, receiving the roasted/boiled meat, and distributing it amongst themselves and the musicians so that they can continue their own duties. The Levites are therefore presented as an essential part of the ritual. v. 13, 'they boiled in the fire' (literal translation from the Heb.); the Chronicler uses this unusual phrase to combine the two contradictory instructions in Ex 12:8–9 and Deut 16:7. '[Q]uickly' emphasizes the Levites' good work whilst simultaneously referring to Exodus' instructions to consume the Passover quickly (Ex 12:11). v. 15, the musicians are first called the 'descendants of Asaph' after their most important ancestor and are then listed according to their families.

vv. 16–17 actually summarize the re-establishment of a religious service which was probably also attended by people from the northern kingdom. The Feast of Unleavened Bread follows immediately after the Passover, though, unlike in Hezekiah's account, is not dealt with in detail.

vv. 18–19, the unique nature of this Passover feast in Kings is due to its central celebration in Jerusalem. This is not the case in Chronicles since Hezekiah's Passover had also been performed in the capital. The unique aspect here is its place in cultic history, since Hezekiah's feast was not correctly prepared for. v. 18, 'since the days of the prophet Samuel' replaces 'since the days of the judges' in the source model. The Chronicler hardly mentions the judges period in general. Since Samuel is regarded as the final judge of the period, the Chronicler is relatively correct in his statement, but is able to simultaneously mention one of the prophets he likes so much.

vv. 20–7, the Chronicler takes the brief note concerning Josiah's death in his source, whilst altering and greatly extending it. Some commentaries have regarded this report as historically more reliable than the source text, although most of its inconsistencies can be explained by the Chronicler's personal perspective. The source model incorrectly states that the Egyptian pharaoh led a campaign against the Assyrians. In fact the pharaoh advanced in support of the Assyrian king, a fact that the Chronicler does not explicitly state. The reference to Carchemish on the Euphrates (v. 20) probably stems from Jer 46:2, since the wording is similar to this passage. However, another interpretation has been suggested: the Assyrian King Ashuruballit founded his new capital city in 610 BCE. The Egyptians supported the Assyrians at this time, as can be seen from the counter-offensive against the Babylonians in 609. Ch. 35 must therefore be regarded in the light of these events. We suggest, however, that the entire section must be understood from the perspective of Josiah's violent death. According to the Chronicler's logic, it is an indication of the king's previous sin. Since there is no mention of such a sin in the source model, the Chronicler is forced to invent one. He has great affection for the king, however, so he places his fall from grace as late as possible, upon the battlefield. Thus he creates the rather unconvincing literary construction by which Josiah rejects the word of God. (The heathen Neco is naturally not permitted to use his name and thus uses the word 'God' instead.) Josiah, who is expected to believe the heathen king's claims (!), insists on meeting him in battle (of which there is no description in the source model) and is killed. His armour, his wounding, and his order to be taken to Jerusalem are not an indication of supplementary information, since the description is based on Ahab's fate. He too dressed for battle, defied God's warning, was wounded, and ordered his men to withdraw (1 Kings 22:30, 34). The astonishing comparison between Josiah and the godless Ahab is probably due to the fact that he was the closest comparable figure who committed a sin on the battlefield.

vv. 24b–25, ultimately, the Chronicler regards Josiah's (only!) sin as not sufficiently grave to deny him an honourable funeral, although this contradicts his own logic. Indeed all Judah and Jerusalem mourn for him, a unique description in Chronicles. Jeremiah even composes a lament to commemorate him which is still included in all laments 'to this day'. Thus the song must be included in all future laments. This may be the biblical parallel to the tradition maintained in the Talmud ascribing Lamentations to Jeremiah. Perhaps the Chronicler is referring to Zech 12:9–14 here, since it also seems to refer to Josiah's death.

The Last Kings of Judah, the Fall of Judah, and Cyrus's Edict (2 Chr 36:1–23)

The Chronicler further reduces his source's rather brief description of the history of Judah's final four kings (to less than half its original length), although he not only deletes material, but also adds a small amount of his own. Above all, he omits the details concerning Jerusalem's destruction, the names of the queen mothers, part of the verdicts on the kings, even certain death announcements (because the relevant kings died in a foreign land), and further Deuteronomistic interpretations of Jerusalem's destruction (as due to Manasseh's sins, 2 Kings 24:3; cf. v. 20). Thus the kings are shifted closely together— forming a kind of indistinguishable *massa perditionis*—giving the story greater unity than its source model. The Chronicler's additions refer to the temple, whose fate is important to the author. His descriptions of the people's responsibility (and their forthcoming downfall) are characterized not so much by colourful details as by strong theological argument.

The deportation of the survivors of Judah is described in one verse (v. 20) which also contains mention of the Persian successors to Babylon. Only v. 21 contains an interpretation (and not a description) of the Exile ('until the land had made up for its sabbaths') and part of the edict of Cyrus as described in the book of Ezra, which allowed deported Jews to return to Jerusalem and rebuild the temple. This description has the effect of concealing the Exile whilst not denying its existence,

allowing the Chronicler to close his work with an image of the temple.

(36:1–4) Jehoahaz The Chronicler's description of Jehoahaz is extremely brief and omits details concerning his journey to the land of Hamath. The concluding judgement upon him is completely ignored (as is the case with Abijah, the only other king to receive such treatment). Is this the result of his short reign, a damaged text, or perhaps the fact that Jeremiah gives him a positive verdict (Jer 22:15–16)?

(36:5–8) Jehoiakim This section contains the usual omissions from the source model. The advance of an alliance of Chaldeans, Arameans, Moabites, and Ammonites (which God had incited!—2 Kings 24:2) is replaced in Chronicles by the claim that Nebuchadnezzar attacked the king, placed him in fetters and deported him to Babylon. The Chronicler probably extracted this information from Dan 1:1–2 and it can hardly be regarded as historically reliable. The last kings of Judah were all deported. Here, Jehoiakim receives the same treatment as Manasseh, though it is unclear whether he is actually deported or whether the Babylonians merely intend to do so, since the Hebrew text allows both interpretations. v. 7, the Chronicler is most interested in the fate of the temple and its equipment (see also vv. 10, 18–19) and uses Dan 1:2 as a source for his description.

(36:9–10) Jehoiachin The source model portrays a comprehensive deportation (597 BCE) which does not differ completely from the second transportation. The Chronicler, however, reduces Jehoiachin's description to an absolute minimum, concentrating on the king's deportation and the (valuable— note the emphasis compared with v. 7) temple equipment.

(36:11–16) Zedekiah The Chronicler applies the same editing principles for Zedekiah as he used for the previous three kings, describing events as briefly as possible. He does, however, introduce new emphases compared with the previous kings. He does not directly report Zedekiah's deportation (cf. the three previous kings), which disappears in the mass of deportations carried out. This is probably an attempt to protect the Davidic monarchy, to which he still clings. Nor is his description of the pillage of the cultic vessels extensive (cf. v. 18 and 2 Kings 25:13–17), since the central issue of importance to the Chronicler is the mere fact of the deportation, rather than individual details. He is of course more extensive in his description of Zedekiah and the people democratically bound to him than in the description of the three previous kings, but there is one reason for this: since each generation and every king is responsible for their own fate, the sins committed by Zedekiah, his notables, and the people must have been great. The source model has little to report here (since the Exile is seen as the result of Manasseh's sin): 'He did what was evil in the sight of the LORD, just as Jehoiakim had done' (2 Kings 24:19). The Chronicler uses this reference to Jehoiakim to make further additions. He (explicitly) points out Zedekiah's disobedience towards Jeremiah (who plays a central role in the background of the entire chapter) and the king's lack of willingness to repent. Furthermore he makes general criticisms, such as that the princes and people were disobedient towards the prophets. This section contains many references to biblical texts, which cannot all be listed here. One reason for this plethora is the notion that what the prophets predicted, based on the law, has come about.

v. 14 underlines the fact that the people and the people's leading ranks (perhaps with the exception of the Levites, who remain unnamed) are responsible for their own exile. The accusations are extremely harsh since active spoiling of the temple—consecrated by God—is described only here. vv. 15–16, apart from Jeremiah, other (unnamed) prophets are mentioned, whose mission is not described by the Chronicler (perhaps because it would in any case have been unsuccessful), but can only be to bring the king and his people to repentance. The motive behind God's invitation to repent is stated, however: compassion for both the people and the temple. It is significant that the people and the temple have the same status here. The language is once again strongly influenced by the book of Jeremiah.

(36:17–21) The End of Judah v. 18, the plundering of the temple reaches a climax: 'All the vessels of the house of God'. In addition, the king's and princes' private treasures are taken. v. 19, Jerusalem's actual destruction is portrayed in a few words. Thus the Chronicler's mention of the 'palaces' is even more striking. v. 20, the Chronicler intentionally omits the source model's mention of vineyard and field workers who remained on the land, concentrating his description of this last phase on Jerusalem, leaving the question of those who remained unanswered. The experience of the Exile is not described at all. v. 21, this sentence combines Jeremiah's announcement of 70 years of exile (Jer 25:11–12) with the warning made in Lev 26, in which the land spits out disobedient dwellers, to restore peace and enable the long-abused sabbath to be observed.

(36:22–3) Cyrus's Edict vv. 22–3, after the extremely brief treatment of the Exile, the Chronicler moves directly on to the Persian King Cyrus's order enabling a return, a central theme of which is his permission to rebuild the temple. The Chronicler bases his text on Ezra here, even quoting it occasionally (cf. Ezra 1:1–3). This is nevertheless no proof that Chronicles, Ezra, and Nehemiah form a Chronicler's history and were only separated at a later date. The Paraleipomena have an open ending, with the appeal, 'Let him go up'. This may encourage the reader to refer to the events described in Ezra and Nehemiah, but can also be regarded as a reference to the future in general.

REFERENCES

Albertz, R. (1992), *Religionsgeschichte Israels in alttestamentlicher Zeit*, Grundrisse zum Alten Testament 8 (Göttingen: Vandenhoeck & Ruprecht).

Avigad, N. (1976), *Bullae and Seals from a Post-Exilic Judaen Archive*, Qedem 4 (Jerusalem: Institute of Archaeology, Hebrew University of Jerusalem).

Cross, F. M. (1975): 'A Reconstruction of the Judean Restoration', JBL 94: 4–18.

Galling, K. (1954), *Die Bücher der Chronik, Esra, Nehemia*, Das Alte Testament Deutsch 12 (Göttingen: Vandenhoeck & Ruprecht).

Japhet, S. (1993), *I & II Chronicles: A Commentary*, OTL (London: SCM).

——(1997), *The Ideology of the Book of Chronicles and Its Place in Biblical Thought*, 2nd edn. BEAT 9 (Frankfurt a.M.).

Junge, E. (1937), *Der Wiederaufbau des Heerwesens des Reiches Juda unter Josia*, Beiträge zur Wissenschaft vom Alten und Neuen Testament 75 (Stuttgart: Kohlhammer).

Knauf, E. A. (1995), 'Zum Verhältnis von Esra 1, 1 zu 2 Chronik 36,20–23', *Biblische Notizen*, 78: 16–17.

Noth, M. (1944–5), 'Eine palästinische Lokalüberlieferung in 2. Chr. 20', *Zeitschrift des Deutschen Palästina-Vereins*, 67: 45–71.

Rad, G. von (1958), 'Die levitische Predigt in den Büchern der Chronik' in *Gesammelte Studien zum Alten Testament*, Theologische Bücherei 8 (Munich: Christian Kaiser), 248–61.

Rudolph, W. (1955), *Chronikbücher*, HAT 21 (Tübingen: Mohr [Siebeck]).

Tarn, W. W. (1941), *Hellenistic Civilisation*, 2nd edn. (London: Edward Arnold).

Wellhausen, J. (1886), *Prolegomena zur Geschichte Israels*, 3rd edn. (Berlin: Georg Reimer).

Welten, P. (1973), *Geschichte und Geschichtsdarstellung in den Chronikbüchern*, WMANT 42 (Neukirchen-Vluyn: Neukirchener Verlag).

Willi, T. (1972), *Die Chronik als Auslegung: Untersuchungen zur literarischen Gestaltung der historischen Überlieferungen Israels*, FRLANT 106 (Göttingen: Vandenhoeck & Ruprecht).

Williamson, H. G. M. (1987), *1 and 2 Chronicles*, NCB (Grand Rapids: Eerdmans).

15. Ezra–Nehemiah
DANIEL L. SMITH-CHRISTOPHER

INTRODUCTION

A. Text and Language. 1. Originally one work (*b. B. Bat.* 14b–15a); Eusebius, *Hist. eccl.* 4.26.14), the books of Ezra and Nehemiah share themes, and even specific texts (the most obvious being what is called the Golah List, Ezra 2 || Neh 7, *gôlâ* meaning 'exile'). In addition, the main character changes from Ezra, then to Nehemiah, and then back to Ezra, etc. The short books are composed largely in late biblical Hebrew, but contain significant sections (Ezra 4:8–6:18; 7:12–26) written in what is often referred to as imperial or official Aramaic (Rosenthal 1974). By general consensus, the texts are well preserved (Rudolph 1949: p. xix). There are fragments of Ezra among the Dead Sea scrolls (4QEzra) which are quite close to the Hebrew and Aramaic sections of the MT (only 4:2–6 in Heb.; 4:9–11; 5:17–6:5 in Aramaic). The text occasionally reflects Old Persian vocabulary (for a list: Fensham 1982: 22), but there is little significant influence from Greek.

2. There are two translations in Greek, known as Esdras *alpha* (1 Esdras) and Esdras *beta*. Esdras *beta* is quite close to the canonical work, but 1 Esdras is an independent work which reproduces *only* the Ezra materials (including the reading of the law which appears in MT Neh 7:72–8:13 (1 Esd 9:37–55; see the helpful discussion in Myers 1974: 1–19)). 1 Esdras includes a charming court tale of Zerubbabel very much in the Daniel tradition. Certain readings in 1 Esdras can be used to correct difficulties in the MT (note list in Rudolph, 1949: p. xvi) but in general it is considered a later text featuring a free rendering into Greek.

B. Subject-Matter and Literary Genre. Contemporary scholarship has formed an uneasy consensus around the notion that Ezra and Nehemiah had their origin in two separate 'memoirs' from the two historical figures in *c.*460–440 BCE. But why were they written? Some have suggested comparisons with official reports written to the Persian monarch (Blenkinsopp 1988: 262), while others have suggested that, at least in the case of the Nehemiah memoirs, they were originally written as a defence against accusations of sedition. Others have suggested biblical precedents such as psalms of lament or defence (so Kellermann 1967). To these memoirs were joined two sorts of supporting materials. First, older correspondence and documents involving both local and imperial Persian authorities provided the material for Ezra chs. 1–6. Secondly, a series of lists was added (the dates are debated), most prominently the Golah List of Ezra ch. 2 || Neh ch. 7. The many lists form one of the most perplexing features of the work.

C. The Religious Teaching. The main issue in Ezra and Nehemiah is the restoration of the post-exilic Judean community. There is a contrast established between the 'official' methods and attitudes of Nehemiah, whatever his title or authority may have actually been, and the more theologically based authority of the priest/scribe Ezra. Nehemiah's focus is on the physical infrastructure—particularly the city wall around Jerusalem. Ezra, on the other hand, is intent on the restoration of the Mosaic law as the spiritual centre of the post-exilic community. Otherwise, both are Jewish officials or leaders (Ezra 7:1–10; Neh 2:1–2) who become concerned about the state of affairs amongst the Jews in Jerusalem; both seek permission from the Persian monarch to carry out their mission (Ezra, implied in 7:6; Neh 2:1–4); both preside over a number of significant reforms in the Jewish communities in Jerusalem; both write of their experiences in the first person. Noting this, Eskenazi (1988) points out that the editorial tendency is towards a preference for Ezra: 'The Omniscient narrator...corroborates Ezra's assessment of reality by repeated references to divine support for Ezra' (ibid. 134). The contrast between the two figures can, however, be taken in other directions. Kapelrud (1944) based his doubts about the very existence of a historical Ezra on this same literary parallelism. Smitten (1973: 88; echoing the earlier work of Torrey (1970)) agrees, considering Ezra a pious fiction created from priestly imagination in order to contrast proper religious conduct against that of Nehemiah (objections include Williamson 1985: 115–16, and Blenkinsopp 1988: 216).

D. Date and Place of Composition. 1. Despite the fact that many of the scenes of the Ezra and Nehemiah story take place in the eastern diaspora in the Persian empire (so reminiscent of court stories such as Daniel and Esther), the movement of the narratives is clearly towards the resettled community in Judah. The narrative ends rather suddenly after the rededication of the temple in Neh 11–12, followed by some afterthoughts in ch. 13. We do not know the fate of either Ezra or Nehemiah.

2. Although we know of important events in the Persian period from Greek sources (pre-eminently Herodotus, *Hist.*), none of these is explicitly referred to in Ezra or Nehemiah. This is particularly problematic given that this was a notably unstable era in the Persian empire (Dandamaev 1989: 351–4). Despite this, the memoirs surely arose within a short time of the work of both Ezra and Nehemiah, and the correspondence between local and imperial Persian officials in Ezra 1–6 may well date from the time of the Persian emperors named. Thus, the events mentioned give us an earliest possible date for the traditions, beginning with the conquest of Babylon by Cyrus in 539 BCE. The last clear reference, Neh 12:22–3, is to Jaddua, high priest at the time of Alexander the Great, according to Josephus, and dated to roughly 323 (Clines 1984: 222; Blenkinsopp 1988: 340), but this reference is almost universally considered to be an insertion by a very late hand, in order to bring the list down to the editor's time. It would therefore be hazardous to use this as an indication of the completion of most of the book, which was undoubtedly in more or less present form by the late fifth century (430–400 BCE).

E. Literary and Historical Problems. 1. Among the more vexed problems of Ezra–Nehemiah scholarship is the problem of determining the historical relationship of the presumed historical figures of Ezra and Nehemiah: Who came first? Did their time in Judah overlap? Another problem has been the possible relationship to the writings of the Chronicler. We can only briefly review these questions here, beginning with the latter question on the relationship to Chronicles.

2. Chronicles ends with the same phrases with which Ezra begins—the suggestion has often been made that they are originally intended to be parts of one work. Among modern commentators, Blenkinsopp (1988: 47–54) defends this unity on both lexical and thematic grounds (David as founder of temple, interest in the details of temple construction and worship, etc.). But as Williamson (1985: pp. xx–xxii), in agreement with the arguments of Japhet (1968), concludes, there are good historical grounds for considering Ezra–Nehemiah as a single work that predates the creation of 1 Esdras, and therefore 1 Esdras cannot be used as an argument that Ezra–Nehemiah were originally the ending of a large work that included Chronicles. These arguments tend towards surveys of lexical comparisons between the two works, including stylistic features. Williamson further argues that Ezra–Nehemiah was completed in three stages: (1) the writing of the primary memoirs of Ezra and Nehemiah, close to their actual lifetimes; (2) a combination of materials that resulted in Ezra 7–Neh 13 (with some parts added later); and (3) the final addition of Ezra 1–6. Although admittedly without great confidence, the presumption of this commentary on Ezra–Nehemiah tends towards reading it separately from Chronicles, except for some thematic and historical similarities which need not depend on common authorship, but simply common historical and sociological circumstances.

3. The problem of when Ezra and Nehemiah arrived in Jerusalem is also complex, and made more so by the number of rulers named Artaxerxes, and the popularity of similar Jewish names among the exilic communities! In short, the same name cannot always be taken to be the same person. For example, the seventh year of Artaxerxes I would be the traditional date for Ezra of 458 BCE, before the date of Nehemiah's opening memoirs, which would be 446 BCE (there is little debate that Nehemiah served under Artaxerxes I). But if it is

Artaxerxes II, then the major alternative argument suggests that Ezra arrived in Jerusalem years after Nehemiah, in 398 BCE. Arguments between these options are not decisive, but more recent trends have accepted that Nehemiah's actions make more sense *following* the precedent of Ezra's legal reforms, rather than preceding them. Nehemiah's reforms on mixed marriage, for example, seem more focused than Ezra's general actions, and tend towards heightening the severity of Nehemiah's judgement against local authorities who still did not comply with what the local population had already dealt with! Williamson (1985: p. xliv), too, notes that Nehemiah's actions did not raise the local controversies that Ezra's actions did, suggesting that by Nehemiah's time these were not generally perceived as controversial actions. Still, Ezra 9:9 raises questions about whether a wall had already been built. Again, risking a position on shifting sands, this commentary will presume that Ezra arrived before Nehemiah, and both engaged in their work (or, to be more precise, the text represents their work) during the reign of Artaxerxes I Longimanus (465–424 BCE) as opposed to the later Artaxerxes II Arsakes (405–359 BCE).

F. The Sociology of Reading Ezra and Nehemiah. 1. Recent work on Ezra and Nehemiah has focused on the presumed relationship between the post-exilic returning Golah community, and the Persian administration. Nehemiah's mission was part of Persian attempts to shore up their western flank in the face of growing Greek involvement in Egyptian rebellions (Hoglund 1992). Berquist (1995) goes further in arguing that the Jewish officials were enthusiastic supporters of Persian goals, and that the court of Darius may have been the workroom for the Torah itself as a civil code for the Jewish subjects. Related to this, Richards (forthcoming) argues for a recognition of 'the ideological collusion of the Ezra-Nehemiah text with Persian colonial ideology'. To a greater or lesser degree, these recent statements share an assumption of complicity with Persian imperial policy in both Ezra and Nehemiah. But it is possible to read Ezra, particularly, in a different light.

2. If one reads from an assumption of the social realities of occupied Judah under Persian imperial power, then one ought to read with attention to the vastly underestimated varieties of ways in which subordinated peoples resist a militarily superior force other than open confrontation (cf. Scott 1985). Reading Ezra's prayer (Neh 9) surely gives one pause ('Here we are, slaves in our own land!'). Further, the only occasion in Ezra–Nehemiah that actually gives us a reason for drawing up a list of personal names is Ezra 5:4, where the situation is of a Persian official wanting to report specific names because he suspects them of rebellious activity. When read in the context of minority strategies of resistance and circumstances of colonialism (see also Fanon 1963; Raboteau 1978; White 1983; Lanternari 1963, and Memmi 1965), Ezra and Nehemiah can be understood quite differently, and it is precisely this postcolonial sociology of resistance that informs the critical reading of Ezra and Nehemiah that is presumed in this commentary.

G. Nehemiah and the Persian Court. Neh 1:1–2:8, normally read as part of the 'Memoirs' of Nehemiah, is surely fanciful legend. Nehemiah's relationship with the emperor is another example of a standard element of Hebrew diaspora legend, so reminiscent of the tales of Daniel, Joseph, and Esther. Cook (1983: 132) reports that 'The King lived largely in seclusion; he is said by Xenophon to have prided himself on being inaccessible'. Georges (1994: 49) discusses that fact that the Persian court fascinated the Greeks—mainly because of the mystery of court life—the Persians in general remained a 'tabula rasa upon which the Greeks drew a portrait in their own idiom'. Persians kept aloof from their subjects 'by the gorgeous and impermeable carapace of formal protocol'. When the few Greeks that did attend court were there, they were 'buffered by courtiers and interpreters' to maintain the remove of the emperor surrounded by the symbols of power and control over his slaves or bondsmen (as all subjects were considered: Cook 1983: 132, 249 n. 3). Indeed, Xenophon (*Cyro.* 8.2.7) admired such power, 'Who else but the King has ever had the power to punish enemies at many months distance?' Georges comments that even Ctesias, who supposedly had close connections to the emperor as a court physician, probably reads like so much harem gossip precisely because his contact with the court (even if authentic) was not so direct as we may imagine (Georges 51). Finally, Dandamaev (1989: 12) raises the prospect of court tales being concocted within the Persian court itself to discredit former royal lines or figures in order to justify changes in administration or policy. One is left with the impression of a Jewish lower official, whose actual relationship to the emperor (if any of the court tale is historical) has become at the very least highly exaggerated in ancient Hebrew imagination—and thus we are more alert to the more negative elements of this story, such as Nehemiah's fear before the emperor, and the reference to God's protection when he stood before 'this man'.

H. The Walls of Jerusalem. 1. Discussions about the possible royal associations of Nehemiah often overlook the fact that wall-building is seen as royal responsibility *par excellence* in the late historical work of the Chronicler (2 Chr 8:5; 11:11; 14:6; 17:2; 26:9; 27:3–4; 32:4–5; 33:14, 34; cf. Ps 51:18 and 1 Macc 4:60–1; 12:38; 14:32–4). Further, breaches in the walls of Jerusalem are causes for painful reflection (2 Kings 25:4; Ps 144:14; Lam 2:8, 18). Visions of peace speak of Jerusalem without walls, or with doors always open (Ezek 38:11; Zech 2:5; less certainly Isa 60:11). In his classic study, Mumford (1961) writes of the significance of the wall as part of social and political symbolism: 'what we now call "monumental architecture" is first of all the expression of power...the purpose of this art was to produce respectful terror'.

2. A great deal of effort has been expended on the geographical references in Nehemiah, but Avigad (1983: 62) concludes: 'no generally accepted solution for the problem of Nehemiah's wall has emerged'. The importance of wall-building for city defence is reviewed in the classic work of Yadin (1963: 19, 70–1, 313–28). Notably, city gates were the most vulnerable section of the wall, not only because of the weakness of the fortification, but also because battering-rams could cross hostile terrain without siege ramps. Nehemiah's later attention to the gates, therefore, was a necessary precaution (Neh 7:3). Their vulnerability may also explain why gates change location and name frequently (which is a difficulty of

precisely locating Nehemiah's geographic references around the wall).

I. Outline

COMMENTARY

Ezra

The Edict of Cyrus and Preparations to Return (Ezra 1)

(1:1–12) vv. 1–3, the opening scene of the book of Ezra connects clearly to the end of 2 Chronicles (36:22), which is taken by many (Rudolph 1949: 2–3) to be another indication of the original unity between the books of Chronicles and Ezra/Nehemiah (*contra* Japhet). The emphasis of this introduction is on the *first* year of the reign of Cyrus of Persia (b. 590/589, d. 530). However, this must certainly refer to the first year of his rule of the Babylonian territory, thus 539. The reference to the predictions of Jeremiah is an indication of the beginnings of a textual canon, and its interpretation. The term 'to fulfil/accomplish' can refer to completed time (Gen 41:53, Jer 8:20; Isa 10:25; 24:13; Ruth 2:23; 2 Chr 29:28) or to finished work (1 Kings 6:38; 1 Chr 28:20; 2 Chr 8:16. Note especially Dan 11:36, 'period of wrath is *completed*'). Williamson (1985) argues that the fulfilment of the word refers not to Jeremiah's 'seventy years' but rather to Deutero-Isaiah's prediction of a victor from the east (Isa 41:2, 25; 45:13). God's 'stirring' of Cyrus ought not to be taken as sympathetic to Persian rule—rather it represents God's control of what appears to be human events (see

Isa 41:2; 45:13). This is also clear in the use of the term *p-q-d*. That God 'entrusts/charges' the Emperor *can* be seen as some kind of endorsement of Cyrus, but it can also be a somewhat subversive statement about who is, in fact, in charge despite appearances (note also Neh 7:1; 12:44).

The use of 'God of heaven' has been taken by some to be a Persian equivalent of the concept of Ahura-Mazda, the central deity in Zoroastrianism, although it is controversial whether Cyrus was already Zoroastrian (Boyce 1975–82). The phrase 'God of heaven' is only used in Persian contexts in the Bible, thus affirming a possible parallel in the Persian mind between the two deities. Finally, the mention of the tribes of Judah and Benjamin is probably based only on the fact that they are the majority group here.

v. 4, on the possibilities of *š-ʾ-r* as a technical term see Hasel (1972). *nādab* || *nĕdābâ* is a reference to freewill-offerings of the temple (Ex 35:29; 36:3; 2 Chr 31:14; Ezra 8:28, and negatively in Am 4:5). Japhet (1993: 503–5) notes the emphasis on these freewill-offerings in the Chronicler (1 Chr 29:5, 6, 9, 14, 17) as part of the Chronicler's emphasis on the whole-heartedness of the community.

It is widely accepted that Ezra 1 represents an oral form of the edict of Cyrus, which appears in written form in ch. 6. The latter is the more historically reliable text, ch. 1 being a summary (Bickermann 1976; Smitten 1972–4: 171).

v. 5, interest in the temple had significant economic implications (Weinberg 1992). v. 6, *sĕgîgîm* (lit. the ones around) means 'foreign peoples' (Ps 50:3; 76:12; 97:2; Jer 48:17; Lam 1:17; Ezek 16:57; 28:24; Dan 9:16). This is part of the 'despoiling Egyptians/new Exodus' motif of Ezra 1–6 (Williamson 1985: 16; Blenkinsopp 1988: 135–9). An awareness of the watchful eyes of the surrounding peoples is prominent in exilic and post-exilic writings. This awareness of wider society, of the presence of others who may laugh or ridicule, is a significant aspect of colonized societies who are sensitive to all aspects of their humiliation (Fanon 1963; Memmi 1965). v. 7, the humiliation theme continues with the mention of Nebuchadnezzar's placing of the vessels 'in the house of his gods', suggesting that even the gods of the defeated peoples are subservient to Marduk (2 Chr 36:10, 18 suggested that all the temple vessels were taken).

v. 8, Cyrus releases the vessels to a certain Mithredath (Persian) who is called *gizbār* (treasurer? from the Persian *ganzabara* (Fensham 1982: 46)). There are problems with interpreting the inventory. References to gold and silver basins and bowls are followed by 'knives'(?)—a difficult translation. The total does not match the enumerated items. The numbers are corrected in 1 Esd 2:2–11. Here is the first mention of Sheshbazzar, who remains the somewhat enigmatic leader of the first group of returnees soon after Cyrus's conquest of Babylon. Most scholars reject the equation of Sheshbazzar with Zerubbabel, simply considering Sheshbazzar to be the leader of the earliest, and unsuccessful, mission back to Judah (but see Galling 1961). Sheshbazzar is called here *nāśîʾ*, which is not necessarily a royal figure (but cf. Ezek 40–8). Moreover, it is probable that many different journeys have been collapsed into one Exodus-type return in chs. 1–2.

(2:1–70) The Golah List v. 1, the term *š-b-h* (take captive) and *šĕbî* (captivity) are used in combination with *gôlâ* (exile) also elsewhere (Nah 3:10, Ezek 12:11). The LXX is sometimes confused as to pointing of the term *šěbî* which can be either 'exiles' or 'elders' in the Aramaic sections. In this context, the meaning is clearly a reference to exiles, but in other cases it is not so clear, since the *leaders* of the community are also referred to. The reference to *hammědînâ* has provoked a continued debate with regard to the nature of the geographical/political entity in question. Was this a province of the Persian empire, or were the Jews administratively under the province of the much larger land-area of Samaria (Abernahara, 'Across the River')? Was 'Yehud' officially designated?

vv. 3–58, the list of the leaders of the community is arranged differently in Neh 7:7. There are suggestions that there was an intention to list leaders in parallel columns, as if to indicate the two leaders of various time periods, e.g. Zerubbabel (political leader) with Jeshua (priestly leader), and Nehemiah (political leader) with Seraiah (Ezra?), but such a plan breaks down because of our lack of knowledge of other periods of time. Who, for example, are 'Reelaiah || Ramiah' or 'Mordecai || Nahumiah'? Alternatively, 1 Esd 5:8 understands the names following Zerubbabel and Jeshua to be *proēgoumenōn* (those who go before) (in Deut 20:9 they are officials who address troops). This is a term used in later Christian literature of exemplary individuals.

When we get into the list of *bêʾ ābôt* (lit. house of the Fathers) itself, there is further confusion between the parallel accounts in Ezra, Nehemiah, and 1 Esdras. The total numbers are problematic as well. The grand total of the laity alone is 24,141 in Ezra, 25,406 in Nehemiah, 'not unreasonable' for a population of the province of Yehud (Blenkinsopp 1988: 85). Galling (1964: 89–108) had earlier argued that this list represented many groups of returnees. Carter (1991) has proposed a small population for Yehud at 17,000. The Golah List, in such a case, must represent not only a succession of time periods added together, in Carter's estimation, but also population from outside the confines of his proposed 'Yehud'. Note, however, that precise numbers may not be as important as the mere fact of counting, as a significant concern in itself. Galling, noting the struggle with those who sought to assist the returning community, wants to add elements of racial consciousness, or racial continuity with the past, on the part of the the returning community ('the purified community', so Galling 1951).

vv. 59–63, the words 'and these' clearly mark this section as separate from the list as a whole. It is possible that further reflection on this episode may help to determine the original meaning of the list. For whom are such lists of significance? 'Counting' is administrative, suggesting responsibility to higher officials—occupied peoples are familiar with the ubiquity of forms, numbers, rolls, registrations, etc. The terms used to describe these people in addition to those related to priestly families, are all place-names. The terms Tel-melah, Tel-harsha, Cherub, Addan occur only here. Immer refers elsewhere to a priestly family (Jer 20:1; Neh 3:29; Ezra 10:20). The presence of those claiming priestly descent would be an unusual claim if it were not authentic (2 Sam 17:27; 19:31–4, 39; 21:8; 1 Kings 2:7). The final decision awaits the reestablishment of the high priest.

It is often pointed out that the numbers do not tally (totals are: 31,351 in Ezra 2; 31,089 in Neh 7; and 30,142 in 1 Esdras).

Would women make up the difference? If so, does this partially explain the mixed marriage crisis? Rudolph (1949: 25) suggests that few women travelled with the returning community, leading some of the exiles to seek marriage partners among the people left in the land.

Two different forms of authority and power are contrasted in the early chapters of Ezra. The political leaders are the Persians and those delegated by them ('governors', *tirshata*, etc.), who represent the military élite, but of greater importance for the returned community of exiles is *charismatic* authority—the divinatory authority of the Urim and Thummim, and the prophets (on magic and myths among occupied people, see Fanon 1963: 55)

vv. 64–7 note the relative value of the animals that are listed, when divided amongst the total people counted in this list: 736 horses represents one for every 57 community members; 245 mules, one for every 172; 435 camels, one for every 97; 6,720 donkeys, one for every 6. Mules are associated with royalty in the Bible, and are the prized and rare possession among the community members (2 Sam 13:29; 18:9; Isa 66:20; Zech 14:15; 1 Kings 10:25 || 2 Chr 9:24, mules among gifts to Solomon). Horses, interestingly, are most frequently associated with warfare (pulling chariots only, stirrups were not used in the ancient Near East), so the number of horses would be of obvious interest to Persian officials. Most of the community members could not afford the long-distance trade animal, the camel (Firmage 1992: vi. 1136–7). Donkeys are clearly the common person's pack animal of choice.

vv. 68–9, the enumeration of financial gifts to the temple is intended to repeat the attitude of freewill-offerings noted already in ch. 1. It is often claimed that this amount of money indicates a wealthy community who had possibly benefited from financial success in the Persian heartland. However, there is reason to question this. These verses tell us that the community managed to donate 61,000 darics of gold, and 5,000 minas of silver to the work of rebuilding the temple. Is the mention of 'daric' anachronistic? Dandamaev believes that 'it is completely possible' that Cyrus issued coins (Dandamaev and Lukonin 1989: 196; and cf. Davies 1994).

Working with weights and measures in the HB is a vexed problem (see Betylon 1992: vi. 1076–89; Zograph 1977; Morkholm 1991), but we can generalize to get the following picture. Basing our calculations on a Persian gold daric at 8.4 g., and a mina as 50 shekels of silver (but 60 in the Babylonian standard), we can convert to metric weights: 512,400 g. of gold and 1,337,500 g. (Babylonian standard, 1,605,000 g.) of silver. This results in an average of 8.04 to 9.64 silver shekels per person, and 1.96 darics of gold per person (the relative *value* of gold to silver would have been 13.3 : 1). Is this a great amount of wealth? Zech 11:12 refers to 30 shekels paid to a shepherd, presumably for an entire season of work, and Jeremiah bought the field in Anathoth for 17 shekels (Jer 32:9). Hosea bought his wife (presumably Gomer) for 15 shekels of silver. As late as 1 Macc 10:42, there is a reference to a 5,000 shekel tax on the temple (which would be a significant percentage of the total given in Ezra 2). The donations, when calculated per person, are rather meagre. A question remains, however, whether we are to consider these figures as donations to the work of the temple, or intended for the wider economic life of the community.

The dimensions of the inner sanctum (Holy of Holies) were 20 × 20 × 20 cubits (1 Kings 6). A cubit is generally held to be approx. 50 cm., and thus, in order to even begin to reproduce Solomon's temple, they needed sufficient gold to gild 500 sq. m. of wall space in the inner sanctum alone. Both Ezra 6 (Darius's instructions) and 1 Kings 6 (Solomon's temple) suggest that the stone walls were first lined with wood and then gilded. Gold, with a basic weight of 18.88 g. per cu. cm., could be applied to a thickness of .001 cm. (based on Egyptian art; thanks to Dr David Scott, Getty Museum, Los Angeles, for figures on gilding). A square metre of gilt, therefore, requires at least 188.9 g. of gold. Just the inner sanctum would minimally require 94,450 g.—about one-fifth—of the 512,400 g. available. However, are we to believe that this community had over a ton of gold available to it (about $1\frac{2}{3}$ cu. m. of gold) besides Persian gifts? The disparity between silver and gold resources in this list, given their relative values, would otherwise seem hard to explain.

We obviously cannot be confident about the historicity of these figures, but the general indications of both the amounts and the tasks required indicate a relatively modest budget with which to try and reproduce Solomon's great achievement. Clearly, we are not dealing with a tremendously wealthy group of returning exiles, and probably must think in terms of a smaller percentage of those able to give larger amounts to achieve the per-capita average that we have indicated.

(3:1–13) The Beginning of the Temple Reconstruction under Zerubbabel Some scholars have suggested that ch. 3 is an independent account of the reconstruction of the temple (combined with 6:19–22? Blenkinsopp 1988: 96). The work establishes the altar, the sacrificial system, and then the shrine that housed it, in that order. The writer wishes to emphasize continuity with what had gone on before. Clines (1984) even writes of the community described here as 'reactionaries' and 'conservatives'. Surely this comes close to blaming the victims! The obsession with rules and regulations may reflect a certain conservatism bordering on reactionary attitudes, but it more probably reflects the fear of taking an unauthorized step. The unity of the people is represented by acting 'as one' or 'as one person' (as the Heb.; also at Judg 20:11; Neh 8:1). The indication 'seventh month' may be left over from the Golah List (ch. 2) being originally from the Nehemiah materials, and transposed to its present location in Ezra. v. 3, related to the community's sense of urgency is the theme of fear of foreigners—'dread' (*'êmâ*) of the neighbours—enemies (*gĕ'ēbâ*) (see Gen 15:121; Ex 15:16; Isa 33:18; Josh 2:9; Prov 20:2; Ps 55:5); but 'neighbours' can mean 'enemies' as the LXX adds: 'for all the peoples of the land were hostile to them, and were stronger than they' (1 Esd 5:50). v. 7, there are echoes of Solomon's project here, particularly in the specific mention of dealings with Sidonians and Tyrians (cf. Solomon and Hiram of Tyre, 1 Kings 5).

vv. 11–13, the throngs give a great shout (*tĕrû'â gĕdôlâ*). This exact phrase occurs at the battle of Jericho (Josh 6:5, 20). Although it can be read as shouts of joy in connection with the movements of the ark (1 Sam 4:5, 6 and 2 Sam 6:15), the ark as war palladium would render these passages much closer to the more frequent reference to such great shouts as acts of warfare (Am 1:14; 2:2; Zeph 1:16; Ps 27:6; 47:6). When seen in the context of the fear of their enemies, the dedication of the temple was thus an act of spiritual warfare—they are shouts to God their Divine Warrior—and the shouts were heard 'far away' (as the Philistines heard the shouts around the ark, 1 Sam 4:5–6). Such a theme of deliverance from enemies fits with the predominant use of *hesed*, the delivering love of God.

Although it is not expressly stated, it is widely assumed that some elders wept at the sight of the new temple because of great disappointment (cf. Hag 2:3; Zech 4:9–10). Sociologists haved noted the phenomenon of exiles whose memory of home becomes quite stylized over the years, with streets paved with gold, and valleys perpetually green and inviting (Baskauskas 1981). The return home is inevitably a disappointment—and we know that the temple was definitely a subject of exilic imagination and longing (Ezek 40–8).

(4:1–24) History of Opposition to the Temple vv. 2–3, other people approach Zerubbabel and Jeshua and say that they, also, 'seek' (*d-r-š*) God. Their reference to a deportation during the time of Esar-haddon may be credible (Williamson 1985: 49; Fensham 1982: 66; cf. Oded 1979). But the leaders make claim to the exclusive right to build the temple. The 'adversaries' appeal on the basis of religion, and the Israelites respond on the basis of permission. In any case, we must reject the identification of these people as '*the* Samaritans', a much later Jewish sect who do not emerge until the Hellenistic period (and would be noted for their conservatism, and interest in an alternative temple site!). Blenkinsopp (1988: 105) argues that an emphasis in Ezra on external problems may effectively avoid mentioning the internal struggles that are noted elsewhere (Hag 1:2–4; Isa 58:4; Zech 8:10; Isa 66:1–2).

vv. 4–5, the response of the surrounding peoples was to discourage the Jews from building their temple, particularly through bribery to 'frustrate/break' (*p-r-r*) the work (2 Sam 15:4; 17:14; Ps 33:10; Isa 14:27). The means used by the opposition is more explicit here than in 1 Esdras, which gives a somewhat more startling series of terms that appears to intensify the conflict: *epiboulas* (plots); *episustaseis* (insurrections); *dēmagōgias* (lit. leading crowds/mobs of people). This suggests far more social instability surrounding the activities of the Jewish community than does the MT of Ezra. Fensham (1982: 68) thinks that the text is speaking of Persian-appointed officials who were bribed, and we know that bribery was a significant Persian tactic (Darius boasted that, 'I will conquer Greece with my archers', an ironic reference to the archers appearing on gold darics and silver sigloi (Davies 1994: 66)). v. 6, Xerxes, we know, moved large numbers of troops through Judah to quell a major revolt in Egypt in 485. v. 7, from 1 Esd 2:16, we read *Beelteemos* (NRSV: Beltethmus), from Aramaic 'one who issues decrees', as a signatory of the letter. At this point the book of Ezra switches to the imperial language of the Persian empire, Aramaic, and continues until 6:18. This section deals largely with correspondence between local officials in Judah and the royal court. vv. 8–10, Rehum is called *b'l š'm* (NRSV: royal deputy; from Akkadian, 'official in charge'), an office which turns up regularly in Persian period biblical literature (Ezr 5:5; 6:14; 7:23; Dan 3:10 and 6:3), perhaps a civilian leader or chancellor (Blenkinsopp 1988: 112). The word used for 'letter' is *'igrâ*, a term used only in Ezra. The list of peoples involved in sending the letter is difficult. The first term, for example, 'ăparsatkāyē', is taken to be 'Persians' or 'generals/envoys'. The ending y' in Aramaic came to be understood as Gentilic, instead of referring to officials, which in the first three cases is more likely (e.g. generals, envoys, secretaries, then Erechians, as well as Babylonians, Susians, Elamites). The impression given is of a large number of peoples arrayed in opposition to the returning Jewish exiles, perhaps even implying the threat of insurrection or instability in the region. The list of various officials could also be a typical Persian-period guarantee against subversion by having all witnesses indicate their presence and agreement and confirm the contents.

vv. 12–13, Jerusalem, this 'wicked' and 'rebellious' city, is resurrecting itself! If it is completed, the worry is that the empire will lose their collections of 'tribute, custom, and toll' (v. 13; all Akkadian loanwords, *mandattu, biltu, ilku*—three types of tax: Fensham 1982: 74), thus 'the royal revenue will be reduced' and the king will suffer loss (cf. Dan 6:3*b*). The term *n-z-q* means 'loss-making', or 'unprofitable' (NRSV: hurtful) (v. 15). The greatest treachery in the eyes of imperialism is always loss of profit; despite flowery rhetoric about national interests. Scholars debate whether a precise rebellion is being alluded to here, but the general historical circumstances, including the Inaros Rebellion in Egypt in 460 BCE, and the later rebellions of the satrap Megabyzus in 448, make the accusations all the more dangerous. v. 14, the reference to eating the salt of the palace is taken by Williamson (1985: 56) to mean, 'in the pay of the court'. Perhaps it relates to an oath of office (Num 18:19; 2 Chr 13:5).

vv. 15–16, the accusations against Jerusalem continue—this time including a Persian loanword *eštaddûr* (Rosenthal 1974: 59) which refers to a 'breach of the peace'. Because of these troublesome activities, the city was 'laid waste' (*h-r-b*). The appeal to the Persian authorities is based on royal interests; historical precedent (note v. 16, 'rebuilt', i.e. built as before); common interest in maintaining authority and order. vv. 19–20, the suspicions about Jerusalem are confirmed. It *was* once a rebellious and powerful city—the centre of a regime; for the Persians the implication is clear: it is a dangerous threat. Note the particularly incriminating evidence (v. 20): they once collected taxes for themselves. vv. 21–4, the work stoppage is backed up by military force. The chronology is confused here. Williamson (1985: 57) argues that v. 24 is a resumption of the narrative that was interrupted by vv. 6–23. The passage inserted was intended to justify the harsh treatment of the foreigners by pointing out that the Jews did, in fact, have some justification in being worried about them. The argument, however, would be strange, justifying their earlier action by what actually happened much later.

(5:1–17) Clarification of Persian Permission to Rebuild v. 3, a

certain Tattenai is considered *paḥat* (governor), and supported by another official, *Sĕtar Bozenai* (NRSV: Shethar-bozenai). The questions appear to be directed at the use of timber rather than religious matters: structures, money, and authority, and ultimately the threat of a competitive power centre. v. 4, the officials' request for the names implies a threat. Indeed, when Tattenai asks for the names of the people, this is the only occasion in Ezra–Nehemiah when a reason is given for drawing up a list of names. Perhaps commentators have missed this clue for the presence of lists running throughout Ezra–Nehemiah. Lists serve the occupying power by keeping constant record of every move, and reveal an atmosphere of control and caution, particularly where there are threats of punishment and warnings that orders must be carried out 'diligently'. They also give a sense of unity and cohesion, of pedigree and authenticity, to the people themselves.

v. 5, the 'eye of . . . God' was on the exiled community. Williamson (1985) trenchantly suggests that the eye of God is to be contrasted to the famous Persian spies throughout the empire known as 'the king's eyes' (cf. 'eye of God' in Ps 33:16–18; Ps 34; Job 36:7). Some classical scholars argue that the 'king's eye' existed only in Greek imagination, although that does not prevent Israelites from having a similar imagination (Hirsch 1985: 101–31). vv. 8–10, Tattenai refers only to elders, which led Zucker (1936: 20) to state that Zerubbabel must not have been appointed governor as yet. The leaders of the apparent insurrection in Jerusalem were questioned. The empire would be interested in removing the apparent cause of the trouble, i.e. the leaders. As with empires everywhere, it is assumed that the leaders are responsible for inciting the otherwise obedient and peaceful masses, apparently incapable of comprehending a people's movement based on principles other than hierarchy. vv. 11–12, in response to this challenge, the exiles respond with *their* understanding of power—'We are the servants of the God of heaven and earth'. The political question is given a theological answer. The phrase 'God of heaven *and earth*' is telling when one recalls a common claim of ancient Near Eastern emperors to be 'Kings of the four corners of the earth', of 'all the lands', etc. Thus, the Persian officials are taught a lesson in religious and Jewish history—in effect, 'we were taken away *because of our sin*, and not because of the powers of this world'.

vv. 13–17, only now do we arrive at the issue that the local governors are truly interested in—permission, documents, and authority. A probable impatience with religious notions gives way to attention when Cyrus and an exchange of commodities is mentioned. The *real* issue, for the Persian officials, is whether Cyrus wrote such a document or not. A search must be made. This is a matter of the 'pleasure' (cf. Kraeling (1953), AP 27:21, 22; 30:23) of the king. Like St Paul (Acts 22:25–6) finally appealing to his Roman citizenship, official wheels are set in motion with this claim.

The disappearance of Zerubbabel without explanation is often grounds for speculation. Was Zerubbabel the centre of an attempt to restore a Davidic leader to the Jewish community, and eventually deposed in disgrace by the Persians? (Waterman 1954: 73–8; Galling 1961: 80–4; Sauer 1967; Fensham 1982: 78). Others deny a conspiracy, and speak only of a mystery surrounding Zerubbabel's fate (Williamson 1985: 76). The speculation is heightened by the confusing language in Zech 6:9–14, which seems to imply the crowning of a king, although the high priest Jeshua has replaced Zerubbabel (a move possibly aimed at hiding the messianic speculation of the original passage).

(6:1–22) Search of the Archives and Completion of the Temple vv. 1–4, Darius makes the search (cf. the legendary Persian obsession with unchangeable law: Dan 3:28; 6:8, 15) and

the document is found. Xenophon noted that Cyrus wintered in Babylon, spent the spring in Susa, and summered in Ecbatana (*Cyr.* 8.6.22). Many scholars now insist, on the example of Elephantine letters (Kraeling 1953: AP 30) that the Persians *would* have been interested in exact details (Blenkinsopp 1988: 124; Williamson 1985: 80–1, especially citing Hallock (1960) where payments are carefully noted; Fensham 1982: 87–9). v. 6, the local officials are told, 'keep away'. Although Williamson (1985: 81) protests that local officials must surely have retained rights of inspection, the authoritarian nature of this order is certainly in keeping with Persian style (Olmstead 1933: 159–60) and seems in the same spirit as the language of threat in the rest of this communiqué. v. 8, the response was surely a humiliating reversal for the local officials, whose initiative stopped this work in the first place. Now they appear to be insubordinate to the authority of Cyrus himself! Furthermore, these 'insurrectionist Jews' are even to be supported from the tax coffers.

vv. 9–10, the provisions emphasize 'whatever . . . the priests . . . require . . . given day by day without fail'. One reason for the Persian interest in the religious life of the subordinate peoples is clear: they insist on 'pleasing [soothing] sacrifices' to accompany prayers offered for the Persian royal family (contrast this with the behaviour of Cambyses with regard to the Apis Bull: see Depuydt (1995), who concludes that Cambyses did kill the Apis Bull, as Herodotus suggested). Williamson (1985: 82), citing Jer 29:7 and AP 30 (Kraeling 1953), claims that the Jews would not have been 'averse to complying with such a request'. And Blenkinsopp (1988: 129) adds, 'The author . . . accepts the possibility of a genuine religious life under foreign rule'. Both statements, however, are constructed out of a telling silence in the text on this matter. If the Jews were so sanguine about such prayers, where are they in the biblical tradition?

v. 11, the benevolence of Persian rulers is ironically backed by the threat of powerful military response if the Persian ruling is disobeyed. Now we recognize the rhetoric of power—anyone who transgresses this law will have a beam pulled from his home, and he will be impaled on it, and his house becomes a refuse heap. v. 12, the message is not subtle, the warning is not merely to individuals. The second part seems cleverly aimed at preventing the Jews themselves from having any independent ambitions, as well as at other political entities in the area. To whom is it directed? Foreign kings? Usurpers? Keep in mind that the Persian authorities have not necessarily forgotten that Jerusalem was 'that rebellious and wicked city', and that all around them is the threat of rebellion. v. 13, the king's orders are carried out 'with all diligence'. The term *'osparna* (exactly, perfectly: Rosenthal 1974: 58) is the language of obedience, translated variously as 'without delay', 'in full', 'with all diligence'—the message is clear—a powerful authority has spoken (Ezra 5:8; 6:8, 12, 13; 7:17, 21, 26; cf. Deut 4:6; 5:1; 6:3). vv. 14–15, if the temple was completed in 515, as is widely argued, then it was completed some 70 years after its destruction in 587–6, and thus perhaps comes close to Jeremiah's predicted seventy years of exile. v. 17, the impressive array of sacrifices is supplied by Persian order, at Persian expense, and thus should moderate hasty conclusions about the alleged wealth of the exiled community.

vv. 19–21, the text reverts to Hebrew at this point, and we find the reference to the 'sons of the exile' (*běnê-hagôlâ*) (NRSV: returned exiles) for the first time here (see Smith 1989: 197). The emphasis on the rededication of the temple now shifts to a celebration of the main Exodus event—the Passover rites. v. 21 specifically notes that some from the surrounding peoples separated themselves from the 'pollutions of the nations of the land (*gôyê-hā'āres*)' (the use of *gôy* is somewhat less typical than that of '*am*, 'people'), and joined with the returned exiles. That there were proselytes among the exiles may mitigate harsh judgements about their xenophobia (Fensham 1982: 96; Blenkinsopp, 1988: 133), although they may simply have been Jews who had 'joined them'. v. 22, the festival of Unleavened Bread is celebrated in the context of God's 'turn[ing] the heart' of the king of Assyria. The MT lacks an explicit air of friendliness here—God was acting in the interests of the Jews. Many scholars have noted the Chronicler's arrangement of important celebrations of Passover to mark deliverance from threat (2 Chr 30, 35, in the context of deliverance from Assyrian threat).

(7:1–28) Ezra Given Permission to Return to Jerusalem

vv. 1b–5, the story of Ezra begins with a geneaology, in the classic Priestly tradition. Part of the significance is the association of Ezra with Moses. Note that Ezra is from Babylonia, a different source community from Nehemiah. We are left to speculate about the precise nature of Ezra's role *vis-à-vis* the Persian authorities. Fensham argues that *spr* is an official Persian title (Fensham 1982: 99; Williamson 1985: 100 sees the phrase 'Scribe of the Law of God in Heaven', from v. 12 as the title); while Blenkinsopp (1988) is cautious, suggesting on the basis of Herodotus 3. 128 (dealing with officials under the Persian authorities) and AP 17 (Kraeling 1953), that Ezra may have occupied an office in the Babylonian satrapal court. It is going too far, however, to argue with Fensham (1982: 98) that the fact that 'Ezra was entrusted with such an important mission indicates that the Jews prospered in Babylon and were well educated'. It can be argued, on the contrary, that Ezra's relationship with the Persian authorities is left vague precisely to contrast his authority with that of Nehemiah, who was an insider. vv. 6–8, Ezra is described as *māhîr* (skilled). Note that this is from the root *m-h-r* (hasten) (cf Ps 45:1 (HB 2); Prov 22:29). Ezra is 'skilled in the law of Moses'. Since the 'hand of . . . God was upon him' (a phrase that typically expresses good fortune in relation to the occupying powers) he was granted what he sought from the Persian authorities. 1 Esd 8:4, typically, goes further by stating that Ezra was held in 'honour' and 'favour'. The third-person account states that the king granted all that Ezra asked for, although there is no narrative account of Ezra appearing before the Persian monarch (as in Nehemiah). The seventh year of Artaxerxes would be *c.* 458 if we presume this to be Artaxerxes I. The occasional suggestion of 398 (thus a later Artaxerxes) raises more questions than it answers.

vv. 10–13, note 'statutes and ordinances' as a way of referring to the laws of Moses (Ex 15:25; Josh 24:25; Deut 4:1, 5, 8, 14; 5:1; 1 Chr 7:17). Ezra's pre-eminent concern with Mosaic law, not Persian backing, is the source of his authority. Note, in v. 13, the implications of power in the ironic terms used to describe the composition of Ezra's travelling part+y: Jews are authorized to 'freely offer' by the ones who command! v. 14, Artaxerxes' authority is vested in the 'seven counsellors'. The reference here is to the seven aristocratic ruling families or houses of the Achaemenid period that supported Darius's rise to power (Berquist 1995: 51–2; however, we note in Xen. *An.* 1.6.4–5 that Cyrus also had seven counsellors). vv. 15–16, silver and gold are found in Babylon for the express purpose of the temple in Jerusalem. In addition to the 'despoiling the Egyptians' theme, perhaps operating here, is a sense of compensation. After all, Babylon's gold consisted in part of the gold and silver stolen by Nebuchadnezzar from Jerusalem in 586, and provided for by tax payments ever since (according to Herodotus 3.90–1, the annual tax for the entire satrapy of Abernahara is 350 talents of silver)—a matter hardly to be missed by writers of the post-exilic community. vv. 17–21, the emphasis on the temple and temple rites is further elaborated in the instructions to provide sacrificial materials, 'bulls, rams, lambs...grain-offerings and drink-offerings' which are to be offerred to 'your God in Jerusalem'. The apparent nonchalance about the remaining funds is clarified by vv. 19–20—any withdrawal from the king's treasury would obviously have required careful accounting.

With v. 22, we are back to the detailed accounting, although the constant use of 'one hundred' probably intends merely to convey large amounts (100 talents of silver is a massive amount, greater by far than the amount mentioned in the Golah List). Williamson (1985: 103), considering this to be about a two-year supply, wonders if that was the original length of Ezra's mission, while Blenkinsopp (1988: 149) considers the mention of wheat, wine, and oil to be 'clear indication of a Jewish redaction' in the light of Num 15:1–16. v. 24, included in this purchase of the loyalty of religious leaders is a release of taxation on the major parties involved in the temple. This would support Weinberg's (1992) arguments about the economic centrality of the temple in the community. v. 26, if Ezra's authority is rooted in scholarship of the religious literary tradition, the Persian's basis for authority is the threat of: death; banishment (*šĕrōš*, uprooting); confiscation of property (note Nebuchadnezzar's confiscation: cf. Wiseman (1956: 35); *ANET* 546; cf. 1 Kings 21:13–15); and imprisonment (*'ĕsûrîn*) (on imprisonment as a *late* form of punishment in the ancient Near East, usually associated with debt, cf. Smith 1989: 171–4). vv. 28–9, lest one be overly sanguine about what has occurred in v. 27, vv. 28–9 add a darker colour—Ezra was protected by God's *ḥesed* before the king, counsellors, and the 'mighty officers'. The suggestion here is clearly the contrast of apparent Persian power, and God's actual power.

(8:1–36) The Journey to Jerusalem, Delivery of Royal Funds

vv. 1–14, in this list, we are intended to see a parallel with the famous Golah List of Ezra 2 || Neh 7. Note the predominance of priestly associations before any Davidic identification. The mention of Hattush as a Davidide makes any other date than 458 difficult (he would be the fourth generation after Zerubbabel, cf. Blenkinsopp 1988: 162). v. 15, the gathering camped by the River Ahava. The camp (associated with the Exodus in Ex 13:20; 14:2; Num 9:18–20) is also used in connection with military campaigns (Josh 10:5; 2 Kings 25:1). vv. 16–17, the absence of Levites is a matter of concern— a note revealing an interesting openness on the part of a

Zadokite priest such as Ezra. Two of the leaders (Joiarib and Elnathan) are selected, according to the LXX, as 'men of understanding' (almost always used of Levites, so Blenkinsopp 1988: 165). There is considerable speculation on the nature of 'the place' at Casiphia. Scholars widely assume that some form of institution for worship, or perhaps religious instruction, must have existed there. In Deuteronomic thought, the 'place' (*māqôm*) often refers to the temple.

vv. 21–4, Ezra is clearly contrasted with Nehemiah, who accepted an armed guard. Ezra proclaims God's protection (cf. 2 Kings 6:17; Mt 26:53). Contemporary scholarly attempts to belittle Ezra's faith at this point ('embarrassing', 'humiliating', 'he made a mistake', and similar) miss the context of divine warfare of the type indicated in Ex 14:14 and illustrated in Judg 7 (Lind 1980). v. 21, the fast (*ṣom*) was proclaimed in order to call on God, an action frequently associated with preparations for warfare or preparing to face crises (1 Chr 16:11; 2 Chr 11:16; 15:4; 20:3–4; Ps 40:16 || Ps 70:5; Jer 29:13; 50:4; Jon 3:5; Zech 8:21, 22). God will provide 'a straight path' (NRSV: safe journey), a term associated with second Exodus themes of the return from exile (Isa 26:7–19; 40:3; Jer 31:9; Ps 107:6–7).

v. 22, who are the ones who 'forsake' God? In Judg 10:10 it refers to apostasy—by those who serve Baal (cf. Deut 28:20; 31:16; Jer 1:16; 2:19; 5:19; 17:13; 22:9). The formulaic saying is intended to mean, in paraphrase, 'If we call on God, God will protect us, *but if we forsake him*, his anger will be on us (by means of enemies, ambushes, etc.)'. Given the association of so many of these terms with YHWH war language, it is clear that what we have here is another element in spiritual warfare—i.e. the necessity to *believe* in the protection of God. Ezra's fast was part of his belief in God's miraculous fighting on the side of those who trust in God's protection, as opposed to the faithlessness of depending on actual armaments (see Smith-Christopher 1993: 269–92). vv. 23–30, the actual amounts given in vv. 26–7 are dramatically higher than the amounts of silver and gold in the Golah List: 650 talents of silver and 100 talents of gold. The reality of these figures can be questioned when they are translated into contemporary weights and measures—the amount of gold mentioned in the Golah List was already nearly a ton—$1\frac{2}{3}$ of a cubic metre of metal. Either there is corruption in the amounts given here, or they are totally fanciful. In any case, these are *Persian* resources, not Jewish. Dandamaev and Lukonin (1989: 205) note that, at the time of the fall of the Achaemenid state, Alexander seized no less than 7,000,000 kg. of gold and silver hoarded in the official treasuries. vv. 30–4, the travel is reported carefully, as well as the distribution of the financial assets of the mission, with proper notification that all has been written down. It is hard to escape the strong sense of Persian officials looking over the shoulders of the Jewish officials. v. 35, the twelve sets of animals are symbolically offered 'for all Israel', i.e. representing the twelve tribes (bulls and goats; cf. 2 Chr 29:20–4). v. 36, the satrap was the highest official of the province. More likely some lower officials, perhaps 'governors' is intended here.

(9:1–15) Ezra Discovers the Problem of Mixed Marriage: The Prayer of Confession

vv. 1–2, it is likely that Neh 8 originally appeared between Ezra 8 and 9. The actions and reactions in ch. 9 ought to follow a reading of the law, as in Neh 8 (William-son 1985: 127; Fensham 1982: 123).

No sooner had Ezra cleared his royal obligations, than he faces a crisis. The complaint here is that the people have not 'separated themselves' (*b-d-l*) from the 'peoples of the lands'. The term 'separation' is deeply significant to the heightened purity consciousness of the Holiness Code/Priestly redaction of the Bible (Smith 1989: 139–51). The priesthood was com-mitted to separation of pure from impure, and the people themselves are violating this passionate concern.

The 'peoples of the lands', are associated with *tôʿēbōt* (abom-inations), the most common cultic term for idolatrous prac-tices, but also of objectionable actions and behaviour. Note, however, the list of peoples: Canaanites, Hittites, Perizzites, Jebusites, Ammonites, Moabites, Egyptians, Amorites. Por-tions of this list are clearly anachronistic (Jebusites and Peri-zzites) and are intended to refer, with obvious revulsion, to the peoples traditionally driven out of the promised land by Joshua. The implication is that the planned second exodus is not being carried out with the same attention to purified peoples as the original Exodus. An argument can be made that Ezra is referring as much to fellow Jews who are not part of the 'sons of the Golah' as any ethnic non-Hebrews at this point (Smith-Christopher 1994). Blenkinsopp (1988: 175–6) comments that Ezra has combined ideas from Deut 7:1–5 with regard to the seven nations, and Deut 23:4–8 with regard specifically to Ammonites and Moabites, although Egyptians and Edomites are allowed after a minimum amount of time. Williamson (1985: 130), too, protests that many heroes of the faith contracted mixed marriages: Gen 16:3; 41:45; Ex 2:21; Num 12:1; 2 Sam 3:3. To understand this action, we must think in terms of minority consciousness of perceived threat and the response to insulate themselves from threatening influences. Mal 2:10–16 even suggests that some of the Jewish women were *first* abandoned so that the men could take on the foreign wives (presumably they were not economically wealthy en-ough simply to take on a second wife), which has led some modern feminist readers of this episode to note the interest-ing silence of the Jewish women of the exiled community, who may well have sided with Ezra!

v. 3, Ezra's attitude is that he is 'appalled (*š-m-m*, desolated: a strong term). Ezra's behaviour is to violate the carefully pre-scribed decorum of priests, who must not, according to Lev 10:6, unbind their hair or tear their clothing (cf. Lev 21:10 and Ezek 44:20; 2 Sam 13:19; 2 Kings 22:11). Ezra's abandonment of proper behaviour, rather like Ezekiel's, is a measure of his reaction to the events at hand. His actions have been com-pared to mourning for a death (Williamson 1985: 133; Blen-kinsopp 1988: 177). vv. 5–6, Ezra rose from fasting: the position of praying on one's knees begins only in the exile (Blenkinsopp ibid.). Ezra's great prayer of confession begins with his recognition of the 'iniquities' of the people (cf. Ps 38:4; 40:12; 79:8). The prayer of confession is reminiscent of other famous prayers of confession known in Hebrew litera-ture—Ps 78, 106, Dan 9, and 4QDibHam. v. 7, reflecting Deuteronomic theology of blaming sins especially on the leadership of monarchical Israel, Ezra refers to the kings and priests of the past. Their sin led to the following threefold punishment—the people given over to the sword; exile and captivity; plunder (*b-z-z*: to spoil, plunder, cf. Ezek 5:12).

vv. 8–9, the Jewish community are called 'slaves' (Deut 6:21; Esth 7:4; 1 Sam 8:17; Add Esth 7:4/14:8). This starkly negative term represents one of the most forthright judgements on Persian rule that we have in post-exilic literature (except Neh 9:36). The 'little sustenance in our slavery' is surely ironic in Ezra, although once again, the LXX transforms this into much more positive language, speaking of the Persians 'giving us food' (1 Esdr 8:80). Finally, to refer to God not 'forsak[ing] us in our slavery' clearly compares the Persian period to the Egyptian period before the Mosaic liberation. Fensham (1982: 130) clarifies that the *ḥesed* is from God, not the Persian rulers. It is often objected that *all* Persians considered them-selves slaves to the emperor as a mere euphemism (the Gk. sources use *doulos*: Cook 132, 249 n. 3) but the context of this use in Ezra 9 is clearly not encouraging us to read this as a neutral term.

v. 11, the language of impurity is reminiscent of Ezekiel (18:6; 22:10; 36:17; cf. Lev 12:2; 15:19, 20, 24). As all of these earlier Priestly references are to the impurity of women dur-ing menstruation, the sexual innuendo may foreshadow the issue of mixed marriages. v. 12, the prohibitions against mixed marriage are taken beyond their textual validity (Deut 7:2–3). In none of the older passages prohibiting mixed marriages is there the further command not even to seek the peace of these peoples. Do we have here an argument with the more open legacy of Jeremiah's letter to the exiles in Jer 29, where the exiles were instructed to 'seek the *šālôm* of the city'? A major concern with mixed marriage is the problems of inheritance and the economic survival of the exclusive community (Eske-nazi and Judd 1994: 266–85). This event, so obviously dis-tasteful for modern commentators, must be read within the context of sociologically informed suspicions about perceived advantages of 'marrying up' into wealthier local families, and our further suspicions that the 'foreigners' may have been Jews who were not part of the exilic community.

(10:1–44) The Mass Divorce of Foreign Wives by Group Covenant v. 2, sections of ch. 10 appear to have been dis-placed. Blenkinsopp (1988: 187) wonders why 10:1–5 would contain the oath of the assembly to act on Ezra's concerns, yet in vv. 6–8 Ezra continues to complain. Williamson (1985: 148), too, notes that the differences between the first-person and the third-person narratives suggest a later editor of the Ezra memoir material. The phrase 'broken faith' (been trea-cherous) has Priestly, and other late use (Lev 5:21; 26:40; Num 5:6; Josh 22:16; 1 Chr 10:13; 2 Chr 28:19; Ezek 17:20; 20:27; 39:26; Dan 9:7). Despite this, 'there is hope' (Ps 33, 119, esp. 147:11). v. 5, Ezra makes the leaders, priests, Levites, and all Israel 'swear' to abide by this covenantal agreement. Despite the fact that Ezra has apparently been given Persian authority, his actions reflect internal politics, unlike Nehemiah, whose tendency is to command and order. v. 6, an interesting debate in the secondary literature involves the person Eliashib named here. It is often argued by those who assign Ezra to a later date (e.g. 398, following the missions of Nehemiah) that this is the Eliashib of Neh 3:1, and thus Ezra is in Judah when this Eliashib's son, Jehohanan, is active. But Blenkinsopp (1988: 190) points out that the Eliashib in Nehemiah is con-demned by Nehemiah for defiling the priesthood—and thus one wonders if Ezra would associate himself with a family with such a reputation. Williamson (1985), on the other hand, notes that Neh 13:4 seems carefully to identify the Eliashib related to Tobiah as a different person. Names are often repeated and can become fashionable in an era, and so it is hazardous to assume that all occurrences of a person with the same name are, in fact, the same individual.

v. 8, the threat to those who do not participate in the community reformation is serious—they are to be banned *ḥ-r-m* (using the strong term of total annihilation from the period of conquest) and forfeit their *rĕkûš* (property). That the temple contingent can take such steps implies their economic power in the community. vv. 11–12, the community agrees to these conditions *en masse*, but then proceeds to ask for clarifications, stipulations, and conditions. Some members ask for more time, better weather conditions, and patience with the problems created by the number of people involved. v. 15, we are not privy to the basis of the objection by some who protested, and whether it was an objection to the process, or the entire issue of breaking up the mixed marriages. As we have evidence of more open-minded attitudes to foreigners elsewhere in the HB (Smith-Christopher 1996) it seems quite likely that they opposed the entire action. On the other hand, Blenkinsopp (1988: 194) refers to these as 'rigorists', because they oppose the *delay* in taking action that the process agreed upon implies. 1 Esdr 9:14 transformed the opposition into a passage about those who carried out the work!

vv. 25–43, the secondary literature carries on an extended discussion about attempts to work out the names in this list toward the expected twelve. v. 44, the foreign women are sent away *with the children*. Children, of course, are the main threat in the issue of inheritance, much more so than the women themselves. This ending of the book of Ezra appears to many commentators to be abrupt, leaving the reader with an uncomfortable sense of reading a book with missing pages.

Nehemiah

Nehemiah's Memoirs (Neh. 1–8)

(1:1–2:9) The Court Narrative of Nehemiah 1:1, Ezra uses the nomenclature of the Torah—that is, numbered months, while Nehemiah uses Babylonian calendrical names (Demke 1996). 1:2, 'brothers' is to be taken figuratively, given the context of Nehemiah's presence in a foreign court, but Williamson (1985: 171), noting Neh 7:2, takes this literally. 1:3, the news of the state of Jerusalem is troubling to Nehemiah partly because of the 'shame' (*ḥerpâ*) of this circumstance (on taunts of foreigners, Ps 69:20, 21; 71:13; 89:51; 119:22; Isa 51:7; Jer 51:51; Lam 3:61; Zeph 2:8). But what is the devastation that Nehemiah is reacting to? It seems unlikely that he would be shocked to hear about the destruction that remained from the Babylonian conquest in 586, so perhaps he is hearing about the results of the events described in Ezra 4:23. It is possible, on the other hand, that we should infer from Nehemiah's reaction that he is surprised that the walls are *still* down, even after the temple has been rebuilt. 1:6, 'let your ear be attentive and your eyes open' (cf. Ezra 5:5). Requests for God to hear and see are common. There are appeals to the ear of God at Ps 5:1; 17:1, 6; 31:2; 54:2; mention of the eye and ear in Isa 37:17; Lam 3:56, and note the special emphasis on the eyes of God in Ezek 5:11; 7:4, 9; 8:18; 20:17; Zech 12:4. Attention to the

eyes of God, especially in time of exile, is further indication of awareness of other eyes of a more hostile nature. For a courtier, the 'agents of the secret police' (Dandamaev and Lukonin 1989: 111) would be all too familiar.

1:10–11, restoration from exile: see also Jer 31:11; Zech 10:8; Isa 35:10 = 51:11. The phrase 'this man' has engendered considerable discussion. Its disrespectful tone contradicts the generally held assumption that Nehemiah's relationship with Artaxerxes was something other than the conquered to the conqueror. Given the realities of Persian rule, Nehemiah's disdain is understandable and his fear is prudent. 'I was cupbearer' (see also Gen 40:1; 41:9) gave rise, in the LXX, to a variant that suggests Nehemiah was a eunuch—cf. *oinochoos* of Alexandrinus to *eunouchos* found in Vaticanus, Sinaiticus, and Venetus—all strong texts. Most scholars reject the variant tradition, and Williamson (1985: 174) further argues that being a eunuch would have created difficulties in exercising authority in Jerusalem. Many scholars suggest that 'cupbearer' meant one who tasted wine for poison (Xen. *Cyr.* 1.3.9; see Yamauchi 1990: 259), and note that Ahiqar was also a cupbearer (Tob 1:22). It must be said, however, that the arguments *against* Nehemiah's physical mutilation tend to be motivated, once again, by the myth of Persian beneficence. Isa 56:4–5, for example, suggests that the notion should not be dismissed lightly, and sociological studies lend further weight to the probable folklore elements involved in the Nehemiah court tale, including the tradition of his being a eunuch (see Balch 1985; Cozer 1972).

(2:1–2) The words of the emperor strike fear in Nehemiah. He is worried about offending the king, despite what sounds like comforting concern. The emperor asks why he appears this way. Fensham (1982: 160), among others, comments that this concern is a 'reflection of his humane character'. Humane indeed! If Nehemiah is the official wine-taster, then the emperor might well be worried if Nehemiah looks sick! 2:3–6, burial in Jerusalem is associated with kings (2 Kings 21:26; 23:30; 2 Chr 16:14; 35:24). The association with tombs of ancestors and Jerusalem strongly suggests royalty, and Nehemiah's reference to 'the place of my ancestors' graves' further supports the royal implications of Nehemiah's concern with Jerusalem (Kellermann 1967: 156–9). In any case, the story seems less compatible with the idea of Nehemiah as governor of a province than a courtier being allowed to run an errand. 2:8, the word translated 'king's forest' is 'paradise' (from Persian), and would normally refer to royal woodland or a forest reserve. Dandamaev (1989: 144–5) concludes that paradises were parks with fruit trees, animals, and other agricultural resources that could belong to king or nobility. 2:9, in stark contrast to Ezra, there is no description of the journey or elaborate preparations. Nehemiah has letters and a military escort consisting of officers (*sārê*), army (*ḥayil*), and cavalry (*pārāšîm*). That Persian soldiers were certainly present in Judah is proven by the presence of cist-type tombs otherwise found in Persian archaeological sites (Stern 1982).

(2:10–20) Reconnaissance and Opposition vv. 10–12, the local resentment recalls Ezra 1–6. Sanballat is called 'the Horonite'. Blenkinsopp (1988: 216) argues that this is undoubtedly a reference to Beth-Horon (Josh 16:3, 5), northwest of Jerusalem (not the Horonaim of Moab, Isa 15:5; Jer

48:3), and that Sanballat would have considered himself a YHWH worshipper after a fashion (Blenkinsopp 1988: 216). There is considerable evidence for Tobiad connections to Ammon. Perhaps this opposition explains Nehemiah's concern for secrecy. vv. 13–15, there is an interesting amount of detail in the locations mentioned by Nehemiah, which invites attempts at close analysis. The Valley Gate would have led west (500 m. from the Dung Gate), and Nehemiah would then have turned south. The Dragon Gate is often associated with the Serpent Stone which is known also as Job's Well, 200 m. south of Ophel. The Fountain Gate would be the south-east corner towards En-rogel, and the King's Pool could be a reference to the Pool of Shelah or the Lower Pool, although Williamson (1985) identifies the King's Pool with the Pool of Solomon. In any case, the tour would have consisted largely of the south-east and south-west sections of the wall. Nehemiah is not able to traverse portions of the wall. Are we to presume that he rode *on* the wall, and therefore could not go further? Nehemiah travels by night to complete his survey. With Nehemiah, however, the reader is also left in the dark with regard to whether Jerusalem was in this state from the devastation of 587/6—the Babylonian destruction—or whether this is the result of a more recent difficulty.

v. 19, the enemies now include Geshem the Arab. A bowl from Ismailia mentions a Geshmu—King of Kedar (for Kedarites see Gen 25:13; Isa 21:16–17; 42:11; 60:7; a 'King of the Arabs' is noted in Herodotus 3.4.88). Thus, Blenkinsopp (1988: 225–6) notes that Nehemiah is surrounded by opponents: Samaria to the north, Tobiads to the east, and Kedarites in the south. They 'mocked and ridiculed' (*l-ʿ-g*, Ps 59:9; Isa 37:22, and *b-z-h*, Ps 15:4; 119:141) but their tangible accusation is that Nehemiah is inciting a revolution against Persian authority. Note the number of times that forms of the verb *m-r-d* (to rebel) will appear in the discussions between Nehemiah, Sanballat, and Tobiah (see NEH 6:4 and following). v. 20, the term 'share' (2 Sam 20:1; 1 Kings 12:16) refers to political association, 'claim' suggests jurisdiction, or legal rights, and 'historic right' (*zikkôr*) refers to a traditional claim resulting from participation in the cult (Williamson 1985: 192). Although neither Sanballat nor Tobiah has asked to participate in building, one notes the influence of the events in ch. 4. There is a significant suggestion, then, that Nehemiah is finishing what Zerubbabel started—and both have messianic associations.

(3:1–32) v. 1, Eliashib and the priests rebuild the Sheep Gate. Williamson (1985: 195; following Ehrlich 1914) reads not *qidĕśûhû* (they consecrated), but *qirĕśûhû* (they boarded it). Commentators have noted that vv. 1–15, working on the north and west sections, have names linked by 'next to', with locations given. But in vv. 16–32, on the east and south sections of the wall, the link is 'after him', and groups are given according to places in the city. Blenkinsopp (1988: 232) speculates that vv. 16–32 focus on the more devastated part of the wall. Indeed, twenty-one work details were on the east side of the wall, and workers on the Fish Gate 'built' rather than 're-paired' the wall. The north would have suffered the brunt of most attacks on Jerusalem, for those arriving from Mesopotamia (famously, Jer 1:13–15).

v. 7, the names of Gibeon and Mizpah, territories apparently outside the parcel of land-area granted to the exilic community, are mentioned as under the authority of the governor of Beyond the River. The term of authority is literally, 'to the throne' (*lĕkisseʾ*) (NRSV 'under jurisdiction'). Ch. 3 presents us with six districts: Jerusalem, Beth-zur, Keilah, Beth-haccherem, Mizpah, which was the administrative centre of the area after the fall of Jerusalem to the Babylonians, and obviously retained its importance to this time, and Jericho. (Simons (1959: 392–3) warns that mentioning a place-name need not imply actual residence, but merely the use of a location as a group identification.) v. 16, the 'house of warriors' (*bêt haggibbôrîm*) may be the Persian garrison.

(4:1–23) Militarizing the Wall Building v. 1, Sanballat was 'greatly enraged' and 'mocked the Jews' (cf. Ps 44:14; Ezek 23:32). 'What are these feeble Jews doing?' The adjective here is rare; *ʾĕmēlāl* is usually translated 'languish/ed': 1 Sam 2:5; Isa 16:8; 24:4; 33:9; Jer 15:9; Hos 4:3; Nah 1:4. v. 3, the language about the fox on the wall has been troublesome. Some see the term as a reference to a siege weapon, but Williamson (1985: 214) sees it as a sarcastic reference to a small animal being able to break apart what the Jews are putting together. vv. 4–7, after asking God to 'hear' Nehemiah says that the Jews are being 'despised' (*b-z-h*); the focus moves to their 'taunt' and reproach (cf. 1 Sam 17:26; Ps 69:20, 21; 71:13; 89:51; 119:22; Prov 18:3; Isa 51:7; Ezek 21:33). They are to be given over as 'plunder' (*bizzâ*) in a land of captivity. In short, the curse calls for a reversal of fortune—God, do to them what they did to us! The opposition includes traditional enemies.

vv. 10–13, the fear, it appears, comes from the threat of guerrilla-type assassinations amongst the piles of rubble, not from large-scale attacks. The murmurings get so serious among the 'Jews who lived near them' (i.e. enemies), that Nehemiah arms the population. vv. 14–15, 'Do not be afraid' (*ʾal tîrĕʾû*: fear not!). This is the great battle-cry of ancient Israelite YHWH War (Deut 20; von Rad 1991; Lind 1980). But as quickly as the crisis builds, it disappears in a single sentence. v. 16, more than mere hand weapons are referred to here: there are shields and body armour ('Persian weapons', Blenkinsopp 1988: 252). vv. 17–18, the concern for defence is emphasized—one hand on a tool, one hand on a weapon. Nehemiah also keeps the trumpeter close at hand so that he can rally the troops at a moment's notice. v. 20, with the blowing of the shofar, a YHWH War was declared—complete with the belief that 'Our God will fight for us' (cf. Judg 3:27; 6:34; 7:18; 1 Sam 13:3). vv. 21–3, there continues the great emphasis on preparation for war. The final phrase (lit. 'a man his weapon the water') is quite impossible. If *hammayim* (water) is emended to *hayyāmîn* (right hand), then it makes sense! 'each [man] kept his weapon in his right hand'.

(5:1–19) Nehemiah's Reforms v. 1, *ṣaʿăqât hāʿām* (outcry of the people), the cry of oppression against their Jewish neighbours. The cry against Pharaoh, the cry against enemies, is here raised up against their own people (cf. Ex 14:10; 22:23, the cry to God for deliverance from injustice and abuse; Ps 107:6, 19–20). Some have suggested (Neufeld (1953–4) that the time of the wall building was before the olive and grape harvest, and thus hit local society at an economically weak point. We also know that the imperial tax burden went up during the time of Darius, and again in the time of Xerxes, in order for the latter to pursue his military campaigns against the Greeks (Blenkinsopp 1988: 257). But the bitterness here seems directed towards fellow Jews. vv. 2–3, 'With our sons and daughters, we are many', and in 5:3 'We are having to pledge our fields, our vineyards, and our houses in order to get grain during the famine' (cf. Gen 47:13–26). Besides the obvious connection to the enslavement narratives of the Exodus, there is also close parallel in image to the laws of divine warfare in Deut 20 where Israelites are exempt from warfare if they have not yet enjoyed the fruits of peace: namely marriage, gardens, and houses. The implication, then, is a protest against Nehemiah's militant enlistments for his building campaign: 'How can we carry on *your* battles, when we haven't even enjoyed the fruits of peace?' vv. 4–5, now the accusation is directed at the emperor. The Persian tax requirements are also oppressive. The tax had to be paid in silver by the time of Darius (on the exploitative result of using silver for taxation, see Kippenburg 1982). This suggests that the main danger is from fellow Jews who would exploit the condition of the the new administration. vv. 6–8, Nehemiah 'brought charges' (*r-y-b* 'disputes', suggests legal action; cf. Ex 23:2, 3, 6; Deut 21:5; 25:1). On the theme of the 'sold ones', 'our Jewish kindred . . . sold to other nations', (cf. Gen 37:27; Lev 25:47–55; Ps 105:17; Isa 50:1; 52:3; Jer 34). The accusation of Nehemiah seems tantamount to saying, 'you are exiling your fellow Hebrews at precisely the time we are trying to ransom the exiles *back* from foreign control'. v. 10, Nehemiah points out that these exploiters are even taking advantage of the fact that they have been helped from *his* funds as a royal representative. Fensham (1982: 194–5), on the other hand, sees this as a confession by Nehemiah that he, too, was involved in this financial exploitation.

v. 15, the previous governors took bread, wine, and 'forty shekels of silver'. This per-diem amount places Nehemiah in a social category far above the per-capita holdings of silver of the average Israelite, if the numbers in Ezra ch. 2 are to be taken seriously at all. This passage has been taken to prove the existence of Judah before Nehemiah, with previous governors before him (the case is hardly closed. See McEvenue 1981; Lapp and Lapp 1974: 81; Stern 1982; for an earlier Judah, Blenkinsopp 1988: 264; Williamson 1985: 243). v. 16, the work on the wall is implied to be of benefit to all the people, but this point can be questioned. Note that in Lev 25:29–31, the year of Jubilee and redemption does *not* apply to houses *in walled cities*! There, a person has only *one* year to redeem a house. The monied rights of the urban aristocracy defeated even the radical measures of the Jubilee redistribution of land (Weinfeld 1995: 176). By rebuilding the wall, Nehemiah also guarantees the financial rights of the wealthy class of Jerusalem—in a sense creating economic opportunity zones within the boundaries of the administrative city that he is trying to rebuild (as a royal figure?). Note the similar impact of Josiah's reforms in 2 Kings 23 (see Nakasone 1993). vv. 17–19, it is so with all the privileged in history—their over-indulgence is justified by their presumed self-importance, and further, the claim that their exploitative practices are for the good of all.

(6:1–19) Continued Opposition, Internal and External vv. 1–2, the suggested meeting-place, the plain of Ono, is surely either on the border (Fensham 1982: 200, Blenkinsopp 1988: 268), or outside Judah altogether, although Williamson places it in Judean territory (Williamson, 1985: 255). vv. 4–7, a rebellion must have a leader, and Sanballat writes that Nehemiah proposes to 'become their king'. Sanballat is well aware of the possibility that popular sentiment will stand behind a claim to restore an independent Judah, and accuses Nehemiah of sponsoring prophetic support (note the importance of prophetic authority in Ezra–Nehemiah). The reason for the open letter is now clear. Sanballat warns that the Persian monarch will soon hear of these plans. We have seen that Nehemiah's activities mirror royal authority and activities to such a degree that Sanballat's accusation, to say the very least, is rational and well founded! v. 10, scholars have suggested that Shemaiah proposes that Nehemiah *openly* proclaim his kingship by closing the doors of the temple (Ivry 1972: 35–45; cf. 2 Chr 23). The temple, it must be recalled, is the administrative centre of the Judean settlement under the Persians. To close the doors of the temple is to declare oneself in charge over that institution, which would apparently declare open sedition against the Persian authorities. Yadin (1963: 95) also notes that the temple was often fortified as a final retreat after the walls of a city were broken. Others have argued that the temple was a site for asylum, and that Nehemiah was being warned of a conspiracy. This would seem to square with his reply about being afraid. A certain Noadiah is also named as a female prophet hired by Sanballat (this accusation, however, is doubted by Carroll 1992). Nehemiah, in his report to God (rather like a report to the Persian monarch) names those who sought to do him harm. v. 17, 'nobles' (*hōrîm*) of the Jews continued to correspond with Tobiah, apparently because they were actually intermarried with Tobiah's family. While Sanballat appears defeated by the completion of the wall, Tobiah continues to be a threat, indicating that Tobiah is more closely related to the people with whom Nehemiah must deal (see Neh 13).

(Ch. 7) The Golah List v. 2, the joint appointments of Hanani and Hananiah over Jerusalem 'and the citadel (military garrison?)' raises some questions. Is Nehemiah preparing to complete his work and return to the Persian heartland? v. 3, the verse is difficult. Many commentators cite the practice of the siesta which is typical in warm climates. Thus, it would be a time for particular vigilance. v. 5, the second appearance of the Golah List is introduced by the idea that Nehemiah wanted to register everyone by their lineage. The editor is clearly aware of this secondary use by his introduction. Many scholars believe that the original purpose of the list is best tied to its location in Nehemiah rather than in Ezra chs. 1–6. In vv. 43–5, gatekeepers and singers are enumerated with the Levites. This serves as one of a few reminders that not *all* difficulties with the list are solved by dating it to 460–430 BCE.

(8:1–18) The Study of the Law v. 1, the presence of Ezra and the virtual absence of Nehemiah support the argument that ch. 8 is among the displaced chapters from the Ezra material. According to the date given, the 'seventh month', this episode is often placed *before* the marriage crisis in the ninth month as noted in Ezra 9–10. Thus, the original place for ch. 8 would logically have been between Ezra 8 and 9. The action of bringing 'the book of the law of Moses' (Torah) (note 2 Chr 23:18;

30:16; Ezra 3:2; 7:6; Dan 9:11, 13; Mal 3:22; Ps 119, 'Torah of YHWH') and reading from it reminds many contemporary scholars of the later synagogue service, and suggests that some aspects of the later service have their roots in a formal ceremony of reading and teaching Torah (on the presence of a service format here see Blenkinsopp 1988: 285, and the variant in Fensham 1982: 215; Clines 1984: 183 and Williamson 1985: 281 disagree). **v. 2**, the phrase 'hear with understanding' (lit. understood to hear) (Neh 10:28; Ps 119:10, 32, 34, 73) can be compared to the teaching of the wise in Dan 10:12; 11:33—the wise who give understanding to the many. **v. 3**, Ezra reads facing the square: 'In a society defined by ethnicity and nationality, the square concentrates a potentially diffuse, and therefore, difficult to control, population into a small geographical space. From this place, the royal/governmental power may keep its hegemony over the elite, while creating an ideology of participation and equality' (Wright 1990). Cf. Josiah's hearing of the law, 2 Kings 22–3.

v. 6, there is an interesting series of actions described here, which reminded Rudolph (1949: 147) of Islamic prayer rites. **v. 8**, yet another term is used here: 'the book, the law of God (*'ĕlōhîm*)'. The Levites read 'with interpretation' (cf. Lev 24:12; Num 15:34; Esth 4:7; 10:2; Ezek 34:12). They 'gave the sense' (cf. Dan 8:25 'cunning'!; 1 Chr 22:12; 2 Chr 2:11; Ps 111:10; Ezra 8:18). 1 Esd 9:55 has the people understanding the reading by using *emphusiaō* (to infuse life into) (cf. LXX Gen 2:7; Wis 15:11). **v. 9**—'The governor[*tirshata*]...said', MT adds Nehemiah's name here, but the LXX omits it. Some scholars have noted that the use of the singular verb, also at v. 10, indicates that Ezra acted alone in the original account. **vv. 10–13**, this admonition to give to those who are poor may not be simply an obligatory piety, but speak to actual conditions among the returning community (cf. Neh 5). As is the pattern, the command is followed by the description of its fulfilment. **vv. 17–18**, the reference to Joshua lends further nationalist overtones to the celebrations.

(9:1–38) Ezra's Confessional Prayer; Mixed Marriage Crisis vv. 1–3, the people stand and proclaim their sins and iniquities, and those of the fathers—as in v. 3—'making confession' (see Lev 5:5; 16:21; 26:40; Num 5:7; 2 Chr 30:22; Ezra 10:1; Neh 1:6; Dan 9:4, 20). **vv. 4–6**, the general prayer of confession follows set patterns established throughout the late biblical material. The theme of God as Creator is a theme that is typical of post-exilic theological reflection (Isa 40–8; although Amos 4:13; 5:8–9; 9:5–6, see Blenkinsopp 1988: 303). God as Creator effectively trumps the claims of universal rule of the Persian emperors as well—note the same theme in the face of Babylonian claims in Daniel (Dan 9; cf. Baruch 1:15–3:8; 1 Kings 8; Ezra 9: all post-exilic confessional prayers). **v. 7**, the historical events are certainly not chosen arbitrarily. The Persians are presumed to be listening. God is identified as Creator, who exercises the military-political tactic of name-changing—the privilege of the conqueror. **vv. 8–11**, note that the beginning of this prayer makes these strong statements: (1) The land is given *outside* Persian authority (i.e. by God); (2) The claim is based on God's sanction, not Persia's; (3) The claim is *prior* to Persian claims. Also, note the reference to sinking 'like a stone' (Ex 15:15)—God's defeat of Pharaoh.

v. 15, for hunger there was manna from heaven (Ex 16; Ps 78; 2 Esd 1:19;) and for thirst, water from rock (Num 20; Ps 78; 105; 114; Isa 48; Wis 11:4; 2 Esd 1:20; 1 Cor 10:4). By the end of v. 15, Ezra has established that God was fully capable of delivering the people from physical, earthly rule, ordering their daily lives, and providing their basic necessities. The obvious implication is, 'What do we need the Persians for?' **v. 16** turns the corner. The people reject God's care because they are 'determined to return to their slavery' (v. 17). It can hardly mean anything other than the implication that their present circumstances are part of the slavery of rejecting God's good care in the past! The stubbornness of the people is contrasted to the 'wonders' performed by YHWH (Ex 3:20; Judg 6:13; 1 Chr 16:9; Jer 21:2; esp. Ps 9:1; 26:7; 105; 106; 107).

vv. 22–3, Sihon and Og (1 Kings 4:19; Neh 9:22; Ps 135:11; 136:19—note that Ps 135, 136 are passionately nationalist) represent kings that were defeated at the initial stages of the conquest of Canaan. Might we have a historical reference to the territories of Sanballat and Tobiah here? The kings of Heshbon and Bashan are, at the very least, symbols of those who resisted the Jewish conquest under God's leadership (Deut 1:4; 29:7, and as a saying in current use, cf. Deut 31:4; Ps 135, 136). **v. 24**, 'Doing...as they pleased' is royal prerogative in late biblical literature, often linked with Persian rulers (Esth 1:8; 9:5; Dan 8:4; 11:3, 16, 36). **vv. 32–4**, 'hardship' or weariness is *tĕlā'â* (Ex 18:8; Num 20:14; of exile, Lam 3:5; Mal 1:13). The use of 'Assyria' implies, even if not stated explicitly, 'that there was not much to choose between the Assyrians and their imperial successors: the Babylonians and Persians' (Blenkinsopp 1988: 307). These events, including Persian rule, are seen as punishment. **vv. 36–7**, the central point is this: 'we are slaves' followed by 'the land'. The people *and the* land are in slavery. The rich yield (Lev 25:20; Prov 10:16; 14:4; 15:6; 16:8) goes to foreign kings. As one might expect in a prayer of confession, the central theology here is Deuteronomic 'God's punishment' theology. There is a possible wordplay on *rāṣôn*, the king's 'pleasure', and the *ṣārâ* (difficulty) of the Jews—in other words, their 'pleasure' is our 'pain'. Blenkinsopp (1988: 30) reminds us, 'One of the worst aspects of imperial policy under the Achaemenids was the draining away of local resources from the provinces to finance the imperial court, the building of magnificent palaces, and the interminable succession of campaigns of pacification or conquest.'

(10:1–39) Crisis Resolved; People's Covenant vv. 1–27, the list interrupts a narrative beginning with v. 1, and continuing with vv. 29–30. Note that Nehemiah is called 'tirshata'. Nehemiah may have carried such a title. **v. 28**, the people are referred to as 'the rest', or remnant, but this includes 'all who have separated themselves from the peoples of the lands'. Presumably these are people from the groups that did not go into exile, or from earlier returns. **vv. 29–31**, the movement of *females* is stressed here (lit. 'our daughters not to them; their daughters not to us'). Foreign daughters coming into the group may result in inheritance passing out of the community on the death of the male. Both directions, however, are an economic threat.

v. 33, the rows of shewbread are noted in Lev 24:5; 1 Chr 9:32; 23:29; 2 Chr 2:4, 11; 29:18. The regular burnt-offerings for priests are noted in Num 15:1–10. The breakdown of the following suggests the divisions of 'holy time': sabbaths (weekly); new moons (monthly); and festivals (annually). v. 35, the casting of lots is clearly to seek fair distribution (1 Chr 24:5, 31; 25:8; 26:13, 14; Ps 125:3) of the wood-offering—by ancestral houses. Cf. the emphasis on fair distribution in Ezek 40–8 on land, weights, and finances. vv. 39–40, the term 'chambers' of 'storehouses' (NRSV: storerooms) is found in previous texts: 1 Chr 9:26, 33; 23:28; 28:11, 12; see also Deut 28:12; 2 Kings 20:13, 15; 2 Chr 32:28; Job 38:22; Ps 33:7; 135:7; Jer 38:11; Mal 3:10. Fensham (1982: 241) suggests that we may have a picture of Persian tax collecting policies, with the temple at the centre. The people will not 'neglect' ('-z-b) the house of God, because God has not neglected them.

(11:1–36) Repopulating Jerusalem v. 1, the military overtones of this entire episode, surely resulting from Nehemiah's Persian commission, have been noted in the literature (Kellermann 1967; Wright 1990; Hoglund 1992). The unusual term for Jerusalem this early (lit. holy city), is found in various forms in 19 other places in the HB, and alluded to in the NT. v. 12, volunteering to live in Jerusalem continues the military theme (cf. Judg 5:2, 9, and esp. 1 Chr 29:5–6). v. 4, 'Judahites and . . . Benjaminites' become symbolic of the majority, rather than exclusive of those from other tribal backgrounds. vv. 4b–36, the sources of this list are usually considered early, given that gatekeepers and singers are not yet listed with levitical status (so Williamson 1985: 347; Blenkinsopp 1988: 325–7). The listing of persons follows the order: (1) vv. 4–6, Judahites; (2) vv. 7–9, Benjaminites; (3) vv. 10–14, priests; (4) vv. 15–18, Levites; (5) v. 19, gatekeepers; (6) vv. 20–1, 'the rest of Israel', those who live each on *naḥălātô* 'his inheritance'. Special mention is made of *nětînîm* (temple servants) (Weinberg 1992: 75–91).

v. 25, there is an unusual combination of terms used here: 'villages' and 'fields' (*ḥăṣērîm, biśědôtām*). Generally, Williamson (1985: 350) considers the role of villages to be a utopian view of post-exilic geography, although we have noted that this list is taken from Josh 15, and thus intended to mimic the conquest of the land (Simons 1959: 393; Blenkinsopp 1988: 330). v. 36, the term used for 'divisions' is typical of the Chronicler (1 Chr 23:6; 24:1; 26:1, 12, 19) and almost always of priests and Levites (see, however, Josh 11:23; 12:7; 18:10).

(12:1–47) Processional Dedication of the Wall vv. 1–21, the first half of this chapter consists of a record of priestly and levitical families, including a record of high priests that, although incomplete, takes us down to the time of Alexander the Great (Jaddua, v. 22; see Jos. *Ant.* 11.302). Nehemiah is mentioned as if the narrator is writing from beyond his time (note the two historical figures David and Nehemiah in v. 46). The chapter shows considerable editorial activity, in the late additions found in vv. 6, 19, 22, and 23. v. 23, the importance of records read to the king further supports the view that the lists throughout Ezra–Nehemiah are evidence of the constant watch of the authorities. v. 26, Joiakim could hardly be Jehoiachim, king after 605 BCE in Judah. v. 27, the term *ḥănukkâ* (dedication) is only late, of dedications in P and other later biblical books. All the instruments must have been carried during the procession, which may affect how we imagine the size of the various specific instruments (Williamson 1985:

372). v. 30, *ṭ-h-r* (purify), predominantly used in P (Lev 13:6, 34, 58). Purification, of course, has been a central concern throughout the exile (Smith 1989: 49–65, 139–51).

v. 31, two or three people abreast could walk on top of Jerusalem's walls, according to Kenyon's excavations (Avigad 1983: 23–63). v. 36, 'the scribe Ezra' is almost certainly a later addition to the text. vv. 38–9, the places named are confusing: Tower of the Ovens; Broad Wall; Gate of Ephraim; Old Gate; Fish Gate; Tower of Hananel; Tower of the Hundred; Sheep Gate; Gate of the Guard. The number of gates around Jerusalem has always been in flux, and named for either direction, particular event, or destination of those who travel from that gate (e.g. Ephraim Gate—cf. the modern Damascus Gate). In the light of the weakness of gates (H.2) this variation in names and locations for gates and towers is rational. v. 43, of joy in Jerusalem, cf. 2 Chr 20:27; 30:26; Esth 8:16, 17; Ps 35:37; 105:43; Tob 13:10, 17; esp. Isa 65:18. The hearing of joyful celebration, especially at a distance by enemies, is an interesting theme (Isa 15:4; 1 Sam 4:6; Ruth 1:6; enemies hearing in Ezra 3:13; Neh 2:10, 19; 4:1, 7, 15; 6:16; and 9:9, 27, 28; of God hearing, see Isa 66:19; Jer 40:11; 49:21; 50:46; 1 Macc 14).

(13:1–31) Nehemiah's Second Visit: Further Reforms It has often been observed that ch. 13 seems an afterthought—a collection of issues that a later editor considered to be loose ends that required tying up. The chapter easily breaks up into separate episodes: vv. 1–9, the presence of Tobiah in the temple; vv. 10–14, levitical duties; vv. 15–22, concerning trade and commercial activities on the sabbath ('In those days I saw . . .'); vv. 23–9, further concerns on mixed marriage issues ('In those days I saw . . .'); vv. 30–1, summary of entire chapter. It is possible, furthermore, that vv. 6–7 provide the reason—they seem to point to an addition from a second term of Nehemiah's responsibilities in Judah.

v. 1, the introduction to the reading of the books of Moses leads to the emphasis on the Ammonites and Moabites (Gen 19:38; Deut 23:3; Neh 4:7; Amos 1:13; Zeph 2:8; Jdt 6:5—a racial slur?). Note, however, that Ruth is a Moabite, and Isa 56:6–8 looked to an era when foreigners would be welcome in the 'house of prayer'. v. 2, Balak and Balaam are recalled here (Num 22–3; cf. Isa 15–16; Jer 48). The tradition becomes a code to speak of issues of contemporary economic and political tension. v. 4, Tobiah was 'close' (*qārôb*) in the sense of related by family ties (cf. Lev 21:2, 3; 25:25; 2 Sam 19:43). v. 5, Tobiah's storehouse was a base of operation. Commentators compare the commercial problems in vv. 15–22, concluding that Tobiah was using a privileged position in the temple economy to pursue advantageous business arrangements (Blenkinsopp 1988: 354; Williamson 1985: 386). v. 6, notably, Nehemiah is not present, and Artaxerxes is called 'King . . . of Babylon'. vv. 8–9, Nehemiah states that he threw out 'vessels [NRSV: household furniture] of the house of Tobiah'. The possibility of rendering the term 'vessels' suggests that Tobiah had religious utensils in the temple. There are suggestions here of Josiah's (and Hezekiah's) cleansing of the temple (again implying royal activities for Nehemiah). They 'cleansed [*ṭ-h-r*] the chambers' (for Holiness Code see Lev 15:13, 28; 22:4; 13:6). The implication is to make clean from idolatry (Jer 13:27; Ezek 24:13). v. 14, Nehemiah's phrase, 'Remember me, O my God' is helpfully noted by Eskenazi (1988), who reminds us to contrast this first-person request to be honoured, with the editor's third-person report that God, in fact, honoured *Ezra*.

v. 16, the Tyrians (Phoenicians), of course, were renowned tradesmen in the ancient Near East. vv. 17–18, regarding the sabbath, economic activity is considered polluting in the ritual sense. There is an interesting interrelationship of ritual profanation and economic social issues, here. We must guard against the stereotype that priestly concerns are often 'empty ritualism' without connection to justice issues. v. 21, Nehemiah's threat is to 'lay hands on' these sellers! (cf. Esth 3:6; 9:2; Add Esth 6:2; 12:2.) v. 22, Levites must purify themselves. Once again, terms of ritual, purity, 'purify' and 'holy' are used in the arena of finance and economics. v. 23, there is considerable discussion about the relation of Josephus, *Ant.* 11:306–12, to these events. Some have suggested that Josephus is speaking of another event entirely, or at the very least a garbled version of these events. It is now rare for modern commentators to argue that Neh 13 has garbled events of which Josephus has more accurately written.

v. 24, what *was* the language of Ashdod? Some have suggested that it simply means 'foreign language' and not a specific, known dialect at all, while others argue for an Aramaic or Philistine (or Gk.?) dialect. Blenkinsopp (1988: 363) is surely correct, however, in stating that the real issue is the inability to speak Hebrew, not the specific language they *did* speak! Political considerations seem predominant in Nehemiah, giving the impression of treacherous power-grabbing in both temple and government through strategic marriages. The example that Nehemiah chooses to illustrate the problems of foreign marriage is an example of political leadership: Solomon. From Nehemiah, much more clearly than from Ezra, we gain the strong impression that the problem of foreign marriages is centrally a political problem, involving the Jewish aristocracy and local governmental leadership. The politics of associating with the descendants of Ammon and Moab is also much more explicitly a reference to local leadership than is the case with Ezra, where the ethnic categories in use seem more pejorative than informative. In the Nehemiah case, the guilty are males who are presumably attempting to 'marry up' to exchange their low status of 'exiles' for participation in aristocratic society. Sociological inferences lead one to conclude that the mixed marriages are built on the presupposition that the exile community was the relatively disadvantaged one of the two (or more) groups involved in the marriages (cf. Smith-Christopher 1994: 243–65). v. 31, the final word regards provisions for the temple's wood-offering (cf. Gen 22; Lev 1; 6:12; Jos 9:21–7; Ezek 39:10). With the final words, 'Remember me!', this additional word about wood supplies must surely qualify as among the least conclusive final sentences of the Bible.

REFERENCES

Avigad, N. (1983), *Discovering Jerusalem* (Nashville: Nelson).

Balch, S. (1985), 'The Neutered Civil Servant: Eunuchs, Celibates, Abductees, and the Maintenance of Organizational Loyalty', *Journal of Social and Behavioural Structures*, 8/4: 313–28.

Baskauskas, L. (1981), 'The Lithuanian Refugee Experience and Grief', *International Migration Review*, 15/1: 276–91.

Berquist, J. (1995), *Judaism in Persia's Shadow: A Social and Historical Approach* (Minneapolis: Fortress).

Betylon, J. W. (1992), 'Weights and Measures', *ABD* vi: 897–908.

Bickermann, E. (1976), 'The Edict of Cyrus in Ezra 1', *Studies in Jewish and Christian History*, 1 (Leiden: Brill).

Blenkinsopp, J. (1988), *Ezra-Nehemiah*, OTL (London: SCM).

Boyce, M. (1975–82), *A History of Zoroastrianism*, Handbuch der Orientalistik (Leiden: Brill), i, ii.

Carroll, R. (1992), 'Coopting the Prophets: Nehemiah and Noadiah', in J. Wright, R. Carroll, and P. Davies (eds.), *Priests, Prophets and Scribes (Festschrift for J. Blenkinsopp)*, JSOTSup 149 (Sheffield: Sheffield University Press).

Carter, C. (1991), 'A Social and Demographic Study of Post-Exilic Judah', diss., Duke University, NC.

Clines, D. (1984), *Ezra, Nehemiah, and Esther*, NCB (Basingstoke: Marshall, Morgan, & Scott).

Cook, J. M. (1983), *The Persian Empire* (New York: Schocken).

Cozer, L. (1972), 'The Alien as Servant of Power: Court Jews and Christian Renegades', *American Sociological Review*, 37: 574–81.

Dandamaev, M. (1989), *A Political History of the Achaemenid Empire*, tr. W. J. Vogel (Leiden: Brill).

——and Lukonin, V. G. (1989), *The Culture and Social Institutions of Ancient Iran*, tr. P. L. Kohl (Cambridge: Cambridge University Press).

Davies, G. (1994), *A History of Money* (Cardiff: University of Wales Press).

Demke, A. (1996), 'Who Returned First: Ezra or Nehemiah?', *Bible Review* (Apr.), 28–33, 46–8.

Depuydt, L. (1995), 'Murder in Memphis: The Story of Cambyses's Mortal Wounding of the Apis Bull', *JNES* 54/2: 119–26.

Ehrlich, A. B. (1914), *Randglossen zur hebräischen Bibel* (Leipzig: J. C. Hinrichs).

Eskenazi, T. (1988), *In an Age of Prose: A Literary Approach to Ezra-Nehemiah*, SBLMS 36 (Atlanta: Scholars Press).

——and Judd, E. (1994), 'Marriage to a Stranger in Ezra 9–10', in T. Eskenazi and K. Richards (eds.), *Temple and Community in the Persian Period*, Second Temple Studies, 2 (Sheffield: Sheffield University Press), 266–85.

Fanon, F. (1963), *The Wretched of the Earth* (New York: Grove).

Fensham, F. C. (1982), *The Books of Ezra and Nehemiah* (Grand Rapids, Mich.: Eerdmans).

Firmage, E. (1992), 'Zoology of the Bible', *ABD* vi: 1109–67.

Galling, K. (1951), 'The "Gola List" According to Ezra 2 Neh. 7', *JBL* 70.

—— (1961), 'Serubbabel und der Wiederaufbau des Tempels in Jerusalem', *Verbannung und Heimkehr: Beiträge zur Geschichte und Theologie Israels im 6. und 5. Jahrhundert v. Chr. (Festschrift für W. Rudolph)* (Tübingen: Mohr).

—— (1964) *Studien zur Geschichte Israels im persischen Zeitalter* (Tübingen: Mohr).

Georges, P. (1994), *Barbarian Asia and the Greek Experience* (Baltimore: Johns Hopkins University Press).

Hallock, R. T. (1960), 'A New Look at the Persepolis Tablets', *JNES* 19.

Hasel, G. (1972), *The Remnant* (Berrian Springs: Andrews University Press).

Hirsch, S. (1985), *The Friendship of the Barbarians* (London: Tufts University Press).

Hoglund, K. (1992), *Achaemenid Imperial Administration in Syria-Palestine and the Missions of Ezra and Nehemiah*, SBLDS 125 (Atlanta: Scholars Press).

Ivry, A. L. (1972), 'Nehemiah 6:10: Politics and the Temple', *JSJ* 3: 35–45.

Japhet, S. (1968), 'The Supposed Common Authorship of Chronicles and Ezra-Nehemiah Investigated Anew', *VT* 18: 330–71.

—— (1993), *I and II Chronicles* (London: Westminster).

Kapelrud, A. S. (1944), *The Question of Authorship in the Ezra Narrative: A Lexical Investigation* (Oslo: Dybwad).

Kellermann, U. (1967), *Nehemia: Quellen, Überlieferung und Geschichte*, BZAW 102 (Berlin: Töpelmann).

Kippenburg, H. (1982), *Religion und Klassenbildung im antiken Judäa* (Göttingen: Vandenhoeck & Ruprecht).

Kraeling, E. G. (1953) (ed.), *The Brooklyn Museum Aramaic Papyri* (New Haven: Yale University Press).

Lanternari, Vittorio (1963), *The Religions of the Oppressed*, tr. L. Sergio (New York: New American Library of World Literature).

Lapp, P. W., and Lapp, N. L. (1974), *Discoveries in the Wadi el Daliyeh*, AASOR 41: 81.

Lind, M. (1980), *Yahweh is a Warrior* (Scottdale, Pa.: Herald).

McEvenue, S. (1981), 'The Political Structure in Judah from Cyrus to Nehemiah', *CBQ* 43/4: 353–64.

Memmi, A. (1965), *The Colonizer and the Colonized* (New York: Beacon).

Morkholm, O. (1991), *Early Hellenistic Coinage* (Cambridge: Cambridge University Press).

Mumford, L. (1961), *The City in History* (New York: Harcourt Brace Jovanovich).

Myers, J. M. (1974), *I and II Esdras*, AB 42 (New York: Doubleday).

Nakasone, S. (1993), *Josiah's Passover: Sociology and the Liberating Bible* (Maryknoll, NY: Orbis).

Neufeld, E. (1953–4), 'The Rate of Interest and the Text of Nehemiah 5.11', *JQR* NS 44: 194–204.

Oded, B. (1979), *Mass Deportations and Deportees in the Neo-Assyrian Empire* (Weisbaden: Reichert).

Olmstead, A. T. (1933), 'A Persian Letter in Thucydides', *AJSL* 49: 154–61.

Raboteau, A. (1978), *Slave Religion* (Oxford: Oxford University Press).

Rad, G. von (1991), *Holy War in Ancient Israel*, tr. M. Dawn (Grand Rapids: Eerdmans).

Richards, R. (forthcoming), 'The Role of the Imperial Decrees in Ezra-Nehemiah', diss., University of Cape Town.

Rosenthal, F. (1974), *A Grammar of Biblical Aramaic* (Wiesbaden: Harrassowitz).

Rudolph, W. (1949), *Esra und Nehemia*, HAT 20 (Tübingen: Mohr).

Sauer, G. (1967), 'Serubbabel in der Sicht Haggais und Sacharjas', *Das ferne und nahe Wort*, BZAW 105 (Berlin: Töpelmann).

Scott, J. C. (1985), *Weapons of the Weak: Everyday Forms of Peasant Resistance* (New Haven: Yale University Press).

Simons, J. (1959), *The Geographical and Topographical Texts of the Old Testament* (Leiden: Brill).

Smith, D. L. (1989), *The Religion of the Landless: The Sociology of the Babylonian Exile* (Bloomington, Ind.: Meyer-Stone).

Smith-Christopher, D. L. (1993), 'Hebrew Satyagraha: The Politics of Biblical Fasting in the Post-Exilic Period', *Food and Foodways*, 5/3: 269–92.

—— (1994), 'The Mixed Marriage Crisis in Ezra 9–10 and Nehemiah 13: A Study of the Sociology of the Post-Exilic Judean Community', in T. Eskenazi and K. Richards (eds.), *Temple and Community in the Persian Period*, Second Temple Studies, 2 (Sheffield: Sheffield University Press), 243–65.

—— (1996), 'Between Ezra and Isaiah: Exclusion, Transformation, and Inclusion of the "Foreigner" in Post-Exilic Biblical Theology', in M. Brett (ed.), *Ethnicity and the Bible* (Leiden: Brill), 117–42.

Smitten, W. in der (1972–4), 'Historische Probleme zum Kyrosedikt und zum Jerusalemer Tempelbau von 515', *Persica*, 6: 171.

—— (1973), *Esra: Quellen, Überlieferung und Geschichte*, SSN 15 (Assen: Van Gorcum).

Stern, E. (1982), *Material Culture of the Land of the Bible in the Persian Period 538–332 BC* (Warminster: Aris & Phillips; Jerusalem: IES).

Torrey, C. C. (1970), *Ezra Studies* (New York: Ktav). Original edn. 1910.

Waterman, L. (1954), 'The Camouflaged Purge of Three Messianic Conspirators', *JNES* 13: 73–8.

Weinberg, J. (1992), *The Citizen-Temple Community*, JSOTSup 151 (Sheffield: Sheffield University Press).

Weinfeld, M. (1995), *Social Justice in Ancient Israel and in the Ancient Near East* (Minneapolis: Fortress).

White, R. (1983), *Roots of Dependency* (Lincoln, Nebr.: University of Nebraska Press).

Williamson, H. G. M. (1985), *Ezra, Nehemiah*, WBC (Waco, Tex.: Word).

Wiseman, D. J. (1956), *Chronicles of Chaldean Kings (626–556 B.C.) in the British Museum* (London: British Museum).

Wright, J. (1990), 'A Tale of Three Cities: Urban Gates, Squares, and Power in Iron Age II, Neo-Babylonian, and Achaemenid Israel', unpub. essay read at Society for Biblical Literature, Chicago.

Yadin, Y. (1963), *The Art of Warfare in Biblical Lands* (New York: McGraw Hill).

Yamauchi, E. (1990), *Persia and the Bible* (Grand Rapids: Baker Book House).

Zograph, A. N. (1977), *Ancient Coinage*, Br. Arch. Rep. Sup. Ser. 33/1 (Oxford: British Archaeological Reports).

Zucker, H. (1936), *Studien zur jüdischen Selbstverwaltung im Altertum* (New York: Schocken).

16. Esther

CAROL MEYERS

INTRODUCTION

A. Overview. 1. The Book of Esther, or Scroll of Esther as it is called in Jewish tradition, is part of the third major section, known as the Writings, of the Hebrew Bible (OT). One of the two books in Hebrew Scripture to bear the name of a woman, its title is the name of the book's heroine. The name is not Hebrew, but its origin is uncertain. It may come from Persian *stara* ('star'), Akkadian *ištār* (the goddess of love), or even a hypothetical Median word *astra* ('myrtle'). The last possibility is related to the fact that Esther also has a Hebrew name (see 2:7), Hadassah, which means 'myrtle'.

2. That the leading character has two names is indicative of the cultural situation that determines the setting and the plot of this exciting and fast-moving tale. The book of Esther is concerned with the often precarious situation of any minority people within a dominant majority culture. In this case, the Jews are dispersed within the Persian empire and face almost certain annihilation through the whim of a power-mongering bureaucrat (Haman). Only through the courageous and creative deeds of a Jewish woman, Esther, along with her mentor, Mordecai, do they escape harm and actually improve their status, though still remaining a subject people. The two names and identities of Esther—as both Jew and Persian—represent the political and ethnic problems facing people who live simultaneously in two cultures.

3. The ostensible reason for the inclusion of this book in the canon of the HB is that it purports to provide the historical origins for a festival known as Purim ('Lots'), a popular and raucous Jewish celebration held on the 14th and 15th of Adar

(Mar.–Apr.). Yet the book's historicity, as well as its legitimacy as a part of both the Jewish and Christian canon, have been the subject of serious disagreement since antiquity.

B. Ancient Versions. 1. The ancient concerns about the legitimacy of what appears in the received Hebrew text of Esther gave rise to a series of six midrashic supplements to the book that appear in the Septuagint version of the late second or early first century BCE. Those Greek Additions, lettered A to F, are interspersed throughout the book (see ch. 42, Esther (Greek)). They were placed together at the end of the canonical book, however, in the fourth century CE by Jerome in his revision of the Old Latin translation. English translations today place those Additions in the Apocrypha, although recent Roman Catholic editions integrate them with the Hebrew Esther.

2. The Septuagint text of Esther, with its additions as well as its omission of the many repetitive words and phrases of the MT, is probably the final stage in a complex process of tradition formation in which two component tales (one about Mordecai, another about Esther) were gradually brought together and elaborated in three successive stages of the Hebrew text (the latest being virtually identical with the present MT), and then the Septuagint stage. This last stage is faithful to the content of the Hebrew but less so to the wording (Moore 1971: lxi–lxiv; see also Clines 1984 and Fox 1990). Esther also exists in another ancient Greek version (the Lucianic recension, or A-text). The Vulgate and Syriac translations are both based on the Hebrew and are quite close to it, although Jerome's translation is a little freer than in most other parts of his work. Two Aramaic translations are quite expansive.

C. Provenance and Date. 1. The tale's focus on the Jewish community in Persia, along with its intimate knowledge of Persian customs and its total lack of interest in Judean life and institutions, indicates that Esther was composed in the eastern Diaspora. Jews who lived as a minority near the locus of power in the post-exilic period would have been the natural audience for this tale of Jewish accommodations and accomplishments in a foreign setting.

2. Extensive textual analysis in the last decade has established that the final Hebrew stage of the book would have been formed by the second century BCE. That it lacks any Greek words or evidence of Greek culture pushes it back to the pre-Hellenistic period for most scholars, although that absence is possibly the result of deliberate archaizing (so Berg 1979: 170–1). The earliest date would be that of the only identifiable historical figure in the book, the Persian ruler Ahasuerus, or Xerxes I (486–465 BCE). Some late fifth-century elements are possible, but the story shows some distance from Xerxes and probably did not reach its present form until some time in the fourth century. In vocabulary and syntax, its Hebrew has much in common with that of the Chronicler (*c.*400 BCE); and its sense of Jews widely and comfortably—though not necessarily securely—settled throughout the empire suits the Persian II period (see Hoglund 1992).

D. Interpretative Problems and Canonicity. 1. Esther is the only book in the Hebrew canon for which no fragments have been discovered at Qumran. Its absence from the corpus of Dead Sea scrolls attests to the difficulty it had in reaching canonical status in early Judaism; and the fact that the Western Fathers merely mention it while the Eastern Church did not accept it as part of the canon until the eighth century CE is indicative of its controversial nature in early Christianity. For both Jews and Christians, the most prominent reason for its disputed status is its lack of explicit religiosity. God is never once mentioned, nor are basic biblical concepts such as covenant, Torah, and temple. Also absent are standard elements of Jewish piety such as dietary laws, sacrifice, and prayer; and virtues such as mercy and forgiveness are not present. The reasons for such omissions are only speculative (see the summary in Moore 1992: 636–7), but the fact that many of these 'missing' elements appear prominently in the Additions to Esther demonstrates clearly how deficient the canonical Esther seemed. Not only are its deficiencies troubling but so also are some of its features, such as the apparent vindictiveness with which the Jews avenge those who would have destroyed them, although that particular aspect may be part of the peripety (unexpected reversal of fortunes) that characterizes the literary structure of the book.

2. Controversy has also surrounded the value of Esther and her deeds as a female role model. Some biblical scholars have downplayed her activities, making Mordecai into the true hero of the tale (see Moore 1971: lii) and questioning Esther's sexual ethics (as Paton 1908: 96). Some radical feminist critics would rather make Vashti the heroine (Gendler 1976); they object to Esther's use of sexuality and food to achieve her ends (as Fuchs 1982). Others writing with a feminist perspective (e.g. LaCocque 1990; White 1989; 1992) are respectful of such tactics of indirection, which serve as models for the powerless, whether individuals or communities, who struggle to establish and maintain a semblance of agency in their lives. For those who view her positively, Esther becomes a sage in her own right: she dominates the action, surpassing Mordecai and subordinating the king to her will (Hallo 1983: 24–5). The characterization of Esther in postbiblical Jewish tradition, such as the Additions (see Day 1995) and rabbinic literature (as Bronner 1994), is another aspect of feminist interest in this biblical book.

E. Genre and Purpose. 1. The blatant historical difficulties, the internal inconsistencies, the pronounced symmetry of themes and events, the plenitude of quoted dialogue, and the gross exaggeration in the reporting of numbers (involving time, money, and people) all point to Esther as a work of fiction, its vivid characters (except for Xerxes) being the product of the author's creative imagination. Recognizing that it is not historical, although it reflects actual conditions and problems of the post-exilic Jewish Diaspora, has allowed scholars to appreciate many of its literary features and to compare its thematic aspects with those of certain other canonical, deuterocanonical, and extracanonical pieces.

2. Esther has long been called a 'Diaspora novella' (Meinhold 1969; 1975–6). Like the Joseph story in Genesis and the book of Daniel, it is a fictional piece of prose writing involving the interaction between foreigners and Hebrews/Jews. In all these works, the Jews have low status, are threatened, and at the end achieve success and a rise in status. The plots of these tales depict only one series of events, all occurring within a limited time period. Esther's similarity to Daniel and to the Joseph tale, especially with many lexical connections to the latter, may be the result of all three of these novellas also being 'royal courtier tales' (see Humphreys 1973). That such tales contain many elements of wisdom literature is also a compelling consideration (Talmon 1963).

3. An important dimension to the wise-courtier aspect of Esther and other biblical pieces is added by noting its folkloristic features (Niditch and Doran 1977). Recognizing the presence of certain elements that are known cross-culturally, outside biblical tradition, broadens the consideration of literary traits and genres to include awareness of the social setting. The type of folk-tale exemplified by Esther involves status difference as a critical element. The interplay and tension between high- and low-status persons and/or groups, with the lower-status character or community prevailing, constitute a kind of resistance literature (Smith 1989: 162–4). The creation of such tales in many cultures uses similar themes and elements because those features, whereby a minority hero/heroine rises above and achieves some sort of victory over the dominant power, allow the oppressed group to maintain identity, self-respect, and hope. Through her cleverness and patience, Esther thwarts a superpower. The official culture's dominance is thereby contested, and traits (wisdom, piety, cleverness) available to even the powerless are shown to have empowering value.

4. In the case of the Book of Esther, as in many other such folk-tales, the outcome does not mean that the dominant power is toppled. Rather, the achievement of the hero/heroine is to establish the integrity of the minority group within the larger culture. That is, Judaism cannot and thus will not overtly oppose its imperial masters; but it can maintain its core identity while subscribing to most of the Persian regulations and structures. More broadly, Jews can be loyal to two masters; they can live successfully in the Diaspora.

F. Outline. 1. As a well-constructed narrative tale, Esther has a clearly demarcated beginning ('exposition', chs. 1–2), middle ('complication', chs. 3–9), and end ('resolution', chs. 9–10), with these three parts each having a number of discrete sections (Clines 1988).

Introducing the Setting (1:1–2:23)
    The Vashti Incident (1:1–22)
    Esther's Accession to the Throne (2:1–23)
The Plot Unfolds (3:1–8:17)
    Struggle between Haman and Mordecai (3:1–4:3)
    Esther Becomes Involved (4:5–5:8)
    The Mordecai–Haman Problem Escalates (5:9–6:14)
    Haman is Overcome and Replaced (7:1–8:17)
The Crisis is Resolved (9:1–10:3)
    Events of the 13th of Adar (9:1–19)
    Purim Becomes a Festival (9:20–32)
    Conclusion (10:1–3)

COMMENTARY

Exposition (1:1–2:23)

(1:1–22) The Vashti Incident The opening four verses provide the setting for most of the book: the sumptuous court of the Persian ruler Ahasuerus (Xerxes), the only historical figure in the book. The exaggerated vastness of the kingdom ('over one hundred and twenty-seven provinces from India to Ethiopia', v. 1) and of the initial banquet, which lasts for the improbably long period of 180 days, emphasizes imperial power and thus prepares the way for the enormity of the reversal that will take place at the end of the book, when Persian political privilege becomes accessible to a subject people. The Hebrew root *m-l-k* ('to rule') appears for the first time in the first verse in designating the king's rule; except for the introductory term 'happened', 'ruled' is the first verb in the book and establishes a major theme. The word appears in various noun and verbal forms some 250 times in Esther, thereby emphasizing the royalty of the governing power, a dominant motif in the book (Berg 1979: 59–72).

The initial use of the term 'banquet' also appears at the beginning of the book (vv. 3, 5, 9). That word (*mišteh*) appears 20 times in Esther but only 24 times in the entire rest of the HB. The importance of official feasts, of which there are eight altogether in Esther (three called by the king, one by Vashti, two by Esther, and two by the Jews), is thus introduced. The symmetry of the book, with feasts at the beginning, middle, and end, is also thereby established. The two feasts called by the king at the outset, with the second one (vv. 5–8) described in exceptionally lavish detail, are mirrored at the end by the two Jewish feasts. In the first instance the imperial power indulged its wealth; and in the second instance, after a series of breathtaking reversals, the Jews in all 127 provinces celebrate their survival.

Another important feature of Esther emerges in the language of the first chapter. The importance of law and the related issue of obedience versus disobedience is obvious from the repeated use of the term *dāt* (vv. 13, 15, etc.). This Persian word, meaning 'law' or 'decree', appears about 20 times in Esther (elsewhere only twice in the HB). Other words for edicts, orders, customs, commands, and proclamations abound. The frequent use of *dāt* and other such terms introduces the problem of Jews adhering to an external legal and cultural system while remaining faithful to Jewish tradition. The recurrent vocabulary of governance highlights the continual tension experienced by any subject group, with its own codes of behaviour, struggling to survive in a land not its own, in a culture with codes and procedures at variance with its own.

Although the king's royal power and palace munificence are important introductory themes of the first chapter, the book's plot is initiated by an incident involving the queen, Vashti, who gave her own banquet at the same time as the king's second one. The announcement (v. 9) of the queen's feast, which appears almost as an aside, establishes the legitimacy of official banquets being offered by the queen of the realm and anticipates the meals to be hosted later by Esther at a critical point in the tale. Certainly the fact of Vashti hosting a banquet for women does not seem essential for the incident that next occurs—except that it may indicate that Vashti was too busy to respond to her husband's request that his beautiful queen be paraded before the king, his officials, and all the people in attendance at the king's second banquet. She survives her disobedience by losing only her position (v. 19). The calm assertion of autonomy by Vashti results in royal rage and then a ridiculous royal decree—that all men should be master in their own homes—which adds a comic touch in that it could hardly be enforced, and indicates that men were not actually dominant in their households.

(2:1–23) Esther's Accession to the Throne When Ahasuerus' anger abates, he again takes action, authorizing the search for a new queen. The idea of his ire dissipating occurs once more, using the same verb (*š-k-k*), in 7:10, when the king is calmed after another royal order is carried out. In both cases his wrath emerges from a spouse problem; in the first case the queen (Vashti) threatens his authority, whereas in the second case, his chief officer threatens the queen (Esther). The king apparently experiences intense anger only in matters of the heart.

In introducing Esther, the narrator informs us of her relationship to Mordecai, her cousin, adoptive father, and mentor. Mordecai's name, which is probably a Hebraized form of a Babylonian name with the theophoric element Marduk, contains an idolatrous element; but he may have had (as did Esther) a true Hebrew name as well (Moore 1971: 19). If his name is suspect, his lineage is not. The genealogical information in vv. 5–6 puts him in the family of Saul, the first Israelite ruler. This brief genealogy accomplishes three things. First, it gives Mordecai a royal identity, fitting his eventual high position in the Persian court (8:2, 8, 10, 15; 9:4). Yet, as a Saulide rather than a Davidide, his royal heritage poses no threat to Persian dominance; it is the Davidic line and not the Saulide one that is expected one day to regain power. Second, it sets up the opposition between Mordecai and his nemesis Haman, the king's chief official. Haman is an Agagite (3:1), a descendant of the Amalekite king who opposed King Saul (1 Sam 15:32). Mordecai and Haman thus echo the historic confrontation between Saul and Agag. Third, it gives a sense of Jewish continuity in presenting Mordecai's family as having survived since the days of Saul. Saul the Benjaminite preceded David the Judahite, and his descendant Mordecai now outlasts Davidic rule.

The beautiful Esther is chosen for the king's harem and receives special food and seven serving maids. These two benefits anticipate an important reversal at the turning-point of the story, when Esther and her maids fast for three days (4:15). Obeying Mordecai's charge, though later she will disobey even the king, Esther does not reveal her Jewish identity (vv. 10, 20). It is not that her identity would have disqualified her from the harem; rather it would preclude the plot development that will enable her to act on behalf of her people. The king must not know her national or ethnic origins ('her people or kindred').

Esther's beauty wins the approval of the king, who crowns her queen (v. 17) even though she requests no special attire or adornment (see vv. 13, 15) when she first enters the king's presence. Her role in saving the king's life in this opening section of the book is just as important as is her beauty in sealing her favoured position. Through her informant Mordecai, she learns of a plan to assassinate the king and warns him of it (vv. 21–2). The would-be assassins die on the gallows, and the motif of the hanging of the king's enemies enters the narrative. All the elements necessary for the central problem of the story are now in place, and the plot begins to unfold in ch. 3.

The Plot Unfolds (3:1–8:17)

(3:1–4:3) Struggle between Mordecai and Haman The only major character not yet on the scene appears in the first verse of this section: Haman the Agagite, linked by his genealogy to Israel's archetypal enemy and historical foe of King Saul, from whose father, Kish, was descended Mordecai (see 2:5–6), who will be his opponent and nemesis in this tale. The issue of obedience is immediately raised, this time in relation to Mordecai. Having elevated Haman to a lofty position in the court, the king has ordered everyone to bow down to him. Mordecai refuses to do so (3:2). This act of defiance is not directly explained, but the servants who witness it and who fail to convince Mordecai to honour Haman then inform Haman of Mordecai's Jewish identity. Perhaps it is implied, as Jewish commentaries from the rabbinical period onwards have suggested, that Jews would bow down only to their God (cf. Dan 3). If so, the tension of binational loyalty, i.e. the problem of diaspora Jewry, appears directly in the story, and a religious dimension is indirectly introduced.

Even if Mordecai's Judaism is not the cause of his refusal to do obeisance, it becomes the reason for Haman's response: a monumental overreaction to a snub. His revenge would be the destruction not simply of Mordecai but of his entire people (3:8). The vastness of Haman's plan to relieve his malice towards Mordecai in some ways recapitulates the outrageous scale of Ahasuerus' response to Vashti's snub, whereby he subordinates all women to their husbands. The parallel between Jews and women is clear. They both must be dealt with in their entirety to rectify the impropriety of one of them towards the royal power. Perhaps, too, both women and Jews have greater potential power than their apparently subordinate status would indicate.

Haman then casts a lot, or *pûr*—an act well-documented as a tool of ancient imperial decision science (see Hallo 1983)—to select the day for this genocide. This procedure is to become the *raison d'être* for the festival of Purim (9:24–6). That the date selected—the thirteenth day of the twelfth month, Adar (3:7, 13)—involves the number 13 (thought to be unlucky already in biblical antiquity) perhaps prefigures the fateful turn of events when that day finally arrives. Haman's plan is approved, at least in part because he makes a donation to the king's treasury of 10,000 talents of silver, a highly inflated sum indicative of the fictive quality of the tale.

Ahasuerus then acts in equally grandiose fashion, allowing Haman to use his signet ring, the ultimate instrument of authority. Because of this preposterous if temporary transfer of royal power to Haman, the ultimate death of the villain will mean that the subject people will have overcome the 'ruler', who is not the actual ruler; and Ahasuerus, the somewhat bumbling good-hearted monarch, will maintain the respect and loyalty of his subjects. The Jews will reverse their subordinate status by disposing of their oppressor while remaining loyal subjects to the real king.

Now it is time for reactions to the evil decree. First the city of Susa itself is 'thrown into confusion' (3:15; cf. the reversal of this situation in 8:15). Then, upon hearing the news, Mordecai and all the Jews throughout the empire go into mourning by donning 'sackcloth and ashes', by crying out, and by fasting (4:1–3). This last act, fasting, is mentioned twice more, when

Esther and her maids fast (4:16), and again in the proclamation of future fasts (9:31). The emphasis on abstention from food as a reflection of and response to the impending death sentence provides a stark contrast to the joyous consumption of food at the various banquets and feasts that punctuate the tale. At the same time, the appearance of fasting may be the one possible example of Jewish religious observance in the entire, rather secular, book of Esther. Fasting together with weeping has good biblical precedent as an individual intercessory attempt to plead with God and thus save a life; the story of David's actions on behalf of his first son by Bathsheba is notable in this regard (2 Sam 12:15–17). Also, as a community-wide response to disaster, the events surrounding the sixth century BCE destruction of Jerusalem and the temple apparently produced several fast days (see Zech 7:4; 8:19).

(4:5–5:9) Esther Becomes Involved The story at last turns towards Esther's response, which will ultimately lead to a reversal. She sends the eunuch Hathach, who is one of her attendants, to Mordecai to find out about Haman's decree. Replying through this messenger, Mordecai charges her to approach Ahasuerus, in order 'to make supplication to him and entreat him for her people' (4:8). Now we hear Esther's voice directly for the first time (4:11–12). This first instance of reported speech for her, followed soon by a second (4:16) as she informs her cousin that no one can approach the king unbidden under threat of death, signals two important shifts. First, Esther has her own voice and is now acting in her own right, no longer under her mentor's direction. Second, her words mark her explicit involvement in her people's dilemma and in the rescue she will orchestrate. Esther's two statements in ch. 4 provide the turning point of the tale; they draw attention to her potential power evident in her astute reading of the palace rules.

In learning of Esther's response, Mordecai presses her further: she will ultimately die anyway, and she must go to the king. Mordecai's words suggest that help may come 'from another quarter'. The Hebrew term here, *māqôm* ('place'), is sometimes a euphemism for the divine presence; if so, the word provides a hint of religiosity and of the salvific working of divine providence. Similarly, the fact that Esther proclaims a fast for herself bespeaks a supplicatory or prayerful attitude, perhaps an indication of the queen's Jewish piety. In any case, Mordecai's immediate obedience to Esther's command (4:17) is an explicit reversal of her earlier acquiescence to his instructions.

In accordance with the information she sent to Mordecai, Esther takes the courageous step of approaching the king unbidden at the end of the three-day fast. She disobeys royal law in appearing before him, yet her risky behaviour is richly rewarded, for he generously offers to give her whatever she wants, 'even to the half of my kingdom' (5:3). But Esther cleverly asks for nothing more than an opportunity to entertain her husband and his chief officer. They are both pleased at her hospitality; and the king again offers her half the empire. This time she requests only a second banquet, thereby demonstrating to the king that her requests are easy and pleasant to fulfil. Her strategy of making the king eager to agree to whatever she wishes is in place.

(5:9–6:14) The Mordecai–Haman Problem Escalates Happy as Haman was to have been entertained by the queen, he becomes intensely distressed when Mordecai once more refuses to do obeisance. At the bidding of his wife Zeresh, he erects monumental gallows intended for Mordecai; only then can Haman feel relaxed enough to look forward to Esther's second banquet. Meanwhile, to pass the hours of a sleepless night, Ahasuerus makes the unlikely but fortuitous move of having his court annals read aloud, thereby discovering that he had failed to reward Mordecai for passing on the information about the assassination plot. In a marvellously ironic scene (6:4–11), as the tale moves inexorably to its ultimate reversal, Haman appears on the scene and is asked what a king should do to honour someone. With his arrogance and egomania, Haman believes he is the one deserving such honour and constructs a reward—parading the honoured man, on horseback and in royal garb, to the city square—that is then given to Mordecai. Haman must lead the horse and proclaim the king's favour for Mordecai. Understandably devastated, Haman is now the one who exhibits mourning behaviour. Once more his wife takes note, this time with the pessimistic notion that Haman's intent to destroy Mordecai may end up with the opposite result. The reason for this? Mordecai is Jewish (6:13). Zeresh's response conveys a powerful notion underlying the book—that the Jews are ultimately inviolable and will somehow survive.

(7:1–8:17) Haman is Overcome and Replaced At the queen's second banquet, when the king is determined to grant her any request, Esther speaks to Ahasuerus in a way that signals her readiness to take advantage of his goodwill. In 7:3 she addresses him for the first time in the second person, saying 'If I have won your favour', rather than using the third person, 'If I have won the king's favour', as in 5:8. She is now ready to be direct in her petitions as well as in her identity. In 7:4 she paraphrases Haman's edict, written in the name of Ahasuerus, to destroy the Jews (3:13). In so doing she identifies herself for the first time as a member of the people to be killed and then requests that the lives of all this group be spared. Incredibly, the king seems ignorant of the decree. Perhaps, because Esther mentions an alternative scenario—that the order might have been to enslave the Jews rather than annihilate them—he had thought he was authorizing a servitude plan. In any case, when Esther identifies Haman as the perpetrator of the projected genocide, the king stomps out to his garden in a rage but says nothing about reversing Haman's edict.

Left alone with Esther, the terrified Haman falls upon the couch where she is reclining to plead for mercy. At that moment the king returns and sees what appears to him to be a sexual assault on his queen. This at last precipitates the climactic reversal of the tale. But it occurs on a personal level. Even with the knowledge that all the Jews were to be slaughtered, the king does not act until his own wife's sexuality is apparently threatened by Haman, just as his proclamation that all men are to be masters in their homes (1:22) is the result of the defiance of his own wife. Now his orders are first to hang Haman—with delicious irony, on the very gallows intended for Mordecai—rather than to reverse Haman's edict. The immediate threat to his wife having been removed, the king's anger is abated (7:10, as in 2:1 when he dealt with Vashti).

Yet the ultimate reversal has still not been accomplished; Haman has been hanged, but his order to destroy the Jews has not been revoked. The next two acts of the king do nothing to change this situation. He continues to respond on a personal level, awarding Haman's household to Esther and giving Mordecai Haman's signet ring. Mordecai and Esther thus together assume ownership of their enemy's holdings, a development hardly satisfactory to Esther, now openly connected with the Jew Mordecai (8:1). Consequently, Esther abandons all guile and falls to the king's feet in tears. Both Esther and the honoured Mordecai are in the king's presence, but it is Esther who speaks out, reverting to the third person in beseeching Ahasuerus to order Haman's decree invalid and in asking that the calamity awaiting her 'people' and her 'kindred' be averted (8:6). Her use of those two terms, in the reverse order to that of ch. 2, finalizes the reversal. Her previously concealed identity is asserted, changing the situation noted in 2:10, which states that Esther 'did not reveal her people or kindred' when she entered the harem.

Just as Ahasuerus had given Haman the authority to issue an edict in the name of the king, he now provides for a symmetrical ending by giving a parallel right to Esther and Mordecai (8:7-8). In the language of formal royal activity, which reflects that of 3:12 when Haman formulated the terrible decree, the narrator tells us about a new irrevocable edict to be sent out to all the Persian provinces. The multicultural nature of the empire was duly noted in the account of the earlier edict, which was sent to 'all the peoples, to every province in its own script and every people in its own language' (3:12), a situation that accords with documented Persian policy allowing peoples comprising the empire to maintain a significant amount of political and economic autonomy. In the reprise in ch. 8 of the stereotyped language of edict promulgation, however, the Jews are singled out; the new orders are of course sent to all those peoples in their own scripts and languages 'and also to the Jews in their script and their language' (8:9).

The new decree, interestingly enough, does not directly revoke Haman's edict; royal edicts issued with the king's signet could not be overturned (8:8). Instead, it authorizes the Jews to annihilate those who, in trying to carry out the terms of Haman's decree, would attempt to slaughter them. In other words, the peculiarity of Persian law in this tale forces the Jews to survive by engaging in the very kind of deadly physical assault to which they are objecting. The official statement, in which the Jews are instructed to assemble and to kill not only their attackers but also the families of their attackers, is a troubling sanction for Jewish violence. But its context, an edict that must overpower an unremovable earlier one, along with the absurdity of the presumably unarmed and militarily untrained Jews overwhelming the imperial forces charged with their slaughter, should ameliorate the horror of the retributive actions to take place at the appointed time. That moment, of course, is to be the thirteenth day of the twelfth month of Adar (8:12), the very day earlier selected by lot for carrying out Haman's edict (3:7).

Accompanying the new edict is the garbing of Mordecai in stunning royal apparel, with a 'great golden crown' (8:15). The leading Jewish male in the kingdom now joins the leading Jewish female (cf. 2:17) in wearing the kind of royal headgear so coveted by Haman (6:7). This vivid reversal is accompanied by a similar sea-change in the response of the people. The citizens of Susa had been 'thrown into confusion' (3:15) by Haman's decree; in contrast they respond with great joy to Mordecai's edict (8:16). The Jews are similarly ecstatic and initiate festive activities. This whole turn of events, in which certain Jewish annihilation has been replaced with greatly elevated Jewish status along with royal power placed in the hands of a Jewish official, leads to the astonishing statement that many of the peoples in the empire 'professed to be Jews, because the fear of the Jews had fallen upon them' (8:17). Whether or not this is to be taken as a description of the conversion of some groups to Judaism, the statement does convey the fact that people are inexorably drawn to the security of siding with those in power and that concepts of ethnicity are complicated by the dynamics of political privilege.

The Crisis is Resolved (9:1-10:3)

(9:1-19) Events of the Thirteenth of Adar The opening verse of this section is explicit in describing the power reversal that ensues. On the very day that the Jews' enemies were to have vanquished them, the opposite would happen: 'the Jews would gain power over their foes' (9:1). That the fear of the empowered Jews mentioned at the end of ch. 8 and repeated in 9:2 (with an additional statement about Mordecai's high standing in the court) was warranted became clear on the thirteenth of Adar, when the Jews struck down their enemies—75,000 in the provinces (9:16) and 500 in the citadel of Susa (9:6)—defined as all who hated them (9:5). They refrained, however, from plundering. This point must be an important one, because it appears three times (9:10, 15, 16). Perhaps it resumes the parallel set up between Mordecai/Saul and Haman/Agag. When Saul defeated the Agagites, he slaughtered men, women, and children but kept the best sheep and cattle as spoils. He earned divine disapproval for the latter act, with God regretting the choice of Saul as king. The echo in Esther of the 1 Sam 15 narrative clearly stops at the plunder issue. Mordecai and the Jews will refrain from taking booty and, unlike Saul, maintain their favoured status (with God?).

The issue of restraint in the taking of plunder, therefore, is not so much an indication of noble character as it is a narrative intent to complete the Saul/Agag parallel with an improvement over the 1 Samuel episode. Yet the vindictiveness of the Jews again seems problematic in their treatment of the people of Susa. A special additional edict is provided directly by the king at Esther's behest, allowing the Jews to kill their 300 remaining enemies in the city of Susa (as opposed to its citadel, which presumably contained the palace and government complex). They do this on the following day, the fourteenth of Adar. At the same time, also in accord with the additional royal edict Esther requested, they hang the bodies of the ten sons of Haman on the gallows. This final gratuitous act may also be an echo of the Agag narrative, which ends with Agag himself being hacked to pieces, his lineage thus symbolically destroyed (1 Sam 15:33). Putting the bodies of Haman's sons, tantamount to pieces of his body, on the gallows has a similar effect. A literary purpose is achieved at the expense of the humanity of the Jews of Susa.

The fictive nature of the slaughter appears not only in the account of Haman's sons, but also in the specification of the huge numbers of Persians struck down by the Jews. Those incredibly large figures are hyperbole designed to emphasize the reversal of the Jews' expected fate and the fact that they have enormous power despite their second-class status. Similarly, the notion that the Jews had enemies everywhere flies in the face of the details of the story, in which Haman alone is the foe. Assigning large numbers to the people slaughtered by the Jews represents the paranoia of the powerless; everyone of higher status has the potential to do them harm and thus *de facto* is a foe.

The immediate consequence of the acts of the thirteenth and fourteenth of Adar is celebration. In the villages of the provinces, the Jews rest on the fourteenth day from the exertions of the previous day (9:17, 19), whereas in Susa the Jews do not celebrate until the fifteenth day because they were engaged in overthrowing enemies on the fourteenth as well as the thirteenth days (9:18). Regardless of the date, the day of rest is a day of joy and yet another occasion for feasting. This set of holidays held by Jews constitutes the final reversal of the tale; the pivotal fasts of 4:3 and 16 become feasts, echoing the two royal banquets that initiate the tale. They not only recall earlier banquets held by the king, as well as those of Vashti and Esther, but also introduce a new element. In the celebratory banquet of 9:19 (cf. 9:22), the Jews hold feasts and at the same time send food around to each other, intensifying the notion of well-being for all.

(9:20–32) Purim Becomes a Festival The momentous events of Adar certainly deserve commemoration by future generations. vv. 20–32 provide for just that. Perhaps an addition to the coherent narrative of 1:1 through 9:19, this section recapitulates the core reversals: relief from persecution, turning 'sorrow into gladness' and 'mourning into a holiday' (9:22). The rehearsal of the reason for the celebration takes us back to Haman's casting of lots (*pûrîm*), thereby providing an etymology for the festive days. The holiday is, of course, to be held for two days, in the light of the fact that the original feasting and rejoicing took place on the fourteenth of Adar in the provinces and a day later in Susa.

A touch of formality is lent to the newly instituted festival by another set of letters, said to be sent to Jews in 'all the provinces' (v. 20; cf. v. 30) and thus using the same language as in the accounts of earlier royal edicts (1:22; 3:12–13; 8:9). Mordecai writes these official letters enjoining Jews to celebrate Purim; and Esther writes them with him (vv. 29, 31), perhaps even writing a second letter (v. 29). Her royal authority in establishing Purim is reaffirmed at the end of this section, where she is the one said to have established the customs of the holiday (v. 32).

(10:1–3) Conclusion If there is reason to consider ch. 9 an addendum meant to institute the festival of Purim, there is good cause to view ch. 10 as another, briefer addition. Ch. 9 ends with the accomplishments of Esther, and ch. 10 is an encomium to Mordecai. But Mordecai's power is here set alongside that of the king. That is, with a Jew as second in command to a Gentile king, the interests of both groups—Persians and Jews—are well served. The ideal diaspora situation is achieved and serves as a model for all diaspora communities.

REFERENCES

Berg, S. B. (1979), *The Book of Esther: Motifs, Themes, and Structures*, SBLDS 44 (Missoula, Mont.: Scholars Press).

Bronner, L. L. (1994), *From Eve to Esther: Rabbinic Reconstructions of Biblical Women*, Gender and the Biblical Tradition, 4 (Louisville, Ky.: Westminster/John Knox).

Clines, D. J. A. (1984), *The Esther Scroll: The Story of the Story*, JSOTSup 30 (Sheffield: JSOT).

—— (1988), 'Esther', *HBC*, 387–94.

Crawford, S. A. W. (1989), 'Esther: A Feminine Model for the Jewish Diaspora', in Peggy L. Day (ed.), *Gender and Difference* (Philadelphia: Fortress), 161–77.

—— (1992), 'Esther', in Carol A. Newsom and Sharon H. Ringe (eds.), *The Women's Bible Commentary* (Knoxville, Ten.: Westminster John Knox).

Day, L. (1995), *Three Faces of a Queen: Characterization in the Book of Esther*, JSOTSup 186 (Sheffield: JSOT).

Fox, M. V. (1990), *The Redaction of the Book of Esther* (Atlanta: Scholars Press).

Fuchs, E. (1982), 'Status and Role of Female Heroines in the Biblical Narrative', *Mankind Quarterly*, 23: 149–60.

Gendler, M. (1976), 'The Restoration of Vashti', in Elizabeth Koltun (ed.), *The Jewish Woman: New Perspectives* (New York: Schocken Books), 241–47.

Hallo, W. W. (1983), 'The First Purim', *BA* 46: 19–29.

Hoglund, K. (1992), *Achaemenid Imperial Administration in Syria-Palestine and the Missions of Ezra and Nehemiah*, SBLDS 125 (Atlanta: Scholars Press).

Humphreys, W. L. (1973), 'A Lifestyle for Diaspora: A Study of the Tales of Esther and David', *JBL* 92: 211–23.

LaCocque, A. (1990), *The Feminine Unconventional: Four Subversive Figures in Israel's Tradition* (Minneapolis: Fortress).

Meinhold, A. (1969), *Die Diasporanovelle—eine alttestamentliche Gattung*, Th.D. diss., Ernst-Moritz-Arndt Universität, Greifswald.

—— (1975–6) 'Die Gattung der Josephsgeschichte und des Estherbuches: Diasporanovelle, I, II', *ZAW* 87: 306–24; 88: 79–83.

Moore, C. A. (1971), *Esther: A New Translation with Introduction and Commentary*. AB 7B.

—— (1992), 'Esther, Book of', *ABD* 2. 633–43.

Niditch, S. and Doran, R. (1977), 'The Success Story of the Wise Courtier: A Formal Approach', *JBL* 92: 179–93.

Paton, L. B. (1908), *A Critical and Exegetical Commentary on the Book of Esther*, ICC (Edinburgh: T. & T. Clark).

Smith, D. L. (1989), *The Religion of the Landless: The Sociology of the Babylonian Exile* (Bloomington, Ind.: Meyer-Stone).

Talmon, S. (1963), 'Wisdom in the Book of Esther', *VT* 13: 419–55.

17. Job

JAMES L. CRENSHAW

INTRODUCTION

A brief narrative informs the reader that the hero is subjected to a divine test as a means of ascertaining whether or not he serves the deity without thinking about profiting from it. A poetic debate between Job and three friends follows, in which they discuss Job's suffering and the broader issue of divine justice. This debate opens with Job's powerful lament; from then on, a friend speaks and Job responds. This happens for three cycles of debate, except that Bildad's last speech is quite brief and Zophar's is missing. Job then remembers his happy past, contrasting it with his miserable present. A poetic interlude asks where wisdom can be found, and Job pronounces an oath of innocence aimed at evoking a divine response. Instead of the anticipated deity, a youthful Elihu appears and criticizes the friends for failing to answer Job effectively and Job for the nature of his complaints. God finally arrives in a tempest, rebukes Job, and praises the wonders of nature, both heavenly and earthly. In the face of such majesty, Job relents—although the text is ambiguous at this point. The book concludes with a short narrative telling about Job's restoration.

A. Composition. **1.** The book of Job receives high praise from critics of every persuasion—literary, philosophical, psychological, and religious—despite its flaws. One interpreter uses the phrase 'a blemished perfection' (Hoffman 1996), comparing the book to *Venus de Milo* and August Rodin's *Torso of a Woman*. Another appreciative reader observes that 'Here, in our view, is the most sublime monument in literature, not only of written language, nor of philosophy and poetry, but the most sublime monument of the human soul. Here is the great eternal drama with three actors who embody everything: but what actors! God, humankind, and Destiny' (Alphonse de Lamartine, cited in Hausen 1972: 145).

2. Such accolades persist partly because of the book's ambiguity, its capacity for ironic readings. A book at odds with itself, the combination of prose and poetry leaves numerous unanswered questions. The story depicts a blameless Job who patiently accepts grievous loss, persists in his integrity by worshipping the one who gives and takes away, and in the end receives everything back—with new children. The poetic debate presents an entirely different hero, one who lacks patience and openly attacks the deity for injustice. This section of the book rejects the hypothesis of a universe operating on a principle of reward and punishment, whereas the prose implies that YHWH does act towards the friends and Job on the basis of merit. Moreover, the names for deity differ in the prose, which uses YHWH, and the poetic debate, where the more general names El, Eloah, and El Shaddai occur, with a single exception, itself a stereotypical expression ('hand of YHWH', 12:9).

3. Other indications of disjointedness give the impression of imperfection. An Adversary (*haśśāṭān*) is featured in the prologue as the heavenly accuser of Job, but the epilogue proceeds without mentioning this character. YHWH's praise of Job for speaking truthfully about the deity suggests that the author of the epilogue had no inkling as to the nature of Job's speeches in the poetry. The youthful Elihu, whose expansive speeches delay the expected appearance of YHWH interminably, is ignored both by YHWH and by the author of the epilogue. This angry young man alone addresses Job by name, frequently quoting his earlier speeches. At the same time, Elihu anticipates major themes in the divine speeches, in a sense stealing divine thunder.

4. A poem (ch. 28) also offers a premature answer to the question it poses: 'Where can wisdom be found?' Having celebrated human achievement in prospecting for and mining precious gems, the poem denies access to wisdom, with the sole exception of God. Strangely, it concludes on a traditional note: God grants wisdom to faithful worshippers. In addition, this poem interrupts Job's final speech, necessitating a repetition of the formula in 27:1 ('Job again took up his discourse and said') in 29:1.

5. This introductory formula differs from the usual one ('Then Job answered'), suggesting that its initial occurrence in 27:1 resulted from textual dislocation, some of Bildad's final speech being attributed to Job and all of Zophar's speech dropping out. It has been suggested that the author used this subtle means of announcing that Job's friends have run out of anything to say; but Elihu's failure to discern the point makes this view unlikely. Job's unexpected comments in ch. 27 could be explained as sarcasm or irony; textual dislocation is more probable.

6. Even divine speeches indicate disjointedness. First, there are two divine speeches and two 'repentances' on Job's part, giving the appearance of browbeating. Second, the references to the ostrich and mighty war-horse differ markedly from previous celebrations of wild creatures. According to 40:5, Job vows to remain silent from this point, but 42:1–6 disregards this promise and has him speak once more.

7. Various theories have been advanced to explain these phenomena, but no consensus exists. The assumption underlying this commentary is that a poet used an existing popular story as the framework for exploring the possibility of disinterested righteousness and the different answers to the problem of innocent suffering. Removing an original section of the story that can only be implied now, that daring poet wrote three cycles of debate, the last of which became dislocated, and concluded them with Job's address to God (chs. 29–31) and YHWH's response (chs. 38–41). At a later time, someone added the poem in ch. 28 and the speeches of Elihu, along with the prose introduction to them (chs. 32–7). Alternative readings cannot be ruled out: ch. 28 retards the action and assuages human emotions; Elihu serves as an ironic foil to the deity, and his citations constitute literary foreshadowing and anticipation; stylistic variety is a mark of literary craft; the book abounds in irony; Job's first repentance was incomplete, requiring further rebuke by God; the breakdown of the friends' speeches declares Job the victor; Job's restoration was an act of grace entirely unrelated to his repentance.

B. Structure. 1. The structure of the book depends on the perspective from which it is viewed, whether on the basis of diction, or dramatic movement, or individual components in sequence. By eliminating brief prosaic introductions and observations, the first approach yields two distinct sections, a narrative and a poetic debate. Stressing the prose introductions, and in some instances conclusions, leads to three divisions within the book (1:1–2:10; 2:11–31:40; 32:1–42:17). Attention to content alone suggests a quite different arrangement (1–2; 3–31; 32–7; 38:1–42:6; and 42:7–17).

2. A striking feature of the book is the use of a framing story to enclose the poetic debate. Widely employed in the ancient Near East, this practice enabled authors to provide essential data for understanding philosophical reflections and for appreciating proverbial sayings. Just as a simple frame enhances a work of art, these brief narratives focus attention away from themselves and offer a perspective from which to view the poetic debate. Twice the narrator passes independent judgement on the hero (1:22; 2:10), one confirmed by YHWH and Job's wife, then withdraws to allow other voices to be heard in the poetry. A story begins, only to be interrupted by poetry that fashions a story within a story, and then resumes so as to bring closure. The prologue evokes dialogue, and the epilogue terminates it, at the same time suppressing the voice within the poetry that rejects the kind of optimism represented by Job's friends and by Proverbs. A story that opens in heaven concludes on earth, where the principle of *do ut des* ('I give in order to receive') is still alive and well. Viewpoints collide everywhere, and the one source of a definitive answer dodges the issue entirely, as YHWH drones on about meteorological phenomena and wild creatures, especially the two favourites, Behemoth and Leviathan.

3. The dramatic development suggested by the three prose introductions in 1:1–5, 2:11–13, and 32:1–5 points to distinct episodes of conflict: YHWH afflicts Job, Job challenges God, YHWH rebukes Job. Alternatively, one may speak of hidden conflict, conflict explored, and conflict resolved (Habel 1985). In this view, the fundamental category of the book is prose, with poetry serving to retard the movement of the plot and heightening the emotions. This understanding of the book encounters considerable difficulty: the narrator's comments mark two closures in the prologue (1:22 and 2:10); the third section has two 'endings'; Elihu's speeches do not resolve the conflict between Job and God; and that resolution occurs in the poetic section.

1. The obvious structure of the book consists of (1) a story about Job's affliction, (2) a debate between him and three friends, (3) the speeches of Elihu, (4) divine speeches leading to Job's submissions, and (5) a story about Job's restoration. Rather than viewing the poetry as a retardation of the plot, one may see it as a way of introducing multiple responses to the problem of evil. Progress does occur, however, with Job gradually moving away from welcoming death and closer towards imagining a judicial resolution, one made possible by a third power, variously understood as umpire, arbitrator, or redeemer.

C. Historical Setting. 1. A second-century BCE Targum on the book of Job discovered at Qumran and the translation into Greek in the Septuagint require an earlier date for the biblical text than the third century. Linguistic evidence seems to point to the sixth century or later (Hurvitz 1974), and certain other features also indicate the Persian period (539–332), for example the language for administrative bureaucracy (3:14–15, kings, counsellors, and princes), the probable allusion to the Behistun Rock, with lead inlay depicting the achievements of Darius the Great (19:24), the reference to caravans from Teman and Sheba (6:19), and the form of the title for the Adversary (the definite article with *śāṭān* as in the sixth-century text of Zechariah and unlike the later form in Chronicles).

2. Several other factors may not settle the debate, but they fit into this general period: the numerous Aramaisms, the similarity with laments in the Psalter, as well as sections of Deutero-Isaiah and Jeremiah, the theological similarities with Ps 73, and the emerging monotheism and monogamy. Less convincing are the sociological conclusions of Crüsemann (1980) and Albertz (1981) that the oppressive conditions reflected in the book of Job point to the time of Nehemiah. Such abuse of power by the *nouveaux riches* may have occurred at various periods in ancient Israel and Judah.

D. Ancient Near-Eastern Parallels. 1. The closest extant parallels to the book of Job come from Mesopotamia. The Sumerian *Man and his God* (2nd millennium) tells about a sufferer who complains to the gods, although conceding that none is born sinless. In the end he confesses his guilt and is restored by the righteous shepherd. The Babylonian *I Will Praise the Lord of Wisdom* denies that anyone can discern the will of the gods; nevertheless, this sufferer trusts in divine mercy, acts in the proper cultic manner, and experiences restoration. This text concludes that the gods have a different system of values from the human one. The *Babylonian Theodicy* (c.1100 BCE), an acrostic, or alphabetic, poem of twenty-seven stanzas with eleven lines each, comprises a debate between an innocent sufferer and a friend. It accuses the gods of endowing humankind with lies. The two debaters maintain a polite tone, while disagreeing with one another, and in the end the complainant prays that the shepherd will once again 'pasture his flock as a god should'. A fourth text, The *Dialogue between a Master and his Slave*, resembles Ecclesiastes more than the book of Job, although both texts reflect similar social turmoil that generated acute personal misery. The master sees no reason to follow any particular course of action, and the slave commends first one thing then its opposite, until the thought of suicide surfaces, followed by the threat of murdering the slave, who seems to say that the master will not survive him three days.

2. Texts from the Egyptian Twelfth Dynasty (1990–1785) with a similar theme demonstrate the extent of intellectual unease resulting from suffering that was perceived to be unjust. The *Admonitions of Ipuwer* conjectures that the divine herdsman either loves death or has fallen asleep. Social turmoil forces the author to reflect on the appropriateness of traditional teachings, for how can the gods possess authority, knowledge, and truth when they permit such chaos in society? The *Dispute of a Man and his Ba* consists of an attempt by a person, overwhelmed by life's misery, to persuade his soul to join him in suicide. The *Eloquent Peasant* depicts the suffering inflicted on a peasant by a governmental figure. These latter two texts abound in positive similes for death, e.g. death is like recovering from illness, like the fragrance of myrrh, like an infant's mouth reaching for milk.

3. A text from Ugarit, the *Epic of Keret*, tells about a hero who loses his wife and children but eventually finds favour with the gods and receives a new wife and more children. The Greek myth of 'Prometheus Bound' has been compared with Job, but Prometheus, a Titan, brought down Zeus's wrath through a wilful act. An Indian tale of a divine discussion leading to a test of the hero, Harischandra, by the god Shiva that demonstrates his virtue shows how the problem of evil pressed itself on thinkers far and near.

4. None of these texts provides an exact parallel to the book of Job, which adapts the traditional genre of debate and framing narrative from the *Babylonian Theodicy* and *I Will Praise the Lord of Wisdom* respectively, adding more friends and enhancing the theophany by incorporating it into the debate. In addition, the biblical author uses extensive catalogues, or lists, hymnic texts, a negative confession, and laments. In the end, the book of Job stands alone, like the hero of the book.

E. Canon and Text. 1. At least one Christian theologian, Theodore of Mopsuestia, questioned the authority of the book of Job, and Job's historicity was called into question in a rabbinic tractate (*B. Bat.* 15a). The exact position of the book of Job in the canon was a matter of dispute. Jewish tradition designates the two different views by acrostic abbreviations, *'mt* (truth) for Job (*'iyyôb*), Proverbs (*mišlê*) and Psalms (*tĕhillîm*) and *t'm* (twin) for the sequence Psalms, Job, and Proverbs.

2. The Greek text of the book of Job, much shorter than the Hebrew, often amounts to a paraphrase. It shows definite theological bias at a few places, e.g. the repointing of a negative particle in 13:15 to affirm trust in God when confronted with the prospect of death at the hand of the deity (Pope 1973: 95–6). The *Targum of Job* from Qumran has the same disorder in chs. 24–7 as that in the MT. Surprisingly, the Targum seems to conclude the book at 42:11 instead of 42:17.

F. History of Interpretation. 1. The *Testament of Job* (1st cent. BCE?) is characterized by zeal against idols, extensive speculation about Satan, cosmological dualism, interest in women, burial customs, magic, mysticism, angelic glossolalia, and patience. The author diverges from the biblical story in a number of ways: (1) Job destroys Satan's idol and incurs his wrath, but when Satan disguises himself to trick Job, an angel reveals his identity; (2) Job's possessions and virtuous deeds are magnified in haggadic fashion (i.e. with sermonic or pious exposition); (3) Job's wife, Sitis, demonstrates her loyalty by begging for bread and selling her hair to obtain food; (4) Satan concedes defeat in the conflict with Job; (5) Bildad poses 'difficult questions' and Zophar offers royal physicians to Job, who relies on the one who made physicians; (6) Sitis expresses concern for her children who have not received proper burial, and Job tells her that God took them; (7) God condemns the friends for not speaking the truth '*about Job*'; (8) Job's daughters inherit magical items and a gift of glossolalia; and (9) Job is transported into heaven by means of chariots.

2. The author of the Epistle of James emphasizes Job's patience, but *'Abot de Rabbi Nathan* accuses Job of sinning *in his heart* and Rashi faulted Job for excessive talking. According to Glatzer (1969), later Jewish interpreters called Job a rebel (Ibn Ezra, Nachmanides), a dualist (Sforno), a pious man searching for truth (Saadia Gaon), one who lacked love (Maimonides), an Aristotelian denier of providence (Gersonides), one who confused God's work with Satan's (Simeon ben Semah Duran), a determinist (Joseph Albo), one who failed to pacify Satan, a scapegoat, an isolationist (the Zohar), one who suffered as a sign of divine love (the Zohar, Moses ben Hayyim). A Jewish legend states that God turned Job over to Satan, called Samael, to keep him occupied while the Jews escaped from Egypt; then God rescued Job from the enemy at the last moment.

3. The early church emphasized Job's suffering as a moral lesson and included readings from the book of Job in the liturgy of the dead. Gregory the Great wrote thirty-five books of sermons on Job, and Augustine read the book as an example of grace. Thomas Aquinas used the book as a starting-point for discussing the metaphysical problem of divine providence (Damico and Yaffe 1989). Calvin wrote 159 sermons on the book of Job, mostly polemical defences of providence (Dekker 1952). In the seventeenth and eighteenth centuries, the emphasis fell on Job as a rebel. Voltaire viewed Job as a representative of the human condition (Hausen 1972).

4. Modern critics also tend to view the book in the light of prevailing intellectual or religious sentiment. Carl Jung (1954) used psychology as the key to interpreting the book. In his view, the marriage of the powerful but unreflective deity to *hokmâ* (wisdom) resulted in the cross, an attempt to provide a more reasoned response to the problem of evil. Jack Kahn (1975) draws on psychiatry to trace the process of grief through which Job passed. Goethe's *Faust* and Archibald MacLeish's *J. B.* (1956) approach the problem of evil from a literary perspective, whereas Girard (1987) stresses the universal desire to establish order through identifying and murdering a scapegoat, and Gutiérrez (1987) identifies the problem as that of speaking properly about God in the midst of poverty.

5. A philosopher emphasizes Job's bitterness of spirit (Wilcox 1989); artists depict Job's suffering in the light of Greek mythology (William Blake) and the holocaust (Fronius 1980); and a Yiddish interpreter uses Goethe's *Faust* as a lens through which to view Job positively (Zhitlowsky 1919). A contemporary novelist and survivor of the Nazi concentration camps likens the Jewish fate under Hitler to Job's affliction (Elie Wiesel) but is opposed by a humanist who contrasts Job's survival with the victims of Auschwitz and Dachau (Rubenstein). Existentialists use Job as an example of the human situation (Camus, Kafka), and a Marxist philosopher sees him as an exemplary rebel against theism and the abuse of power by religious establishments (Ernst Bloch).

6. Within the circles of biblical scholarship, interpreters provide various literary readings of the book: a feminist, a vegetarian, a materialist, a NT ideological critique (Clines 1989). An older reading of the book as drama has been revived (Alonso-Schökel 1977), together with a shift to viewing it as comedy. The modern silencing of ancient dissent in the Roman Catholic liturgy (Rouillard 1983)—in which only affirmative passages are read publicly—and interpretation (Tilley 1989) has evoked dismay. A contemporary poet has provided a fresh translation, removing its sting by omitting crucial verses (Mitchell 1987). In short, interpreters of the book of Job have used it as a convenient means of putting forth their own understandings of reality.

COMMENTARY

The Prologue (1:1–2:13)

In five scenes of elevated prose (1:1–5; 1:6–12; 1:13–22; 2:1–6; 2:7–13 (3:1)) the narrative introduces the main characters in dramatic conflict and the theological issue that will be explored. Part of the problem is the heavenly backdrop of two scenes, for this information is hidden from the hero and his detractors. The Adversary poses the issue in a terse question: Does Job serve God (*'ĕlōhîm*) for nothing? Its staccato rhythm expresses impudence, as does the laconic answer in 2:2 (Gordis 1978: 15). A series of calamities puts Job to the test, and he emerges as a faithful servant despite excruciating circumstances. The arrival of Job's three friends advances the conflict to a different level, one occasioned by poetic debate.

(1:1–5) The five scenes alternate between earth and heaven. The story opens with a description of an exceptional man, Job, who had a full quota of children (seven sons, three daughters; both 7 and 3 are complete numbers) and possessions (7,000 sheep, 3,000 camels, 500 each of oxen and she-asses; 7 and 3 again, equalling 10; 5 and 5 equals ten, a complete number). The description moves outward, from the most intimate to the most distant (Newsom, 1996: 349). v. 1, the reversal of normal order for the verb calls attention to the predicate, Job. A complete (*tām* has this meaning rather than 'perfection') man of integrity, he was also morally straight, religious, and ethical. A non-Israelite, his home was Transjordanian Uz, a name probably chosen as an audial pun on the sages' word for counsel, *'ēṣâ* (Weiss 1983: 23). v. 3, none surpassed him in the East, just as no king rivalled Solomon in wisdom, according to 1 Kings 4:30 [MT 5:10]. v. 4, 'in turn' (lit. each on his day) probably refers to the several birthdays of the sons, not to constant rounds of feasting. The brothers' inclusion of their sisters in these festivities is extraordinary for the ancient culture; their unusual generosity is matched by their father in the epilogue (42:15). v. 5, the narrator views Job's offering of sacrifices as another positive attribute. Job worries that the children may have missed the mark and blessed Elohim without recognizing their guilt. Alternatively, the verb *b-r-k* is used euphemistically, in place of *g-l-l*, hence 'cursed'. Ironically, Job's goodness brings about his terrible misfortune, including the death of his children.

(1:6–12) The idyllic setting, except for Job's unease about his children, shifts, both in location and tenor. An Adversary (*haśśāṭān*, a title rather than a proper name) joins the assemblage of divine beings and responds to the deity by means of a pun on his name (*śûṭ*, to wander). This heavenly Adversary is a counterpart to Job, suspecting everyone just as Job suspected his sons (Weiss 1983: 40). In a rhetorical question indicating ongoing rivalry, YHWH brings up Job's name and vouches for his integrity, using the same language as v. 1, but the cynical

Adversary accuses Job of serving God because it pays well to do so. To determine who has correctly seen into Job's heart, the Adversary proposes to put him to a test by removing all indications of divine favour, here understood as possessions (including children). YHWH agrees to the test, turning Job's possessions over to the Adversary, with a single restriction, that he not harm Job's person.

(1:13–22) The third scene begins on a happy note but quickly descends to the depths of human suffering. Successive messengers inform Job and the reader simultaneously of four calamities, two of heavenly origin and two inflicted by human foes (note the symbolism, four for completion, heaven and earth for the entirety of space). Repetition gives the awful news a stupefying effect. One by one the lone survivors tell Job of his losses: marauding Sabeans killed his oxen and donkeys, a heavenly fire consumed his sheep, Chaldeans stole his camels, and a mighty wind demolished the house in which his children were feasting, killing all of them. These messengers mirror the heavenly ones reporting to YHWH; only the fourth interjects a sign of emotional distress (*hinnēh*). The Sabeans were probably northern Arabians rather than people from the south or Africa. Chaldeans were semi-nomads, not the later Neo-Babylonians of the seventh and sixth centuries BCE, who conquered Judah in 587 BCE and took many citizens of Judah into exile. As this tale of woe unfolds, 'Satan lurks, waiting for the blasphemy' (Dhorme 1967: p. xxx).

Job responds to this litany of destruction in the manner of a faithful servant; he mourns according to custom and quotes a proverb, adding his resolve to bless YHWH. Job does not say he will return to his mother's womb—not even mother earth. The Hebrew word *šammâ* is a euphemism for Sheol, the land of the dead (cf. Eccl 5:15; Sir 40:1). The proverb uses synonymous and antithetic parallelism (naked/came from || naked/return to), while Job's addition limits itself to antithetic parallelism (gave || took away). v. 22, the narrator intrudes long enough to pronounce judgement on Job, whom he declares blameless.

(2:1–6) The fourth scene opens like the second, as if nothing has intervened, although YHWH concludes with an indictment of the Adversary. The word *ḥinnām* (tr. 'for no reason') repeats the word that the Adversary singled out as Job's flaw 'Does Job serve God for nothing [for no reason]?' v. 4, 'Skin for skin' implies a culture characterized by barter rather than monetary exchange, but its meaning is unclear. It may suggest equal value, or the expression may refer to exchanging one kind of skin for another kind. Job's possessions accord with the (pre-)patriarchal setting, but his sons dwelt in houses, not tents. The Adversary incites YHWH to intensify the test by striking at Job's health. When referring to the deity, the stretched-out hand signifies misfortune. This time, too, YHWH limits the Adversary; Job's survival was essential to the story's dramatic unfolding.

(2:7–13) Smitten with a disease of the skin that cannot be identified on the basis of the poetic allusions in the dialogue, Job scrapes himself with a piece of broken pottery, either to ease the itching or as a sign of self-mortification. In his isolation, Job's wife repeats YHWH's affirmation of her husband but turns it into a question: 'Do you still persist in your integrity?' What she urges him to do is unclear. The verb *bārak* may be undecipherable (Linafelt 1996). In favour of translating it 'curse' is Job's harsh reply. He likens her to foolish or vulgar women. The LXX attributes a longer speech to Job's wife, and the *Testament of Job* presents her in a much more favourable light, giving her an actual name, Sitis (the Targum at 2:9 calls Job's wife Dinah). Job reminds his wife that we receive both good and evil from God. He implies that if people receive good they cannot reject the bad. The narrator enters the story for a second time, changing the language ever so slightly. Later Jewish interpreters seized this opening to accuse Job of sinning in his heart while outwardly uttering devout sentiments. The visit by Job's three friends (kings in the LXX) from Edom and Arabia provides a transition from prose to poetry, one appropriately characterized by profound silence. Their stated purpose in coming was pastoral—to bring consolation—and their long silence (only here does the phrase 'seven nights' occur) as they sat with him on the ash heap confirms that positive intention. Their act of throwing dust heavenward may have been apotropaic, to frighten away evil powers. The name Eliphaz occurs in Gen 36:15; the names Bildad and Zophar are not found elsewhere in the Bible. Teman was in Edom; the location of Shuah and Naamah is uncertain. The final scene of this popular narrative appears in 42:7–17, which tells about Job's restoration.

The Poetic Debate (3:1–42:6)

The familiar folk-tale about a virtuous man who loses everything for no apparent reason (cf. Ezek 14:14, 20 where Job is mentioned along with Noah and Dan'el (of Ugaritic legend)) occasions a debate about the relationship between goodness and suffering. A poem about wisdom follows; then Job contrasts his glorious past with his ignoble present and utters an oath of innocence aimed at forcing God to respond (chs. 28–31). Instead, Elihu answers (chs. 32–7) but evokes silence until YHWH speaks from the whirlwind (38:1–42:6), reducing Job to two brief responses (40:3–5; 42:1–6). The poetry is some of the most difficult in the Bible, due partly to the number of rare words but also to the distinctive syntax and grammar. Multiple readings are inherently necessary, both because of the rhetorical strategy and the poetic language. Perhaps also the emotional intensity contributes to unintelligibility at crucial points (e.g. 19:25–7; 42:5–6).

(3:1–26) Job Curses his Birthday A lament is Job's way of opening the debate; instead of cursing God he pronounces a curse on the day of his birth and the night of his conception (the beginning and end of gestation), as if wishing it to be obliterated from the calendar. The verb for curse (*g-l-l*) differs from that of the prologue, where *b-r-k* occurs. In 3:3–10 the curse encompasses the whole creation, seeking to reverse the favourable conditions set into place by God in Gen 1:1–2:4a. A similar anticosmic description occurs in Jer 4:23–6, where the prophet seems to behold a reversal of conditions that rendered life on earth possible, and a curse of one's birthday can be found in Jer 14:14–18 (with an allusion to the destruction of Sodom and Gomorrah). The reference to an infant as a *geber* (elsewhere used of much older boys, even a soldier) contains a pun on the word for grave, *geber*. Poetic parallelism between Leviathan and Yam (the Sea) favours this reading over 'day'; in an unpointed text the Hebrew words for 'day' and 'sea' are

identical. The poet echoes the myth of a chaos-dragon in the ancient Near East (Tiamat in Mesopotamia, Lotan and Yamm at Ugarit), one that was also at home in several biblical texts, where various names for the monster occur (Rahab, Leviathan, Tannin, cf. Isa 27:1; 51:9; Ps 74:14). Professional cursers recall Balaam (Num 22–4; a non-biblical text from Deir Alla mentions this prophet whose reputation became tarnished in biblical memory). In 3:12 Job alludes to a ritual by which a parent acknowledged a newborn by holding it on the knees (cf. Sir 15:2). The threefold use of *šām* ('there') in 3:17–19 recalls the euphemism for Sheol in 1:21. The image of grave-robbers informs 3:20–2, where Job ironically compares their excitement in digging for treasure, buried along with the dead, with his own fantasy of death. The word for 'fenced in' (3:23) differs from that in 1:10 (*sûk* and *śûk* respectively). Tenses in Hebrew are notoriously difficult, making it impossible to know whether or not Job's fear expressed in 3:24 was habitual; if the verbs designate the past, they undercut Job's extraordinary piety (Good 1990: 208). Three parallel expressions (no ease, quiet, rest) contrast grammatically with the fourth (dread) and the verb 'come' links this verse with the previous one. By this means the poet indicates that Job's character is more complex than the prose acknowledges.

Job's lament combines a number of grotesque images: a perpetually pregnant woman, Job's mother; a day robbed of its essence, light; two personified lovers, night and dawn, awaiting one another and condemned to an absence of sexual ecstasy; former enemies, oppressors and the oppressed, at rest together; and an instance of divine mockery, the giving of light to the blind. YHWH's speeches from the tempest will return to this notion of divine largesse; there, too, the gift does not benefit the human population.

(4:1–5:27) Eliphaz Introduces the Parameters of the Debate The only one of Job's three friends whose character is rounded, or fleshed out, Eliphaz sets forth the different arguments that will be explored in the course of the debate: you can trust in God to restore you (here Eliphaz uses two words that earlier characterized Job, 'blameless' and a 'God-fearer', 1:1, 8; 2:3); wickedness is punished; human beings are naturally culpable; the prosperity of the sinful will be cut short; the best course is to seek God; suffering is an indication of divine discipline; you will attain a ripe old age. Beginning on a positive note (unless 4:10 cruelly refers to the death of Job's children through the metaphor of a lion), Eliphaz mildly rebukes Job for impatience when personally victimized. The charge of duplicity weakens his positive affirmation of his friend, one who strengthened others in misery. The rich vocabulary permits the poet to use five different words for lion in 4:10–11 (cf. Joel 1:4 for similar richness). Convinced that a principle of reward and punishment governed the universe, Eliphaz is oblivious to the pain resulting from this dogma (4:7–9, where a divine wind brings destruction like the tempest that killed Job's children). According to Gen 2:7 the breath of YHWH animated the first human; now that wind wields devastation.

(4:12–5:8) The closest thing in wisdom literature to the mantic wisdom of the book of Daniel, a type of wisdom widespread in Mesopotamia, this section resembles a theophany, particularly the divine manifestation to Elijah in the cave at Mt.

Horeb (1 Kings 19:11–18) and to Abraham in Gen 15:12–17. Like Abraham, Eliphaz receives the divine visitation while in a deep sleep (tardēmâ). An elusive word steals past, quiet like a whisper; the prophet Elijah experienced YHWH's word as a faint echo, in contrast to the spectacular phenomena of wind, fire, and earthquake preceding it. Whereas Job felt dread as a result of the calamities that befell him, a sleeping Eliphaz encountered it when a wind (rûaḥ) glided past his face. It is not stated whether or not Abram saw the smoking fire-pot and flaming torch that passed through the severed pieces and secured the covenant with a powerful promise, but Eliphaz is said to have been unable to make out the exact appearance of the deity. He does grasp the brief word that follows an eerie silence: 'Can a mortal be more righteous than God (Eloah)?' This reading takes into consideration the broader context where the issue becomes that of Job's claim to be pure at the same time as he indicts God for crimes against humanity. Those translators who read 'Can a mortal be righteous before God?' emphasize the immediate context, which stresses human vulnerability, as well as angelic fallibility. The irony of this reference to God's lack of trust in his servants is missed by Eliphaz, who does not know about the Adversary. Does Eliphaz also miss the irony of his own counsel? If humans really die without ever attaining wisdom, what does he dispense? Folly? Eliphaz appeals to consensus (4:7), expecting Job to concur in the common dogma of retribution; he also appeals to individual experience (4:8, 'As I have seen'), to special revelation (4:12–21), to collective experience (5:27a, 'See, we have searched this out; it is true'), and to the obvious insights encapsulated in proverbial sayings (4:8, 'those who plough iniquity and sow trouble reap the same'; 5:2, 'Surely vexation kills the fool, and jealousy slays the simple'). In 5:3–5 Eliphaz's remarks border on cruelty, for Job had 'taken root' only to have his dwelling cursed and to discover that his children lacked safety. Does his precipitous fall mark Job as a fool like those scorned by Eliphaz? It appears that Eliphaz considers finitude a breeding-ground for trouble (5:7, where the Heb. words tr. 'sparks' are literally 'sons of Resheph'; in Canaanite mythology Resheph was the god of plague and pestilence). There may be a clever pun between the Hebrew words for ground (ʾădāmâ) and mortal (ʾādām) in 5:6–7 as in Gen 3:17. A striking feature of 5:8 is the initial aleph (the first letter of the Heb. alphabet) in eight of the nine words; the last word breaks the pattern. In this verse, too, the reader encounters two general words for deity, ʾēl and ʾĕlōhîm.

(5:9–13) Participles set this brief unit apart as a doxology, a hymn extolling God whom Job is urged to seek. The language is traditional. Beginning with a reference to innumerable wonders, the hymn then highlights an important specific action, the sending of rain, an oft-mentioned vital necessity in the ancient Near East. It moves on to consider the activity of God in exalting the lowly and bringing down wicked schemers. v. 13, this is the only passage from Job that is cited in the NT (cf. 1 Cor 3:19).

(5:14–27) v. 17, two names for deity occur here, ʾelôah (Eloah) and šadday (Shaddai). The meaning of the latter is often taken to be related to the Akkadian word for 'mountain' or to mean 'destroyer'. The ideas expressed in vv. 17–18, that God disciplines the ones he loves, are widespread in the Bible (cf. Deut 32:39; Ps 94:12; 107:42; Prov 3:11; Hos 6:1). A significant metaphor for YHWH in the story of the Exodus, the healer (Ex 15:26), informs Eliphaz's advice in v. 18. Here, as in Exodus, this metaphor vies with its opposite, that of the warrior (Ex 15:3). Eliphaz understands both wounds and healing as acts of the one deity. Both parental discipline and teachers' punishment of students in Egypt and in Mesopotamia included corporal punishment. Its purpose was to instil reliable teaching in the minds of youth and thus to form character. This motive behind harsh discipline explains Eliphaz's 'macarism' (an expression, frequent in Psalms, that begins with 'Happy', Heb. ʾašrē), 'Happy is the one whom God [Eloah] reproves'. v. 19, numerical parallelism, rarely found in Mesopotamian and Egyptian literature, occurs more often in the Bible and in Ugaritic texts. Biblical usage varies, at some times referring to a total number symbolizing fullness (as in the Epic of Keret from Ugarit) but at other times actually specifying the higher number of items, with emphasis on the final number. The former occurs in Am 1:3–2:16 ('For three . . . indeed for four . . . ') and the latter is exemplified by numerous proverbial sayings (Prov 6:16–19; 30:15–16, 18–19, 21–31). Eliphaz uses the numerical saying for fullness: 'he will deliver you from every trouble'. v. 22, the allusion to destruction may conceal a play on the divine name Shaddai. v. 23, elsewhere the Bible does not mention a covenant with stones, but Isa 11:6–9 gives poetic form to the anticipated peaceful relationship between animals and humans. v. 25, the usual biblical similes for Israel's countless progeny, 'like the stars' or 'like the sands of the sea shore' (cf. Gen 15:5), give way here to an appropriate image for a desert nomad: 'like the grass of the earth'. v. 26, Job does not share this comforting view of death, for in his miserable state he cannot imagine that he will reach old age. Eliphaz's prediction is precisely what happens in the epilogue. How differently the author of Ecclesiastes viewed old age and death (cf. Eccl 11:7–12:7).

(6:1–7:21) Job's Response to Eliphaz Employs both Sarcasm and Parody The participants in this debate seldom respond to the issues raised by the previous speaker, making it difficult to track the development of ideas. Job excuses his bold language by appealing to the deep agony enveloping him at the moment. He thinks it would outweigh the heaviest thing he can imagine: the sand of the sea. The image is striking; psychological and physical suffering in one side of the balance, all the sand of the sea in the other half of the scale. v. 4, no evidence of poison arrows has survived in the ancient Near East, although the dipping of arrowheads in poison was known to Virgil (Aeneid, 9.773) and Ovid (Epist. ex Ponto, 1.2.17–18). The expression may be Job's rhetorical manner of emphasizing the devastating effect of the divine arsenal. Job uses familiar imagery of a divine warrior; ancient peoples, biblical and non-biblical, understood their deities as accomplished fighters. The epithet, YHWH of hosts, probably alludes to heavenly hosts who did battle at YHWH's behest, later coming to mean also Israelite soldiers. Job uses the divine name Shaddai in this instance. vv. 5–6, two 'difficult questions' emphasize the appropriateness of Job's complaint. An animal does not bray when its mouth is full; Job would have no reason to complain if he were contented like well-fed oxen. Life has become for him like tasteless food; he has no more appetite for either food or life. v. 10, following a kind of imitation prayer, the best Job can muster at the moment, he identifies the deity as the Holy One (cf. Isaiah, who often called YHWH the Holy One of Israel). In 5:1 Eliphaz had asked Job which of the holy ones he would turn to; the reader knows about one member of the divine assembly, the Adversary, who would be a poor choice indeed.

(6:14–21) Job imagines a wadi in the wilderness that has so much water that caravaneers have come to rely on it. To their dismay, the stream-bed has dried up in the heat of summer, precisely when they need water most. Sixth-century texts mention traders from far-off Tema and Sheba, apparently travelling a lucrative trade route. The application of this image to Job's circumstances is obvious; he expected comfort from friends, only to get a rebuke. A pun between similar Hebrew words occurs in v. 21, *rā'â* ('to see') and *yārē'* ('to fear').

(6:22–30) vv. 22–3, the language derives from more than one context. A gift implies that Job's deepest need is economic; bribe suggests that he is facing a judicial trial; the reference to saving him fits into a context of attack; ransom refers to a situation in which the opponents have taken Job hostage. By using these different ideas, he hopes to cover all possibilities. v. 24, Job's appeal to be taught anticipates the divine speeches, which succeed in silencing him. An Egyptian proverb states that 'There can be no instruction where love is absent' (Papyrus Insinger, 8:24). The intent is ambiguous: love of the teacher, the student, the subject? In Job's case, the evidence persuades him that the friends do not love, for they speak dishonestly. v. 26, the word for desperate (*nō'āš*) may play on the word for humankind (*'ĕnôš*). vv. 28–9, a rhetorical ploy aims at converting—turning around—the friends. Alternatively, Job watches as they start to walk away, concerned that he could not be vindicated in their eyes unless they remain, he appeals to them to turn back.

(7:1–10) Job portrays human existence in an entirely negative manner, culminating in a graphic image of a weaver's shuttle that speedily comes to an end without hope. The Mesopotamian myth of creation, *Enuma Elish*, states that the gods created humankind to serve their makers. Job refers to sleepless nights occasioned by bodily sores infested with worms. The *Testament of Job* uses this idea to illustrate Job's complete willingness to bear his suffering patiently. In this version, he picks up a worm that has dropped to the ground and places it on his sore from which it had fallen. He rejects Eliphaz's optimistic view that hope remains for him (6:20); in doing so, Job creates a pun on the Hebrew words for hope and thread (*tiqwâ*). v. 8, the one to whom Job directs these remarks is unclear, but the following verses will reveal that he has turned away from Eliphaz momentarily to address God. Job does not expect to live long.

(7:11–21) Job's distress prompts him to utter bold concepts and even to parody traditional hymnody. v. 12, unlike the monster in the myth of chaos, either Yam (the Sea) or Tannin, Job presents no threat to the deity. Why, then, does the deity find it necessary to set a guard over him? Both Yam and Tannin echo the Canaanite myth of chaotic forces that are ultimately defeated by Baal. The enemy is also called Mot; the Hebrew word for death is the same (*môt*, or *māwet*, 7:15).

vv. 14–16, the usual time for resting from one's labour offers no comfort to Job, whose nights are full of terrifying dreams. (The idea of psychological anxiety as punishment for sin is developed further in Sirach and Wisdom of Solomon.) Does Job refer to Eliphaz's allusion to a frightening nocturnal visitor? Breath (*hebel*) as a metaphor for life goes beyond the image of wind in 7:7 (*rûaḥ*). The author of Ecclesiastes uses *hebel* in this way thirty-eight times; its meaning is generally 'futile' or 'absurd', occasionally 'ephemeral'. vv. 17–21, these verses sound like a parody on Ps 8. In this psalm the author expresses wonder that the majestic creator thinks so highly of humankind and watches over the vulnerable creatures with extraordinary solicitude. In contrast, Job views the divine attention as entirely unwanted, a test rather than comfort. Such divine surveillance interferes with Job's need to swallow his spittle. In v. 20 he gives voice to wholly unconventional theology: human sin does not affect God. Moreover, the epithet, 'watcher of humanity', contains an accusing tone, whereas traditionalists often spoke enthusiastically of YHWH's providential care, a shepherding of the people. In Job's view, the guardian has turned villainous. The last verse in this unit may contain an ironical allusion to an ancient worthy, Enoch, who is said to have walked with God and 'was no more, because God took him' (Gen 5:24). Job has suggested that God's watchful eye cannot prevent his lapsing into death (7:8); now he thinks of the deity searching for him after he has descended into Sheol.

(8:1–22) **Bildad Makes God's Character the Issue** The fundamental premiss of Bildad's argument is stated in the form of a rhetorical question: 'Does God [*'ēl*] pervert justice? Or does the Almighty [*šadday*] pervert the right?' (v. 3). Such distortion is unthinkable to Bildad, who consequently deduces that Job's children were terrible sinners and that their father's sins were less serious, since he survived divine retribution. With this cruel conclusion, Bildad actually states the central problem that will exercise the imaginations of the four friends throughout the debate: is God at fault? The reader knows that the answer to this haunting question is a resounding 'yes'. A clearer answer can scarcely be found than the deity's concession that the Adversary had provoked him to afflict Job without cause (2:3). Lacking any knowledge of the heavenly proceedings, Bildad relies on traditional belief that one's external conditions accurately reflect inner states. Good people prosper and wicked people do not; this axiom lies behind everything he says. v. 2, the Hebrew expression for 'great wind' differs from that employed by the narrator in describing the death of Job's children (*rûaḥ kabbîr* in v. 2, *rûaḥ gědôlâ* in 2:19). v. 3, the twin concepts, justice and righteousness (*mišpāṭ and ṣedeq*), are central to many biblical texts describing the Lord's activity. The earth is established on these two principles, as is God's throne (Ps 97:2). God requires these qualities of Israel (Isa 5:7), and the covenant is grounded in justice and righteousness (Hos 2:19). The prophet Amos singles out these two concepts as the Lord's requirement for Israel (Am 5:24). vv. 4–7, Bildad's language implies that sinful deeds possess an inherent power to destroy those perpetrating them. Such language has led to the hypothesis that an automatic principle governed human lives, punishing the guilty and rewarding the virtuous. YHWH's only role, according to this theory, was to act as a kind of midwife assisting in the birth of disaster or its opposite (Koch 1955). Each of the first three verses in this unit begins with the same Hebrew particle, 'im (if). In its first use, the hypothetical aspect is attenuated, giving the sense of 'although', for Bildad has no doubt about the guilt of Job's children. Ironically, Bildad's speculations about Job correspond with reality. He does seek God, but not in the manner intended by Bildad, and is restored. Bildad's description of Job's beginning as 'small' hardly accords with the narrative (1:1–3) or with Job's own account of his previous fortune (29:1–25). Nevertheless, Bildad's assessment of things is not far off, for Job's possessions are doubled in the end (cf. 42:12). vv. 8–10, Bildad appeals to ancient tradition, a sure corrective to individual insight. The accumulation of knowledge over the years is reliable, he thinks, and offsets human ephemerality. Whereas several psalms emphasize life's brevity as a decisive difference between humankind and deity (Ps 90:5–6; 103:14–16), Bildad uses the contrast to call into question knowledge acquired by a single individual. The lengthening of a shadow as the sun slowly goes down provides a vivid image of life itself. vv. 11–15, two impossible questions (Crenshaw 1980) introduce the theme of this unit: just as one cannot expect papyrus to grow without marshy conditions or reeds to flourish away from water, so those who turn away from God cannot thrive. Initial promise quickly fades, as hope proves to be no more substantial than a spider's web. This difficult text is understood differently in the LXX, where 'destiny' replaces 'paths'. Perhaps the author intended a wordplay between 'orḥôt and 'aḥĕrît ('path' and 'end, destiny'). vv. 16–19, this section can be understood in directly contrasting ways. Unlike the flimsy web of a spider, plants with roots firmly penetrating the rocky ground can endure. Alternatively, such plants do not last because the roots lack adequate nourishment. It seems that Bildad returns to his earlier remark about Job's hope and a promising latter end, the word 'aḥēr (behind) recalling 'aḥĕrît (another plant arises). vv. 20–2, Bildad does not know that God has declared Job to be blameless. Ironically, Job will later reject (mā'as) something unspecified in his second response to God (42:6). The last word of Bildad's speech and the last word in Job's previous speech are the same, except for the pronominal suffix ('ēnennû/'ēnennî). Bildad and his other two friends will become Job's enemies and will experience shame.

(9:1–10:22) Job Wishes to Enter into a Lawsuit with God In 9:2–4 Job either agrees with Bildad's concluding remarks or insists on the truth of the rhetorical question: 'how can a mortal be just before God ['ēl]?' If the former, Job speaks ironically; if the latter, he emphasizes the utter impossibility of being vindicated before God. The verb ṣ-d-q carries two senses, 'to be just' and 'to be legally in the right'. The prophet Jeremiah also despaired of receiving a fair trial, because YHWH acts as prosecuting attorney and judge (Jer 12:1). Eliphaz has asked, 'Can a mortal be more just than Eloah' (4:17a, see NRSV marg.), but Job uses different language ('im, before). A decisive shift occurs in v. 3, one from morality to legality. Job introduces an entirely different metaphor, of the heavenly Judge. He uses the technical word for a lawsuit (rîb) but quickly acknowledges the absurdity of such an idea. The expression 'once in a thousand' occurs elsewhere to imply that

trustworthy men are rare and comparable women non-existent (Eccl 7:28), and with reference to childlessness, which Ben Sira understands as preferable to having ungodly children (Sir 16:3). The phrase also occurs in Egyptian wisdom literature.

(9:5–11) Job employs a traditional hymn (vv. 5–10) and gives his own bewildered response to an invisible deity (v. 11). In 5:9–16 Eliphaz used hymnic material to emphasize the orderly universe and the power of its creator. In Job's deft fingers this imagery carries an opposite stamp, connoting the chaotic aspects of reality: earthquakes, a sun that does not rise, stars that exhibit no light. The claim in v. 4 that El is wise finds no support in the doxology that follows (vv. 5–7). The next four verses of the unit do, however, reinforce the identification of El as powerful. Job alludes to the chaos myth in which Marduk conquers Tiamat, the linguistic equivalent of the biblical tĕhôm (great deep) in Gen 1:2. The expression, 'trampled the waves of the sea' derives from military combat and signifies victory over an enemy (Crenshaw 1972: 39–53). The sea is personified as in Canaanite myth. v. 9, which refers to four constellations, resembles the doxological fragment in Am 5:8–9, where two, possibly four, constellations are named. v. 10, Job uses conventional views to increase the shock-value of his conclusion in vv. 11–12. Yes, God's deeds defy understanding and cannot be counted, but this concession brings little comfort. For Moses (Ex 33:18–23) and Elijah (1 Kings 19:11–12) God's passing by was revelatory. Job experiences El as elusive and concludes that God is beyond challenge when seizing someone's possessions (v. 12).

(9:12–24) v. 13, Job despairs of facing an angry El who conquered the chaos-dragon, here called Rahab as in Ps 89:10 (MT 11). v. 15, the universe is fundamentally twisted when an innocent person is obliged to appeal for mercy. v. 16, Job does not subscribe to the traditional credo in Ex 34:6–7; indeed, he does not believe he could obtain a hearing even if he were successful in catching El's attention. v. 17, the rabbis understood this verse as a foreshadowing of God's appearance to Job in a tempest (B. Bat. 16a). In the light of Job's addition of the particle ḥinnām (without cause), which functions thematically in the Prologue, some interpreters emend the Hebrew word for a tempest (sĕ'ārâ) to a similar word for hair (śa'arâ) and obtain a better parallel for ḥinnām. The meaning would then be that El crushes Job for a trifle and multiplies wounds gratuitously. v. 21, confident that he is blameless, although lacking any knowledge of higher confirmation of this fact (God's, 1:8; 2:3; the narrator's, 1:1; Job's wife's, 2:9), Job does not recognize himself. Therefore he rejects life itself (in contrast to 7:16, Job now supplies the object of his loathing). v. 22, the logic of Job's reasoning leads him to reject the concept of individual retribution, the comforting belief that God rewards the virtuous and punishes the wicked. Job now believes that God makes no distinctions between the innocent and the guilty. The Mesopotamian Erra Epic, which deals with a similar collapse of the moral order, has the god of Pestilence confess: 'The righteous and the wicked, I did not distinguish, I felled.' vv. 23–4, even worse, God has taken sides with the wicked, gleefully mocking the innocent when they fall and blinding judges so that they cannot distinguish between guilt and innocence. Because Job subscribes to a modified monotheism, he must attribute both good and evil to the one deity. The question in v. 24 functions rhetorically: God alone has done it.

(9:25–35) For the first time, Job addresses God directly. Convinced that God would besmirch him even after his hands are washed, Job returns to the idea of a trial but imagines that he has an advocate (an arbitrator or umpire). The odiousness of divine perversity has resulted in the ridiculous notion of a neutral figure powerful enough to force God to act fairly towards Job. Such an umpire does not exist for Job, who must hope for God's partial relenting. Meanwhile, his days are swiftly running out; the three images in v. 25 from land, water, and air refer to movements of increasing swiftness.

(10:1–7) v. 1, in 9:21 Job complained that he no longer understood himself and thus loathed his life; in 10:1 he returns to the earlier conclusion, but he uses a different verb here (*nqṭ* or *qûṭ*). Because he despises life, he will speak freely to God. v. 3, Job thinks of God's behaviour as cruel, irrational, and immoral: cruel because God enjoys oppressive conduct, irrational because God destroys what he has fashioned with care, immoral because he gives preferential treatment to the wicked. vv. 4–5, Job underscores the absurdity of God's behaviour by implying that God has forgotten the fundamental difference between ephemeral mortals and the eternal Creator. In v. 7 Job acknowledges that God's eyes have no fleshly components that would make them fallible, so God knows that Job is innocent.

(10:8–22) Returning to the idea of humans as works of God's hands (v. 3), Job develops this theme in some detail. He employs three basic images (a potter, a cheesemaker, the force behind gestation). According to the tradition in Gen 2:4*b*–3:24, the return to dust was a result of human choice, a refusal to obey the divine command. Either Job understands the curse as unfair, or he thinks of premature death. According to v. 12, the Creator bestowed life, compassionate love, and providential care on the finished product of the creative force (cf. 2:6). v. 14, the thought of God keeping watch over newly formed humans leads Job to object that in his case the scrutiny has been oppressive, as he did at 7:20. v. 16, Job understands God in terms of ancient Near-Eastern concepts of royal sport. God, the King of Heaven, hunts the vulnerable lion, Job. vv. 20–2, the dreary picture of Sheol as unrelenting gloom, chaos, and darkness concludes with an oxymoron ('light is like darkness') that is the mirror image of 'That day, let there be darkness' in 3:4*a* (Good 1990: 229).

(11:1–20) Zophar Thinks that God is Lenient The link between excessive talk and sin was acknowledged in a biblical proverb: 'In a multitude of words, sin is not lacking' (Prov 10:19). In v. 2 Zophar describes Job as a 'man of lips' (NRSV 'one full of talk'), a person of superficial speech. Such an one, he thinks, can never be vindicated. He goes one step farther, accusing Job of mocking his friends. Clearly, Job's sarcasm and parody have not escaped Zophar's attention. Such talk falls under the category of senseless babble, Zophar believes, and deserves an answer. Although failing to recognize the real reason for Job's extreme language, Zophar does possess the ability to see what is at stake, for he returns to the theme of vindication that Job has brought into the discussion (v. 2). v. 4,

for Job the decisive issue was moral rectitude, and that issue applied to God as well as to him. Zophar sees things differently; he concentrates on ritual purity (cf. also v. 15 where he uses the word 'blemish'). His inaccurate quotation of Job's words puts the emphasis on external matters rather than moral integrity. vv. 5–6, this expression of a wish that God would answer Job is an example of literary foreshadowing, one filled with irony at Zophar's expense. God will indeed answer Job, but in a tirade of words and without divulging wisdom's hidden qualities. That topic will be addressed in a different fashion (ch. 28), and its meaning will be considerably less ambiguous than Zophar's comment about wisdom (cf. Sir 6:22, 'For wisdom is like her name; she is not readily perceived by many'). Zophar takes offence at Job's certainty that he is blameless; taking up his language of knowing, Zophar turns on him: '*Know* then that God [Eloah] exacts of you less than your guilt deserves.' Israel's sages were reluctant to reckon with the notion of divine compassion, for it seemed to place in jeopardy their belief in a principle of moral retribution. In this scheme, an individual received the appropriate reward or punishment for conduct, and there was no place for mercy. One's destiny lay in one's own hands. Historical circumstances eventually undermined such optimism and prompted the sages to incorporate traditional teachings about divine compassion (cf. the ancient creed in Ex 34:6–7, which occurs with some frequency in later liturgies, e.g. Neh 9:17, 31; Ps 86:15; Joel 2:13; Jon 4:2, always in truncated form). The struggle to keep both sides of the equation, justice and mercy, in tension required constant watchfulness (Fishbane 1985: 335–50). vv. 6–12, Zophar's attempt to match the earlier hymnic passages falls short. He does succeed in pointing to the mystery beyond human grasp, but the thoughts quickly descend to the mundane. Ironically, Zophar has just claimed to know the nature of Eloah: that God acts leniently towards Job. Now, however, Zophar implies that Job, and presumably no one else, can discover the mystery that God withholds (cf. Deut 29:29 (MT 28), 'The secret things belong to the Lord our God, but the revealed things belong to us and to our children forever, to observe all the words of this law').

The verb *ḥāqar* means 'to probe deeply', and the noun *ḥeqer* refers to the act of searching as well as the result, as here. Having used this nominative form of the verb for intellectual inquiry, Zophar seems at a loss for a suitable parallel to *māṣā'* (to find), which he uses twice. v. 8, Ben Sira makes a similar point ('The height of heaven, the breadth of the earth, the abyss, and wisdom—who can search them out?', Sir 1:3). v. 10, the language of theophany, already used by Eliphaz and Job, appeals to Zophar also, but he places it in the context of a judicial trial. v. 12, a proverbial impossible saying, like Ovid's remark, 'Then will the stag fly,' seems to accuse Job of stupidity in addition to iniquity. An echo of Gen 16:12 may be detected; there Ishmael is described as a wild ass of a man. As Zophar employs it, the proverb views ignorance rather than morality as the dividing line between humanity and deity. v. 13, like Ps 73, which identifies the heart (mind) as decisive in determining purity, Zophar understands Job's problem as a misdirected heart, which he can correct through prayer. v. 18, having repented and been cleansed of impurity (v. 15), Job will finally have hope and confidence (a recurring theme thus far). v. 20, Job has longed for death; Zophar threatens him with loss of an escape route and the death of hope unless his guilt is removed.

(12:1–14:22) Job Reflects on the Nature of Wisdom and Life's Brevity 12:2 reeks of sarcasm as Job suggests that the total accumulation of human wisdom is concentrated in his three friends and will die along with them. 12:3, twice in this section (cf. also 13:2) Job claims equality with his friends with respect to knowledge. 12:4–6, before resuming the ideas expressed in the first three verses, Job contrasts his own situation with the divinely protected life of marauders. Although he once enjoyed a special relationship with God, one characterized by prayer followed by divine response, Job has now become an object of scorn. In this setting Job once more characterizes himself in the language of the narrator and God: a just and blameless man. The reference to a vital relationship with God stands in tension with Job's later confession that his previous knowledge of God was derivative, information based on hearing rather than sight (cf. 42:5), if that is what the later text implies. The meaning of v. 6 is not entirely clear. Does it refer to idolatry? Or should one understand the subject as God, who empowers egregious sinners? 12:7–9, Israel's sages believed that the movement of heavenly bodies, the activity of the weather, and the actions of animals contained hidden knowledge about ways of coping with life. By studying these phenomena, one discovered truth that, by analogy, applied to human conduct. Job recognizes the significance of this avenue to knowledge. His use of the plural form, *běhēmôt*, anticipates the description of the partly mythic creature in 40:15–24. Otherwise the singular *běhēmâ* would have sufficed (note the singular verb that follows). 12:9, Job's point is that such knowledge is readily accessible, not hidden beyond human grasp. In making this point, Job uses a cliché: 'For the hand of the LORD [YHWH] has done this'. Here alone in the poetic dialogue between Job and his three friends does the divine name YHWH appear; in some MSS it also occurs in a familiar cliché in the poem about wisdom (28:28). 12:11 emphasizes the importance of possessing powers of discrimination. As the palate distinguishes between appetizing and unappetizing foods, so the ear discriminates between wisdom and folly. 12:12, the accepted view that only the aged possess wisdom appears here in interrogative form; Job will deny its accuracy shortly (v. 20).

(12:13–25) In royal ideology the king was thought to have wisdom, strength, counsel, and understanding (cf. Isa 11:2, where an additional dimension, religious devotion, occurs). Job attributes these four characteristics to God, who frustrates human efforts at being wise. Kings, counsellors, priests, judges, and elders—the entire ruling class of society—are mere pawns in a divine game aimed at exposing human stupidity. This game also involves whole nations, whose fortunes depend on God's whim, and whose leaders are reduced to staggering in darkness like drunkards.

(13:1–3) vv. 1–2, having completed his parody of the friends' claim to possess wisdom and of conventional hymnic descriptions of divine power, Job now insists on his own ability to observe reality and draw accurate conclusions on the basis of experience. The difference between Job and his friends with respect to epistemology is striking. Eliphaz relied

on a revelatory disclosure; Bildad appealed to ancestral tradition; Zophar deduced the facts from a preconceived notion about divine knowledge. v. 3, frustrated over his friends' inability to comprehend Job's viewpoint, he contemplates a bold alternative: he will argue his cause with Shaddai. The debate will take a different turn as Job gradually moves away from addressing his friends and directs his words to God, but first he will express his contempt for the way they have treated him.

(13:4–12) He accuses them of hypocrisy and ineptitude; they have covered the real situation with an attractive façade and offered him worthless medicine. These are strong accusations, given the prophetic language about false prophets who whitewash their lies and the dubious status of physicians in a society that viewed sickness as divine punishment for sin (cf. Ben Sira's valiant effort to salvage the medical profession in Sir 38:1–15). v. 5, in Egyptian wisdom silence was so important that the expression 'Silent Person' came to signify anyone who embodied the virtues. Job's use of the verb *ḥāraš* has a narrow sense ('stop talking'). Elsewhere the mere withholding of one's tongue is seen for what it is, for it may be an indication of ignorance. v. 6, he who has been called 'a man of lips' (11:2) proudly describes his appeal to the friends as 'pleadings of his lips'. In vv. 7–11 Job's questions contain irony that will not become clear until the Epilogue, where the Lord rebukes the friends for failing to speak the truth about the deity.

(13:13–19) Once more Job asks his friends to keep silent, and he begins to muster courage as he contemplates the consequences of taking his life in his own hands. The ambiguity of the text matches his own uncertainty. Is he essentially a Promethean rebel who shakes his fist in God's face or 'a person wracked by the paradoxes of God' (Newsom 1996: 435)? The body of the text has a negative in v. 15 ('I have no hope'), but a marginal note reads differently ('I will hope in him'). The verse can be read as determination: 'See, he may slay me; I cannot wait, for I must argue my ways to his face.' v. 16, this verse focuses the dramatic action of the book: Job argues that only a virtuous person can survive a face-to-face encounter with God. If Job can appear before God and live to tell it, he will have been vindicated. That is true regardless of how 42:6 is understood. Job's use of *yěšû'â* (salvation) instead of the earlier *tiqwâ* (hope) emphasizes the finished deed, a reality as opposed to an anticipated event. vv. 18–19, judicial terminology abounds here: *mišpāṭ*, *ṣedeq*, and *rîb*. Job imagines that he will achieve vindication through litigation, acting in his own defence, and then he welcomes death.

(13:20–7) Job makes an appeal to God lest divine majesty overwhelm him but concludes that he is being treated like an enemy. This allusion to an enemy may be a pun on Job's name (*'ōyēb*, enemy; *'îyyôb*, Job). v. 20, the prayer attributed to the foreign sage Agur (Prov 30:7–9) has a request that two things be granted: that deception be banished from him and he be given neither poverty nor riches. v. 23, in the Prologue Job fretted over the possibility that his children had unconsciously sinned; here he may wonder if he himself is unaware of guilt that is obvious in God's eyes, or he challenges God to identify a single transgression. v. 26, God was believed to have kept a ledger containing the names of virtuous people (Ex

32:32). Does Job imply that God also keeps a record of one's sins? Or that God jots down the punishments that will be directed against sinners?

(13:28–14:6) The simile (13:28–14:1) for the brevity of life fits better with what follows than with what precedes it. Job characterizes life as both short and miserable. Youthful vigour (a flower) soon fades, and disappears like a shadow. 14:4, Eliphaz's low estimate of mortals seems to have found a parallel in Job's ruminations about extracting something clean from an unclean thing. The Sumerian parallel to Job, *A Man and his God*, states that no sinless person has been born of a woman. This expression has nothing to do with any supposed taint involving the birth canal; instead, it merely means 'everyone'.

(14:7–17) Drawing on his knowledge of horticulture, Job contrasts the fate of trees and human beings. The trunk of a felled tree will sprout new growth if given adequate water, but mortals die and cease forever—just as the water in a lake or river dries up. In Job's view, death is final. Not everyone in ancient Israel shared his opinion, and gradually a belief in an afterlife emerged (cf. Isa 26:19 (collective Israel), Dan 12:2, and Ps 73:23–8). v. 13, Job fantasizes about a kindly deity who would hide him in Sheol until his anger waned, a God who really longed for the work of his hands and who would not monitor his actions in search of transgressions.

(14:18–22) The inevitability of death is foreshadowed by the effect of water on seemingly impenetrable rock. The mighty mountains waste away, and so do mortals. Job ascribes this destructive activity to God: 'so [in like manner] you destroy the hope of mortals' (v. 19). In Sheol the dead do not know the events transpiring on earth; here Job reverses the customary talk about remembering the dead. The isolation of the dying (v. 22) seems misplaced; perhaps Job uses this language to emphasize the thin line between the dying and the dead.

(15:1–35) Eliphaz Defends Conventional Wisdom Eliphaz now appears convinced that his friend is an inveterate sinner, for Job's speech confirms this conclusion. Arguing on the basis of age and consensus, Eliphaz makes two points: Job has sinned, and the punishment for sinners is certain. v. 2, Eliphaz accuses Job of being full of hot air (which comes from the east). v. 4, this is the only instance in the debate of anyone other than Job using this Hebrew word for meditation (*śîḥâ*). In Eliphaz's view there was no place for honest expression of doubt. v. 7, Job was not the only one capable of sarcasm; Eliphaz responds to his challenge that the friends consult earth's creatures in search of knowledge by asking if Job were the firstborn of the human race. Rarely does the HB refer to the primal couple outside Genesis. A shift occurs in the early second century, for Ben Sira alludes to the story twice (Sir 25:24; 49:16). v. 8, as illustrated by the Prologue, the destiny of mortals was determined by a divine council. The prophets Amos and Jeremiah claimed to have listened to YHWH's council (Am 3:7; Jer 23:21–2; cf. also the story about the prophet Micaiah ben Imlah preserved in 1 Kings 22:1–28). v. 10, youth was generally understood as a period of immaturity and rashness (cf. 1 Kings 12:1–6), whereas old age was viewed as a time of wisdom. Neither Job nor Elihu accepted this understanding of things, but Eliphaz and his two companions took it for granted. Under Hellenistic influence, this

traditional view changed radically (Crenshaw 1986). vv. 14–16, this linking of purity and morality results in a low opinion of humankind, for Eliphaz assumes that everyone drinks iniquity like water. If he is right, Job's effort to obtain vindication does not stand a chance. vv. 17–19, Eliphaz will give Job the benefit of his own experience, coupled with ancestral tradition. In v. 18 the Hebrew reads (nonsensically): 'which the wise have declared and have not concealed from their ancestors'. The gift of land and an absence of foreigners (v. 19) confirms the sages' wisdom and goodness, in Eliphaz's logic. The desire to dwell among kindred people arose from suspicion of foreigners (cf. Joel 4:17). For the author of Prov 1–9, the strange, or foreign, woman represented the greatest threat to youth. vv. 20–35, Eliphaz uses a traditional topos about the fate of sinners, including psychological anxiety. The primary visual image is that of faded blossoms (cf. 8:12) and wilted plants, corresponding to human isolation (living in ruins). In vv. 31–2 a failed commercial transaction focuses the concept of futility that underlies this entire unit.

(16:1–17:16) Job Identifies God as his Attacker and Abandons all Hope Job accuses his friends of failing as comforters in the same way they did not succeed as physicians. He claims that he could do better than they, although in his present state speaking out brings no solace. He imagines that God has singled out Job as his personal target, coming against him with exceptional brutality. His archers hit their mark, and God disembowels the fallen Job. At 16:15 Job thinks of his mourning as a permanent condition, for it seems as though he has sewn sackcloth to his skin. Such material was worn during mourning and periods of grief associated with repentance and calling upon God for deliverance. 16:17, Eliphaz's assumption that everyone carries a taint (15:14) is not shared by Job, who insists on the purity of his prayer. Not all who lifted their hands and voices in prayer could make such a claim, as various prophets recognized (cf. Isa 1:15). 16:18–19, according to Gen 4:10, the blood of an innocent victim cried out to YHWH for revenge. Job addresses the earth and asks that it leave his own blood exposed until vindication is assured. In v. 19 his imagination soars to new heights as Job envisions a heavenly vindicator—in 9:33 he had dismissed such hope as wishful thinking. Beginning with 16:22, and ending in 17:16, Job concentrates on the grave and the present conditions that will hasten his arrival there. Surprisingly, he thinks in terms of years instead of days or weeks; but when referring to his broken spirit, he shortens the time span to days, as if to emphasize the grave's readiness to receive him. 17:3–4, the appeal seems to be directed to God, whom Job wants to provide surety for him. Because he attributes the friends' closed minds to divine intervention, he thinks God owes him something. 17:10, again Job urges his friends to come back, although he believes that they will do him no good. 17:11–16, returning to the temporal language of 16:22 and 17:1, Job views his life as over. The description of Sheol as a house gains force when one realizes that ossuaries were shaped like houses. The other images are readily comprehensible; in death one appears to be sleeping, and the lifeless body is soon inhabited by worms. Job's fertile imagination portrays him as an intimate of the personified underworld and its denizens, personified worms. In such circumstances, he laments, hope has vanished. Hence the rhetorical question in v. 15 with its repetition of the word 'hope'. The obvious answer to the questions in v. 16 is 'no'. Hope will not accompany Job into Sheol, the land from which no one returns.

(18:1–21) Bildad's Horrifying Description of the Fate of Sinners The plural verbs in vv. 2–3 may be an error for the second person singular; it is much more likely that Bildad addresses Job rather than his two friends. v. 4, from Bildad's perspective, Job's demands would require the suspension of the moral order of the universe, which guarantees that the wicked are punished. Job wishes to be an exception to this rule, Bildad argues, even if it means catastrophic changes on earth. vv. 5–6, in the Bible light often serves as a metaphor for life, as in Othello's famous speech: 'Put out the light, and then put out the light' (cf. the extended metaphors for death in Eccl 12:6–7, as well as the symbolic use of light in Prov 6:23–30, which contrasts parental teaching with lust that burns within). vv. 8–10, Bildad thinks that an intricate network of traps has been laid out to capture the wicked who wander unsuspectingly into the snares like wild animals. v. 13, death was frequently personified in ancient Near-Eastern literature. No record of Mot's firstborn has survived in Canaanite texts, but the Mesopotamian god of plague, Namtar, seems to have been the firstborn of Erishkigal, queen of the underworld. Bildad's meaning is unclear, but it should probably be translated 'Death, the firstborn'. v. 15, according to a practice mentioned by Homer (*Odyssey*, 22.480–1, 492–4), sulphur was sprinkled over a site to purge it from contamination by corpses. In the Bible salt and sulphur were spread over a location to make it unfit for habitation (Deut 29:23 (MT 22); cf. Judg 9:45 (salt alone)). vv. 16–20, a double merism occurs in v. 16 (above/below; branches/roots). Bildad denies that the wicked enjoy either of the two means of surviving death available in popular thought: survival in others' memory and permanence through offspring. The author of Ecclesiastes extended the argument, making it universal with respect to memory and meaningless where descendants were concerned. The reference to inhabitants of west and east may be symbolic; if so, it signifies past and future generations. v. 21, this summary-appraisal expresses Bildad's certainty that the wicked will dwell in darkness—precisely what Job has said characterizes his own existence.

(19:1–29) Job's Imagination Scales New Heights The conviction that he is being persecuted relentlessly by God leads Job to wish the impossible: either that a redeemer would avenge his death on the basis of a permanent record or that he would actually live to behold his vindication. Here for the first time Job concludes his speech with something other than a meditation on death. In its place is a threat aimed at his friends. v. 3, thus far the friends have spoken only five times; the reference to ten times may be taken as a round number or it may indicate Job's impression that his friends have talked excessively (cf. Gen 31:7 and Num 14:22 for references to a full quota of tests). The verb *kālam* (to humiliate, insult) indicates that Job thinks of his friends' words as insulting. vv. 4–6, the conditional sentence does not implicate Job for sins of some kind; he reasons that even if such were true, the consequences would settle on him. Instead, Job argues, Eloah has perverted

things and imputed the guilt to him. The image of God as a fowler hurling a net to capture prey occurs in ancient Near-Eastern political treaties as a deterrent against rebellion. vv. 7–12, Job's innocence contrasts with Eloah's guilt. He calls for help and God pays no attention (cf. Hab 1:2 and Lam 3:8); instead Eloah's violent conduct towards Job escalates. The elaborate preparations to attack his tent, more appropriate for laying siege to a city, suggest the personal animus that Eloah has towards Job. The idea of a divine enclosure in v. 8 differs greatly from Satan's understanding of YHWH's protective fence around the prosperous Job. In vv. 9–10 he accuses God of stripping away his wealth and honour (the Heb. noun *kābôd* has both senses), removing his crown, and uprooting his hope. Unlike the earlier image of a tree-stump left in the ground and capable of regeneration, the complete removal of the roots from the source of nourishment rules out all hope. vv. 13–22, this description of social reversals resembles a literary topos from ancient Egypt and Mesopotamia. An individual complains that society has been turned upside down, with slaves riding horses and nobles walking. Friends have become enemies, and no one can be trusted. Job's servants consider him a foreigner (contrast 31:13–15); the irony in this conception may be lost on those who do not know that most slaves were foreigners acquired through warfare or purchase. Job's loss of control over his slaves means total humiliation within the intimacy of the home. Even his wife finds his breath unpleasant; the Hebrew can also mean: 'my spirit is alien to my wife'. The reference to 'children of my belly' (NRSV: 'my own family') in v. 17 presents difficulty, inasmuch as children would be more appropriately designated as products of his wife's womb and, moreover, Job's children are dead, according to the Prologue. Ancient sexist views may explain such language, which would assume that ownership of a wife gave Job the right to claim her belly as his own (cf. the awful punishment imagined for his wife if he were guilty of adultery, 31:10). Alternatively, Job may refer to his brothers, 'my belly' implying the one from which he emerged, that is, his mother's womb. The topsy-turvy world extends to Job's body; his bones cling to his skin and flesh, instead of the reverse (v. 20). Like El, the friends pursue him relentlessly. The *imitatio dei* is here understood as an undesirable trait; God sets a bad example for them. The simile, 'like God [ʾēl]', stands out in v. 22, as does the negated verb, 'to satisfy'. Job has escaped with nothing ('by the skin of my teeth') and now his friends want more than his flesh. vv. 23–7, Job gives voice to an impossible wish, that his words be inscribed as a perpetual testimony to his innocence (cf. Isa 30:8). Precisely in what medium remains unclear. He may refer to three different forms of preserving words, representing progressively more enduring media: a scroll, a lead tablet, and a stone with lead inlay, like the famous Behistun Rock on which the Persian king, Darius, boasts of his exploits. More probably, Job indicates a single medium for displaying his words, a stone with lead inlay. Textual difficulties render it impossible to interpret vv. 25–7 with any confidence, and familiarity with Handel's *Messiah* gives the impression that one already understands the verses. The word *gōʾēl* ('redeemer') derives from family law. According to Num 35:19 and Deut 19:6 this avenger of blood, the nearest male relative, would vindicate a wronged member of the family. The *gō'ēl* also redeemed property (Ruth 4:4–6; Jer 32:6–7; cf. Lev 25:25) that had been sold because of economic distress, recovered stolen property (Num 5:8), bought back a family member reduced to slavery (Lev 25:28), and married a childless widow to perpetuate the dead husband's name. Job's use of this term indicates that he has given up on justice and begins to hope for revenge. The idea that a redeemer could call God to account for his actions may derive from Mesopotamian religion, where one's patron deity intercedes on behalf of a person in distress, but Job seems to attribute more power to the figure of the redeemer than intercession implies. Job's cry of assurance recalls a Ugaritic text in the Baal cycle: 'And I know that Aleyan Baal is alive', a confession of the god's revivification according to an agricultural calendar. What does Job imply? Three possibilities present themselves: (1) a heavenly figure, like the witness (16:18–21), will champion Job's cause after his death; (2) a heavenly figure will enable him to arise from the dead, or as a disembodied shade Job will witness his vindication; and (3) vv. 25–6a refer to vindication after Job's death, but what he most desires (vv. 26b–27) is that this event occur prior to his demise. The threat to his existence has prompted speculation about heavenly intermediaries: an arbitrator (9:33), a witness (16:18), and a vindicator (19:25), but none of these will accomplish what he truly desires, as expressed in 13:16. Only seeing God and surviving that experience will satisfy Job. From this point on (19:25), Job will not refer to heavenly mediators; instead, he will press his case for an audience with God.

(20:1–29) Zophar's Confidence in the Moral Order This description of the fate of the wicked corresponds to normal expectations in the psalter and in the book of Proverbs. A similar optimism characterizes one of the oldest Egyptian instructions, *Ptahhotep*, which observes that wickedness never brings its goods into safe harbour. Zophar thinks of a principle established in the beginning of time, one that guaranteed justice in the world. The wicked flourished only momentarily, whereas good people enjoyed lasting prosperity. v. 6 may contain an allusion to the story of the tower of Babel in Gen 11:1–9. The idea that the wicked are obliterated like a dream also appears in Ps 73:20. The images that Zophar uses suggest the extent to which the formerly rich have fallen: like dung, unseen, begging from those who have nothing themselves, dust. The popular idea that wickedness had a pleasant taste (cf. Prov 9:17) has left an impression on Zophar, but he thinks God changes the food into poison. This whole section, vv. 12–19, resembles futility curses. The mistreatment of the poor was considered a serious offence throughout the ancient Near East, and legislation aimed at protecting marginalized citizens is widespread. The image of poison-induced vomiting and gastric illness continues in the concluding section of Zophar's speech, vv. 20–9. Both heaven and earth turn against the wicked; their legacy is fire, darkness, and utter deprivation. This picture contrasts sharply with traditional understandings of the Lord or the land as the heritage of the faithful. Like Am 5:19, flight from one danger leads to yet another form of death (v. 24, where bronze bow functions as synecdoche for bow and arrow).

(21:1–34) Job's View of an Immoral Universe Job utters words that must surely have horrified his friends, for he denies the moral order of the universe, which they take for granted. In his considered opinion, the wicked enjoy the pleasant life that Job's friends believed was reserved for good people. He realizes how outrageous his remarks will sound; hence he anticipates their mockery (v. 3). Indeed, he urges them to use a gesture indicating shock; placing one's hand over one's mouth could also express respectful speechlessness, but Job does not hope for this type of response from his erstwhile friends. vv. 7–16, this picture of the prosperity of the wicked contrasts with Job's own misery and serves as self-justification. The particularities of the account constitute a powerful indictment of God, who fails to act even when the wicked ignore him. They reach old age, their children thrive, their cattle multiply, the wicked rejoice. The *Babylonian Theodicy* has the sufferer complain that he has not profited from serving his personal god, whereas 'those who do not seek the god go the way of prosperity while those who pray to the goddess become destitute and impoverished'. vv. 17–18, the fourfold rhetorical question in the NRSV, 'How often?' is represented by a single *kammâ* with sequential verbs. Job asks his friends to test the traditional theory that God punishes the wicked. How often have they witnessed it? vv. 19–26, here Job addresses a possible response: that God punishes the children of evildoers (cf. Jer 31:29 and Ezek 18:2). Job assumes that such scoundrels as he has been describing will lose no sleep over their children's destiny. v. 22, beginning with a common cliché ('Will any teach God knowledge . . .?'), Job proceeds to argue that God does not distinguish between good and evil people (vv. 23–6). In life and in death God makes no distinction. vv. 27–34, Job urges his friends to test his theory by consulting travellers who have observed things far and near. He is certain that they will confirm his conclusion that the wicked are spared when calamity strikes the innocent. The beginning and end of this section reveals Job's distrust of his friends. The semblance of dialogue has completely vanished; insults have taken its place.

(22:1–30) Eliphaz Accuses Job of Great Wickedness Job's extreme sufferings, coupled with his intemperate language and untraditional views, convince Eliphaz that his friend is guilty of the most heinous offences imaginable. Therefore, Eliphaz calls them to mind, after first insisting that God who sits above the human scene cannot be affected by either good or evil. Eliphaz accuses Job of taking advantage of members of his family and of mistreating the naked, widows, and orphans, and (implicitly) of strengthening the hand of powerful oppressors. vv. 12–20, Eliphaz mocks the wicked who imagine that God cannot see through the thick clouds, a motif that is also found in Psalms (Ps 10:11; 73:11; cf. Isa 29:15; Jer 23:23–4; Ezek 8:12). In v. 15 the Hebrew word *'ôlām* (ancient) can be pointed differently to indicate concealment, which continues the thought of the previous verse. Like those who deceive themselves that God cannot see, will you also walk along hidden paths? In v. 18a Eliphaz concedes that God bestows good gifts on the wicked, but such an admission prompts him to reject their schemes as odious, and to cast his allegiance with the righteous who laugh at the perishing wicked. vv. 21–30, Eliphaz has not given up on his friend, whom he urges to make peace with God. The Mesopotamian parallel text, *I Will Praise the Lord of Wisdom*, recommends correct ritual and repentance as a means to restoration. Eliphaz's promising account of what will happen if Job repents comes close to what actually occurs in the Epilogue. v. 24 is laden with word-plays: the Hebrew word for treasure resembles the word for 'like the stones' and that for 'dust' recalls the word for Ophir. v. 27, neglecting to fulfil one's vows was considered a serious offence (cf. Eccl 5:4 and the Canaanite *Epic of Keret*). v. 30, Eliphaz cannot know the irony in this statement, for he—the guilty one—will actually benefit from Job's intercessory prayer (42:8).

(23:1–24:25) The Turmoil within Job's Soul Job may have abandoned belief in a moral order, but he cannot bring himself to give up on God completely. Somehow he still thinks that the judge of all the earth would act fairly if only Job could track him down. Mistakenly, Job believes God would not argue on the basis of power. At this point he still thinks in terms of a lawsuit, despite his earlier insistence that God makes a mockery of justice.

(23:8–9) In Ps 139:7–12 the psalmist takes comfort in the knowledge that one cannot wander beyond God's watchful eye. That soothing feeling is not shared by Job, who despairs of finding God anywhere. He mentions all four directions; in the Bible directions are indicated by picturing someone standing and facing the rising sun. Forward is east, backward is west; to the left is north, and to the right is south.

(23:10–17) v. 10, the understanding of suffering as a divine test was widespread; Job briefly recalls this explanation for his misery and expresses confidence that he will emerge from the smelting process as pure gold. He has no idea how accurate this assessment of things really is. Dread of God returns, along with a renewed wish to be hidden. Unlike the wicked, he knows that one cannot hide from God.

(24:1–12) One can hardly imagine a more powerful indictment of God's ways than this brief section. Job begins by asking why Shaddai does not adhere to times of judgement; he proceeds by giving specific examples of dereliction in the office of judge. In a word, the offences strike at the very foundation of society, its concern for the well-being of those who were unable to fend for themselves. Crimes against widows, orphans, and the needy do not move God to action. These unfortunates are forced to eke out a living and to sleep without protection from the elements. Their clinging to a rock for shelter is Job's shattering blow against traditional belief that the Lord was a protective rock. Job portrays God as totally oblivious to such misery. Job does not stop here but goes on to describe the oppression of the poor and to finish with a rhetorical flourish (v. 12). The dying pray for help, but Eloah ignores the groaning.

(24:13–27) Whereas the author of Ps 104:20–3 rejoices over the orderly creation in which nocturnal animals restrict their movements to the dark hours, Job describes human villains who use the darkness of night to conceal their criminal acts from others. The futility of such clandestine behaviour is proclaimed in Prov 7:6–23.

(24:18–20) The sentiments expressed here do not accord with Job's attitude and must be a caricature of his friends'

view, or they represent his wish that they be punished. Contrasting images appear in v. 20, the womb symbolizing life and the worm symbolizing death.

(24:21–5) Job returns to his indictment of God for empowering the wicked to oppress the widow; he accuses God of watching over such criminals (v. 23). In Job's mind, providence has turned lethal. Again he wishes that God would exact judgement against such criminals (v. 24). Job concludes with an open challenge to his friends: 'prove me wrong'.

(25:1–6) Bildad's Low Opinion of Humanity Several features of chs. 25–7 indicate disarray: the brevity of Bildad's third speech and the absence of Zophar's; the attribution of specific material to Job that expresses views elsewhere rejected by him but articulated by the friends; and the presence of introductory formulas for speeches different from all previous ones ('Job again took up his discourse and said' (27:1; cf. 29:1) as opposed to 'Then Job answered'). In addition, the isolated nature of ch. 28 and the longer introductory formula in 29:1 suggest either an editorial hand or an effort to set apart this material for some unknown reason. It has been surmised that the author never actually completed the third cycle of speeches but merely provided provisional notes for future reference. Inasmuch as the narrator gives no clue that the friends have run out of anything to say, and nothing subsequent to this section suggests a conversion on Job's part at this stage, and arguments for an unfinished debate have little merit, the probable cause of the present disarray is textual transposition. In all likelihood, the insertion of 26:5–14 has brought about this dislocation, one accentuated by the addition of ch. 28. In 25:1–4 Bildad stresses God's governance of the heavens, keeping that domain safe in the face of revolt (cf. 1 *Enoch* 6–11 and Dan 10; cf. also Isa 14:12–21). In Bildad's opinion, God's purity dwarfs everything, from moon and stars to those born of woman, here called maggots and worms.

(26:1–27:23) Job's Integrity Compromised (?) The mixture of untraditional views and orthodox sentiment seems to compromise Job despite his protests otherwise. Did his closing responses to Bildad and Zophar so anger readers that they replaced them with palatable views? What could he have said that went beyond the stinging indictment of God in 24:1–12? Clearly, his anger has reached the boiling point here, and one would expect even harsher observations to follow.

(26:1–4) As usual, Job comments on his friends' failure; the remarks contain bitter sarcasm and are addressed to Bildad alone. Furthermore, the syntax permits one to take the negatives as references to Bildad: 'How you have helped, without strength! . . . How you have counselled, without wisdom!' Job even questions the divine source of such banalities, risking blasphemy.

(26:5–14) This hymn has mythical elements (the reference to Abaddon, a name for the underworld probably derived from the verb '-b-d, 'to perish'; the name Zaphon, the mountain of Baal in the north similar to Mt. Olympus in Greek mythology; the chaos-monster, here identified as Sea and Rahab—cf. Isa 27:1 for a reference to the fleeing serpent, Leviathan). A naked Sheol stands exposed before God, who proceeds to cover it with the cosmic mountain and the earth. One expects it to be 'the heavens' that God stretches out (cf. 9:8; Ps 104:2; Isa

40:22). The language in v. 7 echoes the myth of creation in Gen 1:2 (*tōhû*, 'formless'; *belî-mâ*, for nothing; *bōhû*, 'waste', 'void'). The waters are envisioned as waterskins (v. 8), and the word for moon actually is pointed as 'throne'. v. 14, an appropriate reminder that one can only comprehend a tiny portion of God's majesty concludes this hymn. Those who proclaim the remarkable story of a cosmogonic battle and an ordering of the universe have succeeded in describing the 'outskirts' of his way and have heard only a 'whisper'.

(27:1–6) The new introductory formula in v. 1 uses the noun *mĕšālô*, usually translated 'proverb', 'likeness', 'analogy', and occasionally 'parable'. Job swears by God, whom he has rejected, that he will not give up his integrity. The oath in the name of the deity who has demonstrated total disregard for justice, in Job's view, corresponds to Job's relentless seeking to face God in a trial, although convinced that the divine Judge twists the truth. Such inconsistency grows out of the enormity of Job's suffering and his reluctance to abandon the sole possibility than his friends. Contradictions are part and parcel of daily existence. Thus Job thinks that God afflicts him on every side and pursues him relentlessly, but Job also claims that he can find God nowhere.

(27:7–12) If spoken by Job, this section begins with irony and ends in insult (his friends blow wind; the noun *hebel* in v. 12, as well as the verb from the same root, *h-b-l*, means 'breath', hence lit. 'breathes a breath,' blows wind). Between these sharp barbs rest rhetorical questions that emphasize God's arbitrary power and complete indifference to sinners by God and to God by them. There, too, is a promise to instruct the friends more fully about God's actions.

(27:13–23) The opening verse, which repeats Zophar's conclusion in 20:29, signals the imitative quality of this unit. Job appears to say that he can make Zophar's speech more effectively than the Naamathite can. In the light of the reference to the death of children by a sword and the allusion to a whirlwind (vv. 14, 20), this speech makes more sense when attributed to Zophar. v. 16, the parallelism of silver and clothing is striking, as one expects the pair 'silver' and 'gold'. v. 19, the fleeting nature of wealth was a common topos in the ancient world; according to the *Instruction of Amen-em-ope*, it takes wings like geese and flies away (cf. Prov 23:4–5); Hag 1:6 mentions wages placed in a bag with holes. vv. 20–3, the recurring theme of a wind recalls the sharp attack on the friends for producing empty wind (v. 12, *hebel* and the verb *hābal*, 'to become futile, ephemeral').

(28:1–28) Where Can Wisdom be Found? This exquisite poem functions as an intermezzo, an interlude that enables readers to pause long enough to weigh the arguments on both sides of the debate and to prepare for what follows. The poem consists of two parts, vv. 1–11 and 12–27, with a concluding statement in v. 28. This chapter resembles the divine speech in ch. 38, particularly the cataloguing of facts lying beyond human ken and the use of rhetorical questions (Geller 1987).

(28:1–11) The author of this section marvels at human achievement in searching for (prospecting) and extracting (mining) precious metals from remote depths. The exact meaning of v. 4 is more hidden than the gems being sought,

partly because of ignorance about ancient mining techniques and partly because of obscure language. Its central point can be captured in the expression, 'far from'. Whatever activity is described takes place in virtual isolation.

The phrase in v. 8, 'children of pride', used in 41:26 in association with Leviathan, stands as a parallel to *šaḥal*, which occurs elsewhere in 4:10 in parallelism with *'aryēh* (lion). Its meaning in 4:10 is indisputable, for it represents one of five different words for lion. The reference in v. 11 to probing the sources of the rivers echoes Canaanite myth, which locates the abode of the god El 'at the sources of the two rivers, in the midst of the channels of the two seas'. Several phrases in this section suggest cosmic activity rivalling the achievements of deity: overturning mountains by their roots (9:5; cf. Hab 3:6), opening channels in rocks (Hab 3:9; Ps 74:15), and exposing hidden things to light (12:12; Dan 2:22).

(28:12–19) v. 12 continues the thought of v. 1 by providing its contrast; it does this by means of a sophisticated wordplay between 'mine' (*môṣā'*) and 'find' (*māṣā'*), while repeating the word 'place' (*māqôm*). The Hebrew word for wisdom, *ḥokmâ*, is a supernym indicating a quality of knowledge for which as many as nine nouns stand in parallel cola (*bînâ* as here seems to be the preferred parallel). 'Wisdom' is the general term; *bînâ* is the more specific one for intellectual discernment. Nothing in vv. 12–28 resembles the personification of *ḥokmâ* as depicted in Prov 8:22–31 and Sir 24:1–22, among other texts. Four different words for 'gold' and seven different gems give this text a distinctive character, 'suggesting a connoisseur's familiarity with rarities among rarities' (Newsom 1996: 531). The negative particle *lō'* introduces vv. 15–17, 19; in v. 18 it appears as the third word. The four different words for purchasing ('weighed out', 'given', 'be paid for', and 'valued') in vv. 15–17 contrast with the understatement, 'no mention', in v. 18. The exceptional value placed on wisdom elevates it just as effectively as the author of Prov 8:22–31 does in quite a different way, by imagining her as pre-existent artisan or witness to the act of creation.

(28:20–7) The opening verse repeats the question in v. 12, with one change (the verb 'come' replaces 'be found'). The personification of Abaddon and Death in v. 22 provides smooth transition to the emphatic 'God' in v. 23 ('He' is also in the emphatic position). According to Isa 43:13, YHWH laid claim to the ancient epithet, *hû'* ('He', 'That One'). The personal pronoun in v. 23 may echo this tradition rooted in stories about divine self-manifestations that evoked an ecstatic shout, 'O He'. The emphasis shifts from spatial language (v. 24) to temporal expressions in vv. 25–7 ('when' . . . 'when' . . . 'then'), resembling ancient Near-Eastern stories about creation (cf. also Prov 8:24–30*a*). The poem claims that Elohim recognized wisdom during an act of creativity. Educational terms describe the deity's intellectual pursuit of wisdom: 'Then he *saw* it and *declared* it, he *established* it, and *searched* it out.' Observation led to articulation of the facts as perceived; the positing of a theory followed, with further probing of its accuracy or inaccuracy (cf. Eccl 7:23–5; Sir 6:27). The conclusion of this majestic poem is something of a let-down. One expects a profound statement; instead, a cliché brings readers back to earth. Wisdom is encountered in the mundane choices one makes, specifically in religious devotion. (Using this criterion for wisdom, Job already possessed it and more, according to 1:1 and repeated citations of this fourfold description of his character.) Interpreters have expressed disdain for this formulation of things subsequent to the debate in chs. 3–27, which surely undercuts such simple answers to complex issues, and have insisted that any resolution at this juncture is premature. The unique appearance of the name Adonai in this verse is noteworthy; in Jewish tradition this name was pronounced instead of the sacred name, the Tetragrammaton YHWH. This special name for God was left unuttered out of profound respect.

(29:1–31:40) Job Challenges God In ch. 29 Job remembers an idyllic past, contrasts it with his miserable present in ch. 30, and pronounces an oath of innocence in ch. 31. Much of the material in this section comes from stock expressions in the ancient world, which explains its apparent lack of fit with Job's circumstances in some instances. Reaching historical conclusions about Job's precise role in the community on the basis of this material misconstrues its typical nature. Exaggeration belongs to autobiography; so do self-exoneration and considerable fabrication. Accordingly, Job understands himself in royal categories.

(29:1–25) Job begins his nostalgic reminiscence on a level of intimacy, then moves outwards from this family scene to his role in society and its rewards. When contemplating his activity as champion of the downtrodden, Job returns once more to his most intimate thoughts (vv. 18–20). The reference to autumn days in v. 4 (tr. as 'my prime' in NRSV) strikes Western readers as peculiar, but in the Near East the autumnal New Year signalled a time of regeneration after the drought of summer. The picture of divine care while Job and his entire family sat under his tent contrasts with the following image of an urban dweller (v. 7). The desert sheik was content with cream and oil; the city-dweller takes the leading role in judicial disputes at the gate. Job recalls that he silenced everyone (young and old, prince and nobles) because he embodied the values of the group as expressed in looking out for the interests of the weak. He overlooks none of them, for the list of persons receiving his help includes the usual categories—widows, orphans, poor, stranger—as well as the blind and lame. According to royal ideology, kings were charged with ensuring the well-being of these lowly members of society, and failure to abide by this rule was viewed as grounds for abdication of the throne in the Canaanite story of Aqhat. vv. 18–20, the Hebrew of v. 18 reads 'sand', which makes sense in context and is not excluded by the earlier 'nest'. The mixture of metaphors in this brief reflection argues against reading 'phoenix', for Job thinks of a bird, sand, roots, dew, and a warrior's bow. These images may be placed alongside the more familiar prophetic scene of sitting peacefully under one's vine and fig tree. With the exception of the initial metaphor (dying in one's nest), all Job's images symbolize vitality; the final one, a fresh warrior's bow, has sexual overtones in the tale of Aqhat, where the goddess Anat covets the prince's bow and offers her love in exchange for it. vv. 21–5, unlike Job's miserable comforters, he insists that he actually brought comfort to the needy.

(30:1–31) Job's description of his present circumstances comprises four sections, the first three beginning with a contrasting particle, 'but now', and the fourth with 'surely'. He demonstrates his remarkable skill at insulting others (youth insult me, whose fathers are not even good enough to accompany my dogs; cowering in wadis, they bray like cattle). Such contempt for the poor contrasts with the attitude expressed in 29:12–17 and 31:16–23, although Job's description of their feeble attempts to survive in harsh economic conditions shows that he has internalized their needs. Job acknowledges the principle that religious people tend to identify those whom God has ostracized and to count them as their enemies too (v. 11). In vv. 16–19 Job returns to his earlier suspicion that God personally attacks him. This unpleasant thought gives way to direct address of God for the first time since ch. 16. He imagines that God ignores his cries for help and tosses him about on the wind (vv. 20–3). Job concludes this section with observations about his psychic distress. Together, chs. 29 and 30 effectively describe Job at the pinnacle of success and the nadir of his isolation from society. At one time the aged and nobles stood in awe of him; now children of a no-name mock him (cf. 30:8, 'senseless', lit. children of a fool, 'disreputable', lit. children of a no-name). In previous days he presided over the judicial assembly; now he calls jackals and ostriches his companions. Such ostracism is aptly symbolized in the words that conclude the chapter, 'a sound of weeping'.

(31:1–40) Job's final speech in the debate takes the form of a negative confession reinforced by an oath. Similar oaths of innocence are known from ancient Mesopotamian and Egyptian liturgical texts. Although the context of Job's oaths is a lawsuit, the offences listed are not subject to legal remedy. Job uses two kinds of oath, the complete oath with the consequences specified, and an abbreviated oath that stops short of mentioning any punishment. Interpreters differ in estimating the exact number of oaths and, in a few instances, their specific nature. The latter point applies to the opening reference to looking on a virgin. On the basis of Canaanite mythology of the perpetual virgin goddess Anat, some scholars think Job denies having participated in idolatrous worship. To them, this offence seems more appropriate at the head of a list of wrongs, especially since lust and adultery are treated later (vv. 9–12). The offence, lust (whatever its object, whether a foreign goddess or an ordinary virgin), marks this code of ethics as special, going as it does beyond the actual act to the prior intent as in Jesus' later formulation of the issue. The second and third oaths concern ethics generally—deceit and greed—while the fourth returns to sexual ethics (adultery). The oath in v. 7 refers to hands, feet, heart, and eyes, indicating that Job's total being is devoid of fault (Habel 1985: 433). The first stated punishment in v. 8 resembles a futility curse ('let me sow and another eat'); unlike the next one (v. 10), it does not conceive of the punishment as an appropriate 'fit' to the crime. The prescribed punishment for adultery would fall on Job's wife (others would turn her into a prostitute), but that harsh treatment accorded with the ancient understanding of a wife as the husband's property. The anomaly is that sexual ethics could simultaneously generate the exalted view in v. 1 and the reprehensible attitude of v. 10. The language describing adultery and its punishment is rich in double entendre, with 'door' representing the entrance to the womb and the paired verbs 'grind' and 'kneel', signifying the sex act.

The next four oaths consider the matter of social ethics (vv. 13–15, slaves; vv. 16–18, the poor; vv. 19–20, the needy again; vv. 21–3, the orphan again). Job acknowledges that social distinctions between masters and slaves are human contrivances, for God created both (cf. Prov 22:2 and 29:13 for the same attitude with reference to rich and poor). In v. 22 the full form of the oath occurs for the third time; in this instance the punishment fits the crime; aggression leads to further aggression, the abusive fist to a broken and useless arm. The three oaths in vv. 24–8 deal with various forms of idolatry (gold, wealth in general, worship of heavenly bodies) but lack a specific punishment. The gesture mentioned in v. 27, the mouth kissing the hand, may allude to a Babylonian expression for a gesture of obeisance in which the hand touches the nose. The modern 'blown kiss' involves a somewhat similar gesture. Two oaths in vv. 31–3 concern the obligation of providing hospitality to strangers on a journey (cf. the stories about Abraham's hospitality to the divine messengers in Gen 18:1–15 and its sequel about Lot in a similar role in 19:1–11, as well as the scandal involving the Benjaminites living in the town of Gibeah as told in Judg 19). The language of v. 31 suggests homosexuality; Job denies that anyone in his tent ever abused strangers in such a manner. At this point Job utters an aside (vv. 35–7) in which he expresses a wish to be heard and openly challenges Shaddai. He juxtaposes the thought of his own mark over against a non-existent indictment written by his adversary. The word for 'mark' is the last letter of the Hebrew alphabet, a *taw* resembling an x. In Ezek 9:4, 6, it signified persons to be spared God's judgement. Job imagines that he would wear the indictment for all to see (cf. Hab 2:2 for a prophetic message being publicly displayed). The image of a prince with an indictment for a crown corresponds to Job's ambiguous situation itself. The final oath (vv. 38–40) touches on his relationship with the land. The ancients viewed society and land reciprocally; crimes against one another affected the land adversely. Furthermore, respect for the land required proper treatment, including a practice of periodic release from cultivation. Job's oath seems to echo the story about unavenged blood crying out to God. The full form of the oath once again envisions an appropriate punishment, an unproductive field. The narrator enters for a brief moment to observe that Job's words have come to an end (cf. Ps 72:20); the verb *tammû* echoes the adjective describing his integrity, *tām*.

Elihu Attempts to Answer Job (32:1–37:24)

A youthful figure, previously unmentioned, comes forward and angrily rebukes all four of those engaged in debate. This individual is called Elihu, which means 'He is my God' (cf. Isa 41:4, 'I am He'); he alone is given an impressive Jewish pedigree (cf. Gen 22:21, there Buz is identified as a son of Nahor, Abraham's brother). The name of Elihu's father, Barachel, means 'El has blessed', a significant appellation in the light of the dispute within the prologue over whether or not Job would *bārak* God. Elihu's long address, uninterrupted by responses from anyone, is divided into four parts by prose introductions at 32:1–6; 34:1; 35:1; and 36:1. The speeches appear intrusive for several reasons: Elihu's sudden appearance without previous mention, his Jewish ancestry, his distinctive style and language, his familiarity with the rest of the

book, and his disappearance without a trace after 37:24. He alone addresses Job by name, and he quotes liberally from the book, even anticipating the divine speeches. He prefers the divine name El, the short form of the personal pronoun 'I' (*'ānî*), and the word for knowledge (*dēa'*) missing elsewhere in the book. His vocabulary has more Aramaisms than used by other characters, and he seems determined to tie up loose ends in the arguments against Job. Interpreters generally view Elihu as an intruder, an attempt by a later Jewish author to provide a more orthodox answer to the issues being addressed in the book. Elihu's youth may signal the lateness of this section (Zuckermann 1991: 148, 153). The similarities between Elihu's ideas and certain Hellenistic texts has also confirmed the lateness of these chapters for some critics (Wahl 1993: 182–87). Others insist that both style and content argue for the integrity of the unit and view its anomalous features as artistic skill. While some interpreters consider Elihu a buffoon, a self-destructing upstart, others see him as a bearer of remarkable insight into the nature of suffering and divine majesty.

(32:1–5) The narrator provides a glimpse into the minds of the three friends who have given up on Job, convinced that he was deluding himself (cf. Prov 12:15; 26:5, 12, 16; 38:11; 30:12). The phrase, 'innocent in his own eyes', means that in a legal sense Job saw himself as not guilty; from the friends' perspective, that assessment of things had no firm basis in fact. The narrator characterizes Elihu as angry, repeating the idea four times in as many verses (vv. 2–5). An ideal among the sages was the control of the passions (lust, greed, anger, appetite), but the young Elihu remains very much in their grip. His anger flared at Job and his three friends—at Job because he justified himself and at the friends for their inability to answer him successfully. The narrator explains Elihu's belated remarks as required by ancient protocol: youth must wait for age to speak first. Would ancient readers have expected much from an angry young man? In v. 3 the Masoretes, guardians of the ancient manuscript tradition, inserted a rare change in the text; the original read 'declared God to be wrong'. Elihu's perception of their responses does not instil confidence in his reading of things.

(32:6–14) Not content with the introduction accorded him by the narrator, Elihu provides further justification for his remarks. He does so by juxtaposing two fundamental principles, the first, that age deserves precedence, and the second, that every person has direct access to the divine spirit. For him, the second principle took precedence over the first. He dutifully awaited his turn to speak but became convinced that age does not necessarily imply wisdom. Elihu's ambiguous remark about the breath of the Almighty seems to suggest special inspiration (v. 8, 'bestows understanding on them'). Similar ambiguity surrounds this concept elsewhere in the Bible (cf. Gen 2:7 where the breath of YHWH animates humankind and Isa 11:2, where it suggests special knowledge on the part of a chosen ruler). The author of Ps 119:99–100 expresses the rare notion that meditation on the Torah and obedience to it endows youth with more wisdom than their teachers and elders possess. In v. 13 Elihu hints that he already knows the development of the plot, for he attributes to the friends the idea that God will refute Job. Elihu's protestations to originality do not dissuade interpreters from viewing his contribution to the argument as minimal.

(32:15–22) The final section of Elihu's self-introduction uses the image of a wineskin about to burst from the pressure of fermentation. The sages were aware of a sense of urgency in speaking; they even made clever jokes about the desire to spread gossip, insisting that the words would not explode within one's belly (Sir 19:10). Prophetic literature also recognizes the necessity to express oneself (Jer 20:9). Elihu's language provides a pun on the narrator's description of him as angry (*'ap 'ănî*, also I'/*wayyiḥar 'ap*, *ḥārâ 'ap*, 32:10, 17, 2, 3, 5). A twofold irony underlies vv. 21–2, for Elihu will certainly show partiality to God and, from the perspective of the plot and its development, will cease to exist.

(33:1–13) Elihu offers further rationale for daring to speak, addressing Job by name and citing him almost verbatim. By means of a teacher's summons to attention (v. 1), Elihu shifts the focus from himself to Job momentarily, but quickly reverts to the earlier concentration on his own unique qualifications to refute Job and his friends. No chasm exists between Elihu's mind and words, for he is both upright and pure (v. 3, *yāšār* suggests moral integrity; *bārûr* connotes the lack of any blemish). In v. 4 Elihu uses the ideas of God's spirit and Shaddai's breath in a general sense; as such, they do not reinforce his unique claim. They do, however, function to assure Job that he faces an ordinary mortal in debate. Elihu's citation of Job's fourfold affirmation of innocence and fourfold charge against God (vv. 9–11) is inexact but reliably summarizes what Job has said at some point (9:20–1; 27:4–6; 30:1–40; 33:24b–27a). To refute Job on all counts, Elihu voices a principle that will undergird everything he says: God is greater than any mortal (v. 12). Why then, Elihu asks, do you contend (*rîbôtā*) with God? Mere mortals, he thinks, cannot enter into a lawsuit with Eloah.

(33:14–30) An *inclusio* connects v. 14 with v. 29 (one, two/twice, three times); between these numerical expressions Elihu's argument becomes expansive. He claims that God communicates by different means, sometimes through nocturnal visions and at other times through suffering. Both types of communication come as warnings to stem the natural emergence of pride. As a paragon of virtue, Job was particularly subject to this form of sin, for morally good people tend to recognize their superiority over the masses. Elihu admits that the recipients of divine warnings by night seldom perceive them for what they are (contrast Eliphaz's astute grasp of his divine visitor's message in 4:12–21). The stated purpose of these warnings is to prevent an early departure into the realm of the dead. Does Elihu envision death as crossing a river like the Greek notion of crossing the river Styx? The second type of warning results in emaciated bodies that elicit compassion from a mediating angel (*mēlîṣ*). The term denotes an interpreter (cf. Gen 42:23) and a mediator (Job 16:19 (MT 20)). In later Jewish literature the heavenly mediator becomes an intercessor for devout persons (*1 Enoch* 9:3, 15:2 and the *T. 12 Patr.*). The idiom 'one of a thousand' indicates rarity. The mediator does not offer any information about the nature of the 'ransom' that covers the sins of the person being spared the Pit. In Elihu's extraordinary scenario, the intercessor declares the guilty person innocent, and this

in turn prompts the sinner to confess and receive God's forgiveness. To conclude this remarkable account of a compassionate God who warns sinners and responds favourably to mediators, Elihu praises the divine generosity, insisting that God acts this way repeatedly so that mortals may experience light rather than the darkness of Sheol.

(33:31–3) Again Elihu resorts to a teacher's appeal for an attentive audience; while inviting Job to respond, he states that his sole intention is to justify Job. In v. 33 Elihu promises to convey wisdom to Job (his choice of the verb *'ālap* provides a pun on the earlier expression, 'one of a thousand' (*'eḥād minnî-'ālep*).

(34:1–37) In some ways this chapter resembles the rhetorical conceit of the later Wisdom of Solomon, which also addresses an imaginary audience and offers philosophical reflection on God's just governance of the universe. In Elihu's case, only four persons are present, and he does not consider any of them wise. After a brief rhetorical appeal to the audience (vv. 2–9), Elihu proceeds to defend God's justice on two counts, God's absolute sovereignty and respect for justice (vv. 10–20). Then Elihu shows how God effectively punishes the wicked (vv. 21–30), which makes Job's claim of innocence appear ridiculous (vv. 31–3), as intelligent people will undoubtedly recognize (vv. 34–7). Elihu does not shrink from allowing his imaginary audience to join him in addressing Job by name.

(34:1–9) Elihu quotes a popular proverb (v. 3) reflecting his oral culture; the ear, not the eye, tests words. Ancient sages recognized the need to evaluate what was spoken in the same way one's palate discriminated between desirable and undesirable food. Three of the six occurrences of the noun *mišpāṭ* (just, right) in the larger section (vv. 12, 17, 23), mark the significance of vv. 4–6. Over against Job's charge that God has taken away his right, Elihu places the desired collective conclusion of his audience. They, not Job, have the responsibility of choosing *mišpāṭ*, here used in poetic parallelism with *ṭôb* ('good'). In vv. 7–9 Elihu accuses Job of standing out above all others, but not in goodness (contrast 1:3). He drinks mockery like water (habitually), associates with sinners, and blasphemes, i.e. he denies the fundamental principle that the universe is moral. In Elihu's opinion, whoever delights in God receives an appropriate reward; Job's experience taught him otherwise.

(34:10–15) Elihu appeals to intelligent listeners, reminding them of God's sovereignty. Such a one has no reason to pervert justice, he argues; the unspoken contrast is the human judge whose greed renders him subject to a bribe and whose vulnerability before the powerful leaves him open to showing partiality. vv. 14–15 allude to the ancient story of creation (Gen 2:7; 3:19).

(34:16–20) Appealing to his listeners again, this time in the singular to designate them individually, Elihu points out that God, who loves justice, chose to govern. It follows that God cannot pervert justice; the same person cannot be both *ṣaddîq* and *rešaʿ* (wicked). Does Elihu's understanding of God leave room for the traditional belief that the poor occupied a special place in God's affection?

(34:21–30) God's overthrow of the wicked is made possible by keen sight, according to Elihu, for God sees everything they do. Despite Job's claims to the contrary, God punishes the wicked and pays heed to the cries of the oppressed. Having accepted as a reality the orthodox belief about God's just governance of the world, Elihu concludes that divine silence does not make the deity culpable.

(34:31–7) The meaning of this brief section is obscure. Does Elihu advise Job to repent in vv. 31–2, or does he contrast Job's obdurate conduct with one who repents when confronted with guilt? In v. 33 the verb reject (*māʾas*) lacks an object; a similar phenomenon occurs in Job's actual response to God's second speech from the whirlwind (42:6). Elihu cannot know the conditions governing the Adversary's test of Job—unless he really is a later intruder—and his wish that Job be tested to the limit violates the stipulation that his life be spared. The accusation that Job speaks without knowledge anticipates YHWH's words in 38:2. Here the Lord appears to corroborate Elihu's harsh assessment of Job.

(35:1–16) This entire chapter is structured around two of Job's objections: that in his case it has not paid to serve God and that God pays no attention to his cry for justice (vv. 3, 14–15).

(35:1–8) In the previous chapter Elihu invited rational people to judge for themselves; now he asks the embittered Job to reconsider his complaints against God. At issue is the justice of God as manifested to Job. Elihu thinks any sensible person will conclude that God is just; Job, therefore, has lost his capacity to reason when he says, 'I am more just (innocent) than God' (my tr.). Job's verdict is based on the failure of God to deliver appropriate rewards for faithful service. Job reckons that he has been treated by God like one who has not rendered loyal obedience. In short, religion does not pay. Elihu answers this charge by emphasizing the divine self-sufficiency, an approach that Job's friends have already taken. In Elihu's view, neither virtue nor vice affects God whatever, for God dwells in the remote heavens. Human deeds, both good and bad, relate solely to other mortals (v. 8). This answer does not really address Job's complaint, for even a self-sufficient deity can reward goodness and punish evil for purely altruistic reasons.

(35:9–16) How does Elihu's response to Job's other complaint fare? In this instance Elihu holds the citation from Job's speeches in abeyance until he has dealt generally with the problem it raises. Oppression among mortals compels the less fortunate to raise a cry to the heavens, but they do not cry out in prayer. That seems to be the meaning of vv. 10–12. Instead of searching for their Maker and expressing gratitude for the gift of songs during the night (the Heb. word *zĕmirôt* can mean either 'strength' or 'songs') and acknowledging that the divine teacher instructs by means of animals and birds, they swell with pride. Here Elihu mocks Job's earlier observation that God teaches through animals and birds; in addition, Elihu implies that Job, like the unnamed evildoers, has surrendered to the powerful temptation of pride. The antecedent of the phrase, 'because of pride', is unclear; it can be either the verb 'cry out' or 'does not answer'. If the former, it explains their reluctance to pray; if the latter, it states the reason for God's disregard. Now Elihu has prepared the way for yet another onslaught against Job's character. Thus he cites Job again, this time indirectly and in general (vv. 14–15). Job's firm conviction that God ignores his just cause has been robbed of

its potency by Elihu's clever artifice. It has become obvious to Elihu that Job's talk lacks substance inasmuch as it consists of many words devoid of knowledge. Here Elihu anticipates YHWH's rebuke of Job in 38:2, which uses the same words. Has the later author of Elihu's speeches found a way to authenticate his own views?

(36:1–37:24) Elihu's View of God The conclusion to Elihu's speeches slowly moves away from Job's flaws to concentrate more fully on God's character and majesty. Accordingly, citations of Job's troubling view recede into the background as Elihu reinforces his own authority to speak correctly about God (36:1–4). Returning to earlier themes, Elihu emphasizes God's power, justice, and salvific activity (36:5–15), but in the process Elihu interprets the mystery of disciplinary suffering as an occasion to warn Job (36:16–21). Beginning at 36:22, a decisive shift in the tenor of the speeches takes place, one that anticipates the divine disclosure in ch. 38. The similarities between the two discourses suggest that Elihu intentionally steals a major share of divine thunder. The speech opens with an expansive introduction (36:22–33) divided into three distinct sections by the exclamation 'see' (*hēn*) in vv. 22, 26, and 30. The topics of this unit (divine majesty, God's control over rain and lightning) mark a transition (37:1–5) to the theme of a thunderstorm (37:6–13). Elihu asks several rhetorical questions like those soon to be ascribed to YHWH (37:14–20) and ends with a flourish (36:1–4). Elihu's final self-presentation indicates that he understands exactly what the issue is from Job's perspective: divine justice or, more correctly, its absence. Elihu differs, however, on whether or not it exists. He intends to bring his knowledge to bear on this matter, hoping thereby to refute Job's denial of God's justice. For Elihu, God is innocent and Job is guilty. Moreover, Elihu boasts, my knowledge is both accurate and sound (*tāmîm*).

(36:5–15) The twofold use of the adjective 'mighty' (*kabbîr*), together with another word for strength (*kōaḥ*), in v. 5 demonstrates Elihu's theological starting-point. God is great! When sovereignty and intelligence join hands, as here, one has truly happened upon the best of all possible worlds. Elihu offers a subtle hint of another dimension, compassion, for he claims that God does not reject (*māʾas*...). This verb has no object and therefore it must be supplied by readers. Presumably, Elihu means that God has no predisposition to despise anyone, and by implication God's treatment of individuals is fully determined by human conduct. Pressing the point further by means of a proverbial saying (v. 6), Elihu affirms both sides of the principle of reward and retribution. God destroys the wicked and exacts justice for the afflicted. Among the sages the usual pair of contrasting groups was righteous/wicked, but here *rāšāʿ* is matched with *ʿăniyyîm* (wicked/afflicted) as frequently in psalms of lament. The following verse brings the vocabulary more into line with customary sapiential speech, for it refers to these afflicted ones as righteous (*ṣaddîq*). The origin of the notion that the *ṣaddîq* and the poor were identical is difficult to trace, but it surfaced as early as the eighth century (cf. Am 2:6), becoming normal in later psalms, and evolving into a theological axiom in some post-biblical literature. Indeed, the name of the earliest Christian movement, Ebionites (the poor), reflects this understanding of the lowly as God's special people. Elihu relates divine power to human decisions; the arrogant wicked are overthrown by it, and the lowly afflicted are exalted. Against Job's claim that God looks away from the needy, Elihu boldly asserts the opposite (v. 7). Moreover, he interprets affliction as God's discipline aimed at restoring individuals. Their fate, he insists, lies in their own hands; if they heed divine instruction, they will be lifted up, but if they refuse to listen, they will perish. Here Elihu resorts to a play on words between the verbs for serving God and being destroyed ('ābad/'ābar). Elihu's virtual fixation with right thinking leads him to add 'without knowledge' (cf. 35:16, the same words YHWH will use with reference to Job in 38:2). In vv. 13–14 Elihu describes the punishment of people like Job who become angry because of divine affliction rather than imploring God's mercy. Such stubborn sinners die while young, ending up in the company of reprobates. The Hebrew word for male prostitutes associated with the temple occurs in v. 14. Despite biblical references to this practice in ancient Israel, its scope and nature remain obscure. Apparently, both men and women served as sacred prostitutes (qĕdēšîm), their earnings going into the temple treasury despite intense opposition in Deuteronomistic circles (Deut 23:17–18 (MT 18–19); 2 Kings 23:7). In v. 15 Elihu sums up his teaching about the positive use of discipline; by means of affliction, God opens the ear of the afflicted. An Egyptian proverb states that the teacher opened a student's ear by striking him on the back. It should be remembered that ancient educators made liberal use of corporal punishment. Curiously, Elihu uses the noun 'ānî rather than mûsār, so prominent in Proverbs and Sirach; the verb 'ānâ carries a harsher connotation than yāsar.

(36:16–21) Elihu begins this unit by harking back to God's initial kindness to Job; the three images picture a person at one with the world (wooed from distress, a wide space, a table filled with rich staple foods). Two of these words recur in vv. 18–19 (sût and sar, woe and distress). In other words, God has overcome Job's restrictive limitations and replaced them with wide streets and plenty of 'fat', a delicacy in the ancient world. God's generosity contrasts with Job's niggardliness, his anger. Elihu seems to warn Job against being enticed by his distress to pointless fury and mocking. His near obsession with justice (dîn) will backfire, in Elihu's view. Ultimately, dîn and mišpāt will overwhelm him. By this he probably means 'divine judgement'. The allusion to a great ransom (v. 18) echoes the remark by the mediating angel in 33:24, 'I have found a ransom'.

(36:22–37:24) The final section of Elihu's speech begins with a declaration of God's might and poses three rhetorical questions for Job's consideration (vv. 22–3). Each of the questions functions to negate the answers: no one compares with God as teacher, or tells God what to do, or can accuse God of wrong. The idea of God as teacher (cf. 33:14–22; 34:32; 35:11) reached beyond the sages such as Elihu to prophetic figures as well. In Isa 30:20–1 the themes of YHWH as afflicter and teacher come together in the same way they do in Elihu's discourse. Moreover, both Isaiah and Elihu put forth these ideas as a response to concern that God is hiding. For the prophet, the moment a person starts to veer off course, YHWH speaks up and points out the way to be travelled. Elihu's assurance that the one who afflicts the sinner uses adversity to teach a moral lesson lacks the emotional depth of the related prophetic text,

but at least Elihu's understanding of divine activity has a moral dimension. That cannot be said for YHWH's speeches about the interrelationship between Creator and creature. The second rhetorical question also resembles a text from the book of Isaiah (40:12–14), which asks who has instructed the majestic Creator or taught him the path of justice. The implied answer to these rhetorical questions is 'no one'. Elihu's third question, like his second, underscores the absurdity—from his perspective—of Job's onslaught against the sovereign teacher. For him 'might' comes mightily close to representing 'right'.

(36:24–37:5) The proper response to God's grandeur, Elihu urges Job, is hymnic praise. To reinforce his point, Elihu extols the awesome power unleashed in thunder and lightning, with their accompanying rains that produce abundant food for all living creatures. Not every image in this description of heavenly fireworks is intelligible; for example, 'ēd in v. 27 actually refers to a primordial underground stream, at least in ancient mythology (cf. Gen 2:5–6), and the phrase 'covers the roots of the sea' in v. 30 seems strange. Perhaps it suggests that bright flashes of light expose the roots. On the basis of similarities between this text and Ps 29, some interpreters emend the verb 'cover' to a noun with a possessive pronoun ('his throne'; cf. Ps 29:10, 'The LORD sits enthroned over the flood; the LORD sits enthroned as king for ever'). The last verse of ch. 36 presents greater difficulty; Gordis (1978: 424) revocalizes it to read: 'His thunderclap proclaims His presence; His mighty wrath, the storm'. In 37:1–5 the point of view shifts from God's electrifying display to the human response. The same shift takes place in Ps 29:9 ('all say, "Glory!" '). In v. 2 Elihu uses repetition to effect a breathtaking pause in the action ('Listen, listen') as he invites others to share his excitement. The point of view in vv. 2–5 begins and ends on the human level but soars to the heavens in the interval. Elihu stands in awe of divine power, but he is not alone in failing to comprehend God's niplā'ôt and gĕdōlôt ('wondrous' and 'great' deeds).

(37:6–13) Turning to a less noisy but nevertheless spectacular display of a different kind, Elihu points to the formation of ice and snow, inclement conditions that force animals to seek shelter. The image of thick clouds and lightning prompts him to discern a moral in all this movement. In his view, such phenomena convey divine intention, but one may choose among three possibilities: for correction, for his land, or for love. Although Andersen (1976: 266) emends land ('ereş) to acceptance (rāṣâ), the broad focus in this section on people and animals speaks against emending the text. Elihu views such grandeur as aimed at disciplining wayward humans, nurturing all God's creatures, and as a general display of love. Here, too, Elihu's understanding of divine power is more comforting than YHWH's own interpretation of the same phenomena. Strikingly, Elihu makes minimal use of mythical images in this description. By way of contrast, YHWH will squeeze every ounce of mythic symbolism from the same activity.

(37:14–24) The speech of Elihu ends where it began, but the rebuke of the four men has narrowed to one, providing a smooth transition to YHWH's rebuke of Job. Just as Elihu's earlier rhetorical questions and description of meteorological phenomena anticipate one type of YHWH's speeches, the kind of questions that make up vv. 15–18 prefigure the other type of questions YHWH hurls at the beleaguered Job. These queries ('Do you know?', 'Can you?'), together with the sarcastic 'Teach us', may be understood over against the earlier concept of God as teacher. Elihu prepares Job to face a barrage of questions from the heavenly instructor whose knowledge is perfect (*tām*, cf. Elihu's similar claim about his own knowledge in 36:4). Mocking Job's wish to confront God (v. 20) as an automatic death-wish, Elihu reminds Job that God is far brighter than the sun (cf. Sir 43:1–5), on which none can look without harm. One would think that such brilliance could not be hidden from humankind, but just as the sun has its own hours of concealment, so Shaddai sometimes resides outside human perception. God chooses when to be seen and moves from the north, the mythic abode of the gods (v. 22). Elihu's parting moralism poses a problem. The first colon is clear: 'Therefore mortals fear him'. The second colon reads literally: 'He does not look on any person of intelligence'. Andersen (1976: 268) emends the verb 'see' to a similar verb, 'fear' (*rā'â* to *yārē'*), understands the negative *lō'* as *lû* ('surely'), and takes 'every intelligent person' as the subject (cf. the LXX). This attractive interpretation yields a sense equivalent to that in 28:28, and has Elihu concluding on a high note: 'Surely all wise of heart fear him.'

YHWH's Two Speeches and Job's Responses (38:1–42:6)

The dramatic climax to the book of Job finally arrives, after an interminable delay, at least from Job's perspective. In a sense, his eagerly awaited audience before the Creator contains no surprise, for he expected to encounter power; still, the divine speeches do not measure up to advanced billing. Instead of resolving the matter of Job's innocence, they completely ignore the problem that has exercised Job and his four detractors for so long. Nor do the divine speeches from the whirlwind throw any light on the suffering of innocent persons. YHWH's entire discourse ignores humankind, except in mocking questions addressed to Job. Instead, YHWH expresses exhilaration over meteorological phenomena and animals that dwell outside the ordinary habitat of humans, with one notable exception, the warhorse. Most importantly, YHWH reserves pride of place for two partly mythological creatures, Behemoth and Leviathan. The two speeches (38:1–39:30; 40:1–41:34 (MT 26)) begin with narrative introductions (38:1; 40:6), present direct challenges to Job (38:2–3; 40:7–14), and examine specific themes already articulated in the rebuke of Job (the divine plan, 38:4–39:30; *mišpāṭ*, 40:15–41:34 (MT 26)). Each speech has two distinct parts. The first speech takes up cosmological and meteorological phenomena (38:4–38) and then discusses five pairs of animals (38:39–39:30). The second speech is limited to two special creatures. After each divine speech, Job responds (40:3–5—following a specific invitation from YHWH to answer in 40:1–2—and 42:1–6). The content of the divine speeches resembles the exquisite poetry of Isa 40:12–31 and Ps 104. Readers react variously to the divine speeches; some consider them sublime irrelevance, others think they succeed in forcing a self-centred Job to take a less egocentric view of the universe, and still others discern an unpleasant fact beyond the playful(?) mockery: a world devoid of morality (Tsevat 1966: 73–106). Perhaps the poet chose the wisest course, to leave Job's problem

unresolved, for no answer would have sufficed, whether spoken by YHWH or anyone else. This ambivalence suggests that the dominant genre, disputation, served the poet well, for its strength lies in its ability to present alternative viewpoints.

(38:1–40:5) The Divine Plan of the Universe YHWH's *'ēṣâ* (plan, counsel) includes the cosmos and the realm of wild animals. The initial speech focuses on these two topics, highlighting the argument with periodic questions directed at Job ('Who? Where? On what? Have you? Can you? Where?').

(38:1–3) v. 1 derives from the narrator, who has framed the discussion thus far and made important judgements about Job's character. That the name YHWH occurs here, as in the prose framework (1:1–2:13; 42:7–17), comes as something of a surprise, for it has been avoided in the poetic discourses except for the cliché in 12:9. This name, together with the information that YHWH speaks from a whirlwind (*se'ārâ*), reintroduces the additional problems posed by the interaction between the Adversary and YHWH. Does disinterested piety exist? Will anyone serve God gratuitously, *for nothing*? Furthermore, the destructive power of the whirlwind, its capacity to renew Job's gut-wrenching memory of ten dead children, does not bode well for him. Biblical theophanies usually bring solace along with the inevitable sense of awe; in this instance, form and content clash (Crenshaw 1992). Job has his wish, but not on his own conditions. vv. 2–3 make this fact painfully clear; YHWH rejects Job's reasoning as senseless, an obfuscation of the divine plan. YHWH has no intention of capitulating before human charges of injustice; instead, he will expect far more intellectual rigour from the accuser. The initial question, 'Who is this?' has the tone of 'How dare you?' Job has demanded that God tell him the specific wrongs he has committed (10:2; 13:23), promising an answer for each breach of trust (13:22). This stance quickly becomes meaningless in the type of universe described by the divine speeches. YHWH does not encourage Job to hold on to his conviction that a moral principle governs the world. In the light of this radically different world-view, the situation has suddenly reversed. Instead of YHWH being obligated to answer Job (13:2), Job must now come up with an appropriate response to new revelations about the nature of the universe. The image, 'Gird up your loins like a man', probably refers to tucking the ends of one's robe into a belt to permit quick movement.

(38:4–7) The creation of the earth is described as if it were a huge temple; YHWH designs and constructs the edifice, to the jubilation of interested onlookers (cf. Prov 8:22–31, where the emphasis falls on wisdom's presence and excited reaction). The allusion to heavenly singing echoes the liturgical dedication associated with the construction of an earthly temple. The dedication of YHWH's temple evoked singing from the morning stars and divine beings. The final phrase of 38:5, 'surely you know!', occurs elsewhere in the related sayings attributed to the foreign sage, Agur (Prov 30:1–14, specifically in v. 4).

(38:8–11) Once earth has been established, YHWH sets about to contain the boisterous sea, which represented primeval chaos in ancient Near-Eastern myths. Acting as midwife, YHWH assists in its birth and cares for the newborn infant. At the same time he provided clothing for the sea (clouds and darkness), YHWH determined its limits, here envisioned as doors imposed by divine command. The image is that of parental discipline, a prohibition aimed at the infant's well-being. Behind this language of bursting forth and containment lie numerous biblical and non-biblical stories about primordial chaos, but that hostile power is here circumscribed (cf. Ps 74:13–14; 89:10–13 (MT 9–14); Isa 51:9–10; *Enuma Elish*). The allusion to proud waves points beyond itself to an important topos in the second speech (see 40:10–14).

(38:12–15) YHWH's description of dawn's power to renew creation each day echoes Job's earlier curse (3:9) and complaint about reversals of dawn and darkness (24:13–17). In YHWH's graphic image, a personified dawn takes hold of earth's corners like a bedsheet and shakes out the wicked like bedbugs. Their natural fondness for darkness becomes a self-fulfilling curse, light being denied them and their strength being checked (38:15). In YHWH's world, the wicked have a place just like the good, but dawn limits their destructiveness.

(38:16–21) Turning to the remote regions of the universe, YHWH asks Job about the extent of his progress in reaching the deep recesses, whether above or below. The prophet Amos mentions similar remote areas, along with hiding-places closer to home and a little more distant (Am 9:1–4, Sheol, the depths of the sea, heaven, caves on Mt. Carmel, exile). Whereas Amos emphasizes YHWH's ease in following and punishing anyone who might flee his wrath, the divine speech in Job 38:16–21 concentrates on Job's inability to make such a journey. Twice in this brief section YHWH mocks Job (vv. 18, 21). YHWH reminds him that his life span is but a speck on the eons of time.

(38:22–4) At this point, YHWH shifts from cosmology to meteorology. At least two, possibly three, of these items cause harm (hail, east wind, lightning (?)). The use of the Hebrew word '*ôr* (light) instead of the usual word for lightning (but see 37:11), and the reference to snow, suggest that the speech alludes to two positive and two negative phenomena. Only in one instance does YHWH elaborate: hail is associated with warfare (cf. Ex 9:22–6; Josh 10:11). Late Jewish literature describes heavenly journeys during which angels disclose esoteric knowledge to favoured individuals (cf. *1 Enoch* 41:4; 60:11–12 for a journey to heavenly storehouses).

(38:25–30) YHWH asks Job if he knows pertinent facts about the rain, dew, hoarfrost, and ice. According to the ancient Israelite cosmogony, the firmament was thought to resemble hard metal, hence the language of cutting channels for the rain and making openings through which lightning could pass. YHWH goes to some lengths to emphasize the divine prodigality where rain was involved (cf. Am 4:7–8). Twice YHWH states that rain fell where no human being lived, in the desert waste. vv. 28–9 use images of begetting and birthing; rain and dew are referred to the male act of procreation, whereas ice and hoarfrost are associated with the womb. The formation of ice is further described as water hiding on a rock (cf. Sir 43:20, ice is viewed as a lake's breastplate).

(38:31–3) Unlike the rest of the sections dealing with meteorological phenomena, this one has nothing directly to say about water. Perhaps it was thought that the movements of constellations affected what transpired on earth, even influencing rainfall. The identity of the constellations mentioned here is not certain; a case has been made for the following: Pleiades, Orion, Sirius, and Aldebaran (de Wilde 1981: 366–7). He notes that the last three in this list appear when Pleiades is 'bound,' i.e. hidden from sight.

(38:34–8) The chapter concludes with questions about Job's ability to summon the rain and command lightning during a severe drought. YHWH asks Job if he possesses the requisite skill to handle containers holding precious water, skins and jugs. Although the Hebrew of v. 36 is difficult, it may refer to the ibis and the cock; ancient Egyptians thought the ibis announced the Nile's rising and the cock predicted the approach of rain. Divine sarcasm in v. 35 stands out above the constant ridicule of the rhetorical questions; YHWH imagines the ludicrous: lightning bolts address Job obediently, 'Here we are.'

(38:39–39:30) Beginning in v. 39, YHWH calls Job's attention to wild animals: lion and raven, mountain goat and deer, wild ass and ox, ostrich and horse, hawk and vulture. Scenes from the ancient Near East depict kings hunting many of these wild creatures. Such royal sport contains an element of control; as lord of all creatures, the King of the Universe subjects wild animals to his wishes. Two irreconcilable symbolic gestures rest behind these descriptions; YHWH protects his kingdom from all threat posed by wild animals, and he rules over the animals' well-being. The rhetorical questions continue throughout these descriptions, with the exception of the reference to the ostrich, where one also finds God mentioned in the third person.

(38:39–41) For some unknown reason the lion is paired with the raven. The terror inspired by lions prompted the prophet Amos to speak of the divine calling to prophesy as an inescapable summons, just as the roar of a lion brings terror (Am 3:8). YHWH asks Job if he can provide food for hungry lions and ravens when they cry out.

(39:1–4) In this section YHWH recalls an earlier stage, that of gestation and birth. He asks whether or not Job could watch over these intimate moments in the lives of mountain goats and deer.

(39:5–12) YHWH turns to discuss two wild animals with domesticated equivalents. The wild ass, or onager, lived in the steppe or in salt flats; its preference for living away from human presence gave rise to proverbial sayings (e.g. 'Ishmael is a wild ass of a man'). The strength of the wild ox, possibly the extinct aurochs, was an occasion for marvel. The questions regarding this animal approach the ludicrous: will it serve you, sleep in your crib, submit to your ropes, and plow a straight furrow?

(39:13–18) Like the wild ass, which laughs at noisy cities (39:7), the ostrich laughs at the horse and its rider. YHWH claims to have withheld wisdom from the ostrich, with unfortunate consequences for its offspring. In perpetuating this misconception about ostriches, YHWH gives voice to popular lore at the time of the author. In this matter, as in all others, the author faced enormous difficulty the moment he decided to allow YHWH to become one participant among several in a debate.

(39:19–25) The horse is the only domesticated animal in this list of ten, but what a majestic creature! YHWH can hardly contain the excitement over the warhorse. Completely devoid of fear, the mighty horse laughs as it charges into the heat of battle. The language of a 'warrior god' serves to characterize this horse (might, thunder, majesty, terror; so Habel 1985: 547). The horse's desire for battle rivals the drive for water or sex (Newsom 1996: 612).

(39:26–30) The final pair of animals, hawk and vulture, watch from above as a grim scene unfolds on the battlefields below. From their perspective, corpses provide food for them and their young. This section reaches a conclusion by harking back to the provision of food for the raven and its offspring. Beginning with the description of the horse in battle, YHWH views the conflict of armies from the perspective of the horse and the vulture, rather than from war's effect on human history.

(40:1–5) YHWH demands that Job respond. The former critic acknowledges his lack of honour (social status) over against YHWH and gestures that he will be silent. The earlier boast that he will approach God like a prince gives way now to a numerical saying. The expected disputation has not materialized.

(40:6–42:6) The Mystery of Divine Governance The second divine speech resembles the earlier description of the warhorse, only with considerably more detail. YHWH boasts about two powerful creatures, Behemoth and Leviathan. Partly animal and partly a product of a mythical imagination, these two liminal beasts cavort on land and in water. YHWH's world makes room for such beasts, indeed he glories in their freedom and strength. Although a threat to any mortal who dared to challenge them, they, too, enjoy YHWH's protection.

(40:6–14) The narrator repeats the introduction from 38:1 and the command to Job from 38:3, while explicating the accusation of 38:2 (40:6–8). Finally, YHWH comes to the point of the debate as Job understands it. God is guilty, and Job is innocent. Instead of accepting this view of things, YHWH bristles at such impertinence. To silence Job, YHWH challenges him to perform specific tasks that fall to the deity. First, to manifest his splendour, then to overcome pride (*gēʾeh*), and vanquish the wicked. If Job can successfully perform these duties, YHWH will concede. Does the poet permit YHWH to indulge in a minor confession that even the Creator finds these tasks something of a challenge? By focusing on pride as the fundamental form of rebellion, YHWH shifts the issue from the realm of legality to that of inner attitude. The question is no longer guilt or innocence, whether Job's or YHWH's, but a correct assessment of one's place. In YHWH's view, Job's helplessness when confronted with something as basic as pride renders his charges against the Creator null and void. The divine judge, as it were, has issued a verdict. YHWH, the accused, is innocent.

(40:15–24) The task of overcoming pride becomes concrete in the two descriptions that follow. Both Behemoth and Leviathan demonstrate what it means to encounter pride near at hand. The word Behemoth is a plural form of the usual word for cattle; it may be a plural of majesty, representing cattle *par excellence* (cf. the plural form of wisdom, *ḥokmôt*,

in Prov 9:1). The description of this animal suggests either the hippopotamus or the water-buffalo. In Egyptian myth, the god Horus hunts Seth in the form of a hippopotamus (Keel 1978: 138–9). Ugaritic myth mentions bull-like creatures, and the Mesopotamian *Epic of Gilgamesh* records an incident in which Gilgamesh and Enkidu slay a 'Bull of Heaven'. The comparison of Behemoth's *zānāb* in v. 17 to a cedar derives from the role of bulls in fertility religion; the word *zānāb* (tail) is a euphemism for penis. This powerful creature is called 'the first of the ways of God'; the same thing is said of Wisdom in Prov 8:22. With slight repointing of the Hebrew consonants in v. 19*b*, it may be translated 'made to dominate its companions', in context preferable to 'its maker approaches it with his sword', for elsewhere the description of Behemoth has no suggestion of a struggle between gods and chaos.

(41:1–34 (MT 40:25–41:26)) In contrast to Behemoth, an animal in repose, Leviathan stands before Job as a creature of violence. YHWH begins the description by posing rhetorical questions to Job that illustrate the absurdity of attempting to control this terrifying creature, visualized as part crocodile and part mythical monster (41:1–12) (MT 40:25–41:4). The images for hunting and fishing are not entirely clear, but the practice of controlling captured slaves by inserting a cord through the nose or cheek is mentioned in the Bible (e.g. 2 Kings 19:28; Isa 37:29). The idea of this powerful creature begging for mercy, or submitting to girls' play, or even providing meat for bartering tradesmen approaches the ridiculous. Even the gods dare not engage Leviathan in battle (41:9 (MT 41:1)). Although difficult, vv. 10–12 (MT 2–4) may represent God's indication that none can withstand Leviathan, the creature's arrogant boast, and God's decision not to silence such boasting. Leviathan boasts only about his own domain, unlike Job.

(41:13–24 (MT 41:5–16)) The description of Leviathan begins with its skin, resembling an impenetrable coat of mail, and moves from this general panoramic view to a close-up of the face, neck, and chest. Power and beauty combine to make this creature godlike; it has eyes like the dawn which emit a beam of light, and breathes fire like a dragon. The association of fire and smoke with the gods (cf. Ps 18:8 (MT 9)) is a common feature of ancient lore.

(41:25–34 (MT 17–26)) Before this awesome creature the gods cower, especially when it surfaces so that its impenetrable shield becomes visible. Weapons of war bounce off like harmless straw (sword, spear, dart, javelin, arrows, iron and bronze clubs). Laughter links this powerful creature with the wild ass, ostrich, and warhorse, but Leviathan's ability to distance itself in raging water, disappearing in its white wake, makes it king over all the proud. In 40:11*b* YHWH challenged Job to 'look on all who are proud and abase them'; here Leviathan 'looks on all that are proud' (41:34 (MT 26)).

(42:1–6) The exact meaning of Job's response to YHWH's discourse is unclear, perhaps intentionally so. He certainly acknowledges YHWH's power, but that is not new. Job also quotes YHWH twice (42:3*a*, 4) and responds to each citation; he concedes that he has spoken without understanding, but his second concession is capable of several interpretations. In fact, even his statement in v. 5 is ambiguous. Does he say that his previous knowledge of YHWH was second-hand (obtained through a rumour) or that he has just now really listened, in obedience to the divine command to hear, so that he is prepared to understand the meaning of the theophany, a seeing also? The next verse has built-in problems. The verb *mā'as* requires an object but has none, as has occurred earlier in the book; likewise, *weniḥamtî 'al* may carry opposite meanings. The range of interpretation includes, among others, the following possibilities: (1) 'Therefore I despise myself and repent upon dust and ashes'; (2) 'Therefore I retract my words and repent of dust and ashes'; (3) 'Therefore I reject and forswear dust and ashes'; (4) 'Therefore I retract my words and have changed my mind concerning dust and ashes'; and (5) 'Therefore I retract my words and I am comforted concerning dust and ashes'. The first translation implies humiliation; the second and third refer to symbols of mourning; and the fourth and fifth signify the human condition (Newsom 1996: 629). Some interpreters think the remark carries heavy irony; Job conceals his rebellion to the end. Others believe that he abandons his lawsuit, acknowledges his finitude, and finds comfort in the simple fact of having come before God and survived, his own stated condition for full vindication (cf. 13:16).

The Prose Epilogue (42:7–17)

The conclusion consists of two parts: YHWH's rebuke of Job's three friends (vv. 7–9) and the restoration of Job (vv. 10–17). Astonishingly YHWH commends Job for speaking correctly about him. It is difficult to imagine Job's rebellious speeches struck YHWH as truth, so interpreters assume a different story, one that must have been removed to make room for the poetic debates. Moreover, the restoration of Job comes as something entirely unexpected after the poetic debate, which shattered the concept of a moral order. One could argue that the truth behind Job's remarks was his honesty and that the restoration is an act of grace, but significant problems remain. This suggests that irony lies at the heart of the book. The happy ending uses the rare Hebrew word *šibʿānâ*, which the LXX takes as a doubling, to specify the number of Job's sons. If this is correct, the narrative subtly indicts YHWH for criminal action, for which twofold restoration was mandated (cf. Ex 22:4, 7, 9 (MT 3, 6, 8)). YHWH's treatment of Job's friends on the basis of the retributive principle adds further irony. How can an arbitrary deity who treats Job in the manner described in the prose and poetry be the source of moral order? Furthermore, the happy ending confirms the truth of what Job's friends predicted. Repentance brought restoration in the end. Job completes his life surrounded by a wife, fourteen (or seven) sons, three beautiful daughters, and plenty. In favour with God and people, he lives two additional lifespans and sees four generations of descendants. Like the patriarchs, he dies 'old and full of days'. A moral order is alive and well, at least for the author of the prose. Or is it? Those who have read the poetic debate can no longer be content with such a simple answer to life's deepest enigma. Divine mystery remains, along with a human inability to comprehend the suffering of innocents. Job has succeeded, however, in that the *Deus absconditus* has become the *Deus revelatus* (the hidden God has become manifest).

REFERENCES

Albertz, R. (1981), 'Der sozialgeschichtliche Hintergrund des Hiob-buches und der "Babylonischen Theodizee"', in J. Jeremias and L. Perlitt (eds.), *Die Botschaft und die Boten: Festschrift für H. W. Wolff* (Neukirchen-Vluyn: Neukirchener Verlag), 349–72.

Alonso-Schökel, L. (1977), 'Toward a Dramatic Reading of the Book of Job', *Semeia*, 7: 45–59.

Andersen, F. (1976), *Job: An Introduction and Commentary* (Downers Grove, Ill.: InterVarsity Press).

Clines, D.J.A. (1989), 'Job', in B. W. Anderson (ed.), *The Books of the Bible*, (New York: Scribners), 181–201.

Crenshaw, J. L. (1972), '*Wedōrēk 'al bamotê 'āreṣ*', *CBQ* 34: 39–53.

——— (1980), 'Impossible Questions, Sayings, and Tasks', in J. D. Crossan (ed.), *Gnomic Wisdom* (Chico, Calif.: Scholars Press), 19–34; repr. in Crenshaw (1995), 265–78.

——— (1986), 'Youth and Old Age in Qoheleth', *HAR* 10: 1–13; repr. in Crenshaw (1995), 535–45.

——— (1992), 'Job, Book of', *ABD* iii. 858–68; repr. Crenshaw (1995), 426–68.

——— (1995), *Urgent Advice and Probing Questions* (Macon: Mercer University Press).

Crüsemann, F. (1980), 'Hiob und Kohelet: Ein Beitrag zum Verständnis des Hiobbuches', in R. Albertz *et al.* (eds.), *Werden und Wirken des Alten Testaments: Festschrift für Claus Westermann* (Göttingen: Vandenhoeck & Ruprecht), 373–93.

Damico, A., and Yaffe, M. D. (eds.) (1989), *Thomas Aquinas: The Literal Exposition on Job* (Atlanta: Scholars Press).

Dekker, H. (ed.) (1952), *Sermons from Job: John Calvin* (Grand Rapids: Baker Book House).

Dhorme, E. (1967), *A Commentary on the Book of Job* (London: Nelson).

Fishbane, M. (1985), *Biblical Interpretation in Ancient Israel* (Oxford: Clarendon).

Geller, S. A. (1987), 'Where is Wisdom? A Literary Study of Job 28 in Its Setting', in J. Neusner, B. Levine, and E. S. Frerichs (eds.), *Judaic Perspectives on Ancient Israel* (Philadelphia: Fortress), 155–88.

Girard, R. (1987), *Job: The Victim of his People* (Stanford: Stanford University Press).

Glatzer, N. N. (1969), *The Dimensions of Job* (New York: Schocken).

Good, E. M. (1988), 'Job', *HBC* 407–32.

——— (1990), In Turns of Tempest: A Reading of Job with a Translation (Stanford: Stanford University Press).

Gordis, R. (1978/5738), *The Book of Job* (New York: Jewish Theological Seminary of America).

Gutiérrez, G. (1987), *On Job: God Talk and the Suffering of the Innocent* (Maryknoll, NY: Orbis Books).

Habel, N. C. (1985), *The Book of Job* (Philadelphia: Westminster).

Hausen, A. (1972), *Hiob in der französischen Literatur* (Berne: Herbert Lang).

Hoffman, Y. (1996), *A Blemished Perfection* (Sheffield: Sheffield Academic Press).

Hurvitz, A. (1974), 'The Date of the Prose Tale of Job Linguistically Reconsidered', *HTR* 67: 17–34.

Jung, Carl (1954), *Answer to Job* (Cleveland: World).

Kahn, J. H. (1975), *Job's Illness: Loss, Grief and Integration* (Oxford: Pergamon).

Keel, O. (1978), *Jahwes Entgegnung an Ijob*, FRLANT 121 (Göttingen: Vandenhoeck & Ruprecht).

Koch, K. (1955), 'Gibt es ein Vergeltungsdogma im Alten Testament?' *ZTK* 52: 1–42; ET in J. L. Crenshaw (ed.), *Theodicy in the Old Testament* (Philadelphia: Fortress), 57–87.

Linafelt, T. (1996), 'The Undecipherability of BRK in the Prologue to Job and Beyond', *Biblical Interpretation* IV 154–72.

MacLeish, A. (1956), *J.B.* (Boston: Houghton Mifflin).

Newsom, C. (1996), 'Job', *NIB* (Nashville: Abingdon), iv. 319–637.

Pope, M. E. (1973), *Job*, AB 15 (Garden City, Doubleday).

Rouillard, P. (1983), 'The Figure of Job in the Liturgy: Indignation, Resignation, or Silence?', in D. Duquoc and C. Floristan (eds.), *Job and the Silence of God*, Concilium, 169 (New York: Seabury).

Tilley, T. W. (1989), 'God and the Silencing of Job', *Modern Theology*, 5: 257–70.

Tsevat, M. (1966), 'The Meaning of the Book of Job', *HUCA* 37: 73–106.

Wahl, H.-M. (1993), *Der Gerechte Schöpfer*, BZAW 207 (Berlin: de Gruyter).

Weiss, M. (1983), *The Story of Job's Beginning* (Jerusalem: Magnes).

Wilcox, J. T. (1989), *The Bitterness of Job: A Philosophical Reading* (Ann Arbor: University of Michigan Press).

Wilde, A. de (1981), *Das Buch Hiob*, OTS 22 (Leiden: Brill).

Zhitlowsky, C. (1919), 'Job and Faust', in P. Matenko (ed.), *Two Studies in Yiddish Culture* (Leiden: Brill), 75–162.

Zuckerman, B. (1991), *Job the Silent: A Study in Historical Counterpoint* (New York: Oxford University Press).

18. Psalms

C. S. RODD

INTRODUCTION

A. Problems of Interpretation. 1. Interpretation of the Psalms is not simple. This will surprise many people, for some of the psalms are the best loved parts of the OT. Poetry in every language, however, is less easily understood than prose. The formalized structure, the use of rare words, the many metaphors and other figures of speech, all contribute to the difficulty. The problems are increased when the language is not one's mother tongue, and it is not possible to be immediately aware of overtones of emotion and fine nuances of meaning in words and phrases. With the Psalms these difficulties become even more severe because of the nature of the Hebrew language and the forms of Hebrew poetry.

2. If several English translations of the psalms are compared, differences, sometimes quite startling, will quickly be found, and the reader may well wonder how learned scholars can arrive at such different interpretations of the meaning. NRSV translates Ps 12:4: 'our lips are our own—who is our master?' (cf. GNB: 'We will say what we wish, and no one can stop us'), and REB: 'With words as our ally, who can master us?', but NIV marg., rather startlingly offers: 'our lips are our ploughshares'. Instead of NRSV's version of Ps 58:7: 'like grass let them be trodden down and wither', REB provides: 'may he aim his arrows, may they perish by them', and NIV: 'when they draw the bow, let their arrows be blunted'. In Ps 77:4 NRSV reads: 'You keep my eyelids from closing (cf. GNB's banal: 'You keep me awake all night'), while REB has 'My eyelids are tightly closed'.

3. Like English, Hebrew possesses no case endings. In prose the word order and a particle which marks the object of the verb normally make the sense entirely clear. Hebrew poetry, on the other hand, is highly compressed. The poetic lines are short. The sign of the object is rarely used. Word order is varied. It means that often the three or four words in a line can be construed in more than one way. In Ps 143:10 the problem lies in knowing what is the relation between 'your spirit' and 'good', and what is the subject of the verb 'leads me'. If the Hebrew accents are followed the meaning is probably as RV: 'Thy spirit is good; lead me . . .'. To take the words as 'Your good spirit' involves unusual Hebrew syntax. The verb can either be the third person, 'she will lead (she leads, may she lead) me', or second person, 'lead me'. Hence NRSV translates the phrase: 'Let your good spirit lead me on a level path' (following a few Heb. MSS in the last word rather than the main MT tradition), REB has: 'by your gracious spirit guide me on level ground', and GNB offers the paraphrase: 'Be good to me, and guide me on a safe path'.

4. The meaning of some of the words which the poets use is occasionally uncertain. There are three aspects of this. First, some words appear only once in the whole Hebrew Bible. When this occurs it is not possible to compare different contexts in order to gain an insight into the exact meaning of the word, and recourse has to be had to such things as similar words in other related languages (Akkadian, Aramaic, Ugaritic, and Arabic are the main ones), how the ancient versions understood the word, and the meaning in Jewish tradition. In Ps 58:8 NRSV offers 'snail' for a word that is found only here in the OT, but REB derives it differently as meaning 'an abortive birth', which is certainly a better parallel to 'stillborn child' in the second line. Secondly, there are a large number of homonyms in Hebrew (words in the same form but with different meaning). Scholars are sometimes not sure which of two or more possible words was intended by the poet. Sometimes, indeed, a rare word may be the same in form and sound as a fairly common word, and the common word has driven out the rarer one. Only careful study of the related languages and the versions enables scholars to recover the lost meaning. The word which NRSV translates 'company' in Ps 24:6 is the normal word for 'generation'. REB takes it to be a homonym with the meaning 'fortune'. One reason why NEB contains so many novel translations is that a large number of new meanings of Hebrew words was adopted, many of them rejected by REB. Thirdly, no word has exactly the same meaning in any two languages. At most there is only a large area of overlap. This means that often a range of English words may be needed to express what the poet intended, and it is impossible to be absolutely certain that the correct one has been selected. When the poet uses the verb 'to judge', is the sense to pass a sentence on someone who is accused, or to vindicate him? NRSV translates it by 'vindicate' in three psalms (Ps 26:1; 35:24; 43:1), and in Ps 72:4 has 'may he defend the cause of the poor', but elsewhere it sticks to 'judge', 'pass judgment', 'do justice' or 'try'. The other modern versions offer a somewhat wider range of translations. In each case the translators had to decide what the nuances of the verb were in each context, and they may have been right or they may have been wrong. 'Righteousness' is even more difficult, since it is almost entirely a churchy word in modern English. Although NRSV retains 'righteousness' in many places, REB prefers 'justice' and NJB has a number of synonyms, including 'right' and 'upright'. Sometimes, however, the Hebrew word has a bias in favour of the helpless (Snaith 1944: 68–74; in post-biblical

Hebrew it came to mean 'almsgiving, benevolence'), and translators have tried to capture this. Hence Ps 65:5: 'deliverance' and 35:28: 'saving power', REB. Moreover, the meaning of the word also approached ideas of victory (cf. Isa 41:2), and NRSV translates it in this way in Ps 48:10 (REB adds Ps 65:5; 118:19; 119:123). Further the familiar 'sacrifices of righteousness' (Ps 4:5; 51:21) probably does not mean offering righteousness as a sacrifice and in place of an animal offering but sacrifices offered with the correct ritual or in the right spirit, or even such sacrifices as are YHWH's due, as most modern translations recognize. And the overtones of goodness must probably go from Ps 23:3: the 'paths of righteousness' are simply 'right paths' by which the shepherd leads the flock to pasture.

5. The Psalms have been copied and recopied over the centuries, and although very great care was taken by the later Jewish scribes (the Masoretes) to ensure the absolute accuracy of the scrolls, errors had crept in earlier. Such textual corruptions sometimes make it impossible to determine the poet's meaning, and occasionally the Hebrew defies translation. At one time scholars resorted to wide-scale emendation of the text. Today this is much rarer, and normally support from the ancient versions is demanded for any changes that are made. Few would deny that some emendation is necessary, however, but all such changes introduce some uncertainty as to the poet's meaning. A stock example is Ps 49:11, where all modern translations present the sense of NRSV: 'Their graves are their homes for ever' (transposing two Heb. letters), instead of the AV 'Their inward thought *is, that* their houses *shall continue* for ever' (the italics reveal how much had to be read into that translation). Usually the Eng. versions inform the reader that the text has been altered, and supply the support from the ancient versions, but not always (cf. Ps 27:8, where NRSV makes several changes to produce: ' "Come," my heart says, "seek his face" ', without any footnote; the Heb. appears to be lit. 'To you (masc. sing.) my heart said, "Seek (masc. plur.) my face" '). Some passages are so corrupt that it is impossible to obtain any sense without emendation, and even then the meaning is doubtful.

6. Hebrew letters express only the consonants: the vowels are represented by various signs placed round or in the letters, and these vowel signs came in fairly late in the history of the text, although they express the traditional pronunciation. It is not always certain that the vowels were those intended by the poet, and alternative vowels can often produce a better sense. NRSV frequently makes such changes without drawing attention in a footnote and GNB hardly ever tells the reader.

7. An even greater difficulty in many of the psalms is the tense of the verbs. English possesses a very large number of tenses, simple and compound, most of which indicate the time when the action takes place, though some point to additional features, such as whether the action occurs only once at a single point in time or is continuous. Even in English, however, tenses do not always express the time or the aspect of the action that they appear to. The verb in 'I am going to Scotland on Wednesday' is present continuous, but means something like, 'Next Wednesday I shall go to Scotland' (or even 'I intend to go'). Hebrew possesses only two main forms of the verb, which primarily express aspect rather than tense. The verbal system is highly complex, however, and no one

would profess to understand it completely. In prose the context makes the sense relatively clear. This is far from the case in poetry. One of the most striking differences between the English translations of the Psalms is the way the verbs are translated. Is Ps 63:9–10 an expression of the psalmist's confidence in future destruction of his enemies, or a prayer (contrast NRSV/NIV and REB/NJB)? Should the verbs in 67:7 be past (NRSV/REB/NJB), future (NIV), or is the verse perhaps a prayer? Is Ps 120:1–2 a description of a prayer for divine help in the past (so REB), or part of the present petition (as NRSV/NIV)? On one view of the tenses Ps 8:5–6 should be translated: 'But you have made him a little less than God, | and you will crown him with glory and honor | You will make him master over the work of your hands; | you have set everything beneath his feet' (Craigie 1983: 105).

This is possibly the most serious difficulty in interpreting the psalms. (For a brief account of the issues see ibid. 110–12.)

8. But no translation exists on its own. The translation is linked inextricably with the way the translator understands the whole background of the psalm—when it was written, how and where it was sung, whether it formed part of a cultic activity or was the work of a solitary poet, who it is written for or about, and many other questions. There is never a translation that is not at the same time an interpretation, and a large part of that interpretation depends upon the wider view of the place of the psalm in the life of ancient Israel. Indeed, translation and understanding of the entire religious life of ancient Israel are intertwined so intimately that they cannot be separated.

9. One further feature of modern translations should be noted. Every translation loses part of the richness of the original, but increasingly modern translations have sloughed off vital details. Hebrew verbs express gender as well as number and person. No English translation can represent this for the second person, since 'you' is used for both singular and plural, masculine and feminine, and this disguises important distinctions and changes of person in the Hebrew Psalms. Further, the attempts by NJB, NRSV, REB, and NIV Inclusive Language Edition to avoid sexist language have introduced a wide range of paraphrases which remove the reader even further from the original poet. Thus masculine singulars are very frequently translated by plurals, and even by 'we' or even more extensive modifications. Sometimes it is of little moment, as in Ps 1 where 'those' replaces 'the man', although it obscures the patriarchal society in which the psalm was written. Often, however, such rewriting distorts the original psalm. Most people today accept that women are fully equal to men, and that language can reflect and reinforce a male domination. What is more contentious is whether the Scriptures should be *rewritten* in order to eliminate such language. Ancient Israelite society was plainly patriarchal, despite the presence of some forceful women. In this it was even more extreme than some of the surrounding countries. For example, all the other law codes from the ancient Middle East that have been discovered include arrangements for inheritance of the property by widows. In ancient Israel widows could not inherit property from their husbands, and daughters could only do so if there were no sons. Within the Psalter, in Ps 45 the king's bride is told that her husband is her master and she must bow down to him. The masculine language found in all the psalms is a feature of that society. Sometimes, of course, male terms are used to include both men and women, as was common in English until recently, and in such places modern English requires the removal of purely masculine forms. On the other hand, most of the references to men were intended to apply to men alone, and a proper understanding of the psalms in their original context requires the retention of male terms there (cf. Gerstenberger 1988: 32). The use of patriarchal texts in modern worship is a quite different issue, and cannot be discussed here, vitally important though it is.

B. History of Interpretation. **1.** Over the centuries the way Christians have used, studied, and interpreted the Psalms has changed.

2. Prophecy. The first Christians regarded the Psalms as prophecy, and searched for phrases and verses which foretold events in the life of Jesus. This can be seen in the NT itself. Indeed, some scholars have suggested that the passion narrative has been moulded by reference particularly to Ps 22 and 69. In the second century Justin Martyr argued for the truth of the Christian faith on the grounds that the Messiah had been foretold many centuries before the time of Jesus, and this interpretation persisted up to modern times. It is reflected in the description of several Psalms as 'messianic' (e.g. Ps 2; 101; 110).

3. Allegory and Typology. A somewhat modified form of this view of the relation between the OT and the NT is found in allegorical interpretations and typology. Allegory need not be totally uncontrolled, and rules were developed about the various levels of meaning of the text: literal, moral, allegorical, and anagogical (see PS 114). Often the Psalms retained their spiritual value for those Christians who sang them because they were allegorized. Typology became another method for relating the Testaments, and again, OT figures and ideas were perceived as types of later Christian characters and thought.

4. Historical Interpretation. These approaches existed alongside historical interpretations, and one of the 'senses' which Scripture was believed to possess was the historical, even when greater value was placed upon the other interpretations. Attempts at providing historical occasions for the creation of the psalms, often in the life of David, can be seen in the headings of many of them. It is probable that these are not original but were added later (the LXX contains headings which are absent from the Heb., or additions to headings, in some forty-four psalms: e.g. Ps 70 (MT 71): 'Of (by) David, of the sons of Jonadab, and of the first who were taken captive', and Ps 143 (MT 144): 'Of (by) David, concerning Goliath'). Some of the traditions found in these titles are echoed in the Mishnah (e.g. *M. Tamid* 7.4 sets out the seven psalms which 'the levites used to sing in the Temple' on each of the days of the week: Ps 24 (LXX 'A psalm of (by) David on the first day of the week'); 48 (LXX 'on the second day of the week'); 82; 94 (LXX 'on the fourth day of the week'); 81 (the Old Latin has 'fifth day of the week'); 93 (LXX 'on the day before the sabbath when the earth was inhabited; praise of a song of David'); 92, where the MT has 'A Song for the Sabbath Day', showing that they are genuinely Jewish and not peculiar to the Old Greek version. When, according to Mark, Jesus quoted Ps 110 (Mk 12:36), both he and his hearers accepted that David had written the psalm and that its meaning was to be found in that

context. The historical interpretation came to the forefront of psalm study from the time of the Enlightenment, and much modern study has been devoted to determining the date and authorship of individual psalms. Conservative scholars presented arguments for Davidic authorship, while liberal ones proposed a wide range of datings, some as late as the second century BCE.

5. Form Criticism. It is now generally agreed that it is possible to determine the historical origin of very few of the psalms because of the lack of evidence—who, after all, would be able to discover when and by whom a nineteenth-century hymn was written simply from the hymn itself? A new approach was needed, and a decisive step in the study of the psalms came with the work of Hermann Gunkel (Gunkel and Begrich 1933), who is generally regarded as the father of form criticism. First classifying the psalms according to their type or genre, he then looked for the ways the various types of psalm were used in ancient Israel (see E below for the main types of psalm). Gunkel argued that the original psalms were hymns that were sung in Israelite worship, although he regarded the psalms in the OT as written by poets in imitation of these earlier psalms. Later scholars have tended to limit their attention to the formal structure of the psalms, but Gunkel himself had a sensitive appreciation of Hebrew literature and paid attention to such features as mood and content as well.

6. The Cult. The next important stage in the interpretation of the psalms was taken by Sigmund Mowinckel (1921–4), who argued that the OT psalms were in fact cultic hymns, and on this basis set out to reconstruct the festivals at which they were sung. But as with the earlier approaches, the evidence has proved insufficient for this to be carried through convincingly. It is highly probable that many, perhaps most, of the psalms belong to Israelite worship rather than being compositions of individual 'romantic' poets, but the rubrics are lacking, and the other books of the OT provide few glimpses of how they were used. The historical books might be thought to favour a historical interpretation (see e.g. 2 Sam 22, where Ps 18 has been inserted into the text, and the catena of psalm quotations in 1 Chr 16). On this view the titles provide a context within which the psalms can be read, while the psalms offer personal responses by David that can be taken into the narratives, somewhat like the speeches that Greek historians inserted into their narratives.

7. Literary Approaches. In the light of the failure of these attempts to interpret the psalms within historical Israel, it is no surprise that some scholars today, influenced by movements in general literary studies, have virtually abandoned the quest and have treated each individual psalm as a literary artefact in its own right. The particular interpretation varies, whether structuralism, rhetorical criticism, reader-response criticism, deconstruction, or other methods that have become fashionable. Emphasis has been placed upon the structure and wording of the psalms, and often little attention is paid to the cultural context of ancient Israel. Jonathan Magonet (1994) has pointed out that such an approach has antecedents in rabbinic study. (For a study of Ps 18 which incorporates textual, form-critical, rhetorical, and reader-oriented approaches see Berry (1993); cf. Mays's similar exposition of Ps 3 (Mays, Petersen, and Richards 1995: 147–56).)

8. Canonical Criticism. In stark contrast to the atomistic approach of much literary analysis of the psalms, some scholars have emphasized that the only reason why the OT has been preserved and is still read and studied is because it is canonical Scripture. No interpretation, therefore, is valid which does not take this into account. The emphasis is placed upon the completed book of Psalms and their use in other parts of the Bible, including the NT. Indeed, the key to the interpretation of any passage is found in this 'final form' of the writing. Brevard S. Childs (1979: 504–23) stresses this. He argues that the placing of Ps 1 as the introduction to the Psalter leads to the psalms, which originally were human songs and prayers, being taken as God's word itself. The compilation of psalms (e.g. in Ps 108) is a factor in their movement from a cultic setting towards their apprehension as sacred Scripture. Similarly the fact that the royal psalms are scattered throughout the Psalter, with special prominence given to Ps 2, is a transformation of cultic psalms into messianic ones, and the increased eschatological emphasis in many of the psalms is another mark of this changing theology. Most interestingly, he finds in the relating of thirteen psalms to specific incidents in the life of David a shift of emphasis from the original cultic function to understanding the king as a human being who has the same troubles and joys as ordinary people, thus enabling all kinds of people to relate to them. (For an assessment of Childs's work see Noble 1995.)

9. Each of these stages has importance for an appreciation of the psalms.

10. Prophecy. While most Christians outside the conservative evangelical, pentecostal, and charismatic groups no longer accept that the truth of their religion is confirmed by OT predictions of incidents in the life of Jesus, they accept that the God of the NT is the same God as that of the OT. It might be expected, therefore, that there will be a certain congruence between the Testaments. This is what lies behind typology. Moreover, whenever Christians spiritualize such features of the psalms as the condemnation of enemies or the calls for support in war, features which have now become morally unacceptable, this is akin to the earlier allegorizing, though now no longer with an explicit *raison d'être*. It might even be argued that without such spiritualizing it would be impossible to continue to use the psalms within Christian worship. Many of the hymns of Watts and the Wesleys explicitly reinterpret the psalms in a Christian sense, as, for example, Charles Wesley's fine hymn based on Ps 45, 'My heart is full of Christ, and longs | Its glorious matter to declare'.

11. Cultural Setting. Everyone today is strongly influenced by the historical awareness which is one of the major gifts of the Enlightenment. Today it is often claimed that the meaning of a historical text cannot be limited to the meaning which its author intended and some would go further and argue that the author's intentions are both impossible to discover and irrelevant to the meaning. While the author's meaning may seem central to the understanding of some kinds of literature, with the psalms authorship is of less importance, and it is no devastating loss if we are unable to identify the writers. What is important is that the cultural setting is recognized. Here historical criticism and form criticism meet. Both direct the reader's attention to the original setting of the psalms, although travelling to that point by different routes. It is now fully recognized that simply to repeat words in a different historical situation (and twenty-first century Europe or North America is far removed from ancient Israel) is to say something vastly different from the psalmist's original meaning. The modern congregation comes to the Psalter with its own presuppositions, attitudes, memories, and emotions, and the psalm, sung to Anglican or Gregorian chant, in the Gélineau version or as a metrical psalm, will resonate in very different ways from those which the Israelite attending worship at the Jerusalem temple experienced. Historical criticism, therefore, is vital, not because it alone provides the key to the 'real' meaning of the text, but because it provides another way of reading the psalms and enables modern readers to move to and fro between the world of ancient Israel and the culture of today, expanding their vision of God.

12. Modern Translations. Modern, and modernizing, translations of the Psalms become a hindrance here, for they give the impression to the reader that the words of the psalms are immediately related to present Western society. The removal of much masculine-oriented language from NRSV tends to obscure the fact that ancient Israel was a patriarchal society, and the paraphrasing interpretation of GNB destroys much of the poetic imagery. These translations may be more accessible to the hearers, but they imprison them in a twenty-first-century world, when what the Psalms (and indeed all Scripture) should be doing, among other things, is to open up spiritual and moral dimensions of life which the modern world has crippled or destroyed.

13. Literary Approaches. What then of literary criticism? The presence of eight acrostic psalms within the Psalter (E.14) is an indication that some, perhaps all, of the psalms are self-conscious poetic creations. Certainly an awareness of the skill of the poet will add to our appreciation of the psalms. There is, nevertheless, a danger that modern conventions and fashions will misrepresent the intentions and art of the poet. Once again we are faced with the 'then' and the 'now', and every literary approach needs to be tempered with a sense of the historical.

14. It will be seen that the demands made upon the commentary writer are immense. Certainly it is quite impossible to include all the methods that have been outlined. No single approach applied to all the psalms will be attempted here, although some emphasis will be placed upon genre and setting, since only if we know what kind of text we are reading can we grasp its meaning. In this commentary each psalm will be discussed on its own, using whatever approach appears to offer the greatest insight into its meaning, but always with an awareness that we are reading poetry written in a foreign language and coming from an alien culture and a distant time.

C. The Titles of the Psalms and *Selâ*. 1. Although the titles of the psalms are not part of the original poems, they are important as revealing some of the earliest interpretations, and NEB was mistaken in omitting them (REB has put them back; GNB includes abbreviated, and misleading, forms of the titles as footnotes). The main details supplied by the titles are names (David, Solomon, Moses, Asaph, the sons of Korah, Heman the Ezrahite, Ethan the Ezrahite, and perhaps Jeduthun), situations in the life of David, descriptions of the type of psalm (psalm, song, prayer, song of ascents, *maskîl*, *miktām*), an expression of unknown meaning which NRSV translates as 'To the leader', and a number of varied words and phrases which are usually thought to be the titles of the tunes to which the psalms were sung (e.g. 'the Dove of the Dawn'), or the accompanying instruments (e.g. 'with stringed instruments', 'for the flutes') (Anderson 1972: 43–51, Mowinckel 1962: ch. 23, and Kraus 1988: i. 21–32 provide good surveys).

2. The titles probably have little historical value. The phrase translated 'of David' (*lĕdāwid*) almost certainly intends authorship, despite claims that it means 'on behalf of' or 'for' David (i.e. dedicated to the Davidic king at the time) or 'belonging to the Davidic collection of songs'. (For the tradition of David as a musician and author of psalms see 1 Sam 16:15–16, 23; 2 Sam 1:17–27; 3:33; 6:5; 23:1–7; 1 Chr 23:5; Am 6:5; Sir 47:8–10; 2 Sam 22 ascribes Ps 18 to David; in the Mishnah a casual reference speaks of the 'Book of Psalms by David' (*m. 'Abot* 6.9), and the same belief is reflected in Mk 12:36–7; Rom 4:6–7; 11:9–10. According to 1 Chr 6:39; 15:17; 16:5–6; 2 Chr 5:12 Asaph was one of David's chief musicians, a further example of the Davidic tradition.) Since, however, nothing is known about David outside the OT, there is no way of determining whether he wrote any of the psalms, and, indeed, the date of most of them is unknown. The editors of the Psalter appear to have searched the books of Samuel and Chronicles for suitable occasions in which to place the psalms, and added such references to thirteen psalms (Ps 3; 7; 18; 34; 51; 52; 54; 56; 57; 59; 60; 63; 142: only one title (Ps 7) cannot be readily linked with the biblical narratives.

3. Within the length of this commentary it is not possible to comment on all the terms found in the titles, but the following brief notes discuss some of them. Where a word or phrase occurs only once it is noted in the commentary.

4. *Psalm* (*mizmôr*), found in the titles of fifty-seven psalms, occurs only in the Psalter and probably denotes a religious song accompanied by harp or other stringed instruments. The LXX translated it by *psalmos*, hence our word.

5. *Song* (*šîr*) (Ps 18; 30; 46; 48; 65–8; 75; 76; 83; 87; 88; 92; 108) is the normal word for religious and secular songs. It occurs with 'psalm' in all but two psalms (Ps 18; 46), and the difference between the two terms is unknown.

6. *Prayer* (*tĕpillâ*) (Ps 17; 86; 90; 102; 142; in the rubric in Ps 72:20, and in Hab 3:1) is the normal Hebrew word for prayer. It has been suggested that it denotes laments, although there are far more laments in the Psalter than those with the title.

7. *Miktām* is found in Ps 16; 56–60. The meaning is unknown. The LXX and Targum translated it by 'pillar inscription'. Luther's 'golden jewel' linked it with the Hebrew word for gold. Mowinckel (1962: ii. 209) connected it with atonement.

8. *Maskîl* occurs in the titles of Ps 32; 42; 44; 45; 52–5; 74; 78; 88; 89; 142, and Ps 47:7; 2 Chr 30:22). The Hebrew root from which this word comes is usually taken to mean 'to have insight, to teach, to prosper', and hence 'efficacious song', 'didactic song', 'meditation', 'artistic song' have been suggested.

9. *A Song of Ascents* (*šîr hamma'ălôt*). This is usually held to indicate a pilgrim psalm, but some think (improbably) that it refers to their 'step-like' structure, others connect the fifteen psalms with a reference in the Mishnah (*m. Middot* 2.5) to the fifteen steps from the court of the women to the court of Israel

in the temple and infer that this is where they were sung, although the Mishnah does not say that they were, and others again take it to refer more generally to festal processions.

10. *For the leader* (*lammĕnaṣṣēaḥ*) is the NRSV and REB translation of a term of very uncertain meaning, found in the titles of fifty-five psalms and also in Hab 3:19. The LXX appears not to have known what it meant and rendered it 'To (for) the end'. The Targum offers 'for praise'. Mowinckel (1962: ii. 212) proposed 'for the merciful disposition (of YHWH)', 'to dispose YHWH for mercy', or even 'for homage (to YHWH)', linking the word with a verb in 1 Chr 15:21, but the meaning there is probably 'to make music'. Possibly the meaning is 'for musical performance'. RSV has 'To the Choirmaster', as does NJB, and NIV's 'For the director of music' gives the same sense, all linking the word with a verb meaning 'to excel, lead, be at the head, direct' in 1 Chr 23:4 and 2 Chr 2:2. The meaning is really unknown.

11. *To (according to) Jeduthun* (*lîdûtûn*) (Ps 39; 62; 77). Jeduthun is the name of one of David's musicians in 1 Chr 16:41, and while it may refer to him in the psalm titles it has also been proposed that the word signifies 'confession'.

12. *For the memorial offering* (*lĕhuzkîr*) (Ps 38 and 70). Mowinckel (1962: ii. 212) thinks the psalm is to 'remind' YHWH of the psalmist's distress, and it may be linked with the memorial sacrifice (Lev 2:2; 5:12).

13. *With stringed instruments* (*binĕgînôt*) (Ps 4; 6; 54; 55; 61; 67; 76) refers to accompaniment with harp and lyre, probably in contrast with other noisier instruments.

14. *The Gittith* (*'al-haggittît*) (Ps 8; 81; 84) is of unknown meaning. The LXX translated it 'for the wine-press'. Other suggestions are 'a vintage melody', 'according to the Gittite melody', 'with the Gittite lyre', and even that it refers to Obed-edom, the Gittite (2 Sam 6:10–11), and hence is related to a procession with the ark.

15. *Do not destroy* (*'al-tašḥēt*) (Ps 57–9; 75). Mowinckel (1962: ii. 214) notes that all four psalms contain references to pagan oppressors and suggests that it may refer to some rite which the psalm accompanied. It is often supposed that it is the name of a tune (cf. Isa 65:8).

16. *Selâ* is found within the body of thirty-nine psalms, seventy-one times in the MT and ninety-two in the LXX (details in Kraus 1988: 29). Outside the Psalter it is found in the psalm in Hab 3:3, 9, 13. The meaning is totally unknown, but various guesses have been made. Aquila, Jerome, and the Targum translated it 'always, for ever', and the LXX *diapsalma* (presumably, 'interlude'). If it comes from a verb meaning 'to lift up', it might refer to 'lifting up' one's voice ('sing louder'), 'lifting up' one's eyes ('repeat the verse'), or 'lifting up' the music (with loud instruments or an instrumental interlude). An alternative derivation suggests that it indicated points when the congregation fell prostrate in worship. Kraus (1988: 28) draws attention to the LXX translation of Ps 9:16, 'song of *diapsalma*', which seems to suggest the 'singing' or 'sounding' of the 'interlude' and may point to a musical intermezzo or a doxology.

D. The Development of the Psalter. 1. While the titles provide little historical information about the individual psalms, they are important evidence for the development of the Psalter as a collection.

2. The division into five books (Ps 1–41; 42–72; 73–89; 90–106; 107–50) could hardly have been made before the collection was complete. If, however, Ps 41:13, 72:18–19, 89:52, and 106:48 are doxologies inserted when the arrangement was made, this must have been before the time of the Chronicler, since 1 Chr 16:36 includes Ps 106:48 in the quotation of part of that psalm.

3. Before this fivefold arrangement was made (possibly in imitation of the five books of the Torah) some smaller collections of psalms were already in existence. The most obvious of these is Ps 120–34 which all have the title 'A Song of Ascents'.

4. Eleven psalms are attributed to 'the sons of Korah' (Ps 42; 44–9; 84–5; 87–8) and twelve to Asaph (Ps 50; 73–83), and these were probably separate collections. Why some of the psalms became separated in the completed Psalter is unknown. 'The prayers of David son of Jesse are ended' (Ps 72:20) seems to have stood at the end of a collection of Davidic psalms. In the present form of the Psalter the psalms ascribed to him are not so neatly arranged. 'Of David' is found in the MT titles of Ps 3–9; 11–32; 34–41; 51–65; 68–70; 86; 101; 103; 108–10; 122; 124; 131; 133; 138–45, and in a further fifteen psalms in the LXX. It is commonly supposed that two main collections of Davidic psalms consisted of Ps 3–41 (probably without 33), and 51–71 (possibly even including the Solomonic Ps 72). Whether all the Davidic psalms originally formed a single collection is uncertain, and the titles of these psalms after Ps 72 may be due to the tendency to ascribe ever more psalms to David. There seem to have been smaller collections or groupings of *maskîl* and *miktām* Davidic psalms in Ps 52–5; 56–60. Cutting across these collections, however, are Ps 42–83, the so-called Elohistic Psalter, in which YHWH is found relatively seldom and the Hebrew word for God (*'ĕlōhîm*) much more frequently, almost certainly due to the work of an editor (cf. Ps 53 where 'God' has been substituted for the YHWH of Ps 14, and the curious 'I am God, your God' in Ps 50:7, where the original would appear to have been 'YHWH, your God').

5. Whether it is possible to discover the principles upon which the Psalter was put together is doubtful. Delitzsch (1887) suggested that catchwords (e.g. 'shall never (not) be moved', Ps 15; 16), similarities of theme (Ps 50; 51 both think sacrifice of little value; Ps 12–14 are lamentations, general—personal—general), psalm pairs (e.g. Ps 3–4, morning and evening prayers), or the grouping of similar psalms, such as the 'Hallelujah' psalms (Ps 111–13; 146–50), could explain the ordering, but this is a piecemeal approach. The psalms in praise of the law (Ps 1; 19; 119) have been seen as markers of one stage in the growth of the Psalter. Wilson (1985) points to the presence of royal psalms at the main divisions of the first three books (Ps 2; 72; 89), and traces an overarching scheme of YHWH's covenant with David (bks. 1–2), the failure of that covenant (bk. 3), and the answer to this in the kingship of YHWH (bk. 4), with book 5 as an answer to the plea for restoration from exile in Ps 106:47. To combine form-critical criteria with ancient Israelite intentions appears rash. (For details of other attempts to identify small collections within the Psalter and to account for its growth see Day 1990: 109–22; Gillingham 1994: 232–55, McCann 1993b.)

6. It must be concluded that it is impossible to trace the development of the Psalter, although there is clear evidence of smaller collections that may have existed independently at some stage, and there is a general movement from laments, which dominate the first two books, to praises at the end of the Psalter. Such ignorance is not unexpected, given the long period of use and reuse of the psalms and the wide range of situations in which they have been sung and prayed.

E. Classifying the Psalms. 1. Despite some scepticism as to the value of classifying the psalms and then attempting to determine the original situations in which the types of psalm were sung (cf. Rogerson and McKay 1977: 8), no study can neglect this approach. The evidence is quite insufficient for us to discover the original historical contexts (even such an apparently clear reference to the Exile as Ps 137 is not unambiguous), and similarities in structure, content, and mood between groups of psalms immediately suggests that classifying by the type of psalm may be a valuable way of treating them. This does not mean that there were any rigid structures to which each type of psalm had to conform, and those textbooks which set out the supposed forms are liable to mislead. Few psalms manifest the ideal structure of the types which scholars have proposed. Gunkel was right to adopt a more flexible approach than some later advocates of form criticism. Moreover the types are not rigidly distinct, and it is less than helpful to suppose that any development from 'pure' forms to 'mixed' ones occurred. In this commentary the types will be treated very generally.

2. Laments of an Individual. These form the largest class of psalms. Similarities with the Laments of the Community (E. 6) have led some scholars to group both types as Laments or Complaints. The worshipper is in distress and calls on God for deliverance. Usually the suffering is described in very general terms, and often different kinds of trouble are included in the same psalm. Illness (e.g. Ps 6; 22; 38; 88) and attacks from enemies (e.g. Ps 3; 5; 17; 109) are frequently mentioned. Who the 'enemies' are is uncertain (see G.2). It has been suggested that some of these laments were prayers by those who had been unjustly accused of some offence, were appealing to a higher court, perhaps the temple priesthood, or were awaiting an ordeal to test their guilt (e.g. 7; 26; 27). In some of these psalms the tone changes dramatically towards the end, and the psalmist affirms his confidence that God has heard his prayer (e.g. Ps 6:8–10; 13:5–6; 31:19–24). This has been interpreted in four ways: (1) it may be that a fragment from a different psalm has been attached to the lament; (2) it may be the prayer of the psalmist after his prayer has been answered; (3) it may reflect the alternating moods of the sufferer; or (4) between the two parts of the psalm the psalmist may have received a sign that his prayer had been heard, perhaps through an oracle by a cult prophet, or some indication that his sacrifice had been accepted by God. In some psalms the note of confidence is extended so greatly that the psalm may really be a prayer of thanksgiving, in which the psalmist recalls his suffering and his earlier prayer. Confidence dominates a few psalms (e.g. Ps 11; 23; 62; 131), and here it hardly seems correct to count them as laments: some treat them as a separate type of psalm.

3. Thanksgiving by an Individual. When the psalmist received an answer from God or was delivered from his distress, he would offer thanksgiving, often accompanied by a sacrifice. Such psalms sometimes contain an account of the distress from which the psalmist has been saved, and it is often not easy to determine to which of the two types a psalm belongs (e.g. Ps 30; 32; 34; 66; 116).

4. Hymns. These normally consist of a call to praise YHWH, followed by an account of the reasons for worshipping him, usually introduced by 'for' or 'because' (e.g. Ps 29; 33; 100; 103; 104; 117; 145–50). There seems no need to distinguish between those psalms which describe YHWH's character (e.g. Ps 33:4–5) and those which relate his actions in creating the world or saving his people Israel (e.g. Ps 136:4–25). The hymn often ends with a renewed call to offer praise. Some of these hymns have similarities with Canaanite religion (see PS 29) or Egyptian hymns (see PS 104).

5. Within this general class two groups of psalms have been singled out, and have led to striking proposals for reconstructing the worship of the Jerusalem temple:

a. Songs of Zion, where the main theme is YHWH's deliverance and protection of Jerusalem (Ps 46; 48; 76; 84; 87; 122). Opinion is divided over whether these psalms belong to the Jerusalem cult and express a faith in divine protection of the city, possibly as part of a cultic drama, or were occasioned by a spectacular deliverance of the city, perhaps at the time of Sennacherib's siege (2 Kings 18:13–19:36; Isa 36–7).

b. Enthronement Psalms which are characterized by a phrase which has been variously translated as 'The LORD is king', 'The LORD reigns', 'The LORD reigns (now)', and 'The LORD has become king' (Ps 47; 93; 96–9). The different translations reflect different interpretations. Some follow Mowinckel in positing a great New Year Festival in the autumn as part of the Feast of Tabernacles (Ingathering) in which the kingship of YHWH was celebrated and he was enthroned anew. Others question whether such a festival existed in Israel, and argue that to assert that YHWH *became* king implies that he had ceased to be king, rather like the dying and rising gods of other cultures in the ancient Middle East. But to say that his enthronement was celebrated annually need not imply this, and the psalms certainly gain in vividness if some such annual celebration is imagined.

6. Laments of the Community. When famine or defeat in war threatened the nation, a fast would be called and the people would express their grief and call upon YHWH for help (cf. 1 Kings 8:33–40). Ps 44; 74; 79; 80 are examples of the prayers that would be offered. Whether these were general petitions or were evoked by specific historical events, such as the fall of Jerusalem in 586, is impossible to determine.

7. Royal Psalms. These are psalms of various forms which have the king as the central figure, either as the one for whom the prayer is offered or the one who makes the prayer. There is intense debate about the number of such psalms. The absolute minimum number is Gunkel's list of Ps 2; 18; 20; 21; 45; 72; 101; 110; 132; 144:1–11, with doubts expressed about 89:47–52 (Gunkel and Begrich 1933: 140). At the other extreme Eaton (1986) argues that in principle all the Davidic psalms belong to this group, which are characterized by 'royal' language and motifs, are in first-person form (or use the third person rather like the royal 'we'), and combine individual and corporate features, indicating that the psalmist is in some way the representative of the community. He supports this by stress-

ing the importance of the king in ancient Israelite society. On this understanding a large number of psalms are held to be certainly royal psalms, with others probably belonging to this category. It is difficult to decide between these two positions. Not all of Eaton's arguments are equally convincing, such as the claim that the enemies are always foreigners or Israelite rebels or that there was a distinctive royal style, and a decision ultimately depends on whether the reader is convinced by the reconstruction of the cultic worship into which the psalms are fitted. (See F for a discussion of the New Year Festival.)

8. Smaller Classes of Psalms. Besides these main types of psalm a number of smaller classes have been posited.

9. Wisdom Psalms have similarities with the wisdom writings in the OT (Job, Proverbs, Ecclesiastes, Sirach) and those from Egypt and Babylon. The exact number of psalms to be included in this category depends upon what criteria are used to define wisdom. Many accept Ps 1; 37; 49; 73; 112; 127; 128; 133. Like the wisdom writings they fall into two main types, collections of proverbs, mainly optimistic and expressing a philosophy that goodness will be rewarded and evil punished (e.g. Ps 1; 112), and meditations on what may be termed the problem of theodicy (cf. Job; Ps 49; 73. Ps 37 is more like the first group but recognizes that life does not always work out neatly).

10. Torah Psalms. The great psalm in praise of the law is Ps 119, an elaborate acrostic, each of its twenty-two stanzas consists of eight lines, each line beginning with the appropriate letter of the alphabet. The law is referred to under eight synonyms. Ps 19:7–11 (or 7–14), which may be a separate psalm or psalm fragment, also praises the law under a range of expressions. Ps 1 is often placed in this category rather than among the wisdom psalms.

11. Entrance Liturgies. The question and answer in Ps 15; 24:3–6 suggests that these two psalms may have been the catechism of pilgrims as they approach the temple, whether on an ordinary occasion or, perhaps more probably, for one of the great annual festivals. Isa 33:13–16 has similarities with these liturgies.

12. Pilgrimage Psalms. It is commonly accepted that the title 'Song of Ascents' in Ps 120–34 indicates psalms which pilgrims sang as they made their way to Jerusalem. Possibly Ps 84 and 122 also belong to this type, although Ps 84 has some of the features of an entrance liturgy and a hymn of Zion, and Ps 122 seems clearly related to the latter.

13. History Psalms. Accounts of events in Israel's history play such a large part in Ps 78; 105; 106 that they are often described as history psalms. Each, however, has its own features. Ps 78 has some of the characteristics of wisdom, Ps 105 is a hymn of praise, and the stress on the past sins of Israel in Ps 106 makes it a corporate confession. There is considerable debate as to whether these psalms (or any of them) are dependent on the narratives of the Pentateuch. In the past they were regarded as examples of 'salvation history' theology, but some scholars now question whether this is an adequate term, regarding it as ambiguous and meaning nothing more than that Israel survived when the historical circumstances made it unlikely. It is better to refer simply to Israel's history.

14. Acrostics. Eight psalms are acrostics, each line or verse beginning with the letters of the Hebrew alphabet in correct sequence (Ps 9–10; 25; 34; 37; 111; 112; 119; 145). This is difficult to reproduce in translation, but NJB has followed the letters of the English alphabet in the initial words of each verse of Ps 25, beginning with 'Adoration I offer, Yahweh' and ending with the additional v. 22, 'Ransom Israel, O God'. Of the most recent translations only NJB indicates the Hebrew letters in all eight, though NIV does so in Ps 119. The purpose of the acrostic form is debated. It is unlikely that it was an aid to the memory, or had magical significance. An attractive suggestion is that it expressed completeness, the A to Z, as it were, of the theme. Alternatively it may simply be an artistic device. Acrostics are found both in OT writings outside the Psalter (e.g. in Lam 1–4 and Prov 31:10–31) and in Babylon (though these are not *alphabetic* since cuneiform is syllabic). Moreover, there is evidence of deliberate art in the construction of many of the other psalms. This, therefore, seems to be the most likely explanation.

F. The Pre-exilic New Year Festival. 1. It is quite impossible to reconstruct the rites and liturgy of the worship in the pre-exilic temple. The Torah is largely limited to sacrificial practice and the broad outline of the main pilgrimage feasts, and the psalms neither reveal whether they formed part of the worship nor give sufficient details to enable that worship to be recovered. Nevertheless, the work of Mowinckel (1962), Johnson (1967; 1979) and Eaton (1976/1986) has produced an attractive picture of a cultic drama involving the king and celebrating the enthronement of YHWH, which may also have had an eschatological aspect within it, or alternatively have been essentially sacramental. The main difficulties with such reconstructions lie in the sparsity of corroborative evidence outside the psalms themselves, and the circular argument of reconstructing the cultic drama from the psalms and then fitting the psalms into that worship. On the other hand it has to be admitted that the hypothesis has succeeded in bringing the psalms to life in a vivid way, which few other proposals have managed to do. (For an excellent discussion of the issues see Day 1990: 67–108.) Here only the broadest outline of the rites and some of the evidence which has been drawn upon will be set out.

2. New Year Festival. It is clear from Ex 23:16; 34:22; Deut 16:13; Lev 23:34–43; 1 Kings 8:2; 12:32 that the most important feast at the time of the monarchy was Ingathering. It took place at the 'going out' (Ex 23:16) or the 'turn' (Ex 34:22) of the year, and these terms, plus the later links with the horn-blowing of New Year (Lev 23:24–5; Num 29:1–6) suggest that part of the festival may have been the celebration of the New Year. The late passage in Zech 14:16–17 links the coming of the autumn rains and the kingship of YHWH, and may provide some support for the connection of the enthronement psalms with the festival.

3. YHWH as Lord of Nature. The main celebration appears to have been the worship of YHWH as the Lord of nature, the one who secured the autumn rains and hence prosperity for the coming year. This is described in Ps 29; 93; and 95 in terms of his victory over the cosmic sea and his being proclaimed as king.

4. Procession with the Ark. A prominent feature in the ceremonies seems to have been a procession in which the ark, symbol of YHWH's presence, was carried up the hill of Zion to the temple, and YHWH entered his temple as victor over his foes (Ps 24; 47).

5. Ritual Combat. At some unknown point in the festival there was a ritual combat in which YHWH defeated his enemies, pictured both as the cosmic forces of chaos and the enemies of Israel (Ps 46:8–11; 48:8–9; 149:5–9).

6. YHWH as Lord of Morality. YHWH was also worshipped as Lord of universal morality. This is presented in two ways: he saves his people only as they are loyal to his covenant, and at the festival they renew their vows (Ps 24:1–6; 95:7–11; 97).

7. Defeat of the Gods. YHWH's victory over the kings of the nations has its counterpart in heaven. The gods of the nations have been guilty of rebellious misrule, but YHWH will subdue them and himself take over the rule over the world (Ps 82), leading to universal peace (Ps 46:8–10; 98).

8. The King. The Davidic king played a central part in this celebration. The historical books portray the king, God's anointed, as sacrosanct and the representative of the nation, the welfare of which depends upon his righteousness (1 Sam 9:16; 10:1; 24:6; 26:9; 2 Sam 1:14; 21:1; 24; 1 Kings 18:18). The covenant between YHWH and the Davidic monarchy (2 Sam 23:5; Ps 89:28–37; 132:11–18) was described as 'everlasting', and the king is sometimes referred to as the (adopted) son of God (Ps 2:7; 89:26–7), revealing the lofty place the king held in Israelite thought.

9. Humiliation and Rescue. Like the Babylonian king at the *Akitu* festival, it has been suggested that the Israelite king was almost defeated by his 'enemies' and ritually humiliated, before being saved by YHWH on account of his loyalty and faithfulness to the covenant (cf. Ps 89:38–51; 18; 118). After his vindication the king seems to have been proclaimed as the adopted son of YHWH and enthroned supreme over his enemies to rule them as God's vicegerent (Ps 2; 21; 110).

G. Concepts from a Different Culture. 1. If the culture of Israelite society and the meaning of some common terms used by the psalmists are not appreciated, there is a danger that the psalms will be misread. Out of a large number of words and concepts which might be considered, three are of special importance: enemies, the poor, and life after death.

2. Enemies. No reader of the psalms can fail to notice how often the psalmists complain to God about their enemies. Several different Hebrew words are used, as well as longer descriptions of their actions. A term found in thirteen psalms (Ps 5:5; 6:8; 14:4; 28:3; 36:12; 53:4; 59:2; 64:2; 92:7, 9; 94:4, 16; 101:8; 125:5; 141:4, 9) was formerly translated 'workers of iniquity' but modern translations favour 'evildoers'. Outside the Psalter it is limited to Isaiah, Hosea, Job, and Proverbs. Mowinckel (1921; 1962) argued that it referred to sorcerers, but few have followed him completely, although several accept that in some of the psalms this may be the connotation.

3. To understand why there should be so many references to enemies and who these enemies are is difficult. A useful approach is to note where the terms occur.

4. In hymns, laments, and other psalms of the community the enemies are obviously foreign nations or kings (e.g. Ps 44:10; 74:3–8). In royal psalms the enemies are the king's foes, either actual or ritual (e.g. Ps 2:1–3; 45:5; 110:1, 5–6; some think that 21:8–10 is addressed to the king rather than to

YHWH), and since the king is the representative of his people, his enemies are also the nation's.

5. In some psalms the enemies are described as the enemies of YHWH (e.g. 66:3; 83:2; 92:9), and are linked with mythological actions (e.g. 89:10; cf. 74:12–17).

6. The majority of references to enemies, however, are found in individual laments and thanksgivings, and this causes the greatest difficulty. Those who attribute many of the individual laments to the king naturally treat the enemies as foreign nations or rebels within the king's own people. This is supported by the fact that in some psalms of the individual (e.g. 3:6; 27:3; 55:18; 56:1; 59:3; 62:3) they are depicted as an attacking army, but this is not totally convincing for all the psalms that have been claimed as 'royal'.

7. If some of the psalms are prayers by men who believe themselves to be wrongly accused, the 'enemies' will be their accusers.

8. A group of psalms remains, however, where sickness and enemies occur together. Here the enemies might be those whom the psalmist believes to have resorted to sorcery. Alternatively, or perhaps in different psalms, the enemies may be those who condemn the psalmist as a sinner and hold that his illness is God's punishment for his sin. Even so the vehemence of the psalmist's reaction to his enemies seems extreme, the way he describes them as actively attacking him rather than engaged in a whispering campaign, or refusing to consort with him, and many of the metaphors which are used to describe the actions of the enemies (laying snares, lying in wait, attacking him like dogs and wild animals, sharpening their teeth) hardly seem suitable to apply to those who, after all, are only expressing the orthodox belief in the connection between sin and suffering.

9. Perhaps, therefore, these psalms are intended for use by many different individuals, and the troubles from which they seek God's deliverance are deliberately expressed in general terms that can be applied to a variety of situations. Even so, the wide extent of the references to enemies (they are absent from relatively few psalms), and the presence of illness and enemies in many psalms, is curious. (*DCH* provides an analysis of *'ōyēb* and 'doers of iniquity'; Kraus 1988: 95–9 has a good discussion of 'enemies'.)

10. The Poor. The psalmists frequently refer to themselves as 'poor'. Several different Hebrew words are used for the poor, translated with various English synonyms (four of them occur in Ps 82:3–4: 'weak', 'lowly', 'destitute', and 'needy'; for 'lowly' REB substitutes 'afflicted', and NJB 'wretched'; NIV has 'weak', 'poor', 'oppressed', and 'needy'). The Hebrew word used most frequently in the Psalter for 'poor' possesses active and passive forms, but whether these signify any distinction between 'humble' and 'humbled, oppressed' is doubtful. Even if it does, the text is ambiguous in many places, and sometimes the *qěre* and *kětîb* record the active and passive forms.

11. There has been much debate about the meaning of these terms. Outside the Psalter they normally refer to those materially poor, who, in the same way as widows and the fatherless, are likely to be oppressed by wealthy and more powerful members of the village society (cf. Am 2:6; 4:1; 8:4, 6). This may be the meaning in many of the psalms (e.g. Ps 112:9), especially when they are found together with widows,

the fatherless, and the resident alien (Ps 94:6, cf. 10:17–18), but the interpretation is complicated by two things: the poor are commonly regarded as 'righteous' (even in Am 2:6), and there is evidence both in the OT and in the other countries of the ancient Middle East that 'poor' possessed overtones of 'pious'. Thus an Egyptian votive stele describes the god Amun as 'lord of the humble man' who listens to the voice of the 'poor', and a Hittite king prays to the god Telepinus as father and mother of the oppressed and the lowly.

12. Certainly YHWH is expected to protect the poor and defend the oppressed (e.g. Ps 140:12), and the king, as his vicegerent, does the same (e.g. Ps 72:2–4, 12–14). But equally it has to be kept in mind that 'poor', and even 'oppressed' may be part of the language of piety, without any implications that the psalmist is destitute (e.g. Ps 37:14 places side by side the 'poor and needy' and 'those who walk uprightly'; while Ps 40:17; 86:1, and many other psalms use 'poor and needy' much as in the Egyptian prayers). In ancient Israel the poor would also be illiterate; it is surely doubtful whether those who composed and wrote down the psalms intended them as the prayers of those who were destitute. If many of the laments are the king's prayers the language is even more likely to refer to religious piety rather than economic poverty. On the other hand, there are those who remain firmly confident that the poor in the psalms are indeed the poor (Kraus 1988: 92–5).

13. Life after Death. Despite the weakening of classical culture upon modern society, most people today probably think of human beings either as no different from the animals or as possessing a material body and a spiritual 'soul'. Ancient Israel was closer to the first than the second. Human beings were seen as animated bodies, physical beings into whom God breathed life (cf. Gen 2:7–8). At death the unit of life was broken up and the individual became 'like water spilled on the ground, which cannot be gathered up' (2 Sam 14:14). Although a few scholars (Schofield 1951; Dahood 1966–70) have argued otherwise, it seems almost certain that for most of the period of the OT no happy life after death was envisaged. It was only with the Maccabean martyrs and the apocalypses that hopes of a resurrection appeared (cf. Dan 12:2). Certainly within the Psalter the normal belief was that the shades of the dead went down to Sheol (corresponding to the Greek Hades, and Babylonian concepts of the 'land of no return', cf. Job 8:9–10; 10:21; 16:22). This was pictured as a cavern under the earth, or more exactly under the waters beneath the earth, which stood upon pillars (Ps 18:4–5, 69:1–2, 14–15; Jon 2:2–9; for the cosmology see Ps 24:2; 75:3; 136:6). There the dead continued a weak existence in a region of darkness, dust, silence, and forgetfulness, unable to praise God, and beyond his power (Ps 6:5; 88:3–6, 10–12; 94:17; 115:17; Job 3:13–19. Ps 139:8 does not necessarily contradict this view of Sheol, since it may be a figure of speech describing the power of YHWH and his care for the psalmist.). Three other terms are found for this land of the dead, all translated in NRSV by 'the pit' (Ps 28:1; 30:3; 40:2; 88:4, 6; 143:7; 16:10; 30:9; 55:23; and 69:15). This is the background to all the psalms. It is possible that occasional leaps of faith in a future life are found in Ps 16:9–11; 49:15; 73:24, but these do not constitute an established belief and their interpretation is uncertain.

14. This comes as a shock to many Christians, who have taken it for granted that the Bible teaches life after death. The

dominance of the resurrection of Jesus in the NT has often
made it difficult to realize that Israelite worshippers of
YHWH had a very different belief. The limitation of life to
this world was probably one reason for the importance of
retribution being worked out before death and the devising
of a satisfactory theodicy. Christian use of the psalms, of
course, has imposed Christian ideas upon them, so that beside the messianic interpretations have come readings which
see in many phrases beliefs in resurrection, immortality, and
life after death, while 'soul' came to be understood in the
Graeco-Christian sense of that part of the human being which
survived death (cf. Peter's quotation of Ps 16:8–11 in Acts
2:24–32).

15. Soul. As has been mentioned, alongside these beliefs
about life and death went a particular understanding of
human personality. The older translations, with their frequent mention of 'soul', give the impression that the Israelites
thought in terms of body and soul. This is plainly incorrect, as
Gen 2:7 shows: when God breathed life into the little clay man
that he had made, the man 'became a living *being*' (Heb.
nepeš). Often 'soul' (*nepeš*) is used for a person's inner being
or vitality, virtually the equivalent of 'life' or 'individual'.
Commonly 'my soul' is a way of saying 'I myself'. The Hebrew
word *nepeš* can also express emotions, such as greed, desire,
and courage. In addition, many think that in a few places it
carries the physical meaning of 'neck, throat', as the cognate
word does in Akkadian, and this has been adopted by most
modern translations in Ps 69:1; 105:18, and by REB in 7:2 (and
31:9 marg.) in addition. It may have this meaning in Ps 63:5;
107:9, 18 and a few other places. (For a full discussion see
Johnson 1964.)

16. NRSV often retains 'soul', especially when it is the
subject of a verb or is in the vocative (cf. Ps 42:1–2; 103:1–2).
REB has 'soul' in only seven psalms, presumably where the
English would otherwise be awkward or synonyms for parallel
words needed to be found (Ps 19:7; 42:4; 74:19; 103:1, 2, 22;
104:1, 35; 130:6, 146:1). Various methods are adopted by modern translations to avoid using 'soul'. The most common is to
have the simple pronoun (e.g. Ps 3:2 'to me'; 124:7 'we have
escaped'; the practice is much more common in REB than in
NRSV). Alternative concepts are sometimes adopted, such as
'life' (e.g. Ps 35:4; 38:12); 'heart' (Ps 10:3; 78:18); and 'will' (Ps
27:12, where REB has 'greed' and NIV 'desire'; 41:2). Short
phrases sometimes represent the sense, again more often in
REB (Ps 35:25 'we have got our wish' REB; 105:22 'at his
pleasure'; 107:26 'courage'; 138:3 'bold and strong' REB).
This is to return to the meanings which the psalms had in
ancient Israel. Whether Christians are justified in retaining
the 'soul' of AV and BCP in their use of the psalms in worship,
interpreting it as the immortal part of the individual, is another question.

H. Imagery in the Psalms. 1. As has been seen, poetry is always
seasick when it is ferried to another country. Translation
cannot convey the rhythms, overtones, resonances, sounds,
alliteration, and plays on words in the original. Metaphor and
simile play a very large part in the appeal of the psalms, and
the ultimate horror of the ability of translation to destroy the
poetry is seen in GNB. 'Steps' and 'path' are frequent metaphors for life and conduct. The psalmist says that the 'law of

his God' is in the good man's heart and 'their [Hebrew 'his']
steps do not slip' (Ps 37:31; they 'never depart from it' GNB).
For 'nor have our steps departed from your way', GNB has 'we
have not disobeyed your commands' (Ps 44:18; cf. also 56:6;
73:2). The vivid concrete metaphor of Ps 73: 'But as for me, my
feet had almost stumbled, my steps had nearly slipped', is
replaced in GNB by abstract nouns: 'But I had nearly lost
confidence, my faith was almost gone'. The accusation against
the wicked that 'their throats are open graves; they flatter with
their tongues' is rendered 'Their words are flattering and
smooth, but full of deadly deceit' (Ps 5:9), and the picture of
God gathering the waters of the sea 'as in a bottle' becomes
'into one place' (Ps 33:7).

2. Animal Imagery. One of the delightful features of the
psalms is the very large number of references to animals. Not
only are they God's creatures, who offer to him their own
praise (cf. Ps 104; 149), but they provide images for many
different human and divine characteristics and actions. God is
pictured as a mother bird, sheltering his worshippers under
his wings (Ps 17:8; 36:7; 57:1; 61:4; 63:7; 91:4). The psalmist
wishes he were a sparrow or swallow nesting within the
temple (Ps 84:3). In his distress he likens himself to an owl
in the wilderness, and a lonely bird on the housetop (Ps
102:6–7), and longs for wings like a dove to escape (Ps 55:6–
8). God's goodness and forgiveness renews his youth 'like the
eagle's' (Ps 103:5). His longing for God is like the deer's longing for flowing streams (Ps 42:1), and he urges his fellows to
walk in God's way, and not to be like horses and mules which
are restrained only with bit and bridle (Ps 32:8–9). Some of the
most vivid similes are reserved for the psalmist's enemies.
They attack him like lions (Ps 7:2; 10:9; 17:12; 22:13, 21; 57:4)
and he asks God to tear out their fangs (Ps 58:6). They are like
bulls (Ps 22:12) and the wild ox (Ps 22:21), like snakes, venomous and deaf (Ps 58:4–5; 140:3) and dogs (Ps 22:16, 20; 59:6,
14), and he wishes that they would dissolve into slime like
snails (Ps 58:8, if that is the meaning). The king, if it be the
king, describes himself as surrounded by foreign nations as if
by bees (Ps 118:12). In an elaborate simile which compares
Israel to a vine, its attackers are compared to the wild boar (Ps
80:13). In a different image, the mountains skip like rams and
lambs before YHWH's theophany (Ps 114:4).

3. Hunting. A favourite way of depicting the enemies'
actions is hunting. In Sumerian the sign for the hunt signified
an enclosed space and originally meant 'to surround'. Hunting in the OT was mainly practised with traps and snares.
Frequently the psalmists speak of traps, nets, and pits (Ps
9:15–16; 31:4; 35:7–8; 57:6; 64:5; 69:22; 141:9–10; 142:3). In
Ps 124:7 the Israelites describe their rescue from their enemies who 'would have swallowed up us alive' in the image of
a bird escaping from a broken snare. Keel (1978) illustrates
many of these similes from reliefs from the ancient Middle
East.

4. Images of YHWH: Shepherd. YHWH is described under
a wide range of metaphors and similes. Despite the familiar
'The LORD is my shepherd', the image of a shepherd occurs
only in Ps 23 and 80:1, although his worshippers are referred
to as sheep in a number of other places (Ps 74:1; 78:52; 79:13;
95:7; 100:3). Sheep also represent the weakness of the
psalmists in face of their enemies (Ps 44:11, 22). The
psalmist declares that he has gone astray 'like a lost sheep'

(Ps 119:176), while in Ps 49:14 the shepherd is death, in grim contrast to Ps 23.

5. Father, Rock, Fortress. Not unexpectedly YHWH is never described as the mother of his people, but it is perhaps surprising that he is only rarely called father (Ps 68:5; 89:26; 103:13), though the king is his adopted son (Ps 2:7). More common metaphors are rock (Ps 18:2, 31, 46; 61:2; 71:3; 89:26; 144:1–2), fortress, strong tower, or stronghold (Ps 9:9; 18:2; 31:2; 61:3; 71:3; 91:2; 144:2), and shield (Ps 3:3; 28:7; 33:20; 59:11; 115:9, 10, 11; 144:2). YHWH is a warrior (Ps 24:8; 78:65–6), who takes up his shield (Ps 35:2) and fights for his people. Vivid imagery describes the theophany (Ps 18:7–15; 77:16–20; 97:2–5; 98:7–8). While not exactly a metaphor, the title 'YHWH of hosts' (Ps 24:10; 46:7; 48:8; 69:6; 84:3, 12; cf. 'YHWH, God of hosts', 59:5; 80:4, 19; 84:8, 89:8), is often linked with military language, although there is debate as to whether the 'hosts' are Israel's armies or the heavenly host (the stars). It seems to have been a special title given to YHWH in the Jerusalem cult.

6. The Righteous and the Wicked. Other metaphors light up the character of the righteous and the wicked. The good man is like a flourishing tree (Ps 1:3; 52:8; 92:12), and Israel is depicted as a vine (Ps 80:8–13), while the wicked are like chaff which is blown away (Ps 1:4; 35:5; 83:13; two different Heb. words are used). The shortness of human life is but 'a few handbreadths' (Ps 39:5). The sick man shrivels as quickly as grass (Ps 90:5–6; 102:4; 103:15–16); the image is used as a curse on the psalmist's enemies (Ps 129:6). The days of human beings drift away like smoke (Ps 102:3), and their life is poured out like water (Ps 22:14; 58:7). The wicked are depicted as wearing their evil devices and dishonour like clothes (Ps 73:6; 109:18–19, 29).

7. Wife and Sons. Finally in this selection of images, a man's wife, like Israel, is pictured as a fruitful vine, his children as olive shoots (Ps 128:3), while sons are like arrows in the hand of a warrior (Ps 127:4–5; providing Anthony Trollope with Mr Quiverful!).

I. The Theology of the Psalms. 1. Most commentaries include a discussion of the theology of the Psalter and whole books have been written on the subject (e.g. Gunn 1956; Ringgren 1963; Kraus 1986; McCann 1993a). It is deliberately omitted here for two reasons.

2. First, there is no unitary theology of the psalms. Rather what is found is a number of different theologies and series of theologies. On the one hand, the theology of Ps 1 is very different from that of Ps 73 or 88; the universalism of some of the hymns is different from the intense nationalism of others; even the three history psalms present differing views of God's activity in Israel's history and Israel's response to God. On the other hand, the interpretation of the psalms, and hence their theological teaching, has changed over the centuries. It is doubtful whether we can recover the theology of those who wrote the psalms, even if 'theology' is the correct term to describe their ideas about God, for practice and worship were probably more important than explicit beliefs, and each stage in the editing and compilation of the Psalter introduced fresh theological ideas. Later, the psalms have been used by Jews and Christians in different contexts and with different meanings.

3. Secondly, and even more importantly, the psalms are the poetry of prayer and praise, not the prose of dogma. The attraction and power of the psalms lies in imagery and language, rather than in a set of theological ideas. They kindle religion rather than define it. It is possible to derive a theology from liturgy and worship, but a better way is to allow the psalms to inspire and express religious devotion. But they come from a distant age, and a few problems remain.

J. Problem Features in the Psalter. 1. James Russell Lowell's comment that 'Time makes ancient good uncouth', applies as much to truth as to goodness. One change of attitude in modern times, the rejection of patriarchal society and language, has already been noted (A.9). So strong are feelings about this, that the psalms have been rewritten in all the most recent translations in order that 'masculine-oriented language should be eliminated as far as this can be done without altering passages that reflect the historical situation of ancient patriarchal culture' (NRSV: xv). Two other features often cause distress to Christians today: attitudes towards enemies and assertions of innocence.

2. Attitudes towards 'Enemies'. The most striking form of the hostility and even outright cruelty towards enemies is found in Ps 137:7–9 and 139:19–22, where psalms which have great appeal are wrecked by calls for vengeance (cf. Ps 104:35, with its call for the destruction of the wicked). Ps 69 and 109 contain long imprecations against the psalmist's enemies, Ps 35 and 52 are largely taken up with an appeal to God against an enemy, Ps 58 describes the wicked in violent terms and seeks divine punishment that is even more violent, Ps 83 contains a long section seeking vengeance, and other psalms contain similar expressions. Several of these psalms also find pleasure in contemplating the punishments and disasters that befall the wicked and the enemies (e.g. Ps 52:6–7; 58:10–11). Various devices have been adopted to deal with this.

3. Editing out. Frequently in worship the offending verses (in the case of Ps 137 and 139) are deleted, or the psalm is never sung (in contrast to BCP, where the practice of singing through the whole Psalter is followed). Modern hymn-books, such as the Methodist *Hymns and Psalms*, severely limit the number of psalms they include, and even edit these with deletions.

4. Quotations. Some modern translations try to alleviate the difficulty by their punctuation. Thus NRSV, REB, and NJB express the view that the curses in Ps 109:6–19, or some of them, are those of the psalmist's enemies, not his own (the first two even insert 'They say' at the beginning of v. 6).

5. The Nature of the Psalms. But these expedients are no answer to the problem, which concerns the way in which Scripture is understood and interpreted. Six general comments about the nature of the psalms may be made first. (1) In some psalms the words may be the defence of those maintaining their innocence against criminal charges and thus be part of the legal setting. (2) Even if 'workers of iniquity' is not a technical term for sorcerers, sometimes the psalmist may feel threatened by sorcery, and the curses may have the character of counter-spells. (3) If some psalms were actually composed by men who were seriously ill and not by priests for them, the mental strain of the illness must be taken into account. (4)

The easiest answer is to interpret most of the individual laments as the king's psalms, when his enemies will be the enemies of Israel and ultimately of God, so that the curses are an expression of the psalmist's opposition to evil, and part of the cultic expression of Israel's faith. (5) In the absence of any hope of a happy life after death, evil has to be defeated in the present world if right is to be triumphant. Illness and misfortune are regarded as signs of the psalmist's sin, and only restoration and the discomfiture of his 'enemies' will prove his innocence and God's just rule over the world. (6) It is sometimes also observed that the psalmists make no distinction between the sin and the sinner, whereas Christians are often taught to do so. (See Zenger 1996.)

6. Morality and the Culture. Behind these comments lies a recognition that ethical decisions cannot be made without reference to the society in which the actors live. Morality is part of the overarching culture. This means that ethical ideas change over the years as societies change, and moral judgements cannot be absolute. Even if complete relativity of morals is rejected, it can hardly be maintained that human ethical standards at any one time are the immutable will of God. This means accepting that we too are children of our age; and our consciences are also imperfect and moulded by the society in which we live. The psalmists belonged to their own age, and part of the problem of Scripture lies in the fact that it is the very human word of very frail and sinful human beings. No longer is it possible to defend a view of biblical authority which sees it as the infallible word of God, and attempts to do so lead to grotesque apologetics (see Kaiser 1983: 292–7, with its conclusion that 'neither Ps 137 nor any of the other seventeen imprecatory psalms present a sub-Christian . . . ethic').

7. Assertions of Innocence. An older and more morally sensitive age was troubled by the way in which many of the psalmists claimed that they were righteous, and demanded divine support on this ground (cf. Ps 7:8; 17:1–5; 18:20–4; 26). Now, in an age of advertising, self-assertion, and the ubiquitous *curriculum vitae*, perhaps this is viewed less harshly—indeed, it may even pass unnoticed. Yet it stands in stark contrast to the humility and recognition of human sinfulness that the NT and much of the OT teaches.

8. One answer lies along the lines of the previous section. In some psalms the plaintiff may be presenting a legal case that he is innocent of some particular charge, and the declarations of innocence are not to be taken as assertions of complete sinlessness. Or the king may be confessing his loyalty to the covenant and seeking God's help in the ritual combat with his (and God's) enemies. Moreover, the underlying belief that reward and punishment have to be worked out in this life increases the urgency of the plea.

9. Confession and the Penitential Psalms. It has to be admitted that the psalms are rather short on confession. Of the church's seven 'penitential psalms', only two (Ps 32; 51) clearly express a sense of the psalmist's own sin, with brief glimpses in Ps 130:3–4; and 143:2, and less certainly than NRSV suggests in Ps 38:18. They are mostly to do with the afflicted ones, rather than with those confessing their sins (Snaith 1964: 12). All the psalmists are much more ready to impute evil to their enemies and to castigate 'the wicked'. That we expect to find all the religious emotions in the Psalter is perhaps an inheritance from an age when the Psalter was sung in its entirety as the centre of monastic prayer (Bradshaw 1995).

K. The Numbering of the Psalms. 1. The numbering of the psalms differs between the Protestant and Catholic/Orthodox traditions. The reason is that the LXX combined Ps 9 and 10 as a single psalm, Ps 9 (probably correctly), joined 115 to 114 (as Ps 113), and divided Ps 116 into Ps 114 (= vv. 1–9) and Ps 115 (= vv. 10–19), and Ps 147 into Ps 146 (= vv. 1–11) and Ps 147 (= vv. 12–20). It inserts 'Alleluia' before Ps 116:10, and repeats its expanded form of the title to Ps 147 before v. 12. This means that for most of the Psalter the psalm numbers in the LXX and the Vulgate, and hence the Catholic English versions (Douai and Ronald Knox) are one behind those of the Hebrew/Protestant text. JB and NJB, however, follow the Hebrew numbering.

2. In the Hebrew the titles of the psalms are treated as part of the text. This means that where the title is longer than a few words it is counted as a separate verse (or even two verses in Ps 51; 52; 54; 60). For many of the psalms, therefore, the Hebrew verse numbers differ from the English translations. Some commentaries give both numbers, but in this commentary the English numbering is followed.

COMMENTARY

Psalm 1 The first two psalms lack titles, which is unusual in Book 1 of the Psalter, and it is probable that they provide an introduction to the whole book of Psalms. Whether they originally formed a single psalm is very doubtful, however, in spite of an ancient Jewish saying that the first psalm begins and ends with a beatitude (v. 1 and 2:11). A few manuscripts of Acts 13:33 refer to Ps 2 as the 'first' psalm, which suggests that among some Christians either the two psalms were combined or they knew of texts which began with the present Ps 2. Certainly it seems likely that Ps 1 was placed here after Book 1 or the entire Psalter was completed.

It is similar to Ps 19:7–14 and 119 in its delight in the 'law', and probably is post-exilic. Whether it is correctly termed a 'wisdom' psalm, and whether it was intended for use in the cult are both uncertain. Perhaps it is best understood as a poem to encourage faithfulness to the religion of the Torah. Although often described as 'The Two Ways' (cf. v. 6) its tone is set by the initial, 'Happy are those . . .'. The poet is convinced that the way of goodness is an attractive way, and it would be wrong to regard it as presenting a moralistic religion in which goodness is pursued for reward.

The structure is clear: vv. 1–3 describe the righteous, closing with the simile of a tree planted beside an irrigation canal, a comparison found in ancient Egypt and in pictures from the ancient Middle East. Although the phrases in v. 1 might ascend to a climax ('walk', 'stand', 'sit'; 'wicked', 'sinners', 'scoffers') they may be simple poetic parallels. If the psalm is post-exilic, the reference to the 'law' may be to the written Pentateuch. The picture is of the pious reader speaking the words of the law half aloud until they become part of his being, rather than of silent and passive meditation. The point of the tree simile is that it flourishes, not that the fruit is a 'reward', despite the last line of v. 3, which speaks of the prosperity of the good man.

The wicked are described more briefly in vv. 4–5: the godly man is described in detail; the side glance at the wicked is but to light up the blessing of his life by contrast. The picture is of winnowing the corn, throwing it up into the air after it has been threshed by a flail or a threshing sledge, so that the wind will blow away the straw and the husks and allow the heavier grains to fall to the ground. v. 5 is uncertain. Most translations render the verbs as futures, although they do not differ from the form of many of the verbs earlier in the psalm, implying that the judgement is a future judgement by God. Some early Christian commentators saw a reference to the resurrection by translating the verb as 'rise up', perhaps influenced by the LXX. Since the general OT belief was that the dead went to Sheol and remained there (see PS G.13), this is unlikely unless the psalm were very late indeed. The reference appears to be to day-by-day judgements either by the elders in the gate, or possibly by God himself, and continues the description of the two types of people. This would form a better parallel to 'nor sinners in the congregation of the righteous'. The verb translated 'watches over' in v. 6 is 'knows', with the sense of 'takes care of': other psalmists and the writer of Job will have to question whether life is always as simple as this.

Psalm 2 The first Christians interpreted this psalm as messianic prophecy and v. 7 is quoted in Acts 13:33 and Heb 1:5; 5:5 as referring to Jesus, reflected in the capital letters for 'Anointed One', 'King', and 'Son' in NIV. The older critical scholars connected it with an Israelite king who had recently ascended the throne, and discussed the claims of David, Solomon, or some other king. Form criticism classifies it as a 'royal psalm', but there is no agreement as to the way in which it may have been used in ancient Israel—at the Davidic king's enthronement, or at an annual celebration of his accession, as the new king's first proclamation to his subjects, or spoken by a cultic prophet. Many set it within a cultic drama, in which the king is attacked by his (and God's) enemies and finally is delivered by God. Those more attracted to literary and canonical interpretations point to the concluding beatitude which forms an *inclusio* with that in Ps 1:1, and to the repetition of some words, such as 'meditate' (1:2) and 'plot' (2:1, the same Hebrew verb), and suggest that the two psalms form a double introduction to the Psalter and represent two ways of understanding it, as teaching and as Davidic or messianic. Following the approach adopted in this commentary, the psalm will be interpreted as a poem in its own right.

The psalm falls into four sections: vv. 1–3 describe the rebellion of the 'kings of the earth' against YHWH and his anointed king; vv. 4–6 depict God's mockery and support of his king with a bold anthropomorphism; in vv. 7–9 the king sets out the divine proclamation which established him as God's adopted son and promised him victory over his enemies; and vv. 10–12 give a final warning to the hostile kings to submit to YHWH. The closing benediction stands apart from the rest of the psalm and some have suggested that it is an addition, fitting the psalm into later worship.

Two verses present difficulties of translation. The 'decree' in v. 7 probably declares what YHWH is performing—the act of making the king his son—and should be translated: 'I myself beget you today' (cf. REB, 'this day I become your father'). The sonship is through adoption: unlike other monarchs in the

ancient world, the Israelite king was not regarded as descended from God. In the Hebrew the emphasis is upon 'I myself' rather than 'this day' as Eng. versions.

NRSV follows a common conjectural emendation in vv. 11–12. The Hebrew appears to mean literally: 'and rejoice with trembling. Kiss (the) son lest he should be angry and you perish with regard to the way' (i.e. the way you are behaving). Apart from the word for 'son' being Aramaic (the Hebrew word is used in v. 7) this makes tolerable sense, kissing the king being understood as an act of homage. Kissing the feet would be an even humbler grovelling, and accords with a practice well known in the ancient world. The LXX had a different text: 'and rejoice for him in trembling. Take hold of instruction (or chastisement, correction) lest the Lord should ever become angry and you perish from a (the) righteous way.' Some of the ancient versions understood the word translated 'son' to be a different word meaning 'pure' or 'purity', hence 'worship in purity'. The pronouns also present problems if 'kiss the son' is abandoned, for it becomes uncertain who the subject of the verbs in v. 12 is. NRSV apparently accepts the very striking metaphor of kissing God's feet. Some adopt a change of reference: Serve YHWH, kiss (the king's) feet, lest YHWH be angry. Probably the original text and meaning are irrevocably lost and all that remains certain is that the rebellious kings are warned to submit to God and his representative, the Israelite king.

Psalm 3 The psalm is a prayer to God for help against enemies, with a strong expression of confidence in his protection (vv. 3–6). vv. 1–2 describe the psalmist's situation, v. 7 is the call to God for help (probably the whole verse should be translated as a plea, 'Rise up . . . Deliver me . . . Strike all my enemies . . . break the teeth . . .', cf. NIV). The final verse widens the perspective to the whole congregation or nation. The introductory verses are held together by a threefold 'many', and three words derived from the same Hebrew root, 'help', 'deliver', and 'deliverance' link the first and last sections of the psalm.

So much is clear. Problems begin when we ask who the psalmist and the enemies might be. If the enemies are military foes, it is natural to see the Israelite (Davidic) king as the one who is appealing to God. If the title is not allowed to influence the reader, the psalmist may be an Israelite who faces attacks by fellow Israelites, a man who has been (falsely) accused of some crime (with the enemies as his accusers), or even a sufferer who regards his illness as owing to attacks by enemies, although the last interpretation is less likely. In any case there is poetic exaggeration in the 'ten thousands of people who have set themselves against me all around' (v.6).

Less certain is the situation. If the psalm is taken as a royal psalm, it is still impossible to decide whether the psalm was composed in (or perhaps more probably, for) an actual battle or whether the attacks are part of a ritual combat in a cultic drama. If it was originally a cultic prayer for those suffering from hostility from other people, v. 5 might refer to spending the night in a sanctuary in order to receive a divine oracle, though the more natural way of taking the verse is as a mark of such total trust in God that the psalmist can sleep without fear. The early Christians found a reference to the resurrection of Jesus in the sleep and awakening. Later liturgical use has treated it as a morning psalm.

The title probably comes from a scribe who has searched through the books of Samuel for a suitable occasion in David's life in which to place the psalm, and came up with his flight from his son Absalom (see 2 Sam 15–17, esp. 15:12, 14). Certainly there is much that fits the account in Samuel, and it might even be that the psalm was composed by a scribe as a literary response to the narrative, although the general view is that the titles were added to existing psalms rather than indicating the inspiration of them. Or it may have been written for any of the kings of Judah. The date is less certain on more general interpretations of the psalm.

From a literary perspective attention may be drawn to the threefold reiteration of 'many' in vv. 1–2, and the theme of 'help', 'deliver', 'deliverance' (the same Heb. root) in vv. 2, 7, 8.

Psalm 4 At first sight this is a happy, confident little evening psalm. The many small differences among the main translations and the wide range of interpretations offered by commentators show that it is difficult to be certain about how it should be read. It offers few clues as to the speaker, the persons addressed, and the occasion on which it was spoken or sung, and although there are not a great number of textual problems, the exact meaning of several phrases is not clear.

Some see it as a companion to Ps 3: a king's psalm, which the older scholars placed in the time of Absalom's rebellion and explained as expressing David's faith in YHWH and a rallying call to his dispirited followers. There is little firm evidence to support this. More recent royal interpretations prefer a cultic interpretation, with YHWH's anointed king and representative addressing his opponents and proclaiming his glory over against those who worship false gods. The reference to harvest fits this theme, since the faithfulness of the king is linked with the prosperity of the land (cf. Ps 72). Others, however, find little evidence to refer the psalm to the king, and suggest that it belongs to rulers in general, whether secular or priestly, and see the occasion as a time of drought or bad harvest. Yet others see in it confidence in the face of false accusations or the vicissitudes of life. Even form criticism is uncertain whether the dominant theme is lament or confidence. Repetitions of words ('call', vv. 1, 3; 'right', vv. 1, 5; 'hear' vv. 1, 3; 'heart' vv. 4 (NRSV 'ponder', lit. 'say in your heart'), 7; 'bed'/'lie down' (related words in Heb.), vv. 4, 8; 'trust'/'in safety' (verb and noun), vv. 5, 8; and 'many'/'abound' (noun and verb), vv. 6, 7) point to literary skill but are less helpful in revealing the structure of the psalm. vv. 2–5 stand out as addressed to an opposing group, while vv. 1, 6–8 are a prayer to God. Possibly, like many Christian hymns, the very ambiguity and lack of definite allusions make it more possible for many different people to make its confident appeal to God their own.

In v. 1 the middle line either expresses the confidence upon which the two petitions are based (as most translations) or the Hebrew should be taken as a further petition ('give me relief from my distress', NIV). v. 2 appears to refer to the respect due to the psalmist within the community, although some take it to be a reference to God ('how long will you dishonour my glorious one', REB, cf. NIV marg.), who is dishonoured by worship offered to other gods. The meaning of the Hebrew in v. 3a is very uncertain (cf. the variety of modern translations); perhaps it should be read, with a small emendation, 'Know

that YHWH has shown me his marvellous love' (cf. NEB). 'Right sacrifices' (v. 5, literally 'sacrifices of righteousness') are probably sacrifices offered with correct rites or in a right spirit, although some regard them as sacrifices which acknowledge YHWH's justice, and a very ancient Christian interpretation thought of righteousness itself as a metaphorical sacrifice.

Psalm 5 Usually defined as an individual lament, this psalm is clearly a petition to God. Uncertainties about the status of the psalmist, the nature of the enemies, and precisely what the psalmist is presenting 'in the morning', make it difficult to be certain about its origins and use in ancient Israel.

The title probably intends to ascribe it to David, and some scholars interpret it as a royal psalm, sung in a cultic rite. This is held to fit the identification of the enemies as also rebels against God. Those who find no evidence of authorship or original usage in the titles of the psalms commonly see it as the prayer of someone faced with false accusations, the enemies being the hostile and vindictive accusers. The situation might then be either a prayer for a just outcome to a forthcoming 'trial', or an appeal to God for a verdict (perhaps through a priestly oracle) at a hearing in the temple.

The reference to the 'morning' in v. 3 has led to the psalm being used as a morning hymn, While the references to the morning are clear, it is uncertain what action is being performed. The Hebrew has no object to the verb 'set in order, arrange'. The older English versions (and NIV) supplied 'my prayer', 'my requests', but this is unlikely since the verb is never linked with prayer in the OT. It is regularly used for presenting a case in a lawsuit and for ordering a sacrifice, hence NRSV's 'plead my case' and REB's 'prepare a morning sacrifice'.

The mention of the temple in v. 7 is equally ambiguous. It might refer to any of the local sanctuaries, but most probably is the Jerusalem temple. This is partly supported by the psalmist's address to God as 'my King', which has been widely seen as a characteristic of the Jerusalem cult. Whether the psalmist is actually present at the morning worship or describes his intention to present his case or offer sacrifice there cannot be determined.

The structure of the psalm may be analysed in several different ways. If NRSV is followed, vv. 1–3 are the invocation to God and statement of the psalmist's intention, vv. 4–6 describe God's character, vv. 7–8 express the psalmist's confident approach to God, vv. 9–10 set out the wickedness of the enemies and call upon God to condemn and destroy them, and vv. 11–12 form a concluding invitation to the righteous to rejoice. Possibly the final verse should be taken as a call to God to give his blessing and defend them.

In the title, 'for the flutes' is the most probable interpretation of a phrase that is unique here, and presumably intends the psalm to be accompanied by flutes. The Babylonians had a special kind of lament called 'flute psalms of lamentation'. The LXX referred it to a different Hebrew word and translates 'concerning her that inherits'. It is possible, though unlikely, that it was the name of a melody, 'To "Inheritance"'.

Psalm 6 That the psalmist is gravely ill appears obvious. Less certain is the relation of the illness to the 'enemies'. It has been suggested that it was the enemies who brought about the psalmist's illness, perhaps through sorcery, but few accept this explanation, partly because the usual Hebrew word for sorcery does not occur in any of the psalms, chiefly because the psalmists regularly, as here, see God as the cause of their suffering. The suggestion that the term 'workers of evil' (v. 8) refers to sorcerers has slight support. Usually, therefore, the enemies are regarded as members of the psalmist's community who interpret his illness as divine punishment for wrongdoing, much as Job's friends did (e.g. Job 11:6; 15:4–6; 22:5–11), and by their hostility increase his sufferings. Even so the psalmist's reaction in v. 10 strikes modern readers as extreme. Might it not be that, with the illogicality to which we are all prone, the psalmist accepts both that the illness has been inflicted by God and also that the enemies are responsible for it?

Two features in this psalm are notable. First, the psalmist fears that he is near to death. Sheol is the abode of the dead, who live on in a feeble and miserable existence in the land of no return, outside of the reach of God's love, a land of dust and darkness and silence (for other descriptions of Sheol see Ps 30:9; 88:6–12; 94:17; 115:17; PS G.13). It seems that in ancient Israel all sickness was seen as a form of 'death', and the psalmist probably regarded himself as partly in Sheol already—hence his anguish.

Second, there is a marked change of tone at v. 8. This has been called the 'certainty of hearing', and has been variously interpreted. Some suggest that vv. 8–10 are the real heart of the psalm, the earlier part recounting the suffering from which the psalmist has been delivered and now expresses his thanksgiving. The balance of the psalm hardly supports this. Others suppose that the psalmist's thanksgiving after he had been healed has been attached to the earlier petition, but there is no evidence for this. There is equally little evidence to support the claim that two separate psalm fragments have been combined in the one psalm, although Ps 40 (vv. 13–17 = Ps 70); Ps 108 (vv. 1–5 = Ps 57:7–11; vv. 6–11 = Ps 60:5–12) shows that this could occur. A popular theory is that a temple prophet or a priest uttered an oracle of assurance between the two parts of the psalm. Such oracles are found in Isa 40–55, often beginning, 'Fear not...', and cf. Ps 12:5. Possibly the change in mood is produced by the prayer itself: having uttered his plea the psalmist becomes confident that God has heard it and will answer his request. This would be the most likely view if it is thought that the psalmist is too ill to go to the temple to make his prayer to God. The answer has not yet been fulfilled, however, for the shaming of the enemies lies still in the future.

The psalm is one of the seven 'penitential psalms' of the church (the others are 32, 38, 51, 102, 130, and 143; PS J.9), although there is no confession of sin but rather an appeal from frailty and humility. The reliance upon God's 'steadfast love' (v. 4) should be noted.

'According to The Sheminith' in the title is found only here and in Ps 12 (cf. 1 Chr 15:21). The meaning is unknown. The term is usually linked with the word for 'eight'. Some have proposed that it refers to singing in octaves (but the octave does not seem to have been known in ancient Israel) or by male voices. Other suggestions are that it refers to some element in the ritual, perhaps an eighth stage, or to an instrument with eight strings.

Psalm 7 The title describes this psalm as a 'Shiggaion of David' and links it with 'Cush, a Benjaminite'. The meaning of 'Shiggaion', found only here and in a different form in Hab 3:1, is unknown. Scholarly guesses as to its meaning include a song of irregular form or varied mood, and a psalm of lamentation. One suggestion is that the word is a corruption of 'Higgaion' (Ps 9:16; 92:3), perhaps 'melody' (as NRSV in Ps 92:3) or 'meditation'. The LXX has simply 'a psalm'. The author of the title seems to have linked it with the Cushite of 2 Sam 18:19–33, or one of David's Benjaminite enemies such as Shimei (2 Sam 16:5–14; 19:16–23, 1 Kings 2:36–46). This is the only reference in the psalm titles which cannot be traced to the biblical narratives about David, but it seems unlikely that he drew upon lost traditions in just one psalm.

The psalm belongs generally to the class of individual laments. Greater precision depends upon the interpretation placed upon three features, the references to enemies, who are described with animal metaphors (vv. 1–2, 5, 6), the oath of innocence (vv. 3–5), and the ascription of vv. 12–16, which NRSV divides between God (simply 'he' in the Hebrew) and the wicked (shown by the use of the plural, although the Hebrew has singulars throughout). Those favouring royal origins note the military references in vv. 4, 10, 12–13, and regard the enemies as national enemies of the Israelite king, possibly being portrayed in the cult, while those who place greatest emphasis upon the oath and the description of God as judge (vv. 6, 11) interpret the psalm as the plea of someone accused of some crime, possibly coming to the temple for a divine verdict through priestly decision, prophetic oracle, or an ordeal, or as a court of appeal (cf. 1 Kings 8:31–2). Some think that v. 1 shows that he sought asylum there, but in the biblical narratives asylum is sought only in cases of manslaughter and this does not seem to be the accusation in the psalm. Later use of the psalm will have separated it from the temple and generalized it into a plea for help in time of distress.

The structure is well set out in NRSV, apart from vv. 12–16, where God has been gratuitously introduced, changing the meaning—the whole section should probably be referred to the psalmist's enemy or read as a general description of the wicked. After a call to God for help (vv. 1–2), the psalmist protests his innocence (vv. 3–5; for the form of the oath cf. Job 31), repeats his call to God and seeks divine judgement, (vv. 6–8 and 9–11, perhaps to be taken as a single section with hymnic descriptions of God in vv. 8 and 9c–11), sets out his conviction that evil rebounds upon the wicked (vv. 12–16), and concludes with thanksgiving (v. 17). Whether the thanksgiving is the result of a successful verdict or is a vow to offer praise when his innocence is declared is impossible to determine.

Psalm 8 This well-known and greatly loved psalm presents several exegetical problems. It is usually classified as a hymn, but it is unusual in having no initial call to worship God and in containing features, such as the question, 'What are human beings that you are mindful of them?' which are akin to wisdom teaching (cf. Job 7:17; 15:14, though some see the Job passages as a bitter parody of the psalm, and the book of Job itself has close links with psalmic forms). The first person passages are also unusual in hymns and are somewhat reminiscent of individual laments. It is difficult, however, not to regard it as essentially a hymn that opens with the actual praise of YHWH.

There is a textual difficulty in v. 1c, which NRSV has solved by emendation. An alternative suggestion is that the Hebrew letters should be read as: 'I will serve [worship] your glory'. This problem is linked with the question of the correct sentence division. The NRSV apparently takes v. 2 to mean that God is so powerful that the words of children are sufficient as a rampart of defence, but the meaning is not clear. Perhaps the difficult Hebrew verb should be taken as in REB, with different phrasing: 'Your majesty is praised as high as the heavens, from the mouths of babes and infants at the breast'. This has the advantage of making sense of the reference to the 'bulwark' (usually 'strength'), but at the cost of an uncertain rendering of the Hebrew verb as 'is praised'. The LXX translated v. 2: 'from the mouth of babes and sucklings you prepared praise for yourself', hence the form of the quotation in Mt 21:16.

In v. 5 the LXX translated the Hebrew word 'ĕlōhîm, which means either 'God' or 'gods', as 'angels', possibly to avoid the idea that human beings are almost equal to almighty God. Scholars are divided as to whether the Hebrew means 'God' or 'the gods' as members of his heavenly court.

The structure is transparent: The shout of praise, addressing God by his name, YHWH, envelops the psalm (vv. 1 and 9): vv. 1c–2 enlarge upon the majesty of God; and in vv. 3–8 the psalmist expresses his wonder that creatures as insignificant as human beings should have been given dominion over all the rest of creation (cf. Gen 1:26–8).

The quoting of verses from the psalm in the NT (Mt 21:16; 1 Cor 15:27; Eph 1:22; Heb 2:6–8) reveals that it was interpreted as messianic, but this was hardly its original meaning. Some have regarded it as a royal psalm, seeing the king beneath the references to 'man'. At the other extreme are those who find it difficult to relate the psalm to the worship of the Jerusalem temple, and see in it marks of scribes and rabbis in the post-exilic community.

Psalms 9–10 These two psalms are combined as a single psalm in the LXX and the Vulgate, which accounts for the differences in the numbering from Ps 10 to Ps 148 between the Protestant and Catholic/Orthodox traditions, the latter following the LXX. Despite some differences in the type and emphasis between the two parts of the psalm it was probably originally a single psalm. This is supported by LXX, the acrostic form, the lack of title to Ps 10 (rare in Book 1 of the Psalter), the selâ in 9:20, which never elsewhere comes at the end of a psalm, and a number of unusual words common to both psalms. A few Hebrew MSS also treat the psalms as a single poem.

The acrostic is incomplete. The main pattern is to start each two verses with the appropriate letter of the Hebrew alphabet, but the d verse is missing, and the regular pattern is disturbed at the end of Ps 9 and the first eleven verses of Ps 10, being resumed only with q (Ps 10:12), when it continues perfectly until the end of the psalm. Strikingly each half line in 9:1–2 begins with the first letter of the Hebrew alphabet. Since difficulties in some verses show that textual corruption has occurred, and small changes in the verse division restore some of the missing letters, it seems likely that originally the acrostic was complete; but it cannot now be recovered.

Ps 9 is predominantly thanksgiving by an individual while Ps 10 is closer to individual laments. Possibly due to the acrostic form, there is no clear development of thought. Leading ideas are the call to thanksgiving, YHWH as judge of the nations and of the wicked and defender of the oppressed, and pleas for deliverance from enemies and the wicked.

The setting of the psalm is equally uncertain. Those who hold that many of the psalms are to be linked with the Jerusalem king see in the references to the 'nations' (Ps 9:5, 15, 17, 19, 20; 10:16), who appear as the psalmist's enemies (cf. Ps 9:3, 6), support for their interpretation. Other evidence for this view is the care of the orphan and the oppressed (Ps 9:18; 10:14, 18), a duty of the king as God's representative, and God's universal judgement (Ps 9:7–8, 12; 10:15, 17, 18), claimed to be a feature of the Jerusalem cult. At the other extreme, the psalm has been linked to the post-exilic synagogue as the prayer of the oppressed congregation, but there is little firm evidence for this, especially as the extent to which the synagogue was a place of worship rather than teaching and meeting is contested (McKay 1994). Certain links with wisdom teaching on the retribution coming to the wicked, together with the acrostic form, may indicate that it is a late psalm, possibly written as an art form or for instruction.

One of the main words for 'the poor' in the Psalter occurs here for the first time (Ps 9:12, 18; 10:2, 9, 12; PS G.10–12). The psalmists join with the prophets in asserting that God will defend the poor, and this is one of the duties of the king (cf. Ps 72).

'Muth-labben' means literally 'Death to [of] the son'. Most regard it as the title of the melody to which the psalm was sung. The LXX, with a slight change in the text, has 'For the secrets of the son', and it has been suggested that this might refer to a royal ritual. Alternatively it might be a corruption of 'According to Alamoth' (see PS 46).

Psalm 11 This psalm is usually classified as a psalm of confidence. YHWH is not addressed in prayer but spoken of in the third person. vv. 1–3 set the scene, and vv. 4–7 express the psalmist's trust in God. It is not easy, however, to discover a more precise setting.

Those who try to link it with the life of David point to his flight from Saul or the time of Absalom's rebellion. Others see it as a royal psalm, noting the psalmist's sense of authority, his claim to be 'righteous', and the threat of enemies, and either set it within the Jerusalem temple worship or find a reference to a foreign invasion. Yet others describe it as the plea of one falsely accused, despite the lack of direct prayer, seeing the psalmist as seeking refuge in the temple (v. 1) and trusting in God to defend him. Confidence is largely restricted to the second part of the psalm (vv. 4–7) and this has suggested to some that a prophet or priest declared YHWH's acquittal of the psalmist at this point. The fact is, we simply do not know. How the psalm is interpreted largely depends on the reader's view of the historical and social background into which the psalms are to be placed.

Despite the surface clarity of NRSV there are some uncertainties. Does the speech in v. 1 continue to the end of v. 3 (as most translations, regarding vv. 2–3 as the reason the speakers give for flight), or is it limited to v. 1b, with vv. 2–3 as the psalmist's response as he rejects the call to flee, or does the speech consist of vv. 1b–2 (as REB)? Is the temple in v. 4 the Jerusalem temple, so that YHWH is depicted as present with his people and also the transcendent God, or it is a reference to heaven? Should we press the form of the Hebrew verb in v. 5 and translate, 'May the LORD test the righteous', thus introducing the element of prayer? And is the final clause to be constructed as, 'He [lit. 'his face'] beholds the upright', i.e. accepts the upright with his favour, rather than being taken as referring to the psalmist's experience of God? NRSV has tacitly emended the text in v. 6, where the Hebrew has 'snares, fire' (see RV) instead of 'coals of fire'.

Psalm 12 Prayers both by an individual and the community appear in this psalm, and it is uncertain which predominates. The divine promise in v. 5 suggests that perhaps those are right who call it a prophetic liturgy: opening with petition, having at its centre the comforting words of the prophet, to which the congregation responds with the note of certainty in vv. 6–7. If this is so it may have had its origin in some temple rite. Beyond this it is impossible to go with any assurance. Perhaps the emphasis upon words, both of human beings (vv. 2–4) and YHWH (vv. 5–6), has led some to imagine the psalmist as the target of malicious comments, possibly even of threats and curses (which were thought to have their own power to effect the evil they declared). The psalm may come from a time of moral decadence, when honesty and truthfulness were no longer regarded as the basis of social life.

The structure is fairly clear: appeal to God, with an account of the evil from which the psalmist seeks deliverance (vv. 1–2); plea for divine judgement on the speakers of lies and flattery (vv. 3–4); divine oracle of salvation (v. 5, 'safety' is related etymologically to the verb 'help' in v. 1); an expression of confidence in God's protection (v. 7); and a reiteration of the evil situation in which the psalmist is placed (v. 8), possibly set as a foil to the protection God gives, unless v. 7 is to be taken as a return to petition: 'Do thou, LORD, protect us and guard us ...' (NEB, cf. RSV).

Psalm 13 The fourfold 'How long?' is striking. A feature of both individual and communal laments (Ps 6:3; 74:10; 79:5; 80:4; 90:13; 94:3), it is also found in Babylonian prayers, such as a remarkably similar prayer to Ishtar: 'How long, O my Lady, wilt thou be angered so that thy face is turned away? How long, O my Lady, wilt thou be infuriated so that thy spirit is enraged?' The psalmist appears to be ill (cf. v. 3 with its fear of death), but his main emotion is anguish because he feels abandoned by God.

In spite of a Jewish tradition that the psalm describes Israel's suffering at the hands of hostile neighbours, the intensely personal tone has convinced most commentators that it is the lament or prayer of an individual. The enemies will then not be national foes or the king's enemies, but fellow Israelites who see in the psalmist's illness divine punishment. Probably the alternation between a singular 'enemy' and the plural 'foes' (vv. 2, 4) is stylistic, though it has been suggested that in v. 2 the enemy is death. The book of Job perhaps provides the best commentary on this psalm, with the psalmist's deep sense of loss in the face of God's silence.

For the change of tone from urgent petition to confident trust and rejoicing at v. 5 see PS 6. Was an oracle spoken by a temple prophet at this point? Or has the outpouring of prayer in itself led to a sense of calm joy?

The LXX has a different text at two points: in v. 2 it reads 'day and night' (adopted by NEB), and adds at the end of the psalm: 'I will sing to the name of the Lord, the most high'.

Psalm 14 This psalm must have been widely popular, for it was included in the first Davidic collection (Ps 1–41) and the Elohistic collection (Ps 42–83). The differences between the two versions are relatively minor apart from 14:5–6/53:5. It is usually supposed that both go back to a single original and the differences are due to textual corruption or editorial changes. If they spring from variant traditions, it may be that the evildoers in Ps 14 are Israelites while those in Ps 53 are foreigners. v. 7 was commonly supposed to be post-exilic when the phrase which is correctly rendered 'restores the fortunes' in NRSV was held to mean 'brings back the captivity [captives]'; some still find it distinct in tone and theme and treat it as a liturgical addition.

Even if the psalm was well loved in ancient Israel, the present-day reader finds great difficulty in knowing how it should be read. It has been described variously as a prophetic liturgy, a mixture of prophetic and wisdom literature, a wisdom psalm, communal instruction, perhaps even an early synagogue speech, and an individual lament. Medieval Jewish interpreters saw it as reflecting Jewish national sufferings. Certainly the first phrase is reminiscent of the wisdom writings, where several different words for 'fool' occur, all referring to moral depravity rather than intellectual feebleness or folly, alongside 'any who are wise' (v. 2), a word commonly used in this sense in Proverbs. On the other hand the prediction of coming terror in v. 5 has the ring of a prophetic denunciation of those who oppress the poor. With such a range of possible genres to choose from, it is little wonder that there is no agreement on how it was used in ancient Israel. If it is instruction it fits naturally with Proverbs, but since there is no certainty about the existence of scribal schools in Israel or the position and function of 'the wise', this gives little help. Its presence in two collections of psalms, which presumably were connected with the temple, perhaps points to a cultic prophet uttering his oracle in some rite. If Ps 53 is a prophetic taunt song against foreigners it might have its place during some hostile attack on Jerusalem, but it is by no means certain that the two traditions are to be separated so widely.

The structure at least is clear. vv. 1–3 describe the universal godlessness and wickedness, vv. 4–6 present a threat of punishment, and v. 7 is a wish for the restoration of the nation's prosperity.

It is almost a commonplace to stress that the 'atheism' of the 'fool' is practical—he acts as if God did not exist—and not religious or philosophical, on the grounds that pure atheism would have been impossible in Israelite society, and that the psalmist stresses the moral faults of 'fools'. But how different is 'practical atheism' from a denial of the existence of God?

Paul quotes vv. 1–3 in Rom 3:10–18 in an abbreviated form, followed by a series of quotations from other verses from the OT. At some point these additions found their way into the

LXX and from there into the Vulgate. Curiously the catena is also found in two Hebrew MSS.

Psalm 15 This psalm is similar to Ps 24, and also Isa 33:14–16, while listings of sins and virtues are found in Jer 7:5–7, Ezek 18:5–9, and Mic 6:6–8. It may be that the words of the prophets were modelled on psalms such as this. To call it a 'torah psalm', however, adds little to our understanding, and even if ten moral requirements are found in it, it is not closely similar to the Decalogue. It is commonly described as an 'entrance liturgy', with the worshipper's question in v. 1, followed by the conditions for entering the sanctuary in vv. 2–5b (presumably spoken by a priest), and a closing promise in v. 5c. Elsewhere in the ancient Middle East temple inscriptions set out similar demands, but the two OT psalms differ in that they include no ritual requirements. Another suggestion is that the psalm sets out the conditions for those seeking asylum in the sanctuary, but this seems unlikely in view of the apparent limitation of asylum in the OT to unpremeditated homicide.

The meaning is plain apart from two phrases in v. 4. 'In whose eyes *the wicked* are despised', imports too strong a sense into a word which means 'despised, rejected'. Possibly the sense is 'the one rejected by God', but the Targum rendered it: 'He is despised in his own eyes, and rejected', hence the Prayer Book's 'He that setteth not by himself, but is lowly in his own eyes'. At the end of the verse the NRSV's 'who stand by their oath even to their hurt' involves a forcing of the Hebrew, which is literally: 'he swears to do evil and does not change', a meaning that is hardly possible, despite Lev 5:4. It has been suggested that the Hebrew has a negative sense, 'he swears *not* to do evil', but this does not seem likely. The LXX (apparently reading *lĕhāraʿ* as *lĕhārēaʿ*) has: 'who swears to his neighbour and does not set it aside', which is attractive.

Psalm 16 This is a good example of the extreme difficulty in discovering the original use and meaning of many psalms. vv. 8–11 in the LXX version are quoted by Peter in Acts 2:25–8, who interprets the psalm as messianic prophecy, fulfilled in the resurrection of Jesus. Few today would accept this as the psalmist's own intention, and most classify it as a psalm of confidence, but then unanimity fails. Is it a royal psalm, expressing the Israelite king's confidence that God protects him? Or does the reference to the allotment of land in vv. 5–6 point to the psalmist as a Levite of whom it was said that YHWH is their inheritance (Deut 10:9)? But it might be the whole land that is intended, and hence the psalm would belong to the whole people of Israel. Or might it be the confession of an individual worshipper? Even the description as a psalm of confidence is not quite certain, since the petition of the first verse is closer to laments. Is the psalmist looking back on a past deliverance, and praying for God's continuing protection, or is the danger still threatening? Interpretation is not assisted by the chaotic state of the text in vv. 2–4, and occasionally later in the psalm, where emendation is inevitable. So obscure are these verses that some have found traces of dialogue, or a quotation from the words of a fellow Israelite, who worships other gods as well as YHWH. The psalmist himself is utterly devoted to God.

The meaning of vv. 10–11 is disputed. While some find a reference to life after death, others believe that such a belief was alien to most of the OT, and see only confidence that God

will protect the psalmist until his death at the end of a long life. Perhaps here is a leap of faith. The psalmist holds the bleak Sheol belief with his mind, but his delight in his fellowship with God moves beyond this to the hope that such intimacy cannot be ended by death.

Psalm 17 The structure of this psalm is relatively clear, although the text is uncertain in a number of places, making the exact meaning doubtful. vv. 1–2 are an appeal to YHWH; in 3–5 the psalmist protests his innocence; 6–12 is a further prayer, especially referring to the psalmist's enemies, against whom he seeks YHWH's help in 13–14; a final note of confidence is expressed in v. 15.

The way the enemies are described raises difficulties for a more precise interpretation than the general ascription as a 'declaration of innocence'. The psalmist may be making an appeal to the supreme tribunal in the temple (cf. Deut 17:8–13), or the background may be an ordeal (see *ABD* v. 40–2; the only description of an ordeal is Num 5:11–31, however, and despite the widespread use of ordeals in the ancient Middle East, it is uncertain how far it was a normal practice in Israel). On either view the enemies of the psalmist would be those who accuse him of some wrong—falsely, as he claims. vv. 3 and 15 possibly indicate that the psalmist spent the night in the sanctuary awaiting God's verdict. Christian tradition saw in the final verse a foreshadowing of the believer's resurrection, the sleep being the sleep of death, but this was hardly the psalmist's own meaning.

The severe punishments which are invoked against the enemies appear extreme if they are simply those presenting a legal case against the psalmist, and it has been suggested that this, together with the heading, points to its being the prayer of a king faced with a military invasion, possibly a punitive expedition on the grounds of some accusation of disloyalty or a wrong committed against another state.

Psalm 18 The outline of this long psalm is relatively clear. vv. 1–3: praise of YHWH; 4–6: the distress which has befallen the psalmist; 7–19: a great theophany in which God comes to save his servant; 20–4: the ground of this salvation, the 'righteousness' of the psalmist; 25–30: a wisdom type generalization that God saves those who trust him; 31–45: God has saved (or will save) the psalmist from the attacks of his enemies who will be defeated; 46–50: concluding praise of YHWH. The explicit reference to the king, YHWH's anointed, in v. 50 has convinced most commentators that this is a royal psalm, but there agreement ends. Differences between the sections suggest to some that at least two psalms have been combined, only vv. 31–50 clearly referring to the king. Others suggest that the theophany may have been separate originally. The wisdom features of vv. 25–30 also mark this section off from the myth of the theophany and the defeat of the king's enemies. And as so often the tenses present a problem, as can be seen in the past description of NRSV in vv. 32–48, the present and past tenses of NIV, the predominant presents of GNB, and the presents and futures of NEB and REB.

A cultic interpretation manages to include most of the features of the psalm. The king is supposed to be the main actor in a ritual drama, in which he is almost defeated, cries out to YHWH for help on the grounds of his faithfulness and righteousness, and is both delivered and secures a crushing victory over his enemies. The mythic features are readily accommodated into this pre-exilic worship, since the theophany is central to Israelite faith (cf. Ex 19), while the extravagance of the triumph over the king's enemies fits more easily into a rite than as a reflection of some historical victory. The wisdom expressions of vv. 25–30 fit less easily into this interpretation, but they can be viewed either as a reminder to the listening people that the lesson is for them as well, or as a later transformation of a psalm that originally referred to the king into a more general thanksgiving. There seems no need to regard the whole psalm as coming from the post-exilic synagogue, an expression of hope and encouragement, drawing on past expressions of faith and worship.

The complete psalm is found in 2 Sam 22, with only minor textual differences, an indication of the way the psalms and the life of David were linked by later editors, the psalms expressing the emotions of the king and the narrative providing a setting within which they could be interpreted.

Psalm 19 Is this one psalm or two? The subject-matter, form, and metre mark off vv. 7–14 from 1–6, and Ps 108 shows that portions of psalms were joined together (108:1–5 = 57:7–11; 108:6–13 = 60:5–12) in the Psalter. It may be that the first section of the psalm is part of a hymn praising God as creator, and the second is a prayer to YHWH with wisdom features, centred on the law, which is referred to under six synonyms in vv. 7–9. Support for this is found in the contrasting names for God (El and YHWH) in the two parts of the psalm, and the possibility that the first part is very ancient while the second part may reflect post-exilic piety. (The sun was worshipped in the ancient Middle East as a god, and even in Israel there are hints of this, see 2 Kings 23:5, 11; Jer 8:2; Ezek 8:16, although in this psalm its 'tent' has been set in the sky by God, who is unambiguously the creator of the universe.)

On the other hand modern emphasis upon the completed text of the Bible would suggest that even if the sections of the psalm were originally independent, a unity has been imposed upon them. Nature and law are both needed for a full revelation of God. Indeed, some believe that the psalm was a unity from the first, the psalmist adding his own prayer to a fragment of an ancient hymn. Some find a link between the sections in the fact that the sun was regarded in the ancient world as the giver and sustainer of justice, thus pointing forward to the law, but there is no hint of this in the text of the psalm. It is strange that there is no call to praise, the psalm opening immediately with a description of the praise uttered by the dome of the sky and by the day and the night. In the second part contemplation of the law leads the psalmist to confess his sins and pray that his words and meditation may be acceptable to God. (Some regard vv. 12–14 as an independent prayer.)

In v. 4 REB and NJB retain the uncertain Hebrew word *qawwām* (which seems to mean lit. 'their string, line'), translating it as 'their sign' and 'the design'. NRSV and NIV adopt a common emendation *qôlām*, 'their voice', making a parallel to 'their words' (see *HALOT* (1996), iii. 1081 for other proposals). The paradox of silent speech is unique in the OT.

NRSV interprets v. 13 as a reference to 'the insolent' rather than the familiar 'presumptuous sins' (cf. marg. 'from proud thoughts')—the word elsewhere refers to people. The psalm-

ist may be referring to those whose self-confidence might shake his faith, but the switch to persons is rather abrupt.

'Redeemer' (v. 14) has special overtones for the Christian. In Israel it referred to the next of kin who had the duty to protect any member of the family in trouble, avenging wrongs, giving support in time of poverty, and buying back the relative from slavery (see Lev 25:25, 47–9; Num 35:19–28). YHWH as redeemer is a favourite theme of Deutero-Isaiah (see ISA A.1, 11; Isa 41:14; 43:14; 44:6, 24; 47:4; 48:17).

Psalm 20 The mention of 'his anointed' and 'the king' (vv. 6, 9) have convinced most commentators that this is a royal psalm, and the references to victory (vv. 5, 6; in Hebrew the words are 'salvation' and 'save', but these often refer to victory in war) suggest that it is a prayer that accompanied sacrifice before battle. The only disagreement is whether it is a real battle (see e.g. 1 Sam 7:9; 13:9–12; 1 Kings 8:44–5; 2 Chr 20:1–19) or part of a cultic drama, and there appears to be no way of deciding between the two. Perhaps there is not so much difference between them, since the offering of prayer would be within the setting of worship, while if the psalm was part of a cultic drama, that itself was performed in the expectation that God would save his anointed in actual war in the same way that he was depicted as saving him in the ritual. The change to confidence in v. 6 is probably the result of some expression that God has heard the prayer, either through some symbol or the words of a cultic prophet (cf. ps 6).

Psalm 21 The references to the king in vv. 1 and 7 lead most to treat this as a royal psalm, but the situation to which it refers is not clear. It may be before battle (as Ps 20, pointing to the hope of future victories in vv. 8–12), after victory (with emphasis upon the confidence in vv. 1–7), at the king's coronation (cf. v. 3), or at an annual celebration of his accession (noting the reference to the king's trust in YHWH and the mention of God's 'steadfast love', v. 7). Since the rites performed at the Autumn Festival are unknown, it is impossible to determine more precisely the way the psalm was used.

To whom vv. 8–12 are addressed is a major problem of interpretation—is it God or the king? Possibly these are the words of a prophet who gives this promise to the king during the liturgy. If YHWH is the subject, the reference may be to covenant curses directed against the king's (and Israel's) enemies.

The Hebrew word 'to save', which was translated as 'victory' by NRSV in Ps 20 is here rendered 'help', but REB has 'victory' in both psalms. The salvation which God gives the king is primarily the conquest of his enemies.

The Aramaic version of the psalm rendered 'king' by 'king Messiah', treating it as messianic prophecy, but this is unlikely to have been its original meaning.

Psalm 22 The many quotations from this psalm in the New Testament, especially within the passion narratives, show that the early church regarded it as messianic prophecy (see Mt 27:39 || Mk 15:29 (v. 7); Mt 27:43 (v. 8); Mt 27:35 || Mk 15:24 || Lk 23:34 || Jn 19:24 (v. 18); Heb 2:12 (v. 22); Jesus may have been quoting from this psalm in his cry from the cross, Mt 27:46 || Mk 15:34).

Jewish tradition read the psalm as a reflection of the experience of Queen Esther, who is likened to the 'hind of the dawn' in the title, the Midrash suggesting that 'When the dawn awakes the stars set, and so in the court of Ahasuerus, as Esther awakened the stars of Haman and his sons set' (though this might have been adopted to counter Christian use of the psalm, see Magonet 1994: 111).

Those who adopt a wide view of royal psalms ascribe the psalm to the king, usually in the setting of the rites of the annual festival, but others restricting such psalms to a minimum identify the psalmist as a sufferer who is ill and near to death. A royal interpretation permits the scope to be extended to include the Israelite people whose representative the king is.

There is a marked change of tone from petition to thanksgiving at v. 22 (or 21b if the NRSV is followed—the Hebrew is ambiguous and possibly corrupt). Have two psalms been combined? Does this represent the 'certainty of hearing', which perhaps followed a prophetic oracle or some symbolic action, or even a direct divine revelation? Or is it the words of the psalmist's vow? Verbal links and the many changes of mood and style throughout the psalms are commonly seen as evidence that the psalm is a liturgy.

As often we do not know how the psalm was originally used or in what context, and therefore what its original meaning was. It is, however, the greatest of the laments within the Psalter, akin to the book of Job. More than most psalms the sense of personal experience floods through it. Despair almost drives out hope, yet two things support the psalmist: he remembers that God saved his people, and he looks back on the way God cared for him from his birth.

The structure is relatively plain: in the first part prayer and complaint alternate with expressions of confidence (vv. 1–2, 3–5, 6–8, 9–10, 11–21), and in the second vows (vv. 22, 25) mingle with hymns of thanksgiving and praise.

The animals in vv. 12, 16, 21 may be the psalmist's enemies (if he is the king, the enemies of Israel), but some regard them as demons, as in Babylon, where sickness is often attributed to demons pictured in the form of animals. The last line of v. 16 is difficult. The familiar 'They have pierced my hands and my feet' (retained by NIV) comes from the LXX. The Hebrew is literally: 'like a lion my hands and my feet'. Instead of the NRSV's 'My hands and feet have shrivelled' REB reads 'they have bound me hand and foot'. Curiously the verse, which many see fitting the crucifixion of Jesus perfectly, is not quoted in the New Testament.

The title may refer to the morning sacrifice, although the LXX translated 'the hind of the morning' as 'the help [which comes at] morning' (picking up 'help' in v. 19). But it may be the name of the melody to which it was sung.

Psalm 23 The happy confidence of this psalm, coupled with the comfort that it has given to those in 'the valley of the shadow of death' (v. 4, AV), have made it the best known and best loved of all the psalms. Later usage has taken over from the original meaning, which is clouded in uncertainty.

The most obvious structure divides the psalm at v. 5, making the depiction of God as shepherd and host. The two ideas do not easily sit side by side, however, and (unsuccessful) attempts have been made to retain the pastoral metaphor throughout the psalm, usually by emending 'table' (v. 5) into some kind of weapon. Another proposal finds three metaphors, with YHWH as guide of a wanderer in vv. 3–4. It may

be that the 'paths of righteousness' should be seen as processions to the temple, 'table' as a symbol of the covenant, and 'goodness and mercy' as referring to the qualities of God's reign.

Royal maximalists see the psalm as the prayer of the king, pointing to the metaphor of God as shepherd which normally relates to the nation in the OT, and would be more appropriate in the mouth of the king as representative of the nation, and the royal implications of God's protecting his vassal against his enemies. The psalm is thought to have been used either in cultic ritual or in an act of worship reflecting the king's confidence. But the evidence is far from clear, and it is not legitimate to see in the anointing in v. 5 an allusion to the anointing of the king, since a different word is used.

Alternative interpretations range from regarding the psalm as the (non-cultic) prayer of a pious Jew to ascribing it to the nation in exile in Babylon. There are also differences of opinion about the banquet, some regarding it as metaphorical, others as a reference to a literal sacrificial meal. Even the classification as a psalm of confidence has been challenged, and it has been interpreted as the psalmist's thanksgiving after he has been 'delivered' from his enemies or even acquitted from false accusations.

In fact the original meaning and setting of the psalm are completely unknown, and we are left with hypotheses and the more certain later use by Jews and Christians.

Two translation difficulties may be noted. The traditional 'valley of the shadow of death' assumes the existence of a rather unusual Hebrew word. Many change the vowels and produce 'valley of darkness' (cf. NRSV). In v. 6 'and I shall dwell' follows the LXX and Syriac versions. The Hebrew appears to mean 'and I shall return', possibly a vow or a hope that the psalmist will be able to keep on coming to the temple to worship rather than remaining there permanently for the rest of this life.

Psalm 24 The structure of this psalm is beautifully clear. vv. 1–2 are hymnic, declaring that the world was created by God; vv. 3–6 is an 'entrance liturgy', similar to Ps 15 and Isa 33:14–16; and vv. 7–10 contain a dialogue at the gates of the city or temple, repeated, as often in liturgies, and reaching a climax with the declaration of YHWH as 'YHWH of hosts', 'the king of glory'. While some believe that the three parts were originally separate, the whole fits together easily into a single liturgical movement.

The LXX adds 'of [for] the first day of the week' to the title, reflecting later Jewish usage, which linked the psalm to the story of creation in Gen 1. Those who try to set it within the life of David connect it with the bringing of the ark into Jerusalem (2 Sam 6). Within the worship of the pre-exilic temple it may have been used during the annual Autumn Festival, with the celebration of YHWH as creator, and as warrior who returns to his temple in triumph after the defeat of the powers of chaos (possibly with the ark symbolizing his presence carried in a procession, although there is no explicit mention of the ark). If the psalm is post-exilic it may be a hymn which reflects features from earlier rituals. Paul quotes v. 1 to defend the eating of meat that had been sacrificed to idols (1 Cor 10:26), and later Christian tradition linked the entrance of 'the LORD of hosts' through the gates with the entrance of Christ into heaven at the ascension. In such varied ways was this psalm reused and reinterpreted.

v. 6 is textually difficult. On its own the Hebrew would be most naturally translated: 'those who seek thy face, Jacob', but this seems impossible. The LXX apparently read: 'those who seek the face of the God of Jacob', hence NRSV.

Psalm 25 The acrostic form of this psalm is well preserved, although there are a few irregularities. In v. 2 NRSV follows the verse division of the Hebrew, but 'O my God' should be taken with v. 1 to enable v. 2 to begin with the letter b. The w verse is missing, but is easily restored by inserting 'and' before 'for you I wait' (v. 5; there may be a further corruption since vv. 5 and 7 consist of three lines, while the restored w verse would possess only one). There are two r verses (18 and 19); perhaps the first originally began with a q word, but it is possible now only to guess what it might have been. An additional p verse stands at the end. There are two striking similarities with Ps 34, which also lacks a w verse and concludes with an extra p verse. Some suggest that both psalms come from the same writer.

The acrostic form tends to isolate the individual verses, and an overall structure is difficult to discern. Broadly, vv. 1–7 are a prayer for help, guidance, and forgiveness; vv. 8–15 reflections on the character of God and the blessedness of those who serve him; and vv. 16–21 further prayers for deliverance, with v. 22 expanding the mainly individual lament into a prayer for the nation. While some regard this verse as a late addition to fit the psalm for congregational worship, the similar feature in Ps 34 suggests that it may well have been original.

Confession of sin is rare in the Psalter, and this makes the confession in vv. 7 and 11 the more notable.

Psalm 26 The psalmist protests his innocence and asks God to examine his integrity. The precise occasion for reciting this psalm, however, is far from clear. A common view points to similarities with Ps 7 and 17, and posits an appeal to a temple court or an ordeal. The doubts expressed in the notes on those psalms apply equally here. Those who link a majority of the psalms with the king, find here a royal psalm of confidence, but despite the stress upon 'steadfast love' and 'faithfulness', armed enemies are lacking and the general mood would seem more suited to an ordinary Israelite. The declaration in vv. 4–5 recalls Ps 1, and it has been suggested that the psalm stands closer to Ps 15 and 24 than to 7 and 17. To see it as the worshipper's declaration as he seeks entry into the temple and faces the priest's questioning, may provide the best guide to the spirit of the psalm, with praise and worship dominating over legal declarations, and the hand-washing (cf. Deut 21:6) and procession round the altar reflecting ritual actions (cf. Ps 118:27).

The themes of innocence, prayer, and confidence in God are intertwined and it is not easy to analyse the psalm rigidly; none of the Eng. versions offers a convincing structure.

'Vindicate' (v. 1) is perhaps too strong in the light of v. 2 and while 'judge' may not express the psalmist's confidence that when God examines him he will find that he is innocent, the psalmist's plea is for a hearing. NRSV takes 'faithfulness' in v. 3 to be that of the psalmist, but the parallel line suggests that REB represents the sense better by referring to God's faithfulness which sustains his worshippers. The 'blood-

thirsty' (v. 9) is literally 'men of blood', i.e. murderers (cf. 2 Sam 16:7–8).

Psalm 27 This seemingly simple and confident psalm presents the interpreter with three problems: is it a unity? who is the speaker? and how are the Hebrew tenses to be translated? vv. 1–6 speak about YHWH as if addressing an audience, expressing confidence in his protection from future dangers, or possibly thankfulness for past deliverance. In vv. 7–12 the psalmist addresses YHWH directly with a plea not to reject him or abandon him to his enemies, but the psalm ends with a renewal of confidence (v. 13, the Heb. is difficult, however, and the translation of NRSV involves either emendation or paraphrase) and a call to wait for God's deliverance in hope (v. 14).

Those who accept that some psalms have been wrongly separated (cf. Ps 9–10 and 42–3) and others deliberately combined (Ps 19, 108: the LXX also combines 114 and 115) solve the problems of the differences in tone and address by treating the two parts independently, as a psalm of confident trust and a prayer for help. Those who prefer to keep to the present text explain the changes of tone and form as derived from liturgy: by expressing trust in God before offering his urgent prayer, the psalmist makes it more difficult for God to refuse his request.

Royal maximalists see the speaker as the king, pointing to the references to battle in vv. 2–3, treating v. 10 as an allusion to the king's adoption by God, and regarding the overall style as 'royal'. The setting will then be in worship, either as part of the ritual at a festival or in response to the attacks by national enemies. Others take the military allusions to be metaphorical, and interpret the psalm as spoken by an ordinary Israelite, possibly facing accusations (cf. v. 12) and seeing the action of the psalmist's parents as their rejection of a son they hold to be guilty.

In a striking metaphor YHWH is described as 'my light' (v. 1), a phrase found only here in the OT, although in Isa 10:17 he is the 'light of Israel' and in Isa 60:19, 20 he is the 'everlasting light' of his people.

NRSV has adopted a common emendation in v. 8 without comment. The Hebrew seems to be literally: 'To thee my heart has said, "Seek [plural] my face"', although it has been suggested that it could mean: 'From thee my heart conveys the message "Seek my face"' (Eaton 1986: 176).

Psalm 28 The psalm falls into three distinct sections. In vv. 1–5 the psalmist utters a passionate plea to God to hear his prayer and not remain silent and unresponsive, but rather punish the wicked. NRSV shifts to a future tense in v. 5cd, but the plea may continue: 'may he strike them down' as REB (the LXX has 'you (sing.) will pull them down and not build them up'). The tone changes to 'certainty of hearing' (cf. ps 6), or possibly thanksgiving at v. 6. vv. 8–9 return to prayer, but now for the king and the nation. While some regard the third part as an addition to an original psalm by an individual, the whole may be a liturgical unity, with petition followed by two responses, as the psalmist both expresses his own confidence and includes his people in his prayer.

To define the setting more closely is difficult. Some hold that the psalmist is the king, interpreting the enemies as rebels or even foreigners, and placing the psalm within the temple ritual. The reference to God's 'anointed' (v. 8, almost certainly the king rather than the post-exilic high priest), however, does not require that this is a royal psalm, since the individual may well have included king and people together in his final prayer. The distress of the psalmist is, as often, vague and complex. Is the psalmist ill and near to death? Has plague broken out, affecting both good and evil people, and he fears it may strike him? Or is his suffering largely caused by hostile and deceitful neighbours? The suggestion that the 'workers of evil' (v. 3) are sorcerers has been generally abandoned, but given the nature of small-scale societies the possibility that the psalmist fears that his illness is caused by sorcery should not be completely ruled out.

Psalm 29 This is a majestic hymn of praise to YHWH, the God of the thunderstorm. After an initial call to the 'sons of gods', the lesser gods who are members of YHWH's court (vv. 1–2, cf. Ps 82, Job 1:6; 2:1), the main body of the psalm echoes with the voice of YHWH, repeated seven times, as he thunders against (rather than 'over') the primeval waters, breaks the cedars, makes the mountains quake, flashes flames of fire, shakes the wilderness, and strips the forest bare (vv. 3–9). The conclusion probably describes his enthronement as king over the flood, and as the protector of his people (vv. 10–11).

Less certain are the date and original occasion of the psalm, and the precise meaning of the beginning and the end.

Similarities with Ugaritic poems have led some to date the psalm very early in the history of Israel, possibly as an adaptation of a hymn to Baal or Hadad, the storm god. At the other extreme, by taking the final verse as a petition on behalf of Israel, it has been suggested that, at least in its present form, the psalm is a congregational hymn, possibly quite late in Israel's history. The psalm may have been sung in the Autumn Festival, as the LXX addition to the title, 'at the closing festival of tabernacles' indicates. Later Jewish tradition linked it with the Feast of Weeks. If the Autumn Festival included the celebration of YHWH's enthronement, this may be reflected in v. 10.

'In holy splendour' (NRSV) or 'in holy attire', may seem a disappointment after the AV's 'in the beauty of holiness'. The splendour is probably God's, the attire that of the worshippers. But perhaps the Hebrew word is connected with a Ugaritic word meaning 'vision' and hence a reference to the 'theophany'. The LXX has 'in his holy court', but there is little other evidence for this text. Sirion (v. 6) is Mount Hermon, to the north of Israel.

The tenses in the last verse present a problem. NRSV takes them as an invocation of blessing. The REB's futures make the verse an expression of confidence that the majestic God who is now enthroned as king will protect his people. NIV continues the descriptive present tenses of the previous verses. It is difficult to decide between these three interpretations.

Psalm 30 There is fairly general agreement that this is the thanksgiving of a man who has recovered from a serious illness. The Israelites thought of illness as sinking into Sheol, and this is the image behind v. 3. vv. 6–10 are best seen as a flashback to the time of the psalmist's distress, rather than a present prayer, and the note of joyous thanksgiving sounds out clearly in the two final verses. Although some have attempted to draw this psalm into their group of royal psalms, most find here words said by an individual Israelite.

With such a strong sense of individuality, it is strange to find 'a song of [at] the dedication of the house [temple]' in the title. Most probably it was added at a late date when the psalm was linked with the rededication of the temple in December 164, after it had been desecrated by the Greek king Antiochus Epiphanes (1 Macc 4:42–59), and the festival of Hanukkah ('dedication') was inaugurated. Alternative suggestions of the dedication of David's palace or the dedication of the rebuilt temple in the time of Haggai and Zechariah are less probable. The major difficulty lies in understanding how such an individualistic psalm could be applied to a public ceremony. Perhaps the strong note of thanksgiving and the psalmist's call to the congregation to join in praise led to its use.

In v. 3b the NRSV text and margin represent two Hebrew traditional readings. The stress in v. 5 is upon the merciful favour of God rather than the brevity of his anger. The Hebrew is extremely terse, and REB's 'In his anger is distress, in his favour there is life' is a possible way of taking the words.

Psalm 31 Although rich in isolated spiritual phrases, when viewed as a whole this psalm presents grave difficulties. Urgent prayer for deliverance from a variety of troubles, quiet trust in YHWH, and glad thanksgiving mingle in what may be a many-layered liturgy. On the other hand two, three, or even four psalms may have been combined (vv. 1–8 and 9–24, or 19–24 may be divided off as a separate thanksgiving, or three laments may be distinguished: vv. 1–8, 9–12, and 13–18). The distress from which the psalmist seeks deliverance is equally uncertain, and illness, unjust accusations, and the attacks of enemies have all been proposed. Since illness was commonly seen in ancient Israel as divine punishment, it is possible that this is the background to the whole psalm, explaining the whispers and ostracism to which the psalmist is subjected (vv. 13–15) and even the 'lying lips' of v. 18. The address to the 'saints', those in a covenant relation with God, in vv. 23–4 indicates that the prayer was offered publicly within an act of worship, although not necessarily in the Jerusalem temple. The striking change to confident thanksgiving at v. 19 may be a further example of the 'certainty of hearing' which followed the giving of a favourable sign or prophetic oracle, but some interpret the whole psalm as a thanksgiving, the apparent prayers for deliverance being descriptions of the dangers from which the psalmist has been saved. Those favouring psychological interpretations see the wavering between petition, complaint, and confidence as varying emotional moods. In the MT the psalmist confesses his 'iniquity' in v. 10 (cf. NRSV marg.), but since this is the only mention of sin in the psalm and the LXX has 'destitution', most make the small emendation adopted by NRSV.

Those who posit a royal background to most of the individual laments ascribe this psalm also to the king, pointing to the psalmist's strong sense of privileged position before God, the stress on the covenant relationship, the covenant virtues of faithfulness, righteousness, and 'steadfast love', and the designation of the psalmist as YHWH's 'servant' (v. 16). 'I was beset as a city under siege' (v. 21), usually taken metaphorically, is treated as an actual attack by foreign enemies.

According to Lk 23:46 (= v. 5), 'Into your hand I commit my spirit' were the last words of Jesus on the cross, a further example of the way the psalms were linked with the passion narrative in Christian tradition.

Psalm 32 The structure and general sense of this psalm of joyous thanksgiving for healing and sin forgiven are clear, even though the text is in disarray in several places (cf. NRSV marg. at vv. 4, 6). The psalm opens with a twofold beatitude (vv. 1–2), followed by a description of illness, seen as divine punishment (vv. 3–4), and an account of the psalmist's confession (v. 5). In v. 6 the psalmist addresses the assembled congregation and in the following verse reverts to his own thanksgiving. It is not clear who the speaker in vv. 8–9 is: if it is not the psalmist, these verses may contain divine teaching, perhaps through a prophet or, more in accord with the style, one of the 'wise' teachers. The final two verses (perhaps to be taken with vv. 8–9) express the common idea of retribution, and call the righteous to rejoice in YHWH.

The date and original setting of the psalm are difficult to determine. The wisdom style in vv. 1–2 and 8–9 may point to a post-exilic date, and it has been suggested that the whole psalm fits synagogue practice better than pre-exilic worship in the temple. But it is not impossible that the psalm was intended to accompany the sin or guilt offering.

To be noted are the three words for sin in vv. 1–2, etymologically derived from rebellion, missing the way, and crookedness, combined with three words for forgiveness, lifting the sin from the sinner, covering it up, and no longer accounting the sinner as guilty. But etymologies are fascinatingly deceptive, and use is a better guide to the meaning of words than derivations. Above all the repetitions reveal the psalmist's horror of his sin and underline his happiness.

In Christian tradition this is one of the seven penitential psalms, though it is really thanksgiving for sin forgiven.

Psalm 33 Apart from Ps 10, this is the only psalm in the set of Davidic psalms 3–41 lacking a title. The LXX has 'To David', and Qumran evidence suggests the longer, 'To David, a song, a psalm'. A few MSS join it to Ps 32, but the form of these two psalms makes it certain that they are separate poems, in spite of a few common features.

This is a good example of the hymn form. vv. 1–3 contain the call to praise; 'For' in v. 4 introduces the central section (vv. 4–19), setting out the motivation for offering praise and declaring the greatness of God; and vv. 20–2 express the response of the congregation. The psalm contains the same number of verses as the letters of the Hebrew alphabet, and although it is not an acrostic, this probably is more than chance (cf. Lam 5). The kinship with acrostics is further seen in the great regularity in the length and metre of the verses of the psalm, and the lack of clear structure, reflected in the considerable variation in the way it has been set out (contrast NRSV, REB, and NIV). Instruction, exhortation, and beatitude mingle with the descriptions of God as creator and defender of his people (cf. vv. 8, 10–11, 12, 16–17 with 4–7, 9, 13–15, 18–19). God watches over those who trust in his love—the psalmist thinks of safety from death and famine. As with most of the psalms, the original setting is uncertain. The pre-exilic New Year Festival, worship in the second temple, and late synagogue worship have all been suggested.

The 'new song' (v. 3, cf. 96:1; 98:1; 149:1) hardly means that it was specially composed for this occasion. Perhaps it refers to the 'renewal' of the covenant, or the 'new' creation celebrated at the beginning of the year. Less probably it looks forward to the future age when God works 'new things' (Isa 42:10). More generally the praises of the eternal God are timelessly new. The seer picked up the phrase in Rev 5:9.

Psalm 34 This is another acrostic psalm. Two peculiarities link it with 25: both psalms lack a w verse and both end with an additional p verse. Despite the constraints of the acrostic, it has a clear structure: vv. 1–3 are a call to praise, vv. 4–10 express the psalmist's thanksgiving, and vv. 11–21 are closer to wisdom instruction.

The heading presents problems. If the reference to the incident in David's life recorded in 1 Sam 21:10–15 was added by a later editor it is odd that the name of the Philistine king is given as Abimelech and not Achish. Attempts at an explanation include the unlikely suggestions that Abimelech was the dynastic name, a royal title, or the Semitic name for Achish. The error is surely too blatant to be a simple scribal error, though it is surprising that it was not corrected later. Content of the psalm has little connection with the Achish incident, and some see the reason for the ascription in the occurrence of two similar Hebrew words in 1 Sam 21:13 (HB 21:14) (*ta'mô* 'behaviour') and the psalm (*ta'ămû*, v. 8, 'taste').

The central problem lies in the twin notes of thanksgiving and instruction, and decisions about its origin depend on which is taken as dominant. If thanksgiving, then some liturgical setting is required, though whether the links with wisdom place it within synagogue worship may be questioned. On the other hand, if the wisdom element is stressed it may be that a scribe took a thanksgiving psalm as the basis for his teaching.

It is easy to value the psalm lightly as expressing a superficial view of retribution. If, however, stress is placed upon the distress from which the psalmist has been delivered, it gives the psalmist authority to utter his teaching about God's goodness.

Psalm 35 Three times the psalmist utters a prayer for help (vv. 1–10, 11–18, 19–28), each time concluding with a vow to praise God. While some find here three originally separate psalms, the changes may reflect liturgical movement, and other analyses of the structure are possible. More difficult is to determine the occasion of the psalm and the identity of the 'enemies', and, as often, the presuppositions of the interpreter determine the interpretation. Some point to the military phraseology in vv. 1–3 and find here a king's prayer against his enemies, perhaps vassals who have supporters among the king's own people. Others note the allusions to witnesses, defence, and judgement in vv. 11, 23–4, 27 and describe the psalm as the petition of the falsely accused. Others again regard all such language as metaphorical, and prefer to take the psalm as a more general prayer to be used by any upon whom trouble has fallen, whether illness or more general misfortune (it is difficult to be more precise). In this case the enemies would be those within the village community who see the disasters that have befallen the psalmist as evidence that he has been abandoned by God, and an occasion to mock and take advantage of him.

Several features of the psalm are striking. 'I am your salvation' (v. 3) might be the type of priestly or prophetic oracle that many believe was given to the sufferer when he came to the sanctuary to pray. The appeals to God to help (vv. 1–3, 17, 22–4) are very forthright and strongly expressed, with bold, almost irreverent, imperatives. And the promises to offer thanksgiving and praise are both part of the appeal to God and an expression of the psalmist's own confidence.

Psalm 36 The divisions into which this psalm falls are strikingly clear: vv. 1–4 are a wisdom-type description of the wicked, vv. 5–9 praise God in a hymn, and vv. 10–12 are a prayer for help against evildoers. Some think that the sections are so distinct that three separate psalms have been combined. Others, noting the reference to the wicked in the first and last sections (although the only common term for those who are evil is 'wicked') take the whole psalm to be an individual lament, with the hymnic section as part of the appeal to God by stressing his faithfulness and righteousness. Those who link many of the psalms with the king, find here another of the royal psalms, though with somewhat less confidence than with many other psalms. The sparse use of the first person singular (only in v. 11; the Heb. has '*my* heart' in v. 1, but most follow a few Heb. MSS and the Syriac to read 'his', cf. NRSV 'their') has led some to give the psalm a communal reference, taking it as a national prayer, a view which links easily with the king as representative of the nation. How the psalm originated and in what situation it was used is quite uncertain. This, however, does not impair its religious value.

The text in several sections is corrupt. v. 1 begins with the noun *něʾum* that is frequently found at the end of oracles in the books of the prophets, where it is conventionally translated 'says the LORD' (e.g. Am 1:15). It is linked with transgression only here. (Is the idea that rebellion, personified, speaks to the wicked as YHWH speaks to the prophets?) Hence the emendation 'Transgression is *pleasant* to the wicked' has been proposed. The different translations of vv. 3 and 6–7 among the Eng. versions indicate the difficulty in interpreting the Hebrew words. NRSV has taken 'mountains of God' in v. 6 as 'mighty mountains', but since 'the great deep' is the primeval ocean in Gen 7:11 the psalmist may be using mythological ideas to stress the greatness of God's righteousness.

Psalm 37 The acrostic in this psalm has been preserved almost perfectly. In v. 28c the "*ayin*' verse is easily restored with the help of the LXX as 'The unrighteous will perish for ever' (cf. REB; NRSV has inserted an interpretative 'the righteous' absent from the Heb., contrast NIV). Since the pattern is two double-line (*stich*) verses to each letter of the alphabet, the longer vv. 14 and 20 are suspect, but there is no textual evidence to support deleting a line.

All agree that the psalm is related to wisdom teaching, some classifying it as a wisdom psalm which has no connection with the cult, others rejecting that it is by an individual and relating it in some way to liturgy, possibly, it has been suggested, within the synagogue (although those who make this connection usually date the rise of synagogues earlier than is often allowed now). The acrostic form tends to produce poems without any obvious structure, and the lack of agreement about how it is to be divided (vv. 1–7a, 7b–11, 12–15, 16–26, 27–33, 34–40, and 1–11, 12–20, 21–31, 32–40 are two proposals) indicates how difficult it is to find any progression of thought. Five themes may be singled out: a warning against

envying the prosperity of the wicked, certainty that the good prosper and the wicked will soon suffer disaster, faith that God is active in his world, the conviction that goodness is valuable in itself, and the practical aim of persuading the hearers to commit themselves to God. Especially striking are the frequent imperatives (vv. 1, 3, 4, 5, 7, 8, 27, 34, 37). While v. 25 might imply a superficial confidence in exactly proportioned reward and punishment, the fact that the psalmist feels a need to expound this teaching may point to the beginning of doubt, such as appears more strongly in Ps 49 and 73.

Psalm 38 Illness, sin, divine punishment, and the hostility of enemies and former friends dominate this psalm, which is one of the traditional penitential psalms of the Christian church. Confession is neither as central as that tradition suggests nor as plain as the NRSV translation 'I am sorry for my sin' (v. 18) appears to say (the verb means 'I am anxious, troubled', cf. REB, NIV). Nevertheless, sickness and sin are clearly related, as in the book of Job, and this sufferer accepts that he has sinned and that his illness is divine punishment.

The intensely personal tone has convinced many that this is the prayer of an individual sufferer. Others set it within the cult or some healing rite. If cultic the prayer may have been offered in the sanctuary by a friend or representative of the sufferer rather than in person; if a healing rite it may have been performed at home, perhaps in the presence of some religious expert.

The psalmist's friends, companions, and neighbours who distance themselves from him (v. 11) probably see his suffering as a proof that he has sinned. Who those are who seek his life (v. 12) is not clear. Perhaps they are only those who demand that he should be punished for the wrong he has done rather than 'enemies', although later the psalmist is more bitter against them (vv. 19–20; the emendation adopted by NRSV and REB is very plausible). Whether the psalmist's deafness and silence (vv. 13–14) are his refusal to answer the accusations of his enemies or represent his humility before God is uncertain.

'For the memorial offering' in the title is a possible interpretation of the Hebrew which is more literally 'to call to remembrance' and has been taken as 'to confess one's sins'. The Targum supports the reference to an offering; the LXX adds '[for remembrance] concerning sabbath'.

Psalm 39 To understand this poignant psalm it is necessary to remember the basic convictions of the psalmist. He believes that sickness is divine punishment for sin, and he has no hope of any life beyond the grave.

NRSV takes vv. 1–3 as the psalmist's musings—he tries to keep silent and avoid questioning God, but he finds no relief. At v. 4 he begins his prayer. It is unusual in individual laments to find wisdom-type references to the brevity of human life in general; here the psalmist's pessimism approaches that of Qoheleth. In vv. 7–10 he affirms his trust in God and reiterates his refusal to question him before making his plea for healing. Then after a renewed acceptance of retribution, he utters a further passionate prayer (vv. 11–13).

In v. 12 the psalmist describes himself as God's 'passing guest' and 'an alien' (NRSV). The translation carries false overtones. The Hebrew word, rendered 'sojourner' by the older translations in many of the legal passages (e.g. Deut

24:17–22), refers to the non-Israelite who has settled in the land. Lacking the protection of the head of the family, he was liable to be taken advantage of and oppressed. The laws single out the 'sojourner' as enjoying God's special protection, alongside other vulnerable persons, such as the fatherless and widows, and call upon the full members of the Israelite community to love them as themselves, remembering that they were 'sojourners' in Egypt (Lev 19:33–4; Deut 24:18, 22). The psalmist is putting himself under God's protection rather than stressing the brevity of his life.

As with Ps 38, the intensely personal character of this psalm has led some to regard a cultic setting as impossible. Those who think all the psalms have liturgical use compare somewhat similar laments in other countries of the ancient Middle East. Ultimately it has to be admitted that the origins of this psalm are lost to us.

Psalm 40 vv. 13–17 of this psalm recur as Ps 70. This, together with the sharp difference between the thanksgiving for deliverance in the first part of the psalm (vv. 1–10) and the plea for help in the second (vv. 11–17) suggests to many that two psalms have been combined. Others, however, treat the psalm as a unity, the thanksgiving leading into the petition. In support of this they point out that there are links in vocabulary between the two parts (cf. 'steadfast love' and 'faithfulness' in vv. 10 and 11), and that the division in Ps 40 does not coincide with the beginning of Ps 70, which looks like a fragment ('Be pleased', v. 13, is missing from the Heb. of Ps 70:1).

Royal maximalists include this psalm among the royal psalms, interpreting the ethical stress in vv. 6–8 as fitting an annual festival or an enthronement ceremony. The lament following expressions of God's favour would equally well suit a royal prayer in time of national distress, perhaps the attack of an enemy. Even if the psalm is taken as the prayer of an individual Israelite, a cultic background seems assured from the references to the 'great congregation' (vv. 9–10), the tone of bearing witness to past help from God, and the more general declaration of divine support for those who trust in YHWH, in the thanksgiving section.

The early Christians understood the psalm as messianic prophecy. vv. 6–8 are quoted in Heb 10:5–7 in the LXX version where the somewhat curious Hebrew 'ears you have dug for me' (NRSV 'you have given me an open ear') is replaced by 'you have prepared a body for me', which was then taken to be a reference to the incarnation. The origin of the LXX phrase is uncertain; it may have been internal Greek corruption (the Gk. words for 'ears' and 'body' are not too dissimilar, but could hardly have been confused except in a damaged MS) or a part of the body ('ears') may have been taken to represent the whole.

The apparent rejection of sacrifice in v. 6 is in line with some prophetic words (cf. Am 5:21–4), but the intention is probably to stress the greater importance of ethical obedience. The identification of 'the scroll of the book' (v. 7) is uncertain and suggestions are linked with the general view of the psalm that is taken: the document of the covenant demands presented to the king at his enthronement, the Torah with its laws that the individual accepts, and the heavenly record of the psalmist's deeds have been proposed.

Psalm 41 Sickness and enemies lie behind this psalm. Beyond this, interpretations vary widely. Although complaint and lament have a large place, some classify it as the thanksgiving of the individual, treating vv. 4–10 as a description of the illness from which the psalmist has been healed by God. Others hold that it is a prayer for healing; the confidence in vv. 1–3 expresses the psalmist's faith in wisdom-style language, and the concluding vv. 11–12 the 'certainty of hearing' found in several laments (e.g. Ps 6:8–10).

The setting of the psalm is equally debated. Royal maximalists ascribe it to the king. The care of the poor (v. 1) is a standard duty of the king, when the king is ill his enemies, even courtiers ('who ate of my bread', v. 9), are likely to plot against him, and the revenge of v. 10 is the common sequel to the defeat of such plots. Care of the destitute and orphans and the accusation that those who ate the writer's food raised up troops against him is found in the Egyptian Instruction of Amen-em-het. Others, however, see here family or village services in the home for those who are ill, the enemies being those friends and neighbours who regard the psalmist's illness as divine punishment. In vv. 7–8 there may even be a hint of sorcery and the belief that the psalmist is subject to a curse.

It is very probable that v. 13 is the closing doxology to the first book of the Psalter.

Psalms 42–3 This was almost certainly a single psalm, despite its division into two by both MT and LXX. Some Hebrew MSS join them together, although a few others add the title 'Of David' to Ps 43, where the LXX has 'A psalm of David'. The refrain (42:5, 11; 43:5; NRSV has slightly modified the end of Ps 42:5 to agree with the later forms, probably rightly), and similarities of thought and language across both psalms confirm their original unity.

Opinions on the nature of the psalm and the psalmist differ widely. The intensely personal descriptions, mood, and petitions persuade some that it comes from an individual Israelite poet, expressing his inner thoughts and feelings. Ps 42:6 has often been taken to show that the psalmist was living in the north of Israel, perhaps in exile, perhaps at home but too far from Jerusalem to go frequently to the temple. The references to the psalmist leading the festal procession in the temple (42:4) suggest to others that it is a royal psalm, sung either when the court was absent from Jerusalem, perhaps on a military campaign, or when the king was on the way to pay tribute to his overlord. If the references in 42:7 are mythical and the descent into Sheol figurative (the repetition of the exact phrase in Jon 2:3 points to this), the king may be seriously ill. Yet others place the psalm in the worship of postexilic Israel, as the Jews, suffering in the midst of a pagan empire, seek comfort and reassurance in a congregational liturgy. Whichever interpretation is adopted, the psalmist's eager longing for God, expressed in the simile of a deer searching for water in a barren desert (42:1–2), his memories of happier days in the past (42:4), and his delight in the temple worship (42:2, 4; 43:4) are plain to see. Like other psalmists he is not afraid to accuse God of forgetting him (42:9) and abandoning him (43:2). Yet hope remains and becomes the refrain. He prays that the day will come when he can once again worship God in Jerusalem (43:3–4).

Psalm 44 The kind of occasion on which this communal lament may have been sung can be found in 2 Chr 20. Israel has been defeated in battle. The people come to the temple in great distress, unable to understand why God has not given them victory and beseeching him to help them.

The first part of the prayer is almost a hymn (vv. 1–8), recalling the way God had defeated the Canaanites and given his people the land of Israel. The people proclaim their trust in God and not in their armies and their own weapons. The tone changes completely at v. 9. God has allowed them to be defeated, even to be killed and taken prisoner. Neighbouring peoples scoff at their humiliation. They reiterate their trust in God and deny that the defeat is punishment for any sin. With great boldness they call upon God to awake from sleep and save them.

The occasional singular verses (4, 6, 15) may indicate that this is another royal psalm, the king being the leader and representative of the nation. Some of the Church Fathers took the psalm to be messianic prophecy, and v. 22 is quoted in Rom 8:36.

Psalm 45 Although some have interpreted this as a popular wedding song in which the bridegroom and bride are addressed as king and queen, and others treat it as referring to YHWH's 'marriage' with Israel (cf. Isa 62:4–5), it is most probably a psalm for a royal wedding. Because 'the daughter of Tyre' in v. 12 was taken to refer to a Tyrian princess, some have linked it with Ahab's marriage to Jezebel (1 Kings 16:31) and seen it as a northern Israelite psalm, but the phrase may refer to the 'people of Tyre', as NRSV. It may, therefore, have been used regularly at royal weddings. Less likely is the suggestion that it is evidence for a 'sacred marriage' in the annual festivals at Jerusalem.

After an introduction (v. 1), the poet addresses first the king (vv. 2–9) and then the princess (vv. 10–15), finally promising to the king both sons who will become princely rulers, and world-wide fame (vv. 16–17).

From early times the psalm was regarded as messianic prophecy. The Targum paraphrased v. 2 as 'Thy beauty, O King Messiah, exceeds that of the children of men', and the writer to the Hebrews quotes vv. 6–7 to show the superiority of Jesus over the angels (Heb 1:8–9). In Christian liturgical tradition it is sung on Christmas Day.

The text is in disorder in a number of places, hence the different renderings by modern Eng. versions. The meaning of v. 6 has been hotly debated. The most natural way of taking the Hebrew is as NRSV, with the king addressed as God. Because this would be unique in the OT (although the future king of Isa 9:6 is called 'mighty god'), alternative ways of interpreting the Hebrew have been sought. The NRSV marg. is one possibility, another is 'Your throne is everlasting like that of God'.

Psalm 46 Three stanzas, each ending with a refrain (vv. 7, 11; it seems to have fallen out after v. 3) and 'Selâ', give this psalm a clear structure. Each section is marked by mythological features: the shaking of the earth, the river (akin to the river of Eden), YHWH as warrior. The divine name 'the Most High', probably rooted in Canaanite mythology (for the title 'the LORD of hosts', see PS H.5). There is no river in Jerusalem, only the spring of Gihon, but the idea, expressing the life-giving presence of God, was picked up frequently in the OT (cf. Isa 33:21; Ezek 47; Zech 14:8).

The psalm has been understood in four ways. (1) Historically, it has been linked with the failure of Sennacherib to capture Jerusalem in 701 BCE (2 Kings 18:9–19:36). (2) As cultic, it has been seen as part of the Jerusalem New Year Festival (v. 8 may call the worshippers to see the ritual drama). (3) Eschatologically, it has been treated as prophecy, looking forward to God's final salvation of Israel. (4) Liturgically it has been understood as part of the worship of post-exilic Judaism, the divine protection of Zion in past history or mythology providing assurance in the present. Of these the second seems most likely. There is insufficient detail to link it with any historical event, and while Zech 14 points to the use of cultic mythology in prophetic vision, it is more natural to see in the psalm the cult behind the prophecy rather than prophecy itself. The psalm has provided reassurance to anxious worshippers in the period after the Exile and beyond (Luther's great Reformation hymn, 'A safe stronghold our God is still', is based upon it), but this does not determine its origin.

NRSV has retained the traditional 'a very present help in trouble' (v. 1). The meaning is more probably, 'a well-proved help'. In v. 9 'shields' involves a change in the Hebrew vowels, and is widely accepted. MT has 'carts, wagons', a word which is never used of war-chariots.

The meaning of 'To Alamoth' in the title is completely unknown. Aquila and Jerome took it as 'young women', hence as sung by sopranos. The LXX has 'hidden things', i.e. religious mysteries. Another suggestion is that it is the name of the tune to which it was sung. In 1 Chr 15:20 the harpists play 'according to Alamoth'.

Psalm 47 This is the first of the 'enthronement psalms' (47; 93; 96–9; see PS E.5b, F.4). Its interpretation depends upon general conclusions about the existence of a New Year Festival at which YHWH was annually enthroned, the relation of this group of psalms to Deutero-Isaiah, the precise translation of the phrase 'God is king', whether a procession carrying the ark, symbol of YHWH, into the temple is implied by v. 5, the extent to which the allusion to the conquest of Canaan in vv. 3–4 emphasizes the covenant and controls the meaning rather than ideas of YHWH's enthronement, and how far ideas of a future divine rule are present. The dominant view today is that the psalm celebrates God's kingship at the New Year Festival, but there is less assurance that he was annually enthroned. In Christian tradition the psalm was linked to the celebration of the ascension, owing to v. 5 being taken as an ascent to heaven.

The structure is not entirely clear. NRSV accepts the 'Selâ' as marking a major break, and introduces another break at v. 7. Alternatively the renewed call to praise in v. 6 may be the beginning of the second section of the psalm.

The translation 'with a psalm' (v. 7) takes the word maskîl to be the same as that found in several psalm titles (e.g. Ps 32). Alternatively it may be verbal: 'to him who deals wisely', referring to God.

Psalm 48 This is the second of the Zion psalms (PS E.5a) and forms a pair with 46, praising God for his defence of Jerusalem. The main interpretations take it either historically, as the thanksgiving after the lifting of a siege by Israel's enemies, or within the cult, most probably as part of the New Year Festival. A few hold that it belongs to the worship of post-exilic Judaism.

vv. 1–3 express the praises of God and of his city, Jerusalem. The assembly, attack, and flight of the hostile kings who have come to seize the city is described in vv. 4–7. In vv. 8–9 the worshippers recall the deliverance they have witnessed and God's 'steadfast love' which secured it. Praise is again taken up in vv. 10–11, followed by a call to take good note of Zion so that the divine deliverance may be reported to future generations (vv. 12–14).

Probably 'in the far north' (v. 2) is mythological (cf. NIV 'Like the utmost heights of Zaphon'). At Ugarit ṣāpôn was the sacred mountain, the dwelling-place of the gods. The word does mean 'north' in Hebrew, but it is difficult to extract a satisfactory sense from it, despite attempts to show that Jerusalem was most beautiful when viewed from the north, that the psalm is really northern and does not refer to Jerusalem, or that it comes from the far south of Judah, from where Jerusalem would be in the north. Possibly the difficult closing words of the psalm express the same mythological ideas. NRSV has altered the vowels of MT to produce 'forever'. Others, with a small emendation, read 'According to Alamoth' (see the title of Ps 46), and take it as part of the title of Ps 49. With other vowels it may mean that YHWH is his people's leader and protector 'against Mot (death)', Baal's enemy in Ugaritic myths. Such use of mythology, together with what is apparently a religious procession in v. 12, and the claim to have 'pondered' (perhaps 'pictured', 'seen portrayed') these events *within* the temple, support the cultic interpretation of the psalm. No occasion when an enemy was defeated inside the city is known, and on a historical interpretation the procession would seem to be a tour of inspection after the enemy had retreated. The reference to the destruction of the 'ships of Tarshish' (probably Tartessus in Spain) may be a further indication that the ideas were taken over from Ugarit.

The LXX adds 'for the second day of the week' to the title, presumably indicating its place in the worship of the Jews in Egypt.

Psalm 49 This is usually described as a wisdom psalm, and there are similarities with the wisdom books both in theme and vocabulary. Nevertheless, it is included within the Psalter and may have been sung within the liturgy in post-exilic times. The imagery, e.g. death the shepherd (v. 14), and the contrast between the inability of humans to ransom their life and the divine ransom (vv. 6–7, 15), is striking.

The text is difficult and certainly corrupt in places (hence the many footnotes in all the Eng. versions). vv. 12 and 20 look like a refrain, but there are significant differences, retained only in NIV among recent translations. NRSV assimilates both to the form in v. 12, without a footnote, while REB emends both verses. The LXX reads both as: 'Man being in honour does not understand; he is compared to senseless animals and is like them.'

The poem consists of three parts: vv. 1–4: introduction; vv. 5–12: musing on universal death of rich as well as poor; vv. 13–20: confidence in divine 'ransom' from Sheol despite universal human mortality. If the differences between vv. 12 and 20 are significant, the second part of the psalm becomes yet more positive, distinguishing those with religious understanding from the impious rich.

The meaning of v. 15 is uncertain. Possibly the psalmist accepts the general OT belief that there is no life beyond death, and looks simply for God's protection from premature death. The overall sense of the psalm, however, with its contrast between the wealthy oppressors who are unable to 'ransom' their 'brother's' life, or perhaps their own (v. 7), and the divine 'ransom' suggests that here is a leap of faith: God will 'receive' the psalmist, perhaps in the same way that he 'took' (the same Heb. word) Enoch (Gen 5:24; cf. Elijah in 2 Kings 2).

Psalm 50 The links with prophecy are clear (see the judgement scene in Isa 1:2; Mic 1:2–4; 6:1–2; the teaching about sacrifice in Isa 1:10–15; Am 5:21–5; Mic 6:6–8; and the demands for righteousness in Isa 1:16–17, 21–6; Hos 4:1–3; Am 2:6–16; 5:24), suggesting to some that this psalm should be termed a 'prophetic liturgy', coming from a prophet within the regular cultic worship. Others propose a setting within the New Year Festival or posit a festival for the renewal of the covenant (cf. vv. 5, 16). Another view places the psalm in post-exilic Israel and terms it a levitical sermon.

The introduction depicts God coming in a majestic theophany, reminiscent of the appearance on Sinai (Ex 19:16–20), though now coming from the temple in Zion, and calling heaven and earth as witnesses in his lawsuit against his people Israel (vv. 1–6). The rest of the psalm falls into two parts. vv. 7–15 proclaim, with mocking irony, that God rejects sacrifice that is not offered in the right spirit. It is unlikely that ideas of sacrifice as food for the gods still survived openly in Israel, but the psalmist recalls the people to more spiritual ideas: the call in v. 14 is probably to offer a 'thanksgiving sacrifice', rather than to substitute thanksgiving for animal offerings. vv. 16–21 move on to a demand for righteousness. Stealing, adultery, and slander in vv. 18–19 bring to mind the Ten Commandments, but the phrasing is different and it is unlikely that they are a direct call to obey the Decalogue. The two final verses are akin to the curses and blessings found e.g. in Deut 28. v. 23 must express the same sense as v. 14: 'He who sacrifices thank-offerings honours me', NIV.

Running right through the psalm is a sense of the majesty of God, from the initial piling up of 'The mighty one, God, YHWH' (the Heb. could be equally well rendered 'YHWH, the greatest God'), through the imagery of the theophany and God's power as creator and owner of the universe, to the final threat of punishment and promise of salvation.

Psalm 51 The title links this, the greatest of the penitential psalms of the church, with the David and Bathsheba story (2 Sam 11–12). Although some attempt to justify this ascription, and others think that it was composed with David's sin in mind, it is more probable that the editor was led to make the connection because he thought it was generally suitable and noted certain similarities of language. Proposed settings for the psalm include penitential rites within the Jerusalem New Year Festival performed by the king as representative of the nation, corporate confession by survivors of the destruction of Jerusalem in 586 BCE, and early synagogue worship. The use of 'your holy spirit' and priestly sin and atonement language perhaps point to a date after the Exile.

Appeals for divine forgiveness, cleansing, and renewal (vv. 1–2, 6–12) lead into confession (vv. 3–5), joyful thanksgiving (v. 8, cf. v. 12), vows (vv. 13–15), and the acknowledge-ment that God desires contrition rather than sacrifice (vv. 16–17). vv. 18–19, with their prayer to God to rebuild the walls of Jerusalem and, in an apparent reversal of vv. 16–17, declaration that God will then delight in animal sacrifices, are often considered a later addition to the psalm. Some of those who link it with the pre-exilic temple cult accept an original unity, treating the rebuilding of the walls as simply strengthening them and interpreting vv. 16–17 as asserting no more than that God does not accept sacrifice without true penitence as sufficient in itself for atonement; once the people are penitent God will again delight in their offerings.

The psalm is notable for its deep understanding of sin and forgiveness. The psalmist realizes that all wrongdoing is sin against God and that the most serious consequence of sin is alienation from him, not any punishment that the sinner may receive. He knows that repentance requires not only knowledge of wrongdoing but also knowledge of God's grace (v. 1). Then repentance will not be a gloomy thing but full of gladness.

v. 5 has had a long, unhappy history of misunderstanding as providing evidence for original sin and the 'sinfulness' or impurity of sexual intercourse. Since ancient Israel rejoiced in marriage and the birth of children, this is hardly likely to be the true meaning. Rather the psalmist acknowledges that he belongs to a sinful race, and confesses the depth of the sinfulness he feels.

Psalm 52 The genre and background of this psalm are uncertain, and the text in vv. 1–2, 7, 9 is difficult. The title, with its reference to 1 Sam 22:9, is an example of the way the editor has searched the stories about David in the books of Samuel to discover suitable occasions for the composition of a number of the Davidic psalms. The psalm fits the narrative badly, since Doeg is an informer rather than a liar.

vv. 1–4 address the evildoer, v. 5 appears to express confidence that God will punish him, though it can be read as a prayer, and this confidence is continued in vv. 6–7. In vv. 8–9 the psalmist expresses his trust in God's steadfast love and concludes with a vow.

Those adopting a maximalist position on royal psalms explain this psalm as the king's speech to a powerful enemy, perhaps in the style of mockery before the actual combat. The 'righteous' and 'faithful' in vv. 6 and 9 may be the king's supporters. Others describe it as the prayer of a man accused by a perjured witness, even as a curse uttered against the wicked man before he is expelled from the community. Yet others link it with wisdom teaching, and see it as communal instruction. The denunciation is similar to that of the prophets (cf. Isa 22:15–19), and the psalm may have come from one of the prophets employed in the temple. If the main emphasis is placed upon vv. 5–9 the psalm may be taken as a thanksgiving after a slanderer has been discovered and condemned. With such obscurity about its nature and origins, the psalm may belong to any period of Israelite history.

The attitudes of the psalmist are hardly fitting for Christian worship, yet the psalm expresses divine judgement upon evil, bears witness against the sins of lying and slander, and is suffused with trust in God.

Psalm 53 This psalm appears to be a variant of Ps 14. The general interpretation is given there, but a few additional points need to be added.

Two extra phrases appear in the title: 'A *Maskîl [of David]*', found in the group of psalms 52–5 and '*according to Mahalath*', which may refer to a flute accompaniment or a flute-playing ceremony, or be the name of a melody. Another suggestion is that it is a reference to illness. *Mahalath* occurs only here and in Ps 88 (as *Mahalath Leannoth*, perhaps meaning 'to humiliate', i.e. for penitence), and while illness is appropriate there, it is not in Ps 53.

The differences in the text between the two psalms are relatively small, apart from the substitution of 'Elohim' for YHWH (a feature of this group of Elohistic psalms), and v. 6, where Ps 14 reads: 'There they shall be in great terror, | for God is with the company of the righteous. | You would confound the plans of the poor, | but God is their refuge.' The attention is focused on the destruction of the wicked in Ps 53, but on God's protection of the poor in Ps 14. This suggests that the two traditions developed independently and that different factors influenced them. If the differences are purely textual, the state of the Hebrew text in the Psalter is worse than is commonly supposed.

Psalm 54 Here, as with Ps 52, the close resemblance of the historical part of the title to 1 Sam 23:19—almost a direct quotation—points to an editor searching through the historical books for a suitable setting for the psalm.

Here, as always, the interpreter's presuppositions determine the description of the psalm. Those who believe that a number of psalms were prayers against false accusations, perhaps linked with an ordeal, the taking of an oath, or an appeal to the 'higher court' of the temple, find support in v. 1 with its 'vindicate me'. A royal perspective finds foreign enemies or cultic opponents in the 'strangers' (v. 3; NRSV emends to 'the insolent'), 'the ruthless' (v. 3), and 'enemies' (v. 5), and supports this as the prayer of the king before battle or in a cultic drama by the appeal to God as personal saviour, and the covenant 'faithfulness' (v. 5). Others more generally describe it as the lament, prayer, or complaint of an individual.

From appeal (vv. 1–2) the psalmist moves to description of the danger facing him (v. 3), and on to confidence in God (vv. 4–5). Finally the psalmist promises to sacrifice a free-will offering, the one sacrifice which expressed the voluntary gratitude of a thankful heart (vv. 6–7, another example of the 'certainty of hearing').

Psalm 55 Several unique words of uncertain meaning, textual problems, doubt about the tenses in some verses, sudden changes of thought, and an alternation between a single enemy and groups of oppressors (somewhat obscured in NRSV) make this a difficult psalm to understand. It is commonly taken to be the prayer of an individual. Those attracted to royal interpretations ascribe it to the king, beset by foreign enemies and hostility within his own city, and with the head of a neighbouring state now become his adversary. The wider corruption depicted in the psalm may indicate that it is a prayer for the community, but the intense individuality found especially in vv. 4–8, 12–14 makes this less likely.

After an appeal to be heard (vv. 1–2a), the psalmist describes his anguish (vv. 2b–5; the verse division of NRSV is probably right). He has contemplated flight (vv. 6–8), for the city is full of violence, and he utters a curse (vv. 9–11: it may be that poetically 'violence and strife' are depicted as going round the walls, whether as watchmen or demons, but the subject of the verb may revert to the evildoers). Even his close friend has turned against him (vv. 12–14), and the psalmist utters a renewed curse (v. 15). Taking up his complaint, this time with greater confidence (vv. 16–19), he once again reverts to the treachery of his friend (vv. 20–1). In v. 22 he may recall the assurance of a temple prophet, and he closes the psalm with fresh trust in God who will destroy his enemies (v. 23).

Verses of great beauty (cf. 6–7, 16, 22) may appear to be immersed within desires for vindictive revenge, but the psalmist is concerned for righteousness and faithfulness, and it is this which determines the overall tone of the psalm.

Psalm 56 This is another prayer for help against enemies. Beyond that little can be said for certain. There seems small reason to class it with the prayers of those falsely accused, though some have proposed this. Those who ascribe many psalms to royal rites interpret the 'peoples' of v. 7 as foreign enemies, find references to national war in vv. 1–2, 9, and regard the vows and thank-offerings (v. 12) as particularly suitable for the king. They link the references to 'death' and the 'light of life' (v. 13) to royal imagery, perhaps related to a cultic drama. Alternatively it has been suggested that the psalm comes from one of the Jews of the dispersion who had to face anti-Semitism.

The similarities between vv. 4 and 10–11 may point to a division into two stanzas, with a concluding section vv. 12–13. But the certainty of hearing seems to begin at v. 9, which cuts across this scheme.

Special interest attaches to the title. The editor who linked Davidic authorship with events recorded in the historical books related the psalm to David's flight to Gath in 1 Sam 21:10–15. NRSV's 'according to The Dove on Far-off Terebinths' involves a change in the vowels of MT, which appears to mean 'a dove of silence, distant ones'. The phrase is a reference to a melody, although it has been explained as a reference to a dove sent into the distant desert, rather like the scapegoat of Lev 16:20–2. The LXX has 'for the people far off from the holy places (or holy people)', while the Targum reads 'concerning the congregation of Israel, which is compared to a silent dove at the time when they were far from their cities, and turned again and praised the Lord of the world'. Both of these show that in later tradition the psalm was treated as a national psalm spoken by the personified people.

Psalm 57 vv. 7–11 recur in Ps 108:1–5, and this, together with the change of theme between vv. 1–6 (a prayer for deliverance from enemies) and 7–11 (a confident thanksgiving which almost turns into a hymn), has suggested to some that two psalms have been combined. Against this is the refrain in vv. 5 and 11, and the probability that Ps 108 is a liturgical combination of psalmic pieces (108:6–13/Ps 60:5–12).

Some interpret this psalm as an individual lament (with the certainty of hearing having a more prominent place than usual), an individual thanksgiving (the first part describing the dangers from which the psalmist has been saved), or the prayer of a man falsely accused (who may have spent the night in the temple precincts while awaiting the decision on his

case, cf. 'I will awake the dawn', v. 8). Others see it as a royal psalm, the shelter of God's 'wings' (v. 1) and the divine title 'elyôn ('God Most High', v. 2) linking it with the Jerusalem temple, while 'steadfast love' and 'faithfulness' (vv. 3, 10) reflect God's covenant with the king. On this last view the reference to the king's 'glory' (v. 8; NRSV translates as 'my soul') perhaps indicates casting off his ritual humiliation. The title shows that the editor linked the psalm with the stories in 1 Sam 22–4.

Psalm 58 This psalm does not easily fit into any of the main categories. The dominant theme is confidence that YHWH's justice will prevail over present evil. An obscure text, which is probably corrupt (all the modern translations introduce some emendations) makes the details uncertain. A major difficulty is a word in v. 1 which appears to mean 'silence' (cf. RV 'Do you indeed in silence speak righteousness', apparently meaning that the judges or rulers fail to maintain justice). The LXX and Jerome read it as 'but', hardly possible in the context. Most change the vowels to read 'gods' (cf. Ps 82), either the lesser gods charged by YHWH with maintaining justice in the world, or the rulers, who are acting wickedly instead of upholding the law. The psalm is commonly regarded as a communal lament, but it is unusual to begin with an address to those who are causing the evils to which the righteous are being subjected. The description of the wicked in vv. 3–5 has suggested to some that it is instruction, perhaps given in the synagogue alongside the reading of the law, but there is little evidence for this. The calls for fierce punishment in vv. 6–9 (akin to the prophetic invective of Ps 52) and the rejoicing of the righteous when they see vengeance being taken (vv. 10–11) strike the modern reader as brutal. Attempts to soften the harshness include stressing the social situation where evil appears to call into question God's authority and justice, the need in ancient Israel for justice to be vindicated in the present world, the danger of divine punishment on the covenant community when the covenant laws are flagrantly broken, and the use of curses as a protection and a way of affirming the covenant demands (see PS J.2–8).

Psalm 59 This vigorous plea for the destruction of the psalmist's enemies has been interpreted in several different ways. The least likely is that it is the prayer of the man who has been accused of some wrong, despite the protests of innocence in vv. 3–4. The clear references to foreign enemies (the word translated 'nations' in v. 5 is rarely used of Israel) and the general impression of hostile attacks in war possibly point to national prayer. This could be incorporated in a royal psalm, where the king is the leader and representative of his people and the one against whom the enemy's attacks are primarily directed. Royal covenant ideas, such as steadfast love and fidelity (vv. 10, 16, 17), are noted by those who champion this interpretation.

The structure is not clear. What might appear as two refrains (vv. 6–7, 14–15, and 9, 17) have differences in wording that are hardly textual errors, and they do not divide up the psalm in any very obvious way, as an outline reveals: petition (vv. 1–2), description of the ambush (v. 3ab), declaration of innocence (vv. 3c–4a), renewed appeal (vv. 4b–5), comparison of the enemies as scavenging dogs (vv. 6–7), declaration of confidence that God will give victory over the enemies whom he holds in derision (vv. 8–10), plea for the destruction of the enemies (vv. 11–13, with some ambiguity as to whether the enemies are to be totally destroyed or simply weakened), repeated refrain (vv. 14–15), and a vow to offer praise or a closing thanksgiving (vv. 16–17).

The editor perhaps linked the psalm to the incident in 1 Sam 19:11–17 (part of v. 11 is quoted in the title) because the psalmist says he is surrounded by enemies who lie in wait for him.

Psalm 60 Although part of this psalm (vv. 5–12) is repeated in Ps 108:6–13, there is no reason to suppose that it is not a unity. It is usually classed as a corporate lament. The Israelites have been defeated in battle, and they express their complaint to God and pray for future victory in vv. 1–5. Then the divine promise of conquests is expressed, perhaps by a prophet, a section notable for the listing of parts of Israel and neighbouring lands over which God is to be sovereign (vv. 6–8). Complaint and petition are resumed in vv. 9–11, and the psalm ends with an expression of confidence that God will give his people victory (v. 12). The belief that military defeat was due to God's anger or rejection was common in the ancient world: King Mesha of Moab expresses similar sentiments on the Moabite stone: 'Chemosh [the Moabite god] was angry with his land' and allowed Omri to oppress Moab.

The title links it with 2 Sam 8:3–14 (cf. 10:6–14) but the details differ and since the account in 2 Samuel describes only victories the ascription is hardly apt, unless a previous defeat is assumed. The places mentioned in vv. 6–7 lie mainly, though not exclusively, in the area of northern Israel (Ephraim and Manasseh were the chief tribes). Moab, Edom, and the Philistines (vv. 8–9) were Israel's traditional enemies, who had been defeated by David. Hostility towards Edom increased after the fall of Jerusalem in 586 BCE, when the Edomites encroached on Israelite territory, hence many place the psalm after that date. 'Lily of the Covenant' (or 'Lily of Testimony') is probably the name of the melody to which the psalm is to be sung, though it has been suggested that it refers to using lilies as a means of divination.

Psalm 61 Despite the explicit reference to the king in vv. 6–7 those who restrict the number of royal psalms to a minimum regard this as the prayer of an individual Israelite, who includes among his petitions a plea on behalf of the king, such as is found in some Babylonian prayers. (There is little reason to suppose that the verses are a later interpolation.) Royal maximalists describe it as the king's psalm, and explain the reference to the king in the third person by pointing to similar changes from first to third persons in an inscription from King Yehawmilk of Byblos, arguing that the manner of speech is a way of stressing the privileges granted to the king, here long life and perhaps continued prosperity for his dynasty ('to all generations').

Despite some difficulties in the Hebrew text, the general sense is fairly clear. A plea to God for protection is linked with a promise to sing continual praise and pay daily vows. Unusually there is little indication of the dangers from which the psalmist is seeking deliverance. 'From the end of the earth' (v. 2) has been variously interpreted as showing that the psalmist was an exile, that the king was on a distant campaign, or even that the writer of the psalm depicted himself as at the

entrance of Sheol. The references to God's 'tent' and the 'shelter of your wings' (v. 4) may refer to the Jerusalem temple.

Psalm 62 Royal maximalists treat this as a king's psalm, pointing to the references to God as 'my rock', 'my salvation', and 'my fortress' (vv. 2, 6), seeing in v. 3 a warning by the king, noting the exhortations to the people in vv. 8–10, and finding behind vv. 11–12 a divine oracle given to him. Others classify it as a psalm of confidence, even one of the clearest examples of this genre, with trust in God expressed in vv. 1–2, 5–8, 11–12; they explain the remaining verses, which describe attacks by enemies and teach the insignificance of human power and wealth, as a foil to this assured faith. The suggestion that the psalmist has taken refuge from his enemies in the temple, which some infer from vv. 2, 6, 7, seems rather precarious.

The almost exact repetition of vv. 1–2 in 5–6 sounds like a refrain. It has been suggested that it marks off the first, more personal, part of the psalm (vv. 1–7); 'Selâ' would then be misplaced, and vv. 8–12 would form the second part, which adopts a more direct teaching stance and contains language and ideas that are akin to wisdom. This does not mean that two psalms have been combined, for the note of trust is maintained throughout.

Psalm 63 Although confidence appears to dominate this psalm, most class it as an individual lament, largely due to the opening verses. Who the psalmist is and what called forth his prayer are far from certain. The reference to the sanctuary (v. 2) and to the liars who seek his life (vv. 9, 11) may point to criminal accusations from which the psalmist seeks to clear himself by an appeal to the higher court, through an ordeal, by uttering an oath of innocence, or by a divine oracle. The mention of the king in v. 11 does not necessarily make it a royal psalm, for the psalmist may include the king in his prayer (cf. Ps 61:6), but some features support this interpretation: the opening words may indicate the close covenant relationship with God that the king enjoys, vv. 9–10 perhaps refer to a battle with the slain left to be eaten by jackals, and the confident language, including references to God's steadfast love and protection, are thought by some to be more suitable in the mouth of a king than of an ordinary Israelite.

Tenses present some uncertainties, as variations between the Eng. versions show. Are vv. 9–10 an expression of what will happen to the enemies or should they be taken as a prayer (so REB)?

What incident in the life of David the editor had in mind is less clear than in some other psalms. 'When he was in the Wilderness of Judah' may refer to David's flight from Absalom (2 Sam 15–16), but the time when Saul was pursuing David has also been suggested (1 Sam 23:14; 24:2).

Psalm 64 Problems with the tenses in vv. 7–9 make the interpretation of this psalm difficult. The verbs would normally be translated as a description of past events. If this is adopted, the whole of vv. 2–9 is an account of the actions of the evildoers and the punishment which God has inflicted on them, and the psalm would be an individual thanksgiving, or a testimony to divine judgement. v. 1, however, looks like the introduction to a lament. If the psalm is treated as such a prayer for deliverance from the enemies, it would be most natural to see vv. 7–9 as an expression of confidence in the protection which God is going to give to the psalmist, and to translate the verbs as future (so NRSV; REB gives the same sense with presents and futures), either treating the tense as 'perfect of certainty' or making slight changes in the vowels. A third possibility is to regard the verbs as expressing a wish or prayer ('precative perfect'), in which case the petition of v. 1 is picked up at the end of the psalm, after the description of the activities of the psalmist's enemies.

The metaphors in vv. 2–5 appear to point to slander, false accusations, or, possibly, curses or spells. They hardly refer to foreign enemies, and it is unlikely that they are to be taken literally, as if the psalmist's enemies were planning to mug him. This does not make their attacks any less fearsome, however, since the ancient Israelites regarded words as possessing their own power to achieve what was spoken (Isaac could not recall or alter the blessings which he had mistakenly pronounced upon Jacob, Gen 27).

Psalm 65 This psalm is commonly associated with harvest thanksgiving, possibly due to the overtones which 'you crown the year' (v. 11) has in English and the references to the flocks and grain in v. 13. It may have been a hymn of praise sung at the Feast of Booths (Tabernacles), but the emphasis upon the rains (though a feature of the Autumn Festival) may indicate that it belonged earlier in the agricultural year, perhaps at the beginning of the barley harvest (at the Feast of Unleavened Bread), or simply looking forward to the promise of a future plenty now that the rains have come. Others have suggested that it was intended as thanksgiving after a time of drought when the crops had begun to grow again (cf. 1 Kings 8:35–6; the linking of lack of rain and sin may be reflected in v. 3).

The three sections of the psalm are clearly defined: vv. 1–4, praise to God who answers prayer and forgives sin; vv. 5–8, a hymn to God, the mighty creator, which is rich in mythological ideas; and vv. 9–13, containing references to the rains and the harvest. The verbs, especially in vv. 11–13, present difficulties. The Eng. versions use English present tenses, describing the rains and the fruitfulness which God has given. The LXX took many of the verbs as imperatives and others as futures, thus making the psalm a prayer for forgiveness and a good harvest.

There seems no reason to think that the sections form separate psalms, as some have supposed. Praise, forgiveness, creation, and present providence fit easily together, especially when it is remembered that in ancient Israel creation was viewed as a recurring annual event, when God once again overcame the raging waters and secured the order of the world for another year.

Psalm 66 This psalm divides into three sections: vv. 1–7 are a hymn of praise to God in which the crossing of the Red Sea and the Jordan are referred to (v. 6; if 'the river' is parallel to 'the sea' the whole verse speaks of the Exodus deliverance); vv. 8–12 are a national thanksgiving for some more recent deliverance from foreign conquest; and vv. 13–20 are in the form of the thanksgiving of an individual, coming to the temple with sacrifices in payment of vows he had made when he was in distress.

Several different interpretations have been offered. (1) It may be that an editor has combined three originally separate psalms (or two, if vv. 1–12 originally formed one hymn of national thanksgiving). (2) An individual psalmist may have prefaced his own thanksgiving with hymns drawn from the temple worship, or the first two parts come from a temple festival within which the individual's thanksgiving was recited. (3) The whole psalm is national, the 'I' of the last part being Israel. (4) It is a royal psalm, in which the communal hymn and thanksgiving finds its focus in the king's thanksgiving. The last of these reconstructions has the advantage of explaining the large number of sacrifices offered, which otherwise has to be regarded as poetic exaggeration (v. 15), as well as providing a setting for the whole psalm taken as a unity, but it still leaves unresolved whether the psalm was originally sung at some festival commemorating the Exodus and Conquest, perhaps at Gilgal, was part of the annual New Year Festival, or was a liturgy of thanksgiving after victory against foreign enemies.

Psalm 67 The meaning of the Hebrew tenses presents great difficulties for the interpretation of this psalm, as a glance at the ways the Eng. versions translate v. 6 shows. NRSV takes the first Hebrew verb in its natural sense: 'The earth has yielded its increase'. On this view the psalm is a thanksgiving for the harvest. The verb in the second line of the verse, however, would not normally be translated 'God has blessed us' (NRSV), but rather as 'God will bless us' or 'may God bless us'. Moreover, exactly the same verb is used in v. 7a, so that there is little justification for the NRSV's 'May God continue to bless us' there, and the verbs in the rest of the psalm are most naturally taken as expressing prayers or wishes.

The refrain in vv. 3 and 5 divides the psalm into three sections, the first two being broadly parallel, seeking God's favour and salvation, leading to joy among all the nations as they see God's blessing—a universalism that is somewhat rare in the Psalter. It is against this background that the two final verses have to be interpreted. It would produce consistency if the anomalous verb were taken as a petition, 'May the earth yield its harvest', a possible sense for this tense. An alternative view is that it expresses a repeated experience, represented by a present tense in English, 'The earth yields its increase', forming the basis for the petitions in vv. 6b, 7a, which should be taken as 'May God continue to bless us'. NIV treats all the verbs in vv. 6, 7 as future, with 'has yielded' taken as a 'prophetic perfect' and expressing confidence that the prayer of the earlier sections of the psalm will be answered. This is possibly best of all.

Psalm 68 This is the most difficult of the psalms and the space available here is quite insufficient to offer a detailed discussion. The problems arise from the large number of words which are found only here in the OT, the difficulties in determining the meaning of the tenses, probable textual corruption in many verses, the lack of clear structure and sequence of thought, uncertainty as to the meaning of some phrases even where the words and surface translation are fairly obvious, and ignorance of the way the psalm was used in ancient Israel. A comparison between the Eng. versions shows up the difficulty of understanding the meaning very clearly.

The first words appear to be a quotation from Num 10:35, though not exact, and some believe that the author of Numbers used cultic material such as is found in the psalm. Here they can be translated in at least four ways: 'O that God would arise and his enemies be scattered', 'God will arise . . . ', 'God arises . . . ', 'When God arises his enemies are [or will be] scattered'. The similarities with Num 10:35, together with the vivid account of 'solemn processions' in vv. 24–5, have often been taken to show that the psalm accompanied a procession carrying the ark in the Autumn Festival. Other possible settings are as a battle song, or a ritual at Gihon or Mount Tabor. The disjointed nature of the psalm, however, has led others to suppose that several different psalm fragments have been combined, even that it is a kind of index in which the opening verses of a large number of poems are listed. Many of the ideas reflect the myths of other religions in the ancient Middle East, such as the accounts of YHWH riding on the clouds, as Baal did, the giving of rains, the defeat of 'Death', and battle scenes (at Ugarit the goddess Anat waded in the blood of her defeated enemies). These are intertwined with themes derived from the historical traditions of Israel: the Sinai theophany, the wilderness wanderings, victories over Israel's enemies, and the confederation of tribes (though only four are named in v. 27).

If an attempt is made to treat the psalm as a unity, it may be divided into eight sections: vv. 1–3, God victorious over his enemies; vv. 4–6 God, the protector of the needy; vv. 7–14, God's victory (with reminiscences of the Song of Deborah in Judg 5); vv. 15–18 (or 20), YHWH's choice of Zion as his dwelling; vv. 19 (21)–23, God's victory brings salvation to his people; vv. 24–7, a description of the procession; vv. 28–31, the subject peoples bring gifts and submit to YHWH; vv. 32–5, a triumphant hymn of praise to God.

Psalm 69 This psalm has some similarities with Ps 22, and both are quoted frequently in the NT (cf. Jn 15:25 (v. 4); Jn 2:17; Rom 15:3 (v.9); Jn 19:28–9 (v. 21); Rom 11:9–10 (vv. 22–3); Acts 1:20 (v. 25)). vv. 1–29 are a plea for help, while vv. 30–6 read like a hymn of thanksgiving and praise. The change of tone and form is often regarded as indicating the expression of a favourable oracle or some other sign that God has heard the psalmist's prayer, but some see the final verses as an attempt to fit an earlier psalm into the post-exilic situation.

The background to the psalm is uncertain. The reference to the waters reaching up to the psalmist's neck (v. 1, cf. 14–15) probably indicates severe illness in which he feels that he has almost sunk down into Sheol. More prominent are the accounts of enemies (vv. 4, 9–12, 14, 18, 19–21; even his family are estranged, 8), followed by the psalmist's curses on them (vv. 22–8). Perhaps they believe that he is being punished by God. It may be, therefore, that this is the prayer composed for those who are sick, to be offered by the sufferer, or on his behalf, in the temple. Those who believe that many of the psalms are to be ascribed to the king point to communal aspects, the lofty position which the psalmist appears to hold, and the psalmist's plea as that of the nation's representative. The curses are felt to be appropriate to the royal office. To regard restoring what he did not steal (v. 4) as a reference to the payment of reparations after military defeat seems to be going beyond the natural sense of the verse: the enemies are more naturally taken as fellow Israelites, most probably members of the psalmist's own village or small town. Others include the psalm among the prayers of those accused of some crime, connected with an ordeal, an appeal to the higher court in the temple, or part of an oath ceremony, but this does not seem to fit the overall mood of the psalm.

It is impossible to explain the curses in vv. 22–8 as a quotation of the words of the psalmist's opponents, since they are addressed to more than one person, and they have to be accepted with their full force as what the psalmist wished upon his enemies (see PS J.2–8).

Psalm 70 This psalm repeats Ps 40:13–17, and most treat it simply as a doublet, the minor differences in the text being due either to corruption or deliberate alteration. Opinion is divided between taking Ps 70 as the original, which has been combined with another psalm to form a liturgy in Ps 40, and treating Ps 40 as the earlier psalm, possibly a royal psalm, vv. 13–17 here being offered as a short plea for the use of ordinary Israelites. The lack of 'Be pleased' in Ps 70:1 (NRSV adds it) perhaps favours the second view, but it is possible that 'make haste' serves both halves of the verse (as REB and NIV, despite their different renderings in the two parts, 'Make haste'/'Hasten' and 'come quickly'). The LXX takes the first line as part of the title, rendering it very literally, 'that the Lord may save me'.

As it stands, Ps 70 is a terse and urgent prayer for God's help to save the psalmist from enemies who wish to harm, even kill him.

Psalm 71 In the first two books of the Psalter there are four psalms which lack a title, this being one. Of the others the LXX joins 9 and 10, which the acrostic confirms, and the refrain links 42 and 43. Whether 70 and 71 were treated as one psalm is uncertain. Some Hebrew MSS join the two psalms, but the LXX provides a title for Ps 71: 'By David, of the sons of Jonadab and the first ones taken captive'.

vv. 9, 17–18 suggest that the psalmist is an old man. The distress from which he seeks relief may be severe illness and the approach of death (v. 20), and, as so often in the psalms, his 'enemies' assert that God has abandoned him (v. 11). He speaks of the faith in God which has sustained him all his life (vv. 5–6, cf. 17), prays that God will not reject him (v. 9), and asks for renewed health (vv. 20–1) and the discrediting of his enemies (v. 13, cf. v. 4). Then he will renew his praises (vv. 14–16, 22–4).

Royal maximalists interpret it as the king's psalm, perhaps towards the end of his reign, when there are attempts to supplant him. They point to the close relationship with God that the psalmist affirms, and see royal declarations in his witness to God's salvation (vv. 15, 18) and his praises. Other speculations are that the psalm is a call for protection from impending danger, the prayer of one who has fled to the sanctuary (cf. vv. 1–3), and a plea by faithful Israelites in the post-exilic community. If, however, the references to old age are given primary emphasis, the psalm appears to be much more the work of an individual poet than a liturgical piece for repeated use.

A feature of the psalm is the frequent allusion to other psalms, even almost direct quotation (e.g. vv. 1–3/Ps 31:1–3; vv. 5–6/Ps 22:9–10; v. 11 (NRSV reverses the clauses)/Ps 22:1; vv. 12–13/Ps 35:22; 38:21; 40:13–14; v. 24/Ps 35:4, 26; 40:14). Might it be that the elderly psalmist strengthens his faith and expresses his petition through well-known and greatly loved psalms?

Psalm 72 The obvious reference to the king secures agreement among the commentators that this is a royal psalm. Differences appear only when the original setting is considered. The marked idealism suggests to many that it is appropriate for the king's coronation or enthronement, though it may have been sung at the annual celebration of his accession. Key themes are the just rule which the king will exert, especially in his care for the poor and oppressed (vv. 1–2, 4, 12–14), and the prosperity which his righteousness will bring to his people (vv. 3, 6–7, 16), together with the submission of foreign nations, who will bring tribute (vv. 8–11, 15).

As with many psalms, the tenses prove troublesome. The LXX treats them all as future apart from vv. 3a, 17a. NRSV and REB regard vv. 2–11, 15–17 as prayers or wishes, with vv. 12–14 as descriptive and providing the grounds for the favour which God shows to him and his people, and this may well be right. NIV keeps futures apart from vv. 15–17a, perhaps from conservatism, since AV has future tenses throughout, but possibly because it takes the psalm as messianic prophecy. It was treated as messianic in Jewish and early Christian tradition, the Targum paraphrasing v. 1 as 'O God, give the precepts of thy judgement to King Messiah, and thy righteousness to the son of king David', and v. 17 as 'His name shall be remembered for ever; and before the sun existed his name was prepared; and all peoples shall be blessed in his merits'. It is never quoted in the NT, however, though at an early period it was adopted as the special psalm for Epiphany.

The ascription to Solomon in the title, found also in Ps 127, may have been suggested to the editor by vv. 1, 10, 15 (cf. 1 Kings 10:1–10, 22). In the LXX the form is different from the common 'Of David' normally expressed, and possibly 'for Solomon' rather than 'by Solomon' was intended—a Davidic psalm which he composed for Solomon.

It is generally agreed that vv. 18–19 are a doxology at the end of Book 2 of the Psalter and are not an integral part of the psalm. For v. 20 see PS D.4.

Psalm 73 This psalm has some affinities with the wisdom writings, but its strongly personal tone and references to the temple have led many to hesitate about classing it simply as a wisdom psalm. Possible genres range from an individual lament or thanksgiving, a meditation or psalm of confidence, to a royal psalm. While a case can be made out for the last (Israel is mentioned in v. 1 (NRSV emends), v. 15 seems to imply that the speaker is someone in authority, the intimate trust in God is suitable for a king, the evildoers, probably apostate Israelites, might just possibly be foreign oppressors, and the psalmist's loss of faith would fit the king's humiliation in the cult) most think that its intensely individualistic stance, coupled with the wisdom elements, make it unlikely. Form-critical approaches are less helpful than concentrating on its thought.

The psalmist declares that he almost lost his faith in God when he saw how prosperous the wicked were, and he wondered whether his hard struggle to maintain his personal integrity was worthwhile. His first bulwark against apostasy is the effect that such unbelief would have on others (vv. 15–16). But the turning-point in his experience was a visit to the temple (v. 17). There an oracle, taking part in religious rites, or an experience of God's presence, restored his faith. He realizes that evildoers will meet sudden divine judgement (vv. 18–20) and finds the blessing of knowing God (vv. 21–6), and the psalm ends, as it began, with the supreme 'good' (v. 28).

Some verses appear to be corrupt, and others are difficult to interpret, reflected in the considerable variations between the Eng. versions. In v. 1 NRSV and REB divide the Hebrew letters differently to produce '[good] to the upright'. This provides a good parallel to 'pure in heart', but lacks any textual support, and 'to Israel' should probably be retained. In v. 4 whether the wicked avoid suffering during their lifetime or at the moment of death in uncertain. v. 10 seems to be beyond recall. The meaning of the important v. 24 is uncertain not because of a corrupt text but because the meaning of several words is ambiguous. The issues are: (1) does 'afterwards' refer to the psalmist's present troubles or to death? (2) what connotation should be given to 'glory'—'with honour' or the glory of God's presence? and (3) does 'you will receive' relate to the experience of Enoch and Elijah, who were 'received, taken up' by God, presumably to be with him for ever, or is it divine acceptance in this life? The general lack of any belief in an afterlife throughout the OT except in the very latest writings makes it uncertain whether the psalmist envisages a happy life after death. But the hope seems so important in the thought of the psalm that perhaps it should be seen as a leap of faith.

Psalm 74 Although it has been suggested that this psalm has no historical links but belongs to a ritual desecration of the temple in the cult, almost everyone agrees that it celebrates the destruction of the temple by the Babylonians in 586 BCE. This is the only occasion when the temple was actually burned, and similarities with the poems in Lamentations which commemorate the event provide support. Whether it was composed soon after the events it describes or later, perhaps as part of an annual remembrance of the destruction, is less easy to decide. On the other hand the reference to the enemy having 'burned all the meeting places of God in the land' (v. 8) has sometimes been seen as a reference to synagogues (so Aquila and Symmachus), and the psalm has been interpreted as a reaction to the desecration of the temple by Antiochus Epiphanes in 167 BCE. The Targum paraphrased 'the impious' (v. 22) as 'this mad king', apparently thinking of Antiochus Epiphanes, who was nicknamed by his enemies 'Epimanes', 'madman', which possibly indicates that the psalm was used later to commemorate the Greek desecration of the temple. It may even be that it was modified at that time, but the description in the psalm fits the Babylonian attack more closely than any other. It is very uncertain whether synagogues were built as early as the Maccabaean period, and the LXX reads 'Come, let us abolish the feasts of the Lord from the land' in v. 8, as do the Targum, Syriac, and Vulgate.

The main structure of the psalm is clear: vv. 1–11 and 18–23 are prayers to God to come to the people's aid, while vv. 12–17 recall the power of God in creation in hymnic fashion, using mythical ideas similar to those in Ugarit and Babylon (some find a reference to the Exodus in this section, and the NRSV may intend to support this with its translations 'You divided the sea' and 'creatures of the wilderness', but the whole passage more naturally refers to the divine battle that preceded creation). It has been suggested that the verbs show that the psalm has a more elaborate, chiastic form: vv. 2–3 being matched by 18–23 (imperatives), 4–9 by 12–17 (perfects), and 10–11 (imperfects) forming the central section, with v. 1 as an introduction. Other word-plays, matching words, and the sevenfold repeated 'You' in vv. 12–17 reveal the artistry behind the poetry.

Psalm 75 The rapid changes of speech and style make it difficult to fit this psalm into any of the main categories. It begins as a thanksgiving by the community (v. 1). vv. 2–5 in the first person have been described as a prophetic oracle or the words of the king, declaring divine judgement on the wicked. God is the Creator who established the foundations of the world and maintains justice. The next section (vv. 6–8) describes the future judgement, of which the 'cup of foaming wine' is a symbol, perhaps taken from the old ordeal in which the accused was made to drink a potion that would prove poisonous only to the wicked (for the figure cf. Ps 11:6; Isa 51:17). In v. 9 the psalmist (individual, king, or the community) vows to utter praise to God, and the psalm ends with a renewed promise, in a divine oracle or the words of the king, to destroy the power of the wicked (v. 10).

The psalm fits naturally into some cultic festival. Those who treat a maximum number of psalms as royal regard this also as the king's psalm. Others note the oracles and describe it as a prophetic liturgy. Whether it ever had a historical background such as the failure of Sennacherib to capture Jerusalem (2 Kings 18–19, cf. 19:35) is doubtful, as is the suggestion that it looks forward to the last judgement.

Psalm 76 This psalm has similarities with Ps 46 and 48, and like them has been interpreted as the celebration of some Israelite victory over their enemies, as part of the New Year Festival in Jerusalem, as a prophecy of God's future victory, and more generally as post-exilic praise. The addition to the title in the LXX, 'to (concerning) the Assyrian' indicates that the first of these was adopted in some Jewish traditions, and the psalm related to Sennacherib's attack and defeat as described in 2 Kings 18–19. REB adopts a common emendation of v. 10 ('Edom, for all his fury, will praise you | and the remnant left in Hamath will dance in worship'), finding in the verse an allusion to David's victories, but some who accept the change of text reject a historical interpretation. Linking it with the pre-exilic Jerusalem Autumn Festival is probably more likely, though its presence in the Psalter shows that it continued to be sung in later worship.

NRSV follows the usual division of the text: vv. 1–3 praise God who chose Zion as his dwelling and defended his city; vv. 4–6 describe that victory in more detail; vv. 7–9 change the metaphor into that of judge who saves the humble; and the final section, vv. 10–12, which is less of a unity, declares that human beings will worship YHWH, even those most hostile to him, and calls on them to perform their vows. The 'Selâ' in vv. 3 and 9 adopts a threefold structure by treating the middle sections as a description of God.

Psalm 77 Difficulties in understanding the tenses in vv. 1–12 make the interpretation of this psalm uncertain (contrast NRSV's present tenses with the predominantly past tenses of REB and NIV). Is it the anguished prayer of an individual in distress that is made greater by his nation's suffering? On this view vv. 11–20 sustain the psalmist by recalling God's power as the Creator (or perhaps as the God who saved Israel at the Red Sea (Ex 14:10–31) at the time of the Exodus). Or is it a psalm of thanksgiving which also recounts the troubles from which the psalmist has been delivered? The contrast between vv. 1–10 and 11–20 has suggested to some that two psalms have been combined, a lament and a hymn of praise, the abrupt end in v. 20 possibly indicating that the second part is only a fragment of the original hymn. Yet there are striking similarities of vocabulary between the two parts, and indeed it has been suggested that there are deliberate parallels forming an *inclusio*, e.g. 'voice' of lament in v. 1 ('aloud') and 'voice' of God's thunder in v. 17, the 'hand' of the psalmist (v. 2), the 'hand' of Moses and Aaron (v. 20), and 'remember' in vv. 3 ('think'), 5, 11. However the psalm is understood, the urgent questions in vv. 7–9 lie at its heart.

Taken as a unity, the psalm has been classified in many different ways: the prayer of an Israelite (possibly from the northern kingdom, if any weight is to be placed on 'Jacob and Joseph' in v. 15); a national lament; communal thanksgiving for deliverance from some national distress; a royal psalm in which the king is representative of his people, bearing the nation's suffering, and offers his intercession for the nation, with the final verse perhaps pointing to the king's office as shepherd of his people. It has even been suggested, rather improbably, that this is another of the prayers by a man falsely accused of some wrong.

In the absence of much secure evidence, this is an excellent example of the way interpretation is controlled by the presuppositions that are brought to the psalm.

Psalm 78 This is the first of the three great history psalms (PS E.13). The writer begins like one of the wisdom teachers ('teaching', 'parable', and 'dark sayings' are wisdom vocabulary, and the emphasis on teaching the next generation reflects the aims of the wise men). But unlike Proverbs or Job, this writer chooses to express his teaching by recounting incidents in Israel's history. The broad structure is clear. The history is worked over twice, first concentrating on events during the period of the wilderness wanderings (vv. 12–41), then pointing more directly to the Exodus (vv. 42–53), but continuing the history up to the time of David (vv. 54–72). The emphasis is upon God's continuing protection and forgiveness of Israel, contrasted with Israel's constant rebellion and lack of trust. Past failures are told in order to urge the people to remember God's goodness and obey him. How far the introduction extends is not obvious: a narrow view limits it to vv. 1–4, but since the survey of history begins at v. 9 (or even 12), it may extend to v. 8.

Whether it is profitable to attempt to fit the psalm into any of the major categories is doubtful. It is not obviously either a hymn or a confession, and the sharp differences which mark it off from the wisdom books of the Old Testament make its description as a wisdom psalm unsafe, though it is plainly didactic.

Many attempts at dating the psalm have been made. The chief pieces of evidence that have been drawn upon are: the mention of the destruction of Shiloh, the ending of the history with David, the criticisms of the northern kingdom without any reference to its destruction in 722; the apparent existence of the Jerusalem temple, comparisons of the plagues with the lists in the 'sources' of the Pentateuch, and similarities with the Deuteronomistic interpretation of history. Most arguments are indecisive, and while very early dates have been suggested (the time of David or Solomon), and many are willing to concede a pre-exilic date, in a sense all the psalms are post-exilic since this is the period in which they were edited and collected.

Whether the psalm was used in worship is equally uncertain. Some have suggested that it was sung at the Autumn Festival as an expression of salvation history that formed part of the covenant renewal. Various speakers at such a celebration have been proposed: the king, a Levite, or a prophet. The general didactic tone of the psalm, however, may mean that it was never linked with worship.

Psalm 79 Everyone agrees that this is a communal lament, and most accept the early Jewish tradition that it refers to the fall of Jerusalem in 586 and the destruction of the temple, even though the language is so allusive that other historical incidents might be suggested. It may well have been recited on the fast day that commemorated that event (cf. Zech 7:3, 5; 8:19, and Ps 74 for a similar lament).

Complaint at God's inaction, urgent prayer, confession, and imprecations on the enemies of Israel are interwoven so that it is difficult to produce a clear structure for the psalm. vv. 1–4 describe the disaster, and the petition of the worshippers follows in vv. 5–12, the psalm concluding with a vow to offer thanksgiving and praise (v. 13).

If the prayers for vengeance offend modern sensitivities, we should perhaps be less ready to find relief in the (correct) assertion of earlier scholars that the psalmists saw the defeat of his people as an insult to God himself, now that we are aware of the ease with which religion adds to the evils of war.

Psalm 80 This is another communal lament. It is unusual in having a refrain (vv. 3, 7, 19), and having northern Israel as its main concern. An addition to the title in the LXX referred it to the Assyrian attacks, and it has been suggested that this is correct and that the period towards the end of the northern kingdom, perhaps in 733, is the subject of the plea to God. Alternatively it may come from Judah (the cherubim (v. 1) are usually associated with the Jerusalem temple) and there are some links with Isaiah, who uses a similar image of a vineyard whose wall God breaks down (Isa 5:1–7), while Jeremiah and Ezekiel both refer to YHWH as shepherd, although the exact phrase 'Shepherd of Israel' is unique here, and both show an interest in the northern kingdom. It is impossible to be certain, however, and it has been argued that the psalm is post-exilic and has picked up earlier traditions in a renewed lament.

A refrain (vv. 3, 7) marks off the first two sections of the psalm: vv. 1–2, a call to God for help; vv. 4–6, an urgent plea and complaint at God's treatment of his people. The rest of the psalm then forms a final section, describing God's past care of Israel, referring in the figure of the vine to the Exodus and conquest, and the present distress (vv. 8–13, did the refrain originally follow v. 13 as well?). Petition is renewed in vv. 14–17, with a vow to return to God in v. 18, and a repetition of the refrain in the last verse.

Psalm 81 A reference to the renewal of the covenant has often been found in this psalm (cf. v. 7b, possibly an allusion to Sinai, and the similarities of vv. 9–10 with the beginning of the Decalogue, Ex 20:2–5, together with the kind of teaching found in Deut 4:1; 5:1; 6:4; 9:1, and the reference to a seven-yearly ceremony of covenant renewal in Deut 31:9–13). Whether such a ceremony was part of the New Year Festival has been questioned; the reference to the new moon and full moon in v. 3 and the blowing of the trumpet perhaps reflect the celebration of New Year and Tabernacles. Although the teaching of vv. 9–10 are similar to the Decalogue, the words for 'strange' god and 'foreign' god are different from the 'other gods' of Ex 20 and Deut 5, as is the verb 'brought [you] up', and the order of the phrases is reversed.

The psalm begins like a hymn (vv. 1–5b), and this is followed by an oracle (vv. 5c–16). This is probably a feature of the liturgy and does not indicate that two separate psalm fragments have been combined, although that may be how the liturgy was developed. vv. 6–10 describe God's deliverance of his people from Egypt, while vv. 11–16 remind them of their past disobedience and promise victory over their enemies if they obey him. v. 10c fits oddly and has often been transposed to follow v. 5c as the announcement to the prophet of the oracle that God is giving him. Some see in the changes between third and second person (note NRSV marg. in v. 6) an indication of further disarrangement, the two oracles being vv. 6, 11–16 and 7–10.

Psalm 82 Jewish tradition, seen in the Targum and reflected in Jn 10:34–6, interpreted this psalm as the condemnation of the human rulers of Israel, similar to Isa 3:13–15, but v. 7 makes no sense on this interpretation and it is almost universally accepted today that the picture is of YHWH's heavenly court (cf. 1 Kings 22:19–22; Job 1:6–12; 2:1–7), similar to the pantheons of other nations, with YHWH presiding as Marduk or El did. The gods were apparently charged with maintaining justice in their client kingdoms, but they have shown partiality to the wicked and have not defended those who are exposed to oppression, orphans and the poor. vv. 2–4, 6–7 set out YHWH's judgement. His sentence is that the gods will die like human beings. v. 5 may refer either to the wicked or the gods. The verse stands out within the divine judgement, and some have suggested that the psalm is in chiastic form:

The psalm ends with a prayer that YHWH will undertake universal rule and bring in universal righteousness. This has suggested to some that rather than a prophetic oracle or vision the psalm is really a lament, but it is possible to regard the verse as an exclamation, as in Isa 21:5 and Mic 4:13.

Psalm 83 The extended list of enemies who have leagued themselves together against Israel (vv. 6–8) has given rise to many attempts at dating. Theodore of Mopsuestia (350–427 CE) suggested the time of the Maccabees (cf. 1 Macc 5). Other dates range from pre-exilic times (the reign of Jehoshaphat, cf. 2 Chr 20) to after the Return (cf. Neh 4). The list contains ten names, which perhaps indicates that it is symbolic and that the psalm is a cultic lament (cf. Ps 2:1–3; 46:6; 48:4–8).

After calling upon God to remain inactive no longer (v. 1), the onslaught of the enemies is described (vv. 2–8). The rest of the psalm is an appeal to God to destroy these enemies, and the victories of Deborah and Barak over the Canaanite leader Sisera (Judg 4–5) and of Gideon over the Midianites Oreb and Zeeb, and Zebah and Zalmunna (Judg 7:25; 8:13–21) are recalled as examples. Those looking for literary patterns point to the chiastic arrangement of vv. 3–6, with the enemies of Israel flanked by the enemies of God.

Psalm 84 This is usually termed a pilgrim psalm, and the happiness which the godly Israelite finds as he makes his way to the temple for the Autumn Festival shines through. Other suggestions are that it is an entrance liturgy or simply a hymn of Zion. Several different types of prayer appear in it: expressions of joy and confidence that would fit a hymn of praise (vv. 1, 10, 12), longing, rather in the style of a lament (2, cf. 10*a*), prayer for the king (vv. 8–9; 'our shield' refers to the king), and a description of the pilgrimage as the autumn rains are falling (vv. 5–7). The whole psalm is bound together by the first and last verses, both addressing 'YHWH of hosts' and expressing delight and happiness. Most—even of those who find a maximum number of royal psalms—draw back from ascribing this psalm to the king himself, preferring to think of a cultic soloist.

In v. 7 the MT seems to mean: 'he appears before God in Zion' (cf. RV); NRSV follows the LXX. Behind the psalm may be worship in which God was represented by an image which the worshippers 'saw' in the temple. No image of YHWH existed in Israel, but the phrase may have taken this over conservatively in the liturgy. Later scribes, anxious about orthodoxy and reverence, altered the verb into 'appear before'.

Psalm 85 The surface structure of this psalm is clearer than its exact interpretation. vv. 1–3 describe a past forgiveness and salvation; vv. 4–7 are in the form of a communal lament, a prayer for an end to God's anger and renewed deliverance; in vv. 8–13 a prophet tenses himself to hear God's word and proclaims the promise of rich spiritual and material blessing.

Problems of the meaning of the Hebrew tenses, coupled with uncertainty about the date of the psalm and hence its historical or cultic background, make interpretation difficult. There are three main ways of interpreting the psalm.

Some place it in the period after the Exile, perhaps later than the time of Haggai and Zechariah. vv. 1–3 express the same sentiments as Isa 40–55, while the next section reflects the hardships which the returned exiles experienced, so different from their hopes. They still need the promise of vv. 8–13.

Others think that it belongs to the pre-exilic temple worship, the first section referring to the Exodus salvation, and the emphasis on righteousness suiting their understanding of the thrust of the New Year Festival, or perhaps v. 11 contains the hint of a bad harvest as the disaster from which God's help is sought.

Rather differently, others, sensitive to the contrast between the joyful account of an apparently past deliverance and the following prayer, take the Hebrew tenses in vv. 1–3 either as prophetic, the whole psalm then becoming confident prophecy, or as petition, which turns the whole psalm into a lament, perhaps ending with the certainty of hearing.

Psalm 86 All agree that this is the prayer of an individual, and many describe it as almost a mosaic of quotations. The 'quotations', however, may simply be traditional phrases which the psalmist is reusing. There is less unanimity about the identity of the psalmist. The maximalists hold that it is a royal psalm, probably linked with the ritual humiliation of the king in the cult. They point to the extravagance of v. 9 which seems to go beyond what could be expected from an ordinary Israelite, and note the attacks by the enemies, the association of divine power with the king as YHWH's servant, and the stress on God's faithfulness and his great name, ideas that are linked elsewhere with kingship. On the other hand, some include it among the pleas of those unjustly accused or seeking divine acquittal, but there seem to be few grounds for this proposal. Perhaps it is a post-exilic psalm based on early traditional phrases, possibly taking over some features that previously belonged to royal psalms. The psalmist says so little about the distress from which he seeks God's rescue that it is difficult to determine what it is: enemies, false accusations, illness, even sin, are all hinted at.

The three-part structure is transparent: vv. 1–7, a plea for help, based on the psalmist's piety (vv. 1–4) and the character of God (vv. 5–7); vv. 8–13, a hymn-like section, interrupted by a call on God to teach the psalmist (v. 11) and ending with thankful confidence that his prayer is answered, or a vow to offer praise, perhaps even to sacrifice a thank-offering (vv. 12–13); vv. 14–17, renewed prayer, ending with a request for a 'sign', either some ritual or an oracle, or the salvation itself.

Frequent parallels and repetitions, such as an eightfold 'for' in vv. 1, 2, 3, 4, 5, 7, 10, 13, the repeated 'Lord' (vv. 1, 3, 4, 5, 6, 8, 9, 11, 12, 15, 17), and the description of the psalmist as YHWH's 'servant' (vv. 2, 4, 16), have led some to look for literary patterns. A chiastic structure, with v. 11 in the centre receiving the main stress, has been detected.

```
1–4
      5–6
            7
                  8–10
                            11
                        12–13
                  14
            15
      16–17
```

Psalm 87 This short psalm is one of the most difficult in the Psalter. Short phrases and possible textual corruption, together with lack of clear sequence of thought have led to widespread emendation and rearrangement of the verses (cf. NEB). The only safe approach, however, is to retain the MT (REB has reversed many of the changes in NEB), even if this is not as the poet intended.

To classify it as one of the Songs of Zion takes the interpretation only a small way. The date and original setting are completely uncertain. The reference to dancing in v. 7 perhaps indicates that it was linked with a festal procession. The difficult middle section (vv. 4–6) may be taken in many different ways: as looking to the future when Jerusalem would be the centre of universal worship; as listing some of the nations from which Jewish proselytes have come to the festival; as a reference to Jews who come from different countries in the dispersion. The universal perspective may point to a post-exilic date, but it is impossible to be sure. The other countries might simply be a foil to YHWH's choice of Jerusalem.

'Rahab' (v. 4), the primeval monster quelled by YHWH in ancient story (cf. Ps 89:10), represents Egypt. The 'springs' (v. 7) may symbolize divine blessing, or Zion may be thought of as the source of the streams of Paradise.

Psalm 88 This is the bleakest of all the individual laments. The last word expresses its mood. The wonder is that the psalmist prays at all.

The full horror of Sheol is found here. After death there is nothing but the land of darkness and forgetfulness, beyond God's care, outside the reach of his salvation, where the shades no longer offer praise (vv. 5, 10–12, cf. Ps 6:5; 30:9; 115:17; Job 7:8–10; 10:21–2; see PS G.13). The only spark of faith which glimmers through the darkness is v. 1: 'O LORD, God of my salvation'. Three times he makes his plea to God (vv. 1–2, 9, 13), but always he is met with silence; the final line of the psalm should perhaps be translated as REB, 'Darkness is now my only companion.' We are reminded of Job.

The structure of the psalm is not clear. The three appeals to God mark some divisions. The descriptions of the psalmist's afflictions mark others: so ill that it seems he draws near to Sheol (vv. 3–7); rejected with horror by his friends (v. 8); an account of Sheol (vv. 10–12); seriously ill from his youth he is abandoned by God, subject to his wrath; and once again God seems to have caused his friends to shun him (vv. 15–18). And the psalm breaks off in darkness, the mystery of suffering unsolved, the silence of God unexplained. Traditionally the psalm has been read on Good Friday.

Psalm 89 After an introduction (vv. 1–4), this long psalm falls into three easily discerned sections. vv. 5–18 are a hymn of praise to YHWH, proclaiming his greatness among the gods, his power as creator, and his righteous rule; happy are his covenant people. It ends with a reference to the Israelite king, the nation's 'horn' and 'shield'. vv. 19–37 tell of YHWH's covenant with David and appear to be related in some way to Nathan's prophecy in 2 Sam 7:1–17; most probably both go back to traditions with a long history behind them and perhaps influenced each other. The final section of the psalm (vv. 38–51) is a lament. The king had been defeated and humiliated: he may even have lost his life (cf. v. 45), although the plea in vv. 46–8, if by the king himself, would imply that he was only gravely threatened.

With so many clear references to the king, it is strange that Gunkel (id. and Begrich 1933: 140) is hesitant about including it among his ten royal psalms. He regarded the combination of forms as pointing to a late date and reflecting the fall of the Davidic dynasty in 586. Some think it is a combination of separate psalms, but the overall unity seems assured, as is its being a king's psalm.

It is possible that it is related to some historical defeat, and the death of Josiah (2 Kings 23:29–30) or the Exile and imprisonment of Jehoiachin (2 Kings 24:8–17) have been proposed. Another suggestion places it after 520 BCE, at a time when hopes of the restoration of the Davidic monarchy were current (cf. Zech 4:6–14). On a cultic interpretation the psalm would accompany the ritual humiliation of the king, somewhat similar to that known in Babylon. To see it as part of an annual covenant festival is less likely. If used in a ritual it must have been followed by the king's salvation by God.

Christian tradition has linked it with Christmas, God's covenant promise being fulfilled in Jesus. Typology might find parallels between the king's humiliation and Christ's humble birth, death, and final triumph.

v. 52 is the doxology at the end of Book 3 of the Psalter (PS D.2).

Psalm 90 This is the only psalm ascribed to Moses, and while no one today would accept that Moses was the author, possible reasons for the title can be discovered. There are certain similarities with the Song of Moses (Deut 32), and only Moses calls on God to 'repent' (the word translated 'have compassion on' in v. 13; Ex 32:12).

The psalm does not fit easily into any of the standard categories. It is often classed as a communal lament, but this suits only vv. 13–17. The teaching in vv. 3–12 has many wisdom features, though the main wisdom writings, apart from Job, do not address God in this way, and at v. 7 features of a lament appear (God's anger, references to sin, and the call 'How long?'). The psalm opens like a hymn of praise (vv. 1–2). To divide it into two, or even three, separate psalms, however, is a counsel of despair. While it is possible that a post-exilic scribe compiled the psalm, using some earlier psalmic fragments and other material, what was produced is a single poem which deserves to be treated as a whole. Like Ps 73 it begins with a statement of faith—YHWH has proved himself the security and support of each generation. vv. 3–12 emphasize the brevity of human life, made more bitter by toil and grief. 'How long?' (v. 13) is the familiar cry of lament (cf. Ps 6:3; 74:10; 79:5; 80:4; 94:3); the only ground for prayer is God's unwavering love (vv. 13–17). In this way the eternity of God (v. 2) is contrasted with the fleeting life of human beings (v. 10), and our sin (v. 8) is answered by divine love (vv. 14, 17). Perhaps the scribe wished to compose a psalm that could be used in services of prayer and penitence (cf. Jdt 4:9–12), or even for private devotion.

Psalm 91 Many and varied are the interpretations of this psalm. Royal maximalists find in the assurances given to the psalmist decisive evidence: the king alone can be the recipient of such divine protection. Other suggestions range from a form of entrance liturgy spoken by the priest to the worshipper at the temple, to part of the rites for a convert, who now sets himself under the protection of YHWH. The LXX added a title ascribing the psalm to David, while the Targum found in it a dialogue between David and Solomon. Similarities with Job 5:19–24 have led to proposals to link the psalm with wisdom writings, but Job itself may have been influenced by psalm forms. Reading 'pestilence' (v. 3) as 'word' (i.e. spell, rather than slander) and 'that wastes' (v. 6) as 'and a demon', the LXX reflects the interpretation of the psalm at the time of the translators as a defence against spells and demons. If it is a royal psalm it might have been recited before the king went out to battle, unless it formed part of temple ritual. The quotation of vv. 11–12 in the temptations narrative (Mt 4:6;

Lk 4:10–11) may reflect messianic interpretations of the psalm.

The structure of the psalm is more complicated than appears from the NRSV's emendations and rewriting (see RV for a more literal translation). The main sections are vv. 1–13, 14–16, the latter being in the form of an oracle. Whether there is a dialogue in the first part is uncertain, but changes of person and exclamations interrupt the flow of the narrative.

Psalm 92 Although this psalm begins with thanksgiving, its form is not entirely clear. Teaching, akin to that found in the wisdom writings (vv. 6–7), and individual thanksgiving (vv. 10–11) are also found. Royal maximalists ascribe it to the king, pointing out that the psalmist's victory is also God's, that he is anointed, and that the community flourishes alongside the king. The title presents it as a sabbath psalm, and the Talmud states that it was sung at the offering of wine that accompanied the first sacrifice of a lamb (Num 28:9–10), while the Targum renders the title: 'a psalm of praise and song which the first man uttered upon the day of the Sabbath'.

Those looking for literary patterns find an elaborate chiasmus, with v. 8 at its centre:

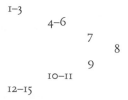

parts of which are more convincing than others. It requires that the ignorance of the 'dullard' (v. 6; all the Eng. versions fail to represent the overtones of evil that are part of the meaning of the Heb. word) refers backwards to v. 5, rather than forwards to vv. 7–8 or 7–9 (as Eng. versions apart from JB and NJB). If this is rejected as too fanciful, a somewhat complicated structure may be seen as: a call to praise God in the form of a reflection on the way such praise is morally good or fits the divine plan for human beings (vv. 1–3); the grounds for this praise (vv. 4–5); a wisdom-type section of teaching, with hymnic elements (vv. 6–8); thanksgiving for deliverance from enemies (vv. 9–11); the blessedness of the righteous (vv. 12–15).

Psalm 93 For a discussion of the enthronement psalms (47; 93; 96–9) see PS E.5b. This psalm celebrates YHWH's kingship, creation, his power over the primeval waters, and his ethical decrees (v. 5), which were probably related to the covenant (cf. Ps 99:7; 132:12).

There is no title in the MT, and some argue that this shows that the editor linked it closely with Ps 92, and also with Ps 94. Despite some common features, this appears unlikely. The LXX provides the title: 'For the day before the Sabbath, when the earth was inhabited; a psalm, a song of David'. This tradition, with its allusion to Gen 1:24–31, is also found in the Mishnah (*m. Tamid* 7.4).

Psalm 94 Although some divide this psalm into just two sections (vv. 1–15, 16–23, or 1–11, 12–23), holding the first to be a communal lament and the second the prayer of an individual, it appears to be more complex than this. vv. 1–7 are a prayer for the punishment of the wicked, whose crimes strike at the heart of the Israelite ethic of care for the poor and oppressed; vv. 8–11 are akin to wisdom teaching, and use the wisdom vocabulary of 'fool', 'teach', and 'an empty breath'; vv. 12–15 are a blessing on the righteous; and vv. 16–23 are either an individual lament or the thanksgiving of an individual, according to how the tenses in vv. 22–3 are understood. This does not mean that fragments from different psalms have been combined, since it is possible to find an overall unity in the theme of divine vengeance on the wicked, and there are similarities in vocabulary between the parts of the psalm (e.g. 'heritage', vv. 5, 14; 'discipline' and 'teach', vv. 10, 12; 'turn back', vv. 2 ('give'), 15 ('return'), 23 ('repay'), the same Heb. word). Maximalists include the psalm among the king's psalms, claiming that it reflects 'royal' language, and finding the reference to the individual and the nation most suitable for the king who is the representative of his people. It was the king's duty to care for widows, the fatherless, and other oppressed members of society, including resident aliens (cf. Ps 72:2–4, 12–14).

The LXX adds the title: 'A psalm of David, for the fourth day of the week', a tradition which accords with the Mishnah's allocation of psalms for each day of the week (*m. Tamid* 7.4).

Its position in the Psalter is odd, since it appears to break a sequence of enthronement psalms. Some have noted eight terms common to Ps 93 and 94, suggesting close links between them, but some are very common words and others (e.g. 'majesty' (Ps 93:1)/'proud' (Ps 94:2), and 'roaring' (Ps 93:3/'crush' (Ps 94:5), although the same roots, are not very convincing). It would, however, be less out of place if it were a royal psalm.

Psalm 95 The striking difference between vv. 1–7c and 7d–11 led some commentators to hold that two separate psalms have been combined. While this is not impossible, most today treat the psalm as a unified 'prophetic liturgy' (cf. Ps 81). In the first part a call to praise is sounded twice, first based on the kingship of God as the great creator (vv. 1–5), then as the shepherd of his people Israel (vv. 6–7c). Some have pointed to an additional call in v. 2, and have suggested three stages in a movement of the worshippers into the temple. In the second part a prophet speaks, uttering a warning from YHWH himself to remember the disobedience of their ancestors (Ex 17:1–7; Num 20:2–13; Meribah means 'strife', 'dispute', and Massah 'testing') and to obey him 'today'. It may have been connected with Tabernacles or the New Year Festival (note the themes of creation and the kingship of YHWH).

In Jewish tradition the psalm was linked with sabbath worship (*b. Šabb.* 119a). From early times it has been sung as an invitation to worship in the Christian church. Athanasius tells of this practice in Constantinople, Benedict directed that the whole monastery should sing it when they first arose from sleep, and it has been included in Anglican mattins since 1549. The modern practice of omitting the second part removes God's moral demands and presents an inauthentic picture of God.

Psalm 96 For the 'enthronement psalms' (47; 93; 96–9) see PS E.5b. This psalm reiterates the central themes of this group of psalms, with special stress on YHWH's universal sovereignty over the nations and his righteous judgement of the whole world. vv. 1–3 sound the call to praise God. The reasons for offering praise are set out in vv. 4–6, and this is followed by a renewed call to worship God in vv. 7–10. In the final section of the psalm (vv. 11–13) the whole of creation is summoned to rejoice before YHWH, who comes as righteous judge. 'Worship the LORD in holy splendour' (v. 9) see PS 29:2; 'new song' (v. 1) see PS 33.

The LXX's title, 'When the house was built after the exile; a hymn of David', indicates the tradition that the psalm was written by David and used later to celebrate the rebuilding of the temple. It forms part of a composite psalm inserted into 1 Chr 16 for the bringing of the ark into Jerusalem by David. A notable Christian gloss in the Old Latin translation produced 'The Lord has reigned from the tree' in v. 10, and many of the Church Fathers from the time of Tertullian and Justin Martyr regarded the psalm as a prophecy of the cross, an interpretation reflected in the hymn *Vexilla regis*.

Psalm 97 Many of the features common to the 'enthronement psalms' (Ps 47; 93; 96–9, PS E.5b) recur here, especially YHWH's kingship as universal lord, upholder of 'righteousness', and saviour of his faithful followers. The most striking feature is the theophany in vv. 2–5, which may reflect the appearance of God on Sinai (Ex 19), although similar phenomena revealing his appearance are found elsewhere in the OT, e.g. Hab 3. It has been suggested that if the psalm was part of the temple worship, features of the theophany may have been experienced in the smoke of incense and the sacrifices accompanied by the blowing of the ram's horn, but there is no reason to treat the imagery so literally.

Many phrases in the psalm are found elsewhere in the Psalter and the prophetic books, leading some to see it as the work of a post-exilic poet who formed it from earlier traditions, but there seems to be no need to deny that it could be earlier. The LXX title, 'By David, when his land was established' reflects the editor's view, though it has been interpreted, like the title to Ps 96, as indicating two traditions, that it goes back to David and that it was used after the Exile to celebrate the restoration of the Jews to their land.

Psalm 98 This psalm begins and ends like Ps 96, and contains many features common to the 'enthronement psalms' (47; 93; 96–9, PS E.5b). It has been suggested that this tremendous hymn marked the climax of the festival, but nothing is really known about its origins or use. A call to praise YHWH for his 'salvation' (vv. 1–3, NRSV 'victory', see PS A.4) is followed by a second call to 'all the earth', first from the people and then from the primeval deep, the mountains, and all the inhabitants of the world because he is coming to exert his just rule (vv. 4–9). For 'a new song' see PS 33.

It is the only psalm with just 'A psalm' as the title. The LXX adds 'of David', and the Syriac translation relates it to the deliverance from Egypt. In Anglican tradition it has been sung as an alternative to the Magnificat in Evensong, seeing Christ as the Lord who comes with salvation.

Psalm 99 The last of the 'enthronement psalms' (47; 93; 96–9; PS E.5b), begins with the familiar cry, 'YHWH is king'. It contains references to justice and righteousness (v. 4), and perhaps the covenant, with its moral demands (vv. 4, 7), and is centred upon Zion (v. 2; cf. 'his holy mountain', v. 9), yet it stands somewhat apart from the others in this group by having

few similarities with Deutero-Isaiah, by calling on the foreign nations to tremble before God instead of joining in his praise, and by directly naming Moses, Aaron, and Samuel, the three great intercessors (cf. Ex 32:11–14, 31–4; Num 12:13; 14:13–19; 16:44–8; 1 Sam 7:7–11).

The text may be corrupt in places and the structure is not clear. vv. 5 and 9 form a kind of refrain, although the wording is not exactly the same, but the threefold 'Holy' (vv. 3, 5, 9), an outstanding feature of this psalm, may equally well mark the intended divisions. God's 'footstool' (v. 5) reflects a feature of ancient Middle-Eastern royalty; the ark (1 Chr 28:2), the temple, Jerusalem (Lam 2:1), or the whole earth (Isa 66:1) may be intended by the term.

The LXX provides a title: 'A psalm of David'.

Psalm 100 This hymn of praise is marked by its seven imperative verbs ('make a joyful noise', 'worship', 'come', 'know', 'enter', 'give thanks', 'bless'). Similar to Ps 95, it is often held to have been sung at the entrance to the temple. The structure is transparent: the call to offer praise to God is made twice (vv. 1–2, 4), each time followed by the motivation, first because YHWH is creator and shepherd of his people, then because of his goodness, love, and faithfulness, the last two words having strong associations with the covenant (vv. 3, 5).

In v. 3b the text and margin of NRSV represent two traditions retained in the MT and reflected in the ancient versions. The Hebrew words 'his' (lit. 'to him') and 'not' are identical in sound but differ in spelling. Aquila, the Targum, and Jerome have 'his', as do all the most recent English translations, while the LXX, Symmachus, and the Syriac follow the alternative meaning, 'and not we ourselves', made familiar through the AV and BCP. A modern proposal is to take the word as a note of emphasis, producing: 'and we are indeed his people'.

Psalm 101 The declaration of the psalmist that he will destroy all evildoers from the land, and especially from YHWH's city (v. 8), has convinced most commentators that this is a king's psalm, even though there is no specific mention of the king in it. Beyond this, however, there is little consensus. Some regard it as an expression of the king's vows at his enthronement, a view supported by the translation of the verbs as future (as in NRSV). This would not exclude its repetition on the annual celebration of his accession. Others point to the cry 'Oh when wilt thou come to me?' (v. 2 RSV; NRSV interprets the phrase differently, against most modern translations), and the metre, which is often used in laments, arguing that the psalm belonged to the New Year Festival in which, they believe, the king played a central part. He was ritually humiliated, like the king in Babylon, and appealed to God for deliverance on the basis of his righteousness and his just rule. The Babylonian king also confessed his innocence and declared that he had removed evildoers from his land. Whether this was depicted in terms of a battle is doubtful: there is no hint of such a conflict in this psalm. Even on this interpretation it is possible to see a future reference, the king vowing to continue his past practice.

The structure of the psalm is not immediately apparent, although repetitions of words and phrases suggest that it was carefully crafted. The simplest outline is to divide the psalm at v. 5, vv. 2–4 setting out the king's own righteousness and vv. 5–8 his rule over his people. v. 1 (or possibly vv. 1–2*a*, if the Heb. verb translated 'I will study' is really 'I will make my theme' or 'I will sing a *maskîl* psalm') forms the introduction. Phrases which may point to more elaborate structuring are 'within [in] my house' (vv. 2, 7, the same Heb. phrase), 'the way that is blameless' (vv. 2, 6); 'before my eyes', 'in my presence' (vv. 3, 7, identical Heb.), 'I will destroy' (vv. 5, 8). Similar but not exact parallels are 'the faithful in the land' and 'the wicked in the land' (vv. 6, 8), and 'integrity of heart', 'perverseness of heart', and 'an arrogant heart' (vv. 2, 4, 5). Whether these form two sets of *inclusio*, or some other pattern, is difficult to determine.

Psalm 102 The urgent prayer of an individual, hymn, and prophecy intermingle in this psalm. Some have held that two psalms have been combined, though there is some uncertainty about the precise extent of each (perhaps vv. 1–11 with 23–4 and 12–22 with 25–8). Less drastic is the view that an earlier lament was adapted into a community prayer, maybe during the Exile. Royal maximalists wonder whether it might not be a king's psalm, the communal aspects showing the king as representative of the nation, and the hymnic features being part of the Autumn Festival. Others who retain the unity of the psalm ascribe the communal features to the use of the psalm within the temple worship or suppose that the psalmist adopted elements of praise from the cult. The final section has been seen as an alternative to the common vow to offer praise that is a feature of many individual laments.

Those who look for patterns within the structure of the psalms note examples of *inclusio* and word plays: 'my days' (vv. 3, 11), 'withered like grass' (vv. 4, 11), the collection of similes (vv. 3, 4, 6, 7, 9, 11) within vv. 3–11; and, less convincingly, within vv. 12–22 the sixfold repetition of YHWH plus one mention of YH (vv. 12, 15, 16, 19, 21, 22, and 18), 'name' (vv. 12, 15, 21, although in v. 12 the word translated 'name' is more literally 'memorial'), Zion (vv. 13, 16, 21), 'servants' and 'to worship' (vv. 14, 22, the same Hebrew verb), and 'generation' (vv. 12, 18). The final sections of the psalm appear to be linked to the two earlier parts by vocabulary: 'your years' (vv. 24, 27), 'long ago' and 'in your presence' (vv. 25, 28, the same Heb. word, slightly modified), 'my days' (vv. 23, 24 ('at the mid-point of my life', lit. 'in the half of my days', cf. 3, 11), 'He has broken' (v. 23) is a homonym of 'answer' (v. 2) in the Hebrew; 'your servants' (vv. 14, 28), 'heaven' (vv. 19, 25), 'to/throughout all generations' (vv. 12, 24), and the similes in v. 26 recall those in vv. 3–11. Some of these features are more convincing than others, but they suggest that the psalm was carefully crafted as a unity.

The psalmist appears to be gravely ill (the suggestion that this is the prayer of one unjustly accused, which some propose, appears unlikely), and the 'enemies' seem to be those who regard his disease as punishment for sin. This is confirmed by the unusual title. Jewish tradition linked the psalm with the days of fasting (*m. Ta'an.* 2.3), and in Christian tradition it is one of the seven penitential psalms, perhaps seeing in the reference to God's anger (v. 10) an implicit expression of penitence, for there is no open confession.

Psalm 103 Although this psalm is often described as a hymn of praise, it differs from many other hymns in the intensely personal character of its opening, and it might well be treated as the thanksgiving of an individual, possibly after recovery from some illness (cf. vv. 3–4) unless this is simply part of a general description of God's goodness.

The main divisions are vv. 1–5, a self-exhortation by the psalmist to praise YHWH, vv. 6–18, a description of YHWH's character and goodness, notable for the stress on divine forgiveness, compassion, and faithful love, and vv. 19–22, a renewed call to praise, now directed to the heavenly beings and the whole of creation. (v. 19 may belong to the middle section, instead of providing the basis for the final call to praise.) In the second part of the psalm the singular subject of the opening is replaced by the plural 'us', and the tone becomes didactic and reminiscent of wisdom teaching, although the characterization of YHWH has parallels in the Torah and the prophets (cf. v. 8 with Ex 34:6; Num 14:18; Joel 2:13; Jon 4:2; v. 5 with Isa 40:31; and v. 11 with Isa 55:9), as well as in other psalms. Whether the psalm was sung within pre-exilic cultic worship, or comes from the time after the Exile within a circle of the pious who 'fear God' (vv. 11, 13, 17) is uncertain.

Those favouring a literary approach note several verbal links: 'benefits'/'deal' (vv. 2, 10, the same Heb. root), 'your/our iniquity/iniquities' (vv. 3, 10), 'steadfast love' and 'mercy' (vv. 4, 8, 11, 13, 17), but these form no clear pattern and may be unintentional repetitions.

Psalm 104 This great hymn praising the creator God is remarkable for its similarities with Gen 1 and an Egyptian hymn to Aten, the sun's disc, by the Pharaoh Akhenaten in the fourteenth century BCE. The similarities with Gen 1 include the general order of creation and vocabulary (with some unusual Heb. forms). Yet there are differences, the most notable of which is the lack of some of the psalm's mythological features in Genesis, such as traces of YHWH's conflict with the waters (vv. 6–9), direct mention of the sun and moon (v. 19; they are 'lights' in Gen 1:14–18), and the naming of Leviathan (v. 26; 'sea-monsters' in Gen 1:21). Moreover the psalm ranges more widely in its description of the world. Examples of similarities with the Egyptian hymn are lions roaming at night, the provision of pasture for the animals, ships sailing up and down, and the god as creator, but again there are differences: night is more sinister in the Aten hymn; several features, such as care of the foetus in the womb and the chicken in the egg, are absent from the psalm; and above all it is YHWH who exercises providential care in the Israelite poem, not the sun. Whether there has been direct contact between Ps 104 and either Gen 1 or the Aten hymn must be regarded as doubtful, though all three may have been influenced by common ideas and even traditions, and it is not impossible that the writer of Gen 1 knew the psalm.

The structure of the psalm can be set out as: vv. 1–4, the introductory self-exhortation of praise, beginning like Ps 103:1; vv. 5–9, YHWH as creator; vv. 10–18, YHWH's care of all creatures; vv. 19–23, moon and sun, and their influence; vv. 24–30, a further account of God's providence, upon which life itself depends; vv. 31–5, a renewed call to praise, including a prayer for sinners to be destroyed, and ending with a repetition of the opening exhortation. The call that sinners be consumed offends many today, but it has been suggested that 'No one who has reckoned with the evil which man has wreaked on animals, trees and waters could think this prayer super-fluous'—it is indeed an essential part of the psalm that 'the spoilers should be brought to the end of their existence *as spoilers*' (Eaton 1995: 73).

The verb 'to make' and the noun 'work' occur at strategic places in the psalm (vv. 4, 13, 19, 24, 31), and it may be that beside the *inclusio* of vv. 1*a* and 35*c* ('Hallelujah' in 35*d* stands outside the psalm itself), there is a concentric structure of vv. 1–4, 5–13, 14–23, 24–30, 31–5, with vv. 14–23 forming the centre.

The theme of the psalm may connect it with the Autumn New Year Festival, but there can be no certainty, as is shown by such diverse suggestions as that it originated at the dedication of Solomon's temple and that it is post-exilic. In the end the origins matter little for an appreciation of the magnificent hymn.

Psalm 105 This is the second of the three great history psalms (Ps 78; 105; 106; PS E.13). The tone throughout is of praise, and it is usually regarded as a hymn, but with such an extended historical section form-critical considerations break down.

Date and original setting are uncertain. The inclusion of vv. 1–15 in the composite poem which the Chronicler has inserted at 1 Chr 16:7 fixes the relative date for its completion and may indicate an original cultic use, although it provides no evidence for linking the psalm with the time of David. The Chronicler was probably influenced by the liturgical practice of his own day or he may have introduced the psalm for literary reasons. Some note the references to the covenant and suggest that the psalm was related to its renewal at an annual festival. Much depends upon the relation of the psalm to the Pentateuchal narratives. Some argue that the historical allusions are derived from the completed Pentateuch, and that the psalm is therefore post-exilic. If so it might be non-cultic, possibly related to wisdom writings. The psalm differs from Exodus, however, in several respects, particularly the number and order of the plagues, and the omission of any reference to Sinai, leading others to claim that similarities with the Old Testament narratives are due to both drawing on common traditions rather than to literary borrowing.

Most base their analysis of the structure of the psalm on the historical sequence, with vv. 7–41 set between an extended call to praise (vv. 1–6) and a concluding section which expounds the covenant faith and calls for Israel's ethical response to election and deliverance (vv. 42–5). The central section is often divided into vv. 7–11, 12–15, 16–23, 24–36(38), 36(39)–41, in a sequence of historical allusions. Those looking for literary devices point to elaborate *inclusio* (e.g. the covenant with Abraham in vv. 9, 42, and 'strangers'/'alien' in vv. 12, 23) and chiasmus (e.g. in vv. 2–5: 'wonderful works', 'seek', YHWH : YHWH, 'seek', 'wonderful works').

Psalm 106 The third of the great history psalms takes a very different view of Israel's history from the other two psalms. The stress now is upon Israel's faithlessness and disobedience, despite the persistent grace and forgiveness of YHWH. Form-critical classifications are uncertain. The opening verses read like a hymn of praise (vv. 1–3), but swiftly turn into the style of an individual lament (vv. 4–5), and then from v. 6 corporate confession dominates, though mixed with hymnic accounts of God's salvation, ending with a vow to offer praise (v. 47). v. 48 is usually regarded as the doxology at the end of Book 4 of the Psalter, but it is included in the extracts from the psalm which the Chronicler quotes in 1 Chr 16:34–6, and it is somewhat bold to claim that the Psalter was complete and divided into five books by that time. To relieve sharply contrasting forms within the psalm, it has been suggested that vv. 1–3 are the conclusion of Ps 105, but this is unnecessary, given the style of many of the psalms, and Ps 105:45 forms a fully satisfactory end to that psalm.

It is widely accepted that vv. 27 and 47 refer to the Exile and the dispersion, and provide a means for dating the psalm. This would not preclude an early form, however, and some are prepared to set it in the pre-exilic period, perhaps as part of a covenant renewal ceremony at New Year. It is intriguing that a ceremony at the Feast of Weeks included recitations of the righteous acts of God by the priests and of Israel's sins by the Levites (1QS 1:21, 23). Perhaps more lies behind the juxtaposition of Ps 105 and 106 than simply the fact that they are history psalms.

Psalm 107 This appealing psalm is unique among the thanksgiving psalms. The central part (vv. 4–32) consists of four sections in which different groups of those who have been rescued by YHWH are called upon to thank him. There are two refrains. The first in vv. 6, 13, 19, 28, which has slight variations, describes the way the unfortunates 'cried to' YHWH, who then 'delivered' (v. 6) or 'saved' (vv. 13, 19) them, or 'brought them out' (v. 28), while the second in vv. 8, 15, 21, 31 urges them to offer thanks, the first two followed by different motivations suited to the trouble into which they had fallen, the last two with extended exhortations (vv. 22, 32). The introductory call to give thanks (v. 1) is followed by what appears to be a reference to the returning exiles (vv. 2–3). vv. 33–43 form a hymn praising God who controls nature and maintains justice among human beings, ending with a wisdom-style admonition.

Not unnaturally many suppose that two separate psalms have been combined, some also regarding vv. 2–3 as a post-exilic adaptation of an earlier psalm (cf. Isa 43:5; 49:12). Since such composite psalms are found both in the Psalter (e.g. Ps 108) and in the historical books (e.g. 1 Chr 16), this is not out of the question. It is possible, however, to read the psalm as a liturgy of thanksgiving, the final hymn summing up the congregation's praise.

How the psalm might have been used is unknown. It has been suggested that it might have had its origin at a mass thanksgiving festival, and was picked up later and slightly modified by pilgrims from the Diaspora. There is also disagreement about the nature of the dangers from which the worshippers have been saved, some taking the language literally and seeing actual travellers, prisoners, sick persons, and sailors, others treating the whole as allegorical of the nation, freed from bondage in Egypt and Babylon, restored to new life and health, and delivered from the 'stormy' attacks of foreign nations.

Psalm 108 This psalm has been formed by combining 57:7–11 and 60:6–12 with only very minor differences in the text. But rather than simply referring to the comments on these two psalms, it is worth looking carefully at the new psalm which has been created, for the thrust and mood have been radically altered.

Ps 57 begins with urgent petition by an individual, and the section which has been taken up in Ps 108 is the concluding expression of confidence that the prayer has been heard and self-exhortation to offer praise. Ps 60 also begins with a complaint against God, because he has rejected his people, but the editor of Ps 108 omits this part of the psalm, takes up the divine promise to give Israel victory over the surrounding nations, especially over Edom, the call for help, and the final note of certainty that God will enable the Israelites to defeat their enemies. Thus the tone of Ps 108 is more assured and joy predominates. The combination of individual and communal prayers presents the psalmist as the representative of the nation (royal maximalists suggest that this is a king's psalm). If the sources are disregarded the structure of the psalm now appears as vv. 1–4, a vow to praise God or the expression of that praise; vv. 5–9, prayers for help linked to the divine promise (perhaps a prophetic oracle); and vv. 10–13, a further appeal, ending in an expression of trust or confidence that God will support his people. Throughout the emphasis is upon the steadfast love, faithfulness, and promises of God. Whether it reflects the experiences of the Exile and Return cannot be determined, but it is a fine example of the way that past liturgies continue to live on into a later age.

Psalm 109 This appeal to God is notable for the comprehensive curse in vv. 6–19. It is probably the prayer of an individual, who is perhaps a man who has been falsely accused, or who is making an appeal to the temple authorities, or who is having to undergo an ordeal, although some find national overtones and link it with the king's psalms. The psalmist makes his plea in vv. 1–5, and this is followed by the extensive imprecation (vv. 6–19, concluded or summed up in v. 20). Pleading is renewed at v. 21, with appeals on the grounds of YHWH's steadfast love, the psalmist's misery, and the attacks and curses of the enemies. The lament ends with the vow to offer praise, so common in this type of psalm (vv. 30–1).

NRSV and REB insert 'They say' in v. 6, taking the following words as a quotation of the enemies' curse, while NJB adopts the same interpretation by the use of quotation marks. NJB continues the quotation to the end of v. 15, and NRSV to v. 19, but REB holds that only v. 6 is the word of the enemy, the rest of the imprecation being uttered by the psalmist against the perjured accuser put up by the enemies. NIV and GNB give no indication of any change of speaker in the text, although NIV offers a marginal alternative similar to NRSV.

Although there seem to be quotations in other psalms (e.g. Ps 52:7), the quotation of such a lengthy imprecation appears unlikely, since the psalmist utters a curse in v. 29, and would surely have been fearful of repeating his enemies' curse in such detail. In support of the theory it is pointed out that outside these verses the enemies are spoken of in the plural (but the imprecation may be against their leader), that the psalmist states that they resorted to curses (v. 28), and that v. 21 may signal the return to the psalmist's own plea. It is doubtful whether the psalm was ever part of normal worship, although if it was a royal psalm it may have been.

Psalm 110 This is one of the irreducible minimum of royal psalms and because of the divine oracle in v. 1 has often been assigned to the king's coronation (cf. Ps 2). The first words of the psalm are found very often in the prophetic books, where they usually come at the end of an oracle and are commonly translated 'says the LORD'. They are found only here in the Psalter (but cf. 'Transgression speaks', Ps 36:1). A further oracle is given in v. 4, where the king is also declared a priest. Melchizedek was the king-priest of Jebusite Jerusalem in Gen 14:18–20, and it has been suggested that when David captured the city he took over many features of the old Canaanite religion. Although NRSV does not insert quotation marks, v. 2b may be a further divine promise.

Unfortunately the text is difficult and almost certainly corrupt in several verses (cf. the varied translations of v. 3 in the Eng. versions), possibly an indication of the great age of the psalm, and its reuse in different situations across the centuries. Some accept that it goes back to the time of David, others relate it to the New Year Festival, either at the beginning, when it is part of the king's preparation for the ritual battle with his enemies, or after his humiliation and victory. The speaker may have been a temple prophet. The mysterious v. 3 may refer to an enacted 'rebirth' within the ritual. Alternative suggestions link it with Solomon's coronation, or the time of Josiah. Others take the military language literally and relate the psalm to actual battles.

Christian interpretation, going back to the first century and building on Jewish tradition, regarded it as messianic, and vv. 1 and 4 are frequently quoted in the NT, where they support the belief in the reign of Christ after the resurrection and ascension (cf. Mk 12:36; Acts 2:34–5; Heb 1:13; 5:6; 7:17, 21).

Psalm 111 This and Ps 112 form a pair of acrostics, each having twenty-two short lines beginning with the letters of the Hebrew alphabet. The present psalm has the features of a hymn of praise or thanksgiving. Whether it was intended to be sung in worship (cf. v. 1) or was a poetic meditation on such worship is impossible to decide. The main themes relate to the Exodus deliverance, possibly linked even more closely to Ex 34 (cf. v. 4b with Ex 34:6, and other similarities of vocabulary with Ex 34:5, 10, 11).

How far the acrostic hinders logical development of the ideas is much debated. Some find reiterated thoughts on the covenant God. Others detect two strophes, vv. 2–7a fastening on YHWH's saving deeds, and vv. 7b–10 on covenant and law. Whether more intricate word patterns are visible as some have claimed, seems doubtful. Certainly this is no drab exercise but a vibrant account of the saving God to whom Israel responds with thanksgiving, reverence, and obedience, for the psalmist is confident that the everlasting graciousness of God will be matched by everlasting praise.

Psalm 112 This psalm is either by the same author as Ps 111 or was modelled on it, as the acrostic form and similarities of vocabulary suggest, but here the poet speaks more like one of the wise men, telling of the blessing which comes to the godly man, rather like Ps 1, though with only a glance at the fate of the wicked in the final verse. The tightly compressed style makes the translation of some verses uncertain, e.g. is the subject of v. 4 light, God, or the righteous man? All the words are singular (the 'they' of NRSV is accommodation to inclusive language). LXX inserted 'the Lord' to make the meaning clear, cf. RSV, probably wrongly in view of the general tenor of the psalm.

A striking feature of this psalm is the way virtues ascribed to YHWH in Ps III are transferred to the good man: like YHWH he is gracious and compassionate and his righteousness is of the same nature as God's. Although the psalm lacks a logical structure, the psalmist pointing to many different ways in which goodness leads to prosperity, its attractiveness lies in its portrait of the righteous man, giving to the poor, always ready to lend to the needy, governed by absolute integrity, and with a life based on trust in God, in whose law he delights.

Psalm 113 Ps 113–18 form the 'Hallel' ('Praise', cf. the frequent 'Hallelujah', 'Praise Yah') or the 'Egyptian Hallel' (cf. Ps 114:1) to distinguish it from the 'Great Hallel' (Ps 136, or 120–36, or 135–6; the name was also given in Jewish tradition to Ps 146–50). These six psalms were the only ones sung at the great festivals, according to the earliest sources. At Passover Ps 113–14 were sung before the meal and 115–18 after it (*m. Pesaḥ.* 10:6, 7, cf. Mk 14:26).

Ps 113 is a hymn of praise. It opens with a thrice-repeated imperative, and this is followed by ascriptions of praise to YHWH (vv. 2–3) and further descriptions of his greatness and goodness (vv. 4–9). v. 9 may have been intended literally of a childless woman; later Judaism found in it a reference to Zion (cf. Isa 54:1–8), and the Targum paraphrased the verse: 'Who makes the congregation of Israel, which was like a barren woman mourning for the men of her household, to be full of crowds, like a mother who rejoices over sons.' Whether the psalm was sung antiphonally, a leader shouting the call to praise and the congregation, or another choir, responding with vv. 2–9, is conjecture.

Psalm 114 Despite the narrative form, this psalm is usually classed as a hymn of praise, in stanzas of two verses, the inner two (vv. 3–4, 5–6) matching each other. Incidents in the account of the Exodus and Conquest are referred to: God's choice of Israel, crossing the Red Sea and Jordan, the provision of water in the desert, and the Sinai law-giving (though some see either parallels to creation myths or a specific reference to creation). Changes of verbal forms have led NRSV and NJB to introduce vivid present tenses in vv. 5–6. The LXX moves 'Praise the LORD' from the end of Ps 113 to the head of this psalm, perhaps rightly, since it then provides an antecedent for 'his' (NRSV 'God's') in v. 2.

In Dante's *Divine Comedy* the spirits sing this psalm as they draw near to the island on which the mountain of purgatory stands. In another place Dante explains the medieval method of exegesis: 'If we regard *the letter alone*, what is set before us is the exodus of the Children of Israel from Egypt in the days of Moses; if the *allegory*, our redemption wrought by Christ; if the *moral* sense, we are shown the conversion of the soul from the grief and wretchedness of sin to the state of grace; if the *anagogical*, we are shown the departure of the holy soul from the thraldom of this corruption to the liberty of eternal glory.' It was on such grounds that the psalm has been used both on Easter Day and at the burial of the dead. While such interpretations may appear far removed from the 'real' meaning of the psalm, modern literary theory warns against supposing that meaning is limited to the author's intention.

Psalm 115 vv. 4–11 recur as Ps 135:15–20, with some differences in the text; many Hebrew MSS, including the Leningrad codex, the LXX, Syriac, and Jerome join the psalm to Ps 114; and many Hebrew MSS begin a new psalm at v. 12. This confusion is increased by the inclusion of the psalm within the Hallel, for it begins like a lament rather than a hymn of praise. It will never be possible to trace its past history, and it is best to try to understand the meaning of the completed psalm on its own.

vv. 1–2 is a cry for deliverance, at a time when God appears to have deserted Israel and his people and foreigners ask for proof of his activity. The next section (vv. 3–8) is a hymn, in which the power of YHWH is contrasted with the impotence of idols. A threefold call to Israel, priests ('Aaron'), and those who 'fear the LORD' (possibly proselytes, but more probably a comprehensive term for all the faithful) to trust in YHWH follows (REB, hardly correctly, follows the LXX, Syriac, and Jerome in taking the verbs as indicative). At this point a prophet or priest confidently affirms that God will bless his people (vv. 12–13) and a priest gives a blessing (vv. 14–15). The liturgy ends with a vow to praise YHWH (vv. 16–18).

Presumably the psalm was intended for worship, and if it reflects the teaching of Deutero-Isaiah it belongs to the time of the second temple.

Psalm 116 This psalm has often been seen as a textbook example of the individual thanksgiving psalms. vv. 1–2 express the psalmist's love of God because he has saved him (other thanksgiving psalms begin with a call to give thanks); a narrative follows (vv. 3–11), in which the psalmist recounts his past distress and describes how God delivered him; and the psalm ends with the repayment of the vows which the psalmist made and the psalmist offers a thanksgiving sacrifice (vv. 12–19; unless this is a vow promising to do all these things).

The trouble from which the psalmist was saved was most probably serious illness: he feels that he had almost entered into Sheol, its cords had gripped him and he felt he would be swept away to destruction. v. 11 does not seem sufficient evidence for supposing that this is another psalm of one falsely accused, and the 'cup of salvation' is more probably a libation accompanying the sacrifice than an ordeal (cf. Num 5:15–28). Royal maximalists take it as the king's psalm, holding that he would be the most likely person to offer sacrifices in the temple and finding a parallel to the libation in a stele of Yehawmilk of Byblos on which the king is depicted standing before the goddess Ba'alat, cup in hand, and uttering his prayer. It is held to be especially appropriate for the king to call himself YHWH's servant (v. 16), and the occasional plurals may show that the royal psalmist is the nation's representative. Aramaisms in the language may point to a post-exilic date, however, and the psalm was perhaps intended for use by any Israelite who came to the sanctuary to offer his thanksgiving.

The LXX begins a new psalm, with a fresh heading of 'Alleluia', at v. 10, but there is no reason to suppose that two psalms have been combined. The tradition in this part of the Psalter appears to have been uncertain about the psalm divisions generally.

Psalm 117 This tiny psalm expresses the perfect form of a hymn of praise, with the call to praise (v. 1), the motivation for that praise, introduced by 'for' (v. 2ab), and a repeated call to praise (v. 2c). The universalist invitation to the (foreign) nations to worship YHWH, a couple of Aramaisms, and possibly the influence of Deutero-Isaiah, have suggested a post-exilic date. Paul quotes v. 1 in support of his belief that God's loving purpose reaches out to the Gentiles (Rom 15:11). It is not impossible, however, that the psalmist thought of the nations as coming in subservience to Israel's God.

The uncertainty about the psalm divisions continues, many Hebrew MSS joining this psalm to Ps 116 (which royal maximalists find appropriate as the conclusion of the king's psalm), and other MSS taking it as the beginning of Ps 118. But Ps 116 is complete in itself, and Ps 118 opens in a different style, so that the tradition of the LXX, and the majority of Hebrew MSS, which treats it as a separate psalm is probably correct.

Psalm 118 The interchange between singular and plural, and apparent dialogue, coupled with apparent references to the temple gates and a procession, suggest that this is a liturgy. In vv. 1–4 the community is called to offer thanksgiving. An individual appears at v. 5 and describes the way YHWH has saved him (vv. 5–18). The call to open the gates (v. 19) with a response in v. 20 is similar to Ps 24:7–10, and has led some to see in the psalm an 'entrance liturgy'. The final verses contain varied elements: thanksgiving (v. 21), possibly in response to the opening of the gates, a proverbial statement (v. 22), praise of YHWH (vv. 23–4), a plea for salvation (v. 25), a blessing, probably by a priest (v. 26), a call to join in the procession round the altar (v. 27), and a vow to praise God (v. 28). The psalm ends, as it began, with a call to thanksgiving (v. 28).

Interpretations vary. Many believe that it is a royal psalm, either after actual victory in war, or as part of the temple ritual, when the king was attacked by his enemies and almost defeated before being 'saved' by YHWH. Some argue that the phrase 'house of Aaron' points to the time after the Exile when this was how the priesthood was known, while 'those who fear the LORD' were proselytes; they refer the psalm to a national leader, or even to the whole nation. Jewish tradition linked it with the feast of Tabernacles, and the Mishnah (m. Sukk. 3:9; 4:5) records that the lûlāb (bunch of palm, myrtle, and willow branches) was shaken at the beginning and end of the recital of the psalm, and that willow branches were set up over the altar.

The psalm was regarded as messianic in early Christian circles and is quoted extensively in the NT (Heb 13:6 (v. 6); Mk 12:10–11; Acts 4:11; 1 Pet 2:7 (vv. 22–3); Mk 11:9 (v. 26)), but whether this interpretation had Jewish antecedents is uncertain.

Psalm 119 This great acrostic consists of twenty-two stanzas of eight lines, each line beginning with the appropriate letter of the Hebrew alphabet (cf. Lam 3). While the stanzas are separated in most English versions, only NIV and NJB mark the Hebrew letters as AV and RV did. GNB is misleading in suggesting that each stanza expresses a special theme. In addition to the alphabetic structure the writer uses eight words to represent the law, visible in most modern translations (cf. NRSV: 'law', 'promise', 'word', 'statutes', 'command-

ments', 'ordinances', 'decrees', 'precepts', but with occasionally different renderings), although GNB varies the translations of all the words apart from 'law' with a wanton promiscuity. It has been suggested that originally all eight words were included in each stanza, and some scholars have emended the text to secure this, but there is so little obvious corruption that it is most unlikely that this is right. Most of the words are found in all the stanzas but only four contain all eight used once each (vv. 57–64, 73–80, 81–8, 129–36). Although the words have different connotations, differences of meaning are hardly important in this psalm, where the psalmist ponders the divine teaching, eagerly looking for it to mould his life. It was a happy chance that the word expressing beatitude begins with the first letter of the alphabet: it is found in the first two verses of the psalm.

Each verse expresses an independent idea, although there is some grouping (e.g. vv. 98–100) and features from different types of psalm appear within the poem: hymn of praise (e.g. vv. 89–91, 172), thanksgiving (e.g. v. 7), lament (e.g. vv. 107, 153–60), references to enemies (e.g. vv. 23, 51, 86–7, 95, 157), confession and assertion of innocence (e.g. vv. 11, 30–2, 97–104, 163), vow (v. 33), wisdom saying (e.g. vv. 9, 130). Although it is difficult to imagine a setting in Israelite worship for this amalgam, the psalmist is deeply versed in the hymns of the temple, and other OT writings, especially Deuteronomy, Proverbs, and Jeremiah.

While it is often described as a Torah psalm, apart from vv. 1–3 and 115 every verse is addressed to God. Perhaps it would be better to regard it as a meditation in the form of a prayer to God (somewhat like Augustine's Confessions). If the beginning and end mark his intention, the psalmist wished to stress the happiness that comes from following YHWH's teaching and to 'walk in his ways', and, despite some assertions of his own righteousness, he seeks the divine help which he knows is necessary if he is to obey God's law.

Psalm 120 The tenses in v. 1 present the main difficulty in the interpretation of this psalm. NRSV changes the pointing and treats the verse as the opening of a prayer for deliverance. The MT should be translated as REB: 'I called to the LORD in my distress, and he answered me'. If this is correct, the psalm would appear to be a thanksgiving which includes the prayer which the psalmist offered and the distress from which he has been delivered. The psalm seems very fragmented, with v. 2 the actual prayer, v. 3 a rhetorical question answered in v. 4, vv. 5–7 an account of the enemies who refuse appeals for peace.

The dangers besetting the psalmist are uncertain. It might be the prayer of one falsely accused, making his appeal in the temple, the references to warfare being metaphorical. Royal maximalists treat it as the prayer of the king, attacked by enemies, and possibly the victim of the breaking of an alliance ('lying lips'). Meshech and Kedar refer to a country or people near the Black Sea and a tribe in the Syro-Arabian desert, places so far apart that the names are often taken metaphorically to represent bitter and implacable foes rather than the actual exile of the psalmist. If 'Song of Ascents' is a reference to pilgrimage (see PS C.9, E.12), the names may have been understood as areas from which the pilgrims have come.

Psalm 121 This psalm is in the form of a dialogue. Unless 'my help' (v. 2) is arbitrarily emended to 'help' or 'your help', the response to the question in v. 1 begins at v. 3. But then v. 2 rather hangs in the air, since it would imply that the questioner offered his own answer before receiving the assurance of vv. 3–8 (probably by a priest). It is just possible that v. 2 as it stands is the beginning of the priest's assurance, expressing his own experience. The AV followed Jerome and Luther in wrongly taking 'from where' (v. 1) as a relative.

The situation in which the psalm may have been recited is uncertain. A cultic setting is more probable than that the psalmist converses with himself, or a father with his son. Some have taken 'your going out and your coming in' (v. 8) as indicating the priest's blessing to pilgrims as they leave the temple after one of the festivals and look to their return for the next, but the phrase is used of the ordinary activities of daily life (cf. Deut 28:6; 1 Kings 3:7) and this seems to be its meaning here. The reference to the Keeper of Israel in v. 4, has convinced others that the promise is given to the king as representative of Israel, who has YHWH at his right hand, with the going out and coming in referring to his leadership in war (cf. Josh 14:11; 1 Sam 18:16).

Psalm 122 It is difficult to decide whether this pilgrim song, which is related to the songs of Zion (Ps 46; 48; 76; 84; 87), was sung when the pilgrims had just arrived in Jerusalem or were preparing to leave after the festival. Whichever it was, the psalmist expresses the great joy he had felt as he set out in the company of others to come up to Jerusalem (vv. 1–2; 'when they said to me' involves a change in the vowels; NIV keeps closer to the MT: 'I rejoiced with those who said to me'). After praising the holy city (vv. 3–5), he prays for its welfare (vv. 6–8; 'peace' is more than just absence of war), and concludes the psalm with a vow (v. 9). There is probably a play on the name Jerusalem, the name of which probably means 'the foundation of Salem', a god's name related to šālôm ('prosperity', 'peace'; the word occurs three times in these verses).

'Of David' is added to 'A Song of Ascents' in the title of this psalm, as also in Ps 124; 131. GNB marg. is misleading in making no reference to the title in Ps 120–34, apart from 'HEBREW TITLE: By David' in these two psalms. 'Of David' is omitted by two Hebrew MSS, LXX MSS, and the Targum. It is another example of the extension of Davidic psalms in later editing.

Psalm 123 Despite the title and its position within the Psalter, this is probably not a pilgrim psalm. Rather a group of persecuted Jews plead for help. The singular of v. 1 may indicate antiphonal chanting, with a representative of the community speaking first. vv. 1–2 express confidence in God (some find a chiastic structure, a b b' a'), while vv. 3–4 are the prayer, supported by a description of the contempt which is shown them. In v. 2 'hand' may represent the master's power, or the sense may be that the servants watch their master's hand so that they can obey every gesture.

The last line has been taken to be either dittography or (following the qere, 'proudest oppressors' or even 'proudest Greeks') a gloss from the Greek period. There seems no reason for rejecting the ketib; the verse may have three lines.

Psalm 124 This communal or national thanksgiving opens with strong emphasis upon the fact that it was YHWH who was on his people's side (vv. 1–5). Had he not been they would have been overwhelmed by the danger, depicted as the attack of a savage animal or a devastating torrent. 'Let Israel now say' (v. 1b) is probably a call to the assembled people to take up the theme. In v. 2 the Hebrew word behind 'enemies' normally refers to humanity in general (e.g. the word is translated 'human beings' in Ps 8:4), but here it appears to be used to contrast the weakness of human enemies compared with the power of YHWH. vv. 6–7 praise God who has delivered his people, and the final verse expresses confidence in YHWH, the great creator.

Certain peculiarities in the Hebrew may point to a late date, but it is impossible to fasten upon any historical situation which called forth the psalm.

Psalm 125 Uncertainty about the verb 'will lead away' in v. 5 partly affects the classification of this psalm. If it is to be translated as a future (so NRSV, NIV) it reiterates the confidence of vv. 1–3, and the psalm appears to be a national psalm of trust in YHWH. If, however, it is taken as expressing a wish (cf. REB: 'may the LORD make them go the way of evildoers'; NJB and GNB render with an imperative) the psalm looks much more like a national lament, the initial expressions of confidence leading up to urgent prayer for help. Most Eng. versions smooth out v. 2, but NJB expresses the vigour of the Hebrew: 'Jerusalem! The mountains encircle her: so [Heb. "and"] Yahweh encircles his people.'

It appears that the Jews are oppressed in their own land by foreigners (cf. v. 3) and most place it in the post-exilic period, during the Persian (or even Greek) empire.

Psalm 126 Four uncertainties in meaning make this apparently simple little psalm one of the most difficult.

1. The opening phrase is now usually translated as NRSV: 'When the LORD restored the fortunes of Zion', rather than as the margin: 'brought back those who returned to Zion', and does not unambiguously refer to the return from exile. Its relation to v. 4, however, remains uncertain. In v. 4 the verb is an imperative, opening up alternative possibilities for the relation of this verse to v. 1. Probably v. 4 is a prayer for a further deliverance (only NJB takes it as a release from captivity, though NIV and GNB offer this as an alternative, both reversing text and margin from v. 1 and presumably taking v. 1 as a reference to the return from exile and v. 4 as a later deliverance), or vv. 1–3 might be a meditation on the future.

2. The tenses in vv. 1–3 are uncertain, as is the meaning of 'we were like those who dream'. If that phrase is interpreted in a modern sense of being almost unbelievable (cf. GNB: 'it was like a dream'), the whole section probably refers to the past (as most Eng. versions). On the other hand, the verbs in v. 2 might refer to a hypothetical future, the sense being that when (almost 'if') God restores Jerusalem's fortunes, the people would be filled with joy, but it is only a dream. On this view 'we are like dreamers' is a parenthesis. The difficulty with this interpretation, however, is that v. 3 appears to refer to YHWH's past actions (unless the verbs are taken as 'prophetic' perfects or as a petition).

3. But 'dreamers' may not be the correct meaning of the Hebrew. The LXX's 'we became as those comforted', the Syriac 'as those who rejoice' and the Targum's 'like sick people who are cured', point to a different tradition, probably sup-

ported by a Qumran text (cf. REB: 'people renewed in health', cf. NIV marg.).

4. The meaning of vv. 5–6 is also uncertain. They look like proverbial statements, but may go back to ideas of a dying and rising god, symbolized by the sowing of seed (his burial) and its growth (his resurrection). Here they appear to be a promise uttered by a prophet or a declaration of confidence (cf. Ps 85). NRSV, however, regards v. 5 as a continuation of the petition in v. 4, and only v. 6 as expressing a note of confidence.

The psalm may belong to the Autumn Festival (cf. God's salvation, reference to rain, and sowing and reaping), and be a prayer for blessing on the coming agricultural year. On the other hand, it might have a historical setting, possibly during the distress that followed the return from exile.

Psalm 127 The wisdom features of this psalm are clear, and it is unlikely that it was related to the cult, although some have associated it with the Feast of Tabernacles, the rededication of the temple, or the birth of a son (later Christian tradition used it in the service of thanksgiving for women after childbirth). The different themes in vv. 1–2 and 3–5 have led to the suggestion that two separate psalm fragments have been combined, but a Sumerian poem also combines the gift of palace, city, and children. This makes it unnecessary to take 'house' (v. 1) as 'household, family'. Sons were important for building up the power and prestige of the family, and v. 5 refers to their support in lawsuits which were judged in the city gate. Sons of a man's youth (v. 4) would be in their prime when he came to rely on their support.

The meaning of 'he gives sleep to his beloved' (v. 2) is very uncertain. The NRSV marg. 'he provides for his beloved during sleep' is doubtfully possible as a translation, since 'gives' requires an object, but neither is particularly suitable in a wisdom context, with its warnings against sleep (cf. Prov 6:6–11; 20:13). Hence other meanings for the word have been sought, such as 'prosperity' or 'honour', but the ancient versions support 'he gives sleep'.

An editor searching for allusions in the historical books ascribed the psalm to Solomon in the title (absent from some LXX MSS), probably through taking the 'house' as the temple, relating 'beloved' with Solomon's other name, Jedidiah (2 Sam 12:25), and maybe seeing in 'sleep' an allusion to Solomon's dream (1 Kings 3:10–15).

Psalm 128 This happy psalm begins with a beatitude and ends with a benediction. Usually classed as a wisdom psalm, from the language and sentiments, it is not impossible that it was used in the worship, perhaps to welcome pilgrims or to bless them as they depart from the temple. The stress on fertility may point to the Autumn Festival. Even these are guesses; still more precarious are suggestions that it is the blessing given to a host at the door of his house, and Luther's description of a 'marriage song'.

It is in two parts, but whether the division is after v. 3 or v. 4 is uncertain. v. 4 could round off the first part or introduce the second. Notable is the combining of prosperity for the pious man and the welfare of Jerusalem.

Psalm 129 The two parts of this psalm stand out fairly clearly. In vv. 1–4 Israel is called upon to affirm YHWH's continual protection against its enemies from the time of the Exodus ('my youth', cf. Hos 11:1). vv. 5–8 are an imprecation on Israel's enemies. It is possible that v. 4 belongs with the second part of the psalm, and that the verb should be taken as precative: 'may he cut', but this is less likely. v. 8c may be an independent blessing, this time invoked on 'those who pass by' or the worshippers who recite the psalm.

Type and setting are quite uncertain, although it seems very probable that the psalm was used in the cult. Classifications include communal psalm of confidence, communal thanksgiving, communal lament, or a mixture of forms: national thanksgiving and psalm of revenge or judgement. Perhaps it is best to admit that it does not fit easily into preconceived categories. The opening and much of the subject-matter link it with Ps 124.

Psalm 130 This is commonly regarded as a lament, although the usual account of the distress of the supplicant is lacking, possibly replaced by the indirect confession of sin (vv. 3–4). For this interpretation the verbs in vv. 1 and 5 need to be translated as present (as NRSV). They may, however, indicate the psalmist's actions in the past ('I have called', REB), when the psalm would more naturally be seen as a thanksgiving which looked back to the earlier distress and prayer. The call to Israel (vv. 7–8) is perhaps odd in the petition of an individual. Some regard it as a later addition to adjust the psalm to the community. Others propose that a priest at this point addressed the assembled worshippers, among whom the individual psalmist had come to the temple.

The depths are the watery deeps, and probably indicate that the psalmist is gravely ill and feels he has sunk into the underworld of death (cf. PS G.13); illness and sin go together, as often in the OT. The watchmen (v. 6) may be military sentinels, but the Targum identifies them as Levites who watch for the first moment of the dawn to offer the morning sacrifice.

A few claim it as a royal psalm, but there is little to support this. While most assume that it was sung within the cultic worship, this also is uncertain. Some view it as a personal prayer, unconnected with the cult, but whether such poems were composed in ancient Israel, even after the Exile, is unknown. It is one of the seven penitential psalms of the church, and was an especial favourite of Luther, who called it one of the 'Pauline psalms' and based his great hymn 'Out of the depths I cry to Thee' on it.

Psalm 131 The brevity of this psalm makes interpretation difficult. It is usually regarded as a psalm of confidence by an individual, v. 3 being either an addition to fit it for corporate worship (cf. Ps 130:7–8), or the widening of the psalmist's devotion to include the community. Even maximalists shrink from suggesting that it is a royal psalm, despite 'Of David' in the title (omitted by some LXX MSS), though this has been proposed, royal traits being found in the references to pride and similarities with Ps 62:1, 5. Other suggestions are that it was a form of entrance liturgy (cf. Ps 15; 24), that the speaker was a teacher in the temple addressing an assembly of Israel, even that it was sung by a woman pilgrim carrying her child. The exact meaning of 'weaned child' is not clear; possibly the weaned child was less fretful than the child just before it was weaned, when its mother's milk was drying up. Whatever the precise meaning and origins, the psalm expresses a quiet confidence in God.

Psalm 132 This is among the essential group of royal psalms. It falls into two clear sections: vv. 1–10 are a prayer for God's blessing on the Davidic king, vv. 11–18 an affirmation of God's promises to David and an assurance that YHWH will remain faithful to his covenant with David and grant blessings on Jerusalem; David's descendants ('one of the sons of your body', 'a horn to sprout up', vv. 11, 17) will enjoy prosperity and will triumph over their enemies. Vocabulary and ideas link the two parts closely together: e.g. 'turn away/back' (vv. 10, 11); 'anointed one' (vv. 10, 17); the clothing of the priests with righteousness/salvation (vv. 9, 16); Jerusalem as God's dwelling-place (vv. 7–8, 13, although the Heb. words are different); the correspondence between David's oath and YHWH's (vv. 2, 11); vv. 13–16 form the response to vv. 6–9. The psalm is commonly described as a liturgy in which king and prophet take part. The linking of Zion (vv. 5, 13–15), the ark (v. 8, and probably v. 6: REB boldly identifies 'it' as the ark), and the Davidic dynasty would all be suitable to the New Year Festival.

There is clearly some connection with the account of David's bringing of the ark into Jerusalem and Nathan's oracle in 2 Sam 6–7. Some accept that the narrative in Samuel is historical, and see in the psalm later cultic celebration. Others regard the psalm and the accompanying cultic worship as primary, the writer of the history having filled out his narrative from the ritual of his own day. This appears to have happened in 2 Chr 6, where the writer concludes his version of the story he has taken from Samuel with vv. 8–10 of this psalm.

Ephrathah (v. 6) probably refers to Bethlehem, where David came from. Unless 'fields of Jaar' is really 'fields of the forest, woodland', it is apparently a reference to Kiriath-jearim from where David brought the ark into Jerusalem (1 Sam 7:1–2; 2 Sam 6:2), and it has been suggested (less probably) that Ephrathah referred to the same area.

Psalm 133 To most people the first line of this psalm is appealing, but to some the second verse may seem grotesque—which shows how difficult it is to enter into the culture and emotions of ancient Israel.

Three main interpretations are generally offered. (1) It is a wisdom psalm concerned with family life, which has been adapted to cultic use by the addition of references to Aaron and Zion. (2) It has a historical setting and perhaps comes from a post-exilic time when attempts were being made to unite the Jews in Judah. (3) It belongs to one of the festivals and sees in the worship of YHWH the true unity of the nation. None of these is particularly convincing, and we have to confess that the psalm is so foreign that we cannot guess at its true meaning.

The dew of Hermon in Syria falling on Jerusalem is a strange concept. Perhaps 'dew of Hermon' was a phrase for heavy dew. Some emend Zion to 'dry', but this is simply to rewrite the psalm. The oil is probably the sacred oil of consecration. It may be that it is not the oil which runs down on the collar but Aaron's long beard, which 'flows' down.

There are carefully crafted repetitions and plays on words in the Hebrew: 'running down' in vv. 2 and 3 ('falls' is the same word); Zion and 'ordained' (vv. 3, 4); and 'brothers (NRSV 'kindred') and 'life' (vv. 1, 3) have a similar sound.

MT has 'Of David' in the title (as REB, NIV), but one LXX MS, the Coptic, and the Targum, as well as two Hebrew MSS

omit the phrase (so NRSV, NJB), perhaps sensing its incongruity. Some think it has been misplaced from Ps 132.

Psalm 134 Ignorance about the worship in ancient Israel makes it difficult to reconstruct the way this psalm was sung. Are there two voices, or one? Are vv. 1–2 addressed to the priests or the laity? Were they actually 'standing in the temple' at the time the psalm was sung, or are they 'attendants' in the temple? What were the night-time practices? (There appear to have been nocturnal rites at the Feast of Tabernacles.) The opening is curious: literally 'Behold, bless YHWH', a unique phrase in the OT—the 'Come' of NRSV, REB, and NJB is not a legitimate translation—and 'Behold' may be wrongly repeated from Ps 133.

While the details are obscure, the general sense is plain: a call to worship God is followed by a priestly blessing. Blessing, indeed, controls the psalm: 'Bless YHWH' opens and closes the first part, and is picked up at the beginning of the last verse.

Psalm 135 Many allusions to other psalms and OT passages (e.g. Ps 134 in vv. 2, 21; Deut 32:36 in v. 14; Ex 19:5 and Deut 7:6 in v. 4), and a close similarity between vv. 15 20 and Ps 115:4–11, suggest that the psalmist either drew his inspiration (and some phrases) from earlier liturgical pieces, or was deeply attuned to living tradition. Perhaps because of this the structure is somewhat complex: vv. 1–4 are hymnic, with calls to praise and motivations introduced with 'for'; vv. 5–7 and 8 12 proclaim YHWH's greatness, first as Lord of nature, then as deliverer of Israel from Egypt and the one who gave the promised land to Israel; vv. 13–14 form another hymnic section, first addressed to YHWH and then describing his protection of Israel; vv. 15–20, apparently drawn from Ps 115:4–11, but with some differences, repudiate idols and call on Israel, priests, Levites, and those who reverence YHWH to praise him; and the concluding verse, possibly a later addition, praises YHWH as the God whose earthly home is Jerusalem.

It is better to try to understand the completed psalm than to worry about the sources from which it has been drawn. The changes of form and address possibly point to antiphonal singing, although it is not easy to determine which verses to ascribe to two or more voices. The tone throughout is of ardent and confident praise. It is apparently post-exilic. Whether it was intended for cultic singing is uncertain: Tabernacles and Passover have both been suggested as suitable occasions for its use.

Psalm 136 The reiterated refrain sounds monotonous to us. It probably points to antiphonal chanting, either between soloist and choir, or priest and people. Possibly it was added to an original psalm which consisted only of the first line of each verse (cf. the additions made to Ps 145 in the Qumran MS).

The form is a hymn. vv. 1–3 are a call to give thanks to YHWH; vv. 4–9 offer praise of YHWH as creator; vv. 10–22 praise YHWH as the one who delivered his people from Egypt and gave them the promised land; vv. 23–5 express a more general praise for God's deliverance of his people, perhaps in the present, and his care of all creation, introduced differently from the earlier part of the psalm; v. 26 is a renewed call to praise YHWH. The psalm forms a companion to Ps 135, and although both are often described as history psalms, both are really hymns (note especially vv. 1–3, 23–5). 'O give thanks' is assumed before vv. 4, 5, 6, 7, 10, 13, 16, 17. The dependence on Gen 1 (cf. vv. 7–9; Gen 1:14–18) makes a post-exilic date almost certain.

Psalm 137 'The tender pathos of the opening verses enlists our sympathy: the crash of bitter denunciation in the closing stanza shocks and repels' (Kirkpatrick 1901: iii. 779). The date of the psalm is variously taken to be during the Exile, when the mockery of vv. 1–3 were a present experience, or soon after the return from exile when the psalmist looked back on past suffering. The key issue is whether v. 6 implies that Jerusalem is restored or faith is holding on to a ruin. Usually described as a communal lament or complaint, the emphasis on Zion is reminiscent of the Songs of Zion, and it may be that the psalmist is reusing features from those songs in a new way. Similarly he expresses his curse on Babylon in the form of a beatitude. The structure is either as in NRSV (vv. 1–3, 4–6, 7–9) or v. 4 belongs to the first stanza, and the rest of the psalm divides into 5–6, 7, 8–9.

History may help us to understand, if not to condone, the final curses. Edom was the traditional enemy of Israel, and at the time of the Exile the Edomites pressed into Judah, and brought upon themselves the undying hatred of Israel (cf. Isa 34; 63:1–6; Lam 4:21–2; Ezek 25:12–14; Ob). On one level it represents the ordinary features of ancient warfare; on another, the Babylonians were accounted the enemies of YHWH and not just of Israel, for they had destroyed his city and his temple.

The LXX gives 'Of David' as a title, and one LXX textual tradition added 'through Jeremiah', possibly noting similarities with Jer 49:7–22; 50:1–51:58, and the verbs 'pay back' and 'dash' (vv. 8–9) in Jer 51:20–4.

Psalm 138 The structure of this psalm is clearer than its type. vv. 1–3 express thanksgiving for answered prayer, vv. 4–6 call on the kings to praise YHWH, and vv. 7–8 conclude the psalm with confidence in YHWH's steadfast love. Perhaps the most natural understanding is that this is an individual thanksgiving, but the universal reference in the middle section has convinced some that it is a royal psalm, offered by the king either when absent from Jerusalem or, more probably, from within the temple court and facing the temple itself. Others propose that it is corporate, the 'I' being either a representative of the nation or symbolizing it. Support can be found for each of these interpretations, but this only reinforces the uncertainty. For example, the call to the foreign kings fits a royal psalm, but might equally be a late 'democratizing' of the style when it was taken over by individuals. In the same way 'lowly' in v. 6 can be understood as a mark of an ordinary Jewish worshipper, but kings, both within Israel and in other countries of the ancient Middle East, described themselves as poor and lowly. Moreover, while there are some resemblances to Deutero-Isaiah (e.g. cf. v. 6 with Isa 57:15) these are hardly close enough to prove dependence on the prophet, and both may well have been calling upon traditional liturgical language. Some LXX MSS add 'of Zechariah' to the title, perhaps finding similarities between the message of this prophet and vv. 4–6. Finally, the tenses in vv. 4–5 present some difficulties. NRSV takes the verbs as future, declaring the homage that the kings will offer, but it is unusual to find such hymnic descrip-

tions directly addressed to God, and it may be that the verbs should be taken as modal ('Let all the kings of the earth praise you', REB; NIV also takes the verbs as modal).

All in all we are left with a somewhat elusive psalm of thanksgiving, which nevertheless expresses as attractive a joyful thanksgiving and trust as any in the Psalter.

Psalm 139 The uncertain meaning and probable corruption of several verses in this psalm, coupled with uncertainties about its type, make interpretation very difficult. No space is available to discuss individual verses, but the wide differences between the chief modern translations, especially in vv. 11, 14, 16–18, 20 should be noted. The original text and meaning of these verses is probably beyond recovery.

The structure of the psalm as set out in NRSV is accepted by many. In vv. 1–6 the psalmist recognizes God's intimate knowledge of all his actions and thoughts. He then confesses God's omnipresence through rhetorical questions showing that nowhere could he escape from God's presence (vv. 7–12, contrast Jonah). The next section (vv. 13–16) refers either to divine foreknowledge of the psalmist, even before he was born, or draws on mythological ideas about the creation of the first man from the womb of the earth; vv. 17–18 are a more general sense of wonder at God's omniscience. The prayer against the wicked and expression of the psalmist's hatred of those who oppose God in vv. 19–22 strike a harsh and possibly alien note, but the opening call for God to examine his thoughts and actions is picked up in the two concluding verses.

A decision about whether vv. 19–24 (or 19–22) are part of a separate psalm is not easy. The echo 'you have searched'—'search me' (vv. 1, 23) is a strong pointer to unity, the sudden imprecation on the wicked and the difference between the types (they appear to be an individual thanksgiving, rather akin to a hymn, and a lament) speak for two separate psalms or parts of psalms.

Royal maximalists, who regard this as a royal psalm, see vv. 19–24 as the goal of a prayer in which the king invites God to search his inner being and prays for the slaughter of his enemies. (Many readers wish that vv. 19–22 were not there, and it is important to remember that for the psalmist the wicked were God's enemies and that for him God's honour was at stake; see PS J.2–8.) An alternative interpretation ascribes the psalm to a man who has been acquitted of the charges made against him (God has *already* searched out his thoughts and deeds, vv. 1–3), and offers his thanksgiving. This is preferable to taking it as the prayer of one who has been accused and awaits judgement, a view that involves seeing vv. 1–18 as a kind of 'negative oath', akin to Job 31. All these interpretations assume that the psalm belongs to cultic worship, but some think it is too personal for this, and, pointing to wisdom features, regard it as a meditative poem.

The date of the psalm cannot be determined, but does not matter for an appreciation of the reverence before the mighty God which shines out.

Psalm 140 This appears to be the prayer of a man accused by slanderers, whose attacks are described under a variety of metaphors: war, snake poison, setting traps, and plots. The difficulties of knowing whether the situation is an appeal to a higher court, an ordeal, a counter-curse against sorcery, or a plea for direct divine aid and a right judgement are the same as in all similar psalms. A few attribute the psalm to the king (largely on the grounds of the references to war in vv. 2, 7, which most treat as part of the figurative language). The text is almost certainly corrupt in vv. 8–9, and the Eng. versions make various attempts to arrive at some sense.

The structure is not entirely clear. vv. 6–7, 12–13 are somewhat parallel in expressing confidence in God, most obviously in 12–13, which may be a response to a priestly or prophetic assurance that the prayer has been heard. This leaves vv. 1–5 as a prayer for help and vv. 8–11 as an imprecation against the enemies.

Psalm 141 vv. 5–7 of this psalm are so corrupt that it seems impossible to gain any certain sense (cf. the differences in the Eng. versions). In the psalm as a whole the psalmist prays that he may be delivered from the enticements and the oppression of the wicked, and seeks divine support to live a sinless life. Royal maximalists take it to be the king's psalm, perhaps offered during a military campaign far away from Jerusalem (v. 2 is taken to mean that he cannot offer sacrifice in the temple, while v. 7 is seen as a lament over battle losses). More probably it is a prayer of an ordinary worshipper, even a prayer outside cultic worship altogether, although most question whether v. 2 implies the substitution of prayer for sacrifice. While vv. 8–10 express the common plea for help against enemies who are persecuting the psalmist, in terms similar to Ps 140 (cf. 35:8), other parts of the psalm are closer to wisdom teaching, especially the request for help against wrong speech (v. 3) and to be kept away from bad company (v. 4, cf. Ps 1). The structure of the psalm is difficult to determine owing to uncertainties about the text. The NRSV divisions are probably as good as any: an opening call to God to hear his prayer (vv. 1–2), a petition to be enabled to avoid sin and sinners (vv. 3–4), and two sets of petitions against the enemies (vv. 5–7, 8–10), but v. 5 may belong to the second section.

Psalm 142 The title, references to enemies, the psalmist's close bond with YHWH, and the celebration of the people around him, perhaps even crowning him (v. 7, cf. REB: 'The righteous will place a crown on me') have led royal maximalists to include this as one of the king's psalms. On the other hand if 'prison' (v. 7) is taken literally, it will be more naturally regarded as the prayer of a man awaiting the divine decision as to his guilt (cf. Lev 24:12; Num 15:34). It may, however, be figurative, either for distress, or, less probably, for exile, turning the psalm into a prayer for Israel.

The simplest structuring of the psalm is to divide it into two strophes, vv. 1–4, 5–7, although the smaller divisions of NRSV point to further developments in the thought: the opening call to YHWH, a description of the distress, and renewed prayers, coupled with expression of trust in God and a final vow to offer thanksgiving for the deliverance.

The title reveals the way the editor searched the historical books for a suitable setting for the psalm. The cave may be that at Adullam or En-gedi (1 Sam 22:1; 24:3). It has been pointed out that he may have found links with the former in the references to 'refuge' (v. 5) and 'stronghold' (1 Sam 22:4), and to the latter through three words in v. 7 and 1 Sam 24:17–18 from the same Hebrew roots, though this is not apparent in

the English: 'prison' (YHWH 'put me [shut me up] into your hands'); 'righteous'; and 'deal bountifully' ('repaid').

Psalm 143 This psalm is clearly the prayer of an individual, but who the psalmist might be is uncertain. Royal maximalists include it among the king's psalms, pointing to the title, the language, references to enemies, including possibly death as the supreme enemy, and similarities with the previous psalms, which are also regarded as royal. Others include it among the psalms of those falsely accused, pointing to its legal phraseology (e.g. vv. 1–2), seeing in v. 3 a reference to imprisonment while awaiting a decision, and relating v. 8 to the divine decision at dawn; the lack of the usual protestations of innocence perhaps counts against this interpretation. On either view, it is more likely that v. 5 refers to YHWH's deliverance of Israel rather than his past dealings with the psalmist. As with many of these individual laments, most of the allusions are too general to make any reconstruction fully convincing. One of the most striking characteristics of this psalm is the writer's eager longing for God himself and not just his gifts (v. 6), and his prayer to be enabled to obey him (vv. 8, 10).

The structure is not entirely clear because of the repetition of some of the ideas. Most simply it can be divided into an introduction (vv. 1–2), a description of his troubles (vv. 3–6), and further petitions (vv. 7–12), but within the second section there are references to enemies, the psalmist's own depression, a memory of the past, and a longing for God, while in the third death seems imminent, and the psalmist makes several requests for God's steadfast love and divine instruction, as well as deliverance from enemies, and their destruction.

Within Christian tradition this is one of the seven penitential psalms, Paul quoted v. 2 in Rom 3:20 to show universal sinfulness. The LXX's enlargement of the title with 'when his son (one MSS adds Absalom) pursued him' (cf. 2 Sam 15–18) shows how later editors looked for incidents in the books of Samuel with which to link the psalms, in this way providing an interpretation both of the narratives and the psalms.

Psalm 144 At least vv. 1–11 of this psalm are a king's prayer and must be included in the irreducible minimum of royal psalms. vv. 12–15, however, with their plural 'our' and theme of fertility and prosperity, are commonly held to be a fragment of a different psalm. The unity of the psalm can be maintained if it is taken to be liturgical, part of the ritual drama of the humiliation and restoration of the king, rather than a prayer before battle. The celebration of prosperity is the expected consequence of YHWH's salvation of his anointed servant and viceroy (cf. Ps 72). vv. 1–11 contain many reminiscences of other psalms, Ps 18 especially, but also Ps 8 and 33. This may indicate a late date, but the similarities might equally be the result of common liturgical language.

The meaning of v. 14 is uncertain. NRSV takes the first line as a continuation of the agricultural scene in the previous verse, with a change to an attack by a foreign enemy and exile in the second line (cf. NIV). REB, however, makes the whole verse refer to fertility among the animals.

To the Davidic title the LXX adds, 'concerning Goliath' (cf. 1 Sam 17), a further example of a late editorial ascription to David.

Psalm 145 This psalm is an acrostic, each verse beginning with the appropriate letter of the Hebrew alphabet. The n verse is missing from the MT, but is supplied by the Qumran scroll and the LXX and Syriac versions. It is included after v. 13 in all the modern Eng. versions.

Despite the limitations which the form imposes on the writer, the psalmist has produced a hymn with a firm structure. Three times the invocation to worship YHWH is followed by descriptions of his power and goodness (vv. 1–2 + 3; 4–7 + 8–9; 10–12 + 13–20), and the psalm ends with a renewed call to worship which links the individual and 'all flesh' (v. 21). If this is the correct analysis, the verbs in vv. 4–7 and 10–12 should be treated as modal, 'May one generation laud your works to another...', not recognized by modern translations (unless the 'shall' of NRSV is intended to express this sense).

The psalm is notable for reminiscences of other psalms; e.g. v. 3/Ps 96:4; and vv. 15–16/Ps 104:27–8. The description of YHWH in v. 8 is found in Ps 103:8 and Ex 34:6, while individual phrases occur elsewhere. It is possible that such phrases are derived from a common liturgical tradition rather than by direct borrowing, although the change of person in vv. 15–16 favours close contact between the two psalms.

Whether the psalm was ever part of cultic worship is uncertain, although the addition in the Qumran MS of 'Blessed is YHWH, and blessed is his name for ever and ever' after each verse may show that it was sung with a congregational response in late Jewish liturgy. The early church sang it at the midday meal, while Chrysostom associates it with the eucharist because of vv. 15–16. Some, however, regard acrostics as purely poetic, or as wisdom exercises which have no connection with the cult.

Psalm 146 Usually described as a hymn of praise, this psalm has several unusual features. It is by an individual. Instead of the call to praise (vv. 1–2) leading into a description of YHWH's greatness, the psalmist introduces a wisdom-style warning against reliance on human aid (vv. 3–4). This is followed by a beatitude (v. 5) which opens out into the expected description of YHWH as creator and protector of the oppressed (vv. 6–9). Striking in this section are a series of relative clauses setting out the character of God and a group of five sentences each beginning with the name YHWH. The psalm ends with YHWH's reign as king of Zion (v. 10), akin to the Zion hymns (cf. also v. 5). As in Ps 145, phrases from other psalms or from liturgical tradition are taken up and adapted for new use.

The LXX title ascribes this psalm, as well as Ps 147 (divided into two, each with the same title), to Haggai and Zechariah, without any obvious reason. Most regard it as post-exilic, however, on the grounds of its apparent use of other psalms and its language.

Psalm 147 This psalm consists of three sections, each of which is in the form of a complete hymn of praise, with call to worship and description of YHWH's character and deeds upon which that praise is based (vv. 1–6, 7–11, 12–20). He is worshipped as the God of Israel who has restored Jerusalem after the Exile (vv. 2, 13), has shown himself as the mighty creator who controls the stars and the forces of nature, especially the winter frost and snow (vv. 4, 8, 16–18), provides food for human beings and animals (vv. 9, 14), and cares for the brokenhearted (v. 3) and the oppressed (v. 6). This raises the question of the unity of the psalm, doubts about which are increased by the LXX's division into two psalms, vv. 1–11, 12–20. While some accept this, or even argue for a combination of three separate psalms, similarities of vocabulary and themes across the whole psalm, and possible structural patterns, such as the mention of Israel at the beginning and end, have convinced others that the MT tradition is the correct one.

The LXX adds to the title 'of Haggai and Zechariah', as in Ps 146, and inserts this full title before v. 12. Possibly the references to the restoration after the Exile are responsible for this, although it is difficult to determine what controlled its decision. In a further departure from the MT, the LXX adds a second 'Praise the Lord' in v. 1 (in these last five psalms in the Psalter 'Hallelujah' stands outside the main poem), which would make the rest of the verse into the 'for' clause of hymns.

Psalm 148 The structure of this hymn is interesting. The call to praise is expressed with imperatives in vv. 1–4, 7, and with jussives ('let them praise') in vv. 5a, 13a, while what is normally the main content of hymns of praise, the description of YHWH's nature and deeds, introduced with 'for', is limited to vv. 5b–6 and 13b–14a. Moreover, in vv. 1–4 the imperative 'praise him' begins every line, whereas in vv. 7–12 the opening verb is followed by a series of vocatives. The unity is confirmed by the careful construction, which moves from the heavenly bodies (possibly thought of in mythological terms rather than merely poetic imagery), to features of the earth (natural forces, plants and animals, human beings), and finally to what is almost a little hymn to God in itself. v. 14bc is rather awkward and it has been suggested that it is an editorial footnote stating that this is a hymn of praise.

The listing of the various parts of the natural world have been compared to Egyptian lists, but these are longer and the psalm sounds more like a hymn than a scribal collection of animals. Others point to the hymnic tradition from Babylon as well as Egypt. There seems no need to go outside the OT, however, for the closest similarities are with Gen 1, even down to some items of vocabulary.

The 'Song of the Three Young Men' (an addition to Daniel inserted between Dan 3:23, 24 in the Gk. and Lat. versions), and the *Cantemus Cuncti* are further developments of this kind of hymn. Job 38, with which it is also often compared, is less close.

Psalm 149 Some divide this hymn into two sections, vv. 1–4, 5–9, others into three, vv. 1–3, 4–6, 7–9. In favour of a twofold structure is the call to praise followed by the grounds for this praise (introduced by 'for') in the first part, and the call to the people to execute divine vengeance in the second. Support for a three-part division is seen primarily in the triad of infinitives, in vv. 7–9, which marks off these verses; its weakness lies in the rather motley collection of themes in the middle part.

The psalm is marked by the martial tone and the look towards the future, and various situations have been proposed for it. The description of YHWH as king (v. 2) suggests that it may be one of the 'new songs' of the Autumn Festival (cf. Ps 96), the battle being cultic, and the eschatology part of the New Year rites. Others suggest an actual battle situation, the psalm being either a hymn of victory that looks forward to still greater triumphs, or as a prayer sung while preparing for the fight.

Many are appalled at the way this psalm has been used to stir up martial passions in the past. It may alleviate their distress to remember that Israel's enemies were also those of YHWH. On the other hand that may be seen to intensify hatred of the nation's enemies.

Psalm 150 This expansion of the cry, 'Praise the Lord', forms a noble conclusion to the book of the praises of Israel. Ten times the cry 'Praise him' (once 'Praise God') rings out. This may be accidental, or it may reflect the ten words of creation in Gen 1 (cf. *m. 'Abot* 5.1: 'By ten sayings was the world created'). These forge the psalm into a unity and it is unnecessary to try to divide it into stanzas, such as vv. 1–2, 3–4, 5–6, or, more realistically, vv. 1–2 expressing where and for what God is to be praised (by 'the sanctuary' is probably meant both the Jerusalem temple and God's heavenly dwelling), vv. 3–5 listing the various musical instruments (presumably those played in temple worship), and v. 6 uttering a final call to all living things to praise YHWH.

The psalm is often regarded as an extended doxology at the end of the Psalter, corresponding to the doxologies which mark each of the first four books. It is, however, a joyful hymn in its own right, distinguished by the dominance of the call to praise, and lacking the 'for' clauses that describe God's greatness (the brief motivation in v. 2 is a different construction in the Heb.).

REFERENCES

Anderson, A. A. (1972), *Psalms 1–72, Psalms 73–150*, NCB Commentary (London: Marshall, Morgan & Scott; Grand Rapids, Mich.: Eerdmans).

Berry, D. K. (1993), *The Psalms and their Readers: Interpretive Strategies for Psalm 18*, JSOTSup 153 (Sheffield: JSOT).

Bradshaw, P. (1995), *Two Ways of Praying* (Nashville: Abingdon; London: SPCK).

Childs, B. S. (1979), *Introduction to the Old Testament as Scripture* (London: SCM).

Craigie, P. C. (1983), *Psalms 1–50*, WBC 19 (Waco, Tex.: Word Books).

Dahood, M. J. (1966–70), *Psalms*, Anchor Bible Commentary (3 vols.; Garden City, NY: Doubleday).

Day, J. (1990), *Psalms*, Old Testament Study Guides (Sheffield: JSOT).

Delitzsch, F. (1887), ET of *Biblischer Kommentar über die Psalmen* (London: Hodder & Stoughton).

Eaton, J. H. (1986), *Kingship and the Psalms*, SBT, 2nd ser. 32; 2nd edn. (Sheffield: JSOT).

—— (1995), *The Circle of Creation* (London: SCM).

Gersterbenger, E. S. (1988), *Psalms Part I with an Introduction to Cultic Poetry*, The Forms of the Old Testament Literature, 14 (Grand Rapids, Mich.: Eerdmans).

Gillingham, S. E. (1994), *The Poems and Psalms of the Hebrew Bible*, Oxford Bible Series (Oxford: Oxford University Press).

Gunkel, H., and Begrich, J. (1933), *Einleitung in die Psalmen* (Göttingen: Vandenhoeck & Ruprecht).

Gunn, G. S. (1956), *God in the Psalms* (Edinburgh: St Andrew).

Johnson, A. R. (1964), *The Vitality of the Individual in the Thought of Ancient Israel*, 2nd edn. (Cardiff: University of Wales Press).

—— (1967), *Sacral Kingship in Ancient Israel*, 2nd edn. (Cardiff: University of Wales Press).

—— (1979), *The Cultic Prophet and Israel's Psalmody* (Cardiff: University of Wales Press).

Kaiser, W. C., Jr. (1983), *Toward Old Testament Ethics* (Grand Rapids, Mich.: Academie Books, Zondervan).

Keel, O. (1978), *The Symbolism of the Biblical World: Ancient Near Eastern Iconography and the Book of Psalms*, ET (New York: Seabury; London: SPCK).

Kirkpatrick, A. F. (1901), *The Book of Psalms* (Cambridge Bible for Schools and Colleges) (3 vols.; Cambridge: Cambridge University Press), iii.

Kraus, H.-J. (1986), *Theology of the Psalms* (Minneapolis: Augsburg; London: SPCK).

—— (1988), *Psalms 1–59*, BKAT; ET (Minneapolis: Augsburg).

McCann, J. C., Jr. (1993a), *A Theological Introduction to the Book of Psalms* (Nashville: Abingdon).

—— (ed.) (1993b), *The Shape and Shaping of the Psalter*, JSOTSup 159 (Sheffield: JSOT).

McKay, H. A. (1994), *Sabbath and Synagogue: The Question of Sabbath Worship in Ancient Judaism* (Leiden, New York, Cologne: Brill).

Magonet, J. (1994), *A Rabbi Reads the Psalms* (London: SCM).

Mays, J. L., Petersen, D. L., and Richards, K. H. (eds.) (1995), *Old Testament Interpretation, Past, Present, and Future: Essays in Honour of Gene M. Tucker* (Nashville: Abingdon; Edinburgh: T. & T. Clark).

Mowinckel, S. (1921–4), *Psalmenstudien* (6 vols.).

—— (1962), *The Psalms in Israel's Worship*, ET (2 vols.; Oxford: Basil Blackwell).

Noble, P. R. (1995), *The Canonical Approach: A Critical Reconstruction of the Hermeneutics of Brevard S. Childs* (Leiden, New York, Cologne: Brill).

Ringgren, H. (1963), *The Faith of the Psalmists* (London: SCM).

Rogerson, J. W., and McKay, J. W. (1977), *Psalms 1–50, Psalms 51–100, Psalms 101–150*, Cambridge Bible Commentary (Cambridge: Cambridge University Press).

Schofield, J. N. (1951), *Archaeology and the Afterlife* (London: Lutterworth).

Snaith, N. H. (1944), *The Distinctive Ideas of the Old Testament* (London: Epworth).

—— (1964), *The Seven Psalms* (London: Epworth).

Wilson, G. H. (1985), *The Editing of the Hebrew Psalter*, SBLDS 76 (Chico, Calif.: Scholars Press).

Zenger, E. (1996), *A God of Vengeance? Understanding the Psalms of Divine Wrath* (Louisville, Ky.: Westminster/John Knox).

19. Proverbs   K. T. AITKEN

INTRODUCTION

A. The book and its background. 1. The book of Proverbs presents itself as a textbook designed to educate humans in general and the young in particular in wise living (1:2–7). It divides into two main parts: a series of didactic discourses comprising parental instructions and speeches by personified Wisdom in chs. 1–9, and collections of chiefly short proverbial sayings in chs. 10–31. The discourses in 1–9 serve as an extended introduction to the collections that follow. The major theme of these chapters is the surpassing value of wisdom and it is in them that the theological character of wisdom is most pronounced. Wisdom is founded on the 'fear of the LORD' (1:7; 9:10), and is the gift of God (2:6). Through its personification, wisdom is also presented as mediating God's revelation in creation to humankind (8:22–31). The question of how far the theological aspects of wisdom in the book represent a later religious or 'Yahwistic' reinterpretation of an earlier 'secular' wisdom has been the subject of much debate (see Wilson 1987: 313–33).

2. The similarity between the instructions in Proverbs and Egyptian texts used in the education of royal princes and state officials (see PROV 1:8–16; 22:17–24:22) has often been observed. It has been argued that court schools also existed in Israel and that Proverbs has its roots in these schools as an adaptation of Egyptian wisdom and its educational context (McKane 1970). But while the book contains observations on kings and royal officials, the majority of its sayings deal with everyday matters of family, community life, and personal relationships. Others have therefore stressed the importance of the family and community as settings for the instruction of the young and the transmission of proverbial sayings, maintaining that the book has its origins in a more popular oral tradition predating the monarchy (Westermann 1995). None the less, the court was evidently an important setting in the course of the literary development of the book (cf. 25:1). Given the variety in the contents of the book and the nature of the wisdom it inculcates, it seems reasonable to think that wisdom flourished in various settings in Israel and had a corresponding variety of exponents—all of which have left their imprint on the book.

B. Date and Authorship. 1. The book comprises a number of separate collections each of which, save the last one, is introduced by its own heading (see the outline below). The heading in 1:1 may be intended to refer to the book as a whole and Solomon is traditionally regarded as its author. But while its major collections are assigned either directly (10:1) or indirectly (25:1) to him, the remaining collections are ascribed to other 'authors'. It is also clear that the book can be no older than the time of Hezekiah (25:1). If the Solomonic origin of some sayings should not be excluded, neither can it be demonstrated. The headings are best seen as a reflection of the association of wisdom with the royal court in pre-exilic times (cf. 25:1), together with the tradition of Solomon as the paradigm of the wise king (1 Kings 4:29–34).

2. The dates of the individual collections are difficult to determine. It is likely that chs. 10–31 largely emerged during the pre-exilic period. Chs. 1–9 are commonly regarded as the latest section of the book. They may have been put together and edited to form an extended introduction to chs.10–31, and it was probably in the post-exilic period that the book received its final shape.

C. Outline
Didactic Discourses: 1:1–9:18
  Introduction (1:1–7)
  Avoid Evil Men! (1:8–19)
  Wisdom's First Speech (1:21–31)
  Wisdom as a Guard and Guide (2:1–22)
  Trust in God (3:1–12)

  Wisdom's Benediction (3:13–18)
  Wisdom and Creation (3:19–20)
  Kindness and Neighbourliness (3:27–35)
  Get Wisdom! (4:1–9)
  The Two Ways (4:10–27)
  Avoid the Seductress! (5:1–22)
  Four Warnings (6:1–19)
  The Price of Adultery (6:20–35)
  The Wiles of the Seductress (7:1–27)
  Wisdom's Second Speech (8:1–36)
  The Two Banquets (9:1–18)
The First 'Solomonic' Collection: 10:1–22:16
Sayings of the Wise: 22:17–24:22
Further Sayings of the Wise: 24:23–34
The Second 'Solomonic' Collection: 25:1–29:27
The Sayings of Agur: 30:1–33
The Words of Lemuel: 31:1–9
The Good Wife: 31:10–31

COMMENTARY

Didactic Discourses (1:1–9:18)

(1:1–7) Introduction These verses state the purpose and value of the book and the basis upon which its teaching rests. 'Wisdom' basically means 'skill, ability'. The term is used, for example, of the manual skills of craftsmen (Ex 35:35; cf. Isa 40:20) and the navigational skills of sailors (Ezek 27:8). To learn about (lit. know) wisdom means to become equipped with the skills necessary to live a good and successful life. 'Instruction' (lit. discipline) often refers to the training received in wise living under the authority of a parent or teacher (e.g. 4:1–5). Here it means 'disciplined living' as the outcome of this training. The good and successful life is the disciplined life (cf. 25:28).

Wisdom promotes 'righteousness, justice, and equity'—i.e. right conduct and right relationships—within the community (v. 3). It equally promotes 'shrewdness' and 'prudence' based on a practical knowledge of the ways of the world (v. 4). A related form of the word 'shrewdness' is used pejoratively of the craftiness of the serpent (Gen 3:1; cf. Josh 9:4). Its good sense is captured in Mt 10:16. Those most in need of this wisdom are the 'simple', i.e. uninstructed youth. The word derives from a root meaning 'to be open'. As portrayed in Proverbs, the simple are 'open' to persuasion, and so easily manipulated (cf. 14:15). They are accordingly the primary targets for the beckoning of Folly (9:16; cf. 7:7, 21).

Following a parenthetic observation that through attending to Proverbs the wise can become wiser, v. 6 highlights the importance of an understanding of the literary forms in which wisdom is expressed. This includes not only intellectual penetration but also the ability to apply the right saying at the right time (cf. 26:7). A 'proverb' (*māšāl*) may originally have meant a short saying drawing a comparison, later extended to include other kinds of 'artistic' sayings (e.g. prophetic discourse, Num 23:7; allegory, Ezek 17:2; taunt song, Isa 14:4). In 1:1 it embraces the varied literary contents of Proverbs. A 'figure' is an enigmatic saying whose meaning lies beneath the surface and has to be teased out.

In v. 7 'fear of the LORD' is presented as the prerequisite of true wisdom. The verse is repeated in 9:10 by way of a literary inclusion for chs. 1–9, and forms a central theme of the book. Fear of the Lord embraces both reverence for God (cf. Isa 8:13) and obedience to him (cf. Deut 10:12–13; Eccl 12:13). 'Beginning' may imply first in order (Gen 1:1), or importance (Am 6:1), or the 'best part' (Am 6:6).

(1:8–19) Avoid Evil Men! This is the first of several instructions addressed by a father to his son in this section of the book. The characteristic features of the instruction are: an appeal for attentiveness (cf. v. 8); the directive expressed as a command or prohibition (cf. vv. 10b, 15), and motivation clauses explaining why the directive should be heeded (cf. v. 9, 16–19). The address by a teacher to his pupils as a father to his sons was a common practice in the wisdom schools of Egypt and Babylonia. However, the parallelism between father and mother (v. 8) suggests that the instructions in Proverbs may reflect the less formal setting of parental instruction within the home.

To 'hear' (v. 8) implies both to listen and to obey (cf. Isa 1:19). Obedience will adorn the child's life and character with charm and beauty (v. 9; cf. 4:9). Though invoking parental authority, the motivation clauses show that the instruction appeals as much to the child's good sense as its duty to obey its parents.

The child is warned against joining in the activities of a professional gang of robbers and murderers. 'Entice' (v. 10) comes from the same Hebrew root as the 'simple' (v. 4), and the passage illustrates the dangers of their 'openness' to persuasion. The gang holds out to the young person the attractions of a life of adventure, comradeship, and easy money. In v. 12 they liken themselves to Sheol swallowing its victims whole. The imagery of Sheol—the abode of the dead—as a devouring monster with an insatiable appetite for human victims (cf. also 27:20; 30:15–16; Isa 5:14; Hab 2:5) probably derives from the depiction of the god Mot (Death) within Canaanite mythology. Their appetite for violence and murder cannot be satisfied and they destroy their victims just as ruthlessly.

vv. 16–19 explain why the child should avoid such companions: they are evil (v. 16 = Isa 59:7a) and foolish (vv. 17–19). Their crimes are self-destructive and they are their own victims. Like a senseless bird that swoops down to the baited trap, these men are oblivious to all signs of their own danger and plunge mindlessly to their destruction. To join in their company is to share in their fate. The passage concludes with a summary statement of the operative principle of retribution (v. 19).

(1:21–31) Wisdom's First Speech In this passage wisdom (a fem. noun in Heb.) is personified as a woman. Though here Wisdom appears to be essentially a dramatization of the wisdom taught by the father, reinforcing the appeal to heed his instruction, she speaks not only like a wisdom teacher but also like a prophet. This implies that Wisdom speaks with a divine authority. To reject her is to reject the fear of the Lord (v. 29). The basis of her authority is expounded in 8:22–31.

Like a prophet, Wisdom takes her stand in public places and cries out to passers-by to accept her counsel and reproof.

Street corners, squares, and the city gates were the centres of the juridical, business, and social life of the city and form an appropriate setting for Wisdom to make herself heard. Wisdom bears on all human activity and has to compete not only with cynicism and wilful folly but also with the distractions of everyday life. 'Give heed' (v. 23) is literally 'turn'. The same word is used in prophetic exhortations to (re)turn to God (cf. Isa 44:22; Jer 3:22; Hos 6:1). The translation of Hebrew *rûaḥ* by 'thoughts' (cf. Ezek 20:32, 'mind') rather than the more usual 'spirit' is supported by its poetic parallelism with 'words' in the next line.

There is an awkward transition between the exhortation in v. 23 and the reproach and threat in vv. 24–8, and this has led some to construe v. 23 as also condemnatory (cf. Murphy 1998: 7, 10). The reproach centres on the continued spurning of Wisdom's counsel (cf. 'how long', v. 22). The language has close parallels in prophetic indictments (cf. Isa 65:1–2, 12; Jer 6:19). The consequences of rejecting Wisdom are spelled out in vv. 26–8. The imagery of the storm or whirlwind is a common metaphor of judgement (Isa 17:13; Am 1:14), particularly in connection with a divine theophany (Ps 18:7–15; Nah 1:3–5). 'Panic' describes the 'terror' evoked by the day of the Lord in Isa 2:10–21. Wisdom's role will be simply that of an amused onlooker (v. 26; cf. Ps 2:4; 59:8). Too late they will realize the folly of spurning her and will be spurned by her. The repetition 'cry/call out' points the irony (vv. 21, 28). The same motif of futile entreaty occurs in the prophets (Isa 1:15; Hos 5:6).

The note of reproach is resumed in vv. 29–30. Echoing the motto in 1:7, v. 29 makes clear that the rejection of Wisdom is tantamount to rejection of the fear of the Lord. The announcement of doom represents the fate of the foolish as the natural outflow of their own folly: the boomerang of their own waywardness and complacency. 'Waywardness' evokes a contrast with 'give heed'. It derives from the same Hebrew root and likewise has echoes in prophetic passages, where it is used of Israel's backsliding and apostasy from God (Jer 8:5; Hos 11:7).

The concluding promise (v. 33) contrasts the security and peace of mind enjoyed by those who pay heed to Wisdom (cf. 3:21–6). This serves to temper the note of doom in the preceding verses, so that the passage as a whole functions as a warning to embrace Wisdom before it is too late.

(2:1–22) Wisdom as Guard and Guide This instruction presents wisdom as a human quest (vv. 1–5) and a divine gift (vv. 6–8), which guards its recipients from the way of evil men and loose women (vv. 9–19), and guides them in the way of good men (vv. 20–2). The alphabetizing shape of the passage, together with its rehearsal of themes developed in later instructions, suggests that it has a deliberate, programmatic character (cf. Skehan 1972: 9–10).

Wisdom must be pursued with diligence. The first step is to be attentive to the father's words and to 'incline the heart' (i.e. 'mind') to understanding wisdom (vv. 1–2). The dual application of ears and heart is reflected in Solomon's prayer for a 'listening heart' (1 Kings 3:9; NRSV 'understanding mind'). There must also be a fervent desire to find wisdom (v. 3), matching the fervency of Wisdom's desire to be found (cf. 1:20); and it must be pursued with the strenuousness and perseverance of miners tunnelling for precious ores (v. 4; cf. Job 28). For wisdom seeker and miner alike, the prize is worth the toil (v. 5). The quest for wisdom is a quest for knowledge of God and his ways, and fear of the Lord is not only the beginning of wisdom (1:7) but also its ripest fruit.

The seeker finds wisdom given by God himself (v. 6). Solomon's prayer (1 Kings 3:7–9) came to typify the prayerful attitude required of the wisdom seeker (cf. Wis 8:18, 21; 9:4). The present passage calls rather for concerted intellectual and moral application. vv. 7–8 characterize the wisdom God gives as 'sound wisdom', i.e. effective. It maintains God's moral order ('paths of justice') by preserving the upright from the pitfalls and snares of evil. The 'shield' may either be 'God' (NRSV) or 'sound wisdom' (NEB 'as a shield'). The upright are God's 'faithful ones' (ḥăsîdîm). This is the only occurrence of this term in Proverbs. It refers to those who are loyal to God and his covenant (cf. Ps 31:23; 37:28; 97:10). The wisdom God gives conserves the right ordering of his people.

Echoing the introduction in 1:2–7, vv. 9–11 elaborate on wisdom as a guide and a guard, and this is applied in vv. 12–19 to two particular cases: evil men and loose women. Evil men (vv. 12–15) are perverted characters who invert the moral order (cf. Isa 5:20). They abandon straight and level paths for ways of darkness, and they go about their evil for profit and for pleasure (v. 14). More dangerous than what they do is what they say (v. 12), for by their words they seek to entice others in the moral chaos of their ways. The instruction in 1:8–19 serves as a parade example of such men, and illustrates both the wickedness of their conduct and their enticement to evil.

The theme of the loose woman (vv. 16–19) is developed at length in 5:1–14, 6:20–35, and 7:1–27. The words translated 'loose woman' and 'adulteress' are literally 'strange woman' and 'foreign woman', neither of which are the normal terms for an adulteress or prostitute. Various explanations of her 'foreignness' have been given—both literal and metaphorical—sometimes linked to participation in the sexual rites of fertility cults. Camp (1985: 116) suggests that the figure functions symbolically for 'the attractions and dangers of any and every sexually liminal woman'. Warning against illicit sexual entanglements was a standard topic within Egyptian wisdom instruction. But whereas the Egyptian sages warned that it could ruin a promising career, here the seductress is a threat to life itself. 'Death' (v. 18) is a further allusion to the Canaanite god Mot and 'shades' (rĕpā'îm, a term for the departed, cf. Isa 26:14; Ps 88:10) to the Repha'im, the underworld deities and minions of Mot. The house of the seductress is as the mouth of the god (cf. 1:12).

(3:1–12) Trust in God Among the instructions in chs. 1–9, this passage stands out by reason of its pronounced religious tone. It may be seen to develop the motto of the book (1:7). Wisdom consists in complete trust in and submission to the Lord. It is introduced by the customary appeal to obey the father's teaching and a statement of the benefits that obedience brings (vv. 1–4; cf. 1:8–9). 'Teaching' (cf. 1:9) translates Hebrew tôrâ (lit. guidance, direction), in parallelism with 'commandments'. Both terms commonly refer to God's law but are

equally at home in wisdom instruction (cf. 'my teaching'). 'Loyalty and faithfulness' can refer to relationships between human beings and God (cf. Jer 2:2; Hos 6:4) or to human relationships (cf. Ps 109:16; Hos 4:1; Mic 6:8). Both may be intended. They are to be worn as an adornment around the neck (cf. 1:9; Deut 6:8; 11:18) and written on the heart (cf. Jer 31:33).

vv. 5–8 form the kernel of the instruction. They contrast trust in God with self-reliance. The Hebrew word 'trust' is related to the words rendered 'securely' in 3:23 (cf. 1:33) and 'confidence' in 14:26. At stake is the basis for security in life, with the confidence to walk boldly without anxiety between the pitfalls and snares that lurk at every step. For this, complete commitment and submission to God ('all your ways') is the key. The medicinal analogy of healing and health to the benefits of wisdom (v. 8) recurs elsewhere in Proverbs (cf. 15:30; 16:24; 17:22).

The admonitions to honour God with the first fruits (vv. 9–10) and to submit to his discipline (vv. 11–12) exemplify trust in God in the contrasting situations of prosperity and adversity. The offering of first fruits was an expression of dependence on and gratitude to God for the gift of the land and its harvests (cf. Deut 26:1–11). But even those who honour God may sometimes suffer adversity. This should be accepted as a divine chastisement and a proof of God's fatherly love (cf. Job 5:17–18; 33:14–30; Heb 12:5–6).

(3:13–18) Wisdom's Benediction These verses form a hymnic celebration of the 'happiness' of those who find wisdom. While Wisdom is again personified (cf. 1:20–33), the hymn takes up and reinforces the benefits claimed for obedience to the father's instructions (cf. 1:8; 3:1–4) and serves the didactic purpose of commending his teaching.

To find Wisdom is to possess an asset of great value. Wisdom unfailingly pays a higher dividend than silver or gold (v. 14), and is a rare and priceless treasure beyond comparison (v. 15). Wisdom also bestows long life, riches, and honour on her devotees (v. 16) and leads them along pleasant and peaceful paths (v. 17). v. 16 probably owes something to depictions of the Egyptian goddess Ma'at, the goddess of truth and justice, who is portrayed with a symbol of long life in one hand and a sceptre symbolizing wealth and honour in her other. The 'long life' bestowed by Wisdom implies not only longevity but also quality of life. This is expressed in the metaphor of 'the tree of life' in v. 18: Wisdom is the vital source that nourishes growth and fruitfulness and promotes fullness of life (cf. 11:30; 13:12; 15:4). The expression recalls the tree of life in the garden of Eden (Gen 2–3).

(3:19–20) Wisdom and Creation In their present context, vv. 19–20 present the credentials for the claims made by Wisdom in the preceding verses. The wisdom by which humans are blessed is the wisdom by which the world was created and is sustained (cf. 8:22–31). The water imagery is suggestive of wisdom as fructifying life.

(3:27–35) Kindness and Neighbourliness The final section returns to the form of instruction and brings together a number of topics. The theme of vv. 21–6 is the secure and tranquil lives of those who hold fast to wisdom (v. 21) and trust in God (v. 26; cf. vv. 5–8). vv. 27–30 inculcate kindness and neighbourliness, with the avoidance of malicious actions and unnecessary quarrels. vv. 31–5 warn against envy of evil men and the imitation of their ways. God's judgement ('curse', cf. Deut 27:15–26) rests on their house and they will be utterly disgraced, while the upright will enjoy divine blessing.

(4:1–9) Get Wisdom! This short passage centres on the value of wisdom and the need to acquire it at all costs (v. 7). The father reinforces the appeal to his children (vv. 1–2) by recounting his own experience as a child when he was taught the lesson by his own parents (vv. 3–4). Here the importance of the home as a setting for wisdom as an educational discipline (cf. Ex 12:26–7; Deut 6:6–7, 20–5), together with its transmission from one generation to the next, is particularly well illustrated. His precepts are 'good' (RSV 'sound', v. 2) because they have been proved by experience, but each new generation must choose to receive them and prove them for themselves.

In vv. 6–9 wisdom is personified as a bride to be wooed, and who will in return love and honour those who embrace her. The garlanding (v. 9) may be an allusion to a wedding feast. This portrayal of Wisdom is evidently intended to counter the spurious love and deadly embrace of the seductress. According to McKane (1970: 306), the representation is rather of Wisdom as an influential patron offering protection and preferment to her protégés.

(4:10–27) The Two Ways The metaphor of life as a road with two ways plays an important role in the teaching of Proverbs. It has already occurred a number of times (cf. 1:15, 19; 2:8–22; 3:17, 23, etc.). In vv. 10–19 it becomes the main theme of the instruction as the father counsels his child to adhere to the way of wisdom and avoid the path of the wicked. 'Paths of uprightness' (v. 11) implies not only paths that are morally upright, but also paths that are straight and level (cf. 3:6). Hence the way of wisdom is not only the good path (cf. 2:9) through life but also the secure path (cf. 3:23). It is a road along which the traveller can progress with firm, measured strides and even run without fear of stumbling (v. 12; cf. Ps 18:36). A further reason why it is the secure path is that it is brightly illuminated. In v. 18 it is compared with the steady increase of brightness from the first flickers of dawn to the full splendour of the noonday sun. No loose stones or potholes can lurk in the shadows to catch the traveller unawares.

The contrasting description of the path of the wicked recalls the description of their activities in 1:8–19 and of their twisted paths in 2:12–15. Wrongdoing and violence come as naturally to them as eating and drinking (v. 7). Their path is shrouded in 'deep darkness' (v. 19). The term is used of the plague of darkness that enveloped Egypt (Ex 10:22), and also recurs in descriptions of the consequences of the day of the Lord (e.g. Joel 2:2; Am 5:20). It suggests the extent of their moral blindness, but more especially it points to the inevitable consequence of walking along a treacherous, twisting path in utter darkness. Intent on the destruction of others ('cause to stumble', v. 16) they make victims out of themselves ('stumble', v. 19). In the darkness of their deeds, they will not even see what their feet strike on that final, fatal step (cf. Job 18:7–12; Jer 13:16; 23:12).

The final paragraph (vv. 20–7) resumes the appeal (v. 10) to accept the father's words, since they are 'life' and 'healing' (cf. 3:8). To walk in the way of wisdom (cf. vv. 26–7) requires

constant vigilance, self-discipline, and singleness of mind and purpose. This is set out in a review of parts of the body: the heart, mouth, eyes, and feet. These may be sources of evil and death (cf. 6:16–18) or sources of goodness and life. If they are healthy, the whole body is healthy.

(5:1–22) Avoid the Seductress This instruction continues the warning against the loose woman introduced in 2:16–19 (see also 6:20–35; 7:1–27). It begins with a typical appeal to the child to listen carefully to the warning so that he might receive the prudence and knowledge necessary to avoid entanglement with her (vv. 1–2).

The danger posed by the loose woman is compounded by her seductive wiles. While making use of her natural sex appeal (cf. 6:25), it is on her seductive speech that she relies most (cf. 7:14–20). Her words are like honey and are smoother than oil (v. 8). Honey was proverbial for its sweetness (cf. 16:24; Judg 14:8, 14). The figure is used in Song 4:11 of the bride's kisses. Smoothness can denote flattery (cf. 29:5) and hypocrisy (cf. Ps 5:9). The seductress thus holds out promise of pleasure and enjoyment. But the reality is quite different ('in the end'). This is brought out by the contrast in vv. 3–4 between honey and wormwood and between smooth and sharp. Wormwood was equally proverbial for its bitterness (cf. Jer 9:15; Am 5:7). Her honeyed words leave a bitter taste and her smooth words are as the thrusts of a double-edged sword (cf. Ps 55:21). Disregarding the path of life, the seductress travels the path to Sheol (v. 5; cf. 2:18–19; 7:27) with the unsteady steps of a drunkard ('wander', cf. Isa 28:7) as she staggers from one lover to another unmindful of the harm she brings either on herself or on her victims (cf. 7:21–7; 30:20).

Following the resumptive appeal for attentiveness and obedience (v. 7), the father offers the same succinct advice as in 1:15 (cf. 4:15), here emphasized by a wordplay between 'far' and 'near' (v. 8). This advice is then reinforced by spelling out the consequences of liaison with her (vv. 9–14): the loss of dignity and honour (v. 9), of hard-earned wealth (v. 10), and of vigour and health (v. 11). This is the antithesis of Wisdom's benediction in 3:13–18. The phrase 'your years to the merciless' (v. 9) is obscure. The Hebrew word 'years' may rather be connected with an Arabic word meaning 'honour, dignity'. This gives a good parallel to the first line. 'Merciless' is masc. sing. and could be an allusion to Death as the cruel, merciless one. With the support of the LXX, it is sometimes emended to the plural, which might then be a reference to the seductress and her associates. 'At the end of your life' is literally 'at the end'. It echoes v. 4 and more probably means 'afterwards', i.e. when the effects of vv. 9–10 are felt. The lament of the victim in vv. 12–14 illustrates the theme of rejecting wise counsel and learning the lesson too late (cf. 1:24–8). The reference to ruin before the public assembly (v. 14) might be a specific reference to punishment meted out by the lawcourt or may refer more generally to public denunciation and disgrace. Possibly behind the scene is the woman's husband (cf. 6:34–5), denouncing the offender in public (v. 14) and pressing for compensation (v. 10).

Whereas the preceding verses primarily have in view young unmarried men, vv. 15–21 address the married man. They counsel that the best way of avoiding the temptation of the seductress is that he remain in love with his wife and derive sexual satisfaction from her. Drawing on imagery of water and its sources (cf. Song 4:15), v. 15 expresses the pleasure which a man should obtain through sexual intercourse with his wife. In v. 16 the 'springs' and 'streams' could allude to the waste that results from extramarital affairs or to the encouragement of the wife to infidelity through neglect. The image of the wife as a 'graceful doe' is symbolic of her beauty (v. 18; cf. Song 2:7), with which the husband should be intoxicated.

Reinforcing the appeals for a prudent weighing up of the consequences of liaison with the seductress, in v. 21 appeal is made to the scrutinizing eyes of the Lord (cf. 15:3; Job 31:4; 34:21) and his guardianship of the moral order. None the less, the concluding summary of the consequence of such indiscipline and folly is again expressed in terms of reaping what has been sown (cf. 1:19; 2:20–2). 'Toils' is literally 'cords'. By threading a path to folly's door, a man is threading a noose around his own neck, like a senseless bird weaving the net that will ensnare it (cf. 1:17–19).

(6:1–19) Four Warnings The four miscellaneous sayings in these verses are more reminiscent of the proverbial sayings in chs. 10–31 than the discourses in chs. 1–9. Though the form of instruction is reflected in the first, it lacks the characteristic parental appeal for attentiveness.

vv. 1–5 warn against acting as guarantor for debts. 'Neighbour' and 'stranger' (v. 1; cf. NSRV fn.) perhaps refer to the friend on whose behalf security is pledged and to the creditor, respectively. The expression 'to give a pledge' is literally 'to strike hands' (cf. 2 Kings 10:15). If a pledge has been given, no time should be lost and no effort spared in seeking to be released from it. Not only penury (cf. 22:26–7) but also slavery threatened the unwise guarantor (cf. 2 Kings 4:1–7; Neh 5:1–8).

vv. 6–11 warn against laziness and encourage diligence. The drawing of analogies with the natural world was common in wisdom circles (cf. 30:15–16, 24–31). The ant is a model of diligence and foresight in that it prepares its food for winter without having to be goaded. Wedded to slumber and indolence, the lazy person makes no such provision (cf. 20:4) and will suffer poverty and want. v. 11 should perhaps be rendered like a 'vagrant' and a 'beggar'.

The description of the scoundrel (vv. 12–15) recalls the evil men in 2:12–16. 'Scoundrel' is literally 'man of bĕlîyaʻal' (from which comes 'Belial') (cf. 16:27; 19:28). The derivation of the word is obscure. It may be a compound word meaning 'worthless' (lit. not-profit), or may derive from a verb meaning 'swallow, engulf' or the like. The scoundrel is characterized by his malicious undermining of harmonious relations within the community (v. 14). v. 13 may imply the casting of magic spells to accomplish his evil designs (McKane 1970: 325) or may simply refer to the covert way he and his associates go about their business.

vv. 16–19 form a graded numerical saying of a type common in the HB (cf. 30:15–31; Job 5:19; Am 1:3) and in the literature of the ancient Near East. It was particularly useful within wisdom circles, both as a means of classification and as an aid to memorization. The saying complements vv. 12–15 by

listing different kinds of malicious and disruptive activity through a review of the unhealthy body: 'eyes … tongue … hands … heart … feet' (contrast 4:23–7). The 'false witness' and 'one who stirs up strife' complete the seven items.

(6:20–35) The Price of Adultery This passage returns to the form of instruction and to the theme of the seductress. vv. 20–4 emphasize the need to hold fast to parental teachings: they are light and life and will protect against her enticements. Though the reference is to parental teaching, vv. 21–2 closely echo the role of divine teaching in Deuteronomy 6:6–8 (cf. 3:3, 24). In v. 24 'wife of another' rests on a change on the vocalization of Hebrew 'evil women' following the LXX and v. 29. Here the seductress is explicitly a married woman. Alongside her seductive speech (24; cf. 5:3), warning is given against being captivated by her eye make-up and inviting glances (cf. Sir 26:9). 'Desire' is the word translated 'covet' in the tenth commandment (Ex 20:17).

In vv. 26–33 the case against the adulteress is closely argued through comparison with a prostitute, fire, and a thief. The Hebrew text of v. 26a is obscure. The English versions are divided between the sense that a prostitute costs only the price of her fee (cf. NSRV; NEB) and that a prostitute brings a man to poverty (NIV). In either case the point is that the adulteress exacts a heavy price: 'a man's very life'. vv. 26–7 appear to be popular maxims. The point of the comparison is reinforced by a wordplay in Hebrew between 'wife' (ʾēšet) and 'fire' (ʾēš). v. 30 may be construed either as a question (RSV; NEB) or as a statement (NRSV; NIV). In the former case, the point of vv. 30–3 appears to be: how much more will the adulterer be despised than the thief and how much more dearly will he have to pay since he has no excuse? In the latter case, the cost to the adulterer is the same, but it would be contrasted with the lenient view taken of a thief in these circumstances. The concluding verses (vv. 34–5) envisage a jealous and enraged husband seeking revenge and demanding a higher price than money.

(7:1–21) The Wiles of the Adulteress The body of this passage is formed by an example story on the wiles of the adulteress (vv. 6–23). It is enclosed by parental instruction to accept teaching (vv. 1–5) and avoid the adulteress (vv. 24–7). The appeal to the child in vv. 1–5 closely echoes 6:20–4. In v. 4 'sister' probably means 'bride' (cf. Song 4:9–10), again presenting Wisdom as a counter-attraction to the adulteress for the love and fidelity of the child (cf. 4:6–9).

The story is cast in the form of the personal reminiscence of what the narrator observed through the lattice of his window. In the LXX it is the woman who looks out of the window seeking her prey, and this reading has been preferred by some scholars. The story unfolds with a young man making his way through darkening streets towards the house of the adulteress (vv. 6–9). The impending darkness becomes symbolic for the story as a whole. He is accosted by a woman dressed like a prostitute and practised in the art of seduction (vv. 10–13). vv. 14–20 illustrate the 'smoothness' of her words (v. 5)—the chief weapon in her arsenal (cf. 2:16; 5:3; 6:24). She flatters him and invites him to spend a night of sexual pleasure with her, reassuring him it is perfectly safe since her husband is away on a business trip. The significance of the cultic reference in v. 14 and its function in the seduction scene are quite unclear (cf. Murphy 1998: 43–4). In any case, unable to resist her advances and oblivious to the real cost he will have to pay, the young man follows her: one more beast to the slaughter; one more bird caught in her snare (vv. 21–3). The final paragraph (vv. 24–7) reinforces the lesson by exhorting the child to avoid the paths of the adulteress and warning of the deadly effects of consorting with her. Her house is the vestibule to Sheol and leads down to death (cf. 2:18–19; 5:8).

(8:1–36) Wisdom's Second Speech Personified Wisdom again takes her stand in public places and invites all who would learn from her to receive her instruction. In vv. 1–11 she assumes the role of a wisdom teacher. The prophetic note of reproach and threat characteristic of her first speech (1:20–33) is lacking. The setting in vv. 2–3 is reminiscent of the 'patch' of the seductress in 7:11–12. It has emerged that Wisdom has to compete not only with the distractions of everyday life and wilful folly (1:20–33) but also with the enticements of the seductress. The emphasis on the character of Wisdom's words in vv. 6–9 can be seen in this light. While the words of the seductress are marked by duplicity and fraudulence, the words of Wisdom are marked by candour and integrity. Wisdom speaks in plain language, which is intelligible to all who find her (v. 9). vv. 10–11 are very similar to 3:14–15.

In vv. 12–21 she extols her providential role in the good and orderly government of the world (vv. 12–16) and as the giver of wealth (vv. 17–21). vv. 12–14 closely echo the language of the prologue (1:2–7). The terms 'advice' and 'strength', however, anticipate the manifestation of the various qualities of wisdom in the government of kings and rulers (cf. Isa 11:2). The role claimed by Wisdom is comparable to that of a royal counsellor (cf. 2 Sam 16:23) and even to God himself (1 Kings 3:1–15). vv. 17–21 (cf. vv. 10–11) are a variation on the theme of 3:13–18. Wisdom bestows not only the intimacy of her embrace but also wealth and prosperity upon her lovers. The connection between vv. 12 and 14 is interrupted by v. 13 and it should perhaps be transposed to vv. 6–9.

The hymn of self-praise by Wisdom in vv. 22–31 falls into two parts: Wisdom's origins before creation (vv. 22–6), and her place at creation (vv. 27–31). As rendered by the NRSV, Wisdom variously describes herself as created by God (v. 22), set up or installed (v. 23; with royal overtones, cf. Ps 2:6) and as born (vv. 24–5). However, the significance of the first two terms in the Hebrew is disputed. The first translates Hebrew *qānāh*, which besides 'create' (cf. Gen 14:19, 22) could also mean 'procreate' (cf. Gen 4:1). Likewise the second term, of uncertain derivation, may be connected with a root meaning 'to be fashioned [in the womb]' (cf. Job 10:11; Ps 139:13). Hence Wisdom may be consistently representing herself as a child of God. None the less, the emphasis of the verses is not the manner of Wisdom's origins but her priority over the created world. Although v. 22 alludes to the creation narrative in Genesis ('beginning'), the language of the passage stands closer to hymnic celebrations of creation (cf. e.g. Ps 104:5–13; Job 38:4–18).

During the creation of the world, Wisdom was 'there' (v. 27), 'beside' God (v. 30). The particular part she played is obscured by the uncertainty of the meaning of Hebrew *ʾāmôn* in v. 30. The translation 'master workman' (NRSV) is based on

Jer 52:15 and has the support of the LXX. In this case, Wisdom actively participated in the design and construction of the world. The apocryphal Wisdom of Solomon explicitly represents Wisdom as 'the fashioner of all things' (7:1). Alternatively, the word may mean 'little child', connected with 'those reared' in Lam 4:5. This suits the metaphor of birth in the preceding verses, while vv. 30–1 read more like a child at play than a craftsman at work. 'Rejoicing' is elsewhere used of children playing in the street (Zech 8:5). The picture is of Wisdom playing at her father's feet and bringing him pleasure and then making the world her playground. As her ways brought pleasure to God, so they now bring pleasure to humankind.

The final vv. 32–6 form a resumptive conclusion looking back to the appeal in vv. 3–4. The 'happiness' of the man who finds wisdom recalls the theme of 3:13–18. To neglect and miss Wisdom spells injury and death.

The identity of the Woman Wisdom in chs. 1–9 and especially in 8:22–31 has been extensively debated (see Camp 1985: 23–70). While some view the figure as a personification or hypostatization of a divine attribute, others find her origins in goddess figures within the ancient Near East or within Israel itself. Von Rad (1975: 148) argued rather that she was an attribute of the world, signifying 'something like the "meaning" implanted by God in creation'. Certainly, she is an ambivalent and enigmatic figure. She belongs at God's side, but she is also at home in the world (8:31–3). This ambivalence conceals her identity as much as it reveals her place as the link between heaven and earth and the mediatrix of divine revelation and divine blessing.

(9:1–18) The Two Banquets In the first and last sections of this chapter, Wisdom and Folly are contrasted as rival hostesses inviting the simple to enter their house and dine with them (vv. 1–6, 13–18). Though Folly is portrayed in terms of the seductress, her description as 'woman of foolishness' (v. 13) implies that she personifies every kind of folly. Hence, the contrast reinforces not so much the earlier warnings against adultery as the teaching on the two ways (cf. 4:10–27).

The significance of Wisdom's seven-pillared house is uncertain. Among other things, it has been taken to symbolize the world as fashioned by Wisdom; the cosmic temple of Wisdom (Perdue 1994: 94–7), or to be simply a stately mansion. Correspondingly, the pillars have been thought to have cosmic or mythological significance; to reflect temple architecture, or to indicate that Wisdom's house is a rather splendid one which can accommodate all who accept her invitation. The invitation of Wisdom (vv. 3–4) echoes her earlier appeals (cf. 1:20–1; 8:1–5). It is addressed to the 'simple', i.e. to those who most need to dine with Wisdom but who can be most easily induced to dine with Folly (cf. 1:4). In v. 5 food and drink is used figuratively of Wisdom's instruction (cf. Isa 55:1–3; Sir 15:3; 24:19–21). 'Bread' may be better translated 'meat' (cf. v. 2).

The brash manner in which Folly invites the simple to her house (vv. 13–16) recalls the solicitations of the seductress (7:11–12) and contrasts with the formality and decorum of Wisdom's invitation. That the provision of Folly is water and bread (v. 17) may be intended to compare unfavourably with the sumptuousness of Wisdom's spread. However, it is likely that Folly is citing a popular proverb on the magnetic power of forbidden fruit. Whereas the banquet of Wisdom promotes and celebrates life (v. 6), to dine with Folly is to banquet with the 'dead' in Sheol (cf. 2:18–19; 5:5–6; 7:27).

The middle section (vv. 7–12) is digressive and is regarded by some commentators as a later intrusion. In its present context it may be intended to contrast two different responses to Wisdom's invitation—the one represented by the scoffer (cf. 15:12; 21:24) and the wicked, and the other by the wise and the righteous. It is those who are responsive to discipline and who fear the Lord who will partake of Wisdom's banquet.

The First 'Solomonic' Collection (10:1–22:16)

This is the largest collection of proverbial sayings within the book—some 375 in all. Differences between chs. 10–15 and 16:1–22:16 have often been observed. Most notably, while the vast majority of sayings in chs. 10–15 are in the form of antithetic parallelism, in 16–31 other kinds of poetic verse forms predominate. Chs. 10–15 also have a certain coherence through the prevalence of sayings on the righteous and the wicked. This section of the book may therefore have arisen through the combination of two originally independent collections.

For the most part sayings appear to be randomly organized with only the occasional small topical grouping. Recent studies have suggested the significance of catchwords, sounds, and various other rhetorical devices in the formation of sub-units within the collection, which provide a context for the individual saying. However, it is seldom evident that such sub-units display a corresponding thematic coherence, and the individual saying still seems to be the significant unit (Martin 1995: 54–61).

(10:1–32) *Wise and foolish children.* Following the parental appeals in chs. 1–9, this section appropriately begins with a proverb observing the effect on parents of the wisdom or folly of their child (v. 1; cf. 15:20; 17:21, 25). Not only is the joy or sorrow of parents at stake, but also the family's reputation (cf. 28:7) and its prosperity (cf. 29:3).

The righteous and the wicked. The sayings on the righteous and the wicked in this part of the book reinforce the earlier teaching of the two ways and the theory of retribution on which it rests (cf. esp. 2:9–22; 4:10–19). In some sayings retribution is presented as part of the natural order of the world (e.g. 11:5–6), while in others God himself acts to uphold his moral order by punishing the wicked and rewarding the righteous (e.g. 10:29; 12:2).

The righteous will enjoy a long and fulfilled life with the satisfaction of their needs and desires, while the wicked will be frustrated at every turn and will in the end meet with an untimely death (vv. 3, 24, 27–8). The 'dread' of the wicked (v. 24) may refer to divine punishment or reflect a basic sense of insecurity—fearing the worst (cf. 25). It contrasts with 'fear' of the Lord (v. 27). After their deaths, the reputation of the righteous will live on and be prized by the community, while the name of the wicked will rot with their bones (v. 7).

Several sayings centre on the difference between the speech of the two groups. The words of the righteous are of great value (v. 20) and win acceptance (v. 32), for they are characterized by wisdom (v. 31), bring nourishment (v. 21), and promote life (v. 11). On the other hand, the wicked have nothing of value to say (v. 20) and what they do say is characterized by perversity (v. 32) and duplicity, concealing their malicious intent to cause harm (v. 11b; cf. v. 6b). By their words, therefore, the righteous contribute to the well-being of the community, whereas the speech of the wicked undermines it. On a more general note, vv. 14 and 19 imply that the words of the wise and righteous will be few (cf. 13:3; 21:23). Garrulousness is a hallmark of the fool (v. 8).

Poverty and wealth. v. 15 contrasts an advantage of wealth with a disadvantage of poverty. Wealth provides protection and security against the vicissitudes of life (cf. 18:11), whereas the poor have no resources to fall back on. For this the poor may sometimes have only themselves to blame (v. 4). But not all wealth is advantageous. How it is acquired is the test of whether it is an asset or a liability (v. 2). The instruction in 1:8–19 illustrates the liability of ill-gotten gain (cf. also 20:17; 21:6; 28:20). By contrast, the wealth that accrues through 'righteousness', i.e. honesty and integrity, is a mark of divine blessing and provides for a long, secure, and anxiety-free life (v. 22; cf. 11:4).

Hatred and strife. v. 12 observes the disruptive effect of hatred on social relationships. The 'covering' of offences by love is commensurate with forgiveness (cf. Jas 5:20). In v. 18a the LXX reads 'Righteous lips conceal hatred', which gives a contrast with 18b (cf. NEB). If the Hebrew text is retained, the thought is either that the ill-will concealed through lies is as bad as open slander, or that lies and slander are both expressions of a deep-seated hatred (cf. 6b).

(11:1–31) *Commercial malpractice.* The use of false weights and measures (v. 1, cf. 16:11; 20:10, 23) is condemned in the law (Deut 25:13–16) and the prophets (Am 8:5; Mic 6:11). Ancient Near-Eastern law codes also prescribed against it. 'An abomination to the LORD' conveys the strongest possible displeasure (cf. 6:16). v. 26 appears to have in view traders who stockpile grain in times of scarcity to force up the prices and increase their profit. Their selfishness invites a curse upon their heads from their customers.

Pride and humility. v. 2 observes that pride goes before a fall (cf. 16:18; 18:12; 29:23) and commends the wisdom of humility. 'Disgrace' is literally 'lightness' and suggests both the contempt for and the lack of importance people of good sense will attach to the self-important. 'Humble' is a rare word. It is found again (as a verb) only in Mic 6:8 of 'walking humbly' with God.

The righteous and the wicked. Several sayings in the chapter are further variations on the theme of the fate of the righteous and the wicked. vv. 3, 5–6, recall the benefits of wisdom as a guide and guard in 2:8–11. While the righteous walk securely along straight paths, the wicked become victims of their own Machiavellian schemes and devices (cf. 2:12–15). vv. 4, 28, are further reflections on the profitlessness of wealth without righteousness (cf. 10:2). v. 7 is difficult. Following the LXX, it has been proposed to emend the first line to read 'when the righteous die their hope does not perish'. If this were to be the correct reading, the notion of an afterlife need not be implied (see 10:7). v. 9 returns to the malicious and destructive speech of the wicked (cf. 10:6). It is unclear whether 9*b* means that the righteous will be delivered from their malevolence or will deliver others from it (cf. NEB). The social consequences of the words (and deeds) of the righteous and wicked for the body politic are summed up in v. 11—making v. 10 self-evident. For the metaphor of the 'tree of life' (v. 30) see PROV 3:18.

Gossip. Those who speak disparagingly of a neighbour show a lack of sense (v. 12), and those who betray his confidence a lack of trustworthiness (v. 13). Both disrupt good relations between friends and neighbours, and as 'whisperers' are close companions of the perverse man who spreads strife (16:28).

A gracious woman. In v. 16 the NRSV adopts the longer text of the LXX. The Hebrew text contains only the first and last lines (cf. RSV). The saying seems to contrast the honour that a woman obtains through her natural disposition with the effort men must expend to acquire wealth (McKane 1970: 431). With a humorous note, v. 22 observes the incongruity of the beauty of a woman who lacks 'sense' (lit. taste).

Generosity. v. 24 points to the paradox between generosity and enrichment and miserliness and impoverishment. In v. 25 'enriched' is literally 'made fat', a figure for abundance and prosperity (cf. Deut 32:15). The sayings may have giving to the poor in view (cf. 28:27).

(12:1–28) *The fool.* The sayings in vv. 1, 15–16, 23, reflect on central characteristics of the fool as portrayed in Proverbs. By reason of his innate stupidity and self-conceit, the fool is as impervious to a word of advice as to a word of rebuke (vv. 1, 15; cf. 18:2; 28:26). The sense to recognize sound advice and to act upon it—not least by those used to giving it (v. 26)—is a mark of wisdom. The fool also lacks self-control, both of his temper (v. 16; cf. 14:17, 29; 29:11) and his tongue (23; cf. 10:14; 15:2; 18:6–7). The eagerness with which he speaks his mind and offers his opinions (cf. 18:2) advertises his folly, and contrasts with the disciplined, restrained speech of the wise ('conceals knowledge') (cf. 10:19; 17:28).

The good wife. 'Good' (v. 4) is literally 'strong, firm'. It is the word that occurs in the expression 'men of valour' (e.g. Josh 1:14). In Ruth 3:11 it describes the heroine. Here it means strength and nobility of character, embracing both her capabilities as a housewife (cf. NEB) and her integrity (cf. NIV). This is a wife who enhances her husband's honour and reputation (cf. 31:10–31). Her opposite is a wife whose behaviour brings her husband into disrepute and saps his energy like a wasting bone disease.

Slander. The metaphor of the words of the wicked as 'a deadly ambush' (lit. ambush of blood, v. 6) echoes the words of the robbers and murderers in 1:11. Here, the reference is to their false and slanderous accusations. Through their wisdom and knowledge, the righteous have the verbal skills to defend themselves—or perhaps to defend others ('them')—against their attacks (cf. 11:9). Going a step further, v. 13 observes that the words of evil men weave a web of intrigue in which they themselves will be ensnared (cf. 1:18; 11:6).

Rash words. Potentially just as dangerous and destructive are rash words (v. 18; cf. 29:20). However well intended, words hastily spoken are apt to wound. It is the judicious, considered speech of the wise that brings healing in a difficult situation. The healing property of a well-chosen word is also remarked in v. 25 (cf. 16:24).

Lying. As already in 6:17, 'lying' is condemned as an 'abomination to the LORD' (v. 22). The thought of v. 19 is not so much that the liar will be quickly found out and punished, but that lies are short-lived and ephemeral since they have no basis in reality. Only the truth endures.

False witnesses. v. 17 is the first of a number of sayings on giving false witness (cf. 14:5, 25; 19:5, 9, 28; 25:18). Perjury is the sin condemned in the ninth commandment (Ex 20:16). It is the worst form of lying, since it mocks (19:28) and defeats the ends of justice (25:18).

Laziness. Diligence is the path to the top of the social ladder and laziness the path to the bottom (v. 24). 'Forced labour' is possibly a reference to debt slavery (cf. Deut 15:12; Lev 25:39–40). The sense of v. 27 is uncertain. Drawing on the imagery of hunting, it may be a comment on the inability of a lazy person to carry a project through to its successful completion (cf. 19:24). Again diligence is the path to success.

(13:1–25) *Parental discipline.* The expression 'loves discipline' (v. 1) rests on an emendation of the Hebrew 'instruction of [his] father'. The Hebrew text lacks a verb and possibly 'heeds' should rather be supplied as understood from its occurrence in the parallel line. The verse reinforces the parental appeals of chs. 1–9. Refusal to heed correction places wisdom beyond reach of the 'scoffer' (cf. 9:7–8; 14:6; 15:12). Though always having more to do with a listening ear, the word 'discipline' is also used of physical chastisement (v. 24), which is viewed as an essential component in the upbringing of a child. The contrast between 'hate' and 'love' underlines the importance the wise attached to it (cf. 20:30; 23:13–14).

Rash speech. v. 3 is a warning against garrulousness or rashness of speech. Not only can it be harmful to others (12:18), but also it can land the speaker in trouble (cf. 10:14; 21:23).

Poverty and wealth. The general point made by v. 7 is that appearances can be deceptive. Behind it may lie the thought that ostentation is as reprehensible as miserliness or that true richness and poverty are not measured by a person's possessions. The first line of v. 8 points to an advantage of wealth. A rich man has the resources to pay what is demanded when kidnappers or robbers threaten his life. The second line is literally 'but a poor man does not heed rebuke', which the NRSV probably rightly takes to mean that the poor are never threatened in this way, since they have nothing worth extorting. Here—but ironically—the advantage lies with the poor. In v. 11 wealth gained through manual labour is contrasted with the kind of wealth that is achieved overnight. The reference is perhaps to the returns on speculative investments in trade and commerce rather than to dishonest gain. The first kind of wealth is substantive and enduring, while the latter is fleeting and ephemeral (cf. 27:23–7). v. 18 is one of several sayings in Proverbs which view poverty as a consequence of folly (cf. 10:4; 21:17, 20). If the NRSV rendering of v. 23 is sustainable (cf. McKane 1970: 462–3), this verse observes that the poor do not always have themselves to blame. The poor may reap a good harvest from their meagre plot of land only to have it extorted by greedy, unscrupulous men (cf. 22:16; 30:14).

Desires fulfilled. v. 12 reflects on the psychology of human desire and its disappointment or realization. The thought recurs in the first line of v. 19, but the second line of this verse seems quite unconnected.

The teaching of the wise. The expression 'fountain of life' in v. 14 (cf. also 10:11; 14:27; 15:4) is perhaps a distant echo of the rivers that watered the garden of Eden (Gen 2:10–13; cf. Prov 3:18). Wisdom teaching is the source of life's vitality and growth for those who heed it (cf. v. 13). The imagery of the second line is of Death as a hunter laying traps to ensnare the unwary and uninstructed (cf. PROV 1:12).

(14:1–35) *Wisdom's house.* As rendered by the NRSV, v. 1 seems to be a comment on the value of the good wife as homemaker, and may be so (cf. 31:10–31). But the phrase translated 'the wise woman' raises difficulties, and 'the foolish' is literally 'folly'. The verse is most reminiscent of personified Wisdom building her house in 9:1 as the antithesis of Folly and her house in 9:14 and may be making much the same point: what Wisdom is at pains to build, Folly is at pains to demolish.

The fool. Whereas the words of fools get them into trouble, the judicious and economical speech of the wise keeps them safe (v. 3). 'Rod for their backs' is an emendation of the Hebrew 'rod of pride'—an obscure image, which, if retained, would make the first line a comment on the arrogance underlying what a fool says. The most natural sense of 'misleads' (lit. 'is deception') in v. 8 is to mislead others, but the parallelism suggests that here the word may mean to mislead oneself ('is self-deception'). By contrast, the wise give careful thought to the course of their conduct and have a clear understanding of its consequences. v. 16 draws a similar contrast between the cautious and prudent conduct of the wise and the arrogant recklessness of the fool. Since the speech of a fool is not informed by knowledge, his company should be avoided (7; cf. 13:20). The meaning of v. 9 can only be guessed (cf. the English versions).

Joy and sorrow. vv. 10, 13, are pensive reflections on joy and sorrow in human experience. Others cannot share the depths of an individual's sorrows and joys; and even the most joyous moments are clouded by sorrow with grief never far away.

The simple. v. 15 contrasts the prudent conduct of the wise (cf. v. 16) with the credulity of the simple (see PROV 1:4). Without the benefit of instruction in wisdom, the simple are on the way to becoming fools (cf. v. 18, NRSV fn.).

Anger. The antithesis between the quick-tempered and the schemer in v. 17 does not seem very apt. It is perhaps better with the RSV to follow the LXX and translate the second line 'but a man of discretion is patient'. v. 29 makes the same point (cf. 12:16). The word 'passion' in v. 30 is a fairly general word for deep emotion, including envy and jealousy (6:34; 27:4) as well as anger. This verse shows insight into the effect of the state of the mind on the health of the body (cf. 3:8).

Rich and poor. v. 20 points to a social advantage enjoyed by the rich over the poor. The saying is not a sardonic comment on the dubious value of wealth's new-found friends (cf. 19:6) but a frank comment on human nature. In v. 31 the social obligation of caring for the poor (cf. v. 21) is grounded in the common humanity of rich and poor alike as the creatures of God. To oppress the poor is to show contempt for their creator (cf. 17:5), while to show kindness and generosity towards them is to honour him.

(15:1–32) *Words.* v. 1 contrasts the conciliatory reply that soothes a situation and makes for reasoned discussion and the acrimonious reply that inflames it and makes intelligent discussion impossible. 'Gentle' (v. 4) points either to the conciliatory or to the healing quality of words. Such speech promotes life, in contrast with twisted or perverse speech, which causes injury and brings death (cf. 18:21). v. 23 expresses the satisfaction that comes from a timely word for both the one who gives it and the one who receives it. Out of 'season' the best of words are ineffective and counter-productive. In v. 26 'pure' expresses God's approval of gracious words, i.e. words spoken to promote harmony and well-being, over against his abhorrence of evil and malicious schemes. The second line is often emended to read 'but the words of the pure are pleasing to him' (so RSV; cf. NIV).

God's scrutiny. Echoing 5:21, the theme of v. 3 is the all-seeing eye of God, from which nothing can be hidden. The implication is that the good will receive his blessing and the evil will be condemned and punished (cf. 22:12). v. 11 makes much the same point. 'Abaddon' (lit. destruction) is a poetic synonym for Sheol. If the depths of Sheol are 'naked' before God (cf. Job 26:6), how much more are the thoughts, motives, and intentions of the human heart exposed to divine scrutiny (cf. Ps 44:21).

Prayer and sacrifice. v. 8 is one of the few sayings in Proverbs that deal with cultic practice. The point is not the superiority of prayer, but that only sacrifices offered in sincerity are acceptable to God. So in v. 29 the prayer of the wicked likewise falls on deaf ears. Though v. 8 closely echoes prophetic passages on the theme (e.g. Isa 1:10–17), it also has parallels in Egyptian wisdom literature.

Joy and sorrow. vv. 13, 15, are further comments on joy and sorrow (cf. 14:10, 13). The first contrasts the inner joyfulness that makes for a healthy body and a glowing complexion (cf. 17:22) with the sorrow (lit. painfulness of heart) that debilitates the body and leaves its etchings on the face. v. 15 comments on the inner happiness that can overcome adversity.

True enrichment. While wealth may be good and advantageous in many respects, it can lead to 'turmoil' and breed moral and spiritual blindness (cf. 11:28; 30:8–9). Fear of the Lord (v. 16), righteousness (16:8) and a good name (22:1) are better things—things that truly enrich.

Planning and counsel. v. 22 states the principle that the key to a successful venture is sound planning and wide consultation. The saying most of all has in view the rulers and leaders of the nation. In 11:14 it is applied to affairs of state, and in 20:18 to the conduct of war.

Divine justice. God champions the cause of the widow by protecting her boundaries and breaking down the house of the proud (v. 25). Here the proud are those whose estates have been built up through their appropriation of the property of the poor and needy. Removing the landmarks marking the boundaries of the family inheritance was a serious offence (Deut 19:14; 27:17; cf. Prov 22:28; 23:10–11).

(16:1–33) *God's purposes.* vv. 1–9 (except v. 8) form a small group of sayings dealing with divine providence over human affairs. Over against sayings commending careful planning as the key to successful undertakings (e.g. 15:22; 20:18; 21:5), vv. 1, 9, observe its limitations along the lines: 'Man proposes, but God disposes'. Only plans which coincide with God's purposes will succeed (v. 3; cf. 19:21). The prevailing of God's purposes is also the theme of v. 33. The reference is to the casting of the sacred lot (cf. 1 Sam 10:20–1) perhaps in the settlement of legal disputes (cf. 18:18). The saying asserts that though men cast the lot—and however much a matter of chance the procedure may appear—it is God who makes the decision (lit. judgement).

v. 2 observes the defective evaluation people make of themselves. They are unable to penetrate their deepest motives and have a capacity for self-deception. God alone can properly evaluate and judge ('weigh') a person's character and conduct (cf. 21:2; 15:11). The word translated 'weigh', however, could also mean 'fix to a standard' (cf. NEB). In that case the point of the saying would be the poor standards by which men evaluate themselves. The meaning of v. 4 is obscured by the ambiguity of the expression 'for its/his purpose' (lit. answer, response). The expression might be better rendered 'with its counterpart'. The saying asserts a divinely created order in which actions and their consequences have been made to correspond. The day of trouble is the appropriate counterpart to the wicked person. Alternatively, it could mean that even the punishment of the wicked is part of the divine plan. v. 6 implies that atonement for sin is not a matter of sacrifice but of 'loyalty and faithfulness' towards God (cf. Hos 6:6). In the second line 'avoids evil' could refer either to doing evil (cf. 8:13) or to suffering harm.

The king. vv. 10–15 (except v. 11) form another small group of sayings dealing with the king. The word translated 'inspired decisions' (v. 10) is elsewhere used only in the bad sense of 'divination, soothsaying'. Here it points to the uncanny perceptiveness underlying the king's legal pronouncements—as though they were divine oracles (cf. 2 Sam 14:17, 20). The first line of v. 12 might better be translated 'Kings detest wrongdoing' (NIV), the reference being to wickedness by the king's subjects, which, left unchecked, will undermine the stability of his throne (cf. 25:4–5). vv. 14–15 contrast the king's displeasure with his favour. They may have originally been sayings advising royal officials and courtiers of the hazards and rewards of employment in the king's service. The hazards are illustrated by the stories of Joseph (Gen 39–50), Daniel (Dan 1–6), and Esther (cf. also 1 Kings 2).

Pleasant speech. In vv. 21, 23, 'persuasiveness' is literally 'learning'. The wise teacher speaks in a pleasant and judicious manner, which enhances the appropriation of his teaching by his pupils. In so doing, he will also enhance his reputation for perceptiveness. The sweetness and health-giving properties of pleasant words (v. 24) evoke a contrast particularly with the seductive words of loose women (cf. 5:3–4).

Evil and slanderous speech. The sayings in vv. 27–30 give particular emphasis to slanderous speech. On the 'scoundrel' (v. 27) see 6:12–14. He 'digs up evil' (lit.) and spreads his slanders with devastating effect. v. 28 observes the strife and divisions caused by slanderers and gossips (cf. 6:14; 26:20). The wink and compressed lips (v. 30) may signify slander by insinuation (cf. 6:13) or that the facial expression betrays a malicious intent.

Old age. v. 31 reflects the thought that longevity is the reward of a righteous life. Old age is the fitting climax and fulfilment of a life well lived (cf. 17:6; 20:29).

(17:1–28) *Quarrelling and strife.* A modest meal with peace and harmony round the table is better than a sumptuous spread with resentments and rivalries smouldering away and breaking out into open quarrels (v. 1; cf. 15:17). 'Feasting with strife' is literally 'sacrifices of strife'. The allusion is perhaps to the 'peace offering', giving added force to the saying. The first line of v. 19 observes the disruptive effect of the quarrelsome. The meaning of the second line is unclear. It is perhaps an unrelated comment on the self-destructiveness of arrogance. Drawing on the imagery of a dam springing a leak, v. 14 advises to stop a quarrel before it gets out of control. McKane (1970: 505) suggests legal disputes are particularly in view. These should be dealt with before they go to court.

The prudent servant. Despite his lowly status, a household servant who serves his master well will disinherit a worthless child who brings disgrace (v. 2)—a happy acknowledgement that ability counts for more than privilege (cf. 27:18; see 2 Sam 16:1–4). vv. 21, 25, are further observations on the grief caused by foolish offspring (cf. 10:1).

God tests the heart. v. 3 is a companion saying to 16:2. As an assayer tests silver or gold, God 'tests' the heart to determine its genuineness and purity.

Bribes. v. 8 is one of several proverbs that remark the benefits of giving a bribe. It smooths the path to social advancement (18:16), wins friends and influences people (19:6), and extricates the giver from difficult situations (21:14). Such sayings read strangely against the condemnation of bribery in 15:27. A distinction is sometimes drawn between a bribe and a gift to explain the difference. However, while both terms are used in these sayings, no clear distinction is drawn between them. They are equated in 21:14, and the word translated 'gift' there is translated 'bribe' in 15:27. The sayings simply observe how things are and do not necessarily recommend or condone the practice. In v. 23 the 'wicked' is a corrupt judge. 'Concealed' is literally 'from the bosom', i.e. the fold in a garment at the breast, from where money could be slipped surreptitiously. The corruption of justice is also the theme of vv. 15, 26. To justify the wicked and condemn the righteous means to pronounce the guilty innocent and the innocent guilty.

Friendship. The second line of v. 9 may refer to spreading tales (lit. repeats a matter) about friends behind their backs or continually harping on to them about their shortcomings (cf. NEB). Friendship thrives on forgiveness. In v. 17 'friend' is probably equated rather than contrasted with 'brother'. It is in times of adversity that friendship and kinship are displayed.

Rebels. v. 11 is probably a warning of the consequences of plotting sedition against the king rather than of rebellion against God. The 'cruel messenger' is a reference either to the king's executioner or to death (cf. 16:14).

The fool. A few sayings centre on the inability of the fool to learn wisdom. The fool is intellectually deficient and unable to benefit from instruction (v. 16). He also lacks the concentration of mind and purpose demanded (v. 24), while even the rod makes not the slightest impression on him (v. 10).

Restraint in speech. v. 27 observes the restraint in speech and in temper of the wise. The 'cool in spirit' is the opposite of the 'hot-tempered' in 15:18. Since silence is a mark of wisdom, a fool who remains silent can conceal his folly and enjoy the esteem afforded to the wise (v. 28)—a lesson, however, that the fool seems incapable of learning (cf. 12:23; 15:2).

(18:1–24) The meaning of v. 1 is unclear. As rendered by the NRSV, it appears to be a comment on the contempt that goes hand in hand with a misanthropic isolation (lit. one separated) from society.

The law court. Partiality in judgement is condemned in v. 5. The Hebrew idiom is 'to raise the face'. This probably reflects the custom of the ruler raising the face of a prostrate subject as a sign of his favour (cf. Mal 1:8). v. 17 also seems to be concerned with the legal process. It cautions against reaching a premature verdict on the basis of the eloquence with which the case against a defendant is presented. Only when the defendant has submitted this case to careful cross-examination can a fair and balanced judgement be reached. To use the lot to settle cases the legal processes could not resolve was to submit them to divine arbitration (v. 18; cf. 16:33).

Rich and poor. v. 11 describes the security and protection provided by wealth from the point of view of the rich and need not imply that it is illusory (cf. 10:15). The juxtaposition of v. 11 with v. 10, however, underlines that the protection afforded by wealth is not absolute. It is relative to the vulnerability of the poor (cf. 11:28). In v. 28 the deferential words of the poor as they ask for charity are contrasted with the harsh reply of the rich, who have become hardened to their incessant appeals. This is expressed simply as a fact of life.

Quarrelling. The Hebrew text of v. 19 is quite obscure. The thought seems to be that the closer the relationship (ally is lit. brother), the greater the alienation a quarrel causes and the more difficult reconciliation becomes.

Words. The power of the tongue is summed up in v. 21. It may deal in death and destruction or in life and healing. The point of the second line is perhaps that those who love to talk must bear the consequences of their words for better or worse. Alternatively, the thought may be that the words of those who respect the power of the tongue and cultivate wise speech bear fruit. The satisfaction to be derived from productive and beneficial speech is stated in v. 20. v. 4 is better translated: 'the words of a man's mouth are deep waters, a flowing brook, a fountain of wisdom'—a wise man is implied. The metaphors express the profundity of his words, and the abundance and inexhaustibility of the refreshment and blessing they bring. Contrasting with the productive use of the tongue, a small group of sayings deal with destructive uses of it. Through his malicious and slanderous words, the fool creates disturbance and dissension around him and sows the seed of his own ruin (vv. 6–7). The last phrase of v. 7 could also be translated 'a snare to his life'. v. 8 comments on the fact that it is a weakness of human nature to find pleasure in listening to gossip. Already 17:4 has implied that listening to slander and gossip is as bad as spreading it. v. 2 remarks the eagerness of fools to air their ignorance. Disdainful of the opinion of others, they take every opportunity to express their own. Much the same thought underlies v. 13.

(19:1–29) *Rich and poor.* v. 1 is almost identical with 28:6, but there the poor are contrasted with the rich (some emend the verse accordingly, cf. NEB). Compared to the fool who has lied

and cheated his way to success, the poor person who has maintained his integrity is better off (cf. 16:8). While the second line of v. 22 makes a similar contrast between the poor and the liar, the meaning of the first line and its connection with it are uncertain. Wealth attracts friends while poverty repels them (v. 4; cf. 14:20). Friendship with the poor is too demanding. While their relatives may have little choice but to support them, their friends and neighbours will do all they can to avoid them (v. 7a). The text of v. 7b is obscure and may form the remains of a separate saying (cf. NEB, following the LXX). Over against this matter of fact observation, v. 17 commends generosity to the poor. To be kind to the poor puts God into debt and he will pay his debts in full (cf. 14:31; 22:9).

Zeal without knowledge. In v. 2 'desire' connotes vitality and drive. The saying complements those that counsel careful planning (e.g. 15:22; 21:5). Zealous and impulsive activity carried out without careful forethought and a clear objective will achieve nothing.

Anger. vv. 11, 19, return to the topic of anger (cf. 14:17). The text of v. 19 is difficult, but the general sense seems to be that to bale the violent-tempered out of the consequences of their actions will be counter-productive and will only encourage them.

The king. v. 12 repeats the thought of 16:14–15 with a change of imagery.

Wives and children. v. 13 adds 'ruin' to the grief caused by a foolish child (cf. v. 26; 10:1). The second line may be tongue in cheek or from the heart. The following verse (14) is evidently placed here to contrast the nagging wife with the good wife (cf. 12:4; 18:22). The point of the saying seems to be that marriage is an uncertain affair. Whereas house and wealth inherited from parents are known quantities, a newly wed wife is not. Only time will tell whether she is a good or bad wife, and therefore whether she is from the Lord (cf. 18:22). The necessity to 'discipline' children is emphasized in v. 18. Discipline includes both 'instruction' (cf. vv. 20, 27) and the 'chastisement' of the rod (cf. 13:24). The second line of the verse means that discipline will save the child from following the paths of folly and wickedness that lead to death.

Laziness. A humorous description of a lazy person is given in v. 24. It reflects an incapacity to take in hand even the simplest of projects and carry it through to a successful end (cf. v. 15; 6:6–11).

(20:1–30) *Drunkenness.* Excessive drinking turns a person into a mocker and a brawler (v. 1; cf. 23: 29–35). It befuddles the senses and excites belligerence. The last phrase may mean to drink to excess is not wise or that it makes a person act unwisely.

Laziness. v. 4 shows again the inevitable step from laziness to want (cf. 12:27; 13:4). Perhaps citing the wet and the cold of autumn ('in season') as his excuse for not ploughing (cf. 26:13), the farmer foolishly expects a harvest for which he has been too lazy to work. v. 13 encapsulates the instruction in 6:6–11 (cf. 19:15; 24:30–4).

The purpose of the heart. The point of v. 5 is evidently that the deepest thoughts and intentions of the heart can be fathomed through the patient probing of the wise and discerning. Alternatively, it could mean that the wise man's skills of articulation and clarification are required before a profound plan can be carried into effect (McKane 1970: 536–7).

Loyalty. When put to the test, loyalty and faithfulness (cf. 3:3) become scarce commodities (v. 6; cf. 19:22; 25:19; Job 6:14–23).

The king. Drawing on the same imagery, vv. 8, 26, remark the king's exercise of justice. The wise king will have the discernment to see through the schemes concocted by miscreants to cloak their evil and pull the wool over his eyes, to separate truth from falsehood, and his punishment will be 'crushing'. v. 28 recalls 16:12 (cf. 25:4–5). Here, however, the reference could be to God's 'loyalty and faithfulness' as expressed in his covenant with the Davidic house (cf. 2 Sam 7:15; Ps 89:33–4).

Purity of heart. v. 9 reinforces the deficiencies of human evaluation of character and conduct when set beside God's weighing of the heart (see PROV 16:2). Against this, v. 27 seems to imply that conscience is an inner, divine illumination of the deepest motives of the heart, so that people need not be self-deceived (but cf. NEB). v. 11 makes the quite separate point that the character of the adult is already revealed in the conduct of the child.

Eyes and ears. The point of v. 12 may be either that the wisdom learned through experience is reliable, since it was God who created the eyes and the ears, or that they should be used to learn wisdom, since that was what they were created for.

A good bargain. v. 14 gives a humorous picture of the buyer who complains he is being offered inferior goods to get a reduction in the price, and then boasts about how clever he was.

Going surety. v. 16 (cf. 27:13) is perhaps an ironic warning that the guarantor need expect no mercy from the creditor if the debtor defaults. Alternatively, it may be advising the creditor to take security from the guarantor when he is underwriting the debts of a foreigner, since they are a high risk. Garments were commonly given as security for loans (cf. Ex 22:25–7; Deut 24:10–13; Am 2:8).

Acquiring wealth. v. 17 returns to the theme of ill-gotten gain (see PROV 10:2). It is not clear whether v. 21 has in view seizing the property before the proper time through fraudulent or violent means (cf. 19:26; 28:24) or illustrates the principle 'easy come, easy go' (cf. 13:11; 27:24).

Rash vows. v. 25 is a case in point of the folly of rash speaking (cf. 29:20). Failure to fulfil a vow was a serious matter (cf. Num 30:2; Deut 23:21–3), while fulfilling a rash vow could be costly (cf. Judg 11:30–40).

The rod. v. 30 provides the justification for the counsel of Proverbs not to spare the rod (cf. 13:24; 22:15; 23:13–14).

(21:1–32) *God disposes.* v. 1, 30–1, are further sayings on God's sovereign control of human affairs. God controls the actions and decisions of the king to achieve his own purposes (v. 1; cf. 16:1, 9)—whether as his willing (Ps 78:70) or his unwitting servant (cf. Jer 25:9). The 'streams' are irrigation channels, which can be directed to where they are needed. The best-laid human plans and intentions that do not conform to God's purposes will come to nothing (v. 30; cf. Ps 33:10–11).

Sacrifices. The priority of righteousness and justice over sacrifices (v. 3; cf. 15:8) is a common prophetic theme (see PROV 15:8; cf. Isa 1:11–17; Jer 7:21–6; Hos 6:6; Am 5:21–7; Mic 6:6–8), and is illustrated by Saul (1 Sam 15). The 'evil intent' compounding the offensiveness of the sacrifices in v. 27 is best known to the wicked.

Pride. v. 4 is a difficult text. The connection between the first and second lines is obscure. 'Lamp' follows the LXX (Heb. 'ploughing'). The general sense seems to be the sinfulness of pride (cf. 6:16–17; 16:5), complementing such sayings as 16:18 and 18:12, which underline its folly (but cf. McKane 1970: 558–9).

Wealth. Wealth obtained fraudulently is both 'fleeting' and lethal (v. 6)—in contrast with Wisdom's wealth, which is 'enduring' (8:18) and life-enhancing (3:16–18). 'Snare of death' follows the LXX. v. 20 contrasts the thrift of the wise with the profligacy of the fool, of which the extravagant self-indulgence remarked in v. 17 may serve as a case in point.

The righteous and the wicked. v. 12 is obscure, but probably means that God takes note of the house of the wicked and brings it to ruin. 'The Righteous One' occurs as a divine title in Job 34:17. If 'ransom' is taken literally, v. 18 would seem to mean that the punishment of the wicked discharges the liability of the righteous to punishment. This seems an improbable thought. The point of the saying 'remains an enigma' (Murphy 1998: 160).

Contentious wives. v. 19 suggests that the roof of the house (cf. v. 9; 25:4) is still too close for comfort! The point both sayings make is that any kind of discomfort and privation is preferable to the comforts of home where there is domestic strife (cf. 19:13; 27:15–16).

Wisdom v. strength. The superiority of wisdom over strength is the subject of the anecdote in v. 22 (cf. 24:5–6, also 16:32). The saying reinforces the advice on waging war in 20:18. The wisdom of the strategy implemented and the tactics employed secures the victory.

False witnesses. v. 28 is a further saying on the topic of false witnesses (cf. 12:17). The meaning of the second line is obscure. The Hebrew is literally 'a man who hears will speak for ever'. The English versions go different ways in wresting sense out of this as a contrast to the first line.

(22:1–16) *A good reputation.* In v. 1 the NRSV rightly supplies the word 'good' from the context. Behind the verse lies the thought that a name is an expression of the inner character and worth of its bearer (cf. Gen 32:28) and that it survives his or her death (cf. 10:7).

Rich and poor. v. 2 makes the observation that rich and poor are to be found side by side and that they are equally the creatures of God (cf. 29:13). No moral is drawn. Similarly, v. 7 simply notes that the poor end up as slaves of the rich because of their inability to repay their debts. v. 9 returns to the theme of showing generosity to the poor (cf. 14:31). The Hebrew of v. 16 is cryptic and its meaning elusive (cf. McKane 1970: 571–2).

Parental discipline. v. 6 emphasizes the importance of parental instruction in the home (cf. 19:18). The Hebrew simply reads 'according to his way'. This could mean the training must be tailored to the individual child, but the NRSV is doubtless correct in interpreting it as the way in which the child ought to go. v. 15 again reinforces the value of the rod in educating children (cf. 3:24).

Laziness. The lazy person's inventiveness in making excuses for doing nothing is quite remarkable (v. 13; cf. 26:13).

The seductress. v. 14 resumes a central theme of the first section of the book. 'Mouth' recalls the seductive speech of the loose woman (cf. 5:3), but in conjunction with 'pit' it may also imply the entrance to the underworld (cf. 1:12; 2:18–19; 5:5, 27).

Sayings of the Wise (22:17–24:22)

This section is primarily in the form of a series of short parental instructions (cf. 23:15, 22; 24:13, 21). It has affinities with the Egyptian Instruction of *Amen-em-ope* (see examples below) and is widely held to be dependent on it, with its 'thirty sayings' (22:20) modelled on the 'thirty chapters' of *Amen-em-ope*. However, the parallels extend only as far as 23:11 and the nature and extent of the dependence is a matter of debate. In the course of its adaptation the material has been made to serve the wider educational goals of Proverbs, including inculcation of trust in the Lord (22:19).

(**22:17–29**) vv. 17–21 are an *introduction*. The heading has been extracted from the Hebrew 'hear the words of the wise', generally assumed to have been incorporated into v. 17 by mistake for 'hear my words' (LXX). *Amen-em-ope* begins with a similar appeal for attentiveness: 'Give thy ears, hear what is said, Give thy heart to understand them.' There is also a striking parallel between v. 21 and the statement of the purpose of *Amen-em-ope*: 'to know how to return an answer to him who said it, and to direct a report to one who has sent him'. vv. 22–3 concern the oppression of the poor. They warn against using the legal system ('at the gate') as an instrument for the exploitation and oppression of the poor (cf. Isa 10:1–2; Am 5:12). God is their protector and will take up their cause (cf. Ex 22:22–4). vv. 24–5, concerning hotheads *Amen-em-ope* gives the same advice: 'Do not associate to thyself the heated man, Nor visit him for conversation'. It also contrasts the heated man (cf. 15:18) with the cool or silent man (cf. 17:27) in language reminiscent of Ps 1: the one will flourish like a 'tree growing in a garden' while the other will be cut down and used as firewood. The 'ways' of hotheads are strewn with snares and are ultimately the way of death.

vv. 26–7 warn that penury beckons the imprudent guarantor. See PROV 6:1–6; 20:16. v. 29, the term rendered 'skilful' means a scribe in Ps 45:1 and Ezra 7:6. The saying advises that the scribe who carries out his duties efficiently and judiciously may expect the highest promotion in the king's service. *Amen-em-ope* similarly observes: 'As for the scribe who is experienced in his office, He will find himself worthy to be a courtier.'

(**23:1–35**) vv. 1–3 give some further advice about table manners to aspiring royal employees. To 'put a knife to your throat' is a forceful expression for 'curb your appetite'. The description of the royal fare as 'deceptive food' (lit. bread of lies) may imply that an ulterior motive lies behind the king's hospitality or may simply mean that it can prove a courtier's undoing. The king will take note of the glutton and assume he is just as uncouth in carrying out his duties. vv. 4–5, to make accruing

wealth the chief goal in life is to pursue a mirage: no sooner here than gone. *Amen-em-ope* likewise advises: 'Toil not after riches ... They have made for themselves wings like geese, And have flown into the heaven.' vv. 6–8, 'the stingy' is literally 'one with an evil eye' (cf. 28:22), as contrasted with the 'generous' ('one with a good eye', 22:9). While the miser affects to be a generous host ('eat and drink') his hospitality is insincere. When his guests see through him they will 'vomit' with disgust and rue every friendly word wasted on him. The expression rendered 'like a hair in the throat' is uncertain. An alternative rendering is 'like one who is inwardly reckoning' (RSV).

vv. 10–11 warn against the appropriation of the land of the defenceless through the removal of the boundary stones (cf. 15:25; 22:28). Where there is no human kinsman to defend their rights (cf. Lev 25:25; Ruth 4), God himself will become their redeemer (cf. 22:23). *Amen-em-ope* likewise warns: 'Do not carry off the landmark at the boundaries of the arable land ... Be not greedy after a cubit of land, Nor encroach upon the boundaries of the widow.' vv. 13–14, yet again the value of the rod in the disciplining of children is affirmed (cf. 13:24; 20:30; 22:15). That the child 'will not die' could mean that it will not suffer irreparable harm. However, the parallelism with 'Sheol' suggests it means that the rod will save the child from following the paths that lead to death and direct him along the path of life (cf. 13:14; 15:24). vv. 19–21, the child is warned to avoid the company of drunkards and gluttons. Excessive eating and drinking are marks of indiscipline and sure routes to inertia and ultimately to poverty.

vv. 26–8, once again warning is given against the seductress. She is portrayed both as a huntress who traps her victims (cf. 7:22–3) and as a robber who lies in wait for them (cf. 7:12). The depth and narrowness of the 'pit' ensures her victims will be well and truly caught (cf. Jer 38:6–13). The pit probably also represents the gateway to Sheol (cf. 2:18–19; 5:5, 27; 22:14). vv. 29–35 give a portrait of the drunkard comparable in its vividness to the portrait of the seductress in chs. 1–9. 'Sparkles' (v. 31) is literally 'gives its eye'. The 'eye' and 'smoothness' (cf. Song 7:9) of wine has the same seductive power to bewitch and captivate as the glances and smooth words of the seductress (cf. 6:24–5). In both cases the reality belies the promise of pleasure and enjoyment ('at the last', v. 32; 'in the end', 5:4). vv. 29, 33–5, describe the degenerative effects—both physical and mental—on its victims.

(**24:1–22**) vv. 3–4 echo the building of the house by the woman Wisdom in 9:1. While the primary meaning of the saying is that wisdom is the key to the prosperity of the family, it might also imply that it is the key to healthy and harmonious family relationships. vv. 5–6 compare wisdom and strength. See PROV 21:22; cf. also 20:18. v. 7 observes an occasion when the silence of fools is indicative of their character (cf. 17:28). At assemblies to debate the affairs of the community the fool is out of his depth, with nothing of value to contribute. So he keeps silent.

vv. 11–12 speak of divine scrutiny. The situation envisaged in v. 11 is not altogether clear (cf. McKane 1970: 400–2). The reference may be to prisoners who have been wrongfully condemned to death. Every effort should be made to secure their release. Feigning ignorance of their plight will be exposed as callous indifference under the scrutiny of the one 'who weighs the heart' and judges accordingly (cf. 16:2; 21:2). If v. 10 belongs with vv. 11–12—as presupposed by the NRSV—then neither would the claim to be powerless to intervene bear examination. However, it is more likely that this is a separate saying counselling perseverance in adversity. vv. 13–14, the eating of honey is commended for its sweetness and health-giving properties and then becomes an analogy for the pleasure and benefits of wisdom (cf. 16:24; contrast 5:3). vv. 15–16, this instruction recalls 1:8–19. Violence against the righteous is self-destructive. While the righteous may fall down any number of times under the onslaughts of the wicked, they will always recover. The wicked will not (cf. vv. 19–20). vv. 17–18 warn against gloating when misfortune befalls an enemy. This is as displeasing to God as their enmity and may provoke God to divert his anger from the enemy to the one who gloats. vv. 21–2, the final saying counsels respect for God and king. In 21b the NRSV follows the LXX. The Hebrew text reads 'do not associate with those who change', where 'to change' may have the sense of advocating change. It may therefore be a warning not to take part in conspiracies against the king. The LXX contains a further five verses mainly on the wrath of the king.

Further Sayings of the Wise (24:23–34)

This short collection evidently forms an appendix to 22:17–24:22, though in the LXX the sayings of Agur in 30:1–14 come between vv. 22 and 23.

Judges and witnesses. vv. 23–5, 28, warn against the corruption of justice through the partiality of the judges (cf. 18:5; 28:21) or the false testimony of witnesses. The expression 'without cause' (v. 28) could mean 'without necessity' (mischievously) or 'without grounds' (falsely). Either way it amounts to perjury (v. 28b). v. 29 may be an independent saying on taking revenge (cf. 20:22) or may uncover the motive for the perjury. v. 27 advises the young farmer to ensure that he is financially secure before he begins to build a house and raise a family. The advice is widely applicable. vv. 30–4 form an example story (cf. 7:6–23) reinforcing the lesson drawn from the industry of the ant in 6:10–11. They also provide a good example of how instruction may be received through the eye as well as the ear ('saw . . . considered . . . received instruction', v. 32).

The Second 'Solomonic' Collection (25:1–29:27)

According to the heading in 25:1, these chapters form a further collection of Solomonic proverbs, transmitted and edited by royal scribes (if that is what the rather vague 'copied by the men' implies) during the reign of Hezekiah. As with the first collection in 10:1–22:16, differences in style and subject-matter suggest it may have been compiled from two originally separate collections: chs. 25–7 and chs. 28–9. The first part is characterized by its many similes—often drawing comparisons with nature—and its 'earthy' tone. Antithetic parallelism is rare. The second part contains a high proportion of antithetical sayings and is predominantly moral and religious in tone after the manner of chs. 10–15. The question

concerning the context of individual sayings raised in connection with 10:1–22:16 arises here also, though topical or thematic groupings are now more evident, especially in chs. 25–6.

(25:1–28) vv. 2–7 form a short series of sayings centred on the king (cf. 16:9–15). While God is appropriately surrounded in mysteries no one can fathom, the king must take steps to investigate all that goes on in his kingdom (v. 2; cf. 2 Sam 14:20). v. 3 points to the profundity of the king's mind and so to the unpredictability of his decisions—which enhance his power and authority. The next saying (vv. 4–5) reiterates the point of 16:12 through a comparison between refining silver and rooting out the wicked. Further advice is given to royal officials in vv. 6–7a (cf. 23:1–3). On state occasions, the best strategy is that they take their place with the lower ranks, for then they may receive a public acknowledgement of their worth to the king if they are asked to join the higher ranks (cf. Lk 14:7–11). v. 15 probably has in view royal counsellors. Gentle but persistent persuasion will break down even the hardest resistance to their advice.

vv. 7b–8 warn against impetuous litigation. It is not clear whether vv. 9–10 also refer to litigation or to pursuing a quarrel in public through slanderous accusations and breaches of confidence. This will earn the culprit a bad reputation as one who is disloyal and untrustworthy. The wise course is to keep a quarrel private and to settle it in private. A word 'fitly spoken'—i.e. well expressed and well timed—is a product of great artistry, beauty, and value (v. 11; cf. 15:23). The artistic design envisaged is unclear. In v. 12 a similar comparison is made with the marriage between a wise rebuke and a listening ear. An 'earring' is perhaps meant. v. 16, even healthy things (cf. 24:13) in excess can become harmful. The application of the imagery in v. 27 is obscure. The NRSV assumes a slight emendation of the Hebrew text, which makes little sense as it stands ('searching out their honour is honour'). Too much honour can be too much of a good thing. v. 17, a neighbour's hospitality should not be abused. The *Instruction of Ani* likewise counsels, 'Do not go freely to your neighbour's house, but enter it only when you are invited.'

The significance of the 'coals of fire' in v. 22 is unclear. It may reflect an Egyptian ritual practice in which a brazier of burning charcoal was held on the head as a sign of shame and remorse. In any event the point of the saying is probably that by meeting hostility with kindness (v. 21) the enemy will have a change of heart and be reconciled (cf. 16:7) and not that it will heap punishment upon them. Cf. *Amen-em-ope*: 'Fill his belly with bread of yours, so that he shall be satisfied and ashamed' (cf. Rom 12:20–1). v. 25 reflects on the refreshment and revitalization that comes with the receipt of good news (cf. 15:30; Gen 45:25–8. In 13:12 the 'healing' brought about by a faithful messenger (cf. v. 13) is contrasted with trouble caused by a bad messenger.

(26:1–28) The first twelve verses (except v. 2) form a series of sayings on the 'fool'. vv. 1, 8, probably have in view the promotion of the fool to a position of public responsibility in the community. This is a gross distortion of what is right and proper (v. 1) and utterly absurd (v. 8), for fools are neither worthy of such honour nor capable of discharging their duties responsibly. vv. 4–5 point to the dilemma of how best to respond to a fool. To speak up runs the risk of descending to his level (v. 4), while to keep silent means their conceit will go unchecked (v. 5). It is a test of wisdom to know whether silence or reprimand is the lesser of two evils in the circumstances. To send a message with a fool is counter-productive (v. 6). Instead of receiving the help of their legs, it is like cutting off one's own legs and will have harmful consequences. While the text of v. 10 is difficult, it too appears to warn of the dangers of employing a fool, comparing the damage the fool will do to that of an archer firing arrows indiscriminately. Both vv. 7 and 9 make the point that the fool is incapable of the effective use of proverbs. The proverb will invariably be misapplied or mistimed, and fall 'limp' to the ground. The imagery of v. 9 is less clear. The rendering of the NRSV implies that the fool's proverb wreaks havoc and causes injury. Alternatively, the point may be that the proverb makes not the slightest impact—any more than a drunkard feels a thorn piercing his hand (cf. RSV).

The law made provision for the pronouncing of curses, particularly in cases where the guilty might escape detection (Deut 27:15–26). v. 2 adds that a malicious curse targeting an innocent victim will fly harmlessly past.

vv. 13–16 centre on lazy people, sketching with humour their attachment to their beds, the preposterous excuses they make for doing nothing, and their inability to finish what they started—while all the time deluding themselves that they are wiser than any number of intelligent people. The 'meddler' in v. 17 is probably not a well-intending peacemaker but the quarreller of v. 21. To 'meddle' is literally 'become excited'. This kind of person thrives on strife and enjoys pouring fuel on quarrels—whether those of their own making or by interfering in the quarrels of others. v. 20 observes the role of talebearing in fuelling and perpetuating a quarrel (cf. v. 22). In v. 23 'smooth lips' follows the reading of the LXX, referring to flattery (cf. 28; 29:5). The Hebrew reads 'burning lips', perhaps meaning warm protestations of friendship. Either way it is speech that lacks honesty and cloaks malice. Thus, vv. 24–6 warn against the kind of enemy (lit. one who hates) who conceals his malice behind a veneer of friendly words. 'Seven abominations' may look back to 6:16–19, but more likely it means that the enemy harbours any number of malicious thoughts and intentions. Sooner or later, however, the duplicity and treachery will be publicly exposed.

(27:1–27) v. 1 is directed against an arrogant confidence in one's ability to control the future, and so reinforces the theme of the limitations of human planning (cf. 16:9; 19:21). Amen-em-ope expresses a similar thought: 'Man knoweth not what the morrow will be, The events of the morrow are in the hands of God.' Jealousy is more overwhelming and destructive than anger (v. 4; cf. 6:34–5). The image is of floodwaters sweeping all before it (lit. a flood of anger; cf. Isa 28:2).

In vv. 5–6 a frank and sharp word of censure, however hurtful at the time, is contrasted with a misguided love which turns a blind eye to the faults of others (cf. 10:10; 28:23), and with hypocritical expressions of affection, however profuse. 'Well meant' might be better rendered 'trustworthy' (cf. NIV,

'can be trusted') as compared to the deceitful kisses of a Judas. The second line of v. 9 is difficult: literally, 'the sweetness of his friend from the counsel of the soul', which may mean that the counsel of a friend sweetens the soul. The NRSV follows the LXX, making it a reflection along the lines of 15:13. v. 10 is another difficult verse, seeming to contain three sayings. The second is at odds with 17:17. The sense may be 'don't pester them with your problems' (cf. 25:17). The NEB omits the line. The loud and untimely greeting in v. 14 could be a mark of inconsiderateness, but it is more probably of insincerity—akin to the profuse kisses of v. 6. v. 17 observes the necessity and value of social interaction with friends and adversaries alike to sharpen the mind and shape the character (lit. face).

v. 15 repeats the thought of 19:13b. With most modern versions, the translation of v. 16 in the NRSV is an attempt to wrest sense out of a difficult Hebrew text—which is probably meaningless as it stands—on the assumption that it is connected with the preceding verse. Such a wife is as uncontrollable as a gust of wind or oil grasped in the hand. As construed by the NRSV, the point of v. 19 seems to be that knowledge of one's character comes through observing the character of others. The Hebrew is enigmatic, however, and could equally mean that the heart reflects the character or that self-knowledge comes through self-examination. The image in v. 20 is of Sheol as a monster with a voracious appetite for human victims (cf. 1:12; 30:16). Human desires and ambition are just as insatiable. It may also be implied they are just as ruthless. Just as the value of silver or gold is tested in the crucible, so the worth of a person's character is tested by their reputation (v. 21; cf. v. 2). The instruction in vv. 23–7 commends the pastoral life as providing the best and most enduring kind of wealth. Whereas riches are fickle and fleeting (cf. 23:4–5), flocks are assets which do not dwindle but are renewed each spring at the lambing season, and they will provide for all the household needs. According to Van Leeuwen (1988: 137), the instruction is 'addressed to the king (and his court) as "shepherd" of his people'.

(28:1–28) v. 1 takes up the theme of the confidence of the righteous to walk securely through life with unfaltering step in contrast with the fearfulness of the wicked, who are weighed down by a guilty conscience and dread of the inevitable punishment (cf. vv. 10, 18). In v. 14 the contrast may be between those who 'fear' the Lord and the impious or wicked (cf. RSV), though a different Hebrew word for 'fear' is used. The NEB renders 'scrupulous in conduct', which may imply fear of sin and its consequences. The theme of vv. 12, 28, is the consequences for good or ill within the body politic when either the righteous or the wicked hold the reins of power (cf. 11:10–11). The verb translated 'go into hiding' in v. 12 is literally 'are sought out', which probably means 'are hunted down', providing the reason why they hide themselves (v. 28).

The Hebrew text of v. 2 is obscure, especially the second line. As translated by the NRSV it compares the political instability of the land during times of rebellion—with its succession of rulers and different factions vying for power—and its stability under a good and capable ruler. The NEB follows the LXX in making it a saying about quarrelling. In

v. 3 'ruler' rests on a slight emendation of the Hebrew for 'a poor person', which makes better sense. v. 15 makes the same point with different imagery, while v. 16 observes that rulers who abuse their power in this way will be as short-lived as they are short-sighted. Poverty with integrity is preferable to riches with perversity (v. 6; cf. 15:16; 16:8; 22:1; see also 19:1). The rich may be inflated by a sense of their own importance, but a poor person with intelligence will see through their pretension (v. 11).

The charging of interest (v. 8) on loans to fellow Israelites was condemned in the law (cf. Ex 22:25; Lev 25:36–7). 'Exorbitant interest' is literally 'interest and increase', the former indicating interest deducted from the loan and the latter interest added to the loan. The saying asserts that the wealth thereby amassed will pass to a kind person, who will share it among those from whom it was taken. vv. 20, 22, are directed against those who 'hasten to be rich'. The 'miser' is literally 'one with an evil eye' (v. 22; cf. 23:6). The phrase probably implies not only their greed and self-ishness but also their lack of moral scruples in their pursuit of wealth. It is the 'faithful' (v. 20) who will be blessed with wealth, while they will be punished (cf. also v. 25). In v. 9 'law' probably refers to the divine law rather than the teaching of wisdom (cf. v. 4). God will turn a deaf ear to the prayers of those who turn a deaf ear to him (cf. 15:8, 29). The person who confesses and repents of their sins will receive divine mercy and forgiveness (v. 13). The verse is unique in Proverbs.

(29:1–27) When the wicked are in power, the people groan under an intolerable burden as injustice and violence flourish unchecked (vv. 2, 16). But righteousness will in the end prevail (cf. 11:10–11; 28:12, 28). v. 6 is a further reflection on the confidence of the righteous in contrast with the snares the wicked weave for themselves through their evil activities. In a similar vein, v. 25 contrasts the snare of 'fear of others'—which breeds anxiety and may also breed wrongdoing—with the security to be found in trusting God (cf. 3:5–8). To 'know the rights of the poor' (v. 7) means to actively promote justice for the poor. The wicked care nothing about their rights. The 'men of blood' (v. 10) recalls the robbers and murderers of 1:8–19. The 'blameless' may be their innocent victims (cf. 1:11) but more probably those who oppose them and seek to bring them to justice. The English versions go different ways in making appropriate sense of the second line (lit. and the upright seek his life). The Hebrew implies an antithesis, so that here, unusually, to 'seek his life' may mean to 'seek to preserve his life' or to 'seek his well-being'.

Justice is the key to the stability of the king's throne and of his kingdom (vv. 4, 14). The king whose main preoccupation is to build up and enhance the splendour of his kingdom through crippling taxation sows the seeds of its dissolution (cf. 1 Sam 8:11–18; 1 Kings 12). The king who listens to lies will be quickly surrounded by corrupt officials (v. 12)—and his throne will be equally undermined (cf. 16:12; 25:5). The first line of v. 26 may refer to currying royal 'favours' (lit. face) or to seeking an audience for a legal decision. In the latter case, the second line either reaffirms that God's decisions underlie those of the king (cf. 16:10; 21:10) or reflects that kings are

not always just: God alone is the unfailing source of justice. 'Flatters' (v. 5) is literally 'makes smooth'. The flatterer's words are in the same debased currency of deceit and duplicity as the words of the seductress (cf. 2:16; 5:3; 26:23, 28).

To enter into litigation with a fool is not worth the trouble (v. 9). A fool is incapable of calm and reasoned debate and it is not likely that the matter will be satisfactorily resolved (cf. 26:4–5). v. 13 is a variant on 22:2. The first line of v. 18 affirms that without prophecy (lit. (prophetic) vision) social anarchy prevails, and the second line pronounces blessing on those who obey the law of God. Divine revelation through prophecy and law is essential to the harmony and well-being of society and of individuals within it. McKane (1970: 640–1) suggests the saying proposes obedience to the law as the solution to the indiscipline resulting from the cessation of the age of prophecy. v. 24 deals with the failure of a person to step forward as a witness when publicly adjured (lit. hears the curse, as in Lev 5:1) because they are an accomplice of the thief and will only implicate themselves. In this way they bring the 'curse' on their own heads.

The Sayings of Agur (30:1–33)

This collection is ascribed to an otherwise unknown sage. In the heading, the word 'oracle' translates Hebrew *maśśā'*. While this could describe the sayings as a prophetic type 'revelation' (cf. Hab 1:1) it is more likely that it designates the tribe or place of Massa in northern Arabia (Gen 25:14) to which Agur belonged (RSV). In that case, Proverbs has preserved the sayings of a non-Israelite sage (cf. also 31:1). It is possible that Agur's sayings do not extend beyond v. 14. These verses are separate from vv. 15–33 in the LXX—vv. 1–14 following 24:22 and vv. 15–33 following 24:34. Opinion is divided on whether they end before v. 14 (at vv. 4, 6, or 9).

v. 1b in the Hebrew is very cryptic and obscure. However, the rendering of the NRSV is preferable to the RSV ('The man says to Ithiel, to Ithiel and Ucal'—presumably his sons or disciples). In vv. 2–3 Agur confesses his lack of knowledge of God and his lack of wisdom. While 'holy ones' could refer to the divine council (cf. Ps 89:5–7), it is better taken as a reference to God himself, the Holy One (cf. 9:10). Agur's words may be in part ironic, directed against the wise who professed a deep understanding of God and his ways (cf. Eccl 8:17). The rhetorical questions in v. 4, like those in Job 38–41, emphasize the inscrutability of God's ways. To ascend and descend to and from the heavens is a biblical and ancient Near-Eastern motif for the arrogant attempt to attain knowledge of eternal truth and become like the gods (cf. Perdue 1994: 117–19). The ironic challenge at the end of v. 4 is to produce such a person. God alone has the power and wisdom to rule his creation and is enveloped in mystery which human wisdom is unable to fathom. While it is not clear whether vv. 5–6 originally belonged with the preceding verses, they give reassurance that God has made himself known through his 'word'. This may refer to the canonical Scriptures. The term rendered 'proves true' is used of refining metals (Ps 12:6) and means that God's word is unalloyed or that it has stood the test. The warning not to add to or subtract from it echoes Deut 4:2; 12:32 (cf. Rev 22:18–19). In the form of a prayer (unique in Proverbs), vv. 7–9 counsel contentment with God's provision of the basic necessities of life. Wealth can lead to self-sufficiency and the denial of God, while poverty is just as likely to lead to stealing and the profanation of God's name. vv. 15–16 contain two related sayings on unsatisfied desires. The first (15a) is a comment on human greed. That might also be the point of the second saying or it may be a comment on the barren womb. Like the desire of Sheol for human victims (cf. 1:12), the earth for water, and the fire for fuel, the desire of barren women for children is never satisfied. It is not clear what the 'way' of the eagle, the snake, and the ship on the high seas have in common with one another, and even less clear what the 'way' of a man with a woman has in common with them (vv. 18–19). That human sexuality is mysterious and marvellous may dilute the point. vv. 21–3 describe as earth-shattering events four inversions of the social order. The point could be that people who experience a dramatic change in fortune become unbearable or that social upheaval threatens cosmic order. The general theme of vv. 24–8 is 'small but wise'. Ants are commended for foresight (cf. 6:6–8); badgers for ingenuity; locusts for discipline; and the lizard for adeptness at getting into places. Wisdom and not strength is the key to success (cf. 16:32). vv. 29–31 evidently compare the majestic bearing of a king in procession with the proud gait of the lion, the strut of the rooster and the he-goat. The second animal is literally 'one girt of loins', i.e. 'the strutter', usually taken with the LXX as referring to the cock, though other animals such as the warhorse have been proposed. The Hebrew text of the last line (v. 31b) is obscure.

The Words of Lemuel (31:1–9)

In this passage the queen-mother instructs her son on his duty to administer justice. King Lemuel is otherwise unknown. As in 30:1, 'oracle' translates Hebrew *maśśā'* and may designate a tribe or region in northern Arabia. This gains some added support by the presence of Aramaic words in the text (e.g. *bar*, 'son', for Heb. *ben*). Although the role of the queen-mother is unusual, the vocational intent of the passage brings it particularly close to Egyptian instruction, especially those concerned with the training of future monarchs (e.g. the *Instruction of Merikare*).

Appealing to his filial respect as a son for his mother and his birth as an answer to prayer (v. 2; cf. 1 Sam 1:11), the queen-mother warns her son against sexual promiscuity and drunkenness (vv. 3–5). One will sap the strength and the other will anaesthetize the mind, rendering the king physically and morally incapable of administering justice. While the wretched seek oblivion in alcohol (vv. 6–7), a king cannot afford to become oblivious to their wretchedness. Rather he must speak on behalf of the 'dumb', i.e. those unable to make their own voice heard in defence of their legal rights: the poor and needy and the destitute (vv. 8–9).

The Good Wife (31:10–31)

These verses are in the form of an acrostic poem, in which each one begins with a successive letter of the Hebrew alphabet. As characterized in the poem, the good wife is an industrious housewife; a shrewd businesswoman; an enterprising trader; a generous benefactor (v. 20); and a wise teacher (v. 26). Her husband has complete confidence in her, since he knows that his wealth and his reputation are safe in her hands (vv. 11–12; cf. 23). The key to her industry, acumen, kindness, and wisdom is that she 'fears the LORD' (v. 30). Like Wisdom herself, such a wife is a priceless treasure who is worthy of praise (vv. 10, 28–31; cf. 3:13–18).

In view of the emphasis given to the dangers of loose women in chs. 1–9, it would be fitting for the book to end by directing the attention of prospective bridegrooms to the ideal wife. Certainly, to have such a wife would be a gift from God (18:22)! It is probable, however, that the passage does not merely sum up the ideal wife but also the ideals of wisdom. The good wife may be a final personification of Wisdom, completing the portrait of the woman Wisdom as housebuilder in 9:1–6: 'In chapter 31 Wisdom is a faithful wife and skilled mistress of her household, finally settled down with her own' (McCreesh 1985: 46).

REFERENCES

Camp, C. V. (1985), *Wisdom and the Feminine in the Book of Proverbs* (Sheffield: JSOT).

McCreesh, T. P. (1985), 'Wisdom as Wife: Proverbs 31:10–31', *RB* 92: 25–46.

McKane, W (1970), *Proverbs: A New Approach*, OTL (London: SCM).

Martin, J. (1995), *Proverbs*, OTG (Sheffield: Sheffield Academic Press).

Murphy, R. E. (1998), *Proverbs*, WBC (Nashville: Thomas Nelson).

Perdue, L. G. (1994), *Wisdom and Creation: The Theology of the Wisdom Literature* (Nashville: Abingdon).

von Rad, G. (1972), *Wisdom in Israel* (London: SCM). German original, 1970.

Skehan, P. W. (1972), *Studies in Israelite Poetry and Wisdom*, CBQMS 1 (Washington: Catholic Biblical Association).

Van Leeuwen, R. C. (1988), *Context and Meaning in Proverbs 25–27*, SBLDS 96 (Atlanta: Scholars Press).

Westermann, C. (1995), *Roots of Wisdom: The Oldest Proverbs of Israel and Other Peoples* (Edinburgh: T. & T. Clark. German original, 1990).

Wilson, F. M. (1987), 'Sacred and Profane? The Yahwistic Redaction of Proverbs Reconsidered', in K. G. Hoglund (ed.), *The Listening Heart*, JSOTSup 58 (Sheffield: JSOT), 313–33.

20. Ecclesiastes
STUART WEEKS

INTRODUCTION

A. Author and Date. Most of this book takes the form of a monologue, spoken by a character called '(the) Qoheleth' ('the Teacher'): its author has adopted the common ancient habit of setting philosophical discussion within speeches, and he probably comments on his own character's words in 12:9–10. We know little about this author, but the book's language does include a number of Aramaic terms and loanwords from Persian, and has certain characteristics which are more common in post-biblical Hebrew than in the Bible. Despite some attempts to explain these as dialectal, it is widely agreed that they point to a late date of composition. Since the work seems to have been known by Ben Sira, a date between about the fifth and second centuries BCE seems probable, and it is most likely to have been composed in the latter part of this period. The lack of an ancient Septuagint version may be telling in this respect: the Greek 'Ecclesiastes' is probably the work of Aquila or his followers. The Greek title reflects an early attempt to translate 'Qoheleth': the original meaning of this name or title is uncertain, although it may be connected with ideas of 'summoning' or 'gathering'.

B. Content. Qoheleth's ideas are notoriously confusing and contradictory, but some continuity is visible across the book. Qoheleth views the world as changeless, with humans unable to comprehend its workings or to make any lasting impact upon it; within their society, moreover, injustice is rampant and the future unpredictable. All this is attributed to God's deliberate design, but leads Qoheleth to ask just what humans should do to get the best from life in such a world. His answer, after reflection on his own experiences, is that humans should simply enjoy what they have: they are in no position to seek more, and greater comprehension is a source only of unhappiness.

Set against all this, though, is an attempt to justify God, and to affirm the reality of divine judgement. This sits uncomfortably beside the book's other assertions, leading many scholars to suspect either that the book has undergone secondary editing by a more orthodox writer, or that the views of others are being quoted. Either is possible, but it is no less likely that this disharmony is original, and it is explicable in two ways. First, several ancient works show a strong interest in inconsistency as a phenomenon: the demotic instruction on Papyrus Insinger, most famously, juxtaposes contradictory 'truths' to argue, like Qoheleth, that divine power is supreme and unknowable. Secondly, Qoheleth's monologue is presented as the conclusions of a wise man reflecting on his experience, but the book seems suspicious of such claims to wisdom: self-contradiction is, therefore, embedded at its deepest level, and the work's aims may include a critical, ironic look at the limitations and contradictions of wisdom represented by Qoheleth and his speech.

In his commentary upon the world and his own observations, Qoheleth resorts frequently to a single word, *hebel*.

Conventionally translated 'vanity', the literal sense of this term is probably 'a breath of wind', but it is more often used metaphorically, to suggest transience, uselessness, or deceptiveness. No single implication seems to suit all its occurrences in this book, where it is closely associated with another expression: *rĕ'ût rûaḥ* (1:14, 2:11, 17, 26; 4:4, 6; 6:9; cf. the similar *ra'yôn rûaḥ* in 1:17; 4:16). A comparable phrase in Hos 12:1 suggests that this latter means 'pursuing the wind', and it is probably used here to evoke the sense of frustration inherent in attempts to achieve the impossible (cf. Fox 1989).

COMMENTARY

'All is Vanity' (1:1-11)

(1:1) Qoheleth is described as a Davidic king, and this is picked up in 1:12, which claims that he ruled Israel from Jerusalem: if the term 'Israel' here is meant to include the northern kingdom, then, since the only descendants of David to rule it were Solomon and the far-from-wise Rehoboam, a claim to Solomonic authorship is apparently intended, though never stated outright. However, sometimes Judah is referred to as 'Israel'.

(1:2) The motto, 'vanity of vanities', appears again in 12:8, at the end of the teaching, while the key term 'vanity' (*hebel*) recurs frequently as a comment on situations described in the book.

(1:3–11) The rhetorical question in v. 3 picks up the claim that all is *hebel*, and the poem that follows portrays a world which is impervious to human effort. While human generations each pass into oblivion, nature continues regardless, and itself reaches no fruition or consummation. Without change, there is no novelty, and without effect, no satisfaction. Qoheleth describes a world without progress or culmination, where everything has been done before, but, unremembered, will be done again. This is not an assertion that the world follows cycles or patterns. although the sun, rather comically, hurries panting back to its starting place, the other phenomena are not cyclical, merely ceaseless. v. 8 suggests the inadequacy of human speech and senses for any comprehension of this endlessness: 'All words are exhausted: a person will never manage to speak [of it], an eye will never see enough, and an ear will never be filled as it listens' (my tr.). Qoheleth rejects not only any actual human progress in innovation and understanding, but the very possibility of such progress.

Memoir (1:12–2:26)

This fictional memoir describes Qoheleth's own, futile quest for understanding, which leads him to conclude that humans can do no more than enjoy what they have been given. The generalities of the introductory section now give way to a style more characteristic of the book as a whole, in which Qoheleth takes claims of personal experience as the context or basis for his assertions. He begins by associating himself with the famously wise and wealthy Solomon, which allows him to claim that he had the power and resources necessary for the subsequent experiments. We hear no more of this royal status after the device has served its purpose, but the equally implausible claim in 1:14, that Qoheleth has seen 'all the deeds that are done under the sun', is echoed several times in the book.

(1:12–18) The section begins with a pair of units, in each of which Qoheleth presents his credentials for undertaking a specific enquiry, then summarizes the result of that enquiry before finishing with a short aphorism. In the first he sets out to observe all that is done in the world, using his wisdom, and concludes that all is *hebel* and *rĕʿût rûaḥ*. The unit finishes with an aphorism which again denies any human ability to affect the world. In the Egyptian *Instruction of Ani*, which includes a debate about the efficacy of education, the principal character asserts that a crooked stick *can* be straightened: any direct reference to that text here is unlikely, but it does emphasize Qoheleth's distance from more optimistic ideas of human effectiveness. The second line of the aphorism seems so patently obvious that some scholars have suggested emendation, but it does sum up Qoheleth's enquiry: he searches out all deeds, but finds nothing to measure. The unit vv. 16–18 follows the same pattern as vv. 12–15, but Qoheleth's enquiry is now into wisdom itself, which was the tool he used in the first enquiry, and into its opposites. His conclusion is again pessimistic: wisdom and knowledge merely enhance vexation and sorrow.

(2:1–11) After this presentation of results, the section moves on to a more detailed memoir. Disappointed by wisdom, Qoheleth decides to sample pleasure, and tells himself to have a good time. Ever the intellectual, though, he finds laughter irrational and pleasure useless, and puzzles over how to become drunk while staying wise, and over how to become foolish. He does succeed, though, in building an establishment geared to beauty and sensual pleasure, becoming great and retaining his wisdom while indulging himself unstintingly. This brings him to a crucial observation: his efforts are rewarded by the irrational pleasure that he gains from them, even though, on consideration, they seem still to be *hebel*, and a chasing after wind.

(2:12–21) As in 1:17, Qoheleth now turns to wisdom, madness, and folly. His initial conclusion seems conventional, and is in line with ideas found elsewhere (e.g. Prov 4:18–19). It immediately becomes clear, though, that the saying in v. 14 has a double edge: the ability of the wise to see where they are going does not affect their route; they are going the same way as the fools, and are merely more aware of it. Both the wise and the foolish, Qoheleth realizes, are doomed to oblivion, and this realization causes him to hate life, exemplifying the conclusion in v. 18. With the wisdom to look forward, Qoheleth also realizes that all he has worked for will be left in the hands of another, who may be wise or foolish, and who will have done no work for it. This leads him, retrospectively, to hate his own efforts.

(2:22–6) As the section nears its conclusion, Qoheleth echoes the question originally asked in 1:3, adding emphasis by the observation that humans suffer for their work. Now he offers an answer of sorts: all that he has found rewarding is pleasure in work, and he proposes that mortals can do no better than to eat, drink, and enjoy what they do. At this point, though, he attempts to explore a theological justification for his *carpe diem* conclusion: the ability to enjoy life, or perhaps the ability to know that one should enjoy life, is a divine dispensation granted only to those who please God; those who do not are condemned to toil on their behalf. That implies, though, a social analysis with which Qoheleth later shows himself to be uncomfortable: those who are suffering and working on behalf of others are the sinners, and those who enjoy themselves, while others work for them, are the righteous.

'Everything Suitable for its Time' (3:1–15)

After his foray into kingship, Qoheleth now returns to the ideas of 1:3–11, but retains the interest in divine action found at the end of the last section. A poem in vv. 2–8 illustrates the claim of v. 1, that every action or event will come to pass, and v. 11 further explains that God has made each 'suitable for its time'. Although the poem is often taken as a celebration of this fact, with each and every action given its own appropriate hour, the context suggests that, for Qoheleth, it is more a source of resignation. In vv. 14–15, the point originally made in 1:9–10 is picked up: what has happened will happen again, and there can be no innovation. Now, though, this situation is explicitly attributed to divine action, with God creating and maintaining a scaled system, in which nothing has a beginning or an end, but everything has its day. It is against this background that Qoheleth repeats his now familiar question: 'what gain have the workers from their toil?' God has given humans business to do, and a sense of past and future, but they lack any ability to comprehend the divine activity. Again, then, the best that they can do is to enjoy life, and the ability to do so is made available to all by God. Upon the world itself, though, they can make no impact: its unchangeability is a deliberate device that ensures that humans will stand in awe of God (1:14).

Wickedness and Oppression (3:16–4:3)

Such a perception of the world raises an obvious problem: despite the divine jurisdiction, wickedness seems to triumph over justice and righteousness. Qoheleth tackles the problem of theodicy with reference to the ideas that he has put forward already, and declares his belief in some ultimate judgement on the basis that, since there is a divinely appointed time for everything, there must be a time for divine judgement. The Hebrew of 3:18 is very obscure, and the text may be corrupt; the gist of 3:18–21 seems to be, though, that God permits humans no understanding of their eventual fate that would allow them to distinguish themselves from animals. Their inability to comprehend, or to foresee the future, leads, again, to the conclusion that the best they can do is to enjoy their work. Qoheleth seems to be claiming, then, that there are grounds for believing in some sort of judgement after death, but that this is deliberately hidden by God, who prevents human comprehension of the world. The argument is followed, in 4:1–3, by a more emotional reaction to the seemingly perverted nature of the world, as Qoheleth declares it better to be dead or unborn than to have to experience the horror of oppression. He emphasizes the lack of any comforter for the oppressed, and the passage as a whole seems to react against the preceding argument: the obscurity of the divine purpose is all very well, but offers little solace to the oppressed, who are in no position to enjoy themselves.

'All their Toil' (4:4–12)

The loneliness of the oppressed provides a transition to Qoheleth's next, rather different topic. He begins with the observation that competition is the sole motive for work and skill, a fact which is *hebel* and a chasing after wind. He then presents, in v. 5, an aphorism suggesting that laziness is the vice and the downfall of fools, leading them to eat themselves instead of their produce; folding of the hands is elsewhere associated with sloth (cf. Prov 6:10; 24:33), and the saying may be a conventional one. A second aphorism, in v. 6, is set against this, suggesting that rest is better than toil, and establishes the first of the two themes in this section: a condemnation of pointless greed. The second theme, that co-operation is better than competition, sits alongside this in vv. 7–8, and is further elaborated in vv. 9–12. The discussion finishes with a further saying, about the strength of a plaited cord, which resembles an ancient proverb found in the *Epic of Gilgamesh*.

Wise Youth, Foolish King (4:13–16)

The meaning and relevance of this next section are quite obscure, and there have been many attempts to identify a particular historical situation to which it might refer. The principal problems are a certain ambiguity in the syntax, and the possibility that the 'second' youth of v. 15 is simply the same youth as in v. 13. It seems probable that Qoheleth is again setting one idea off against another: a wise youth is better than a foolish king, whatever his background, *but* that youth will be followed by another and ultimately forgotten. Gordis (1968) interprets the term that NRSV paraphrases as 'whom he led' in a temporal sense, so that v. 16 places the fragment of succession illustrated here in a much broader context: these characters were preceded by a whole host of others, and will be forgotten by those who follow. In any case, Qoheleth seems to be drawing out an implication of 1:11, that what seems true and important at a particular moment will only be swallowed up in the forgetfulness and repetition of time.

Fear of God (5:1–9)

(5:1–7) Moving to a quite different theme again, Qoheleth advocates caution in dealings with God, emphasizing the risks rather than the benefits of such dealings: 'fear of God' often has a more general implication of piety and fairness in the OT, but in v. 7 its sense is literal. The particular risks here involve speech: hasty words and unfulfilled vows may both incur divine displeasure, and there is specific reference to the Torah (v. 4 is a paraphrase of Deut 23:21–3, and 'mistake' in v. 6 is a technical term for an unwitting sin). Such speech may lead to the divine destruction of one's work. In vv. 3, 7, a plethora of words is associated with dreaming. The former is a straightforward comparison, probably suggesting that a fool's voice is as much a product of too much speech as dreams are of too many cares. The syntax and meaning of the latter, though, are very obscure. v. 6 mentions a 'messenger', and the reference is probably to an angel. The particularly literal Septuagint rendering, though, has 'God', and this is likely to be the original reading (cf. Fox 1989).

(5:8–9) This passage is notoriously difficult, and no very satisfactory interpretation has yet been proposed. The first verse probably explains oppression either in terms of the protection offered to each level of officials by their superiors, or else as a result of the demands made by such a vast bureaucracy. Just conceivably, though, it is suggesting that one should not be too concerned by such oppression, as God is in a higher position than the officials (Ogden 1987). The sense and relevance of the second verse are all but impenetrable; it might possibly be an ironic comment on the hierarchical system, which gives every field a ruler. Some scholars take these comments to have been inspired by experience of a particular historical bureaucracy, perhaps that of Ptolemaic Egypt.

The Problems and Inadequacies of Wealth (5:10–6:12)

(5:10–20) vv. 10–12 make three concise points about financial greed: those who love money never have enough; financial commitments grow in proportion to resources; too much wealth, without compensating work, makes for indigestion. vv. 13–17 point out the potential ephemerality of wealth: those who have refused to spend it may yet lose it, making all they have been and done pointless. In vv. 18–20 Qoheleth reiterates his earlier conclusion about the importance of enjoyment. God gives not only wealth, but the capacity for its enjoyment, which enables humans to focus on pleasure.

(6:1–9) vv. 1–6 elaborate on the theme, highlighting the case of those to whom God gives wealth and its trappings, without the capacity for enjoyment; they may live long and have much, but it is someone else who will ultimately enjoy their riches. They themselves are worse off than the stillborn child, which at least finds rest. vv. 7–9 close the discussion, but the place and meaning of v. 8 are unclear. The verse may be simply parenthetical (cf. Fox 1989), but it is possible to take it as a continuation of the point in v. 7, if *nepeš* there means something more than physical appetite. Qoheleth would then be arguing that humans are left unsatisfied because there are important questions to be answered: what is the point of wisdom, and what reason is there for the poor to find a role in life? It seems more likely that v. 9 condemns the desire to go beyond what one already sees, than that it is a further affirmation of death over life (cf. Whybray 1989), and in the section as a whole, then, Qoheleth acknowledges the human desire to answer questions that go beyond the obvious, but sees it as *hebel*.

(6:10–12) This point is explained in a summary passage that picks up earlier themes and provides a transition to the next main section. Since everything has been defined, humans are known to be inherently incapable of pleading or contesting a cause with whoever is stronger than they. Words, therefore, are futile: no one can tell mortals what they should do in their brief lives, or what will follow them.

Collection of Aphorisms (7:1–14)

The style of this section imitates that of the 'sentence literature' collections (e.g. Prov 10:1–22:16), and the sayings are linked, as normally in such collections, by catchwords and thematic links with their predecessors. The overall theme is broadly temporal: wisdom is associated with the need to look forward rather than focusing upon the good or bad times along the way. v. 14 sets this point in context: God has made bad times as well as good, to prevent humans from knowing what will follow them.

vv. 1–4 begin with a stylish play on words, but then present death and mourning as better than life and celebration. vv. 5–7 pick up the wise/foolish contrast and the rejection of celebration, with a comment on the transience of fools' laughter (again involving a play on words), but this is itself rejected as *hebel*, with a comment on the potential impermanence of wisdom. vv. 8–10 deal with the need to take a long-term view of life when reacting to adversity: it is not wise to react quickly or to question the passing of prosperity. vv. 11–12 commend wisdom as a source of protection, presumably taking it in the sense outlined above. The ideas are reminiscent of Prov 8, where wisdom, better than gold, promises life. Given Qoheleth's earlier comments on the insecurity of wealth, this is a two-edged commendation. v. 13 is similar to 1:15, and again emphasizes the impossibility of human influence on the world. Its expression, though, is more daring, with 'crookedness' directly identified as the work of God. v. 14 gives a general conclusion, but its affirmation of joy in times of prosperity seems to contradict vv. 1–4. Qoheleth advocates an approach that incorporates wisdom's long-term view when contemplating adversity, but rejects it for those times in which one can rejoice. The view of divine action picks up his earlier conclusions.

Neither Too Wise nor Too Foolish (7:15–22)

(7:15–20) This advice, to adopt some parts of wisdom but not others, is now generalized and made explicit. The best course is to be neither too wise and righteous, nor too foolish and wicked, but to be a bit of both; whoever fears God will succeed in both (or escape the consequences of doing neither: the Heb. is ambiguous, but the basic meaning clear). These remarkable assertions do need to be put in context: they arise not only from the observations of the previous section, but from the experiences asserted in v. 15, and so there is, perhaps, a wry or bitter edge to them.

(7:19–22) These three sayings are puzzling. The second clearly relates to the theme of 7:15–18, and the third may be an attempt to illustrate its point. Fox (1989) and others reposition the first after 7:12, which is drastic, but reflects the difficulty of finding a context for it here. The intention, however, is possibly another ironic comment on wisdom, exaggerating the idea in such sayings as Prov 24:5–6: to have ten rulers is to have nine too many, just as wisdom itself goes too far.

The Search for Integrity (7:23–8:1)

The key problem here is to reconcile what Qoheleth claims to have found with his claims to be seeking wisdom, a knowledge of folly and wickedness, and, above all, a *ḥešbôn*—an accounting or reckoning. In this quest for the abstract, all he finds, though, are people: the dangerous woman of 7:26, the one man in a thousand of 7:28, and the human behaviour described in 7:29. As it stands, furthermore, 7:28 is absurd: the traditional interpretation, that Qoheleth found no 'good' or 'wise' women, has no basis in the text, but, equally, he can hardly be claiming that he encountered no women at all. It may be helpful to think in terms of the influential personifications of wisdom and folly as women in Prov 1–9, not least because the woman in 7:26 here is strongly reminiscent of wisdom's dangerous counterpart in that work. His discovery of this woman therefore satisfies the second part of Qoheleth's stated quest, the recognition of folly, leaving him to find wisdom and the *ḥešbôn* (the sum); in 7:29 he recognizes the human capacity to create *ḥeššĕbōnôt* (schemes), which is probably a play on *ḥešbôn* (reckoning). Only wisdom is left, then, and 7:28 may be an acknowledgement of Qoheleth's failure to find her. The section as a whole, then, suggests that it is not so easy to find either wisdom or any definitive explanation of the world.

8:1*a* may be a gloss, if it is not the author's or Qoheleth's own ironic commentary. The term *pēšer* refers, in late Hebrew and Aramaic, to the interpretation of texts and dreams, and the line effectively doubts that anyone is wise enough to interpret what has been said; the secondary Hos 14:9 is a similar, though more positive comment. 8:1*b* has no obvious relevance to what precedes, or, despite Fox (1989), to what follows. Elsewhere, the shining of a face expresses contentment or favour, not intelligence, and is used of God (e.g. Num 6:26), while the LXX legitimately understands the second clause to mean 'and the man shameless in his face will be hated'. If the saying originally followed straight after 7:29, we might read: 'A human's wisdom makes him (God) favourable, but the impudent will be hated.'

Human and Divine Authority (8:2–9)

Qoheleth uses conclusions drawn from the observation of human authority as the basis for an understanding of divine authority. There are several difficulties in the first two verses, and the sentence division is unclear. The sense may be that one should watch out for royal anger, and flee as soon as it happens, or, more probably, that one should avoid both hurrying to leave the king and joining conspiracies against him (cf. Whybray 1989). The key point is in v. 5: it can do no harm to obey a command, while the wise mind will be aware that a reckoning is coming (*mišpāṭ* means 'justice' or 'judgement' rather than 'way' here); the thought is similar to that of 3:17. Qoheleth once again stresses, though, the impossibility for humans of knowing outcomes: there is no one to tell them. Equally, no human has control over the wind (or 'spirit') or over his or her death. There is no release from the situation in which people find themselves: v. 8 probably means that battle offers no more possibility of deliverance than does wickedness. Qoheleth, then, restates his views on human ignorance and impotence, but commends obedience to a secular ruler as the safest course.

Fear of God is the Wisest Course (8:10–17)

This idea is now applied in the religious context, in a passage which echoes the thoughts of 3:16–17. The lack of any immediate punishment of the wicked, along with their apparent prosperity, leads others to follow their example. But Qoheleth affirms again that the appearance is deceptive: it is still safer to 'stand in fear before God'. He goes on further to note, though, that the righteous are sometimes treated as though they were wicked and vice versa, a *hebel* which drives him again to commend enjoyment. He finishes by once more claiming that human comprehension of the world is deliberately prevented by God, and he now explicitly rejects the claims of the wise to know such matters.

(8:10) is difficult. Most commentators emend *qĕburîm*, 'buried', to *qĕrēbîm*, 'draw near', and see a reference to worship; Fox (1989) retains the idea of burial, and envisages burial processions from the temple or synagogue. 'Praised' reflects an alternative reading in some MSS and versions: MT has 'forgotten', suggesting that the second part compares the more forgetful attitude towards those who have done good.

(8:13) uses ambiguous imagery: 'like a shadow' refers either to the transience of the wicked, or to the stretching out of their lives.

(8:16) does not make clear whether the sleepless eyes are a part of the general human business, or a parenthetical exclamation, referring to Qoheleth's endless observation.

The Common Destiny (9:1–10)

The theme continues. The righteous and wise are under God's control, but even they cannot know his attitude towards them; all that is obvious is that the same end seems to come to all, whatever their behaviour or religious conscientiousness. This again drives humans to evil and to madness. In 3:16–4:3 such ideas led to the conclusion that it was better to be dead or unborn, but Qoheleth's thought has moved on: the living still have some knowledge—if only the knowledge that they will die. The dead can take nothing more from the world, and what they gave is now gone. The section ends with Qoheleth's fullest expression of his exhortation to enjoy life to the full, while it is still possible to do so.

(9:1–2) is difficult in MT, and the NRSV translation reflects a common emendation. Some scholars (e.g. Gordis 1968; Crenshaw 1988) retain MT and understand 'everything is before them, everything the same for everybody'. The reference is probably to what they can observe. In v. 2, 'and the evil' is lacking in the Hebrew, but its presence in the LXX suggests that it is original.

(9:4) probably refers not to 'hope' as such, but to the confident knowledge outlined in the next verse. Dogs are not highly regarded in most ancient literature, and it is interesting to note the use of 'dead dog' in expressions of self-abasement or insult (e.g. 2 Sam 9:8; 16:9).

(9:7–9) resembles a number of passages in ancient texts, but has particularly close links with the imagery of a passage in the *Epic of Gilgamesh*, where the hero is advised to abandon his quest for immortality. A direct dependence on this text is possible, but indirect knowledge of it, through other sources, is at least as likely. Such behaviour is here justified as something pre-ordained by God.

(9:10) refers to Sheol, the underworld, to which all humans were believed to descend after death. Biblical descriptions envisage it as a place of weakness (e.g. Isa 14:9–11), and as a leveller of the dead (Ezek 32:17–31). The shades who dwell there are impotent, miserable creatures.

Unpredictability and Injustice (9:11–16)

(9:11–12) After stressing death's lack of discrimination, Qoheleth turns briefly to its unpredictability. Those who should win or gain things have no control over them, but are at the mercy of events. Humans can no more foresee disaster than can animals foresee the traps in which they are caught. There is no suggestion that this is a matter of random misfortune, though: 'time and chance' is a hendiadys, meaning something like 'the turn of events', and the point is not that humans are lucky or unlucky, but that they cannot know what will happen.

(9:13–16) Qoheleth now returns to the theme of wisdom, and this will remain his principal topic until 11:6. He begins with a short anecdote, the point of which is unclear: many commentators think it tells the story of a wise man who could have saved a town had he been heeded, but the Hebrew reads more naturally as a claim that he really did save the town. The various elements are best explained on the assumption that he saved it, but that his contribution went unrecognized. The role of this anecdote is also difficult to pin down. Described as a 'great example' of wisdom, it lacks both the detail that would make it convincing evidence, and the symbolic aspect that would encourage us to view it as a parable. It seems most likely, then, that Qoheleth is summarizing a story familiar to his readers. He picks up the story's intended message, that wisdom is superior to might, but then puzzles over the failure to respect the poor man's wisdom.

Sayings and Counter-Sayings (9:17–11:6)

The issue raised in Qoheleth's mind by the story leads on to the book's most curious section. In 7:1–13, Qoheleth employed the sentence-literature style to make some key points of his own. Now he uses it as, effectively, a witness against itself. How far he is citing sayings that already existed is unclear: he may simply be inventing new sayings with the right style and tone. In any case, the basic technique is to set sayings together in such a way that they are undermined or reduced to absurdity. So 9:17–10:1 follows the story by initially proclaiming wisdom's superiority, but ends with the observation that it is outweighed by even a little folly. In 10:3, the metaphorical imagery of the saying in 10:2 is taken literally, to conjure up the comic image of fools walking differently from everyone else. The career-orientated advice in 10:4 is set against the observation in the next verse of a society in which rank has no basis in reason. The dangers and difficulties in 10:8–10*b* can patently not be overcome by wisdom, as 10:10*c* asserts, even if there were any chance to apply it in time (10:11). The claim in 10:12, that fools will be consumed by their speech, is enlarged upon in 10:13, but abruptly deflated in 10:14 by the observation that, nevertheless, they talk on and on; Qoheleth draws out the implication that the future is simply unpredictable, before recalling the comic image of the fools on the road. In 10:16–20, condemnations of revelry, drunkenness, and sloth are met by the claim that the first two are good things, while the third is no problem if one has money. The very notion of criticizing the rich and powerful in this way is itself condemned by the flight of fancy in 10:20, which would seem to have its tongue firmly in its cheek. 11:1–2 again stresses Qoheleth's concern with the impossibility of knowing the future. Finally, 11:3–6 sums up his point: the phenomena in 11:3 are not only absurdly obvious, but inevitable and uncontrollable; instead of wasting time watching for such things, which are beyond one's comprehension, it is better to get on with one's work, and to cover ones bases. Inherent in this is a more general criticism of any endeavour to comprehend the world through wisdom: it is not only foredoomed, but a waste of valuable time.

(9:18) contrasts wisdom with the *ḥôṭẽ'*, 'bungler' in NRSV, but more literally 'sinner'. Given the usage of this term elsewhere in the book, it is unlikely to be devoid of moral or religious connotations here.

(10:1–2) v. 1 presents several problems. 'Flies of death' is a curious way to say 'dead flies': it might mean 'dying flies', but it is best to follow an old suggestion, and redivide the text to read 'a fly dies' (cf. Fox 1989). NRSV leaves untranslated a reference to the flies making the ointment 'bubble', or 'ferment'; this might be a gloss, or a corruption of some term meaning 'preparation' or 'container' (cf. LXX). For 'wisdom and honour' (lit. weight) we should read 'a great weight of wisdom'. v. 2 assumes the common metaphor of a 'way' through life, which the next verse takes literally; right and left have moral connotations in later Jewish literature.

(10:4–7) v. 4 probably commends 'soothing' rather than 'calmness'. vv. 5–7 are strongly reminiscent of a theme popular in some much earlier Egyptian literature: the topsy-turvy society brought about by a failure of leadership. The error in v. 5 is probably ascribed to the ruler, not just compared with a ruler's error.

(10:10) is notorious for its obscurity. The form shows that it is paired with v. 11, while the theme links it to the preceding sayings: 'iron' is a cutting instrument or axe (cf. 2 Kings 6:5). The sense 'edge' for *pānîm* is improbable: we should probably emend *lō'-pānîm* to *lĕpānîm*, point *qlql* as passive, and read: 'If the axe is blunt but is sharpened beforehand, then it increases in strength.' The syntax of the second part is difficult, but most commentators agree that it refers to wisdom being advantageous. The saying refers, then, to the benefits of wisdom in forearming one: a claim undermined by the next verse's observation that that is not always possible.

(11:1) is similar to a saying in the late Egyptian *Instruction of 'Onchsheshonqy* (19.10), where a good deed is to be thrown in the water and recovered when dry: it may have been a familiar metaphor. As in the next verse, the issue is cautious preparation for the uncertain times ahead.

Youth and Age (11:7–12:8)

The end of Qoheleth's monologue offers a summary of his advice: life is good and to be enjoyed, especially by the young who can enjoy it best. Against that enjoyment, though, must be set the recollection that darkness is to follow, and that deeds will be judged: to remember one's creator is also to remember one's judge. Although these two ideas seem very different, there is no real contradiction here. Qoheleth has already rejected any idea that humans can know the criteria against which they will be judged, and so his advice to bear in mind

the coming judgement is not an exhortation to behave in a particular way. Rather, it is both a simple warning, on which one cannot act to any effect, and a spur to proper enjoyment of what one has now. In 12:1, this requirement to enjoy oneself is again picked up, but now with an emphasis upon one's inability to do so in old age.

(12:2–5) has been taken by most ancient and modern commentators to contain a series of symbolic, metaphorical descriptions of the physical degeneration which accompanies old age. This interpretation is not without its problems, and there is some disagreement about details, but it remains more persuasive than alternative readings (e.g. Fox 1989). It is bolstered, furthermore, by the existence of a Sumerian poem that applies the same technique to the same theme, albeit in a more obvious way: this supplies an analogy and suggests, perhaps, that the poem belongs to a particular genre. In any case, the symbolic interpretation should not be rejected because the symbolism is sometimes obscure: the passage has an enigmatic character, which may be as deliberate as in a riddle. Taking this approach, v. 2 refers to growing blindness, and v. 3 to trembling limbs, a bent back, the loss of teeth, and poor sight. v. 4 presents greater problems: we should translate 'Doors are shut on the street when the sound of the mill grows low, but it rises to the sound of a bird while all the song-notes are brought down'; the references may then be to the ears and voice: hearing fades as the voice grows quiet, and the latter rises to the pitch of bird-song, though that can no longer be heard. v. 5 begins with the frailty of the old, for whom falling and going out become more dangerous. The second half is more obscure: the almond tree blossoms, the grasshopper 'makes itself heavy', and the caper (which NRSV misleadingly translates as 'desire') either fails or bears fruit (depending on the derivation of the verb). These may be references to nature's ability to renew itself, in contrast to the inevitability of human death (cf. Job 14:7–10), but the locust would be an odd component for such an image, while the caper is not known for its fruit (the 'capers' used in cookery are pickled buds from the bush). If they continue the symbolism of old age, then the almond tree may be the whitening of the hair, and the grasshopper the impotent penis (as suggested in early rabbinic exegesis); the symbolism of the caper is obscure, although it, too, has white flowers. v. 5b returns to Qoheleth's initial point, that death is coming, at the end of old age.

(12:6–7) vv. 6–7 pick up the 'remember…before…' structure of 12:1–2, and this marks them as a separate subsection. The imagery in v. 6 is usually taken to refer to death, but conceivably we have moved back to old age here, and the reference is again to parts of the body, perhaps the genitals and bladder. In any case, v. 7 certainly concerns death, and seems to have in mind the ideas of Gen 2:7 and 3:19. The breath here is not a 'spirit', but the animating breath lent to humans for the duration of their lifetime. v. 8, the monologue closes with an echo of the motto which began it, in 1:2.

Epilogue (12:9–14)

The book finishes with an epilogue attached to Qoheleth's speech, which is probably the work of the author rather than a secondary addition. This falls into three parts: a brief description of Qoheleth's work (vv. 9–10), a comment on study

(vv. 11–12), and a closing admonition (vv. 13–14). In the first, the emphasis is on Qoheleth's literary activity, and he is portrayed as a collector and arranger of sayings. The second is more obscure, but it seems to compare such sayings to goads—which leads to the mischievous suggestion that too much study wears out one's flesh. The final admonition seems to draw on some of Qoheleth's conclusions—that one should fear God, and that there will be a judgement (cf. esp. 11:9). The advice to obey God's commandments, however, lends the saying an orthodox tone which is quite absent in the monologue.

(12:11–13) v. 11 uses a double comparison: the sayings are like ox-goads, and the individual parts of a collection like the nails stuck in a stick by a shepherd. The shepherd is not God, nor is there any admonition to heed only one writer—'one' here is simply an indefinite article. v. 12 is an additional comment: we should translate 'furthermore', rather than 'beyond these'. For the first and only time, the writer uses the address 'my son', which is common in the instructional literature of Proverbs. v. 13 does not describe keeping God's commandment's as the 'whole duty' of everyone, but as something applicable to everyone.

REFERENCES

Crenshaw, J. L. (1988), *Ecclesiastes* (London: SCM).

Fox, M. V. (1989), *Qothelet and his Contradictions* (Sheffield: Almond).

Gordis, R. (1968), *Koheleth—The Man and his World*, 3rd edn. (New York: Schocken).

Ogden, G. (1987), *Qoheleth* (Sheffield: JSOT).

Whybray, R. N. (1989), *Ecclesiastes* (London: Marshall, Morgan & Scott).

21. The Song of Solomon   ATHALYA BRENNER

A. Introduction. **1.** The Song of Songs, as the first two words of its superscription (1:1) imply, is lyrical poetry (Heb. sing. *šir*: song, poem; pl. *haššîrîm*: of songs, of poems), originally intended to be performed, i.e. sung to music, on suitable occasions. The meaning of the name is variously explained further as 'the most sublime', the 'best' song (a superlative construction) or collection of songs (one song or poem constructed of a plurality of poems). On the rest of the superscription, 'of', 'by', 'for', or '[dedicated] to' Solomon, see below (B.2).

2. The second verse (1:2) conveys the subject-matter:'Let him kiss me from the kisses of his mouth! For your love is better than wine.' ('From' is the literal meaning of the Heb. text, rather than NRSV 'with'.) The songs/poems are secular love poems about heterosexual, erotic, passionate relationships. Indeed, the songs *celebrate* love between unmarried, seemingly young, female and male lovers. The form is, mostly, that of monologues, dialogues, and chorus rejoinders delivered in the first person mode: the voice of the narrator(s) *per se* is not directly heard. The predominant speaking voice is female. There are no direct references to religious, ethical, or national values. YHWH is never mentioned (although some interpreters find a reference to him in the component *-yâ*, added to the Heb. word for 'flame', in 8:6). The geographical settings vary, as do the implied economic and social settings. Urban, sophisticated backgrounds interchange with nature and natural and rural settings. Imagery of food, drink, flora and fauna interchanges with metaphors of fortifications and military phenomena. In short, and in spite of the mention of place-names (such as Jerusalem, Tirzah, Gilead, Lebanon, Hermon), the universal phenomenon of erotic love is communicated in a largely universal manner, hence its appeal.

B. Place in the Hebrew Canon, Date, and Text. **1.** The Song is one of the Five Scrolls, a collection of short texts (also Ruth, Lamentations, Ecclesiastes, and Esther) placed within the third and latest division of the HB (the *kĕtûbîm*: Writings). These texts are called 'scrolls' since, in this form, they are used for reading as part of the liturgy of various holy days. In the case of the Song it is read on Passover, either in the synagogue or as part of the family ritual, in accordance with the customs of the Jewish community concerned.

2. The placing of the Song in the Hebrew canon testifies to its lateness:the mention of Solomon in the superscription, as well as in other passages of the book (1:5; 3:7–11; 8:12), is ambiguous. It does not necessarily uphold the traditional Jewish view, probably shared by the editor who added the superscription, that King Solomon was the author of the book. The language, which is varied and sometimes contains Aramaisms, is relatively late biblical Hebrew. This points to a date of composition, or at least collection and editorship of the final text, not earlier than the Second Temple era. Therefore few modern scholars, with the notable exception of Rabin (1973–4), argue for a tenth-century (possibly Solomonic) date. On the other hand, the attribution to Solomon was probably influential enough for accepting the Song as a canonical text. Discussions in Jewish sources (*m. Yad.* 3:5; *'Abot R. Nat.* 1; *t. Yad.* 2:4; *Sanh.* 12:10; *b. B. Bat.* 14–15; *Sanh.* 101a) show that acceptance of the Song as a sacred text was problematic and largely conditioned by two factors: its acceptance by Rabbi Aqiba and the Hillel school; and its understanding not as secular erotic lyrics, but as an allegory of the historical love between God and his people, the Jewish nation. This allegorical understanding, which completely disregards God's absence from the Song by way of positing it as its hidden but true subject, is already fully developed in the Aramaic *Targum* of the Song and was subsequently taken up by all mainstream Jewish commentators (see *Song Rab.*, and Rashi, for instance), to be further elaborated in mystical works (cf. the *Zohar* and *Hekhalot* literature). Christianity took the allegorical principle in different directions, first Christological (an allegory for the relationship between Christ and the individual believer's soul, or Christ and the church) and later Mariological (between Mary and the believer, or Mary and the church community). Works on the Song by Christian mystics such as Teresa of Avila, St John of the Cross, Bernard of Clairvaux, and Gregory of Nyasa, continue to witness its evocative power, interpreted as a celebration of mystical divine–human union rather than human erotic love.

3. At any rate, it is clear that, through divorcing the Song from its original setting and understanding it as religious poetry, a trend which has continued until modern times, both the emerging Judaism and Christianity of the second century CE had already accepted it as sacred literature. But the text's popularity is attested as earlier by its existence among the Qumran MSS. Four MSS of the Song were found in Qumran, three in Cave 4 and one in Cave 6.4. The first three (4QCant[a], 4QCant[b], 4QCant[c]) contain larger or smaller fragments of Song 2:1–5:1. The fourth MS (6QCant) contains verses of ch. 1. The Qumran texts are somewhat shorter than the MT texts: Tov (1995: 89) defines them (at least the first three) as abbreviated texts, based on one similar to or identical with the MT. If Tov's position is accepted, the Song already existed as a well-formed text quite early, in the second century BCE. Given the nature of the Qumran community, the Qumran Song texts perhaps also attest to its popularity even then as a secretive religious text. (In addition to the Jewish sources mentioned, see also the indirect evidence of 1st-cent. CE 4 Ezra 4:24, 26, and the *Ta'anit* scroll.)

C. Style and Structure. 1. The Song is best viewed not as one single poem but a collection. To begin with, there is no unified style. Conventional poetic devices are certainly much in evidence. Parallelisms, refrains, alliteration, word- and sound-play, puns and repetitions are rife, but not in any way that could be considered typical to the Song. Metaphors and symbols derived from many areas of human experience are heavily used in a combination of conventionality and originality but, once more, it is difficult to attribute any specificity of single authorship, place, and time to this variety. In addition, while a structural unity is discernible, no narrative plot sequence—in the sense of a story, a linear trajectory leading from beginning through to end—is obtainable. In short, the Song is best viewed as an anthology of love lyrics. This is the position adopted here, although from ancient times until this century, many exegetes and scholars (Exum 1973; Goulder 1986; Landy 1983) have preferred to view the Song as a unified composition containing a single, ongoing love story.

2. Even so, some problems remain concerning the boundaries of individual songs—there are no rhymes and, in most MSS and printed editions, no indications of lines. Change of speaker, from female to male or vice versa, do not necessarily constitute a departure or a new unit. Neither do changes of settings, places, times, and so on. In short, the principles of unit boundaries and organization as well as the organization of the whole are not easy to uncover. The fact that some passages are repeated verbatim or almost so (cf. 3:1–4 with 5:6–7, or 4:1–3 with 6:5*b*–7) is best interpreted as a structural (editorial) device, rather than a repeated stage in a plot sequence. Nevertheless, some songs do combine, by verbal and narrative association, into a larger mini-story—such as the sequence beginning in 5:2: a woman refuses to admit her lover; he departs and she seeks him, without success (5:2–7); she asks the daughters of Jerusalem to find him (5:8), they want his description (v. 9), she complies (vv. 9–16); they agree to look for him (6:1) but, by that time, the lovers are reunited (6:2–3).

3. At the beginning of the Song, 1:2–8, it is clearly a woman's or women's voice that we predominantly hear.

Possibly, there are three songs strung together here. The first (vv. 2–4) sets out the subject: the love of a woman for a man. In the second (vv. 5–6) a woman defiantly explains that she is 'dark and [or: but] beautiful' (NRSV: 'black and beautiful') as a result of being assigned to outdoor occupations by her maternal brothers, presumably in a vain effort to preserve her sexual modesty. In the third we watch her search for her male lover (v. 7), who—and this is the first male voice we hear—teases her to try and find him (v. 8). Exactly at the collection's centre, 4:8 (HB 4:9)–5:1, a seduction scene takes place. It is metaphorical, gentle, and polite. Unmistakably, though, at its end a young man has obtained a young woman's consent to have sexual relations. Consummation is followed by a celebration, with food and drink. At the end of the collection, ch. 8, maternal brothers set out their concern for their sister's chastity, and the means they will employ to preserve it when that becomes necessary (vv. 8–9). A woman's voice responds, defiantly (v. 10 or vv. 10–12). After an unclear interlude (v. 13) the book ends when a woman's voice sings to her lover: run away, jump like a deer on the fragrant mountains (v. 14). Thus, at the end of the Song readers, and lovers, are precisely where they were at its beginning. Although a poignant personal credo of what love is about is voiced by a female to a male, and is placed in 8:6–7, it does not end the whole. At the end lovers are, once more, apart. They look, search, depart and go—especially the female lovers, who are more active than the males. And yet, a clear act of consummation has occurred in the exact quantitative centre of the book. The collection's movement, then, is not linear (as in a regular narrative plot) but circular, with its presumed climax situated at its middle rather than at its end. This, and the fact that parallels are chiastically placed on either side of the climactic 4:8 (HB 4:9)–5:1 passage, once again signify editorial rather than authorial intent. In other words, the cyclical 'plot' seems to be the result of a plan to unify the whole by means of its structure.

D. Contents and Set of Characters. 1. In attempting to divide the Song into individual songs, let us remember that boundaries between individual pieces are fluid and also blurred; and that many passages have been artfully organized, so that they run into each other and form larger sequences. The following, therefore, is a feasible division only: other divisions are conceivable. The songs will be labelled 'female' or 'male' if the speaker is clearly one or the other. 'Dialogue' is between female and male lovers unless otherwise indicated.

(**1:1**) Superscription.

(**1:2–6**) Two female songs (see above).

(**1:7–8**) Dialogue: female searches for male, he teases.

(**1:9–17**) Male praises female; dialogue; seem to be meeting in the open air.

(**2:1–3**) Dialogue, in the open air.

(**2:4–17**) Several female poems, 'reciting' embedded male voices. Main imagery is again of flora and fauna. Includes the first appeal for help to the 'daughters of Jerusalem', for the speaker is lovesick.

(**3:1–5**) A tightly constructed female song: she looks for her lover in the city streets, at night (or in a dream), is not helped by the city guards but manages to find him and bring him to her 'mother's house'. Second appeal to the 'daughters'.

(3:6–11) One or two poems describing King Solomon's train, and bed or palanquin, coming out of the desert surrounded by his mighty men; and his wedding, at which his mother is present but not his father. The speaker's gender is unclear.

(4:1–7) (cf. 6:3b–7; a male's *wasf* (see SONG E.1) describing his female lover from head to breasts. Imagery mainly of flora and fauna, also of fortifications and military weapons.

(4:8–5:1) A dialogue, the 'seduction and consummation' scene (see SONG C.3). Male seduces female, with extravagant images of food and aromatic herbs and flowers; she consents; the male closure (5:1) and the call to eat and drink imply consummation.

(5:2–9) (cf. 3:1–5); female refuses to welcome male into her room at night (in reality or a dream); when she changes her mind he disappears. She looks for him in the city and the guards beat her up. She appeals to the daughters of Jerusalem to help her lovesick condition.

(5:9–6:2) The daughters want to know what the male lover looks like. A female lover describes him in a *wasf*, from head to toe. The imagery is of fauna and flora for the head; minerals, metals and precious stones for the rest of his body. The daughters agree to look for him but, meanwhile, he is found and seems to be enjoying his 'garden' again (see SONG E.3). If 6:3 belongs here, it contains a female affirmation of her love.

(6:4–9) A male song of praise for a female lover, partly parallel (vv. 5b–7) to the *wasf* of ch. 4.

(6:10–12) Either a male monologue—male praises female in a garden—or a dialogue, with a questionable voice attribution for v. 11 and the difficult v. 12.

(7:1–10) *Wasf*, probably in a male voice, calling to a female (the Shulamite) to dance and then describing her body from toe to head (vv. 2–7). A response indicating male desire (vv. 8–9), perhaps followed by a female retort (v. 10) rounds off this passage.

(7:11–14) One song, or several songs in a female voice, seductively inviting a male lover to go outdoors where she will give herself to him (cf. 4:9–14).

(8:1–7) A female passage, again probably or possibly more than a single song: a woman would like her lover to be her brother, so that they can be together in her 'mother's house' (vv. 1–2; cf. 3:4); they embrace (v. 3; cf. 2:6); another appeal to the daughters of Jerusalem (v. 4); two fragments (v. 5; cf. 3:6a, 2:3). vv. 6–7 are, once again, in a female voice:

Set me as a seal upon your heart, | as a seal upon your arm; | for love is strong as death, | passion fierce as the grave. | Its flashes are flashes of fire, | a raging flame. | Many waters cannot quench love; | neither can floods drown it. | If one offered for love | all the wealth of one's house, | it would be utterly scorned.

This declaration, surely, might have constituted a suitable end for the whole book. Nevertheless,

(8:8–14) (see SONG C.3); maternal brothers decide how to keep their sister's virginity, when necessary (vv. 8–9). She answers mockingly (v. 10 or 10–12; cf. 1:5–6). An unclear verse is followed by the very last verse: a female voice calls to her male lover to run away, like a gazelle or deer, to the distant never-never land of the perfume hills. Thus, love's game can begin afresh, suspended in timelessness and moving cyclically.

2. This survey shows that the Song can be understood as a collection of love lyrics, performed by one couple and two choruses ('daughters' and 'maternal brothers'). However, variety and the repetitions point in the direction of multiplicity of settings, backgrounds, moods—and cast of characters. That is, if we agree that a structural 'plot' only is in evidence, then there is no reason to assign *all* female lines to a *single* female textual speaker, or *all* male lines to a *single* textual male speaker. This has been done in some older translations, dividing the lines between 'bride' and 'bridegroom', or some similar arrangement. However, notwithstanding a description (3:9–11) of Solomon's wedding (which might be a satire or parody, see Whedbee 1993), nothing in the Song points to a marital setting or conclusion for lovers, as we have seen. Furthermore, there is no compelling reason to assume that one couple only is reflected in the Song, or even a love triangle (as in some older scholarship, where a triangle of Solomon–Shulamite–shepherd lover is found). Rather, a multiplicity of voices is heard in the Song, as befits such an anthology on a universal topic. Looking for a comprehensive, all-embracing interpretation for the book may form a link with allegorical renderings of it (since those depend on a comprehensive reading, with a single, well-defined pair of lovers), but seems unwarranted by the text itself.

3. Clearly, though, the female voices far outstrip the male voices in the Song. Female voices search; male voices tease and escape. Females become lovesick; males allow themselves to be found and led to the 'mother's house' (fathers are as absent from the Song as the figure of a God.) Females are articulate (they have almost two-thirds of the text!), unconventional, risk-takers. Males are loving but less adventurous. Therefore, whereas Trible (1978) maintains gender equality in the Song, perhaps we should do better to recognize female superiority in it. Whether this signifies female authorship, or an original background of female performance, remains uncertain (see Goitein 1988 for female authorship and performance). At any rate, also from this perspective of gender affairs, the Song is an exception in the HB. Although traces of a patriarchal framework are apparent in it (the brothers' role as custodians of female sexual modesty; the guards' beating up of a woman searching at night), nowhere else in the HB do women roam and make love so freely, outside the framework of marriage, in the open, without chaperones. Nowhere are 'they' allowed such outspoken voices on erotic love and desire (as is the case in other ancient cultures too; and see SONG C). It is perhaps worthwhile, therefore, to read the Song *as if* it contained traces of female voices (Brenner and van Dijk-Hemmes 1993), not just *as if* it contained male voices (which is the biblical norm).

4. What, then, can we say about the kinds of love described and celebrated in the Song? Erotic yearnings are complementary, never in contrast, to emotions and feelings. In a sense, love in the Song is unproblematic: although pre- or non-marital, no complications of unwanted pregnancies result from sexual relations. Joy and exaltation indeed interface with heart-sickness and despondency: much depends on lovers' availability for each other. High seriousness interchanges with humour (3:7–11; 7:1–10). Passion can be painful as well as uplifting. Socio-moral norms prohibiting non-marital sexual unions are ignored or disregarded. Lovers exist

in a world of their own creation, as they would. One spectrum of emotion and behaviour is conspicuous by its absence, however. Jealousy, betrayal, violence borne out of frustration, infidelity—the negative facets of love are simply not in evidence. Idealization? Perhaps, although not fully, when the suffering and difficulties recounted (especially for female lovers) are noticed.

E. Poetics, Forms, Imagery. 1. As noted at SONG A.2, the Song is composed of monologues (or soliloquies), dialogues, and choruses. These are sometimes combined into composite poems (5:2–6:2; and see Falk 1982). A special poetic genre is the *wasf* (from Arabic: description). In this type of song the lover's body, be it a male's (5:10–16) or a female's (4:1–7 with a partial parallel in 6:3–7; 7:1–7 MT), is referred to by means of a series of delightful and sensuous images and in a certain order: from head to toe in chs. 4 and 5, and from toe to head in ch. 7. Pope (1977) cites many examples of *wasf*-type parallels from Arab and other sources.

2. The imagery of the Song draws on many areas of human experience: natural phenomena, zoology, botany, agriculture, art, trade, precious materials, architecture, and much more. It appeals to all senses, even floods them. A recurrent, deceptively simple simile/metaphor, 'your eyes are doves' (1:15; 4:1) invokes a synesthetic response of sight, sound, and emotive content—as does the more explicit elaboration of this metaphor in 5:12, 'His eyes are like doves'. Or the praise, 'your breasts are like young twin gazelles' (4:5; 7:4), that signifies colour, movement, size, texture, shape, perhaps smell—all of these, or at least several. Translations of the Song that attempt to convey this sensuous imagery, together with the rhythm and spirit of its poetry, are no simple tasks. Two such recent translations, by Falk (1982) and by Bloch and Bloch (1995), are recommended for their poetic quality.

3. Perhaps the most astounding and complex are metaphors relating to nature, especially as it reawakens in springtime. The image of the orchard, or garden, will serve as an example. On the first level, much of the action in the Song—lovers meeting, lovers departing, lovers talking—happens outdoors. The garden or orchard, then, is the natural backdrop, and represents realism as well as an optimistic setting for love meetings. On the second level, gardens and orchards—especially in spring—symbolize an option of love's flowering and growth. On the indexical level, their flowering and fruitfulness are akin to sexuality in the human world. Ultimately, then, the garden/orchard are metaphorized into human sexuality (fourth level). And finally, by way of specification, the garden/orchard stand for female sexuality, especially female erogenous zones: in other words, on the fifth level of meaning (or signification) female sexuality is metaphorized into a garden/orchard. This symbol/image/indexical notion/metaphor is sensuously rich: it appeals to sight, sound, smell, touch, and taste. The richness is especially apparent when a perfume garden is invoked, as in the central seduction scene of 4:9–5:1. There, by naming plants and gardens and foodstuff and aromatics, a male lover manages to talk his female lover into having sexual relations—without ever speaking directly. 'They' are in a physical garden (outside), they are a garden, love is a garden, the woman is a garden, her anatomy is a perfumed garden. And when the male lover receives the woman's permission to enter 'his garden' and eat its fruit (4:16; cf., more articulately, 7:13–14), it is quite obvious what transpires through the use of garden/orchard/aromatics imagery.

F. Ancient Extrabiblical Parallels. Pope (1977) supplies exhaustive lists of Song parallels in the ancient and pre-modern world, especially the Mesopotamian, Indian, and Islamic worlds. Fox (1985) does the same with Egyptian love poetry. Rabin (1973–4) and others draw attention to parallels in Tamil. A curious feature is that, in most if not all parallels, women's voices are quite pronounced in the context of premarital love poetry (in distinction from their situation in marital contexts). However, the subject-matter and experience of heterosexual love and passion is so universal as to render the parallels less significant than they would otherwise have been.

G. Biblical Intertexts. 1. In prophetic books such as Hosea, Jeremiah, Ezekiel, Isaiah 40 ff, and Malachi there obtains a metaphor of divine–human marriage covenant. The male partner is YHWH; his wife is variously Jerusalem (or Samaria, or both cities), the land of Israel, or the Israelite or Judahite people. The divine husband is presented as constantly and ceaselessly loyal to his spouse, of whom he takes care. The wife is presented as a creature who is adulterous, fickle, and prostitutes herself, and who keeps looking for fresh lovers and fresh sexual sensations (in the plural). The husband punishes his wife, who stands accused but mostly does not get a chance to defend herself.

2. When the Song is interpreted allegorically, the situation is reversed. Here it is clear that the woman searches for her man and remains faithful to him. This reversal, theologically interpreted, is significant: for theological thinking, it might afford hope to the post-Roman conquest nation. It might have provided at least part of the motivation to interpret the Song as religious rather than secular love poetry—despite the fact that such allegories require sacralization of a secular text and its transformation by interpretation into a comprehensive unit focused on only one male and one female lover. It also requires a displacement of the female lover to a secondary position relative to the male's (now divine) position, and an introduction of the missing divine element into the Song in the guise of a divine (male) lover. The early Jewish allegories which, in turn, mutated into Christian allegories, are thus rooted not only in practical theology (a response to the politically troubled times of the Roman conquest and the loss of land, political organization, and autonomy) but also in biblical intertexuality.

H. Epilogue: Directions for Reinterpretation. 1. In contemporary scholarship various trends can be discerned. Some scholars re-examine the possibility of an early, perhaps even Solomonic, provenance for the Song in the light of extrabiblical parallels (Rabin 1973–4; Fox 1985). Others attempt to reconcile allegorical and surface (Heb. *pešat*: simple) meanings. According to Rabin, Murphy (1990), and others, the possibility that the Song was, from its very inception, a double-tiered composition relating to both human love and divine–human love should be explored. Yet other scholars, such as Pope, look for a goddess in the Song, again an allegory, if of a modern kind.

2. Feminist critics have paid a lot of attention to the predominance of female voices in the Song. Understanding this phenomenon and its implications, even though it reflects similar phenomena in the love lyrics of cognate cultures, requires further deliberation. Already there is a backlash against feminist appropriation of female voices by way of reclaiming male authorship for the Song (Clines 1995).

3. Ultimately, it is the sheer beauty of the poems, the unadulterated strength of the lyrics and imagery, that keeps it so attractive, be its interpretation secular or religious. Regrettably, part of the experience, the musical aspect of the performance—for songs are there to be performed to music rather than merely recited—is lost to us. Fortunately, in the newly minted traditions of Zionism and modern Israel, many of the songs of the Song have been set to music afresh. I grew up on this music, these lyrics: for me they are inseparable—and intrinsically secular.

REFERENCES

Bloch, A., and Bloch, C. (1995), *The Song of Songs: A New Translation with an Introduction and a Commentary* (New York: Random House).

Brenner, A., and van Dijk-Hemmes, F. (1993), *On Gendering Texts: Female and Male Voices in the Hebrew Bible* (Leiden: Brill), 1–11.

Clines, D. J. A. (1995), *Interested Parties: The Ideology of Writers and Readers of the Hebrew Bible*, JSOTSup. 205 (Sheffield: Sheffield Academic Press), 94–121.

Exum, J. C. (1973), 'A Literary and Structural Analysis of the Song of Songs', *ZAW* 85: 47–79.

Falk, M. (1982), *Love Lyrics from the Bible: A Translation and Literary Study of the Song of Songs* (Sheffield: Almond).

Fox, M. V. (1985), *The Song of Songs and the Ancient Egyptian Love Songs* (Madison: University of Wisconsin Press).

Goitein, S. D. (1988), 'Women as Creators of Biblical Genres', *Prooftexts*, 8:1–33, tr. M. Carasik.

Goulder, M. D. (1986), *The Song of Fourteen Songs* (Sheffield: JSOT).

Landy, F. (1983), *Paradoxes of Paradise: Identity and Difference in the Song of Songs* (Sheffield: Almond).

Murphy, R. E. (1990), *The Song of Songs*, Hermeneia (Minneapolis: Fortress).

Pope, M. H. (1977), *The Song of Songs: A New Translation with Introduction and Commentary*, AB 7C (Garden City, NY: Doubleday).

Rabin, C. (1973–4), 'The Song of Songs and Tamil Poetry', *Studies in Religion*, 3: 205–19.

Tov, E. (1995), 'Three Manuscripts (Abbreviated Texts?) of Canticles from Qumran Cave 4', *JSS* 46: 88–111.

Trible, P. (1978), *God and the Rhetoric of Sexuality* (Philadelphia: Fortress), 144–65.

Whedbee, J. W. (1993), 'Paradox and Parody in the Song of Solomon: Towards a Comic Reading of the Most Sublime Song', in A. Brenner (ed.), *A Feminist Companion to the Song of Songs* (Sheffield: Sheffield Academic Press), 266–78.

22. Isaiah   R. COGGINS

INTRODUCTION

Overview. 1. It may come as a surprise to some readers to discover that the whole book of Isaiah is being dealt with in one article. One of the success stories of the historical-critical method of biblical study has been to establish that the 66 chapters of the book come from a variety of backgrounds, and the custom has been to treat chs. 40–66 independently of the earlier part of the book. These chapters are said to come from 'Deutero'- or 'Second Isaiah' (40–55), usually with chs. 56–66 further isolated and ascribed to 'Trito'- or 'Third Isaiah'. It is argued that historical references and stylistic features alike enable them to be distinguished from the Isaiah of the earlier chapters, and it might seem perversely old-fashioned to go back to treating the whole book as a unity.

2. It may be helpful to rehearse briefly the relevant findings of historical criticism with regard to the different elements in the book. Broadly speaking they fall into three categories: historical, stylistic, and theological.

3. Historical. Many references in the early part of the book (e.g. ch. 7, chs. 36–9) as well as places in 2 Kings where Isaiah is mentioned by name (e.g. 19:2) make it clear that the prophet's life and activity were envisaged as taking place during the last third of the eighth century BCE, when Judah was under threat, first from its Northern neighbours, Israel and Damascus, and then from the Assyrians. But from ch. 40 all this has changed; the people addressed are pictured as being in Babylon, and Cyrus of Persia, who overthrew the Babylonian empire, is mentioned by name (44:28; 45:1). Cyrus became king in 550 BCE, and if we are to use any of the normal criteria of

historical assessment the words referring to him must have been written after that date. It is generally agreed, therefore, that chs. 40–55 come from a Babylonian setting and should be dated in the 540s. Chs. 56–66 offer fewer clear indications of date, but the general consensus has been to place these chapters later still, perhaps in Jerusalem in the time when the work of restoration was going slowly forward in a disillusioned and demoralized community.

4. Literary. In terms both of detailed vocabulary and more generally of style there are important differences which come over clearly even in translation. Numerous phrases and expressions characteristic of the earlier chapters ('briers and thorns', 'remnant') are not found in the later sections, whereas such terms as 'create' and 'redeem' are peculiar to the later chapters. Again, there are marked stylistic differences, the sharp, brief, and often bitterly condemnatory oracles of the early chapters (e.g. the 'woes' of 5:8–23) contrasting markedly with the repetitive, dignified style of 40–55, where many Psalm-like passages are addressed to God rather than to a human audience.

5. Theological. From ch. 40 onwards major theological themes emerge which have played little or no part earlier: concern with the Exodus and wilderness deliverance, clearly pictured as the model for a new return from exile to the promised land (40:3–5); the restoration of a destroyed Jerusalem as a symbol of renewed divine favour (ch. 52); the concentration on creation, with the use of the distinctive Hebrew verb *bārāʾ*, used in Gen 1 but rare elsewhere, to speak of divine creative action; the concern with the role of a servant. All these themes have no obvious parallel in the earlier chapters.

6. Until a decade or so ago these considerations were generally regarded as sufficient to justify treating the book of Isaiah as two, or three, separate and unconnected blocks of material. Some of the points made by historical critics may be less securely based than might at first sight appear; in particular their tendency to treat poetry as if it had precise reference to historical events can give a false sense of security. We shall note this particularly when we look at the 'Babylonian' chapters, 40–55. Nevertheless the substance of their work has not been challenged. Yet despite this, the agenda of Isaiah studies has changed dramatically, so that a recent survey of such studies can speak of 'the current focus' of scholarly attention being 'the final form of the book of Isaiah as a whole' (Sweeney 1993: 141), an issue barely touched on in most historical-critical work.

7. A number of reasons for this shift can be put forward, but it may be helpful at the very outset to distinguish between two basic approaches, each concerned with the final form of the book. One approach looks for its unity in and through the circumstances in which it developed. It will envisage an Isaiah 'tradition' or a 'school', and seek to discern some basic elements holding the whole block of material together through differing historical circumstances. The other regards the concerns of this kind of historical approach as largely illusory; what we have is a book, so let us treat it as a book, regardless of the particular circumstances which are alleged to have led to its composition. We read and can appreciate a classic novel without enquiring into the background of its composition; similarly, it is argued, Isaiah can be read as a whole without exploring what are regarded as irrelevant details. There are obvious differences, for Isaiah is mainly poetry, without any storyline. Nevertheless certain basic themes run through the whole book which are of intrinsic importance.

8. The two approaches to which we have referred may for convenience, though with some ambiguity, be described as 'historical' and 'literary'. They seem to be radically different; whether they can be reconciled to one another, as some have claimed, must remain doubtful. In the commentary which follows more attention will be paid to the second approach, partly because it has been less prominent in commentaries on Isaiah. It is hoped, however, that the important concerns of the first approach have not been ignored.

9. There are some issues which the two views have in common. We may accept that the various parts of the book of Isaiah are diverse in their origin. What next should be examined is the fact that this heterogeneous material has been brought together into one book. In this connection we must first of all remember the unanimous testimony of the ancient witnesses to the unity of Isaiah. The book of Sirach (Ecclesiasticus), in the Apocrypha, refers to Isaiah in an eighth-century context, but also ascribes to him the theme of comforting 'those who mourned' (Sir 48:24), a clear reference to Isa 40, i.e. the later part of the book. The chronological problem is resolved by the supposition that the prophet himself 'saw the future'. That evidence comes from the second century BCE. From roughly the same period the scrolls of Isaiah from Qumran, among the earliest found and best preserved of the Dead Sea scrolls, do not reflect any division

between chs. 39 and 40. From a somewhat later period it is clear that the New Testament regards Isaiah as one book. Among many passages which could be quoted, perhaps the most striking is Jn 12: 38–41, because of the way in which it links material from different parts of the book of Isaiah.

10. All the ancient testimony, therefore, points to Isaiah as being *one* book. It seems improbable, though the possibility cannot be totally ruled out, that that oneness consists simply in the bringing together of wholly disparate blocks of material, a merely accidental juxtaposition. Again, such theories as those which propose that the shortage of material in exile led to the reuse of existing scrolls, or that the prophet called Deutero-Isaiah was actually named Isaiah, and so had his work linked with that of his illustrious forebear and namesake, reflect more on the ingenuity of those who propose them than on any historical likelihood. There are, indeed, certain features which recur throughout the whole book of Isaiah (the characteristic description of God as 'the Holy One of Israel' is a case in point), which also make any suggestion of mere accidental linkage a most unlikely one. We are left with the conclusion that, though an *authorial* unity of the book of Isaiah, in the sense of it all going back to one individual, is most unlikely, there is a real sense in which we may view it as a *redactional* unity, that is, a work which has been brought together as a deliberately structured whole. It is to the nature and purpose of that redaction that much recent scholarly attention has been devoted.

11. Was there a School of Disciples? One theory which has been a good deal discussed in recent years is that Isaiah's own words were gathered together and handed down by his disciples over a period of perhaps two or three centuries. Some of those disciples, it is argued, were among those exiled to Babylon, and they included among them the great poet who came to be known as Deutero-Isaiah, who was responsible for chs. 40–55 of our present book. There are certain clues which seem to favour this line of interpretation. 8:16 is a difficult verse, but a typical translation is that of NRSV 'Bind up the testimony, seal the teaching among my disciples.' (For other ways of understanding this verse, see the commentary.) Various scholars have supposed that this is an indication of the beginning of a process that lasted at least 200 years. Eaton, for example, detects a 'definite connection of master and disciples with the centre of worship (i.e. Jerusalem), yielding a disciplined succession into and beyond the exile' (Eaton 1982: 59). On this view there was a clearly structured tradition, owing its origin to the historical Isaiah of the eighth century (sometimes rather misleadingly described as 'Isaiah of Jerusalem'), closely linked in its concerns and manner of expression with the worship of the Jerusalem temple, and reaching new theological and liturgical insights as its conviction grew that the days of exile were coming to an end (Eaton 1979. Albertz 1990: 253–5 recognizes the force of these links, but notes also that the later stages of the Isaianic tradition drew on sources other than words attributable to Isaiah himself).

12. The existence of such a school is certainly possible, but other scholars have not been slow to point out some of the difficulties of this view. Clements, for example, notes that we know little of how such a school of authors (for whose existence there is, in any case, no certain testimony in the book of Isaiah and no independent evidence from other sources) would have evolved, or what kind of connection between different parts of the book is implied. His own proposal is that the material in chs. 40–55 was 'intended to develop and enlarge upon prophetic sayings from Isaiah of Jerusalem' (Clements 1985: 101). He then illustrates this point by drawing attention to a number of themes which are common to different parts of the book, in which it is possible to see a development throughout. We are in the world of redaction criticism; less interested in authors and precise historical circumstances, more concerned with the way in which particular themes and motifs developed within a specific literary tradition.

13. One important element in this development has its roots in the work of the historical critics. As we have seen, the conventional division was between chs. 1–39 and what followed, with 1–39 described as 'Isaiah of Jerusalem'. But it has long been recognized that a large part of chs. 1–39 could not simply be ascribed to the eighth-century Isaiah. Much in the foreign nations oracles (13–23) seemed to come from a period later than that of Isaiah. Chs. 24–7 betray some of the features of the apocalypses, and have usually been thought of as the latest part of the whole book. Chs. 33–4 have characteristics which again suggest a late date, while 35 has so much in common with 40–55 that it has sometimes been attributed to Deutero-Isaiah. Chs. 36–9 are substantially identical with 2 Kings 18–20, and the dependence has usually been held to be on the side of Isaiah. Detailed critical study, therefore, has found material going back to Isaiah himself only in chs. 1–12 and 28–32.

14. Even in those chapters, however, the tendency has been to discern a radical process of development. Kaiser at the outset of his commentary makes it clear that only 'the earliest prophecies, contained in chs. 28–31, should be identified with sayings of Isaiah' (Kaiser 1983: 2). The remainder of this material only began to be collected in the fifth century, that is, at a time later than the traditional date for Deutero-Isaiah! Vermeylen engaged in a detailed study of the stages by which the book reached its present form, and suggested that the influence of those responsible for chs. 56–66 can also be traced in 1–39, again reversing the conventional order of composition (Vermeylen 1977–8: 757). The subtitle of Vermeylen's work gives a good indication of his view of the process of composition: 'Isaïe I–XXXV, miroir d'un demi-millénaire d'expérience religieuse en Israël'. An analogous approach is that of Ackroyd (1987), who examines some of the issues involved in the gradual development of the complete book of Isaiah, and then goes on to look in greater detail at chs. 1–12, in which he is able to discern 'the presentation of a prophet'—the reflection of a later generation on how the ideal prophetic figure should be delineated.

15. The above studies, and others that could be listed, retain something of a historical concern, but with a difference. Whereas in earlier writings questions of historicity related to the amount of material which could plausibly be traced back to Isaiah himself and the circumstances of the eighth century, now the historical concerns are those relating to the process of redaction and editing. Kaiser, for example, sees much of Isa 1–39 as an attempt to come to terms with and offer a satisfactory explanation for the downfall of Judah and the exile of its leading citizens in the sixth century. In a comparable way

Vermeylen claims that one redactional 'layer' was a process of anti-Samaritan polemic which cannot be dated earlier than the fourth century.

16. More recently, however, a number of studies have rejected this historical concern out of hand. These represent what we have already referred to as a 'literary' rather than a 'historical' standpoint. In this approach what we have is a piece of literature, which should be read and appreciated like other pieces of literature, without constantly breaking off to speculate about the historical circumstances from which its elements emerge, either in their original form or in the process of editing. The title of Conrad's book (1991) is significant: *Reading Isaiah*. 'Isaiah' here clearly refers to the book; now only minimal attention is paid to the 'historical Isaiah', the eighth-century figure of whom we can in any case know very little. Indeed there is a real sense in which Isaiah becomes a fictional figure. We need not doubt that such a person did indeed exist, but it would be misleading to suppose that the book gives us access to his actual words and thoughts. But the other word in his title is also highly significant: it is the reading, and the reader who engages in that exercise, that take centre stage. For an approach of this kind it is a book to read, to savour as a piece of literature, to reflect upon its message. But this scarcely says enough. 'To reflect upon its message' may imply that there is an objective 'message' there, equally accessible to all. Much traditional interpretation of Scripture has indeed claimed just that, that it refers to something beyond itself. The emphasis on the reader, to which reference has been made, is inevitably much more subjective. For a start, it will ask: Who is the reader? Is it a man or a woman? There is much feminine imagery in Isaiah, some of it dismissive (3:16–4:1) but some of it much more positive. Sawyer (1989) offers an interesting and illuminating comparison between the 'servant of the Lord' and the 'daughter of Zion' imagery in the second half of the book. Or again: From what social and economic background does the reader come? The book speaks harshly against those who 'join house to house … until there is no more room' (5:8). One's attitude to that might differ according to whether one were involved in the property market, or were anxious to alleviate a housing shortage. Or again: What is the reader's attitude towards religious practice? Many readers of the Bible might be thought to be favourably disposed towards it; how then will they react to the fierce criticism of religious practice in 1:11–15?

17. In this kind of reading of the text not only the concerns of historical criticism, but also those of redaction criticism, are now dismissed as of no more than marginal relevance. Such an approach is a far cry from that of most traditional commentaries upon Isaiah. It is too early as yet to say whether it will become the norm, or whether it will itself be regarded as a curious sidetrack. Unclear also is the extent to which the historical and the literary approaches are totally independent of, and perhaps even hostile to, one another.

18. However that may be, it will be clear from the above brief survey that many of the questions habitually raised in introductions of this kind no longer seem to be as central as once they were. As recently as 1989, the excellent commentary by J. Jensen and W. H. Irwin on Isa 1–39 in the *NJBC* began with a section devoted to 'The Prophet and his Times', outlining the history of Judah in the last third of the eighth century and placing the activity and oracles of Isaiah within that context. Such an approach has become steadily more difficult, and will not be attempted here. It is likely that the final redactors of the book of Isaiah drew on something akin to our present 2 Kings as one of their sources, and the modern reader who wishes to find out how much we can know about Judah in the second half of the eighth century BCE must do the same. By the time that Isaiah reached its final form the time of the monarchy, the pre-exilic period, was a distant memory.

19. That is not to say that little or nothing of what has been preserved for us in the final form of the book goes back to Isaiah himself. Rather, it implies that the process of editing and shaping the collection of material, and then the composition of a completed book, gives us a different perspective, one which stretches over several centuries of the growth and development of the Jerusalem community. It has the simple practical consequence for this commentary that the word 'Isaiah' will, unless otherwise stated, refer to the book rather than to the figure of an individual. (Indeed the paucity of references to Isaiah as an individual within his book is striking; there are 16 such references, compared with more than 130 to Jeremiah in the book that bears his name (Conrad 1991: 34). It also means that more attention than has been usual will be paid to linkages within the whole of Isaiah, the sense in which the whole book is a unity. As has already been made clear, that need not have any implication that the individual Isaiah son of Amoz was not himself responsible for particular sayings; it does emphasize the clearly patterned overall structure of the book. For believers in particular the question may become acute. Is their concern as they approach the book of Isaiah a desire to find out the underlying historical circumstances of each part of the book, and to discover a specific point of reference—historical, doctrinal, ethical—in each passage? Or is it rather to come to the text as literature and let it speak to them as a 'holy text'?

20. It is appropriate to end this introduction with an outline of what we shall be studying. It is a book, mostly of poetry, which begins by warning a religious community of the dangers inherent in its failures, dangers which must lead to punishment. These warnings occupy much of chs. 1–33. There follows the triumphant proclamation that the time of punishment is now over, and that the way to restoration lies ahead; this theme is found in chs. 34–5, and clearly underlies the stories in chs. 36–9, chapters which function as a hinge upon which the whole book turns. As has long been recognized, the announcement of restoration predominates in chs. 40–55. But the book ends with renewed notes of warning; the community must not suppose that in future 'anything goes'. There are still dangers to be guarded against, patterns of behaviour which are incompatible with their religious claims. These warning signs are prominent in chs. 56–66. Sometimes there are clues which suggest a particular historical background for particular passages, but they are subsidiary to the main thrust of the book and liable to misinterpretation. We may be wiser to read Isaiah as a structured collection of religious verse, keeping this broad thematic progression in mind.

COMMENTARY

(Ch. 1) provides a good illustration of the way in which interest in the literary structure of the whole has replaced some of the older historical questions. It concludes (v. 31) with a reference to the burning of those who trust in their own strength, in a fire which cannot be 'quenched' (Heb. root: *k-b-h*). This relatively rare word is also found in the last verse of the whole book (66:24: 'their fire shall not be quenched'), linking together beginning and ending of the book. But it is also used of the servant in 42:3, of whom it is said, by contrast, that 'a dimly burning wick he will not quench'. Again, the fire devouring Edom will be quenched (34:10), and those who oppose the LORD's path are 'quenched like a wick' (43:17). It is obviously possible that these uses are coincidental, but even if that were true the reader is surely invited to see and reflect upon this linkage. It will be noted, of course, that the five examples which have been given take in all three of the parts into which Isaiah has customarily been divided.

Other links between ch. 1 and the last part of the book have been noted. Clements (1980a: 28) expressed this as 'a selection of the prophet's sayings in order to provide a general preface and guide to his teaching', but it may be more appropriate to envisage this 'selection' in terms of an introduction to some of the main themes of the whole book. The issues of sin, judgement, and hoped-for restoration are those with which the community of Israel as a whole and the prophetic writings were deeply concerned, and they form the overarching structure of the book of Isaiah.

(1:1) The introductory verse is closely comparable to the opening of the books of Jeremiah, Hosea, Amos, Micah, and Zephaniah. It is sometimes supposed that all ancient Israelites were necessarily expert in knowing which king reigned when, in the way in which children of an earlier generation were required to learn lists of the kings of Judah and Israel. Much more probably this is a literary device at one stage in the editorial process of the Isaiah collection, linking it with the account of the people's history given in the books of Kings. Since those books are usually described as part of the Deuteronomistic History this verse is then regarded as evidence for one of the redactions of Isaiah's words being Deuteronomistic. (Kaiser 1983: 1–2 suggests that this implies a fifth-century date, but there is little unambiguous evidence for dating.) It is not even possible to offer exact dates for the kings listed, but they all ruled in the second half of the eighth century BCE. What follows is described as 'a vision which (Isaiah) saw'. Part of the reference here must surely be to the great vision in ch. 6, but we should also bear in mind that vision (what we might describe as 'second sight' or 'insight') was an important element in the prophetic role. Another way of describing prophets was as 'seers', and the two terms seem in practice to have been synonymous. Indeed, from the visions of Amos onwards the prophetic collections emphasize the importance of visions, and the books of Obadiah, Habakkuk, and Nahum, like that of Isaiah, are described in their opening verse as 'visions'. The distinction between words and visions, which to us may appear fundamental, may not have seemed so basic to the compilers of these oracles. Perhaps this is a pointer, one of many we shall notice, that much of what follows is poetry, and is not to be treated in the precise manner in which we approach prose.

(1:2) The form used here appears to be that of a lawsuit, with witnesses being summoned. We have no means of knowing how closely the book's language is based on actual legal practice; some may feel that poetry and legal usage are at opposite ends of the spectrum. Indeed no legal system could tolerate the duplication of roles here envisaged, for YHWH speaks both as prosecuting counsel, here summoning his witnesses, and as judge, whose verdict, though implicit, is inevitable (Nielsen 1978: 27–9, though her reading of a covenant context underlying the lawsuit seems doubtful—the idea of 'covenant' is not prominent in the early chapters of Isaiah). It seems clear that 'heavens' and 'earth' are envisaged as a totality; the whole created order is summoned to witness the verdict that God is about to announce. 'I reared children': this is the first example of what will become a frequent and increasingly explicit feature of Isaiah, the picture of God as parent (both father and mother) of wayward children. The language may be that of adoption rather than of direct parentage (Melnyk 1993: 252), but we know too little of adoption procedures in ancient Israel to be certain of this.

(1:3) This verse has played an important part in Christian tradition. Much of Isaiah came to be regarded as pointing forward to the time of Christ, and the reference here to the ox and the ass recognizing God's presence came to be interpreted in connection with the stories of the birth of Jesus. The animals in the Christmas crib are not a biblical tradition, but are first mentioned in the Gospel of Pseudo-Matthew, thought to date from the eighth or ninth century CE, where it is said that Mary 'put her child in a manger, and an ox and an ass worshipped him. Then was fulfilled that which was spoken through the prophet Isaiah: "The ox knows his owner and the ass his master's crib"'' (Hennecke 1963: 410). It is interesting that the Hebrew word translated 'master' is ba'al, the same word as is used elsewhere of a god regarded as a rival to YHWH. There is no suggestion of a rival deity here, or any feeling that the use of this word posed problems.

The same theme, of animals recognizing what is hidden from God's own people, is found again in Jer 8:7, but the 'stork, turtledove, swallow and [?]crane' of that verse might not seem so appropriate to a Christmas crib. The remainder of the verse introduces themes basic to Isaiah. The people are described as 'Israel'. But Israel in the time of the prophet Isaiah meant the northern kingdom, which was absorbed into the Assyrian Empire around 722 BCE. It is likely that the use of the term in a religious sense, to describe the worshippers of YHWH, only became predominant at a later period. The expression 'my people' is also used, here in a strongly condemnatory sense. There is a clear cross-reference here with the usage in 40:1, with its cry to 'comfort my people'. In this opening chapter the people's sins are described in detail and the inevitability of punishment spelt out; in ch. 40 it is made clear that the punishment, though thoroughly deserved, had now been completed and that the people might now contemplate restoration.

(1:4) The section from v. 2 onwards is rightly set out in most modern translations as poetry, and one of the characteristics of Hebrew poetry is parallelism: the repetition in slightly different words in the second line of what has already been said in the first. Often such parallelism is described as 'synonymous', with the implication that there is no additional nuance of meaning to be discerned in the second line. But this conflicts with a deeply held traditional Jewish belief, shared also by some Christians, that every word of Scripture must have its own in-built significance. This verse provides a good example of the tension. Are 'children' and 'deal corruptly' simply synonyms of 'offspring' and 'do evil', or do they add details which might otherwise be overlooked? The usual view in modern scholarship has been that they are no more than synonyms, but the other view has been vigorously upheld by some scholars (Kugel 1981: 289–92). Similarly with the words gôy and 'am, translated 'nation' and 'people'. These can certainly be understood as synonyms; but it is also possible to suppose that the wickedness of YHWH's own 'am is somehow more culpable than that associated with a gôy, a term used of any nation.

The verse begins with the characteristic Isaianic word hôy, translated 'Ah', but in reality somewhat stronger than that implies: 'Alas!' It is followed by a characteristic reproach, a form in which the reasons for God's condemnation of the people are set out. The third-person usage in the second half of the verse is somewhat unexpected, and has led some commentators (Kaiser 1983) to regard it as a later clarification; without it the whole section to v. 7 can be taken as a direct address of condemnation. The point is of some importance for our understanding of Isaianic usage, because this part of the verse contains the first instance of the designation of God as 'the Holy One of Israel', an expression found 28 times in all parts of the book of Isaiah, but rare elsewhere, only 5 occurrences in the rest of the HB (van Selms 1982). 'Israel', as we have already seen, came to be used as an overall term for the worshippers of YHWH, but it is disputed whether the term was already in use in that sense in pre-exilic times (when it also designated the northern kingdom) or, as is perhaps more probable, only developed at a later time. If the latter view is correct, the term 'Holy One of Israel' may be seen as a characteristic marker of a fairly late stage in the redaction of the Isaiah material. Holiness, which at an earlier stage meant that which is separate, set apart, has now come to be an appropriate designation of God.

(1:5–7) These verses illustrate well the perils inherent in trying to interpret poetry in a precise historical fashion. In vv. 5–6 it is clear that a vivid metaphor is being used, with the people's condition set out in terms of a desperately sick body. The language here used of the community will be picked up again in the description of the suffering of the servant in ch. 53; the rather rare word ḥăbûrâ (bruise) is found in Isaiah only here and at 53:5. In v. 7 the metaphor changes, to that of a land lying desolate, and many interpreters have attempted to discover some precise historical 'reality' underlying this description. There has been discussion about whether the devastation of Sennacherib and the Assyrians in 701 BCE is the setting, or whether only the even greater devastation of the Babylonian armies in the early sixth century was in mind. We may be wiser to take this description, like that of the sick body in the preceding verses, as a vivid way of describing the general punishment inflicted on a people who are perceived to have abandoned the right way.

(1:8) The phrase *bat ṣîyyôn* has traditionally been translated 'daughter of Zion', but NRSV is surely right in its rendering 'daughter Zion'. It is Zion itself whose fate is here being described, not its daughter (however that expression may be understood). In the social world of ancient Israel daughters were pictured as their father's possession, and so to describe the city as a 'daughter' implies that it was God's possession. Sometimes in the ancient Near East cities were pictured as being married to their gods, but that particular mode of expression is not often found of Jerusalem and YHWH (though cf. 54:5 and 62:1–5) (Pfisterer Darr 1994).

The verse also brings out another characteristic theme of Isaiah: that of the remnant. There is an inherent ambiguity in this theme: it may be a means of expressing vividly the magnitude of a disaster. Only a remnant is left. Indeed, sometimes the scale of a disaster can only be grasped by the fact that there are a few survivors, as is recognized nowadays by the media when they heighten their account of an earthquake, an aeroplane crash, or a fire, by letting the few survivors tell their story. But a remnant can also be a hopeful sign; there *are* those who have lived to tell the tale, and on them a better future can be built. Both usages of the theme are found in Isaiah, sometimes in close relation to one another (see 10:20–3 and commentary), but here there is no doubt that the underlying notion is of disaster. There has been much discussion as to which of the two ideas inherent in the theme of remnant is primary, a commonly held view being that 'remnant as threat' goes back to Isaiah himself, while 'remnant as promise' is secondary. It may be more appropriate to understand the whole motif as a theodicy: the community in the Second Temple period were very aware of themselves as a remnant, those who had survived great disasters. But those disasters had been part of God's purpose for his people, who might, as a purified remnant, look forward to a more confident future under his guidance.

The word *mĕlûnâ*, here translated 'shelter', occurs in only one other place in the HB: Isa 24:20 (NRSV: 'hut'). The idea is very much that of a temporary and insecure place of refuge. Less certain is the meaning of *neṣûrâ*. NRSV's 'besieged' is doubtful as a rendering of the word and is in any case scarcely appropriate for the context. Kaiser (1983) deletes the reference to a 'city', to obtain the meaning 'like a refuge in the sheepfold', but this seems purely speculative. REB's 'beleaguered' may bring out the sense, but it seems doubtful whether we should follow the example of many commentators (most recently Stacey 1993) in claiming that the language here 'changes abruptly from image to harsh reality'.

(1:9) The community's self-recognition as a remnant is now brought out. The use of 'we' suggests the existence of a group with which the prophetic tradition could identify which regarded itself as the surviving remnant. The image of Sodom and Gomorrah is based on Gen 19, with special emphasis on the totality of destruction; in the next verse the same image will be used in a rather different sense.

(1:10) The theme of Sodom and Gomorrah is now used to emphasize the wickedness of the community as a whole, and of its leaders in particular. They have become totally alienated

from 'the word of the LORD', and from his 'teaching'. This represents Hebrew *tôrâ*, the term which came ultimately to be used for the gathered collection of Scripture. It scarcely has that formal sense here, but already we can see that a body of teaching is envisaged which the community could be expected to recognize and adhere to. The roots of *tôrâ* may be in the wisdom tradition (Jensen 1973), but its usage in the final form of the book goes significantly beyond that base.

(1:11–15) There follows a fierce denunciation of wrong ritual practice, comparable to other such attacks in the prophetic books (Am 5:18–24; Hos 6:6; Mic 6:6–8). Some modern writers have claimed that this indicates a complete 'rejection of the sacrificial cult, a momentous break with the past' on the part of the prophet (Heaton 1994: 96). There are difficulties with this view. First, it imposes a very modern, Western approach on an ancient text. Secondly, it ignores the fact that in the sweeping denunciations used here the actual terminology of the sacrificial cult seems not to be employed, as we should expect if the practices laid down in e.g. Leviticus were here being condemned. More probably we should discern a twofold purpose underlying these words. On the one hand the community needed to be warned against complacency; even the glories of the Jerusalem cult-tradition, amply illustrated in Isaiah, cannot be taken as a guarantee of worship acceptable to God. On the other hand there were dangers inherent in a false understanding of what worship could achieve. To set these out offers the beginning of an explanation of the humiliations which the community had experienced.

In what way should we understand these condemnations? Some have simply taken them at face value, and supposed that the whole cultic structure had become decadent. But we need to remember that there is no polemic as bitter and violent as religious polemic, and it may well be that this passage illustrates rivalries within the Jerusalem community, of which there is a good deal of evidence scattered through Isaiah, illustrated in particular in chs. 56–66.

One way in which this condemnation is more all-embracing than the comparable passages in the other prophetic collections is that all forms of religious activity are here condemned; even prayer (v. 15). There is no sense here of private religious observance being acceptable and the condemnation being limited to public worship. The development within the passage is also striking. From v. 11 it would appear that it is sacrificial worship of any kind which is rejected, but in the following verses the words 'you' and 'your' become increasingly prominent, so that the climax in v. 15 is a clear condemnation of the offerers rather than of their practice in itself: 'Your hands are full of blood'.

This in turn raises important interpretative questions. Those being condemned are apparently those in positions of authority; they are the 'rulers of Sodom'. At one level, therefore, Isaiah is condemning the community's leaders. At another level, however, the book claims authority for itself; 'the vision' mentioned in 1:1 is clearly a vision of God, empowering the prophetic group. This tension, whereby Isaiah both condemns the rulers and claims authority for itself, runs all through the book and is especially prominent in chs. 56–66. It is a tension still characteristic of modern religious leaders, who both exercise positions of authority and feel free to condemn those in authority.

(1:16–17) It is important to recognize that what has preceded leads directly into these verses. Until the commands set out here are observed there can be no true worship. The commands here may be understood as a *tôrâ*, the term understood now in a slightly different sense. Here it implies a set of commands, comparable to the Ten Commandments (though those here are all positive) or the briefer statement in Mic 6:8. The material itself is part of the common stock of ancient Near-Eastern texts. It is sometimes supposed that concern for the oppressed, the orphan, and the widow was peculiar to Israel, but exhortations of this kind were widespread. Thus in the Aqhat epic from Ugarit, the achievement of Dan'el as ruler was that 'he judged the cause of the widow and tried the case of the orphan' (Gibson 1978: 107). This Canaanite evidence should remind us that it was not Israel alone in the ancient world that had an awareness of justice.

(1:18–20) We return now to the language of the lawsuit. The people are summoned; their offences are set out; and the alternative possibilities laid down ('If you are willing...'; 'if you refuse...'). Clearly repentance is envisaged as a possibility. Repentance is not a prominent theme in the eighth-century prophets such as Amos, but it later came to be of major importance, e.g. in Jeremiah. This may be an indication that this passage is a relatively late element in the complete collection.

(1:21–3) This passage is usually characterized as a lament. The metre, at least at the beginning of the poem, has three stresses in the first part of the line and two in the second, as is usual in such laments. Some scholars wish to delete 'but now murderers' to preserve the form throughout the verse, but we do not know enough of the details of Hebrew poetry to be confident in doing so. The opening word *'êkâ* (how) is also typical of the lament (cf. 2 Sam 1:19, 25, for one of the most famous laments, that of David over Saul and Jonathan). Jerusalem is not named in the Hebrew text, but it is clearly the subject here, as is made explicit by the Greek translation, and this concern with Jerusalem, both its great potential and its wickedness in practice, will run throughout the whole book. *Mišpāṭ* (justice) and *ṣedeq* (righteousness) should have characterized the city and especially its rulers, but they are nowhere to be seen. The passage ends with further reference to the orphan and the widow (cf. v. 17), as those in whose interest justice and righteousness should in particular be exercised. The theme of the corruption of justice is one which runs through the whole prophetic tradition, but is specially characteristic of Isaiah, and is one of the elements which hold the whole book together.

(1:24–5) These verses comprise one unit with what has preceded; they are introduced by the characteristic 'therefore' of judgement. The wrongs which have been outlined in previous verses here have their inevitable consequences spelt out, and metaphors based on metallurgy provide a link between vv. 22 and 25. God is here described as 'the Mighty One of Israel', a term distinct from but closely related to the more usual Isaianic term, 'the Holy One of Israel'; the present phrase is not found elsewhere but the almost identical 'mighty One of Jacob' occurs at 49:26; 60:16. The piling up

of divine titles here is in general more characteristic of the second part of the book.

(1:26) But the picture is not all of gloom; the punishment is to be followed by restoration. The phrase 'faithful city' provides an *inclusio* (that is, the repetition of an opening word or phrase at the end of a section) with v. 21, where that status had been lost, and the use of *ṣedeq* not only offers a link with v. 21, but also gives a reminder of the importance of this *ṣ-d-q* root in Jerusalem's tradition. Perhaps originally concealing a divine name, it reminds us of Melchizedek in Gen 14 and of Zadok the priest in the story of David, and of the frequent use of the root in the Psalms.

We are here introduced to a theme which has caused much discussion: that of the 'inviolability of Zion'. It has been widely held that there was an ancient tradition, traces of which may be found for example in Ps 2, that Zion was impregnable and could not be captured by its enemies. On the other hand Clements (1980*b*) has argued strongly that the tradition found its origin in the interpretation in Isaiah and elsewhere of the Assyrian king Sennacherib's failure to capture the city in 701 BCE. However that may be, it proved to be a powerful theme, being retained often in the teeth of historical evidence to the contrary.

(1:27–8) Religious polemic is clearly again at work here. Those of whom the writer approved are offered sweeping promises; there are others whose behaviour leads them to be condemned as forsaking the Lord. This is very reminiscent of the divisions highlighted in chs. 56–66. Various attempts have been made (notably by Hanson 1979) more precisely to identify different groups within the Second Temple community, but they founder for lack of sufficiently detailed knowledge.

(1:29–31) Reasons for the rejection of one group are now offered, and they are to be found in some form of idolatrous practice the details of which are not clear to us. The closest links are again with chs. 56–66. In addition to the link between v. 31 and 66:24 already noticed, we may see in particular the reference to the 'oaks' in 57:5 and to the 'gardens' in 65:3. What is here condemned seems to be some form of pagan worship; it is apparently quite different from the misuse of the temple referred to earlier in the chapter. The variety of condemnations and of hopes expressed in this first chapter have led a number of scholars to see in it a summary of the message of the book as a whole (Fohrer 1967). One must not push this idea too far—there are important elements in the book which are not reflected here—but in general terms it is a valuable concept, particularly if it is divorced from largely sterile debate about how much of its contents can plausibly be said to go back to Isaiah himself.

(Chs. 2–4) The majority of commentators have seen these chapters as consisting of a variety of short and largely unrelated oracles but the attempt has been made to discern in them 'a coherent and functional literary unit' (Wiklander 1984, p. ix) a theory based on an elaborate text-linguistic foundation. On this reading the basic theme is the 'restoration of the covenant by means of a lawsuit involving Yhwh, Judah and the nations' (ibid. 114). It is an interesting theory which anticipates some more recent literary readings, but suffers from the serious weakness that the word covenant does not occur in these chapters! Nevertheless the theory that a unifying structure can be discerned in this material, beginning (2:2–4) and ending (4:2–6) with a vision of a glorious future for Jerusalem, is a valuable one.

(2:1) Somewhat unexpectedly a new superscription is introduced here. Various suggestions have been made to account for this unique feature. It might wish to stress that the following oracle, found also in Micah, is genuinely Isaian; if ch. 1 is seen as a later summary of the book as a whole this could be seen as the original introduction to the oracles of Isaiah himself; it may be intended as an introduction to chs. 2–12 (NB the comparable introduction to the 'foreign nations' section at 13:1), or to chs. 2–4 on the view outlined above.

(2:2–4) The most remarkable feature of these verses is that they are also found in Mic 4:1–3, with very minor internal differences and a different conclusion. It is obviously possible that one prophet, or the collector of his oracles, borrowed from the other; if this is so, there are no certain criteria for deciding on which side the dependence lay. But it may also be that there has been a tendency to lay too much stress on the supposed 'originality' of prophets. As we work through the whole Isaiah collection we shall come across a number of places where there are very close similarities with material found in other prophetic books. The present example is a well-known one and has therefore attracted much attention; the others are mostly in the foreign nations oracles which have been the subject of less attention. The use and reuse of existing prophetic oracles may be a subject which deserves more attention than has customarily been devoted to it. Whatever its origin, the striking feature of this oracle is the glorious future held out for Jerusalem, in stark contrast to what has preceded in ch. 1. The vision is to be fulfilled 'in days to come'. Later in this chapter we shall find frequent references to the day of the Lord, pictured as a day of disaster. This oracle, in common with much else in Isaiah, seems to be saying that beyond the disaster there will be a genuine hope of restoration and new prosperity. 'The highest of the mountains': the theme of the 'cosmic mountain' is a widespread one in the ancient Near East and in the Hebrew Bible in particular (Clifford 1972 offers a useful survey of the main relevant texts). The theme is frequent in the Psalms (cf. e.g. Ps 48:1–3; 68:15–16), and both in this passage and in the Psalms the claim is made that Mount Zion, in fact not at all a spectacular mountain, will be established as 'the highest of the mountains'. The mythical features of this picture show us that this is theological geography. It is also noteworthy that, despite the importance for much of Israel's tradition of Mount Sinai and the Torah given there, in the Isaiah tradition the 'holy mountain' is consistently Mount Zion.

Remarkable also in view of later developments within the book is the place here given to 'the nations'. Elsewhere, especially in chs. 13–23, they are presented as the recipients of the judgement of YHWH. Here, a much more positive future is held out for them. It is in the light of this passage, the first dealing with foreign nations, that later judgements will naturally be read. (Davies 1989 makes an interesting comparison between this passage near the beginning of the whole book and 66:18–24, which rounds it off.)

(2:3) A particular concern of the Second Temple community was the position of the worshippers of YHWH *vis-à-vis* those who worshipped other gods (cf. Zech 8:20–3; 14:16). That concern is very prominent in Isaiah, and a variety of attitudes can be found, ranging from the extraordinary openness of 19:24–5 to the bitterness of some of the foreign nations material and the opposition to Edom in ch. 34 and elsewhere. Here a measure of openness can be seen, but it is clear that Israel is envisaged as playing a superior role as the nation from which others might profitably learn.

It is striking that here *tôrâ* (law) and 'word of the LORD' are treated as synonymous. The word of the Lord is characteristically that which was uttered through prophetic mouthpieces; *tôrâ*, as we have seen, had a variety of meanings, but here it may be comparable to the kind of summary of divine guidance found in 1:16–17.

(2:4) Ancient Israel lived in a world where war was a fact of life. The vision of the cessation of war in this verse is a remarkable one, and it is perhaps not surprising that it proved too remarkable for a later prophetic voice. In Joel 3:10 we find the vision being reversed; there ploughshares and pruning hooks are to become swords and spears, in recognition of the need for continued conflict.

(2:5) This brief appeal has no equivalent in Micah. It is an exhortation of the kind more commonly found in Deuteronomy, inviting the community to amendment. It is couched in the first person plural (cf. 1:9), suggesting the identity of a group to whom Isaiah is making special appeal.

(2:6–21) An extended passage, the precise meaning of whose details is not always clear owing to textual uncertainties, is devoted to the 'day of the LORD' theme. The Hebrew word *kî*, with which it begins, can indeed mean 'for' as in the NRSV translation, but it is more likely here to be asseverative, that is making an assertion rather than spelling out a condition, and should be translated 'surely'. It is a new start, not a direct continuation of v. 5, to which it is linked only by the phrase 'house of Jacob'. Already there is a difficulty in the condemnation here: the word translated 'of diviners' is missing in the Hebrew text, and is supplied from a later tradition, which presumably already felt that the gap needed to be filled. In any case the idea seems to be another condemnation of false worship comparable to that found in 1:29–31. There is no other evidence that the Philistines were especially gifted as 'soothsayers'. The point of the address to YHWH is that intercession is useless; doom is inevitable. The condemnation is largely formulaic, with two refrain-like phrases giving a structural unity to the whole. One is found in vv. 9, 11, and 17, and speaks of humanity being humbled; the other in vv. 10, 19, and 21 pictures those who are left hiding among the rocks in the hope that they might thereby escape God's anger. As can readily be seen the two sets of passages are not identical, as a modern refrain would be; this may imply that the poem is not a unity but has been developed over an extended period (Vermeylen 1977–8), but it may also be a characteristic of Hebrew poetry to tolerate greater variation than would be acceptable in most modern Western traditions. The passage as a whole brings together two basic Isaianic themes: the vanity of human self-confidence and the folly of worshipping false gods.

(2:11) The poem reaches a climax with the assertion of God's sole power 'in that day'. Here the way in which the 'day' is spoken of differs sharply from the picture of the latter 'days' in v. 2. There it was a time of the vindication of Zion and its worshippers, here it is an occasion of unmitigated disaster.

(2:12–19) The idea of a 'day of YHWH' when his enemies would experience his power seems to have been a common one. Am 5:18 presents the idea of the 'day of YHWH' as one to which the people looked forward in eager anticipation. In this Isaiah passage the idea that YHWH will indeed have a day of punishment of his enemies is again set out, but with the disturbing difference that the enemies are now pictured as those who claimed to be his worshippers. In particular, as frequently in Isaiah, the most severe condemnations are reserved for those who trust in their own strength. The imagery used is not always clear, but an important place is found for the storm-wind, a recurring image of divine power in the HB, from the description of Mount Sinai down to the apocalyptic writings.

(2:22) This last verse is missing from the Greek translation (LXX). Its presence illustrates the way in which the tradition developed. It functions as a kind of brief sermon to the readers of the final form of the book, warning them of the dire consequences of the kind of behaviour outlined above.

(3:1–5) As at 2:6 the word *kî*, translated 'for' in NRSV and elsewhere, is really asseverative: 'Surely'. What is sure is the complete break-up of the established structure of society. Among the prophets it is Jeremiah who is often pictured as endangering the very basis of the society in which he lived, but this charge is less often brought against Isaiah. Here, however, it is clear that the whole established order is at risk. The words translated 'support and staff' in NRSV function in two different ways within the announcement of judgement. They refer to the structure of the society without which there would be chaos. But they also refer to the need for sustenance: bread and water. (NEB/REB omit the reference to bread and water as a later gloss, but this kind of double allusion seems well suited to the basic Isaiah tradition.) The list of leaders of society undergoes an interesting development. At first it appears as purely neutral description ('warrior', 'soldier', and so forth); but as it develops it becomes steadily more derogatory ('skilful magician', 'expert enchanter'). It is an entirely male-dominated structure, and age is also regarded as an important prerequisite for ability to rule. Notice particularly in this respect v. 5, where the parallelism suggests that 'youth' is equivalent to 'base' and 'elder' to 'honourable'.

(3:6–9*a*) NRSV makes the section end at v. 8, but it may be better to take the first part of v. 9 (down to 'do not hide it') with what precedes. This brings out more clearly the link, already familiar to us from ch. 1, of Jerusalem with Sodom, regarded as a gloss by *BHS* and Vermeylen (1977–8), but quite understandable in the larger context of the book.

(3:9*b*–11) These rather generalizing verses have often been regarded as additions to the original context, but if we pay less attention to which words may be original to the prophet Isaiah himself, we can see that this section fits well as an overall verdict on different kinds of behaviour, and the rewards that each brings. The word 'verdict' is deliberately chosen, for the legal context is clear to see.

(3:12) The whole section ends with a statement of a society in confusion, expressed in a way which shows all too clearly the values of ancient Israelite society. It is regarded as a sign of disaster that children or women, bracketed together in the parallelism, should be in positions of authority. It will be for the reader to decide whether he or she can accept the prophet's assessment in such a matter.

(3:13–15) In these verses we return to the lawsuit language already found in ch. 1, and the problem already expressed there returns even more clearly. Here YHWH is both the prosecuting counsel (v. 13) and the judge (v. 14). Whatever we may think about the legal proprieties of such a situation the prophet's intention is clear; he continues his attack upon the leaders of the community, regarding them as the real perverters of justice through the oppression of the weaker members of society. The section ends with the messenger formula ('says the Lord GOD of hosts') showing the prophet's claim to divine authorization.

(3:16–23) There follows an extraordinary male chauvinist attack upon the women of Jerusalem. There were women prophets in ancient Israel (e.g. Huldah, 2 Kings 22), but those prophets whose words have been handed down in written form seem for the most part strongly misogynistic (Hos 1 and 3; Am 4, as well as this passage and Isa 32: 9–11). Whether this tells us more about the women of the time or about the prophets to whom such words are attributed must be left open. The form of 16–17 is a reproach, describing female behaviour from a male point of view; it leads into a prose expansion, vv. 18–23, which reads like a catalogue from some ancient fashion store. Several of the terms are found only here, and not all of them can be identified; the larger commentaries must be consulted for fuller details (Wildberger 1972: 135–45).

(3:24–4:1) In one sense this is a reversion to the reproach of 3:16–17, but there is a shift of emphasis. Instead of the attack upon the women of Jerusalem the stress shifts so that the reference is to Jerusalem itself, pictured, as cities often were, in feminine terms. The 'sitting on the ground' as a symbol of mourning undergone here by Jerusalem will be used in the same way of Babylon in 47:1. But the passage reverts at its close to the picture of individual women, eagerly seeking the respectability which being called by a man's name promises.

(4:2–6) The degradation and desolation of Jerusalem might appear to be complete, yet it is now contradicted by the great hope expressed in these verses. In historical-critical terms it is certainly a late addition, and has been disparagingly described as a 'mosaic of clichés from different sources' (Bentzen 1957: ii. 108); in the context of the book as a whole, however, it functions as showing that the ordeal suffered by Jerusalem at the hands of its enemies was not the whole story. There was a glorious future to look forward to. Remarkable, too, is the transformation of the 'on that day' theme, so negative in ch. 2, such a powerful symbol of hope here. The use of *ṣemaḥ*, 'branch', here introduces a term which elsewhere (Jer 23:5; Zech 3:8; 6:12) is associated with a hoped-for figure in terms that can be called messianic. (In Isa 11:1 the word rendered 'branch' in NRSV is a different Heb. word.) Another theme, rare in these early chapters of the book, introduced here is that of the Exodus and the wilderness journey, evoked in v. 5 by the 'cloud by day and smoke and the shining of a flaming fire by night' (Sweeney 1988a: 18–19). This forms an important link with the later part of the book. We also note in this passage a positive use of the theme of the remnant: those who are left are to be 'recorded for life'.

(5:1–7) Though the literary form is very different the thrust of this passage is essentially that of the kind of lawsuit of which we have already seen examples: the evidence, in the form of God's kindness to his people, is set out in vv. 1–4; the verdict—guilty—is assumed and punishment follows in vv. 5–6. Then v. 7 supplies a kind of key to the dramatis personae of the story, offering the opportunity for a characteristic play on words. In form it may be regarded as a parable, a rare literary form in the prophetic writings, though some prophetic actions can certainly be regarded as parabolic: Isa 8:1–4 offers an example (Westermann 1967: 201–2). The parable may itself be based on a vintage-song, though we know too little of these to be confident. It would be unwise to interpret the details of the action described in an allegorical fashion, with specific meanings being given to watchtower, wine vat, and so on, though this kind of literary reading, so much despised by historical critics, has had something of a renaissance in recent years. v. 1 is one of the places where NRSV has modified the RSV translation, rendering 'my' rather than 'a' love-song. If this is correct, vv. 1–2 could be seen as providing the setting, with the song actually starting in v. 3 (Petersen and Richards 1992: 82–3). The more usual view is that the song is found in vv. 1b–2, with 3–6 providing the reflections of the owner of the vineyard (Emerton 1992, who also suggests rendering v. 1 'a song about my friend'). v. 2, 'wild grapes'. Literally 'stinkers'! v. 4 at first looks like the defence to the lawsuit. It takes the form of two questions. The first simply invites a sympathetic answer; the second expresses bewilderment at the unforeseen and unwanted harvest. But then we realize that it is not really a defence at all, for the 'I' of this verse continues to speak in v. 5, now passing judgement. In v. 7 'house of Israel' and 'people of Judah' are treated as synonymous. This may be a pointer to a late date for the final form of this parable, when Israel referred to the whole religious community, not simply the northern kingdom. The passage closes with the kind of wordplay that defies acceptable rendering in English. God looked for *mišpāṭ* (justice) but found *miśpāḥ* (bloodshed), for *ṣĕdāqâ* (righteousness) but found *ṣĕʿāqâ* (a cry). The parable, having begun with the prophet himself as speaker, ends with proclamation from YHWH.

(5:8) A new section begins here; this is not made very clear in many editions of NRSV. We have a series of woes, introduced by the word *hôy* (cf. 1:4). For a reason which is not clear NRSV here translates this word with the very neutral 'Ah', whereas in a similar series in Amos 'Alas' is used. Whether the origin be in a mourning-cry or in some form of cultic usage its impact is powerful. Sometimes the punishment is implicit in the woe itself, sometimes a threat is added, introduced by the word 'therefore'. There is a link between the series of woes here and that which follows in 9:8–10:4, best illustrated by the common refrain found in 5:25 and several times in the later passage. This initial verse illustrates a common characteristic of this section; it is complete in itself, but has probably been elaborated in the course of transmission to emphasize the

point being made. In itself the point of v. 8 seems to be that land is to be held in trust, and encroachment by enlarging it infringes that principle. The story of Naboth in 1 Kings 21 may illustrate the same point.

(5:9–10) The image here is of the prophet being admitted to the heavenly council (cf. Jer 23:18, 22) to hear the divine verdict on unacceptable behaviour. An ephah is one-tenth of a homer (de Vaux 1961: 199–200), and so the point of the decision seems to be that in future those condemned will harvest only a tenth of what they sow—a less severe threat than one might have anticipated.

(5:11–17) vv. 11–12, the condemnation of excessive drinking, with the picture of the accompanying merriment, is reminiscent of Am 8. Were the prophets somewhat Puritan in their approach, or was the excess of some people's behaviour an open scandal? v. 13, 'therefore' is a characteristic word of threat, binding this spelling out of the consequences to the woe which has preceded. The tense of the verb 'go into exile' would normally be rendered by an English past, and this makes good sense in the final form of the book: its compilers knew what their community's history had been, and interpreted it as divine punishment. The reason for the exile is striking: NRSV 'without knowledge' might imply mere ignorance, but the Hebrew really means 'for lack of knowledge'—a failure to grasp what God really wanted of his people. v. 14, the threat is elaborated with another 'therefore'. Sheol, the place of the dead from which there was no return, eagerly awaited the offenders—the rulers of Jerusalem, so frequently condemned in these opening chapters. v. 15 is almost identical with 2:9 and functions in a way similarly dismissive of human aspirations. v. 16 is a key text for the appreciation of much of Isaiah. It brings together three key terms: the holiness of God, which will play an important part in the vision of ch. 6; and the qualities of *mišpāṭ* (justice) and *ṣĕdāqâ* (righteousness), which are claimed as characteristic of divine action and are required of God's worshippers also. One of the most important features of the teaching of the Israelite prophets is this claim that divine characteristics and human behaviour should in some way reflect one another. Where justice and righteousness are lacking the whole of society, from the leaders down, is at risk.

(5:18–25) The series of woes continues, rounded off with a threat. The basic charge is that those condemned are imposing their own standards of right and wrong (v. 20), corrupting the legal structure (v. 23), and confident that God is either ignorant of or uninterested in their behaviour (v. 19). In the light of these sweeping condemnations the charge of drunkenness (v. 22) seems a relatively trifling matter. It is disputed whether the references to wisdom in v. 21 imply any specific link with a wisdom movement in Israel, as proposed by McKane (1965: 65–7). Speculation about Isaiah himself having once been a member of such a wisdom movement is probably best avoided (Whybray 1974); to be 'wise in one's own eyes' means that one is conceited or a fool, and has nothing to do with membership of a wisdom group. All we can say with fair confidence is that these passages are aimed against the policy-makers who were convinced, as is not unknown with politicians, that they were the special recipients of wisdom. By contrast, as the threat in v. 24 makes clear, the Isaiah tradition regards them as having rejected the *tôrâ* (instruction) of the Lord. This whole section brings out very clearly the tension between those who rely upon human political skills and those who seek a superior religious authority.

v. 25 provides a second threat, and here we are confronted with a methodological problem. Those who have attempted to trace the redactional process underlying the book have noted the identity of the last part of this verse ('For all this his anger . . .') with the conclusion of each section of 9:8–10:4, and have concluded that some displacement, deliberate or accidental, has led to this arrangement (NEB placed 5:24–5 after 10:4 but REB reverts to the order of MT). Some scholars (Clements 1980a: 66) have regarded the displacement as intentional, whereas older commentators supposed an accidental dislocation. But as we saw in the introduction there is a strong case for the view that it is the book of Isaiah as it has been handed down to us that is the subject of attention, and that we should not attempt rearrangement to conform with an original authorial or redactional intention which is no longer accessible to us. As it stands, therefore, this warning of God's continuing anger forms an important frame to the passages dealing with the hope of a glorious royal figure who features in chs. 7–9. The destruction envisaged here is cosmic in scope.

(5:26–30) The approach of an oppressing army is vividly portrayed, but perhaps the most important point comes at the outset: this oppressor has been summoned by God himself, in terms of signalling to the nations, a metaphor which will be used again in 11:12 and 49:22. (The Heb. here has 'nations', though NRSV has changed it to the singular 'nation', without note, in view of the context.) Here it connotes threat; in the later passages the signal will herald deliverance. What follows is a conventional description of an army on the march, and it would be unwise to limit its applicability to the Assyrians or any other enemy force. Its universal reference is shown most clearly at v. 30, where the devastation is directly linked back to the 'on that day' language of ch. 2 and elsewhere.

(Ch. 6) With this chapter, one of the best-known in the whole book, acute differences of interpretation arise. Clements summarized a widely held view of the whole of the following section when he wrote, 'Undoubtedly we have in 6:1–8:18 a memoir written by the prophet himself' (Clements 1980a: 70). On this view ch. 6 is autobiographical: the prophet's own account of his calling, precisely dated and vividly set out in the context of the worship of the Jerusalem temple. More recently, however, a number of scholars have been much more cautious. They note the increasing tendency within the prophetic tradition to personalize the experience of individuals by attributing first-person accounts to them, and see this as idealizing by a later generation rather than a reliable guide to personal experience. (Such an approach is characteristic of the work of R. P. Carroll on Jeremiah; it has not yet been applied in so systematic a way to Isaiah, but the principles laid down are very similar, and were indeed outlined by Carroll himself in an earlier work. See Carroll (1979) for basic discussion.) It may be appropriate to see in this chapter part of the 'presentation of a prophet' (Ackroyd 1987) rather than an item from an autobiography. In particular the disasters that the community had experienced since the time of Isaiah himself

are shown in this chapter to have been inevitable, having already been spelt out in his very call. The point is clearly put by Kaiser (1983: 115): 'The first-person account serves to transpose the narrative fictitiously into the time of Isaiah, using his ministry to reflect the fact that Yahweh was also present beforehand in the history of disaster . . . and therefore to make clear and credible his abiding power over the future of this people.'

The other question often asked concerning this vision, whether or not it should be regarded as inaugurating Isaiah's ministry, loses much of its force if the whole passage is seen as a literary device. It is nevertheless worth bearing in mind that this account does bear striking similarities in its overall shape with those in Jer 1 and Ezek 1. In each case a specific date is given. There follows an account of the divine presence with the prophet, a theophany. This leads the prophet to acknowledge his unworthiness, from which he is purified and then given a commission. The accounts end with an indication of the content of the message that the prophet is to deliver. There are minor differences of order and of degree of elaboration, but the similarities are so great as to raise the possibility that the accounts are based on some known form of commissioning.

(6:1) 'In the year that king Uzziah died'. The year of death of Uzziah (known also as Azariah) is unknown, but a date around 740 BCE is likely. More striking is the manner of describing the year. Why is the accession of the new king not mentioned? It is possible that this is a way of dismissing Ahaz, who for the Isaiah tradition, as for the Chronicler, embodies all that could go wrong with the Davidic dynasty. In any case, as the following words make clear, it is the Lord himself who is the real king. He wears a *śûl*, a robe elsewhere associated with the priestly garments (Ex 28:33–4).

(6:2) There have been many conjectures concerning the seraphim, who are here pictured as messengers in the divine council. The root *ś-r-p* might make it appropriate to think of them as 'burning ones'. Alternatively they have been likened to snakes; but when one notes that they had wings and genitalia (here euphemistically 'feet'), could call out, and could carry things the similarities diminish. There are no real biblical parallels; the same root is used in Isaiah at 14:29 and 30:6, but these links do not seem to shed much light on this passage. With visionary language of this kind, attempts at precise description, or at finding a specific cultic context, are likely to be misguided.

(6:3) This is the only direct example in the HB of the Trisagion, the threefold cry of 'Holy'. It has, of course, been taken up in almost all Christian eucharistic liturgies as the Sanctus. One of the nearest parallels to it in the HB is Ps 99:3, 5 with its cry of 'Holy is he!' There (v. 1) cherubim rather than seraphim were the divine attendants. We are not sure of the difference. God is here described as 'the LORD of Hosts'; it can be taken in this context simply as a divine title, whether its origin is to be sought among the hosts of heaven or in some kind of military usage. It is striking as the only context in which the divine name is used in a genitival ('YHWH of . . .') relation with another noun; the HB was very dismissive of the Baals of this place and that.

'The whole earth is full of his glory': is this a claim to universalism, or would 'land' be a better translation than 'earth'? Whatever the original intention, the larger claim soon came to be established. *Kābôd* (glory) is also a significant word, being closely associated with the Jerusalem temple and its worship: 'in his temple all say "Glory"' (Ps 29:9; cf. 72:19).

(6:4–7) v. 4, the language here is very characteristic of the theophany, the manifestation of the divine presence to humanity: the shaking, the smoke. v. 5, appropriate to the theophany, too, is the human response, expressing fear and inadequacy in the divine presence: cf. Moses in Ex 3:33, Samson's parents in Judg 13. Both points are brought out in 'my eyes have seen the king': human limitations in the presence of the divine, but also fear, since to be brought into the presence of any king might be a situation of danger. The literary input becomes clear with the reference to 'a people of unclean lips'. The prophet himself will have his uncleanness purged, but in this vision at least there is no such reprieve for the people. It needs the whole book, and the promise of the end of punishment in ch. 40 in particular, to bring about any such remission. vv. 6–7, there follows the rite of purification. Though the details of the language and actions described are quite different, there are similarities here with the accounts of the call of Jeremiah and of Ezekiel. No particular theory of atonement for sin is here implied; it is the fact of such cleansing that is all-important.

(6:8–10) Here we see a difference from Jeremiah and Ezekiel; they express reluctance, whereas here the prophet is pictured as actively volunteering. There is an obvious link with another passage describing the divine council, 1 Kings 22 with its volunteering spirit, and this similarity extends to the content of the message. In the 1 Kings passage the recipients are misled because the spirit is lying; here again the messenger is to prevent the people from receiving the true import of the message. If this passage *were* autobiographical we should have to suppose that the prophet was speaking with heavy irony; much more likely these are the reflections of a later editor, seeking to find a possible explanation for an otherwise incomprehensible series of events leading to the exile and accompanying disasters. So v. 10 emphasizes that every possible way by which 'this people' (here, as often, used in a dismissive way) could have grasped the message has been blocked. There was then no way in which disaster could be avoided. But that is, of course, not the end of the story; in 43:8 and elsewhere in the latter part of the book we shall hear of a glorious future for this people who are so blind and deaf.

(6:11–12) To use a further question is a frequent stylistic device (cf. Moses in Ex 3), here used less as a request for information than as a way of stressing the totality of the inevitable disaster. The form of the question, 'how long', reminds us of the lament Psalms (e.g. Ps 79:5), as the community begins to realize the full impact of the disaster. The reference to exile, implicit in what has preceded, becomes explicit with v. 12. As in 2 Chr 36 the exile is here pictured as total, with 'emptiness in the midst of the land'. This is a poetic way of expressing the seriousness of what occurred rather than a precise statement of prosaic fact.

(6:13) This verse presents a major textual problem which cannot be dealt with in detail here (see Emerton 1982 for a 34-page study of this one verse which apologizes for its super-

ficiality). The problem is not just a modern one, for the last part of the verse is omitted by the ancient Greek translation, the Septuagint, and interpreters through the ages, including modern translations, have differed sharply in their understanding. (NEB bracketed part of the verse and omitted the last phrase entirely.) In the first part of the verse it seems as if the disaster outlined in the preceding verses is intensified: even if a tenth survived they would be subject to further destruction. The last phrase introduces a note of hope for the 'holy seed'. Though no doubt a later addition this chimes in well with the hopefulness of the final form of the book as a whole.

(7:1–9) The difference between commentators, already noted at the beginning of ch. 6, continues here. Whereas this narrative account has traditionally been seen as part of the Isaiah *Denkschrift*, or memorial, deriving substantially from the prophet himself, others have seen here a late narrative, dependent on 2 Kings for its outline, and part of an Isaiah 'legend' found also in chs. 20; 36–9. Its particular concern is to show Ahaz as an unworthy member of the Davidic line in sharp contrast to his much more worthy son and successor Hezekiah.

v. 1, the reference to the attack by foreign kings on Jerusalem is based on 2 Kings 16:5; the episode is often referred to as the 'Syro-Ephraimite war'. It is often supposed that the objective of the two kings was to draw Judah into a coalition which might resist the Assyrian threat, but this remains speculative—there is little direct evidence in support of this interpretation (Tomes 1993). In the last phrase the Hebrew actually says 'he [i.e. presumably Ahaz] could not fight for it', which might imply that Jerusalem had been captured, but the Dead Sea scrolls Isaiah and most of the versions read 'they could not fight against it', bringing out the idea that Jerusalem was inviolable. v. 2, there are difficulties in translation also with this verse. 'Allied itself with' is not at all the normal meaning of Hebrew *nāḥâ* (guide), and most translations have been shaped by their general sense of the overall context. There is actually no reference to Ahaz in this verse; it is the 'house of David' whose heart shook. v. 3, 'Shear-jashub' means 'a remnant shall return', an expression found also in 10:21. The name is significant as showing that there will be those who survive the inevitable disaster. It is striking that the encounter with Ahaz takes place at exactly the same spot as that with Hezekiah in 36:2. While it is obviously possible that this was a recognized place for diplomatic business to be carried out, it seems much more likely that the link was a literary one, aimed at bringing out the contrast in subsequent behaviour between Ahaz and Hezekiah.

vv. 4–6, the message 'be quiet, do not fear' in many ways encapsulates the Isaianic message; cf. 30:15, where the same word for 'quietness' is used. It is making religious claims, as against the 'evil plotting' of the community's enemies. Pekah is referred to dismissively as 'the son of Remaliah' and not given his own name: perhaps a sign of southern hostility to northern pretensions. We know nothing for certain of 'the son of Tabeel', but it is at least possible that he was a member of the Tobiad family, referred to in various post-exilic texts (cf. Neh 2:10) and known as rivals of the Jerusalem establishment (Mazar 1957). The original form of this pretender's name is uncertain (perhaps Tab-el, 'God is good'), but it is—surely deliberately?—misspelt in the MT to mean 'son of a no-good'.

vv. 7–9, the poetic oracle in v. 7 is so generally worded as to be applicable to a variety of situations, and the particular point of the passages naming the 'head' of the different countries is not clear, though it is surely derogatory. Inserted in the middle is what is usually taken to be a prose gloss, alluding to an event which took place 65 years after the Syro-Ephraimite war. Possibly the reference is to the campaigns in Palestine of Esar-haddon of Assyria c.669 BCE (cf. Ezra 4:2). An alternative understanding of this and other passages that specify a period of time for their fulfilment (e.g. 7:16; 8:4) is to note their similarity with the Mesopotamian divinatory texts known as *adannu*. These laid down a period of time during which the 'prophecy' could be regarded as valid (Cryer 1994: 293).

The obscurities of the first part of these verses suddenly clear away with the categorical statement in v. 9. The Hebrew is even more dramatic than an English translation can be, with a wordplay which NRSV does hint at. The verb (the same in each clause) translated 'stand firm' and 'stand at all' is that from which the word 'Amen' derives: 'If you will not be firm, you will not be confirmed.' The sentence is taken up by the Chronicler and made the basis for a sermon (2 Chr 20:20).

(7:10–17) Here we have a new section in which Isaiah is not mentioned by name at all. NRSV refers to him at v. 13, but as the margin makes clear he is not named in the Hebrew text; the 'he' of that verse is YHWH. The whole of this section, together with vv. 18–25, is a reflection on a common theme rather than a continuous narrative. v. 11, if a link with vv. 1–9 is intended the sign envisaged will have been something to show the discomfiture of the two kings. The biblical use of 'signs' is a complex one: they are sometimes regarded as an important way of showing the divine intention, whereas at other times (not least in the NT) they are regarded with suspicion (Mt 12:39!). Zechariah asks for a sign (Lk 1) and is struck dumb for it. v. 12, Ahaz's answer here appears to be wholly admirable; one might expect that Hezekiah would be condemned for asking for a sign (38:22) yet his action is apparently commendable. Quasi-psychological explanations claiming that Ahaz had the wrong mental attitude are not based on anything in the text. The whole episode is extremely artificial in historical terms. It is, as it were, pre-determined that Ahaz's attitude will be wrong.

vv. 13–14a, the strongly negative wording in this section prepares us for as strongly threatening a sign: the condemnation of the 'house of David' (cf. v. 2); the 'wearying' of God, with the implication that the divine patience will soon run out; the 'therefore', often used to introduce a threat. All these features suggest that a negative outcome will follow. v. 14b, in line with what has just been said some scholars have attempted to construe the original meaning of the sign in negative terms. The name Immanuel could be translated 'May God be with us', a prayer for deliverance; and the food ('curds and honey') be taken to imply all that was available in a devastated land. Overwhelmingly, however, the interpretative tradition has taken this sign as one of promise and hope for the future, and it is that tradition that will be followed here. (Werlitz 1992: 241, lists 29 different issues which have divided critical scholars in their interpretation of this verse, and that is quite apart from the division between conservative and critical scholars which is here very deep-seated.)

If the passage is seen as a contemporary memoir, then it would most naturally refer to a young woman who was pregnant at the time it was uttered, and this in effect means the wife of either the prophet (so Clements 1980a) or the king, with the possibility that Hezekiah, as the child to be born, is being alluded to. If, as is suggested here, the passage originates from a later period, then precise reference to a particular young woman is not required, and it may be better to translate 'a young woman' with the sense of 'any young woman'. The word 'almâ may well have reference to the social status of the woman referred to, but it does not imply virginity. The Greek translation of Isaiah, for reasons which are still unknown, here used the word *parthenos*, which does mean 'a virgin', and it was that tradition which was followed by Mt 1:23, and has been of enormous importance in the Christian interpretative tradition; its use in countless Christmas services still attests its evocative power. If historical-critical criteria are to be paramount this should be regarded as a *mis*-interpretation; if a reader-response approach is accepted it is presumably a perfectly proper way to read the text.

vv. 15–17, 'curds and honey' could imply a desperate search for food in a devastated land, but they could be royal food (as is perhaps better implied by the 'butter and honey' of AV) (Ringgren 1956: 27 for the idea of this as food of the gods in Babylonian texts). v. 16 is difficult, and it looks as if in part at least an addition has been made to provide an explicit link with the Syro-Ephraimite conflict. There is no obvious sense in which the two kings could be said to have 'a' land. In v. 17, too, there has been elaboration, particularly in the abrupt reference to the king of Assyria. We can see in these verses a tension between a historicizing approach, wishing to give the section a specific rooting in the events of the eighth century, and a thematic understanding more concerned with the hope for the future of the community.

(7:18–25) These four short oracles bring back the 'in that day' theme, but our approach to it is inevitably affected by the context. The 'day' is no longer simply the unpredictable 'day of the LORD' of ch. 2. Now the understanding is shaped by, on the one hand, the threat posed by Assyria and other foreign enemies, and on the other by the hopes expressed through the birth of the child. But the predominant note is one of threat. v. 18 envisages threats from both Assyria and Egypt—the latter, often a hoped-for ally, is unexpected in the context. The verse should be read in the light of the much more optimistic picture in 19:23–5. It has been suggested (Matthews and Benjamin 1993: 104) that the reference to shaving the 'hair of the feet' (i.e. genitalia) (v. 20) is a euphemism for castration. There is irony in the suggestion that Assyria, traditionally hired as Ahaz's protector (2 Kings 16:7) should treat its dependant thus. vv. 21–2 offer the possibility of reading either a threat or a promise; 'curds and honey' reflects back to the similar ambiguity of v. 15, and the remnant theme could be either hopeful or threatening. But there is no ambiguity in vv. 23–5: general dereliction is inevitable. We are reminded of the 'briers and thorns' of 5:6, and recognize that the passage offers its fullest sense in the context of the devastation of the exile.

(8:1–4) We revert here to the first-person material, found in ch. 6 but not in 7. The general sense of the requirement here is clear, though the detail is obscure. The expression translated 'in common characters' is literally 'with the pen of a man' (thus AV, RV). It may imply ordinary human writing, or a very slight emendation would give 'unerasable writing' (*DCH* 344). Of the two cited as witnesses Uriah is mentioned also in 2 Kings 16:10, Zechariah is more confusing. The same parentage is attributed to the prophet Zechariah (1:1, 7) and to the Zechariah referred to in the NT as an innocent martyr (Mt 23:35). The present passage may be the historical original, or itself part of the literary development. vv. 3–4 show striking similarities with 7:14–15, so much so that it has been argued that this is a variant version of the same story. But the heavily symbolic name given to the unsuspecting child has markedly different overtones: 'the spoil speeds, the prey hastens'.

(8:5–8) What follows is printed in prose in NRSV but as poetry in REB and some other translations. This has two implications. We are reminded of the uncertainty of our criteria for determining poetry. Perhaps more important, our approach may be different; we expect factual information from prose, whereas poetry is recognized as allusive and opaque. This passage starts with the idea of rejection, though it is not made clear in what sense the people have rejected Shiloah, the local Jerusalem stream. But 'melt in fear' depends on an emendation of the Hebrew text, which has 'rejoice in' (so RSV; NRSV rather disingenuously has 'Meaning of Hebrew uncertain'). Perhaps the condemnation is of those in Jerusalem (dismissively 'this people') who believe that political solutions of their problems are feasible. But with v. 7 we find the contrast between the gentle stream and God's judgement pictured as a mighty river, destroying all before it. The metaphor becomes a mixed one as the river turns into a bird with wings, and the section ends with a puzzling reference to Immanuel. Whatever its original force the term here has connotations of judgement.

(8:9–15) vv. 9–10 (poetry in NRSV as well as in other versions) scarcely fit the context; they are an oracle of judgement warning all those who conspire against the community that the presence of Immanuel ('God is with us') will overthrow their plans. vv. 11–15, the theme of conspiracy is taken further, but this time it is addressed against the community itself (or at least some element within it). Though there are details in the passage which are obscure, the general thrust is clear. Political solutions to the community's problems are no solutions; they are to trust in YHWH. 'Let him be your fear, and let him be your dread.'

(8:16–18) These verses have played an important part in shaping theories about the composition of Isaiah; indeed they have been required to bear more weight than they can legitimately stand. They have been read as requiring the 'sealing' of the prophet's words among his disciples, with the implication that they were to guard them and in due course publish them. Isaiah himself, it is argued, withdrew from public ministry, committing his testimony to his followers. Even where so sweeping a conclusion as this has been avoided, it has still been customary to see here the end of the supposed autobiographical *Denkschrift* which extended from 6:1. Such interpretations seem to read too much into the

material. In the context of claims to political solutions to the community's problems the Isaiah tradition is maintaining that the prophetic testimony and teaching (*tôrâ*) will in God's good time be seen as offering the true solution to problems, even if it is necessary to wait for and hope in the Lord, whose presence seems to be hidden. This theme of the hiddenness of God as compatible with saving power will be taken further at 45:15, but remains a problem for the faithful community throughout the book (64:5). Meanwhile, both the prophet himself and the children who have been referred to (Shearjashub; Maher-shalal-hash-baz; perhaps also Immanuel) are clear signs that God's presence remains in Jerusalem. This fairly standard religious message may be less exciting than the elaborate compositional theories, but seems better to express what is actually said. It also fits the context of the following verses better; there is no need to take 8:18 as a major closure.

(8:19–22) This passage serves as a kind of appendix to the main unit just completed, expressing in new language the familiar Isaianic theme of the right resources to use to ensure God's favour. Ruled out here is any kind of necromancy, magical practices which claimed that the dead could somehow give them solutions to the uncertainties of life. The last part of v. 19 can be seen as a continuing search by the people for answers by turning to false gods, or it may be part of the answer, in which case we should read 'God' for 'gods'. However that may be it is clear that the answer is found in v. 21: it is in the *tôrâ* and the instruction of the prophetic tradition (cf. v. 16) that God's will can be found. An awkward transition leads into a warning: nowhere else can deliverance be found. The climax of the threat, in v. 22*b*, is very similar to that already expressed in 5:30.

(9:1) is 8:23 in the Hebrew; the natural division comes within this verse. Its first part (down to 'anguish') relates to the threat that has preceded. But the difficulty with this verse is in what follows. Some contrast is clearly implied between 'former' and 'latter' time. One understanding that has been very influential (Alt 1953) is that this was an introduction to the poetry that follows. Where once Zebulun and Naphtali, in the north of Israel, had been oppressed, soon there would be a glorious deliverance. Whether so precise a historical reconstruction is feasible must remain doubtful (Kaiser 1983). Part of the problem arises from the fact that the two verbs ('brought into contempt', 'will make glorious') could be understood quite differently, because the basic meaning of the second verb (*k-b-d*) is to 'make heavy', and so it would be possible to read this verse as saying that the burden already imposed on the far north will become even heavier as it spreads south, into the 'way of the Sea', Transjordan, and Galilee. These names may be those of Assyrian provincial districts. If that reading is right the transformation from threat to glorious promise does not begin until v. 2.

(9:2–7) How much of this Psalm-like poem refers to earlier passages must remain doubtful. Are the 'people who walked in darkness' those described in 9:1? Does the child bear any relation to the one mentioned in 7:14? What is certain is that this is a psalm of thanksgiving, closely comparable to such a poem as Ps 2. v. 2, 'deep darkness'; the Hebrew word(s) *ṣal māwet* are the same as are found in Ps 23 and traditionally translated 'shadow of death'. 'Death' should probably not be taken literally, the expression is a kind of superlative, meaning 'deepest shadow'. v. 3, this is one of the most famous 'mistranslations' of the older versions, which introduced a misleading negative: 'and not increased the joy'. This nonsensical reading can still commonly be heard in Christmas services, though all later translations, such as NRSV, have followed the alternative form of Hebrew which is literally 'increased joy to it'. A successful harvest and the time of dividing the spoil after a battle had been won were the traditional times of rejoicing.

vv. 4–5 are printed as poetry but may rather be a prosaic addition, linking the scenes of joy in the poem with comparable occasions from the people's history. 'The day of Midian' is most probably a reference to the story of Gideon in Judg 6–8, a rare example for Isaiah of such a cross-reference. Though the joy has been compared to the gaining of booty, this verse somewhat illogically looks for an end to any such fighting in the future.

v. 6, here is the climax of the Psalm. If, as is quite likely, God is the speaker, then what seems like an announcement of a birth may more properly be understood as a coronation or enthronement of an earthly king (cf. Ps 2:7), where the king is proclaimed as God's son. What follows is a series of titles, possibly comparable to the titles given to Egyptian pharaohs (von Rad 1966a). Four throne-names are given to the newly crowned ruler: 'Wonderful Counsellor' speaks of the potential achievements of the king: the word translated 'wonderful' comes from the same root as that regularly used of God's mighty deliverance at the Exodus. 'Mighty God' may imply divine kingship, for which there is some evidence in ancient Israel (cf. Ps 45:6), or 'God' here may be a kind of superlative: 'Divine Warrior'. 'Everlasting Father' brings out the theme of the king as protector, 'father', of his people; and 'Prince of Peace' implies both freedom from war and the prosperity implicit in šālôm. In traditional Judaism, these oracles were applied to Hezekiah, around whom an elaborate series of legends developed. In Christianity, the belief of the early followers of Jesus concerning his status made it natural for these words to be applied to him also, though NT allusions are only implicit (Jacob 1987: 141).

v. 7, the Egyptian titles comparable to this were usually fivefold, and the unusual form of the Hebrew words at the beginning of this verse has led some scholars to suppose that there are traces of a fifth title here, which has been lost either accidentally or through deliberate rearrangement. In any case the Davidic link, hitherto implicit, is now brought out clearly. There are close links with 2 Sam 7, emphasizing the permanence of the covenant with David's house and with Ps 72:1, where justice and righteousness are stressed as royal qualities. The last phrase in the verse is found again at 37:32, surely a deliberate cross-reference emphasizing the certainty of God's protection of his chosen ones against enemy assault.

(9:8–12) The tone changes dramatically as we return to a passage of threat similar to those found in ch. 5; indeed, it has often been held that 6:1–9:7 is to be seen as an insertion into a series of threats. The refrain at v. 12 has already occurred at 5:25. This section seems to use the fate of the northern kingdom of Israel as an awful warning to the south. It looks as if the basic poetry of the oracle, which could apply to a variety of situations, has been made more explicit by a number of specific additions, referring to the north ('Ephraim and the inhabitants of Samaria') as the victims and the Arameans and Philistines as the attackers. At a later stage a redactor has linked this with the preceding passage by referring to the enemies of Rezin of Damascus, but NRSV dismisses this part of the text to the margin.

(9:13–17) Another oracle, closely related to what has preceded, sets out one view of the reasons for disaster. The people did not 'turn' (the same root šûb, as is used of the child Shear-jashub, 7:3) and therefore the whole structure of society was at risk. A particular concern was the danger from prophets; with conflicting messages, all claiming prophetic inspiration, whom was one to believe? The hostile way in which prophets are referred to here (and cf. 28:7) must make it questionable whether the individual Isaiah was himself a prophet. Would he have spoken so slightingly of a group to which he himself belonged? Perhaps it was only later, possibly Deuteronomistic, shaping which brought all the great figures together under the heading 'prophets' (Carroll 1992: 90–1).

(9:18–21) The briers and thorns, so frequent as an Isaianic image of desolation, are recalled here, though this time they are themselves consumed rather than symbolizing the destruction of others. v. 21 might refer to some specific historical event in the former northern kingdom, but seems more likely to be a general picture of the kind of anarchy portrayed throughout this section.

(10:1–4) This section functions as a bridge between the series of passages ending with the same refrain (here in v. 4), and the attack on Assyria, with which it shares an introduction (NRSV, rather blandly, 'Ah'). As so often in these early chapters of the book, it is the deprivation of justice and of mišpāṭ (here 'right') that is the main gravamen of the prophetic condemnation.

(10:5–11) A new section, which stretches throughout the chapter, is here introduced. All the major prophetic books are concerned not only with Israel but also with the surrounding nations, and Isaiah is no exception. The book is anxious to establish the point that the downfall of Israel and Judah does not thereby validate Assyrian or Babylonian claims. They are no more than the rod used by YHWH in his anger. Whereas other prophets, such as Amos, referred in general terms to the inevitability of destruction, Isaiah is quite specific in its reference to Assyria. vv. 5–7 bring out the double point that Israel fully deserved her punishment as a godless nation, and that this was inflicted by Assyria as God's own instrument. The 'spoil' and 'plunder' of v. 6 remind us of the child Maher-shalal-hash-baz in 8:1–4, where the same words are used. But from v. 8 the fairly standard form of invective takes a new direction. This is not just another attack on YHWH's own people; instead it is the Assyrian who is to be condemned out of his own mouth. vv. 8–11 picture the Assyrian plans to 'cut off nations not a few', and a list is provided climaxing in Samaria and Jerusalem, yet with the Assyrians themselves imagining that the nations they have already conquered (Calno, Carchemish, and the rest, all cities in northern Syria) are more significant than Samaria and Jerusalem. This type of comparison is an important theme in the Isaiah tradition, with its great esteem for Jerusalem; it will recur again in another 'Assyrian' speech at 37:15. In effect a double charge is aimed against the Assyrians. Their boasting is what the

Greeks would call hubris, a falsely based pride in one's own capacity. To it is added blasphemy, the supposition that Jerusalem has nothing more than idols. (Unless, of course, this is to be seen as an Isaianic dig against false worship in Jerusalem.)

(10:12–15) The two speeches by the Assyrian are linked by v. 12, which serves to remind the reader that there is a deeper purpose underlying the devastation which Jerusalem has undergone. The claim in vv. 13–14 is close to the claims actually made in Assyrian victory-inscriptions; it is turned upsidedown by the saying in v. 15, a close parallel to which, in both form and substance, is found in a widespread collection of wisdom-sayings known as the sayings of Ahiqar, warning against the danger involved in human pride (*ANET* 429a). Though the Assyrian reference is not lost, the next section develops it in different ways. A continuation of the present theme is found in 14:24–7.

(10:16–19) In its present context this threat, introduced by the characteristic 'therefore', has to be understood as directed against Assyria. But there is little specific to Assyria in it, and it may have have originated as another of Isaiah's many threats against Judah, and been transformed at a later stage (Eissfeldt 1965: 312). Alternatively, the sheer scope of destruction here gives the passage an eschatological dimension which some will see as a late development within the tradition. There is clearly little room for hope in the picture of a remnant with which the passage ends.

(10:20–3) But as we have already seen the notion of a remnant can be interpreted in more than one way, and this passage provides the classic example of such a double reading. In 20–1 there is clearly a note of hope, and the passage is linked in a way that is not immediately obvious from the English translation to the hopes expressed in the Immanuel section. 'A remnant will return' is Shear-jashub, as in 7:3; 'the mighty God' is El Gibbor, one of the titles given to the newly crowned king in 9:6. Historical-critical interpreters have been very aware of the tension between the two parts of this passage, the hope of 20–1 being directly followed by the dire threat of 22–3, and have felt it necessary to dismiss one part (usually the first) as a late, secondary addition. But a reading of the book as a whole may not be so disconcerted by this tension. A remnant could imply both destruction and a hope beyond that destruction; this was an important message for the Second Temple community.

(10:24–7a) This prose passage links back both to the Assyrian theme of 10:5–15 and to 9:2–7, with its reference to Midian and the throwing off of the yoke (cf. 9:4). The introductory 'therefore' on this occasion does not herald a threat; rather the people are told not to be afraid. The Hebrew phrase is identical with that used to Ahaz in 7:4 (who rejected the opportunity) and to Hezekiah in 37:6 (who will be more responsive). We find a reminder of the deliverance at the Exodus (a rare allusion in the early chapters of Isaiah) as a paradigm for what the community can expect when present, temporary afflictions are past.

(10:27b–32) v. 27 is very difficult to follow in the Hebrew, and the division proposed by NRSV offers as likely a solution as any. It takes the first part as the conclusion of the preceding prose, the last phrase as an introduction to the following poem, though the reference to Rimmon is entirely conjectural. The poem is a vivid account of the supposed progress of an army attacking Judah from the north; how the foe 'from the north' of Jer 4 and elsewhere might actually manifest itself. It would be unwise to base military strategy on such a list of names, some of which are chosen for their sound and opportunities for word-play rather than their strategic significance. For this reason the discussions in some commentaries as to whose campaign is here described should be treated with scepticism. The shaking of the aggressor's fist (v. 32) is, perhaps deliberately, ambiguous. It is certainly a threat, but may also be understood as a gesture of frustration because of inability to capture the holy city.

(10:33–4) Many passages in Isaiah depend for their understanding upon the context in which they are found, and this is one such. Placed elsewhere it could readily have been understood as a condemnation of the community's own leaders with their arrogant pretensions (cf. 2:13, where this same comparison with trees is made, the word there translated 'lofty' being here rendered 'tallest'). Following the account of an enemy army it is much more natural to read it as a warning to that enemy, that its failure was determined. It will be disturbing for ecologists to find this destruction of trees attributed to God's own action.

(11:1–9) A third passage, following 7:14 and 9:2–7, which has been interpreted messianically, and which certainly speaks of aspirations for the future of the Davidic line. We know little of such aspirations in the Second Temple period, but this passage seems to come from that time, with its reference to the cut-down stump of Jesse most likely implying the end of the monarchy in 587 BCE. In any case the poem as a whole draws out the ideal characteristics to be envisaged in a royal figure. vv. 1–3a, as indicated the most natural reading of the 'shoot from the stump' is that the Davidic line had been cut down, presumably at the exile, but that some among the community were convinced that that was not the end of the story. The child to be born would be imbued with God's spirit, as was David himself in 1 Sam 16:13. The Christian tradition has spoken of 'sevenfold gifts of the Spirit' and used vv. 2–3a as a basis, but only six gifts are in fact mentioned here. They are the characteristic charismatic qualities of the king, and of all those pictured as being especially close to YHWH (e.g. Moses and the elders, Num 11:25–30; Elijah and Elisha, 2 Kings 2:15). There are also close links with the wisdom tradition, shown not only by the use of the word 'wisdom' itself but also by 'understanding', 'counsel', and 'fear of the LORD'—all terms particularly associated with, for example, Proverbs. But here they are God's direct gift, not dependent on the skills of human counsellors. vv. 3b–5, what is meant by being endowed with the divine spirit is then spelt out. As often in Isaiah there are close links with the royal Psalms. The stress on just judgement, with particular concern for the poor and meek, and the display of ṣedeq (righteousness) and ĕmûnâ (faithfulness) are characteristic both of the Isaiah tradition and of such a Psalm as 72:12–14. In v. 4 a very minor emendation, adopted by REB but not NRSV, would give 'smite the ruthless (ʿārîṣ)' for 'strike the earth (ʾereṣ)', and this would both improve the parallelism (with 'kill the wicked') and give better general sense. vv. 6–9, but the just rule of YHWH goes further than the establishment of true Davidic rule in Jerusalem. There follows an eschatological picture, looking forward to a restoration of paradise conditions in which the primeval way of life would be restored. There are important links here with 65:25, showing how these aspirations draw the whole book together. The ancient Israelites come down to us in their writings as pretty hard-headed people, but such passages as this show that they had the capacity to dream of a better world, and this capacity is particularly illustrated by the prophets. In addition to various passages in Isaiah, Hos 2:18 and Am 9:13 breathe something of the same spirit. Murray (1992: 103–14) offers a sensitive spelling out of the implications of this passage, both in its larger biblical context and in terms of human duties towards animals. He notes the link with the creation stories of Genesis provided by the vegetarian habits of the lion (v. 7), and the way in which the passage brings out both peace *from* the threat of wild animals and the prospect of living at peace *with* animals.

(11:10) 'On that day' language is again used, but now in a hopeful sense. The 'root of Jesse' figure, thought of in vv. 1–9 as imminent, will be part of the manifestation of the great day of YHWH.

(11:11–16) This passage displays close links with chs. 40–55, with the raising of a signal to the nations (cf. 49:22 and also 5:25) and the more general theme of the gathering of dispersed exiles (Williamson 1994). The reference to the 'coastlands' and the expression 'outcasts of Israel' are also reminiscent of the later chapters of the book. Here exile is no longer a threat but a reality, and it can be seen as a prelude to future promise of restoration. As in Ezek 37, part of the promise for the future is the removal of hostility between north (Ephraim) and south (Judah). The theme of a highway linking the lands where the people had been scattered is an important one throughout Isaiah (cf. 19:23; 49:11), and is a valuable illustration, not only of the unity of the whole book, but also of the way in which what had once been a threat—a means of deportation—can be transformed into a promise of peace between formerly rival nations. The word here used for a 'highway', *měsillâ*, is especially used of religious, processional ways.

(Ch. 12) This brief chapter consists of one, or possibly two, short psalms which round off the first part of the book. Much of the language used is that typical of the Psalms, with their emphasis on giving thanks to and praising God. But v. 2 deserves special attention for its similarity to Ex 15:2, the Song of the Sea. Just as that poem rounded off the account of God's salvation of his people at the Exodus, so here the first part of the story is rounded off. And the word 'salvation' (*yěšûʿâ*) is striking, because of its close similarity to the name Isaiah (*yěšaʿyāhû*). The words of Isaiah are potentially words of salvation. (Ackroyd 1987: 94–7, rightly characterizes this as part of the 'portrait of a prophet.') In addition some have seen links with the royal material earlier in these chapters by claiming this section as part of an enthronement ceremony. However that may be, the links between prophetism and the cult, once thought of as bitterly opposed, are clearly brought out.

(Chs. 13–26) The theme of YHWH's dealings with his own people, in terms both of punishment and of salvation, is now

set aside, and a fresh section dealing with other nations begins with the formal introduction in 13:1. Each of the major prophetic collections in the HB has a group of 'Oracles against Foreign Nations', traditionally the most neglected part of those collections. To some extent this neglect is understandable—not everyone will want to explore the history of Moab in the eighth century BCE—but it has unfortunate consequences. It overlooks what must have been perceived as an important element in the prophetic vocation, most clearly expressed in Jeremiah when he was appointed a 'prophet to the nations' (Jer 1:5), and it also fails to recognize that these oracles contain major themes (not always very palatable ones) in the understanding of God and his relation not only to Israel, but to the world beyond the nation's boundaries. The origin of such passages may lie in ritual curses against enemies in times of war, but that context has been largely overlaid, and the oracles against the nations now fulfil a predominantly literary function. (Davies 1989 offers a useful discussion of these oracles, considering their place within Isaiah and their larger significance.)

(13:1) This formal introduction, though it might refer only to chs. 13–14, is almost certainly intended to relate to the whole section to ch. 23. It is described as an oracle (*maśśāʾ*), a term used several times in these chapters to introduce passages relating to the different nations (e.g. 15:1; 17:1). It is striking that this first and much the longest passage relates to Babylon. Some have maintained that material originally relating to Assyria has been reapplied to Babylon, for in the eighth century Babylon was a potential ally rather than a threat, and it was only later that it became the great enemy. But if literary rather than historical considerations are introduced the significance of this title within the book as a whole becomes apparent; in chs. 40–55, the climax of the book, Babylon was indeed the great enemy, and here we are being introduced to that point in the very beginning of the material dealing with foreign nations. It is striking also that Babylon seems already to have been taking on symbolic significance as the representative enemy, in a way that Nineveh, the Assyrian capital, did not, except in Jonah.

(13:2–22) There seems to be nothing specific to Babylon in the opening section, vv. 2–5, or indeed through much of this chapter. There are numerous similarities between this section and Jer 50–1, and it has been suggested that each of these sections functions as a general expression of divine judgement alongside the more specific accompanying oracles against particular nations (Vermeylen 1989: 31–2). This might help to explain the relation between this general passage and the more specific oracle concerning Babylon in ch. 21. The point is stressed that war is inevitable, and that God himself is involved. The picture of universal destruction is that associated with the apocalypses, and many have therefore argued that this is a very late passage, from the time when apocalyptic language was becoming widespread. Certainly this passage is not concerned with any empirical Babylon; it has become the symbol of human pride and imperialism (Gosse 1988: 167). The passage reaches its climax with the destruction of 'the whole earth'. vv. 6–16, the nature of the destruction is now spelt out in greater detail. First, it is associated with the 'day of the LORD', a theme already often found in chs. 2–11. The form of words seems to have been widely used, for the same expression is found at Joel 1:15 and (partially) at Ezek 30:3 and Zeph 1:7. A rich variety of expressions is then used to describe the destruction regarded as inevitable; it would be rash indeed to try to tie them to any specific historical circumstances. At the end of this section we come across a ghastly image familiar from another part of the Bible: the 'dashing in pieces' of the infants (v. 16) is reminiscent of Ps 137:9: different verb, same appalling sentiments.

vv. 17–22, this last part of the chapter contains expressions making the reference to Babylon more specific. The Medes played an important part in the overthrow of the Assyrian Empire in the late seventh century BCE and were a powerful force in warfare and politics until the rise of Cyrus c.550 BCE. At some point in the Isaiah tradition it was envisaged that the Medes would be more important in the overthrow of Babylon than in fact proved to be the case. The legend of 'Darius the Mede' as victorious over Babylon in Dan 5:31 may owe its origin to this passage. It is possible that the references in the later part of the book of Isaiah to things prophesied in 'former times' and 'long ago' are to passages of this kind (North 1964: 161, makes this suggestion with regard to Isa 45:21). The dramatic tension of the book is increased by the likening of Babylon's fate to that of Sodom and Gomorrah. Previously (1:9–10) it was Jerusalem that had been compared with Sodom and Gomorrah; now that fate, symbolic of total destruction, is transferred to Babylon, as the implications of God's 'day' are more widely realized. Babylon did eventually become desolate, but not until much later than any possible dating for Isaiah. During much of the Second Temple period it remained an important, though no longer a capital, city. The imagery of vv. 20–2 should be recognized as such, without any attempt to relate it to historical developments.

(14:1–2) A prose passage takes the opportunity to give encouragement to Israel by contrasting its fate with that just described as awaiting Babylon. This is a passage comparable to the more nationalistic sections of chs. 40–55 (e.g. 49:22–6), which gloat over the expected doom of the oppressors.

(14:3–4a) Still in prose, this section invites Israel to take up a māšāl (taunt) against Babylon, and more specifically its king. A māšāl is a poem setting out 'some form of retribution which will make the person concerned an object-lesson in the abuse of power' (A. R. Johnson 1955: 166). It is basically a prophetic form, warning of the inevitability of disaster; only by concentrating on the effect rather than the purpose can it legitimately be described as a taunt. The basic theme in the poem which follows is a common one, both in the HB and in the ancient world more generally: the attempt of a human being, often as here an enemy king, to make himself like God, and the inevitable fate which attends such presumption. Ezek 28 and 31 are variants on the same theme, found also in prose form in the story of Nebuchadnezzar's madness in Dan 4. It has sometimes been suggested that a similar theme underlies the Garden of Eden story in Gen 3.

(14:4b–21) The word 'insolence' provides a good example of the way in which the Dead Sea scrolls have helped in the interpretation of Isaiah. The Hebrew text gives no clear meaning, and older English versions had 'golden city' here. But a slight change, already suggested by some scholars and sup-

ported by the Dead Sea scrolls, offers an excellent parallel. In the following description of the fate which awaits the fallen ruler it would be unwise to try to offer any link with particular individuals; this is what is in store for all who make such arrogant claims. Sheol (v. 9) is the place of the dead. It is not in itself a place of punishment, though it is striking that in the HB it is most commonly those who are disapproved of who are described as coming to Sheol (Barr 1992: 29). Here all earthly distinctions are ironed out. Part of the taunt is that the rĕpaʿîm, the 'shades', can treat the king of Babylon as on a level with themselves. The inhabitants of Sheol are clearly not extinct; they are fully conscious of what is happening and are able to taunt the fallen king.

v. 12 has played an important part in the history of interpretation, being understood as an illustration of the theme of Lucifer, the fallen angel. (The theme actually owes more to the influence of Milton's *Paradise Lost* than to any direct biblical references.) The whole passage, vv. 12–21, has a widespread mythological background, reflecting stories about Venus, the 'day-star', visible just before dawn, and driven away by the power of the rising sun. The 'heights of Zaphon' is the holy mountain mentioned also in the Ugaritic texts as the assembling-place of the gods. In Ps 48:2 the same words are used to identify Mount Zion as the true divine dwelling-place. The 'Most High' of v. 14 is ʿelyôn, a divine title also claimed by the HB as appropriate for YHWH (Gen 14:18; Ps 91:1). These pretensions are then contrasted with the certain fate of Babylon, which will not even be granted proper burial-rites (v. 20), a matter of very deep concern in the ancient world.

(14:22–3) This brief prose note is usually taken with what precedes, underlining the point that the poem has been addressed to Babylon. It is possible, however, that it is placed here as a deliberate link between the known fate of Assyria, the subject of the following verses, and the still future threat against Babylon (Clements 1989).

(14:24–7) Assyria is now mentioned, though the bulk of this extended section has related to Babylon. Assyrian power will be broken: v. 25b has a clear allusion to the breaking of the yoke from the shoulders as in 9:4 and 10:27. But 'all the nations' (v. 26) are under threat. The picture is of the prophet 'overhearing' what YHWH has decreed. This is one of a number of passages which have been described as 'summary-appraisals' (Childs 1967), offering an outline, in didactic fashion, of YHWH's intended purpose ('This is the plan . . .').

(14:28) The reference to the death of Ahaz (which should be retained in the text, despite the proposals of many scholars to emend it) is reminiscent of that to the death of Uzziah in 6:1. The date of Ahaz's death is unknown, but it may be significant that he was succeeded by Hezekiah, in whom such great hopes were placed. It is not easy to see any link between the maśśāʾ (oracle) announced here and the passage which follows.

(14:29–32) The Philistines were ancient enemies of Israel from the time of Saul and David, but little is known of their later history. Here an unknown occasion of rejoicing is said to be only transitory; worse troubles will come, and Judah should avoid becoming entangled with the Philistines. v. 32 looks like a later addition, stressing in psalm-like fashion the inviolability of Zion as a sure refuge (cf. Ps 132:13–15).

(15:1–16:12) These two chapters are directed against Moab, Judah's neighbour east of the Dead Sea, and they pose problems for the interpreter of Isaiah because much of the material in them is found again, with minor variations, in the comparable oracles against foreign nations in Jeremiah: specifically Jer 48. It raises the question of whether much material of this kind was used as required in the Jerusalem cult and could be taken up into different prophetic collections as 'independent adaptation of traditional material' (Jenkins 1989). Much of it reads like a gazetteer of contemporary Moab, but many of the place-names are chosen to bring out specific wordplays. Many of the places referred to are of uncertain location; those seeking more precise details must refer to the larger commentaries (Wildberger 1978: 604 ff.). In comparison with the gloating over the anticipated fate of Babylon in 13–14 here a note of sympathy can be found (15:5; 16:11), alongside a recognition that even worse disasters may be anticipated (15:9). The most striking section in the passage is one which has no parallel in Jeremiah: another messianic passage (16:4b–5) looking forward to a time when devastation will have ceased and a ruler concerned with mišpāṭ (justice) and ṣedeq (right), those two key Isaianic terms, will rule 'in the tent of David', an expression without exact parallel elsewhere in Isaiah. Moab's worship is condemned (16:12), but less harshly than the false worship of Israel itself (1:12–17).

(16:13–14) This postscript to the Moab oracles illustrates the development of the tradition. Earlier material was indeed valid, but in a later situation a further devastation of Moab could be anticipated. We have no means of precise dating: we do not know to what the 'three years' refers, though this could be an adannu of the kind we noted as a possibility for 7:8. The same phrase, referring to 'the years of a hired worker' is found in a similar context at 21:16.

(17:1–3) The introductory maśśā' refers only to Damascus, but the following threat takes in the area of northern Israel also; we are back in the hostilities typified by the Syro-Ephraimite conflict of ch. 7. Indeed if the Hebrew is followed there is a link also with Moab, but 'Aroer' in v. 2, a place in Moab, is usually emended, as by NRSV. It is not clear why some of Israel's neighbours are referred to by the country's name (e.g. Moab), whereas for others the capital is seen as personifying the country (as here, Damascus, the capital of the Aramean kingdom). Damascus fell to the Assyrians in 732 BCE, and many commentators see in this oracle a genuine survival from the eighth century. But Kaiser (1974) points out that it was equally applicable to the condition of Damascus in the fourth century; possibly an earlier nucleus has been reapplied and expanded. The difficult phrase in v. 3 may be intended ironically; the Arameans will be reduced to a remnant (and here surely the theme implies a threat) comparable to the once glorious northern kingdom of Israel.

(17:4–11) There is no further reference to Damascus; instead, the theme of 'that day' is reintroduced, linked with what precedes by the reference to 'glory'. There will be a rich harvest, but the people are at risk of not benefiting from it. The 'Valley of Rephaim' is known from 2 Sam 5:18 as a place near Jerusalem, but the name may be deliberately chosen here: rĕpaim is the word translated 'shades' in 14:9, and it may be implied that the people will be no better off than the shades. Deut 24:19–20 paints a beautifully generous picture of harvest and gleaning, with the alien, the orphan, and the widow allowed to join in; one may doubt whether such idealism normally prevailed. A further 'in that day' passage, this time in prose, brings out the theme of idolatry, with the hope that in due course the attractions of rival worship will be set aside. The terms used are all part of the standard vocabulary for attacks upon false worship. The 'sacred poles', Heb. ăšērîm, will have been wooden representations of the goddess Asherah. In v. 9 the Hebrew text is very uncertain, as can be seen by comparing the text of NRSV with the footnote. NRSV follows the Greek, which may itself have been trying to make sense of a difficult form. However that may be, the section ends by recalling once again the twin themes of a harvest which cannot be shared and of idolatrous worship.

(17:12–14) A fresh oracle on a new theme. The repetition of the last part of 12 at the beginning of 13 may be for emphasis, but is more likely to be an erroneous repetition, and some translations (e.g. REB) omit it. This is a vision of an eschatological battle, comparable to that fought against Gog of Magog in Ezek 38–9, with emphasis on the inviolability of Zion. The passage ends with another summary-appraisal of the type already noted in 14:26. It rounds off the section dealing with Israel's neighbours with an assurance that God would protect his people against those who had plundered them.

(Ch. 18) This chapter lacks the usual introduction, but its application soon becomes clear. Ethiopian dynasties ruled in Egypt from time to time, and this passage concerns them. It is highly artificial: the messengers are apparently from the Ethiopians themselves, but it is odd to describe a people to their own messengers, and no indication is given of the contents of the message or of how it might be answered. Ethiopia was a symbol of distance and strangeness (Am 9:7), and that may well be part of the point here. The passage quickly becomes an oracle of judgement, threatening destruction on a scale usually reserved for the Babylonians and Assyrians. But the chapter ends with a prose addition, picturing the distant Ethiopians acknowledging the supremacy of YHWH on Zion. This theme is found several times in the prophets; we may compare Zech 8:23, and the more specific application to Egypt in Zeph 3:10 and Zech 14:18, and also Ps 68:31. The bringing of gifts from afar is also reminiscent of Isa 60:5–7. During the Second Temple period we know of links between the Jerusalem community and the Jewish colony at Elephantine on the Nile—such links may underlie passages such as this and the others noted.

(Ch. 19) contains some of the most remarkable and neglected material in the whole book of Isaiah. It well illustrates the development of the tradition, from the essentially negative picture found in the opening verses to a remarkably positive assertion concerning both Egypt and Assyria in the conclusion.

(19:1–4) There is no hint of any positive development in this opening oracle. Egypt's idolatrous practice is condemned in terms very similar to those used against Israel (8:19). The Egyptians were famous for their skill in wisdom and counsel; here by contrast they are reduced to internal division and desperate measures to find out what action to take. The 'hard master' and 'fierce king' of v. 4 may well be a reference to the protracted claims to rule over Egypt by the Persian rulers. A striking omission throughout this section is of any reference to the Exodus tradition. As we have seen (e.g. 4:5; 12:2) this was not totally ignored in the first part of Isaiah, but it is not as prominent as it becomes in the latter part of the book, and here, where allusions might have been expected, there appears to be nothing of the kind.

(19:5–15) vv. 5–10 are much more specific than other passages depicting future desolation. Here the applicability of the threats to the civilization which was so heavily dependent upon the Nile for many aspects of its life is abundantly clear. The Nile would dry up, and daily life would be thrown into chaos. The implication is certainly that YHWH was regarded as the effective ruler of Egypt; the Egyptian gods themselves were envisaged as powerless to maintain the life of their own country. vv. 11–15, again a very specific application to Egyptian tradition is found. The 'princes' referred to here are pictured as a kind of cabinet of expert counsellors who could provide the Pharaoh with the appropriate answers to all the problems which confronted him. Despite their hereditary background and their training in wisdom techniques they are reduced to being no more than fools. Egyptian wisdom was famous and elsewhere in the HB is treated in a neutral way; here it is mocked as quite incapable of guiding those who trusted in it. In v. 15 the reference to head and tail, palm-branch and reed is a—surely deliberate—allusion to 9:14, where the same expressions are used in describing the downfall of Israel.

(19:16–25) Five short prose passages are appended, each headed 'On that day' but differing markedly from one another in content and tone. We have not attempted in this commentary to offer precise dates for most of the passages discussed, but it is striking that many commentators have seen here some of the latest material to be added to the whole book, perhaps reflecting the political situation of the Ptolemies and Seleucids of the third century BCE, after the conquests of Alexander the Great.

vv. 16–17, the theme here is fear. Whereas Israel is often encouraged not to fear, the warning is given that Egypt will have real cause for fear—even of Judah itself, by comparison apparently so insignificant.

v. 18 presumably refers to the phenomenon of the diaspora, the development whereby increasing numbers of Jews came to be settled in Egypt and other parts of the Mediterranean world. Hebrew is here called 'the language of Canaan', an important corrective to the picture found in Deuteronomy and elsewhere which pictures Israel and Canaan as bitterly opposed entities. Hebrew is a Semitic language, very close to what is known of different Canaanite dialects. There are interesting variants in the name of the city: NRSV 'City of the Sun' is the well-known Egyptian city of Heliopolis. But the Greek translation (LXX), which originated in Egypt, has 'city of righteousness', the name given to Jerusalem (1:26), and many Hebrew MSS have 'city of destruction'! We are warned that the notion of a fixed, unchanging biblical text can be illusory.

vv. 19–22, again a different stress from that characteristic of Deuteronomy is found here. Instead of the single place of sacrificial worship, understood to be the Jerusalem temple, required by the Deuteronomistic tradition, here an altar and a maṣṣēbâ (pillar) in Egypt are treated as positive signs. There was in fact a temple of YHWH at Leontopolis in Egypt in the second century BCE; whether an allusion to that is here intended cannot be certain. Just as in Gen 31:48, 52 (Jacob and Laban), the maṣṣēbă is a 'witness' between two neighbouring and potentially rival communities. Even more remarkable is the promise that a messianic figure, a 'saviour', will be sent, whose mission extends beyond the holy land itself. There are important anticipations of some of the later chapters of the book here. The 'striking' of the Egyptians is a theme already found in the earlier passages; here, however, it is the prelude to 'healing', and we have the picture, hinted at in ch. 18, but now expressed more specifically, of Egyptians turning to the worship of YHWH and being welcomed.

vv. 23–5. These last two passages take that openness even further. In the first, Israel will live at peace with the great powers of the day: Assyria is probably here, as in Jonah, symbolic of the current Mesopotamian great power, or may stand for Syria, if the passage be dated in the Seleucid period (3rd cent.). In the second passage Israel is not only at peace with Egypt and Assyria but is regarded as their equal, and it is stressed that all are part of YHWH's favoured creation. It would be instructive to hear a contemporary exposition of this passage, but at least in the Christian tradition it is curiously neglected by most lectionary schemes.

(Ch. 20) This short prose section differs markedly from what has preceded. The link which presumably accounts for its inclusion at this point is the reference to Egypt and Assyria, but they are mentioned in a spirit very different from that of ch. 19. Commentators concerned with the historical setting of the passage differ sharply in their judgement. For some it is a primary piece of eighth-century material, reflecting a time of rebellion against Assyria when it seemed to be in difficulties elsewhere. The rebellion was brought to an abrupt end when Sargon's tartān (NRSV: 'commander-in-chief') captured Ashdod and so ended any hopes of a successful stand against Assyria by an Egyptian-led coalition. Others note that this historical reference is confined to v. 1 and that the main thrust of the episode is what can be described as the development of an Isaiah legend, the story of the prophet specially attuned to the divine will and able to interpret the signs of the times. It is noteworthy that there is no first-person material here; like ch. 7 it is a story about Isaiah rather than one directly attributed to him. As we saw in the introduction there are many fewer stories about Isaiah than about Jeremiah.

The 'sackcloth' of v. 2 appears to be characteristic prophetic clothing; this is the nearest we come to a portrait of Isaiah as a professional prophet. We need not suppose that he was literally naked; the removal of his outer garments, symbolic of his office, was sufficiently shameful for the 'sign and portent' to make their point (cf. Mic 1:8, though there in a poetic context it is difficult to know how literally the words are to be understood). The action is best seen in the context of the other symbolic actions in Isaiah, such as the naming of children. It is certainly not to be understood simply as a kind of 'teaching aid'; the sign is set out as an effective prefiguring of action which is determined by God. It is noteworthy, in view of the importance of 'servant' language in the latter part of the book, that Isaiah is here described as 'my servant'. 'Three years' is curious, not least in the way that this period is only mentioned in the subsequent explanation (Stacey 1990: 123–4). There may be a cross-reference here to the 'three years' of 16:14. It is striking, and very unusual, that the passage ends with a question; we are presumably meant to look for at least part of the answer in what follows.

(21:1–10) The reference in the body of this oracle is clearly to Babylon, but that is not indicated by the heading. Once again there are links with Jer 49, suggesting the common use of cultic material. Indeed the problems in making sense of this chapter have led one scholar to describe it as a 'palimpsest', in which 'the text has been reworked in order to make it relevant to a later situation' (Macintosh 1980: 75). Such a theory is difficult either to prove or to disprove; we may simply note that we seem once again to be in the world of 'theological geography'. Like the 'valley of vision' of 22:1, 'the wilderness of the sea' does not appear on any map. The passage is, as v. 2 makes clear, a vision of utter destruction. The prophet speaks in the first person, spelling out the anguish which his vision causes him, in a way without close parallel elsewhere in the book; little attention is normally paid in Isaiah to the psychology of the messenger, though in both Jeremiah and Ezekiel this feature is more prominent. But he has no alternative but to carry out his mission of summoning the nation to their task of destruction. Only in v. 9 is the object of this destruction made clear: Babylon. The proclamation of the fall of Babylon is found also in Jer 51:8, and is picked up in the NT by the seer of Revelation (Rev 14:8; 18:2).

v. 8 is one of several passages in the prophetic books which picture the prophet as a watchman (cf. Ezek 3:17; Hab 2:1), an important office in the ancient world, where the safety of cities might well depend upon the vigilance of their watchmen. The likening of a prophet to a watchman is a revealing one; each had to be able to make sense of and interpret correctly obscure and mysterious signs. NRSV's correction of the Hebrew 'a lion' to 'the watcher' is based on the Qumran scrolls. It is probably correct—the same letters are used but in a different order—though it entails losing a possible cross-reference to 29:1.

(21:11–12) is linked to what precedes by the watchman theme. Dumah is elsewhere linked with the Ishmaelites (Gen 25:14), but here an otherwise unknown association with Edom is supposed—'Seir' is frequently found in poetry for Edom. The message given is extremely cryptic: it looks as if the prophet has no certain answer to give to those who question him; they are to return for further guidance.

(21:13–17) Again it seems doubtful whether 'the desert plain' is an identifiable spot; this is one of the passages which is closely linked with Jeremiah (cf. Jer 49:8). The picture is of the need to give some succour to refugees from disaster, but whether this was a specific historical situation, or a more general plea, we have no means of knowing. The geographical area involved is usually thought to be Arabia, but this may be because of the symbolism involved in its remoteness and the threat implicit in the desert.

(22:1–4) Though included in the series introduced by the word 'oracle' which has mainly been concerned with foreign nations, the 'valley of vision' here must surely be Jerusalem itself. The whole theme of the book relates to the ultimate deliverance of God's people, but that deliverance must not be falsely anticipated by premature rejoicing. There must be destruction before there can be legitimate hope for restoration. (This assumes that NRSV is correct in its reference to the 'exultant town'; other translations, notably the REB, do not find such reference here.) A characteristic Isaian theme is the uselessness of the normal human agencies of self-reliance; the 'rulers' in whom trust might be put had fled ignominiously. There is ambiguity, perhaps deliberate, in the use of personal pronouns here: the 'you'/'your' clearly refers to Jerusalem and its inhabitants, but the 'I' of v. 4 can be understood either of Isaiah or of God himself.

(22:5–8a) Two themes characteristic of Isaiah are brought together here. The 'day of the LORD' may be future, but it can be prefigured by events that have already taken place. Secondly, YHWH is pictured as using foreign armies as the instruments by which he punishes his own people; so it is with two enemies from the East here, 'Elam' and 'Kir'. As elsewhere in these chapters there is evidence that material found also in Jeremiah is used here; cf. Jer 49:34 ff.

(22:8b–11) This prose passage comes somewhat unexpectedly in the middle of the series of poems, and has been much used as a basis for historical information concerning Hezekiah's attempts to render Jerusalem impregnable. The Assyrian king Sennacherib in his Annals referred to Hezekiah strengthening his city, and both 2 Chr 32:2–8 and Sir 48:17 have approving references to such work by Hezekiah. But recent archaeological and literary study has cast doubt on the extent of this work which actually goes back to Hezekiah's time—much may more properly be dated to the Hasmonean period—and these later passages may more probably be seen as part of the development of a Hezekiah legend. There is in any case no reference to Hezekiah in our passage, and the tone is sharply condemnatory as against the praise of Hezekiah in the other passages. Here by contrast we have the familiar Isaian theme of legitimate planning being a divine prerogative; whatever was done by its inhabitants to protect Jerusalem 'on that day' could have no success against God's decisions.

(22:12–14) If there was doubt whether vv. 1–4 referred to the rejoicing of the inhabitants of Jerusalem which the authors of the prophetic book regarded as inappropriate, there can be no such doubts here. v. 13b is quoted in the NT (1 Cor 15:32) and has survived into modern times as a popular proverb; its origin is unknown. It may have been coined by the redactors of Isaiah, or—more probably—already have been in widespread use.

(22:15–25) This passage is unique in Isaiah as a judgement aimed at an individual; Ahaz is treated in a somewhat similar way, but nowhere else is someone not a member of the royal family so addressed. It is also one of the most difficult passages to explain for the view taken in this commentary that in the form we have it Isaiah is essentially a poetic collection from the Second Temple period concerned with God's dealings with king and community. However, we may note first that, though NRSV prints the whole passage as prose many (e.g. REB) regard vv. 15–19 as poetry, and others (e.g. *BHS*) extend the poetic section to the end of v. 23, leaving only

vv. 24–5 as a prose addition. Further, Kaiser has shown that its composition is a good deal more complex than a first glance might lead one to suppose (Kaiser 1974: 149–59); he concludes that we may well see here a trace of the final editor, 'holding up the mirror to a hated contemporary'.

There is no obvious reason offered in vv. 15–19 why Shebna should be so fiercely condemned. To prepare a tomb does not seem to be a particularly heinous offence, and Abraham is praised for such foresight in Gen 23. No doubt the virulent attack is to be seen as part of a larger condemnation of human officials whose pretensions went beyond what the prophetic community regarded as acceptable. The imagery employed, of 'hurling' the victim into another land, is found also in Jer 22:26, where it is applied to the unfortunate king Jehoiachin (Coniah). It is noteworthy that Shebna is not named in the body of this passage (vv. 16–18), and it may be that that should be taken as a more general condemnation of human presumption, as in vv. 11–14, which has been made specific to Shebna for reasons beyond our present knowledge. Shebna is also referred to in 36:3, still in royal service. In the 1950s there was much speculation whether a tomb inscription dating from about the eighth century BCE might have referred to Shebna, but the name was not fully preserved, and this link must remain speculative. It is also possible, though again only a matter for speculation, that important offices in the community were handed down in particular families, and that descendants of Shebna (and perhaps of Eliakim also) were still in positions of power in the Second Temple period. Certainly the nepotism condemned in v. 24 would support such a view. We may compare the Tobiads, whom we met in ch. 7.

In v. 19 YHWH is pictured as speaking in the first person, and this continues in vv. 20–3, concerned with another figure mentioned also in 36:3: Eliakim, who apparently succeeded Shebna as 'master of the household'. It is striking that he is referred to as 'my servant', as if we are being given various inadequate models of the servant of YHWH before the true one is described in chs. 52–3. For inadequate Eliakim is shown to be. The picture in vv. 21–4 is reminiscent of a royal accession, with the theme of the 'key of David' that was picked up by the author of Revelation in the NT (Rev 3:7). But Eliakim is shown to be unable to sustain the burden (v. 25). The limitations of human aspirations are once again set out.

(23:1–12) The composite nature of the material in this chapter is well illustrated by the fact that it refers sometimes to Tyre (vv. 1, 5, 8), sometimes to Sidon (vv. 2, 4, 12). But even those commentators most concerned with detailed historical analysis have recognized the difficulty of teasing out an 'original' nucleus from the present poem which is skilfully constructed and in no sense a mere patchwork. Tyre and Sidon, in the modern Lebanon, were trading ports on the Mediterranean, and here, as in Ezek 26–8, that is the main theme of the prophecy of lament, much of it in the distinctive form of 3 + 2 stresses often found in prophetic laments.

'Ships of Tarshish' are frequently referred to as sea-going vessels; it remains disputed whether the reference is to a kind of ship, or to Tarshish as their characteristic destination. The place-name seems the more natural explanation, but there is a difficulty in that sometimes such ships seem to have reached it in the Mediterranean, as here (and cf. 1 Kings 10:22), some-

times from the Red Sea (e.g. 1 Kings 22:48). In any case the main point here is the widespread nature of the trade engaged in by Tyre and Sidon and the confidence it engendered. Once again it is the 'plan' of YHWH (vv. 8, 9) that will be decisive against all human aspirations.

(23:13) This interesting prose note, comparable to the addition at 7:8b, gives a glimpse of the way in which the redaction of the Isaiah material developed. Assyria had never conquered Tyre; at a later period a member of the tradition was convinced that the destruction implicit in vv. 1–12 would indeed come about, but at the hand of the Chaldeans (Babylonians). In fact, as far as our knowledge goes, the Babylonian siege of Tyre was unsuccessful, and it was not until the campaigns of Alexander the Great that Tyre was captured.

(23:14) v. 1 is repeated, either as an accidental gloss, or—more likely in the context of a reading of the book in its final form—as an indication of the completion of that poem.

(23:15–18) The section is rounded off by further elaborations, mostly in prose, on the theme of 'seventy years', symbolic here as elsewhere in the Bible of a whole lifetime. Some older scholars tried to identify the 70-year period with some specific episodes in history, but that seems to be a false exegetical move: the arrival of a new generation seems to be the point of the usage. When that new generation arrives it will be involved in the service of YHWH, but only in a subsidiary role. The openness of 19:24–5 is scarcely present here.

(Chs. 24–7) These chapters, taken as a unit and often called 'the Isaiah apocalypse', have attracted much attention. They are not introduced by a separate heading, so in the present form of the book they can be taken to continue chs. 13–23, which have themselves not been devoid of features more usually associated with the apocalypses. The earlier chapters were for the most part addressed to specific nations; here their message of doom is universalized. But these chapters have enough distinctive features for it to have been widely supposed that they form a distinct block. Stress has been laid upon their eschatological concerns, their envisaging of the possibility of a future life beyond death, and their extensive use of mythological themes, to claim that the closest links of these chapters are with Daniel (dated in the 2nd cent. BCE) and with the even later apocalypses. Dates ranging from the exile (Millar 1976; D. G. Johnson 1988) down to the second century (Ludwig 1961) have been proposed, with the consensus, in so far as there is one, settling on the fourth or third centuries. Though it may indeed be appropriate to see a certain unity holding these chapters together, we should also note that they contain a variety of forms, which have usually been broken down into two main categories: lyrical, Psalm-like passages primarily addressed to God, and oracles of a prophetic or apocalyptic type concerned with the fate of the community. Another characteristic feature, present to some extent in chs. 13–23 but now carried much further, is the frequency of allusions to and sometimes direct quotations of, other biblical material, both elsewhere in the book of Isaiah and in other books. Sweeney (1988b) lists seven passages which display links with other parts of Isaiah, often being given a different sense from that in their other context, with the emphasis here more universal or even cosmic, while Day (1980) draws attention to strong thematic links between 26:13–27:9 and a passage in Hosea (13:4–14:10), which again illustrates the phenomenon of Scripture interpreting itself. Our attempt to discern overarching structures running through the whole book of Isaiah will gain important insights from these chapters, where several themes touched upon elsewhere are developed more fully.

(24:1–6) The theme of inevitable destruction comes to the fore at once. In chs. 1–12 the basic concern had been with the fate of Judah; in chs. 13–23 with that of Assyria, Babylon, and the other foreign nations. Now the destruction becomes universal, raising interesting questions about the psychology of those who were so convinced that such devastation could only be understood as an inevitable part of God's dealings with his creation (v. 3). The list of the different constituent elements of society in v. 2 is in general reminiscent of wisdom literature, with its penchant for lists, but the closest parallel is in another prophetic text, Hos 4:9, and these chapters in fact contain a number of apparent allusions to Hosea (cf. 24:4 with Hos 4:3). There is no mention here of a king, which might well be a pointer to a period when the priesthood was the leading social group. v. 5 contains a reference to 'the everlasting covenant'. 'Covenant' is not a common theme in the early chapters of Isaiah, but we may perhaps see reference here to the 'cosmic covenant' which holds together the whole order of creation and is put at risk by human behaviour (Murray 1992: 16–22; he suggests that the word in v. 5 translated 'inhabitants' by NRSV may refer to kings). The lament of vv. 4–6 is in many ways reminiscent of the communal laments in the Psalms. Devastation has struck the community in a way that has induced total bewilderment.

(24:7–13) v. 7 is also found with slight modification in Joel 1:10, 12. This provides an example of that reuse of biblical material in a new context which characterizes these chapters. Unfortunately since the dates both of Joel and of the final form of Isaiah are unclear it is not certain which text made use of the other. The theme of lack of wine is then linked with one of the recurring motifs of chs. 24–7: that of a city, usually in terms of its destruction. Historical critics have assumed that the actual ravaging of a specific city underlay these references, and have devoted much energy to identifying it: Jerusalem, destroyed in 587, or Babylon, captured by Cyrus in 539, or the overthrow of some other city to which allusion is made in our sources of ancient history? That some actual historical event has played its part in shaping the poetry need not be denied; it is much more doubtful whether it is useful to read this as a description of an actual historical event. Rather, much of the language may legitimately be taken as future (the proper rendering of Hebrew 'tenses' is a notorious difficulty), and as a reflection upon the nature of God's manifestation of power (D. G. Johnson 1988: 11–14). What had already happened had provided the stimulus to continuing reflection on God's ways, symbolized by his destructive power (Henry 1967). With those provisos it seems right to assume that the 'typical' city whose fate is here envisaged is, as so often in the book of Isaiah, Jerusalem. These chapters will offer differing perceptions of that city: here (v. 10) a 'city of chaos'; in 26:1 a 'strong city' wherein God 'sets up victory'. The passage ends with imagery already used in 17:6, an example of that reuse of

the same motifs which we have found to characterize the Isaiah tradition.

(24:14–16) This section begins as another of those universalist passages of which we have already found examples scattered through the book of Isaiah. The group with which the prophet is associated (the 'we' of v. 16) hear the universal praise of God, but are far from satisfied; instead 'I pine away' because of treachery. This verse is closely linked in language to 21:2, and will be further developed in ch. 33 (Wildberger 1978: 937). As we saw there the cause of the desolation is not clear, but this passage suggests the opposition of different groups within the community, as we shall see more fully in the climax of the book, chs. 56–66.

(24:17–20) We have noticed several links with the 'foreign nations' oracles of Jer 46–51. This is one of the closest, since vv. 17–18 appear to be almost a direct quotation of Jer 49:43–4. There is an important difference; what was in Jeremiah applied specifically to Moab is now universalized into destruction for the inhabitants of the whole earth. This is expressed in particularly vivid language: *paḥad wāpaḥat wāpāḥ* sounds even more threatening than 'terror and the pit and the snare'. Another example of universalizing earlier material may be found at v. 20. In 1:8 Zion was reduced to a mere 'shelter'; now the same word, here translated 'hut' is applied to the whole earth. Similarly Am 5:2 spoke of Israel as fallen, no more to rise; here that warning is applied to the whole earth.

(24:21–3) The 'on that day' language links this closely to the many other passages in Isaiah that begin thus. YHWH is proclaimed as king in Zion, as in many Psalms; all rival claims, whether of earthly kings or of sun and moon, will be put down. This is language which would be developed in the later apocalypses; in the HB, Dan 10, with its picture of the 'guardian angels' of different nations being overthrown, provides the closest parallel.

(25:1–5) The divisions suggested by NRSV are here followed, though many other proposals have been made. On this reading these verses form another hymnic section, a psalm-like thanksgiving. The theme is the destruction of a city. If this were prose we should be required to try to identify the city, but in a poetic passage such as this it seems legitimate to maintain that the poet sees as part of the divine purpose both the destruction of Jerusalem at the time of the exile, with the sweeping away of the corruption that had set in, and also the destruction of Babylon, symbolized as the oppressor, when it too had fallen to the Persians. Each destruction could be hymned as evidence of God's overarching power, since they presaged greater things to come. After that the picture of Zion as a refuge and a shelter, already used in 4:6, becomes appropriate.

(25:6–10a) Something of the extent of the divine victory is now spelt out. First, it will be celebrated by a banquet, a theme which may embarrass the well-fed West, but which in a subsistence economy is surely a legitimate aspiration. The theme of the banquet is often associated with judgement and victory over enemies (as in ch. 24), including death (so v. 7 here), and often (though not in this passage) features the presence of an individual who can be identified as the messiah. (See 'Messianic Banquet' in *ABD* iv. 787–91.) It becomes prominent in the later biblical material and in the extra-biblical apocalypses. The Feeding of the Five Thousand is a characteristic NT example (Mk 6:30–44), though with a less exotic menu than the present one.

It would be hazardous to base a specific belief in individual resurrection on the phrase 'he will swallow up death forever'. As in ancient Canaanite mythology, death (môt; here māwet) was an enemy whose overcoming was a sign of the triumph of proper order. Here the 'shroud' and 'sheet' are mourning garments, for which there will be no more need in the joy that is envisaged. The passage as a whole may properly be compared with 2:2–4, with its great anticipation for the holy mountain, and with the expectation of salvation in ch. 12.

(25:10b–12) This conclusion is unexpected, since it goes against the usual universalizing tendency of these chapters. Some commentators have seen it as a gloss, others as the historical key to the whole section. It is printed as poetry in NRSV, but it may be wiser to see it as basically prose, possibly with some poetic phrases based on the threats found in 2:9–17. It is linked thematically to chs. 15–16, but there are no obvious links of vocabulary or of geography with that passage. It may well be that some otherwise unknown episode from the time when this material reached its final form provoked this outburst against Moab, which is reminiscent of the hostility displayed in Deut 23:3, excluding Moabites from ever participating in the worship of YHWH. The book of Ruth shows that this attitude toward Moabites was not universally shared.

(26:1–6) Another Psalm-like poem follows, with the city now a matter of pride. Here there can be no doubt that a purified Jerusalem is in mind, with v. 2 reminding us of the 'entrance liturgies' found in some Psalms, where only those who are righteous are allowed through the gates to the holy place beyond (cf. Ps 15; 24). The entry may be that of the ark, symbolic of the divine presence, and it is possible to envisage this as an example of the 'divine warrior hymn' held by some to have accompanied such a procession (Millar 1976: 82–90, summarizes the issues involved). More widely it is possible to see in this one of the Songs of Zion referred to in Ps 137:3, and exemplified by Ps 48; 76. Links with the Psalms are also provided by the themes of faith and trust, šālôm (peace), and confidence in the overthrow of enemies.

(26:7–19) Again the extent of the next passage is not very clear, but it is probably artificial to attempt any division within this section, characterized as a 'community lament' (D. G. Johnson 1988). A feature of such laments is the entreaty of YHWH's favour at a time of distress (e.g. Ps 74; 79) and that is certainly appropriate for the climax of the passage in vv. 16–18. The picture is of the faithful community under alien rule, but still expressing its confidence that deliverance will come. If we are strict in applying logical criteria, then further subdivision within the section will be necessary, for some verses are expressed in first person singular, some in first person plural forms. We may notice, however, that this alternation occurs elsewhere in Isaiah (e.g. 63:7—'I will recount . . . all that the Lord has done for us'). vv. 14–15 clearly express the conviction that though individuals die the whole community survives to glorify God. The anguish of childbirth, used as a threat against enemies in 13:8, here too symbolizes human inadequacies, but this time inadequacies which will be gloriously trans-

formed. In the light of this poetic imagery it is probably wise not to regard the much-discussed v. 19 as a straight assertion of belief in a blessed future life, as has often been done when the verse has been taken out of context. It expresses hope in a continuing national restoration. However when the book of Isaiah had reached its final form 'this is a reference to the resurrection of the dead which no-one but a Sadducee, ancient or modern, could possibly misconstrue' (Sawyer 1973: 234). When it had achieved the status of Holy Scripture, liable to be ransacked for guidance in later problems, then its use as an affirmation of belief in resurrection was scarcely surprising— though less use was made of this particular verse than might have been expected; it is, for example, not quoted in the NT.

(26:20–1) This brief section functions as a link between the preceding lament and the more mythological material in ch. 27. Use is made of the images either of the universal flood of Genesis, or of the Exodus tradition, or both, to symbolize the totality of destruction. The shutting of the doors here may call to mind Gen 7:16 and the hiding of the Israelites behind closed doors when the angel of God passed by in Egypt (Ex 12:22–3).

(27:1) provides the clearest example of links with the ancient mythological traditions best known to us in the Ugaritic texts from Ras Shamra. Leviathan was the chaos-monster, described already at Ugarit as 'the wriggling serpent' (Gibson, 1978: 50). Creation in Genesis is pictured as a matter of no more than the divine word bringing about what is commanded, but elsewhere the theme of creation as struggle is found. Ps 74:14 provides a particularly vivid parallel to this verse; cf. also Ps 104:26. The importance of the serpent in creation accounts, familiar to us from Gen 3, also emerges here. It is an anticipation that 'on that day' there will be a new creation when the forces of chaos will be destroyed.

(27:2–6) Here a very different image of what is anticipated 'on that day' is offered. It is perhaps the clearest example from these chapters of the reuse of material found elsewhere in Isaiah—in this case the 'song of the vineyard' in 5:1–7. The theme of the vineyard (kerem) is the same; in each case briers and thorns pose a threat to the vineyard; YHWH is the protector of the vineyard, which is identified as his own people. But it is by no means a repetition of the earlier passage. Now YHWH acts as the guard who ensures that the vineyard comes to no harm, and by clinging to YHWH for protection Jacob/Israel (the juxtaposition of these two words is reminiscent of the usage in chs. 40–55) will be given a universal reward. Now, in an almost deterministic way, the possibility of the people falling away is removed. They will be protected from the briers and thorns by YHWH himself. The strongly-rooted future of the people is reminiscent of 37:31, the story of the deliverance from the Assyrian threat.

(27:7–11) This difficult passage has been very variously interpreted by different commentators (D. G. Johnson 1988: 88 summarizes the difficulties, some of which, such as the awkward shifts in tense and gender, are obscured in English translations). Many have supposed that a city other than Jerusalem (Samaria?) is referred to in v. 10, but it seems better to take the passage, with all its obscurities, as a warning that, despite the promise of better things to come for the faithful community, there are also those who can expect no mercy.

God's 'fierce blast' (v. 8) implies that he will not have compassion on them or show them favour (v. 11). Our ignorance of the divisions within the community precludes us from being more precise about who is thus excluded.

(27:12–13) This section of the book ends with another eschatological passage looking forward to 'that day'. Here the imagery is of a harvest being gathered, those exiled in the diaspora being gathered to their own land. The symbol used is that of a trumpet-blast, which would become a favoured symbol in later apocalyptic writings (cf. the trumpets of Rev 8–11), but there may be a closer link here with the trumpet blast for the Day of Atonement prescribed in Lev 25:9. In the Second Temple period this day took on increasing significance in the life of the community.

(Chs. 28–31) In this section we turn from the obscurities and allusions of chs. 24–7 to a much more straightforward series of oracles, mainly of woe against a series of offenders. As noted earlier NRSV 'Ah' at 28:1 and elsewhere is too bland a translation for the force of the Hebrew *hôy*. (REB has 'Alas' at 28:1 and 'Woe' in later occurrences of the same word.) For historical critics this section has been the one part of the book where a significant body of material is held to go back to Isaiah himself in the eighth century BCE, though these chapters make no direct reference to him.

There are, however, some structural problems. The difference from what precedes has to be inferred from the different content; there is no heading to indicate a fresh start. Nor is it clear how far the passage extends. Certainly chs. 28–31 belong together, but whether the section should be extended further is not clear; chs. 32, 32–3, and 32–5 have all been proposed as integral elements of this section. Nor is there any obvious reason why these chapters should be placed at just this point in the book as a whole. Both in assumed dating and in content they are close to much of the material in chs. 2–12.

One helpful way of looking at the organization of this material has been suggested by Williamson (1994: 184–7). He notes that there is no separate heading for this section, which invites us to read it as a continuation of what has preceded, and suggests that the best analogy may be, not the self-contained bodies of 'Oracles against Foreign Nations' found in Jeremiah and Ezekiel, but the collection in Am 1–2, which uses condemnation of foreign nations to lead up to even sharper condemnation of Judah and Israel. Here that final order is reversed: Israel (the northern kingdom) is condemned in 28:1–4, then follows material directed against Judah and Jerusalem.

(28:1–4) The form of this oracle is clear, with its statement of wrongdoing followed by an announcement of judgement introduced by *hinnēh* ('behold' in the older Eng. versions; NRSV 'see'). Less clear is the meaning of 'the proud garland of the drunkards of Ephraim'. If it is simply an accusation of drunkenness the punishment seems remarkably severe! In fact it is the garland rather than the fact of drunkenness which seems to be condemned, and there is surely some symbolism here, which largely escapes us. Kaiser (1974) suggested that the wearing of garlands was a Hellenistic custom and that we are introduced here to the tension between traditional Judaism and the spread of Hellenistic culture.

(28:5–6) Characteristic of these chapters is the interspersing of the predominant note of threat with short passages of a much more hopeful tenor. Historical critics have for the most part taken the hopeful interludes as later insertions; those concerned with the final form of the book will see this as a literary device, maintaining the tension between threat and promise so characteristic of the book of Isaiah. Here the key words from the earlier passage ('garland', 'glory', 'beauty') are picked up and applied to the faithful remnant—here clearly a hopeful symbol. The stress on 'judgement' and 'justice' (the same word, *mišpāṭ*, in the original) recalls a frequent theme of the Isaianic tradition.

(28:7–13) We return now to the announcement of judgement using language closely comparable to vv. 1–4; some commentators have seen this passage as a continuation of those verses, but they were complete in themselves. The earlier theme of drunkenness is taken up again and made the basis of a divine judgement speech condemning the nation through its leaders. Priests and prophets are condemned together. This should warn us against setting the two groups over against one another as natural opponents; as noted earlier it may suggest that at some stage in the tradition Isaiah was regarded as opposed to, rather than an integral part of, the prophetic movement. At v. 9 NRSV provides quotation-marks. This is speculative, for there is no equivalent in Hebrew, but it seems to make best sense of the passage to understand what follows as the imagined response of the priests and prophets, the 'he' being Isaiah. If this is so it is natural to see here, as often in chs. 56–66, dispute between rival claims to access to the divine will, a dispute carried on in strongly polemical terms. The 'priests and prophets' sarcastically ask whether the Isaianic group has any sure basis for imparting the wisdom of the tradition. NRSV then rightly says of v. 10 that its meaning is uncertain. It is very doubtful whether the words *ṣaw* and *qaw*, translated 'precept' and 'line' are intended to have any formal meaning. They may be a suggestion of drunken muttering, with the implication that Isaiah is no better than they are; or of prophetic glossolalia; or of teaching children their equivalent of the ABC, as may be implied in v. 9. If this is right, then *ṣaw* and *qaw* would simply be forms of successive letters of the Hebrew alphabet. If what has preceded is the challenge, v. 11 provides the Isaianic response to it. The right language has been one of the basic concerns of Judaism through history, and here an ominous challenge to that concern is set out. God's will is to be achieved through those of an 'alien tongue'. If we wish to envisage an 'original' setting for this threat, then the Assyrian invaders of the eighth century would fill the bill. But this was a threat which continued to exercise the community as it lived first in the Persian and then in the Hellenistic world (cf. Neh 13:23–5). YHWH's control of the nations might have the unpalatable consequence that the community might have to learn God's will by very strange means. But in the first instance that control has threatening implications. True rest lay in confidence and trust in YHWH, which the community had refused—hence the inevitability of desolation, spelt out in v. 13 by a repetition of the terms in v. 10. This idea of rest given by God to his people is a basic theological theme of much of the HB (von Rad 1966b).

(28:14–22) offers a very clear example of the way in which a basic message of threat has a hopeful element interwoven with it. v. 16 in that sense differs from the surrounding material, but as the passage stands it provides an important indication of a basic theme of hope beyond disaster. v. 14, the application to Jerusalem and its rulers is now made explicit. Even the word 'scoffers' is very similar to the name 'Zion' and is probably intended as a wordplay. The expression 'this' (rather than 'my') alerts us that a threat is imminent. v. 15, we have noted that specific covenant language is rare in the early chapters of Isaiah, and this verse may provide part of the reason. The only covenant that the leaders understand is actually one made with death (māwet). There was a Canaanite divinity called Mot, but such worship is probably not in mind here. Isaiah's opponents' words are certainly not accurately reported on this occasion, but the underlying theme seems to be of false trust; they are held to suppose that the power of death can be set to one side—Isaiah is confident that the hollowness of such claims will soon be exposed.

vv. 16–17a, into this threat has been incorporated an oracle of salvation promising YHWH's lasting protection of Jerusalem. There is dispute whether the 'stone' is the foundation-stone or the headstone, but perhaps we need not suppose Isaiah to have been concerned with architectural niceties. The phrase 'One who trusts will not panic' is placed in quotation-marks by NRSV, and we may follow its implication that this will have been an inscription on the stone. Here as elsewhere in Isaiah we are very close to the language of the Zion Psalms (e.g. 46; 48). Those who put their trust in YHWH could be confident that Zion was a place of true safety. There is also a close link with 7:9, the words addressed to Ahaz, with the same demand for trust. The connection is closer in Hebrew than appears from NRSV, which translates the same Hebrew verb (the one from which the word 'Amen' is derived) as 'stand firm' at 7:9, but 'trust' here. The idea of the 'inviolability of Zion', if not explicit here, is clearly not far removed from the thought of the passage, which ends with a reiteration of the characteristic Isaianic themes of mišpāṭ and ṣĕdāqâ. A link with the previous oracle is provided by the word qaw (line). As against the false trust mockingly set out there the basis of true trust is now shown.

vv. 17b–22, the remainder of the oracle of threat spells out its implications, in the first part by making much use of the same phrases as have already been used—another characteristic Isaianic technique. The last two verses introduce new points of comparison. Two episodes from the Former Prophets are alluded to: David's victory over the Philistines at 2 Sam 5:20, and Joshua's defeat of the Amorites in Josh 10. Now, however, the holy war which YHWH had earlier waged on his people's behalf will become a war against Jerusalem itself—a 'strange' and 'alien' work. This theme of YHWH as the divine warrior, normally expected to fight on Israel's behalf against its enemies, but quite capable of turning against his own people, plays a prominent part in the Isaiah tradition. There is clearly an acute tension between that understanding and the theme of the inviolability of Zion which we found in vv. 16–17a.

(28:23–8) What follows in these verses has no close formal parallel elsewhere in the book of Isaiah. It is a kind of parable, using farming techniques as a model for bringing out the significance of God's work in creation. There is no suggestion that it is a divine oracle; the 'my' of v. 23 refers to the human author. It has a markedly didactic character, which may remind us of wisdom literature rather than of the prophetic writings. While in general terms it is not difficult to see the various operations described as symbolizing God's dealings with his people, it is less certain that each of the particular tasks is intended to relate to the varying fortunes of Israel as it experienced now success and now humiliation. Several of the agricultural terms are of uncertain meaning; what is clear is that the poem is claiming a meaningful rhythm in God's dealings with his created world.

(28:29) Another of the summary-appraisals (Childs's term; see above on 14:26) scattered through the book, offers a kind of reassurance that all that is being revealed is indeed in accordance with God's overall plan.

(29:1–4) One of the most basic themes running through the whole book of Isaiah is the fate of Jerusalem, the place of greatest promise and of greatest hope. Whereas 28:16–17 envisaged Zion as inviolable, here we have a threat of utter destruction. 'Ariel' seems to stand for Jerusalem; the word means 'altar-hearth' (cf. Ezek 43:15), but, divided into two words, Ari El, it would mean 'lion of God', and there may well be a deliberate wordplay here, with God's destructive power in mind. That is still further strengthened by the imagery of a siege. Jerusalem was under siege at the very beginning of the book (1:8); here it is made clear that it is YHWH himself who is besieging the city. The reference to David in v. 3 is not in the Hebrew text (cf. NRSV marg.), and REB 'I shall encircle you with my army' makes it more explicit that YHWH himself is the besieger. In v. 1 the allusion is to David's capture of Jerusalem described in 2 Sam 6; now in v. 3 it is YHWH himself who is the city's enemy, reducing its inhabitants to ghostly status.

(29:5–8) As so often in these chapters the picture is miraculously reversed. Even in these verses the theme of threat is not wholly lacking, for the theophany described in v. 6 would normally imply God's displeasure with his people, as if he were waging war against them. But in its present context that potential threat has been overridden; it is not Jerusalem but its enemies who will be scattered like dust. As elsewhere (cf. 10:32), the passage ends with the expression of frustration by Jerusalem's opponents. Dreams in the HB are often thought to have religious significance; v. 8 reminds us that, as in the modern world, they can be simply an illustration of frustration.

(29:9–10) It is not clear whether this passage is to be taken as self-standing, or as a continuation of the words of threat in vv. 1–4. In any case the threat is now once again directed to the community itself. The references to 'prophets' and 'seers' may well be a later addition, making the general threat of incomprehension even more specific. In any case we see once again the hostility of much of the Isaianic tradition to these religious groups.

(29:11–12) A brief prose section interrupts the sequence of poetic oracles. The breakdown of the established structures of the community is reminiscent of 4:1 and 8:16–20. Those who shaped the book of Isaiah continued to proclaim their faith in God's continuing power, but there were those in the community who either could not or would not read the signs of the times.

(29:13–16) vv. 13–14, the placing of the prose section is surely deliberate to bring out the ironic contrast with this poetic oracle. There the problem was ignorance; here it is assumed wisdom. The people claim to have access to the mind of God, with their pattern of festivals and the alleged wisdom and discernment of their 'experts'. It will all be shown to be a false claim. vv. 15–16, this theme of false claims to wisdom is carried further. Excessive self-belief has led the wise among the people, falsely so-called according to Isaiah, into turning the truth upside-down. The theme of the thing made disowning its maker occurs again in 45:9, and this verse may well underlie Paul's argument in Rom 9:19–21.

(29:17–21) In this rather fragmentary section we find another oracle of promise, very different from what has preceded. Now the picture is of a complete transformation of earthly conditions into a restoration of paradise. Not just Jerusalem, but the whole created order is here transfigured. Lebanon had previously (2:13) been regarded as the first victim of the impending 'day of YHWH'; now it will become a fruitful field. Similarly the deaf and the blind of v. 18 remind us of the deaf and blind people of 6:10. There is a hope beyond that threat. In vv. 20–1 we cannot be certain whether those condemned reflect a general aspiration towards justice, or whether particular groups in a divided society are targeted.

(29:22–4) In the Judaism of the Second Temple period the patriarchs, who played little or no part in earlier traditions, come to increasing prominence. To be children of Abraham and of Jacob was an important theological claim as is amply illustrated in the New Testament. In these verses we find a more generous hope than in the previous oracle. Even those who err and grumble may now, it is hoped, come to a true understanding.

(30:1–5) We return to another passage of threat, on a theme which may have been relevant in the eighth century BCE, and thus go back to the earliest traditions embodied in Isaiah, but which continued to raise important issues at different times in the people's history. In the face of threats from elsewhere was Egypt to be a valued resource, or was trust in Egypt no more than an illusion? vv. 1–2 are an accusation put in the mouth of YHWH himself. The plans of those who rely on Egyptian support are rebellion, a human plan which it is claimed is a vain attempt to thwart the larger divine plan. NRSV 'against my will' in v. 1 gives the sense, but obscures the fact that a more literal translation would be 'not of my spirit' (so RSV) with the sense that conformity with the spirit of YHWH is far more important than human counsel. To 'go down into Egypt' was an exact reversal of the divine action in bringing the people up out of Egypt in the Exodus. This accusation leads by way of a characteristic 'therefore' into an announcement of judgement showing that the very forces which the people hope will offer them protection will lead to their greater discomfiture. In v. 4 'Zoan' may stand for Egypt (cf. 19:11, 13), but 'Hanes' is otherwise unknown.

(30:6–7) This passage looks to have been misplaced. Its formal structure, introduced by the word *maśśā'* (oracle) is reminiscent of the oracles against foreign nations in chs. 13–23. The Negeb is probably not the specific area south of Judah, but rather evokes any distant and little-known southern land. The passage has presumably been placed here because of its thematic links with the preceding verses, stressing that supposed help from Egypt is useless. It brings out a theme which will be taken up again at 51:9. Egypt is identified with the chaosmonster Rahab. The exact force of the comparison is not clear, but Clements (1980a) proposes a minor emendation to the Hebrew to achieve the translation 'Rahab that is stilled', the implication being that the powers of chaos have been rendered powerless by YHWH's creative act. Ps 87:4 suggests that the identification of Egypt as Rahab was a well-known one.

(30:8–11) The next unit extends to v. 17, but is readily divisible into three smaller sections, of which this is the first. Taken as a whole it may well be one of the most important basic elements in the book. Historical-critical scholars have been almost unanimous in seeing material here which goes back to the eighth century BCE. In v. 8 there is little point in speculating what may have been inscribed on the tablet; more fruitful is a comparison with 8:16–18, which shares with this passage the concern that the words of God through his messenger should be inscribed and handed down to future generations. The theme of YHWH as 'father' of Israel, touched on in v. 1, is then further developed in a way strikingly similar to Deut 21:18–21, where a 'stubborn and rebellious (*sōrēr ûmōreh*: both terms used to describe Israel in this chapter) son' may receive the punishment of death (Pfisterer Darr 1994: 61). We are reminded that the situation described in 1:2 shows as yet no signs of improvement. The *tôrâ* (instruction) of YHWH, here as so often the touchstone of obedience, is still being ignored. As we have noted seers and particularly prophets are often condemned in Isaiah. Here the blame for their inadequacies is placed on the community as a whole.

(30:12–14) Two announcements of judgement follow, each introduced by the characteristic 'therefore'. In the first the recurring theme of trust, true and false, reappears. In the second two vivid similes are used to picture the inevitable break-up of the community: first an insecurely built wall whose weakness causes it to collapse; secondly, a pot smashed into fragments.

(30:15–17) A further accusation and announcement of judgement follows, with an important statement of a basic Isaianic theme. God had laid down how they might be saved from their troubles, and they had refused. There are two Hebrew verbs some forms of which are very similar: *šûb*, to turn or return; *yāšab*, to sit or dwell. Most translations take the verb here as the first (thus NRSV 'in returning'), but various Jewish scholars have put forward a case for supposing that it might be the second, which would involve only minor changes and give a better parallel: 'in stillness' (Uffenheimer 1994: 179). In the light of the community's failure to offer such trust the remnant theme reappears in v. 17 as an undisguised threat.

(30:18) is printed in NRSV as a poetic conclusion to what has preceded, but it can also be taken as introducing the very varied material which follows. It points forward to the latter part of the book in its emphasis on God's saving justice (*mišpāṭ*), while the last phrase provides a link back to 25:9. These links are important warnings against dividing the book into small isolated fragments.

(30:19–26) These verses are held together by the common element of promise, but their detailed content is very varied. Vermeylen (1977–8: 418) proposes that they are intended as a 'relecture' of the preceding material in this chapter offering a much more hopeful future. Thus instead of blinding their seers (v. 10) the people will see for themselves (v. 20). The deafness of v. 9 will give way to the ability to hear the message in v. 21; instead of straying from the way (v. 11), they will walk securely in it (v. 21). The condemnation of idolatry is less prominent in these chapters than attacks on the false worship of YHWH, but here (v. 22) the community are assured that idols will be a thing of the past: a sharp contrast with 1:27–31 on a similar theme. The last verses of the section introduce once more the vision of 'that day', now expressed in eschatological terms as a restoration of paradise, when the anxieties of an agricultural community living a marginal existence will be totally dispelled. These pictures of an ideal future constantly recur throughout the book of Isaiah.

(30:27–33) There are a number of textual problems in these verses, which account for the variety within modern translations. vv. 27–8 seem to be a powerful description of a theophany, but whereas in other such passages God's anger is directed against his own people, here 'the nations' and 'the peoples' are the victims of his anger. This is the language of YHWH as divine warrior. The prose passage that follows this warning first offers reassurance to the people of God that Zion (the 'mountain of the LORD') will remain inviolable, and then identifies the enemy to be overthrown as the Assyrians. It is doubtful whether we should take this as a historical reference with a specific eighth-century setting, when the Assyrians were attacking Israel and Judah; rather it should be grouped with other passages (Jon; Ezra 6:22) which see Assyria as the typical oppressive force—a role which came to be taken over by Babylon. The chapter ends with a highly unattractive, but no doubt understandable, picture of the community gloating over the ruin and degradation of a hated enemy. The picture of a triumphant cultic occasion here should dispel any notion, based on such passages as 1:10–17, that the book of Isaiah is opposed to cultic worship. v. 33 seems to embody a pun; the Assyrian king (*melek*) will meet his end in the Topheth, or burial place where human sacrifice was alleged to have been carried out in honour of the god *mōlēk* (Molech).

(31:1–3) The theme of the futility of turning to Egypt for help, found already in 30:1–5, is resumed. The reference to 'chariots and horsemen' is evocative of the accounts in Exodus, where 'Pharaoh's chariots and his army were cast into the sea' (Ex. 15:4). v. 2 interrupts the condemnation for a brief hymnic fragment in praise of God. 'He too is wise' has been interpreted by some as a claim that wisdom, previously primarily understood as human shrewdness, was a characteristic that was also to be attributed to God. However that may be, the claim is clearly being made that purely human skills were not enough to see the whole truth of any situation. An idea is developed in v. 3 which was to have momentous consequences in the history of theology: the contrast between 'flesh' and 'spirit', apparently in parallelism with 'human' and 'God' in the previous line. What is stated here as simply a warning about human inadequacies came, in the New Testament and elsewhere, to be formative of a complete anthropology that is a doctrine of human nature.

(31:4–5) The thrust of this passage is difficult to determine. As translated in NRSV it is a promise, with YHWH coming down 'to fight upon Mount Zion', that is, on behalf of his people. But this then offers a curious set of images: YHWH is pictured as a lion fighting for his people against their shepherds. While this is not impossible—leaders as unworthy shepherds is a common idea in the HB—it is unusual, and the more natural sense of the preposition translated 'upon' would be adversative: 'against'. Perhaps this passage originated as a threat, with YHWH pictured as a lion intent upon attacking his own people for their faithlessness. Only in later tradition has it been transformed to allow an element of promise, which becomes explicit in v. 5.

(31:6–9) A prose passage follows. It begins with something unexpectedly rare in the book of Isaiah: a call to repentance ('turn back', using the characteristic verb *šûb*). Then it looks forward to the destruction of all idols, as in 30:22; this is a point which will be elaborated in greater detail in the 'Babylonian chapters', especially 44–7. It leads into a renewed threat against the Assyrians (cf. 30:31), making clear that it is the Divine Warrior and not any human agency that overthrows alien powers.

(32:1–8) These verses return to a theme last found in ch. 11—the hope of an ideal king. Though less widely used as a messianic prophecy than the passages in chs. 7, 9, and 11, this section puts the hope of an ideal ruler in the context of other Isaianic themes. The plural 'princes' in v. 1 indicates that the hope is not of a specific ruler but rather an idealized picture of the true nature of monarchical rule. It embodies *ṣedeq* (righteousness) and *mišpāṭ* (justice), two recurrent Isaianic concerns. When these are present, the ruler will provide true protection for his people (v. 2). As in 30:20–1, the blindness and deafness imposed upon the people for their stubbornness in ch. 6 and elsewhere will now be removed; a well-ordered and properly structured society will be inaugurated. There are links with the wisdom literature in the condemnation of the fool (vv. 5, 6) and the stress on proper planning (the verb *yaʿaṣ* (plan) in v. 8).

(32:9–14) Unexpectedly there follows another attack upon women. The presentation of women in those usually counted as the 'eighth-century prophets' (Amos, Hosea, and Isaiah) is by and large not an attractive one. In these verses the condemnation is in juridical style, inviting witnesses to come forward (cf. 1:2). But what begins as a taunt, apparently aimed against the women, gradually changes character, and the women come to be seen as examples of those who will be forced to mourn the imminent disaster. Instead of a vintage festival, rites of mourning will be the order of the day. The image of 'thorns and briers' (v. 13) is reminiscent of the two songs of the vineyard in 5:1–7 and 27:2–6, though the word here translated 'thorns' is different from that used in the other passages. As the following verses will show this is one more example of the recurrent Isaianic pattern of inevitable and imminent disaster to be followed by restoration.

(32:15–20) As so often in Isaiah words of warning suddenly give way to a promise which radically transforms the thrust of the whole passage. Conventional historical criticism has taken most of these hopeful sections to be later additions. This may be true, though we have no sure means of knowing. In any case to dismiss some material as 'secondary' in this way is to weaken the thrust of the message in the form in which we now have it. Here the expectation of justice and righteousness is taken up once more, as a means of transforming the desolation described in the preceding verses. Now righteousness will lead to šālôm, peace or wholeness, and a picture of paradise is offered, analogous to that found in 11:6–9. The whole passage ends with a 'beatitude', comparable in form with those found in the New Testament, in the Sermon on the Mount (Mt 5).

(Ch. 33) is one of the most disputed chapters in Isaiah. It fits into no obviously recognizable category, and has been interpreted in a variety of ways. Some have seen it as reflecting a particular historical crisis; others, following an influential article of 1924 by Gunkel, have characterized it as 'liturgical', though that description has itself led to further dispute as to what that term should mean. A coherent analysis on the basis of form is almost impossible. The chapter contains an initial 'woe', a lament by the community addressed to God in vv. 2–9, interrupted by a prophetic oracle addressed to the community in vv. 3–6. Further oracular material is in its turn interrupted by a question-and-answer passage in vv. 14–16 enquiring who may properly live in God's presence, and offering an answer closely analogous to Ps 24:3–6. (Childs (1967) offered an analysis of the chapter in terms of a possible historical development; Murray (1982) notes previous discussions and makes his own proposals.) As elsewhere in Isaiah there are important links with the Psalms in language and theme.

(33:1–6) The introductory 'woe' in v. 1 is aimed at a 'destroyer' and a 'treacherous one'. The two roots are each used four times in one verse: NRSV brings this out but at the expense of a very ponderous rendering (42 words in Eng. as against 16 in Heb.). The repetition may be intended as a curse-formula (Murray 1982); it is certainly powerfully allusive, though many of the allusions now escape us. We seem to be in the presence here of more than human enemies. vv. 2–6, however powerful the enemies the confidence is expressed that YHWH's power is greater. In 'the morning', so often the time of hoped-for salvation from the powers of darkness, God will offer protection. The passage which follows in vv. 3–6 offers reassurance in the by-now familiar terms of justice and righteousness; these will be the basis of lasting stability.

(33:7–12) There are close similarities in vv. 7–9 with 24:4–8 (Murray 1992: 16–25). In each passage the 'covenant' is 'broken' (NRSV obscures this rare reference to běrît by translating 'treaty' here in v. 8); in each the inhabited land 'mourns and languishes'; in each normal human activity has ceased (NRSV at 33:8 'left' for the verb translated 'ceased' in 24:8). Whether or not we follow Murray's view of the breakdown of a cosmic covenant it seems clear that the disorder here described is more than the usual damage imposed by human enemies. There are links with the Song of Deborah (Judg 5:6), a passage which celebrates the victory over Sisera but expresses in cosmic terms the threat which he posed. Here again we are confronted with a real dread of the whole inhabited order breaking down, returning to its original chaos. vv. 10–12, as in the Song of Deborah, the threatened breakdown into chaos is the preliminary to a reassertion of the exalted status of YHWH (cf. v. 5). The language used to assert the fate of all enemies seems shocking, but it may be appropriate if those condemned to destruction are envisaged as supernatural beings threatening order.

(33:13–16) The cosmological threat of the preceding verses is now applied to a more domestic situation. The community is summoned to acknowledge the effective power of YHWH. As so often in Isaiah it appears that the Jerusalem community is divided; some ('the godless') express their anxiety as to their fate. But the terms of admission to the true fellowship are spelt out in ways reminiscent of such Psalms as 15 and 24. Those who satisfy such terms can look forward to security and the assurance of food and drink.

(33:17–22) Another passage put in the mouth of the prophet offers reassurance to Jerusalem. The 'king in his beauty' might be a reference to YHWH as king, but it is also possible that there is a linkage with the ideal ruler depicted in 32:1–2. In any case the basic theme is of deliverance from oppression, symbolized by the use of an alien, barely understood language (v. 19; cf. 28:11, where the same rare root l-ʿ-g, translated 'stammering', is found; it will appear again in 37:22, there translated 'scorns'). The passage reaches a climax with the promise of the restoration of the proper liturgical round and the assurance of continuing divine protection.

(33:23–4) v. 21 had used the image of a ship, and this brief appendix takes that image further, though in a very obscure way. The spacing in NRSV suggests a link with the following chapter, and this is possible, but it may be that the passage is misplaced (so Clements 1980a; cf. REB, which places 23a in square brackets). If this is so of 23a, the remainder of the passage may be read as a continuation of the picture of restoration set out in the preceding verses. The 'spoil' and 'plundering' remind us of the child Maher-shalal-hash-baz of 8:1–3, for the same words šālāl and baz are here used.

(Chs. 34–5) Most scholars argue that these two chapters originated as a pairing (though for a contrary view see Steck 1985). Certainly they develop a theme found several times elsewhere in the HB. The glorification of Mount Zion corresponds with the punishment of Edom. This point is made in summary form in Am 9:11–12, Ob 21, and Mal 1:2–5; it is developed more fully both in our present chapters and in Ezek 35:1–36:15. No doubt the course of historical events contributed to this theme, but it goes beyond the historical, so that Edom becomes symbolic of the enemies of God. We shall see a further development of this theme in ch. 63. In ch. 35 in particular we shall also see close links with later chapters in the book.

(34:1–7) The horrifying picture of vv. 1–4 offers no suggestion that Edom is to become the focus of attention. After an introductory summons which recalls Ps 49:1, a picture of cosmic disaster is set out in a way that has led to this chapter being described as an apocalypse. Not just the enemy nations but also the very 'host of heaven' and the skies themselves are to be brought to an end. In vv. 5–7 the judgement is made specific to

Edom, in terms which show the bitter hatred which developed between the two communities who, according to the tradition of Gen 25:29–34, should have seen one another as brothers. Instead of the kind of banquet envisaged by God for his own people in 25:6, we have the horrors of a community described as the potential sacrificial victims. No polemic is as bitter as religious polemic.

(34:8–15) The preceding theme is now elaborated in terms of 'day of the LORD' language, used so often with reference to the Jerusalem community, but now gloatingly reapplied, while Zion itself is triumphantly vindicated. The Septuagint Greek translation (LXX) introduces here the idea of a 'day of judgement', an expression not found in the HB but characteristic of later Jewish literature, including the NT. 'Zion's cause' (*rîb*) has the same legal term which is often used against YHWH's disloyal followers. At v. 9 the NRSV footnote should be borne in mind; there is no specific mention of Edom in the Hebrew text, and there is a sense in which the reference to Edom in vv. 5–7 is only a more specific application of the general theme of radical destruction of all alien forces. The word 'alien' is deliberately chosen; we are in a world comparable to that of modern science fiction, with hostile forces barely kept at bay. Thus in v. 11 'confusion' and 'chaos' are *tōhû wābōhû*, the 'formless void' of Gen 1:2. In the same verse the animals are part of a bestiary rather than those familiar from daily encounters. There are links here with 13:21–2 where several of the same creatures were invoked in the description of the destruction of Babylon. Indeed Vermeylen (1977: 440) went further and, drawing attention to similarities of structure, suggested that this chapter is modelled on the eschatological destruction of Babylon portrayed in ch. 13. (Williamson (1994: 216–17) adds further details of linguistic similarities.) v. 14 reminds us that below the surface of belief in one God there lurked fears of demons. 'Lilith' seems to have been an aggressive female demon known also from Mesopotamian incantations; she was not a 'night hag' (so RSV, a rendering based on false etymology). She has been brought to life again in recent years in some radical feminist work.

(34:16–17) These verses are very different in tone from what has preceded, and the linkage with the rest of the chapter is widely regarded as minimal. The reference to 'the book of the LORD', more properly a 'scroll', suggests a period when the gathering of particularly valued texts had begun, a process which would lead to the formation of 'Scripture'. The chapter ends with a word of reassurance for those for whom the divine lot had fallen favourably.

(Ch. 35) This chapter poses a major problem for the view of a threefold division of Isaiah outlined in the introduction. Though part of Isa 1–39 it displays very close links with chs. 40–55. Some have supposed that it must have originated with those chapters, became detached and 'by some roundabout way reached the collection of First Isaiah independently' (McKenzie 1968: 12). Others regard it as a much later development: 'a later development, probably separated from (Deutero-Isaiah) by centuries' (Kaiser 1974: 362). The greater concern with Isaiah as a book that we have tried to develop in this commentary means that these historical issues will be less important though they cannot be ignored. We must certainly be aware that themes and actual expressions used in this chapter will come to greater prominence in what follows. But there are important links also with earlier chapters; thus in 29:17–18 Lebanon is restored, the deaf hear, the blind see—the central motifs of vv. 2–5 here.

(35:1–4) Whereas at 33:9 Lebanon, Carmel, and Sharon had faced destruction, in vv. 1–2 they are typified as those who will see the glory of YHWH. It is important to recognize this literary link between two chapters which historical critics usually treat as quite separate. The threat posed in the preceding chapters is now to be reversed. Occasionally in the HB the wilderness is pictured as a place where Israel enjoyed a kind of honeymoon period (Hos 2:14), but the usual theme is of the wilderness as a place of threat. To transform that into fertility was a sure sign of restoration. 55:12 shares this motif, and the universal revealing of God's glory is found also at 40:5. vv. 3–4, another theme found very frequently in chs. 40–55 is that of restoration of health and strength, though the promise of salvation is accompanied by the warning of vengeance and recompense.

(35:5–7) A riot of imagery runs through these verses. The basic concern is for restoration of wholeness, whether (5–6a) to those human beings who were deprived of the fullness of their humanity—the blind, the deaf, the lame, the speechless—or (6b–7) to those parts of the natural world which seemed comparably to be deprived. This 'good news' was seen by the Gospel writers as an obvious pointer to the good news which they wished to proclaim, and so it is no surprise to find that this chapter as a whole and these verses in particular are alluded to in the NT (e.g. Mt 11:5). In the Isaiah context we remember that the blind and the deaf are the community themselves (6:10), so that this section plays an important part in proclaiming the restoration of that community to full humanity.

(35:8–10) As in 40:3 and 62:10 a highway through the desert is promised. Chs. 40–55 are sometimes spoken of as 'universalist', but they display a strong concern for ritual purity (e.g. 52:1), and that is also expressed here. Indeed the very title 'the Holy Way' implies separateness from that which is unclean; it is specifically for those who are 'redeemed'. The final verse is virtually identical with 51:11; the two uses may be seen as a kind of refrain, in each case bringing a hymn of triumph to a joyful conclusion in the restoration of Zion and its community.

(Chs. 36–9) These chapters have often been somewhat neglected in commentaries on Isaiah. They are substantially identical with 2 Kings 18–20, with one significant addition (38:9–20) and two omissions (2 Kings 18:14–16 and 20:6b–8), and the usual assumption has been that the redactors of the book of Isaiah utilized this material from 2 Kings, in which Isaiah himself is named, as an important element in the tradition about 'their' prophet. Only very conservative scholars, anxious to hold Isaiah himself responsible for the whole of chs. 1–66, have rejected this approach. Detailed commentary, and an exploration of the considerable historical problems here raised, has therefore usually been undertaken in the context of 2 Kings.

In recent years, however, this situation has changed, and a number of scholars have argued that these chapters were first composed within the Isaiah tradition and then taken into 2 Kings. Williamson (1994: 189–211) offers a 'lengthy discussion'. Whatever the circumstances of composition it is clear that these chapters play a very important part in the structure of the book of Isaiah as a whole. The community was under threat. That arose first of all from the Assyrians. God in his graciousness had destroyed that threat. But that did not mean that the people were henceforth out of danger. God might raise up another and greater threat—the Babylonians. These chapters tell of the overthrow of the Assyrians and warn of the greater danger lying ahead. Chs. 38–9 can therefore legitimately be seen as, in the title of Ackroyd's essay, 'An Interpretation of the Babylonian Exile' (Ackroyd 1987: 152–71).

In what follows attention will primarily be directed to that material in these chapters which seems to have played a significant role in the shaping of the Isaiah tradition. For more general considerations, see the commentary on these chapters in 2 Kings.

(36:1–3) We know of Sennacherib's exploits from his own records, e.g. the 'Taylor Prism' in the British Museum (*DOTT*: 67); the campaign here referred to took place in 701 BCE. 2 Kings 18:14–16 describes Hezekiah's admission of defeat and payment of substantial reparations. The absence of those verses here gives a radically different picture, both of Hezekiah himself and of the fate of the community. Hezekiah, unmentioned by name since 1:1 but perhaps hinted at in the oracles looking to an ideal Davidic ruler, will be portrayed in idealistic terms contrasting markedly with the description of Ahaz his father (Ackroyd 1987: esp. 175–6). The 'fortified cities of Judah' may fall and Jerusalem be confronted 'with a great army', but YHWH has yet to reveal his will for his own city. The confrontation takes place at the same place as that between Isaiah and Ahaz in 7:3. We are being prepared for the great contrast between the renegade behaviour of Ahaz and the appropriate response from Hezekiah.

(36:4–10) With a nice irony the Assyrian king's envoy, the Rabshakeh, is pictured as echoing Isaiah's words (cf. chs. 30–1): to rely on Egypt is to put one's trust in a broken reed. There has been no reference in Isaiah to the removal of 'high places and altars', but it is entirely consonant both with Isaiah's stress on Jerusalem and with the idealization of Hezekiah. Again there is irony in the words put into the Rabshakeh's mouth, 'The LORD said to me, Go up against this land', for we know that Assyria is nothing more than a rod in God's hand sent against a godless nation (10:5–6).

(36:11–12) We have seen already that the issue of proper language is a concern of the book of Isaiah (28:9–13). Aramaic and Hebrew are closely related languages, and some parts of the 'Hebrew' Bible, particularly of Daniel and Ezra, are written in Aramaic. If the words here quoted had actually been spoken by Eliakim it would suggest that he and his colleagues were extraordinarily poor diplomats, revealing in this way the weakness of their position. Much more likely we have here a concern that the sacred language should not be heard in the mouth of the hated Assyrians.

(36:13–21) As in ch. 10 the Assyrians do not know the real truth of the situation. Their words are a blasphemous parody of the real situation. Hezekiah *will* be able to deliver the city through his trust in YHWH's deliverance. The promises of the Assyrians are a mockery of the truth. Of course the gods of the nations had not delivered their lands from the Assyrians, for they were no-gods, powerless to achieve anything. In the catalogue in vv. 18–19 the inclusion of Samaria may be a thrust against the alleged apostasy of the northern kingdom of Israel. The only appropriate response to such arrogance is silence (v. 21) (Ackroyd 1987: 112).

(37:1–4) Hezekiah's response is a model of correctness. He acknowledges his human weakness, he enters God's temple, he turns to the prophet of YHWH, Isaiah, asking for his prayers. The description of Isaiah as a 'prophet' here is the first of its kind; the few previous references in the book to prophets have been of a very disparaging nature. It may well be that Isaiah was 'enlisted' as a prophet only in much later tradition, when prophetic words were perceived as *the* way in which God guided the people.

(37:5–20) As at 7:4 the word of YHWH to the king conveyed through Isaiah is 'Do not be afraid' (7:4 has 'do not fear' for the same Heb. expression). Ahaz had failed to stand firm; Hezekiah is pictured as putting his trust in divine protection. (Conrad 1991: 36–40 draws out the parallels between the two narratives.) We need to remember, here as elsewhere, that this is the verdict of a particular religious tradition. It would not be difficult in political and historical terms to praise Ahaz for coming to a successful *modus vivendi* with the Assyrians and to condemn the foolhardiness of Hezekiah which led to an extended period of vassalage.

The promise in v. 7 is not taken up again until vv. 36–8, and it is often held that a second account of the same events is inserted between the promise and the account of its fulfilment. If this is correct the break comes after 'fight against you' in v. 9a. Childs (1967: 69–103) discusses the historical and literary problems; Clements (1980b) offers a theological appraisal of the two narratives. For discussion of the historical problems, in particular those relating to Tirhakah, see the commentary on 2 Kings. Many of the themes of the first narrative recur again in vv. 9b–20, with stronger theological emphasis. In particular Hezekiah's prayerful response is brought out (vv. 14–20). Though it is prose it has many of the characteristics of a psalm of lament. The uniqueness and the creative power of YHWH are stressed, along with the impotence of other so-called gods, in a way that clearly anticipates chs. 40–8.

(37:21–9) Hezekiah's prayer is followed by words put into the mouth of Isaiah, but they are scarcely an 'answer'. Instead, they are addressed to the king of Assyria. They bear comparison with the divine response to Assyrian boasting in 10:15–19, and also (NB v. 26 in particular) with the recurrent motif in chs. 40–55 that contemporary events are the fruition of what has been the plan of YHWH for long generations.

(37:30–5) Like Ahaz (7:11), Hezekiah is offered a 'sign'. Ahaz had refused it; that possibility is not even envisaged for Hezekiah. The land is to undergo a kind of Sabbath year (cf. Lev 25:5). Then in language closely reflecting earlier passages in the book (cf. esp. 4:2–6; 27:6 and the earlier usage of 'remnant' language) the survival of the city is promised. The certainty that this will happen is underlined in the same way as the enthronement oracle in 9:2–7; v. 32b is identical with 9:7b.

The ideal picture of Jerusalem's security in vv. 33–5 seems somewhat to outrun historical fact. It is by no means clear that Jerusalem was as immune from attack as is suggested here. YHWH is pictured as asserting that this is to be done 'for my own sake', a phrase characteristic of the later chapters of Isaiah (e.g. 43:25).

(37:36–8) For the historical issues arising from these verses, see the commentary on 2 Kings. In their context in Isaiah they fulfil the warnings against the proud boastings of the Assyrians in 10:5–19 and elsewhere. One threat against the community has been removed, but it is not yet the time for unthinking rejoicing. Another threat is looming.

(38:1–6) The introductory 'in those days' is very imprecise; we need not suppose that the events described in this chapter occurred later than the Assyrian attack just described. More important is the picture of Hezekiah that is conveyed. Modern ideas of modesty and self-control admired in some parts of the West should be set to one side; Hezekiah can announce his own virtues and can also weep. He asserts his own 'faithfulness', a word from the same root as the warning to Ahaz to 'stand firm' in 7:9, and in the response is recognized as a true son of David. The tradition asserts that Hezekiah reigned for 29 years (2 Kings 18:2), so that the promised addition of 15 years to his life and the promise of freedom from the Assyrian threat invite us to consider this event in close association with the deliverance already described. The relatively rare verb *gānan*, to defend, links v. 6 here with 31:5 (NRSV 'protect') and 37:35. (At this point there are significant differences between Isaiah and 2 Kings, both in what is contained and in the order of the material; Sweeney (1988*a*: 14–15) and Williamson (1994: 202–8) offer comments on these divergences.)

(38:7–8) Whereas God's own words were reported in the preceding verses, now Isaiah speaks. Once again a sign is given to Hezekiah. In 2 Kings he bargains with God for a more convincing form of the sign; here that form is directly offered. Presumably what is described was regarded as in some way remarkable or even miraculous, but problems of translation (cf. NRSV fn.) make this uncertain. The mention of Ahaz makes us wonder whether some comparison is again intended, but it seems likely that 'the dial of Ahaz' was a recognized feature of the palace–temple complex.

(38:9–20) This 'Psalm of Hezekiah' has no parallel in the 2 Kings account. It is of a form readily recognizable in the Psalms: the Individual Thanksgiving. v. 9 provides the context of recovery from illness, and this may well have been one of those settings for which Psalms of Thanksgiving were provided. vv. 10–15 are in the form of a lament, spelling out with a variety of imagery the ill fate which has befallen the psalmist. Up to that point there are close similarities with Ps 88, but that psalm has no happy ending, whereas here the plea for deliverance in v. 16 is followed by the confident cry of those who have recovered from their troubles. The assumption in v. 18 is that death cuts one off from the opportunity to praise God; Sheol and the Pit are isolated from the presence of God. This is a different picture from that which we found in chs. 25 and 26, but, like the closely related Ps 115:16–18, it makes important theological assertions about the value of this life. But this is more than a purely individual thanksgiving. The restoration can be seen as that of the whole community, able to worship once more at its holy place after the disaster of exile. 'The illness of Hezekiah and the death sentence upon him become a type of judgment and exile' (Ackroyd 1987: 165). The 'stringed instruments' of v. 20 are unexpected; such a reference is more usually found in the heading of Psalms (e.g. Ps 4:1) and may serve the same purpose here.

(38:21–2) In the 2 Kings parallel these verses, in substantially identical form, appear earlier, and REB has placed them after Isa 38:6 (cf. also *BHS*, which makes the same proposal). NRSV resolves the tension by translating the verbs as pluperfects ('had said'). But, awkward though it may be for translators, it is likely that the present order is intentional. Hezekiah had been shown to be faithful even before the sign of healing had taken place. The motif is similar to that expressed in the words of Jesus to Thomas (Jn 20:29). Again, Hezekiah's request for a sign that he 'may go up to the house of the LORD' relates now not to the sundial (as in 2 Kings 20) but to the hope for restoration of its true place of worship to the whole community. The king may legitimately be seen as representative of the larger community.

(39:1–4) A Babylonian theme is now introduced. Merodach-baladan (Marduk-apla-iddina) is known to have been a long-standing threat to Assyria's assured control of Babylon, but he functions here in effect as a symbolic figure. His envoys come 'from a far country, from Babylon', which is surely symbolic of the threat of exile. Similarly the emphasis on their seeing all that is in the storehouses—a quite unnecessary detail in historical terms—is a clear hint of the despoliation of palace and temple by the Babylonians.

(39:5–8) The forewarning of the exile becomes even more explicit. Hezekiah's response has often been taken as a deplorably complacent reaction, washing his hands of any responsibility for such a disaster, but it seems most unlikely that that is how we should read v. 8. It begins with the obedient king acknowledging that all that will happen is within God's providence. Then he asserts his confidence in God's *šālôm* (peace). It is likely that a deliberate contrast is being made here between the *šālôm* of Hezekiah with the repeated assertion in the following chapters (48:22; 57:21) that 'there is no peace for the wicked' (Williamson 1994: 210).

Traditionally, historical-critical studies of Isaiah have made a sharp division at this point, with commentaries often assigned to two different authors working independently. On any showing it seems an unusual place for a division, with ch. 39 ending as it does with a look forward to the threat of the Babylonian exile in the context of the book as a whole which sees hope beyond that threat.

(Chs. 40–55) In critical orthodoxy these chapters are regularly referred to as Deutero-Isaiah, with the underlying assumption that there was a prophet who could be referred to in that way who was active among a group of exiles from Judah in Babylon in the 540s BCE. Attempts have been made to reconstruct some of the obscure details of Babylonian history on the basis of these chapters (see esp. Smith 1944). In German scholarship in particular one comes across references to the 'book of Deutero-Isaiah'; thus Kratz (1991), and, regrettably, Albertz (1990) in an otherwise very perceptive article concerned with the whole book of Isaiah. Kratz is also one of several scholars who have attempted to discern different redactional levels within these chapters, so that the picture of this material as one coherent block is no longer part of the scholarly consensus. In particular, attention is paid to differences between chs. 40–8 and 49–55 (Merendino (1981); see also the notes in this commentary at the end of ch. 48).

There is certainly no book of Deutero-Isaiah, only some anonymous chapters within the larger collection which we are studying. Attempts to structure history on the basis of poetry are notoriously difficult. But does the substantive point remain? Was there really a poet-prophet among a community of Jews in Babylon in the last years before its overthrow by Cyrus? It may be so. But we should recognize that the evidence is much less secure than is often supposed. In the first place the existence of a substantial community of Jewish exiles, living and presumably worshipping together, is assumed. But it is surely a very unlikely assumption. All that we know of ancient imperial practice in such matters suggests that they would have been dispersed, particularly if they were regarded as posing any kind of threat to good order. The idea of the massive deportation of a community which was able to remain together and in due course to return together owes more to ideology than to the known facts of history.

Secondly, there are very few historical allusions in these chapters which allow us to place them with confidence. In effect they amount to the two specific references to Cyrus (44:28; 45:1), and several less certain but likely allusions to him. Cyrus is a known figure of history whose career reached its climax with the seizure of Babylon in 539 BCE. This only establishes that these chapters (if they are taken as a unity) cannot have been written before that date; they could perfectly well be later. In fact so much attention has been given to the task of showing that these chapters cannot be earlier than the sixth century that little attention has been paid to the possibility that they could be later. (Two scholars who have explored this possibility are Torrey (1928) and Simon (1953); their views have won little support among more recent studies.) This is not the context to explore in detail an alternative reading; we should at least be open to the possibility that, in the context of the whole book of Isaiah, Cyrus is mentioned in the same way as Sennacherib, as a figure from the distant past who was perceived as having played a significant role as God's will for his community took shape. Cyrus is given favourable attention in 2 Chr 36:22–3 and in Ezra 1–6; those references, or the source on which they were based, may provide the origin of the similarly favourable attention to Cyrus here. There is no independent historical evidence to support the view that Cyrus knew anything of YHWH and his worshippers, or that he singled out a Judahite group for favourable treatment. In this context it may also be worth noting that specific references to Babylon in these chapters are very few; indeed, Duhm, who did so much to establish modern study of 'Deutero-Isaiah', gave these chapters a Phoenician rather than a Babylonian setting (Schramm 1995: 22).

We shall look at these chapters as poetry which continues to explore the mystery of God's dealings with his worshippers. There are important links and parallels with what has preceded, but also some characteristic new developments, both in style and in theological viewpoint, which must not be neglected. While the *historical* arguments for isolating these chapters as a separate unit dating from the 540s may be less strong than has sometimes been supposed, the distinctive features which led to the postulating of a 'Deutero-Isaiah' remain and should not be ignored.

(40:1–2) The end of ch. 39 has supplied the geographical context: Babylon. The next few chapters will retain their concern for Jerusalem, as v. 2 makes clear, but the immediate setting is Jerusalem in exile. By the time that these poems were brought together it had become clear that the punishment brought about by the Babylonians, including the deportation of many of Jerusalem's leading citizens, had not been the end of the story; some at least of their descendants had been able to return. And since that return had taken place during the period of Persian rule, the Persians here as elsewhere in the HB are looked upon with favour. Presumably they were still ruling the community when this material reached its final form.

The message of comfort in these verses and the clear intimation that the time of punishment is over suggests a comparison between this chapter and ch. 6. There the prophet had been summoned to make clear the extent of forthcoming judgement; here the equivalent announcement is that the time of punishment is past. 'Double for all her sins' sounds unjust, and has often been taken as no more than a deliberate exaggeration; Phillips (1982) suggests that the 'doubling' may refer to an innocent generation of those who had undergone exile. In this way the idea of suffering on behalf of others, which plays a prominent part in these chapters, is already introduced. There are uncertainties in these first verses as to who is speaking. What begins as a divine word (v. 1) refers to YHWH in the third person in v. 2, and this uncertainty persists through much of ch. 40, beginning with the unidentified 'voice' of v. 3.

(40:3–5) Each of the first three Gospels saw in this passage a prefiguration of John the Baptist, and applied it accordingly, though at the expense of the parallelism, for they have the voice 'crying in the wilderness' (Mt 3:3; Mk 1:3; Lk 3:3). But there are also important links within Isaiah: the expression *qôl qōrē* (NRSV 'a voice cries out') is virtually identical with 6:4 ('the voices of those who called'). Just as in 6:3 'the whole earth is full of his glory', so here the glory of YHWH is to be revealed so that 'all people shall see it together'. As elsewhere in these chapters there is an ambiguity in the interpretation of such a phrase. It can be construed universalistically, with the God of Israel being known by all the world, and much Christian theology has favoured this understanding. But it can also be interpreted in terms of YHWH as the triumphant warrior, putting all his enemies to rout.

The transformation of the wilderness also played an important part in ch. 35. Underlying these allusions is the tradition of the Exodus and wilderness wandering, when God had led the people to the promised land. The deliverance from Babylon will frequently be pictured in these chapters as a new and greater Exodus.

(40:6–8) A further reference to a voice suggests that the setting of this whole section may be the divine council, and this would provide another link with ch. 6, a link which is still further strengthened when we note that the phrase *qôl 'ōmēr* ('a voice says') is found in 6:8. Only here and in ch. 6 in the whole Bible are the two expressions, 'a voice cries out' and 'a voice says' juxtaposed (Williamson 1994: 38). In the light of these similarities it is natural to interpret 'the word of our God' (v. 8) as referring to the book of Isaiah itself. 'I said' might seem to contradict what has been said of the anonymity of these chapters, but (though unacknowledged by NRSV) this is an—admittedly very widely followed—emendation of the Hebrew text, which has 'and he said' (Albertz 1990: 247).

The basic theme of these verses is human transitoriness. In the Near East the summer heat quickly withers the grass, and that is the image used here. But there may also be a literary cross-reference. At 28:4 the people were described as a 'fading flower'; here an almost identical expression is used ('the flower fades') to remind the people of their parlous state before the divine rescue had been undertaken. The word translated 'constancy' is Hebrew *ḥesed*, usually 'steadfast love' or the like. There is much dispute whether that meaning is acceptable here, or whether an emendation should be made (cf. RSV 'beauty').

(40:9–11) Jerusalem is now directly addressed, a warning against giving too specifically 'Babylonian' a setting to this section. As frequently in Isaiah (and, of course, in the Psalms), Jerusalem is the place of the divine self-revelation. Though different imagery is used, this passage is strongly reminiscent of the promise to Zion in 2:2–4 and of the return of the dispersed in 11:11–12. Here it is clear that God is pictured as a conquering king; the image of the king as shepherd of his people is a common one (cf. Ps 23; 78:70–2).

(40:12–17) A series of questions follows, a form characteristic of these chapters, especially the early ones. They are legal in character, based on the questions in a trial as to the truth of a disputed issue. Each set of questions is followed by an answer. For the poet the answers are not really uncertain; the answer is of course that YHWH is responsible for the whole order of creation. This will become a fundamental claim in the chapters that follow, and provide the basis for the often-made claim that these chapters are legitimately described as 'monotheistic'. This is an issue to which we shall need to return.

In vv. 12–14 the answer to all the questions is clearly 'Nobody'. YHWH himself is responsible for the ordering of creation, seen as a supreme example of skilful planning. This concern for creation, though not absent in the earlier chapters of the book, is one of the distinctive features of this section, especially chs. 40–5. Underlying the questions may be the idea of a divine council, with the implication that YHWH, who achieves all by his own power, is superior to the Babylonian gods who needed the advice of others (Whybray 1971); as we have seen, however, the idea of a divine council in attendance upon YHWH is also found in this chapter.

The questions are rhetorical and are not directly answered, but vv. 15–17 balance them by making statements which assert that all the nations are as nothing by comparison with the power of YHWH. Lebanon may be chosen as a specific example because of its fertility and the richness of its forests, but we should also remember the reference to Lebanon when a similar but false claim was put into the mouth of the Assyrians (37:23–5).

(40:18–20) The questions continue, addressed now to a 'you' who will be identified in v. 27 as 'Jacob' and 'Israel'. They take up a theme which was already raised in the Hezekiah narrative (37:18–19) and will recur several times. Whenever these poems were composed, they have as part of their background a community tempted by the worship of human-made representations of the divine. Such 'idols' are fiercely condemned as no more than human workmanship. There is no recognition that they might stand for something greater than themselves. Given the prominence of artistic representation in the Christian tradition it is surprising that these chapters, with their harsh denigration of such representation, have been esteemed as highly as they have. vv. 19–20 have been widely held to be an interpolation (Whybray 1975: 55), but there is no textual evidence to support their omission.

(40:21–4) The address to Jacob/Israel becomes more specific, with a note of accusation. The community should have recognized the creative power and achievement of YHWH. Another motif already touched upon in 37:26 is reapplied: the mysterious and apparently meaningless development of history is in God's control. More specifically, and relevant to the overall thrust of the book, those 'princes' and 'rulers of the earth' who imagine that they control the world's destinies are 'as nothing'. v. 24 sees a reuse of the imagery already employed in v. 7.

(40:25–6) By a kind of *inclusio* the questions here are closely similar to those in v. 18, strongly implying that God's creative power is beyond any comparison. The use of the characteristic Isaianic phrase 'the Holy One' binds this section into the larger structure of the book. We notice also the use of the verb *bārā'*, 'created', a word virtually confined in its usage to the divine as creator and rare outside the Priestly account of creation in Gen 1. It is used 19 times in Isa 40–66; its one usage in 1–39 (at 4:5) seems not to offer any special link.

(40:27–31) The series of questions reaches a climax, being now directly addressed to the community. The overarching power of God in no way implies that he has no concern for his own worshippers, and this is shown by the way in which the same form of question, already put to the Assyrian ruler (37:26), is used both at v. 21 and here, v. 28. The complaint of Jacob/Israel that they are neglected or ignored by God is answered with the twofold assertion, of the universal creative power of God, and of his continuing concern for the faint and powerless.

(41:1–7) These verses take up a literary form which we have seen to be characteristic of Isaiah from 1:2 onwards: the trial scene. But whereas in that first poem it was the people of YHWH who were themselves accused, now it is rival gods whose claims are under scrutiny. The trial begins with the summons to universal silence, and the invitation to the witnesses to come forward for judgement (*mišpāṭ*, a typically Isaianic word, as we have frequently seen). Then with v. 2 the first main speech, setting out YHWH's claim, begins (Schoors 1973). It has been widely supposed that there must be a specific reference to an individual in the 'victor from the east', and opinion has been divided between the traditional interpretation, which from the Targum onwards has understood this of Abraham, and the usual modern scholarly view, which sees here an implicit reference to Cyrus, who will later be mentioned by name (Jones 1971 sets out some of the strengths and weaknesses of each approach). But there is an underlying issue which has been less often addressed: how far is it proper to see specific reference to particular individuals and events in poetry of this kind? In the most general terms it is from the east (as in this verse) and the north (so v. 25) that the threats to Israel's safety emerged. What underlies this poem is the conviction that those areas of greatest danger were also those of great promise: YHWH's power was at work.

NRSV 'who has roused a victor' is rather free, and misses the point that the word translated 'victor' is actually *ṣedeq*, a frequent Isaianic word which is usually better understood as 'righteousness' or the like. Though 'victory' (so RSV) is a possible translation, the connotations are not exclusively military. v. 4 emphasizes that YHWH has been active since the very beginning, a clear allusion to his creative role. The following phrase can be literally translated 'and with the last I am he'. 'I am he' is a designation of YHWH, which may play on the form of his name and is found several times in these chapters. We are reminded that this is poetry rather than a transcript of an actual trial by the fact that the coastlands, summoned as witnesses in v. 1, are now referred to in the third person. vv. 5–7 describe one—ineffectual—human alternative to the claims made by YHWH. They suppose wrongly that diligence in the making of idols may bring them a reward.

(41:8–13) These verses serve as a contrast to what has preceded, but they also introduce a new theme which will be of great importance. The idea of a 'servant' played a small part in the earlier chapters, being used as a designation of the unworthy Eliakim in 22:20 and of the figure of David in 37:35, but it now comes to the fore as a description of major significance, the noun being used more than 20 times in chs. 40–55. Its first usage is obviously important in establishing the sense in which we are to understand it, and here it is clear that the community of Israel/Jacob is so described. We shall need to consider later, especially when the suffering of the servant is described, whether all the occurrences of the term can be so understood, but in Jewish tradition this interpretation has been the dominant one. In the present context the people are reminded that, just as YHWH has control over enemy forces from the east and north, so in the past he has brought them from distant lands.

They are bidden not to fear. This is the same expression as was used to Ahaz (7:4) and Hezekiah (37:6); it is as if the community is here addressed in the same way as kings had been, offering them assurance, setting out the reasons why their confidence is warranted, and giving them orders for their future behaviour (Conrad 1985: 104–5). Just as YHWH has called other kings from earth's farthest corners, so he has summoned his own worshippers as if they too should enjoy royal status. 'Victorious' again conceals a reference to *ṣedeq*, as in v. 2—an important reminder that victory must be accomplished by the proper ordering of the conquered world. The reference to those who 'contend with' and 'war against' the people is a further warning against interpreting the beginning of this chapter too specifically of Cyrus, who came to be perceived as a support for Israel.

(41:14–16) Another 'do not fear' oracle follows, but with an important difference in the way that it describes the community. By contrast with the exalted relation to God set out in vv. 8–9, Jacob/Israel (there seems to be no significance in the inversion in order of the two terms) has become a 'worm' and an 'insect'. The latter description is based on an emendation (cf. RSV 'men of Israel') but is likely to be original—it may well have been too offensive for later copiers, because the Akkadian word on which the emendation is based means 'a louse'. God is again described as 'the Holy One of Israel', but a new description is also applied: Redeemer, *gōʾēl*. In modern usage this word has a predominantly religious sense, but in ancient Israel it was used of a kinsman who owed duty to relatives who through bereavement or other circumstances needed help. This is a strong metaphor to use of God, and bears comparison with the picture of God as mother which we also find in these chapters. The rather confused figurative language of vv. 15–16 stresses that Israel has itself an important part to play in the carrying out of God's purposes. The analogy with 'chaff' (*môṣ*) reminds us of 29:5.

(41:17–20) But whatever part Israel had to play, the decisive acts of deliverance were those of YHWH himself. As in the story of the wandering through the wilderness in Exodus and Numbers it is YHWH himself who will supply water and make the land fruitful. The oracle is a further elaboration of the journey on which YHWH was to lead his people (40:3–5), and the consequence would be that an even wider audience ('all', v. 20) would see YHWH's mighty acts.

(41:21–4) We return to the legal language which has pervaded this chapter. The challenge is now put to other gods and their adherents in a way which will be of considerable importance for the understanding of these chapters and of the book of Isaiah as a whole. The gods are challenged to produce evidence of their capacity to predict the future or explain the past, indeed to do anything at all. It soon becomes clear that this is not a real trial; no opportunity is given for the other side to offer a defence. The poem ends with a dismissive condemnation, not only of the gods themselves but even more basically of those who trust in them.

(41:25–9) Now the contrasting position is set out: the claim made by YHWH of the effectiveness of his action. He has the capacity to summon conquerors from both north and east ('from the rising of the sun'). 'He was summoned by name' (NRSV) follows the Dead Sea scroll text, where RSV, following MT, had 'he shall call on my name'. NRSV is to be preferred; the idea of YHWH personally summoning those whom he wishes to do his will is characteristic of Isaiah. By contrast with the so-called gods, YHWH has made his purpose clear 'from the beginning' and 'beforehand'. In their present context it seems natural to read these words as referring to the earlier part of Isaiah, which has spread out YHWH's purpose in one great panorama. The theme of the 'herald of good tidings', already hinted at in 40:1–2, will be developed more explicitly in 52:7–10. The section ends with further polemic against the uselessness of other gods. This is expressed so frequently and with such vehemence in these chapters that the threat they presented must have seemed to be a real one.

(42:1–4) These verses have attracted much attention since their isolation by Duhm, more than a century ago, as one of four distinct poems known as Servant Songs. (The others are 49:1–6; 50:4–9; 52:13–53:12.) Duhm held that these poems make specific reference to a suffering individual and originate from an author different from the Deutero-Isaiah of chs. 40–55. His theory has generated a vast literature; North (1948) and Rowley (1952) offer surveys of interpretation up to the mid-century, and the spate has shown little sign of abating since. (Whybray (1983: 68–78 and bibliog.), offers a briefer outline of later views.) Several recent scholars (e.g. Mettinger 1983 and Barstad 1994) have, however, questioned the notion of a distinct collection of Servant Songs. The approach we have tried to follow here renders the notion of a distinct body of Servant Songs problematic on two accounts. First, it has not seemed possible to be specific about authorship of individual sections within the whole poetic library which we call the book of Isaiah. Secondly, the idea of particular poetic sections referring to specific individuals, in principle identifiable, has seemed a very doubtful one. Better, surely, to try to understand this poem, like the others, in the context in which we find it. If that be accepted, we shall immediately think of the servant as the community (cf. 41:8), an assumption that goes back at least as far as LXX which has 'my servant Jacob . . . my chosen one Israel'. A further link with the earlier passage is provided by the use of the verb tāmak, 'uphold', both in 41:10 and in 42:1.

The community is here described in royal terms. The 'servant of YHWH' is an appropriate description for the king himself (e.g. Ps 89:3). As with the hoped-for king in ch. 11 the spirit of God is upon the servant; as in both chs. 9 and 11 the servant's task is to 'bring forth justice to the nations'. This conviction that the king would exercise world-wide justice is found also in the Psalms (e.g. 72); it would be unwise to argue from this, as is sometimes done, to a new understanding of universalism in these chapters. The importance of justice is underlined by the threefold repetition of mišpāṭ in the four verses. Not only is it an important part of the royal role, it also is significant in the light of the 'trial' speeches which have preceded this poem. Less obvious is the meaning of vv. 2 and 4; some form of ritual humiliation undergone by the king has been suggested, but there is no independent support that such a ritual was ever practised. It has been linked with the theme of suffering and this has led to the servant of these poems being described as 'the suffering servant', but such an association is at best only very indirect.

(42:5–9) The next oracle is introduced by what is often described as the 'messenger formula', 'Thus says God, the LORD'. In some prophetic collections this leads directly into a—usually very harsh—message. Here by contrast the whole of v. 5 is given over to identifying the source of the message, and when the message itself does emerge it is largely in the form of divine self-praise. It is a literary device of which we shall see many examples in these chapters. God is the universal creator, and the breath and spirit with which the servant-community was endowed come from him. vv. 6–7 address the servant once more, first as God's people, then 'as a covenant to the people' (NRSV translation, which is accompanied by the footnote, 'Meaning of Hebrew uncertain'). The words are familiar enough; the uncertainty arises as to their precise force. One possible solution lies in the fact that the Hebrew word běrît does not always have the bilateral force associated with 'covenant'. It may sometimes denote an obligation laid upon an individual or a community. It may

therefore be right to see the sense here as a reminder of the obligation laid upon Israel as God's servant-community (so Whybray 1975: 74–5).

The phrase 'a light to the nations' has powerful resonances in the Christian tradition, not least from its liturgical use in the Nunc Dimittis, the evening canticle based on Lk 2:32. But it is unlikely that any 'missionary' requirement is here being laid upon the servant. Rather, the confident expectation is that the nations at large will come to see the work that YHWH has wrought on behalf of his own people, and realize thereby the contrast between their own ineffective gods and the capacity of YHWH. Whereas in 14:17 the now impotent earthly ruler had tried to prevent his prisoners from gaining their freedom, here prisoners will be released from captivity. That contrast may be implicit in the 'former things'/'new things' comparison in v. 9.

(42:10–13) What follows is a psalm, bearing striking similarities to the Psalms in praise of YHWH as king found in Ps 93; 96–9. We are reminded once again of the close links between the poetry of this collection and what is known of the liturgical tradition of Jerusalem expressed in the Psalms. After an opening identical with Ps 96:1 and 98:1, NRSV follows a very widely favoured emendation to 'let the sea roar', a phrase again found in those Psalms, rather than the Hebrew 'those who go down to the sea', which, though found in Ps 107:23, does not give good sense here. The naming of geographical areas which follows has no precise Psalm parallel, though the theme of universal praise is a common one there. The poem ends with the assertion, again common in the Psalms, of the warlike character of YHWH. The poets of the Hebrew Bible found no difficulty in expressing their belief in this aggressive manner.

(42:14–17) The imagery of a woman about to give birth is frequent in the HB, but it usually signifies mortal fear. It is used here uniquely to describe the feelings of YHWH, and its association with the saving acts described in the following verses is a vivid simile. (Pfisterer Darr 1994: 104 argues that vv. 10–17 should be taken as one unit, which would juxtapose the themes of YHWH as warrior and as travailing mother even more powerfully.) Here again a figure of speech previously used in the oracle against Babylon is now reused and reapplied in a remarkable way.

The poem goes on to spell out God's saving acts in a way that at first seems negative ('lay waste', 'dry up') but is rapidly transformed into a powerful picture of transformation in language filled with imagery from the description of the Exodus. All this is to be done for YHWH's own people; the poem ends with a renewed warning against those who continue to put their trust in useless human-made images.

(42:18–25) The inherent ambiguity of the servant's status is brought out here. We know from 6:10 and later allusions that those who are deaf and blind are the community themselves, imprisoned in their own obstinacy by divine decree. The servant is to be the means of deliverance from these afflictions (cf. v. 7), yet the servant is also the community itself—stricken with blindness and deafness. (In v. 19 the threefold repetition of 'blind' is unexpected, and the word translated 'my dedicated one' is of uncertain meaning—Westermann 1969: 108 leaves it untranslated—but the general sense is clear.)

The latter part of the poem addresses these inconsistencies. The unhappy fate to which the community had been reduced is spelt out, and it is made clear that this was all part of the divine purpose—a theme which runs right through Isaiah, and indeed through much of the HB. God's anger had been vented against his people, but they had failed to grasp the true meaning of their plight. The shift from first to third person is in places confusing, and it is not always immediately clear to whom each repetition of 'him' refers, but what has been said above seems to reflect the main thrust of the passage.

(43:1–7) An oracle of salvation follows, with the elaborate structure characteristic of these chapters. (The repetition of 'Do not fear' in vv. 1 and 5 has led some to suppose that two originally separate oracles have been joined here, but we may properly take it as one passage, with the repetition designed to emphasize the message.) The message is a very straightforward one of reassurance. There is no mention of the wrongdoing of the community, or of divine punishment. Instead YHWH is completely in charge. He had created them; he had made them part of his family (the root g-ʾ-l, as we have already seen (ISA 41:14–16) has strong family implications); in both past experience and future hope he was active in delivering them from every kind of danger. There have been a few comparable passages earlier in the book (11:11–16 is one such, Williamson 1994: 126–8), but the unconditional confidence of this passage is striking. The references to Egypt, Ethiopia, and Seba in v. 3 have been understood as allusions to the expected conquest of those lands by the Persians, but it seems more likely that they function to express distant, alien territory. Together with the four compass-points in vv. 5–6 they show the totality of YHWH's expected triumph.

(43:8–13) We return to the language of a trial with the demand for witnesses. As in 42:18 Israel itself is blind and deaf, yet it retains the capacity to bear witness to YHWH's acts on its behalf. Indeed, all the nations can offer no different witness. This concern for reliable witnesses reminds us of 8:2, and points to the internal consistency of the very diverse elements which make up Isaiah (Clements 1985: 107). Thus in these verses the three themes of the blind and deaf, the community as servant, and the need for witnesses are all interwoven, with the purpose of bringing out yet another assertion of the incomparability of YHWH. Again we may feel that the perceived need for so constantly reiterating this theme may suggest that there were many who questioned it. In particular, the reference to 'no strange god' in v. 12 may suggest that there were or had been those within the community itself who upheld the claims of gods other than YHWH.

(43:14–21) The reference of chs. 40–55 to a group exiled to Babylon has been very widely assumed, but this is the first explicit reference to Babylon in these chapters. In fact Babylon was last mentioned at ch. 39, and this passage may be taken as an indication that the triumph of the Babylonians there implied will not be a lasting one. The reference to 'lamentation' in NRSV is a speculative emendation of the text, said in the footnote to be uncertain. The Hebrew text and older translations have a reference to ships ('in ships is their rejoicing', RV); it may be the inappropriateness of this to Babylon that has led to the emendation. Perhaps it is not too fanciful here to see a link with the condemnation of false trust in ships found

earlier (2:16; 23:1). It certainly offers a more natural connection to the following passage stressing the control of YHWH over the sea and the mighty waters. The command not to remember the former things is unexpected, since elsewhere that is precisely what the hearers of these oracles are commanded to do. One can only assume that the point is that former things—whether perceived as the earlier oracles in Isaiah or past deeds of history—will pale into insignificance before 'the new thing' that can be expected in the future. That is expressed once again, as in 40:3–4, in terms of 'a way in the wilderness'. In all these references there may be an allusion back to the wilderness wandering described in Exodus and Numbers, but they go beyond that; the wilderness is chaos, uncreation, all that is basically most resistant to YHWH's saving power.

(43:22–4) An unexpected development follows. There have been many passages in which the community was described as blind and deaf, and ultimately that was due to their failure (6:9–10). But for many chapters there have been no charges against the community for their limitations. Even more surprising is the nature of the accusation now made. Whereas earlier in Isaiah (1:10–17) misplaced enthusiasm for worship had been condemned in terms similar to that of the other prophetic collections (Am 5:18–24; Hos 6:6; Mic 6:6–8), here it is failure to participate in worship that is condemned. One explanation (Whybray 1975) is to stress the word 'me' (repeated 8 times in 3 verses) and to suppose that the passage is concerned with the worship of other gods. In any case this passage should serve as a warning against the supposition that chs. 40–55 have a purely Babylonian setting; presumably there would have been no opportunity there for worship of the kind whose absence is here deplored.

(43:25–8) These verses make it clear that the unexpected condemnation of Israel is to be seen in the context of the trial, no doubt in order to stress that the community must not regard itself as free from blame. Now an assurance is given that past sins will not be held against the people, despite their constant proclivity to sin. The 'first ancestor' may be Jacob, also called 'Israel' and thus in a real sense the founder of the people. If, as some have supposed, this is a reference to Adam in the Garden of Eden it would be a rare example of such an allusion in the Hebrew Bible. But it is not clear who are the recipients of the condemnation here; NRSV 'interpreters' might refer to those responsible for the tôrâ (cf. 8:20), or if RSV 'mediators' is preferred the reference might be to prophets who had failed to pass on YHWH's words with integrity. Again something more than ordinary priests seems to be implied by 'princes of the sanctuary', but the detailed nuances escape us.

(44:1–5) Though we have expressed doubts about the adequacy of the evidence to identify a prophet active among the exiled Jews of sixth-century Babylon ('Deutero-Isaiah') it seems very likely that the same poet was responsible for most of the material at least in chs. 40–5. The same themes are repeated, the same literary style used. Yet again in these verses, after an introductory summons to the servant Jacob to 'Hear', we find the assertion of the creative power of YHWH and another oracle of salvation characterized by 'Do not fear'. Again the theme which illustrates this care of YHWH for his people is the transformation of the wilderness. The metaphor is then modified, so that the people themselves are likened to a wilderness which may look forward to renewed prosperity. Jeshurun is a rare synonym for Israel, found elsewhere in the HB only in Deut 32 and 33. Unusually, v. 5 appears to envisage those not of Israelite origin claiming to join the community of Israel, and this is likely to be what underlies the reference to writing on the hand. Though it would give a misleading impression to describe these chapters or any other part of the HB as missionary-minded, there are occasional references to foreigners being so impressed by YHWH's work for his own people that they wish to join them (cf. Zech 8:20–3; 14:16–19).

(44:6–8) It is possible that this is part of a larger oracle, with its completion in vv. 21–2, the intervening prose section being regarded as an insertion. However there is no textual support for this view, and it seems best to treat the material in the form in which it has been handed down. These verses repeat forms and themes already familiar: the messenger-formula; the use of 'redeemer' language; the assertion by YHWH of his own incomparability; the demand for evidence in support of rival claims; the salvation formula 'Do not fear' (though in this case it is a different verb which is so rendered). YHWH is here (and again at 48:12) described as 'the first and the last' and Williamson (1994: 69–70) has drawn attention to the links with 9:1. The same words are there found (NRSV 'the former time'/'the latter time'), and it may be right to read this passage in the light of the claims there made for YHWH's saving power.

(44:9–20) This extended section is printed as prose by NRSV and most versions, and this is probably right, though part of it is regarded as poetry by *BHS*. As we have noted previously the distinction between prose and poetry in biblical Hebrew is not always a clear-cut one. However that may be, the theme is a clear and familiar one: the mockery of those engaged in the manufacture and worship of idols. The point is made in general terms in vv. 9–11, after which there follows a description of idol-making and its absurd consequences in vv. 12–17, and a conclusion poking fun at those who are so deluded as to engage in such practices in vv. 18–20. The reference to their blindness in v. 18 reminds us of previous such descriptions of the Israelite community, and suggests that that may be the intended application here. The reference to 'witnesses' in v. 9 provides a link with what has preceded. Whereas YHWH's own community were true witnesses (v. 8), these witnesses are ignorant and will be put to shame. 'The artisans are merely human' (v. 11) is a possible rendering of the Hebrew but seems odd in context: who would have supposed that workmen were anything other than human? An emendation is possible which would read 'incantations' for 'artisans', aptly bringing out the point that all the claims associated with idols are of merely human creation. This would then lead naturally into the—perhaps rather laboured—account of the actual making of the idol. How far it is possible to read these verses as a reasonably accurate description of manufacturing processes in the ancient world is disputed; vivid effect rather than precise description seems to have been the concern of the writer. In any case the point is that what is worshipped as a god is actually no more than a left-over piece of wood. If one were to say the same of a crucifix venerated by Christians great

offence would be caused, but these verses seem to have been accepted without question in both the Jewish and the Christian tradition. The last three verses (18–20) sum up the points already made, emphasizing the folly of those who suppose that objects made by human hands can have saving power.

(44:21–2) Poetic forms are resumed, with this passage, as we have seen, being possibly the original completion of vv. 6–8. The emphasis is on remembrance, not a mere calling to mind of past deeds, but their application as present reality. Servant language is used, and the overall message is close to that of 40:1–2. Past wrongdoing was real enough, but its impact has now been put completely out of sight.

(44:23) A psalmlike passage comparable to 42:10–13 follows. As in that earlier passage the whole created order is summoned as witness to God's past ('has redeemed') and expected future ('will be glorifed') work.

(44:24–8) The messenger-formula at the beginning leads us to expect a prophetic oracle, but there is no message in the usual sense. 'I am YHWH' in the opening verse is followed by no fewer than 14 participial clauses (in NRSV relative clauses introduced by 'who') characterizing the mighty acts of the Lord. They begin with further assertions of his creative power. More specific claims follow, with v. 25 reminding us of earlier rejection of earthly wisdom (cf. 29:14). The reference to 'his servant' in parallelism with 'his messengers' in v. 26 is unexpected, and it may be that we should follow Greek and other versions which have 'servants', a general reference to the prophetic succession. But it is also possible either to interpret 'the word of his servant' in terms of the commissioning set out in 42:1–4, or, following a suggestion of Clements (1985: 108), to see here a reference back to 6:11 which had warned of the laying waste of cities. That had taken place in accordance with the word of God's servant who had proclaimed that threat; now restoration could confidently be anticipated. v. 27 retains the cosmic note, but it is surrounded by images of restoration. Both before and after it we have a renewed promise for the future of Jerusalem; this should not be taken as implying a specific date for this passage, since we know that as late as the mid-fifth century Nehemiah still had the task of rebuilding the city's walls. Here also we find specific reference to Cyrus, king of Persia 550–529 BCE. He extended Persian rule into much of Asia Minor and the surrender of Babylon in 539 was the climax of his reign. Whether Persian rule was also effective in Palestine during his lifetime remains unknown, but there was a strong tradition that he gave permission to the Jerusalem community to restore its temple (Ezra 6:3–5), and that seems to be the picture which dominates this poem. Though never a worshipper of YHWH (despite the impression given by 2 Chr 36:23; Ezra 1:2) he became something of an idealized figure in the tradition of Israel, even to the extent of supposing that he authorized a mass return of exiles. (See Kuhrt 1983 for an account of Cyrus's policy which notes the extent of this idealization and attempts a more balanced picture of his policy.) It seems appropriate therefore to take the treatment of Cyrus here as a reflection from a later period and as the mirror-image of the account of Sennacherib in chs. 36–7. Each was equally under the control of YHWH, Sennacherib as a warning to the community of the threats involved in their sinfulness, Cyrus as the beneficent instrument through whom God's goodness to the community could be shown.

(45:1–7) The role of Cyrus as YHWH's instrument in furthering the good of the community is now developed in greater detail. His work is described in such positive terms that we might be tempted to identify him as YHWH's servant, if we did not already know that Israel was that servant, a point reiterated in v. 4. Meanwhile, just as the Assyrians had been enabled by YHWH to carry out their destructive work (ch. 10), so Cyrus is given power to restore wholeness. He is first described as the anointed one, the 'messiah' (*māšîaḥ*). The evocative power of this title was tragically illustrated as recently as 1993, when the leader of the Branch Davidian sect who was killed at Waco, Texas, took the name David Koresh (Koresh is the Heb. form of Cyrus) as part of his claim to divine endorsement. To those who first heard Cyrus thus described it must have seemed as astonishing a claim as that which described Nebuchadrezzar of Babylon as 'the servant of YHWH' in Jer 27:6. Yet all the military victories which tradition credited to him were simply 'for the sake of my servant Jacob'. The tradition embodied here recognizes that Cyrus knew nothing of YHWH; he was an unwitting instrument of the divine purpose, which, in a way left unspecified, would be recognized in Cyrus's achievements. The poem ends with a strong assertion of YHWH's uniqueness as creator. The poet evidently saw no problem in describing YHWH as the creator of woe; indeed it is implicit in the way that divine agency has been put forward as the reason for the people's misfortunes.

(45:8) Christian liturgical use of this verse, especially in the season of Advent, has given it an eschatological dimension. In its Isaianic context, however, it is a brief interjected hymn of praise. Righteousness (*ṣedeq*) and salvation (*yešaʿ*), those key words through so much of Isaiah, are envisaged as flowing out from God's created order.

(45:9–17) The theme of the prose section, 44:9–20, is now taken up from a different angle. There it was taken for granted that a piece of wood was available for the ironsmith and carpenter to use as they wished. Here, using a different but very popular metaphor, that of the potter, the absurd situation is envisaged of the pot arguing with its maker. NRSV obscures the link with 5:8–23 and other earlier passages by translating the same word as 'Ah' there and 'Woe' here. There are very close links also with 29:16 (and there the same introductory word in v. 15 is translated 'Ha!'!). Then in v. 10 for the first time in these chapters YHWH is directly referred to as 'father'. This way of referring to God has become so basic in later Jewish and especially Christian tradition that we are apt to forget that it is a comparative rarity in the HB itself. Nearly all the texts that use the term are late ones; perhaps by the later period the danger of using obvious sexual imagery in the description of God seemed less acute. Then, even more strikingly, YHWH is referred to as a mother bearing a child. In vv. 11–13 the rather general reference of the 'woe' passages becomes specific: the community is still tempted to question YHWH's purpose and his capacity to carry out that purpose. There is no specific reference to Cyrus in v. 13 (MT has 'him'), but it is natural in this context to suppose the reference to be to Cyrus, without forgetting the larger capacity of YHWH to use any instrument deemed appropriate to carry out his will. vv. 14–17 can be seen

as part of the one larger unit, but they also have their own internal coherence. The theme hinted at in 44:5, of other nations being so impressed by what YHWH has achieved for Israel that they wish to share in the benefits, is now made more specific. Both the idea expressed and the geographical allusions show links with Ps 72:8–10, and these lands have already been mentioned in 43:3. The Egyptians, the oppressors of Israel up to the Exodus, will now come as a subject people. The Sabeans were probably also an African people; in Ps 72:10 they are distinguished from 'Sheba' (whose queen was Solomon's famous visitor), but one wonders whether the difference went beyond different spellings of the same far-off and largely unknown land. In v. 15 a theme first set out in 8:17 is picked up again. There God's hiddenness was a cause of bewilderment and uncertainty, alleviated only by the 'signs' of his continuing presence. Here the 'God who hides himself' is also the Saviour. The link with vv. 16–17 is not an obvious one—these last verses return to the theme of the folly of idol-worship. It may be that in the poet's mind these foreigners were associated with such false worship.

(45:18–19) The section extending to the end of the chapter has been understood as another of the trial-scenes found in these chapters (Schoors 1973: 233–8). As so often the messenger-formula is used, but there is no real message. Instead we have words put into the mouth of YHWH asserting once again his incomparable status as creator, carrying out creative acts with a deliberate purpose of overthrowing chaos and establishing a properly inhabited land. In a characteristically Isaianic way this is specified as *ṣedeq* (NRSV 'the truth').

(45:20–1) Witnesses are now invited to challenge this claim, but before they can do so they are dismissed as ignorant worshippers of false idols. Once again we are reminded that this is religious polemic, not an attempt to arrive at some impartial, balanced judgement. 'Who told this long ago?' may well here, as in other comparable rhetorical questions in this part of the book, represent a claim that the warnings made in the earlier part of Isaiah had been vindicated. This leads to the assertion of YHWH's uniqueness; he alone is *ṣaddîq* ('righteous').

(45:22–3) The trial is in effect over; what hope is there for the nations who have been found guilty of worshipping false gods? The answer given in v. 22 has been interpreted in very different ways. Many Christian commentators have seen this as a message of universal salvation offered to all people and have built elaborate doctrinal structures on such a basis, but there seems little justification for this in the main thrust of the book of Isaiah. Others have seen here an invitation to the dispersed Jews, exiled to distant parts of the world, to return to the true centre of the worship of YHWH. This is not impossible, but such a meaning owes much to imaginative reconstruction. More probably 'all the ends of the earth' is to be understood cosmically; the whole created order will recognize YHWH as having vindicated his people (Whybray 1975: 112). The same phrase is found at 52:10, where this cosmic understanding comes over more clearly. 'Vindicated' is a less theologically charged translation than 'saved'; 'the English versions have been produced under strong universalist influence' (Snaith 1967: 160). The passage is quoted in Rom 14:11

and alluded to in Phil 2:10, in senses that seem far removed from their understanding in their present context.

(45:24–5) The final and predictable verdict of the trial is now announced. Once again 'righteousness' (this time in the curious plural form ṣĕdāqôt, possibly suggesting the translation 'victory/ies'), is to be ascribed to YHWH.

(46:1–2) We shall divide this chapter according to the paragraphs of NRSV, but there is a real sense in which it forms a unity. The condemnations of idols, previously very generalized, now become more specific. Bel, the Akkadian equivalent of Baal, was another title regularly applied to Marduk the chief Babylonian god. Nebo was another Babylonian god, particularly honoured in the sixth century, whose name can be seen as an integral part of the imperial names Nebu-chadrezzar and Nabo-nidus. The processions in their honour are here mocked. Those who associate these chapters with a specific prophet active among the exiles in Babylon (Deutero-Isaiah) have to suppose that this part of the prophecy was an underground satire (*ABD* i. 653); a more natural view is that this poem originates from a later period, when the veneration of these gods was a thing of the past. Cyrus attributed his victories to Marduk, but among his successors Zoroastrianism took hold, and against that religious belief there is no satire in the HB. As elsewhere (cf. 40:19) it is simply assumed that the idols *are* the gods. There is no victory for them; instead of bearing their worshippers' burden, they themselves become that burden.

(46:3–4) The use of remnant language, rare in these later chapters, offers a direct link back to the beginning of the book. The element of threat in the idea of remnant found in some passages (e.g. 10:22–3) is now completely overlaid by the notion of the vindicated remnant. Where Bel and Nebo were totally incapable of bearing any burden, YHWH will do this throughout their lives. The word 'bear' here is from the same root as 'burden' in v. 2.

(46:5–7) The comparison thus made leads into a rehearsal of some familiar themes: the incomparability of YHWH, and the folly of trusting in human-made idols. There are close similarities both of theme and of language between v. 5 and 40:18 and between vv. 6–7 and parts of 44:9–20. The poet(s) of these chapters certainly believed that the message needed to be hammered home.

(46:8–11) v. 8 is suspect textually, as the verb translated 'and consider' is of uncertain meaning, and it is not clear who the 'transgressors' are who are addressed at its end (though cf. v. 12). The remainder of the passage has similarities with 44:21–8, beginning with the summons to 'remember', then spelling out the incomparability of YHWH, and concluding with a reference to the summoning of those who will carry out the divine purpose. In ch. 44 that was specifically identified with Cyrus; here no specific reference is made, though 'bird of prey' is a regular metaphor for military conquerors, and there is no difficulty in identifying 'the man for my purpose from a far country' with Cyrus. It is all to be understood as part of God's purpose.

(46:12–13) So far the community has been addressed as those who needed persuasion of YHWH's ability; here (and possibly in v. 8 above) their attitude seems more negative. They are 'stubborn of heart', refusing to believe that YHWH's deliverance (or 'victory'; once again the word is ṣĕdāqâ) could be imminent. It is obviously possible that this refers to the release of Babylonian exiles, but the reference to 'salvation in Zion' makes it more natural to think of a community established in Jerusalem but still uncertain of the carrying out of YHWH's promises spelt out in the whole book of Isaiah.

(47:1–4) There has already been one taunt directed against Babylon, in chs. 13–14. The mockery there was mainly of the king of Babylon; here the city itself is the victim. As Begg (1989: 124) notes, chs. 14 and 47 reflect the same gloating over the fate of Babylon, a fact which is the more remarkable in that in some other parts of the HB the presentation of Babylon is neutral or even positive. Here, just as daughter Zion had once been apparently abandoned to its fate (1:8), so now daughter Babylon will be put to shame. Daughter Zion was restored (37:22); no such hope can be entertained by Babylon. Demeaning labour and sexual humiliation is to be its fate. Though the exact meaning of 'I will spare no one' is uncertain, the overall picture is clear, of gloating revenge against oppressors, for which the credit is to be given to the 'Holy One of Israel'. The title is another link with the earlier chapters of the book.

(47:5–7) The following sections elaborate further on the miserable fate awaiting Babylon. Just as YHWH delivered his own people from darkness (42:7), so Babylon would be cast into darkness. It had not recognized that its success had been due to YHWH's own decree; its cruelty and pride would now reap their own reward.

(47:8–9) The image of the city as a 'daughter' is now taken further by picturing the greatest losses which could come upon a woman: widowhood, and the loss of children. It was an inevitable fate, for Babylon had made claims which were proper only to YHWH (cf. the 'I am' saying here with 43:11). This picture is linked in a somewhat arbitrary way with renewed condemnation of false religious practice. Though in line with the condemnations of idolatry in earlier chapters, there has been no specific reference previously to 'sorceries and . . . enchantments'.

(47:10–11) Confidence in human wisdom is once more condemned, and associated with the same blasphemous claim as was found in v. 8. Babylonian expertise in magical arts is useless; they have failed to foresee the inevitable disaster.

(47:12–13) The tone turns to mockery, analogous to the way in which Elijah mocked the prophets of Baal (1 Kings 18:27). But the 'perhaps' is heavily ironical; there is no doubt at all in the poet's mind—all the supposed expertise of the Babylonians will in fact be useless. The point has been reiterated that gods other than YHWH cannot tell what will happen, and so attempts to predict the future by means of heavenly observations will achieve nothing. (The expertise of the Babylonians in astronomy was in fact considerable, but that is another story which cannot be pursued here.)

(47:14–15) With a reference back to the (mis)use of wood in ch. 44, and the implication that Babylon might be destroyed by burning, the mockery reaches its climax. This marks the end of an important element in Isaiah: the words directed against foreign nations. They have played a prominent part from ch. 10 onwards. There will be virtually no further concern for nations other than Israel in the latter part of the book. (An apparent exception to this, the references to Edom in ch. 63, is not a true exception, as we shall hope to show when we reach that point in the commentary.) One obstacle in the way of the community has been removed; the remaining difficulties in its becoming the true people of God are internal.

(48:1–2) The next development is an unexpected one, so much so that many commentators in the historical-critical tradition have doubted whether the whole of this chapter can originate from 'Deutero-Isaiah'. From ch. 40 on the tone in address to the community has been one of comfort. There have been several trial scenes in these chapters; perhaps the poet was anxious to avoid giving the impression that Israel was never more than an innocent victim and witness. Here, in a way reminiscent of the earlier part of the book, the community is itself accused of falsity in their commitment to YHWH. False trust, a theme often mentioned in the earlier chapters, appears to be the cause of complaint here.

(48:3–5) A familiar mode of address, stressing YHWH's control of 'former things' is here put to new use: as an attack on the community itself. They themselves are guilty of the kind of idolatry which has been so harshly condemned in other nations. It is scarcely possible to engage in detailed sociological analysis in a commentary of this nature, but it may well be that we have one of those pointers to divisions within the community which called itself Israel, signs of which become more marked in chs. 56–66.

(48:6–8) Themes characteristic of the preceding chapters are again used here but with very different emphases. At one level it would be possible to take the openings of vv. 6 and 8 as flatly contradicting one another and to decide that one must be a later insertion. But that only raises the question of why a later inserter should have produced this contradiction. Better to see here a poetic technique analogous to that used in ch. 6, where the people's initial failure to hear had led to their consequent inability to do so. We should also remember that the servant-community was described as deaf and blind in 42:18–25, yet that did not exclude its use as God's instrument.

(48:9–11) The stress in this section is on what is done 'for my name's sake'. 'Name' may simply stand for nature or character, as it appears to do in Ezekiel, where this imagery is frequently found. But it is also possible that there is reference to the use and abuse of the divine name YHWH, again with different groups claiming to be his true worshippers. One could envisage, though there is no proof, that this was the kind of situation which led in the later biblical period to the abandonment of use of the name itself.

(48:12–13) A fresh summons to attention, again using the language of the lawcourt, reminds the hearers of YHWH's incomparability and his creative power.

(48:14–16) This reads like a reminder of some of the themes in the preceding chapters. It is natural to read the 'him' of vv. 14–15 as referring to Cyrus; Babylon's overthrow is reasserted; and the whole series of events is claimed to be in accordance with the divine plan.

(48:17–19) A different strand of thought is introduced. YHWH is here pictured as bewailing the people's stubbornness, in a form of words ('O that...') more usually put into human mouths as a prayer imploring YHWH himself to take action (cf. 64:1). Whereas in vv. 9–11 the imperishable name of YHWH himself had been at the centre of concern, now it is that of the people. Their folly had led to the real possibility that they would no longer be remembered.

(48:20–1) We return to more characteristic modes of expression, with the hope for a return from exile in Babylon comparable with the Exodus from Egypt. It is dangerous to mistake these prophetic longings for a statement of historical fact; there is no independent evidence, and little inherent likelihood, that such a return ever did take place. In poetic form, however, this section forms an *inclusio* with 40:1–5, the redemption of God's servant pictured in terms of the wasteland being made fertile and prosperous.

(48:22) This verse may be regarded as a kind of editorial comment. It serves at least two purposes. First, it warns against any complacency that the promises spelt out in the preceding chapters might have induced. Secondly, it has an important structural function. It is repeated in almost identical words at 57:21, and, as we noted at 39:8, has an important link with Hezekiah's confident expectation of *šalôm*. This has the result of inviting us to see chs. 40–8 and 49–57 as blocks of material with their own integrity, even though important cross-references to other parts of the book are by no means to be excluded.

(Chs. 49–55) As we have just noted, there are indications within the book itself that the next section to be considered should be chs. 49–57. Historical-critical scholarship, however, has often regarded 49–55 as the next unit. It is usually regarded as part of Deutero-Isaiah, even though there are important differences from 40–8: for example, no more references to Cyrus or the supposed historical situation of the exiles, and much less use of 'new Exodus' language. The speeches of judgement against the gods play no significant further part, and there are also some noteworthy stylistic differences (Merendino 1981: 2–9). From now on Jerusalem rather than Babylon becomes the centre of attention.

(49:1–4) The first six verses of this chapter were identified by Duhm and those who have followed him as the second of the Servant Songs. We look first at vv. 1–4, not only because of the NRSV paragraphing, but also because there is an inherent tension between v. 3 and v. 5 in the matter of the relation of Israel to the servant. The servant has previously been described in the third person; here words are put into his mouth, a literary device which has certainly strengthened the impression that an individual is being spoken about. The first two verses certainly lend support; the claim that the call of YHWH went back to the time before birth is strongly reminiscent of accounts of a prophetic call; NB particularly Jer 1:5. This impression is strengthened by the reference to 'my mouth' in v. 2, for the prophet was essentially a speaker. Yet in v. 3 we find the unambiguous identification of the servant with Israel. Textual criticism is normally thought of as a strictly objective exercise, but it has been employed here in a very dubious fashion to get rid of the word Israel, either by claiming that it is superfluous to the metre (a notoriously uncertain guide) or by following a single manuscript, otherwise of no special importance, which omits the word. On all normal criteria, 'Israel' must be accepted as a defining part of the text in the account of the servant. (For a contrary view, persuasively set out though in my judgement not finally convincing, see Whybray (1983: 71–2).) It is by means of what God has accomplished in and through Israel that he will be glorified. We have seen various occasions (e.g. in ch. 48) when God's dissatisfaction with Israel was expressed; here, correspondingly, the servant's own dissatisfaction is put into words. All the loyal service which Israel claims to have offered to its God seems to have been in vain, nothing better than chaos (*tōhû*; NRSV 'for nothing'). But the passage ends with the expression of confidence that despite outward appearances the servant's *mišpāṭ* (NRSV 'cause'; notice the use once again of legal language) is in God's care.

(**49:5–6**) An additional reason for dividing these verses from what precedes is that they are presented as a divine answer to the servant's plea. Here, by contrast to v. 3, a distinction seems clearly to be made between the servant and Israel, since the servant apparently has a mission to Israel. This may well be a further pointer, in addition to those already noted, towards divisions within the community. The author(s) of these poems saw it as part of the servant's role to restore all Israel to what was perceived to be the true service of YHWH. As in 42:6 what God has achieved through his victory (which may give the sense better than NRSV 'salvation') will be seen as a light by distant nations, even to what was poetically described as 'the end of the earth'.

(**49:7**) The theme of the previous verse is here developed. Westermann (1969) and other commentators have proposed elaborate rearrangements of this and the following verses to provide an overall structure which may indeed seem more logical to us, but does not necessarily reflect the less tidy literary views of the original author(s). This verse starts from the 'despised' and 'abhorred' state to which Israel had been reduced. Its 'servant' status meant simply doing the bidding of other rulers. NRSV stresses this by translating *'ebed* here as 'slave', but it is the same word as that regularly rendered 'servant' and it is better with RSV to retain that translation here. By contrast to that status the saving acts of YHWH will lead to the rulers of the nations acknowledging Israel as their superior.

(**49:8–12**) There are striking similarities between this poem and 42:5–9, and links also with those other passages which have envisaged the transformation of the wilderness (cf. 40:3; 41:18). The most striking new development occurs in v. 12, where we find references to the gathering together of those of the community who had been dispersed to distant lands. MT *sînîm* was taken in traditional interpretation as a reference to China (Skinner 1910: 93), but the Dead Sea scroll has given added weight to an old hypothesis that we should read here *sĕwēnîm*, that is 'Syene', modern Aswan in Egypt—a less romantic but much more plausible identification. There is evidence of Jewish groups in Egypt from the sixth century onwards.

(**49:13**) The technique, already employed at 42:10 and 44:23, of interjecting a brief psalm-like passage into the series of oracles, is here used again. In terms very close to 44:23 heavens and earth are called upon to witness God's concern for his people.

(**49:14–18**) A different literary form is now employed: the lament of Zion is quoted with the divine response following. Closely analogous forms will be found in vv. 21 and 24. Laments in the Psalms and in Lamentations frequently call upon God to 'remember' (Ps 74:2; Lam 5:1); here is expressed the obvious corollary, that in the past he has forgotten (cf. Ps 42:9; Lam 5:20). Ancient Israelites were more prepared to make direct accusations against God than are most modern believers, especially in the Christian tradition. The charge of forgetfulness is indignantly denied in words which many will recall from their use in Cowper's hymn 'Hark, my soul, it is the Lord'. The metaphor of Zion as inscribed on the palms of God's hands has no obvious parallel elsewhere in Isaiah, but we should probably see a link with 54:11–13, and both passages may be linked with the idea that a God might be 'crowned' by the walls of his own favoured city (Pfisterer Darr 1994: 200–2). In v. 17 NRSV has 'builders' (*bōnayik*) for the 'sons' (*bānayik*) of the Hebrew text; this gives a better contrast with 'destroyers', but the idea of the children of the city, already referred to in v. 15, being under the divine protection is also appropriate. Perhaps we have here a deliberate wordplay. The command to 'lift up your eyes and see' is found again at 60:4. As we near the end of the book greater emphasis comes to be placed upon the unfolding of God's work to human vision.

(**49:19–21**) The transformation theme, found frequently in these chapters, is developed further. The land was reduced to desolation, Israel itself bereaved and separated from its homeland, yet now the very first command of the Bible, to 'Be fruitful and multiply' (Gen 1:28) has been fulfilled in an unbelievable way. It would probably be a misreading of a poetic passage to see behind the 'too crowded' language of these verses disputes about land rights between those who had been in exile and those whose forebears had never left Israel and Judah. More natural is to see in these verses the reversal of the threat in 6:12. There the emptiness was 'vast' and the inhabitants of the land were sent 'far away'. Now the land is crowded and it is the destroyers who are sent 'far away' (Williamson 1994: 53–4, who also draws attention to links with 5:8–10).

(**49:22–3**) Again it is natural to read this passage as a deliberate reversal of a threat found earlier in the book. At 5:26 God had raised a signal to a distant nation, calling it to carry off Israel like prey. The promise of a reversal of that threat, already implicit at 11:12, is now carried a stage further—instead of acting as oppressors, foreign rulers are now to grovel before Israel. There is no universalism here; the once enemy nations are to be reduced to impotence. Such a vision has never been achieved historically; we are moving into the kind of visionary language which can be called eschatological.

(**49:24–6**) This vision is taken a stage further. The theme of prey, already used at 5:29 (though with a different Heb. word; cf. Davies 1989: 115), is reused to show the magnitude of YHWH's achievement. Most translations, including NRSV, follow the Dead Sea scroll Isaiah and many ancient versions in reading 'tyrant' for the 'righteous one' of the Hebrew text. This makes a natural balance with v. 25, where 'tyrant' is found in all forms of the text, but MT is also possible, with YHWH himself being regarded as the mighty and righteous one whose captives cannot be taken away. The chapter ends with a revolting picture of cannibalism, a desperate way of declaring the saving and redeeming power of YHWH.

(50:1–3) Though this reads like a new start it can also be seen as a continuation of what has preceded. YHWH speaks as if to answer a legal challenge against him. The 'children' of Zion are addressed; they, not he, have been responsible for the 'divorce' of their mother. Their own sinful behaviour had led to the parting, but the power of YHWH brings about restoration, pictured once again in language appropriate to a new Exodus deliverance.

(50:4–6) The passage extending usually to v. 9, sometimes to v. 11, has regularly been characterized as another Servant Song. The word 'servant' is not used, but there are obvious similarities in presentation with 49:1–6, so that for those who maintain the theory of a distinct collection of songs, it is a natural inference to include this passage within it. But it is also perfectly possible to continue to take Israel, or some constituent part of Israel, as the servant (the links with ch. 49 are valid, and justify us in seeing implicit reference to the 'servant' here) and to see these verses as setting out the community's understanding of its situation before God. There is tension in much of the Hebrew Bible between the sense that the people were themselves responsible for their own unhappy history because of their sins (thus the Deuteronomistic History, Joshua–2 Kings), and the feeling that they had been unjustly used through no fault of their own (thus many Psalms and the book of Lamentations). Each side of that tension is represented in Isaiah; the preceding verses have stressed 'sins' and 'transgressions'; here innocence is affirmed. The servant has been punished as a means of increasing his awareness of God's redemptive activity. Whether or not NRSV is right in correcting the first 'those who are taught' to 'a teacher', the phrase occurs again at the end of the verse, and provides a link back with 8:16. We saw then (see ISA 8:16–18) the hope that in God's good time solutions to the anxieties facing the community would be revealed; now that conclusion has come a significant stage nearer. Again, in 8:17 the complaint was that God had hidden his face; here the servant avows that he has not hidden his face, even though the exposure subjected him to 'shame and spitting'. Language of this kind may well reflect the experience of an individual who had been the subject of insulting treatment; that does not preclude its applicability to a larger group. This may be strengthened by the contrast drawn between the 'rebellious people' of 30:9 and the claim here that the servant was not rebellious. There is much repetition in these verses, and it is difficult to know to what extent that is intended as a deliberate poetic device, and how far errors have crept into the text.

(50:7–9) But the servant's obedience in the face of insult is not to be understood apart from the aid provided by YHWH. These verses are clear assertions of the confidence that such aid will be forthcoming; they are less clear in specifying how it will take place. Perhaps that is not surprising in view of the rich imagery used in the surrounding chapters to describe the saving work of YHWH. We may note only that the series of rhetorical questions and the use of such words as 'adversaries' suggest that the context is still the lawsuit.

(50:10–11) Reference to the servant, implicit in vv. 4–9, now becomes explicit. Here, more clearly than previously, divisions within the community are indicated. The difficulty in interpretation rests largely in knowing who is addressed as 'you'. Two groups seem to be envisaged. One is the godfearers, identifiable as the servant community, trusting in God despite the lack of present light. The other is condemned in general terms in v. 11. They have lit a fire which will in fact destroy themselves. Whether some specific point of dispute underlies this metaphor, or whether it is better understood in more general terms as rival views of the community's standing, cannot be established on such slender evidence. We have a pointer forward to the last chapters of the book where this rivalry between different groups will become still more acute.

(Ch. 51) There is dispute here as to the extent of the units. Kuntz (1982) has made a persuasive case for seeing vv. 1–16 as a complete unit, but that involves calling vv. 9–11 an 'interlude'. There is also a sense in which the natural unit is vv. 1–8, a structured poem with three parallel introductions in vv. 1, 4, and 7, though what follows is certainly closely linked. We shall follow the NRSV divisions.

(51:1–3) This is not regarded as a Servant Song but the introductions are strikingly similar to 49:1, which is so reckoned. Within this larger framework we may look at each element separately. Summons to recall the past are common in the prophets; much rarer are specific references to individuals as here in v. 2. The recall of Abraham features prominently in the NT; much less so in the HB outside Genesis. Perhaps the Abraham stories did not reach their normative form until the Second Temple period. Divine blessing and the hope of progeny were the basis of the Abraham story (Gen 12:1–3) and so they can be the basis for restoration as envisaged here (Van Seters (1975: 275–6), though he makes nothing of the remarkable fact that Sarah is also specifically mentioned here). The 'making many' of Abraham was obviously an important element in the tradition concerning him; it is also picked up, negatively, in Ezek 33:24. The use of Genesis themes goes further with the reference to Eden; there is an increasing sense, strengthened by the references to the Exodus, of a body of sacred traditions to which the poet could allude.

(51:4–6) 'Listen' in v. 4 is a different word (NRSV translates it 'pay attention' in 49:1), but the form is the same. Here once again is the theme of YHWH's deliverance being recognized by 'the peoples' (cf. 42:4, 6), but it is placed in an eschatological context. The existing order may come to an end, but God's salvation has no end.

(51:7–8) This brief strophe aptly rounds off what has preceded, with a number of phrases and themes repeated from the earlier verses. The one different element is the metaphor of the moth and the worm, but the first has already been used in 50:9. The word *sās*, translated 'worm', is of uncertain meaning and occurs in the HB only here.

(51:9–11) The passage begins with a double imperative; this stylistic feature is characteristic of this part of the book (cf.

v. 17, and 52:1, 11). Once more we have the recall of God's saving activity as the clue to the confident expectation of his continuing power to save. We last met Rahab in 30:7, where Egypt was mocked for its incapacity. That reference is now taken up into a much larger context. The overthrow of Egypt is linked not only with the Exodus but with the whole act of creation. It is quite impossible to decide whether the 'waters of the great deep' refer to primordial chaos or to the waters of the sea in which the Egyptians were drowned; both pictures are present. We have seen that these later chapters of Isaiah stress YHWH's activity as creator; here that is pictured, as in some Psalms (e.g. 74:12–17, where the same word *tannîn*, 'dragon', is used) as a victorious struggle against evil monsters. The theme is the same as that of Gen 1; the way in which it is expressed differs greatly. All this is translated in NRSV with past tenses, and that may be inevitable in English. But it is noteworthy that the verbs are participles, as if YHWH is envisaged as continuing to carry out these saving acts. In any case they are seen as a foretaste of the anticipated act of salvation: the pilgrimage to Zion of those who have been ransomed by God. This theme which has run right through the book from 2:2–4 onwards here reaches its climax.

(51:12–16) God is now pictured as speaking to his people, but in terms different from those we have experienced so far. He offers encouragement in their anxieties with words of 'comfort' (cf. 40:1). The people's enemies, the 'oppressor bent on destruction' are no more than mere mortals, just as was the Assyrian in ch. 10. The creative power of YHWH is not something abstract; it is integrally bound up with his commitment to his own people.

(51:17–20) Another double imperative introduces the next divine word, addressed directly to Jerusalem, but in significantly different terms from what has preceded. What was briefly expressed in ch. 12, of comfort following divine anger, is now elaborated more fully. God's anger is often regarded as the result of human sin, but that element is not prominent here; it is regarded as an unpredictable burden which human beings, Israel not excepted, may have to bear. The image used is that of the 'cup of wrath', a theme found elsewhere (e.g. Zech 12:2) as a warning against Jerusalem itself, but here applied to its enemies.

(51:21–3) Divine anger does not disappear, but it may be transferred. In the legal case which is again alluded to here God and Israel are on the same side; God's anger will therefore be transferred from his own people to those who have been their tormentors. They will have to experience the punishment they have inflicted upon Israel.

(52:1–2) Yet another double imperative, a feminine form of the same verb *'ûr*, to awake or be roused, as was used in 51:9, 17, is addressed to Zion. The exclusion of the uncircumcised and the unclean warns us that we should not stress too greatly the supposed universalism of this part of Isaiah. The Judaism of the Second Temple period laid much stress on the need for circumcision as a distinctive feature of the holy people; and the exclusion of the unclean is strongly reminiscent of Leviticus. If in v. 2 the Hebrew is followed (see NRSV fn.) it will consist of an invitation to Jerusalem to be enthroned.

(52:3–6) This brief prose passage, with its fourfold use of 'says the LORD' (in two slightly different Heb. forms), is unusual in this overwhelmingly poetic block of material. Whereas previously Zion was addressed in the feminine, here 'you' is masculine. The passage links Egypt and Assyria in a manner found in 11:15–16 but rarely elsewhere. Assyrian oppression is a frequent theme in the earlier part of the book (e.g. ch. 10), though there it was made clear that there was indeed 'cause' for the Assyrian invasion: the sin of the people. That is now treated as a matter of the past. The reference to the rulers howling has not been satisfactorily explained. REB understands it as illustrating the misery of those carried into exile; others have supposed that it is the Babylonian rulers who are here referred to.

(52:7–10) This hymnic passage is strongly reminiscent of Nahum 1:15 (MT 2:1), where its cultic context emerges even more markedly. As in the parallels with Micah in ch. 2 and those with Jeremiah in ch. 15 and elsewhere, so this passage reminds us that there must have existed bodies of traditional material which could be taken up and used as appropriate in different prophetic collections. The messenger announces YHWH's entry into his holy place, thus symbolizing the downfall of Assyria. The cry of triumph, 'Your God reigns' also reminds us of those Psalms (93; 96–9) which proclaim the kingship of YHWH; the word *mālak*, here translated 'reigns', is found in the Psalms as 'is king'. The whole passage is a song proclaiming the victory achieved by YHWH. Read in the context of the book as a whole, it asserts that the redemption of Jerusalem, adumbrated as early as 1:27, is now being achieved.

(52:11–12) Yet another repeated imperative pictures God as the protector of the purified community in its 'going out'. If these chapters are regarded specifically as composed by an exiled Deutero-Isaiah it will be natural to see them as envisaging return from Babylon. In a larger Second Temple setting the whole theme of a diaspora one day being able to join together in Jerusalem will commend itself.

(52:13–53:12) No passage in Isaiah, or indeed the whole HB, has attracted more attention than this the fourth and last of Duhm's Servant Songs. It is disputed to what extent it was the subject of speculation and interpretation within Judaism before the Common Era. Certainly the portrayal of the servant here was applied to Jesus within the NT, most notably in Acts (cf. 8:32–5) and in 1 Peter (e.g. 2:22), and probably in many other places as well; in view of what we have said in the introduction about the importance of the reader, it would be quite wrong to dismiss such understandings as illegitimate. This is what the Christian reader may well discern in these verses. Characteristically Jewish tradition has given a corporate interpretation to this poem, seeing it as prefiguring the persecution undergone by the Jewish community. Until the last century Christians in general followed the NT in applying it to Jesus. The rise of critical scholarship has led to an enormous variety of suggested 'identifications' of the servant (North 1948 and Rowley 1952 offer surveys of scholarship). More recently the tendency has been to suggest that 'historical-critical scholarship is bound to *mis*treat a cryptic poetic text when it regards it as a puzzle to be solved' (Clines 1976: 25). In its place different literary readings have been proposed.

As we shall see these have particular value in recognizing the ambiguity of much of the language: questions such as 'Who is the servant? Did he die?' and still more such loaded theological issues as 'Should the suffering be seen as atoning for the sins of others?' may not be as readily susceptible of an unambiguous answer as interpreters have often supposed. In particular we need to consider the placing of this poem within the book as a whole. Unless Isaiah is seen as a completely random anthology there will be significance in its present placing within the book. But here more than anywhere else in Isaiah one must acknowledge that space limitations exclude many considerations one would like to pursue. A century ago a great scholar, S. R. Driver, abandoned his commentary on Isaiah, not just for space reasons but 'because this part of his subject overwhelmed him' (North 1948: 1). The problems in writing on these verses have not diminished since then.

(52:13–53:3) Some scholars (e.g. Whybray 1975) have regarded 52:13–15 as distinct from the 'song of thanksgiving' which follows, but the majority view has been to see a larger unity. The specific reference to the 'servant' at 52:13 seems to be balanced by the only other such reference, at the climax of the poem, in 53:11. At the outset the established identity of the servant with Israel poses no problems; the theme of the restoration of Israel following humiliation is a familiar one in these chapters. v. 15 makes it clear that recognition of what is being achieved by and through the servant extends well beyond the community ('many nations', 'kings'), but this theme has been implicit in much of Isaiah and explicit in references such as those to Cyrus. The verb translated 'startle' in NRSV has been rendered in many different ways: the traditional 'sprinkle' (so KJV) seems unlikely and the most probable meaning is that conveyed by LXX: 'many nations shall be astonished at him'.

The following verses take further the theme of the servant and the unpromising circumstances of his rearing. The language used is vividly personal, but does not prevent its application to the community. We need to remember that this is poetry, and that precise reference is not to be expected. In one sense 53:1–3 does clearly differ from what has preceded; there is now reference to a 'we', a group reflecting on the significance of the experiences of the servant. They have been very variously identified: the disciples of the prophet; a group of faithful Israelites; and so on. But perhaps the traditional interpretation should not be neglected—the nations and kings who were so amazed by what was referred to in 52:15 are now given voice. The language used is that of the Psalms, in particular the 'individual Psalm of Thanksgiving' (Whybray 1978: 109 ff.), in which a description of suffering and rejection is followed by a cry of thanksgiving for God's restorative power. As in the Psalms it is difficult to decide how far the description of sickness and rejection is to be taken literally, and how far it is figurative language, regularly employed in this particular literary genre.

(53:4–6) Here there arises the question of vicarious suffering. These verses have played a prominent part in Christian expositions of doctrine, applying the sufferings of the servant to Jesus, and understanding his sufferings as effective for the whole range of human sin. For many who may not themselves be committed Christians the use of vv. 3–6 in Handel's *Messiah* will still have familiarized them with such an interpretation. In its original context, however, mundane as this may seem, a less exalted interpretation may be appropriate. As Whybray (1978: 58) has noted, the words translated 'infirmities' and 'diseases' are 'eminently suitable to express the broken state of the nation after the destruction of Jerusalem in 587 BC'. Indeed, as he points out, the word *ḥŏlî*, here 'infirmities', was already found in 1:5 in the description of the ravaged state of the community: 'the whole head is sick (*ḥŏlî*)'. The servant at one level *was* the suffering community; at another level the figure was used of that part of the community which was being restored through God's saving power. The poet goes well beyond literal attention to detail in his fancy that Gentile observers would picture themselves as sheep going astray, but here, just as in the references to the supposedly God-fearing Cyrus, we are reminded of the power of poetry to stretch the imagination in ways it had never previously considered.

(53:7–9) The picture in these verses is clearly of the death of the servant, and the appropriateness of the NT application to Jesus is clear enough, given the presuppositions of its writers. Less impressive have been the efforts of historical-critical scholars in their arguments as to whether or not someone's literal death is here implied. Too often they have tried to ignore the poetic context and to make the lines refer to some, in principle, identifiable individual. In any case as Whybray (1978: esp. 92–106) has shown, much of the language here used is that found in Psalms of Thanksgiving as a means of expressing the desperate plight of the sufferer before God's saving action became apparent. Indeed such expressions as 'they made his grave with the wicked' tell us more about the expectations of the servant's enemies in plotting his death than about the 'actual' fate of the servant.

(53:10–12) Finally we reach the point of the thanksgiving: God's wonderful deliverance of the faithful servant. Comparison is appropriate with another individual Psalm of Thanksgiving embodied in Isaiah: the Psalm of Hezekiah in 38:9–20. That was expressed in the first person, being placed in the mouth of Hezekiah, against the third-person usage here. But the sentiments, of the wonderful providence of YHWH in delivering his servant from the power of death, are basically similar. In this passage, however, the language used is wider-ranging. The servant is likened to an *'āšām* (offering for sin), a term most frequently found in Leviticus, though it should be noted that the text here has often been thought to be corrupt (Whybray 1978: 63–6; cf. *BHS* and NRSV marg., noting the uncertainty of the meaning). If it is accepted as it stands the poetic fancy of the writer envisages the suffering of the servant as comparable to that of a blameless animal victim, like the lamb of v. 7.

There are again textual uncertainties in v. 11, but the striking point here is in the use of the root *ṣ-d-q*, 'righteous'. In the first part of the book this theme was overwhelmingly used as a requirement of human behaviour, whereas from ch. 40 onwards it has been descriptive of God's action (Rendtorff 1994: 162–4). Here the two are combined: God's righteousness is now to be a characteristic of the whole community. This whole section needs to be seen as a dramatic reversal of the state of affairs described in 1:4. There the people were 'laden with iniquity' ('āwôn); now the servant will 'bear their iniquities' ('ăwōnōtām). There are other correspondences with earlier material which repay detailed study, such as the 'division of the spoil' motif found in v. 12 and in the Davidic oracle of 9:3. Whatever the historical origin of this poem, at a literary level it fulfils a very important function in the development of the book of Isaiah as a whole. One might indeed suppose that such a note of triumph would make an appropriate point at which to complete the book (the four Gospels would provide an obvious parallel to such a structure), but the remaining chapters make it clear that warnings must continue to be intermingled with the note of confidence.

(54:1–3) This is the beginning of a poem, perhaps extending to v. 10, with a feminine subject corresponding to the masculine servant. (Sawyer 1989 offers some reflections upon this juxtaposition as well as a more detailed discussion of this poem.) Barrenness was a cause of shame in ancient Israel, and so many stories, in Genesis and elsewhere, focus on this theme; indeed the word 'ăqārâ, 'barren one' is never found elsewhere in the Prophets, but is used to describe Sarah, Rebekah, Rachel, Manoah's wife (Judg 13), and Hannah (Pfisterer Darr 1994: 179). Here the poem offers hope for the barren one, just as the suffering of the servant had not been the end of his story. As elsewhere in these chapters the community is to look forward to a time when the alien nations will be part of their own possession—again a warning against too readily seeing an undifferentiated universalism here.

(54:4–8) Here some remarkable claims are made. For YHWH of hosts to be called the people's 'maker' and 'redeemer' is not unexpected; more striking is his description as 'husband'. It is probably right to see an implied reference to Zion or to the community at large, but in the first instance, as in the servant poems, the language is individual, and here clearly refers to a woman. Still more astonishing is the assertion that the troubles which have befallen her are the result of YHWH casting her off, abandoning her, hiding his face from her. Frequently in the Psalms the claim is made that YHWH has neglected his people's plight; here such an acknowledgement is both expressed in more personal terms and put into the mouth of God himself.

(54:9–10) The poem ends with another of the allusions to earlier traditions, now probably regarded as what would later be called Scripture, which are characteristic of this part of the book (cf. 51:2). Here the comparison is with the great flood and more specifically with Noah, but it is made in a way which significantly changes the emphasis from that found in Genesis. The focus here is on the postscript to the Genesis story, the promise that there would never again be such a flood. Admittedly this impression is strengthened by an unacknowledged emendation in the NRSV text, which reads 'days of Noah' where the Hebrew twice has 'waters of Noah'. The flood itself is regarded as no more than the occasion for God to promise the continuance of his steadfast love (ḥesed) and of peace (šālôm).

(54:11–17) Whereas in the previous poem the reference to Zion was allusive, here the address is more directly to the city. So far the city is 'not comforted', but that will now be put right. The theme of glorious restoration, touched on in

33:20–2, is now elaborated; the 'righteousness' which had once lodged in her (1:21), will be restored once more. Links with the servant poems are provided by the description of the city as 'afflicted' (v. 11; cf. 53:4), and by the theme of those who are taught (v. 13; cf. 50:4). Another familiar theme is picked up in vv. 16–17: that of YHWH as the ultimate creator, whose power lies behind all human creating. Whereas earlier the stress had been on the creation of idols, here it is weapons that are fashioned by human hands. They will be of no use against God's community. The chapter ends with a summary reminiscent of those we have noted in 14:26 and elsewhere. Unusually here the reference is to the plural 'servants of the Lord'. ṣ-d-q language is again used, but is somewhat obscured in NRSV by the translation 'vindication' for the word rendered 'righteousness' in v. 14.

(55:1–5) This section of the book concludes with a poem which is formally unique in Isaiah. It has been compared with the cry of the water-seller, or perhaps more plausibly with the invitation of Woman Wisdom in Prov 9:1–6 (Whybray 1975: 190). At first it would seem as if the invitation is to all and sundry, but as the poem proceeds it becomes clearer that it is specifically addressed to the Israelite community. A characteristic theme in the prophetic literature of the exilic and Second Temple periods was the assurance of a new or renewed covenant (Jer 31:31–4; Ezek 34:23–31). In literary terms it is noteworthy that these promises occur at very similar points in the overall structure of the prophetic book. They are united also by the fact that in each case there is a strong Davidic link. (In Jeremiah this is found in the fuller development of the covenant theme in ch. 33.) Here the point had already been mentioned in 54:10; now it is taken further. NRSV, like most modern translations, makes the Hebrew expression ḥasdê Dāwīd refer to God's love for David, but it could equally mean (and the Hebrew usage would be more natural) the mercies of David. In any case it appears as if the covenant with David, described for example in Ps 89, will now be extended to the whole community (Eissfeldt 1962). This 'democratization' (Williamson 1994: 112) is a characteristic theme of Isaiah, with its concern for the community, but it does not necessarily exclude hopes centred in the Davidic line as well. If we are to read the book as a whole we shall need to see this in the light of 9:2–7. In the present context, however, the main stress is the summons to the community to fulfil a role comparable with that which God had allotted to David.

(55:6–9) The basic notion of 'seeking' and 'calling upon' YHWH implied engaging in the appropriate cultic worship. Some, emphasizing the links between Isaiah and the Jerusalem cult, would suppose that is the underlying meaning of v. 6; others would see a more generalized sense. In this unit it is still assumed that the wicked and the unrighteous, perceived as such by the prophetic author, may change their pattern of belief and behaviour. In the last chapters of the book that hope seems to fade away, and those from whom the prophet differed are more harshly rejected.

(55:10–11) The theological reflection begun in vv. 8–9 is here continued, with special emphasis on the word of YHWH. An obvious way to understand this is to take it as a claim by the prophetic author to be the recipient of God's word. However that may be, we have here the beginnings of what seems to have been a new understanding of God's word, which would assume major importance in later writings such as the prologue to the Gospel of John. The theme of these verses is closely comparable to 40:8, and in so far as chs. 40–55 form a distinct unit within the whole book, these two sections form an *inclusio*, the end matching the beginning.

(**55:12–13**) A recurring theme running throughout the book of Isaiah is that of paradise regained (Whybray 1975: 195). In 11:6–9 it was animal life that was transformed; here we are reminded of the 'briers and thorns' of the early chapters (5:6 and elsewhere), though the actual words used here are different. In the present vision such threats to agriculture will be replaced by cypress and myrtle, symbols of God's transformation of the wilderness (41:19). Then, in a way which contributed to the vision of St Francis, the trees can join mountains and hills in praise of God. Not all apocalyptic visions are as attractive as this.

(**56:1**) Though conventionally regarded as the beginning of 'Trito-Isaiah' there are few signs of a new start here. The summons to maintain justice (*mišpāṭ*) and do right (*ṣĕdāqâ*) are reminiscent of the early chapters of the book, where the lack of these qualities had led to the city's degradation (1:21). But there is an important linkage here which is very difficult to bring out in translation. The word translated 'my deliverance' in NRSV is *ṣidqātî*—the same word but now used, as for example in 46:12–13, in the sense of YHWH's saving power. Such a wordplay is surely not accidental. Here, more clearly than anywhere else in the book *ṣĕdāqâ* as a human requirement, parallel with *mišpāṭ* (justice), and as a divine blessing, parallel with *yĕšûʿâ* (salvation), are brought together (Rendtorff 1994: 185–9).

(**56:2**) After the theological heights of the first verse this may seem to be something of a let-down. The only specific example offered of the ideal behaviour demanded is to keep the sabbath. Very clearly the sabbath was an important identifying mark for Second Temple Judaism, and the solemnity of Jeremiah's 'Confessions' is similarly broken with a bitter attack on those who fail to keep the sabbath (Jer 17:19–27).

(**56:3–5**) In fact, of course, for members of a specific religious grouping within which the Isaiah tradition was handed down, the issue of who were legitimate members of that community was a sensitive one. Sabbath-keeping was one marker; now the issue arises of the status of eunuchs and foreigners. First mentioned is 'the foreigner joined to the LORD', presumably forerunners of the Godfearers of later times, but reflection on the status of foreigners comes in the next stanza. Here the concern is with eunuchs. According to Deut 23:1 they were to be excluded from the covenant community, but here they are envisaged as being able to keep the covenant, pictured once again primarily in terms of sabbath observance. The reference to 'house' and 'walls' may imply the existence of the Second Temple, but as we have seen throughout Isaiah it is dangerous to base dating on allusions in poetry. Clearer perhaps is the link between v. 5 and 55:13; the hope for the eunuchs is comparable to the paradise picture set out in the earlier passage.

(**56:6–8**) Attention now turns to the status of foreigners. Down to the exile Israel and Judah had been nation-states among other like states, but in the later period their descendants were essentially a religious community, bound by the laws of membership of that community. What was to be the attitude to those from outside? The literature of Second Temple Judaism offers the whole spectrum of answers to that question; here is one of the most open and affirmative responses. It is possible for foreigners to be the 'servants' of YHWH, an important acknowledgement in view of the status of the servant set out in earlier chapters. They must of course keep the sabbath, but they are thereby rendered able to maintain the covenant. In these circumstances they can bring offerings for sacrifice in the same way as native-born Israelites. The passage reaches a climax with the promise of the availability of the temple to those from any nation. Quotation of this passage is of course attributed to Jesus in his dispute with the temple authorities of his time (Mk 11:17). The bringing in of foreigners is pictured as being on a par with the restoration of exiled Israelites.

(**56:9–12**) This passage comes as something of a shock after the edifying sentiments which have preceded it. This bitter condemnation of the inadequacies of the community's leaders reminds us of the attack on the rulers in ch. 1, and some scholars have thought it likely that this oracle originated in pre-exilic days (see the discussion in Emmerson (1992: esp. 16, 21)). The leaders are likened to watchmen ('sentinels'), a term most commonly used of prophets, who were expected to warn the people of imminent dangers, and to shepherds, applied to political leaders in Ezek 34 and elsewhere. The point seems to be that the hope for deliverance and salvation must not obscure the need for proper leadership.

(**57:1–10**) NRSV here departs from its usual practice and prints an extended section as a single paragraph. In fact vv. 1–2 are extremely difficult, with awkward shifts between singular and plural, largely masked by the NRSV translation. It seems that a contrast is being drawn between a group of whom the prophetic tradition approves and others who are strongly condemned. The word *ṣaddîq*, righteous, comes from the same *ṣ-d-q* root as we have been considering; at a later stage it was used of particular strictly observant religious groups; whether that is the case here cannot certainly be established. But this group is in any case mentioned only briefly; as is usual with religious polemic, those being attacked receive far more detailed attention, and their evil practices are now spelt out at length and in unattractive terms. Their parentage is attacked (v. 3); then they are accused of apparently childish behaviour (v. 4); finally unspecified sexual offences and even child-sacrifice are attributed to them (v. 5). Not surprisingly Hanson (1979: 186) headlines his discussion of this passage 'The Conflict grows acrimonious'! It seems unlikely that we can gain any objective picture of those being attacked; these are the standard terms of religious abuse. It looks as if the following verses may yield more sense, but this hope proves unwarranted when we discover that the 'you' of NRSV is sometimes masculine plural and sometimes feminine singular. All we can say is that various practices were regarded as idolatrous by those from whom these oracles originate, and that in the structure of the book as a whole we are reminded that the prostitution of the city described in 1:21–3 is a continuing danger. The promise of divine deliverance so vividly set out in the preceding chapters is not unconditional.

(57:11–13) These verses seem to continue the preceding condemnation. v. 12 must surely be ironic, a point rather obscured by NRSV 'concede' for RSV 'tell of'. 'Concede' suggests a genuine lawsuit, but the poet can scarcely have seriously accepted the *ṣĕdāqâ* (righteousness) of those who have just been condemned so bitterly. The poem ends with a mockery of idols reminiscent of chs. 44 and 45, and an assertion of the impregnable position of those who take refuge in YHWH. The 'holy mountain' reminds us not only of 56:7, with its aspirations for the temple, but also of 11:9, with its picture of paradise restored.

(57:14–21) The double imperative reminds us of the series of such usages found in chs. 49–55, and this stylistic indication of a new start is borne out by the consoling contents of this passage, a strong contrast with what has preceded. The 'high and lofty one…whose name is Holy' offers an obvious link with 6:1–3, and there follows an assurance of God's continuing presence with the contrite and humble. This positive approach to the humble is somewhat unexpected; the root involved, *š-p-l*, has been used several times in Isaiah but always previously in the negative sense of being humbled (e.g. 2:9). The theme will recur again (cf. 66:2); some scholars would see in it a pointer to the socially excluded status of those responsible for this part of the book (Hanson 1979: 78–9). The most natural reading of the following verses is to suppose that those now being praised had turned from unacceptable ways, rather than that a different group is spoken of in v. 17. But in vv. 19–20 a clear contrast is made between those accepted by God and 'the wicked', and in this context the refrain, encountered already at 48:22, fits naturally into its context. (See the comment on 48:22 for the function of this refrain.)

(58:1–5) We have seen that proper observance of the sabbath was important for the Isaiah community. Another characteristic religious observance, fasting, receives a more qualified endorsement. It is most conspicuously practised by those described in 57:20 as wicked, and in these verses their devotion—to outward appearance at least—seems manifest. It seems unlikely, therefore, that they should simply be identified with the idolaters of 57:3–10, unless, as some scholars have supposed, relations between two groups which were at first no worse than strained deteriorated rapidly so that all kinds of attacks could be launched. There is evidence from Zech 7–8, Joel, and Ezra that the desirability of fasting was an issue in the early Second Temple period (and many have supposed that this part of Isaiah originated at that time). Joel 1:14 and Ezra 8:21 approve of fasting, whereas as in Zech 8:19 fasting is apparently rejected. So here fasting is seen as too readily accompanied by unacceptable behaviour.

v. 3 raises two important points. First, this passage stands within the prophetic tradition, best known from Amos but well exemplified as a major theme in Isaiah (cf. 1:10–17), which warns that religious practice is worse than useless if not accompanied by true social justice. Secondly we are reminded that prophetic words were characteristically addressed to the upper strata of society—presumably those who had sufficient leisure to attend to them: it is the one who oppresses the workers rather than the workers themselves who is addressed.

(58:6–9a) Fasting is no longer the subject of concern. Instead, the theme of social justice is taken a stage further, in a passage which has become a classic as an expression of one vital side of the prophetic movement. Not least among its attractions for religious people down the ages is the fact that it is couched in the form of an exhortation, with a powerful promise attached, rather than in terms of condemnation. Again it is clear that it is the upper strata of society who are being addressed; those who have bread and a house, as against the hungry and the homeless poor.

(58:9b–12) This and the following passage (vv. 13–14) are similar in form: a series of conditions followed by a spelling out of the results which will follow obedience to those conditions. The contents, however, differ. Here we have a continuation of the promise already made in vv. 6–9a. Active concern for the needs of others will ensure that God's saving activity becomes available. It is doubtful how far the language of restoration in v. 12 is to be applied literally, for example as picturing the restoration of ruined Jerusalem. It is at least as likely that this is a metaphor for the renewal of the community, a theme which runs through so much of Isaiah.

(58:13–14) It might seem logical that, having rejected the need for fasting, sabbath-observance could also be considered otiose. But poetry and religious practice have a habit of resisting logical demands. As in ch. 56, sabbath-keeping is to be an essential feature of the community. It is the 'holy day of YHWH', and we have seen enough of the importance of holiness in Isaiah to know that this is a guarantee of its status.

(59:1–8) After the encouragement implicit in the exhortations of ch. 58 the harsh condemnations of these verses provide a striking contrast. The theme of YHWH as saviour, implicit already in the name Isaiah itself, has run right through the book from ch. 12 onwards, yet salvation still seems afar off. This is not due to any lack of capacity on YHWH's part. It is the result of the iniquities (once again the word used is *ʿāwôn*) of the community, or at least of those opposed by the Isaiah group. A whole catalogue of wrongdoing follows. For some of the items a literal understanding is possible, though not required (false dealings in the lawcourts, v. 4). Other accusations defy precise interpretation ('They hatch adders' eggs and weave the spider's web', v. 5).

vv. 7–8 are quoted by Paul in Rom 3:15–27, following a quotation from Ps 14, and then by a curious error these verses came to be incorporated in the Book of Common Prayer version of Ps 14, with which they have no original connection.

(59:9–15a) A lament follows. It is not easy to decide whether we are to envisage the 'they' of v. 8 as now speaking in the first person, or whether this reflects tensions within the community. The latter is perhaps easier: the lack of *mišpāṭ* (justice) among those condemned has had an invasive effect, and this leads to the true worshippers feeling themselves to be deprived of *mišpāṭ* and *ṣĕdāqâ*. In the Psalms most laments are in effect protestations of innocence, with the fault for present troubles lying elsewhere. Here, by contrast, there is a confession of sin (vv. 12–13).

(59:15*b*–19) YHWH's response to these troubles is now set out. This describes YHWH as the Divine Warrior, an image running through much of the HB from Ex 15:3 on, and frequently used in Isaiah (e.g. 51:9–11). Here the conflict is spelt out in greater detail. The threat to peace is found in the lack of justice; there is no one else to intervene, so YHWH himself, pictured as clad like a warrior, brings a retribution which will be acknowledged in world-wide terms (Hanson 1979: 124). The wording provided the author of Ephesians with the basis for his picture of the Christian's warfare, but it is a theme which was to have an ominous future in the history of religion, as various fanatical groups have identified themselves with God's supposedly warlike purposes.

(59:20–1) The first verse is better seen as the climax of the preceding poem, stressing that Zion, so prominent in the Isaiah tradition, will be the locale of the divine triumph manifested to those who 'turn from transgression'. It is not specified who is involved here. The following verse, one of the rare prose elements in this part of the book, seems unrelated to its context. It is not clear who is being addressed; it may be an assertion of the lasting validity of the words of YHWH spoken through prophets, and the promise of the spirit provides a link with 61:1.

(60:1–3) Chs. 60–2 are often regarded as the high point of the last part of Isaiah, providing many links back with 40–55. Certainly we shall see themes here which encourage us in our reading of the book as a whole. The promise of salvation, muted in chs. 56–9, now comes strongly to the fore once again, not least in these opening verses. In some ways it almost seems as if the vision in ch. 6 undergoes significant modification. There the whole earth was full of the glory of YHWH; here the glory appears over the saved community, whereas darkness covers the earth. We are warned against too easy a universalism; light and brightness come to other nations and kings only by way of Israel. This last theme is strikingly similar to 2:4.

(60:4–7) The gathering of the nations is now described in greater detail, though throughout this chapter it is noteworthy that the nations described are not those who had ruled over Israel (Assyria, Babylon, Persia), but those referred to in its traditions, especially Genesis. Within Isaiah itself there are literary links, first between v. 4*a* and 49:18, which are identical, and then more generally with such passages as 49:22, spelling out the privileged status of the community's offspring, and also with some Psalms, notably Ps 72 with its description of the bringing of tribute. The gold and frankincense of v. 6 provide part of the literary background to the story of the wise men in Mt 2. Only in its conclusion, with its emphasis on the temple, is the stress somewhat different from the other passages.

(60:8–16) As this extended section moves forward it becomes increasingly clear that it is the holy city Zion which is being apostrophized. v. 10*b* could serve as a summary of a large part of the book as a whole, spelling out how God's wrath against his city and people has turned to favour. In all this foreigners, the former oppressors, have their part to play, so that v. 12 strikes an unexpectedly harsh note. It is often understood as prose (*BHS*), and some regard it as 'a secondary interpolation' (so Emmerson 1992: 42), but it does represent one strand in

the book which speaks of divine vengeance on enemies (cf. 63:1–6). The remainder of the present passage, however, is more concerned with spelling out the exalted state of Zion than with the fate of its enemies. It is unwise to try to use poetry of this kind as a guide to the rebuilding of Jerusalem after its destruction; Williamson (1989: 149) has noted that v. 13 has been used as a proof that the temple both has been and has not been built. In a vivid figure of speech at the climax (v. 16) Zion is pictured as a suckling infant—a remarkable transformation of the whore of 1:21. But though still at the breast (of kings!) Zion is mature enough to know what 'the Mighty One of Jacob' has done for her. The verse is clearly meant to be read with 49:26. What had there been shown to 'all flesh' is now perceived by Zion herself.

(60:17–22) *šālôm* and *ṣĕdāqâ*, such prominent terms throughout Isaiah, are now pictured as in full control, guiding the fortunes of the restored city. With such overseers and taskmasters oppression is far away and *yĕšûʿâ* ('salvation', another constantly recurring expression) and *tĕhillâ* ('praise', a much less frequently found term, though cf. 42:10, 12; notice also that the Hebrew name for the Psalms, with which Isaiah has so much in common, is *tĕhillîm*) will become the basis of trust. It is clear that here a tendency already implicit in what has preceded is taken further: we are moving into the world of apocalyptic imagery, in which the realities of daily living are swept up into a vision of divine possibilities. In 65:17 this is taken even further into the thought of new heavens and a new earth. Perhaps equally visionary and removed from everyday reality is the hope that 'your people shall all be righteous (*ṣaddîqîm*)', but the prophetic vision extends even to this possibility. Finally, in words reminiscent of Gen 12:2, a population explosion is envisaged. What might today seem a threat was in the ancient world an occasion of joy.

(61:1–4) 11:2 had promised that 'the spirit of the LORD' would come upon God's chosen one; here in language reminiscent of the servant passages in chs. 40–55 the claim is made to indwelling by that spirit and through God's anointing—*māšaḥ*, the word from which 'messiah' is derived. Not surprisingly, therefore, the figure here depicted has been understood as an ideal king (Eaton 1979: 90), though the bringing of good news suggests that prophetic elements are also present. As in 11:4 the role of this spirit-filled figure is to bring about justice, particularly to those most liable to be the victims of injustice. It was natural that Luke should find this an appropriate passage on which to base his presentation of the ministry of Jesus (4:18–19). The themes of 'release' and of a particular 'year of favour' recall the Jubilee described in Lev 25, whereas 'the day of vengeance' has already been mentioned in Isaiah (34:8). But whereas the earlier passage described that vengeance in gruesome detail, here it is no more than a passing allusion, perhaps introduced as a wordplay with the following promise of comfort. (The words for 'vengeance', *nāqam*, and 'comfort', *nāḥam*, are very similar in Heb.) The comforting provides a link with 40:1, and it is then elaborated using a variety of metaphors. The destruction which has played so prominent a part early on in the book will now be restored.

(61:5–7) The ambivalent attitude to foreigners which has run through the whole book is found again. Here strangers and foreigners are welcome, but only in a subordinate role; it is the community itself which will enjoy the wealth and riches of other nations. The community itself is to be given priestly status; and here difficulties of interpretation arise. Is this to be taken literally, for example as providing scriptural warrant for the belief held by some Christian bodies in the 'priesthood of all believers'? Or is a sociological reading appropriate, so that the thrust of this passage is against those who claimed an exclusive priestly status in Second Temple Israel? Or is it better simply to see here a metaphor, comparable to many others in these chapters, a way of expressing the favoured status of the true community? v. 7 is difficult; there seems to be a link with 40:2 (which would argue against the NRSV emendation of Heb. 'your' to 'their'), but the exact force of the language is not easy to capture ('quite unintelligible', Whybray 1975: 243).

(61:8–11) v. 8 is put into the mouth of YHWH himself, but in the rest of the section the 'I' is the prophetic voice. The need for justice (*mišpāṭ*) is again reaffirmed. NRSV then follows some ancient versions and the majority of modern commentators in reading 'robbery and wrongdoing', and this may be right. But MT 'robbery with a burnt offering' is not to be ruled out; it would tie in well with 1:11, and serve as a warning to the community that justice must accompany their sacrifices. The covenant theme is then picked up from 55:3. As in v. 5 foreigners have a subordinate position, as those who will acknowledge Israel's blessed condition. The chapter ends with the Zion community expressing its thanksgiving to God in psalm-like language and with very varied metaphors for the blessings that have been promised.

(62:1–3) There has been much dispute as to the identity of the 'I' in v. 1; is it a prophetic voice or YHWH himself? The same problem arises later in the chapter (Emmerson (1992: 76–8) provides a brief survey). We must ask, however, whether we should expect poetry to yield an objective answer to such a question. Clearly the poem sees as essential to the divine plan the 'vindication' (*ṣedeq* once again) and 'salvation' (*yĕšûʿâ*) of Zion. Here the nations are no more than witnesses of the astonishing transformation that is envisaged. A series of blessings for Zion is spelt out: a new name and royal status. The first of these will be spelt out more fully in the next oracle.

(62:4–9) The giving of a new name did not necessarily mean the abandonment of the old one; Jacob was called Israel (Gen 32:28; 35:10), but still continued to be known as Jacob. The destruction of Jerusalem in 587 seems to have led all the main prophetic traditions to envisage a new name for the restored city (Jer 33:16; Ezek 48:35), and the renaming here is in line with that pattern (Pfisterer Darr 1994: 198–200). The 'desolate' land described in 1:7 is now transformed. Here, perhaps more clearly than anywhere else in the book, the picture of YHWH as the marriage-partner of the city emerges. With v. 6 the imagery changes once more to that of a city and its inhabitants (and the issue of the first-person reference emerges again). Now the foreigners are no more than witnesses of all that YHWH is achieving for his own community.

(62:10–12) We return to the double imperatives which have been a marked feature of the book from ch. 40 onwards. The link with ch. 40 is strengthened by the building of the highway, the processional way leading up to the restored city, and

by the identity of the last part of v. 11 with 40:10. The restoration proclaimed as it were from a distance in the earlier chapter is now coming more sharply into focus. This is emphasized by the names given to the community in v. 12. The transformation begun in v. 4 is complete; what once was called 'forsaken' shall be so no longer.

(63:1–6) From these rarefied heights it seems a steep descent to the bloodthirsty language of this passage. The nineteenth-century hymn-writer may have found himself able to read these verses in terms of Christ's passion ('Who is this with garments gory | Triumphing from Bozrah's way?'), but such an understanding is alien to a natural reading of the passage. (The poem also underlies the American 'Battle Hymn of the Republic', which links it with Christ's triumph, but in terms closer to the original: 'Mine eyes have seen the glory of the coming of the Lord; | He is trampling out the vintage where the grapes of wrath are stored'.) The poem portrays YHWH as the Divine Warrior, as does 59:15–19, with which there are several links: cf. 59:16 with v. 5 and 59:18 with vv. 4 and 6. The form used at the outset is that of the watchman demanding to know the identity of the fearsome figure approaching the city. His questions provide the opportunity for a divine warrior hymn, exulting in the victory that has been won. Edom, referred to in v. 1, was assigned typical status as *the* enemy in Second Temple Judaism (cf. Ps 137 and Obadiah), and later symbolized such enemies of Judaism as the Roman Empire and the Christian church (Dicou 1994: 204). In this passage the symbolic element is already present, for the hymn is concerned with any hostile nation, not just Edom. But ch. 34 has already shown that this anti-Edom strand is an important element in Isaiah, and the references to Edom and Bozrah should certainly be retained, against the widely held emendation, still suggested by *BHS*, to words meaning 'stained red' and 'one who treads grapes' (Whybray 1975: 253). The reply takes up once again the theme of 'vindication' (*ṣĕdāqâ*), thereby providing a strong link with what has preceded. The metaphor of the winepress is reused in Rev 19:15.

(63:7–9) It is widely and probably rightly held that 63:7–64:12 constitute a single extended unit, comparable to the community laments found in such Psalms as 44 and 74. We shall look at the constituent elements, while trying to bear in mind the presence of a larger context, a context which reminds us once again of the close links between the language of Isaiah and that of the Jerusalem temple. The lament begins with the characteristic recall of past times, when God had been personally active in protecting his people (cf. Ps 44:1–8). As in 61:10 the 'I' seems to denote a prophetic voice, but it plays no further part in the lament.

(63:10–19) A very characteristic feature of this and of the laments in the Psalms is the vivid description of the disasters that have befallen the community. There are links also with Lamentations, but there the disaster is largely regarded as inexplicable; here the context is immediately provided by the acknowledgement of the people's rebellion (v. 10). The usage, 'holy spirit of God' is rare in the HB, and this passage was seized upon by the writer to the Ephesians (4:30) in the development of a distinctive Christian understanding. The references to Moses are unique in Isaiah; it would be unwise to build anything on the NRSV description of Moses as 'servant'; this is based on an emendation to the Hebrew text, and a more natural modification would offer 'Moses and his people' (Hanson 1979: 84). The example of the deliverance at the Exodus is used, both because it was the paradigm of God's saving power, and also because it was so closely juxtaposed in tradition with the community's wilderness rebellion. With v. 15 we reach the next stage of the lament; the complaint that God is taking no notice of his people's fate. It is as if he has forgotten them. v. 16 has been understood by some (esp. Hanson 1979: 92–3; Achtemeier 1982: 115–18) as indicative of a division within the community, with the names 'Abraham' and 'Israel' standing for a rival group. But this is surely to read too specific a reference into allusive poetry. More naturally we may suppose that the poet is hoping that though Abraham and Israel (Jacob) are long gone, the continuing power of YHWH could and should be used on the people's behalf. In v. 18 it is natural to see a reference to the destruction of the Jerusalem temple, and to identify that with the Babylonian attack of 587/6 (2 Kings 25:9), but once again we should be aware of the danger in attempting precise cross-reference; poetic allusions and historical statements occupy different frames of reference.

(64:1–12) This extended section continues to reflect the characteristic features of the communal lament. There is a good deal of repetition, but that is not to be regarded as a weakness in this kind of poem. So v. 1 reflects 63:15; vv. 2–4 recollect God's past mighty deeds in a way analogous to 63:7–14. Then comes the renewed acknowledgement of the people's sin, now made more direct by the use of the first person plural (v. 5; cf. 63:10). This description of sin is further elaborated here, with the interesting logic in v. 7 that they have ceased calling on God because he doesn't listen. The notion of God hiding his face is most characteristic of the Psalms (cf. Ps 44:24), but we should also see a link with Isa 8:17 and with 45:15 where the 'hiddenness' of God allowed a measure of hope which is scarcely present here. But amid this despair the community still has a claim upon God as its father, recalling the theme of 63:16, and the poem ends with a final plea that God will be so moved by the unhappy state into which the places of his worship have fallen that he will stir from his apparently unending silence. Questions of God feature frequently in lament psalms, but usually in the body of the psalm (Ps 44:24; 74:10–11); here the lament ends with the question still being asked. We are warned against supposing that the confidence of many of the later chapters of the book tell the whole story.

(65:1–7) This is the first part of a longer unit, which extends to v. 16. YHWH himself is now pictured as speaking, and in that sense this provides an obvious response to the anxious pleas of the previous chapter. We are invited to see that idolatrous practices are the cause of the people's continuing rejection. In many ways, that is to say, we are back in the situation depicted in ch. 1, though with an important development. Ch. 1 seemed to offer hope to those who would mend their ways (e.g. vv. 18–20); here it seems as if that door has been closed, and there is now no alternative to punishment (Carr 1993: 73–4). However that may be, the links between these verses and ch. 1 are striking. The 'gardens' of v. 3 recall those in 1:29, a verse in which the themes of choosing and delighting are picked up

here in vv. 12–13 (Sweeney 1988a: 23). This section is clearly a picture of a community rejected because of practices regarded as idolatrous. Less certain is the attempt to reconstruct what those practices actually were. We are back in the world of religious polemic, in which any practice, however appalling, can be attributed to one's enemies.

(65:8–16) Whereas the first part of the unit 1–16 was concerned only with the looked-for fate of idolaters, here a series of contrasts is drawn, introduced at vv. 8 and 13 by the prophetic messenger formula 'says the LORD'. On the one hand is the promise to those who are judged to have remained faithful (vv. 8–10); on the other further idolatrous practices are listed, ensuring the condemnation of those engaged in them (vv. 11–12). Following the second prophetic introduction the contrast becomes even sharper as it sets out the different fates awaiting 'my servants' (here regularly in the plural; a divided community cannot be addressed as 'servant') and 'you'. The third-person references of vv. 1–7 are now pictured as spoken directly to the offenders. This contrast is an important difference from the early chapters of the book, where the community as a whole was apparently condemned (though even there there were presumably those who shared the standpoint of the author of the poems and expected to escape judgement). In v. 11 NRSV translates the Hebrew words *gad* and *menî* as 'Fortune' and 'Destiny'; this is the only direct biblical reference to their worship, though Gad is frequent as one element in place names. The theme of delighting and of right and wrong choice in v. 12 provides another link with 1:29, and strengthens the impression of a deliberate rounding-off of the completed collection.

(65:17–25) The bitterness of the preceding poem gives way to a new promise. 'For' at the outset suggests a link with what has preceded, but this may be an asseverative usage: 'Surely I am!' YHWH as creator has been a recurrent theme since ch. 40, and the last two chapters of the book take this to a climax with a complete renewal of heaven and earth (cf. 66:22). The 'former things' played an important part in the lawcourt-like material of ch. 41; now, as in 43:18, they are to be set aside. The cosmic picture of v. 17 then narrows down to hopes for Jerusalem in 18–19, but perhaps in view of the way the city is idealized in Isaiah the shift is less dramatic than it seems. The blessings promised in the following verses are characteristic of the hopes of an agricultural community in the ancient world. The allusion to a tree in v. 22 may be a deliberate contrast to the rejected trees of 1:29–31, in view of other allusions to that section in these final chapters (Sweeney 1988a: 23). However that may be, it is clear that v. 25 offers deliberate allusions to 11:6–9, several phrases from which are brought together in an idealized description of Jerusalem, 'my holy mountain'. The prophetic formula is added as in vv. 8 and 12 to provide additional authenticity to the vision. It is a picture akin to, but not yet fully developed into, the apocalyptic visions of a later period.

(66:1–2) Another messenger formula introduces an oracle which begins conventionally enough, but then develops unexpectedly. Where is God's dwelling? It is natural, particularly in the light of the immediately preceding reference to 'my holy mountain' to speak of God as dwelling in heaven and not confined to an earthly house (cf. 57:15). Much more unusual is the apparent rejection of the temple at the end of v. 1. It is most unlikely that there is a reference here to a sanctuary other than the Jerusalem temple. It is possible that deliberately exaggerated language is being used, but in any case it is likely that we have a warning, comparable to 1:10–17, against excessive trust in any earthly building—even the very temple itself (Emmerson 1992: 58). That God is indeed pictured as speaking from the temple emerges clearly from v. 6. Just as the earlier passage went on to spell out what was required of God's true worshippers, so here v. 2 emphasizes what God really looks for.

(66:3–5) The dangers of false worship are now spelt out more fully, though unfortunately not more clearly. The Hebrew consists of a series of four pairs of statements, the first in each pair describing normal cultic practice, the second an offensive action. There is no indication of the connection between them. Thus 3a could be translated 'The one who slaughters an ox, the one who kills a human being'. Most ancient versions and most modern translations (e.g. NRSV) insert a comparison ('is like'), with the implication that all sacrificial worship is unacceptable. This scarcely seems likely. Perhaps more plausible is to suppose that those in charge of the cult are being condemned, their legitimate actions being no better than the grossest syncretism. (There is a helpful discussion in Schramm 1995: 166–70.) v. 5 seems to stand somewhat apart from what has preceded, and acts as a summary. It is introduced by the solemn formula 'Hear the word of the LORD' found in a similar context at 1:10. The divisions within the community seem less sharp than in the preceding verses, difficult though those are. Here those who are being opposed are still 'your own people', even if they hate and reject you.

(66:6) is taken by NRSV as an isolated verse, but it is perhaps best seen as linked with the preceding, and claiming that God will denounce from the temple those whom the poet regards as his enemies. The contrast with the doubts about the temple in v. 1 is striking.

(66:7–9) The theme of Zion as the mother of children is taken up again, as in 54:1–3. But the most striking contrast is with 37:3. There children came to the birth, but there was no strength to bring them forth. Now, by means of a rhetorical question, YHWH gives assurance that he will bring to birth (NRSV: 'open the womb', the same verb as in 37:3). By an extraordinary metaphor YHWH is pictured as a midwife—so effective in the task that there will be no labour pains.

(66:10–11) There have been many references to daughter Jerusalem in the book; now Jerusalem as mother is the centre of celebration. Whatever divisions the community may display, the holy city is pictured as the kind of faithful city envisaged at 1:26.

(66:12–16) The promise to Jerusalem is underlined by the introductory messenger formula, with a message of comfort reminiscent of ch. 40. But the comfort is not universal. As is too often the case in the ancient and the modern world, the reassurance of one group bears with it the assurance of punishment on those perceived as enemies, and the language of the last two verses, using once again the motif of the divine warrior, is as harsh as anything we have found in the whole

book. It is also poetry, which reminds us that we should not take 'all flesh' literally.

(66:17) A curious prose note is inserted. Someone felt it necessary to be more explicit about what were regarded as abominable practices carried on in the 'gardens' to which 65:3 has already referred. The avoidance of food which is not kosher is a widespread religious concern.

(66:18–21) Another prose passage, but this time of a very different temper. If v. 17 stressed what seems to us a negative viewpoint, here the positive attitude to foreigners found in ch. 56 is taken further. Though the reference to the coastlands is characteristic (cf. 11:11), the actual list of foreign places in v. 19 is unexpected, owing more to Ezek 27 than to anything in Isaiah (though cf. Davies (1989: 95) for links within Isaiah). Still more astonishing is the thought, underlined as being a divine oracle, that some of these foreigners might be enrolled as priests and Levites—a far cry from what is found elsewhere in the HB, e.g. Num 18:7 (Emmerson 1992: 106).

(66:22–3) The last poem in the book takes up again the 'new heavens and new earth' theme of 65:17, linking it first with the idea of perpetuity ('shall remain'), then with the concern for new moon (not otherwise characteristic of Isaiah) and sabbath (much emphasized in 56 and 58), and finally universalizing it. In v. 16 'all flesh' was to be destroyed by the sword; here it is to come to worship. We are reminded for a last time of the dangers of too literal and referential a reading of poetry.

(66:24) The high note of v. 23 might have seemed an appropriate closure, and indeed in synagogue readings it is customary to read v. 23 again after v. 24. For in this last prose note we have a sombre warning, of the possibility of lasting judgement on the rebellious, with the same rare word 'quenched' as we found in 1:31. The HB is often thought of as harsh, so it is ironic to note that this is virtually the only passage in all its contents to speak of lasting judgement—and that it is a passage seized upon by the New Testament (Mk 9:48).

It seems appropriate as we reach the end of the book briefly to reflect upon what we have been reading. As with most collections of poetry it is inappropriate to ask for a 'meaning', but we can readily see that certain themes recur: the hope of salvation, expressed in the name 'Isaiah' (= God saves) and repeated through the book; the need for God's ṣedeq to be expressed in the community of his worshippers; the concern for Zion as potentially the best and too often in practice the worst of God's creation. This linkage with Zion is underlined by the many allusions to and cross-references with the Psalms. Dating of all this material is difficult, and is most unlikely to follow the order of the complete book, but a period of 200–300 years may well be implied. Within all this poetry are a number of prose passages, linking it with Isaiah and using episodes from his life as providing a structure for the whole. Some of these passages may well have been taken from 2 Kings; to what extent they enshrine reliable tradition or whether any of the poems go back to Isaiah himself we have no means of knowing. Readers will differ in their perception whether or not this uncertainty is a serious loss. What we do have is a collection of superb poems driven by their authors' conviction that God was active in all the ups and downs which the community had experienced and must continue to anticipate.

REFERENCES

Achtemeier, E. (1982), *The Community and Message of Isaiah 56–66* (Minneapolis: Augsburg).

Ackroyd, P. R. (1987), 'Isaiah 1–12: Presentation of a Prophet', 'Isaiah 36–39: Structure and Function', 'An Interpretation of the Babylonian Exile: A Study of II Kings 20 and Isaiah 38–39', and 'The Death of Hezekiah', in his *Studies in the Religious Tradition of the Old Testament* (London: SCM), 79–104, 105–20, 152–71, and 172–80.

Albertz, R. (1990), 'Das Deuterojesaja-Buch als Fortschreibung der Jesaja-Prophetie', in E. Blum, C. Macholz, and E. W. Stegemann (eds.), *Die Hebräische Bibel und ihre zweifache Nachgeschichte: Festschrift für Rolf Rendtorff* (Neukirchen-Vluyn: Neukirchener Verlag), 241–56.

Alt, A. (1953), 'Jesaja 8, 23–9, 6: Befreiungsnacht und Kronungstag', in *Kleine Schriften zur Geschichte des Volkes Israel*, 1st edn. 1950 (Munich: C. H. Beck), ii. 206 ff.

Balentine, S. E. (1983), *The Hidden God* (Oxford: Oxford University Press).

Barr, J. (1992), *The Garden of Eden and the Hope of Immortality* (London: SCM).

Barstad, H. M. (1994), 'The Future of the "Servant Songs"; Some Reflections on the Relationship of Biblical Scholarship to its own Tradition', in S. E. Balentine and J. Barton (eds.), *Language, Theology, and the Bible: FS James Barr* (Oxford: Clarendon), 261–70.

Begg, C. T. (1989), 'Babylon in the Book of Isaiah', in J. Vermeylen (ed.), *The Book of Isaiah*, BETL 131 (Leuven: Leuven University Press), 121–5.

Bentzen, A. (1957), *Introduction to the Old Testament* (Copenhagen: Gad).

Carr, D. (1993), 'Reaching for Unity in Isaiah', *JSOT* 57: 61–80.

Carroll, R. P. (1979), *When Prophecy Failed* (London: SCM).

—— (1981), *From Chaos to Covenant* (London: SCM).

—— (1992), 'Co-opting the Prophets: Nehemiah and Noadiah', in E. Ulrich, J. W. Wright, R. P. Carroll, and P. R. Davies (eds.), *Priests, Prophets and Scribes: FS J. Blenkinsopp*, JSOTSup 149 (Sheffield: Sheffield Academic Press), 87–99.

Childs, B. S. (1967), *Isaiah and the Assyrian Crisis*, SBT 2/3 (London: SCM).

Clements, R. E. (1980a), *Isaiah 1–39* (NC Bible Commentary) (Grand Rapids, Mich.: Eerdmans).

—— (1980b), *Isaiah and the Deliverance of Jerusalem*, JSOTSup 13 (Sheffield: JSOT).

—— (1985), 'Beyond Tradition History: Deutero-Isaianic Development of First Isaiah's Themes', *JSOT* 31: 95–113.

—— (1989), 'Isaiah 14, 22–27: A Central Passage Reconsidered', in J. Vermeylen (ed.), *The Book of Isaiah* (Leuven: Leuven University Press), 253–62.

Clifford, R. J. (1972), *The Cosmic Mountain in Canaan and the Old Testament*, HSM 4 (Cambridge, Mass.: Harvard University Press).

Clines, D. J. A. (1976), *I, He, We, and They: A Literary Approach to Isaiah 53*, JSOTSup 1 (Sheffield: JSOT).

Conrad, E. W. (1985), 'The Community as King in Second Isaiah', in J. T. Butler, E. W. Conrad, and B. C. Ollenburger (eds.), *Understanding the Word: FS B. W. Anderson*, JSOTSup 37 (Sheffield: JSOT), 99–111.

—— (1991), *Reading Isaiah* (Minneapolis: Fortress).

Cryer, F. H. (1994), *Divination in Ancient Israel and its Near Eastern Environment*, JSOTSup 142 (Sheffield: Sheffield Academic Press).

Davies, G. I. (1989), 'The Destiny of the Nations in the Book of Isaiah', in J. Vermeylen (ed.), *The Book of Isaiah* (Leuven: Leuven University Press), 93–120.

Day, J. (1980), 'A Case of Inner Scriptural Interpretation: The Dependence of Isaiah xxvi.13–xxvii.11 on Hosea xiii.4–xiv.10 (Eng. 9) and its Relevance to Some Theories of the Redaction of the Isaiah Apocalypse', *JTS* NS 31: 309–19.

Dicou, B. (1994), *Edom, Israel's Brother and Antagonist: The Role of Edom in Biblical Prophecy and Story*, JSOTSup 169 (Sheffield: Sheffield Academic Press).

Eaton, J. H. (1979), *Festal Drama in Deutero Isaiah* (London: SPCK).

—— (1982), 'The Isaiah Tradition', in R. Coggins, A. Phillips, and M. Knibb (eds.), *Israel's Prophetic Tradition* (Cambridge: Cambridge University Press), 58–76.

Eissfeldt, O. (1962), 'The Promises of Grace to David in Isaiah 55:1–5', in B. W. Anderson and W. Harrelson (eds.), *Israel's Prophetic Heritage: FS J. Muilenburg* (London: SCM), 196–207.

—— (1965), *The Old Testament: An Introduction* (Oxford: Blackwell).

Emerton, J. A. (1982), 'The Translation and Interpretation of Isaiah vi. 13', in *Interpreting the Hebrew Bible: Essays in Honour of E. I. J. Rosenthal* (Cambridge: Cambridge University Press), 85–118.

—— (1992), 'The Translation of Isaiah 5:1', in F. Garcia Martinez, A. Hilhorst, and C. J. Labuschagne (eds.), *The Scriptures and the Scrolls: Essays in Honour of A. S. van der Woude* (Leiden: Brill), 18–30.

Emmerson, G. I. (1992), *Isaiah 56–66*, Old Testament Guides (Sheffield: Sheffield Academic Press).

Fohrer, G. (1967), 'Jesaja 1 als Zusammenfassung der Verkündigung Jesajas', in his *Studien zur alttestamentlichen Prophetie*, BZAW 99 (Berlin: de Gruyter), 148–66.

Gibson, J. C. L. (1978), *Canaanite Myths and Legends* (Edinburgh: T. & T. Clark).

Gosse, B. (1988), *Isaïe 13, 1–14, 23 dans la tradition littéraire du livre d'Isaïe et dans la tradition des oracles contre les nations*, OBO 78 (Fribourg: Universitätsverlag).

Hanson, P. D. (1979), *The Dawn of Apocalyptic*, 2nd edn. (Philadelphia: Fortress).

Heaton, E. W. (1994), *The School Tradition of the Old Testament* (Oxford: Clarendon).

Hennecke, E. (1963), *New Testament Apocrypha* (London: SCM), i.

Henry, M.-L. (1967), *Glaubenskrise und Glaubensbewährung in den Dichtungen der Jesajaapokalypse* (Stuttgart: Kohlhammer).

Jacob, E. (1987), *Esaïe 1–12*, CAT 8a (Geneva: Labor et Fides).

Jenkins, A. K. (1989), 'The Development of the Isaiah Tradition in Isaiah 13–23', in J. Vermeylen (ed.), *The Book of Isaiah* (Leuven: Leuven University Press).

Jensen, J. (1973), *The Use of tora by Isaiah*, CBQMS 3 (Washington: Catholic Biblical Association).

—— and Irwin, W. H. (1989), 'Isaiah 1–39', in *NJBC*.

Johnson, A. R. (1955), 'Mashal', in M. Noth and D. Winton Thomas (eds.), *Wisdom in Israel and in the Ancient Near East*, VTSup 3 (Leiden: Brill), 162–9.

Johnson, D. G. (1988), *From Chaos to Restoration: An Integrative Reading of Isaiah 24–27*, JSOTSup 61 (Sheffield: JSOT).

Jones, G. H. (1971), 'Abraham and Cyrus: Type and Anti-Type?', *VT* 22: 304–19.

Kaiser, O. (1974), *Isaiah 13–39*, OTL (London: SCM).

—— (1983), *Isaiah 1–12* OTL (London: SCM). This is the 2nd English edn.; in the first edn. (1972), much more of the material was regarded as originating from Isaiah himself.

Kratz, R. G. (1991), *Kyros im Deuterojesaja-Buch*, FAT 1 (Tübingen: Mohr[Siebeck]).

Kugel, J. L. (1981), *The Idea of Biblical Poetry* (New Haven: Yale University Press).

Kuhrt, A. (1983), 'The Cyrus Cylinder and Achaemenid Imperial Policy', *JSOT* 25: 83–97.

Kuntz, J. K. (1982), 'The Contribution of Rhetorical Criticism to Understanding Isaiah 51: 1–16', in D. J. A. Clines, D. M. Gunn, and A. J. Hauser (eds.), *Art and Meaning: Rhetoric in Biblical Literature*, JSOTSup 19 (Sheffield: JSOT), 140–71.

Lindblom, J. (1958), *A Study on the Immanuel Section in Isaiah* (Lund: Gleerup).

Ludwig, O. (1961), *Die Stadt in der Jesaja-Apokalypse* (Bonn: Rheinische Friedrich-Wilhelms-Universität).

McKane, W. (1965), *Prophets and Wise Men*, SBT 44 (London: SCM).

McKenzie, J. L. (1968), *Second Isaiah*, AB 20 (Garden City, NY: Doubleday).

Macintosh, A. A. (1980), *Isaiah XXI: A Palimpsest* (Cambridge: Cambridge University Press).

Matthews, V. H., and Benjamin, D. C. (1993), *Social World of Ancient Israel 1250–587 BCE* (Peabody, Mass.: Hendrickson).

Mazar, B. (1957), 'The Tobiads', *IEJ* 7: 137–45, 229–38.

Melnyk, J. L. R. (1993), 'When Israel was a Child: Ancient Near Eastern Adoption Formulas and the Relationship between God and Israel', in M. P. Graham, W. P. Brown, and J. K. Kuan (eds.), *History and Interpretation: Essays in Honour of John H. Hayes*, JSOTSup 173 (Sheffield: Sheffield University Press), 245–59.

Merendino, R. P. (1981), *Der Erste und der Letzte: Eine Untersuchung von Jes. 40–48*, VTSup 31 (Leiden: Brill).

Mettinger, T. N. D. (1983), *A Farewell to the Servant Songs: A Critical Examination of an Exegetical Axiom* (Lund: Gleerup).

Millar, W. R. (1976), *Isaiah 24–27 and the Origin of Apocalyptic*, HSM 11 (Missoula, Mont.: Scholars Press).

Miscall, P. D. (1993), *Isaiah* (Sheffield: Sheffield Academic Press).

Murray, R. (1982), 'Prophecy and the Cult', in R. Coggins, A. Phillips, and M. Knibb (eds.), *Israel's Prophetic Tradition* (Cambridge: Cambridge University Press), 200–16.

—— (1992), *The Cosmic Covenant* (London: Sheed & Ward).

Nielsen, K. (1978), *Yahweh as Prosecutor and Judge* JSOTSup 9 (Sheffield: JSOT).

North, C. R. (1948), *The Suffering Servant in Deutero-Isaiah* (Oxford: Oxford University Press).

—— (1964), *The Second Isaiah* (Oxford: Clarendon).

Petersen, D. L. and Richards, K. H. (1992), *Interpreting Hebrew Poetry* (Minneapolis: Fortress).

Pfisterer Darr, K. (1994), *Isaiah's Vision and the Family of God* (Louisville, Ky.: Westminster/John Knox).

Phillips, A. (1982), 'Double for all her Sins', *ZAW* 94: 130–2.

Rad, G. von (1966a), 'The Royal Ritual in Judah', in *The Problem of the Hexateuch and Other Essays* (Edinburgh: Oliver & Boyd), 222–31.

—— (1966b), 'There Remains Still a Rest for the People of God: An Investigation of a Biblical Conception', ibid. 94–102.

Rendtorff, R. (1994), 'The Composition of the Book of Isaiah', and 'Isaiah 56:1 as a Key to the Formation of the Book of Isaiah', in his *Canon and Theology* (Edinburgh: T. & T. Clark).

Ringgren, H. (1956), *The Messiah in the Old Testament*, SBT 18 (London: SCM).

Rowley, H. H. (1952), 'The Servant of the Lord in the Light of Three Decades of Criticism', in his *The Servant of the Lord and other Essays* (London: Lutterworth), 1–57.

Sawyer, J. F. A. (1973), 'Hebrew Words for the Resurrection of the Dead', *VT* 23: 218–34.

—— (1989), 'Daughter of Zion and Servant of the Lord in Isaiah: A Comparison', *JSOT* 44: 89–107.

Schoors, A. (1973), *I am God your Saviour: A Form-Critical Study of the Main Genres in Isaiah xl–lv*, VTS 24 (Leiden: Brill).

Schramm, B. (1995), *The Opponents of Third Isaiah: Reconstructing the Cultic History of the Restoration*, JSOTSup 193 (Sheffield: Sheffield Academic Press).

Selms, A. van (1982), 'The Holy One of Israel', in W. C. Delsman *et al.* (eds.), *Von Kanaan bis Kerala: FS J. P. M. van der Ploeg* (Neukirchen-Vluyn: Neukirchener Verlag), 257–69.

Simon, U. E. (1953), *A Theology of Salvation* (London: SPCK).

Skinner, J. (1910), *The Book of the Prophet Isaiah Chapters xl–lxvi*, Cambridge Bible, 1st edn. 1898 (Cambridge: Cambridge University Press).

Smith, S. (1944), *Isaiah Chapters xl–lv: Literary Criticism and History*, Schweich Lectures, 1940 (London: British Academy).

Snaith, N. H. (1967), 'Isaiah 40–66: A Study of the Teaching of the Second Isaiah and its Consequences', in H. M. Orlinsky and N. H. Snaith, *Studies on the Second Part of the Book of Isaiah* VTS 14 (Leiden: Brill).

Stacey, W. D. (1990), *Prophetic Drama in the Old Testament* (London: Epworth).

—— (1993), *Isaiah 1–39*, Epworth Commentaries (London: Epworth).

Steck, O. H. (1985), *Bereitete Heimkehr*, SBS 121 (Stuttgart: Katholisches Bibelwerk GmbH).

—— (1991), *Studien zu Tritojesaja*, BZAW 203 (Berlin: de Gruyter).

Sweeney, M. A. (1988a), *Isaiah 1–4 and the Post-Exilic Understanding of the Isaianic Tradition*, BZAW 171 (Berlin: de Gruyter).

—— (1988b), 'Textual Citations in Isaiah 24–27', *JBL* 107: 39–52.

—— (1993), 'The Book of Isaiah in Recent Research', *Currents in Research: Biblical Studies*, 1: 141–62.

Tomes, R. (1993), 'The Reason for the Syro-Ephraimite War', *JSOT* 59: 55–71.

Torrey, C. C. (1928), *The Second Isaiah* (Edinburgh: T. & T. Clark).

Uffenheimer, B., 'Isaiah's and Micah's Approaches to Policy and History', in Reventlow, H. G., Hoffman, Y., and Uffenheimer, B. (eds.) (1994), *Politics and Theopolitics in the Bible and Postbiblical Literature*, JSOTSup 171 (Sheffield: Sheffield Academic Press), 176–88.

Van Seters, J. (1975), *Abraham in History and Tradition* (New Haven: Yale University Press).

Vaux, R. de (1961), *Ancient Israel* (London: Darton, Longman & Todd).

Vermeylen, J. (1977–8), *Du prophète Isaïe à l'apocalyptique*, 2 vols. (Paris: Gabalda).

—— (1989), 'L' unité du livre d'Isaïe', in Vermeylen (ed.), *The Book of Isaiah* (Leuven: Leuven University Press).

Werlitz, J. (1992), *Studien zur literarkritischen Methode: Gericht und Heil in Jesaja 7, 1–17 und 29, 1–8*, BZAW 204 (Berlin: de Gruyter).

Westermann, C. (1967), *Basic Forms of Prophetic Speech* (London: Lutterworth).

—— (1969), *Isaiah 40–66*, OTL (London: SCM).

Whybray, R. N. (1971), *The Heavenly Counsellor in Isaiah xl 13–14*, SOTSMS 1 (Cambridge: Cambridge University Press).

—— (1974), *The Intellectual Tradition in the Old Testament*, BZAW 135 (Berlin: de Gruyter).

—— (1975), *Isaiah 40–66*, New Century Bible (London: Marshall, Morgan & Scott).

—— (1978), *Thanksgiving for a Liberated Prophet*, JSOTSup 4 (Sheffield: JSOT).

—— (1983), *The Second Isaiah*, Old Testament Guides (Sheffield JSOT).

Wiklander, B. (1984), *Prophecy as Literature: A Text-Linguistic and Rhetorical Approach to Isaiah 2–4*, CBOT 23 (Lund: Gleerup).

Wildberger, H. (1972), *Jesaja 1–12*, BKAT 10/1 (Neukirchen-Vluyn: Neukirchener Verlag).

—— (1978), *Jesaja 13–23*, BKAT 10/2 (Neukirchen-Vluyn: Neukirchener Verlag).

—— (1989), 'The Concept of Israel in Transition', in R. E. Clements (ed.), *The World of Ancient Israel* (Cambridge: Cambridge University Press), 141–61.

Williamson, H. G. M. (1994), *The Book Called Isaiah* (Oxford: Clarendon).

23. Jeremiah

KATHLEEN M. O'CONNOR

INTRODUCTION

A. 1. To read the book of Jeremiah is to enter a colloquy of voices. These voices contend with one another to give meaning to a national tragedy so devastating that it defies simple explanation and rational analysis. Poetry and narrative, metaphor and myth, sermonic exhortation and theological defiance converge in what can seem like a cacophony of non-melodic speech. When expectations of linear development and the search for historical origins are set aside as primary criteria of interpretation, however, a multifaceted conversation emerges from the book. By its very open-ended nature, that conversation moves towards healing and hope for a radiant future.

2. In current Jeremiah scholarship, issues of critical introduction are greatly disputed and thoroughly intertwined. Unsettled matters include aspects of the book's historical background, audience, dating, history of composition, and relationship to the historical Jeremiah. Summary discussions of these matters follow. Herrmann (1986) provides a detailed survey of introductory questions.

B. The Tragedy. 1. From the beginning to the end of its fifty-two chapters, the subject of Jeremiah is the fall of Judah to Babylon in the sixth century BCE. This national catastrophe and subsequent struggles for survival were the catalysts that produced the book, and they haunt every chapter. Events reflected here reach a climax in the siege and fall of Jerusalem in 587 BCE, but international and internal troubles afflicted the nation well before and after that defining period (Herrmann 1986: 7–27; Hayes and Miller 1986: 416–36; Ackroyd 1968: 50–61).

2. The waning of the Assyrian empire in the late seventh century BCE opened the door to competition between Egypt and the emerging neo-Babylonian (Chaldean) empire for dominance in the region. In response to international pressure, Judah divided into political factions that supported Egyptian or Babylonian alliances. Many in the Judean governing classes were pro-Egyptian, whereas Jeremiah and his followers, including some leading families, supported Babylon. A decisive victory over Egypt at Carchemish in 605 gave Babylon control of the region but did not quiet the political strife in Judah.

3. In 597, Judah revolted against Babylonian sovereignty. This resistance provoked an invasion of Jerusalem, the capital city, and led to the deportation of King Jehoiachin and other leaders, and the installation of puppet King Zedekiah upon the throne (2 Kings 24–5; Seitz 1989a). A second Judean revolt under Zedekiah caused an even more disastrous attack on Judah and Jerusalem ten years later. After a long siege, the Babylonians breached the city walls in 587/6. They burned the king's palace, destroyed the temple, and exiled more citizens to Babylon. The Babylonians then appointed Gedeliah governor of conquered Judah, but a group led by a surviving member of the royal family assassinated him and massacred his entourage. Inner anarchy triggered a third invasion and deportation in 582.

4. Historians judge that exilic life in Babylon was not as onerous by ancient standards as it might have been (Hayes and Miller 1986: 430–5). Judean exiles settled, married, and may even have engaged in business dealings with the native population. Rather than submit to Babylon, however, some Judean survivors escaped to Egypt and forced Jeremiah and his companion Baruch to accompany them (Jer 43). About life in Egypt and in occupied Judah little is known, though the book of Lamentations is traditionally ascribed to a remnant in Judah.

5. Many aspects of this version of Judah's history evoke heated debate among historians. One problem is that the chief sources of information about these events are biblical texts that receive scant corroboration from other sources and which themselves are fragmentary, contradictory, and interpretative rather than descriptive and referential. Biblical texts are not historical documents in the modern critical sense. They do not narrate events to tell precisely what happened. As theological literature, they portray events to interpret and explain them, to persuade the community to act in particular ways, to challenge and shape its identity, and to sow seeds for a new future (Perdue 1994: 7–11).

6. What this brief narrative does reveal, however, is that the book of Jeremiah emerged from perilous, chaotic, and conflictual times (Seitz 1989a). Prior to 587, Judah experienced occupation by foreign powers who interfered in internal affairs, exacted tribute and political allegiance, and created long-lasting internal divisions. The Babylonian siege of Jerusalem in 587 caused starvation and death for many, destroyed national and family life, and shook theological and political foundations of the people's identity. Survivors lost loved ones, land, and livelihood; many were deported. Beyond physical and emotional devastation, there was also symbolic wreckage. The destruction of palace and temple meant the collapse of political, ideological, and theological symbols that had long provided identity and stability for the nation (Stulman 1995). Because national identity had been linked to YHWH's promises to dwell in the temple and to protect the Davidic monarchy (2 Sam 7; Isa 1–12), the loss of these institutions and of the promised land led to profound upheaval. Nor did conflict abate after the invasion during the exilic period. Events called out for interpretation; survival of the community was in serious doubt; new leadership and symbolic understandings needed to emerge.

7. From this maelstrom of suffering and confusion came questions of ultimate meanings. Where was the covenant God who gave them land and promised to be with them? Had God abandoned them, abused them, forgotten them, or was God merely powerless to prevent the crushing of the chosen people? The book and its multiple voices compete to explain events, to argue about divine justice, and to point the way to survival.

C. Audience and Dating. 1. Various passages and blocks of material in the book addressed many different audiences in the process of its composition. The audience of the book's final form, however, was probably survivors of the Babylonian invasion, particularly exiles in Babylon (Seitz 1989a; Overholt 1988; but see Carroll 1986 and Goldman 1992). To propose the exilic community as the primary audience does not preclude later additions, nor does it deny the likelihood of an earlier audience in pre-exilic Judah. Although the historical setting of the book's final form cannot be established with certainty, a number of elements point to an exilic provenance. These include overriding concern with the nation's fall and with survival, reserve regarding restoration, vague promises of return (chs. 30–3), the absence of Cyrus and the Persians who were historical agents of the return, and the limited attention given to temple rebuilding.

2. In addition to thematic elements pointing to an exilic audience, reader-response analysis provides tools for examining the 'implied audience' dramatized in the text. The text itself provides clues about the audience it wishes to influence (Suleiman and Crosman 1980; Thompson 1980). The book's early chapters (2:1–4:2) address the children of YHWH's unfaithful wife and invite them to repent (3:14–25). With liturgical praises they confess their sins and return to YHWH in fidelity (3:21–15; Diamond and O'Connor 1996). This same first-person plural liturgical voice reappears in a number of places (10:1–25; 14:7–9; 31:18–20), suggesting that the text brings its audience in by dramatizing them in the voice of the children. The children are the survivors of YHWH's cast-aside wife (Jer 2:1–4:2). The book artfully constructs imaginative symbolic worlds that seek to elicit response and to create new worlds for the exiles. It invites them to repent by presenting models of repentance; it provides theological and political explanations of the nation's collapse; and it assures their survival and a future, if they do repent.

D. History of Interpretation. 1. Modern readers often find Jeremiah difficult. Its wide variety of literary materials, contradictory themes, and abundant imagery create the impression of chaos and dissymmetry. Poetic oracles, prose narratives, and prose sermons overlap, contradict, and interrupt one another. Chronological confusion compounds literary and thematic disarray. Although the book contains occasional headings that date events to reigns of particular kings, these dates do not follow chronological order. Modern interpretation of Jeremiah tries to make sense of these difficulties.

2. Nearly all interpretations of Jeremiah in the twentieth century begin from the work of Bernhard Duhm (1901) and Sigmund Mowinckel (1914). Good summaries of their theories appear in Stulman (1986: 7–14); Carroll (1986: 39–42); and Holladay (1989: 11–12). Duhm and Mowinckel made sense of the book by understanding it as the result of a long compositional process during which distinct written sources or traditions from different times were joined together by editors. The sources were thought to be: (1) poetic sayings from Jeremiah himself; (2) biographical prose narratives attributed to Jeremiah's scribe, Baruch; (3) prose sermons, attributed to Deuteronomistic writers; (4) salvific oracles in chs. 30–1 and other miscellaneous blocks of material including the Oracles Against the Nations (Jer 46–51). According to this theory, literary evidence enables interpreters to separate the book's strata from one another and arrive at the earliest, most authentic layer (Rudolph 1947; Weiser 1960).

3. After nearly a century of interpretative labour, little of the Duhm–Mowinckel consensus remains though it still greatly influences the conversation (see Herrmann's 1986 discussion). Challenges have come from several directions with no new agreement yet emerging. Hyatt (1958), Nicholson (1970), Thiel (1973), and Carroll (1986), for instance, have accepted a late Deuteronomistic layer in the book, but rather than discrediting it as secondary, they have considered it to be creative theological and redactional activity with its own integrity (Goldman 1992).

4. By contrast, building on studies by Weippert and Bright, Holladay (1986) disputes Deuteronomistic influence. This line of interpretation holds that much of the prose and nearly all the poetry contains Jeremiah's own words or the gist of his message. Sharp changes in style and theme reflect changing situations in the prophet's life, not redactional activity. McConville (1993) makes a similar case for Jeremianic authorship on theological rather than linguistic and stylistic grounds. He finds crucial differences between Jeremiah and the Deuteronomistic books regarding visions of the future.

5. From yet another direction, Wanke (1971) denies the existence of a single Baruch document, finding at least three tradition complexes within the so-called Baruch material, while McKane (1986) dispenses with written sources altogether (cf. Reitzschel 1966). He proposes, instead, that an original core of Jeremiah's words generated expansions and developments over the years in an unsystematic fashion. The result was a rolling corpus that grew gradually into a complex, diffuse, and untidy book without overarching redactional intention. McKane finds little possibility of distinguishing compositional layers within the text. He argues correctly that dating of various pieces and additions cannot be easily accomplished. Carroll (1986: 50) joins him in emphasizing the complexity of the final text, although Carroll (1986) and Thiel (1973; 1982) hold to strong Deuteronomistic redactional activity.

E. Jeremiah. 1. Traditional interpretation has long held that the book contains a biographical account of Jeremiah's life and work. Many contemporary scholars still operate from this assumption and even understand the book to contain a narrative of its own historical beginnings (Jer 36). Holladay (1989), Skinner (1922), Bright (1965), and recently, Seybold (1993) and McConville (1993) view the book this way. A rising choir, however, opposes the notion that the book provides access to the historical Jeremiah at all. McKane (1980) believes it begins with a core of Jeremiah's words, but they cannot be located with reasonable certainty. Carroll (1986) doubts the prophet's historicity altogether. In his view, Jeremiah is an 'editorial link' between different parts of the tradition, that is, largely an imaginary character. Brueggemann (1988; 1991) is agnostic on the historical Jeremiah and, in agreement with Polk (1984), speaks of the literary persona rather than the historical figure. Whether the text records historical events, reflects theological and ideological imagination, or both, is simply not clear, nor have we the evidence to make it clear (Perdue 1994: 7–11).

2. A Symbolic Figure. Rather than search for the historical life of Jeremiah or for precise historical origins of the book's many elements, helpful as those approaches have been in the past, this commentary attempts to understand the book's final form. Such an interpretive procedure recognizes that the figure of Jeremiah plays a major role in the book, unlike any prophet in any other prophetic book. Although Jeremiah may not be a character in the modern literary sense, the portrait of Jeremiah presented in the book cannot be dismissed. Jeremiah appears in the call narrative of ch. 1, is the presumed or identified speaker of many oracles, sermons, and first-person prayers called 'confessions', and he is the subject of numerous narrative accounts. Impressions of his life, whether historical or imagined, are an important feature of the book and provide one key to its interpretation. Jeremiah plays a critical symbolic role in meeting the needs of the exilic audience. As symbolic and imaginative construction, Jeremiah's life is iconic of the fate of the exiles, even as he represents YHWH as the prophet who announces their fate (Polk (1984), *contra* Biddle 1996: 6). But YHWH, too, suffers with the people as the book progresses.

F. Synchronic Interpretation. 1. While it is evident that the book is vastly complex literature composed over a long period of time by many hands, the text's unreadability may be overstated in some theories of composition. By concentrating on origins of texts and placing greater historical and theological value on the oldest texts, interpreters often overlook theological and literary power embedded in the text as it stands. Synchronic approaches are beginning to address these issues. Brueggemann (1994); Clements (1993); Seitz (1989a); Biddle (1996); Liwak (1987); Stulman (1995); Diamond and O'Connor (1996); and Kessler (1997) are employing new approaches to investigate literary unity across many parts of the book. (See Perdue 1994 on new methods.)

2. When the search for origins of texts is set aside, the book emerges as a conversation among many voices in an open-ended structure (see also Biddle 1996). Voices overlap, echo and re-echo, debate, rage, and grow quiet. Often a narrative, symbolic logic appears in the book's circular and discordant symphony. Voices portray different characters in poetry and different narrators in prose. Unity comes from the dominance of the divine voice across the book (Biddle 1996) and from the central role given to Jeremiah. His words and actions help structure the book, create emotional and theological power, and draw readers into his struggles as both foil and mirror to their own. Synchronic interpretation attends to the unifying effects of root metaphors in poetry and prose, notices narrative devices and symbolic meanings of events and dates, and considers rhetorical functions of text.

3. Diachronic questions cannot be dismissed entirely, however. The relationship of text to historical context remains central to interpretation (Liwak 1987). Rather than seeking original contexts of small units, however, synchronic interpretation seeks to understand the relationship of the final form of the text to its audience in exile. Past, present, and future time frames criss-cross one another as if temporal boundaries were permeable. Linear chronology is absent because for exiles the pre-exilic past and hoped-for future merge with present realities as they struggle to survive.

G. The Versions. 1. A further complication in interpretation comes from differences between the Hebrew (MT) and Greek (LXX) versions of the text of Jeremiah. Reversing the usual relationship of the MT to LXX, the Hebrew text of Jeremiah is significantly longer than the Greek. It adds titles and epithets to names, makes explicit pronouns left implicit in the Greek, and adds more complex expansions (Janzen 1973: 127). In addition, the arrangement of the two texts differs significantly. The MT places the Oracles Against the Nations near the end (chs. 46–51), whereas the LXX locates them in the centre (25:14–31:44) and arranges them differently. Soderlund (1985) presents a clear discussion of theories to explain the differences between the two texts.

2. Four fragments of the text of Jeremiah were found among the Dead Sea scrolls at Qumran: from cave 4, 4Q Jer[a], 4Q Jer[b], 4Q Jer[c] and from cave 2, 2Q Jer. One of these fragments (4Q Jer[b]) points to a shorter Hebrew text that may have been the basis (*Vorlage*) for the LXX translation. Janzen (1973) (see also Cross 1964 and Tov 1976) argues that the LXX is both an older and a superior text to the MT. This view is challenged, however, by Soderlund (1985: 193–248), and Bogaert (1981). It may be argued that the LXX and MT must represent two separate recensions, arising in different circumstances to meet different communal needs. At the very least, the differences between the versions show that the text received complex and lively scribal attention, and this is testimony to the significance accorded to the Jeremiah tradition (Carroll 1986: 50–5; McKane 1986: pp. xv–xli). This commentary treats the MT as a version of Jeremiah with its own literary and theological integrity.

H. Structure. 1. Jeremiah has two major subdivisions, chs. 1–25 and 26–52.

Book One, chs. 1–25:
Cosmic Destruction (chs. 1–10)
　Superscription and Call (1:1–19)
　Broken Marriage (2:1–4:2)
　Cosmic Battle (4:3–6:30)
　Temple Sermon (7:1–8:3)
　Weeping (8:4–10:25)
Covenant Destroyed (chs. 11–20)
　Covenant Curse (11:1–17)
　Jeremiah's Protest and God's Reply (11:17–12:25)
　A Loincloth, a Winejar, and a Rape (13:1–27)
　Drought (14:1–22)
　No Future, Yet a Future (15:1–16:21)
　Hope for Some (17:1–27)
　Captivity (18:1–20:18)
Aftermath (chs. 21–5)
　Siege of Jerusalem (21:1–10)
　Collapse of Royal Power and Promise of Restoration (21:11–23:40)
　Figs (24:1–10)
　Babylon's Fall (25:1–38)
Book Two, chs. 26–52:
Blame and Hope (chs. 26–36)
　Prophetic Discord (26:1–29:32)
　Book of Comfort (30:1–33:26)
　A Bad King and a Good Community (34:1–35:19)
　Two Scrolls (36:1–32)

The 'Baruch Account' (37:1–45:5)
Oracles Against the Nations (46:6–51)
The End (ch. 52)

2. Jeremiah has the reputation of unremitting doom, relieved only by the book of comfort buried near the centre (Jer 30–3). Such an assessment is not entirely accurate. The book does contain a river of accusation, destruction, and weeping, but across its complex literary composition there flows a steady spring of hope and renewal. Read synchronically as a document for exiles, Jeremiah is a book of life.

COMMENTARY

Cosmic Destruction (chs. 1–10)

Largely poetic in form, these chapters announce Jeremiah's commission (Jer 1) and contain accusations and judgements against Judah and Jerusalem (Jer 2–10). They progress from a description of the broken marriage between YHWH and the people to announcements of invasion by a mythic army, to massive weeping at the inevitable cosmic destruction. Amidst this material appear short liturgical expressions of repentance that symbolize the voice of the exiles and provide them with models of repentance.

(1:1–3) The superscription introduces the book by making authoritative claims for its contents. Jeremiah prophesied for forty years, from the thirteenth year of King Josiah (627 BCE) until Jerusalem's capture (587 BCE). Holladay (1989: 25–7) and Carroll (1986: 89–92) provide maximalist and minimalist historical opinions of these dates. Theologically, the superscription points to an intimate relationship between Jeremiah and YHWH who alone is the source of Jeremiah's words (1:1–2; Craigie, Kelley, and Drinkard 1991: 1–2; Liwak 1987: 54–103). Politically, the superscription sets the book within the context of royal rule that is about to collapse (Brueggemann 1988: 20). Symbolically, it links Jeremiah's forty-year ministry to Moses' leadership in the wilderness. (On Jeremiah's many parallels with Moses, see Seitz 1989a.) The superscription's details, therefore, serve to persuade readers that this book comes from Jeremiah, can be trusted, and must be heeded. Such a defence suggests an audience in conflict.

(1:4–19) The Call The call account introduces Jeremiah and certifies him to be a true prophet. (For history of composition, see Rudolph 1947: 21–31 and Thiel 1973: 63–79.) The chapter divides into two scenes, poetic audition (vv. 4–10) and prose visions (vv. 11–19). Both scenes contain dialogue between prophet and deity in which Jeremiah speaks in the first person and quotes divine speech (vv. 4, 7, 9, 11, 14). Elements of the conventional call narrative appear in the text (Habel 1965), but here also are introduced major themes and motifs of chs. 1–25 (O'Connor 1988: 118–23). YHWH names Jeremiah 'prophet to the nations', warns him about the people's resistance, and promises divine assistance. YHWH also announces disaster from the north that will bring judgement upon Judah and Jerusalem. For the exilic audience, the call narrative implies that the disaster that has already befallen them was in the divine plan to 'pluck up and to pull down', and equally that YHWH can be relied upon to 'build and plant' (v. 10).

In memorable poetry, the opening scene (vv. 4–10) creates a portrait of the prophet as YHWH's indisputable agent. Jeremiah himself provides a first-person account of his dialogue with YHWH who called him before his birth (v. 5); this pre-natal commission indicates that YHWH alone established him as prophet. Jeremiah resists (v. 6) with vocational hesitancy that evokes Moses' call (Ex 3:11; 4:10–11). Like Moses, Jeremiah receives divine assurance. Were there still any doubt about the source of Jeremiah's message, YHWH touches Jeremiah's mouth and puts there divine words (v. 9; McKane 1986). Creating an emphatic climax to the poem, v. 10 circles back to and expands the commission announced in v. 5c. Jeremiah's mission extends beyond Judah to include the nations in a divine plan of destruction and rebuilding, of uprooting and planting.

An astonishing theological assertion of this book is that Jeremiah is sent 'to the nations'. His mission has global significance. The God for whom he speaks governs the fall and rise of nations, a theme that receives reprises at both the middle (25:15–38) and end of the book (chs. 46–52). For an exilic audience, even the prophet's commission may intimate hope because it reveals that the nations who have destroyed Judah are also the subject of divine governance.

Prose visions (vv. 14–19) provide the content of Jeremiah's message, narrow its recipients from the nations to Judah and Jerusalem, and reassure Jeremiah that YHWH is with him to deliver him (v. 19, cf. v. 8). Dialogue predominates over vision in the narrative about the almond tree (vv. 11–12). When YHWH asks Jeremiah what he sees, Jeremiah replies literally, 'the branch of an almond tree'. YHWH, not Jeremiah, interprets the vision, playing on the Hebrew word for almond tree (šāqēd). 'I am watching (šōqēd) over my word to perform it' (v. 12). The conversation reassures both prophet and audience that the prophetic word is relentless and irreversible because its divine speaker utters it and 'does it' (laʿăśōtō).

The context of the divine word is metaphorical. A boiling pot tilts 'away from the north' and from the north will come disaster upon Judah and Jerusalem for their idolatry (vv. 13–16). The northern location of the boiling pot, and later in the book of 'the foe from the north', poses interpretative difficulties because Babylon is east of Judah. Literal interpretations of this language have led to many historical identifications of the enemy, including the ancient Scythians (McKane 1986: 20). But Childs (1959) and Perdue (1994: 141–6) show that the 'foe from the north' is language that comes from a myth of a transcendent enemy who brings chaos in a great battle. Borrowed from Israel's neighbours, this language expresses the theological conviction that Israel's disaster has cosmic significance and arises from YHWH's fierce anger. The mythic foe from the north is eventually historicized in Jeremiah but not until 20:4–6 where Babylon appears by name for the first time.

The absence of a historical referent for the 'boiling pot, tilted from the north', at the beginning of the book strikes an ominous note and is all the more fearsome for its lack of specificity. The threat from the north is greater than any human enemy. Boiling, burning fluid, tipped over and uncontrolled, advances upon Judah and Jerusalem with unstoppable horror in the form of attacking tribes from unknown kingdoms. They, 'all of them', will establish hegemony over Judah for its idolatry (1:16).

YHWH speaks directly to Jeremiah to prepare him for battle (vv. 17–19). Imperatives replace dialogue. Jeremiah must gird his loins and announce everything YHWH commands. He must be implacable in face of resistance or YHWH will 'break' him. Yet Jeremiah will prevail for YHWH has already strengthened him as 'a fortified city, an iron pillar, and a bronze wall', and is with him to deliver him. This encouraging assurance is often thought to refer exclusively to the prophet and his mission, but it may also have resonances for an exilic audience. In some parts of the book Jeremiah's sufferings seem to gather up those of the community. Even as nations fight against them, YHWH is with them.

(2:1–4:2) A Broken Marriage Many interpreters find unifying thematic threads in the poetry and prose collected here (Biddle 1990: 82; McKane 1986: 82; DeRoche 1983; Carroll 1986). Study of the literary devices of direct address, grammatical gender of characters, and the nature of divine accusations reveals strong literary coherence in the material. The broken marriage of YHWH and his unfaithful wife serves as an organizing or root metaphor (Ricoeur 1975, 1976; McFague 1982) that closely unites the chapters (Diamond and O'Connor 1996; Brueggemann 1988: 46–7). In its present form, 2:1–4:2 dramatizes the ending of the marriage (2:1–3:5) and depicts its aftermath of recrimination and partial familial restoration (3:6–4:2). This metaphor functions as a second prologue to the book by providing a symbolic interpretation of the nation's fall and of the crisis facing the exiles.

Borrowed from Hosea 1–3 (see Holladay 1989: 45–7) and significantly modified (Diamond and O'Connor 1996), the marriage metaphor allows the poet to introduce YHWH's wife Judah or perhaps Jerusalem (Biddle 1990: 68–73) as a parallel persona to male Israel. Direct address alternates between the two personae in 2:1–3:5. Hebrew feminine singular grammatical forms address the wife in 2:2; 2:17–25; and 2:33–3:5; and masculine singular and plural forms address male Israel in 2:3; 2:4–16; and 2:26–32. At first the two personae appear to be distinct characters, but they are one entity, addressed under different guises. The opening poem (2:1–3) equates them symbolically, and 2:19–20 makes literal that identification. Both male and female personae receive the same rhetorical and thematic treatment. YHWH addresses each directly, interrogates them with similar rhetorical questions, accuses by quoting their words, and charges each with abandonment and pursuit of other allegiances.

These poetic devices in 2:1–3:5 amass legal evidence against wife/Israel. Reluctantly, husband/YHWH recognizes the hopelessness of the marriage and divorces the wife (2:1–3:5). The symbolic identity of the wife is fluid at this point in the book, though she will later be identified as Jerusalem or daughter Zion (4:31). Here, however, she represents Israel from the earliest days in the wilderness (2:2). After the divorce (3:6–4:2), the husband declares wife Judah worse than her northern sister, his first wife, whom he invites to return to him (3:6–12). The second wife, like the first, remains silent or absent, so he turns to the children and invites them to return

instead (3:14–18). They accept by proclaiming repentance and return to him with a liturgical declaration of fidelity and loyalty (3:22b–25).

(2:1–3:5) The Divorce The poem that introduces the story of the marriage (2:1–3) begins with the same formula as 1:4, but here Jeremiah is commanded to proclaim the word to Jerusalem. The husband's monologue begins with direct address to his wife (2:2b, fem. sing.). Nostalgically he recalls her past devotion and loyalty in the wilderness. v. 3 explicates v. 2 (Fishbane 1985: 300), even as it shifts the subject to male Israel who is 'holy to the LORD, the first fruits of his harvest'. In this verse, wife and male Israel converge symbolically; both are 'totally devoted to' (Brueggemann 1988: 32), and exclusive property of, YHWH. Subsequent poems alternate in addressing the two personae, equally guilty of betrayal and pursuit of idols.

(2:4–16) An introductory formula, different from 2:1, opens the first poem addressed to male Israel, called here the houses of Jacob and Israel (v. 4). Some scholars explain the shift from a Judahite to an Israelite audience historically by arguing that Jeremiah originally preached on the subject of the northern kingdom that had fallen to Assyria in 721, over a century earlier than Jeremiah's own time (Holladay 1986: 68). Of more interest is the rhetorical import of address to the northern kingdom (Carroll 1986: 122). Jacob is the eponymous ancestor and unifying patriarch of all Israel (Gen 29–30), who figures here as symbol of united Israel. The poems in 2:1–4:2 accuse both north and south of heinous betrayal and envision a reunified future. They interpret theologically the fall of both kingdoms. The materials concerning the north may carry further rhetorical import for, by contrast, Judah appears far more guilty (3:6–12) and by implication, faces a similar fate (cf. 7:12–15).

Rhetorical questions (2:5, 6, 8, 11, 14) structure 2:4–16 and convey YHWH's shock at the ancestors' treatment of him (vv. 5–6), despite his generosity in bringing them into a 'plentiful land' (v. 7). Leaders fail to ask the right questions, abandon him, and pursue others (v. 8). YHWH accuses Israel of forsaking him, 'fountain of living water' (v. 13), and of substituting their own useless cisterns (v. 14). The husband invites the heavens to participate in his shock (v. 12) for this betrayal has cosmic implications. Subjugation to Egypt, identified by its cities, becomes inevitable (v. 16).

(2:17–25) Feminine singular forms appear without explanation. Accusatory questions (vv. 17, 18, 21, 23) and charges of betrayal continue from the previous poem but with a qualitative difference. Betrayal is no longer only theological, national, and cosmic; it is also intimate, domestic, sexual, pornographic (Weems 1995; O'Connor 1992). To build his case against his wife, the husband quotes her (v. 20a) and accuses her with her own words (v. 25). He describes her lewd behaviour (v. 20b), portraying her as a harlot, bestial in her sexuality, a lust-driven animal wildly out of control (vv. 23–4).

(2:26–32) Male Israel's shame, by contrast, compares to that of a captured thief and to idolators who relate to trees and stones (vv. 26–7). The male persona turns his back on YHWH and resists correction. Again YHWH quotes (vv. 27, 31) and heaps questions upon the accused (vv. 28, 29, 31, 32). The poem reeks of scorn for idols and their addle-brained devotees

(vv. 27–9) to evoke sympathy for YHWH/husband who cannot understand this treachery (v. 31).

(2:33–3:5) Formally, this section may contain two poems (2:33–7 and 3:1–5; Nicholson 1973: 40), unified by the feminine form of address and by a return to themes of adultery and promiscuity. The adulterous wife now becomes a madam of whores who teaches other women her ways (2:33). Her husband characterizes her as a murderer of the innocent poor (2:24) and quotes her declaration of innocence and false estimates of his anger (2:35). Other lovers will shame her (2:36–7). Then comes the climactic question of this account of the marriage; will a husband return to his wife after a divorce? (3:1; see Holladay 1986: 112–13 and McKane 1986: 58–9 on translation difficulties). The marriage is over. For her to return is legally impossible and would pollute the land (Deut 24:1–4).

Multiple partners compound her adultery. She lurks at roadsides in search of them (3:2). Her distorted sexuality brings barrenness upon the land (3:3). The husband quotes her misperception of his anger (3:4) and charges her with full responsibility for the marriage's failure.

(3:6–4:2) The Aftermath The subsequent collection of poetic (3:12b–14, 19–23) and prose materials (3:6–12a, 15–18, 24–5) depicts the immediate aftermath of the divorce, but the text's formal divisions no longer correspond with shifts in addressee. Direct address of female (3:12b–13, and 19) and male (3:20) continues but other characters, hardly noticed before, become important here. Jeremiah, mentioned only in 2:1, becomes part of the narrative as sympathetic friend of the husband (3:6–12). A second wife appears (3:7–10) and male children assume the climactic role in the story of this marriage (3:14–18, 21–5).

(3:6–11) In a dramatic aside, the furious husband confides to Jeremiah the story of his wife's harlotry (vv. 6–7). The passage dates to the time of Josiah, further anchoring the marriage metaphor in the history of Judah and indicating that Jeremiah's prophecy of national collapse significantly predated the event. The husband muses out loud about his past hopes for the marriage. Readers receive a shock when the husband admits he had a previous wife, Israel, sister of his second wife, who also cuckolded him. Compared to Judah, who should have learned from her sister's treachery, however, first wife Israel is less guilty. YHWH sends Jeremiah to intercede with her (vv. 8–11).

(3:12–18) To the north, Jeremiah proclaims, 'Return, faithless Israel' (v. 12). But there is a condition; she must take responsibility for the failure of the marriage by acknowledging her guilt (v. 13). The text narrates no reply from her, and a decisive shift occurs in relationships. Husband/YHWH turns attention on the children, offering them the same invitation to 'return'. The Hebrew verb *šûb* carries the nuance of turning from sin (Holladay 1958). For the children there are no preconditions. Instead, they are coaxed to return with promises of a splendid future in the land, joined together north and south under one shepherd after YHWH's own heart (vv. 15–18).

(3:19–20) Yet YHWH's unfaithful wife lingers in his thoughts as he muses sadly about his past plans for her and for their relationship. At this bitter moment, the divine speaker steps out of the role of husband to elucidate the meaning of the marital metaphor: 'as a faithless wife leaves her husband, so have you been . . . O house of Israel' (v. 20).

(3:21–5) A mysterious voice introduces a major motif of the book, the heartbreaking sound of children weeping (v. 21). They repent of their sins that echo their mother's; they, too, have forgotten their God (vv. 23–5). But unlike their mother whose silence implies refusal to repent, the children repent emphatically after hearing promises of healing the mother never heard (v. 22). The narrative closes in a dramatic reunion of father and children. Surprisingly, YHWH does not quote them, they speak for themselves. For the first time in the book, YHWH becomes the addressee and the speakers use liturgical prayer (Blank 1961: 102; Biddle 1996: 138). 'Here we come to you; for you are the LORD our God' (v. 22). Monologue becomes dialogue and chastised hope emerges (Diamond and O'Connor 1996).

The broken-marriage metaphor creates a highly effective introduction to Jeremiah's prophecy. Through it, the book invites readers to side with YHWH in the collapse of the nation. YHWH's portrayal as a betrayed, broken-hearted, and faithful husband creates an emotional claim upon readers that encourages them to view the marriage from the husband's perspective. What happens to wife/Israel is not YHWH's fault, but hers. The metaphor explains the fall of the nation as punishment for the infidelity of the pre-exilic generation that experienced divine rejection (ibid.). Male and female personae represent the fallen Judah and Jerusalem, and the first wife from the north represents the fallen northern kingdom. For them there is no future because they do not repent. The children in this troubled family are the implied audience, the exilic community given voice at the story's climax (vv. 22–5). The marriage metaphor spins a theological narrative that encapsulates the destruction of the two Israelite kingdoms, promises unconditional restoration to their offspring, and portrays the implied audience in the book as children of the cast-aside and abandoned wife. In miniature, 2:1–4:2 conveys the accusation, judgement, and hope of the entire book.

Despite the extraordinary artistic effectiveness of Jeremiah's version of the broken marriage, contemporary readers must approach this text with caution. The account's most rhetorically winning and theologically pregnant feature is its portrayal of God as an abandoned, heartbroken husband, betrayed by faithless, nymphomaniac wives. Readers cannot avoid taking his side. Hidden in this account, however, is a rhetoric of blaming in which the failure of the marriage is placed on the women with whom male Israel is symbolically identified. Men are dishonoured by being called faithless 'women', and the metaphor projects onto women the sins of the nation (ibid.; O'Connor 1992; Weems 1995). When viewed against cultures that subtly or blatantly vilify women and deify men, this metaphor requires careful treatment.

(4:1–4) bridges the collections of the broken marriage and the cosmic battle (4:5–6:30). Thematically, the poem reaches back to repeat the invitation to 'return' (v. 1) in the marriage (3:12–14), and it extends forwards by promising YHWH's wrathful judgement if they refuse to turn (v. 4; see 4:8, 26). The children have returned (3:21–5), but vv. 1–4 ignore the family reunion. The marriage metaphor symbolically enacts the entire course of Judah's history from the perspective of divine–human relationship. But vv. 1–4 and the chapters that follow shift the temporal perspective of the text to the pre-exilic period. The text assumes that repentance is uncertain and reissues conditions of repentance and loyalty to avoid disaster (vv. 1–2; on syntactical problems, see Holladay 1986: 122–3). The temporal shift places readers in the psychic and spiritual world of the implied audience who exist in a limbo between the nation's destruction and return from exile. Whatever their earlier functions may have been, poems of threat and warning appropriate to the pre-exilic period aid the exilic audience by interpreting their plight and underscoring the necessity of repentance and fidelity.

The consequence of Israel's hoped-for loyalty confirms the book's exilic context; its allegiance will redound to the benefit of the nations (v. 2; Carroll 1986: 156). Like Jeremiah, Israel has a mission among the nations, and like Abraham, the mission is to be a blessing (Gen 12:3). vv. 3–4 transform YHWH's conditional invitation to Israel in vv. 1–2 into a threat, addressed to Judah and Jerusalem. Circumcision of the heart must replace cultic circumcision, or divine wrath will burst forth like unquenchable fire. The text's demand for circumcision of the heart echoes Deut 10:16 (Holladay 1986: 129–30), and highlights again the text's male audience. Metaphorical interpretation of circumcision as spiritual commitment, however, makes possible the inclusion of females in the worshipping community, albeit as spiritual males (O'Connor 1992).

(4:5–6:30) Cosmic Battle No narrative unifies the poems collected here, but the metaphor of the impending cosmic battle with the mysterious 'foe from the north' looms over the chapters and grants them a unity of swirling, menacing drama (Condamin 1920: 28; Perdue 1994; Brueggemann 1988: 49–73). The voices of YHWH, Jeremiah, a narrator, the people, the northern kingdom, daughter Zion, and the foe—all announce, respond to, and dispute YHWH's role in the coming siege.

The battle poems use great artistry in portraying war. Scenes of approaching armies vividly appeal to the senses and give the suprahuman enemy from the north shape in the imagination. With a few well-chosen details of sight and sound, they transport readers into the thick of battle. 4:5–31 announces the battle's approach; 5:1–31 reveals the battle to be inevitable; 6:1–30 names Jerusalem as the place of siege (Clements 1988: 40–1). Major themes and images overlap and weave together to defend YHWH from charges of injustice and arbitrariness in the fall of the nation. The principal rhetorical purpose of these chapters is to persuade the readers that YHWH was forced to punish the people. Dissenting and interrupting voices connect the chapters to the implied audience in exile (4:27; 5:18–19). Lament themes (4:8, 19) link these chapters to 8:4–10:25, and threads from the broken-marriage metaphor (4:16–18, 29–31; 5:7–9) connect them to 2:1–4:2.

(4:5–8) Battle Announced Opening the battle sequence (4:5–6:30), this poem announces major themes to appear in the poetry of chs. 4–10. It assumes that the people have not repented (*šûb*) and proclaims that YHWH's anger has not

'turned' (*šāb*) from them (v. 8). v. 5 asserts a divine origin for the prophetic message addressed to Judah and Jerusalem. Symbols of war, details of sight and sound, evoke the terror of the impending siege. A trumpet, shouting, and the raising of the military standard imaginatively create the scene of battle and signal the urgency of seeking safety (vv. 5–6). In fierce anger (v. 8) YHWH claims sole agency for the approaching catastrophe, 'for I am bringing evil from the north' (4:6b). Reference to the mythic foe adds to the unearthly terror advancing upon the nation. The enemy is a lion, magnified into a 'destroyer of nations' (v. 7). Bourguet 1987: 117 observes that the demonic power of the enemy from the north expresses the disproportionate supernatural resources amassed against Judah. The battle is already lost, so lamentation and wailing are the only suitable response (v. 8).

(4:9–11) Interrupting prose voices indicate conflict in interpretation of the nation's fall as blame changes hands and the temporal perspective shifts to the future (vv. 9, 11). A narrator blames the leaders. Their courage will fail, implying their astonishment, and perhaps their ineptitude, and imputing to them responsibility for the disaster (v. 9, Brueggemann 1988: 51–2). In the first person Jeremiah accuses YHWH directly (v. 10): divine deception caused the catastrophe. Then YHWH speaks to defend divine action. The disaster will be total, and it is a judgement against them (v. 11).

(4:13–31) comprises four poems that employ an array of metaphors but together depict and respond to the battle announced in 4:5–8. vv. 13–18 continue to announce the coming battle, and in vv. 19–22 YHWH grieves over the battle. vv. 23–8 interpret the battle's meaning and vv. 29–31 continue to describe it. To escalate the horror of impending siege, vv. 13–18 use many speakers. A frenzied command opens the poem, 'Look, he comes up like clouds' (v. 13). In a cosmic epiphany, an unidentified, superhuman foe advances like clouds, with chariots 'like the whirlwind', and horses 'swifter than eagles'. The community voices its dismay, 'woe to us for we are ruined'. A voice from northern Israel broadcasts the siege to the nations (vv. 15–16), and YHWH speaks to Judah in feminine singular forms as to the wife who betrayed him (v. 18; cf. 2:1–3:25; Biddle 1996: 20).

(4:19–22) With poignant effect, YHWH witnesses the battle's destruction and expresses uncontrollable anguish (vv. 19–20) (*contra* Craigie *et al.* 1991: 78–9). The conventional question of the lament form, 'how long?' combines with images of standard and trumpet to set the speaker in the centre of an endless battle (v. 21). That God is the speaker becomes clear in the accusation of 'my people' who 'do not know me' (v. 22). Like the previous poem, this one also interprets the national disaster as the people's fault, but here YHWH is deeply anguished by it.

(4:23–8) Uncreation YHWH or Jeremiah describes a terrifying vision of the destruction of creation that reverses and adapts the creation account of Gen 1. Four times the speaker 'looked' and 'lo' the earth and its creatures disappear before YHWH's 'fierce anger' (vv. 23–6). YHWH interrupts the vision to announce that destruction will not be total (v. 27), but the poem continues relentlessly describing the earth's return to *tōhû wābōhû*, 'waste and void' (4:23, see Gen 1:2). Earth will mourn and heavens be lightless because the ineluctable divine word undoes them (v. 28).

The terrifying vision of uncreation that turns the earth into a lunar surface or a bombed city does not deviate from the cosmic battle; uncreation interprets it (Perdue 1994: 142). Theologically, politically, socially, the Babylonian invasion of Judah and Jerusalem meant the end of the world and the cessation of the created order for the community. Life in the land is over; no humans are present (v. 25); cities are in ruins (v. 26). In this mythical conception, earth, animals, and cities form an organic, interdependent whole, and their destruction by YHWH's angry decree is the result of human evil (4:22; Habel 1995: 87). The divine promise in v. 27 not to make a 'full end' addresses the implied audience who have survived the desolation.

(4:29–31) returns to the battle itself, the noise, the attack, the empty cities (v. 29), but the speaker addresses Jerusalem, personified as daughter Zion. On this poetic figure see Dobbs-Allsopp (1955). Zion is YHWH's divorced wife (2:1–3:5; 4:16–18) who continues to play the whore and whose predicament has worsened. Her lovers now despise her and want to kill her (v. 30). The speaker hears her 'voice' (qôl) as of a 'woman in labour'. She gasps and writhes not from giving life but in fear of death, finding her voice for the first time to bemoan her fate (v. 31; cf. 3:14).

(5:1–31) contains closely woven materials, making it difficult to distinguish literary units (Nicholson 1973: 56). In the chapter's present arrangement, it portrays YHWH's reluctance to bring judgement, explains why the cosmic battle is inevitable, and defends the Divine Warrior from charges of cruelty and arbitrariness (Carroll 1986: 174).

(5:1–17) Divine Reluctance YHWH's desire to avoid disaster dominates the opening poem. To find one just person in the city, YHWH sends Jeremiah on a search, 'so that I may pardon Jerusalem' (v. 1; for covenant lawsuit elements, see Brueggemann 1988: 59). But the people refused to turn (šûb) from their hypocritical ways (v. 3). After initial failure, Jeremiah decides he is searching among the wrong people; the poor do not know justice (mišpāṭ). He then searches among the rich, but they are no better. Like the adulterous wife (2:20) all break their yoke (vv. 4–5). Less successful than Abraham searching Sodom for ten just people (Gen 18:23–33), Jeremiah fails to find even one. With Jeremiah's help, YHWH did everything possible to avert punishment (Carroll 1986). Destruction by beastly enemies is a fitting result (v. 6).

(5:7–11) The rhetorical question of v. 7, addressed to a female, suggests YHWH still desires to pardon his former wife. But the adultery of her male children (v. 8) leads to a second question that brings the reader to YHWH's side of the argument. 'Shall I not punish them?' (v. 9). YHWH does not wish to punish, but how could God do otherwise? (cf. 5:29). YHWH will destroy her vineyards for both Israel and Judah have been faithless (vv. 10–11).

(5:11–17) Further accusations against Israel and Judah follow (vv. 11–13). Because of their false (v. 12) and belittling words about prophetic speech (v. 13), YHWH puts devouring fire into Jeremiah's mouth (v. 14). His prophetic counterspeech is as destructive and sweeping as fire, for it announces the coming of an unnamed nation for the cosmic battle. A suprahuman military machine will devour the nation's children, their sources of life, and their false security (vv. 15–17).

(5:18–29) YHWH speaks in prose to the implied exilic audience in a temporal shift to the future that again promises an incomplete end. YHWH then quotes the exile's most salient theological question. 'Why has the LORD our God done all these things to us?' (v. 19). YHWH's answer shows proportionate retribution and deflects blame to the people. Idolatry in their own land results in service in a foreign land. vv. 20–9 show how YHWH's reluctance to punish was overcome. Neither Jacob nor Judah sees, hears, or fears the Creator. Despite impenetrable boundaries established in the created world (vv. 20–2), the people know no boundaries in their wickedness (v. 28). The Creator questions, accuses, and quotes the people to reveal their sin (vv. 22–5). Scoundrels among them rob and trick the people and oppress the orphan and the needy, while they themselves grow sleek and fat (vv. 26–8). The refrain of 5:9 (cf. 9:9) reappears to persuade the implied audience of the necessity of the punishment (v. 29). The last two verses of the chapter act as an expansive codicil to the previous poem. Though religious leaders engage in lies, the people want it that way (vv. 30–1).

(6:1–30) Attack on Daughter Zion This chapter gathers metaphors of the cosmic battle, the foe from the north, and Daughter Zion into a collection of poems from a chorus of speakers. The mythic nature of the battle sharpens when the text identifies daughter Zion as the object of attack. A ferocious military nation wages war against Jerusalem portrayed as a weak, wanton woman, defenceless in the face of her foe. From the viewpoint of the ancients, the feminine character of the city heightens its weakness and the hopelessness of resistance (Bourguet 1987: 117).

vv. 1–9, the first-person speaker in this poem appears to be YHWH (see v. 8). Imperatives warn the children of Benjamin to flee as trumpet and warning signals herald evil looming from the north (v. 1). Nostalgically, YHWH describes how lovely and safe Zion was thought to be (vv. 2–3). Voices of the enemy intrude, shouting preparations for attack among themselves (vv. 4–5). In a brilliant stroke of imagination that further indicts Zion, the poet portrays the enemy's thoughts. They believe they are acting on divine orders against a city deserving judgement (vv. 6–7). Warnings of v. 1 become a threat in v. 8 that YHWH will turn from Jerusalem in disgust. Divine abandonment will cause the city's collapse because she did not attend to her own inner sickness (v. 7). v. 9 returns to the vineyard metaphor that appeared in 5:9–10, where it is also connected to punishment of the faithless female. There the vineyard was simply to be pruned, but here the 'remnant of Israel' is to be gleaned thoroughly. Survivors of the destruction, the exiles perhaps, face still further suffering.

vv. 10–12, Jeremiah laments the people's recalcitrance. They are not even capable of hearing the prophetic warning. He is weary of holding back divine wrath (vv. 9–11). Only Jeremiah stands between them and destruction. YHWH responds with a command to pour divine wrath on the people, young and old, male and female (v. 12). vv. 13–15, 'no peace': a refrain that recurs in 8:10–13 distributes guilt throughout the community from the people to the leadership and justifies YHWH's punishment of them. Everyone is greedy and the leaders lie. Denial characterizes their speech. Though priests and prophets are particularly guilty, the whole people deserve punishment (v. 15), and by implication, YHWH appears fully justified in bringing it upon them. vv. 16–21, to vindicate YHWH's judgement and to embellish the significance of the people's sin, YHWH brings them before witnesses. Two parallel accusations open the poem (6:16c and 17). In both YHWH speaks to direct and to warn and then dramatically quotes the people's blanket refusal to co-operate (vv. 16–17). YHWH appears to have no choice but to assemble the nations and the earth itself as legal witnesses in a trial of cosmic import. The people bring the verdict upon themselves, despite rich liturgical offerings that merely reveal their duplicity (v. 20). All will perish (v. 21) in the cosmic battle to which the next poem returns.

vv. 22–6, the foe approaches. The voice of YHWH describes the advance of the mythic nation, a merciless military force crossing the earth, their sound 'like the roaring sea' (v. 23b). Their target is 'you, O daughter Zion!' (v. 23c). The people themselves speak, fearful and helpless. They urge each other to hide from the 'terror…on every side', māgôr missābîb (vv. 24–5, see Jer 20:3, 10). Jeremiah then speaks to the 'daughter of my people' (my tr.), urging her to begin ritual lamentation in sackcloth and ashes, as if on behalf of an only child, for the destroyer is coming with such certainty that lamentation must begin. Divine commands to lament link this section with 8:4–10:25. vv. 27–30, the collection dominated by the metaphor of the cosmic battle (4:5–6:30) closes with YHWH speaking to Jeremiah about his prophetic role. He is the assayer of fine silver with a hopeless task (McKane 1986: 154). The people have failed the refiner's test. Dross cannot be separated from the pure metal, so they become 'rejected silver' (v. 30). Divine, prophetic, and human speakers have voiced horror, resistance, and finally certitude that disaster is unavoidable.

(7:1–8:3) Temple Sermon The relationship of the temple sermon and other prose sermons to the rest of the book and to Deuteronomistic editors are troubling questions (see Holladay 1988: 244–82; Stulman 1986; McKane 1981; Nicholson 1970). Ascribed by Mowinckel to the Deuteronomists, this first lengthy prose segment disturbs the poetic flow of chs. 2–6. Those chapters confront readers with multiple images, metaphors, and poetic figures that intrude upon and interrupt each other to create a rich literary soup. By contrast, the prose sermons appear as a thin broth of repetitive and stereotypical language. The temple sermon focuses on worship practices, seeming to change the subject from the cosmic battle and broken marriage in chs. 2–6. The sermon, however, provides one more interpretative voice in the book's debate about the nation's collapse.

The temple sermon is not extrinsic to the poetry, but comments upon it, and in the view of Stulman (1995) simplifies and tames it. The nation's arrogant complacency depicted in the poetry receives precise focus in the sermon. Judah and Jerusalem, monarchy and temple fell to Babylon because of hypocritical and obscene worship practices that violated the nation's own symbolic and theological perspectives. From the time of David, monarchy and temple had been inextricably bound together in the symbolic order. God would establish David's throne forever, and David's son would build YHWH's temple (1 Sam 7:1–3). When Jerusalem was invaded by Assyria a century earlier, some Isaianic passages interpreted the Davidic promises as unconditional assurance of Jerusalem's safety (Isa 36–7; Ollenburger 1987; Brueggemann 1988: 74). Perhaps because Jerusalem avoided destruction at that time, Isaiah's message solidified in the national consciousness as a promise of eternal security for the temple and the entire religious-political system. They thought they were safe no matter what they did. Judah's temple ideology was based on wrong notions of God as eternally fixed by former promises no matter how the people acted.

In the temple sermon Jeremiah speaks a terrifying counter-word that challenges an entire world-view and reveals why it had to fall. The sermon insists that YHWH is an untamed deity, a wild being not reducible to theological formulae, who can bring the temple to ruins like Shiloh, the destroyed northern sanctuary (Stulman 1986; see Keown, Scalise, and Smothers 1995: 16–19 on Shiloh). The temple sermon, therefore, draws on different theological and symbolic traditions to make claims similar to the poetry. Israel is guilty and divine judgement justified. The sermon adds to the poetry a specific charge that the people failed to 'listen' (7:13, 26, 27), a theme that appears frequently in the prose passages. By implication, if the people in exile are to regain their place, their land, their temple, they must 'listen' now (8:3).

Some interpreters limit the temple sermon to 7:1–15, seeing the rest as later accretions (Weiser 1960). Although the history of its composition remains obscure, the sermon (7:1–8:3) exhibits linguistic patterns and thematic links that create inner coherence (Isabell and Jackson 1980). It moves in a downward spiral to report and mock idolatry within legitimate temple worship (7:1–15) and across a range of foolish idolatrous practices (7:16–8:3).

(7:1–15) opens with an undated superscription that presents Jeremiah as the speaker of divine words. A principal motif of the sermon is the multivalent phrase 'in this place' (bammā-qôm hazzeh; Carroll 1986: 207). The phrase refers to the temple (7:3, 7, 10, 11), the land (3:7, 15), and perhaps also the city (cf. Jer 26). The 'place' is symbolic of false national pride, blind devotion to the monarchy, and complacent arrogance. Frequent use of the phrase in the sermon emphasizes displacement of trust from the deity to the place where the deity dwells (vv. 3, 7). The narrator places Jeremiah at the gates of the temple to announce that its fate will be like Shiloh, another 'place' where YHWH made the divine name to dwell (vv. 12, 15).

Exhortations to amend reveal the depth of the problem (vv. 4–7). The people trust in a lie, 'the temple of the Lord' (v. 4). Repeated three times like a mantra, this phrase parodies the people's confidence in the 'place'. The true threat identified in this sermon, therefore, is not the enemy from the north but the enemy within the community (Stulman 1995). Insiders oppress the alien, the widow, the orphan. They kill and follow after idols. They have made 'this place' a robbers' den (v. 11) where they hide from the truth of their behaviour. They will not listen (v. 13). Only if they amend can they avoid the fate of Shiloh and the northern kingdom (14, 15).

(7:16–17) No Intercession Before adding to Judah's cultic infractions, YHWH addresses Jeremiah, forbidding him to intercede on the people's behalf (vv. 16–17). Wilson (1989) argues that this prohibition protects Jeremiah from charges that he failed as intercessor to avert the fall of Jerusalem. The prophet's role included intercession to avoid disaster, and it was not avoided. Rather than see this as a failure of Jeremiah, the prose writer interprets Judah's fall as YHWH's unwillingness to hear the prophet's intercession. YHWH prohibits intercession because of the outrageous infidelities described in the sermon.

(7:18–8:3) Downward Spiral YHWH accuses the community of increasingly heinous offences. Entire families worship the queen of heaven, an astral deity. (See Ackerman 1987; O'Connor 1992; and cf. 44:15–19, 24–30.) The passage's insistence on the involvement even of the children in the worship may simply depict the all-pervasive nature of the sin, reaching even to the offspring. But it may also encode the exilic audience, the next generation who continue in the idolatry of the generation that was expelled from the land. 7:21–6, next YHWH rejects all burnt offerings on the grounds that they were never required. Instead, YHWH commanded obedience from the time they came out of Egypt, but they did not 'listen' (vv. 24–6). Their sins are even worse than those of their ancestors. 7:27–34, YHWH accuses them of even more horrible sins, of child sacrifice at Topheth in the valley of Hinnom. A poetic interruption orders the nation to begin ritual lamentation for the generation that will die (v. 29). This verse connects the sermon to the weeping and official lamentation that follows in 8:4–10:25. For the ritual sacrifice of children, the people deserve to die. Their corpses will remain unburied, and life in the land will end (v. 34). Jerusalem will become a silent, joyless place, a dead place, a wasteland of shame, where bodies of leaders and people are exhumed and spread like dung upon the ground (8:1–3).

The temple sermon interprets the national catastrophe as the result of injustice and idolatry within Judah and ultimately calls for repentance. It offers a theodicy that interprets the past and addresses the exiles (8:3). Justice and covenant living within the community, obedience and total allegiance to YHWH, expressed in proper worship, are the requirements for covenant relationship (7:23). That did not happen in the past, consequently only a remnant survive where YHWH has driven them (8:3). But for the exiles the call to 'listen', to obey the voice of YHWH spoken through the prophets, to heed the book itself, is still before them.

(8:4–10:25) Weeping The poems assembled here fall into four groupings: 8:4–17 continues to explain why the cosmic battle must come; 8:18–9:25 begins mourning rites in face of the siege and includes a prose comment; 10:1–16 is a communal liturgy that proclaims loyalty to YHWH and the foolishness of idols; 10:17–25 announces exile as the enemy from the north comes closer. A number of metaphors, themes, and poetic devices connect these poems with earlier poetic materials in the book. 8:10*b*–12 repeats the refrain of 6:13–15, and 8:13 returns to the metaphor of the vineyard (2:21; 5:10–11; 6:9). The cosmic battle, its sounds and approaching destructiveness (8:16–17; 10:17–18, 22) explicitly links this material with chs. 4–6. The approach of the foe provokes the only

response possible, lamentation and weeping for the dying nation.

As in earlier chapters, multiple voices speak to announce, comment upon, or respond to the disaster. This section of the text acts as a conclusion to chs. 2–10, drawing together voices, themes, and perspectives from throughout the section. Voices of lamentation and weeping that appeared earlier (3:21; 4:19; 6:26; 7:29), erupt here into cascades of tears that envelop God, the prophet, and the people. Liturgical expressions of fidelity that mock other gods (10:1–16; and perhaps 8:14–15) repeat the form and themes used by the children in the marriage metaphor (3:22–5). If the first-person plural liturgical voice symbolizes the implied exilic audience, prayers dramatize their voice to offer them a model of proper confession of sin (Biddle 1996: 27).

(8:4–17) returns to poetry as if never interrupted by the temple sermon. YHWH speaks to Jeremiah in continued perplexity at the people's failure to return (*šûb*, 8:4–5) and compares their behaviour to that of wild creatures (vv. 6–7). They are like a horse plunging headlong into battle, blind to the dangers facing them. And unlike birds who know their times, the people are unnatural beings who 'do not know the justice (*mišpaṭ*) of YHWH' (8:7, my tr.). YHWH quotes them to accuse them of arrogance and denial. They claim to be wise but they have rejected the word of YHWH (vv. 8–9). Then YHWH depicts their punishment, not by invasion but by naming an effect, the capture of wives and fields by others (v. 10). The refrain of accusation from 6:13–15, repeated here, explains why invasion must occur. Every one is greedy; priests and prophets fail to see the depth of the wound; no one is ashamed. YHWH expresses bitter disappointment because the vineyard is barren (8:13; cf. 5:10–11; 6:9; and Isa 5:1–6).

In the midst of this crisis the people speak, using first-person plural forms (vv. 14–15). Befuddled and confused, they blame YHWH for poisoning the water they drink. Though they confess their sin (v. 14), they speak in a tone of innocent misgiving. They looked for peace and healing but found neither (v. 15). It is as if the community recognizes the truth of accusations against it but finds itself still in circumstances of terror. This voice may characterize the implied audience, set poetically before the invasion but also expressing the dilemma and theological confusion of exile. In reply, YHWH calls attention to the sounds of the approaching battle. The snorting and neighing of horses and the quaking of the land signal the close proximity of a huge cavalry (vv. 16–17). YHWH orchestrates the invasion, as if uncontrollable and deadly snakes are let loose.

(8:18–9:22) The weeping of God, the earth, and the mourning women signify the imminence and inevitability of the destruction, for 'death has come up into our windows' (9:21). But the poetry of weeping connotes something more. It joins God with the people and the earth in vulnerability, pain, and grief. Divine tears make healing possible.

(8:18–9:3) The speaker, the demarcation of units, and meaning of these verses bring no consensus among interpreters, yet these lines contain some of the most extraordinary poetry in the book. Particularly disputed is the speaker of 8:18–9:1. Because the English text numbers 8:23 of the Hebrew as 9:1, the English verse numbers are one ahead of the Hebrew throughout ch. 9. Who is the 'I', and who says 'my poor people' (8:19, 21, 22; 9:1, 2)? A sampling reveals vast disagreement. Carroll (1986: 235) assigns these verses to personified Jerusalem; Condamin (1920: 84) attributes them to the people; Craigie, Kelley, and Drinkard (1991: 136), and Clements (1988: 59) believe Jeremiah is the speaker. Holladay (1986: 288–9) finds three voices including YHWH's in 19b and 22a.

There is a strong possibility, however, that the speaker throughout the lament is YHWH, weeping at the destruction of the people; 8:19c and 9:3 clearly identify YHWH as the poem's speaker. Elsewhere in Jeremiah, YHWH is most often the speaker of the words 'my people' ('ammî, cf. 2:11, 13, 32; 6:14, 30; 8:7, 11; 9:7; 15:7; 18:15; 23:22; less clearly, 6:26; 14:17). Brueggemann (1988: 88) observes that divine pathos structures 8:18–23. Roberts (1992) corroborates this view by observing that Mesopotamian laments use the motif of the weeping God and exhibit similarities to 8:18–9:3. Perhaps commentators avoid identifying YHWH as speaker because this tearful metaphor appears too contradictory of the powerful, wrathful warrior deity in much of the book; or perhaps they think weeping too vulnerable a characteristic to be attributed to the deity.

The decision as to the divine identity of the principal speaker, by no means certain, is theologically crucial. To recognize that YHWH speaks in this poem is to see a temporary but massive turning. The imagery returns to a portrait of divine suffering already begun in the broken-marriage metaphor, but rather than distancing YHWH from the people as in the divorce of his wife (2:1–3:25), this poem unites YHWH with the people in their weeping (9:17–22). God's tears mean that there may be a balm in Gilead, healing may be possible, for in such a metaphorical depiction, God joins in the people's suffering. Tears heal because they stir 'all living souls', bring people together in suffering, and reveal them to one another in their vulnerability (Song 1981: 40–5). YHWH's tears are more powerful even than the armies under divine command because, for a poetic moment at least, God, people, and cosmos articulate a common suffering. The pathos of God, as Heschel (1962) named God's intense suffering, offers an alternative interpretation of the suffering of the exiles. It puts aside punishment, eschews questions of causality, and understands God in radically different terms from much of the rest of the book.

The poem begins with divine proclamation of grief and joylessness (8:18; see Holladay 1986: 287–8 and McKane 1986: 194 on translation problems). YHWH quotes 'daughter of my people' (bat 'ammi, my tr., and in 8:21, 22, 23 Heb.), a term for the city. Her question expresses either smug confidence in YHWH's presence or a sense of abandonment at divine absence (8:19–20). YHWH questions in turn, expressing hurt and dismay at her idolatry. But it is the hurt of the daughter that overwhelms YHWH, not the provocation to anger (8:21). YHWH calls for healing. Is there no balm, no physician, no return to health? The implied answer is 'no'. But YHWH does not abandon her; he weeps with her. 'O that my head were waters and my eyes a fountain of tears that I might weep day and night for the slain of the daughter of my people' (my tr.; 9:1; 8:23 MT). YHWH desires to become weeping, to turn into tears, to weep unceasingly over the slain.

9:2 changes the mood and may be a separate poem (Thompson 1980: 307) but similar phrasing links it to 9:1. YHWH now wants to escape the infidelities of the people. 'O that I had a lodging-place in the desert to escape their betrayal, their adultery, their lies, for they do not know me' (9:2–3, my paraphrase).

8:18–9:3 echoes the broken-marriage metaphor of 2:1–3:25, in its accusations of idolatry and adultery, in its attention to city personified as female, and in the grief of YHWH over the failure of people to know him. Though accusation is still part of the poetry, grief and tears predominate, bringing the reader again to side with YHWH, but here YHWH's grief joins him with the suffering woman, at least temporarily.

(9:4–9) continues divine speech. YHWH speaks to the people directly to warn them against treacherous neighbours and to announce that they will be tested and refined (cf. 6:27). The language of refinement and testing provides yet another interpretation of exile for it suggests something less than the complete destruction promised in the material in chs. 4–6 and would undermine the prophet's earlier message. Hence, the refinement and testing motif suggests hope to the implied audience in exile. They will emerge purified. The question of v. 7, repeated from 5:9 and 27, however, indicates that divine hesitancy exists, as if YHWH needs confirmation of the appropriateness of punishment, and expects to receive it.

(9:10–11) Weeping Whether the speaker, who is probably YHWH, does the weeping or commands it is not clear (McKane 1986: 203). The weeping is on behalf of the earth itself, the mountains and the pastures of the wilderness, for their destruction and the absence of life upon them (v. 10). Lamentation is for the world that has been uncreated and returned to chaos (4:23–8). The world of Judah and Jerusalem will become a barren heap of ruins.

(9:12–16) A prose voice interjects a further interpretation of the tragedy with undisguised questions about the meaning of events. 'Who is wise enough' to interpret these happenings? 'Why is the land laid waste . . .?' (v. 12). Clearly the writer of these verses claims to be wise enough to answer them. The people did not obey tôrâ, they did not listen to YHWH's voice, and they worshipped the Baals. That is why they are in exile (v. 16).

(9:17–22) Official Weeping This two-stanza poem (9:17–19, 20–2) formalizes the weeping and makes it official, public, and massive. In the first stanza of the MT (vv. 17–19), YHWH commands that the mourning women be summoned. But it is the people or Jeremiah speaking in the rest of the stanza. The official task of the keeners was to begin the public rituals of mourning for funeral rites (O'Connor 1992). Their presence indicates that a death has occurred. Their wails will release the tears of the people whose eyes will 'run down with tears' and their eyelids 'flow with water' (v. 18). The people of Zion have already begun their keening over the death of the city (v. 19). In the second stanza (vv. 20–2), the speaker gives instructions to the women. The weeping will be so extensive that they must teach other women their professional skills. The community speaks again in v. 21 to announce that death like an invading force or an intruding person has 'come up into our windows'. The funeral to which the people are invited is their own. Life is over (v. 22).

(9:23–5) returns to the motif of wisdom in another prose comment which seems to take up the prose remarks of vv. 12–16 rather than the poem of vv. 17–22, where people are weeping, not boasting. The wise must not boast about wisdom but about the knowledge of God who is loving, righteous, and just. An eschatological future promises judgement against the worship of Israel's uncircumcised neighbours whom Israel resembles in heart.

(10:1–16) Confession of Sin These verses contain a hymn presented as prophetic word (vv. 1, 11), the subject of which is the foolishness of worshipping other gods and the loyalty of the speakers to YHWH the true God. This liturgical song, a many-voiced choir of witnesses (Seybold 1993) perplexes interpreters on a number of grounds (Margaliot 1980; Craigie, Kelley, and Drinkard 1991: 157–61). v. 11 is in Aramaic; the order of the MT differs from the LXX, and the poem's themes of loyal monotheism intrude abruptly upon poems of accusation and weeping in the previous chapters. The order of the MT passage, however, makes sense as it stands (Craigie, Kelley, and Drinkard 1991; Thompson 1980: 325), and, of greater interest, the sentiments of this hymn, loyal monotheism and derision of idols, as well as its liturgical style, evoke the voice of the repentant children in 3:21–5. It may be placed after the injunction to the people to weep for their imminent death (9:1–22) so as to serve as a model of repentance and reconciliation for the exilic survivors of that death. The exiles are brought into the text as the voice of the community that has been refined in the fire, and they are provided with language to reconcile them with the one true God. The hymn's location in the book transposes exilic conflict from the historical world to the divine. The gods of the nations are powerless and ridiculous, and so they and their people will be punished and perish (v. 15). Only the Creator God of Israel can give life, and by implication provide the community with a future.

The parody and disdain for the gods of the nations expressed here (vv. 1–5, 8–9, 14–15) have close parallels with other exilic texts (Isa 40–8, esp. 44:9–20; Craigie, Kelley, and Drinkard 1991; Blank 1961: 243). Whereas syncretism and idolatry were always part of Israel's struggle in the land, idolatry was a particular temptation for the assimilating community in Babylon. These liturgical materials, moreover, draw on creation theology of the wisdom tradition rather than on covenant terminology. The hymn of praise (vv. 12–16) reverses the chaos of the cosmic battle, connecting it with the defeat of the mythic foe from the north (Perdue 1994: 141–50).

Brueggemann calls the text a 'litany of contrasts' between true and false gods (1988: 98). Commands not to learn from the nations nor to be afraid of their idols surround the first stanza (vv. 2–5). The people should not become like the nations among whom they live nor adopt their idolatrous customs. Those peoples and their deities are foolish and powerless (vv. 3–5b). The second stanza (vv. 6–10) begins and ends with praise and awe of the one true God. In direct address to YHWH, v. 6 declares the greatness of the divine name and the fear owed to the true King of the nations (vv. 6–7). By contrast, the gods of the nations are stupid, human productions (vv. 8–9). These gods will perish (v. 11), says the prose comment. The third stanza (vv. 12–16) provides the reason for their demise. YHWH is the Creator whose wisdom established the world, whose voice (Gen 1) brings potent upheaval (v. 13), while idols are delusions (vv. 14–15). In this poem of praise, relationship with the One who formed all things is re-established (v. 16). The Creator is unmatched by any pretenders to deity and chooses Israel for a special inheritance (v. 16).

(10:17–25) Exile We are brought back dramatically to the temporal threshold of exile through the voices of at least two speakers. YHWH (vv. 17–18 and probably in v. 22) announces the exile and the siege. Daughter Zion (vv. 19–21 and probably vv. 23–5) comments on the personal significance of the disaster for her and pleads for justice. YHWH's commanding voice (vv. 17–18) orders the people to pick up their bundles; the siege has begun. YHWH will 'fling away the inhabitants of the land' with relish, indeed, with vindictiveness, 'so that they shall feel it'.

vv. 19–21, in terminology of 'hurt' and 'wound' that makes her a figure of sympathy rather than scorn, Daughter Zion laments her fate (see Isa 54:1–3). She has no one to help expand her tent and no need to do so for she is bereft of children (v. 20). Her leaders have wounded her; her people are scattered (v. 21). She sees at last what faces her and humbly acknowledges the severity of her wound. Exile is a punishment she must bear. From her own words we learn again that YHWH is not the cause of the tragedy (v. 19). If the female character here is YHWH's divorced wife of 2:1–4:2, she has undergone a transformation from a silent, unreconciled cast-off to a repentant and long-suffering figure of lament, deprived of her children. But the cosmic battle approaches anyway: 'Hear', the noise of battle comes from the north (v. 22).

Daughter Zion appears to speak again in vv. 24–5, although Holladay (1986: 338) identifies the speaker as the people rather than as the personified city, and Brueggemann (1988: 103) thinks the speaker is Jeremiah. The speaker prays that God punish in 'just measure' and not in anger (cf. 10:19b). She begs, instead, for YHWH to pour anger on the nations that have laid waste and devoured Jacob (vv. 24–5). Clearly speaking from exile, this voice echoes the repentance themes of 3:21–5 and 10:1–16. Exile is punishment that must be borne, but YHWH, God of all nations, may, in turn, punish those who have devastated Israel, if Israel repents.

Covenant Destroyed (chs. 11–20)

A frame of curses surrounds these chapters. Covenant curses upon those who do not 'listen' to YHWH's word appear in the opening prose sermon (11:1–17), and Jeremiah's curses on his birth (20:14–18) conclude the section. Between the two curses, poetic threats and accusations, as well as prose sermons (11:1–16; 17:19–27), continue to appear, but new literary elements change the shape of the literature and give movement to the chapters. In contrast to chs. 2–10 where Jeremiah's prophetic pronouncements appear chiefly in poetry, these chapters add dimension to the character. Prose descriptions of symbolic events that feature Jeremiah (chs. 13, 18, 19, 20:1–6) and poetic laments or 'confessions' of Jeremiah (11:18–12:6; 15:10–21; 17:14–18; 18:18–23; 20:7–14) bring the prophet himself into the foreground as a significant character who had barely been visible in chs. 2–10. These new elements show him in action and portray his inner suffering.

By the end of ch. 20, Jeremiah's fate and the fate of the nation converge symbolically so that what happens to him evokes and mimics the suffering of the people. In this section Jeremiah represents both God and people. He stands as prophet against the people who reject him, yet he symbolically embodies their grief, doubt, anger, and finally their hope (Polk 1984) once they are in exile. The community's rejection of Jeremiah contributes to the massive theodicy this book is building. By rejecting Jeremiah as prophet and covenant mediator the people bring the tragedy upon themselves. But later, Jeremiah's suffering and lamentation become iconic of the pain and hopelessness of the exilic audience. Finally, disputation among voices, particularly between YHWH and Jeremiah, intensifies, offering dissenting interpretations of the catastrophe.

(11:1–17) Covenant Curse In the book's second major prose sermon, similar in language and style to the temple sermon (7:1–8:3), Jeremiah announces a curse upon anyone 'who does not heed the words' of the Mosaic covenant (vv. 3–4) (on the Deuteronomistic flavour of the sermon and for other views as to the identity of the covenant, see Stulman 1986: 63–6 and Carroll 1986: 267). If Jeremiah himself were the author of this sermon, then it would have prophesied the fall of the nation in advance of events. If the sermon is the work of later followers of Jeremiah, then it would explain the nation's fall after the fact. In either case, this sermon has one point and presents it with astonishing simplicity: possession of the land hinges entirely upon obedience to the covenant (v. 5).

Like the temple sermon (7:1–8:3), the covenant sermon demands that the people 'listen' to YHWH's voice (vv. 4, 7–8; cf. 7:13, 23–6), and prohibits Jeremiah's intercession on behalf of the people (v. 14; cf. 7:16). The covenant sermon, however, describes the people's failure to listen in vague formulaic terms different from those of the temple sermon which castigates the worshipping community for specific social and religious infractions. By contrast, the covenant sermon accuses the ancestors (vv. 6–8) and the present generation (vv. 9–13) of walking 'in the stubbornness of an evil will' (v. 8), and going after other gods to serve them (vv. 10, 12–13). Both sermons, however, undercut fundamental symbolic understandings of ancient Israel. The temple sermon proclaims the end of the royal temple ideology, and the covenant sermon announces the collapse of the Mosaic covenant because of human disloyalty. The covenant curse will fall upon them and Jeremiah is powerless to change it.

vv. 1–5, narrated in solemn ritualistic fashion, the announcement of the curse occurs in a prose dialogue between God and Jeremiah. YHWH explains what will activate the curse. It will fall upon those who disobey the covenant made with the ancestors brought from Egypt. The covenant formula, 'I will be your God and you will be my people' (v. 4), encapsulates the intimacy of covenant relationship and gains expression in YHWH's oath to give them a land 'flowing with milk and honey'. At stake in YHWH's pronouncement, therefore, is the entire future of the community in the land. Jeremiah's formal response, 'Amen' (v. 5, reading the Heb. literally) makes him legal witness to the solemn statement of the curse. vv. 6–13 continue the divine speech, narrated by Jeremiah, that recounts the nation's history as a failure to 'listen' (vv. 6–8), a failure of ancestors and of Jeremiah's contemporaries (vv. 9–13). In quid pro quo fashion, YHWH refuses to listen to them, nor will the idols to whom they cry (vv. 11–13). Not listening is all-pervasive, spreading like vindictiveness on a playground. No one will listen to anyone, and above all, YHWH will not listen to any word from Jeremiah on their behalf (v. 14).

Although the sermon's theme is simple, it contains a complex, artistic reperformance of Israel's history and serves as a comment upon the poetry that precedes it (Stulman 1995). The cosmic battle already underway and the weeping that marks it are, according to this sermon, the result of covenant infidelity by the insiders. Mosaic covenant language becomes another symbolic lens for interpreting the loss of the land. Other than 3:16, this is the first explicit mention of covenant in the book (Carroll 1986: 267). The absence of blessings that usually accompany covenant curses underscores the inevitability of the disaster ahead (O'Connor 1988). But why does the sermon simply announce the curse as an unalterable course of events? From the perspective of the book's exilic audience, the disaster has already happened. The sermon blames it on covenant disloyalty of their ancestors, distant and immediate. The implicit call to them as survivors is that they must hear and obey. Redactionally, the covenant sermon introduces chs. 11–20 within which the last appeals to 'turn' are made to the nation and by the end of which the curse is enacted.

vv. 15–17 are corrupt (see Holladay 1986: 354–6; Carroll 1986: 272–4). As translated in the NRSV, however, their language and imagery reach both forwards and backwards. YHWH's query about the beloved in v. 15 is echoed in his challenge to the beloved in 12:7, creating a frame around the confession of Jeremiah in 11:8–12:6. YHWH's rebuke of her activity in the temple sacrifice connects these verses with ch. 7, and the tree planted by YHWH evokes the planting language of Jeremiah's call (1:10) and the tree in Jeremiah's confession (11:19). The green tree that YHWH planted will be destroyed, as Jeremiah's enemies seek to destroy him. Linguistically, these difficult verses link the prophet's fate to that of the nation.

(11:18–12:25) Lament and Response The first lament or 'confession' of Jeremiah (11:18–12:4; see also 15:1–21; 17:14–18; 18:18–23; 20:7–13) gains a divine response (12:5–6). Akin to psalms of individual lament in form and style (Baumgartner 1987), these first-person prayers are more akin to psalms than to prophetic literature. In each lament an unidentified speaker addresses YHWH to complain bitterly about threats to his life, acute loneliness and isolation, and failure in his prophetic role. Only by deduction or from prose comments is it clear that the speaker is Jeremiah. Although many interpreters find in the confessions a window into the inner life of the prophet (von Rad 1984; Hubmann 1978; Ittmann 1981), the relationship of the poems to a historical person cannot be known (see Gunneweg 1970; Gerstenberger 1963; Reventlow 1963). None the less, the poems' intense portrayals of the prophet's inner life are immensely important on a number of levels.

The confessions defend Jeremiah against the charge of false prophecy (on which see Meyer 1977, Carroll 1981:

158–97). Like the call narrative (Jer 1), the confessions portray Jeremiah as one who spoke under divine compulsion, who stood in the council of YHWH to receive the message, and who faithfully executed his role as mediator at immense cost (Diamond 1987; O'Connor 1988). In potent language that portrays an inner anguished self, the confessions also portray Jeremiah in combat both with God whose word he speaks and with the people who reject that word. Identified with both God and people, yet distinct from them, Jeremiah embodies the pain and anger of both. By revealing an inner life, by 'going behind' the character into internal struggles, the confessions help create a character whose life symbolizes his message (Polk 1984: 125). Whatever else it is, Jeremiah's life is a metaphor of the pain of God and of the people. For the implied audience in exile, Jeremiah's life, with its anger and resistance, its suffering and captivity, is a symbol that interprets their reality.

(11:18–12:6) presents formal problems, for it is not certain whether the verses comprise one (O'Connor 1988) or two confessions (11:18–23 and 12:1–6; Diamond 1987; Smith 1990). In the present text, however, the two parts of the poem form two panels of complaint (11:18–20 and 12:1–4) and response (11:21–3 and 12:4–6) that interpret and nuance one another as a single composition (Hubmann 1978: 165–78). 11:18–23 opens with an unidentified voice. The speaker uses *yādaʿ* (to know), a covenant verb of intimate relationship (O'Connor 1988: 90–1), but he does not divulge the content of what YHWH has revealed to him (11:18). The point is that the prophet speaks on the authority of relationship with YHWH. The speaker is an innocent 'lamb led to the slaughter'. He quotes enemies who want to cut him down like a tree (11:19); he appeals to YHWH, who 'judge[s] righteously', to judge his case (*rîb*). A prose voice interrupts the poet to identify the enemies as people from Jeremiah's home town, to explain why they attack him, and to promise their punishment (11:21–3).

The second panel (12:1–6) reuses images and themes from the first but inverts them. No longer confident that justice will be done, Jeremiah doubts his success in a legal case (*rîb*) against YHWH (12:1). Why, Jeremiah asks, do 'the guilty prosper' and the 'treacherous thrive?' And Jeremiah answers his own question: because YHWH plants and nourishes them (12:2). Jeremiah protests his innocence and claims that YHWH knows (*yādaʿ*) his innocence as well. He asks for vengeance against his enemies in terms that echo their plans for him in 11:19. Then he shifts to the cosmic consequence of their evil, 'How long will the land mourn?' (12:4), recalling the poetic uncreation of the world (4:23–8), as the land shrivels and grieves with Jeremiah. YHWH's response to Jeremiah's attack against divine justice brings neither resolution nor comfort (12:5–6). Instead, YHWH promises that things will get worse. Like 11:21–3, 12:6 personalizes the escalating difficulties for Jeremiah. Even his own family is treacherous.

This confession invites interpretation at more than one level. As a defence of the prophet, Jeremiah's resistance indicates that YHWH alone has designated him a prophet. As an indictment of the wicked, even his own kin, it shows that the people bring sword and famine upon themselves by rejecting the prophet (11:22). As an attack on the justice of God, it protests the suffering of the innocent and implicates God in that suffering. What is uncertain is who the innocent are. Surely it is Jeremiah, but for the exilic audience, it may appear that their suffering is out of proportion to their guilt. In that case, Jeremiah the rejected prophet also becomes the paradigm of the innocent sufferer (Craigie, Kelley, and Drinkard 1991; Polk 1984), struggling to be faithful, yet uncomprehending. The primary issue in these verses is divine justice. The prominence of this theme evokes the conditions of exile where theodicy became the central theological question (Carroll 1986; Raitt 1977). YHWH's reply to the prophet (12:5–6) indicates that things will become harder before they improve. Treachery, conflict, and betrayal will continue in their midst, and no satisfactory explanation of their suffering emerges.

(12:7–13) YHWH's Lament YHWH continues to speak, first in a tone of 'exhausted grief' (Brueggemann 1988: 115), and then of destructive rage. In love language that suggests the broken marriage of 2:1–3:25, YHWH announces that he has forsaken his heritage (*naḥălâ*, vv. 7, 8; Habel 1995; Clements 1988: 84), the beloved of his heart (cf. 11:14). His heritage has again gone wild like the animals. Sexual overtones are absent here, but the turn in the relationship is no less shocking than was the beloved's behaviour in the marriage. 'Therefore I hate her', says YHWH, who calls for the animals to devour her (vv. 8–9). In vv. 10–13 YHWH continues to speak, but the object of indictment shifts from the beloved to the many shepherds of the vineyard. Their destructiveness (vv. 10–11*a*) and fruitless actions (v. 13) frame the mourning of the personified land, desolate, uncared for, and abandoned (v. 11). YHWH's sword devours (v. 12).

Like Jeremiah, YHWH also voices pain and fierce anger (v. 13) but in this case provoked by the intimate betrayal of a loved one, who 'has lifted up her voice against me', and by the feckless leadership of kings. The language of betrayed love (11:15 and vv. 7–8) surrounds Jeremiah's more cautious anger in a rhetorical battle between prophet and deity. YHWH's betrayal by the beloved, the most intimate of treacheries, is certain. Jeremiah merely asks indirectly if YHWH has betrayed him (12:1–2). Jeremiah's meek rebellion holds its ground but not without encroachment from the more justified divine fury.

(12:14–17) YHWH continues speaking, but now in prose and in a temporal shift to the exile. YHWH corrects the previous poems and looks toward the future (Craigie, Kelley, and Drinkard 1991: 183). With language from the call narrative (1:10), YHWH promises to 'pluck up' those who touch his inheritance (*naḥălâ*). From amongst those plucked nations, YHWH will 'pluck up' Israel to return them to their inheritance. For the nations, too, there is hope, if they will learn to swear by YHWH's name. If they will not listen, a major theme of the prose materials, then YHWH will 'uproot and destroy'. This prose comment, therefore, qualifies YHWH's rage, hatred, and destruction from 12:7–13.

(13:1–27) Symbolic Acts Connections among the prose and poetry sections collected here are neither narrative nor formal but thematic; destruction must come on account of the nation's foolish pride. The certainty of destruction is expressed by Jeremiah's first 'symbolic action' (vv. 1–11), by a second symbolic act to be performed by the people (vv. 12–14), and by poetic pieces that announce the exile.

Symbolic acts are dramatized speech that involve more than the drama of street theatre (Carroll 1986: 293–7). Within ancient Israel symbolic prophetic acts were understood as enacted speech forms that embody the divine plan (Overholt 1989: 86–91). Many of the book's narratives portray Jeremiah engaging in symbolic acts (16:1–4; 19:1–2; 25:15–29; 27:1–3; 32:1–15; 43:8–13; 51:59–64), but others also perform acts for Jeremiah to interpret (13:12–14; 18:1–11; 51:59–64). Competing claimants to divine authority use symbolic acts to cancel Jeremiah's message (28:10–11; 36:20–4; Lundbom 1995: 191). So many narratives in Jeremiah describe events and deeds rife with symbolic meanings that the symbolic act as a specific genre of prophetic literature becomes a blurred category (cf. 20:1–6; 35:1–19). What seems important to note is that the ancient world, and some contemporary cultures, ascribe to events far more revelatory significance than do Western 'scientific' cultures.

(13:1–11) The Ruined Loincloth Two major problems bedevil interpretation of this passage. The first is the difficulty in determining the event's location and historical status. Because the Euphrates is a great distance away from Jerusalem, it becomes hard to imagine Jeremiah actually performing the act. Some interpreters, therefore, emend the text to name a site near Jerusalem or understand the narrative as entirely fictional. The problems are unresolvable (Condamin 1920: 114–17; Holladay 1986: 396; Carroll 1986).

The second, equally thorny problem concerns the meaning of the symbolic action. Jeremiah narrates the story in the first person and describes his obedient responses to a sequence of divine commands that result in the burial and disintegration of a loincloth (vv. 1–6). Apart from portraying him as an obedient servant, the action itself is nearly opaque. Who or what is being buried and destroyed? If Euphrates is the location of the event, then the text suggests that the exiles, symbolized by the loincloth and buried in Babylon, are ruined by the experience. The symbolic act, then, might be a critique of the exilic community, ruined in their captivity. Or, since burying a cloth by a river will undoubtedly destroy it, the act could stand as a protest against YHWH's abandonment and neglect of the community by burying them in exile. But the interpretative speech that follows (vv. 8–11) suppresses both these possibilities. What is being buried and destroyed is the pride of Judah and Jerusalem (v. 9). Because they would not listen and because they followed other gods, Israel and Judah have failed to realize their true identity (vv. 10–11; Brueggemann 1991: 121–3). They are utterly useless.

(13:12–14) The Wine-Jars A second symbolic and equally destructive event follows, though it is not Jeremiah but YHWH and the people, presumably of Judah and Jerusalem, who will perform the future act. And it is not Jeremiah but YHWH who interprets that act in a divinely scripted conversation. Jeremiah's role is to mediate between the two parties. The filling of the wine-jars does not, as expected, symbolize feasting and joy but drunkenness. The people's forced drunkenness leads to self-destruction of all the land's inhabitants, particularly royal and religious leadership (v. 13). YHWH will neither spare nor have compassion. By its juxtaposition with 13:1–11, this passage seems to describe Judah's punishment for its pride (13:9). It blames the national catastrophe on Judah, but it also places the fall within divine punishment of the nations by leading forward to 25:15–29 where all the nations drink of the same cup of destruction.

(13:15–19) Attack and Exile These verses explicate YHWH's announcement, 'I will not have pity...' (13:14). Announcements of exile and divine commands (vv. 15–16, 18, 20) unify the verses. vv. 15–19, Jeremiah orders the people to listen (v. 15) and announces the consequences of not listening (v. 17). By contrast with YHWH who has no compassion (13:14), Jeremiah will weep bitterly for their pride and captivity (v. 17). The king and queen mother must become 'lowly' for the attack is underway and the towns of the Negeb are cut off (vv. 18–19).

(13:20–7) Zion's Rape This poem addresses personified Jerusalem and returns to the theme of the cosmic battle, here imagined in terms of a rape. YHWH warns Jerusalem to look because the enemy from the north advances. (See Holladay 1986: 411 on gender of pronouns.) Rhetorical questions highlight Zion's plight and her guilt (vv. 20–3). As in the broken-marriage metaphor (2:19), YHWH quotes speech he imagines she might say. If she asks herself why these things have happened to her, he tells her it is because of her own sin that she is raped (v. 22). She cannot help herself (v. 23). Then in one of the most horrible lines in the book, YHWH tells her, 'I myself will lift up your skirts over your face' (v. 26). Her rape is punishment in kind for her animal-like adulteries (v. 27). Rape as a metaphor for military invasion is widespread (Washington and Gordon 1995) in the ancient and modern world. Here it is particularly awful because YHWH is credited with the deed (O'Connor 1992). Zion learns how truly without compassion and pity YHWH can be.

(14:1–22) Drought and Wound Various possibilities exist for dividing the chapter on formal and thematic grounds (Carroll 1986: 307–8). Many commentators find two communal laments, one on the drought (vv. 1–16) and one on the wounds of war (vv. 17–22), with thematic and formal links between the two (vv. 9, 22; Craigie, Kelley, and Drinkard 1991: 200). Some see the drought and the war materials as referring to two separate historical catastrophes, but the two panels of poetry (vv. 1–10 and 17–22) interpret one another (Holladay 1986: 422) and speak of the same subject alternately imagined as meteorological and military events. Despite possible connections to an actual drought, the drought serves as a metaphor for the shattering of the nation in the cosmic battle and the uncreation of the world associated with it.

Both communal laments contain confessions of sin (vv. 7, 20) and statements of loyal praise (vv. 8–9, 22). The latter dramatize the voice of the implied exilic audience, children of the unfaithful wife of YHWH (3:22–5; 10:1–16; McKane 1986 also places these prayers in exile). The purpose of these liturgical pieces is to invite the audience to repent and to find in YHWH their only hope (vv. 8, 22). Wedged between the two panels of poetry is prose material (vv. 11–16) that explains the cause of grief and lamentation as the consequence of the prophets' false discernment of reality (Brueggemann 1988: 128). Together the laments summon the exilic community to learn from the disaster and repent, while simultaneously moving the narrative thread of the book towards the disaster.

vv. 1–10, an undated superscription identifies the setting of the poem and chapter as a drought (v. 1), but more than the absence of rain threatens the community. Israel has forsaken the 'fountain of living waters' and dug their own cisterns, broken cisterns that cannot hold water (2:13; 17:13). The drought symbolizes the consequences of Israel's infidelity (Jer 4:27–8; 12:4; 23:10; O'Connor 1988: 20). A third-person narrator describes the drought's impact (vv. 2–6). Animals, humans, and the earth suffer together. Affliction binds everyone from nobles to servants (v. 3; Brueggemann 1988). In first-person plural forms, vv. 7–9 introduce the voice of the people. They confess their sin and petition YHWH for help in repentant and humble terms. It is YHWH's distance and inaction that perplexes them. 'Why should you be like a stranger... like someone confused, like a mighty warrior who cannot give help?' (vv. 8–9). They confess their loyalty, none the less, and beg YHWH not to forsake them.

Interpreted as a pre-exilic text, this first panel of lament implies that the community finally expresses repentance, but it is insincere or too late (McConville 1993: 68). As an exilic text however, the poem raises a theological phantom that haunted the defeated nation. Where is God in their pain? Is God absent, confused, powerless? By giving exiles dramatic voice, the poem models how the exilic community should respond to the crisis. The speakers confess their sins and turn to YHWH, their hope (v. 8). But YHWH rejects their repentance (vv. 10–11), switching back from the world of the reader to the pre-exilic world. Repentance is too late; punishment will come. vv. 11–16 remain in a pre-exilic time-frame, but they too address issues of exile. The first prose comment (vv. 11–12) prohibits Jeremiah's mediation on behalf of the people no matter what liturgical rite they offer. Prohibition of Jeremiah's intercession defends him against accusations of failed prophecy (Wilson 1989). His mediation did not fail; it was not even permitted, because YHWH had already decided to send the invasion. The second prose comment (vv. 13–16) derides speech of prophets who invent their word, send themselves, and by contrast to Jeremiah, promise šālôm 'in this place' (v. 13). Two prophetic views of reality compete, but it is clear which one should be chosen—the Jeremianic interpretation of the tragedy.

vv. 17–22, this second lament panel also ridicules religious leadership (v. 18) and resumes the theme of weeping over destroyed daughter Zion. YHWH commands Jeremiah to express the divine 'pathos' (Seybold 1993: 134) at the destruction of virgin daughter Jerusalem who has been struck in war with a mortal wound (vv. 17–18; cf. 13:20–7). The people cry out again (vv. 19–22) to continue their protest against YHWH's neglect of them. The implied audience faces its catastrophe and asks if YHWH hates Zion, why YHWH has struck them, why there is no healing. For their part, they accept their sin and the sins of their ancestors and beg YHWH to remember the covenant (v. 20). Unlike YHWH the idols cannot bring rain; YHWH is their only hope (v. 22).

Although this chapter and other communal liturgical fragments in the book have often been seen as secondary, they play a key role in bringing the audience into the Jeremianic programme for the nation's renewal. (For post-exilic dating, see Biddle 1996: 97–8.)

(15:1–16:21) No Future, Yet a Future 15:1–4 parallels 14:11–12 in its expression of divine rejection of Jeremiah's intercession. In another defence of Jeremiah as a true mediator foiled in preventing disaster by divine command, the prose commentator announces that no mediation would work, not even by Moses or Samuel. The people's fate is sealed. Terms of catastrophe are less mythic than in chs. 2–10 where the foe from the north was advancing upon Jerusalem. In chs. 11–20 the foe appears only in 13:20. Instead, the modes of tragedy become more realistically precise: pestilence and sword, famine and captivity (15:2; 11:22; 14:15; 21:8), as well as unburied bodies (14:16). The destroyers are no longer a mythic army whose noise can be heard from afar, but the sword that kills and the beasts and birds that scavenge upon corpses (15:3). Nor is it the people who are held responsible here, but former King Manasseh (2 Kings 21:10–15). Clements (1988: 94–6) discusses the dislike of Manasseh shared by the book of Jeremiah and the Deuteronomistic history.

(15:5–9) Divine Lament YHWH grieves over doomed Jerusalem with a poignant rhetorical question that brings readers into divine anguish and portrays Jerusalem's pitiful isolation (v. 5). The subject of YHWH's lament is divine reluctance to destroy the city, described after the fact. Personified Jerusalem is abandoned, but as pathetic as her condition is, she has brought it upon herself in a now familiar complaint against her. She rejected him, so he destroyed her (v. 6). YHWH and female Jerusalem cannot yet be reconciled (see Jer 2:1–3:25). He alone puts effort into the relationship and is 'weary of relenting' (v. 6). Although the poem does not comfort Jerusalem, it invites pity for her (vv. 7–9). In a reversal of promises to Abraham and Sarah (v. 8), Jerusalem's widows and childless mothers augur the death of the nation, for they have no offspring to create a future.

(15:10–21) Jeremiah's Lament The juxtaposition of Jeremiah's second confession with YHWH's lament over Jerusalem creates subtle interactions between them. As YHWH doomed the mothers to childlessness (15:9), Jeremiah's mother doomed him to a life of suffering by giving him birth (v. 10). Prophetic anguish (v. 18) replaces divine weariness (15:6). Jeremiah's lament identifies him with grieving YHWH by defending Jeremiah's prophecy as divinely imposed. But the confession also identifies Jeremiah with the people against God (Polk 1984; McConville 1993). Jeremiah's confession is an act of protest in which he embodies the questions of the exiles even as he complains about his people (v. 15). He challenges divine governance of the universe and ultimately charges YHWH with the destruction of daughter Jerusalem (Diamond 1987: 78). He suffers unjustly, his wound is incurable, YHWH has abandoned him, and if he repents (šûb, v. 19), he will be delivered from 'the hand of the wicked' (v. 21).

vv. 10–14 are problematic on textual and formal grounds, and many earlier commentators excised verses (Diamond 1987; O'Connor 1988; Hubmann 1978: 245; Ittmann 1981: 44–9). These prose verses introduce the confession, however, by showing Jeremiah's resistance to a prophetic vocation imposed on him from before birth (v. 10, see 1:5). They distinguish him from false prophets from whom he did not borrow, and in YHWH's voice, they restate the certainty of exile (vv. 13–14).

This confession begins like the previous one (11:18). Jeremiah reminds YHWH of divine knowledge (yādaʿtā) and appeals for justice against persecutors (v. 15). He fears divine tolerance will result in disaster for himself. He claims to be so identified with the divine words that he ate them, and they became his joy (v. 16). By choice, he faced extreme loneliness for the sake of his vocation (v. 17). Then, trapped and betrayed, he asks, 'Why is my pain unceasing?' He answers his own question with anguished accusation of YHWH who is 'a deceitful brook . . . waters that fail' (v. 18). Jeremiah himself experiences abandonment like daughter Zion (15:5) and blames YHWH because Jeremiah is innocent. YHWH responds (vv. 19–21) by inviting him to return (šûb, 3:12, 14; 4:2). If he is faithful to his prophetic mission, he will remain YHWH's spokesperson, and though enemies fight against him, YHWH will deliver him (vv. 20–1).

This many-levelled poem depicts Jeremiah as a person who suffers because of his undesired prophetic vocation. It shows him to be a true prophet of YHWH, rejected by his own people. His persecution and sense of divine abandonment, however, resemble the suffering of the exiles, and the invitation for him to repent repeats the book's frequent invitation and expression of repentance voiced by the implied audience. YHWH's promise to deliver Jeremiah from the 'ruthless' (v. 21), therefore, implies hope for the audience.

(16:1–21) Jeremiah's Celibacy Ch. 16 is divine speech related largely in prose by Jeremiah. It opens with an account of Jeremiah's celibacy and its interpretation (vv. 1–9). vv. 10–21 comprise four units that raise the question of theodicy (vv. 10–13), promise restoration (vv. 14–15), reiterate promises of exile (vv. 16–18), express communal repentance in poetry (vv. 19–20), and end with a divine threat (v. 21). The chapter gives the impression of a conversation among many voices debating the meaning of exile, all presented through divine speech.

vv. 1–9, Smith (1990: 36) believes the superscription in v. 1 introduces a new unit, but the verse's purpose is merely to underscore divine origins of Jeremiah's celibacy. YHWH's command that Jeremiah neither marry nor beget children (v. 2) embellishes Jeremiah's complaint of social isolation in 15:17. The prophet's celibacy is symbolic action akin to the burying of the loincloth (13:1–11). Jeremiah's spouseless, childless life announces Judah's fate and continues his characterization as a symbol of the people's plight. Life in the land is over; there is no future. In the picture that unfolds here, all remnants of communal and domestic life cease. vv. 3–4 describe the fate of children and parents who die of sword, famine, and disease, unlamented and unburied. The scene resembles the aftermath of battle with corpses littered everywhere. The world has become utterly silent. There will be no mourning rituals, no feasting. There will no sound of mirth or gladness, no voice of bride or bridegroom (vv. 5–9). Jeremiah's celibacy signifies the total obliteration of daily domestic life.

vv. 10–13 ask the questions that lie at the heart of the book and belong to the experience of exile: why has God done this to us? What is our sin? In Deuteronomistically phrased prose, the answer is clear and familiar. They and their ancestors betrayed YHWH by following other gods and breaking tôrâ. This is why they are hurled out. vv. 14–15 interrupt threats of exile to announce hope to the implied audience. Their resi-

dence in the land of the north will not be permanent for the God of the exodus will return them to their land in the unspecified future. By retrieving the Exodus tradition, the text imaginatively links the audience's captivity to bondage in Egypt. God will again bring them to their land. vv. 16–18 return to the theme of exile and stress its inescapability. YHWH will send fisherfolk and hunters to drag off idolaters who have polluted the land and filled YHWH's inheritance (naḥălâ) with abominations.

In vv. 19–20, a first-person liturgical voice breaks into divine speech to address YHWH in loyalty and confidence (v. 19c). 'Our ancestors have inherited (nḥl) nothing but lies' (v. 19). Again the liturgical voice brings the implied audience into the text and provides them with a model of repentance. They proclaim the gathering of all nations around YHWH and the futility of idols (v. 20). YHWH's response in v. 21 ignores the people's praise and repentance to interpret suffering as pedagogy that will at last succeed despite the people's recalcitrance. The entire chapter defends YHWH from charges of injustice.

(17:1–27) True Worship Many voices combine in this chapter. YHWH speaks in prose accusation (vv. 1–4) and wisdom sayings (vv. 5–11). The people speak in liturgical praise (vv. 12–13), Jeremiah speaks in his third confession (vv. 14–18), and then speaks on behalf of YHWH in a prose sermon on proper sabbath decorum (vv. 19–27). Most commentators view the chapter as a miscellaneous collection (Diamond 1987: 165), but recent scholarship has begun to locate unifying features. Craigie, Kelley, and Drinkard (1991) find a chiastic structure in vv. 1–13, and Polk (1984: 143–50) identifies links between vv. 1–13 and 14–18. Viewed synchronically, ch. 17 contains a collection of prose and poetic voices that attack false worship (vv. 1–4), exemplify proper worship (vv. 12–13, 14–18), and display attitudes of the heart (lēb, vv. 1, 5, 9) that underlie worship (vv. 5–11).

The text of vv. 1–4 is corrupt (Holladay 1986: 484) and its genre uncertain (prose, NRSV; poetry, NEB), but the general import of the verses is clear. Israel's sin has been written (k-t-b, see v. 13) with unusually hard and precise instruments and engraved ineradicably on heart and altar (v. 1). The horns of the altar, symbols of cultic protection (Carroll 1989: 349), here signify sins of idolatrous worship (v. 2). The people have provoked YHWH's fierce anger, so they will lose their heritage (naḥălâ) and go into exile (vv. 3–4).

vv. 5–8 contain a poem of two stanzas with strong resemblances to Ps 1, a wisdom psalm (Holladay 1962), recast in Deuteronomistic terms of covenant blessing and curse (Polk 1984: 145) and put in YHWH's mouth. In an unusual arrangement, curse precedes blessing (cf. Ps 1). Those who are cursed trust what is human and turn from YHWH. Although the poem does not mention idols explicitly, the attitude of the cursed heart (lēb) is idolatrous (v. 5). People with such a heart will die from lack of life-giving water. By contrast, those who trust in YHWH will flourish like a tree planted by water (vv. 7–8). vv. 9–11, YHWH adds comments in proverbial wisdom style on the mysterious and devious nature of the human heart. YHWH, Just Judge, tests and searches the heart and dispenses justice. The language of v. 10 plays upon and reinterprets Jeremiah's first confession (12:1–4) where he protests divine injustice and asks YHWH to test his heart (*lēb*) and establish his innocence (12:3). YHWH meets Jeremiah's demand (v. 10) by announcing a reversal of fortunes for the unjust (v. 11, cf. v. 3).

vv. 12–13, the divine promise brings forth praise from the congregation (Craigie, Kelley, and Drinkard 1991: 230). Text and translation are difficult (O'Connor 1988; Diamond 1987), but the communal liturgical voice, in form and language similar to other communal liturgies in the book, gives expression to the implied exilic audience. The praise casts them as the blessed who trust in YHWH (vv. 7–8), their *miqwēh*, meaning both 'hope' (see 14:8, 22) and 'pool' (Holladay 1986: 502). Their praise (v. 13) links them with the tree planted by the water (vv. 7–8) and with the ones who seek the fountain of living water (v. 13). They curse those, once among them, who have forsaken the fountain of living water (see 2:13). Those enemies will be recorded (written: *k-t-b*) in the underworld (v. 13; see 17:1). The cursed ones may suggest internal enemies or perhaps the previous generation whose infidelity led to exile.

vv. 14–18, Jeremiah's confession; next in the sequence of speakers, Jeremiah is at once distinct from, and identified with, the suffering audience. His tone changes from his earlier one where he challenged YHWH's fidelity and was urged to 'turn' (15:10–21). Instead of continuing the challenge here, Jeremiah begs for healing and salvation (v. 14). Like the people in vv. 12–13, he trusts YHWH and exemplifies true worship: 'you are my praise' (v. 14). Like the people, he is wounded and in need of healing, and like them, he has enemies (v. 15) upon whom he wishes vengeance (v. 18). But the prophet's chief complaint also separates him from the people and identifies him with YHWH. He has been a faithful prophet whose enemies doubt his word (v. 15). He pleads for the persecution of his persecutors. Jeremiah is a model worshipper and innocent sufferer who seeks refuge and justice from YHWH (vv. 17–18). Within the book's pre-exilic narrative movement towards the fall of the nation, his request for vengeance will result in the destruction of his people. For the implied audience already in exile, however, the confession invites wholehearted repentance as exemplified by Jeremiah's prayerful attitude.

vv. 19–27, the sabbath sermon: Jeremiah delivers this prose sermon as divine speech that appears to undermine earlier parts of the book (4:4; 7:1–8:3). Proper sabbath behaviour, rather than attitudes of heart, itself becomes a sign of obedience to YHWH. YHWH demands negatively that the people refrain from carrying a burden or working on the sabbath, and positively that they sanctify the sabbath (vv. 21–2, 24, 27). Failure to keep sabbath law will cause Jerusalem's destruction (v. 27), whereas keeping it will bring Davidic rule and the reunification of Israel as a worshipping community in Jerusalem (vv. 25–6).

In contrast to the temple sermon (Jer 7), this passage specifies proper cultic behaviour, but like the temple sermon and other prose passages (11:1–14; 13:1–14; 16:1–13; 18:1–12; 19:1–15), the central requirement is to 'listen' (17:23, 24, 27; Brueggemann 1988: 160). The sabbath sermon interprets Jerusalem's fall as a failure to obey, evidenced by breaking the sabbath. But the sermon is more concerned about the future than about the past. Restoration of monarchy and city hinges on obedience to sabbath *tôrâ* (O'Connor 1988: 141–3). Many

see the passage as a post-exilic addition (Carroll 1986) because sabbath-keeping marked post-exilic life, but it may also have characterized life in exile (von Rad 1965: 79–84). The king's triumphant entrance through the city gates and the unification of Israel in common worship were surely an exilic hope.

(18:1–20:18) Captivity These chapters are more closely woven than previous units in chs. 11–20 (O'Connor 1988; Diamond 1987; Smith 1990: 56–60; Carroll 1986: 371) and form the climax of the first half of the book (Jer 1–25). Symbolic events and their sermonic interpretations (18:1–12; 19:1–15; 20:1–6), a divine lament (18:13*b*–17), laments of Jeremiah (18:18–23; 20:7–13), and a curse of his birth (20:14–18) create a symbolic narrative with multiple meanings. Jeremiah visits the potter whose work serves as a simile for divine power and occasions the final invitation to repent before the catastrophe. The people adamantly refuse to repent (18:12). God laments in horror and dismay (18:13–27); Jeremiah begs for fulfilment of the word (18:19–23) and breaks the potter's jug to signify the nation's imminent destruction (19:1–14). Babylon appears by name for the first time as the mythic foe from the north, concretized as a real historical invader. Just as Babylon is about to capture Jerusalem, Jeremiah is imprisoned in the temple and released. He utters his final confession in vindication (20:7–13) and then curses his birth (Jer 20:14–18). The covenant curse (11:1–13) has befallen the nation.

These chapters interpret the nation's fall as divine justice, a deserved punishment after relentless efforts by YHWH and Jeremiah to evoke repentance. Within the horizon of the implied exilic audience, however, the course of events offers a glint of hope. YHWH is not implacable. If they repent, divine building and planting are possible for their God is God of all nations (18:8–9). Jeremiah's own beating and imprisonment does not end in death but in release and in the proclamation of praise for YHWH who 'delivered the life of the needy from the hands of evildoers' (Jer 20:13).

(18:1–12) The Potter's Hand YHWH commands Jeremiah to go to the potter's house where the potter, not Jeremiah, performs a symbolic action (vv. 1–4) that Jeremiah interprets in his sermon (vv. 5–11). The event itself is rife with metaphorical connotations that vividly portray divine power. YHWH's hand and the potter's hand have symmetrical capabilities. Both can destroy their own creations at will (vv. 4, 6*b*). As the potter can crush the pot, so YHWH can destroy a nation or kingdom (v. 7). But YHWH's threat of destruction is conditional; repentance and obedience will induce YHWH to build and plant instead of destroying (vv. 9–11). The sermon concludes with YHWH's direct appeal to the nation: 'Turn now...from your evil way' (v. 11). But the people reply, 'It is no use!' (v. 12). Narratively, their emphatic refusal sets in motion further symbolic events.

(18:13–17) Divine Lament YHWH's lamentation is not grief-stricken but angry and appalled. Who can imagine behaviour like that of virgin Israel? (v. 13). YHWH's people, who are portrayed like the wife in 2:1–3:25, have forgotten him and gone after false gods (v. 15). As a result of their behaviour the land will become a horrifying example to others; they will go into exile. YHWH will turn from them and be beyond imprecation, beyond sympathy, beyond helping. For the exilic audience, this poem may convey their experience of God's absence, but it does not accuse God of abuse. It implies, instead, that God acted justly in scattering them before the enemy.

(18:18–23) Jeremiah's fourth confession corresponds to the spirit of YHWH's lament in the preceding poem. Like YHWH, Jeremiah has given up on the people after trying to avert divine wrath from them (v. 20b). Like YHWH, Jeremiah has been rejected by the people (vv. 20, 22, 23). And like YHWH, Jeremiah now wants war and its appalling consequences to come upon his enemies (vv. 21–2). He begs YHWH not to forgive, not to blot out their sin: 'deal with them while you are angry' (v. 23). Jeremiah's fourth lament, therefore, moves the larger narrative thread of the book forwards. In the scene at the potter's house, the people decisively refuse the final invitation to listen (18:12). Then both YHWH and Jeremiah utter laments that propel the narrative towards invasion by the still unnamed but no longer mythical enemy. They are of one mind; YHWH must act now.

At the same time, Jeremiah's confession marks him again as the innocent sufferer, one trapped by enemies who dug a pit to ensnare him (vv. 20, 22, 23). They entrap him because of his fidelity to the prophetic mission that he long resisted. He is a true prophet who does not send himself or speak for himself. If the implied audience is exilic, however, more is suggested in this portrayal. Jeremiah is the model of the faithful sufferer who, like his people, is entrapped by plots to destroy his life and who turns to YHWH for justice against enemies.

(19:1–15) The Broken Jug The story about the smashing of the potter's jug combines prose sermon and symbolic event to drive the book inexorably towards Jerusalem's destruction (v. 15). The chapter responds to Jeremiah's request for vengeance (18:18–23) and completes the punishment threatened in 18:13–17 and throughout the book thus far. Rather than narrate the actual invasion of the city (21:1–10; 39:1–10; 52:1–27), the text portrays it symbolically. YHWH commands Jeremiah to break the jug in front of the power structure of elders and priests (vv. 1–2; Brueggemann 1988: 167) to constitute the event as a legal act. YHWH then orders the invasion to be enacted symbolically. The jug's destruction signifies and embodies the smashing of the nation (v. 10; Carroll 1986: 386–7; O'Connor 1988: 144). The community's offences are cultic (see 13:1–11 and 7:1–8:3). Leaders and people alike have forsaken YHWH, profaned 'this place' and gone after the baals. They have killed the innocent and sacrificed children (vv. 4–5). Invasion by those 'who seek their life' (vv. 7, 9), therefore, will yield equally hideous results. Corpses will remain unburied; the city will be a horror (cf. 18:16); its people will become cannibals (vv. 7–9). A familiar accusation of the prose material concludes the chapter; the people refused to hear YHWH's word (v. 15). The end has come.

(20:1–18) Imprisonment In vv. 1–6 the chief priest Pashur beats Jeremiah and imprisons him in the stocks at the temple gate. Pashur's release of Jeremiah the next morning serves as the occasion for Jeremiah's brief prose sermon (vv. 4–6), his final confession (vv. 7–13), and his curse of the day of his birth (vv. 14–18).

vv. 1–6, the brief story of Jeremiah's incarceration is of decisive importance for narrative developments in the book. The chief officer of YHWH's house repudiates YHWH's message (v. 1) and abuses YHWH's messenger (v. 2; O'Connor 1988: 145); thus Pashur signifies the nation's total rejection of the divine word, and with great irony, he shows his disdain within the temple itself. As a consequence, he and all his allies will fall by the sword, go into captivity in Babylon, and lose their wealth (vv. 4–6). It is remarkable that the text names Babylon only now: in chs. 2–10, the threat came from the mythic 'enemy from the north', advancing for cosmic battle. In chs. 11–19, the enemy was less mythic, described by metonymy as sword, famine, pestilence, and captivity, but without historical specificity. In vv. 4–6 Babylon is mentioned four times. Historical identification has replaced mythic and poetic allusions.

Whereas Pashur represents both the people in their rejection of the prophet and the religious leaders who have led the people astray by prophesying falsely (v. 6), Jeremiah also represents more than the rejected prophet. Except for Jeremiah's confessions (11:18–12:6; 15:10–21; 17:14–18; 18:18–23; 20:7–13) and the call narrative (1:3–19), this is the first passage that portrays Jeremiah as a suffering prophet. Here his fate parallels that of his people; he is beaten and taken captive just as they will be, and he is released as they ultimately will be. Jeremiah's suffering and release portends their own. His captivity symbolizes their captivity and offers a glimpse of survival (McConville 1993; Polk 1984).

vv. 7–18, unlike Jeremiah's previous confessions, the final one is unaccompanied by divine speech. In ch. 20, YHWH does not speak because he has spoken insistently throughout the first twenty chapters either directly or through the prophet (but see von Rad 1984). In the symbolic accomplishment of the prophetic word, YHWH withdraws from the scene.

The literary limits of Jeremiah's confession are much disputed. Many interpreters include vv. 14–18 in the confession as a second complaint (von Rad 1936). Formally, however, they curse the prophet's birth and create an inclusio with the covenant curse (11:1–17; O'Connor 1988; Craigie, Kelley, and Drinkard 1991). Without vv. 14–18, Jeremiah's confession contains all the elements of a conventional lament: complaint (vv. 7–10), statement of assurance (v. 11), petition (v. 12), and praise (v. 13; O'Connor 1988; Baumgartner 1987: 19–38).

Jeremiah accuses YHWH of enticing and overpowering, of seducing and raping him (v. 7; Craigie, Kelley, and Drinkard 1991; O'Connor 1988; Diamond 1987). He complains again of rejection and mockery (vv. 7b–8). In anguish, he decides to stop speaking, but he cannot withhold the fire in his bones (v. 9). He quotes his enemies who call him the same name he gave Pashur, māgôr missābîb, 'terror all around' (20:3). His enemies use the same verbs against him that he used to accuse God of trickery; they want to 'entice' him and to 'prevail' over him (v. 11). But then Jeremiah remembers that YHWH is with him, a 'dread warrior'. His enemies will not 'prevail' (v. 11; cf. 15:20). His petition for vengeance appeals to God who tests and sees (v. 12, cf. 12:4). The confession closes with a statement of praise in which Jeremiah confidently announces that God has 'delivered the life of the needy from the hands of evildoers' (v. 13). In the narrative context of chs. 11–20, Jeremiah's trust rests in the confidence that the divine word, 'Violence and destruction!' (v. 8) is about to be realized. The prophetic mission is accomplished, and Jeremiah is vindicated as a true prophet.

From the perspective of the implied audience, however, Jeremiah's praise and confidence exemplify proper attitudes for captives. Just as some among the exiles begin to understand themselves as relatively innocent sufferers at the hand of Babylonian captors (Isa 40:1–2), so Jeremiah claims innocence and begs to be vindicated in face of enemies. His concluding praise voices not only confidence about his own fate but ultimately represents the trust to be evoked from the implied exilic audience who are the 'needy', seeking deliverance from the hands of evildoers.

Jeremiah's praise evaporates into a curse upon the day of his birth (vv. 14–18). This poem has long been recognized as similar to Job's curse (Job 3). Both biblical figures would prefer death in the womb to the toil, shame, and sorrow life brings them (v. 18). Jeremiah's curse makes sense in the pre-exilic temporal setting of the book's narrative thread where he faces the devastating consequences of his prophetic vindication. His nation, people, land, and way of life are destroyed. Had he never been born, he could not have delivered such a message. Because his prophetic vocation preceded his birth (1:5), it would have been better if his mother had aborted him, or if he had been stillborn (v. 17). In a kind of reverse symbolic action, he imagines a cancellation of his ministry. He wishes to unmake his life so that he would not have to deliver such a message and see it fulfilled. He wants the deliverer of the news of his birth to be like 'the cities the Lord overthrew without pity' (v. 16), a category that must include Jerusalem, symbolically destroyed already. The prophet's curse of his birth expresses horror and despair at the consequences of his message. Its closing questions extend beyond the prophet's own life to embrace the sorrow of the nation (v. 18).

Aftermath (chs. 21–5)

These loosely connected chapters assume that the nation has already fallen, although to this point it has been presented only in symbolic terms. Even when the invasion is finally reported (21:1–10), the focus is upon the choice facing survivors in the siege's aftermath. Prose narratives give them advice (21:1–10; 24:1–10). Poems explain how the invasion occurred by blaming the royal establishment of kings and prophets (21:11–23:40). Prose materials point beyond exile to a future of national survival (25:1–14) and ultimately of international justice (25:15–38).

The character of the literature changes markedly in 21:1 from that of the preceding chapters. Explicit conversation and debate by poetic and prose speakers is overtaken by a narrator's controlling voice that more obviously frames and orchestrates the speakers. And for the first time, the narrative is historically referential, although the material is no less interpretative than earlier symbolic and metaphoric passages. 21:1–10 dates to the reign of King Zedekiah during the siege of Jerusalem by Nebuchadrezzar, the first such dating since 1:1–3 and 3:6. (See Holladay 1986: 571 on the Babylonian ruler's name and Seitz 1989b: 214 on Zedekiah's importance.) The book has moved from announcements of the cosmic battle with the mythic foe from the north, through symbolic enactments of the destruction of Judah and Jerusalem, to depictions of the historical siege and burning of the city (21:1–10). The point of 21:1–10 is not historical narration, however, but

theological, political persuasion. (See Rudolph 1947 and Craigie, Kelley, and Drinkard, 1991: 284–5 for different views of the contrast between chs. 20 and 21.)

(21:1–10) Life King Zedekiah sends two named messengers to ask Jeremiah to 'enquire of the Lord' in the 'hope that Nebuchadrezzar might be turned away from Jerusalem (vv. 1–2), as were the Assyrians during Hezekiah's time (Isa 36–7). (On the literary relationship of ch. 21 with chs. 24 and 37, see Pohlmann 1978: 44 and Seitz 1989b: 253.) Jeremiah returns a terrifying message. Instead of sending the Babylonians away, YHWH will bring them into the city, thwart Judah's defence, and fight against Judah. YHWH is indeed the dread warrior of Jeremiah's prayer (20:11). YHWH heads the attack (vv. 5–6, 10), and Nebuchadrezzar will kill survivors without pity (v. 7). In the face of this interpretation of events, the people have to choose, in Deuteronomistic terms (Deut 30:11–20), between life and death (v. 8). To survive, their only choice is surrender to Babylon.

Political and theological perspectives of the narrator are absolutely clear. Only one path will lead to life: surrender and co-operation with the invaders. This alone will enable the community to gain their lives as the 'prize of war' (v. 9). Any other political or military course will bring death, 'For I have set my face against this city', says YHWH (v. 10). While appearing to report history, the narrator seeks to persuade the audience that survival hinges upon right relationship with Babylonian invaders. Not to side with them is to choose death. There can be no confusion about loyalties because Babylon is acting as YHWH's agent. This means that those who escape to Egypt or remain in the land have chosen death. The truly faithful among surviving groups are the Babylonian exiles alone. More hidden in the text is its implicit criticism of Zedekiah whose question reveals his complacency regarding divine protection (v. 2). Zedekiah is only the first of the royal establishment to come under attack in these chapters.

(21:11–23:40) Collapse of Royal Élites Attention to the monarchy in chs. 1–20 is sparse and general (1:1–3; 3:6; 3:15; 4:9; 8:1; 13:18–19; 15:4; 17:19–25). This section, by contrast, gives sustained attention to the royal institution and interprets the national tragedy as the consequence of corrupt and unjust leadership by kings (21:11–22:30), as well as by prophets and priests (23:9–40; Carroll 1986: 404). Although the monarchy will be restored after exile by divine action (23:1–8), no such restoration is promised for priests and prophets.

Some of the poems in the section 21:11–23:8 appear to be associated with royalty by prose introductions and juxtaposition with material critical of the monarchy rather than by addressing kingship directly (21:12b–14; 22:6b–7; 22:10). 22:20–3 mentions kingship only briefly in an address to female Israel. The poems and prose pieces are short and concern the last kings of Judah. Together they charge the nation's collapse to the complete failure of the monarchy and describe its imminent demise. Only later will it be reconstituted by divine action in a new form (23:1–8; McConville 1993: 54–8).

(21:11–14) Do Justice A prose introduction addresses the entire house of David (vv. 11–12a). The poem itself turns the oblique attack on monarchy (vv. 1–10) into a devouring fire (vv. 12c, 14). YHWH is the speaker who describes the monarchy's primary responsibility and attacks it for complacency

(21:12–13). What the king should do is expressed in positive and negative terms, 'execute justice' and prevent oppression (v. 12). If kings fail in this duty, the fire of divine wrath will devour all around it (v. 14). YHWH is the angry critic whose address to the whole house of David (v. 12) implies that the entire dynasty of kings caused the national wreckage.

(22:1–6) is a prose elaboration of monarchical duties in which YHWH continues to speak. Addressees expand from the 'house of David' to include an unnamed present king, servants, and people (vv. 1–2). v. 3 adds to kingly responsibilities, prohibitions against oppression of the alien, widow, or orphan and against shedding innocent blood. The principal duty of the king that summarizes all others and joins this text with prose throughout the book is the king's responsibility to 'listen' (vv. 4–5). The future of the monarchy depends upon obedience to the word, an appeal that has double meaning for the implied audience. Because the kings failed to listen, the kingdom was lost, but if kings, servants, and people listen, then kings will again sit on the throne (v. 4). The future depends upon the repentance of all.

(22:6–12) contains a loose collection of pieces associated with monarchy by prose directions to readers (vv. 6, 11). Like the rich forests of Gilead and Lebanon (Holladay 1986: 584), the kingship is about to be cut down. Prose verses (8–9) shift attention from monarchy to the destroyed city in an imagined conversation that blames the destruction on idolatry and abandonment of the covenant, presumably by the monarchy. vv. 10–11 combine poetry and prose to comment on the double tragedies of King Josiah and his son, Jehoahaz, also known as Shallum (Honeyman 1948). Beloved King Josiah died in battle (2 Kings 23:28–30), but more lamentable is the fate of his son, exiled forever from the land.

(22:13–19) contrasts actions of an unidentified bad king (vv. 13–14, 17) with that of a good king (vv. 15–16) who is the first king's father. v. 18 identifies them as Josiah and his son Jehoiakim. Jehoiakim builds his house, that is, both his monarchy and his palace, without righteousness and justice, using the forced labour of his people. YHWH uses rhetorical questions to ask Jehoiakim about the essence of monarchy: true kingship is not manifested in the display of wealth but in the doing of justice and righteousness as did Josiah (v. 15). This is what it means to 'know God' (v. 16; Brueggemann 1988: 193), precisely what is absent in Jehoiakim's rule (20:13, 17; cf. 21:12; 22:3; 2 Kings 23:31–24:6). Thus Jehoiakim will not be mourned but buried like a beast (22:18–19; Craigie, Kelley, and Drinkard 1991: 307–13 discuss literary features of this passage).

(22:20–3) addresses a female but her identity is uncertain. Carroll (1986: 434–5) believes this poem to be an oracle originally addressed to Lebanon, but some of the language echoes poems against the bride of 2:1–3:25, who has been unfaithful from her youth, though here her specific crime is 'not listening' (v. 21; Brueggemann 1988: 195; Carroll 1986: 436). Her trysts are over because her lovers are crushed, but why she lives in Lebanon is unclear (v. 23). v. 22 links the poem to the material on kings for her shepherds will be shepherded by the wind, referring either to Israel's captivity or to punishment of the wife's lovers-turned-enemies. (In the ancient Near East, shepherd imagery referred to leaders, particularly kings, whose task was to protect and guide their people as a shepherd cares for the flocks.)

(22:24–30) combines prose and poetry to portray YHWH's attack on Coniah, also called Jehoiachin, and to announce the monarchy's end. Even if he were a precious signet ring on YHWH's hand, 'I would tear you off, and hurl you away', says YHWH (vv. 24–6). And in a sadder poetic voice, YHWH asks if the king is a despised and broken pot to be thrown away. Both Jehoiachin and his offspring will be hurled into a foreign land. A lamenting voice invites the personified land to witness the monarchy's end (v. 29), for the house of David is finished (v. 30).

Chs. 21–2 announce and explain the end of the monarchy and provide a theo-political explanation for the fall of the nation. The kings failed to listen, oppressed the weak and vulnerable, and sought counsel from lying prophets. In the exilic search for causes and explanations of the national tragedy, the greed, injustice, and infidelity of the monarchy loom large. Because of kingly misdeeds, the Davidic dynasty is finished and with it the nation.

(23:1–8) But in the pattern of composition typical of the book of Jeremiah, here it contradicts the former picture of destruction, death, and definitive end, doing so without preparation or explanation. YHWH simply announces the future reconstitution of the dead monarchy. Both past and future continue to impinge on the exilic present. To the implied audience, divine promises of restoration and new shepherds may not have appeared to contradict Jeremiah's prophecies of doom, for the latter had already been fulfilled. Jehoiachin was being held captive (Jer 52:31–4); other kings had died ignominious deaths; people were in exile. Temporally the audience was situated after the nation's destruction and the seeming end of monarchy. The monarchy had failed them, and its re-establishment as an institution of wisdom and justice (v. 5) could occur only by divine intervention. In vv. 1–4, YHWH chastises the shepherds who have scattered the sheep and promises to raise up new shepherds for the remnant (v. 4) and a 'righteous Branch', who will embody the royal ideal (vv. 5–6). In that future day, all the dispersed community will return to their own land (vv. 7–8).

(23:9–40) Prophets This set of prose and poetic pieces attacks claimants to prophetic office who presume to have a divine word but, in the estimate of these poems, speak lies. (On false prophets, see Overholt 1970; Meyer 1977; and Osswald 1962.) That the book contains so much material about competing prophetic visions suggests great conflict in the rhetorical battle to envision the future. This chapter sets Jeremiah apart from false prophets. It belittles and demeans them in order to dismiss their interpretation of the national crisis in favour of Jeremiah's (Carroll 1981: 196). Prophets and priests are as culpable as the kings in leading the people astray and bringing the community to its tragic demise. There is no promise of a renewed prophecy in the future because that role is already played by the Jeremiah tradition. Jeremiah's word, the vision he creates with his prophecy alone, has power to create a new future.

(23:9–15) uses shocking and potent rhetoric to discredit priest and prophet in two poetic panels of accusation and punishment (vv. 9–12 and 13–15). In a dramatic lament Jeremiah describes his emotional state and claims the true prophetic message for himself. His heart is 'crushed' because of YHWH's 'dread' words (v. 9, NEB). On account of unidentified adulterers, the land mourns and dries up. v. 11 announces the surprising source of evil. Priest and prophet are ungodly, so disaster will come upon them (v. 12). Equally harsh language appears in the second panel (vv. 13–15) where a first-person voice describes the 'disgusting' sight of prophets prophesying by Baal, but the prophets of Jerusalem are even more shocking. They are adulterers, liars, conspirators in evil, as bad as the legendary Sodom and Gomorrah (vv. 13–15). They will be poisoned for they have spread 'ungodliness' throughout the land.

(23:16–22) Prose verses (16–17) urge the audience to reject the prophets. They are bad leaders who delude the people and confect their own messages of pseudo-peace and complacency. The two-stanza poem that follows reveals the depth of their deceit. In vv. 18–20 Jeremiah appears to be the speaker who asks the central question that distinguishes prophets from one another: 'Who has stood in the council of the LORD so as to see and to hear his word?' Only such a one can proclaim the divine word, but YHWH's wrath goes forth, presumably upon the false prophets (vv. 19–20). In the second stanza YHWH speaks to deny the prophets' claims. If they had stood in the divine council, they would have proclaimed a truthful message (vv. 21–2). The 'council of the LORD' refers to a heavenly gathering of beings who surround YHWH. Prophets claim to have access to this divine council (1 Kings 22:19–23; Jer 23:18–22; Dan 7:9–14, 23–7).

(23:23–40) YHWH continues to deny claims of false prophets in a prose diatribe against them. Their dreams and their words are not divinely given but self-invented. YHWH is against them (vv. 23–31). These false prophets are no different from those of the pre-exilic period who prophesied by Baal, leading the people astray. vv. 33–40 continue the critique of false prophets with a play on words. A prophetic term for oracle, maśśā', also means 'burden' (McKane 1980: 597–603). When they ask, 'What is the burden of the LORD?', meaning the prophetic message, Jeremiah is to reply, 'You are the burden', meaning that they impede the divine word (v. 33).

In this section, accusation undermines professional competitors who battle for the hearts of the people. Should any in the audience doubt the veracity and divine origin of Jeremiah's message, this collection makes the case that Jeremiah alone can be trusted. It interprets the nation's fall as caused by duplicity of priests and prophets who have lied to the people. But also at stake is the fidelity of the present generation. By implication, they must avoid listening to false prophets and, instead, follow the voice, visions, and dreams of Jeremiah, the one true prophet. Their survival hinges upon listening to his message alone.

(24:1–10) Figs Jeremiah appears as first-person narrator in this prose chapter, dated to the first deportation of exiles in 597 BCE. Jerusalem has been invaded, Jehoiachin is in captivity (v. 1), and Zedekiah rules in the not yet destroyed Judah (v. 8). Although the chapter is set ten years earlier than 21:1–10, it continues directions for survival begun there: co-operate with the invaders (Pohlmann 1978: 44). Jeremiah's vision of two

baskets of figs resembles his vision in 1:11–13. In both narratives, Jeremiah relates a vision that YHWH interprets to give both accounts the double authority of deity and prophet. The figs symbolize two groups of survivors. Those in captivity in Babylon are very good and those remaining in the land or who have escaped to Egypt are rotten. To the former is promised a future in language adopted from the call narrative (1:10). The exiles will be planted and built. They will receive a new heart, know YHWH, and return (šûb, vv. 6–7). This chapter honours the exilic community as the elect, the special, the carriers of true Yahwism. It is they who are obedient, repentant, and possess a future. Nicholson (1970: 81) notes the absence of conditional terms in the promise. Divine preference for the exiles is absolute. The vision of the fig baskets marks a major shift in the message thus far. This vision no longer warns the people to repent in order to avoid calamity, but instead addresses a community that has experienced and survived the tragedy, and in those circumstances offers them hope.

The chapter divides the survivors into two groups, exalting one and belittling the other. The bad figs who remain in the land or go to Egypt will be utterly destroyed (vv. 8–10). The effect of this vision is to delegitimate the rule of Zedekiah and those who remained in the land (Brueggemann 1988: 211). Carroll (1986: 487) places the chapter's contest for supremacy among survivors in post-exilic times, but the chapter may be an attempt to bolster the confidence and responsibility of despondent exiles by identifying them as the chosen. Since the text describes restoration in vague theological and relational terms, omitting political or institutional arrangements, it appears to be urging an exilic audience towards an open future, albeit at the cost of their compatriots elsewhere.

(25:1–38) Babylon's Fall Ch. 25 is an important but problematic chapter. It is here that divergences between the MT and LXX versions of the book are most marked, with LXX inserting the Oracles Against the Nations at v. 13 and omitting many of the references to Babylon found in the MT, to yield a shorter chapter (Craigie, Kelley, and Drinkard 1991: 363). Fischer (1991), Holladay (1986: 665), and McKane (1986: 618–23) have thorough discussions of differences between the versions. Many commentators recognize links between this chapter and ch. 1 and understand ch. 25 to close off the first major division of the book. Kessler (1997) calls it a 'hinge' chapter that reaches backwards and forwards across the book. Here, for instance, Jeremiah acts at last as 'prophet to the nations', a task assigned him in the call narrative (1:5, 10) and completed in the Oracles Against the Nations (chs. 46–51). In its present shape ch. 25 announces punishment against Judah's invaders (vv. 1–14), enacts the promise symbolically (vv. 25–9), and concludes the book with a poem on the devouring anger of the lion-like God (vv. 30–8).

(25:1–14) A Global View A third-person narrator dates the chapter to the fourth year of Jehoiakim and the first year of Nebuchadrezzar. The year is 605 when Babylon gained hegemony in the ancient Near East. The date's significance in this passage is to show that Jeremiah prophesied the fall of Judah to Babylon well in advance of events and that his prophecy of the exile's end is equally reliable. In v. 3 Jeremiah takes over as narrator, declaring in Deuteronomistic terms (Carroll 1986: 491) how persistently he has preached throughout his entire career from the thirteenth year of Josiah (v. 3, cf. 1:2) to the year 605. For twenty-three years Jeremiah continued the work of prophets before him (v. 4), calling Judah to repent of its idolatry. But they did not listen, provoking YHWH's anger (vv. 1–7). Many interpreters correctly understand these verses as a summary of Jeremiah's preaching in chs. 1–25 (Craigie, Kelley, and Drinkard 1991: 363), but they also serve other theological and literary purposes. They interpret the nation's fall as a refusal of Judah to listen to YHWH's prophets, and they introduce the broader global and temporal framework in which this chapter views the catastrophe.

In vv. 8–14 YHWH replaces Jeremiah as speaker to provide greater authority for the prophecy that follows. Expanding motifs from earlier passages, the divine voice spells out consequences of not listening (vv. 8–11). YHWH will again send the tribes of the north, but for the first time they are explicitly identified with Babylon (v. 9). As YHWH's agent of destruction, Nebuchadrezzar acquires the shocking sobriquet, 'my servant' (v. 9; 29:10; Thompson 1980: 512). Newly emphasized in this divine speech is that the invasion to come will not only be against 'this land' but against 'all these nations around' (v. 9). Remarkably, Judah's fate is not singular. Babylon will destroy domestic life, indeed, all life on an international scale (vv. 9–10). Nor will Judah serve Babylon alone, for all these nations will serve Babylon for seventy years, a symbolic number for 'many years' (v. 11; Thompson 1980: 515). The temporal frame extends even further into the future than previously. After seventy years, YHWH will also punish Babylon. The invader will be invaded and be repaid according to its deeds (v. 14). All the words 'written in this book' will be brought against them (v. 13).

Rhetorically, this passage gives hope to the exiles. It closes the first 'book' upon a promise—vague, indefinite, but certain—that the exilic community has a future. The three voices in this narrative—unknown narrator, Jeremiah, and YHWH—do not debate. Each builds upon the previous speaker with increasing authority, for it is, perhaps, the words of hope that most need bolstering for the exiles. The text does not call for political action or rebellion; it encourages endurance (Kessler 1997) until YHWH brings about a reversal of fortunes (v. 14). Why Babylon will meet the same fate it metes out is not explained; YHWH simply asserts it. A transformed, barely imaginable future will come to pass.

(25:15–29) The Cup of Wrath If readers should doubt the promises of 25:8–14, the following prose narrative enacts them symbolically, thereby setting the divine purpose in motion. Jeremiah is again cast as narrator who reports YHWH's command for him to act as wine steward. Instead of presiding over a joyous feast, Jeremiah delivers the cup of wrath to all nations beginning with Judah and Jerusalem (v. 18). They are the first to drink from the 'fiery wine' (NEB) of YHWH's anger; indeed, they have already drunk from it (13:12–14). Following Judah comes the list of Judah's enemies beginning with Egypt (v. 19) and concluding with Sheshach, a term for Babylon (v. 26; Holladay 1986: 675). All will drink of YHWH's wrath, and should they refuse, Jeremiah must insist (vv. 28–9). Reversal of fortunes, therefore, has already occurred in the symbolic sphere. All that remains is for events to unfold.

(25:30–8) Against the Nations Poetry replaces prose in an oracle against all the nations (v. 30). (See Carroll 1986: 497–508 for a thorough discussion of Oracles Against Nations.) Jeremiah continues as speaker of poems that focus on divine anger and judgement against unnamed nations. The metaphor of YHWH as roaring lion out to devour all the earth's inhabitants frames the poem (vv. 31, 38). No particular crimes are attributed to the nations who are merely 'guilty', or 'wicked' (v. 31 NEB). The poem attends, instead, to the certitude of their punishment. A prose comment uses language previously used for Judah to describe devastation of the entire earth (v. 33). vv. 34–8 then narrow the attack to the 'shepherds', the kings who are responsible for provoking divine anger (25:35–7). YHWH, the attacking lion, has already left his 'covert' to begin the attack.

Chs. 1–25 use mythic, metaphorical description to magnify the threat to Judah as superhuman and inexorable. They charge the people with heinous crimes and obscene infidelities. They portray Jeremiah as isolated and absolutely alone. All these facets of the text bolster its theodicy. The people were warned with dramatic visions of their foe, by constant reminders of their sins, but they rejected the prophet and his words. In effect, they forced YHWH to punish them. The complex collections of materials in chs. 1–25, therefore, attempt to explain why the tragedy happened. The second half of the book (chs. 26–52) focuses on how to survive the tragedy.

Introduction to Book Two (chs. 26–52)

Kessler (1968) views this second section of the book as a history of Israel's rejection of the prophetic message. Pohlmann (1978) finds evidence of conflict between hope and judgement upon those who went to Egypt. Seitz (1985) also sees conflict within the community after 597 in an exilic redaction. While these thematic elements are present in the second half of the book, they are subsumed into larger rhetorical purposes. Chs. 26–52 develop issues of survival and consider the place of Judah's tragedy in the divine plan for the future of the nations.

The prophetic message in contention in the second half of the book is no longer whether Judah will repent in time to avert collapse. The book's audience lives with Judah's failure to do so. In fits and starts, all the chapters in the second half address the community's survival. In doing so, they seek to evoke repentance from the exiles, to instruct them to endure through the unavoidable suffering they face (Kessler 1968), and to have confidence that God will bring them into a future they can barely imagine. In service of these purposes, Jeremiah appears as an iconic presence, not only as a prophet rejected, but as the model of the faithful sufferer whose behaviour exiles must emulate to gain their lives as 'the prize of war'. The chapters reveal enormous tensions within the communities of survivors over how to proceed (Seitz 1989b).

Although many different actual speakers may stand behind these texts (Reitzschel 1966), two 'implied' narrators appear in them. The first and most prominent is an omniscient third-person speaker who is authoritative and descriptive, often identified with Jeremiah's scribe Baruch, and who relates events in many of these chapters (26, 29, 32, 33, 36, 37–45; Holladay 1989: 16; but see Carroll 1986: 662–8; Clements

1988: 153; Nicholson 1970: 17). He describes events and quotes YHWH, Jeremiah, and other characters whose voices are filtered through his own. The theological, political, and ideological perspectives of this implied narrator are both obvious and conflictual. Jeremiah and his adherents alone carry YHWH's intentions for the survivors. Life will come through submission to Babylon. Sufferings of exile cannot be escaped but must be embraced. The second narrator is Jeremiah (chs. 27–8, 35). In the few chapters where he is principal speaker, additional authority accompanies the narrating voice by the impression that the prophet himself addresses readers.

Poetic voices reappear in a significant way in chs. 30–1 and in the Oracles Against the Nations (chs. 46–51). The sparsity of poetry sets it apart and gives it prominence. The poetic voices promise more than survival; they point to a radiant future and to divine overthrow of aggressive enemy nations. This part of the book, therefore, concerns hope, muted and distant, but as certain and ineluctable as tragedy was in chs. 1–25.

Chs. 26–36 concern blame and hope. Chs. 26 and 36 create a literary frame around sub-units devoted to prophetic conflict (chs. 27–9), the 'little book of consolation' (chs. 30–3), and an example and counter-example for faithful living (chs. 34–5). Chs. 26–9 are loosely connected chapters concerning prophetic discord, and address disputes over which prophetic vision of the future will ensure the nation's survival message is true. Ch. 26 defends Jeremiah as the true prophet whose credentials are reaffirmed in the face of rejection and threats upon his life. Chs. 27–8 make the same point through Jeremiah's confrontations with lying prophets, and ch. 29 affirms Jeremiah's advice to the exiles over that of lying prophets. Hananiah, Ahab, Zedekiah, and Shemaiah die for their false prophecy. By contrast, Jeremiah's mysterious escapes from death (26:24; 36:26) witness to the truthfulness of his prophecy. But discernment of the true prophetic word, a major issue in exile, is a means to an end, not the end itself. Only correct discernment of and obedience to true prophecy ensure the community's survival. The content of the prophetic word in this sequence of texts is as important, therefore, as the debate over the true messenger. Narratives progress logically from the proclamation of Jerusalem's destruction and Jeremiah's survival (ch. 26), to directions to submit to the invaders (chs. 27–8), to advice for settling in for a long exile (ch. 29). The primary issue, therefore, is not prophecy itself (*contra* Kessler 1968), but survival.

(26:1–24) A Second Commission Ch. 26 continues a midrashic reinterpretation of Jeremiah's temple sermon (7:1–8:3) and functions as a second call narrative (O'Connor 1989: 619). Some in the community accept Jeremiah's word, whereas priests, prophets, and especially King Jehoiakim reject it. A chronological note typical of the second half of the book dates the story to the beginning of Jehoiakim's reign (v. 1). Many interpreters use these dates to construct chronologies of the prophet's life but frequently overlook the date's symbolic import. The date indicates that, from the beginning of his reign, Jehoiakim rejected the prophetic word. Ch. 26 divides into three parts: vv. 1–16, the trial; vv. 17–23, the elders' intervention; v. 24, rescue. (On the many differences between LXX and MT, see Carroll 1986: 551.)

(26:1–16) The implied narrator reports a command to Jeremiah to preach in the temple (cf. 7:2) but adds that he is not 'to trim a word' from the prophetic message for the people might still 'listen' (v. 3). This divine command parallels commissions to Moses (Deut 4:2; 13:1), except that Moses was prohibited from adding to the message. Jeremiah receives no such prohibition because this narrative does precisely that; it adds to the message. It adapts Jeremiah's preaching to the circumstances of exile assumed in the second half of the book. A radically abridged version of the temple sermon follows the commission (vv. 4–6), revealing a process of selection and elaboration in the transmission and updating of prophecy, omitting the cultic delinquencies central to ch. 7, and attending, instead, to the consequence of the people's refusal to listen. For the audience that consequence has already occurred. The temple has become like Shiloh (see Jer 7). The exilic community itself must heed the call to repent (O'Connor 1989).

Multiple responses from the community follow in vv. 7–16 and culminate in Jeremiah's trial. Initially, priests, prophets, and all the people respond to Jeremiah's threats to temple and city (v. 6) by capturing him and pronouncing a death sentence upon him (vv. 7–9). A trial begins with priests and prophets acting as prosecutors and 'officials' and with the people acting as jury (vv. 10–11). To charges against him, Jeremiah courageously reaffirms that YHWH sent (š-l-ḥ) him and calls again for repentance (vv. 12–13). He also comments on his own predicament. He is in their hands and they can do as they wish with him, but he is innocent for YHWH has sent him (vv. 14–15). The trial concludes with the 'officials and all the people' proclaiming his innocence (v. 16). Thus far, the narrative reaffirms Jeremiah's commission, reintroduces the call to repent, and reveals that Jeremiah has support among officials and people but not among religious leaders. Jeremiah himself, under a threat of death, remains steadfast and is vindicated.

(26:17–23) muddies the narrative. Though the trial is finished, new speakers appear, 'elders' who continue the debate by presenting examples of two other prophecies of Jerusalem's destruction and their contrasting reception by kings. The first prophet is Micah (Mic 3:12) whose message was received by Hezekiah as a call to repent (vv. 17–19). By contrast, the prophet Uriah's message was not simply rejected by Jehoiakim. The king sent a death squad into Egypt to extradite Uriah, killed him, and abused his corpse (vv. 20–3). This comparison between kings underscores Jehoiakim's heinous disregard for the prophetic word from the beginning of his rule (v. 1). Jehoiakim joins priests and prophets as enemies of the word, and by implication, they are together responsible for the fall of the nation.

Mysteriously Ahikam then rescues Jeremiah from death (v. 24). Some interpreters argue that the purpose of this verse is to illustrate the danger Jeremiah personally confronts as prophet (Hossfeld and Meyer 1973 35; Weiser 1960: 235; Thompson 1980: 528). But the people have already declared Jeremiah's innocence (v. 16) so that his rescue seems unnecessary. However, it creates a parallel to another account of Jeremiah's endangerment and rescue in ch. 36. These two chapters contain many similarities and thereby create a literary frame around chs. 27–35 (O'Connor 1988; Nicholson 1970: 55). Moreover, Ahikam is the first of a list of named rescuers in the 'second book', among whom the Shaphan family is central (Wilson 1989: 62–8; Boadt 1982b: 15). Jeremiah is no longer alone. Named supporters probably point to a group in the exilic community who stand firmly in the Jeremiah tradition and resist monarchic authority (Brueggemann 1991: 12). Their support and rescue of Jeremiah is also support and rescue of his tradition. His rescue indicates that he is a true prophet because he does not die after its announcement as do false prophets (Deut 18:20).

Ch. 26 introduces the second book, therefore, by announcing themes central to the following chapters. It blames King Jehoiakim, priests, and prophets for resisting the prophetic word and failing to repent. It invites the implied exilic audience to join supporters of the prophet against the leadership and invites them to repent now. It presents Jeremiah as a model of exilic obedience who, while in the hands of his captors, holds steadfast in his confidence in YHWH's word. His rescue symbolically heralds a mysterious and surprising future rescue of the repentant exilic community and contrasts him with numerous false prophets in chs. 27–9 who come under the sentence of death for their lying ways.

(27:1–28:17) The Yokes In a prose account of symbolic actions Jeremiah narrates his conflict with other prophetic groups. At issue is how Babylon will control Judah, the exiles, and captured temple vessels. Conflict over interpretation of the divine will for Judah and the nations crystallizes in the encounters between Jeremiah and Hananiah. What is at stake between Jeremiah and the prophets is the imaginative envisioning of the future in order to affect behaviour in the present. The text contains three narrative panels that increasingly narrow the conflict from an international disagreement to a personal dispute between two prophets. The first panel contains Jeremiah's message to the nations and the contrary view of their prophets (27:1–11); the second narrows to Jeremiah's message to King Zedekiah and the opposition of Judah's prophets (27:12–22); the third funnels further down to the specific clash between Jeremiah and Hananiah (28:1–17). (But see Carroll 1986: 523 for whom ch. 28 is a variant of ch. 27.)

(27:1–11) The story begins in the first year of Zedekiah's reign, immediately after the first invasion of Judah by Babylon in 597. The date signifies the truth of Jeremiah's words. At the time of the first invasion, Jeremiah prophesied Babylon's triumph and eventual overthrow. His word was reliable regarding Babylon's ascent to power and will be equally reliable regarding Babylon's fall. The story of the yokes enacts and dramatizes this message. Jeremiah himself relates that he put a yoke around his neck at YHWH's command and delivered a message to the envoys of neighbouring kings. The yoke symbolizes enslavement of the nations to Babylon. As Creator of the earth, YHWH can direct events at will (Clements 1988: 162). Describing YHWH's creative activity, Jeremiah announces that Babylonian rule will extend through three generations and then will end (vv. 2–7). Nations that do not comply with Babylon will lose their lands. They are forbidden to listen to their own prophets and mediators who counsel lies (vv. 8–11).

(27:12–22) Next Jeremiah interprets the yoke for Judah. He addresses the king but uses plural forms (v. 12), urging him to accept Babylon's yoke and not to listen to the prophets. They lie, for YHWH did not send them (vv. 12–15). The prophets' lies become specific in a dispute over temple vessels carried to Babylon in 597 (vv. 16–22; Seitz 1989b: 184–9). The prophets promised quick restoration of the vessels to the temple (v. 16), but Jeremiah contends that they and additional vessels and people will remain in Babylon indefinitely, until YHWH decides to think of them (vv. 19–22). Strong ideological claims are being made here with the authority of Jeremiah's own voice. Prophets who anticipate a quick end to exile and oppose Babylon are not only wrong, they are liars who stand against God. The community must resist their vision or it will not survive (v. 17; see 21:8).

(28:1–17) Interpretative conflict turns into a personal showdown in Jeremiah's encounter with Hananiah. In the same year, before priests, prophets, and all the people (vv. 1–2), Hananiah announces a countermessage. YHWH will destroy the yoke of the king of Babylon and return vessels, king, and exiles within two years (vv. 3–4); captivity will be short. Jeremiah reports his own ambivalence in response. He wishes it were so, but tradition stands against Hananiah's interpretation. Only time will tell if the message of peace is from God (vv. 5–9). Hananiah parries with a symbolic act of his own. He breaks Jeremiah's yoke (vv. 10–11) in an action designed to cancel Jeremiah's word and set a different word inexorably towards fulfilment. Jeremiah himself indicates that the true word is difficult to discern. He departs for some time (v. 12), then YHWH sends him back with an iron yoke (vv. 13–14). Revelation cancels indecision. Hananiah's word is a lie and his death within the year stands as irrefutable Deuteronomistic proof (vv. 12–17; Deut 18:20) To Jeremiah, Hananiah's message is more than wishful thinking; it is a theological and political path to death. Only by accepting Babylonian rule and enduring the suffering that accompanies it will they ultimately escape exile and find a future. Babylonian hegemony will surely end but not quickly. The text labels the anti-Babylonian leanings in the surrounding nations, in Judah, and among exiles as vicious lies. For those living in exile, the story of Jeremiah's yoke offers instructions about survival. In their present circumstances, exiles must persist and endure, for the Creator who made the earth and its inhabitants will eventually bring about a reversal of fortunes. Hope, historically unspecific but theologically grounded, rests in the power of the Creator.

(29:1–32) Letters This chapter develops themes of the previous two, but takes the form of letters reported by the third-person narrator. From Jerusalem Jeremiah writes to the exiles (vv. 1–23) and responds to a letter about him from Shemaiah (vv. 24–32). The epistolary literary device allows Jeremiah to remain the authoritative source of the prophetic message even though he is not present among the exiles. He becomes the author of written prophecy addressed to elders, priests, and prophets, to everyone taken to Babylon after the deportation of 597 (vv. 1–2). Emissaries of Zedekiah, both among families of Jeremiah's supporters, are couriers (v. 3; Brueggemann 1991: 31). The letter's message is precise regarding the exiles' relationship to Babylon. Not only are they not to resist Babylon, they are actively to seeks its welfare (šālôm). They are to settle there, to set up daily life and domestic relationships, and to seek the welfare of the city in which they are captive. In its shalom is their shalom (vv. 4–7). This surprising advice, delivered at the very beginning of exile (v. 2), indicates that there is no escape, no way out, despite contradictory interpretations of the prophets among them. The prophets are lying (vv. 8–9).

The letter encourages long-suffering and discourages rebellion or false confidence in an early release. Rescue will come, but only after seventy years (v. 10, cf. 25:11–12). Clements (1988) thinks that seventy years means one generation, but it probably means the symbolic long time of biblical numerology (Newsome 1984: 121), since 27:7 promises three generations of Babylonian rule. What the narrator claims to be Jeremiah's own view, however, is that Babylon is acting as YHWH's agent and therefore their only choice is to co-operate actively. Eventually their suffering will end because YHWH has plans for their shalom (v. 11). Then YHWH will relate to them differently, no longer hiding from them. YHWH will restore their fortunes and return them from the diaspora of exile (vv. 10–14).

In this letter, the exiles alone are the fortunate, the chosen. Jeremiah promises curses of 'sword, famine, and pestilence' upon those who stay in Judah (vv. 15–18; see 24:8–10). Two false prophets among the exiles, Ahab and Zedekiah, will die like Hananiah under the Deuteronomic curse (28:17). The letter totally discredits prophets of the anti-Babylonian group and of people who remained in the land. Nor will subsequent texts support those who stay in the land, a group that strangely includes Jeremiah himself (chs. 40–1). His choice to remain in the land (40:1–6) contradicts his advice to survivors.

vv. 24–32, Shemaiah's letter: the narrator relates the contents of a second letter, written by one of the exiles named Shemaiah to the high priest in Jerusalem. Shemaiah demands that the priest silence the madman Jeremiah because of his letter (29:1–23). When the high priest reads Shemaiah's letter aloud, Jeremiah curses Shemaiah and his family for false prophecy (vv. 31–2).

The altercations in chs. 26–9 create a marked contrast with the harmony and contentment envisioned in chs. 30–3.

(30:1–33:26) The Little Book of Consolation contains collections of poetry (chs. 30–1) and prose (chs. 32–3) that depict a complete reversal of fortune for the destroyed and exiled people. Using themes and motifs from previous parts of the book, these chapters envision an alternative future of healing, restoration, and renewed relationship between God and the people. Keown, Scalise, and Smothers (1995: 84–5) review efforts to determine and date core texts collected here. The placement of these chapters at the relative centre of the MT version of Jeremiah is puzzling. Texts that are largely accusatory and conflictual surround them, seeming to bury joyous hope in a cloud of terror and suffering, as if to dim the enthusiasm they are designed to inspire. The book's arrangement, however, like that of Lamentations, tempers hope for the exilic audience for whom restoration is not an imminent possibility (Kessler 1968). The universe imagined here does not offer a programme for escape. Rather, the text seeks to restore the community by recasting its narrative world. The 'narrative wreckage' (Frank 1995: 53) of their communal life

begins to heal in the creation of a new future, a new narrative. Chs. 30–3 are not the book's conclusion, as modern readers might wish, but a glowing centre, a hidden life, yet to emerge in historical specificity.

(30:1–31:40) Restoration YHWH is principal speaker in these poetic passages. The convergence of divine voice, poetic genre, and themes of hope set the chapters apart from surrounding materials, and draw attention to their presence at the book's centre. Because of their frequent use of the names Jacob and Israel some scholars assume that these poems originally addressed the northern kingdom alone (Rudolph 1947: 159; Lohfink 1981; but see Carroll 1986: 571–2; McKane 1986: 752). In their present location, however, these titles contribute to a rhetoric of unity and harmony for a unified nation. Jacob/Israel was the eponymous ancestor of all twelve tribes (Gen 29–30). Whatever the original provenance of these poems, they are here closely linked with poems addressed to Judah and Zion (30:3, 4, 12–17; 31:6, 12, 27, 31). After an introduction (30:1–4), the poems depict reversals of fortune (30:5–17), celebration (30:18–24), the journey home (31:1–14), the garden of delights (30:10–14), and in poetry and prose, the comforting of Rachel and the restoration of the broken marriage and family (31:15–40).

(30:1–4) A narrator reports that Jeremiah wrote YHWH's words in a book or scroll. The device of the revelatory book allows the character of Jeremiah to speak to the implied exilic audience even though he is not among them, and it allows Jeremiah's traditionists to expand the message under his authority (25:13; 36:1–32; 45:1; 51:60; McKane 1986: 750 accepts the scroll's contents as 30:4–31:40). Using imagery from other parts of the book (Odashima 1989: 98–138), the 'little book' witnesses to the days when YHWH 'will restore the fortunes of Israel and Judah' (v. 3). The poems collected here shift between addressing male Jacob/Israel, and virgin/daughter Israel/Rachel in a manner reminiscent of the account of the broken-marriage metaphor (JER 2:1–3:25). Here that broken family is healed and renewed.

(30:5–17) Two poetic panels, the first addressed to male Israel and the second to daughter Zion, depict reversals of fortunes in literary movements from panic (vv. 5–7) to fearlessness (vv. 10–11) and from incurable wounds (vv. 12–15) to restored health (vv. 16–17). In both instances, the reversal occurs without transition or explanation. Both panels imagine reversal as a change within YHWH, not within Jacob or Zion.

vv. 5–11, in the opening verse a speaker announces the sound of a terrifying voice (qôl). Pain grips men as suddenly as it does a woman in labour. An 'awful' (NEB) day of distress is upon them (see Carroll 1986: 574–5 on the day of YHWH). A prose comment (vv. 8–9) inexplicably replaces terror with future hope and links this passage to the account of the two yokes (27:1–28:19). YHWH will remove the yoke of servitude, restore relationship with them, and raise up a king. In vv. 10–11, YHWH comforts Jacob in the second person and responds to the panic and terror of vv. 5–7. Like a woman who finally gives birth, male Jacob will survive. The appropriation of labour imagery for male terror appears elsewhere (4:31; 13:21; 49:24; 50:43), but only here does it lead to life rather than death (O'Connor 1992). From far away YHWH will save them and punish the nations. Rescue is a complete surprise, but it comes with sobering caution for YHWH will also punish them justly (v. 11). Exile still means just punishment for sin.

The second poetic panel (vv. 12–17) also moves unexpectedly from desperation to salvation, but the metaphor shifts from panic to woundedness, and the addressee changes from male Jacob to female Zion (v. 17). vv. 12–13 and 15 return to language of Zion's incurable wound (8:21–2) and to her isolation, for all her lovers have abandoned her (v. 14). Daughter Zion is YHWH's unfaithful wife (2:1–3:25), and her wound is the consequence of her guilt (3:15). Like the previous panel, this poem explains destruction and exile as punishment for sin (v. 15). But rather than continuing with the expected description of her punishment, the poem reverses itself. It is her destroyers who will be punished (v. 16), and she who will be healed and restored to health. YHWH pities her in her abandonment (v. 17).

In vv. 18–22 YHWH continues to speak, first about Jacob and then to him (v. 21, second-person masculine plural). Jerusalem may be included in the poem indirectly as the city and citadel rebuilt on the mound (v. 18; Thompson 1980: 561). If so, north and south are reunited in a burst of thanksgiving and new life. In a book particularly attuned to sounds, cries of battle, shouts of grief, panic, and terror, this poem creates a startling sonic reversal. A great crowd of merrymakers will make joyous noises of thanksgiving as they exchange shame for honour (v. 19). To counter fears that the people would dwindle and disappear in exile, YHWH promises to establish the children of merrymakers in the liturgical assembly. Besides signifying the certainty of a future for the community, mention of 'their children' also identifies the implied audience as children of the exiled generation (v. 20). Clements (1988: 176) points to the conspicuous absence of temple restoration in these promises of hope for the exiles. The community will, none the less, be restored as a worshipping people. YHWH will punish their oppressors; foreigners will no longer rule them. Divine initiative alone will restore covenant relationship for 'who would otherwise dare to approach' YHWH? (v. 21).

vv. 23–4 close the chapter with a summary interpretation of national tragedy. YHWH's wrath came upon them as a raging tempest that will accomplish YHWH's plan (cf. Isa 55:10–11). Addressed directly, readers learn that they will understand 'in the latter days'. These verses suggest that there is little present understanding, only continued conflict among exiles regarding the meaning of events.

(31:1–14) Return The next three poems (31:2–6, 7–9, 10–14) envision and celebrate the journey home as a utopian restoration of the entire people of Israel. A superscription (v. 1) links this chapter to the previous one by continuing the motif of the eschatological future (30:24c) and by reusing the covenant formula (30:22). v. 1 explicitly names the human covenant partners as 'all the families of Israel'.

The first poem (vv. 2–6) continues the expansive vision of the restored community in which people of Samaria and Ephraim (vv. 5–6) prepare to return to Zion (v. 6). Resonant with echoes of other texts, the poem continues divine speech from the previous chapter. The subject of the poem is the future survivors (v. 2), personified as female Israel (vv. 3–5,

second-person feminine singular object pronouns). Using references to the journey out of Egypt and to Israel's devotion as a bride (Jer 2:2), YHWH reinterprets history. From 'far away', and despite having divorced her and her sister Judah (3:1–10), YHWH declares his 'everlasting love' and 'continued faithfulness' to her (v. 3). YHWH's words disregard her sordid past and transform her very being. She is no longer a faithless harlot but bĕtûlat, (virgin) Israel (v. 4). YHWH promises to 'build' her and she will plant (vv. 4–5), recalling promises to Jeremiah (1:10). In joyous celebration, female Israel will sing and dance like Miriam and the women after the escape through the sea (31:4b, cf. Ex 15:20–1). Sentinels will call them and the people will return 'to the LORD our God' (v. 6). Before exile, female Israel refused to return, but at that time there had been conditions (JER 3:11–13). Here there are none.

The second poem describes the procession home (vv. 7–9). YHWH invites song on behalf of, and perhaps by, Jacob (McKane 1986: 788) and provides words for intercession, 'Save, O LORD, your people, the remnant of Israel' (v. 7). This liturgical refrain may again dramatize the voice of the exilic community, bringing it into the text as expectant and hopeful. The poem assumes covenant relationship and YHWH's willingness to grant the request. Then YHWH announces the divine plan (vv. 8–9). YHWH will bring them back from the place to which they had been sent, the land of the north and the farthest parts of the earth. YHWH will gather them and lead them by water on easy pathways. What is most significant is the description of the company. Among them are the most vulnerable people, the blind, the lame, the pregnant, and those giving birth. As vulnerable or disabled, this procession embodies the whole community, humbled and broken yet bringing forth new life. On their journey, YHWH will accompany them as the father of Ephraim, his firstborn. The broken family of 2:1–3:25 reappears here, restored and made whole. Ephraim symbolizes the generation of exiles, the faithless children who have repented and returned (3:22–5).

The third poem (vv. 10–14), summed up by 'a watered garden' (v. 12), breaks out in lyrical celebration as the captive community returns to Zion. YHWH calls the nations as witnesses to, and proclaimers of, the new order imagined here. Gathering replaces scattering; bringing in overtakes thrusting away; the divine punisher becomes the redeemer who buys back the helpless slave (v. 11). The returnees will sing, radiant over divine goodness, unanticipated, hardly believable. In this imagined future, life will be a watered garden, an oasis of refreshment, an Eden of delights. Land and flocks will be fertile. Women and men, old and young shall dance and be merry. Priests and people, all will be satisfied. As YHWH turns mourning into joy, sorrow into comfort, the painful realities of the present world will be totally reversed.

The visions of these poems must have been shocking to exiles and their reversals barely conceivable to a people held under Babylonian sovereignty. But even if Babylonian hegemony had already begun to weaken under pressure from Persia, these poems envision more than mere survival for Israel. They speak of a prodigal transformation of reality, of an eschatological Utopia that restores divine–human relationship, reaffirms Israel as the chosen people, and recognizes that Israel itself has been changed by its suffering.

(31:15–30) Rachel's Comfort Rachel and her son, historically her grandson, Ephraim, symbolize this transformation on many levels. They appear in a poem (vv. 15–22; Trible 1978 140–50), which is followed by three prose comments that interpret its ambiguous conclusion (vv. 23–30). Many scholars argue for an original northern provenance of this text because Ephraim symbolizes the northern kingdom (Thompson 1980: 573). But whatever its origins, Rachel is the quintessential bereaved mother who cannot recover from the loss of her children (v. 15). As Jacob's most beloved wife (Gen 29), she is matriarch of all Israel, and her two sons, Joseph and Benjamin, become fathers of northern and southern tribes (Holladay 1989: 187). Rachel's motherhood of northern and southern offspring suggests that she weeps not only for Ephraim but for all the children of Israel for whom there is no future (Brueggemann 1991: 64). Her characterization recalls the 'faithless' (3:22) first wife of YHWH, the wife from the north (3:1–13) who fails to repent. In 3:6–25, it is her offspring, not she, who return to the father, as does Ephraim here. She signifies the generation whose children are in exile, who face extinction as a people. Ephraim personifies the next generation, the implied exilic audience who gain in his portrayal another model of true repentance. He is their imagined future, but mysteriously she, too, is included.

Like many other characters in this book, Rachel's grief is unceasing and her weeping voice (qôl) can be heard (v. 15). In the vignette created by this much discussed poem (Trible 1978; Anderson 1978; O'Connor 1992; Weems 1995), YHWH comforts her, seeks to dry her tears, recognizes her labour, and finally promises her a heart-stopping reward. The mother who believes her children are dead will see them return from the land of the enemy (vv. 16–17). A more poignant announcement can hardly be imagined as the poet climbs into the persona of the mother who learns that, miraculously, her children live.

YHWH hears another voice, a voice of shame and repentance, a voice of pleading (vv. 18–19). The mother weeps, but the child speaks. Ephraim interprets his suffering as his father's discipline of an untrained son. In the liturgical language that forms a leitmotif across the book (3:22–5; 8:14–15; 10:1–16, 22–5; 14:7–9, 19–22; 16:19–20; 17:12–23) Ephraim begs to be brought back 'for you are the LORD my God' (vv. 18–19). The stanza re-enacts and embellishes the scene where the children admit their shameful youth and return repentant to their Father (3:22–5). Unlike the earlier version, however, this account of repentance and return evokes a response from YHWH, who expresses delight in his son and insists with promises of mercy that he never forgot him (v. 20, Trible 1978; Anderson 1978).

Reversing the broken marriage (2:1–3:25), YHWH also invites grieving mother and still 'faithless' virgin Israel to return (vv. 21–2). YHWH will create yet another surprise, 'a new thing on the earth: a woman encompasses a man' (v. 22). This is a difficult and astonishing verse. Translation of těsôbēb is only part of the difficulty. It can mean 'protect', 'encompass', 'surround'. Holladay (1989: 195); Carroll (1986: 602–4); and McKane (1986: 807) discuss the problems. In addition, there remains the problem of understanding the 'new thing' God has created. In part that decision rests on who the woman and man symbolize. In the context of the poem they seem to be

Rachel and Ephraim. If so, then mother and son, the older unrepentant generation and the present exilic generation, are reunited; mother again surrounds, encompasses her child, thought dead but now living. Woman encompassing man is the mother and son reunited as she embraces her child. Alternatively this may be a biological promise in which bereaved Rachel encompasses a man sexually to give birth to a new generation (vv. 27–8). Or the woman may be Jerusalem encompassing the returned nation (vv. 23–6).

vv. 23–30 contain three prose pieces that, by juxtaposition, interpret the woman surrounding a man and continue promises for the days that are coming. Rather than pinpointing meaning, they accumulate multiple interpretations of v. 22. vv. 23–6 appear as a revelation in a dream of a restored Jerusalem, though the city is not named. It will be a place of rest and replenishment for the weary. By juxtaposition with v. 22, these verses suggest that the woman surrounding a man symbolizes Jerusalem, the holy hill that protects and encompasses her returned inhabitants. By contrast, vv. 27–8 promise human and animal fertility in the planting of seed, thus providing offspring and food for the nation. The woman encompassing a man to become pregnant personifies the future of the destroyed people. Finally, vv. 29–30 offer yet another interpretation of v. 22. The proverb comments on the generational divide by insisting that children are responsible for, and suffer for, their own sins. The exiles cannot blame their parents' generation exclusively for their predicament. They themselves are accountable for their behaviour and, by implication, they must repent. Woman does not encompass a man; mother does not include child in her guilt. The children's guilt is their own.

The prose comments of vv. 23–30 seek to tame the radical, open-ended poem that precedes them, but the power of the text still breaks out. Whatever it may denote, it also reverses gender imagery from earlier parts of the book. Rachel, weeping mother, virgin daughter, faithless daughter, is invited home again by God/husband who divorced her. She symbolizes a new future. She is the restored Israel, mother of north and south, reunited with her children, laughing, not weeping, protecting, surrounding, embracing them, and finally leading them into a utopian future of harmony and equality. The prose comment on the new covenant portrays that future.

(31:31–4) The New Covenant Following Ephraim's enactment of repentance, YHWH's acceptance of it, and the restoration of the broken family, YHWH proclaims a new covenant, a new way of relating within the reconstituted family. (For reviews of modern interpretations, see Herrmann 1986: 146–62 and McKane 1986: 817–27.) Among Christians, the new covenant passage is perhaps the most well-known and misread of Jeremianic texts. The new covenant prophecy does not cancel YHWH's covenant with Judaism in favour of Christianity (Brueggemann 1991: 69–71). Christians will, of course, place great significance on this short passage, using its language to express their faith that the newness of divine revelation in Jesus Christ stands in continuity with YHWH's covenant with Israel. When the book of Jeremiah speaks of the new covenant, however, it is referring to renewed relationship between Israel and YHWH.

That renewed relationship will differ from YHWH's covenant with Israel's ancestors rescued from Egypt (v. 32). They broke covenant even though, YHWH says, *bāʿaltî*: 'I was master over them' (Holladay 1989: 198), or 'I was their husband' (Carroll 1986: 609 cf. NRSV, NIV). This covenant language reaches back to the broken marriage and divorce between YHWH and his faithless wife (JER 2:1–3:25). The new relationship will be stronger than the previous marriages because YHWH will inscribe *tôrâ* on their hearts (v. 33; Polk 1984: 35–57). YHWH, not the community, will create love and fidelity so that everyone from the 'least...to the greatest' will know YHWH (v. 34). The new covenant, therefore, manifests itself as an egalitarian religious vision that embraces everyone in the community without hierarchical preferences of any kind. The new covenant restores the broken marriage, heals the wounded family, and creates a new story from Israel's narrative wreckage. Finally, the new covenant continues the development of the book's theodicy by inviting the implied audience to recognize their sufferings as discipline by a loving father and husband. YHWH will forgive them and remember their sins no more (v. 34).

(31:35–7) The Covenant's Endurance In a spectacular reversal of the cosmic undoing of creation caused by sin (JER 4:23–8), this brief poem finds, in the permanence of the created order, assurance that Israel's offspring will receive divine acceptance forever (v. 36). In images that echo Gen 1 and Job 38:4–7, the Creator threatens to reject Israel's offspring (*zeraʿ*, 'seed', vv. 36c, 37c), but not until the fixed order of creation fails and the cosmos can be measured. Since this will never happen, YHWH promises an eternal covenant with restored Israel.

(31:38–40) Jerusalem Rebuilt By returning to the image of the restored Jerusalem, this prose comment forms a frame with 31:23–6 (Keown, Scalise, and Smothers 1995). As the focus of exilic hope, the city will be rebuilt beyond its former borders to accommodate the population explosion among its inhabitants. Jerusalem will never again be uprooted or overthrown (v. 38).

(32:1–33:26) In these two chapters, prose narrative supplants poetry; Jeremiah replaces YHWH as main actor; a narrator replaces YHWH as speaker. Both prose chapters prophesy a radical change of fortunes for the exiles; both are set during Jeremiah's confinement as the Chaldeans (Babylonians) invade Jerusalem; and both appeal to YHWH as all-powerful Creator whose portrayal changes unexpectedly from angry punisher to loving redeemer and healer (Perdue 1994: 145).

(32:1–44) Jeremiah Redeems a Field In the previous two chapters Jeremiah appears only in the superscription (30:1–2) and as unnamed recipient of a revelatory dream (31:26). Both notices lend Jeremiah's prophetic authority to the message of renewal and restoration found there. In ch. 32, however, Jeremiah is chief agent and central character, and for the first time he has a companion, Baruch, to act as witness (v. 12; Brueggemann 1994). Jeremiah's symbolic action (vv. 1–5) and sermon-like prayer (vv. 16–25), to which YHWH responds (vv. 26–44), confirm and give concreteness to the hopeful poetic vision of the previous chapters. During Jeremiah's imprisonment in the palace, he again serves as an exemplar for exiles by acting with obedient hopefulness in the face of

invasion and captivity. Clements (1996: 128) believes that the land purchase holds a central position in Jeremiah's vision of hope. To the extent that the story serves as first step towards restoration, the narrative begins the fulfilment of the visions of 30:1–31:40.

(32:1–15) The Purchase A superscription places Jeremiah's symbolic act in the reigns of Zedekiah and Nebuchadrezzar (v. 1), during Babylon's most devastating invasion of Jerusalem (588/87 BCE; on dating, see Holladay 1989: 212 and Keown Scalise, and Smothers 1995: 150; on historical inconsistencies, see Carroll 1986: 622; McKane 1986: clxi). The chief importance of this chronological note is symbolic. It places Jeremiah's foolhardy purchase at the nadir of Judah's history. During the bleakness of invasion, Jeremiah acts and prays in ways that embody and announce a new future (Seitz 1989b: 244). The dating of the narrative, therefore, assures the exilic audience that the seemingly unrealizable promises are already active in the divine plan.

The narrative itself is highly symbolic. Jeremiah prophesies Babylonian triumph and the resultant capture of Zedekiah for an indefinite period, until YHWH 'attends' to him (vv. 2–5; cf. 27:19–22). To repress this treacherous message, Zedekiah, himself about to be imprisoned, imprisons Jeremiah. YHWH tells Jeremiah that his cousin Hanamel will ask him to redeem his uncle's field in Anathoth (vv. 6–8). As next of kin, Jeremiah's responsibility is to redeem family property in case of debt (Lev 25:23–8; Ruth 4:1–10), but under the circumstances of the invasion such an act appears pointless. The narrative offers no details of the family predicament, but rushes, instead, to describe legal and monetary components of the transaction (vv. 9–15). These details underscore the public, legal nature of the event. As executor, Baruch places the deeds in a jar to preserve them (vv. 12–14). The last verse explains the meaning of the purchase. Life will resume in the land (v. 15), for YHWH will redeem it just as Jeremiah redeems the land of his kin.

The story of Jeremiah's land redemption affirms to the implied audience that life in the land will resume in a new future. Although the promise originated with Jeremiah, Baruch witnessed it, served as executor, and thus emerges as a reliable interpreter and developer of the Jeremiah tradition (Carroll 1986: 61–2). The narrative portrays no quick end to exile (v. 5), but only a promisory deed. In the meantime, Jeremiah emerges as a paragon of faithful obedience and hope in the midst of captivity.

(32:16–25) Jeremiah's prayer elaborates upon and parallels the story of the redemption of land. The prayer also revisits the grim hour of invasion as fulfilment of YHWH's word and finds in the reliability of earlier messages the basis for new hope. In first-person direct address, Jeremiah reminds YHWH of past divine treatment of Israel that distributed love prodigally and punishment sparingly (vv. 17–19). Jeremiah addresses YHWH as Creator of the earth and Sovereign of history (Perdue 1994: 144). The 'impossibilities' God performed on behalf of the people in the past (Brueggemann 1991: 83) brought no obedience from them (vv. 20–3). Jeremiah begs YHWH to 'see' that the promised invasion is underway (vv. 20–4). In the thick of the siege, YHWH orders Jeremiah to buy the field in front of witnesses (v. 25). Hints of conflict in the exilic community concerning the future float beneath the surface of this prayer. For some, resumption of life in the land is unthinkable. It is this hopelessness that the prayer seeks to overturn.

(31:26–44) Divine Assurance If readers are not yet convinced that they will return to the land, YHWH's reply to Jeremiah's prayer assures them that they will. A third-person narrator introduces the divine speaker who tells Jeremiah that the God of all can do anything (vv. 26–7). The passage parallels the narrative of land purchase and Jeremiah's prayer in describing the disaster (vv. 28–9a) and the sins that provoked it (vv. 29b–35, cf. 7:1–8:3), and in shifting to the good fortune ahead (vv. 37–44). Even as the city falls into the hand of Babylon, YHWH announces the gathering of exiles (vv. 36–7), their safe return, and the making of an everlasting covenant (cf. 31:31–4). YHWH's responsibility for the national tragedy is unusually explicit in this prayer (v. 42), but divine agency in the disaster provides confidence in promises regarding YHWH's new activities. YHWH will plant them, delight in them (v. 41), and restore their fields (vv. 43–4).

All three units of this chapter follow the same literary and theological movement. They plunge down into invasion and devastation before turning upwards in hope. Narratively they meet the exiles in their hopelessness and insist on a transformation grounded in divine initiative. YHWH commands the land redemption (32:1–5). YHWH is the mighty Creator who loves and does impossible things (32:16–25). YHWH will restore their fortunes (vv. 37–44). In its attack on the people's sin and failure to listen, the passage defends God against charges of injustice, but YHWH also accepts responsibility (v. 42). YHWH undergoes a change of heart, reaffirms loving fidelity to the people, and in this part of the text, asks for nothing in return.

(33:1–9) Restoration of Fortunes A superscription joins this chapter to the previous one for Jeremiah is still imprisoned (v. 1). Reversing earlier prohibitions against intercession (11:14; 15:1–15), the Creator now invites prophetic mediation and promises to reveal things hitherto hidden (v. 3). This invitation reopens relationship between YHWH and the people, and the new revelations suggest further development of the tradition. The cause of the invasion and destruction was divine anger at the people's sinfulness. YHWH turned the divine face away, a momentary lapse during which the enemy wreaked havoc upon the city. Though the people's sin remains the root cause of the tragedy, divine inattentiveness suggests that punishment for the people's sin became excessive. But after that turning away, YHWH has made a full reversal by promising recovery, healing, and abundance for north and south (vv. 6–7). YHWH will rebuild, cleanse, forgive. The city's glory will evoke awe from nations at the transformation YHWH will accomplish (v. 9).

(33:10–14) Two brief comments emphasize the drama of the future transformation by describing the land as an empty wasteland (vv. 10–11, 12–13). Because the land was never empty after the invasion nor at any point during exile, some commentators judge the depiction of the land as unpeopled to be propaganda on behalf of Babylonian exiles. The claim that they alone are left of Judah makes them heirs of the true Israel. Those remaining in the land become invisible. But the

text's historical referrents cannot be determined. Rather, the poetic evocation of an empty, hostile wasteland sharpens the contrast between the seemingly hopeless present reality and the bustling, noisy, domestic, and worshipful future (Carroll 1986: 636).

(33:14–26) Davidic Monarchy Restored The book of consolation closes with an eschatological promise that a descendant of David will once again rule all Israel, a rule characterized by justice and righteousness (vv. 14–16). The people will never again lack kings or levitical priesthood for eternal worship (vv. 16–17). The new covenant is as eternal as the created order (vv. 19–22). Nor will YHWH ever again reject the two families of Israel.

(34:1–35:22) A Bad King and a Good Community The prose narratives of chs. 34 and 35 shift the temporal frame back abruptly from the eschatological, utopian future to the reality of the recent past. Both chapters are set during the Babylonian invasion, but the behaviour they describe concerns survival in the exilic present. Ch. 34 portrays the failures of king and all the people to obey the divine word wholeheartedly, and it underscores the desolate consequences of those failures. Ch. 35, by contrast, narrates the dogged obedience of a small group of faithful Rechabites whose righteousness gains them a future. Together these chapters set forth an implicit choice between attitudes and behaviours from which readers must choose. The rhetoric is not subtle. Half-hearted obedience of king and people caused the nation's destruction; only heroic obedience in the present will issue in the survival of the faithful few. In both chapters a third-person narrator presents the speech of Jeremiah who, in turn, uses divine speech.

(34:1–22) Half-hearted Obedience After Zedekiah makes a covenant with all the people (vv. 8–20), they first obey and then disobey YHWH's word. The king's fate (34:1–7, 21–2) frames the failure of the community (34:8–20) during the invasion, described in both hyperbolic (v. 1) and concrete terms (vv. 6–7). Jerusalem is under attack from 'all the kingdoms of the earth' and all the peoples under Nebuchadrezzar's dominion (v. 1). Only Lachish and Azekah remain among Judean cities (vv. 6–7). (Archaeologists have found letters at Lachish, dating to the time of the Babylonian invasion.) This time-frame is critical for Jeremiah's prophecy (v. 8) for, at a truly grim moment, YHWH commands Jeremiah to announce the city's destruction and Zedekiah's capture and exile (vv. 2–3). The story, however, modulates the terror for the king who will not be killed but will die in peace and be lamented with proper royal rituals (vv. 4–5; cf. 52:1–11). Holladay (1989: 233–4) and Brueggemann (1991: 105) believe the passage relates an implicit choice for Zedekiah to surrender or die, while Carroll argues that the passage must mean that the royal burial will occur in Jerusalem, not in exile, since such treatment of captives is unthinkable.

The text is not conditional in its prophecy of Zedekiah's survival, however, nor does it refer to burial in Jerusalem. Instead, the text offers a picture of a slightly mitigated disaster, discerning in the royal survival a glimpse of the community's survival. That is the 'word' that Jeremiah speaks (v. 5, cf. v. 4). This passage, therefore, treats Zedekiah somewhat differently from other texts (21:1–7; 37:1–38:28), not only form-critically (Keown, Scalise, and Smothers 1995: 178) but also narratively.

That Zedekiah might save his life by surrendering to Babylon is clearer elsewhere (Carroll 1986: 641–2). It is the certainty of his exile that this narrative stresses (vv. 3, 21). It emphasizes the reliability of the prophetic word. In the larger context of chs. 26–36, Jeremiah's words of muted hope are as reliable in the midst of the siege as were his words of exile before the invasion. In the rest of this passage Zedekiah makes an attempt at righteousness that is thwarted by the citizens remaining in the land.

vv. 8–22, a broken covenant: Zedekiah makes a covenant with the people of Jerusalem, apparently enforcing the release law for Hebrew slaves (Lev 25:10). The legal and historical backgrounds of this text are obscure (Keown, Scalise, and Smothers 1995: 185–8), but they are not the main concerns of the narrative. The story uses the law of release, first, to indict the people for failure to listen and, second, to interpret exile as a reversal of the release law. Rather than depicting Zedekiah's vacillation (37:1–38:28), this text portrays the people's fickleness. At first the officials and 'all the people' obey the covenant, signifying their repentance (v. 15), but they reverse their course by taking back their slaves. In a form of poetic justice, therefore, YHWH will release them to the sword, pestilence, and famine (v. 17).

YHWH then describes an enactment of covenant ritual in which all the officials and people (v. 19) walk between the parts of a butchered calf (see Gen 17). Because that act signifies commitment to the covenant and brings a curse upon all who break it, YHWH announces the curse's fulfilment. Everyone in the community will be butchered like the sacrifical calf (vv. 18–20). Although Zedekiah acts well in this story, vv. 21–2 reiterate his fate and the fate of the city. For the book's implied audience, the account illustrates the consequence of insincere repentance.

(35:1–19) The Rechabites By contrast to officials and people of Judah in ch. 34, the Rechabites are utterly steadfast. Their identity is uncertain (see Keown, Scalise, and Smothers 1995: 195–6), but what is clear is that they provide a counter-example to Judah's faithlessness in ch. 34. The narrative takes place during Jehoiakim's reign (v. 1), earlier than events in ch. 34. Sequential chronology is not what binds these chapters.

The Rechabite event follows the style of a symbolic act. Jeremiah receives a command to go to the house of the Rechabites and bring them to the temple. There he is to offer wine to a community that abstains from drinking (vv. 1–3) and that disdains urban, settled ways such as house-building and agriculture (vv. 6–10). Out of loyalty to their ancestor Jonadab, they refuse the wine and explain their presence in the city as a security measure during the Babylonian invasion (vv. 6–11).

vv. 12–19 explain the Rechabites' temperance. It teaches a lesson to the people of Judah and Jerusalem (v. 13). Stalwartly, the Rechabites refuse to break their traditions for the sake of loyalty to a mere human ancestor. By contrast, the people of Judah persistently disobey YHWH despite continual divine efforts to speak to them through the prophets. Their failure to listen will bring disaster (vv. 12–16), but the Rechabites will survive in God's presence for all time (vv. 18–19). The text unequivocally calls for repentance as the only path to survival.

(36:1–32) The Two Scrolls The long-held scholarly assumption that the story of the scrolls is a historical report of the origins of the book of Jeremiah led to a diligent search for the contents of the *Urrolle*, the original scroll. Efforts to reconstruct the scroll's contents and thus to recover Jeremiah's original words have yielded little consensus (Perdue 1984: 21–2; Holladay 1989: 253). Carroll (1986: 662–8) has broken the interpretative log-jam by proposing that the scrolls are fictional elements of a narrative, based on 2 Kings 22:8–13 and designed to legitimate Baruch's scribal authority. Baruch himself, in Carroll's view, represents Deuteronomistic scribes who expand the Jeremianic tradition (see Dearman 1990 for a contrary view). Carroll is correct in insisting that the story's historical roots are not recoverable. The story's importance is symbolic, theological, and literary. Narrative parallels with ch. 26 suggest that the two chapters create a literary frame around chs. 27–35. Parallels between the two chapters include dating, the prophet's audience, lists of supporters, threats to Jeremiah's life and mysterious rescues, and virulent indictments of King Jehoiakim (O'Connor 1989: 626).

Ch. 36 authorizes developments in the Jeremianic tradition begun in ch. 26, partly by portraying Baruch as a faithful agent of that development. It may be best to think of Baruch as a reader of an earlier Jeremiah tradition who writes himself into the narrative to continue the story for new circumstances. In ch. 36, Baruch broadcasts Jeremiah's message in the temple and faithfully excludes nothing from the preaching of Jeremiah's entire career (v. 2). He is a reliable conduit of Jeremiah's prophetic message (McKane 1986: 912). The goal of his activity, directed by Jeremiah, is to bring about repentance in the community (v. 3). Besides providing Baruch with credentials, ch. 36 also validates the writing of the book (Brueggemann 1991: 129), itself designed to evoke repentance in the community. Finally, the story indicts royalty for rejecting the word, interprets the nation's fall as the monarchy's failure to listen, and explains the monarchy's collapse.

The superscription (v. 1) sets the story in Jehoiakim's fourth year. The narrative, related by a third-person narrator, unfolds in four scenes of intensifying drama that attend closely to the production of the scrolls and their fate. In the first scene (vv. 4–10), Jeremiah dictates the scroll to Baruch, indicating that Jeremiah, not Baruch, was the source of the scroll's contents (cf. v. 17). Because Jeremiah is barred from the temple, Baruch must read on his behalf to 'all the people' on the chance they may repent and thereby avert the promised disaster (vv. 5–8). The second scene (vv. 9–18) occurs a year later. Baruch reads the scroll 'to all the people' in the temple chamber of Gemariah, a member of the Shaphan family of Jeremiah supporters (JER 26:1–24). Another member of the Shaphan family hears the reading, seeks out named officials, and reads the scroll to them. Alarmed by the scroll's contents, they in turn decide to read it to the king, but not before sending Baruch and Jeremiah into hiding (vv. 11–18). The written text, that is, the book, must carry the full power of the prophetic message, since neither its speaker nor its writer are present.

The third scene (vv. 20–6) reveals that writing has not dulled the power of the prophetic word. The officials who are among Jeremiah's protectors leave the scroll and report to the king who, in turn, sends Jehudi to get it and read it to him. These minute arrangements for the king to hear the scroll highlight his agency in the unfolding events. The scroll must be brought to his attention, he must consent, and then he must send for the document (vv. 20–1). As it is read to him, he deliberately cuts off the columns and, despite efforts to stop him, casts them into the fire until the entire scroll is consumed. The king's cutting and burning of the scroll is a symbolic act designed to cancel the uncontrollable power of the written word by making it disappear. As further evidence of the king's disobedience, he orders the arrest of Jeremiah and Baruch, whom YHWH miraculously protects from discovery.

The final scene of the narrative (vv. 27–32) forms a frame with the first (vv. 4–10). Jeremiah receives a divine command to write a second scroll, containing the words of the first. Only now are the king's words upon the burning of the scroll revealed, and they provide the only clue as to the scroll's message. Babylon will destroy the land and the life in it (v. 29). This short verse summarizes 'all the former words' (v. 28), the entire prophetic message, in highly abstracted, reduced form. In this narrative, it is not the potent images, metaphors, calls for repentance, and lamentations that matter, but only the fact of invasion by Babylon. The king's rejection of the scroll means the end of the monarchy and disaster for all (vv. 30–1).

The king cannot cancel the prophetic word, for Jeremiah and Baruch create a second scroll and add 'many similar words' as well. Brueggemann (1991: 129) calls the scroll 'emblematic' of the canonical book. This story validates the scroll as scribal expansion of the tradition and keeps that tradition alive so that later generations can read it. Ch. 36 also introduces the narrative complex, traditionally ascribed to Baruch, that continues through ch. 45 (Reitzschel 1966: 95–110).

The Baruch Account (chs. 37–45)

In these chapters a third-person narrator, identified as Baruch (45:1), relates events that occur in the land during and after the Babylonian invasion. Chs. 37–8 contain two stories of Jeremiah's imprisonment and meetings with Zedekiah during the invasion, and ch. 39 describes the invasion and Jeremiah's release. Chs. 40–1 portray anarchy in the land under Gedaliah, and chs. 42–4 relate events surrounding the forced exile of Jeremiah and Baruch to Egypt. The chapters close with the commissioning and comforting of Baruch (ch. 45). Interpretation of the chapters has focused on historical matters of Baruch's authorship and the invasion and on the search for unifying themes of the chapters. Brueggemann (1991: 121–8) provides a succinct survey of viewpoints. The narratives, whatever their historical content, are richly symbolic.

Although Baruch is portrayed as writer of the tradition (45:1; 36:32), he receives little attention in the intervening chapters. In ch. 45, however, Jeremiah disappears from the story and Baruch replaces him as sufferer, survivor, and bearer of the community's hopes and traditions. Baruch is an underdeveloped character whose function is to interpret and preserve the Jeremiah tradition in the absence of Jeremiah (see Carroll 1986; Brueggemann 1994).

Efforts to find thematic unity in the chapters have not reached consensus because the collection of narratives is quite multifaceted. Kremers (1953) offered the most controversial interpretation by calling chs. 37–45 a 'passion narrative' of Jeremiah's suffering and rejection in the manner of Jesus' passion. Kremers's approach has been rightly criticized for imposing Christian language and thought on the OT without first letting the text stand on its own. Jeremiah's absence from chs. 40–1 and 45, moreover, make it difficult to see his portrayal as a primary key to the narratives. Opposition to Kremers's view, however, has obscured the immense symbolic import that stories of Jeremiah's suffering, imprisonment, and rescue would have had for an exilic audience.

Taken together, the chapters show the exilic audience how to survive the suffering brought on by the invasion and its aftermath. In doing so they provide a history of rejection and fulfilment of the prophetic word (Kessler 1968; Nicholson 1975) and reveal conflictual interpretations among survivors about both the nature of prophecy (Diamond 1993) and how to face the national crisis (Seitz 1989b). Jeremiah's instruction to submit to Babylon cuts through the political alternatives. Survival cannot be achieved in their own land nor in Egypt but only by submission to Babylon (Brueggemann 1991: 121–8). The stories characterize Jeremiah as a model of faithful submission who faces utter hopelessness but once again survives with his life (cf. 26:24; 36:26). His suffering is iconic of the suffering of the exilic people. His support and rescue by Ebedmelech and the Babylonians creates hope of rescue for exiles. Like them, Jeremiah is imprisoned and carted off to exile against his will. He keeps his life and promises those who submit to Babylon that they will keep their lives as a prize of war (38:2; 39:18; 45:5). Both his word and actions in the midst of suffering signify their possibilities of survival.

Holladay (1989: 286–7) notices the great amount of realistic detail found in these stories. He also observes that Jeremiah is not portrayed as a hero, nor his enemies as villains, nor is Jeremiah's death reported. If, however, the accounts are not biography in a modern sense but concerned with showing exiles a way into the future, a report of Jeremiah's death would destroy the narrative's effect. It is Jeremiah's survival in captivity and his confidence that justice will be done among the nations that are central to the prophet's portrayal in these final narrative sections of the book. Whereas the little book of consolation promises that future life will be radiantly idyllic, the Baruch document focuses on immediate problems of brute survival.

(37:1–39:18) Life as a Prize of War King Zedekiah imprisons Jeremiah on two separate occasions (chs. 37–8), but ironically the two characters exchange places when the Babylonians invade the city (ch. 39). Puzzling similarities between chs. 37 and 38 have led some interpreters to see them as duplicate accounts of the same story (Condamin 1920: 275). In both chapters Jeremiah is arrested, accused of treason before princes, imprisoned, and released, and in both he consults with Zedekiah in similar terms (Thompson 1980: 636). The chapters are not identical, however: ch. 38 advances the narrative by increasing the gulf separating king and prophet and by setting into motion the fulfilment of the prophetic word. An unidentified third-person narrator, presumably Baruch, relates events and portrays dialogues between characters but provides no lengthy speeches in the voices of either YHWH or Jeremiah. Although divine speech moves to the background in these stories, it is, none the less, the potent force behind events.

(37:1–21) The superscription (vv. 1–2) dates the two chapters to Zedekiah's rule during the siege. This date reveals that, from the beginning of his reign, Zedekiah was no better than his predecessor Jehoiakim. He neither obeys the prophetic word (Carroll 1986: 671) nor fulfils his responsibility to lead the nation to listen (v. 2). Ch. 37 contains three scenes: two of Zedekiah's consultations with Jeremiah (vv. 3–10, 17–21) frame the scene of Jeremiah's imprisonment (vv. 11–16). Even the chapter's literary structure, therefore, artistically hints at the king's efforts to squeeze a desirable word from the prophet and to suppress the true word.

vv. 3–10 (Consultation), on the occasion of Egyptian efforts to deflect the Babylonian army from Jerusalem, Zedekiah sends messengers to request prayer from Jeremiah. This international power struggle gives Zedekiah hope that Egypt will overcome Babylonian hegemony and avert the threat to Judah. Jeremiah's reply to Zedekiah is unequivocal. Babylon will prevail because that is YHWH's plan. Even if the Babylonian army had no one left but the wounded, they would miraculously rise up and burn the city (v. 10). vv. 11–16 (Captivity), after this emphatic crushing of false hope, Jeremiah attempts to leave Jerusalem to visit his property in Benjamin (JER 32). A sentinel believes Jeremiah is deserting (v. 13). When the sentinel refuses to listen, he illustrates the point made in 37:2. Officials, even more disrespectful of the prophet and the word, beat and imprison Jeremiah and thereby attempt to repress the divine word (vv. 15–16). vv. 17–21 (Consultation), Zedekiah's second consultation with the prophet is held in secret. The king claims to desire a word from YHWH but not the word Jeremiah offers. Faithful to his mission despite the danger he faces, Jeremiah does not waver in his message (v. 17). Instead, he protests his illegal imprisonment (v. 18; Diamond 1993), chides the king regarding his lying prophets, and survives with his life.

(38:1–28) does not flow easily from the previous chapter because there Jeremiah is captive, but here he is freely preaching to the people and taken captive again without being released in between. Although 38:9 implies a lapse of time between arrests, chronological depiction of events is clearly not a purpose of these chapters. Chapter 38 contains three scenes: capture, rescue, and consultation.

vv. 1–6 (Capture), four officials hear Jeremiah's admonitions to the people about survival. Any one who stays in the city will die, but those who surrender will save their lives 'as the prize of war' (v. 2). The officials charge Jeremiah with lowering morale and seeking harm instead of shalom (v. 4). Diamond (1993) observes that the story contains conflicting views of prophecy. The officials believe that the prophet's role is to secure the state's safety, but Jeremiah's intercession secures its doom. The king, in turn, listens to the officials rather than to the prophet and allows them to imprison Jeremiah in a cistern, where he sinks in the mud (v. 6). The literary detail of the mud reveals that Jeremiah has reached the nadir of suffering and humiliation. All is lost. Death awaits and future hopes are extinguished. vv. 7–13 (Rescue), inexplicably and with no prior narrative intimations, an Ethiopian servant of the king, named Ebed-melech, dramatically rescues Jeremiah from certain death. Using ropes made of rags from the king's wardrobe, perhaps a signal of the mon-

archy's true condition, Ebed-melech gets help and lifts Jeremiah out of the cistern. Jeremiah does not gain immediate freedom but against all expectations has gained his life. Ebed-melech's name, meaning 'servant of the king', is probably ironic here. What king does he serve, Zedekiah or YHWH? As a non-Israelite and an African slave, without explanation Ebed-melech risks his own life to save Jeremiah. Does his intervention indicate the possibility of survival (Carroll 1986: 690) for the exiles? Does his deed signify that rescue of exilic captives will occur with equal surprise from quarters they can barely imagine?

vv. 14–28 (Consultation), prophet and king meet for secretive conversation. Both are in danger: Jeremiah from Zedekiah and Zedekiah from the invaders. Zedekiah secretly swears by the God who 'lives' to protect Jeremiah's life (*nepeš*, v. 16). Jeremiah, in turn, promises Zedekiah that he will save his own life (*nepeš*) and city, if he surrenders to Babylon (vv. 17–18). Zedekiah is afraid of the Babylonians and Jeremiah assures him of his safety (*nepeš*) if he surrenders (vv. 19–20). Jeremiah then reports a vision that reveals the consequences of refusal and foreshadows the reversal of fortunes that occurs in ch. 39. The women of the king's house will be captured and will taunt the king with poetry that echoes the language of Jeremiah's enemies. The king's friends have seduced and overcome him (cf. 20:7–11). Now the king's feet are stuck in the mud (v. 22). In Jeremiah's vision, he and Zedekiah exchange places. The one who caused Jeremiah's capture will himself be captured and sink in the mud. Consultation ends in a stalemate. The king orders Jeremiah to keep their exchange secret and Jeremiah obeys, remaining in the court of the guard until Jerusalem falls. At this point, the narrative appears to drift off in indecision, but in quiet understatement the last phrase announces the king's failure and the prophet's triumph (v. 28). The fall of the city results in Jeremiah's release, the king's capture, and the fulfilment of the prophetic word.

(39:1–18) The Fall of Jerusalem Ch. 39 follows ch. 38 chronologically and thematically. In unadorned prose it describes Babylon's invasion of Jerusalem and its consequences, particularly for Zedekiah (vv. 1–10) and Jeremiah (vv. 11–18). Anticipated role-reversals occur here. In this narrative the invasion serves as background to larger issues (Carroll 1986; see Jer 52:4–16 and 2 Kings 25:1–12).

vv. 1–10 (Zedekiah captured), vv. 1–3 telescope events from the invasion's beginning in the ninth year of Zedekiah to the capture and occupation of the city by Babylonian officials two years later. The narrative's main interest is not the battle but the king's cowardly behaviour, escape, and capture (vv. 4–5). The prophetic word proves inescapable. Zedekiah's offspring are killed and he is blinded, thus marking in his flesh what had already been true of his spirit. The fate of city and inhabitants follows that of the king. Houses are burned and people are exiled. Only the poor remain, and Nebuzaradan, captain of the guard, then gives them land (vv. 8–10). vv. 11–18 (Jeremiah freed), as Zedekiah is imprisoned by Nebuzaradan, Jeremiah simultaneously gains release and protection from the same captain at the command of Nebuchadrezzar (vv. 11–13). Jeremiah is put under the protection of Gedaliah, the Jewish governor appointed by Babylon, and son of

Ahikam (see JER 26:24). Jeremiah goes home with his people (v. 14), contradicting the report that all but the poor were left in the land (v. 10). But the importance of Jeremiah's release and return home are symbolic. Jeremiah's behaviour illustrates how to survive. By submitting to Babylon, he has escaped with his life as the prize of war and returned home (vv. 11–14). The Ebed-melech sequel (vv. 15–18) lends strength to this interpretation. After his release, Jeremiah receives a divine message for his Ethiopian rescuer (see 38:7–13). Although the fate of the city is sealed, Ebed-melech will escape with his life as a prize of war because he trusted in YHWH (v. 18). It is that confidence that the exiles must emulate, and they too will gain a future. The many themes of these narratives unite in this rhetorical effort to persuade the exiles to submit to Babylon as the only avenue forward.

(40:1–41:18) The Monarchy's Perversity These chapters describe events in the land after the Babylonian invasion. They continue to urge submission to Babylon and depict chaos in the occupied land.

(40:1–6) retells the story of Jeremiah's release (39:11–14) with significant alteration and elaboration of detail, indicating again the narrative's lack of concern for precise biographical reporting. In this version, Jeremiah is released, not from the court of the guard (39:14) but from among the fettered captives in Ramah who are about to be exiled. With great prescience, Nebuzaradan interprets the fall of Judah in Jeremianic terms, treating Jeremiah as if he were one of the sinners responsible for the nation's fall rather than the one who called for repentance (vv. 2–3). This passage fully identifies Jeremiah with the exiles. Nebuzaradan gives him the choice of remaining in the land or going into exile, but if he stays in the land he must give his loyalty to the Babylonian appointee, Gedaliah (vv. 4–5). Unlike ch. 24 where Jeremiah portrays those who stay in the land as bad figs, here Jeremiah chooses to be among them, and they are portrayed as faithful people, except for the remnants of the royal family and followers. Submission to Babylon, however, remains a constant requirement for survival.

(40:7–12) Peace in the Land Numbers of people, poor and notable, as well as a remnant of the troops, come under Gedaliah's protection and experience temporary prosperity and peace in the land (vv. 7–9). In terms reminiscent of Jeremiah's letter to the exiles (29:4–6), Gedaliah urges the survivors to serve the Chaldeans without fear. Returnees from neighbouring countries gather under Gedaliah's protection and live with abundance of wine and summer fruit (vv. 10–12). Once again survival and a future depend upon submission to Babylon whether in the land or out. But Ishmael, a descendent of the royal family, destroys the possibility of peace in the land (vv. 13–16). When Gedaliah learns about Ishmael's plot against him, he shows himself to be trusting and loyal. He disbelieves the threat and defends Ishmael. The contrast between the Babylonian appointee and the monarchical family survivor could not be more pointed, lending credence to Pohlmann's view that these narratives support the Babylonian exiles over those who remain in the land.

(41:1–17) Chaos in the Land In graphic terms, this chapter portrays treachery, conflict, and betrayal within the Jewish community after the fall. Details of the narrative reveal Ish-

mael's craven wickedness as he brutally assassinates Gedaliah and massacres pilgrims on the way to offer worship (vv. 4–7). Although Jeremiah is under the protection of Gedaliah, he is conspicuously absent from this narrative and appears again only in ch. 42. Were the narrative to portray Jeremiah's death, he would not save his life as a prize of war, and would not function·as a clear model for the exiles. Whatever historical memories underlie this narrative of conflict among survivors, the intentions of the text are to ridicule the anti-Babylonian survivor of the royal family whose 'crimes' (v. 11) reveal his brutal resistance to the prophetic word.

Ishmael and his followers assassinate Gedaliah and his companions at Mizpah. They choose a mealtime for their deed, when covenant community is celebrated and the guard is down (vv. 1–2). Next they murder 'all the Judeans' and Babylonian soldiers at Mizpah (v. 3). Then they slaughter eighty Israelites on pilgrimage to the temple and desecrate their bodies by dumping them in a cistern with an ancient sacred tradition, thus also desecrating the cistern (vv. 4–9). Opportunist that he is, Ishmael spares only men with food stores (v. 8). After making hostages of people remaining at Mizpah, the royal claimant tries to escape to his foreign supporters in neighbouring Ammon (v. 10; cf. 40:11). Johanan son of Kareah and military forces pursue him and rescue the happy hostages (v. 13), but Ishmael escapes to Ammon (v. 15). The bloodbath leaves its survivors in terror of the Chaldeans (v. 18) and sets in motion forces that are played out in the next chapters. The remnant intends to escape to Egypt (v. 17).

(42:1–44:30) Emigration to Egypt Divine rejection of emigration to Egypt unifies these chapters. Paradoxically, Jeremiah and Baruch are forced to join the condemned group. Pohlmann (1978); Nicholson (1975); and Carroll (1986) view these chapters as propaganda in favour of the Babylonian exiles over against groups that remained in Judah or went to Egypt. McKane (1986: 1064) proposes that the text attacks Egypt, not the exiles, but ch. 44 argues against that view. These chapters create close parallels between the fate of the Egyptian émigrés and the fate of the citizens of Judah before the fall (Keown, Scalise, and Smothers 1995: 250–2). They refuse to listen, engage in idolatry, and serve the queen of heaven, and they are promised a dreadful fate even as they search for safety. At the same time Jeremiah and Baruch, though faithful, suffer forced exile. Ch. 42 portrays the survivors' rejection of the prophetic word (Brueggemann 1988: 174–5); ch. 43 portrays Jeremiah's forced emigration, and ch. 44 denounces idolatry.

(42:1–22) Jeremiah's Intercession All the survivors of Ishmael's bloody devastation, 'from the least to the greatest', including Johanan, go to Jeremiah for advice regarding their planned escape to Egypt. The story begins with the survivors' request that Jeremiah intercede on their behalf. They make a dramatic oath to 'obey' whatever message they receive, setting a curse upon themselves if they do not (vv. 1–6) and underscoring their subsequent disobedience.

Jeremiah does not reply hastily to the request but goes away for ten days and returns with the divine response (vv. 7–22). The response repeats themes and motifs that occur earlier in the book but which are used here in the new conflict between life in the land and escape to Egypt. YHWH promises to 'build' and to 'plant' the survivors only if they remain in the land. Since Jeremiah had previously advised exiles that they would prosper only in Babylon, this is puzzling counsel. Now life in the land under Babylon is a preferred alternative to escape to Egypt. And another new element enters the narrative. YHWH grieves over the disaster 'I . . . brought upon you' (v. 10). This verse portrays YHWH as repentant of divine action against the people and uses YHWH's empathy to further motivate submission to Babylon. Submission will gain mercy and restoration to their native soil (vv. 11–12). But if the Judeans go to Egypt where they expect to escape suffering, they will find sword, famine, and pestilence (vv. 13–15). vv. 18–22 continue divine advice to the remnant of Judah against the fatal mistake of escape to Egypt. There is no escape from Babylon.

(43:1–13) Jeremiah and Baruch Become Exiles Suddenly Johanan, who acted heroically in ch. 42, speaks insolently. He and other leaders of the remnant accuse Jeremiah of lying, and they charge Baruch with inciting Jeremiah to betray them to the Babylonians (vv. 1–3). In Brueggemann's terms (1994), the opponents accuse Baruch, not Jeremiah, of socio-political bias in favour of Babylon. This suggests that Jeremiah's memory is too sacred to attack but that his scribal successors, represented by Baruch, are in open contest over the control of the future. Then Johanan, the leaders, and the remnant, described in terms that seem to ignore the massacres of ch. 42, disobey Jeremiah, forcing him and Baruch to escape with them to Egypt (vv. 4–7). In a massive contradiction of his own preaching, Jeremiah meets a fate similar to the Babylonian exiles. He and Baruch are taken from the land against their will and forced where they do not wish to go. They escape none of the pain of their people. They disappear with their lives to a place already condemned.

In Egypt Jeremiah continues to prophesy, and directs rather than performs a symbolic action (vv. 8–13). In full view of the Judeans, the directee, presumably Baruch, is to bury stones at the gate to Pharaoh's palace at Tahpanhes (vv. 8–9) and then explain the action. The dreaded King Nebuchadrezzar of Babylon will come to Egypt and establish his throne over those buried stones. What YHWH promised in 42:15–17, 22 will happen at the hand of Nebuchadrezzar (v. 11) who will destroy the Egyptian deities (vv. 12–13).

(44:1–30) Idolatry in Egypt Jeremiah delivers a final message to Judeans living in Egypt. A preamble explains the recent disaster that befell Jersualem and Judah as the consequence of the wickedness of its inhabitants (vv. 1–6). vv. 7–10 continue the harangue but speak directly to the circumstances of the remnant in Egypt who are threatened with extinction because of idolatry and forgetfulness of their history of sin. Their sin will cause all but a few fugitives to perish (vv. 11–14). vv. 15–30, worship of the queen of heaven exemplifies the idolatry that causes the destruction of the Egyptian refugees. (On the identity of the queen of heaven see Ackerman 1987; Keown, Scalise, and Smothers 1995: 266–7; and Smith 1990: 145, 55). Jeremiah accuses the people of Jerusalem of this crime in the temple sermon (7:1–8:3), but in that text it is entire families that are engaged in idolatry. Here women are the chief practitioners and defenders of idolatrous practices. The narrative intends to reveal the depth of idolatrous thinking, but it also

shows women with minds of their own and spiritual resources to which they hold fast (O'Connor 1992). The women speak for themselves reporting that life collapsed when they stopped worshipping the queen of heaven. They would, therefore, continue to make cakes for her and offer libations. The text portrays the women as brazen violators of the covenant who implicate their husbands in their practices, revealing the husbands to be weak but not idolators themselves (vv. 15–19).

Jeremiah replies that it is exactly that history of idolatry that led to the destruction of the city (vv. 2–23; see Keown, Scalise, and Smothers 1995: 263 on parallels with Ezekiel). Furthermore, they can surely continue these wicked practices in Egypt and with the same certainty of extinction. Upon them will settle the curses of YHWH. Pharaoh will meet the same fate as Zedekiah at the hands of Nebuchadrezzar (vv. 24–30). This chapter announces the end of Judean life in Egypt. The believing community will disappear, for YHWH's name will never again be pronounced on their lips (v. 26). They have no future because they have turned from YHWH, disregarded the prophets, and engaged in deliberate, calculated idolatry. They are inheritors of idolatry and their departure from the land plunges them further into the family perversity. They, not YHWH, have created the end of their own history. The divine word will triumph (Carroll 1986: 743). Despite Jeremiah's attacks on the Egyptian exiles, a thriving and productive Jewish community continued.

(45:1–5) Baruch and the Scroll Ch. 45 concludes chs. 26–44 by asserting that the prophetic word will survive because Baruch will 'gain his life as a prize of war' (v. 5). The chapter contains a lament by Baruch and reassurance by Jeremiah. The date is the fourth year of Jehoiakim 'when he wrote these words in a scroll at the dictation of Jeremiah' (v. 1). The scroll probably refers to the second scroll that Jeremiah and Baruch created after Jehoiakim burned the first (36:32). The scroll contains Jeremiah's original message and additional words as well. As the written expansion of Jeremiah's message for later audiences, the scroll survives and Jeremiah's prophetic mantle has been handed on.

Like Jeremiah, Baruch utters a lament of sorrow, pain, and weariness (vv. 2–3) that follows upon the utterances of curses upon his own people (ch. 44). Through Jeremiah, YHWH replies, using the principal motifs of the book, 'I am going to break down . . . and pluck up . . . the whole land' (v. 4). Deconstruction and demolition of the land, of the way of life, of the symbolic world of Judah cannot be avoided, not even by escape to Egypt. The only way out of suffering is through its very centre. Baruch is then admonished not to seek 'great things' for himself. This probably means that he should not consider himself to be Jeremiah's replacement but only the conduit of Jeremiah's message. Baruch's reward is not grand but it is precious. He will survive. He will gain his life 'as a prize of war', wherever he goes (v. 5).

With this lament and response, the main part of the book closes on a sombre note. Baruch is the world-weary survivor who is promised only his life, not escape, not return, not restoration of fortunes. Only life, endurance through difficulties, that is the prize in the midst of exhaustion from the disaster that will come 'upon all flesh' (v. 5). The Baruch narratives end with a most chastened hope that leaves the lyrical utopian vision of chs. 30–3 far from sight. The mood is of subdued trauma, emotional devastation after cascading catastrophes, quiet after the passing of divine wrath. There is not yet energy for rebuilding or planting. There is little space for dancing or laughing. Now there is only waiting.

But survival is assured by the stories in chs. 37–45. Jeremiah, Baruch, Ebed-melech, and a remnant survive. Yet survivors must still obey Jeremiah's message or further destruction awaits. The next section of the book, the Oracles Against the Nations, confirms survival of the faithful who wait in obedience. It implies a reversal of fortunes for them because YHWH is 'going to bring disaster upon all flesh' (v. 5). Israel and Judah are no longer the target as all present power arrangements are about to be overthrown (Brueggemann 1991: 210).

(46:1–51:64) Oracles Against the Nations Common in prophetic literature (Isa 13–23; Ezek 25–32; Am 1–2; and Zeph 2:2–15), the Oracles proclaim unequivocally that YHWH is ruler of the nations. In the book of Jeremiah, this complex genre gains special importance from Jeremiah's title, 'prophet to the nations' (1:10; McKane 1986: clxv). The LXX places the Oracles at 25:13 in the centre of the book, following the drinking of the poisoned cup by Israel and the nations. By contrast, the MT makes the Oracles the penultimate section of the book and presents them in a different order from the LXX. Carroll (1986: 751–9) and Herrmann (1986: 163–5) have good discussions of these differences as well as genre and themes, and Clements (1988: 245–7) draws attention to the significant differences in tone, theme, and theology among the Oracles.

Despite modern resistance to theological themes of vengeance, anger, and retribution, Bellis (1995) shows that the Oracles in Jeremiah, particularly those against Babylon, serve important rhetorical, literary, and theological functions. They seek to build up the weak faith of Israel, and they defend God against charges of injustice. Located at the book's conclusion, they bring satisfactory closure to the captive nation's hopes. YHWH is the principal speaker throughout the poems, giving them the authority of divine speech. YHWH's voice announces that foreign nations had been instruments of divine punishment of Israel and Judah, but soon tables will turn to create a different future. The Oracles address Judah's neighbours first (chs. 46–9) and culminate in oracles against Babylon (50–1).

(Chs. 46–9) Oracles Against Judah's Neighbours The predominant metaphor across these texts is that of the cosmic battle. As Carroll (1986: 754) points out, this is one of many shared poetic elements between the Oracles and chs. 4–6, 8–10. Now the mythic enemy from the north will stalk Israel's neighbours.

(46:1–25) Oracles Against Egypt This chapter contains poems against Egypt that bring to fulfilment Jeremiah's prophecies to the Judean remnant that escaped to Egypt (chs. 43–4). Babylon will destroy their safe refuge. v. 1 introduces the entire collection of Oracles Against the Nations. The remainder of the chapter comprises three poems, two concerning Egypt (vv. 3–12, 14–24) and one concerning Israel (vv. 27–8). Prose comments link the poems (46:2, 13, 25–6).

v. 2 dates the first poem (vv. 3–12) to the year 605, the fourth year of Jehoiakim and a code for the year of judgement (Taylor 1987). In that year Babylon defeated Egypt at Carchemish, gaining control of Syria–Palestine and destroying Egypt's power in the region. This dating, therefore, places Jeremiah's interpretation of Egypt's history well in advance of events about which it prophesies. It implies that YHWH has plans, long known and foretold, that will determine the fate of nations and reverse Israel's fate. For an exilic audience, the oracle's date confirms its reliability and offers hope that their enemies will be defeated and their God will triumph. vv. 3–12, the day of YHWH begins with a battle scene (vv. 3–6) in which a voice, presumably YHWH's, calls to military troops to prepare for battle. It is not clear which army is being addressed, the Egyptian for the defence or the Babylonian for the attack. Parallel commands in the second stanza (v. 9) suggest that Egypt is called to battle only to face defeat. Babylon is never named in this poem because, as Carroll (1986: 763) points out, the real enemy is YHWH. A few vivid words describe defeat in the north as they stumble and fall (vv. 5–6).

vv. 7–12, the famed swelling and waning of the Nile describes the rise and fall of Egypt, the foreign power that intended to 'cover the earth' with destruction, but which is now under attack in the day of YHWH. Egypt again prepares for battle but has no possibility of defending itself. The enemy is not human but divine. YHWH gains 'vindication' for foes, offering a sacrifice in the 'land of the north' (vv. 9–10). In mocking reuse of the poem of Judah's wound (8:22), Egypt is sent to Gilead for a healing balm, but there is no healing for her (v. 11). Female imagery reappears in describing the wounded nation's reversal of fortunes. Egypt is 'virgin daughter', vulnerable and shameful (vv. 11–12). vv. 13–25, Egypt's exile: a prose frame that specifies Egypt's human assailant as Nebuchadrezzar of Babylon (vv. 13, 25) encompasses the second oracle against Egypt. Because the battle is in the divine sphere, the human agent Babylon remains in the margins of both power and poem (vv. 13, 25). In the poetry itself the battle is cosmic and heavenly. On the mythic day of YHWH the deities of Egypt and Israel enact the siege. A command to announce the battle in Egypt's major cities opens the poem (v. 14). Egypt's defeat is certain, for YHWH has 'thrust down' Egypt's bull-god, Apis (v. 15; on Egyptian deities and cities, see Thompson 1980: 691–4). Nor is the deified Pharaoh, called 'King Bombast' (NEB), a match for the true king YHWH (v. 18). Pharaoh's power is mere braggadocio; YHWH's power is genuine and international. YHWH sends the agent of destruction to advance upon Memphis and send Egypt into exile (v. 19). Female metaphors again describe Egypt's vulnerability and shame (vv. 20–4). She is a beautiful heifer, and like her, her soldiers are fat and well-paid. They cannot withstand 'the gadfly from the north' (vv. 20–1). Egypt makes a noise like a retreating snake in front of her enemies (vv. 22–3). Daughter Egypt is shamed and taken captive by the mythic enemy from the north (v. 24).

The historical prose frame makes no promise of Egypt's survival (v. 25). Egypt's great crime in these poems is not equivalent to the crimes of Israel and Judah in the book of Jeremiah. Its offences are hubris, personified in its pharaoh (v. 17), and false claims to power over the earth and its civilizations (v. 8). Its gods are not declared false, but before powerful YHWH they are powerless. YHWH rules the world (v. 18). For exiles, these would be hope-restoring words. vv. 27–8, comfort for Israel: Israel/Jacob, by contrast to exiled Egypt, will return. This poem promises comfort, restoration, and a quiet, fearless future for the dismayed exiles of Israel (v. 27). Jacob is YHWH's servant; YHWH is with him (v. 28). Retribution and the turning of the tables is at hand, for YHWH will make an end of all the nations 'among which I banished you' for punishment (v. 28). This short poem of reversal offers redactional clues to the interpretation of the whole collection of Oracles Against Nations. The poem assumes restoration of covenant relationship between YHWH and Israel and interprets the national tragedy as divine punishment that will soon end. It affirms that YHWH is just. The poem promises an international reversal of fortunes, punishment for the punishers. It asserts divine control of history and obliquely suggests that the nations were out of hand and now, in turn, deserve punishment. Hence, the audience of the oracles is Judah, not the nations themselves. The oracles function to give hope, encourage endurance, and reassert the justice of God who continues to elect them as a special people among all the nations. What is at stake here is identity politics, a global vision that places the survivors of the destroyed nation of Israel at the head of YHWH's people.

(47:1–7) Oracle Against the Philistines This poem presents historical perplexities, not the least of which relates to the superscription that describes the attack as coming from Egypt in the south (v. 1), whereas the poem describes the mythic attack from the north (Carroll 1986: 777). Why Philistia is included at all in the list of enemies is not clear (Keown, Scalise, and Smothers 1995: 299). What is certain is that the attack ultimately comes from warrior YHWH. The invasion is like an overflowing, raging river that will destroy all in its path (v. 2; cf. 46:7–8). The day of YHWH has come. People scatter at the noise of the army and abandon children in fear. The poem provides no clear reason for the attack, but it ends with the 'song of the sword'. In a poignant personification of YHWH's weapon, an unidentified speaker begs the sword to be still but recognizes that the sword is unable to countermand YHWH's plans for it (vv. 6–7).

(48:1–47) Oracles Against Moab This chapter, comprising a loose collection of prose and poetry, contains the book's second lengthiest description of attack against a foreign nation. Only the poems about the destruction of Babylon are longer (chs. 50–1). (See Keown, Scalise, and Smothers (1995: 308–10) for a discussion of literary forms, division of passages, and Moabite place-names.) Moab's status as a traditional and bitter enemy of Israel may explain the rancorous tone of these Oracles. There is significant echoing of texts from several other OT passages in this chapter, and numerous parallels with Isa 15–16 (Holladay 1989: 346; Thompson 1980: 700). Despite textual difficulties, the general argument of the chapter is clear. YHWH will visit punishment upon Moab.

In vv. 1–2 YHWH announces the invasion of Moab's major cities, plots against the nation, and destruction by the sword. Another voice cries out in alarm that great desolation, destruction, and wild fleeing for safety is occurring in Moab (vv. 3–6). Moab's crime arises from its own arrogance concerning its power and wealth (Brueggemann 1988: 243). For this idolatrous hubris, its god Chemosh will go into exile (v. 7). There will be no escape and salt will cover the desolate country to make it a barren place (v. 9). Known for its viniculture (Keown, Scalise, and Smothers, 1995), Moab has a history of complacency described in terms of a wine that will soon be decanted (vv. 11–12). v. 14 returns to language of warfare. Soldiers speak through the ventriloquism of the poet who mocks them. They think they are mighty warriors but YHWH, 'LORD of Hosts', the head of armies, has sent the destroyer (v. 15). Readers are to mourn over Moab for its great power is broken (v. 17).

In vv. 18–20, YHWH addresses the city, daughter Dibon, for she too is under attack and put to shame. A prose comment in vv. 21–7 names the destroyed cities to illustrate the destruction of Moab's power. In retaliation for its mockery of innocent Israel, Moab will be forced to drink until sick with drunkenness (cf. 25:22).

YHWH next speaks to Moab's inhabitants, urging them to flee and accusing them, with repetitive insistence, of false pride (vv. 28–33). YHWH wails for Moab as gladness, joy, and wine presses are removed from the land (vv. 31–3). In prose, vv. 34–9 elaborate on YHWH's lament by naming the cities crying out in the disaster. In poetry again, YHWH announces that an eagle will swoop down on Moab to terrify and destroy 'because he magnified himself against the LORD' (vv. 40–2). No one among them can escape the pit (vv. 43–4); all will perish (vv. 45–6). But the oracles against Moab come to a truly surprising conclusion for, in the last line, YHWH promises to restore the fortunes of Moab (v. 47). Carroll (1986: 796) interprets this reversal of fortune as a simple recognition that Moab survives. Theologically the verse affirms divine desires for the well-being of nations beyond Judah.

(49:1–39) contains a series of short Oracles against several peoples: Ammon, Edom, Damascus, Arab tribes, and Elam.

(49:1–6) Against the Ammonites The history of relations between Israel and Ammon was bitter. The book of Jeremiah implicates the Ammonites in Gedaliah's assassination (40:13–41:3; Thompson 1980: 715–16 provides a history of the relationship). The major theme of the poem is punishment of Ammon for land-grabbing. In a disingenuous rhetorical question, YHWH asks if Israel is without an heir. The next verse provides motivation for the question: why has Ammon's capital city taken over Gad, presumably from Israel? For the crime of wrongful land acquisition, YHWH will invade the city of Rabbah, reduce it to ruin, and give the land back to Israel (vv. 1–2). Mourning and exile will follow as Ammonite locations are destroyed. Like other nations, Ammon's pride and false boasting will bring disaster upon the 'faithless daughter' (v. 4). Female imagery again underscores the terror and vulnerability of a people about to be attacked. But like Moab (48:47), Ammon will later have its fortunes restored (v. 6).

(49:7–22) Against Edom Two poems (vv. 7–11, 14–16) and two prose comments (vv. 12–13, 17–22; but see Thompson 1980: 719) portray YHWH's obliterating punishment of Edom. On the troubled history of relations between Israel and Edom, see the book of Obadiah and ibid. 720. The Edomites are the offspring of Jacob's brother Esau (Gen 36). YHWH questions the disappearance of wisdom from Edom, perhaps a wisdom derived from its ancestral connection to Jacob. YHWH will be the one to bring calamity upon them (vv. 7–8). Unlike grape-gatherers or thieves who leave something after they work,

YHWH will completely pillage Edom, here called Esau (vv. 9–10). Orphans and widows alone will remain, signifying the end of the people (v. 11). vv. 12–13 are a prose comment that links this text with the destructive drinking bout (25:21). If even the innocent must drink the cup of punishment, how can Edom expect to escape? Who might be innocent is not revealed, but perhaps the prose writer believes that Judah's exiles are innocent of the totality of the disaster that befell them.

vv. 14–16 announce in poetry the sending of an unnamed messenger among the nations. By implication, Jeremiah is the messenger, sent to announce the cosmic battle in which YHWH will reduce Edom to the least among the nations. A lengthy prose comment compares Edom's destruction to the ruin of the wicked Sodom and Gomorrah (v. 18, cf. Gen 19) and to the decimation of a flock (vv. 20–1). The agent of this apocalyptic catastrophe (v. 29) is YHWH who will attack like a lion (v. 19) and swoop down like an eagle, turning warriors into frightened women (v. 22). The poem never names Edom's sin.

(49:23–7) Against Damascus The poem against Damascus also uses female imagery to reveal the weakness, panic, and grief that will befall Syria's capital city. This poem also omits the sin that provokes the destroying fire (v. 27).

(49:28–33) Against Kedar and Hazor In the list of Nebuchadrezzar's triumphs in the Oracles (v. 28), Kedar and Hazor join Egypt among those attacked (46:2; see Thompson 1980: 726–7 on peoples and places). The superscription identifies Nebuchadrezzar as the addressee of the poem's commands to attack. He is to 'rise up, advance' against both the tribe of Kedar (v. 29) and the people of Hazor (v. 31). As the human agent of the attack, Nebuchadrezzar merely followed YHWH's commands (v. 30). Kedar and Hazor will lose their herds of camels and cattle (vv. 29, 32) and both peoples will be dispersed (vv. 30, 33). No reasons for their fate appear in the poem, unless being at ease (v. 31) implies a profligate arrogance.

(49:34–9) Against Elam A prose passage interprets theologically the international turmoil created by Babylon's imperialism. The comment is set in the reign of Zedekiah, just after Babylon's first invasion of Judah in 597, and describes Elam's devastation in cosmic and meteorological terms. The four winds of heaven, not historical agents, will be YHWH's instruments in Elam's destruction. After this colossal disaster, YHWH will restore its fortunes (v. 39).

(50:1–51:64) Against Babylon Long thought to be misplaced, derivative, and monotonous, these two chapters contain Oracles that form a fitting theological conclusion to the book (Bellis 1995; Reimer 1993). Here the punisher is punished; the destroyer is destroyed; the inflicter of pain receives pain. Although previous texts understood Babylon as YHWH's agent and Nebuchadrezzar as YHWH's servant, these chapters see them as perpetrators of evil against innocent, oppressed Israel. No longer does the text emphasize Israel's sinfulness, though that theme does not disappear entirely (50:7; 51:5).

Chs. 50–1 portray the deity as a God of recompense, the warrior God, who sets right the world's injustices and restores the well-being of the chosen people. Despite the vengeful nature of the material and theological difficulties created by

a seemingly fickle divine reversal in relation to Babylon, these passages are good news for the exiles. They no longer explain why Judah's tragedy occurred, but, like chs. 30–3, they look beyond the tragedy to a new future. In them is expressed a biblical hope, a glimpsed confidence, that the present reality does not exhaust reality, that just out of sight, beyond comprehension, dwells the God of justice (Brueggemann 1991).

Keown, Scalise, and Smothers (1995) summarize problems in interpretation, particularly in delimiting literary units. Carroll (1986) dates the poems to the post-exilic period and suggests that they may have functioned as songs of celebration upon Babylon's defeat. Bellis (1995) and Aitken (1984) find structural and thematic unity among the poems. Bellis (1995: 216–27) and Keown, Scalise, and Smothers (1995) identify similar poetic units: 50:2–20, 21–32, 33–46; 51:1–33 (Bellis divides at v. 19); 34–58 (Keown, Scalise, and Smothers divide at v. 44). The great difficulty in agreeing upon a structure reveals the complicated nature of the collection. It is perhaps best viewed as a loose unity of voices, an interpretative conversation that moves from promises of attack on Babylon, through preparations for military onslaught, to a portrayal of Babylon's ultimate doom. The cosmic battle, this time between the enemy from the north and Babylon, between YHWH and the Babylonian deity Bel/Merodach, serves as an organizing metaphor for the chapters. Interwined with poetic imaginings of Babylon's fate, are poetic and prose accounts of Israel's escape from captivity. Rhetorically, the chapters seek to create hope by inverting the fate of the exiles over that of Babylon.

(50:1–46) The Enemy from the North An undated superscription emphatically relates 50:2–51:64 to Babylon (v. 1). vv. 2–20, whether this material is all poetry (Bellis 1995, Keown, Scalise, and Smothers 1995), or partly prose (NRSV; Carroll 1986) is not certain. A simple declaration of celebration by YHWH opens the poem. Coming after this long book in which Babylon has dominated Judah and the nations around it, the words compress immense feeling. Babylon is taken; her gods are shamed (v. 2). Using verbs of completed action, the text pictures already accomplished destruction. The agent of that destruction is the mythic foe from the north, an unnamed enemy that will reduce Babylon to a wasteland (v. 3).

In vv. 4–10 YHWH continues to speak but shifts the subject from Babylon to Israel. The fates of Israel and Babylon are connected, for the coming attack on Babylon will signal the return of Israel and Judah. They will come weeping to seal the everlasting covenant with YHWH (cf. Jer 30–3). YHWH refers to the people with empathy. They are lost sheep, led astray by their shepherds/rulers, and attacked by enemies who think themselves guiltless as they punish sinful Israel (vv. 6–7). But now the exiles must flee from Babylon. The enemy from the north comes again as a company of plundering nations that YHWH will bring against Babylon (vv. 8–10). vv. 11–16, direct address shifts to the plunderers of YHWH's heritage. Though they 'frisk about' now, their mother will be shamed, made desolate, and left without inhabitants. YHWH commands the cosmic army to take position for the attack, to raise the shout, to cut off from Babylon the sower and the harvester. In the world of poetry, Babylon's destruction is accomplished and celebration has begun (vv. 14–16).

vv. 17–20, YHWH again speaks about Israel, reinterpreting its history as a series of destructive attacks upon hunted sheep. Perhaps as sheep they are innocent or stupid, but certainly they are helpless and vulnerable, despite guilt ascribed to them by enemies (v. 7). In a reinterpretation of invasions by Assyria and Babylon, YHWH will prevent any one from finding sin among the remnant. They will be pardoned. Earlier interpretations of tragedies of Israel and Judah as the result of sin are not denied, but they are transcended by divine fiat. vv. 21–34, preparations for battle continue and descriptions become more vivid (vv. 20–2). Babylon, 'the hammer of the whole earth', is itself cut down. YHWH addresses Babylon directly. The nation is caught in a snare of its own devising (vv. 23–4), so YHWH will conduct the military campaign against it (vv. 25–7), making Babylon's fall inevitable. v. 28 shifts attention from Babylon and the armies attacking it to the fugitives escaping from it. Already approaching Zion to announce the achievement of divine vengeance, they act as a chorus commenting upon the action. vv. 29–32 return to the scene of battle preparations. Babylon has arrogantly defied the Holy One of Israel so YHWH plans retaliation. Speaking directly to Babylon, YHWH takes a stand against it, the arrogant one (vv. 31–2). Babylon has exceeded its divine commission. Israel's suffering is no longer entirely of its own making.

Interpretation of international events has come full circle within the book itself. History has a different face in these chapters, for here Israel and Judah are oppressed people, not guilty people. They have a future, unexpected and barely imaginable. Their strong Redeemer, the one who buys back captives, will take their side and give 'rest' to the whole earth (v. 34).

vv. 35–40 (The Sword), this curse-like poem gloats over the reversal of fortunes about to take place, as if an incantation of the sword would activate thrusts into the heart of Babylon. The song of the sword involves intricate literary weaving of phrases and forms. The phrase, 'a sword against', appears five times and its object is always an element of Chaldean society: the inhabitants, officials, diviners, the military, and the nation's treasures (vv. 35–7). The second and third verses of the poem (vv. 36, 37) break the monotony of sword imprecations by adding curses that continue through v. 38a. The final verse changes the instrument of attack from sword to drought. The artistically crafted poem concludes with a motive for the devastation to come. For its rampant idolatry, Babylon deserves the sword (v. 38b). A prose comment (vv. 39–40) finds in the poem cause for the destruction that will reduce Babylon to an uninhabited land like Sodom and Gomorrah.

vv. 41–6 (The Foe from the North), the sword approaches in this poem that uses imagery familiar from earlier parts of the book and forms a frame with v. 3. A speaker announces the imminent approach of a people from the north. They are cruel, noisy, and arrayed for battle against daughter Babylon. The king is like a terrified and pain-struck woman in labour (v. 43). Prose verses (44–6) divulge the identity of the agent of destruction. It is YHWH, coming like a lion, sovereign and unbiddable, coming with a divine plan that will make the earth tremble.

(51:1–64) Opposing fates of Babylon and Israel continue to interweave and echo one another in this chapter. For the first time in the book YHWH orders the implied exilic audience to flee Babylon and return to Zion (vv. 6–10, 45–51). Divine power dominates the passages. YHWH, creator of all the earth, alone has the power and wisdom to set the world aright for Israel and all the earth's peoples. The vengeful violence of captives and their gloating delight at the fall of their vanquishers converge in a theology of divine governance of nations and of divine power to create a future out of nothing which will overturn systems of domination.

vv. 1–5, military preparation: underscoring divine agency, YHWH uses first-person verbs to plan the siege against Babylon. Cosmic and human elements will participate in the invasion (vv. 1–2) to destroy utterly the military power of the Chaldeans (vv. 3–4). Although the poem's final verse appears to change the subject, it announces the conclusion to be drawn from the promised attack. Despite the guilt of Israel and Judah, YHWH has not abandoned them (v. 5). vv. 6–10, urgent appeals to the exiles follow. To save their lives from the divine vengeance about to engulf Babylon, exiles must flee. Now Babylon, not Judah, is guilty. Although Babylon had been a golden cup in YHWH's hand (cf. 25:15–29), she has fallen from her insider status (vv. 6–7; Stulman 1995). A voice calls for balm to heal the nation's wound (cf. 8:23–9). The exiles themselves speak. They had tried to heal Babylon, but it is too late; the patient is dying (v. 9). In a poetic crescendo of urgency and excitement, the captives advise each other to flee to Zion where they will declare their vindication by their God (v. 10).

vv. 11–14, war preparations continue with divine commands that echo preparations for the cosmic battle against Judah in chs. 4–10. YHWH orders the armies to sharpen arrows, raise the standard, post sentinels, and prepare ambushes (vv. 11–12), but here the nameless, perhaps mythic, armies receive historical identification in a prose comment. The Medes will destroy Babylon in YHWH's retaliation for the temple (v. 11). Victory is assured (v. 14). vv. 15–19, praise of the Creator: perhaps the hymnic language of this poem is voiced by the exiles. The divine agent of battle is the Creator, wise and understanding, whose powerful voice creates tumult and pyrotechnic meteorological events (vv. 15–16). Compared to the Creator, the idols are worthless, a delusion (cf. 3:23; 10:15). The battle between Jacob's God and the lifeless gods of goldsmiths is already over (vv. 17–19). vv. 20–3, this poem repeats the violent first-person verb and preposition, 'I smash with you' (wĕnippaṣtî bĕkā) eight times to create a staccato rhythm of destruction. Babylon is the assumed addressee, the divine hammer used to destroy kingdoms, warriors, and ordinary people (McKane 1986: 1310). vv. 24–33, war planning and preparations continue. In first-person speech, YHWH declares divine opposition to superpower Babylon, the 'destroying mountain' (vv. 24–5). Nations muster for war (vv. 27–9) and Babylon trembles in panic and fear (vv. 29–33).

vv. 34–44, accusations of Babylonian wrongdoing accelerate. YHWH imagines the speech of the people in Zion describing Nebuchadrezzars's violence against them and their request for vengeance (vv. 34–5). YHWH promises to take vengeance, drying up Babylon, sending lion-like attackers, making Babylon drunk for its arrogance, and punishing the engorged Babylonian god, Bel. vv. 45–58, again YHWH calls the exiles to depart, to save themselves. They must overcome the fear created by the rumours among them (vv. 45–6). In the eschatological future, YHWH will destroy Babylon. The cosmos will shout for joy (vv. 47–8). But now it is urgent that the exiles do not linger but remember YHWH in Jerusalem (v. 50). The people speak of their shame and the desecration of the temple (v. 51), and YHWH promises punishment of Babylon no matter how mighty it becomes (vv. 52–3).

vv. 54–8, the poetry of the book closes with an imagined portrayal of the attack. There is a cry, a crashing, massive noise, for the destroyer has come against Babylon (v. 56). Her leaders will be made drunk, will sleep never to wake, and Babylon will fall to the ground. vv. 59–64, a symbolic act, described in prose by a third-person narrator, closes the Oracles Against the Nations. The action is performed neither by Jeremiah nor by Baruch but by Baruch's brother Seraiah. Jeremiah sends Seraiah to Babylon with the scroll containing the prophecies against it. Seraiah is to read the scroll aloud, attach a stone to it, and sink the scroll in the Euphrates. The sinking of the scroll mimics the way Babylon itself will sink from its high position. The symbolic act embodies the divine will. It waits only to come to completion.

(52:1–34) The End The end of the book reports in prose the end of national life in Judah, but curiously, neither Jeremiah nor YHWH appears in it. The temporal and geographical setting is exile, and Babylonian defeat is far from sight. The chapter is nearly identical to the account of the nation's fall that concludes the second book of Kings, the final book of the Deuteronomistic history (2 Kings 24:18–25:30). The Jeremiah chapter substitutes an enumeration of exiles for the description of Gedaliah's governorship and assassination (2 Kings 25:22–6). Jer 40:5–41:8 describes the Gedaliah era far more fully. Keown, Scalise, and Smothers (1995) propose that the book of Jeremiah uses a pre-existing narrative because it would have more authority than a newly minted one. Carroll (1986) and Clements (1988) see in the borrowing the signature of Deuteronomistic editors.

The narrative divides into six vignettes: failure of kings (vv. 1–3); Zedekiah's failed escape (vv. 3b–11); deportation of people (vv. 12–16) and of temple vessels (vv. 17–23); execution of officials (vv. 24–7); numbers of exiles (vv. 28–30); Jehoiachin's survival (vv. 31–4).

At first the chapter appears to be a superfluous addition to the book, but it actually functions as vindication of Jeremiah's message (Carroll 1986: 858; Clements 1988: 268). In it Jeremiah's words of judgement against kings, priests, temple, and people find tragic fulfilment. The closing chapter, moreover, describes the destruction of the regnant symbols of the nation. The holy city is invaded. The cowardly king and 'all the soldiers' escape only to be caught; the king's sons are murdered; the king, blind to the word, is himself blinded; and the temple is burned. Many citizens and temple vessels are deported. Officials are executed. The numbers of exiled are listed. The counting of exiles in Jeremiah differs markedly from the enumeration in 2 Kings 24:14 where 10,000 people are said to have been deported rather than the 4,600 in v. 28. The numbers in Kings may be inflated, or the numbers in Jeremiah may count only men (Keown, Scalise, and Smothers 1995: 381). Whatever historical data underlie the account, the narrative simply and vividly depicts the collapse of the nation just as Jeremiah promised. Every element of life that sup-

ported and sustained community identity is destroyed by this catastrophe. The promises of Jeremiah's call (Jer 1) have been accomplished.

The bleak narrative of this chapter implies that Israel and Judah will disappear from history, but perhaps a glimmer of hope remains. King Jehoiachin gains his life as a prize of war. Though still captive, he receives honour at the king's table, and an allowance. Like the exiles in Babylon, he survives. The king's release may be symbolic. The book does not end with a triumphal procession back to Zion but with dignified existence in captivity. How to survive the tragedy has been the subject of the book. Its many conflicting voices—of warning and accusation, defending and attacking divine justice, urging submission or resistance to Babylon, blaming the people for their sufferings, and of brief but translucent hope—all give the exiles instructions for survival. They must endure for the future day. Jeremiah's words will not fail.

REFERENCES

Ackroyd, P. R. (1968), *Exile and Restoration: A Study of Hebrew Thought of the Sixth Century B.C.* (London: SCM).

Ackerman, S. (1987), ' "And the Women Knead Dough": The Worship of the Queen of Heaven in Sixth Century Judah', in Peggy L. Day (ed.), *Gender and Difference in Ancient Israel* (Minneapolis: Fortress), 109–24.

Aitken, K. (1984), 'Jeremiah', *Daily Study Bible* (Edinburgh: St. Andrew's Press)

Anderson, B. W. (1978), ' " The Lord Has Created Something New ": A Stylistic Study of Jer 31:15–22', *CBQ* 40: 463–77.

Bak, D. H. (1990), *Klagender Gott-Klagende Menschen: Studien zur Klage im Jeremiabuch*, BZAW 193 (Berlin: de Gruyter).

Baumgartner, W. (1987), *Jeremiah's Poems of Lament* (Sheffield: Almond). German original, BZAW 32, 1917.

Bellis, A. O. (1995), *The Structure and Composition of Jeremiah 50:2–51:58* (Lewiston, NY: Mellen).

Biddle, M. E. (1988), 'The Literary Frame Surrounding Jeremiah 30, 1–33, 6', *ZAW* 100: 409–15.

—— (1990), *A Redaction History of Jeremiah 2:1–4: 2*, ATANT 77 (Zurich: Theologischer Verlag).

—— (1996), *Polyphony and Symphony in Prophetic Literature: Rereading Jeremiah 7–20* (Macon: Mercer University Press).

Blank, S. H. (1961), *Jeremiah: Man and Prophet* (Cincinnati: Hebrew Union College).

Boadt, L. (1982a), *Jeremiah 1–25* (Wilmington, Del.: Michael Glazier).

—— (1982b), *Jeremiah 26–52, Habakkuk, Zephaniah, Nahum* (Wilmington, Del.: Michael Glazier).

Bogaert, P. M. (1981) (ed.), *Le Livre de Jérémie: Le Prophète et son milieu, les oracles et leur transmission* (Leuven: Leuven University Press).

Bourguet, D. (1987), *Les Métaphores de Jérémie*, EBib 9 (Paris: Lecoffre).

Bright, J. (1951), 'The Date of the Prose Sermons of Jeremiah', *JBL* 70: 15–35.

—— (1965), *Jeremiah*, AB 21 (Garden City, NY: Doubleday).

Brueggemann, W. (1988), *To Pluck Up, To Tear Down: A Commentary on the Book of Jeremiah 1–25* (Grand Rapids, Mich.: Eerdmans).

—— (1991), *To Build, To Plant: A Commentary on Jeremiah 26–52* (Grand Rapids, Mich.: Eerdmans).

—— (1994), ' "The Baruch Connection": Reflections on Jer. 43:1–7', *JBL* 113: 405–20.

Carroll, R. P. (1981), *From Chaos to Covenant: Prophecy in the Book of Jeremiah* (New York: Crossroad).

—— (1986), *Jeremiah*, OTL (Philadelphia: Westminster).

—— (1989), *Jeremiah* (Sheffield: JSOT).

Childs, B. (1959), 'The Enemy From the North and the Chaos Tradition', *JBL* 8: 187–98.

Clements, R. E. (1988), *Jeremiah* (Atlanta: John Knox).

—— (1993), 'Jeremiah 1–25 and the Deuteronomistic History', in A. G. Auld (ed.), *Understanding Poets and Prophets: Essays in Honour of George Wishart Anderson* (Sheffield: JSOT), 93–113.

—— (1996), *Old Testament Prophecy: From Oracles to Canon* (Louisville, Ky.: Westminster/John Knox).

Condamin, A. (1920), *Le Livre de Jérémie* (Paris: Lecoffre).

Craigie, P. C., Kelley, P., and Drinkard, J. F. (1991), *Jeremiah 1–25*, WBC 26 (Dallas: Word Books), i.

Cross, F. M. (1964), 'The History of the Biblical Text in Light of Discoveries in the Judean Desert', *HTR* 57: 281–99.

Dearman, J. A. (1990), ' "My Servants the Scribes": Composition and Context in Jeremiah 36', *JBL* 109: 403–21.

DeRoche, M. (1983), 'Jeremiah 2:2–3 and Israel's Love For God During the Wilderness Wanderings', *CBQ* 45: 364–75.

Diamond, A. R. P. (1987), *The Confessions of Jeremiah in Context: Scenes of Prophetic Drama*, JSOTSup 45 (Sheffield: JSOT).

—— (1993), 'Portraying Prophecy: Of Doublets, Variants, and Analogies in the Narrative Representation of Jeremiah's Oracles—Reconstructing the Hermeneutics of Prophecy', *JSOT* 57: 99–119.

—— and O'Connor, K. M. (1996), 'Unfaithful Passions: Coding Women Coding Men in Jeremiah 2–3 (4:2)', *Biblical Interpretation*, 4/3: 288–310.

Dobbs-Allsopp, F. W. (1955), 'The Syntagma of *Bet* followed by a geographical name', *CBQ* 57: 451–70.

Duhm, B. (1901), *Das Buch Jeremia*, KHCAT 11 (Leipzig: Mohr).

Fischer, G. (1991), 'Jer 25 und die Fremdvölkersprüche: Unterschiede zwischen hebräischem und griechischem Text', *Bib* 72: 474–99.

Fishbane, M. (1985), *Biblical Interpretation in Ancient Israel* (Oxford: Clarendon).

Frank, A. (1995), *The Wounded Storyteller: Body, Illness, and Ethics* (Chicago: University of Chicago Press).

Fretheim, T. E. (1984), *The Suffering of God* (Philadelphia: Fortress).

Gerstenberger, E. (1963), 'Jeremiah's Complaints: Observations on Jer 15:20–21,' *JBL* 82: 393–408.

Goldman, Y. (1992), *Prophétie et royauté au retour de l'exil: Les origines littéraires de la forme massorétique du livre de Jérémie*, OBO 118 (Göttingen: Vandenhoeck & Ruprecht).

Gunneweg, A. H. J. (1970), 'Konfession oder Interpretation im Jeremiabuch', *ZTK* 67: 395–416.

Habel, N. (1965), 'The Form and Significance of Call Narratives', *ZAW* 77: 297–323.

—— (1995), *The Land is Mine: Six Biblical Land Ideologies* (Minneapolis: Fortress).

Hayes, J. H., and Miller, J. M. (1986), *A History of Ancient Israel and Judah* (Philadelphia: Westminster).

Herrmann, S. (1986), *Jeremia*, BKAT 12 (Neukirchen-Vluyn: Neukirchener Verlag).

Heschel, A. J. (1962), *The Prophets* (2 vols.; New York: Harper Colophon).

Holladay, W. L. (1958), *The Root šubh in the Old Testament, with Particular Reference to its Usages in Covenantal Contexts* (Leiden: Brill).

—— (1962), 'Style, Irony, and Authenticity in Jeremiah', *JBL* 81: 44–54.

—— (1980), 'The Identification of the Two Scrolls of Jeremiah', *VT* 30: 452–67.

—— (1986; 1989), *Jeremiah*, Hermeneia (2 vols.; Philadelphia and Minneapolis: Fortress).

—— (1990), *Jeremiah: A Fresh Reading* (New York: Pilgrim).

Honeyman, A. M. (1948), 'The Evidence for Regal Names among the Hebrews,' *JBL* 67: 13–26.

Hossfeld, F. L., and Meyer, I. (1973), *Prophet gegen Prophet. Eine Analyse der alttestamentlichen Texte zum Thema: Wahre und falsche Propheten*, Biblische Beiträge 9 (Schweizerisches Katholisches Bibelwerk).

Hubmann, F. D. (1978), *Untersuchungen zu den Konfessionen: Jer. 11, 18–12, 6 und Jer. 15, 10–21*, FB 30 (Würzburg: Echter).

Hyatt, J. P. (1958), *Jeremiah: Prophet of Courage and Hope* (New York: Abingdon).

—— (1984), 'Jeremiah and Deuteronomy', in L. G. Perdue and B. W. Kovacs (eds.), *A Prophet to the Nations: Essays in Jeremiah Studies* (Winona Lake: Eisenbrauns), 113–27.

Isabell, C. D., and Jackson, M. (1980), 'Rhetorical Criticism and Jeremiah VII 1–VIII 3', *VT* 30: 20–6.

Ittmann, N. (1981), *Die Konfessionen Jeremia: Ihre Bedeutung für die Verkündigung des Propheten*, WMANT 54 (Neukirchen-Vluyn: Neukirchener Verlag).

Janzen, J. G. (1973), *Studies in the Text of Jeremiah*, HSM 6 (Cambridge, Mass.: Harvard University Press).

Jones, D. R. (1992), *Jeremiah*, NCB (Grand Rapids, Mich.: Eerdmans).

Keown, G. L., Scalise, P. J., and Smothers, T. G. (1995), *Jeremiah 26–52*, WBC 27 (Dallas: Word).

Kessler, M. (1968), 'Jeremiah Chapters 26–45 Reconsidered', *JNES* 27: 81–8.

—— (1997), 'Jeremiah XXV 1–29: Text and Context, a Synchronic Study', *ZAW* 109: 44–70.

Klein, R. W. (1979), *Israel in Exile: A Theological Interpretation*, OBT (Philadelphia: Fortress).

Kremers, H. (1953), 'Leidensgemeinschaft mit Gott im Alten Testament', *EvT* 13: 122–40.

Lindars, B. (1979), 'Rachel Weeping For Her Children: Jeremiah 31:15–22', *JSOT* 12: 47–62.

Liwak, R. (1987), *Der Prophet und die Geschichte: Eine literar-historische Untersuchung zum Jeremiabuch* (Stuttgart: Kohlhammer).

Lohfink, N. (1981), 'Der junge Jeremia als Propagandist und Poet: Zum Grundstock von Jer 30–31', in P. M. Bogaert (ed.), *Le Livre de Jérémie: Le Prophète et son milieu, les oracles et leur transmission* (Leuven: Leuven University Press), 351–68.

Lundbom, J. R. (1995), 'Jeremiah 15, 15–21 and the Call of Jeremiah,' *SJOT* 9: 43–55.

Margaliot, M. (1980), 'Jeremiah X 1–16: A Re-examination', *VT* 30: 295–308.

McConville, J. G. (1993), *Judgement and Promise: An Interpretation of the Book of Jeremiah* (Leicester: Apollos).

McFague, S. (1988), *Metaphorical Theology: Models of God in Religious Language* (Philadelphia: Fortress).

McKane, W. (1980), 'משׁה in Jeremiah 23:33–40', in J. A. Emerton (ed.), *Prophecy: Essays Presented to Georg Fohrer* (Berlin: de Gruyter), 35–54.

—— (1981), 'Relations between Poetry and Prose in the Book of Jeremiah with Special Reference to Jeremiah iii. 6–11 and xii. 14–17', *SVT* 32: 220–37.

—— (1986; 1989), *Jeremiah*, ICC (2 vols.; Edinburgh: T. & T. Clark).

Meyer, I. (1977), *Jeremia und die falschen Prophete* (Göttingen: Vandenhoeck & Ruprecht).

Miller, P. D. (1984), 'Sin and Judgment in Jeremiah 34:17–19', *JBL* 103: 611–23.

Mowinckel, S. (1914), *Zur Komposition des Buches Jeremia* (Kristiana: Dybwad).

Newsome, J. D. (1984), *The Hebrew Prophets* (Atlanta: John Knox).

Nicholson, E. W. (1970), *Preaching to the Exiles: A Study of the Prose Tradition in the Book of Jeremiah* (Oxford: Blackwell).

—— (1973), *Jeremiah 1–25*, CBC (London: Cambridge University Press).

—— (1975), *Jeremiah 26–52*, CBC (London: Cambridge University Press).

O'Connor, K. M. (1988), *The Confessions of Jeremiah: Their Interpretation and Role in Chapters 1–25*, SBLDS 94 (Atlanta: Scholars Press).

—— (1989), 'Do Not Trim a Word: The Contributions of Chapter 26 to the Book of Jeremiah', *CBQ*: 617–30.

O'Connor, K. M. (1992), 'Jeremiah', in Carol A. Newsom and Sharon H. Ringe (eds.), *The Women's Bible Commentary* (Louisville, Ky.: Westminster/John Knox), 169–77.

Odashima, V. T. (1989), *Heilsworte im Jeremiabuch: Untersuchungen zu ihrer vordeuteronomistischen Bearbeitung* (Stuttgart: Kohlhammer).

Ollenburger, B. C. (1987), *Zion the City of the Great King: A Theological Symbol of the Jerusalem Cult*, JSOTSup 41 (Sheffield: JSOT).

Osswald, E. (1962), *Falsche Prophetie im Alten Testament* (Tübingen: Mohr).

Overholt, T. W. (1970), *The Threat of Falsehood* (Naperville, Ill.: Allenson).

—— (1979), 'Jeremiah 2 and the Problem of "Audience Reaction"', *CBQ* 41: 262–73.

—— (1988), 'Jeremiah', *HBC* (San Francisco: Harper & Row), 597–645.

—— (1989), *Channels of Prophecy: The Social Dynamics of Prophetic Activity* (Minneapolis: Fortress).

Perdue, L. G. (1984), 'Jeremiah in Modern Research: Approaches and Issues', in Perdue and Kovacs (1984).

—— (1994), *The Collapse of History: Reconstructing Old Testament Theology*, OBT (Minneapolis: Fortress).

—— and Kovacs, B. W. (1984) (eds.), *A Prophet to the Nations: Essays in Jeremiah Studies* (Winona Lake, Ind.: Eisenbrauns).

Pohlmann, K. (1978), *Studien zum Jeremiabuch: Ein Beitrag zur Frage nach Entstehung des Jeremiabuches*, FRLANT 118 (Göttingen: Vandenhoeck & Ruprecht).

—— (1989), *Die ferne Gottes—Studien zum Jeremiabuch: Beiträge zu den 'Konfessionen' im Jeremiabuch und ein Versuch zur Frage nach den Anfängen der Jeremiatradition*, BZAW 179 (Berlin: de Gruyter).

Polk, T. (1984), *The Prophetic Persona: Jeremiah and the Language of the Self*, JSOTSup 32 (Sheffield: JSOT).

Rad, G. von (1936), 'Die Konfessionen Jeremia', *Erth* 3: 265–76 (1965), *Old Testament Theology* (New York: Harper & Row), ii.

—— (1984), 'The Confessions of Jeremiah', in Perdue and Kovacs (1984: 339–48). German original, 1962.

Raitt, T. M. (1977), *A Theology of Exile* (Philadelphia: Fortress).

Reimer, D. J. (1989), 'The "Foe" and the "North" in Jeremiah', *ZAW* 101/2: 223–32.

—— (1993), *The Oracles Against Babylon, Jeremiah 50–51: A Horror Among the Nations* (San Francisco: Mellen Research University Press).

Reitzschel, C. (1966), *Das Problem der Urrolle: Ein Beitrag zur Redaktionsgeschichte des Jeremiabuches* (Gütersloh: Mohn).

Reventlow, H. G. (1963), *Liturgie und prophetisches Ich bei Jeremia* (Gütersloh: Mohn).

Ricoeur, P. (1975), *The Rule of Metaphor: Multidisciplinary Studies of the Creation of Meaning in Language* (Toronto: University of Toronto Press).

Roberts, J. J. M. (1992), 'The Motif of the Weeping God in Jeremiah and Its Background in the Lament Tradition of the Ancient Near East', *Old Testament Essays*, 5: 361–74.

Rudolph, W. (1947), *Jeremia* (Tübingen: Mohr[Siebeck]).

Seitz, C. R. (1985), 'The Crisis of Interpretation over the Meaning and Purpose of Exile: A Redactional Study of Jeremiah xxi–xlii', *VT* 35: 78–97.

—— (1989a), 'The Prophet Moses and the Canonical Shape of Jeremiah', *ZAW* 101: 3–27.

—— (1989b), *Theology and Conflict: Reactions to the Exile in the Book of Jeremiah*, BZAW 176 (Berlin: de Gruyter).

Seybold, K. (1993), *Der Prophet Jeremia: Leben und Werk*, Urban-Taschenbucher, 416 (Stuttgart: Kohlhammer).

Skinner, J. (1922), *Prophecy and Religion, Studies in the Life of Jeremiah* (Cambridge: Cambridge University Press).

Smith, M. S. (1990), *The Laments of Jeremiah and Their Contexts: A Literary and Redactional Study of Jeremiah 11–20*, SBLMS 42 (Atlanta: Scholars Press).

Soderlund, S. (1985), *The Greek Text of Jeremiah: A Revised Hypothesis*, JSOTSup 47 (Sheffield: JSOT).

Song, C. S. (1981), *The Tears of Lady Meng: A Parable of People's Political Theology*, Risk, 11 (Geneva: WCC).

Stulman, L. (1986), *The Prose Sermons of the Book of Jeremiah: A Redescription of the Correspondences with Deuteronomistic Literature in the Light of Recent Text-Critical Research*, SBLDS 83 (Atlanta: Scholars Press).

—— (1995), 'Insiders and Outsiders in the Book of Jeremiah: Shifts in Symbolic Arrangement', *JSOT* 66: 65–85.

Suleiman, S. R., and Crosman, I. (1980) (eds.), *The Reader in the Text: Essays on Audience and Interpretation* (Princeton: Princeton University Press).

Taylor, M. A. (1987), 'Jeremiah 45: The Problem of Placement', *JSOT* 37: 79–98.

Thiel, W. (1973), *Die deuteronomistische Redaktion von Jeremia 1–25*, WMANT 41 (Neukirchen-Vluyn: Neukirchener Verlag).

—— (1982), *Die deuteronomistische Redaktion von Jeremia 26–45*, WMANT 52 (Neukirchen-Vluyn: Neukirchener Verlag).

Thompson, J. A. (1980), *The Book of Jeremiah*, NICOT (Grand Rapids, Mich.: Eerdmans).

Tov, E. (1976), *The Septuagint Translation of Jeremiah and Baruch: A Discussion of an Early Revision of the LXX of Jeremiah 29–52 and Baruch 1:1–3:8*, HSM 8 (Missoula, Mont.: Scholars Press).

Trible, P. (1978), *God and the Rhetoric of Sexuality*, OBT (Philadelphia: Fortress).

Wanke, G. (1971), *Untersuchungen zur sogenannten Baruchschrift*, BZAW 122 (Berlin: de Gruyter).

Washington, H., and Gordon, P. (1995), 'Rape as a Military Metaphor in the Hebrew Bible', in A. Brenner (ed.), *A Feminist Companion to the Latter Prophets*, Feminist Companion to the Bible, 8 (Sheffield: Sheffield Academic Press), 308–25.

Weems, R. J. (1995), *Battered Love: Marriage, Sex, and Violence in the Hebrew Prophets* (Minneapolis: Fortress).

Weippert, H. (1973), *Die Prosareden des Jeremiabuches*, BZAW 132 (Berlin: de Gruyter).

Weiser, A. (1960), *Das Buch Jeremia*, ATD 20/21 (Göttingen: Vandenhoeck & Ruprecht).

Wilson, R. R. (1989), 'Jeremiah', in Bernhard W. Anderson (ed.), *Books of the Bible* (New York: Charles Scribner's Sons), i. 281–302.

24. Lamentations

P. M. JOYCE

INTRODUCTION

A. Subject-Matter and Literary Genre. The English title of the book, Lamentations, sums up very well its subject-matter. As is commonly the case, the Hebrew title is taken from its first word, *'ēkâ*, meaning 'how!' The book consists of a series of complaints about a disaster, which has struck the city of Jerusalem and her people. It comprises five poetic laments, in style similar to many in the psalter. The *qînâ* or lament metre (classically three beats followed by two) characterizes much of the poetry of the book, and is best seen in ch. 3 (Shea 1979). Four of the five chapters are acrostic poems; acrostics typically begin each verse with a different letter of the alphabet, in sequence (Freedman 1986). Some have thought that this elaborate literary form reflects a long development and prolonged polishing (cf. Kaiser 1992). However, it is more likely that this feature is evidence of the drive to establish order in a time of traumatic loss, and so is quite compatible with composition during the immediate aftermath of a great catastrophe.

B. Authorship, Date, and Place of Composition. 1. The work is traditionally ascribed to the prophet Jeremiah (cf. 2 Chr 35:25, and affinities with the so-called 'Confessions of Jeremiah'). We read in the Babylonian Talmud (*B. Bat.* 14b–15a) that 'Jeremiah wrote the book which bears his name, the book of Kings and Lamentations'. This view is rarely defended today, since the style and thought are somewhat different from the book of Jeremiah. Nevertheless, the consensus view remains that the work takes its starting-point from the fall of Jerusalem to the Babylonians in 587 BCE. A minority of scholars have looked to the Maccabean period (e.g. Treves 1963), whilst Morgenstern (1956, 1957, 1960) proposed a date of 485 BCE. More recently, Provan has adopted an agnostic view with regard to dating (Provan 1991a: 7–19; cf. S. J. D. Cohen 1982).

2. The work was probably written in Jerusalem during the months and years immediately following the destruction of the temple in 587. There is evidence that people gathered to mourn on the site of the ruined temple during this period (Jer 41:5; cf. Jones 1963; Ackroyd 1968: 26, 47); it is likely that the work was shaped by liturgical use in such a setting (cf. Zech 7:2–5; Joel 2:15–17).

C. Theological Themes. 1. It is clear that the work expresses many questions about the recent disaster and its meaning. There have been various attempts to present the religious teaching of the book in a systematic way. The most influential have been those of N. K. Gottwald and B. Albrektson. Gottwald (1962) proposed that the theological key to the work is provided by Deuteronomistic theology, which presented a 'just deserts' pattern; he argued that the problem in Lamentations is that the disaster, coming so soon after the reforms of the ideal king, Josiah, is perceived as undeserved (cf. 2:20; 5:7). Albrektson (1963), on the other hand, interpreted the book in the light of the old belief in the inviolability of the city of Jerusalem, a belief apparently falsified by the present disaster (cf. 2:15; 4:12). He found this dilemma resolved in the Deuteronomistic view of the catastrophe as a divine judgement (cf. Deut 28:64–5). Both Gottwald and Albrektson gave a clear place to hope in their overall interpretations, and Gerstenberger (1971) argued that the complaint (in contrast to the lament of resignation) is in fact an act of hope. However, it must be recognized that the place of hope is at best ambiguous and fleeting (the clearest cases are found in 3:19–39 and 4:22).

2. The inconsistencies of theme prompt the question as to whether the book will indeed yield a coherent overall message. This (together with inconsistencies of form, especially in chs. 3 and 5) has led some, such as Brandscheidt (1988), to assert that the book is composite. Joyce (1993) has argued that the book's lack of theological consistency is not surprising, drawing upon the insights of pastoral psychology to show that such lack of coherence is typical of human reaction to the perennial experience of radical loss.

D. Text. The received Hebrew text (MT) of Lamentations is relatively well preserved and raises fewer problems than much OT poetry (examples are found in 1:14; 3:22; 5:5). The evidence of the ancient versions, such as the Greek LXX, is rarely very helpful, since for the most part they seem to reflect a Hebrew text close to the MT. The Dead Sea scrolls have yielded a range of remains from Lamentations (Fitzmyer 1990: 232), of which the most important is 4QLam^a (Hillers 1992: 41–8). For detailed discussion of the text of Lamentations, see especially Albrektson (1963) and Gottlieb (1978).

E. Scriptural Status. This has never been a matter of dispute. This short work is found with four others (Ecclesiastes, Song of Songs, Ruth, and Esther) comprising the Megillot ('little scrolls'), which occur among the Writings of the HB. In the order found in the English Bibles used by Christians (deriving from LXX, which was followed by the Latin Vulgate), the book is placed among the Prophets, after Jeremiah, in recognition of its traditional association with him. That supposed link may well have played its part in securing scriptural status. The primary factor, however, appears to have been its liturgical use, particularly in the annual commemoration of the fall of the first temple, on the 9th day of Ab, in the late summer. The profound impact of the fall of the second temple to the Romans in 70 CE would have consolidated the book's place in a period when the process towards closure of a scriptural canon was under way in Judaism. Mintz (1984) has explored the ongoing role of the book in the long story of Jewish response to catastrophe, and this is mirrored in the important role played by the book in Christian liturgy down the centuries.

F. Ancient Near-Eastern Parallels. However important the immediate crisis for shaping the biblical book, it is profoundly conditioned also by existing oral and literary convention, not only within Israel itself but also in the wider ancient Near-Eastern world. Particularly important are comparative materials from Mesopotamia (Pritchard 1969: 455–63, 611–19; M. E. Cohen 1988). Assessments range from McDaniel (1968), who plays down the alleged Sumerian influence, to Gwaltney (1983), who argues that returning exiles brought back and applied Mesopotamian models.

COMMENTARY

(1:1–11a) A Dirge over the Ruined City We are immediately introduced to the city, Zion, the major focus of the book. The Hebrew word for 'city' is feminine, and this encourages the use of female personification—though the language of humiliation (as in v. 8) raises pressing ethical questions for some readers (O'Connor 1992). The city is often presented as the wife of YHWH in the OT (cf. Galambush 1992), and the motif of the 'widowed city' (v. 1) is found outside Israel too (C. Cohen 1973); it is not unreasonable to understand Zion here as bereaved of YHWH himself. 'Daughter Zion' (v. 6) is a key phrase in the book, as also in Isaiah (e.g. 1:8; 52:2; cf. Sawyer 1989). The Hebrew has 'daughter *of* Zion' (as in RSV), but the NRSV's 'daughter Zion' captures well the sense, namely the city personified. The formula is used also of Jerusalem and Judah, sometimes designated as 'virgin' (e.g. 1:15; 2:13).

As is commonplace in such dirges (cf. Isa 1:21–3), v. 1 contains several contrasts between a former positive situation ('full', 'great', 'princess') and the present negative one ('lonely', 'widow', 'vassal'), and in this it sets a pattern for the whole book. The language of grief pervades the work, vv. 2 and 16 providing notable examples. That Zion 'has no one to comfort her' (v. 2) is a recurrent theme (cf. vv. 16, 17, 21). Reference to Zion's deceptive lovers (vv. 2, 19) probably stands, as often, for false political allies (cf. 4:17). The chapter features two related motifs: 'The foe looked on mocking' (v. 7; cf. v. 21; the historical circumstances described in 2 Kings 24:2 may be in mind); and 'all you who pass by' (v. 12; cf. 2:15, where passers-by mock).

v. 3 provides the first mention of exile. Some have noted that explicit reference to the actual destruction of the temple (in 587) seems to be lacking in this chapter; indeed Rudolph argued that ch. 1 was written shortly after the first capture of Jerusalem in 597 (Rudolph 1962: 209–11). Provan (1990) contends that the precise historical background to ch. 1 is unclear, but that this is not crucial for its theological interpretation. The references to festivals and priests (v. 4) highlight the cultic concern which will mark the whole book. As we learn in v. 10, the nations have invaded the sanctuary (the theme is similar to Psalms such as 74 and 79). 'Her priests groan; her young girls grieve' (v. 4): the emphasis here is on the reaction to events; RSV's 'her maidens have been dragged away' unnecessarily follows LXX, presupposing a different Hebrew verb. v. 5 provides the first of many theological explanations of the disaster. In the course of the book as a whole some inconsistent accounts are given, but in ch. 1 it is made clear that YHWH is in charge (vv. 12, 14) and that he has acted on account of Judah's sin (vv. 8, 18). v. 9b introduces the first use of the first person. In this it anticipates the section which begins at v. 11b, and for this reason NRSV presents these words as a quotation. However, such movement from one grammatical person to another, found throughout the book, is not at all unusual in Hebrew poetry. Lanahan (1974) reflects imaginatively on the 'voices' that speak at various points in the book.

(1:11b–22) A Lament Uttered by Zion With 11b, there begins a passage consistently in the first person (through to the end of the chapter, with the exception of v. 17). 'Is it nothing to you?' (v. 12): the Hebrew has merely 'not to you'. It is perhaps preferable to take this as an assertion, 'This is none of your business', part of Zion's inconsistent emotional reaction to her tragedy. The end of v. 12 echoes 'day of the LORD' language, as does v. 15 (cf. 2:1, 21, 22); in the present circumstances, it is clear that the day of the Lord means bad news for Israel (cf. Am 5:18). In a bloody image, 'The Lord has trodden as in a wine press the virgin daughter Judah' (v. 15; cf. Isa 63:1–6). 'My transgressions were bound into a yoke' (v. 14): the Hebrew word translated 'were bound' here is found nowhere else in the OT, but the context (esp. the following words) seems to demand some such sense. It is unnecessary to follow those, ancient and modern, who have suggested significant alternatives, e.g. LXX, 'watch was kept over my sins'. The chapter ends with a call for vengeance upon Zion's enemies; it is noteworthy that the same theme is found at the end of chs. 3 and 4. 'Bring on the day' (v. 21): the Hebrew actually has 'You

have brought on the day', which makes perfect sense as a reference to Zion's fate, before the appeal that the same should befall her enemies is introduced in the following clause, 'let them be as I am'.

(2:1–22) The chapter begins with the exclamation 'How!', as do chs. 1 and 4, and takes the form of another dirge over the ruined city. The divine anger is a recurrent theme, found here in vv. 1–4, as is the statement that YHWH acts 'without mercy' (cf. vv. 17, 21). He has 'humiliated' daughter Zion: the Hebrew verb is found only here in the OT and its meaning is uncertain; the main alternative interpretation is represented by the RSV's 'set under a cloud'. His 'footstool' is the Jerusalem temple (cf. Ps 99:5); 'he has broken down his booth like a garden' (cf. Isa 1:8) and 'has destroyed his tabernacle' (v. 6): a truly shocking claim! In other ways too expectations are overturned. In v. 3 'he has withdrawn his right hand from them', the hand of protection in this case, whilst in v. 4 he has 'his right hand set like a foe' against Israel, in an apparent inversion of the holy war tradition. In v. 7 festal acclamations are turned into the shouts of war within the temple itself (cf. v. 22).

In vv. 7–9, the physical features of the city are listed; rampart and wall 'languish together', a strange image perhaps, but not so unusual for the poetry of the OT! YHWH has stretched the measuring line in judgement (v. 8; cf. Job 38:5; Am 7:7–9). All sources of authority are removed: kings, princes, prophets, elders (vv. 9–10); 'guidance is no more', that is, the teaching given by the priests (as in Jer 18:18; Mal 2:5–8). v. 10 illustrates Judean mourning rites (cf. Bloch-Smith 1992), whilst vv. 11–12 highlight another central issue of the book, hunger (1:11, 19; 4:4–5, 9–10; cf. 2 Kings 25:3). Wine is mentioned in v. 12 because water would have been too polluted to drink. The famine theme culminates in the grim reality of cannibalism, here in v. 20 and at 4:10 (cf. 2 Kings 6:28–9).

'What can I say for you, to what compare you?': these moving words of v. 13 recall the comparison in 1:12, but the voice is different here, possibly even that of mocking irony, for the question 'who can heal you?' implies of course the answer 'no one' (cf. Isa 1:5–6). Certainly the prophets cannot help; as in v. 9, so now in v. 14 they are the butt of stern criticism (cf. Ezek 13:1–16; Jer 23:9–32). We should not worry about whether Jeremiah himself has been overlooked, even if he was a contemporary of the poet, for these words are the stuff of rhetorical hyperbole. Mockers 'clap their hands' (v. 15): in ancient Israel, this was a sign of derision; they 'hiss and wag their heads' (cf. Ps 69:9–12, 19–21). 'Is this the city that was called the perfection of beauty?': a poignant question indeed; we are reminded of Zion Psalms such as 46 and 48. 'The LORD has done what he purposed' (v. 17): he is indeed responsible for the catastrophe, which 'he ordained long ago' (cf. Deut 28:64–5; 1 Kings 9:6–9).

'Cry aloud' (v. 18): this is an emendation followed by many modern translations and commentators; the Hebrew actually has 'Their heart cried'. v. 19 introduces the language of prayer, even repentance; and in this anticipates themes of ch. 3. And yet in v. 20 even God is rebuked, anger towards God being one of the many inconsistent reactions to events in this book. 'Should priest and prophet be killed in the sanctuary of the Lord?': a terrible fate, but 4:13 implies that they deserve to be!

The chapter culminates in v. 22 with reference to an invitation to the enemies to come and slaughter the Judaeans (the language shares something with Ezek 38), a judgement so total that 'no one escaped or survived' (cf. Am 5:19).

(3:1–66)

This is the most elaborate chapter in the book, and the most important. One way in which this is signalled is in the intensification of the acrostic form, with three verses to each letter of the Hebrew alphabet. This chapter is characterized by the frequent use of the first person singular voice. It is a unit, but may be read in four parts.

(3:1–18) An Individual Lament This section has many similarities to Ps 56. There is little specific reference to the fall of Jerusalem or the sufferings which followed. It opens with the puzzling words 'I am one who has seen affliction': NRSV here masks the decidedly masculine Hebrew word *geber*, 'man', and indeed also a definite article (RSV: 'I am the man'). The identity of the speaker here is much disputed. Is the 'I' who speaks a collective personality who represents the people as a whole (similar to Zion in chs. 1–2) or an individual? And if an individual is intended, who is it? Suggestions have included Jeremiah, Jehoiachin, the poet himself, or an anonymous typical sufferer (Hillers 1992: 120–3). There are parallels here with the debate over the identity of the 'servant' in Isa 40–55; and, as in that case, it may be wrong to seek one consistent identity (see the rhetorical reading in Mintz 1984: 32–3). A grim picture is painted of the man's suffering, with many parallels with Job (e.g. v. 4, 'He has made my flesh and my skin waste away'; cf. Job 7:5; 30:30). He sinks to a despairing low point (v. 17). All hope has gone: 'Gone is my glory, and all that I had hoped for (RSV: "my expectation") from the LORD' (v. 18).

(3:19–39) A Glimmer of Hope It is interesting that it is in the middle sections of the middle chapter of this book that the most positive material is to be found. Many have puzzled over the lack of closure at the end of the book and over the ambiguous place of hope. Johnson (1985) argued that here in the middle of ch. 3 we have the keystone to the work, the section which provides the positive answer to the theological questions it raises. v. 21 is where the positive note is first struck, but vv. 19–20 serve as an introduction (and indeed the *zayin* section of the acrostic begins at v. 19). In affirming hope, v. 21 (like v. 24) uses the same Hebrew root as was used in the denial of hope in v. 18. 'This I call to mind' (v. 21): 'this' refers to the grounds for hope to be detailed in vv. 22–4. The text of v. 22 is disputed: NRSV has it that the steadfast love of the Lord 'never ceases', following the Syriac and the Aramaic Targum (and a single Heb. MS). But the Hebrew MT actually has 'we are not cut off' (rather than '[it] never ceases'); this does yield tolerable sense, for it can be understood as a celebration of survival in spite of all. 'The LORD is good to those who wait for him' . . . 'wait quietly for the salvation of the LORD': the idea here in vv. 25–6 is similar to Isa 30:18, which may well itself be exilic (so Clements 1980: 250). 'It is good for one to bear the yoke in youth' (v. 27): 'one' here translates *geber* (man), as in v. 1, to which there may well be an allusion. The 'yoke' refers to suffering; 'to put one's mouth to the dust' (v. 29) was a sign of submission. 'Although he causes grief, he will have compassion according to the abundance of his steadfast

love' (v. 32): as in v. 22, the important Hebrew word *ḥesed*, 'steadfast love', is used. 'For he does not willingly afflict or grieve anyone' (v. 33): 'willingly' here is literally 'from his heart'.

NRSV is right to regard vv. 34–9 as continuing the positive theme, in the voice of the same speaker. The disasters listed in vv. 34–6 are followed by a rhetorical question 'does the Lord not see it?' (v. 36). In contrast, some (such as Rudolph 1962: 240–1) have taken vv. 34–6 as an objection from an interlocutor, culminating in the statement 'the Lord does not see'. A similar issue arises in vv. 37–9: NRSV rightly has three rhetorical questions, rather than the three assertions (denying divine involvement) proposed by Gordis (1974a: 181–3). The first of the questions 'Who can command and have it done, if the Lord has not ordained it?' is strikingly similar to Am 3:6: 'Does disaster befall a city, unless the LORD has done it?' The second, 'Is it not from the mouth of the Most High that good and bad come?', reminiscent of Isa 45:7, raises profound theological questions (cf. Lindström 1983: 214–36). The last question, 'Why should any who draw breath complain about the punishment of their sins?' (v. 39) carries the theme of accepting catastrophe to its conclusion, but, like vv. 25–33, prompts the question whether there is not here the danger of a naïve, even masochistic, denial of the reality of tragedy (a line powerfully pursued by Miller 1991).

(3:40–51) A New Start v. 40 marks a fresh departure: 'Let us test and examine our ways, and return to the LORD'. The 'us' in question must be the nation Israel. For Mintz (1984: 37), this first use in ch. 3 of such a plural 'stunningly enacts the very moment of release from aloneness'. v. 41 introduces a summons to prayer, as in 2:19; the contrast between externals and the 'heart' is a familiar one in the OT, e.g. Joel 2:13. A summary explanation of events is given in v. 42: 'We have transgressed and rebelled, and you have not forgiven'; and then in vv. 43–4 a darker note is again struck, as is typical in this ambiguous book, the words 'you have wrapped yourself with a cloud so that no prayer can pass through' recalling v. 8 (cf. Isa 45:15).

(3:52–66) An Individual Prayer for Vindication There are many features here typical of the laments of the psalter, for example the enemies of vv. 52–3, 60–3, and the appeals of vv. 55 and 64–6. v. 54 reminds one of Jonah's cry from the belly of the fish (cf. Jon 2:3–6). NRSV (like RSV) takes the perfect tenses in vv. 56–61 to refer to the past, recalling blessings received. But Provan (1991b) argues, probably correctly, that the perfects in this passage are better rendered by imperatives in English (known as the 'precative perfect'), e.g. in v. 56, not 'you heard' but 'hear', or again, in v. 60, not 'you have seen' but 'see'. Such plaintive appeals imply a situation very close to that of vv. 1–18 and so, after the lighter interlude provided by the central sections of the chapter, we are brought full circle, as is further indicated by the way v. 59 stands in sharp contrast to v. 39. The chapter ends on a vengeful note (vv. 64–6), echoing again the language of the psalter (e.g. Ps 17:13, 14; 35:26).

(4:1–22)

This dirge over the ruined city begins with the temple treasures, now desecrated, another example of the cultic emphasis of this book. 'The precious children of Zion' are said to be 'worth their weight in fine gold', a lovely statement with human values transcending cultic ones; yet now even these are as earthen pots. Such a contrast (as again in vv. 5, 7–8) reminds us of ch. 1. Compared to the jackals, 'my people has become cruel' (v. 3; cf. Isa 1:3), as exemplified by the cannibalism of v. 10. A grim situation—indeed 'the chastisement of my people has been greater than the punishment of Sodom' (v. 6). The words used here for 'chastisement' and 'punishment' could instead mean 'iniquity' and 'sin', but the context suggests that NRSV is right to take them to refer to the people's tragic state. Sodom is said to have been overthrown in a moment, 'though no hand was laid on it'. The meaning of the Hebrew here is uncertain: the basic idea of the verb is 'turn', but it could be 'turn against', as in NRSV's 'no hand was laid on it' (implying that God acted directly), or 'turn towards', as in the NIV's 'without a hand turned to help her'. A similar problem arises in v. 7: the meaning of the rare Hebrew noun translated '[their] hair' by NRSV is uncertain. The root has to do with cutting: RSV has 'the beauty of their form', based on the idea of a carved object, whereas NRSV envisages the cutting of hair. The latter is the more likely since lapis lazuli (to be preferred to 'sapphire') was used in the art of the ancient Near East to represent hair.

'The kings of the earth did not believe . . . that foe or enemy could enter the gates of Jerusalem' (v. 12; cf. 2:15). The perceptions of the nations are highlighted again in v. 15 (cf. Ps 79:10). According to Albrektson (1963) the fall of the supposedly inviolable city is the central theological problem of the book. vv. 13–16 give a clear explanation of this disaster as the result of Judah's sin, presenting the nation's leaders as moral lepers. As so often in the OT prophets, moral and cultic sins occur side by side: they 'shed the blood of the righteous', they are 'defiled with blood'. v. 17 makes reference to 'watching eagerly for a nation that could not save': ironically 'watching eagerly' is just the kind of attitude one should have towards God himself, according to 3:25–6. Instead, the people have looked vainly to political alliances, as also in 5:6. It is possible that Egypt is in view here (cf. Jer 37:5–10). In spite of all, 'The LORD's anointed, the breath of our life, was taken in their pits' (v. 20; perhaps the capture of Zedekiah by the Babylonians is in mind; cf. 2 Kings 25:4–7). The poignant v. 20b is reminiscent of royal psalms such as Ps 72; judgement upon the monarchy is mentioned also at 2:6, 9 and 5:16.

v. 21 declares: 'Edom . . . to you also the cup shall pass': Edom is often regarded with particular enmity in the OT, especially it seems in relation to the events of 587 (cf. Ps 137:7; Ob 8–14). For the cup of judgement, cf. Isa 51:17–23 (esp. vv. 22–3); Jer 25:15–29. v. 22 announces good news of a kind unparalleled elsewhere in the book: 'The punishment of your iniquity, O daughter Zion, is accomplished, he will keep you in exile no longer' (cf. Isa 40:1–2). The OT elsewhere too features a see-saw motif whereby the fortunes of Israel rise as those of the nations decline (and indeed vice versa), as in Ezek 35–6, which again concerns Edom. As before in Lamentations (cf. 1:22; 3:64), the fate of the enemies is related to their sins and is thus not in any way merely arbitrary.

(5:1–22)

This relatively short chapter is in the form of a communal lament and has affinities with Ps 44, 74, and 79, usually seen as liturgies for times of national calamity. Alone of the five chapters, it is not an acrostic, though its twenty-two verses perhaps echo that form. It is treated by some as separate from the rest of the book (e.g. Lachs 1966–7 assigned it a 2nd-cent. date); but there is no overwhelming reason to regard the chapter as anything but integral to the book.

The poem begins with a classic lament formula, 'Remember, O LORD!', and goes on to paint a sorry picture of the nation's disgrace. This is done in part by reference to the loss of some of the very special gifts of God: 'Our inheritance'—the land granted to Israel in ancient times—'has been turned over to strangers' (v. 2; cf. Num 26:53). One of the great things about living in the promised land was rest from enemies (cf. Deut 12:10), but now 'we are given no rest' (v. 5; cf. 1:3). The NRSV's words 'With a yoke' (v. 5) are supplied from the Greek of Symmachus; the Hebrew in fact lacks them, but yields adequate sense none the less: 'on our necks we are hard driven'. Provan (1991a: 126–7) finds hunting imagery here, the metaphor being one of close pursuit (which has a place in the second half of ch. 4). v. 6 speaks of political alliances (as did 4:17). 'Egypt and Assyria', being to the south and north of Judah respectively (at least in terms of travel routes), represent all nations, rather than referring to a precise historical circumstance. The reason for such pacts is said to be 'to get enough bread', straitened circumstances further indicated in v. 4 ('We must pay for the water we drink; the wood we get must be bought') and v. 9 ('We get our bread at the peril of our lives'). If Lamentations comes, as is probable, from the period immediately after 587, the reference to alliances is likely to be retrospective, alluding to events leading up to the fall of the city.

v. 7 declares: 'Our ancestors sinned; they are no more, and we bear their iniquities.' It would be possible to take the word used here (lit. fathers) to mean leaders rather than ancestors, which would cohere with the blaming of leaders in 4:13–16, but it is more likely that 'ancestors' are indeed meant. Such an idea of suffering for the sins of one's forebears is assumed elsewhere in the OT (e.g. 2 Kings 23:26), but interestingly this is precisely the belief rejected in Ezek 18:1–4, which could well be contemporary with these words. The verse also stands at odds with the acknowledgements of responsibility found elsewhere in Lamentations (e.g. 1:8; 3:42, and, strikingly, v. 16 here). 'Slaves rule over us' (v. 8): important posts were sometimes given to the slaves of kings, but the real point is similar to that in Isa 3:4–7, namely that the proper ordering of society has been destroyed. Further dimensions of the tragedy are spelled out in vv. 15–16: 'The joy of our hearts has ceased' (cf. 3:17–18). 'The crown has fallen from our head': as before, judgement on the monarchy is in view (LAM 4:20), and perhaps also an allusion to the dancer's garland (cf. Isa 28:1), picking up the reference to dancing having 'been turned to mourning'. Zion has been the focus of the book, and as we approach its end v. 18 portrays the once noble city lying desolate, with jackals prowling over it (cf. Mic 3:12; Jer 26:18).

'But you, O LORD, reign forever; your throne endures to all generations' (v. 19): it is hard to know how to take these very affirmative words, coming so close to the downbeat conclusion of the book. Could this be an ironic, even cynical, snatch of quotation from the temple liturgy (cf. Ps 93:1–2; 103:19)? In v. 20, we are straight back to pessimistic questioning, then in v. 21 comes the final appeal, which echoes

Jerusalem's recalling of her former days of glory (1:7): 'Restore us to yourself, O LORD, that we may be restored; renew our days as of old'. The word 'unless', with which NRSV introduces the final verse, conveys perfectly (far better than the 'even though' proposed by Gordis 1974b) the way in which this perplexing book tails away into renewed doubt: 'you have utterly rejected us, and are angry with us beyond measure'. The book ends on anything but a confident note (contrary to Kraus 1968: 91); in fact, such is the bleakness of this conclusion that it is difficult to follow Johnson (1985) in judging even the book as a whole as essentially positive. Rather its greatness is to be found precisely in the honesty with which it articulates the ambiguities of the fate of Zion and indeed of the human condition itself.

REFERENCES

Ackroyd, P. R. (1968), *Exile and Restoration: A Study of Hebrew Thought of the Sixth Century BC* (London: SCM).

Albrektson, B. (1963), *Studies in the Text and Theology of the Book of Lamentations*, Studia Theologica Lundensia, 21 (Lund: Gleerup).

Bloch-Smith, E. (1992), *Judahite Burial Practices and Beliefs about the Dead*, JSOTSup 123, JSOT/ASOR MS 7 (Sheffield: JSOT).

Brandscheidt, R. (1988), *Das Buch der Klagelieder*, Geistliche Schriftlesung, Altes Testament, 10 (Düsseldorf: Patmos).

Clements, R. E. (1980), *Isaiah 1–39*, NCB (London: Marshall, Morgan & Scott).

Cohen, C. (1973), 'The "Widowed" City', *JANESCU* 5: 75–81.

Cohen, M. E. (1988), *The Canonical Lamentations of Ancient Mesopotamia* (2 vols.; Potomac, Md.: Capital Decisions).

Cohen, S. J. D. (1982), 'The Destruction: From Scripture to Midrash', *Prooftexts: A Journal of Jewish Liturgy*, 2: 18–39.

Fitzmyer, J. A. (1990), rev. edn., *The Dead Sea Scrolls: Major Publications and Tools for Study*, SBLRBS 20 (Atlanta, Ga.: Scholars Press).

Freedman, D. N. (1986), 'Acrostic Poems in the Hebrew Bible, Alphabetic and Otherwise', *CBQ* 48: 408–31.

Galambush, J. (1992), *Jerusalem in the Book of Ezekiel: The City as Yahweh's Wife*, SBLDS 130 (Atlanta, Ga.: Scholars Press).

Gerstenberger, E. (1971), 'Der klagende Mensch', in H. W. Wolff (ed.), *Probleme biblischer Theologie* (Munich: Chr. Kaiser), 64–72.

Gordis, R. (1974a), 3rd edn., *The Song of Songs and Lamentations* (New York: Ktav).

—— (1974b), 'The Conclusion of the Book of Lamentations (5.22)', *JBL* 93: 289–93.

Gottlieb, H. (1978), *A Study on the Text of Lamentations*, Acta Jutlandica, Theology Series, 48/12 (Aarhus: Det lærde Selskab).

Gottwald, N. K. (1962), 2nd edn., *Studies in the Book of Lamentations*, SBT 14 (London: SCM).

Gwaltney, W. C., Jnr. (1983), 'The Biblical Book of Lamentations in the Context of Near Eastern Lament Literature', in W. W. Hallo, J. C. Moyer, and L. G. Perdue (eds.), *Scripture in Context*, ii. *More*

Essays on the Comparative Method (Winona Lake, Ind.: Eisenbrauns), 191–211.

Hillers, D. R. (1992), 2nd edn., *Lamentations*, AB 7A (Garden City, NY: Doubleday).

Johnson, B. (1985), 'Form and Message in Lamentations', *ZAW* 97: 58–73.

Jones, D. R. (1963), 'The Cessation of Sacrifice after the Destruction of the Temple in 586 B.C.', *JTS* NS 14/1: 12–31.

Joyce, P. M. (1993), 'Lamentations and the Grief Process: A Psychological Reading', in *Biblical Interpretation: A Journal of Contemporary Approaches*, 1/3: 304–20.

Kaiser, O. (1992), 4th edn., 'Klagelieder', in H.-P. Müller *et al.*, *Das Hohelied, Klagelieder, Das Buch Ester*, ATD 16/2 (Göttingen: Vandenhoeck & Ruprecht), 91–198.

Kraus, H.-J. (1968), 3rd edn., *Klagelieder (Threni)*, BKAT 20 (Neukirchen-Vluyn: Neukirchener Verlag).

Lachs, S. T. (1966–7), 'The Date of Lamentations V', *JQR* NS 57 (1966–7): 46–56.

Lanahan, W. F. (1974), 'The Speaking Voice in the Book of Lamentations', *JBL* 93: 41–9.

Lindström, F. (1983), *God and the Origin of Evil: A Contextual Analysis of Alleged Monistic Evidence in the Old Testament*, ConBOT 21 (Lund: Gleerup).

McDaniel, T. F. (1968), 'The Alleged Sumerian Influence upon Lamentations', *VT* 18: 198–209.

Miller, A. (1991), 'The Mistreated Child in the Lamentations of Jeremiah', *Breaking Down the Wall of Silence to Join the Waiting Child* (London: Virago), 114–26.

Mintz, A. (1984), *Hurban: Responses to Catastrophe in Hebrew Literature* (New York: Columbia University Press).

Morgenstern, J. (1956), 'Jerusalem—485 B.C.', *HUCA* 27: 101–79; (1957), 28: 15–47; (1960), 31: 1–29.

O'Connor, K. M. (1992), 'Lamentations', in C. A. Newsom and S. H. Ringe (eds.), *The Women's Bible Commentary* (Louisville, Ky.: Westminster/John Knox), 178–82.

Pritchard, J. B. (ed.) (1969), 3rd edn. with suppl., *ANET* (Princeton: Princeton University Press), 'Lamentation over the Destruction of Ur', 455–63; 'Lamentation over the Destruction of Sumer and Ur', 611–19, both tr. S. N. Kramer).

Provan, I. W. (1990), 'Reading Texts against an Historical Background: The Case of Lamentations 1', in *Scandinavian Journal of the Old Testament* 1: 130–43.

—— (1991a), *Lamentations*, NCB (London: Marshall Pickering).

—— (1991b), 'Past, Present and Future in Lamentations iii 52–66: The Case for a Precative Perfect Re-examined', *VT* 41/2: 164–75.

Rudolph, W. (1962), 2nd edn., *Das Buch Ruth—Das Hohe Lied—Die Klagelieder*, KAT 17 (Gütersloh: Mohn).

Sawyer, J. F. A. (1989), 'Daughter of Zion and Servant of the Lord in Isaiah: A Comparison', *JSOT* 44: 89–107.

Shea, W. H. (1979), 'The *qinah* Structure of the Book of Lamentations', *Bib.* 60: 103–7.

Treves, M. (1963), 'Conjectures sur les dates et les sujets des Lamentations', *Bulletin Renan*, 95: 1–4.

25. Ezekiel   J. GALAMBUSH

INTRODUCTION

A. Composition and Style. 1. Commonly considered the most difficult of the major prophets, Ezekiel's perceived obscurity actually reflects a tantalizing combination of obscurity and clarity. The book combines precise dating and clear, logical structure with bizarre imagery, opaque historical references, abrupt changes in subject-matter and literary style, and numerous grammatical and textual difficulties. Anchored in a specific historical context and well-documented events, but presented via a series of weird visions and grotesque metaphors, the book is above all, tantalizing. Whereas a reader might easily despair of comprehending every reference in Hosea or Jeremiah, Ezekiel continually holds out the elusive potential for order and precision.

2. As early as the first century CE, Ezekiel's structure impressed the historian Josephus, who commented that the prophet had left behind 'two books', probably the oracles of chs. 1–39 and the temple vision of 40–8. Ezekiel's structure and composition have continued to be debated by commentators up to the present day. Recurring themes and key words and a readily apparent overall structure give the work a striking appearance of unity (see Greenberg 1983). At the same time repetitions, the use of a broad range of genres and literary styles, and seeming anachronisms have raised the question of whether the book's apparent unity is simply the work of an especially talented redactor of earlier fragments or even of a succession of such redactors (see esp. Zimmerli 1979).

3. Writing in 1924, Gustav Hölscher concluded that only 144 of the book's 1,273 verses (all of them poetry) were attributable to the ecstatic prophet Ezekiel, while the rest of the book derived from a tedious and legalistic post-exilic priest. Such radical minimalism represented the form-critical conventions that (1) all prophecy was originally oral; (2) the original oracles consisted of brief, formulaic utterances; and (3) a change in genre could generally be taken to indicate a change in author. In addition, anti-Jewish sentiment tended to idealize the Israelite prophets while decrying the 'decline' represented by early Judaism. Brief, poetic oracles were considered 'authentic' prophetic utterances, and thus superior to legal or didactic material, all of which was considered late and spurious. As academic assumptions changed over the course of the twentieth century, particularly the rejection of strict form-critical categories and heightened awareness of literary techniques, scholarly assessment of Ezekiel underwent a marked change, so that in 1983 Greenberg could create what he called a 'holistic' reading of the prophet and Davis (1989) explore Ezekiel as the first writing prophet. At the beginning of the twenty-first scholars, focusing on the book's complex and interlocking literary patterns, tend to attribute as much as possible to the original prophet. While additions are acknowledged (all of chs. 40–8 are frequently considered an addition), the book's substantial unity is widely accepted. Agreement on Ezekiel's unity, however, does not settle the question of authorship. Relative literary unity may indicate that the book derives substantially from the sixth-century prophet Ezekiel or that the work is largely the achievement of a later redactor so thoroughgoing as virtually to have authored the book.

4. Ezekiel displays a wide range of literary styles, from the intense disjointedness of Ezekiel's first vision (chs. 1–3) to the systematic dryness of his last (chs. 40–8). Perhaps its most striking literary feature, however, is its use of symbolic language. In addition to visions comprising approximately a third of the book, Ezekiel employs vivid extended metaphors to bring his charges against Judah and its neighbours. The metaphors are chiefly ironic, playing on and subverting commonly used symbols of national pride and identity (see EZEK 15:1–8). Thus, the lion of Judah becomes a rabid man-eater; Judah the luxuriant vine a dried-up twig; Jerusalem the faithful bride a perverse prostitute; and Tyre the merchant ship a foundering wreck. Throughout Ezekiel a strong visual sensibility predominates. Ezekiel sees visions that in turn contain seeing eyes and old men gazing at pictures, while he himself is instructed to observe carefully all that he sees. The extended metaphors are graphically intense, with the depictions of Jerusalem (exposing herself to all passers-by) and her lovers bordering on the pornographic. The emphasis on seeing builds on Ezekiel's role as witness to Judah's depravity and to YHWH's acts of self-vindication, and enlists the reader as witness alongside the prophet.

B. Historical Background. 1. Ezekiel is set in Babylon, beginning in the fifth year of Judah's Babylonian exile (593 BCE). Ezekiel was apparently brought to Babylon with the first group of exiles following Nebuchadrezzar's 597 BCE capture of Jerusalem. Zedekiah, the monarch chosen in 597 by Nebuchadrezzar to replace the rebellious and now exiled Jehoiachin, remained loyal to Babylon for only a few years, and in 594 BCE hosted an international meeting of regional leaders in Jerusalem, apparently to plan rebellion against Babylon. In 593 BCE Zedekiah was summoned by Nebuchadrezzar to Babylon, presumably to account for his actions and to renew his loyalty oath. Zedekiah's planned rebellion and subsequent reprimand by Nebuchadrezzar may have formed the occasion for Ezekiel's inaugural vision and call to speak against the 'rebellious nation' of Israel (2:3). Ezekiel considered Zedekiah's oath of loyalty to Babylon binding. According to 2 Chr 36:13, the oath had been sworn in the name of God (YHWH), and thus its abrogation violated YHWH's honour and constituted rebellion against YHWH.

2. Zedekiah seems to have continued to court illicit alliances, and in 592 BCE the Egyptian Pharaoh Psammeticus II (595–589 BCE) toured Palestine in a show of military power, clearly violating the Judean–Babylonian covenant. In addition to violating Zedekiah's covenant with Nebuchadrezzar (the covenant described in Ezek 17 as YHWH's own covenant), evidence from the Rylands IX Papyrus (Griffith 1909) indicates that Psammeticus stationed Egyptian priests in the land of Israel, thus compounding Judah's treaty violation with ritual abomination. The defilement of both name and temple represented by Psammeticus's 592 visit may have occasioned Ezekiel's vision, dated to the same year, of abominations taking place in the Jerusalem temple (chs. 8–11). Sometime following Psammeticus's visit Zedekiah withheld tribute from Babylon, relying on an Egyptian alliance for protection. In 588 BCE Nebuchadrezzar campaigned through Judah, destroying several large towns before laying siege to Jerusalem. The Egyptian army under the command of Pharaoh Apries (Hophra; 589–570 BCE) offered token resistance before withdrawing, leaving Jerusalem to the Babylonians, who in 586 BCE captured and burned the city. Zedekiah escaped by night, but was overtaken by the Babylonians at Riblah and forced to witness the killing of his two sons before being himself blinded. Massive deportations followed Nebuchadrezzar's victory, and Zedekiah was replaced by Gedaliah, a non-Davidic overseer whose title is not specified in either Israelite or Babylonian sources. Nebuchadrezzar continued his attempt to subdue the eastern Mediterranean seaboard, undertaking a siege of Tyre that was to last thirteen years (586–573) and

ultimately fail. The latest dated oracle in Ezek (29:17–21, dated to 571 BCE) promises Nebuchadrezzar Egypt as compensation for his ill-fated efforts in besieging Tyre. Nebuchadrezzar apparently shared Ezekiel's hopes regarding Egypt; Babylonian texts report a battle between the Babylonian and Egyptian armies in Egypt in 568 or 567 BCE, but no more is known about Nebuchadrezzar's Egyptian campaign(s).

3. The living conditions of the exiled Israelites are widely debated. Scholars have tended to emphasize either the individual and communal trauma entailed in the loss of family members and homeland or the exiles' ability to maintain their communal identity and social structures while in Babylonia. Both aspects of the exilic experience must be held in tension: the community was allowed to preserve its language, religion, and some forms of internal governance (i.e. elders). This same community, however, bore the scars of war and displacement, and many in Babylon were conscripted into forced labour corvées. Ezekiel, a priest of sufficient prominence to have been included in the deportation of the 'upper stratum' in 597, appears to have retained some status within the exiled community, as evidenced by the formal visits from the elders described in 8:1; 14:1; and 20:1. Ezekiel's primary concern is with theology rather than with subsistence, and his oracles tend to be directed to (or against) elders, princes, and other prophets. Even the likelihood that Ezekiel was a writing prophet would suggest that he lived in relative security and stability.

The relationship between the exiled community and those in the homeland seems to have been a complex one. Ezekiel's preoccupation with Jerusalem and Judah reveals not only his priestly concern over the temple and its destruction, but also the people's questions as to how to understand their own experiences vis-à-vis those of the population still in Israel. Popular concern for the welfare of family and friends back home was tempered by a sense of competition over which segment of the divided community now held hegemony over the Israelite land and cultural identity. Ezekiel, though critical of both the exiles and those in the land, sees the exiles, whose number includes figures such as himself who represent the *status quo ante*, as retaining God's favour and thus a claim to prominence in any future reconstruction of Israel.

C. The Person of the Prophet. 1. Ezekiel is identified in the book's superscription as a priest, and his deportation with the first exiles to Babylon in 597 BCE suggests his prominence, either because of family connections or because he was a priest of some importance. Whether Ezekiel functioned as a prophet as well as a priest before his vision of 593 BCE (chs. 1–3) is unknown. Ezekiel was recognized as a prophet by the Judean community in exile, and was apparently highly enough regarded that the elders assembled before him, perhaps even on a regular basis, to enquire of YHWH (Ezek 8:1; 20:1). Although the book provides some autobiographical information it is difficult to form a clear picture of the prophet or of how he was perceived by his contemporaries. To the modern reader Ezekiel seems to exhibit symptoms typical of mental illness. He experiences disorienting and overwhelming visions, undergoes paralysis and muteness, and attributes these debilitating occurrences to YHWH's direct intervention in his life. Attempts to diagnose the prophet's condition (see

esp. Halperin 1993), while intriguing, fail to engage the question of how such a figure, however bizarre by modern standards, would have functioned or have been understood within his own society. Ezekiel himself expresses misgivings about his role as prophet (20:49 [MT 21:5]; cf. 9:8), but his concern seems to stem from people not taking his words seriously enough, rather than from resistance to taking on the prophetic role *per se*.

2. Ezekiel is remarkable for his personal involvement in accomplishing numerous symbolic actions. At times playing the role of the people (eating meagre food as if during a siege; 4:9–15), Ezekiel more often plays the part of YHWH himself, setting his face against Jerusalem (4:3), and even experiencing his own wife's death as a sign of YHWH's temple's demise (24:15–24). Most frequently, however, Ezekiel is called upon to act as YHWH's witness, observing and certifying, first the people's abominations (thereby justifying their destruction; 8:1–18), then YHWH's command for Jerusalem's annihilation (9:5), and finally, each detail of YHWH's new and purified temple (chs. 40–8). Ezekiel is a witness in an almost legal sense, noting and attesting YHWH's actions (cf. the calls for Ezekiel to 'judge' in Ezek 20:4; 22:2). In this regard Ezekiel's appointment as sentinel over Israel in 3:16–21 is apt. Ezekiel is literally appointed to 'look out', to warn Israel against YHWH's wrathful approach, and he is told that his own life depends on his watchfulness.

D. Ezekiel and the Prophetic Tradition. 1. Ezekiel shows a number of affinities with earlier prophetic texts. Depiction of the prophet's personal experience most closely parallels descriptions of the early prophets Elijah and Elisha (see Carley 1975). In particular his experience of the 'hand of the Lord' as a compelling force (1:3; 3:22; etc.; cf. 1 Kings 18:46; 2 Kings 3:15) links him with this earlier tradition, as do reports of being physically transported by the spirit (3:12–14; 8:3; cf. 1 Kings 18:12; 2 Kings 2:16). Ezekiel's vivid sign-acts lend his persona a dramatic intensity similar to that of Elijah and Elisha, but whereas the earlier prophets' symbolic actions are generally depicted as having immediate, visible effects (e.g. calling fire from heaven in 1 Kings 18:30–9), Ezekiel's actions (with the possible exception of 11:13) are not transmuted into external events. Ezekiel's sign-acts, while clearly understood as setting in motion the events they portray, often precede their fulfilment by a period of years. Though presumed to be efficacious, Ezekiel's actions are not miraculous in the same sense as the deeds of Elijah and Elisha.

2. While Ezekiel's experience seems most directly modelled on that of Elijah and Elisha, the content of his prophecy owes more to the prophets of the eighth to the sixth centuries. Thus Ezekiel's announcement in ch. 7 that 'the end (*qēṣ*) has come' depends on Am 8:2 and the smelting of Israel in 22:17–22 reflects Isa 1:22–5. It is Jeremiah, however, with which Ezekiel is most intimately connected, to the extent that many of Ezekiel's most striking images seem like extended meditations on themes introduced in Jeremiah. Like Jeremiah, Ezekiel opens with a vision coming 'from the north' (1:4; Jer 1:13), a vision followed in Ezekiel's case by the eating of a divine scroll (3:1–3), an action styled on the metaphor of Jer 15:16. YHWH must then fortify each prophet against Israel's angry resistance to his words (Ezek 3:8–9; Jer 1:18–19).

Ezekiel's condemnation in ch. 13 of prophets whom YHWH never called seems to draw on Jeremiah's oracles against false prophets in 23:23–40; 29; the compelling image in Ezek 16 and 23 of Jerusalem and Samaria as degenerate sister-cities expands on the conceit introduced in Jer 3:6–14; the 'sour grapes' proverb cited in Jer 31:29, in Ezek 18 forms the basis for an extended debate over individual responsibility and the possibility of repentance; YHWH's claim in Jer 21:5 to fight with outstretched arm against his own people reappears in Ezek 20:33; and the depiction of YHWH as shepherd in Jer 23:1–8 is expanded upon in Ezek 34. Finally, Ezekiel appropriates Jeremiah's promise of renewal in 31:31–3, but with a characteristically ironic twist. Whereas Jeremiah shows YHWH inscribing his law onto the people's hearts as if onto so many stone tablets, in Ezek 11:19–20 and 36:26–7 YHWH must remove the people's hard, stony hearts altogether, replacing them with hearts of flesh before endowing them with his spirit. The question of how Ezekiel came to have such extensive knowledge of Jeremiah's words remains unresolved. It is entirely possible that a written edition of Jeremiah's prophecies was available to him in Babylon (cf. Jer 29:24–32 in which Jeremiah counters an exiled prophet's response to his letter), though this raises the further question of why, despite his detailed commentary on the situation in Jerusalem, Ezekiel makes no mention of Jeremiah.

E. Textual Problems. 1. The MT of Ezekiel is unarguably replete with grammatical lapses, repetitions, and inconsistencies. On the question of how to deal with these difficulties, however, little agreement has been reached, largely because no clearly superior text exists. LXX, while smoother, clearer, and containing fewer repetitions, can easily be interpreted as responding to the difficulties presented by MT rather than preceding them. In addition, LXX itself appears not to be a homogeneous translation but a composite text, and one that exists in widely differing versions. The Ezekiel scroll from Qumran cave 11 cannot be unrolled, and additional fragments of text cannot be argued conclusively to favour either LXX or MT. The Targum follows MT closely, thereby offering early interpretations of MT's difficult passages but no assistance in reconstructing a *Vorlage*. MT generally serves as a scholarly 'default text' with the versions used sparingly as correctives.

2. Divergent stands regarding Ezekiel's composition history have also affected the way commentators have viewed the book's textual difficulties. Zimmerli (1979; 1983), for example, who considered Ezekiel the product of several generations' accrued reflections, could assign many doublets to the hands of Ezekiel's earliest interpreters. Greenberg (1983: 275–6), however, exploring the complexities of a presumed literary prophet, considered even an awkward repetition such as the doubled 'I said to you, "In your blood, live!"' of 16:6 not dittography, but a deliberate stylistic device.

F. Themes. 1. The Temple. Ezekiel's passionate concern with the Jerusalem temple—its defilement and destruction—has long been considered a central focus of the book. As a priest of sufficient stature to have been among the first exiled, Ezekiel may be assumed to have had more than a passing interest in both worship practices within and the ultimate fate of the Jerusalem sanctuary. In fact, both the structure and content of the book point to the temple's centrality in Ezekiel's

thought. A growing horror at the temple's defilement dominates the oracles of doom in chs. 1–24, and the temple's destruction, symbolized by the death of Ezekiel's wife (24:15–24), marks the ultimate satisfaction of YHWH's rage against Jerusalem and the beginning of his forgiveness. In the book's final chapters YHWH's eventual restoration of Israel is signified by the building of a new temple and YHWH's renewed residence within it (43:1–5). The existence or destruction of the Jerusalem temple serves as a cipher for the existence or non-existence of Israel. Israel's life is defined for Ezekiel, not by political independence, the Davidic monarchy (which receives scant notice in the book), or even the people's possession of the land (the second, more extensive exile of 586 BCE is barely mentioned in Ezekiel), but by the presence or absence of the temple, and by YHWH's acceptance or rejection of the temple as his home. The temple thus forms the emotional core of the book, representing Israel's ritual purity or impurity, its political and theological fidelity or infidelity, and YHWH's presence or absence among his people.

2. The Divine Name. The exile of YHWH's chosen people to Babylon, as well as their own flagrant disobedience to his laws, could easily be seen as compromising YHWH's reputation as a god worthy of the name. Ezekiel, like other exilic authors, is concerned to vindicate YHWH's offended honour. Exile in itself was sufficient to defile YHWH's divine name, as it implied either YHWH's impotence or his violation of his covenant oath made to Israel. As recorded in 36:20, the nations' observation that 'These are the people of the Lord, yet they had to leave His land' (NJPS) impels YHWH to act in defence of his holy name. The violation of Zedekiah's vassal oath sworn in YHWH's name similarly amounted to defilement of the name, and so YHWH in Ezekiel appears caught between the need to avenge himself *against* Judah and the competing need to manifest his power by bringing the people back from exile, both of which seem necessary to defend the sanctity of his name. Ezek 20 retells the entire history of Israel as a struggle between YHWH's desire to punish Israel's disobedience and his unwillingness to defile his own name by destroying the covenant people. Ezek 16 and 23 cast YHWH's defilement in the emotionally charged terms of male sexual honour, depicting YHWH as a sexually shamed husband whose honour has been devastated by his wife's (the personified Jerusalem's) infidelity. YHWH's vindication of his honour, first by punishing Israel for its infidelity and then by re-establishing his potency and authority over the people, emerges as a dominant theme over the course of the book. The repeated phrase, 'Then they will know that I am YHWH' (my tr.; see *inter alia* 6:7, 10, 14), sometimes employed as a threat of punishment and sometimes as a promise of restoration, emphasizes the concern for the divine name that motivates YHWH throughout Ezekiel. This 'recognition formula' (Zimmerli 1979: 37–41) occurs with variations some seventy-two times. In Ezekiel, to 'know YHWH' denotes not merely recognizing the deity, but specifically acknowledging his sovereignty. Not only the Judeans but ultimately all nations must come to 'know the LORD', that is, to recognize his dominion over all the earth. The climax of Ezekiel thus comes at the moment when YHWH is fully 'recognized'. After vanquishing his ultimate enemy and so vindicating his holy name in chs. 38–9, YHWH is at last enthroned in 43:1–5 on his holy mountain, overlooking the city whose name declares his sovereign presence at the centre of the world: YHWH is There (48:35).

3. The Divine Warrior. Ezekiel's concern with the sanctity of both temple and divine name manifests itself in the book via the symbolic complex associated with the Israelite celebration of YHWH as Divine Warrior (see *ABD*, 'Warrior, Divine'). In Israel, the New Year celebration apparently included a ritual in which YHWH (symbolized by the ark) went forth from the temple in an annual battle against cosmic enemies. While the ritual battle was taking place the temple was cleansed, and upon YHWH's victory a triumphant procession celebrated the renewal of the temple and reaffirmed YHWH's reign as well as that of his regent, the earthly monarch (see *ABD*, 'King and Kingship'). In the opening chapter of Ezekiel the prophet reports seeing a vision of YHWH as Divine Warrior, seated on his chariot-throne. Ezekiel then looks on in chs. 10–11 as YHWH mounts his chariot and rides forth from the temple to the Mount of Olives, the traditional goal of the New Year's ark procession. YHWH then engages in battle, first against Jerusalem itself, and then against the enemies of Judah. The wars of YHWH culminate in chs. 38–9 with the battle against Gog, depicted as a cosmic foe. Following his victory over Gog YHWH calls for the purification of the land and a sacrificial banquet, after which he returns in triumph to take his throne as king in a renewed and purified temple. For Ezekiel, writing in Babylon during a period when YHWH's power and kingship could not be affirmed by military, political, or ritual means, the visionary mode provides a venue through which to vindicate YHWH's honour and assert his continued sovereignty.

4. Sin and Repentance. Ezekiel is widely noted for his assertions, primarily set forth in ch. 18 (cf. 33:10–20) that, contrary to the perspective expressed in Ex 34:7 and elsewhere, YHWH does not visit the sins of the parents upon the children; rather, each person is judged on the basis of individual merit. Moreover, each person's merit is determined solely by their current actions. Past sins do not count against a repentant individual, nor does past righteousness count in favour of a person who has turned to evil ways. Ezekiel thus presents a distinctive perspective on the individual as a moral agent and on the present moment as the moment of moral significance. YHWH stresses that he takes no pleasure in the death of the wicked, but desires repentance and life for each person (18:23, 32).

5. In contrast to the focus on the ongoing responsibility of each individual, YHWH's actions toward the community are designed solely to punish past sins and to purify the people as a whole, regardless of their present moral inclinations. At the communal level YHWH's concern is with the ritual defilement created by Israel's sins and his goal is to vindicate his name and his holiness (see EZEK F.2; *ABD*, 'Holiness (OT)'). The community must at all costs be fitted to these ends. Thus, much of Ezekiel describes YHWH's plans precisely to visit the consequences of the community's sins upon it so as to purify people, land, and temple and re-establish YHWH as sovereign. In his wholesale purgation of land and people YHWH will punish 'both righteous and wicked' (21:3–4 [MT 21:8–9]). Regardless of whether they choose repentance YHWH will replace their corrupt hearts with organs inclined to obedience

(11:19–20; 36:26–7), thus ensuring his ability to rule undefiled by the people's sins. Here purification and return (the word 'forgiveness', *slḥ*, does not occur in Ezekiel) take place not as an act of grace, but of necessity, a required step in the vindication of YHWH's sovereignty. Ezekiel's concern presses far beyond the restoration of the people, to climax in ch. 43 with YHWH's own restoration as king. Within this overarching and impersonal scheme focused on YHWH's vindication, however, rests Ezekiel's almost pastoral attention to the moral life of the individual. In the midst of the calamity of the exile comes a firm rejection of despair and moral defeatism. Righteous action is far from pointless, as some in the exilic community claim (33:10), nor does hope lie in the vague notion that the righteousness of the ancestors will suffice for the present (14:12–20). Instead, even as he announces YHWH's inevitable destruction of Israel Ezekiel articulates a responsibility and opportunity for each person to 'turn and live' on the basis of new choices and righteous acts.

G. Outline

Oracles of Destruction against Judah (1:1–24:27)
   Ezekiel's Inaugural Vision and Commissioning (1:1–3:27)
   Signs and Oracles of Doom (4:1–7:27)
   The Vision of the Defiled Temple (8:1–11:25)
   Rulers, Elders, Prophets, and a Few Virtuous Individuals
      (12:1–14:23)
   The Twisted Symbols of Judah's Pride (15:1–20:44)
   The End Approaches (20:45–24:27 [MT 21:1–24:27])
Hope for the Future (25:1–48:35)
   Oracles against Foreign Nations (25:1–32:32)
   Images of Restoration and Return (33:1–39:29)
   YHWH's Re-enthronement (40:1–48:35)

COMMENTARY

Oracles of Destruction against Judah (1:1–24:27)

Ezekiel's Inaugural Vision and Commissioning (1:1–3:27)

(1:1–3) Superscription The book begins with a superscription informing the reader of the identity of the prophet and the time and place that the prophecy was received and delivered. Ezek 1–3 actually includes two such introductions, one in the first person (v. 1) and one in the third (vv. 2–3). vv. 2–3 are the only two verses in the book written in the third person, and the first-person superscription of v. 1 is probably the original. v. 1 announces that the writer saw 'visions of God' while among the exiles 'by the river Chebar' in 'the thirtieth year'. The introduction is obscure, assuming the reader's knowledge of which year is 'the thirtieth' and who it was who were exiled 'by the river Chebar'. The second superscription (vv. 2–3) seems designed to clarify the first, identifying the speaker and the location of the Chebar, and restating the date in terminology consistent with that employed elsewhere in the book. vv. 2–3 follow the typical form of prophetic superscriptions, providing a date in terms of the reigning monarch, identifying the prophet both by his own name (Ezekiel) and his father's name (son of Buzi), and announcing that 'the word of the Lord came' at this time. In this case Ezekiel's profession as a priest is also noted (cf. Jer 1:1), as well as the location in which he prophesied: in the land of the Chaldeans (Babylonia), by the river Chebar. Finally, the superscription contains the notice that 'the hand of the Lord' was upon him there (v. 3).

The significance of the 'hand of the Lord' (cf. 8:1), and how this term differs from the 'word of the Lord' in the same verse or the 'visions of God' mentioned in v. 1, is not clear, although the terminology seems to link Ezekiel's experience with that of earlier prophets such as Elijah (1 Kings 18:46) and Elisha (2 Kings 2:15; see EZEK D.1). The correlation between the year specified in v. 2 (593 BCE) and the thirtieth year of v. 1 has long puzzled interpreters. Speculation has included the possibility that Ezekiel himself was 30 years old (in his thirtieth year) when he began to prophesy, or that the call actually occurred (or the book was composed) in the thirtieth year of the exile, 568 BCE. The Targum of Ezekiel, however, suggests that Ezekiel received his call in the thirtieth year after Josiah's reform, a dating that would yield 593, and so correlate with the date given in v. 2. This early understanding has gained little credence among scholars, but given that Josiah's reform took place in a Jubilee year (cf. Hayes and Hooker 1988), Ezekiel might well be reckoning his vision according to the Jubilee. In this case, both his initial and his final vision are dated according to their relation to the Jubilee (EZEK 40:1).

(1:4–28a) The Vision of the Throne-Chariot Ezekiel watches as a stormy wind blows in from the north, bringing with it a shiny cloud that in turn contains YHWH's chariot borne by supernatural creatures (identified in 10:20 as cherubim). YHWH's approach from the north carries implications ranging from the mundane to the mythical. Although summer storms do in fact come into Babylon from the north, Ezekiel more probably reflects the Ugaritic traditions according to which the storm-god Baal made his home in the far north (cf. Ps 48:2 [MT v. 3]) or to a tradition describing an unnamed 'enemy from the north' (cf. Jer 1:13; Ezek 39:2) arriving to destroy Israel. In the light of YHWH's appearance riding his war chariot and Ezekiel's role warning Israel of YHWH's approach, the northerly storm wind of 1:4 probably foreshadows the approaching destruction of Israel. Ezekiel sees in the storm a shining cloud containing fire and 'something like ḥašmal' (v. 4). The identity of ḥašmal is not known, though the Akkadian cognate elmešu is also used in describing a god's shining appearance (see Greenberg 1983: 43). The details of Ezekiel's vision, while tantalizing, are also intentionally obscure. Ezekiel claims only to see 'the appearance of the likeness of the glory' of YHWH (v. 28), and while the vision is described in minute detail, it is likewise understood that what the prophet describes so fully remains essentially indescribable.

In vv. 5–14 Ezekiel sees 'something like four living creatures' in the midst of the cloud. The designation of the creatures as ḥayyôt, living beings, may emphasize that he is not experiencing a vision of the temple furniture, the carved cherubim bearing the ark, but of the living original (cf. the seraphim of Isa 6:1–8). The description of the four creatures is garbled in MT, with repetitions, sentence fragments, and even changes in the creatures' gender. While the uncertain prose creates translational difficulties, and may well reflect a corrupt text, the result is a strangely enhanced sense of awe and bedazzlement built up over the course of the vision. The creatures have four faces—each face having the likeness of a different animal, with a human face in the front—and four wings. The effect is that the creatures face in all directions simultaneously, and are thus able both to move in any direction and to guard the blazing substance around which they stand. In vv. 15–21 Ezekiel describes four shining wheels accompanying the four creatures. The construction of the wheels, 'a wheel within a wheel', may indicate either concentric circles in the same plane or wheels at right angles to one another, thus facing, like the living creatures, in all directions at once. The wheel rims are full of eyes so that, like the creatures, they may be both omniscient and all-seeing. Whereas the living creatures move at the impulse of 'the spirit' (of YHWH) the wheels are themselves moved (vertically as well as horizontally) by the spirit of the creatures.

In vv. 22–8a Ezekiel sees a crystalline dome stretching over the creatures' heads (cf. Gen 1:6), and notes the sound made by the creatures' wings as they move, 'like the sound of mighty waters, like the thunder of the Almighty' (v. 24). A voice sounds from over the firmament; the creatures halt and let down their wings. Ezekiel now looks above the dome to see the 'likeness of a throne' with what appears to be 'something that seemed like a human form' (v. 26). The form shines as if with ḥašmal, fire, and even a rainbow (vv. 27–8), and upon seeing it Ezekiel falls prostrate, recognizing 'the appearance of the likeness of the glory' of YHWH (v. 28).

Ezekiel's vision report, for all its claims to describe only the remotest representations of things divine, employs what for an Israelite reader would have been unmistakable symbols of YHWH's presence. Zoomorphic throne guardians formed part of both Israelite and Babylonian iconography, as did the transformation of the divine throne into a war chariot, borne by its winged guardians and accompanied by fire, storm, and the thundering voice of the god (Ps 68; 77:16–19 [MT vv. 17–20]). The throne's location above the crystalline dome reflects YHWH's location 'above the heavens' (Ps 8:1 [MT 8:2]; 11:4; 57:11 [MT v. 12]), while the repeated emphasis on the mobility of the creatures and wheels may serve to explain YHWH's unexpected presence in Babylonia.

(1:28b–3:15) Ezekiel's Commissioning Ezekiel hears a voice addressing him, commanding him to rise. Ezekiel is called 'son of man' (2:1 RSV) here and throughout the remainder of the book, not as an honorific title, but as a mark of the distance between this 'mere mortal' and his divine interlocutor (see Vermes 1981; ABD, 'Son of Man'). The prophet is then set on his feet by the spirit (cf. 37:10), moving, like the living creatures, only at YHWH's behest. Ezekiel receives a commission to go to the 'rebellious house' of Israel and speak for YHWH. YHWH's emphasis on Israel's stubborn rebellion, and even his reassurance that Ezekiel need not fear the people's words and looks, suggest that Ezekiel's message will be rejected; none the less he will serve as evidence of YHWH's will, so that the people 'will know that there has been a prophet among them' (2:5). Ezekiel is now shown a scroll containing 'words of lamentation and mourning and woe' (2:10) and instructed to eat it (cf. Jer 15:16). Henceforth, Ezekiel speaks YHWH's words, which have literally been put into the prophet's mouth. The scroll's contents, lamentation and woe, confirm the earlier suggestion that YHWH has come as an enemy from the north: Ezekiel will prophesy destruction to Israel. In 3:4–11 YHWH offers Ezekiel the ironic consolation that he will not be sent to foreigners whose speech he cannot understand. Rather than going to foreigners, who might listen despite the language barrier, Ezekiel will go to his fellow exiles, who, understanding his words, will simply refuse to listen.

Ezekiel then reports that as the divine chariot departed he himself was lifted up by the spirit and returned to the exiles living at the Babylonian settlement of Tel Abib (3:12–15). Ezekiel depicts his visionary experience as entailing pain and consternation. The intensity of YHWH's hand upon him causes Ezekiel 'bitterness' and 'rage' (3:14, my tr.). Following the vision Ezekiel sits stunned for seven days. Ezekiel is not unique in experiencing the prophetic role as galling (cf. Moses in Ex 4; and Jeremiah in Jer 15:15–18); Ezekiel feels the burden even before receiving orders or learning the community's response. 'Rage' (*ḥēmâ*) in Ezekiel is most often characteristic of YHWH (see *inter alia* 5:13, 15; 6:12; 7:8) and it may be that Ezekiel is overwhelmed by his empathic experience of YHWH's fierce emotion. In his later sign-acts (beginning with 4:1–3) the prophet frequently takes on YHWH's role. Ezekiel is thus stunned not only by the fact of his encounter with the divine glory, but also by his internalization of divine rage.

(3:16–21) The Sentinel (See also EZEK 33:1–9.) After his seven days' recuperation, Ezekiel receives in effect a second commissioning, this time couched in metaphoric language. Ezekiel is to serve as the sentinel for Israel. The sentinel is posted on the city wall to watch for and give warning of enemies without. The metaphor refers obliquely to Jerusalem, the walled capital whose 'rebelliousness' (2:5) should give it reason to expect retaliation by Babylon. In fact, however, YHWH is the enemy approaching the city, and although YHWH, speaking through Ezekiel, warns the people, it is also YHWH against whom the people must be warned. The image of YHWH attacking the city is consistent with Ezekiel's vision in ch. 1 of YHWH riding on his war chariot, confirming the uneasy possibility that it is Israel against whom the Divine Warrior rides. Ezekiel's commission as sentinel employs military imagery to convey Israel's moral accountability. As sentinel Ezekiel is responsible for conveying YHWH's warning to the people. While it is the people who will be judged, the passage focuses on Ezekiel and his own accountability as sentinel. Thus, if Ezekiel warns the wicked to repent but they do not, they bear responsibility for their own sins. Should Ezekiel fail to warn them, however, they will receive the death sentence for their actions, but he will be held responsible for their death. Regardless, then, of the people's response, Ezekiel's own life is at stake as he is charged with a message of life-and-death importance.

(3:22–7) Binding and Dumbness In the final episode of Ezekiel's call the prophet is sent out to 'the valley', where he again sees the divine glory. As in the earlier vision, Ezekiel falls prostrate but the spirit stands him upright. YHWH now restricts both Ezekiel's mobility and his speech. He is to confine himself to his house, where he will be bound with cords, and YHWH will strike him dumb and thus unable to reprove

the people. YHWH's command is puzzling, as its effect is to render Ezekiel incapable of communicating with the people, and thus seemingly to negate his commission as prophet. The restriction is particularly alarming in the light of 3:16–21 in which Ezekiel is told that he *must* warn the people on peril of his life. The problem is compounded by the fact that immediately following the announcement of his binding and dumbness YHWH commands Ezekiel to perform symbolic actions requiring both mobility and speech. While Ezekiel rarely reports his own fulfilment of YHWH's command the problem remains as to why YHWH would command actions he himself has rendered impossible to perform. One traditional solution has been to label vv. 22–7 a late addition, or out of place in its current setting. Such a solution merely introduces the new problem of what the difficult passage is in fact doing out of place—how it got there and how it functions now. One less radical possibility is that Ezekiel's confinement and dumbness symbolize his status as a writing prophet. If in fact Ezekiel's prophecies were produced substantially in writing (while seated, silent and immobile, indoors) rather than orally, this novel practice might have required both explanation and theological justification in a culture regarding prophecy as primarily an oral genre. In v. 27 YHWH declares that when he addresses Ezekiel he will open the prophet's mouth to tell the people, 'Thus says the Lord God'. This emendation could refer to YHWH's removal of the dumbness in 33:21–2 but more likely means that YHWH will relieve the prophet's dumbness *whenever* YHWH gives Ezekiel oracles to deliver in YHWH's name.

Signs and Oracles of Doom (4:1–7:27)

(4:1–8) The Siege of Jerusalem Ezekiel is commanded to perform his first sign-act, a symbolic representation of Jerusalem under siege. After inscribing a map of Jerusalem on a mud brick (examples of mud maps are known from the ancient Near East) Ezekiel is to construct a model siege apparatus surrounding the model city. Finally, he is to set up an iron plate as a wall between himself and the city, set his face against the city, and lay siege to it. Ezekiel's action straightforwardly predicts a siege against Jerusalem, but the siege is not initiated by Babylon. Rather, it is YHWH, as represented by Ezekiel, who is setting his face against the city, and, intent on Israel's destruction, erecting a barrier between himself and them. Ezekiel, appointed in 3:16–21 as lookout against YHWH's attack, now changes roles, playing the part of YHWH. The iron plate between Ezekiel's face and the city recalls the hardening of the prophet's face in 2:8–9. The hardness that kept Ezekiel from being harmed by the people's rejection apparently also keeps YHWH from being softened by their pleas. YHWH now commands Ezekiel to lie, first on his left side and then on his right, symbolically bearing the punishment of Israel and Judah respectively (vv. 4–6). The prophet is to lie 390 days on his left side, signifying 390 years of punishment for the Northern Kingdom, and 40 days on his right side, signifying 40 years of punishment for Judah. The numbers are baffling. While Judah's 40 days may predict 40 years of exile (cf. Jeremiah's prediction of 70 years, Jer 25:11; 29:10), creating a symbolic correlation to the wilderness wanderings (cf. Ezek 20:36), a corresponding 390-year exile for Israel (beginning in 722 and lasting until 332 BCE?) is not easily explained. In vv. 7–8 YHWH recapitulates 4:1–3 and 3:25, namely that Ezekiel is to set his face against Jerusalem and that YHWH will bind and so immobilize him during the siege. This summary implies that it is the siege, not the exile, that will last 40 days (a day for each of forty years' iniquity), corresponding to a 390-day siege of Samaria. Unfortunately, neither Assyrian nor Israelite records permit the kind of close dating that would prove or disprove this possibility.

(4:9–17) Famine Ezekiel, now acting out the part of Jerusalem's citizens, is commanded to eat meagre rations during the time that he lies on his side. He is to bake cakes made of a mixture of poor grains, baking them on defiling human excrement in public as a sign of the coming siege conditions. The discrepancy between the public actions prescribed in 4:9–17 and the seclusion and immobility commanded in 3:24–5 and 4:8 may be the result of editorial insertions here or may simply reflect modern scholarship's continued failure to penetrate the meaning of Ezekiel's dumbness and binding. In v. 14 Ezekiel emerges briefly as a character independent of YHWH's actions and words, to resist carrying out YHWH's defiling commands. YHWH relents, allowing Ezekiel to bake the cakes on animal dung instead of human, thereby maintaining his ritual purity.

(5:1–17) The Coming Judgement In ch. 5 Ezekiel is assigned a sign-act that both summarizes the eventual fate of Jerusalem and introduces the theological questions to be worked out over the remainder of the book. The prophet is told to shave his hair, an action that in itself symbolizes wartime captivity (cf. Isa 7:20) and then to divide the hair into three sections, one for burning, one for destruction by sword, and one for scattering. From the third section a tiny remnant is to be preserved, though some even from this will be burned. vv. 5–17 explain that the hair represents the citizens of Jerusalem, some of whom will be consumed by plague and famine within the besieged city, others of whom will be slain after the city falls, and the rest of whom will be 'scattered' in exile where further destruction will pursue them. Although YHWH gives no explanation of the preserved fragments of hair, they presumably represent some small fraction of those sent into exile who will be kept safe throughout the ordeal. Jerusalem, meanwhile, will be subjected to famine, plague, wild beasts, and the death of children, the punishments prescribed in Lev 26 for breaking YHWH's covenant. YHWH's description of Jerusalem's rejection of the law and of its shame at being punished in sight of other nations prefigures the lengthy account in EZEK 20:1–44 of YHWH's futile attempts to establish his rule over Israel and his ultimate decision to expose the nation to public humiliation in order to vindicate his divine name. v. 13 marks the first occurrence of YHWH's assertion repeated in various forms throughout Ezekiel, that the goal of Jerusalem's destruction is recognition of YHWH and his name: 'They will know that I, the LORD, have spoken' (see EZEK F.2).

(6:1–14) Judgement against Israel's Mountains In ch. 6 Ezekiel is directed to prophesy against the mountains of Israel, a message of destruction that will be mirrored by promises of restoration directed to the mountains in 36:1–15. Ch. 6 consists of variations on themes introduced in ch. 5, as the earlier judgement against Jerusalem is extended throughout the

Israelite countryside, in which idols are worshipped 'on every high hill, on all the mountaintops, under every green tree and under every leafy oak' (v. 13; cf. e.g. Jer 2:20; for discussion of these practices see Ackerman 1992). As in 5:13, YHWH will spend his rage against the people (v. 12), dividing them as in 5:1–4 into three parts (vv. 11–12) to be destroyed by famine, by plague, and by the sword (cf. Jer 14:12; Lev 26). The judgements against the mountains (and the people who worship there) continue to be depicted, like those of ch. 5, as a fulfilment of the covenant curses set forth in Lev 26. In addition to the levitical stipulation of punishment by famine, sword, and plague, ch. 6 predicts the fulfilment of the prediction in Lev 26 that the idolaters will be slain at the feet of the very idols they serve (vv. 5, 13), thus simultaneously destroying the worshippers and defiling the idolatrous altars (cf. 2 Kings 23:20).

YHWH stretches forth his hand (v. 14), a gesture invoking his triumph over Pharaoh in the Exodus (see e.g. Ex 3:20; Deut 4:34), but here emphasizing that YHWH will fight not for, but against, his own people (cf. Jer 21:5; see EZEK 20:33). As in ch. 5, the goal of YHWH's punishment is acknowledgment of YHWH's person and sovereignty. The recognition formula (they/you shall know that I am YHWH) appears four times in this brief chapter (see EZEK F.2). Structurally, ch. 6 provides an excellent example of the 'halving' technique described by Greenberg (1983: 25–6) with vv. 1–10 forming the primary and 11–14 the related, secondary section of a two-part oracle.

(7:1–27) Judgement against the Land Judgement by sword, pestilence, and famine, pronounced against Jerusalem in ch. 5 and against the mountains of Israel in ch. 6, is extended to every corner of the land in Ezek 7. Building on the emotional intensity of the previous two chapters, Ezek 7 announces urgently that the expected judgement has now arrived. The MT is difficult, written in strong but sometimes erratic poetic metre, riddled with *hapax legomena*, repetitions, and untranslatable phrases. As with the chariot vision of Ezek 1, however, so also here the disjointed syntax lends an uncanny urgency to the passage, so that both form and content express Ezekiel's (and the people's) panic at YHWH's approach.

The chapter consists of three sections, vv. 1–4, 5–9, and 10–27, each announcing Israel's doom and concluding with the recognition formula. The three sections seem to build on Amos's announcement (Am 8:1–10) of the day of YHWH (*ABD*, 'Day of the Lord'), a day traditionally celebrating the Divine Warrior's conquest of his enemies, but which the prophets re-envisioned as a day of judgement against Israel. Thus, Amos's declaration that 'the end' (*qēṣ*) had come upon Israel (8:2) reappears in Ezek 7:2. The second doom saying begins in v. 5 with the addition of 'disaster after disaster' before the repeated notice that 'the end' has arrived. Images drawn from Ezek 5 and 6 are built into a concatenated recital of YHWH spending his anger, spilling out rage against the people (v. 8; cf. 5:13; 6:12), mercilessly punishing their abominations (v. 4, 8–9; cf. 5:9, 11; 6:9, 11). 'Then,' says YHWH, 'you will know that it is I, the Lord, who strike' (v. 9). God's revelation is one of naked power, a warrior unleashed in battle. The final section, vv. 10–27, opens with the explicit announcement of 'the day' (v. 10). People are paralysed with fear as YHWH brings the sword, plague, and famine upon them (vv. 14–18).

vv. 19–23 predict in veiled language the Babylonian capture and desecration of the Jerusalem temple. YHWH speaks first of silver and gold which were the occasion of the people's sin, out of which they had made 'abominable images' and *šiqqûṣîm* (in this context 'idols', v. 20), using YHWH's treasures for idolatry. YHWH will make these objects 'like a menstruant woman' (*lĕniddâ*, v. 20; cf. v. 19), that is, repulsively unclean to the people, a prefiguration of YHWH's rejection of Jerusalem as an unclean wife in ch. 16 (and cf. 36:17). YHWH will bring foreigners into his 'treasured place' to profane it (vv. 21–2), an oblique reference to the Babylonian destruction of YHWH's private abode within the Jerusalem temple. YHWH explains in v. 23 that destruction will occur because of the people's violent crimes (not their idolatry), and goes on in vv. 26–7 to describe the breakdown of established order. In vain will people seek a vision from the prophet, law from priests, or advice from elders. This triad of religious leaders in v. 26, all now defunct, is paralleled in v. 27 by a secular order, similarly dismantled: the king mourns, the prince despairs, and the people of the land shake with fear. All of society is in chaos. Ezekiel's mention of the people of the land is intriguing, as they are structurally parallel to 'the elders' in the list of religious authorities, a usage suggesting that the term meant 'petty officials' rather than the more widely accepted meanings of either 'peasantry' or 'landed gentry' (see *ABD*, 'Am Ha'arez'). The third section of the chapter, like the two preceding, concludes with the recognition formula: YHWH's violent attack against people and temple will ultimately result in acknowledgment of YHWH (v. 27).

The Vision of the Defiled Temple (8:1–11:25)

(8:1–18) The Temple Tour Ezek 8 begins with a date formula, introducing a new section of the book. The date is September 592 BCE. The timing, approximately three weeks after the 390 days of immobility prescribed in 4:5, may indicate the prophet's release from confinement and renewed ability to prophesy, although the 40 days prescribed in 4:6 would not yet have elapsed. Historical circumstances may also have provided the occasion for the oracle (see EZEK B.2). Pharaoh Psammeticus's victory tour of Palestine, bringing along the priests of the 'great gods' of Egypt, took place during the second half of 592, and this violation of both cultic and political loyalties may lie behind Ezekiel's vision of depravity at the heart of Jerusalem.

Ezekiel is depicted sitting in his house with the elders of Judah seated before him, a scenario repeated in 14:1 and 20:1; apparently the community recognized Ezekiel's prophetic status and regularly sought YHWH's oracles through him. On this occasion Ezekiel experiences 'the hand of the Lord' in much the same form as in his inaugural vision. A form made of gleaming *ḥašmal* (MT's *'ēš* 'fire' is probably an error, corrected by LXX's reflection of *'îš*, 'human') appears, reaches out, and lifts Ezekiel by the hair, transporting him within the vision to the Jerusalem temple (vv. 2–3). Physical translocation seems to have been an accepted element of prophetic experience in some Israelite circles (cf. 2 Kings 2:16 and Obadiah's complaint to Elijah in 1 Kings 18:12). In Ezekiel's case the divine spirit's actions range from merely setting the prophet upright (Ezek 3:24) to transporting him into exclusively

visionary realms (37:1; 40:1–2). Here Ezekiel's experience is ambiguous since he seems to describe both actual conditions and activities in the Jerusalem temple (8:5–16) and also divine responses such as the work of the heavenly executioners in 9:5–8, that seem to be occurring only at a visionary level.

Ezekiel's vision begins just outside the north gate of the temple's 'inner court', a phrase reflecting the double courtyard of the late monarchic temple (see *ABD*, 'Temple, Jerusalem'). Ezekiel identifies the spot as the location of 'the image of jealousy which provokes to jealousy' (v. 3). The idol's identity is uncertain, though Asherah (see Olyan 1988; *ABD*, 'Asherah') is generally assumed (and cf. 2 Chr 33:7, 15). The fact that Ezekiel need not name the idol, but refers to its location as a means of orienting the reader, suggests that this figure was not a shocking innovation, but a familiar and perhaps longstanding feature of the Jerusalem temple (cf. NJPS 'that infuriating image').

Ezekiel notes that 'the glory of the God of Israel was there' (v. 4). The precise relationship between the *ḥašmal* figure, the glory of YHWH, and YHWH himself is not entirely clear, though the former two figures seem to make visible the invisible presence of YHWH. As in the inaugural vision (1:28), however, the voice of YHWH himself addresses Ezekiel, in this case describing four scenes in different parts of the temple, each more offensive than the last. YHWH begins in v. 5 by directing Ezekiel's attention to the 'image of jealousy' Ezekiel himself had just noted. This statue, according to YHWH, is among Israel's 'great abominations' that 'create distance' (my tr.) from YHWH's sanctuary (v. 6). The object of the verb *rḥq* (to make distant) is not specified, and the phrase could suggest that the people are distancing *themselves* (either spiritually, through idolatry or literally, via their exile) from YHWH's temple, or that YHWH will distance himself from his temple, i.e. by his departure in chs. 10 and 11. Interpretation is further complicated by the apparent *inclusio* formed with 11:15–16, in which the current exiles are described as 'distanced' from YHWH.

Having condemned the jealousy-provoking statue, YHWH informs Ezekiel that he will see 'still greater abominations' (v. 6) and leads him into the north gateway. Ezekiel now burrows through a hole in the outer wall of the inner court, into a room (or series of rooms) whose walls are covered with engravings depicting unclean animals. Seventy elders, symbolically representing all Israel (cf. Ex 24:1, 9) offer incense before the images. The hidden rooms engraved with animal figures recall the iconography of Egyptian tombs but the reference in 23:14 to Judah's infatuation with engraved images of Babylonians may indicate that the elders are in fact practising a Babylonian ritual. Among the seventy elders Jaazaniah ben Shaphan is named, probably because of his family's prominence (2 Kings 22:3; Jer 29:3; 36:12). YHWH now brings the prophet to 'the entrance of the north temple gate' (v. 14), a location not otherwise known (for an attempt at reconstructing the temple layout assumed in 8:1–18 see Zimmerli 1979: 237–43), but clearly another step closer to the temple itself. The sanctity of the location and the gravity of the abomination progress simultaneously, so that the worst offences take place in the holiest areas. The third abomination consists of women weeping for Tammuz (*ABD*, 'Tammuz'), the Sumerian god whose descent into the underworld and subsequent return to life represented the annual renewal of the earth's fertility. The cult of Tammuz was widespread throughout the ancient Near East, though the god's death and rebirth were re-enacted during the fourth month, not the sixth, as represented in Ezekiel's vision.

The final abomination takes place between the sacrifice altar and the temple entrance, where men are worshipping the sun in the east, thus presenting their backsides to YHWH. Sun worship could be either Egyptian or Babylonian in provenience (see *ABD*, 'Sun'; Smith 1990). YHWH emphasizes to Ezekiel the gravity of all Judah's abominations, and adds the unexpected charge of violence. Finally, YHWH concludes, 'they are putting the branch to my nose' (v. 17). This last accusation is entirely enigmatic, but clearly represents the ultimate affront to YHWH. MT reads (and NRSV follows) 'they put the branch to *their* nose', but this almost certainly reflects a *tiqqûn sōpĕrîm* (see *ABD*, 'Scribal Emendations'), a scribal emendation, apparently intended to defend YHWH against the insulting gesture. While the specific rituals alluded to in ch. 8 remain obscure, the overall effect is that the full gamut of religious cults is present in the Jerusalem temple, from the local Canaanite Asherah (presented as the least offensive) to Mesopotamian and Egyptian rituals. As a result, YHWH will show no mercy in punishing the people.

(9:1–11) The Divine Avengers As Ezekiel looks on, YHWH summons seven executioners to carry out his sentence against the city. Meanwhile, the divine glory moves from the holy of holies out to the threshold of the temple. In a recapitulation of the Exodus narrative, those to be spared are given an identifying mark (the Hebrew letter *taw*) to protect them as the destroyers pass through the city. The destroyers are explicitly told to defile the temple with corpses and then proceed outwards, killing throughout the city (vv. 5–6). In a rare instance of self-expression Ezekiel protests (v. 8) that YHWH will destroy all that remains of Israel, but YHWH remains implacable. This vision of Jerusalem's destruction is a symbolic, not literal, fulfilment of YHWH's judgement. It may be, however, that here the prophetic vision has the same efficacy elsewhere attributed to the prophetic word (cf. Isa 55:11), so that the vision itself seals the fate of Jerusalem.

(10:1–22) Reappearance of the Chariot After the avengers have completed their killing, Ezekiel sees again the chariot vision that he earlier received by the Chebar river. While occasional details differ from those of ch. 1, the living creatures, now explicitly called cherubim, the wheels, and their motion are again described in exhaustive detail. Now, however, the divine throne chariot assumes a role in the ongoing drama of Ezekiel's temple vision. One of the destroyers is instructed to bring coals from the midst of the cherubim and scatter them over the city. The coals may represent either the city's destruction following the death of its inhabitants or the beginning of purification (cf. Isa 6:6–7). The avenger takes the coals but no account of the city's destruction (or purification) follows. Instead, the prophet focuses on the cherubim bearing the divine throne and on the movement of YHWH's glory out of the temple. The details of this second chariot vision are confusing, making it impossible to follow precisely where the glory is (if the glory begins its journey in the holy of holies, who is seated above the firmament carried

by the cherubim?), and the relative movements of the glory and cherubim. The overall effect of the vision is clear: the glory leaves its seat within the holy of holies and mounts the living chariot, departing in stages from the temple. By the chapter's end the glory of YHWH is mounted over the cherubim, stationed at the door of the temple's east gate, and poised to depart.

(11:1–25) The Glory Departs The Twenty-five Men (vv. 1–13): the spirit now carries Ezekiel to the temple's east gate, following the progress of the divine glory on its chariot. At the gateway Ezekiel sees twenty-five men (v. 1), apparently a separate group from those described in 8:16. These are accused of giving 'wicked counsel' (v. 2), probably advocating revolt against Babylon and reliance on Egypt. They are quoted as saying, 'It is not time for building houses; the city is the pot and we are the meat' (v. 3). The second half of the saying is given as the reason not to build houses and the metaphor seems to have clear implications for Ezekiel's original audience. Unfortunately, the meaning is no longer self-evident. Some interpret the meat as the choice portions chosen for inclusion. In this case the speakers would disdain to build more housing for the less 'select' members of society, since they themselves, having been spared exile, are now the élite of the city. Such an interpretation is precarious given the metaphor's obvious extension (made explicit in 24:1–5), that even the most select cuts are in the pot only to be cooked, clearly not a desirable fate. The saying, then, must reflect the men's dismay at inhabiting a 'cauldron'. No time now for building houses or any other peacetime pursuit (cf. Jer 29:4–6); all energy must go to defence lest they be 'cooked' in an upcoming siege. YHWH answers in effect that cooking is too mild a fate for these men. The city is indeed a pot, but it is the bodies of those whom the speakers have killed (whether as a result of their 'wicked counsel' or through some other abuse) that will be the meat. Whether Ezekiel is here holding the twenty-five men responsible for people already killed or anticipates the people's death during the siege (for which the 'counsellors' are indirectly responsible) is uncertain. The men, however, will be removed from the city and judged at the border of Israel (v. 11). The reference to judgement at the border may be a later addition, reflecting Nebuchadrezzar's punishment of Zedekiah and his entourage at Riblah following the siege of Jerusalem in 586 BCE. Ezekiel then reports that even as he was delivering this prophecy Pelatiah, one of the twenty-five men, fell dead, at which point Ezekiel again (v. 13, cf. 9:8) objects that YHWH seems to be destroying even the remnant of Israel.

The Chariot Departs (vv. 14–25). YHWH responds to Ezekiel's protest of v. 13 with an oracle directed to the exiles. Although all Ezekiel's oracles are perforce delivered to the exilic community, this is the first directly addressing their fate. The current residents of Jerusalem, says YHWH, claim that having been spared the exile they are the (righteous) inheritors of the land, while the (unrighteous) exiles have been removed from YHWH's presence (v. 15; cf. 8:6; cf. Jer 24). YHWH, however, refers to the exiles as 'the whole house of Israel', and says that though the exiles have been removed, he has in fact been to some extent their sanctuary in exile (v. 16). The image is striking. Not only does YHWH claim to have been present outside the land of Israel, but he identifies his presence as itself a sanctuary (*miqdāš*) in the temple's absence. YHWH then promises that the exiles will in fact return and be given the land. Moreover, YHWH will replace their heart of stone with a new and unified heart, a heart of flesh willing to follow YHWH's covenants and ordinances (vv. 19–20; cf. 36:26). YHWH then invokes the covenant formula, 'They will be my people and I will be their God', promising a new covenant with Israel upon their return. The promise combines elements from Jer 31:31–4 and 32:36–41. Strikingly, while YHWH in Jer 32:39 gives the people a 'single', i.e. unified, heart and in Jer 31:33 inscribes the law on the people's hearts, in Ezekiel YHWH must replace the people's heart altogether. Humankind must be recreated if they are to be capable of obedience.

Following this complete repudiation of Jerusalem and the corresponding promises to the exiles, in vv. 22–3 YHWH departs the temple and city altogether, flying to 'the mountain east of the city', the Mount of Olives. Commentators widely assume that the divine glory merely pauses at the Mount of Olives on its way to Babylonia, but such an assumption is without textual support. On the contrary, the Mount of Olives was the traditional goal of the ark's procession at the New Year Festival and the site from which the Divine Warrior waged his battles (see *ABD*, 'Olives, Mount of'). YHWH has left the Jerusalem temple riding on his war chariot, having effectively declared war against Judah and Jerusalem. Ezekiel concludes with the notice that after the glory's departure the spirit returned Ezekiel to Babylon, the vision ended, and he reported to the exiles what he had seen (v. 25).

Rulers, Elders, Prophets, and a Few Virtuous Individuals (12:1–14:23)

(12:1–16) Escaping the City Ezekiel is now commanded to perform a sign-act directed at 'the rebellious house who have eyes to see but do not see and ears to hear but do not hear' (v. 2). The reference to the people's wilful incomprehension recalls similar characteristics in Isa 6:9 and Jer 5:21. Ezekiel is to prepare 'baggage for exile', presumably the barest necessities, then dig through the wall and depart at night, covering his face so as not to see the land. In v. 7 Ezekiel carries out the symbolic action. The action seems to represent a resident of Jerusalem during a siege who has decided to escape the city by night rather than suffer siege conditions or be forcibly removed by the attacking army. The symbolism of covering the face so as not to see the land is enigmatic, especially since the action is undertaken at night, when the land would not be visible in any event. Most likely the gesture represents the successful escapee's new condition—safe, but no longer able to see the land.

In vv. 8–16 Ezekiel responds to the people's questions regarding his actions. Ezekiel explains, 'As I have done, so shall it be done' to the residents of Jerusalem (v. 11). This response deviates somewhat from the action itself, since Ezekiel has represented someone escaping the city furtively, while the niphal *yē'āśeh* ('it shall be done') indicates that the exile will be imposed upon the people. Ezekiel's response focuses on 'the prince in Jerusalem' (v. 10), that is, Zedekiah, who will pack a bag, dig through the wall, and cover his face

(v. 12). YHWH will capture him, however; he will be taken to Babylon 'but shall not see it' (v. 13). The prophecy gives a substantially accurate description of Zedekiah's fate in the upcoming siege of Jerusalem. According to 2 Kings 25:4–7 (Jer 52:4–11), after the Babylonians took the city Zedekiah escaped via a gate near the palace. He was captured, taken to Nebuchadrezzar at Riblah, and witnessed his own sons' execution before being blinded and taken to Babylon. The details of Zedekiah first escaping, then being captured and taken to Babylon, but unable to see, match the actual events of 586 BCE so closely that the passage is commonly considered 'prophecy after the event', a later addition posing as a prediction. The case, however, is far from simple, since in fact Zedekiah did *not* burrow through the wall, and the blinding of rebellious vassals was common and perhaps even stipulated in Zedekiah's vassal treaty. The oracle gives a plausible description of what might happen *should* Zedekiah attempt to escape the impending siege. The sign-act ends with the recognition formula: those who survive will acknowledge YHWH in their exile (v. 16).

(12:17–20) Quaking with Fear Ezekiel performs a second sign depicting the siege of Jerusalem: this time not an escape scene but a symbolic portrayal of those remaining during the siege. He is to eat bread and drink water while trembling. Similar to the sign-act of 4:9–17 demonstrating the people's deprivation, eating and drinking while trembling shows the extent to which all of life will be dominated by fear of the upcoming destruction. Here, as in 8:17 and 9:9, it is violence rather than cultic or treaty infidelity for which YHWH will punish Judah (v. 19).

(12:21–8) Prophecy and Fulfilment The final section of ch. 12 addresses the people's self-serving belief that prophetic oracles and visions are fulfilled only in the distant future if at all, and their resulting complacency in the face of Ezekiel's prophecy. Twice YHWH cites the people's words: first, a proverb indicating that longstanding prophecies remain (and presumably will continue to remain) unfulfilled (v. 22), and second, the opinion that Ezekiel's prophecies deal only with the distant future (v. 27). The two sayings dovetail conveniently, allowing people to write off new prophecy as not yet due for fulfilment and ancient prophecy as having 'expired'. YHWH responds to both sayings with the grim assurance that no prophecy will be delayed any longer; all will soon be performed.

(13:1–23) Varieties of False Prophecy Following YHWH's defence of authentic prophecies that remain embarrassingly unfulfilled, in Ezek 13 he condemns three separate groups of false prophets in Israel: self-appointed men who prophesy despite having heard nothing from YHWH; men who create a false sense of security through platitudinous promises of well-being; and women whose magical practices endanger their clients' lives. vv. 2–9 are directed against men who prophesy 'from their own imagination' (v. 2), who fabricate prophecies, having in fact seen nothing. In implicit contrast to Ezekiel, stationed in 3:16–21 as lookout on the city walls, these prophets are scavengers in the ruins of Jerusalem, having neither filled in the breaches nor erected a wall on which to stand on the 'day of the Lord' when the Divine Warrior attacks. Instead they announce, 'Says the LORD', when YHWH has not spoken (v. 6). These prophets receive ironically fitting punishment. YHWH responds to their false prophecy with a genuine oracle (appropriately beginning, 'thus says the LORD'; v. 8), announcing that his hand is against (*'el*) these prophets (not, as in Ezekiel's case, 'upon them'; cf. 1:3), and they will be expelled from both the people and the land of Israel. The recognition formula in v. 9 wryly attests that only after their complete rejection will these prophets 'know the LORD'.

The second group of prophets (vv. 10–16) predict only peace when in fact destruction awaits the people. These so-called 'peace prophets' are documented throughout the book of Jeremiah as a major presence in Jerusalem, a group whose message is understandably better received than are Jeremiah's predictions of disaster (Jer 6:14; 8:11; 14:13–16, *et passim*). These prophets, like the deluded prophets of vv. 2–9, are also depicted via imagery contrasting their actions with Ezekiel's role as lookout on the city wall. In this case the people build a patently insubstantial wall, namely their hope of successful rebellion, and the prophets, whitewashing the mudbrick wall, validate the people's false hopes. YHWH counters by declaring that he will bring rain and wind, attributes of the Divine Warrior, and wash away the wall and the prophets with it. Only in their death will these prophets acknowledge YHWH, who will shower, not peace, but rage upon the city (vv. 13, 15).

Finally, in vv. 17–23 YHWH directs Ezekiel to prophesy against a group of women charged, like the men of vv. 2–9, with making up their own prophecies and also with practising divination. The women sew items of fabric to be placed on the people's arms and heads, either as amulets or for divination. The women are further accused of 'profaning' YHWH by means of barley and bread (v. 19). The exact nature of the women's activities is debated; whether the grain represents a payment for divination or an offering, and if an offering, to what deity. Because the grains are able to 'profane' (*ḥll*) YHWH, they were probably offered to him, but in a manner capable of profaning his name. Divination, a practice forbidden in Ex 22:18 and Deut 18:10, might have been understood to defile YHWH if performed in his name. The women who in Jer 44:17–19 report having offered cakes to the queen of heaven (probably Astarte) during this period may provide a parallel. Not only is this divination a forbidden practice; it also serves the opposite purpose from Ezekiel's own prophecy. While he is commissioned to warn the wicked and support the righteous (3:16–21), the female prophets' divination encourages the wicked while discouraging the righteous (vv. 19, 22). If Ezekiel's authentic prophetic calling places his own life at stake (EZEK 3:16–21), how much more so the lives of these diviners who work at cross-purposes to YHWH. YHWH announces that he will tear off the female prophets' magical coverings and release the people whose lives have been captured by these false prophets (vv. 20–1). Then, says YHWH, they will acknowledge him.

The prophets currently in Israel are uniformly depicted by means of a negative comparison with Ezekiel, prophesying in Babylon. Whereas in his commissioning in 3:16–21 Ezekiel is posted on the wall to deliver YHWH's word, these prophets refuse either to build or to stand on the wall, and have received no word from YHWH. While Ezekiel must warn the wicked to repent and the righteous to stand firm, Israel's prophets re-

assure the wicked and dishearten the righteous. Ironically, it is the prophet farthest from Jerusalem's walls and apparently in the least danger who must stand guard on the walls and risk his life.

(14:1–11) The Idolatrous Elders Ezekiel is approached, as in 8:1 (and cf. 20:1) by a group of elders, this time having come to 'enquire' of YHWH. That is, rather than simply receiving whatever word of YHWH Ezekiel might speak, here the elders engage in the traditional practice of using the prophet as mediator to convey specific questions to YHWH (cf. Judg 18:5). YHWH, however, refuses to co-operate in the enquiry because of the seriousness of the elders' idolatry (cf. 20:3–4). Remarkably, the elders are not condemned simply for idolatry, but for 'lifting up' their idols 'into their hearts' (v. 4, my tr.). This accusation is far from clear, but seems to focus on the depth of the elders' attachment to idolatrous images (cf. the Jerusalem elders described in 8:9–12, who maintained secret 'picture rooms' inside the temple itself). YHWH's only response to the elders' enquiry is to warn them to turn back from idolatry or suffer death at his hands (vv. 6–8). When the idolater is 'cut off', an expression denoting sudden death as a punishment for sin, then the people will acknowledge YHWH (v. 8). YHWH goes on to say that if a prophet should in fact deliver a response to the idolater's enquiry, that response would be a deceitful one, planted by YHWH. The oracle thus serves as a warning to the prophet as well as a rebuke to the elders. Should a prophet persist in presenting the idolatrous elders' enquiry, which YHWH has already refused to hear, then that prophet would in fact receive a word in response, but the word would be an intentional lie sent by YHWH. YHWH would then destroy the prophet as well as the enquirer. YHWH's threat to entrap the people by sending deceitful oracles foreshadows the 'bad laws' of 20:25. Here and in ch. 20, however, YHWH's deceit and punishment of the people is not absolute, but preparation for his renewed rule over the covenant people (cf. 20:33, 40–4; 11:20).

(14:12–23) Noah, Dan'el, and Job In the second half of the chapter YHWH addresses the question of individual responsibility for sin. The issue was touched on in ch. 9 when the righteous Jerusalemites were marked so as to escape the city's destruction (9:4; and see EZEK 18:1–30). The number of citizens to be spared was apparently quite small, as Ezekiel protests that YHWH is destroying the last remnant of Israel (9:8). Now the question arises of whether a few righteous individuals might not suffice to save an entire city (as proposed by Abraham in Gen 18:22–33) or at least members of their own family (as Abraham was able to do; Gen 19:29). YHWH therefore puts forward for consideration the hypothetical example of a land inhabited by three legendary paragons of virtue: Noah, Dan'el, and Job. Noah was the most (or only) righteous person of his generation (Gen 6:9), and was consequently spared along with his family in the Flood. Dan'el is known from the Ugaritic Epic of Aqhat (the biblical Daniel's name does not occur in Ezekiel), in which Dan'el is a king famed for his wisdom and righteousness (see *ABD*, 'Daniel, Book of '). Job was 'blameless and upright, one who feared God' (Job 1:1), but his offerings on his children's behalf failed to save them. YHWH next posits a hypothetical land that has committed trespass (*m'l*, v. 13) against him, that is, defiled sancta (objects dedicated to temple service and therefore holy; see *ABD*, 'Holiness, OT') or broken an oath sworn in YHWH's name (see Milgrom 1976). YHWH further posits that should the three aforementioned paragons of virtue inhabit this land, even they would be helpless to save their own children from YHWH's punishment of famine, wild beasts, sword, and plague. It is allowed to go without saying that the prospects for anyone saving the current generation are slim indeed.

The scenario recalls YHWH's predictions in ch. 5 and 7 that he is about to bring these four levitically prescribed punishments against Jerusalem and Israel. The use of the technical term for trespass against sancta (*m'l*, translated 'acting faithlessly' in NRSV) suggests Jerusalem's own defilement of YHWH's sanctuary by idolatry and his name by treaty violation. The chapter's conclusion thus comes as no surprise: Jerusalem (which is patently not inhabited by Noah, Dan'el, or Job) will not be spared, whether for the sake of some few righteous citizens, or by the righteousness of those exiles whose children will now share in the city's doom (v. 21). YHWH adds the ironic note that some will in fact survive the city's destruction and be brought into exile. These will serve as consolation to the exiles, not because they were spared, but because their obvious wickedness will make it clear that YHWH did not destroy the city without reason (vv. 22–3).

The Twisted Symbols of Judah's Pride (15:1–20:44)

(15:1–8) The Useless Vine Ch. 15 ironically subverts the traditional metaphor of Israel as a luxuriant vine, lovingly tended by YHWH (cf. Isa 5:1–7; Gen 49:22; Jer 2:21). The chapter marks the first in a series of bitter parodies based on Israel's national symbols: Israel as a vine (here and in ch. 17), as the bride of YHWH (chs. 16 and 23), and as a proud lion (ch. 19). This deconstruction of Israel's national identity climaxes in ch. 20, where even the Exodus story is transformed into a history of Israel's degradation and YHWH's rejection. YHWH begins in 15:2 by posing a riddle to Ezekiel: how does the vine wood differ from any other wood? He continues with a series of rhetorical questions, proving that vine wood is distinctive only in its utter uselessness. Thus, this inferior wood serves only to be burned, or perhaps merely charred, a process rendering it even less useful than it had been initially. The figure of the vine wood's complete inutility patently contradicts Israel's self-styling as a fruitful vine. YHWH's comment on the further uselessness of charred vinewood is explained in vv. 6–8 as a metaphor for Jerusalem which has now been partially burned by Babylonia. Like the charred vinewood, Jerusalem will be burned again. The punishment, says YHWH, will result from the people's trespass (*m'l*). v. 8, the defilement of holy objects or of the divine name already condemned in 14:13.

(16:1–63) YHWH's Unfaithful Wife In Ezek 16 YHWH takes up the metaphor of Jerusalem as the bride of YHWH, declares her to be thoroughly unfaithful, and passes the death sentence upon her. Thus, as in the metaphor of the vine in ch. 15, so here too a symbol of national pride is transformed into a symbol of national shame. The chapter is divided into three sections: vv. 1–43, a biography of Jerusalem; vv. 44–52, an unfavourable comparison of Jerusalem to Samaria and Sodom; and vv. 59–63, in which YHWH promises at last to

forgive Jerusalem. The metaphor of the city as wife has deep roots in the ancient Near East. Capital cities were routinely considered goddesses, often the consorts of resident male deities and mothers to their inhabitants. The Israelite prophets continued to personify both Israelite and foreign capitals, but ordinarily presented them as debauched and unfaithful (Galambush 1992; cf. Hos 1–4; Isa 1:21–6; 23; 54; Jer 2; *et passim*).

YHWH commands Ezekiel to inform Jerusalem of the accusation brought against her, and in vv. 3–34 provides a 'biography' for his bride. Jerusalem, he says, is Canaanite, the daughter of an Amorite and a Hittite (v. 3; Jerusalem's Canaanite origins are well attested in OT: Jebusites, as per Judg 1:21; 2 Sam 5:6–10). The reference to Amorites and Hittites is best taken as in apposition to 'Canaanite' (and thus referring to the Hittites of Palestine (Gen 15:20), not those of Anatolia), an example of Canaanite peoples generally rather than a specific claim about the city's founders. As an infant Jerusalem was abandoned in a field, a common method in antiquity for disposing of unwanted children. YHWH finds her lying in the field, still covered with placental blood. His command for her to live apparently constitutes legal adoption (see Malul 1990), though he gives her no care until she reaches adolescence. When YHWH visits the girl again she has reached puberty; YHWH provides a graphic description of the still-naked and still-bloody girl's breasts and pubic hair (v. 7). YHWH now covers and bathes the girl, entering a marriage covenant. The imagery is disturbing to the modern reader; YHWH's behaviour seems lecherous, even incestuous, and the reader, like the prophet, is enlisted as a witness to Jerusalem's perverse sexual history. YHWH adorns his new bride lavishly, and her clothing of linen and *tāḥaš*, a material mentioned elsewhere only as a covering for the tabernacle, reflects the true significance of the city as bride: she is home to YHWH's holy of holies, the sanctuary in which YHWH's honour will be either maintained or defiled.

YHWH bestows perfect beauty upon his regal bride, but she has plans of her own. In vv. 15–22 Jerusalem systematically takes YHWH's gifts—clothing, food, gold, even children—and uses them for idolatrous purposes, described in the metaphor as prostitution. The charge of child-sacrifice is supported by similar charges in Jeremiah (e.g. 7:31, and see EZEK 20:25–6). In addition to 'adulterous' relations with other gods, Jerusalem seeks liaisons with other nations, the sexually potent Egyptians and the Babylonians. The charge that Jerusalem's foreign alliances constituted infidelity to YHWH is rooted, not in the marriage metaphor, but in the metaphor of YHWH as king. Israel has entered a vassal treaty (see *ABD*, 'Covenant') with YHWH and is therefore forbidden to give loyalty to any other king. Here the competing kings are pictured as Jerusalem's lovers, copulating with YHWH's bride and thereby violating his sexual honour. Jerusalem, meanwhile, is portrayed as a 'perverted prostitute' who pays her clients; that is, she pays tribute to the foreign nations with which she consorts (v. 34). The sequence of events roughly corresponds to Jerusalem's political history. Jerusalem entered an anti-Assyrian alliance with Egypt in 705 BCE (v. 26), after which Sennacherib in 701 BCE awarded Judahite territory to Philistia (v. 27). 'Unsatisfied' by the Assyrians (v. 28), Judah became a Babylonian vassal in 605 BCE (v. 29), but remained unsatisfied (v. 29), as witnessed by her numerous attempts at revolt.

In vv. 35–43 YHWH announces his wife's punishment: exposure and stoning, common punishments for adultery in the Bible and ancient Near East (Hos 2:10 [MT v.12]; Jer 13:22; and cf. Westerbrook 1990). The punishing agents, however, are not the husband or community as would be expected, but Jerusalem's former lovers. Here Ezekiel must shape the metaphor to suit historical reality. YHWH's rivals, the foreign nations, now become his agents in Jerusalem's destruction. In addition to being exposed and stoned, Jerusalem is hacked with swords and her houses burned (vv. 40–1), actions reflecting actual warfare. This, says YHWH, will satisfy his rage, ease his jealousy, and leave him calm. The husband's visceral satisfaction over his wife's death is presumably appropriate in its ancient Near-Eastern context, and the vocabulary parallels that used elsewhere in Ezekiel to describe YHWH's satisfied rage (cf. 5:13). To the modern reader, however, the scene is horrifying, the more so because the wife-killing husband is God.

In vv. 44–58 YHWH describes Jerusalem's place within an entire family of sinful women (cf. Jer 3:6–11). Her Canaanite mother, says YHWH, hated her own husband and children, just as Jerusalem has hated hers. YHWH goes on to claim that Jerusalem is the second of three sister cities, of which Samaria is the eldest and Sodom the youngest. The anachronism of portraying Sodom as 'younger' than Jerusalem may reflect the former city's relative unimportance or may be an adjustment necessary to preserve Samaria as Jerusalem's immediate role model (cf. ch. 23). Compared with two infamously wicked cities Jerusalem is found to be the worst. Contrary to the account of Gen 19, here the sin of Sodom is described as neglect of the poor despite the city's prosperity (cf. Isa 1:10–17), while Samaria is accused simply of 'abominations' (v. 51). Both sisters, however, look righteous in comparison to Jerusalem. Surprisingly, YHWH goes on to say he will *restore* all three cities and their daughters (suburbs or dependent towns), but that Jerusalem will be shamed before her two sisters (v. 54). Just as Sodom had been a byword connoting wickedness in the past, so now Jerusalem serves as an infamous object-lesson to her neighbours (vv. 56–7).

In vv. 59–63 YHWH summarizes Jerusalem's sin and both his punishment and his restoration of the city. Here Jerusalem's sin is described simply as 'showing contempt for the oath by breaking covenant' (v. 59, my tr.). All Jerusalem's sin fits under the rubric of covenant-breaking, but the specific charge of contempt for the oath introduces an issue that will be more fully explored in EZEK 17, namely, that in breaking his treaty oath to Nebuchadrezzar, Zedekiah has committed a trespass (*mᶜl*) against YHWH. 'I will deal with you as you have done', says YHWH (v. 59), that is, ignore his own covenant obligations to Jerusalem just as she has ignored hers to him. Yet, he goes on, he will ultimately establish an eternal covenant with Jerusalem. Although Samaria and Sodom will become her 'daughters', Jerusalem herself will be overcome with shame when at last she acknowledges YHWH (vv. 61–3).

(17:1–24) The Allegory of the Cedar In this chapter Ezekiel is instructed to 'propound a riddle', another in a series of extended metaphors. The metaphor is easily understood already in vv. 1–10, but a point-by-point explanation in vv. 11–21 becomes the occasion for YHWH to give his own perspective on the events described. Finally, in vv. 22–4 YHWH provides a new ending for the story, an allegory predicting YHWH's restoration of Judah.

In the allegory of vv. 1–10 a great eagle takes the top off a cedar of Lebanon and transports it to another land. He then takes some of the local seed and plants and waters it until it grows into a luxuriant vine spreading towards him. When a second eagle arrives, however, the vine turns and grows towards him, and he in turn transplants and waters the vine. Ezekiel's original audience would have had no trouble following the story. The first eagle is Nebuchadrezzar and the head of the cedar (considered a royal tree) is Jehoiachin, taken to Babylonia. Meanwhile, some of the royal 'seed', Zedekiah, is planted in Jerusalem. Zedekiah initially shows loyalty to Babylon (growing in his direction), but when Psammeticus of Egypt arrives he abandons Babylon for Egypt (see EZEK B.2). Ironically, whereas Jehoiachin was depicted as the top of a cedar, Zedekiah remains a creeping vine (cf. ch. 15). YHWH asks rhetorically whether such a vine will survive or be pulled out by its planter and desiccated by the harsh 'east wind'.

In vv. 11–21 YHWH explains the oracle as depicting Nebuchadrezzar's capture of Jehoiachin and Zedekiah's wavering loyalty, again concluding with a series of rhetorical questions: Can Zedekiah succeed, breaking covenant and yet escaping? Now YHWH gives explicit answers to his questions. Zedekiah will die in Babylon, the land of the king for whose oath he had contempt by breaking covenant (vv. 16, 18; cf. 16:59). Indeed, says YHWH, it was '*my* oath that he despised, and *my* covenant that he broke' (v. 19, emph. added), committing trespass (*mᶜl*, v. 20; cf. 14:13, *et passim*) against YHWH. It is YHWH whose honour has been defiled and he who will avenge it. Finally (vv. 22–4), YHWH adds his own ending to the story: himself will take a sprig from the top of the cedar and plant it on a high mountain of Israel. This plant will at once bear fruit (as the vine, Zedekiah, did not) *and* grow into a towering cedar (like Jehoiachin). What earthly kings attempted YHWH will accomplish, and Israel will thrive under an upright ruler of the Davidic house. If Israel's destruction vindicated YHWH's power before his own people (v. 21), Israel's restoration will demonstrate his sovereignty before the world (v. 24). This idyllic ending to the allegory, while unexpected in the midst of oracles of punishment, may none the less be original to Ezekiel, as it fits the pattern that will be repeated over the entire course of the book: YHWH will first destroy and then restore, both destroying and restoring in order that his sovereignty might be acknowledged (v. 24; cf. 20:1–44; 36:16–32).

(18:1–30) On Individual Responsibility In this chapter Ezekiel responds to the Israelite tradition that 'the sins of the parents are visited upon the children' (cf. Ex 34:7; Jer 32:18), arguing instead that each individual is responsible for his or her own sins. The question of responsibility would have been crucial during the Exile, and Ezekiel has already touched on the subject in the commissioning in 3:16–21 where the relative responsibility of Ezekiel and his hearers is discussed, and in ch. 14, in which YHWH denies that one person's virtue might save another. The chapter is a rhetorical *tour de force* formulated in response to a proverb current in Israel (see Jeremiah's citation of it in 31:29) and presumably among the exiles as well: 'The parents have eaten sour grapes, and the children's teeth are set on edge' (v. 2). The proverb deflects responsibility for the exile away from the current generation and into the past, a view of history shared by the editors of 2 Kings, who held both Manasseh (ch. 21) and Hezekiah (20:17–18) responsible for the Babylonian Exile. The proverb, whether used by those still in the land or by the exiles, serves simultaneously as complaint and reassurance; YHWH may be punishing us for sins we did not commit, but at least we are not to blame for our condition. The prevailing tone is one of complacent self-pity.

YHWH responds with an oath, forbidding the proverb's use and announcing that only 'the person who sins shall die' (v. 4). He then (vv. 5–20) describes a family of three generations: a righteous father, an evil son, and a righteous grandson. The righteous father, says YHWH, having kept the commandments, shall live; the violent, idolatrous son shall die bearing sole responsibility for his own death; the righteous grandson shall live, free from responsibility for his father's sins. Ezekiel's audience challenges this distribution of justice, asking, 'Why *shouldn't* the son suffer for the father's sin?' (v. 19, my tr.). The objection reflects both the people's comfort with the tradition of retribution and their discomfort at the most obvious application of YHWH's words: if the exile does not reflect their parents' sins, it must reflect their own. YHWH, however, reiterates that if the son has done what is right, then he shall live; the person that sins shall die (vv. 19b–20).

YHWH next changes the terms of the argument, taking up in vv. 21–4 the question of how a person is to be judged who turns within their own lifetime from wickedness to righteousness or from righteousness to wickedness. That is, instead of discussing retribution from generation to generation YHWH moves to the case of a single generation. Within a culture focused not on individuality but on tribal continuity YHWH's separation of the generations in vv. 5–20 might well have raised the question of how and when, if not from generation to generation, YHWH did in fact parcel out retribution for sins (cf. Job 18:19; 20:10; 21:7–13, 19). In the specific context of the exile, however, the change in topic from cross-generational behaviour to sin and repentance within a single lifetime effectively ends the people's speculation about who sinned in the past and focuses the argument squarely on their own choices in the present. A wicked person, says YHWH, who repents, keeping YHWH's laws and statutes, shall not die but live (v. 21). YHWH's goal is not the death of the wicked but their repentance. A righteous person, however, who turns from righteousness to sin will be held responsible for their trespass (*m'l*, v. 24) and shall die.

The people complain in v. 25 that YHWH's conduct as set forth in this passage is 'unruly' (*lō yittākēn*, my tr.), presumably because it does not conform to established standards governing sin and its punishment. YHWH responds that it is not his conduct but theirs that is unruly. Re-emphasizing the logic of punishing a righteous person who turns to evil but sparing a wicked person who turns to righteousness, YHWH repeats that it is not his conduct, in judging the people, that is unruly, but theirs (v. 29). The people's discomfort reflects only their suspicion that judged by these standards they deserve not only exile but death. In vv. 30–2 YHWH abandons theoretical discourse about hypothetical behaviour—whether each

person should be judged by their own actions—and announces that he will now judge his hearers, each according to *their* deeds. The rhetorical shift marks the climax of a speech that has progressed from discussion of multiple generations to evaluation of individuals within a generation, and finally to the current behaviour of the specific individuals at hand. 'Turn', says YHWH, 'from all *your* evil deeds . . . Why would you die, O house of Israel?' (vv. 30–1, my tr.). Whereas the people have implicated themselves by their own objections to YHWH's judgements, YHWH has proved not only his justice but Israel's guilt and the very real danger of punishment facing the people. Urging them to get themselves 'a new heart' (v. 31; note the contrast with 11:19 and 36:26 in which YHWH himself must replace the people's heart), YHWH reminds them that he has no stake in their death, which now seems inevitable according to the standards he has just delineated. Like the wicked person of vv. 21–2, however, YHWH's hearers face not simple condemnation but a decision. 'I have no pleasure in the death of anyone,' says YHWH (v. 32). 'Turn, then, and live.'

(19:1–19) The Dirge for the Rulers of Israel In ch. 19 Ezekiel is instructed to sing a dirge for Israel's ruler (emending MT's *něśî'ě* to sing. with LXX). Israelite prophets frequently employed the dirge (*qînâ*) form, with its distinctive 3–2 metre (cf. Am 5:2), addressing the dirge directly to the person being 'mourned', thus simultaneously predicting his or her downfall and lamenting it as an accomplished fact (cf. Ezek 26:17; 27:2, *et passim*). This dirge has two sections, each describing the ruler's mother. In vv. 2–9 she is presented as a lioness and in 10–14 as a vine, both common symbols for Judah and the Davidic dynasty.

The 'prince' addressed is probably Zedekiah, not Jehoiachin, as Ezekiel ordinarily calls Jehoiachin 'king' (*melek*) and Zedekiah 'prince' (*nāśî'*). The dirge focuses on the prince's mother, probably the city of Jerusalem as seat of the royal family and 'mother' to her inhabitants (cf. Ezek 16:1–63) rather than on an actual or idealized queen mother. The dirge depicts the Judean royal house as lions, a tradition established in Gen 49:9. The mother lion raises a cub to maturity; he learns to hunt and, we learn, becomes a man-eater. This grotesque distortion of Judah's national symbol follows the pattern set in chs. 15–17. The luxuriant vine is worthless and charred (EZEK 15:1–8); the bride sleeps with every passer-by (EZEK 16:1–63); and the proud lion now devours human beings. The lion, having turned man-eater, is captured and led off to Egypt. The lioness now takes another cub and raises him to maturity, at which point he, too, becomes a man-eater. Indeed, this lion ravages cities (the difficult term 'widows' in v. 7 occurs in parallel with 'cities', and probably reflects application of this term to devastated cities; cf. Cohen 1973) and terrorizes the coutryside. Soon he, too, is apprehended and taken to Babylon (v. 9). The identity of the first lion cub is clear: Jehoahaz, the son of Josiah, crowned by the people in 609 BCE but immediately deposed and deported by Pharaoh Necho II (610–595 BCE) is the only Judean monarch exiled to Egypt. The second cub is more difficult to identify; Jehoiachin and Zedekiah are both possibilities, but Jehoiachin is the more likely candidate. Jehoiachin had indeed been led before the king of Babylon, though he ruled only three months during which time he was hardly the international threat depicted here. Commentators who seek a literal queen of Judah as the two cubs' mother rather than the personified Jerusalem identify the second cub as Zedekiah because his mother, Hamutal, was also mother of Jehoahaz (2 Kings 24:17–18).

The second half of the dirge (vv. 10–14) is based, like chs. 15 and 17, on the vine as a symbol of Israel. Now the prince is told that his mother was like a vine, fruitful and lush, bearing boughs from which sceptres were made (unlike the useless wood of ch. 15). The vine climbed to a tremendous height, but was then uprooted, thrown to the ground, desiccated by the east wind, and then burned. Now, says YHWH, she has been transplanted in the wilderness and no bough remains from which to make a sceptre. As in vv. 2–9, the mother is Jerusalem. Her strong boughs, made into sceptres, represent the Davidic dynasty. The proud city, however, has now been torn down, stripped, and burnt with fire. Her prominent citizens exiled, she has been 'transplanted' to Babylon. The figure could describe Jerusalem's condition following the Babylonian capture in 597 BCE or could look forward to devastation yet to come. The prophetic convention of 'mourning in advance' allows either possibility, though the references to the devastating east wind (v. 12) predicted in 17:10 and to a time when no Davidic ruler remains (v. 14) suggest that the dirge predicts Zedekiah's downfall and the destruction of Jerusalem.

(20:1–44) Israel's Perverse Exodus Ezek 20 opens with a date formula (v. 1), the first since 8:1, dating the oracle to August 591 BCE, just over a year after the temple vision of chs. 8–11. As in 14:1 (and implied in 8:1) a group of elders has approached Ezekiel, hoping to enquire of YHWH. As before, YHWH refuses, this time by solemn oath (v. 3), to participate in their enquiry. Instead, he commands Ezekiel to judge them. YHWH proceeds by retelling the story of Israel's sojourn in and exodus from Egypt. The story forms a climax to the allegories in chs. 15–17 and 19, in which symbols of Israelite national identity are ironically recast into emblems of national shame. In ch. 20 the nation's founding myth, the Exodus narrative, undergoes an analogous subversion, becoming a tale of YHWH's endless rage against an Israel that cannot be ruled. The narrative is framed by YHWH's solemn oath in vv. 5 and 31 that he will not allow the elders to enquire of him. The problem of YHWH's oath and the honour of his name, prominent throughout Ezekiel, forms the core of this twisted history of Israel.

The history of Israel is depicted as a repetitious cycle in which YHWH first acts on the people's behalf and then sets out laws for them to follow. The people, however, rebel against YHWH, who considers destroying them, but instead acts for his 'name's sake', that is, for the sake of his honour, bound by the covenant with Israel. The history begins in v. 5, on the day YHWH chose Israel. Remarkably, Israel's election is said to have taken place in Egypt. The earlier covenants with Abraham, Israel, and Jacob are not mentioned, suggesting either that Ezekiel deliberately changes the traditional story or, equally likely, that he is acquainted with an alternative version, still current in the period before the Pentateuch's canonization. YHWH emphasizes his early vow to Israel,

repeating three times in two verses (5–6) that he took an oath (lit. raised my hand) declaring that he was their God and would bring them out of Egypt into their own land. YHWH demanded that his people discard their Egyptian idols, but his demands were ignored. Ezekiel's claim of Israel's initial election and subsequent rebellion while still in Egypt is unique, but consistent with strands in the Exodus narrative suggesting that the Israelites in Egypt were not acquainted with YHWH as their god and were reluctant to follow him, even in exchange for freedom (Ex 6:9; 14:11–12).

YHWH, faced with Israel's rebellion, decides to destroy the people already in Egypt (v. 8). Upon realizing, however, that by breaking his oath he would profane his own name—and that in plain sight of all the surrounding nations—he instead leads Israel out into the wilderness, where he provides statutes and ordinances for Israel's benefit (vv. 10–12). Israel shamelessly violates YHWH's statutes; YHWH again considers destroying them but again chooses not to profane his own name by doing so. Instead, he swears a new oath, namely, that he would not bring the people into the land (v. 15). This decision to reject the wilderness generation parallels the punishment decreed in Num 14, though the causes for YHWH's anger differ there. YHWH next commands the generation of the children not to emulate their parents, but to follow his statutes. The children also rebel, and once again YHWH considers destroying them but relents because of the danger to his own honour. Instead, YHWH devises a solution to the difficulty in which his loyalty oath has placed him. First, YHWH swears that rather than giving the people the land he will actually scatter them into exile in other lands (v. 23). YHWH then gives the people bad— even deadly—statutes. YHWH entraps the people by commanding them to sacrifice their firstborn to him, thereby justifying his destruction of Israel (vv. 25–6). The logic is not entirely clear, but seems to argue that child-sacrifice to YHWH was such a grave offence that it justified YHWH's violation of his covenant with Israel. The historical data is incomplete, but supports Ezekiel's claim here and elsewhere (16:20–1; 23:39) that child-sacrifice was practised in Jerusalem during this period. The ambiguous wording of Ex 22:29 [MT v. 28] may reflect a period in which Israelite law demanded or at least permitted such sacrifices, and YHWH's passionately repeated denial in Jeremiah (7:31; 19:5; and 32:35) that he ever commanded (or even dreamt of commanding) child-sacrifice seems calculated to respond to worshippers' claims that YHWH had indeed commanded the sacrifices they offered. YHWH's description of the sacrifice in Ezek 20:25–6 serves as the ironic climax to a perverse retelling of the Exodus. Instead of sparing Israel's firstborn YHWH now commands their slaughter; in place of liberation he decrees new enslavement for the people.

In vv. 27–38 YHWH concludes his bitter historical survey by addressing the current generation of Israel. Despite his vow not to bring the people into the land (v. 15), YHWH here describes the behaviour of those whom he did in fact bring into the land of Israel. This apparently is the generation who received the 'bad laws' of vv. 25–6, and the charge of child-sacrifice is repeated in v. 31. The current generation, says YHWH, continue their parents' sins, and YHWH vows, as he did at the recital's beginning (v. 31; cf. v. 3), not to honour their enquiries. Nevertheless, Israel's involvement with

YHWH is far from ended. On the contrary, any fantasy on Israel's part that they can now freely engage in idolatry is rejected. YHWH once again enters a solemn oath, swearing that 'with a mighty hand and outstretched arm', in rage he will at last rule over Israel (v. 33). Israel's joyful acclamation of YHWH's rule announced in Ex 15:18 now becomes the Warrior's conquest of his own people. In a reversal of the first Exodus YHWH will gather the people out of exile and judge them in the wilderness. Those who rebel against YHWH will be purged, but the rest included in YHWH's covenant (vv. 37–8; cf. Lev 27:32).

In vv. 39–44 YHWH portrays Israel's future after YHWH has established his reign. YHWH harshly dismisses those who persist in idolatry: 'Go serve your idols . . . if you will not listen to me; but my holy name you shall no more profane with your gifts and your idols' (v. 39). Those continuing to practice idolatry will no longer defile YHWH's name in so doing, having been excluded from the covenant. This expulsion of the idolaters seemingly contradicts YHWH's insistence in v. 32 that he will never allow Israel simply to 'be like the nations . . . [worshipping] wood and stone', and may mark v. 39 as a late addition to the book. Faithful Israel is described in vv. 40–4, serving YHWH with acceptable offerings on his 'holy mountain', Zion. YHWH's sanctity (not, as before, his dishonour) will be revealed before the nations after he has vindicated his name (cf. EZEK 39). Indeed, YHWH will act, not for Israel's sake, but for the sanctity of his name (cf. 36:22). Israel will be overwhelmed with shame (cf. 16:59–63) as it acknowledges YHWH.

The End Approaches (20:45–24:27; MT 21:1–24:27)

(20:45–21:32; MT 21:1–37) Fire and Sword against the Land A series of four brief oracles all announce the impending destruction of Judah and Jerusalem. The description of YHWH's punishment as a raging fire in 20:45–9 (MT 21:1–5) is followed by three oracles focusing on the sword by which YHWH will destroy the people. In 20:45–9 (MT 21:1–5) Ezekiel is commanded to set his face and prophesy against the forests of the Negeb ('Negeb' here refers to southern Palestine generally, rather than the modern Negeb). YHWH is sending a fire that will consume the green and the dry trees alike; that is, every tree. Ezekiel objects, pointing out that the people call him a 'metaphor maker' (v. 49; MT v. 5; my tr.; cf. NJPS, 'riddlemonger'). The prophet's complaint may be that people do not take his oracles seriously; Ezekiel is 'only' making metaphors, which will not come to pass. Such a complaint would be consistent with the people's earlier attitude towards prophecy expressed in 12:22 and with YHWH's observation in 33:31–2 that Ezekiel is treated as a mere singer of love songs. Alternatively, Ezekiel may be expressing the people's complaint that since he speaks only metaphors he cannot be understood.

The oracle of 21:1–7 (MT vv. 6–12) seems to come in response to Ezekiel's complaint in 20:45–9 (MT 21:1–5), whether to enforce the seriousness of the prophet's words or to explain their subtlety. Ezekiel is instructed to prophesy against the sanctuaries of Jerusalem and the land (ʾădāmâ, not ʾereṣ) of Israel, announcing that YHWH himself is drawing his sword to kill both the righteous and the wicked, 'all

flesh', from south to north. The image of YHWH wielding his sword recalls again the mythology of YHWH as Warrior, introduced in the vision of chs. 1–3. YHWH will destroy righteous and wicked alike, a startling inversion of the judicious discrimination promised in ch. 18 (and cf. Gen 18). Here, however, Ezekiel draws an image of cosmic war, in which 'all flesh', that is, all creation must be subdued before coming to acknowledge YHWH (cf. Gen 6:12–13). The puzzling image of YHWH destroying people in order to gain their fealty is presumably not to be taken literally, but assumes a scenario in which 'all flesh' as a whole suffers divine retribution, after which 'all [remaining] flesh' acknowledges YHWH's sovereignty (cf. the analogous claims in Ex 14:17–18; Ezek 25:7, inter alia). As in 12:17–20, Ezekiel is instructed in vv. 6–7 (MT vv. 11–12) to act out the response to YHWH's actions, in this case moaning pitifully in order to provoke the people's curiosity and so provide further opportunity to warn them of the coming disaster.

In 21:8–17 (MT vv. 13–22) Ezekiel is commanded to deliver an oracle in the form of a poem describing a sharpened sword. Israel has despised the rod, the traditional punishment for disobedient children (Prov 13:24; Isa 1:5–6). The sword is presumably YHWH's own, and it is handed over to a 'slayer' (understood as Nebuchadrezzar). Ezekiel is to wail over Israel (v. 12; MT v. 17) but also to clap his hands together and to chop and slash with the sword (v. 14; MT v. 19), acting out the enemy's satisfaction (cf. 6:11; 25:6) as he slaughters the people. Israel's true enemy, however, is not the 'slayer' to whom the sword is given, but YHWH himself, who in v. 17 (MT v. 22) joins Israel's attacker in clapping his hands as he satisfies his rage against Israel.

In 21:18–32 (MT vv. 23–37) Ezekiel is commanded to erect a signpost designating two roads: one to the Ammonite capital of Rabbah and the other to Jerusalem. The signpost represents the decision currently faced by Nebuchadrezzar of which of these two capitals to attack. Nebuchadrezzar engages in divination to determine his course, shaking arrows, consulting teraphim, and inspecting a sheep's liver (v. 21; MT v. 26). The arrows apparently functioned like lots, first labelled and then shaken together in a quiver, after which one was drawn out. The exact use of teraphim, though attested in the OT (Gen 31:19; 1 Sam 19:13–16; Hos 3:4), is unknown. Hepatoscopy, divination based on the analysis of sheep livers, was widespread in the ancient Near East (see ABD, 'Omens in the Ancient Near East'). Jerusalem is chosen for destruction. v. 23 (MT v. 28) is difficult, claiming that some unspecified group ('they') will doubt the results of divination, having sworn oaths. Most likely, this describes the Babylonians' initial reluctance to believe that they are in fact to destroy Jerusalem, 'having sworn oaths', i.e. entered a covenant with Zedekiah. However, says YHWH, Israel's guilt will be remembered, an event that will result in their capture. YHWH then addresses the Jerusalemites in v. 24 (MT v. 29), repeating to them that their transgression (presumably their violation of the vassal oath with Nebuchadrezzar) will indeed become known and they will be taken.

A brief oracle (vv. 25–7; MT vv. 30–2) is then directed specifically against the 'prince' (Zedekiah), whose downfall is foretold (cf. 17:24). A final note in v. 27 (MT v. 32) hints at a postexilic restoration of the Davidic dynasty, a promise made explicitly in 37:24–5. Following the oracles against Judah and Jerusalem, the sword song of vv. 9–12 (MT vv. 14–17) is recapitulated in vv. 28–32 (MT vv. 33–7), but this time in an oracle addressed to Ammon, predicting that the Ammonites, too, will be destroyed. The oracle, which may be a later addition, recalls the divination performed in vv. 18–22 (MT vv. 23–7) in which Jerusalem was designated for the Babylonian attack. Ammon's reprieve was temporary; it will now be so utterly devastated as to be 'remembered no more' (v. 32; MT v. 37). In fact, Nebuchadrezzar destroyed Ammon shortly after the fall of Jerusalem in 586 BCE. The oracle against Ammon prefigures the Oracles Against the Nations in chs. 25–32, describing YHWH's destruction of a nation that was spared momentarily during Judah's destruction, but now will feel the full weight of YHWH's wrath.

(22:1–16) Indictment of the Bloody City Ezekiel is called upon in v. 2 to indict Jerusalem for her abominations (cf. 20:4). A general announcement of the city's crime and punishment appears in vv. 3–5, followed by a detailed list of accusations in vv. 6–12, and the city's sentences in vv. 13–16. All the crimes of the 'bloody city' are described in terms of bloodshed: social injustice (vv. 6–7); cultic impurity (vv. 8–11); and abusive financial practices (v. 12). The list of Jerusalem's wrongs resembles the list of sins committed by the evil man and avoided by the righteous in the legal test case of ch. 18. Jerusalem is accused of the entire gamut of social and cultic sins. Consequently, YHWH will scatter the people in exile, purifying Jerusalem but in the process defiling himself. The reading of the versions in v. 16, 'I shall be profaned', is almost certainly preferable to the MT's 'you (fem. sing.) shall be profaned'. The niphal form should probably be translated even more strongly as a reflexive: 'I shall profane myself'. By exiling Israel YHWH can purify land, temple, and people, but the concomitant violation of his covenant oath defiles the divine name even as it vindicates and ultimately purifies it (cf. EZEK 16:59–60; 36:16–38).

(22:17–22) The Smelting of Israel The image of YHWH as smelter and refiner was used as early as Isa 1:21–5 to describe YHWH's purification of the corrupt city (and cf. Jer 6:27–30). This oracle, apparently delivered shortly before the beginning of the siege of Jerusalem (24:1–2), employs the image of a smelting furnace, in which metals are brought together and heated to the melting-point, to describe the populace crowded into the city, which is about to undergo the Babylonian attack (cf. the image of the city as a cooking pot in 11:3–7; 24:3–13). The metaphor, which aptly depicts the upcoming ordeal, is ironic, since YHWH announces at the outset that all the people have become dross (v. 18), the base metals discarded at the end of the process. They will be heated to the melting-point, but no silver will emerge. The recognition formula in v. 22 provides the oracle's only positive note; in their own destruction the people will recognize YHWH's wrath at work.

(22:23–31) Jerusalem's Destructive Leaders YHWH condemns Jerusalem's offences as committed by various groups of leaders: princes, priests, rulers, prophets, and people of the land (cf. the similar list in 7:26–7). The princes (reading, with LXX, 'whose princes' for MT's 'a conspiracy of its prophets') are the ravening man-eaters described in 19:1–9. The priests have defiled YHWH's sancta and failed to teach his ways. The

rulers prey like wolves upon the people (v. 27). The prophets embody the faults described in ch. 13, covering over reality with whitewash, seeing and divining messages YHWH never sent (v. 28). The people of the land (see EZEK 7:27) have oppressed the powerless (v. 29). No one has built up or stood in defence on the wall (see EZEK 13) to stave off the coming disasters. YHWH now claims that his rage *has been* poured out upon Jerusalem; Jerusalem's destruction is no longer a threat, but has already been set in motion.

(23:1–49) Oholah and Oholibah: YHWH's Faithless Wives Like ch. 16, Ezek 23 catalogues the behaviour of YHWH's unfaithful wife. Here, however, the conceit of 16:44–63 (also used by Jeremiah, 3:6–10) that Samaria is Jerusalem's elder sister is developed at length. The two cities are portrayed as 'daughters of one mother' who spent their youth in Egypt, where they were sexually molested. The verb *znh*, used extensively throughout the chapter, should not be understood in its literal sense, 'to act as a prostitute', but as a pejorative describing any illicit sexual behaviour, and thus secondarily, as a metaphor for cultic infidelity to YHWH. The two girls, already accustomed to illicit sexual practices in their youth, become YHWH's wives and bear him children. The women's Egyptian origin and history of illicit behaviour predating YHWH's election accords with the account of Israelite origins provided in 20:5–7.

The two sisters are given names: Samaria is Oholah and Jerusalem Oholibah. The names probably refer to the women's 'tents', that is, the cities' sanctuaries. Oholah ('she has a tent') represents the northern kingdom, with its own worship centres, and Oholibah ('my tent is in her') represents the southern kingdom, which contained YHWH's chosen dwelling in Jerusalem (cf. the renaming of the city as YHWH *šammâ*, 'YHWH is There', in 48:35). Oholah was unfaithful to YHWH, becoming infatuated with the Assyrians and their gods, a reference to Samaria's alliance with Assyria beginning in 842 BCE. As in ch. 16, both foreign alliances and idolatry are considered 'infidelity', though here the emphasis is on the political liaisons. Idolatry is described as merely a side-effect of these alliances, while the strong and handsome foreigners are described with a tone bordering on envy. Egypt, which for centuries encouraged both Samaria and Jerusalem to revolt against their Mesopotamian overlords, is depicted as a constant temptation to the two women. Their early experiences of abuse are seen as addictive, creating a constant desire for repeated encounters with Egypt. Thus, Oholah is unfaithful to Assyria, having continued her sexual contact with Egypt (on whom the northern kingdom did in fact rely in Hoshea's 725 BCE revolt against Assyria), and YHWH hands Oholah over to her offended Assyrian lovers for revenge. The death of Oholah and her children recapitulates Samaria's destruction by Assyria in 722/20 BCE.

Oholibah (Jerusalem) witnesses her sister's fate, but instead of amending her ways becomes even worse than Oholah had been (vv. 11–35). Oholibah continues to lust after the handsome Assyrians, but soon becomes distracted by etchings depicting Babylonians from Chaldea. Oholibah invites the Babylonians to her bed, but soon tires of them also. The description of Oholibah's liaison with Chaldeans is reminiscent of the Chaldean Merodach-Baladan's visit of 714 BCE, cited in 2 Kings 20:12–18 as the cause of the temple's destruction in 586 BCE. The following description of Oholibah's return to the Egyptians (vv. 19–21), however, represents Jerusalem's illicit alliance with Egypt both before and after the Exile of 597 BCE. In retaliation YHWH will now enlist both Babylonians and Assyrians along with their allies to punish Oholibah's infidelity. Like ch. 16, so also ch. 23 is alarming to the modern reader. Sexually abused young women are labelled tainted, and their later sexual deviance punished by still further sexual violence against them.

In vv. 32–4 Oholibah is sentenced to drink from Oholah's cup, i.e. to undergo her punishment (cf. Jer 25:15–19; Hab 2:16). YHWH then begins a new indictment (vv. 36–49), now directed simultaneously against Oholah and Oholibah. Oholah's inclusion is unexpected within the terms of the metaphor (she was killed in v. 10), but may reflect the historical reality of displaced northerners present in Jerusalem and active in the cult. The crimes described in vv. 36–49 are primarily cultic, defined as adultery (*n'p*, the technical term for adultery, is used) and bloodshed. The women are said to have committed adultery with their idols, sacrificing their children to them. Moreover, the child-sacrifices were carried out in conjunction with worship in the Jerusalem temple (vv. 38–9), thus defiling the sanctuary. YHWH then describes a scene in which foreign men were invited into the sanctuary (vv. 39b–42) and lavishly entertained by the women, probably a reference to Psammeticus's entourage (see EZEK B.2; EZEK 44:7), whose presence in the Jerusalem sanctuary simultaneously defiled the temple and violated YHWH's covenant. In v. 46 YHWH calls for the avenging Babylonians to advance, thus setting the stage for the announcement in 24:1–2 that the siege of Jerusalem has begun. The notice (v. 48) that Oholah and Oholibah will serve as warnings to 'all women' should be understood within the terms of the metaphor; other cities will be warned against rebellion.

(24:1–27) Jerusalem under Siege The Cooking Pot (24:1–14). The chapter opens with a date formula, January 588 BCE, the beginning of Nebuchadrezzar's siege of Jerusalem. Ezekiel is instructed to record the date, either to underscore its significance, or as evidence of his prescience. He then delivers an oracle in which the besieged city is figured as a pot on the fire (vv. 3–14), after which he performs the sign-act of stifling his grief when his wife is stricken dead (vv. 15–27).

Ezekiel is commissioned to recite a song for the exiles, in which a pot is filled with choice meat and water and then boiled (vv. 3–5). The context of Jerusalem's siege makes the song's meaning self-evident: the residents of Jerusalem are currently being 'pressure cooked' within the city walls (cf. 11:3). YHWH next announces doom to the pot itself (vv. 6–13), that is, the destruction of the personified city rather than the death of its inhabitants. The 'bloody city' is described as a 'diseased' pot (v. 6). Whether the disease symbolizes mere corrosion or an actual infirmity such as the leprosy that infects clothing and houses in Lev 13:47–59 and 14:34–53, the pot is ritually unclean, and so the meat must be removed from it. YHWH identifies bloodshed as the source of Jerusalem's impurity, and he now exposes the shed blood and punishes the city for its crimes (cf. Lev 17:11–13; see ABD 'Blood'). In vv. 9–14 YHWH describes the pot's purification. After its contents

(the residents of Jerusalem) have been cooked and burned, then the pot itself must be purified in the fire. The gruesome metaphor aptly describes YHWH's double concern: the punishment of Jerusalem's sinful inhabitants and the purification of the holy city and its sanctuary. YHWH laments in vv. 12–13 that previous attempts to purify the sanctuary have failed; only after his rage has been fully spent upon it will the city again be cleansed.

Ezekiel's Wife's Death (24:15–27). YHWH now informs Ezekiel that 'the delight of [Ezekiel's] eyes' is to be taken away, in response to which Ezekiel is to refrain from mourning. Ezekiel relates this word to the people 'in the morning' and that evening his wife, the delight of his eyes, dies. The people ask for an interpretation of Ezekiel's sign-act and YHWH responds that he is about to profane his own sanctuary and kill the exiles' children in Jerusalem (v. 21). Ezekiel thus acts out both YHWH's and the people's loss. The use of Ezekiel's wife to symbolize the Jerusalem sanctuary recalls the personification of Jerusalem as YHWH's wife, as depicted in chs. 16 and 23, where the death sentence has already been passed upon her. With Jerusalem's destruction the people will suffer both the loss of the temple and the death of beloved children, yet they are commanded not to mourn. Ezekiel's sign-act, including the countermand against mourning (v. 22) implies that it is not only the prophet and the people but also YHWH who will stifle his natural grief over the city, knowing the justice of its fall. The sign-act simultaneously evokes both the intimacy of YHWH's loss and his implacable determination. With the exception of a simile in 36:38 recalling the temple flocks, Jerusalem is never again mentioned by name in Ezekiel.

Finally (vv. 25–7), YHWH informs Ezekiel that after the city and temple have been destroyed a fugitive will bring him the news, after which the prophet's dumbness will be removed. The motif of dumbness connects the passage with Ezekiel's call in 3:24–7, creating a loose *inclusio* and concluding the first half of the book. The prediction regarding the fugitive similarly creates a bridge to ch. 33, which relates the fugitive's arrival and marks the resumption of prophecies regarding Israel after the oracles against the nations in chs. 25–32.

Hope for the Future (25:1–48:35)

Oracles against Foreign Nations (25:1–32:32)

Collections of oracles against foreign nations appear in all three major prophets (cf. Isa 13–23; Jer 46–51) as well as some minor prophets (e.g. Am 1–2). Such oracles, delivered before an Israelite audience and announcing YHWH's judgement on enemy nations, served primarily as oracles of reassurance for Israel (see ABD, 'Nations'): YHWH could and would act on Israel's behalf to punish his people's enemies. In Ezekiel the oracles serve as a transition between the first half of the book (chs. 1–24), which is preoccupied with YHWH's judgement against Judah and Jerusalem, and the second half (chs. 33–48), in which promises of restoration predominate. Spanning the gap between the announcement in 24:1–2 that Jerusalem is under siege and the notice of the city's fall in 33:21, the oracles reveal the universal reach of YHWH's power. Having first gone forth against his own people, the Divine Warrior will not stop until *all* nations have been brought to justice. The oracles thus place Jerusalem's destruction within the larger context of YHWH's authority over all the earth. Each of the oracles against a foreign nation includes YHWH's claim, 'You shall know that I am YHWH'; each nation in turn will be brought to acknowledge his sovereignty.

Of the seven nations singled out in chs. 25–32, five (Edom, Moab, Ammon, Tyre, Sidon), are known to have participated in rebellion against Babylon, while a sixth, Egypt, provided support for this rebellious activity. Ezekiel's concern not to defile YHWH's honour by a revolt violating 'YHWH's covenant' with Nebuchadrezzar (EZEK 17) is often considered sufficient justification for labelling all the rebellious nations enemies of YHWH and appropriate objects of his wrath. Two problems mar this interpretation. First, in their rebellion against Babylon, the foreign nations do *not* violate YHWH's covenant as Judah does, but covenants presumably sworn in the names of their own gods. Second, nowhere in chs. 25–32 are the foreign nations condemned for joining in rebellion against Babylon; rather, they are punished for their misconduct towards Judah and Jerusalem. Even as he orchestrates Jerusalem's destruction by Babylon, YHWH is shown avenging the scorn shown to his people (and, presumably, himself) by their lesser enemies, who gloat over the city's fall.

(25:1–7) Against Ammon Ezekiel delivers a two-part oracle against Ammon (vv. 3–5, 6–7; cf. 21:28–32). In each, Ammon is accused of malicious glee at the temple's destruction and the exiles' deportation. Ammon, itself a Babylonian vassal, will therefore also be utterly destroyed by these 'people of the East'. Each section of the oracle concludes with the recognition formula; after being themselves vanquished, the Ammonites will acknowledge YHWH. Note that the reference to the temple's desecration (v. 3) requires that the oracle be dated to 586 BCE or thereafter.

(25:8–11) Against Moab Moab is accused simply of considering Judah to be 'like all the other nations' (v. 8). The claim may represent a Moabite response to the destruction of the Jerusalem temple: the Davidide claim to YHWH's special protection of Zion (see ABD, 'Zion Traditions') has been proved false. As punishment for its gloating, Moab will be given along with Ammon to 'the people of the East' (v. 10). Particularly, the area of northern Moab (Beth-jeshimoth, Baal-meon, and Kiriathaim) whose possession was a subject of dispute between Moab and Judah, here referred to as 'the glory of the country' (v. 9), will now belong to foreigners. Having denied Judah's special status, Moab will lose its own 'glory'. Even its punishment will not be unique to it, but shared with Ammon, its neighbour. Then, says YHWH, the Moabites will recognize his sovereignty.

(25:12–14) Against Edom The oracle against Edom is especially vehement (cf. an additional condemnation of Edom in ch. 35). Edom is apparently singled out because, having joined with Judah in rebellion against Babylon (Jer 27:3), it then acted as a Babylonian ally, perhaps taking over Judean holdings in the Negeb (cf. Jer 49:7–22, Ob 1–14; but see the discussion in ABD, 'Edom'). The 'āšām (grievous offence) referred to in v. 12 presumably refers to Edom's violation of the oath forming the anti-Babylonian alliance. YHWH thus hands Edom over, not to the Babylonians (whose newly loyal vassal they have be-

come), but to the Israelites themselves. Israel will act as YHWH's agents in devastating Edom, after which they will 'know my vengeance' (v. 14), says YHWH.

(25:15–17) Against the Philistines Like the Edomites, the Philistines are accused of 'taking vengeance' against Judah. The Philistines are not recorded in Jer 27 as participating in the anti-Babylonian alliance nor is their vengeance against Judah described, like Edom's, as an 'āšām (see EZEK 25:12–14). It is therefore likely that the Philistines had continued as loyal Babylonian vassals (they had been conquered by Nebuchadrezzar as recently as 601 BCE) and had been rewarded for this loyalty with a gift of Judean territory. In any case, their treatment of Judah is described as vicious, and YHWH swears to take vengeance against them. The mention of the Cherethites in v. 16 probably refers to the Philistines' origins from the island of Crete (see ABD, 'Philistines'). After he takes vengeance on them, says YHWH, the Philistines also will acknowledge his sovereignty.

(26:1–28:19) Against Tyre Tyre's Downfall (26:1–21). Ezekiel devotes nearly three chapters to oracles against the Phoenician city-state of Tyre. An island fortress located off the coast of Lebanon, Tyre was the immensely prosperous centre of a vast Mediterranean trade network. Although paying tribute to Babylon, Tyre had thus far avoided outright conquest by Nebuchadrezzar. Nevertheless, Tyre was among those plotting rebellion as per Jer 27 against even this nominal submission. Tyre's apparent exemption from the harshest consequences of Babylonian rule and its continued prosperity, both due to its commercially and strategically favourable location, seem to have singled Tyre out (along with Egypt) for Ezekiel's particularly harsh judgement.

Ezek 26 consists of a four-part oracle in which the first two sections (vv. 1–14) describe the city's destruction while the latter two (vv. 15–21) describe the aftermath of Tyre's fall. The oracle opens with an incomplete date formula, placing the oracle sometime in 587/6 BCE. A date towards the end of the year would be appropriate since the oracle implies (v. 2) Nebuchadrezzar's successful capture of Jerusalem, and probably anticipates his siege of Tyre, begun around this time. Nebuchadrezzar maintained his siege for thirteen years before reaching a negotiated settlement (see Jos. Ant. 10.11.1).

The oracle opens quoting Tyre's satisfaction with Jerusalem's capture. The merchant city sees Jerusalem's destruction in strictly economic terms; Jerusalem's loss will become Tyre's gain. YHWH responds that he will hurl ships like so many waves against the island fortress. Tyre (Heb. ṣōr) will be scraped down to the bare rock, a punishment that plays indirectly on the Hebrew ṣûr, 'rock', after which Tyre will acknowledge YHWH's sovereignty (v. 6). YHWH continues in vv. 7–14 with a more detailed and literal prediction of Nebuchadrezzar's siege of the city. After destroying Tyre's coastal dependencies, the Babylonian monarch will muster his impressive battery of horses, troops, and siege equipment. The city will be taken and plundered; the comparison between Tyre and a bare rock reappears to conclude the oracle (v. 14).

In vv. 15–18 YHWH describes the horror of the coastlands and 'the princes of the sea' (v. 16), probably Tyre's coastal settlements and its Mediterranean outposts. Tyre's bereaved allies raise a lament (vv. 17–18) over the ruin of the once-glorious city. Finally, in vv. 19–21 YHWH explains Tyre's demise in cosmic terms. It is he who has vanquished the city, covering the maritime capital with 'the great waters' (v. 19) of chaos and bringing it down to Sheol. Thus, not only will Tyre 'never again be rebuilt' (v. 14); it will vanish and 'be no more' (v. 21).

The Shipwreck of Tyre (27:1–36). The whole of ch. 27 constitutes a single oracle, an extended allegory describing Tyre as a ship. Like the allegories against Judah in Ezek 15, 16, 17, and 19, so also in the case of Tyre Ezekiel employs stock symbols of national identity, ironically transforming them into symbols of national shame. The city, bordered on all sides by the sea, making its living by commerce, is depicted as a merchant ship, setting forth on a voyage. As Tyre enjoyed luxury goods from all corners of the world, so also the ship is fitted out with the finest materials from Senir, Lebanon, Bashan, Cyprus, and Egypt (vv. 5–7). An international crew sails the ship, which is 'perfect' in its beauty. The ship trades with numerous lands, from Tarshish to Arabia, and carries a cargo of exotic wares. After lovingly describing the Good Ship Tyre's embarkation Ezekiel abruptly informs her that her rowers have brought her into deep water, where she has been shipwrecked (v. 26). Riches, crew, army, and cargo sink together into the sea. All the mariners on shore lament the great ship's utter devastation.

Against the Ruler of Tyre (28:1–19). Ezekiel delivers an oracle against the ruler (něgîd) of Tyre (vv. 1–10) followed by a lament over the destruction of the king (melek) (vv. 11–19). In the initial oracle the prince is accused of calling himself a god (perhaps playing on the theophoric name of Ittoba'al III (man of Baal), who ruled Tyre from 590–575 BCE). Although he is indeed wiser than the legendary king Dan'el (v. 3; see EZEK 14:14) and has prospered through his wisdom, yet YHWH will bring 'the most terrible of the nations' (Babylonia, v. 7) against him. Tyre's prince will be relegated to Sheol, where he will be unable to boast divine status. The ensuing lament over the king of Tyre strikingly combines imagery drawn from the Israelite cult and from the Eden tradition, depicting the monarch simultaneously as the first man and as high priest. Like the primordial man (cf. Gen 2:4b–3:24) he was in Eden, until, having become corrupted, he was cast out by the guardian cherub. Like the Israelite high priest (Ex 28:6–14; 24:13), he wore a breastplate encrusted with precious stones and resided on the holy 'mountain of God'. Having profaned his sanctuaries, however, he was consumed by fire. The king of Tyre is thus depicted as having enjoyed God's favour to an unprecedented degree, having become corrupted by his immense wealth, and finally being destroyed forever. The oracle's symbolism is puzzling, as no known tradition links Tyre directly with either the Eden or the priestly traditions.

(28:20–3) Against Sidon A brief oracle announces YHWH's judgement against Sidon, another member of the anti-Babylonian alliance mentioned in Jer 27. No direct accusation against Sidon is made, and its punishment is described in the most general terms. More significant than either Sidon's sin or its punishment, however, is YHWH's ultimate goal, repeated twice in this brief oracle: they shall acknowledge YHWH's sovereignty.

(28:24–6) Promises to Israel The catalogue of Israel's smaller neighbours concludes with two brief oracles of promise to Israel. First (v. 24), Israel will cease to be provoked by these contemptuous neighbours. Second (vv. 25–6), having punished Israel's neighbours, YHWH will then restore Israel to its land and his presence to Israel. As in vv. 20–3, YHWH twice repeats his goal: that the nations will acknowledge his sovereignty. This first group of oracles against the nations thus fulfils the traditional role of reassuring Israel of YHWH's favour. At the same time the oracles reaffirm that Judah's current humiliation is taking place within the wider context of YHWH's self-vindication before all the world.

(29:1–32:32) Against Egypt The seven oracles against Israel's smaller neighbours in chs. 25–8 are balanced in chs. 29–32 by seven oracles directed against Egypt. The object of condemnation equal to that directed against all other nations combined, Egypt is represented as the great enemy of Israel and of YHWH. Unlike the other nations, however, Egypt is nowhere accused of mocking Israel or of taking advantage of its destruction. Rather, Egypt is condemned for its grandiose pretensions—the power that rendered it a fatal lure for Israel (see EZEK B). As described in chs. 20 and 23, Israel had since earliest times demonstrated a weakness for 'the idols of Egypt' (20:7; cf. 23:8, 19). More recently, Judah had repeatedly depended on Egypt to support rebellion against Babylon. Egypt, then, is the enemy making possible Judah's violation of YHWH's covenant with Nebuchadrezzar. Egypt has presented itself as protection against the wrath of Nebuchadrezzar and of YHWH, and YHWH must therefore avenge his honour against the challenge of Egypt.

Pharaoh the Sea-Serpent (29:1–16). In an oracle dated to January of 587 BCE, YHWH addresses Pharaoh as a great sea-serpent (tannîn; reading sing. for MT's pl.) stretched out in the Nile surrounded by fish (vv. 3–4). Like the king of Tyre, Pharaoh is condemned for claiming divine status (in this case, as the Nile's creator), and YHWH announces that he will fish out the serpent along with its dependent fishes (Egypt's allies) and fling them out to rot in the field (vv. 4–5). Thus, says YHWH, the Egyptians will acknowledge YHWH's sovereignty.

In vv. 6b–9a a new metaphor describes the political background for the oracle. Egypt is a reed on which Israel has leant for support, but which has broken and injured those who trusted its strength (cf. Isa 36:6). The image encapsulates Israel's political and military situation. The January 587 BCE date locates the oracle in the aftermath of Pharaoh Hophra's aborted attempt of 588 BCE to lift Nebuchadrezzar's siege of Jerusalem. The staff on which Judah had depended for support had broken easily under Babylonian pressure. YHWH will punish Egypt for the harm done to Judah, with the result that the Egyptians will acknowledge YHWH. In vv 9b–16 YHWH repeats Pharaoh's pretensions as the Nile's creator, responding that Egypt and the Nile will be devastated, and the land made uninhabitable. Like Judah (4:6; cf. Num 14:34), Egypt will be exiled for forty years and then restored as only a minor kingdom (vv. 13–15). Israel, recalling its former reliance on this now humble nation, will then acknowledge YHWH's sovereignty.

Nebuchadrezzar's Consolation Prize (29:17–21). This oracle, dated to January 571 BCE, is the latest-dated oracle in Ezekiel (the 573 BCE date assigned to the concluding vision of chs. 40–8 is the next latest). Separating oracles dated to

January 587 BCE (29:1–16) and April 587 BCE (30:20–6), 29:17–21 seems to disrupt the chronology thus far established in Ezekiel. The oracle can, however, be dated with some certainty to 571. The oracle's message is peculiar in that it depends on the *inaccuracy* of Ezekiel's earlier oracles against Tyre. In chs. 26–8 (dated to 586 BCE) Ezekiel had predicted Tyre's downfall in a series of oracles, including specific notice in 26:7–14 that YHWH's agent for Tyre's destruction would be Nebuchadrezzar of Babylon. Nebuchadrezzar had in fact mounted a prolonged siege against Tyre following his successful campaign against Jerusalem. After a thirteen-year siege, however, in 572 Nebuchadrezzar proved unable to take the island fortress. Apparently in response to Nebuchadrezzar's failure (and so also the failure of his own earlier predictions), Ezekiel now offers Egypt to the Babylonian king as compensation for his fruitless efforts on YHWH's behalf in the aborted siege of Tyre. Egypt, says YHWH, will serve as Nebuchadrezzar's payment for services rendered during the siege of Tyre (v. 20). Egypt's demise will bring honour to Israel, who in turn will recognize YHWH. Ezek 29:17–21 is remarkable for its open acknowledgement of unfulfilled prophecy. In fact, Nebuchadrezzar did invade Egypt in 568 BCE (*ANET* 308), but even his own annals do not claim victory. While disrupting Ezekiel's overall chronology, the oracle's contents—predicting Nebuchadrezzar's conquest of Egypt—explain its insertion into a collection of oracles condemning Egypt and announcing Nebuchadrezzar's triumph over Pharaoh.

The Day of YHWH against Egypt (30:1–19). This oracle announces YHWH's judgement on Egypt in three sections. In vv. 1–5 YHWH announces that the day of YHWH (see EZEK 7:10) has come for Egypt. YHWH's sword will be unsheathed and the nation will be utterly destroyed. The final section, vv. 13–19, presents YHWH as an ancient Near Eastern monarch publishing his conquest list—the list of cities vanquished during a successful military campaign. The oracle's central section, vv. 6–12, announces the instrument by which YHWH will devastate Egypt; YHWH will conquer Egypt 'by the hand of King Nebuchadrezzar of Babylon' (v. 10). This central section combines the cosmic imagery of vv. 1–5 (YHWH will dry up the life-sustaining waters of the Nile; v. 12a) with descriptions of normal, human warfare and its consequences (vv. 11, 12b). The oracle thus reinforces its claim that victory over Egypt belongs to the Divine Warrior. Nebuchadrezzar's army represents merely the human aspect of YHWH's triumphant day.

Pharaoh's Broken Arm and Nebuchadrezzar's Strong Arm (30:20–6). In an oracle dated to April 587 BCE YHWH reiterates both his condemnations of Pharaoh (see ch. 29) and his announcement that he will place his own divine sword in Nebuchadrezzar's hand (cf. 30:10–11; ch. 21). The date, like that of 29:1, locates the oracle in the aftermath of Apries's withdrawal from Jerusalem. The current oracle may reflect Nebuchadrezzar's renewal of the siege. YHWH claims that, having already broken one of Pharaoh's arms, he will now shatter the other. By contrast, he will strengthen Nebuchadrezzar's arms, arming him with YHWH's own sword. As Babylon is fortified and Egypt dispersed into exile, the nations will acknowledge the sovereignty of YHWH.

The Fall of the Great Cedar (31:1–18). This oracle, dated to June of 587 BCE, consists of an extended metaphor comparing Pharaoh to a great cedar. The point of comparison is actually between Egypt and Assyria, depicted here as a cedar of cosmic proportions. Despite the common scholarly practice of emending ʾaššûr (Assyria) to tʾaššûr (cypress tree) with the result that Pharaoh is likened to the cosmic cedar tree, MT's ʾaššûr should be maintained; Pharaoh's power is compared to that of Assyria, which despite its former glory has now been laid low by Babylon. The comparison between Egypt and Assyria is intriguing, since towards the end of the sixth century BCE Egypt had gained influence on the eastern Mediterranean seaboard as Assyria's influence in the region waned (see Miller and Hayes 1986: 383–5). Egypt could therefore style itself as heir to the western portion of the Assyrian empire. Ezekiel plays out this flattering comparison. Assyria, he says, was not only great among all other 'trees'; it surpassed even the trees of Eden (v. 8). Assyria is depicted as the 'world tree', known from Babylonian and Sumerian sources as a tree connecting heaven and earth, with roots extending down into the cosmic waters. Beautiful and fruitful, this tree provided shade in which all the nations flourished. The tree's greatness, says YHWH, was its downfall. Because of its excessive pride, YHWH handed over this greatest of all trees to 'the most terrible of nations' (v. 12), Babylonia. Now the tree lies broken, stretched out across the countryside. Indeed, says YHWH, the tree has descended into Sheol, along with all its allies (vv. 14–17). The unrivalled splendour of Assyria is matched only by the shock felt among the nations over its utter collapse. The moral of the story is tersely stated in v. 18: And you, asks YHWH, which of the trees of Eden were *you* like in *your* splendour? No matter; you will have plenty of company among the many trees of Eden in Sheol. 'This', says YHWH, 'is Pharaoh and all his horde.'

Concluding Laments over Egypt (32:1–32). Ezekiel's final oracles against Egypt are assigned a range of dates in the various MSS, with most locating them in March of 586 or 585 BCE. The oracles thus address Egypt in the context of Jerusalem's destruction, whether immediately following the event, or on the first anniversary of the city's fall. In either case, Ezekiel's oracles against Egypt cover a span of over two years (excluding 29:17–21, which reflects the situation over a decade later). The oracles thus begin during the siege of Jerusalem, condemning Egypt for misleading Israel into rebellion (29:6–7), and conclude after the city's fall with two 'laments' (32:1–16, 17–31), one summarizing all the preceding oracles, the other celebrating in advance Egypt's arrival in Sheol. The concluding oracles address an Egypt that has apparently emerged unscathed after luring Israel to its destruction, and express the prophet's determination that YHWH (and therefore Nebuchadrezzar) has yet to conclude his dealings with Pharaoh.

vv. 1–16 present a recapitulation of the punishments designated for Egypt over the course of the previous three chapters. YHWH begins in vv. 1–6 by saying that although Pharaoh considers himself a lion, he is in fact a sea-serpent, fouling the waters of the Nile. As in 29:1–5, YHWH will trap the serpent and fling it out to die in the open field. The earlier image of animals feeding on Pharaoh's corpse appears here in even greater detail. YHWH's victory over Pharaoh will, like the day of YHWH described in 30:2–5, reverberate throughout the cosmos, as YHWH blots out the light of the sun, moon, and stars (vv. 7–8). Egypt, as predicted in 29:9b–12, will be exiled from its land (vv. 9, 13) because of YHWH's sword and the sword of Nebuchadrezzar (vv. 10–12; cf. 29:8; 30:2–12, 20–6). In the aftermath of Jerusalem's destruction YHWH renews his earlier threats against Judah's attractive but deceitful ally. The oracle departs from the course set by earlier condemnations of Egypt only in its depiction of Egypt's restoration. Whereas the oracle dated to 587 BCE could envision Egypt's humble return following its forty-year 'exile' (29:13–16), in the aftermath of Jerusalem's destruction Ezekiel promises only that the land itself will be restored. After Egypt's land has been 'stripped' of its inhabitants, YHWH will restore its luxuriant streams (vv. 14–16). The oracle concludes with the recognition formula (v. 16), the seventh and final declaration within the oracles against Egypt that finally, in their utter devastation, the Egyptians will recognize YHWH.

In vv. 17–32 Ezekiel laments Egypt's descent into Sheol (see ABD, 'Dead, Abode of the'). No longer a great sea-serpent or a mighty tree, Egypt is assigned to share the fate of all other former military powers; namely, the leaders and warriors who fill the vast underworld, each in its assigned corner of the Pit. After introducing in vv. 18–21 the theme of Egypt's descent, in vv. 22–30 Ezekiel enumerates the nations with whom Egypt will share the grave: Assyria, Elam, Meshech and Tubal, Edom, and Sidon. Each of these nations was once able to create terror in the land of the living. Now they populate the land of the dead, their graves laid out in orderly array, rank upon rank, shamed, murdered, sharing an unclean grave. Pharaoh, the most recent arrival in this realm (vv. 31–2), will be 'consoled' for the loss of his army, presumably when he perceives that his fate is not unique, but shared with many who were once proud and powerful. Ezekiel's final oracles against Egypt, 'lamenting' Egypt's downfall at a period when Egypt appeared impervious to Babylonian incursions, serve as predictions, celebrating in advance the destruction YHWH would finally bring against Egypt, the power whose alliance with Judah had proved disastrous for the smaller nation.

Images of Restoration and Return (33:1–39:29)

(33:1–33) Ezekiel's New Commission Following Ezekiel's condemnations of Judah and Jerusalem in chs. 1–24 and his announcement in chs. 25–32 of YHWH's wrath against nations variously implicated in Judah's destruction, in ch. 33 Ezekiel begins a series of oracles (chs. 33–9) promising YHWH's restoration of the people and land of Israel. This new beginning is signalled in ch. 33 by a complex interweaving of themes imported from the first twenty-four chapters of the book. Specifically, the chapter addresses in various forms the question of responsibility, both Ezekiel's responsibility as prophet and the people's responsibility for their own moral and religious choices. The question of how to assign moral responsibility takes on special poignancy in the light of the announcement in the middle of the chapter (vv. 21–2): the city has fallen.

Ezekiel as Sentinel over Israel (33:1–9). Ezekiel was first commissioned in 3:16–21 as sentinel over Israel in the context of Judah's rebellion against Nebuchadrezzar (and thus also against YHWH). The prophet's role was to warn the people against YHWH's impending attack in hopes that

they would abandon their sins in time to avert YHWH's judgement against them. In ch. 33 YHWH again asserts, now in the aftermath of Jerusalem's destruction, that Ezekiel is to stand as sentinel over Israel (v. 7). Ezekiel must warn the people to repent, lest when destruction comes he should bear responsibility for their death, having failed to warn them. The people, for their part, must heed the sentinel's warning and repent, lest they die and, having been forewarned, bear responsibility for their own deaths (vv. 8–9). The image of Ezekiel as sentinel is startling in context, since it assumes that the sentinel will be posted on the wall of a city that has already been destroyed. Some scholars assume the oracle is intended for an audience that does not yet know of Jerusalem's destruction, an event not announced until 33:21. The large block of oracles against foreign nations, however, which immediately precede ch. 33, depend on the reader's knowledge of Jerusalem's fall (see e.g. 25:3; 26:2). Thus, in the current arrangement of chapters, whether Ezekiel's own or an editor's, the reader hears Ezekiel commissioned to watch over a city that has already been destroyed. Such a commission is ironically apt for Ezekiel, who even while Jerusalem and its temple were standing could deliver his prophecies only to those who had already been exiled. In ch. 33 Ezekiel hears that just as earlier he was called to prophesy despite his distant location in Babylon, so now he must continue in his calling despite the city and temple's destruction. Israel's moral responsibility and Ezekiel's prophetic role remain, even in exile, even after Jerusalem's fall.

The Possibility of Repentance (33:10–20). Ezekiel is given specific instructions on how to warn the wicked; in effect, the content of the warning he was commissioned to deliver as sentinel in vv. 1–9. The warning rephrases the argument of ch. 18 regarding individual responsibility for moral behaviour. In ch. 33, however, the implicit debate concerns not whether one generation bears the punishment for another's sins, but whether repentance has any effect. 'Our transgressions and our sins weigh upon us', say the people, 'and we waste away because of them' (v. 10). The Judeans now accept that they are being punished for their own sins. Acknowledging the justice of their punishment, however, they continue to see no use in repentance. If judgement has already been passed, then repentance must be futile. As in ch. 18, YHWH asserts that his goal is not the death of the wicked but precisely their repentance. 'Turn back, turn back!' YHWH calls (v. 11), assuring the people that although prior righteousness will not help righteous people who turn to wickedness, neither will past wickedness trip up the wicked who turn to the path of righteousness. As in ch. 18, so here also YHWH attempts to shake the people out of moral lassitude and awaken belief in their present accountability. Despite YHWH's obvious judgement against Judah and Jerusalem, he urgently claims, 'I will judge all of you according to your ways!' (v. 20). YHWH's judgement is ongoing and so, therefore, is Israel's responsibility.

Jerusalem's Fall (33:21–2). Following the notices in vv. 1–9 and vv. 10–20 of Israel's continued moral responsibility—and hence its ongoing relationship with YHWH—in vv. 21–2 Ezekiel learns of Jerusalem's destruction. In January 585 BCE, nearly six months after Nebuchadrezzar had breached the city walls and five months after the city's burning (cf. Jer 52:12–13; 2 Kings 25:8–9), a refugee reaches Ezekiel to inform him of the city's fall. Babylonian messengers would presumably have carried the news back to Babylon prior to this date, but the refugee's arrival and report of events fulfils the prophecy of 24:26. Also in accordance with the earlier prophecy, Ezekiel's mouth is 'opened' after the refugee's arrival. The meaning of Ezekiel's newly regained speech is no more clear than the meaning of the dumbness imposed on him in 3:26–7. The strongest possibility remains that now the prophet is able to speak in his own right, rather than uttering exclusively oracles relayed to him by YHWH (see EZEK 3:26–7).

The Sinful Remnant in Judah (33:23–9). In vv. 23–9 YHWH responds to the Judean survivors' claim to be the new heirs to the land of Israel. Just as Abraham, though only one man, was given the entire land, so now the few remaining Judeans have been given the land to possess (v. 24). The survivors' claim is the logical extension of the argument reported in 11:14–21 that YHWH had expelled the exiles from the land, rejecting them in favour of those who remained. Whereas earlier YHWH had responded with an oracle of promise to the exiles, now he pronounces its converse: judgement against the Judean remnant. Enumerating their various sins, YHWH swears that even those who have survived thus far by hiding in the desert or in caves, he will now hand over to be killed by sword, plague, and wild animals (v. 27). The sins of the Judean survivors—bloodshed, idolatry, adultery, eating blood—recall the list of abominations committed by the 'wicked son' of 18:10–13, who is condemned to die for his sins. YHWH's judgement against the Judean remnant in vv. 23–9 thus mirrors his call in vv. 10–20 for the remnant of Israel to avert further condemnation by turning from their sins.

Ezekiel the Minstrel of Israel (33:30–3). These verses afford an unusual glimpse (albeit from the hand of Ezekiel or his sympathetic editors) of how an Israelite prophet was perceived by the people. Remarkably, Ezekiel was popular among the people, even a source of gossip (v. 30), and a trip to sit and hear a word of YHWH takes on the flavour of a social event. The problem with this amiable state of affairs is that the people 'hear [Ezekiel's] words, but they will not obey them' (v. 31, NJPS). Indeed, the prophet who was commissioned in vv. 1–9 to blow the warning trumpet for his people finds that the people enjoy his musicianship (v. 32) but ignore his message. None the less, says YHWH, when judgement comes, then the people will realize the prophetic significance of Ezekiel's word.

Ch. 33 displays a chiastic pattern:

A (vv. 1–9) Ezekiel, as sentry, warns the people, who may or may not listen.
   B (vv. 10–20) The wicked can escape judgement if they abandon their sins.
      C (vv. 21–2) Ezekiel receives word of Jerusalem's fall.
   B′ (vv. 23–9) The wicked Judeans continue to sin.
A′ (vv. 30–3) The exiles fail to hear Ezekiel's warning.

News of Jerusalem's fall in vv. 21–2 is thus surrounded by oracles certifying that the people, both the exiles and those remaining in the land, have been fully warned but have refused to listen. They thus bear full responsibility for Jerusalem's destruction, an accountability that continues beyond the city's fall.

(34:1–31) **Judgement of Shepherds and of Sheep** This chapter combines several oracles based on the metaphor of Israel as a flock and its leaders as shepherds. The image of a god, king, or other ruler as shepherd was traditional throughout the ancient Near East, and is extended in the OT to include YHWH as shepherd of his people (see Ps 23:1–4; 95:7; ABD, 'Sheep, Shepherd').

Against the Shepherds of Israel (34:1–16). Ezekiel is instructed to prophesy against the shepherds of Israel; that is, the leaders, now presumably in exile in Babylon. Ezekiel distorts the traditional metaphor to highlight the Israelite leaders' abuse of their power (cf. his use of the same technique in chs. 15–17; 19–20). Far from caring for the sheep, these shepherds have slaughtered and eaten them (v. 5). The Israelite leaders' callous harshness left the people with 'no shepherd', and in consequence they were scattered, first on to 'every high hill' as idolaters (see 6:13; Jer 2:20) and then 'over the face of the earth' in exile (v. 6). YHWH, meanwhile, casts himself as the owner of the sheep, who will demand from the shepherds an accounting for their neglect and loss of the sheep (vv. 8–10). The rulers will be held accountable for Israel's destruction, and will be removed from leadership. Instead, YHWH will himself act as shepherd, seeking the lost and scattered sheep and returning them to their own land. The metaphor is a complex one, combining images of YHWH as shepherd with the implicit, underlying image of YHWH as king. The reference in v. 12 to a day of clouds and thick darkness recalls the day of YHWH with its imagery of YHWH as Warrior (cf. 32:7–8; Ps 77:17–18 (MT 18–19); 97:2–5). Finally, literal language clearly anticipates a return from exile to the land of Israel (v. 16).

Israel as YHWH's Flock (34:17–31). Having dismissed Israel's previous shepherds in vv. 1–16, YHWH addresses his flock in vv. 17–31. Speaking now not as shepherd but as judge, YHWH announces that he is about to judge the sheep for their abuse of one another (v. 17). The fat sheep have taken the best pasture, trampled the remainder, and shoved out the weaker sheep to be scattered (vv. 18–21). The location of this mixed flock of weak and strong sheep, whether Judah or Babylon, is uncertain. The metaphor is often taken to describe inequities within the exilic community; if this is accurate, then 34:17–31 is the sole occasion upon which Ezekiel addresses struggles among the exiles. Imagery depicting YHWH feeding and watering his flock, however, is strongly associated with the land of Israel as YHWH's pasture (Ps 78:52–5; Isa 49:9–13; Mic 7:14; cf. Jer 13:17), and the passage is probably best understood in this sense. Thus, in vv. 23–4 YHWH promises to restore (a descendant of) David as Israel's shepherd, and in vv. 25–31 pledges to provide blessings and security for the sheep in the land, rather than return to the land. The consequent picture of conditions within the land of Israel is bleak, with the stronger citizens bullying the poor, who wander homeless (cf. vv. 21, 27), 'consumed with hunger' (v. 29). YHWH claims only the weak as his 'flock', and pledges a běrît šālôm (v. 25) with them. In context, this 'covenant of peace' assures šālôm in the sense of general well-being and prosperity. When those who remain homeless in Judah can dwell secure in their land, they will acknowledge YHWH (v. 27), that he is among them, and that they, his flock, live under his care (vv. 30–1).

(35:1–36:15) **Mount Seir and the Mountains of Israel** Two oracles in chs. 35–6 pair judgement against Mt. Seir in

Edom with promises of restoration to the mountains of Israel. The oracles effectively reverse the judgements pronounced against Israel's mountains in Ezek 6. The choice of Mt. Seir (35:1–15) as the counterpart to the mountains of Israel is puzzling. Ezekiel's oracle against Edom in 25:12–14 is a brief, virtually pro forma condemnation of Israel's neighbour for taking advantage of Israel's broken condition. The motivation for locating a second, more vehement condemnation here is obscure. Edom is accused in ch. 25 of 'handing over' Israel to its enemies, a possible reference to a last-minute shift in Edomite loyalties (see EZEK 25:12–14). Edom is here further berated for planning to take possession of YHWH's own homeland following the Israelites' deportation. YHWH's reminder that he has been present in Israel all along (v. 10) may provide a clue as to why Mt. Seir is singled out for condemnation. Ancient traditions, both biblical and extrabiblical, associate YHWH with Seir as his residence (see Judg 5:4; ABD, 'Seir') and YHWH's emphatic rejection of Seir and blessing of Israel's mountains (36:1–15) may serve to refute any Edomite claim to YHWH (or to his land). YHWH's determination to 'desolate' Seir is repeated five times in this brief oracle, reflecting an acute awareness that in fact it is Israel's mountains that have been desolated (vv. 12, 15; cf. 6:14), while Seir remains inviolate. The Edomites are informed that once they too have been desolated, they will then acknowledge YHWH (v. 15).

In 36:1–15 Ezekiel is instructed to deliver an oracle of consolation to the mountains of Israel. YHWH cites the humiliation endured by Israel's mountains as the reason for his special promise to restore them. Specifically, Edom's gloating and its encroachment on Israel's territory are cited. Whether or not Edom annexed parts of Israel following Jerusalem's destruction is debated (see EZEK 25:12–14), but YHWH's point is clear; whatever humiliations the land suffered will now be turned against those who celebrated Israel's fall. Israel's mountains, by contrast, will grow luxuriant and fruitful branches to sustain the people soon to return. In a final promise (vv. 13–15) YHWH assures the personified mountains that they will no longer cause Israel to stumble by devouring the nation's children. The reference is awkward, but seems to recall Ezekiel's charge elsewhere (16:20–1; 20:25–6; 23:37–9) of child-sacrifice practised in the period immediately preceding Jerusalem's destruction.

(36:16–38) YHWH's Honour Restored In vv. 16–38 YHWH moves from a bitter reminiscence on Israel's pre-exilic sinfulness to promises of its restoration. The predominant concern voiced throughout the passage, however, is not for Israel's history, but for YHWH's. Whether punishing or forgiving, YHWH acts, not for Israel's sake, but to protect the sanctity of his name. In v. 17 YHWH summarizes Israel's past behaviour with a single phrase: they acted lĕniddâ, like a menstruant woman. The simile is intended to capture the intense defilement characterizing all of Israel's actions (cf. 7:20), but the image also recalls the striking personification of ch. 16 in which Jerusalem begins life weltering in placental blood (v. 6), matures to menarche (vv. 7–9), and finally sheds the blood of her own children (vv. 20–2). The designation 'like a menstruant' thus aptly recapitulates the deeds of the 'bloody city' (22:2) Jerusalem.

YHWH then explains (v. 19) that he punished the people for their sins by scattering them in exile. Unfortunately, this punishment itself involved additional defilement of the divine name, in that YHWH was made to appear either weak or unfaithful in allowing his own people to be exiled (cf. EZEK F.2). 'These', say the nations, 'are the people of the LORD, and yet they had to go out of his land' (v. 20). YHWH is therefore forced to act yet again to vindicate his name.

In vv. 22–32 YHWH enunciates not only his promise to restore Israel to the land, but also his motives for doing so: 'It is not for your sake, O house of Israel, that I am about to act, but for the sake of my holy name' (v. 22). YHWH's assertion that he is not acting for Israel's sake is repeated in v. 32, creating an *inclusio* framing YHWH's discussion of his motives. YHWH's holy name—his honour—has been profaned 'among the nations' by Israel's exile (v. 21); therefore he will now display his holiness before the nations by bringing Israel back from exile and restoring a purified people to a fruitful land. The underlying logic is consistent with the discussion of Israel's history in ch. 20 (and cf. 22:16): by allowing Israel to be exiled YHWH violates his own covenant and injures his reputation. YHWH is apparently incapable of protecting his people or even his own temple, and his land has been devastated. It is therefore imperative that YHWH restore land, temple, and people, not for their sake, but for his own. Here Ezekiel's overriding concern with the divine honour (EZEK F.2) comes to the fore. Whatever tenderness might be evident in images such as the 'good shepherd' of Ezek 34, Ezekiel's urgent task remains the vindication of YHWH's honour, power, and holiness. Just as in 20:33–5 YHWH announces that he will rule over the people whether they will or no, so here YHWH re-establishes his people, not only regardless of their worthiness, but, indeed, regardless of their needs or desires. It is YHWH's stature, not theirs, that is at stake and that must be confirmed. YHWH will bring back his people from exile and, before returning them to the land, will first purify them and then render them incapable of defiling his name further (vv. 25–7). Whereas Jeremiah had promised that God's law would be inscribed on the people's hearts (31:33), Ezekiel requires that the people's hearts be replaced altogether (cf. 11:19). YHWH will make the people obey his laws by means of new hearts directed by YHWH's spirit (v. 27). Then Israel will again become YHWH's covenant people (v. 28), and inhabit a land blessed with fertility (vv. 29–30). The restoration that vindicates YHWH's name, however, will cause shame for Israel (cf. 16:63) as they realize the gravity of their sins.

Proof that Israel's cleansing and restoration have been effective is found in the new reputation YHWH enjoys among 'the nations that are left' (v. 36), presumably those remaining after the day of YHWH described in the preceding oracles against the nations. The nations will credit YHWH with making the desolate land 'like the garden of Eden' (v. 35) and so will acknowledge his sovereignty. YHWH will favour Israel by increasing its population, making it 'like the flock at Jerusalem during her appointed festivals'—that is, both multitudinous and holy—so that Israel also may acknowledge YHWH's sovereignty (v. 38).

(37:1–14) The Vision of the Dry Bones As in Ezekiel's earlier visions (1:3; 3:22; 8:1–3) the prophet experiences the 'hand of the Lord' and is transported in a vision. The vision of 37:1–14 is unique in that YHWH's chariot does not appear. The focus is not on heavenly realities but on Israel's despair and God's response. Ezekiel is placed in a valley (or 'plain'; cf. 3:22) filled with bones. As in his vision of the defiled temple in chs. 8–11 (and cf. chs. 40–8) Ezekiel is led about as a witness, in this instance a witness to the number of bones and their desiccated condition. YHWH asks the prophet whether the bones can live; given Ezekiel's role certifying the bones' utter lifelessness, the obvious answer is 'no'. Ezekiel, however, answers, 'O Lord GOD, you know' (v. 3), an ambiguous response that can signify either, 'You already know they cannot', or more likely a more open-ended deference to YHWH's sovereignty: 'You alone know what is possible.' YHWH then instructs Ezekiel to prophesy to the already dead and desiccated bones, assuring them that YHWH will cause them to live, and, living, to acknowledge YHWH (vv. 4–6). The prophecy has ironic overtones in context: for years Ezekiel prophesied to living Israelites who proved as unable to respond as any dry bones. Now he must prophesy to the bones themselves.

Ezekiel prophesies and at once the bones come rattling together. Sinews, flesh, and skin cover them, effectively reversing their decayed state (vv. 7–8). The bodies are still lifeless, however, and YHWH commands Ezekiel to prophesy now to 'the breath' (v. 9), calling it to bring life to the corpses before him. Again Ezekiel prophesies, the breath enters the bodies, and they stand, alive, before him. Wordplay based on the word *rûaḥ* (breath, wind, spirit) lends a mystical ambiguity to the scene. A wind blowing across the valley floor enters the bodies to endow them with breath. This breath, however, is in fact YHWH's own spirit, which will not only enliven the Israelites, but make possible their fidelity to YHWH (vv. 13–14; cf. 36:27; 39:29). In vv. 11–14 YHWH explains the vision to Ezekiel. The bones are Israel in its current, hopeless condition (v. 11; cf. 33:10). The image of unburied corpses, now turned to parched, dislocated, and scattered bones, simultaneously evokes the remains of Israelites killed in the Babylonian invasions, the dislocated and disoriented Israelites still living in the land, and the exiles whose hopes have at last been utterly crushed. To this devastated people YHWH promises that he will act beyond their despair; he will open their very graves in order to give them life and restore them to their land (vv. 13–14). Although later interpreters, both Jewish and Christian, saw in Ezek 37:1–14 a promise of the resurrection of the dead (see *ABD*, 'Resurrection (OT)'), here the image is clearly metaphorical. The people who find themselves 'cut off completely' (v. 11) will be rejoined and given a new life in the land.

(37:15–28) The Two Sticks Connected YHWH commands Ezekiel to take two sticks, inscribing one 'for Judah' and the other 'for Joseph', that is, one for the southern and one for the northern kingdom, and to join the sticks in his hand. YHWH goes on in vv. 19–28 to explain the meaning of the symbolic action and to deliver further promises to Israel. The two sticks represent the northern and southern kingdoms of Israel. Though both kingdoms have now been destroyed, YHWH says he is about to make them one 'in my hand' (v. 19). The sticks are thus sceptres. YHWH will not only restore the two kingdoms, but will rule over both. He will appoint David (that is, a descendant of the Davidic house) as 'shepherd', reigning over the reunited kingdom of Israel. The purified people will follow YHWH's laws and inhabit the land (v. 25). YHWH will establish an eternal covenant of peace with the people and will dwell in his sanctuary in their midst (v. 26). The oracle combines images from previous oracles of promise and then extends those promises still further: the appointment of David as 'shepherd' and the promise of the covenant of peace echo YHWH's promise of ch. 34. The cleansing of the people, who will then follow YHWH's laws, recalls 36:25–7 (and cf. 11:19–20). YHWH's promised restoration of northern Israel as well as Judah is foreshadowed in the restoration of Oholah (Samaria) in 16:53–5 and perhaps already in the instructions for Ezekiel to 'bear the punishment' of both kingdoms in 4:4–6. YHWH's promise to restore the northern tribes none the less comes as a surprise here, it being nearly 150 years since the northern kingdom's destruction. YHWH's restoration, however, is primarily the restoration of his own kingdom, not Judah's, and he will reign over his entire land and his entire people. The final sign of YHWH's renewed sovereignty is the re-establishment of his sanctuary, the throne-room from which he will reign over the land. The promise of a new sanctuary looks forward to the vision of chs. 40–8, in which YHWH is at last re-enthroned forever over an obedient Israel.

(38:1–39:29) Gog of Magog Chs. 38–9 form the climax of Ezekiel's promises of restoration in chs. 33–9. Vividly depicting the Divine Warrior's victory over his ultimate enemy, the triumph of Ezek 38–9 paves the way for YHWH's re-enthronement in the restored temple of chs. 40–8. The two chapters comprise two related oracles (38:1–23 and 39:1–29) against Gog of Magog, a figure otherwise unknown from biblical or extrabiblical sources (though providing the basis for the Gog *and* Magog of Rev 20:7–10). The oracles envision a period after Israel has been restored to the land, at which point YHWH will incite Gog to attack them (38:4; 39:2). YHWH will then engage and defeat Gog in battle, thus displaying his glory and holiness before the nations. Once the land has been cleansed following the carnage a sacrificial feast will be celebrated, the people will receive YHWH's long-promised spirit, and the nations will recognize YHWH.

One of the most vexed questions in the interpretation of Ezekiel remains the identity of Gog. The seventh-century king Gyges of Lydia has often been suggested but is not a convincing candidate. Gyges had been dead over a century by Ezekiel's time and had never commanded power anything like that attributed to Gog. The only points of connection are the similarity in names and the location of each in (different areas of) Anatolia. Recent scholarship prefers to see Gog as an embodiment of chaos, a designation that suits his role as the ultimate force opposing YHWH's people and defying his universal sovereignty. A third possibility is that Gog represents Nebuchadrezzar of Babylon, elevated here into an enemy of cosmic significance. Several factors support reading Gog as a cipher for Nebuchadrezzar. First, the role played by Nebuchadrezzar elsewhere in Ezekiel poses serious dissonances within Ezekiel's overall theological outlook. Nebuchadrezzar is depicted in exclusively positive terms in Ezekiel, as YHWH's covenant partner (see Ezek 17) and his agent in destroying both Israel and its smaller neighbours (see e.g. Ezek 21:18–23; 26:7–14; 29:17–20). Nebuchadrezzar's role parallels that played in Isaiah by Assyria, who is employed by YHWH as 'the rod of [YHWH's] anger' against Israel (Isa 10:5–11). In Ezekiel, Babylonia's role as ally and agent of YHWH reflects the reality of YHWH's invocation as guarantor of Zedekiah's vassal-treaty, as well as providing YHWH with a human agent to carry out his warfare in the world. Nebuchadrezzar's capture of YHWH's land and destruction of his temple, however, imply the *de facto* superiority of the Babylonian god Marduk over the Israelite YHWH. 'These', say the nations, 'are the people of the Lord, but they had to leave his land' (NJPS), a situation that in and of itself defiles YHWH's holy name (Ezek 36:20). Nebuchadrezzar's military superiority together with the implicit supremacy of Marduk over YHWH thus continue to compromise YHWH's honour despite all claims that the Babylonian monarch acts only as YHWH's ally or agent. Isaiah had faced the same theological problem in his use of Assyria and resolved it by claiming that ultimately YHWH would punish the over-proud king of Assyria for believing himself YHWH's conqueror rather than his servant (Isa 10:12–19; 30:19–33). Ezekiel, writing in Babylon, would have had strong reasons to seek a means of predicting YHWH's triumph over Nebuchadrezzar. As a Babylonian vassal living in Babylonian territory, however, he would have had equally strong reasons for predicting this triumph covertly rather than, as Isaiah had, overtly.

Gog's true identity as Nebuchadrezzar of Babylon is supported by strong verbal parallels between the description of Gog in chs. 38–9 and depictions of the Babylonian monarch elsewhere in Ezekiel. Like Gog, Nebuchadrezzar is described as coming from 'the north' (23:24; 26:7; cf. 38:6, 15; 39:2; Jer 25:9). Both monarchs are rulers over 'many peoples' (26:3; 31:11; cf. 38:6, 9) and arrive with horses and riders bearing shield, buckler, and helmet (23:23–4; 26:10; cf. 38:4–5) to terrify and devastate their enemies. For Ezekiel the 'king of kings' (26:7), leader of 'the worst of the nations' (7:24) is Nebuchadrezzar of Babylon. Gog's title of *nĕśî' rō'š mešek wĕtûbāl* (38:2; NRSV 'the chief prince of Meshech and Tubal') may point indirectly to Nebuchadrezzar. Traditional designation of Gog as 'chief prince' ignores the construct relation, *nĕśî'rō'š*, that literally yields 'prince *of* the head', that is, ruler over the leader of Meshech and Tubal. The location of Gog's home, Magog (cf. Gen 10:2), is unknown, but Meshech and Tubal were regions of north-central Anatolia. Early in the sixth century Nebuchadrezzar gained control over Cilicia in southern Anatolia, and so functioned as a leader in the region. When a dispute broke out between the Lydians and Medes over control of Meshech and Tubal Nebuchadrezzar's deputy successfully brokered a peace in the region (Wiseman 1956). Gog's designation as 'prince over the leader' of Meshech and Tubal could thus covertly designate the Babylonian Nebuchadrezzar in his role as the principal powerbroker in northern Anatolia.

The final factor pointing to Gog as a cipher for Nebuchadrezzar is the former's role in YHWH's vindication and in paving the way for his enthronement in Ezek 43. In 36:20–32 YHWH admits that Israel's exile has caused defilement of the divine name. He therefore announces his intention to act for his name's sake, to sanctify his name, display his holiness, and gain recognition from the nations. He will then cleanse his people and put a new spirit within them, thereby creating a people worthy of his name. In Ezek 38–9 it is precisely Gog's defeat that will accomplish YHWH's self-vindication, removing the stigma of the exile. YHWH will display his holiness (38:16, 23; 39:7, 21–3, 27–8), causing nations to acknowledge his sovereignty. Israel will be cleansed (39:11–16) and gifted with YHWH's spirit (39:28–9). Gog is the monarch whose power continues to defile YHWH's name and whose destruction opens the way for YHWH's re-enthronement. Gog is the enemy who cannot be named but must be overcome: Nebuchadrezzar of Babylon.

Both Ezek 38 and 39 depict Gog's destruction; ch. 38 focuses on events leading up to YHWH's battle with Gog while ch. 39 centres on the aftermath of YHWH's victory. In 38:1–16 YHWH informs Gog as to the circumstances surrounding Gog's attack against Israel. Even before the predicted battle Gog will be YHWH's vassal; YHWH will put a hook through Gog's nose to lead him and his minions out to war. At the time of Gog's invasion Israel will already have been 'restored from war', a land where people have been 'gathered from many nations' (v. 8). This gathering of Israel from 'many nations' may well envision the restoration of the scattered northern tribes (cf. 37:15–23; 48:1–7) as well as Judah. The restoration is apparently not contingent on the prior destruction of Israel's enemies, and so YHWH's final battle against Israel's enemies and his own takes place in the land of Israel, 'at the centre of the earth' (v. 12). Like Pharaoh in the Exodus narrative (Ex 14:4, 17–18), Gog will serve as a foil whose real purpose is to demonstrate YHWH's prowess. YHWH himself will instigate Gog's attack in order to gain renown and display his holiness by crushing the enemy. YHWH announces that Gog is the enemy whom YHWH had for years prophesied that he would bring against Israel (v. 17). If Gog is to be understood as Babylon, then Ezekiel may in part be referring to his own earlier prophecies. Now the battle with Gog is revealed as 'that day', the day of YHWH's wrath, on which the earth will quake and YHWH will rain down fire and sulphur (vv. 17–23). Gog's defeat is thus not so much a literal, military victory as the day of YHWH, the triumph of the Divine Warrior.

Ezek 39 opens as did ch. 38 with an announcement to Gog that YHWH is about to lead him 'against the mountains of Israel' (v. 2), where he and his troops will die and be devoured by wild beasts. This, says YHWH, will remove the defilement from YHWH's holy name and vindicate him before both Israel and the nations. 'This', says YHWH, 'is the day of which I have spoken' (v. 8). The day of YHWH is no longer a 'distant vision' (12:27); 'It has come! It has happened' (v. 8; cf. 7:2, 5–6). YHWH's announcement has rendered Gog as good as dead. In vv. 9–16 YHWH describes the aftermath of Gog's defeat. The invaders' weapons will suffice for firewood for seven years, not only providing for the people's needs, but also sparing the trees (cf. Lev 19:23–5; 26:34–5). Meanwhile, seven months will be required to cleanse the land from the pollution created by the slaughtered army's corpses (vv. 11–16). The people will search out the corpses and bury them in a mass grave in the 'Valley of Gog's Multitude' (v. 11, NJPS).

In vv. 17–20 Ezekiel is commanded to assemble the birds and animals, inviting them to a sacrificial banquet to be held on the mountains of Israel. The animals will eat and drink their fill of human flesh and human blood—the flesh and blood of YHWH's slaughtered enemies. The victorious god's sacrificial banquet on the mountain was a stock element of the Divine Warrior traditions of both Canaan and Mesopotamia. Here, however, the image is distorted to make human sacrifices, not animal, the main course. At first glance YHWH's grisly banquet would seem to defile both the participants and the land, as it violates the levitical prohibition against 'eating blood' (see Lev 17:11). In this case, however, the utter defilement of YHWH's enemies (whose corpses are fed to the birds and animals; cf. 32:4) serves to restore the mountains that earlier had been defiled by idolatrous sacrifices (6:1–7). Textually, the banquet of vv. 17–20 seems out of place since the corpses of Gog's army are already burned in vv. 11–16. It is possible that either vv. 11–16 or vv. 17–20 are later additions, as is commonly assumed. It is equally possible that logical consistency is set aside here in order to depict the events normally preceding the god's enthronement: the cleansing of the land (vv. 11–16); the sacrificial banquet (vv. 17–20); the triumphant procession into the temple (43:1–5); and last, the enthronement (43:6). The description of YHWH's triumph over Gog concludes (vv. 21–9) with YHWH's explanation of the theological significance of his triumph. YHWH's victory manifests his glory (v. 21) and holiness (v. 27) before all nations; both the nations and Israel will acknowledge YHWH's sovereignty. Moreover, with Gog's defeat the nations will at last understand that 'Israel went into captivity for their iniquity', because of their treachery (m'l) against YHWH (v. 23) and not because of weakness or infidelity on YHWH's part. After YHWH has restored Israel to its land and displayed his holiness by destroying Gog, then the people will be allowed to forget their sins and their shame (vv. 25–8). When the people fully understand YHWH's control over both exile and restoration, then he will pour out his spirit upon Israel (vv. 28–9), promising never again to abandon them.

YHWH's Re-enthronement (40:1–48:35)

The last nine chapters of Ezekiel comprise a single vision, the last of Ezekiel's three visions of YHWH on his chariot (cf. chs. 1; 8–11). The vision parallels the vision of chs. 8–11 in which Ezekiel is led on a tour of the defiled temple before watching the Divine Warrior's departure. In chs. 40–8 Ezekiel tours the restored, pure temple and then watches the Warrior's return and re-enthronement. In each case Ezekiel seems to serve as a witness, certifying both the abominations committed in the old temple and the purity maintained in the new, and then perceiving YHWH's response as he first departs warlike from the old and finally returns victorious to the new temple. Sometimes considered Ezekiel's blueprint for a new, post-exilic Jerusalem temple and cult (a blueprint ignored or rejected by the post-exilic community), in fact the vision gives no instructions for building the temple. Rather, the new temple is revealed as completed, whole and pristine, awaiting only YHWH's formal accession to his throne. Israel's role will be to observe the 'law of the temple' (43:12), not to build it. While the vision's arid details of architecture and ritual praxis often lead commentators to consider chs. 40–8 a secondary addition, the vision's crucial role in completing the plot of YHWH's return and re-enthronement argues for its original congruence with the rest of the book (see EZEK A.3).

(40:1–42:20) The Temple Measurements Ezekiel reports receiving his final vision 'in the twenty-fifth year of our exile' (40:1), 573 BCE. Although often interpreted as a 'half-Jubilee' (that is, half of a theoretical jubilee cycle taking the exile as its starting-point), the year should be understood as a Jubilee year. Just as the vision of ch. 1 was dated according to the Jubilee ('in the thirtieth year' (of the Jubilee) = the fifth year of the exile; see EZEK 1:1), so this climactic vision of restoration takes place in the Jubilee year, the twenty-fifth year of Judah's exile. The further specification, 'the beginning of the year, on the tenth day of the month' (v. 1) confirms the year's Jubilee status, the Jubilee being the only year beginning on the tenth rather than the first of the month (see Lev 25:9), that is, on the Day of Atonement. The date, in October of 573, is thus the proper moment to declare both the enthronement of YHWH as king and Israel's restoration to the land according to the law of Jubilee (Lev 25:10).

As in 8:3 Ezekiel is transported in his vision to the land of Israel. He is placed on 'a very high mountain, on which was a structure like a city to the south' (v. 2). The mountain is evidently Mount Zion, now exalted as in the prophecies of Isa 2:2 and Mic 4:1. The unnamed city replaces the devastated Jerusalem. A man gleaming 'like bronze' (v. 3; cf. 1:7 and the figure of ḥašmal in 1:27; 8:2), evidently the heavenly guide from the vision of chs. 8–11, appears with a measuring rod and instructs Ezekiel to pay close attention so as to be able to pass on what he sees to the Israelites. The whole of 40:5–42:20 comprises a tour in which Ezekiel witnesses as his guide measures the various dimensions of the temple complex, beginning at the outer wall, proceeding inwards to the holy of holies, and then returning to the complex's outer wall. Unlike the Solomonic temple, Ezekiel's is provided with two courtyards, thus allowing an additional buffer-zone separating the holy from the common. Both the outer and inner courtyards include gates on the north, east, and south sides. Within the inner courtyard are various chambers for the washing and slaughter of sacrificial animals and for the use of Levites and other temple servants. Ezekiel's tour of the new temple, witnessing its structures and dimensions, parallels his tour of the defiled temple in ch. 8. Now, however, he watches as his guide measures and thus certifies the perfection of the new structure. Everything is quite literally in order, creating a physical boundary between sacred and profane space (42:20).

(43:1–12) The Enthronement of YHWH Following his tour of the temple precincts Ezekiel is brought to the outer east gate, where he sees the glory of YHWH coming from the east. Ezekiel identifies this vision specifically as being 'like the vision that I had seen when [YHWH] came to destroy the city, and like the vision that I had seen by the river Chebar' (v. 3), that is, like his earlier visions of YHWH as Warrior. Following the pattern of the Israelite enthronement ritual, the triumphant Warrior returns in procession to take his throne within the holy of holies. Ezekiel is brought only as far as the inner court, while, recapitulating YHWH's first possession of the newly built wilderness sanctuary (Ex 40:34–35; cf. 1 Kings 8:10; Isa 6:1), the glory of YHWH fills the temple.

In v. 6 Ezekiel is addressed by YHWH himself, who proclaims his own enthronement within his eternal dwelling, the place of his footstool (v. 7; cf. Ps 99:5). YHWH announces both his eternal presence among the people and the condition making that presence possible: Israel will cease to defile YHWH's holy name. Israel's past offences are described as its 'whoring' (*zĕnût*, cf. chs. 16; 23) and its royal *pĕgārîm*, both in close proximity to the temple (v. 8). The *pĕgārîm* are probably not royal corpses (as e.g. in NRSV) but royal memorial stelae (see Neiman 1948), perceived as threatening YHWH's exclusive kingship over Israel. Israel's 'whoring' comprised idolatry and foreign alliances, both of which violated YHWH's honour (cf. Ezek 16). Here Israel's exaltation of its own (former?) kings is grouped with idolatry and foreign alliances; all are seen as compromising YHWH's sovereignty and thus his honour; none may be allowed in the restored temple precincts.

In vv. 10–12 YHWH instructs Ezekiel to explain the temple's layout to the house of Israel in order to bring about their repentant shame. The causal relation posited between knowing the temple plan and obedience, seemingly implies that the people (perhaps as a result of YHWH's outpoured spirit; 39:29) are now fully ready to obey and need only instruction as to 'the law of the temple' (v. 12).

(43:13–46:24) Laws Governing Land and Cult Following the sequence displayed by Exodus and Leviticus, Ezekiel first describes the temple itself and then witnesses the arrival of the divine glory before detailing the routine of ritual observance (much as the laws of Leviticus follow immediately upon Ex 40:34). With YHWH enthroned in his new sanctuary, Ezekiel proceeds in 43:13–17 to describe the sacrificial altar and in vv. 18–27 to detail the procedures for its purification. The altar consists of three square tiers with 'horns' at its four corners (see *ABD*, 'Altar'). Its purification, performed by Zadokite priests, follows the procedures set out in Lev 8:14–15 and Ex 29:36–7.

Ezekiel is next (44:1–3) brought from the inner court to the east gate of the outer court. Here he is informed that the east gate is to remain closed because YHWH, 'the God of Israel, has entered by it' (v. 2). Although the commandment suggests the special holiness attributed to, so to speak, YHWH's private entrance, the permanently locked gate also symbolizes the permanence of YHWH's presence in the temple. Having vanquished his final enemy and established an obedient people, YHWH will have no further need either to conduct full-scale purification of the temple or to re-establish his supremacy in an annual battle beginning with his departure from the temple. The 'ruler' (*nāśî*', or prince), who is never called 'king' in Ezek 40–8, is alone permitted to enter the east gate (from the courtyard side) in order to 'eat food', presumably taking part in a ritual meal (v. 3).

In 44:4 Ezekiel again approaches the temple and is again overwhelmed by the glory of YHWH present in the sanctuary. This additional notice of YHWH's presence probably serves to reinforce the instructions of vv. 1–3; YHWH no longer processes out or in; his location is known and it is eternal (cf. 43:7).

In 44:5–9 YHWH prescribes that no foreigners are to be admitted to the temple. This prohibition is specifically in response to Israel's former 'abominations', including breaking YHWH's covenant and failing to watch over the temple sancta, instead giving foreigners charge of the temple. The charge is obscure, but may refer to the Egyptian ruler Psam-meticus II, who in 592 BCE visited Palestine and stationed his priests there, thereby breaking YHWH's covenant with Nebuchadrezzar (see EZEK 17; Galambush 1992).

YHWH goes on in 44:10–31 to outline the respective duties of the Levites and Zadokites (see *ABD*, 'Levites and Priests'). The Levites, designated as priests in Deut 18:1–18 but 'given' as assistants to Aaron and his descendants in Num 3:5–10, are here presented as being demoted to the rank of servant as punishment for previous idolatry. The Zadokites, however, are designated 'levitical' priests (v. 15) and alone are authorized to present offerings and to enter the temple proper. Regulations governing the dress and conduct of the priests generally follow the prescriptions of Lev 10 and 21, though with some variation. The priests are charged with teaching the people the distinction between clean and unclean, and with maintaining the holiness of feasts and sabbaths (vv. 23–4). As also specified in the Priestly legislation, the priests will inherit no land but will be maintained from temple offerings.

In 45:1–8 the land surrounding the temple is allocated; the Zadokite priests live in a 'most holy' area immediately adjacent to the temple with the Levites to their north and the city to their south. The areas to the east and west of these holdings will be royal property. The royal holdings are strictly limited by a sharp command in v. 8 for the prince to allow the people their land. The prince is commanded to establish justice and righteousness, the traditional responsibility of divine and human rulers. Legislation in vv. 10–17 specifying legal weights and measures as well as the prince's duty to supply various offerings seems aimed at curbing abuses by the ruler.

The ritual calendar is set forth in 45:18–25, beginning with the cleansing of the temple in 'the first month' (v. 18), apparently assuming a spring new year. This annual cleansing of the temple is similar to the Yom Kippur of Lev 16, but with important differences. First, the cleansing is confined to the court and exterior of the temple, perhaps indicating that grave sins that would contaminate the temple proper are not committed in the restored community. Second, the cleansing is linked to the observance of the Passover two weeks later (vv. 21–4) rather than to the New Year or enthronement festival. In v. 25 offerings are prescribed for 'the seven days of the festival' in the seventh month (cf. 1 Kings 8:2–11), apparently a reference to the old New Year/enthronement festival. No Yom Kippur cleansing of the temple is envisioned, and no ark procession (indeed, the east, processional gate was sealed in 44:1–3). The Autumn Festival's apparent truncation may reflect simultaneously the desire to de-emphasize the role played by the human king (cf. 43:6–9) and to accentuate the unchallenged kingship of YHWH. Following Gog's defeat in chs. 38–9 YHWH no longer needs annually to re-establish his reign by subduing his enemies. YHWH is now enthroned continuously within the temple.

In 46:1–18 the logistics governing the access of ruler and people to the temple are laid out. On occasions when the ruler is required to offer sacrifice he is allowed to enter the east gate of the inner courtyard (not the outer, as in 44:3) and stand 'by the post of the gate' (v. 2; cf. 2 Kings 11:14; 23:3) while the priests present his offering. While the east gate is standing open the 'people of the land' (v. 9) are to pass by it and so (albeit obliquely) 'come before the Lord'. vv. 16–18 provide for royal property to remain in royal hands, meanwhile prohibiting the ruler from 'thrusting' the people off their own property. The various rules in Ezek 40–8 prohibiting the ruler from abusing the people (45:8–9) and limiting his cultic function (43:8; 44:3) as well as the avoidance of the title 'king', suggest Ezekiel's distrust of the monarch and his determination not to allow secular authority to erode YHWH's sovereign power. Concern to advance cultic over secular authority may, of course, also have motivated this priest-in-exile.

(47:1–12) The Life-Giving River In 46:19–24 Ezekiel is shown various outbuildings in the inner and outer courts and in 47:1 he is returned to the temple door. Water flows out from the south side of the temple threshold and then heads eastward from the temple complex, deepening into a great river that finally empties into the Dead Sea. Along the river's banks grow trees always laden with fruit and medicinal leaves (v. 12; cf. Rev 22:1–2). The river itself 'heals' the Dead Sea (v. 8) so that it becomes full of fish and thus able also to sustain human life. This life-giving river recalls not only the rivers of Eden in Gen 2:10–14 and the Gihon spring originating from the Jerusalem temple mount (1 Kings 1:33), but also the widespread ancient Near Eastern traditions of rivers flowing from a cosmic mountain to the ends of the earth (see Clifford 1972). As in the Psalms, YHWH sits enthroned 'above the waters' (Ps 29:3; 104:3), having both defeated chaos and ordered the fruitful world. Fruitful trees similarly characterize Eden (Gen 2:9) as well as the gardens of ancient Near-Eastern gods generally (see *ABD*, 'Garden of God'; Levenson 1976).

(47:13–48:35) Boundaries and Tribal Allotments Following the outward movement of the miraculous river, the vision's focus turns outwards. Like the plan of the temple complex in chs. 40–2, the regular division of the land expresses the rule of divine order. In 47:13–23 the boundaries for all of Israel are laid out: the Brook of Egypt (Wadi el-'Arish) on the south, the river Jordan on the east, the Mediterranean on the west, and a line running through Lebo Hamath on the north (cf. the similar boundaries of Num 34:1–12). No trans-Jordanian holdings are envisioned and the northern border is drawn not far north of Dan (see *ABD*, 'Hamath, Entrance of'). The borders are apparently realistic rather than idealized, as is often asserted. That is, if the location of Lebo Hamath at the southern end of the Anti-Lebanon mountains is accepted, then the territory outlined is considerably smaller than that claimed in various other texts (Gen 15:18; 1 Kings 4:21 (MT 5:1)).

The land is divided into twelve equal portions, excluding that allocated for the temple, Zadokites, Levites, and ruler (45:1–7). Each of the tribes is to receive a strip of territory extending across the entire land from west to east, with seven to the north and five to the south of the central, holy portions. Judah, located immediately north of the Levites' territory, occupies the holiest position among the twelve tribes, followed by Benjamin to the immediate south of the city and its territory. The city itself is described last (vv. 30–5). The fate of the holy city, which preoccupied Ezekiel throughout the first twenty-four chapters of the book, returns to centre stage at the book's conclusion. The restored city, however, is not given the name 'Jerusalem', a name made infamous by the wild infidelities of YHWH's earlier 'bride' (Ezek 16; 23). The purified city is as far removed as possible from the defilement of its pre-exilic counterpart. The city's twelve gates, one for each of the twelve tribes, are described in vv. 30–4. Here the tribes of Manasseh and Ephraim, listed as separate tribes in the boundary list (48:4–5), are replaced by Joseph in order to allow for the inclusion of Levi as one of the twelve tribes. This apparent inconsistency may reflect the very practical need for the Levites and Zadokite priests (considered descendants of Levi in 44:15) to enter and exit the city despite their lack of tribal inheritances *per se*.

Ezekiel concludes with the naming of the city in 48:35. The new name, 'YHWH is There', plays on the name 'Jerusalem' (*YHWH šammâ* instead of *yĕrûšālaim*), but proclaims the central triumph of the temple vision: YHWH is present, reigning from his temple and dwelling amid his people forever.

REFERENCES

Ackerman, S. (1992), *Under Every Green Tree: Popular Religion in Sixth Century Judah* (Atlanta: Scholars Press).

Carley, K. W. (1975), *Ezekiel among the Prophets* (Naperville, Ill.: Alec R. Allenson).

Clifford, R. J. (1972), *The Cosmic Mountain in Canaan and the Old Testament*, HSM 4 (Cambridge, Mass.: Harvard University Press).

Cohen, C. (1973), 'The Widowed City', *JANESCU* 5: 75–81.

Davis, E. F. (1989), *Swallowing the Scroll: Textuality and the Dynamics of Discourse in Ezekiel's Prophecy* (Sheffield: Almond).

Galambush, J. (1992), *Jerusalem in the Book of Ezekiel: The City as Yahweh's Wife*, SBLDS 130 (Atlanta: Scholars Press).

Greenberg, M. (1983), *Ezekiel 1–20: A New Translation with Introduction and Commentary*, AB 22 (Garden City, NY: Doubleday).

—— (1997), *Ezekiel 21–37: A New Translation with Introduction and Commentary*, AB 22A (New York: Doubleday).

Griffith, F. L. (1909) (ed.), *Catalogue of the Demotic Papyri in the John Rylands Library* (3 vols.; Manchester: Manchester University Press).

Halperin, D. J. (1993), *Seeking Ezekiel: Text and Psychology* (University Park, Pa.: Pennsylvania State University Press).

Hayes, J. H., and Hooker, P. K. (1988), *A New Chronology for the Kings of Israel and Judah* (Atlanta: John Knox).

Hölscher, G. (1924), *Hesekiel: Der Dichter und das Buch. Eine literarkritische Untersuchung*, BZAW 39 (Giessen: Töpelmann).

Levenson, J. D. (1976), *Theology of the Program of Restoration of Ezekiel 40–48*, HSM 10 (Missoula, Mont.: Scholars Press).

Malul, M. (1990), 'Adoption of Foundlings in the Bible and Mesopotamian Documents: A Study of Some Legal Metaphors in Ezekiel 16:1–7', *JSOT* 46: 97–126.

Milgrom, J. (1976), 'The Concept of *ma'al* in the Bible and the Ancient Near East', *JAOS* 96: 236–47.

Miller, J. M., and Hayes, J. H. (1986), *A History of Ancient Israel and Judah* (Philadelphia: Westminster).

Neiman, D. (1948), '*Pgr*: A Canaanite Cult-Object in the Old Testament', *JBL* 67: 55–60.

Olyan, S. M. (1988), *Asherah and the Cult of Yahweh in Israel*, SBLMS 34 (Atlanta: Scholars Press).

Smith, M. S. (1990), 'The Near Eastern Background of Solar Language for Yahweh', *JBL* 109: 29–39.

Vermes, G. (1981), *Jesus the Jew: A Historian's Reading of the Gospels* (Philadelphia: Fortress).

Westerbrook, R. (1990), 'Adultery in Ancient Near Eastern Law', *RB* 97: 542–80.

Wiseman, D. J. (1956), *Chronicles of Chaldaean Kings (626–556 B.C.) in the British Museum* (London: British Museum).

Zimmerli, W. (1979), *Ezekiel*, tr. R. E. Clements, Hermeneia (Philadelphia: Fortress), i; German original, 1969.

—— (1983), *Ezekiel*, tr. J. D. Martin, Hermeneia (Philadelphia: Fortress), ii; German original, 1969.

26. Daniel

P. R. DAVIES

INTRODUCTION

A. The Two Forms of the Book of Daniel. 1. Daniel exists in a Hebrew–Aramaic version, that of the Hebrew (Jewish) Bible which forms the basis of most modern English translations; and also in Greek versions: an Old Greek translation and the one which became the standard Christian text, ascribed to Theodotion. The HB, of which fragments have been found among the Dead Sea scrolls, does not include certain passages and stories that are found in the Greek versions. These Greek additions are usually found in English Bibles in the Apocrypha, as three separate books, under the names Prayer of Azariah, Susannah, and Bel and the Dragon. In the Greek versions, however, Azariah's prayer comes after what is 3:23 in the canonical book of Daniel, while Susannah and Bel and the Dragon form chs. 13 and 14. Apart from these, however, the Old Greek text often differs significantly from the HB (e.g. in chs. 4 and 5) implying more than one Hebrew–Aramaic text of Daniel at some stage.

2. Another major difference between the two forms of Daniel is that the (canonical) HB version belongs with the third section, Writings, while in the Greek (and Eng.) Bibles it occupies a pivotal point in the prophetic section of the canon, between the three major prophetic books and the twelve minor prophets. It is the shorter HB version that is being dealt with here.

B. Original Language. The HB version of Daniel opens in Hebrew, the original language of the Old Testament, but switches in 2:4 to Aramaic, a related language increasingly spoken and written by Jews from the Persian period onwards (from the middle of the 7th cent. BCE). But chs. 8–12 revert to Hebrew. It is unclear whether the book was originally written in one language only and partly translated; if so, then the Aramaic is more likely to be the original because chs. 2–7 seem to contain the older parts of the book. But no one explanation of this curious feature has yet been generally accepted.

C. Literary Form and Structure. 1. Two genres are contained in Daniel. One is the story, narrated in the third person, represented by chs. 2–6; the other is the vision report, narrated in the first person (with Daniel the speaker). Ch. 4 is unusual in being a story narrated in the first person by Nebuchadnezzar, king of Babylon, and ch. 1, which contains a little story about Daniel and his friends, seems to have been composed especially to link Daniel with the biblical history and to introduce the characters in the following stories.

2. *The stories* fall into two types: deliverance stories and interpretation stories. Deliverance stories (chs. 1, 3, 6) relate some miraculous preservation or rescue of the hero or heroes. Interpretation stories (chs. 2, 4, 5) focus on the hero's remarkable ability to explain a puzzling sign, whether a dream or writing on a wall. The two genres combine in important ways to present a single theme: the God of Daniel is the omnipotent lord who controls history, setting up and removing earthly rulers and empires, but also rescuing his people from the power of those kings and teaching them the limits of their sovereignty. He is thus the only sure source of knowledge about the future, and through him Daniel can predict what will happen in the future. All these stories, set in a foreign court and concerning the success of a wise courtier over his rivals, represent a well-known genre in the ancient Near East (see Wills 1990). In the Bible the genre is also represented in the stories of Esther and Joseph.

3. *The visions* of chs. 7–12 focus on that future. Already in ch. 2 Daniel has foretold a sequence of four mighty kingdoms which will culminate in a great and everlasting kingdom. In four visions (chs. 7, 8, 9, and 10–12) he narrates how he saw visions which are subsequently interpreted to him by a heavenly being as being symbolic of the rise and destruction of these kingdoms. The one exception here is ch. 9, where Daniel is puzzled not by a vision but by a word of the prophet Jeremiah concerning the length of the desolation of Jerusalem. The final vision consists for the most part of a monologue from the interpreting heavenly messenger, Gabriel, about the history of the last kingdom, which will culminate in great distress for Daniel's people, though they will in the end be saved—or at least the righteous of them.

4. The visions, at any rate, may accurately be called 'apocalypses', the main feature of which is the revelation of heavenly secrets, usually to a great figure of the past. These secrets may be about the origin of evil, the workings of the universe (sun, stars, winds), or the future. The prime example of this in the Bible is Revelation, which draws some of its inspiration from Daniel. However, Daniel *as a whole* is not an apocalypse.

5. Of the history of the composition of the book we have numerous clues but little consensus. Most of the stories appear once to have been independent compositions. One attractive theory is that chs. 2–7 formed an Aramaic collection (in a concentric pattern, ch. 2 matching ch. 7, ch. 3 matching ch. 6, and ch. 5 as a centre). There are signs of editorial expansion in most chapters, and linking between them, such as the addition of ch. 1, and the provision of datings to each chapter, so that both stories and visions run from Nebuchadnezzar to Cyrus. Chs. 8–12 must have come from a fairly narrow period, between the desecration of the Temple (167 BCE) and its restoration (163).

D. Historical Context. 1. After the Exile, and the return of exiles to Judah, the Judeans lived under Persians (until 331) then under Alexander the Great and the Hellenistic-Egyptian kingdom of the Ptolemies. In 199 Judah was captured by the Hellenistic-Syrian kingdom of the Seleucids. Daniel deals simultaneously with the beginning and end of that timespan. Daniel's lifetime lasts from the beginning of the exile of Judeans under Nebuchadrezzar (always called Nebuchadnezzar in Daniel) until the reign of Cyrus. Daniel's actual dates of birth and death are not given, but the fact that his life coincides with the exile of the Judeans is the significant point. The other period is that which the visions clearly point to: the time of the last kingdom, the final persecution and ultimate deliverance of the righteous: in other words, the end of history. Is the book, then, a prediction of events centuries ahead of its time, or a history veiled in the form of prediction? Those who dislike the idea of what one commentator called a 'fraud' argue for a sixth-century BCE date, and a real Daniel as the author. The majority of scholars, however, accept that the visions, at least, betray a knowledge of the time at which the 'end' is set, which can be deduced as the reign of the Seleucid (Syrian) king Antiochus IV, known as Epiphanes. Antiochus banned Jewish practices, desecrated the temple, and provoked a war of resistance under the leadership of the Maccabees which, after his death, succeeded in restoring the temple and traditional Jewish religious practices.

2. The main reasons for assigning a Maccabean date to the book (at least in its final form) are (a) some inaccuracies that a sixth-century writer ought not to have made, (b) the presence of a *genuine* prediction at the end of the book which we now know to be incorrect, and (c) the popularity of a kind of pseudo-historical writing among Jews of the Maccabean period and later, in which figures of antiquity were made to foretell the future (e.g. Enoch, Noah, the twelve sons of Jacob).

3. However, it seems probable that while the visions come from the second century BCE, the stories (chs. 2–6) may be a good deal earlier. For they represent foreign kings as foolish but ultimately persuaded, while Jews are promoted to high office at court. The climax of the tale is usually the king learning his lesson. In the visions, however, we are presented with an ever-increasing hostility towards the Jewish God and his people, which only their total destruction will solve. The perspective of the stories seems to be that of Jews living under a relatively benign rule (the Persians?) while that of the visions suggests Jews in Judah under a malign ruler. It is therefore likely that the book of Daniel has a long and complex history. This possibility is supported by the discovery of a story about an unknown Jewish exile and the Babylonian king Nabonidus, found among the Dead Sea scrolls and remarkably similar to the story of Daniel and Nebuchadnezzar in Daniel ch. 3 (4QPrNab). Yet, the story of Belshazzar's feast (ch. 5) marks a contrast to the theme of the other stories with its negative portrayal of the king who dies for his insolence, and may well have been inspired by the figure of Antiochus.

4. Finally, it is worth contrasting the relatively serene and optimistic mood of the stories, in which one High God is in supreme control and succession from one kingdom to another passes smoothly with the very different world-view of the visions, where the succession of power is violent—not just on earth but in the heavenly realm too, as the celestial patrons of each nation fight it out among themselves. The departure of the one supreme God from participation in this scenario (marked by ch. 7 where he hands power to another figure) is both remarkable and disturbing, suggesting an underlying view of the world's subsequent history that is rather pessimistic.

E. Structure. Despite the differences between the two halves of the book (language, form, setting, mood), there are features that bind the book together. The two most obvious are the chronological settings: the stories are assigned individually to the kings from Nebuchadnezzar to Cyrus, and the visions recapitulate this sequence. An important structural role is also played by ch. 7, which is bound to the preceding stories through its language (Aramaic) and its similarities with ch. 2, while it shares the same form as chs. 8–12 and indeed sets the agenda for the visions that follow. Hence the HB book of Daniel seems to have an intentional unity—obscured by the Greek book with its closing 'detective stories'.

COMMENTARY

Setting the Scene (1:1–21)

(1:1–7) The 'third year of the reign of Jehoiakim' is hard to reconcile with 2 Kings 24:1–6, Jer 25:1, and the *Babylonian Chronicle*, and may be based on a misunderstanding of other biblical texts. But the point here is to note the vessels taken (ch. 5), the Babylonian names of the four youths (ch. 3), and their introduction to the court, thus anticipating key elements of the stories, as well as Daniel's knowledge of Aramaic. Note also how the theme of 'the Lord' (Heb. *'ădōnāy*: 'YHWH' is used in Daniel only in ch. 9) giving kings into the power of other kings is introduced immediately.

(1:8–21) Many scholars think that the issue here is the observance of Jewish dietary laws, but no Jewish laws prescribe vegetarian diet. Either meat (and wine) are avoided for fear that it has been offered to Babylonian gods (thus implicating the youths in idolatry) or as a demonstration that the youths do not need the favours of the king, for they serve another heavenly king. Note how, although they have been educated in the Babylonian school (v. 5), they are said to have learned from God (v. 17), and in the case of Daniel, specifically the understanding of 'visions and dreams'. Thus, the theme of conflict between earthly and divine kingship and wisdom is neatly brought out, and the chapter has served its purpose as an introduction either to the whole book of Daniel or at least to a cycle of Daniel stories that may have once existed independently.

Daniel's First Success (2:1–49)

This story does not quite hang together. Is Daniel known to the king or not? And why does Daniel's interpretation of the dream introduce new details? Is it the original interpretation? The story shows signs of some editing (Davies 1976).

(2:1–12) In Daniel dreams typically leave the dreamer troubled (cf. 4:5; 5:6; 5:9; 7:15, 28). The list of interpreting professions is also often repeated (cf. 1:20; 2:27; 4:7; 5:11), perhaps to contrast the single figure of Daniel. The requirement to tell the dream as well as the interpretation is a unique element, and the underlying message, that this cannot be done through human wisdom but only through 'the gods', is emphasized in vv. 10–11; the Babylonian interpreters are made to confess that they are not truly inspired from heaven.

(2:13–23) According to this section, Daniel is one of the royal wise men, and a companion of Hananiah, Mishael, and Azariah. He is thus sought to be killed with the rest, presupposing the events of ch. 1. But why was he not summoned at first or, if he was, could not give the interpretation? And why does v. 24

repeat v. 14? The reason is probably that the writer of ch. 1 has inserted vv. 13–23. The original story presented Daniel as a hitherto unknown Jewish exile who had to be introduced to the king by one of his officers. It seems, then, that this story was once an independent tale, which has been integrated by means of this inserted passage. As the story now stands, Daniel and his friends act to preserve their lives and those of the wise men, and to pray for the 'mystery' from God. 'Mystery' here refers to the secret message (given by dream or any other means) which needs interpreting, and such a scheme reflects the mantic culture of Babylonia in which various guilds of diviners attempted to learn the will of the gods by means of the interpretation of natural phenomena taken as signs. Although the book of Daniel apparently opposes Babylonian mantic practices, it in fact adopts them. The prayer (20–3) nevertheless stresses that such interpretation is not an art but is possible only by direct intervention from the true God.

(2:24–45) Presented now as a hitherto unknown 'exile of Judah', Daniel surprises the king by telling him both dream and interpretation. The sequence of metals may reflect an ancient belief in which the ages of the world were symbolized by metal, the course of time showing a gradual deterioration in quality. Interpreting the successively baser metals as kingdoms contrasts with chs. 7–8 where each kingdom is more powerful than its predecessor. The interpretation flatters Nebuchadnezzar, and the statue may originally have referred to his own dynasty, which degenerated quickly under his successors until it fell to Cyrus. That makes better sense of the destruction of the statue in one moment. If so, the story is indeed an old one. As it stands, the interpretation offers the only hint in the story part of the book that human kingdoms will eventually be supplanted by a final eternal one. But it also shows some differences from the account of the dream, such as 'and the toes' (v. 41) and the stone being cut *from* a mountain instead of becoming one.

(2:46–9) It is characteristic of wise-courtier stories that the hero's success leads to advancement at court. Such an ending in the Daniel stories serves to show (a) that Jews may legitimately seek high office in foreign courts, (b) Jews can contribute to the welfare of non-Jewish regimes, and (c) Jews will be rewarded by their God for loyalty to him (a theme taken up on a grander scale in ch. 12). The use of the Babylonian names (contrast v. 17) is an editorial device to prepare us for these names in the next chapter.

The Golden Image and the Fiery Furnace (3:1–30)

This is not a story about Daniel. His inexplicable exclusion is probably due to this being originally an independent story adapted for the Daniel cycle. v. 12 may indicate its having been edited for this purpose.

(3:1–18) The golden image resumes the golden-headed statue of ch. 2. The lists of officials in vv. 2–3 echo the lists of interpreters in other stories. The phrase 'all . . . peoples, nations, and languages' (vv. 4 and 7) is picked up in subsequent stories (4:1; 5:19; 6:25; 7:14) and emphasizes the Babylonian kingdom as the first of several world empires. The king is depicted here as a foolish and arrogant self-idolater, but the enmity of rivals is also a factor, as in ch. 6. 'Chaldeans'

originally meant the Babylonians of Nebuchadrezzar's time, but under the Persians came to mean a class of mantic interpreter. It is generally used in this later sense in Daniel (1:4; 2:2, 4, 5, 10; 4:7; 5:7, 11) but in 5:30 and 9:1 has its earlier meaning. vv. 17–18 are important in raising the uncertainty of being rescued, perhaps hinting that the story arose or was applied to a time of persecution when not every loyal Jew could be sure of escaping suffering and death. (It is perhaps to meet this case that the hope of resurrection is finally raised in ch. 12.)

(3:19–27) v. 22, punishment of persecutors also needs to be included! Cf. 6:24 and Esth 7:9–10. v. 25, the fourth person having the 'appearance of a god' suggests one of the heavenly emissaries such as found in the visions (the Greek text here has an angel quenching the flames). Note that it is this fourth person (whom Nebuchadnezzar identifies as an angel), as much as the preservation of the other three, that amazes the king and prompts him to summon the youths out.

(3:28–30) The king's reaction is told in as exaggerated a manner as the rest of the account. He does not yet convert to the Jewish God (see the end of ch. 4), but makes another royal decree, involving equally violent sanctions—for he remains a typical foreign king!—prohibiting offences against the God of the youths. Their promotion to even higher office is part of the genre (see DAN 2:46–9).

Nebuchadnezzar Learns a Lesson (4:1–37)

Written in the form of a royal decree, this story may well have its origin in the activities of Nabonidus, the last king of Babylon, who withdrew to the desert oasis of Teima, provoking strange rumours about him in Babylon. A text from Qumran called the *Prayer of Nabonidus*, also written in the first person, tells how the king had a disturbing dream, and how he was 'afflicted . . . for seven years . . . and an exorcist pardoned my sins. He was a Jew . . .' When the story was incorporated into the Daniel cycle, and expanded, the lesser-known king was replaced by a better-known one, and the anonymous Jew became Belteshazzar and then Daniel.

The story contains two episodes: the king's dream with its interpretation (vv. 1–27), and the fulfilment of the interpretation (vv. 28–37).

(4:1–27) The opening doxology starts where the stories usually end, with the king praising the power of the Jewish God (usually given the title Most High, 'elyôn). v. 8, the story presumably originally featured another hero named Belteshazzar, whose name occurs in this chapter 6 times, 4 times on its own without 'Daniel'; elsewhere, the two names (always together) are to be found once in each of chs. 1, 2, 5, and 10. Belteshazzar has the position of 'chief of the dream interpreters' (2:48 uses entirely different terms of Daniel). 'Spirit of the holy gods' (vv. 8, 9, 18) is also confined to this story, except for 5:11 (which recapitulates this story). v. 10, the 'tree at the centre of the earth' is a well-known and worldwide mythic motif, here perhaps representing the power of the king who rules the world, providing for his subjects (animals, birds). Cf. Ezek 31:3–9, which likens Pharaoh to a cedar of Lebanon, or 17:10, similarly of the Davidic dynasty. v. 11, 'reaching to heaven' invokes the tower of Babel and human ambition, the reason for Nebuchadnezzar's collapse. v. 13, 'a holy watcher': both 'holy' and 'watcher' are terms for heavenly beings in

Jewish writings of the Hellenistic period, especially the 'Book of the Watchers', *1 Enoch* 1–36. 'Decree of the watchers' reinforces the deterministic outlook of the book of Daniel as a whole: all that happens in human history is the result of heavenly dictates. This is the basis of both mantic lore and apocalyptic writing. vv. 19–27, the interpretation makes it clear that Nebuchadnezzar's kingdom is not to be destroyed (v. 19, and the meaning of the stump, vv. 26–7), but the king needs to learn a lesson; the summons to atone for his pride (v. 27) recalls the *Nabonidus* text. As with the previous stories, the aim and outcome is the conversion of the king from arrogance to recognition of the complete power of the god *'elyôn*. During this interpretation, the image of the tree fades and the focus moves to the animal-like fate of the king.

(4:28–37) The decree comes about at the moment when Nebuchadnezzar, apparently forgetful of the dream, is at his most arrogant. Appropriately he comes to resemble the very opposite of power and splendour, losing his human form and his human reason, his palace, his food. The lesson is learned when the king 'lifts his eyes' (v. 34) and his reason returns; also 'when the period was over' exactly! The coincidence of human free action and divine decree, the core difficulty of any theory of predestination, is glossed over. Does Nebuchadnezzar confess his arrogance because his reason is restored, or vice versa? The repetition in v. 36 'my reason returned' creates the ambiguity. In v. 37 the king appears at last to become a *worshipper* of the 'king of heaven' (a term found only here in the OT, but cf. the NT expression 'kingdom of heaven').

Desecration Brings Death (5:1–31)

This story's allusions to preceding chapters (borrowing the same phrases), in vv. 10–12 and 17–21 may be editorial passages intended to integrate this story into the cycle. But they go well beyond what is required, and this factor, together with the killing, rather than persuading or converting, of the king and also the clear allusion to temple desecration suggest it may have been composed after the story cycle was in existence (with or without ch. 6), in the time of Antiochus IV who desecrated the temple and whose death is predicted in 11:45.

(5:1–4) For a long time Belshazzar was regarded as one of the fictions of this book. But he is now known from Babylonian texts as the son of Nabonidus the last king of Babylon, who ruled in the city while his father was in Teima (see ch. 4), though he was apparently not ever the king as he is named here. The impious act of the king is cleverly and economically set out. The plunder of the vessels alludes to the opening of Daniel, and the gold and silver vessels are used in the worship of gods of gold and silver but also of bronze, iron, wood, and stone, consciously or not invoking the idolatrous statue of ch. 2. The mention of *women* touching these holy Jewish vessels only compounds the horror!

(5:5–12) 'Next to the lampstand' suggests the illuminated spectre in a semi-darkened room but also perhaps hints at the temple lampstand, the menorah, symbol of the presence of God in the Holy of Holies. There is a wonderfully comic pun (in Aramaic) in the phrase 'his limbs loosened' (lit.), since the same phrase means 'solving riddles' and is so used in vv. 12 and 16. Thereafter we are given the familiar ingredients: the king summons all the varieties of interpreter and prom-

ises political advancement; but they are unable to deliver. The queen (his mother and wife of Nebuchadnezzar, who, as said, was *not* the father of Belshazzar) is the vehicle for the reintroduction of Daniel, who is presumably no longer among the court favourites. The interpreters (v. 8) are unable even to *read* the writing, let alone interpret it. Here is an echo of ch. 2; both sign *and* meaning have to be constructed.

(5:13–30) In vv. 17–23 Daniel rejects the king's offer of reward (but see v. 29!), and before he interprets the writing proceeds to admonish the king by comparing him with Nebuchadnezzar, whose story (ch. 4) he relates. The writing is deciphered as MENE, MENE, TEKEL, and PARSIN. The words are Aramaic but their meanings are ambiguous. All three terms might denote measures of weight. It is interesting to speculate about meanings other than those given; the authors may well be playing (as in vv. 12 and 16) with multiple meanings. Daniel's interpretation is linguistically possible: the verb *m-n-'* can mean 'number'; *t-q-l* (Heb. 'shekel') 'weigh'; and *p-r-s* can mean 'divide'. But other allusions may also be present: *t-q-l*, for instance, might suggest *q-l*, which means '(s)light' and hence 'wanting'; while *parsin* also means 'Persians'. The king's reaction seems untypical of a despot: he rewards the bearer of the bad news as promised! We are not told how Belshazzar was killed, whether by human or divine means. 'Darius the Mede', despite ingenious attempts by some scholars to identify him with some other historical character, is a mistake. Darius was the name borne by several kings of Persia. It is not a Median name. There was a Median empire, which Cyrus incorporated in his own Persian realm (we might accurately speak of a Medo-Persian empire). In the four-kingdom scheme of Daniel Media comes between Babylon and Persia, which is chronologically correct. But the Medes never ruled Babylon, and the city passed from Belshazzar directly to Cyrus. This notice is therefore not from the hand of a contemporary, or even a reliable historian. But that hardly matters; the point being made is that the one divine kingdom has been transferred by its owner from one king and nation to another, and all Darius has to do is 'receive' it.

The Den of Lions (6:1–28)

The last of the stories about Daniel introduces a benign king deceived by jealous officials (as in Esther), who is delighted when Daniel is rescued. Hence the political setting of this story is of a benevolent regime, where the only danger to Jews comes from those resentful of their success. The Darius of this story looks more like a Persian monarch (see v. 1—his description as 'the Mede' (5:31) is not mentioned in this chapter). If so, his portrait conforms to that of Persian kings throughout the OT (Isaiah, Nehemiah, Ezra, Esther): neither they nor their gods are attacked, and they are consistently well-disposed towards the Jews.

(6:1–9) According to Herodotus, Darius organized the Persian empire into twenty satrapies (later enlarged by Xerxes; see Esth 1:1). A position such as Daniel's is implausible, since the empire was centrally governed by a small number of families. But Daniel's ever higher office is a uniting thread in the stories. The word for 'law' in v. 5 does not mean the Torah, the book of Moses, but is a general word for 'religion' or 'religious custom'. 'Prays for thirty days': 'pray' here is better translated as 'make a request', whether of gods or humans. Why not a permanent ban? Presumably because Jews were known to pray daily in any case, while a permanent ban on requests to gods or humans besides the king would be impractical. We know nothing about any practice of keeping lions in dens to kill people under any ancient Near-Eastern regime.

(6:10–28) v. 10 describes Daniel as praying three times a day in an upper room, facing Jerusalem. We have little information about Jewish praying customs from the Persian period. The Mishnah prescribes three times a day, and synagogue architecture suggests an orientation of prayer and worship towards Jerusalem. But the point is that Daniel did not make his habit secret; the conspirators knew when and where to find him. vv. 14–15, the portrait of a benign king duped into making an edict which, according to the 'law of the Medes and Persians' is irrevocable, recurs in Esther. The issue presented here, then, is a conflict between two sets of irrevocable laws, one Medo-Persian, the other the law of 'the God of Daniel'. Prominent in Esther, too, is the theme of the 'law of the Medes and Persians' by which the king is trapped into acting. In vv. 16–20, the king's virtue is strongly emphasized: he prays for Daniel's deliverance by his God, spends the night fasting, and hurries back, calling out *as if he expects Daniel to be delivered*. vv. 22–4 repeat the motifs of the rescuing angel and the punishment of the instigators (see 3:22, 28), with the added ingredient of the wives and children. The final decree (vv. 25–7) is a feature of chs. 2–6; a comparison will show that they successively broaden their acclaim of the Jewish God. This doxology is a fitting climax to the sequence of stories, encapsulating its recurrent theme: eternal kingship, power to deliver. v. 28 extends Daniel's lifetime into the next kingdom (according to the book's historical scheme), that of the Persians. No story, but the final vision (chs. 10–12) is set under Cyrus.

The Vision of the Four Beasts and the Final Judgement (7:1–28)

In this chapter the narrative passes from third person to first, and instead of interpreting signs given to others, Daniel receives the signs and has them interpreted by a heavenly being, in the manner of the book of Zechariah. The first vision takes up the four-kingdoms sequence of Dan 2 and focuses on the final judgement and annihilation of these kings/kingdoms. Again, however, we find signs of an earlier account being revised, particularly with regard to the 'little horn' on the fourth beast, suggesting a more ancient story being updated to fit the time of Antiochus IV. The chapter utilizes many mythical themes, possibly of Judean rather than Babylonian origin.

(7:1–8) v. 1 links the vision to the preceding stories with its smooth transition to first person, and its reuse of the phrases 'visions of your head as you lay in bed' (see 2:28; 4:5, 10, 13). Since the apocalyptic visions of chs. 7–12 are pseudonymous, due care must be taken to explain how Daniel's words were preserved, so 'he wrote down the dream'; see 12:4 also. The four winds ... the great sea' (v. 2): the sea symbolizes chaos before creation (see Gen 1:2), and the winds may represent (a) the four corners of the earth, from which the kingdoms come, (b) forces stirring up a storm, and/or (c) a divine creative force

(see Gen 1:2). We are perhaps meant to be witnessing the beginning of time and history (as well as, later, their end). The description of the four beasts (vv. 3–8) no doubt also draws on mythological resources. The myth of dragon(s) in the sea is alluded to in Isa 27:1, 51:9–11, and is pre-Israelite in origin. Hos 13:7–8, mentioning a lion, a leopard, a bear, and a 'wild beast', has been noticed by Collins (1993: 295). Hellenistic astrology is another suggestion (Caquot 1955).

(7:9–14) 'Ancient One' (lit. ancient of days) is a title used of the 'father of the gods' El in the Ugaritic texts. His description fits closely with that of the deity in Ezekiel's vision (Ezek 1), and was possibly drawn from older mythology (see Emerton (1958), and for the mythological motifs in general, Day (1985: 151–78)). The heavenly king sits enthroned in the court surrounded by the other gods and by attendant heavenly servants. The 'books' are those in which sins (and good deeds) are recorded (see 12:1). The last and most vicious beast is condemned to immediate death, while the others have a stay of execution. The implication of this judgement is unclear. 'One like a human being' receives the kingdom from the 'Ancient One'. Is this second figure a symbol of the nation that will exercise the dominion (the Jewish people), depicted as a human rather than an animal? Or is he a divine figure (such figures represented as in human form, Dan 8:15; 10:5)? If so, is he Michael, who 'stands' for the Jews in 12:1? The title (lit. son of man) was adopted in the NT as a title for Jesus Christ, though how far it derives from Daniel alone is disputed. Since we are dealing with a book that has a long literary history, both interpretations may be valid; and in any event the ambiguities of this book are not always best served by insisting on one exclusive meaning. Surrealism is no respecter of logic.

(7:15–28) In the visions it is Daniel's turn to be perplexed and dismayed and to seek the interpretation. The beasts are said to be kings and not kingdoms—whereas the 'little horn' on the fourth beast is clearly one king and the beast a kingdom! Is this a sign of an earlier story about *kings* (as suggested for ch. 2)? Another question is whether the 'holy ones of the Most High' who 'receive the kingdom' are human or heavenly. 'Holy one' is often applied in biblical and post-biblical writings to angelic beings. Is the envisaged final kingdom earthly or heavenly? Chs. 10–12 portray each nation as having its own angelic 'prince', suggesting that kingdoms have both heavenly and earthly aspects. What would a kingdom of *all* the angels mean in this context? But Daniel is not consistent throughout and plays with different conceptions of the government of the earth and also of the final state of affairs. The focus quickly moves to the fourth beast (v. 19). Several discrepancies with the vision report also appear. The beast has now acquired bronze claws, and the 'little horn' wages war with the 'holy ones' (v. 21). In v. 26 it is the little horn that is judged, not the fourth beast. We have details of this king's career intended, no doubt, to identify him as Antiochus IV. There are many candidates for the 'three kings' of v. 24 depending on whether succession or conquest is meant; the 'changing of sacred seasons and the law' presumably refers to Antiochus' imposed reforms of the Jerusalem cult, and the 'time, two times and half a time' (the first of a series of oblique reckonings in the book) predicates three and a half years for his domination of the 'holy ones'.

The Vision of the Ram and Goat (8:1–27)

(8:1–14) Curiously, although dated to the reign of Belshazzar, ruler of Babylon, the vision is set in the capital of the subsequent *Persian* empire (see Esth 1:2, 5; 2:3, 5), and describes conflict between two beasts, one with two horns from the east (?) charging north, west, and south, the other from the west. The goat overcomes the ram (vv. 5–7), and, following ch. 7, horns representing kings sprout from its head, with one little horn distinguished for its aggression, especially towards the 'beautiful land', i.e. Judah (vv. 8–9). It defies the 'host' (the heavenly beings). In particular this horn confronts the 'prince of the host', removes his daily sacrifice and overthrows his sanctuary: a clear reference to the Jerusalem cult, of which the twice-daily offering (the *tāmîd*) was the regular basis—and which figures prominently in the remainder of the book. Also prominent will be the question of the duration of the desecration, here defined in an angelic conversation (vv. 13–14). The calculation is expressed in *tāmîd* sacrifices (which were offered morning and evening): 2,300 means 1,150 days, or three years and about three months (not quite the three and a half years of 7:25, and different from subsequent calculations in ch. 12).

(8:15–27) The interpreting angel is now named as Gabriel, depicted in human form (*g-b-r* in Hebrew can mean 'man', though the whole name means 'God is my strength'). As in Zech 2:8 he is instructed to speak by a second voice. The two animals are interpreted as the kingdoms of (Media-)Persia and Greece, who warred from the sixth to the fourth centuries, until Alexander the Great (d. 323; the goat's one horn) conquered the whole Persian empire. He had four successors, reducing to three and finally two kingdoms, Egypt (Ptolemies) and Syria (Seleucids). The 'prince of the host' of v. 11, interpreted as the 'prince of princes' is probably Michael, not the High God himself (see 10:21–11:1; 12:1); see also v. 25 'prince of princes'. Two meanings of 'people of the holy ones' are possible: (a) the nation belonging to the angels (angels = 'holy ones') or, more probably, since all the nations have their angels, (b) nation of holy people. But in attacking the Jews he rises up against their patron Michael and will be destroyed by heavenly force (v. 25). The vision is referred to (v. 26) as 'the vision of the evenings and mornings', alluding to the twice-daily *tāmîd* sacrifice, and Daniel is told to 'seal up' the vision, i.e. to roll up the scroll on which it is written and fasten it, to be opened only at the time to which it refers (see 12:9).

The Mystery of Jeremiah's Prophecy (9:1–27)

(9:1–3) In 5:31 'Darius the Mede' takes the kingdom from Belshazzar; here he is said merely to be Median 'by descent' and succeeds Xerxes (Ahasuerus), the name borne by several Persian kings (as was Darius). Nevertheless, since ch. 10 dates from Cyrus, the first Persian king, the book is still dealing with a Median empire between the Babylonian and the Persian. The mystery to be solved here lies not in a vision but in a scroll of Jeremiah's prophecies which Daniel is studying and which contains a prediction that Jerusalem's devastation will last seven years (see Jer 25:11–12; 29:10). Daniel seeks an answer by praying, using symbols of penitence.

(9:4–20) The prayer is thought by many scholars to be a later insertion because its theological attitude is unique in Daniel,

and deals with confession of sin rather than a request for illumination. Here distress appears to be due not to a preordained plan but to Israel's sin, and divine intervention will occur not when the timetable prescribes but once Israel has repented. The importance of the dating (v. 1) is that Darius comes to the throne after seventy years have passed from Jerusalem's destruction. The prayer, in better biblical Hebrew than found in the rest of Daniel, is similar in content and structure to the prayer contained in 1 Kings 8:15–53, Ezra 9:6–15, Neh 9:6–37, and in other early non-biblical Jewish texts as well as in the present Jewish Day of Atonement liturgy. Apart from 1:3 'Israel' occurs in Daniel only in this prayer. However, vv. 3, 21, and 23 make it clear that a prayer (whether or not actually recorded) belonged to the story. Whether originally incorporated or inserted later, it was probably composed independently. The prayer expresses a typical Deuteronomic theology: Israel has ignored the warnings of prophets, abandoned the covenant, and been exiled accordingly. The curses of Deut 27 are referred to in v. 11. The reference to the Exodus (v. 15) is also a Deuteronomic theme, as is the notion of the divine 'name' being present (v. 18).

(9:21–3) Again, 'the man' Gabriel is the messenger and as in ch. 8 comes at the time of the second twice-daily temple sacrifice. The explanation involves interpreting a week of seven days as a 'week' of seven years. The total period is thus 490 years. This formula is implicit in the notion (Deut 15, Lev 25) of a 'sabbath year' in every seven. Calculations of epochs in history according to sabbath-years are found in other contemporary Jewish literature such as *Jubilees* (a jubilee is seven such cycles, forty-nine or fifty years).

(9:24–7) marks the seventy years with crucial events: a problem is that the calculation that follows begins only with the decree of Cyrus (by which time Jerusalem had been desolate for about fifty years. Even then the total number of weeks is seventy and a half ($493\frac{1}{2}$ years)! The end of seven weeks (forty-nine years) pass before a high priest ('anointed prince') is installed (since there were no kings, only high priests were anointed). After 434 more years a high priest is killed (this would seem to refer to the murder of Onias III, recorded in 2 Macc 4:23–8), and the sanctuary destroyed. For seven years the destroyer, who is to be identified with Antiochus IV (Epiphanes) makes a pact with 'many' and for three and a half years the temple is desolated. The 'abomination that desolates' is the altar to Zeus that Antiochus has erected in place of the altar. 9:27, the end itself is not described, but it represents the end of Jerusalem's desolation, and of the sin that brought it, the beginning of eternal goodness, the fulfilment of prophecy, and the reconsecration of the temple: this is equivalent to the end of the historical sequence foreseen in chs. 2 and 7, but focused on temple, holiness, and Jerusalem, not on world empires.

The History of the World as a Heavenly Conflict (10:1–12:13)

This final section is in poor Hebrew, and may represent a rather poor translation from an Aramaic original. Several difficulties in interpretation may be due to translational errors. The section, covering three chapters, barely sustains the vision-interpretation scheme, and runs more like a lightly disguised narrative of historical events, which the modern historian (and ancient reader, no doubt) can identify. But it also offers an interpretation of history as a 'great conflict' (10:1) that combines the idea of a preordained sequence and a struggle between nations: heavenly beings representing each nation fight for the supremacy of their people. The idea of each nation having its own divine patron is found in Deut 32:8–9 (following, with most scholars, the reading of the LXX 'sons of God' rather than 'sons of Israel'), and the idea that heavenly politics determine events on earth is also found in several Jewish writings of the Graeco-Roman period. For example, according to *1 Enoch* 1–6 and *Jubilees* 5:1–11, sin came into the world as a result of rebellion in heaven and the descent (voluntary or enforced) of some angels to the earth (see also Gen 6:1–4). That human fate is determined by heavenly events is in any case generally a common notion in the ancient world, though in monotheistic Judaism it acquired particular features, such as the emergence of an arch-rebel or opponent, variously called Satan, Mastema, and Belial. But in Daniel this figure makes no appearance; his role is taken by the rebellious human king. However, the effective agent on Israel's behalf is now no longer God but its own angel, Michael.

(10:1–9) vv. 1–4 date the final vision from the first Persian king, Cyrus (see 1:21 and 6:28) after a three-week fast. The bank of the river as the site of revelation may depend on Ezek 1:1. The description of the heavenly messenger (vv. 5–9) is influenced by various texts in Ezekiel (especially chs. 1 and 9); Acts 9:7 may in turn be influenced by the account of Daniel's reaction here.

(10:10–11:1) vv. 10–12 point out that understanding of mysteries is given only to those who desire it and prepare for it, whether by praying or fasting. It is not bestowed without merit. Even though wisdom according to Daniel does not mean acquisition of knowledge by study or instruction (as in Proverbs) but by revelation of heavenly secrets, it none the less demands a religious discipline (as already shown in ch. 9). The first hint of heavenly warfare comes in v. 13: the angel (Gabriel, according to 11:1) was prevented from coming (for the same time Daniel was fasting!) by the Persian 'prince' (angel), now fighting against Israel's patron Michael (who appears only here in the OT). Thus, while in chs. 1–6 the one divine kingdom is that which passes from nation to nation, here sovereignty is continually contested, now between Jews and Persians and soon between Jews and Greeks (v. 20). vv. 15–20 perhaps relate a commissioning of Daniel in a quasi-prophetic role (cf. Isa 6:7 for the touching of lips). Daniel is to assume a prophetic role as writer of a book of predictions (12:4). 'Do not fear' and 'be strong' are frequently reassurances in time of war (e.g. Deut 31:6, Josh 10:25); war, as Daniel learns, is now the perpetual state of things until the end. v. 21 introduces the 'book of truth' in which all preordained history is inscribed (see 12:1).

(11:2–4) mentions three more Persian kings after Cyrus: although historically there were many more, the OT mentions only four in all. The last, who campaigns against Greece, may be Xerxes.

(11:3–9) clearly refers to Alexander the Great, who died in 323 and from whose empire evolved (v. 4) the two kingdoms of the Seleucids (Syria) and Ptolemies (Egypt), whose kings Daniel refers to as respectively the 'king of the north' and 'king of the south'. Judah was first ruled by Ptolemies, though the Seleucid kingdom was larger (v. 5); in about 250 BCE an alliance by marriage of the two kingdoms was made (v. 6) but later Ptolemy III (called Euergetes) made huge inroads into the Seleucid territory (vv. 7–8). Seleucus II recovered the territory (v. 9).

(11:10–13) describes the efforts of Seleucus II and Antiochus II ('the Great') to conquer the Ptolemaic kingdom. In 200 BCE Antiochus defeated the Ptolemies and took Samaria and Judah.

(11:14–19) In the struggle over control of Judah, Judeans were divided in their allegiance. Who the 'violent' or 'lawless' of v. 14 are is unclear, and what they tried to do ('fulfil the vision'); but the writers of Daniel (who may have been pro-Ptolemaic) presumably opposed them. vv. 16–17 allude to Antiochus' arrival in Jerusalem as its ruler and another marriage alliance with Egypt. Antiochus' ambitions were frustrated by the Romans who forced him to leave Asia Minor (the 'coastlands', v. 19).

(11:21–9) Antiochus IV is the 'contemptible person' of v. 21, who tries to restore the kingdom reduced by the Romans. The 'ruler/prince of the covenant' (v. 22) is probably the high priest Onias III, murdered by a pro-Seleucid rival (see 9:26). His campaign against Egypt is referred to in v. 25, and the abortive peace negotiations in vv. 26–7. Peace will not come because the allotted time for the denouement of history has not come (v. 27). At the centre of this denouement is the 'holy covenant' (v. 28). But the final events are taking place as and when decreed: 'at the time appointed' (v. 29).

(11:30–5) records Antiochus' measures against Judah. After being driven from Egypt by the Romans (Kittim, v. 30), he stopped the twice-daily burnt-offering sacrifice, dismantled the altar and replaced it with one to Zeus (the 'abominating desolation', as in 9:27), and forbade practice of traditional Jewish religion, making alliances with like-minded Jews (whom the writer calls 'violators of the covenant', v. 32). However, those who remained loyal, led by 'the wise' (who must include the writers of Daniel), would resist, suffering punishment and death (vv. 32–4). The 'little help' they received (v. 34) may have been the violent (and ultimately successful) resistance led by the Maccabees. But the writers are not interested in such military actions. The end would come about by divine intervention, and meanwhile the 'wise' suffered so as to be 'purified' (v. 35). The goal of history, earlier in the book identified with the supremacy of the nation (ch. 2) is now focused on the destiny of righteous individuals.

(11:36–45) merely summarizes the preceding account. The account of the end of Antiochus' career (vv. 40–5) does not correspond to the actual course of events. 'At the time of the end' (v. 40) appears to denote what for the authors still lies immediately ahead. It envisages an attack from the 'king of the south' (Egypt), with huge retaliation. The 'king of the north' will enter the 'beautiful land' (Judah, v. 41), and though Judah's traditional enemies will be spared, he will extend his power into and beyond Egypt (vv. 42–3), but reports of trouble from the north and east will force him angrily to retrace his steps. Pitching his war-tent in Judah, between the Mediterranean and Jerusalem (v. 45) he will meet his end. In fact Antiochus died campaigning in Persia and did not conquer Egypt. On the basis of this passage scholars assign the composition of Daniel to between 167, when the 'desolating abomination' was set up, and 163, when Antiochus' death must have been known in Jerusalem. (But for evidence that the book was updated during this period, see DAN 12:5–13.)

(12:1) The death of the great and final oppressor and the end of the last kingdom is no longer of interest. Rather, the final resolution now concerns the respective fates of righteous and wicked and the calculation of the time when the end will come. On the death of Antiochus, the patron angel Michael will 'stand' or 'arise', which may mean not more than 'appear' or 'act'. Reference to a 'time of distress' *following* this is curious, but may refer to prophecies of such a time in Isa 33:2; Jer 14:8; 15:11; 30:7, all of which associate the phrase with a decisive divine rescue, and intend to identify Michael's rise with that promised divine intervention rather than predict fresh misery. But the deliverance will only be for some, not all: 'everyone found written in the book', presumably in a heavenly record of the names of the righteous. The possibility that these names were written *beforehand*, the righteous being predestined, cannot be ruled out, given Daniel's strong attraction to predetermination.

(12:2–4) Resurrection is explicitly affirmed only here in the OT, though belief subsequently spread, until it finally became orthodox Jewish doctrine. But who is to be revived? 'Many' appears to mean only 'some', but it includes righteous and wicked. The scenario makes best sense if we see the problem being addressed as one of justice. There are those who have suffered undeservedly and those who have sinned without punishment. Both groups must be revived so that justice can be administered. But those outside these two categories will remain dead. The 'land of dust' (as the Heb. has it) may be a poetic expression for the grave (Gen 3:19 has both words) or mean Sheol, the place where the dead exist as shadowy spirits (see Ps 16:10; 55:15; 86:13). Among those to live forever the 'wise' have a special place, for they are the religious leaders. The language of 'wise' (Heb. *maskil*) and 'making many righteous' is derived from the description of the Servant in Isa 52–3. Wisdom and righteousness are virtually equated (Daniel being the paragon of each). 'Like the stars' is probably a metaphor rather than indicating an angelic status, since it is parallel to 'shine like the brightness of the sky'—though the idea of the righteous dead being like angels is found in 12:25 (Mt 22:30; Lk 20:35). The notion of a hidden book, revealed just before the end time, is a common feature of apocalyptic and apocryphal literature in which books attributed to authors of antiquity appear only recently to have been publicized. Hence the author is commanded to hide the book until its contents need to be known, and thus is Daniel commanded in v. 4 (and v. 9). In the meantime, evil will increase, and few will understand what is happening; if 'run to and fro' is taken from Am 8:12, it probably refers to a lack of divine guidance.

(12:5–13) The other theme of ch. 12, 'how long?', occupies most of vv. 5–13. Ch. 9 suggested three and a half years from

the 'desolating abomination'. In vv. 5–13 Daniel witnesses, then joins, a conversation about the calculation of the remaining time. At first he overhears it (as if it were a secret not to be directly told to humans, even to him). Although only one of the persons he sees is explicitly said to be 'clothed in linen' (angelic dress, see 10:5) both are presumably heavenly beings. For the 'bank of the stream' see DAN 10:4. The formula 'a time, two times, and half a time', repeats 7:25 and corresponds to the last half-week (three and a half years) of ch. 9. True to the character of the book, Daniel does not understand this (fairly transparent!) calculation and so yet another interpretation is asked for. The rather puzzling question (we would expect him to ask for the 'explanation' rather than the 'outcome') is one possible instance of a defective translation from an original Aramaic text into Hebrew. In fact we get a repeat, though not just of the conversation in vv. 6–7. First come the contents of v. 4, reiterating the sealing of the book (v. 9), then a repetition of the 'refining' of 11:35, then a resumption of 12:4 where the 'running back and forth' and increase of evil is changed so that now the wise *do* understand, but not the wicked, while the wicked continue to act wickedly. Finally comes a more detailed calculation of the time of the end, in terms of days, and dating from the day on which the *tāmîd* sacrifice was abolished and the 'abominating desolation' set up. But there are two different answers in vv. 11 and 12, and both differ from the 1,150 days of 8:14 and at least one differs from the three and a half years of 9:27 (and 12:7). An obvious explanation is that someone, after 1,290 days had elapsed, recalculated, while still hoping (or insisting) that the time was near. The sense of a disappointment is perhaps conveyed by the phrasing of v. 12: 'Happy is the one who waits' (cf. Ps 1:1).

(12:13) The exilic past with its author Daniel, and the future are finally sewn together in v. 13 as Daniel himself is told to go and die, awaiting his reward as he rises along with his successors, the 'wise' of the present (i.e. end) time. For Daniel, of course, serves throughout this book as the archetype of the authors, the *maskîlîm*, of the time of distress under Antiochus, who saw their duty, as had Daniel, in withstanding persecution and 'making many righteous'.

The book of Daniel is generally thought to have bequeathed to its obviously literate and knowledgeable second-century BCE readers, whether or not they were supposed to accept its ancient origin and recent 'discovery', an affirmation that an end had been set and that suffering was not in vain. Yet the lack of specific information about the manner and time of the end, the disappearance of the orderly regime of chs. 1–6, and with it the High God who made and sustained order, and the retreat from historical triumph into trans-historical vindication all seem to betray an anxiety that suggests hope, rather than conviction, in an imminent happy ending. Paradoxically, in a book compiled in the middle of a confrontation between Hellenistic and traditional models of Judaism, the notion of a personal ethical responsibility, an interest in the meaning (or lack of it) of history, and a hope for personal survival beyond death mark it as anything but a reactionary and conservative book; its authors were learned and innovative, and very much a product of the age of cultural change which Hellenism brought to Judah as well as to the rest of the ancient world.

REFERENCES

Caquot, A. (1955), 'Sur les quatre bêtes de Daniel VII', *Semitica* 5: 5–13.

Collins, J. J. (1993), *Daniel*, Hermeneia (Minneapolis: Fortress).

Davies, P. R. (1976), 'Daniel Chapter Two', *JTS* 27: 392–401.

Day, J. (1985), *God's Conflict with the Dragon and the Sea* (Cambridge: Cambridge University Press).

Emerton, J. A. (1958), 'The Origin of the Son of Man Imagery', *JTS* NS 9: 225–42.

Wills, L. M. (1990), *The Jew in the Court of the Foreign King* (Minneapolis: Fortress).

27. Hosea

JOHN DAY

INTRODUCTION

A. Historical Background. 1. Hosea prophesied in the second half of the eighth century BCE from the reign of Jeroboam II of Israel (*c.*787–747) to that of Hoshea (*c.*731–722), the last king of Israel. Although ch. 1 and perhaps ch. 4 reflect the long, peaceful reign of Jeroboam II, much of the book dates from the period of *coups d'état* which afflicted the northern kingdom in its last decades following his death. Cf. 7:7, 'All of them are hot as an oven, and they devour their rulers'.

2. Jeroboam II was succeeded by his son Zechariah, who was murdered after only six months' rule (*c.*747–746) and this ended the dynasty of Jehu, which had ruled for almost a century. His slayer Shallum was himself struck down after only one month (*c.*746) and was succeeded by Menahem (*c.*746–737), who paid tribute to the newly aggressive Assyrian ruler Tiglath-pileser III (745–727). His son Pekahiah ruled *c.*737–736, but was assassinated by his captain Pekah, who reigned *c.*736–731. This event is probably reflected in 6:7–9, with its reference to bloodshed in Gilead, since Gilead is where the rebellion started.

3. Pekah made an alliance with Rezin, king of Syria (the Syro-Ephraimite alliance) in order to besiege Jerusalem under King Ahaz with the intention of putting on the throne one willing to join an anti-Assyrian alliance. Ahaz (rejecting Isaiah's advice, cf. Isa 7) appealed to Tiglath-pileser III, who intervened, annexing Galilee, Gilead, and much of the coastal plain from Israel and exiling part of the population in *c.*733, as well as destroying Damascus in 732. The internecine strife between Judah and Israel then is reflected in 5:8–15.

4. Next Hoshea (*c.*731–722) assassinated Pekah, and pursued a pro-Assyrian policy for a few years, paying tribute to the Assyrian king, Shalmaneser V (727–722), but later paid tribute to 'So king of Egypt' instead (2 Kings 17:4). Consequently, the Assyrians invaded Israel, imprisoned Hoshea (possibly alluded to in 13:10), and besieged Samaria for three years, capturing it in 722. Thus ended the northern kingdom of Israel; 27,290 prisoners were exiled by Shalmaneser V's successor, Sargon II, in 720. These last years of the northern kingdom are echoed in Hosea's references to the changing shift of alliances between pro-Assyrian and pro-Egyptian policies, e.g. 7:11, 'Ephraim has become like a dove, silly and without sense, they call upon Egypt, they go to Assyria'.

5. The northern kingdom's end was predicted by Hosea, who saw this as YHWH's judgement on Israel's sin. Hosea has often been compared with Amos, who a little earlier (*c.*760–750) likewise prophesied judgement on Israel. Whereas Amos had little hope for the future (Amos 9:11–15 is a later addition) and concentrated his invective on social injustice, corruption, and hypocritical religiosity, Hosea hoped for restoration after judgement and concentrated his anger on the religious syncretism of the Baalized YHWH cult and the political follies of *coups d'état* and foreign alliances. Whilst the differing historical circumstances of the two prophets partly explain these differences, some of them are attributable to their differing temperaments.

B. Hosea's Marriage and Its Meaning. 1. One important question the book of Hosea raises is the problem of the prophet's marriage: how do chs. 1 and 3 relate to one another? Ch. 1 is a third-person narrative in which God commands Hosea to take a wife of whoredom and have children of whoredom. He subsequently marries Gomer, who bears three children, their sign-names symbolizing judgement for Israel. Ch. 3 is a first-person narrative in which Hosea is told to 'love a woman who is beloved of a paramour and is an adulteress, just as the Lord loves the people of Israel, though they turn to other gods and love cakes of raisins' (RSV). The woman is unnamed. We then read that the prophet bought her and put her under discipline for a while (prior to the full restoration of the relationship).

2. An explanation common among the Church Fathers and medieval Jewish rabbis, but no longer followed, was that Hosea's marriage was not a literal event, but purely symbolic, either an allegory or a dream. However, it does not read like an allegory or a dream, and some details, such as the name Gomer, have no obvious symbolic significance.

3. One minority view maintains that chs. 1 and 3 are parallel narratives, one concentrating on the children, the other on the wife. But against this (1) 3:1 seems to represent this chapter as the sequel to ch. 1. Whether we read 'The LORD said to me again, "Go, love a woman..."' (NRSV) or 'The LORD said to me, "Go again, love a woman..."' (RSV), we seem to have a reference back to ch. 1, suggesting that ch. 3 follows on from it. (2) The analogy between YHWH's love for Israel, though the people have been faithless to him, and Hosea's love for the woman in 3:1, makes sense only if the woman had previously been his wife and subsequently been unfaithful to him. This implies that 3:1 is not describing the beginning of the marriage, which the view that it is parallel to ch. 1 requires. (3) In 3:3–4 the woman undergoes a period of discipline before the marriage is (re)consummated, which does not fit ch. 1 (cf. 1:2–3, which reads as if sexual relations were established immediately).

4. Another minority view holds that Hos 3 describes Hosea's relations with a woman other than Gomer (Rudolph 1966; Davies 1992). This seems unlikely, again in view of

3:1. Hosea's loving the woman is parallel to YHWH's loving Israel, though they turn to other gods. Therefore, for the symbolism to work, the woman must have been Hosea's wife and previously unfaithful to him.

5. The most commonly accepted and natural view is that ch. 3 is the sequel to ch. 1 (Rowley 1963; Mays 1969; Wolff 1974; Macintosh 1997). Hosea, we are to understand, married Gomer and had one or more children by her. At some stage she committed adultery, but eventually Hosea succeeded in wooing her back, though the marriage was not reconsummated until after a period of discipline. The theological significance of these events for Israel is spelled out in ch. 2, which depicts Israel as YHWH's wife, who goes whoring after her lovers (the Baals), bearing children of whoredom, but eventually YHWH succeeds in wooing her back, whilst imposing a disciplinary period before the relationship is fully restored.

6. Hosea has been much studied recently by feminist scholars (see Brenner 1995). The prophet's references to 'whoring' have been much criticized, but his use of this image is not anti-women, since it is applied to the nation as a whole (e.g. Hos 5:3, 6:10), and presumably had particular reference to the male political and religious leaders.

C. The Book and its Redaction. 1. Probably most of the book of Hosea goes back to the prophet himself, his words having been first gathered together either by himself or his disciples. The book is in the form of poetic oracles apart from the two narratives about Hosea's marriage in 1:2–9 and 3:1–5, and the introductory and concluding verses 1:1 and 14:9. The third-person narrative in ch. 1 clearly betrays the hand of an editor. The book falls into two broad sections, chs. 1–3 relating to the prophet's marriage and what it symbolized for Israel, and chs. 4–14, which contain oracles of judgement (and later salvation) for Israel. Chs. 4–14 may have some broad chronological basis for their ordering.

2. After the fall of Samaria Hosea's words were preserved and edited in Judah. A first stage of redaction was added, probably sometime after 700 BCE, indicating that unlike Israel, Judah was still faithful and would be preserved (1:7; 11:12b). Then, either after or just before the fall of Judah in 586, a few glosses were added proclaiming that Judah too would fall because of its sins. Hosea's original words of judgement were thus given a new lease of life by being applied specifically to the southern kingdom (4:15a; 5:5b; 6:11a; 10:11b; 12:2a). Other glosses envisage a future united kingdom of Judah and Israel under a Davidic monarchy, clearly betraying a Judean outlook (Hos 3:5; cf. 1:10–2:1, esp. 1:11), and were presumably added in the sixth century or later. Other additions are the superscription (1:1), believed to derive from Deuteronomistic circles; 11:10c, predicting the return of the western exiles, an idea surprising in the eighth century; and the Wisdom-type saying concluding the book in 14:9. It has occasionally been supposed that passages expressing future hope for northern Israel after judgement in Hosea are also later editorial additions, and not authentic to the prophet himself. However, the passages do not stand out awkwardly like the happy ending in Amos or the pro- and anti-Judean glosses in Hosea itself. (For some different ideas on the redaction of Hosea see Emmerson 1984.)

3. The Hebrew text of Hosea has often been thought one of the most corrupt in the OT. Nowadays, the amount of emendation thought necessary is less than was often believed in the past. However, we should not go to the other extreme, like Macintosh (1997), who avoids emendation at all costs.

COMMENTARY

(1:1) Superscription This is a typical editorial addition to the beginning of a prophetic book. The divine origin of Hosea's message is affirmed, and Hosea's ministry is dated to the reigns of Judean and Israelite kings. The Judean kings are listed first, even though Hosea was a northerner, suggesting Judean redaction. Strangely, Jeroboam (II) is the only northern king listed; Hosea prophesied many years after his death down to the 720s. But Jeroboam's successors had short reigns and to have listed them all would have required adding another six names.

(1:2–9) The Children of Hosea's Marriage with Gomer Here Hosea marries Gomer and three children are born bearing sign-names of judgement for Israel. Gomer is described (v. 2) as a wife of whoredom bearing children of whoredom. v. 2, probably the description of Gomer as 'a wife of whoredom' is proleptic and describes her future behaviour. Cf. 2:4, where the term is applied to Israel following her abandonment of YHWH. Another view is that Hosea married a common or cult prostitute. In 1:3 Hosea's wife is called Gomer, the daughter of Diblaim. Neither name has any apparent symbolic significance, which supports their historicity and argues against a merely allegorical or visionary understanding of the events. The first child, Jezreel, is the only one explicitly stated to be Hosea's (cf. vv. 6, 8), which may or may not be significant. Jezreel, the first son (v. 4), is named after the city of Jezreel, the scene of Jehu's bloody massacres, c.842, that ended Omri's dynasty (2 Kings 9:1–37; 10:1–11). Jehu's actions were supported by the prophet Elisha and his followers, but Hosea condemns this sanctified murder. Jezreel (modern Zer'in) has been excavated.

Lo-ruhamah, the name of the daughter, means 'not pitied' (v. 6). v. 7 is a pro-Judean gloss. Its reference to God's saving Judah without military force may well reflect Jerusalem's deliverance from the Assyrians in 701 (cf. 2 Kings 19:35–7). Lo-ammi, the name of the second son, means 'not my people' (v. 9).

(1:10–2:1 (MT 2:1–3)) Oracle of Salvation: The Reversal of Judgement These verses primarily reverse the negative meanings of the names of Hosea's children and apply them to the nation. They resemble the hopeful message of 2:21–3, though, unlike the latter, are generally considered redactional. The promise in 1:10 of numerous progeny echoes the promises to the patriarchs (Gen 22:17; 32:12). The name of Hosea's son, Lo-ammi, 'not my people', is now reversed and the people are to be 'children of the living God'; cf. 2:23. v. 11 predicts 'one head' for Judah and Israel. Cf. 3:5, where another Judean redactional addition anticipates a future united Davidic monarchy, which could be in mind here. Although it is sometimes supposed that v. 11 reflects Hosea's own ideas, it is more probably redactional, since Judah is mentioned first and the idea is absent in Hosea's salvation oracles in chs. 11 and 14. 'For great shall be the day of Jezreel' reflects Hosea's reversal of the negative implications of the name for the nation—cf. 2:22–3. In 2:1 the names Lo-ammi, 'not my people', and Lo-ruhamah, 'not pitied', are reversed to Ammi, 'my people', and Ruhamah, 'pitied', and applied to the people as a whole; cf. 2:23. The people addressed, following LXX, are 'your brothers' and 'your sisters', i.e. the nation, not 'your brother' and 'your sister' (NRSV, etc.), which might suggest simply Hosea's children.

(2:2–15 (MT 4–17)) Indictment of Israel, the Unfaithful Wife YHWH's relationship to Israel is here depicted as one of husband and wife. Israel has been unfaithful to YHWH and gone whoring after her lovers, the Baals, from whom she expects to receive grain, wine, oil, and other products, not realizing these come from YHWH (vv. 5, 8). Consequently, YHWH will strip her naked (vv. 3, 9–10), block the way to her lovers so she cannot find them (vv. 6–7), withdraw the grain, wine, etc. (v. 9), and put an end to her religious festivities (vv. 11, 13). She will then seek to return to him and YHWH will allure her in the wilderness, cause her to respond to him there, as at the Exodus, and bring her into Canaan anew (vv. 14–15). Some think the more hopeful note in vv. 14–15 implies that it belongs rather with vv. 16–23, but against this stand the third-person form of address found also in vv. 2–13 and the 'Therefore' in v. 14 (cf. vv. 6, 9). Furthermore, hope is already anticipated in v. 7. The words of v. 2, 'for she is not my wife, and I am not her husband', are not a divorce formula, contrary to the view of some. There would be no point in divorce, since the point of the proceedings was to regain the wife (v. 2b, 'that she put away her whoring from her face').

Stripping a wife naked (v. 3) was a punishment the wronged husband could inflict, mentioned also in vv. 9–10. The phrase 'children of whoredom' (v. 4) occurs at 1:2, of Gomer's children, but now it refers to the Israelites. Some scholars place vv. 6–7 between vv. 13 and 14, but though this position might seem more logical, it is unjustified; Hosea's thought sometimes flits around.

Grain, wine, and oil (v. 8) were the chief agricultural products of Israel but the people did not realize they came from YHWH, attributing them rather to Baal who was the great Canaanite storm and fertility god, believed to be dead during the hot, dry summer season and risen from the dead in the wet, winter season. The words 'that they used for Baal' are probably a gloss, because we have 'Baal', not 'Baals' here, and the third-person plural verb is foreign to the context. The Baals (v. 13) were local manifestations of the god Baal, also mentioned in 2:17, 11:2. This is the first time Hosea alludes to Israel's 'lovers' as the Baals. v. 15, the Valley of Achor (lit. trouble) was associated with the stoning of Achan (Josh 7:24–6). Its precise location is uncertain, but it was near Jericho, at the entrance into Canaan, and is perhaps at Wadi Qilt.

(2:16–23 (MT 18–25)) YHWH's Remarriage with Israel and the Restoration of Well-being Here, the imagery of YHWH and Israel as husband and wife continues, but the dominant note is hope. YHWH will renew his marriage bond with Israel and everything will be well. There are three units here, each containing the words 'on that day'. The first predicts that Israel

will no longer call YHWH 'my Baal', but 'my husband', and the names of the Baals will be mentioned no more (vv. 16–17). The second speaks of YHWH as the mediator of a covenant with the animals and the abolition of war from the land, when YHWH will take Israel as his wife forever (vv. 18–20). Finally, the implications of the names of Gomer's three children are reversed, thus signifying the restoration of fertility to the land, YHWH's pity, and Israel as YHWH's people (vv. 21–3).

In v. 16 the future Israel will call YHWH 'my husband' ('îšî), not 'my Baal' (ba'ălî). This indicates that in Hosea's time YHWH could be called 'Baal' and was in danger of being confused with him. Cf. the personal name Bealiah, 'Baal is YHWH' (1 Chr 12:5). In v. 18 YHWH is the mediator of a new covenant with the animal world. This could imply either the banishment of wild animals from the land (Ezek 34:25–8; Lev 26:6), or the paradisal transformation of wild animals (Isa 11:6–9). 'Take as wife for ever…', v. 19: the verb refers to the legally binding agreement that preceded the wedding. In vv. 22–3 the significance of the names of Hosea's three children is reversed, so as to symbolize hope for Israel (cf. 1:10–2:1). Jezreel ('God sows') will betoken fertility for the land. YHWH will have pity on Lo-ruhamah ('not pitied'), and will say to Lo-ammi ('not my people'), 'You are my people'.

(3:1–5) Hosea and his Wife This chapter is a first-person narrative (unlike the third-person ch. 1) in which Hosea is told to love an adulterous woman, just as the Lord loves Israel, though they turn to other gods. As noted (HOS B.3, 4), the parallelism here only makes sense if the woman had previously been married to Hosea and gone astray from him, i.e. she was Gomer. That she is unnamed, unlike in ch. 1, is not significant, since the first-person ch. 3 comes from a different hand from the third-person ch. 1. Hosea bought the woman and put her under discipline for a while, symbolizing Israel's lack of cultic paraphernalia (cf. God's luring Israel, bringing her into the wilderness in 2:14).

v. 1 can be translated either 'The Lord said to me again, "Go love a woman…"' (NRSV) or 'The Lord said to me, "Go again, love a woman…"' (RSV). Either way there is a clear reference back to ch. 1. 'Other gods' corresponds to 'Baals' in 2:13, 17; 11:2, whilst the raisin cakes that Hosea condemns must have been associated with Baal worship. In 2 Sam 6:19 they are eaten in a Yahwistic cultic context. The reference in v. 2 to Hosea buying the woman probably alludes to the bride-price. A homer equalled 10 ephahs (between 15 and 40 litres). NRSV, REB, NEB 'a measure of wine' is based on LXX; MT has 'a lethech of barley' (RSV etc.). A lethech was half a homer. v. 4 describes Israel's temporary deprivation of king, prince, sacrifice, pillar, ephod, and teraphim. Scholars debate whether Hosea considered them legitimate or not, but the parallel deprivation of God's good gifts (2:9, 11) suggests that at least some, and maybe all, were held legitimate. The ephod is here probably an object used in divination (cf. 1 Sam 23:6; 30:7). Elsewhere it can be the name of a priestly garment (1 Sam 2:18; 22:18), and eventually it became part of the high priest's dress (Ex 25:7). Teraphim were figurines of gods in human form used in divination, at first regarded as legitimate (1 Sam 19:13, 16), but later disapproved (2 Kings 23:24). v. 5 finally describes Israel's return to YHWH, and corresponds to the hopeful conclusion of ch. 2. Israel's return to 'David their king' is probably a Judean redactional addition, since the northerner Hosea is unlikely to have supported the Davidic monarchy. Also, 'in the latter days' probably reflects later Judean eschatology.

(4:1–19) YHWH's Indictment of Priest and People This chapter begins (vv. 1–3) with a general divine indictment against Israel for its lack of knowledge of God. The indictment is continued in vv. 4–6 specifically against the priests, who are blamed for the people's lack of knowledge of God, and a further oracle against the priests continues in vv. 7–10. vv. 11–14 focus on the cult, which is condemned for being pervaded by a spirit of whoredom as well as literal cult prostitution. vv. 15–19 also condemn Israel's whoredom, manifested in the cult and idolatry.

'Indictment', v. 1 (*rîb*) is a legal term. The absence of knowledge of God in the land is an important theme in Hosea (4:6; 5:4; 6:6). 'Knowledge of God' is not mystical knowledge of God (as in the NT), but an awareness of his basic moral laws, and a practical keeping of them—summed up in *ḥesed*, 'steadfast love'. v. 2 castigates 'murder', 'stealing', and 'adultery', the same terms used in the sixth, eighth, and seventh commandments of the Decalogue (Ex 20, Deut 5); also mentioned are 'swearing' and 'lying', equivalent to the sins found in the third and ninth commandments. Scholars debate whether Hosea refers specifically to the Decalogue. If it is older than Hosea (and Ex 20 has traditionally been ascribed to the Elohist source, *c*.750), he could have done so, but recently some scholars have dated it later. By way of judgement 'the land dries up'—'dries up' is a better translation of the verb *'bl* here than the usual 'mourns'. v. 5, 'the prophet also shall stumble with you by night' is probably a gloss; prophets are nowhere else mentioned in this chapter and some other glosses contain 'also' (5:5; 6:11).

'Thing of wood' or 'staff', v. 12 (RSV) is probably an abusive description of a wooden idol used in divination, possibly the Asherah. Though sometimes seen as rhabdomancy (divination by sticks), this is unlikely since it is only rarely attested in the ancient Near East. REB 'diviner's wand' and NRSV 'divining rod' are unlikely. v. 13 alludes to the sanctuaries known in the OT as 'high places' (Hos 10:8) and the description of sacrifices taking place on mountains and under trees recalls the frequent phrase 'on every high hill and under every luxuriant tree' (cf. Jer 2:20; NRSV's 'green tree' is incorrect). Continuing with the high places, v. 14 alludes to 'cult prostitutes' (RSV) there. The word literally means 'holy ones' (*qĕdēšôt*) and the parallelism with 'harlots' (*zōnôt*) here and elsewhere (Deut 23:17–18; Gen 38:15, 21–2) establishes the meaning as 'cult prostitutes'. We cannot say much about their precise role, but they seem to have had some connection with the Baal fertility cult. There is no reason to doubt their existence, as some scholars have done recently—in addition to the OT we have references to them in many (admittedly mostly late) classical sources, as well as in Mesopotamia, where they were particularly associated with the goddess Ishtar. In v. 15 Hosea rejects Gilgal and Beth-aven (i.e. Bethel), both sites of sanctuaries. Gilgal (Khirbet el-Mefjir, near Jericho) is also condemned in 9:15 and 12:11, there specifically in connection with sacrifices. Beth-aven, literally 'house of evil', is a derogatory name for Bethel (modern Beitin; cf. 5:8, 10:5), the leading sanctuary

associated with the calf-cult (10:5). The words 'Do not let Judah become guilty' are probably a gloss. In v. 16 Israel is like a stubborn heifer: this is one of a number of Hosea's sayings employing nature imagery. The text of vv. 17–19 is uncertain in parts.

(5:1–7) Judgement on a Faithless Nation and its Leaders vv. 1–7 continue ch. 4's description of the apostasy of the leaders and nation. vv. 1–2 condemn not only the priests (mentioned in ch. 4), but also the 'house of the king'. vv. 3–7 then describe the apostasy of the whole nation.

v. 1 oddly includes the 'house of Israel' between the specific groups of the 'priests' and the 'house of the king'. vv. 1–2 employ hunting images to describe the leaders' entrapping the people at Mizpah, Tabor, and Shittim. Probably there were sanctuaries at these sites and cultic sin is alluded to, though precise information is lacking. Mizpah is probably Tell en-Naṣbeh in Benjamin. Tabor is a striking dome-shaped mountain in Galilee. Shittim in Transjordan was associated with apostasy to Baal of Peor (Num 25:1–5), with which Hosea was familiar (9:10). vv. 3–7, the leaders having set a bad example (vv. 1–2), Hosea now describes apostasy amongst the whole people. v. 5b extends the judgement to Judah, and is doubtless a gloss.

(5:8–6:3) Israel's Sickness unto Death and Hosea's Exhortation to Repentance This section concerns the period of the Syro-Ephraimite war (735–733 BCE) and its aftermath (733–731) (see HOS A.3). In 5:8–15 Hosea describes the internecine strife of that period between Judah and Israel and expresses divine judgement on both. YHWH will inflict sickness and death on the nation, but in 6:1–3 predicts it will revive if they accept his exhortation to repent.

5:8–10 reflects the movement north of Judean troops into northern-Israelite/Benjaminite territory during the Syro-Ephraimite crisis, and this is condemned. At the same time, the northern kingdom is condemned for its self-inflicted wound in going after 'vanity' (Heb. uncertain), which refers to its attack under Pekah (with the Syrians under Rezin) on Judah in the time of Ahaz. At 5:12 translate 'Therefore I am like a *moth* to Ephraim', as traditionally (RSV), not 'maggots' (NRSV) or 'festering sore' (NEB, REB), which have been proposed for *'āš* on the basis of an alleged Arabic cognate. Certainly *'āš* means 'moth' in Job 13:28, where it is parallel with *rāqāb*, 'rottenness', as here. The thought is compressed: just as a moth is to a garment, so will YHWH be to Israel. 5:13 mentions Ephraim's going to Assyria, which refers to Hoshea's submission to Tiglath-pileser III in 731. Judah under Ahaz appealed to the Assyrians too (even though this is not explicit here), following the northern Israelite and Syrian invasion of Judah (2 Kings 16:7–8; cf. Isa 7). The Assyrian ruler is referred to as 'the great king' (similarly Hos 10:6): the Hebrew is unusual (*melek yārēb*), rendered incorrectly by AV and RV as 'King Jareb'.

Israel's hoped-for restoration is depicted in 6:1–3, which raises two highly debated questions. First, with regard to who is speaking it has been suggested: (1) that these are the words of the Israelites, but that they are insincere. However, the language is so full of genuine Hoseanic images and the sentiments so similar to Hosea's exhortation to repentance in ch. 14, that it is difficult to regard the words as insincere. (2)

Some suppose these are the words that Hosea hopes the Israelites will say, but 'saying' (RSV) is lacking in the Hebrew at the end of 5:15 and the parallel with ch. 14 also tells against it. So (3) is most likely—this is Hosea's own exhortation to the people, like 14:1–3.

The second debated question is whether Hosea's imagery is of resurrection from death or simply healing of the sick. In favour of the former are: (1) elsewhere when the verbs 'revive' (hiphil of *ḥyh*) and 'raise up' (hiphil of *qûm*) appear together, they denote resurrection (Isa 26:14, 19; Job 14:12, 14); (2) 6:5 speaks of Israel as slain; (3) there are impressive parallels between chs. 5–6 and 13–14 (lion image, 5:14, 13:7–8; exhortation to return, 6:1; 14:1; dew or rain imagery, 6:3; 14:4), and since in ch. 13 it is clearly a case of death (vv. 1, 9, 14), this should also be the case in chs. 5–6 (cf. Ezek 37 for death and resurrection as symbolic of exile and restoration). Probably Hosea has appropriated the imagery of Israel's death and resurrection from the dying and rising god Baal. This is supported by 13:1, 'he incurred guilt through Baal and died', and the association of the resurrection with rain in 6:3. 'After two days... on the third day' means 'after a short while'; cf. *'etmôl šilšōm*, 'formerly', literally, 'yesterday, the third day'.

(6:4–7:16) Israel's Corruption, Political and Religious This section contains loosely connected oracles mostly concerned with Israel's political, but also religious, corruption. 6:4–6 enunciates Israel's failure to live up to YHWH's demand for steadfast love and knowledge of God; 6:7–10 recalls crimes perhaps associated with Pekah's rebellion; 6:11*a* is a Judean gloss, applying YHWH's judgement to the southern kingdom; 6:11*b*–7:2 explains how Israel's corrupt deeds prevent YHWH from restoring her; 7:3–7 describes vividly the court intrigues leading to the overthrow of a king; 7:8–12 rejects foreign alliances; finally, 7:13–16 condemns religious apostasy.

The statement at 6:4–6 has often been thought to be YHWH's response to Israel's insincere repentance in 6:1–3, but, as noted, it is not insincere, but contains Hosea's own exhortation to repentance. Rather, 6:4–6 reflects Hosea's response to the people's current plight prior to any possible repentance such as that depicted in 6:1–3. Hosea's famous words in 6:6 elevate the importance of right moral behaviour above ritual. As in similar passages in other prophets (Isa 1:10–17; Jer 7:21–3; Mic 6:6–8), it is probably not sacrifice *per se* that is rejected, but hollow and meaningless worship (and syncretistic worship in Hosea's case). 'Not this but that' can mean, 'That is more important than this'. Obscure allusions to crimes at various locations are contained in 6:7–10. Gilead (v. 8) was in Transjordan and Adam (v. 7, read with NRSV 'at Adam', not 'like Adam') was a town in the Jordan valley in the region of Gilead. Since Pekah's rebellion in *c*.735 started in Gilead (2 Kings 15:25), we may have allusions to it here. v. 7's words, 'But at Adam they transgressed the covenant' are significant, since, together with 8:1, we have here the only explicit reference to YHWH's covenant with Israel in any of the eighth-century prophets. It has sometimes been supposed that the covenant referred to here is rather a political treaty, but against this note that elsewhere 'transgress a (political) treaty' is *hēpĕrû bĕrît*, not *'ābĕrû bĕrît* as here. (See Day 1986.) v. 11*a* is an anti-Judean gloss. Other glosses also contain 'also' (cf. 4:5 and 5:5) and its lame brevity challenges its genuine-

ness. The words reapply Hosea's message to Judah at a later date. 'Harvest' is an image for judgement. In 6:11*b*–7:2 YHWH states his willingness to restore the fortunes of Israel, but cannot because of their wickedness. Samaria (7:1), first mentioned here in Hosea, was the capital of the northern kingdom since the ninth-century King Omri (it has been excavated); sometimes it stands for the remaining rump northern kingdom (cf. 10:5).

The treachery involved in one of the *coups d'état* is reflected in 7:3–7, possibly when Hoshea overthrew Pekah (*c*.731). The passionate intrigue of the conspirators is compared to the heat of a baker's oven (cf. 7:4, 6, 7). It has sometimes been supposed that Hosea was opposed to kingship in principle, but it is more likely that it was the behaviour of contemporary kings that he opposed.

The section 7:8–12 returns to condemning Israel's foreign alliances. These devour Israel's strength (7:8), a probable allusion to Assyria's annexing some of Israel's territory in 733. The fact that Israel calls upon Egypt as well as Assyria (7:11) probably indicates a date after Hoshea's appeal to Egypt in *c*.725. At 7:13–16 Israel's religious apostasy is again condemned. There is an interesting reference in 7:14 to the ritual practice of people gashing themselves for grain and wine. (The translation 'they gash themselves' follows LXX and some Heb. MSS instead of MT, 'they assemble themselves'.) Lacerating oneself is prohibited in Deut 14:1 (cf. 1 Kings 18:28), but was part of the Baalistic cult. The beginning of 7:16 is unclear: perhaps emend to 'They turn to Baal', which fits the context, though other suggestions have been made.

(8:1–14) A Catalogue of Israel's Sins Here Hosea recounts the sins which will lead to judgement on Israel. vv. 1–3 begin in general terms, proclaiming that Israel has broken God's covenant and transgressed his law. The specific sins are unauthorized changes of rulers (v. 4*a*), making of images, especially the (golden) calf cult (vv. 4*b*–6), Israel's foreign alliances (vv. 8–10), sacrificial worship (vv. 11–13), and trust in fortifications rather than YHWH (v. 14).

v. 1 is significant because, along with Hos 6:7, it contains the only explicit mention of the word 'covenant' (Heb. *bĕrît*) to describe YHWH's relationship with Israel in the eighth-century prophets. Although some have argued that the notion of covenant was a later invention of the Deuteronomists, there are good grounds for seeing it as authentic to Hosea here and in 6:7 (Day 1986). Also in v. 1 'trumpet' is better rendered 'ram's horn'. 'One like a vulture' is the probable translation (retaining MT) and seems to be an image for the invader's swiftness. v. 4*a* refers to the frequent *coups d'état* of Israel's final years after the death of Jeroboam II. Then, in 8:4*b*–6, in condemning images, Hosea focuses especially on the calf cult, claiming that the calf is not a god and will be destroyed (cf. 10:5–6; 13:2). In referring to the calf as Samaria's (vv. 5, 6) the prophet probably means the province of Samaria (i.e. the northern kingdom), not the capital city (cf. 10:5). Jeroboam I had set up golden calves in Bethel and Dan in *c*.930 (1 Kings 12:28–30) to lure the north away from the Jerusalem temple. The calf cult at Dan probably ended in 733 when Assyria annexed part of the northern kingdom. Probably the golden calves were originally symbols of YHWH, not a pagan god, and had been acceptable to many Israelites. It is sometimes maintained that they were merely pedestals of the deity, but this is unlikely. Hosea insists, 'it is not God', which would be meaningless if everyone regarded it as simply a pedestal. Probably the calf image goes back to the supreme Canaanite god El (called 'Bull El' in the Ugaritic texts) with whom YHWH was equated (cf. Bethel, 'house of El'). Aaron's golden calf (Ex 32) is probably a back projection from 1 Kings 12:28–30.

vv. 8–11 condemn Israel's foreign alliances, a repeated theme of Hosea's (5:13; 7:8–9, 11; 12:1; 14:3). In particular he condemns the alliance with the Assyrians: this probably refers to Hoshea's submission to the Assyrian king Tiglath-pileser III in 731. This fits v. 9, 'Israel is swallowed up; now they are among the nations as a useless vessel', as Tiglath-pileser III exiled part of Israel in 733 (2 Kings 15:29). The translation of 8:10b is uncertain: RSV follows LXX, 'And they shall cease for a little while from anointing king and princes.' vv. 11–13 reject Israel's sacrifices on account of the people's sin; probably sacrifices are not rejected *per se* (cf. HOS 6:6). Finally, v. 14 rejects Israel's trust in fortifications rather than in YHWH.

(9:1–9) Exile will Bring an End to Israel's Festal Worship These verses form a prophetic diatribe, unlike 9:10–13, 15–16 and most of ch. 8, where YHWH speaks in the first person. The prophet condemns the festal worship and predicts that exile in Assyria and Egypt will bring it to an end. Hosea's words lead the people to think he is a mad prophet (v. 7), to which he replies in v. 8. Israel's return to Assyria and Egypt is predicted in v. 3, whilst v. 6 emphasizes simply the return to Egypt. This latter verse's detail suggests it is meant literally, not symbolically. In the light of Hosea's message of doom, v. 7b quotes the popular view of him as a mad prophet. (Cf. 2 Kings 9:11 and Jer 29:16 for the perception of other prophets as 'mad'.) v. 8 then presents Hosea's response to this charge with his claim that, as a prophet, he is rather God's watchman over Ephraim. Interestingly, this passage challenges the proposal of some recent scholars that the pre-exilic prophets did not actually see themselves as prophets and that this was a later Deuteronomistic understanding. The reference at v. 7 to Hosea as 'the man of the spirit' is also of interest, since unlike the 'word' of God, the 'spirit' is mentioned only rarely in the *pre*-exilic canonical prophets.

The reference to the people as corrupt 'as in the days of Gibeah' (v. 9, cf. 10:9) probably alludes to the outrage in Judg 19–20, when a Levite's concubine was raped and murdered in Gibeah, which made a notable impression (Judg 19:30). The combination of violence and sexual sin makes it appropriate for this to be paradigmatic for Hosea. A reference to Saul, whose capital was at Gibeah, is less likely.

(9:10–17) Israel's Sinful History Begets a Barren Future These verses are primarily in first-person divine speech, unlike the preceding and following sections. They describe how, though YHWH found Israel in the wilderness like grapes or the first ripe figs, they committed apostasy with Baal-peor (v. 10), and following in the same train ever since, they are destined to infertility (cf. vv. 11–14, 16). Since Baal was a fertility god, there is evident irony here.

v. 10 speaks of Israel's apostasy to Baal-peor, recalling Num 25:1–5. 'Shame' (*Heb. bōšet*) is a euphemism for 'Baal'. v. 13a is difficult and various renderings have been given. v. 15, 'Every

evil of theirs began at Gilgal; there I came to hate them.' It is uncertain whether we should translate as past tense (as NRSV) or with present tense. Also, the evil referred to at Gilgal is unclear. Elsewhere Hosea refers to cultic misdemeanours there (4:15; 12:11) so that may be the case here. If the tense is past, the reference may be to the Baal-peor incident alluded to in v. 10, which Mic 6:5 says extended 'from Shittim to Gilgal'. Others envisage political misdemeanours, whether referring in the past to Saul, who was made king at Gilgal (1 Sam 11:14–15), or to some contemporary event, as might be suggested by 'all their officials are rebels'.

(10:1–8) The Coming Downfall of Cult and King Hosea here anticipates the downfall of the nation's institutions, both religious and political. Characteristically, he flits from one to the other: vv. 1–2, 5–6, 8 envisage the end of the cult and vv. 3–4, 7 highlight the futility of the monarchy and its foreign alliances and anticipate the end of Israel's king.

For the image of Israel as a vine (v. 1), cf. Isa 5:1–7, Ps 80:8–16 (MT 9–17). The 'pillars' (*maṣṣēbôt*) of vv. 1–2 were sacred pillars at the high places, and symbolic of the male deity. Originally they were acceptable (Gen 28:22), but later they were condemned (Deut 16:22). The covenants opposed in v. 4 are probably treaties made with foreign nations (cf. 12:2). vv. 5–6 predict judgement on the calf of Beth-aven, i.e. Bethel (see HOS 8:5–6). 'Calf' (v. 5) follows Greek and Syriac—Hebrew, strangely, has feminine plural, *ʿeglôt*. For v. 6's 'great king', see HOS 5:13. The 'high places' (Heb. *bāmôt*) of v. 8 were local sanctuaries where the syncretistic practices condemned by Hosea took place. Strangely, in Hosea the term occurs only here. Some (e.g. NRSV) take *ʾāwen* as a place-name (Aven, short for Beth-aven, i.e. Bethel), but more likely it has its normal meaning 'wickedness', because of the plural 'high places'.

(10:9–15) Predictions of War and Disaster This section begins and ends with judgement oracles (vv. 9–10, 13b–15); in between are sayings about Israel, using agricultural imagery (vv. 11–13a).

For 'the day of Gibeah' (v. 9) see HOS 9:9. vv. 11–13a illustrate Hosea's fondness for agricultural images. Within v. 11 the reference to 'Judah' is probably a gloss, extending the words to the southern kingdom. Some think v. 14 refers to an invasion of Irbid (Arbela) in Transjordan by King Salamanu of Moab, whilst others identify Beth-arbel with a place in northern Israel and see Shalman as the Assyrian King Shalmaneser V. The latter would be a more effective image, since Shalmaneser V eventually destroyed the northern kingdom as anticipated by Hosea (HOS A.4). In v. 15 MT has 'Bethel', but the context of vv. 13–15 supports 'house of Israel' with LXX. 'At dawn' (NRSV follows MT): RSV 'in the storm' is based on debatable emendation.

(11:1–11) YHWH's Inextinguishable Love for Israel and Israel's Ingratitude This is one of the high points in the OT, depicting God's love in the face of Israel's continued ingratitude. vv. 1–11 appear to be a unity, apart from v. 10, which is probably a later addition. vv. 1–4 depict YHWH's love for Israel from the Exodus and Israel's ingratitude, sacrificing to the Baals. vv. 5–7 prophesy the divine judgement and Israel's exile. vv. 8–9 then mark a shift, not only in the move from YHWH's speaking of Israel in the third person to addressing it directly, but in its poignant depiction of the anguish of YHWH's love so that he cannot totally destroy Israel. Finally, vv. 10–11 depict Israel's subsequent deliverance from exile.

v. 1 speaks of YHWH's call of Israel, his son, at the time of the Exodus (cf. Ex 4:22; Deut 14:1). In vv. 3–4 YHWH's tender care for the infant Israel is more characteristic of a mother, and feminist scholars have suggested YHWH is depicted with female imagery (cf. Isa 66:12–13). This may be, though the OT never directly calls YHWH mother, but only father. v. 5, the threat of exile in Egypt and Assyria is a repeated theme in Hosea (7:16; 8:8–10, 13; 9:3, 6). v. 7 contains a textual problem: NRSV has 'To the Most High ('al) they call', but 'al is possibly a corruption from ba'al (Baal).

In vv. 8–9, one of the most moving passages in the OT, YHWH struggles with himself, and the anguish of his love finally dictates that he cannot totally destroy Israel as he did Admah and Zeboiim (these being two cities of the plain destroyed alongside Sodom and Gomorrah: Deut. 29:22–3; cf. Gen 10:19; 14:2, 8). This does not negate the promise of judgement, but means that Hosea foresees it as not final; rather it has a chastening effect on Israel. In the literal sense this contradicts some other passages where YHWH says he will destroy Israel (13:9, 16), but even there subsequent restoration is envisaged (ch. 14). Interestingly, Hosea implies a degree of divine suffering; contrast the denial of divine suffering in some early Church Fathers. v. 10 is probably a later addition, alluding to a return of Israel's western exiles: other prophetic references to an ingathering of western exiles are post-exilic (Isa 11:11; 60:9; Joel 3:6–7; Ob 20). v. 10 is probably a later amplification of Hosea's authentic prophecy of return from exile in v. 11 (reversing the threat of v. 5).

(11:12–12:14 (MT 12:1–15)) Israel's Perfidy and Kinship with its Ancestor Jacob In the MT ch. 12 begins with 11:12 of the English versions and this represents a better chapter division. Allusions to Israel's lies and deceit in 11:12 clearly belong with ch. 12 (cf. vv. 1, 3, 7). Much of ch. 12 is pervaded by Israel's deceit and unfaithfulness, and interestingly, Hosea associates this with the character of Israel's ancestor, Jacob (vv. 2–4, 12). Hosea here shows knowledge of traditions about Jacob very similar to those contained in the J source in Genesis. In contrast stand God's prophets (12:10), including Moses, who led Israel out of Egypt (12:13). The chapter is essentially a unity, though there are later glosses, both pre- and anti-Judean, in 11:12b and 12:2a. The translation of 11:12b is uncertain, but it seems to contrast Judah's faithfulness with Israel's infidelity. That 'Judah' is a gloss in 12:2 is supported by the play on the name Israel as well as Jacob in v. 3, which supports 'Israel', not 'Judah' being original in v. 2. In 12:1 the oil carried to Egypt probably alludes to an Israelite gift to induce Egyptian support, rather than being part of the ritual of treaty-making. 12:2 introduces the verses about Jacob with 'The Lord ... will punish Jacob according to his ways', indicating the remarks about Jacob are intended to be critical. Jacob's overweening ambition was first manifested in the womb when he sought to supplant his brother Esau (12:3a). The word 'supplant' (ya'ăqōb) here plays on the name of Jacob. Cf. Gen 25:26 (J), where Jacob takes Esau by the heel ('ăqēb), and 'āqab (supplant) is used rather in connection with Jacob's taking Esau's birthright and blessing in Gen 27:36

(J). A second allusion to Jacob's ambition comes in 12:3b–4a, recalling Jacob's wrestling with God/an angel at Penuel (Gen. 32:22–32), though Hosea's reference to Jacob's weeping there is unattested in Genesis. The third allusion is to God's meeting with Jacob at Bethel (12:4b), attested in both Gen. 28:10–22 (J) and 35:9–15 (P).

At 12:7–8 the theme of Israel's deceit is continued, but without explicit allusion to Jacob. With their condemnation of Israel's commercial corruption these verses are reminiscent of Amos. 12:11 condemns two sites, Gilead, perhaps as in 6:8 for its part in Pekah's rebellion, and Gilgal for its sacrificial cult. 12:12 returns to citing the tradition about Jacob, this time in connection with his flight to Aram (Syria), where he served for his wives (Rachel and Leah—cf. Gen 29:15–30). The point is not wholly clear, but it probably hints at Israel's embroilment in foreign alliances and exile, since 12:13 contrasts Moses' leading of Israel out of Egypt. Moses is called a 'prophet' (taking up the theme of prophets in 12:10), the first time in the OT he is so called. Moses is later called a prophet in Deut 18:15, 18; 34:10, one of a number of instances in which Deuteronomy stands in the tradition of Hosea.

(13:1–16 (MT 14:1)) Death for Israel Ch. 13 is pervaded by Israel's death. This is primarily future, but in v. 1 is already present. This is a metaphor for Israel's end, specifically with reference to exile. The chapter divides into three sections, vv. 1–3, 4–8, and 12–16, beginning with a historical retrospect establishing Israel's guilt (vv. 1–2, 4–6, 12–13) and concluding with a declaration of judgement (vv. 3, 7–8, 14–16). To the second oracle is appended a mocking condemnation of the monarchy (vv. 9–11).

The statement in v. 1 that Israel 'incurred guilt through Baal and died' is ironical. Baal was a dying and rising fertility god, and Israel has died through worshipping him (to be followed, after repentance in ch. 14, by resurrection). The current 'death' probably alludes to Tiglath-pileser III's exile of part of the northern kingdom in 733. The end of v. 2 is a little uncertain: NRSV is probably right, with partial LXX support, to read ' "Sacrifice to these", they say. People are kissing calves!' For the calf cult, cf. 8:5–6 and 10:5–6. In devouring Israel (vv. 7–8) YHWH is compared with various wild beasts. YHWH as a lion (vv. 7–8) is found also in the similar passage in 5:14. v. 10 possibly refers to the period after c.725 when King Hoshea was imprisoned by the Assyrians. There may be a play on his name (meaning 'salvation') in the words 'that he may save you'.

In v. 14 YHWH declares he will hand Israel over to the power of Death (Sheol). The interrogative particle hă is lacking, so the ancient versions (followed by Paul in 1 Cor 15:33) understood the sentiments positively: 'I shall ransom them from the power of Sheol ...', but this does not fit the context (cf. 'compassion is hid from my eyes' at end of verse). In v. 14 Israel is in the grip of Death (māwet) and Sheol, whilst in v. 15 Israel's 'fountain will dry up, his spring will be parched'. This ultimately reflects Baal mythology, for in the Ugaritic Baal myth, after Baal goes down into the realm of Mot (Death), the land becomes dry and parched.

In v. 15, read probably 'among the rushes' ('āḥû) with NRSV rather than MT's 'among the brothers' ('aḥîm), as it fits the nature-based imagery better.

(14:1–8 (MT 2–9)) Repentance and Restoration As is characteristic of OT prophetic books, the final chapter of Hosea ends happily, anticipating Israel's future repentance and restoration. vv. 1–3 are the prophet's exhortation to the people to repent. Following this, in vv. 4–8 YHWH promises to restore Israel; the passage employs striking images from the blossoming of nature to depict this.

In vv. 1–3, following the prophecy of Israel's death (exile) in ch. 13, there is a call to repentance, just as 6:1–3 has a call to repentance following the description of Israel's illness/death in 5:12–16. In repenting, the people are to confess their guilt to YHWH, renouncing their faith in Assyria, military might, and idolatry (v. 3). Following its repentance, v. 4 gives a beautiful depiction of Israel's future national restoration, depicted under the imagery of the growth and blossoming of nature. Somewhat similar imagery is used of the restoration of Israel in Isa 27:2–6, which is probably dependent on Hos 14 (see Day 1980).

The passage has several textual problems. In v. 5 probably retain MT 'Lebanon' (NRSV, etc.) rather than reading *libneh*, 'poplar' (RSV, etc.). In v. 7 probably retain 'his shadow' rather than emending to 'my shadow' (*contra* NRSV, etc.), and also in this verse read 'they shall grow grain' with MT (similarly REB) rather than emending to 'they shall flourish as a garden' (*contra* RSV, NRSV); also, *zikrô* should be rendered 'their fame' (cf. REB), not 'their fragrance'. v. 8 is best translated 'What has Ephraim to do with idols? It is I who answer and look after him. I am like a luxuriant cypress, from me comes your fruit.' It is unique in the OT for YHWH to be compared to a tree. The fact that idolatry is rejected in the same context and that the Canaanite goddess Asherah, worshipped by the Israelites, was symbolized by a stylized tree, may indicate that Hosea is appropriating her role as a source of fertility to YHWH. The words 'It is I who answer and look after him' (*'ānîtî wa'ǎšûrennû*) could be a word play on the names of the goddesses Anat and Asherah.

(14:9 (MT 10)) Epilogue This is an editorial postscript in the style of the Wisdom writers, reflecting on the message of the book. It implies that, rightly understood, its words bring blessing, but to the wicked they bring disaster.

REFERENCES

Brenner, A. (1995) (ed.), *A Feminist Companion to the Latter Prophets*, A Feminist Companion to the Bible, 8 (Sheffield: Sheffield Academic Press), 240–1.

Davies, G. I. (1992), *Hosea*, NCB (London: Marshall Pickering).

Day, J. (1980), 'A Case of Inner Scriptural Interpretation', *JTS* NS 31: 309–19.

—— (1986), 'Pre-Deuteronomistic Allusions to the Covenant in Hosea and Psalm lxxviii', *VT* 36: 1–12.

Emmerson, G. I. (1984), *Hosea: An Israelite Prophet in Judean Perspective*, JSOTSup 28 (Sheffield: JSOT).

Macintosh, A. A. (1997), *Hosea*, ICC (Edinburgh: T. & T. Clark).

Mays, J. L. (1969), *Hosea*, OTL (London: SCM).

Rowley, H. H. (1963), 'The Marriage of Hosea', in *Men of God* (London: Nelson), 66–97.

Rudolph, W. (1966), *Hosea*, KAT (Gütersloh: Mohr).

Wolff, H. W. (1974), *Hosea*, ET, Hermeneia (Philadelphia: Fortress).

28. Joel   CARL-A. KELLER

INTRODUCTION

A. Structure. We may divide the book into twelve literary units. Units are identified by two criteria: subject-matter and the identity of the speaker. The style of prophetic oracles is quite particular in so far as sometimes God himself is the speaker of a message, the prophet being nothing but his mouthpiece, whereas on other occasions it is the prophet who explains the plans and actions of his Master. In the first case, the 'I' of the text refers to God, and in the second, the 'I' is the prophet, who refers to God in the third person. With the aid of these principles we obtain the following units:

The Prophet Announces Destruction by Locusts (1:2–4)

The Prophet Describes the Invasion of a Strange 'Nation' and Exhorts People to 'cry to YHWH' (1:5–14)

The Prophet Describes the Drought Caused by the Day of the Lord (1:15–18)

The Prophet's Prayer (1:19–20)

The Prophet Praises the Day of the Lord: the Lord is Coming at the Head of his Army (2:1–11)

The Prophet Explains a word of YHWH (2:12–14)

The Prophet Summons the People to Fast (2:15–17)

God and the Prophet Announce Mercy and Prosperity (2:18–27)

God Announces the Effusion of his Divine Energy Amidst Disruptions of Cosmic Order; the Prophet Adds an Exhortation (2:28–32)

God Announces the Restoration of Judah and Jerusalem, and Judgement over the Nations (3:1–8)

God and the Prophet Describe the Final Battle Against the Nations (3:9–17)

The Prophet Announces a Glorious Future for Judah and Jerusalem (3:18–21)

The first eight units, mostly words of the prophet, concern Jerusalem and Judah, whereas the last four, mostly words of God, treat the relationship between God and all the nations. They are divided up differently in the HB: 3:1–5; 4:1–8; 4:9–17; 4:18–21. The book is made up of two parts: is it a unity or the work of at least two authors? But the idea of the day of the Lord is central to both parts and establishes a strong link between them; moreover, there are some expressions and ideas ('Judah and Jerusalem', 'to sanctify'; the question of fertility) which occur in both sections. So we may consider the whole as one in thought and speech. There is no reason either to doubt that it is a single author's work.

B. Background. Nothing is known about Joel (which means 'YHWH is God'), son of Pethuel (which perhaps means 'Man of God'). Most scholars think that he lived in the middle of the fourth century BCE, but their arguments are open to criticism. The following observations point to a date shortly before 600. Israel, the northern kingdom, has disappeared, but Judah and Jerusalem still exist (3:1): this detail agrees with the situation of the seventh century BCE. Moreover, the expression 'Judah and Jerusalem' alludes to the political status of the city and the countryside which were not the same: the city, conquered by David, was more closely related to the reigning dynasty than the province which had freely submitted to David and his successors (see Alt 1953: 116–34). The absence of an allusion to the king is not surprising, as there are many oracles which do not mention a king (though see the collection in Isa 1:1). On the other hand, 3:1–8 offers arguments which suggest the end of the seventh century (between 630 and 600). During the final years of the seventh century, the declining power of the Assyrians encouraged the small states along the Mediterranean coast, Tyre, Sidon, and the Philistine towns, to join hands in order to make incursions into Judaean territory, to carry away whatever they found and to sell the booty, including men, women, and children, to the Greeks (3:4–6). Archaeological evidence testifies to trade relations between Phoenicia and Greece at the end of the seventh and the beginning of the sixth century. The language of the book is a final and decisive argument in favour of an early date. It is throughout classical, living, pre-exilic Hebrew. The Hebrew of the fourth century (Nehemiah; Ecclesiastes) is rather rigid and gives the impression that it was no longer a living idiom. We consider the Book of Joel in its entirety as a piece of creative prophetic discourse (see JOEL D. 1). Other interpretations have also been offered. Some scholars divide the book into at least two parts. They think that chs. 1–2 contain the reactions of the prophet to an invasion of locusts, whereas 2:28–3:21 was added by a later author who belonged to the 'apocalyptic' tradition, describing events of the end times. This 'apocalyptic' author is also thought to have enriched chs. 1–2 with allusions to the Day of the Lord. But the divide between prophetic and apocalyptic discourse is extremely tenuous and the notion of the Day of the Lord is an ancient one found also in pre-exilic prophecy. On the other hand, Joel features none of the characteristics of the great apocalyptic texts such as books of *Enoch*: ascensions and periodizations of history. The announcement of a judgement is not specifically apocalyptic, it is rather an essential part of prophetic literary resources. Other scholars read Joel as a liturgy used on the occasion of an invasion of locusts. There are undoubtedly liturgical elements in it (see JOEL D. 2), and the book (at least chs. 1–2) might indeed have been used as a liturgy, but there is no indication that this was actually the case.

C. The Message of Joel. 1. The pivot of the prophet's message is the announcement of the day of YHWH. Many scholars think that this latter notion is rooted in the ideology of YHWH's holy wars; according to this view, the 'day' is the great day when YHWH vanquishes his enemies. This hypothesis being admitted, we must insist that the Day is above all a theophany, a glorious and intruding manifestation of God and his uncanny army (2:1–11) which creates feelings of awe and fear. Joel has splendid and awful visions of this manifestation which strikes the people of God and all the nations. Moreover, the theophany has cosmic dimensions: it is 'thick darkness' and brings about the disappearance of the sun, the moon, and the stars (2:10; 3:3–4; cf. 3:16). On earth, it causes drought, famine, and sheer anguish. Similar descriptions of the 'day' are found in Am 5:18–20; Zeph 1:7–18; Isa 13:6–16; Ob 15–16; Mal 4:5).

2. The effusion of divine energy (of the spirit of YHWH) 'on all flesh' is one of the phenomena which concur with the divine manifestation, and causes profound changes to the minds and behaviour of humans (see JOEL 3:1–2).

3. But with Joel, the destructive power of the manifestation is merely the unavoidable background for renewed blessings. The theophany is an invitation to 'return to God', to pray and to implore God's mercy (1:13–14; 2:12–14). And God responds faithfully to faithful prayer. Thus Joel confirms the central structure of OT thought: the experiential movement which leads people from darkness to light, from suffering to joy, from death to life.

D. The Abiding Value of the Book. 1. The prophecy of Joel was probably occasioned by the devastating incursion of a huge swarm of locusts (1:2–12), but the oracles are essentially the utterances of a man whose word has the creative power to make things happen (see JOEL 1:2–4). Many incidents of Israelite history prove that prophetic discourse was a means to change destinies. It aroused fear and repulsion when it was gloomy, and happiness when it promised a bright future. Joel's prophetic word *creates* calamities; it is effective when it describes the day of the Lord, and when it indicates the path to salvation.

2. In that sense, Joel stands as a creative word which overrules all contingencies. Not dependent on a particular event, it is non-historical and can exercise its powers anywhere and at any moment. Later readers internalized this and found that it led them from suffering and feelings of deprivation, through repentance and prayer, to the joy of renewed communion with the merciful Lord.

COMMENTARY

(1:1) For the names, see JOEL B. The word of the Lord 'came': it is active, and even the prophet's own words are powerful because the Lord's word is acting through them.

(1:2–4) The Locusts The 'elders', citizens with full rights, and the entire population must listen: the prophetic word concerns everybody. 'Has *this* [Heb. *contra* NRSV 'such a thing'] happened in your days': no, it has never happened but it happens *now*, through the very word of the prophet. This newly created event is a thing to be remembered (and thus re-enacted) by future generations. v. 4 presents an unsolved riddle: do the four terms for 'locusts' stand for four varieties of insects, or for various stages in the development of one, or do they represent vernacular differences? Whatever the answer, it is clear that the accumulation of terms creates the certainty of total devastation.

(1:5–14) Incursion of a Strange 'Nation' The prophetic word evokes the havoc wrought by a swarm of locusts and asks drunkards, farmers, growers of fruit-trees, and priests to 'awake', to fast, to assemble in the temple, and to pray. The devastation is undoubtedly attributed to locusts, none the less the swarm is called a 'nation' (v. 6), perhaps on account of its strict 'political' organization, but more probably in order to suggest something more than locusts: the attack by a strange power of which the locusts are but the visible forms. In 2:25, this 'nation' is, in almost mythological terms, called 'the great army of God'. 'Sanctify a fast' (v. 14): the fast is a holy rite which requires mental preparation, an attitude of prayer, and the fully assumed intention to consecrate oneself entirely to communion with God.

(1:15–18) The 'Day of the LORD' Causes Drought and Despair The 'day of the LORD', the awful manifestation of God (see JOEL c), elicits a sigh of despair even from the prophet who is compelled to evoke it: 'Alas!' In normal times, rich harvests fill the temple with joyful songs and dances; the manifestation of the 'day' transforms laughter into subdued groaning.

(1:19–20) A Prayer of the Prophet The prophet experiences pain along with all those who suffer. The desolation he had helped to bring about by his prophetic word stirs up feelings of compassion and he is moved to prayer. The prophetic ministry had two sides: to address the people in the name of God, and to talk to God on behalf of the people. Joel does not fail in this twofold task. He acts in communion with the animals (v. 20); prophetic prayer never ignores the moaning of the animal world (cf. Jer 14:5–6; Rom 8:19).

(2:1–11) The Lord at the Head of his Dreadful Army This is the most vivid description of the 'day of the LORD', that is, of the Lord's theophany or manifestation (see JOEL B). It is like a terrifying army marching against Jerusalem under the cover of cosmic darkness (v. 2: the 'thick darkness' mentioned in another foundational theophany, Ex 20:21; Deut 4:11; 5:22; cf. also Zeph 1:15). God's action and the action of his army are invisible to human eyes stricken with blindness. The army is a mysterious one. The prophet does not dare to give a clear description of it. It is anonymous, 'like blackness spread over the mountains' (v. 2), surrounded by fire burning in front of it and behind it (v. 3); the 'soldiers' are something like horses or like war-chariots (vv. 4–5). The prophet avoids clear terms, everything is vague and suggests an event which eludes human language. But these ghastly warriors are everywhere, on the roofs, on the walls, through the windows, in the houses (v. 9), everyone his own commander, resisting all attempts to halt him (vv. 7–8). Heaven and earth tremble, sun, moon, and stars lose their light—darkness everywhere (v. 10). But a voice is heard in the night and amidst the terrors: the voice of the divine commander, the Lord himself (v. 11). Scholars wonder whether Joel is speaking of a human army or of locusts. This question seems out of place. In the passage under discussion the prophet tries to describe or rather to provoke a supra-human and cosmic event which is beyond human imagination. In so doing, he chooses language which seems to allude to the activities of soldiers and of locusts.

(2:12–14) A Sermon Based on a Word of God This passage represents a literary form which we find elsewhere in the prophetic books: the prophet quotes a word of God (v. 12) and unfolds the meaning of it in his own words (vv. 13–14). In the midst of the terrors of his manifestation, the Lord invites his people to 'return to him'. The repentance he is asking for is a total engagement of the human being: fasting, weeping, and mourning as over one's own death. vv. 13–14, the prophet, expatiating on this invitation, encourages the people and develops some very pertinent theological considerations.

(2:15–17) The Prophet Organizes the Ritual Mourning Not content with a general sermon on God's mercies, the prophet orders precise action: a holy ceremony uniting the whole people, including children and infants, sanctified by holy rites and by holy intentions, assembled for prayer in the temple, under the leadership of the priests (vv. 15–17a). The prayer he suggests (v. 17b) corresponds to the prayers of collective mourning found in the Psalms.

(2:18–27) With One Voice, the Lord and the Prophet Announce Salvation This passage introduces the final reversal of things. The Lord who has manifested the terrible effects of his coming, announces now his mercy in favour of Judah and Jerusalem. The main thrust of his revelation comes to its end: abundant blessings and joy. The proclamation is pronounced alternately by the prophet (vv. 18, 21–4, 26a) and the Lord (vv. 19–20, 25, 26b–27). The prophet introduces the statements by declaring that the Lord has felt 'passionate love' (rather than 'jealousy'—a term which does not render the real meaning of the Heb. verbal root q-n'). His promise of blessings is the answer to the people's ritual mourning.

The Lord confirms the prophet's sayings and announces the blessings the people are waiting for. Moreover, he is going to 'remove the northern army [northerner] far from you [from over and against you]' (v. 20). The 'northerner' (the Heb. does not have 'army'!) is a mythological term which designates a superhuman power (note its gigantic dimensions: from sea to sea!) residing on a mythological mountain somewhere in the 'north'. Here, the term refers probably to the mythological forces accompanying God's theophany.

In vv. 21–4 the prophet enlarges on God's promises, inviting soil, animals, and trees (note again his solidarity with the non-human world, as in 1:20) not to fear but to rejoice over God's loving-kindness. He then addresses the same exhortation to the inhabitants of Jerusalem (vv. 23–4). In v. 25, God declares that he will 'repay' (cf. 3:18–21) the damage caused by the swarms of locusts, his 'great army', during several years: the catastrophe is not a momentary one, it strikes serious and lasting blows. In vv. 26a–27, which may have received additions by a later hand, God reveals the true intention of all his actions: that his people may come to know him and his faithfulness. This is expressed with the ancient formula which sums up the covenental relationship: YHWH is Israel's God, none other.

(2:28–32) The Outpouring of the Lord's Energy The Hebrew word rûaḥ usually translated by 'spirit', means first of all 'wind' or even 'storm-wind'; rûaḥ is an energy whose effects can be felt and seen. Theologically, this energy is the very life-energy of God. In OT history we learn that this divine life-energy may suddenly fall on a human—a military hero or a prophet—and enable him to work extraordinary things. Whenever God pours out his divine energy, people are transformed; they behave like madmen, they dance frenziedly; seized by ecstasy they undress and lie naked on the ground. Moreover, they have visions and enter the heavenly realms. In our text, this divine energy is poured 'on all flesh', on every member of the chosen people; or on all humans? perhaps even on animals? For this event is a new manifestation of the 'day of the LORD' (v. 31) and it leads up to yet another manifestation which will be the final judgement over all the nations (3:14). This universal action of God colours the outpouring of his energy 'on all flesh'; it changes radically the mind and the behaviour of those who are touched by it. 'Sons and . . . daughters' will 'prophesy': possessed and pushed on by this energy, they will do strange things—things which we see Saul and his servants do when they are seized by the same divine energy (1 Sam 10:10–13; 19:20–4). Old people will have dreams heavily laden with meaning, and young men visions giving fresh spiritual insight (v. 28). The social order will be disturbed or rather abolished as everybody, including male and female slaves will suffer the same transformations of mind and behaviour (v. 29). While the outpouring of the divine energy produces mad behaviour and social disorder on earth, the whole cosmos undergoes frightening transformations: 'blood, fire, and columns of smoke' (v. 30); the sun loses its light and the moon is changed into blood (v. 31). The 'great and terrible day of the LORD' brings the world order to its end.

In the context of the whole passage, the outpouring of divine energy is an ambiguous event. People are filled with divine presence and God is revealed to them, but nothing is said about the contents of the dreams and visions. The prophecy inspires embarrassment and awe. Perhaps we ought to understand the story of the first Christian Pentecost (Acts 2, where our text is quoted) more in the light of eschatological revolutions than in that of the current Christian concept of the Spirit.

The revelation of the Day being terrifying, the prophet feels compelled to give some concrete advice (v. 32). He proposes a two-sided attitude. First, in the midst of the disturbances, continue to invoke the name of the Lord, remain faithful, and trust in YHWH. Secondly, stay in Jerusalem, for there the Lord will save those whom he chooses. Even this advice is thus tainted with uncertainty: who will be chosen?

(3:1–8) The Judgement in the Valley Called 'YHWH judges' This passage gives concrete information about the historical background of Joel (see JOEL B). The Lord assembles 'all the nations' in the valley Jehoshaphat ('YHWH judges' or 'YHWH is judge'): the Assyrians who have dispersed Israel, broken up the northern country, and ill-treated boys and girls; and the small nations along the Mediterranean coast who have pillaged Judah and Jerusalem and who are guilty of selling prisoners as slaves to the Greeks. God has decided to release the victims and to punish the guilty according to the principle of the *lex talionis*.

(3:9–17) The Final Battle in the Valley Called 'YHWH judges' The programme mentioned in the preceding passage is being carried out: YHWH assembles the armies of all the nations and rouses them to fight against his own warriors (v. 11). These latter are probably the mythological soldiers described in 2:1–11. The prophet (it is he who speaks in vv. 9–11) calls upon YHWH to bring down this army again, at a specific place: 'there'. Further, he does not hesitate to reverse the prophecies announcing the transformation of swords into ploughshares (Isa 2:4; Mic 4:3), for now the atrocious final battle is unavoidable: YHWH has decided to manifest his triumph. In v. 12 YHWH adds a word to say that he 'will sit to judge' while the battle is raging: the judgement determines the outcome of the fight. In vv. 13–17 the prophet gives a terrifying picture of the contest which is nothing less than the manifestation of the day of the Lord with its cosmic dimensions (vv. 14–15). Finally, he reminds his audience that YHWH is definitely dwelling in Zion and that he will manifest this fact to all who survive the battle (v. 17). In passing he quotes an exclamation which is also found in Am 1:2, probably a liturgical formula.

(4:18–21) Final Benediction It is a message of prosperity, happiness, and peace for Judah and Jerusalem, whereas there is no hope for the enemies of the people of God (v. 19; see JOEL B).

REFERENCE

Alt, A. (1953), *Kleine Schriften zur Geschichte des Volkes Israel* (Munich: C. H. Beck), ii.

29. Amos

JENNIFER M. DINES

INTRODUCTION

A. Canonical Context. 1:1 sets Amos the prophet in the eighth century BCE, just prior to Assyria's conquest of Israel (Soggin 1987: 1; Andersen and Freedman 1989: 18–19). Further internal evidence (e.g. 6:13–14) suggests a period slightly antedating Hosea and Isaiah (cf. Hos 1:1; Isa 1:1); hence Amos is often called the earliest 'writing' prophet. But in the Twelve ('Minor') Prophets, the book of Amos never comes first, either following Hosea and preceding Micah (LXX) or following Hosea and Joel and preceding Obadiah (MT). MT's canonical order is perhaps by supposed historical period (Amos is contemporary with all prophets from Hosea to Micah) but not chronological priority. Books are linked verbally and thematically; Amos dovetails with Joel (Am 1:2; Joel 4:16) and Obadiah (Am 9:12; Ob 1–4); Am 9:13–15 resembles Hos 14:4–8, Joel 4:18; Am 9:2–3 echoes Jon 1:3. These and other links suggest deliberate arrangement (Collins 1993; Nogalski 1993; Coggins 1994).

B. Outline. From Jerusalem, YHWH judges surrounding nations, Judah, and Israel for 'transgressions'; Israel's crimes include oppressing the poor, perverting justice, and resisting prophets (1:1–2:16). Mistaken religious attitudes are exposed (3:1–4:13). Israel's only hope lies in 'seeking' YHWH through justice and compassion (5:1–27). Mistaken confidence is exposed (6:1–14). Visions, threats, and narrative reinforce YHWH's judgement; eventually restoration is promised (7:1–9:15).

C. Style and Structure. Amos is mainly poetic in form; see especially 1:3–2:6; 3:3–8; 4:6–11; 9:2–4; other sections are held together by various literary devices (e.g. 3:9–15; 5:1–17; 6:1–7). Later passages often echo earlier ones (e.g. 6:1–7||4:1–3; 7:15–16||2:11–12; 8:4–6||2:6–8; 9:3||1:2), with many cross-references (e.g. 9:7||1:5; 3:2; 9:14||5:11), suggesting deliberate symmetry (Smalley 1979). Other comprehensive structures have been suggested (e.g. Andersen and Freedman 1989: 26; Paul 1991: 6–7; Bovati and Meynet 1994: 237–8); none exhausts all the possibilities. The outline followed here is:

Judgement on Nations, including Judah and Israel (1:1–2:16)
Indictment of, and Appeal to, Israel (3:1–6:14)
Visions, Interpretations, Words of Judgement and Salvation (7:1–9:15)

D. Composition. The present surprising form of the text (it emphasizes judgement, but ends with salvation) has been accounted for by several theories. (1) It reflects Amos's real preaching. His oracles were preserved by disciples; almost everything dates from the eighth century (e.g. Paul 1991). (2) An eighth-century stratum of judgement oracles against Samaria has been progressively expanded, particularly by a pro-Judean, anti-Bethel redaction in the seventh century, and an idealistically hopeful redaction in post-exilic times (e.g. Wolff 1977; Coote 1981). This is the majority position. (3) Most of the writing was done in the post-exilic period, utilizing earlier (possibly anonymous) poetic collections and traditions; historical and biographical information is not necessarily to be taken at face value (e.g. Davies 1989: 278, 289). Option (1) seems unlikely, given Amos's integration with the Twelve which must belong, finally, to the post-exilic period. Option (2) is plausible, though difficult to establish in detail (e.g. the same verses in 1:3–2:6 have been assigned to different editorial stages by different scholars). Option (3) plausibly emphasizes the creative role of post-exilic editors; but marked differences between individual prophetic books, and circumstantial details (e.g. the description of Amos as *nōqēd* in 1:1) perhaps point to the survival of ancient historical elements. This commentary takes the position that the received text is essentially a post-exilic literary work, produced, in the form in which we have it now, during the Persian or early Hellenistic period (6th–4th cents. BCE); it assumes that there are traces of earlier sources and traditions within 'the words of Amos' (1:1), but is agnostic as to whether, or how much, these can be identified. In what follows, it is assumed that 'the words' are understood by the book's author to apply to the whole text.

E. Method. A step-by-step reading of the received text highlights its verbal and thematic interconnections, and its shifting moral and theological perspectives. As far as possible, the text is interpreted within its own literary context, in an attempt to do justice to it as a whole. Historical issues, although addressed where appropriate, are not the main focus. This is not because they are unimportant but because they interrupt the sequence of the text, and also because, within the limits of a short commentary, it is impossible to discuss them thoroughly. For further information see e.g. Wolff 1977; King 1988: Andersen and Freedman 1989. Speculation about compositional process is, for the same reason, generally avoided. As part of the Twelve, Amos necessarily reflects Second Temple shaping; an understanding of the text against this background is a necessary preliminary to considering questions of historical origins and redactional development.

COMMENTARY

Judgement on Nations, including Judah and Israel (1:1–2:16)

(1:1) Title Uzziah (Azariah) of Judah reigned (including co-reigns) *c.*783–735 BCE; Jeroboam II of Israel *c.*786–746 (Soggin 1987: 1; King 1988: 8). Uzziah's literary priority indicates a Judean perspective: Amos's prophecy 'concerning Israel' involves both kingdoms. The referent for 'Israel' is often unclear; alone, 'Israel' properly refers to the northern kingdom, but wider usage, denoting all descendants of Jacob/Israel, means that Judah is often included, or intended (Andersen and Freedman 1989: 98–139). NRSV's 'shepherd' is a guess; MT's *nōqēd* perhaps means 'sheep-farmer' (cf. 2 Kings 3:4). Effectively, Amos is presented as a Judean countryman (cf. 7:14–15). 'Saw' (*ḥāzâ*) is a technical term in prophecy (cf. 7:12, 'seer' *ḥōzeh*). Formally, visions occur only in chs. 7–9; chs. 1–6 consist of speeches ('words'): both are prophetic. Zech 14:5 echoes this verse, but there is no firm external evidence for dating the earthquake. Earthquake imagery is, however, important throughout Amos, symbolizing YHWH's judgement.

(1:2) Epigraph Amos's first 'word', a hymnic couplet, is partly shared with Joel 4:16, melding the two books and setting Amos's theme: YHWH's supremacy. YHWH's 'roar' is lion-like (cf. 3:8); 'utters his voice' suggests thunder (cf. Ps 29). Emanating from Jerusalem, this 'voice' reinforces the Judean perspective. The effect is devastation of naturally fertile countryside; 'the top of Carmel' (cf. 9:3) is explicitly contrasted with Zion/Jerusalem, YHWH's power-base.

(1:3–2:16) Oracles against the Nations (cf. Num 21:27–30; Isa 13–23; Jer 46–51; Ezek 25–32; Zeph 2). 1:3 initiates a collection of eight quasi-legal arraignments for war-crimes (Barton 1980); six nearby nations are accused (see map), then Judah and Israel. The numerical expression is idiomatic, probably indicating an unspecified, cumulative number. The composition-history of this passage is disputed; the judgements on Tyre, Edom, and Judah are often thought to be later than the rest. Literary features, however, show that the whole poem is carefully constructed. Even if individual oracles were composed at different times, starting in the eighth century, the passage can be read as an integrated whole where Tyre, Edom, and Judah play significant roles. The historical allusions are obscure, as are reasons for geographic and ethnic sequence (Andersen and Freedman 1989: 208–10; Paul 1991: 11–15), but the Oracles against the Nations significantly shape what follows: YHWH's control of historical destinies.

(1:3–5) Damascus Capital of Israel's traditional enemy Aram, Damascus represents the whole country (v. 5). Its crime, real or metaphorical, is an atrocity against the fertile Transjordanian territory fought over by Israel and Aram in the ninth/eighth centuries BCE, and prominent again in Maccabean times. 'Threshing sledges' symbolize military victory also in Isa 41:15, where Israel is to do what Am 1:3 condemns! Punishment is imprecise; 'fire' may be metaphorical for warfare, or suggest supernatural intervention (cf. 1:7, 10, 12, 14; 2:2, 5). 'House of Hazael' is a *double entendre*: 'house' represents both building and dynasty (cf. 7:9). Hazael and Ben-Hadad were ninth/eighth century Aramean kings. The 'strongholds' (a recurring term in chs. 1–6), belong to powerful leaders in Israel and abroad; they are special targets for YHWH's anger. The word translated 'inhabitants' could also mean 'ruler', matching 'the one who holds the sceptre' (cf. 1:8). 'Valley of Awen' (lit. of nothingness, futility) and 'Beth-eden' (House of Pleasure) are sarcastic punning allusions, perhaps to real places. 'Awen' appears again (5:5) describing Bethel (NRSV: nothing). 'Eden' perhaps hints at luxurious living (cf. 4:1; 6:1–7). The threat of mass deportation ('go into exile') introduces an important theme. In 9:7 Kir (location unknown, probably in Mesopotamia) is Aram's place of origin (cf. 2 Kings 16:9; Ezek 21:30).

(1:6–8) Gaza 'Carried into exile' links vv. 6–8 with 1:3–5: the reference is probably to Philistine slave-raids (cf. NJB). Ironic-ally, what YHWH does to punish Aram (1:5) is Gaza's cause of punishment! The unidentified victims are destined for Edom, the nation traditionally descended from Esau (Gen 36). In pre-exilic times Edom lay south-east of the Dead Sea (slavers used the port of Ezion-Geber on the Gulf of Aqaba); but later Edom/Idumea occupied the south of erstwhile Judah, close to the Philistine cities. Ashdod, Ashkelon, and Ekron are other Philistine city-states; Gath is not mentioned till 6:2. Philistia's punishment is severer than Aram's. A remnant which itself is devastated recurs elsewhere (esp. 9:4; cf. Isa 6:11–13).

(1:9–10) Tyre Of the Phoenician cities, only Tyre is men-tioned; by implication all are probably covered. The crime resembles Gaza's; in addition, some contract or treaty has been broken; the word *běrît* (covenant) occurs, but not theo-logically of a 'contract' between God and Israel. The deportees are not explicitly Israelites, though Judeans might remember dealings between Solomon and Hiram (1 Kings 5; 9:11–14). Historically, Tyre survived until Alexander's conquest. If this is *ex eventu* prophecy, it dates from after 332 BCE at the earliest. Otherwise, it may express traditional convictions about na-tional enemies, as with the rest of the Oracles against the Nations, and could be earlier.

(1:11–12) Edom Twice implicated in others' crimes, Edom now faces judgement. The catchword is 'brother', but the atrocity does not refer to dealings with Gaza and Tyre; nor do tradi-tions in Gen 27:41 or Num 20:14–21 really fit. Edomite expan-sion during the sixth century (Ezek 25:12–14; Ob 10–14; Ps 137:7) provides a likely context, if 'brother' means 'Israel' (i.e. Judah, cf. 9:12); v. 11*b* underlines Edom's continuing aggres-sion. 'Cast off' is literally 'destroyed'; the word translated 'pity' possibly means 'womenfolk' (Paul 1991: 64–5; cf. LXX), which would create a link with 1:13 (cf. 1:3 LXX; 5Q Amos). 'Anger' and 'wrath' (virtually personified) are better taken as subjects; the verb rendered 'maintained' (*ṭārap*) is used of wild beasts tearing their prey (cf. 3:4). Teman (N) and Bosra (S) represent the whole of Edom/Idumea.

(1:13–15) Ammon 'Gilead' knits Ammon's crime with 1:3, so Israelites are victims. For Ammon's kinship with Israel, see Gen 19:30–8. The motive is territorial gain, through a form of genocide (cf. 2 Kings 8:12; 15:16; Hos 13:16), doing to Gilead what YHWH threatens to do to the Philistines. Military action becomes a tempest (suggesting YHWH as the epiphanic war-rior), a merging of themes typical of Amos. 'Says the Lord', and 'exile' constitute an *inclusio* with 1:5, tying 1:3–15 together.

(2:1–3) Moab (cf. Gen 19:30–7); despite this literary closure, the poem continues, suggesting a larger pattern ('sound', v. 2, is *qôl*, cf. 1:2). The catchword is 'king'; surprisingly, Edom is victim of an atrocity. The crime probably hinges on sacrilege (cf. Jer 8:1–3; cf. 2 Kings 23:16–20). Bones figure again in 6:9–10 (also obscure). Burning the bones 'to lime' (NJB: ash) precludes burial, or suggests savagery. v. 2*b* echoes 1:14*b*. The trumpet reappears in 3:6, in a similar context (cf. Ex 19:13, 16, 19).

(2:4–5) Judah Little links this oracle with what precedes but, as it separates two blocks (1:3–2:3; 2:6–16), it may reflect the post-exilic writer's central interest (Bovati and Meynet 1994: 59–62). Formally, it follows the standard pattern. Judah's sin, however, is religious not political. 'Lies' suggest idolatry; 'an-cestors' extend it backwards in time (cf. 1:11).

(2:6–16) Israel Finally, Israel is accused like the rest (v. 6). The mention of Judah (2:4–5) defines Israel as the northern king-dom, though the distinction soon blurs. This 'transgression' too differs from that of the foreigners; it is primarily social. The 'righteous' (*ṣaddîq*) is either 'an honest man' (cf. REB), sold into debt-slavery, or the 'innocent' party (Soggin 1987: 47–8), unjustly convicted. The reference to 'sandals' is ob-scure (see Andersen and Freedman 1989: 310–13 for sugges-tions). vv. 7–8, instead of sentence immediately being passed, Israel's crimes are elaborated. The verdict comes in vv. 13–16, but from v. 7 on, the form of the Oracles against the Nations dissolves. There are difficulties in v. 7*a*, but the link between economic poverty and corrupt legal practice seems to be maintained (cf. NJB; 8:4). v. 7*b* is obscure (lit. a man and his father go to a/the girl), but the accusation appears to be sexual. The juxtaposition with v. 7*a* perhaps suggests exploitation. The result is profanation of YHWH's name: there is a reli-gious dimension (cf. 2:4). 'On garments taken in pledge' (v. 8; cf. Deut 24:12–13; Ex 22:26–7) implies a night-time setting and a wrong done to the poor. Drinking the proceeds of fines is not obviously illegal; the objection is presumably to callous-ness. 'House of their God/god/gods' (*'ĕlōhêhem* permits all three interpretations) indicates a sanctuary setting; the ac-cused are wealthy and powerful over against those from whose plight they profit. vv. 9–10, YHWH reminds Israel of his benefits when they entered the land. 'Amorites' is a blan-ket term for the original inhabitants of Canaan who, under many names, are often described as giants (e.g. Deut 2:10, 20–1; 9:2; Num 13:32–3); though only here are the Amorites in general so described. As in the Oracles against the Nations YHWH controls the destinies of all. The past annihilation of the Amorites balances 1:8, the future annihilation of the Philistines. History is extended even further back, to the Exodus (v. 10, cf. 3:1; 9:7) and the Wilderness Period (cf. 5:25). 'Inheriting' recurs in 9:12, where the restored Davidic kingdom will 'inherit' the 'remnant of Edom'. There is no mention of the lawgiving at Sinai/Horeb (evoked only in 2:4).

vv. 11–12, prophets and nazirites were further divine gifts (cf. Deut 18:15–19; the same verb, 'raise up', occurs). They are the central element in vv. 6–16 (Bovati and Meynet 1994: 45). For the nazirite vow, see Num 6:1–21. The rhetorical question leads the addressees to condemn their own actions (cf. 5:14; 9:10): Israelites (the inclusive 'people of Israel' occurs for the first time) stand accused of corrupting nazirites and silencing prophets (the two groups are linked only here), i.e. neutralizing potential saviours. Nazirites are not mentioned again; prophets are central to chs. 3 and 7. vv. 13–16, YHWH's verdict, expected since v. 6, is of a new kind: instead of fire, an obscure picture involving a wagon. The verb (NRSV: press down) may mean 'tremble' or 'split', and refer to an earthquake (Soggin 1987: 49); if so, this resembles the Oracles against the Nations' supernatural fire. An ominous use of apparently positive imagery is typical (cf. 8:1). What impresses is the initial vagueness of Israel's punishment. The image of a defeated army (vv. 14–16) is clearer: no escape, no survival (cf. 9:2–4). The situation is, however, quite general: many historical events could fit. Nor is the victor named: perhaps Assyria, perhaps Babylon, certainly YHWH. MT contains much assonance and wordplay: repetitions create a sense of inexorable doom, dramatically ending 1:3–2:16.

Indictment of, and Appeal to, Israel (3:1–6:14)

'Hear this word', introducing chs. 3–5 (3:1; 4:1; 5:1; cf. 3:13; 8:4), creates one literary unit (3:1–5:17). Two 'woes' (5:18; 6:1) structure another (5:18–6:14).

(3:1–5:17)

(3:1–8) YHWH's Control of Israel's History, and the Role of Prophets, Reinforced (cf. 2:9–11). The 'family' of Israel (vv. 1–2) is distinguished from other national 'families' (cf. Gen 12:3); this is contradicted in 9:7. The logic of Israel's punishment now depends on the exclusivity of the historical relationship with YHWH, not on violations of human rights (2:6–8, though from either perspective Israel stands condemned). Aphoristic questions (vv. 3–8) draw obvious conclusions (vv. 3–6) until an important theological point is made (vv. 7–8). NRSV's 'made an appointment' (v. 3) interprets the Hebrew verb 'know' again (v. 2; 'know each other' perhaps). The lion's 'roar' (v. 4) echoes YHWH's (1:2). The 'young lion' literally 'gives its voice', again cf. 1:2. 'Prey' (*terep*) comes from the same root as the verb in 1:11 (NRSV: kept); the implications are menacing. 'Taken' is the same word as 'caught' in v. 4, linking both situations. The trumpet is a siren, proclaiming enemy attack; it recalls the panic in 1:14, 2:2. YHWH's control of history is again underlined (cf. 1:3–2:16; vv. 1–2). The solemn title 'my Lord YHWH' (NRSV: the Lord GOD), last met in 1:8, suits imagery of the divine council: YHWH in his heavenly palace discusses plans (NRSV: secret) with his ministers. To this cabinet meeting prophets are occasionally admitted (e.g. 1 Kings 22:19–23; Isa 6:1–8). The prophet as servant (i.e. high-ranking minister or ambassador) occurs only here in Amos but is presupposed by the 'messenger-speech' form ('Thus says YHWH') from 1:3 onwards. v. 7 is crucial for the theme of prophecy, introduced in 1:1; 2:11–12 (cf. 7:14–15). However, it undermines the point made in vv. 3–6, that God's action is self-evident; different views of revelation are combined, perhaps reflecting earlier stages in composition (Auld 1986: 31–2.) or an ongoing debate on the nature of prophecy (Carroll 1983: 26). v. 8 links YHWH's roar (1:2) with the divine/prophetic speaking of 1:1; 1:3–2:16, and forms an *inclusio* with the beginning of v. 1. The parallelism equates the inevitability of prophecy (cf. Num 11:29) and of Israel's punishment. However, in the light of 2:11–12, the implication may be that YHWH's speech is not heard because prophets have been ignored.

(3:9–15) Destruction for Powerful Oppressors The threat of 3:8 unfolds (vv. 9–12). Enemies are summoned for a grandstand view, or as witnesses in a trial. Some scholars emend 'Ashdod' to 'Assyria' (e.g. Andersen and Freedman 1986: 406; cf. LXX); this is possible: together, Assyria (N) and Egypt (S) would imply 'all foreign powers' (cf. 1:12; 6:14). Egypt was named in 2:10; 3:1, in connection with the Exodus; here it is a contemporary. This is also the first naming of Samaria, the northern capital. The situation is ironic: instead of foreigners contemplating their own crimes (1:3–2:3), they are now to witness Israel's. The simile in v. 12 suggests the situation covered by Ex 22:13, but now the shepherd finds only scraps as evidence. The point is not that there will be survivors, but that practically nothing will remain at all. v. 12*b* is obscure; NRSV adopts a plausible conjecture, implying that only scraps of luxury items enjoyed by Samaria's warlords survive as evidence of their demise.

vv. 13–15, a further summons again presumably addresses foreigners. 'House of Jacob' occurs for the first time, probably involving all Judah/Israel (Andersen and Freedman 1989: 410); it recurs only in the pivotal 9:8*b*. A new theme appears: YHWH's decision to destroy the northern sanctuary of Bethel. Cutting off the 'horns' of altars (for illustrations, see King 1988: 93) means that blood cannot be smeared on them to make sacrifices valid (Lev 4:30; 16:18); nor can they be grasped for sanctuary (1 Kings 1:50–3; 2:28). No explanation is given for the threat. Perhaps the link is with 2:8, where sins are committed in the 'house of their God/god(s)'; Bethel means 'House of El/God'. The desecration of Bethel is recounted in 2 Kings 23:15. Coote (1981: 46–53) connects this and other passages with a seventh-century redaction; Soggin (1987: 65) thinks an earthquake is intended. 'Falling' is an important motif (5:1; 8:14; 9:11). 'Winter house' and 'summer house' (v. 15) are conjectures; MT's 'house of ?harvest' and 'house of ?fruit' possibly have cultic overtones, which would fit well with v. 14; most, however, suppose the magnificent houses of the rich are meant (see King 1988: 64–9). 'Great' could also be 'many'; the word is that used in v. 9 of 'tumults', effectively providing an *inclusio*: the 'tumults/oppressions' come from 'houses' (cf. v. 10, 'strongholds').

(4:1–13) The Fate of Wealthy Women and Religious Enthusiasts vv. 1–3, wealthy women: their crimes recall 2:7 (cf. 6:1–7); 'oppress' echoes and makes specific 3:9. 'Cows of Bashan' suggests affluence (Deut 32:14; Ezek 39:18; cf. Ps 22:12). 'Let's drink' (*ništeh*; cf. 2:8, 12) is countered by 'has sworn' (*nišba'*, 4:2). This wordplay introduces YHWH's first oath (cf. 6:8; 8:7). YHWH swears by his 'holiness' (cf. 2:7), rendering the outcome inevitable, although the time-formula is imprecise (cf. 8:11; 9:13). MT is difficult, but 4:3 pictures women being deported. The imagery suggests warfare, perhaps also earthquake; the fall of Samaria in 722 BCE is related in 2 Kings 17:6, but other similar situations could be evoked. The final threat is obscure: 'the Harmon' appears to be a place-name, perhaps a mountain. 'Flung out' is the verb used in the Oracles against the Nations of YHWH 'sending' fire. The savage punishment predicted for these guilty women contrasts with 1:13, where perpetrators of atrocities against women are condemned.

vv. 4–5, a summons to sin. The command (countermanded in 5:5) is a trick: obedience leads to 'transgression', sin equivalent to that of the Oracles against the Nations. Gilgal's location is uncertain; it is again paired with Bethel in 5:5. Cultic *faux pas* are highlighted, or excesses are mocked; the latter suits Amos's style, and the context. The offerings are voluntary, additional to the major sacrifices, but sin-offerings are conspicuously absent (cf. Lev 1–7); the ironic exclamation in v. 5*b* suggests religious fervour which may be genuine; its uselessness is underlined in 5:21–4. Further irony is suggested by 'proclaim', used in 3:9 to advertise Samaria's sins. vv. 6–11, fruitless warnings: this poetic set-piece functions as YHWH's response to the enthusiasm of vv. 4–5 and suggests the attitude which should have prevailed (cf. Joel 2:18–27, where people do, apparently, 'turn'). The point is that Israel failed to grasp the meaning of the five disasters instigated by YHWH (cf. 3:3–6), i.e. their dependence on YHWH's favour. (1) Famine (v. 6; cf. 8:11). 'Places', paired with 'cities', may indicate cult-centres (cf. Gen 13:3–4; 28:18–19); if so, 'lack of bread' includes sacrificial offerings (cf. Joel 1:9, 13). 'Return' perhaps suggests public mourning rituals (demanded in 5:16) to elicit YHWH's mercy. (2) Drought (vv. 7–8; cf. 8:13). 'Drinking' is no longer the heartless indulgence of 2:7; 4:1 (cf. 6:6), but a matter of survival. (3) Other natural disasters (v. 9). Curiously, locusts are mentioned only in passing; they usually constituted a major disaster (cf. 7:1–3; Joel 1–2). (4) Plague (v. 10). 'Pestilence' either emanates from the rotting corpses or is a supernatural attack (cf. 5:3; Isa 37:36). The reference to Egypt is obscure; possibly an allusion to the plagues tradition; possibly a proverbial saying. Typically, the imagery switches from agriculture to war, another area where Israel should have recognized YHWH's hand (cf. 6:13). (5) Earthquake (v. 11). The climactic event is of a different order: the allusion to Sodom and Gomorrah suggests punishment rather than warning. As in Gen 19:24–9, where only Lot and his daughters escape, the emphasis is on the few survivors. 'Snatched' (*muṣṣāl*) echoes 3:12 ('rescues', *yaṣṣîl*). In Gen 19:24 YHWH 'rained' sulphur and fire (cf. Am 4:7; 7:4). In the context of Amos, an earthquake may be intended; but any 'act of God' is possible. 'Overthrow' (*hāpak*, cf. Gen 19:25, 29) introduces an important new verb.

v. 12, summons to Israel: the solemn address suggests a cultic occasion (cf. vv. 4–5). 'Your God' (*ʾĕlōhêkā*) reinforces this; the title is used for the first time (cf. 8:14; 9:15; contrast 2:8). But the God awaiting them is not a benevolent deity gratefully accepting gifts. The true nature of the religious situation, with its reversal of expectations, merely hinted at here, is spelled out in 5:18–20. v. 13, doxology: in the style of a liturgical praise-song, YHWH is celebrated as Creator and his 'name' evoked (cf. 2:7). This is the first of three 'hymnic/judgement doxologies' (Crenshaw 1975; cf. 5:8; 9:6). Provenance and dating are disputed; they function to demonstrate YHWH's supremacy over nature, as well as in history. v. 13 is so structured that the central element, flanked by two powerful acts, is YHWH's 'revealing' of his 'thoughts'. This universalizes 3:7 (although with different vocabulary). 'Darkness' prepares for the Day of YHWH in ch. 5.

(5:1–17) Death and Life This complex chiastic passage (de Waard 1977; Smalley 1979: 121–2), Amos's literary and theo-

logical centre, begins and ends with mourning, around exhortations to possible survival through justice and compassion. vv. 1–3, lament for Israel. v. 1 introduces a funeral dirge (cf. 2 Sam 1:19–27; 3:33–4). The image is startling: Israel (masculine) is a dead girl, with no one to bury her! This image of the fallen nation is reversed only in 9:11. The decimated armies (v. 3) recall the remnant of 3:12, reinforcing, rather than contradicting, v. 2 (cf. 6:9). The end of v. 3 (omitted by NRSV) reads 'for the House of Israel'. This phrase is functional: it clinches the identity of the 'cities' and forms an *inclusio* with v. 1. vv. 4–9, seeking YHWH; 'live' (i.e. 'survive') slightly tempers the language of death; 'seek', a technical term for visiting a cult-centre with a request, resumes the cultic language of ch. 4, but with a contradiction in terms: Israel is not to go to cult-centres! An explicit distinction is made between YHWH's presence and the doomed sanctuaries. The addition of Judean Beer-sheba is puzzling. It is not threatened with destruction, although its literary centrality may mean it shares the others' fate; it is mentioned again, negatively, in 8:14. 'House of Joseph', supposedly referring to the northern kingdom (Andersen and Freedman 1989: 99), is unique to Amos (cf. v. 15; 6:6). In v. 7 cultic yields to legal language (cf. 2:6). Two important words appear: 'justice' (*mišpāṭ*) and 'righteousness' (*ṣĕdāqâ*, cf. *ṣaddîq*, 2:7); together, they suggest 'universal order' (Murray 1992: 42–3; Barton 1995: 56). 'Turn' is *hāpak*, the opposite of order (cf. 4:11, 'overthrow'). This creates powerful associations: 'they' are doing to 'justice' what YHWH did to Sodom and Gomorrah. The second doxology (vv. 8–9; cf. 4:13; 9:6) again highlights YHWH's activity in creation and human affairs. The catchword with v. 7 is again 'turns' (*hāpak*). The phenomena evoked are natural, although *hāpak*, the imagery of darkness and light, and the suggestion of a flood (cf. 8:8; 9:5), are menacing. There is also irony: YHWH transforms elemental forces; people overthrow justice.

vv. 10–13, the wages of sin: perversion of justice (v. 7) becomes explicit. The gate(way) is where, in an Israelite walled town, legal cases were conducted (cf. Ruth 4:1–12). The objects of 'their' hatred are not the innocent poor, as in 2:6–7, but honest judges. 'Hate' recurs later with YHWH as subject (5:21). The consequence of disregard for honest speaking is that the poor continue to be exploited (v. 11); it is for this, ultimately, that punishment is decreed. The form is connected with treaty and law-code curses (e.g. Deut 28:30; Murray 1992: 62–7). 'Gate' forms an *inclusio*, so that vv. 10, 12 frame v. 11, with its assurance of punishment for oppressors. v. 13 is enigmatic. It may be related to what precedes, i.e. honest men know they will not succeed in giving or receiving justice ('evil' (*rāʿâ*) implies 'disastrous'); or a general comment, perhaps from the writer's perspective (it is Amos's central verse; contrast Hos 14:9). vv. 14–17, 'it may be…': YHWH and 'good' are now equated, so Bethel and Gilgal constitute 'evil'. Israel's complacent 'speaking' contrasts with YHWH's words of judgement. v. 15 sums up the situation: hating bad and loving good do not require cultic acts, but justice. The tentative hope for mercy (v. 15*b*) is reminiscent of Jon 3:9. 'It may be' occurs in Amos only here and may be ironic: historically, the northern kingdom did not survive. Alternatively, it may point forward to 9:8*b*–10, the survival of a (Judean) 'remnant', 6:1, 6 having universalized the scope of 'house of Joseph'. If so, this verse is of crucial importance to the thought of the book of Amos. vv. 16–17, a penitential ceremony (cf. Joel 1–2): the theme of mourning is resumed, forming an *inclusio* with vv. 1–2. The Hebrew could mean '*let there be* wailing'; this makes sense of 'therefore' (v. 16) and reinforces 'perhaps' (v. 15). Punishment, certainly, is unavoidable (v. 17). YHWH's presence, confidently presumed in v. 14, is now terrifying (cf. Ex 12:12, 23).

(5:18–6:14) Cultic and Political Triumphalism Attacked Although there is continuity, a new section is established by two 'woe' exclamations (5:18; 6:1; cf 5:16*b*).

(5:18–20) The Day of YHWH This originated as a cultic celebration of YHWH as Israel's victorious king (see *ABD* ii. 82–5). But triumphalist expectations are reversed. As in 2:13, normal and abnormal combine. 'Fled' (v. 19) echoes 2:14. The simile suggests inescapability (cf. 9:2–4), reinforced by the repetition (5:18, 20) of the light/dark motif (cf. 4:13; 5:8).

(5:21–7) Repudiation of Heartless Religion (cf. Isa 1:11–17). If the day of YHWH belonged with the cult, the abrupt return to rituals makes sense. 'Despise' has occurred before (2:4), of Judah's 'despising' (NRSV: reject) YHWH's law. The annual pilgrim feasts are categorically rejected, although in other texts they are said to be divinely ordained (Ex 23:14–17; Deut 16:16); the technical term *ḥag* (implied in 4:4–5; 5:4–5) occurs for the first time (cf. 8:10). The text of v. 22 is uncertain, but rejection of various sacrifices continues, together with accompanying hymns and music, anticipating 6:4–6, especially 6:5. The lessons of 5:4–7, 10–15 are again summed up in an all-embracing demand for justice and righteousness (v. 24; cf. 5:7). vv. 25–7 are often regarded as an intrusion, presupposing a different cultural and historical background, but in the literary organization of both section and book they are significant. With vv. 21–3 they form a cultic envelope, within which v. 24 is central. 'Exile' recalls the defeat of 5:1–3. v. 25 mentions the Exodus period, midway between 2:10 (cf. 3:1) and 9:7. Clear references to idolatry occur only here and in 2:4; 8:14. In v. 25 YHWH addresses the 'house of Israel' directly, as in 5:4. The problem is whether the answer 'yes' or 'no' is expected (cf. Ezek 20:10–26, a positive evaluation; Jer 7:21–3, a negative one; Exodus and Leviticus suppose all legislation to have been given at Sinai; cf. Ex 24:3–8). As Jer 7:22 is the only text which could be taken to deny a desert cult, it is likely that a post-exilic writer/reader would understand v. 25 as inviting the answer 'yes'. The Hebrew word order makes 'sacrifices and offerings' emphatic ('was it *only* sacrifices . . .'). In the wider context of Amos this may reinforce the motif of orthodox practices rejected by YHWH because they were not backed up by 'justice and righteousness' (vv. 23–4; cf. 4:4–5; 5:5). So apparently virtuous activities have only merited a grimly appropriate punishment (the chiastic structure of vv. 25–6 equates 'Sakkuth' and 'Kaiwan' with 'sacrifices' and 'offerings'). But the verb-tense in v. 26 and the thrust of the sentence remain unclear and much debated (see Harper 1904/1979: 136–8). NRSV understands a future judgement oracle: Israel will worship foreign deities as a punishment (cf. Deut 4:28). Others understand a past tense, suggesting idolatry in the post-wilderness period (e.g. Stuart 1987: 355); there could even be a hint of the 'sin in the desert' motif (cf. Num 25:1–5). But judgement may come only in v. 27. A statement about the present is more likely in v. 26: '*nowadays* you take up

Sakkuth . . .' (cf. Harper 1904/1979: 137). There may be a deliberate link with 2:4: 'your images which . . .' perhaps supplies names for Judah's 'lies'. The identity of the deities is uncertain. NRSV's 'Sakkuth' assumes an Akkadian astral deity perhaps associated with Saturn (Borger 1988; Paul 1991: 195); 'Kaiwan' is better attested as Saturn; both names require us to repoint MT. The picture is probably of carrying statues in a procession. v. 27 gives the most explicit statement of Israel's fate so far (contrast with 2:13). 'Beyond Damascus' is, however, still vague, suggesting somewhere north-east of Samaria/Jerusalem, appropriate to both an Assyrian and a Babylonian deportation.

(6:1–7) Callous Carousing and its Outcome In 1:2 YHWH's 'roar' reverberated from Sion; now, Sion merits YHWH's anger: both kingdoms commit the same sins (contrast 2:4 with 2:6). v. 1 repeats the 'woe' of 5:18, with a vivid picture of a feast; the theme of misused wealth is resumed (2:6, 4:1). v. 1*a* accuses the complacent: 'feel secure' suggests ill-judged confidence ('trust', cf. Hos 10:13; Ps 146:3). v. 1*b* is difficult; it perhaps suggests ordinary Israelites approaching their leaders for justice. 'First of nations' (*rē'šît haggôyîm*) is sarcastic; 'nation' recurs with great effect in 6:14. In 3:9 foreigners were summoned to 'see' Samaria's sins. Now (v. 2), Israelites are to go abroad ('*ābar*, cf. 5:5, 'cross over'; 7:8; 8:2, 'pass by') and 'see' foreign places (cf. 1:3–2:3). Calneh and Hamath are (northern) Aramean city-states, Gath a (southern) Philistine city: a new all-inclusive 'pilgrimage' balances the three forbidden shrines (two northern, one southern) of 5:5. The Hebrew is uncertain; probably the idea is that Israel should learn from the downfall of once powerful nations (Calneh, Hamath, and Gath fell to Assyria in 738, 720, and 711 respectively; see NJB note). As in 1:3–2:6, Israel is assessed as other nations (cf. 9:7). The reference to David (v. 5) is obscure, but may suggest hubris. Wine flows freely (cf. 4:1); 'bowls' suggest drinking 'by the bowlful' (REB) or sacrilegiously using containers reserved for sacrificial drink-offerings. 'Finest' (*rē'šît*) echoes v. 1 (NRSV: first) and anticipates v. 7 (*rō'š*, 'head'; NRSV: first); it provides a *double entendre*, as *rē'šît* are often 'first fruits' (e.g. Ex 23:19). This concentration of vocabulary capable of cultic usage suggests that the 'orgy' is a *marzēaḥ*, a ceremonial meal associated with funerals (Barstad 1984: 128–42; King 1988: 137–61; cf. Andersen and Freedman 1989: 566–7). A funeral-feast here should be for the 'ruin' of Joseph/Israel (5:1–2, 16–17; cf. 5:15; ?Gen 37:23–8), but this feasting is, again, at the expense of the most vulnerable. The punchline (v. 7) delivers the verdict expected since v. 1. The theme of exile reappears; punishment fits crime through wordplay and assonance: 'revelry' (*mirzaḥ*) puns on 'bowls' (*mizrĕqê*); the 'loungers' (vv. 4, 7) are the 'first to go into exile' (*bĕrō'š gōlîm*); this echoes 'first of nations' (*rē'šît haggôyîm*, v. 1) and forms an *inclusio* for the whole passage.

(6:8–14) Futile Success v. 8, YHWH's second oath (cf. 4:2); Jacob's 'pride' (only here, and, differently, 8:7; see Andersen and Freedman 1989: 410) is probably the arrogance of the addressees of 6:1–7. YHWH specifically 'hates' (cf. 5:21) the 'strongholds' (their final appearance), the symbols of oppression last mentioned in 3:11 (hence 'pride' is made specific). YHWH's action, 'delivering up' the whole city, resembles the act for which Gaza was to be annihilated (1:6). Realistically, guilty and innocent perish together (contrast with 9:10). vv. 9–10, bringing out the dead (cf. 5:3). It is unclear how many people are trying to remove 'bones' (MT; NRSV: body), and why (some think, unconvincingly, of plague); what 'burning' implies (cf. 2:1?); and why YHWH's name may not be invoked (contrast 4:13; 5:8; 9:6); but evidently burial proceedings are involved. 'Taking up' recalls 'taking away' in 4:2; perhaps also 'taking up' the dirge in 5:1 (nāśā' each time).

Linked to vv. 9–10 by the catchword 'house', v. 11 expands v. 8. The destruction of the houses, suggesting earthquake, fulfils 3:15: 'great' and 'little' are a merismus, meaning 'every'. vv. 12–14 resume the themes of political overconfidence and perversion of justice. The questions in v. 12 (formally matching 3:3–6, the second involving an emendation) suggest self-evidently stupid activity. Perverting justice is equally counter-productive: it turns things upside-down (hāpak, again, cf. 4:11, 'overthrew'; 5:7, 'turn'). 'Poison' is rō'š, a homonym of the word for 'head' or 'first', which dominated 6:1–7: a grim pun. The perverters of justice (v. 13) are apparently boasting about military successes. Lo-debar and Karnaim are Transjordanian towns recaptured from Aram in the eighth century by Jeroboam II (cf. 2 Kings 14:25–8). For an evaluation of this period of Israelite recovery, in which Amos's activity is set (1:1), see Miller and Hayes (1986: 307–9). Lo-debar sounds like 'Lo-dabar', 'No-Word/Thing' (MT's vocalization); Karnaim means 'horns', a symbol of strength (cf. 1 Kings 22:11). There is a blasphemous ring to the first-person forms; such hubris discounts YHWH's responsibility for Israel's success (cf. 2:9–10). 'Strength' recalls 2:14 where Israel's army is already doomed. Punishment is by surprisingly normal means: instead of intervening personally, YHWH incites another 'nation' (gôy). Lebo-hamath and the Wadi Arabah represent the northern and southern limits of Israelite territory, encompassing both Israel and Judah (2 Kings 14:25). The 'nation' is unnamed (only with hindsight to be identified with Assyria or Babylon; but see AM 7:1). Also surprising is the relatively mild punishment: Israel will be 'oppressed', not annihilated. The end of national expansion is, however, certain. The dramatic placing of gôy forms an inclusio with gôyîm (6:1), marking the end of the immediate section and, with the stress on foreigners, perhaps the wider one (chs. 1–6).

Visions, Interpretations, Words of Judgement and Salvation (7:1–9:15)

First four interpreted visions explore Israel's fate (7:1–9; 8:1–3; a 'mantological anthology', Fishbane 1985: 447–59; 520–1; cf. Jer 1:11–14; Zech 1:7–6:8; Dan 7–12). A central narrative (7:10–17) demonstrates why judgement is irrevocable.

(7:1–3) Locusts Amos now speaks in his own voice. The setting is late spring; with no rain expected until autumn (cf. 4:7), locusts are catastrophic. If the 'king's mowings' were a tax, it would ruin the rural population; but the king's advantage is short-lived (7:9). Although starting a new section, v. 1 connects with 6:14. There is assonance between 'oppress' (lāqaṣ, 6:14) and 'latter growth' (leqeš, v. 1), between 'nation' (gôy, 6:14) and 'locusts' (gōbay, v. 1). Here, the connection is more than aural: the locusts could be the gôy; they symbolize invading armies (and vice versa) in Joel 1:4, 6–7; 2:2–11 (esp. 1:6 where they are called gôy). v. 1 perhaps functions as immediate

fulfilment of 6:14. In v. 2 the locusts have done their worst (for 'eat', 'ākal, cf. 1:4, 7, 10, 12, 14; 2:2, 5). Amos considers the affliction excessive. Previously he has been YHWH's ambassador to guilty Israel; now he is Jacob/Israel's ambassador to an angry God. 'Jacob' deserves pity, like 'Joseph' (6:6). Amos sees 'Jacob' as 'small'—very different from the nation's self-perception (6:13). 'Stand' (lit. arise) recalls 5:2; also 6:14, where YHWH 'raises' not Israel but a foe. The result of Amos's intercession is the cancellation of what might have happened (cf. Moses, Ex 32:9–14), reversing previous threats. Scholars who assign the visions to a historical Amos usually date them before the prophecies in chs. 1–6 (e.g. Andersen and Freedman 1989: 65–9); there are, however, no temporal links with what precedes; the visions, whatever their prehistory, are satisfactorily read as parallel accounts of Israel's judgement.

(7:4–6) Fire NRSV's 'shower of fire' adopts a plausible emendation of difficult Hebrew. 'Fire' may represent summer heat, drought, or lightning, but is also YHWH's punishing fire, promised in the Oracles against the Nations (cf. 1 Kings 18:38; Ex 9:23–4). Here, not merely buildings are 'devoured' but the world-ocean ('the great deep'), the source of the waters (cf. 5:8; 9:6). The dialogue in 7:1–6 is something new in Amos: previously YHWH has either made decisions or explained actions. Now Amos glimpses YHWH's forward planning (cf. 3:7) and intervenes to object. YHWH gives no reasons for his (temporary) change of heart: Amos's reasoning suffices.

(7:7–9) Tin YHWH resumes control; there is no further intercession or reprieve. The Hebrew is difficult to interpret; MT's 'ănāk probably means not 'plumbline' (NRSV) but 'tin' (Auld 1986: 18–20). YHWH stands 'near' or 'on' a city wall (cf. 1:7, 10, 14), plated with metal (?). The wall suggests supernatural strength (cf. Jer 1:18; 15:20; Zech 2:5), but the actual substance in YHWH's hand is the puzzling focus. Auld (1986: 20) suggests that as 'ănāk is a Mesopotamian loan-word, not the usual Hebrew word for tin, it might suggest military capability of an invader. Tin was a precious metal needed for the manufacture of bronze weapons; here, God has the potential to destroy his people. But the vision's interpretation may also involve punning on similar sounding words for 'groaning', so that 'I am setting 'ănāk' might sound like 'I am setting groaning in the midst...' (Andersen and Freedman 1989: 756–9; Stuart 1987: 373); this interpretation is reinforced by the wordplay in 8:1–3, verses which are formally close to vv. 7–8. v. 9 switches to the cult-centres, destined for destruction in 3:14. 'High places', originally Yahwistic shrines, became synonymous with forbidden practices; 'sanctuaries' suggest major cult-centres (7:13). Tradition associates Isaac with Beersheba (cf. 5:5; 8:14). v. 9 ends with an explicit threat, different from earlier ones. The dynasty of Jeroboam II (cf. 1:1) foundered in c.745 BCE (Soggin 1993: 238). In line with the Oracles against the Nations (but unlike 6:14), YHWH himself is the aggressor.

(7:10–17) Amos and Amaziah Alternating first- and third-person material occurs also in Hos 1–3; Isa 6–8. Such narratives, in their received form, are literary rather than (auto)biographical; they are a recognizable genre, functioning to establish a prophet's authority (Auld 1986: 25), though they may, of course, be based on earlier, and authentic, material. An 'adversarial centrepiece' also occurs in other mantological anthologies (e.g. Zech 3:1–10; 11:4–16; see Larkin 1994: 223–33); for the relationship of these verses with 1 Kings 13, 2 Chr 25:14–16, see Ackroyd (1977: 71–87). Here, the confrontation between Amos and Amaziah justifies YHWH's decision to punish. The central theme is again opposition to prophets (cf. 2:12). In v. 10 'sent' contrasts with what YHWH intends to 'send' in chs. 1–2. Ironically, Amaziah places Amos 'in the very centre' of the kingdom, YHWH's position in 5:17; 7:8. Amaziah introduces Amos with the 'messenger' formula ('Thus . . . has said'), giving his words prophetic authority. He acknowledges Amos's prophetic standing, addressing him as 'seer' (cf. 1:1), but by forbidding him to prophesy at the national shrine (v. 13), Amaziah effectively silences him in the very place about which the prophetic word was given. Amos's refusal (v. 14) of the name 'prophet' (nābî'—not used by Amaziah, nor in 1:1; cf. Hab 1:1; Hag 1:1; Zech 1:1) is disconcerting, whether the ambiguous Hebrew refers to present (NRSV, NJB) or past (REB). In 2:12 a nābî' is one of YHWH's greatest gifts; he knows YHWH's thoughts (3:7). Amos seems to distinguish between prophecy as paid profession (cf. 'earn your bread', v. 12), and individual call (v. 15; cf. 2:11–12; 3:8; Zech 13:5; Auld 1986: 34), though he accepts the activity of 'prophesying' (v. 15). His occupations situate him outside court and cult (cf. 1:1). The shepherd called from his flock has intertextual echoes with Moses (Ex 3), perhaps also David (Ps 78:70; 2 Sam 7:8); cf. Elisha (1 Kings 19:19–20). But a tension remains between this passage and chs. 2–3. This is characteristic of other places in OT which deal with the nature and role of prophets; at the time of the formation of the prophetic corpus the problem was evidently not resolved (see Carroll 1983: 25–31; Overholt 1990: 3–29, 51–4; Auld 1990: 31–2, for an ongoing debate.) Amos's commission is surprising: he must prophesy to 'my people' (rare in Amos, cf. 7:7), yet the addressees of 2:6–6:14 are the powerful rich, not the whole people (contra Carroll 1992: 38, 275). Finally (vv. 16–17), Amos demonstrates the effects of opposing YHWH's prophet: he prophesies! Amaziah must 'hear' (cf. 3:1, 13; 4:1; 5:1): his own words, echoing 2:12, convict him. His children suffer the fate prophesied for Jeroboam's family ('house', 7:9); their 'fall' recalls 5:2. His own exile will take him where he (rather than the land) will be ritually unclean (cf. his wife's defilement), incapable of exercising priesthood. His own words (v. 11) form an inclusio with v. 17: Israel will indeed be exiled.

(8:1–3) Ripe Fruit Formally and thematically this vision matches 7:7–9. 'Summer [i.e. ripe] fruit' (qāyis) sounds positive (cf. 2:13). But 'end' is qēs; the pun on qāyis effects the meaning. 'Songs' recalls 5:23; 6:5, but are now shrieks over the dead (cf. 5:16–17). 'That day' suggests the day of YHWH (5:18–20). 'Be silent!' recalls 6:10, suggesting a scene so terrible that even mourning must cease.

(8:4–14) Judgement Re-Emphasized

(8:4–6) Sharp Practice Condemned 'Hear' links v. 4 with 3:1, 13; 4:1; 5:1, but, by picking up vocabulary from 2:7, also recalls Israel's first indictment (cf. 5:11). Self-condemnation is typical of this book (5:14; 6:13; 7:10). Impatience with cultic constraints contrasts with enthusiasm for religious observance (4:4–5). 'Be over' is 'ābar, cf. YHWH's refusal to 'pass by' (7:8; 8:2). The practices envisaged are illegal (Lev 19:35–6; Deut

25:13–15), another perversion of justice. v. 6 quotes 2:6; more self-condemnation.

(8:7–10) YHWH's Final Oath (cf. 4:2; 6:8), 'pride' is probably a divine title, so meaning 'himself'; but it also ironically echoes 6:8 where YHWH 'hates' Jacob's 'pride' (i.e. arrogance). 'Never' occurred in 1:11 (Edom's undying enmity); again YHWH exhibits a trait elsewhere condemned (1:9, 6:8). YHWH's oath establishes cosmic order (Murray 1992: 1–13); here, sin undoes this order with disastrous effects: earthquake ('tremble') and flooding (cf. 5:8; 9:6). v. 9 picks up 4:13; 5:8, 18–20, perhaps evoking a solar eclipse. The mourning theme reappears (v. 10; first in 1:2, where 'wither' could also be 'mourn'; so NJB, cf. 5:16b). 'Turn' is hāpak, cf. 4:11; 5:7, 8; 6:12. 'Feasts' (haggîm) are those repudiated in 5:21, so it is cult-centres that are overthrown. A different kind of ritual results (cf. Joel 1:5–14; 2:12–17; burlesqued in Jon 3:4–9); praise-hymn becomes dirge (cf. 5:1). The inclusion of 'baldness' (i.e. shaving of forelocks) indicates a stance different from Deut 14:1. For 'mourning for an only child', cf. Jer 6:26; Zech 12:10.

(8:11–14) A Theme Reworked Drought and thirst are now related to prophetic silence and misdirected oaths. The time-formula of v. 11 recurs only in 9:13 (see Wolff 1977: 324–5). 'Send' echoes 1:4, 7, 10, 12; 2:2, 5; 'famine' evokes 4:6–8. But this famine is spiritual, not physical, perhaps to be connected with 2:12, 7:12–13, a powerful comment on the importance of the prophetic words without which YHWH's designs cannot be known (3:7). vv. 12–14 rework 4:6–11 (cf. 'wander', 4:8). 'Seeking' interprets 5:4, 6, 14, and identifies 'living' with YHWH's prophetic word. But, as often in Amos, people come to their senses too late. Those destined for punishment are not perverters of justice (8:4–8), but 'young women' (bĕtû-lôt, cf. 5:2, 'maiden') and 'young men' (bahûrîm, cf. 2:11, 'youths'). Their 'fall' recalls 5:2. They, like YHWH, have been swearing oaths (in reaction to YHWH's silence?). NRSV's 'by Ashimah' adopts an emendation giving the name of an Aramean goddess, cf. 2 Kings 17:30 (Barstad 1984: 157–81). MT has 'ašmat, 'sin/guilt(-offering)'; this also fits, either suggesting the 'calves' at Bethel and Dan (1 Kings 12:28–30); or constituting a sarcastic Judean comment on the ineffectiveness of any northern sin-offerings. In any case, 'ašmat would sound like 'ăšîmâh (NJB). Dan appears only here in Amos (cf. Judg 18). For 'your god', cf. 2:8. For Beersheba, cf. 5:5. 'Way' (derek) is obscure; emendations give 'beloved' (a divine title) or 'pantheon'. If derek is retained, it could mean either 'power' (another divine title, Soggin 1987: 140–1), 'processional route' (REB), or 'pilgrimage' (NJB). The general sense is clear: heterodox or idolatrous practices at sanctuaries (even southern ones) lead to death: a new emphasis.

(9:1–10) Final, but Mitigated, Judgement

(9:1–4) A Fifth Vision (cf. Ezek 9), this differs formally from the others, though there are links with 7:7–8 (cf. Isa 6:1–4; 1 Kings 13:1); cf. 2:8. The sanctuary is unnamed, so could be either Bethel or Jerusalem, or both. 'Shake' is the verb from which earthquake (1:1) is derived. YHWH's attack on survivors recalls 1:8; the impossibility of escape 2:14 (cf. 9:8a). vv. 2–4 are comparable in artistry to 1:1–2:6; 3:3–8; 4:6–11. The language is hyperbolic (cf. Ps 139:7–12), with many cross-references. 'Carmel' recalls 1:2, its 'top' (rō'š) as vulnerable as the 'heads' (*rōʾš*) in v. 1. 'Taking' (v. 2) contrasts with 7:15, where YHWH 'took' Amos. The 'sea-serpent' recalls the 'snake' in 5:19 (both *nāḥāš*). For YHWH 'commanding', cf. 6:11. YHWH's gaze for 'harm' (*rāʿâ*) and not 'good' recalls 'good' and 'evil' (*raʿ*) in 5:14–15. For YHWH's eyes cf. 9:8 (usually a sign of favour, e.g. Ps 33:18–19; 34:15; their withdrawal spells disaster, e.g. Isa 8:17). This passage intensifies the theme of YHWH's all-embracing power (cf. the Oracles against the Nations and doxologies).

(9:5–6) Final Doxology The appropriate response to 9:1–4 is 'mourning' (cf. 5:16). v. 6*a* is obscure but has creation elements. 'Upper chambers' requires emendation (MT lit. stairways). In Hebrew cosmology this is the region above the sky, where YHWH lives and controls the waters. v. 6*b* repeats 5:8*b*; cf. 4:13.

(9:7–8*a*) Exodus Revisited Key moments from earlier sections are reworked. Israel is addressed directly for the first time since 6:14. 'People of Israel' last occurred in 4:5; before that only in 2:11; 3:1. The comparison with the 'Ethiopians' subverts 3:2, as do the exodus stories, relativizing Israel's trump card. Israel's exodus recalls 2:10; 3:1; Aram's 1:5. Philistine origins have not appeared earlier ('Caphtor' is usually identified with Crete). v. 7 reinforces chs. 1–2: Israel will be treated no differently from other nations (does this also annul 3:1's rationale for punishment, opening the way for v. 8*b*'s escape-clause?). v. 8*a* echoes 9:2–4. 'The 'sinful kingdom' may be Israel (cf. 7:13) or, generically, any sinful kingdom (cf. 6:2).

(9:8*b*–10) Selective Punishment v. 8*b*, with the abrupt and unique 'except' fulfils the hope of 'it may be . . .' (5:15*b*). The 'House of Jacob' (cf. 3:13), the 'remnant of Joseph' (5:15), will, after all, survive. Harvest imagery reappears (cf. 2:13). 'Shake' is *nûaʿ* as in 4:8; 8:12 ('wander'). The image is of winnowed grain (cf. 1:3) passed through a sieve which retained pebbles and dross (Sir 27:4); v. 10 explains the 'sieving' as war. A distinction is now made between sinners ('pebbles') and (by implication) the innocent. The 'sinners' are those of 6:1–6 ('overtake' is the same verb as 'bring near', 6:3); cf. 8:4–6.

(9:11–15) Future Glory

(9:11–12) National Restoration Judgement now unequivocally yields to salvation. When 'on that day' last occurred (8:14; cf. 2:16; 8:3), the sinful young people had 'fallen', never to 'rise'. Here, YHWH himself 'raises' the 'fallen', reversing 5:2, 8:14. Hence, the mysterious 'booth of David' matches 'maiden Israel'; both represent the nation. Perhaps restoration of the united kingdom is suggested (2 Sam 8; cf. Hos 1:11; 3:5). 'Booth' may continue the harvest motif, referring to temporary shelters at harvest-time (Isa 1:8; cf. Jon 4:5); but a military context is also possible (2 Sam 11:11; 1 Kings 20:12). 'Breaches' (cf. 4:3), 'ruins' and 'rebuild' suggest reconstruction of a city. 'Rebuild' is the same as 'build' in 9:6: YHWH constructs places for himself on earth as in heaven. The purpose (v. 12) is to 'possess' (lit. inherit, cf. 2:10) the territory of others. The situation of chs. 1–2 is radically changed. Edom (cf. Ob 1–4; in post-exilic times a quite substantial 'remnant'!) replaces the 'Amorites' (2:10). 'All the nations' echoes 9:9, reversing that situation. 'Calling by name' can be a legal formula expressing ownership: as all nations are YHWH's, he has them in his gift.

'Who does this' perhaps authenticates a daring eschatological prophecy (cf. Isa 9:7?).

(9:13–15) Paradisal Promise v. 13 chiastically reverses 8:11 (cf. 9:11; 8:13). Finally, harvest language is entirely positive. For unending fertility cf. Lev 26:3–6 (where, however, obedience to Torah is required). For the richness of the promised land cf. Deut 8:7–10; for 'overtake', now used positively, cf. 6:3; 9:10. 'Flow' comes from the same root as 'melt' in 9:5; again, a peaceful image substituted for a terrifying one (cf. Hos 14:5–7; Joel 4:18). v. 14 reverses 9:4: 'my people' are no longer objects of wrath. YHWH restores, but the people rebuild (contrast with 9:11); the curse of 5:11 is annulled ('cities' replace 'houses'); the replanting of vineyards brings the drink motif to a happy conclusion. The third promise puts right all the damage detailed in 4:9; 'eat' loses its menace. Finally (v. 15) YHWH himself 'plants' Israel; a farmer God balances a herdsman prophet (1:1). 'Upon their land' reverses 7:17. Resettlement is permanent (cf. Ezek 39:25–9); the gift of the land recalls 2:10. The final prophecy (salvation) is authenticated by 'says YHWH' as was the first prophecy (judgement 1:3, 5). The ultimate word is 'your God' (*ʾĕlōhêkā*). This title first occurred in 4:12, a summons to a terrifying encounter. In 8:14, it was addressed blasphemously to other deities. Now it can be used without presumption or fear.

Epilogue From the perspective of post-exilic Jews, centred on the Jerusalem cult, the northern kingdom had been destroyed for ever, Judah was part of the Persian empire, but life beyond judgement had been experienced, and better things were hoped for (even if 5:13 hints at the reality; cf. Neh 9:36–7?). Yet the past remains relevant; hence, in this prophetic book, judgement is not softened with unconditional hope until the end (unlike Hosea, Micah), although it is hinted at occasionally. By reading their own history as an eighth-century prophecy about the northern kingdom, those responsible for Amos as we know it were able to express convictions about past, present, and future. Amos is a brilliantly crafted text; when it is read backwards from its post-exilic closure (whatever its earlier stages), and outwards from its theological centre (ch. 5), it works on several levels simultaneously; this, despite tensions and ambiguities, substantially makes sense of its unique blend of warnings, exhortations and promises.

REFERENCES

Ackroyd, P. R. (1977), 'A Judgment Narrative between Kings and Chronicles: An Approach to Amos 7.9–17', in G. W. Coats (ed.), *Canon and Authority* (Philadelphia: Fortress Press), 71–87. Repr. in P. R. Ackroyd, *Studies in the Religious Tradition of the Old Testament* (London: SCM Press, 1987), 196–208.

Andersen, F. I., and Freedman, D. N. (1989), *Amos: A New Translation with Introduction and Commentary*, AB 24A.

Auld, A. G. (1986), *Amos*, Old Testament Guides (Sheffield: JSOT).

—— (1990), 'Prophecy in Books: A Rejoinder', *JSOT* 48: 31–2.

Barstad, H. (1984), *The Religious Polemics of Amos: Studies in the Preaching of Am. 7b–8; 4, 1–3; 5, 1–27; 6, 4–7; 8, 14*, VTSup 34 (Leiden: Brill).

Barton, J. (1980), *Amos' Oracles Against the Nations: A Study of Amos 1.3–2.5*, SOTSMS 6 (Cambridge: Cambridge University Press).

—— (1995), *Isaiah 1–39* (Sheffield: Academic Press).

Borger, R. (1988), 'Amos 5,26, Apostelgeschichte 7,43 und šurpu II, 180', ZAW 100/1: 70–81.

Bovati, P., and Meynet, R. (1994), La Fin d'Israël: Paroles d'Amos (Paris: Cerf).

Carroll, R. (1983), 'Poets not Prophets', JSOT 27: 25–31.

—— (1990), 'Whose Prophet? Whose History? Whose Social Reality? Troubling the Interpretative Community Again: Notes Towards a Response to T. W. Overholt's Critique', JSOT 48: 33–49.

Carroll R., M. D. (1992), Contexts for Amos: Prophetic Poetics in Latin-American Perspective, JSOT Sup 132 (Sheffield: JSOT).

Coggins, R. J. (1994), 'The Minor Prophets: One Book or Twelve?' in S. Porter et al. (eds.), Crossing the Boundaries: Essays in Biblical Interpretation in Honour of Michael D. Goulder (Leiden: Brill), 57–68.

Collins, T. (1993), The Mantle of Elijah: The Redaction Criticism of the Prophetical Books (Sheffield: JSOT), 59–87.

Coote, R. B. (1981), Amos among the Prophets (Philadelphia: Fortress).

Crenshaw, J. L. (1975), Hymnic Affirmation of Divine Justice: The Doxologies of Amos and Related Texts in the Old Testament, SBLDS 24 (Missoula, Mont.: Scholars Press).

Davies, P. R. (1989), 'Prophetic Literature', in J. Rogerson and P. R. Davies (eds.), The Old Testament World (Cambridge: Cambridge University Press), 274–92.

Fishbane, M. (1985), Biblical Interpretation in Ancient Israel (Oxford: Clarendon).

Harper, W. R. (1904/1979), A Critical and Exegetical Commentary on Amos and Hosea (Edinburgh: T. and T. Clark).

King, P. J. (1988), Amos, Hosea, Micah—An Archaeological Commentary (Philadelphia: Westminster).

Larkin, K. (1994), The Eschatology of Second Zechariah: A Study of the Formation of a Mantological Wisdom Anthology (Kampen: Kok Pharos).

Miller, J. M., and Hayes, J. H. (1986), A History of Ancient Israel and Judah (London, SCM).

Murray, R. (1992), The Cosmic Covenant, Heythrop Monographs, 7 (London: Sheed & Ward).

Nogalski, J. (1993), Literary Precursors to the Book of the Twelve (Berlin: de Gruyter), 74–122.

Overholt, T. W. (1990), 'Prophecy in History: The Social Reality of Intermediation', and ' "It is Difficult to Read" ', JSOT 48: 3–29, 51–4.

Paul, S. M. (1991), Amos, Hermeneia (Philadelphia: Fortress).

Smalley, W. A. (1979), 'Recursion Patterns and the Sectioning of Amos', The Bible Translator, 30/1: 118–27.

Soggin, J. A. (1987), The Prophet Amos: A Translation and Commentary (London: SCM).

—— (1993), An Introduction to the History of Israel and Judah, 2nd edn. (London: SCM).

Stuart, D. (1987), Hosea–Jonah, WBC 31 (Waco, Tex.: Word), 274–400.

Waard, J. de (1977), 'The Chiastic Structure of Amos V 1–17', VT 27: 170–7.

Wolff, H.-W. (1977), Joel and Amos, Hermeneia (Philadelphia: Fortress), 89–392.

30. Obadiah

REX MASON

INTRODUCTION

A. The Prophet. 1. The Man. Perhaps it is fitting that the prophet who has given his name to the shortest book in the OT has the briefest Press Notice—merely his name. Indeed, we might not even know that, since it means 'One who serves (or worships) YHWH', and so it might be a descriptive title. Perhaps this brevity is because he was unknown to the latest editors of the book, or they thought he was so well known to his readers that no details were necessary (Ben Zvi 1996: 14–19). It is also possible the title was given to an anonymous prophecy to bring the number of the smaller prophetic collections up to twelve (Ackroyd 1992).

2. His Times. No biographical or chronological details are given to us. Nor is it easy, for reasons explained below, to deduce the historical situation of his activity from the contents of the book.

B. The Book. 1. Genre. The title 'The vision of Obadiah' places the book firmly within the category of 'prophecy' in the Old Testament canon (e.g. Isa 1:1; Nah 1:1). The phrase 'concerning Edom' allies it with the Oracles Against the Nations (OAN), a type of prophetic oracle which occurs in most of the prophetic books of the OT. The fact that at v. 15 the book switches to promises of salvation for Jacob in no way conflicts with this designation since oracles of judgement upon Israel's foes and salvation for them frequently occur together and, indeed, the OAN is (usually) a form of 'salvation oracle' for the people of God (Barton 1980: 3–7). If they were sometimes used in a cultic setting they may not only have been intended to announce such promises but actually to help bring them about (see Bič 1953 and, more temperately, Coggins 1985).

2. Literary Connections. One of the remarkable features of Obadiah is the number of connections with other biblical books. The closest is between vv. 1b–5 and Jer 49:9, 14–16 with more general connections between v. 9 and Jer 49:22 and v. 16 and Jer 49:12. For a synoptic arrangement of these passages see Mason (1991: 89–90). Scholars have often debated which one of these is the original. However, it is now recognized that it is much more likely that there was a stock of prophetic oracles (perhaps current in temple worship) and that prophets drew from such a common source and adapted it for their own use. This is the view of Ben Zvi who has most fully and recently explored the issue (Ben Zvi 1996: 99–114). Another close parallel is between v. 17 and Joel 2:32 (HB 3:5). Other echoes of more general prophetic concepts are examined in the commentary.

3. Allusive and Ambiguous Characteristics. Apart from actual textual problems (dealt with as they occur in the commentary) there is a strange 'allusive', sometimes even ambiguous quality to Obadiah. It was said above that it is difficult to pinpoint historical events from the text. This is partly because it is often unclear whether a past or future event is being described. The tenses of the Hebrew verbs are not much help here since a perfect tense, usually denoting an event completed by the time of speaking, can be used in the sense of a 'prophetic perfect', a future event which is seen by the prophet as so certain that it can be described as if it has already happened. Again it is not always easy to know if a future tense is alluding to what is yet to happen, or is a colourful way of describing a past event. We shall see this is a particular problem in vv. 12–14 where the Eng. versions differ considerably in their rendering. Nor is it always clear who is addressing whom. Further, attacks on apparently particular peoples such as Edom/Esau turn out to be attacks on very general human attitudes such as self-confidence, boasting of one's own wisdom, betraying promises, while a specific nation appears to be taken as some kind of symbol for pagan nations in general. Ben Zvi makes a good deal of this aspect of the book arguing that it means we cannot use it for making historical inferences (1996: esp. 260–7).

4. Contents and Structure. There is some disagreement on the subdivisions to be found within this short text, but the plan I follow is set out in the commentary. This, broadly, agrees with Snyman's divisions (1989). Slightly different analyses may be found in Dick (1984), Clark (1991), and Ben Zvi (1996). These are based on their recognition of literary and rhetorical markers. It is open to question whether or not, where earlier prophetic material is being used later, some of these markers may have achieved a purely conventional force, and so it seems better to divide by the development of the argument as far as this can be traced. Whatever the date and origin of the individual sections, they have been crafted together skilfully by means of link-words and other literary devices, probably well on in the post-exilic period.

5. Theology. The book of Obadiah has often been dismissed as purely a piece of vindictive hate against Edom, a hatred incited by memories of Edom's failure to help when Judah was in trouble. We may presume this certainly lies behind some of the original prophetic material which has been incorporated into the book, but we shall see how the issues have been broadened out, so that 'Edom' has become a symbol, not only of all pagan nations, but of certain sinful human characteristics (Coggins 1985; Cresson 1972; Mason 1991; Ben Zvi 1996). Ultimately, what is hoped for is the rule, not so much of Israel as a nation, but of God, in whose kingdom such things will have no place.

6. Place in Canon. In the HB the book is placed immediately after Amos and this is often thought to be because it was seen as a commentary on Amos 9:11–12.

C. Israel and Edom. The relations between Judah and Edom were turbulent over a long period, yet there was a strong note in the patriarchal traditions of their relatedness. Here, and elsewhere, Esau and Jacob are depicted as brothers (Bartlett 1977). David is said to have subdued Edom (2 Sam 8:12). There is a record of their successful rebellion in the time of Jehoram in the ninth century BCE (2 Kings 8:20–2). Some early conservative scholars dated Obadiah to this occasion (e.g. Keil 1866; von Orelli 1893). The Chronicler records Edom as taking advantage of pressure on Ahaz in the eighth century (2 Chr 28:16–19). A sense of betrayal by Edom when the Babylonians invaded Judah and captured Jerusalem in 586 BCE is marked in some exilic and post-exilic literature, e.g. Ps 137:7, Lam 4:21. A considerable number of commentators have assigned Obadiah to this occasion, usually dating it shortly after the event (e.g. Rudolph 1971; Weiser 1974; Allen 1976). Later, the Edomites were subject to pressures from the incursions of the Nabateans and were pushed up into the region of the Negeb, a region therefore later known as Idumea. Some scholars have dated Obadiah to this time in view of the (future, as they see it) threat to Edom in vv. 1c–10 and

especially the reference about being 'driven to the border' by her enemies (v. 7). So e.g. Wellhausen (1892); Bewer (1911). Wellhausen's suggestion that Obadiah might be 'commentary' on Mal 1:2–5 is interesting. For a detailed history of Edom and the Edomites see Bartlett (1989), and for the place of Edom in the biblical literature see Dicou (1994). The fact is, as has been said, that the text is not detailed enough to locate its historical context, and we have to allow for a development of the text in which material that once related to one situation is found to have relevance and force in others, and in which the lessons of one incident are found to have more general and even universal significance.

COMMENTARY

(1 ab) Superscription See OB B.1. 'Vision' is a technical term meaning 'prophetic revelation' or 'prophetic message'.

(1c–5) An oracle threatening (or reporting) an attack against an apparently impregnable enemy.

(1 bcd) Although the parallel in Jer 49:14 and LXX have the singular, 'I have heard', the plural 'we' suits this context better. It may suggest the sense of the prophet's identity with his hearers but is far more likely to be an allusion to the 'council of Heaven', admission to which was the sign of a true prophet (cf. Jer 23:22; 1 Kings 22). The call to battle is a literary device (Bach 1962).

(v. 2) First-person speech of YHWH shows it is he who is actually attacking the power: the human confederates, 'the nations', are only his instruments.

(v. 3) This human power typifies human pride. The height and apparent inaccessibility of its strongholds which God brings down is a familiar prophetic theme, particularly of Isaiah (2:6–19, cf. Ezek 35). The power is unnamed in these verses but some see in the use of the word 'rock' an allusion to the name of the Edomite city Sela (cf. 2 Kings 14:7). Irony marks the question of the power 'Who will bring me down to the ground?'—the answer comes in v. 4.

(v. 4) For the same imagery see Num 24:21 and cf. Isa 14:12–15.

(v. 5) NRSV follows many when it marks a break between vv. 4 and 5 because of the 'concluding' prophetic formula at the end of v. 4, 'says the LORD'. Yet see OB B.4. v. 5 really continues the thought of the threatened downfall of the apparently impregnable city. There is a play on words here. The verb which gives the noun 'grape-gatherers' also means to fortify a city or, literally, to make it 'cut off, inaccessible'. It also forms the first three letters of the name 'Bozrah', an Edomite town (Am 1:12; Isa 34:5–7).

(vv. 6–9) The application of the threat to Edom The tenses throughout are past, but see OB B.3, C. v. 6, Edom is here called 'Esau' just as Judah/Jerusalem is referred to as 'Jacob' thus linking the relations between the two countries to the patriarchal stories which portray them as brothers. In these Esau is the 'elder brother' and it is Jacob who cheats him. Yet this book shows that God 'chooses' the younger and the trickster, and why. It is a theme also found in Mal 1:2–5 and in the NT (Rom 9:6–13 and, in a general way, in the parable of the Prodigal Son). vv. 7–9, it is an irony that Edom's allies betray them.

Edom, for all its wise men (v. 8) has shown extraordinary folly in its military alliances, the futility of which in the face of YHWH's judgement is another familiar prophetic theme (e.g. Isa 31:1–3). The Hebrew has only 'your bread' in v. 7d. NRSV follows a suggestion of Davies (1977) here, but the word alone may suggest this anyway. The meaning of the word 'trap' is uncertain but there is no doubt of the general thrust. The last phrase, 'There is no understanding of it', is another ironic dig at Edom's vaunted wisdom, and is echoed in v. 8, which says that God will destroy such wisdom and understanding as might be there. 'Teman', another Edomite town, gives its name to Edom as a whole here.

(vv. 10–14, 15b) The reasons for Edom's fate Usually the grounds of accusation are given before the announcement of judgement in prophetic oracles of this nature (Westermann 1967: 142–62), but this order gives added dramatic force. v. 10, NRSV follows many in seeing the last word from v. 9, 'for the slaughter' as really the beginning of v. 10. Note that it is the betrayal of fraternal obligations which is at the heart of the accusation. This opens up a wider concern of YHWH's judgement than any merely one-off historical incident between two nations. The irony is that Edom's 'allies' behave in the same way to her. v. 11, Edom is charged with *lack* of action so perhaps the 'slaughter and violence' done to Jacob (v. 10) was that Edom allowed it to happen by such callous indifference. vv. 12–14 have a series of lines all beginning with a construction which would normally be rendered as a prohibition, 'Do not gloat' etc. (see REB, JB, and NIV). Since most commentators feel that this reflects a situation which *has* happened and of which the prophet was an eyewitness they translate it as NRSV has, 'You should not have gloated'. Again, however, there may be a studied ambivalence here suggesting that this now embodies a timeless truth about just and compassionate behaviour towards 'brethren' (see Ben Zvi 1996: 144–6).

Note also the recurrent theme of 'the day' in these verses. In this case it is YHWH's 'day' of judgement against Judah for their sins. But that in no way excuses Edom or the 'nations' who will know their own 'day' (vv. 8, 15a), which will also be a 'day' of salvation for God's people ('*my* people', v. 13a, my emphasis). v. 15b, the simplest explanation is that this summarized vv. 10–14 with its theme of a divine *lex talionis* against Edom.

(vv. 15a, 16–18) The day of YHWH Now 'the day' is a day of judgement for 'the nations', of which Edom is taken as typical, and of salvation for the people of God. v. 16, Judah is now addressed. The imagery of judgement as 'drinking a cup' is a familiar one, cf. Ps 75:8 (HB 9). In a reversal of roles it will now be 'the nations' which drink it. v. 17 parallels Joel 2:32 (HB 3:5). The Hebrew word for 'remnant' is a feminine singular noun. By rendering it as 'those who escape' NRSV makes 'it shall be holy' refer to the city. The text, however, here and in Joel, suggests that it is the 'remnant' which will be holy. Thus the reader is not being incited to wallow in a sense of nationalistic revenge and superiority but in a belief in the overthrow by God of all that is represented by Edom/the nations, that is of all evil, and the establishment in his kingdom of only that which is holy. The same Hebrew word, pointed differently, can mean either 'will possess their possessions' or 'dispossess

those who dispossessed them' (so NRSV). v. 18, God, in his judgement against 'Esau' and all she stands for will make use of 'the house of Jacob' and (for the first time in this book) 'the house of Israel'. Perhaps this is to suggest that the 'remnant' will represent the 'true Israel'.

(vv. 19–20) Geographical details of the possessions of God's people This is a prosaic and laboured addition to the book trying to give the readers some details of just what will be 'their possessions'. NRSV renders the text as it stands, but it appears to be in such disorder that it is very difficult to know just what is being predicted. There is a similar expansion in Zech 14:10–11, in a chapter which also stresses the 'kingship of YHWH' as v. 21 does here. Parallels with Joel and Zech 9–14 may suggest that this represents the latest part of Obadiah.

(v. 21) Conclusion Again a Hebrew word may be pointed differently to mean 'those who have been saved', so NRSV, or 'saviours' (NRSV marg.). It is interesting that the author, in his picture of the future, goes back to the era of the Judges before the monarchy in Israel. The only king here is YHWH. The kingdom is his, not Israel's.

REFERENCES

Ackroyd, P. R. (1992), 'Obadiah, Book of', *ABD*, v. 2–4.

Allen, L. C. (1976), *The Books of Joel, Obadiah, Jonah and Micah*, NICOT (Grand Rapids, Mich.: Eerdmans).

Bach, R. (1962), *Die Aufforderungen zur Flucht und zum Kampf im alttestamentlichen Prophetenspruch*, WMANT 9 (Neukirchen: Neukirchener Verlag).

Bartlett, J. (1977), 'The Brotherhood of Edom', *JSOT* 4: 2–27.

——(1989), *Edom and the Edomites*, JSOT Sup 77 (Sheffield: JSOT).

Barton J. (1980), *Amos's Oracles against the Nations*, SOTSMS 6 (Cambridge: Cambridge University Press).

Ben Zvi, E. (1996), *A Historical-Critical Study of the Book of Obadiah*, BZAW 242 (Berlin: de Gruyter).

Bewer, J. A. (1911), 'Obadiah,' in J. M. P. Smith, W. H. Ward, and J. A. Bewer, *Micah, Zephaniah, Nahum, Habakkuk, Obadiah and Joel*, ICC (Edinburgh: T. & T. Clark).

Bič, M. (1953), 'Zur Problematik des Buches Obadja', *Congress Volume, Copenhagen*, VTS (Leiden: Brill), 11–25.

Clark, D. J. (1991), 'Obadiah Reconsidered', *Bible Translator*, 42: 326–36.

Coggins, R. J. (1985), 'Judgement between Brothers: A Commentary on the Book of Obadiah', in R. J. Coggins and S. P. Re'emi (eds.), *Israel among the Nations: A Commentary on the Books of Nahum, Obadiah, Esther*, ITC (Grand Rapids, Mich.: Eerdmans, and Edinburgh: Handsel), 65–100.

Cresson, B. C. (1972), 'The Condemnation of Edom in Postexilic Judaism', in J. M. Efrid (ed.), *The Use of the Old Testament in the New and Other Essays: Studies in Honor of William Franklin Stinespring* (Durham, NC: Duke University Press), 125–48.

Davies, G. I. (1977), 'A New Solution to a Crux in Obadiah 7', *VT* 27: 484–7.

Dick, M. B. (1984), 'A Syntactic Study of the Book of Obadiah', *Semitics*, 9: 1–29.

Dicou, B. (1994), *Edom, Israel's Brother and Antagonist*, JSOT Sup 169 (Sheffield: JSOT).

Keil, C. F. (1866), *Commentary on the Minor Prophets*, BKAT 4. ET (1880).

Mason, R. (1991), *Micah, Nahum, Obadiah*, Old Testament Guides (Sheffield: JSOT).

Orelli, C. von (1888), *Die zwölf kleinen Propheten ausgelegt*. ET (Edinburgh: T. & T. Clark, 1893).

Rudolph, W. (1971), *Joel, Amos, Obadja, Jona*, KAT 13/2 (Gütersloh: Mohn).

Snyman, S. D. (1989), 'Cohesion in the Book of Obadiah', *ZAW* 101: 59–71.

Weiser, A. (1974), *Die Propheten Hosea, Amos, Obadja, Jona, Micha*, ATD 24 (Göttingen: Vandenhoeck & Ruprecht).

Wellhausen, J. (1892), *Skizzen und Vorarbeiten*, v. *Die Kleinen Propheten* (Berlin: Reimer).

Westermann, C. (1967), *Basic Forms of Prophetic Speech*, tr. H. White (London: Lutterworth); German original, 2nd edn. (Munich: Chr. Kaiser, 1964).

31. Jonah

PETER J. M. SOUTHWELL

INTRODUCTION

1. We read in 2 Kings 14:23–7 of a Galilean prophet called Jonah, son of Amittai, who successfully predicted a national expansion for Israel in the reign of Jeroboam II (786–746 BCE). The book of Jonah, which appears on literary, linguistic, and historical grounds to have been written in the fourth century, tells a story about this prophet designed to show the limits of mere nationalism as an expression of the purposes of God. Faced with the challenge of addressing God's word to the great Assyrian city of Nineveh, Jonah flees the task. Brought back and recommissioned by God he at length undertakes it, only to be dismayed by the comprehensive repentance of the Ninevites and consequent forgiveness by God, whose nature is always to have mercy. Jonah's error was to magnify God's wrath at the expense of his compassion.

2. Passages of the Old Testament known to our author appear to include Jer 18:8 ('if that nation, concerning which I have spoken, turns from its evil, I will change my mind about the disaster that I intended to bring on it')—cf. Jon 3:10—and Joel 2:13–14, which significantly includes the phrase 'and relents from punishing' cited in Jon 4:2 (cf. 3:9) despite its being absent from the original Hebrew formulation of God's character in Ex 34:6–7. There are also echoes of the Elijah story (1 Kings 19:4–5, cf. Jon 4:6–8) and of Ezekiel's lament over Tyre (Ezek 26:16, cf. Jon 3:6; Ezek 27:25–9, cf. Jon 1:3–6). That the book is hazy about the details of the city of Nineveh and also contains a sufficient number of Aramaic expressions to locate it comfortably after the period of Ezra (see below) both indicate, as also do its quotations, a context in the post-exilic era, more particularly in the period of Judah's increasing awareness and acceptance of foreigners in and after the fourth century. This book is of a different order from the other prophetic books, having the form of a story rather than being a collection of prophetic oracles.

COMMENTARY

(1:1–16) Like the book of Joel and unlike those of e.g. Hosea and Amos this book lacks any biographical or chronological background to the divine commission. The word of the Lord came: how, when, and where are less important than its startling content—Jonah is to preach judgement to Nineveh. At the time of Jeroboam II Nineveh was not the capital city of Assyria, though later (in the reign of Sennacherib, 704–681) it became so, but in the mind of our author it stood for all the wickedness which had been endemic in the Assyrian empire. Its 'king' (3:6) is not named and its size (3:3) is expressed in appropriately exaggerated terms. The text here is focused not on history but on morality.

Other prophets had addressed foreign nations (cf. Am 1:3–2:3; Jer 46–51, etc.) but none had been sent in person to preach exclusively to a powerful foreign city. For our writer, God's concern is not with the Jews only but with Gentiles also (cf. Zech 8:23; Mal 1:11). However, the task was daunting: 'arise', Jonah was told, and so he did, but only to flee in the opposite direction (1:3)! Tarshish may have been Tartessus in Spain, in the far west, and there is humour in the way the writer depicts the outcome of the prophet's encounter with God, in such contrast with e.g. Isaiah (6:8 'Lord, here am I; send me').

The humorous note is maintained as the chapter develops, depicting a constant succession of descents. Thus the Lord 'hurled a great wind' down to the sea (1:4); the cargo was hurled into the sea (1:5); Jonah had gone down to Joppa, then down into the heart of the ship (1:2, 5) and was thrown down into the sea (1:15), only to descend into the belly of a great fish (1:17; 'the belly of Sheol' 2:2), all to indicate the invincible power and purpose of the Lord in heaven over the lives of those who disobey him. The sailors begin to discern this, for Jonah was not reticent about telling them of his God 'the LORD . . . who made the sea and the dry land' (1:9, a bold statement of faith under the circumstances), and when the tempest ceased they worship Jonah's God with vows and sacrifices offered not in the sanctuary in Jerusalem but (by traditional Heb. standards irregularly) on board ship—the reluctant prophet's first 'converts' (1:16), whose allegiance to his God he had won by his willingness to offer his life for them (1:12). Gradually the character of his God was becoming clearer to, and delineated in, the prophet himself.

The world of our writer is a cosmopolitan one, in which fleeing from one's god (v. 10), offering prayers to many gods (v. 5), casting lots (v. 7), propitiatory human sacrifice (v. 14), and offering heterodox worship to an alien deity (v. 16) are all part of the life of the seagoing people of whom he writes with such sympathetic insight and perhaps also with experience of the life of a busy port. Little of the narrative of the OT relates to life at sea—the Hebrews were not a seafaring nation (cf. 1 Kings 9:27 where Phoenicians had to teach them seafaring skills)—but it is the author's aim to tell his readers that amidst all the superstition and, by Jewish standards, religious irregularity of such a way of life, the God of Israel, maker of sea and dry land alike, is sovereign over the affairs of men, and may attend to their prayers.

(1:17–2:10) As we might expect with this God who is gracious and merciful, deliverance from the sea was provided for the runaway prophet (v. 17), in the form of a 'large fish' which swallowed him. This is the best-known of all the episodes in the story, and the one which occasions Jesus' prediction in Mt 12:38–41 that the Son of Man would also be delivered after three days and nights in the heart of the earth, as a sign to his generation of God's favour upon him. Jesus' imagery, and that of Jonah here, is brutal in its intimation that before deliverance there may come humiliation and agony, but though 'weeping may linger for the night...joy comes with the morning' (Ps 30:5). God is perceived in his role of creator both here (of the fish) and in 4:6–7 (the bush and the worm), ever active in achieving his redemptive purposes for the human race, just as he is perceived in Deutero-Isaiah (Isa 43:1) and in Jn 5:17 ('My Father is still working, and I also am working'). 'He who keeps Israel will neither slumber nor sleep' (Ps 121:4).

Jonah's ensuing prayer presupposes his deliverance (2:2, 6) and has been thought by some to be a later insertion into the book. Certainly, its poetic structure interrupts the prose narrative sequence of 2:1, 10. There are precedents, however, for proleptic anticipations of deliverance in the Hebrew psalter itself (e.g. Ps 40:1, 13), and this provides an appropriate indication of the prophet's new, grateful, and ultimately more obedient frame of mind in the ensuing sections of the story. The language of his song of thanksgiving is derived largely from existing psalms (e.g. cf. 3:4; 120:1; 118:5 with Jon 2:2, and Ps 31:22 with 2:4; 69:1 with 2:5, etc.) thus reminding the reader that the God of our deliverance is the God whose promises were daily sung in Zion.

The phrase 'the belly of Sheol' (meaning the very depths of the earth, where the shades of the dead are assembled) is not to be found elsewhere in Hebrew poetry, and vividly expresses the poet's despair in his life-threatening predicament. Even there, however, God has heard him (cf. Ps 139:8 'if I make my bed in Sheol, you are there'). In vv. 3–6 the writer piles metaphor upon metaphor to accentuate the horror and terror of his plight, echoing some traditional formulae (e.g. Ps 88:7, 'you overwhelm me with all your waves'; Ps 69:1, 'the waters have come up to my neck'; Ps 103:4, 'who redeems your life from the Pit') as well as his own vivid imagery. His faith stands in contrast to that of other psalmists, who doubt God's ability to reach into the realm of death (cf. Ps 6:5; 88:5–7, 10–12). Our writer believes that God dwells in the temple in Jerusalem (v. 7) and from there hears those who pray towards his house (for this practice cf. Dan 6:10, where thrice-daily prayer is offered), a view particularly appropriate to the scattered Jewish communities of the post-exilic Diaspora. Idolatry (v. 8) was a mark of apostasy amongst Jews living abroad, but vows and sacrifices could still be offered to the God of Israel in Zion (v. 9), just as the mariners had done in 1:16, and as Jonah appears to be intending here. He echoes Ps 50:14 ('Offer to God a sacrifice of thanksgiving, and pay your vows to the Most High'), with its ensuing note of deliverance ('Call on me in the day of trouble; I will deliver you, and you shall glorify me') and its prior dismissal of the necessity of animal sacrifice ('Do I eat the flesh of bulls, or drink the blood of goats?'). 'Deliverance belongs to the Lord' (v. 9) is an echo of Ps 3:8 and is a triumphant climax to this remarkable expression of faith against all the odds. All this God heard; he spoke to the fish (this is not the only place in the OT where he uses a sub-human creature to achieve his purposes, in the life of a recalcitrant prophet, cf. Num 22:28–30), and Jonah is,

in the narrator's vivid phrase (reminding us of the depths to which the prophet had been sent by God), spewed out upon the dry land, presumably near his Galilean home (v. 10).

(3:1–10) We now reach the heart of the story. God persists in his gracious purpose towards sinful Nineveh and again calls Jonah to the task of warning its people of impending judgement. This time he obeys the call and reaches the outskirts of the fabulously large city (vv. 1–3), 'a three days' walk' across. Our writer has already exhibited considerable narrative skills, using irony, humour, assonance, and alliteration, and to these he now adds hyperbole. Faced again with so vast a task, this time Jonah, undaunted, faithfully proclaims the message he was given in what must be the shortest prophetic oracle on record (and the only one in this book): 'Forty days more, and Nineveh shall be overthrown' (v. 4). Interestingly, the Greek tradition here reports 'three more days' but is unsupported by any other versions or Hebrew MSS. The variation may be caused by the Greek translator's awareness of the three-day journey with which Jonah was faced. (For a suggestion that 4:5 belongs here see below.) His preaching had its effect (v. 5) in city-wide repentance indicated by a fast. Even the city's king (vv. 6–9), whom the narrator may have believed to have been one of Assyria's emperors (though he never says so), sits in sackcloth and ashes ordering repentance, fasting (even for animals), and prayer, to attract the compassion of Israel's God and to avert his wrath. In Mt 12:41 Jesus cites this story to shame his own impenitent Jewish contemporaries. The result here was, as Jer 18:8 would lead the post-exilic reader to expect, that God 'changed his mind about the calamity that he had said he would bring upon them; and he did not do it' (v. 10). The king's words in v. 9 ('Who knows? God may relent and change his mind...') echo those of the only slightly earlier Joel, where (2:13–14) we learn that because God 'relents from punishing' there is hope for the penitent and fasting sinner. Jonah's mission, which was God's also, was a success, despite his original fears and the narrow nationalism ascribed to his prophetic ministry in 2 Kings 14:25, upon which the rest of this story depends for its dramatic effect.

(4:1–11) This nationalism, however, has not yet been cured, for Jonah is hurt and angry at the non-fulfilment of his prediction (vv. 1–3) and, in a rebuke to his God reminiscent of Jeremiah's daring accusations (e.g. 20:7), he claims that from the beginning he had known that God's proverbial compassion (Ex 34:6–7) detracted from his justice. Unfulfilled prophecy is a problem addressed by biblical writers in a number of places, but it is unwarranted to see it as the principal subject-matter of the book, the climax of which (4:11) is about God's universal compassion. Like Elijah (1 Kings 19:4) he prays for death, but his reasons are less noble than Elijah's, being marked by self-pity and petulance. There is also a hint of sheer exhaustion in v. 5, which some have thought to transfer between 3:4 and 5 as it suits that context well, whereas here it interrupts the narrative sequence (God himself is about to create a shelter for him, v. 6) and we have already been told (3:10) what Jonah is here waiting to learn. No surviving manuscript or version makes the transposition, however, and if accepted it would be a copying error at a very early stage of the story's literary transmission.

God, however, challenges Jonah to review his attitude (v. 4), and, being Lord both of the sea and of the dry land by Jonah's own admission (1:9), now uses the fruits of the dry land ('a bush', v. 6, which translates a Heb. word of uncertain meaning, though attested in Assyrian also; and a worm, v. 7) as he had earlier used a creature of the sea, to teach Jonah a lesson. The lesson was that Jonah cared more about his pleasure in the sheltering plant which he had not cultivated than about God's concern for a huge city of people and their livestock which he had cared about for years (vv. 9–11). As claimed for Assyrian kings (and attested on their building inscriptions), the Lord is the good shepherd of all his sheep, as the Hebrew kings themselves recognized (e.g. Ps 23), and Jonah here, like Jesus' followers in Jn 10:16, needs to learn he has sheep in other folds also. Their sin is born of ignorance ('who do not know their right hand from their left', v. 11), and their repentance was welcome to a merciful God. Such theology is also present in the NT (e.g. Lk 23:34 'Father, forgive them; for they do not know what they are doing'; 1 Tim 1:13 'I received mercy because I had acted ignorantly in unbelief'), and implied in Ezek 18:28 'because they considered and turned away from all the transgressions that they had committed, they shall surely live; they shall not die', where the word 'considered' implies seeing the truth of the situation at last. The prophet's task, as that of all God's people, is simply to speak his message wherever he may be sent. The outcome, so the book of Jonah is telling its readers, is God's responsibility, and his alone. As another Jewish writer with a similar theological problem was led to conclude, 'O the depth of the riches and wisdom and knowledge of God! How unsearchable are his judgements and how inscrutable his ways! "For who has known the mind of the Lord? Or who has been his counsellor?"' (Rom 11:33–4, cf. Isa 40:13).

32. Micah   H. G. M. WILLIAMSON

INTRODUCTION

A. The Man and his Message. 1. Very little can be deduced from the book of Micah about the man who stands behind it. There is no account of a 'call', and at 3:5–8 he even seems to deny to himself the title of prophet. From the few details at 1:1 (see Commentary) and elsewhere we may surmise that he spoke on behalf of his fellow landowners and elders of a typical country town against the excessive burdens which the centralized militarizing policy of the Jerusalem establishment was imposing upon the people. Against surface appearances, he denounces these policies as leading to injustice (2:1–2; 3:1–3) and so interprets them as 'transgression' and 'sin' (1:5; 3:8). Appeal to only one aspect of the nation's religious traditions (2:6–11; 3:11) will not prevent them from receiving their just deserts.

2. Such a message fits most comfortably in the first part of the reign of Hezekiah, when intensive preparations for rebellion against Assyrian domination were undertaken. Yet it seems that Micah may earlier have spoken out against the northern kingdom (1:6), whose capital Samaria fell some twenty years previously. An extended ministry may thus be envisaged (again, see MIC 1:1), but the way in which such earlier material is reused to address the later situation in ch. 1 suggests that what we have now of Micah's words comes from a relatively brief period at the very end of the eighth century BCE.

B. The Book and its Formation. 1. Much of the book as we now have it comes from periods long after Micah's day. This is not based on a dogma that someone like Micah could not envisage any future hope, but rather on the style and thematic content of the work which suit later periods best. (Recent attempts, such as Hillers (1984) and Shaw (1993), to defend authorial unity do not seem convincing.) Micah's uncompromisingly negative message (3:12) was still remembered at the time of the fall of Jerusalem to the Babylonians and the exile of part of its population (cf. Jer. 26:17–19), and his words began to be read as having found fulfilment at that time, leaving its mark at a number of points in the text (Jeremias 1971). Such a living 'word of the LORD', however, could never be exhausted by a single event, and so new material which looked beyond the judgement (not instead of it) came to be added. The explicit development and reversal of Micah's own themes (see esp. ch. 4) indicate that this was not an arbitrary extension, but was regarded as a development of what lay already latent in the book.

2. Finally, the whole was set in a universal and proto-apocalyptic context (see esp. 1:2 and 5:15), the word to Judah now being applied to the whole earth and all its peoples. It is in this final context that the book reaches us, and we do best to read it from that perspective. It is not that later additions to Micah's words need to be stripped away, but rather that the words of Micah need to take their place as a historical example of the timeless 'word of the LORD' (1:1), which is the book's true title.

C. Outline

God and Israel (6:1–7:20)
   God's Requirement (6:1–8)
   Crime and Punishment (6:9–16)
   Lament for the Loss of Society (7:1–7)
   Concluding Confession, Appeal, and Confidence (7:8–20)

COMMENTARY

Title (1:1)

Although Micah often appears to speak on his own authority (e.g. 3:1), the book as a whole is characterized by its editor as 'The word of the LORD'. 'Micah' is a shortened form of *mîkāyâ* (cf. Jer. 26:18), meaning 'Who is like Yah?', a name possibly echoed at the end of the book (7:18). His identification by domicile, Moresheth(-gath; cf. 1:14), suggests that his ministry was mainly conducted away from home, almost certainly in Jerusalem. On the basis of the material which can most plausibly be ascribed to him, it has been suggested that he was a local elder, responsible in particular for justice (Wolff 1990: 6–8), and perhaps also one of the *'am-hā'āreṣ*, 'the people of the land' (Rudolph 1975: 22), a conservative group of small landowners with a particular concern for constitutional stability (e.g. 2 Kings 21:24). The remainder of the title seems to be deduced from the information in ch. 1 in particular, and is unlikely to be of independent historical value.

God's Dealings with his People as a Warning to the Nations (1:2–5:15)

(1:2–16) One Nation's Judgement is Another Nation's Warning Although this lengthy passage includes material of diverse origins, it has been developed by stages into a single literary unit with clear connections between the various parts (e.g. 'For lo', v. 3; 'All this is for', v. 5; 'For this', v. 8). The prophecy against Samaria (v. 6) is likely to be the earliest part, but its fulfilment is already reused by Micah (vv. 8–9 with 10–16) as background to his warning that a similar fate awaits Judah and Jerusalem. His words were partially realized at the time of Sennacherib's invasion of Judah in 701 BCE (cf. 2 Kings 18–19) but, as Jer 26:18–19 reminds us, it was not until the fall of Jerusalem to the Babylonians in 587 BCE that Micah's words found complete vindication, and this may be reflected in v. 16. Finally, by extension of the same process and in the light of this vindication, v. 2 (post-exilic) elevates these lessons from history into a warning to all the nations. This universal perspective then gives shape to chs. 1–5 as a whole, with the words of Micah to Jerusalem in chs. 2–3 giving way to an emphasis on the nations in 4–5, and concluding (5:15) with a clear reprise of v. 2. Thus the historically bound words of Micah become in later reflection a timeless and universal word of the Lord. vv. 3–4 are a characteristic description of a theophany, but unlike earlier passages, where this theme heralds God's deliverance (e.g. Judg 5:4–5; Ps 18:6–19), here it presages judgement (v. 5). Appropriate to an introduction to the book, v. 5*a* reflects Micah's basic message (cf. 3:8*b*). Elsewhere, 'transgression' and 'sins' apply particularly to the ruling élite, while 'Jacob' and 'the house of Israel' invariably refer to Judah (e.g. 2:7, 12; 3:1, 8, 9), and both may originally have done so here. In line with the theme of this chapter, however, they have

been reinterpreted in the second half of the verse to apply to the northern and southern kingdoms respectively (see too v. 13*b*), while the sin is described as more narrowly religious (vv. 5*b*, 7), thus aligning it with the causes of the eventual Babylonian Exile as perceived by the Deuteronomists. vv. 8–9 are the hinge on which the chapter turns. 'For this' refers back to the fall of Samaria, but Micah's lament is due to the fact that a like fate awaits Judah and Jerusalem (v. 9), as vividly portrayed in vv. 10–16. The Hebrew text of vv. 10–16 is exceptionally difficult (cf. the different Eng. translations), but its general sense is clear enough; cf. Na'aman (1995). About twelve towns in the vicinity of Micah's home in Moresheth in the Judean Shephelah are listed, and threatening remarks made about them on the basis of wordplay, e.g. 'in Beth-leaphrah' (*'aprâ*) roll yourselves in the dust (*'āpār*)'. This feature probably accounts for the selection of towns, so that it would be hazardous to try to construct a military line of advance out of them. In 701 BCE Sennacherib destroyed most of the towns of Judah and threatened Jerusalem (vv. 9, 12), so that Micah's distress (v. 8) at this impending doom is intelligible. There was a partial exile to Assyria at this time (v. 16), but inevitably later readers will have seen a more complete fulfilment of this prophecy in the Babylonian Exile.

(2:1–3:12) Judah and Jerusalem Condemned These two chapters basically comprise five paragraphs in which various groups within the Judean population are condemned for social injustice and rejection of the prophetic word. In substance they derive from Micah himself and form the securest basis for reconstructing his historical message. Within the broader structure of the book (see MIC 1:2–16), however, they function more in retrospect as background to the broader international vision of chs. 4–5.

Man Proposes, but God Disposes (2:1–5). Accusation (vv. 1–2) and threat ('therefore', vv. 3, 5) are here perfectly balanced: as the accused 'devise . . . evil' (v. 1), so does God in return (v. 3); 'they covet fields' (v. 2), while God parcels out theirs to others (v. 4); they seize others' 'inheritance' (v. 2) only to bewail the loss of their own (v. 4). But who are 'they'? Rather than simply avaricious capitalists, who dispossess the small landholders of their supposedly inalienable property, they may rather be official administrators under the crown (cf. 3:1, 9) who were obliged to tax the rural population heavily and sometimes to appropriate land and property as part of Hezekiah's military preparations for Sennacherib's invasion (cf. Isa 22:7–11), which struck Micah's home territory first (cf. Dearman 1988; Wolff 1990: 74–5). For Micah, 'I was only doing my job' is no excuse: his ethical interpretation of their exercise of power is that it amounts to a breach of the Ten Commandments (v. 2). The threat is therefore directed initially against a relatively small circle in Judean society, who will have no part in the future reconstruction after the Assyrian devastation is over (v. 5). Again, however, the later addition of 'against this family' (v. 3; cf. Am 3:2) suggests that the passage has subsequently been reread after the Babylonian exile in terms of national sin and judgement.

A Prophetic Disputation (2:6–11 with 12–13). The plural imperative 'do not preach' indicates that a new paragraph starts here (and obviously concludes with the use of the same verb in v. 11). Nevertheless, it follows closely on the preceding, and illustrates how Micah and his associates were opposed by those whom they condemned. There are considerable obscurities in the Hebrew text, so that it is not always clear where a change of speaker occurs; the following outline (which differs from NRSV) can only be tentative.

Micah's preaching is rejected (vv. 6–7) on the basis of an orthodox view of God's patience and promises (cf. 3:11b) (read 'his words' instead of 'my words' in v. 7). Micah retorts (vv. 8–10) that such confidence is misplaced because his opponents do not, in fact, 'walk uprightly'. They violently seize what is not theirs (v. 8, not a reference to the law of Ex 22:26–7; Deut 24:10–13), and again, perhaps because of the national emergency (see MIC 2:1–5), they appropriate others' property. v. 10a is the heartless command of the evictors, while 10b, 'because of [your] uncleanness [= moral defilement; cf. Isa 6:5; Am 7:17] you will be destroyed . . .' (my tr.), is Micah's riposte. v. 11 is a sarcastic conclusion. 'Wine and strong drink' are an attractive part of the covenant blessings (e.g. Am 9:13); these people like preachers who focus on the promises without reference to the conditions of obedience which accompany them. vv. 12–13 are usually interpreted as a promise of God's restoration of his exiled people, in which case their present setting remains a puzzle, awkwardly anticipating the sharp change in mood between chs. 3 and 4. However, there has always been a minority of commentators (recently Mays 1976: 73–6; Hagstrom 1988: 51–7, 85–6; Brin 1989) who see them rather as an announcement of judgement: the 'gate' of v. 13 naturally suggests Jerusalem (hardly Babylon!), where the people have been gathered by God for a siege (v. 12). It is he who breaks down the defensive wall (cf. Ps 80:12; 89:40) and who, in a reversal of the Exodus, leads his people away into exile. On this view, 4:6–7 deliberately reverses this judgement saying, just as 4:1–5 reverses 3:9–12.

Cannibalism in Court! (3:1–4). Three closely related paragraphs in ch. 3 bring the catalogue of judgements to a climax in v. 12. In this section, the 'heads' and 'rulers' (the ruling élite of Judah and Jerusalem) are condemned for manipulating the judicial process in a manner which results in a denial of true 'justice' (v. 1), a fundamental term in Micah's critique (cf. 3:8, 9). As in 2:1–5, neither they nor the courts regarded their actions as illegal, but if the outcome is an intolerable oppression of the ordinary citizen (so the grotesque metaphor of vv. 2–3), then the system itself stands condemned. As a result, they themselves will call to God at some time of unspecified distress (v. 4, perhaps amplified by 3:12), only to find that he will no more answer them than they have the people.

Prophets for Profit (3:5–8). Just as 3:1–4 has a certain parallel in 2:1–5, so too does 3:5–8 in 2:6–11. Now, however, the objects of Micah's polemic are explicitly called 'prophets' (vv. 5–6), 'seers', and 'diviners' (v. 7)—and there seems to be little difference between them; the latter are no worse than the former (indeed, in 3:11 the prophets 'divine'), but all alike are condemned because the substance of their message is determined solely by their wages (v. 5). The judgement, therefore, is another case of poetic justice (vv. 6–7): 'vision', 'revelation', and an 'answer from God' will all be withdrawn, leaving them looking foolish and ashamed. Micah adds a concluding and contrasting note about himself (v. 8), which implies that he does not regard himself as a prophet. As already noted, the verse is a succinct summary of the basis of his condemnation (see MIC 1:5; 3:1), just as 3:12 will epitomize its consequences.

Concluding Judgement (3:9–12). This paragraph gathers up the themes of chs. 2–3 as a whole: form, addressees, and accusations are broadly the same. v. 10 may well reflect for Jerusalem the same circumstances as 2:1–5 did for the countryside. v. 11 refers to the same misplaced confidence as 2:6–7, 11, but clarifies that this was based on the so-called tradition of Zion's inviolability; see especially Ps 46, which is more or less quoted here. Micah's uncompromising judgement is therefore appropriate (v. 12) and was remembered more than a century later as the epitome of his preaching (Jer 26:18). The fulfilment of his words at that time doubtless stimulated renewed attention to his work, leading to its reworking in redaction, as already seen, and in development, as follows immediately.

(4:1–5:15) Israel among the Nations This section presupposes the reality of the judgement already described, but opens up the prospect of a glorious restoration beyond it. While several of the previous themes are thus reversed, a consistent new element is the effect of Israel's restoration on the nations, whether for good or ill. This connects with ch. 1 and sets the words of the historical Micah in a more universal context. The material is of diverse origin and date, but it has been welded together to show how the vision for a new order (4:1–5) will be realized through the rule of God (4:6–7), exercised by a restored monarchy in Israel (4:8–5:6). For this to come about, both the nations and Israel will need to be forcefully purged (5:7–15).

Peace at the Last (4:1–5). The section opens with a vision (of late-exilic origin at the earliest) of universal, eschatological peace. Several verbal associations with the concluding paragraph of ch. 3 demonstrate that God's destruction of Zion is not his last word, but rather the necessary first step in his far-reaching purpose. It should be emphasized that the peace of verses 3b–4 can only be achieved as the nations willingly submit to God's instruction: 'The theological integrity of the prophecy lies in its unity' (Mays 1976: 93). A concluding (liturgical?) response (v. 5) invites the people of God to exemplify just such a submission. vv. 1–3 have a close parallel in Isa 2:2–4, and each passage concludes with a verse (Isa 2:5; Mic 4:5) which integrates the material into its new context. Mic 4:4 (lacking in Isaiah) is probably an original part of the oracle, and has Isaianic characteristics. It therefore looks as though the material has come independently into each book from a common original which was developed in Isaianic circles.

A Positive Role for the Remnant (4:6–7). The realization of the vision (cf. 'in that day') will begin by God's rule in Zion over the restored remnant. As 4:1–5 reverses 3:9–12, so here the judgement of 2:12–13 is overturned (see too Zeph 3:11–20). This absolute use of the word 'remnant' is post-exilic, and helps to locate the setting of the redaction of this section as a whole.

The Instrument of God's Rule (4:8–5:6). This passage has a clear and balanced structure. 4:8 and 5:2 (introducing 5:2–6) are exactly parallel, and between come three short paragraphs introduced by 'now' (4:9, 11; 5:1). The whole is closely tied to the preceding by way of detailed development of the theme of God's rule. 4:8 makes clear that God's rule over Zion will be exercised through a restoration of 'the former dominion', which 5:2–6 confirms will be in the person of a new Davidic figure. His insignificant place of origin parallels that of the remnant among the nations; in neither case does God's rule follow the normal course of power politics. Whether or not the reference to the Assyrians in 5:5–6 points to a pre-exilic origin for 5:2–6 (in part, at least), its redactional setting and hence use in the book as a whole are clearly post-exilic. For readers at this later time, 'Assyria' will be a sobriquet for the world powers in general (cf. Ezra 6:22 etc.), an interpretation reinforced by the unprecedented use of the parallel 'land of Nimrod' (cf. Gen 10:8–12). The period of suffering which precedes his rule (5:3) is thus the Exile (cf. 4:10); as throughout this section, restoration follows, and does not replace, judgement. This emphasis is also the focus of the three short paragraphs in 4:9–5:1. The first two (and so probably also the third, 5:1; the Heb. text, however, is too obscure for certainty) may have their origin in the immediate aftermath of the fall of Jerusalem to the Babylonians (so Wolff 1990), but they are developed by future promises which loosen them from any strictly bound historical setting. The gathering of the exiles (4:10b) and the overthrow of enemies (4:12–13; 5:1 is developed by the promises of 5:2–6) link up with what has been seen elsewhere in the section, so that again God's 'thoughts' and 'plan' (4:12) are to use his now judged people as his agents and instruments of eventual universal rule.

A Negative Role for the Remnant (5:7–9). In 4:6–7 the remnant was restored as a sign of the positive benefits of God's rule. Here, we see the other side of the coin—as his instrument of judgement on the nations which oppose it. For this use of the 'dew' image (v. 7), see 2 Sam 17:12 (Rudolph 1975; Hillers 1984); the two similes of vv. 7 and 8 are thus closely parallel in both structure and thought.

No Peace for the Wicked (5:10–15). A probably pre-exilic oracle in 10b–14 (which some scholars ascribe to Micah) is here reused to stress again that 'in that day' the rule of God will not be thwarted by either military or religious opposition. As 5:7–9 was the negative counterpart of 4:6–7, this may be regarded as the downside of 4:1–5. (With 4:8 and 5:2 in parallel, the whole of chs. 4–5 thus displays a certain symmetrical arrangement.) The content of vv. 10–14 points to Israel as the object of God's judgement here, but v. 15 extends this to the nations. The clear echo of 1:2 ('obey' in 5:15 is the same word as 'hear' in 1:2) is the clue to the purpose of the whole, and shows again that the final form of Mic 1–5 is ultimately concerned with God's dealings with all the nations, to whom Israel is presented as an example. The prospect of peace and blessing is set before them (4:1–4), but persistence in their rebellion will lead to their overthrow. As with Israel, however, this need not be God's last word, for 'that day' (4:6 and 5:10) can include his rule over a remnant just as much as vengeance on the disobedient.

God and Israel (6:1–7:20)

A major new section of the book begins at 6:1. Like chs. 1–5, its general shape is of warning and threat (6:1–7:7) followed by promise (7:8–20), but in contrast the latter refers to the na-

tions only as a foil to Israel, not as a subject in their own right. At the same time, it is Israel as a collective whole which is addressed rather than particular sections within the population. Whatever the material's origins (most of 6:1–7:7 could be as early as Micah), these features certainly suit its later use within the worshipping community, towards which the closing verses of the book clearly point.

(6:1–8) God's Requirement In vv. 2–5, God takes his people to court to accuse them of ingratitude. His treatment of them over the course of their long history is characterized as 'saving acts' (v. 5), some examples of which are supplied (vv. 4–7b). They, however, consider only that he has 'wearied' them (v. 3); they focus exclusively on his demands without seeing them as a response to his prior grace. This is unnatural behaviour, as the call to the mountains and foundations of the earth to act as witnesses implies (v. 2).

The first verse is a separate introduction, characterizing the text as 'what the LORD says'. As we saw in 1:1 and 1:2–16, no matter who the speaker was in the original text (and there are frequent changes in person throughout chs. 6–7), it is now all presented as God's word to the reader or hearer.

Although there is a sharp change of form at v. 6, it cannot be read in isolation from what precedes: an unidentified individual is chastened by God's indictment, and in order to put the relationship right offers a crescendo of cultic responses. God's reaction (v. 8) is in effect to say, 'It is not *what* I want, but *whom* I want, that counts'. It is a summary of early prophetic and Deuteronomic ethics (cf. Deut 10:12–13). 'Justice' was the key theme of Micah's preaching (3:1, 8, 9), so that the earlier chapters have given specific examples of what is here elevated into an abstract principle. 'Kindness' is its frequent partner elsewhere (though not in Micah), and refers primarily to the necessary conditions for the forging of a community which justice then regulates. 'To walk humbly' would be better translated as 'to walk carefully, prudently'; it includes humility, but goes very much further (cf. Eph 5:15).

(6:9–16) Crime and Punishment The main thrust of this textually difficult passage is clear. The accusation (vv. 10–12) is of dishonest business practices which result in the amassing of ill-gotten gain. The punishment (vv. 13–15), which closely imitates ancient Near-Eastern forms of treaty curses, is that God will ensure that this activity will all be in vain. v. 16 repeats this two-part form, summarizing and extending it now in terms reminiscent of the Deuteronomic History. Judah has imitated the evil ways of the northern kingdom of Israel, and so will share her fate of national disaster. The development of thought is closely comparable with 1:3–7, just as the prophet's response in 7:1 echoes 1:8–9.

(7:1–7) Lament for the Loss of Society The description in vv. 2–6 of a society which has lost all sense of cohesion has so many parallels in the book of Proverbs that in itself it could stem from almost any point in the later pre-exilic or earlier post-exilic periods. Here in Micah, however, it is closely integrated into its surrounding context. First, it illustrates the consequences of ignoring the requirement of 6:8. Secondly, it follows as a prophet's lament on the announcement of national disaster in 6:16, just as 1:8 follows 1:7, so that it may be applied in particular to the consequences of life in such a time of dire emergency. Thirdly, v. 7 provides a transition to the last part of the book; even now, there are those who maintain faith, and that faith will be vindicated (cf. Isa 8:17–18). The first person speaker of vv. 1, 7 could thus be the respondent of 6:6, the personified figure of Zion (6:9 and especially 7:8–10), or the prophet. The ambiguity may be conscious, since all three embody or represent the community of those who 'look to the LORD' (v. 7) in contrast to the unrighteous. The reader, of course, is thus drawn in to identify him- or herself with the speaker and so to appropriate personally and in community the faith of the concluding psalm-like passage (7:8–20).

(7:8–20) Concluding Confession, Appeal, and Confidence
The four short paragraphs in this passage can each be paralleled formally by elements found in the psalms of lament, so that the suggestion has often been made that the piece is liturgical. It lacks rubrics, however (contrast Hab 3), the changes of person of the participants (e.g. from first person singular in vv. 8–10 to plural in 19–20) are liturgically awkward, and the order of paragraphs (esp. vv. 11–13 before 14–17) is not what would be expected (Wolff 1990). The arrangement is thus more likely to be literary and redactional, though intended to draw the reader in, as seen already at 7:7 (Mays 1976).

The first-person speaker in vv. 8–10 is feminine, and so probably Zion/Jerusalem as a personification of the community. The setting is one of defeat, distress, and darkness (which applied to Jerusalem as much after as during the Exile), but for the first time in Micah this is acknowledged as being due to sin, which is frankly confessed. This is a first step on the road to the repentance which so many of the prophets saw as a precondition for restoration.

Appropriately, this is met by a reassuring oracle (vv. 11–13) which promises a regathering of the dispersed exiles and political rehabilitation. The community (cf. 'our God' in v. 17) presses this with a petition that this restoration should be as glorious as at the time of the Exodus when the nation knew God's care and when their enemies were overwhelmed. The closing verses (18–20) reflect the calm of a restored relationship with God (contrast 6:1–8), no matter what the external circumstances. 'Iniquities', if not enemies, may be trodden 'under foot', and 'sins', if not Egyptians, cast 'into the depths of the sea' (v. 19). The members of the assembly have repositioned themselves as the spiritual heirs of the patriarchs, and so anticipate a return to the experience of God's 'faithfulness' and 'unswerving loyalty'.

REFERENCES

Brin, G. (1989), 'Micah 2, 12–13: A Textual and Ideological Study', *ZAW* 101: 118–24.

Dearman, J. A. (1988), *Property Rights in the Eighth-Century Prophets: The Conflict and its Background*, SBLDS 106 (Atlanta: Scholars Press).

Hagstrom, D. G. (1988), *The Coherence of the Book of Micah: A Literary Analysis*, SBLDS 89 (Atlanta: Scholars Press).

Hillers, D. R. (1984), *Micah*, Hermeneia (Philadelphia: Fortress).

Jeremias, J. (1971), 'Die Deutung der Gerichtsworte Michas in der Exilszeit', *ZAW* 83: 330–54.

Mays, J. L. (1976), *Micah: A Commentary*, OTL (London: SCM).

Na'aman, N. (1995) ' "The House-of-No-Shade Shall Take Away its Tax from You" (Micah i 11)', *VT* 45: 516–27.

Rudolph, W. (1975), *Micha—Nahum—Habakuk—Zephanja*, KAT (Gütersloh: Mohn).

Shaw, C. S. (1993), *The Speeches of Micah: A Rhetorical-Historical Analysis*, JSOTSup 145 (Sheffield: JSOT).

Wolff, H. W. (1990), *Micah: A Commentary* (Minneapolis: Augsburg); German original BKAT 14/4 (Neukirchen-Vluyn; Neukirchener Verlag, 1982).

33. Nahum   JULIA M. O'BRIEN

INTRODUCTION

The superscription of Nahum bluntly and tersely confronts its reader with the theme and tone that will dominate the book. The sole focus on Nineveh underscores that the book will pointedly address the fate that is to befall Assyria, and indeed all who stand in opposition to YHWH and YHWH's people. Its self-description as a 'burden' (*maśśā'*, usually translated 'oracle'), well describes a collection that is textually, historically, and theologically 'heavy', one filled with difficulties, ironies, and harsh pronouncements.

A. Text. Textually, Nahum is notoriously difficult, as notes to the NRSV and other translations attest. Its vocabulary is uncommon, its text at times seems ill-preserved, and its pronouns shift repeatedly in number and gender with rare indication of their antecedents.

B. Redaction. Most commentators have attributed the book's disjointedness to an extensive redactional history. Several clues indicate editing. The semi-acrostic in 1:2–8 bears little connection to the rest of the material but does serve to offer the book a more universal frame, shifting the exclusive attention on the downfall of Nineveh to a larger vision of God's awesome power. Numerous links with other parts of the prophetic corpus, especially Deutero-Isaiah, suggest a late exilic or perhaps post-exilic editing. Given Nahum's catchword connections to Micah and Habakkuk (which envelope it in the canon) (see Nogalski 1993), redaction may have been undertaken with an eye to the book's canonical placement. Clearly, a book so focused on a single enemy would need to be generalized in some way for later generations to appropriate its message.

C. Dating. The recognition of the multilayered character of the book complicates its dating. While most scholars accept a general time-frame between 663 BCE (the fall of Thebes, Nah 3:8) and 612 BCE (the fall of Nineveh), the final form of the book is probably exilic or even post-exilic, given allusions to Isa 40–55 and other prophetic materials. Further problematizing the dating of Nahum is the possibility that Assyria may represent less a historical entity than a symbolic enemy, much as Edom serves as a symbol of evil in many of the prophets, and Babylon stands for Rome in Revelation. The readiness with which Nahum's language could be read symbolically is attested in the Nahum pesher from Qumran, in which the writers' contemporary foes are labelled 'Assyria'.

D. Literary Features. 1. Disagreements regarding the material that would have constituted the 'original' Nahum also relate to discussions of the book's genre. Those who maintain that the semi-acrostic in 1:2–8 was composed for, or incorporated early into, the book often attribute it to cultic circles. The tone and vocabulary of Nahum also indicate affinities with the Oracle against the Nations genre utilized by other prophets. A succinct discussion of the history of scholarship on Nahum is found in Mason (1991).

2. Despite its textual difficulties, Nahum manifests evident literary skill. Its acrostic—whether original or not—demonstrates literary playfulness. Assonance, alliteration, repetition, and wide-ranging metaphors abound.

E. Theological Concerns. 1. Engendering perhaps even more discussion, however, is what readers are to make of a book dominated by anger and violence. While late nineteenth-century commentators lambasted the book's bloodthirsty celebration of revenge, mid-twentieth-century scholars attempted to vindicate the book, by arguing (1) that a god who did not punish evildoers would not be a good god; and/or (2) that the book's final form reframes the original celebration of revenge into a call for celebration of God's universal sovereignty. Recent feminist critiques have found these latter rationalizations of the deity's behaviour in Nahum unsatisfying and have pointedly focused attention on the graphic sexual violence of Nah 3, directly attributed to YHWH the Divine Warrior.

F. Outline. While the clearly composite nature of Nahum precludes agreement on the delineation of its sections, a thematic outline is as follows:

Superscription (1:1)
Theophanic Hymn in Semi-Acrostic Style (1:2–8)
The Futility of Assyria's Resistance (1:9–11)
The Contrasting Fates of Judah and Assyria (1:12–2:2) (HB 2:3)
The Assault of Nineveh (2:3–13) (HB 2:4–14)
An Oracle against Nineveh (3:1–19)

COMMENTARY

(1:1) The designation of this anti-Assyrian prophecy as a 'burden' (*maśśā'*) parallels closely the similar designation of Oracles against the Nations in Isa 13–23, as well as the superscriptions of Zech 9:1; 12:1; and Mal 1:1. 'Nahum', which means 'comfort', echoes the beginning of Deutero-Isaiah, a somewhat ironic designation for the harsh voice to follow. The significance of the description of the prophecy as a 'book' is debated, but may indicate final redaction in a period in which prophetic books (and perhaps collections) were being formed.

(1:2–8) That Nahum opens with an acrostic has been noticed at least since the mid-nineteenth century, though its origin is debated. The acrostic's incomplete state (it continues only as far as the letter *kap* and manifests two breaks in the alphabetic

sequence) has enticed many commentators to emend it to various degrees. Nogalski (1993: 104–7) convincingly argues that a redactor incorporated and altered a 'loose' acrostic in order to apply an earlier Nahum corpus to a new situation in the exilic or post-exilic period; the effect of its inclusion is to stress God's universal sovereignty beyond the book's specific historical context. This powerful poem imputes to YHWH strong feelings and awesome power. Alluding to the credo found in Ex 34:6–7 and elsewhere, the author highlights the deity's insistence on vindicating his friends and ensuring that his enemies do not escape punishment. The dichotomy of the fate of friends and enemies is especially strong in v. 3: God is 'slow to anger' *and* 'will not acquit'. Similarly, vv. 6–7 explain that no one can withstand the inferno of God's anger *and* that he is a place of safety for those who take refuge in him. YHWH's ability to effect his will is underscored by the strongly mythological language of the passage. Ancient Near-Eastern motifs of storm gods and geological upheaval, as well as epithets commonly used for other deities, reinforce the image of the powerful, vindicating God.

(1:9–11) The shift from the previous hymnic description of God to an address to 'you', as well as cryptic references to concrete events, indicates the beginning of a new section. According to Nogalski (1993), these verses serve as a transition from the imported acrostic to the original Nahum corpus which begins in 1:11–14. The 'you' of v. 9 is the first of many unspecified pronouns in this section and the next. Ambiguity attends v. 11 ('from *you* an evil plotter came out') both in terms of the pronominal antecedent and in the identification of the 'plotter', though Isa 10's designation of Assyria as the 'plotter' may serve as a close parallel. 'Belial', both in 1:11 and 1:15 (HB 2:1), seems a generic reference to evil rather than indication of a personified demonic power. The lack of antecedents to the many pronouns of this section, as well as the lack of any reference to Assyria so far (apart from the superscription), has been variously assessed. It may indicate that much traditional, generic material has been gathered for later application to the Assyrian context; or, conversely, it may indicate that the superscription itself is presupposed by and integral to the remainder of the book. v. 10 introduces a literary technique frequent in Nahum: the concatenation of similes/metaphors. Within the course of one verse, 'they' are interwoven thorns and drunkards who will be burned like chaff.

(1:12–2:2) (HB 2:3) While 'you' in 1:12–13 refers to Judah ('I will afflict *you* no more,' 'I will break off his yoke from *you*'), in 1:14 God addresses an individual 'you' whom most commentators identify as the king of Assyria. 1:15 (HB 2:1) again addresses Judah, while 2:1 (HB 2:2) announces to Assyria that a 'scatterer' (variously considered an epithet of YHWH or an allusion to the Babylonians) has arrived. This volley of addressees betrays, as do earlier verses, the book's extended redactional history. 1:15 is a clear reference to Isa 52:7, one of the many connections between Nahum and Deutero-Isaiah.

(2:3–13) (HB 2:4–14) This unit portrays the attack of Nineveh, identified in 2:8 (HB 2:9) for the first time since the superscription. Well-dressed warriors storm the city, their chariots dash in madly, and the city walls cannot hold them back. While some mythological motifs are evident in this section ('waters run away', 2:8, HB 2:9), various literary devices attempt to capture the feel of an actual siege: staccato sentences, some without verbs; and alliteration in 2:10 (HB 2:11) (*bûqâ ûmĕbûqâ ûmĕbullāqâ*, 'Devastation, desolation, and destruction'). 2:7 (HB 2:8) has proved problematic for interpreters. The MT reads '*she* is exiled'. While NRSV links 'she' to the city Nineveh, Sanderson (1992: 218) relates the reference to Ishtar, the city goddess of Nineveh. Others have suggested that the reference to 'handmaids' later in the verse suggests that 'she' is an Assyrian princess. The lion imagery in 2:11–12 (HB 2:12–13) draws upon the iconographic connection of Assyria with the lion.

(3:1–19) v. 1 begins with *hôy* ('woe'), a form-critical marker of the 'woe-oracle'. While this genre often bears funerary connotations, Roberts (1991: 118) well demonstrates its utilization in other contexts. As in Nah 2, literary devices attempt to capture the feel of attack; 3:2–3 strings together phrases without verbs, heaping up images of the devastation of Nineveh. While other prophets frequently compare sinful Israel and/or Judah to a prostitute, Nahum directs this imagery towards Nineveh in 3:4. The sexual violence in 3:5–6 is graphic: YHWH himself uncovers the woman's genitals for all nations to see and throws filth upon her. vv. 8–11 taunt Nineveh, asking it to compare itself to Thebes, a well-defended Egyptian city conquered by the Assyrian king Ashurbanipal in 663 BCE. *Even* Thebes went into exile, *even* her children were dashed to pieces, and Assyria can expect to fare no better than its own victim. v. 13 again turns to derogatory feminine imagery: Assyrian warriors are shamefully compared to women, and the *double entendre* of 'gates opened wide to your enemies' promises the horror of sexual violation. Sanderson (1992: 219), who explains both the social setting from which the

rape/war connection arises and its problematic character for modern readers, highlights the irony of this passage: Assyria's brutal warfare was perpetrated by men, and when women were involved at all they were victims. Facetiously, vv. 13–14 encourage the Assyrians to try to defend themselves, though v. 15 makes clear that all resistance is futile. Locust vocabulary is used extensively in vv. 15–17, where three different Hebrew words are used to describe these devourers. In this regard, Nahum shares with Joel (esp. ch. 1) the comparison of invading armies with locust plagues.

Nahum ends with a mock funeral dirge for the Assyrian king in vv. 18–19, in which the Assyrian leaders are called 'shepherds' (cf. Jeremiah, Ezekiel, and Zech 9–14). v. 19 performs an important theological function, forcefully reminding the reader that the preceding exultation in Assyria's downfall issues not from free-floating hatred but from the community's own suffering. This concluding rhetorical question leaves the reader with another, implicit one: is delight in an oppressor's defeat morally justified?

REFERENCES

Mason, R. (1991), *Micah, Nahum, Obadiah*, Old Testament Guides (Sheffield: JSOT), 56–84.

Nogalski, J. (1993), *Redactional Processes in the Book of the Twelve* (Berlin: de Gruyter).

Roberts, J. J. M. (1991), *Nahum, Habakkuk, and Zephaniah: A Commentary*, OTL (Louisville, Ky.: Westminster/John Knox).

Sanderson, J. E. (1992), 'Nahum', in Carol A. Newsom and Sharon H. Ringe (eds.), *Women's Bible Commentary* (London: SPCK; Louisville, Ky.: Westminster/John Knox), 217–21.

34. Habakkuk   DONALD E. GOWAN

INTRODUCTION

A. The Subject of the Book. 1. Habakkuk is different from all the other prophetic books, in subject-matter and in its choice of forms of literature. It questions whether the earlier prophets' explanation of the disasters that befell Israel and Judah can be true: that YHWH has sent the armies of foreign nations to punish them for their crimes. The crimes of those armies are manifestly worse than those of Israel or Judah, so how can this be called God's just judgement?

2. The reference to the Chaldeans (the ruling class that established the Neo-Babylonian empire in the late 7th cent.; *ABD* i. 886–7) in 1:6 suggests that the book is a reaction to the approach of Nebuchadnezzar's army as it made its way through Syria and Phoenicia, and it shows no awareness of the fall of Jerusalem in 597 BCE, so may be dated in approximately 600 BCE. Jehoiakim was king of Judah (2 Kings 23:34–24:7; Jer 22:13–19) and it may have been the injustice of his reign that led to the complaints in Hab 1:2–4, although some think the wicked in these verses are the foreign armies. For the history of the period, see Miller and Hayes (1986: 402–15). Neither the wicked in 1:4, 13; 2:4–19 nor the righteous in 1:4, 13; 2:4 are explicitly identified, and this has led to much debate over the date and setting of the book, but the fact that it speaks

in general terms (Childs 1979: 447–55) may perhaps make it all the more valuable as an early contribution to the perennial question of theodicy (*ABD* vi. 444–7): whether God's justice can really be seen at work in the world.

B. Unity and Method. 1. We know nothing about Habakkuk except that 1:1 gives him the title 'prophet' (elsewhere only Hag 1:1; Zech 1:1). This, plus the extensive use of liturgical forms and wisdom terminology, suggests that he may have been a 'cult prophet', functioning in some formal way in the worship of the Jerusalem temple (Murray 1982: 200–16; Coggins 1982: 77–94). The book begins with the language used in the psalms of lament (cf. 1:2–4 with Ps 13:1–2; 74:10; 89:46; and 1:12–13 with Ps 5:4–5), indicates that the prophet could seek an oracle from YHWH (cf. 2:1 with 2 Kings 3:11–20), speaks explicitly of YHWH's presence in the temple (2:20), and concludes with a psalm that uses technical terms found also in the Psalter (3:1, 9, 13, 19), all showing that the prophet knew well the language of worship and may have even been an official participant. He was also well acquainted with the concerns and vocabulary of the sages in Jerusalem: his questions about the justice of God remind us of Job and

Ecclesiastes, and he uses favourite words of the sages, such as 'complaint' (2:1), 'taunt', 'mocking riddles' (2:6), and others (Morgan 1981: 63–93). The only uniquely prophetic form in the book is the 'woe' (or 'alas') poem in 2:6–19.

2. The book is clearly divided into three parts: 1:2–2:5 is a complaint of the prophet, quoting two oracles from God (1:5–11; 2:4–5); 2:6–20 is a poem consisting of five 'woes' over some unnamed tyrant; 3:1–19 is a psalm of thanksgiving. Since ch. 3 has its own introduction many have suggested it did not originally belong with chs. 1–2, but most commentators now agree that even though it may once have been used separately it now forms an appropriate conclusion to the book (Roberts 1991: 141; Robertson 1990: 212; Smith 1984: 95).

COMMENTARY

(1:1) The oracle was a word from God directly spoken to an inspired person. Habakkuk is said to have 'seen' it (also Isa 2:1; Am 1:1) because it was known that sometimes revelation came to the prophets via visions (cf. Hab 2:2; Isa 1:1; Ob 1:1), even though no vision is recorded in this book.

(1:2–2:5) Whereas other prophets announced that God was about to bring judgement upon his people because of the injustice in their society (e.g. Isa 5; Am 5:11–12; 8:4–8), Habakkuk complains to God, using the language of the psalms of lament (Westermann 1981: 165–213), that God appears to have done nothing to alleviate the violence he sees around him (1:2–4). Without introduction a new speaker appears in 1:5–11. The speaker is clearly God himself, as 1:6 reveals. This is usually taken to be a response to the complaint, with a new message that God intends to use the Chaldeans as his agents of judgement for the sins of his people, the way he had used the Assyrians in the eighth century (Isa 10:1–19; Mic 1; etc.). If so, this is a dialogue between the prophet and his God, similar to the complaints of Jeremiah that God answered (Jer 11:18–20, 21–3; 12:1–4, 5–6; 15:10–18, 19–21). Isaiah and Micah may have accepted the idea of Assyria as agent of judgement, but Habakkuk knows too much about what an invading army does to conquered people to accept that as evidence for God's justice. His rejoinder in 1:12–17 puts the issue bluntly: how can a righteous God do nothing about wrongdoing, treachery, and wickedness? Rather than a dialogue, 1:2–2:1 may be a single complaint, however, in which Habakkuk quotes an oracle he had received earlier (1:5–11). If so, this oracle was already the cause of the protest in 1:2–4.

The MT's 'we shall not die' (1:12) is identified in the rabbinic literature as one of the *tiqqûnê hassōphěrîm* (emendations of the scribes), a few very early changes of texts that were offensive for some reason. Rabbinic tradition recalled that the original reading was 'you shall not die', a good parallel to 'Are you not from of old . . . ?' in 1:12a, and NRSV has adopted that tradition. Apparently the scribes found the very thought of the death of God to be shocking enough to alter the sentence, even though it negated the idea. 1:12–13 represents one of the OT's starkest contrasts between belief in a just and holy God and the realities of this violent world, comparable to some of Job's speeches (Job 21, 24). Habakkuk elaborates on the impossibility of accepting the cruelties of an invading army as God's way of establishing justice on earth, likening the enemy to a fisherman and the defeated to his catch (1:14–

17). But like Job, Habakkuk does not give up on God, and insists there must be an answer, using the imagery of the watchman on a tower to represent his persistence (2:1). NRSV has emended 'what I will answer' to 'what he will answer ', but the MT is understandable as a reference to the way Habakkuk may react to the answer he awaits from God. His reaction is recorded in 3:17–19.

God's answer (2:2–5) is brief, and in many respects cryptic. He affirms the need for persistence, assuring Habakkuk that waiting will not be futile (v. 3), and speaks of writing a vision (without indicating what its contents will be) on tablets (v. 2), one of the few references in the prophetic books to putting their words in written form (cf. Isa 8:1; 30:8; Jer 36). 'So that a runner may read it' (NRSV and most trs.) suggests a message written large, but the Hebrew literally says 'so that one who reads it may run'. Royal messengers normally carried a written copy of the text they were to declare, and since the prophets functioned as messengers of God (cf. the frequent occurrence of the 'messenger formula': 'Thus says the Lord'; Westermann 1967: 98–128) this may be an allusion to the delivery of God's message by his prophet.

2:4 is the thematic centre of the book, but the first half of the verse is difficult. NRSV paraphrases, using 'proud' to represent a word that occurs only here in the OT, but which seems to be formed from a root meaning 'to swell', so others translate it 'puffed up'. 'Spirit' is not the best choice for *nepeš*, which is better rendered 'life'. 2:4a must be a contrast of some sort to 2:4b, but every translation proposed so far involves some guesswork. 2:4b is composed of three potent words in Hebrew. According to Habakkuk the righteous have been suffering unjustly (1:4, 13) and the issue is when and whether God will do something about it. As used in ch. 1, 'righteous' would seem to mean 'innocent', as in many other occurrences of the word (*ABD* v. 724–36). Here, God does not say what he intends to do for them, but assures them that life is possible in the meantime, and in Hebrew to be alive means more than merely to exist or survive; it connotes full vitality, health, and even reputation (*IDB* iii. 124–6; *TDOT* iv. 324–44). The last word is more appropriately translated 'faithfulness' than 'faith' since that is its usual meaning in the OT (cf. 2 Chr 19:9; Hos 2:20), and the root has the sense of 'belief' only in Isa 7:9 (*ABD* ii. 744–9). Paul thus used the verse in an original way in Gal 3:11: 'Now it is evident that no one is justified before God by the law; for "The one who is righteous will live by faith"' (cf. Rom 1:17). Faith and faithfulness are not to be sharply distinguished, for one can scarcely be faithful without faith, and mere belief without faithful behaviour would be a mockery, as Paul makes clear in Rom 6 and elsewhere. God's brief answer insists the puffed up (proud or presumptuous) will not endure, but offers no explanation for their present success in a world supposedly ruled by a just God. The answer, so far, is an existential one, putting the responsibility on the shoulders of the righteous, but containing the promise that they may live by their faithfulness. The pronoun with 'faithfulness' is singular in Hebrew (not 'their', NRSV). The usual translation has been 'his faithfulness', referring to the righteous, but some prefer 'its faithfulness', i.e. the reliability of the vision promised in 2:2 (Janzen 1980: 53–78; Roberts 1991: 104).

(2:5) serves as a transition verse between the first and second major sections of the book. It introduces the theme of 2:6–19; the inevitable downfall of the arrogant who (like the Chaldeans) 'gather all nations for themselves'. It may thus be an elaboration of 2:4a. MT reads 'wine is treacherous', which does not seem a natural move from 'the righteous live by their faith', and NRSV has preferred the reading 'wealth', found in the commentary on Habakkuk at Qumran. The reference to wine in MT may look ahead to 2:15–16, however. The metaphor of Death as a monster with a gaping mouth was well known in the ancient Near East (Prov 27:20; 30:15–16; Isa 5:14; also in the Baal epic found at Ugarit in Syria; ANET 1955: 138).

(2:6–20) Clearly this is a distinct section of the book, with an introduction in 6a and with v. 20 making the transition to ch. 3. It is a poem of five stanzas, the first four of which are introduced by hôy ('woe' or 'alas'). The same word occurs in the middle of the fifth stanza (v. 19). It may be that v. 18 originally followed v. 19 and became dislocated in the copying of the text, or perhaps the poet chose to vary the shape of the last stanza. In Hebrew the entire poem speaks of a tyrant in the third person; NRSV has changed the references to second person. The exclamation hôy was originally a cry of grief, as 1 Kings 13:30 shows. The element of grief appears in some prophetic uses (Jer 22:18; 30:7; 34:5; Am 5:16), but the word is used here in a context of rejoicing over the death of a tyrant, and Isaiah uses it to introduce a series of accusations (5:8–23; 10:1–4). Some have claimed the word was just a cry to get attention, like 'Hey!', but that scarcely explains its uses in mourning the dead and the fact that it is usually followed by a third-person reference (ABD vi. 945–6; TDOT iii. 359–64). Other elements in Habakkuk's poem show that he had constructed a mock funeral song, using the traditional cry of grief in a new way, and emphasizing the theme of reversal of fortune that is typical of dirges (cf. 2 Sam 1:19–27). The introduction, with the words 'taunt' and 'mocking riddles', alerts us that Habakkuk is making a radically new use of a traditional genre. God has thus told the prophet to authorize his suffering people to celebrate the death of the tyrant in advance, for his downfall is inevitable.

Five of the ways the tyrant has brought suffering to many people will soon rebound upon him, the prophet says. He has enriched himself by impoverishing others; soon his own debts will be called in (vv. 6b–8). He has sought to ensure his own security at the cost of others; his own palace will testify against him (vv. 9–11). He thought the greatness of his building programmes justified bloodshed and iniquity; when the earth is filled with the knowledge of the Lord that will be shown to be folly (vv. 12–14). The use of drunkenness to accomplish his purposes (vv. 15–17) may be literal (cf. Isa 28:7; Prov 31:4–5), but the cup in v. 16b is the metaphorical cup of wrath found also in Jer 25:15–19. The violence done to Lebanon (v. 17) refers to the frequent invasions of Phoenicia by Mesopotamian conquerors in order to obtain its valuable cedars (cf. Isa 14:8; 37:24). The gods who have authorized the empire-building of the tyrant are mocked as mere idols (vv. 18–19), using wordplays in Hebrew, one of which may be echoed in English as 'stolid statues'. Then the rude mockery is brought to a sudden end with the call to silence (v. 20), for Habakkuk is about to speak of the way YHWH comes to save his people.

(3:1–19) The separate title given to this poem, similar to those attached to some of the Psalms (Ps 7:1; 17:1; 86:1; 90:1), suggests that this may originally have been a separate piece, a psalm produced for use in temple worship, but it now forms an appropriate conclusion to the book (Hiebert 1986). Its use of theophanic language is similar to that of Ps 18, and it may thus have been written as a psalm of thanksgiving. Several lines are extremely difficult to translate, because of their use of rare words. Apparently Habakkuk either quoted extensively from earlier poetry, or deliberately chose to use archaic language to express the awesomeness of the coming of the Lord. v. 2 is an effective introduction, including a prayer for divine intervention recalling ch. 1, a confession of awe (lit. fear) at God's work, anticipating the terrifying theophany of vv. 3–15, and the key words 'wrath' and 'mercy'.

vv. 3–15 are one of the impressive theophanies (ABD vi. 505–11; OCB 740–1) of the OT, a term used of descriptions of the appearance of God that make extensive use of the most awe-inspiring of natural phenomena in order to convey the sense of God's overwhelming power (cf. Ex 19; Ps 18:7–19; 50:3; 77:16–20; Nah 1:2–8). Its archaic character is reflected not only in its vocabulary, but also in the echoes of ancient Near-Eastern myths involving conflict between a hero god, such as Marduk or Baal, and the watery chaos, Tiamat or Yam (ANET 1955: 60–72, 129–31; and cf. Ps 74:13–15; Isa 27:1; 51:9). Habakkuk also used the old traditions of YHWH as a warrior in order to speak of God's coming to save his people. Teman and Mount Paran (v. 3) are places south-east of Judah and are probably intended to recall the Sinai tradition, as in Deut 33:2. Cushan may be a poetic shortening of Cushanrishathaim, one of the oppressors of Israel during the period of the Judges (Judg 3:8–10), and Midian may thus refer to the story of Gideon (Judg 6–8). Israel's use of terrifying language to describe the saviour God, as in vv. 5–15, may be disturbing to modern readers, but it is properly understood as an effort to convey the awareness that God is 'wholly other', whose presence is both daunting and intensely attractive; the religious experience best described by Rudolf Otto as the 'numinous' (Otto 1958; Gowan 1994: 25–53). These two aspects of the sense of God's immediate presence then appear in Habakkuk's description of his reaction, in vv. 16–19. He is physically shaken by it (v. 16a), but the presence of God has given him not only the ability to endure trustfully (v. 16b) but a sense of rejoicing that transcends all suffering. In the economy of ancient Israel, the failure of all that is listed in v. 17 would mean starvation, but in vv. 18–19 Habakkuk affirms that he has found in the saviour God the strength to become 'more than conqueror' (Rom 8:37; cf. 2 Cor 4:8–10). He has not found rational answers to the 'Why?' and 'How long?' questions with which the book began, but he has learned how to live without the answers, and how to live rejoicing.

REFERENCES

Childs, B. S. (1979), *Introduction to the Old Testament as Scripture* (Philadelphia: Fortress).

Coggins, R. (1982), 'An Alternative Prophetic Tradition?', in Richard Coggins, Anthony Phillips, and Michael Knibb, (eds.), *Israel's Prophetic Tradition: Essays in Honour of Peter R. Ackroyd* (Cambridge: Cambridge University Press).

Gowan, D. E. (1994), *Theology in Exodus: Biblical Theology in the Form of a Commentary* (Louisville, Ky.: Westminster/John Knox), ch. 2.

Hiebert, T. (1986), *God of My Victory: The Ancient Hymn in Habakkuk 3*, HSM 38 (Atlanta: Scholars Press).

Janzen, J. G. (1980), 'Habakkuk 2:2–4 in the Light of Recent Philological Advances', *HTR* 73: 53–78.

Miller, J. M., and Hayes, J. H. (1986), *A History of Ancient Israel and Judah* (Philadelphia: Westminster).

Morgan, D. F. (1981), *Wisdom in the Old Testament Traditions* (Atlanta: John Knox).

Murray, R. (1982), 'Prophecy and the Cult', in Richard Coggins, Anthony Phillips, and Michael Knibb (eds.), *Israel's Prophetic Tradition: Essays in Honour of Peter R. Ackroyd* (Cambridge: Cambridge University Press).

Otto, R. (1958), *The Idea of the Holy: An Inquiry into the Non-Rational Factor in the Idea of the Divine and its Relation to the Rational* (Oxford: Oxford University. Press).

Roberts, J. J. M. (1991), *Nahum, Habakkuk, and Zephaniah: A Commentary*. Old Testament Library (Louisville' Ky.: Westminster/John Knox).

Robertson, O. P. (1990), *The Books of Nahum, Habakkuk, and Zephaniah* (Grand Rapids Mich.: Eerdmans).

Smith, R. L. (1984), *Micah-Malachi*, Word Biblical Commentary (Waco, Tex.: Word Books).

Westermann, C. (1967), *Basic Forms of Prophetic Speech* (Philadelphia: Westminster).

—— (1981), *Praise and Lament in the Psalms* (Atlanta: John Knox).

35. Zephaniah

REX MASON

INTRODUCTION

A. The Prophet. 1. For all the lengthy pedigree given for Zephaniah in 1:1 we know nothing about him. His descent is traced back to 'Hezekiah'. Commentators offer the mutually cancelling views that either Hezekiah was so well known he did not need to be called 'king' or that, if it were really *the* Hezekiah he would have been called king! We cannot use either view for evidence as to why Zephaniah did not criticize the king in his prophecy (e.g. at 1:8). It is, perhaps, difficult to believe that one who criticized the political and religious establishment of his day so severely was of the royal line. Zephaniah seems to know Jerusalem well and to be familiar with the language and practices of its temple worship. The deduction from this that he was a 'cult prophet' runs into the same difficulties as the view that he was royal: could an official temple servant have been so devastating in his critique of it? He draws on very similar prophetic traditions to those found in Amos, Hosea, and Isa 1–39. The suggestion that he is to be identified with an exiled priest of the name (2 Kings 25: 18–21, Williams 1963) lacks both foundation and probability.

2. The superscription sets Zephaniah's ministry in the time of King Josiah (640–609 BCE). Many commentators have accepted this and seen his attacks especially on the religious syncretism of Judah as predating Josiah's reform of 621 BCE. It is argued that such abuses would not have existed after the clean-up described in 2 Kings 23:4–24 (e.g. Roberts 1991: 163). We may suspect that the account of Josiah's reform has been somewhat exaggerated, especially in the light of the subsequent fierce attacks of Jeremiah and Ezekiel on the religious life of Judah. Even if that is so, however, it is true that the book would suit a general movement of unrest following the period of Assyrian domination in the time of Manasseh such as gave rise to the Deuteronomic reform movement. (For a brief survey of the history of the period and assessment of the account of Josiah's reform, see Mason 1994: 35–43; for a recent questioning of the account of Josiah's reform in Kings, see Clements 1996: 10–13.) Some have argued for a post-reform Josianic date, or even a date in the reign of his successor Jehoiakim, sometimes on the grounds of 1:4 with its

reference to the '*remnant* of Baal', which suggests Josiah had done his work, or on the identification of the prophet with the exiled priest of the same name, or on the basis of Deuteronomic parallels in the book (e.g. Hyatt 1948, Williams 1963, Robertson 1990). However, the phrase in 1:4 may just mean 'every vestige of Baal' (Ben Zvi 1991: 67) while the Deuteronomic parallels arc general and we do not know which influenced the other. The identification of the two Zephaniahs is purely hypothetical. The most extreme dating of Zephaniah in the second century BCE (while allowing for a 6th-century origin for 1:4–13, Smith and Lacheman 1950) has received little support. However, many would argue for a post-exilic date for the present form of the *book* (e.g. Ben Zvi).

B. The Book. 1. The outline and division of contents which we follow in the commentary is one which is generally and broadly accepted (variations are noted). The book, small as it is, shows the whole range of prophetic material including oracles of judgement against Israel/Judah, oracles against the nations, oracles of salvation for Israel or a remnant within her, and more cosmic or universal pictures of YHWH's future action tending towards what is sometimes called 'apocalyptic'. General prophetic themes, especially as found in Amos, Hosea, and Isa 1–39, include the 'day of the LORD', whether seen as a day of darkness and judgement for God's people or as salvation for Israel and judgement of the nations; a critique of both social injustice and religious apostasy; and calls for repentance in humble submission to and dependence upon YHWH. In addition, there are echoes of psalms and other worship material from the temple cult. There is a dearth of unambiguous references to historical events and, as we shall see, there appears to be a tendency towards a more generalizing interpretation of earlier prophetic material, which may suggest a complex redactional process as earlier oracles were edited, exegeted, and found to have relevance in new situations. It is difficult to be precise about the exact stages of such redaction. Some commentators see the book as mainly the work of the seventh-century prophet Zephaniah (e.g. Keller 1990, Roberts 1991). Many assume a redaction process, usually incorporating what they view as an exilic or Deuteronomic stratum and later post-exilic material, especially in 3:9–20 (e.g. Renaud 1987, Irsigler 1977, Krinetzki 1977). Ben Zvi (1991) has argued strongly that the book, while incorporating earlier material—he identifies three compositional levels—must be read as a post-exilic literary work from which we can deduce nothing certain of the historic prophet or his ministry. House (1988) attempts to read the book as a 'prophetic drama' based on alternating speeches of YHWH and the prophet, but this founders on the dubiety of his distribution of some of the speeches between the protagonists and the lack of any obvious dramatic plot or, indeed, any literary parallel for such a form.

2. The text itself does not present major problems. The more important difficulties are noted in the commentary.

COMMENTARY

(1:1) Editorial Superscription See A1, 2.

(1:2–18) The Day of YHWH's Judgement against Judah and Jerusalem The main indictments of the Judean community and warnings of YHWH's judgement appear in vv. 4–16. These are now set in a framework, vv. 2–3 and 17–18, which extends God's judgement against Judah and Jerusalem on to a universal, more cosmic stage. vv. 2–3, what is announced is a complete reversal of the act of creation as described in Gen. ch. 1. All the main aspects of the created order will be swept away. To drive the point home, the word rendered in NRSV as 'humans' and 'humanity' is 'ādam (as in Gen. 1:26–7), and there is the same paronomasia with the word 'earth', 'ădāmā, as in Gen. 2:5, 6, 7, 9. In a general reversion to chaos from created order human beings will lose their divinely given rule of the earth (see de Roche 1980). vv. 4–6, for the phrase 'remnant of Baal' see A.2. The word rendered in NRSV as 'idolatrous priests' is rare and relates only to those who serve other gods (2 Kings 23:5; Hos 10:5). This may have led a glossator to add an explanatory 'with the priests' showing that, in his view, God would judge his own priests as well. v. 5 links this with astral worship (see 2 Kings 23:4–5 for an account of how this cult was overthrown in Josiah's reform). 'Milcom', NRSV, is a version of the name of the Ammonite god (1 Kings 11:5 etc.). The Hebrew is pointed to read 'their king' (malkām), which might refer to Baal worship. The point is that Judeans combine worship of YHWH with that of other deities. Either these are contrasted with yet others (v. 6) who have simply abandoned the worship of YHWH without embracing that of any other god, or religious syncretism is seen as in fact abandoning YHWH anyway.

vv. 7–9, the day of YHWH: the call 'Be silent' was used in the cult to announce the theophany (Hab 2:20; Zech 2:13) but here YHWH's appearance among his people is not for salvation but for judgement. There will be a festal sacrifice but the people of Judah will find no substitutionary victim, they themselves will be the victims (whoever the 'guests' may be). But just as the priests were singled out for attack in v. 4 so here the royal establishment is held responsible. The failure to specify the king might be because Josiah was still a minor (so several, e.g. Roberts 1991: 178), but the phrase 'the king's

sons' may be a generic term like 'sons of the prophets', here signifying the whole royal establishment. Sabottka's (1972) idea that 'the king' is Baal and the reference is to his priests whose 'foreign attire' is their officiating robes is unlikely. Their fault seems to be that they are a foppish and effete wealthy class, whose wealth is obtained (v. 9) by robbery and violence. Whether they leap out of their own doors on unsuspecting passers-by or leap into the houses of their victims is not clear. vv. 10–12, it seems to be the city of Jerusalem which will bear the brunt of YHWH's judgement 'on that day'. Priests, royals, and now wealthy merchants and traders are singled out (v. 11). Various places in the city are specified, and its inhabitants are addressed as those who live in 'mortar', i.e. buildings within a walled city. God will search out the complacent and indifferent who are virtual (if not theoretical) atheists. God may exist but they do not think they need take him into the reckoning of practical life and politics. They are like wine which deteriorates if it is never disturbed (Jer. 48:11). They will reap no long-term profit from their oppression (v. 13). vv. 14–16, the day of wrath: this passage, the basis of the medieval hymn 'Dies Irae', stands in the tradition of the teaching of Amos and Isaiah about the day of YHWH as a day of darkness, a day which sees invasion and defeat. It may already mark a widening of the original attacks on Jerusalem by its threat to 'cities' in the plural. Its description of them emphasizes them as places of strong fortifications and security. All human might is helpless before God's power, however. vv. 17–18, the threats here have become quite general, against 'humanity', the same word 'ādām as in v. 3, NRSV masking the 'framework' effect of this with its translation, 'people'. Now no specific crimes are mentioned, they have 'sinned against the LORD'. Again, it seems to be those who confide in human resources—here their wealth—who are singled out, but the threat is now universal, to 'all the inhabitants of the earth'. The effect of vv. 2–3 and 17–18 is therefore to make the threats of vv. 4–16 against the people of Jerusalem for specific sins applicable to all people of all times.

(2:1–3) A Call to Penitence There have been those who see this oracle as belonging with the oracles against the nations which follow (J. M. P. Smith 1911: 211). This would be more likely if v. 3 were the late addition many have argued (Taylor 1956: 1022; Elliger 1964: 69; Seybold 1991: 103). However, although a call to penitence might seem illogical to us coming after such threats of total disaster, it is quite normal in the prophetic books (e.g. Am 5:4–5). The book of Jonah is concerned to show that penitence can avert even a prophetic prediction of disaster. Further, Zephaniah may articulate something which may well be implicit elsewhere in the prophetic canon. While the 'organized state' will disappear there is hope for 'the humble' if they seek YHWH. v. 1, the verb rendered 'Gather together' is related to the word for gathering stubble. The adjective 'shameless' seems to be from a verbal root meaning 'to desire' and so mean 'undesired'. In God's eyes the nation and its establishment have become as worthless, and little wanted, as stubble in a harvested field. v. 3, note that the prophet's call is to the 'poor' or 'humble' as opposed to the priests, the royal establishment and the wealthy merchants and traders. The word 'humble' is almost a technical term in the psalms for the downtrodden and oppressed, those who have no hope of help from any but God. The 'perhaps' suggests that his mercy is sovereign.

(2:4–15) Oracles against the Nations (OAN) Many commentators have spent a lot of time trying to ferret out the historical context of these oracles. The reason for their widely differing conclusions is that references are of the most general kind. This renders dubious the claim of those such as Christensen (1984) that they all fit neatly into the year 628 BCE. Even the apparent allusion to the fall of Nineveh (v. 13) must be treated with caution (see below). The nations represent Israel's enemies at the four points of the compass. In the ancient Near East new kings had to earn by their victories the right to call themselves 'Lord of the Four Quarters of the Earth' (Liverani 1981). One function of these oracles may therefore be to establish YHWH's claim to be Lord of the whole world. (For a detailed study see Ryou 1995.) vv. 4–7, no special crime of Philistia is mentioned. Perhaps it symbolizes 'the uncircumcised' *par excellence*. v. 7 introduces the idea of the 'remnant', one way of easing the tension between threats of judgement against the nation of Israel and yet of God's purpose for future salvation. vv. 8–11, note that the crime of Moab and Ammon is human pride and enmity against God's people. God's judgement against all human pretensions is a familiar prophetic theme, and it may well be the function of this oracle to express this truth rather than recall some specific historical occasion. v. 12, the brief mention of the Ethiopians is a mystery. Perhaps it is a fragment of a longer oracle. vv. 13–15, Nineveh fell in 612 BCE and it might be that this oracle, or some form of it, was once uttered by the prophet Zephaniah in the early period of Josiah's reign. But note again it is her pride and confidence in her own power (v. 14) which is the reason for her downfall. In later times Nineveh could, and did, become a symbol of all that is opposed to God, as in Jonah.

(3:1–8) Further Indictments against the Jerusalem Community The switch to Jerusalem in v. 1 is so abrupt, with only the introductory 'Woe' of the judgement oracle in the form of a lamentation (Westermann 1967: 189–94), that some have taken it as a continuation of the threat against Nineveh. But the paralleling may well be deliberate (Renaud 1987: 235–6). Jerusalem is no better than these 'pagan' nations. This would echo Amos's use of OAN (Barton 1980: 3–15). It further strengthens the view that the 'nations' now typify that kind of sin which God will judge, wherever he finds it. vv. 3–4, note again the attack on the figures of the establishment, both civil and religious. v. 5, the contrast is between YHWH who gives real justice 'in the morning' (when the king heard legal appeals, Jer 21:12) and the corrupt exercise of power by those who claim his authority. The statement 'The LORD within it is righteous' may well parody the claims of the Jerusalem cultus, 'God is in the midst of her' and 'The LORD of hosts is with us' (Ps 46:5, 7, 11, HB vv. 6, 8, 12). vv. 6–7, YHWH's actions against other nations should have shown Israel his power and his demands for righteousness (again, the function of the OAN in ch. 2), but they refused to pay any heed. v. 8 is a totally unexpected denouement. One would expect vv. 1–7 to culminate in the announcement of God's judgement against Jerusalem for all her sins, but instead, v. 8 appears to switch to the theme of the announcement of his judgement against the

nations. If originally it was his intention to gather nations to act as his agents of judgement (a familiar prophetic theme, e.g. Ob 1, Zech 14:2) we would expect the verse to read 'to pour out upon *you*', an emendation some have suggested (e.g. Renaud 1987: 243). Roberts (1991: 215) suggests that the verse is addressed to 'the faithful' and the 'them' on whom YHWH is to pour out his wrath are the faithless, corrupt officials of vv. 3–4).

(3:9–13) Salvation for Judah and the Nations v. 9, this is unexpected and seems far removed from the threat in v. 8 of judgement against the nations, which suggests that v. 8 was read, at least by some, in one of the ways suggested above. The idea that the nations will be given a 'change of speech' (cf. Isa 6:5–7; 19:18) so that they call on YHWH suggests a somewhat late universalism. Its position here probably shows an editor's view that the salvation of Israel will have universal consequences. vv. 11–13 return to the strong contrast drawn throughout this book between the 'proud', and the 'humble' and 'lowly', or 'poor', another term from the Psalms. Note the complete reversal of the state of such people from that described in 1:4–13 and 3:1–4.

(3:14–20) YHWH's Reign as King in Jerusalem Again in familiar cultic terms the faithful are called upon to rejoice already in YHWH's victorious kingship (cf. Isa 12:6; Zech 2:10; 9:9 etc.). Now judgements are taken away and YHWH really is in their 'midst' (v. 15, cf. the irony of 3:5). Many have pointed to the strong parallels between this whole passage and the 'Psalms of YHWH's Enthronement' (e.g. Ps 47, 93, 96–9). He alone will be king—there is no mention of any renewed experiments with human kings—and it is again stressed that it is the 'lame' and the 'outcast' whom he will bring in as his subjects, having ousted their 'oppressors' (v. 19). Zephaniah is a thoroughly radical prophetic book—a charter for the 'little people' of all corrupt societies. v. 20 is probably a later addition whose purpose is to extend to Jews living in all kinds of difficulty the assurance that God will bring them back from their own particular 'Babylon'.

REFERENCES

Barton, J. (1980), *Amos's Oracles against the Nations*, SOTSMS 6 (Cambridge: Cambridge University Press).

Ben Zvi, E. (1991) *A Historical-Critical Study of the Book of Zephaniah*, BZAW 198, (Berlin: de Gruyter).

Christensen, D. L. (1984), 'Zephaniah 2:4–15: A Theological Basis for Josiah's Program of Political Expansion', *CBO* 46: 669–82.

Clements, R. E. (1996), 'The Deuteronomic Law of Centralization and the Catastrophe of 587 B.C.', *After the Exile: Essays in Honour of Rex Mason* (Macon, Ga.: Mercer University Press), 5–25.

Elliger, K. (1964), *Das Buch der zwölf Kleinen Propheten*, ATD 25/2 (Göttingen: Vandenhoeck & Ruprecht).

House, P. R. (1988), *Zephaniah: A Prophetic Drama*, JSOTSup 69, (Sheffield: Almond Press).

Hyatt, J. P. (1948), 'The Date and Background of Zephaniah', *JNES* 7: 25–9.

Irsigler, H. (1977), *Gottesricht und Jahwetag: Die Komposition Zef 1, 1–2, 3, untersucht auf der Grundlage der Literarkritik des Zefanjabuches*, ATAT 3 (St Ottilien: Eos).

Keller, C. A. (1990), *Nahoum, Habacuc, Sophonie*, CAT 11b 2nd edn. (Neuchâtel: Delachaux et Liestle).

Krinetzki, G. (1977), *Zefanjastudien. Motiv- und Traditionskritik + Kompositions- und Redaktionskritik*, Regensburger Studien zu Theologie, 7 (Frankfurt: Lang).

Liverani, M. (1981), 'Critique of Variants and the Titulary of Sennacherib', in F. M. Fales (ed.), *Assyrian Royal Inscriptions: New Horizons* (Rome: Istituto per l'Oriente).

Mason, R. (1994), *Zephaniah, Habakkuk, Joel*, Old Testament Guides, (Sheffield: Sheffield Academic Press).

Renaud, B. (1987), *Michee-Sophonie-Nahum*, SB (Paris: Gabalda).

Roberts, J. J. M. (1991), *Nahum, Habakkuk and Zephaniah*, OTL (Louisville, Ky.: Westminster/John Knox).

Robertson, O. P. (1990), *The Books of Nahum, Habakkuk and Zephaniah*, NICOT (Grand Rapids, Mich.: Eerdmans).

Roche, M. de (1980), 'Zephaniah 1:2, 3: The "Sweeping" of the Creation', and 'Contra Creation, Covenant and Conquest (Jer. viii 13)', *VT* 30 (1980), 104–9, 280–90.

Ryou, D. H. (1995), *Zephaniah's Oracles against the Nations: A Synchronic and Diachronic Study of Zephaniah 2:1–3:8*, Biblical Interpretation Series, 13 (Leiden: Brill).

Sabottka, L. (1972), *Zephanja, Versuch einer Neuübersetzung mit philologischem Kommentar*, BibOr 25 (Rome: Pontifical Biblical Institute).

Seybold, K. (1991), *Nahum, Habakuk, Zephanja*, ZB, (Zurich: Theologischer Verlag).

Smith, J. M. P. (1911), 'Zephaniah', in *Micah, Zephaniah, Nahum, Habakkuk, Obadiah and Joel*, ICC (Edinburgh: T. & T. Clark), 159–263.

Smith, L. P., and Lacheman, E. R. (1950), 'The Authorship of the Book of Zephaniah', *JNES* 9: 137–42.

Taylor C. L. (1956), 'The Book of Zephaniah', *IB* 6 (New York: Abingdon), 1007–34.

Westermann C., (1967), *Basic Forms of Prophetic Speech*, tr. White (London: Lutterworth); German original, 2nd edn., (Munich: Chr. Kaiser, 1964).

Williams, D. L. (1963), 'The Date of Zephaniah', *JBL* 82: 77–88.

36. Haggai

D. L. PETERSEN

INTRODUCTION

A. Historical Background. 1. Haggai is one of the shortest of the prophetic books. Still, these thirty-seven verses offer a significant vantage point from which to observe a nodal moment in Israelite history, the creation of the Second Temple community out of which Judaism emerged. The book's chronological markers (1:1; 2:1; 2:10) fix the literature to one year, 520 BCE, and to the issues of restoration for those in Persian-period Judah (also known as Yehud).

2. Many prophetic books begin with references to Israelite or Judahite kings during whose reign the prophet was active (e.g. Isa 1:1; Jer 1:3; Hos 1:1; Am 1:1). Haggai could not commence with such references since there was no longer a king in Israel. Still, the author/editor of this book decided to situate the literature with reference to a king's reign. The natural candidate was Darius, the Persian emperor, who reigned from 522 to 486 BCE.

3. The Persian empire was vast, reaching from the Mediterranean sea to territory far beyond the eastern borders of the classical Mesopotamian civilizations (Assyria and Babylonia). The empire was divided into larger and smaller administrative areas, called satrapies and districts. Whether the territory known as Judah was a province separate from a larger district, Samaria, during the time of Haggai is disputed. That dispute affects our understanding of the title 'governor of/for Judah', which is applied to Zerubbabel (Hag 1:1 *et passim*). The phrase could in theory refer to either a temporary assignment or a more permanent office.

4. Darius was not the first Persian king to affect the fate of those who venerated YHWH. Cyrus, whom the exilic Isaiah viewed as a messiah (Isa 45:1), had issued an edict that enabled the restoration of communities destroyed and displaced by the Babylonians (Kuhrt 1983). During his reign, some Yahwists had apparently returned from exile to Judah and attempted to rebuild the temple. But the efforts associated with their leader Sheshbazzar in *c*.538 BCE came to nought (Ezra 1:8; 5:14–16).

5. Things changed with Darius. Soon after he acceded to the throne there were rebellions throughout the empire. Though he was able to quell most of them readily, such activity represented a problem, namely, security at the empire's perimeter. All the dates in the book of Haggai refer to 520 BCE, a year during which Darius was making plans for a campaign against Egypt (Meyers and Meyers 1987; Berquist 1995). It was in the Persians' interest to have a secure and stable Judah. Having the local populace focused on the rebuilding of their temple, supported in part by the Persians, would have placated some of their dismay at imperial overlords. The Persians needed food for their armies, and it is probably no accident that Haggai refers more than once to food supplies. Hence, one should understand the rebuilding of the Jerusalem temple as consistent with and supported by Persian imperial policy. As governor, Zerubbabel was, after all, a Persian official.

B. Date and Place of Composition. Although the book of Haggai refers explicitly to Persian chronology, it was almost certainly written in Judah. Haggai himself may well have been among those Yahwists who remained in the land during the Babylonian Exile. Since the book includes chronological formulae, all of which refer to the year 520 BCE, it is difficult to imagine that the book was written much later than this pivotal moment. Given the special prominence of the temple for Haggai, one would have expected him to refer to its completion, which took place in 515 BCE. Since the book does not refer to this event, it was probably written between 520 and 515 BCE.

C. The Literature and its Formation. 1. Haggai is an odd book, difficult to characterize. If one consults the NRSV, one finds a text translated entirely as prose. Were such the case, Haggai and Malachi would be the only prophetic books to include no poetry (at least according to NRSV). By contrast, the editors of the MT deem 1:4–11; 2:3–9, 14, and portions of vv. 22–3 as poetry, a judgement also followed in part by NAB. Although the boundary between poetry and prose in classical Hebrew is notably difficult to discern, it is reasonable to follow those who have identified some poetry in the book, notably, many of those verses in which Haggai or others are speaking (cf. Christensen 1993).

2. The book initially appears to be a collection of oracles, e.g. 1:7–11 or 2:21–3, that have been integrated by complex dating formulae, e.g. 1:1; 2:10. But there is also material very much like a chronicle, i.e. 1:12–14. It is possible to view the entire book as a brief historical account (Petersen 1984). This account memorializes the building of the temple and emphasizes the importance of Haggai, along with Zerubbabel and Joshua, in accomplishing this task.

3. Scholars have offered various theories about the composition of the book. Beuken (1967) thinks the oracles were edited by someone such as the Chronicler. Mason (1977) pursues a similar argument, though without equating the redactor with the Chronicler. Wolff (1988) discerns three stages of growth: the prophetic speeches, sketches of scenes (e.g. 1:12b–13), and the word occurrence formulae (e.g. 2:10). Meyers and Meyers (1987) and Tollington (1993) think similar hands were responsible for both Haggai and Zechariah 1–8, whereas Bauer (1992) and Pierce (1984a, 1984b) see Haggai and Zechariah 1–8, together with Malachi, as forming a compositional group. Although there is no scholarly consensus, most discern a rather complicated process of literary formation, according to which Haggai's own words have been preserved and edited by others.

D. Religious and Theological Issues. **1.** To speak of Haggai is to speak of the temple and its manifold significance (cf. Clines 1993). To read the Hebrew phrase, 'YHWH's house', and to contemplate a time without such a house presents the problem with which this book is concerned. How is YHWH to be present with the people if the deity's residence is in ruins? To be sure, God could not be encapsulated by the temple, but without that earlier and powerful religious symbol, Israel's notions of both the immanence and transcendence of the deity stood in crisis. Further, Haggai reveals that there was a debate about whether 520 BCE was the time for such a crisis to be resolved, so Hag 1:2 (see Bedford 1995).

2. Haggai refers at numerous points to the weal that will ensue when the temple is rebuilt. Such promises encourage the leaders and the populace to undertake the task of rebuilding the temple. According to this prophetic historical account, Haggai was successful; the temple was rededicated during his period of prophetic activity. One can only surmise about the reaction of the people to the various promises uttered by the prophet (2:6–7, 19, 21–2). Still, both the exilic Isaiah (Isa 40–55) and Haggai offered exuberant rhetoric on behalf of the return and reconstruction of Judah; and both prophets' words remain in the canon even though Jerusalem's gates were not made of jewels and her walls of precious stones (Isa 54:12).

E. Outline

Build the House (1:1–11)
They Worked on the House of the Lord (1:12–15a)
Take Courage (1:15b–2:9)
Holy—Unclean (2:10–14)
A Stone in the Lord's Temple (2:15–19)
Zerubbabel, my Servant (2:20–3)

COMMENTARY

(1:1–11) Build the House Haggai addresses two individuals, both of whom were Yahwists sent to Judah by the Persian authorities (cf. Ezra 2:2). Zerubbabel held the political title of governor, while Joshua bore the religious title, high priest. They symbolize a new governance structure in Israel. Both offices were new ones. Zerubbabel may have been a member of the Davidic house, though this matter is the subject of scholarly debate (see Berquist 1995). He was governor of or for Judah, which means he was a Persian official. Both Joshua the high priest and Zerubbabel are mentioned by Haggai's contemporary, Zechariah (Zech 3:1–10; 4:6–7). Joshua's grandfather was chief (but not 'high') priest just before the defeat of Jerusalem in 587 BCE (2 Kings 25:18–21). Zerubbabel and Joshua are harbingers of a religious and political pattern attested also in the later Persian period, one in which major leadership and power are exercised by those who had been in, or could trace their roots to, the Exile. The genealogies provided for both these individuals enable them to affirm this exilic heritage.

Although it begins with the formulaic 'thus says the LORD of Hosts', thereby suggesting that a divine speech will follow, the text itself provides a report about what people are saying, questions based on such talk, and admonitions. Everything focuses on 'the LORD's house', the temple in Jerusalem. For whatever reason, the populace has demurred at rebuilding Yahwism's central shrine. Worship was taking place, so they may have found the status quo acceptable. Haggai's question (v. 4) implies, though does not state explicitly, that the people have worried about their own houses, and not YHWH's house. This indictment is made specific in v. 9. The imperative admonition, 'Consider how you have fared' might be translated literally, 'Set your heart upon your ways', a phrase repeated in v. 7. Haggai challenges the people to reflect about their material existence, which must have been meagre (v. 6). The language is that of a fulfilled futility curse (cf. Deut 28:38; Hos 4:10; Petersen 1984). v. 8 challenges the people to rebuild the temple. But immediately thereafter the prophet resumes his analysis of the current plight. The people now learn that their difficulties are not due to simple crop failure but to YHWH's punitive action, namely, a drought. (In the ancient Near-Eastern flood story, the angry deity calls for a drought before summoning the deluge.)

(1:12–15a) They Worked on the House of the Lord This prose section chronicles the impact of Haggai upon those who heard him. That group is, however, larger than his initial audience. Along with Zerubbabel and Joshua, the text refers to 'all the remnant of the people' (vv. 12, 14; 2:2). The word 'remnant' requires comment. By implication, the author claims that not everyone in Judah participated in the work of temple rebuilding. But who did? Based on texts such as Zech 6:9 and Ezra 2:1, both of which highlight the special role exercised by those who had been in Babylon, one may theorize that the remnant refers to those who had only recently returned to Jerusalem (cf. Wolff 1988). Such an inference is consistent with Ezra 3:8, 'and all who had come to Jerusalem from the captivity', and the more general prominence of 'the congregation of the exiles' (Ezra 10:8) or 'returned exiles' (Ezra 8:35). The chronicle is stylized using traditional religious vocabulary: 'the people feared the LORD' (v. 12), 'the LORD stirred up the spirit of...' (v. 14). The date formula in v. 15a has vexed scholars. Such formulae in Haggai normally occur at the beginning of a section in the book. Hence some have suggested that v. 15a be relocated to precede 2:15–19, which is prefixed by no such formula (so initially Rothstein 1908). However, one may read the formula in its canonical position with benefit. The formula at this place indicates that some time elapses between the utterance of Haggai's words and the actual work on temple reconstruction. The people do respond, but it takes time, a little over three weeks. This is no utopia in which the prophet's words are immediately efficacious. Still, Haggai ranks as a 'successful' prophet, since his words inspire the people to rebuild the temple.

(1:15b–2:9) Take Courage Almost a month passes before Haggai's next utterance. His public is the same as that in the previous chronicle: Zerubbabel, Joshua, and the remnant. Moreover, he uses interrogative rhetoric as he did earlier (1:4, 9). 2:3 presents questions that surely explore the sensibilities of those who were in a position to compare the emerging Second Temple with the Solomonic Temple. The new structure must have seemed a pale copy. Ezra 3:12 notes that reaction was mixed to the dedication of this rebuilt temple; some shouted for joy while others 'wept with a loud voice'. Haggai is addressing the latter audience and their apparent concerns about the glory (kabôd) of the temple. 1 Kings 6–7 make clear that the 'glory' refers to the ritual ornamentation of the temple. After offering general admonitory language 'take courage' (v. 4), Haggai avers that YHWH is with Israel even now, before the temple has been completed: 'I am with you ... My spirit abides among you'. Allusion to the Exodus tradition is apt (v. 5), since that too was a time when YHWH was with Israel, but not with benefit of a temple.

vv. 6–7 strike a new note, YHWH's forthcoming action on behalf of the temple. The scale is cosmic, as the diction of heavens and earth, sea and dry land suggest. However, the shaking of the nations will prove pivotal, since it is from them that riches to endow the temple will come. (The word kābôd, variously translated as 'glory' and 'splendour', occurs in vv. 3, 7, 8.) Haggai defines such splendour through the symbolism of various metals, though the silver and gold are ambiguous. They might signify the use of these metals in the decoration of the temple (cf. 1 Kings 6). They might refer to ritual objects made from these metals (e.g. Ezra 1:6–11; Zech 6:9–11). Or they might signify the wealth of the temple treasury (cf. Ezra 2:68–9). Whatever the case, Haggai promises greater glory for the second temple than there was in the Solomonic version. As if to modify the language of precious metals, Haggai concludes by proclaiming that šālôm, the Hebrew word translated by 'prosperity', will be present in this place, presumably the temple.

(2:10–14) Holy—Unclean A little over two months passes before Haggai speaks again as prophet. Now the audience is limited to the priests. Haggai makes use of questions again, and of a sort that requires special knowledge about Israel's ritual norms. Haggai asks for a priestly ruling (tôrâ). Offering such rulings was one of the basic tasks of priests, cf. Deut 33:10; Lev 10:10–11. However, Haggai's questions are odd. He asks whether something is holy (v. 12) and then whether something is unclean (v. 13). One normally thinks about holy v. profane, and clean v. unclean. In any case, the first question (v. 12) involves the power of the holy. Does holy food

make a garment holy, i.e. is holiness contagious in this case? The priests negative answer is appropriate, given what we know about Israelite ritual. However, the second case is different. v. 13 broaches corpse uncleanness, cf. Num 19:13. Here the uncleanness is more powerful than the aforementioned holiness. Haggai uses this dialogue with the priests to make a point. The people are now worshipping at the temple site. However, it had been profaned and hence is unclean. Without the purification of that holy place, all that the people of Judah now offer is, from Haggai's perspective, unclean (cf. Unger 1991). Rebuilding the temple would solve the problem, since the rebuilding of a holy site involves rituals of purification (see HAG 2:15–19). (This text does not condemn Samaritans or any other particular group for their participation in the work of temple construction, e.g. Rothstein 1908; Wolff 1988.)

(2:15–19) A Stone in the Lord's Temple If the book of Haggai has a climax, it occurs in this section. These verses attest building activity of a special form, the laying of a foundation stone (vv. 15, 18; see Petersen 1974). Texts from other ancient Near-Eastern cultures describe a ritual (kalû), which was used for the rededication of destroyed sanctuaries. At one point in the ritual—'this day' (vv. 15, 18)—a foundation stone or deposit was placed in the building being purified or rededicated (cf. Zech 4:9; Ezra 3:10–11). Haggai takes this ritual moment as an occasion to ask more questions (vv. 16, 19). The first question, 'how did you fare?', refers back to the discourse in the first section (vv. 1–11). But Haggai again reminds the people (though they are not so identified) of the specific agricultural problems that they have encountered (v. 16) and that YHWH caused these misfortunes (v. 17). Their cursed existence is destined to change after 'this day'. The second question (actually two questions) alludes to the day when there will be seed in the barn and the various vines and trees will yield abundantly. A time of blessing rather than curse will ensue due to the rebuilding and rededication of the second temple.

(2:20–3) Zerubbabel, my Servant The twenty-fourth day of the sixth month in 520 BCE was doubly important, as this second oracle from that day signifies. Whereas earlier oracles had been delivered to both Zerubbabel and Joshua, this one is addressed only to Zerubbabel. The oracle begins with language very similar to that in 2:6–7. However, the consequences of the 'shaking' of the nations are now made more concrete. The nations are to be destroyed. v. 22 picks up the traditional imagery of YHWH's holy war, in which the enemy self-destructs ('every one by the sword of a comrade'). Just as the shaking of the nations in 2:6–7 had an impact on Judah—the provision of material wealth—so too the shaking in v. 22 has an effect: the creation of a power vacuum that will allow for a political leader to arise in Israel. v. 23 commences with the enigmatic 'on that day', a phrase that elsewhere in late prophetic literature refers to what YHWH will do at an eschatological moment, cf. Zech 14. However, in Haggai, with all its references to specific days, this phrase bears special import. It cannot be too far off. Moreover, unlike all the previous days in Haggai, this one will not be a day of Darius; it will be YHWH's day.

Zerubbabel, as an apparent member of the Davidic line, is heir to promises of a lineage that many Israelites believed would last forever. The book closes with language redolent of Israel's monarchic traditions. Kings could be called 'servant' (see 2 Sam 6:5; Ps 132:10), the 'signet ring' could refer to the special status of the king (see Jer 22:24; Ezek 28:12), and the verb 'take' (*b-ḥ-r*) was used earlier to describe YHWH's choosing of both David (Ps 78:70) and David's city (Isa 14:1). In sum, Haggai appears to propound a special role for the house of David. He does not call outright for the coronation of Zerubbabel, since such an act might have antagonized the Persians as well as Judah's neighbours. Still, Haggai envisions a Judahite polity quite different from the Persian status quo.

REFERENCES

Bauer, L. (1992), *Zeit des Zweiten Tempels: Zur sozio-ökonomischen Konzeption im Haggai-Sacharja-Maleachi-Korpus*, BEATAJ 31 (Berlin: Peter Lang).

Bedford, P. (1995), 'Discerning the Time: Haggai, Zechariah and the "Delay" in the Rebuilding of the Jerusalem Temple', *The Pitcher is Broken: Memorial Essays for Gösta W. Ahlström*, JSOTSup 190 (Sheffield: Sheffield Academic Press), 71–94.

Berquist, J. (1995), *Judaism in Persia's Shadow: A Social and Historical Approach* (Minneapolis: Fortress).

Beuken, W. (1967), *Haggai-Sacharja 1–8: Studien zur Ueberlieferungsgeschichte der frühexilischen Prophetie*, SSN 10 (Assen: Van Gorcum).

Christensen, D. (1993), 'Poetry and Prose in the Composition and Performance of the Book of Haggai', in J. de Moor and W. Watson (eds.), *Verse in Ancient Near Eastern Prose*, AOAT 43 (Kevelaer: Butzon & Bercker), 17–30.

Clines, D. (1993), 'Haggai's Temple, Constructed, Deconstructed, and Reconstructed', *SJOT* 7: 51–77.

Kuhrt, A. (1983), 'The Cyrus Cylinder and Achaemenid Imperial Policy', *JSOT* 25: 83–97.

Mason, R. (1977), 'The Purpose of the "Editorial Framework" of the Book of Haggai', *VT* 27: 413–21.

Meyers, C., and Meyers, E. (1987), *Haggai, Zechariah 1–8*, AB 25B (Garden City, NY: Doubleday).

Petersen, D. (1974), 'Zerubbabel and Jerusalem Temple Reconstruction', *CBQ* 36: 366–72.

—— (1984), *Haggai and Zechariah 1–8*, OTL (Philadelphia: Westminster).

Pierce, R. (1984a), 'Literary Connectors and a Haggai/Zechariah/Malachi Corpus', *JETS* 27: 277–89.

—— (1984b), 'A Thematic Development of the Haggai/Zechariah/Malachi Corpus', *JETS* 27: 401–11.

Rothstein, J. (1908), *Juden und Samaritaner: Die grundlegende Scheidung von Judentum und Heidentum: Eine kritische Studie zum Buche Haggai und zur jüdischen Geschichte im ersten nachexilischen Jahrhundert*. BWAT, 8 (Leipzig: Hinrichs).

Tollington, J. (1993), *Tradition and Innovation in Haggai and Zechariah 1–8*, JSOTSup 150 (Sheffield: Sheffield Academic Press).

Unger, T. (1991), 'Noch einmal: Haggais unreines Volk', *ZAW* 103: 210–25.

Wolff, H. (1988), *Haggai: A Commentary*, trans. M. Kohl (Minneapolis: Augsburg).

37. Zechariah

KATRINA J. A. LARKIN

INTRODUCTION

A. Text and Language. The oldest complete MS is a second-century leather scroll of the Minor Prophets from Wadi Murabba'at in the the Judean desert (DJD 2). Fragments of seven older Hebrew MSS of the Minor Prophets were found at Qumran in cave 4, but only three are sufficiently well preserved to offer meaningful comparison with the Masoretic Text (*OCB* s.v.), and no significant variants emerge. A Greek translation ('Translations, Ancient Languages', *OCB*) of the second century CE found at Nahal Hever confirms the above picture. However, Zechariah is a cryptic book, and the fact that the MS tradition is reliable and textual problems are few does not mean that it is always easy to translate.

B. The Two Main Parts. William Newcombe in 1785 first noted that the second half of Zechariah (chs. 9–14) differs from the first in authorship, date, and circumstances. Proto-Zechariah comprises an anthology of visionary material in 1:7–6:15, surrounded by an editorial frame in 1:1–6 and chs. 7–8 containing oracles and preached material. The whole concerns the restoration of Jerusalem and its temple after the Exile, and is dated over a brief period, 520–518 BCE, though the editorial additions may not have been completed until 450 BCE. Zech 9–14 opens with a secondary heading in 9:1 and is subdivided by another at 12:1. The same occurs at Mal 1:1. This may indicate that three small booklets were appended to Proto-Zechariah at different dates. In literary genre Zech 9–14 looks at first sight more akin to classical prophecy than to Proto-Zechariah, but closer inspection reveals that it is very hard to

relate to history, and that the messenger formula 'Thus says the LORD' introducing first-person speech from YHWH is hardly used. Much is in the third person, and the whole of ch. 14 is an extended descriptive piece. The forms of classical prophecy are breaking down. The interest in Jerusalem and the leadership is maintained, but there are no references to the temple building programme, and the hopes of the immediate restoration period appear to have been soured; there are tensions within the community, and hope is deferred until the final day of the Lord, which must be preceded by further suffering. No dates are given, and a great range of historical contexts has been suggested, from the seventh century (chs. 9–11 only, Otzen 1964) to the third century, after the conquests of Alexander the Great ('Alexander III', *OBC*). The latter view, put forward by Stade (1881–2), is probably now the majority view. Certainly nothing predates 450 BCE. For a full study of the continuities and discontinuities between the two halves of Zechariah see Mason (1976).

C. The Social and Religious Context. Proto-Zechariah can fairly be called a 'theocratic' or establishment work because of its institutional subject-matter and occasionally its tone, particularly in the oracular additions to the visionary material. It has sometimes been accused (e.g. by Hanson 1979) of complacently assuming that the promises made in classical prophecy were completely fulfilled in the restoration of Jerusalem in the sixth century, leaving nothing further to be hoped for. In contrast Zech 9–14, which contains controversy material criticizing the leadership, has been characterized as anti-establishment and dissatisfied with the restoration (Hanson 1979; Plöger 1968); it is more eschatological in outlook ('Eschatology', *OCB*). However, if the two halves really had such opposing interests it would be odd that the work is as unified as it is. Rather they are complementary: Proto-Zechariah knows his own time is the 'day of small things' and his work does have an eschatological dimension. Zech 9–14 stems from a later time in which the community required to be challenged rather than consoled, and much of chs. 12–14 in fact has a liturgical background; according to Plöger (1968) in ch. 12 the establishment criticizes itself. One plausible explanation for the ambivalence of Deutero-Zechariah is that it was written and edited over an extended period of perhaps two centuries (450–250?) by and for the kind of traditionists who would later emerge into the light of history as the community at Qumran: separatists who criticized mainstream Judaism for its perceived loss of purity and its political compromises.

D. Relation to Apocalyptic. Some scholars regard the visions of Proto-Zechariah as proto-apocalyptic because their literary form is similar to that of the later apocalypses such as the second half of Daniel ('Apocalyptic Literature', *OCB*): they are clearly revelatory literature ('Revelation', *OCB*). A contrary school of thought says that Proto-Zechariah does not have the dramatic and calamitous eschatological content normally associated with apocalyptic. Rather, 9–14 has the better claim to be proto-apocalyptic because it does have this type of content, especially in ch. 14. The background of controversy detectable in 9–14 is the seedbed of this type of thinking on the part of disadvantaged groups in a situation of political crisis. Clearly in this debate the framing and handling of definitions is very important. Each school of thought has perhaps detected one of the origins of apocalyptic (North 1972), but it has many origins. A third origin, studied more recently (Larkin 1994; Tigchelaar 1996), is in the learned, interpretative tradition which underlies both halves of Zechariah. There are numerous allusions to older parts of the prophetic tradition, particularly Jeremiah, Ezekiel, and Isaiah, and some allusions to the Pentateuch and Psalms; familiarity is also shown with Ugaritic literature ('Ugarit', *OCB*).

E. The Relation to Older Prophecy. Zechariah affirms the validity of the words of the 'former prophets' (1:6), either explicitly or implicitly throughout, but particularly in the non-visionary material. A new exegetical principle can be seen to have emerged: that all prophecy should be read as a unity, and that it holds the key to understanding any political situation. For a study of the new character of prophecy in Proto-Zechariah and Haggai see Tollington (1993); for Zech 9–14 see Larkin (1994). The ultimate outcome of these changes can be seen in the Qumran commentaries or pesharim (see under 'Interpretation', *OCB*) which treat all Scripture as cryptic and its interpretation as requiring a special gift of insight. The motif of the 'eye' which is the ancient symbol of the interpreter and seer (e.g. Num 24:3–4) now occurs 16 times throughout Zechariah (it is not always apparent in translation, either because it is not idiomatic in English, e.g. at 2:1, or because the text is corrupt, e.g. 5:6; but see 4:10; 9:8; 11:17; 12:4), and this is a further sign of the text's editorial unity.

F. The Religious Teaching. Zechariah develops a theology that is eschatological and ultimately hopeful. Proto-Zechariah's picture of the restored Jerusalem, its temple and leadership, feeds into the later concept of the New Jerusalem, and chs. 12–14 contribute to the developed picture of the final day of the Lord. Zechariah contains important material on the subject of the Messiah (*OCB*). A number of passages which may refer to such a person or role are found in both parts. The historical-critical tendency to limit the reference of such passages to specific historical settings has recently been challenged (Duguid 1995). Zechariah offers a number of different pictures of leadership and of the relationship between the leader and the led, so that their relationship to Christian doctrine is not straightforward. However, ideal leadership is shown as intimately related to the problem of how to break the hold of sin and be free from the endless repetition of a sin, punishment, repentance, restoration cycle. The problem is not, however, fully resolved within the OT.

G. Outline

The Restoration of Jerusalem (1:1–8:23)
    Preface (1:1–6)
    The Vision Cycle (1:7–6:15)
    Oracles and Sermons (chs. 7–8)
Hope Amid Conflict and Sin (9:1–14:21)
    Foreign Nations Oracles (9:1–8)
    The Hopes of Judah and Israel (9:9–10:12)
    The Shepherd Allegory (ch. 11)
    Judah and Jerusalem on the Day of the Lord (chs. 12–13)
    The Cosmic Day of the Lord (ch. 14)

COMMENTARY

The Restoration of Jerusalem (1:1–8:23)

(1:1–6) Preface With chs. 7–8 this forms an editorial frame (Beuken 1967). Darius the Persian has allowed the Jews to return home from exile. The date is mid-October to mid-November 520 BCE. In recent history the covenant curses have justly been invoked, the land is unclean, the glory departed, and the community still partially disbanded. The fathers of the present generation and the prophets who admonished them are all dead, but their words and their experience stand as a lesson for all time. Zechariah is concerned with full restoration: his very name means 'YHWH has remembered', which is foundational to the book. On the human side, returning and repenting (the Hebrew is the same) are equally basic. Zechariah is a contemporary of Haggai and comes of a priestly line that had been exiled. There are two other Zechariahs in the OT (Isa 8:2 and 2 Chr 24:20–2) and biblical tradition sometimes confuses them; 'son of Berechiah' may be part of this confusion. His oracles often reinterpret the 'former prophets' (v. 4); he may have had access to the early collections of prophecies from Jeremiah and Ezekiel.

(1:7–6:15) The Vision Cycle Zechariah's eight night visions (perhaps originally seven) are his primary and most distinctive feature. They exist betwixt and between the mundane world and the heavenly world where history is made and where Jerusalem's restoration is being ordained. The visionary form is highly literary and has a standardized format; the cycle is structured in a concentric pattern (though Butterworth (1992) argues for caution in looking for, and finding, detailed literary structures). In contrast to his predecessors the prophet has an angelic interpreter as intermediary between himself and God, whose communications have become cryptic. Much of the imagery has cultic roots, drawn particularly from the liturgies of temple foundation ('Temple', *OCB*) and with a general background in Ugaritic (*OCB*) texts. The vision cycle is now studded with brief oracles, in more than one redactional layer, preoccupied with leadership and temple. These, like the editorial frame, could be summaries of relevant sermons by the prophet and reuse themes from older prophecy (Mason 1990). The cycle is dated mid-January to mid-February 519 (v. 7).

(**1:8–17**) In the first vision the earth is peaceful and expectant. The four patrolling horsemen ('Number Symbolism', *OCB*) are the first of numerous symbols (*OCB* s.v.) from Zechariah which would be reused in Revelation. The seventy years of the Lord's withholding mercy (cf. Jer 25:11) are over (the Exile is loosely held to have lasted from 587 to 519 BCE); he has returned and the temple is to be rebuilt.

(**1:18–21**) The second vision bizarrely symbolizes both the powerful nations that have terrorized the chosen people, and the counterforces (blacksmiths) raised by YHWH; blacksmiths are supposed to be skilful in spells (Tigchelaar 1996).

(**2:1–5**) The third vision shows the restoration of Jerusalem in the cosmic realm which must precede mundane restoration (cf. Ezek 40:3–4; Isa 49:19–21); it points forward to the New Jerusalem of Rev 21:15–17. The formerly negative image of a city without walls becomes a positive one, and the symbolism of Sinai (the fire, cloud, and direct vision of God) is added to that of Zion (see 'Glory', *OCB*). The appended oracles (vv. 6–13) are still encouraging a return to Jerusalem after Zechariah and his community were already there; possibly not everyone had returned, and possibly the oracles have an eschatological dimension. For 'apple of the eye' (v. 8) see *OCB*. With v. 10 cf. Zech 9:9–10. v. 13 is thought to be liturgical.

(**3:1–10**) The fourth vision shows the high priest Joshua accused by Satan (lit. the Satan, or the Adversary, i.e. the prosecuting counsel in the heavenly court) but acquitted (for a contrasting confrontation see Am 7:10–17). His subsequent cleansing ('Purity, Ritual', *OCB*) signifies the renewal of the temple services which make provision for the cleansing of the community. The high priest has expanded powers and duties in the functioning of a temple without a king, and these are sanctioned in the appended oracles (vv. 6–10). Arguably v. 8 is a messianic reference ('my servant the Branch'), and does not merely refer to the Davidic governor of the time. Although the complete 'removal of guilt' is also promised (v. 9), the mechanism is unclear and the matter is actually left unresolved by Proto-Zechariah and returned to in an atmosphere of some bitterness in Zech 12; meantime, it appears that priests and sacrifices will still be needed.

(**4:1–14**) The fifth vision, of the golden lamp and the olive-tree people, uses seal imagery to symbolize joint leaders who can be identified from the context as Joshua and the Davidic governor Zerubbabel (*OCB* s.v.). The primary function of the latter (vv. 6–10a) is to build the second temple, just as Solomon (*OCB* s.v.) founded the first. The two leaders are both 'anointed ones' (v. 14; lit. sons of oil, vocabulary from the same root as 'messiah'; see 'Anoint', *OCB*). Although there is realized eschatology here, the people and events of the restoration are not mistaken for those of the golden age; Zerubbabel's is the 'day of small things' (v. 10) and he is utterly reliant on the work of the Lord's spirit. The Lord's favour is still contingent on the fitness of his people (v. 7) and therefore the fullness of blessing is still deferred.

(**5:1–4**) The sixth vision of the flying scroll, shows the word of the Lord in materialized form, i.e. 'scripture' beginning to emerge as a concept, a gold standard by which to assess and cleanse the community. The invocation of the covenant curse shows that the covenant does remain in force despite having once been broken.

(**5:5–11**) The seventh vision is of a woman in a basket (Heb. 'êpâ,) personifying the people's iniquity (Heb. 'eye'; the emendation only requires the alteration of one consonant for another which looks similar). It is no coincidence that a feminine idol (*OCB* s.v.) (to be stood 'on its base' in a 'house', i.e. a temple), should be symbolically exiled to Babylon (*OCB* s.v.) just as Judaism truly became a YHWH-alone religion, abjuring feminine deities such as the Queen of Heaven, about whom Jeremiah complained (see 'Women, Second Temple Period', *OCB*).

(**6:1–8**) The eighth vision forms an *inclusio* with the first; it specifies the pacifying of the north country because that is the direction from which the majority of attacks on Israel were made (cf. Jer 1:14).

(**6:9–15**) To the visions is appended a sign-act of the crowning of a 'messianic' leader or leaders, which concludes the whole cycle. The text has been altered at the cost of some ambiguity. Originally, a blatant presentation of Zerubbabel as the promised leader probably occurred here (esp. vv. 12–13); but if so his name has been removed, possibly to square the record with the facts of history; only that of Joshua remains, though confusingly a second priest stands beside his throne, and he is the wearer of two crowns. This is one of the roots of the concept of a priestly Messiah and of joint messiahship. On 'peace' (v. 13) see *OCB*.

(**Chs. 7–8**) **Oracles and Sermons** The epilogic editorial frame returns to the mixture of oracles and condensed sermons seen in the prologue (the sermon forms of Chronicles are comparable). It has grown from an enquiry to the prophet about fasting (*OCB* s.v.) (7:2–3). The date is mid-November to mid-December 518 BCE (7:1) and the temple is presumably complete. The question arises whether the fast of the fifth month commemorating the destruction of the first temple is still necessary. There are two views as to the meaning of the answer (7:4–7; amplified in 7:8–14), which is negative and sweeps in the fast of the seventh month also (v. 5): it could be anti-cult, but that would be alien to the spirit of Proto-Zechariah; more likely it means that in the ideal world which the prophet envisages, fasting, like punishment, should no longer be necessary. For 'the alien' and 'the poor' see *OCB*. Zech 8:1–8 returns to the renewal theme of earlier oracles in the vision cycle (cf. 1:14, 16); likewise 8:9–13 returns to temple building (cf. Hag 2:15–19). 8:14–17 emphasizes the need for right living. In 8:18–19 the fasting theme resurfaces and now two more fasts are added (those of the fourth and tenth months) with exhortations to rejoice reinforcing the view that the prophet is speaking idealistically and positively. The booklet closes with a picture of universal pilgrimage to Jerusalem (8:20–3), forming an *inclusio* with 7:2 and indeed the more universalistic 2:11 and 14:16. This is one indication that it is legitimate to read Proto-Zechariah, as edited, in the light of the more developed eschatology of chs. 9–14. 'Ten men' (v. 23) is the number required to form a synagogue; for 'Jew' see *OCB*.

Hope Amid Conflict and Sin (9:1–14:21)

(9:1–8) Foreign Nations Oracles The heading 'An Oracle' (Heb. *māśśā'*) appears again at 12:1 and Mal 1:1 suggesting that three separate booklets have been appended to Proto-Zechariah. Some wisdom influence is apparent in this section (Larkin 1994: 54–67; 'Wisdom Literature', *OCB*). It makes numerous allusions to older prophets including Amos, Ezekiel, and Isaiah. v. 1 may allude to a tradition later developed by the community at Qumran, that Damascus (*OCB* s.v.) would be the place of God's eschatological sanctuary (i.e. be merged with the concept of Zion); however, NRSV's 'capital of Aram' (v. 1b) is an emendation of the Hebrew 'eye of man', i.e. another corrupt 'eye' reference. The other places referred to have symbolic or typological rather than historical significance ('Typology', *OCB*). If this is a 'foreign nations' section, such as appears in the majority of prophetic collections, then it is the only passage of its kind in the whole of the Haggai, Zechariah, Malachi corpus. It contains a summing up of thought on the future of the foreign nations, in surprisingly positive terms (e.g. the Philistines in v. 7b; *OCB* s.v.), while also guaranteeing the safety of the holy land and city. The motif of the 'eye' which binds the book together, appears not only in 9:1 but also in 9:8, which draws on the wisdom tradition (Job 42:5); the anonymous successor to Proto-Zechariah claims that he has received revelations of his own, which he reports together with his reinterpretation of traditional material.

(9:9–10:12) The Hopes of Judah and Ephraim 9:9–10 is the first of several linking passages which bind chs. 9–14 together. Like 10:1–2; 11:1–3; 11:17; and 13:7–9 it is compact, metrical, uses opening imperatives and vocatives, and links the material that precedes and follows it. It pictures the king of peace, in terms drawn partly from Jacob's blessing of Judah (Gen 49:10–11) (quoted in Mt 21:1–9 and par.), and partly from the royal theology of Ps 72:8. The adjectives used to describe the king are significant for later Christology and it should therefore be noted that several are capable of more than one translation. 'Triumphant' (Heb. *ṣaddîq*) could be rendered 'righteous' (see *OCB* s.v.), 'vindicated', or even 'legitimate'; it is also used of the Branch (referring to a Davidic ruler) in Jer 23:5, and of the Servant in Isa 53:11. 'Victorious' could equally be 'saved'. 'Humble' (or 'poor', see *OCB*) is found on a victory inscription of King Zakar of Hamath; though evidently part of the ancient kingly ideal, its exact significance is not known. This king is evidently a numinous figure. The whole reiterates an important promise made to the tribe of Judah, which had seemed subverted by history.

The next picture is that of God as a warrior (9:11–17), who will bring ultimate victory to his oppressed people against the Greeks (an indication of date). The imagery is reminiscent of the enthronement psalms. 10:1–2 is a link passage containing controversy material (in common with 11:1–3; 11:17; 13:7–9; and the whole of ch. 11). It is critical of the community's leaders (symbolized as shepherds) whose guidance is false ('Dreams', *OCB*); such tensions would surface later in the formation of the Qumran community. The passage shows Deuteronomic influence, in common with the passage of Scripture it harks back to (Jer 14:14). Polemic against the 'bad shepherds', continuing a tradition found in Jer 23 and Ezek 34, persists into the first verse of the next unit, 10:1–3. It denies their ultimate authority and affirms the Lord's control of history, and care for Judah and Ephraim. Ephraim (named after one of the two sons of Joseph) was the principal tribe of the old northern kingdom of Israel (*OCB* s.v.). The principal promise made to him in Jacob's blessing (Gen 49:22) was that of fruitfulness, but for that to remain valid the principal need of Ephraim was to be restored to existence after their dispersion by the Assyrians in the eighth century. Such restoration is here promised. It has been called the most conspicuous example of false prophecy in the OT; but the references to the great hostile powers of Assyria (*OCB* s.v.) and Egypt (*OCB* s.v.) are not historical so much as typological and should not be interpreted too literally. As the passage unfolds it contains a mixture of first-person and third-person speech. In older prophetic collections this is often an indication of exegesis being added to the original revelation at a later date. Here, however, the exegesis may be contemporary and the passage a literary unity. In chs. 9–10 overall the future is pictured as an improved version of Israel's past in which everything will be made new. Eschatology cannot be solely a question of deferred ideals, since utter failure is unlikely to provide a picture of the ideal future. History therefore provides some of the content of eschatology.

(Ch. 11) The Shepherd Allegory 11:1–3 is a link passage (the 'stitch words' are 'Lebanon' (cf. 10:12; 11:1) and 'shepherds' (10:3; 11:3, 4). It alludes to Jer 25:36. It is in the form of a taunting song against the leadership and probably the temple itself: in rabbinic tradition 'Lebanon' can signify the temple (as it often does in the Dead Sea scrolls). The passage was certainly understood to refer to the second temple after that was destroyed in AD 70. 11:4–14 is the major controversy passage and is central in the anthologizing process that brought chs. 9–14 together. It has baffled interpreters more than any other part of the OT, because it cannot be pinned down historically (there have been over 40 different identifications of the three shepherds of v. 8), and its symbolism is no longer fully comprehensible. Even its literary genre is unclear, neither purely allegorical (though it is often called an allegory), nor visionary, nor parabolic. It is most like an acted parable, and is certainly a learned piece. vv. 4–6 introduce the *dramatis personae*, namely the prophet who plays a shepherd and is strongly identified with YHWH ('shepherd' is a description normally reserved for YHWH or the king, though Moses, who is the prototype of the good prophet, is also called shepherd); the people of Israel who are the flock; and their leaders who are merchants. The passage is written with Ezek 37:15–28 in mind, though the nature of the relationship is controversial. In turning Ezekiel's image of unity into one of threefold disunity (vv. 9, 10, 14) Zechariah could be repudiating the complacency of a theocratic leadership pictured as greedy and ruthless (Hanson 1979); or reflecting contemporary tension between Jerusalem and Samaria ('Samaria', OBC) (a possibility favoured in German scholarship); or simply picturing the relationship between God, prophet, and people typologically. A prophet's mission is, as here, typically both divinely supported and also frustrated. The negativity of the imagery then stems from this propet's intuition that the people do not in fact welcome good shepherding, and that prophetic leadership therefore entails suffering in which God himself partakes. Israel repudiates grace, and as a result there is no unity even among the people of God, but unfitness for the task of mediating grace to the nations. Thus Zechariah may not be repudiating Ezekiel's ideas so much as explaining why, in the face of the 'givens' of human nature, those ideals have not been, and will not be, actualized. The report of the action over the prophet's derisory wages in vv. 11–12 (possibly fragmentary; 'Money', OCB) contains a phrase ('Then you will know...') that links this material with the oracles of Proto-Zechariah (2:13, 15; 4:9; 6:15). v. 12 is wrongly attributed by Mt 27:9 to Jeremiah. vv. 15–16 contain a horrifying image of an antitype to the good shepherd. Because the passage seems deliberately to pervert the imagery of Ezek 34:3–4, which pictures Davidic leadership as good, it has been called anti-establishment as well as anti-messianic. This time, however, the prophet is not asked to perform the role assigned to him. v. 17 counteracts vv. 15–16 with an oracle of woe against the worthless shepherd. Zechariah's favourite 'eye' motif reappears. Blindness (OCB s.v.) symbolizes loss of spiritual sight and spiritual potency (cf. 12:4). The withered right arm symbolizes loss of might, and would render the person unable to hold sacred office. The verse is another one of the link passages, and rounds off the little anthology of passages with a theme of shepherding that now forms Zech 11.

(12:1–13:9) Judah and Jerusalem on the Day of the Lord 12:1, the heading 'An Oracle' seems to cover the whole of the rest of the book; the doxology on creation, which is possibly liturgical in origin, provides an example of ideas about creation and origins (the *Urzeit*) being projected forwards onto the end of time (the *Endzeit*). 12:2–13:6 comprises the next major section of the book, compiled on different principles from chs. 9–10 or 11, and relying on introductory and continuation formulae containing the phrase 'in that day', whose origin is controversial. It has a range of meanings, although in Zechariah it is eschatological, referring to the coming 'day of YHWH' (OCB). This is a relatively late usage. Further distinctive features of chs. 12–13 are their cultic flavour, using motifs from the autumn festivals, especially Booths; their focus on Judah (OCB s.v.), Jerusalem, and the house of David (OCB s.v.); universalism; and the lateness of the three major themes: the final onslaught of all nations on Jerusalem (12:2–9), the outpouring of the spirit (12:10; see 'Holy Spirit', OCB) and of cleansing water (13:1; see 'Water', OCB); and the end of true prophecy. However, the interest in leadership shown in ch. 11 is maintained with mysterious references in vv. 8 and especially 10–14. The motivation behind chs. 12–13 is controver-

sial; they have been held to spring from intra-community conflict (perhaps Judah v. Jerusalem), but if so there is no agreement as to whether the establishment or an alienated group is behind them (Hanson 1979 v. Plöger 1968). Actually there is a strong possibility that an originally Jerusalemite vision has been elaborated with references to Judah. The most theologically distinctive material is in v. 10. The Zechariah tradition here returns to the problem of how to remove human guilt (cf. 3:9). The people beholding the death of a martyr are moved by a spirit of grace (OCB s.v.) from YHWH, enabling them to mourn their sinfulness unselfishly, thus preparing them for cleansing ('Mourning', OCB). The verse contains an interpretative crux: literally 'when they look *on me, on him* whom they have pierced'. This is both ambiguous and implies a paradox, i.e. that it is God who is pierced; both ambiguity and paradox are probably deliberate. It is possible that there is an echo here of a ritual of the humiliation and vindication of the king, from the autumn New Year festival of monarchical Israel (e.g. Day 1985). However, there is no direct evidence for this in the OT. One can only say with certainty that the scene combines elements from mythology (Hadad Rimmon, v. 11, is the Syrian name for the dying and rising vegetation god Baal); from history (e.g. the good king Josiah (OCB s.v.) died at Megiddo (OCB s.v.)); and from older prophecy (so Lamarche 1961; cf. the fourth Servant Song, Isa 52:13–53:12). The apparently arbitrary names of the mourners in vv. 12–14 are in fact all found in the stories about Absalom (who died leading a rebellion against his father David, see 2 Sam 15–19), and are predominantly priestly and royal. The final picture of the fountain cleansing the people's sin (13:1, see 'Sin', OCB) harks back to Ezek 36. 13:2–6 attacks prophecy, remarkably bracketing together 'the prophets and the unclean spirit', though it is usually interpreted as applying to false prophecy. Person (1993) argues that Zechariah shows Deuteronomic influence, including hostility towards false prophecy (Deut 18:15–11) and that it was the disillusion of this movement with the temple authorities that led to the mission of Ezra. Deutero-Zechariah is himself a prophet, but one who sets great store by tradition. He may in consequence regard the ability to pronounce anything new as restricted to a learned class who can ensure its consistency with tradition. Such an attitude contributed to the closing down of prophecy. 13:7–9 is the last of the controversy passages which link the main blocks of material and is not to be relocated after 11:17 as attempted by the editors of the NEB. Its description of the stricken shepherd is quoted in Mt 26:31 and par. Its severity towards the sheep, the remnant (OCB s.v.) who appear to be martyrs as much as sinners, is remarkable.

(Ch. 14) The Cosmic Day of the Lord This chapter, like 12–13, depicts the day of the Lord but in more cosmic terms; it has a liturgical dimension and is related to the Festival of Booths (vv. 16, 18, 19). It is learned and resonates with older Scripture, having a special preference for earlier 'apocalyptic' material (Ezek 37–8; Joel; Isa 60), from which scattered references to the final day of YHWH are gathered into a coherent programme, though it is not known whether this is an authorial or an editorial achievement. Mention of David or Judah disappears, but Jerusalem has an honoured place founded on cult and law, and the New Jerusalem is pictured as the focal point of all the nations, and indeed of creation. The chapter is written almost entirely in third-person prophetic discourse, punctuated with references to 'that day' seven times. The arrangement gives prominence to the centre of the chapter rather than to the end: in v. 9 the fourth use of 'in that day' accompanies an affirmation of the coming to reign of YHWH. vv. 1–5 picture the coming of the 'day' with YHWH summoning the nations to attack Jerusalem, terrifying upheavals in the natural world, and a theophany (cf. Am 9:1–4; see 'Theophany', *OCB*) on the Mount of Olives (*OCB* s.v.) as YHWH enters the city in triumph. 'Azal' is mysterious and not to be confused with Azazel (*OCB* s.v.). It is not apparent whether the remnant that will be saved from Jerusalem consists of the righteous (ethical dualism) or is simply a *de facto* remnant such as would be historically realistic. vv. 6–8, picturing changes in the laws of nature, have been said to contain ontological dualism, i.e. a complete abrogation of the old natural order as established in Genesis, to be replaced by something totally new, with the implication that the old order was too hopelessly corrupt to be redeemable. Such an extreme intention seems improbable bearing in mind that historical realities (such as the importance of the city of Jerusalem) have been allowed to shape the picture of the day of the Lord. There is a two-era view of time such as is characteristic of full-blown apocalyptic, but there is not complete discontinuity with what has gone before. v. 9 acclaims the universal kingship of God (see 'Kingdom of God', *OCB*) and vv. 8, 10–11, describe the New Jerusalem in terms drawn both from mythology (its imaginary height and the river of life flowing from it) and from history (the description of its gates and boundaries). vv. 12–19 consider the fate of the nations, and here it is more obvious than elsewhere in the chapter that it is the righteous who are to be saved and to enjoy the privilege of making pilgrimage to Jerusalem to take part in the eschatological Feast of Booths (at which the coming of rain is celebrated). vv. 20–1 describe Jerusalem crowded with pilgrims at the Feast. These verses are comparable to the ending of the book of Isaiah.

REFERENCES

Beuken, W. A. M. (1967), *Haggai-Sacharja 1–8: Studien zur Überlieferungsgeschichte der frühnachexilischen Prophetie* (Assen: Van Gorcum).

Butterworth, M. (1992), *Structure and the Book of Zechariah* (Sheffield: JSOT).

Day, J. (1985), *God's Conflict with the Dragon and the Sea: Echoes of a Canaanite Myth in the Old Testament* (Cambridge: Cambridge University Press).

Duguid, I. M. (1995), 'Messianic Themes in Zechariah 9–14', in P. E. Satterthwaite, R. S. Hess, and G. J. Wenham (eds.), *The Lord's Anointed: Interpretation of Old Testament Messianic Texts* (Carlisle: Paternoster).

Hanson, P. D. (1979), *The Dawn of Apocalyptic: The Historical and Sociological Roots of Jewish Apocalyptic Eschatology* (Philadelphia: Fortress).

Lamarche, P. (1961), *Zacharie IX–XIV: Structure littéraire et messianisme* (Paris: Gabalda).

Larkin, K. J. A. (1994), *The Eschatology of Second Zechariah* (Kampen: Kok Pharos).

Mason, R. A. (1976), 'The Relation of Zechariah 9–14 to Proto-Zechariah', *ZAW* 88: 227–39.

—— (1990), *Preaching the Tradition: Homily and Hermeneutics after the Exile* (Cambridge: Cambridge University Press).

North, R. (1972), 'Prophecy to Apocalyptic via Zechariah', *SVT* 22: 47–71.

Otzen, B. (1964), *Studien über Deutero-Sacharja* (Copenhagen: Prostant Apud Munksgaard).

Person, R. F. (1993), *Second Zechariah and the Deuteronomic School* (Sheffield: Sheffield Academic Press).

Plöger, O. (1968), ET, *Theocracy and Eschatology* (Oxford: John Knox).

Stade, B. (1881–2), 'Deuterozacharja: Eine kritische Studie', *ZAW* 1: 1–96 and 2: 151–72, 275–309.

Tigchelaar, E. J. C. (1996), *Prophets of Old and the Day of the End: Zechariah, the Book of Watchers and Apocalyptic* (Leiden: Brill).

Tollington, J. E. (1993), *Tradition and Innovation in Haggai and Zechariah 1–8* (Sheffield: Sheffield Academic Press).

38. Malachi   J. ROGERSON

INTRODUCTION

1. 'Malachi' in Hebrew means 'my messenger', from which many commentators have concluded that the book stems from an anonymous prophet to whom its editors gave the name 'my messenger' on the basis of Mal 3:1. Meinhold (1991) maintains that the actual name is found on an Ostracon from Arad from the seventh century (Davies 1991: no. 2.097). If Malachi is a name it is a shortened form of Malachiah, meaning 'messenger of YHWH'.

2. Little can be said with certainty about the date and setting of the book, except that it belongs to the Second Temple period. It is common to place it in the early part of the fifth century BCE on the grounds (1) that it mentions abuses that were later dealt with by Ezra and Nehemiah (i.e. before *c.* 458), (2) that it assumes, with Deuteronomy, that there is no difference between priests and Levites and generally seems to be closer to the spirit of Deuteronomy than the later Priestly Code, and (3) that linguistic analyses of Malachi show the book to have closest affinity with other texts of around 480 BCE. All of these claims can be—and have been—contested. In any case, so little is known about the history of Hebrew language and society in the Persian period that any date down to 350 BCE is possible. There is also uncertainty about the social setting of the book, with plausible suggestions as widely opposed as seeing Malachi as a priest or as an eschatological prophet addressing the aspirations of an oppressed underclass. A radical view, expressed by Utzschneider (1992), is that Malachi is *Schriftprophetie*, that is, prophecy by means of the literary interpretation of older traditions.

3. What is certain is that Malachi contains a unique set of dialogues in which the complaints and fears of the people are expressed, and in which God reproves the people, answers their complaints, and stresses his trustworthiness.

The Hebrew and English chapter divisions diverge at the end of the book, with 3:19–24 in Hebrew being 4:1–6 in English.

COMMENTARY

(1:1) The heading: cf. Zech 12:1. Both headings are the work of a later editor or editors, which is why some commentators hold that the name Malachi is taken from Mal 3:1.

(1:2–5) First Disputation The charge that God has not loved his people is answered in two ways. First, appeal is made to the story of Jacob and Esau in which Jacob, the ancestor of the Israelites, outwits his elder brother Esau (Edom, cf. Gen 25:19–34). Second, an apparent recent disaster that has befallen Edom is cited as evidence for God's control of human affairs, backed by the promise that, if Edom rebuilds its ruins, God will destroy them. Scholars who date Malachi early in the fifth century see a reference to Babylonian campaigns against southern Jordan (which had been occupied by Edomites) after 552 BCE (see Bartlett 1992) but this is too distant from the early fifth century to be convincing. The uncomfortable saying that God hates Esau is softened by some commentators to mean simply that God loves Esau/Edom less than Jacob/Israel—an interpretation hardly supported by v. 4. Yet as the oracles continue it becomes clear that if God indeed has a special love for Israel it will not spare the people from forthcoming judgement (cf. 3:5).

(1:6–2:10) Second Disputation The implications of God's special love for Israel are now worked out in a powerful condemnation of the priests. They are charged with dishonouring God by offering polluted food (Hebrew *leḥem*, a general term for offerings including animal sacrifices) on the altar. This surprises them. The answer to the question 'How'? (v. 6) in vv. 7–8 is not easy to understand. They are accused of saying (NRSV 'thinking') that the altar may be despised; but presumably this 'saying' is not speech but actions, as they allow blind or sick animals to be sacrificed. Against NRSV, 'is not that wrong?' in v. 8 (twice) should be translated 'it is not wrong'. Either the priests give this advice to ordinary worshippers, some of whom may be unable to offer healthy animals, or the priests deliberately procure for the temple service animals that do not conform to the rules (cf. Lev 22:22–4). Whatever the motivation, such an attitude values God less highly than the (probably foreign) governor (v. 8). If the priests cannot honour God properly, how can they mediate between God and the people (v. 9)? It would be better to have no offerings than dishonourable ones (v. 10).

At this point a later addition to the text (vv. 11–14) seeks to clarify the situation. The main criticism is now directed towards the ordinary people who bring stolen as well as sick animals as offerings, when they have healthy animals (reading *zākeh* 'clean' for *zākār* 'male', v. 14) available. But the criticism is preceded by the noble statement (v. 11) that God's name is great among the nations and that incense and pure offerings are (or will be) made to him 'in every place'. Most commentators deny that this envisages the worship of the God of Israel by all the nations, and see a reference to the worship of Jews in the Diaspora, or to the worship of the God of heaven in the Persian empire (cf. Ezra 6:9). However, as Rudolf (1976) points out, the idea that foreign nations recognize the God of Israel is not unknown in the OT (cf. Jonah). The seemingly obvious sense of the verse should not be dismissed too hastily, and it becomes a corrective to the exclusivist tendency of Mal 1:2–5.

vv. 2:1 and 3–9 (v. 2 is secondary) continue the original dispute from 1:10, and contain a rebuke to the priests. v. 3 implies that the priests and their descendants will be removed from office and Levi, the ancestor of the tribe from which all priests come, is held up as the true example of the mediator of a covenant between God and his people. Commentators are divided over whether the background to these verses is Deut. 33:9 or Num 25:10–13 (see Glazier-McDonald 1987). What is at issue is whether or not Malachi is aware of the distinction between priests and Levites, the point being that the book would be early fifth century if it could be shown that, with Deuteronomy, Malachi knows no such difference. In fact, 2:4–9 emphasizes the teaching and not the sacrificial role of Levi. Does the prophet envisage the suspension of the sacrificial cult until the coming of his messenger (3:1)?

(2:10–16) Third Disputation Attention shifts from the priests to Judah and Jerusalem as a whole (Israel in v. 11 is a later gloss). The accusation is that the people have not lived out the implications of having one God and father, in two ways. First they have profaned the covenant and the temple by worshipping a goddess (NRSV 'daughter of a foreign god'). Most commentators take v. 11 to refer to marriages with foreign wives, but this is not obvious from the text nor from the continuation in vv. 13–16. The reference is to a female consort for YHWH. Although the idolatry interpretation is not free of difficulties—it implies that Judah is a bridegroom and that therefore God is the rejected bride—it makes best sense of vv. 10–12. The words 'any to witness or answer' (v. 12) have yet to be convincingly translated or explained.

The second charge is that men have been too ready to divorce the wives that they first married (i.e. wives who are now old), that this violates the notion that man and wife are one flesh (v. 15, cf. Gen 2:24) and undermines the loyalty to the covenant expected by God from his people. The text of vv. 13–16 contains many difficulties. 'I hate divorce' (v. 16 in NRSV and many modern trs.) is a correction of the Hebrew 'he hates' without any support from the ancient versions, and cannot be correct. In fact, the ancient versions took the words to mean that God approved the divorcing of wives who were hated! The Babylonian Talmud (*b. Giṭṭin* 90b) rightly understands the logic of the passage (if not its Heb.) by arguing that it means that God hates the man who divorces his first wife. The Hebrew is best repointed and rendered 'if one hated [his wife and] divorced [her]...he covers his garment with violence' (cf. Redditt 1995).

(2:17–3:5) Fourth Disputation The complaint that evildoers prosper materially in a world in which, according to covenant ideas, they ought to suffer misfortune, is common in the OT (cf. Deut 28:15–44 and Ps 73). Here, it gives rise to the charge that the complainants have wearied God, and occasions the promise that God is about to act decisively. His messenger will prepare for God's coming, which will result in judgement against the evildoers (v. 5). Two later expansions of the text blur the focus of the passage, while indicating that the promise was taken seriously by the users of Malachi. The second expansion (v. 3 from 'and he will purify' to v. 4) concentrates the divine coming upon a purification of the temple cult, and in connection with v. 5 implies that a reform of the temple will have to precede the divine judgement of social abuses. The first expansion (v. 1 from 'The messenger of the covenant') is an attempt to clarify who is meant by the Lord (Hebrew *'ādôn*). Although certainty is impossible here, it is likely that the original oracle envisages the imminent coming of God, while the expansion implies that the Lord will be a heavenly being (cf. the angel of God in the Exodus narratives, Ex 14:19–23:20, the Hebrew *mal'āk* meaning both 'messenger' and 'angel'). This introduces us to the central problem in Malachi that is taken up again in ch. 4. The book in its first main draft and in its final form urges faithfulness to God upon a society in which there were social abuses, indifferent worship, and even idolatry, and in which a speedy divine intervention had not materialized. How those who advocated faithfulness to God coped with the situation is indicated in the remainder of the book.

(3:6–12) Fifth Disputation A new strategy is brought into play. In direct address by God it is implied that the people's misfortunes are due not to God's indifference but to Israel's failure to observe God's laws. It is because God does not change that the children of Jacob (the name is a pun on a root that can also mean 'trickster' or 'crooked') still survive despite their waywardness. The people are challenged to show that they have returned to God by fulfilling their obligations to render tithes to the temple. They are invited, indeed, to put God to the test (v. 10), who promises that he will then bless their agricultural labours (vv. 10–11). This is a positive attitude to the temple compared with 1:7–2:3, but not necessarily at variance with it. Tithes could be used for social purposes (Deut 14:28–9) and if the people who had something were, through the tithe, to provide for the socially oppressed (v. 5), this would show practical commitment to the implications of being the children of one creator father (2:10).

(3:13–4:3) Sixth Disputation The complaint first heard at 2:17, that God is indifferent to justice, is taken up again and expressed even more forcefully. Not only do the evildoers prosper; those who try to keep God's commandments see no benefit. The day belongs to those who treat the things of God with dismissive arrogance. It would be wrong to suppose that the complainants are interested in religion merely for what they can get out of it. We have here rather the anguished cry of those who want to live in a world where goodness and not evil is paramount. The second-person dialogue between God and the people is broken at 3:16–17 by a prose passage in the third person. While switches from second to third person and back are not necessarily signs that verses have been interpolated, the logic of the passage becomes clear if it is assumed that v. 18 originally followed v. 15. The God-fearers are assured that they will see a difference between themselves and the wicked. The occasion will be the coming day of the

Lord (4:1) that will destroy the evildoers and bring healing and life to the faithful (4:2).

The fact that this may have not been entirely reassuring brings us to the expansion in vv. 16–17, which has the effect of bringing the hope of future vindication into the present. The opening word 'then' makes no logical sense in its context, and has been emended to 'thus' (i.e. in this way) but this is unnecessary if v. 16 is regarded as an expansion. The faithful are reassured that even now their names are being recorded in a book (cf. Esth 6:1–3) and that they are a special possession. Thus, their words of complaint do not occasion God's anger, but his mercy.

(4:4–6) Closing Words The last three verses are a later conclusion to Malachi and the Book of the Twelve. The reference to the coming of Elijah both amplifies 3:1, which expects a forerunner to precede the day of the Lord, and subverts 3:16–4:3, which envisages an imminent day of judgement which will spare those whose names have been written in the book of remembrance. The reference to Moses (v. 4) echoes Deut 34:5, where Moses is called the Lord's servant. Tradition dislikes anonymity, which is why the anonymous 'messenger' of 3:1 has become the named Elijah here. Elijah has been chosen because of the tradition that he did not die but was taken up to heaven (2 Kings 2:11). On the other hand, the designation 'messenger of the covenant' and the picture of him coming to the Jerusalem temple (3:1) hardly fits the Elijah of 1 and 2 Kings.

In the IIB Malachi concludes the Law and the Prophets, which is why the references to Moses and Elijah in 4:4–6 are apposite. In the Christian Bible Malachi ends the Old Testament, and the reference to the coming of Elijah is taken up in the story of the Elijah-like figure of John the Baptist.

REFERENCES

Bartlett, J. R. (1992), 'Edom', *ABD* ii. 287–95.

Davies, G. I. (1991), *Ancient Hebrew Inscriptions, Corpus and Concordance* (Cambridge: Cambridge University Press).

Glazier-McDonald, B. (1987), *Malachi: The Divine Messenger*, SBLDS 98 (Atlanta, Ga.: Scholars Press).

Meinhold, A. (1991), 'Maleachi/Maleachibuch', *Theologische Realenzyklopädie* (Berlin: de Gruyter) xxii. 6–11.

Redditt, P. L. (1995), *Haggai, Zechariah, Malachi*, New Century Bible (Grand Rapids, Mich.: Eerdmans).

Rudolf, W. (1976), *Haggai, Sacharja 1–8, Sacharja 9–14, Maleachi*, KAT 13/4 (Gütersloh: Mohn).

Utzschneider, H. (1992), 'Die Schriftprophetie und die Frage nach dem Ende der Prophetie. Überlegungen anhand von Mal 1, 6–2, 16', *ZAW* 104: 377–94.

39. Introduction to the Apocrypha   MARTIN GOODMAN

A. Definition. 1. The term 'apocrypha' was never used in antiquity to denote the separate corpus of disparate books which are printed under this heading in some modern Bibles. The current use of the term was popularized through the practice of Protestant scholars during the Reformation in distinguish-

ing these books, which were standard in Catholic Bibles, from canonical biblical writings. This use reflected more general uses of the term in late antiquity.

2. The Greek word 'apocrypha' means books that have been hidden away in some sense. The term was sometimes used in antiquity to refer to books that contained mysterious or secret teachings, but although many such esoteric writings were known and highly regarded by both Jews and Christians (cf. 2 Esd 14:45–6) the description of them as apocryphal was rare. Other Christian writers described as 'apocrypha' those books which were reckoned to be spurious or heretical and thus unfit for Christian use (e.g. Athanasius and Rufinus, both in the 4th cent. CE). The use of the term to refer to the corpus of books that now forms an appendix to the OT began with Jerome in the early fifth century. Jerome was concerned to define the limits of the OT canon and elected to exclude those books found in the Greek and Latin versions but not in the Hebrew. He did not condemn these books as unworthy but only as non-canonical and hence useful for general edification rather than to define church dogma.

3. Since the MSS of Greek and Latin Bibles do not all contain precisely the same works, but all contain the writings included in the OT as defined by Protestants, the extent of the Apocrypha is not entirely fixed. Some biblical MSS include 3 and 4 Maccabees and Ps 151 which, since they are not part of the HB, have therefore sometimes been treated as part of the Apocrypha. Conversely, during disputes in the Reformation about the religious importance of the Apocrypha, some theologians declared unfitting for the corpus those writings that seemed to them to lack value; thus Luther excluded from his version of the Apocrypha both 1 and 2 Esdras. The books discussed in this Commentary are those commonly found in those Protestant English Bibles in which the Apocrypha is printed.

B. History. 1. Septuagint. The creation of the Apocrypha is part of the history of the translation of the HB into Greek. The Septuagint, so-called because of the foundation legend that it was the work of seventy (or seventy-two) translators, was produced gradually during the third and second centuries BCE. According to the *Letter of Aristeas*, the translation of the Pentateuch was produced by translators sent to Alexandria from Jerusalem by the high priest Eleazar at the behest of King Ptolemy II Philadelphus (283–246 BCE) and, although the detailed historicity of this legend is dubious, and it is more likely that the work was commissioned by Greek-speaking Jews, the Alexandrian origin of the work is plausible since a festival to celebrate the translation was held there regularly in the first century CE (Philo, *vit. Mos.* 2.7 (41)). But the other books were translated piecemeal and quite possibly in other parts of the Greek-speaking diaspora. All that is certain is that the main body of the Writings and the Prophets were available by the late second century BCE, when the grandson of the author of Ecclesiasticus, Jesus son of Sira, referred, in the prologue to his translation of his grandfather's work, to the existence of Greek versions of 'the Law, the prophecies and the rest of the books'. In the same passage the grandson of Jesus son of Sira referred to the impossibility of precise translation: 'What was originally expressed in Hebrew does not have exactly the same sense when translated into another language.' In this he was quite correct, and the translators of different books in the Septuagint varied between those who aimed at a very literal rendering and those who apparently aimed more at reproducing the mood of the original. In the latter case the Greek version often necessarily included a great deal of interpretation and (to a lesser extent) elaboration; the authors both inspired and were part of a much wider movement of translating Jewish texts into Greek in this period, often producing work so distinctly Hellenic that they should be treated as compositions in their own right. It is in this context that the material now found in the Apocrypha was composed.

2. The transmission of the Septuagint in antiquity was almost entirely through Christian rather than Jewish copyists. Some fragments of the Pentateuch, the minor prophets, and indeed some of the apocrypha survive in Jewish MSS from pre-Christian times, and further papyrus fragments including parts of Wisdom and Sirach from the second to third centuries CE was found at Antinoopolis in Egypt, but the main witnesses to the text are the Christian MSS of the fourth century, the Codex Vaticanus and the Codex Sinaiticus, and the rather later (between the late fourth and early sixth centuries) Codex Alexandrinus. Christians from the beginning treated the Septuagint as a sacred text in its own right and not simply as a translation of the Hebrew.

3. At the time when the Septuagint translations and the apocrypha were composed, books were written on papyrus or leather scrolls and each book would normally have been written on a separate scroll. Thus the issue of what was to be included together with the other books of the Greek Bible only really arose with the Christian adoption of the Codex. Most of the books of the apocrypha are to be found in each of the great codices of the Septuagint from late antiquity without any indication that they are not part of the canon of Scripture, but they are found in different places within the text and not all are consistently included. Thus, for example, the Prayer of Manasseh is not in any of our ancient copies of the Septuagint, but some Septuagint MSS include 3 and 4 Maccabees and Ps 151, which were not to be treated as part of the Apocrypha when the corpus was defined in the Reformation, and by contrast 2 Esdras is not found in any Greek codex of the Septuagint. From all this it is clear that Christians in late antiquity on the whole treated the Apocrypha as part of the canon of sacred Scripture, but since the limits of the canon were still disputed, some books were more consistently treated in this way than others.

4. Confirmation of this view can be found in the lists of canonical works of the OT compiled by Christian authors in late antiquity, in which the books of the apocrypha are found in varying numbers and order. Many Greek Christian writers of the second and third centuries regularly cited apocryphal books, using the same formulas to introduce quotations that they used to cite texts from the OT. However, a few Christian authors, such as Melito of Sardis in the second century and Origen in the third, were aware that although the apocryphal books were to be found in the Septuagint and were therefore 'Scripture' they were not in use among Jews as part of the HB, and in the fourth century Cyril of Jerusalem, Gregory of Nazianzus, and Amphilochius did not include any of the apocrypha in the lists of canonical books that they drew up.

C. Use of the Apocrypha in the Early Church. 1. There is no direct quotation from the apocrypha in the NT, and it is difficult to be certain whether parallel expression and allusions, of which many can be identified, show use of the apocrypha by the authors of the NT or the influence of a common tradition. Thus, for instance, many expressions in the letters of Paul and in Hebrews use imagery close to that in Wisdom of Solomon (e.g. Heb 1:1–3 = Wis 7:25–7), and Heb 11:35–7 alludes to the martyrdom story found in 2 Macc 6–7. Direct borrowing is not, of course, impossible, but these themes may have had much wider currency than just the surviving literature.

2. In contrast numerous quotations from the apocrypha can be found in patristic writings. Among Greek-speaking Christians, Wisdom of Solomon was quoted by 1 *Clement* at the end of the first century and in the *Epistle of Barnabas* from the early second; Ecclesiasticus and 2 Esdras were also quoted by *Barnabas*; Tobit was quoted by Polycarp in the mid-second century; the stories of Susanna and the other apocryphal Additions to Daniel were included by Hippolytus of Rome in his commentary on Daniel. These citations generally treated the text of the apocrypha as inspired like the rest of Scripture. In the fragmentary Muratorian Canon, to be dated probably to *c.*200, the Wisdom of Solomon actually appears as part of the NT, albeit with an indication that this is not certain. Among Latin Christians, such as Tertullian and Cyprian, the apocryphal books were accorded even higher esteem, doubtless encouraged in the view by their inclusion in the Old Latin version of the OT, which was translated from the Septuagint. The main dissenting voice was that of Jerome, who made much use of the HB in creating his new Latin translation, the Vulgate, in the early fifth century. Jerome was persuaded to include some of the apocrypha in the Vulgate on the grounds that these were popular books, but in the margins he marked as missing in the Hebrew the Additions to Daniel and Esther, and, although he translated Tobit and Judith, later MSS of the Vulgate imported into Jerome's corpus the Old Latin versions of the other books. This ambivalent attitude was best summed up by Jerome himself in the Prologues to a number of these books: in his view the apocryphal books might be read by Christians and contained much of value, but they were not canonical and thus should not be used to establish the doctrines of the church. This view coexisted unhappily among Latin Christians with the powerful advocacy of the canonical status of these books urged by Jerome's contemporary Augustine. Among Greek Christians canonical status was generally taken for granted, but early Syriac patristic authors used an OT even more restricted than the Hebrew—of the apocrypha they knew only Ecclesiasticus, which they treated as canonical.

D. Identification of the Apocrypha as a Distinct Corpus. 1. Treatment of the apocryphal books as quasi-Scripture precluded recognition by patristic authors of these books as constituting a distinct literary corpus. Even Jerome, who applied the term 'apocrypha' to these writings (above, A.2), treated them only negatively: the apocrypha were defined as the books found in Greek and Latin Bibles but not in the Hebrew. The insights of Jerome were for the most part ignored during the Middle Ages. Most Christians treated all the books found in the Septuagint and the Vulgate as of equal value, and many of the books of the apocrypha were widely read and popular. None the less some scholars continued to distinguish the apocrypha from the distinctive authority of the books found

in the Hebrew OT, from Nicholas of Lyra and Wycliffe in the fourteenth century to Cardinal Ximenes, editor of the Complutensian Polyglot edition of the Bible in 1514–17.

2. The attitude of Protestant scholars in the Reformation was thus not entirely a break with recent Christian practice. In 1520 Andreas Bodenstein of Karlstadt published a tracture distinguishing the apocryphal books from those in the Hebrew OT and dividing the apocrypha itself into two groups of non-canonical but holy books (e.g. Tobit, Wisdom, and Sirach) and foolish writings 'worthy of the Censor's ban' (i.e. 1 and 2 Esdras, Baruch, the Prayer of Manasseh, and the Additions to Daniel). Following this lead, many Protestant Bibles in the vernacular, most influentially Luther's German translation completed in 1534, placed the books of the Apocrypha in a separate appendix after the books of the OT, with a preface stating that these books 'are not held equal to the sacred scriptures, and yet are useful and good for reading'. The treatment of the Apocrypha as a separate corpus became standard in Protestant Bibles, although there continued to be rare exceptions, such as the place of the Prayer of Manasseh in the Geneva Bible published in English in 1560, between 2 Chronicles and Ezra, with a note about its apocryphal status.

3. This attitude in Protestant churches provoked a vigorous response by the Catholic church, with the declaration in the Council of Trent in 1546 of an anathema on anyone who did not recognize as sacred and canonical all the books found in the Vulgate, although the same Council rather inconsistently denied the canonical status of the Prayer of Manasseh and 1 and 2 Esdras; as a result, these books were after 1593 regularly printed as a separate appendix, while the rest of the books treated by Protestants as the apocrypha continued to be printed as part of the biblical text as in older editions of the Vulgate. None the less it remained useful for Catholics to distinguish the Apocrypha as a separate corpus and these books were thus often termed by Catholics 'deutero-canonical'.

4. The books of the Apocrypha do not play a major role in contemporary Christianity even among Roman Catholics. Among Protestants the lower status given to these books early led to their omission altogether in many printed Bibles. Among Calvinists the Apocrypha was rejected altogether as wholly without authority, and arguments about the value of these books continued among Protestants in many countries through the nineteenth century. Among the Protestant churches, the most positive attitude towards the apocrypha is found in the Anglican church, in which extensive use is made of these books in the liturgy.

E. Jewish Attitudes to the Books of the Apocrypha. 1. The late Second Temple period, when the apocrypha were written, was a time of intense literary activity among Jews (see below, G.16). The basis of that activity was the books now found in the HB, but it is unclear when and how precisely Jews came to agree on the limits of a canon of inspired Scripture. Thus it is entirely possible that soon after their composition the writings now found in the Apocrypha were treated by Jews as similar in nature and authority to the books in their Bible. On the other hand the statement by Josephus (*Ag. Ap.* 1.43) that 'there are not with us myriads of books, discordant and discrepant, but only twenty-two, comprising the history of all time, which are justly accredited' almost certainly refers to the biblical books and shows that, even if a fixed canon was not yet generally agreed, the idea that there might be such a canon was familiar. The discovery among the Dead Sea scrolls of fragments of Ecclesiasticus (also found at Masada), the Letter of Jeremiah (in Greek), and Tobit shows that these books were read by some Palestinian Jews before 70 CE, and the lack of the other apocryphal books among the finds may be accidental, although it is worth noting in contrast the discovery at Qumran of parts of every book of the HB except Esther. Josephus used 1 Esdras, 1 Maccabees, and the additions to Esther, but his failure to refer to the other books of the Apocrypha may in some cases be only because they were not sufficiently historical to be of use to him. It should be noted that, if Josephus really meant to insist that Jews used a fixed number of historical texts (see above) but himself follows the version of Jewish history in 1 Esdras, either he did not possess the biblical books of Ezra and Nehemiah or he believed 1 Esdras to be canonical and the biblical books to be lacking in authority.

2. Early rabbinic literature shows no awareness of any of the books of the Apocrypha apart from Sirach. This is unsurprising for those books that existed only in Greek, but more surprising for Tobit and Judith, which certainly existed in Aramaic and perhaps in Hebrew, and 1 Maccabees, which was probably originally composed in Hebrew; at any rate a Hebrew version was known to Origen and to Jerome (see below, F.6). Citations of Sirach (under the name 'Ben Sirah') in early rabbinic texts are quite frequent and are sometimes preceded by the same introductory formula ('as it is written') which was used to introduce passages from the Writings, the third part of the OT (cf. b. B. Qam. 92b). It is clear from this that Sirach was highly regarded, but not that the rabbis treated this text as equal in status to those in the biblical corpus; the rabbinic discussions over which texts 'render the hands unclean' reveal doubts about the status of a number of books that are included in the biblical corpus (e.g. Song of Songs and Ecclesiastes), but not about Sirach. The rabbis may not have used most of the apocryphal texts but they were aware of some of the traditions referred to in those texts. Most important was the festival of Hanukkah, which celebrated the events described in 1 and 2 Maccabees, but there are also occasional rabbinic references to the martyrdom story of Hannah and her sons found in 2 Maccabees (cf. b. Git. 57b) and to the stories found in the Additions to Daniel.

3. The contents of some of the books of the Apocrypha came back to the attention of Jews in the Middle Ages through the wide dissemination of Hebrew versions of some of the stories. The narratives of Tobit and Judith were popular, as was *Megillat Antiochus*, which repeated in outline some of the material found in the books of Maccabees. Ecclesiasticus, known to the rabbis as Ben Sira, was presumably still known to some Jews in the original Hebrew even in the high Middle Ages, since large portions of the text were found in the Cairo Genizah in 1896, but the uniqueness of this manuscript find, and the scarcity of references to the work in rabbinic literature after antiquity, suggests that the book was not widely read, although the composition in the medieval period of a new work, the *Alfabet of Ben Sira*, demonstrates the continuing prestige thought to attach to the work of Ben Sira himself. The real revival of Jewish interest in the apocrypha came in the Renaissance, when scholarly Jews became aware of the existence of a large Jewish literature in Greek, and a translation of the apocrypha into Hebrew was published in the early sixteenth century. Since then Jewish scholars have made much use of these books in the study of Jewish literature and history, but these writings have never reverted to their original status as sources of religious edification.

F. Description of the Books of the Apocrypha. 1. Size The corpus of the Apocrypha is about one-fifth of the length of the OT and over two-thirds that of the NT. The books are of very unequal length. Sirach is the longest, almost as long as Exodus. The Prayer of Manasseh consists of one brief chapter.

2. Genres The books included in the Apocrypha show no generic uniformity. 1 Esdras, 1 Maccabees, and 2 Maccabees are, or purport to be, historical works. Tobit, Judith, and the Additions to Daniel are essentially moralizing romances. Sirach is a work of wisdom literature similar to Proverbs; Wisdom of Solomon is a more high-flown and philosophical instance of the same genre. 2 Esdras is apocalyptic. The Prayer of Manasseh is an example of devotional literature.

3. Dates of Composition The only book in the Apocrypha whose date of composition can be ascertained fairly precisely is Sirach, since the grandson of the author, who translated the book into Greek, stated in the prologue to the translation that he had arrived in Egypt 'in the thirty-eighth year of the reign of Euergetes', i.e. in 132 BCE; his grandfather must therefore have composed the original Hebrew in the first half of the second century BCE. For some of the other writings (1 Esdras, the Additions to Esther, 1 Maccabees) a final *terminus ante quem* is the end of the first century CE because Josephus knew and used them; the date of the translation of the Hebrew book of Esther into Greek is given by a colophon which probably fixes it to 114 BCE, but it is possible that the Additions that are found only in the Greek text (and hence are now found in the Apocrypha) were composed separately after the completion of the main translation and were only later inserted into the narrative. Composition before c.100 CE is also likely for the bulk of 2 Esdras since the book was early cited by Christians. It is in any case unlikely that any Jewish writing would have been adopted by Christians with the enthusiasm accorded to the Apocrypha if it had been composed much after that date.

4. The earliest date that most of these books could have been written is in most cases less easy to state. 1 and 2 Maccabees cannot have been composed before the events they describe; the author of 1 Maccabees thus wrote after 134 BCE, the author of 2 Maccabees after 163 BCE. In theory all the other books may have originated much earlier, in the Persian period; this is entirely possible, for instance, of Tobit. Arguments for a later date, after c.300 BCE, are commonly advanced, but they rely upon the general nature of these writings, and especially alleged reflections of political events, rather than any specific temporal indication in the texts, and they are thus only hypothetical.

5. Places of Composition There is no reason to assume that all these books were either written or (in some cases) translated in the same place; only the translation of Sirach can be confidently located in Alexandria in the Egyptian delta. Those writings originally composed in Hebrew or Aramaic (see c.5) may have been written either in the Land of Israel or in

Babylonia or Syria or even in Egypt (e.g. Tobit). Those written in or translated into Greek may originate from any part of the Eastern Mediterranean world, including quite possibly Judea, since some knowledge of Greek can be presumed among educated circles in Jerusalem from at least the third century BCE (see below, G.15).

6. Original Languages Because of the process of transmission of this corpus of texts (see B.1, 3–4), all of them have been preserved in Greek, but this does not mean that all were therefore originally composed in Greek. The Hebrew or Aramaic origin of the book of Tobit is now certain because of the discovery of five Tobit MSS, four in Aramaic and one in Hebrew, among the Dead Sea scrolls. In contrast the original Semitic version of Judith and of 1 Maccabees can only be hypothesized from the nature of the Greek text, although an Aramaic version of Judith was known to Jerome in the early fifth century and a Hebrew text of 1 Maccabees was known to Origen in the third century. There is no reason to doubt that both 2 Maccabees and the Wisdom of Solomon were originally written in Greek, but for the rest of the Apocrypha the original language is uncertain. In the third century CE Julius Africanus argued that the play on words in the Greek text of Susanna shows that this narrative was originally composed in Greek, but it is also possible that this was the work of an ingenious translator.

7. Authors Most of the authors of the apocryphal books are anonymous or pseudonymous and their identities can only be surmised from the contents of their writings. The exceptions are Jesus ben Sira, author of Ecclesiasticus, who identified himself in the text (50:27) as a Jerusalemite, and his grandson, who translated his work and, according to his statement in the prologue, wrote in Egypt. 2 Maccabees is an abridgement of a larger work in five volumes by a certain Jason of Cyrene (2 Macc 2:23), but beyond the facts that his name indicates that he came from Cyrenaica (modern Libya) and that the details in the narrative suggest (if they derive from Jason) that he had spent some time in Judea, nothing else can be said about him. Despite the preservation of the Apocrypha eventually through Christian rather than Jewish copyists since the end of the first century CE (see B.2), there is no reason to doubt that most of what is found in these books was written by Jews except for 2 Esd 1–2; 15–16; these passages, which are found in the Latin Vulgate, are missing in the oriental translations and appear to be additions by a Christian author. Christian interpolations into the texts of other books of the Apocrypha are possible but seem to have been rare, presumably because these texts were from early on treated as Scripture.

8. Readership So far as is known, everything in the Apocrypha, apart from the Christian interpolations (see C.6), was written originally primarily for a Jewish readership. Only in the case of the Wisdom of Solomon is it reasonable to speculate that the author may in part have had in mind also Gentile readers: the address to the 'judges and kings of the earth' (Wis 1:1; 6:1) is a literary fiction, but the attack on the foolishness of idolatry (chs. 13–15) may have been genuinely aimed at Gentile pagans, although its prime intention may more plausibly have been to guide Jews away from any temptation to indulge in such worship, and the book as a whole contains so many veiled allusions to biblical history that only Jewish readers could have appreciated it fully. In any case, and whatever the aims of the authors, there is no evidence that any ancient pagan in fact read any of these works.

G. Historical Background. 1. Political Events In the Hellenistic World The political event of most significance in the shaping of the Apocrypha was the conquest of the Levant by Alexander the Great of Macedon in 331 BCE. For nearly two centuries before the arrival of Alexander, the Land of Israel lay under Persian rule. The Persian state was on the whole content to interfere little with the lives of its subjects, and the small province of Judah was allowed to develop its own distinctive culture around the temple city of Jerusalem. This quiet, parochial existence was shattered by Alexander, who brought Greek culture in all its forms to the Jews.

2. Alexander inherited the throne of Macedon from his father Philip at the age of 20 in 336 BCE and almost immediately embarked on an ambitious campaign to conquer the Persian empire. Astonishing success in a series of battles brought him by the time of his death in 323 BCE control of the whole of the Near East up to the borders of India. Within his new empire lay not just the Jewish homeland and temple but also the great centre of Jewish exile in Mesopotamia. For the next 200 years Jewish history was continually affected by the intrigues and ambitions of Alexander's Macedonian successors. After a period of turmoil following Alexander's death, his generals eventually parcelled out his huge conquests among themselves. Of the great dynastic empires that thus came into existence by 301 BCE, the two most to affect the Jews were the dynasty founded by Ptolemy I Soter, with its base in Egypt, and the rival dynasty of Seleucus I Nicator, which had essentially two main bases, one in Mesopotamia and the other in northern Syria.

3. From 301 to 198 BCE Jerusalem lay under the rule of the Ptolemys, lying at the northern fringes of the Ptolemaic state, but the territory of the Land of Israel was disputed by the Seleucids in six wars in the course of the third century, and eventually the Seleucid king Antiochus III in 198 BCE wrested control of the southern Levant into his own hands as part of a general expansion of his kingdom. The result was a change in the method of state control of Judea. In essence the Ptolemaic dynasty ruled through a large bureaucracy, in part a necessity because of the reliance of Egyptian agriculture on irrigation which depended on state regulation; in contrast the much more diffuse empire of the Seleucids relied heavily on co-operation by local élites, who were given incentives to administer their regions on behalf of the state. Hence in the Seleucid empire there were more (or more openly recognized) routes to advancement for non-Greeks than in the Ptolemaic state, but with the proviso that non-Greek élites were expected to behave in Greek fashion if they were to be granted such control over their own communities. In Jerusalem the Jewish ruling élite was essentially the high priest and his associates. During the course of the first quarter of the second century BCE some members of this élite proved sufficiently attracted to the prospect of power to adopt Greek names and some Greek customs. It is possible (although it is hard to tell whether this was actually their intention) that the gradual adoption of this alien culture would have led in time to the end of a distinctively Jewish culture and religion. In any case the process was abruptly halted by the Maccabean revolt.

4. The Maccabean Revolt In 168 BCE the Seleucid king Antiochus IV Epiphanes ordered the abolition of the ancient cult in the temple in Jerusalem and the conversion of the shrine to pagan worship. Neither the new divinity to whom the temple was dedicated nor the precise causes of this highly unusual attack by a Hellenistic king on an ancestral religion can be stated with certainty; the main sources of evidence are the books of Maccabees in the Apocrypha, which provide as explanation the internal divisions within the Jewish ruling class, and in particular the desire of some high priests to embrace Hellenism as a route to political power, but the wider policy of Antiochus, who first expanded his power through a dramatic campaign south into Egypt and was then compelled to withdraw by the threat of Roman intervention, may have been equally or even more responsible. At any rate this attack provoked an uprising led by Mattathias, a priest from Modiin, north-west of Jerusalem, and his five sons, of whom Judas Maccabee emerged in the course of the struggle as supreme leader. By 164 BCE guerrilla warfare had succeeded and the temple was purified and rededicated.

5. Hasmonean Rule Control of the temple did not automatically bring political independence. There continued to be a Seleucid garrison in Jerusalem until probably 129 BCE. Nor did the family of Mattathias and Judas immediately reap in full the fruits of their victory: when the temple cult was restarted by Judas, the new high priest was a certain Alcimus, an associate of the high priest from before the war; Mattathias died during the war and Judas himself was killed in battle in 161 BCE. On the death of Alcimus in 159 BCE there was a hiatus in the high priesthood until 152 BCE, when Judas's brother Jonathan had himself appointed to the post. From that date to 37 BCE all the high priests came from this family. The dynasty was called by the name 'Hasmonean', a reference back to an ancestor of Mattathias. At first the Hasmoneans ruled Judea as vassals, in effect, of the Seleucid kings, but they took advantage of the disintegration of the Seleucid state through internal dissension and the machinations of the Romans, whose interest in the eastern Mediterranean increased during the second century BCE. By the 120s BCE the Hasmonean high priest John Hyrcanus was sufficiently independent to commence campaigns to expand the region of Jewish rule outside Judea, and by 112 BCE the whole region of Idumea, to the south of Judea, had been forced by him to convert to Judaism. A similar policy of expansion and incorporation was followed by his son Aristobulus, who in 104–103 BCE compelled the Itureans who lived in Galilee to become Jews.

6. The brief rule of Aristobulus (104–103 BCE) marked something of a shift in the nature of Hasmonean rule. Aristobulus was still high priest, and his right to power was still justified by the dynasty's role as the leaders of the revolt in the 160s, but he liked to be known as 'philhellene' (a lover of Greek culture) and he had himself declared king. In his rule, and that of his successor Alexander Jannaeus (103–76 BCE), the Hasmonean dynasty behaved much like other Hellenistic rulers, using mercenary soldiers to establish themselves as a regional superpower. When Jannaeus died, his widow Alexandra Jannaea Salome became queen (76–67 BCE), in a fashion found elsewhere in the Hellenistic world but not previously among Jews. In the process the relationship of the Hasmoneans with their Jewish subjects at times became stormy.

7. The decline of the Hasmonean dynasty was a direct product of the ambitions of Rome. During the 70s BCE the remnants of the Seleucid state fell into Roman hands and in 63 BCE the Roman general Pompey the Great took advantage of quarrels between Hyrcanus and Aristobulus, the two sons of Alexandra Jannaea Salome, to intervene ostensibly on the side of Hyrcanus. Thus Pompey besieged Jerusalem and inaugurated the ensuing history of misunderstandings between Jews and Romans by desecrating the Holy of Holies in the temple simply out of curiosity to know whether it was true that there was no cult image in the shrine. From that date Judea lay in effect within the Roman empire, although for much of the next century Rome preferred to exercise control through proxy Jewish rulers, a procedure common in Rome's administration of her empire elsewhere.

8. Herodian Rule The transfer of Roman patronage from the Hasmonean dynasty to Herod the Great in 40 BCE was not a result of standard Roman policy, for Rome usually sought client kings from within the ranks of existing native dynasties. Nor was it remotely to be expected on the Jewish side, since Herod was an Idumean, descended on his father's side from the people converted to Judaism less than a century before by John Hyrcanus and on his mother's side from a Nabatean Arab, and thus ineligible for the high priesthood. Herod was proclaimed king of Judea by the Roman senate and consuls out of desperation caused by the internal disintegration of the Roman state.

9. The period of civil war that had first engulfed the Mediterranean world in 49 BCE with the struggle of Pompey and Julius Caesar did not abate until the victory of Octavian, the future emperor Augustus, in the battle of Actium in 31 BCE. In the meantime the Roman state was in turmoil and in 40 BCE the Parthians, whose empire in this period was based in Mesopotamia, took advantage of Roman disarray to invade the southern Levant. The Hasmonean ruler and high priest Hyrcanus (67–40 BCE) was carried off into exile in Babylonia and replaced by his nephew, the pro-Parthian Antigonus. The Romans, who had no Hasmonean adult male to put forward in opposition, chose Herod instead simply because he had already proved himself an energetic aide to Hyrcanus and a loyal friend to Rome.

10. Herod's first act once proclaimed king was to join his Roman patrons in a sacrifice to Jupiter on the Capitol, and when he eventually captured his capital in 37 BCE it was through the efforts of Roman legionaries commanded by a Roman general. It is not surprising that, after this inauspicious start, Herod's relationship with his subjects was never easy. He ruled until 4 BCE through repression, constantly fearful of plots, not least by members of his own family. His grandiose building plans, which included the massive reconstruction of the Jerusalem Temple, did not succeed in endearing him to his people. His success in ruling through fear was demonstrated by the eruption of widespread revolts when he died. His son Archelaus, appointed ethnarch of Judea by the Roman emperor Augustus, proved incapable of imposing control in the same way, and in 6 CE he was sent by Augustus into exile in the south of France. Judea came under the direct rule of a Roman governor.

11. Roman Rule Judea was controlled directly by Rome for many centuries from 6 CE, with the exception of the glorious three-year rule from 41 to 44 CE of Agrippa I, Herod's grandson, who owed his throne to his machinations in Roman politics and his role in bringing to power the new emperor Claudius, and the periods of Jewish revolt in 66–70 and 132–5 CE.

12. There was a revolt in 6 CE when a census was imposed as part of the organization of the new province, but this phenomenon can also be observed in other provinces in this period. Despite a mass protest in 40 CE when the emperor Gaius Caligula attempted to have a statue of himself erected in the temple, and occasional disturbances in Jerusalem at the times of mass pilgrimage on the festivals, the Romans left Judea lightly garrisoned down to 66 CE and evidently did not consider the Jews a particular threat. The revolt in 66–70 CE may thus have come as something of a surprise. At any rate it appears that Roman war aims changed during its course: a war which began as an attempt to make the Jews give sacrifices in their temple on behalf of the emperor ended with the total destruction of the temple. It is probable that the exceptional ferocity of the final Roman assault on the temple owed much to the need of the Roman commander Titus to win rapid prestige in Rome for himself and his father Vespasian, since Vespasian had seized power in a bloody civil war the previous year and, lacking any other qualifications for supreme office, used the victory over the Jews as evidence of his beneficence to the empire. Hence the superfluity of monuments in Rome to commemorate the defeat of the Jews, and the impossibility of an immediate rebuilding of the temple.

13. The destruction in 70 was a terrible disaster for all Jews, but the temple had been destroyed before and eventually rebuilt, so it is wrong to imagine universal Jewish despair. The institution of national Jewish leadership, the high priesthood, was now gone, and the Roman state probably saw no need for any new Jewish spokesman. Most Jews probably continued in their old beliefs and hoped for the temple to be restored. Eventually the rabbis evolved a new type of Judaism which could flourish without a temple, and the Roman state formally recognized the rabbinic patriarch as the political leader of the Jews, but, so far as is known, neither of these processes took place until long after the temple's destruction.

14. Jewish Settlement Judea was the homeland of the Jews throughout this period, and by its end Jerusalem was one of the greatest cities of the eastern Mediterranean, but there was also a large Jewish population in the diaspora. Some of these Jews had been carried into captivity in Babylonia at the time of the destruction of the First Temple and the Babylonian community remained considerable throughout the Second Temple period, although little is known of its history. The diaspora in the eastern Mediterranean world outside Israel grew rapidly from the third century BCE to the first century CE, partly because of the settlement of descendants of slaves taken captive in the numerous wars which affected the region, partly because of the use of Jews by Hellenistic monarchs as mercenaries settled in Asia Minor and in Egypt, partly through economic migration in the face of overpopulation in the homeland, and partly (but to an unknown degree) through the accretion to Jewish communities of Gentile proselytes. By the early first century CE Jewish communities were to be found in all the coastal areas in the eastern Mediterranean from Greece round to Cyrene in Libya as well as in the city of Rome, in the interior of western Asia Minor on the Anatolian plateau, and in large numbers in the countryside in Syria and in Egypt, while the largest diaspora communities were in the great Hellenistic capital cities of Alexandria and Antioch. After the defeat of 70 CE Jews were ever more dispersed, but the emergence of a diaspora in the western Mediterranean cannot be attested until late-Roman times.

15. Cultural Developments Jews in this period were profoundly affected both in the Land of Israel and in the Mediterranean diaspora by the Greek culture spread and promoted by Alexander the Great and his successors. In this respect Jews were part of a much wider phenomenon in which native cultures throughout the Near East fused to a greater or lesser extent with the culture of the Graeco-Macedonian dynasties which ruled over them; the amalgamated cultures which resulted have been termed 'Hellenistic' by scholars since the nineteenth century. Thus the use of the Greek language was widespread in the Land of Israel by the first century CE, although it was probably in more common use in towns and in cities. Jews also adopted Greek architecture, political forms, literary genres, and, to a limited extent, philosophical ideas. Much of this adoption was apparently both gradual and unselfconscious: Hellenistic culture was simply the milieu in which Jews from the time of Alexander found themselves living. Only with regard to the events preceding and during the Maccabean revolt did the adoption of Greek culture and opposition to it acquire wider significance because of the preference of the Seleucids to give greater political power to natives who Hellenized (see above G.4). It is thus only in the books of the Maccabees that Judaism is explicitly contrasted to Hellenism. The Hasmonean rulers themselves, despite their dynasty's founding myth based on their opposition to Hellenism, adopted much of Greek culture. It is probable that the degree of Hellenization varied among Jews of different places of origin and different classes of society. Richer Jews, and those from big cities, especially Jerusalem, were more likely to speak Greek and operate easily within Greek cultures. In most diaspora communities, apart from Babylonia, Greek was probably the main language of religious as well as secular discourse, and there was little knowledge of Hebrew or Aramaic. In the Land of Israel, both Hebrew and Aramaic were in general use down to the end of the Second Temple period, but the native Jerusalemite Josephus proved capable at the end of the first century CE of writing complex literary works in Greek, albeit in a style for which he felt it necessary to apologize (Jos. Ant. 20. 263–4).

16. Religious Developments By the time the books of the Apocrypha were composed there had emerged many different varieties of Judaism, but Jews did have a common core to their religion. All pious Jews had in common their devotion to the one God who was worshipped in Jerusalem, and the belief that God had both chosen his people for care and (all too often) chastisement, and that God's instructions for the correct way for a Jew to live were contained within the Torah, which was itself encapsulated within the Pentateuch. Judaism had become a religion of the book, and there was a general (but not universal) consensus that real prophetic inspiration was no longer possible. The main grounds for disagreement lay in differing interpretations of what precisely the Pentateuch requires, and religious leaders, whether priestly or lay, tended to gain their authority from their expertise in such interpretation.

17. Many of the disputes attested in writings of this period concerned the conduct of the temple cult in Jerusalem. Since Jews held that there should be only one such temple (although in fact a second temple existed in Leontopolis in Egypt down to 72 CE), the correct performance by the priests of the sacrifices and other offerings made in the temple was of immense importance to all. There was widespread interest in, and disagreement about, the notion of physical purity both as a requirement for worship in the temple and as a metaphor for spiritual purity. Among some Jews this led to high value being placed on an ascetic lifestyle. Jews debated also more philosophical and theological questions such as whether there is life after death (a tenet in which most but not all Jews came to believe from around the mid-second century BCE); the nature of the events to precede the end of the world towards which history was generally agreed to be leading; the nature and role of a messianic figure in those events; the relationship between human free will and divine intervention; the role of angels as intermediaries between man and God; the extent to which customary interpretation of the Pentateuchal laws could itself be taken to reflect the divine will. These debates were sometimes acrimonious but by no means always so, since the areas of agreement among Jews far outweighed the areas in dispute: thus Josephus (*Ag. Ap.* 2.179–81) could state that, in contrast to Greeks, a characteristic of Jews was their 'admirable harmony... Unity and identity of religious belief, perfect uniformity in habits and customs, produce a very beautiful concord in human character. Among us alone will be heard no contradictory statements about God... Among us alone will be seen no difference in the conduct of our lives.'

18. The Emergence of Sects It is all the more surprising that this same author, Josephus, provides the best evidence that a characteristic of Judaism in this period which distinguished it from the biblical age was the emergence within the religion of groups or parties that defined themselves by their distinctive theologies. In many passages he referred to the three, or sometimes four, *haireseis* (lit. choices) among the Jews, which he defined as the Pharisees, the Sadducees, the Essenes, and the Fourth Philosophy (about which Josephus is the sole witness). These groups were not strictly sectarian, since they all appear to have participated in mainstream Jewish life, but they all had special doctrines of their own; at least in the case of the Essenes they had a strong communal organization; and in each case they defined themselves as different from other Jews. More clearly sectarian in the sense that they viewed themselves as legitimate in contrast to the rest of Israel were the group which produced the communal writings among the Dead Sea scrolls found at Qumran. It is possible that these Dead Sea sectarians are to be identified with one or other of the groups known from the classical sources, but it is no less possible that this group was a separate sect unknown until the chance discovery of the scrolls in 1947. These groups are first attested in the Hasmonean period. This may be through chance, and the groups may have existed before this time since the narrative in Josephus' histories

becomes so much more detailed from precisely this period, but it is also possible that the development of sectarianism was a product of the complexities of Jewish life in the land of Israel during the second century BCE.

19. Literary Developments The new kinds of literature produced by Jews in this period were, like the religious innovations of the time, mostly the product of an intense attachment to the biblical text on the one hand, and the influence of the wider Hellenistic world on the other. The books contained within the Apocrypha comprise only a very small portion of the total literary output of Jews in this period. Many other Jewish writings were preserved by Christians for religious edification and instruction independently from the biblical corpus; such texts included the writings of Josephus and Philo as well as the heterogeneous collection of other works known to modern scholars (rather misleadingly, since not all are pseudepigraphic) as the 'Pseudepigrapha'. A quite different body of writings in Hebrew and Aramaic were handed down through the Jewish rabbinic tradition; although none of the extant rabbinic texts, including the Mishnah, the foundation document of rabbinic Judaism, originated in its present from before *c*.200 CE, they incorporate much earlier literary material. Since the writings preserved by Christians and those preserved by Jews overlap to such a small extent, it is a reasonable assumption that both traditions selected the material they found valuable from a much larger pool. That this is so was confirmed by the discovery at Qumran of the Dead Sea scrolls which included many religious texts about whose existence there had previously been no trace. This highly fluid literary tradition provides the background for understanding the literary and religious aims of the authors of the Apocrypha.

20. Some at least of the works composed in the late Second Temple period continued within the genres to be found in the HB; thus there was religious poetry in the style of the Psalms, wisdom literature comparable to Proverbs, and so on. But there were also new kinds of writing The main literary innovations in the post-biblical period were the development of different types of commentary on the Bible, including rewritten versions such as the book of *Jubilees*, systematic expansions of biblical lemmata, as in some rabbinic midrashim, and many other forms of bible interpretation; the genre of apocalyptic, in which a story is told of the revelation of a divine message to a sage; philosophical treatises, most notably in the writings of Philo of Alexandria; the composition of tragedies in the Greek style but on Jewish themes, of which only one, a play on the Exodus by a certain Ezekiel, is partially extant; the development of communal rules, as at Qumran; and, perhaps most importantly, the adoption of Greek genres of historiography to describe the past. In all these cases it is probable that the literary form had some connection to the ideas expressed in the text—so, for instance, it is not accidental that eschatological speculation is to be found quite frequently, although by no means always, in apocalyptic writings. Similarly, the transmission of many quasi-prophetic texts in this period either under a pseudonym ('pseudepigrapha') or anonymously must be connected to the belief that genuine prophecy belonged to an earlier age.

H. The Apocryphal Books and History. 1. Our lack of precise knowledge about the date and place of composition of many of the books of the Apocrypha (F.3–5) precludes any certain deduction about the relationship between most of these writings and the historical background outlined in G. It is thus possible that the Additions to Daniel, Tobit, and the Letter of Jeremiah should be understood against the background of the Babylonian Diaspora, and that Wisdom of Solomon and the additions incorporated in the Greek Esther were products of the Jewish community in Egypt in the late Hellenistic age (so e.g. Nickelsburg 1981), but since the circumstances in which these writings were produced can only be deduced from their contents, any argument that the contents reveal the impact of the circumstances in which they were composed is dangerously circular.

2. However, some books in the Apocrypha can be more precisely located. Thus Sirach was composed in the Land of Israel in the first quarter of the second century BCE when the country lay under Seleucid control and Greek culture was being enthusiastically adopted by the upper class of Jerusalem for whom Jesus ben Sira wrote. It is thus significant that, although his thought contains elements apparently derived from Hellenistic philosophy, and especially Stoicism, ben Sira wrote in Hebrew and within the traditional Jewish genre of wisdom literature. On the other hand the book contains no explicit polemic against Greek culture, so if he wrote in opposition to Hellenism he did so only indirectly. From the period following the Maccabean revolt originate of course both 1 and 2 Maccabees. 1 Maccabees appears to be an attempt by a Judean Jew to justify the assumption of power by the Hasmonean dynasty by referring back to their great deeds at the time of the rebellion. 2 Maccabees contains an edifying reminiscence for diaspora readers of the heroic deeds of the rebels, putting these comparatively recent events into the same category of the revelation of divine care for Israel to be found in biblical stories about the distant past. The book of Judith, with its interest in political as well as religious freedom, may also belong to this period, but the evidence is uncertain. The only other work in the Apocrypha for which a moderately sure origin can be postulated is 4 Ezra, the Jewish apocalypse incorporated into 2 Esd 3–14, which appears to have constituted a reaction by a Judean Jew to the destruction of the temple in 70 CE.

I. The Apocrypha and the Bible.

1. Some of the works in the Apocrypha derive their literary form primarily from their relationship to biblical texts. In no case is this relationship in the form of a phrase-by-phrase commentary, unlike some rabbinic midrashim (see above, G.19), but the types of association are different in each case.

2. **Rewritten Bible** 1 Esdras is a Greek translation of a version of the biblical book of Ezra incorporating material from Chronicles and Nehemiah. It is uncertain whether it is best to explain the book by suggesting that the author possessed something like the Masoretic Hebrew text of Chronicles, Ezra, and Nehemiah before he wrote and then adapted it for his own purposes, or that he translated an independently preserved Hebrew text of the biblical books, but if the former is the case, 1 Esdras constitutes a free reworking of the biblical account similar to the relationship of the book of *Jubilees* to Genesis and relationship of the *Temple Scroll* found at Qumran to Deuteronomy.

3. **Additions to Biblical Books** The passages inserted into the Hebrew book of Esther and now found in Greek Esther serve to enhance the dramatic and religious appeal of the original version and to bolster its historicity through the citation of verbatim copies of royal edicts. The author of these additions has made no attempt to alter or comment on the biblical story, but only to increase its impact in the spirit of the original. The Prayer of Manasseh, in which the king admits his sins and begs forgiveness from God, was similarly intended to supplement the biblical account in 2 Chronicles because 2 Chr 33:18–19 mentions that such a prayer is recorded elsewhere. The difference in this case is that the prayer was not preserved in the text of Chronicles in the Septuagint but only as a separate text.

4. **Imitation of Biblical Books** Baruch is a hortatory prophecy so similar in tone and content to the Hebrew book of Jeremiah that it was treated by some Christians from the second century CE as a supplement to the biblical book. This notion was doubtless aided by references in the book of Jeremiah to Baruch as the prophet's secretary and references to the Babylonian exile in Baruch itself. The book of Baruch contains rather disparate material (narrative, prayer, instruction in the form of a poem about Wisdom, and comfort for the people in a poem about Zion), but all the elements are familiar from the prophetic books of the Bible.

J. The Apocrypha as Independent Compositions.

1. Most of the books in the Apocrypha are self-standing compositions and can be appreciated without reference to the Bible; this includes even those stories, like that of Susanna, which survive only through incorporation into a Greek translation of a biblical book. These works thus reflect many of the literary developments attested in Jewish society in the late Second Temple period (see G.19–20), although it is worth noting that many of the religious concerns expressed in other Jewish texts of this time (an interest in purity, temple ritual, asceticism, life after death, and so on, see G.16–18) are not as prominent in the Apocrypha as might be expected.

2. **Wisdom Literature** Sirach can be assigned to the same wider genre of wisdom literature to which the biblical book of Proverbs belongs, but although it is close both in form and in content to the biblical model, it includes also much that is novel. Like other Jewish wisdom texts, Sirach deals with practical advice and religious problems, but this work is the earliest extant writing of its kind explicitly to identify divine wisdom with the Torah (24:8–29) and to provide a historical perspective by alluding to the laudable deeds of previous generations in Israel (chs. 44–9).

3. **Philosophy** On the surface, the Wisdom of Solomon appears to be another offshoot of the biblical genre of wisdom literature, but it often diverges from that genre into philosophical rhetoric, using sophisticated Hellenistic rhetorical devices in order to present both a general attack on godlessness and a novel picture of Wisdom as an independent hypostasis alongside God. In the process of describing the nature of this hypostasis and in his picture of the nature of mankind the author makes use of concepts borrowed from Stoicism and perhaps Middle Platonism. The result is a work of philosophy, albeit on a level rather unsophisticated in comparison to, for example, the writings of Philo.

4. Historical Works 1 Maccabees is a straightforward narrative history, and in that sense it is similar to and undoubtedly deliberately imitates biblical historiography, but in contrast to the biblical books the author of this work emphasizes the competence and wisdom of the human figures in the study, especially those of the Maccabean dynasty, rather than the effects of divine intervention. 2 Maccabees is a work firmly within the Greek tradition of 'pathetic' history in which dramatic events were written up in an attempt to induce the reader to empathize with the characters, although this work too is specifically Jewish in the moral and religious lessons explicitly derived by the author from his story; how many of these characteristics were the work of Jason of Cyrene and how much the work of the epitomator who produced the current text of 2 Maccabees is unknown.

5. Didactic Stories The Apocrypha includes a number of stories which, despite their historical setting, seem to have been intended not for instruction about the past so much as to give ethical and religious guidance, and to instil in readers an awareness of the power of divine providence, despite the problems faced by even the most pious. Among such stories are the book of Judith (which deals with the delivery of Jerusalem from the Assyrian Holophernes through the intrigues of the beautiful and good eponymous heroine) and the book of Tobit, which deals with the trials and tribulations of the charitable and pious hero and his son Tobias.

6. Of the Additions to Daniel, the story of Susanna and the story of Bel and the Dragon have similar qualities as edifying fictions. Neither tale is particularly well integrated into the biblical text of Daniel, and these writings thus served a very different purpose to the additions found in the Greek Esther (see 1.3.). The story of Susanna illustrates the wisdom of Daniel, who saves her from the wicked lechery of the elders who accused her of adultery, and the correctness of her decision to trust God even when she appeared doomed. The narrative of Bel and the Dragon reveals the foolishness of idolatry; in this case the story may have originated not just in the imagination of its pious author but also in midrashic extrapolation from verses in Jeremiah or Isaiah. The third Addition to Daniel, the Prayer of Azariah and the Song of the Three Jews, is a rather different writing from the other two. It consists of two poetic compositions, both of which probably existed as separate works before their insertion into the Daniel corpus.

7. Apocalyptic 2 Esdras is the sole example in the Apocrypha of a literary genre whose popularity in this period has been confirmed by the discovery of fragments of apocalyptic texts among the Dead Sea scrolls (see G.19–20). The original Jewish part of the extant text (2 Esd 3–14) is divided into three dialogues and four visions, all described by Ezra himself. Ezra is taught by an angel a divine theodicy for the world which makes sense of the disaster of the destruction of the temple by reassuring him of the coming judgement and the beginning of a new age.

K. The Impact of the Apocrypha. The books of the Apocrypha have been little read in any tradition over recent centuries, particularly because they are no longer printed in most translations of the Bible, but their influence is pervasive (Metzger 1957: 205–38). In particular, European art, literature, and music contain numerous allusions to the stories of Tobit, Judith, Susanna, Judas Maccabee, and the Maccabean martyrs, and sententious sayings culled from Sirach have become clichés in many languages. Among Jews the most obvious impact of the Apocrypha, apart from the festival of Hanukkah which celebrates the events described in 1 and 2 Maccabees (but without most Jews knowing the original books), has been in the popularity among Jews from medieval to modern times of the names Judah, Susanna, Judith, and Raphael.

REFERENCES

Metzger, B. M. (1957), *An Introduction to the Apocrypha* (New York: Oxford University Press).

Nickelsburg, G. W. (1981), *Jewish Literature between the Bible and the Mishnah* (London: SCM).

40. Tobit

JOSEPH A. FITZMYER, SJ

INTRODUCTION

A. Text and Language. 1. The book of Tobit is preserved in four fragmentary Aramaic texts (pap4QTob[a] ar, 4QTob[b] ar, 4QTob[c] ar, 4QTob[d] ar) and in one fragmentary Hebrew text (4QTob[e]), which together preserve about one-fifth of the book. These copies date roughly from mid-first century BCE to mid-first century CE. The full form of the book is preserved mainly in Greek and Latin versions, but also in various derivative versions (Arabic, Armenian, Coptic (Sahidic), Ethiopic, and Syriac). Derivative forms are also found in medieval Aramaic and Hebrew versions of the book.

2. The Qumran fragmentary Aramaic and Hebrew texts have been published in DJD 19. In general, these Semitic forms of the book are related to the long recension of the Greek and Latin versions.

3. The Greek version of Tobit is known in three forms: (*a*) The Long Recension (G[II]), preserved in the fourth-century Codex Sinaiticus (discovered in 1844), and part of it in both the eleventh-century MS 319 (Vatopedi 513), and sixth-century MS 910 (Oxyrhynchus Papyrus 1076). Sinaiticus has two major lacunae, 4:7–19*b* and 13:6*i*–10*b*, the first of which is covered by MS 319; also a number of minor omissions of phrases or clauses, which sometimes make the comprehension of its context difficult, but which can be supplied from other Greek forms or the Old Latin version. This recension is used in the NRSV; the numbering of verses here follows that of this recension in the critical text of Hanhart (1983). (*b*) The Short Recension (G[I]), preserved mainly in the fourth-century Codex Vaticanus, the fifth-century Codex Alexandrinus, and the eighth-century Codex Venetus, and also in a host of minuscule MSS. This form of the Greek text was used before the discovery of Sinaiticus. (c) The Intermediate Recension (G^III), preserved in MSS 44, 106, 107. It may have some pertinence for Tob 6:9–13:8; for the rest it reproduces the text of Vaticanus.

4. The Latin version is likewise known in two forms: (a) The Long Recension, preserved in the Vetus Latina (VL), for which there is no modern critical text. One must use the eighteenth-century text of P. Sabatier and supplement it with readings from MSS that have subsequently been published or come to light. This long recension is related to G^II, but sometimes it is closer to the Qumran Aramaic and Hebrew texts than that Greek recension. (b) The Short Recension, preserved in the Vulgate (Vg) and found in the critical edition of the Monks of San Girolamo (1950). The relation of this form of the book, long used in the Roman Catholic tradition, to a Greek version is problematic; at times it differs considerably from the VL and Greek recensions. Jerome admitted that he dashed off the translation of it in one day (*unius diei laborem arripui*), having found a Jewish interpreter who could read Aramaic and translate it for him into Hebrew, which he then rendered in Latin (*Ep. ad Chromatium et Heliodorum; PL* 29. 23–6). As a result it differs notably from the Qumran Aramaic form known today and from G^II.

5. Other versions of Tobit and the medieval Aramaic and Hebrew forms are considered secondary because they seem to be derived from G^I.

6. The book was probably composed originally in Aramaic, because the Qumran Hebrew form now known has peculiarities relating it to a late post-exilic form of the language and contains words and syntagmemes that argue for an Aramaic substratum. This issue is debated, and some have been trying to maintain that the original was Hebrew. The matter is still unresolved.

B. Subject-Matter and Literary Genre.

1. The book is named after its principal character, Tobit, a model of Jewish piety. He was a law-abiding Israelite, who had been captured and deported with his wife Hannah and his son Tobias from the northern kingdom of Israel to Nineveh. There he suffered in various ways and was finally blinded. Praying to die, but recalling in his old age that he had deposited a considerable sum of money in far-off Rages in Media, he decided to send Tobias to get the money. At the same time at Ecbatana in Media, a young relative, Sarah, was also praying to die, because she suffered from the vituperation of maidservants, since all seven men to whom she had been given in marriage were slain by an evil demon Asmodeus, as they sought to approach her. In answer to the prayers of the two of them, Tobit and Sarah, God sent the angel Raphael to Nineveh. Raphael accompanied Tobias on his journey to Media to get his father's money. *En route*, when Tobias bathed in the Tigris, a large fish tried to swallow his foot. Raphael told Tobias to catch the fish and extract its gall, heart, and liver for use as medicine. At Ecbatana in Media Tobias married his kinswoman Sarah and used the fish's heart and liver to smoke the demon away on his wedding night. Tobias then sent Raphael on to Rages to fetch the money. When Raphael returned, Tobias took the money and Sarah his wife and

came back to Nineveh, to his father's house, where he used the fish's gall as a medicament to remove white films from Tobit's eyes. Then, when Tobit and Tobias wanted to pay Raphael for his aid, the angel revealed who he was and disappeared, having instructed Tobit to offer thanks to God. Tobit composed a hymn of praise, instructed Tobias to leave the wicked city of Nineveh, once his mother had died, and then passed away. After Tobias buried his mother beside his father, he departed with Sarah for Media, where he continued to dwell with his parents-in-law. There he learned of the destruction of Nineveh.

2. Though some modern scholars (Miller 1940) have argued for a historical kernel in the story, most commentators regard the Book of Tobit as a Semitic novel composed for an edifying and didactic religious purpose. Its fictional character is seen in various historical and geographical improbabilities (see comments on 1:2, 4, 15, 21; 6:2; 9:2; 11:1; 14:15) and in its use of folkloric motifs ('The Grateful Dead' and 'The Monster in the Bridal Chamber').

C. The Religious Teaching.

The purpose of the book is clearly didactic edification. Jews faithful to God, to obligations imposed by the Mosaic law, and to their ancestral customs, even in the time of persecution and deportation, are rewarded for their loyalty and fidelity. God is thus seen not to have abandoned his faithful servants. The book inculcates the teaching of Deuteronomic retribution (see Deut 28), mutual respect for tribal relations, support for family life, monogamous marriage, and the giving of alms. It incorporates numerous maxims characteristic of wisdom literature.

D. Date and Place of Composition.

The Aramaic of the Qumran form of Tobit relates it to other second/first-century Aramaic compositions known from the Dead Sea scrolls. The Qumran copies thus support the generally recognized date of composition of the book in the early second century BCE. Although the Tobit story recounts events of the eighth-century deportation of Jews from Israel, the post-exilic customs of tithing, the recognition of prophetic writings as sacred, and the absence of any awareness of the Maccabean revolt support that dating of the composition of the book. Whether it was composed in the Mesopotamian diaspora or in Judah itself, or even elsewhere, cannot be determined.

E. Canonicity.

Tobit is not part of the canon of the Hebrew Scriptures or of the Protestant OT canon. It is found in the collection of Alexandrian Jewish writings (LXX), and is regarded as a deuterocanonical book in the Roman Catholic church; it is also used as canonical in Eastern Orthodox churches. Jerome did not regard it as canonical and dashed off his Latin version of it only at the insistence of two bishops (who apparently did consider it canonical).

F. Outline

COMMENTARY

The Double Situation in Nineveh and Ecbatana (1:1–3:17)

(1:1–2) Tobit *Tōb(e)it* is the Greek form of Aramaic *Ṭôbî*, the father's name, which is a shortening of *Ṭôbīyāh*, the son's name, meaning, 'YHWH is my good'. The name characterizes what God does for both in the book. *Tobiel*, the name of Tobit's father, means, 'El (God) is my good'. The tribe of Naphtali was named after its eponymous ancestor, son of Jacob and second son of Bilhah, the maidservant of Rachel (Gen 30:8). The tribe resided in northern Galilee, near Beth-shemesh and Beth-anath (Judg 1:33). 'Shalmaneser' (Gk. *Enemessaros*): the Assyrian king Shalmaneser V (727–722 BCE) began the siege of Samaria, capital of the northern kingdom (2 Kings 17:5), but it capitulated only after his death (721), to his successor, the usurper Sargon II (722–705), who eventually deported Israelites to captivity in Assyria (2 Kings 17:6; cf. 18:9–13). Thisbe was a Galilean town otherwise unknown. Kedesh Naphtali was a town in Upper Galilee, mentioned in Josh 20:7. From it Tiglath-pileser III (745–727) had earlier (733–732) deported Jews to Assyria (2 Kings 15:29). Asher was probably Hazor (Josh 11:1; 2 Kings 15:29). Phogor was another Galilean town otherwise unknown.

(1:3–22) Tobit's Background Until 3:6 the story is recounted in the first person singular. Tobit tells of his piety and struggle to lead an upright Jewish life both in Israel and in exile. v. 3, the ancient city of Nineveh became the capital of Assyria under Sennacherib (705–681) and functioned as such during the last decades of the Assyrian empire. It was located on the east bank of the Tigris River, a site today opposite part of the town of Mosul in northern Iraq. See Jon 1:2; 3:2–7; 4:11; Nah 2:7–8; 3:1–19; Zeph 2:13. v. 4, 'deserted the house of David and Jerusalem', according to 1 Kings 12:19–20 the revolt of the northern tribes occurred in the days of Jeroboam in 922 BCE, but Tobit speaks of it taking place in his youth. 'Chosen from . . . all the tribes', see Deut 12:1–14; 2 Sam 6:1–19; 1 Kings 5:5; 2 Kings 23:23. v. 5, 'on all the mountains', high places are mentioned in Hos 10:5, 8; Ezek 6:1–14. 'Calf', see 1 Kings 12:26–33, where Jeroboam set up shrines in Dan and Bethel so that people would not have to go to Jerusalem to celebrate feast-days. The calf was probably intended as a base for YHWH's throne, but soon it came to be an object of worship itself. Jeroboam also encouraged the offering of sacrifice on high places (1 Kings 14:9). v. 6, 'everlasting decree', see Deut 12:11, 13–14; 2 Chr 11:16. To such a decree Tobit affirms his fidelity, whence arises his loneliness in the face of the apostasy of the rest of Israel; 'first fruits of the crops', see Ex 23:16; 34:22; Num 18:21–30; Deut 14:22–3; 18:4; 'firstlings of the flock', see Ex 13:2; 34:19; Lev 27:26; Deut 14:23. The first and best part of crops and flocks were to be dedicated to God and his service. v. 7, 'the tenth', or 'the tithe', mentioned in Num 18:21–30; Deut 18:1–5; 26:12; Lev 27:30–1; 'second tenth', this tithe could be converted to money and brought to Jerusalem every seventh year and spent there (Deut 14:24–6). v. 8, 'third year' tithe, see Deut 26:12; 14:28–9; cf. Josephus, *Ant.* 4.8.22 §240. Tobit is depicted as religiously carrying out the tithe-regulations as they were interpreted in post-exilic Israel; 'Deborah', Tobit credits his grandmother with his religious training. v. 9, 'Anna', called *Ḥannāh* ('grace') in Qumran Aramaic texts; 'Tobias' is the Greek form of the son's name, *Ṭôbīyāh*, see TOB 1:1. v. 10, 'food of Gentiles', Mosaic law prescribed what foods were clean and unclean for Jewish people (Lev 11:1–47; Deut 14:3–20). Unclean food, eaten by Gentiles, caused ritual impurity for Jews. So Tobit is depicted faithfully observing dietary regulations even in captivity. v. 12, 'mindful of God', Tobit is motivated in his fidelity by the Deuteronomic ideas of divine retribution (Deut 28:1–68); whence his prosperity and prominent status in Assyria. v. 13, 'Shalmaneser', see TOB 1:2. v. 14, Media was a realm south-east of Nineveh, situated today in northern Iran. It was under Assyrian domination 750–614 BCE; 'ten talents', this great sum of money becomes an important motif in the story, providing the background for Tobias's journey to Media, his catching of the fish, and his marriage to Sarah, who along with Tobit is eventually cured by the fish's innards. Rages was a town in Media; it is not mentioned in Sinaiticus, but read in G[I]. Its ruins are found today about 5 miles south-east of Teheran in Iran. v. 15, 'his son Sennacherib', Sennacherib (705–681 BCE) was actually the son of Sargon II, who succeeded Shalmaneser V. v. 16, 'many acts of charity', lit. 'I made many alms'. v. 17 makes it clear that *eleēmosynai* has to be understood in a broad sense, including food, clothing, and even burial. Tobit's generosity is extolled, for he practised it even when it was dangerous for him, in his status as a captive. His activity in burying the dead reflects the Jewish horror of corpses left unburied, especially those of fellow Jews. v. 18, 'when he came fleeing from Judea', i.e. Sennacherib, who had unsuccessfully attacked Jerusalem (2 Kings 18:13–19:37; cf. Isa 36:1–37:38). Sennacherib's fate is duly ascribed to a decree of heaven; 'put to death many Israelites'. This was done in retaliation for the king's failure to take Jerusalem. 'Looked for them'. Perhaps to expose them to further ridicule and disgrace. v. 21, 'forty days', or 'forty-five days' (VL), or 'fifty days' (G[I], Peshitta); 'killed him', see 2 Kings 19:37, where his sons are named as Adrammelech and Sharezer; 'Ararat', also mentioned in 19:37, the traditional spot where Noah's ark landed (Gen 8:4) is today in modern Armenia; 'Esar-haddon', another son of Sennacherib (2 Kings 19:37), he reigned 681–669 BCE. Rightly named in 4QTob[a] *'srḥdwn*, he is called *Sacherdonos* in Greek versions and *Archedonassar* or *Archedonosor* in VL; 'Ahikar', in Aramaic *'Aḥîqar,* a well-known counsellor of Assyrian kings. See *Story and Wisdom of Ahiqar*, partly preserved in fifth-century Aramaic papyri from Elephantine (*ANET* 427–30); and in later legends of many languages (*APOT* ii. 715–84). Tobit here makes him a 'son of my brother [kinsman] Hanael', thus giving him a Jewish background. v. 22, 'appointed him as Second to himself' (my tr.). The Greek *ek deuteras* is unclear; NRSV renders it, 'reappointed him'. However, 4QTob[a] reads *tnyn lh*, 'second to him(self)', i.e. made him an Assyrian *turtānu/tartānu*, an official mentioned in 2 Kings 18:17; Isa 20:1.

(2:1–3:6) Tobit's Troubles and Prayer 2:1, 'Pentecost', the Greek name for the wheat-harvest feast that followed 'fifty days' or 'seven weeks' after Passover (Ex 23:16; 34:22; Lev 23:15–21; Deut 16:9–11). 2:2, 'poor person', Tobit shows his concern to carry out the injunction of Deut 16:11 about strangers, widows, and orphans on the feast. 2:3, 'lies there strangled', another Israelite executed, see 1:18. 2:4, burial after sunset would be less likely to be detected. 2:5, 'washed myself', to remove the ritual defilement from contact with a corpse (Num 19:11–13). 2:6, see Am 8:10. 2:10, 'white films', a primitive description of a cause of blindness; 'four years', see 14:2; *Elymais*, the Greek name for ancient Elam, a district north-east of the head of the Persian Gulf; see 1 Macc 6:1. 2:12, 'Dystrus', the Macedonian month *Dystros* corresponded to the Jewish winter month of Shebat, roughly Jan.–Feb. of the modern calendar. 2:14, 'flushed with anger against her', Tobit, otherwise so righteous, could get angry with his wife, even over a supposed theft, in which she might have been only indirectly involved; 'your righteous deeds', Anna's rebuke of Tobit and his righteousness reminds one of the taunt of Job's wife (Job 2:9). Her vituperation finds a parallel in that of the maid in 3:8. 3:1–6, Tobit's prayer: in this first formal prayer of the book, Tobit begs God for pardon from offences unwittingly committed and for release from this life, which he finds so greatly burdened with affliction, distress, and insult. 3:6, 'eternal home', i.e. Sheol, described in Job 7:9–10; 10:21–2; 14:12 as an abode from which no one returns; 'it is better for me to die', cf. Jon 4:3, 8; also Num 11:15 (Moses); 1 Kings 19:4 (Elijah); Job 7:15 (Job).

(3:7–15) Sarah's Troubles and Prayer The narrative shifts to the third person. v. 7, 'on the same day', this temporal note will dramatically join various parts of the story together (see 3:16, 17; 4:1). Ecbatana was the capital of ancient Media, on the site of modern Hamadan in northern Iran. 'Sarah', her name means 'princess'. Her plight parallels that of Tobit in Nineveh. *Ragouēl* is the Greek form of Aramaic *Rĕʿûʾēl*, 'friend of El (God)', the name of Moses' father-in-law (Ex 2:18); 'reproached', in this case the vituperation comes from a maid, who blames Sarah for the death of seven husbands-to-be. v. 8, 'wicked demon Asmodeus', probably a Persian name (*Aešma daeva*, 'demon of wrath') used for the spirit that afflicts Sarah; cf. the folktale, 'The Monster in the Bridal Chamber'. See Tob 6:14–15. v. 10, 'intended to hang herself', Gen 9:5–6 was usually understood as a prohibition of suicide. Sarah thinks better of it, realizing the reproaches that would come upon her father; 'in sorrow to Hades', Sarah echoes a biblical refrain; see Gen 37:35; 42:38; 44:29, 31; 'pray the Lord that I may die', her prayer parallels that of (Tobit 3:6). v. 11, 'With hands outstretched towards the window', Sarah prays facing Jerusalem, as does Daniel (Dan 6:11); cf. 1 Kings 8:44, 48; Isa 28:2; 'Blessed are you', she uses the traditional beginning of Jewish prayer, as will Tobias (8:5) and Raguel (8:15); cf. Ps 119:12; 1 Chr 29:10; Jdt 13:17. In this second formal prayer, Sarah

protests her innocence, her purity, and her lack of responsibility for the death of the seven husbands, begging God to deliver her from continued life and vituperation. v. 15, 'I should keep myself as a wife', Sarah apparently does not know of Tobias, but recognizes the duty, emphasized in this book (1:9; 4:12–13; 6:12; 7:10) to marry within her ancestral family; cf. Gen 24:4, 38, 40; Num 36:6–8.

(3:16–17) God's Commission of Raphael to Go to Their Aid v. 16, 'At that very moment', see 3:7. The prayers of Tobit and of Sarah are heard simultaneously by God. v. 17, the angel's name, *Rāpāʾēl*, means 'God has healed', a name indicating the source of the cures to come to Tobit and Sarah; 'At the same time', again the note of simultaneity.

Preparations for Tobias's Journey (4:1–6:1).

(4:1–21) Tobit's Speech v. 1, 'That same day', the simultaneity is joined with the motif of the money (1:14). v. 2, 'I have asked for death', see 3:6. vv. 3–19, to Tobias Tobit delivers a speech, which is a cross between a farewell discourse (so DiLella 1979) and a sapiential exhortation, with a group of maxims inculcating the virtues of the life that Tobit has himself been leading. These maxims recommend filial duty to parents (4:3–4), pursuit of uprightness (4:5–6), giving of alms (4:7–11, 16–17), avoidance of fornication (4:12), marriage within the ancestral family (4:12), love of kindred (4:13), avoidance of pride, sloth, and drunkenness (4:13, 15), prompt payment of wages (4:14), the Golden Rule (4:15), and the praise, reverence, and trust of God (4:5, 19). Many of these counsels can also be found in Proverbs, Sirach, and other collections of ancient Near-Eastern wisdom. v. 3, 'Honour your mother', cf. Ex 20:12. v. 6, 'will prosper in all', the Deuteronomic doctrine of virtue rewarded by earthly prosperity and of sin recompensed by disaster (Deut 28:1–68; cf. Ps 1:1–3; Prov 10:27–30). v. 7, a lacuna in Sinaiticus begins here and lasts until v. 19; 'give alms', this counsel constitutes a major teaching of this book (see 12:8–9; 14:10–11), as also of Sirach (4:3–5; 7:10b; 29:9–13; 35:9–10; 40:17, 24); 'your face', cf. Sir 4:4–6; Prov 19:17; Deut 15:7–8. v. 9, 'treasure', cf. Sir 29:11–12. v. 10, 'darkness', Sheol; see TOB 3:6. v. 12, 'marry a woman', see comment on 3:15; 'Noah, Abraham, Isaac, and Jacob', Noah's wife is not named in the OT, but in *Jub.* 4:33: 'Her name was Emzara, daughter of Rakeel, his father's brother.' Abram married Sarai/Sarah (Gen 11:29); Isaac married Rebekah (Gen 24:67; 25:20); and Jacob married Rachel (Gen 29:28). v. 13, 'pride', see Prov 16:18; 'idleness', see Prov 19:15; Sir 22:1–2. v. 14, 'pay them at once', see Lev 19:13c; Deut 24:15. v. 15, 'what you hate', a negative form of the Golden Rule; 'Do not drink wine to excess', see Prov 23:29–35; Sir 31:25–31. v. 17, 'bread on the grave of the righteous', the meaning of this counsel is disputed. It seems to recommend what is otherwise prohibited: the pagan practice of putting food on graves (Deut 26:14c; cf. Sir 30:18). Yet it may be an echo of *Wisdom of Aḥiqar*, Syriac A 2.10 (*APOT* ii. 730): 'My son, pour out your wine on the graves of the righteous rather than drink it with evil people.' Hence it is sometimes understood to refer to meals brought to mourners (the 'cup of consolation', Jer 16:7) as a sign of sharing in their grief at the death of a good person (cf. Ezek 24:17, 22). Others think that it recommends the giving of alms in honour of the deceased. v. 19, 'bless the Lord God', Tobit commends prayer to his son as the basis of a good and upright life, realizing that God freely disposes of his creatures. v. 20, 'ten talents', the speech ends with the money motif, see comment on 1:14.

(5:1–6:1) Raphael Engaged to Accompany Tobias to Media v. 3, 'bond', Greek *cheirographon* denoted a 'handwritten document', often composed in duplicate, which could be torn in two so that it might guarantee the obligation to repay and later be matched on payment. v. 4, 'found the angel Raphael', as the reader realizes, Tobias does not recognize him as an angel; this folkloric technique is used also in Gen 18:2–22 (cf. Heb 13:2). v. 6, 'two days', from Ecbatana to Rages was actually about 185 miles. Arrian tells that Alexander took 11 days of forced march to go from one to the other (*Anab.* 3.19.8–3.20.2). The storyteller uses 'two days' to imply a far-away place. v. 12, 'Why do you need to know', heavenly messengers were reluctant to reveal their identity; cf. Gen 32:29. v. 13, 'Azariah', his name means, 'YHWH has helped', a covert identification of his role, which will be played out in the story; 'son of...Hananiah', the patronymic means, 'YHWH has been gracious'. v. 14, 'Nathan', a shortened form of Nathaniah, 'YHWH has given', a form found in some MSS; 'Shemeliah', probably a corrupted form of Shelemiah, *Šelemyāh(û)*, 'YHWH has recompensed'; other texts read Shemaiah, *Šĕma'yāh(û)*, 'YHWH has heard'; 'Jerusalem', see 1:6. v. 15, 'drachma', a craftsman's normal daily wage. v. 18, 'his mother', again Anna does not approve of Tobit's decision to send Tobias to Media. Her disapproval will play itself out in the rest of the story. v. 19, the meaning of this verse is disputed. *Peripsēma* may mean, not 'ransom' (NRSV), but 'refuse'. VL: 'Nunquam esset pecunia illa, sed purgamento sit', to which MS G adds 'filio meo'. v. 21, 'my sister', a term of affection, used even by husbands of their wives; see 7:11, 15; 8:4, 7, 21; 10:6. v. 22, 'a good angel', i.e. a guardian angel. Tobit does not recognize what Raphael is.

Tobias's Journey to Media (6:2–18)

v. 2, 'The dog', the dog appears again in the story only when Tobias begins to come home (11:4), probably acting there as a herald of the return of the travellers. The Tigris was actually west of Nineveh (see comment on 1:3) and would not have been crossed *en route* to Media. v. 3, 'large fish', Tobias's wrestling with the fish is part of the romantic thrust of the story; the fish is subdued, and its heart, liver, and gall become vital elements in the narrative, which uses folklore about the curative qualities of fish organs. v. 6, 'ate', in the Qumran texts and G[II] the verb is singular. In many of the other forms of the story it is plural, meaning that the angel also ate; see 12:19. v. 9, 'the gall', Pliny notes that fish gall 'heals scars and removes superfluous flesh about the eyes' (*Nat. Hist.* 32.24.69). v. 11, 'Sarah', Tobias now first learns of Sarah as his kinswoman; see TOB 3:15. v. 12, 'who loves her dearly', this clause is omitted in G[I], G[II], and the Peshitta, but is found in 4QTob[b] and VL instead of the last clause in NRSV. v. 12. v. 13, 'book of Moses', see Num 36:6–8, which does not mention a death penalty. v. 14, 'demon...killed them', see 3:8. v. 15, 'to bury them', a major concern of this book (1:17; 4:3–4; 14:2, 10). v. 16, 'your father's house', see 4:12–13. v. 18, 'pray', prayer too may be needed to get rid of the demon, but the author is more con-

cerned to set marital intercourse in a proper perspective; 'she was set apart for you', i.e. in God's providence; cf. Gen 24:14, 44; 'You will save her', i.e. from a lonely and unmarried future.

Marriage of Tobias and Sarah (7:1–10:14)

(7:1–16) Tobias Arrives at Raguel's House and Marries Sarah The arrival scene may be modelled on that of Jacob at Haran (Gen 29:4–6). v. 2, 'Edna', she is called Anna in VL, a confusion with Tobit's wife's name. v. 5, 'in good health', no mention is made of Tobit's blindness, even though Raguel later speaks about it in 7:7. To get around this discrepancy, vv. 4–5 are omitted in the Peshitta and Vg; G[I] adds in v. 7: 'Hearing that Tobit had lost his sight, he was griefstricken and wept.' v. 11, 'seven...kinsmen', see 3:15; 'she is your sister', see comment on 5:21. v. 12, 'gave her to Tobias', in marriage. v. 13, 'marriage contract', this ancient Jewish custom is not mentioned in the OT. For an example, see the Elephantine contract of Mibṭahiah's marriage (Cowley 1923: 44 §15; *ANET* 222): 'She is my wife, and I am her husband from this day forever'; 'to which he affixed his seal', this clause is omitted in G[I], abridged in G[II], but read in VL at the end of the verse; 4QTob[a] has preserved one word of it, *wḥtm*, 'and he sealed [it]'. v. 16, 'the Lord of heaven', God, in whose providence Sarah has been kept for Tobias, will assure the joy of their marital life; 'Take courage', lit. 'be brave', an encouragement used in the book in contexts mentioning healing (5:10; 11:11).

(8:1–21) Sarah is Cured of the Demon v. 2, 'incense', used domestically to fumigate or perfume a house. In obedience to Raphael's instruction (6:17), Tobias burns the fish's heart and liver on its embers to create a smoke that will drive Asmodeus away. v. 3, 'Egypt', the demon flees to Egypt, traditionally considered the home of magic (see Ex 7:11; 1QapGen 20:20), where Raphael, having pursued Asmodeus, binds and renders him ineffective. vv. 5–7, Tobias's prayer, the third formal prayer, is uttered in obedience to Raphael's instruction (6:18): he praises God, the creator and author of human marriage (Gen 2:24), and begs the grace of a long life together with Sarah. v. 5, 'Blessed', cf. Song of Thr 3. v. 9, 'went to sleep', the presumption is that they consummated the marriage. The Vg of 8:4 speaks of three nights of continence before consummation: 'Sarra, exsurge; deprecemur Deum hodie et cras et secundum cras, quia istis tribus noctibus Deo iungimur; tertia autem transacta nocte in nostro erimus coniugio.' That addition is not found in the Qumran texts, Greek versions, Peshitta, or VL but corresponds to another addition in the Vg of 6:18. 'Dug a grave', for Tobias, in fear that he too might have succumbed to Asmodeus, for Raguel knows nothing of the flight of the demon. vv. 15–17, Raguel's prayer, the fourth formal prayer, on learning of Tobias's safety, begins as Sarah's did; see TOB 3:11. Raguel thanks God for his mercy and compassion. v. 20, 'fourteen days', Raguel doubles the usual time of a wedding celebration; see 11:18; cf. Judg 14:12. In Gen 24:54–5 Rebekah's brother and mother insist on her staying for ten days after the marriage; from it probably comes the 'ten days' in some MSS of the Peshitta here.

(9:1–6) Raphael is Sent to Get Tobit's Money v. 2, 'Travel to Rages', this was a lengthy journey (see TOB 5:6), but Tobias trusts Azariah. v. 3, 'oath', see 8:20. In the NRSV and some other Bibles v. 3 follows v. 4. v. 5, 'counted out...the money bags', so Gabael is depicted as another trustworthy and dependable person in the story. v. 6, 'wedding celebration', the author gives the impression that it was but a short distance to the wedding in Ecbatana; 'blessed him', Gabael repeats the blessing of Raguel; see 7:7.

(10:1–14) Tobias Prepares to Return to Nineveh v. 1, 'kept counting', Tobit knows nothing of Tobias's marriage and the two-week wedding celebration but speculates about the delayed return of Tobias. v. 4, 'My child has perished', Anna gives the most pessimistic interpretation of the delay. Again, she rebukes Tobit; cf. 2:14; 5:18. v. 7, 'Tobias', he understands his parents' fears, even as Raguel tries to dissuade him from departing so soon. v. 10, 'half of all his property', Tobias, as the husband of Sarah, Raguel's only child, has become his heir. Thus the story has joined the two families, of Tobit and Raguel. v. 11, Raguel's farewell includes a prayer, invoking 'the Lord of heaven', a title often used of God in the post-exilic period (see 10:13–14; Ezra 1:2; Jdt 5:8). The farewell prayers of Raguel and Edna sound yet again the religious chords of the entire story, as Tobias undertakes his return journey with joy and happiness.

Homecoming of Tobias and Cure of Tobit's Eyes (11:1–18)

v. 1, 'Kaserin…opposite Nineveh', G[II] omits a preceding sentence that VL has: 'They set out and travelled until they came to Haran', a place half-way between Ecbatana and Nineveh. G[I] gives Nineveh itself as the place they have reached and the scene where Raphael, not mentioned in ch. 10, reappears. The diversity of location is probably owing to the problematic 'Kaserin opposite Nineveh'. No such place is known. Torrey (1922) argued that Kaserin and Nineveh were respectively Ctesiphon and Seleucia, towns farther south on the Tigris on the caravan-route from Mesopotamia to Media. If he were right, Tobias and Raphael would have travelled from a town on the west bank and would have had to cross the Tigris; see TOB 6:2. v. 4, 'the gall', Tobias is to use it on the eyes of Tobit; 'the dog', see TOB 6:2. Sinaiticus reads rather *ho kyrios*, 'the Lord'. The Peshitta of 11:6 depicts Anna seeing the dog coming, and the Vg of 11:9 reads: 'Then the dog that was with them on the road ran ahead and coming on as a herald took delight in the charms of its tail.' So Anna was apprised of the coming of her son. v. 5, 'the road', see 10:7. Despite her belief that Tobias has perished (10:4), Anna continued her vigil. v. 7, 'Raphael', again the angel's instructions are important, and Tobias obediently does what he has been told: he uses the fish's gall to restore Tobit's sight. v. 9, 'Anna ran up to her son', reading *Hanna edramen* instead of *anedramen*. v. 11, 'blew into his eyes', so Tobias cures his father's blindness, and the peak of the story is reached; 'Take courage', see TOB 7:16; 'made them smart', G[II] reads *epedōken* (corrupt); read rather *epedakē*, which would agree with *momordit* (VL). v. 14, 'light of my eyes', said of Tobias, it sums up the sense of the entire story, in which the contrast of darkness and light has played a significant role; recall 2:10; 3:17; 5:10; 10:5; 11:8; 14:10. vv. 14b–15, Tobit's prayer of praise, the fifth formal prayer of the book, ascribes both affliction and cure to God, and ends, 'Now I see my son Tobias!' v. 15, 'reported to his father', Tobias's report sums up the success of his trip: he has brought the money, he has married Sarah, and she is on her

way here. v. 17, 'Tobit acknowledged that God', this expresses the expected reaction of the upright Tobit, who now understands that the affliction of blindness has led only to good for him and his whole family. v. 18, 'Ahikar', see TOB 1:21; 'his nephew Nadab', 4QTob[d] bears the correct form of Ahiqar's nephew's name, *Nadin*. It so appears also in the Elephantine version of the Ahiqar story. G[I], however, reads *Nasbas*; G[II], *Nadab*; the VL, *Nadab* or *Nabal*; the Peshitta omits the name; 'seven days', see TOB 8:20.

Revelation of Raphael's Identity (12:1–20)

v. 1, 'see to paying the wages', Tobit had advised prompt payment of wages (4:14); now he summons Tobias to carry out that counsel, and with a bonus (recall 5:15–16). v. 4, 'half of all that he brought back', this is usually regarded as a folkloric motif derived from 'The Grateful Dead', in which a guide is rewarded with half of all the hero acquires. vv. 6–10, Raphael's answer begins with a didactic, sapiential discourse, in which he urges Tobit and Tobias to praise God (cf. Isa 38:16–20), to pursue good and not evil, to pray, fast, and give alms, and practise righteousness. v. 8, 'Prayer with fasting', so G[I] and VL; but G[II] reads, 'Prayer with fidelity'. v. 9, 'almsgiving saves from death', see 4:7–10, 16 and comment there. v. 10, 'their own worst enemies', Raphael's closing verdict on sinners. vv. 11–15, Raphael reveals his identity as one of the seven Angels of the Presence; so he appears in 1 Enoch (Gk.) 9:1; 20:3. The other six are Michael (Dan 10:13, 21; 12:1), Gabriel (Dan 8:16; 9:21), Uriel (2 Esdr 4:1), Sariel, Raguel, and Remiel. The seven names appear together in 1 Enoch (Gk.) 20:2–8, where they are called 'archangels'. v. 12, 'I who brought', Raphael functions as the intercessor for praying mortals and as one who tests them. vv. 16–18, Raphael seeks to dispel fear of himself by ascribing all to God, whose messenger he has been. v. 19, 'a vision', the text of this verse is garbled in the versions. G[II] has: 'You saw me that I ate nothing'; G[I]: 'I was seen by you all the days as neither eating nor drinking anything'; VL: 'You saw that I was eating, but you saw with your sight.' Fragmentary 4QTob[b] preserves only, 'I did not drink'. v. 20, 'acknowledge God', i.e. give God the praise that is due.

Tobit's Song of Praise (13:1–18)

The sixth formal prayer in the book imitates Ex 15:1–18. Tobit obeys the angel's instruction to praise and thank God for his deliverance. He expresses concern for deported Israelites still in Assyria and prays for the restoration of Jerusalem. All of this is done with words and phrases echoing Psalms and Deutero- and Trito-Isaiah (esp. 54:11–12; 60:1–4; 66:10–14). The song has two parts: vv. 1–8 laud God's mercy and sovereignty; vv. 9–18 proclaim the rebuilding of Jerusalem. Some commentators have thought that chs. 13–14 were a later addition to the book, but they appear in both the Aramaic and Hebrew copies from Qumran; so they must be an original part of the composition. v. 2, 'Afflicts, and…shows mercy', God is recognized to be in control of all. v. 3, 'before the nations', Israel is called on in its exile to acknowledge God even there. v. 6, Sinaiticus lacks vv. 6i–10b, for which one must follow G[I]. vv. 5–6, the theme of Deuteronomic retribution reappears; see comments on 1:12; 4:6. v. 9, 'Jerusalem, the holy city', cf. Isa 52:1; 48:2; Neh 11:1; 'deeds of your hands', idols. v. 10, 'tent',

God's tabernacle, the temple. vv. 12–14, Tobit utters a curse and a blessing on people as they will react to the future of Jerusalem. vv. 16–17, 'Jerusalem will be built', Tobit's song echoes the vision of the new Jerusalem in Isa 54:11–12.

Epilogue (14:1–15)

The conclusion recounts the last advice given by Tobit before he dies. v. 2, 'Fifty-eight years old', so his age is given in 4QTob[a], 4QTob[b], VL, and G[I], whereas G[II] reads 'sixty-two years old'; 'after regaining it', G[II] gives no length of time that Tobit lived, but VL reads 'fifty-four years', which seems to be what 4QTob[e] once read; 'giving alms', again Tobit's life is so summed up. v. 3, 'seven sons', so the VL, which may be supported by 4QTob[a] and 4QTob[c]; but this is not clear, because the final t could also be the ending of 'six', which would then agree with G[I], 'six sons'. G[II] omits the number. v. 4, 'Nahum', see Nah 1:1; 2:8–10, 13; 3:18–19; cf. Zeph 2:13. Tobit is made to speak from the eighth-century perspective about the coming destruction of Nineveh and the exile of 'all the inhabitants of the land of Israel' (after 587 BCE). G[I] substitutes 'Jonah' for 'Nahum'. 'Samaria and Jerusalem', the capitals of Israel and Judah are mentioned in 4QTob[c] and G[II], whereas G[I] omits Samaria, and VL omits both. The theme of desolation and rebuilding emphasizes what has happened in Tobit's own life. v. 5, 'the temple', its rebuilding is foretold in Isa 66:7–16; Ezek 40:1–48:35; Zech 14:11–17. v. 6, 'will all be converted', Tobit reflects a widespread post-exilic Jewish conviction (see Isa 45:14–15; Zech 8:20–3). v. 9, 'leave Nineveh', Tobit repeats his advice (14:3); v. 10 explains why. v. 10, 'Nadab', or Nadin; see TOB 11:18; 1:21. As the villain of the Ahiqar story, Nadin epitomizes what is wrong with Nineveh. Ahiqar had educated his nephew Nadin to succeed him as counsellor of Assyrian kings, but he treacherously plotted to have his uncle put to death. Ahiqar hid and was finally vindicated (came into the light), whereas Nadin died in a dungeon (in darkness). Again the motif of light/darkness is used to characterize the relation of good Ahiqar and evil Nadin; see comment on 11:14; 'gave

alms', this sums up Ahiqar's life, as it did Tobit's (14:11); see TOB 4:7–10; 12:9; 14:2. v. 12, 'Buried her', Tobias obeys Tobit's last instructions. v. 14, 'One hundred and seventeen', some VL MSS read 118. v. 15, 'destruction of Nineveh', in 612 BCE Nineveh fell after a three-month siege to the combined forces of Babylonians and Medes, under kings Nabopolassar and Cyaxares. The fall of Nineveh likewise exemplifies Deuteronomic retribution: the wicked are punished. See TOB 1:12; 4:6. 'Cyaxares', Sinaiticus and G[I] strangely read Ndbouchodonosor kai Asouēros; Hanhart (1983) reads Achiacharos, reflecting the VL Achicar, which seems to be a confusion of the name with Ahiqar.

REFERENCES

Brooke, A. E., McLean, N., and Thackeray, H. St J. (1940), *The Old Testament in Greek* (3 vols.; Cambridge: Cambridge University Press, 1906–40), iii. 123–44 (VL of P. Sabatier).

Cowley, A. (1923), *Aramaic Papyri of the Fifth Century B.C. Edited with Translation and Notes* (Oxford: Clarendon; repr. Osnabrück: Zeller, 1967).

DiLella, A. A. (1979), 'The Deuteronomic Background of the Farewell Discourse in Tob 14:3–11', *CBQ* 41: 380–9.

Gerould, G. H. (1908), *The Grateful Dead: The History of a Folk Story*, Publications of the Folklore Society, 60 (London: D. Nutt; repr. Folcroft, Pa.: Folcroft Library Editions, 1973), 45–7.

Hanhart, R. (1983), *Tobit*, Septuaginta: Vetus Testamentum graecum, 8/5 (Göttingen: Vandenhoeck & Ruprecht).

Miller, A. (1940), *Das Buch Tobias übersetzt und erklärt*, Die Heilige Schrift des Alten Testaments, 4/3 (Bonn: Hanstein), 1–116.

Monks of San Girolamo (1950), *Biblia Sacra iuxta latinam Vulgatam versionem ad codicum fidem... cura et studio monachorum Sancti Benedicti... edita* (Rome: Vatican Polyglot), viii.

Porten, B., and Yardeni, A. (1933), *Textbook of Aramaic Documents from Ancient Egypt Newly Copied, Edited and Translated into Hebrew and English*: iii. *Literature, Accounts, Lists* (Jerusalem: Hebrew University; distrib., Winona Lake, Id.: Eisenbrauns), 23–57 (Story of Ahiqar).

Torrey, C. C. (1922), '"Nineveh" in the Book of Tobit', *JBL* 41: 237–45.

41. Judith   AMY-JILL LEVINE

INTRODUCTION

By combining theological convictions and narrative motifs familiar from the HB with Hellenistic literature's increasing attention to character development, pathos, and personal piety, the book of Judith epitomizes Second Temple Judaism's attempt to define itself in the light of Greek culture. Along with other Jewish narratives in the OT Apocrypha such as Bel and the Dragon, Susanna, and Tobit, the book of Judith provides instruction on Jewish identity even as it inspires and entertains.

A. Genre. 1. Whether labelled novella, novel, historical fiction, or romance (see details in Wills 1995), Judith should be regarded as fiction, as the opening lines clearly signal. The more blatant errors include the identification of Nebuchadnezzar as ruler of Assyria rather than Babylon, and of his capital as Nineveh (1:1), which had been destroyed by the Babylonians in 612 BCE, before Nebuchadnezzar ascended

the throne. The same chapter claims that Ecbatana was captured by Nebuchadnezzar; it fell instead to Cyrus of Persia in 550 BCE. Disrupting even the internal attempts at verisimilitude, the Ammonite Achior's recitation of Jewish history includes reference to both the destruction of the Jerusalem temple by Nebuchadnezzar and its rebuilding, following Persia's defeat of Babylon.

2. Consistent with the fictional genre is the absence from any other ancient sources of several major figures, of whom Arphaxad the ruler of the Medes (1:1–6) is the most conspicuous example, as well as of several nations, such as the Cheleoudites (1:6) and the Rassites (2:23). Although Judith includes several specific dates and times, such as the year of a king's reign (1:1, 13) and the number of days of a particular siege (7:20; 15:11), the enumerations function more to convey a sense of verisimilitude—this is what ancient historiography looks like—than they do to demonstrate historicity.

B. Date. 1. The date by which the book of Judith must have been written is the late first century CE; its first external reference is not, as might be expected, the Jewish historian Josephus nor any of the Dead Sea scrolls. Rather, it is in the Christian text, *1 Clement* 55:4–5, which lists Judith as among several women empowered by divine grace to accomplish 'many manly deeds' and who 'asked from the elders of the city permission' to enter the enemy camp.

2. Establishing the date of composition is more difficult, in part because of the book's genre. The first three chapters may show knowledge of the Achaemenid king Artaxerxes III Ochus (358–338 BCE), who did mount western campaigns (in 350 and 343), did attack Sidon (cf. Jdt 2:28), and had both a general named Holofernes and a courtier named Bagoas. Yet knowledge of such events does not preclude the author's adapting this information for a fictional retelling.

3. The majority of today's scholars who regard the volume as fiction offer much later datings than the fourth century. While Volkmar argued that the book reflects the events of 70 CE, with Nebuchadnezzar representing Trajan and Judith the faithful Judean population, and Gaster associated Nebuchadnezzar with Pompey's entry into Jerusalem in 63 BCE, Ball's association of Judith with Judah Maccabee and Nebuchadnezzar with Antiochus IV Epiphanes is probably correct (details in Moore 1985).

4. The Maccabean connection is supported by several plot motifs. First, whereas Antiochus Epiphanes and his supporters banned circumcision, Achior, Holofernes' erstwhile general, submits to the operation in his conversion to Judaism. Second, and more suggestive, the death of Holofernes resembles Judah Maccabee's defeat of the Syrian general Nicanor; 1 Macc 7:47 states, 'Then the Jews seized the spoils and the plunder; they cut off Nicanor's head and the right hand that he had so arrogantly stretched out, and brought them and displayed them just outside Jerusalem' (for additional connections, see Moore 1985).

5. The geographical centre of the book of Judith, the town of Bethulia, is another possible clue to the book's Hasmonean date. Bethulia appears to be located in Samaritan territory, which was annexed by the Hasmonean ruler, John Hyrcanus, in 107 BCE. By this time, Hyrcanus had destroyed the capital, Shechem, and torched the Samaritan temple on Mt. Gerizim. Given the positive attitude the book of Judith displays towards Samaritan territory, the book's date may well be several generations after the conquest.

By invoking the outrages of Antiochus and his minions and the successful insurrection against his forces, Judith celebrates Jewish independence, praxis, and theology. As a new Judah (whose name means 'Jewish man'), Judith ('Jewish woman') corrects the priestly leaders' weak theology, defeats the Syrian king, and preserves the temple for Jewish worship. Unlike Judah's successors, the Hasmonean dynasty that eventually assumed the roles of both king and high priest, however, Judith serves more in the model of the biblical judges than she does either as monarch or cleric. Dying childless, she passes on no dynastic legacy. Perhaps then the volume praises Judah even as it subtly critiques his heirs. That Judith's age at her death, 105 years (16:23), is the number of years of independent Jewish rule may be a clue to a first-century BCE dating for the volume.

As a fictional study rather than a historical report, Judith obtains its value in great measure because it can represent problems faced by the covenant community throughout the ages. The almost supernatural evil of Holofernes, a general who marched his army from Nineveh to Cilicia, a 300-mile journey, in three days, permits him to become the model of any villain. Moreover, detached from history, the volume serves various allegorical purposes; Martin Luther, for example, regarded the book of Judith as an allegory of Jesus' Passion.

C. Language and Culture. 1. Best preserved in two of the three major uncial Greek codices, Vaticanus and Alexandrinus, as well as in the uncial Basiliano-Vaticanus (the third major codex, Sinaiticus, shows signs of later editing), Judith may have an Aramaic or Hebrew original (Moore 1985); scholars have argued that in preparing his translation of the book into Latin for his Vulgate, the Christian author Jerome utilized an Aramaic source: he speaks of translating only the texts found in 'Chaldean'. However, one could equally argue that the author of Judith wrote in an elegant, Hebraicized Greek (Craven 1983).

2. Other ancient versions rely either upon the Septuagint (e.g. the Old Latin) or upon the Vulgate (e.g. various Hebrew versions as well as, from the Middle Ages, midrashic iterations).

3. Whether Second-Temple Aramaic or Greek, the book of Judith is permeated by Hellenistic motifs. In the wake of Alexander the Great (d. 323), Jewish communities in both Israel and the Diaspora developed new forms of self-definition under pressures to assimilate and acculturate. Such struggles are noticeable in the OT Apocrypha; the volumes reflect intense concerns for Jewish practices (e.g. dietary observances, circumcision, conversion), relationship to the Gentile world, and personal piety. Yet the books are also preserved in the Greek language and reflect Greek culture. For example, in the book of Judith, Greek culture underlies the wearing of olive wreaths (15:13) and the custom of reclining to dine (12:15). The *thyrsus* Judith carries recollects Bacchantes, who, like Judith, confound gender roles, take heads from unwitting men, and celebrate their god, despite threats against their practice, through dancing and prayer. Scholars have even found allusions in the book to Herodotus' account of the Persian invasions of Greece in the fifth century BCE (Camponigro 1992).

4. The location of composition is, like the date, debated. Most scholars argue for a Palestinian provenance; if the original version were in Aramaic rather than Greek, this argument would be strengthened. However, just as the fictional nature of the tale foils any secure attempt at dating, so its fictional depictions of geography undermine any secure attempt at establishing provenance.

D. Religious Beliefs and Practices. 1. Although the book of Judith has few references to divine intervention (4:13), theological concerns are paramount. Sounding somewhat like Rahab (Josh 2), Achior the Ammonite gives a relatively complete summary of God's relationship to Israel and concludes with the warning, 'their Lord and God will defend them' (5:21).

2. Notable are the volume's depiction of personal piety and struggle for a faithful approach to the problem of theodicy.

Concerning the former: Judith, like her sisters in the OT Apocrypha (Susanna, Esther of the Greek Additions, Sarah of the book of Tobit) prays; like them as well, she is pious, well schooled in the traditions of her community, and chaste even in the presence of lecherous threat.

3. The innocence of these women leads directly to the question of theodicy. Esther, Susanna, and Sarah are all tested and are all found worthy; so too, Judith argues against the Deuteronomic theology mouthed by Uzziah, the Bethulian leader, which insists that the onslaught of the enemy general Holofernes is punishment for the people's sins. Judith responds that the Assyrian campaign is not a punishment but the means by which God proves the people's fidelity. More, she condemns Uzziah's willingness to put God to the test by stating that, if divine help does not come within five days, he will surrender.

4. Like Greek Esther and, especially, the book of Daniel (a work probably composed during or immediately after the Maccabean revolt), the book of Judith emphasizes Jewish self-definition by accentuating dietary concerns: Greek Esther speaks of avoiding the Persian king's libations; Daniel refuses to dine at Nebuchadnezzar's table (Dan 1:8) and so, along with his friends, resorts to a vegetarian regime; Judith eats only kosher food (10:5; 11:13; 12:2). Finally, like the story of Tobit, the book of Judith emphasizes the Jerusalem Temple (4:2–3, 12; 8:21, 24; 9:8, 13; 16:20) as a place to be protected, to be entered undefiled, and to serve as the location for votive offerings, celebrations, and worship.

5. Such concerns for piety have been regarded both as indicative of Pharisaic piety and as in contravention of it. The former suggestion can also be supported by Judith's calendrical observances and ritual washings; the latter suggestion is premised upon the conversion of the Ammonite Achior, despite Deuteronomy's prohibition of Ammonites (and Moabites) entering the covenant community (Deut 23:3). However, lack of secure information on Pharisaic thought of the Hasmonean period makes any suggestion tentative.

6. Similar problems apply to explanations for Judith's absence from the canon of the synagogue. Justifications ranged from the conversion of the Ammonite, to his conversion apart from ritual immersion, to the volume's universalism seen as incompatible with (hypothetical) Pharisaic exclusiveness, to the (more likely) arguments that the book was known to be late (Daniel gained entry because of its back-dating to the Babylonian Exile), fictional, and/or composed originally in Greek. Again, any argument on the absence of Judith from the canon of Judaism must remain tentative.

E. Aesthetics and Ethics. 1. Because the titular heroine does not appear until midway through her story, the volume has been regarded as unbalanced. However, closer reading indicates substantial connections and correctives between the first and last seven chapters (Craven 1983). Paragraphs 2–4 below are examples of the balance:

2. Chs. 1–7 emphasize military campaigns, fear engendered by overt show of strength, and success based on armaments, numbers of soldiers, and male dominance; at the end of this section, Achior appears condemned, Nebuchadnezzar triumphant, and the Bethulians doomed. Chs. 8–16 provide the corrective by emphasizing Judith's personal history (e.g. her genealogy), clever strategizing, deception, and the power of the individual. For these reasons and others, commentators typically divide the book between the first and second eight chapters (Craven 1983). One notable exception is the theory of Ernst Haag (1963), which suggests the Book of Judith forms a tripartite structure (1–3; 4–8; 9–16).

3. Characterization serves to yoke the two parts. In the first seven chapters, Achior provides the transition. His speech relates Assyrian plans and Jewish abilities, and his forced removal from the military camp to the outskirts of Bethulia shows the division between the two areas both geographically and ideologically. This most unlikely of heroes will enter Israel not only as an involuntary exile, but as a willing convert, as his circumcision attests. Judith is Achior's opposite: the second section of the book depicts her traversing from Bethulia to the enemy camp, but through her own will rather than as an outcast. Whereas Achior truthfully summarizes Jewish history and is not believed, Judith dissembles about plans for the temple sacrifices and is believed. While Achior undergoes circumcision and therefore changes both identity and appearance, Judith only feigns change: her make-up can be washed off and her festive clothes replaced by sackcloth.

4. Judith is also the opposite of Holofernes. The Assyrian general insists that everyone worship Nebuchadnezzar as divine, although the king had not actually given this order (Craven 1983). That is, Holofernes interprets his task theologically. Judith does the same: she invokes God through prayer, but her actions are of her own devising. Furthermore, unlike Greek Esther, Susanna, or Tobit's Sarah, who explicitly receive divine aid, Judith's prayers are answered by the machinations of the plot rather than the entry of the supernatural.

5. Just as the book of Judith is frequently regarded as aesthetically uneven, so it is often condemned as ethically untenable. Interpreters have excoriated the heroine, who lies, who lulls her victim into a false sense of security, who kills. Such a focus misses the narrative's irony even as it displays sympathy for Holofernes, who is a ruthless butcher. The irony accompanies the assassination motivated by self-defence: Judith decapitates the general, with his own sword no less, by the 'hand of a woman' (the phrase appears several times). Nothing could be more ignominious (see Judg 9:53). Enhancing the irony are the numerous *doubles entendres*, the fainting of the seasoned soldier Achior at the sight of Holofernes' head, and the name of the theologically weak Bethulian leader, Uzziah, which means 'God is my defence'.

6. Yet irony and self-defence do not preclude the fact that the book, and its heroine, can be regarded as dangerous. More cunning than Jael (Judg 4–5), who dispatches the enemy general Sisera by tucking him into bed, giving him milk, and then pounding a tent peg into his temple, Judith seeks out her victim, takes the head as a trophy, and then facilitates the slaughter of the Assyrian army and the looting of their camp (White 1992). More dangerous than Jael, the 'wife of Heber the Kenite' and therefore distanced from the covenant community, Judith is 'one of us'. More threatening to traditional gender roles than Deborah, who is aided by Barak and is called a 'mother in Israel', Judith as book and as character subverts the social expectations for men and women. Judith remains independent, her female slave runs her estate, she refuses all sexual advances, the men she encounters are at best inept, even her donkey is female (Craven 1983). Perhaps then it is not surprising that the book insists upon its fictional status, that Judith finally retires to her house, and that she does not produce children.

7. The connection of the books of Judith and Judges is, however, a helpful corrective to those who find her story unethical or unladylike. Judith is, in terms of narrative genre and character development, in the model of the judges: she is resourceful and brave like Jael; she is a mother figure in her protection of the community, like Deborah; she is sly (and even conveys a possible hint of sexual scandal) like Ehud. As with the judges, the land remains at peace until her death.

8. The book of Judith evokes more than the stories of the judges, and herein lies a major part of its aesthetic import. Throughout, by drawing upon other texts, it adds to its own literary richness even as it contributes to the tradition-history of its literary predecessors. Most significant is Judith's connection to Gen 34, the rape of Dinah. From the (probably) Samaritan setting of Bethulia, to Judith's descent from Simeon, to her promise to protect the 'virgin' (Heb. *bĕtûlâ*), to the deceitful conquest, and even to the suggestions in each story of castration, the Apocryphal narrative recapitulates the earlier story. Indeed, the character of Judith redeems that of Simeon (as do two other Second-Temple texts, *Jubilees* 30, and the *Testament of Levi*), condemned for his violence by Jacob (Gen 49:5–7).

9. Like Jacob, Judith travels from her home, cleverly defeats an enemy who has been feigning friendship, and escapes enemy territory unnoticed. Judith may also be compared to Moses: both faced lack of water and a suffering people with weakening theological grounding (Ex 17; Num 20; Deut 33); both, with divine help, preserve and strengthen the covenant community (Van Henten 1995). Like Abigail, Judith descends a mountain, takes her own food, humbles herself before a military leader (David), and is involved with a drunk man who dies (Nabal); see 1 Sam 25 (Van Henten 1995). Like Esther, with whom she is typically paired in both ancient manuscript collections and modern interpretation, Judith uses her physical charms along with her clever words and loyalty to her people to defeat a genocidal enemy. Like the Maccabees, she rescues her people from false worship as well as military conquest.

10. Given Judith's composition during the Hellenistic era, it is not inappropriate to compare her also with Greek figures. Like Medusa, her looks prove deadly (see Bal 1994 for art-historical and literary connections); like Euripides' Bacchae, she carries a *thyrsus* and produces the decapitated head of a ruler. For more on connections between Judith and Greek fiction, see Wills 1995.

COMMENTARY

Nebuchadnezzar's Threat (1:1–16)

Judith opens with an overtly fictional conceit: Nebuchadnezzar, the infamous king of Babylon who destroyed the Jerusalem temple in 587 BCE, is named the ruler of Assyria, the

empire which in 722 destroyed the northern kingdom of Israel. He is depicted as ruling from Nineveh, the Assyrian capital which his father had sacked in 612 BCE. This mythic setting makes the story always relevant: Nebuchadnezzar represents any who seek to obliterate the Jewish community. The conceit also allows the horror of the scene to be contained; from the opening sentence, irony and not the destruction of Jews will be the dominant motif.

Reinforcing this pattern, the first chapter continues to mitigate the ominous references to Nebuchadnezzar by means of exaggeration. Arphaxad, identified as the king of Media but unknown to history, prepares to defend his lands against Nebuchadnezzar by constructing major fortifications around his capital, Ecbatana: the towers are 150 ft. high, with foundations 90 ft. thick; the gates, 60 ft. wide, permitted entire armies to parade through. Contributing to the exaggeration of the fortifications is the language: the opening sentence in Greek is several lines long, which English translations typically break up.

Nebuchadnezzar also seeks strength in numbers: he rallies much of what is now southern Turkey. However, the populations from Persia to Jerusalem to Egypt to Ethiopia refuse to join him, for they regarded him as 'ordinary' or, literally, 'as an equal' (v. 11). The irony continues: Nebuchadnezzar is more than the average king, as recognition of his name even today demonstrates. Increasing the irony, Holofernes will insist that Nebuchadnezzar be worshipped as a god.

Prompted by Arphaxad's insult to his military strength, Nebuchadnezzar seeks revenge; among his targets are Judea, Egypt, Moab, Ammon; thus Judea is now threatened together with, rather than by, its traditional enemies.

The battle begins with the despoliation of Ecbatana. The Greek literally states that the city's beauty was 'turned to shame' (v. 14). Here the motif of shame appears for the first time (recurring at e.g. 4:12; 5:21; 8:22; 9:2), anticipating Judith: by placing herself in a situation of seduction that would traditionally be considered shameful for a woman, she will succeed in humiliating the Assyrian men.

Nebuchadnezzar's army returns to Nineveh for four months of recuperation. With the fall of Ecbatana, the fate of the rest of the Mediterranean and Asia Minor is, apparently, sealed.

Nebuchadnezzar's Plan (2:1–13)

Irony continues as Nebuchadnezzar broadcasts his 'secret strategy' (v. 2) to his ministers, nobles, his general Holofernes, and the readers. His self-appellation, 'Great King, lord of the whole earth', continues the hyperbole of ch. 1 even as it establishes the theological challenge of the book. Holofernes is ordered to take 'experienced soldiers' (v. 5; lit. men confident in their own strength; the inference is that one should be confident in God's strength (Moore 1985)) to occupy all the territories, slaughter the rebellious, and capture the rest for Nebuchadnezzar to kill later. The general, ordered to follow his 'lord's' commands (v. 13) is thus a parallel to Judith, who will follow her 'lord's' commands. That the number of infantry soldiers Holofernes takes, 120,000, matches the number of Antiochus' troops (1 Macc 15:13) appears more than coincidental.

Nebuchadnezzar orders Holofernes to have 'all the land to the west' prepare for him 'earth and water' (v. 7), traditional

Persian tokens of submission. Should they fail, he promises, again hyperbolically, the destruction of their peoples until the rivers overflow with corpses. The repetition of terms concerning water anticipates again the second half of the book, where Holofernes attempts to enforce Bethulia's submission by severing its water supply. The king concludes his orders first by taking the oath, 'as I live, and by the power of my kingdom', and then by promising that he will accomplish his plans 'by [his] own hand' (v. 12). The oath is reminiscent of the divine proclamation of Deut 32:39–41; Nebuchadnezzar is again seen to be setting himself up as a false god. The promise augurs Judith's repeated point that vengeance will be taken 'by my hand'—that of a woman (8:33; 12:4).

Holofernes' Campaign (2:14–3:10)

Holofernes begins his campaign by mustering an army comparable in its exaggerated description to the fortifications of Ecbatana (1:2–4). Contributing to the numbers, and the threat, of his army, are its multifarious followers; like a locust plague (2:20) they demolish all in their path: Put and Lud, the Rassisites and Ishmaelites, Cilicia and Arabia, Midian and Damascus. Their amazing feats are matched by their miraculous, or at least humorously exaggerated, feet: the army traverses 300 miles, from Nineveh to Cilicia, in three days (2:21). Hearing of Holofernes' victories, the coastal cities, including Tyre and Sidon, Jamnia and Ascalon, petition for peace. The reference to Jamnia (2:28) may recall Judah Maccabee, who burned the city in 164 BCE. The local populations offer everything: land, livestock, even the people as slaves. They greet Holofernes with garlands (Gk. 'crowns'), dancing, and tambourines. He, however, mercilessly demolishes their sanctuaries and 'woods' (groves dedicated to a goddess?) so that all nations worship Nebuchadnezzar alone, 'that all their dialects and tribes should call upon him as a god' (3:8). This scene will be reversed in ch. 12, when Judith, with garlands, dancing, and tambourines, brings Holofernes' head to Jerusalem and her God. Holofernes next advances towards the Esdraelon plain, near Dothan. Camping for a month between Geba and Scythopolis, he readies his army to attack Judea.

Israel Threatened (4:1–15)

Hearing of Holofernes' attacks, including his sacking of sanctuaries, the Israelites in Judea are terrified; in particular they are 'alarmed both for Jerusalem and for the temple of the Lord their God' (v. 2). The concern is, moreover, poignant: the people had recently returned from exile and recently rededicated the temple (v. 3). Although some scholars look on this verse as a gloss, its date is consistent with the purification of the temple by Judah Maccabee and his supporters (1 Macc 4:36–61; 2 Macc 10:3–5).

That the Judeans warn their neighbours, including 'every district of Samaria' (v. 4), poses another historical quandary. Samaria, the former northern kingdom of Israel, was in the post-exilic period commonly Judea's enemy (Neh 4, 13; Ezra 4). The Hasmonean John Hyrcanus conquered Samaria in 107 BCE; it remained in Judean hands until 63 BCE, when Roman hegemony began.

The Judeans together with the neighbouring peoples fortify their villages and stock food, but given Arphaxad's unsuccessful preparations their efforts appear hopeless. Joakim the high priest, together with the Jerusalem council (Gk. gērousia) orders the populations of Bethulia and its environs to guard the hill-country passes and thereby protect Judea. This Joakim is otherwise unknown. Neh 12:26 mentions a high priest Joiakim, but he did not have the military authority that this figure does. The first leader of the post-exilic period with both temple and military control was the Hasmonean Jonathan (see 1 Macc 10:18–21). The indication that the high priest was in Jerusalem 'at the time' (v. 6) would be gratuitous except during Hasmonean times, when priest-kings involved with military manœuvres did leave Jerusalem. That the gērousia (see also 11:14; 15:8) is replaced by the Sanhedrin (Synedrion) under John Hyrcanus II in about 67 BCE may narrow the date of composition.

The Israelites comply with Joakim's request. The men, women, and children of Jerusalem and the resident aliens and servants also fast, don sackcloth, prostrate themselves before the temple, and drape the cattle and even the altar (v. 10) with sackcloth. This public expression of religiosity, especially fasting, becomes increasingly common in the post-exilic period, as Esth 4:1–3 and 1 Macc 3:44–8 attest. The people's prayers are both personal and communal: they seek protection lest children be carried off, women raped (lit. for booty), towns destroyed, and the temple profaned. However, reference to cows in mourning is probably here, as it is in Jon 3:8, a touch of humour.

The Lord hears their prayers, but it will take several chapters before the people recognize this response. Meanwhile, they continue to fast and wear sackcloth while the priests make burnt as well as votive and voluntary offerings for the house of Israel.

Achior Recounts Jewish History (5:1–24)

Holofernes is furious upon learning of the Israelite fortifications, including the closing of mountain passes, the garrisoning of hilltops, and the laying of traps in the plains. Summoning the rulers of Israel's traditional enemies, Moab and Ammon, he seeks information from these 'Canaanites' concerning the resistance: their identity, numbers, the size and resources of their army, the source of their power, and their king (v. 3). Achior the Ammonite leader responds with a recitation of Jewish history. However, aside from identifying the people, he answers none of the other questions. The omission is pregnant: their numbers are irrelevant given what one woman can accomplish; their king and the source of their power is, as readers well know, God.

Locating Israel internationally, Achior begins by recounting its Chaldean origins, its rejection of local gods in favour of the 'God of heaven' (v. 8), and its consequent expulsion. He recounts that, fleeing to Mesopotamia the people, upon divine command, settle in Canaan where they prosper. Next, moving to Egypt because of a famine, they again prosper until their numbers prompt the king to enslave them. Answering their prayers their God afflicts Egypt with plagues. Israel's divine protection will continue as a theme through the speech: it is again confirmed when, as the Israelites flee Egypt, God dries up the Red Sea and leads the people through the Sinai. Driving out the desert peoples, the Israelites inhabit Amorite land. They then cross the Jordan, take the hill country, and expel the Canaanites, Perizzites, Jebusites, Shechemites, and Gergesites (v. 16). With the exception of the Shechemites, the list matches the summary statements of Gen 15:20; Ex 3:8, 17; Deut 7:1; Josh 9:1; 11:3; Ezra 9:1; and Neh 9:8. Perhaps the inclusion of the Shechemites is meant to anticipate Judith's reference (9:2) to Simeon's conquests in Gen 34. Ironically, the existence of Achior, the Ammonite narrator, along with his Canaanite allies, belies any total conquest.

Achior observes that the Israelites are protected as long as they remain faithful to their God. When they sin, they are defeated and taken into exile; their temple is destroyed, and their towns occupied by enemies. Having repented, the people have returned to their lands. Thus Achior advises that, if the Israelites are faithful, Holofernes should change his plans lest he be defeated and his army become a laughingstock. Although Achior spoke truthfully, Holofernes' officers reject his advice: viewing Israel as weak they assert to 'Lord Holofernes' that his army 'will swallow them up' (v. 24). Ironics abound. First, the people do lack military strength; the officers are correct. Second, it is an Ammonite general, rather than the Israelite high priest, who recognizes the connection between faithfulness and security, sin and war. Third, Achior proves prophetic: his comments foreshadow the plot. Fourth, the image of the rapacious army plays upon the trope of food common throughout the book: the people in Bethulia fear starvation, but Judith will avoid Holofernes' table and her servant will transport Holofernes' head in a food bag. Finally, whereas Achior's truthful statements are not believed, Holofernes and his troops will trust the deceiving Judith.

Achior's Fate (6:1–21)

Holofernes' reaction ironically recalls biblical traditions. First, he questions not only Achior's advice, but his association with Ephraïmite mercenaries (v. 2). Ephraim is another name for the northern kingdom of Israel, destroyed in the eighth century by Assyria. Rhetorically, Holofernes thus begins reconstituting the covenant community. Second, he accuses Achior of playing the prophet; whereas biblical prophets typically encourage the repentance of Israel, Achior seeks the protection of the Assyrian general; yet both speak the truth and are usually not believed by rulers. Finally, Holofernes asks, 'What god is there except Nebuchadnezzar?' (v. 2). This god, Holofernes insists, will erase the memory of Israel. Thus Holofernes threatens even more than Nebuchadnezzar commanded.

For his words, Achior is banished from the Assyrian camp and delivered (v. 7, lit. 'they will bring you back') to the hill country of Israel; perhaps the expression indicates that Holofernes thought Achior was already on the Judeans' side. Holofernes then vows to kill him during the siege. The conversation ends with the general's snide observation that if Achior believed his own words he would not be depressed. The Greek is literally 'do not let your face fall' (v. 9); Holofernes unknowingly prophesies his own fate. Achior's presence in Bethulia will in turn prove fortuitous: he will be able to identify the severed head (14:6–8).

Under a rain of stones from the Israelites, Holofernes' slaves bind Achior and leave him near the springs below Bethulia. Achior is then taken by the Israelites to their rulers, Uzziah the Simeonite, Chabris, and Charmis. The rulers summon the elders, and all the young men and women assemble as well. Questioned by Uzziah, Achior relates Holofernes' plans and his own recitation of Israelite history. The Bethulians respond by praying that the enemy's arrogance be punished and the people's plight be pitied. They also commend Achior; Uzziah takes him home and gives a banquet (v. 21, lit. drinking party; one that will stand in contrast to Judith's encounters with Holofernes) where, together with the elders, he prays for help.

Bethulia under Siege (7:1–32)

Holofernes' forces, 170,000 infantry and 12,000 cavalry, as well as soldiers with the baggage train, begin the siege; the Israelites stand guard in fear. On the second day, Holofernes secures the city's water source. Returning to his main forces, he is then visited by the rulers of Israel's traditional enemies, the 'children of Esau' (v. 8), the Moabites, and others who urge him to forgo a battle. (The reference to Esau probably refers to the Edomites, who were defeated by Judah Maccabee in 164 BCE (see 1 Macc 5:1–5) and then converted to Judaism under John Hyrcanus around 120 BCE.) They advise that he wait until thirst and starvation leave the Bethulian men, women, and children dying in the streets. Prolonged death will be, in the enemy's view, appropriate punishment for the city's rebellion. Agreeing, Holofernes places the area surrounding Bethulia under guard by thousands of Assyrians, Ammonites, and the children of Esau. The plan was to prevent any man (Gk. andros) from leaving (v. 13); keeping the gender-specific Greek permits irony, for no man will leave Bethulia, but only Judith and her female slave.

As Holofernes' generals predicted, the children grow listless, and young men and women faint in the streets. Their courage depleted, and convinced that God has abandoned them for their (unnamed) sins and the sins of their ancestors, the population condemns Uzziah and the elders for not making a treaty with the Assyrians. Better to be slaves, the men insist, then to watch their wives and children die from thirst. The choice of slavery or death evokes the Exodus generation (Ex 14:10–12; 16:3) as well as that of the Jews facing the campaign of Antiochus Epiphanes (1 Macc 1:52–3). The cry that 'God has sold us into their hands' (v. 25; see Esth 7:4) will be corrected by the saving ability of Judith's hand. As the people cry to heaven, Uzziah exhorts courage. He promises that if there is no rescue after five days, he will accede to their wishes. Dejected, the men return to their posts, the women and children to their homes. For the moment kept apart from men and military concerns, the women will later join Judith as well as their male relatives in the celebration of victory (15:12–13).

Judith's Introduction (8:1–36)

News of the siege finally reaches the widow Judith; separate from the community, she has not been affected by the lack of water nor involved in the political discussions. The narrative keeps her even more detached by inserting a very long genealogy, the longest of any biblical woman, immediately after her introduction: interest shifts from the dying population, who believe they suffer for the sins of their ancestors, to Judith's (righteous) forefathers. With names among the sixteen generations such as Merari, who was a son of Levi (Gen 46:11); Shelumiel, a Simeonite leader who aided Moses (Num 1:6; 2:12; 7:36, 41; 10:19); Gideon, a judge; Elijah, a prophet; Hilkiah, a prophet; Nathaniel, a prophet; and Israel, Judith appears destined for greatness. However, the majority of these names do not represent the well-known figures; at best they are evocative. It is Judith herself who brings the glory to her line.

Even Judith's name, meaning 'Jewish woman', is portentous: this only named woman in the story will both protect and embody the covenant community (Levine 1992). A widow, Judith recalls the God known as the protector of widows (Ps 68:5; Sir 35:15), even as the covenant community is depicted as a widow (Isa 54:4; Lam 1:1; 5:3–4). However, Judith's mourning, unlike that of the Judeans in Babylon, is not caused by sin; rather, her husband Manasseh, also from the tribe of Simeon, had died from sunstroke while supervising his servants as they bound barley sheaves. His inglorious death will be repeated by Holofernes, who is also wounded in the head, takes to his bed, and dies (cf. 8:3; 13:2). Manasseh's disgrace may be exacerbated by his name, which he shares with the Judean king to whom is attributed Jerusalem's destruction (see 2 Kings 21:12–15; 23:26–7; 24:3–4).

By marrying endogamously, Judith conformed to recommended practice (Num 36; Tob 1:9). She does not, however, submit to levirate marriage, even though she is childless and the Bethulian leader, Uzziah, is a fellow Simeonite. Yet Uzziah is weak, and Judith neither needs nor desires a spouse. Given her actions, perhaps her widowhood is fortunate; the shame her actions might cause a husband would be enormous. Judith's mourning epitomizes radical piety. She lives in a rooftop shelter, wears sackcloth around her waist, and dresses in widow's clothes. Every day save sabbaths, new moons, and Jewish festivals, she fasts. Nevertheless, she remains 'shapely and beautiful' (v. 7; see Gen 29:17 concerning Rachel) as well as rich in gold and silver, male and female servants, livestock and fields, all inherited from her husband. Finally, so well known was her piety that 'no one spoke ill of her' (v. 8). This too is ironic; few maintain such spotless reputations. The specified length of her mourning, three years and four months (v. 4) or forty months, may suggest the number of years Israel spent in the wilderness; it also parallels the thirty-four days of the siege of Bethulia (7:20) even as Judith's sackcloth mirrors that of the townspeople (and cattle).

Upon hearing of the people's protest and Uzziah's response, Judith sends her slave, the one in charge of all her property, to summon the town elders. Stereotypical gender roles are reversed: a female slave commands a major estate; a widow demands obedience from city officials. The Bethulian elders receive from Judith strong rebuke: how do they dare test, place conditions upon, or presume to know the thoughts of God? Rather, the people should continue to pray and await deliverance. Then, like Achior, Judith recites the history of Israel: their ancestors had been punished for worshipping idols, but the present generation has remained faithful. Consequently they must have hope. Judith next observes that,

given Bethulia's strategic location, its fall would entail the sack of Jerusalem and the destruction of the temple. Were the people then taken captive, they would become a disgrace in the eyes of all. Therefore, she concludes, Bethulia must be an example for the rest of Judea: the people should thank God for putting them to the test, just as Abraham was tested at Isaac's near-sacrifice (Gen 22) and Jacob at Laban's house (Gen 28).

Uzziah acknowledges Judith's wisdom yet fails to recognize the import of her words: he first makes the excuse that he was 'compelled' (v. 30) to acquiesce by the people, and then he urges her, perhaps condescendingly, to pray; since she is a 'God-fearing woman' (v. 31), God will send rain at her request. Judith does not deign to respond to these comments. Instead, she announces she will do something memorable 'through all generations' (v. 32). But she refuses to divulge her plans. Again, the leaders acquiesce; whether out of desperation, because they are cowed by her resolve, because they trust her judgement, or because, as some more cynical commentators suggest, they are happy to be rid of her, is unclear; saying, 'may the Lord God go before you, to take vengeance on our enemies', they depart for their posts. That Judith acts while the ostensible leaders react reverses gender roles; psychoanalytic readers would even suggest that the leaders were symbolically castrated. They will, of course, find a better application for this insight a few chapters later.

Judith's Prayer (9:1–14)

Extended prayers, particularly by women, feature prominently in Hellenistic-Jewish literature; examples include Susanna, Esther (in the Greek Additions), Sarah of the book of Tobit, and the martyr mother of 2 and 4 Maccabees; comparable models include the prayers of Daniel, his friends, and Tobit.

Judith prays at the time of the incense offering in the Jerusalem temple; the note anticipates her pilgrimage there following Holofernes' defeat. The prayer begins by invoking the God of her ancestor Simeon, omitted from her genealogy. Just as Simeon took revenge on the 'strangers who had . . . polluted [a virgin's] womb' (v. 2)—the reference is to the sacking of Shechem following the rape of Dinah (Gen 34)—so Judith seeks to protect Bethulia: the city's name evokes the Hebrew word bĕtûlâ, meaning virgin, even as it sounds like bêt-ʾēl ('house of God') and bêt-ʿāliyâ (house of ascents). Dinah's name goes unmentioned, and this omission highlights the connection to Bethulia even as it places increasing emphasis on Simeon. Finally, in a reversal of the episode of Dinah, who 'went out' (Gen 34:1) to visit the women of the land but instead was attacked by Shechem, the local prince, Judith will go out to the Gentile camp, where she will 'unman' the general who had planned her seduction. The mention of deception in v. 3 (the prayer utilizes forms of the term 'deceit' four times) hints at Judith's yet unnamed plan.

Her unabashed celebration of the rape (see 4:12) of the Shechemite women, the selling of their daughters into slavery, and the distribution of their property among the Israelites recollects the fear of the Bethulians. That such militaristic ideology appears in the context of theological egalitarianism

(Judith notes that God 'strikes slaves as well as princes', v. 3) is typical in ancient narrative.

Following the recitation of Simeon's victory, Judith prays that God now help her, not a warrior but a widow (v. 4), since God is the ally of the weak (v. 11). Then, typical in Hellenistic–Jewish prayers, she celebrates God's omnipotence, omniscience, and creative powers. Against these attributes, the boasts of the Assyrians are empty and insulting. Because, Judith says, the Assyrians plan to desecrate the temple, to knock off the horns of its altars with a sword, so God should strike them down. Like Esther, who asks for 'eloquent speech' (Add Esth 14:13), Judith asks for a beguiling tongue ('deceitful words', v. 13). Deceit will be her weapon, so that Holofernes will be killed 'by the hand of a woman' (v. 10; the 'hand' motif appears 9 times more: 2:12; 8:33; 9:2, 9; 12:4; 13:14, 15; 15:10; 16:5), as was Sisera by the deceitful Jael (Judg 4–5, see 9). To emphasize the insult, in the Greek Judith speaks not of a 'woman' but uses the generic 'female' (see also Judg 9:54 on Abimelech's fear of the shame of being killed by a woman).

Judith's Plan (10:1–17)

As Esther transforms from mourning to magnificence (Add Esth 15:1), so Judith removes her sackcloth, bathes (how she obtained water given the siege is unexplained), applies perfume, dons a tiara, and puts on the clothes she wore when she celebrated with her deceased husband. Among her accessories are chains, typically translated as 'anklets' (v. 4); Judith may be wearing a step-chain, designed to shorten her stride and make her appear more 'feminine' (Moore 1985; see Isa 3:16). The connection to Isaiah may also suggest that 'earrings' should be translated 'nose-ring' (Moore 1985). Thus she presents a picture of pampered helplessness. On the other hand, perhaps she should be seen as arming herself for battle. Bedecked with jewellery and dressed to kill, she intended to draw the attention of any man who saw her. Then, accompanied by her maid, who carried a skin of wine, jug of oil, and bag with roasted grain, fig cakes, and bread, she ventured to the city gate. Seeing her, Uzziah and the elders are struck by her beauty. Judith orders the gates open, and as she and her maid journey to the enemy camp, the leaders stare after her.

Caught by an Assyrian patrol, Judith is questioned about her nationality. Honestly she replies she is a Hebrew; by using that term rather than 'Israelite', perhaps Judith sought to evoke the time when the people were enslaved in Egypt. Dishonestly she adds that she is fleeing from the Assyrian onslaught and to Holofernes, to whom she will tell the way (v. 13; the term could refer either to the means or to the path) by which he can conquer the hill country. The soldiers, struck by her beauty, promise her protection and flounder in attempts to find the lucky one-hundred to escort her to the general (v. 17).

Judith's Promises to Holofernes (10:18–11:23)

Judith's arrival stirs the enemy camp; the soldiers, judging by her, speculate that they had best destroy all the Israelite men; with 'women like this among them . . . they will be able to beguile the whole world!' (10:19). Holofernes rises from his ornate bed to greet Judith. He and his attendants are also struck by her beauty. After accepting her obeisance, Holo-fernes exhorts her to courage (11:1), for he has never hurt anyone who chooses to follow Nebuchadnezzar. The comment is disingenuous, given his earlier massacres (2:10; 3:7–8). He apparently assumed, mistakenly, that she would be afraid of him. As for the siege, he asserts that the Israelites, refusing such loyalty, have brought about their own situation.

Judith's response is a masterpiece of *double entendre*. She states she will speak nothing false to '[her] lord'; she claims that if he follows her advice, 'my lord will not fail to achieve his purposes' (11:6). She then moves to mocking, in stating that because of Holofernes, not only people, but also beasts, cattle, and birds, serve Nebuchadnezzar (11:7). Mentioning Achior in the one verse of this dialogue in which she does not in some degree dissemble, Judith acknowledges the truth of his statements; however, she lies in stating that the people have resolved to sin by eating the first fruits and tithes consecrated to the priests, which the people are forbidden even to touch; they are but waiting for permission from the Jerusalem council (11:12–13). No law forbids such touching, but Holofernes would not know in any case.

Finally, Judith states that God sent her to accomplish with Holofernes 'things that will astonish the whole world' (11:16). Claiming loyalty to the God of heaven who has given her foreknowledge, she tells Holofernes that she will withdraw to the valley every night to pray, and that God will tell her when the Israelites have transgressed. At that time, she will guide Holofernes to victory. The general along with his attendants is so delighted by Judith's words, and beauty, that he promises her, upon the completion of her prediction, that her God will be his God (see Ruth 1:16), she shall dwell in Nebuchadnez-zar's palace (hardly something Judith desires), and her fame shall encompass the world.

Judith in the Assyrian Camp (12:1–9)

Holofernes invites Judith to dine on his 'delicacies' (v. 1, a term not found elsewhere in the LXX, and perhaps suggestive of self-indulgence (Moore 1985)), but she insists on eating her simple meal of kosher food. The general is concerned for her well-being, since there are no other Jews in his camp who might replenish her supply, but Judith, echoing her prayer (9:10), assures him that the Lord will accomplish by her 'hand' what is planned before her supplies are exhausted. Judith's comments reinforce Holofernes' trust: surely someone so faithful to diet would not lie regarding the Bethulians' transgressions.

Escorted by Holofernes' attendants to her tent, Judith begins the first of a three-day pattern. She sleeps until midnight and at the morning watch, leaves for the valley of Bethulia to bathe herself from the uncleanness of the Gentile camp and pray; ritually pure, and giving the Assyrians no reason to distrust her, she returns to her tent (v. 8).

Judith Serves her Lord (12:10–13:10)

The fourth night, Holofernes holds a drinking party (see 6:21). He asks Bagoas, the eunuch in charge of his personal affairs, to persuade the 'Hebrew woman' (12:11) to join the party; were she not to do so, he and his associates will be disgraced. Were Judith able to refuse his advances (the term refers to sexual intercourse; see Sus 54), she would make him a laughing-stock.

Bagoas' request is itself of double meaning. Addressing Judith as *paidiskē* (12:13), he could be complimenting her as 'maiden' or insulting her as 'serving girl' or even 'prostitute'. With his invitation that she become as the women who serve Nebuchadnezzar in the palace (11:4) the sexual undertone continues. Unlike Vashti's response to the eunuchs who invite her to the king's banquet (Esth 1), Judith affirms that she will do whatever is pleasing in the eyes of '[her] Lord' and that will be something to boast of until the day of her death.

Seeing Judith reclining on lambskins, Holofernes' appetite becomes uncontrolled: having planned to have intercourse with her from the moment he saw her, he can almost taste conquest. He encourages her to enjoy herself (12:17) and to 'be with us' (see Gen 39:10; Tob 3:8; Sus 20–1); the sexual implications become increasingly overt. Judith feeds his fantasy by accepting his invitation to drink, for 'today is the greatest day of my whole life' (12:18). So delighted is Holofernes that he drinks more than he had ever before consumed. As it is growing late, his retinue leaves, and Bagoas closes the tent from the outside. Dead drunk, Holofernes lies sprawled on his bed. Judith, alone with him (for the full ten verses of 13:1–10), offers one final prayer for strength (she always prays before her major undertakings), yanks the general's sword from the bedpost, grabs his hair, and with two strokes beheads him. This new Jael, who struck the temple of Sisera after giving him something to drink and lulling him into a false sense of safety (Judg 5:26), or new David, who felled Goliath and then decapitated him (1 Sam 17:51), Judith has rescued her people by striking the head of the enemy force. Holofernes' death is, as Judith had prayed, by the hand of a female.

The decapitation has been interpreted both as a perverse sacrifice and as a scene of castration. Regarding the former, Judith does appear to function in a priestly manner: she wears special clothes, bathes for ritual purity, is sexually abstinent, painlessly slits the throat of the victim, receives the aid of a helper in disposing of the victim's parts, and retains a portion for communal (visual) consumption (see 16:18–20). Regarding the latter, the connection of the story of Judith to Gen 34 already provides a reference to genital wounding, and modern commentators read the symbolic value of Judith's action by connecting decapitation to castration (Dundes 1974; Levine 1992).

Quickly leaving the tent, Judith hands Holofernes' head to her waiting servant, who puts it in the food sack. Then the women leave, as they had done the previous nights, 'to pray'. The female donkey, laden excessively with the spoils from Holofernes' tent, will later prove just as doughty as her mistress (Craven 1983).

Return to Bethulia (13:11–20)

Returning to Bethulia, Judith calls the sentries to open the gate, for 'God is with us' (13:11). The entire town, surprised that she has returned and thus, apparently, not as secure in their faith as she, welcomes the woman. Then Judith publicly praises God, and in testimony to divine protection displays Holofernes' head and the canopy from his bed. Celebrating her action, she repeats her prayer now as thanksgiving, 'The Lord has struck him down by the hand of a women' (v. 15).

Preserving her reputation, she also avers that nothing sinful, defiling, or disgraceful occurred. The people, in response, bless God.

Uzziah then praises Judith as most blessed of all women (see Judg 5:24 and Lk 1:48); his prayer is that her story redound to everlasting honour, for she risked her life to avert disaster. His calling her 'daughter' (v. 18) may be a continuation of his paternalism; it may also indicate her young age. Saying 'Amen', the people assent.

Judith's Military Instructions (14:1–10)

Judith, taking control of military strategy, instructs Bethulia's leaders to hang Holofernes' head from the battlements of the town wall; the heads of Goliath (1 Sam 17:54), Saul (1 Sam 31:9–10); Ahab's family (2 Kings 10:7–8); Nicanor (1 Macc 7:47; 2 Macc 15:35); and John the Baptist (Mt 14:8) were similarly displayed. Then, at dawn, they are to prepare for battle but not descend to the plain. When the Assyrians see the attack forming, they will rush to Holofernes, only to find a decapitated corpse. While they panic, Israel will strike.

Summoned by Judith, Achior faints (lit. falls on his face; see 6:9) at the sight of the head. Revived, he prostrates himself before Judith, blesses her 'in every tent of Judah' (v. 7; see Judg 5:24), and asks her to relate her experiences in the Assyrian camp. When she finishes, the entire town cheers. Achior, seeing what the God of Israel had accomplished, submits to circumcision; his descendants, although Ammonites (see Deut 23:3), remain among Israel 'to this day' (v. 10; see Josh 6:25). Achior is reminiscent of Ruth who, as a Moabite, should also have been prevented from joining Israel. Both leave their people, their gods, and their land, and both affiliate not only with the covenant community but also through a female, maternal representative. Achior has also been seen as an expression of the ideology of proselytism and a type of Abraham (Roitman 1992), as well as a type of Barak (White 1992).

Assyrian Defeat (14:11–15:7)

The Israelites, bolstered by Judith's deed, set out to the mountain passes; the Assyrian generals, so convinced of their opponents' weakness that they view the incursion as suicidal (14:13), go to wake Holofernes. Bagoas, expecting to find Holofernes sleeping next to Judith, begins the panic: seeing the headless corpse and then finding Judith's tent empty, he rushes out crying that the Hebrew woman has shamed the house of Nebuchadnezzar. Headless, the Assyrian soldiers flee to the hills; there the waiting Israelites kill many and pursue the rest to the Damascus borders. Other Israelites, those who had not directly engaged the Assyrian army (the women? the weak?) loot the camp; there being so much booty, every village prospers.

Israel Celebrates Victory (15:8–14)

Joakim the high priest, with the council, arrives to bless Judith, the 'great boast of Israel' who by her own hand (v. 9) rescued Israel. Having looted the Assyrian camp, the people present Judith with Holofernes' tent, silver dinnerware, and equipment. Judith loads the spoils on carts and hitches them to her mules. As the women of Israel come to praise her and perform a dance in her honour (see 3 Macc 6:32, 35; 7:16), she distributes branches (*thyrsus*; see 2 Macc 10:7) to them. These branches were also carried by the Bacchantes, the worshippers of Dionysus. The book of Judith may even be read as a parody of the worship of the wine god: here the decapitated head is of Holofernes, not Pentheus, yet gender roles are still muddled and drunkenness leads to downfall.

Then all the women crown themselves with olive leaves and, with Judith at their head, dance; the men, armed and with garlands, follow her to Jerusalem.

Judith's Hymn (16:1–18)

Judith's hymn, sung also by all the people, is an amalgam of Hebrew and Greek ideas. For the Hebrew tradition, women's celebration of victory in song is a common motif (Ex 15:20–1; Craven (1983) proposes that Jdt 16 parallels Miriam's Song at the Sea; Judg 11:34; 1 Sam 18:6–7). Like the Song of Deborah (Judg 5), Judith's hymn invokes the God who crushes wars and delivers Israel, personalizes the enemy in terms of its threats, and celebrates the heroine's role. Reflecting its Hellenistic context even as it highlights Israel's supremacy, the hymn compares the captivating and successful Judith with the inability of the Titans as well as the Medes and the Persians to defeat Holofernes.

Judith then sings a 'new song' to the invincible God, who can move mountains and melt rocks, whom no one can resist. Emphasizing her maternal role, she speaks of the threats to *her* infants, children, young men and women (v. 4). Highlighting again the Hellenistic setting, she exalts herself even over the Titans (v. 6). Celebrating the Israelites' miraculous victory, she contrasts the Assyrian might with their defeat by 'sons of slave girls' (or young women, v. 12). She ends with the wisdom motif that fear of the Lord is more precious than sacrifice and the apocalyptic image of the eternal vengeance taken by God against those who rise against Israel.

The image of consigning flesh to fire and worms (see Sir 7:17; 2 Macc 9:9 on the fate of Antiochus Epiphanes; Mk 9:48) may suggest a belief in life after death and so be another indication of a relatively late date.

Celebration at the Temple (16:18–20)

In Jerusalem, the parade of people worship; once purified, they sacrifice their burnt offerings, votive offerings, and gifts. While entry into the temple would require worshippers to be in a state of ritual purity, the explicit mention of this ritual highlights two motifs of the book: the concern for Jewish piety and the defeat of the Gentile forces. Judith dedicates Holo-

fernes' property: the bed canopy becomes a votive offering, much like Goliath's sword (1 Sam 21:9) and Saul's armour (31:10). For three months, the celebration in Jerusalem continues.

Epilogue (16:21–5)

Returning to Bethulia but not to her rooftop, Judith's fame does not abate. Many men seek to wed her, but she remains celibate until her death at the age of 105. At this time, she frees her slave (thereby belying artistic renditions which typically depict the slave as much older than Judith) and distributes her property to her near relatives and to those of her husband. Judith is interred in the same burial cave as Manasseh. The people mourn for her seven days (see Sir 22:12), a Second-Temple innovation.

The last line recollects the stories of the Judges: no one threatens Israel again during her lifetime, or for a long time after her death.

REFERENCES

Bal, M. (1994), 'Head Hunting: "Judith on the Cutting Edge of Knowledge"', 63: 3–34.

Camponigro, M. S. (1992), 'Judith, Holding the Tale of Herodotus,' in VanderKam (1992: 47 59).

Craven, T. (1983), *Artistry and Faith in the Book of Judith*, SBLDS 70 (Chico, Calif.: Scholars Press).

Dundes, A. (1974), 'Comment on "Narrative Structures in the Book of Judith"', in W. Wuellner (ed.), *Protocol Series of the Colloquies of the Center for Hermeneutical Studies in Hellenistic and Modern Culture*, 11: 28–9.

Haag, E. (1963), *Studien zum Buche Judith: Seine theologische Bedeutung und literarische Eigenart*, Trierer Theologische Studien, 16 (Trier: Paulinus-Verlag).

Levine, A.-J. (1992), 'Sacrifice and Salvation: Otherness and Domestication in the Book of Judith', in VanderKam (1992: 17–30).

Moore, C. A. (1985), *Judith. A New Translation with Introduction and Commentary*, 40 (Garden City, NY: Doubleday).

Roitman, A. D. (1992), 'Achior in the Book of Judith: His Role and Significance', VanderKam (31–45).

VanderKam, J. (1992) (ed.), *'No One Spoke Ill of Her': Essays on Judith*, Early Judaism and its Literature, 2 (Atlanta: SBL).

Van Henten, J. W. (1995), 'Judith as Alternative Leader: A Rereading of Judith 7–13', in Athalya Brenner (ed.), *A Feminist Companion to Esther, Judith and Susanna* (Sheffield: Academic Press), 224–52.

White, S. (1992), 'In the Steps of Jael and Deborah: Judith as Heroine', in VanderKam (1992: 5–16).

Wills, L. (1995), *The Jewish Novel in the Ancient World* (Ithaca: Cornell University Press).

42. Esther (Greek)

ADELE REINHARTZ

INTRODUCTION

A. Background. Vivid testimony to the popularity of the story of Esther in the Hellenistic Jewish milieu is the presence of a lengthy Greek version in the Septuagint (LXX Esther). This is generally considered to be a free translation of a Hebrew text similar to, or perhaps even identical with, the later Masoretic version (MT Esther) included among the Writings of the Tanak. Greek Esther shares with its Hebrew counterpart the engaging characters of Vashti, Ahasuerus, Mordecai, Esther, and Haman, its basic story-line concerning Haman's anti-Jewish plot and the means by which it is thwarted, as well as many of the details of setting, dialogue, and description. Yet the presence of six major sections (the Additions) not attested in the MT (or presumably, its Heb. *Vorlage*), the many smaller additions and omissions, and, most strikingly, the presence of over fifty references to God, transform LXX Esther into a different story. This story contrasts with MT Esther not only in portraying the inner spiritual struggles of its main characters but also in attributing the outcome of the plot to the divine hand.

B. Textual History. 1. In addition to LXX Esther, the story of Esther exists in another Greek version, often referred to as the Alpha Text (ΛT). The AT is similar though not identical to LXX Esther in the content and wording of the six Additions, but differs substantially from it in those sections that are paralleled in MT Esther. AT Esther is shorter than LXX Esther, due in part to the absence of many personal names, numbers, dates, and repetitive elements. Differences in content also abound. For example, AT omits the theme of the unalterability of Persian law, as well as the aetiology of the Purim festival and the lengthy instructions for Purim observance (cf. AT Esth 8:30, 47). Equally striking is its ending. In contrast to the LXX, in which Addition F concludes the book with a colophon, and the MT, which ends with a testimonial to the greatness and popularity of Mordecai, AT's version of F ends with Mordecai's interpretation of his initial dream (cf. A).

2. How does one account for the similarities and differences among the Hebrew and Greek versions of Esther? The body of LXX Esther is similar to MT Esther (and therefore presumably to the Heb. version available to the Gk. translator) in the content and structure of its story. These similarities support much of LXX Esther being based on a Hebrew original similar to the MT. Significant differences in wording, however, suggest that LXX Esther was a rather free translation of the Hebrew original. Some of the differences reflect stylistic or theological changes, as in 2:20, in which Mordecai's words to the newly chosen queen include not only the instruction to keep her Jewish identity a secret but also to maintain the fear of God and keep God's laws. A number of substantive differences also exist. For example, MT Esth 2:19 refers to the king's 'gate'. Assuming that the translator found 'gate' in his Hebrew version, the Greek should have read *pulē*. The fact that *aulē* (court) appears instead, however, suggests copyist error

(Moore 1977: 175). A similar conclusion emerges from discrepancies within AT and Greek Esther concerning the date of the anti-Jewish pogrom: the thirteenth of Adar, reflecting the Hebrew original (3:12; 8:12; 9:1; E 16:20), or the fourteenth (B 13:6; Moore 1977: 192–3). To the free rendition of Hebrew Esther were added six sections, four of which appear to have been translated from a Hebrew source or sources independent of the Hebrew *Vorlage* of the MT (Additions A, C, D, F) and two of which were probably composed in Greek (Additions B, E).

3. More complex is the relationship between the AT and LXX. Paton (1908: 38) considered AT to be a recension of some form of the LXX, arguing that there were too many parallels between them to view the latter as an independent translation of the Hebrew. Bickerman (1950) suggested that the AT was a recension of an abbreviated Greek Esther, as was Josephus' paraphrase, *Ant.* 11 §§183–96, which lacks the first and sixth of the Additions which are present in both AT and LXX. More recently Emanuel Tov (1982: 25) has contended that the AT is a translation or more accurately, perhaps, 'a midrash-type of rewriting of the biblical story' which corrects the LXX towards a Hebrew or Aramaic text which differed from the later MT. Fox (1992: 209–10) suggests a similarly complex theory. He posits the existence of a proto-AT, as the Greek translation of an original Hebrew text that differed from the Hebrew text used by the translator of LXX Esther. Proto-AT was then redacted by someone who had access to LXX Esther. Comparing proto-AT and LXX, this redactor drew on the latter to supplement the former. Hence the redactor did not set out to borrow the deutero-canonical Additions but rather moved sequentially through the two texts, transferring material from the LXX to fill the gaps perceived in proto-AT. Most scholars, however, hold to the view that AT is a separate Greek translation based upon a Hebrew or Aramaic text quite different from the MT (Clines 1984: xxv). The Additions in AT were borrowed directly from the LXX, as indicated by the strong verbal agreement between their respective forms of these sections. Hence the AT has become an important factor not only in the textual history of the Greek versions but also in the composition history of the Hebrew Esther (Fox 1991*b*; Clines 1984; Wills 1990; 1995).

C. The Additions: Introductory Issues. 1. The six major Additions are as follows:

- A. Mordecai's dream and the plot of the two eunuchs against the king.
- B. The text of the king's edict authorizing the destruction of Persian Jewry.
- C. The prayers of Mordecai and Esther.
- D. Esther's approach to the king.
- E. The edict reversing the decree of destruction.
- F. The interpretation of Mordecai's dream, followed by the colophon.

2. There is little doubt that the Additions are secondary to the body of the text, that is, not present in any Hebrew *Vorlage*. The Additions are not found in any of the standard versions of Esther, except those that are recognized as having been based on the LXX, such as Old Latin, Coptic, and Ethiopic as well as *Sefer Jossipon*, a tenth-century work in which Hebrew translations of Josephus' versions of the Additions are present (Moore 1977: 154). Origen (185?–254), in his *Epistle to Africanus*, 3, testifies that several Additions, namely the prayers of Esther and Mordecai (C) and the royal letters (B, E), did not appear in the Hebrew texts current in his own day. Because of their absence from the Hebrew, Jerome (340?–420) placed the Additions at the end of the canonical portion of his own Latin translation rather than in the locations in which they are found in LXX Esther. Finally, Additions A and F (Mordecai's dream and its interpretation) are not present in Josephus' paraphrase of Esther, though this is not evidence that they were not yet in existence at this time.

3. Four of the Additions (A, C, D, F) give clear internal evidence of having been translated from Hebrew (though no Heb. source is extant) while Additions B and E, the royal edicts, are Greek compositions (Moore 1977: 155; 1982: lxx). All six Additions, however, probably had a Jewish origin (Moore 1977: 160), betraying the concerns and perspectives of diaspora Jewry. Their presence in the LXX and the Vulgate led the Christian church to regard them as canonical, and they were sanctioned by the Council of Carthage in 397 CE and by several later councils, including Trent in 1546. Luther and later Protestants, however, considered the Additions to be apocryphal rather than canonical.

D. Date and Provenance. 1. The earliest possible date is that of the final form of the Hebrew version, probably the early Hellenistic period, though earlier versions may have gone back to the late Persian period. The latest possible date is c.93–4 CE, when Josephus used Additions B, C, D, and E in his paraphrase. LXX Esther, however, ends with a colophon, which, if authentic, provides the basis for a more precise dating. The colophon attributes the translation to one Lysimachus son of Ptolemy, in Jerusalem, and claims that it was brought to Egypt by a priest and Levite named Dositheus in the fourth year of the reign of Ptolemy and Cleopatra. Questions have been raised about the authenticity of the colophon, based on its content. How can Dositheus be both priest and Levite? Why would the translation have been done in Jerusalem and for whom (Enslin 1972: 19)? Many scholars, however, accept the colophon as authentic. Moore (ibid. 161) for example, argues that the body of the story as well as all the Additions were translated by Lysimachus except B and E, whose original language is Greek. Because Greek was present in Graeco-Roman Palestine, notes Bickerman (1944: 357), LXX Esther is a remarkable and unusual example of Palestinian Greek.

2. If the colophon is authentic, then identifying the reigning Ptolemy provides a date for the Greek translation as a whole. Several Ptolemies had a reign of at least four years and wives named Cleopatra, including Ptolemy XII (77 BCE), favoured by Bickerman (1944), Ptolemy XIV (around 48 BCE), and Ptolemy VIII Soter II, who lived in around 114 BCE, favoured by Moore (1977: 250). In general terms, therefore,

LXX Esther may be dated to the late second or early first century BCE.

3. Provenance is difficult to determine, and is directly related to the assessment of the text's purpose. Moore (ibid. 167) suggests that the royal edicts, Additions B and E, may have originated in some sophisticated non-Palestinian centre such as Alexandria, whereas the others may have originated in Palestine, since their theological content is compatible with that of other Palestinian texts of this period such as Daniel, Judith, and some of the Qumran material. Linda Day (1995: 231–2) suggests that the AT, which does not emphasize the Purim festival, may be the product of a Hellenized Jewish community in a diaspora setting, facing the challenge of living Jewishly among a Gentile (i.e. non-Jewish, polytheistic) majority. In contrast, LXX Esther, which retains the MT's emphasis on the aetiology and celebration of Purim, may have been shaped by a Jewish community in Palestine itself or, alternatively, a traditionally observant diaspora Jewish community experiencing increased tension or discrimination at the hands of non-Jews. Such tension would account for the anti-Gentile sentiments expressed in Additions A, C, and F. If so, the story's intent may have been to underscore the necessity of, and dangers inherent in, working with the Gentile power structure while maintaining a primary allegiance to the Jewish people (Wills 1995: 120).

E. Purpose and Genre of LXX Esther. 1. Why did the translator include the six Additions and make the numerous other changes that distinguish LXX Esther from its Hebrew prototype? Most answers to this question reflect upon LXX Esther's inclusion of over fifty references to God, in contrast to MT Esther in which direct divine references are absent. Divine titles and other references to God are found primarily in the Additions. Addition C, which conveys the prayers of Esther and Mordecai, mentions God in virtually every verse, as does Addition F, the interpretation of Mordecai's dream. But the LXX translator has added a number of references to God in the canonical material as well. For example, 2:20, which describes Esther's obedience to Mordecai in her decision not to divulge her ethnic identity, also indicates that she is to fear God and keep his laws even as she commences a new life in the harem of a Gentile king. In 4:8 Mordecai calls upon Esther not only to go to the king but also to call upon the Lord in her effort to avert the evil decree instigated by Haman. Artaxerxes' insomnia is attributed to the Lord in 6:1, while the premonition of Haman's wife concerning Haman's downfall is ascribed to the fact that the living God is with Mordecai (6:13). The Greek word used most frequently in reference to the divine is *theos* (God), with *kyrios* (Lord) as the next most frequent term. Other descriptive terms are 'king' (*basileus*, C 13:9, 15; 14:3, 12), and 'saviour' (*sōtēr*, 15:2). Phrases, such as 'the living God, most high and mighty' (E 16:16), 'the God of Abraham' (C 13:15; 14:18) and 'the all-seeing God' (D 15:2; 16:4) are also employed.

2. The effect of these references, both in their variety and quantity, is to insert God very securely into the story as the one through whom the salvation from danger occurred. God's prominence in the plot is in contrast to the MT's emphasis on the human agents, Mordecai and Esther (Fox 1991a: 273). Moore comments, however, that LXX Esther's religious concerns are reflected not only in the addition of references to God but also in the emphasis on particular themes, such as God's providential care of Israel (A, F), God's miraculous intervention in history (D 15:8), the efficacy of prayer and fasting (C), and the importance of cult and temple (C 14:9).

3. Clines, however, argues that the function of the Additions is not wholly or even primarily to introduce the explicit language of divine causation into a deficient Hebrew original, but to recreate the book in the mould of post-exilic Jewish history, as exemplified by the books of Ezra, Nehemiah, and Daniel. Just as God stirs up the spirit of Cyrus in Ezra 1:1 and of returnees in 1:5, so does he change the spirit of the king to gentleness in LXX Esther D 15:8 and keep him from sleeping in 6:1. In Dan 2, as in Additions A and F, the meaning of history is conveyed through dreams and their interpretations, while Ezra 9, Neh 1, and Dan 9 contain exemplary prayers of supplication similar to the prayers of Mordecai and Esther in Addition C (Clines 1984: 169–70).

4. In addition to religious motivations and concerns, the Greek translation may have been intended to increase the story's dramatic appeal (Moore 1977: 153). The aura of authenticity is strengthened by Additions B and E which in florid Greek purport to be the texts of royal edicts authorizing (B) and repealing (E) the mass destruction of Persian Jewry. Moore (ibid. 220–2) suggests that Esther's prayer (C) and the detailed description of her emotions and behaviour upon approaching the king (D) combine to make Esther a more realistic character and to suggest a similarity to Judith, a link frequently made by the Church Fathers as well as by contemporary scholars (Day 1995: 222–5). Certainly LXX Esther differs from its Hebrew *Vorlage* in describing the inner thoughts and feelings of its principal characters.

5. Such observations have led some scholars to conclude that LXX Esther is a Hellenistic Jewish novel, influenced by the Graeco-Roman novel genre (Wills 1990; 1995). This suggestion does not rule out a didactic purpose or a historical kernel, but does emphasize the imaginative and entertaining aspects of the book, including its fanciful setting, adventurous tone, and detailed portrayal of its central figures (Wills 1995: 1). Day's (1995: 215–22) study, which focuses on the characterization of Esther in MT, LXX, and AT, argues that there is not enough direct correspondence between these Esthers and the heroines of Greek novels to conclude that LXX and AT were intended as explicit reworkings of their Hebrew prototypes towards the Greek novel genre.

F. Procedure in the Commentary. 1. This commentary will focus on LXX Esther, which is the basis of the NRSV translation. The attempt will be made to see it in its own terms, as a text which is coherent in and of itself. Some comparative comments will be made throughout, however, both with respect to the AT and, more frequently, with respect to the MT. Relatively greater attention will be paid to the Additions, but the material which parallels the MT will also receive comment. In keeping with the judgement that LXX Esther is a novel, the primary emphases in the commentary will be upon the development of plot and character. The Additions will be referred to by letter (Additions A to F), but the chapter and verse designations of the NRSV, which are based on Jerome's

placement of the Additions at the end of his translation, are also included.

G. Outline

Addition A: Mordecai's Dream (11:2–12); The Eunuchs' Plan (12:1–6)
    Setting the Stage (1:1–3:13)
Addition B: The King's Edict against the Jews (13:1–7)
    The Plot is Revealed (3:14–4:17)
Addition C: The Prayers of Mordecai and Esther: (13:8–14:19)
Addition D: Esther's Approach to the King: (15:1–16)
    The Villain is Unmasked (5:3–8:12)
Addition E: The Official Repeal of the First Edict: (16:1–24)
    Events of Adar (8:13–10:3)
Addition F: Interpretation of Mordecai's Dream (10:4–13); Colophon (11:1)

COMMENTARY

Addition A (11:2–12; 12:1–6)

(11:2–12) Mordecai's Dream LXX Esther begins with an introduction to Mordecai and a description of his dream. Mordecai is described in terms of his lineage (son of Shimei, son of Kish, of the tribe of Benjamin), ethnic identity (a Jew), home (Susa), status (a great man), occupation (serving in the court of the king), and, perhaps most important, his personal history. This history, repeated in 2:6, links him strongly with the national history of Israel: he was a captive of King Nebuchadnezzar after the Babylonian conquest of Judea in 597–6 BCE. It also, however, poses a chronological difficulty. Even if Mordecai were only a year old at the time of the Conquest, he would still have been about 115 years old in the third year of Xerxes (1:3) and about 119 years old at Esther's ascension to the throne, when Esther herself would have been approximately 60 years old (1:6). The problem may be resolved in several ways. Perhaps the one exiled was not Mordecai but Kish, his great-grandfather (cf. NRSV translation of MT Esth 2:6). Alternatively, the text may have disregarded historical accuracy in order to connect this story to the larger biblical framework of exile and redemption. Similar 'errors' occur in other Jewish novels from this period, as in Jdt 1:1, in which Nebuchadnezzar is described as the ruler of Assyria based in Nineveh.

This lengthy and detailed introduction to Mordecai serves two purposes. First, it impresses upon the reader his importance, both as a character in the story and as a player in the king's court. Here is a Jew who spends much time in contact with Gentile royalty and officialdom. Second, it indicates that he had previously experienced suffering at the hands of Gentile kings, having been exiled from the land of Israel to Babylonia. The story therefore immediately raises the question of Gentile–Jewish relations and evokes the historical tensions in that relationship.

It is this information, then, that we carry into our reading of Mordecai's dream. In images similar to the prophecies against the Gentiles in Joel 3:2, Zeph 1:15, and Zech 14:2 (Moore 1977: 180), this dream describes a battle between two dragons, and the persecution of 'the righteous nation' at the hands of 'the nations'. When the righteous nation calls for help, however, God intervenes. A great river springs forth, there is light, sun, and the exaltation of the lowly who devour those held in honour. Mordecai realizes that this dream is a foretelling of God's plan, and he continues to ponder it after he awakes.

The dream provides an interpretative framework for the book which it introduces, encouraging us to see it as an apocalyptic battle in which the Gentiles' attempt to destroy the Jews will be thwarted by God, resulting in salvation and the reversal of the status quo in which the Jewish nation is in a subordinate position to others. The broad context of danger and salvation is provided not only by the reference to the Babylonian Exile, but also by the date of Mordecai's dream, namely, the first of Nisan. The main event of this month in the Jewish calendar is the festival of Passover, which celebrates God's incursion into history to redeem the Israelites from slavery in Egypt. The Exodus is traditionally seen both as the finest example of God's providential care for Israel and as the prototype of future salvation. The allusion to the Exodus is strengthened by the reference to Israel's outcry (11:10), which calls God into action in Mordecai's dream as it does in Ex 3:7 (cf. also Jdt 4:9). Finally, the dream, which is similar to other late biblical dreams such as Dan 2:19, readjusts the focus of the story from that of conflict between Haman and Mordecai, or between Haman and the Jews, or between the Jews and their enemies, to a wider focus, namely, a cosmic conflict between Israel, which is God's righteous nation, and the rest of humankind (Clines 1984: 171–2).

(12:1–6) The Eunuchs' Plan The transition to the second episode is abrupt. Mordecai overhears two of Artaxerxes' eunuchs plotting to lay hands on the king; they confirm their plan to him, and he informs the king, who cross-examines the eunuchs, extracts a confession, and then executes them. Mordecai is rewarded by the king and given a position in the royal court. The entire event is then portrayed as the cause of Haman's grudge against Mordecai. The episode therefore introduces Haman as Mordecai's adversary and provides a rationale for his hatred as well as for Mordecai's position as a courtier, essential for the rest of the story.

In doing so, however, the episode also differs from MT Esther as well as from the LXX story itself as it develops in subsequent chapters. Puzzling is the designation of Haman as *bougaios* (Bougean), a term repeated in 3:1 but completely distinct from the MT identification of Haman as an Agagite. Also unclear is the precise nature of Mordecai's position in the royal court. Is he a courtier before the story begins, as the first episode (11:3) might imply, or does he become so only in this episode (12:5)? Furthermore, the incident contradicts 3:3–6, which attributes Haman's hatred to Mordecai's refusal to bow down. Finally, what is the connection between this episode and the dream? Though the AT 1:11 claims that the eunuchs' plot makes plain to Mordecai the significance of his dream, its full meaning will become clear only as the book proceeds, to be confirmed in Addition F with which the narrative concludes. Nevertheless, the AT 1:18 version of this episode may foreshadow the plot structure of the story as a whole, by referring to the hatred of Haman and his desire to take revenge on Mordecai and his people (cf. 12:6). Similarly, the otherwise curious comment in AT 11:17 that the king 'gave'

(*edōken*) Haman to Mordecai as part of his reward for revealing the plot may intimate Mordecai's later replacement of Haman as the king's right-hand man (AT 8:52; cf. NRSV 8:15; 10:3).

Setting the Stage (1:1–3:13) After these prefatory incidents, LXX Esther begins with the story proper, paralleling the opening episodes of MT Esther. The setting is Susa, the capital of the Persian empire, in the third year of Artaxerxes' reign, that is, one year after the dream recounted in Addition A. The king's lengthy and decadent drinking party is described in lavish detail (1:1–8), with brief mention of the drinking party that Queen Vashti holds in the king's palace for her friends (1:9). Vashti's refusal to answer the king's call to display her beauty before his guests leads in this version, as in the MT, to a lengthy and farcical flurry concerning the potential threat that her insolence poses to family harmony and male authority throughout the kingdom (1:16–22). Only by banishing Vashti and issuing a solemn declaration ordering women to obey their husbands can the king alleviate this threat.

But whereas the Ahasuerus of the MT later remembered, and perhaps regretted, Vashti's fate (2:1; for the rabbis' views on the king's remorse see *Esther Rab.* 5:2), the Artaxerxes of the LXX forgets about her, and, as in MT, proceeds to choose her successor by means of a contest among the eligible young women in the kingdom (2:2–5). Mordecai is reintroduced by his lineage and personal history as a captive of Nebuchadnezzar, but the narrative focus shifts quickly to Esther, Mordecai's beautiful niece and foster-child. Esther immediately begins the elaborate and lengthy preparations which will result in her selection as the new queen. Throughout this process Esther remains silent about her Jewish identity, as instructed by Mordecai (2:10). Her selection as queen is celebrated by the remission of taxes, and predictably, by a lengthy banquet reminiscent of the feast which had led to the banishment of Esther's predecessor.

Three discrepancies between MT and LXX Esther may be mentioned briefly. According to Moore (1977: 186), the translator failed to see the three phrases in MT 2:1 ('he remembered Vashti', 'what she had done', and 'what had been decreed against her') as parallel to one another, and instead thought the latter two to be explanations of the first, concluding therefore that the king remembered Vashti herself no longer. A second difficulty occurs in 2:7. According to the MT, Mordecai took Esther to be his daughter, a more reasonable statement in light of the narrative context than the LXX's assertion that he took her as a wife. In this case too Moore (ibid.) posits the LXX translator's misreading of the Hebrew consonants (*bt*), which are the same for 'daughter' as for 'house'. A third discrepancy, concerning the length and timing of each candidate's 'audience' (or audition) with the king, does not permit a similar solution. Whereas both the MT and the AT describe the young woman as spending the night with the king, that is, from the evening (MT: *'ereb*; AT: *hespera*) of one day to the morning (MT: *bōqer*; AT: *prōi*) of the next, the LXX uses less specific temporal designations that may imply that she spent from the afternoon (*deilē*) of one day to some unspecified time the following day (*hēmera*) (2:14). From this language Day (1995: 42–3) concludes that the choice of queen was made on more than sexual ability, since the longer time together would have included meals, conversation, evening's entertainment, possibly a palace tour in addition to a sexual encounter at night. This suggestion seems highly speculative, however, given the indeterminate meaning of the Greek terms and the questionable assumption that the king's sexual activity was limited to the nocturnal hours.

Whether or not other activities took place, it is clear from the processes of preparation and selection that the main criteria for the king's choice were beauty and sexual satisfaction. Hence Esther's success emphasizes not only her beauty but also the fact that she had sexual relations with a Gentile king. Both of these points will be addressed later on in the story (Addition C).

This section also introduces a narrative thread concerning the relationship between Mordecai and Esther. From the beginning of Addition A, it is clear that Mordecai, as Esther's elder and a man, dominates this relationship, a position that is reinforced by his role as her guardian, her obedience to his command not to reveal her people or her country (2:10), and his monitoring of her welfare in the courtyard of the harem (2:11). Her ascension to the throne, however, is a potential threat to Mordecai's dominant position in their relationship. The threat is defused, for the moment, by the narrator who goes beyond the MT in emphasizing that Esther continued to obey Mordecai's word not only in this matter but in all matters pertaining to faith and lifestyle: she was to fear God and keep his laws, 'just as she had done when she was with him' (2:20). Though her wordly status may now surpass Mordecai's, the essential structure of their relationship remains unchanged. At the same time, however, her royal role, along with his own still-vague status as a courtier, provides occasion and justification for Mordecai's continued presence in the king's courtyard.

Mordecai's presence in the royal precincts sets the stage for his discovery of the plot by two of Artaxerxes' eunuchs to kill their master, a fact which Mordecai divulges to Esther who in turn informs the king. The king investigates and hangs the two, and writes a memorandum praising Mordecai, to be put in the royal library. This episode, which parallels closely MT Esther 2:19–23, points to the secondary nature of the similar plot recounted in the second part of Addition A. In this section, however, as in the MT, the intrigue is conveyed to the king by Esther and not by Mordecai directly as in Addition A. This point may be further indication of the adjustment in their relationship wrought by Esther's new role. The reward for Mordecai is, as yet, no more than appreciative recognition.

At this point Haman is again introduced, this time as the newly appointed chief Friend (MT: minister) of the king. His plot against the Jews has its roots in the enmity between Mordecai and Haman. Although this enmity had been attributed in Addition A to Mordecai's action *vis-à-vis* the two eunuchs, in 3:2–6 it is portrayed as a consequence of Mordecai's refusal to do obeisance to Haman once the latter has been elevated to chief Friend of the king (3:1). Because Mordecai's refusal is apparently related to the fact that he is a Jew (3:4), Haman's (rather exaggerated) response is to plot to destroy all the Jews under Artaxerxes' rule. The fourteenth day of Adar is chosen by lots as the date for the pogrom, and the king is persuaded that the destruction of these people, who observe different laws and 'do not keep the laws of the king', would be

to his benefit. Of even greater benefit, perhaps, are the ten thousand talents of silver which Haman offers to the king's treasury. Although the king's comment: 'Keep the money' might be taken to imply altruism, it is not in fact a refusal of the money but rather has the force of 'if you really want to spend your money that way, be my guest' (Moore 1977: 189). The king takes the bait and gives his signet ring to Haman, authorizing him to do whatever he wished with 'that nation' (3:10–11).

Addition B (13:1–7): The King's Edict against the Jews

Addition B purports to be the letter sent throughout the kingdom to put Haman's plan into place. Though broadcast in the king's name, the context, particularly 3:12, makes it clear that the letter has been written by the king's secretaries in accordance with Haman's instructions. The letter features three main themes: first, the ostensible desire of the king to restore peace and tranquility to the land (v. 2), second, the aggrandizement of Haman, the king's second in command who through his superior judgement, goodwill, and fidelity has determined the course of action to assure this result (v. 3), and finally, the vilification of the Jews, that alien and disobedient people wilfully preventing the kingdom from attaining stability (vv. 4–5).

Florid and bombastic in style, Addition B has been compared to various other purported edicts recorded in biblical and apocryphal works. Clines (1984: 173) sees B's closest parallel in the letter to King Artaxerxes written by the Samaritans against the inhabitants of Judah and Jerusalem in Ezra 4:11–16. Moore (1977: 199) points out similarities between B and Ezra 4:17–22, the reply of Artaxerxes to the Samaritans (cf. also Ezra 1:2–4; 6:3–12; 7:11–38). He argues, however, that B is closest to, and may have been modelled after, Ptolemy Philopator's letter in 3 Macc 12–29, though LXX Esther as a whole predates 3 Maccabees. Whether or not B drew directly from any of these sources, its effect is to deepen the impression of historicity and strengthen the royal Persian setting of the story (ibid. 159).

The tone, style, and content emphasize Haman's hand in the matter. To a diaspora Jewish reader, however, the accusations against the Jews may have sounded quite familiar, echoing views expressed by various Graeco-Roman writers (e.g. Diodorus; cf. Stern 1974: 180–4). The edict permits the (Graeco-Roman Jewish) audience to compare their experience with that of the Jews in Esther's story, and therefore implicitly encourages a belief that divine deliverance will come to them as it does to the Jews of Artaxerxes' Persia by the end of the story.

The Plot is Revealed (3:14–4:17) The posting of the document throws Mordecai and the Jews of Susa into mourning. Mordecai is not permitted to enter the court in mourning garb, and refuses Esther's offer of other clothing. Under these conditions, the two protagonists must formulate and communicate a plan of action through the good offices of Esther's eunuch Hachratheus. In MT Esther, Mordecai's initial message to Esther is not conveyed in direct speech but is summarized briefly by the narrator who focuses on the courtier's charge that Esther entreat the king on behalf of her people. In LXX Esther, however, the words of Mordecai are given.

While the substance is the same as the summary in MT, in the LXX Mordecai takes this opportunity to remind Esther of 'the days when you were an ordinary person, being brought up under my care', an admonition intended to give greater force to his command to 'Call upon the Lord; then speak to the king on our behalf, and save us from death' (4:8). This speech serves both to maintain the 'proper' hierarchy of relationship between Mordecai and Esther and to emphasize that an appeal to God through prayer is essential if tragedy is to be averted.

The exchanges that follow are similar to those in the MT. Esther expresses her fears of entering the king's presence unbidden, fears that are countered by Mordecai's warning that she herself will not escape; if she does not co-operate, he threatens, help will come to the Jews 'from another [no doubt divine] quarter', but she will perish. Furthermore, Mordecai notes, Esther's ascension to royalty may have been intended for this express purpose. Esther agrees to go, asking only that the Jews of Susa gather and fast for three days and nights, as will Esther and her maids.

Addition C: The Prayers of Mordecai (13:8–18) and Esther (14:1–19)

These prayers were presumably uttered during the three days of fasting stipulated by Esther. Mordecai's prayer, in 13:8–18, praises God as Lord and Creator of the universe and saviour of Israel, and clarifies—perhaps more for the reader's sake than for God's—that his refusal to bow down to Haman was not due to insolence or desire for personal aggrandizement but to a conviction that humans are not to be honoured above God. Mordecai begs God to save Israel, and invokes the memory of the Exodus as the time-honoured paradigm of salvation. After the prayer the narrator notes that all Israel cried out mightily, 'for their death was before their eyes'. This final remark, and indeed the prayer as a whole, are reminiscent of Mordecai's dream in Addition A. The fact that the outcry of 'the righteous nation' inspired God's intervention in the prophetic dream assures the readers that Israel's outcry in Artaxerxes' Persia will also be followed by divine salvation.

These themes are repeated, though in a different context and at greater length, in Esther's prayer (14:1–19). Before praying, Esther changes her royal apparel for 'the garments of distress and mourning', anoints herself with ashes and dung instead of her usual perfumes, and thoroughly debases her physical body (v. 2). More than a sign of mourning, the change in clothing is consistent with her profound feelings of fear and despair as well as with her identity as a daughter of Israel. In contrast to Mordecai's prayer, which focused upon the past and God's love for and redemption of Israel, Esther's prayer is much more personal even when it refers to the same saving events of Israel's history. Esther places her fate directly in God's hands, speaking of what she has heard from infancy concerning God's election of Israel and God's fulfilment of the divine promises to Israel. Attributing Israel's dispersion to sin, she describes the impending destruction as an intensification of Israel's 'bitter slavery' under Persian rule.

The nations, declares Esther, magnify a mortal king. She pleads with God not to surrender the divine sceptre to that which has no being, apparently in oblique reference to Artaxerxes, although no direct claims for the king's divinity are made in LXX Esther. Hence the current crisis is portrayed as a conflict between God, the true king, and Artaxerxes, who claims to be God. Finally, Esther prays for eloquent speech, in what may be an allusion to Ex 3 and Moses, who similarly desired eloquent speech in order to speak to a foreign king (Ex 4:10).

The justification of her behaviour that Esther includes in her prayer seems, like Mordecai's, to be directed more towards the reader (or listener, as during Purim) than to God. An audience dismayed and puzzled by the marriage of a pious Jewish maiden to a decadent Persian king may have been heartened by Esther's declaration of abhorrence of the 'splendour of the wicked', 'the bed of the uncircumcised and of any alien' (v. 15), and the royal crown, which she likens to a 'filthy rag' (lit. menstrual rag) not to be worn on days of leisure. Esther's royal life is a masquerade. Though she has slept with the Persian king, however reluctantly, she has not violated the dietary laws by eating at the royal table or by drinking the wine of libations to the gods. In this manner readers are reassured that she has maintained her resolve to fear God and keep the divine commandments, as she had been instructed by Mordecai (2:20).

These prayers not only speak of Israel's cry for help, but actually constitute the means by which Israel's representatives, Mordecai and Esther, do so. For this reason Addition C functions as a turning point in the story, just as in Mordecai's dream the nation's outcry is followed by salvation. Secondly, the prayers constitute a blueprint for Jewish behaviour in the Diaspora: Jews should refrain from bowing down to human dignitaries, and should continue to maintain dietary laws, but may compromise even basic principles when necessary for survival, as Esther did in sleeping with an uncircumcised man. Third, the prayers provide a point of comparison with other texts. Clines (1984: 173) compares them to the exemplary prayers of supplication in Ezra 9, Neh 1, and Dan 9, but perhaps more telling are the prayers in Jdt 9 and Tob 3:11–15 in which faith in God's saving acts is a central theme. Judith, like Esther, is a woman of prominence, the only person capable of saving her people from annihilation. Her act too is preceded by a prayer, and involves mortal danger, as well as a (potential) erotic connection to the Gentile leader, Holofernes, whom she must confront and deceive. There are differences, of course. Judith's act is more dramatic; Esther's enemy is not the king whose anger she fears but his viceroy, who engineered the plot to kill the Jews. Nevertheless, these two women protagonists are cut from similar cloth (cf. Day 1995: 222–6; Moore 1977: 167; Enslin 1972: 15–21).

Addition D (15:1–16): Esther's Approach to the King

This Addition is an expansion of the brief description of Esther's approach to the king in MT Esth 5:1–2. After three days of fasting and prayer, Esther prepares herself by changing her clothing. In this act Esther is similar to the Tamar of Genesis (34:14, 19), as well as to Judith (Jdt 10:3–4) and Asenath (*Joseph and Asenath*, 14:14–15) who change their clothing as deliberate strategies in their encounters with the men who figure prominently in their plans. Just as she had to wear humble clothes when approaching God, her true King, so must Esther wear resplendent clothing to approach the earthly king whom she feared more, despite her own royal status.

After invoking God's aid, Esther, supported by two maids, approaches the king, who, seated on a royal throne, clothed in the full array of majesty, and covered with gold and jewels, appears 'most terrifying' to her (v. 6). Initially, her fears about approaching him unsummoned seem to be justified: he responds to her approach with fierce anger. Esther saves her skin by behaving like the genteel woman she has dressed herself to be: she faints and collapses. God then changes the king's spirit to gentleness. Artaxerxes takes her in his arms till she comes to, comforts her with gentle words, and reassures her that she will not die 'for our law applies only to our subjects' (v. 10). Perhaps in explanation of her collapse, Esther describes the king as an angel of God who inspires fear at his glory, wonderful, and with a countenance full of grace, and promptly faints a second time, inspiring further attempts to revive and comfort her.

The king's reference to himself as Esther's 'brother' (LXX; NRSV marg.) in this exchange is taken by most interpreters as a general term of warmth, though Brownlee (1966: 168) argues that in Egypt married couples referred to each other as brother and sister. In addition, there may be some irony in this form of address, given their ethnic differences and her extreme fear in approaching him.

A more pressing question, however, is why indeed did Esther faint, not once but twice? Moore (1977: 218; cf. Day 1995: 102), reasonably, comments that three days of fasting may indeed have weakened Esther, rendering her inadequate to the challenge of overcoming her fear, the challenge for which she had begged for divine assistance. Noting the parallels between Esther's description of the king and biblical portrayals of kingship, including Gentile monarchs (1 Sam 29:9; 2 Sam 14:7, 20; 19:27; Ezek 28:2), Brownlee (1966: 164–70) suggests that despite the disclaimers in her prayer, Esther may have felt herself to have been in the presence of the angelic or divine, in which case fainting was not an inappropriate response. A final suggestion, plausible in light of the book's soteriology, is that Esther's fainting may be attributed to God, who may have required some human act as a catalyst for overcoming the king's anger and gaining her the sympathetic hearing necessary for turning the plot of the story.

(5:3–8:12) The Villain is Unmasked The conflict between Haman and Mordecai comes to a head in this section. Just at the moment that Haman is ready to ask the king for permission to hang Mordecai on the giant gallows that he has prepared, the king, during a bout of insomnia, comes across the memorandum concerning the assassination plot which Mordecai had foiled and seeks Haman's advice on how to honour his saviour. Instead of executing Mordecai as planned, Haman must honour him as he himself would have wished to be honoured (6:1–13). Recognizing that Mordecai has the living God with him, Haman's friends and wife see this act prophetically, as a sign of Haman's future downfall. Shortly thereafter Esther unmasks Haman as villain at the second of two dinners at which the king and Haman are her only guests. Like her prayer in Addition C, Esther's plea to Artaxerxes is phrased in terms which emphasize that Haman's wicked plot threatens not only the Jewish people, but also Esther herself, as a Jew. Both plot lines are neatly resolved when Haman is hanged on the gallows which he had prepared for Mordecai and the king authorizes Esther to write a decree replacing the one dictated by Haman (7:7–10, 8:1–12).

In a reprise of 3:12–13, the secretaries are summoned to write an edict, to be broadcast throughout the empire. The date, the twenty-third of Nisan, recalls both the month of the Exodus and that of Mordecai's dream in Addition A, and hence is associated with the theme of divine salvation. The edict is written with the king's authority, sealed with his ring, and conveys his command that the Jews observe their own laws and give themselves free rein in defending themselves against attack. The context makes it clear, however, that the letter was initiated by Esther (8:5), and written by her and Mordecai in the king's name (8:8), a point which seems to have been overlooked by scholars (such as Moore 1977: 234; Wills 1995: 126) who attribute the letter directly to the king.

In this section, as in its parallel in MT Esther, the king gives Mordecai Haman's ring and his position as the king's right-hand man, and Esther gives him authority over Haman's estate (8:2). Although the king's command to write a new edict and seal it with his ring is addressed only to Esther (8:7; in contrast to the MT in which both Esther and Mordecai are named), the fact that the verbs 'write' and 'seal' in 8:8 are in the plural indicates that both Esther and Mordecai are intended. In this section, therefore, Mordecai not only replaces Haman in relationship to the king, but also achieves parity with Esther, thereby eliminating the discrepancy between their relative status in the social realm and their father–child relationship in the private and religious spheres. The portrayal of Esther also changes, however. No longer fearful and coy, Esther is given a measure of royal power, which she exercises along with Mordecai in the composition of the edict.

Addition E (16:1–24): The Official Repeal of the First Edict

Similar in style to Addition B, Addition E undoes the substance of the earlier edict and carries forward the divine plan for the rescue of the Jews. Most of the Addition is devoted to the discrediting of Haman, beginning with a lengthy reflection on the fact that some people who receive great honours respond by plotting evil against their benefactors and the innocent (vv. 2–6). The real threat to the peace and stability of the kingdom comes not from the Jews but from Haman. Haman was not a Persian by birth but an alien devoid of Persian kindliness, whose real goal was to use his position of power to transfer the kingdom of the Persians to the Macedonians (v. 14). The second theme, the role of the Jews, is dealt with rather quickly, by dismissing Haman's earlier charges and emphasizing the righteousness of the Jews' laws and their status as 'children of the living God, most high, most mighty', who also directs the affairs of the Persian kingdom (vv. 15–16). Finally, the edict orders the populace not to put the earlier letters into execution, since their author himself has been executed. This new edict, which must be circulated and displayed, allows for the Jews to live under their own laws, and to be given reinforcements so that they may defend themselves from attack. The thirteenth day of Adar is to become a day of joy rather than destruction. The edict concludes by specifying this day as a festival day not only for the Jews but for the entire empire, as 'a reminder of destruction for those who plot against us' (v. 23) and promises swift punishment for those who transgress its stipulations (v. 24).

Though ostensibly addressed to the Persian empire by Artaxerxes, the edict, like the prayers of Mordecai and Esther, is more plausible as a message from the implied author to the diaspora Jewish audience of Greek Esther itself. As such it sanctions the celebration of Purim, celebrates the reversal of fortunes and the fulfilment of Mordecai's dream, and, perhaps most important, stresses that Jews should live by their own excellent laws even in the Diaspora. This focus on the reader may also explain the edict's references to Haman as a Macedonian, which contrast with the earlier, obscure descriptions of Haman as a *bougaios* (A, 12:6; 3:1). Moore suggests that this variation is an updated term of reproach, meant not to provide historical accuracy but to identify Haman as a despised person from the point of view of the reader. The label can be used to support a Hasmonean date for the book, since the term 'Macedonian' would have been a term of disparagement familiar to readers in this period (Moore 1977: 178, 236).

(8:13–10:3) Events of Adar This section describes the posting of the letter, the elevation of Mordecai, and the conversion of many Gentiles, albeit out of fear. The narrator apparently delights in the Persians' fear of the Jews, and of Mordecai in particular, whose name was to be held in honour throughout the kingdom (9:3). Esther continues to exercise a role as royal counsel, advising the king to let the Jews continue their killing on the morrow, and to hand the bodies of Haman's sons over to the Jews for hanging. These two points are responsible for Esther's post-biblical reputation as a bloodthirsty woman on a par with Jael of Judg 4–5 (ibid. 242). The narrator notes that on the next day 300 people were killed but no looting occurred, while in the countryside 15,000 Gentiles were killed (compared to 75,000 according to the MT), without plundering. The description, institution, and validation of the annual festival, whose main features are merrymaking and the giving of gifts to friends and to the poor, are associated with both Mordecai and Esther, implying their parity not only *vis-à-vis* the Persian kingdom but also as leaders of Persian Jewry.

Addition F: Interpretation of Mordecai's Dream (10:4–13); Colophon (11:1)

The explanation of Mordecai's dream in its general outlines is no doubt superfluous to the reader/listener who has been led to recognize the Purim story itself as the fulfilment of that dream. Nevertheless the interpretation of its details provides a satisfying closure to the narrative. The river in the dream is Esther, while the two dragons are Haman and Mordecai. These identifications lead Moore (ibid. 181) to conclude that Esther is the human hero of the piece, rather than Mordecai, whom he sees as the hero of the MT Esther. The righteous nation is Israel; the surrounding nations—the Gentiles—are her enemies. The Lord rescued Israel, an event which led to joyous celebration on the thirteenth and fourteenth days of Adar. The dream and its interpretation, as introduction and conclusion, therefore provide a soteriological framework for the story as a whole, placing the events in the context of God's love for Israel and the divine propensity to come to Israel's rescue from persecution and destruction at the hands of idolatrous enemies.

Addition F concludes with a colophon that purports to provide the details of the text, its date, and its translation. Whether or not the colophon is authentic, and can therefore be used for dating the text, it, like Additions B and E, creates an aura of authenticity as well as providing explicit acknowledgement of the status of this story as a translation of a Hebrew original. The colophon is absent from AT, which follows the interpretation of Mordecai's dream with a concluding statement concerning the joyous celebration on the fourteenth and fifteenth days of Adar.

Conclusion

LXX Esther, like any translation, is also an interpretation of its sources. The six Additions as well as numerous smaller changes redraw the main characters, amplify some of the details, and, most noticeably, explicitly situate the story-line in the context of the covenantal relationship between God and Israel. While comparisons of LXX Esther with the versions of the Esther story in the MT and the AT are fruitful (cf. Day 1995; Moore 1977), LXX Esther repays consideration in its own right, clearly reflecting the Hellenistic Diaspora situation and commonality of genre and concerns with other narrative works from the last two centuries BCE. The social dilemmas faced by Jews in the Diaspora, the importance of family, group identity, religious practice, the theological conviction that God continues to care for God's people in exile, and the necessity of compromise all figure in this story, contributing to its ancient popularity and its continuing relevance.

REFERENCES

Bickerman, E. J. (1944), 'The Colophon of the Greek Book of Esther', *JBL* 63: 339–62.

—— (1950), 'Notes on the Greek Book of Esther', *PAAJR* 20: 101–33.

Brownlee, W. H. (1966), 'Le Livre Grec d'Esther et la Royauté Divine', *RB* 73: 161–85.

Clines, D. J. A. (1984), *The Esther Scroll: The Story of the Story* (Sheffield: JSOT).

Day, L. (1995), *Three Faces of a Queen: Characterization in the Books of Esther* JSOTSup 186 (Sheffield: Sheffield Academic Press).

Enslin, M. S. (1972), *The Book of Judith* (Brill: Leiden).

Fox, M. V. (1991a), *Character and Ideology in the Book of Esther* (Columbia, SC: University of South Carolina Press).

—— (1991b), *The Redaction of the Books of the Esther: On Reading Composite Texts* SBLMS 40 (Atlanta: Scholars Press).

—— (1992), 'The Redaction of the Greek Alpha-Text of Esther', in Michael Fishbane et al. (eds.), *Sha'arei Talmon: Studies in the Bible, Qumran, and the Ancient Near East presented to Shemaryahu Talmon* (Winona Lake, Ind.: Eisenbrauns), 207–20.

Moore, C. A. (1977), *Daniel, Esther and Jeremiah: The Additions*, AB 44 (New York: Doubleday).

—— (1982) (ed.), *Studies in the Book of Esther* (New York: Ktav).

Paton, L. B. (1908), *The Book of Esther*, ICC (Edinburgh: T. & T. Clark).

Stern, M. (1974) (ed.), *Greek and Latin Authors on Jews and Judaism*, i. *From Herodotus to Plutarch* (Jerusalem: Israel Academy of Sciences and Humanities).

Tov, E. (1982), 'The "Lucianic" Text of the Canonical and the Apocryphal Sections of Esther: A Rewritten Biblical Book', in Shemaryahu Talmon (ed.), *Textus: Annual of the Hebrew University Bible Project*, 10 (Jerusalem: Magnes) 1–25.

Wills, L. (1990), *The Jew in the Court of the Foreign King: Ancient Jewish Court Legends*, HDR 26 (Minneapolis: Fortress).

—— (1995), *The Jewish Novel in the Ancient World* (Ithaca, NY: Cornell University Press).

43. The Wisdom of Solomon

WILLIAM HORBURY

INTRODUCTION

A. Teaching. 1. This book, preserved in Greek and in versions made from the Greek, forms a high point not only in ancient Jewish literature but also in Greek literature as a whole; yet it belongs above all to the sapiential stream of Jewish biblical tradition, and crowns the series of earlier biblical wisdom-books: Proverbs, Job, Ecclesiastes, Ecclesiasticus (Sirach). In the early church it was one of the books linked with Solomon, together with Proverbs, Ecclesiastes, the Song of Songs, and the non-canonical *Psalms, Odes*, and *Testament of Solomon* (ET in Sparks 1984: 649–751); but Solomonic authorship was often questioned, and some ascribed Wisdom to the author of Ecclesiasticus (Jesus son of Sirach of Jerusalem, early 2nd cent. BCE), or to the Jewish philosopher-exegete Philo of Alexandria (*c*.25 BCE–*c*.50 CE) (Horbury 1994*a*; 1995).

2. The Wisdom of Solomon begins with instruction to kings on wisdom, as regards the suffering and vindication of the righteous (see chs. 1–5); the doctrine of immortality is presented as the confirmation of the righteousness of God. From these chapters, which are close to the judgement scenes in *1 Enoch* and the *Psalms of Solomon*, and opposed to the this-wordly emphasis of Ecclesiastes and Sirach, the church drew a theology of martyrdom and an interpretation of the passion of Christ. Then in chs. 6–10 King Solomon emerges by implication as the speaker, telling the Gentile kings how he prayed when young for the heavenly gift of wisdom, as is related in 1 Kings 3 and 2 Chr 1. Recollections of his ardent love for wisdom are mingled with praise for her in terms that appropriately suggest 'the spirit of wisdom and understanding' promised to the Davidic king (Isa 11:2); she is an all-pervasive loving spirit issuing from God, the fashioner and guardian and renewer of all things as well as the giver of knowledge and the guide of life. Wisdom is set in the divine realm, following Prov 8 with the young Solomon; these chapters differ markedly from Eccl 1–2, in which the old king views wisdom as an ultimately pointless human acquisition. Lastly, chs. 11–19 praise God through a meditation on the Exodus that inculcates repentance and faith and defends providence (14:3; 17:2) and the election of God's 'people' (12:19, etc.); a digression (chs. 13–15) on the origins of Gentile idolatry has affinities with the beginning of Romans. Throughout chs. 11–19 the writer continues the address to God, rather than the kings of the earth, which was begun in ch. 9, and wisdom is named only in one passage (14:2, 5); these chapters recall Sirach in their theodicy (Crenshaw 1975) and in their dependence on the biblical histories, but otherwise they show less kinship with the sapiential books than with Jewish exegesis of Exodus and Christian paschal homily (17:1).

3. Four great characteristics of Wisdom's teaching can be discerned throughout. First, it has an element of mysticism, in the sense of the soul's quest for the divine (WIS 2:13; 13:6), especially divine wisdom (7:10; 8:2); conversely, the immanent deity is the lover of souls (1:4; 7:27; 11:26–12:1; 16:21).

Secondly, to some extent by contrast, it is also focused on the people of God (9:7; 12:19, etc.), although Israel is not named—much as in 1 Peter the church is central, but the word *ekklēsia* is lacking. A link with the mystical element is formed by verses on inspired or ecstatic communal praise (10:21; 19:9). Thirdly, it is permeated by zeal for righteousness (WIS 1:1) in collective and individual morality; God helps the righteous, divine punishments are just (5:20; 12:15; 16:24), and God's people and their heroes are exemplars of virtue. Lastly, in accord with its emphasis on the nation (Barclay 1996: 181–91), Wisdom shows deep familiarity with Scripture and interpretative tradition; artistic allusion is pervasive (Chester 1988). Many biblical characters are portrayed, but, like Israel, they are all unnamed (WIS 4:10).

4. In biblical style, but with a tinge of philosophical language, Wisdom welcomes a number of Greek philosophical conceptions. Broadly speaking, the book sounds both Platonic and Stoic. Its mystical strand has affinities with Plato; 'understanding [*phronēsis*, cf. 7:7] would arouse terrible love [cf. 7:10; 8:2], if such a clear image of it were granted [cf. 7:22–8:1] as would come through sight' (Plato, *Phdr.* 250D). Wisdom is more particularly indebted to Plato, perhaps through intermediaries, on the virtues, pre-existence, primal matter, and beauty (8:7, 19; 11:17; 13:3), and in the treatment of the soul (WIS A.3; 8:20; 9:15–17; 15:8); but Plato's theory of archetypal ideas (Stead 1994: 18–21), which is central in Philo's theology, here stays in the background (9:8; 13:7). Wisdom's own central conception of a beautifully ordered world guided by immanent spirit (WIS 1:7; 8:1; 19:18) has antecedents in the biblical sapiential tradition (WIS A.1; A.3), but comes mainly from Plato as interpreted by the Stoics.

5. The book defends providence, afterlife, and the reward of virtue. These Platonic themes became central in the Stoic and Epicurean philosophies of the second and first centuries BCE (ACTS 17:18; Stead 1994: 40–53). Philosophers then nurtured by the Greek cities of Syria and Palestine include the Stoics Poseidonius of Apamea and Antiochus of Ascalon, and the Epicurean Philodemus of Gadara; all drew upon the classical philosophers, and were influential among educated Romans as well as Greeks (Hengel 1974: 86–7). Wisdom takes, broadly speaking, the Stoic side; Stoics argued for a universe pervaded and directed by a vital force (WIS 1:7), and the survival of righteous souls, but Epicureans envisaged non-intervening deities and souls which perished with the body. In the first century CE Josephus (*Vita*, 12) compares the Pharisees to the Stoics, and his outline of Sadducaic opinion recalls Epicureanism.

6. 'Wisdom' itself (Gk. *sophia*, Lat. *sapientia*, 1:4, etc.) was a weighty term in philosophical vocabulary. In Plato it included morality and the art of government (*Rep.* 4.6, 428B–429A), in Aristotle it was identified with abstract philosophy and knowledge of principles as opposed to practice (*Eth. Nic.* 6.7, 1141^b), but its practical moral association was strong among the Stoics. They linked *sophia* and *sapientia* with their ideal figure of the imperturbably virtuous Wise, the true king among mortals, who goes 'where heavenly wisdom leads' (Horace, *Epistles*, 1.3.27).

7. Platonic and Stoic *sophia* therefore readily converged with the moral as well as intellectual portrayal of *sophia* in the biblical wisdom-books (WIS A.3; A.9). Educated Jews were aware of possible associations between Judaism and the Greek schools of thought, as can be inferred from Josephus. Thus Aristobulus, in the Egyptian Jewish community of the second century BCE, mentions Pythagoras, Plato, and the Aristotelians in his fragmentarily preserved Pentateuchal comments, and urges that the philosophers drew on Moses (Hengel 1974: 163–9; Collins 1985; Barclay 1996: 150–8; WIS 6:12). Wisdom does not give names, but shows similar awareness, especially with regard to Stoicism. Like Aristobulus, but implicitly, it urges that the wisdom of biblical tradition anticipates and includes the philosophical truths and virtues (7:17–27; 8:7); at the same time it implicitly modifies biblical tradition, and integrates it fully into Hellenic culture (Chester 1988: 164). In the church this aspect of the book led to assertions (in line with the earlier Jewish argument seen in Aristobulus) that Wisdom itself was the original source of Platonic and Stoic doctrines (WIS 7:24; 11:17).

8. The philosophy of Wisdom leads it also to differ, on points debated by early Christians, from what in the end became the most approved church teaching. The soul is pre-existent and not originated in connection with conception (WIS 8:19); the world is made from pre-existent matter rather than *ex nihilo* (WIS 11:17); and the soul's future life is described (A.9) without reference to the body (Stead 1994: 29–30).

9. Within the Apocrypha the philosophical theology of Wisdom recalls 2 Maccabees, which is likewise concerned with martyrdom and afterlife, but speaks of resurrection (*anastasis*) rather than immortality (*athanasia*); Wisdom expresses future hope just as vividly, but seems to expect a spiritual rather than carnal revival of the righteous (WIS 3:7). The personified wisdom of WIS 7–10, linked with the wise king of Israel, compares and contrasts (WIS 7:22) with that of Sir 24 and Bar 3:9–4:2, linked with the Jerusalem temple and identified with the Pentateuchal law; all three passages are patriotic Israelite developments of the goddess-like figure of cosmic wisdom in Prov 8–9 and Job 28, could have been associated by Greek-speaking readers with the philosophical and moral overtones of *sophia* noted above, and owe something to contemporary portrayals of Isis (Knox 1939: 69–81; WIS 7:22). The cosmos in Wisdom is a world of spirits, good and bad, including 'the spirit of the Lord' (1:7), 'angels' (16:20), and 'the devil' (2:24), as is already the case in the LXX, and wisdom herself is spiritual, as already noted (7:22–7); correspondingly, human beings are envisaged above all as 'souls' (2:22, etc.; WIS A.3), which are probably held to be pre-existent, as in Plato and Philo (WIS 8:19). In assessment of this spiritual aspect of Wisdom it is noteworthy that, for Stoics, the world-soul and individual souls were material, even if superfine (7:22–4; Hengel 1974: 199–200). Philosophy had links with widespread conceptions of energetic good and evil spirits (P. Merlan in Armstrong 1970: 32–7), and spiritual immortality (WIS 3:7) need not have seemed insubstantial by contrast with

resurrection, which could itself be envisaged spiritually (Mk 12:25).

10. Among the NT books Wisdom has affinity not only with Romans (WIS A.2) but also with the speeches in Acts on repentance and faith, with the sapiential morality of James, and with the vindication of righteous suffering in 1 Peter. In the treatment of wisdom and *logos* as intermediaries (WIS 7:22; 9:1) Wisdom also shows kinship with the Christology of word, spirit, radiance, and image in John, Paul, and Hebrews. From a wider range of ancient Jewish literature, Philo's philosophical exegesis of Scripture, Josephus's presentation of the Jewish schools of thought as philosophies, and 4 Maccabees on Jewish martyrdom as adherence to true philosophy, all broadly resemble Wisdom as Jewish expositions of Judaism using Greek philosophical terms. It should be stressed, however, that all these NT and other works are written in Greek prose, and are far removed from Wisdom's adherence to biblical poetic style (WIS B.1). The portrayal of Christianity as a philosophical school by the Apologists, such as Justin Martyr (later 2nd cent.) and Tertullian (early 3rd cent.), adapts the philosophical interpretation of Judaism attested in Wisdom (WIS A.4–8). Similarly, rabbinic biblical exposition current in third–fifth-century Galilee and embodied in the Talmud and Midrash, although it is handed down in Hebrew and Aramaic rather than Greek, evinces a debt to philosophical vocabulary and Greek conceptions of a spiritual cosmos which once again recalls Wisdom.

11. Affinities between Wisdom and Christian books later than the NT emerge in 1 *Clement* (WIS 4:10) and in the mythopoeic treatment of wisdom's love for the Father (cf. 8:4; 9:9) by Valentinus and his school, as recounted in the later second century by Irenaeus (*Haer*. 1.2). Signs of Wisdom's direct influence on the church are evident from this time onwards (WIS C.1). Wisdom helped to mould not only dogmatic and moral theology, but also baptismal instruction, hymnody, and prayer. The philosophic and exegetical treatment of wisdom as intermediary in Wisdom 7–10 was joined with the Pauline view of Christ as the wisdom of God (WIS 10:1); Christological indebtedness to Wisdom is especially striking in the early third-century Origen (WIS 1:4; 7:22). Wisdom also formed the clearest biblical source for the notion of pure universal love permeating and ordering the cosmos (WIS 7:22–8:1; 11:20–12:1; 14:3; 16:7, 12).

12. In the fourth century Athanasius (*Festal Letter*, 39) put Wisdom first among those books which (he says) are not canonical, but were approved by the fathers for reading to newcomers (catechumens). Jerome (WIS B.1) likewise stressed that Wisdom was outside the canon, but endorsed the reading of this and other approved extra-canonical books for edification, as is recalled in the sixth of the Thirty-Nine Articles (1562). Augustine, by contrast, worked for church recognition of these approved books as canonical, and noted Wisdom's prophetic witness to Christ (*De civ. dei*, 17.20). The later Christian West found Wisdom congenial, as medieval commentaries show (Smalley 1986); the book's influence on forms of prayer (WIS 1:7; 3:7; 8:1; 9:1; 11:24; 16:6, 20) appears at its most famous in the antiphon *O Sapientia* (8.1). The old acclamation of Christ as the wisdom of the Father's heart, echoed in the poems of Prudentius (end of 4th cent.), was reunited with mystical passages of Wisdom in the warm

Christ-mysticism of the Swabian Henry Suso (Seuse) (c.1295–1366); in the language of courtship as well as piety he called himself 'servant of the eternal wisdom' (WIS 7:10; 10:9).

B. Form. 1. 'The very style has a scent of Greek eloquence', as Jerome noted in the letter introducing his Latin translation of the books of Solomon from the Hebrew (Weber *et al.* 1975: ii. 957, lines 17–18). The scent arises mainly from literary and philosophical vocabulary (WIS A.4), occasional patches of rhetorical style, and thematic contacts with such typically Greek concerns as consolation (3:13–4:19). Nevertheless, the form of Wisdom belongs chiefly to Hebrew literature. It recalls the third- to first-century BCE Judean continuation of Hebrew wisdom poetry attested in the Dead Sea scrolls, including the apocryphal Ps 154 (Vermes 1997: 302–3, 393–425; van der Woude 1995), and it is comparable with the form of the Greek *Psalms of Solomon* (c.60–40 BCE), for it resembles the translations of Psalms, Proverbs, and Sirach preserved in the LXX, and replicates in Greek the stressed parallelistic verse of the HB. This would not necessarily be expected of a Jewish poetical book current in Greek. Jews loved Greek verse in the quantitative metres of classical poetry, as literature and inscriptions composed or sponsored by Jews attest (Horbury and Noy 1992: pp. xx–xxiv); the moral hexameter *Sentences* of Ps.-Phocylides (van der Horst 1985; Barclay 1996: 336–46) form a metrical Jewish work broadly comparable with Wisdom. The classical metres are set aside in Wisdom, however, for a form redolent of ancestral Jewish Scripture, in line with the book's strong national feeling (WIS A.3). Indeed, it is not impossible that Wisdom 1–10 is a version of a text also issued in Hebrew or Aramaic. On the other hand, Wisdom's occasional transitions from biblical parallelism to hymn-like prose, such as the list of epithets in 7:22–3, sometimes give it a mixed Hebraic and rhetorical style like that seen on a small scale in the hymn of Rev 15:3–4.

2. A formal feature visible throughout the book is correspondence between speeches or descriptions. Within sections, units of text have been arranged to show parallels of sense and to return to an opening theme (as with the two speeches of the ungodly, 1:16–2:24; 5:1–23, and perhaps also with the four distinct passages that can be discerned between them). Suggested divisions naturally differ, but there is a good case for some intentional correspondence. The prevalence of this structural care (Grabbe 1997: 18–23) then recalls the prevalent consistency of style, but it does not cancel the marked thematic variation between chs. 1–10 and 11–19 (WIS A.2). These sections probably represent at least two separate compositions (WIS 9 introduction; 11:2), following the same conventions but not necessarily written by the same author.

3. It is correspondingly difficult to name a Greek literary genre to which the book in its present state belongs, although Jewish wisdom literature in general has some kinship with the proverbial and moralistic literature of the Greeks (WIS A. 4–8). If lack of Greek metre is overlooked, Wisdom broadly recalls the didactic poetry on philosophical and moral subjects which flourished in Hellenistic authors such as Aratus (3rd cent. BCE), found a Jewish echo in Ps.-Phoc, and was later imitated by Roman poets such as Lucretius, Virgil, and

Horace (WIS A.4). The biblical allusions of Wisdom roughly correspond to classical dependence on Homer and the mythical tradition. Didactic compositions in prose or verse could inculcate virtue and knowledge through exhortation (protreptic, cf. Wis 1–6) and praise (encomium, cf. Wis 7–10). In the twentieth century Wisdom was identified with protreptic and encomium in turn. The book can be loosely classified in Greek terms as a protreptic work, but it differs as a whole from the kind of Greek prose or verse composition which this classification evokes. Aspects of the book recalling Greek and Roman didactic poetry, including moral exhortation, are perhaps less important as indications of genre than as clues to the popularity of Wisdom in antiquity and the Middle Ages (A.12), when classical didactic literature was also relished.

4. The genre seems better classified in biblical terms as 'sapiential'; the book furthers the literary tradition followed in the wisdom-books of Proverbs, Job, and Ecclesiastes, but it does so in a more consciously Israelite and biblically oriented manner, in this respect resembling Sirach (WIS D). Unlike the Hebrew and Greek Sirach, however, Wisdom presents itself as wisdom of the inspired Solomon (7:7). Might it therefore be classed as pseudepigraphic prophecy, and be called an apocalypse, like 1 Enoch which it seems to echo? No, even though Wisdom declares the future and interprets Scripture in prophetic fashion, and exemplifies the thematic overlap between wisdom-books and apocalypses (2 ESD); for the centrality of wisdom in chs. 1–10 makes the book as a whole more sapiential than apocalyptic.

C. Setting. 1. Wisdom echoes the Septuagint of the Prophets as well as the Pentateuch, and probably draws on 1 Enoch 1–36 and 91–108 (WIS A.2). It is therefore unlikely to be earlier than the second century BCE. It was valued in the early church, but its lack of Christian allusion suggests that it is not a Christian work. In the second century CE it was known to Irenaeus, as Eusebius notes (*Hist. eccl.* 5.8.8), and was named with comment in the Muratorian Canon (Horbury 1994a); it also received a Latin translation, later incorporated by Jerome into the Vulgate, which forms the earliest surviving interpretation of Wisdom. Wisdom was explicitly quoted by Christian writers from Clement of Alexandria (c.150–215) onwards. Earlier allusions in Paul, 1 Clement, and Justin Martyr are probable but not certain. Wisdom is therefore likely to have been current by the early years of the first century CE, at latest. The vocabulary includes Greek words not otherwise attested before the first century CE, but the body of extant Greek literature from the previous century is not large.

2. A date in or near Caligula's principate (37–41 CE) has often been suggested, in line with the old ascription to Philo (WIS A.1) that Jerome notes (in his comment cited in WIS B.1). This date is one of those which might suit address to the kings of the earth (6:1) and opposition to ruler-cult and idolatry (chs. 13–15), with the depiction of persecution (chs. 1–6), for these are themes of Philo's defence of the Alexandrian Jews under Caligula; but the academic tone of the remarks on ruler-cult is less urgent than would be natural under Caligula, and this date allows less time than would be expected for the book to gain the high esteem implied by its Christian usage. The first-century BCE date which has also often been suggested for

Wisdom seems preferable. Address to kings and a theory of pagan cult would suit the Greek as well as the Roman period of Jewish history. In chs. 1–6, on persecution, the argument seems to be directed against internal foes, as in *1 Enoch* and the *Psalms of Solomon*. These chapters can then be tentatively associated with Sadducaic-Pharisaic strife, in which afterlife was a prominent topic (WIS 3:1); persecution of those who defended it figured in the bloody repression of the Pharisees under Alexander Jannaeus in the early first century BCE. The Egyptian Jewish community, in close touch with Judea and probably including Judean refugees, seems the likeliest cradle for the Greek text of the whole book, perhaps between 100 and 50 BCE; these dates are speculative, but they would suit the points of contact with both Sirach and the *Psalms of Solomon* noted above. Sirach was put into Greek probably in 132 BCE, with what seems (especially but not only in the longer form of the Greek text) a fresh recognition of reward and punishment hereafter, specifically for circulation among Egyptian Jews. Their Greek epitaphs attest a difference of opinion on after-life like that evinced between the Sadducee-like Ecclesiastes and the Hebrew Sirach on the one side, and the Pharisee-like Wisdom and *Psalms of Solomon* on the other (Horbury 1994*b*). The young and still righteous Solomon of Wisdom endorses the Pharisaic-Stoic preaching of 'justice, self-control, and the coming judgement' (Acts 24:25). Sirach was translated to aid Jewish education (Prologue), and Wisdom will have been valued for this reason as well as for its special doctrine. Its Christian educational use (WIS A.11–12) probably had Jewish antecedents.

D. Character. The special contribution of Wisdom to Jewish sapiential literature and the Christian sacred library is high-lighted by its contrasts with the often comparable book of Sirach. Sirach is scribal wisdom in mainly proverbial form, but its author gives his name in accord with Greek conven-tion; Wisdom is hortatory and expository rather than proverb-ial, but is anonymously presented as royal wisdom from the mouth of Solomon, in the manner of post-biblical prophecy like *Enoch* (WIS B.4). Sirach is not unaffected by the Greek world, but sticks to ancestral Jewish modes of expression; Wisdom shows equal pride in Jewish tradition, but manifestly incorporates Greek terminology and thought (WIS A.4–9). Sirach is a Judean book translated for Egypt, Wisdom probably arose in Egypt but in contact with Judea (WIS C.2). Sirach depicts the social round of a wise scribe, but Wisdom looks with royal and prophetic eye on scenes of martyrdom, divine judgement, and biblical story (WIS A.2). Sirach in Hebrew sounds mainly sceptical of afterlife, Wisdom preaches immor-tality (WIS A.9; C.2). In Sirach biblical knowledge subserves proverbs and poems, in Wisdom expanded biblical narrative shapes the structure of the book (WIS A.2). In Sirach wisdom takes root in the people and is identified with the law (ch. 24), in Wisdom she is known to the king, and not identified with the law (WIS A.9); she is seen above all as a world-soul bringing individual souls to God. In Sirach wisdom herself speaks (ch. 24), in Wisdom her ardent disciple (chs. 6–9). Both books present her as loving and beloved, but only Wisdom clearly links this mystical theme with afterlife and the divine and human spirit.

COMMENTARY

Love Righteousness, for Unrighteousness Cannot be Hidden and Leads to Death (1:1–16)

(1:1–5) Righteousness, the Great Virtue Needed by Kings, Must be Sought in a Whole-Hearted Quest for the Divine Spirit of Wisdom With the exhortations characteristic of wis-dom herself (Prov 2:20; 8:1; 9:3) and her prophetic 'children' (Lk 7:35; 11:49; Wis 7:27), the writer addresses those 'who judge the earth' (1:1, my tr.); they are 'rulers' (NRSV), being 'kings' as well as 'judges' (6:1–2), but their judicial office is in view, as with Solomon (1 Kings 3:3–28). 'Love righteousness' echoes psalms of kingship (Ps. 2:10–11; 45:7; 72:1–4). This hint at the form of a manual for kings commended Wisdom to an intellectual Jewish public, given the keen current interest in political and moral philosophy (WIS A.4–7). The signifi-cance gained by the first line in Christian political thought emerges when Dante sees its letters displayed by heavenly spirits (*Paradiso*, 18.70–117).

Righteousness, the characteristic virtue of the Israelites and their martyrs and heroes in Wisdom (as at 2:12; 3:1; 5:1; 10:4; 18:7), was exalted in Greek tradition as the principle of civic life and a cardinal virtue (WIS 8:7), indeed as 'the entirety of virtue' (Arist., *Eth. Nic.* 5.1.19, 1130ª8); these views converged with the prominence of righteousness in the OT, there too as a civic principle, but with emphasis on conformity to the will of a righteous deity (Isa 11:4–5; Ps 11:7; 45:7; Wis 15:3). Here this emphasis marks the quick transition in 1:1 to advice on seek-ing the God of Israel, who is named, as often in Wisdom, by the royal title 'lord' (*kyrios*) used in the LXX. He must be sought wholeheartedly (Deut 4:29), by inward 'goodness', a term used for the unqualified zeal of Phinehas (Sir 45:23) and the generosity of Solomon (Wis 8:15, 19), and by sincerity (*haplotes*, REB 'singleness') of heart, a phrase linked with the kingly large-heartedness of David (1 Chr 29:17 LXX). Single-ness of heart ranked high as a virtue (1 Macc 2:60; Col 3:22; 1 *Clem.* 60:2); the 'double-minded' must 'purify the heart' (Jas 1:8; 4:8).

The great example of divine 'manifestation' to those who do not tempt or distrust (v. 2) was Moses (Ex 33:13, 18–19), by contrast with the rebellious children of Israel in the wilder-ness (1:10–11). 'Thoughts' (*logismoi*, v. 3) are also the main obstacle in Prov 15:23 LXX ('an unrighteous thought is an abomination to the Lord'), 2 Cor 10:4–5. 'The power' (RV; NRSV adds 'his') is the divine manifestation itself (Mk 14:62), the spirit identified with wisdom (Wis 1:4–6) and probably also with the angelic spirit of the divine presence who led the Exodus and met rebellion (Ex 3:2; 32:34; Isa 63:9–14; WIS 10, introduction). v. 3 also takes up Isa 59, where perverse ways separate sinners from God (Isa 59:2, 8, quoted at Rom 3:15), and he appears as a warrior to punish them (Isa 59:16–21, also echoed in Wis 5:18).

Wisdom (WIS A.6–7) is named with reverent emphasis at the end of v. 4*a* in Greek (WIS 6:12). If not excluded by sin (cf. 4:10–12) it can 'enter' the soul (v. 4; 7:27) as a 'spirit' (vv. 5–6); the soul likewise enters a body (8:19; WIS A.4; 8). Origen (WIS A. 11), thinking on these lines, held that the Logos entered the pre-existent soul of Christ (Origen, *On First Principles*, 2.6.3–7;

4.6.4–5). For the body in bond to sin (v. 4) cf. Rom. 6:12–14; 7:14; 8:23.

'Disciplined spirit' (v. 5) seems to imply the human spirit, but the more exact rendering 'spirit of discipline' (RV, REB) is preferable, for divine wisdom ('holy', cf. 7:22) is probably the subject, as in vv. 3–4 and 6. For its flight from iniquity cf. Ps 51:10–11. 'Discipline' (*paideia*)—training with instruction—was constantly linked with wisdom (so Prov 1:2; Wis 3:11); here too Jewish and Greek thinking converged.

(1:6–11) The Universal Spirit of Wisdom Conveys All Unrighteous Speech to the Lord
The spirit of wisdom is *philanthrōpos* (v. 6; 7:23), 'kindly' to humanity in particular, for she delights in human company (Prov 8:31; Bar 3:37); but this epithet unexpectedly subserves the ruling theme of vv. 6–11, the omnipresence of a *judicial* spirit aware of all thought and speech (Ps 139:1–12, 23–4; Wis 9:11; divine omniscience linked with wisdom, 1 Enoch, 84:3). Likewise, v. 7 recalls the Stoic conception (WIS A.2) of a universe in which 'one common soul inspires and feeds and animates the whole' (Virg., *Aen.* 6.725–6, tr. Dryden); but the spirit is pictured as a world-soul in order to show that it has 'knowledge of the voice' (*phōnē*, see RV), hears all, and knows all languages (1 Cor 14:10–11a REB). In the medieval and later Christian West v. 7 was therefore aptly recited at Pentecost (see Acts 2:4), but throughout vv. 7–11 the spirit's linguistic and other knowledge is judicial; the ungodly are detected (v. 8), heard (vv. 9–11) by divine jealousy or zeal (v. 10; 5:17; Isa 59:17 RV, REB), and punished (vv. 8, 9, 11) by unfaltering justice (*dikē*, 8; 2 Macc 8:11; Acts 28:4). As the Greek deities were *epopsioi*, 'watchers' (Callimachus fr. 85), so the eyes of the Lord run to and fro everywhere (2 Chr 16:9; Prov 15:3; Zech 4:10). 'Know what is above thee: a seeing eye, and a hearing ear, and all thy doings written in a book' (*m. 'Abot*, 2.1). The famous 'grumbling' (vv. 10, 11) of the wilderness generation was strictly punished (Num 14:27–35; 1 Cor 10:10); the soul's destruction (v. 11) is then probably seen as the penalty as well as the consequence of untruth.

(1:12–16) Do not Court Death by Going Astray, for the World is Made for Life through Righteousness
vv. 12–16 expand Prov 8:35–6, the end of the speech by wisdom already echoed in v. 6. In v. 12 'error' (*planē*, 'straying'; WIS 12:24) has overtones of idolatry, the root of all vice. 'Death' (v. 12), coupled with 'destruction' (vv. 12, 14), is personified according to an old biblical tradition probably influenced at various stages by Syrian and Greek myths of a god of death, and exemplified at Job 28:22; Isa 28:15 (taken up in v. 16, below); Hos 13:14. In v. 13, accordingly, death was not divinely created, but came in 'through the devil's envy' (2:24); all created things, by contrast, were made for life and health (v. 14; WIS 2:23). Because of this contrast between the created and the intruded, 'creatures' (v. 14, NRSV marg.) is preferable to 'generative forces' as a rendering of *geneseis*; created things have the sap of life in them, not the 'poison of destruction' (RV), the principle of death. 'Hades' (v. 14) usually represents Hebrew *šĕ'ōl* in the LXX, and can therefore be personal (Isa 5:14) as well as topographical; here, where death is personified, Hades is probably imagined as a godlike figure whose 'dominion' is underground, on the lines of Greek myth, as in the Egyptian Jewish epitaph CIJ 1508 (Horbury and Noy 1992: pp. xxiii–xxiv, 63). The single-line

v. 15 can be viewed together with the last two lines of v. 14 as forming a triad, on the pattern of vv. 1, 5, 9; in the OL it is followed by the line 'but unrighteousness is the obtaining of death', but this is probably an early expansion. The characteristically Greek term 'immortal' (WIS 3:4) here adorns a maxim found in other words in the Psalms (111:3; 112:3, 9; 119:142, 144). The 'ungodly' are pictured (v. 16) as in Isa 28:15 LXX (also echoed at Sir 14:12) 'we made a covenant with Hades, and a bond with death'; 'him' (NRSV marg.) is perhaps more likely to be Hades, just mentioned, than 'death' (text), but the diabolical power of death (2:24; Heb 2:14) is in view in either case. This Isaianic 'covenant' became in medieval thought the pact with the devil in witchcraft, as when Dr Faustus made Lucifer 'a deed of gift of body and of soul', conditionally on 'all covenants and articles between us both' (Marlowe, *Doctor Faustus*, ll. 89–91). The covenanters deservedly belong to the 'portion' (*meris*) of Hades, death, or the devil (v. 16; 2:24 RV; NRSV 'company'), implicitly opposed here to 'the Lord's portion' (Deut 32:9, 2 Macc 1:26), (righteous) Israel, wisdom's home (Sir 24:12); an explicit contrast is drawn in Qumran rule literature between those who belong to 'the lot of Belial' and 'the lot of God' (1QS ii 2–5). For the movement of thought from the infernal covenant to the two portions compare 2 Cor 6:15, where Christ has no concord with Belial, and a believer no *meris* with an unbeliever.

The Ungodly Declare their Falsely Argued Philosophy, and their Resolve to Use their Time in Revelry and Oppression (2:1–20)
This speech, 'full of a kind of evil grandeur rhythmically expressed' (Deane 1881), follows the expressions of doubt or lawlessness imagined by biblical writers (as at Isa 22:13; Ps 10:4–11; 14:1; Prov 1:10–14). These were later developed, with hints at Epicureanism as popularly represented (1 Cor 15:32; 1 Enoch 102:6, 'they [the pious] like us have died'; *Ps. Sol.* 4:11 (14) 'There is none that sees and judges'). Similarly, Cain was pictured as saying to Abel, in a dispute before he killed him, 'Did nature create pleasures for the dead?' (Philo, *Det.* 33), or 'There is no judgment, no Judge, and no other world' (*Tg. Ps.-J.* Gen. 4:8). The evocation of both sides of the argument in Wis 2–5 sounds like an echo of the judgement scene in 1 Enoch 102–3.

In vv. 1–5, as in Job 14:1, we have 'but a short time to live, and are full of misery', for there is no 'remedy' (RV 'healing') for death (v. 1, line 3); OL 'refreshment' (*refrigerium*, also at 4:7; often used of afterlife) prematurely introduces the denial of happy immortality implied in the following line, but well displays the link of 'healing' with new life (Deut 32:39; Ps 30:3–4; Hos 6:1–2) which leads to the coming denial (v. 1, line 4). None was known to 'return' from Hades or, transitively, to 'give release' (RV); the latter seems preferable for its sharper polemic. It implicitly negates the myths of Orpheus and Heracles, the miracles of Elijah and Elisha (Sir 48:5, 14), and the hope of rescue by the supreme deity himself (Hos 13:14); its feeling is both biblical (Ps 89:48) and classical: 'Nor virtue, birth, nor eloquence divine Shall bid the grave its destin'd prey resign: Nor chaste Diana from infernal night Could bring her modest favourite back to light' (Horace, *Odes*, 4.7.21–8, tr. P. Francis).

The materialism of v. 2–4 comparably blends biblical and Hellenic reminiscence, following the more sceptical and mocking the more hopeful side of both traditions. Our birth is haphazard, as Epicureans held cosmic origins to be: 'not by design did the first beginnings of things station themselves' (Lucretius, 5.419, tr. H. A. J. Munro); on the other side, like a refutal of the ungodly, 'Not to blind hazard or accident is our birth and our creation due' (Cic. *Tusc.* 1.118, tr. J. E. King). The philosophers' 'spark' of reason is as temporary as the associated heart-beat (v. 2); Heraclitus' view that the soul was a 'spark' of ethereal fire (Macrobius, *In Somnium Scipionis*, 1.14) is cited as well known by Tertullian, *De Anima* 5.2. When the body dies, the spirit is dispersed (v. 3; Eccl 3:21), and (as in Horace, *Odes*, 4.7.16) 'our best remains are ashes and a shade'. Lastly, the sealed end without 'return' (*anapodismos*, v. 5) for the passing of our shadow seems implicitly to negate Isaiah's miracle of the shadow on the dial, when the sun 'went back' (*anepodisen*, Sir 48:23 REB) and life was regained.

The call to enjoy life (vv. 6–9) was often underlined in poetry by a reminder of death: 'Live, says he, for I'm coming' (Virg. App. *Copa*, 38, tr. H. Waddell); but here death has been the first consideration (vv. 1–5), and 'Gather ye rosebuds while ye may' (v. 8) leads not simply to wine or love but to robbery, torment, and murder (vv. 10–20). Heartless sensuality, 'making use of the creation' (v. 6), is vividly evoked through concentration (vv. 7–9) on the spring flowers grabbed for the soon-discarded crowns of the drunkards (contrast the decorous bestowal of a wreath at a well-conducted symposium, Sir 32:2); Isa 28 (1–4) is echoed again, as in 1:16 above. In accord with this floral theme, in v. 9 probably read *leimon* (meadow) for *hēmon* (of us), as suggested by an additional line in the OL which otherwise corresponds to v. 9, line 1 NRSV (Kilpatrick 1981: 216; Scarpat 1989–96; see Gregg 1909), and render 'Let no meadow fail to share in our revelry'.

In vv. 10–20 the series of hedonistic group exhortations starting with 'let us enjoy' turns, with a sinister unveiling of purpose, into the tyrannical 'let us oppress . . . lie in wait . . . test . . . condemn'; for this sequence compare Jas 5:5–6, perhaps an echo of Wisdom. Now the speech recalls Prov 1:10–14, cited above, an enticement by the 'ungodly' (LXX) to rob and murder the 'righteous' (LXX). In Wisdom also the victim is the 'righteous' (*dikaios*, Lat. *iustus*, vv. 10, 12, 16, 18; 3:1), taken by early Christians (WIS A.11–12) to be Christ amid his enemies prophetically foreseen (so among others, with reference to v. 12 onwards, Cyp. *Test.* 2.14; Aug. *De civ. dei*, 17.20); the scene recalls Plato on the inevitable torture and judicial murder of the *dikaios* (*Rep.* 2.5, 362A, also referred to Christ by Clem. Al. *Strom.* 5.14), and biblical accounts of the suffering righteous (Ps 37:12–13; Isa 53:11; *Ps. Sol.* 13:6–12), from 'righteous Abel' onwards (Mt 23:25; 1Jn 3:12; Philo and Targum as cited above; in 1 Enoch 22:5–7 Abel leads the spirits' cry for vengeance). The whole of 2:1–3:11 recalls Isa 57:1–3 LXX: 'See how the righteous perishes, and none takes it to heart . . . from the face of unrighteousness the righteous was taken away; his grave shall be in peace, he was taken from the midst. But draw near, you lawless children . . . in what did you take delight, and against whom did you open your mouth?' In the much-quoted verse 12, for 'lie in wait' see Prov 1:11 and Ps 10:8–9; 'inconvenient' echoes Isa 3:10 LXX, a verse which Christians also applied to the passion (*Barn.* 3:7, etc.).

Israel collectively are usually the 'child of God' (18:13; Ex 4:22), but suffering individuals apply this to themselves (Deut 8:5, using the second person singular; compare *Ps. Sol.* 13:8 'he will admonish the righteous as a child of love'; Heb 12:5–7); here then (Wis 2:13, 16, 18; 14:3 is collective) the *individual* righteous is the child claiming God as Father, probably with satirical reflection of the near-mystical piety (cf. 7:27; 8:2; WIS A.3) which became characteristic of wisdom and martyrology (5:5); see Sir 23:1, 4, 'O Lord, Father . . .'; 4Q417 (Sapiential work) fr. 1 ii, 'you will be His first-born son' (tr. Vermes 1997: 405); 'These wounds caused me to be beloved of my Father in heaven', *Mekilta*, *Yithro*, *Bahodesh* 6, on Ex 20:6 (tr. Lauterbach 1933: ii. 247).

The righteous 'will be protected' (v. 20), for (rendering more closely with RV margin) 'there will be a visitation of him' with immortality, as at WIS 3:7.

The Ungodly, Reasoning Thus, were Blinded to God's Gift of Life (2:21–4)

God's purposes (v. 22, *mystēria*, RV 'mysteries'), hidden (Mk 4:11) from the impious by a judicial blinding (Isa 6:9–10) brought on by their wickedness (v. 21; cf. 2 Cor 4:4) are indeed to give the worthy their 'wages' (*misthos*, as 5:15 and Mt 5:12, where NRSV has 'reward'); so at 1 Cor 3:7–9 it is similarly said that the rulers responsible for the crucifixion would have refrained if only they had known what God prepares for them that love him. 'Incorruption' (v. 23; 6:18–19) hints, as its Pauline usage suggests (Rom 2:7; 1 Cor 15:42, etc.), at the hope for immortality expounded in the sequel and expressed here in the bold view of human creation as the image (7:26; GEN 1:26) of divine 'eternity' so in the Parables of Enoch, from near the end of the Second Temple period, human beings were created like angels, and 'death would not have touched them' (1 Enoch, 69:11). The technical term 'devil' in English renderings of v. 24 is in origin a transliteration, perhaps derived through Latin *diabolus*, of Greek *diabolos*, 'slanderer', found here; the English technical term is apt because by the time of Wisdom '(the) Slanderer' was already used in Septuagintal Greek, in a comparably special sense, to interpret Hebrew *sāṭān*, 'Accuser' (1 Chr 21:1; Job 1:6; Zech 3:1; cf. Rev 12:9). The serpent in Paradise (GEN 3:1) is here probably identified with Satan, as in REV 12:9 (RV 'that old serpent, he who is called the Devil and Satan'); comparably, a fallen angel tempts Eve in the passage of the Parables of Enoch just quoted (1 Enoch, 69:6). 'Death entered the world', echoed in Rom 5:12, recalls not only Gen 3:3, 19, 22, but also Gen 4:3–8 (Abel's murder), quoted after a citation of Wis 2:24 in 1 Clem. 3:4–4:6; yet the allusion in v. 24 should not be restricted to Cain. The devil's 'company' is none other than death's company (see WIS 1:16).

The Suffering of the Righteous is Rewarded by Immortality (3:1–9)

The consolation now offered evokes such biblical judgement scenes as Deut 32:39–43; 33:26–9; Isa 66:10–24. The doubts addressed (vv. 2–4) are also specified in other literary development of these scenes, for example Mal 3:13–21 (4:3) 'it is vain to serve God'; 1 Enoch, 102–3, *Ps. Sol.* 4:11 (14), quoted on WIS 2:1. 'The Sadducees said: It is a tradition among the Pharisees to afflict themselves in this world; yet in the world to come they will have nothing' (*'Abot R. Nat.* A, 5; tr. Goldin 1955: 39). Here, however, 'the souls of the righteous' are safe (4:17, 5:16) 'in the hand of God' (verse 1), as in Deut 33:3 LXX, 'all the sanctified are under his hands' (applied to Jewish martyrs in 4 Macc 17:19); Wisdom is closer to MT 'in thy hand' (RV). The righteous souls or spirits are kept in hollow places (1 *Enoch*, 22:9; cf. 2 Esd 4:35, 'in their chambers'; 1 Pet 3:19, in 'prison' or safeguard; Rev 6:9, 'under the altar') until their 'visitation' (vv. 7, 9, 13), but can also be pictured in Jerusalem above (3:14; Heb 12:23), blessing the Lord (Song of Thr 64). The 'torment' (*basanos*) that they are spared will not just be that already inflicted (2:19–20), to which OL 'torment of death' or 'torment of malice' (3:1) and 'suffered torments among men' (3:4) probably allude, perhaps with martyrdom in view; but the judgement-scene context suggests that 3:1 also envisages punishment after death, like the *basanos* of the rich man in the parable (Lk 16:23–8; cf. Isa 66:24; Sir 7:17).

The strikingly Hellenic 'seemed to have died' (v. 2; contrast 1 Cor 15:3) recalls Socrates in Plato: 'when death comes to a man, his mortal part, it appears, dies, but the immortal part goes away unharmed . . . the hope is great [cf. v. 4] . . . after I drink the poison I shall no longer be with you, but shall go away to the joys of the blessed' (*Phd.* 106E, 114C, 115D). With 'in peace' (v. 3 RV) cf. Isa 57:2 LXX (WIS 2:10–20). The apparent punishment of the righteous (v. 4) is not only their suffering (WIS 3:1), but the divine 'sentence' of death itself (Sir 38:22; 41:2–4); cf. Hos 13:14 LXX, 'O Death, where is your judgment?', and the Egyptian Jewish epitaph *CIJ* 1513 (Horbury and Noy 1992: no. 36), 'If it was decreed that I should live but a short time, yet I have a good hope of mercy.' 'Hope' has the link with afterlife found in Plato as quoted above on v. 2 and suggested by LXX (Ps 16:9–10, quoted in Acts 2:26; Sir 2:9).

The Hellenic term 'immortality' (v. 4, *athanasia*, 5 times in Wisdom) could be used together with the more typically biblical language of 'resurrection' (*anastasis*), as shown by 1 Cor 15:52–4 and Ps.-Phocylides 102–15. Wisdom's vivid sketch of the righteous departed shining in eschatological war and judgement (3:7–8; 5:16) was applied in medieval exegesis to the agility of the glorified risen body (so Aquinas, *Summa contra Gentiles*, 4.86); and together with the term 'visitation' (WIS 3:7) it has been held to suggest that resurrection was not alien to the outlook reflected here (Puéch 1993: 92–8, 306). Yet Wisdom and 4 Macc speak of immortality without mentioning resurrection, whereas Paul and Ps.-Phocylides both combine the two, and 2 Macc uses equally Hellenic vocabulary but speaks solely of resurrection (WIS A.9); and Wisdom also avoids the imagery of waking (Dan 12:2–3, echoed in other respects). Wisdom then probably reflects preference for the notion of spiritual immortality—no insubstantial form of life (WIS A.9). Contrast the common epitaph-formula 'no one is immortal' (attested at the first-century BCE tomb of Jason in Jerusalem, *SEG* 33.1276).

To interpret martyr-like suffering as probative or sacrificial (vv. 5–6) was traditional (Job 23:10; Song of Thr 17), to cite afterlife in support (v. 7) rather less so. 'Visitation' (v. 7, taking up 2:20) renders *episkopē*, Old Latin *respectus*, a 'looking upon' or 'inspection'; in LXX *episkopē* and the cognate verb (echoed in old prayers, for instance on Good Friday, for the deity to 'look upon' or 'behold' the church) answer to Hebrew commonly rendered 'visit, visitation' (Gen 50:24–5, etc.). Divine

'visitation' could bring good or ill (19:15) here and hereafter (1QS iv 6–14, tr. Vermes 1997: 102; *Ps. Sol.* 9:4–5), but the term was used, with echoes as here of its biblical links with 'day' and 'time' (Isa 10:3; Jer 6:15), particularly for final judgement (*As. Mos.* 1:18; 1 Pet 2:12). Linked too with the human spirit (Job 10:12 RV), it was readily seen as a 'visitation of souls' (Wis 3:13 RV; cf. 1 Pet 2:25 *episkopos* of souls'), with special reference to afterlife as in 3:7 and (on resurrection, WIS 3:4) in *Ps. Sol.* 3:11–12 'when he visits the righteous . . . they that fear the Lord shall rise to life eternal'. Here (vv. 7–8) the righteous, agile in glory (5:16–17; Dan. 12:3), burn sinners like stubble (Ob 18) and judge the world (Dan 7:22; 1 Cor 6:2; WIS 5:16) under the Lord. The 'truth' (v. 9) hidden by false reasoning (1:3; 2:1; 3:10) is now clear; 'at the time of visitation he will destroy it (iniquity) forever and truth will go forth' (1QS iv 18–19). Wisdom's reticence perhaps sharpens the hint at vengeance (3:7), but vv. 1–9 are justly prized for explicit attention to peace, hope, brightness, and the kingdom of God.

The Wicked and their Children are Punished, but the Virtuous, though Childless, are Happy (3:10–4:20)

Reassurance that the wicked will be punished is prominent in judgement-scenes (WIS 3:1; 1 *Enoch*, 102–3). Here the advice 'Do not despair of retribution' (*m. 'Abot*, 1.8) is entwined with the biblical and classical theme of consolation for childlessness (WIS B.1). The wicked and their seemingly hopeful offspring are doomed (3:10–13, 16–19, following wisdom-texts such as Ps 37:28), and their unlawful issue will not thrive (4:3–6, which has exerted a not always salutary influence as the main biblical comment on illegitimacy); whereas the chaste woman or man without children (3:13–14) can look for fruit at 'the visitation of souls' (3:13 RV; WIS. 3:7) and a place in the heavenly temple (3:14; WIS 9:8)—and for present honour, an immortal memory and the propagation of virtue here below (3:15; 4:1–2). The man's consolation develops that given to the righteous eunuch in Isa 56:3–5, and the train of thought is anticipated in Ps 17:14–15 LXX 'They were satisfied with children . . . I shall be satisfied when thy glory is seen'; but the emphasis in Wisdom is on the day of judgement (3:13, 18; 4:6).

(4:7–20) The Righteous who Die Young are Happy, but the Wicked End Miserably Comfort for childlessness now leads to another great theme of classical consolation (WIS B.1), the untimely death (cf. 4:3; 14:15) of 'boys and unmarried maids . . . and youths entombed before their fathers' eyes' (Virg. *Aen.* 6.307–8, tr. Dryden). The universality of this theme, touched in epitaphs throughout the centuries but not so explicitly addressed elsewhere in the Bible, has helped to win special esteem for Wisdom. The premature decease of the righteous is viewed (4:7–16) as the rest (v. 7; OL *refrigerium*, as WIS 2:1) or translation to heaven of those who, like Enoch, soon reached perfection (v. 13; WIS 6:15), being beloved of God, and receive the 'visitation' (WIS 3:7) accorded to the 'holy' or pious (v. 15, *hosios* (3:9), frequent in *Ps. Sol.*); the despisers will themselves be dishonoured and forgotten (vv. 17–20). Allusion to Enoch becomes plain in v. 10, echoing GEN 5:24 (in vv. 10, 13–14 the Gk. has the singular, despite NRSV 'they'); 1 *Clem.* 9:3 'having been found righteous he was translated' is probably indebted to Wisdom, but in any case sums up the view of Enoch set out here. This is the first in a series of unnamed biblical portraits (WIS A.3); didactic as well as artistic, they stimulate biblical knowledge, and present the characters as exemplars of virtue. Similarly nameless allusions characterize the Hebrew liturgical poetry (*piyyut*) of Byzantine Palestine. The lapidary v. 8–9, 13, recall Greek grave-epigrams, and have found many later applications; 'that which the wise man hath said concerning Enoch [v. 13] . . . the same to that admirable child [king Edward VI] most worthily may be applied' (R. Hooker, *Ecclesiastical Polity, 4.14.7*). Virtuous youth condemning age (v. 16) is a commonplace (Ps 119: 99–100; *Jub.* 23:16; Sus 45,52), relevant later on (8:19–21). Even the dead scorn the ungodly (vv. 18–20; Isa 14:16–19).

The Judgement of the Righteous and the Unrighteous (5:1–23)

(5:1–14) **The Righteous have Assurance in the Unexpected Judgement but the Unrighteous Lament their Folly** With 'boldness in the day of judgement' (1 Jn 4:17, perhaps echoing Wisdom), the righteous (WIS 1:1) will 'stand', as later envisaged for the vindicated Christ (Acts 7:55–6) and his followers (Lk 21:36; Eph 6:13); the unrighteous cannot (Ps 1:5).

The unrighteous repent (v. 3) 'too late and without fruit' (Aug. *En.* 2 on Ps 48 (49), s. 4, one of his many quotations of 5:3); any earlier chances (12:19–20) were lost. Repentance after death is also viewed as impossible in Lk 16:19–31 and in much rabbinic teaching (so *Ruth Rab.* 3.3, on 1:17, Montefiore and Loewe 1974: no. 864). The importance of repentance in Wisdom (WIS A.2), as in the Synoptic Gospels and rabbinic teaching, reflects its general prominence in ancient Jewish piety (PR MAN; Philo, *Virt.* 175–86; the Fifth Benediction of the *Amidah*).

vv. 3–5 recall earlier mockery of the 'child of God' (WIS 2:13, 16, 18) and the 'lot' (WIS 1:16; Acts 20:32; Col 1:12) of the 'saints'—*hagioi*, 'holy ones', sometimes angels (Dan 4:17, etc.), but here probably true members of the holy nation (18:9, cf. 17:2), ultimately triumphant over sinners (Ps 149:5–9); Christians are entitled *hagioi* in this sense by Paul (2 Cor 1:1, etc.). Light fails (v. 6) those who leave 'the way of truth' (Ps 119:30 AV; Prov 4:18–19). After 'sun' (v. 6) probably supply 'of understanding', with some Latin witnesses; cf. 7:26, and 11QPs^a xxvii 2–4 'David son of Jesse was wise, and a light like the light of the sun . . . and the Lord gave him the spirit of understanding and illumination' (my tr.; Vermes 1997: 307). 'Arrogance' (v. 8) typified Sodom (Ezek 16:49–50), and tyrannical Jews or Gentiles (*Ps. Sol.* 17:26, 46).

Nine largely biblically inspired short and long similes of transitoriness (vv. 9–12, 14; Job 9:25–6; Prov 30:19; Ps 1:4; Jer 14:8) evoke the fleeting world of the unrighteous and their desires (cf. 1 Jn 2:17); in 9*b* REB 'messenger galloping by' gives the sense better than NRSV. Archery (v. 12, cf. v. 21) was practised by Jews (Hecataeus in Jos. *Ag. Ap.* 1.201–4). These verses, like those on repentance, will have helped to commend Wisdom for use in baptismal instruction (WIS A.11–12; C.2).

(15–23) **The Righteous Receive their Kingdom, and Divine Vengeance on the Unwise Overtakes the Nations** The 'reward' (*misthos*, WIS 2:22) sketched in 3:7–9 now appears as a truly royal benefit (3:5) 'in (*en*) the Lord' (v. 15 RV; cf. Gen 15:1), that is, in his power to give, but perhaps with the overtone that it is constituted by communion with him; cf. Phil 3:14, 'the

prize of the upward call of God *in* Christ Jesus'. 'Crown' for *basileion* (v. 16*a*) matches 'diadem' (v. 16*b*), but 'kingdom' (OL, AV) seems a better translation in 16*a*, for *basileion* as 'kingdom' is linked with Israel and the saints (Ex 19:6 LXX; cf. Rev 1:6; Dan 7:22 LXX). The whole phrase 'the kingdom of fair majesty (*euprepeia*) and the diadem of beauty' (v. 16, my tr.) then perhaps hints at enthronement (Dan 7:9; Mt 19:28) followed by crowning, at the same time suggesting the indescribability of God's gift. 'In the world to come there is neither eating nor drinking . . . but the righteous sit enthroned, their crowns upon their heads, and enjoy the lustre of the Shekhinah' (Rab [early 3rd cent. CE] in *Ber.* 17a; Montefiore and Loewe 1974: no. 1658). Hope for a 'kingdom' of the saints (Dan 7:18, 22, 27) in the 'holy land' (12:3) is unmentioned here, but was indicated in 3:8 on their international dominion, and is not precluded by the leaning in Wisdom towards the spiritual (WIS 3:4; A.9); later Christian chiliasm could keep a spiritual emphasis by stressing the descent of a *heavenly* Jerusalem (Rev 21:2; Tert. *Adv. Marc.* 3.24.6 'changed into angelic substance . . . we shall be translated into that heavenly kingdom').

In this final conflict the righteous are safe (v. 16; WIS 3:1; cf. 19:8; 2 Thess 1:7). Their part in it (3:7) is here neglected in favour of the marshalling of the elements for divine vengeance (vv. 17, 20–3), a familiar thought (Sir 39:28–9) developed in WIS 16:17, 24; 19:6–22; this ethical interpretation of OT storm-theophanies helps theodicy (WIS A.2), and fits Wisdom's Stoic-like conception of an ordered 'cosmos' (*kosmos*, v. 20, better rendered 'world' (REB) than 'creation' (NRSV), WIS A.4). vv. 17–23 (like Eph 6:13–17; 1 Thess 4:8) take up Isa 59:16–19 on the avenging deity and his panoply of judicial virtue; in the background are the influential hymns to the Divine Warrior put in the mouth of Moses, Ex 15:1–18; Deut 32:1–43 (22–5, 35–43). The unwise, *aphrones*, already denounced for perversity of thought (WIS 1:3) are now (5:20), since they resist divine power, *paraphrones*, the 'frenzied'. AV 5:20 'against the unwise' keeps the link with 1:3; later versions add 'his' and 'foes' in amplification.

Kings are Exhorted to Learn Wisdom (6:1–25)

The exhortation to kings takes up the similar speech in 1:1–16, already echoed (5:20), and introduces the great expansion of Solomon's prayer for wisdom (chs. 7–10) which can be viewed as the second main section of the book (WIS A.2).

(6:1–11) **Kings Must Give Heed, for Their Power is from God** Kings are reminded (vv. 1–2; cf. Ps 2:10; *Ps. Sol.* 2:32) that they rule by the grace of God as ministers of his 'kingdom' (vv. 3–4) under his scrutiny (vv. 3–11; WIS 1:6–11; 3:7); so Solomon sat 'on the throne of the kingdom of the LORD over Israel' (1 Chr 28:5), or, later, God gave Ptolemy Philadelphus the hegemony in Egypt (*Ep. Arist.* 219). Near vv. 3–4 in wording are Rom 13:1–7; 1 *Clem.* 61:1; and Jos. *J.W.* 2.140 on the Essene oath 'to keep faith with all, especially those in power, since no ruler attains office apart from God'. The OT view took classic form in the Danielic scheme of four successive God-given world-empires (DAN 2:38–40); with and through Paul it influenced the church (Caesar 'was appointed by our God', Tert. *Apol.* 33.1), and it was not far from Greek and Roman thought. 'Monarchs on earth their power extend, Monarchs to Jove submissive bend, And own the sovereign God' (Horace,

Odes 3.1.1–3, tr. P. Francis). Many Jews served the Seleucids and Ptolemies professionally (Williams 1998: 88–91), but the sentiment led (vv. 3–11; cf. Dante's use of WIS 1:1) to assessment as well as confirmation of human rule. 'Behold, great ones of the earth, the judgment of the Lord, for he is a great king' (*Ps. Sol.* 2:32). God 'takes thought' (v. 7, *pronoei*) providentially (WIS 14:3). 'Holy' (v. 10, *hosiōs*; WIS 4:15) here verges on 'righteous' or 'blameless', as at Lk 1:75; 1 Thess 2:10.

(6:12–25) Wisdom is Soon Found, Kings should Honour her, and her Nature shall be Declared In chs. 1–10 any attempt at describing Wisdom herself is reserved until now, when hearers or readers have been purified by stern narratives of judgement; 1:4–6 stressed that she flees from sin. In 6:12*a* (Gk.) the place of *sophia* at the end (as in 1:4, 6) is natural, but conveys emphasis and awe: 'Bright and unfading is Wisdom' (12*a*, tr. Goodrick). With the recurrent light-imagery (5:6; 7:22–6), here placed first, compare Aristobulus (WIS A.7), frag. 5: all light has its origin in wisdom (Collins 1983–5: 841; Hengel 1974: 167). The praise of wisdom (vv. 12–20) first takes up (vv. 12–16) Prov 1:20–1; 8:1–17 (she utters her voice in the streets, loves those who love her, and is found by those who seek early); v. 21 takes up her guidance to kings (Prov 8:15–16).

In vv. 12–16 the themes from Proverbs are reordered into an emotional and intellectual mysticism (WIS A.I; A.II; D): wisdom is first of all to be loved and desired (vv. 12*b*–13; cf. 21 OL; 7:10; 8:2; Sir 4:12; 24:19, 24), and reflection upon her (vv. 15–16; cf. Sir 14:20–1) is the perfection of understanding.

vv. 17–20, rising to this intellectual challenge with an argument in Greek style (WIS B.I), form a chain-syllogism with six links, in the widely admired manner (cf. Rom 5:3–5; 2 Pet 1:5–7) termed 'heap-like' (sorites, from *soros*, 'heap'). It is urged that desire for instruction in wisdom (vv. 17, 20) ultimately leads to the kingdom constituted by nearness to God (vv. 19–20; cf. 5:16). This conclusion associates the general Stoic view that wisdom brings a kingdom (WIS A.6) with Wisdom's special emphasis on immortality (vv. 18–19, more exactly 'incorruption', RV; WIS 2:23) as the consequence of virtue.

Kings then should 'honour wisdom' (v. 21; cf. Prov 8:15–16); the advice sums up all they have been told since 1:1–4. OL here 'love wisdom', and then (in a continuation not in the Gk.) 'love the light of wisdom', re-emphasize vv. 12*b*–13. The royal preacher will now (v. 22) declare her nature and origin from the very beginning (NRSV 'creation' represents *genesis*, 'beginning') without hiding secrets, or rather 'mysteries' (*mystēria*; OL adds 'of God' in explanation, following 2:23 and evoking the sacred aura of this word and wisdom herself (1 COR 2:7). Here this combines with the sense of the mysteries of a guild, imparted without envy or grudge (v. 23; WIS 7:13), lest salutary wisdom and wise kingship be lacking (vv. 24–5).

The Wise King Starts to Recount his Prayer and Quest for Wisdom, and Speaks in Her Praise (7:1–8:1)

In the genre termed 'rewritten Bible', exemplified at length in *Jubilees* or Josephus's *Antiquities* (Alexander 1988), a far-reaching expansion of the narratives of Solomon's prayer for wisdom (1 Kings 3:4–15; 2 Chr 1:1–13) begins now (WIS 6:1) from the verses on his tender years.

(7:1–7) Since I Shared the Beginning and End which Come to All, I Prayed The young Solomon (1 Chr 29:1) called himself 'a little child' (1 Kings 3:7), and now speaks memorably of his share in the plight of each crying (v. 3) newborn descendant of the 'first-formed', i.e. Adam (v. 1; WIS 4:10); so at birth the baby 'lies naked on the ground' with 'rueful wauling' (Lucretius 5.224–7, tr. H. A. J. Munro). Gestation lasts ten months (v. 2), as in many sources including 4 Macc 16:7, but not 2 Macc 7:27 (nine); NRSV 'pleasure of marriage' reworks the less restricted euphemism of the Greek, 'pleasure that came with sleep' (RV, similarly REB). Despite the detail, the soul is not mentioned separately (WIS 8:19). Kings have the same entrance and exit as the rest (vv. 5–6). 'Know whence thou camest: from a fetid drop; and whither thou art going: to worm and maggot...' (*m.* '*Abot*, 3.1). The king therefore prayed (v. 7*a*), and received understanding (*phronēsis*); he called (NRSV adds 'to God', but perhaps wisdom is invoked, cf. Song of Thr 37, 64) and a spirit of wisdom came (1 Kings 3:12 LXX, 'an understanding and wise heart'; Isa 11:2 'spirit of wisdom and understanding'; WIS A.2); he was like the young disciple who prays for wisdom in Sir 51:13–22; cf. 39:5–6 ('spirit of understanding' given in answer).

(7:8–14) I Preferred Wisdom to Everything Else For the sake of his deep love (8:2) he preferred wisdom to the enjoyment of wealth (vv. 8–9, with 1 Kings 3:11; 2 Chr 1:11; cf. Prov 8:10–11), and also to health, beauty, and light (v. 10); perhaps arduous study (6:14, 17; Sir 39:1) away from broad daylight made him like a pale sickly disciple of the wise, but in any case he looked like a disconsolate lover. The unsought good things in fact came together with wisdom (1 Kings 3:13; 2 Chr 1:12), but, loving her for herself (contrast WIS 8:17–18), he did not think of her as producing them (vv. 11–12). He simply learned without guile and taught 'without envy', in generous abundance (v. 13; 6:23); compare Plato's abundant 'philosophy without envy' arising from contemplation of the beautiful (*Symp.* 219D). She opens (v. 14) the possibility of 'friendship with God' (WIS 7:27).

The mystical aspect of 7:8–8:18 appears in Henry Suso's *Life* (14th cent.; WIS A.12); when he longed to see wisdom, as far as he could see her with the inner eye through Scripture, she showed herself to him. 'She shone like the morning star, and burnt like the glowing sun (7:29)...she spread out herself powerfully from end to end of the earth, and gently ordered all things (8:1)...His face became so happy, his eyes so kind, his heart so jubilant, and all his inner senses sang: Above all happiness, above all beauty, I have loved thee, my heart's joy and beauty...' (7:10) (Clark 1952: 23–4).

(7:15–22a) God, the Guide of Wisdom and Corrector of the Wise, Grant me to Speak Aright; he Gave me All my Universal Knowledge, for Wisdom Taught me Once more (WIS 6:12) an attempt to describe wisdom is reverently deferred, here (v. 15) for prayer to wisdom's own guide (cf. Prov 8:22–3, 30). God 'gave' the king's encyclopedic knowledge of the natural world (vv. 17–20; 1 Kings 4:33), but wisdom the fashioner (8:5; Prov 8:30) was in fact the teacher (vv. 21–2), as implied in 1 Kings 4:29–30, 34; God acted through her (9:1–2) as through an intermediary angelic spirit (9:17). The 'powers' (v. 20), better 'violences' (RV), of demonic 'spirits' (alternatively, 'winds'; OL attests both) were quelled by the king (*T. Sol.*), sometimes through 'roots' (v. 20). Josephus, in his own retelling of 1 Kings 4, relates how Solomon's name and a root and charm prescribed by him were effectually used in the presence of Vespasian for an exorcism; Solomon's wisdom was thus made plain (*Ant.* 8.44–9).

(7:22*b*–26) Wisdom's Attributes and Essence Now at last Wisdom is portrayed, in a hymn-like philosophic enumeration of her glories. Twenty-one (3 × 7, a felicitous number) epithets of her spirit (vv. 22–3) show her understanding, subtlety (WIS A.9), goodness and might and lead to a series of clauses on her name and titles: *sophia*, breath, emanation, brightness, mirror, image (vv. 24–6).

This passage extends the biblical line of sketches of personified Wisdom (WIS A.9); an intellectually-focused portrait by the loving disciple, it is the counterpart of Sir 24:1–22, a mainly sense-oriented self-portrait by wisdom herself (WIS D). It also recalls verses on a divine spirit (1:7) as inspiring or pervasive (Ex 31:3; Isa 11:2; 63:10–11; Ps 139:7); but its distinctively Hellenic vocabulary underlines its extrabiblical connection with the Stoic world-soul (WIS A.4; WIS 1:7; Knox 1939: 71–7). Clement of Alexandria (WIS C.1) indeed held that the Stoics, identifying the Deity too closely with nature, 'were misled by what is said in Wisdom, Pervades and passes through all...' (v. 24), not understanding that this refers to wisdom rather than God himself (*Strom.* 5.14; cf. 2.19; WIS A.7). vv. 22*b*–26 heap up epithets and titles like a hymn, and praise a goddess-like cosmic figure; hence with 7:27–8:16 the passage is compared (Knox 1939: 77–9; Kloppenborg 1982; WIS A.9) with Greek hymns to Isis from the Ptolemaic period, known mainly from inscriptions and forming examples of aretalogy (*aretalogia*), recital of the virtues and wonders of a deity. These include statements in the third person, as here, as well as first-person statements by her (cf. 8:3, and wisdom's self-praise, Sir 24:1–22; Knox 1937) and second-person addresses to her (perhaps cf. 7:7*b*, but contrast prayer to God for wisdom, 9:4). In philosophical interpretation Isis was the female principle of nature (Plut. *De Is. et Os* 53. 372F) and the mother of the universe (Ap. *Met.* 11.5), and so, like wisdom, came to resemble the world-soul (Hengel 1974: 163).

Wisdom's derived qualities (vv. 25–6) excel just because they flow from 'the Almighty' (v. 25). Her five great titles use current ancient metaphors of outflow or 'emanation' (*aporrhoia*, v. 25); so the order in the universe is 'the emanation (*aporrhoē*) and image of Osiris' (Plut. *De Is. et Os.* 49.371B). Christians at first applied the titles to the Holy Spirit as well as to Christ as spirit (Athenagoras, *Leg. pro Christ.* 10.3; Malherbe 1969), but they are discussed christologically by Origen, *De princ.* 1.2.9–12 (WIS 1:4), and in Latin became part of medieval Christ-devotion. 'Breath', RV marg. 'vapour' (v. 25), recalls Sir 24:3 (from the mouth, like mist); 'reflection' (v. 26, *apaugasma*), better 'radiance' (REB), recurs in Heb 1:3, probably not an echo. OL 'majesty' for 'working' (v. 26, *energeia*, Jn 5:17) reflects noble but less pointed, probably secondary, variant Greek. 'Mirror' (v. 26), later viewed together with 1 Cor 13:12; 2 Cor 3:18; Jas 1:23, held special fascination: 'the Lord is our mirror' (*Odes of Solomon* 13:1); 'through Solomon the saviour is called the spotless mirror of the father, for the holy spirit, the son of God, sees himself redoubled, father in son and son

in father, and both see themselves in each other' (Ps.-Cyprian (3rd cent.), *Sinai and Zion*, 13).

(7:27–8:1) Wisdom's Energy and Scope One yet universal (v. 27; 8:1), like the world-soul (WIS 1:7) and the omnipresent Isis (Ap. *Met.* 11.5), she renews all, and mediates between God and the soul by continually 'entering' (WIS 1:4) 'holy souls' (6:10; WIS A.3). 'Friends of God' (6:14) recalls the Hellenistic concept of royal 'Friends' (1 MACC 2:18), and became the title of medieval mystical and prophetic groups (*Gottesfreunde*). Wisdom can do this since (it is implied) her beauty, surpassing light (5:6; 6:12), is dear to God (vv. 28–9; cf. 8:3*b*). She conquers vice (v. 30) and everywhere (8:1), again like a world-soul 'stretched through the whole' and 'enveloping the heaven in a circle from without' (Plato, *Tim.* 34B, 36E), orders (more exactly 'manages'; WIS 11:20) all things 'well'; OL 'sweetly' (AV) forms a link with 16:20–1; Sir 24:15. The Advent antiphon *O Sapientia* (WIS A.12), in use by the eighth century, chiefly consists of 8:1 prefaced by Sir 24:3 (close to WIS 7:25*a*).

From Youth I was in Love with Wisdom, through Whom All Good Things Come; Pondering this I Sought her, and Perceiving that God Alone could Give her, I Prayed (8:2–21)

Turning back from wisdom's portrait to his own youth, the king again recalls his ardent love (7:10); he sought a mystical marriage (v. 2*b* WIS A.2–4). 'Enamoured' (v. 2*c* renders the strong word *erastēs*, AV 'lover'. vv. 3–4 echo wisdom's self-praise (Prov 8:22–30; Sir 24:2–4); she is near and dear to God (v. 3), initiated into his mind and promoting his work (v. 4), like the most noble Friend (v. 3; 7:27) in a king's privy council (v. 4). The king then justifies his youthful passion by recalling with mature worldly wisdom that she is also (vv. 5–16), as again she herself says (Prov 8:10–21, 34–5), the giver of wealth, righteousness, knowledge, kingship, happiness, and honour; this is why he sought her when young (vv. 9, 17–18). The young king, however, fell in love simply with her beauty (7:12; 8:2), but was then also able to rationalize his choice. The differing attitudes of youth and middle age are tactfully sketched; his first love recalls the Aristotelian exaltation of pure over applied science (WIS A.6).

Righteousness (v. 7; WIS 1:1) here takes the philosophic form of the Greek cardinal virtues (WIS A.7); 'there are four aspects of perfect virtue; prudence, justice, fortitude, and temperance' (Diogenes Laertius, 3.90, summarizing Plato; cf. Plato, *Phd.* 69C). The Mosaic law was held to teach these virtues (e.g. 4 Macc 1:18), and is here perhaps implicitly viewed as the sum of the 'righteousness' taught by wisdom (with whom the law is identified in Sir 24:23, Bar 4:1; WIS A.9). By 'foreknowledge' (v. 8) 'signs and wonders' like the Egyptian night (18:6) are both expected and rightly interpreted in advance. 'Immortality' (vv. 13, 17) is the immortal memory rather than (WIS 3:4) life; 4:1 includes both senses, but in this section the latter is conveyed by 'incorruption' (WIS 6:18–19 RV). Rest with her (v. 16; Sir 6:28) in the palace of Israel's king matches wisdom's own expressed desire for rest, fulfilled in Jerusalem (Sir 24:7–12); this 'friendship' (v. 18) leads to friendship with God (7:27–8), but now the stress falls on earthly benefits; contrast Sir 24:24, part of the longer Greek text (WIS C.2;

NRSV marg.), beginning similarly from 'beautiful love', but going on spiritually to fear, knowledge, and holy hope (WIS 3:4).

A youth of parts and purity (vv. 19–20), the king was a 'holy soul' with whom wisdom might live (7:27–8); but even so he had, as he discerningly saw (v. 21), to ask the bride's father. vv. 19–20 are best understood as self-identification with a noble pre-existent soul (WIS A.4), as envisaged by Plato (immortal souls fall from the heavenly regions into mortal bodies, those who have seen the most being embodied as lovers of wisdom or beauty, *Phdr.* 248c–e); compare Philo, *Gig.* 6–16 (the air is full of unseen souls, some descend into bodies, and soul, demon, and angel are different names for one thing) and Essene belief according to Josephus, *J.W.* 2.154 (souls from the subtlest ether become entangled in prison-like bodies; WIS 9:15). v. 21 uses the adjective *encratēs*, OL *continens*, 'in possession of', or alternatively 'continent'. This sense suits v. 20b, and v. 21 was often held to speak of prayer for 'the gift of continency' (preface to the marriage service in the English Prayerbooks of 1552 and 1662); 'give what thou commandest' (Aug. *Conf.* 10.29, quoting v. 21).

Give me Wisdom, without which Even the Perfect are of No Account, and Let her Teach me the Mind of God (9:1–18)

This prayer up to v. 12 has formed a model (WIS A.12), for example in the primers of private prayer issued under Elizabeth I (Clay 1851: 96, 195, 310). It can be taken to end at v. 12, where the petition closes, or with the chapter (so NRSV); but the whole of chs. 10–19, throughout which the Deity is still being addressed (10:20; 11:4, etc.), can also be taken as its continuation in meditative praise. Chs. 9–19 would then be an extended instance of prayer and praise alluding to a series of deliverances in the Exodus and conquest, like Neh 9:5–32 (prayer) or Ps 136 (praise). It seems possible that 10:1–11:1 has been added to ch. 9, and that 11:2–19:18 has then been added to form a more discursive continuation of this Pentateuchally based praise (WIS A.2; B.2).

The prayer in ch. 9 (divisible into vv. 1–6, 7–12, but thematically continuous) is focused on two petitions for wisdom (vv. 4, 10), echoed in v. 17; reasons for asking are given in vv. 5–9, 11–12, and in the semi-detached vv. 13–18 (matching vv. 1–6, 7–12 in length, but in essence meditation, not petition). The address (v. 1a) echoes David's recent prayer (1 Chr 29:18) and adds an anticipation of Solomon's later claim on promised 'mercy' (2 Chr 6:14, 42 RV). Following a familiar prayer-pattern the request begins (vv. 1b–3) from the making of all things (Neh 9:6; Ps 136:5), including viceregal humanity (vv. 2–3; Gen 1:26), by intermediary 'word' (*logos*; Ps 33:6) and 'wisdom' (Ps 136:5 'understanding', Prov 8.30 'I was beside him', Gen. 1:26 'let *us* make'). Logos (v. 1b; 16:12; 18:15) seems to function separately beside wisdom, contrary to Christian identification of both with Christ, but as later seen in part of the Targumic tradition: 'By wisdom the Lord created . . . and the word of the Lord said, Let there be light' (*Frg. Tg.* Gen. 1:1–3); the Logos is an angel-like spirit (18:16) in and probably before Philo (*Conf.* 146; H. Chadwick in Armstrong 1970: 143–5), as JN 1:1 also suggests.

Wisdom (v. 4) has one of the divine 'thrones' (RV marg., pl., as 18:15; Dan, 7:9; cf. David's 'thrones', v. 12 NRSV marg.; Ps 122:5), like an assessor beside the judge, as befits her uniquely close association with the Deity (vv. 9–11; Prov 8:22–30); the young king asks for her in his insufficiency (cf. 7:1–5; 1 Kings 3:7–8; 2 Chr 1:10), also recalling 1 Kings 3:7–8 with 'servants' (v. 4), alternatively 'children' (RV marg.). He dares to ask, for (v. 7) God himself made him king (1 Kings 3:7; 2 Chr 1:8–9) of the chosen people (1 Kings 3:8–9; 2 Chr 1:9; WIS 10:15; A.3), God's 'sons and daughters'. The latter come to the fore in 1 Kings 3:16, just after the prayer; the phrase therefore suits Solomon, but its general familiarity is suggested by Pentateuchal and prophetic attestation (Deut 32:19; cf. Ex 15:1, 20–1; Isa 43:6), and confirmed by 2 Cor. 6:18. God also (v. 8) commanded the building of a temple (by Solomon, 1 Chr 28:6) on the holy hill (Mount Moriah, 2 Chr 3:1; WIS 12:3), a copy of the heavenly tabernacle (1 Chr 28:11–19). The return to the underlying biblical narrative in vv. 7–8 is typical of the 'rewritten Bible' genre (Alexander 1988: 117). The notion of a pre-existent divinely prepared heavenly temple met in 8c (see also Ex 15:17 (LXX 'ready dwelling'); 25:9; Heb 8:5; cf. WIS 16:20 'ready') pervades the LXX versions of Solomon's temple-prayer (1 Kings 8:39, 43, 49 LXX; 2 Chr 6:30, 33, 39 LXX), and also suits a general awareness of Plato's doctrine of ideas (WIS 13:3; A.4).

vv. 13–18 (cf. 1 Cor 2:11–16; 2 Cor 5:4–9) combine the biblical conviction that we need God-given wisdom (v. 17) because we cannot know God's mind (vv. 13–14; Isa 40:13; 1 Cor 2:16) with Plato's view (WIS A.4) that the soul is weighed down (v. 15) by the body (*Phdr.* 81c; 2 Cor 5:4), 'entombed in the body. . . in which we are imprisoned like an oyster in its shell' (Plato, *Phdr.* 250c); cf. Plato and Josephus, quoted on WIS 8:19. v. 18 leads easily to examples of those 'saved' (10:1–11:1); OL 'healed' exemplifies a widespread OL rendering of Greek *so(i)zein* which strengthened the conception of salvation as cure (WIS 2:1), and links wisdom here with *logos* (WIS 9:1) in 16:12. The Latin continuation 'whoever pleased thee, O Lord, from the beginning' (cf. 4:10) is close to clauses in the Greek liturgies (Deane 1881) but is probably an addition; it echoes v. 18b, forms a link with 10:1, and stresses that wisdom helps the saints (7:27).

Wisdom Saved Adam, Noah, Abraham, Lot, Jacob, Joseph, Moses and the Israelites (10:1–11:1)

This series of Pentateuchal examples, of course unnamed (WIS 4:10), still follows biblical conventions (WIS 9, introduction) of prayer (Neh 9:5–32) or praise (Ps 136). It can also be read (Knox 1939: 80–1) as a sketch, in the manner of a philosophic Greek historian, of the growth of civilization from world catastrophe (the Fall, the Deluge, and the destruction of the cities of the plain; vv. 1–8) to a righteous monarchy (Jacob, Joseph, vv. 9–14), preserved by the Exodus (10:15–11:1). This meditation addressed to God (v. 20) is therefore still suitable as instruction to kings (1:1; 6:1).

Wisdom's guidance (10:1–2, 4, etc.) forms an interpretation and development of the biblical portrayal of an angelic spirit who guided patriarchs and people, especially in the Exodus and conquest (Gen 18:2; 19:1; 31:11; 48:16; Ex 3:1; 14:19; 23:23; 33:2; Num 20:16; Josh 5:13–14; Neh 9:20; Isa 63:9–14; Bar 6:7; cf. WIS 1:3). Identification of this spirit with wisdom was already known; in Sir 24:4 the angel's pillar of cloud (Ex 14:19) is wisdom's throne (10:17). Yet wisdom was present, and hence active as mediator, from the beginning (9:9; Prov 8:22–30). Hence in 10:1–11:1 the guidance of the patriarchs by the angelic spirit of wisdom simply continues wisdom's earliest guidance. Christians, uniting pre-existent wisdom with the angelic spirit in the same way, understood both wisdom and spirit as the pre-existent Christ; so (later 2nd cent.) Justin Martyr, *Dialogus*, 61.1, on a power begotten as a beginning (Prov 8:22) and called Glory, Son, Wisdom, Angel, Lord, Word, and Commander-in-Chief (Josh 5:13). Jn 12:41; 1 Cor 10:4, 9 already attest this line of thought.

(10:1–3) Adam's deliverance (1–2) from his 'transgression' (*paraptōma*, as Rom 5:15) reflects contemporary emphasis on his glory (2:23; Sir 49:16) and salvation; in the *Life of Adam and Eve* (Sparks 1984: 141–67) they find mercy after penitence, cf. v. 1*b*. Cain (v. 3), thought to favour views like those of the ungodly in WIS 2:1–20, perished not precisely 'because . . . he killed' but rather 'in fratricidal passions' (my tr.); he is seen as a soul, lost in irrational anger (WIS A.9; 1 Jn 3:15). Concern with individual morality and the career of the soul marks the whole series of examples (vv. 1, 5, 7, 9, 11, 13, 17, 21), and is promoted by their labelling with epithets of virtue.

(10:4–11:1) From Noah (cf. 14:6) to Joseph (vv. 4–14) the unnamed heroes are 'righteous' (WIS 4:10). Wisdom's inward voice is probably credited with Noah's shipbuilding, Abraham's steadfastness, and Joseph's kingship (vv. 4, 5, 13–14; cf. 7:16; 9:11; 8:10–15, respectively); but she came as an angel to Lot (v. 6; Gen 19:15, 17), Jacob (vv. 10–12; in dreams, vv. 10–11; cf. Gen 28:12; 31:11), and the Israelites (v. 17; Ex 14:19). She entered into Moses' soul (v. 16; cf. Ex 4:12), having first appeared to him (Ex 3:1), and made him a 'holy prophet' (11:1; cf. Deut 18:15); cf. 7:27.

A high doctrine of Israel (vv. 15, 17, 20; WIS A.1) is reinforced, first when the kingdom of God (v. 10) kept in heaven (Mt 3:2; 6:9–10; 1 Pet 1:4) is revealed (Gen 28:12) to Jacob/Israel (v. 12*c*–*d*; Gen 32:28); and secondly when (v. 21) wisdom inspires the congregational song at the sea (Ex 15:1–21). Allusions to the wilderness song of the dumb (v. 21*a*; Isa 35:6) and the praise offered by babes (v. 21*b*; Ps 8:2 LXX) suggest the miraculous and hint at ecstatic hymnody (WIS A.1; 19:9); men and women alike, 'filled with ecstasy' (*enthousiontes*), formed one choir to sing hymns of thanksgiving (Philo, *Vit. Cont.* 87). Similarly in rabbinic exegesis 'the holy spirit rested upon Israel and they uttered the song'; babes and sucklings (Ps 8:2) and embryos in the womb all sang with the angels (*Mekilta, Beshallah, Shirata* 1, on Ex 15:1; Lauterbach 1933: ii. 7, 11–12).

The Israelites were Saved, and the Egyptians Punished, by Water; the Egyptians were Punished Also through the Same Irrational Creatures which they had Revered in Idolatry; God could have Acted More Terribly, but His Justice is Measured, and He Loves All that Is (11:2–12:1)

11:2–19:22 continue the Exodus theme of 10:15–11:1, and the address to God begun in 9:1 (WIS 9, introduction), but contrast as a whole with 6:1–11:1, and can be regarded as forming the third main section of the book (WIS A.1). The structure is no longer governed by the biblical narratives of Solomon's prayer for wisdom, its antecedents and sequel; instead, the narratives of the Exodus are determinative. The figure of Wisdom ceases to be central, and the hints at a manual for kings, sustained ever since 1:1 (WIS 10, introduction), are given up; instead, a discursive and homiletic exegetical meditation is addressed to

the deity. Elaborate and sometimes laboured, it ranges from the sweet and noble to the grim and grotesque; but it lacks as a whole the depth of the sections focused on the suffering righteous and the wise king. It seems likely to be a separate composition, perhaps by another author, added to 10:1–11:1 (WIS 9, introduction; 10, introduction; A.1, B.1).

11:2–12:1 forms a coherent passage, but comprises the beginnings of two separate sequences within 11:1–19:22 as a whole. First, vv. 1–14 open a series of seven contrasts between Egyptians and Israelites; the remaining six constitute chs. 16–19. The first six contrasts begin from the Egyptian plagues, the seventh from the Egyptian pursuit of Israel to the Red Sea. The series echoes the contrasts between Egypt and Israel which were drawn in the biblical accounts of the ten plagues and the Exodus (see Ex 8:21–3; 9:4–7, 25–6; 10:22–3; 11:4–7; 12:27; Ps 78:50–3; Neh 9:11), and received additions later on (WIS 11:6–10); contacts with Philo's account suggest that some of the developed material may already have been traditional at the time of Wisdom. In form, however, the series is primarily indebted to the currency of antithetic comparison as a Greek literary device. Secondly, 11:15–16 discerns the principle that as we sin, so are we punished; this, added to the principle already noted (vv. 5, 13), that the ungodly in the form of Gentile foes are punished by the very things that benefit the holy people, leads to praise of God's love and tempered judgement (11:17–12:27) on idolatrous sinners and then to concentrated examination of the root sin of idolatry, its causes and consequences (chs. 13–15). After this bipartite digression (11:15–12:27; 13:1–15:19), linked with its context especially by the theme of Gentile sin (*Jub* 23:23–4; Gal 2:15) and united throughout its two parts by the theme of idolatry in particular, the series of contrasts between Egypt and Israel begun in 11:1–14 is resumed (16:1–19:22).

11:2–14, taking up the Exodus narrative from 10:20–11:1 (cf. Ex 14:31–15:21) recalls (11:2–3) the wilderness march and battle (Ex 17), focusing like Ps 114:8; 1 Cor 10:4 on the gift of water from the rock (Ex 17:6); this suggests the insight that the people benefit from the very things that punish their foes (11:5), who themselves feel extra chagrin and awestruck terror at the thought (11:13). 11:5 thus brings in the first of the seven contrasts, between (11:6–7; Ex 7:17–18) the never-failing Nile turned into blood (itself a fitting penalty for the 'infanticidal decree' (11:7, 14; 18:5; Ex 1:22) against the Israelite male children) and (11:7–10) the unlooked-for abundance of fresh water from hard stone after thirst (itself a fitting paternal chastening (WIS 2:13) which also showed the righteous the torments of their foes, the ungodly. This contrast was later current in the form that the Nile water was bloodied for the Egyptians, but sweet and drinkable for the Hebrews (Philo, *Vit. Mos.* 1.144; Jos. *Ant.* 2.294–5; 3.17).

11:15–16 could start a second contrast, but that is deferred to 16:1. Instead, the plagues of frogs, lice, and flies (Ex 8:6, 17, 24) are taken with some freedom to have been educational punishments (11:16) by the very things with which the Egyptians sinned when, astray through insensate 'thoughts' (*logismoi*, WIS 1:3), they revered worthless 'animals' (*knodala*, 11:15*b*; 16:1; the word covers the range of size from AV 'vile beasts' to RV 'wretched vermin'). Cats or crocodiles, with which deities were indeed associated, would have led more naturally than frogs and unpopular insects to this interpretation; but

Wisdom gives out standard anti-Egyptian polemic: 'they have put their trust in . . . creeping things and vermin' (knodala) (Ep. Arist. 138); 'be ashamed of deifying polecats and brute beasts (knodala)' (Sib. Or. frag. 3, 22, tr. J. J. Collins; Charlesworth 1983–5: i. 471).

11:17–20: the strikingly measured character of divine retribution, on the principle set out in 11:16, is now brought out by a flight of fancy found also in Philo (Vit. Mos. 1.19). The almighty hand that shaped the cosmos (11:17) could have sent truly fearsome beasts (11:18–19). 'Formless matter' (11:17), from the philosophical vocabulary, will have been held by the author to agree with Genesis (WIS A.2); 'it was from our teachers that Plato [cf. Tim. 30A, 51A, (69BC)] borrowed his statement that God, having altered formless matter, made the world . . . the prophetic spirit . . . said [Gen 1:1–2 LXX]: In the beginning God made the heaven and the earth, but the earth was invisible and unwrought' (Justin (WIS A.10), I Apol. 59.1, approving Plato and perhaps echoing Wisdom). The pre-existence of matter is probably allowed in 17 (WIS A.8), for divine power is being asserted, yet words like 'did not make them out of things that existed' (2 Macc 7:28) are not used; these words too could be reconciled with pre-existence, for in Greek thought non-existence tended to signify lack of definite character rather than utter nullity (Stead 1994: 66–8, 107–8), but with fair probability they can be taken as an intended protest against any challenge to divine power implied by pre-existence. Growth of objection to the notion of pre-existent matter among Jews in the first two centuries CE is implied by the revised Greek versions of Gen 1:2: the LXX as quoted through Justin Martyr above is replaced by 'nothing and nothing' (Theodotion) or 'emptiness and nothing' (Aquila) (Salvesen 1991: 1–2). 11:17, treated by Origen as a seeming witness to views of pre-existence matter that he opposed (De princ. 4.6), was reconciled with creation from nullity by the suggestion that prior creation of matter is assumed; 'we read " . . . from formless matter " . . . but that matter itself is made from what is altogether nothing' (Aug. De Gen. c. Manich. 1.5).

11:20 passes from uncanny creatures to wind or spirit (7:20) of divine power (5:23); this was indeed reserved for the Egyptians' ultimate punishment (Ex 15:10). Such tempered and proportionate justice marks (11:20c) the divine ordering (diatassein; to dispose or ordain, cf. 1 Cor 7:17); the similar 8:1 uses dioikein, 'manage', but OL disponere and AV, RV, REB 'order' unite 11:20c with 8:1. The triad 'measure and number and weight' would suit Solomon as builder (1 Kings 7:9–12), but 11:20c, with Philo, Somn. 2.192–4, on the Deity as the weighing, measure, and number of all things, and 2 Esd 4:36–7, on weighing the world and measuring and numbering the times, primarily echoes a current formula derived from Plato, 'an equality which is equal in measure, weight and number' (Laws, 757B). Plato here goes on to speak of the best equality, which is the judgement of Zeus, and the phrase is applied to divine judgement in Wisdom; but it also resembles biblical verses on creation (Job 28:25; Isa 40:12), and T. Napht. 2 praises the beautiful order of creation and the human constitution, made 'by weight, measure and rule' (v. 3). Origen correspondingly applied 11:20c to divine creation of the right number of creatures and the right amount of matter; 'he made all things by number and measure; for to God there is nothing either without end or without measure' (De princ. 2.9, 4.4).

Links with creation and providence (strengthened by association with 8:1) as well as judgement gave 11:20c broad influence as a summary of divine action; it is cited over 30 times by Augustine, for example on the importance of number in Scripture and in the work of creation (De civ. dei, 11.30, 12.19).

(11:21–12:2) 11:20, on power and moderation, expands into an equally influential hymn on God's power and love (11:21–12:2; comparably hymn-like are 12:12–18; 15:1–6; 16:13–14). At its heart it claims (11:23) not simply that 'as his majesty is, so also is his mercy' (Sir 2:17 RV), but rather that he is merciful just because he is almighty, cf. 12:16. 11:23a is echoed in the old collect (before 8th cent.) beginning 'O God, who declarest thy almighty power most chiefly in showing mercy and pity' (Gelasian Sacramentary; English Prayerbook (1662), Trinity XI; Tridentine Roman Missal, Pentecost X). As in Acts 17:30; Rom 2:4, his overlooking of sins appeals for repentance (12:10, 19; WIS 5:3).

11:24–12:1 is governed by the remarkable declaration that he loves all things that are, hating nothing that he has made, sparing all things, and immanent in all things. The emphasis lies on all created things, rather than (as in Jon 4:11) on all human beings or living creatures; compare the divine love for 'the world' (kosmos) in John (3:16, soon passing to humanity in particular), perhaps also hinted at in Paul on 'the creation' (Rom 8:20–1). Platonic and Stoic views of the cosmos as a living organism (WIS A.4) will have assisted this way of thinking. Plato stressed the benevolence of the maker who shaped the world and its soul; 'he was good . . . and desired that all things should be as far as possible like himself' (Tim. 29E). In Ps 145:9, Ps. Sol. 18:1, not dissimilarly, the Lord's mercy is upon all his works, yet thought is immediately focused on his people in particular. Within the biblical tradition, therefore, 11:24–12:1 forms a landmark in the history of the notion of a God of love, combining Greek universality of scope with the strength of the OT imagery of divine love. They are summed up in the epithet 'lover of souls' (11:26 AV; philopsychos), taken up in Charles Wesley's hymn 'Jesu, lover of my soul'; cf. wisdom's entrance into souls (7:27), and the divine 'visitation of souls' (WIS 3:13). NRSV, REB 'who love the living' (similarly RV) does less than justice to the importance of the soul (psyche) in Wisdom (A.9). Although souls in human bodies are primarily in view, the thought need not be restricted to them (WIS 8:19). 12:1 finally praises the Deity's omnipresence through his incorruptible (RV, cf. 2:23) spirit; perhaps wisdom (WIS 1:4–6), but, strikingly, wisdom is not named (WIS 11:2). In view of the fresh emphases of 11:2–19:18 it seems unlikely that the identification is assumed.

12:2 spells out the moral of gradual reformative correction that was suggested by 11:15–20, and is now to be further illustrated.

God did not Destroy the Canaanites at Once, as he Might have Done; in Sparing them he Taught his Own Children, but he Scourged the Unrighteous Egyptians with a Terrible Judgement (12:3–27)

(12:2–18) The national consciousness (WIS A.3) of the 'children of God' (v. 7, NRSV marg.), the righteous who worthily inherit his dear and holy land (vv. 3, 7), is at its fiercest here. Destruction at their hand (v. 6) was ordained for the Canaanites, cannibals whose murderous superstition deserved it (vv. 3–5; cf. Lev 18:21; Ps 106:28, 37–8, respectively forbidding and condemning adoption of these customs); but judgement came little by little (vv. 6–10; Ex 23:30), allowing time for repentance (v. 10; WIS 11:23; 5:3) even though they were an accursed race, and divine power fears no enemy (vv. 10–11). The curse of Canaan (v. 10; Gen 9:25–7, predicting servitude; destruction is added in *Jub.* 22:20–1) is reinforced by the list of capital crimes (vv. 3–6) to justify (cf. v. 13) the divine judgement (and implicitly also the conquest, v. 7), and to show the great clemency (v. 10) of gradual retribution—even if it took the form of hornets (v. 8; Ex 23:28). In v. 5*c* NRSV, with REB v. 6*a*, follows a probable division of Greek letters which in many MSS have suffered confusion. 'Opportunity to repent' (v. 10), more exactly 'place of repentance' (RV), recurs towards the end of the first century CE in the apocalypses of Ezra and Baruch (2 Esd 9:11; Syriac *Apoc. Bar.* 85:12, ET in Sparks 1984: 895); Heb 12:17; 1 *Clem.* 7:5. It is attested in Latin from Livy 44.10 (late 1st cent. BCE) onwards, and Acts 25:16 'opportunity to make a defence', literally 'place of defence', suggests similar Greek use outside the Jewish and Christian communities. Wisdom probably therefore uses a current non-Jewish phrase which gained wide Jewish and Christian circulation through the prominence of repentance.

vv. 12–18 form another hymnlike address to God (WIS 11:21); his absolute sovereignty sets his sentence of destruction above question, but is in any case manifested in righteousness and forbearance; by contrast yet similarly, his seeming forbearance raises questions in Romans, but still no one is qualified to ask (Rom 3:25–6; 9:20–2). 'Those who know' (v. 17) know God, but do not honour him (Rom 1:21).

vv. 19–22 teach repentance and Godlike forbearance. His suffering 'people' (v. 19; 15:14; 16:2, 20; 18:7, 13; 19:5) are being prepared for mercy; their prosperous foes are being given time to repent before a scourging far harsher than God's discipline of his children. The imitation of God (v. 19) was also taught in Plato, the Stoics, and Philo, cf. Lev 11:44; Deut 13:4; Mt 5:45; Eph 5:1; 1 Pet 1:15–16; 1 *Clem.* 30:1; Abrahams (1924). 'A man highly esteemed says in the *Theaetetus* [176AB] . . . Flight [to heaven] is to become like God, as far as this is possible; and to become like him is to become righteous and holy (*hosios*), with understanding' (Philo, *Fug.* 63, quoting Plato).

vv. 22–7, revert to the Egyptians, who ignored the relatively mild rebukes of the earlier plagues (11:15–16; 12:2), but under sterner judgements were angry with their idols and recognized the true God, even as they received his final condemnation. This conclusion balances 11:15–16; in unrighteousness (11:15; 12:23) they were led astray (11:15; 12:24), worshipping ignoble creatures (11:15; 12:24), and punished through the things in which they sinned, holding them to be gods (11:16; 12:24). A weighty term in 11:15–15:19 which gains fresh force through this resumption is 'error' (*planē*, v. 24; cf. Rom 1:27), with the cognate verb 'go astray' (v. 24; 2:21; 5:6; 13:6; 14:22; 15:4; 17:1). Through the LXX it is specially linked with idolatry; images of the heavenly host are forbidden lest 'being led astray, you should worship them' (Deut 4:19 LXX), the false prophet spoke 'to lead you astray from the Lord' (Deut 13:5 LXX), and the holy people dally with but reject error and idolatry (Isa 30:10, 19–20, 22 LXX).

Those who Worshipped God's Works were not Excused; but Yet More Miserable are Those who Worship what Human Hands have Made (13:1–19)

Idolatry has been the sin underlying the various crimes detailed since 11:15. Now its nature as the root sin is examined (13:1–15:19). Gentile observances posed practical problems for adherents of the God of Israel living near or among non-Jews (see 1 Cor 8, the Mishnah tractate 'Aboda Zara, and Tertullian *On Idolatry*; inscriptions and documents in Williams 1998: ii. 46–8, v. 47–55); but chs. 13–15, true in their fashion to the philosophic bent of Wisdom, include not wholly unsympathetic speculation on the origins of idolatry (13:1–9; 14:12–31; WIS C.2), and deal with practical problems only implicitly, by polemic and ridicule (13:10–14:11; 15:1–19; WIS 11:16). The continuation of biblical idol-satire in the Letter of Jeremy (Bar 6) and Bel and the Dragon had been adapted in Greek with a philosophical tinge like that of Wisdom in *Epistle of Aristeas* 134–8 (2nd cent. BCE) and *Sib. Or.* 3 (mainly 2nd and 1st cents. BCE).

vv. 1–9, to which Rom 1:18–23 are close, hail and mournfully condemn as *mataioi* 'foolish', that is 'vain' (RV) or 'empty' (v. 1; Isa 44:9 LXX; cf. Rom 1:21) all who seek (v. 6; Acts 17:27; WIS A.10), yet fail to pass from things seen (v. 8) to 'him who is' (v. 1)—a title (from Ex 3:14 LXX 'I am he that is') 'implying that others lesser than he have not being, as being indeed is'(Philo, *Det.* 160)—and fail to rise from the power and beauty of creation to 'the author of beauty' (v. 3). Plato's doctrine of ideas is in view, as at WIS 9:8 (A.4), with particular reference (vv. 3, 5, 7) to the ascent from 'what has the name of beauty here' to 'beauty itself' (*Phdr.* 250E; cf. *Symp.* 211C); LXX shows that the thought of divine beauty implied in the Hebrew OT found increasingly explicit expression among Jews (Ps 50:2, 11 LXX; 96:6 LXX; Isa 63:1 LXX; WIS 7:28–9; 8:2, on wisdom's beauty).

vv. 10–19, with contrasting sarcasm, follow Isa 44:9–20 and kindred texts in drawing a cartoon of the wretched heathen (v. 10; cf. v. 1; 3:11), whose hope is on or (OL) among 'dead things' (vv. 10, 18; Bar 6:32, 71). He whittles an image out of waste wood, not even wanted for the fire (Isa 44:15–17), to fill up his spare moments (vv. 12–13), fixing it safely in a niche (Isa 41:7), and then petitioning it for health and wealth (vv. 17–19). The piquant contrast between helpless image and divine power was equally familiar to non-Jews, who could likewise treat it satirically; 'the carpenter, in two minds whether to make me into a stool or a Priapus, decided that I should be a god' (Horace, *Satires*, 1.8.1–3). Greek dedications can indeed mention the material and the making of an image with humorous pride before formulating a prayer, precisely in the sequence mocked in vv. 10–19; but they also show an ability to differentiate between image and deity which is ignored in satire like that of Wisdom: 'pray that the herald of the gods may be kind to Timonax, who set me up . . . in honour of Hermes the lord' (*Palatine Anthology*, 6. 143, 5th–3rd cent. BCE; the image of Hermes addresses the passer-by).

Wooden Ships, not Wooden Images, Save Seafarers, and Idols are Accursed like their Makers; How Idolatry Began, and How it Brings in Sin and Judgement (14:1–31)

vv. 1–11, still on wood, move to ships and the yet frailer wood of the images of their patron deities (v. 1; ACTS 28:11). The sea between Judea and Egypt is the scene of *T. Zeb.* 6:1–3 (Egypt reached in a fishing-boat), *T. Napht.* 6 (storm off Jamnia). Wisdom, named (vv. 2, 5) here uniquely in 11:2–19:22 (WIS A.1; B.1; 11:2), is the divinely inspired art of the shipwright and navigator; no clear link is made between v. 2 and 7:16 on wisdom as 'fashioner', or vv. 5–6 and 10:4 on the wood of the ark.

Divine 'providence' (*pronoia*; v. 3; 17:2, cf. 6:7) is first mentioned in the biblical books here and in 3 Macc (4:21; 5:30). *Pronoia* was a quality of rulers (2 Macc 4:6; 14:9; Acts 24:3) discerned by Plato in the divinity who brought cosmic order out of disorder (*Tim.* 30BC), denied by Epicurus to his tranquil deities, but ascribed by Stoics to the world-soul (WIS A.2; Stead 1994: 42–51, 146–7); divine providence becomes prominent in Philo, Josephus, and 4 Macc (9:24; 13:19; 17:22). Later Jewish references to *pronoia* in synagogue inscriptions from Sardis (3rd–4th cent.; Rajak 1998) are contemporary with Christian defence and praise of divine providence in Origen (*C. Cels.* 6.71; 7.68) and Eusebius (*Hist. eccl.* 2.14.6). 'Father' (v. 3) is said on behalf of the righteous people of God collectively (contrast the individual, WIS 2:13), as suggested by vv. 6–7 on Noah, who set sail when God 'changed the dry land into sea' (Jos. *Ant.* 1.75) and the giants died (Gen 6:4, 17; Sir 16:17; 3 Macc 2:4); he is perhaps the unskilled navigator of v. 4*b*. 'World' in v. 6*b* renders *kosmos*, but in 6*c aiōn*, a future age (WIS 18:4). Blessing (v. 7) on the wood 'by which righteousness comes', applied in the church to the cross (as by Ambrose, *Sermones* 8.23; *PL* 15.130) and in modern study sometimes (improbably) ascribed to Christian authorship, well fits the ark (v. 6) and sharpens the ensuing curse on idols (vv. 8–11); they shall have their prophesied 'visitation' (v. 11; Jer 10:11, 15 (RV 'visitation'); WIS 3:7).

(14:12–31) The causes (vv. 12–21) and consequences (vv. 22–31) of idolatry are sketched in the conviction that it is the root of sin (vv. 12, 21, 27); 'fornication' (v. 12) has the biblical overtone of disloyalty in religion (Ex 34:15; Ps 73:27 RV). The devising of idols (vv. 12–14) was an innovation (perhaps in the time of Serug, Abraham's great-grandfather, as in *Jub.* 11:4–6, cf. Ps.-Philo, *LAB* 4.16); it will not last for ever (cf. v. 11). vv. 15–21 gain force through touches of sympathy (vv. 15, 17–20; cf. 13:6–7) and echoes (vv. 15, 20) of the Greek Euhemerus (end of 4th cent. BCE; followed in *Sib. Or.* 3:105–61; translated into Latin by Ennius, 2nd cent. BCE), who held that the gods had once been honoured mortals. The link suggested in v. 15 between this view and the cult of the departed child was consciously made by Cicero after the loss of his daughter (45 BCE): 'We see that many former human beings of either sex are among the gods . . . Best and most accomplished of women, with the blessing of the immortal gods themselves I shall set you in your consecrated place among them' (*Consolation*, quoted by Lactantius, *Divinae Institutiones* 1.14). Ruler-cult (vv. 6*b*–21), flourishing throughout the Greek world from the fourth century BCE onwards (Walbank 1984: 84–100), could be seen as evidence on the side of Euhemerus; the composed brevity of Wisdom here contrasts with Philo's vehemence on Caligula's cult (*Legatio* 75–118; WIS c.2).

This error (v. 22) brings, under the name of the 'peace' sought from gods and rulers, what is really internecine war arising from ignorance; for idolatry causes not just the crimes clearly related to it (v. 23; cf. 12:5–6), but the whole range of

social evils (vv. 24–6; Rom 1:28–31; *Barn.* 20, where the catalogue starts with idolatry). What appears in idolaters to be ecstatic joy (WIS 10:21; 19:9) is madness, and prophecy falsehood; they live by unrighteousness and false oaths, which will not go unpunished.

The True God is Hailed. The Ambitious Maker of Clay Idols Hopes in Vain, but the Enemies of God's People yet more Childishly Take all the Heathen Idols for Gods, Even Beasts without Sense or Beauty (15:1–19)

(15:1–6) These hymn-like verses (WIS 11:21), used as an Elizabethan model prayer (Clay 1851: 363), begin by varying the formula 'pitiful and merciful, long-suffering and plenteous in mercy, gracious to all' (Ps 145:8–9 LXX) with the significant designations 'true' (*alēthēs*), over against idols (cf. 1 Thess 1:9; 1 Jn 5:20, *alēthinos*) and 'mercifully ruling' (more exactly 'managing' or ordering, as 8:2) 'all things'; cf. Ex 34:6 LXX; Num 14:8 LXX; Ps 86:15 LXX 'long-suffering, plenteous in mercy, and true (*alēthinos*)' Ps 86:5 LXX 'gracious, gentle, and plenteous in mercy'; 2 Macc 1:24 'only king and gracious one, only supplier of our needs' (my tr.). 'Gracious' (*chrēstos*), not in the LXX Pentateuch, became a solemn and valued description (Ps 25:8 LXX; 34:8 LXX, etc.; 'gracious and merciful', *Ps Sol.* 5:2; 10:8); it is the most frequent epithet for the departed in second-century BCE to first-century CE Egyptian Jewish epitaphs (Horbury and Noy 1992: 272).

v. 2 can perhaps be paraphrased 'If we sin we will not give up our loyalty to our God, for we fear his power [*kratos*, probably punitive, as at 2 Macc 3:34; 7:17]; but knowing that our repute reflects on our God, out of love we will not sin.' 'Immortality' (v. 3) is again future life (contrast WIS 8:13), for (Ps 115:4, 8 are echoed) we are not deceived by 'art or man's device' (Acts 17:29, close to v. 4) into Pygmalion-like desire for an image (v. 5); those who make or desire or revere them are worthy of them.

(15:7–13) in a variation on the amateur wood-carver (13:11–19) and the famous sculptor (14:18–20), depicts the maker of clay figures, whose own borrowed soul (v. 8; WIS A.4; 8:19; Ps.-Phoc. 106) must be returned (Lk 12:20; Jos *J.W.* 3.374: do not commit suicide, but return the loan (*chreos*, as here) when it is claimed); and who thinks only of gain (v. 12; Jas 4:13) despite awareness of guilt (v. 13). Jewish potters are attested in second- to first-century BCE Egypt (Williams 1998: i. 71), and perhaps v. 13 implies criticism of some who sold images.

(15:14–19) turns to Gentile oppressors who adopt all heathen gods without discrimination (Ps 115:5–7 is echoed). The gibe suits Ptolemaic government in Egypt; returning to Milton's 'brutish gods of Nile' (11:15), it prepares for resumption of the series of contrasts between Egypt and Israel which was broken off at 11:14 (WIS 11:2).

Egyptian Animal-Worshippers were Punished by Vermin, but Creatures of Rare Taste were a Benefit to God's People; Egyptians were Slain by Insects, but God's People were Healed after Chastisement by Serpents, the Brazen Serpent Betokening Divine Salvation; Heat and Cold Changed their Nature to Punish and Starve the Ungodly, but to Delight God's People with Angels' Food (16:1–29)

(16:1–4) The second contrast (WIS 11:2, 15–16) sets the fitting torment of *knodala* (v. 1; WIS 11:15) over against the toothsome

quails (19:11–12; Ex 16:13); Egyptians lost their appetite, Israelites relished exotic food like epicures. The wonder is recalled
with the happiness of Ps 106:40 rather than the shame of Ps
78:26–31.

(16:5–14) The third contrast adds (v. 9) the locusts (Ex 10:14–
19), which constituted a 'death' (Ex 10:17 RV; LXX *thanatos*), to
the flies, by which Egypt was 'destroyed' (Ex 8:24 (RV marg.,
LXX), used in the second contrast). These tiny insects sufficed
to kill the oppressors (vv. 4, 8–9); but when (Num 21:6–9)
God's children (vv. 10–11) were bitten by writhing serpents
(vv. 5, 10), like the dread 'writhing serpent' to be slain by God's
own sword (Isa 27:1; RV, REB retain the full echo), it was just a
'warning' (v. 6) wherein they were saved (v. 11) 'sharply'
(*oxeōs*). NRSV (v. 11) adds 'then' to 'and', without express
warrant in the Greek, but perhaps affliction itself is viewed
as salvific, and *oxeōs* means 'cuttingly' as well as (NRSV)
'quickly'; cf. 1 Cor 3:15; 5:5; 11:32.

The brazen serpent (vv. 6–8; Num 21:8–9) showed the
enemy God's power (v. 4a; Deut 32:24b, 26–7); it was a symbol
of salvation (OL *signum salutis*, through Jn 3:14 a designation of the cross; in the medieval and later Western divine
office vv. 6, 7, and 8 formed antiphons for Holy Cross Day, 14
September.) Not effectual in itself, it recalled the commandment (v. 6b, cf. Mal 4:4; including Deut 6:16 'Ye shall not
tempt', cf. 1 Cor 10:9) and the healing divine word (vv. 11–12;
Ex 15:26; Ps 107:20); in later Jewish teaching, as here, they
looked and were saved *if* their hearts were fixed on God's name
(*Tg. Ps.-Jn.* Num 21:8, adding this condition). 'Saviour' (v. 7,
sōtēr, here only in Wisdom) is a Hellenistic royal title applied to
God in LXX (Deut 32:15; Ps 95:1, etc.); 'of all' (probably all
things, as v. 12, not, as 1 TIM 4:10, people only) gives v. 7
universalist potential (WIS 11:24; A.11), despite particularist
stress (v. 10).

(16:13–29) The hymn-like vv. 13–14 (WIS 11:21), developing
Deut 32:39, bring in the fourth contrast (see vv. 1, 5; on
16:15–17:1a, Dumoulin 1994). In the plague of hail and thunderbolts (v. 16; Ex 9:22–34; Ps 78:48) fire and water seemed to
change their nature; fire in the midst of water spared the
pestilential frogs, lice, and flies, yet scorched the crops
(vv. 17–19), whereas God's people received 'ready' (pre-
existent, WIS 9:8) heavenly manna, food of angels (WIS A.9)
which, snowlike though it was (19:21) remained and took on
any taste desired (vv. 20–1). This interpretation, not in Philo,
first occurs in Wisdom, perhaps from comparison of Ex 16:31
(honey) with Num 11:8 (fresh oil); so later, in the name of
Eleazar of Modin (early 2nd cent. CE), 'anyone who liked
what is baked could find in it the taste of anything baked
in the world; anyone who preferred cooked food could find
in it the taste of any cooked dish' (*Mekilta, Beshallah, Wayassa,*
5; Lauterbach 1933: ii. 118). In the church v. 21 was applied
both to word and sacrament (especially through Mt 4:4; Jn
6:57–8; 'the manna is the word of God, and whatever taste
is rightly desired when it is taken is immediately there in the
mouth when it is eaten' (Gregory the Great, *Moralia in Job,*
31.15); 'O may my mind for ever live from thee, And thou, O
Christ, its sweetness ever be' (Aquinas, *Rhythm on the Blessed
Sacrament*).

vv. 24–5 (with vv. 17, 23; 19:6, 18–21) allow for miracles in
the providential order by envisaging a transmutation of the

elements, in accord with Stoic teaching ('the four elements
are changed and transmuted up and down', Epictetus frag. 8;
Sweet 1965). Harmony wherein even apparently destructive
forces work together for good (Judg 5:20; Wis 5:20; 16:17; Rom
8:28) is depicted in Sir 39:16–35 (Crenshaw 1975; WIS 5:17). In
Wisdom the harmony can embrace a change of notes (v. 24;
19:18).

v. 28 earnestly commends thanksgiving before dawn and
petition 'towards the sunrise' (*pros anatolēn*, perhaps hinting
at orientation as well as time). The Essenes comparably
prayed 'as though beseeching [the sun] to rise' (Jos. *J. W.*
2.128). Thanksgiving each day 'when it is beginning' was
generally viewed as a Mosaic ordinance (Jos. *Ant.* 4.212); the
morning Shema is said when it is light yet before sunrise,
according to a Mishnaic teaching resembling Wisdom (in the
name of Eliezer b. Hyrcanus, end of 1st cent. CE), but later
recitation was also acceptable (*m. Ber.* 1:2).

*Darkness and Terror Shrouded the Lawless, but Light
Guided the Holy (17:1–18:4)*

The fifth contrast (Mazzinghi 1995; cf. 16:13) expands Ex
10:22–3, under the heading of 'error' (17:1; WIS 12:24)
punished by 'providence' (17:2; WIS 14:3), into a heightened
depiction of the haunted darkness that fell upon Egypt
(17:2–21), although light shone from the fiery pillar and a
temperate sun on God's holy children (18:1–4). Its style is
followed in an eerie passage of Melito, *On Pascha* (16–33;
late 2nd cent. CE; WIS A.2). The spectres (17:3–6, 18) perhaps
are or come from the 'evil angels' who afflicted Egypt (Ps
78:49). 'Inner chamber' (17:4) is a bland rendering of *mychos*,
OL here 'cave', used also of hellish 'recesses' (17:14). Lurid
flashes of fire, which themselves could not be properly
seen, made what *could* be seen by their light seem still worse
(17:6, following OL; cf. Goodrick 1913). The wizards of Egypt
were humbled (17:7–8, 14–15; Ex 9:11; 2 TIM 3:8–9); their
night (v. 14), like Hades (WIS 1:14) whence it came, was
adynaton, perhaps in the less well attested sense 'intolerable'
(AV) rather than 'powerless'. Light shone (18:1–3) on
those through whom the light of the law (Prov 6:23) would
shortly dawn on the 'world' (*aiōn,* 18:4; a future age, as
in 14:6); in the time of Moses 'the lamp of the eternal law
shone on all those in darkness' (2 *Apoc. Bar.* 59:2; Sparks 1984:
877).

*The Enemies' Firstborn were Utterly Destroyed, but the
Plague on the Righteous was Stayed (18:5–25)*

The sixth contrast (cf. 17:1) juxtaposes the death of the firstborn (vv. 5–19; Ex 12:12–14, 21–31) not with the sparing of the
righteous (vv. 7–9) 'that night' (v. 6), as in Ex 12:12–13, 27, but
with Israel's later plague, when after experiencing death (v. 20)
they were spared through the person and office of the high
priest (Num 16:41–50); compare the third contrast, between
the Egyptian plagues of 'vermin' and the later Israelite plague
of serpents (16:5–14). Pharaoh's 'infanticidal decree' is here
(v. 5, differing from 11:6) requited by the slaying of the firstborn and then of the Egyptian host. The saints (vv. 6–9) were
aware beforehand (v. 6; WIS 8:8); v. 9, with *Jub.* 49:6 and Philo,
Spec. Leg. 2.148, anticipates the Mishnah's emphasis on passover hymnody: 'therefore are we bound to give thanks, to
praise, to glorify, to honour, to exalt, and to bless . . . so let us

say the Hallelujah' (Ps 113–18) (*m. Pesaḥ.* 9.5). The destroyer (Ex 12:23) is in vv. 14–15 the divine word (*logos*), pictured (v. 16) as a great angel (WIS 9:1); this electric description (a Christ-mastide antiphon in medieval and later service-books, cf. Jn 1:14) helped to form the concept of Christmas as 'silent night'.

The 'blameless' Aaron (vv. 21–5) stood between dead and living with his censer (Num 16:46–8); Wisdom adds to Numbers an explicit mention of 'prayer', associated with incense (Ps 141:2; Rev 5:8), and Aaron's 'word' recalling the ancestral covenants, an insertion perhaps modelled on Ex 32:13. His vestment, breastplate, and mitre (v. 24; Ex 28:2–39; 39:1–26) display respectively the cosmos, the glories of the patriarchs, and the divine name itself. This interpretation is spelt out later in Philo (*Vit. Mos.* 2.117–35; *Spec. Leg.* 1.84–97) and Josephus (*J. W.* 5.232–5; *Ant.* 3.184–7).

Sinners Justly Met a Strange End in the Sea, but the Righteous were Saved there, for the Elements are Governed in Favour of God's People (19:1–22)

The seventh and last contrast (19:5), from Ex 14:1–15:19, is between the doom that justly filled up the torments of the ungodly by a strange death in the Red Sea (vv. 1, 4–5), and the safe passage of God's people amidst a series of wonders (vv. 6–12). The same interchange of elements (vv. 6, 18–21; WIS 16:24) punished the sinners (vv. 13–17) and saved God's servants (vv. 5–12, 22). 'Fate' (v. 4) represents *ananke*, 'necessity', a word here as in Paul (e.g. 1 Cor 9:16) thought compatible with divine predestination. The 'grassy plain' (v. 7), seemingly peculiar to Wisdom, suits the ecstatic gambols of v. 9 (WIS 10:20–1); vv. 7–9 draw not only on Ps 114:3–4 but also on Isa 63:13–14, where the people at the sea are led like a horse in the wilderness or like cattle in a valley (LXX 'plain').

(19:10–21) brings in hitherto unmentioned points from narratives already considered. vv. 10–13 recall 16:1–2 (lice, frogs, quails), then (v. 13) probably 16:16–19, on the plague of hail and lightning which also brought the 'violence of thunder' (v. 13; Ex 9:23, 28–9, 33–4); the thunders that were prominent in this relatively early plague can more naturally be viewed as a 'prior sign' (v. 13) of warning than the thunder just before the Egyptians were drowned (Ps 77:18–19; Jos. *Ant.* 2.343). Worse than the inhospitable Sodomites (vv. 14–17; WIS 10:6; Ezek 16:49) awaiting punishment (v. 15; *episkope*, WIS 3:7), they too were struck with blindness (17:2, 17; 18:4; Ex 10:23). vv. 20–1 recall 16:17–18, 22–3, but more clearly depict the solidity of the snowlike manna (v. 21; Artapanus 3.37, 3rd–2nd cent. BCE, tr. J. J. Collins, in Charlesworth 1983–5: ii. 903; Jos. *Ant.* 3.27). 'Heavenly' (v. 21; *ambrosios*, RV 'ambrosial') underlines 'angels' food' (16:20) with an allusion to the food of the Olympian gods.

v. 22 concludes the address to the Lord taken up in WIS 11:2; as shown by the seven contrasts discerned in the Exodus, his 'people' (WIS A.3; 12:19) have been 'exalted' (Ps 20:6, 8 LXX) and 'glorified' (18:8; Isa 43:4; 44:23 LXX; Sir 24:12; Rom 8:30) by his observant assistance 'at all times' (*Ps. Sol.* 16:4) and 'in all places' (Prov 15:3). Just so (perhaps it is remembered) his 'people' pray 'at all times' (Ps 34:1, 1 Macc 12:11) and 'in all places', at home and abroad (Mal 1:11).

REFERENCES

Abrahams, I. (1924), 'The Imitation of God', in I. Abrahams, *Studies in Pharisaism and the Gospels*, 2nd ser. (Cambridge: Cambridge University Press), 138–82.

Alexander, P. S. (1988), 'Retelling the Old Testament', in Carson and Williamson (1988), 99–121.

Armstrong, A. H. (1970) (ed.), *The Cambridge History of Later Greek and Early Medieval Philosophy* (corr. repr. Cambridge: Cambridge University Press).

Barclay, J. M. G. (1996), *Jews in the Mediterranean Diaspora* (Edinburgh: T. & T. Clark).

Carson, D. A. and Williamson, H. G. M. (1988) (eds.), *It is Written: Scripture Citing Scripture: Essays in Honour of Barnabas Lindars, SSF* (Cambridge: Cambridge University Press).

Charlesworth, J. H. (1983–5) (ed.), *The Old Testament Pseudepigrapha* (2 vols.; London: Darton, Langman, & Todd).

Chester, A. (1988), 'Citing the Old Testament', in Carson and Williamson (1988), 141–69.

Clark, J. M. (1952), *The Life of the Servant*, by Henry Suso (London: James Clarke).

Clay, W. K. (1851), *Private Prayers put forth by Authority during the Reign of Queen Elizabeth* (Cambridge: Cambridge University Press).

Collins, A. Yarbro (1985), 'Aristobulus', in Charlesworth (1983–5), ii. 831–6.

Crenshaw, J. L. (1975), 'The Problem of Theodicy in Sirach', *JBL* 94: 47–64.

Day, J., Gordon, R. P., and Williamson, H. G. M. (1995) (eds.), *Wisdom in Ancient Israel* (Cambridge: Cambridge University Press).

Deane, W. J. (1881), *The Book of Wisdom* (Oxford: Clarendon).

Dumoulin, P. (1994), *Entre la manne et l'eucharistie: Étude de Sg 16, 15–17, 1a*, Anbib 132 (Rome: Pontificio Instituto Biblico).

Goldin, J. (1955), *The Fathers According to Rabbi Nathan*, Yale Judaica Series 10, (New Haven: Yale University Press).

Goodrick, A. T. S. (1913), *The Book of Wisdom* (London: Rivingtons).

Grabbe, L. L. (1997), *Wisdom of Solomon*, Guides to Apocrypha and Pseudepigrapha (Sheffield: Sheffield Academic Press).

Gregg, J. A. F. (1909), *The Wisdom of Solomon* (Cambridge: Cambridge University Press).

Hengel, M. (1974), *Judaism and Hellenism*, ET (London: SCM).

Horbury, W. (1994a), 'The Wisdom of Solomon in the Muratorian Fragment', *JTSNS* 45: 149–59.

—— (1994b), 'Jewish Inscriptions and Jewish Literature in Egypt, with Special Reference to Ecclesiasticus', in J. W. van Henten and P. W. van der Horst (eds.), *Studies in Early Jewish Epigraphy* (Leiden: Brill), 9–43.

—— (1995), 'The Christian Use and the Jewish Origins of the Wisdom of Solomon', in Day, Gordon, and Williamson (1995), 182–96.

Horbury, W., and Noy, D. (1992), *Jewish Inscriptions of Greco-Roman Egypt* (Cambridge: Cambridge University Press).

Horst, P. W. van der (1985), 'Pseudo-Phocylides', in Charlesworth (1983–5), ii. 565–82.

Kilpatrick, G. D. (1981), review of Thiele, *Sapientia*, Fascicles i–iv, *JTS* NS 32: 214–16.

Kloppenborg, J. S. (1982), 'Isis and Sophia in the Book of Wisdom', *HTR* 75: 57–84.

Knox, W. L. (1937), 'The Divine Wisdom', *JTS* 38: 231–7.

—— (1939), *St Paul and the Church of the Gentiles* (Cambridge: Cambridge University Press).

Lauterbach, J. Z. (1933), *Mekilta de-Rabbi Ishmael* (3 vols.; Philadelphia: Jewish Publication Society of America).

Malherbe, A. J. (1969), 'The Holy Spirit in Athenagoras', *JTSNS* 20: 538–42.

Mazzinghi, L. (1995), *Notte di paura e di luce: esegesi di Sap 17, 1–18, 4*, An bib 134 (Rome: Pontificio Istituto Biblico).

Montefiore, C. G. and Loewe, H. (1974), *A Rabbinic Anthology*, repr. with Prolegomenon by R. Loewe (New York: Schocken).

Puech, E. (1993), *La Croyance des esséniens en la vie future: Immortalité, résurrection, vie éternelle?* (2 vols; Paris: Gabalda).

Rajak, T. (1998), 'The Gifts of God at Sardis', in M. Goodman (ed.), *Jews in a Graeco-Roman World* (Oxford: Clarendon), 229–39.

Salvesen, A. (1991), *Symmachus in the Pentateuch*, JSS Monograph, 15 (Manchester: University of Manchester).

Scarpat, G. (1989–), *Libro della Sapienza*, i–ii (in progress; Brescia: Paideia).

Smalley, B. (1986), *Medieval Exegesis of Wisdom Literature*, ed. R. E. Murphy (Atlanta: SBL).

Sparks, H. F. D. (1984) (ed.), *The Apocryphal Old Testament* (Oxford: Clarendon).

Stead, C. (1994), *Philosophy in Christian Antiquity* (Cambridge: Cambridge University Press).

Sweet, J. P. M. (1965), 'The Theory of Miracles in the Wisdom of Solomon', in C. F. D. Moule (ed.), *Miracles* (London: Mowbray), 115–26.

Vermes, G. (1997), *The Complete Dead Sea Scrolls in English* (London: Allen Lane).

Walbank, F. W. (1984), 'Monarchies and Monarchic Ideas', in F. W. Walbank *et al.* (eds.), *The Cambridge Ancient History*, vii. *The Hellenistic World* (Cambridge: Cambridge University Press).

Weber, R. *et al.* (1975), *Biblia Sacra iuxta Vulgatam Versionem*, 2nd edn. (2 vols.; Stuttgart: Württembergische Bibelanstalt).

Williams, M. H. (1998), *The Jews among the Greeks and Romans: A Diasporan Sourcebook* (London: Duckworth).

Woude, A. S. van der (1995), 'Wisdom at Qumran', in Day, Gordon and Williamson (1995), 244–56.

44. Ecclesiasticus, or The Wisdom of Jesus Son of Sirach

JOHN J. COLLINS

INTRODUCTION

A. Title and Author. 1. The book of Ben Sira is known by various names in Jewish and Christian tradition. The Greek MSS usually provide a title at the beginning and again at the end: The Wisdom of Jesus, son of Sirach. The Latin is similar: The Book of Jesus son of Sirach. The beginning of the book is not extant in Hebrew, but MS B from the Cairo Geniza refers to the book as The Wisdom of Simon son of Jeshua son of Eleazar son of Sira (51:30; cf. 50:27). The name Simon is probably introduced by mistake, because of the praise of the high priest Simon in ch. 50. The author's grandson, who translated the book into Greek, refers to his illustrious ancestor as 'my grandfather Jesus'. The full name was presumably Jeshua ben Eleazar ben Sira. The 'ch' in the form Sirach derives from the Greek Sirachides, son or grandson of Sira, and so the Greek and Latin 'son of Sirach' is redundant; here we will use Ben Sira or Sirach. In many MSS of the Latin Vulgate the book is called simply 'Ecclesiasticus', or 'church book'. The medieval Jewish commentator Saadia calls it The Book of Instruction.

2. Ben Sira was evidently a scribe, and he provides a eulogistic account of his way of life in 39:1–11. In his view, the ideal scribe is a man of piety, devoted to the study of the law and to prayer, but also concerned with the wisdom of all the ancients. He also appears before rulers and travels in foreign lands. The book concludes with a quasi-autobiographical poem (51:13–30), in which the author refers to travels in his youth and invites the uneducated to 'lodge in the house of instruction'. The first part (vv. 13–20) of this poem, however, is found independently in 11QPsª and its authenticity as a composition of Ben Sira is disputed (J. A. Sanders 1965: 79–85; but see Skehan and DiLella 1987: 576–80, who take it as autobiographical). Regardless of the authenticity of this passage, however, it is likely that the author of the book was a teacher and that it preserves a sample of one kind of instruction offered to the youth of Jerusalem in the period before the Maccabean revolt.

B. Date. The book is exceptional among the wisdom books of the Bible and Apocrypha in disclosing the name of the actual author. The approximate date of composition is also disclosed by the grandson's preface to the Greek translation. The grandson, we are told, arrived in Egypt in the thirty-eighth year of King Euergetes. The reference can only be to Ptolemy VIII (VII) Euergetes II (Physcon), and the date of arrival is 132 BCE. The translation was completed some years later, probably after the death of Euergetes in 117 BCE. If we assume that the grandson was an adult when he moved to Egypt, and that the grandfather's prime was about half a century earlier, we may infer that Ben Sira's book was compiled somewhere in the first quarter of the second century BCE. Since it claims to present accumulated wisdom, it can scarcely be the work of a young man. Consequently, a date towards the end of that period is likely. The glowing praise of the high priest Simon in ch. 50 suggests that he was a contemporary of Ben Sira, although the eulogy was probably written after his death. Simon II was high priest from 219 to 196 BCE. The book shows no awareness of the upheavals of the time of Antiochus IV Epiphanes (175–164). The prayer in ch. 36 is so alien to the thought world of Ben Sira that it must be regarded as a secondary addition, possibly from the Maccabean period.

C. Genre. Ben Sira's book stands in the tradition of Proverbs, which in turn stood in a tradition of wisdom instruction that is best represented in Egyptian literature. The basic genre of wisdom instruction includes a blend of observational sentences and commands and prohibitions. Sir 3:1–16 is a typical example: 'Those who respect their father will have long life ... Honour your father by word and deed.' Traditional wisdom forms of speech in Sirach include comparisons (Sir 20:31: 'Better are those who hide their folly than those who hide their wisdom'), beatitudes (26:1: 'Happy is the husband of a good wife'), numerical sayings (50:25–6: 'Two nations my soul detests and the third is not even a people ... '), and hymns in praise of wisdom (1:1–10; 24:1–34). But Sirach also incorporates literary forms that are not part of the repertoire of Proverbs. These include hymns of praise to God (39:12–35; 42:15–43:33) and at least one prayer of petition (22:27–23:6; 36:1–22 is probably a later addition). Some departures from Proverbs have precedents in Egyptian wisdom literature, notably the use of autobiographical narrative (33:16–18; 51:13–30) and the critique of the trades (38:24–34). The most striking formal departure from biblical wisdom, however, is found in the Praise of the Fathers (chs. 44–50) which uses the history of Israel as a source of instructional examples.

D. Ben Sira and Biblical Tradition. 1. One of the hallmarks of the biblical wisdom tradition, as found in Proverbs, Ecclesiastes, and Job, is the lack of reference to the distinctive traditions of Israel. The concern is with humanity as such, not with the special status of one people. Sirach, in contrast, pays considerable attention to Israel and its Scriptures. The grandson, in the preface, says that Sirach 'devoted himself especially to the reading of the Law and the Prophets and the other books of our ancestors', and implies that he envisaged his own book as comparable to the ancestral writings. This interest in the Scriptures cannot be explained simply by the spirit of the times. Ecclesiastes may be close to Sirach in date, but makes no mention of the law and the prophets. Sirach, however, says that all wisdom is 'the book of the covenant of the Most High God, the law that Moses commanded us' (24:23) and he describes the sage as 'one who devotes himself to the study of the law of the Most High . . . and is concerned with prophecies' (39:1–2). It has been claimed that he cites or alludes to all the books of the HB except Ruth, Ezra, Esther, and Daniel (Skehan and DiLella 1987: 41). This claim is misleading, however. Most of the allusions occur in the Praise of the Fathers. Elsewhere there are frequent allusions to Proverbs and to Genesis, and several to Deuteronomy. But many of the alleged allusions are loose, and may be coincidental. For example, when Sirach writes 'The rich speaks and all are silent, his wisdom they extol to the clouds' (13:23), an allusion to Job 29:21 is often suggested: 'They listened to me, and waited, and kept silence for my counsel.' But the saying is a truism, and the allusion is accordingly doubtful. Despite Sirach's reverence for the law, his teaching remains in the form of wisdom instruction. It is neither legal proclamation nor legal interpretation. He subsumes the law under the rubric of wisdom, as its supreme example. He does not subsume wisdom under the law. Moreover, he ignores certain sections of the law, particularly the cultic and dietary laws of Leviticus. Not all biblical laws are equally useful as illustrations of wisdom, and there remain other avenues to wisdom besides the law of Moses.

2. The extent to which Sirach drew on non-biblical, non-Jewish sources is also controversial. The maximal view (Middendorp 1973) finds over 100 passages where Ben Sira betrays dependence on Greek sources, but here again there is difficulty in distinguishing between imprecise allusion and coincidental commonplace. Many commentators grant an allusion to Homer's *Iliad* 6. 146–9 at Sir 14:18: both passages use the figure of leaves on a tree to express the transience of human life. Even if the allusion be granted, however, we can no more conclude that Sirach had read Homer than that someone who ponders 'to be or not to be' has read Shakespeare. The strongest evidence for Sirach's use of non-Jewish sources concerns the sayings of Theognis and the late Egyptian wisdom book of *Phibis*, preserved in Papyrus Insinger (J. T. Sanders 1983). In both cases, the material bears a strong resemblance to traditional Jewish wisdom.

There is also evidence of Stoic influence in the notions of complementary opposites (33:14–15), teleology (39:21), and in the striking affirmation about God that 'He is the all' (43:27). There may be an echo of Epicurean teaching in 41:1–4. Sirach certainly shows no aversion to foreign wisdom, but he seems to have favoured Hellenistic material that resembled Jewish traditions and conversely pays little attention to the most distinctive aspects of Judaism such as the levitical laws.

E. The Text. 1. The textual history of Ben Sira's book is exceptionally complicated. We know from the grandson's prologue that the book was composed in Hebrew, but it has not survived intact in the original language. For many centuries the Hebrew text was known only from rabbinic citations (Schechter 1890–1). At the end of the nineteenth century, however, several fragments were found at Cambridge University, in the collection of MSS recovered from the Cairo Geniza (Schechter and Taylor 1899). These fragments represented four distinct MSS, A, B, C, and D. More leaves of MSS B and C were discovered later. Fragments of another manuscript (MS E) were discovered in the Adler Geniza collection at the Jewish Theological Seminary in New York and yet another (MS F) at Cambridge (see Skehan and DiLella 1987: 51–3). All these Geniza fragments are of medieval origin. They include most of chs. 3–16 and fragments of chs. 18–36. The Dead Sea scrolls yielded further, much older, fragments, from around the turn of the era. Two fragments from Cave 2 (2Q18) contain only four complete words and some letters from ch. 6 (Baillet, Milik, and de Vaux 1962) but 11QPs^a contains Sir 51:13–20, and the last two words of verse 30b (J. A. Sanders 1965). Then 26 leather fragments were found at Masada (Yadin 1965). These dated to the first century CE and contained portions of chs. 39–44. In all, about 68 per cent of the book is now extant in Hebrew (Beentjes 1997). For a time, some scholars expressed doubts about the Hebrew text preserved in the medieval Geniza fragments, and entertained the possibility that it might have been retranslated from Syriac. The Masada fragments, however, confirmed the antiquity of Geniza MS B, and indirectly enhanced the credibility of the other fragments. The present consensus is that the Geniza fragments faithfully preserve a text from antiquity (DiLella 1966; Skehan and DiLella 1987: 54).

2. The Hebrew fragments bear witness to two textual recensions. The second recension is distinguished from the first primarily by additions (e.g. 15:14b, 15c). These passages can be recognized as secondary because they are not found in the primary MSS of the Greek translation, and in some cases they are reflected in overlapping Hebrew fragments. There is also a second Greek recension, which expands the text in a way similar to the second Hebrew recension. The second Greek recension is also reflected in the OL. One of the distinctive features of this recension is the belief in eternal life and judgement after death. The textual situation is further complicated by the fact that the Greek text is poorly preserved. The edition of the Greek text by J. Ziegler contains more emendations and corrections than any other book of the Septuagint (Ziegler 1965).

3. In all extant Greek manuscripts 30:25–33:13a and 33:13b–36:16a have exchanged places, probably due to the transposition of leaves. The Greek order of these chapters is often given in parentheses. Only the Hebrew order is given here.

F. Structure and Composition. 1. Attempts to discern a literary structure in Ben Sira have met with only limited success. In the judgement of A. A. DiLella 'the book manifests no particular order of subject matter or obvious coherence' (Skehan and DiLella, 1987: 4). In contrast, an elaborate structure has been proposed by M. H. Segal (1972) and W. Roth (1980). These authors distinguish an original book in 1:1–23:27 and 51:1–30. This book was made up of four sections: 1:1–4:10; 4:11–6:17; 6:18–14:19; and 14:20–23:27 + 51:1–30. Each section was introduced by a prologue: 1:1–2:18; 4:11–19; 6:18–37, and 14:20–15:10. Three additional sections were subsequently added: 24:1–32:13; 32:14–38:23; 38:24–50:29. (So Roth 1980. Segal 1972 distinguishes the Praise of the Fathers as an additional section.) Each of these also has a prologue: 24:1–29; 32:14–33:15, and 38:24–39:11. The key to this structure is provided by five passages on wisdom (1:1–10; 4:11–19; 6:18–37; 14:20–15:10, and 24:1–34). These passages seem to mark stresses in the first part of the book, but they have no discernible effect on the passages that precede or follow them (Gilbert 1984: 292–3). There are some indications that the book grew by a series of additions. The personal reflection in 24:30–4 appears to be the conclusion of a section rather than the beginning of the second half of the book. A similar autobiographical note is found in 33:16–18. First-person statements at 39:12 and 42:15 may also mark new beginnings, and the Praise of the Fathers in chs. 44–9 is formally distinct. There is a concentration of hymnic material in chs. 39–43. These observations render plausible the hypothesis that the book grew gradually, but they do not amount to proof.

2. In this commentary the structure proposed by Segal and Roth is modified to yield the following division: Prologue; Part I: 1:1–4:10; 4:11–6:17; 6:18–14:19; 14:20–23:27; 24:1–34. Part II: 25:1–33:18; 33:19–39:11; 39:12–43:33; 44:1–50:29; 51:1–30.

3. Sirach differs from Proverbs in so far as its material is not a collection of individual sayings, but consists of several short treatises. Some of these are devoted to traditional practical wisdom (e.g. relations with women, behaviour at banquets). Others are theological reflections on wisdom and on the problem of theodicy. Even when the material is largely traditional, Sirach often concludes his reflections by commending the fear of the Lord or observance of the law (e.g. 9:15–16; 37:15).

4. The prayer for the deliverance and restoration of Israel in 36:1–22 contrasts sharply in tone and style with the remainder of the book. It may have been added during the upheavals of Maccabean times. Another prayer, in 51:13–30, is attested independently in 11QPs[a] and evidently circulated separately in antiquity. Whether it was composed by Ben Sira remains in dispute.

G. Major Themes. 1. The major theme of the book is the pursuit of wisdom. In accordance with Proverbs (1:7) and Job (28:28), wisdom is identified as 'fear of the Lord': 'The whole of wisdom is fear of the Lord, and in all wisdom there is the fulfilment of the law' (19:20). Wisdom finds its objective expression in 'the book of the covenant of the Most High God, the law that Moses commanded us' (24:23). Yet Ben Sira's emphasis is not on the fulfilment of the specific commandments of the Torah. It is rather on wisdom as a discipline: 'My child, from your youth choose discipline, and when you have grey hair you will still find wisdom' (6:18). The discipline involves meditating on the commandments of the Lord (6:37) but also requires that one 'Stand in the company of the elders. Who is wise? Attach yourself to such a one. Be ready to listen to every godly discourse, and let no wise proverbs escape you' (6:35). The hymn in ch. 51 informs us that wisdom is to be found in 'the house of instruction', but it can also be sought by travel and requested in prayer. Fear of the Lord, then, is an attitude which requires obedience to the commandments but reaches beyond this. It entails reverence towards received tradition, and towards the elders who transmit it. It is a conservative attitude to life. It is often said to be opposed to the Hellenistic wisdom that attracted many in Jerusalem in the pre-Maccabean period (Hengel 1974: i. 131–53). Ben Sira does not polemicize against Hellenism, and is not averse to borrowing Hellenistic notions on occasion. He has little sympathy, however, for the spirit of adventure and innovation and does not appear to advocate new ideas consciously. In so far as Hellenization led some people to reject established Jewish traditions, as eventually happened in the reign of Antiochus IV Epiphanes (cf. 2 Macc 4), Ben Sira would surely have opposed it.

2. The Lord revered by Ben Sira is all-powerful and little short of overwhelming. The hymnic passages in chs. 39 and 42–3 affirm that 'all the works of the Lord are very good, and whatever he commands will be done at the appointed time'. He is closely identified with the power of nature. The climactic declaration 'He is the all' sounds close to pantheism, but Sirach quickly adds that 'he is greater than all his works' (43:28). In these passages Sirach seems to affirm that all that is, is good. God has made everything for a purpose. The world is constituted by complementary pairs, so that evil is necessarily the opposite of the good, and as such contributes to the harmony of the cosmos. All humanity can do is submit to the will of God. Sirach would seem to be influenced by Stoic philosophy here, if only unconsciously. In other passages, however, Sirach affirms a more traditional, Deuteronomic theology of free will: 'Do not say "It was the Lord's doing that I fell away"; for he does not do what he hates. Do not say, "It was he who led me astray"; for he has no need of the sinful' (15:11–12). When Sirach is praising God's creation, even evil has a purposeful role, but when the focus is on human behaviour it is an abomination to be rejected.

3. The problem of theodicy, or the justice of God, recurs intermittently throughout the book. It is made more acute for Sirach by his steadfast rejection of any belief in reward or punishment after death, beliefs which appear in apocalyptic literature around the time that Sirach wrote. 'Whether life lasts for ten years or a hundred or a thousand, there are no questions asked in Hades' (41:4). Having ruled out the possibility of retribution after death, Sirach offers a range of considerations, from simple submission to the divine will to the unconvincing claim that death and bloodshed fall 'seven times more' heavily on sinners than on others (40:8–9;

see Crenshaw 1975). There is, of course, an inevitable tension between the affirmation of the omnipotent goodness of God and the reality of evil in the world. While he is less than consistent, Sirach generally insists on human responsibility. When God created humanity, 'he left them in the power of their own inclination [NRSV: free choice]. If you choose, you can keep the commandments, and to act faithfully is a matter of your own choice' (15:14–15). Sirach does not pause to ponder the origin of the human inclination, a subject that fascinated later writers such as 4 Ezra (cf. 2 Esd 3:20–6).

4. Ben Sira breaks with the tradition of biblical wisdom by devoting extensive attention to the history of Israel. This history is not presented, however, as the history of the acts of God, or even as a sequential narrative. Instead it is cast as the praise of famous men, who stand as examples for future generations. The examples are chosen primarily because of leadership in their exercise of the offices of priest, king, judge, or prophet (Mack 1985: 11–65). Aaron is praised at greater length than Moses, and Phinehas is singled out for his role in securing the covenant of the priesthood. The whole series ends with a eulogy of Simon the Just, who was high priest at the beginning of the second century BCE. It seems fair to conclude that Sirach was an admirer and ally, and perhaps a protégé, of the high priest Simon. History for Sirach is not a process leading to a goal but a storehouse of examples from which the scribe may draw lessons that are essentially ahistorical.

5. Much of Sirach's instruction is taken up with the traditional wisdom concerns of family and social justice. The social teaching is quite conventional. Sirach has a keen sense of class distinctions: 'What peace is there between a hyena and a dog? And what peace between the rich and the poor? . . . Humility is an abomination to the proud; likewise the poor are an abomination to the rich' (13:18, 20). Observations of this sort are commonplace in Proverbs and in Egyptian wisdom literature. More distinctive is Sirach's negative characterization of merchants: 'A merchant can hardly keep from wrongdoing, nor is a tradesman innocent of sin. Many have committed sin for gain, and those who seek to get rich avert their eyes' (26:29–27:1). Martin Hengel has argued that such passages reflect the conditions of the early Hellenistic period in Palestine, as exemplified in the story of the Tobiad family in Josephus (Ant. 12.154–236; Hengel 1974: i. 138). But Sirach's admonitions lack historical specificity, and his remarks on merchants must also be read in the context of his general condescension to the trades in ch. 38.

6. The family ethic is also grounded in tradition, but here again Ben Sira strikes some original notes, especially in his negative view of women (Trenchard 1982). He affirms the authority of mothers as well as fathers, and is aware of the benefits of a good wife. He discourses at greater length, however, on the bad wife. His most distinctive utterance is found in 25:24: 'From a woman sin had its beginning and because of her we all die.' There is no precedent in the biblical tradition for this interpretation of Genesis. He regards daughters as occasions of anxiety, lest they lose their virginity before marriage or having married, be divorced (42:9–10). In part, Ben Sira's worries reflect the reality of life in ancient Judea. Honour and shame loom large in the value system of the society, and the danger of shame through a daughter's

indiscretion was all too obvious (Camp 1991). If a woman should be divorced, she would return to her father's house, and become, again, his responsibility. Yet Ben Sira is exceptional in so far as his worries are not relieved by any joy or delight in his daughters. In part this may be attributed to his anxious personality—compare his view of the human condition at 40:2: 'Perplexities and fear of heart are theirs, and anxious thought of the day of their death.' But for whatever reason he also shows a personal antipathy for women that goes beyond the prejudices of his society: 'Better is the wickedness of a man than a woman who does good; it is a woman who brings shame and disgrace' (42:14). Negative statements about women are more plentiful in Greek literature than in the Hebrew scriptures (see Lefkowitz and Fant 1982). Familiarity with Hellenistic views may have been a contributing factor of Ben Sira's view of women, but he was quite selective in his borrowings from Hellenistic culture, and so a deeper explanation must be sought in his personality.

H. Canonicity and Influence. Of all the pre-Mishnaic writings that were eventually excluded from the Hebrew canon, the book of Ben Sira was the most widely used. The fragments found at Qumran and Masada show that the book was widely used in antiquity. (Nothing about it was especially congenial either to the Essenes of Qumran or to the Zealots.) Although its use was reputedly banned by R. Akiba, it was venerated by many rabbis in the subsequent generations. Verses from the book are often cited as popular proverbs, and it is also often cited by name (Leiman 1976: 92–102). None the less, the Hebrew text was eventually lost. In Christian circles, the status of the book was ambiguous, like that of the other Apocrypha. On the one hand it was widely cited, and included in some canonical lists; on the other hand some authorities, most notably St Jerome, limited the canonical scriptures to those found in the HB (see Box and Oesterly 1913: 298–303). Unlike the Hebrew text, however, the Greek and Latin versions of Sirach were transmitted continuously with the other scriptures.

COMMENTARY

The Prologue

The prologue was written by Ben Sira's grandson, who translated the book into Greek. It establishes approximate dates for both the original Hebrew book and the translation. The grandson arrived in Egypt in the thirty-eighth year of Ptolemy Euergetes, or 132 BCE. Assuming that the grandson was a young adult at this time, the grandfather would have been in his prime some fifty years earlier. It has been argued that the translation was made after the death of Euergetes in 117 BCE, since the grandson uses the aorist participle synchronisas to indicate that he lived through the remainder of that king's reign (Smend 1906: 4; Skehan and DiLella 1987: 134).

The prologue falls into two parts, the first addressing the grandfather's purpose in composing the book, the second dealing with the translation. The grandfather, we are told, was well versed in the law, the prophets, and the other writings, and wished to add to the tradition. His goal was to help people live according to the law. The translation is undertaken in the same spirit, presumably for the benefit of the Jewish community in Egypt. The prologue attempts to deflect possible criticism of the translation by asking the readers' indulgence. In fact, the corrupt state of the text probably has its root cause in the difficulties of the Hebrew, which often result in a Greek translation that is less than felicitous.

The most controversial point raised in the prologue concerns the formulaic reference to 'the Law, the Prophets and the other books of our ancestors'. By the time of Sirach, there can be little doubt that the Torah had taken its definitive shape. There was evidently also an authoritative collection of prophets, although we cannot be sure where the boundary line was drawn between the prophets and the writings. (David, the putative author of the Psalms, is often regarded as a prophet in the NT era.) The collection of writings that eventually became canonical was certainly not current at this time. The book of Daniel had not yet been completed. Ben Sira does not refer to Ruth or Esther, and surprisingly fails to mention Ezra in the Praise of the Fathers. It is not apparent that Ben Sira's collection of Scriptures included any book that did not eventually become part of the HB. Early sections of 1 Enoch, which seem to have been authoritative for the Qumran sect, would not have been congenial to Sirach, but most of the books now classified as apocrypha and pseudepigrapha had simply not been composed when he wrote.

Part I. Chs. 1–24

(1:1–4:10)

(1:1–10) The Source of Wisdom The book begins with a short hymnic passage in praise of wisdom. Similar passages are found in 4:11–19; 6:18–37; 14:20–15:10, and at greater length in ch. 24 (Marböck 1971; Rickenbacher 1973). The opening affirmation is characteristic of Sirach: all wisdom is from the Lord. On the one hand, this sentence affirms the priority of Yahwistic revelation over all philosophy and wisdom. On the other hand it co-opts all philosophy and wisdom into divine revelation. Wherever wisdom is to be found, it is the work of the Lord.

Two biblical passages come directly to mind here. Prov 8 asserted that the Lord created wisdom as the beginning of his way. Temporal priority here bespeaks primacy of importance. The midrash on Genesis, *Genesis Rabbah*, ascribes this priority to the Torah, which was supposedly created 2,000 years before the creation of the world. In Proverbs, and also later in Sirach, wisdom then becomes God's implement in creation. The second biblical passage that comes to mind here is Job 28, which emphasizes that no one but God knows where wisdom can be found. Unlike Job, Sirach does not consider wisdom to be hidden: God has poured it out upon his works. Sirach does, however, pick up the conclusion of Job 28:28: 'the fear of the Lord, that is wisdom'. The fear of the Lord becomes the *leitmotif* of the following passage in Sirach. A few Greek MSS read 'he lavished her on those who fear him' in v. 10, instead of 'those who love him'.

(1:11–30) Fear of the Lord This passage begins and ends with reference to the fear of the Lord. The motif recurs over 60 times throughout the book. (For a tabulation, see Haspecker 1967: 48–50.) Fear of the Lord is constitutive of wisdom, and

as such it pertains to the central theme of the book, which is laid out here in the opening chapter.

Fear of the Lord is primarily an attitude of reverence towards God and respect for received tradition. Some of its practical implications will become clear as the book unfolds. One fundamental requirement is noted here: 'if you desire wisdom, keep the commandments' (v. 26). Even though Ben Sira pays scant attention to the ritual commandments of Leviticus, their observance is probably taken for granted. We may compare the attitude of Philo of Alexandria, who was far more strongly inclined to emphasize a spiritual meaning than was Ben Sira. None the less, Philo faulted those who neglected the literal observance of the laws, and argued that Jews should be 'stewards without reproach . . . and let go nothing that is part of the customs fixed by divinely empowered men greater than those of our time' (*Migr. Abr.* 89–93). For Sirach, too, fear of the Lord entails diligence even in matters to which he does not otherwise accord importance.

Beyond observance of the commandments, fear of the Lord entails patience (v. 23), discipline, trust, humility (v. 27), and sincerity (vv. 28–9). These are age-old virtues of Near-Eastern wisdom. They offer a pointed contrast to the behaviour of profiteers such as the Tobiads in the Hellenistic period, but there is nothing peculiarly anti-Hellenistic about them. The fruits of wisdom and fear of the Lord are often described in rather vague terms, such as glory and exultation. vv. 12–13 are most specific. Wisdom leads to a long life and happiness even in the face of death. This is the traditional view found in the HB, especially in the Deuteronomic and sapiential books. By the time of Ben Sira, however, its inadequacy was widely perceived. Within the wisdom tradition, Job and Ecclesiastes had pointed out the all too obvious fact that wisdom does not guarantee a long life, and that those who ignore the counsels of the sages often prosper. The religious persecution of the Maccabean era would put a further strain on the traditional theology of retribution. Accordingly, notions of retribution after death were gaining credence in Judaism by the time of Ben Sira (cf. 1 Enoch, 1–36, which may date from the 3rd cent. BCE) and would become widespread in the apocalyptic writings of the Maccabean era (e.g. Dan 12).

At least one commentator has argued that Sir 1:11–13 implies a belief in retribution after death (Peters 1913: 13–14). He points to the parallel in the Wisdom of Solomon 3:1–11 ('The souls of the righteous are in the hand of God . . .'). Cf. also the eschatology of the *Rule of the Community* from Qumran. The children of Light, who walk in the way of humility, patience, and goodness, are rewarded with 'great peace in a long life, and fruitfulness, together with every everlasting blessing and eternal joy in life without end, a crown of glory and a garment of majesty in unending light' (1QS 4). But Sirach lacks the specific references to eternal life that are explicit both in Wisdom (Wis 3:4: 'their hope is full of immortality') and in the *Rule of the Community*. Since Sirach states unequivocally in ch. 41 that there is no retribution after death, there is no justification for importing ideas of an afterlife into ch. 1. However problematic Sirach's belief in this-wordly retribution may be, even for his time and place, he holds to it consistently.

(2:1–18) Trust in God In one MS this passage has the title 'On Patience'. The address to 'My child' suggests the paradigmatic setting of wisdom instruction, a father speaking to his son. The testing in view here consists of the normal trials and setbacks of life. It does not imply persecution with the threat of death, as it does in Dan 11:35 and in Wis 3. Sirach echoes the language of older Scripture to make his point. The questions in vv. 10 and 11 recall the arguments of Job's friends (e.g. Job 4:7; 8:8) and the assertion of the psalmist that he has never seen a righteous man go hungry (Ps 37:25). Since Job's friends are eventually rebuked by God, we might have expected more reticence on the part of Sirach here. He could, of course, point to the restoration of Job to support his point. The scriptural warrant for Sirach's confidence is found in Ex 34:6–7: the Lord is 'a God merciful and gracious'. This appeal to divine mercy is exceptional in the wisdom literature of the Hebrew tradition, where God does not normally interfere in the workings of the universe, but lets the chain of act and consequence take its course (Koch 1955; this view seems applicable to Proverbs and Ecclesiastes, though not to Job). Sirach's view of God is informed by the Torah and the prophets in a way that the earlier wisdom books were not. The result is a more personal view of God, which also opens up a space for prayer in the world-view of the sage.

vv. 12–14 are cast in the form of 'Woes', a form also found in prophecy (Isa 5), apocalyptic literature (1 Enoch, 98–9), and Luke (6:24–6).

The notion of the Lord's visitation (v. 14) is also exceptional in the Hebrew wisdom literature. In Wis 5, the visitation in question clearly takes the form of judgement after death. This is not the case in Sirach. (Sir 2:9c, which promises an everlasting reward, is an addition and belongs to the second Greek recension.) The Hebrew prophets often speak of a day of the Lord which does not involve a judgement of the dead, but brings about a dramatic upheaval on earth (e.g. Am 5:18; Joel 1:15; 2:1; Mal 3:2). Sirach seems to have something less dramatic in mind, but he insists that each individual must sooner or later face a reckoning with the Lord. The chapter concludes by recalling the words of David from 2 Sam 24:14, that it is better to be judged by God than by human beings.

(3:1–16) Honour of Parents The command to honour father and mother is found earlier, in the Decalogue. In Lev 19:2 this commandment follows immediately on the command to be holy, before the injunction to keep the sabbath. It occupies a similarly prominent place in the moral instructions of Hellenistic Judaism. Pseudo-Phocylides, 8, tells the reader to 'honour God first and foremost, and thereafter your parents'. Josephus, in his summary of the Jewish law in Ag. Ap. 2.206, likewise links honour of God and parents. (For further references see van der Horst 1978: 116.) The 'unwritten laws' of Greek tradition likewise demand honour first for the gods and then for parents, and this injunction is ubiquitous in Greek gnomic poetry (Bohlen 1991: 82–117). Ben Sira is the first Jewish writer to offer an extended discussion of the subject. In this, as in several other respects, he parallels the late-Egyptian wisdom book of Phibis, found in Papyrus Insinger (Bohlen 1991: 138–9; J. T. Sanders 1983: 81).

Sirach is in accordance with the Decalogue when he suggests that honouring parents leads to well-being (cf. Ex 20:12; Deut 5:16). The logic of this suggestion is shown by v. 5:

one who honours his parents can expect to be honoured by his own children in turn. There is then a very practical reason for admonishing the son to be kind to the father who is old and senile (vv. 12–13). The son may find himself in the same position one day. Sirach does not rely entirely on the reciprocity of human behaviour, however. He also offers that one who honours his parents atones for sins (vv. 3, 14). This idea is in accordance with the tendency in Second-Temple Judaism to associate atonement for sin with good works (cf. Dan 4:24). Sirach attributes potency to the blessing of a father (cf. the blessing of Isaac in Gen 27) but also to the curse of a mother (v. 9; the parallelism of the verse implies that both cursing and blessing are effective on the part of both parents).

Throughout this passage, mothers are honoured equally with fathers, although the sage mentions the father more often. This is also true in the wisdom text 4QSapA. This Qumran work also promises 'length of days' to one who honours his parents, and exhorts children to honour parents 'for the sake of their own honour' (Harrington 1994: 148; cf. Sir 3:11). Here again the honour of the parent is linked to the self-interest of the son, as his honour too is at stake. The theme of honour and shame will recur frequently in Ben Sira.

(3:17–29) Humility and Docility Exhortations to humility are common in Jewish writings of the Hellenistic period. It is a recurring theme in the Rule of the Community (e.g. 1QS 2:23–5; 3:8–9; 5:24–5), and a posture of humility is characteristic of the Thanksgiving Hymns or hodayot. Cf. also the beatitudes in Mt 5. Sirach, however, goes on to urge intellectual modesty and to polemicize against speculation. We are reminded of the redactional postscript to Ecclesiastes, which discourages the pursuit of books and study and recommends the fear of the Lord instead (Eccles 12:12–13).

It is possible that Ben Sira is polemicizing here against Greek philosophy, and the inquisitive pursuit of knowledge that it represented (so Skehan and DiLella 1987: 160–1). It is equally possible that he wished to discourage the kind of speculation found in rival Jewish wisdom circles, such as those represented in the apocalyptic writings of 1 Enoch, which frequently speculate about the matters beyond the range of human experience. It is also possible, however, that what we have here is simply the attempt of a teacher to keep inquisitive pupils in line. This passage must be read in conjunction with the rebuke of stubbornness in vv. 25–9. Ben Sira wants his pupils to accept what he says and not question it. This is not good pedagogy by modern standards (nor by those of a Socrates or an Ecclesiastes) but it is typical of much wisdom instruction in the ancient world.

(3:30–4:10) Charity to the Poor Sirach rounds out this introductory section with exhortations to almsgiving and social concern. For the notion that almsgiving atones for sin, cf. Dan 4:24; Tob 4:10–11. Concern for the poor, specifically for the orphan and the widow, is a staple of ancient Near-Eastern wisdom literature. In Proverbs, God is the guardian of the poor: cf. Prov 14:31, 'those who oppress the poor insult their Maker'. The rights of the poor rest in their status as creatures of God: 'The poor and the oppressor have this in common: the LORD gives light to the eyes of both' (Prov 29:13). Accordingly,

Sirach argues that God will hear their prayer (4:6). For the idea that one who spurns the poor is cursed, cf. Prov 28:27. Sir 4:10 promises that one who is like a father to the orphan will be like a son to God. The phrase recalls the covenantal relationships between God and Israel (Ex 4:22) and between God and the Davidic king (2 Sam 7:14). In Sirach, however, the relationship does not derive from a covenant but from a style of behaviour. Cf. Ps 68:5, where God is called 'Father of orphans and protector of widows'. Similarly, the righteous man is called son of God in Wis 2:16, 18. For God as father, see further Sir 23:1.

There is a significant textual variant in 4:10c–d. The Hebrew reads: 'God will call you son, and he will show favour to you and rescue you from the pit.' The Greek reads: 'You will be like a son of the Most High, and he will love you more than does your mother.' The Hebrew reading is more likely to be original (Smend 1906: 38). The Greek attempts to improve the parallelism, possibly with an eye to Isa 49:15; 66:13 which compare God to a mother. The translation may also be influenced by the reference to 'their mother' in 10b.

(4:11–6:17)

(4:11–19) The Rewards and Trials of Wisdom The second in the series of wisdom poems falls into two parts. vv. 11–16 discuss the rewards of wisdom. vv. 17–19 describe, in metaphorical terms, the process by which wisdom is acquired. The 'children' addressed by wisdom are her pupils. Cf. Lk 7:35. Wisdom is associated with the love of life (cf. Prov 3:16; 8:35). The terminology suggests an absolute, unlimited life, but the word 'life' is used in Proverbs and Psalms in a sense that is qualitative rather than quantitative (von Rad 1964). Cf. Ps 84:10: 'For a day in your courts is better than a thousand elsewhere.' For the term 'glory' in v. 13, cf. Ps 73:23–6. In v. 14, wisdom is a virtual surrogate for God. The verb to serve, or minister, often has a cultic connotation. The elusive relationship between wisdom and God is explored at greater length in ch. 24. The notion that the wise will judge the nations is found in an eschatological context in Wis 3. It is not clear what form this judging will take in Sirach, except that it affirms the superiority of those who serve wisdom to the rest of humanity. vv. 16–19 make clear that wisdom is not acquired without a period of testing. Wisdom is not mere knowledge, but is a disciplined way of life that involves the formation of character.

(4:20–31) True and False Shame The notions of honour and shame were fundamental to the value system of the ancient Mediterranean world (Moxnes 1993. See further 10:19–25; 20:22–6; 41:16–42:8). Sirach seeks to modify commonly accepted notions of shame, by suggesting that one should not be ashamed to admit ignorance or confess sin. The notion of the proper time received its classic expression in Eccl 3:1–8, but is intrinsic to ancient wisdom. Ben Sira here uses the concept in a more restricted sense. He is concerned with the proper time for speech. It is typical of Ben Sira's cautious approach to life that bold exhortations to fight to the death for the truth are tempered by warnings not to be reckless in speech. v. 31 is cited in *Did.* 4.9 and *Barn.* 19.9.

(5:1–6:4) Cautionary Advice This ethic of caution is also in evidence in ch. 5. For the thought of 5:1–2, cf. Prov 16:1; 27:1. vv. 1, 3–4, 'say not . . .' make use of a literary form that can be

traced back to old Egyptian wisdom (the *Instructions of Ani* and *Amen-em-ope*, ANET 420, 423) and is still found in the late-Egyptian *Instruction of Onchsheshonqy*. It is rare in the biblical wisdom books (but see Eccl 7:10). In most cases, but not all, the form is used to forestall questions about divine justice. Sir 5:1 has a parallel in the *Instruction of Onchsheshonqy*: 'Do not say: I have this wealth. I will serve neither God nor man' (Crenshaw 1975: 48–9).

vv. 5–6 qualify the emphasis on divine mercy in 2:11. A similar warning is found in the Mishnah: 'If a man said, "I will sin and repent, and sin again and repent," he will be given no chance to repent. If he said, "I will sin and the Day of Atonement will effect atonement," then the Day of Atonement effects no atonement' (*m. Yoma*, 8:8–9; Snaith 1974: 32). For the 'day of wrath' (v. 8) cf. 2:14 above. The reference is not to an eschatological day of judgement, but to a day of reckoning for the individual, within this life. 5:9–6:1 deals with duplicitous speech, with emphasis on its shameful character. A good reputation is of fundamental importance for the sage. vv. 10–12 guard against even inadvertent duplicity by deliberation. Cf. Jas 1:19: 'Let every one be quick to hear, slow to speak, slow to anger.' Cf. also Jas 3:1–12 on control of the tongue. The expression 'put your hand over your mouth' indicates restraint. It occurs in Prov 30:32b in the context of exalting oneself, and in Job as a gesture of respect in the presence of superiors (Job 29:9b; 40:4b; cf. Wis 8:12). In Sirach, the restraint is for the sake of discretion.

This section concludes with a warning against desire. The text of 6:2 is uncertain. The Hebrew is corrupt, and the Greek is also problematic ('lest your strength be torn apart as a bull'). Skehan and DiLella (1987) restore 'lest like fire it consume your strength', which makes good sense but lacks textual support. The original text seems to have involved comparison with the raging of a bull. Sirach suggests that desire is self-destructive. The expression 'a dry tree' is taken from Isa 56:3, where it refers to a eunuch. Control of the passions was a trademark of Stoicism but the ethic of restraint was typical of Near-Eastern wisdom. We may compare the various warnings against adultery and the 'loose woman' in Prov 1–9. Cf. also Prov 23 on control of the appetite, and see further Sir 18:30–19:3.

(6:5–17) On Friendship Friends should be chosen carefully and trusted slowly, but a true friend is invaluable (see further 22:19–26). The theme of true and false friendship is sounded briefly in Prov 18:24 (cf. Prov 19:4, 7). Job complains that his friends have failed him (7:14–23; 19:19–22). The closest parallels to Ben Sira, however, are found in the Greek gnomic poet Theognis and in the late-Egyptian *Instruction of Phibis* (J. T. Sanders 1983: 30–1; 70–1). *Phibis* is especially close to Sirach in warning against premature trust. On Sir 6:13 cf. Theognis 575: 'It is my friends that betray me, for I can shun my enemy.' Theognis also says that the trusty friend outweighs gold and silver (cf. Sir 6:15). Sirach strikes his own distinctive note, however, when he says that one who fears the Lord should seek a friend like himself.

(6:18–14:19)

(6:18–37) The Pursuit of Wisdom The third poem about wisdom resembles the second (4:11–19) in focusing on the process of acquiring wisdom, but does not speak in wisdom's name. Several analogies and metaphors are used to convey the need for discipline. The student is like a farmer who ploughs and sows, but who must be patient if he is to reap. (Cf. the NT parable of the sower in Mark 4 and par.) Wisdom is like a stone in the path, and the short-sighted fool casts it aside. Finally, wisdom is compared to various restraining devices—a net, a yoke, or bonds. Cf. the image of the yoke in the teaching of Jesus in Mt 11:28–30 and the yoke of the law in *m. 'Abot*, 3:5. Cf. also Sir 51:26, a passage found independently at Qumran. Another set of images describes the delight of wisdom for one who perseveres: garments of gold or purple, and a crown. A crown is often a symbol of immortality, but here it represents the glory of wisdom.

vv. 32–7 give more straightforward advice to the pupil. He should frequent the company of the elders and attach himself to a teacher. Cf. the call in 51:23 to enrol in the house of instruction. He should also reflect on the law of the Most High. It appears then that the student has two sources to study, at least initially: the discourse of the elders and the book of the Torah. Neither is simply equated with wisdom here. Rather, they have the character of a propaideutic. Wisdom is a gift of God, over and above what one can acquire by study. It is a disposition of the mind and character, and as such it can not be equated with any collection of sayings or laws, although these are indispensable aids in the quest for wisdom.

(7:1–17) Humility and Piety This passage is noteworthy in two respects. First, the sage discourages the pursuit of public office. We find later that the role of the scribe was to serve high officials, not to hold office himself (Sir 39:4). This advice acquires added relevance in the time of Antiochus Epiphanes, when first Jason and then Menelaus sought the office of high priest by bribing the king (2 Macc 4). Both men subsequently came to grief. Hengel (1974: i. 133–4) has suggested that these verses fit Onias III, the high priest deposed by Jason, who had pleaded his case already before Seleucus IV, before Epiphanes came to power. It is more likely that Sirach is articulating his general approach to life, rather than responding to any specific occurrence. None of the high priests had sought to become judges. While we may admire the modesty of the sage this passage shows a serious limitation in his political commitment. While he holds strong views on such matters as social justice, he is unwilling to take the personal risks that might put him in a position to implement them.

The second noteworthy aspect of this passage is the attention given to the subject of prayer, which was scarcely noted in Proverbs. Ecclesiastes has a few comments that accord in substance with those of Sirach (cf. Eccl 5:2). Proper behaviour at prayer is essentially the same as in public speech. One should not be curt, but neither should one run on (v. 14; cf. Mt 6:7).

Respect for physical work (v. 15) is grounded in the divine command in Gen 3:17–19. According to the Mishnah: 'Study of Torah along with worldly occupation is seemly; for labour in the two of them makes sin forgotten. And all Torah without work ends in failure and occasions of sin' (*m. 'Abot*, 2:2). The same Mishnah also parallels Ben Sira's reflection in v. 17 on death as the demolisher of human pride: 'Be exceedingly humble, for the hope of mortal man is the worm' (*m. 'Abot*, 4:4). The Greek changes this verse in Sirach to read 'fire and worms,' thereby implying punishment for the wicked after death (cf. Isa 66:24).

(7:18–36) Social Relations Similar manuals on social relations can be found in *Pseudo-Phocylides*, 175–227, Jos. *Ag. Ap.* 2. 198–210. The household codes in the NT differ in so far as they often prescribe the duties of wives, children, and slaves as well as those of the master, husband, and father (e.g. Col 3:18–4:1; see Balch 1988). None of the relationships is discussed in detail here, but several are treated at greater length elsewhere (friends in 6:5–17 and 22:19–26, wives in 26:1–4, 13–18, slaves in 33:25–33, sons in 30:1–13, and daughters in 26:10–12 and 42:9–14). All the relationships here are viewed in the light of the interest of the patriarchal male, with the unfortunate consequence that wives, slaves, cattle, and children are all on the same level (cf. the tenth commandment, Ex 20:17; Deut 5:21, where wife and animals are grouped together as possessions).

The advice not to 'reject' (v. 19) or 'abhor' (v. 26) one's wife probably concerns divorce (but see the objections of Trenchard 1982: 26–8, who points out that this is not the usual divorce terminology). Divorce appears to have been widespread in Second-Temple Judaism. We have several divorce documents from Elephantine in Upper Egypt in the fifth century BCE and from *Naḥal Ḥever* near the Dead Sea from the early second century CE. Divorce was the prerogative of the husband. According to the Mishnah, 'A woman is divorced irrespective of her will; a man divorces of his own accord' (*m. Yebam.* 14:1). Notoriously, Hillel ruled that a man was entitled to divorce his wife even if she spoiled a dish for him and Akiba allowed it even if he found a fairer woman (*m. Git.* 9:10; Archer 1990: 218). The Jewish community at Elephantine was apparently exceptional in allowing women to initiate divorce. There has been much debate as to whether women could initiate divorce in the Roman era, but the evidence is at best ambiguous (Collins 1997a). Ben Sira here cautions against gratuitous divorce, but he does not challenge the right to divorce as such. Such challenges first appear in the Dead Sea scrolls (CD 4:20–5:2) and then in the NT (Mk 10:2). Sir 7:26b is ambiguous. The Hebrew literally reads 'do not trust a woman who is hated'. Skehan and DiLella (1987) render 'where there is ill-feeling, trust her not'. The verb 'to hate', however, is often used in the sense of 'divorce' (e.g. at Elephantine). Ben Sira here is most probably advising against trusting a divorced woman, probably on the pragmatic grounds that 'Hell hath no fury like a woman scorned.' So the advice is: be slow to divorce, but do not trust a woman you have sent away.

On the subject of slaves, Ben Sira counsels kindness, but again he does not question the institution of slavery. His ethic is based on enlightened self-interest. Slaves and animals are more profitable when they are well treated. It has been suggested that 7:21b is an allusion to the biblical law that Hebrew slaves should be released after six years (Ex 21:2; Skehan and DiLella 1987: 205), but Sirach only recommends freedom for a wise slave (cf. Paul's plea for Onesimus in the letter to Philemon).

Ben Sira takes a somewhat stricter view of children than does Pseudo-Phocylides, who counsels 'be not harsh with your children but be gentle' (Ps.-Phoc. 207). But he shares with the Hellenistic Jewish author the concern for the chastity of unmarried daughters (cf. Ps.-Phoc. 215–16). See SIR 42:9–14. The debt to one's parents, and especially to one's mother, is often noted in Egyptian wisdom literature (J. T. Sanders 1983: 65).

Sirach departs from the conventions of wisdom literature when he dwells on the honour due to priests (vv. 29–31). Sirach's admiration for the priesthood is clear especially in praise of the high priest Simon in ch. 50. Deut 14:28–9 associates the Levites with the aliens, orphans, and widows as people who need support. Sirach, however, does not view the offerings to the priests as charity, but as the fulfilment of a commandment.

It is not clear what kindness to the dead (v. 33) is supposed to entail. The simplest explanation is that it means a decent burial for the poor (cf. Tob 1:16–19; 2:4, 8). It is possible that it entails the placing of offerings at the graveside, a custom noted in Sir 30:18, but with apparent disapproval. Cf. also Tob 4:17. Sirach concludes this section by reminding people of their own latter days, when they too may be in need of kindness. The thought of death reminds us of our common humanity. Cf. m. 'Abot, 3:1: 'Keep in mind three things and you will not come into the power of sin: whence you come, whither you go, and before whom you are to give strict account.'

(8:1–19) Prudential Advice Caution and prudence are fundamental virtues in the wisdom tradition. This passage warns against contention with the powerful, the rich (vv. 1–2), or a judge (v. 14), since in each case there is an imbalance of power. It also warns against becoming embroiled with people of a foolish or violent disposition (vv. 3–4), sinners (v. 10), the ruthless or the quick-tempered (vv. 15–16), because the situation can get out of control. The dangers of dealing with a 'heated' man figure prominently in the Egyptian *Instruction of Amen-em-ope* (ANET 421–4, esp. ch. 9). Cf. Prov 22:23. The image of fire in v. 10 captures both the way in which anger flares up and its destructive consequences. This image is more commonly used to describe sexual passion (cf. Job 31:9–12; Sir 9:8). The warning against giving surety beyond one's means is another time-honoured piece of sapiential advice, nicely captured in Prov 22:27: 'why should your bed be taken from under you?' In all of this the concern of the sage is not with principles of right and wrong but with practical consequences.

Two of the admonitions in this chapter are of a different kind. vv. 4–7 warn against making fun of others or treating them with disdain. Here as in 7:36 mindfulness of one's own mortality is the key to the sage's ethics. The Talmud also forbids reproaching the reformed sinner (y. B. Meṣ. 4:10). The warning not to slight the discourse of the sages (vv. 8–9) is also positive advice, of a line of action to be pursued rather than one to be avoided. Warnings against revealing one's thoughts (v. 19) can be traced back to old Egyptian wisdom (e.g. the Instruction of Ani, 4:1; 7:7; ANET 420). The Egyptian instruction warned not to reveal one's thoughts to a stranger. Sir 8:19 (lit. do not reveal your mind to all flesh) should

probably be read in the same vein as a warning against indiscretion, rather than as against ever confiding in anyone at all.

(9:1–9) On Women Ben Sira now applies his ethic of caution to the subject of women. The meaning of 9:1 is disputed. It is usually taken to mean that the husband's jealousy might suggest the idea of infidelity to the wife (so Snaith 1974: 50: 'and so put into her head the idea of wronging you'). Trenchard (1982: 30) suggests that the wife might then become jealous of the husband and discover infidelity on his part. Camp (1991: 22) takes the verb qn' to refer to ardour rather than jealousy, so that 'the evil the wife learns from the husband is sexual ardor itself'. Against the latter suggestion, it must be said that the sense of 'jealousy' is far better attested. Cf. the notorious ritual for the woman suspected of adultery in Num 5, and the use of the word in Prov 6:34; 27:4. The word qn'h most probably means sexual passion in Song 8:6, however (although even there the nuance of jealousy may also be present). Ardour provides a better parallel than jealousy to 9:2 ('do not give yourself over to a woman'; the Hebrew text is corrupted by dittography of the word qn') and the theme of the following verses is the danger of yielding to sexual attractions. The notions of jealousy and excessive passion are not unrelated. In view of the usual usage of the word, the meaning 'jealousy' should probably be retained in 9:1. For the general sentiment of this passage cf. Ps.-Phoc. 194: 'For "eros" is not a god, but a passion destructive to all.'

Sirach follows Proverbs in his warnings against the 'strange woman' (cf. Prov 5:1–6; 7:1–27; note esp. the motif of wandering the city streets in Sir 9:7 and the decline to the pit or destruction in 9:9). The danger of losing one's inheritance (9:6) recalls Prov 5:10. Sirach's admonitions also bear the stamp of the Hellenistic age. The enticements of the singing girl (9:4) recall the story of Joseph the son of Tobias, who allegedly fell in love with a dancing girl during a visit to Alexandria (Jos. Ant. 12.186–9). The motif of gazing at a virgin recalls the elders in the story of Susanna, but cf. earlier Job 31:1 where Job protests his innocence in this respect. Descriptions of female beauty become somewhat more common in Hellenistic Jewish writings than in the HB—e.g. contrast the description of Sarah in the Genesis Apocryphon from Qumran (1QapGen 20) with the text of Genesis. Public banquets and symposia were a feature of Hellenistic life (cf. Sir 31:12–32:13), but married women were normally excluded from them (Corley 1993: 24–79). The only women found at such gatherings were courtesans and dancing girls. Roman women enjoyed more liberty in this regard, but even they were often criticized for participating in public meals. Roman practice, however, can scarcely have made an impact on Ben Sira in the early second century BCE. It is all the more remarkable then that such socializing with married women appears as a problem in his historical setting. There was a precedent for married women who revelled in wine in ancient Israel (Am 4:1) but they are not said to have done so with men other than their husbands.

(9:10–16) Heterogeneous Advice On the subject of friendship, see SIR 6:5–17. On loyalty to old friends cf. Theognis, 1151–2: 'Never be persuaded by men of the baser sort to leave the friend you have and seek another.' Ben Sira often reassures himself that the wicked will yet be punished: cf. 3:26; 11:28. 'Those who have power to kill' (v. 13) are presumably rulers. Cf. the advice against seeking office in 7:4–7, but the advice here would seem to be in tension with the sage's desire to serve before the great and mighty (39:4). The tales of foreign courts in the books of Esther and Daniel typically portray the king as erratic and the courtiers in danger of sudden death (cf. the king's peremptory decision to put all the wise men of Babylon to death in Dan 2). The importance of making friends with the righteous was already noted in 6:16–17. Contrast Mt 5:43–8, where Jesus reminds his disciples that their Father in heaven makes his sun shine on the wicked and the righteous alike. The reference to the 'law of the Most High' in v. 15 is not found in the extant Hebrew text, which reads 'let all your counsel be among them' (i.e. the wise). For an example of dinner-table conversation that a Hellenistic Jewish writer considered edifying see the *Epistle of Aristeas*, 187–294.

(9:17–10:18) On Rulers and Pride 9:17 contrasts the skill of the tradesman with the wisdom of the ruler (cf. ch. 38). The Hebrew of 9:17b is corrupt. Read *bînâ* instead of the unintelligible *bîtâ*, so the ruler of the people is wise in understanding. Wisdom is associated with kingship in Prov 8:15–16. Cf. also Plato's ideal of the philosopher king. Skehan and DiLella (1987: 223) assume that Ben Sira is thinking of the high priest, the ruler of Jerusalem at that time, but this passage is more likely to be a traditional wisdom reflection on the nature of authority. Cf. the discussion in the *Epistle of Aristeas*, 187–294. (The need for discipline on the part of the king is emphasized in 205, 211, 223.) The motif of the loud-mouthed person, who is hated by all, is also found in Theognis, 295–7.

The discussion of kingship passes over into a discussion of arrogance. It is because of human hubris that sovereignty passes from nation to nation. The belief that God brings low the proud and exalts the lowly is widespread in both Testaments: cf. 1 Sam 2:1–10; Lk 1:46–55. For the notion that God disposes of kings and kingship, cf. Dan 2:20–3; Wis 6:1–8. The motif that God overthrows nations and raises up rulers at the proper time is common to wisdom and apocalyptic literature, and this led von Rad (1972: 281–2) to speculate that apocalypticism developed out of wisdom tradition and the activities of the sages. But the similarity between Sir 10 and Dan 2 is quite limited. Daniel envisages a historical progression, with a climactic conclusion. Sirach sees no such progression, but only a principle that is always at work. This principle, moreover, applies to individuals as well as to kingdoms. The fundamental critique of pride is that human beings are only dust and ashes, living under the shadow of death. Nations are like individuals writ large.

(10:19–11:6) Honour and Shame Cf. SIR 3:1–16 and 4:20–31. Honour should attach to the fear of the Lord, and there should be no shame in poverty. Appearances are often misleading. Yet Sirach does not entirely abandon conventional wisdom. He acknowledges that one who is honoured in poverty will be honoured much more in wealth, and vice versa (v. 30). In part this is simple realism, a recognition of the way honour is actually conferred in his society, but there is an undeniable tension between this realism, which tends to

accept things as they are and adjust to them, and the more idealistic affirmation that the intelligence should be honoured even in poverty (cf. Camp 1991: 9–10). Hengel (1974: i. 151–2) has argued that this passage constitutes a social commentary on Hellenistic Judea, where people such as the Tobiads won honour and glory by opportunistic disregard for law and traditional ethics. Ben Sira is not so specific, and he surely intended to formulate general principles that would apply to any situation. None the less, it is not unreasonable to assume that he was influenced to some degree by the events of his time.

The virtue of humility, extolled in 10:26–31, is quite alien to the Greek sense of honour. In part this is the mentality of the sage, who does not want to occupy centre stage but gains honour through the service of others. In part it is a strategy to guard against humiliation: cf. Prov 25:6–7; Lk 14:7–11; cf. further Sir 13:8–13. 11:1–6 refers back to 10:6–18 for the notion that God brings low the proud, even kings and rulers. It also barely mentions a theme that will be treated at length in chs. 39–44, the wonderful works of the Lord.

(11:7–28) Patience and Trust vv. 7–8 involve elementary courtesy as well as being a prerequisite for wisdom: cf. Prov 18:13; *m. 'Abot*, 5:10. The advice in v. 9 is expressed more pungently in Prov 26:17: 'Like somebody who takes a passing dog by the ears is one who meddles in the quarrel of another.'

In much of this section Sirach expounds a theme that is surprisingly reminiscent of Ecclesiastes: the futility of toil and effort. Success is determined by the favour of the Lord (cf. Eccl 2:26). Even if someone thinks he has acquired wealth, the acquisition is not secure. God can change a person's fortune, and whatever has been accumulated must eventually pass to another when the person dies (cf. Eccl 2:18–22; 6:1–3 and the parable of the rich fool in Lk 12:16–21). These observations lead to an attitude of resignation. The principle enunciated in v. 14, that all things, good and bad, life and death, come from the Lord, will be developed in Sir 33:14–15 into a systematic theory that the world is constituted by pairs of opposites. A similar view leads to resignation in the face of death in ch. 41. While Sirach has no place for judgement after death, he accords great significance to the manner of death. The sentiment expressed in 11:28 is a commonplace of Greek tragedy (e.g. Aesch. *Ag.* l. 928; Soph. *Oed. Rex*, l. 1529; see further Skehan and DiLella 1987: 241).

vv. 15–16 were added in a secondary recension, apparently by way of theological correction. v. 14 ascribes both good and evil to the Lord. v. 15 ascribes various good things to the Lord, but v. 16 goes on to say that error and darkness were formed with sinners from their birth. Cf. WIS 1:13, 16, which denies that God made death, and claims that the wicked brought it about by the error of their ways.

(11:29–12:18) Care in Choosing Friends Sirach here picks up the theme of true and false friendship, already broached in 6:5–17, but here the tone is more directly imperatival. The Hebrew text of 11:29–34 is garbled: see Skehan and DiLella (1987: 244). Much of the advice is practical. One must exercise some caution in inviting people into one's home, and beware of the friendship of an old enemy. The notion that prosperity attracts false friends is nicely illustrated in the book of Job, where his friends suddenly reappear after he is restored (Job

42:11; cf. Prov 19:4, 6). Theognis, 35–6, also counsels against mingling with the bad. For the image of the snake charmer, cf. Eccl 10:11.

What is most striking about this passage, however, is the vigorous insistence that one should only do good to the just, and give no comfort to the wicked (12:2–3) and even that God hates sinners (12:6). Cf. the Qumran *Rule of the Community*, where those who enter the covenant commit themselves to hate all the sons of darkness, with the implication that God detests them (1QS 1:4, 10). A similar proverb is found in *Midr. Qoh. Rab.* 5. 8f. §5 (Soncino edn.): 'Do no good to an evil person and harm will not come to you; for if you do good to an evil person, you have done wrong.' The contrast with the teaching of Jesus in the NT is obvious (Mt 5:43–8; Lk 6:27–8, 32–6). But the idea that God hates sinners is also exceptional in Jewish literature. Contrast Wis 11:24: 'For you love all things that exist, and detest none of the things that you have made, for you would not have made anything if you had hated it.' This idea is illustrated in a colourful way in *T. Abr.* 10:14, where God tells the archangel Michael: 'Abraham has not sinned and has no mercy on sinners. But I made the world, and I do not want to destroy any one of them.' Ben Sira presumably could not claim to be as innocent of sin as Abraham was.

(13:1–23) The Rich and the Poor v. 1 continues the theme of selective friendship. This saying became a popular proverb and is quoted by Shakespeare (*Much Ado About Nothing*, III. iii. 61, and *1 Henry IV* II. iv. 460). The passage goes on to speak of the inequities of rich and poor. These inequities are often noted in wisdom literature—e.g. Prov 14:20; Eccl 9:16; *Sayings of Ahikar*, 55. The need for caution in dealing with the rich and powerful is also commonplace. The Egyptian *Instruction of Ani* warns against indulging oneself at the table of a rich man (*ANET* 412) and the warning is repeated in the *Instruction of Amen-em-ope*, ch. 23 (*ANET* 424) and in Prov 23:1–3. vv. 9–13 have a parallel in the late-Egyptian *Phibis* (J. T. Sanders 1983: 92–3). Similar warnings are found in *m. 'Abot*, 2:3: 'Be cautious with the authorities, for they do not make advances to a man except for their own need.' The subject of proper behaviour when invited by the mighty is taken up at length in Sir 31:12–18. The notion that a powerful person may test his guests by conversation is illustrated (somewhat artificially) in the *Epistle of Aristeas*, 187–294.

None of these parallels, however, express the antagonism of rich and poor as sharply as vv. 17–20. The wolf and the lamb may be reconciled in eschatological prophecy (Isa 11:6) but not in historical experience. Sirach uses vivid imagery to express the violence of the rich towards the poor. They are lions; the poor are their fodder. (Cf. Job 24:4–5 for the poor as wild asses.) It is reasonable to assume that this picture is coloured by the social context in which Sirach wrote, in which families such as the Tobiads grew rich at the expense of the common people (Tcherikover 1970: 146–8). The general picture is reminiscent of the Epistle of Enoch (*1 Enoch*, 94–105), which may have been written about the same time. The Epistle pronounces woes against the rich and tells them that they will not have peace (94:6–8). Sirach's tone, however, is detached. He observes the antagonism of the classes as if it were an unalterable fact of nature. The wise man will avoid the excesses of this situation, but he will not attempt to overthrow it.

v. 14 has the character of a pious gloss, and belongs to the secondary Greek recension.

(13:24–14:19) Miserliness and Generosity For Sirach, wealth is good in itself (13:24); the guilt which is often attached to it is not intrinsic to it. Conversely, while a good person may be poor, poverty is not good in itself. Even though Sirach qualifies his condemnation of poverty by attributing it to the proud, he does not contradict it. The value of wealth is undercut, however, if the person has a guilty conscience or is a miser. For the notion that the heart is reflected in the countenance (13:25–6), cf. Prov 15:13; Eccl 8:1. The implication of 14:2 is that a person with a guilty conscience has no hope, presumably because of Sirach's belief that retribution must strike sooner or later. Cf. Ps. 1.

Sirach's exhortation to generosity is, again, in the spirit of Ecclesiastes. Since there is no joy in the netherworld, one should treat oneself well in the present. Cf. Eccl 8:15: 'So I commend enjoyment, for there is nothing better for people under the sun than to eat and drink and enjoy themselves,' and, centuries earlier, the advice given to Gilgamesh by the ale-wife Siduri: 'When the gods created mankind | Death for mankind they set aside | Life in their own hands retaining. Thou Gilgamesh, let full be thy belly, | Make thou merry by day and by night...' (*ANET* 90). Sirach's endorsement of enjoyment, however, is limited to the correct use of wealth. It is not a goal to be pursued in its own right.

None the less the inferences drawn from mortality here provide an interesting contrast with the reasoning of the Wisdom of Solomon. In Wis 2:1–11, it is the wicked who reason 'unsoundly' that life is short and sorrowful and that therefore we should 'crown ourselves with rosebuds before they wither'. They go on to argue that might is right in a world where there is no post-mortem retribution. Sirach, in contrast, insists that there is retribution in this life. The lack of judgement after death, then, gives no licence to sin. But neither is there any reason for asceticism. Life has its fulfilment in the present and should be enjoyed. Moreover, wealth and enjoyment should be shared, since there is no reason to hoard it.

The comparison of generations to leaves (14:18) is found in Homer, *Iliad*, 6:146–9: 'As is the generation of leaves, so is that of humanity... So one generation of men will grow while another dies.'

(14:20–23:27)

(14:20–15:10) The Pursuit of Wisdom This wisdom poem resembles 6:18–37 in so far as it describes the quest for wisdom in poetic images, and adds a brief comment associating wisdom with the law of the Lord (cf. 6:37; 15:1). The poem falls into two halves: 14:20–7 describes the quest of the student for wisdom, 15:2–10 describes wisdom's rewards. 15:1, which associates wisdom with the law, stands as an editorial comment by Ben Sira, repeating a recurring theme in the book.

14:20–7 has the form of a beatitude or makarism, a form found about a dozen times in Sirach and almost as frequently in Proverbs (Rickenbacher 1973: 83). The wisdom text 4Q525 declares blessed 'the man who attains wisdom and walks in the law of the Most High' (García Martínez

1994: 395). There is probably an allusion in 14:20 to Ps 1, which pronounces blessed those who meditate on the law of the Lord, with the implication that wisdom can be substituted for the law. Ps 154, previously known only in Syriac but now found in Hebrew at Qumran, commends those whose meditation is on 'the law of the Most High' (García Martínez 1994: 305). The passage goes on to describe wisdom as bride and mother. The pursuit of wisdom has a mildly erotic connotation in Prov 4:6–9, while wisdom is cast as the nourishing mother in Prov 9:1–5. Erotic motifs will appear more prominently in 51:13–28. Here the imagery of peering in at the window recalls Song 2:9; cf. also Prov 8:34. The maternal side of wisdom is expressed through the images of tent and tree, both of which give shelter. For the image of the tent or canopy, cf. Isa 4:6.

The identification of wisdom with the Torah in 15:1 is a favourite theme of Ben Sira, but it has little impact on the way in which wisdom is described. Rather, the poem continues with the images of bride and mother, but shifts from the agency of the student/suitor to that of wisdom. The imagery of food and drink (15:3) will be developed in ch. 24. In the HB the support of the righteous is usually the Lord (Ps 18:19; 22:5; 25:2). Here wisdom acts as the surrogate of the Lord. This notion too will be developed in ch. 24. The crown (15:6) is often a symbol of a blessed afterlife (see SIR 1:11). Sirach's hope, however, is for an everlasting name. This is *not* a standard expectation in the wisdom books of the HB. It does not appear at all in Job or Ecclesiastes. According to Prov 10:4, the memory of the righteous is a blessing but the name of the wicked will rot, but the motif is far more prominent in Sirach (Rickenbacher 1973: 95–8). This interest reflects Sirach's heightened sense of honour and shame and reflects his Hellenistic milieu. It appears prominently in the Praise of the Fathers in chs. 44–50.

It is not immediately clear to what the 'praise' of 15:9–10 refers. Smend (1906: 141) takes it as the praise of God. Peters (1913: 129) thinks the reference is to the preceding praise of wisdom. In either case, the point is that the sinner cannot secure prosperity by reciting hymns; they must arise from wisdom if they are to be efficacious.

(15:11–16:23) Freedom and Responsibility The discussion of freedom of choice in 15:11–20 is complemented by a long discourse on the punishment of sinners in ch. 16. The closing unit (16:17–23) harks back to 15:11–12 in its use of the formula 'Do not say'. (See the comments on the form at SIR 5:1–4.) The passage on worthless children (16:1–4) appears abruptly after the discussion of free will, but leads into the theme of punishment, which rounds out this treatise on sin. Sirach returns to the theme in 17:1–24. 15:11–12 testifies to a lively debate on the origin of sin and evil. One current explanation was provided by the Book of the Watchers in *1 Enoch*, 1–36, which expanded the story of the sons of God in Gen 6 and attributed various kinds of evil (violence, fornication, astrology) to the intervention on earth of the fallen angels. Even within the Enoch literature, however, this explanation of evil was questioned. In the Epistle of Enoch, which may be roughly contemporary with Ben Sira, we read: 'I swear to you, you sinners, that as a mountain has not, and will not, become a slave, nor a hill a woman's maid, so sin was

not sent on the earth, but man of himself created it' (*1 Enoch*, 98:4). In the next generation, the Qumran *Rule of the Community* would adopt a new proposal, with overtones of Persian dualism, according to which God created two spirits within humanity, and so was ultimately the source of evil as well as good (Collins 1995).

In this passage, Sirach comes down unambiguously on the side of free will, with echoes of Deuteronomy. Cf. Deut 11:26–8; 30:15–20; Sir 15:17 alludes directly to Deut 30:15. The entire wisdom tradition represented in Proverbs presupposes free will. The clear-cut assertion that the Lord hates evil (15:13) accords with what we have read in 12:6. But Sirach is not consistent. He also maintains that God has made both good and bad (11:8) and reckons the sinner among the works of the Lord (33:14–15). There is evidently some tension between the belief that all the works of the Lord are good (39:33) and the actuality of sinners, whom God allegedly hates.

The origin of human sin is addressed most directly in 15:14. Sirach echoes Genesis in saying that God created man in the beginning, but then adds, according to the Hebrew, 'and set him in the power of his plunderer (*hōtĕpô*) and placed him in the power of his inclination (*yēṣer*)'. There is evidently a doublet here. The plunderer is most probably Satan (Peters 1913: 130; cf. Sir 50:4, where the same word is parallel to *ṣār*, enemy) and this phrase is probably inserted as a theological correction. It has no equivalent in the Greek. The word 'inclination', however, becomes a loaded term in rabbinic literature, according to which human nature was endowed with both a good and an evil inclination. The Talmud attributes to R. Jose the Galilean the view that 'the righteous are ruled by the good inclination … the wicked are ruled by the evil inclination … average people are ruled by both' (*b. Ber.* 61b; Urbach 1975: 475). The potency of the evil inclination (or 'evil heart') is recognized in 4 Ezra, written at the end of the first century CE (2 Esd 3:20–1). 4 Ezra stops short of saying that God created the evil heart, but the Sages are explicit on the point (Urbach 1975: 472). The notion of an evil inclination is now attested close to the time of Sirach in a fragmentary wisdom text from Qumran (4QSapA), where we encounter such phrases as 'the inclination of the flesh' and 'the thoughts of evil inclination' (Elgvin 1994: 187). The reference to 'the inclination of the flesh' follows a statement 'so that the just man may distinguish between good and evil' (García Martínez 1994: 383). The *Damascus Document* attributes the recurrence of sinful behaviour throughout history to following 'the thoughts of a guilty inclination' (*yēṣer ăšāmâ*), which seems to be equated with stubbornness of heart. The Greek text of Sirach also refers to the evil inclination in 37:3, but the Hebrew does not support this reading. In view of the history of the term 'inclination', the usual translation here as 'free choice' (NRSV) is inadequate. To be sure, Sirach emphasizes free choice in the following passage, but the exercise of that choice is conditioned by the inclinations with which human nature is fitted at creation. Sirach stops a long way short of the teaching of two spirits that we find in the Qumran *Rule of the Community*, but we can see that he is wrestling with the same problem, in attempting to explain the presence of evil while preserving the sovereignty of the creator God.

The worthlessness of impious children is also emphasized in Wis 4:1–6. In ancient Israel, children provided a kind of immortality. The Wisdom of Solomon could dispense with this, because it preached personal immortality. Sirach maintains that the wicked come to grief in this life. On 16:4, cf. Wis 6:24: the multitude of the wise is the salvation of the world, but cf. also Eccl 9:15.

For the examples of divine punishment in 16:3–14, cf. CD 2:15–3:12. The sinners in CD follow their guilty inclination. Sirach seems to imply a similar view, in the light of 15:14. Both Sirach and CD also note the role of stubbornness. A similar tendency to view history as a series of examples is found in Wis 10–19. Wisdom underlines the typological character of the events by suppressing all names; cf. the reference here to 'the doomed people' in 16:9.

On the impossibility of hiding from the Lord (16:17–23), cf. Wis 1:6–11, which explains that the spirit of the Lord, which is closely associated with wisdom, fills the whole world and hears whatever is said.

Two additions to the Greek text of this chapter have theological significance: 16:15 recalls that God hardened Pharaoh's heart, by way of illustrating that God's mercy is balanced by severity towards sinners. The point is of interest, however, because of the preceding discussion of free will. 16:22 adds that 'a scrutiny for all will come at death', which is one of several attempts by a Greek redactor to introduce a belief in judgement after death into the text of Sirach. Contrast Sir 41:4.

(16:24–18:14) Wisdom and Creation The direct call for attention in 16:24 marks the beginning of a new section. Such calls are rare in Sirach after chs. 2–4. In v. 25, Ben Sira appropriates words attributed to Wisdom in Prov 1:23 when he says that he will pour out his spirit. 16:26–30 develops the theme of creation which had been touched on briefly in the preceding section. Here the emphasis is on the order of nature. Cf. Ps 104, or, closer to the time of Sirach, 1 Enoch, 2–5, 73–82. There are several allusions to Gen 1–3: from the *beginning* (16:26); he filled it with *good* things (16:29); all living creatures must return to the earth (16:30; 17:1; cf. Gen 3:19). In 17:1–10 the focus shifts to the creation of humanity, following the order of the biblical text. (The same progression is found in a fragmentary paraphrase of Genesis and Exodus from Qumran, 4Q422.) Again, there are several echoes of Genesis. Human beings are granted authority and dominion over the other creatures. They are made in God's image, an idea which is explained by juxtaposition with the statement that they are given strength like that of God. (The Gk. redactor adds a reference to the senses at this point.) Perhaps the most noteworthy aspect of this meditation on Genesis is that it ignores the sin of Adam completely. (Sir 25:24 ascribes the original sin to Eve.) Death is not here considered a punishment for sin. God limited human life from the start (17:2). In contrast, the sin is highlighted in other second-century retellings of the Genesis story, notably *Jubilees*, 3. Cf. also the Words of the Heavenly Luminaries (4Q504 8; García Martínez 1994: 417). Sirach chooses instead to emphasize here that the first human beings were endowed with wisdom and understanding.

The 'law of life' in 17:11 is most probably the Mosaic law. Cf. 45:5, where 'the law of life and knowledge' is given to Moses on Sinai. The designation 'law of life' is derived from Deut 30:11–20. In the context, the 'eternal covenant' of v. 12 must also refer to the Sinai covenant, although 44:18 uses this phrase for the covenant with Noah. Cf. Bar 4:1, where the Torah is 'the law that endures forever'. v. 13 refers to the revelation at Mt. Sinai; cf. Ex 19:16–19. In 17:17, the rulers of the nations are angels, or 'sons of God', cf. Deut 32:8. 17:19–20 recapitulates the theme of 16:17–23. Nothing is hidden from God. On the value of almsgiving, cf. SIR 3:30.

The call to repentence in 17:25 is more characteristic of prophetic than of sapiential literature. Here again Sirach uses the ambivalence of death for his purpose. No one sings the praise of God in the netherworld (cf. Ps 30:9; 88:11–13; 117:17; Isa 38:18–19). For the Wisdom of Solomon, the lack of a significant afterlife would undermine the demand for a moral life. For Sirach, it rather adds urgency to the present and so supports the appeal for repentance. The concluding verses of ch. 17 and 18:1–14 constitute a hymn praising the mercy of God. Sirach emphasizes the surpassing power of God and the insignificance of humanity. 18:8 echoes Ps 8:5 (cf. Ps 144:3) but Sirach will not conclude that human beings have been crowned with glory and honour, only that God has mercy on them. The estimate of life expectancy is slightly higher than Ps 90:10, but the difference is inconsequential. (In contrast, Isa 65:20 promises that in the new creation death before the age of 100 years will be premature.) Just as Sirach regards the imminence of death as a reason that people should be moral, he also regards it as a reason for divine mercy. 18:13, which extends the divine compassion to every living thing, is in sharp contrast to 12:6, where God has no pity on the wicked, but is in accordance with Hos 11:8–9; Wis 11:23: 'you are merciful to all because you can do all things'. Sir 18:14, however, seems to restrict God's compassion to those who submit to his law. The latter notion is more typical of Sirach, and is likely to reflect his own view over against a more generous tradition.

(18:15–19:17) Caution and Restraint After the extensive theological reflections in 14:20–18:14, Sirach now reverts to practical advice and admonitions. The sage guards against impulse and anticipates what needs to be done. The first admonition in 18:15–18 is an exception to this theme, and indeed to the usual moralism of Ben Sira. Even he recognizes, however, that there are times when admonition is inappropriate. On the spirit of giving, cf. 2 Cor 9:7 (God loves a cheerful giver) and Jas 1:5 (God gives ungrudgingly). 18:19–27 gives various examples of prudence and caution. The advice on vows in 18:22–3 recalls Eccl 5:4–5: it is better not to vow at all than to make a vow and not fulfil it. Characteristically, Ben Sira undergirds his advice with a reminder of the day of death, seen as the day of reckoning when God settles accounts.

Sirach goes on to admonish against self-indulgence and against gossip. The main argument put forward against licentiousness is that it leads to poverty. Cf. Prov 5:10; 21:17; 23:20–1. There is also the threat of disease and early death (19:3; cf. Prov 2:16–19; 5:3–6, 11–12; 7:27). The argument against gossip is likewise grounded in self-interest. It may cause someone to hate you (19:9). Cf. Hesiod, *Opera et Dies*, 721: 'If you say a bad thing, you may hear a worse thing said about you.' This subject evokes a rare flash of humour from Ben

Sira, when he compares the gossip to a woman in labour. Cf. Jas 3:1–12 on the need to bridle the tongue.

Both the Qumran *Rule of the Community* and the Gospel of Matthew advocate pointing out faults to offenders rather than rejecting them out of hand. Cf. 1QS 5:24–6:1; Mt 18:15–17. This procedure has a biblical warrant in Lev 19:17–18. Cf. Prov 27:5; 28:23. Sirach differs from all those passages, however, in leaving open the question of the person's guilt, and allowing that there may a mistake or a case of slander.

(19:18–30) Wisdom and Fear of the Lord Like some other passages on the fear of the Lord (e.g. 15:1), this passage stands out from its context and has the character of an editorial comment by Ben Sira. vv. 18–19 belong to the second Greek recension, and include a trademark reference to immortality. v. 20 is ambiguous in principle. It could mean that the person who acquires wisdom, from whatever source, thereby fulfils the law, or it could mean that the fulfilment of the law constitutes wisdom, even if one draws on no other source (cf. Bar 3:4: 'Happy are we, O Israel, for we know what is pleasing to God'). v. 24 makes clear that Ben Sira intends the latter interpretation. Better a person with little understanding who keeps the law than a learned and clever person who violates it. Ben Sira would probably contend that a truly wise person will keep the law in any case, so there is no necessary conflict between the two interpretations. But he recognizes that a person may have many of the attributes of wisdom without the fear of the Lord. Keen but dishonest shrewdness was always a problem in the wisdom tradition. Cf. the advice of Jonadab to Amnon in 2 Sam 13, which leads to the rape of Tamar. Already in Gen 3:1 the serpent is recognized as crafty. The Hellenistic age offered several models of wisdom to the people of a city such as Jerusalem. The resourcefulness of v. 23 is illustrated in the tale of the Tobiads in Josephus, *Ant.* 12, and appears again in the enterprising ways in which Jason and Menelaus secured the high-priesthood shortly after the time of Ben Sira. Sirach evidently does not restrict wisdom to the observance of the Torah, but he regards the rejection of law and tradition as incompatible with wisdom. He thereby stakes out a conservative position in the spectrum of Jewish opinion in the period before the Maccabean revolt.

The discussion of duplicitous behaviour in vv. 25–8 is suggested by the topic of false wisdom in vv. 22–3. vv. 29–30, however, are at odds with this passage, as they seem to disregard the possibility of being duped by appearances. Proverbial wisdom does not lend itself easily to consistent, systematic thought. In the book of Proverbs, contradictory maxims are sometimes placed side by side (Prov 26:4–5). Similarly, Sirach here brings together traditional advice on a topic, even though it is somewhat inconsistent.

(20:1–32) Miscellaneous Advice Like much proverbial wisdom, the maxims in this chapter are only loosely connected. The general theme is true and false wisdom. vv. 1–3 reprise the topic of admonition. Timely silence (vv. 5–8) is a favourite theme of prudential literature. Cf. Prov 17:28; Eccl 3:7; Plutarch's *Moralia*, 5.2 (for further examples see Skehan and DiLella 1987: 300–1). vv. 9–11 reflect on the variability of fortune. vv. 13–17 comment on the fool's lack of perspective, and impatience. The fate of the fool is to be laughed to scorn.

While the fool is not guilty or subject to divine punishment, he incurs shame.

v.18 echoes a proverb attributed to Zeno of Citium, founder of Stoicism: 'Better to slip with the foot than with the tongue' (Diog. Laert. 7.26). v. 20 shows the crucial importance of timing in the wisdom tradition. The principles laid out in Eccl 3:1–8 are fundamental to the application of all proverbs. Cf. Prov 26:7, 9. vv. 21–3 point out ambiguities in some commonly accepted values. Poverty is not desirable, but if it keeps one from sinning it can be beneficial. Honour is a good to be sought, but it can also mislead a person and lead to downfall. These comments, however, do not put in question Ben Sira's acceptance of conventional wisdom on these subjects; they merely allow for exceptions.

Condemnations of the liar (vv. 24–6) are ubiquitous in moral literature (cf. Prov 6:17, 19; Sir 7:13). The particular nuance that Sirach brings to it here is the shame that the liar incurs. For the comparison with the thief, cf. Prov 6:30: 'The thief is not despised who steals only to satisfy his appetite.' None the less, neither sin is excused. The most notable advice in vv. 27–31 is that the wise should please the great. This advice contrasts with that given in 9:13, which warns people to keep their distance from the powerful, but accords with Sirach's account of the sage in 39:4, and is likely to reflect his own opinion. The wise courtier was a stock character in ancient wisdom literature (cf. Ahikar, Joseph, Daniel, etc.). Most remarkable is the statement that those who please the great atone for injustice (v. 28). It is not clear for whose sin the wise person would atone. The question of atonement for sin comes up in Dan 4 in the context of a wise man serving the mighty. In that case, Daniel advises the king that he can atone for his (the king's) sin by almsgiving. Smend (1906: 188) assumes that the phrase 'who pleases the great' is copied carelessly from the previous verse, so that the text is corrupt.

(21:1–12) Sin and Forgiveness Ben Sira differs from Proverbs and Ecclesiastes in his concern for atonement and forgiveness for sin. The serpent in v. 2 is not the tempter of Gen 3 but is avoided because it bites; cf. Am 5:19. Mention of the serpent here may be prompted by Prov 23:32 which compares a drunken hangover to the bite of a snake. 1 Pet 5:8 compares the devil to a roaring lion. The pit of Hades in v. 10 is not the hell of Christian tradition but Sheol, abode of all the dead. vv. 11–12 repeat the association of wisdom with the Torah, but here a new rationale is given. The law is an instrument for controlling impulses. This understanding of the law is developed at length in 4 Maccabees, which was written in Greek, probably in Antioch or Alexandria, more than two centuries after Sirach. Cf. 4 Macc 1:13–17, which sets out the enquiry of the book as to whether reason is sovereign over emotions, and then associates reason and wisdom with education in the law. Control of the passions was a matter of high priority in Greek philosophy, especially in Stoicism. As in 19:25, Sirach distinguishes wisdom from mere shrewdness, but he acknowledges that resourcefulness is a necessary component of wisdom.

(21:13–22:18) Wisdom and Folly The sayings in this section are not overtly theological, and may well be part of the traditional lore that Ben Sira passed on. 21:13–28 contrasts the wise person and the fool, a contrast that is ubiquitous in Proverbs. For the comparison of the wise to a spring, cf. *m. 'Abot*, 6:1. The fool is like a broken vessel because he cannot retain instruction. On the chatter of fools, cf. Eccl 10:13–14. Sir 38:32 notes that artisans are not sought out for the assembly. Presumably, the prudent man who is sought out in 21:17 must also be educated in wisdom. Education in itself, however, does not suffice. It has quite a different effect on the fool and on the wise person (21:18–21). 21:22–6 describes the impetuosity of the fool, especially regarding lack of verbal restraint (cf. 19:8–12). In 21:27, the Greek 'Satan' reflects the Hebrew *sāṭān*, adversary. The reference is to an ordinary human adversary, not to a demonic figure, although the Hebrew term is used to designate a specific supernatural figure in Job 1–2 and in 1 Chr 21:1.

22:1–2 characterizes the sluggard, who is the target of barbed wit i Proverbs (6:6–11; 24:30–4; 26:13–16). Sirach's analogies are crude. The 'filthy stone' is one that has been used as toilet paper (Smend 1906: 196; Skehan and DiLella 1987: 312). Hence the parallelism with 'a lump of dung' in v. 2. The Syriac adds: 'and everyone flees from the stench of it'.

22:3–5 comments on sons and daughters. On the unruly son, cf. 16:1–5. 22:3 may be influenced by Prov 17:21, which says that the father of a fool has no joy. Sirach switches the reference from the apparently male fool to a daughter (Trenchard 1982: 135). He appears to regard the birth of any daughter as a loss; cf. his comments on daughters in ch. 42. Later, the Talmud says that a man should bless God for not having made him a woman or a slave (*b. Menaḥ* 43b), and blesses the man whose children are male rather than female (*B. Bat.* 16b). The misogyny of Sirach's statement is modified only slightly by the concession that a daughter may be sensible and obtain a husband (v. 4). It is clear from 7:25 that the daughter does not get the husband on her own initiative. She is given in marriage. Ben Sira's great fear about daughters is that they will bring shame on their fathers (or husbands) by 'shameless' behaviour. He will urge precautionary measures in 26:10–12 and 42:11. The second Greek recension adds the interesting comment that children who are well brought up can hide the ignoble origins of their parents (22:7).

22:7–12 is a scathing dismissal of the fool, whose life is said to be worse than death. The seven-day mourning period is observed by Joseph for Jacob (Gen 50:10), by all Israel for Judith (Jdt 16:24), and by orthodox Jews today. 22:13–15 counsels against the company of a fool; cf. the advice to avoid the wicked in ch. 12. In 22:13*b* the Syriac reads 'and do not travel with a pig', and this reading is preferred by Smend (1906: 199) and some others. The second Greek recension seems to presuppose this reading when it warns 'you may ... be spattered when he shakes himself' (13*d*). 22:16–18 stresses the importance of steadfastness and resolve in contrast to the fool's lack of conviction.

(22:19–26) On Friendship This section on friendship continues the sequence of advice on assorted matters; cf. SIR 6:5–17. The concern in vv. 19–22 is with dangers to friendship. v. 23 is an attempt to overcome a common pitfall—friendship that is contingent on prosperity. Cf. Sir 6:8–12 and the parallels cited there. vv. 25–6 are cast in the first person in the

Greek. Thus the author reassures himself that his friend's reputation is at stake in the friendship. Many scholars think, however, that the first person here is a corruption, influenced by the following section (22:27–23:6) and that the reader was warned that his or her reputation was at stake in friendship (Smend 1906: 202). Friendship for Sirach is grounded in mutual self-interest, and in this he is typical of the wisdom tradition. This cautious approach can legitimately be contrasted with the NT commandment to love one's enemies (Skehan and DiLella 1987: 317; Lk 6:27–38), but the same NT passage contains the maxim: 'Do to others as you would have them do to you' (Lk 6:31). This suggests that mutual self-interest may none the less also have a part to play in Christian ethics.

(22:27–23:27) Verbal and Sexual Restraint It is rare indeed to find a prayer of petition in a wisdom book. The only other example in this book, the prayer for national restoration in ch. 36, is very different in spirit and is probably not the work of Ben Sira. The prayer here introduces the themes that follow in ch. 23: sins of speech and of lust. The section concludes with another affirmation of the fear of the Lord and obedience to the commandments.

For the opening of the prayer in 22:27 cf. Ps 141:3. The main concern of the prayer is protection from sin but it is noteworthy that Sirach's concern for honour and shame intrudes in v. 3 (but cf. Ps 13:4; 38:16).

The most noteworthy feature of the prayer is undoubtedly that God is addressed as 'Father'. God is only rarely called father in the HB, and is never so addressed by an individual. (God is called father of the people of Israel in Isa 63:16; Mal 2:10, and possibly in 1 Chr 29:10, where 'our father' could refer to either God or Israel.) In the Apocrypha, God is addressed as father in 3 Macc 5:51 and 6:3 and in Wis 14:3, passages that were composed in Greek. The Hebrew text of the psalm in Sir 51:10 reads: 'Lord, you are my Father', although the Greek has a confused reading 'Lord, father of my Lord'. The Hebrew of ch. 23 is not extant. Joachim Jeremias argued that there was no evidence for the use of 'my father' as a form of direct address to God in Hebrew before the Christian era (Jeremias 1967: 29) and suggested that ch. 23 originally read 'God of my father'. The direct address, however, is now attested in the Prayer of Joseph (4Q372), which is dated tentatively about 200 BCE (Schuller 1990). The Prayer begins, 'My father and my God'. In view of this parallel there is no reason to question the authenticity of the Greek text of Sir 24:1, 4. The familial title 'father' balances the appellation 'Master', which emphasizes rather God's power (Strotmann 1991: 83). For Sirach's understanding of the fatherhood of God, cf. SIR 4:10.

The phrase 'instruction of the mouth' in 23:7 is lifted out and set as a heading for this section in several MSS. The subject of loose talk has been treated in 19:4–12 and 20:18–20. The present passage, however, is not concerned with gossip but with swearing (vv. 9–11) and coarse talk (vv. 12–15), which are matters of Jewish piety rather than common Near-Eastern wisdom. Avoidance of swearing is a matter of respect for the divine name. Cf. Ex 20:7; Deut 5:11; Mt 5:34–7; 23:18–22; Jas 5:12. Sirach evidently believes that oaths have consequences, even if they are sworn inadvertently (v. 11). The reference of 23:12 is not clear. Some commentators take it to refer to blasphemy (Smend, Skehan and DiLella), for which the death penalty is prescribed in Lev 24:11–16 (cf. Mt 26:65–6; Jn 10:33). Others think the 'speech comparable to death' is that which is described in the following verses (so Peters 1913). It is more likely, however, that v. 12 refers to a separate offence, and that Ben Sira deliberately avoids mentioning it directly. On respect for parents, see SIR 3:2–16. To curse the day of one's birth is the depth of despair. Cf. Job 3:3–10; Jer 20:14. The point here is the acute embarrassment of the person who disgraces himself or herself in the presence of the mighty. Remembering one's parents is a way to keep on guard.

The treatise on adultery (23:16–26) is introduced by a numerical proverb. For a cluster of such proverbs see Prov 30:15–31. Other examples are found in Sir 25:1–2, 7–11; 26:5–6, 28; 50:25–6 (see Roth 1965). The form 'two kinds … and three' invariably introduces the latter number. So in this case there are three kinds of sinner: the person of unrestrained passion, the person guilty of incest, and the adulterer.

Sirach gives equal time to the adulterer and adulteress. The discussion of the adulterer can be viewed as an extrapolation from Prov 9:17, which refers to the sweetness of stolen water and bread eaten in secret. Sirach speaks of sweet bread and dwells at length on the issue of secrecy. On the futility of hiding from the Lord, cf. 16:17–23 above. Here Sirach adds that God knows everything even before it is created. Cf. 1QH 9:23 (formerly numbered 1:23): 'What can I say that is not known?' In the Qumran theology, however, God not only knows what will happen but determines it (1QS 3:15–16; 1QH 9:19–20). Sirach is closer to the position attributed to Akiba in *m. 'Abot*, 3:19: all is foreseen, but free will is given. Sirach does not specify how the adulterer will be punished. Proverbs implies that the adulterer will be beaten up by the wronged husband and publicly disgraced and that he will have to pay a heavy fine (Prov 6:31–5: 'sevenfold', 'all the goods of his house'). Sirach evidently envisages public disgrace. Neither Proverbs nor Sirach make any mention of the death penalty for the adulterer prescribed by biblical law (Lev 20:10; Deut 22:22).

The treatment of the adulteress differs from that of the adulterer in several respects. Her sin is said to be threefold—the offence against God and her husband and the fact that she produced children by another man. Sirach implies that the adulterer sins against God (v. 18), although he does not say so directly. There is no implication, however, that the adulterer sins against his wife. The imbalance in this regard reflects the common ancient tendency to group the wife with the possessions of her husband (see SIR 7:22–6). The sin against the husband is that she has violated his rights and his honour. The production of children by adultery is considered a separate offence. Sir 23:23 does not imply that the woman's adultery was prompted by the desire to have a child (against Trenchard 1982: 99). Neither is there any reason to think that the woman acts out of economic necessity (so Camp 1991: 27–8). If an adulterous affair ended in pregnancy, the woman would have little choice but to try to pass the child off as her husband's offspring. One of the main reasons for prohibiting adultery was to guarantee the legitimacy of a man's children. At issue here is the right of inheritance, and

so the adultery has economic consequences, which are deemed to constitute a separate, third, offence.

While the adulterer will be punished in the streets of the city, presumably by the cuckolded husband, the adulteress is led to the assembly. Sirach is not explicit as to what action the assembly may take. The story of Susanna, which may be roughly contemporary, comes to mind. Since Susanna is not married, she is accused of fornication rather than adultery, but she is sentenced to death. The death sentence is also proposed for the woman taken in adultery in Jn 8. It is very unlikely, however, that these stories reflect actual practice in the Hellenistic or Roman periods. In the Elephantine papyri (5th cent. BCE), the punishment for adultery is divorce, with loss of some property rights. The extension of punishment to the children recalls Ezra 10: 4, where the foreign wives were sent away with their children. Ben Sira, however, seems to indicate a divine punishment rather than a human one. His contention is that the children of an adulteress will not prosper. Cf. Wis 3:16–19. Sirach does not provide any human mechanism to ensure that this punishment will be effected.

Sir 23:27 brings this section to a conclusion by making the disgrace of the adulteress into a moral lesson that it is better to keep the law. It is noteworthy that his discussion of the punishment of the adulteress does not call for literal fulfilment of the law. Sirach's concern is with conformity to the tradition in principle, with the attitude of reverence rather than with legal details. The second Greek redactor adds a gloss (v. 28), which promises great glory and length of days to one who follows after God. In accordance with the usual theology of this redaction, 'length of days' probably means eternal life (so Skehan and DiLella 1987: 326).

(24:1–33) The Praises of Wisdom The great hymn to wisdom in ch. 24 may be regarded as the centrepiece of the book. It is often regarded as the introduction to the second part of the book (e.g. Segal 1972; Roth 1980; Skehan and DiLella 1987), with a view to finding a symmetrical structure in the book as a whole. Since each of the wisdom poems in 1:1–10, 4:11–19, 6:18–37, and 14:20–15:10, introduces a section, so it is argued does ch. 24. Against this, however, the second half of the book is not punctuated by wisdom poems as the first had been. The only true wisdom poem in the remainder of the book is found in 51:13–30, which serves as a conclusion, and may be added as an epilogue. That passage is cast as a personal declaration by Ben Sira; vv. 30–4 are also a personal declaration. It seems better then to see ch. 24 as the conclusion of the first part of the book (Marböck 1971: 41–3). It sums up the theme of wisdom that has been treated intermittently in chs. 1–23, and will be paralleled by the concluding poem on wisdom in ch. 51.

Ch. 24 differs from other wisdom poems in Sirach in so far as vv. 3–22 constitute a declaration by Wisdom in the first person. As such, it is most accurately designated as an aretalogy, and is properly compared to the aretalogies of the Egyptian goddess Isis (Marböck 1971: 47–54). There is an obvious biblical precedent in Prov 8, which may itself be influenced by Egyptian prototypes. The argument that Sirach drew directly on the aretalogies of Isis has been made especially by Conzelmann (1971: 230–43). In addition to the formal similarity, there are also thematic parallels. Both Wisdom and Isis are of primeval origin, exercise cosmological functions, and claim dominion over the whole earth. Isis claims to have established law for humanity. v. 23, which stands outside the first-person aretalogy, equates wisdom with the law of the Lord. It is quite likely then that the concept of Wisdom singing her own praises, in both Sirach and Proverbs, is indebted to the Egyptian Isis hymns. Sirach, however, also draws heavily on biblical phraseology, and so adapts the aretalogy form for his own purpose (Sheppard 1980: 19–71).

vv. 1–2 provide the setting for Wisdom's speech. v. 2 clearly locates her in the heavenly council (cf. Ps 82:1), with the implication that she is imagined as a heavenly, angelic being. It is possible that 'her people' in v. 1 refers to this heavenly assembly (so Smend 1906: 216), but it is more likely to refer to Israel, among whom Wisdom settles in vv. 8–12. She speaks, then, on both earthly and heavenly levels simultaneously. vv. 3–7 describe the origin and nature of Wisdom. The first-person pronoun (Gk. *egō*) is especially characteristic of the Isis aretalogies, but cf. also Prov 8:12; 17. Even though the Hebrew text is not extant, the original Hebrew is clearly reflected in the idiom of v. 1, lit. 'Wisdom praises her soul'. The divine origin of Wisdom is also stressed in Prov 8:21 and Sir 1:1. The idea that Wisdom proceeds from the mouth of God may be suggested by Prov 2:6 ('For the Lord gives wisdom; from his mouth come knowledge and understanding'). This motif lays the foundation for the identification of Wisdom with the *word* of God, which also proceeds from the mouth (cf. Isa 45:23; 48:3; 25:11). The identification is clear in Wis 9:1–2. The Greek word *logos*, however, had far-reaching connotations in Greek, especially Stoic, philosophy, where it referred to the rational spirit that pervades the universe. This concept was also developed by the Jewish philosopher Philo (Mack 1973). The fusion of the Jewish wisdom tradition and Greek philosophy on this point is essential background to the use of the Logos/Word in Jn 1:1. The notion that Wisdom proceeds from the mouth also invites association with the spirit/breath of God (Gk. *pneuma*) which had similar philosophic connotations in Stoic philosophy (cf. the use of *pneuma* in Wis 1:7). The association with the spirit is suggested here in the statement that Wisdom covered the earth like a mist, which recalls Gen 1:2, although the allusion is not precise.

The statement that Wisdom lived 'in the heights' is suggested by Prov 8:2, but here, unlike Proverbs, the heights should be understood as heavenly. What is most striking about the following verses is how language used of God in the HB is now applied to Wisdom. The pillar of cloud of the Exodus (Ex 13:21; 33:9–10) is also identified with the Logos by Philo (*Quis Heres*, 203–6) and Wisdom is given a key role in the Exodus in Wis 10. Here, however, it is removed from the Exodus context, and associated with the primordial enthronement of Wisdom. While Prov 8:27 says that Wisdom was there when God established the heavens, Sir 24:5 has Wisdom circle the vault of heaven *alone*. Cf. rather Job 9:8, where God alone stretched out the heavens. In Job 38:16 God challenges Job whether he 'has walked in the recesses of the deep'. Rule over the sea is a divine prerogative in the HB (Ps 65:8; 89:10; 93:3–4, etc.). Wisdom is never said to be

divine, but it appears to be the instrument of God's presence and agency. The quest for a resting place has been compared to the wandering of Israel in the wilderness (Sheppard 1980: 39). Ben Sira however shows no interest in the historical process by which Israel settled in its land. Wisdom's quest for a resting place completes the process of creation. There is an enigmatic passage in 1 *Enoch*, 42:1–2, that dramatically reverses Sirach's account: Wisdom found no place to dwell and so withdrew to heaven.

vv. 8–12 describe how Wisdom settles in Israel. The command to settle in Israel may be compared to the command given to Israel to seek out the designated place of worship in Deut 12 (Sheppard 1980: 42). But Sirach implies that Wisdom had settled in Israel before Israel settled in its land. So Wisdom ministered already in the tabernacle, the tent-shrine of the wilderness (Ex 25:8–9). v. 9 suggests that the association of Wisdom with Israel is primordial. The most apt parallel to this passage in Sirach is found in Deut 32:8–9, which says that when God divided the nations among the 'sons of God' he took Israel as his own portion. Sirach has God exercise the election of Israel through Wisdom. The passage is remarkable, however, for its cultic emphasis. Wisdom finds expression in the cult of the Jerusalem temple. This idea is exceptional in the wisdom tradition, but it accords with Sirach's high esteem for the priesthood (cf. 44:6–26; 50:1–21). The notion of Wisdom making its dwelling in Israel is picked up in Jn 1:14, where the Word comes to dwell with humankind.

vv. 13–17 compare Wisdom to the luxuriant growth of various trees and plants. Such imagery is not found in Prov 8, but is familiar from other parts of the HB. Cf. Ps 1, which compares the righteous man to a tree planted by water, and in general Num 24:6; Hos 14:5–7. The cedar of Lebanon is the most celebrated tree in the Bible (Ps 92:12; Song 5:15). v. 15 changes the imagery to perfumes, and again evokes the cult by mentioning the incense in the tabernacle. vv. 19–22 compare Wisdom to food and drink. Cf. John 6:35, where Jesus says that whoever eats of him will never hunger and whoever drinks of him will never thirst.

v. 23 introduces a short commentary on the words of Wisdom, drawn in part from Deut 33:4. The word 'inheritance' also picks up a motif from vv. 8, 12. The fact that the verse has three cola is exceptional in Ben Sira, and has led to the suggestion that the first colon, which refers explicitly to the book and which is not paralleled in Deut 33:4, is a secondary addition, influenced by Bar 4:1 (Rickenbacher 1973: 125–7). Sirach was certainly familiar with the Torah in its written form (cf. 38:34), but this is the only passage that identifies wisdom specifically with the book. The identification of wisdom with the law is implied again in the hymn at the end of Sirach, by the metaphor of the yoke in 51:26. The repeated association of wisdom with the Torah is one of the principal ways in which Ben Sira modifies the wisdom tradition he had received. It has its basis in Deut 4:6, but is never hinted at in Proverbs or Ecclesiastes. Yet for Sirach, in contrast to Deuteronomy, wisdom is the primary category which is the subject of hymnic praise. The Torah is mentioned secondarily, by way of clarification. Wisdom is older than Moses, having been created 'in the beginning'. Later, rabbinic authorities would claim that the Torah too was created before the world, and was even the instrument with which the world was created (Urbach 1975: i. 287). On this understanding, the law revealed to Moses was implicit in creation from the beginning (Marböck 1971: 93–4; for a contrary interpretation see Schnabel 1985). Cf. Rom 1:20, although Paul evidently did not regard all details of the law as part of the law of creation. Sirach also ignores most of the levitical laws, and does not address the question whether the whole law was implied in Wisdom from the beginning.

Sirach proceeds to compare Wisdom/Torah to the four rivers associated with Eden in Gen 2, and also to the Nile and the Jordan. The comparison with foreign rivers may be significant. Wisdom was always an international phenomenon, and its character is not changed in that respect by the identification with the Jewish law. The reason that the first man did not know wisdom fully (v. 28) is not because it was not yet revealed (so Skehan and DiLella 1987: 337). Sir 17:7 claims that when God created humanity he filled them with knowledge and understanding and gave them knowledge of good and evil. Besides, the last man is no wiser (25:28). No human being can fully comprehend Wisdom (cf. Job 28, which has a decidedly more negative view of human wisdom).

The chapter closes with a stanza in which Sirach compares himself to an offshoot of the great river of Wisdom. For the metaphor of light, cf. Prov 6:3. He also compares his teaching to prophecy, without claiming to be a prophet. Sirach views prophecy as part of the textual lore to be studied by the sage (39:1). It is not apparent that he recognized any active prophets in his own time. The specific point of comparison with prophecy here is that it remains for future generations. Sirach concludes with a protestation of disinterestedness. He has not laboured for himself alone. Cf. 51:25, where he invites the uneducated to acquire learning without money.

Part II. Chs. 25–51

(25:1–33:19)

(25:1–12) Sources of Happiness The three poems in this section are only loosely connected. The first and third are numerical sayings. The first contrasts three kinds of people of whom Sirach approves with three of whom he does not. Harmony among friends finds its classic expression in Ps 133. v. 1d, on the harmony of husband and wife, is an important corrective to some of Ben Sira's more patriarchal pronouncements on marriage. The adulterous old man is universally despised. Cf. the elders in the story of Susanna. Mention of the adulterous old man leads to a brief encomium on the wisdom appropriate to old age. In the third poem, Sirach lists ten beatitudes; see SIR 14:20. The makarisms here concern very practical matters that are typical of the instruction of Sirach. The joy of a sensible wife is reiterated in 26:1, and contrasts with the bitter denunciations of an 'evil' wife in 25:16–26. All of these sayings on marriage are formulated from the point of view of the husband. Ploughing with an ox and ass together is explicitly forbidden in Deut 22:10. Here it appears to be a matter of wisdom rather than of law. In the context, it may be a metaphor for polygamy (cf. 26:6; 37:11). The blessing of one who finds wisdom (v. 10) is paralleled in 4Q525 2 ii 3–4. The affirmation of the superiority of the fear of the Lord resumes

the theme of 23:27. Fear of the Lord was similarly emphasized at the beginning of Part I in 1:11–21, 28–30. The distinction implied here between wisdom and fear of the Lord recalls the contrast of true and false wisdom in 19:20–5, especially 19:24, which prefers the God-fearing who lack understanding to the clever who transgress the law.

(25:13–26:27) Wives, Bad and Good This passage is Sirach's most sustained treatment of marriage, or rather of the good and bad wife from the husband's point of view. The bad wife receives more than twice as many verses as the good. The first stanza (vv. 13–15) sets the tone by comparing a woman's anger to a snake's venom. Smend (1906: 229) suggested that 'those who hate' and 'enemies' in v. 14 are mistakes by the Greek translator. (The Heb. is not extant.) The original would have read feminine forms, 'hated' (i.e. repudiated, divorced) and 'rival', and so the woman's anger would arise from a situation of either polygamy or divorce. The subject of rivalry between women is explicit in 26:6 and 37:11.

The contentious or nagging wife is a common subject of complaint in folklore, and appears also in Proverbs (21:19; 25:24; 27:15). Sirach's comparisons are more violent. Even if we make allowance for Semitic hyperbole, the statement that any iniquity is small compared to that of a woman (v. 19) is exceptional. This sentiment is developed further in 42:14, which says that the wickedness of a man is better than the goodness of a woman! There is an extreme quality to these sayings that cannot be dismissed as simply part of the culture of the time. (A character in Eur. *Phoen.* 805, refers to women as the wildest evil (Middendorp 1973: 21), but the playwright does not necessarily endorse the view.) The wish that a sinner's lot befall her may mean that a sinner should marry her; cf. Eccl 7:26. vv. 21–2 warn against marrying a woman for either her beauty or her wealth. The deceptiveness of beauty was noted in Prov 31:30. The wealth of a wife might prevent a man from seeking divorce, since the woman could take her own possessions with her. The same sentiment is found in Ps.-Phoc. 199–200; Eur. *Melannipus*, frag. 502 (Middendorp 1973: 21).

No verse in Ben Sira is more pregnant with implications or more controversial in a modern context than v. 24. The notion that the 'strange woman' can lead a man to sin and death is developed in Prov 7, and finds colourful development in 4Q184 (The Wiles of the Wicked Woman). The Qumran text has been adduced as a parallel to v. 24 because it says that 'she is the start of all the ways of wickedness' (4Q184:8; Levison 1985: 622). Ben Sira, however, is not concerned only with the strange or loose woman. (It is clear from the parallels with Prov 7 that this is the figure envisaged in the fragmentary 4Q184.) Sirach does not only speak of the death of the sinner, but why we *all* die. There can be no doubt that v. 24 represents an interpretation of Gen 3, and that it is the earliest extant witness to the view that Eve was responsible for the introduction of sin and death (Meyers 1988: 75, *pace* Levison 1985: 617–23, who argues that the woman in question is the bad wife). Even the view that Adam was the source of sin and death only emerges in literature of the first century CE (Rom 5:12–21; 1 Cor 15:22; Wis 2:23–4; 4 Ezra 4:30; 7:116–21; 2 Bar 17:3; 48:45–6. 2 Bar 54:19, however, contends that Adam is only responsible for himself). Sir 17, which clearly reflects Gen 2–3, contains no mention of an original sin. In the apocalyptic literature roughly contemporary with Sirach the origin of evil was attributed to fallen angels (1 Enoch, 6–11) or to God's design at creation (1QS 3). Sirach elsewhere insists that death is simply the decree of the Lord, with no implication that it is a punishment (41:3–4). None the less, this verse is extant in Hebrew and there is no reason to doubt its authenticity. Sirach's inconsistency on this matter shows only that his argumentation was influenced by the immediate context in which an issue is raised.

There is no precedent in Hebrew tradition for the view that woman is the source of all evil, but there is a clear Greek precedent in the story of Pandora's box (Hes. *Op.* 42–105; Middendorp 1973: 21; Kieweler 1992: 115 insists on the differences in context, but the parallel is none the less significant). It would be too simple to ascribe the misogynist aspects of Ben Sira's thought to Hellenistic influence. Ps.-Phocylides represents a more heavily Hellenized form of Judaism but does not pick up these elements. There is undoubtedly Greek influence here, but Ben Sira's personality also played a part in his selective use of Greek culture.

Ch. 25 concludes with the rather brutal advice that a wife who is outspoken and not compliant should be cut off or divorced. Contrast the advice not to divorce a good wife in Sir 7:26. The Hebrew verb *k-r-t*, cut off, gives rise to the standard word for divorce, *krytwt* (Deut 24:1). Deuteronomy allowed that a man could divorce his wife if she did not please him because he found something objectionable ('*erwat dābār*) about her. This text was invoked in a famous debate between the houses of Shammai and Hillel in the first century BCE. The Shammaites tried to restrict its application to cases of adultery. Hillel ruled that a man was justified in divorcing 'even if she spoiled a dish for him' (m. *Git.* 9:10). Rabbi Akiba went further, saying that it sufficed if he found another woman who was fairer (Archer 1990: 219). The Mishnah also provides that a woman could be sent away without her *kĕtûbâ* (the *mōhar* or bride-price owed by the husband) if she transgressed the law of Moses or violated Jewish custom, even by going out with her hair unbound, spinning in the street, or speaking with a man (m. *Ketub.* 7:6). R. Tarfon also permitted this in the case of a scolding woman, who spoke inside her house so that a neighbour could hear. Ben Sira does not suggest that the dowry can be retained in this case. Smend (1906: 233) explains the expression 'from your flesh' by suggesting that the financial settlement involved would be as painful as cutting off a piece of flesh. It is more likely, however, that the phrase reflects Gen 2:24 (man and wife are 'one flesh' while they are married). The woman had no corresponding right to divorce in Mishnaic law (m. *Yebam.* 14:1).

Sir 26:1–4 turns briefly to the joys of a good wife. She is considered solely in terms of her effect on her husband. The point of this stanza is the converse of 25:19. As the sinner deserves a bad wife, the one who fears the Lord deserves a good one. The good wife here seems to exist to reward the deserving man rather than having a value in her own right. The value of a good wife for a wise man is also noted in the late-Egyptian *Instruction of Phibis*, 8:5 (J. T. Sanders 1983: 86).

26:5–9 repeats the thought of 25:13–20. The jealousy of a wife for her rival raises the question of polygamy. While polygamy is never forbidden by biblical law and is still permitted by the Mishnah (m. *Ketub.* 10:5; m. *Ker.* 3:7), it has often been thought to have died out by the Hellenistic period, except for people in high places such as the sons of Herod. This common assumption has been put in doubt, however, by the Babatha archive from the early second century CE (Lewis 1989: 19–22). Babatha was an illiterate woman from the region of the Dead Sea, who, after her husband's death, was involved in a dispute with another woman who claimed to be his wife, and whose claim is not disputed. While Babatha was not a poor person, she was far removed from the social class of the Herodian family. Polygamy may not have been as exceptional in the Hellenistic and Roman periods as was previously thought.

The Egyptian *Instruction of Phibis* refers to an otherwise unknown book 'Faults of Women' (*Phibis*, 8:10; J. T. Sanders 1983: 86), so we should assume that passages such as this were a topos of Near-Eastern wisdom in the Hellenistic period. On the eyelashes of the adulterous woman cf. Prov 6:25, where they appear to be instruments of seduction. The point here is that a woman intent on adultery makes up her eyelids, while the faithful wife has no reason to do so. On the making up of the eyelids cf. 2 Kings 9:30 (Jezebel); Jer 4:30; Ezek 23:40. In 1 Enoch, 8:1, the art of making up the eyes is taught to human beings by the fallen angel Azazel.

The warning about a headstrong daughter in 26:10 will be taken up at length in 42:9–14; cf. Ps.-Phoc. 215–16. Several Hellenistic Jewish texts indicate that virgin girls were confined to the home (Philo, *Spec. Leg.* 3.169; *Flacc.* 89; 2 Macc 3:19; 3 Macc 1:18; 4 Macc 18:7; see further Archer 1990: 113–15). Sir 26:12 recalls Ezek 16:23–5 in its obscene portrayal of the promiscuous woman, but Sirach attributes this behaviour not to an exceptional individual but to a daughter who is not held in check. The tent-peg and arrow are phallic symbols (Smend 1906: 236; Peters 1913: 217).

Sir 26:13–18 is more explicit than earlier passages on the attributes of the good wife. Although she puts flesh on her husband's bones, this is not the capable wife of Prov 31, who can buy a field and deal with merchants. Sirach's ideal wife is a homebody, characterized by silence, modesty, and chastity. In part, the difference in perspective reflects the transition from a rural to an urban culture. The wife of a scribe in Jerusalem has no occasion to buy a field, and her labour is not needed outside the house. Instead she is portrayed as an ornament in his home. This is the only passage where Ben Sira shows an appreciation of physical beauty (contrast 25:21). It is characteristic of ancient Near-Eastern love poetry to single out parts of the body for praise. Cf. Song 4:1–7; 1QapGen 20:2–7. The description of Sarah in the latter passage comments on the perfection of her legs. Ben Sira differs from the other passages however in drawing his analogies from the furnishings of the temple, and thereby projecting a sense of admiration rather than physical desire.

26:19–27 are found in the second Greek recension and are not extant in Hebrew. They are usually regarded as secondary, but Peters (1913: 218) and Skehan and DiLella (1987: 351) regard them as authentic. They add little to the foregoing discussion. v. 26c, d repeats 26:1a, b. The advice in vv. 19–22 is closely parallel to Prov 5:7–14. The concern in sexual activity is to propagate a line of offspring. Relations with a prostitute are wasted. v. 23 recapitulates 25:19 and 26:3. Some of the analogies in this passage are very crude: a prostitute is like spittle and a headstrong wife is like a dog.

(26:28–27:29) Miscellaneous Maxims The extended discourse on women is followed by a string of short units on traditional wisdom themes, punctuated by pronouncements on the inevitability of retribution (26:28c; 27:3, 29). 26:28 is a numerical proverb, which ends with the condemnation of the relapsed sinner. 28c should read 'wealthy man' (Syriac) rather than 'warrior' (Gk.)—the Greek translator evidently misunderstood the Hebrew 'îš ḥayil, which can mean either man of valour or man of wealth (Smend 1906: 240). For the wise man despised, cf. Job 29:2–30:10. If we allow that the wise man was not always despised (cf. Job), then in each case the person has lost something that he or she had for a time. On the relapsed sinner, cf. Ezek 18:24.

26:29–27:3 gives a remarkably sceptical view of commerce. Traditional wisdom denounced cheating and the use of false scales, which was evidently widespread in the ancient world (Prov 11:1; 20:10), but Sirach goes further in suggesting that dishonesty is inherent in the pursuit of wealth. Cf. Mt 19:23–4 on the difficulty of a rich person entering heaven. This saying is probably a comment on the increase of commerce in Judea in the Hellenistic period. The Tobiads come to mind as the paradigmatic profiteers of the era. According to 2 Macc 3:4, a dispute over the city market was the initial cause of friction that initiated the chain of events that led to the persecution of Antiochus Epiphanes and the Maccabean revolt. 27:3 is typical of Sirach's rather naïve view that sinners suffer retribution in this life.

27:4–7 emphasizes the importance of speech as the reflection of a person's character; cf. 20:5–8. The 'refuse' in v. 4 refers to the dung of the oxen mixed in with the straw. For the comparison with the fruit of a tree, cf. Mt 7:16–19; 12:33. This theme is illustrated in vv. 11–15. The intervening vv. 8–10 emphasize the inevitability of the link of act and consequence, which is typical of ancient Near-Eastern wisdom (Koch 1955), cf. Am 3:3–8. This theme is further developed in vv. 22–9, and is the underpinning of Sirach's belief in the inevitability of retribution. 27:16–21 on the betrayal of secrets illustrates another aspect of indiscreet speech, and is a traditional concern of wisdom literature. Cf. Prov 20:19; 25:9. Finally, the sage turns to hypocrisy and mischief-making. Here again there is a parallel in Prov 6:12–19. Cf. also Theognis, 93–6. 27:25 is a variant of Prov 26:27b, while Prov 26:27a is reproduced exactly in Sir 27:26a. The unit ends with an affirmation of retribution in this life.

(27:30–28:11) Anger, Vengeance, and Strife Mention of the Lord's vengeance recalls Deut 32:35–6. The Qumran *Rule of the Community* also eschews vengeance for the present, but only defers it until the day of wrath (1QS 10:17–20). Sirach here is closer in spirit to the Gospels, especially in linking forgiveness to prayer (Mt 6:12, 14–15; 18:32–5; Mk 11:25; Lk 11:4). Similar sentiments are found in *T. Gad*, 6:3–7; *T. Zebulon*, 5:3, but these passages are of uncertain provenance. In a later Jewish context, cf. *b. Roš Haš.* 17a; *b. Meg.* 28a. Characteristic of Sirach is the reminder of death as an argument for forgiveness: cf. 7:36; 8:7; 14:12; 18:24; 38:20. The point is that everyone is subject to divine judgement in the end, on the basis of the commandments. We have no secure place from which to pass judgement on others (cf. Mt 7:1).

(28:12–26) On Slander The discourse on slander has no real parallel in the earlier wisdom tradition, but cf. the discussion of gossip in 19:7–12. On the ambivalence of speech (v. 12), cf. Jas 3:10. The expression translated as 'slander' in the NRSV is literally 'third tongue', so called because it comes between the subject of the slander and the hearer. So *b. 'Arak.* 15b: 'The third tongue kills three' (the subject, the speaker, and the hearer). In the case of virtuous women (v. 15), slander could lead to divorce and loss of the marriage settlement. v. 17b echoes Prov 25:15b, but the context in Proverbs concerns persuasion. This section ends by reiterating the need for caution in speech, which is typical of ancient wisdom; cf. 20:18–19; 23:7–8.

(29:1–20) Loans, Alms, and Surety This section combines three poems on related themes: loans (vv. 1–7), alms (vv. 8–13), and providing surety or collateral for another (vv. 14–20). There is some tension in Ben Sira's advice on loans. The Torah requires that one help an indigent neighbour, and not exact interest (Ex 22:24; Lev 25:36–7; Deut 15:7–11; 23:19–20). Sirach endorses the commandment. No mention is made of interest. He also urges rectitude in repaying loans, thereby implying that even a scribe or an educated person may need a loan on occasion. The need to repay promptly is also emphasized in 4QSapiential Work A (4Q417 1 i 21–3). But much of the passage dwells on the difficulty of recovering a loan. Cf. Ps 37:21: the wicked do not pay back, the righteous keep giving. So in v. 7 Sirach shows considerable sympathy for those who refuse to lend because of fear of being cheated. On this issue, he is at odds with the spirit of the Gospels. Contrast Lk 6:34–5: if you lend to those from whom you hope to receive, what credit is there for that? Sirach abides by the letter of the commandment, but his pragmatic wisdom favours a more cautious course of action.

In the case of almsgiving, there is no expectation of repayment. Sirach has already treated this subject in 3:30–1. The NRSV translation of 9:11 ('Lay up your treasure . . .') is unduly influenced by the Gospel parallel (Mt 6:10 || Luke 12:33–4: 'Lay up for yourselves treasure in heaven'). The point here is rather 'dispose of your treasure in accordance with the commandments of the Most High' (cf. Skehan and DiLella 1987: 368). The parallel with the NT holds, however, as Sirach goes on to say 'store up almsgiving in your treasury'. Good deeds earn credit with the Lord. Cf. Tob 4:8–9: 'If you have many possessions make your gift from them in proportion; if few, do not be afraid to give according to the little you have. So you will be laying up a treasure for yourself against the day of necessity.' *Pss. Sol.* 9:5 speaks of laying up treasure with the Lord by doing righteousness. *2 Bar* 24:1 speaks of treasuries where the merits of the righteous are stored until the day of judgement. The notion that hoarded wealth rusts (Sir 29:10) parallels the thought of Mt 6:20 on the perishability of wealth. Cf. also Jas 5:2–3.

Proverbs uniformly counsels against going surety for another (Prov 6:1–5; 11:15; 17:18; 20:16; 22:26–7; 27:13). Sirach appreciates the helpfulness implied, but he also dwells on the pitfalls. He also includes a warning for the sinner, who tries to take advantage of such a situation, that lawsuits will follow. Retribution is not left entirely in the hands of God! He concludes with a typical middle way: help your neighbour if you can, but be prudent. The theme of surety also appears in 4QSapiential Work A (4Q416 7) but the passage is obscure (Harrington 1994: 147).

(29:21–8) On Self-Sufficiency The theme of self-sufficiency is illustrated by the misery of one who depends on others for lodging. A longer list of the necessities of life is given in 39:26. Ben Sira's concern is with honour and the lack thereof, the indignity of depending on others; cf. the critique of begging in 40:28–30. Self-sufficiency was widely entertained as an ideal in Greek philosophy, especially by the Stoics (Middendorp 1973: 30), but Prov 12:9 appreciates the advantage of working for oneself (reading 'ōbēd lô rather than 'ebed lô). See further Sir 31:19. Sirach warns, however, against inappropriate self-sufficiency (11:22).

(30:1–13) On Sons The education of sons, which is treated in scattered proverbs in Proverbs, is expanded into a section of 13 verses here. Phibis also devotes a whole instruction (the tenth, Papyrus Insinger 8:21–9:20) to the subject. Both rely heavily on physical punishment, as also does Proverbs (13:24; 22:15; 23:13–14; 29:15). Cf. also the *Sayings of Ahiqar*, Syriac version: 'My son, withhold not your son from stripes, for the beating of a child is like manure to the garden, or like rope to an ass, or like a tether on the foot of an ass' (Skehan and DiLella 1987: 377). The goal is to instil discipline, but also to produce a copy of the father (v. 4; cf. Tob 9:6). The emphasis is on conformity, with little or no place for creativity. A very different emphasis is found in Ps.-Phoc. 207–9: 'Be not harsh with your children but be gentle, and if a child sins against you, let the mother cut her son down to size, or else the elders of the family or the chiefs of the people.' (This passage is based on Deut 21:18–21, but transforms the biblical text into a plea for paternal leniency.) Cf. also Col. 3:21: 'Fathers, do not provoke your children'. Sirach seems to have belonged to the 'old school' in the matter of family discipline.

(30:14–25) Food and Health The value of good health is universally appreciated. The sentiment that death is preferable to life in some circumstances is also found in Tob 3:6, 10, 13 in the prayers of Tobit and Sarah. Cf. also 1 Kings 19:4 (Elijah), Jon 4:3; Job 3:11, 13, 17; Eccl 4:2. Sirach, however, does not speak out of personal misery, nor is he a sceptic like Ecclesiastes. His observation is all the more remarkable for its dispassionate objectivity; cf. Theog. 181–2. Death is characterized as 'endless sleep' in the Greek text. (The corresponding Heb. has 'to go down to Sheol'.) The repose of the dead is commonly called sleep in Jewish epitaphs of the Hellenistic and Roman periods (van der Horst 1991: 114–17) but so also Job 3:13.

Greek MSS variously insert the heading 'About Foods' before v. 16 or v. 18. In either case, the heading is inappropriate. Food is introduced in v. 18 only to illustrate the frustration of sickness. Offerings placed on a grave are viewed as futile here, and are disapproved in Deut 26:14, but appear to be approved in Tob 4:17. See also the comment on Sir 7:33 above. The futility of offering food to idols is the theme of the satirical story of Bel and the Dragon. An ominous note is struck

in passing in v. 19c, which implies that a person in bad health is being punished by the Lord. Compare the theology of the friends of Job, and the assumption of the disciples in Jn 9:2. This line is not found in the Hebrew, which refers instead to 'one who has wealth'. The Greek verse may have resulted from an attempt to make sense of corrupt Hebrew (Smend 1906: 270). The theological position it reflects was widespread, but not explicitly endorsed by Ben Sira. v. 20 is also corrupt. The eunuch embracing a virgin, and the comparison with one who acts under compulsion, are imported here from Sir 20:4. (The reference to the eunuch was apt enough in the context of ch. 30.) The thought of v. 23 is more typical of Ecclesiastes than of Sirach. Cf. Eccl 9:7–10; 11:9, but cf. also Sir 14:11–19 and the comments above. Modern medicine has come to appreciate the wisdom of the sentiment in v. 24.

(31:1–11) Attitude to Wealth The order of chapters in Greek and Hebrew diverges at this point (Gk. ch. 31 = Heb. ch. 34). vv. 1–2 are hopelessly corrupt in the Hebrew, and 30:2 is also corrupt in Greek. The general idea is that a person devoted to the pursuit of wealth suffers insomnia. According to 40:1–11, troubled sleep is an affliction of humankind in general, but sinners are afflicted more than others. Insomnia in itself is not necessarily a moral indictment. The statements in vv. 2–3 are neutral, simple observations of fact. Cf. 13:21–3. Proverbs is similarly realistic on the question of wealth and poverty (Prov 10:15; 18:23; 19:4, 6).

vv. 4–11 move on to moral judgement. v. 5 echoes 27:1 in condemning the inordinate pursuit of wealth. Yet v. 8 suggests Sirach's ideal: a rich person who is found blameless. Such a person may be hard to find, but not impossible. Wealth was traditionally regarded as a reward of wisdom. Sirach was aware that this view was problematic, but he had not given up on it entirely. In defence of his admiration for the blameless rich person, he points out that he had the power to sin, but refrained. Sirach's confidence in the security of the wealth of the righteous person, however, might have been dispelled by a reading of the book of Job.

(31:12–32:13) Eating and Drinking at Banquets Behaviour at banquets is a theme of Egyptian literature from an early time and is treated in the *Instruction of Ptah-hotep*, the *Instruction of Kagemni*, and the *Instruction of Amen-em-ope* (J. T. Sanders 1983: 67). The latter work was probably the source for Prov 23:1–3. Sirach's instruction follows the same pattern. (Cf. also 13:8–13.) The advice is directed towards someone who is inexperienced in such matters, and is likely to be excited by the abundance of food. Sirach counsels moderation, and this is in accordance both with age-old Near-Eastern wisdom and with Hellenistic philosophy (cf. Ps.-Phoc. 69 and the Greek parallels cited by van der Horst 1978: 160–1). vv. 19–20 note the beneficial effects of moderation. The advice on vomiting in v. 21 does not imply the Roman custom of using an emetic so that one could then eat more, but is simply practical advice to relieve distress. The need for such advice, however, is not reflected in the older wisdom literature.

vv. 23–4 shift the focus away from the inexperienced diner to the host of the banquet. Dinner parties were much more common in the Hellenistic world than they had been in the ancient Near East (cf. the passing reference to banquets in 2

Macc 2:27, which assumes familiarity with the practice). They were also a source of prestige for the hosts. The NRSV rendering of v. 24, 'the city complains', reflects the idiom of the Greek translator. The Hebrew speaks of murmuring in the gate, the traditional place of congregation in the Near-Eastern city.

In the Hellenistic banquet, the main course was followed by wine-drinking and entertainment, but this was also the custom in the ancient Near East (cf. Esth 5:6; Dan 5:1–2, which are set in the Persian and Babylonian periods, but, at least in the case of Dan 5, date from the Hellenistic). The eighth-century prophet Amos castigates those who lounge on couches while eating lambs from the flock, and then sing idle songs while drinking wine from bowls (Am 6:4–6. On the Greek banquet see Smith and Taussig 1990: 21–35). Wine-drinking was a problem long before the Hellenistic period. Isaiah taunts those who are 'heroes in drinking wine and valiant in mixing drink' (Isa 5:22) and Amos complains of the drinking of the women of Samaria (Am 4:1). Proverbs paints an amusing picture of drunkenness (23:29–35), but is invariably negative on the subject (cf. also 20:1; 31:4–5). Sirach is more positive, and proclaims wine to be 'life' to humans. Cf. Ps. 104:15; 1 Tim 5:23. He is no less cautionary than Proverbs on the danger of excess, but he recognizes the inadvisability of reproaching a person who is inebriated. The dangers of intoxication at a banquet are vividly illustrated in 1 Macc 16:15–16 and Jdt 13:2–8.

In 32:1–13, Sirach addresses in turn the conduct appropriate to the banquet master, the elder guests, and the younger guests. The position of banquet master or symposiarch reflects the Hellenistic context of this discussion. This person had the responsibility of arranging seating and ensuring good service. Since this was an honorary position, there was danger of self-importance (32:1). The Hebrew of 32:2 is corrupt. Smend (1906: 286) argues that the Greek 'crown' renders Hebrew 'glory' (*kābôd*), adding a distinctively Hellenistic nuance. Sirach acknowledges that older guests have the right to speak but he urges moderation. He discourages speech-making by the younger guests. His preference is that people simply enjoy the music. Cf. Am 6:5. In Plato's *Symposium*, 176E, the flute-girl is dismissed so that the company can concentrate on philosophical discussion. The Greek text of Sir 9:14–16 (but not the Heb.) seems to imply that the righteous should discuss the Torah on such occasions, but ch. 31 envisages a social situation where all the company is not necessarily righteous. The well-educated person should also know how to behave in an urbane manner in such a setting. A fictional account of after-dinner conversation in a Jewish work can be found in the *Epistle of Aristeas*, 187–294, but this is exceptional as it is a royal banquet and the king questions the guests. Cf. however Sir 13:11, where Sirach warns that a powerful person may test a guest by prolonged conversation. Sirach, characteristically, concludes the section with an exhortation to piety. It was also customary at Greek banquets to pour a libation and sing a chant to the gods (Plato, *Symp.* 176).

(32:14–33:6) Prudence and the Law The long section 25:1–33:19, which is mainly taken up with practical advice, concludes with two theological poems (32:14–33:6 and 33:7–19).

The first of these emphasizes observance of the Torah and fear of the Lord, which appear to be interchangeable here. Seeking God here is equivalent to seeking wisdom in other passages (14:22–5; 51:15–22). Those who seek the law are those who genuinely want to conform to it. The sinner who shuns reproof bends it to his own liking. Ben Sira here seems to have in mind people who pick and choose among the stipulations of the law. In contrast, 1 *Enoch*, 99:2, speaks of people who 'alter the words of truth' and seem to undertake a more serious revision or reinterpretation of the Torah. vv. 19–22 dwell on the need for caution. This too leads to keeping the commandments. Sirach recommends conformity to the Torah as the surest means of self-preservation. The comparison with a divine oracle (33:3) only concerns dependability. Sirach is not suggesting that the Torah be treated as prophecy. vv. 4–6 are traditional sayings, only loosely related to the rest of the poem by their characterization of the fool.

(33:7–19) Variety in Creation The final poem in this section addresses the question of theodicy. Why do things turn out differently from one case to another? Sirach takes his cue from the variation between ordinary time and holy days, which he attributes to divine decree. The idea that God controls the times for all things occurs frequently in the apocalyptic literature of the time (Dan 2:21; 1 *Enoch*, 92:2; von Rad 1972: 266–9). So also with humanity. Nothing is said here of Adam's (or Eve's!) sin as a cause for distinctions between people. Rather, God appointed their different ways. The illustration of this principle in v. 12 contrasts the election of Israel with the dispossession of the Canaanites, but both are taken by way of example. The idea that God makes people walk in their different paths sounds remarkably close to the deterministic view of the Qumran *Rule of the Community* (1QS 3:15–16), and is at odds with Sirach's vigorous defence of human responsibility in 15:11–20; 17:1–20. Sirach's thought on the subject seems to be influenced by the focus of his question. In chs. 15 and 17 he was primarily concerned with human behaviour. In ch. 33 he considers the question from the viewpoint of the order of creation, and the problem of theodicy or the justice of God. His solution is to assert that all God's works are in pairs. This notion is very probably influenced by Stoic philosophy (Pautrel 1963; Middendorp 1973: 29). Chrysippus (late 3rd cent. BCE) taught that nothing could be more inept than the people who suppose that good could have existed without the existence of evil, because antithetical concepts must exist in opposition to each other (frag. 1169; the contrast of opposites is also found in Pythagoras and Heraclitus). This doctrine is different from the systematic dualism of the Qumran *Rule of the Community*, which is probably indebted to Zoroastrian dualism. Sirach is not claiming that all things are divided between good and bad, light and darkness, only that everything must have its opposite. He was not a rigorous enough philosopher, however, to try to reconcile this doctrine with his other theological beliefs.

This section ends with an autobiographical passage in which Ben Sira protests his selflessness and asserts his authority as a teacher of wisdom. The image of the gleaner emphasizes his dependence on tradition. This passage is a counterpart to Sir 24:30–4, which concluded Part I of the book. Sir 51:13–30, which concludes the entire book, strikes similar notes. The suspicion arises, therefore, that 24:30–4 and 33:16–19 may have marked the conclusion of the book in earlier stages of its composition.

(33:20–39:11)

(33:20–33) Property and Slaves vv. 20–4 warn against handing over one's property prematurely. This advice accords with Ben Sira's general preference for self-sufficiency. It also protects the honour and dignity of the parent. Ben Sira does not seem to envisage the possibility of making a will in advance that would only come into effect at the time of death. The literary form of testament, as found in the *Testaments of the Twelve Patriarchs*, imagines the father on his deathbed.

The existence of slaves was taken for granted throughout the ancient Mediterranean world. Ben Sira's advice on their treatment vacillates. First, he advocates harsh treatment, comparing the slave to a beast of burden. A slave who is underworked will seek liberty, and idleness creates mischief. This advice is in line with Prov 29:19, 21 and is also paralleled in *Phibis* (Papyrus Insinger, 14:6–11; J. T. Sanders 1983: 95). This advice, however, is severely qualified, if not undercut, by 33:30c, d, which warns against overbearing behaviour towards anyone. Here Sirach is probably influenced by the Torah, which granted slaves limited but important rights (Ex 21:1–11, 20–1, 26–7; Lev 25:39–55; Deut 15:12–18; 23:16–17). Lev 25:39, 46, permits the acquisition of Gentiles as slaves but says that Israelites who are forced into debt slavery should be treated as hired-servants. The Hellenistic Jewish Ps.-Phocylides, 223–6, advocates humane treatment for slaves, as does Sirach also in 7:20–1 and 33:31. Finally Ben Sira takes his characteristic line of self-interest. A slave who is ill-treated will run away. According to Deut 23:15–16, it was forbidden to return a runaway slave to the owner. The need to take good care of a slave is especially acute if there is only one. It seems then that Ben Sira is transmitting a traditional hard line on the treatment of slaves, but recognizes that gentler treatment is more practical.

(34:1–20) On Dreams Dreams were a respected means of revelation in the ancient world, and so also in Genesis (e.g. Jacob's dream in Gen 28; the Joseph story). Close to the time of Sirach, Daniel was honoured as interpreter of the dreams of a foreign king, and received his own revelation in a dream (Dan 7:1). Deuteronomy, however, views dreams with suspicion and groups them with portents and omens (Deut 13:1–5). Jeremiah is derisive towards prophets who rely on dreams (Jer 23:23–40). Proverbs pays no attention to dreams, but Eliphaz in Job reports 'visions of the night' (Job 4:13). Sirach stands in the tradition of Deuteronomy and Jeremiah on this issue. He does not rule out entirely the possibility of revelation through dreams (34:6) but he emphasizes their deceptiveness. His debt to Deuteronomy is evident in 34:8: dreams are not necessary for keeping the law (cf. Deut 30:11–14). This passage shows clearly the gulf that separates Ben Sira from the roughly contemporary apocalyptic writers of 1 Enoch and Daniel. In the apocalyptic writings, some form of additional revelation, over and above the law, is essential. In fact, Sirach's sweeping rejection of dreams is exceptional in ancient Judaism. Josephus often introduces references to dreams where there were none in the biblical text, and the efficacy of dreams

is widely accepted in rabbinic literature (Box and Oesterley 1913: 433).

The dismissal of dreams is followed by two short affirmative poems. First, Sirach stresses the importance of experience and travel, a point reiterated in 39:4. It is unfortunate that he gives no details of his travels. Travel was dangerous in the ancient world. Cf. Paul's litany of dangers in 2 Cor 11:25–6. Second, Sirach balances his acknowledgement of experiential wisdom with an encomium of the fear of the Lord. For the image of God as shelter, cf. Isa 4:6; 25:4–5; Ps 121:5–6.

(34:21–35:26) On Sacrifices Ben Sira is exceptional among the wisdom books of the HB and the Apocrypha in devoting a lengthy treatise to cult and sacrifices (Perdue 1977). The first part of this treatise, 34:21–31, is a critique of the abuse of the cult, in the spirit of the prophets. Especially striking are vv. 24–7, which equate social injustice with murder. Cf. Isa 65:3, which can be read as equating sacrifice with murder, although the text is ambiguous. Sirach is quite clear that the problem is not with sacrifice as such but with the abuse of the poor, but sacrifice cannot compensate for social injustice. Sirach may be commenting on contemporary abuses here, or he may be simply reflecting the teaching of the prophets (cf. Am 5:21–7; 8:4–8). In 34:25, Skehan and DiLella (1987) read 'bread of charity' (reading ḥesed, with the Syriac; the Gk. presupposes ḥeser, 'want/need'). If this is correct, almsgiving is not optional. To withhold it in some cases would be tantamount to murder. vv. 28–31 build an argument against superficial repentance. vv. 28–9 are examples of mutually negating behaviour. The person who fasts and sins again is self-negating. For purification after touching a corpse, see Num 19:9–12.

In 35:1–5 Sirach addresses those things that are most pleasing to the Lord, and insists that the ethical demands of the law are more important than sacrifices. The point of 35:1 is not that the law requires many sacrifices (a point that Sirach would also grant) but that observance is the equivalent of many sacrifices. Sirach displays his familiarity with the different kinds of sacrifice, but the point is that kindness and almsgiving are as effective as sacrifice in pleasing God. This kind of spiritualizing of the cult is found already in the HB, e.g. Ps 51:17. In the Qumran *Rule of the Community* (1QS 8:1–4) righteousness serves as a substitute for the cult. Hellenistic Jews such as Philo also placed their primary stress on the spiritual, symbolic meaning of sacrifice. Ben Sira, however, goes on to say that one should also observe the literal commandments in this respect. Cf. Sir 7:31. The language of the Torah (Ex 23:14; 34:20; Deut 16:16) is echoed by 35:6. This is in accordance with Ben Sira's general insistence on the fulfilment of the law, and also with his criticism of miserliness (14:3–19). Sirach does not, however, attach value to the sacrificial cult in itself, except in so far as it is required by the fulfilment of the law. (For an argument that Sirach attached greater importance to the sacrificial cult, see Stadelmann 1980: 40–138.)

35:14–26 is a poem on the justice of God, related to the preceding passages by the shared theme of prayer. God cannot be bribed by sacrifice to overlook the injustice of the worshipper. The Hebrew of 35:15b reads 'for he is a God of justice' echoing Isa 30:18. (The Gk. reads: 'for the Lord is the judge'.) Concern for the widow and the orphan is a commonplace of ancient Near-Eastern wisdom. Deut 10:18 says that the Lord executes justice for the orphan and the widow. According to Ps 68:5, he is their father; in Prov 23:10–11 he is their redeemer. Cf. also Ex 3:9, where God hears the cry of the oppressed Israelites. The imagery of God as Divine Warrior, coming to wreak vengeance on his enemies, is widespread in the HB; cf. especially Deut 32:35–6. Typically in the HB, the Lord comes to vindicate his people, Israel. This biblical language is borrowed in v. 25, but in the context 'his people' are the poor rather than ethnic Israel.

(36:1–22) A Prayer for Deliverance This is the main passage in Sirach whose authenticity is disputed. Nowhere else in the book does Sirach express antagonism towards foreign nations. If this prayer was composed by Ben Sira, the hostile rulers would have to be the Seleucids, who ruled Palestine from 198 BCE. But Josephus reports that Seleucid rule was initially welcomed by the Jews, and that Antiochus III (the Great) helped restore the city and supported the temple cult (*Ant.* 12.129–53). The high priest of the day was Simon II (the Just), who is eulogized in Sir 50:1–21. The restoration of temple and city are listed as his outstanding achievements. It is scarcely conceivable, then, that Sirach would have viewed Antiochus III as a hostile ruler, or asked God to crush his head. In fact, such sentiments only make sense in or after the time of Antiochus IV Epiphanes, and there is no other reflection of that reign in Sirach's book (Middendorp 1973: 125). (The possibility that the poem was composed before the Syrian take-over, and regards the Ptolemies as the enemy, is unsatisfactory because of the generic denunciation of foreign nations.) The likelihood that this prayer is a secondary addition to the book is overwhelming. It is true that 35:21–6 provides a lead into the prayer (Skehan and DiLella 1987: 420). This explains why the prayer was inserted at this particular point. But the passage in ch. 35 is concerned with the universal judgement of God on the unrighteous, whereby 'he repays mortals according to their deeds' (35:24). The prayer in ch. 36 calls for a highly particular judgement on the enemies of Israel.

In the canonical psalter, communal prayers for deliverance are usually embedded in psalms of complaint, which include some description of the abject state of the community (Ps 44; 74; 79–80; 83; Gerstenberger 1988: 14). Comparable prayers from the Second Temple period also typically include a confession of sin (Ezra 9:6–15; Neh 9:6–37; Dan 9:4–19; Song of Thr (Prayer of Azariah); Bar 2:11–26; 4QDibHam—Words of the Luminaries). There is no confession of sin in Sir 36, and the distress of Jerusalem is only hinted at. Instead it is a direct appeal for divine intervention.

The expression 'God of all' in v. 1 recurs in 45:23*c* (Heb. only) and 50:22*a* (Gk. only; Heb. reads 'God of Israel'). Sir 43:27 goes further, saying that he *is* the all. The fear of God among the nations recalls the original conquest of Canaan. Cf. Ex 15:15–16. The language of manifesting holiness is especially characteristic of Ezekiel. Cf. Ezek 20:41; 28:25; 39:27, where God manifests his holiness in gathering Israel from among the nations. (In Ezek 38:23, the reference is to the judgement on Gog.) Since Sirach

goes on to pray for the gathering of the tribes in v. 13, the display of holiness to the nations probably lies in the punishment of Israel. Sirach asks in effect that the nations be brought low just as Israel was. The goal of the knowledge of God is also characteristic of Ezekiel (cf. Ezek 6:7, 14; 7:28, etc.). Insistence on monotheism is characteristic of Hellenistic Judaism. Cf. *Sib. Or.* 3:11; Wis 13:10–19; *Ep. Arist.* 135–8; Philo, *Dec.* 76–80. The signs and wonders of v. 6 evoke the Exodus (Ex 7:3).

The notion that God determines the times has been encountered already in Sir 33:7–9. In v. 10, NRSV 'day' corresponds to Hebrew 'end' (*qēṣ*), which the Greek renders as *kairos*, time. There is some tension in 36:10 between the belief that God can hasten the day of vengeance and the belief that the time is appointed and God need only remember it. The linking of the terms 'end' and 'appointed time' derives from Hab 2:3, and is reflected several times in Daniel (10:14; 11:27, 35), where it invariably implies that the time is fixed. The idea that God can hasten the end arises from the urgency of prayer. v. 11 calls for complete destruction of the enemy leaving no survivors. For the crushing of the heads of the enemy, cf. Num 24:18; Ps 110:6. The boast of the enemy is taken from Isa 47:8. For Israel as God's firstborn, cf. Ex 4:22; for Jerusalem as the place of God's dwelling, Ps 132:13. Especially noteworthy is the emphasis on the fulfilment of prophecy in vv. 20–1. While Sirach's sage studies prophecies (39:1) we do not get the sense that he expects them to be fulfilled. The fulfilment of prophecy is of urgent concern in Daniel (cf. Dan 9) and in the Dead Sea scrolls (e.g. the pesher on Habakkuk). The *Apostrophe to Zion* from Qumran (11QPs 22:5–6, 13–14) also recalls the visions of the prophets for the restoration of Zion. The final appellation, God of the ages, harks back to the divine title El Olam in Genesis (Gen 21:33).

(36:23–37:15) Discrimination and Friendship The theme of this section concerns the need for discrimination in choosing friends and companions. 36:23 sets the tone by distinguishing between what is tolerable and what is preferred. The pattern is repeated in 36:26, 37:1, and 37:7. In each case Sirach makes a statement about a class (food, men, friends, counsellors) and then says that some members of that class are preferable to others. 36:26 stands out as an exception. Instead of moving from 'any man' (will a woman accept) to 'some men are preferable', he says 'one girl is preferable to another'. It is likely that Sirach has modified a traditional statement, so as to impose a male instead of a female point of view (Trenchard 1982: 20). The woman's willingness to accept any man does not imply promiscuity. It simply reflects the social practice whereby the woman had little choice. Girls were given in marriage by their fathers (cf. Tob 7:10–14; in Gen 24:57–8, Rebekah is consulted as a courtesy, but she has already been given, v. 51). The marriage contract was an agreement between the groom and the bride's father. Moreover, women had little security in life outside marriage (Archer 1990: 125–6).

36:27–8 notes some of the things that make a woman attractive: beauty, kindness, and humility. The following verses digress on the advisability of marriage. Sirach borrows the phrase of Gen 2:18, 20 to refer to the help a wife can give her husband. Moreover, she can give him a 'nest' and prevent him from wandering. Sirach implies that the unattached man cannot be trusted (cf. the language applied to Cain in Gen 4:12). A wife is necessary for social respectability. Most revealing of Sirach's attitude on marriage, however, is the statement that a wife is a man's best possession (v. 29); cf. SIR 7:26. Even while Sirach expresses the high value he places on a wife, he still regards her as a possession of her husband. The patriarchal quality of this statement is not negated by the fact that the language recalls Prov 8:22, which says that the Lord acquired (or created *qānâ*), wisdom as the beginning of his way.

The subject of friends has been treated at length in 6:5–17 and 12:8–13:23, and touched upon in several places. The reference to the evil inclination (cf. 15:14 above) seems to have arisen from a translator's mistake. The Hebrew reads 'alas for the friend who says "why were you fashioned so?"' (Skehan and DiLella 1987: 428).

37:7–15 reviews some of the pitfalls involved in seeking advice; v. 11 probably refers to a polygamous situation, cf. 26:6. Characteristically, Sirach concludes the discussion of friends and associates by recommending the company of those who keep the law. Cf. 6:16–17; 12:13–15; 13:1.

(37:16–31) True and False Friends The theme of true and false wisdom was treated in 19:20–30 in religious terms, emphasizing that the wicked are not truly wise. vv. 16–26 make the contrast in practical terms. A person who is intelligent and a good speaker, but derives no personal benefit from this wisdom, is deficient. Wisdom entails enlightened self-interest. vv. 23–6, however, put the individual in a communal context. The people, Israel, transcends the individuals, whose days are limited. v. 26 expresses one of Sirach's major goals in life: honour among the people and immortality through reputation. This ideal is repeated in 39:9–11; 41:11–13, and 44:13–15. Contrast the pessimistic view of Ecclesiastes that there is no remembrance of wise or fool (Eccl 2:16).

The brief stanza on moderation recapitulates a theme treated at greater length in 31:12–31.

(38:1–23) Attitudes to Physicians and Death The two instructions in this section are related by the themes of sickness and death. vv. 1–15 recommend respect for physicians. In the HB, physicians are rarely mentioned, and regarded as unreliable. King Asa of Israel is condemned because he sought healing from physicians rather than from God (2 Chr 16:12). Job derides his friends as 'worthless physicians' (Job 13:4). Jeremiah points to the uselessness of medicine for certain problems (Jer 8:22–9:6; 46:11; 51:8) but he at least shows familiarity with the practice of seeking balm from Gilead. In view of the Chronicler's comment on Asa, it seems safe to infer that some people in ancient Judaism had a negative view of physicians for religious reasons, and that Sirach's advocacy of the profession is in some part directed against such people. In contrast, Greece had a flourishing medical tradition, associated with the fifth-century figure of Hippocrates, and there was also a venerable medical tradition in Egypt.

Sirach argues that the healing power of God is mediated indirectly by physicians working with balms and herbs. The statement that God created medicine (38:4) is paralleled in *Phibis* (Papyrus Insinger, 32:12; J. T. Sanders 1983: 75). Ex 15:23–5 is taken as an illustration of the use of a balm, since wood was thrown in the water to sweeten it. Contrast the negative view of 'roots', which are taken to be part of the revelation of the fallen angels in the roughly contemporary Book of the Watchers (1 *Enoch*, 8:3).

None the less, Sirach does not rely completely on the ways of medicine. He also advocates prayer and sacrifice. He implies that illness is due to sin (38:10; cf. Deut 28:21–9; Job 4:7; Jn 9:2), which must be cleansed before the physician can be effective. The physician too prays for divine assistance (v. 14). The Greek and one Hebrew reading of v. 15 say that the sinner will be delivered into the hand of the physician, and this reading is preferred by some authorities (Smend 1906: 343; Peters 1913: 311). Yet the negative implication about the physician goes against the thrust of the passage. The reading of NRSV is supported by another Hebrew MS and makes better sense (Skehan and DiLella 1987: 443).

vv. 16–23 treat the subject of mourning for the dead and counsel moderation. On the one hand, custom should be properly observed. The importance of burial is amply illustrated in Tob 1:17–18; 4:3–4; 6:15; 12:12; 14:12–13. Mourning was often performed by wailing women (cf. Jer 9:16–19). Sirach's counsel of moderation is paralleled in Ps.-Phoc. 97–8, and in several Greek authors (e.g. Soph. *El.* 140–2. See van der Horst 1978: 179). Sirach uses the occasion to remind the reader of the inevitability of death, including one's own. The practical tone here is typical of biblical wisdom: what matters is not the intention but the result. In this case, mourning does not help the dead and may injure the living.

(38:24–39:11) The Scribal Profession The contrast between the scribe and various professional artisans bears an obvious analogy to an Egyptian composition called the 'Satire on the Trades', the *Instruction of Kheti, Son of Duauf*, composed in the early second millennium, but copied repeatedly over several centuries (*ANET* 432–4). It is derisive towards all kinds of manual work: the building contractor is dirtier than pigs; the embalmer smells of corpses; the metal worker stinks more than fish. Writing some 1500 years later, Ben Sira is much more diplomatic. He acknowledges that every city needs craftsmen, and that they are worthy of respect. None the less, his tone is condescending and his goal is to proclaim the superiority of his own profession. This superiority is reflected in the positions of honour listed in vv. 32–3, which are beyond the capacity of an artisan, but for which a scribe is well qualified.

The Greek of 38:24a preserves the better reading, as is shown by the parallelism with 24b. The Hebrew ('the wisdom of the scribe increases wisdom') is obviously corrupt. Sirach makes no apology for belonging to a leisured class. How else could he pursue wisdom?

The positive characterization of the scribe begins in 38:34. Pride of place is given to the study of the Torah. Ezra might be considered the prototype here, since he is described as a scribe well-versed in the law of Moses (Ezra 7:6) but Ben Sira singularly fails to acknowledge Ezra in the Praise of the Fathers (chs. 24–50). Unlike Ezra, moreover, Sirach's sage is concerned with the wisdom of all the ancients. His concern for prophecy has been the source of some debate (Stadelmann 1980: 216–46). Despite occasional flourishes, such as his critique of false worship in ch. 35, Sirach breathes little of the prophetic spirit. Apart from the prayer in ch. 36, whose authenticity we have questioned, he is not concerned with predictions of national restoration or doom. For him, the books of the prophets are a source of wisdom just as Proverbs is. His hermeneutic of prophecy appears most clearly in chs. 48–9. The aspiration of the sage to serve before rulers is corroborated by the stories of Joseph, Daniel, and Ahiqar. On foreign travel, cf. Sirach's own claim in 34:12. The sage evidently has other sources of wisdom besides the Law and the Prophets. Sirach concludes, however, by emphasizing his piety. For prayer of petition, he could point to the precedent of Solomon in 1 Kings 3, but Sirach puts the stress on prayer for forgiveness. For the spirit of understanding, cf. Isa 11:2. For the imagery of pouring forth words, cf. Sir 24:30–4. The reward of wisdom is enduring fame, but Sirach also expresses resignation in the face of death.

(39:12–43:33)

(39:12–35) Praise of the Creator The first-person invitation in vv. 12–15 marks the beginning of a new section. Specifically, these verses introduce the praise of God's works in 39:16–35. This is followed by various reflections on human wretchedness. The section is concluded by another, longer, hymn of praise (42:15–43:33). The *Instruction of Phibis* also includes a section on the works of God in creation (24th instruction; J. T. Sanders 1983: 78).

Sir 39:15 characterizes the following passage as a hymn of praise, and the imperative to praise is repeated in 39:35. The passage itself is made up of declarative sentences. The affirmation that the works of the Lord are all good has its biblical warrant in Gen 1:31, but Sirach is aware of the problem of evil. In this passage he offers two suggestions as to how the evil in the world can be reconciled with the goodness of creation (Crenshaw 1975: 47–64).

First, everything will be clarified at the appointed time (v. 17). This solution is not unlike what we find in apocalyptic literature, especially in 4 Ezra, where Ezra's persistent questioning about the justice of God's dealing with Israel is overcome by a series of eschatological visions that shift the focus from past and present to future. But unlike the apocalyptic visionaries Sirach projects no eschatological scenario to silence the critics. The notion of the appointed time, however, is common to sapiential and apocalyptic writings (von Rad 1972: 263–83). So also is the notion of God's synoptic view of history as a unity (v. 20), but again Sirach differs from the apocalypses by not attempting to describe history from a revealed perspective. Sirach would probably agree with Eccl 3:11 that such comprehensive knowledge is not accessible to humanity, but he is content that God knows even if we do not.

Second, everything has been created for a purpose (v. 21). This idea reflects the influence of Stoic philosophy. So Chrysippus is said to have taught that bed-bugs are useful for waking us and that mice encourage us to be tidy (Plutarch, *On Stoic Self-Contradictions*, 1044D). Carneades (mid-2nd cent. BCE) taught that everything is benefited when it attains the end for which it was born. So the pig fulfils its purpose

when it is slaughtered and eaten (Porphyry, *On Abstinence*, 3.20.1, 3). The Stoics also conceded that the usefulness of some plants and animals remains to be discovered (Lactantius, *On the Anger of God*, 13.9–10; for the debates about teleology in antiquity see Long and Sedley 1987: 58–65; 121–2; 323–33). Sirach's elaboration of this notion, however, is somewhat confusing. All God's works are good (vv. 16, 33) but for sinners good things and bad were created (v. 25), or the same things are good for the righteous but bad for sinners (v. 27). In part, the confusion lies in the ambiguity of the term 'bad'. What is bad for sinners is really good. This ambiguity is also in evidence in the doctrine of pairs (33:14–15; 42:24–5). But there is also a reluctance on the part of Ben Sira to admit that bad things can happen to good people. The idea that nature discriminates between the righteous and the wicked is also found in Wis 19:6.

The language of this hymn has occasional biblical overtones. v. 17 alludes to the Exodus; v. 23 to the Conquest; vv. 29–30 to the curses of the covenant (Lev 26:14–22; Deut 28:20–4). Sirach's concern, however, is with the universal working of nature, not with the history of a particular people.

(40:1–41:13) Life in the Shadow of Death This cluster of short poems is framed by two reflections on death. Consistently in Sirach (except for 25:24!), death is viewed as the end for which humanity was created rather than as punishment for sin. Cf. 17:1–2. The language recalls Gen 3:19–20, but here the 'mother of all the living' is the earth, not Eve. The grim picture of life also accords with Genesis. Cf. Job 7:1–2; 14:1–2. The anxiety of disturbed sleep is also noted in Eccl 2:22–3; Job 7:4. The prevalence of anxiety is assumed in Mt 6:25–34; Lk 12:22–31. Sirach modifies the traditional theme, however, by claiming that afflictions befall the sinner 'seven times more' (40:8). The context suggests that the wicked also suffer more from anxiety (Crenshaw 1975: 57) but this is not explicitly stated. Sir 31:1–4 also suggests that anxiety is universal. Sirach is here reiterating the point of 39:28–31, that disasters serve the purpose of punishing the wicked. 40:12–17 expresses a confidence that lawbreakers will fail that seems naïve in the light of general human experience. Cf. the theology of the friends of Job (e.g. Job 8:11–15).

Sir 40:18–27 provides relief from contemplating the misery of life by listing ten things that are surpassingly good. There is a traditional proverbial form, which asserts that one thing is better than another (Ogden 1977: 489–505). Examples can be found in the Egyptian *Instructions of Kagemni* and *Amen-em-ope* as well as Proverbs and Ecclesiastes. Within Sirach cf. 10:27; 20:31; 41:15. The present passage modifies the form by listing two things that are good, and a third that is better. So a good wife is preferred to cattle and orchards (v. 19) and also to friends and companions (v. 23). In passing, Sirach shows appreciation for wine, music, and beauty (vv. 20–2). Characteristically, Sirach concludes with the superiority of the fear of the Lord. 40:28–30 contains a sharp critique of begging. The crucial point is the shame and loss of self-respect that it entails; cf. Sir 29:21–8. 41:1–4 is Sirach's most definitive statement on the finality of death, and leaves no room for resurrection or a blessed afterlife. Sirach's views on this subject are no different than those of Ecclesiastes, except that he holds them with resignation. The attractiveness of death in certain circumstances received classic expression in the Egyptian *Dispute of a Man with his Ba* about 2,000 BCE. Such sentiments are not common in the HB but cf. Sir 30:17 and the references cited at SIR ibid. Closer to the spirit of Sirach here is Epicurus (*Ep. Men.* 124–7; Long and Sedley 1987: 149): death is sometimes a release from the evils of life. Sirach adds that it is the common lot of humanity and it is the good pleasure of the Lord. The denial of judgement after death in this context is also reminiscent of Epicurus. There is no reason to fear death. Neither Sirach nor Epicurus inferred that one could live a life of licentiousness with impunity. Contrast Wis 2:1–20. The denunciation of the children of sinners (41:5–10) resembles Wis 3:13–19, but Sirach carries no implication that childlessness is virtuous in itself. Cf. Sir 23:25. This passage concludes with another consideration mitigating the fear of death. A good name can provide a measure of immortality; cf. Sir 37:26. The same hope is professed in the *Instruction of Phibis*, 20:1 (J. T. Sanders 1983: 84–5).

(41:14–42:8) On Shame Hebrew MS B gives this section the title 'Instruction about Shame'. Honour and shame were pivotal values in Greek society. Homer's epics are dominated by the warrior's search for honour. In the Hellenistic world people gained honour by their benefactions to their cities. Honour and shame were very much at issue in sexual relations. A male was shamed by the loss of chastity on the part of a woman under his control. The pursuit of honour was sometimes criticized by Hellenistic philosophers, especially Epicureans and Cynics. (For a concise summary of current scholarship on this issue see Moxnes 1993.) The categories of honour and shame are much more prominent in Sirach than in earlier books of the HB (Camp 1991: 4–6).

The subject of honour and shame has appeared several times in Ben Sira (3:1–16; 4:20–31; 10:19–25; 20:21–3). In general, he seeks to retain the category, but also to modify it in accordance with his religious criteria. There is no place for false modesty with respect to wisdom (41:14–15, repeated from 20:30–1; cf. Mk 4:21–5; Lk 8:16–19). The catalogue of things of which one should be ashamed gives considerable prominence to sexual offences, even when they only involve gazing (cf. 9:1–9). All forms of lawbreaking are disapproved, but shame also extends to bad manners at table and lack of graciousness (41:19). Not surprisingly, the Torah heads the list of things of which one should not be ashamed. But Sirach also recommends keeping accounts in dealings with a companion, strict discipline for children and slaves, and even locking up an unreliable wife. Sirach here inclines to the practical, hard-headed side of traditional wisdom that has little place for trust (cf. 6:7; 11:29–12:18). While Sirach diverges from Hellenistic mores in his insistence on the honour of the Torah, he retains a quite conventional code of patriarchal control.

(42:9–14) On Daughters Patriarchal control is very much in evidence in Sirach's treatise on daughters (cf. 7:24–5; 22:3–5; 26:10–12). In part, his worries have an economic base. The father has to provide a dowry for his daughter, and if she is divorced it is to his house that she returns. The greater concern for Sirach, however, is the threat of disgrace.

Indeed, Sirach's view of daughters is entirely clouded by the danger of incurring shame. Hence the extraordinary preference for the wickedness of a man over the goodness of a woman (42:14). Contrast the more affectionate picture of family life in Tobit. Despite the fact that Sarah's first seven husbands died on their wedding night, the concern of the parents is simply that God give her joy instead of sorrow (Tob 7:16).

The theme of anxiety in v. 9 must be seen in the context of Sirach's generally anxious view of life (40:1–11). The 'fear that she may be disliked' is really that she may be divorced. (The verb 'hate', *ś-n-ʾ*, clearly has the sense of 'repudiate' in the Elephantine papyri. Cf. Deut 24:3.) Concern for the virginity of unmarried girls is ubiquitous in the ancient world, but especially in Hellenistic Judaism. The draconian laws of the Pentateuch that required the death penalty for a woman who was found not to be a virgin at marriage (Deut 22:20–1; cf. Gen 38:24) were not enforced, but a woman who was not a virgin would be difficult to give in marriage. Ps. Phoc. 215–16 advises that virgins be locked up and not seen outside the house until their wedding day (see van der Horst 1978: 251; Archer 1990: 101–22 for other references to the confinement of Jewish virgins). A lattice (v. 11) offered an opportunity to look out on passers-by (cf. Prov 7:6) but Sirach's main concern is that the young woman not be seen. Most remarkable is the advice that a daughter should not associate with married women. (The Heb. 'in the house (*byt*) of the women' is probably a mistake for 'among' (*byn*), Smend 1906: 394.) From the context, it would seem that Sirach's fear is that the young woman may become aware of her sexuality (Trenchard 1982: 158).

(42:15–43:33) Hymn to the Creator This section of Sirach concludes with a long hymn to the creator. 42:15–20 praises the omniscience of God. 42:21–43:26 lists the works of creation. 43:27–33 concludes the hymn with a call to praise. The praises of nature in ch. 43 recalls Job 28, 38–41, but also Ps 104, 148, and the Song of the Three Jews in the Greek additions to Daniel. It has been argued that the Egyptian genre of onomasticon, which compiled lists of various phenomena as an aid to the scribes, lies behind such passages as Job 38 (von Rad 1966). A more immediate Egyptian parallel to Sirach is found in the 24th instruction in the wisdom book of *Phibis* (J. T. Sanders 1983: 78–9). Cf. also the praise of God as creator in the hymns of Qumran (e.g. 1QH 9:10–14, formerly 1QH 1).

The praise of God's omniscience in 42:15–20 is replete with biblical echoes. On v. 15*a*, cf. Ps 77:11; on v. 15*b*, cf. Job 15:17. On creation by the word, cf. Ps 33:6; Wis 9:1. The NRSV reading of v. 15*d* relies on the Syriac version. On God's knowledge of past and future, cf. Isa 41:22–3; 44:7. God's ability to reveal hidden things is also emphasized in Dan 2:22. The introduction to God's works in 42:22–5, however, introduces some non-biblical concepts. v. 23*a* expresses the teleological, Stoic, view that all things are created to meet a need (cf. 39:21 and SIR ibid.). v. 24 articulates the idea of complementary opposites, which also has its roots in Stoic philosophy (cf. SIR 33:14–15).

The praise of nature in ch. 43 envisages the sun as a charioteer racing his steeds (Heb. *ʾabbîrîm*, see Skehan and

DiLella 1987: 488). The horses and chariots of the sun were familiar in ancient Israel, but were destroyed in Josiah's reform (2 Kings 23:11). The image of the solar charioteer was standard in Greece, and this may have led to its rehabilitation here. The Greek translator (followed by NRSV) missed the reference. In 1 Enoch 72:5, the wind blows the chariots on which the sun ascends. Sir 49:7 is often taken to indicate that Sirach observed a lunar calendar, presumably the one that later became standard in rabbinic Judaism. Calendars were very much in dispute in Hellenistic Judea. A solar calendar of 364 days was advocated by the Astronomical Book of Enoch (1 Enoch, 73–82), Jubilees (esp. 6:32–8), and the Qumran sect. It is possible that Sirach is referring only to the observance of specific lunar festivals such as the new moon (cf. 1 Sam 20:5; Am 8:5). The Hebrew MS B reads 'by them is the appointed time ...' which implies that both sun and moon had a part in determining the festal calendar. The creator's control of the calendar is also noted by *Phibis* (J. T. Sanders 1983: 79). On the permanence of the astral world cf. 1 Enoch, 75:1, but 1 Enoch, 80, anticipates that the order will be disrupted in 'the days of the sinners'. The rainbow is praised for its beauty, but no reference is made to its role as a sign of the covenant of Noah (Gen 9:13–17). The description of lightning and thunder has overtones of the traditional language of theophany (cf. Ps 18:7–15). vv. 23–6 refer to God's mastery over the deep and its monsters (cf. Job 41:1–11). It is possible that the word *rabbâ*, great, in the Hebrew of vv. 23, 25, should be emended to Rahab, a traditional name for the sea-monster (Job 26:12; Isa 51:9).

The most remarkable statement in this hymn, however, comes in 43:27: 'He is the all.' This formulation evokes the pantheism of the Stoics, as we find, e.g. in Cleanthes, *Hymn to Zeus* (Hengel 1974: i. 148; Marböck 1971: 170). Ben Sira is no pantheist, however. His use of the phrase is hyperbolic, and should probably be understood as equivalent to 'God of all' (SIR 36:1). It is likely, however, that his formulation here has been influenced by Stoic notions, even if they were imperfectly grasped. The hymn concludes by emphasizing its own inadequacy.

(44:1–50:29) The Praise of the Fathers

(44:1–15) Introduction The last major section of the book bears the title 'Praise of the Fathers of Old' in the Hebrew and 'Hymn of the Fathers' in the Greek. The long review singles out individuals as examples to be praised, but presents no continuous historical narrative. There is no real parallel to this kind of review of history in the HB. The closest parallels are found in other books of the Apocrypha, 1 Macc 2:51–60; 4 Macc 16:20–3; 18:11–19. Cf. also Heb 11. There are ample Hellenistic precedents, however, for the listing of examples. The genre of the Praise of the Fathers has also been related to the Greek encomium (Lee 1986; Mack 1985: 136 implausibly designates it an epic).

vv. 1–15 are an introductory section. Sirach lists the kind of people he is about to praise. These reflect major categories of the Hebrew scriptures: kings and rulers, prophets and sages. Those who composed musical tunes (v. 5) may be the psalmists. In v. 6, the Hebrew 'stalwart men' is rendered somewhat tendentiously as 'wealthy men' in the Greek and NRSV. One category, the priesthood, that figures prominently in the subsequent chapters, is noticeably absent here. These people have acquired a qualified immortality in either of two ways, either by leaving behind a name or by the continuity and loyalty of their descendants. In the end, their honour is ratified by the congregation.

(44:16–23e) Enoch to Abraham The initial mention of Enoch is textually suspect. It is not found in the Masada MS or in the Syriac, although it is in the Greek and Hebrew MS B. Here he walks with the Lord, rather than with *'elōhîm*, God (or angels) as in Genesis. In the Hebrew he is a sign of knowledge, because of his knowledge of the heavenly world. The Greek makes him a symbol of repentance, probably under the influence of Philo, *Abr.* 17. Sirach shows no awareness of the story of Enoch as amplified in 1 Enoch. Noah was probably the first name on the list because he was the recipient of the first covenant. In some apocalyptic texts the deliverance of Noah serves as a paradigm for the end-time (1 Enoch, 93:4). Abraham's covenant is also emphasized. Abraham is said to have kept the law of the Most High, even though it was not yet revealed to Moses. This may indicate that Sirach associated the law with creation (cf. 17:11; 24:1–7), or it may reflect a tendency that we find in *Jubilees* to retroject the observance of the law back to the beginnings. v. 20d is a passing reference to the sacrifice of Isaac, seen purely as a test of Abraham. No mention is made of Jacob's trickery. Isaac and Jacob are significant as links in the transmission of the blessings.

(44:23f–45:26) Moses, Aaron, Phinehas Moses, predictably, is praised as the recipient of the Torah. In contrast to some Hellenistic Jewish writers, such as Philo, Sirach does not call Moses a lawgiver, and does not attribute any creativity to him. He makes him equal in glory to the angels (holy ones), whereas Philo, following Ex 7:1, makes him a god (*Vit. Mos.* 1.155–8). For 'the law of life and knowledge' cf. 17:11. For 45:5ef, cf. Ps 147:19. The most striking thing about the praise of Moses, however, is that it is less than half as long as the praise of Aaron.

Sirach does not acknowledge the priesthood of Moses (contrast Ps 99:6). Rather he follows the Priestly source in emphasizing the eternal covenant of priesthood with Aaron, but he ignores Zadok, and does not refer to the sons of Zadok (Olyan 1987: 261–86). We can scarcely infer, however, that he was polemicizing against the restriction of the priesthood to the Zadokites. He may have regarded them as the only legitimate Aaronides. The only individual who receives treatment of comparable length is the Zadokite high priest Simon II in ch. 50. The covenant with Aaron, however, extends to all the priesthood, not just the high priest. On the high priest's robe, cf. Wis 18:24, which claims that the whole world and the glories of the ancestors were engraved on it. Sirach touches only briefly on Aaron's role in offering sacrifices, and gives equal time to his teaching authority (cf. Deut 33:10; the teaching role of the eschatological priest is illustrated in 4Q541). Sirach's interest in sacrifices does not match his interest in the priesthood. In the Hellenistic period, the high priest also wielded political power in Jerusalem, and could be a powerful patron for a scribe such as Sirach. Sirach notes how rebellion against Aaron was put down by God. The implications for his own day were obvious. On 45:22, cf. Num 18:20.

Phinehas is third in the priestly line, after Aaron and Eleazar (v. 23). In 1 Macc 2:26, Phinehas is cited as the model for the violent action of Mattathias. Sirach's interest is in the covenant he receives. It is clear from v. 25 that this is not conceived as a separate covenant but is part of the heritage of Aaron. v. 25*d* should read 'so the heritage of Aaron is for all his descendants' (so Heb.; Gk. reads 'also for his descendants'). The contrast with the Davidic covenant (read: 'the inheritance of a man for his son alone', Skehan and DiLella 1987: 510) also implies the superiority of the more inclusive priestly covenant. It does not, however, imply that the priesthood has inherited the promise to David (*pace* Stadelmann 1980: 157). This section ends with a benediction addressed to the priesthood; cf. 50:22–4.

(46:1–20) Joshua to Samuel The extensive praise of Joshua is initially surprising, since there is little militancy in Sirach apart from the disputed prayer in ch. 36. Even more surprising is the statement that he was an aide (Heb.; Gk.: successor) to Moses in the *prophetic* office (neither Moses nor Joshua is said to have delivered oracles). Of primary importance to Sirach is the glory enjoyed by Joshua. In this respect he resembles the high priest Simon (cf. 46:2 with 50:5). He also resembles the priesthood in his role as intercessor (v. 5) although this role might also be deemed prophetic (Josh 10:6; cf. Moses in Num 14:13–19). The decisive role of the hailstones in the battle is already noted in Josh 10:11. Finally, Joshua and Caleb are praised for loyalty, a virtue already commended by Sirach (6:14–17; 26:19–26).

The prayer for the judges in 46:11–12, that their bones sprout from their place, is not found in the Hebrew, but appears apropos of the minor prophets in 49:10. The new life envisaged by Sirach is the immortality of their names in their children.

Samuel is characterized primarily as a prophet, by anointing rulers, judging in the light of the law, and being a trustworthy seer. He is also admired for offering sacrifice (without consideration of his priestly rank), and for his profession of innocence. His apparition to Saul (46:20; cf. 1 Sam 28:19) adds to his glory, with no hint of disapproval of the consultation. Rather it shows how the glory of Samuel transcended his death.

(47:1–25) Nathan to Jeroboam After a brief mention of Nathan, ch. 47 deals with the early kings. David is glorified for his early exploits, with some elaboration. Where 1 Sam 17:34–5 has David rescue animals from lions and bears, Sirach has him play with lions and bears as if they were lambs and kids. Cf. the idyllic scene in Isa 11:6–9, but contrast the more subdued portrayal of David's youth in Ps 151 (11Q5 xxviii); Sir 47:8 reflects David's reputation as author of the psalms. Cf. the list of David's compositions in 11QPsalms (11Q5 xxvii). vv. 9–10 reflect the portrayal of David in 1 Chr 15–26. The most controversial statement about David is found in 47:11, which says that God exalted his 'horn' or strength forever. Some scholars see here an expression of messianic hope (Smend 1906: 452; Skehan and DiLella 1987: 526; Olyan 1987: 282–3), while others disagree (Caquot 1966; Pomykala 1995: 145). Sirach does not cite Nathan's oracle, and expresses no hope or expectation for the restoration of the Davidic line. He does, however, acknowledge the biblical record that everlasting kingship was promised to David. While the word translated 'covenant' in 47:11c is *ḥōq* (statute) rather than the usual word for covenant (*bĕrît*), the latter word is used in 45:25, and so there can be no doubt that Sirach affirmed a Davidic covenant. The perpetuity of the line is also affirmed in 47:22. In short, Sirach acknowledged the promise, but it was far from the centre of his own devotion. He attached far greater importance to the high-priesthood, the actual seat of authority in his time. On the issue of messianic expectation, see further the psalm found between Sir 51:12 and 13 in the Hebrew text.

The Greek translation says that Solomon's security was because of David, but this connection is not made in the Hebrew. Solomon is praised as the one who built the temple and, inevitably, for his wisdom. For the image of overflowing like the Nile, cf. 24:27, 30. But Solomon also illustrates a favourite theme of Sirach, the danger of women. The Hebrew of 47:19b reads 'and you let them rule over your body'. Cf. Prov 31:3; Sir 9:2, and the fear that a woman can trample a man's strength. Sirach makes Solomon's sexual transgressions rather than idolatry responsible for the division of the kingship (cf. 1 Kings 11:11–13, 33). He none the less affirms the enduring validity of the promise to David. While Solomon's record is mixed, Rehoboam and Jeroboam are the only figures in the review who are entirely negative. Sirach follows the standard Deuteronomic line in making the sin of Jeroboam responsible for the exile of northern Israel.

(48:1–15d) Elijah and Elisha The treatment of Elijah dwells on the miraculous and therefore glorious aspects of his career. Cf. the passage on Joshua in ch. 46. His ascent in a chariot of fire (v. 9) fits this theme and is already found in 2 Kings 3:11. Sir 48:10, however, is exceptional in Ben Sira in citing a prophecy as eschatological prediction. The prophecy in question is Mal 3:23–4, supplemented by Isa 49:10. Because there is so little eschatological interest in Sirach, some scholars argue that this verse must be secondary (Middendorp 1973: 134; Mack 1985: 200). But Sirach here is only affirming what he found in the older scripture. There is no implication of imminent expectation. Like the promise to David, Elijah's return was part of the tradition, even if it had little importance for Sirach's overall scheme. The idea of an appointed time is reminiscent of Dan 10:14; 11:29, 40, etc., but is quite compatible with the wisdom tradition (von Rad 1972: 263–83).

Sir 48:11 is much more difficult. The Greek reads: 'Blessed are those who saw you and have fallen asleep in love, for we also shall certainly live.' The Hebrew (MS B) is fragmentary at this point. The first half of the verse reads 'Blessed is he who sees you and dies' (i.e. sees you before he dies). The second half has been restored, plausibly, to read 'for you give life, and he will live' (Puech 1990: 81–90). While granting that Sirach did not believe in a general resurrection, Puech thinks he anticipated a limited resurrection at the return of Elijah. The prophet is often associated with the eschatological resurrection in later tradition (*m. Soṭa,* 9:15; *Pesiqta de Rab Kahana,* 76a). In view of Sirach's emphatic insistence on the finality of death elsewhere, however, it is easier to suppose that this verse is a later addition (cf. Sir 14:11–19; 38:21–2; 41:4). If the

Hebrew text is original, it must have meant something less than eschatological resurrection.

The praise of Elisha is in a similar vein to that of Elijah. The reference in 48:13–14 is to 2 Kings 13:21. As in the case of Samuel, Sirach is interested in the continuing power of the prophet after death, but there is no implication of a lasting resurrection. This passage ends by attributing the fall of the northern kingdom to the lack of repentance.

(48:17–49:16) Kings and Prophets Sirach repeats the Deuteronomic judgement on the kings of Judah (49:4; cf. 2 Kings 18:3; 23:25), using observance of the Torah as his criterion. He emphasizes the miraculous in the accounts of Hezekiah and Isaiah (cf. 2 Kings 20:8–11; Isa 38:7–8). The Hebrew of 48:21 attributes the destruction of the Assyrians to a plague. The Greek substitutes the angel of the Lord, in conformity to the biblical text (2 Kings 19:35; Isa 37:36). It is clear from Sir 48:24–5 that Sirach attributed the whole book of Isaiah to the eighth-century prophet, who is credited with foretelling the future return from the Exile. Cf. the theme of consolation in Isa 40:1–2; for the revelation of hidden things cf. Isa 42:9. The notion that Isaiah had predicted what would happen 'forever' (48:25a) may reflect such passages as Isa 65:17–25, but without any note of imminent expectation.

Jeremiah is credited with foretelling the destruction. Ezekiel is remembered only for his vision, which was influential in apocalyptic circles (e.g. Dan 10) and was also elaborated in 4QPseudoEzekiel (4Q385). Job is mentioned between Ezekiel and the Minor Prophets. It is possible that Josephus also included Job among the prophets when he said that they wrote the history from Moses to Artaxerxes in thirteen books (*Ag. Ap.* 40). The order of the biblical books was not set in the time of Sirach. The Minor Prophets are treated as one book, and are understood to convey a message of hope rather than doom. There is no reference to Daniel, which was presumably not yet composed. There is no mention of Esther, which is also absent from the Qumran scrolls, and may not have been known in Jerusalem at this time. Sirach also ignores Ruth, and fails to single out a single woman for praise. Most striking, however, is the omission of Ezra, especially in view of the inclusion of Nehemiah. It would be rash to conclude that the book of Ezra was not yet written. There is no apparent ideological reason for the omission. The most plausible explanation offered to date is that Sirach preferred Nehemiah because his building activity offered a precedent to that of Simon II (Begg 1988). Cf. the emphasis on the building activities of Hezekiah, Zerubbabel, and Joshua the high priest.

49:14–16 concludes the review of the ancient past. Except for the questionable reference to Enoch in 44:16, none of those extolled here has been mentioned in Praise of the Fathers. Only Adam has figured in the rest of Sirach's book. All except Joseph are antediluvian. (Shem is son of Noah; Gen 6:10.) The authenticity of this passage has been questioned, as it does not fit any pattern of characterization in Sirach (Mack 1985: 201) but this is not necessarily a cogent objection to a concluding stanza. If the passage goes back to Sirach, it represents the earliest reference to the splendour of Adam. This motif was later elaborated (e.g. Philo, *Opif.* 136–41).

Another early reference to the glory of Adam is found in CD 3:20.

(50:1–28) The High Priest Simon Even though 49:14–16 seems to conclude the praise of the ancestors, the passage on Simon is the culmination of all that has gone before. Simon II was high priest 219–196 BCE. He was presumably dead when Ben Sira wrote (cf. 50:1). Under his leadership, Jerusalem welcomed Antiochus III of Syria, and assisted him in besieging the garrison of the Egyptian general Scopas (Jos. *Ant.* 12.129–53). Antiochus, in return, assisted in the restoration of the temple. Sirach does not mention the support of the foreign king, but he takes evident pride in the renewed splendour of the temple. Sirach had already noted building projects under Solomon, Hezekiah, Zerubbabel and Joshua, and Nehemiah. vv. 5–21 describe the splendour of the high priest performing his functions. The curtain in v. 5 *pārōket* normally refers to the veil at the entrance to the Holy of Holies (e.g. Ex 36:31–5; the Greek *katapetasma* can also refer to the outer curtain, between the temple and the forecourt). It is likely, then, that the occasion is the Day of Atonement, the only day the high priest entered the Holy of Holies (but see O'Fearghail (1978), who argues that the reference is to the daily offering). Cf. the account of Aaron's splendour in 45:6–13. A comparable account of the splendour of the high priest is found in the *Epistle of Aristeas*, 96–9. All the sons of Aaron share in the splendour. The recollection of the blessing pronounced by Simon (vv. 20–1) leads into the benediction in vv. 22–4. The Hebrew (MS B) reads 'God of Israel' instead of 'God of all'. It also includes in v. 23 a prayer for Simon, that God fulfil for him the covenant with Phinehas forever. In fact, the line came to an end in the next generation, in the reign of Antiochus IV. Simon's son Onias III was murdered in 172 BCE (2 Macc 4:34) and his son Onias IV fled to Egypt and founded a temple at Leontopolis. We cannot know whether Ben Sira had an inkling of impending problems when he prayed for the preservation of the line. The Greek translator dropped the prayer for Simon and substituted a prayer that God redeem Israel 'in our days'.

It is quite possible that the benediction in 50:22–4 was the conclusion of Sirach's book, except for the subscription in vv. 27–8. The numerical proverb in vv. 25–6 has no relation to the context, and could easily have been added by a scribe. The Edomites of Seir and the Philistines were old enemies of Israel. The thrust of the proverb is to express dislike for the Samaritans. There was conflict between Samaritans and Jews in the time of Ezra (Ezra 4). The books of Maccabees imply that the Samaritans were sympathetic to Antiochus Epiphanes in his suppression of Judaism (1 Macc 3:10; 2 Macc 4:2). At the end of the second century BCE, Shechem was sacked and the temple on Mt. Gerizim razed by John Hyrcanus. We have no evidence for Jewish–Samaritan relations in Sirach's time.

For Sirach's self-characterization as one who poured forth wisdom, cf. 24:30–4; 39:12.

(51:1–30) Appended poems Ch. 51 contains three poetic compositions, of which the middle one is found only in Hebrew MS B. It is generally admitted that this Hebrew psalm was not composed by Sirach, but many scholars defend the authenticity of the other two poems, despite the apparent finality of

50:27–8 (Smend 1906: 495; Skehan and DiLella 1987: 563). The Greek MSS have the heading 'Prayer of Jesus Son of Sirach', but the attribution is none the less doubtful. We know that prayers were added secondarily to other books (Esther, Daniel). The wisdom poem in vv. 13–30, which is closest to the style of Sirach, is found independently at Qumran.

Sir 51:1–12 is a thanksgiving psalm, analogous to Ps 30 or Jonah 2:2–9 (Gerstenberger 1988: 15–16) and to the thanksgiving hymns from Qumran (e.g. 1QH 10 (formerly 2)). The psalmist begins by declaring thanks, and goes on to give his reasons. The Hebrew speaks of deliverance from death, the pit, and Sheol (v. 2). Cf. Ps 30:3; Jon 2:2, 6; 1QH 11:19). The slanderous tongue is an object of frequent complaint in the Psalms (e.g. Ps 69:4–5, 11–12) and in the Qumran thanksgiving hymns (1QH 10:10–17; 13:22–5). The most noteworthy feature of this hymn is the direct address to God as father in v. 10, which echoes Ps 89:27. See SIR 23:1, and Strotmann (1991: 87). The Greek rendering 'lord, father of my lord' is confused. The Hebrew of Sir 51:1 refers either to 'God, my father', or more probably 'God of my father', but this reading is not supported by the Greek.

The Hebrew psalm inserted between vv. 12 and 13 is modelled on Ps 136 in so far as it has the refrain 'for his mercy endures forever'. Two features of the psalm are noteworthy. First, line 9 of the hymn must be understood as expressing hope for a Davidic messiah; cf. 1QSb 5:26. While Sir 47:11 affirmed the covenant with David, it showed no such messianic hope. Second, line 10 affirms the priesthood of the sons of Zadok. Since messianic expectation was conspicuously lacking even in the Maccabean period, it is unlikely that this combination of Davidic hope and Zadokite priesthood dates from pre-Hasmonean times. It is more likely that this psalm originated in the Qumran community, which was staunchly pro-Zadokite and had lively messianic expectations. DiLella suggests that the Hebrew MS B from the Cairo Geniza was one of the documents found by the Qaraites in a cave near Jericho about 800 CE, and had originated at Qumran (Skehan and DiLella 1987: 569).

The wisdom poem in vv. 13–28 is also found in 11QPsᵃ, between Ps 138 and the *Apostrophe to Zion*. (Only vv. 11–17 and the last two words of the poem are preserved.) Like Prov 31:10–31, it is in the form of an acrostic. vv. 13–22 use the language of love to describe the sage's pursuit of wisdom. Cf. Sir 14:20–7. J. A. Sanders, editor of 11QPss (1965: 79–85), has argued for a highly erotic interpretation of the poem, but even those critical of Sanders' interpretation recognize that love imagery is intrinsic to the poem (Muraoka 1979: 167–78). The second half of the poem is an exhortation to the student to submit to the yoke of wisdom; cf. Sir 6:23–37. The themes and language of the poem all have close affinities with other material in Sirach, but it is not certain whether this reflects common authorship or a common tradition of wisdom poetry (cf. in part 4Q525).

We have three recensions of this poem, in the Qumran text, the Geniza text, and the Greek translation. The reference to travel in v. 13 is reflected in the Qumran text ('before I wandered'; Skehan and DiLella take it as 'while I was innocent'); cf. Sir 34:9–13; 39:4. v. 14 of the 11Q text reads 'she came to me in her beauty'. The Greek, and NRSV, eliminated the erotic overtones of this verse. This is also true of v. 19 where both Hebrew texts have readings that indicate desire, but the Greek has 'grappled'. Hebrew v. 19e, 'my hand opened her gate' may be an allusion to Song 5:4, and v. 21, which even in Greek reads 'insides' rather than 'heart' (NRSV), recalls the same verse ('my inmost being yearned for him'). The teacher in v. 17 is God.

The 'house of instruction' (v. 23) is usually taken to refer to an actual school, but the expression could be metaphorical (Wischmeyer 1995: 176; cf. Prov 9:1). There can be no doubt, however, that wisdom is construed as a medium of education, whatever the institutional setting. The Hebrew (MS B) has a reference to 'my yeshivah' in v. 29 (see Smend 1906: 494), which the Greek converts into a reference to God's mercy. For vv. 24–5 cf. Isa 55:1. For the image of the yoke, cf. Sir 6:30; Mt 11:28–30, and *m. 'Abot*, 3:5. The idea that God will give one's reward in due time is not eschatological in the context of Sirach, who consistently affirms this-worldly retribution. The Hebrew MS B has a second subscription at the end of ch. 51. In both cases, the sage's name is given incorrectly as Simon, son of Jesus, son of Eleazar, son of Sira. Simon is presumably introduced by mistake from ch. 50.

REFERENCES

Archer, L. J. (1990), *Her Price is Beyond Rubies: The Jewish Woman in Graeco-Roman Palestine* (Sheffield: JSOT).

Baillet, M., Milik, J. T., and de Vaux, R. (1962), *Les 'Petites Grottes' de Qumrân*, DJD 3 (Oxford: Clarendon).

Balch, D. L. (1988), 'Household Codes', in D. E. Aune, *Greco-Roman Literature and the New Testament* (Atlanta: Scholars Press), 25–50.

Beentjes, P. (1997), *The Book of Ben Sira in Hebrew* (Leiden: Brill).

Begg, C. (1988), 'Ben Sirach's Non-mention of Ezra', *BN* 42: 14–18.

Bohlen, R. (1991), *Die Ehrung der Eltern bei Ben Sira* (Trier: Paulinus).

Box, G. H., and Oesterley, W. O. E. (1913), 'Sirach', in R. H. Charles (ed.), *The Apocrypha and Pseudepigrapha of the Old Testament* (Oxford: Clarendon), i. 268–517.

Camp, C. V. (1991), 'Understanding Patriarchy: Women in Second Century Jerusalem through the Eyes of Ben Sira'. in A.-J. Levine (ed.), *Women Like Us: New Perspectives on Women in the Greco-Roman World* (Atlanta: Scholars Press), 1–39.

Caquot, A. (1966), 'Ben Sira et le Messianisme', *Semitica*, 16: 43–68.

Collins, J. J. (1995), 'The Origin of Evil in Apocalyptic Literature and the Dead Sea Scrolls', in J. A. Emerton (ed.), *Congress Volume, Paris* (Leiden: Brill).

—— (1997a), 'Marriage, Divorce and Family in Second Temple Judaism'. in L. Perdue, J. Blenkinsopp, J. J. Collins, and C. Meyers *Families in Ancient Israel* (Louisville, Ky.: Westminster/John Knox), 104–62.

—— (1997b), *Jewish Wisdom in the Hellenistic Age* (Louisville, Ky.: Westminster/John Knox).

Conzelmann, H. (1971), 'The Mother of Wisdom', in J. Robinson (ed.), *The Future of Our Religious Past* (New York: Harper & Row), 230–43.

Corley, K. (1993), *Private Women: Public Meals* (Peabody, Mass.: Hendrickson).

Crenshaw, J. L. (1975), 'The Problem of Theodicy in Sirach: On Human Bondage', *JBL* 94: 47–64.

DiLella, A. A. (1966), *The Hebrew Text of Sirach: A Text-Critical and Historical Study* (The Hague: Mouton).

Elgvin, T. (1994), 'Admonition Texts from Qumran Cave 4', in M. O. Wise *et al.* (eds.), *Methods of Investigation of the Qumran Scrolls and the Khirbet Qumran Site* (New York: New York Academy of Sciences), 179–94.

García Martínez, F. (1994), *The Dead Sea Scrolls Translated* (Leiden: Brill).

Gerstenberger, E. S. (1988), *Psalms with an Introduction to Cultic Poetry*, Forms of Old Testament Literature, 14 (Grand Rapids: Eerdmans).

Gilbert, M. (1984), 'Wisdom Literature', in M. E. Stone (ed.), *Jewish Writings of the Second Temple Period* (Philadelphia: Fortress), 283–324.

Harrington, D. J. (1994), 'Wisdom at Qumran', in E. Ulrich and J. C. VanderKam (eds.), *The Community of the Renewed Covenant* (Notre Dame, Ind.: University of Notre Dame), 137–52.

Haspecker, J. (1967), *Gottesfurcht bei Jesus Sirach* (Rome: Pontifical Biblical Institute).

Hengel, M. (1974), *Judaism and Hellenism* (2 vols.; Philadelphia: Fortress).

Horst, P. van der (1978), *The Sentences of Pseudo-Phocylides* (Leiden: Brill).

—— (1991), *Ancient Jewish Epitaphs* (Kampen: KokPharos).

Jeremias, J. (1967), *The Prayers of Jesus* (Philadelphia: Fortress).

Kieweler, H.V. (1992), *Ben Sira zwischen Judentum und Hellenismus* (Frankfurt am Main: Lang).

Koch, K. (1955) 'Gibt es ein Vergeltungsdogma im Alten Testament?', *ZTK* 52: 1–42. ET: 'Is There a Doctrine of Retribution in the Old Testament?', in J. L. Crenshaw (ed.), *Theodicy in the Old Testament* (Philadelphia: Fortress, 1983), 57–87.

Lefkowitz, M. R., and Fant, M. B. (1982), *Women's Life in Greece and Rome* (Baltimore: Johns Hopkins University Press).

Lee, T. R. (1986), *Studies in the Form of Sirach 44–50* (Atlanta: Scholars Press).

Leiman, S. Z. (1976), *The Canonization of Hebrew Scripture* (Hamden, Conn.: Archon).

Levison, J. (1985), 'Is Eve to Blame? A Contextual Analysis of Sirach 25:24', *CBQ* 47: 617–23.

Lewis, N. (1989), *The Documents from the Bar-Kokhba Period in the Cave of the Letters* (Jerusalem: Israel Exploration Society).

Long, A. A., and Sedley, D. N. (1987), *The Hellenistic Philosophers* (2 vols; Cambridge: Cambridge University Press).

Mack, B. L. (1973), *Logos und Sophia* (Göttingen: Vandenhoeck & Ruprecht).

—— (1985), *Wisdom and the Hebrew Epic* (Chicago: University of Chicago Press).

Marböck, J. (1971), *Weisheit im Wandel* (Bonn: Hanstein).

Meyers, C. (1988), *Discovering Eve* (New York: Oxford University Press).

Middendorp, Th. (1973), *Die Stellung Jesu Ben Siras zwischen Judentum und Hellenismus* (Leiden: Brill).

Moxnes, H. (1993), 'Honor and Shame', *BTB* 23: 167–76.

Muraoka, T. (1979), 'Sir 51:13–30: An Erotic Hymn to Wisdom?', *JSJ* 10: 166–78.

Ogden, G. S. (1977), 'The "Better"-Proverb (Tôb-Spruch), Rhetorical Criticism, and Qoheleth', *JBL* 96: 489–505.

O'Fearghail, F. (1978), 'Sir 50, 5–21: Yom Kippur or The Daily Whole Offering?', *Bib* 59: 301–16.

Olyan, S. M. (1987), 'Ben Sira's Relationship to the Priesthood', *HTR* 80: 261–86.

Pautrel, R. (1963), 'Ben Sira et le stoicisme', *RSR* 51: 535–49.

Perdue, L. G. (1977), *Wisdom and Cult* (Missoula, Mont.: Scholars Press).

Peters, N. (1913), *Das Buch Jesus Sirach oder Ecclesiasticus* (Münster: Aschendorff).

Pomykala, K. E. (1995), *The Davidic Dynasty Tradition in Early Judaism. Its History and Significance for Messianism* (Atlanta: Scholars Press).

Puech, E. (1990), 'Ben Sira 8:11 et la Résurrection', in H. W. Attridge et al. (eds.), *Of Scribes and Scrolls: Studies on the Hebrew Bible, Intertestamental Judaism and Christian Origins* (Lanham, Md.: University Press of America), 81–90.

Rad, G. von (1964), 'Life and Death in the OT', *TDNT* ii. 843–9.

—— (1966), 'Job XXXVIII and Ancient Egyptian Wisdom', in idem, *The Problem of the Hexateuch and Other Essays* (New York: McGraw-Hill), 281–91.

—— (1972), *Wisdom in Israel* (Nashville: Abingdon).

Rickenbacher, O. (1973), *Weisheitsperikopen bei Ben Sira* (Göttingen: Vandenhoeck & Ruprecht).

Roth, W. M. (1965), *Numerical Sayings in the Old Testament* (Leiden: Brill).

—— (1980), 'The Gnomic-Discursive Wisdom of Jesus Ben Sirach', *Semeia*, 17: 35–79.

Sanders, J. A. (1965), *The Psalms Scroll of Qumran Cave 11 (11Qps^a)*, *DJD 4 (Oxford: Clarendon)*.

Sanders, J. T. (1983), *Ben Sira and Demotic Wisdom* (Chico, Calif.: Scholars Press).

Schechter, S. (1890–1), 'The Quotations from Ecclesiasticus in Rabbinic Literature', *JQR* 3: 682–706.

Schechter, S., and Taylor, C. (1899), *The Wisdom of Ben Sira: Portions of the Book Ecclesiasticus from Hebrew Manuscripts in the Cairo Genizah Collection Presented to the University of Cambridge by the Editors* (Cambridge: Cambridge University Press).

Schnabel, E. J. (1985), *Law and Wisdom from Ben Sira to Paul* (Tübingen: Mohr).

Schuller, E. M. (1990), '4Q372 1: A Text about Joseph', *RevQ* 14: 349–76.

Segal, M. H. (1972), *Sēper ben Sîrā haššalēm*, 2nd edn. (Jerusalem: Bialik).

Sheppard, G. T. (1980), *Wisdom as a Hermeneutical Construct* (Berlin: de Gruyter).

Skehan, P. W. (1971), 'The Acrostic Poem in Sirach 51:13–30', *HTR* 64: 387–400.

Skehan, P. W., and DiLella, A. A. (1987), *The Wisdom of Ben Sira*, AB 39 (New York: Doubleday).

Smend, R. (1906), *Die Weisheit des Jesus Sirach erklärt* (Berlin: Reimer).

Smith, D. E., and Taussig, H. (1990), *Many Tables: The Eucharist in the New Testament and Liturgy Today* (Philadelphia: Trinity).

Snaith, J. G. (1974), *Ecclesiasticus or The Wisdom of Jesus Son of Sirach* (Cambridge: Cambridge University Press).

Stadelmann, H. (1980), *Ben Sira als Schriftgelehrter* (Tübingen: Mohr).

Strotmann, A. (1991), *'Mein Vater Bist Du!' (Sir 51,10)* (Frankfurt am Main: Knecht).

Tcherikover, V. (1970), *Hellenistic Civilization and the Jews* (New York: Atheneum).

Trenchard, W. C. (1982), *Ben Sira's View of Women: A Literary Analysis* (Chico, Calif.: Scholars Press).

Urbach, E. E. (1975), *The Sages: Their Concepts and Beliefs* (2 vols.; Jerusalem: Magnes).

Wischmeyer, O. (1995), *Die Kultur des Buches Jesu Sirachs* (Berlin: de Gruyter).

Yadin, Y. (1965), *The Ben Sira Scroll from Masada* (Jerusalem: Israel Exploration Society).

Ziegler, J. (1965), *Sapientia Jesu Filii Sirach* (Göttingen: Vandenhoeck & Ruprecht).

45. Baruch

ALISON SALVESEN

INTRODUCTION

A. Title. 1. The book is known in Greek tradition as Baruch or the Epistle of Baruch. The name means 'blessed' in Hebrew, and is a shortened form of Berechyahu, 'the Lord blesses'. According to the book of Jeremiah, Baruch was Jeremiah's secretary. He recorded the Lord's words at Jeremiah's dictation, read them out to the people in the temple, was taken to Tahpanes in Egypt along with Jeremiah, and was given a promise from the Lord that his life would be spared wherever he went (Jer 32:12–16; 36:4–32; 43:3–6; 45:1–5). Baruch himself was a historical figure, and a clay seal impression of the late seventh century bears his name, patronymic, and profession: 'Berechyahu, son of Neryahu, the scribe' (Avigad 1986: 28–9).

2. However, there are a number of circumstances that make it very unlikely that this Baruch was the author of the book of Baruch. Given that Baruch was a close associate of Jeremiah and may even have been responsible for parts of the Jeremiah tradition, it is odd that the first part of Baruch does not tie in more closely with statements in Jeremiah: e.g. Baruch's presence in Babylon in Bar 1:1, the return of the temple vessels in Bar 1:9, and the imprecise dating in Bar 1:2. Baruch is a compilation of three very different parts, only the first of which explicitly has to do with the figure of Baruch. There are many similarities of thought and expression between Baruch and works known to date from the Hellenistic period such as Daniel (c.164 BCE), Sirach (mid-2nd cent. BCE) and the *Psalms of Solomon* (probably mid-1st cent. BCE). While it is conceivable that these depend on Baruch, the nature of the book is fundamentally derivative, a 'mosaic of Biblical passages' (Tov 1976: 111). Baruch is more likely to be dependent on them or to have originated in a common milieu. Finally, Baruch was not accepted as canonical by the rabbis, and was never cited by them, as if the the book's pedigree were suspect at an early stage.

3. So why was the name Baruch attached to the book? Baruch as a whole is concerned with problems of faith during the Diaspora, and the outlook of the first part is strongly influenced by the book of Jeremiah. As recorder of the prophet's words, Baruch was no doubt accorded quasi-prophetic status by Jews in the Second Temple period and, later, by Christians. Thus a book bearing his name would have enjoyed a certain prestige. One can compare the high position accorded to Ezra as a scribe of the law in the Second Temple period and the pseudepigraphical works consequently ascribed to him.

B. Text and Language. 1. No fragments of Baruch in any language were found at Qumran, nor does the NT cite it. The earliest preserved text of the book is in Greek: it exists in the Septuagint MSS Alexandrinus and Vaticanus: it may have been part of the missing portion of Sinaiticus. The Latin, Syriac, Coptic, Armenian, Arabic, Bohairic, and Ethiopic versions of Baruch are all translated from the Greek. As for the original language of the book, Origen knew of no Hebrew text of Baruch in the mid-third century CE. Although at Bar 1:17 and 2:3 the Syriac translation of Origen's *Hexapla* notes in the margin that a certain phrase is not found 'in the Hebrew', this must refer back to the biblical sources Baruch is quoting, not to a Hebrew version of Baruch itself. However, there are occasional phrases that must arise from a mistranslation of a Semitic original. For instance, at 3:4 the strange expression in the Greek text, 'hear then the prayer of the *dead* of Israel' must arise from a misreading of the Hebrew *mĕtê yiśrā'ēl* '(people of Israel) as *mētê yiśrā'ēl*' (dead of Israel) (vowels were not represented in ancient Heb. script). Such mistranslations occur mainly in the first part of the book (1:1–3:8). The second and third parts are more generally thought to have been written in Greek (but see Burke 1982).

2. 2 Baruch (Syriac) and 3 Baruch (Greek) are later compositions, also pseudonymous.

C. Subject-Matter and Literary Genre. 1. Baruch is composed of three principal parts, one in prose (1:1–3:8) and two poetic (3:9–4:4, 4:5–5:9), reflecting the separate documents that were combined by a later editor. The first part describes Baruch's reading of a book to the exiles in Babylon, to which they respond by sending money, the looted temple vessels, and a communal confession and prayer to Jerusalem. The second part, which is not obviously connected with the first, is a eulogy of Wisdom and has affinities with sapiential literature in both Hebrew and Greek. The third part consists of Zion's consolation of the exiles and an exhortation to Jerusalem in the manner of Isa 40–66, and to some extent at least answers the concerns of the first part.

2. Thackeray (1923) suggested that Baruch was a compilation that served a liturgical function in a diaspora Jewish community, and he linked it to the seven sabbaths around the ninth of Ab, the fast on which the destruction of the temple was commemorated. While few scholars have accepted his theory, it does at least attempt to explain the association of three such disparate documents. In addition, the first part explicitly provides a communal confession to be read in the temple on behalf of diaspora Jewry, a reversal of the situation in 2 Macc 2:16, where the Judean Jews instruct the Jews of Alexandria to keep the Feast of Dedication.

D. The Religious Teaching. The theology of the book varies according to the section. The first part is strongly influenced by Deuteronomistic thinking, that the Diaspora is caused by Israel's sin and is something to be borne until God brings it to an end. The second part identifies Torah with Wisdom. The third part is close to the mood of Deutero-Isaiah. Interestingly, there are no references to messianism, angelology, or the resurrection, which are themes of some other Jewish literature of the period and might have seemed appropriate in this text also.

E. Date and Place of Composition. 1. The question of the date of Baruch is unusually difficult, partly because it is a compilation of three quite different compositions. However, a time in the second century BCE seems likely for the earliest material, the latest possible date for the work in its present state being within a few years of the destruction of the Second Temple in 70 CE.

2. Tov (1976: 165) argues convincingly that the distinctive revision of the Septuagint of Jer 29–52 also covered Bar 1:1–3:8. Since Sirach's grandson knows the Prophets in Greek in 116 BCE (Sir, Prologue) and quotes from the revised Greek Jeremiah, the first part of Baruch in Greek must have been in existence by that date. The Hebrew original would of course be older.

3. Baruch's assumption that it was still possible to make offerings at the temple in Jerusalem (Bar 1:8–10) may also point to a period before 70 CE, though we cannot be certain to what degree the story reflects the actual historical circumstances of the writer. Another feature which may be consistent with a pre-70 date is the generally positive attitude of the first part towards foreign rulers, especially Nebuchadnezzar, who in rabbinic literature became the archetypal enemy of the Jewish people and was also regarded as the forerunner of the Emperor Vespasian in his destruction of Jerusalem.

4. The book is not attested until the time of the Church Fathers, being cited first by Irenaeus (*Adv. haer.* 5. 35), then Athenagoras (*Apologia*, 69), in the 170s CE.

5. The provenance of the book is as uncertain as its date (Tov 1976: 160). The first part is written very much from the perspective of the diaspora Jews looking towards Jerusalem, but it is possible that this is a deliberate fiction on the part of the writer in order to encourage exiled Jews to regard Jerusalem as their cultic centre. Certainly, if the original language of Baruch was Hebrew, Judea is the most obvious place of composition.

F. Canonicity. 1. If there was a Hebrew original of Baruch, there is no evidence that it ever formed part of the Hebrew canon of the Jews. The Greek and Latin versions of Baruch, along with the Letter of Jeremiah, were generally regarded as part of the book of Jeremiah, and were thus treated as canonical in the early Christian church. The attribution to Baruch, who plays an important role in Jeremiah, also contributed to the book's acceptance in the Christian community. Only Jerome rejected Baruch, since it was not included in the Jewish canon.

2. Today, Baruch is regarded as canonical by the Roman Catholic and Eastern Orthodox churches, as part of the Apocrypha by Protestants, and is disregarded by Jews.

G. Outline.
Narrative Introduction (1:1–14)
Confession and Prayer (1:15–3:8)
Eulogy of Wisdom (3:9–4:4)
Address to Israel (4:5–9a)
Zion's consolation of her children in the Diaspora (4:9b–29),
    and a corresponding exhortation of Jerusalem (4:30–5:9).
    There is no formal conclusion to the book.

COMMENTARY

Narrative Introduction (1:1–14)

The structure and mood of this introduction are strongly influenced by Jer 29:1–2 and Jer 36. There are many historical problems surrounding the events and circumstances as described here.

(1:1) 'these are the words of the book': there are four main theories as to what is meant. (1) It is generally thought that the book of Baruch itself is meant, and that Baruch is envisaged as reading aloud either the whole composition or the first part (1:15b–3:8). However, this would give the response of the hearers to the book (1:5) before the reader knows its contents, which are revealed when the exiles send back the scroll in 1:10 for recitation in the temple. Such a device is far from impossible, and is upheld by Steck (1993: 5–60), who sees 1.1–15a as the introduction which attributes the book as a whole to Baruch. (2) Whitehouse (1913) considered that 1:1, 3 prefaced 3:9–4:4, while 1:2, 3b–3:8 and 3:9–5:9 formed separate documents. (3) Another solution would be to suppose that the order of the biblical books was Jeremiah–Lamentations–Baruch. Thus, 'these are the words' would refer to the book of Lamentations, a response to the fall of Jerusalem written by Baruch in Babylon to be repeated in front of the Jews there. The order Jeremiah–Lamentations–Baruch is not generally found in the Septuagint MSS, though it may have existed in the original form of Codex Sinaiticus (now truncated), and Epiphanius is the only commentator on the canon of Scripture to list the books in this order. But it would explain the response of the exiles and their dispatching of a prayer to be said on their behalf by their fellow Jews in Jerusalem. We would then have a lament sent from Jerusalem to Babylon (Lamentations), and its counterpart of a confession and petition sent back to Jerusalem from Babylon (Bar 1:15b–3:8):

The structure of the book according to this hypothesis would be:
(a. Lamentations sent from Jerusalem to Babylon)
b. Response of exiles: prayer and confession sent from Babylon to Jerusalem (Bar 1:1–3:8)
c. Hymn to Wisdom (3:9–4:4)
a'. Zion's exhortation of the exiles (4:5–29)
b'. Consolation of Jerusalem (4:30–5:5).

(4) An alternative explanation of the opening words is that they may somehow refer to the book of Jeremiah (the normal order in LXX MSS is Jeremiah–Baruch–Lamentations), or to Jeremiah's letter sent to the exiles after Jeconiah's deportation, as described in Jer 29:1–28 (LXX 36:1–28). Jer 29 does not mention Baruch as either the scribe or the messenger of the letter, but it does begin in Greek in exactly the same way as Baruch: 'these are the words' (LXX 36:1). It also counsels the exiles to settle down in Babylon and pray for its welfare. This is exactly the response we find in Bar 1:11–12. On this interpretation, the structure of the whole book would not be very different from that described above, in (3).

'Book' is the Greek *biblion*, here and in 1:3a, 10. The same word is used for the scroll dictated by Jeremiah to Baruch in Jer 36:8, 10, 11, 18 (LXX ch. 43). A slightly different word, *biblos*, is used in Bar 1:3b for what Baruch recites, and in Jer 29:1 for Jeremiah's letter to the exiles (LXX 36:1). The difference is not significant: Jer 29:29 (LXX 36:29) uses *biblion* for a letter. 'Baruch son of Neriah son of Mahseiah son of Zedekiah son of Hasadiah son of Hilkiah': the patronymic 'son of Neriah son of Mahseiah' is found in Jer 32:12, but the other names are unattested as ancestors of Baruch.

'Babylon' refers to the region, and not just the city. According to Jeremiah, Baruch was taken only to Egypt (43:7), but both the book of Baruch and rabbinic tradition say that Baruch went to Babylon. In fact, the Babylonian Talmud improbably states that Baruch taught Ezra there (*b. Meg* 16b)! It is possible that a combination of the Lord's promise to spare his life wherever he went (Jer 45:5), Jeremiah's letter to the Babylonian exiles in Jer 29, and the presence of Seraiah, Baruch's brother, in Babylon (Jer 51:59–64) suggest that Baruch journeyed there. Bar 1:8 may imply that Baruch returned to Jerusalem.

The Syriac version of Baruch says that Baruch *sent* the book to Babylon, but this may be a later change in order to avoid the problem of an unattested journey to Babylon. On the other hand, it may represent an attempt to harmonize Bar 1:1 with 2 *Apoc. Bar.* 77:19, where Baruch is said to send two letters to Babylon.

(1:2–9) 'In the fifth year, on the seventh day of the month', the chronology of v. 2 is unclear, particularly as the month is not specified. The original reading was perhaps 'the fifth year, on the seventh day of the *fifth* month', the second 'fifth' having dropped out in the copying process. The fifth month was Ab (August), and the date is that of the burning of Jerusalem by Nebuzaradan, according to 2 Kings 25:8–9. So Baruch is depicted as writing the book as Jerusalem is being destroyed (586 BCE). But then there remains the problem of which 'fifth year' is meant. It may be an echo of Jer 36:9, where Baruch reads out Jeremiah's words before the people in the temple. Or it may refer to the fifth year after the capture of Jerusalem, which would be 581 BCE. The 'Chaldeans' are the Babylonians. v. 3, for similar public readings, see 2 Kings 23:1–2 (= 2 Chr 34:30), and Neh 8:1–8.

'Jeconiah son of Jehoiakim' (v. 3) is also known as Jehoiachin and Coniah (see 2 Kings 24:8–17, 25:27–30; Jer 22:24–30). According to Jer 52:31, he was in prison for 37 years, rather than dwelling among the other exiles. He is certainly not mentioned in Ezek 8:1.

v. 4, 'the princes', the Greek 'sons of the king'. Jer 22:30 says that Jeconiah will be childless, but 1 Chr 3:17 and Babylonian cuneiform inscriptions (*ANET* 308) say that he had sons. 'The river Sud': there is a reference in the Dead Sea scrolls (4QpJer) to a river Sur in the context of the Exile. The Hebrew letters *r* and *d* are very similar in form, and the Greek translator may have misread Sud for Sur. v. 5, 'they wept and fasted': For a similar response, see Neh 8:9; 9:1, similarly followed by a prayer of national confession (Neh 9:6–37). v. 6, '*the high priest Jehoiakim son of Hilkiah son of Shallum*' is constructed from several biblical genealogies: J(eh)oiakim is a priest in Jerusalem much later, in the days of Ezra and Nehemiah (Neh 12:10, 12, 26, cf. Jos. *Ant.* 11.5.1); the high priest Hilkiah discovered the book of the law in the temple (2 Kings 22:8), and Hilkiah son of Shallum is a progenitor of Ezra in Ezra 7:1. According to 2 Kings 25:18–21, the high priest at the time of the Exile was Seraiah, who was taken to Babylon and executed. It is possible that Jehoiakim is to be understood as a deputy who remained in Jerusalem.

v. 8, Sivan is the third month, corresponding to May–June, evidently in the year following Baruch's reading of the book: 'the vessels of the house of the Lord . . . the silver vessels that Zedekiah son of Josiah . . . had made': according to 2 Kings 24:13 and 25:14–15 all the temple vessels were removed by the Babylonians (in 597 and 586 BCE), and they were not brought back until the end of the Exile (Ezra 1:7–8): Jer 27:22 certainly does not envisage an early return. Zedekiah is not known to have made anything for the temple, so perhaps this is an invention on the part of the writer of Baruch, to explain how an offering could be made in Jerusalem while the vessels were still in Babylon. The 'Lord': throughout the first part of Baruch, the Deity is referred to as 'the Lord' (*kurios*) in contrast to the second and third parts of Baruch, where 'Lord' never appears. The second part uses *theos* (God), and the third part *ho aiōnios* (the Eternal). 1.9, some MSS and versions add 'and the craftsmen' after 'the prisoners'. The Hebrew word for 'prison' is identical to that for 'smith', *masgēr*. The same double translation is found in LXX Jer 24:1 and 36:2 (Eng. versions 29:2).

(1:10–14) v. 10, 'grain-offerings' is Greek *manna*, an error for *manaa*, the transliteration of Hebrew *minḥâ* (offering), a further indication of a Semitic original for the first part of Baruch. '[O]ffer them on the altar': in spite of the burning of the temple, it seems from Jer 41:5 and Lam 1:4 that the temple cult continued in some form. The instruction to 'pray for the life of King Nebuchadnezzar' is an unusual sentiment, particularly in later Judaism where Nebuchadnezzar was regarded as the archetype of the evil ruler, and forerunner of Vespasian and Titus who destroyed the second temple. But cf. Jer 29:7, where Jeremiah tells the Jews taken to Babylon in the first captivity to pray for the land in which they are exiles; cf. also 1 Tim 2:1–3. In fact Belshazzar is not Nebuchadnezzar's son, as Baruch supposes, but the son of Nabonidus (555–538 BCE) whom Cyrus overthrew. The same error occurs in Dan 5:2, 11, 13, 18, 22, which has led some to date Baruch after Daniel (167–164 BCE). However, the error may be due to dependence on a common source and have no bearing on the dating. Some scholars identify Baruch's Nebuchadnezzar and Belshazzar with Antiochus IV (*c.*175–164 BCE) and his son Antiochus V Eupator (164–162 BCE) after the desecration and rededication of the Temple, or with Vespasian and Titus in the years just prior to or immediately after the destruction of the Second Temple (70 CE), and date Baruch accordingly. There is no convincing evidence for either identification.

v. 14, 'and you shall read aloud' is cited by some in support of a liturgical origin for Baruch. Cf. 2 Macc 1:1–2:18. In 'to make your confession', 'your' is not in the Greek text, which has merely 'to make confession'. The 'days of the festivals': the oldest Greek MS has 'day of festival'. It is not at all clear which, if any, specific festival the writer had in mind. Some have suggested the eight-day Feast of Tabernacles, held in the early autumn (Lev 23:33–6), while Thackeray (1923: 93) prefers a period in the summer, leading up to the ninth of Ab, when the burning of the temple was commemorated.

Confession and Prayer (1:15–3:8)

This section is a pastiche of biblical citations. The main parallels are with Dan 9:4–19 and there are many references to Jeremiah. Tov (1975) gives a full list. From 1:13–15a, it seems that the Jews in Judah and Jerusalem are to pray the following words on behalf of those in the Diaspora. Nickelsburg (1984) suggests that the Jerusalem Jews make their own confession in 1:15b–2:5, and then pray on behalf of the Jews in the Diaspora in 2:6–10, but there is no real sign of a change in speaker, and it is easier to assume that 1:15b–3:8 is all part of the prayer sent by the exiles to be recited by the Jews of Jerusalem for the Jewish people as a whole.

(1:20) 'the curse that the Lord declared . . . through Moses: see Lev 26:14–39, Deut 28–31.

(2:1–2) 'against our judges . . . under the whole heaven' . . . is based on Dan 9:12–13.

(2:3) 'Some of us ate the flesh of their sons' . . . is a reference to Lev 26:29, Deut 28:53, and Jer 19:9, which with Bar 2:3 was the origin of the frequent anti-Jewish jibe in early Christian writers that the Jews had eaten their own children. Josephus (J.W. 6.3.4) describes one such incident during the Roman siege of Jerusalem in 70 CE.

(2:17–18) 'the dead who are in Hades . . . will not ascribe glory' is a common theme: cf. Ps 6:5; 30:9; 88:10–12; 115:17; Isa 38:18; Sir 17:27–8. For 'the person who is deeply grieved . . . with failing eyes' see Deut 28:65.

(2:21–6) 'as you declared by your servants the prophets': in fact, the references are all to Jeremiah: 26:5, 27:9; 7:34; 48:9; 36:30; 16:4; 32:36; 11:17.

(2:29–35) a reworking of several passages, principally from Jeremiah (42:2; 24:7; 25:5; 30:3; 29:6; 32:40; 31:33), along with Lev 26:39, 45; Deut 30:1–10. vv. 34–5, there is no explicit request for a return from exile, but the prayer repeats God's promise to end the Dispersion. The wording is based on Jer 30:3; 32:40; 31:33; 1 Kings 14:15.

(3:1–8) a heartfelt plea for mercy ends this first section of Baruch. Although the people of Judah have turned in repentance, they are still suffering the punishment incurred by their ancestors.

The Eulogy of Wisdom (3:9–4:4)

The second section of Baruch commences without preamble, and with no obvious connection with the preceding section. The poem shows indebtedness to the style and ideas of Deut 30:15–19; Prov 1–9; Job 28:12–28; Sir 24.

(3:9) 'Hear the commandments of life, O Israel', or, 'Hear, O Israel, the commandments of life', is deliberate verbal echo of Deut 6:4, 'Hear, O Israel . . .', the Shema, the 'creed' of Judaism, a feature cited as part of the evidence of a liturgical origin for Baruch. The identification of Torah with Wisdom is common in the late-biblical and intertestamental periods, the central text being Prov 1:7, and the idea is developed in Sir 1 and 24.

(3:10–14) Cf. Jer 9:12–16, which says that the wise can discern the reason for the Exile: disobedience to God.

(3:12) The 'fountain of wisdom', i.e. its source, is God: see Jer 2:13; Ps 36:8–9; Sir 1:1–20.

(3:15–16) Cf. v. 15 with Job 28:12, 20. v. 16, 'who lorded it over the animals on earth', is possibly an allusion to Nebuchadnezzar. Cf. Jer 27:6; 28:14; Dan 2:38.

(3:22–4) the repetition of Teman in two different geographical contexts indicates that two locations were originally

intended. The first must refer to Teman of Edom, which was proverbial for wisdom in the Bible, hence Jer 49:7, Ob 8–9. Job's friend Eliphaz was a Temanite (Job 2:11). The second Teman is Tema of Arabia (Job 6:19, Isa 21:14, Jer 25:23). Merran is more puzzling, but may be due to a misreading of Hebrew Midian or Medan (Gen 25:2) by the translator: r and d were often confused (see BAR 1:4). Those who travelled widely were thought to gain much wisdom (Sir 34:9–12; 39:4), hence the association of the desert traders of Midian/Medan, Tema, and the descendants of Hagar with wisdom. v. 24, cf. Isa 66:1.

(3:26) 'The giants', a reference to Gen 6:4. There was much speculation in the intertestamental period concerning these giants: see Wis 14:6; Sir 16:7; Jub. 7:22–3; and especially 1 Enoch 6–7.

(3:33–5) For similar concepts to vv. 33–4 see Job 38:7; Isa 40:26; Sir 43:9–10. v. 35, 'This is our God': comparable expressions can be found in Deut 4:35, 39; Isa 25:9; 43:10–11; 44:6; 45:18; Jer 10:6; Ps 48:14.

(3:37) 'she appeared on earth and lived with humankind', or, 'was seen on earth and moved among humankind'. The personal pronoun 'she' is not represented in Greek and the verb ōftē (appeared), is not gender-specific. Therefore some early Christian exegetes took the subject to be God, following vv. 35–6, and understood v. 37 to be a proof-text for the incarnation. Some modern scholars have dismissed the whole of v. 37 as a Christian interpolation, but Bar 3:8–4:4 is not the most obvious place to insert a Christological text, and it is much easier to understand the verse as original to its setting, describing how the inaccessible divine Wisdom (3:15, 29–31) was given as Torah to Israel and came to dwell on earth (3:36–4:1).

(4:1–4) v. 1, the explicit identification of Wisdom with Torah is also found in Sir 24:23. v. 3, 'Do not give your glory to another', cf. Isa 48:11. v. 4, 'Happy are we', literally, 'blessed (makarioi), are we, Israel, for the things that are pleasing to God are known by us', in the form of a beatitude resembling those in Ps 1:1 and Mt 5:3–11.

Address to Israel (4:5–5:9)

This section consists of encouragement of Israel (4:5–9a), followed by Zion's exhortation of her children (4:9b–29), answered by prophetic words of comfort addressed to Jerusalem (4:30–5:9). The words 'take courage' in 4:5 are repeated in Zion's speech at 4:21, 27, and mark the start of the message of consolation at 4:30. A prominent feature of the third part of Baruch is the personification of Zion as a mother. This is an idea found in the source for much of this section, Deutero-Isaiah (e.g. Isa 49:20–1; 50:1; 54:1–8), and also explicitly in the peculiar LXX reading of Ps 87 (86):5, 'Mother Zion'. Zion is depicted as calling to her female neighbours, paroikoi, in 4:9, 14, 24. These seem to be witnesses of the exile of the citizens and of Zion's grief, and perhaps refer to other Judean cities, since they are portrayed as passive, not hostile, onlookers.

(4:7–8) 'to demons and not to God,' see Deut 32:16–17; Ps 106:37; 96:5 (LXX), 1 Cor 10:20. v. 8, 'You forgot the everlasting God,' see BAR 1:8; 'who brought you up', literally, 'who nursed you' or 'suckled you', a very maternal image of God, cf. Hos 11:4.

(4:15) See Deut 28:49–50.

(4:23) 'I sent you out with sorrow and weeping, but . . . ', cf. Isa 62:3.

(4:35–5:9) A prophetic message of consolation, largely based on Isa 40–66. The wording of Bar 4:37–5:8 is also very close to that of *Pss. Sol.* 11:3–7. 4:35, for Babylon's punishment, see Isa 13:21–2; Jer 51:37, 58. 4:36–7, cf. Isa 49:18; 60:4. For 5:1 see Isa 52:1. The idea in 5:4 of the renaming of Jerusalem in the eschatological future is also found in Isa 1:26; 60:14; 62:4; Jer 33:16; Ezek 48:35. For 5:5 see Isa 51:17; 60:1, 4. 5:7 is close to Isa 40:4. 5:9, cf. Isa 52:12; 58:8; Ex 13:21.

The book has no formal conclusion, but ends on a note of promise and hope.

The Letter of Jeremiah

INTRODUCTION

A. Title. The KJV and Vulgate treat the Letter of Jeremiah as ch. 6 of Baruch. The Septuagint places Lamentations between the two works. The work purports to be a letter sent by Jeremiah to the exiles in Babylon, on the precedent of Jer 29, but is quite different stylistically from the work of the prophet, and must be pseudepigraphical.

B. Text and Language. Although the letter exists only in Greek and in versions based on LXX (Syriac, Sahidic, and Latin), there is linguistic evidence to support a Hebrew or Aramaic original. Crudely put, the Greek is often incoherent, and must indicate an imperfectly understood Semitic base text. Some examples are given in the Commentary below.

C. Subject-Matter and Literary Genre. The Letter is a heavy-handed prose satire on idolatry, rather in the manner of Bel and the Dragon, but it is cruder and less entertaining.

D. Date and Place of Composition. 1. There are several indications of the date of the Letter in Greek (any Semitic original would of course be rather older than the Greek text). There is an allusion to it in 2 Macc 2:1–3, a work composed some time in the second century BCE. The language of the Letter is koine Greek, which again supports a date from the second century BCE onwards. Finally, a fragment covering vv. 43–4 was found at Qumran (7Q486: DJD 3: 143 and pl. xxx), and dated to *c.*100 BCE on the basis of the writing.

2. The work is addressed to the Jewish exiles in Babylon, and this has led some scholars to suggest an eastern provenance such as Mesopotamia. But this is merely a literary device, and it could be aimed at any Jewish community in the Diaspora. Another argument for an origin in the east is the writer's apparent familiarity with Babylonian customs, though this need not have been acquired at first hand. However, if the original language was Hebrew, it would tend to support a Palestinian provenance, and an Aramaic *Vorlage* would indicate a Palestinian, Mesopotamian, or Babylonian origin.

E. Canonicity. 1. Like Baruch, the Letter of Jeremiah was associated by the church with the book of Jeremiah from the second century or earlier, and considered part of that prophetic work. However, with the exception of Aristides, Tertullian, and Cyprian, Christian writers rarely allude to it. This may be in part because the worship of idols became less and less of a threat to the church as time went on, and also because similar ideas are expressed more succinctly in Deut 4:28; Ps 115:4–7; 134:15–17; Isa 44:9–20; 46:5–7; Jer 10:1–16, the very passages from which the Letter drew its inspiration.

2. The Letter of Jeremiah once circulated among Jewish communities, witness its presence at Qumran and the allusion to it in 2 Maccabees, but it was not recognized later by the rabbis.

F. Outline. There is no obvious structure to the work, merely the association of ideas.

Introduction (6:1)
Address to the exiles in Babylon; prophecy of their long stay there and eventual return (6:2–3)
Warning to avoid idols in Babylon and to maintain faith with the Lord (6:4–7)
Satirical denunciation of idols, focusing on their utter impotence and the tainted service offered by their worshippers (6:8–72)
Conclusion, reiterating the warning to keep away from idolatry (6:73)

COMMENTARY

(6:1) Introduction 'A copy of a letter that Jeremiah sent', cf. Jer 29. The Greek word used here, however, is *epistolē* (see BAR 1:1).

(6:3–4) 'for a long time, up to seven generations', in conflict with Jer 25:12; 29:10, in which the Exile is prophesied as lasting seventy years. The implication is that the writer is addressing a Diaspora of long standing. Some commentators have taken the expression literally, and dated the work 7×40 years after the exiles of 597 and 586, to 317–306 BCE. But it is most likely that 'seven generations' is to be understood figuratively, as a long period of time. v. 4, 'which people carry on their shoulders', a possible reference to the Babylonian *akitu* festival at the New Year, which involved solemn processions, though it is more likely to have been influenced by Isa 46:1–2. See also LET JER 6:26.

(6:7) 'My angel is with you', for the concept and expression, see Gen 24:7; 48:16; Ex 23:20, 23; 32:34.

(6:11–12) 'the prostitutes on the terrace', literally, 'on the roof', Greek *stegos* or *tegos*. This is explained in a number of ways. It may refer, as NRSV suggests, to part of the pagan temple where the cult prostitutes operated (Hdt. 1.181). Alternatively, the Greek word is being used in the sense of 'brothel'. Another suggestion is that the Greek translator misread the unvowelled Aramaic 'al 'agrā (for payment, hire), as 'al 'iggār ā (on the roof). v. 12, 'from rust and corrosion', the NRSV has attempted to make sense of the Greek *apo iou kai brōmatōn* (lit. from rust and food), in the light of Mt 6:19, *sēs kai brōsis* ('moth and eating'), rendered as 'moth and rust' in NRSV. Otherwise, there may be a mistranslation behind the Greek: the Hebrew word for 'food' is *'ōkel* or *ma'ăkāl*, whereas the Hebrew for 'from a moth' is *mē'ōkēl* (lit. from a devourer).

(6:22) 'bats ... alight ... and so do cats', Strabo (*Geog.* 16.7) says that bats were a particular nuisance in temples. The verb rendered 'alight' by NRSV has the literal meaning in Greek, 'to fly over, flit', which is hardly appropriate to cats. This has led to many emendations in order to provide another type of bird at the end of the list, but none so far has proved convincing. See Lee (1971).

(6:29) 'touched by women in their periods or at childbirth', in Judaism women were regarded as ceremonially unclean at these times (Lev 12:4, 15:19–20).

(6:31–2) In contrast to the cults of the Babylonian gods, women played very little part in the cult of YHWH. Torn clothes, shaved and uncovered heads were regarded as signs of mourning and unfitting for a supposedly holy place. Israelite priests were forbidden to mourn in the customary way, in order to remain ceremonially clean for the service of God (Lev 21:1–5, 10). The pagan priests described here may be participating in the cult of dying and rising gods such as Tammuz.

(6:36–8) The impotence of the idols is implicitly compared with the compassion of Israel's God (cf. Ps 68:5–6, 146:8; Isa 35:5).

(6:40) The 'Chaldeans' here are not Babylonians; the word is used in the sense of 'astrologers, magicians'. 'Bel' means 'lord', an epithet for the patron deity of a city, in this case Marduk (Merodach), god of the Babylonians. Cf. the apocryphal book Bel and the Dragon.

(6:42–3) Herodotos (1.199) gives a similar account of this practice. He says that once in her life, every Babylonian woman has to sit in the precinct of Aphrodite (Ishtar), and have intercourse with the first stranger who throws a silver coin into her lap. The cords here may refer either to the string that Herodotos says the women wear on their heads, or to the roped-off areas in which they sit. The accounts here and in Herodotos appear to be independent. Burning bran for incense is a strange custom, but perhaps some sort of grain offering or aphrodisiac is meant.

(6:55) 'like crows', this is a strange simile, and it has been plausibly suggested that the Greek translator read the unvocalized Hebrew *'ābîm* (clouds) as *'ōrĕbîm* (crows).

(6:60) For the theme of the obedience of the heavenly bodies, see BAR 3:33–4.

(6:67–70) These verses mirror the thought of Jer 10:2–5, with some reordering. '[A] scarecrow in a cucumber bed' is a vivid image, probably influenced by the similar expressions in Isa 1:8 and especially Jer 10:5, which occurs in a passage on the futility of idols. Since the clause does not appear in LXX Jer 10:5, the writer must have had direct knowledge of the Hebrew. The Greek *probaskanion*, rendered 'scarecrow' here, generally means something that averts witchcraft.

(6:71–3) Gardens were cultivated for food, not for leisure or decorative purposes, so a thornbush in a garden, attracting birds that would feed on the produce, would be a metaphor for uselessness (cf. Judg 9:14, 15). '[a]corpse thrown out in the darkness': corpses were ceremonially unclean, and for a body to be thrown out unburied was a sign of enormous disrespect. For similar expressions, see Am 8:3, Jer 14:16, 22:19, Isa 34:3, Bar 2:25. v. 72, for 'linen' the Greek reads 'marble', apparently having mistaken the Hebrew *šēš* (fine linen) for its homonym. For the combination with purple, describing luxurious attire, see Ex 26:1, Prov 31:22, Lk 16:19. The letter concludes at v. 73 with a recommendation to keep away from idolatry.

REFERENCES

Avigad, N. (1986), *Hebrew Bullae from the Time of Jeremiah. Remnants of a Burnt Archive* (Jerusalem: Israel Exploration Society).

Baillet, M., Milik, J. T., Vaux, R. de (1962), *Les Petites Grottes de Qumrân*, DJD 3 (Oxford: Clarendon).

Burke, D. G. (1982), *The Poetry of Baruch: A Reconstruction and Analysis of the Original Hebrew Text of Baruch 3:9–5:9*, Septuagint and Cognate Studies Series 10 (Scholars Press: Chico, Calif.).

Lee, G. M. (1971), 'Apocryphal Cats: Baruch 6:21', *VT* 21: 111–12.

Nickelsburg, G. W. D. (1984), 'Baruch and Epistle of Jeremiah', in M. E. Stone (ed.), *Jewish Writings of the Second Temple Period* (Assen: Van Gorcum), 140–8.

Steck, O. H. (1993), *Das apokryphe Baruchbuch: Studien zu Rezeption und Konzentration 'kanonischer' Überlieferung* (Göttingen: Vandenhoeck & Ruprecht).

Thackeray, H. St J. (1923), *The Septuagint and Jewish Worship*, Schweich Lectures, 1920; 2nd edn. (London: Oxford University Press), 80–111.

Tov, E. (1975), *The Book of Baruch, Also Called I Baruch (Greek and Hebrew)*, SBLTT 8 (Missoula, Mont.: Scholars Press).

—— (1976), *The Septuagint Translation of Jeremiah and Baruch: A Discussion of an Early Revision of the LXX of Jeremiah 29–52 and Baruch 1:1–3:8*, HSM 8 (Missoula, Mont.: Scholars Press).

Whitehouse, O. C. (1913), '1 Baruch', *APOT* i. 569–95.

46. Additions to Daniel

GEORGE J. BROOKE

INTRODUCTION

A. Background. The book of Daniel in the HB is composite; not only is it written in two languages (Hebrew and Aramaic), but its contents fall into two parts, one containing stories about Daniel as the wise man in the court of the foreign king, the other his visions. The scrolls from Qumran have shown that there were other traditions in the Second Temple period which are most suitably associated with Daniel (4Q242–6; 4Q551–3); notably 4Q242 seems to be an alternative form of Dan 4. It is not altogether surprising that the Greek versions of Daniel contain additions. All three additions are set in Babylon and concern in some way the deliverance of the faithful. For further detail on matters of background see the survey by C. A. Moore (1992).

B. Text and Language. 1. The Greek versions of Daniel are usually divided into two groups. On the one hand the OG is attested in the late second-century CE Papyrus 967 (which places Bel and the Dragon before Susanna), in Origen's *Hexapla* (which survives in a very literal Syriac translation made in the early 7th cent. CE, known as Syh), and in the ninth–eleventh century MS 88 (Codex Chisianus). On the other hand there is the text linked with the name of Theodotion (2nd cent. CE) which very early became dominant in the churches. It is widely agreed that this text predates Theodotion himself (Schmitt 1966). Both Greek versions contain three passages not found in the Hebrew and Aramaic Daniel. Whether the Theodotion text of these additions is a revision of the OG, perhaps in the light of a Semitic text (Moore 1977), or a fresh translation from a Semitic original (Schmitt 1966) is still unclear. There is nothing in the two traditions that distinguishes the Greek of the additions from that of the rest of Daniel.

2. In both Greek traditions the Prayer of Azariah and the Song of the Three Jews occurs between Dan 3:23 and 3:24 (not extant in Papyrus 967). This addition has three parts: the Prayer of Azariah, a narrative link, and the Song of the Three Jews. In Theodotion (and Papyrus 967) Bel and the Dragon form Dan 13 and Susanna comes before Dan 1. In Papyrus 967 Susanna follows Bel and the Dragon but in MS 88, Syh, and Vg Susanna is Dan 13, and Bel and the Dragon Dan 14. The NRSV gives a translation of Theodotion's version of the additions, but they are printed in the order of the OG. The standard edition of the Greek texts is that of Ziegler (1954) which must be supplemented by the work of Geissen (1968).

3. Most scholars suppose that the Prayer of Azariah and the Song of the Three Jews were originally composed in Hebrew (cf. Kuhl 1940: 111–59). If the narrative interlude was original to the text of Daniel it would have been in Aramaic, but if it was composed to introduce the Song of the Three, then it would have been originally in Hebrew. Nothing can be deduced from the Aramaic forms of these additions in the eleventh-century *Chronicles of Jerahmeel* (Gaster 1895; 1896), which are versions produced independently from the Greek versions, probably to make a Hebrew original fit its Aramaic context. The two Greek versions are in close agreement with one another.

4. The differences between the OG and Theodotion are most significant in Susanna. They can be seen in English in some parallel presentations (Kay 1913; Collins 1993) and have been discussed extensively (Moore 1977: 78–80; Steussy 1993). Most scholars suppose that Theodotion supplements the OG either on the basis of oral tradition (Delcor 1971: 260), through redactional activity (Engel 1985: 56–7), or through using a Semitic source (Moore 1977: 83). For the story as a whole a Hebrew original is likely (*kai egeneto* = *wayyĕhî*: vv. 7, 15, 19, 28, 64), though the extant medieval Hebrew forms of the story are probably secondary. Since Julius Africanus in the third century CE (*Letter to Origen*, PG 11.41–8) some have argued for a Greek original because of the puns in vv. 54–5 and 58–9, but the Syh represents the puns easily enough so a Semitic original remains quite possible. Milik (1981: 355–7) has tentatively proposed that a three-part Aramaic fragment from Qumran (4Q551) reflects the story of Susanna. It talks of

the appointment of a judge but there are no clear overlaps and the proper names found in the Aramaic fragment nowhere occur in the story of Susanna.

5. For Bel and the Dragon OG and Theodotion are close, though some argue that Bel is told more effectively in the OG, whilst the Dragon is stylistically better in Theodotion (Moore 1977: 119). The greater number of Hebraisms in Theodotion suggests that the OG may have been based on an Aramaic original, which Theodotion reworked on the basis of a Hebrew text. The Theodotion version seems to be somewhat assimilated to Dan 6 while its OG counterpart may be older than Dan 6 (Wills 1990). The story of the Dragon is known in Aramaic in the *Chronicles of Jerahmeel*, which possibly reflects an early version independent from both Greek and Syriac versions.

C. Subject Matter and Literary Genre. 1. The Prayer of Azariah, though in its present context said by an individual, is a communal confession of sin and plea for mercy similar to Dan 9:4–19 (cf. Ps 44; 74; 79; 106; Ezra 9:6–15; Neh 1:5–11; Bar 1:15–3:8; 4Q504). It is full of the theology of Deuteronomy. The Song of the Three Jews is a hymn of praise; there is no need to suppose that its two parts ever existed separately. It is closely related to Ps 148 and the 'list science of nature wisdom' (Koch 1987: 1.205; Collins 1993: 207; cf. Job 38–41; Sir 43). These additions shift the emphasis in Dan 3 away from the king towards the faithfulness of the martyrs, who thus acknowledge and bless God before Nebuchadnezzar does (Hammer 1972: 213).

2. Susanna is the story of the eventual vindication of an innocent woman who thwarted an attempted rape by two of the elders of her community. Since the refutation of its historicity, the story has been variously categorized: as a moral fable (see Baumgartner 1926: 259–67), as a midrash (on Jer 29:21–32) which either critiques perverted Jewish authorities (OG: Engel 1985: 177–81) or is designed to be an attack on Sadducean court practice (Brüll 1877), as a folktale (Baumgartner 1929; Schürer 1987; LaCoque 1990), as a wisdom instruction (Theodotion: Engel 1985: 181–3), as a parable on Jewish relations with Hellenism (Hartman and Di Lella 1989: 420), as a court legend adapted for the Jewish community (Wills 1990), perhaps with a particular 'democratized' stress on the persecution and vindication of the righteous (Nickelsburg 1984: 38), as a novella (Collins 1993: 437). For all its folkloristic feel, the story is replete with religious terminology and themes. Because Susanna is a woman, there has been some recent interest in the tale from that perspective. Through the contrast of the virtuous woman with the lecherous elders Susanna is subversive of the Jewish establishment (LaCoque 1990); she is also the story's object whose feminine passivity allows God to be the avenger (Pervo 1991). Motifs in the story suggest that Susanna is a new Eve, the one who knows the law and is obedient in the garden (cf. *T. Levi* 18: 10–11; *Pss. Sol.* 14:1–5; Brooke 1992; Pearce 1996). The story is told from a male angle which encourages the (male) reader to be voyeuristic like the elders and Susanna's choice of death rather than rape makes her subscribe to the idea that her purity, the hallmark of her husband's esteem, is more important than her life (Glancy 1995; cf. Steussy 1993: 118). What happens to Susanna challenges through stereotyped

feminine instability the notions of righteousness and true ethnic identity (Levine 1995).

3. Bel and the Dragon are two interwoven court tales about the falsehood of idolatry. They are typologically very similar to the stories of Dan 1–6. Some have supposed them to be historicizations of part of the Babylonian creation myth *Enuma Elish* or to be interpretations of scriptural passages: Jer 51:34–5, 44 (Moore 1977: 122); Isa 45–6 (Nickelsburg 1981: 27). But both tales are principally polemical parodies of idolatry. In both the friendship between the king and Daniel is challenged, in Bel by Daniel mocking his friend's worship of the clay and bronze, in the Dragon by indignant Babylonians casting aspersions on the king's nationalism. In both stories there is a subtle interweaving of themes concerning life, food, and deity. In the story of Bel Daniel shows that the idol does not and cannot eat, and therefore cannot be said to be alive; his God, by contrast, is the living God. In the test it is the priests and their families who take the food offered to Bel. In the story of the Dragon Daniel shows that eating is not a sufficient criterion of divinity; the Dragon eats and dies and as a result Daniel is given to the lions for food, is himself miraculously fed while the lions fast, and those who have been his detractors are in the end themselves turned into the lion's dinner. Though provided with some characteristics of historical verisimilitude, the two tales are polemics not against the Gentile world as such but against idolatry and all the religious attitudes that go with it (Collins 1993: 419). Not only is idolatry attacked (cf. Isa 44:9–20; Jer 10:1–6; Hab 2:18–19; Ps 115), but also the actual destruction of the idols is depicted (cf. *Jub* 12:12–13). Its similarity to Dan 6 suggests that the den episode may have originated as an independent tradition.

D. Date and Place of Composition. 1. About 100 BCE, the *terminus ante quem*, all three additions were incorporated into the Greek text of Daniel; determining actual dates of composition is much more difficult. Most scholars suppose that the Prayer of Azariah and the Song of the Three Jews are so typical in form and content that they are virtually impossible to date (Eissfeldt 1965: 590), but internal clues show that these psalms are post-exilic (as is the very similar Dan 9). It should be noted, however, that while the Prayer of Azariah supposes the destruction of the temple (v. 15), the Song of the Three may presuppose its existence (v. 31). If the description of the king in Prayer of Azariah 9b refers to Antiochus Epiphanes, then the Prayer may have been written during his persecution (167–164 BCE), when effectively there was no temple (v. 15) but a real need to pray for the destruction of one's enemies (v. 21). If Tob 8:5 is dependent on the Song of the Three Jews (Moore 1977: 47), then the Song cannot be later than the third century BCE; at least it was composed before being translated into Greek at the end of the second century BCE.

2. Scholars are divided about the date and origin of Susanna. Those who see it as a Judaized folk-tale suggest that its outline is of Gentile origin and undatable (Eissfeldt 1965: 590). Many of those who see it as a Jewish composition have followed Brüll in locating the tale as a Pharisaic illustration of the dispute between Pharisees and Sadducees at the time of Alexander Jannaeus (103–76 BCE) concerning the application of Deut 19:16–19 (cf. *m. Mak.* 1:6; e.g. Kay 1913: 644). More recently a majority of scholars, while acknowledging that

the story was probably translated at about 100 BCE, see the original Hebrew as belonging to any time in the Second Temple period, probably in Palestine (Collins 1993: 438).

3. There is a historical notice at the start of Bel and the Dragon (see BEL 1–2) but it does not help in dating the story. According to Herodotus the temple of Bel was plundered by Xerxes I (485–465 BCE). The phrase 'become a Jew' (v. 28) reflects an attitude first prevalent in the second century BCE (Collins 1993: 415–16). The tales were part of an extensive Daniel literature.

E. Canonicity. All three additions are clearly secondary, in their earliest form surviving only in Greek. In the early church Justin (d. 165) is the earliest to refer to the additions to Dan 3, Irenaeus (140–c.200) the earliest to refer to Susanna and Bel and the Dragon (Schürer 1987: 726–9). Julius Africanus (d. c.240) was the first to question the canonicity of the additions, as did Jerome, but they remained part of the Greek Bible and the Vg. They are unattested amongst the Jews of antiquity, first appearing fully in the medieval versions of Josippon and in the *Chronicles of Jerahmeel*. Perhaps Susanna was never accepted by Jews either because it appears to contravene certain legal practices concerning witnesses (cf *m. Sanh.* 5:1) or because it undermines the authority of elders, or because it was seen as an inept introduction to Daniel.

F. Outline.
The Prayer of Azariah and the Song of the Three Jews
The Prayer of Azariah
   Introduction (1–2)
   Azariah's Prayer (3–22)
Narrative (23–7)
The Song of the Three Jews
   Introduction (28)
   Blessings (29–68)

Susanna
Introduction (1–4)
The Plot (5–62)
   The opportune day: in the garden (5–27)
   The next day: in the house (OG synagogue) (28–64)
Epilogue (63–4)

Bel and the Dragon
Introduction (1–2)
Two Idol Tales (3–42)
   Bel (3–22)
   The Dragon (23–42)

COMMENTARY

The Prayer of Azariah and the Song of the Three Jews

The Prayer of Azariah (1–22; Gk 3:24–45)

(1–2) Introduction A narrative link explains that Hananiah, Mishael, and Azariah are in the fire, singing to God; this would seem to be the introduction to the Song of the Three Jews. Theodotion has Azariah pray alone; the OG has his two companions join him. The names are Hebrew; in Dan 3 only the Babylonian Aramaic forms of their names occur: Shadrach, Meshach, and Abednego.

(3–22) Azariah's Prayer Like many of the biblical psalms the prayer of Azariah is composite, containing the blessing of God, a confession, and an intercession. Since the three are in the furnace because of their obedience to God in refusing to worship the gold idol, they pray on behalf of fellow Israelites rather than for themselves. vv. 3–5, the blessing of God: the blessing extols God for his righteousness (cf. Deut 32:4), i.e. his justice in judging the people and letting Jerusalem be destroyed. The opening 'Blessed are you, Lord' is common in contemporary prayers (1QH 13:20; 18:14; cf. 4Q414 27 H 2; 4Q504 6 H 20; 3:11). The address to God as 'God of our ancestors' places the prayer in the tradition of Deut (1:11, 21; 4:1, etc.) and Tob 8:5. Mention of 'the name' links this opening with the chiastic intercession (11, 20). The entire blame for what has happened rests with the sinful people, a recognition which leads naturally into confession.

vv. 6–9, the confession neatly declares how those who have broken the law have been justly handed over to the lawless rebels and an unjust king for punishment: the administrators of the punishment fit the crime. v. 9b, the descriptions may have been thought to have suited Nebuchadnezzar well, even though the prayer was not originally composed for its present context; perhaps it originally referred to Antiochus Epiphanes ('a sinful root', 1 Macc 1:10; Hartman and Di Lella 1989: 412b). For this confession cf. Dan 9:5, Ezra 9:6, Neh 9:26.

vv. 10–22, the chiastic intercession has six elements to it. These are arranged chiastically so that the poetry of the prayer has a balance which itself expresses the calm self-realization of the person praying it, whether Azariah in the fire or any other dispersion Jew. (The chiasmas is here indicated as follows: 1, 2, 3, 3', 2', 1'.) (1) God's servants and God's name (10–11). The first element in the chiasm concerns the shame the servants who worship God have become; but the poet requests God, for his name's sake, not to annul his covenant. (2) Call for mercy (12–13). The second and fifth elements in the confession are pleas for mercy. v. 12, Abraham is described as God's friend (*ēgapēmenon*; cf. Isa 41:8; 2 Chr 20:7; 4Q252 2:8; Jas 2:23; *Apoc. Abr.* 9:6; 10:5; *T. Ahr.* A 1:6; 2:3 etc.; Philo, *de Sobr.* 55–6). Isaac, rather than Jacob (Isa 44:1–2; Jer 30:10), is described as the servant (cf. Gen 24:14). The epithet 'holy one' is usually reserved for supernatural creatures, though Israel is called holy (Deut 7:6). v. 13, the promise of descendants derives from Gen 13:16, though the phraseology here is closer to Gen 22:17 (Delcor 1971: 101); the promise of the land is omitted here. (3) No leaders or temple (14–15). The third and fourth elements in the intercession deal with leadership and the temple. This may suggest a likely origin for the prayer: perhaps it was compiled in the post-exilic period by a priestly group in the dispersion who felt the lack of a temple. The lack of prophets would also suggest post-exilic times. Some have suggested that these lines reflect the Maccabean situation (Bennett 1913: 629; Collins 1993: 201). v. 14, Israel is diminished as of old (cf. Deut 7:7), hardly the fulfilment of the promise to Abraham. Similar pleas are made in Jer 42:2, Bar 2:13. (3') Substitute for the temple, and God as leader (16–17). v. 16, in the literary setting in which it now stands Azariah in effect prays that he and his friends may be acceptable to God as martyrs (Koch 1987: 2.54–5). This is a development of the tradition that a contrite heart is acceptable to God in place of

sacrifices (cf. Ps 40:6 (cited in Heb 10:5–6); 51:17; 141:2; 11QPs* 18:7–10 (Syr Ps 154:17–21)). In place of the institutional leaders, God himself will be followed directly. The Greek is difficult to understand here. Theodotion reads 'to complete after you', usually taken as a literal rendering of the Hebrew phrase 'to follow you completely' (*ml' 'ḥrhk*; Num 14:24; Deut 1:36; Josh 14:8; Bennett 1913: 634). OG has literally 'to atone after you', perhaps a rendering of the Hebrew 'to atone for you' (cf. *kpr b'dw*: Lev 16:11). With reference to the Aramaic (*lr'w' mn ydmk* 'to please you'), the OG might be seen as an attempt to render this, and Theodotion as a further inner-Greek corruption (Koch 1987: 2.55–9; Collins 1993: 202). (2') Call for mercy (18–19). The fifth element concludes as the second had begun with a plea for mercy. (1') God's servants and God's name (20–2). The sixth element rounds out the confession. It is a request that God glorify his name by putting to shame all who harm his servants.

Narrative (23–7; OG 46–50)

The narrative link, perhaps part of a Semitic original, serves to heighten the drama in the incident. To avoid contradicting Dan 3:22, the OG distinguishes between those who stoked the fire and those who threw the three Jews in. Though some consider the angel to be present to preserve the transcendence of God, it is just as possible to argue that the angel represents the saving presence of God himself. The angel of Dan 3:25 is identified as Gabriel in later Jewish tradition (*b. Pesuḥ.* 118a–b). The narrative is reflected in 3 Macc 6:6.

The Song of the Three Jews (28–68; OG 51–90)

(28) Introduction The three praise, glorify, and bless (OG: also exalt) God.

(29–68) Blessings The body of this lengthy and elaborate hymn is in two parts, which may have existed separately (Moore 1977: 75–6), the first (29–34) a blessing addressed to God himself, the second (35–68) a call to the whole of creation to bless the Lord. It is unsuitable to let neatness of strophic division control the understanding of the blessings (Christie 1928). The refrains may suggest that the hymn had an independent life as a responsorial psalm (cf. Ps 136; also each verse of Ps 145 in 11QPs* 16:7–17:22 is given the refrain 'Blessed is the Lord and blessed is his name for ever and ever').

vv. 29–34, God is addressed as 'God of our ancestors' as in v. 3 (cf. Tob 8:5). God's name is blessed; he is blessed in the temple; as he sits on his throne on the cherubim (cf. 1 Sam 4:4; 2 Sam 6:2; 2 Kings 19:15 (Isa 37:16); Ps 80:1; 99:1); as he sits on the throne of his kingdom; in the firmament (cf. Gen 1:6–8; Dan 12:3) of the heaven. Each of the six ascriptions of blessing has a refrain. These give structure to the blessing. The first and the fourth are the same: in these two blessings God is described in relation to things outside heaven: the ancestors and the depths. The second and fifth both conclude with the same verb (*huperupsoun*): God's holy name and his kingdom are linked (cf. Mt 6:9–10 || Lk 11:2). The third (*huperumnētos* and *huperendoxos*) and sixth (*humnētos* and *dedoxasmenos*) are similar: the temple on earth (Delcor 1971: 104; Collins 1993: 205; rather than the heavenly temple: Bennett 1913: 635; Moore 1977: 69) is a veritable microcosm. v. 33: cf. Ps. 29:10; 1 Clem. 59.3.

vv. 35–68, the call to blessing, commonly known as the Benedicite from the opening word of the Latin translation, is in two parts, the first addressed to the heavens, the second to the earth. Though encompassing the whole of creation, these two spheres often occur together as witnesses to divine activity (cf. Deut 4:26; 30:19). v. 35, all the works of the Lord are addressed as a whole (Hammer 1972: 221); cf. Ps 103:20–2. vv. 36–51, blessing of heavens: there are sixteen verses in this section. v. 36, it is likely that this is to be considered as the overall address in this section as also v. 52 in the next. vv. 37–51, fifteen verses remain; it is difficult to discern their structure, but five sets of three are possible: 37–9, 40–2, 43–5, 46–8, 49–51. If so, then the following patterns emerge. A half-verse involving water features four times; as the central element in the first and last trio, and chiastically as the last element of the second trio and the first element of the fourth; in the second and fourth trios the sun and moon and stars are balanced by the nights and days and light and darkness (cf. the similar balance in Gen 1:5 and 1:14). The refrain is the same in every verse. v. 37, the angels are called to praise God (cf. 4Q400 1 i 1–2). v. 38, for the waters above the heaven cf. Gen 1:7; Ps 148:4. vv. 39–41, the powers may be the heavenly armies (Delcor 1971: 105) (cf. Ps 103 (Gk. 102): 21; 148:2). The sun, moon, and stars also praise God in Ps 148:3. v. 43, the Vg understands the winds as the spirits of God (*omnes spiritus Dei*). v. 47, night may be mentioned before day because for the psalmist the day began at sunset (cf. Gen 1:5, 8, etc.). v. 50, for snow and frost cf. Ps 148:8. vv. 52–68: blessing of earth. v. 52, the earth is addressed as a whole. vv. 52–9, four verses cover the earth's habitats (mountains (cf. Ps 148:9) and plants; seas and rivers and springs) and three their inhabitants (whales and other swimmers (cf. Ps 148:7; Gen 1:21; Ps 104:26); birds (cf. Ps 148:10); wild animals and cattle (cf. Ps 148:10)). Though echoing Ps 148, the overall order reflects Gen 1:21–6. vv. 60–8: the people of the earth are called upon to bless the Lord. vv. 60–5, first there are three couplets: all people and Israel; priests and servants of the Lord (cf. Ps 134:1); the spirits and souls of the righteous, and the holy and humble in heart. The priestly character of the list is all the more striking when comparison is made with Ps 148 in which it is kings, princes, and rulers who are addressed; there no priests are mentioned. The refrain in all these verses as in the next is the same. v. 66, second comes a verse which Hananiah, Azariah, and Mishael address to themselves. This is extended with the reason why they should praise God: he has rescued them from Hades, saved them from death, and delivered them from the fiery furnace. This verse is commonly regarded as a later interpolation into the hymn. v. 67, this general exhortation is the same as Ps 106 (Gk. 105): 1; 107 (Gk. 106):1; 136 (Gk. 135): 1; Sir 51:12. v. 68, all those who worship the Lord are called upon to bless the God of gods (cf. Ps 136:2).

Susanna

(1–4) Introduction v. 1, the scene is set in Babylon (as in OG 5) in the household of Joachim (meaning 'the Lord will establish'). His name is the same as that of the king mentioned in Jer 29:2 and Dan 1:1. In Jewish tradition the two are identified: when Nebuchadnezzar gives King Joachim's wife permission to visit him for intercourse, she says 'I have seen something like a red lily' (*šwšnh*; menstrual blood; *Lev. Rab.* 19:6) and so

he does not sleep with her. This identification may account for the association of the story with Daniel, who does not appear until v. 44. v. 2, Susanna (meaning 'lily') is introduced after her husband. Nobody else in the HB is named Susanna but the name occurs in Lk 8:3 and in some Jewish inscriptions (*CII* i. 627, 637). She is described first as the daughter of Hilkiah (meaning 'the Lord is my portion'; cf. Jer 29:3), and is thus narratively protected between husband and father, secondly as very beautiful (like Jdt 8:7–8; cf. the tree of knowledge, the object of desire, in Gen 3:6), thirdly as fearing the Lord, the sapiential expression for religious piety (cf. Prov 1:7; 10:27). In one Jewish tradition she is the wife of King Joachim and the daughter not of Hilkiah but of Shealtiel (*Chronicles of Jerahmeel*). v. 3, Susanna's parents are righteous and have taught their daughter in the law of Moses; mention of the law (not in OG) raises the expectation that some commandment may be challenged in what follows. v. 4, like the leading figures of many other Jewish stories (Job, Tobit, Judith), Joachim is very wealthy; wealth is a sign of divine favour, but in itself is no protection from the execution of the law. Perhaps alluding to Jeremiah's letter to the exiles (Jer 29:5), Joachim has a fine garden (*paradeisos*); though often referring to an ordinary garden, the juxtaposition with the keeping of the law suggests that Paradise itself (Gen 2:9) is also at stake. Joachim is also the most esteemed of all Jews.

(5–62) The Plot The plot of Susanna is in two parts (Brooke 1992; Steussy 1993): the first (5–27) takes place in the garden, the second (28–64) in Joachim's house (OG: the synagogue) which acts as a courtroom. The close narrative proximity of garden and court strongly implies that motifs from Gen 3 are being replayed.

vv. 5–27, the opportune day. The scene in the garden has two elements, the prelude (5–14) and the attempted rape (15–27). v. 5, 'That year' may indicate the year of Joachim's marriage. The elders (*presbuteroi*) are introduced as recently appointed judges; the exilic communities seem to have had some considerable autonomy. The quotation is an unknown saying, perhaps based on Jer 29:21–3 (cf. *b. Sanh.* 93a) or Zech 5:5–11. The term used for 'Lord' is *despotēs* (as in OG Dan 9:8, 15, 16, 17, 19). v. 6, because Joachim's house acts as a court, these elders have reason to be hanging around his property (OG: even hearing cases from other cities). v. 7, after court business, Susanna is accustomed to walk in the garden (OG: 'in the evening'; cf. God in Gen 3:8). vv. 8–12, the elders' covetous lust (in breach of Ex 20:17) increases and they turn away their eyes from heaven, a surrogate for God (cf. Dan 4:31, 34). The OG notes that Susanna was unaware of their lewd passions. vv. 13–14, catching each other out, they conspire together to rape Susanna. vv. 15–27, the attempted rape. There are three moments in this scene. vv. 15–18, the bath (cf. 2 Sam 11; *Jub.* 33:1–9; *T. Reub.* 3:11); the opportune moment comes for the rape when Susanna sends her maids to fetch oil and ointments (cf. Esth 2:3, 9; Jdt 10:3) for when she has finished bathing. When they leave they unwittingly shut the elders in the garden with Susanna. This scene is not in the OG. vv. 19–23, the dilemma; the elders threaten Susanna, putting her in a dilemma, which she instantly recognizes: to give in is to be liable for capital punishment for infidelity (Lev 20:10; Deut 22:22), not to give in is to be liable for the same punishment but on the basis of the elders' false witness. She determines not to sin before the Lord (cf. Gen 39:9; 2 Sam 24:14). This complex psychological (and for some, erotic) moment has often been depicted by artists, notably by Rembrandt in 1647 (Gemäldegalerie, Berlin), to suggest even that Susanna is the cause of the elders' lust. vv. 24–7, the false accusation (not in the OG); a shouting battle ensues. The young woman who is sexually assaulted must cry out to attest her unwillingness (Deut 22:24, 27); the elders also shout and are listened to. When they tell their false story, Susanna's servants are ashamed.

vv. 28–64, the next day: in the house. The second part of the overall plot consists of the trial scenes either side of a dramatic interlude. The postlude sees the judgement carried out. vv. 28–41, the first trial is a perversion of justice from which there seems no escape. v. 29, the elders call for Susanna; she is mentioned first, no longer narratively protected by father and husband. v. 30, in the OG Susanna's servants are numbered at 500, and she has four children. Susanna's husband is absent from the trial: her supposed disgrace is his shame (Levine 1995: 312). vv. 31–3, Susanna is made to unveil (cf. m. Soṭa 1:5: accused beautiful women should appear veiled) so that the elders can once again feast their eyes on her great beauty; OG may imply that she was stripped (cf. Ezek 16:37–9; Hos 2:3), the elders pre-empting the judgement. None present discern their self-condemnatory leering gazes. v. 34, as witnesses the elders lay their hands on her head (Lev 24:14), thus finally managing to touch her. v. 35, Susanna looks up to heaven, which the elders had cast aside (v. 9); her appeal to a higher court has already begun. vv. 36–41, the elders give their fabricated testimony, two witnesses being sufficient (Deut 17:6); in the OG the elders refer to a stadium, a symbol of Greek perversity (1 Macc 1:15). There is no cross-examination, nor is Susanna allowed to testify. v. 41, as witnesses the elders cannot themselves pass sentence; the assembly does (cf. Jer 26:9–10; 1QS 6:8–13; 1 Cor 5:4). Adultery was a capital offence (cf. Lev 20:10), stoning the likely means of execution (cf. Deut 22:21; Jn 8:5).

vv. 42–6, before the sentence can be carried out there are two exclamations. vv. 42–4, the first cry is Susanna's prayer (in the OG Susanna's prayer precedes her sentence). She does not intercede for divine intervention on her behalf; she simply declares out loud to the eternal God (cf. Gen 21:33), who knows what is secret (cf. Deut 29:29; Sir 1:30) and what will happen (cf. 1 Enoch 9:11), that she is innocent. The story's audience is put in the privileged position of being able to assess the situation like God himself. The Lord hears the cry of the innocent and righteous one. vv. 45–6, as a result the young man Daniel is stirred into action by God himself (OG: by an angel). Mention of Daniel's youthfulness is often thought to account for why the story is put before Dan 1 in Theodotion and the OL. Daniel makes the second outburst and shouts out his refusal to participate in the execution of the assembly's sentence (cf. Mt 27:24). m. Sanh. 6:1–2 permits people to appeal against a verdict before sentence is carried out (Delcor 1971: 270). Similar sudden interventions by a youth are a common folklore motif.

vv. 47–59, the second trial takes place. vv. 47–9, it is initiated by Daniel railing against the people and urging them to return to court to consider things clearly; cf. Simeon ben Shetach's advice on careful cross-examination (m. 'Abot 1:9; Brüll 1877: 64). v. 50, Daniel's authority is recognized and he is invited to join the elders. vv. 51–9, Daniel undertakes the separate cross-examination of the two witnesses. With little impartiality Daniel lays into the first elder as a 'relic of wicked days', accusing him through Ex 23:7. When asked under which tree he had seen Susanna and her supposed lover he answers 'a mastic tree' (schinos). Daniel declares the sentence: he will be cut in two (schizō). The second elder is addressed equally brusquely, this time as an offspring of Canaan (cf. Gen 9:20–5; Ezek 16:3; 4Q252 2:6–8). A cheap jibe is levelled against the daughters of Israel (perhaps the Samaritans for the author; Engel 1985: 126) who have given in when a daughter of Judah would not; Susanna is also called a daughter of Israel in v. 48. The second elder declares that Susanna and her supposed lover were under an oak (prinos). Daniel declares the sentence: he will be split in two (priō). Two trees also feature in the Garden of Eden story (Gen 2:17; 3:22) as does the sword (Gen 3:24; cf. Num 22:31).

vv. 60–2, postlude. v. 60, the assembly (sunagōgē) blesses God for saving those who hope in him. v. 61, the two elders receive the punishment they had intended for Susanna (cf. Deut 19:16–19). That this law was a matter of dispute between Pharisees and Sadducees in the first century BCE (m. Mak. 1:6; y. Sanh. 6:3:23e) has been used to suggest a likely setting for the story (Brüll 1877) which agrees with the Pharisee position. v. 62, the law of Moses which Susanna had been taught (3) is thus upheld and innocent blood spared.

(63–4) Epilogue The conclusion is a neat inclusio. As at the opening so at the close of the story Susanna is listed between her two male protectors; this time Hilkiah is mentioned first. Though exposed when initially brought to trial (29), she is now protected and redomesticated. Though she has in fact threateningly exposed the weakness of the community's judiciary and shown the community's patriarchal institutions to be flawed, nothing shameful was found in her (cf. Deut 24:1) and she is now neatly put back in her place and the reader is reminded that there are some righteous, law-abiding men around. Whereas vv. 1–4 have described Joachim's reputation, the story closes with a description of Daniel's. In the OG none of the story's participants are mentioned in the conclusion; rather all pious young men are declared 'beloved of Jacob' because of their knowledge and understanding (cf. Isa 11:2–4).

Bel and the Dragon

(1–2) Introduction v. 1, only the OG carries the title: 'From the prophecy of Habakkuk, son of Joshua, of the tribe of Levi'. This identification seems to depend on 33–9. No mention is made in Habakkuk of his tribe; in Lives of the Prophets 12:1 he is of the tribe of Simeon. The historical scene is set by mentioning the death of Astyarges, king of Media (585–550 BCE) and the succession of Cyrus the Persian (cf. Dan 6:28; 10:1), who conquered Babylon in 539 BCE; neither king is named in the OG. v. 2, Daniel is the companion (sumbiotēs) of the king and the most honoured of all his friends (cf. Dan 2:48); in the OG he is also described as a priest and son of Abal (Sabaan was father of Daniel according to Epiphanius, Adv. Haer. 55.3). The full introduction of Daniel suggests that the reader has not met him before and therefore that Bel and the Dragon were originally independent Daniel tales.

(3–42) Two Idol Tales Both stories have a similar structure of three parts in which a friendship is put to the test but emerges strengthened. The two tales are interwoven in as much as the second test (Daniel in the lions' den) relates to both idols (28) and only at the end of the chapter does the king confess Daniel's God.

vv. 3–22, Bel. vv. 3–7, friendship challenged. v. 3, the Babylonian god is introduced as an idol. Bel ('Lord'; short form of Baal) is Bel-Marduk, head of the Babylonian pantheon (cf. Isa 46:1; Jer 50:2; Let Jer 41). Enormous quantities are offered to Bel: twelve bushels (65.5 litres) of flour, forty (OG: 4) sheep, six measures of wine (OG: oil). vv. 4–5, the king worships Bel, but Daniel does not worship handmade idols (cf. Isa 46:6; *Sib. Or.* 3:606, 618) because he worships the living God (cf. Josh 3:10; Dan 6:26; OG: Lord God), the creator and ruler (cf. Gen 1:26) of heaven and earth (cf. Gen 1:1; Jer 10:11). vv. 6–7, the king claims rhetorically that Bel is a living god because he eats and drinks, but Daniel laughs impertinently (also 19) and states simply that the idol is a mere moulded statue (cf. Isa 44:14–17; Let Jer 4; Wis 13:10). vv. 8–18, the test. vv. 8–9, the test is set up and the sentence on those in the wrong agreed. For phrasing similar to Daniel's agreement cf. Luke 1:38. vv. 10–11, the enormous amount of food is consumed by seventy priests and their families. vv. 12–13, OG does not mention the pact again nor the hidden entrance. vv. 14–15, the king alone witnesses the laying of ashes by Daniel's servants. The temple doors are closed and sealed. vv. 16–18, in the morning, the king is assured that the seals are unbroken. When the temple doors are open he sees the empty table and exclaims that Bel is great (cf. 41). vv. 19–22, the temporary outcome. vv. 19–20, Daniel dares to laugh at the king's credulity and points out the footprints in the ashes. vv. 21–2, enraged, the king arrests the priests and their families for eating the food and executes them (OG: hands them over to Daniel). The king does not himself declare Bel a fraud or make a confession of the greatness of Daniel's God, but hands Bel over to Daniel who according to the story destroys the idol and its temple (OG: the king destroys Bel). Herodotus (1:183) has Xerxes I (486–465 BCE) destroy the temple and statue.

vv. 23–42, the dragon. The Greek *drakōn* most probably refers to a serpent. The story of the dragon repeats the motifs of its previous companion tale. vv. 23–30, friendship challenged. vv. 23–4, the king challenges Daniel to recognize the dragon as a living god, for surely it is alive. No Babylonian cult of a live serpent is known from written sources, though there is some iconographic evidence; serpents play various cultic roles elsewhere (cf. Num 21:9; 2 Kings 18:4; cf. Kneph in Egypt; Asclepius in Greece). vv. 25–6, Daniel responds with a confession that the Lord his God is the living God, and with a request that he may be permitted to kill the dragon. The king grants the request. v. 27, Daniel bakes a cake of pitch, fat, and hair to feed to the dragon and explodes the idea of the dragon's divinity. The similarity to the opening up of Tiamat by Marduk is often noted, but no other motifs of that myth have influenced the story (Collins 1993: 414). *Gen. Rab.* 68 has the cake made realistically lethal by lacing it full of nails which perforate the dragon's intestines. vv. 28–30, the Babylonians are

enraged and taunt the king with becoming a Jew (cf. 2 Macc 9:17). They demand Daniel. The king weakly yields to their demands. vv. 31–9, the test. vv. 31–2, with mob rule Daniel is thrown into the lions' den. This is the second time such a fate has befallen him (cf. Dan 6:16–24), where seven lions, fed on a daily ration of two humans and two sheep, are now given nothing so that they might devour Daniel. The punishment, being destroyed by an animal, fits the crime (Koch 1987: 2.195). OG notes that this means that Daniel would not even have a burial place (cf. Tob 1:17). vv. 33–9, Habakkuk is transported by his hair (cf. Ezek 8:3) from Judea with a stew he had just made (cf. Gen 25:29). It has been suggested that Habakkuk is linked to the meal through the Akkadian *hambakuku*, a plant used in soups (Delcor 1971: 288). The *Lives of the Prophets* 12:5–8 knows of his story. The angel transports Habakkuk 'with the swiftness of the wind' which *Gen. Rab.* represents as 'power of his holy spirit' (cf. 1 Kings 18:12; 2 Kings 2:16). Daniel thanks God for remembering him and eats the meal. Habakkuk is returned to Judea. The whole incident is possibly a narrative interpretation of Ps 91:11–13 (Nickelsburg 1984: 40). vv. 40–2, the final outcome. v. 40, on the seventh day the king comes to mourn Daniel but finds him alive. v. 41, the king confesses Daniel's God: 'You are great' (cf. Ps 86:10; Jdt 16:13; 4Q365 6 ii 3), 'there is no other besides you' (cf. Isa 45:18; 46:9). v. 42, those who had thought themselves far from mealy-mouthed are thrown into the den and instantly eaten by seven very hungry lions.

REFERENCES

Baumgartner, W. (1926), 'Susanna—Die Geschichte einer Legende', *ARW* 24: 259–80.

——(1929) 'Der Wiese Knabe und die des Ehebruchs beschuldigte Frau', *ARW* 27: 187–8.

Bennett, W. H. (1913), 'The Prayer of Azariah and the Song of the Three Children', *APOT* i. 625–46.

Brooke, G. J. (1992), 'Susanna and Paradise Regained', in G.J. Brooke (ed.), *Women in the Biblical Tradition*, Studies in Women and Religion, 31 (Lewiston, NY: Edwin Mellen), 92–111.

Brüll, N. (1877), 'Das apokryphische Susanna Buch', *JJGL* 3: 1–69.

Christie, E. B. (1928), 'The Strophic Arrangement of the Benedicite', *JBL* 47: 188–93.

Collins, J. J. (1993), *Daniel*, Hermeneia (Minneapolis: Fortress).

Delcor, M. (1971), *Le Livre de Daniel*, SB (Paris: J. Gabalda).

Eissfeldt, O. (1965), *The Old Testament: An Introduction* (Oxford: Blackwell).

Engel, H. (1985), *Die Susanna-Erzählung: Einleitung, Übersetzung und Kommentar zum Septuaginta-Text und zur Theodotion-Bearbeitung*, OBO 61 (Göttingen: Vandenhoeck & Ruprecht).

Gaster, M. (1895; 1896), 'The Unknown Aramaic Original of Theodotion's Additions to the Book of Daniel', *PSBA* 16: 280–90, 312–17; 17: 75–94.

Geissen, A. (1968), *Der Septuaginta-Text des Buches Daniel: Kap. 5–12, Zusammen mit Susanna, Bel et Draco, sowie Esther Kap. 1, 1a–2, 15, nach dem Kölner Teil des Papyrus 967*, Papyrologische Texte und Abhandlungen, 5 (Bonn: Habelt).

Glancy, J. A. (1995), 'The Accused: Susanna and her Readers', in A. Brenner (ed.), *A Feminist Companion to Esther, Judith and Susanna*, FCB 7 (Sheffield: Sheffield Academic Press), 288–302.

Hammer, R. J. (1972), 'The Apocryphal Additions to Daniel', *The Shorter Books of the Apocrypha*, CBC (Cambridge: Cambridge University Press), 210–41.

Hartman, L. F., and Di Lella, A. A. (1989), 'Daniel', *NJBC*, 406–20.

Kay, D. M., (1913), 'Susanna', *APOT* i. 647–51.

Koch, K. (1987), *Deuterokanonische Zusätze zum Danielbuch: Entstehung und Textgeschichte*, AOAT 38/1–2 (Neukirchen-Vluyn: Neukirchener Verlag).

Kuhl, C. (1940), *Die drei Männer im Feuer*, BZAW 55 (Giessen: Töpelmann).

LaCoque, A. (1990), *The Feminine Unconventional: Four Subversive Figures in Israel's Tradition*, OBT (Minneapolis: Fortress).

Levine, A.-J. (1995), ' "Hemmed in on Every Side": Jews and Women in the Book of Susanna', in A. Brenner (ed.), *A Feminist Companion to Esther, Judith and Susanna*, FCB 7 (Sheffield: Sheffield Academic Press), 303–23.

Milik, J. T. (1981), 'Daniel et Susanne à Qumrân', in J. Doré, P. Grelot, and M. Carrez (eds.), *De la Tôrah au Messie: Mélanges Henri Cazelles* (Paris: Desclée), 337–59.

Moore, C. A. (1977), *Daniel, Esther and Jeremiah: The Additions*, AB 44 (Garden City, NY: Doubleday).

—— (1992), 'Daniel, Additions to', *ABD* ii. 18–28.

Nickelsburg, G. W. E. (1981), *Jewish Literature Between the Bible and the Mishnah* (Philadelphia: Fortress).

—— (1984), 'Stories of Biblical and Early Post-Biblical Times', and 'The Bible Rewritten and Expanded', in M. E. Stone (ed.), *Jewish Writings of the Second Temple Period*, CRINT 2/2 (Assen: van Gorcum), 33–87, 89–156.

Pearce, S. J. K. (1996), 'Echoes of Eden in the Old Greek of Susanna', *Feminist Theology*, 11: 11–31.

Pervo, R. I. (1991), 'Aseneth and Her Sisters: Women in Jewish Narrative and in the Greek Novels', in A.-J. Levine (ed.), '*Women Like This': New Perspectives on Jewish Women in the Greco-Roman World*, SBLEJL, 1 (Atlanta: Scholars Press), 145–60.

Schmitt, A. (1966), *Stammt der sogenannte "θ"-Text bei Daniel wirklich von Theodotion?*, MSU 9 (Göttingen: Vandenhoeck & Ruprecht).

Schürer, E. (1987), *The History of the Jewish People in the Age of Jesus Christ*, iii. pt. 2, rev. and ed. G. Vermes, F. Millar, and M. Goodman (Edinburgh: T. & T. Clark), 722–30.

Steussy, M. J. (1993), *Gardens in Babylon: Narrative and Faith in the Greek Legends of Daniel*, SBLDS 141 (Atlanta: Scholars Press).

Wills, L. M. (1990), *The Jew in the Court of the Foreign King: Ancient Jewish Court Legends*, HDR 26 (Minneapolis: Fortress).

Ziegler, J. (1954), *Susanna, Daniel, Bel et Draco*, Septuaginta Vetus Testamentum Graecum, 16/2 (Göttingen: Vandenhoeck & Ruprecht).

47. 1 Maccabees

U. RAPPAPORT

INTRODUCTION

A. Text and Language.
The textual tradition of 1 Maccabees is in general similar to that of the other books included in the Septuagint. 1 Maccabees is also known in other versions of the Holy Scriptures, such as the Syriac and Latin, which derive from the Greek version, which itself is a translation of a lost Hebrew original. This is evident from its style, which reveals Hebrew idiom (cf. *ABD* iv. 439–40). The original was probably known up to the 3rd and 4th centuries CE, but has not survived even in fragmentary form.

B. Author, Date, and Title.
1. The author of 1 Maccabees is anonymous, and whatever may be surmised about him comes from the book itself. He seems to be attached to the Hasmonean dynasty, both ideologically and personally, and to have some connection with the ruling circles.

2. Most scholars date 1 Maccabees to around 100 BCE. The principal disagreement is whether it was written in the last years of John Hyrcanus or in the days of Alexander Jannaeus. According to Momigliano (1976) and S. Schwartz (1991), 1 Maccabees was written in the beginning of Hyrcanus' rule, before 129 BCE, but it seems to me that the evidence is somewhat too narrow and that the last years of Hyrcanus' rule fit better (and see 16:23–4).

3. 1 Maccabees is named thus according to the Septuagint's textual tradition; obviously it has nothing to do with the original title, which some scholars think can be reconstructed from a reference in Eusebius, *Hist. Eccl.* 6. 25. 1–2, which goes back to Origen (first half of the 3rd cent. CE). There it is cited under the Hebrew name of the book as *Sarbethsabanaiel*. Among the acute proposals to decipher it we will cite the following: 'Book (*sēper*) of the house of the ruler (*śar*) of the sons of God'; 'Book of the dynasty (*bêt*) of God's resisters', where God's resisters should mean 'resisters on behalf of God's cause' (Goldstein, 1975; 1976: 15–17).

C. The Author's Views.
1. Jews and non-Jews: the author takes for granted a sharp dichotomy between Jew and Gentile. This may be rooted in a traditional view, similar to the ideology expressed in the books of Ezra and Nehemiah (5th cent. BCE), but strengthened by the religious persecution under Antiochus IV and the Maccabean revolt. However, though stressing repeatedly the hatred of the nations round about, he is proud of the success of the Jews in forging friendly relations and alliances and in being honoured by various nations and rulers. The incongruency in this attitude towards the non-Jewish world is typical of Hasmonean politics in general—a mixture of national separation (related to religious abhorrence of paganism) with a pragmatic approach to politics.

2. God and the Jews: as in biblical historiography, the author postulates that God directs history according to his will. Yet, though history is directed by God, he does not intervene directly in human affairs, in contrast to some instances in the Bible (cf. e.g. Josh 10:11–14; 2 Kings 19:35) and 2 Maccabees, where miracles abound.

God's intervention is through human beings, in whom he instils courage or cowardice, wisdom or arrogance and stupidity. Success and failure are manifestations of God's will and plan, but this does not efface the human values of courage, devotion, wisdom, cunning, etc. It is similar to some elements of the 'fourth philosophy' described by Josephus, which postulated that God helps those who take action themselves (*Ant.* 18 § 5). Some scholars see these and other views, such as the absence of reference to an afterlife (cf. 9:7–10), as Sadducean. The present writer refrains from such a label, on the grounds that our knowledge of Sadduceanism is extremely poor and because it is not necessary to assume that the expression of every idea should be defined on sectarian lines.

3. The role of Mattathias's family: the author's political views may justify his description as a court historian. His book serves Hasmonean propaganda well, especially for

John Hyrcanus. He attributes to Mattathias's family a divine role to deliver Israel (5:62), thus giving legitimacy to the Hasmonean dynasty in face of the traditional right both of the house of David to kingship and of the house of Zadok to the high-priesthood. In addition to this general message in favour of the house of Mattathias, there is a clear preference for Simon, the father of Hyrcanus and founder of the dynasty, among the sons of Mattathias. To him the author allocates the first and major role in Mattathias's testament. (2:49–64), where it is said that 'he [Simeon] shall be your father' (v. 65).

D. Historiography. 1. Style and Composition: 1 Maccabees is composed in a style and with a vocabulary similar to biblical historiography. It has compositional biblical elements such as poetic passages (including some prayers) interwoven with the narrative, a testament (2:49–70), documents (more than are usually found in the Bible, but see the documents in Ezra and the unhistorical correspondence of Hiram and Solomon, in 1 Kings 5:17–23), and speeches. The Bible is behind many passages in 1 Maccabees, either as explicit citations (e.g. 7:16–17), or implicitly (e.g. 5:48), or as historical exemplary precedents (e.g. 2:49–64). See Dimant (1988). In addition 1 Maccabees adopts biblical geographic and ethnic vocabulary, though most of it is anachronistic. The adoption of names such as Moab, Ammon, Philistines, Canaan, or sentences reminiscent of Joshua's conquest of Canaan, are used not only as literary conventions, but also serve an ideology that compares or assimilates Judas's wars to those of yore. The attachment of 1 Maccabees to the biblical heritage is expressed also by the citation of biblical exempla and precedents, which abound (e.g. 2:51–60). The author's views about God's interventions with humans is also similar to that of biblical historiography (see 1 MACC C.2). Though rooted in this tradition, 1 Maccabees is also a creation of its author's time. His treatment of non-Jewish history is much more ample than in the Bible, although he is Judeocentric as well. In this respect he resembles more the apocalyptic attitude of Daniel than that of the rest of biblical historiography, though the two books belong to completely different genres.

2. The author of 1 Maccabees utilized various sources in his book.

(1) Documents: the documentation in 1 Maccabees begins with the treaty between Rome and Judea, and goes on well into Simon's days. The documents from an earlier period cited in 2 Macc 11 apparently came from another source, probably unknown to the author of 1 Maccabees. It is probable that 1 Maccabees' documentary source was a Hasmonean archive in which the earliest document was the Roman–Judean treaty. This archive may be identical to that of the temple, which from the time of Jonathan's appointment as high priest was under Hasmonean administration, and may have been kept in the temple's treasury (14:4–9).

(2) Oral information: living close to Hasmonean circles— probably a member of court—a generation or less after the most recent events reported in his book, the author of 1 Maccabees was able to collect information from participants or eyewitnesses of various events, and to integrate it into his composition. Some of the oral testimonies could be also hearsay about previous events kept by leading families.

(3) Written sources: from where the author got his knowledge, especially about Seleucid history, is hard to tell. Was it oral information from informants at home in Hellenistic history (such as the Hasmonean diplomats)? Or had he at his disposal a written survey, in either Hebrew or Greek? We cannot tell. Yet, like his contemporaries the author(s) of Dan 7–12, he was interested enough in non-Jewish history to obtain the information he shared with his readers. Some of it is almost common knowledge (1:1–9), and some more specific (Trypho's rise to power; Demetrius II's fall into captivity, etc.).

(4) Parallel sources: for most of the period this book covers, it is the sole extant source. Josephus (*Ant.* 12 § 241–13 § 214) depends almost solely on it, up to 1 Macc 13:42. The main source to corroborate that part of the narrative covering Judas's revolt from its beginning to his last victory over Nicanor (approx. 165 to Adar 162 BCE) is 2 Maccabees. Apart from this we have only a little information about Judea at this time from pagan sources (see Stern, 1974–1984; Diodorus, no. 63 (34–35. 1.3–4); Timagenes, no. 80; Pompeius Trogus, via Justinus, no. 137 (Justinus, 36. 3.8); Tacitus, no. 281 (*Historiae*, 5.8. 2–3), and scanty Talmudic references (see 1 MACC 7:5).

(5) Chronology: the dates given in 1 Maccabees, mostly according to the Seleucid era, raise certain problems because of the difficulty of fitting them all into one system, since the Seleucid calendar did not begin on the same date throughout the Empire (Bickerman, 1968: 71). There is no consensus about the system(s) used in 1 Maccabees, or about the use of any system in a consistent way. For a review of the problem and earlier literature on it, see Grabbe (1991).

(6) Creative writing: current and earlier *Quellenforschung*, though vital for any historiographical enquiry, can divert attention from the writers and historians themselves. 1 Maccabees is a work by a talented historian who composed a historical narrative out of various ingredients, not all of which we can identify. His narrative is coherent, sometimes chronological, sometimes thematic (cf. ch. 5, on wars with the neighbouring peoples). It is supported by documents (most of them authentic) and highlighted by the author's interventions or passages woven into his narrative. Some of them are poetic passages, either written by him or based on suitable sources. His history is human, in the sense that it is activated by human actions, virtues or vices, wise or unwise, and God's share in it is either a *post factum* conclusion of what has already happened, or is shown by the motivation of the actors on the scene.

The author's talents served a political cause, as explained above (1 MACC C.3). Needless to say it diminishes the veracity of his narrative, along with his other apologetic aims and his Judeocentric attitude. Nevertheless he succeeded in producing a historical narrative of high quality, although because the original language was lost, it can only partially be appreciated by us.

E. Outline. 1 Maccabees opens with Alexander the Great (356– 323 BCE) and concludes with the murder of Simon (134 BCE). The first *c.*150 years are dealt with in only nine verses (1:1–9), so that the major parts are:

Introduction: From Alexander to the Revolt (1:1–64)
  Acts of Antiochus IV (1:10–64)
The Revolt Under Mattathias (2:1–70)

On the various proposed divisions of 1 Macc see Martola (1984) and Williams (1999).

COMMENTARY

Introduction: From Alexander to the Revolt (1:1–64)

(1:1–10) 1 Maccabees opens with a short introductory passage about Alexander the Great, whose exploits are concisely and negatively described (vv. 1–4). The author's conception of history is very similar here to Dan 11:2–4. Both saw Alexander's conquest of the East as the inception of a new destructive era in the history of mankind, which culminates in the religious persecution of the Jewish cult. This approach depicts the Hellenistic regime in general as an ungodly phenomenon, and is in line with, and probably influenced by, the general Eastern (Egyptian, Babylonian, Iranian, and Indian) anti-Hellenic world-view (Rappaport 1993). v. 1, 'Kittim,' a generic word for peoples who arrived from the west. It derived from the name of the city Kition in Cyprus. Here it designates Greece. 'Darius' is Darius III, the last Achaemenid king of Persia (336–331 BCE) who was defeated by Alexander. vv. 2–3, on Alexander's conquests there is ample literature (See *ABD* i. 146–50). In general terms Alexander is the prototype of Antiochus IV (Dan 11:36–7 and see on v. 10). vv. 5–6, generally speaking this description is correct, though Alexander's empire was neither divided by him nor according to his will. Alexander did reign for about twelve years (336–323 BCE). vv. 8–9, the author is mainly interested in Antiochus IV, and refers to the intermediate period (323–175 BCE) in an extremely concise way. Nevertheless, he stresses that Alexander's successors 'caused many evils on the earth'. That is, the chain of wickedness is continuous from Alexander to Antiochus IV. v. 10, Antiochus IV is linked here directly with Alexander, though there was no blood relationship between them. This linkage is expressed also in Daniel's visions of the horns (esp. 7:7–8; but also 8:8–9). This conception of Hellenistic history is eastern and based on anti-Hellenic, moralistic, religious, social, and cultural views of the changes that occurred in the Near East with the fall of the Persian empire. 'Hostage in Rome', Antiochus IV was sent by his father Antiochus III as a hostage to Rome after the Roman victory in the battle of Magnesia (190 BCE). He was replaced in 176 BCE by his nephew, Demetrius, and gained the kingship in 175 after his brother, Seleucus IV, was murdered.

The year 137, according to the Seleucid era, is approximately 175 BCE.

(1:11–15) The author does not tell us how the Hellenistic party in Judea came into being. He condenses it all around a 'manifesto' and certain acts ascribed to them. He also avoids mentioning any of their leaders by name. Almost all we know about the Hellenizers and their leaders comes from 2 Macc 3–5. v. 11, 'renegades', Greek *paranomoi*, lit. 'those who do not abide by the law (Torah)', a common designation in 1 Maccabees for the Hellenizers. It may also reflect such nouns as *pārîzîm*, which Dan 11:14 uses to describe them. 'Many' (Heb. *rabbîm*) does not signify the majority but an undefined big number.

'Let us go . . . upon us' sounds like their manifesto, strictly opposed to common Jewish self-perception. v. 13, 'went to the king', this was not a single act by the Hellenizers, but a repetitive one. We are told in 2 Macc 4:7 that Jason met with Antiochus IV soon after his accession and obtained from him the high priesthood and permission to establish a gymnasium and an ephebeion and to enrol the men of Jerusalem as Antiocheans (2 MACC 4:9). This permission is understood by many scholars as sanction for a Greek *polis*, called Antioch-in-Jerusalem (to distinguish it from other Antiochs). See Bickerman (1937), developed by Tcherikover (1959: 161), and accepted by others (Hengel 1974; le Rider 1965: 409–11). v. 13, the concise narrative does not define in clear terms the constitutional changes that took place in Judea, but observation of the ordinances of the Gentiles gives an indication. v. 14, 'gymnasium', there is no doubt that the foundation of the *polis* Antioch-in-Jerusalem caused a most shocking intrusion into the traditional Jewish lifestyle. Especially abhorrent to Jewish sensitivities the performance naked of sporting activities that took place there. v. 15, as a result of exercising in the nude there came about the phenomenon of uncircumcision, which necessitates surgical intervention. This was an extreme act of repudiation of allegiance to Judaism, circumcision being considered the primary sign of being a Jew (Gen 17:11).

(1:16–19) Antiochus IV's invasion of Egypt is a famous event in Hellenistic history. Here it is merely a hinge on which the author suspends Antiochus' invasion and plunder of the Jerusalem temple (vv. 20–8). For Antiochus' expeditions to Egypt see Rappaport (1980: 66–8 (Heb.)).

(1:20–8) It seems that Antiochus entered Jerusalem three times: the first time on an inspection tour, when he was received favourably by the populace and Jason (in 172 BCE, 2 Macc 4:22); the second time after his first invasion of Egypt (in 169 BCE); and the third time after his second invasion of Egypt, from where he was repulsed by a Roman delegation (in 168 BCE, see 2 Macc 5). The second visit to Jerusalem (169 BCE) after the first invasion of Egypt is the one described here; see Rappaport (1980). The absence of any mention of the Hellenized high priests Jason and Menelaus, who play a prominent role throughout the account in 2 Maccabees, should be noticed. This is intentional, as a kind of *damnatio memoriae*, to erase the names of the wicked from Jewish memory. v. 21, the entrance of Antiochus IV into the temple was a breach of Jewish law, since Gentiles were not allowed inside. Cf. 3 Macc 1:10–2:24, and 2 Macc 3. vv. 21–3, Antiochus stripped the temple of its more sacred and valuable objects, mainly those of gold and silver. It was known, as were many other temples, for its riches gathered from obligatory taxes, donations, official contributions, and private deposits. 'Hidden treasures', in addition to the various expensive vessels, there were in the temple other deposits kept in secret places for security. These were either discovered, or divulged by priestly treasurers co-operating with Menelaus' party. The author does not give any reason for this confiscation. It may have had the co-operation of the Hellenized high priest Menelaus, who was perhaps in arrears in paying his tributes, or it may have been caused by the avarice of the king. The common explanation that Antiochus was short of money because of the huge indemnities (12,000 talents) his kingdom still had to pay to Rome is not valid, since this debt was already paid. See le Rider (1993: 49–67). vv. 24–8 are the first poetic passage, but such passages abound in 1 Maccabees. This literary device is not rare in biblical historiography. Naturally it was intended to bear to the reader a certain message.

(1:29–40) This passage deals with measures taken by the Seleucid government to crush Jewish opposition to Menelaus' regime, prior to the religious persecutions. 2 Macc 5 supplies more details for the period of approximately two years that elapsed between Antiochus' second visit to Jerusalem (169 BCE) and the religious persecution (167 BCE). These include another visit of the king to Jerusalem (a third one, see above) and the appointment of Philip the Phrygian (2 Macc 5:22) as governor of Jerusalem. v. 29, 'collector of tribute' may reflect a Hebrew phrase in the original lost version of 1 Maccabees: *sar hammissîm*, may have been wrongly translated into Greek as *archōn phorologias* (officer for tribute collection) rather than 'officer of the Mysians', i.e. of soldiers or mercenaries from Mysia, a region in Asia Minor. The name of this officer is given in 2 Macc 5:24, Apollonius. For the rate of taxes in Judea see 1 Macc 10:29–30. v. 30: the fact that the Seleucid officer entered Jerusalem 'deceitfully' is one of the arguments for the supposition that the city was in the hands of a pre-Maccabean opposition to Menelaus. 2 Macc. 5:25 specifies that Apollonius took advantage of the sabbath to enter the city. See Tcherikover (1959: 188–9). vv. 31–2, Apollonius' behaviour in Jerusalem strengthens the impression that he took the city from the rebels' hands, not from Menelaus and his supporters. These rebels are not mentioned here probably because the pre-Maccabean period is in general abridged by the author, and he endeavours to concentrate on the Maccabean family, and avoid any distraction which might put them off-centre.

v. 33, 'citadel', two questions concern the building of the citadel (*akra*) in Jerusalem: what was its function, and where exactly was it located? In addition to its function in suppressing the Jewish opposition to the regime, it seems that it was (or became) a stronghold for the Hellenizers. Its location depends on the location of the 'city of David' (as understood in the Second Temple period) and on various archaeological–topographical considerations. See Bar-Kochva (1989: 445–65). v. 34, 'renegades' may signify the Hellenizers, in addition to the Seleucid military force. v. 35: see 1 MACC 9:52 about storage of food in fortresses for the purpose of subduing the population. vv. 36–40, in this poetic passage, we learn about the flight of residents from Jerusalem (v. 38), on which cf. 2 MACC 5:27 and 2:1.

(1:41–53) The religious persecution ordered by Antiochus IV is an unprecedented historical event. The main difficulty in explaining the king's policy is that polytheists were generally tolerant in religious matters, and we have no real analogy elsewhere to the events in Judea. Moreover, what we encoun-

ter in Judea is not only the prohibition of a certain cult, but a violent compulsion to transgress its religious laws. There is no consensus at present on an explanation of this problem, yet two suggestions which may contribute to our understanding of it have been proposed. One is that the initiative for the persecution came from Menelaus' circle, either as an ideological repressive act (Bickerman, 1937; 1979) or otherwise. The second is that a revolt in Judea, led presumably by religious leaders, preceded the persecution, which was aimed to subdue it (Tcherikover 1959: 197). For more expanded discussion and bibliography see *ABD* iv. 437–9. vv. 41–3, no such ordinance by Antiochus IV is preserved, and no evidence of interference in religious matters is known elsewhere in the Seleucid empire. 'All the Gentiles' is didactic, and in line with the message of the book, see 1 MACC 2: 19–22. According to Hellenistic royal procedures an order by Antiochus IV must have been issued, though it is not preserved. Otherwise Antiochus III's letter (*Ant.* 12 §§ 138–44), which confirmed the ancestral laws of Judea, would be binding. To invalidate it, there must have been some enactment by Antiochus IV, the contents of which may be reflected in the following verses. vv. 44–50, the compulsion that the Jews must transgress their customs, not merely refrain from the observance of them, has no precedents. vv. 51–3, cf. Esth 1:22; 3:13; 8:11; 9:21, 31.

(1:54–61) The 'fifteenth day of Chislev', that is ten days before the profanation of the altar (v. 59). 'A desolating sacrilege' (Gk. *bdelygma hermōseōs*), evidently represents *siqqûs mĕsômēm* in the lost Hebrew original version (cf. Dan 11:31) but what it was materially is unclear: a pagan altar placed on the temple's altar (cf. v. 59); an effigy of Zeus or of the king; or a sacred stone (*bêt-ʾēl*; Phoenician, *bettilu*). See Bickerman (1979: ch. 4); Rowley (1953); Hengel (1974: 294–5); Millar, (1993: 12–15) (who doubts Bickerman's supposition). vv. 56–7, books of the law, i.e. Torah scrolls. It seems to be the first known historical occurrence of the burning of books. It also shows the centrality of the Torah in Jewish religion, which was well understood by the persecutors. v. 59, 'twenty-fifth day', of the month of Chislev. Some commentators suggest that it was a special day (Abel 1949; Dancy 1954 suggest the birthday of Antiochus), but this view has no basis here or in 2 Macc 6:7, nor elsewhere. vv. 60–1, this horrible event was chosen by the author as an example of the cruelty of the persecutors. It is mentioned also in 2 Macc 6:10, where other events, probably not all of them historical, are told (cf. 2 Macc 6–7).

(1:62–4) v. 62, as many were misled by the Hellenizers (1 MACC 1:10), so many stood firm in Jewish tradition (cf. Dan 11:33–4). A decisive question in the confrontation within Jewish society was which side would be more persuasive and turn the many into a majority. v. 63, this is the first time that a case of martyrdom is mentioned in 1 Maccabees but see another at 2:29–38. Dan 11:33–4; 12:2–3 and 2 Macc (esp. ch. 7) are even more concerned with this theme. The Jewish martyrs, especially the 'Maccabean' martyrs of 2 Macc 7 became models of martyrdom for Christianity (Doran 1980; Bickerman 1951: 63–84).

The Revolt under Mattathias (2:1–70)

(2:1–14) When the religious persecutions became extremely severe, Mattathias and his family appeared on the stage.

The dynastic inclination of 1 Maccabees is clear. It whole-heartedly supports the Hasmoneans, and especially Simon's branch. Former rebels are not mentioned and martyrs are appreciated (1:63), but their example was not followed up (below). 'Joarib', the first priestly division among the twenty-four divisions of priests (see 1 Chr 24:7). 'Jerusalem', 'Modein', it seems that the opulent family of Mattathias was well-established both in Jerusalem and in Modein, where their landed property was. (For doubt about their relation to Jerusalem see Goldstein (1976).) Modein was a village in the region of Lydda, which belonged to the eparchy of Samaria (see 1 MACC 10:30). vv. 2–5, we do not have an explanation for the nicknames of Mattathias's sons. For Judas's nickname, Maccabeus, several proposals have been made, such as that its origin was the Hebrew word *makkebet* (hammer), but though attractive, this view is baseless. vv. 6–14, a lament in poetic form on the dreadful lot of the holy city.

(2:15–18) The decrees of Antiochus are about to be forced on the inhabitants of Modein, beyond the frontier of Judea, at the outskirts of the territories populated by Jews. The persecution is executed by the Seleucid government, through its military forces. Co-operation from the local population, either voluntary or compulsory, is expected. The government encountered the first active opposition to its policy in Modein from Mattathias and his sons. vv. 17–18, the speech of the king's officers is evidently a rhetorical piece which stresses the obedience of all others (Jews and Gentiles) to the king's decrees.

(2:19–28) vv. 19–22, Mattathias's speech is totally opposed to the king's men's speech. Its central point is unconditional faith in God. vv. 23–6, Mattathias's speech could have been terminated by a martyrological conclusion, but at this point the parting of the ways between martyrdom and zealotry comes out clearly. Mattathias prevents by force the breach of the Torah, being ready not only to die but to kill for it. At this moment the Maccabean revolt breaks out. v. 26, 'Phinehas', the priest who acted bravely and decisively when the people of Israel sinned in the plain of Moab (Num 25:8–13) was the model of zealotry. vv. 27–8, the first step of the rebels was to leave the populated area and find shelter in the wilderness. Commentators have assumed that it was in the Judean desert that Mattathias and his followers sought refuge (as with Jonathan and Simon after Judas's death (1 MACC 9:33). Recently it has been suggested that at this stage of the revolt the Maccabees' base was in the desert of Samaria, not far from the thickly populated Jewish area of southern Samaria (see J. Schwartz and Spanier 1991).

(2:29–41) Mattathias's position was taken up against those who co-operated with the persecutors or acquiesced to them. Here the case of martyrdom is dealt with, and though the author's attitude is sympathetic to the martyrs, martyrdom is shown to be no alternative to Mattathias's zealotry. v. 29, the ideological affiliation of those who went to the desert is unknown. Proposals identifying them with the Hasideans, with the Essenes (proto-Essenes), or with the *maskilim* of Daniel, though possible, cannot be substantiated. 'Wilderness', see J. Schwartz and Spanier (1991). v. 32, 'sabbath', that Jews refrained from fighting on the sabbath was known to pagans and sometimes ridiculed by them (see Josephus, *Ant.* 12 § 6; *CA* i. 209–10), as well as used by them to their advantage (the

above reference; 2 Macc 5:25). v. 37, 'heaven and earth testify for us', note that the meaning of the Greek for 'martyr' is 'witness'. No mention is made of afterlife, which is an important motif in 2 Maccabees. vv. 39–40, Mattathias and his supporters are sympathetic to those who died in the caves, but disagree with their ideology. They fear for their own lives and are not expecting an eschatological deliverance or resurrection of the dead (cf. Dan 12: 2–3). This signifies a major difference between the Hasmoneans and various contemporary nascent Jewish sects. v. 41, the decision by Mattathias's party, to take arms and fight even on the sabbath, raised voluminous discussion. On what authority was this decision based? What was the preceding situation? How could Jewish mercenaries (and there were many) serve in imperial armies if they did not fight on the sabbath? Was this an *ad hoc* decision or a permanent and valid legal one? How did it fit with Jewish law and especially with more recent *hălākâ*? See Bar-Kochva (1989: 474–93); Goodman and Holladay (1986: esp. 165–71); Johns (1963).

(2:42–8) The first military act on the part of Mattathias was in Modein (2:1). A second stage in the revolt was when it spread over Judaea (but outside Jerusalem). v. 42, we learn about a growth in the number of Mattathias's supporters. An organized group joined him—the Hasideans (lit. 'the pious'). Scholars differ about their identity. Are they related to those who died in the caves, having changed their attitude to the revolt as a consequence of this horrible event? Or do they belong to the *maskilim* in Daniel, who decided to appeal to arms at the call of Mattathias? Or are they a sect of their own, and if so, when did they come into being? How are they related to the later sects—Pharisees, Sadducees, and Essenes/Qumranites? See Davies (1977). D. R. Schwartz (1994: 7–18) prefers a variant reading of this phrase, 'a company of Jews' instead of 'a company of Hasideans', which is the current reading. See also 1 MACC 7:12–18. 'Mighty warriors' fits both readings: if we take it with Hasideans, it fits the conception of 'sect' (not a very suitable term in any case) or 'order' with some military flavour (cf. some Dead Sea scrolls, esp. *War Scroll*); if with Jews, it signifies the military prowess of those who joined Mattathias. v. 43, 'fugitives', those who lost their property and domicile, and were an important source of recruitment for the rebels. Cf. *J.W.* 2. 588. v. 46, 'circumcised all the uncircumcised', the intention, in line with the destruction of altars (v. 45) is to undo what was done by the persecutors; 'forcibly', might mean against the orders of the Seleucid government, or, in the case of Hellenized families, without their consent. The first explanation is preferable.

(2:49–70) The following testament of Mattathias in poetic rhyme brings to mind Jacob's blessing of his sons in Gen 49. It exposes the author's views and his attitude towards the ruling Hasmonean family, and the ideology and atmosphere at the royal court. vv. 51–60, this section is a series of illustrious examples from biblical history relevant to the actual situation and recommended by Mattathias to his sons. Phinehas, a model of zealotry, is given a special highlight ('our ancestor [father]'; and see v. 26 above); David's inheritance of kingship is interpreted by commentators as either an indication that the book was written before Hyrcanus I's sons put the crown on their heads (i.e. not after 103–104 BCE), or as a criticism of Hasmonean royalty. With Elijah the word 'zeal' (or its derivatives) is repeated again, and the last are the 'saved martyrs' whose acts are told in the contemporary book of Daniel. See Dimant (1988: 394–5). v. 65, 'Simeon . . . he shall be your father', this is explicit propaganda for the Hasmonean dynasty, which indeed was founded by Simeon. To strengthen its legitimacy it is related here to the testament of Mattathias, the ancestor of all the family. v. 66, Judas's military talent and task is stressed here, but in line with the message of v. 65. Though Judas was the leader of the revolt till he fell on the battlefield (165–160 BCE), he is ranked here as second to Simeon. His appointment as leader of the revolt was surely because of his military talent and/or experience, about which we know nothing. v. 70, 146 ES is 166 BCE; 'tomb of his ancestors at Modein' demonstrates clearly that the Hasmonean family had its roots in Modein, though it does not mean that they could not also have been involved in the political life in Jerusalem (see on v. 1).

The First Battles of Judas Maccabaeus (3:1–4:35)

(3:1–9) The acts of Judas begin with a poetic encomium (vv. 3–9) about Judas, the great hero of the revolt. v. 2, the author stresses here, and elsewhere, the unamimity of all the brothers. It may have been a message for his own time. vv. 3–9, the encomium precedes the acts of Judas. Cf. the encomium for Simon (14:4–15) which precedes his appointment by the 'great assembly'. Both serve as a poetic introduction to what follows.

(3:10–12) This is the first military encounter of Judas that we are told about. Formerly, under Mattathias's command, the rebels made surprise attacks on civilian settlements (2:45–8 above). And cf. 2 Macc 8:6–7. v. 10, 'Apollonius', unknown otherwise, but evidently a commander, probably the governor (*stratēgos* according to Josephus, *Ant.* 8 § 287) of Samaria, an important city in the centre of Mt. Ephraim, formerly the capital of Israel (the northern kingdom) and of the Assyrian and Persian province of Samaria. A military settlement was founded there in Alexander the Great's time, and the city served as a principal strategic base under the Ptolemies and the Seleucids (see Rappaport 1995a: 283–4). v. 11, 'killed him', killing the commander of the enemy obviously gave a great advantage to the opposing army. Judas endeavoured to achieve it, since it could compensate for his weaker army and demoralize the enemy (see also I MACC 7:43). v. 12, 'spoils', an important source of arms for the ill-equipped rebel army.

(3:13–26) The encounter with Seron is the second battle of Judas. The author of 2 Maccabees ignores the first two battles of Judas and relates his battles in detail only from the battle of Emmaus (below) onwards. This may indicate that the encounters with Apollonius and Seron were guerrilla clashes not full-fledged battles. v. 13, Seron is not known elsewhere. (See Bar-Kochva 1989: 133.) v. 14, 'I will make a name', a biblical idiom, which signifies Seron's arrogance and strengthens the effect of his defeat at the end. v. 16, 'Beth-horon', the slope of Beth-horon could have turned into a trap for armies invading Judea (the Romans suffered a severe defeat there in 66 CE. See Josephus, *J.W.* 2 §§ 546–50). vv. 17–22, according to 1 Maccabees the result of a battle is from God, and so the few can overcome the many. This idea is different from 2 Maccabees where God intervenes in human actions and changes the

course of events. In 1 Maccabees it is only through the courage of the Jewish fighters that God instils in their hearts, that he may tip the scales of battle. See also I MACC C.2. Actually it does not seem that the rebels were numerically inferior to the Seleucid forces which were sent against them. They also had professional military officers and soldiers in their ranks, though they were inferior in arms, at least in the initial stages of the revolt. This view was recently put forth by Bar-Kochva (1989). v. 24, 'land of the Philistines', a biblical name for the southern coastal plain of the land of Israel.

(3:27–31) Here we have a typical Judeocentric view of Seleucid history. Antiochus IV's plan to reconquer the Eastern satrapies is explained as an offshoot of Judas's victories. Nevertheless some objectively correct points are made, such as the lavishness of Antiochus, emphasized perhaps by the advance payment of a year's salary to the army.

(3:32–7) v. 32, Lysias was regent for Antiochus V, son of Antiochus IV, both in the latter's lifetime (165–164 BCE) and after his death, until Demetrius I conquered the kingdom (162 BCE). v. 33, 'his son Antiochus' was about 7 years old, according to Appian (11.46), or 11 according to Eusebius (*Chronica*, 1.253). Appian seems preferable on this point. See Houghton and le Rider (1985: 27 n. 30). v. 34, the division of the army into two halves is probable, as well as the giving of instructions to Lysias. v. 36, 'settle aliens' is reminiscent of Dan 11:39. The repressive measure of settling foreigners on land confiscated from the local population is well-known under Hellenistic rule. It is less clear whether it was implemented in Judea or mentioned only as a potential threat against the Jews. v. 37, 147 ES is 165 BCE; 'upper provinces' the Seleucid provinces east of the Euphrates.

(3:38–41) v. 38, the appointment of three commanders of the expedition against Judas is misleading. Ptolemy the son of Dorymenes was the governor of Coele-Syria and Phoenicia and supported an anti-Jewish policy (cf. 2 Macc 4:45; 6:8) but did not personally command the forces sent against Judas. According to 2 Macc 8:8–9, the one who called for military support was Philip, the governor of Jerusalem. Lysias is not mentioned there at all, and may be introduced by the author of I Maccabees to increase the importance of the battle. Nicanor was son of Patroclus, according to 2 Macc 8:9. Gorgias was the military expert of the two (see 2 Macc 8:9). v. 39, the numbers of military forces are in many cases exaggerated. The greater the difference between Seleucid and Jewish forces the greater was the victory of the Jews, or their defeat was better explained (see Bar-Kochva 1989: ch. 2). v. 40, Emmaus is a strategic location at one of the main entrances into the Judean mountains. v. 41, merchants accompanied armies, and naturally were eager to gain from slave trade. 'Forces from Syria', probably in the Hebrew original text it was Edom, which was read wrongly by the translator as Aram, the only difference in Hebrew being the letter *resh* instead of *daleth*, which are very similar in form. If so, we are informed here about additional local forces, presumably the militia of the Hellenistic towns of Idumea and the coastal plain.

(3:42–60) This relatively long passage deals with the preparations for battle on the Jewish side, in opposition to those in the Seleucid camp. It is probably in part historical, in part embellished. v. 46, 'Mizpah', for historical reminiscences cf. 1

Sam 7:5–7. Here we see the historical consciousness of the Jewish rebels (beside the historical-biblical awareness of the author), and the use of precedents for the moral preparation of the rebel army for battle. v. 47, the fasting in 1 Sam 7:6 is accompanied here by common mourning customs, mentioned often in the Bible and elsewhere (e.g. 1 Macc 2:14). v. 48, this consulting of the Torah replaces the older way of consulting God, either through a prophet, or a priest who possessed the Urim and Thummim. But at this time there were neither signs nor a prophet (cf. Ps 74:9). v. 49, these are acts which should have been performed in the temple had it not been desecrated, and may be understood as a performance in place of the usual ceremonies, in an attempt to convince the deity to respond to believers who manifest their inability to perform their religious duties properly. v. 54, 'trumpets' (*hă-ṣōṣĕrôt*), were used in warfare (see Num 10:9–10 and the *War Scroll* (1QM ii. 15–iii 11). v. 55, that there would be organization of the rebel army at this stage is very probable, since Judas is turned from guerrilla to more regular warfare and has to manœuvre greater forces; cf. 2 Macc 8:21–2. The division of an army into units of tens, fifties, etc. is common in the Bible. v. 56, Judas is following Gideon (Judg 7:3, according to Deut 20:5–9). vv. 58–60, this short speech of Judas, hardly historical, sums up well the main targets of the revolt and the belief in heavenly succour.

(4:1–5) vv. 1–2, Gorgias adopted new tactics, to avoid the failures of his predecessors, Apollonius and Seron. From a base on the outskirts of the Judean hills, he went with a select column to surprise his opponents, thus taking from them the initiative in choosing the time and place of battle. His audacious step was accompanied by 'intelligence' service, rendered to him by men from the Akra, who knew the Judean terrain. v. 3, Gorgias's audacity was forestalled by Judas. He quickly left his camp, which Gorgias was going to attack by surprise, and moved towards the Syrian base at Emmaus. vv. 4–5, the deserted Jewish camp misled Gorgias into thinking that the rebels fled in panic, and he turned to chase them in the hills. Josephus adds that Judas left unextinguished fires to strengthen this impression (*Ant.* 12 § 306). This information is probably a conjecture of Josephus, based on military tactical textbooks, which he knew well.

(4:6–11) v. 6, 'At daybreak', the appearance of Judas's army was a surprise, as it was thought to be fleeing before Gorgias's stormtroops; 'armour', the shortage of arms was endemic in the rebels' camp in the first stages of the revolt (see 3:12). The lack of arms also increases the impact of the ensuing victory. v. 7, the Seleucid army, like other Hellenistic armies, fortified their camps, even when in use for short periods. vv. 8–11, Judas's harangue before his men repeats the author's ideas about God's power in battle (see 1 MACC c.2).

(4:12–18) v. 13, 'trumpets', see 1 MACC 3:54. About Jamnia see 1 MACC 5:58. vv. 17–18, Judas disciplined his army, not an easy task with guerrilla fighters. Yet as only half of his military plan was achieved, it was necessary in order to achieve a final victory.

(4:19–25) Assuming the details are historical, we have here an illuminating case of the psychological defeat of the Syrian army. Arriving at their camp after a futile night chase after Judas and his men, they saw before them a burnt camp and the rebels drawn up for battle; thus they retreated, morale broken. v. 23, the details of the plunder are embellished, but, strangely, no arms are mentioned. v. 24, hymns, cf. Ps 106:1; 118:1; 136:1.

(4:26–9) The defeat at Emmaus finally brought home to the Syrian government the seriousness of the revolt in Judea. The royal army itself now became involved in the war. v. 28, the numbers here are obviously out of all proportion. At least half the royal Seleucid army went with Antiochus IV to the eastern front, and even from the rest Lysias was obliged to leave some behind. 'Next year', 164 BCE. v. 29, Beth-zur was a strategic point on the border between Judea and Idumea. It lost its importance when John Hyrcanus conquered Idumea.

(4:30–3) In this poetic passage, as elsewhere, the author invokes historical precedents in the prayer he puts in Judas's mouth. The examples cited here are David's victory over Goliath (1 Sam 1:17), and Jonathan's victory over the Philistines (1 Sam 14:1–16).

(4:34–5) The description of this battle is extremely schematic, untrustworthy, and hardly comprehensible. 2 Macc 11:1–16 is more detailed and embellished but also untrustworthy. The only conclusion that can be safely drawn is that Lysias's invasion of Judea was blocked. He probably did not persist in his efforts because of news of the death of Antiochus IV. According to 2 Macc 11:14, Lysias's withdrawal was accompanied by a truce.

The Rededication of the Temple (4:36–61)

(4:36–41) Soon after Lysias's retreat the rebels took over the temple (164 BCE). v. 37, Mount Zion is the Temple Mount. v. 38, 'desolate', this description refers mainly to the results of negligence. The profanation of the altar refers to what happened at the beginning of the religious persecution, not to any ongoing pagan performances at the altar; 'bushes sprung up', various scholars (esp. Bickerman 1979: 72) have interpreted this as a sign of some oriental syncretistic cult, to which a sacred grove was necessary. Yet it seems to indicate simply the negligence and deficient maintenance of the temple's court. v. 41, it is strange that military activity is mentioned only at this stage. It seems therefore that no fighting was involved when Judas took control of the temple.

(4:42–51) Here a detailed description is given about the replacement of the stuff of the temple and of the polluted objects in it. v. 44, 'altar of burnt-offering', the most sacred object in the temple. Dan 12:11 counts the duration of the persecution according to the number of days when there was no daily sacrifice. v. 46, 'until a prophet should come', cf. 1 MACC 3:48 and 14:41.

(4:52–9) A new festival was established which is not mentioned in the Bible (there was one other, Purim). It took some effort (see 2 Macc 1) before it was accepted by Jews everywhere. It was incorporated into the Jewish calendar by the rabbis, although in Talmudic sources it is related to divine miracles and the Hasmoneans are hardly mentioned. (On the attitude of the sages and Pharisees towards the Hasmoneans, see D. R. Schwartz 1992: 44–56.)

vv. 52–3, the renewal of the daily sacrifice at the end of 164 BCE (Chislev is December), three years after the desecration of the temple (v. 54), and half a year earlier than the $3\frac{1}{2}$ years envisaged in Dan 9:27. v. 54, 'songs', music had an important place in the worship at the temple (cf. 2 Chr 7:4). v. 56, 'eight days', the dedication of Solomon's temple was prolonged also for eight days (1 Kings 8:65; 2 Chr 7:9), as was Hezekiah's sanctification of the temple (2 Chr 29:17). In 2 Macc 10:6 the dedication of the temple is compared to Sukkot (Booths), which lasts eight days.

(4:60–1) Judas did not neglect military preparations. He fortified the temple against, probably, the forces in the Akra, but it served him well also when Lysias invaded Judea again. Beth-zur was fortified in view of local skirmishes and possible invasion by Lysias, who has already traversed the same route.

The Wars with the Surrounding Peoples (ch. 5)

(5:1–8) The chronology of Judas's war against the Gentile neighbours of Judea is not clear, because they are arranged thematically. vv. 1–2, 'Gentiles all around', meaning those who lived in the land of Israel. The language and attitude of the author are influenced by the biblical account of the conquest of Canaan by Joshua ben Nun. See Schwartz (1991: 16–38). The Gentiles becoming angry against the Jews because of their success cannot be a historical explanation, but it fits well with the author's idea that the Gentiles drew satisfaction from the desecration of the temple (see 4:45, 58). Now that the situation was reversed, they became frustrated and angry. As opposed to the other wars against the Gentiles, there is no mention here of Jews living among the Idumeans being attacked, and it seems that Judas was tackling marauders (see v. 4). v. 3, 'descendants of Esau', a biblical, anachronistic designation for the Idumeans. 'Akrabattene', despite textual difficulties, usually located in eastern Idumea, south-west of the Dead Sea. For a different location see Goldstein (1976: 294). v. 4, 'Baean', a nomadic tribe, probably located in Transjordan (cf. Num 32: 3), which took advantage of the insecurity of the region for marauding purposes. v. 6, 'crossed over', this shows that the events here are not arranged chronologically, as both the Baeans and the Ammonites were east of the river (i.e. Jordan). Timothy, probably a Seleucid official or commander, is mentioned also in v. 11. vv. 7–8, there is no mention of the Jews here either, though it is to be supposed that Judas came to their succour, both according to v. 2 and to the more detailed account below.

(5:9–13) Here the author returns to the theme of v. 1, the Jews being attacked by their neighbours. v. 9, Gilead is normally the area between the rivers Yarmuk and Arnon, in which Ammon is also included. The location of Dathema is unknown, but probably connected to the 'land of Tob' (see v. 13). It may be that this and other strongholds in which the Jews were seeking shelter were locations which they held as soldiers, or descendants of soldiers, who had served already under the Ptolemies. Cf. v. 13. vv. 10–13, the appeal for help of the Gileadite Jews is in the form of a letter. Though incomplete in its present form, there is nothing in the letter to render it unauthentic. It may be a fabrication, to dramatize the story, or an abridged letter (without the opening and concluding phrases), or a formulation of known events into epistolary form. Timothy is probably the same person who is mentioned above. If so it creates a link between the two

passages vv. 1–8 and vv. 10–13. 'land of Tob', probably the land of Tobiah, where the palace of Hyrcanus the Tobiad was, in Arak el-Emir. Some scholars locate it in the north of Transjordan, but see Gera (1990: esp. 27–9). There was there a military colony (Gk. *katoikia*), headed by the Tobiad family, and composed, at least in considerable part, of Jewish soldiers. The Tobiad family, or dynasty, is known at least from the time of Nehemiah See *ABD*, s.v., vi. 585.

(5:14–19) v. 14: note the dramatization of the story and see 1 Kings 1:42; Job 1:16–18. The attacks on the Jews in Gilead and Galilee seem to be simultaneous, as told here, otherwise there is no point in the division of the Jewish forces (v. 17). v. 15, 'Ptolemais and Tyre and Sidon', these three Phoenician cities were among the first oriental cities in the east to be Hellenized and to become *poleis*. They had territories (Gk. *chōra*) in Galilee, and may have been worried by the success of the Jewish revolt, and its possible repercussions on the local population in Galilee, mostly Semitic and partly Jewish. About Ptolemais see also 1 MACC 10:1, 39, 57, and 2 Macc 13:25–6. 'Galilee of the Gentiles', for this expression see Isa 8:23. In the present context it may simply be a repetition of the three cities mentioned before. See *ABD* ii. 879, 895. v. 17, as usual in 1 Maccabees, Simon, the founder of the dynasty, is described as second in command to Judas, and almost equal to him. Yet Jonathan succeeded Judas as leader of the revolt, and we may assume that he, not Simon, was second in command to Judas at that time. v. 18, 'Joseph . . . Azariah', this is one of the few places where 1 Maccabees raises the curtain and allow us a glimpse of other people who shared the leadership of the revolt. Nothing is known about these two men, except what is told below (vv. 55–62), which is not sympathetic. v. 19, leaving some reserve forces behind accords well with the evidence in the approximately contemporaneous Dead Sea *Temple Scroll* (col. 58).

(5:20–2) Though Simon had the smaller army (3,000 as against the 8,000 of Judas), his exploits are told first. The information about the fighting is very scanty, and the pursuit of the enemy 'to the gate of Ptolemais' may be more poetic than real. The number of the enemy's casualties equals that of Simon's soldiers (3,000) and may be fictitious. (For such equal numbers see v. 34.)

(5:23) There were Jews in Galilee at that time, but it is difficult to tell how many. There are unanswered questions: did Simon rescue all the Galilean Jews, or only those who were at greater risk? How many Jews were then left, and what was their position in Galilee until its conquest by the Hasmoneans about forty years later? Arbatta is identified by many commentators as Arbel in Galilee, yet other proposals compete, and see 1 MACC 9:2.

(5:24–7) v. 24, here again Judas crosses the Jordan, as in v. 6. Maybe it is a double recounting of the expedition? v. 25, the Nabateans were a tribal organization, mentioned already in the time of Alexander of Macedon. They are thought to have been an Arab people, though the epigraphic evidence about them is mostly in Aramaic. (See *ABD* s.v., iv. 1053.) At this period they were friendly towards the Jews because of their common interest in weakening the Seleucid empire. Later they turned into bitter enemies of Judea.

(5:28–34) v. 29, 'of Dathema', a conjecture not found in the MSS, after v. 9. v. 30, the fact that the Jews found shelter in a stronghold outside the city of Bozrah may point to their military task in the region; if they were installed in a fortress which was guarded by them, this will have made it possible for them to hold out against their enemies even though they were outnumbered. v. 34, for the meaning of Maccabeus see 1 MACC 2:2–5. Here the author wishes to tell us that Judas's fame was such that his nickname alone could strike panic among his enemies. 'Eight thousand', here again the number of the enemy casualties equals that of Judas's soldiers.

(5:35–9) v. 37, mention of Raphon helps to place the battlefield in northern Gilead. Raphon became a *polis* in the Roman period, and belonged to the Decapolis. v. 39, 'Arabs', we are not told to which tribe those Arabs belonged. Arabic nomads of Transjordan should not be viewed as enemies of the Jews, but as opportunistically co-operative with whomever they can gain from.

(5:40–4) The description of the battle is influenced by 1 Sam 14:9. v. 43, the city, also known as Ashtaroth Carnaim, was famous because of its temple to Ashtaroth (Astarte). v. 44, the burning of the sacred precincts at Carnaim is the first act of destruction of pagan temples recorded in 1 Maccbees, but not the last (see 1 MACC 5:68; 10:83–4; *Ant.* 12 § 364). Had it been a lone event, it could have been explained as an act of retaliation, but because it was repeated it should be considered as a policy of purification of the holy land from idolatry.

(5:45–51) v. 45 poses the same problems as v. 23. It is unclear how it is to be interpreted: as a proof of Jewish population in Transjordan, or as an evacuation of its Jewish minority. v. 46, Ephron is east of the Jordan on the road to Beth-shan. Mentioned in Polybius (5.70), under the name Gephron (note the interchangeability of the Semitic 'ayin into G in the case of 'Aza = Gaza), it did not seem to exist very long, as was the case with some other contemporary settlements in Israel, such as Tel-anafa and Hargarizim. v. 47, we are not told why the inhabitants of Ephron were inimical towards the Jews. It may be guessed that it was a strategic fortified place, maybe with a Seleucid garrison. Anyhow, this passage is modelled after Num 20:14–21. See Dimant (1988: 407). v. 51, the cruel treatment of the people of Ephron recalls the ruling of Deut 20:10–18.

(5:52–4) v. 52, 'the large plain', the valley of Jezreel, of which Beth-shan is in the eastern part. 'Beth-shan' is a transcription of the Semitic name of the city, which in Greek was called Scythopolis. In contrast, the city of Acco is called by its Greek name Ptolemais. Beth-shan received the passing Jews in a friendly manner according to 2 Macc 12:30 unlike Ephron, mentioned above. Probably 1 Maccabees intentionally refrained from recording an act of friendship by Gentiles. v. 53:2, Macc 12:31 tells that the refugees arrived at Jerusalem on the festival of Pentecost.

(5:55–64) This passage is a clear indication of the dynastic inclinations of 1 Maccabees. The disobedience to Judas's instructions is harshly criticized by the author, and he puts forth clearly his conviction that the deliverance of Israel was deposited with Mattathias's family (v. 62). v. 56, for the two commanders see 1 MACC 5:18. They may have had ambitions of

their own which competed with those of Mattathias's sons. v. 57, the motive attributed to Joseph and Azariah is to 'make a name'. This motive of name or honour is repeated often in 1 Maccabees (see 1 MACC 10:10). Surely had they been successful they could have created competition for the Hasmoneans, but since they failed, they serve as a proof of the divine election of the Hasmoneans. v. 58, Jamnia (see also 1 MACC 4:15) was an important base for the Seleucid forces confronting rebellious Judea. A Seleucid inscription, dated to Antiochus V's reign, was found there. It mentions some co-operation of the Sidonians there with the king, presumably in relation to the rebellion in Judea. See Isaac (1991). vv. 61–2, the dynastic propaganda sounds very loud here.

(5:65–8) The setting of this passage is bizarre. The chapter was nicely concluded with an encomium for Judas and his brothers (vv. 63–4), so the return to the battles against the Idumeans is odd, having been treated at the beginning of the chapter. v. 65, 'descendants of Esau', cf. v. 3 above. Hebron is about 30 km. south of Jerusalem, and in this period was in the heart of Idumea. v. 66, 'land of the Philistines', again a biblical phrase. Marisa was on the western edge of Idumea. It was a Hellenized town, with a Hellenized population of Idumeans and Phoenicians, and some immigrants from the Greek cultural sphere (see Peters and Thiersch 1905; Oren and Rappaport 1984; Kloner, Regev, and Rappaport 1992). The battles carried on by Judas are clearly no more than retaliatory border skirmishes. v. 67, the incident referred to here is enigmatic. It may have been a case of disobedience, which is criticized. v. 68, the idolatrous worship was destroyed in Azotus (the old Philistine city of Ashdod); cf. the case of Carnaim (v. 44).

More Wars of Judas (chs. 6–7)

(6:1–4) On Antiochus' expedition to the east ('the upper provinces') see 1 MACC 3:27–37. For his attempt on the Temple of Nanaia (Artemis) see Polybius, 31. 9; Appian, 11. 6. v. 1, the author is mistaken: Elymais was not a city but a country, bordering south-west Persia. 'Persia' is a common anachronism for Parthia, the rising power, which finally swallowed most of the Seleucid provinces east of the Euphrates. v. 2, Alexander is a famous figure also in Jewish legends, but no story about treasures he left in Elymais is mentioned elsewhere. v. 3, 'the city', other sources speak about a temple. v. 4, 'Babylon' seems to be wrong, because other sources tell that Antiochus went to Tabae (should probably be Gabae, modern Isfahan).

(6:5–7) This report was, needless to say, written by the author, and represents his view of the situation. A report to the king would not refer to the 'abomination'. v. 5, 'someone', probably Menelaus himself. For Menelaus' visit to the king see 2 Macc 11:29, 32, and Habicht (1976: 11, 14). The author refrains from mentioning either Jason or Menelaus anywhere by name; cf. 1 MACC 1:11–15. v. 7, 'abomination', i.e. the 'desolating sacrilege' (*šiqqûs mĕšômēm*) of Dan 11:31, and see 1 MACC 1:54.

(6:8–13) The story of Antiochus IV's death follows a common pattern in Jewish literature. The wicked person becomes arrogant (afflicted by *hybris*, to use a Gk. term), is punished, repents, and then is either pardoned or condemned. To the first group belong the stories in Dan 1–6, and the story of Heliodorus in 2 Macc 3. This belongs to the second group, as does the much more elaborate story of Antiochus' death in 2 Macc 9.

(6:14–17) The appointment by Antiochus IV of Philip as regent, either while in full command of his decisions or not, caused turmoil in the Seleucid empire. To this year (148 ES is 165/4 BCE) are dated two royal letters, the first by Antiochus IV, the other by Lysias (cited in 2 Macc 11:27–33; 16–21 respectively). These events alleviated the Seleucid pressure on the rebels. v. 17, Eupator means 'of a good father', the good father being Antiochus IV.

(6:18–27) The siege of the Akra shows that the rebels became stronger in the course of the war. This first attempt was repeated under Jonathan. Capture was achieved finally by Simon (see 1 MACC 13:50–3). v. 20, 'siege-towers', the use of these and siege-engines shows a professional military knowledge among Judas's followers. It brings to mind the proposals of various scholars that some groups or individuals who had prior military training joined the rebellion. These could have been Jewish veterans of Hellenistic armies, soldiers of the Tobiad troops, or Jewish volunteers from Ptolemaic Egypt. v. 21, in the Akra lived Jewish Hellenizers, probably citizens of the *polis* Antioch-in-Jerusalem, and soldiers of the Seleucid garrison. vv. 22–7, the speech before the king, attributed to the delegation from the Akra, is clearly the work of the author of 1 Maccabees who had in mind both earlier and later events related to the Hasmonean dynasty. v. 24, 'our inheritances' may refer to the allotments (Heb. *naḥălôt*) which were confiscated from the rebels and given to the Hellenizers (see 1 MACC 7:6). v. 27, cf. EZRA 4:12–16.

(6:28–31) The decision to renew the war in Judea and the preparations for the expedition are attributed to the 7-year-old king (see 1 MACC 3:33), but were almost certainly made by Lysias. The numbers of the soldiers are incredible. v. 30, 'elephants', shortly after this war the elephants were destroyed by a Roman delegation (162 BCE), because their use was contrary to the treaty of Apameia concluded between the Romans and Antiochus III, after his defeat at Magnesia in 190 BCE. v. 31, Beth-zur—this time Lysias invades Judea from the south also, probably because he had at his rear the friendly population of the coastal region. The siege of Beth-zur is a new phase in the war, when Judas tries to fight neither in the open field nor by surprise, but from a strategic fortress which he held.

(6:32–41) v. 32, the first achievement of Lysias seems to be that Judas was forced to lift the siege on the Akra. v. 33, Beth-zechariah is on the way from Beth-zur to Jerusalem. v. 34, 'juice of grapes', wine was used to excite elephants before battle. Here we should accept the textual proposal 'saturated' instead of 'offered' (the elephants) (the two words are similar in Heb.). vv. 35–7, the exotic appearance of elephants on the battlefield caused the author to give them the central place in his description, which though dramatic is, generally speaking, plausible. vv. 39–42, the description is very embellished but may reflect an authentic impression made by the Seleucid troops. v. 39, 'shields of gold' is an obvious exaggeration; 'ablaze', since the disposition of the army took place in the morning (v. 33) the blazing of the arms may have been more striking because of the sun shining from the east, that is from in front of them. v. 42, 'the clanking of their arms' might have been an intentional noise meant to strike fear in the enemy.

Gera (1996) thinks the description is not realistic but influenced by military scenes in Greek literature. Bar-Kochva (1998) opposes this opinion, and thinks that the battle's description is credible.

(6:42–7) The main theme of this passage is the heroic deed of Eleazar, Judas's brother. His self-sacrifice is in line with Maccabean tactics, trying to kill the enemy's commander (cf. 1 MACC 3:11–12 and 8:40). The failure of Eleazar to tip the scales of the battle is due not to a lack of courage, but to a wrong guess he made about the whereabouts of the king. Eleazar's death serves as an excuse for Judas's withdrawal. v. 44, 'everlasting name', a typical phrase in 1 Maccabees, similar to 'honour' (Gk. *timē* or *doxa*), to describe the reward for heroic death or deeds. Cf. 1 MACC 9:7–10.

(6:48–54) After his victory at Beth-zechariah Lysias turned to besiege Judas and his men in the Temple Mount. He also forced the Jewish garrison of Beth-zur to surrender, an act which the author explains as a result of shortage of food. Judas's position very quickly becomes desperate. Some scholars stress the fact that Judas's name is not mentioned explicitly in this passage, and doubt the adherence of the beseiged to his supporters. This is one of the arguments for the opinion that there were other rebel groups at this stage of the revolt which are ignored by 1 Macc. v. 49, 'sabbatical year', every seventh year the cultivation of the fields was interrupted according to biblical law (Ex 23:11; Lev 25:3–7). This sabbatical year explains the weakness of Jewish opposition in Beth-zur and the great difficulties in defending Mt. Zion. It seems quite probable indeed that letting the fields lie fallow at the time of war, when many of the farmers were serving in the rebels' ranks, could cause a situation more severe than in a normal sabbatical year, yet it seems that it is also used by the author as an excuse to explain the dire situation of the rebels. v. 52, 'engines of war', their use by the Jews in the siege testifies again to professional elements in Judas's camp (cf. v. 20). v. 53, here an explanation is brought forth as to why the usual preparations for a sabbatical year, such as the storage of provisions in advance, did not help. Yet at the same time it shows the altruistic and brotherly attitude of Judas towards the refugees.

(6:55–63) On the verge of destruction Judas was saved by a turn in the political situation in Syria. Philip appeared in Antioch as the new regent, appointed by Antiochus IV on his deathbed (v. 15). This forced Lysias to return immediately to the capital. The author puts Lysias's decision into a speech attributed to him (vv. 57–9). Judas accepted Lysias's conditions, and Lysias left to attend to more urgent business which awaited him at home. v. 57, 'our food supply is scant', it is very probable that the sabbatical year also made difficult the supply of the besieging army, because it would usually live off the country in which it was camping. Yet at the same time the author tries to depict the Syrian army as being forced to evacuate Judea. v. 60, what were the conditions of this peace? If we follow Habicht's (1976) interpretation, that the letter of Antiochus V preceded the surrender of the rebels at this juncture, then it seems that the rebels' sole benefit was that they were let out with immunity from Mt. Zion. v. 61, according to the most simple reading, the Jews left the Temple Mount as a result of the peace conditions. This is strengthened by the fact that later on the temple was not in the rebels' hands. See 1 MACC 7:33. v. 62, it is hard to say if indeed the king broke his word, or if the author describes the destruction of the wall as a breach of the agreement with the rebels. It seems to me that, as in Beth-zur, the besieged got a free leave from the place and nothing else. By attributing to the king this act the author tries to save the prestige of Judas, who was forced into an almost unconditional surrender. Compare this to the similar blame laid on Antiochus VII when John Hyrcanus surrendered to him (*Ant.* 13 § 247). v. 63, although the king is the subject here, it was Lysias who got the upper hand against Philip—but not for long.

(7:1–5) Demetrius was the son of Seleucus IV (187–175 BCE). When his father was murdered he was young and was kept as a hostage in Rome, while his uncle Antiochus IV (175–164 BCE), took advantage of the situation and usurped the throne. After the death of Antiochus IV Demetrius tried to get permission from the Roman government to return to Syria to try to regain his ancestral throne. As the Romans were reluctant to let him go, he escaped from Rome. When he arrived in Syria he easily dismissed Lysias and his *protégé* the boy-king Antiochus V, and took over the government. In the first years of his rule, and despite Roman enmity, he succeeded in suppressing various rebellions in the empire, among them the one in Judea. v. 1, 151 ES is 162/1 BCE; 'a town by the sea' is Tripolis (cf. 2 Macc 14:1).

(7:5–7) 1 Maccabees does not differentiate any specific groups among the Hellenizers. Yet there were various groups within the Jewish nobility that differed not solely on religious questions, but also on political issues (such as Ptolemaic versus Seleucid orientation) and social issues (such as power struggles between the leading aristocratic families). In contrast to Jason and Menelaus, who were condemned to *damnatio memoriae* by 1 Maccabees, Alcimus is mentioned by name, though very little is told about him (but see below). We do not know his father's name, his priestly tribe, who his supporters were, or their attitude to Menelaus and his policy. Nevertheless it may be guessed that Alcimus did not represent the former Menelaus' party, led probably by the 'house' of Bilga and by what remained of the Tobiads; that he did not support the desecration of the Jewish cult (but 1 see MACC 9:54–7); that he had no pro-Ptolemaic inclination; and that he represented a certain segment of the nobility, who were trying to keep their property in Judea (see v. 6). v. 5, Alcimus may be referred to in a Talmudic story (*Gen. Rab.*, Theodor-Albeck edn., pp. 742–3). There it is told that when Rabbi Yossi ben Yoezer was led to his execution, he was met on the road by his nephew Yakim, who is identified as Alcimus, about whom Josephus told that his Hebrew name was indeed Yakimos (*Ant.* 12 § 385; 20 § 235). v. 6, 'your Friends' is stressing the pro-Seleucid inclination of Alcimus' party. 'Our land' may stress the main grievance of this group, who felt that their property, acquired rightly or wrongly, is jeopardized (see 1 MACC 6:24). v. 7, Antiochus IV was looking for a strong pro-Seleucid government in Judea, but he got the opposite. He was forced militarily to support Menelaus, and if Lysias hoped that by replacing him he would have a supportive leadership in Judea, he was wrong again. The new high priest, Alcimus, also could not rule without the active military support of the government

in Antioch. No wonder, as will be seen below, that the patience of the Seleucid government ran short, till power was transfered to the Hasmoneans, the only ones who were not in need of support, but could even supply troops to their Seleucid overlords.

(7:8–11) v. 8, Bacchides is known only from 1 & 2 Maccabees; a namesake officer is mentioned in 2 Macc 8:30, but this may be a coincidence. At this juncture he is the governor of the western part of the Seleucid empire, anachronistically called Beyond the River (*'eber hannāhār*), as in the Persian period and in the Bible (see Ezra 4:11). v. 9, Alcimus was probably already appointed high priest by Antiochus V, to replace Menelaus (cf. 2 Macc 14:3), and confirmed by Demetrius I. vv. 7:10–11, it is not the only time that peaceful messages are repudiated by Judas (see Nicanor's message to Judas, v. 26). The author tries to present Judas as both a peace-lover and a clever leader who will not let himself fall into a trap.

(7:12–18) This is one of the most discussed passages in the book, the issues being whether the Hasideans deserted Judas, what their attitude was towards the revolt, and so on. The common understanding of this passage is that the cancellation of the religious persecution made the Hasideans reluctant to continue the revolt, which from now on was aimed at political, national, or personal achievements. So they were ready to recognize an Aaronide high priest and to end the war. Their fate is a *post factum* proof for the author that Judas was right in disbelieving Bacchides' and Alcimus' peaceful overtures. Recently D. R. Schwartz (1994) proposed that 1 Macc 2:42 should be read differently (*ioudaiōn* (Jews) instead of *hasidaiōn* (Hasideans)), because of textual and other considerations. If Schwartz's suggestion is accepted, and it seems convincing, then there is no question of the Hasideans deserting the Maccabean camp, but only of their negotiations with Alcimus and Bacchides, which failed for some unknown reason. vv. 12–13, 'Scribes . . . Hasideans', there seems to be no satisfactory answer to the question of whether these two words are synonymous, or, if not, what the relation is of one group to the other. v. 16, no information is given here or elsewhere as to why these Hasideans were butchered. v. 17 is a citation of Ps 79:2–3 (see Dimant 1988: 390–1).

(7:19–20) It seems that Bacchides, on a grand scale, took punitive measures aimed at various groups of the population. v. 19, 'men who had deserted'—why would Bacchides kill deserters who joined him? Perhaps for 'crimes' which he did not forgive. Anyhow Bacchides' punitive expedition was intended to intimidate any potential opposition.

(7:21–5) The struggle between Alcimus and his supporters and Judas and his party seems to be now mainly in the countryside outside Jerusalem, where the interests of many of the Judean nobility were in danger. Probably part of the land had once belonged to their opponents, and had been confiscated by the Seleucid authorities and allocated anew to pro-Seleucid aristocrats, probably citizens of Antioch-in-Jerusalem. Being shut in Jerusalem they could not benefit from their fields, which the rebels tried to regain. v. 25, the opponents of the Maccabees were unable to overcome Judas with their own power, even with some small governmental support. Their constant need of Seleucid help was finally the cause of their desertion by the government in Antioch.

(7:26–32) When, after Bacchides' repressive activity, Judas resumed attacks on the supporters of Alcimus, again help was needed from the central government. For whatever reasons, the force under Nicanor seems to have been relatively small and insufficient. Nicanor's peaceful message is described as treacherous, either rightly so or as an excuse for Judas, for whom the appointment of Alcimus was unacceptable. It is quite possible that the Seleucid government inclined to a peace agreement, as is clear from its policy since the cancellation of the religious persecution. But Judas's demands were unacceptable to it at this stage, though similar conditions were accepted later on, when Jonathan was appointed high priest (see 1 MACC 10:18–20). But to arrive at such a decision the Seleucids needed about ten years more. v. 26, 'Nicanor', the name is a common one, and various Nicanors are mentioned in 1 & 2 Maccabees (see Bar-Kochva 1989: 352–3). vv. 29–30, it is unclear why, if 'the enemy were preparing to kidnap Judas', they did nothing on this occasion, and gave Judas the chance to avoid further meetings with Nicanor. It makes the story about Nicanor's treacherous intentions more apologetic then historic. v. 31, Capharsalama was about 5 miles north-east of Jerusalem. v. 32, nowhere is the number of Nicanor's army given. The number of those who fell in the battle is relatively small, and it seems that Nicanor's force was not a big one. 'The city of David', where the Akra was located. This too shows the limited size of Nicanor's force.

(7:33–8) v. 33, 'priests . . . elders', these two groups seem to represent a kind of institution or representation of the people, probably the gĕrousia, which is mentioned in various documents of this period (see 1 MACC 12:6, 35; 2 Macc 11:27; Ant. 12 § 138, and 'elders', as here, at 1 Macc 13:36). It also shows that the temple and its staff are not under Judas's authority, and it may even be supposed that Alcimus is the chief authority in the temple (a fact, that, even if true, 1 Maccabees is not expected to tell). Anyhow, we have here a component of Judean society which belongs neither to Judas's followers nor to the Hellenizers. 'Burnt-offering', offerings or prayers for the welfare of foreign rulers of Judea are known well before this period (Ezra 6:11), and after it (Josephus, J. W. 2 § 408–17). v. 34, the reason for the anger of Nicanor is told only after his outburst against the priests (v. 35); 'defiled', probably by spitting.

(7:39–50) v. 39, Beth-horon, see 1 MACC 3:16; 'the Syrian army', its arrival shows again that up to now Nicanor's army was small, and the size of this reinforcement was probably also limited, and composed of local recruitments. Even the name of their commander is not mentioned. v. 40, Adasa is located between Beth-horon and Jerusalem. vv. 41–2, as in other cases the author brings historical precedents to encourage the people, i.e. his readers. Here he refers to Sennacherib, king of Assyria, as a very suitable antecedent. v. 43, 'first to fall in the battle', attacking the commander was an effective tactic pursued by Judas (cf. 1 MACC 3:11–12). 'On the thirteenth day', see v. 49. The year is 161 BCE. vv. 44–6, the victory of Judas was complete and Nicanor's army was routed. The description of their débâcle is vivid, and may be realistic. v. 47, for Nicanor's fate cf. 2 Macc 15:30–5. v. 49, 'the thirteenth day of Adar', see also 2 Macc 15:36. This day is included in Megilla Taʿanit (a tannaitic work which preceded the Mishna,

and which lists the days of joy, on which fasting (Heb. taʿanit) is prohibited). In this work the story and its moral are the same as in 1 & 2 Macc, but Judas's name is not mentioned.

Rome and the Treaty between Rome and the Jews (ch. 8)

Chapter 8 deals with the relations between Rome and Judea in Judas's time. It has three parts: (1) what Judas heard about the Romans, which is probably what was common knowledge in Judea when 1 Maccabees was written down; (2) the delegation sent by Judas to Rome; (3) the treaty between Rome and the Jews. It raises many important questions: Is the document of the alliance authentic? What does this initiative mean from Judas's point of view? Is he striving now for political independence? How should this Roman intervention in the internal affairs of the Seleucid empire be understood? These and further questions have been profusely dealt with in the scholarly literature (for further bibliography see Gruen 1984: 748–51).

(8:1–16) This passage includes some mistakes and provides some clues for its own dating and for that of the whole book. The sources for the information are not known, but it may be guessed that it was brought by Jewish diplomats, who visited Rome quite often from the time of Judas Maccabeus until the end of the rule of John Hyrcanus I. Additional sources could have been Roman propaganda, which either influenced such reports, or found its way somehow to Judea. v. 1, 'Judas heard', Judas could not have received the following report because some details in it postdate his time. Nevertheless he was in no way ignorant about Rome. A Roman delegation which passed along the coast of Israel in about the spring of 164 BCE sent a friendly letter to the Jews (2 Macc 11:34–8), probably the rebels under Judas. Also Dan 11:18, 30, written about the same time, or even a little bit earlier, mentions the Romans. So Judas knew enough about Rome to be able to weigh up the situation. 'Pledged friendship', indeed the Romans made many treaties at that period, with both important and small states, and intervened in the internal affairs of independent ones. v. 2, 'Gauls' refers either to the Galatians of Asia Minor, beaten by the Romans in 189 BCE, or to the Gauls of Gallia Cisalpine (modern France). Galatians are also mentioned in 2 Macc 8:20. vv. 3–4, Spain was known for its rich silver mines; the Romans began to infiltrate there in the third century BCE and continued to subdue its various tribes after their victory over Carthage; 'kings', since the kings defeated by Rome are mentioned below, it seems here it must refer to Spanish chieftains, who fought against the Romans. v. 5, 'Philip, and king Perseus', Philip was defeated by the Romans in 197 BCE and Perseus, his son, in 168. v. 6, 'Antiochus the Great', Antiochus III (223–187 BCE) was beaten by the Romans in the battle of Magnesia, in Asia Minor, in 190 BCE. This defeat accelerated the disintegration of the Seleucid empire. vv. 7–8, the details here are wrong. Antiochus III was not taken captive, though the rest of v. 7 is correct. Antiochus was obliged to pay a huge amount of money as war indemnities, and to give hostages, and he lost all the territories held by the Seleucids in Asia Minor, west of the Taurus mountains. 'Eumenes', the closest ally of Rome in this war and a winner at the expense of the Seleucids, but India and Media had nothing to do with either the Romans or Eumenes. vv. 9–10, this war against the Greeks is probably the Achaean war, which terminated with the destruction of Corinth in 146 BCE. If this is so, then it post-dates Judas. It is somewhat astonishing to note the positive attitude of the author towards Roman brutality, especially when contrasted to the critical and negative stance of the Dead Sea sectarians (*Pesher on Habakkuk* (1QpHab), e.g. 3:5–6; 6:6–8, 10–12, etc.). vv. 11–12, this sounds almost like a slogan of Roman propaganda, cf. Virgil, *Aeneid*, 6. 853: 'to be merciful to the conquered and beat the haughty down' (tr. J. W. Mackail). v. 13, there are various cases in which the Romans interfered in the inheritance of thrones in eastern kingdoms. vv. 14–16, some commentators suggest that the admiration for the non-royalist character of the Roman constitution is directed against royalist inclination, or actual king-ship, in the Hasmonean court. I think that it is simply a factual description of the Roman constitution, with admir-ation and a focus on what was extraordinary in it, in the eyes of one who was used to the Hellenistic monarchies of his day. 'Purple' was a sign of royalty, but could be worn by various dignitaries in the Hellenistic courts, as also by Simon (see 1 MACC 14:43–4). The number of senators at that time was 300. At v. 16 we find a surprising mistake by the author of 1 Maccabees, in his description of the Roman constitution; he does not know about the system of two consuls, and thinks that there is only one at a time.

(8:17–22) v. 17, 'Eupolemus . . . Jason', the envoys bear Greek names, as was fashionable among the Hellenizers (cf. to Jason, Lysimachus, Menelaus, mentioned in 2 Maccabees, and Alcimus). Their fathers' names, John (i.e. Yohanan) and Eleazar, are purely Hebrew, which shows that before their generation this custom was not yet fashionable, and that, unlike their fathers, their grandfathers gave Hebrew names to their children. Both were priests: Eupolemus was of the Accos family, a distinguished priestly clan. His father was active in foreign affairs at the time of Antiochus III (see 2 Macc 4:11). Jason was also, very probably, a priest, because his father's name Eleazar was common among priests in the Second Temple period. Their names show some Hellenistic colouring; their mission necessitated at least some knowledge of Greek, international politics, and worldly affairs. So through them we know that Judas had support not only among Judean farmers and shepherds, but also among the Jewish nobility, who may have been to some degree Hellen-ized, but were not of the Hellenizers' party. Some think that Eupolemus is the author of 'On the Kings of Judea', see Holla-day (1983: 93–156; *ABD* s.v.).

'Friendship and alliance', a common Roman terminology; the allies of Rome are often called 'allies and friends' (Lat.: *socii et amici*). v. 18, the author of 1 Maccabees thought, and may have been right, that Judas was already aiming at full political independence at this stage of the rebellion. v. 20, 'alliance and peace', an awkward expression, because there was peace between Judea and Rome. 'Friendship' might have been more suitable here (see v. 17). v. 21, this is the first authentic document cited in 1 Maccabees, and see 1 MACC D.2(I). The original text, perhaps in Latin, was kept on bronze tablets in Rome.

(8:23–30) The majority of scholars today accept the authenti-city of this document. Its oddities are explained by the various translations, from the Latin original into Greek, then to Heb-rew (the original version of 1 Maccabees), then back to Greek (the surviving Gk. translation). v. 23, this opening formula is common in documents of this kind. v. 24, parallel and equal stipulations on both sides (cf. v. 27) were also a convention in this kind of treaty, though the difference in political and military importance between them was tremendous. This convention is best seen in the treaty between Rome and Astypalaea, a small city in the Aegean (see Sherk 1969: no. 16, 94–9). v. 26, 'ships', a convention, as the Jews had neither a harbour nor any exit to the open sea. v. 28, 'without deceit', probably a translation of the Latin formula, *sine dolo malo*. v. 30, this permission to introduce changes to the terms is common in such treaties.

(8:31–2) These verses clearly do not form part of the treaty. They might be a part of an accompanying letter, or oral information brought by the envoys. In any case either Demetrius ignored the message, or it arrived too late to save Judas, or, indeed, it restrained Demetrius from taking extremely harsh measures after Judas's defeat (see 1 MACC 9:19–22).

The Last Stand of Judas (9:1–22)

(9:1–4) Again the Seleucid government is forced to send a considerable army to put down the revolt. Small reinforce-ments and local recruits do not suffice. v. 1, 'the right wing', inexplicable as it stands. For the proper meaning see at v. 12. Dancy (1954: 131) explains it as a gloss, to which explanation Bar-Kochva (1989: 382) also adheres. v. 2 poses great historio-geographical problems. The reading *arbēlois* is certain, and is usually taken to be Arbela in eastern Galilee, overlooking the Sea of Galilee, which argues that there was a Jewish popula-tion in Galilee before its conquest by the Hasmoneans. But then what is the connection of Arbela with the road to Gilgal (further south on the Jordan)? Bar-Kochva (1989: 383–4, 552–9), proposes that the translator wrongly transcribed *har* (mountain) *bêt- êl* in the Hebrew original into Arbelois, and he locates Har Beth-el west of Gilgal and north of Jerusalem. Mesaloth is probably not a place-name but a Hebrew word *mĕsālôt*, meaning 'trails'. v. 3, the date is about April/May 160. v. 4, various readings and locations have been proposed for Berea; Josephus thought it was Beer-zaith (*Ant.* 12 § 422). The numbers of Bacchides' soldiers are acceptable to many scholars.

(9:5–7) Judas's camp is small from the beginning (3,000) and dwindles to 800 soldiers, which are hardly sufficient to op-pose Bacchides' powerful army. Some explain this as a reac-tion of many who, having fought with Judas from religious motives, now deserted him, feeling that the war was becom-ing more and more political and national in character. Bar-Kochva (1989: 388–9) suggests that the final small number given by the author is an excuse for Judas's defeat.

(9:7–10) Judas decided to go to battle to keep his 'honour' (Gk. *doxa*) intact. When the author makes him speak about dying bravely, there is no mention of afterlife or of any reward but honour. See 1 MACC c.3. Also rare in 1 Maccabees is the spirit of resignation on Judas's part, which reflects the author's attempt to cope with the death of his hero, a problem which the author, or epitomizer, of 2 Maccabees avoided by ending his book before the defeat of Judas, with his victory over Nicanor.

(9:11–18) The description of the last battle of Judas is detailed. Bar-Kochva (1989: 64), who assumes its authenticity, thinks that it shows that Judas must have had a larger army, because it would have been impossible for him to accomplish what is described here with only 800 men. Shatzman (1991: 19 n. 42) suggests that the description is more literary than actual. v. 14, it may be that Judas's attack on the right flank, where Bacchides himself had been, was in accordance with his tactics, aiming to hit at the commander of the enemy. v. 15, 'Mount Azotus', no mountain of this name is known and many commentators accept a textual correction, based on an assumed mistranslation of the lost Hebrew original (ʾašĕdôt-hāhār), which should be translated 'the slopes of the mountain'.

(9:19–22) Taking Judas's body for burial could have been done either some time after the battle, when the enemy left the scene, or under truce. Some scholars think that a truce was indeed granted by the Syrians, because of the Jewish treaty with Rome. v. 19, Modein was where the family property was located, and where its mausoleum was later built by Simon (13:25–30). v. 21, this dirge is reminiscent of 2 Sam 1:19. v. 22, 'the rest of the acts of Judas... have not been recorded' is a phrase often repeated, in a positive form, in Kings (e.g. 1 Kings 11:41). It seems then that the author of 1 Maccabees did not have any written sources for Judas's acts.

The First Years of Jonathan (9:23–10:17)

(9:23–7) The extremely sombre situation is a suitable background for the difficult and slow reorganization of the revolt under Jonathan.

v. 23, 'renegades... wrongdoers', all opposition to the Hasmoneans is encompassed in one package, without differentiating the various groups which composed it. v. 24, 'famine' might be connected with the sabbatical year that preceded (see 6:49, 53) and with the continuous war. As Bacchides now ruled the country he could have control of the agricultural produce, and through it dominate the population outside Jerusalem. We assume that the fortresses built by him were also intended to achieve this aim (vv. 50–2). v. 25, 'the godless', cf. v. 23. The word might also reflect the effort of some groups of the nobility to regain or take over land which changed hands in the course of the revolt. v. 27, see 1 MACC 4:46, 14:41; Ps 74:9.

(9:28–31) The election of Jonathan to lead the revolt raises some questions. He was the youngest among the five sons of Mattathias, and so we must assume that militarily he was the fittest for the task among them. The same consideration was valid for Judas's election after Mattathias's death, as he was also younger than John and Simon, but he may have been Mattathias's choice, and now an assembly of the rebels elected his successor. The election of Jonathan also demonstrates that the senior position given to Simon in Mattathias's testament (2:65–6) above does not reflect the actual situation at that time. As for the legal aspects of Jonathan's appointment, it seems to be irregular: the electing body consisted of the warriors who were present at this point in the camp, and they must have been few in number.

(9:32–4) The major achievement of Jonathan in an almost desperate situation was the mere survival of the Hasmonean party. v. 33, Tekoa and Asphar are in the wilderness of Judea, south-east of Bethlehem. v. 34, 'sabbath day... crossed the Jordan', probably there is here some conflation with v. 43.

(9:35–42) This passage gives a good idea of the situation of the rebels at this time. They were forced to fight for their lives at the outskirts of the inhabited land, being supported by the Nabateans, who were already on friendly terms with them (5:25), but were ambushed by another tribe, who took advantage of the unstable conditions in the area (cf. 5:4–5, 35). v. 36, 'family of Jambri', an Arab tribe, acting independently of the Nabateans, though living at Medaba, near the Nabatean territory. See Kasher (1988: 34–5). v. 37, 'Canaan', see 1 MACC D.I. The location of Nadabath is unknown but must be in the approximate area of biblical Moab.

(9:43–9) Jonathan's dire position is clear. His encampment near the Jordan was probably intended to enable him to escape to the other side of the river when in danger, as indeed came to pass. v. 43 is a repeat of v. 34, and resumes the story, interrupted by the sons of Jambri incident, which for some reason was inserted here. 'Sabbath', this detail points to Bacchides' ignorance of Mattathias's decision to fight on the sabbath (see 2:40), which is not very probable. In any case it casts him in a negative light, as one who despises the Jewish religious ordinances and tries to take advantage of them. v. 47, the battle itself is a kind of a skirmish. Jonathan tried to repeat Judas's tactics, and to kill the commander of the enemy, Bacchides— as Judas had done to Apollonius (3:11–12) and Nicanor (7:44–5, 47). Though he failed, it shows that, like Judas, Jonathan took part personally in battle, an activity which is not recorded about Simon, and which may explain the preference given to Judas and Jonathan as leaders of the revolt.

(9:50–3) Bacchides' decision to build fortresses in strategic locations in Judea is the most serious attempt to rule over the Judean countryside, and shows that Bacchides and Alcimus understood well that a basis of power in Jerusalem alone was not sufficient to rule Judea as a whole. The hard core of the revolt was in the land, the chōra of Antioch-in-Jerusalem and the presence of armed forces was necessary to dominate Judea. For the location of the various fortresses see Galil (1992). v. 52, 'stores of food', storing food, which in part at least came as taxes in kind, in royal fortresses helped the government to subdue the population, because it was dependent on those food reserves, especially in years of shortage, like the present time (see v. 24). And see Rappaport, Pastor, and Rimon (1994). Also cf. 1 MACC 13:33. v. 53, 'hostages', this may indicate that the local aristocracy outside Jerusalem was not trusted by the Seleucid government, and was suspected of supporting the Hasmoneans.

(9:54–7) The motivation of Alcimus to destroy the wall of the inner court is not clear. Was it an architectural enterprise described by 1 Maccabees as sacrilege, to blacken Alcimus, or was it a meaningful ideological step, intended to open to the view of all, including Gentiles, the cultic performances in the temple? For an ideological interpretation see Schmidt (1994: 98–9). v. 54, 153 ES is 159 BCE, and the second month is about May. vv. 55–6, the illness (probably a stroke) and death of Alcimus are interpreted as a divine punishment, which put an end to his sacrilegious plan. v. 57, Bacchides' return to Syria after Alcimus' death shows that his arrangements were efficient, and kept the country quiet for two years (approximately from mid-159 BCE to mid-157 BCE). The author of 1 Maccabees does not inform us about the arrangements which took place after Alcimus' death. Was there a *intersacerdotium* period of about seven years (from 159 to the appointment of Jonathan in 152 BCE (see 10:20))? Or was there a high priest, whose name and very existence are concealed by 1 Maccabees for political reasons? And if there was no high priest for such a long period, how did the temple function?

Josephus, when he lists the high priests from beginning to end, mentions a vacancy of seven years between the death of Alcimus (Jacimus in the text there, *Ant.* 20 § 237) and Jonathan's appointment to the high-priesthood. Most commentators follow this statement of Josephus, which is in accordance with 1 Maccabees. In *Ant.* 12 §§ 414, 419, 434, Josephus gives contradictory information, probably wrong. This vacuum in our information has tempted some scholars to propose that the Teacher of Righteousness mentioned in the Dead Sea scrolls was the high priest in these years. Needless to say, no proof can be posited for this ingenious proposal. See Murphy O'Connor (1976).

(9:58–61) The enemies of the Hasmoneans initiated a new attempt to get rid of Jonathan. Their dependence on Seleucid help against the Hasmoneans finally brought about their abandonment by the government, because they became an unbearable burden to it. In spite of what is said about the large force Bacchides assembled, it looks like a limited military operation, the success of which depended mainly on secrecy. v. 61, 'men of the country', it seems that Bacchides was successful in installing (or reinstalling) the pro-Seleucid nobility to their lands in the country, and now Jonathan was trying to undo it. The main struggle took place in the countryside, as in the beginning of the revolt.

(9:62–9) When his plan for a surprise attack failed, Bacchides tried to crush Jonathan in his base in the desert. Clearly he did not muster a big force, and probably the king could not spare great forces for a small war in Judea because of more serious preoccupations. v. 62, Bethbasi is between Jerusalem and Tekoa, not far from Bethlehem. Bacchides' co-operation with his local allies, which did not bring any valuable results, finally led to a reversal of Seleucid policy in Judea. v. 66, 'Odomera . . . Phasiron' are unknown Arabic tribes. Jonathan is again involved in skirmishes with the nomads, or semi-nomads ('in their tents' here), near the scene of battle. vv. 67–8, Bacchides is unable to face the attack on both sides, though performed by a small force (v. 65, Jonathan 'went with only a few men'). Despite the text ('he was crushed by them'), it is clear that he was forced only to give up the siege. v. 69, Bacchides' rage and frustration were turned now against the 'renegades', who called him but did not deliver any valuable goods for the Seleucid government. It is reminiscent in a way of Lysias's reaction towards Menelaus.

(9:70–3) The relations between the Seleucids, represented by Bacchides, and the Hasmoneans are now reversed. Whatever remained of the former Judean nobility, it was almost ignored by the Seleucid government. Jonathan gradually became the real representative of the Seleucids in Judea, and the agreement with Bacchides was the first step in this direction. v. 73, Michmash is eight miles north of Jerusalem; 'to judge the people', a biblical phrase, common in the book of Judges. It associates with the judges of old, and is in line with the style of 1 Maccabees in general. 'Destroyed the godless', the internal war goes on, though now, without Seleucid support, the liquidation of the aristocratic opposition to the Hasmoneans arrives at its almost final stage.

(Ch. 10) The agreement between Jonathan and Bacchides made Jonathan the one who could supply military reinforcements to contending Seleucid pretenders in their internecine wars. The opportunity to exploit Seleucid difficulties for his own aggrandizement came when Demetrius I was challenged by a certain Alexander, who pretended to be Antiochus IV's son. The threat to his rule incited Demetrius to look for support wherever he could get it. To prevent Jonathan from joining Alexander, Demetrius made friendly overtures to him.

(10:1–14) v. 1, 160 ES is 152 BCE. 'Alexander Epiphanes', many ancient sources and most contemporary scholars reject an affiliation between Alexander and Antiochus IV. He was put forward as Antiochus IV's son by the enemies of Demetrius, who utilized for their aim a certain outward similarity between him and Antiochus V, who was a real son of Antiochus IV. Alexander is known by his nickname Balas, the meaning and origin of which is not clear. This nickname is never used in 1 Maccabees. Ptolemais was an important harbour west of Galilee, which became at this period a kind of secondary capital, and served as a base for the invasion of Alexander into Demetrius' realm. On Ptolemais see 1 MACC 5:15. v. 6, the permission to raise and to equip an army was intended to encourage Jonathan to render support to Demetrius in the war against Alexander. vv. 7–11, Jonathan took full advantage of Demetrius' gestures to strengthen his position. The release of the hostages increased his support by various families; he left Michmash and turned Jerusalem into his seat, fortifying the city and the Temple Mount. v. 12, 'fled', actually the withdrawal of most of the Seleucid garrisons from Judea was part of the preparations for the war with Alexander. Their withdrawal made Jonathan the uncontested master of the Judean countryside. v. 14, the remaining forces, in the Akra and Beth-zur, were composed of both Syrian soldiers and Jews, the remnants of the once powerful nobility.

(10:15–17) The great opportunity for Jonathan came when Alexander tried to draw him to his side. Jonathan accepted his proposal to appoint him high priest. It meant the achievement of the highest position in Judea, equal to princely or even royal status, though under Seleucid suzerainty. It surpassed by far Demetrius' proposals, of which Jonathan had already made use. Jonathan's support of Alexander had various goals: to achieve national aims through his own personal advancement; to obtain the high-priesthood; to co-operate with Rome and the Ptolemies (and perhaps also other states) for the weakening of the Seleucids. This last target was already adopted by Judas and was in line with Ptolemaic interests. It was a policy developed constantly by Jonathan, by Simon, and by John Hyrcanus, until Alexander Janneus. For Janneus' change of policy see Rappaport (1968).

Jonathan, High Priest and Ruler of Judea (10:18–12:53)

(10:18–20) This is the first document, beside the treaty with Rome, that is cited in 1 Maccabees. On documents see 1 MACC

D.2(I). The appointment of Jonathan as high priest was a new starting-point for the house of Mattathias, on his way to hegemony over Judea. Yet it aroused criticism from various quarters. It is similar, from a legal point of view, to the appointment of Jason and Menelaus by Antiochus IV, and of Alcimus by Antiochus V, and not in accordance with the laws of the Torah and the traditional inheritance of the high-priesthood by the house of Zadok. It is also quite possible that there were still in Judea supporters of the Zadokite Oniad family, and there may have been others who doubted the moral quality of Jonathan to serve as high priest. It is no wonder then that some Qumranic scholars see Jonathan as the one who is called in the Dead Sea scrolls the Wicked Priest. Cf. I MACC 9:57. v. 20, 'king's Friend', Jonathan was the first Hasmonean to be a Friend (Gk. *philos*), a hierarchical rank in Hellenistic courts. 'He also sent him . . . crown', this sentence is not part of the letter, because it is not in direct speech as is the rest; 'purple robe and a golden crown', both were symbols of royalty or high rank, and under various regimes their use was restricted to privileged persons. See Rheinold (1970).

(10:21–4) v. 21, 160 ES is 152 BCE. Jonathan begins to perform as high priest on Sukkoth (the Feast of Tabernacles or Booths) of that year. vv. 22–4, the disappointment of Demetrius provides an explanation of his letter cited below.

(10:25–45) The authenticity of this long letter is doubtful according to various scholars. Those who accept it explain the difficulties as problems of textual transmission. v. 25, the opening of Demetrius' letter is more formal and less personal than Alexander's letter (v. 18). Jonathan is not mentioned by name, which is strange in a letter which tries to convince Jonathan to join Demetrius. vv. 26–8, the contents of these verses are blatantly untrue, but may serve Demetrius' effort to draw Jonathan to his side. v. 29, 'all the Jews', is this to be understood as an exemption of all the Jews in the Seleucid empire, as some commentators think? It seems unreasonable from a Seleucid point of view and irrelevant for Jonathan. It may refer to all those who are within Jonathan's jurisdiction, or at most to those in the land of Israel.

These three categories of tax are known in the Seleucid empire: tribute (Gk. pl. *phoroi*) was an annual payment by communities and may refer here to taxes in general; tax on salt, a vital product for conservation of food; and the crown (Gk. *stephanos*) tax, which from a voluntary donation on the crowning of a new king became a permanent tax. v. 30, 'third of the grain . . . half of the fruit', this is a very high rate, especially when we consider the relatively low fertility of the land of Judea. Some scholars suppose that it was not the usual rate of taxation, but a punitive measure imposed on Judea because of the revolt. See Mørkholm (1989: 285). The three districts—Aphairema, Lydda, and Ramathaim—are mentioned in 11:34. They were populated mainly by Jews. Modein itself was in the district of Lydda. It is evident that the administrative division of the land did not suit its ethnic division. It is not at all clear when and why these districts were transferred from Judea to Samaria, but be that as it may, they were annexed to Judea by Jonathan's days, and it seems that *de facto* they were already in Jewish hands and under Hasmonean influence. 'Samaria and Galilee', the three districts bordered on Samaria, and the mention of Galilee is either a mistake in the Hebrew original or a mistake by the translator (*gālil* in Heb. means 'district', and this may have caused confusion). vv. 31–2, the complete cancellation of taxation and the evacuation of the Akra were achieved only in Simon's days (see 13:39). The inclusion of these privileges already in a document from Demetrius I's time makes the authenticity of the document suspicious, though those who believe in its authenticity claim that his desperate situation could have brought him to such extreme concessions. v. 33, the release of captives is a common stipulation in post-war arrangements, cf. Josephus, *Ant.* 12 § 144. A tax on cattle is well-known, but mention here seems out of place, belonging better in vv. 29 or 30.

vv. 34–5, the exemption of the Jews from any disturbance on their holidays is quite understandable, but what are the three days before and after, and why is it declared for the whole kingdom? The three days are explained as the time necessary for a journey to Jerusalem (probably from other districts, because in Judea no more than one day was necessary for such a trip). But the exemption to all the Jews of Demetrius' kingdom is incomprehensible. See Wise (1990). vv. 36–7, on the one hand this passage fits well with the need of Demetrius to muster whatever military support he can get, on the other hand the number of 30,000 seems to be far beyond the manpower potential of Judea. Generally speaking the conditions of service proposed to those who register are within the norms of Hellenistic military customs. The Jews often served as mercenaries in Persian and Hellenistic armies, see Shatzman (1991: 14, 17–18, with further lit.). v. 38, the three districts were mentioned in v. 30 in relation to the removal of taxation. Here the king allows them to be annexed to Judea. The high priest is mentioned here, but not his name. v. 39, the annexation of Ptolemais to Judea and its being granted to the temple is either an absurd or a cunning move by Demetrius to incite Jonathan to attack the city, which served as a temporary capital for his adversary, Alexander. On this city see I MACC 10:1. v. 40, royal contributions to temples were common, and we know of such donations given to the Jerusalem temple. See Ezra 6:5; 8:9–10; 7:20; *Ant.* 12 § 138; 2 Macc 3:2–3. vv. 41–2, the details of this account are not clear, yet it seems to be intended to regulate, and add important sums of money to, the temple treasury, which was probably in bad shape after the troubles of the last two decades or more. v. 43, this is reminiscent of the *asylia*, granted to temples and cities by Hellenistic kings. In this case it is limited to debts to the government. vv. 44–5, there are precedents for subsidies by the king to various building projects, as for example by Cyrus (Ezra 6:4) and Darius (Ezra 6:8), and by Antiochus III (*Ant.* 12 § 141).

(10:46–7) This explanation is right, but not full. For additional reasons see vv. 15–17.

(10:48–58) About the international political activity involved in these affairs see Gruen (1984: ii. 585–6, 666–8, 709–11). vv. 51–4, the support Alexander got from Ptolemy VI Philometor and other rulers, with Roman tacit encouragement, is omitted here. The message of Alexander's ambassadors is given in direct speech, as quite often in I Maccabees, but it cannot be taken as authentic. The same is true of Ptolemy's reply. v. 57, on the importance of Ptolemais see I MACC 5:15; 10:1, 39.

(10:59–66) v. 60, Jonathan's meeting with the two kings cemented his participation in the pro-Roman coalition, which included Ptolemaic Egypt, the Attalids, and in this case also Alexander. Yet the pomp and presents of Jonathan remind one of the Tobiads' relations with the Ptolemaic court in the third century BCE, and show Jonathan's urge to take part in political affairs. v. 61, 'malcontents . . . renegades', we do not know who these opponents of Jonathan were. Cf. I MACC 15:21. vv. 62–4, the description of the change in Jonathan's position is reminiscent of that of Mordecai in Esth 6:6–9. v. 65, 'chief Friends', the Greek is *prōtoi philoi*, 'first friends', a rank above Friends. See I MACC 10:20. 'general and governor', Greek *stratēgos* and *meridarchēs*. The second office is known mainly as a Ptolemaic one, and may show a persistence of Ptolemaic terminology in Israel or the strong Ptolemaic influence on Alexander, who was, to some extent, a vassal of Ptolemy VI; or it may be a usage of a translator familiar with Ptolemaic terms (especially so if we suppose that the translation was made in Egypt). The area entrusted to Jonathan is not specified, so that it is reasonable to assume that it was Judea. Later on Jonathan and Simon were appointed as governors of some additional regions.

(10:67–9) In 147 BCE the war between the two branches of the Seleucid dynasty was resumed. The branch of Seleucus IV is represented now by his grandson Demetrius II. v. 69, Apollonius cannot be identified, because it is a very common name. He represents Demetrius against Jonathan, a supporter of Alexander, his adversary.

(10:70–3) The message of Apollonius is a literary invention by the author of I Maccabees or one of his sources. Yet it stresses some interesting points. v. 71, 'come down to the plain', the Jewish forces were well-adapted to fight in the mountainous area of Judea, but deficient in the plain, where the Seleucid forces could use their phalanx and cavalry. The readiness of Jonathan to descend to the plain is a turning-point in Hasmonean warfare, and shows the considerable development of the Jewish army (see Shatzman 1991: 12). The 'power of the cities', Apollonius' force included, or was mainly composed of, the *poleis*' militia. These Hellenistic cities were inimical to the Hasmoneans, and lent their support to Apollonius against Jonathan.

(10:74–85) For this important battle see Bar-Kochva (1975; 1989: 76–81); Shatzman (1991: 19, 23, 311). v. 75, Joppa was an important harbour and the main sea-route out of Judea. v. 77, Azotus was formerly one of the five Philistine cities, and now served as a base for Apollonius. v. 83, 'Beth-dagon' means the house of Dagon, a god whose identity is somewhat unclear. It was once thought to be derived from the Semitic root *d-g* (fish), but a derivation from root *d-g-n* (corn) seems preferable. vv. 84–5, the motivation for this cruel act is not clear. It may have been a savage revenge for the evildoings perpetrated on the Jews in earlier times, or, as sometimes understood, an attempt to clean the holy land from idolatry (cf. I Macc 5:44).

(10:86–9) v. 86, Askalon was the only city towards which the Hasmoneans were friendly, because of the strong Ptolemaic influence on it; this caused it to be immune to Hasmonean expansionist policy. vv. 88–9, the difficult situation of Alexander because of Demetrius II's success in gaining support from within and without his kingdom made Jonathan's alliance even more important to him, and he poured on him even greater benefits. A 'golden buckle' was a symbol of honour in the hierarchic Seleucid order. Ekron was formerly a Philistine city. Probably it was a royal domain (Gk. *gē basilikē*), which was given to Jonathan as a present (Gk. *gē en dōrea*). This is the first known territorial annexation to Judea, seemingly under personal title.

(11:1–12) This passage discusses mainly the relations between the Seleucids and the Ptolemies. In it Ptolemy VI is the bad guy and Alexander the good one. But we should be cautious regarding the author of I Maccabees, who manifests a great sympathy towards Alexander. v. 1, 'like the sand by the seashore', a biblical expression, cf. e.g. Gen 22:17; 'by trickery', I Maccabees attributes to Ptolemy sly intentions (see also v. 8), yet it is doubtful if Ptolemy thought it feasible to annex the Seleucid empire without incurring a collision with Rome, and more so at such an early stage of his intervention in Syria. v. 2, it seems that at this stage Alexander was friendly towards Ptolemy. v. 3, 'stationed forces as a garrison' may show that Ptolemy had in mind the reannexation of southern Syria to the Ptolemaic empire. vv. 4–7, Jonathan's position was strong enough to sustain the blame of the people of Azotus, and Ptolemy was not yet, at least openly, an enemy of Alexander. The Eleutherus was a river north of Tripolis, in what is now Lebanon. v. 8, Seleucia in Pieria was the harbour of Antioch, at the mouth of the river Orontes. vv. 9–12, Ptolemy transferred his support from Alexander to Demetrius, perhaps because of the feeble and weak personality of Alexander, or, conversely, his refusal to give up southern Syria to Ptolemy. In any case, neither was very popular, and Ptolemy was acclaimed by the Antiochians. It should also be remembered that Ptolemy had Seleucid blood in his veins, through his mother, Cleopatra I, daughter of Antiochus III the Great.

(11:13–19) v. 13, it is not credible that Ptolemy made himself king of the Seleucid empire, as he never deposed Demetrius II. According to Josephus (*Ant.* 13 §§ 113–15) and Diodorus (32. 39c), the crown was offered to him, but refused. 'Asia' is a non-official term for the Seleucid empire (cf. I Macc 8:6; 12:39; 13:32). v. 17, Zabdiel was an Arab chieftain in the Syrian desert, called Arabia in v. 16. With the decline of the Seleucid empire, Arab tribes became important all along the fertile crescent. Zabdiel had a Greek name too: Diocles (*ABD* s.v. no. 3, 1031–2, and see I MACC 11:39; 12:31). v. 18, 'Ptolemy died', he was wounded in the battle against Alexander and died after three days. v. 19, the year 167 ES is 146/5 BCE.

(11:20–9) Jonathan appears as an assertive and astute politician, who used brinkmanship in his negotiations with Demetrius II (esp. v. 23). v. 20, 'engines of war' shows the professional and technological advancement of the Hasmonean army. See I MACC 6:20, 52. v. 21, 'renegades', despite its constant failure there remained a hard core of Jewish opposition to Jonathan. The motivation of his opponents is not known. v. 23, three acts of Jonathan are listed here: continuation of the siege of the Akra; choosing of elders and priests; risking his own life by going to Ptolemais. Many commentators follow Josephus (*Ant.* 13 § 124), and assume that the elders and priests went with Jonathan to Ptolemais. It seems to me more probable that they compose the *gērousia*, which Jonathan left in charge of the siege and the state's business, and which is mentioned in various documents, cited below.

v. 25, see v. 21. vv. 26–7, the reinstallation of Jonathan shows his strong position and the weak position of Demetrius at this time. v. 28, waiving of taxes in return for one sizeable instalment was agreed upon by Demetrius II in Simon's days. See 13:37; 'three districts', see v. 34 and I MACC 10:30.

(11:30–7) This letter from Demetrius II to Jonathan contains many characteristics of a genuine Seleucid royal letter. From this aspect it is different from the letter of Demetrius I to Jonathan (10:25–45), which is considered by some scholars to be a forgery, probably influenced by this genuine letter. v. 30, the opening formula is regular, and contains both the ruler and the people, as is true from now on in similar documents (e.g. 15:2). v. 31, 'copy', it was a regular chancellery rule to send copies of relevant orders to various functionaries, and to other interested parties (cf. *Ant.* 12 §§ 138–44). Lasthenes was from Crete, a leader of mercenaries who became prime minister to Demetrius II (Diodoros, 33.4.1). He is ranked as 'kinsman' and 'father' (v. 32), in line with the Seleucid hierarchic order (see *ABD* s.v.). v. 34, 'Aphairema and Lydda and Rathamin'—see I MACC 10:30. 'To all those who offer sacrifice in Jerusalem' differentiates between Jews and Samaritans, who offer sacrifice on Mt. Gerizim (see Rappaport (1995*a*). v. 37, putting important documents in public places was common, and the Temple Mount was such a place. Cf. 14:48.

(11:38–40) v. 38, Demetrius decided to release the regular Seleucid troops, who were recruited from among the military settlers in Seleucis, in northern Syria, either because of pecuniary considerations, or because their fidelity to him was questionable. This aroused the enmity of the core of the Seleucid army, and pushed it to support the rival Seleucid branch of Alexander (issued from Antiochus IV). 'Recruited from the islands of the nations', i.e. the Cretan mercenaries under Lasthenes. v. 39, 'Trypho', an appellation for Diodotus, an officer of Alexander, a native of the region of Apamea in north Syria. Trypho was influential among the soldiers of this region, whom Demetrius had estranged. He began as regent for Antiochus VI, Alexander's son, and later set himself up as a king, the only pretender who was not of the Seleucid dynasty. 'Imalkue the Arab', son of Zabdiel, who killed Alexander (v. 17) but brought up his son.

(11:41–51) vv. 41–4, Jonathan tried to benefit from the difficult situation of Demetrius II, and to achieve more independence. He requested the evacuation of the remaining forces in Judea, especially those in the Akra. Demetrius prudently agreed to Jonathan's demand, but on condition of military help against the rebels. Jonathan accepted, and sent Jewish troops to Antioch. vv. 45–51, the revolt of the Antiochians and its suppression is told also by other historians (Diodorus, 33. 4.2 and others). These do not mention the Jewish involvement, whereas I Maccabees does not mention the involvement of the mercenaries. Josephus (*Ant.* 13 § 137) combines I Maccabees' report with some Hellenistic source, and mentions both the Jewish soldiers and the mercenaries. We see here Jonathan's deep involvement in the internal affairs of the Seleucid state, but at the same time his intention to get advantages for Judea.

(11:52–3) The refusal of Demetrius to evacuate the fortresses in Judea pushed the frustrated Jonathan to support Demetrius' enemies.

(11:54–9) The most natural step for Jonathan was to renew his alliance with the son of Alexander, the child Antiochus VI, who was now under the tutelage of Trypho. This branch of the Seleucids was his reliable ally in Alexander's days. v. 54, despite Trypho's success Demetrius was able to keep some bases in the kingdom. For the chronology and division of the Seleucid empire at this time see Houghton (1992). vv. 57–8, Antiochus VI confirms to Jonathan what was given to him by his father, Alexander. There is no mention of the evacuation of the Akra here, which means that Trypho refused to give up the last vestiges of Seleucid sovereignty in Judea. v. 59, 'from the Ladder of Tyre to the borders of Egypt', the appointment of Simon as a governor of the *Paralia* (Gk. 'the coastal plain'), shows the relative great importance of the Hasmoneans in Seleucid politics, and their progress and involvement in it. Jonathan was already a *stratēgos* (10:65), though the area under his control is not defined. The *Paralia* was one of the subdivisions of southern Syria, and some other governors of it are known (see 15:38; 2 Macc 13:24). The idea behind this appointment was to encourage Simon and Jonathan to take control of this area from Demetrius II's supporters.

(11:60–74) Two fronts now confronted Jonathan and Simon. Jonathan was fighting against Demetrius' supporters in the north and on the southern coastal plain and Simon against Beth-zur in Judea. v. 60, 'beyond the river', see I MACC 7:8; 'the army of Syria', the Syrian army, which supported Antiochus VI, joined Jonathan against Demetrius. Askalon sided with Jonathan as before (cf. 10:86). vv. 61–2, Gaza participated in the eastern commerce of luxuries in co-operation with the Nabateans and in competition with the Ptolemies. On Askalon and Gaza see Rappaport (1970). Damascus was the most important city in southern Syria. Jonathan's arrival there shows his involvement in matters and areas not related to Jewish interests. v. 63, Kadesh was a city in northern Galilee, in the territory of Tyre, which supported Demetrius II. v. 64, the two brothers are not fighting in their respective provinces, and it seems that their activity is functional. v. 65, Beth-zur was the second most important Seleucid base in Judea after the Akra. With its conquest the Akra remained the last Seleucid fortress in Judea. v. 67, 'waters of Gennesaret', the Sea of Galilee. Hazor was in upper Galilee, a city well-known in biblical times (Josh 11:1). v. 70, we do not know anything else about these two officers. The mention of Jewish individuals, other than the Maccabees, is relatively rare in this book. v. 71, here Jonathan's courage and piety are exemplified, as well as the importance of divine help. Yet divine help is not miraculous, but through human acts, that is, through Jonathan's bravery and the return of his men to the battlefield; cf. also 9:47.

Jonathan's Exploits (12:1–53)

(12:1–4) If the order of events here is chronological and not thematic, then Jonathan considered his rule stable enough to embark on diplomatic activity, and to renew and expand Judea's involvement in the political activity of the Mediterranean world. v. 1, since the Roman state and senate were stable and kings and rulers were transitory, they were expected to take the initiative and to renew former alliances with Rome. This was done by Jonathan. v. 2, 'Spartans', see 14:16–23;

'other places', it was common to assign to an embassy more than one destination; cf. 15:22–4. v. 3, 'senate chamber', *bouleutērion* in the Greek, not an exact term, but a suitable one in the transmission of Roman institutions into Greek. We do not know the Hebrew word behind it. v. 4, giving letters of recommendation to envoys for the authorities in the places along their route was a common custom in Hellenistic diplomacy.

(12:5–23) The relations between the Jews and the Spartans have intrigued many scholars, and various explanations have been suggested for the problems raised by this passage, including the historicity of Jonathan's letter to the Spartans; the authenticity of the letter of Arius to Onias, cited in Jonathan's letter (vv. 19–23); and the supposed 'brotherhood' of the Jews and the Spartans. The last problem is the easiest to resolve. Assertion of relations between various peoples was popular in the ancient world (see Gen 10), and was revived in the Hellenistic period, when new connections were invented to suit the new map of the world. It was utilized also to facilitate diplomatic relations, or to forge alliances and friendships between states. v. 6, the letter is addressed to the Spartans by the Jewish authorities of that time. The formula is a common one, including the *gērousia* (the senate) and the people, with a special mention of the priests. 'Brothers', in accordance with the genealogy specified at v. 21. vv. 7–8, for Arius and Onias see at v. 19. v. 8, 'the envoy', Josephus relates that the envoy's name was Demotcles (*Ant.* 12 § 227), but we do not know on what authority this information was based. v. 9, this passage is considered impolite by various scholars, and therefore not authentic. v. 13, 'the kings', this expression is rather strange, but may refer to various kings attacking the Jews not simultanuously, but successively (Antioctius IV, Antiochus V, and Demetrius I). v. 16, here we have the names of the envoys mentioned in v. 1. Numenius is a relatively rare name in Greek, and his father's name, Antiochus, is even more surprising. Yet it could have been given to him in honour of Antiochus III, a benevolent king in Jewish eyes. The name of the other envoy, Antipater son of Jason, may be connected to Judas's envoy to Rome, Jason son of Eleazar (1 MACC 8:17). We may conclude that diplomatic tasks were confided, in some cases at least, to members of families that had provided diplomats for more than one generation (cf. ibid.).

(12:19–23) The authenticity of this letter of Arius is based on even less firm foundations than the letter of Jonathan. Many ingenious proposals were made to support it, but nevertheless it remains bizzare that Sparta would appeal to a small people under Ptolemaic suzerainty. Some scholars have therefore repudiated the authenticity and historical value of this letter, and even of the whole correspondence between Sparta and Judea. If there is any good argument to support the authenticity of this letter, it is, to my mind, the lively interest shown in various quarters at that period in ethnic genealogies, which triggered here and there diplomatic activity as well. Even if the letter is a forgery, it shows an interest, in Jewish circles, in ethnic genealogies and in their potential help in forging relations between oriental peoples and the Greeks. For further bibliography see Schürer (1973–87: i. 184–5). v. 19, Arius is usually identified with the Spartan king Areius II (309–265 BCE); Onias is supposedly Onias II, who began his office *c.* 270

BCE. v. 21, around the figure of Abraham various stories were entwined, which relate him to different peoples. Cf. Josephus, *Ant.* 14 § 255, and further references in Stern (1974–84, nos. 46, 83, 335).

(12:24–32) Jonathan is again active in the service of his Syrian ally, this time Trypho, Antiochus VI's regent. The war is far north of Judea proper, but probably within the borders of southern Syria, of which Jonathan was *stratēgos*. v. 24, Demetrius II, the enemy of Trypho and now also of Jonathan. v. 25, Hamath was probably on the river Orontes, north of Israel; 'his own country', probably not the small Judea of that period, but the greater area encompassed by Jonathan's administration. v. 28, the kindling of fires is a well-known strategem to cover withrawal (cf. 1 MACC 4:5). vv. 30–1; the Zabadeans were one of the Arab tribes on the borders of the cultivated land of the fertile crescent. On other Arab tribes see 1 MACC 5:4, 25; 9:36–7; 11:17. v. 32, Damascus was probably included in Jonathan's *stratēgia*. See 1 MACC 11:62.

(12:33–4) Simon was occupied with defending his *stratēgia*, the *Paralia* (see 1 MACC 11:59) against Demetrius II's supporters, as his brother Jonathan was doing in his own area. v. 33, for Askalon, see 1 MACC 10:86. v. 34, the annexation of Joppa by the Jews was gradual. This time it was the installation of a garrison, but later on the pagan population was replaced by Jews (see 1 MACC 13:11).

(12:35–8) Jonathan and Simon tried at this stage to stabilize their achievements by occupying the Akra and by strengthening the strategic places on the borders of the Jewish territory. v. 35, 'the elders', Jonathan was co-operating with the senate (Gk. *gērousia*; Heb. *zĕqēnîm*), the assembly of elders usually translated 'elders' except in 12:6. The functioning of the *gērousia* gives a glimpse of the internal constitution of Judea at the time, and reflects a certain power base of the Hasmoneans in Judean society. No wonder the elders appear also when Simon is appointed by national decision as ruler and high priest (14:28). v. 36, the Jews could not storm the Akra, and so they resorted to a prolonged siege, which indicates the limits of their military power. v. 37, Chaphenatha was probably a quarter of Jerusalem, but its location is unknown. v. 38, Adida was a village north-east of Lydda (Heb. *hadid*), guarding one of the western entrances to Judea (see 13:13).

(12:39–53) That Trypho resorted to enticing Jonathan into a trap shows the limits of his power to impose his will on the Jews. vv. 39–40, indeed, Trypho did assassinate Antiochus and replace him on the Seleucid throne. Yet Jonathan was not an obstacle for him, and it seems to be a Judeocentric point of view that he had to get rid of Jonathan before murdering Antiochus. It is also interesting to note the persistence of the author of 1 Maccabees in his sympathy for the descendants of Alexander Balas. v. 41, 'forty thousand', the strength of Jonathan's army is considered by many commentators to be exaggerated. v. 47, 'three thousand...one thousand', the numbers may refer to various components of the Hasmonean army: 40,000 may represent the full conscription of Judea, including the reserve; 3,000 may be a unit in the standing army, which may have been composed of two or three similar units; the 1,000 soldiers who remained with Jonathan may have been his bodyguard. Cf. Shatzman (1991: 28–31). v. 48, for the hostility of Ptolemais towards the Jews see 1 MACC 5:15;

2 Macc 6:8; 13:25. The capture of Jonathan may be reflected in the *Temple Scroll*, lvii 9–11, where very strict rules for the king's bodyguard are stated.

Simon's Rule (13:1–16:24)

(13:1–11) These verses are concerned with the transfer of leadership from Jonathan to Simon, which did not follow the usual hereditary pattern. It avoids the problem of the succession of Jonathan's sons, and ignores the fact that Jonathan was still alive at that time. Indeed Simon's position was consolidated about two years later (see ch. 14). Interestingly Simon initiated the proposal that he should take the leadership, and was not called upon by the people (cf. Jonathan's appointment in 9:28–31). To sum up, this seems to be a passage with an apologetic flavour, written by the author of 1 Maccabees under Hyrcanus (see 1 MACC B. 2). v. 6, 'all the nations', a common stereotype in 1 Maccabees (see 5:7 and 12:53). v. 8, 'leader' (Gk. *hēgoumenos*), cf. 14:35, 41. Jonathan was still alive (see above). v. 11, 'Jonathan son of Absalom' was probably a brother of Mattathias son of Absalom, mentioned in 11:70. At this time Simon did not garrison Joppa, but replaced its Gentile population with a Jewish one (cf. 12:33–4, and 14:34).

(13:12–19) This is a very strange passage, which ascribes to Simon action taken against his better judgement. Since Simon inherited from his brother, under very difficult circumstances, it might have given place to various rumours and laying of blame, as well as rivalries and tensions within the ruling family. So we may see in this passage an apologetic or even polemical effort to vindicate Simon, the real founder of the dynasty, from culpability for the fate of Jonathan (and his two sons), murdered by Trypho (see v. 23). v. 13, 'Adida', see at 12:38.

(13:20–4) Trypho failed to invade Judea by surprise, and was unable to overcome Simon's defensive tactics. v. 20, Adora was a Hellenistic town in eastern Idumea, also called Adoraim. Trypho arrived there after encircling Judea, trying in vain to invade it. v. 22, 'heavy snow', indeed, very rare in Judea. 'Gilead', we do not know why Trypho chose this way. v. 23, Baskama was probably in the Golan, but identification is uncertain.

(13:25–30) This passage, like some other passages, stresses Simon's role as the head of the dynasty. v. 27, burial monuments are known all over the Mediterranean world. Similar to this one are the monuments from the Kidron valley in Jerusalem and the tomb of Jason, which are not much later than this period. v. 28, 'pyramids', as in the tomb of Jason, v. 29, 'columns', as in the tomb of Benei Ḥezir. The carvings, or bas-reliefs, are common in Hellenistic art, but less common on Jewish monuments of this period. Yet it does not seems out of place on a royal monument, and it bears neither anthropomorphic nor zoomorphic figures, as was customary in Jewish art of that period. 'Ships', though often signifying death and afterlife, in this case, and in the author's eyes, their message is related to Hasmonean maritime aspirations. Cf. the paintings in the tomb of Jason. v. 30, 'to this day', i.e. some time before Hyrcanus' death in 104/3 BCE (see 1 MACC B.2).

(13:31–40) v. 31, the sympathy of the author is clearly with the branch issued from Antiochus IV, through Alexander Balas;

cf. at 12:39–40. v. 32: 'Asia', cf. at 11:13. v. 33, 'stored food in the strongholds', see at 9:52.

(13:36–40) Simon renewed the alliance with Demetrius II, who issued a royal letter announcing the complete release of Judea from taxation. This was considered to liberate Judea from Seleucid rule and to be the beginning of its independence. v. 36, the letter formally addresses the high priest, the *gērousia*, and the nation in general. v. 37, the release from tribute was not given gratuitously. A lump sum, in the form of a gold crown and palm branch, was paid for it. Cf. at 11:28. vv. 38–40, the sweeping measures of the king's decision included the evacuation of Judea, general amnesty, and an appeal to Jews to join the Seleucid army.

(13:41–2) Our author pauses here in his narrative to declare solemnly the beginning of the independence of Judea. v. 41, 170 ES is 142 BCE. v. 42, dating according to a local ruler is one of the symbols of sovereignty, as is, for example, the issuing of coins (cf. 15:6). Evidence for the use of dating according to Hasmonean regnal years is meagre, but see 14:27, and some coins of Janneus bearing dates (Naveh 1968).

(13:43–7) Simon's policy and military activity were generally directed inwards. Contrary to Jonathan he refrained from intermingling with Seleucid affairs. v. 43, Gazara was on the road between Jerusalem and Joppa. It served as a military base under the command of John Hyrcanus, who lived there (v. 53). 'siege-engine', the Greek has *helepolis* (lit. city taker—a movable tower). It shows the continuation of the military development of the Hasmonean army. See Shatzman (1991: 24).

(13:47–8) The cleaning of Gazara from impurity stresses the religious motivation behind the Hasmonean conquest. See 1 MACC 5:44. v. 48, Simon was severe in replacing the pagan population with a Jewish one (cf. 11:66; 13:11; 14:34). This policy combines military, national, and religious motivations. Later on, in Idumea and Galilee, it was replaced by the enforced conversion of the population.

(13:49–53) The Akra was not taken by storm, as Gazara partially was, but by prolonged siege and starvation (cf. 12:35–7). The procedure of its recovery was similar to that of Gazara, but it served as an occasion for festivity and commemoration, being the last vestige of foreign rule and part of the holy city. v. 51, the date is the 23rd of Iyyar (the second month in the Jewish year, which begins from Nisan), and the year is 141 BCE. This date is also mentioned in *Megillath Ta'anith*, as one of the days on which mourning and fasting are prohibited. v. 53, Simon took measures to assure an orderly succession to his rule, by preparing his successor in advance and giving him enough authority and power to take over the government. His old age played a role in his decision, as shown at 16:3.

(14:1–3) This is a digression, correct in its major lines but its source unknown. v. 1, 172 ES is 140 BCE. The reason given for Demetrius' expedition is incorrect, as it was forced on him because of the Parthian advance westwards. v. 2, 'Arsaces' is a generic name of all Parthian kings. The king at this time was Mithridates I (171–138 BCE). 'Persia and Media', it is because of biblical influence that the Parthian empire is so-called. In Jewish sources it is often called Persia.

(14:4–15) This is one of the most important poetic passages in 1 Maccabees, because of the service it renders to the ruling dynasty. It was composed by the same hand as the rest of the book as can be seen from the common motifs (unlike the decision about Simon's appointment in ch. 14). It is written in a biblical style and includes factual statements. The principal topics mentioned here are: Simon's broadening of the borders of Judea; caring for peace; security and material prosperity; caring for the law and the temple. v. 5, Joppa, see 13:11. v. 10, the supply of food was one of the main concerns of Hellenistic rulers, and cf. 13:33.

(14:16–23) vv. 16–19, the author tries to make of Jonathan's death and Simon's installation as high priest a major international event. Yet this is not supported by his own report, because the Spartan letter is a response to Jonathan's letter, and does not mention, even out of politeness, Jonathan's murder, and the Romans are approached by Simon, not vice versa (see below). vv. 20–3, this letter is taken to be a forgery by various scholars, and as authentic by others. We think that in the light of the author's source for other documents he cites (see I MACC D.2(I)), we should consider the correspondence of Jonathan/Simon and Sparta as authentic, with the exception of Arius' letter (I MACC 12:19–23). v. 22, for the envoys see I MACC 12:16. v. 24 is out of context here, and should be linked with the Roman document later. For its contents see I MACC 15:16–24. A 'gold shield weighing one thousand minas': sending a decorative shield made of precious metal, like a golden crown (see 13:37), was a common custom, and may have been a sign of submission. The weight of 1,000 minas, about 500–1,000 kg., depending to which mina it is equated, is excessive; see I MACC 15:18.

(14:25–49) The document cited here is a most important one for the history and constitution of Hasmonean Judea. It is the only document which tells about the internal procedure of an appointment of a Jewish ruler, his responsibilities, legal standing, titles, and authority. This is the starting-point of the new state, and dynasty, and its consequent history is to be viewed in the light of this document. Its authenticity is undisputed, because, among other reasons, it is not fully in accord with the point of view of I Maccabees. The structure of the document is similar to Hellenistic usage (most parallels are decisions of Hellenistic poleis). Its composition is the following: date (v. 27); place and circumstances (v. 28); motives for the decision (vv. 29–40); the decision (vv. 41–5); the people's and Simon's mutual agreement (vv. 46–7); details concerning its copying, publicizing, etc. (vv. 48–9).

vv. 25–7a, an introduction to the decision, which explains the motivation for it and the whereabouts of the document. v. 27b, there is here a double dating, Seleucid era and Simon's era, and the equation is correct, the date falling on 13 September, 140 BCE. v. 28, 'Asaramel', an incomprehensible combination of letters, thought to be a transcription derived from the Hebrew original. From among the various ingenious suggestions we prefer Azara megale (azara, Heb. 'a court', esp. in the temple, and megalē, Gk. 'big' which becomes Heb. gĕdolâ), as proposed by Schalit (1969: 781). 'Great assembly', some scholars think it refers to the great synagogue, mentioned in the Mishnah ('Abot, 1:1). It is indeed the Greek word sunagōgē, which appears here, but in the Greek of the Septuagint it translates various Hebrew words, so that it is not necessary to restore the Greek into kĕneset haggĕdolâ (great synagogue).

This assembly is supposed to represent the nation (cf. Neh 10:1 for the assembly in his days). When the will of God could not be known, as there were neither true prophets (see v. 41), nor Urim and Thummim, the national assembly is called forth to legitimize the appointment of Simon.

vv. 29–40, the reasons that justify the appointment of Simon are listed here in the form of a review of Hasmonean history. v. 32, 'own money', this detail in the catalogue of Simon's virtues discloses one of his sources of power, which was a direct pecuniary connection with the army. v. 35, this appointment refers either to that by the people immediately after the kidnapping of Jonathan by Trypho (13:8–9), or when independence was declared after Demetrius II's letter (13:41–2). vv. 38–40: Simon's success and prestige abroad are highlighted. The mention of Demetrius II's confirmation of Simon as high priest shows that, in spite of the effort made by Simon to get national legitimation of his position, the royal appointment was not ignored, and even if it did not carry much weight legally it was considered to be prestigious. The alliance with Rome is mentioned for the same reason. v. 41 is the beginning of the decision of the assembly, which is the core of the document. Simon gets two appointments, as leader and high priest. We do not know what was the Hebrew title behind the hēgoumenos (Gk. leader) here (and in 13:8). On some Hasmonean coins of John Hyrcanus I the inscription reads: 'Head of the community of the Jews' (Heb. rō'sh heber hayyĕhudîm, so rō's may be proposed, but nāśi' and mōśēl have a good claim too. As high priest, Simon is not dependent any more on the appointment of a pagan king, yet his nomination by vox populi is not comparable to divine appointment. But this was out of the question at the time, so the national approval was the best he could get. 'For ever', usually understood to mean that Simon's post is hereditary, as indeed it was; 'until a trustworthy prophet should arise', considering the problematic nomination of Simon (at least from a religious point of view), this sentence seems to be a kind of a compromise, to achieve a wide agreement for his appointment. Criticism of his nomination could have come from various quarters, such as Pharisees, supporters of the Oniad dynasty, Essenes, or other sectarian or political groups. Some of them, and especially the Pharisees, could have been positively responsive to such a formula, which theoretically acknowledged the temporariness of Simon's nomination, but in practice did not affect his rule over Judea. vv. 42–3 give a list of Simon's tasks, which are part of his double office as both leader and high priest. His military tasks are part of his leadership, not a third role as a general. vv. 44–5, these stipulations made the decision irreversible, and also show the ephemeral place of the assembly in the Jewish constitution. 'Purple . . . gold', see I MACC 10:29. vv. 46–7, there is here a mutual agreement as to the contents of the decision, and some scholars point out its contractual character. 'Ethnarch' is again a Greek word, chosen by the translator perhaps for the same Hebrew word translated as hēgoumenos in v. 41. vv. 48–9, the arrangements to be taken with the decision are specified here. They may have been a part of the decision, or an authorial expansion.

(15:1–9) v. 1 refers to Antiochus VII Sidetes (so-called because he was raised in Side, in Asia Minor), son of Demetrius I and younger brother of Demetrius II, who fell in Parthian captivity (see 14:1–3). vv. 2–9, this document is considered to be genuine, and to reflect the situation of Antiochus VII at the beginning of his struggle to regain his hereditary kingdom. Trypho was still powerful, and Antiochus needed all the support he could get. His friendly attitude towards Simon changed when his position became more secure (see vv. 26–31). v. 3, 'scoundrels', obviously Trypho and his supporters. v. 5, probably for conciseness' sake, details about tax release are skipped, and the reference is made to former arrangements. v. 6, 'your own coinage', this privilege was one of the more conspicuous symbols of sovereignty in the Hellenistic-Roman world, especially in the case of silver coinage. Nevertheless Simon did not utilize it, and the earliest Hasmonean coinage known is from John Hyrcanus' time. See Rappaport (1976) and Meshorer (1990–1: 106).

(15:10–14) Dor was a Phoenician coastal city south of Acco/Ptolemais. Excavations there revealed some vestiges of the siege by Antiochus, e.g. lead missiles bearing the inscription: obv. 'For the victory of Trypho'; rev. 'Dor, year 5, of the city of the Dorians, Have the taste of sumac'. See Gera (1985). For an alternative reading see Fischer (1992). v. 10, 174 ES is 138 BCE. Antiochus' landing in Syria brought him general support. Trypho, who was a usurper, was quickly driven away and was besieged in Dor.

(15:15–24) According to many commentators, this passage should have come after 14:24, to which it is related. The linkage is not only because it is the same envoy and delegation, with the same golden shield, but also because chronologically it was already mentioned in the document about Simon's rule, from September 140 BCE (14:40). It is reasonable to assume a misplacement of this passage somewhere in the chain of the transmission of 1 Maccabees. v. 15, 'Numenius', see 12:16; 14:22, 24. v. 16, Lucius Caecilius Metellius was consul in 142 BCE. 'Ptolemy' refers to Ptolemy VIII (VII) Euergetes II Physcon (145–116 BCE). The copy of the Roman letter, cited here, is the one sent to Ptolemy, though there were other recipients (vv. 22–4). v. 17, 'renew', see 14:24. v. 18, 'thousand minas', here it is not said that the shield weighed 1,000 minas (despite the NRSV tr.). Various scholars understand it to mean 'of the value of a thousand minas', and correct it and 14:24 accordingly. v. 19, circular letters announcing Roman policy and decisions were an instrument of Roman diplomacy; see at vv. 22–4. v. 21, 'scoundrels', such an extradition clause is not common in our sources, yet some incomplete analogies can be found. See Rappaport (1995b). vv. 22–4, the list of *poleis*, kings, and states, recipients of a letter similar to the one sent to Ptolemy, cited above, has evoked many suggestions, aimed mainly at finding a common denominator for these incongruous political units. Some have suggested that all had Jewish communities; others that the itinerary of the envoys back to Judea passed through these places; others that those states were allied to Rome. But none of these criteria can be applied to all the states on this list. It has also been suggested that it is metaphorical: that such an impressive list is meant to express the whole sphere of Roman influence.

My opinion tends to the list being accurate, that the letter was indeed sent to those addressees, with intent to demonstrate the wide extent of Roman activity and influence,

especially in the east (see Rappaport 1995b: 282). Most of the kings and cities mentioned in the list need no comment. Ariarathes V was king of Cappadocia, 162–130 BCE; for Arsaces see at 14:2. The name Sampsames is unknown and probably corrupt. Among the suggestions made to replace it are Lampsakos and Amisos (in western and northern Asia Minor respectively). The names in this list also include regions, which do not always represent a political entity. v. 24, the copy cited above is the one to Ptolemy, who is properly not mentioned in the list. It would have been superfluous to send copies of every letter, all of them being similar, to Simon. Probably each one of them had an appendix with all the other addressees except himself, like the copy of the letter to Ptolemy.

(15:25–31) Here our author resumes the story of the siege of Dor, cut off after v. 14. The siege is going on (v. 25), and the end of it is told in v. 37 after a digression about Simon. v. 26, Simon, like a faithful vassal, sent aid to Antiochus. v. 27, Simon's support became unnecessary in view of Antiochus' imminent victory over Trypho, and the king's interest was now to curtail his power. v. 28, Athenobius is known only from 1 Maccabees. vv. 28–31, it is important to notice that the king is not trying to restore Judea to its prior position, as a province under direct Seleucid rule, but to curtail its expansion, especially into the coastal region, and to restore it to its former borders. Simon could even have kept these places had he been ready to pay for them. So Antiochus' policy was not to return to the glorious days of his ancestors, but to restore obedience of the vassal princes and to replenish his treasury in preparation for a war against Parthia.

(15:32–6) vv. 33–4, Simon's response to the demands of the king is extremely important. It may not be a verbatim citation, but it reflects, at least, the current opinion in the Hasmonean court or the author's circle. This response is based on the idea of historical right, as an ideological and legal argument, to justify Hasmonean conquests in the land of Israel. It is in contrast to the legal basis of the rule of the Hellenistic dynasties, which was the conquest itself—their kingdoms were *doriktētoi*, conquered by the spear. So it is not a conquest, runs this argument, but a reacquisition of an inheritance. v. 35, typically of Simon, he is not rushing into an armed conflict, and proposes a small sum of money, 100 talents as against 1,000 demanded, to placate the king.

(15:37–41) v. 37, Orthosia was in what today is northern Lebanon. v. 38, Cendebeus was *stratēgos* of the *Paralia*, as was Simon before him. v. 39, for the use of Kedron to put pressure on Simon by harrassing the population see vv. 40–1. 'The king pursued Trypho', Trypho fled further on to Apamea, where, with the support of the Seleucid military settlers, his revolt had originally begun, and was slain there.

(16:1–3) v. 1, for Gazara becoming John's seat see 13:53; now it was on the front line, against Cendebeus. v. 2, we know by name three sons of Simon: John, Judas, and Mattathias (v. 14). All three names are common in the Hasmonean family. John, the successor of Simon, is known also as Hyrcanus in the writings of Josephus Flavius, but not in 1 Maccabees, nor in Talmudic sources, nor on his coins. We do not know Simon's age, but since about thirty years have passed from the beginning of the Maccabean revolt, and at that time Simon was not a young person, he should by now be about 70 years old.

(**16:4–10**) v. 4, the number of soldiers is quite reasonable here. Cavalry in the Hasmonean army is explicitly mentioned here for first time (but cf. 2 Macc 12:35). Bar-Kochva (1989: 68–81) thinks that cavalry was already used by Judas and Jonathan. Shatzman (1991: 19, n. 42, 22) is more sceptical. v. 6, John, following the example of the Maccabees, took part in battle in person.

(**16:11–17**) v. 11, nothing is known about Ptolemy except what is told here. His patronymic may point to an Arabian origin (Habubus/Habib). Was he born Jewish or was he a proselyte? (It is unlikely that he was a non-Jew, as he was the son-in-law of the high priest, Simon, himself.) We may then consider the possibility that Ptolemy was a local chief who accepted Judaism and married into the Hasmonean family. He may have been a prototype of Antipas, Herod's grandfather, but there is no way to prove it.

'Governor', we may learn from this passage that Judea was divided into regions, Jericho and its surroundings among them, under governors (Gk. *stratēgoi*) who might have the power to build fortresses (v. 15), and that they could come from the local nobility (see above). v. 14, Simon attended to the administration of the country by means of inspection tours. The year 177 ES is 134 BCE. v. 15, Dok was a fortress above Jericho to the north-west. v. 16, according to Josephus, who is not relying on 1 Maccabees on this matter (see 1 MACC D.2(4)), Ptolemy murdered only Simon, and took his two sons and wife prisoner (*Ant.* 13 §§ 228–9).

(**16:18–22**) Ptolemy's appeal to Antiochus VII after the murder raises the possibility that the conspiracy itself was co-ordinated with him. His motivation to murder the high priest, his father-in-law, may hint that he was not integrated into Jewish society, and was linked to the Hasmoneans very lightly (see v. 1). Ptolemy tried also to get rid of John, but the men whom he sent to murder him were forestalled. Josephus (ibid.) has some more details, which stress that the popularity of the Hasmoneans caused the failure of Ptolemy's conspiracy.

(**16:23–4**) This passage is very similar to the concluding verses in Kings, at the end of the acts of the various kings (e.g. 1 Kings 14:19, 29; 16:14, 27; 22:40; 2 Kings 1:18; 10:34, etc.). It raises the question of whether there was a book, named 'The Chronicles of the High-Priesthood of John', or whether this is merely an imitation of biblical style, adopted by the author of 1 Maccabees. Since the formula used here is not complete, and does not contain the number of the ruler's regnal years and the name of his successor, it leads to the conclusion that 1 Maccabees was written before Hyrcanus' death in 104 BCE (after Shatzman (forthcoming)).

REFERENCES

Abel, F.-M. (1949), *Les livres des Maccabées* (Paris: Gabalda).
Bar-Kochva, B. (1975), 'Hellenistic Warfare in Jonathan's Campaign Near Azotos', *Scripta Classica Israelica*, 2: 83–96.
——(1989), *Judas Maccabaeus* (Cambridge: Cambridge University Press).
——(1998), 'The Description of the Battle of Beth-Zacharia: Literary Fiction or Historical Fact?', *Cathedra*, 86: 7–22 (Heb.).
Bickerman, E. (1937), *Der Gott der Makkabäer* (Berlin: Schocken).
——(1951), 'Les Maccabées de Malalas', *Byzantion*, 21: 63–84.
——(1968), *Chronology of the Ancient World* (London: Thames & Hudson).
——(1979), *The God of the Maccabees* (Leiden: Brill).
Dancy, J. C. (1954), *Commentary on First Maccabees* (Oxford: Blackwell).
Davies, P. (1977), 'Hasidim in the Maccabean Period', *JJS* 28: 127–40.
Dimant, D. (1988), 'Use and Interpretation of Mikra in the Apocrypha and Pseudepigrapha', in J. Moulder (ed.), *Mikra* (Assen: Van Gorcum), 379–419.
Fischer, T. (1992), 'Tryphons verfehlter Sieg von Dor?', *ZPE* 93: 29–30.
Galil, G. (1992), 'Parathon, Timnatha and the Fortifications of Bacchides', *Cathedra*, 63: 22–30 (Heb.).
Gera, D. (1985), 'Tryphon's Sling Bullet from Dor', *IEJ* 35: 153–63.
——(1990), 'On the Credibility of the History of the Tobiads', in A. Kasher, U. Rappaport, and G. Fuks (eds.), *Greece and Rome in Eretz Israel* (Jerusalem: Yad Izhak Ben-Zwi), 21–38.
——(1996), 'The Battle of Beth Zacharia and Greek Literature', in I. Gafni *et al.* (eds.), *Studies in Memory of Menahem Stern*, 25–53 (Heb.).
Goldstein, J. A. (1975), 'The Hasmoneans: The Dynasty of God's Resisters', *HTR* 68: 53–8.
——(1976), *I Maccabees*, AB (New York: Doubleday).
Goodman, M. D., and Holladay, A. J. (1986), 'Religious Scruples in Ancient Warfare', *CQ* 36: 151–71.
Grabbe, L. J. (1991), 'Maccabean Chronology, 167–164 or 168–165 BCE', *JBL* 110: 59–74.
Gruen, E. S. (1984), *The Hellenistic World and the Coming of Rome* (2 vols.; Berkeley: University of California Press).
Habicht, C. (1976), 'Royal Documents in Maccabees II', *HSCP* 80: 1–18.
Hengel, M. (1974), *Judaism and Hellenism* (2 vols.; London: SCM).
Holladay, C. R. (1983), *Fragments from Hellenistic Jewish Authors* (Chico, Calif.: Scholars Press).
Houghton, A. (1992), 'The Revolt of Tryphon and the Accession of Antiochus VI at Apamea', *RSN* (=*SNR*) 71: 119–41.
——and G. le Rider (1985), 'Le deuxième filo d'Antiochos IV à Ptolémais', *RSN* 64: 73–85.
Isaac, B. (1991) 'A Seleucid Inscription from Jamnia-on-the-Sea: Antiochus V Eupator and the Sidonians', *IEJ* 41. 132–44.
Johns, A. F. (1963), 'The Military Strategy of Sabbath Attacks on the Jews', *VT* 13: 482–6.
Kasher, A. (1988), *Jews, Idumeans and Ancient Arabs* (Tübingen: Mohr [Siebeck]).
Kloner, A., Regev, D., and Rappaport, U. (1992), 'A Hellenistic Burial Cave in the Judean shephela', *Atiqot*, 21: 27*–50* (Heb. with Eng. summary, 175–7).
le Rider, G. (1965), *Suse sous les Séleucides et les Parthes* (Paris: P. Geuthner).
——(1993), 'Les ressources financières de Séleucos IV et le paiement de l'indemnité aux Romains', in M. Price *et al.* (eds.), *Essays in Honour of R. Carson and K. Jenkins* (London: Spink), 49–67.
Martola, N. (1984), *Capture and Liberation* (Åbo: Åbo Akademi).
Meshorer, Y. (1990–1), 'Ancient Jewish Coinage: Addendum I', *INJ* 11: 104–33.
Millar, F. (1993), *The Roman Near East 31BC–AD337* (Cambridge, Mass.: Harvard University Press).
Momigliano, A. (1976), 'The Date of the First Book of Maccabees', *L'Italie préromaine et la Rome républicaine, Mélanges J. Heurgon* (Rome:), 657–61.
Mørkholm, O. (1989), 'Antiochus IV', *The Cambridge History of Judaism*, ii. 278–91.
Murphy O'Connor, J. (1976), 'Demetrius I and the Teacher of Righteousness, I Macc., X, 25–45', *RB* 93: 400–20.
Naveh, J. (1968), 'The Dated Coins of Alexander Janneus', *IEJ* 18: 20–6.
Oren, E. D., and Rappaport, U. (1984), 'The Necropolis of Maresha-Beit Govrin', *IEJ* 34: 114–53.

Peters, J. P., and Thiersch, H. (1905), *Painted Tombs in the Necropolis of Marissa* (London: Palestine Exploration Fund).

Rappaport, U. (1968), 'La Judée et Rome pendant le règne d'Alexandre Jannée', *REJ* 127: 329–45.

—— (1970), 'Gaza and Ascalon in the Persian and Hellenistic Periods in Relation to their Coins', *IEJ* 20: 75–80.

—— (1976), 'The Emergence of Hasmonean Coinage', *AJS Review*, 1: 171–86.

—— (1980), 'Notes on Antiochus' Persecutions as Reflected in the Book of Daniel', in B. Bar-Kochva (ed.), *The Seleucid Period in Eretz-Israel* (Tel-Aviv: Hakibbutz Hameuchad) (Heb.).

—— (1993), 'The Hellenistic World as Seen by the Book of Daniel', *RASHI: Hommage à E. E. Urbach* (Paris:), 71–9.

—— (1995a), 'The Samaritans in the Hellenistic Period', in A. D. Crown and L. Davey (eds.), *New Samaritan Studies: Essays in Honour of G. D. Sixdenier* (Sydney: Mandelbaum Publishing), 281–8.

—— (1995b), 'The Extradition Clause in I Maccabees 15: 21', in K. van Lerberghe and A. Schoors (eds.), *Immigration and Emigration in the Ancient Near East: Festschrift für E. Lipinski* (Leuven: Peeters), 271–83.

—— Pastor, J., and Rimon, O. (1994), 'Land, Society and Culture in Judea', *Transeuphratène*, 7: 73–82.

Rheinold, M. (1970), *History of Purple as a Status Symbol in Antiquity* (Brussels: Collection Latomus).

Rowley, H. H. (1953), 'Menelaus and the Abomination of Desolation', *Studia orientalia J. Pedersen dedicata* (Copenhagen: E. Munksgaard), 303–15.

Schalit, A. (1969), *König Herodes, der Mann und sein Werk* (Berlin: de Gruyter).

Schmidt, F. (1994), *La Pensée du Temple de Jérusalem à Qoumrân* (Paris: Éditions du Seuil).

Schürer, E. (1973–87), *The History of the Jewish People in the Age of Jesus Christ* (3 vols.; Edinburgh: T. & T. Clark).

Schwartz, D. R. (1992), 'On Pharisaic Opposition to the Hasmonean Monarchy', in *Studies on the Jewish Background of Christianity* (Tübingen: Mohr[Siebeck]).

—— (1994), 'Hasidim in I Maccabees 2:42?', *SCI* 13: 7–18.

Schwartz, J., and Spanier, J. (1991), 'On Mattathias and the Desert of Samaria', *RB* 98: 252–71.

Schwartz, S. (1991), 'Israel and the Nations Roundabout: 1 Maccabees and the Hasmonean Expansion', *JJS* 42: 16–38.

Shatzman, I. (1991), *The Armies of the Hasmoneans and Herod* (Tübingen: Mohr[Siebeck]).

—— (forthcoming) *The Hasmoneans in Greco-Roman Historiography and Jewish Sources.*

Sherk, A. K. (1969), *Roman Documents from the Greek East* (Baltimore: Johns Hopkins University Press).

Stern, M. (1974–84), *Greek and Latin Authors on Jews and Judaism* (3 vols.; Jerusalem: Israel Academy of Sciences and Humanities).

Stern, M. (1981), 'Judea and her Neighbors in the Days of Alexander Jannaeus', *Jerusalem Cathedra*, 1: 22–46.

Tcherikover, V. (1959), *Hellenistic Civilization and the Jews* (Philadelphia: Jewish Publication Society), 189–222.

Williams, O. S. (1999), *The Structure of Maccabees* (Washington, DC: CBQ).

Wise, M. O. (1990), 'A Note on the "Three Days" of I Maccabees X. 34', *VT* 40: 116–22.

48. 2 Maccabees

R. DORAN

INTRODUCTION

A. Title. The title, the Second Book of Maccabees, is a convenient tag to distinguish this collection of documents from the other history of the Maccabean revolt known as the First Book of Maccabees. 1 and 2 Maccabees, therefore, are not the titles for a two-volume work on the Maccabean revolt, but are quite distinct.

B. Subject-Matter and Literary Genre. 1. 2 Maccabees is composed of three documents, two letters prefixed to an epitome of a larger historical work. There is no explicit connection between the two prefixed letters and the epitome, although scholars have attempted to show interrelationships (Momigliano 1975; Doran 1981). The first letter (1:1–10a) is addressed to Egyptian Jews and exhorts them to celebrate the Feast of Hanukkah. The second (1:10b–2:18) has a similar addressee and message, but also contains an account of the death of Antiochus IV, and attempts to show the continuity between the first and second temples. The first letter follows the conventions of letters written in Aramaic, while the second does not. The epitome (2:19–15:39) covers the history of the Maccabean revolt from the reign of Seleucus IV Philopator (187–175 BCE) to Judas's defeat of Nicanor in 161 BCE. The epitome therefore covers a different time-period from that of 1 Maccabees. 1 Maccabees in one verse (1:9) notes the time between Alexander the Great and Antiochus IV, and in five verses (1:11–15) the events of Antiochus IV's reign before the persecution of the Jews in Judaea; the epitome, on the other hand, devotes a whole chapter to events under Antiochus IV's predecessor (2 Macc 3) and another chapter to events prior to the persecution

(2 Macc 4). The epitome ends with the defeat of the Seleucid general Nicanor in 161 BCE at the hands of Judas Maccabeus, while 1 Maccabees continues through the death of Judas and the successive leadership of his brothers Jonathan and Simon down to Simon's death in 134 BCE. The two works also differ in style: 1 Maccabees is the translation of an original Hebrew work and its style betrays its translation quality at times; the epitome follows the conventions of Hellenistic historiography, and is written in good Greek style. 1 Maccabees focuses primarily on the heroic exploits of the Hasmoneans: they are the family 'through whom deliverance was given to Israel' (1 Macc 5:62). 1 Maccabees in fact closes with a refrain which echoes those found about the kings of Judah and Israel in 1–2 Kings, e.g. at 1 Kings 11:41. Judas is certainly a warrior hero in the epitome, but victory comes from the epiphanies of the God of Israel and God's mercy is gained through the sufferings of the martyrs. The epitome in fact falls within the genre of epiphanic collections which narrate how a god defends his/her temple.

2. A totally different question is how faithfully the epitomist preserves both the content and the style of the author he is condensing, Jason of Cyrene. The rapid-fire telling of events as at 13:22–6 and 14:25 and the brief mention of characters' names, e.g. Callisthenes at 8:33, without further introduction suggest a fuller fund of narrative events which Jason would have supplied. Did Jason's five-volume work end where the epitome ends, with the victory over Nicanor? Some scholars suggest so, and even go so far as to identify Jason of Cyrene with Jason son of Eleazar who was sent by Judas Maccabeus on an embassy to Rome after the defeat of Nicanor (1 Macc

8:17): Jason therefore would have ended his story with the defeat of Nicanor because that was where his participation in the events ended. Others would argue that the rhetorical style and flourish of the epitome would not have been present in Jason's work. Behind both these suggestions lurks the desire to show that the epitome is based on 'real' history, on the word of an eyewitness who wrote in a sober style. Unfortunately, all we have is the epitome and we simply are not able to say anything about what Jason wrote. The epitome ends where it does because it provides a fitting literary and rhetorical flourish as the blaspheming attacker of the temple is appropriately destroyed.

C. The World-View of the Epitome. The author of the epitome confronts Judaism with Hellenism, particularly emphasizing traditional Jewish values as opposed to innovations such as Jews being educated at Greek gymnasia. Yet the author also stresses that Jews can be good citizens and can interact well with their Greek neighbours. Theologically the epitome is Deuteronomistic in tone: as long as the Jews obey the Torah, God will protect them. Punishment always fits the crime. One particularly important part of the world-view that God rewards the righteous is the author's strong belief in individual bodily resurrection for the pious (2 Macc 7). God will give back to the martyrs all their bodily parts in a new creative act.

D. Date and Place of Composition. In discussing date and place, one has to ask about both the date of Jason of Cyrene and the date of the epitome. The only secure date for Jason's work is that it was written before the epitome. If one assumes that Jason was an eyewitness to the events or that he drew on oral reports from contemporaries, he might have written not long after 161 BCE, the date of the battle against Nicanor. In attempting to date the epitome, one has to decide whether the prefixed letters, particularly the first, were originally joined to the epitome or not. If one does assume this, then one has to decide whether the epitome was written along with the letter or previously. Since the first letter is dated to 124 BCE, then the epitome would have been written on or before that date. If the epitome and the letters were written separately and then joined later, then one has to rely on other clues in the epitome itself. In a work which emphasizes God's defence of the temple, one might suggest that it was written before Pompey the Great entered Jerusalem and the temple in 63 BCE. The chronological differences between 1 and 2 Maccabees have also been used as a clue to argue that Jason/the epitomist wrote to refute 1 Maccabees with its pro-Hasmonean bias, and thus after 1 Maccabees (Goldstein 1976; 1983), but this is unlikely. So no one knows either when Jason of Cyrene wrote his five-volume work or when the epitomist did his shortening, with dates for the latter ranging from around 124 to 63 BCE. Nor can one be sure *where* the works were written. The epitomist has clearly learnt Greek well, and is aware of Greek historigraphical conventions, so he could have written anywhere in the Greek-speaking world. The opposition he shows towards the gymnasium suggests a city where some Jews were beginning to attend the gymnasium, but that again could be anywhere.

E. Outline.

COMMENTARY

The Prefixed Letters (1:1–2:18)

(1:1–10a) The First Letter The first letter follows the normal format of letters in the Hellenistic period as it first indicates who the recipients and senders of the letter are (v. 1), then follows this with good wishes for the recipients (vv. 2–6), the body of the letter (vv. 7–9), and closes with the date (v. 10a). The letter was written in 124 BCE, a year in which a bitter civil war in Egypt had ended. The letter makes no reference to these events, however, nor does it refer to any specific individuals. Rather, it emphasizes that both recipients and senders are all brothers. A somewhat similar greeting is found in the letter of 419 BCE found in the Elephantine papyri (Cowley 1923: 60–5). One wonders who were the senders—John Hyrcanus the high priest and his council?—and who were the recipients—the Jewish community in Alexandria, or the military colony at Leontopolis? The greeting combines a Jewish formula—'true peace'—and a Greek formula—'greetings'.

The initial greetings are followed by a long prayer of blessing which emphasizes the common covenant with the patriarchs, and the role the Torah should play in their lives. Particularly interesting is the stress on God's active role in the following of the Torah. The Greek verb for 'be reconciled' at v. 5 (*katallageiē*) is unusual in the rest of the LXX. It is found with this meaning at 2 Macc 7:33; 8:29, and this may constitute one piece of evidence for seeing a connection between the letter and the epitome. The same notion is found in the prayer of Solomon at the dedication of the first temple (2 Chr 6:19). Some scholars have found in v. 5 an allusion either to the civil war in Egypt or to the need for reconciliation because of the sin of Onias IV in building a temple at Leontopolis (Jos. *Ant.* 13.62–73). The terms are those used for general good wishes, however, and so such specificity need not be present.

The body of the letter contains a quotation of a previous letter. Since there are no quotation marks in Greek, where does the quotation begin? Does the 'critical distress' of v. 7 refer to the time of Demetrius II in 169 of the Seleucid Era, i.e. spring 143 to spring 142 BCE, the time when Jonathan was captured (1 Macc 12:48)? If that were the case, why is Jonathan's capture not mentioned whereas an event over 20 years previously, the withdrawal of Jason, is? Would the body of the letter begin with a quotation of a letter with no indication of the fact? We should probably begin the letter at 'In the critical distress...' It is not exactly sure what event is being described as the time of distress. It is not Jason who is said to have burned the gates, but others (2 Macc 8:33; 1Macc 1:31; 4:38). I suggest that the withdrawal, not revolt, of Jason is being referred to (2 Macc 5:1–9) and the subsequent destruction of the city by the Seleucids is described using the traditional figures of burnt gates and the shedding of innocent blood.

The end of the quotation is marked by the formula, 'And now'. Only here and at 2 Macc 1:18 and 10:6 is the festival of Chislev connected with the Feast of Booths. The date is given at the end of the letter, as is usual.

(1:10b–2:18) The Second Letter The second letter bristles with problems. The first section (1:10b–18) speaks of the death of Antiochus IV and seems about to stop at 1:18 with an invitation to celebrate the festival of the purification of the temple, but then the letter continues on with a digression on the holiness of the second temple until the exhortation to celebrate the festival of Chislev is repeated at 2:16. No date is given. While the first letter had as recipients and senders only the brothers in Judaea, Jerusalem, and Egypt, this letter provides a range of people with Judas and Aristobulus being specifically named. The reference would seem to be to Judas Maccabeus, the leader of the revolt in Judea, and possibly to the Aristobulus whose fragments are preserved by the later Christian bishop, Eusebius of Caesarea (*Praep. Evang.* 7.32. 16–18; 8.9.38–8.10.17; 13.12.1–16). Aristobulus is said to have presented a work to Ptolemy VI Philometor (180–145 BCE), whereas in this letter he is called the teacher of Ptolemy. Most scholars do not regard this letter as genuine. Rather it is creative historiography, wherein an author writes what should have been written. What is in evidence is the attempt to show a close connection between Jews in Egypt and in Judea.

The account of the death of Antiochus IV differs from that in Polybius, 31, and Appian, *Syriaca*, 66, and, more interestingly, from that in 1 Macc 6:16 and 2 Macc 9. All these other sources agree that Antiochus IV did not die at the temple of Nanea. One cannot reconcile the death accounts in this letter and in the epitome, and one must conclude that they were written by different people.

(1:19–36) The Miraculous Fire At 1:18, the text unexpectedly speaks of a festival of fire at the time of Nehemiah. The author has this Nehemiah commissioned by the Persian king (1:20), and seems to refer to the Nehemiah who is the central figure of the book of Nehemiah. However, he sets the scene at the end of the Babylonian exile, when another Nehemiah accompanied Zerubbabel back to Judea (Ezra 2:2; Neh 7:7; 1 Esd 5:8), and so has conflated the two figures. Here Nehemiah, not Jeshua and Zerubbabel (Ezra 3–6), is credited with the restoration of temple worship. Nehemiah is also important at 2 Macc 2:13–14; perhaps his role as governor and temple restorer provided a model for the activity of Judas. The fire on the altar was never to go out (Lev 6:12–13) and so its miraculous preservation emphasizes the continuity between the first and second temple, which some had questioned (Ezra 3:12; 1 Enoch 89:73; 2 Apoc. Bar. 68:5–6).

The prayer of the priests stresses God's election of Israel, and his role as the Divine Warrior who fights for his people and leads them to their home, as in the hymn in Ex 15. The miracle of the fire is verified and acknowledged by the Persian king, and Nehemiah is recognized as the discoverer of naphtha, a kind of petroleum well known to Hellenistic scientists and geographers (Dioscorides, *De materia medica*, 1.73; Strabo, *Geog.* 15.3.15; 16.1.15). He is thus ranked with other 'inventors' of benefits to mankind, as Dionysos of wine and Demeter of grain. Among Jewish Hellenistic authors, Abraham was said to be the inventor of astrology and mathematics (Eus. *Praep. Evang.* 9.17.3) and Moses the discoverer of ships, weapons of war, and Egyptian religion (ibid. 9.27.4–6).

(2:1–15) The Temple and Earlier Traditions The narrative now answers the question of who had ordered the sacred fire to be taken to Babylonia, and the answer is Jeremiah. While that story shows the continuity between the first temple and the second, the hiding of the sacred vessels on Mt. Nebo shows the discontinuity. The sacred vessels are returned to God's mountain until the ingathering of the people when, as during the Exodus (Ex 40:34–8) and at the dedication of the first temple by Solomon (1 Kings 8:10), God's glory will appear again.

v. 4, many traditions clustered around the figure of Jeremiah. He will appear again as an intercessor for his people at 2 Macc 15:14–16. Eupolemus, perhaps the ambassador of Judas Maccabeus, stated that Jeremiah preserved the ark and the tablets from the Babylonians (Eus. *Praep. Evang.* 9.39.5) and the Letter of Jeremiah similarly exhorts the exiles to refrain from idolatry.

vv. 9–12, the reference to Moses and Solomon in v. 8 is further developed. There is no mention of Moses' praying at Lev 9:23–4 when fire consumes the burnt offering, although at Solomon's prayer fire came down (2 Chr 7:1). The saying of Moses in v. 11 is not found in the HB although the event referred to derives from Lev 10:16–20. The command to celebrate the Feast of Tabernacles for eight days given at Lev 23:33–6 seems to be missing before v. 12. These stories all testify to the lively narrative world of Second-Temple Judaism as the traditional stories were told and retold with creative nuances.

vv. 13–15, after discussing the divine fire at the time of Moses and Solomon, the author returns to Nehemiah and his fire exploits. Interesting is the reference to Nehemiah's founding a library and collecting books. After Ptolemy I founded the great library at Alexandria, others imitated him as did the Attalid kings of Pergamum in Asia Minor. Nehemiah is being put in good company! Scholars have puzzled over exactly what is referred to in the list of books. Rather than attempting to align this list neatly with specific books of the canonical HB, one should recognize that, as the finds at Qumran are showing us, Judean society was filled with many more stories, hymns, and retellings of traditional narratives than are extant today. 1 Macc 1:56–7 relates how the books of the law were ripped apart and burnt if found. Judas is said to act similarly to Nehemiah, and so another element of the comparison made at 2 Macc 1:18 is introduced. Does v. 15 suggest a superiority of the library at Jerusalem as regards Jewish books to the one in Alexandria?

(2:16–18) Conclusion The request of 1:18 is repeated here, and interwoven with the themes of God as Divine Warrior (1:25), of the people as God's inheritance (1:26–7), and of the ingathering of the people (1:27–9; 2:3). The reference in v. 18 to God's rescue of his people and his purification of the place provides the appropriate introduction to the epitome. As mentioned in the introduction, we do not know what exactly the relationship is between the two prefixed letters and the epitome. One can suggest corresponding themes, but there is no intrinsic connection.

The Epitome (2:19–15:39)

(2:19–32) Prologue The author writes an elegant preface to his work, outlining his source, the contents of the work, his aims, and his methods. He shows his control of the current historiographical methods and style, and his command of Greek. The source of his work is Jason of Cyrene, of whom we know nothing. Ptolemy I Lagus is said to have settled a group of Jews in Cyrenaica (Jos. Ag. Ap. 2.44) and Jewish inscriptions have been located there. At the time of Sulla (around 85 BCE), Strabo stated that the city of Cyrene was composed of four elements, citizens, farmers, resident aliens, and Jews (Jos. Ant. 14.115). Jason would therefore have been a Greek-speaking Jew from Cyrenaica which was under the control of the Ptolemies.

As for the content of the book, the author says nothing about the events under Seleucus IV which open the book (ch. 3) nor those under Demetrius I which close the book (chs. 14–15). The operative word for the author appears to be the term 'epiphany'/'appearance', a word which the author uses throughout the work, and which appears also in these chapters (3:24; 14:15; 15:27). In this prologue, the author, who loves to play on words, contrasts Antiochus IV Epiphanes and the 'epiphanies' which God gave his people. A further contrast is between Judaism and the barbarian hordes. This is the first known use of the term 'Judaism', seemingly coined to contrast with 'Hellenism' (2 Macc 4:13) and 'allophylism/foreign ways' (2 Macc 4:13; 6:25). The Greeks called those who did not speak their language 'barbarians'. Here the author is calling the Greek-speaking Seleucids the barbarians.

The aims and methods that the author espouses are those standard for Hellenistic historians, as is the motif of hard work undertaken willingly for the benefit of the reader. At v. 24, the author does not really claim to get rid of 'the flood of statistics'; the terms rather mean that the author is concerned to shorten the number of lines, of which there would have been quite a few in a five-volume work.

(3:1–39) The First Attack on the Temple The first attack and the first epiphany are set during the reign of Seleucus IV Philopator (187–175 BCE). The story is similar to other accounts written in praise of a deity who defends his/her temple: the attack, the plea for help, the response of the deity, the rout of the enemy, and the rejoicing of the defenders. One finds such a scheme, for example, in the repulse of Sennacherib from Jerusalem (2 Chr 32:1–22; 2 Kings 18:17–19:36), and in the defence of Delphi by Apollo against the Persians under Xerxes in 480 BCE (Hdt. 8.37–9) and against the Gauls in 179 BCE (Paus. 10.23.2).

(3:1–8) The Problem The city is described as idyllically at peace. The author stresses that peace depends on the piety of the leader, the high priest, a theme found in the books of Kings (1 Kings 9:1–9; 2 Kings 17:7–8; 21:11–15). The behaviour of Onias will stand in sharp opposition to that of his successors in the office. This utopian picture contrasts with the conflict and division described in the history of the Qumran Covenanters (CD 1) and in the narrative of 1 Enoch 1–11. The benign relationship of the ruling powers depicted here is similar to what is found elsewhere as the Persian kings had provided for the sacrificial cult (Ezra 6:9–10; 7:20–3), and Josephus states that the Ptolemies and Antiochus III had bestowed privileges on Jerusalem (Ant. 12.50, 58, 138–44; Ag. Ap. 2.48).

vv. 4–8, this utopian scene is disrupted. One should follow the Latin and Armenian translations which show that Simon belonged, not to the tribe of Benjamin, but to the priestly clan of Bilgah (Neh 12:5, 18; 1 Chr 24:14). Simon's exact position is not known, as the term for 'captain' could cover civil and military as well as religious functions, nor do we know if he had been appointed by the high priest or by Seleucid authorities. Precisely what the conflict was over is not known either: was the disagreement over what the duties of the supervisor of the market were, or who would supervise all aspects of buying and selling? According to the Temple Scroll (11QT 47:7–18), only hides from clean animals sacrificed in Jerusalem could be brought into Jerusalem, whereas the decree of Antiochus III on the temple only forbade the hides of unclean animals and did not require that the hides be from animals sacrificed in Jerusalem (Jos. Ant. 12.146). This purity debate obviously has economic implications. Is this the basis for the conflict, or is it more likely a power-play between two factions in the small city-state of Judea? Such power-plays were earlier evident in Jerusalem in the historical romance of the Tobiads (Ant. 12.154–222). Simon was the brother of Menelaus, the future high priest, and one should see here a struggle between important families for control of the city. Simon makes his move by appealing to the governor, who, not willing to interfere in temple affairs, sends the question to the Seleucid ruler. The Peace of Apamea in 188 BCE had imposed a large indemnity on the Seleucids and so they were looking for funds. Seleucus reasoned that Simon's suggestion did not involve any sacrilege as it was not a question of funds for the actual temple cult, and so sent Heliodorus, chancellor of the realm, who had been brought up with him.

(3:9–14a) The Attack on the Temple The author stresses the friendly reception of the Seleucid minister to underline the unexpectedness of the attack. The high priest cleverly responds, basing his argument on the idea that deposits in temples should not be violated, particularly those of widows and orphans who are particularly protected by God (Ps 146:9; Deut 27:19; Isa 1:23). The mention by the high priest of deposits in the temple by a Hyrcanus, son of Tobias, has led some scholars to suggest that Onias was pro-Ptolemaic and the leader of an anti-Seleucid faction. Within the Tobiad romance preserved in Josephus' Antiquities (12.154–222), the Tobiads and the youngest son Hyrcanus are depicted as closely allied with the Ptolemies. However, such a suggestion seems totally out of place in a context in which the high priest is trying to win over the Seleucid minister. Would he bring his anti-Seleucid leaning to the attention of Heliodorus? More likely, Hyrcanus is simply mentioned as an important personage.

(3:14b–21) The Plea for Divine Help The description of the distress of the citizens is highly emotional. The author stresses the involvement of the whole populace, as married women, usually excluded from public business, and unmarried women, normally hidden out of sight, are included.

(3:22–30) The Response of the Deity The author highlights the sovereignty of God through the title given to him at v. 24 and the reference to God's sovereign power at v. 28. This first epiphany has first a horseman and then two young men and so Bickerman (1979) suggested that there were two intertwined accounts, one with the horseman (vv. 24–5, 27–8, 30) and another with the two young men (vv. 26, 29, 31–4). However, one could also argue that the author is displaying God's power through several agents. The description of the avenging figures as dressed in golden armour and extremely handsome is how divine interveners are usually portrayed in Hellenistic literature.

(3:31–9) The Effect of the Miracle Heliodorus later appeared in history in a plot to assassinate Seleucus IV, and so this story sees his recuperation. His recognition of the power of the God of Israel does not mean that Heliodorus converted, only that he acknowledges the power of the deity who resides there. A similar story is told of Ptolemy IV Philopator in 3 Macc 1–2, but Ptolemy does not repent on his recovery. Recognition of the power of the resident deity is a theme in the story of how the Persian commander Datis was forced to proclaim the power of the goddess Athene who sent a miraculous thirst on the Persian forces when they besieged the isle of Lindos (Faure 1941). The healing of Heliodorus through a sacrifice, possibly a reparation offering about deposits (Lev 6:1–7; Num 5:5–10), and the prayer of the high priest, highlight that Heliodorus was defeated by divine aid, not by some human ambush. Heliodorus in turn offered sacrifice, perhaps a sacrifice of well-being (Lev 7:11–18), as Alexander is reported by Josephus to have done (*Ant.* 11.336). Both sacrifices emphasize the power of the God of Israel and suggest that Jews and Gentiles can live on good terms, as long as the rights of the Jews are respected.

(3:39–10:8) The Second Attack on the Temple The second attack encompasses the time of Antiochus IV. The section has the same structure as in the earlier part of ch. 3: attack against the temple and the traditional way of life (4:1–6:17); the cry for help (6:18–7:42); God's answer (chs. 8–9); the reversal of the effects of the attack (10:1–8).

(3:39–6:17) The Attack on the Traditional Way of Life The traditional way of life is disturbed when the pious high priest Onias is removed from Jerusalem and replaced by an innovative high priest, Jason, and his usurper, Menelaus (4:1–5:10). This internal disruption is then followed by the attack of the outsider, Antiochus IV (5:11–6:10). The author has interspersed his narrative with reflections on the significance of events (4:16–17; 5:17–20; 6:12–17), which evidence the author's belief in the election of Israel by God and the requirement that Jews live according to the laws of the covenant.

(3:39–4:6) The Removal of Onias 3:39 sums up the events in the previous chapter, but 4:1 shows that the underlying problem, the rivalry between families of the ruling élite, still exists. The increase in violence is an index of the breakdown of the polity, but now the new Seleucid governor takes an active role in the political in-fighting by supporting Simon against Onias. We do not know why he would encourage such unrest. Onias' response is to go over his head to the king. The author insists that this is not Onias playing politics, but altruistic concern for the welfare of Jerusalem. This selflessness of

Onias will constrast sharply with the self-seeking motives of his successors.

(4:7–22) The High-Priesthood of Jason The author omits the details of Seleucus IV's assassination, the installation of his young son, and the usurpation of the throne by Seleucus' brother, Antiochus IV Epiphanes, who returned from Rome where he had been a hostage (App. *Syr.* 45; cf. Dan 11:20–1). A new monarch would appoint or confirm rulers in their position, and Jason, Onias' brother, seized the opportunity to grasp for the position of high priest. The annual indemnity imposed by the Romans on the Seleucids at the Treaty of Apamea was 1,000 talents of silver, and so Jason's offer of 590 talents, quite a hefty sum for a small country like Judea, would have been welcomed towards paying the few last instalments.

Exactly what Jason wanted in exchange has long been debated. The gymnasium was the sign *par excellence* of Greek life. Originally designed for physical and military training, the gymnasium normally had a running-track and a wrestling area, and sometimes areas for jumping and javelin- and discus-throwing. There were buildings for changing and bathing, and for storing oil. Later, gymnasia became centres for intellectual training with halls for lectures on various topics, but exactly when this changeover took place is unclear. One does not know how much intellectual training would have been carried on in a city like Jerusalem in the early second century BCE. The group called 'ephebes', translated 'body of youth' in NRSV, were boys who had reached the age of puberty. At Athens for a short period of time in the late fourth century BCE, all young men aged 18–20, the ephebes, had to do compulsory military training for two years before being enrolled as citizens of Athens. In the late second century, ephebes were still doing such military exercises as archery and the use of siege-engines. Few families could afford not to let their sons work for two years, and this period of training, as with education in general, became primarily for the sons of rich families. The ephebate involved the young men in the public life of a city, and they would participate in its religious festivals and processions. It is important to note that education in the Hellenistic world was to fit a student to be a citizen of that particular city with its peculiar civic and religious responsibilities. The physical exercises would remain the same, as would the study of mathematics and the ability to read and write Greek, but such lessons would take place within the context of the city's traditional culture. Even the physical exercises, however, evidenced a desire to be part of the larger world, as athletes from different cities would compete against each other (4:18–20). Construction and maintenance of such a facility would have been costly and one gains a sense of the wealth of these aristocratic families. According to 4:12, the gymnasium lay right under the citadel. If one locates the citadel on the south-eastern hill of Jerusalem, the gymnasium would lie either between the city of David and the temple or in the broad ravine which separated the Lower from the Upper City (Jos. *JW* 5.140).

Jason's further request in 4:9b has been much disputed: should one translate 'to enrol the people of Jerusalem as Antiochenes, i.e. as citizens of Antioch', or 'to enrol the Antiochenes in Jerusalem'? Who were these Antiochenes? Four suggestions have been made: (1) the Hellenized Jews would be made citizens of Antioch of Syria; (2) that Antiochus IV had set up a new republic on the pattern of the Roman one and its citizens were to be called Antiochenes (Goldstein 1983); (3) that a Hellenistic corporation was to be set up in Jerusalem whose members would be called Antiochenes (Bickerman 1979); (4) that Jerusalem itself would now become a Greek *polis*, called Antioch-in-Jerusalem, and its citizens called Antiochenes (Tcherikover 1961). The first three seem unlikely: even a king could not force a city to bestow *en bloc* citizenship on those of another city; Antiochus IV seems to have supported local traditions rather than instituted a new republic; the word for Antiochene always refers, not to members of a corporation, but to citizens. The last suggestion seems the best, although it is intriguing that the author of 2 Maccabees does not complain about such a name change, and 1 Maccabees does not mention it. Many ancient cities received new Greek names, and this seems the best explanation for this verse. What did such a name change involve? Tcherikover (1961) argued that the change had constitutional implications: theoretically the Mosaic law could be overthrown as the law of the city, and Jason would control who became citizens of the city—only those who underwent ephebic training could become citizens of Antioch-in-Jerusalem. However, there is no evidence that a name change meant a change in constitution, nor that ephebic training was the only way to become a citizen. All we can say is that the name was changed, but even that implies that Jason wanted to connect Judea more closely with the Seleucid empire. Jason's position depended on royal favour, and Antiochus not only gained more money but a secure ally on his southern border.

The author of 2 Maccabees uses all his rhetorical skill to condemn what Jason did. As noted above, education was intimately tied to preparation for public life in a city. The author depicts Jason's educational reforms as a denial of traditional Jewish culture. Hellenization, which formerly meant the use of a pure style of the Greek language, is now labelled as foreign, and Jason is said to be a wicked priest. The author mocks concern for physical pursuits rather than spiritual. At v. 13, the Greek hat is the broad-brimmed hat worn by athletes to protect them against the sun, and said to be that of Hermes, the god of athletics. At v. 14, the signal was that given to start activity, not specifically discus-throwing. The reflection of the author at vv. 16–17 shows the author's notion of just deserts, whereby the punishment meted is appropriate to the crime committed (4:26, 38; 5:9–10; 13:8; 15:32).

vv. 18–22 show further how Jason was concerned to integrate Judea into the Seleucid empire. Every four years games were held at Tyre in honour of the god Melqart/Heracles, perhaps in imitation of Alexander the Great's celebration of games to Heracles after capturing Tyre in 331 BCE (Arr. *Anab.* 3.6.1). Jason sends official representatives of Antioch-in-Jerusalem. The author contrasts the action of Jason with that of the envoys who use the 300 silver drachmas, the customary price for a sacrificial ox, to fit out triremes, Greek ships with three rows of oars. Such a fitting-out would seem to go against the stipulations of the Treaty of Apamea. Did Jason reason that such a sacrifice was not against the Torah, in line with the Greek translator of Ex 22:28 who translated 'You shall not revile the gods', a translation which seems to imply that the

gods of other nations could be honoured as subordinate to the supreme God of Israel? The author clearly sees Jason as an apostate. Jason's welcome to Antiochus on his visit to Jerusalem is similar to the ceremonial reception of Hellenistic kings and again emphasizes the friendly relations between Jews and their Greek rulers.

(4:23–5:10) The Rule of Menelaus The Bilgah clan gained control of the city as Simon's brother, Menelaus, successfully outmanoeuvred Jason, who fled across the Jordan. The reader is now informed that there was a Seleucid garrison in the city, perhaps stationed in response to the Ptolemaic threat, and manned by mercenaries from Cyprus. Since Sostratus' duties involved collecting the revenue, there was probably a division of authority within Jerusalem, with a regular royal functionary operating within and above the city's political structure.

Menelaus' tenure is marked by murder and intrigue. Short of cash, he had sold temple treasure perhaps to pay his taxes, as had Hezekiah (2 Kings 18:13–16). Using temple vessels to pay taxes is one thing, using them to connive at murder is quite another matter. Clearly Onias III, as well as the epitomist, thought it wrong to sell temple vessels. Onias is depicted as upholding tradition, but yet appears to take sanctuary in the famous temple of Apollo and Artemis in Daphne. The murder of Onias by the utterly treacherous Andronicus, perhaps the same Andronicus who is said by Hellenistic historians to have murdered the son of Seleucus IV (Diod. Sic. 30.7.2), has the author emphasize the motif of just deserts, and also the fact that non-Jews can have a sympathetic attitude towards Jews unjustly punished.

(4:39–50) Further Charges against Menelaus Whereas Onias had protected the temple, Menelaus and Lysimachus despoil it, and launch an armed attack against the unarmed citizens who protest their actions. Divine help is intimated in the fact that unarmed citizens put to flight the armed followers of Lysimachus, who dies. Where Onias had been slandered by Simon (4:1), the true charges against Menelaus are dismissed and justice is perverted through bribery. Ptolemy son of Dorymenes may already have been governor of Coelesyria and Phoenicia as at 8:8. He certainly continues the favourable attitude to the Bilgah faction that Apollonius is said to have shown (4:4). He acts against the three members of the Jewish council, a body known from a letter of Antiochus III (Jos. *Ant.* 12.142), but whose exact function is unknown. As at the murder of Onias, non-Jews are shown as sympathetic to the unfairly condemned councillors.

(5:1–10) Jason's Uprising The author of 2 Maccabees locates the events after the second invasion of Antiochus IV in Egypt in 168 BCE, while 1 Maccabees places them after his first invasion (170/169 BCE). According to Dan 11:28–30, there were two invasions of Egypt and two attacks against the temple, but Daniel does not explicitly state that Antiochus IV came in person against Jerusalem the second time. The chronology of 1 Maccabees is to be preferred, and the epitomist has perhaps run the two attacks on the temple together. 1 Maccabees gives a precise date for the second attack by the captain of the Mysians (1 Macc 1:29), whereas 2 Maccabees does not (5:24).

Portents are frequently described in non-Jewish literature as occurring before a momentous event (Tacitus, *Histories*,

2.50.2; 78.2). The closest parallel to this passage is found in the narrative of Josephus about events before the destruction of Jerusalem (*JW* 6.298–9). Such portents could be interpreted in different ways: Jason must have hoped that Antiochus' successor would accept the *fait accompli* of his defeat of Menelaus, but he failed. Tcherikover suggested that he did so because a third force of pious crowds as at 4:40 rose up to repel him, but it is more likely that the citadel, well-stocked and defended by the Seleucid garrison, could hold out until reinforcements came. Jason's death is depicted in terms of just deserts. 1 Macc 12:6–18, 20–3 also speaks of a fictive relationship between the Jews and the Spartans. Many Hellenistic cities sought to connect themselves to famous events and cities, as the Romans traced their origins to Aeneas the Trojan.

(5:11–6:17) The Attack on the Temple This section contains Antiochus' own attack on Jerusalem (5:11–20); the repressive measures he imposed on Jerusalem (5:21–7); the new cult imposed (6:1–11). The author includes two reflections on what was happening (5:17–20; 6:12–17).

(5:11–20) Antiochus' Attack The parallel account is found at 1 Macc 1:20–4, but there no reason is given for Antiochus' assault after his first invasion of Egypt. At that time, Antiochus had not captured Alexandria, but had installed his nephew Ptolemy VI Philometor, with himself as Ptolemy's guardian. It is not known why Antiochus withdrew from Egypt, but perhaps he was satisfied with a weakened Ptolemaic empire. A Babylonian text records that Antiochus celebrated his victory with a great festival in August/September 169 BCE, and such a festival suggests that Antiochus was satisfied with his incursion. If Jason's coup attempt occurred after the second invasion, the author of 2 Maccabees makes no mention of the rebuff of Antiochus by the Romans and writes as if the only reason Antiochus left Egypt was to put down the revolt in Jerusalem. He dehumanizes Antiochus with animal-like descriptions—'inwardly raging' is literally 'wild-beast-like in soul'. The author is not concerned with exact chronology or exact numbers so much as with rhetorical polemic. At about the same time, Antiochus was forcibly extracting treasures from a temple in Babylon, so Jerusalem must not be seen as a special act of temple despoliation on the part of Antiochus. His liberal gifts to Greek cities, particularly to Athens where he wanted to complete the magnificent temple of Zeus, made him always on the look-out for more revenue. The contrast between Onias and Menelaus is shown as Onias had defended the deposits in the temple while Menelaus now guides Antiochus in his plunder of the temple.

At 5:17–20, the author reflects on the discrepancy between Antiochus' purpose and that of God: Antiochus is uplifted, thinking himself special, but God is simply using him as the instrument of his anger. This motif is found earlier at Isa 10:5–15 concerning the role of the king of Assyria. The theology is that of Deuteronomy where, if the people disobey God's laws, they will be punished (Deut 11:13–17; 28; cf. Jer 18–19). The hope of restoration expressed in v. 20 looks forward to the events of ch. 8, and reflects the prayer of Solomon at the dedication of the first temple (1 Kings 8:46–53).

(5:21–7) Antiochus' Measures in Jerusalem The arrogance of Antiochus is described as was that of the Persian king Xerxes who dared to bridge the Hellespont and cut a canal through Mt. Athos (Hdt. 7:22–4, 34–7; Aesch. *Pers.* 69–72, 744–51). Philip appears again at 6:11; 8:8 and was perhaps the commander of the Seleucid garrison in Jerusalem. The enemy of the Jews is called a barbarian, as at 2:21. It is fascinating to note how the author of 2 Maccabees binds the Jews and the Samaritans as one people in v. 22 and 6:2, whereas Josephus reports a letter from same Samaritans which forcefully argues that the Samaritans are not like the Jews (*Ant.* 12.257–61).

The account parallels that of 1 Macc 1:29–40. There a purpose for the attack is given—to install and fortify a strong Seleucid garrison in the city. In 2 Maccabees, however, the attack seems unprovoked and senseless, duplicating the action of Antiochus at 5:13–14. The author also dates it to the sabbath, thereby heightening the offence (cf. Jos. *Ag. Ap.* 1.209–12). The author of 1 Maccabees dates the event two years after Antiochus' first invasion of Egypt, i.e. to 167 BCE, and so not long after Antiochus' humiliation by the Romans in Egypt. These further fortifications might be part of an attempt to strengthen Antiochus' southern border.

In the midst of this tragedy the author strikes a hopeful note with the mention of Judas Maccabeus. The author has Judas living in Jerusalem until this. He makes no mention of Mattathias, the father of Judas, who is such an important personage in 1 Maccabees. The author of 1 Maccabees, concerned to highlight the Hasmonean family (1 Macc 5:62), focuses on the reaction of Mattathias to the persecutions but gives little attention to the martyrdoms. The author of 2 Maccabees, on the other hand, views the martyrdoms as the appropriate reaction to persecution and God's mercy comes through the martyrdoms (7:38; 8:5). Judas's story is placed before the persecution to provide hope for the reader. The wilderness was the traditional place of refuge (1 Sam 23:14; 1 Kings 19:1–9). Here Judas escapes from the pollution in the city into the natural world of the mountains (cf. Hos 2:14–15; Mk 1:12).

(6:1–11) The Imposed Cult Further measures are now taken by the king, measures directed against the Jews in Judea, not all Jews in the empire. We do not know why Antiochus took this extremely unusual step of outlawing Jewish religion in Judea. 1 Maccabees blames the megalomania of the emperor who is said to have wanted all nations to be the same and to give up their particular customs (1 Macc 1:41–2). Antiochus is thus portrayed as zealous in the spread of Hellenization. However, all the evidence we possess points in the direction of Antiochus encouraging local customs, rather than attempting to suppress them (Mørkholm 1966). Rather, Antiochus must have considered the cult in Judaea to be the focal point of resistance to his administration, even though the high priest Menelaus was his friend, and its suppression a final step in trying to stabilize conditions in this restless southern border region. The king's agent is Geron the Athenian (NRSV marg.). Jews are no longer to follow the civic institutions of their ancestors, not even privately, as the stories at 6:10–11 show. The first change is to the name. Olympios and Xenios ('the Friend-of-Strangers') are both common epithets for Zeus. The author gives a reason for the name Xenios, but the translation is uncertain. The NRSV accepts an emendation of the text to bring it into line with the petition, known from Josephus (*Ant.* 12.261), of some Samaritans to Antiochus IV requesting that their temple be renamed Zeus Hellenios. However, the author seems to hold no antipathy to the Samaritans but rather links the two together in undergoing oppression from Antiochus (5:22–3), and so one could maintain the present text and translate 'as those who live there are hospitable'.

What exactly was the cult imposed? In posing the question in this fashion, scholars have undertaken to find one particular cult substituted for the cult in Jerusalem. Noticing how the Hebrew expression for 'abomination of desolation', which is used in Dan 9:27; 11:31 and is reflected in the corresponding Greek terms at 1 Macc 1:54, is a play on the name Baal Shamem, i.e. Lord of heaven, scholars such as Bickerman (1979) argued that the cult imposed was a Syro-Canaanite cult. Tcherikover (1961) followed him in this, adding that the cult was that of the Syrian garrison stationed in the citadel, while Goldstein (1983) suggested it was the cult of a heterodox Jewish garrison in the citadel. Bringmann (1983) noted that the sacrifice of pigs and the prohibition of circumcision would be against Syrian religion and so suggested that the cult was created by Menelaus. Rather than looking for one cult to substitute for another, however, perhaps simply the worship of many gods was introduced. 1 Macc 1:47 speaks of many altars, sacred precincts, and shrines for idols, and 2 Macc 10:2 mentions that altars had been built in the public square of Jerusalem and that there were sacred precincts. Besides Zeus Olympios and Dionysos, other gods would have been worshipped.

The description at 6:3–6 differs from the accounts in 1 Maccabees and Dan 7–12. Cult prostitution is prohibited at Deut 23:17; getting rid of cult prostitutes is praised (1 Kings 15:12; 22:46; 2 Kings 23:7), while their presence is a sign of evil (1 Kings 14:24). The author of 2 Maccabees seems to be using stereotypical accusations to point out the barbarism of the actions. Antiochus III had proclaimed that only the sacrificial animals known to their ancestors were to be introduced into Jerusalem (Jos. *Ant.* 12.145–6), and this is now done away with. It is noteworthy that the author does not mention the desolating sacrilege of Dan 11:31; 1 Macc 1:54. Also, one wonders what precisely is meant by 'confess themselves to be Jews'. Does Jew mean more than a geographical designation, i.e. someone who follows the Torah, or does the phrase mean that one had to call oneself an Antiochene? The author insists that the Jews were forced to take part in the pagan festivals, in contrast to 1 Macc 1:52 which states that many were eager to follow the new practices. The attempt to force Jews to follow Greek ways is extended to neighbouring cities, probably those which bordered on Judea so that the Judeans could not slip across the border to practise their religion. v. 8 is difficult: the verb can mean either the less forceful 'suggest' or the stronger 'enjoin'; and the MSS read either 'Ptolemais', i.e. the coastal city, or 'of Ptolemy', i.e. Ptolemy the governor of Coelesyria and Phoenicia (4:45). Ptolemais was later hostile to the Jews (1 Macc 5:14; 2 Macc 13:25), but so was Ptolemy.

Two examples of the persecution are then adduced (cf. 1 Macc 1:60–1; 2:31–8). Women with babies at their breasts, who would normally enjoy privacy at home are paraded publicly through the streets as opponents of Antiochus' ideals for the city. Men who meet outside the city and away from sight are still burnt, their rituals seen as a threat to the state. The ritual

of initiation into Judaism, circumcision (Gen 17:9–14), and the sabbath, the sign of God's delivering his people from Egypt (Deut 5:12–15), are outlawed.

(6:12–17) Reflections of the Author The persecution is interpreted as God's discipline of his people, pre-empting a harsher judgement. As at Deut 8:5, God is seen as a parent who trains and educates his child. In some ways this differs from Wis 11:10–12:27 where God's forbearance towards other nations is to give them time to repent (cf. Sir 5:4–8).

(6:18–7:42) The Cry for Help After providing a reflection on the events, the author focuses on the martyrdoms of Eleazar and the mother and her seven sons. That the two narratives are tied together is shown by the concluding note at 7:42: 'the eating of sacrifices' is a term found in the story of Eleazar (6:18), the term for 'tortures' is found at 7:1, 13, 15. The author sees these events as the pivotal point in turning God's anger into mercy (7:38; 8:5).

(6:18–31) Eleazar The story of Eleazar is retold in greater detail in 4 Macc 5–7. There he is a priest (4 Macc 5:4), here he is a scribe. The exact social meaning of this term is not certain, but it means more than someone who copies or writes documents. He is a leading official, well known to those in charge of the sacrifices. We do not know if they are Jews or non-Jews. As all heroes, Eleazar is handsome, of noble birth, and dignified. Pork was prohibited by the Torah (Lev 11:7–8; Deut 14:8). The method of torture is unclear: *tympanon* is a drum, stick, or wagon-wheel and so the sense is of something turning around, perhaps a rack. The narrative is full of rhetorical flourishes and contrasts, as the last words are designed to arouse emotion in the reader. Eleazar refuses any contradiction betwen his private and public behaviour; consistency, not hypocrisy, is his watchword. He is a model of *aretē* (Simonides, *Lyra Graeca*, LCL ii 359, no. 127), just as Achilles chose death with honour rather than long life without glory (Homer, *Iliad*, 9.410–16). Here a Jew rather than the Seleucid officials symbolizes this classical Greek virtue. What is interesting is that there is no mention of restoration to life in this story. Eleazar asks that he be sent down to the bleak world of Hades. Eleazar is not seeking a reward, only to live nobly.

(7:1–42) The Mother and her Seven Sons After the martyrdom of an important male comes the story of the deaths of a mother and her sons. Stories of whole families perishing under attack are found in Jewish literature, for example in the story of Taxo and his seven sons (*As. Mos.* 9) and in that of the Galilean martyrs (Jos. *JW* 1.312–13; *Ant.* 14.429–30) and in Greek literature, as in the deaths of Theoxena and her sister's children (Polyb. 23.10–11). The particular story of a mother with her seven sons, so laden with emotion, was a favourite one in later rabbinic literature, either before a Roman emperor (*b.Git.* 57b; *Midr. Lam.* 1:16) or more generally in the days of persecution (*Pesiq. R.* 43). The folklore motif of the importance of the youngest son is also found in this traditional tale. The story is loosely connected with the preceding account, and scholars have wondered where it took place. Later tradition, both Jewish and Christian, located it at Antioch. However, there is no indication of a change of scene from the preceding account, and the folk-tale type where a ruler is bested by a wiser underling argues against any search for a specific locale. The wicked character of the emperor is stressed, as the martyrs respond calmly while the emperor loses control of himself.

vv. 3–5, the brothers are all dehumanized, as first the tongue, the instrument of human communication, is cut out and then, with legs and arms lopped off, the first brother is fried like an animal. vv. 6–7, the quotation from Deut 32:36 is apt, as the purpose of the song of Deut 32 is to confront the people as a witness. The quotation is from that section of the song where God, after chastising his faithless people, begins to take vengeance on his instruments of anger who think they have conquered God's people by their own power.

vv. 7–9, the boy uses his last breath to contrast Antiochus' limited power with that of the King of the universe. The mention of a renewal of life evidences the growing belief in a resurrection and judgement after death. As noted, the story of Eleazar only speaks of the traditional shade-like existence in Sheol/Hades. In the psalms, however, there are passages which speak of a longing for a continued enjoyment of God (Ps 73:23–6; 16:9–10; 84:10), and also passages which speak of resurrection in the context of national restoration (Ezek 37; Hos 6:2; the fascinating Isa 26:19). 1 Enoch speaks of an after-death judgement (1 Enoch 22–7; 91:10; 93:2; 104:1–16) and Dan 12:2–3 clearly expresses a belief in resurrection (cf. also 1 Enoch 90:33). The Greek translators of passages such as Isa 26:19; Job 19:24–6; 14:14 seem to speak of individual renewal. The threefold repetition of the first person plural in v. 9 shows that the author of 2 Maccabees is speaking of individual resurrection. There probably was a rich tradition about the shades in Sheol (cf. Isa 14:9–22); they can be brought back, but do not like to be disturbed (1 Sam 28:18–19), and Job 14:7–22 asserts that the shades do not come back to this present existence. The boy about to be martyred, however, is made to proclaim that the dead will be given life again, presumably life on this earth as the description at 7:23 resonates with the description of the first human at Gen 2:7.

vv. 13–19, Antiochus is threatened with punishment. Since kings were granted divine honours, this is a radical statement. Hope for the people as a whole is now expressed: the suffering is attributed to their sins, not to the power of Antiochus. Antiochus is now listed among those who fight against God and therefore sure to lose (Isa 14; cf. Eur. Bacch.).

vv. 20–9, the mother's attachment to her ancestral customs is shown, as earlier by the second son (7:8), in her use of Hebrew. In a patriarchal culture, her nobility is shown by her possessing a man's courage. The origin of human life is unknown (Ps 139:13–16; Eccles 11:5), but the author uses language which resonates with the creation of humans at Gen 2:7 when God breathed life into the human's nostrils. Her wisdom is further shown as she tricks the emperor and tells her last son to recall God's creating power when he shaped the unformed world (Gen 1:2, particularly in the LXX). Later Christian writers, such as Origen (On First Principles, 2.1.5) and the Latin translator of 2 Maccabees, interpreted the phrase at v. 28 to mean that God created out of nothing, but the text states that God did not make them from what already existed as properly formed. vv. 30–8, the last and most impressive speech is given to the youngest brother, as appropriate to traditional literature. Themes already met in 2 Maccabees are spoken again: the Hebrews suffer because of their sins as God disciplines them (5:17–20; 6:12–17); the king

should not be arrogant (4:17, 21; 7:15) as God will punish him (7:14–19). The text of v. 36 is difficult to translate: 'endured a brief suffering in exchange for everlasting life and have fallen under God's covenant' or 'endured a brief suffering and have fallen to everlasting life under God's covenant'. The meaning reflects that of earlier statements that God will renew their life for they have followed his laws (7:9, 23). vv. 37–8 foretell what the following narrative will show: the deaths of the martyrs have turned God's wrath to mercy, and Antiochus learns through sickness to confess the power of God. vv. 39–42, as at the beginning of the chapter, the king loses control of himself. 'In his integrity' is literally 'pure', suggesting not only the separation from unclean actions, but also the purification of the temple which will soon occur. We are not told how the mother died, a classic example of patriarchal neglect. Nothing is mentioned of her husband either, as the author focuses on the maternal role of the woman.

(Chs. 8–9) God's Response The response of God to the cry for help comes quickly as Judas wins the first victory (8), and afflicts Antiochus (9).

(8: 1–36) The First Victory The parallel narrative in 1 Macc 3:10–4:25 describes a series of events and tactical manœuvres with various commanders, whereas the author of 2 Maccabees concentrates on one single battle against one commander. Such a focus heightens the dramatic effect. The main villain in 1 Maccabees is Gorgias, whereas in 2 Maccabees it is Nicanor, no doubt to balance the villain in the final battle in 2 Maccabees 14–15. Both are called thrice-wretched (8:34; 15:3).

(8:1–7) The Rise of Judas Last mentioned before the martyrdoms (5:27), Judas and his companions now gather a force of like-minded followers. They have persisted in following 'Judaism' (2:21; 14:38), not the 'Jewish faith' as NRSV translates. The number 6,000 is repeated at 8:16, although some are reported to have left at 8:13. The group prayer employs traditional language, with the motif of blood crying out from the ground recalling the blood of the innocent Abel (Gen 4:10; cf. Heb 12:24, and Deut 32:43). The mention of the levelling of the city looks forward to Antiochus' vow (9:13). God's aid renders Judas unbeatable, although he first used the tactic of surprise raids and ambushes.

(8:8–11) The Reaction of the Seleucids While the account in 1 Maccabees has the matter dealt with at the highest level (1 Macc 3:27), 2 Maccabees has the governor of Coelesyria and Phoenicia deal with the nuisance and is the more likely account. Many Nicanors are mentioned at this time: one is a royal agent of the middle rank mentioned in the letter of the Sidonians in Shechem to Antiochus IV (Jos. Ant. 12.257–64); one is mentioned as being one of the closest friends of Demetrius, son of Seleucus IV (Polyb. 31. 14.4; Jos. Ant. 12. 402); and there is Nicanor the Cypriarch (2 Macc 12:2). It is unlikely that all these references are to the same person. Gorgias was later governor of Idumea (2 Macc 10:14; 12:32), presumably someone with local experience. The author's estimate of a mixed army of 20,000 is half that of 1 Macc 3:38, but still high. Ninety slaves per talent was cheap, perhaps showing contempt for the Jews. At that rate, Nicanor would need to sell 180,000 slaves, many more than those already taken from Jerusalem (5:41). Nicanor is stated to be the author of the plan to enslave, thereby heightening his evil and preparing for the theme of appropriate retribution at the end of the story where Nicanor has to run away like a fleeing slave (8:35).

(8:12–20) Judas's Preparation While others fear, Judas is unafraid. The Gentiles act arrogantly, like Antiochus at 5:17–21. The 'torture of the derided city' echoes the language used of the martyrs (tortures: 7:1, 13, 15, 42; derided: 7:7, 10). Judas, as every good general would do, exhorts his troops. The unconquerable power of God is captured in the phrase 'with a single nod'. Two examples are adduced. The first is known from the HB, the defeat of Sennacherib in 701 BCE (2 Kings 19:35–6; Isa 37:36), the same as used at 1 Macc 7:41 and again at 2 Macc 15:22. The precise reference of the second example is unclear. The Galatians are the Celts who were forced to travel from western and central Europe towards the east and southeast. In 280/279 BCE some Celts invaded Greece, while others went towards Asia Minor in 278/277 BCE and overran many Greek cities. After a long process they were confined to an area north of Phyrgia later called Galatia. Scholars have suggested three possibilities for the example Judas mentions: (1) a battle of Antiochus I against the Celts in the 270s BCE, although this took place in Asia Minor and the text would have to be emended from Babylonia to Bagadonia, near the Tauros mountains in Cilicia; (2) an incident during the rebellion of Molon, governor-general of the eastern satrapies, in 220 BCE; (3) an incident in the rebellion of Antiochus Hierax in 227/226 BCE in the east against his brother Seleucus III—Antiochus used Galatian mercenaries. The last-mentioned seems the best candidate. This passage shows that there were Jewish soldiers serving under the Seleucids, and supports Josephus who said that Antiochus III transferred Jewish soldiers from Babylonia to Phyrgia and Lydia to maintain the loyalty of the local population (*Ant.* 12:147–53).

(8:21–9) The Battle The actual order of the Jewish army is not certain: some MSS read as if Judas appointed his four brothers, Simon, Joseph, Jonathan, and Eleazar, to be in charge of 1,500 men each while Judas read the Scriptures and led another division, the first, the word for which normally means a phalanx unit of 256 men; others suggest that Eleazar read aloud from the Scriptures. 2 Maccabees has one of the brothers named Joseph, while 1 Maccabees calls him John (1 Macc 2:3–5). Whatever the proper understanding, the author of 2 Maccabees wants to stress that the whole family is involved, and therefore divides the forces in a way that is not paralleled elsewhere. The focus is on the Jews following correct covenantal procedure, and so the Scriptures are read (Deut 20:2), and the sabbath observed. Note how the spoils are given not only to the fighters but to the widows and orphans (Deut 14:29; 26:12–15), and to the tortured, which brings back the role of the martyrs in obtaining God's mercy.

(8:30–3) The Defeat of Timothy and Bacchides The shortened character of the work is evident in this section as names and events are introduced without any preparation, and disrupt the flow of the Nicanor story. In 2 Maccabees, there seem to be two Timothys: one who appears at 9:3 and 10:24–38, where he is killed, and another at 12:10–25, where he escapes. In 1 Maccabees there is only one Timothy, who engages Judas's forces three times (1 Macc 5:6–8, 28–34, 37–44). 1 Maccabees appears to relate the events in the proper sequence, and so the author of 2 Maccabees has misplaced events. v. 31 has Judas in

control of Jerusalem, which otherwise does not occur until 10:1–8. The author of 2 Maccabees tightly connects vv. 30–3 with the rest of the Nicanor story, however. The complex of widows, orphans, and tortured is used, the same word for collecting arms is found at vv. 27, 31, and the appropriate retribution motif appears in both. Perhaps the author wants to show how Judas's men behave after victory and also to heighten interest as to what happened to Nicanor. As for Bacchides, in 1 Maccabees he is a high-ranking Seleucid official (1 Macc 7:8–20) and it is unlikely that he would be listed after such a low-level commander as Timothy. Perhaps another Bacchides is meant than the one in 1 Maccabees. The spoil taken to Jerusalem is probably God's portion as in Num 31:28. At v. 32, *patris* should probably not be translated with NRSV as 'city of their ancestors', but as 'fatherland'. Nothing else is known about Callisthenes except that he is appropriately punished. At 1 Macc 1:31, the city is said to have been burnt by the Mysarch commander.

(8:34–6) The Fate of Nicanor Nicanor's plan to enslave the Jews went awry and he himself had to flee like a runaway slave. The help of the Lord (v. 35) was the watchword of Judas's forces (v. 23); the word for defender at v. 36 (*hypermachōn*) resonates with the word for ally (*symmachōn*) at v. 24. The author returns to themes found in his opening chapter: the Jews are invincible when they follow God's law (3:1), and Nicanor, as Heliodorus before him (3:35–9), proclaims God's power.

(9:1–29) The Death of Antiochus Antiochus IV set out in midto late 165 BCE to consolidate his rule in the eastern satrapies. Early in his reign, a local dynasty of priests and princes had risen to power around Persepolis and won their independence. This account appears confused as to the geography, as Persepolis, the old capital of the Persian empire, lay hundreds of miles south-east of Ecbatana in Media. This account of Antiochus' death is one of many versions (2 Macc 1:13–14; 1 Macc 6:1–16; Polyb. 31.9). According to Polybius, Antiochus died after attempting to rob the temple of Nanaia in Elymais, south of Ecbatana. Antiochus, a well-known plunderer of temples and someone always in need of ready cash, took the opportunity to help finance his eastern campaign.

According to a Babylonian chronicle, news of Antiochus' death reached Babylonia in the month Chislev of 148 according to the Babylonian calendar, i.e. between 20 Nov. and 18 Dec. 164BCE (Sachs and Wiseman 1954). The order of 2 Maccabees, where Antiochus dies before the purification of the temple thus seems confirmed over against the order of 1 Maccabees, where Antiochus dies after the purification, although some scholars still dispute this point. However, the narrative of 2 Maccabees has significantly dramatized history. The author concentrates on the death of the arch-enemy of the Jews and places it as part of the victory of God over Israel's attackers, and ignores the more complex details. 1 Maccabees tells of an invasion by the regent Lysias (1 Macc 5:26–35) and there were negotiations to settle the rebellion as evidenced by the letters in 2 Macc 11 which have been put out of order. These negotiations may have included the replacement of the inimical Ptolemy son of Dorymenes by the more friendly Ptolemy Macron as governor of Coelesyria and Phoenicia (2 Macc 10:12–13). The death of Antiochus is told in gruesome detail to highlight God's power. The threat of 2 Macc 8:3 is repeated by Antiochus at 9:14, and 9:3 ties the narrative to the preceding one so that the two chapters work together to show God's vindication of his people.

(9:1–12) The Punishment of Antiochus The last time the king was mentioned he was in a rage (7:39), so now too he rages like a bully against those weaker than him. The seventh brother had prayed that Antiochus' arrogance be punished (7:36; cf. 5:21), and now it begins to be. The punishment is said to fit the crime. The deeds impossible for a human reflect Isa 40:12 and 2 Macc 5:12, and v. 10 compares with the hymns of the prophets Isaiah (14:4–21) and Ezekiel (28:12–19) against proud kings. The cruel punishment of death by worms is found both in Greek (Hdt. 3.66; Diod. Sic. 21.16.4–5) and Jewish writers (Isa 66:24; Jdt 16:17). As Heliodorus came to confess the power of God when flogged (3:33–9), so Antiochus, 'under the scourge of God', came to understand that one must not fight against God.

(9:13–27) The Repentance of Antiochus Antiochus vows, but he will not be heard. One does not know exactly what freedom Antiochus was going to give to Jerusalem. Freedom in the meaning of autonomy was always a slogan that competing parties would use to gain allegiance as, for example, the counter claims of Antiochus Gonatas and Ptolemy I to set all Greek cities free, as well as the Roman Senate declaring in 196 BCE that all Greeks were to be free. Freedom here did not mean independence from the superior party. Each 'free' city would have been allowed to keep its own traditions and system of government, but the relationship between the monarch and each such city was a special one. Nor is one sure what is meant by making the Jews equal to the Athenians. Athens was relatively prosperous in the second century BCE; the Parthenon was restored and the Agora reconstructed. Antiochus IV promised in 174 BCE to complete the unfinished temple of Olympian Zeus. He certainly promises to restore the status quo as at the time of Onias (3:1), but in what way will he become a Jew? Clearly the meaning here is not geographical, i.e. become a Judean, but religious. Would it mean more than the worship of Naaman (2 Kings 5:1–18), or Nebuchadnezzar's confession (Dan 4:34–6)? Does the author envisage Antiochus being circumcised and following the laws of Torah, or being a 'god-fearer'? Compare the debate in Josephus (Ant. 20.34–48) as to whether Izates, king of Adiabene, should be circumcised.

Even in such pain, the king pens a letter, a deathbed testament. The authenticity of the letter has been questioned: either an original letter has been added to, or this letter has been modelled on the form of a genuine letter, possibly a letter to the army for support in any change in leadership. The present letter, whether authentic or not, has been used by the author to further his own rhetorical plan. The addressees, the Jews, are placed before the king, and are said to be 'worthy', 'esteemed', and even 'citizens', although one does not know what the Jews are being said to be citizens of. The Jews as a whole were not usually given citizen rights in any community where they lived: note e.g. 2 Macc 12:3, where the citizens of Joppa are distinct from the Jews living among them. The phrasing, however, suits the author in his desire to show that the Jews are good citizens, i.e. not antisocial. The

greeting formula is quite extravagant, and then the king is said to remember with affection the Jews' esteem and goodwill. After the description of Antiochus' condition in 9:5–12, to describe himself as suffering an annoying illness is a marvellous understatement to say the least, and it suggests that the letter does not belong in its current context. Antiochus trusts the Jews to help in the successful transfer of power, and Antiochus describes his policy towards the Jews as moderate and kind! The thrust of this letter is clearly to put the Jews in as good a light as possible and as good citizens of the empire, contrary to what was suggested by many anti-Jewish stories which circulated in the Hellenistic world.

(9:28) The Death of Antiochus Antiochus is said to die in a strange land, like Jason (5:9–10), although Antiochus died in his own empire. In 1 Macc 6:55–63, Philip was appointed guardian of Antiochus V but was forced out of Antioch by Lysias, who had been left in charge of Antiochus' son. A revolt led by a Philip is mentioned at 2 Macc 13:23, but the narrative in its extreme brevity seems to distinguish between this Philip and the guardian appointed by Antiochus IV. Ptolemy VI Philometor had been driven out of Alexandria in October 164, just before Antiochus' death, and did not return until mid-163, and so the conflict between Lysias and Philip must have occurred around that time. Lysias is said by Josephus (Ant. 12.386) to have had Philip murdered before he reached Egypt.

(10:1–8) The Result of the Lord's Intervention With the death of the contender against God, Antiochus, the people now regain control of the temple and purify it. As the author has emphasized how the temple was overthrown because of the sins of the people (5:17–20; 6:12–17), he stresses the sin of the people and the cleansing of the temple. In contrast, at 1 Macc 4:36–59 not only the purification is stressed but also the dedication of the temple as at 1 Kings 8:63; 2 Chr 7:5; Ezra 6:16–17. 1 Maccabees also underlines the need to defend the temple from those in the citadel (4:41, 60), whereas the epitomist does not mention it here. Setting altars around the agora reflects Greek custom. The restoration of temple worship shows Judas as following the Torah. 1 Macc 4:52 states it was an interval of three years, Dan 12:7 three and a half years. 1 Maccabees is the more likely: the providential care of God is shown by the renewal falling on the anniversary of the defilement. Judas's flight to the mountains is recalled (5:27) and the connection to the Feast of Tabernacles, as in the prefixed letters, is made. The carrying of branches was commanded at Lev 23:40, but the word used here—*thyrsoi*, ivy-wreathed wands—signified what was carried in processions to the god Dionysos and may have been chosen to show again the reversal of the persecution when Jews were forced to process in honour of Dionysos (6:7). The language at v. 8 is repeated almost verbatim at 15:36 to bind the two festivals together.

(10:9–15:36) Further Defence of the Temple Further attacks against the temple by the successors of Antiochus IV are described in this third section. The first section shows marked signs of condensation, whereas the account of Nicanor's expedition is treated more extensively. The author dramatizes his account by focusing on the attacks of the two Nicanors.

(10:9–13:26) The Attacks under Antiochus V The events in this section seem to be structured in such a way that attacks by local leaders (10:14–38; 12:3–45) alternate with major expeditions (chs. 11, 13). First, however, come changes brought about by the new dynasty. Antiochus V was 9 years old and under the guardianship of Lysias (1 Macc 3:33). Lysias kept the position given him by Antiochus IV (1 Macc 3:32), and appointed Protarchos as governor of Coelesyria and Phoenicia. The NRSV at v. 11 is wrong, as the offices of chief minister and governor of Coelesyria did not overlap. A new governor is appointed at 13:24. Ptolemy Macron, former governor of Cyprus, had been loyal to Ptolemy VI Philometor, but the intrigues at the Ptolemaic court and the victory of Antiochus IV in 170/169 BCE led him to go over to Antiochus IV's side, possibly when Antiochus' fleet besieged Cyprus in 168 BCE. Ptolemy's friendly attitude towards the Jews should not be seen as something personal, but as part of Seleucid policy. The previous governors of Coelesyria and Phoenicia, Apollonius (4:4) and Ptolemy son of Dorymenes (4:45; 8:8), had been hostile to the Jews, and they probably reflected court policy. The appointment of Ptolemy Macron and his friendly attitude would then reflect the changed Seleucid policy after peace negotiations had begun under Antiochus IV (11:27–33) and after the first expedition of Lysias in 164 BCE (1 Macc 4:28–9; 2 Macc 11:14, 16–21). These events have been rearranged by the author of 2 Maccabees as he wished to portray Antiochus, not as someone who negotiated peace with the Jews, but as their arch-enemy till overthrown by God. The restoration of the temple called for a rethinking of this friendly policy before the second expedition of Lysias (1 Macc 6:21–8).

(10:14–38) **Attacks by Local Leaders** Campaigns in Idumea (10:14–23): the author provides sparse details, both as regards geographical location and exact naming of opponents. His main concern is to emphasize that it was not the Jews who initiated the attacks, but the Seleucid forces, and that the Jews pray to God as their ally (see 8:24). The figures in vv. 17, 18, 23 for those killed are high. The parallel account is found in 1 Macc 5:3–5. The names of the three commanders in charge of the siege are most likely two brothers of Judas (8:22) and an otherwise unknown Zacchaeus. Scholars have suggested that this episode is a doublet of 1 Macc 5:18, 55–61 where two commanders, jealous of Judas, attempt to win glory for themselves and are defeated. Moreover, Simon is glorified in 1 Maccabees, but not here in 2 Maccabees (see also 14:17): is this subtle anti-Hasmonean polemic on the part of the epitomist? Rather, the epitomist alludes to many stories of compromise (12:24–5), backsliding (12:39–40), and deception (13:21), so this story here should be taken, not as anti-Hasmonean, but as evidencing as do the others the faithfulness and incorruptibility of Judas. The accusation 'lovers of money' was a regular accusation against opponents (see Lk 16:14). The story here should be compared to the story of Achan in Josh 7.

(10:24–38) **The Defeat of Timothy** This campaign is also told with sparse chronological and geographical detail. It is often compared with the campaign of Judas into Ammonite territory reported in 1 Macc 5:6–8, but there are considerable differences. Whereas Judas attacks the Ammonites in their territory (1 Macc 5:6), here Timothy invades Judea (10:24–5) and the battle seems to take place in Judea, if at a considerable distance from Jerusalem (10:27). Timothy is killed in this campaign in 2 Maccabees, but not in the one in 1 Maccabees,

and the town of Gazara (Gezer) in the Shephelah just outside the border of Judea appears to be captured, whereas it is not so until much later by Simon at 1 Macc 13:43–8.

Given that the author has Timothy die here and another Timothy emerge at 12:17–25, he must suppose there were two Timothys. The author emphasizes the size of the threat by speaking of mercenaries, i.e. trained soldiers, and excellent cavalry. The Jewish forces are pictured around the altar in Jerusalem, supplicating God in the traditional signs of mourning as if buried and wearing sackcloth from which shrouds were made. They refer to Ex 23:22, where God promises to be an enemy to their enemies if they listen to his words. After so praying, the Jews await in calm confidence in contrast to the animal rage of their opponents. The epiphany has many Greek touches. In the *Iliad*, a hero is often protected by a god (e.g. 5.436–7). Gigantic figures pursued the fleeing Persians and later the Gauls who had dared to attack Delphi while thunderbolts crashed about them (Hdt. 8.36–9; Paus. 1.4.4; 10.23.1–6). Zeus was pre-eminently Zeus Keraunos who hurls thunderbolts at his enemies (Homer *Od.* 23.330; Hes. *Theog.* 854). There is no satisfactory explanation of why five figures are involved. The motif of taunting defenders occurs again at 12:14–16, and is reminiscent of what happened at David's siege of Jerusalem (2 Sam 5:6–9). Timothy found a perfect hiding-place in a cistern, a large pit with plastered walls for storing water, but to no avail. The victory hymn, as the army marched back to Jerusalem, may be compared to the song of Miriam at the defeat of Pharaoh (Ex 15:20–1), or that after David's defeat of Goliath (1 Sam 18:6–7).

(11:1–38) **The Campaign of Lysias** As mentioned above, the author of 2 Maccabees, to intensify the dramatic quality of the narrative, recorded only one major battle before the death of the arch-enemy, Antiochus IV, and so places the campaign of Lysias after Antiochus' death. The events as recounted in 1 Maccabees show much more action as the first campaign of Lysias occurs during the time of Antiochus IV. The displacement of the campaign of Lysias by the epitomist has made him place all the correspondence of peace negotiations out of order as well.

(11:1–12) **The Campaign** Lysias is given his full title here, rather than at 10:10, which may suggest some misplacement. He is guardian and in charge of the government, positions to which Antiochus IV had appointed him (1 Macc 3:32–3). 'Kinsman' was a high title in the Seleucid hierarchy (cf. 1 Macc 10:89). The number of his forces exceeds that given in 1 Macc 4:28, and is exaggerated. The description of Lysias's intentions at vv. 2–3 is fascinating given what happened under the high priest Jason (4:7–15). v. 4 shows how the author enjoys contrasts, particularly those between the might of men and the power of God. By the Treaty of Apamea, the Seleucids had been forbidden to use elephants. Lysias approaches from the south, as in 1 Macc 4:29. At v. 5, Beth-zur is located five *schoinoi*, not stadia, from Jerusalem by the author. A *schoinos*, a Persian measure, could equal anywhere from 30 to 60 stadia (Strabo, 17.1.24, 41). Five *schoinoi* of 30 stadia would locate Beth-zur about 30 kms. south of Jerusalem, which is almost right. The prayer is for God to send an angel as he had before the Israelites in the Exodus from Egypt (Ex 23:20; 33:2). The commander of the Lord's army had appeared to Joshua before

Jericho (Josh 5:13–15), and Sennacherib's army had been struck down by an angel (2 Kings 19:35). Within the Greek tradition, Theseus is said to have rushed before the Greeks against the Persians at Marathon (Plut. *Thes.* 35), Athena had helped the citizens of Cyzicus (Plut. *Luc.* 10.3), and the twin gods, the Dioscuri, had led the Roman force against the Latins (Dion. Hal. 6.13). The author has taken over Greek descriptions. Here Lysias makes a disgraceful flight, while in 1 Maccabees he makes an orderly retreat in order to collect an even larger force.

(11:13–38) Peace Negotiations Further, 2 Maccabees has Lysias recognize, as Heliodorus had done (3:38–9) that the Hebrews are invincible while God is their ally, and to start peace negotiations. At this point the author brings in four documents which talk of peace. These letters have been much debated. The same year is given for the first, third, and fourth letters although it seems inconsistent with their contents. The second letter has no date. The month in the first letter, Dioscorinthius (11:21), is not known in the Macedonian calendar. Scholars have set out to find what is the correct setting and date for each letter. Habicht (1976) suggested that the third letter reflects peace efforts by Menelaus before Antiochus IV began his eastern mission. When this fell through, Lysias set out on his invasion and then negotiated with the rebels (first letter). The second letter would come at the accession of Antiochus V and be an amnesty to the rebels on that occasion. Bar-Kochva (1988) suggested that negotiations began after Nicanor and Gorgias were defeated, and the first letter represents an interim report and the fourth a sign of Roman willingness to help. Antiochus IV refused to negotiate with the rebels, but acceded to Menelaus' request for a conditional amnesty (third letter). The second letter would be the official reprieve of the persecution by Antiochus V. I would concede a larger role to Menelaus, and place the third letter after the local initiatives had failed. The amnesty offer was rejected, Lysias invaded and then sought peace (first letter) and the fourth letter is the request of the Roman emissaries for a report on the progress of the negotiations. The second letter would be placed either at the accession of Antiochus V, or after Lysias' second expedition.

(11:16–21) First Letter Lysias uses a neutral term *plēthos*, multitude, mass, sometimes people, to refer to the addressees, not the formal *ethnos*, nation, or *gērousia*, senate (11:27), or *dēmos*, people (11:34). Such an address may be a hint that the letter is not written to a formally recognized group. The envoys, John and Absalom, are otherwise unknown but carry Hebrew, not Greek, names. Two sons of an Absalom, Mattathias (1 Macc 11:70) and Jonathan (1 Macc 13:11), fight with Judas's successors. v. 18 should not read with the NRSV 'agreed to what was possible', but rather 'what lies within my competence, I have agreed to'. The year 148 of the Macedonian Seleucid calendar is from Oct. 165 BCE to Sept. 164 BCE. Dioscorinthius has been interpreted as the first month in the Macedonian calendar, Dios, or the fifth, Dystros, or the eighth, Daisios.

(11:22–6) Second Letter v. 23 is phraseology usual at the death of a king, and suggests a time near the accession of Antiochus V. The change to Greek customs most probably refers to the decrees of Antiochus IV: the same verb *politeuesthai* is found at 6:1 and 11:25. The language of v. 25 is similar to that used by Antiochus III (Jos. *Ant.* 12.142) allowing the Jews to live by their ancestral religion. If this letter is dated to the beginning of Antiochus V's reign with Habicht (1976), the temple was already in Judas's hands and the letter simply recognizes the status quo. If with Bar-Kochva (1988) it is dated to the end of Lysias's second expedition (1 Macc 6:55–62), it contains a real concession as Lysias had retaken Jerusalem.

(11:27–33) Third Letter The *gērousia* is the official municipal body in Jerusalem (4:44). Is the letter addressed only to supporters of Menelaus, as some have suggested? The phrase, 'to the other Jews', seems to make it quite general. The fifteenth and thirtieth Xanthicus refer to the middle and end of March respectively. As Antiochus IV left on his eastern campaign in 165 BCE, the concession must have been granted while he was away from Antioch in March 164 BCE, but the allowance of only 15 days to accomplish the conditions seems to cut things a bit close. At v. 31, one should read 'customs' (*diaitēmata*) rather than 'food' (*dapanēmata*), as the kosher laws would be included in the reference to the Torah. The offer is conditional on the cessation of hostilities and the return home of the rebels; if these conditions are not met, hostilities will break out again. The reference to Menelaus is intriguing: elsewhere in 2 Maccabees he is portrayed as a traitor to Judaism, but here he seems to come across as an advocate for allowing the Jews to return to their ancestral customs.

(11:34–8) Fourth Letter After forcing Antiochus IV from Egypt in 168 BCE, the Romans had kept an eye on him. An embassy had been sent to Antioch in 166 BCE, and another would come in 163/162 BCE. This embassy probably took place in autumn 164. The date in the text should probably be disregarded and seen as copying the date on the third letter. The tacit recognition of the rebels as a *dēmos*, a 'people', is a sign of how Rome liked to cause discomfort to other sovereigns: in 164 BCE, the Roman commissioner C. Sulpicius Gallus publicly invited accusations against Eumenes II of Pergamum in his own city of Sardis.

(12:1–45) Further Local Hostilities The author insists that the Jews are peaceful (10:14–15; 14:25), only wanting to follow their own ancestral customs, but they would not be let alone. Various hostile leaders are mentioned, about whom we know nothing more. This author must see the Timothy here as distinct from the earlier Timothy; Nicanor is not, as NRSV translates, governor of Cyprus as Cyprus was at this time in Ptolemaic hands, but rather the commander of Cypriot mercenaries and of a lower rank that the Nicanor of ch. 8 and chs. 14–15.

(vv. 3–9) Deceit in Joppa and Jamnia This incident is not found in 1 Maccabees. Both these events take place at coastal areas, and are linked through the burning of ships in the respective harbours. As non-citizens, the Jews would not take part in a public assembly, but would they have no inkling of the matter? The author wishes to insist on the peaceful character of the Jews, and stress the hatred of the citizen body of these towns. They stand in marked contrast to the citizens of Scythopolis (12:30).

(vv. 12–16) The Campaign in Gilead The scene shifts quickly from the west coast in a march towards Transjordan. The campaign in Gilead is also told in 1 Macc 5:9–36. Arabs are mercenaries in Timothy's forces at 1 Macc 5:39, but the first encounter between Judas's forces and the Nabateans is a peaceful one at 1 Macc 5:24–5. Judas is shown in this incident in 2 Maccabees to be a pragmatist, not someone completely antagonistic to non-Jews. A town named Chaspo is simply mentioned at 1 Macc 5:36, but here it is given a more prominent role. Here the result is much different from that with the Arabs, as the author stresses the blasphemous insults of the enemy. The image of the blood-filled lake is starkly emotional, and reminiscent of the way enemies are put under the ban in the book of Joshua as, for example, at Jericho (Josh 6:21).

(vv. 17–26) The Pursuit of Timothy The author of 2 Maccabees now has Judas and his men travel south. 1 Macc 5:13 states that all male Jews in the land of the Toubiani had been killed, whereas our author insists that Timothy accomplished nothing. At this point in the narrative of 1 Maccabees, the Jewish forces are divided into three, one for Gilead, one for Judaea, and one for Galilee (1 Macc 5:17–18), whereas Judas in 2 Maccabees keeps his forces together. Most likely this reflects the author's intentions to show that, now that God is on the side of the Jews, nothing untoward can happen to them, and that the Jews are unified. The size of Timothy's forces is exaggerated, but only emphasizes the more the epiphany that takes place. vv. 24–6 stress the deceit of Timothy rather than the gullibility of the Jewish commanders, who are shown as deeply concerned about Jewish lives. Carnaim was where Timothy had sent the women and children for refuge, and one wonders if the slaughter encompassed them as well, i.e. was all that lived put under the ban?

(12:26–31) The Road Back to Judea The parallel story is in 1 Macc 5:45–7. As told here, the narrative has a formulaic quality like that at Caspin (vv. 13–16). v. 27 suggests that Lysias, the chancellor of Syria, had a residence in this Transjordanian town. The incident at Scythopolis shows that the Jews do not hate Gentiles but only wish to live peaceably among them. The piety of the Jewish forces is shown in their desire to be at Jerusalem to celebrate a major feast.

(12:32–42) The Battle against Gorgias Judas now turns south of Jerusalem to Idumea. After stories which show the piety of the Jewish forces comes a story which tells what happens to those who are not pious. The few details provided by the author all dramatize the event: the courage and near success of Dositheus, the weariness of the troops, the rallying prayer and the shouts and hymns in Hebrew, the sudden unexpected success. In the encounter at 1 Macc 5:55–61, Gorgias is victorious against the foolhardy commanders Judas had left behind in Judaea, Joseph and Azariah. In the account of 2 Maccabees, a commander called Esdris is mentioned without any explanation of who he is. Some scholars wish to identify him with the Eleazar of 8:23, but more likely one should recognize that we are dealing with a shortened account. While 1 Maccabees explains the defeat at the hands of Gorgias by the jealous behaviour of the two leaders, Joseph and Azariah (1 Macc 5:55–62), the epitomist sees the deaths as caused by lack of Torah piety. Judas is shown as ever observant, as he and his soldiers purify themselves. So far from the temple, why did they need to become ritually clean so that they could participate in temple service? The purification seems to refer to purifying oneself after coming into contact with a dead body

(Num 19:10–22; 31:24; 1QM 14:1–2). The sacred objects may have been taken on the raid on Jamnia (12:8–9). Greek inscriptions from Delos set up by the people of Jamnia honour two Phoenician deities, Herakles and Horon. Such idolatrous objects were forbidden at Deut 7:25–6, and the transgression of such a command was embodied in the story of Achan (Josh 7). Most likely the soldiers wore amulets which were thought would protect them.

vv. 42–5 are difficult textually and also to translate. The language of v. 45 is similar to that of Lev 4:26, 35 and suggests that the sacrifice is similar to the reparation offering described at Lev 4:13–35 to make atonement for the sin committed. Each man contributes to the sacrifice, and thus the whole community is involved in reparation. As seen in 2 Macc 7, the author believes in resurrection, whereby the martyred brothers hope to live in a new created world. vv. 44–5 offer alternatives: *either* Judas does not think that the dead rise, that it is foolish to pray for the dead, *or* he considers that a reward awaits those who die piously, 'a holy and a pious thought'. In the light of recent research on rituals for the dead in Israel, e.g. those underlying Isa 57, 'to pray for the dead' may reflect a custom of which only traces can be discerned. The dead clearly had an existence in Israel, albeit a shadowy one (1 Sam 28:14–19; Deut 18:11–12; Isa 65:4). What the author seems to suggest is that there is a community which stretches beyond death and that atonement can be made for those who have died so that they gain a more splendid reward. Many of the burial practices among the Greeks and Romans were to help the deceased be properly integrated into the realm of the dead, and suggest that the dead could benefit from actions performed on their behalf by the living. In speaking of a splendid reward, one is reminded of the different regions of the underworld signalling different rewards found in Book 6 of Virgil's *Aeneid*. A similarly obscure ritual is mentioned by Paul at 1 Cor 15:29, where some Christians are baptized on behalf of the dead.

(13:1–26) The Second Invasion of Lysias The author gives no reason for the breaking of the agreements reached in ch. 11, except that the young king wished to do worse than his father (v. 9). Perhaps the author sees the successes of ch. 12 as sufficient reason for this attack. Except for the dates given in the letters in ch. 11, only here and at 14:4 are dates given. They appear to follow the Seleucid Macedonian calendar which would place this event between Sept. 164 and Oct. 163 BCE. 1 Macc 6:20 dates the second invasion to 150 of the Seleucid Babylonian calendar, i.e. to 162 BCE. The force assembled is enormous, and no doubt exaggerated. One wonders in particular what use scythed chariots would be in the hilly terrain of Judea. Instead of both Antiochus V and Lysias each having a separate force, as the NRSV translation suggests, Antiochus came with Lysias as well as a huge force.

(vv. 3–8) The Death of Menelaus Menelaus resumes his role in the narrative as the opposite of the good high priest Onias, as a plotter against his own people. Perhaps the failure of Menelaus' peace overtures or simply the fact that he was a left-over from Antiochus IV's regime caused his death. Josephus (*Ant.* 12.383–5) states that Menelaus died after the expedition. Death by ashes was a Persian punishment (Ctesias, *Persia, FGrH* 688): cold ashes suffocated the criminal, hot burnt him to death. The holiness of the altar fire had caused the death of Aaron's two sons (Lev 10:1–5). Menelaus is appropriately punished.

(vv. 9–17) The Battle at Modein The Greek king is said to be barbarous (2:21; 4:25). The Jewish response to the invasion is for the whole community to pray, as at 3:14–22. The elders with whom Judas consults may be members of the council/senate as at 4:44; 11:27. Judas is portrayed as not acting arrogantly. In the Temple Scroll from Qumran, the king is supposed to have twelve princes of his people, twelve priests, and twelve Levites with him at all times and he should not do anything without consulting them; before going to war he should have the high priest consult the Urim and Thummim (11QTemple 57–8).

The account of this battle is the opposite of that of 1 Macc 6:32–47 where the Jewish forces are defeated at Beth-zechariah. The author of 2 Maccabees is adamant that the loyal Jews cannot be defeated, and so the defeat is turned into a victorious assault at Modein, the home-town of the Maccabees (1 Macc 2:1), an account filled with heroic tales as Judas with twenty men kills over 2,000, creates havoc in the enemy camp, and yet retires unharmed.

(vv. 18–26) Treaty of Antiochus V The contrast with 1 Maccabees is again striking: there the forces at Beth-zur fight courageously but eventually are forced to capitulate (6:31, 49–50). The forces at Jerusalem hold out but survive only because the king withdraws at the news of Philip's return (1 Macc 6:51–62). It looks as if the author of 2 Maccabees has transferred the events at Jerusalem to Beth-zur as he did not want any hint of danger to the temple. The only setback to the Jews comes through a traitor, but even he does not succeed. All in all, the invasion of Antiochus V and Lysias is shown to be completely unsuccessful and the Jews remain undefeated. Both 1 and 2 Maccabees mention the approach of a Philip: in 1 Maccabees, he is the same as the one given charge of affairs at Antiochus IV's death (1 Macc 6:55); in 2 Maccabees, it appears to be a different Philip from that of 9:29.

In 2 Maccabees, the king behaves honourably, and honours the temple (cf. 3:2–3). Antiochus and Judas seem to be on good terms—another sign that the author stresses that Jews and Gentiles can get along. The installation of a new governor perhaps signals the new friendly policy of the Seleucids as the removal of Ptolemy Macron at 10:12 had been a sign of increased hostility. Some scholars place the land of the Gerrenians south of Gaza and west of Beersheba, others as far south as near Lake Pelusium, then under Ptolemaic control, others that it be placed north of Ptolemais at Gerrha, which lies south-east of Beirut. If the area covered by the new governor lay south of Ptolemais, he would have been in charge of Joppa and Jamnia and possibly Idumea, overseeing Gorgias (12:32–7). If north of Ptolemais, he would have overseen Tyre and Sidon. The citizens of Ptolemais, previously shown to hate the Jews (6:8; 1 Macc 5:15), have to be appeased in order to secure the king's rear. In glaring contrast to this rosy account, the author of 1 Maccabees has the king break his oath and tear down the walls of Jerusalem (1 Macc 6:61–2).

(14:1–15:39) The Attacks under Demetrius I The transition to the new ruler, Demetrius I, is made quickly. Demetrius, son of Seleucus IV and nephew of Antiochus IV had replaced

Antiochus as a hostage in Rome in 178 BCE. Demetrius had tried to leave Rome at the death of Antiochus IV but had been refused permission. After the murder of a Roman envoy in Laodicea in 162 BCE, Demetrius had again asked permission to leave, was again refused, but then slipped out of Rome anyway. 2 Maccabees states that he landed in Tripolis with a large force, whereas Polybius (31.12.11–13; 31.14.8–13) and 1 Macc 7:1 state that he arrived with only a handful of supporters. He was quickly successful in overthrowing Antiochus V and Lysias. Given the date at 2 Macc 13:1, the three years at 14:1 must refer to the beginning of the year 151 of the Seleucid Macedonian calendar, i.e. Sept. 162 to Oct. 161 BCE. Demetrius would have landed in 162 BCE, and so the three years must be interpreted as within the third year.

(14:3–25) The Expedition of Nicanor Just as the peace gained at the end of 2 Macc 11 was broken, so now the peace at the end of 2 Macc 13. Josephus states that Alcimus, also called Yakim, had been appointed high priest after Menelaus (*Ant.* 12.385–7). When the new king came to the throne, he had come with the requisite gifts for confirmation of his office (1 Macc 10:60–4; 11:23–7; cf. 1 Macc 13:36–7). 'Olive branches' might be translated by the more general 'gifts'. Scholars have puzzled over what Alcimus had done in the times of separation (v. 3: *amixia*). At 1 Macc 7:12–18, Alcimus is said to have been acceptable to the Hasideans, and so scholars have argued that this 'defilement' of Alcimus could not refer to participation in actions like those of Menelaus. Some have suggested that the defilement refers to the incident in 1 Macc 7:12–18 where sixty Hasideans are executed, others that it refers to the division between the Hasideans and Judas over receiving Alcimus or not (1 Macc 7:10–11). However, the incident in 1 Maccabees takes place after Alcimus has been reappointed high priest by Demetrius, and so this interpretation seems unlikely. Other scholars have accepted another MS reading and translate 'in times of peace (*epimixia*)'. However, the use of *amixia* in the same chapter of 2 Maccabees to describe the loyal Razis (14:38) argues for retaining its use here. The term translated 'defile' can have the general meaning of 'disgrace' as at Sir 21:28; Tob 3:15, and so may not refer to some particular incident. Rather, it contrasts Alcimus with Razis and with Judas who left Jerusalem so as not to share in the 'defilement' (5:27). Alcimus must have been forced out of Jerusalem (1 Macc 7:6). Alcimus acts shrewdly in waiting until the king has a meeting about Judaea, for it would be appropriate for the king to ask someone with local knowledge. The author provides Alcimus with the right speech for the circumstances: he first answers the king by throwing the blame on others while maintaining that he has only the king's and the country's best interests at heart in requesting help. He describes Judas as leader of the Hasideans, a group clearly demarcated from Judas in 1 Macc 2:42; 7:13. Here Alcimus lumps them all together under the term *hasidim* (pious, faithful ones), using it in a derogatory fashion much as people today talk of 'fundamentalists'. These Hasideans are distinguished from the nation (v. 8). The accusation against Judas is the opposite of what the reader knows from the earlier narrative: it is always the non-Jews who start trouble (10:14–15; 12:2). The charge that the state will never know peace while they are around (14:10) parallels the charge made by Onias against Simon (4:6). It is an accusation found also in the Greek Esther (3:13) and in 3 Macc 3:26; 7:4; 6:28.

v. 7 is sometimes interpreted to mean that Alcimus has had the high-priesthood taken away from him, but in this context it probably means no more than that he has left behind his high-priestly duties to come to the king, as Onias did earlier (4:4–6). The glory here would then refer to the glorious robe of the high-priesthood (Sir 45:8; 50:5–11): the verb translated 'laid aside' can mean 'take off a garment' as at Esth 4:4; LXX Esth 4:17k. As at 10:13, the king's counsellors instigate action against the Jews.

No mention is made in 2 Maccabees of the expedition of Bacchides and Alcimus' tenure as high priest told in 1 Macc 7:8–25, as such a defeat would have spoiled his thesis of the invincibility of the Jews. The Jews' response is to pray to God, who is said to uphold his heritage 'with an epiphany' (v. 15). The slight set-back at Dessau is not mentioned in 1 Maccabees. Some scholars have seen in this 'defeat' of Simon an anti-Hasmonean stance, but I see it as in line with the feints and probes that take place before a major engagement. At v. 16 the armies were drawn up in battle array, rather than engaged in battle as NRSV. As in the dealings with Antiochus V, a very different picture emerges in the dealings of Judas and Nicanor from that in 1 Maccabees. Here Nicanor acts honourably, although Judas acts with commendable caution after again consulting with the people. The ambassadors are otherwise unknown, and the scene of the meeting is vividly drawn. In 1 Macc 7:27, Nicanor is pictured as planning treachery, a motif common in 1 Maccabees (1:30; 7:10–18). The author of 2 Maccabees insists on the warm attachment that Nicanor had for Judas, although one might suspect that the Seleucid commander kept Judas close to him for more strategic reasons. The genuineness of the peace is underscored with the image of the battle-hardened Judas married with children and taking part in normal community life.

(14:26–46) The Change in Nicanor Alcimus intervenes to ruin the peace. The account assumes that Alcimus is in Jerusalem, presumably functioning as high priest. Alcimus charges that Judas has been appointed Nicanor's deputy as the word is used at 4:29, not 'successor' as NRSV. If Alcimus is not lying, Judas had become part of the normal bureaucracy of Jerusalem. The slander works. The author notes the distress of Nicanor, an honourable man, at breaking the covenant, but he obeys orders. The scene of Judas carefully observing the change in Nicanor reads like a movie script. No mention is made in 2 Maccabees of the battle at Caphar-salama in 1 Macc 7:31–2, the narrative moves straight to the confrontation of Nicanor with the temple. Why would the priests know where Judas was hiding? Does Nicanor think they will follow the principle that it is better for one man to die than for the nation to be destroyed (2 Sam 20:14–22; John 11:50)? In any event, Nicanor's character changes: from being honourable, he turns into someone who fights against God. The contrast between Nicanor stretching out his hand against the temple (v. 33) and the priests stretching out their hands to God (v. 34) underscores the point. Nicanor, in his threat to level the temple to the ground, is likened to Antiochus (9:13; 8:3). Nicanor threatens to build a splendid (*epiphanēs*) temple to Dionysos, foreshadowing God's manifestation (*epiphaneia*) in

defeating Nicanor (15:27). The prayer of the priests at v. 36 refers back to the purification at 10:4 and is fulfilled in the blessing at 15:34. It is interesting that the term used in v. 35 for 'habitation' is literally 'tenting' (*skēnōsis*), a term which reflects God's tent of meeting in the wilderness (Ex 25:8–9; cf. 1 Kings 8:4).

(14:37–46) The Death of Razis The episode of Razis lies between the threat of Nicanor and his final defeat. Just as the martyrdom accounts in 6:17–7:42 were placed after the desecration of the temple and brought about God's mercy, so now the death of Razis precedes the removal of Nicanor.

vv. 37–40, Razis is an unusual name. He is a lover of his compatriots in contrast to Alcimus who claims to be one. No reason is given why Razis was denounced. Nicanor is now simply said to hate the Jews. Five hundred soldiers to arrest one man emphasizes the importance of Razis. vv. 41–6, the scene takes place in a private house with a tower overlooking a courtyard, in which Razis is surprised. With no escape he kills himself, preferring to die nobly like Eleazar (6:23) rather than be insulted. A code of honour and disgrace is clearly at play here. Plato in Book 9 of his *Laws* had said that suicide was allowable: (1) under judicial constraint; (2) under the constraint of unavoidable misfortune; (3) in order not to participate in a dishonourable deed. Razis chooses not to be humiliated. vv. 43–6, the suicide is drawn out to the last grisly detail. He throws his entrails on the troops so that his blood is literally upon them. His last prayer is similar to that of the martyrs at 7:11, 22–3.

(15:1–5) The Defeat of Nicanor The confrontation between Judas and Nicanor continues. Bordering Samaria lie the Gophna Hills, just north-east of Modein, a favourite hiding-place of the Maccabeans (1 Macc 2:28). The treachery of Nicanor is further emphasized by his desire to attack on the sabbath (cf. 1 Macc 2:29–38). Non-Jews knew how the Jews kept the sabbath and characterized it as a superstition which allowed them to be taken unawares (Jos. *Ant.* 12.4–6; *Ag. Ap.* 1.209–12). The Hasmoneans in 1 Macc 2:40–1 resolved to defend themselves even if attacked on the sabbath. Here Nicanor's wish shows him to be barbarous (cf. 2:21; 4:25; 10:4; 11:9). Nicanor taunts God as Goliath taunted the army of the living God (1 Sam 17:2–10, 26). His foolishness is shown in the fact that the sabbath observance is grounded in God's creating heaven and earth (Ex 20:8–11).

(15:6–19) The Battle Preparations As usual, the author contrasts the arrogance of the Seleucids with the trust in God of Judas and his forces. Following the injunctions for a speech before battle at Deut 20:1–4, Judas cites victories from the law and the prophets, where prophets here would include the books of the HB from Joshua to 2 Kings (Jos. *Ag. Ap.* 1.39–40). The perfidy of the Gentiles refers to Nicanor's breaking of the covenant he had made (14:20–2, 28). Judas then relates a dream. Dreams in antiquity were one means by which humans kept company with the gods. People were aware that not all dreams were heaven-sent, but they were one way by which the gods communicated with humans. The author of 2 Maccabees describes the dream as 'a certain waking reality', reading *hypar ti* instead of *hyper ti* at v. 11. The detail of the description suggests that the elements of the dream were so clear that Judas thought he was awake. The characters in the dream are significant. Onias takes us back to the beginning of the epitome; he is called a perfect Greek gentleman, one trained in *aretē*, excellence, as Eleazar (6:18.23) and Razis (14:37–8, 42) were. As the priests stretched out their hands (14:34), so does Onias. The continuity between the dead and the living is shown by the dead praying for the living, as the living had prayed for the dead at 12:42–5. The second person in the dream is the prophet Jeremiah. Often his message is one of doom, but he is also sent to build and to plant (Jer 1:10). Although before the destruction of the temple Jeremiah had been instructed not to pray for the people (Jer 7:16; 11:14; 14:11), after the destruction he is told to pray for the people (Jer 42). Jeremiah in the dream gives Judas a golden sword. Heavenly weapons are of gold (3:25; 5:2). The giving of special weapons to a hero is a motif found widely in traditional literature. In Egyptian accounts, a god often gives a sword to Pharaoh to defeat his enemy. The giving of the sword thus provides divine assurance of victory. Polybius relates how the Roman general Scipio cynically used the motif of a dream to urge his soldiers on (10.11.5–8). v. 19 suggests that those inside the city could almost see what was happening out in the open, impossible if the location of the battle given in 1 Macc 7:40, Adasa, is correct.

(15:20–7) The Battle The armies are again contrasted. The presence of war elephants is unlikely: the Roman envoy Octavius had had them hamstrung in 162 BCE, just before Demetrius became king. Judas refers, as he had at 8:19 in the battle against the first Nicanor, to the defeat of Sennacherib (2 Kings 18:13–19:35). He asks for an angel as he had at 11:6, as happened against Sennacherib and as promised at Ex 23:20. At v. 25, the battle songs are perhaps those often addressed by soldiers to Apollo, and contrast with the prayers of Judas's forces. The battle is portrayed as a fight between gods. The God of Israel manifests himself (cf. 2:21). The numbers are exaggerated.

(15:28–36) The Feast of Nicanor The use of the ancestral language, as by the martyrs (7:8, 12, 27), signals the victory of the God of the Jews. Judas is described in terms reminiscent of Onias (4:2, 5). Decapitation and cutting off the sword hand, the right hand, is found among the Persians (e.g. Xen. *An.* 1.10.1; 3.1.17; Plut. *Art.* 13.2); dismemberment is also found among the Greeks (e.g. *Cleom.* 38) and Romans (e.g. Plut. *Cic.* 48–9). David had Goliath's head brought into Jerusalem (1 Sam 17:54), the Philistines cut off Saul's head and fastened his body to the wall of Beth-shan (1 Sam 31:9–10), and Judith had the head of Holofernes displayed on the walls of Bethulia (Jdt 14:1, 11). The details of the narrative may have been influenced by such heroic tales as these. Certainly the punishment fits the crime: 15:32 responds to 14:33, 15:34 to 14:36. The author distinguishes those in the citadel from Judas's compatriots. However, the fact that all bless the Lord (v. 34) and that Judas can hang Nicanor's head from the citadel suggests that the citadel is in Judas's control. This is rhetorically powerful but probably incorrect. The citadel remained under the control of the enemies of the Hasmoneans (1 Macc 9:53; 10:9) and was not captured until 141 BCE under Simon (1 Macc 13:49–52). According to 1 Macc 7:47, Nicanor's head and right hand were displayed just outside Jerusalem. It seems unlikely that the dead corpse of an unclean Gentile

could be brought into the view of the priests around the altar. The skins of unclean animals were forbidden in Jerusalem (Jos. *Ant.* 12:145–6; see also 11QTemple 48:11–14), and how much more so a dead Gentile? There is debate among scholars as to whether some later rabbinic texts would allow a corpse into the court of women, although *m. Kelim* 1.7 explicitly forbids burial within towns.

The wording of v. 36 is very close to that of 10:8, and shows how the book was structured. Interestingly, the author identifies the feast by reference to Mordecai's day known from the book of Esther (3:7; 9:20–3). Since the author knows about otherwise unknown events in Babylonia (8:20), he also must know about this popular celebration.

(15:37–9) The Epilogue Even though the author seems to know of later events—e.g. perhaps the embassy of Eupolemus to Rome (4:11; cf. 1 Macc 8:17), although 4:11 may refer to earlier contacts with Rome—he closes at this point. His statement that the city was in the possession of the Hebrews from this time on hardly agrees with what happened: a year after Nicanor's defeat, Bacchides returned and conquered Judea, killing Judas and reinstalling Alcimus (1 Macc 9:1–57). Just as the epitomist suppressed any mention of Bacchides' first expedition, so he ends here with a great victory of the Jews to promote his programme of how the God of Israel defended his temple. 2 Maccabees is propaganda history, and should not be judged by other criteria.

The last verse recall the images the epitomist used in his prologue (2:29–31) as well as his posture of humility (2:26–7). Wines in the ancient world were so strong they were usually mixed with water.

REFERENCES

Bar-Kochva, B. (1988), *Judas Maccabeus* (Cambridge: Cambridge University Press).

Bickerman, E. (1979), ET *The God of the Maccabees: Studies on the Meaning and Origin of the Maccabean Revolt*, SJLA 32 (Leiden: Brill). German original, *Der Gott des Makkabäer* (Berlin: Schocken, 1937).

Bringmann, K. (1983), *Hellenistische Reform und Religionsverfolgung in Judäa: Eine Untersuchung zur jüdisch-hellenistischen Geschichte (175–163 v. Chr)* (Göttingen: Vandenhoeck & Ruprecht).

Cowley, A. (1923), *Aramaic Papyri of the Fifth Century B.C.* (Oxford, Clarendon).

Doran, R. (1981), *Temple Propaganda: The Purpose and Character of 2 Maccabees* (Washington: Catholic Biblical Association).

Faure, P. (1941), 'La Conduite des armées perses à Rhodes pendant la première guerre médique', *Revue historique*, 192: 236–41.

Goldstein, J. A. (1976), *1 Maccabees*, AB 41 (Garden City, NY: Doubleday).

—— (1983), *2 Maccabees*; AB 41A (Garden City, NY: Doubleday).

Habicht, C. (1976), 'Royal Documents in Maccabees II', HSCP 80: 1–18.

Momigliano, A. (1975), 'The Second Book of Maccabees', CP 70: 81–8.

Mørkholm, O. (1966), *Antiochus IV of Syria* (Copenhagen: Gyldendalske).

Sachs, A. J., and Wiseman, D. J. (1954), 'A Babylonian King List of the Hellenistic Period', *Iraq* 16: 202–12.

Tcherikover, V. (1961), *Hellenistic Civilization and the Jews* (Philadelphia: Jewish Publication Society).

49. 1 Esdras

SARA JAPHET

INTRODUCTION

A. Title and Place in Canon. 1. Biblical and apocryphal 'Ezra literature' consists of three works: the Hebrew Ezra-Nehemiah, regarded by early Jewish tradition as one book; the Greek apocryphal book of the Septuagint; and the Ezra Apocalypse, found first in Latin in the Vulgate. The book discussed here is the apocryphal book found in the LXX. There it is called Esdras A (or 1 Esdras). The Latin translation of the book, found in the Vulgate, is there designated 3 Ezra. 1 Esdras has a complex relation to the Hebrew Ezra-Nehemiah and its Greek translation (known in the LXX as Esdras B).

2. 1 Esdras holds a peculiar position in the canon. Common to other works of the Apocrypha, its existence is not attested to by early Jewish sources, but its extensive use by Josephus, next to Ezra-Nehemiah (*Ant.* 11.3), suggests that it was known and appreciated. 1 Esdras was quoted and referred to by early Greek and Latin Christian fathers (Myers 1974: 17–18). However, its position in the Western church was greatly affected by Jerome's harsh criticism (with the Ezra Apocalypse). Its canonicity was rejected by the Council of Trent (1546 CE), although it was printed, in small type, as an appendix to the Tridentine Vulgate (Cook 1913: 3). It thus remained in a unique marginal position within large parts of the Christian world.

B. Nature, Scope, and Relationship to Chronicles and Ezra-Nehemiah. 1. 1 Esdras is a description of the history of Israel from the eighteenth year of King Josiah to the time of Ezra, and forms a parallel history to sections of Chronicles and Ezra-Nehemiah. Broadly ch. 1 is parallel to the two concluding chs. of 2 Chronicles (35–6), and chs. 2 and 5:7–9:55 are parallel to Ezra 1–10 and Neh 7:72–8:13*a* (with some differences in order and detail). Only chs. 3:1–5:6 are unique to this book. When compared with Chronicles and Ezra-Nehemiah, 1 Esdras seems to open at a peculiar point, in the last stages of Josiah's reign, and end abruptly with the first word of Neh 8:13: 'They came together'. These facts determined the literary context in which the book's nature was discussed (cf. *inter alia* Bayer 1911; Pohlmann 1970; Williamson 1977; Torrey 1970; Eskenazi 1986; Schenker 1991): does the present scope of 1 Esdras represent the original format of the work, or is it a fragment of a longer work? If a fragment, what were the boundaries of the original work? And, in any case, how is the book related to the canonical books of Chronicles and Ezra-Nehemiah?

2. It is beyond the scope of this introduction to survey the history of research, in which every conceivable possibility was suggested (see, among others, Pohlmann 1970: 14–31). I will restrict myself to major views and a proposition of my own. Regarding the book's original format, two extreme views have been offered: the prevalent view, that the book is a fragment of a much larger work which originally included the entire so-called 'Chronistic history', from the beginning of Chronicles to the end of Ezra-Nehemiah (e.g. Cook 1913; Pohlmann 1970; Torrey 1945; 1970; Myers 1974; Coggins and Knibb 1979); and the less common view that the work is complete as it is, both at the beginning and end (e.g. Bayer 1911; Rudolph 1949; Williamson 1977; Eskenazi 1986). Within each of these general lines many varieties of opinion were expressed. Most conspicuous is the hot debate, among those who hold that 1 Esdras is a fragment of the Chronistic work, regarding the question of originality: where is the supposed original Chronistic history represented in a superior way, in the canonical Chronicles and Ezra-Nehemiah, or in 1 Esdras? This question was examined mainly in regard to three issues: the story of the three guards, found in 1 Esdras but not in Ezra-Nehemiah; the story of Nehemiah, found in the canonical Ezra-Nehemiah but not in 1 Esdras; and the order of the events at the beginning of the Persian period, where 1 Esdras places Ezra 4:6–24 after Ezra 1. Here too, opinions differ greatly, but it is interesting that within this line of research, although the originality of every other aspect of 1 Esdras was questioned, the originality of the continuity between Chronicles and Ezra-Nehemiah was taken for granted.

3. The consequences of this debate exceed the bounds of literary composition and have great significance for the understanding and evaluation of 1 Esdras. For if it is a fragment, then 1 Esdras may have no identity of its own, no purpose or theology. Consequently, there should be no sense in studying it, except for those aspects judged to be 'more original', or as 'a version' for matters of textual criticism or translation techniques. This attitude is reflected in the book's history of research.

4. In recent years, the existence of a 'Chronistic history', encompassing both Chronicles and Ezra-Nehemiah, has been questioned (Japhet 1968; Williamson 1977; Japhet 1991) and denied by a growing number of scholars. A closer study of both Chronicles and Ezra-Nehemiah has shown that while they certainly belong to what may be termed post-exilic historiography, they are two independent works, written in different periods, with different presuppositions, theology, and purpose. This conclusion, reached independently, also has a bearing on 1 Esdras, for if there is no Chronistic history, 1 Esdras cannot represent a fragment thereof. If this is correct, 1 Esdras may be recognized as a work in itself, with its own purpose, method, and ideology, composed as one more description of the restoration period, the author choosing to gather existing literary excerpts and stitch them together rather than use his own words. The excerpts were taken from three sources: the biblical books of Chronicles and Ezra-Nehemiah, and another, no longer extant, source. The nature of the final work may be compared to Chronicles and best defined as 'corrective history' (Japhet 1996: 140, 148–9): a reformulation of history from a new, 'modern' perspective, responsive to its time. Such a history would provide a new interpretation of the past, be valid for the present, and lay the foundations for the future. For the specific theological features of this formulation, see below.

5. The success of the 1 Esdras effort may be judged by two criteria: his work was translated into Greek and eventually included in the Septuagint, and it was extensively used by Josephus, who followed it faithfully and in great detail, as he did with other biblical works. There still remains the matter of the book's scope. We find no difficulty in its beginning; this is where the author chose to begin his story. As for the end, it is possible that a few words or a short paragraph had accidentally been dropped at this point (see Commentary).

C. Basic Structure and Contents. 1 Esdras can be rightly called 'The Book of Destruction and Restoration'. It describes the history of Israel from the last period of the monarchy, at the eve of its downfall, until the reading of the law and the celebration of the festivals in the time of Ezra, the ultimate expression of restoration. This long period encompasses three historical foci: the last kings of Judah and the fall of Judah and Jerusalem (ch. 1); the material restoration of Jerusalem during the reigns of Cyrus and Darius (chs. 2–7); the spiritual restoration under the leadership of Ezra (chs. 8–9). The details of this structure are:

The Last Kings of Judah and the Destruction of Jerusalem (1:1–58)
    Josiah (1:1–33)
    The Last Kings of Judah (1:34–58)
The Material Restoration (chs. 2–7)
    First Beginnings (2:1–30)
    New Beginnings (3:1–4:63)
    The Return (5:1–46)
    Laying the Foundations (5:47–73)
    New Start and Final Realization (6:1–7:15)
Spiritual Restoration (chs. 8–9)
    Ezra's Return to Jerusalem (8:1–67)
    Dissolving the Mixed Marriages (8:68–9:36)
    Reading the Law (9:37–55)

D. Sources and Composition. 1. The material of 1 Esdras can also be outlined from the perspective of its sources, with the division of paragraphs intending to clarify the different structure and order of the parallel works.

Parallel:		Parallel:	
1:1–22	2 Chr 35:1–19	6:23–34	Ezra 6:1–12
1:25–33	2 Chr 35:20–7	7:1–15	Ezra 6:13–22
1:34–58	2 Chr 36:1–21	8:1–27	Ezra 7:1–28
2:1–15	Ezra 1:1–11	8:28–67	Ezra 8:1–36
2:16–30	Ezra 4:6–24	8:68–90	Ezra 9:1–15
5:7–46	Ezra 2:1–70	8:91–6	Ezra 10:1–5
5:47–66	Ezra 3:1–13	9:1–36	Ezra 10:6–44
5:67–73	Ezra 4:1–5	9:37–55	Neh 7:73–8:12
6:1–22	Ezra 5:1–17		

The remainder, peculiar to 1 Esdras (1:23–4; 3:1–5:6), is composed of two elements: material taken from other sources no longer extant, and editorial notes written by the author. In the absence of comparative material, and with the original language of the work having been disguised by the Greek translation, a precise division between the two elements cannot be made, but some observations may be offered.

2. The Story of the Three Guards (3:1–5:6). The general scholarly consensus that this story was drawn from some Hellenistic source is followed by disagreement on the details: the scope and form of the original story, its original language,

and when it was included in the present context. I will refrain from presenting all the divergent views and propose my own conclusion. An analysis of the story reveals clear signs of literary development: (*a*) The core of the story is a conventional wisdom story, in the form of a riddle: 'Who, or what, is the strongest?' Three candidates compete for the status of 'the strongest': wine, king, and women, in this order or in a different one. In all the answers the concept 'strongest' is viewed from a human perspective: who (or what) in the mundane world has the greatest control over the life of the individual man? (*b*) This original wisdom-riddle was then put in the framework of another wisdom-riddle, revolving around the question: 'Who is the smartest?' and formulated as a court-story: a competition between three of the great king's courtiers for the title 'the smartest'. The long speeches, which are examples of the genre, probably belong to this stage. (*c*) This court-story, formulated around the conventional pattern of 2+1, was again reformulated by the introduction of a fourth element, illustrating the pattern 3+1. The decision is now to be made between wine, king, and women on the one hand, truth on the other. The three are indeed strong, but they are all limited, because they belong to the petty and evil world of human beings. The 'strongest' is what transcends this world, is spiritual and abstract rather than material and concrete, namely, truth.

3. This courtly wisdom story, which seems to be drawn from the universal wisdom lore in its specific Hellenistic garb, also underwent a development of historicization and nationalization. The 'great king' was identified with Darius; the third, winning, guard, with Zerubbabel; and his reward was conceived in national rather than personal terms. This is the final, Jewish form of the wisdom-story, which then continued to describe the historical consequences of the competition (4:49–5:3) and was integrated into the history of the restoration by a new introduction to the list of returnees. Three different literary activities are evident in this final stage: editing an existing wisdom story, composing its sequel, and integrating it into the present context. Although different solutions are possible, we prefer to refrain from speculation and ascribe them all to the author of 1 Esdras.

4. (1:23–4) As will become clear in the commentary, the author of 1 Esdras did not add much to what he took from Chronicles, and intervened in the text only at the level of details. Only this short paragraph can be ascribed to his editorial efforts, in the attempt to express his own view on the changing fortunes in the history of Israel (see the Commentary).

5. Another aspect of the literary composition is the peculiar contents and structure of ch. 2. As illustrated by the comparative table of sources, 1 Esdras presents a different order from that of the canonical Ezra, with Ezra 4:6–24 following Ezra 1. What is the origin of this order? Is it the original order, later changed in Ezra-Nehemiah, or is it secondary? If the latter, who was responsible for it, the author of 1 Esdras or a later 'interpolator'? Although some scholars have argued that the order of 1 Esdras was original and superior (e.g. Schenker 1991; Dequeker 1993), a close scrutiny of the comparable texts makes it clear that the original order—although in itself problematical—is represented by Ezra-Nehemiah, and the general view in this regard should be upheld (e.g. Rudolph 1949:

xii–xiii). The new order of 1 Esdras is not a result of misunder-standing, or a later mishandling of it, but an intentional act of structuring by the author himself. The inclusion of the story of the three guards and the identification of the winner with Zerubbabel, intended to anchor Darius's favourable measures in the cultural milieu of the time and glorify Zerubbabel, demanded a clear distinction between the time prior to 'the second year of Darius' and the time following it. The hostile intervention in the building, which is explicitly circumscribed in Ezra 4:6–23 to 'until the second year of the reign of King Darius' (Ezra 4:24), had to be put before the story of the competition, while the founding of the temple by Zerubbabel (Ezra 3) had to be placed after Zerubbabel's appearance in the time of Darius. The present structure is thus a logical result of these considerations and should be ascribed to the author of 1 Esdras himself. While the general perspective of these changes is easily demonstrated, their practical results for historical cohesion were negative. As will become clear in the commentary, the reorganization was applied only to the major blocks of material and neglected the adaptation of the details, thus demonstrating the secondary character of the work.

E. Language, Translation, and Transmission. 1. What was the original language of 1 Esdras? The prevailing answer, although by no means the only one, is that it was Greek. This view conformed with the other prevalent view that 1 Esdras was a fragment of the Chronistic history, and probably its more original form. The fine Greek idiom in which the book is written led scholars to conclude that it was, from the outset, a Greek work. Another possibility, that it was a rework-ing of Ezra B, was soon disproved, and it was regarded as an independent and much better translation. Torrey's early ob-servation, that the original language of the story of the three guards was Semitic, probably Aramaic (Torrey 1970), did not change his position that 1 Esdras was 'merely a piece of the oldest Greek version of the Chronicler's work' (Torrey 1945: 395), but led him to see in the story a later interpolation into 1 Esdras. This view determined to a great degree the develop-ment of research—the scholarly concentration on the study of 1 Esdras as a 'version', a textual evidence for Ezra-Nehemiah (see e.g. Walde 1913; Bewer 1922; Klein 1966).

2. This view can no longer be maintained. As demonstrated by Torrey (1970), followed by Zimmermann (1963–4) and further by Talshir and Talshir (1995), the peculiar linguistic character of the story of the three guards cannot be explained as a 'Judeo-Greek'. Although the Greek in which it was written seems free-flowing, it is nevertheless a translation Greek, the *Vorlage* of which was certainly Semitic. The scholars men-tioned above suggest Aramaic, but it cannot be excluded that this pericope, like the books of Ezra and Daniel, was itself bilingual, containing both Hebrew and Aramaic sections.

3. Combined with the view that 1 Esdras is not a fragment but a literary work of its own, and that the integration of the story of the three guards and the reorganization of the mater-ial are the work of its author, the consequences of this ob-servation are self-evident: the original languages of 1 Esdras as a whole were Semitic—Hebrew and Aramaic—and as was the practice at the time, the work was then translated into Greek. 1 Esdras cannot be considered merely a version, a textual wit-

ness for the MT of Chronicles and Ezra-Nehemiah, with no further qualification. Its position in this regard may be com-pared to that of Chronicles *vis-à-vis* the MT of Samuel and Kings. While in many cases the source-text was followed literally, and the Greek translation may bear witness to a divergent Hebrew or Aramaic *Vorlage*, in other cases the change was the work of the author and cannot be considered within the framework of scribal transmission, or translation technique.

4. In dealing with the text of 1 Esdras one should try to distinguish between the work of the author at the level of composition, the work of the Greek translator at the level of translation techniques, and the process of transmission, which affected both the MT and the Greek of 1 Esdras at all stages.

F. Provenance and Date. 1. A general consensus sets the prov-enance of 1 Esdras in Egypt in the second century BCE (e.g. Eissfeldt 1966: 576). The basis for this conclusion is the nature of the Greek idiom in which the book is written, which has clear affinities with the language of the Papyri of the second century and some of the Apocrypha, particularly the books of Maccabees (see Myers 1974: 12–13; Talshir 1984), and the assumed literary affinities of the book to the canonical books of Esther and Daniel.

2. Again, the two aspects of the work should be distin-guished. It seems very plausible that the Greek translation was done in the second century BCE in Egypt; there is nothing to contradict this view and many reasons to support it. The original work should be dated earlier, but its date and prov-enance cannot be suggested with precision. The influence of the book of Esther on the story of the three guards (see 1 ESD 3:1–4:41) sets an upper date for its composition, whereas the affinity with the book of Daniel is of a general nature and rather doubtful. The historical reality and general cultural milieu of 1 Esdras seems to be that of the Hellenistic period, with no trace of the Hasmonean period. We would place the composition of 1 Esdras in the third century BCE, and its Greek translation in the second century, probably in Egypt.

G. Purpose and Theology. 1. The most important feature of 1 Esdras is the concept of historical continuity. 1 Esdras bridges the gap between the periods of the First Temple and the Second by the flow of the story, with destruction, exile, and restoration fully integrated into the historical sequence. As a result, the fall of Jerusalem loses the severe meaning it had in Kings, and Cyrus's decree becomes one in a series of events rather than a decisive turning-point. It no longer marks, as in Ezra-Nehemiah, the beginning of the new period nor, as in Chronicles, is it the springboard toward a new future. The realization of the concept of continuity can be seen as the motive for the book's structure. The author does not show any interest in the history of the interim period, as he does not 'fill in' the bridged gap with any additional data—not even ready materials that he may have found in 2 Kings 25 or Jer 39–45, 52. Nor are theological explanations given for the transition from destruction to restoration. A direct and uneventful path leads from the one to the other, through the decree of Cyrus and beyond it.

2. A different historical perspective is seen also in the understanding of the restoration itself. According to

Ezra-Nehemiah the restoration was achieved in two distinct phases, the building of the temple during the reigns of Cyrus and Darius, in which Zerubbabel was the most prominent figure, and the building of the city, initiated and carried out by Nehemiah in the time of Artaxerxes. 1 Esdras 'condensed' this history so that the restoration applied from the outset to both the temple and the city of Jerusalem. Both were undertaken under the same orders of the Persian kings (see e.g. 2:18–20; 4:43–5), and completed together. Therefore, after having transferred Nehemiah's main undertaking, the building of Jerusalem, to the time of Zerubbabel, 1 Esdras had no need for the story of Nehemiah and omitted it—but not before he had moved Nehemiah himself to the time of Zerubbabel (e.g. 5:40), and borrowed motifs from his story for the history of Zerubbabel (e.g. 4:47–8). The result is a different periodization, which is also expressed in the view of the political order in Judah during the restoration period.

3. According to Ezra-Nehemiah, during the two generations of the restoration Judah was ruled by pairs, a secular and a clerical ruler working together (Zerubbabel and Joshua for the first period, Nehemiah and Ezra for the second). This is changed in 1 Esdras in three ways: For the first period of the restoration 1 Esdras augments the role of Zerubbabel without doing the same for the priest Joshua; Joshua is no longer Zerubbabel's equal but acts very much in his shadow. The omission of the story of Nehemiah leaves Ezra as the sole protagonist of his time, following immediately after Zerubbabel. Finally, by beginning the story with Josiah, the entire periodization of Ezra-Nehemiah has been changed.

4. Perhaps the best-known feature of 1 Esdras is his presentation of Zerubbabel, who becomes the major protagonist of the restoration. Although we find in Ezra-Nehemiah a tendency to extend the span of Zerubbabel's office from the time of Darius back to that of Cyrus, we do not find therein any form of glorification of his figure (Japhet 1982–3). This is modified in 1 Esdras in several ways. The Davidic descent of Zerubbabel, which is totally absent in Ezra-Nehemiah, is reaffirmed in 1 Esdras by an explicit genealogy tracing his descent to the tribe of Judah and the house of David (5:5). He is also explicitly referred to as the governor of Judah, a fact that is suppressed in Ezra-Nehemiah, and he is connected with the completion of the temple (6:27). With the introduction of the story of the three guards, Zerubbabel is presented as full of wisdom and piety, devoted to the welfare of his people. He is unquestionably the central figure, 'the governor', perhaps the symbol, of the restoration.

5. On the other hand, while 1 Esdras follows Haggai in calling Zerubbabel 'my servant' (6:27; Hag 2:23), he does not adopt the eschatological perspectives of the restoration prophets. Zerubbabel is not the bearer of any eschatological expectations, not even the hope of political renewal and independence. In this respect, 1 Esdras follows Ezra-Nehemiah, seeing in the Persian rule the 'good hand' of the Lord towards his people. Thus, Zerubbabel's office is subordinate to the foreign rulers and there is no political independence. Nevertheless, he is presented as the legitimate heir of the earlier monarchy and in some way the continuation of the Davidic kings.

COMMENTARY

The Last Kings of Judah and the Destruction of Jerusalem (1:1–58)

1 Esdras begins his story with the last period of the kingdom of Judah, from the eighteenth year of the reign of Josiah (622 BCE) to the destruction of Jerusalem in the time of Zedekiah (586 BCE). Except for a short section in vv. 23–4, it faithfully follows 2 Chr 35–6.

(1:1–33) Josiah (2 Chr 35:1–27) The story of Josiah comprises two major parts, the celebration of Passover (vv. 1–22) and the story of Josiah's end (vv. 25–33), connected by the author's note in vv. 23–4.

(1:1–22) Celebrating Passover (2 Chr 35:1–19) After a brief introduction of the historic event in v. 1—a Passover held by Josiah in Jerusalem at the appropriate date (echoed and elaborated in the conclusion of the story, vv. 19–22), vv. 2–9 begin the detailed description of Josiah's preparations, referring to two matters: the summoning of the cultic personnel for the performance of the ritual (vv. 2–6), and the grant of sacrificial animals (vv. 7–9). Only one verse deals with the priests (v. 2), with special attention to their garments—the external representation of their special status and privileges (see also 7:9 in comparison to Ezra 6:18)—a matter which seems to have been of great import at the time. It is followed by Josiah's long address to the Levites (vv. 3–6), which seeks to legitimize their 'trespass' into the performance of the ritual: the change in circumstances, which freed the Levites from the task of carrying the ark, made them available for other roles, to 'worship the Lord' and 'serve his people'. They are now asked to take upon themselves the main burden of the festival: to prepare the Passover sacrifices for all the people of Israel, according to their organization into divisions.

vv. 7–9 enumerate the sacrificial animals: lambs and kids for the Passover sacrifice, and cattle for the peace-offerings of the festival (Japhet 1993: 1050). The four groups of donors in Chronicles (35:7–9)—the king, his officials, the priestly and levitical heads—here become three, with the omission of the king's officers (see also v. 54 versus 2 Chr 36:18). The levitical heads are unexpectedly changed (a textual corruption?) into 'captains over thousands'. The complex ritual, regarding both the Passover sacrifice and the peace-offering of the festival, is described in 2 Chr 35:10–16 in great detail, relating to the various stages of the sacrifice and the division of work between the Levites, priests, singers, and doorkeepers, from the perspective of the levitical service. This precision is not preserved in ch. 1 (vv. 10–18). With the omission of 2 Chr 35:11–12a and the rephrasing of v. 12b, the details concerning the slaughtering of the Passover sacrifice, the sprinkling of the blood, the flaying of the animals, the removal of the fat parts, and their delivery to the representatives of the people, are not recorded. Due to these changes, the description of the ritual begins with the roasting of the Passover sacrifice (v. 12), the cooking of the other sacrifices, and their distribution. In addition, a completely unknown feature is introduced, namely, the priests and Levites standing 'with the unleavened bread' (v. 10), most probably a result of a textual corruption (*běmiṣwāt*, 'according to the king's command', to *bemāṣot* 'with the unleavened bread'). Each sector of the clergy performed its task with great precision and dedication: the priests offered the fats 'until nightfall', the singers were 'in their place', the gatekeepers were at 'each gate', and the Levites made it all possible, for they prepared the Passover sacrifices for everyone: the people, the priests, the singers, the gatekeepers, and themselves. Even more than Chronicles, I Esdras emphasizes the brotherhood (NRSV: kindred) of the Levites, not only to the singers and gatekeepers (v. 16 || 2 Chr 35:15) but also to the priests (vv. 13, 14).

vv. 19–22 (2 Chr 35:17–19) are a detailed conclusion of the story, summing up the general facts and the significance of the event: the celebration of the Passover and the feast of unleavened bread for seven days, the uniqueness of the festival and, again, the precise date, the eighteenth year of king Josiah.

In all, I Esdras retains the emphases of 2 Chr 35: the innovative character of the Passover, its having been celebrated in Jerusalem as a national festival; the magnitude of the festival, demonstrated by the number of sacrifices; the conformity of the ritual with the prescribed rules, the emphasis on matters of authority: the command of the king, of the Lord, as prescribed, etc.; and the diligence and sense of responsibility displayed by all, particularly the Levites.

(1:23–4) The Author's Comment The author's only explicit theological reflection points to the purpose of the chapter: the transition—in the very glorious days of Josiah—from glory to doom. According to the author's view, the end of Josiah marks the turning-point in the history of Israel and demands an explanation. In 2 Chr 35, the story moves from the Passover to Necho's campaign, with a broadened conventional formula: 'after all this, when Josiah had prepared the house, Necho king of Egypt went up to fight' (v. 20). Although Pharaoh's war is not waged against Judah, its end with the death of Josiah poses a grave theological problem: rather than being rewarded for his zealous dedication to the Lord, Josiah is confronted with a test that he does not pass.

The book of Kings provides the necessary explanation in the form of a special paragraph; it juxtaposes Josiah's unprecedented merits with Israel's accumulated sins, and concludes that God did not repent his decision to destroy Judah (2 Kings 23:25–7). This theological explanation was rejected by the Chronicler, who omitted the passage altogether (for his own theological solution see Japhet 1997: 156–65), but its absence was felt by I Esdras, who supplemented it in the present passage in his own words. The juxtaposition of vv. 23 and 24 draws a contrast between Josiah, whose heart was 'full of godliness', and the 'former times' (NRSV: ancient times), when the people of Israel sinned against God and made him angry. The last statement, 'the words of the Lord fell against [NRSV: upon] Israel' are the necessary introduction to the next paragraph: Josiah's merits could not change the Lord's decision to destroy Israel, which now begins to be carried out with the untimely death of Josiah.

(1:25–33) Josiah's End (2 Chr 35:20–7) Several changes have been introduced in I Esdras to the passage that describes the defeat of Josiah, his death and burial, and the conclusion of his reign. In the phrasing of v. 25: 'After all these acts of Josiah' the reference to the preparation of the temple (2 Chr 35:20) has been omitted, an obvious adaptation to the new literary context, since the 'preparing of the house' has not been told in

I Esdras and a reference to it became irrelevant. In the story itself, the proper name of the king of Egypt is omitted, and more significantly, the theological part of the story—the address of the king of Egypt and the explanation of Josiah's sin— is rephrased. In 2 Chr 35:21 Pharaoh speaks and threatens Josiah in the name of *his* god, '[g]od who is with me', and Josiah is blamed for not listening 'to the words of Neco from the mouth of [g]od'. In I Esdras, Pharaoh speaks in the name of 'the Lord God' (*kuriou tou theou*) or 'the Lord' alone (mentioned altogether four times), which may refer only to the God of Israel. Josiah is blamed outright for not listening to the 'words of the prophet Jeremiah from the mouth of the Lord' (v. 28). These changes overcome the pressing theological difficulty, implied in the Chronicler's phrasing, that Josiah was punished for not obeying Pharaoh's god, and express the belief that the foreign rulers serve as instruments of God's works in history. This universal biblical concept is reformulated here (also elsewhere, e.g. the decree of Cyrus in Ezra 1:1) to say that it was not only the Jews who saw world history in this way but the foreign rulers themselves adopted this view and conceived their task in history similarly.

In Chronicles (in contrast to 2 Kings), the text followed by I Esdras, the devastating significance of Josiah's death was recognized by his own generation as well as by later ones, and was acknowledged in the unprecedented scope and depth of mourning: the people of Judah, the prophet Jeremiah, the princes and their wives (a misreading of *haśśārîm wĕhaśśārôt* for the original *haśśārîm wĕhaśśārôt* 'singing-men and singing-women'), all mourn upon his death 'to this day'. In v. 33 the conclusion to Josiah's reign is recorded in great detail, as appropriate for the last great king of Judah. His fortunes and achievements were recorded in two books rather than one: the mourning over him was written in the 'book of the histories of the kings of Judea', while every one of his deeds and his great virtues were put down 'in the book of the kings of Israel and Judah'.

(1:34–58) The Last Kings of Judah (2 Chr 36:1–21) The story of the last kings of Judah faithfully follows the source in Chronicles and presents a similar historical picture. There are, however, several differences in the names of the kings and their relationship to each other, which do not seem to result from mere textual corruption (an attempt at harmonization is seen in the various MSS). A comparison of the three sources, with the order of reign in parentheses may clarify the picture.

2 Kings 23–5:

```
                    (1) Josiah
        ┌───────────────┼───────────────┐
    (3) Jehoiakim   (2) Jehoahaz    (5) Zedekiah
        │
    (4) Jehoiachin
```

2 Chr 35–6:

```
                    (1) Josiah
        ┌───────────────┼───────────────┐
    (3) Jehoiakim                   (2) Jehoahaz
   ┌───────┴───────┐
(4) Jehoiachin  (5) Zedekiah
```

1 Esd 1:

    (1) Josiah

    ┌──────────────┴───────────┐

(2) Jeconiah   (3) Joiakim

                  │

           (4) Joiakim II (NRSV: Jehoiachin)

The relationship of (5) Zedekiah is not recorded.

In 1 Esdras, Joahaz/Jehoahaz disappears (as in 1 Chr 3:15); Jeconiah, who is elsewhere presented as another name for Jehoiachin (e.g. 1 Chr 3:16–17), the son of Jehoiakim and Josiah's grandson, is placed as Josiah's son and successor; Joiakim/Jehoiakim's son carries the same name as his father, and the relationship of Zedekiah—the son of Josiah in 2 Kings, of Jehoiakim in 2 Chronicles—is not given. Although no precedence should be given to the historical picture created by 1 Esdras, it reveals some independent traditions and an effort at reconciliatory interpretation.

(1:34–8) Jeconiah (2 Chr 36:1–4: Jehoahaz) The clear historical picture drawn in 2 Kings 24:31–4, blurred somewhat in Chronicles by the omission of the death of Jehoahaz, is further obscured here. After having reigned for three months, Jeconiah was removed by the king of Egypt and replaced by his brother, Joiakim. Beyond that, the details are impenetrable: why did Joiakim 'put the nobles in prison'? Who was 'Zarius', whose brother was he, and how did he get to Egypt? Why and how was he taken out of Egypt? It is not clear what part of the picture is a result of textual corruption, and what echoes conflicting traditions, like those of 2 Kings, which were not repeated in Chronicles. In any event, the historical picture of 2 Kings should clearly be preferred.

(1:39–42) Joiakim (2 Chr 36:5–8) 1 Esdras presents the abbreviated and reworked form of the history of Jehoiakim, as drawn in 2 Chronicles. Jehoiakim is the only king in 1 Esdras for whom the standard Deuteronomistic framework is preserved (vv. 39, 42). Recorded within the framework are two matters: (1) Nebuchadnezzar took Joiakim as prisoner to Babylon—a tradition which appears for the first time in 2 Chr 36:6, and then in Dan 1:1. The date given in Daniel for Jehoiakim's exile (the third year of his reign) explains well why 1 Esdras has completely omitted to mention the length of his reign. (2) Nebuchadnezzar took the holy vessels from the temple in Jerusalem and put them in his own temple (rather than his palace—2 Chr 36:7; cf. also Ezra 1:7) in Babylon. Thus, following 2 Chronicles, 1 Esdras views the spoiling of the temple's vessels as a multi-stage process, during the reigns of Jehoiakim, Jehoiachin, and Zedekiah, parallel to the fate of those kings who were all exiled to Babylon.

(1:43–58) Joiakim II and Zedekiah (2 Chr 36:9–21) The strict Deuteronomistic structure of Kings, followed also in Chronicles, in which the descriptions of the kings are clearly distinguished by standard formulas, is disrupted in 1 Esdras. The formulas are abandoned in favour of a more continuous and fluent discourse, which combines the stories of Joiakim II (vv. 43–5) and Zedekiah (vv. 46–58) into one sequel. Contrary to 2 Kings and 2 Chronicles, in all MSS of 1 Esdras the name of Joiakim's son is not Jehoiachin but Joiakim, like his father. It probably reflects the reality of the author's times, in which consequent kings would bear the same name. Other than this

change, the history of the king is described along the lines of 2 Chronicles: the king reigned just over three months and was exiled to Babylon, together with the holy vessels. The history of Zedekiah is the story of the destruction, following the Chronicler and adopting his theological presuppositions. According to the Chronicler's philosophy of history, the destruction was God's reaction to the transgressions of the generation in which it happened—that of Zedekiah and his people. Thus the measure of their sins has been augmented in the necessary proportion. Moreover, since God does not exert punishment without first warning the sinner and trying to make him repent his sin, God's warning through the prophets is described in great detail and the people's rejection of the prophets' rebuke is added to their sins. The destruction relates to Jerusalem and its people: many were killed; all the great buildings were burnt to ashes; the treasures were spoiled and brought to Babylon; and those who survived were exiled. All those who sinned received their due, and the place of their transgression became desolate.

The Chronicler's description assumes a poetic character, while the actual fortunes of the king (reported in detail in 2 Kings 25:4–7), the details of the deported bronze vessels (2 Kings 25:13–17), the fate of the dignitaries from Jerusalem who were deported and killed (2 Kings 25:18–21), as well as some facts regarding the aftermath of the destruction (2 Kings 25:22–30), are all passed over in silence. Jerusalem became desolate, and was to stay in this situation for seventy years, until it had repaid its debt, until the land had enjoyed its sabbaths.

The Material Restoration (chs. 2–7)

(2:1–30) First Beginnings Following the hint of the Chronicler, who concluded his work with the decree of Cyrus, 1 Esdras moves directly from the destruction in the days of Zedekiah, to the new beginnings in the time of Cyrus. The theme of prophecy and fulfilment, found in his sources (esp. Ezra 1:1; 2 Chr 36:21), is further emphasized by the augmented role of the prophet Jeremiah in the time of the destruction (1:28, 32, 47, 57). His prophecies of doom have all come true, and now the time has arrived for the fulfilment of this prophecy of hope, with the first steps towards restoration undertaken by Cyrus, king of Persia. Ch. 2 covers all the events that preceded 'the second year of Darius', that is, Cyrus's decree and the people's response (vv. 1–9), the transfer of the holy vessels to Sheshbazzar (vv. 10–15), the intervention of Judah's enemies and the cessation of the work (vv. 16–30).

Following the literary method of Ezra (cf. Japhet 1996: 127–8; Williamson 1983: 1–26), the chapter's three paragraphs are composed in a similar way: a document, embedded in a narrative framework. The decree of Cyrus (vv. 3–7) is framed by an introduction (vv. 1–2) and a narrative conclusion (vv. 8–9); the list of holy vessels (vv. 13–14) has a narrative introduction (vv. 10–12) and conclusion (v. 15), and the official correspondence with Artaxerxes (vv. 17–24, 26–9) has the necessary introductions (vv. 16, 25) and narrative conclusion (v. 30).

(2:1–9) Cyrus's Decree (Ezra 1:1–6) Cyrus's declaration in his first year as king of Babylon (538 BCE) is addressed to the Jews in Babylon and grants them permission in three matters: to rebuild the house of the Lord in Jerusalem, to return from Babylon to Jerusalem for that purpose, and to take with them money and presents that were to be collected in the Diaspora. Immediately after the decree the people start to effectuate it. They organize the return (v. 8) and collect money and presents from those who remained (v. 9). Another version of Cyrus's decree, in a bureaucratic style and with some differences in content, is recorded in 6:24–6 (Ezra 6:1–3). The relationship between the two documents, and the question of their respective authenticity has drawn the constant attention of scholars (cf. the commentaries on Ezra and the specialized studies), but the existence of such a document seems to be generally accepted. A consistent difference between the text of 1 Esdras and his source is expressed in the representation of the divine names, mainly in two features: the avoidance of the common title in the Persian period, 'God of heaven' (Japhet 1997: 25–6), and its replacement by various other titles (cf. Ezra 5:11, 12; 6:9, 10; 7:12, 21, with 1 Esdras 6:13, 15, 29, 31; 8:9, 19, respectively), and the preference of 'the Lord' (kuriou, usually representing the tetragrammaton) over the more general 'God'. Here, in v. 3, 'the God of Heaven' is replaced by 'The Lord of Israel, the Lord Most high' (see Moulton 1899: 226–30).

(2:10–15) The Return of the Holy Vessels (Ezra 1:7–11) The theme of the holy vessels, pillaged by Nebuchadnezzar, kept in Babylon during the period of the captivity, and returned by Cyrus, is greatly emphasized in the book of Ezra and serves as a concrete symbol of restoration and continuity (cf. Ackroyd 1972). The holy vessels are also prominent in 1 Esdras, but their fortunes are differently conceived. Contrary to the picture given here (= Ezra 1:11) and repeated, although with some rephrasing, in 6:18–19 (= Ezra 5:14–15), according to 4:44 Cyrus took the vessels out of Babylon, but did not send them to Jerusalem. They were transferred to Jerusalem only in the time of Darius, by Zerubbabel.

The list of vessels includes only the small ritual utensils, such as cups, censers, and vials, which were not broken up or damaged during the destruction of Jerusalem. Unlike at Ezra 1, there is full correspondence in numbers between the details and total.

(2:16–30) Disruptions in the Time of Artaxerxes (Ezra 4:6–24) Outside interference with the building begins immediately, during the reign of Artaxerxes, who is conceived here as Cyrus's successor. This obvious divergence from the historical sequel of the kings of Persia is 'corrected' by Josephus, who identifies the king as Cambyses, heir to Cyrus (Ant. 11.2.1–2). However, the problem is not historical but literary, since the whole episode comes at this point as a surprise. According to 1 Esdras, the building has not yet begun and the description of the energetic construction in Jerusalem, as well as its cessation, are all premature. All these are the consequences of the literary reorganization of the material, which dealt with the larger blocks of the story but did not take care of the details. (See 1 ESD D. 1)

After the introduction to the correspondence (v. 16), the heading of the letter is recorded in v. 17, which is a fine example of the author's reworking method. In Ezra 4:6–10 three letters are mentioned: an 'accusation' sent to Ahasuerus (Xerxes), regarding 'the inhabitants of Judah and Jerusalem' (v. 6); a letter written to Artaxerxes by 'Bishlam and Mithre-

dath and Tabeel and their associates' (v. 7), and another letter to Artaxerxes, sent by Rehum the royal deputy, Shimshai the scribe, and a long list of officials (v. 8). The last letter is actually quoted. These complex data have been condensed in 1 Esdras to form one single letter, sent to Artaxerxes. However, rather than writing the new narrative in his own words, the author made use of selected phrases gleaned from Ezra 4:6–11 thus:

In the time of king Artaxerxes of the Persians [= Ezra 4:7, 8], Bishlam, Mithridates, Tabeel [= Ezra 4:7], Rehum, Beltethmus, the scribe Shimshai [= Ezra 4:8], and the rest of their associates [= Ezra 4:8], living in Samaria and other places [= Ezra 4:10], wrote him [= Ezra 4:6, also 7, 8] the following letter [= Ezra 4:11] against those who were living in Judea and Jerusalem [= Ezra 4:6]: 'To king Artaxerxes [= Ezra 4:8, 11] our lord, your servants the recorder Rehum and the scribe Shimshai [= Ezra 4:9] and the other members of their council [= Ezra 4:9] and the judges [= Ezra 4:10, 11] in Coelesyria and Phoenicia [= Ezra 4:9: beyond the river]...'

The letter itself (vv. 18–24) begins by presenting the situation: the Jews who came 'from you to us' are building the city of Jerusalem. It follows with the threat: if the city is built, the Jews will refrain from paying tribute and the income of the king will be damaged. Then comes the basis of this deduction: the city has a record of being rebellious, which was the cause of its initial destruction; and conclusion: if the city is rebuilt, the interests of the king will be greatly damaged. The accusational intent of the letter is revealed already at its beginning, where Jerusalem is described as 'that rebellious and wicked city' (v. 18), and is continued through various rhetorical means, such as the emphatic repetition of 'Judeans' (ioudaioi, NRSV: Jews), who were 'rebels and kept setting up blockades in it from of old' (v. 23; in addition to the parallel of Ezra 4:12 with v. 18).

In structure and contents, the version of 1 Esdras faithfully follows its source in Ezra 4:12–16, but there are some interesting changes in detail, most important of which is the scope of the construction. In Ezra 4 the complaint is directed exclusively against the building of the city and its walls (vv. 12, 13, 16), as is confirmed by the king's answer (v. 21). In 1 Esdras the accusation also refers to the building of the temple: they 'are building that ... city ... and laying the foundation for a temple' (v. 18). The change expresses the author's historical criticism of the original story and his own view that the temple and the city were built at once, and not—as in Ezra-Nehemiah—in two different stages at different periods. However, this change does not do away with the initial difficulty of the new structure, since according to 1 Esdras, the reference to the building of either the city or the temple is premature, from both the literary and historical points of view. Another difference, of less significance, is the accusers' attempt to justify their intervention by pointing to their loyalty and lack of self-interest: 'because we share the salt of the palace and it is not fitting for us to witness the king's dishonour, therefore we send and inform the king' (Ezra 4:14). This is rephrased in 1 Esdras in neutral language: 'Since the building of the temple is now going on, we think it best not to neglect such a matter, but to speak to our lord the king' (vv. 20–1a). Through slight rephrasing, the tone of the king's response (vv. 25–9 = Ezra 4:17–22) has become more strict and final. Rather than leaving the order in the hands of his deputies (Ezra 4:21: 'Therefore issue an order that these people be made to cease'), Artaxerxes issues the order himself, 'Therefore I have now issued orders to prevent these people from building the city' (v. 28). The possibility that this order may be revoked at some point (Ezra 4:21: 'until I make a decree') is omitted, and the general, rather ambiguous, warning (Ezra 4:22), becomes a straightforward reference to the circumstances at hand: 'take care that nothing more be done and that such wicked proceedings go no further to the annoyance of kings' (vv. 28b–29). v. 30 reports the conclusion of the event, its anticipated purpose: the accusers hasten to cause the work to stop 'until the second year of the reign of King Darius'.

(3:1–4:63) New Beginnings The pericope is composed of two units: the competition (3:1–4:41) and its consequences (4:42–63).

(3:1–4:41) The Competition The story of the competition is composed of two uneven units, representing two genres: the wisdom story, in itself comprising 'story' and 'speeches', and the historical narrative. The inclusion of a fully fledged wisdom story seems out of place in a historiographical work, but the literary inclination of the author leads him to retain the wisdom story in its entirety, including the speeches. (Somewhat similar is the inclusion of Esther in the records of Josephus; see *Ant.* 11.b. 1–13.) The structure of the story follows the lines of the plot: the circumstances, terms, and setting of the competition (3:1–17); the speech of each of the contestants (3:18–24; 4:1–12; 4:13–40), and the decision (v. 41).

(3:1–17) Proposition Since the introductory, narrative part of the wisdom story had been already adapted to fit the specific historical situation, it is difficult to say how much of it belongs to the original source and how much was reformulated for the present context. The circumstances as described are somewhat problematic. Following Esth 1:1–3, Darius is described as having held a grand feast for all his courtiers, officials, and subjects, from all the 127 provinces of his empire, after which he went to his chambers but could not sleep (vv. 1–3). Then his three bodyguards brought up the idea of a competition, decided between them on its terms, and took the first steps towards its execution by writing down their answers and putting the written note under Darius's pillow for his decision after he had arisen (vv. 4–12). When Darius got up, he read the writing and accepted the idea, but turned the competition into a public event. The guards were asked to present their case before the assembly. The problematic nature of this exposition seems clear. The 'great feast' which opens the story plays no role in the development of the main theme. The motif of the king's sleeplessness stands in contrast to the sequence, in which the note is put under his pillow during his sleep. Even more difficult are the consequences for the image of Darius, who is presented as totally passive. Indeed, while the idea of the competition might have come from the guards, it is difficult to see how they could decide upon the winner's reward and make the king comply with their terms. All these seem to result from an elaboration of an original story with motifs borrowed from the book of Esther (the feast, the king's sleeplessness, the participants deciding upon the rewards to be extended by the king), but not fully integrated. Josephus's version is smoother in all these aspects (*Ant.* 11.3.2), but seems

to be a secondary adaptation rather than a reflection of the original.

(3:18–4:40) The Speeches The speeches are set in a conventional pattern of openings and conclusions, retouched by small stylistic variations: 'Then the first who had spoken of the strength of wine began and said' (v. 17); 'When he had said this he stopped speaking' (v. 24, and see 4:1, 12; 4:13). Only the conclusion of the third speech deviates from that pattern, probably as a result of the new literary sequel.

3:18–24, the power of wine is presented from various perspectives, individual and social, positive and negative, with some ambivalence. Most important of all, wine is seen as depriving a human being of his greatest advantage, his mind and reason. Wine obliterates the social differences within society because it transfers people from the world of reality to a world of illusion. There, all are equal, all are masters, all are rich, all are happy. This blurring of distinction may lead a person to treat a friend as an enemy, but he cannot be asked to take responsibility for his deeds, for the world under the influence of wine is unreal: when the wine is gone nothing remains of the illusory world, not even memory.

Although this speech is independent of the other themes, it already refers to the next contestant, 'the king'—which might suggest a different original order. The king is mentioned from two different angles: the influence of wine on the king himself, whose wisdom then becomes similar to that of an orphan (v. 19), and its influence on his subjects, who then forget their masters and rulers (v. 21). The king may be strong, but wine overcomes him.

4:1–12, the focus of this speech is the control of the king over his subjects: people may be strong because they dominate nature (v. 2), but the king is the strongest because he masters people (v. 3). The power of the king is then illustrated by several examples: he commands wars in which people kill and are killed, pillage and destroy (vv. 4–5); by means of his tax-system he is a partner of everyone's toil (v. 6); and he demands and receives absolute obedience (vv. 7–10a). The apparent illogical nature of the people's obedience is greatly emphasized: they fulfil the king's command although they themselves are strong, although the king is but one person and they are many, although he may deprive them of their property and even life, and command them to do things that they do not agree with. Thus, while wine controls man by affecting his body and mind, the king subordinates the human will!

Two textual notes: (1) v. 4 describes the army as overcoming 'mountains, walls and towers', 'mountains' being a misreading of the Hebrew 'cities' ('ārîm/hārîm); (2) the absolute obedience to the king's command is expressed in vv. 7–10a in a series of oppositions in a conditional structure. The list has seven items (kill/release; attack; lay waste/build; cut down/plant), and one wonders whether the list originally had four pairs, with one of the items having been lost (attack), or was built originally around the typological number seven.

4:13–33, the third guard takes advantage of his position as the last contestant, and utters two speeches rather than one, on women and on truth. The two speeches are already connected in the present context, together with the identification of the third guard as Zerubbabel (v. 13), but this sequel may still be broken down into its several components. The first speech, about women, is in itself structured in two parts: a general exaltation of the power of women (vv. 14–27, 32), and a secondary concrete example, taken from the court-life of the present king and his mistress (vv. 28–31). The speech opens with a rhetorical question directed at the two earlier contestants: the king is great, people are great (Gk. 'many' is a mistranslation of the Heb. *rabbîm*) and wine is strong—but are they not ruled by a higher master, women (v. 14)? As mothers, women are the origin; they give birth to the king, to the people who master nature, and to the farmers who prepare wine (vv. 15–16). They provide the physical and spiritual needs of men—clothes and honour (v. 17). A man may give away everything that he had amassed for a beloved woman (vv. 18–19); he may leave his parents and country to stay with his wife until his death (vv. 20–1). He may adopt all kinds of lifestyles—good or bad, on sea or land—to satisfy his wife (vv. 22–5). In sum, many men who loved women were led to insanity or slavery, or lost their way (vv. 26–7). Isn't this proof that women rule men and are the strongest (v. 32)?

Into this general praise of women, fully in line with the preceding two speeches, a short passage of the most surprising and dramatic nature was interpolated: a 'hot' story from the king's private chambers. It is an illustration of the general statement that women may lead men to madness and improper behaviour, as exemplified by the person who is supposed to be the measure of all things, the present king. This is in fact a penetrating criticism of the king, almost bringing him to trial, in which the guard betrays the king's trust by exposing his misconduct. This unexpected move is indeed followed by general embarrassment: 'the king and nobles looked at one another' (v. 33). Would the guard's words about the power of women be judged for their value, or would he be punished for his outright criticism of the king? At this point, the guard takes advantage of the general embarrassment and continues his argument, as if saying: 'I told what I did because this is the truth. I speak in the name of truth—the greatest value of all.' This bold and dramatic turn offers the king a way out of the embarrassing situation and brings the guard the longed-for victory.

4:34–40, this speech, too, begins with a comparison to the preceding argument: women are strong, but truth is stronger. Henceforth, the speech goes its own way and moves onto an elevated plane, in both content and style. The speaker refers to the foundations of the world—the earth, the heavens, and the sun (vv. 34–5), and these are but a path towards the highest of all: the Creator. Having made this cursory identification of truth and God, the speaker goes on to eulogize truth, through praise of the earth, the heavens, and everything else (v. 36). The essence of truth is that it has absolutely no injustice, a statement that highlights the concrete, moral concept of truth as 'justice'. With great rhetorical force, and with a fourfold repetition of the word 'injustice' in a parallel rhythm, the speech compares truth with all the other claimants to the throne of 'the strongest'. Wine, king, and women are unrighteous, indeed, all human beings are unrighteous. They are all transitory, having no lasting existence or value (v. 37). The speaker moves from the petty world of mankind to the eternal world of absolute values and ends in a hymnal eulogy, 'to it belong the strength, and the kingship, and the power, and the

majesty, for ever and ever' (v. 40), which leads to what is now self-evident: 'Blessed be the God of truth!' The speech is a mixture of Jewish and Hellenistic elements, but its origin seems to be clearly in the Hebrew psalmodic style, with echoes from Isaiah, 1 Chr 29:11; Ps 148:13, etc., and the repetitious use of keywords: truth, injustice, great, strong.

(4:41) Decision The spirit in which the words were said overtakes the audience; they react to the rhetoric of the speech and are moved by its force. Their reaction, 'Great is truth and strongest of all' is a verbal echo of the keywords of the speech: truth, great, and strong! In its Latin translation, this sentence has become a universal slogan, whose force and validity have not waned.

(4:42–63) The Consequences of the Competition vv. 42–6, the beginning of the king's address continues in the vein of the wisdom story and accentuates the king's generosity toward the guard (v. 43). But the guard's response does not follow this lead, and rather than asking for additional personal favours, he moves boldly from the personal to the political sphere and addresses the king as the political sovereign. The scene seems to have its origins in the book of Nehemiah, where Nehemiah addresses the Persian king Artaxerxes with the request to build Jerusalem (Neh 2:3–9), but the differences are noteworthy. Zerubbabel's request is much longer than that of Nehemiah, and more important, it is presented as if he does not really ask anything new. He only reminds the king of his vow and provides him with an opportunity to be 'righteous'—in line with the spirit of the speech. Darius's vow is not known from any other source, and its historical basis seems doubtful. When did Darius make this vow? Why? How did Zerubbabel come to know about it? And if he made the vow—why did he not fulfil it? Darius's vow is not a historical datum but a literary device, which elevates his dedication to the building of Jerusalem on the one hand, and affords Zerubbabel the opportunity to achieve his goals with no need for explanations on the other. The king had already recognized, by his earlier vow, the need to build the city of Jerusalem, to return the holy vessels, and to build the temple.

The historical picture drawn by Zerubbabel has several peculiar points: (1) The burning of the temple is not ascribed to the Babylonians who conquered the city, but to the Edomites. The participation of the Edomites in the destruction of Jerusalem is attested in several places (e.g. Ps 137:7; Ob 11–14), but the main story in 2 Kings 25:8–10 ascribes its burning to Nebuzaradan, the king's general. Does the information given here reflect the more precise historical facts, or is it one more trick of the speaker, avoiding possible embarrassment on the part of Darius who, as 'the king of Babylon', might find it difficult to revoke an earlier 'Babylonian' deed? (2) The holy vessels were not sent to Jerusalem by Cyrus—who only took them out of Babylon and made a vow to send them to Jerusalem—but were still in the hands of the Persians. This twist of the story (see I ESD 2:15) is another aspect of shifting the credit for the restoration from Cyrus to Darius. Cyrus's decree is not mentioned; what remains is his unfulfilled vow regarding the holy vessels. (3) The story seems to imply that Cyrus actually destroyed Babylon, a fact which is not confirmed from any other source.

vv. 47–57, it seems that Darius was only waiting for the opportunity provided by the guard's request. He turns energetically to the project, issues a bill of rights, and begins to implement it by writing to all the officials who were to be involved. These measures provide for: (1) Permission for Zerubbabel and others to leave Persia and go up to build Jerusalem, to be supported by the officials' help in this matter (v. 47). (2) Permission to build the city, to be supported by the right to transport cedar wood from Lebanon (v. 48). (3) Exemption of the people going up to Jerusalem from taxes (v. 49). (4) Exemption from taxes on the territory under their control (v. 50). (5) Recovery of the land that had been taken over by the Edomites (v. 50). (6) Concrete allowances for the furtherance of the building: twenty talents a year for the construction of the temple (v. 51), and ten talents a year for the maintenance of the temple cult (v. 52). (7) Tax exemption of all those who came from Babylon and their descendants (v. 53). (8) Priestly exemption from taxes (v. 53). (9) Special allowance for the upkeep of the priests and provision of their vestments (v. 54). (10) Special allowance for the Levites, until the completion of the temple and the city (v. 55). (11) Provision of land and wages for the guards of the city (v. 56). (12) Return of the holy vessels that Cyrus 'set apart' (v. 57). (13) A general confirmation of all the rights extended in the past by Cyrus (v. 57). This extensive bill of rights is taken from many sources and goes beyond the original request. For example, it opens with the securing of a safe journey for Zerubbabel and his caravan, although Zerubbabel did not mention that he wanted to go to Jerusalem. This feature, as well as the provision of wood, is certainly taken from the story of Nehemiah (Neh 2:7–8). Issues concerning the taking of land by the Edomites may reflect actual historical facts, but were not relevant to the building of Jerusalem, and are nowhere mentioned in Ezra-Nehemiah. The generous exemption from taxes also seems to reflect some reality of the Hellenistic, rather than the Persian period; in the latter period, only the letter of Artaxerxes refers to this matter and that only concerning the clergy (Ezra 7:24).

No mention is made in this context of the appointment of Zerubbabel as the governor of Judah, and the exact political order envisaged by Darius is not specified. The freedom from taxes and tributes seems to imply a broader concept of self-government than is usually known in the Persian period. In any event, the political terminology of 1 Esdras is very similar to that of Maccabees.

vv. 58–63, the episode is concluded in accordance with the conventions of the time: a thanksgiving prayer of Zerubbabel (cf. Ezra's prayer after he had received the letter of Artaxerxes, Ezra 7:27–8), and the celebrations of the community. The conventional hymnal style of the prayer, as well as its parallel structure, are obvious.

Aware of the historical reality, the competition having taken place in Persia and the Jews living in Babylon, the author concludes by telling of Zerubbabel's journey to Babylon. The people react to the news with thanksgiving and rejoicing. The special emphasis of 1 Esdras that the city and the temple were built together is expressed here too: 'to go up and build Jerusalem and the temple'. With these celebrations, the story of the competition has completed its role as an opening for a new beginning, and comes to an end.

(5:1–46) The Return Due to the new arrangement of the material, the great return to Jerusalem, ascribed in Ezra 2 to the time of Cyrus, is here transferred to the time of Darius, and Ezra 2 is connected to the new sequel by a new narrative introduction (vv. 1–3) and a new preface to the list of returnees (vv. 4–6). The author then resumes his source, and follows it faithfully (with small divergences) from v. 7 onwards (Ezra 2:1–70).

vv. 1–3, the preparations for the return consist of one thing: the choice of returnees. The idea that only a fraction of the people returned from Babylonia to Jerusalem probably represents the historical reality, but the explanation of this fact as a result of 'choosing', namely, that permission was extended only to a minority that was to be chosen from the great multitude, seems to be the author's own. It was probably suggested to the author by the story of Nehemiah's repopulating of Jerusalem, in which he designated by lot one out of ten to live in the city (Neh 11:1–2). The end of the passage refers again to this issue but from a different perspective: the people who accompanied the returnees were so joyful that they too were allowed to go up!

The caravan described is similar to that of Nehemiah who went to Jerusalem with an escort (Neh 2:9: 'the king had sent officers of the army and cavalry with me'), rather than to the caravan of Ezra who 'was ashamed to ask the king for a band of soldiers and cavalry to protect us against the enemy on our way' (Ezra 8:22). 1 Esdras sees the return as a festive procession, a pilgrimage to Jerusalem accompanied by musicians and song (see Isa 30:29), rather than a long voyage through the desert.

(vv. 4–43) The List of Returnees vv. 4–8, the introduction is composed of two parts: the original heading of the list, taken from Ezra 2:1–2, which appears in vv. 7–8 following the author's presentation of the leaders (vv. 4–6). After establishing the fact of the return (v. 4), three leaders are mentioned (vv. 5–6): 'the priests ... Jeshua the son of Jozadak ... and Joakim his son, and Zerubbabel, the son of Salathiel'. (Due to a minor textual corruption in the Heb. *bnw w* to *bn*, the three leaders have become two, both of them priests: Jeshua the son of Jozadak, and Joakim the son of Zerubbabel. For various attempts to explain the text as it is, or to restore it differently, see Cook 1913: 34; Myers 1974: 66.) The leaders are provided with short genealogies which connect them to the constitutive periods of their respective authority. The priests are related to Phineas the son of Aaron on the one hand, and to Seraiah, the last high priest of the First Temple (2 Kings 25:18; following 1 Chr 5:40) on the other. Zerubbabel is connected to the house of David, the family of Perez, and the tribe of Judah, but nothing is said about his descent from Jehoiachin, the exiled king of Judah (cf. 1 Chr 3:17–19), perhaps because of the divergent traditions in this regard, in 1 Esdras as well. Tracing the hero's genealogy to his ancient, tribal origin is a literary mark of the period—see Esth 2:5–6; Tob 1:1; and Jdt 8:1. This is the most elaborate genealogy of Zerubbabel at our disposal; it reflects in an unmistakable way one of the important features of 1 Esdras—the glorification of Zerubbabel and his Davidic lineage. The short note that Zerubbabel was the person who 'spoke wise words before Darius' highlights the sequence of the events. The date of the competition, here added to the story, seems to have been created under the influence of several sources: the date of Nehemiah's approach to Artaxerxes, 'In the month of Nisan in the twentieth year' (Neh 2:1), illustrating again that Nehemiah's memoirs were drawn upon for the story of Zerubbabel; Esth 3:7, 'In the first month which is the month of Nisan'; and perhaps also Ezra 7:9.

In vv. 7–8 the text returns to its source in Ezra 2 and produces the original introduction, with small changes. Most important is the replacement of the term: 'people of the province' with 'people of the land of Judah' (NRSV: the Judeans), which is the term generally used in this book. Also worth noting is the emphatic rendering of 'each to his own town', and the twelve names of the leaders (as in Neh 7:7) rather than the corrupt eleven in Ezra 2:2.

vv. 9–43 (see Ezra 2:2b–67; Neh 7:7b–72), while the literary structure and general contents of the list faithfully follow its source in Ezra 2, there are numerous differences in the details of names and numbers. Some names in Ezra 2 are not found in 1 Esdras, and some names in 1 Esdras are missing in Ezra 2. There are also changes in the order of names, and above all, their forms—as everywhere in the book—are sometimes unrecognizably reshaped. There are also several changes in the numbers, which could be easily explained as a result of corruption, but the original version cannot be determined. In what follows we will not deal with the variant details (see Cook 1913: 35–8), but present only the list's broader lines. It is structured in three main parts: vv. 9–35, register of the people according to their ancestry; vv. 36–40, register of those who lack a genealogical record or could not verify it; vv. 41–3, summary, including servants and property.

vv. 9–35, the register of the people is divided between the laymen (vv. 9–23) and the clergy (vv. 24–35). Among 'those of the nation' (v. 9), the people are registered in groups in two ways: by their ancestral genealogy or by their settlements. From a formal point of view, some are described as 'the descendants of' and others as 'those of', and while in general there is some correspondence between these criteria ('the descendants of Parosh', 'those of Netopha'), the correlation is only partial, and with the obscurity of some of the names, no precise division can be made. It is worth noting, however, that the groups registered according to their ancestry are usually larger than those of the settlements. Also, the settlements, as far as they can be identified, are mostly in Benjamin, with only a few place-names (Bethlehem, v. 17b; Netophah, v. 18a) in Judah. The list does not refer to Jerusalem, and it is hard to say how many of those enumerated were regarded as living in Jerusalem.

The clergy are divided into six groups, representing the temple orders in a declining hierarchy: priests (vv. 24–5), Levites (v. 26), singers (v. 27), gatekeepers (v. 28), temple servants (vv. 29–32), and the descendants of Solomon's servants (vv. 33–4). In matters of terminology, the singers are termed—as throughout 1 Esdras—'the holy singers' (NRSV: temple singers), probably to distinguish them from non-cultic singers, mentioned for instance in v. 42; and the Nethinim (Ezra 2:43 etc.) are consistently defined as 'temple servants' (hierodouloi). In all versions of the list, the priests outnumber all the other orders put together: 4,288 (4,289) priests against 713 (733, 752) for all the others.

vv. 36–40, two groups are mentioned in this supplement to the list of persons without proper record: three families who could not prove their Israelite ancestry (vv. 36–7), and three families of priests, who could not prove their priestly origin and were rejected from service until the restoration of the now lost priestly Urim and Thummim (Ex 28:30; Num 27:21, etc.), that is, indefinitely (vv. 38–40). In listing the Babylonian origins of those without record, 1 Esdras presents three of the place-names, Cherub, Addan, and Immer, as the names of the people's leaders—in harmony with his general tendency to emphasize the role and person of the leaders (cf. above, vv. 5–6, 9). An interesting rephrasing is found in v. 40, which cannot be fully explained on textual grounds. According to Ezra 2:63 the decision regarding the priests was made by the Tirshata, a Persian loanword probably meaning 'his highness', referring anonymously to the officiating governor. In Ezra-Nehemiah 'the Tirshata' is identified twice with Nehemiah (Neh 8:9; 10:2) and this identification is similarly assumed here, introducing Nehemiah at this period, alongside Zerubbabel. However, as a result of misunderstanding or a later corruption, the title 'Tirshata' has been transformed to a proper name and presented in transliteration.

vv. 41–3: the summary provides the final numbers: the free people of Israel and, as against Ezra 2:64, 1 Esdras distinguishes explicitly between freemen and slaves, substituting for the original 'the whole assembly together', 'All those of Israel, twelve or more years of age, besides male and female servants' (v. 41). The age of 12 years as denoting maturity or a change of status, is not recorded anywhere in the Bible; the general age for full membership in the community being 20 (inter alia Num 1:3–46). The specification of age may either reflect a certain reality of the time which is not otherwise attested to (but cf. Lk 2:42), or another typological use of the number 12.

(vv. 44–6) **Arrival and Settlement** The arrival in Jerusalem is not stated explicitly, as in Ezra 8:32 or Neh 2:11: 'We/I came to Jerusalem'; rather, it is stated apropos the principal information: the vows of the returnees to build the temple. An interesting change of contents is introduced by the rendering of 'made freewill-offering' (hitnadbû) as 'vowed' (nādrû). This turn of phrase is evidenced throughout 1 Esdras and may have originated with the Greek translator. The derivations of the root n-d-b are almost consistently rendered with 'vow' (see 2:7, 9, as compared to Ezra 1:4, 6, and more). The actual donation of Ezra 2, made by the heads of the families 'according to their resources' (vv. 68–9, in itself a summary of Neh 7:69–71), is turned into a vow 'that to the best of their ability, they would erect the house . . . and . . . they would give'.

The settlement of the returnees is described somewhat differently in the various versions of the list (Ezra 2:70, Neh 7:72a), but according to 1 Esdras the higher ranks of clergy, the priests and Levites, and some of the people of Israel settled in Jerusalem and 'in the land', whereas the other clerical orders, the singers and the gatekeepers, together with all Israel, settled 'in their towns'. It seems that an original distinction between 'Jerusalem' and 'their towns' has been obscured by the addition of 'in the land' for the first group (NRSV: 'and its vicinity' is a nice way out of the difficulty). Why none of the lower orders of the clergy settled in Jerusalem is not made clear.

Concerning the reality behind the list, it seems self-evident, and indeed is generally accepted, that the list cannot be taken at face value; all these people could not have come up at once from Babylon to Jerusalem. The magnitude of the return would be impossible for the journey assumed here, and it may be compared to the return under Ezra, already of an outstanding size (Ezra 8:2–14, 18–19). On the other hand, there can be no doubt that a return to Judah did occur at that time as both Joshua and Zerubbabel were born in Babylon and their activity in Jerusalem is reflected in the prophecies of Haggai and Zechariah (Hag 1:1, 12, 14; 2:2–4, 21; Zech 3:1–9; 4:6–10). There are two main solutions suggested: that several, separate returns, throughout a longer period of time, hinted at by the twelve leaders at the heading of the list, have been condensed into one record, as if they represented a single event (Williamson 1985: 30–2); or, that a distinction should be made between the list proper and its narrative framework. While the introduction and the narrative section refer to a return, the list itself represents a census of all the inhabitants of the province, returned exiles and non-exiles alike. In this context, all these inhabitants are legitimized as 'returned exiles'. This second view is supported by the archeological data, which estimates the population of the province of Judah in the fifth century BCE to have been around 50,000 (Lipschits 1997: 331–6; for a much smaller estimate see Carter 1994: 133–7), and it is no longer possible to regard them all as returned exiles.

(5:47–73) Laying the Foundations Following his source faithfully, 1 Esdras records the first steps towards the restoration of Jerusalem as the religious centre of the Jews: constructing the altar and establishing the pattern of worship, making preparations for the building of the temple, and laying its foundations in joy and celebrations. This is followed by the intervention of Judah's enemies, which brought the effort to a halt.

(vv. 47–55) Building the Altar and Establishing a Regular Cult (Ezra 3:1–6) With the arrival of the seventh month, the date of the great pilgrimage, the people gather in Jerusalem to perform their duties. The place of the convocation, 'the square before the first gate towards the east', is not mentioned in Ezra 3:1, but is probably influenced by Neh 8:1 in the version of 1 Esd 9:38. Their first step, under the leadership of Joshua and Zerubbabel, is to build an altar on which sacrifices can be offered. As at Ezra 3, it is emphasized that everything was done properly: the altar was built 'in its place' (v. 50), the burnt offerings were 'in accordance with the directions in the book of Moses the man of God' (v. 49); they offered sacrifices 'at the proper times' (v. 50), and kept 'the festival of booths, as it is commanded in the law' (v. 51). In fact, two sets of sacrifices are described here: the daily sacrifices and those of the festivals, as of that specific date (vv. 50b–51), and the regular sacrifices throughout the year from that point onwards (v. 52). The free-will offerings, here termed 'vows' (cf. vv. 44–6 above), were also resumed at that time.

In an interesting rephrasing of his source, the attitude of the 'other peoples' is differently conceived. According to Ezra 3:3 'they were in dread of the neighbouring peoples', alluding to the animosity that accompanied all their actions. According

to 1 Esdras there were two groups among the 'other nations': those who 'joined them from the other peoples of the land' (v. 50a), and others, who were 'hostile to them and were stronger than they' (v. 50b). The stereotypical negative attitude to the 'other nations', characterizing Ezra-Nehemiah, is somewhat qualified.

At the same time, first steps are taken towards the building of the temple, with the provision of building materials: hewn stones, probably found in the immediate vicinity and mentioned cursorily, and cedar wood, brought from Lebanon with the special permission of Cyrus (vv. 54–5). The reference to this permission, as the whole chapter, follows the source of Ezra 3 (v. 7), and although there is no explicit reference to this item in Cyrus's decree (either in Ezra 1 or 6), one may assume that this was one aspect of his general support of the building. However, in the context of 1 Esdras, our chapter is explicitly placed at the time of Darius and follows his explicit order to this effect (4:48); the reference to Cyrus here is a glaring deviation from the new historical sequel.

(vv. 56–65) Laying the Foundations of the Temple (Ezra 3:7–15) Seven months later, at the beginning of the second month of the second year, the work on the temple, the main goal of the return and the symbol of restoration, is begun with a great ceremony under the leadership of Joshua and Zerubbabel. The ceremony is described as a grand liturgy—the priests in their holy vestments with trumpets, and the Levites with musical instruments, accompany the builders in music and song. In a touching scene, the reaction of the people is described: the old people, who had seen the previous temple and witnessed its destruction, react in 'outcries and loud weeping', while the majority of the assembly 'came with trumpets and joyful noise'. These voices mingle together in an indistinguishable loud voice, heard from afar. The inspiration for this story, based literally on Ezra 3:12–13 and somewhat rephrased, comes from Hag 2:3–4. While in Ezra 3 the event occurred in the time of Cyrus, in the present context it is transferred to the time of Darius, where Zerubbabel's return is placed.

(vv. 66–73) Intervention of Judah's Enemies (Ezra 4:1–5) This scene is connected to the previous one in a narrative chain: The noise of the celebrations raised the interest of the neighbouring foreigners and caused them to come to Jerusalem. These people are described in three different ways: the enemies of the tribes of Judah and Benjamin (v. 66); those who were brought to the land by 'king Esar-haddon of the Assyrians' (v. 69); and 'the peoples of the land' (v. 72). Although, even according to this text, they have obeyed and worshipped the Lord for many years, the threefold identification marks them as complete foreigners whose intentions are met with great suspicion. It is generally assumed that the people designated in this way are the inhabitants of the former northern kingdom, but no single ethnic term is used to identify them. This is an authentic reflection of the prehistory of the Samaritans and their early relations with the people of Judah. Their origin and loyalty are questioned and they are totally rejected, but their separate identity in religious and ethnic terms is not yet established.

The natural offshoot of rejection, aggression, does not take long to appear: the rejected people now take every possible measure to obstruct the building, which stopped 'as long as king Cyrus lived...for two years, until the reign of Darius' (v. 73). The insurmountable historical difficulties created by this statement are mainly twofold: (1) There is no direct sequel from Cyrus to Darius; Cambyses, Cyrus's heir, ruled for eight years between them, and so the time gap was longer than two years. (2) According to the context of 1 Esdras, the events described in ch. 5, including the laying of the temple's foundations, took place in the time of Darius, after the second year of his reign (2:30; 5:6). A reference to Cyrus at this point deviates from the historical sequence. These difficulties may be fully understood as a result of 1 Esdras's literary procedure. 1 Esdras has completely reorganized the story by transferring Ezra 4:6–24 to ch. 2 and relocating all the events of Ezra 3 to the time of Darius. However, these have not influenced the phrasing of the original story, which is now continued in its original sequence.

(6:1–7:15) New Start and Final Realization Following Ezra 5–6 with small changes, the story now goes on to tell about the resumption of work on the temple 'in the second year of Darius' under the inspiration of the prophets, and its completion 'in the sixth year of King Darius' (7:5). In Ezra 5:1–2, the resumption of the building stands in outright contradiction to Artaxerxes' command that no work should be executed 'until I make a decree' (Ezra 4:21). With the removal of the correspondence with Artaxerxes (Ezra 4:6–24), the logic of the story in this regard has improved. Nevertheless, the broader historical context remains problematic, since it displays the short memory of everyone involved. According to the historical view of 1 Esdras, 'the second year of Darius', given here as the date of the governor's inspection (vv. 1, 3), is also the date of the competition of the three guards (5:6), which resulted in Darius's extended bill of rights and Zerubbabel's return. On that occasion Darius wrote letters to all the governors in Syria and Phoenicia and instructed them to help Zerubbabel on his way back and aid his projects (4:47–57). All this is completely ignored by the present story; neither the governor, nor the Jews, not even Darius himself, take cognizance of the events described in 4:47–57. This is another result of 1 Esdras's incomplete method of reworking.

(6:1–2) Resumption of Work (Ezra 5:1–2) The data about the role of Haggai and Zechariah in encouraging the people to build are probably dependent on their prophecies as preserved in their books (see Hag 1:1–11; 2:1–9; Zech 4:6–10; 8:9–13), although these prophecies speak about the construction and not its resumption.

(6:3–22) The Governor's Inspection (Ezra 5:3–17) Immediately after the successful resumption of the work, the builders are visited by the supreme authority of the satrapy, but contrary to other interventions, the inspection is described in neutral terms, as part of the governor's routine duties. Nevertheless, the high rank of the visiting officials may suggest an earlier unrecorded act of conspiracy. The circumstances of the inspection are recorded in two forms: briefly, in the introductory narrative passage (vv. 3–6), and more extensively, in the governor's letter to Darius (vv. 8–22). Its purpose is implied in the governor's questions: to investigate doubts regarding the official authorization of the building. The point made at the beginning, that the inspection did not result in an immediate

halt of the work, as would have been expected under such circumstances, is understood as an expression of special divine grace (vv. 5–6).

The letter of Sisinnes (Ezra 5:3: Tattenai) is an interesting example of official correspondence and local politics, structured carefully and phrased in official terminology. It begins with precise information regarding the governor's visit and observation (vv. 8–10), informs the king about the governor's investigation and his demand to be given the names of the responsible leaders (vv. 11–12), and continues with a lengthy recital of the answer he received, presented literally in the first person plural (vv. 13–20). The letter concludes with the governor's request: that the veracity of the elders' claim in the matter of authorization be checked, and that he be given further instructions (vv. 21–2). To the question of authorization, 'at whose command are you building this house..?', the elders of the Jews provide the formal answer by referring to Cyrus's edict in the first year of his reign. However, they set this answer within a long report of the history of the house, before and after Cyrus's command. Their central point is that they were not doing anything new! The house was built 'many years ago by a king of Israel', burned down by Nebuchadnezzar, began to be restored by the command of Cyrus, and had been being built since that time. Their words do not hint at any break in the process of building, nor at any previous intervention to stop it. The elders' answer is marked by strong religious tones, which are absent from the official language of the Persian visitors; they present themselves as 'the servants of the Lord who created the heaven and the earth' (v. 13), and explain the destruction of the temple as divine punishment (v. 15).

The version of the letter in 1 Esdras has undergone several changes from the version in Ezra in both content and style. The term 'God of heaven' has been replaced by other divine titles (vv. 13, 15, as against Ezra 5:11, 12; see 1 ESD 2:1–9); the city of Jerusalem is mentioned right at the beginning (vv. 8, 9, with no parallel in Ezra 5), and the house is glorified in several ways (vv. 9, 10). Also, the king is addressed more formally as 'our lord the king' (vv. 8, 22) and the Jews are defined as those 'who had been in exile' (v. 8, absent in Ezra 5).

A matter of special interest is the addition of the name Zerubbabel to that of Sheshbazzar as the one who received the holy vessels from king Cyrus (v. 18). While the theological goal of this insertion seems obvious—the wish to glorify Zerubbabel by connecting him from the very beginning with the fortunes of the vessels and the restoration of the temple— the historical result is embarrassing. Contrary to the picture drawn in this book, where Zerubbabel makes his first appearance as Darius's guard and receives the holy vessels from him, he is projected here back to the time of Cyrus and the vessels are seen as already delivered in Cyrus's time.

(6:23–34) Darius's Response (Ezra 6:1–12) Darius's response is a precise reaction to the governor's request: he conducts a search in order to find confirmation for the Judeans' claim of authorization (vv. 23–6) and issues his own instructions (vv. 27–34). The search throughout the empire produces an archival record of Cyrus's decree, found in Ecbatana, the king's summer residence in Media. The record confirms the main claim, that the permission to build the temple was granted by Cyrus, but differently from the decree in 2:3–7, it refers to the measurements of the house and the manner of its building, imposes the coverage of the expenses on the royal treasury, and contains an explicit order to return the holy vessels. It does not mention the people's return to Judah. All these create a coherent picture in which the issues that involve the imperial administration are set down, and the features of the house carefully detailed, because the expenses are to be covered by the treasury.

Darius's own instructions (vv. 27–34) are styled somewhat differently from Ezra 6:6–12. In both versions, the instructions are presented as an excerpt from Darius's letter, addressed to the governor in the first person, with the heading of the letter omitted. 1 Esdras turns the one long excerpt into four passages, phrased alternately as direct speech (vv. 28–31, 33–4) and indirect speech (vv. 27, 32). The instructions provide the governor with the answer to his query, but go far beyond that. Their main point is the recognition of the temple as a 'king's sanctuary', under the direct protection of the emperor. The royal treasury assumes responsibility for the provision of the ritual, and the priests are required to make sacrifices and pray for the welfare of the king and his offspring. The orders are upheld by severe penalties to transgressors—death by hanging and confiscation of property—and a general prayer to God to punish anyone who would act against the temple. However, unlike Ezra 6:8, the contribution of the king towards the building is absent in the present version.

Note that contrary to Ezra 6, which refers in a general fashion to 'the governor of the Jews' (v. 7), or ignores him altogether (v. 8), Zerubbabel is mentioned here twice as the governor (vv. 27, 29).

(7:1–9) Completion and Dedication of the Temple (Ezra 6:13–18) The completion of the temple and its dedication are told in a very concise style: the governor and his escort complied with the contents and spirit of Darius's orders and helped the Jews to complete the building. The house was finished on the 23rd (Ezra 6:15: the 3rd) day of the month of Adar, in the sixth year of Darius's reign, and dedicated. Compared with the extravagant dedication of the first temple (1 Kings 8:1–66), the elaborate ceremonies reported in Chronicles (e.g. 1 Chr 15–16; 28–9; 2 Chr 29:20–36), and even some of the events described in Ezra-Nehemiah (e.g. Neh 12:27–44), the conciseness of the description and the modesty of the ceremony and its puristic character are striking. The ritual includes only sacrifices, with no accompaniment of music or song, which had become a hallmark of Second Temple ceremonies. The number of sacrifices—although quite high in itself—is minimal in comparison to the extent of the other ceremonies, and no details at all are provided regarding the actual ritual practice. In Ezra 6, the ceremony is qualified succinctly in two ways: that it was conducted 'with joy' (v. 16), and 'as it is written in the book of Moses' (v. 18). 1 Esdras omits even the single reference to 'joy', and replaces it by another statement that the people did 'according to what was written in the book of Moses' (v. 6). On the other hand, 1 Esdras adds a few details of the ceremony: the priests and the Levites stood 'arrayed in their vestments' (v. 9), the gatekeepers were at their gates (v. 9, cf. 1:16), and the sin offerings were brought according to the

number of the leaders of the tribes, rather than of the tribes themselves.

One more point should be made. According to Ezra 6:14, the complete success of the building was achieved 'by command of the God of Israel and by decree of Cyrus, Darius, and King Artaxerxes of Persia', expressing very loudly the book's view of the role of the Persian kings as the agents of God's will for his people (Japhet 1996: 132–6). Although 1 Esdras generally shares this view, it is softened here in his phrasing of the same verse: 'they completed it by the command of the Lord God of Israel. So with the consent of Cyrus and Darius and Artaxerxes, kings of the Persians, the holy house was finished' (vv. 4–5).

(7:10–15) Passover (Ezra 6:19–22) The pericope is concluded with a short description of the Passover following the dedication. This sequel is clearly an imitation of earlier events, such as the dedication of Solomon's temple followed by the Feast of Booths (1 Kings 8:65), and Josiah's Passover following the restoration of the temple (2 Kings 23:1–20, 21–3). The description of the festival is again very concise, with brief mention of the date of the Passover and the celebration of the feast of unleavened bread after it; no details are provided concerning the sacrifices, the ritual, and the ceremony.

One matter stands out beyond the information of Ezra 6, that of purification, probably under the influence of 2 Chr 30. Ezra 6:20 refers to the general purification of the clergy, 'both the priests and the Levites', and says nothing about the people. 1 Esdras repeats this information, but extends it to relate to the status of the people 'Not all of the returned captives were purified', and repeats again that 'the Levites were all purified together' (v. 11). Another difference regards the composition of the celebrating community. According to Ezra 6:21 the celebrating crowd was composed of two groups: 'the people of Israel who had returned from exile, and also ... all who had joined them and separated themselves from the pollutions of the nations of the land to worship the LORD the God of Israel'. While the identity of the latter group, mentioned in Ezra-Nehemiah only once more (Neh 10:29), may be debated, the note certainly refers to people outside the narrow circle of the returned exiles. This group disappears in the rephrasing of 1 Esd 7:13, where 'those who had separated themselves from the abominations of the peoples of the land' are the same as 'the people of Israel who had returned from exile'.

The peculiar view of the book of Ezra, emphasizing the role of the foreign rulers as the vehicle by which God's grace is extended to his people, is retained here too (v. 15).

Spiritual Restoration (chs. 8–9)

(8:1–67) Ezra's Return to Jerusalem By means of a conventional literary formula, 'After these things', the story now moves from the period of Zerubbabel to that of Ezra, from the physical restoration of Jerusalem and Judah to the spiritual plane. This kind of transition, already found in Ezra-Nehemiah, obscures the chronological gap of about seventy or 120 years (depending on whether Ezra should be placed in the time of King Artaxerxes I or II) between the events and creates the impression of direct continuation.

'The Story of Ezra', taken in full from Ezra-Nehemiah and followed faithfully, centres on religious issues and is composed of three parts: the story of Ezra's return (8:1–67), the issue of the foreign women (8:68–9:36), and the reading of the law (9:37–55). The story of Ezra's return is also composed of three parts: a general introduction (vv. 1–7), the letter of Artaxerxes (vv. 8–27), and the return (vv. 28–67).

(vv. 1–7) Introduction (Ezra 7:1–9) The introduction is to some extent a summary of the following story. It introduces Ezra by his genealogy and qualifications (vv. 1–3, 7), alludes to the letter of Artaxerxes (v. 4), and provides in a few words the bare facts of the return (vv. 5–6).

Ezra's genealogy is based on the common priestly genealogical scheme, which traces the descent of the high priests of Solomon's temple, from Zadok to Seraiah, back to Aaron through Eleazar and Phineas. The most elaborate form of this list is found in 1 Chr 5:27–41, and is abbreviated by the omission of a few generations in Ezra 7:1–5. It is further abbreviated in 1 Esdras, but in both versions (although the evidence of the MSS is not straightforward), Ezra is presented as 'the son of Seraiah', which means 'the descendant of Seraiah', since no matter what view one takes of his time, it is impossible—and nowhere claimed—that he was Seraiah's direct son.

Ezra's official Aramaic title is given in Artaxerxes' letter as 'the priest Ezra, the scribe of the law of the God of heaven' (Ezra 7:12, 21). The second part of the title was interpreted by some scholars as referring to an official position in the imperial court (following Schaeder 1930). In the Hebrew sections of Ezra, the official meaning of the title is less obvious and the connection of Ezra to the learning, teaching, and doing of the law is highlighted (Ezra 7:6, 10, 11; also Neh 8:1, 4, 9, 13; 12:26, 28). This line of interpretation is developed further here, with Ezra described as one who 'possessed great knowledge, so that he omitted nothing from the law of the Lord or the commandments, but taught all Israel all the ordinances and judgements' (v. 7, cf. Ezra 7:10). In several places the title 'scribe' was rendered 'the reader of the law of the Lord' or simply 'the reader' (vv. 8, 9, 19; 9:39, 49), and rather than just 'priest', he is titled 'the high priest' (9:39, 40, 49). All these are meant to elevate his figure, in conformity with his reputation in later Jewish tradition, as illustrated for example by rabbinic sources.

The details of the return are summarized in vv. 5–6: the date of departure, the date of arrival, and the composition of the return, people representing all Israel.

(vv. 8–27) The Letter of Artaxerxes (Ezra 7:8–28) This unit is structured in the same literary manner that we observed before (cf. 1 ESD ch. 2), that is, as a document quoted literally (vv. 9–24) and embedded in a narrative framework, consisting of a short introduction (v. 8) and a conclusion (vv. 25–7). In an interesting manner, the style of the narrative moves from the third person of the introduction to the first person in the conclusion, and continues in this fashion until v. 90 (Ezra 9:15), where the narrative returns to a third-person record (vv. 91–9:36 = Ezra 10:1–5). The letter itself is written in a conventional official style and terminology, but some of the changes introduced clearly reflect the writer's provenance.

The official mission of Ezra, established by the king and his counsellors, is 'to make inquiries about Judah and Jerusalem, according to the law of your God' (Ezra 7:14), or, as it is

phrased in 1 Esdras: 'to look into matters in Judea and Jerusalem' (v. 12). This seems to be a temporary nomination for a limited, distinct purpose, rather than a regular position in the Persian administration or the Jewish religious hierarchy. On the occasion of this mission, Artaxerxes grants Ezra authority in several matters, pertaining first to the return and then to his actions in Jerusalem. Regarding the return, Ezra is invested with authority in three matters: (1) to organize a return of Jews who wish to go with him to Jerusalem, in unlimited number and of all classes (vv. 10–11); (2) to transfer money and gifts from Babylonia to Jerusalem and use it according to his own judgement (vv. 13–16); and (3) to transfer to Jerusalem the vessels necessary for use in the temple (v. 17).

Regarding his activities in Judah, three matters are specified: (1) A special contribution of the imperial treasury for the maintenance of the cult, which should be provided by the local governors (vv. 18–21). However, the letter does not specify whether a regular yearly contribution or just a single donation is intended. (2) Exemption from taxes for all the clergy in whatever task (v. 22). (3) The authority to introduce the Jewish legal system, by the force of royal administrative measures, through the appointment of judges and the teaching of the law (vv. 23–4). Artaxerxes' letter is marked by a religious tone, culminating in the phrasing of v. 21: 'Let all things prescribed in the law of God be scrupulously fulfilled for the Most High God, so that wrath may not come upon the kingdom of the king and his sons.' This spirit, also found in the original version, is further intensified in 1 Esdras by his rendering of the divine titles, changing 'the God of Heaven' to 'the Most High God' and in some instances replacing the general title 'god' by the specific 'the Lord'.

A particular Hellenistic feature is introduced into the letter by the rendering of v. 10. While the original in Ezra 7:13 opens simply with 'I decree that' (lit. an order is issued by me), 1 Esdras precedes it with 'In according with my gracious decision I have given orders'. Officially this may mean that the king's special favour was outside and beyond the common procedure, but the use of the Greek term *philanthrōpia* certainly reflects the spirit of the author's time. With no transition of any kind and no introductory formula, the story now moves to Ezra's thanksgiving prayer after he had received the letter, phrased in the first person. In several MSS this elliptic transition is smoothed over by the interpolation of a preface: 'Then Ezra the scribe said', adopted also by the NRSV. The blessing is centred on one theme: blessed be the Lord who turned the heart of the Persian king and his counsellors towards Israel, the temple, and Ezra.

(vv. 28–49) Registration (Ezra 8:1–20) Ezra regards his caravan as a representative of the whole people, as 'Israel' in a nutshell, and he conducts the organization and registration of the returning people in two stages: the people who have gathered of their own initiative are registered according to their families (vv. 28–40), and then a special effort is made to express the idea of wholeness through the addition of the missing Levites (vv. 41–9). This symbolic aspect of the return also finds expression in the composition and hierarchy of the list. It begins with three individuals, representing the ruling families of Israel: the priesthood—represented by two priests, descendants of Aaron's two sons—and the kingship, represented by a descendant of the house of David. In principle, the same structure may also be found in the list of returnees of Ezra 2, headed by the priest Joshua and the descendant of David's line, Zerubbabel. However, Ezra 2 does not spell out these genealogical lines (this intentional omission is 'corrected' in 1 Esd 5:4–8), whereas here these people are identified in terms of their distinguished origins. The laymen consist of twelve heads of families, listed in a formulaic manner: 'of the descendants of X, Y the son of Z, and with him N men'. This unified formula is modified slightly in two cases, the first (where the name of Zechariah's father is not given, and the word 'enrolled' is added; v. 30), and the next to last, where the descendants of Adonikam are qualified as 'the last ones' and three of them mentioned by name only (v. 39). The basic structure and the main details of the list are the same as in Ezra 8, but there are some differences in names and numbers (1,690 here, 1,496 in Ezra 8). All the families also appear in the list of Ezra 2 (1 Esd 5:9–43), but their order is different and the numbers here are much smaller.

After having gathered the people at the 'river called Theras' (Ezra 8:15: 'the river that runs to Ahava'), Ezra found the composition of the caravan unsatisfactory. The absence 'of the descendants of the priests or of the Levites' (v. 42) meant an incomplete representation of 'all Israel', and Ezra makes special efforts to correct it. (In Ezra 8:15 the missing group are the Levites alone, whereas here it also includes the priests (cf. also v. 46), contrary to his own statement in v. 29 and the results of the search.) The descendants of two levitical families, eighteen and twenty men respectively, together with 220 temple servants, join the people preparing themselves to return.

An interesting misunderstanding is represented by the rendering of the place-name Casiphia as an adjective derived from the Hebrew word 'silver' (*kesep*), as: 'the place of the treasury' or 'the treasurers at that place' (vv. 45–6).

(vv. 50–67) The Journey (Ezra 8:21–36) A peculiarity of the story is seen in its unbalanced structure. The journey itself is described briefly in one verse: 'We left the river Theras . . . and we arrived in Jerusalem' (v. 61), including the date of the departure and a reference to the divine providence. All the rest of the story is dedicated to the preparations before the journey (vv. 50–60), and the people's whereabouts upon their arrival (vv. 62–7). Although the actual arrangements for the journey must have been extensive, as several thousand people were preparing themselves for a four-month journey in the desert, the details provided in this description relate to only two matters: a proclamation of fasting and prayer to the Lord before departure, and arrangements for the transfer of the money and gifts. It is interesting that the general fast of Ezra 8:21 is changed in 1 Esdras to 'a fast for the young men' (v. 50). Does this reflect the reality of the author's time and his presuppositions, or is it merely a result of textual corruption or misunderstanding (*hnhr*, 'the river', to *hnʿr* 'the young man')?

The description of the preparations is dedicated mainly to the transfer of the money and vessels from Babylonia to Jerusalem (vv. 54–60). Twelve priests and twelve Levites (Sherebiah, Hashabiah, and ten of their kinsmen) are nominated as trustees (v. 54), the gold and silver are weighed, the vessels are enumerated, and the transaction is concluded by an inspiring

address of Ezra to the elected men: 'You are holy . . . and the vessels are holy . . . be watchful and on guard' (vv. 58–9). The conclusion of the journey focuses on the same subjects: the deposition of the money and vessels in the hands of the Jerusalem priesthood, including priests and Levites (vv. 62–4), and a religious ceremony revolving around sacrifices (v. 65). The numbers of the sacrifices are basically the same as in Ezra 8:35, and they are all of symbolic value: multiples of twelve, standing for 'whole Israel'. While the number of sacrifices is particular to this context, their composition—bulls, rams, and lambs for burnt offerings, and a male goat as a sin offering—represents the standard procedure for holy day sacrifices as, for example, in Num 28:11–15, 19–22, etc. In 1 Esdras the strict terminology of Ezra 8:35 is not preserved: the specific 'burnt-offerings' is replaced by the more general 'sacrifices', and the distinct 'sin-offering' is replaced by 'peace-offerings' (NRSV: thank- offering). The latter is completely irregular, since male goats were always brought as sin-offerings (e.g. Lev 4:23–4; 9:3, 15, etc.), and probably reflects the distance of the translator from the actual cult in the Jerusalem temple.

The end of the passage creates the frame for the larger unit, by returning to the beginning of the Ezra narrative, to the letter of Artaxerxes. Upon the arrival of the returning exiles, they transmitted the king's orders to the appropriate authorities, who acted upon it. It is interesting that the language here deviates from the first person singular of Ezra to a plural, '*they* delivered the king's orders', as if someone else and not Ezra himself was invested with this power. One should also mention, perhaps, the constant dual presence of God on the one hand and the Persian king, on the other. Although the story is permeated with a religious spirit expressed in every way, the presence of the Persian king is also very strong, and his orders conclude the story.

(8:68–9:36) Dissolving the Mixed Marriages The first thing that Ezra encounters upon arrival in Jerusalem is the problem of mixed marriage, presented to him by the leaders of the community. In Ezra–Nehemiah (chs. 9–10), attention to this problem seems to overshadow the other aspect of Ezra's activity in Jerusalem, namely the reading of the law (Neh 8). This is even more apparent in 1 Esdras, where the reading of the law is abbreviated (9:37–55), and the matter of intermarriage occupies the centre of the Ezra narrative. The story of the mixed marriages is presented in a detailed record:

8:68–9:2: The encounter with the problem (Ezra 9:1–10:6)

    8:68–70 (Ezra 9:1–2): The matter is brought to Ezra's attention

    8:71–90 (Ezra 9:3–15): Ezra's reaction and confession

    8:91–9:2 (Ezra 10:1–6): The decision

9:3–36: The solution (Ezra 10:7–44)

    9:3–14: The assembly in Jerusalem (Ezra 10:7–15)

    9:15–36: Investigation, recording and expulsion (Ezra 10:16–44)

(8:68–9:2) The Encounter with the Problem (Ezra 9:1–10:6) The opening formula, 'After these things had been done', creates the impression of a direct sequel between the conclusion of the ceremonies and formalities involved with the return, and dealing with the matter of intermarriages. However, according to the chronological details of the narrative, Ezra arrived in Jerusalem 'on the new moon of the fifth month' (8:6), while the matter of intermarriages was dealt with four months later, in the ninth month (9:5). It is thus probable that the reading of the law in the seventh month (9:37; Neh 8) antedated the matter of intermarriages and was Ezra's first undertaking in Jerusalem. This original sequence was disrupted in Ezra-Nehemiah (see Rudolph 1949: xxiv); the new structure places the dissolving of the intermarriages—the wholesome purification of the people of Israel from the pollution of the foreign nations—as a necessary precondition for the sacred ceremony of the reading of the law.

(8:68–70), the leaders present Ezra with a grave problem; the people of Israel have mixed with the foreign population of the land by taking their daughters to be their wives, with the leaders of the community in the forefront. The list of foreign peoples is enlightening. Ezra 9:1 mentions two groups of peoples: five of the 'seven nations', the ancient inhabitants of the land of Canaan, about whom Deut 7:2–3 demands: 'you must utterly destroy them. Make no covenant with them . . . Do not intermarry with them', and three peoples (Moabites, Ammonites, and Egyptians), about whom it is commanded that they 'shall [not] be admitted to the assembly of the Lord', either forever or for several generations (Deut 23:3, 7–8). It is obvious that the list is not historical but programmatic, identifying the contemporary foreigners with the forbidden nations. The list of 1 Esdras is different in two specifics: rather than Emorite it has Edomite—probably a better version—and the Ammonite people are omitted. This may be accidental, a result of some corruption, or a wish to keep the list to the number 'seven', the symbolic figure of the 'foreign nations'.

(8:71–90), Ezra's spontaneous reaction is that of the most profound grief and mourning: tearing garments including his priestly mantle, pulling out the hair of his head and beard, and fasting through the day. It culminates in his long confession of guilt, which represents the developing literary genre of prose confessions typical of the late biblical period (see also Neh 9 and Dan 9). The confession opens with the first person singular (v. 74), but moves immediately to the first person plural, 'For our sins . . . and our mistakes have mounted up . . . and we are in great sin . . .' (vv. 75–90). This style is retained to the end, as Ezra identifies himself completely with the iniquities of the people and becomes their spokesman.

The confession (vv. 74–90) is a piece of theodicy of the highest order. It juxtaposes the obstinate disobedience of the people throughout their history with God's unfailing mercy and compassion, and is permeated with the spirit of penitence: profound acknowledgement of the people's sins, and reminder of God's mercy. The argument develops as follows: (1) We are sinful and have always been so. Our sins have put us in a position of constant blame, from of old 'to this day' (vv. 75–6). (2) We were duly punished, and suffered gravely for our sins (v. 77). (3) Then the Lord, because of his mercy, gave us some respite; he brought us into favour with the kings of Persia, and we now see the beginning of some consolation (vv. 78–81). (4) Now, we have sinned again, in the most grave historical sin of mixed marriages (vv. 82–5). (5) In view of our terrible ingratitude, what are our chances now? Would not the Lord's anger be justified? Are we not destined to the worst of all? (vv. 86–90). The confession does not end with a prayer. There is not even a request or a plea for forgiveness, only a confession of sin: you are faithful and we are sinful.

Each of the points made in the confession is expressed with great rhetorical force. The tone of self-accusation is achieved through a constant repetition of keywords denoting sin: 'Our sins have risen higher than our heads, and our mistakes have mounted up to heaven' (v. 75) . . . 'and we are in great sin to this day' (v. 76). 'Because of our sins and the sins of our ancestors' (v. 77). 'We have transgressed your commandments . . .' (v. 82), 'and all that has happened to us has come about because of our evil deeds and our great sins' (v. 86), 'but we turned back again to transgress your law' (v. 87), 'we are now before you in our iniquities' (v. 90). On the other side stands the merciful God: 'And now in some measure mercy has come to us from you, O Lord, to leave us a root and a name in your holy place, and to uncover a light for us in the house of the Lord our God, and to give us food . . . Even in our bondage we were not forsaken by our Lord' (vv. 78–80), 'For you, O Lord, lifted the burden of our sins and gave us such a root as this' (vv. 86–7). 'O Lord of Israel, you are faithful' (v. 89).

This counterpoint of 'we, the sinners', 'you, the faithful' is further accentuated by the description of the extreme consequences of the people's sinful history. Although it may be implied that destruction and bondage were brought on Israel by the Lord, it is not spelled out explicitly. The disasters are described in an emphatic passive: 'Because of our sins . . . we . . . were given over to the kings of the earth, to the sword and exile and plundering, in shame until this day' (v. 77; also vv. 79, 80, 86).

The unique point of the confession lies in the definition of the national sin, the root of all the evil visited upon Israel. Unlike all other biblical sources, it is not the sin of idolatry, the worship of other gods, that evoked God's anger, but the sin of intermarriage. This was, according to the confession, the gist of God's warning before the conquest of the land, and the core of the prophets' rebuke. The conceptual context of this sin is impurity and pollution: 'The land . . . is . . . polluted with the pollution of the aliens of the land, and they have filled it with their uncleanness' (v. 83, also v. 87). The nature and source of this 'pollution' is not specified, but is ascribed to the very essence of these peoples and not to their conduct. The implication is self-evident: the only way for Israel to atone for this sin is to purify themselves, to detach themselves completely from the source of pollution, from 'the peoples of the land'.

Two details deserve attention: although the confession is transmitted faithfully from Ezra 9:3–15, even in the details, there is some rephrasing. The peculiar view of 1 Esdras that the restoration involved the city of Jerusalem from the very beginning, and not merely the house of God, is expressed clearly in the phrasing of v. 81, replacing 'to set up the house of our God, to repair its ruins' (Ezra 9:9) with: 'they . . . glorified the temple of our Lord, and raised Zion from desolation'. The repetitious reference to 'survivor' (Ezra 9:8, 13, 14, 15—sometimes translated as 'a remnant'), is rephrased as 'a root' (vv. 78, 87, 88, 89). The basic formula of theodicy in Ezra 9:15: 'you are righteous' (NRSV: you are just) is rephrased in 1 Esdras to 'you are faithful' (v. 89).

(8:91–9:2), the extremity of Ezra's position and the rhetorical force of his confession set in motion a series of actions, leading to the desired goal: the dissolution of the mixed marriages, and the solution of the problem 'once and for all'. It should be noted that in all that follows, the motivating power is not Ezra but other people, probably laymen, whose position of leadership is not specified. Ezra is described as rather passive, reacting rather than acting. It is a popular movement, under Ezra's inspiration and authority. The first move, following the confession, is the proposition of necessary practical steps. One of the men who surrounded Ezra and witnessed his conduct, someone from Israel (Ezra 10:2: 'of the family of Elam'), takes upon himself to represent the people. In an eloquent address he admits the people's sins, accepts Ezra's authority, and suggests the solution: to expel the foreign women and their children. Ezra acts upon this immediately and makes the people swear to follow this procedure. The scene ends with Ezra's withdrawal to the chamber of Jehohanan the son of Eliashib—probably the officiating high priest. If this identification is correct, it may serve as a chronological mark for the dating of the events—after Nehemiah, in whose time the high priest was Eliashib himself (Neh 3:1; 13:4).

(9:3–36) The Solution (Ezra 10:7–44) The decision made by the leaders of the community, to expel the foreign women and their children, now has to be implemented. This is done in two stages: a general assembly is called in Jerusalem, to have the proposed solution adopted by all those involved, and a procedure is suggested and carried out. The whole process takes about four months: the assembly was called in the ninth month (9:5); the procedure of recording the transgressors and dissolving the marriages began on the first day of the tenth month (9:16); and it was concluded on the first day of the first month (9:17).

(9:3–14), the initial decision is followed by a proclamation throughout the land to assemble all 'who had returned from exile' (lit. those who were of the exile) to Jerusalem. The authority behind the proclamation is that of 'the ruling elders', but the measures undertaken to have the people conform rest on both the imperial authority granted to Ezra to confiscate their property (thus Ezra 10:8; v. 4: their livestock would be seized for sacrifice), and the internal power of excommunication (v. 4). Whether because of their own free will or because of the threats, the people indeed gather in Jerusalem. The fine irony of Ezra 10:9, that the people sat 'trembling because of this matter and because of the rain' is lost in v. 6, where the people are described as 'shivering because of the bad weather'. This sets the tone for the assembly: everything is done directly and efficiently, even with some impatience and perhaps antagonism. In a straightforward statement, with no drama or elaboration, Ezra informs the people of their sin before the Lord, and demands that they confess their sin and separate themselves from their foreign wives (vv. 7–9). The people acquiesce, and since they wish to go home, ask Ezra to settle the matter in a more orderly and less public way, with the help of the judges of every locality (vv. 10–13). It should be pointed out that while administrative measures were taken in order to gather the people in Jerusalem, no authority is exerted to make them separate from their wives. This is left to their own discretion and decision, which

indeed they make with full acceptance of Ezra's spiritual authority. The role of the five individuals mentioned in v. 14 (Ezra 10:15 has 'four'), remains unclear. In Ezra 10:15 it seems that these people formed an opposition to the general trend, while in 1 Esdras they are described as those who took upon themselves the execution of the people's decision. In either case, the actual procedure begins in the next verses, with Ezra appointing his own men for the task.

(9:15–36), the people comply with the proposals. A committee, headed by Ezra and some men of his choice, begins to investigate the matter systematically: to enquire in every settlement about the men who married foreign women, record their names, and dissolve the marriages. The result is a thorough list of people of all classes, from the highest ranking priests to the various families of laymen. The list is organized similarly to the other lists in Ezra-Nehemiah, beginning with the clergy. First mentioned are four individuals of the family of the high priest; they undertake to put away their wives and to offer sacrifices in expiation of their sin (vv. 19–20). This is the only reference to an individual pledge and sacrifice, and one may question whether it should be explained in literary or historical terms. Does the record imply that each of the transgressors was supposed to pledge himself and offer a sacrifice individually, or was a special procedure applied for the family of the high priest, the highest class on the hierarchal ladder?

In Ezra 10:18–43 the version of the list is apparently corrupt, as for example in the listing of the family of Bani (vv. 34–42), where twenty-seven individuals are traced to one family, while the average for the other families is between six and seven. In 1 Esdras the list has been corrupted further, and as in other cases, the names have been reformulated to a great degree. However, the general structure is clear: men of the four priestly families (Ezra 10:18–22; three families in 1 Esdras 9:21); of the Levites, singers, and gatekeepers (vv. 23–5), and of the laymen, the descendants of ten families (Ezra 10; eleven in 1 Esdras)—altogether above 100 individuals in either list. The end of the passage carries its final message: 'All these had married foreign women, and they put them away together with their children' (v. 36). This finality is not clear in the obscure phrasing of Ezra 10:44, which leaves open the possibility that the women were not expelled but merely registered, but the doubt is removed in the straightforward phrasing of 1 Esdras.

As noted above, the matter of the mixed marriages occupies the centre of Ezra's activities in Jerusalem, the focus of his dedication. However, this does not prevent the reader from wondering about the phenomenon as a whole and its details. It seems that the motivation for this initiative was the fear of the returnees of losing their own distinct sense of identity, but was it dealt with in the best possible way? Who were these women who are described here as 'foreign'? How is it possible that what is regarded by Ezra and his followers as the worst possible sin, was practised by everybody in Judah, including the highest clergy? Were these women indeed 'foreign', or did they come from circles other than 'those of the exile' who were relegated to the status of 'foreigners'? Why were the measures suggested by the 'devotees' so strict and extreme? Why were the children expelled together with their mothers? Why was there no expedient, nor even a suggestion, for converting these 'foreign women'? And finally—was Ezra's undertaking really successful? As shown by such works as Ruth or Chronicles, Ezra's position was not the only stance in the Judean community; and, later, Judaism rejected his position altogether and provided a mode of conversion—for women of foreign origin as well as others. All these questions should be left for further reflection and study.

(9:37–55) **Reading the Law** In the book of Ezra-Nehemiah, the reading of the law and the celebration of the festivals form one event in the history of the restoration and one chapter in the course of the narrative. In I Esdras they stand at the end of the book, marking its conclusion. After solving the problem of the mixed marriages and the purification of the people, the time has come for Ezra to fulfil his mission: 'you shall teach those who do not know them' (i.e. 'the laws of your God' (Ezra 7:25)).

One of the matters that has attracted much scholarly attention is the scope of this passage. It opens with a reference to the people's settlement in 'Jerusalem and in the country' (v. 37)—a redundant and meaningless statement in the present context, but of great importance in illustrating the literary procedure of the author. Originally, this verse concluded the list of the returned exiles of Neh 7 (in itself a parallel to Ezra 2); I Esdras borrowed it from Neh 7:72 and rephrased it—a clear demonstration that I Esdras's *Vorlage* was the book of Ezra–Nehemiah as we know it, including the story of Nehemiah (cf. I ESD B).

The end of our passage concludes succinctly with 'and they came together', reflecting the beginning of Neh 8:13. This abrupt ending reflects a Greek rather than a Hebrew syntax for, in the Hebrew, the sentence opens with the time-phrase, 'and in the second day they came together', while in the Greek the subject + predicate came first. Although some scholars would see in this ending an intentional feature of the work (e.g. Eskenazi 1986: 56–9), we tend to accept the more prevalent view that some continuation of the story was lost. How far the story continued is impossible to say at this point. As the text now stands, the passage deals with two matters: the reading of the law (vv. 37–48), and the celebration of the holiday (vv. 49–55).

(vv. 37–49) **Reading the Law (Neh 8:1–8)** The reading of the law on the new moon of the seventh month is, again, the initiative of the people and not of Ezra: 'they told Ezra . . . to bring the law of Moses' (v. 39). It is described in two stages: a general description of the occasion (vv. 37b–41 = Neh 8:1–3), and a more detailed account of the ceremony (vv. 42–8 = Neh 8:5–8), all set forth in unique terms. Indeed, a public, ceremonial reading of the law has no precedent in the Bible and is inaugurated here for the first time (cf. also the cursory note of Neh 13:1). It is not clear from the story whether it remained a unique event, or became an organic part of the religious calendar. However, this is certainly the earliest evidence, in unusual circumstances, of the reading of the law, which became a regular part of later Jewish liturgy.

The details of the event are of interest: Ezra stood on an elevated wooden platform, made for the occasion (v. 42), with two groups of dignitaries, whose descent or status are not mentioned, to his right and left (six or seven on each side). He opened the reading with a blessing of the Lord (mentioned but not quoted), and the people responded in the conventional

gestures of prayer: they 'answered "Amen." They lifted up their hands and fell to the ground and worshipped the Lord' (v. 47). Ezra read aloud from the book for several hours, 'from the early morning until midday' (v. 41), and a group of thirteen Levites taught and explained the reading to the standing crowd (vv. 48–9).

Two matters should be noted: the event is described throughout as having a popular nature, encompassing the gathered crowd, both men and women. The people who attend are 'the whole multitude' (v. 38, also v. 40), both men and women (v. 41). The popular aspect of the ceremony is accentuated by the absence of any sacrificial aspect. One may sense a touch of ritualistic gesture in Ezra's bringing and opening the book (vv. 45–6) and in his prayer and the people's ceremonial response, but the event takes place outside the temple's precincts and with no participation of the clergy, except for the Levites acting as 'teachers'. Although Ezra is titled, as elsewhere in I Esdras, 'the chief priest and reader' (vv. 39, 40, 42, also 49), there is no expression of the priestly aspect of his mission; he is 'the reader of the law'.

(vv. 49–55) **Celebrating the Holiday (Neh 8:9–12)** The people's reaction of mourning, repeated three times (vv. 50, 52, 53), is matched by the statement of the leaders that 'this day is holy' (also repeated three times, vv. 50, 52, 53), and should be spent in joy. Unlike Neh 8:9, where the address to the people comes from Nehemiah the governor (the Tirshata), Ezra, and the teaching Levites, in I Esdras an unknown person, 'Attharathes', addresses Ezra, the Levites, and the people. It must be inferred that he was a person of the highest authority, although his title or position are not specified. In this way, and at the price of some unclarity, I Esdras omits the reference to Nehemiah in this chronological context (cf. also I ESD 5:36–40). Although the day is described emphatically as 'holy', it does not involve any cultic activity. It is described as a popular holiday, in which the expression of festivity is eating, drinking, sending portions to those who have none, and rejoicing. The date of the event, the new moon of the seventh month, is marked in the priestly holiday calendar as 'a day of complete rest, a holy convocation commemorated with trumpet blasts' (Lev. 23:24) and a set of special sacrifices (Num 29:1–6). All these are outside the purview of the present story, which focuses on the new, popular celebration of reading the law.

REFERENCES

Ackroyd, P. (1972), 'The Temple Vessels: A Continuity Theme', *Studies in the Religion of Ancient Israel*, VTSup 23: 166–81.

Bayer, E. (1911), *Das dritte Buch Esdras und sein Verhältnis zu den Büchern Esra-Nehemia* (Freiburg im Breisgau: Herder).

Bewer, J. A. (1922), *Der Text der Buche Ezra*, FRLANT 31 (Göttingen: Vandenhoeck & Ruprecht).

Brooke, A. E., and McLean, N. (eds.) (1935), *The Old Testament in Greek* (Cambridge: Cambridge University Press), ii. pt. 4.

Carter, C. E. (1994), 'The Province of Yehud in the Post-Exilic Period: Soundings in Site Distribution and Demography', in T. C. Eskenazi and K. H. Richards (eds.), *Second Temple Studies*, JSOTS 175 (Sheffield: JSOT), ii. 106–45.

Coggins, R. G., and Knibb, M. A. (1979), *The First and Second Books of Esdras*, CBC (Cambridge: Cambridge University Press).

Cook, S. A. (1913), 'I Esdras', *APOT* i. 1–58.

Dequeker, L. (1993), 'Darius the Persian and the Reconstruction of the Jewish Temple in Jerusalem (Ezra 4:24)', *Orientalia Lovaniensia Analecta*, 55: 67–92.

Eissfeldt, O. (1966), *The Old Testament: An Introduction*, tr. P. R. Ackroyd (Oxford: Blackwell).

Eskenazi, T. C. (1986), 'The Chronicler and the Composition of I Esdras', *CBQ* 48: 39–66.

Hanhart, R. (1974a), *Text und Textgeschichte des I Esrabuches* (Göttingen: Vandenhoeck & Ruprecht).

—— (1974b) (ed.), *Esdrae Liber I*, Septuaginta Vetus Testamentum Graecum, 8/1 (Göttingen: Vandenhoeck & Ruprecht).

Japhet, S. (1968), 'The Supposed Common Authorship of Chronicles and Ezra-Nehemiah Investigated Anew', *VT* 18: 330–71.

—— (1982–3), 'Sheshbazzar and Zerubbabel against the Background of the Historical and Religious Tendencies of Ezra-Nehemiah', *ZAW* 94: 66–98; 95: 218–29.

—— (1991), 'The Relationship of Chronicles and Ezra-Nehemiah', VTSup 43: 298–313.

—— (1993), *I & II Chronicles*, OTL (London: SCM).

—— (1996), 'L'Historiographie post-exilique: Comment et Pourquoi?', in A. de Pury, Th. Römer, and J-D. Macchi (eds.), *Israel construit son histoire* (Geneva: Labor et Fides), 123–52.

—— (1997), *The Ideology of the Book of Chronicles and its Place in Biblical Thought*, tr. Anne Barber, 2nd edn. (Frankfurt: Peter Long 1989), Hebrew original, 1977.

Klein, R. W. (1966), 'Studies in the Greek Texts of the Chronicler', Diss., Harvard.

Lipschits, O. (1997), *The Yehud Province under Babylonian Rule (586–539 BCE): Historic Reality and Historiographical Conceptions*, Ph.D. thesis, Tel-Aviv.

Moulton, W. J. (1899; 1900). 'Über die Überlieferung und den textkritischen Werth des dritten Esrabuchs', *ZAW* 19: 209–58; 20: 1–35.

Myers, J. M. (1974), *I & II Esdras*, AB 42 (New York: Doubleday).

Pohlmann, K. F. (1970), *Studien zum dritten Esra: Ein Beitrag zur Frage nach dem ursprünglichen Schluss des chronistischen Geschichtswerkes*, FRLANT 104 (Göttingen: Vandenhoeck & Ruprecht).

Rudolph, W. (1949), *Esra und Nehemia samt 3 Esra* (Tübingen: Mohr [Siebeck]).

Schaeder, H. H. (1930), *Esra der Schreiber* (Tübingen: Mohr [Siebeck]).

Schenker, A. (1991), 'La Relation d'Esdras A' au texte massorétique d'Esdras-Néhémie', in *Tradition of the Text, Festschrift D. Barthélemy* (Göttingen: Vandenhoeck & Ruprecht), 218–47.

Talshir, Z. (1984), 'The Milieu of I Esdras in the Light of its Vocabulary', in A. Pietersma and C. Cox (eds.), *De Septuaginta: Studies in Honour of John William Wevers* (Mississauga: Benben), 129–47.

—— and Talshir, D. (1995), 'The Story of the Three Youths (I Esdras 3–4): Towards the Question of the Language of its *Vorlage*', *Textus*, 18: 135–57.

Torrey, C. C. (1970), *Ezra Studies*, 2nd edn. (New York: Ktav).

—— (1945), 'A Revised View of First Esdras', *L. Ginzberg Jubilee Volume* (New York: American Academy for Jewish Research), 395–410.

Walde, B. (1913), *Die Esdrasbücher der Septuaginta* (Freiburg in Breisgau: Herder).

Williamson, H. G. M. (1977), *Israel in the Book of Chronicles* (Cambridge: Cambridge University Press).

—— (1983), 'The Composition of Ezra 1–6', *JTS* 34: 1–26.

—— (1985), *Ezra, Nehemiah* (Waco, Tex.: Word).

—— (1996), 'The Problem with First Esdras', in J. Barton and J. Reimer (eds.), *After the Exile: Essays in Honour of Rex Mason* (Macon, Ga.: Mercer University Press), 201–16.

Zimmermann, F. (1963–4), 'The Story of the Three Guardsmen', *JQR* 54: 179–200.

50. Prayer of Manasseh GEORGE W. E. NICKELSBURG

INTRODUCTION

A. Text and Language. 1. The Prayer of Manasseh claims to be the prayer that moved God to forgive the wicked king of Judah and restore him from his captivity in Babylon to his throne in Jerusalem (2 Chr 33:12–13). The text is preserved only in Christian sources, which are of two kinds. The first is the Odes, a collection of hymns and prayers that forms an appendix to the book of Psalms in three Greek biblical MSS (A, 5th cent.; T, 7th cent.; 55, 10th cent.) and in some daughter translations. A few Syriac MSS append the prayer to 2 Chronicles. Two church handbooks provide the second set of sources. The third-century *Didascalia Apostolorum* (*Teaching of the Apostles*) was written in Greek and has been preserved in a Syriac translation and some fragments of a Latin translation. Parts of the *Didascalia* have also been preserved in another church handbook, the 4th-century Greek *Apostolic Constitutions*. Both handbooks set the prayer in a narrative context that conflates and expands the accounts of Manasseh's reign in 2 Kings 21 and 2 Chr 33.

2. It is uncertain whether the Greek of the prayer is the language of its composition or a translation of a Semitic original (*APOT* i. 614–15; *OTP* ii. 625–7). The Greek does have a strong Semitic flavour, but it also uses phrases paralleled in the LXX and has some linguistic constructions that suggest composition in Greek.

B. Literary Genre. This penitential prayer, or confession of sin, spoken in the first person singular, has relatively few counterparts among the individual laments of the canonical psalter. Its closest parallel is Psalm 51, whose language it appears to echo (*OTP* ii. 630). Despite its prevalent concern with the covenant, it differs significantly from such penitential prayers as Ezra 9, Neh 9, Dan 9, Bar 1:15–3:8, Song of Three, the Qumran 'Words of the Heavenly Lights', and Tob 3:2–6. Its focus is consistently personal rather than national, and it lacks the language of the Deuteronomic tradition that permeates these prayers.

C. Narrative Context. Verbal allusions to details of the 2 Kings and 2 Chronicles narratives indicate that the prayer was composed in the voice of Manasseh. A question rarely discussed or even mentioned is whether the prayer was composed as an integral part of the conflated narrative context in which it stands in the *Didascalia* and the *Apostolic Constitutions* or whether it is an independent composition that was later placed in that narrative context (see, however, *APOT* i. 613–14). Two factors may support the former alternative. All but one of the other compositions in the Odes are drawn from biblical contexts (Ode 14 is, however, an expansion of Lk 2:14). The prayer and the narrative share at least one detail (v. 10) that is missing in both 2 Kings and 2 Chronicles. Claiming to recount the story in 2 Kings and 2 Chronicles, the narrative begins with a compressed revision of 2 Kings (with a few details from 2 Chr). Turning to 2 Chronicles, it mentions Manasseh's exile, elaborates the Chronicler's account by detailing the terrible conditions of Manasseh's imprisonment, picks up the report of his prayer and recounts the prayer, describes how a fire miraculously melted his chains, returns to the Chronicler's account of Manasseh's return to Jerusalem, adds that he worshipped God wholeheartedly and 'was reckoned righteous', and concludes with a summary of the Chronicler's report of Manasseh's restoration of the Jerusalem cult. As a whole, the rewritten narrative emphasizes the severity of God's judgement, the sincerity of Manasseh's repentance, God's direct intervention and restoration of the covenantal relationship, and Manasseh's transformation from sinner to righteous, attested by his deeds.

D. The Manasseh Traditions. According to both 2 Kings and 2 Chronicles, Manasseh's sins were mainly related to the cult, and 2 Kings states that these sins caused the destruction of the temple in 587 BCE. Scholars dispute whether the Chronicler's mention of Manasseh's prayer (which he ascribes to a source) and repentance are an attempt to explain his long reign, or whether the author of 2 Kings expurgated the incident from a form of the Deuteronomistic history that was subsequently used by the Chronicler (McKenzie 1984: 191–3). Some later Jewish texts depict Manasseh wholly in a bad light (*Mart. Isa.*; *2 Apoc. Bar.* 64–5; *Apoc. Abr.* 25), while others emphasize his repentance (e.g. *Josephus, Ant.* 10.3.2 §§ 40–6; see Bogaert 1969: ii. 296–304). One Qumran text (4Q381 33:8–11) preserves fragments of a prayer ascribed to Manasseh but it has no certain relationship to Prayer of Manasseh (Schuller 1986: 151–62).

E. Religious Teaching. According to Prayer of Manasseh, repentance is a divine gift that allows the worst of sinners to be accepted back into the covenant and have its curses turned to blessing. Even Manasseh, whose apostasy caused the destruction of the temple and the holy city, could be forgiven and, according to the narrative context, reckoned to be righteous, as was Abraham, the first recipient of the promise (*Ap. Con.* 2.22.16; Gen 15:6). This moralizing focus on the vices and virtues of a biblical figure, implicit in the prayer and explicit in the narrative, is typical of Jewish and Christian literature of the Graeco-Roman period (e.g. *Jub.*, *T. Job*, *T. 12 Patr.*).

F. Date and Provenance. The prayer's presence in the *Didascalia* indicates a date of composition before the third century CE, and the prayer's parallels to LXX Greek may indicate a date in or after the first century BCE. Whether the prayer is a Jewish or a Christian composition is disputed. Every concept and mode of expression in the prayer is paralleled in Jewish texts of the Graeco-Roman period, and nothing in it or its narrative context is demonstrably and exclusively Christian. At the same time, the prayer's attestation and documented usage are exclusively Christian, and it could have been composed by a Christian conversant in the LXX and other post-biblical Jewish traditions.

G. Function and Setting. In the *Didascalia* and the *Apostolic Constitutions*, the story and prayer of Manasseh are part of a long instruction to bishops and provide the basis for an appeal

to accept penitent sinners back into the fold. Alongside this pastoral function, the prayer's inclusion among the Odes suggests a devotional or liturgical use for this text. A similar pair of alternatives can be imagined in a Jewish setting. The prayer and its narrative context should be studied together with an eye towards Jewish texts that recast Scripture (see e.g. 1QapGen 20 and other texts discussed in Nickelsburg 1981: 231–68).

H. Canonicity. Although the prayer is regularly included in editions of the Apocrypha, only Eastern Orthodox churches consider it authoritative. This doubtless reflects its preservation in church manuals of Syrian provenance.

COMMENTARY

Invocation (vv. 1–7)

(v. 1) Address The title 'Almighty' (*pantokratōr*) anticipates vv. 2–3 and the prayer's first major theme, God's power in creation. It sets a tone for the prayer in its very first line, by expressing Manasseh's repentance from his polytheistic worship of rival gods. Taking up the Chronicler's reference to Manasseh's humility 'before the God of his ancestors' (lit. fathers, 2 Chr 33:12), the prayer strikes its second major theme, the covenant with Abraham, Isaac, and Jacob, and their righteous offspring. The appeal indicates Manasseh's repentance from his idolatrous apostasy from the covenant and is ironic, since Manasseh was anything but righteous, having 'shed innocent blood' (2 Kings 21:16).

(vv. 2–5a) God's Power in Creation God's creative power is a traditional topic in Jewish prayers (1 Enoch 9:5; Add Esth 13:10; 3 Macc 2:9). The Greek noun *kosmos* (order) translates the Hebrew *ṣābā'* (host) in Deut 4:19; 17:3; Isa 24:21; 40:26 with reference to the host of heaven (Osswald 1974: 23). Perhaps Manasseh is here acknowledging that the sovereign God created the host whose idolatrous worship he had instituted in Jerusalem (2 Kings 21:3, 5; 2 Chr 33:3, 5). The shackling of the sea and sealing of the abyss alludes to the mythic notion that the Creator brought order from chaos by taming the great sea monster (cf. Job 38:8–11; Ps 89:9–10; 104:5–9; Prov 8:29; Jer 5:22; 1 Enoch 101:6). Depicted here as capture and imprisonment, it may imply the king's concession that his own imprisonment is an act of divine power and judgement. Although vv. 4–5 assert that the *whole* creation fears and trembles in the presence of God's power and majestic glory, these characteristics of God recall descriptions of the divine throne room.

Employing language found in Jewish texts and orthodox and Gnostic Christianity, vv. 5–6 use the Greek alpha privative (a- = 'non-' or 'un-') to describe God in terms of what God is not: 'cannot be borne, unendurable, immeasurable, unsearchable'. This heaping up of adjectives reinforces Manasseh's repentance before the sovereign, almighty, and majestic God.

(vv.5b–7) The Wrath and Mercy of the God of the Covenant The emphasis on God's majesty continues in a description of God's activity within the covenant, which juxtaposes the threat of wrath against the sinner and the promise of mercy to the repentant. In the idiom of the section, the one is *unendurable*, while the other is *immeasurable* and unsearchable. This first major section of the prayer closes with reference both to God's unique power ('Most High') and to God's covenantal activity. The latter is phrased in a quotation of Joel 2:13, which undergirds that prophet's appeal for repentance by allusion to the covenantal description of God in Ex 34:6–7. Thus the author comes to the major point of the prayer and sets the stage for Manasseh's repentant confession of his sins. Although the two earliest Greek MSS of the Odes (A, T) omit most of v. 7 ('O Lord, according to your great goodness . . . be saved') the originality of these lines is attested by their inclusion in a later Greek biblical text (55), in the Vg, and in the *Apostolic Constitutions* and the *Didascalia*. The passage interprets the promise of mercy in v. 6 as the mercy that God promises to those who accept the divinely initiated repentance. Although v. 7b, following Joel 2:13, could refer to the curses of the covenant that fall on sinners ('human suffering'), the present context seems to allude to human wickedness and Manasseh's sins in particular.

Manasseh's Confession of Sin (vv. 8–10)

(v. 8) Introduction The continuation of the description of God in v. 8 reprises themes in v. 1 and thus seems to conclude the prayer's invocation. However, Manasseh's personal reference to 'me, who am a sinner' in the last line links it to the confession that follows. Thus the verse serves as a transition between the first and second parts. Employing the traditional Jewish distinction between the righteous and the sinner, Manasseh contrasts Abraham, Isaac, and Jacob, who have not sinned against God, with himself, who epitomizes the category of 'sinner'. In normal Jewish usage, 'righteous' does not designate a person who never sins, but one who attends to his or her sins and does not let them accumulate; the 'sinner', by contrast, lives in effective rejection of God and the covenant (*Pss. Sol.* 3). The consequences of these two ways of life are the blessings and curses of the covenant. While the present verse is consonant with such usage, it emphasizes God's active role in establishing repentance as a means by which the sinner can become righteous (cf. v. 13).

(vv. 9–10) The Confession Manasseh's confession fits well with the emphasis of the biblical accounts on the quantity and quality of his sins. Although v. 9c recalls Ezra's confession (Ezra 9:6), the combined language of vv. 9a and 9c with reference to the multitude of Manasseh's sins may be an inverted allusion to the covenantal promises about the multitude of Abraham's descendants (Gen 22:17; 15:5). The verb 'they are multiplied' (*eplēthunan*) corresponds to the same verb in 2 Kings 21:6; 2 Chr 33:6, and the doubling of the verb 'I have sinned' (cf. v. 12) emphasizes the point. The vivid reference to the physical conditions of Manasseh's imprisonment ('I am unworthy to look up . . . I am weighted down', lit. bent down, v. 10) complements v. 9c, and his physical condition may be seen to symbolize the spiritual (cf. the variants of v. 10b in Gk. MSS T and 55 and the *Didascalia*). Manasseh's iron fetters are not mentioned in 2 Kings or 2 Chronicles, but the specification of 'iron' in the narrative section preceding the prayer in the *Apostolic Constitutions* (2.22.10) may indicate that the prayer was composed as an integral part of the narrative preserved in that text. Manasseh's lack of 'relief' from his torment also suggests an allusion to

the specific conditions of his imprisonment described in that narrative. This particular complaint and its repetition in v. 13b recalls a similar repetition in the confession of the 'mighty kings' in 1 Enoch 63:1, 5, 6, 8). The language of the second half of v. 10 refers to details in 2 Kings 21:2, 6 and 2 Chr 33:2, 6.

Manasseh's Petition for Relief and Forgiveness (vv. 11–15)

(vv. 11–12) Introduction Like v. 8, these introductory verses provide a transition between what precedes (a double confession of sin; cf. 9b) and what follows (formal petition). The introductory 'And now' is formulaic in Jewish prayer (Add Esth 13:15; 14:6, 8; 3 Macc 6:9; 1QpGenAp 20:13; Tob 3:12; 1 Enoch 9:9–10). Again, external condition symbolizes the internal state. Physically bent down and, presumably, kneeling in prayer, he submits his will (heart) to the God against whom he has sinned. The sentiment again recalls Joel 2:13. The appeal for God's 'goodness' (*chrēstotēs*; cf. *agathosynē* in 14) is a request for the covenantal blessing (Deut 30:15, *ṭôb*, *agathon*), which God promises to those who repent (Deut 30:1–10). The second of the parallel lines in v. 12 is one of several resonances of Ps 51 (cf. Ps 51:3).

(vv. 13–14) Petition The language of v. 13ab with its participle, 'making petition' (*deomenos*), and its doubled verb reprise at vv. 11, 12a. Having twice confessed that he has sinned, he now twice begs for relief (Gk. *anes*) from the suffering (cf. 10c, *anesis*) that is a consequence of his sin. This implies God's forgiveness, although NRSV may overtranslate the verb as 'forgive'; cf. 'relief' in v. 10). The three parallel lines in 13cde expand on the notion in negative form, 'do not destroy, do not be angry, do not condemn me'. Most serious is the possibility of eternal destruction in the underworld. 'Evil things' (Gk. *kaka*), i.e. the covenantal curses (Deut 30:15), contrast with the 'goodness' he seeks in vv. 11, 14a. The rationale is expressed in the climax of a triad of divine appellations: 'Lord the God of our ancestors' (v. 1), 'Lord, God of the righteous' (v. 8), 'Lord, the God of those who repent' (v. 13f). v. 14a may allude to Ex 33:18–19, where Moses asks to see God's glory and is promised a vision of God's goodness, which is epitomized in a reference to the covenantal mercy that is now extended to the repentant Manasseh. On the king's unworthiness and need for 'much mercy', cf. 9cd and his unworthiness due to 'the multitude of my iniquities'. The wording of v. 14b recalls Ps 51:1.

(v. 15) The Praise of God The promise to praise God after relief from present distress is typical of the psalms. More importantly, it corresponds with the Chronicler's account of Manasseh's return to the worship of the true God (2 Chr 33:15–17), and it echoes specifically the wording of the narrative in *Ap. Con.* 2.22.16, 'He worshipped the Lord God alone with all his heart and all his soul all the days of his life.' Parallel to Manasseh's promise to praise God is the statement, 'For all the host of heaven sing your praises.' Coming from one who had instituted the worship of 'the host of heaven' (cf. v. 2), it is a fitting reinforcement of his repentance from polytheism and a suitable reprise of prayer's opening invocation of the 'LORD Almighty'. It remains only to assert the eternity of that God's glory (v. 15c).

REFERENCES

Bogaert, P. (1969), *Apocalypse de Baruch*, SC 144–5 (2 vols.; Paris: Cerf).

McKenzie, S. L. (1984), *The Chronicler's Use of the Deuteronomistic History*, HSM 33 (Atlanta: Scholars Press).

Nickelsburg, G. W. E. (1981), *Jewish Literature Between the Bible and the Mishnah* (Philadelphia: Fortress).

Osswald, E. (1974), 'Das Gebet Manasses', JSHRZ 4:1 (Gütersloh: Mohn), 17–27.

Schuller, E. M. (1986), *Non-Canonical Psalms from Qumran: A Pseudepigraphic Collection*, HSS 28 (Atlanta: Scholars Press).

51. Psalm 151

JOHN BARTON

Ps 151 occurs at the end of the book of Psalms in the Greek Bible, and can also be found in the ancient versions that depend on the Greek: Latin, Syriac—where it is one of a group of five non-canonical Psalms—and Ethiopic. The heading in the Greek indicates that it is 'outside the number' (and some texts add 'of the one hundred and fifty'), but it is regarded as canonical in the Greek and Russian Orthodox churches. As it stands it describes various aspects of the life of David and 'is ascribed to David as his own composition': his work as a shepherd, his musical ability, his choice by God even though his 'brothers were handsome and tall', and his victory over Goliath.

The Qumran *Psalms Scroll* 11 QPsᵃ preserves evidence of an earlier Hebrew version in which there were two separate psalms. The first corresponds to Ps 151:1–5; but the second was evidently a fuller version of Ps 151:6–7, though only two lines of it now remain. The first dealt with David's early career, the second (which originally had its own superscription) with his victory over Goliath. The superscription to the first psalm in Hebrew is 'A hallelujah for David the son of Jesse'. There is no scholarly consensus about the status of 11 QPsᵃ. It may reflect an early 'canon' of the Psalms differing from the later Hebrew one, or it may be a compendium of hymns for worship containing both canonical and non-canonical texts.

Verses 1–5 are based on 1 Sam 16. On David's musical abilities (vv. 2–3) the Hebrew adds, 'And I rendered glory to the Lord; I spoke in my soul. The mountains do not witness to him and the hills do not tell. The trees have cherished my words and the flock my deeds.' Verses 6–7 derive from 1 Sam 17.

52. 3 Maccabees

SARAH PEARCE

A. Text and Title. 1. Despite its title, the content of 3 Maccabees bears no obvious relation to events surrounding the Maccabean Revolt nor to its heroes. Nor does it pretend to do so, since it describes events affecting an earlier generation of Jews under Ptolemaic rule in Jerusalem and Egypt in 217–216 BCE. The title was no doubt attributed to this work on account of its position in the Greek canon where it lies between 2 and 4 Maccabees. However, its concerns with the defence of the sanctity of the Jerusalem Temple, resistance to idolatry, and belief in divine providence link it firmly with the ideology espoused in the other Maccabean stories.

2. 3 Maccabees survives in Greek, the language of its original composition, in the fifth-century uncial MS Alexandrinus and the eighth-century Codex Venetus as well as in minuscules of varying reliability, though the chief textual witnesses show few substantial variations. Otherwise, some sign of its popularity in the Christian east is reflected in fourth-century translations into Syriac and Armenian.

B. Provenance. Both the author and place of writing of 3 Maccabees are unknown. Any sense of the author's identity must, therefore, be surmised from the religious and political ideology and the intellectual influences apparent in this story. As to the author's background, the setting of 3 Maccabees in Egypt, and particularly in Alexandria, as well as clear signs of familiarity with Ptolemaic history and culture, point to Alexandria as home, but this is by no means certain.

C. Language and Genre. The Greek composition of 3 Maccabees is the work of a 'pseudo-classicist', combining both classical and koine forms of the language. Passages of purple prose and other rhetorical devices are employed both to entertain and to elicit strong sympathy for the heroes and villains of the story. In genre, 3 Maccabees is like a number of Hellenistic romances that embroider historical events or personalities with legendary developments characterized by their presentation in a historical framework and by narratives of the miraculous public rescue, by divine intervention, of the hero(es). In its function as an explanation for the origin of a festival, 3 Maccabees also bears some relation to Hellenistic antiquarian histories that seek to provide 'historical' explanations for ancient institutions.

D. Date. 1. A firm date of composition for 3 Maccabees remains elusive. It can be no earlier than the battle of Raphia in 217 BCE, with which the narrative begins. However, in spite of the narrator's efforts at verisimilitude, the overriding fantastic nature and improbabilities of the story, as well as the absence of any other evidence for a real persecution targeted at Jews in this period, cast serious doubt on its historical authenticity. A latest possible date is more difficult to fix, although the story's assumption that the Jerusalem Temple exists and stands at the heart of Judaism suggests (but does not prove) that it was written before the temple's destruction in 70 CE. In spite of the meagre evidence that serves to support any particular date within these boundaries, several specific settings have been proposed for the origins of 3 Maccabees.

2. Of the main proposals, the latest suggested setting for 3 Maccabees relates it to the persecution of the Jews of Alexandria in the time of the emperor Gaius Caligula. However, there is little proper correspondence between the situation described in 3 Maccabees and events in Roman Alexandria from 38 CE. If the story is a veiled criticism of that period of Roman rule, it is very cryptic indeed.

3. A dating to early Roman rule in Egypt under Augustus depends on the significance of the term *laographia*. In 3 Maccabees, this refers to a census imposed by Ptolemy IV for the registration of all Jews unwilling to commit apostasy and who are to be enslaved (2:28). This has been taken as a covert reference to the *laographia* introduced in 24 BCE that subjected the vast majority of inhabitants of Egypt to a poll tax. The Augustan measure was, however, by no means equivalent to enslavement, and certainly not directed exclusively at Jews. It carried no demands for religious observance, and certainly did not offer citizenship in the terms proposed in 3 Maccabees for Jewish apostates. It is quite possible that the term in 3 Maccabees, which also appears in the usage of Ptolemaic papyri, is meant simply to recall the strict taxation imposed under Ptolemy IV as a result of his expensive wars.

4. The author of 3 Maccabees seems to borrow from the Greek Daniel, which, in final form, must belong to a period after 165 BCE. However, the connection depends on just one word (6:6, cf. Dan 3:50), and the fluid nature of the composition of the Daniel corpus must make it impossible to prove our author's dependency on the Greek Daniel. An early first-century BCE date may be indicated by the formulae in the royal letters that appear in 3 Maccabees and reflect the style of late-Ptolemaic papyri. Caution, however, must be urged here too: the formulae might well be the work of a later writer, imitating the style of earlier chancery practice.

5. Finally, 3 Maccabees has been related to a persecution of the Jews of Alexandria under Ptolemy VIII Euergetes (Physcon) (145–116 BCE), which is recorded only in Josephus' *Against Apion*, 2.50–5). Josephus' narrative, though showing no clear dependence on 3 Maccabees, shares some similarities of detail with our story: a Ptolemy's attempt to destroy the Jews of Alexandria with a herd of drunken elephants; his repentance; and the commemoration of the Jews' deliverance by a special festival day. However, the two narratives, as their differences demonstrate, are best seen as different versions of a common folk-tale, adapted for different purposes. From a historical point of view it is not implausible that Physcon may have expressed hostility to Jews at the beginning of his reign, since Alexandrian Jews had sided with his opponent, subsequently his partner and queen, Cleopatra II. However, there is no other evidence for a persecution of Jews at this time. Indeed, Physcon is known from papyrological evidence to have favoured the Jews.

E. The Plot. 1. The story purports to record an otherwise unknown attempt to exterminate the Jews of Egypt under Ptolemy IV Philopator (221–205 BCE). Following his victory over the Seleucid Antiochus III at the battle of Raphia (217 BCE), Ptolemy made a tour of his subject territories, honouring their temples as he went. Responding to a warm invitation from Jerusalem, he also visited the temple there, but insisted on entering the Holy of Holies, to the horror of the Jews. However, following their prayers for deliverance from this violation, God's intervention struck the king unconscious. Full of rage at this rebuff, the king returned to Alexandria, determined on exacting revenge against the Jews. At the instigation of certain courtiers, he issued a decree removing all civil rights from the Jews of Alexandria with the exception of Jewish apostates who, if they embraced the cult of Dionysus, would be treated like citizens of Alexandria. A further royal decree, fuelled by widespread resistance to the first plan and by rumours of Jews' disloyalty to the crown, planned for the extermination of all the Jews of Egypt. The king commanded that they be taken to Alexandria, registered, and executed.

2. As the burlesque dimension of the story unfolds, each attempt to destroy the Jews is foiled as God intervenes to rescue them in answer to their prayers. First, a complete registration fails because papyrus and calami (reed pens) run out after forty days of writing! Then all the king's attempts to kill the Jews in the hippodrome with 500 drunken elephants come to nothing. Thanks to the Jews' prayers and God's action, the king is prevented from carrying out the execution. First he oversleeps; then he forgets completely about his plan; and, finally, two angels appear to the Jews' enemies, paralysing them and forcing the elephants back to crush them and not the Jews.

3. The king is brought to acknowledge the Jews' loyalty and that 'the living God of heaven' protects the Jews (6:28). Ptolemy turns from annihilator to protector of the Jews, commanding their safe return home and decreeing a seven-day feast of deliverance for them which the Jews determine to celebrate as a festival for ever. All ends happily except for Jewish apostates: with the king's permission, the Jews execute 300 who abandoned Judaism under the king's first decree, on the grounds that Jews disloyal to God will also be disloyal to the crown. On their return home, with further celebrations, the Jews can look forward to a secure future: 'They had even greater authority than before among their enemies and were regarded with high esteem and awe; no one at all extorted their property... The great God had accomplished great things for their salvation' (7:21–2; tr. Andersen 1985).

F. Purpose. 1. 3 Maccabees is often seen as a crisis document, hence the attempts to locate the story's origins in persecutions or perceived persecutions of the Jews under Ptolemaic or Roman rule. If so, there is little in the story itself to suggest that it represents the concerns of an alienated community unhappily struggling for survival in the Diaspora. The story does not oppose Alexandrian citizenship for Jews—only when such status is dependent on abandoning Judaism. Alexandrians themselves are depicted as close and loyal allies of the Jews in the time of persecution. Indeed, except when his mind is temporarily clouded by madness or the machinations of his evil counsellors, Ptolemy himself is seen as very positive towards the Jews. While the Jews of Alexandria are presented as the 'countrymen' of the people in Jerusalem who protested against the king's entry into the Holy of Holies, they do not yearn for refuge in Jerusalem. On the contrary, the story celebrates their return to their legitimate homes in Egypt, as does the festival that commemorates their freedom to do so. True, the festival is, we are told, to be held only for as long as the Jews' sojourn (*paroikia*) in Egypt continues, language that recalls the ancestors' toils in pre-Exodus Egypt (cf. Wis 19:10; Lev 26:44), and a hint that this is not their final home. There is, thus, a sense of looking forward to a 'return' to Judea, but this is not at all prominent in the story, and belongs to very common expectations for the future in Second Temple period Judaism.

2. The emphases of the story reveal several main concerns on the part of the author of 3 Maccabees. First, it is emphasized that Jews are loyal to the Ptolemaic monarchy, and that they are vital for the security of its empire. Above all, however, the author seeks to show, in the great tradition of the Exodus and the later history of the Jews, that the supreme king is the God whom the Jews serve and that only this king has power over the fate of the Jews and, indeed, of all things. The message is essentially a declaration of confidence in God's providence, manifested in response to the power of prayer. What is demanded of the story's Jewish readers is to be confident in that providence and to trust that, in all circumstances, loyalty to Judaism will be rewarded with life and security. In this, the author of 3 Maccabees adheres strongly to the Deuteronomic teaching that fidelity to the God of Israel will be rewarded with life, apostasy with death. Finally, the story serves, as does *Esther* for the feast of Purim, to explain and support an existing Jewish festival whose origins had perhaps been forgotten by the Jews of Egypt.

REFERENCE

Andersen, H. (1985), '3 Maccabees', *OTP* ii, 509–30.

53. 2 Esdras

PETER HAYMAN

INTRODUCTION

A. Background. 2 Esdras in the Apocrypha of the English Bible consists of three separate works which are found combined together only in manuscripts of the Latin Vulgate Bible dating from the ninth century CE onwards. It has become conventional amongst scholars to distinguish these three works by designating 2 Esd 1–2 as 5 Ezra, 2 Esd 3–14 as 4 Ezra, and 2 Esd 15–16 as 6 Ezra. The core work in the collection to which the others were subsequently added is 4 Ezra. This was written by a Jew not long after the Jewish War against the Romans in 66–73 CE and the destruction of the temple in 70 CE. The author was devastated by these events and felt that they severely threatened his inherited theological beliefs. His text was composed as a kind of catharsis in which he and the reader travel in the early chapters of the book through the dark night of doubt into the shining light of apocalyptic certainty which pervades the end of the book. But his book seems to have had little impact upon that mainstream of Jewish culture which eventually crystallized into Rabbinic Judaism. Its major impact was upon those groups on the periphery of Jewish life in the first century who eventually crystallized into the Christian church. They alone preserved it for posterity and included it in their collections of sacred and authoritative books.

B. Authorship. The author of 4 Ezra chose to write under the pseudonym of Ezra, apparently the person depicted in the biblical book of Ezra as the bringer of the law from Babylon. There is, however, a problem about identifying precisely whose persona the author is adopting and it emerges in the first verse of the book (3:1). This places Ezra in the middle of the Babylonian exile and identifies him with someone called Salathiel. Salathiel is the Latin form of the Hebrew name Shealtiel and it is taken from 1 Chr 3:17 where Shealtiel is identified as the son of King Jehoiachin who was taken into exile in Babylon in 597; 1 Chr 3:19 makes Shealtiel the uncle of Zerubbabel who led the first return from Babylon in 537. Unfortunately, Ezra the scribe as depicted in the books of Ezra and Nehemiah lived 100 years later than this. Box (1912) regarded 2 Esd 3:1 as a clumsy attempt by the editor of our text to identify these two originally quite separate figures. He did so because in Box's opinion one of the main sources the author utilized for his work was an apocalypse ascribed to Salathiel. So, on his view, the verse is an editorial attempt to fuse together separate sources. Box's view here is part of a much more elaborate source-critical analysis of 4 Ezra which has since fallen out of favour with most scholars; see Hayman (1975), Stone (1990: 11–23). Most recent scholarly work takes for granted that the text is a unitary composition by a single author who yet had earlier sources available to him. The most probable explanation for the identification of Ezra and Salathiel/Shealtiel is that it arises from a misreading of the Hebrew text of 1 Chr 3:17 (Stone 1990: 55–6). Another seductive reason for the identification has often been pointed out. In Hebrew the name Shealtiel means 'I asked God'. Since in the book Ezra spends a good deal of time asking pointed questions of God, the name seems quite appropriate.

C. The Date of 4 Ezra. The book can be fairly securely dated by aligning the known facts of Roman history with the eagle vision of chs. 11–12, just as we can date the book of Daniel by running through its ch. 11 to the point where history ends and prediction begins. The point where the accurate history stops in 4 Ezra and the prediction begins seems to be near the end of Domitian's reign (81–96) towards the middle of the 90s CE. One other factor confirms a date for this apocalypse towards the end of the first century CE: in 3:1 and 3:29 the author sets these supposed visions of Ezra thirty years after the destruction of Jerusalem. In the pseudonymous structure of the book this refers to the destruction of Jerusalem by the Babylonians in 587 BCE. However, the real reference point of the book is to the destruction of Jerusalem by the Romans in 70 CE. The span of thirty years seems to come from Ezek 1:1, but is the author's choice of this date due to his own distance from the seminal event of his lifetime?

D. The Author's Audience and His Social Setting. 4 Ezra is probably to be related to other Jewish works (2 *Apoc. Bar.*, *Apoc. Abr.*, and Ps. Philo, *Bib. Ant.*) which may have been written in the aftermath of the destruction of Jerusalem and the temple in 70 CE. They have in common the urgent need to address the theological crisis occasioned by the recent events and to offer what reassurance they could to the Jewish people. But 4 Ezra clearly has two separate audiences in mind, as ch. 14 makes clear. There are the wise (represented by his five scribes in 14:24)—the ones really 'in the know', and the people (represented in 5:16 by Phaltiel, a chief of the people; see also 12:40–50). It is clear that 4 Ezra is designed for the inner circle of the wise; it is one of the seventy reserved books (14:46). But nevertheless the function of the book is to instruct the wise so that they will be in a position to 'reprove your people' (14:13). This social structure seems to be close to that which began to develop within the Jewish community of refugees from the disaster of 70. Rabbinic texts tell us that a small group of sages led by Yohanan ben Zakkai escaped from Jerusalem during the siege and obtained from the Romans permission to set up in Yabneh (near present-day Tel-Aviv) an academy for the study of the law. They formed a nucleus of order and authority around which at least parts of the Jewish community rallied and which eventually gave rise in the course of the next century to a new social and political order in Judaism based upon rabbinic authority to expound and administer the law. It is very tempting to set 4 Ezra within this nucleus of rabbinic sages at Yabneh. Recent students of 4 Ezra (Grabbe 1981, 1989; Longenecker 1995; Coggins and Knibb 1979; Essler 1994) seem to be succumbing to this temptation. But if this was the locus from which 4 Ezra originated we are left with the question: why, then, was this text preserved only by Christians and not by the rabbis? Could it have originated in a group whose long-term aim became to forge an enduring identity for Judaism that would preserve it from the Christian threat?

E. The Text of 2 Esdras. The original text of 4 Ezra, which was almost certainly written in Hebrew, disappeared at an early stage, as did the Greek translation of the Hebrew. Only a few traces of the Greek have been preserved in isolated quotations by Christian writers. We are dependent now for our knowledge of the text upon translations of this Greek version into Latin, Syriac, Ethiopic, Georgian, Armenian, and Arabic, plus a tiny Coptic fragment. Of these secondary versions the most important is the Latin which is preserved in a number of manuscripts dating from the seventh century onwards. In the Latin version the prevalent name given to 2 Esd 3–14 is 4 Esdras and hence the contemporary scholarly preference for calling this text 4 Ezra. 2 Esd 1–2, 15–16 are found only in this Latin version and there they are always kept separate from chs. 3–14. They are two separate works, now called 5 and 6 Ezra, and consist of Christian material added to the original Ezra apocalypse in the course of the second to third centuries CE. None of the oriental versions contains these additions. The next most important version after the Latin is the Syriac. Apart from a few liturgical extracts this is preserved in only one manuscript, the Codex Ambrosianus, the most important and complete codex of the Syriac Bible, dating from the sixth to seventh century. Most translations of the text are based on the Latin and bring in readings from the other versions (principally the Syriac) only when the Latin does not make sense, is clearly corrupt, or has been altered tendentiously. The clearest example of Christian scribes at work 'improving' the text is 7:28 where the Latin has 'my son Jesus' but the Syriac 'my son the Messiah' and the Ethiopic has just 'the Messiah'. That the readings of none of the oriental versions can be passed over lightly is shown by one very interesting example in ch. 8:23. At the end of this verse nearly all the versions attest to a text which read: 'and whose truth bears witness'. However, a

quotation in the Apostolic Constitutions, a fourth-century collection of liturgical texts, and the second Arabic version read: 'and whose truth stands for ever'. The divergence is neatly explained by different readings of the same consonantal Hebrew text: $l^c d$ read as $l\bar{a}^c\bar{a}d$ (for ever) or $l\check{e}^c\bar{e}d$ (for/as a witness).

F. The Structure of the Text. The text is carefully structured into seven episodes. These episodes are usually called visions although the vision genre only dominates the later parts of 4 Ezra. The divisions between the episodes or visions are clearly marked out by means of a chronological framework—usually, but not always, a seven-day period.

Macrostructure

Vision 1	3:1–5:20	
Vision 2	5:21–6:34	Lament
Vision 3	6:35–9:25	
Vision 4	9:26–10:59	Transformation/Fulcrum
Vision 5	11:1–12:51	
Vision 6	13:1–58	Consolation
Vision 7	14:1–48	

At the deepest level the text is structured by a movement from lament to consolation with the change of mood hinging on the fourth vision (Breech 1973). Visions 1–3 have similar internal structural patterns as (to a lesser extent) do visions 4–7. See the table in Stone (1990: 51). The primary literary genre used to structure the lament section is the dialogue between the prophet Ezra and the angel Uriel; in the consolation section the apocalyptic vision is the mould in which the author chooses to write.

G. 2 Esdras 1–2 (= 5 Ezra). 1. As we have seen, these two chapters are not attested in any of the oriental versions which we have in abundance for 4 Ezra. They are found only in nine Latin manuscripts (eight of which also contain the text of 4 Ezra). These Latin manuscripts clearly divide into two main recensions which have been named the Spanish and French Recensions (Bensley 1895: xxi–xxii, xliv–lxxviii). It is unfortunate that the RSV and NRSV translations of 5 Ezra follow the manuscripts of the French recension since Bergren (1990) has confirmed James's view (Bensley 1895) that the readings of the Spanish recension (mostly confined to marginal notes in the NRSV) are almost always superior. See also Kraft (1986). Readers interested in a text closer to the original would be better to follow Bergren's Eng. translation (1990: 401–5).
2. The general scholarly consensus is that 5 Ezra dates from about the middle of the second century CE and is a Christian work (albeit from the hands of a Jewish Christian). Stanton (1977: 80) has argued that it represents a 'continuation into the second century of Matthean Christianity' and offers a Christian perspective on the recent cataclysmic outcome of the Bar Kochba revolt (132–5 CE). This view is strongly contested by O'Neill (1991) who argues that 5 Ezra is an originally Jewish work, probably of the first century CE, which has suffered interpolations and corruptions at the hand of Christian scribes. As for the original language of these chapters, Bergren (1990: 22), who has studied this at great length, is cautious in his conclusions: '5 Ezra could have been written either in Greek or Latin (with the former option being slightly

preferable)' but 'a Semitic original (at least for parts of the book) also cannot be excluded.'

H. 2 Esdras 15–16 (= 6 Ezra). From internal evidence it would seem that these chapters were composed towards the end of the third century CE as a deliberate attempt to reapply 4 Ezra to a new situation facing, this time, not the Jews but the Christian church in the eastern Roman empire. Like 5 Ezra they are not found in the oriental versions of 4 Ezra. Except for a small Greek papyrus fragment (15:57–9) they are attested only in the Latin version. They were clearly written at a time of political upheavel and probably of persecution of the church (15:21; 16:68–70). Their aim is to encourage the persecuted righteous to stand firm, confident of their eventual vindication by God and the overthrow of their oppressors.

COMMENTARY

2 Esdras 1–2 (= 5 Ezra)

5 Ezra contains two principal blocks of material: (1) a prophetic indictment of Israel and the proclamation of the transfer of its status as 'people of God' to another people (1:4–2:9); and (2) a series of eschatological promises for the new people of God (2:10–48).

(1:1–3) Introduction A better and drastically shorter text of these verses (the Spanish Recension) can be found in n. *b* to the NRSV. The printed text (the French Recension) represents an attempt to bring the earlier version into line with biblical tradition (Ezra 7:1–5). The characterization of Ezra as a 'prophet' (only in the French Recension) contrasts with his biblical titles 'scribe' and 'priest' but agrees with 4 Ezra 12:42 and suits well his role in 5 Ezra.

(1:4–23) God's Actions on Behalf of Israel Like 4 Ezra, 5 Ezra begins with a recital of salvation history. However, the two recitals are used for very different purposes. Here the purpose is to point up the contrast between God's faithfulness to his people and their utter failure to respond as they ought. The text is closely modelled on Ps 78, see especially vv. 17–22, 59–62.

(1:24–40) The Rejection of Israel and the Election of A New People of God Whereas the purpose of Ps 78 is to demonstrate that God rejected the northern tribes (Joseph/Ephraim) in favour of the 'tribe of Judah' and 'David his servant' (Ps 78:67–72), the author of 5 Ezra uses his recital to demonstrate that Israel is entirely rejected in favour of the Christian church—the 'other nations' of v. 24 ('another people'—Spanish Recension) and the 'people that will come' (1:35, 37). The OT texts which he uses are part of a standard repertoire frequently found in Christian anti-Jewish polemic (Simon 1986: 135–78). Cf. v. 26 with Isa 1:15, 59:3, 7, Prov 1:28; v. 31 with Isa 1:14 and Jer 7:22; and v. 32 with 2 Chr 36:15–16. In the OT denunciations such as these were meant to call the people to repentance; Christians used them to demonstrate the final rejection of Israel. This section of 5 Ezra is heavily dependent upon the Gospel of Matthew, especially the notorious ch. 23. Cf. v. 24 with Mt 21:43 (the conclusion added by Matthew to the parable of the vineyard), v. 30*a* with Mt 23:37, v. 32 with Mt 23:34, and v. 33 with Mt 23:38. The purpose clause in v. 24— 'that they may keep my statutes' (see also 2:40) suggests that

the author of 5 Ezra may have been a Jewish Christian (Stanton 1977). For a full treatment of the text and history of the version of v. 32 quoted in n. *n* to the NRSV see Hayman (1973, CSCO 339: 11*–13*).

In vv. 38–9 Jewish hopes for the return of the Dispersion to Israel (particularly in Bar 4:36 and 5:5, but see also 4 Ezra 13:39–40) are reapplied to the new people who will replace them. Mt 8:11–12 is probably responsible both for the reference to the 'east' and to 'Abraham, Isaac, and Jacob'. This passage in Matthew's Gospel precisely summarizes the main theme of 5 Ezra. The reference to Ezra as 'father' is probably based on a misreading of the Greek text of Baruch (Bergren 1990: 290). n. *s* in the NRSV contains the more original Spanish Recension of v. 39; the French Recension in the main text eliminates the obscure elements in the earlier version and provides a correct list of the twelve minor prophets in the Septuagint order.

(2:1–9) Zion Denounces her Children vv. 2–5*a* draws closely on, and is scarcely comprehensible without reference to, Bar 4:8–23; cf. v. 3 with Bar 4:11. The 'mother who bore them' is Jerusalem/Zion as personified in Bar 4; cf. Isa 50:1; 54:1; 4 Ezra 10:7. In Baruch she consoles her children, but here in 5 Ezra she denounces them, a denunciation in which Ezra joins, vv. 5–7. In this latter section the MS tradition is hopelessly confused and the original text scarcely recoverable. However, we should read 'your covenant' at the end of v. 5 with the Spanish Recension. Ezra is the speaker and God the person addressed—'father'. Most commentators take the reference to Assyria in v. 8 as a cryptic allusion to Rome.

(2:10–19) Israel's Blessings Transferred 'My people' (v. 10) refers to the new people of 1:24, 35, 37—presumably the Christian church. The old Israel is blotted out (2:7) and the old covenant promises transferred to the new legatees. Mother Zion now has a new set of children (vv. 15, 17); as the text progresses she seems to be transmuting into Mother Church. The influence of the books of Revelation and 1 Enoch may be perceived in this section. Cf. vv. 12, 16, 18–19 with Rev 2:7; 14:1; 22:2, 14; 1 Enoch 24–5. v. 18 probably refers to the role of Isaiah and Jeremiah as providing the prophecies which Christians applied to the events of Christ's life—a view confirmed by the addition of Daniel in the Spanish Recension.

(2:20–32) Exhortations and Promises Israel's ethical and legal obligations are now incumbent upon the new people of God. These injunctions are found in many places in the OT but for the obligation to bury the dead (v. 23) see Tob 1:17–19. With v. 31 cf. 4 Ezra 7:32.

(2:33–41) Ezra, the Second Moses v. 33*a* is probably modelled on 4 Ezra 14:1 ff. v. 33*b* probably alludes to the incident of the Golden Calf (Ex 32) which became a type of Israel's rejection of Christ in Christian anti-Jewish polemic. The pattern is as before: Israel rejects God, so he turns to a new audience (v. 34). The 'shepherd' (v. 34) could be God but more likely refers to Christ; see Jn 10:11; Heb 13:20; 1 Pet 2:25; 5:4. Like other parts of the 2 Esdras complex, 5 Ezra is marked by an intense expectation that the end of the age is at hand; see 4:26, 14:18, 16:74. The end is at hand because the predetermined number of the saved has been reached. The theme may have been taken from 4 Ezra 4:36–7 but see also Rev 6:11; 7:4. The reference to the 'sealing' of the elect certainly seems dependent on Rev 7:4–8. 'The feast of the Lord' (v. 38) refers to the messianic banquet; see Isa 25:6; Rev 19:9; 2 ESD 6:52. For the white clothing (v. 40) see Rev 3:4; 6:11; 7:13–14.

(2:42–8) Ezra's Vision As frequently in 4 Ezra so here the prophet is granted a vision of the future, but the text breathes the atmosphere of the book of Revelation. See Rev 4:1; 7:9; 14:1, and cf. Heb 12:22–4. The tall young man (v. 43) is identified in v. 47 as 'the Son of God'. A similar figure appears in *Herm. Sim.* 9.6.1 and the *Acts of John*, 90, while in *Gos. Pet.* 40 Jesus is distinguished by his height ('overpassing the heavens') from the two angels who assist him at the resurrection. The description is also reminiscent of the appearance of the Son of Man in *1 Enoch* 46:1–3. The vision seems to be describing the eschatological reward in heaven of the Christian martyrs.

2 Esdras 3–14 (= 4 Ezra): First Vision (3:1–5:20)

This vision consists of four major sections: (1) Ezra's prayer (3:1–36); (2) a dialogue between Ezra and the angel Uriel (4:1–43); (3) a vision (4:44–9); (4) the interpretation of the vision (4:50–5:20). The same basic structuring of the material can also be seen in the second and third visions; in the fourth vision the dialogue element is missing, thus presaging the change of mood as we move into the consolation section of the text.

The principal problem that the author confronts in the first vision is God's apparent failure to carry out his promises to Israel viewed in the light of the distressing situation of the Jewish people after the end of the war against the Romans and the loss of the Temple in 70 CE. In the past Jews had always managed to cope with such crises by regarding the disasters they suffered as God's punishment for their sins, and then by looking forward to a restoration of their national fortunes. 4 Ezra's sister apocalypse *2 Apoc. Bar.*, which probably stems from the same Jewish circles, adopts this traditional response to the Jewish dilemma. But this traditional solution does not satisfy the character Ezra in the dialogue for two reasons: (1) He cannot understand why God deals more severely with his own people than with the Gentiles. After all, Israel has accepted God's law and tried to live up to it. Why then has God not dealt more severely with the Gentiles who now oppress Israel? Behind this complaint appears to lie the widespread Jewish belief that at Mount Sinai God offered the law to all the nations of the world but only Israel volunteered to take on its yoke (see 7:20–4). But all Israel has got for agreeing to fall in with God's plans is one disaster after another. The Gentiles seem to have been rewarded by God for not accepting his law! (2) But Ezra has a deeper reason for finding the traditional explanation for Israel's suffering unsatisfactory. Unlike the OT in general and in contrast to later rabbinic Judaism he seems to believe that humans beings are incapable of keeping God's law because the power of their 'evil heart' is too strong and overwhelms their desire to obey God (3:20–2). Christian doctrine as first formulated by Paul in Rom 5 holds that the power of sin took hold of humanity as a result of Adam's transgression. But the Jewish doctrine to which our author holds is that the 'evil inclination' (*yēṣer hāraʿ*) was placed in humans at the time of creation and it is their task to strive to overcome it; see 4:30–1, 7:92, and Hayman (1976; 1984). The

rabbis held, in line with the implied teaching of the OT, that God had created humanity with the ability to overcome the evil inclination by means of the law. But Ezra surveys the history of Israel and concludes that the facts warrant the opposite conclusion, namely, that the power of the evil inclination is irresistible. But if this is so, then God's justice is impugned because he is making demands which cannot be fulfilled (3:20, 8:35). How then can God with any justice blame Israel for transgressing the law, and why has he punished them so drastically?

(3:1–36) Ezra's Prayer This first speech by Ezra consists primarily of a review of the salvation history from the creation of Adam to the fall of Jerusalem to the Babylonians. The review ends at v. 27 and is then followed by a complaint and appeal to God based on the preceding review. The structure of this chapter is probably based upon the pattern of the communal lament psalms in the Psalter, e.g. Ps 44, 85, and 89. In these psalms we find a review of past history recited in order to motivate God's intervention in Israel's present distress. However, when we look more closely at Ezra's speech considerable differences between it and the communal lament psalms appear. The most striking difference is that in his review of past history there is already an element of complaint about God's actions. It is not only, as in the lament psalms, God's present actions or inactivity that are under attack; the salvation history itself is no longer a secure foundation for faith.

Each of the prayers of Ezra which begin the first three visions in the book has this same structure. 5:23–7 similarly gives us a review of God's past actions, in this case specifically his election of Israel, followed in 5:28–30 by a forthright lament. 6:38–54 offers a review of God's work in creation followed in 6:55–9 by a lament. But in neither of these two later visions is the review of God's past actions marred by any element of complaint. Hence ch. 3, placed at the beginning of the book, presents us with the strongest statement of Ezra's scepticism about the salvation history. This is one way in which the pattern of movement from fierce complaint to eventual acquiescence is built into the structure of the book.

(3:1–11) vv. 1–3 serve as an introduction both to the book and this specific prayer. For the problem of the identification of Ezra with Salathiel, the possible significance of the latter name, and the apparent setting of the book in Babylon see 2 ESD B. vv. 4–11 summarize the biblical story from Adam to Noah. The words 'and commanded the dust and it gave you Adam, a lifeless body' (vv. 4–5) rephrase Gen 2:7 in such a way as to give to the earth an active role in Adam's creation. The author does this elsewhere: in 7:62, in 7:116, which has almost a dualistic tone, and in 10:14. But, as if to immediately counteract any dualistic implications, he goes on to emphasize God's direct involvement in the creation of Adam. This also he does elsewhere: 7:70, 8:7, 8–13, 44. But why use this image of mother earth here? Probably it serves two purposes: first, it enables the author to avoid irreverence when addressing God by making the accusation indirect—God produced the earth but it, in its turn, produced this flawed creature, man; secondly, it enables the author to stress humanity's earthy origins as mitigating its guilt. The latter reiterates a common sentiment of the OT: Job 14:1–2, Eccl 3:19–20, Ps 90:3; cf. also Paul's use of the image in 1 Cor 15:47–9. v. 7 is obviously summarizing the story of Gen 2–3, though whether it is a correct exegesis is another matter. There is nothing in Gen 2 to suggest that Adam was created immortal and that death was his punishment for transgressing God's command. Gen 3:22–3 says that Adam and Eve were driven out of the Garden in order to *prevent* them from becoming immortal (Hayman 1984: 15). However, the author's exegesis of Gen 2–3 is in line with that first hinted at in Sir 25:24, and then more systematically in Wis 2:23–4, and, of course, Paul in Rom 5:12; see also *2 Apoc. Bar.* 23:4. In this tradition of exegesis the way in which Adam's transgression brings death upon his descendants is not spelled out. The connection is stressed elsewhere in 4 Ezra (4:30, 7:11–12, 118) but never explained. 3:21 is the closest we get to an explanation and this is closely parallel to Rom 5:12. Both these texts are factual statements, not explanations. Explanations had to wait for St Augustine. The point made in vv. 9–11 is going to be echoed later in the chapter, for here God is behaving how Ezra thinks he should—punishing the wicked and saving the righteous.

(3:12–19) takes us from Noah to the Exodus. The Abraham presented in v. 14 belongs to the esoteric tradition which is read into Gen 15; see 2 ESD 14:1–18. This is the Abraham of the *T. Abr.* and *Apoc. Abr.*, texts approximately contemporaneous with 4 Ezra. See also *2 Apoc. Bar.* 4:4–5. Emphasizing the miraculous and cosmic significance of God's theophany on Mt Sinai (vv. 18–19) serves the function of stressing the vital importance of the giving of the law. But our author does it not only for this purpose but also to heighten the contrast with the following verse.

(3:20–2) **The Evil Heart** With the Exodus we have reached the focal point of the salvation history as far as Judaism is concerned, and it is just here that Ezra raises his major objection. What was the point of giving the law if God did not first wipe out the 'evil heart' inherited from Adam which made it impossible for the people to keep the law? The author's terminology for the evil component within human beings is not consistent and there is a problem deciding exactly what he has in mind.

evil heart	3:20, 21, 26; 7:48
evil root	3:22; 8:53
grain of evil seed	4:30, 31
evil thought	7:92
mind	7:62–4

The problem is: do all these expressions refer to the same thing? Some scholars think they do, but others distinguish between the 'evil heart' and the other terms which it is admitted refer to what the rabbis called 'the evil inclination' (*yēṣer hā-ra'*). This was implanted in Adam at the time of creation (4:30–1; 7:92). But some scholars argue that in the author's thinking the 'evil inclination' developed into 'the evil heart' as a result of Adam's sin. The evidence for this differentiation is 7:48 and the Syriac/Ethiopic text of v. 21 which Box (1912: 16) translates: 'the first Adam, clothing himself with the evil heart, transgressed', i.e. Adam 'clothed himself' with the evil heart by yielding to the suggestions of the evil impulse. Though none of its proponents clearly states it, the importance of this interpretation is that the irresistibility of the evil inclination dates from after the Fall; prior to that it was just a

potential force. This exegesis aligns 4 Ezra somewhat closer to the specifically Augustinian Christian doctrine of original sin, and away from the general rabbinic view which regards humanity's free will as unimpaired by the Fall. However, there are strong reasons for resisting this line of interpretation: (1) To say that Adam clothed himself with the evil heart and then transgressed but (as 7:48 states) the result of his sin was the emergence or development of the evil heart does not make sense. (2) The Syriac text of 7:48 omits the word 'has grown up' and simply reads: 'for there is in us an evil heart . . .'. If Box and others wish to follow the Syriac in v. 21, why not in 7:48 also? (3) Why does the author revert to the terminology 'evil root' at v. 22 and back to 'evil heart' in 3:26? The natural way is to take these as equivalent expressions for the same phenomenon.

These are weighty objections and it seems unlikely that the author of 4 Ezra had a more complicated and developed view of the effect of the Fall on humanity's constitution than that of the rabbis, or one more closely aligned to the later Christian position. It is undeniable, however, that he uses the metaphor of growth to describe the increasing influence of the evil inclination; see 4:30–1; 7:64; and the Latin text of 7:48. Possibly v. 22 carries this meaning also. The author clearly feels that sin has got a firmer and firmer grip on human beings and the influence of the evil inclination has become more and more irresistible. This fits in with the pessimism he expresses elsewhere in statements such as that in 5:55.

(3:24–7) Ezra now introduces the theme of Zion and its fate which is to play an important role in the book as a focus for his complaints. Again the point is made that each new initiative by God is neutralized by humanity's sin. v. 26 parallels v. 21. Ezra is saying that since God had not dealt with the root of the problem, then failure was inevitable. At v. 27 we reach the supposed author's own time, the Babylonian exile. The real, rather than the implied, readers can draw their own conclusions about the period from 587 BCE to 70 CE—the whole Second Temple period had ended as disastrously as the First.

(3:28–36) This section looks back over the salvation history which has just been recounted and highlights one contrast between the present and the past. At the time of the Flood God had acted as he ought to have done—punishing the wicked and saving the righteous. But now he seems to be doing the exact opposite (v. 30).

(4:1–43) **Dialogue between Ezra and the Angel Uriel** Having been exposed at some length to the complaints of Ezra we now get the response of the other partner in the dialogue, Uriel. The dialogue between them passes through two phases. In vv. 1–21 Uriel provides three illustrations of the limits of human understanding. The point made is very similar to the message Job gets when God appears to him out of the whirlwind (Job 38–41). In the second phase (vv. 22–43) Ezra asserts his right both to ask his questions and to have an answer. Uriel replies that all his problems will be solved, not in this age, but in the age to come. Ezra then asks how long it will be before the future age arrives, and receives a somewhat ambiguous answer, replete with characteristic apocalyptic determinism (vv. 36–7). As this dialogue proceeds Ezra's role gradually diminishes until he becomes no more than a stooge offering appropriate prompting questions to Uriel. Uriel, for his part, only picks up and answers the last of Ezra's questions in vv. 23–5. He ignores the questions for which he has no answer—as often in the rest of the book.

(4:1–25) Uriel (v. 1) is listed as one of the four archangels in *1 Enoch* 9:1 and occurs often in other lists. In *1 Enoch* 20:2 he is said to be set 'over the world and over Tartarus'. vv. 5–8 contain a polemic against the exaggerated claims of part of the apocalyptic tradition. In texts like *1 Enoch* the apocalyptic seer travels to the heavens precisely so that he can acquire the sort of knowledge which here both Ezra and Uriel accept is off limits to human beings. The scepticism of 4 Ezra towards these sorts of claims aligns it with the tradition marked out by Prov 30:1–4 and Sir 3:21–4 (much quoted by the rabbis for the same purpose). The author's reticence over revealing such matters probably accounts for the abrupt end of the fourth vision (10:55). Other apocalyptic works would have treated us here to a full tourist's guide to the heavenly city; we get not a word from Ezra.

(4:26–32) This paragraph presents us with the first systematic statement of 4 Ezra's view of history. In contrast to large parts of the OT (though not all of it) where history is seen as the sphere of God's saving actions, in 4 Ezra salvation is seen as a catastrophic intervention of God to wipe out this present world and to replace it with an entirely new heaven and earth. It is repeated time and again that this present age/world cannot possibly see the realization of Israel's hopes or the fulfilment of God's promises (4:27; 7:12–13). In the previous chapter Ezra looked back over the course of Israel's history and saw it as one long disaster leading nowhere and Uriel does not disagree with this analysis. The present age is evil, full of pain and sorrow, so must be eliminated before God's salvation can come, as must the 'evil heart'; the words 'place' and 'field' in v. 29 have this dual reference. The same general atmosphere pervades the NT and early Christianity; the temptation story presupposes that the devil is in charge of this world, not God (Mt 5:8–9), and Paul goes so far as to describe the devil as 'the god of this world' (2 Cor 4:4). Christianity expresses this in a dualistic fashion alien to Judaism and to 4 Ezra but underlying both is despair of this present world and a concentration on the 'other world' as the real sphere of God's actions and the real goal of the saved.

(4:26) The phrase 'The age is hurrying swiftly to its end' in 4:26 reflects the tone of eschatological urgency which pervades 4 Ezra; see 6:20 and esp. 14:11–12, 18, where a timetable is laid down. However, just at this point the author's literary use of the device of pseudonymity is in real danger of unravelling. He, in the late first century CE, is writing as though he were living in the sixth century BCE. He believes that the tragic events of 66–70 through which presumably he has lived are the woes preceding the coming of the Messiah, an event which he expects to take place very soon. But in the fictional stance of the text the world had at least another 650 years to go! The writer has to suggest in a veiled way that the world will soon come to an end but not so overtly as to rupture his pseudepigraphic framework. This is a hard act to accomplish. Precisely at v. 26 and 14:18 we can feel him stepping out from behind his pseudonym; from the perspective of the implied rather than the real author the arrival of the Roman empire

(whose demise was being predicted) was still several hundred years off.

(4:26–7) Throughout 4 Ezra a sharp distinction is made between this age/world and the next; see especially 6:7–10; 7:29–31, 50, 112–13; 8:1. It is probable that the term used for age/world in the original Hebrew text was *'ôlām*. In biblical Hebrew this almost invariably has an adverbial use in the phrase *lĕ'ôlām* (for ever); by the first century CE it had changed its meaning to 'world'. The rabbis used the phrases *hā'ôlām hazzeh* (this world) and *hā'ôlām habbā'* (the world to come) to distinguish the two time periods; possibly the original Hebrew text of 4 Ezra did likewise.

(4:33–42) 4:34 and similar verses (5:33; 8:47) hint at the 'experiential solution' to Ezra's agonizing that will come in the fourth vision—when he turns from his own, self-absorbed doubting to dealing with the concrete problems of his needy people, and so mirrors God's concern for 'the many'. v. 35, 'storehouse of souls' (NEB) rather than 'chambers' (NRSV) better reflects the Hebrew word *'ôṣār* which probably underlies the Latin and Syriac here. The 'storehouse of souls' (located under the divine throne according to R. Eliezer b. Hyrcanus in *b. Šabb.* 152*b*) was the place where the rabbis believed the souls of the righteous were kept before they were reconnected with their bodies at the resurrection; see 7:32 and cf. 4:41; 7:80, 95. The archangel Jeremiel (v. 36) is mentioned in the *Coptic Apoc. Zeph.* as being in charge of the souls of dead. However, the Syriac here has Ramiel, who is the seventh archangel in *1 Enoch* 20:8 (cf. *2 Apoc. Bar.* 55:3—'the angel Ramiel who presides over true visions'). The idea that the end of the world has been predestined by God (4:36–7; cf. 7:74) is a common one in apocalyptic and other Jewish texts, as also is the idea that he has fixed beforehand the number of human beings that will be born. The two ideas are combined in *2 Apoc. Bar.* 23:4–5 and strikingly in *Gen. Rab.* 24:4 ('The Son of David will not come until all those souls which are destined to be born will be born'). However, the author may intend to refer here to the completing of a fixed number of the righteous, as with the 144,000 in Rev 7:4; 14:1. Locating the chambers of the souls in Hades (4:41) hardly fits in with what the text later indicates is the fate of the righteous after death (7:88–99). It is better to follow the Syriac (supported by the Ethiopic) which reads: 'Sheol and the storehouses of the souls are like the womb'. The alternative is to think of the wicked being separately stored in Sheol away from the righteous (Box 1912: 37).

(4:43–5:25) A Vision and its Interpretation 4:44–6 leads into the actual parabolic vision in vv. 48–9; see 5:50 for a similar leading question. In 5:1–13 the vision is interpreted to show that most of human history has passed, and only a little while remains before the future age comes. All Jewish apocalyptists believed this. It is schematized in 14:10–11 but is a recurring refrain throughout the book. 5:1–13 contains a description of the hard times (conventionally referred to as 'the messianic woes') which will precede the end and by means of which the 'wise' may discern its approach. The list of signs is traditional material and may well have been drawn from a literary source. The beginning of 5:1 looks like a rubric to an already existing collection of material. Many parallels can be cited. See Mk 13 and parallels and the extensive list provided by Stone (1990:

110 n. 15). The signs catalogue the reversal of all order as the end approaches—in nature and in human society. The theme of the reversal of the natural order reaches far back into the OT; see esp. Isa 24. In 5:3 the author alludes to a theme which will be vastly expanded in ch. 11 and 12, namely, the demise of the Roman empire as a sign of the end. In 5:6 he hints, and no more, at another standard theme of Jewish apocalyptic—the emergence of the Antichrist, a belief which is rooted in Jewish experiences at the hands of Antiochus Epiphanes in the Maccabean period. He does not develop this theme later in the book, which reinforces the impression that he is editing traditional material.

We have now had the two responses of Uriel to Ezra's complaints that will dominate the rest of the book: (1) who are puny you to challenge God?—mere mortals cannot understand God's ways; (2) the resolution of the problem can only be sought in the next world, not in this one.

(5:16–20) A transitional narrative that connects the first and second visions. Similar material is placed between the other visions. Phaltiel's rebuke is significant since it points forward to the resolution or assuaging of Ezra's problems by immersing himself in communal service. See 2 ESD 4:33–42. 12:40–5 expands the rebuke, this time on the lips of the people, but in 12:46–8 and esp. 14:27–36 Ezra responds and accepts the role required of him.

Second Vision (5:21–6:34)

This follows more or less the same pattern as the first vision: (1) Ezra's prayer (5:21–30); (2) a dialogue between Ezra and Uriel (5:31–6:10); (3) a vision (6:17–28); (4) conclusion of the vision (6:29–34).

(5:21–30) Ezra's Prayer This time Ezra's complaint has a much narrower focus than in ch. 3. What makes it less acute is the absence of the whole theme of the permanently diseased 'evil heart', though the language of v. 30 ('hates') pulls no punches. As here (v. 21) a period of seven days' prayer and fasting precedes each of the first three visions; see 5:13, 20; 6:31, 34. The pattern is broken at the end of the third vision where seven days of eating flowers replaces the period of fasting (9:23, 27)—a significant symbol of the change of mood in the fourth vision. The prayer is based on a series of seven images which illustrate God's unique choice of Israel, but in v. 28–9 the imagery of 'one out of the many' is neatly reversed by the complaint: the many oppress the one. Why? The series of images is based on traditional symbols for Israel in biblical and Jewish sources; cf. Ps 80:8–19; Hos 14:5; Ps 132:13; 74:1, 19. The use of the language 'love' and 'hate' (v. 30) comes from the biblical comparison of the relationship between Israel and God with human marriage. The tone is reminiscent of Hos 1–3.

(5:31–6:10) Dialogue between Ezra and Uriel This repeats in a different form the content of their previous dialogue. Cf. 5:36–40 with 4:5–11. Again Uriel states that the future age is imminent, that the time when it will come has been completely predetermined from the beginning of creation, and that history is moving inexorably towards this predestined goal.

(5:31–56) Since further dialogue is blocked on the issue of Ezra's competence to understand God's ways in creation, the text carefully creates an opening (v. 40, 'my judgement', 'the goal of [my] love') for the discussion to shift to the topic of eschatology, ground where the angel has answers to offer. We noticed the same technique in 4:23–5. Ezra's question in v. 41 refers back to the angel's future-orientated answer in the first vision to the problem of theodicy. Uriel does not know whether Ezra will be alive when the end comes (4:26, 52). Ezra wants to know if this means that he, and all the righteous born before him, will therefore miss out on part of this promised eschatological reward. If so, its power to soften the problem of theodicy is weakened. The issue raised by Ezra is very similar to that faced by Paul in 1 Thess 4:3–18. Note how in these verses the angel recedes into the background in the author's mind and God directly addresses Ezra. Uriel does not re-emerge until 6:30. This phenomenon occurs regularly in 4 Ezra just as in the OT the Angel of the Lord and the Lord constantly fuse together; cf. also Judg 6:12, 14. The image of the circle (v. 42) is not very clear and the text is uncertain. The point it makes has been aptly compared with 1 Thess 4:15. The general resurrection (7:32) will ensure that all will stand on an equal footing in the future age. v. 45 is a neat rejoinder by Ezra: if all who have ever lived will be resurrected and kept alive for the final judgement, then there is no reason why all who are destined to be born could not be alive now and so the end could come without any delay. With v. 46 cf. 4:40–3 where the deterministic potential of the image of human reproduction is similarly used. The pessimistic view of the world in vv. 50–5 (cf. 4:26–7; 14:10) is a deduction both from the references to the giants in Gen 6:1–4 and the lengths of the lives of the prediluvian patriarchs in Gen 5. But the general sentiment was widespread in the ancient world; see Philo, On the Creation, 140–1, and 2 Apoc. Bar. 85:10.

(6:1–16) The text at the beginning of v. 1 is uncertain; see n. l to NRSV. Possibly Christian scribes in the Latin tradition removed the reference attested in the Syriac to the 'beginning' coming through 'man', feeling that it contradicted the divinity of Christ. If the phrase is original it could have referred either to the Messiah (see 7:28; 11:32–4; 13:37–8) or to the human agents of the messianic woes (5:1–13; 6:24). Here, and in the emphatic wording of v. 6b, there seems to be some polemical intention, perhaps against the heresy of 'the two powers'. On this see Segal (1977). The function of the list of elements in the cosmos in vv. 1b–6 is to reinforce the point made more prosaically in 7:70. The text of vv. 7–10 is much disturbed in the versions, especially in the Latin. Scribes found it difficult to understand and probably made matters worse by trying to 'improve' it. The section presupposes an eschatological interpretation of Gen 25:26 well-attested in later rabbinic texts: Esau = Rome, Jacob = the Jewish messianic kingdom which will seamlessly replace the Roman empire (5:3; 11:38–46; 12:31–4).

(6:17–28) Vision This is not really a vision but an audition. Ezra hears a voice proclaiming the arrival of the End. The messianic woes are again described and also the beginning of the messianic age (6:25–8). We get here in embryo the eschatological timetable that will be spelt out in much greater detail in the next vision. Cf., for example, 6:25 with 7:27–8, 12:34, 13:48–50; and 6:26b with 8:53. vv. 11–12 consciously hark back to 5:1–13, and some scholars have seen in what follows further material from the source the author may have used there. The foundations of the earth shake (vv. 14–16) because the prediction concerns their imminent end and transformation into a new heaven and earth (7:30–1). v. 17 alludes to Ezek 1:24. The heavenly books on which all human deeds are recorded (v. 20) are mentioned in many biblical and extra-biblical books; see Dan 7:10; Mal 3:16; Rev 20:12; *1 Enoch* 47:3; *2 Apoc. Bar.* 24:1. For the trumpet blast (v. 23) see Isa 27:13; Mt 24:31; 1 Thess 4:16 v. 26*a* refers to the OT saints who were assumed to heaven (Enoch, Gen 5:24; Elijah, 2 Kings 2:11, Mal 3:5–6) and who will appear with the Messiah as his companions ('those who are with him', 7:28, 13:52). Ezra himself is elected to this select band—14:9, 49 (Syriac). Other figures, such as Moses and Baruch, were similarly believed to have been assumed to heaven without dying.

(6:29–34) Conclusion of the Vision There is no interpretation of the vision because the message of the audition is fairly comprehensible on its own. Ezra is warned not to misinterpret what has happened in this present age; his attention is being firmly focused on the future, not the past. v. 34 refers back to the agonizing laments of ch. 3 and 5:22–30. The legitimacy of the laments is not denied, otherwise Ezra would not be praised in the terms of v. 32; see also 10:38, 57. This approval of Ezra performs the same psychological function as Job 42:7; it legitimizes the cathartic effect on readers who empathize with Job and Ezra in their railing against the incomprehensibility of God's ways.

Third Vision (6:35–9:25)

In this vision the pattern of the previous two is broken since we get only Ezra's prayer (6:35–59) and then a very long and involved dialogue between Ezra and Uriel (7:1–9:25). There is no vision and interpretation. These elements are replaced here by a series of apocalyptic predictions or monologues (7:26–44, 78–99; 9:1–13).

(6:35–59) Ezra's Prayer The structure of the prayer, like those which begin the first and second visions (3:4–36; 5:22–30), follows the pattern of the lament psalms. On the basis of God's deeds in the past, in this case his work in creation culminating in his election of Israel (6:54), a lament is raised over his inaction in the present (6:57–9). In the earlier prayers the emphasis was on God's acts in history. Here it centres on his work in creation (Gen 1) because the dialogue in this vision is going to confront the issue: if nearly all human beings are sinners and hence shut out of the future age, why did God bother to create them in the first place?

No exact parallel is known to the sevenfold division of the earth in v. 42. v. 49 expands on 'the great sea monster' (Gen 1:21). This is traditional material (possibly incorporated here by the author from another source) which is not utilized elsewhere in 4 Ezra; see *1 Enoch* 60:7–10, and *2 Apoc. Bar.* 29:4. Many OT passages allude to a mythical version of creation (with parallels in the Ugaritic and other ancient Near-Eastern texts) in which God is involved in conflict with a monster (Rahab/Leviathan) which is never really subdued and hence has to be definitively dealt with at the end of the world (Isa 27:1). See Ps 74:13–14; 89:10–11; Job 7:12; 26:12–13; Isa 51:9. Job 40:15–41:34 describes the two monsters and names them as Behemoth and Leviathan. v. 51 is based on Ps 50:10 where the word 'cattle' is in Hebrew *běhēmôt*. In a parallel passage to

6:52 in *2 Apoc. Bar.* 29:4, and in rabbinic texts, Behemoth and Leviathan provide the menu at the messianic banquet (Isa 25:6). It is not explicitly said in the OT that the world was created for the sake of Israel (v. 55) but rabbinic and other Jewish texts took it for granted, as Ezra does here and the angel/God does in 7:11. Note the careful phrasing of vv. 55–7: 'you have said that . . .', 'which are reputed to be . . .' (referring mainly to Isa 40:15, 17). Ezra attributes these views to God; in the subsequent dialogue they represent Uriel's position. In fact Ezra is going to dispute this attitude to the Gentiles on the basis of the doctrine of creation (8:14). The author is bringing to the surface the latent contradiction between the doctrines of creation and election in the OT. This contradiction is not resolved in 4 Ezra.

(7:1–25) First Dialogue The initial speech by Uriel (vv. 3–16) attempts to show that the harsh conditions under which human beings now live are the result of the Fall and that this world now serves as a testing ground, so that those who pass the test can enjoy eternal blessedness. Ezra retorts that this is a bit hard on those who have suffered the pains of humanity's mortal conditions yet will not receive any compensatory reward (v. 18). Behind Ezra's retort lies his concept of the evil inclination which he sees as mitigating the guilt of the unrighteous. Uriel will have none of this and reiterates in harsh terms the criteria by which human beings will be judged (vv. 19–24).

The parables in vv. 3–9 imply that 'the world' in 6:59 is the future world (contrary probably to what Ezra himself had in mind) and that Israel has first to negotiate this difficult world (the narrow entrance) before reaching the spacious future age: cf. Mt 7:13–14. The effects of Adam's sin spread out from human beings (3:7; 7:118) to encompass the whole of creation (9:19–20)—as in Rom 8:20–2. But there is a tension between this 'heavy' view of the Fall and the clear statement that God planned for it all in advance (7:70). What sense does it make to say that God made the world for Israel's sake when he knew that they would never inherit it and when he had planned another future world for at least the righteous Israelites? This tension accounts for the slippery meaning of 'world' in 6:59–7:11. Basically, our author here is up against the old problem of the contradiction between God's foreknowledge and human free will. He does not see the problem clearly, so some degree of muddle in his thinking is inevitable. v. 16 is a significantly placed harbinger of what is to come later in the text; turning his attention to the future is in the end what Ezra does because the issues raised in this vision are never (perhaps can never be) resolved. They are rather sidelined by the change of orientation in the last four visions. Note how in vv. 17–18 Ezra changes from being the spokesperson for Israel (6:57–9) to being 'spokesperson for humanity trapped in sin' (Longenecker 1995: 46). He persists in this role to the end of the vision (9:14–15). The dialogue fluctuates, sometimes confusingly, between having Israel in mind and broadening the scope to encompass the whole of the human race. In 8:15 the author alludes specifically to this double focus of attention.

(7:19–25) The angel states clearly the hard line to which he will stick right to the end of this vision: human beings know the score; they have only themselves to blame if they fail to observe the rules and end up with 'empty things'. Deut 30:15–

20 lies behind the formulation of vv. 20–1. But if the author's scope has widened to include all humanity—'those who come into the world'—then they can hardly be blamed for not observing the law of Moses. Something like the rabbinic notions of the Noachian commandments or the legend that all nations were offered the law at Sinai but only Israel accepted it must lie in the background if the angel's argument is to be coherent (Box 1912: 105). On the other hand, it is more likely that the focus is shifting back to the wicked within Israel, since vv. 22–4 retail the sort of accusations fired in the OT at wayward Israelites. Cf. v. 23 with Ps 14:1; 8:58 shows that the author has this psalm in mind.

(7:26–44) Apocalyptic Prediction This is the clearest and most systematic exposition of 4 Ezra's eschatological time-table. As has often been pointed out, the author combines here two different types of eschatological expectation (the this-worldly and the other-worldly) by placing them in chronological sequence. Here we can observe the fusion of ideas that gave rise, both in Judaism and Christianity, to the concept of the millennium. In principle, these two types of eschatology are distinguishable. They line up with the different possible attitudes to history discussed in 2 ESD 4:26–32. They can be found in isolation in different Jewish texts or, as here in 4 Ezra, in combination. They are similarly combined in the book of Revelation, produced at almost the same time as 4 Ezra, and in 2 Apoc. Bar. In 4 Ezra the two types of eschatology neatly correlate to the two main problems raised by Ezra, namely, the current situation of his people Israel and the problem of the utter corruption of the world and human nature. The this-worldly eschatology responds to the first problem: it will be resolved by the Messiah's removal of the Roman empire and re-establishment of the kingdom of David and a totally renewed city of Jerusalem and land of Israel. The other-worldly eschatology explains how eventually this corrupt and worn-out world will be wiped out and replaced by a new heaven and a new earth. Thereafter the evil inclination will be extirpated from human nature (8:53).

Ezra gets a foretaste of the hidden city (v. 26) in 10:25–7, 55–6. See also 8:52; 13:36; Rev 21. On 'my son the Messiah' see Stone 1990: 208 for a table of the variant readings of the versions and a detailed treatment of the redeemer figure in 4 Ezra. For the most up-to-date survey of scholarship on the topic of the Messiah see Collins (1995). Christian scribal interference with the text of v. 28 is clearest in the Latin but has probably contaminated the other versions as well. The major critical issue is whether or not the term 'son' (if part of the original text) goes back to the Hebrew *ben* (son), or via the Greek *pais* (child, servant) to the Hebrew *'ebed* (servant). The appearance of a Qumran text (4Q246 ii 1, Martinez 1994: 138) which assigns the title 'son of God/of the Most High' to the redeemer figure swings the balance now in favour of the former option. Other references to the Messiah/son of God in 4 Ezra are 12:32–4; 13:25–39, 52; 14:9. The word 'revealed' suggests the pre-existence of the Messiah, a belief which is explicitly affirmed in 13:26, 52; 14:9. The idea that the Messiah is predestined to appear from the beginning of time is well-attested in rabbinic Judaism. However, the rabbis were more careful than our author in the way they phrased it; in their view it was the 'name of the Messiah' which had been fixed at

the beginning of time (Moore 1927, ii: 348–9). Our author seems to believe that the Messiah is ready waiting in heaven. On the phrase 'those who are with him' see 2 ESD 6:26. There is no hint here of the militant role ascribed to the Messiah in chs. 11–13. The 400-year reign of the Messiah is an exegetical deduction from the collocation of Gen 15:13 and Ps 90:15. The same figure is found in some rabbinic texts with explicit reference to these biblical texts. The 1,000-year period (millennium) found in Rev 20 similarly arises out of biblical exegesis of Ps 90:4 (see 2 Pet 3:8) applied to the concept of the day of the Lord.

Cf. v. 27 with 6:25; 9:8; 12:34, and see 2 ESD 5:41. Mention of the death of the Messiah (v. 29) is unique to 4 Ezra in Jewish sources. In 2 Apoc. Bar. 30:1 the Messiah is assumed to heaven at the end of the messianic era. According to v. 30 the clock is wound back through the seven days of Gen 1 to the state of the earth in Gen 1:2. Compare 2 Apoc. Bar. 44:9 and Barn. 15:8. The Gen 1 paradigm shapes v. 43 as well. With v. 31 cf. 7:75 ('renew the creation') and see 2 ESD 6:14–16. v. 32 describes the general resurrection. Cf. Dan 12:2; Rev 20:5, 12–13; and for the 'chambers' see 2 ESD 4:35. With the description of the final judgement (v. 29) cf. Dan 7:9 and 1 Enoch 47:3. That 'compassion will pass away' becomes a matter of fierce dispute later in this vision (7:102–15). Cf. the description of hell here with the parable of Dives and Lazarus (Lk 16:19–31) which also presupposes that hell and Paradise are within sight of each other, as does the setting of Wis 5. The earth as we know it will no longer exist so the promise of Gen 8:22 will no longer hold good (7:38–42). See also Zech 14:6–7 and Rev 21:23.

(7:45–74) Second Dialogue This expands out of the positions adopted by the two protagonists in 7:17–24. Again, as in the earlier dialogues, Ezra is not silenced by the account of the glory to come reserved for the righteous because he feels that there is no one, or at best only a few people, righteous enough to qualify for the future age (vv. 45–8). As ever the bugbear is the 'evil heart'. Uriel replies that God is only really interested in those few who are righteous; the rest can go to hell (vv. 49–61)! Ezra then, not unreasonably, asks why all the wicked (among whom he seems to include himself) have been created at all, if their ultimate fate is eternal damnation (vv. 62–9). The substance of v. 48 is dealt with at 2 ESD 3:20–7; for the textual problem in this verse see Hayman (1975: 54 n. 35). The view in v. 46 (see also v. 68; 8:35), that no human being is without sin, is widespread in the OT (2 Kings 8:42; Prov 20:9; Eccl 7:20) and outside it (*Man and his God, ANET* 590). But Ezra's argument here seems to depend on such texts as Ps 90:3–8 and Isa 40:6–8, the grounds for his appeal being the frailty and weakness of human nature. The doctrine of the 'evil heart' gives this OT idea more precision. However, there is not necessarily a contradiction between this verse and the view with which both Ezra and the angel agree—that there will be at least a few righteous people saved for the future world. It is not sinlessness that qualifies people for the next world but the correct attitude to the law (7:72, and esp. 9:10–12). In vv. 49–61 the angel simply accepts what Ezra says about the righteous being few in number, explaining that that is why God has made not one but two worlds—so that they will get their just reward. For the address to the earth in vv. 62–4 see 2 ESD 3:4–5. What the author means here by the 'mind' is difficult to pin down. Myers (1974: 211) translates the Latin *sensus* as 'reason'. Stone (excursus on inspiration, 1990: 119–24) thinks it means something like 'consciousness'. In the role which he has adopted since 7:18 Ezra identifies himself with the wicked (v. 67; and see 8:31). The angel will have to try and stop him doing this (7:76–7; 8:47). v. 74 seems to be designed to forestall Ezra's subsequent attempts to plead for God's mercy on the wicked (7:132–40). The delay in the end is planned, not a sign that God is being or will be patient with sinners.

(7:75–101) The Fate of Souls after Death In this section the tension of the dialogue relaxes and, as in earlier visions (4:33, 44–6; 5:50; 6:11), Ezra lapses into the role of prompter. This allows the angel to launch into a long explanation of the fate of the soul after death, the purpose of which is to forestall Ezra's question whether there is any hope of repentance for the wicked after death, and whether the righteous will be able to intercede on their behalf (7:70–103). The souls are said to pass through three stages: (1) For a period of seven days after death each soul, whether good or bad, is given a foretaste of its fate after the Last Judgement (vv. 75–101). This state is described as 'separation from the body' (7:78, 88, 100). (2) After these seven days the souls depart to their resting-places to await the Last Judgement. Where the souls are located during this waiting period is difficult to discern. 4:35, 41, and 7:32 suggest that they are all alike in Hades; v. 80 could be read to suggest that the wicked souls are left to wander about (ghosts?) while only the righteous go into their chambers. If it is the former, then the author's view of the intermediate state is similar to that found in *1 Enoch* 22 where Sheol is the place where all the dead go to await the Last Judgement, but where moral distinctions are already made and the righteous enjoy bliss while the wicked suffer preliminary punishment. From elsewhere in the text we know that a privileged few of the saints are taken up immediately into heaven (6:26; 14:9, 48)—reflecting the OT stories of the ascensions of Enoch and Elijah and subsequent Jewish expansion of the number of ascenders. (3) At the Last Judgement all the dead are raised and a final separation is made between the righteous and the wicked. The righteous enjoy all the eternal delights described in vv. 88–99 and 8:52–4. It is not expressly stated, though it may be inferred, that the wicked suffer eternal punishment (7:36–7, 84; 9:10–13). 7:97, 125 reflect the belief that after death the risen righteous join the host of heaven/sons of God/stars (Job 38:7). Cf. Dan 12:3; Wis 3:7; *1 Enoch* 104:3; 4 Macc 17:5; *2 Apoc. Bar.* 51:10. This concept of astral immortality, widespread in the ancient world, also lies behind Lk 20:35–6. These views about the soul and its fate in 4 Ezra mark a considerable change from OT teaching. In the OT human beings are regarded basically as animated bodies; they are made from 'the dust of the earth' into which God infuses the life force/breath of life. But by the first century CE many Jews had come to accept both the ideas of the pre-existence of the soul and that souls could live on after death (at least for an interim period) without their bodies. See Wis 3:1; 8:19; 9:11; *2 Enoch* 23:4–5; Josephus, *J.W.* 2:154–8.

(7:102–8:3) A Duel with Texts! In his efforts to avoid the conclusion that only a few will be saved if the test is full compliance with the law, Ezra seeks for alternative ways by which the vast numbers of the wicked might not be shut out of the future age. Could the righteous intercede for the wicked as they have certainly done in this age? Is it possible that God might not judge by strict justice but exercise mercy in line with the characterization of his nature found in Ex 34:6–7? The angel loads his pistol with Deut 30:19 (7:129) and fires off a firm negative to both suggestions (7:104; 8:3).

A dual numbering of the verses from 7:106 to the end of the chapter appears in the Eng. versions. The printed editions of the Vg, on whose numbering system the AV and later Eng. translations draw, all go back ultimately to one MS, the ninth-century Codex Sangermanensis, from which 7:36–105 had been cut out. Since Bensley published (1875; 1895: xii–xiii) what came to be known as 'The Missing Fragment' modern translations have preserved the old and the new numbering systems side by side.

For the intercessions of Abraham and Moses see Gen 18:22–33 and Ex 32:11–14. For the other biblical allusions in 7:107–10 see Josh 7:6–9; 1 Sam 7:9; 12:19–23; 2 Sam 24:17; 1 Kings 8:22–53; 18:42(?); 17:20–1; 2 Kings 19:15–19. It is difficult to reconstruct the text of v. 112 from the versions. The point seems to be that there is a decisive difference between this world and the next, marked primarily by the intermittent presence of God's glory in this world and his permanent presence in the next. His permanent presence dates from the Day of Judgement (7:33, 113); from that point on everyone's fate is sealed. Only before that time is intercession possible. 7:113–15 spells out in detail how 'the day of judgement is decisive' (7:104).

As before in 6:62–9, when confronted with the angel's blank negatives, Ezra moves into lament mode (7:116–26). This preserves the basic psychological motivation of the lament psalms in the OT, namely, to evoke a merciful response from God by depicting one's miserable condition, often acted out by means of the symbol of sackcloth and ashes (cf. 9:38). It might have worked in OT times; it cuts no ice with Uriel! The substance of the lament harks back to the prayer with which this vision began: what is the point of all God's work in creation if nearly all human beings are fated to go to perdition? For 7:118 see 2 ESD 7:46 and 3:20–2. Ezra appears to be making the same move as before: we frail mortals cannot help sinning—it is all Adam's fault. The implication of the angel's words in 7:129 is that he rejects any notion that human freedom to obey the law was affected by the Fall.

7:132–40 is a midrash on Ex 34:6–7, a frequently used literary topos in both biblical and extra-biblical texts. Most of the elements of the biblical text are cited and expanded, but it is highly significant that everything after 'forgiving iniquity and transgression and sin' (Ex 34:7) is left out. The rest of the verse would not have helped Ezra's case in the present context! 8:2 harks back to 7:52–7 with the point of both sets of comparisons being bluntly stated in 8:3. With the angel summarizing the position he has taken throughout, these three verses mark the conclusion of the major dialogue cycle which began in 7:45.

(8:4–62) Two Prayers and a Subsequent Dialogue Yet again, as in 7:62–9 and 116–26, Ezra responds to the angel with a lament based on creation. The same point is made (v. 14) but this time emphasized by an elaborate description of the process of pregnancy and birth. Why such a marvellous process of birth if the end is only death? There follows the so-called Prayer of Ezra which was excerpted from the book and used in many early Christian liturgies (8:19–36). The wording of v. 19*b* is a result of this practice. In this prayer Ezra appeals to God to forgive those who have no store of good works to their credit. The grounds of the appeal in vv. 27–30 are that a few in Israel have been faithful to God. But this conflicts with what Ezra goes on to say in vv. 31–6, themselves not very internally consistent if we compare v. 33 with v. 35. This apparent inconsistency serves a literary purpose for it allows Uriel to pick up the first part of Ezra's prayer but ignore the second (8:37–40). 'Some things . . . rightly' (v. 37) presupposes 'some things incorrectly'. For the textual variant in 8:23 see 2 ESD E. On the issue of the criteria for salvation in vv. 32–3 see 2 ESD 9:7. The idea of a 'treasury of works' laid up for the righteous in heaven (7:77; 8:33, 36) was widespread in Judaism at the time and appears also in the NT (Mt 6:20). For v. 35 see 2 ESD 7:46.

The angel has no answer to the second part of Ezra's plea (8:31–6) and has to resort rather pathetically to claiming that despite appearances God loves his creation better than Ezra does (v. 47). Ezra is rebuked for identifying himself with the wicked. As always when the argument gets too tough for Uriel he resorts to recounting the eschatological bliss laid up for the righteous (vv. 51–4). This strategy comes explicitly to the surface in 9:13. For v. 47 see 2 ESD 4:33–42. vv. 52–4 give a four-teen-phrase summary of the rewards of the righteous—seven positive items (v. 52) and seven deleted negatives (vv. 53–4). Not only is the 'evil root' removed (cf. Ps.-Philo, *Bib. Ant.* 33.3; 1QS 4:20), hence neutralizing one of Ezra's more agonizing complaints, but all the consequences, material and spiritual, of Adam's sin will disappear. v. 62 hints at a theme to be developed at greater length in 12:36–8 and throughout ch. 14. As for the fate of the wicked, Uriel appeals to the concept of free will to justify their damnation (8:56, 59–60).

(8:63–9:25) Concluding Prediction and Dialogue As with the first and second visions (5:1–13; 6:11–28), so this vision draws to an end with Uriel again describing the messianic woes and the Day of Judgement, and claiming that God is just (9:10–12). Ezra remains dissatisfied (9:14–16), and the discussion ends with yet another justification by Uriel of God's actions.

Commentators vary in their understanding of 9:5–6 which is made difficult by differences between the Latin and Syriac texts. The point seems to be that since observably everything has a beginning and an end, so has the world: it begins with the wonders of creation (referring back to 6:1–6, 38–54) and ends with the signs mentioned in 9:1–3. Note in v. 9:7 the criteria for being one of the saved. Stone (1990: 296) comments on this verse that 'while not asserting that these two concepts, faith and works, are identical, we may say they were not very clearly differentiated and are used interchangeably'. This would seem to be justified by 13:23 where 9:7's 'either works *or* faith' becomes 'both works *and* faith'. Nor does there seem to be much difference between 'treasures of faith' (6:5) and 'treasure of works' (7:77; 8:33). Contrast this with Paul's position in the NT (e.g. Rom 3:20, 27–8; Gal 3:10–11). The Pauline view on the issue of justification fails to take account of one vital ingredient in Jewish theology which our text mentions in v. 11, namely, repentance. In Judaism what mat-

ters is one's attitude to the law, not keeping it perfectly. Fully in line with this Uriel states in vv. 10–11 that it is the refusal to acknowledge God and 'scorning' his law which disqualifies human beings from salvation. For a detailed comparison of 4 Ezra and Paul on these issues see Longenecker (1991). 9:8 refers to the messianic age; see 6:25; 7:28; 12:34; 13:48–9.

Ezra's position, like the angel's, remains unchanged throughout this vision (9:15; cf. 7:45–8). He never explicitly accepts the validity of the angel's views, thus legitimizing the feelings of those who sympathize with his problems. See 2 ESD 6:32 and Hayman (1975: 53). Uriel's words in 9:20–2 seem to hint at a scheme at variance with 7:70, namely, that the second world/age to come and the salvation of only a few righteous people was a rescue plan by God, not something determined in advance.

Fourth Vision (9:26–10:59)

This vision serves as a transition from the tense dialogues of the first three visions to the apocalyptic revelations of the last three visions where the author has turned his attention away from the doubts and complaints occasioned by the current situation of his people in order to reaffirm his eschatological hopes. As was nicely observed by Breech, the change of mood in the fourth vision is comparable with that which we find in the lament psalms (Breech 1973: 271). It is possible that the change of mood in these psalms was occasioned by a cultic oracle (see esp. Ps 60:6–8 and Eissfeldt 1966: 113–20). If so, the vision in 10:25–7 performs the same role in 4 Ezra.

(9:26–37) Ezra's Prayer The introduction in vv. 26–8 contains most of the same elements as in those to the previous visions (3:1–3; 5:21–2; 6:35–7), but the change of venue and location are a hint that this vision will not end like the others. In 10:51–4 we discover the reason for the change of location. The main burden of the prayer is a contrast between the law, in all its glory and immutability, and the perishable human vessels who must keep it (9:36–7). Note that, as elsewhere in the book, there is no criticism of the law itself, only of people's inability to keep it. Although the prayer harks back to issues raised earlier in the book, its tone of complaint is considerably muted in comparison to the prayers which begin the first three visions (Longenecker 1995: 63).

(9:38–10:28) Vision of the Mourning Woman The vision does not respond directly to the issues raised by Ezra's prayer, reflecting the fact that the author has come to see that they are irresolvable in this world. In the vision Ezra sees a woman weeping and, when he asks her what her trouble is, she tells him that her only son, conceived after thirty years of barrenness, has just died on his wedding day. At the end of the vision the woman metamorphoses into the vision of a great city. Ezra's speech to the woman in 10:6–17 plays a crucial role in the transition from complaint to hope in 4 Ezra. The complaint is clearly restated in vv. 6–14 ('almost all go to perdition', v. 10), but in vv. 15–16 Ezra turns to give the woman some stern advice. v. 16 foreshadows what is to follow in the fourth to seventh visions. In effect, Ezra's advice to the woman is self-exhortation by the author to himself: what are your mental agonies worth in the context of the total disaster faced after 70 CE by the whole Jewish people? The author draws back from the chasm opened in the first to third visions. If he denies

God's justice, if this fundamental tenet of the OT and Judaism can no longer be affirmed, then all is lost and there is nothing more to hope for. Despite all his doubts he wills to affirm God's justice because he must. His solution to the problem of evil is experiential, not rational (Hayman 1975: 56). The God whom he knows simply cannot be unjust whatever the evidence to the contrary.

Ezra is transformed by the need to do what religious leaders have to do—hold the community together in times of crisis. Cf. the role of Rabbi Ephraim Oshry in the ghetto of Kovno during the Holocaust (Rosenbaum 1976). Ezra's changed role is expressed symbolically by his move from lamenter to comforter. Only then is he, himself, granted the vision which lifts him in the rest of the book into the realm of eschatological affirmation. Note how in 14:13 Ezra is commanded to do what here he did voluntarily and spontaneously—'comfort the lowly among them'. Ezra has also done what previously Uriel advised (8:55; 9:13). 9:39–40 and 10:5 show him taking this advice, but he only does so when faced by the grieving woman. We have already been prepared for this assumption of a leadership role by Ezra (5:16–18). Ezra is now doing his job as Phaltiel had requested. Progressively hereafter he accepts the 'Mosaic role' (12:40–8; 14:27–36).

The woman's 'thirty years' period of barrenness corresponds to the thirty years Israel has spent in exile in Babylon (3:1). The reference to 'Zion, mother of us all' in 10:7 is a literary hint of what is to follow later in the story. For the image cf. Gal 4:26. On the phase in 10:10 'almost all go to perdition' see 7:48 and Hayman (1975: 54 n. 35); also Thompson (1977: 303–10). 'You will receive your son back in due time' (10:16) refers, on the individual level, to the resurrection of the dead; on the symbolic level this represents the descent of the restored Zion from heaven. The events lamented in 10:21–3 fit in well with Josephus' description of the destruction of Jerusalem in 70 CE, in *J.W. b*. However, most of the items are conventional elements belonging to the lament genre; see Lamentations *passim* and 1 Macc 1:36–40; 2:7–13. The intensity of the lament fits in with the observation that part of the answer to Ezra's troubles is to recognize the legitimacy of lamenting (Humphrey 1995: 74). The graphic account of Ezra's experience in 10:25–8 probably relates in some way to the author's own experience of moving from doubt to faith, but cf. Dan 10:7–9 and 1 Enoch 71:11. In 10:27, 42, 44 the RSV's 'an established city' (following the oriental versions) is preferable to the NRSV's 'a city was being built' (following the Latin). The heavenly city/Jerusalem exists already and needs only to be revealed (7:26; 8:53; 10:54; 13:36). Cf. 1 Enoch 90:29, 2 Apoc. Bar. 4:2–7, and the Description of the New Jerusalem texts from Qumran (Martinez 1994: 129–35).

(10:29–59) Interpretation of the Vision and Dialogue with Uriel Uriel interprets the vision so that the grieving woman represents the real Zion, the heavenly Jerusalem which for 3,000 years had no earthly counterpart (vv. 44–5). Her son is the earthly Jerusalem built by Solomon (v. 45). The son's death represents the destruction of Jerusalem in 587 BCE (v. 48). In his vision (10:25–8) Ezra saw the real Zion which exists in heaven and will be revealed in the last times. This reflects the view of the apocalyptists that the events and personnel of the end-time (city, Messiah, immortality, Paradise, etc.) are pre-existent realities which are only finally revealed to human beings in the future age. In the ancient Near East it was generally believed that earthly realities were but pale copies of heavenly originals (see Ex 25:40 and Ps 11:4; Heb 8:5). In apocalyptic a radical change takes place in that it is believed that at the end of time these heavenly originals will come down to earth. Ezra's consolation consists in the evidence of his own eyes that the heavenly Zion exists now.

There is no parallel known to the dating scheme behind the 'three thousand years' of 10:46, nor are any of the dating schemes hinted at in the book (14:11–12, 48 Syriac) consistent with each other (Stone 1990: 337). For 10:56–9 see 2 ESD 4:5–8. Contrast the Description of the New Jerusalem texts from Qumran and Rev 21–2. The theme of restricted apocalyptic secrets will be developed in ch. 14. Ezra is now placed on the same level as Abraham (3:14) and Moses (14:5–6).

Fifth Vision (11:1–12:51)

The eagle vision of chs. 11–12 is cast in the form of an elaborate allegorical prediction of the history of the Roman empire especially as it impacted on the Jewish people (2 ESD C). Such surveys of history are a common genre within the apocalyptic literature; two good examples are Dan 11 and 1 Enoch 85–90. For their authors they served two purposes: to enable them to demonstrate to their audiences that they were indeed living in the 'end of the times', and also to enhance their claims to speak with veracity and authority. If the presumed authors had been able to predict history so accurately before it happened, surely they must be right about the end of history!

The eagle vision is a reapplication for later times of Dan 7, as the author makes clear in 12:11. The beginning of the dream consciously alludes to Dan 7:1–3. The eagle is identified with the fourth kingdom seen by Daniel in his visions (11:39; 12:11). The eagle symbol was used on the standards of the Roman army and Jewish and Christian exegesis had by the first century CE updated Daniel and shifted the interpretation of this kingdom from Greece to Rome. Our author (unlike many later reinterpreters of Daniel) is aware of the fact that his view is not that of Daniel himself (12:12). His language implies that he knows better than Daniel—a claim to inspiration and authority worked out in detail in the Ezra legend of ch. 14. A similar claim is made by the author of the Habakkuk commentary at Qumran (1QpHab 7:1–8—Martinez 1994: 200). The eagle has twelve wings and three heads, and also eight little wings. All commentators are agreed that the eagle symbolizes the Roman empire but the identification of these wings and heads has been much disputed. There seem to be too many wings for the known Roman emperors and usurpers before the author's time. The problem of identifying them is not helped by some divergences between the vision and its interpretation. However, all contemporary commentators agree on the following identifications: the second wing which reigned for a long time (11:13–17; 12:15) is Caesar Augustus, and the three heads are the Flavian emperors Vespasian, Titus, and Domitian. 11:32 and 12:23–4 clearly reflect a Jewish perspective on the Roman rulers (Vespasian and Titus) who destroyed Jerusalem and enslaved the Jews. All the other wings must be, then, the Roman emperors and the pretenders to the throne who lived between Julius Caesar (the first wing) and Domitian (who reigned from 81–96 CE).

The author predicts the appearance of the Messiah (the lion) and the subsequent destruction of the Roman empire in the reign of the third head, Domitian (11:36–46; 12:31–4). There is a bit of a loose end in 12:2, 29–30 with a reference to two little wings, on the explanation of which scholars do not agree. They do not really fit Domitian's two successors Nerva and Trajan. The latter's reign from 98–117 could hardly be said to be 'brief and full of tumult'. So the point where the accurate history stops and the prediction begins seems to be near the end of Domitian's reign, presumably near the middle of the 90s CE.

The chapters can be divided into four sections: (1) The Dream (11:1–12:3a); (2) Ezra's Prayer for Enlightenment (12:3b–9); (3) The Interpretation of the Dream (12:10–39); and (4) A Dialogue between Ezra and the People (12:40–51).

(11:1–12:3a) For the phrase 'rising from the sea' in 11:1 see 2 ESD 13:1–3 and cf. Dan 7:1–3 and Rev 13:1. What is most noticeable about the role of the lion in 11:36–46 is the absence of the use of military force or violence. His function is judicial and his speech to the eagle reads like a legal indictment, a characterization of his role that is continued in the interpretation in 12:31–4. As we shall see, this makes it all the more likely that the militant 'man from the sea' in 13:9–11 has roots in an earlier mythical tradition of cosmic conflict. 11:39 shows that, despite his gloomy view of this world, the author still conceives of God as in charge of human history. 'Laid low the walls' in 11:42 is probably a reference to the Roman destruction of Jerusalem in 70 CE. 11:46 hints at the messianic kingdom; its interpretation in 12:34 alludes to the eschatological timetable in 7:26–44.

(12:3b–9) Ezra's prayer in 12:3b–9 is parallel in structure and function to 13:13b–20; cf. 10:29–37 and Dan 7:15. The seer's reaction to the dream is a conventional element in the genre of the apocalyptic vision. For 12:9 see above on 10:59 (Ezra being placed on the same level as Abraham and Moses).

(12:10–39) For the implied pre-existence of the Messiah in 12:32 see 2 ESD 7:26–44. It is unfortunate here that the reference to the Davidic descent of the Messiah is missing in the Latin version where there seems to be a lacuna in the text; see the translation in the NEB. The textual basis for this belief is actually rather sparse in earlier Jewish texts outside the NT. Knibb claims it is widespread but cites only *Pss. Sol.* 17:23 in support (Coggins and Knibb 1979: 252). However, the image of the lion here does seem to connect the Messiah with David and the tribe of Judah; see Gen 49:9–10 (interpreted messianically in the Targums and rabbinic texts) and Rev 5:5. 12:37–8 adumbrates a theme that will be developed at length in ch. 14. The purpose of the injunction is to explain how a revelation received during the Babylonian Exile remained secret until the end of the first century CE. The authors of other apocalyptic books had to use the same device; see Dan 12:4, 9; 1 Enoch 82:1, 104:11–13; *As. Mos.* 1:16, 10:11–12.

(12:40–51) For Ezra's changed role in 12:40–51 see on 9:38–10:28. 12:47 reveals the purpose for which 4 Ezra was written: to provide consolation and hope for the author's people, to assure them that, in the aftermath of 70, God had not forgotten them. Note that Ezra gives no indication to the people

of what has really been going on while he has been out in the field, thus observing the injunction of v. 38.

Sixth Vision (13:1–58)

This chapter divides into three sections: (1) The dream of the Man from the Sea (Dan 13:1–13a); (2) Ezra's response to the dream (Dan 13:13b–20); and (3) the interpretation of the dream (13:21–58). The dream can likewise be divided into three sections:

(13:1–4) The Origin of the Man v. 1 immediately calls to mind Dan 7:1, and we know from 12:11 that our author consciously intended to update and rewrite Dan 7. By v. 2 we know that this is precisely what is happening here; cf. Dan 7:2. In Daniel the 'great sea' is an allusion to the old creation myth, probably in its Babylonian form (the *Enuma Elish*), in which the god Marduk, armed with the four winds of heaven, attacks Tiamat, the chaos monster and personification of the primeval ocean. So, given this background, we would expect the sea here to be the source of evil as it is in 11:1; Dan 7:3; and Rev 13:1 (also rewriting Daniel). That is why v. 3 comes as such a surprise for, instead of the chaos monster, it is the eschatological hero, the Man, who rises out of the sea. The continuation of the verse makes it quite clear that this figure is being equated with the figure of the Son of Man in Dan 7:13–14; cf. also 1 Enoch 37–71. But what can it mean that he rises 'out of the heart of the sea'? The best explanation is that it symbolizes the victory of the Man over the sea, the image of chaos in the OT. This would parallel YHWH's defeat of Leviathan (Ps 74:12–17; 89:9–10). The subsequent 'flying with the clouds of heaven' also aligns this figure with YHWH, the 'rider on the clouds' (Ps 68:4; 104:3; 18:6–11; Isa 19:1). v. 4 is likewise drawn from the standard imagery used to depict the theophany of YHWH in the OT (Ps 68:2; 97:5; 104:32; Mic 1:4). But the imagery here has deeper roots in ancient Canaanite mythology. 'Rider on the clouds' is Baal's title in the Ugaritic texts, and one of the important roles of Baal is to defeat and trample on Yam (Sea). 4 Ezra 13:1–4 represents the resurgence of myth at the heart of apocalyptic. But here the Man's victory lies before him, not behind him. The great battle against the forces of evil has still to take place. This is precisely the shift discernible as we move from Ps 74 to Isa 27:1. Jews such as the author of our text believed that the forces of chaos had not been defeated at the time of creation; they had come back and ruined God's world. The battle would have to be fought once again but this time with a definitive result.

(13:5–11) Armageddon/The Last Battle The final battle of the forces of evil against the Divine Warrior is an idea as old as the Gog and Magog narrative in Ezek 38–9; cf. Ps 2:1–2; Joel 2:1–11; and Zech 14. vv. 8–11 are full of allusions to the OT traditions of the Holy War and of YHWH's theophany. The effortlessness with which the Man defeats his enemies, the stream of fire he emits, the great storm, etc. are all conventional elements of this tradition; see Ps 97:3; 2 Sam 22:9 || Ps 18:9; Is 11:4. The cosmic mountain (vv. 6–7) is, on one level, an allusion to Dan 2:34, 45. But although the author intended it as a reference to Mt. Zion (13:35–6), behind it lies the ancient Near-Eastern idea of the cosmic mountain, the centre of the earth, the home of the gods. In the Ugaritic texts it is called Zaphon as Zion is in Ps 48:2. Baal has a house built for him on

Zaphon after his victory over Yam. In ancient Israel the king sits on this mountain (Ps 2:6), but in Isa 31:4b the Man's eschatological role here is assigned to the Lord of Hosts.

(13:12–13a) Salvation for the People of God This is the final act in the eschatological drama and it corresponds to Dan 7:22, 27; Rev 20:4. v. 13 picks up some elements of Isaiah which were taken into the apocalyptic tradition; cf. Isa 11:10–12; 49:22–3; 66:18–20, and also Hos 11:10–11. There in v. 13a the original vision ends. It is a crucial text for confirming the correctness of the view that the Son of Man figure in Dan 7 and the NT represents the continuation in another form of a very old Israelite way of picturing YHWH, the Divine Warrior (Emerton 1958; Hayman 1991; 1998).

(13:13b–58) Ezra's Response and the Interpretation of the Dream After a paragraph recording Ezra's response to the dream (for vv. 18–20 see 2 ESD 5:41) there follows a lengthy interpretation extending to the end of the chapter. But the interpretation greatly expands on the dream; it both ignores parts of it and reads into it elements such as the return of the lost ten tribes which have only a very tenuous basis in the original vision. Moreover it is clear that the author does not understand parts of the dream. He has three unsatisfactory attempts to explain why the Man arises from the sea (vv. 25–6, 32, 51–2). All the cosmic phenomena which accompany the Man are reduced to not much more than symbols of the law (v. 38). Hence it looks as though he has incorporated in his work a much older text closer to the world of Daniel and then provided a kind of midrash or expansionary exegesis of it, both updating it and infusing it with his own concerns (Stone 1990: 396–400, and *contra* Casey 1979: 124–9). In the interpretation the supernatural and mythological overtones of the Man are downplayed and he looks more like the Messiah pictured in chs. 7, 11, and 12. However, he is never called the Messiah in this chapter; rather he has the title son/servant of God like the Israelite king (vv. 32, 37, 52: cf. Ps 2:7; 89:26–7; and see 2 ESD 7:28).

v. 24 refers, like vv. 48–9, to the 400-year messianic era; see 2 ESD 7:28. vv. 37–8 refer to the denunciation of the Messiah's enemies already mentioned in 12:32–3, not the Last Judgement which God conducts (7:33). The purpose of spinning out the long tale of the lost ten tribes (vv. 39–47), which has such a tenuous base in the dream (13:12–13), is to set them up as a model for the author's contemporaries (vv. 41–2). Josephus, writing at about the same time as 4 Ezra, also knows of this legend (*Ant.* 11 § 133). The figure of nine and a half tribes in the oriental versions of v. 40 is found also in *2 Apoc. Bar.* The variant readings derive from disagreements as to how much of, or whether, the tribe of Levi went into exile with the other northern tribes. 'Arzereth' (v. 45) is derived from the Hebrew for 'another land'; see end of v. 40. vv. 57–8 show how the revelation of the visions in chs. 11–13 has transformed the anguished Ezra of the first three visions in the way that, presumably, the author hoped his work would impact on his contemporaries.

Seventh Vision (14:1–48)

This chapter is based upon the Jewish legend, well-known to the early Christian fathers, that Ezra, like a kind of second Moses, restored the law to Israel after it had been destroyed

along with Jerusalem by the Babylonians. The author has adapted this legend to further his own purposes of stressing the equal antiquity, inspiration, and authority of the secret apocalyptic writings alongside the publicly known and accepted books of the Old Testament. The chapter divides into three main sections: (1) A theophany of God to Ezra out of a bush which is deliberately modelled on the experience of Moses (14:1–26); (2) Ezra's last address to the people (14:27–36); and (3) the climax of the book recording Ezra's supernatural inspiration which enables him to dictate, to five scribes over a period of forty days, ninety-four books, of which twenty-four are the canonical books of the Old Testament and seventy the corpus of apocalyptic writings (14:27–48).

The theophany in 14:1–26 divides into an introduction setting the scene (vv. 1–2), the address to Ezra (vv. 3–18), Ezra's response (vv. 19–22), and God's instructions to Ezra (vv. 23–6).

(14:1–18) The parallel with Moses is sustained by describing what happens here as a waking experience in which God deals directly with Ezra; Uriel has disappeared from the scene (vv. 1–2). In vv. 3–6 the author rewrites Ex 3 and locates Moses within the esoteric tradition to which he clearly feels that he himself belongs. This picture of Moses as a secret apocalyptist appears elsewhere in such earlier works as *Jubilees* and the *Assumption of Moses.* The author of 4 Ezra traces the tradition as far back as Abraham (v. 14); other authors took it back to Enoch or even as far as Adam (*Adam and Eve*, 50:1–2; 51:3–9). Other references in 4 Ezra to this esoteric tradition are 9:4; 12:37–8; and 14:26. Ch. 14 of 4 Ezra is the clearest statement we have of how the 'wise men' who wrote and preserved the apocalyptic texts saw their undertaking in relation to the overt biblical tradition. vv. 8 and 13 show our author aligning his book with this esoteric tradition. For the reference to the pre-existent Messiah in v. 9 see 2 ESD 7:28.

vv. 10–12 set out a kind of eschatological timetable. It is not certain that they were originally part of the text since the Syriac and Armenian versions leave out vv. 11–12 entirely. Even if they were there originally, the text has suffered badly from scribal attempts to revise the timetable. Violet (1924: 192) has argued convincingly that the Ethiopic has preserved the original division of the times into ten parts with nine and a half already passed. For the veiled hint here and especially in v. 18b that the world will soon come to an end see 2 ESD 4:26. vv. 14–15 provide reinforcement from the mouth of God himself for the injunctions of the angel in 6:34 and 7:16. Through them the reader is addressed: ignore the inglorious past and the dismal present; look to the future for hope!

(14:19–26) develop the claim for Ezra's authority based on the parallel with Moses. Like Moses he has to separate himself from the people for forty days (Ex 24:18) while the command in v. 26 parallels that to Moses in v. 6. The forty-day period is crucial for understanding what is going on in this chapter. If we add up all the indications of time for the events recorded from the beginning of the book to this point it comes to forty days (Stone 1990: 373–4). The reader thereby receives a hint that 4 Ezra itself is part of the secret revelation. Jesus' forty-day sojourn in the wilderness represents the same sort of claim to an authority like that of Moses (Mk 1:13 and par.). Ezra's claim to authority is also bolstered by the reference to inspiration by the holy spirit in v. 22. Two images are used to illustrate the

experience of inspiration: 'lighting the lamp of understanding' in Ezra's heart (v. 25) and the cup of fiery liquid (14:38–
40). See the excursus on inspiration in Stone (1990: 119–24).

(14:27–36) For the function of this speech in the book as a
whole see above on 9:38–10:28; cf. 12:40–51. The contrast
with the way Ezra depicts the salvation history in ch. 3 could
not be more clear.

(14:37–48) Here we come to the climax of the book. The
commands given in 14:23–6 are carried out. The five scribes,
like Ezra inspired by God, copy out all the ninety-four books
(12:42). The phrase 'using characters that they did not know'
refers to the square Aramaic script which replaced the old
Hebrew (Phoenician) script after the Exile (b. Sanh. 21b). At
the end of the forty days Ezra is told to make public the twenty-
four books but to keep back the seventy to be read only by the
wise. The scale of the author's claims for the authority of the
esoteric books is noteworthy—'for in them is the spring of
understanding, the fountain of wisdom, and the river of
knowledge' (v. 47). Only the wise understand these books
and only they really explain what the overt biblical tradition
is about and what God is doing and will do in the world. By
implication their authority exceeds that of the publicly known
and acknowledged biblical books. Beneath the cover of his
pseudonym our author is claiming greater authority for what
he says than for any other biblical figure. We have already seen
in 12:12 a striking example of his assumed superiority over
biblical figures when he blithely tells us that Daniel misunderstood his vision of the four world empires.

The chapter concludes with an account of Ezra's assumption to heaven which was cut out of the Latin version when
chs. 15 and 16 were added, but preserved in the oriental
versions. 14:9 shows that something like the Syriac text in
the margin of the NRSV originally concluded the book. But
this too is an overt claim to inspired authority. The Bible states
that Enoch and Elijah were assumed into heaven and by the
first century this was claimed also for Moses. A far more
important figure such as our author makes of Ezra must also
have been assumed into heaven. So we are assured that he was.

2 Esdras 15–16 (= 6 Ezra)

These chapters are composed of two main types of material:
(1) apocalyptic predictions of political, social, and natural
upheavals and disasters (15:1–16:34); and (2) exhortation of
the righteous to remain faithful in the face of persecution
(16:35–78).

(15:1–63) The text begins with the commission of the prophet
who, being unnamed, must be presumed to be Ezra (vv. 1–4).
Behind the long denunciation that follows scholars have seen
allusions in vv. 12–13 to a great famine in Alexandria at the
time of the Emperor Gallienus (260–8 CE), and in vv. 28–34 to
the political upheavals of the period 259–67 in Asia. In the
latter section the 'dragons of Arabia' have been identified as
the Palmyrenes under Odenathus who prevented the Sassa-
nian King Shapur I (the Carmonians of v. 30) from detaching
Asia from the Roman empire. The name Carmonians comes
from Carmania (Kirman), the southern province of the
Parthian empire. v. 33 could be an allusion to the death of
Odenathus in 267. vv. 46–63 are seen by Myers (1974: 351–2)
as a denunciation of Odenathus's wife Zenobia who for a brief

while took advantage of Roman weakness to establish Palmyr-
ene hegemony over the eastern empire. These allusions are
the strongest evidence we have for dating 6 Ezra sometime
after 268 CE.

(16:1–78) Like most of the material in ch. 15, the apocalyptic
woes in vv. 1–34 consist mainly of a mosaic of material taken
from the OT prophets. Similar material can be found in the
'messianic woes' sections in 4 Ezra (5:1–13; 6:18–34) and in the
NT (Mk 13 and par.). The exhortation section in vv. 35–78 has a
marked tone of apocalyptic urgency (v. 52). Not much compassion is expressed for those who fail to meet the test (vv. 77–8),
just as in the earlier section the rule of 'an eye for an eye'
prevails (15:21).

REFERENCES

Bensley, R. L. (1875), The Missing Fragment of the Latin Translation of the
   Fourth Book of Ezra (Cambridge: Cambridge University Press).
—— (1895), The Fourth Book of Ezra, with an introduction by M. R.
   James, Texts and Studies, 3/2 (Cambridge: Cambridge University
   Press).
Bergren, T. A. (1990), Fifth Ezra: The Text, Origin and Early History,
   Septuagint and Cognate Studies, 25 (Atlanta: Scholars Press).
Box, G. H. (1912), The Ezra Apocalypse (London: Isaac Pitman & Sons).
Breech, E. (1973), 'These Fragments I Have Shored Against My Ruins:
   The Form and Function of 4 Ezra', JBL 92: 267–74.
Casey, M. (1979), Son of Man: The Interpretation and Influence of Daniel
   7 (London: SPCK).
Coggins, R. J., and Knibb, M. A. (1979), The First and Second Books of
   Esdras, Cambridge Bible Commentary on the NEB (Cambridge:
   Cambridge University Press).
Collins, J. J. (1995), The Scepter and the Star: The Messiahs of the Dead
   Sea Scrolls and other Ancient Literature, B. Reference Library (New
   York: Doubleday).
Eissfeldt, O. (1966), The Old Testament: An Introduction (Oxford: Basil
   Blackwell).
Emerton, J. A. (1958), 'The Origin of the Son of Man Imagery', JTS
   9: 225–42.
Essler, P. F. (1994), 'The Social Function of 4 Ezra', JSNT 53: 99–123.
Grabbe, L. L. (1981), 'Chronography in 4 Ezra and 2 Baruch', SBL
   Seminar Papers, ed. K. H. Richards (Missoula, Mont.: Scholars
   Press), 49–63.
—— (1989) 'The Social Setting of Early Jewish Apocalypticism', JSP 4:
   27–47.
Hayman, A. P. (1973), The Disputation of Sergius the Stylite Against a
   Jew, CSCO 338–9.
—— (1975), 'The Problem of Pseudonymity in the Ezra Apocalypse',
   JSJ 6: 47–56.
—— (1976), 'Rabbinic Judaism and the Problem of Evil', SJT 29: 461–
   76.
—— (1984), 'The Fall, Freewill and Human Responsibility in Rabbinic Judaism', SJT 37: 13–22.
—— (1991), 'Monotheism—A Misused Word in Jewish Studies', JJS
   42: 1–15.
—— (1998), 'The Man from the Sea in 4 Ezra 13', JJS 49: 1–17.
Humphrey, E. M. (1995), The Ladies and the Cities: Transformation and
   Apocalyptic Identity in Joseph and Asenath, 4 Ezra, the Apocalypse and
   the Shepherd of Hermas, JSP Suppl. Ser. 17 (Sheffield: Sheffield
   Academic Press).
Kraft, R. A. (1986), 'Towards Assessing the Latin Text of "5 Ezra": The
   "Christian" Connection', HTR 79: 158–69.
Longenecker, B. W. (1991), Eschatology and the Covenant: A Comparison
   of 4 Ezra and Romans 1–11 (JSNTSup 57 (Sheffield: Sheffield Aca-
   demic Press).

—— (1995), *2 Esdras* (Sheffield: Sheffield Academic Press).

Martinez, F. G. (1994), *The Dead Sea Scrolls Translated: The Qumran Texts in English* (Leiden: Brill).

Moore, G. F. (1927), *Judaism* (2 vols.; Cambridge, Mass: Harvard University Press).

Myers, J. M. (1974), *I and II Esdras*, AB 42.

O'Neill, J. C. (1991), 'The Desolate House and the New Kingdom of Israel: Jewish Oracles of Ezra in 2 Esdras 1–2', in *Templum Amicitae: Essays on the Second Temple presented to Ernst Bammel*, ed. W. Horbury, JSOTSup 48 (Sheffield: Sheffield Academic Press), 226–36.

Rosenbaum, I. J. (1976), *The Holocaust and Halakah* (New York: Ktav).

Segal, A. F. (1977), *Two Powers in Heaven: Early Rabbinic Reports About Christianity and Gnosticism*, SJLA (Leiden: Brill).

Simon, M. (1986), *Verus Israel*, trans. H. McKeating, Littman Library (Oxford: Oxford University Press); original edn. (Paris: 1964).

Stanton, G. N. (1977), '5 Ezra and Matthean Christianity in the Second Century', *JTS* 28: 67–83.

Stone, M. E. (1990), *Fourth Ezra*, Hermeneia: A Critical and Historical Commentary on the Bible (Minneapolis: Fortress).

Thompson, A. L. (1977), *Responsibility for Evil in the Theodicy of IV Ezra*, SBL dissertation series 29 (Missoula, Mont.: Scholars Press).

Violet, B. (1924), *Die Apokalypsen des Esra und des Baruch in deutscher Gestalt*, GCS 32 (Leipzig: Hinrichs).

54. 4 Maccabees   DAVID J. ELLIOTT

A. Introduction. 4 Maccabees is a Jewish book vehemently opposed to the oppression and suppression of Jews in the Graeco-Roman world whilst simultaneously exhibiting some of the latter's most distinctive features. The work was well established in Christian circles some time before Eusebius wrote his *Church History*, where he refers to it under the title 'On the Supremacy of Reason' (*Hist. eccl.* 3.10.6). It can be divided into three main sections: a prologue (1:1–3:19), a narrative of the martyrdoms of the priest Eleazar and the seven brothers and their mother, and finally a third section from 17:2 that is a eulogy for the martyrs. This last section ends at 17:22, and the remainder of the book appears to be an addition to the original.

B. Outline.

Introduction and the Purpose for Writing (1:1–3:19)
  Outline of the Author's Intentions (1:1–12)
  Discourse on Reason (1:13–35)
  Reason and the Law (2:1–24)
  The Ability of Reason to Conquer Emotions (3:1–19)
Narrative of the Martyrdoms (3:20–17:1)
  Punishment and Deliverance of Apollonius (3:20–4:14)
  Antiochus' Treatment of the Jews (4:15–26)
  Antiochus' Conversation with the Priest Eleazar (5:1–38)
  Eleazar's Steadfastness under Torture (6:1–35)
  Panegyric on Eleazar (7:1–23)
  Antiochus' Conversation with the Seven Brothers (8:1–9:9)
  The Torture of the Seven Brothers (9:10–12:19)
  Panegyric on the Seven Brothers (13:1–14:10)
  The Mother Unwaveringly Sacrifices Herself (14:11–17:1)
The Martyrs as Examples (17:2–22)
  Panegyric on the Mother (17:2–6)
  The Importance of the Martyrs' Sacrifice (17:6–22)
The Martyrs' Faith is at One with the Faith of their Forefathers (17:23–18:23)

C. Sources. 1. Two major sources can be cited for the book of 4 Maccabees. The narrative part is clearly an embellishment on 2 Maccabees. 4 Macc 5–7 is an expanded version of 2 Macc 6:18–31; the same can be said of 4 Macc 8–12 in relation to 2 Macc 7, while the historical preamble in 2 Macc 3:6–11 has been expanded in 4 Macc 3:20–4:26. These transformations have been achieved in two main ways: as Breitenstein (1976) has noticed, by means of characterization via the construction of speeches; secondly by didactic insertions to link the main

illustrative narrative to the introduction. Without these two devices the narrative in 4 Maccabees would even more closely resemble that of 2 Maccabees.

2. The second major source is Plato's *Gorgias*. When 4 Maccabees embroidered the martyrdom of Eleazar he equated it to the death of Socrates. Eleazar, like Socrates, is controlled by his allegiance to his previous career and refuses to be swayed by an ultimate weakness. As in the case of Socrates, there are no supernatural interventions at the end. Both are old men revered as teachers by their followers, and for that reason mistrusted by the authorities who regard their teachings as suspect. They cling to their systems of thought and treat with disdain the option of extending their lives by denying their prior teachings.

D. Authorship, Provenance, Date, and Occasion. 1. Authorship. 4 Maccabees is clearly a Jewish book written by a Jew for Jews. There are not only several references to figures from the OT (e.g. 2:2, 17, 19; 14:20; 16:3, 20–1), but in 4:20 there is an explicit reference to the citadel in Jerusalem, 'of our native land'. Whether the book was read orally, or by individuals in private, the book assumes the reader will have previous knowledge of its author's work. The author implies the existence of such works when he says in 1:12b: 'as my custom is, I shall begin by stating my main principle, and then I shall turn to their story, giving glory to the all-wise God'. This appears to indicate that the recipients can be assured the book is authentic because it exhibits the same style as his previous works.

2. Provenance. The reference in 4:20 to 'our native land' rules out Palestine as a place of composition. Other centres such as Alexandria and Athens are possible, but the strongest candidate is Antioch. The most immediate indicator is the person of the arch-villain Antiochus IV Epiphanes, who naturally had a close connection with his capital city of Antioch. John Chrysostom testifies that the Christians believed the tomb of the Maccabean martyrs to be situated at Antioch, in the quarter of the Kerateion, near the synagogue (*Fourth Homily on the Maccabean Martyrs*).

3. Ignatius of Antioch sent seven epistles from Antioch *en route* to Rome where he was martyred in 107 CE. He thought in the same sacrificial terms as the Jew responsible for 4 Maccabees. Perhaps the most striking example is his use of the Greek word *antipsychon*. Ignatius uses the word (*Smyrn.* 1.2; *Eph.* 21.1) to express the idea of ransom, which is mirrored in its use in 4 Maccabees. The word is exceptionally rare, and appears in neither the LXX nor the NT, though it does appear twice in 4 Maccabees (6:29; 7:21). It is not unlikely that the Ignatian letters and 4 Maccabees are related. Both are concerned with the idea of martyrdom, use the rare word *antipsychon*, and display a direct and vivid style. Due to the rifts in Antioch between Jews and Christians, and the fact that none of Ignatius' letters remained in Antioch, a common source may be the best solution. This may also explain the abundance of sea imagery found in 7:1; 13:6–7; and 15:31.

4. Date. For Christians to have appropriated the work from Judaism, the book must have been extant in Jewish circles at a time when the two groups had cordial relations. The most desirable date would be a time when the majority of Christians still formed a Jewish sect. Incidentally, nowhere in the ancient world would the Christians be in a better position to appropriate the work than in Antioch. Acts 11:19–20 states that the church in Antioch was second only to Jerusalem. The main evidence for dating the book is the title assigned to Apollonius in 4:2: 'governor of Syria, Phoenicia, and Cilicia' (Bickerman 1945). There was only a single short period in early imperial Rome when Cilicia was associated with Syria for administrative purposes: 18–54 CE. There is no convincing reason why this title should be given to Apollonius rather than the one given in 2 Macc 4:4: 'governor of Coelesyria and Phoenicia', unless it was written in these years. Within this period there are two particular moments when the book may have been written. Three sources tell of angry Jewish reaction to Caligula's reign (38–41 CE), especially concerning the proposed erection of his statue in the Jerusalem Temple. Malalas chronicled in 39–40 that the animosity between Jews and Greeks in Antioch was at flashpoint (see also Philo, *Leg. ad Gaium*, and Jos. *Ant.* 18.8). The initial impetus for protests was probably at the seat of the governor himself: Antioch. The narrative of 4 Maccabees would have been quite pertinent at this juncture. The Jews are here exhorted not to compromise their faith, but to imitate their forefathers in defying the oppressive power.

5. Another contemporary allusion may be found in 4:15: 'When King Seleucus died, his son Antiochus Epiphanes succeeded to the throne, an arrogant and terrible man'. The author's source, 2 Maccabees, states correctly that Antiochus was Seleucus' brother. This is usually dismissed as an authorial error, but it is more likely that an author who is not afraid to use allusions is employing the same device again, perhaps with reference to the Roman emperor of his own time. In the period 18–54 CE, there were four emperors. Neither Caligula nor Claudius was the son of his predecessor, but Tiberius and Nero were. Both their predecessors had adopted them, and were their stepfathers. In Nero's case he came to the throne late in 54 CE, the year in which the governor's title reverted. Besides this, the case for Tiberius' reign is very strong. His predecessor Augustus was tolerant towards the Jews, as is demonstrated by the edict he promulgated, recorded by Josephus (Ant. 16.6.2). Tacitus and Suetonius similarly maintain his benevolence towards Jews (see e.g. Suetonius' *Augustus*, 2.93). In a striking contrast the same three authors describe how Tiberius disliked the Jews. The first persecution of Jews began when the Jews in Rome were expelled in 19 CE: four thousand were shipped to Sardinia where they were 'employed in suppressing brigandage' (Tac. *Ann.* 2.85). In add-

ition Josephus reports Tiberius' incitement of Jewish feelings in Jerusalem itself, when through Pilate he introduced effigies of the Caesar (*J.W.* 2.9.2). It is clear that Tiberius had an axe to grind against the Jews and other so-called mystery cults. The reign of Tiberius therefore may provide the most congenial backdrop to the writing of 4 Maccabees.

6. Occasion. The majority opinion prefers the idea that 4 Maccabees was written for oral delivery at an annual festival in memory of the deaths of the Maccabean martyrs, probably at the site of their tombs. However the book is of such a philosophical nature that it makes more sense if it were read in private where the terms could be inwardly digested rather than speedily passed over in speech. Commentators have pointed to 3:19 and 1:10 as the best proof that it was prepared for oral delivery on a day of commemoration. The Greek text of 3:19 reads: *ēdē de kai ho kairos hēmas epi tēn apodeixin tēs historias tou sōphronos logismou.* Hadas (1954) translated this passage: 'But the season now summons us to the demonstration of the theme of temperate reason.' Hadas claimed that 'the season' refers to a specific time of the year, but a better rendering of *kairos* may be 'time', referring to contemporary events. Whichever view is accepted will dictate the importance attributed to difficult parts of the book's narrative. The natural corollary of the commemoration theory is that the arguments put forward in 1:1–3:19 and 17:2–22 are subordinate to the narrative describing the martyrdoms. However, the author claims the narrative is an illustration of his ideas, and is subsidiary to the rest of the book: 'I could prove to you from many and various examples that reason is dominant over the emotions, but I can demonstrate it best from the noble bravery of those who died for the sake of virtue, Eleazar and the seven brothers and their mother' (1:7–8). By the author's own admission the narrative supplements the argument and not vice versa. If the argument is the main focus, it is unwise to assume that the book was written for an annual commemoration of the martyrs.

E. Theological Points of Interest. 1. The author of 4 Maccabees uses philosophy to further his arguments. If philosophical Jewish texts of this period were graded on a line of philosophical sophistication with Philo Judaeus at one end and the Wisdom of Solomon at the other, 4 Maccabees would sit half-way along. Whilst much of the theology of 4 Maccabees is inextricably bound up with its philosophy, certain areas remain untouched. These are the classical theological areas of eschatology, salvation, and atonement, the latter being the linchpin for the whole narrative. Atonement in ancient Jewish and Christian literature is occasionally dominated by the debate between propitiation and expiation, and 4 Maccabees has much to offer in this area. Three short texts in 4 Maccabees provide the best way to understand the theology of the author as a whole.

2. (4:10–14) A Case of Gentile Propitiation. This passage is essentially derived from 2 Macc 3:22–34. The starkest change is that the account in 4 Maccabees is considerably shorter and concerns Apollonius, not Heliodorus. Despite this, the eschatological element is still present and this is essential to the episode as a whole for it ushers in the manifestation of God's power to earth in order to confront Israel's enemy. Apollonius is all but dead at the hands of the heavenly host when he begs 'the Hebrews to pray for him and propitiate the wrath of the heavenly army' (v. 11). The idea of propitiation expressed here is important for the theology of 4 Maccabees. Of primary significance is the Greek word used to describe this form of atonement: *exeumenisōntai*, from the verb *eumenizō* (cf. the Eumenides, Latin Furies). This form of the verb is in the third person plural (to agree with the plural Hebrews) aorist subjunctive. With *hopōs*, it is clearly a purpose clause, but the voice used is middle. It is apparent from the narrative that in the process of propitiation, Apollonius can play no part but must ask the Hebrews to propitiate the wrath of their God on his behalf. In the author's view, the Gentiles have no means of contact with the Jewish God, but rather any petition must come from the Jews. By using *exeumenisōntai* the author is diverging from the mother passage in 2 Macc 3:33 where the common word *hilasmos* is used. 4 Macc reserves the concept of *hilastērion* for 17:22 (see 4 MACC E.4). Here is a distinct dichotomy between Jew and Gentile in the mind of the author; these two groups are respectively represented by expiation and propitiation. It is clear that in Jewish thought the word *hilastērion* was not synonymous with *exeumenisōntai*. The author of 4 Maccabees is making a distinction between propitiation that pertains to Gentiles, and expiation that is reserved for Jews. Another observation on this passage reveals that in comparison to 2 Macc 3:32, Onias does not sacrifice but prays for the life of the Greek. This points towards practice in the Diaspora rather than the homeland.

3. (6:27–9) Eleazar's Atonement for the Nation. In this death-scene of Eleazar, attention is drawn to the salvific nature of the shedding of blood. This is reminiscent of the sacrificial language found throughout the HB where blood played such an important part (Isa 52:13–53:12; Lev 23:27–8). The portrayal of the martyrdom of Eleazar was intended as a vicarious sacrifice

along the lines of the Day of Atonement ritual. Eleazar says, 'make my blood their purification, and take my life in exchange for theirs' (v. 29). It is the shedding of blood that seems to be the guarantee of the Jews' purification and expiation.

4. (17:20–2) Martyrdom and Expiation. As in 6:29 *antipsychon* is used in v. 21 to express the idea of 'ransom'. The blood motif reappears here in connection with 'their death as an atoning (*hilastērion*) sacrifice' (v. 22). Through their deaths the martyrs were able to pardon the sins of all Israel as well as themselves. They achieved this by not compromising their faith, but instead living their lives according to the law and by reasoning through divine wisdom. Encapsulated in these three verses is the kernel of the author's earlier assertion: 'reason is sovereign over the emotions' (1:1b). These verses, with 6:27–9, also express the three essential tenets of Judaism: the Jewish belief in God, their election, and their partaking of the covenant. While they are elect, Apollonius must ask the Jews to intercede for him. Even when they do intervene he does not receive the full pardon of God, but merely a temporary reprieve. The Jews propitiated the wrath of God for Apollonius, but they themselves were able to effect expiation through these acts of vicarious suffering.

REFERENCES

Bickerman, E. (1945), 'The Date of the Fourth Book of Maccabees', in *Louis Ginzberg: Jubilee Volume on the Occasion of his Seventieth Birthday* (New York: American Academy for Jewish Research).
Breitenstein, U. (1976), *Beobachtungen zu Sprache: Stil und Gedankengut des Vierten Makkabäerbuchs* (Basle: Schwabe).
Hadas, M. (1954), *The Third and Fourth Books of Maccabees* (New York: Harper).

55. Essay with Commentary on Post-Biblical Jewish Literature

PHILIP S. ALEXANDER

INTRODUCTION

This anthology offers selections from post-biblical Jewish texts which are not dealt with elsewhere in the Commentary. The Jewish texts that were accepted as canonical or deutero-canonical by the synagogue and the church are only a portion of the Jewish literature that has survived from antiquity. The non-canonical literature is of the utmost importance in understanding early Judaism and in putting the Bible into its historical context.

The anthology is arranged according to very broad genres, Bible interpretation, law, apocalyptic, wisdom, hymns and prayers, rules of religious associations, and hagiography, which often cut across the extant texts, so that some texts will be found quoted under more than one genre. The comments appended to the extracts in the Anthology proper are intended to elucidate only the passage quoted. More general discussion of the texts from which the passages have been taken is given in the discussion of the Major Genres which

precedes the Anthology: a system of cross-references leads the reader from one section to the other.

Most of the texts included in the anthology were written in the Second Temple period, but not all. Also found here are selections from early rabbinic literature, composed mainly between the third and sixth centuries CE. This literature has been included because, though written later, it contains early material and is often cited in discussions of the earlier texts. Students of the OT, the Apocrypha and Pseudepigrapha, and the NT should have at least a nodding acquaintance with the rich and important rabbinic texts, while bearing their later date and the dangers of anachronism in mind. They should also bear in mind that many Second Temple period texts survive only in much later versions, often translated into other languages. Even when there are good grounds for believing that a given text originated in Second Temple times, it may be well-nigh impossible to be sure of its Second Temple form.

Strictly speaking the only absolutely primary evidence for Jewish religious literature of the Second Temple period is the Dead Sea scrolls, but it would be extreme to confine our study to the scrolls and ignore the other Jewish texts that have survived from antiquity, however problematic their transmission.

The Introduction to the Apocrypha (INTRO.APOC) provides the wider historical setting of the texts excerpted in the anthology. Bibliographical information on the texts will be indicated at the appropriate points and expanded in the References. A more general bibliography on the literature will be found in the Main Bibliography.

The texts have all been newly translated for the anthology (though existing renderings were gratefully consulted) in order to embody the latest research, and to ensure maximum intelligibility and evenness of style.

MAJOR GENRES

A. Bible Interpretation. 1. All texts require interpretation, but Scripture, since it contains the words of the living God, requires it more than most. Scripture is created by canonization which inevitably engenders a secondary literature of commentary. Much of the literature of Second-Temple Judaism can be loosely classified as interpretation of Scripture. The interpretation was presented in a variety of literary forms.

Commentary

2. There were commentaries in the strict sense of the term, which took a section of Scripture and worked more or less systematically through it, quoting phrases or verses and glossing them with explanations. The earliest representatives of this subgenre, whose basic form is lemma (i.e. biblical quotation) followed by comment, are the Qumran Pesharim (Anthology (ANTH A.I)). Written in Hebrew, the Pesharim take certain biblical texts and find in them predictions of events in the Pesharist's own times, particularly events affecting his own religious community. He treats the words of the biblical prophets as a code which can be deciphered only by inspired exegesis (1QpHab 2:8–10; 7:4–5). Hence his description of this mode of interpretation as *pēsher*—a technical term derived from the interpretation of enigmatic dreams (cf. Akkadian *pašaru*, 'to interpret a dream'; Dan 4:6, 9). This type of fulfilment-exegesis was adopted by the early Christians and probably also by other eschatologically oriented groups in early Judaism. The 'searching of the Scriptures', undertaken by the post-Resurrection church in order to integrate the death of Jesus, and the events that followed it, into God's purposes as revealed by the prophets was largely a programme of pesher-exegesis (cf. Lk 24:25–7, 44–8). Pesher-style exegesis sometimes occurs also in the later rabbinic Midrashim. The Pesher Habakkuk, though palaeographically dating from the late first century BCE (comparatively late in the history of the Dead Sea community), is probably one of the earliest of the Qumran Pesharim. (Text García Martínez and Tigchelaar (1997: i. 11–21); tr.: Vermes (1997: 478–85); commentaries: Brownlee (1979); Horgan (1979: 10–55).)

3. For the Pesharists the key to biblical prophecy lay in the history of their own times. For Philo of Alexandria (c.20 BCE–

c.50 CE), however, a major representative of Hellenistic Judaism, the key to Scripture lay in the writings of Plato. Moses and Plato, he believed, were fundamentally saying the same thing: Plato had almost the status of an inspired prophet; he was 'Moses writing in Attic Greek'. Philo, who seems to have known the Bible only in Greek translation, composed in highly sophisticated Greek two great series of interpretations of the Torah of Moses, the Exposition and the Allegory, in which he expounded the text in the light of Platonic philosophy. Neither of these is now complete and their original extent is unclear. The Allegory is largely in the lemma plus comment form, whereas the Exposition comprises a series of discursive exegetical essays, which may go back to the style of lecturing that Philo used in his school. In addition he seems to have written a series of notes on Scripture in the catechetical form of question and answer (his *Questions on Genesis* and *Exodus* have been preserved in Armenian). This was a type of exegesis widely practised in the Greek schools. In order to achieve his exegetical ends, Philo, like the Qumran Pesharists, had to treat the text of Scripture as being, at times, in code: there is a deeper meaning than appears on the surface. This method of reading texts, which was well known in the Greek world (where it was applied especially to Homer), was called *allegorēsis*, and the reading which resulted from it *allegoria*. ANTH A.2 quotes an extract from Philo's *On the Creation of the World*. For text and tr. see Colson and Whitaker (1971: i. 6–137); tr. alone: Yonge (1993: 3–24). For introductions to Philo see Sandmel (1979); Runia (1990); Siegert (1996: 162–89).

4. The most extensive and intellectually impressive corpus of Bible commentary in early Judaism emerged from the rabbinic schools of Palestine between the third and seventh centuries CE. This corpus, written in rabbinic Hebrew, embodies a close and endlessly inventive engagement with the biblical text, the purpose of which was to demonstrate that the Bible supported the rabbinic world-view, particularly as expressed in the Mishnah (c.200 CE), the law-code which served as the manifesto of the rabbinic party (see further Major Genres (MAJ GEN B.II)). The most general term for this style of exegesis is 'midrash', and the commentaries that embody it are known as Midrashim. The rabbis, to a degree unparalleled in early Judaism, believed that the text of Scripture is polysemic, that is to say, it contains multiple levels of meaning, all of which are simultaneously true. Thus they will sometimes interpret a text according to its simple, surface meaning; at other times they will find hidden in it allegorical, or homiletic, or even mystical senses. They divided the text of Scripture into two broad categories: aggadah (narrative) and halakah (law). Midrash aggadah could be freer and more fanciful than midrash halakah, though there was a strong tendency to insist that the simple sense (the *pešat*) should always be given primacy, and that no one should attempt to disclose meanings in Scripture that are contrary to halakah.

5. By the early Middle Ages the rabbinic schools had produced commentaries on almost the whole of the HB. The most worked parts of the Scripture are the Pentateuch, and, perhaps somewhat surprisingly, the Song of Songs. A classic example of a rabbinic Midrash is the *Mekilta of Rabbi Ishmael* (ANTH A.3), a commentary on Exodus that dates in its present form to no earlier than the 3rd century CE, but which traditionally is attributed to the school of the early 2nd century CE

Palestinian scholar Rabbi Ishmael. (Text and tr.: Lauterbach (1933–5); introduction: Stemberger (1996: 251–7); see further Neusner (1988).) Though the Midrashim were produced long after the biblical period, they are of immense importance for the understanding of the Bible. The exegetical reasoning which they explicitly express often appears to be implicit in earlier interpretations of the Bible, and a knowledge of rabbinic Midrash is essential for an understanding of the whole tradition of Jewish Bible exegesis. Midrashic methods have been found operating within the HB itself in the reinterpretation of earlier layers of tradition, and they throw light on the use of the Old Testament in the New.

Rewritten Bible

6. Another well-represented subgenre of Bible interpretation is 'Rewritten Bible'. In Rewritten Bible the interpreter retells the biblical story in his own words with explanatory insertions and additions, some of which can be very extensive. Rewritten Bible mirrors the literary form of the Bible itself, so that, without comparing the retelling with the original the reader will usually be unable to discover what is actually found in the Bible and what has been added by the interpreter. Thus Rewritten Bible differs from Commentary proper, in that in the latter the interpretation is clearly demarcated from the biblical text, whereas in the former it is not. Rewritten Bible is also selective: it emphasizes through expansion certain episodes in the Bible, and totally omits others, and it sometimes rearranges the order of the narrative. It spins a new story out of the Bible, one with its own distinctive message. It can, therefore, appear to be challenging or even replacing the Bible. However, this was probably not the intention. All the Rewritten Bible texts indicate in subtle ways their dependence on the Bible and were meant to be read in dialogue with it.

7. There are important elements of Rewritten Bible in 1 Enoch, perhaps the single most important non-canonical Jewish text to have survived from Second Temple times. This has been preserved more or less intact only in Ge'ez, the liturgical language of the Ethiopian church. The Ethiopic version, which was made probably in the sixth century CE, was derived from a Greek version that is partially extant in MS fragments and quotations. The Greek was in turn translated (possibly in the 1st cent. CE) from an Aramaic original, substantial fragments of which, from multiple copies, have now been found among the Dead Sea scrolls. (Ethiopic text: Knibb (1978); Gk. text: Black (1970); Aram. text: Milik (1976); trs.: Knibb (1978); Milik (1976); see also Charles, APOT ii. 163–281; Knibb, in Sparks (1984: 169–320); Isaac, OTP i. 5–89; commentaries: Charles (1912); Black (1985).) However, 1 Enoch was not composed by the Qumran sect. Rather, it was a non-Qumranian work which the Qumran community held in high esteem. It has long been recognized that the current 1 Enoch is a highly composite work made up of separate treatises originating at very different periods. The earliest of these, the Book of the Heavenly Luminaries (chs. 72–82; ANTH D.5), probably goes back to the Persian period (early 4th cent. BCE). The latest, the Similitudes of Enoch (chs. 37–71; ANTH C.3), which is unattested at Qumran, probably dates from the late first century CE. The Book of the Watchers (chs. 1–36; ANTH A.4, C.2), dating probably to the second half of the third century BCE,

is rich in Rewritten Bible. 1 Enoch incorporates not only different sources, but also different genres: it includes apocalyptic and wisdom material (ANTH C.2–5, D.5), as well as Rewritten Bible. It claims to go back to revelations granted to the antediluvian sage Enoch, to whom only brief and enigmatic reference is made in the Bible (Gen 5:18–24). In choosing as a patron for their teachings a figure who lived well before the time of Moses and the revelation at Sinai, the original Enochic circles may have been quite deliberately challenging the primacy of Moses and of the Mosaic paradigm of Judaism.

8. Another text which can be classified basically as Rewritten Bible is the Book of Jubilees (ANTH A.5), which retells the story of Genesis and part of Exodus. (Ethiopic text: Charles (1895); Gk. text: Denis (1970: 70–102); Heb. text and tr. (1Q17–18, 2Q19–20, 3Q5, 4Q176, 4Q216–24, 11Q12): García Martínez and Tigchelaar (1997, i. 22–5, 214–15, 226–7, 360–3, 458–79; ii. 1204–7); trs.: Vermes (1997: 507–10); Charles, APOT ii. 1–82, rev. ch. C. Rabin, in Sparks (1984: 1–140); O. S. Wintermute, OTP ii. 35–142; commentary: Charles (1902); see further: VanderKam, (1977); Alexander (1997: 147–58) on the Jubilees' Mappa Mundi). Jubilees, like 1 Enoch, survives in its entirety only in an Ethiopic version, which was translated from the Greek. Although it seems to have been popular among Greek-speaking Christians, who knew it as The Little Genesis, only portions of the Greek version now survive in the form of citations in patristic authors. That this Greek version, as scholars long ago postulated, was a translation of a Hebrew work written in the Second Temple period has been confirmed beyond any doubt by the discovery of fragments of the original Hebrew, surviving from multiple copies, among the Dead Sea scrolls. Though the Qumran community regarded Jubilees as important (they were influenced by its advocacy of a solar calendar: cf. ANTH D.5), there is general agreement that, like 1 Enoch and the Aramaic Genesis Apocryphon (another retelling of Genesis found among the Scrolls; text García Martínez and Tigchelaar (1997: i. 28–49); tr: Vermes (1997: 448–59)), it was not composed by the Qumran sect. It is usually dated to the mid-second century BCE, to the time of the Hasmonean revolution. Jubilees gets its name from the fact that it imposes on the biblical narrative a schematic chronology that divides it into a series of 49-year periods or jubilees, each comprising seven 'weeks of years'. Of all the Rewritten Bible texts, Jubilees defines most clearly its relationship to the Scripture. It claims to be a second Torah written by an angel, or rather (alternatively) dictated by him to Moses on Sinai, the first Torah being the well-known canonic text, which was written by God himself (Jub. 1:4–6, 26–9; 6:22). Thus it claims high authority for itself. Jubilees' doctrine of the two Torahs recalls the latter rabbinic doctrine of the dual Torah (which effectively raised rabbinic Bible interpretation to the level of inspired Scripture), save for one significant difference: the Second Torah in rabbinic teaching was, at least in principle, an Oral Torah, that is to say, one transmitted by word of mouth down through an accredited line of tradents from Moses (cf. Mishnah 'Abot, 1:15), whereas Jubilees seems to have envisaged the Second Torah as having been written down from the very beginning.

9. An extensive retelling of the biblical story can also be found in Josephus' Antiquities of the Jews (ANTH A.6). Josephus

(c.37–c.100 CE) was a Palestinian Jew of priestly family who went over to the Roman side during the First Jewish War against Rome (66–74 CE). Later in life he lived in Rome, where he enjoyed imperial patronage. He adopted the role of apologist for the Jews and attempted to explain Jewish history, belief, and practice to the educated Gentile world of his day. His *Jewish Antiquities* is modelled on the great history of Rome—the *Roman Antiquities*—by Dionysius of Halicarnassus. Written in very competent Greek, the *Antiquities of the Jews* was probably composed in Rome in the 90's of the first century CE. Like the works of Philo, Josephus' writings were preserved by the church, which found them of inestimable value for apologetic purposes, and, indeed, interpolated them with a famous testimony to the more-than-human status of Jesus (*Ant.* 18.63–4). (Text and tr.: Thackeray *et al.* (1965: iv–ix); tr. Whiston (1737); introduction: Rajak (1983); see further Feldman (1998).)

Testimonia

10. In the Second Temple period the standard form of the book was the skin or papyrus scroll. Scrolls, however, are bulky: a complete copy of the Bible amounted to 22 or 24 scrolls, and, as the copy of the Isaiah[a] scroll from Qumran shows, just one of those scrolls could be well over 20 ft. long. Scrolls are also inconvenient to use: if one is looking for a particular passage, it can be hard to find in a scroll. It was probably a combination of these factors that led from the second century CE onwards to an ever-increasing use of the codex, the forerunner of the modern book, as an alternative to the scroll. It is possible to pack more writing into a codex (since both sides of the skin or papyrus are used), and in general codices are easier than scrolls to handle and consult. A complete Bible in the form of a set of scrolls would have represented a very considerable outlay of money, and few individuals in antiquity, even scholars, are likely to have possessed one. It is hardly surprising, therefore, that anthologies of biblical texts were produced. The existence of such anthologies is well known from later Christian practice, and some had deduced from the recurrence of certain key proof-texts in the NT that they were used by the first Christians (note e.g. the quotation of Ps 118:22 in Mt 21:42; Mk 12:10; Lk 20:17; Acts 4:11; Eph 2:20; 1 Pet 2:7). But it was only when actual examples of biblical anthologies were discovered among the Dead Sea scrolls that their existence in Second Temple times was finally proved. The anthologies consist of verses from Scripture, with or without commentary, grouped around a theme or motif. A good example, dated palaeographically to the early first century CE, is 4Q175, which contains a collection of messianic testimonia (Deut 18:18–19; Num 24:15–17; Deut 33:8–11). Another example, 4Q174, dated palaeographically to the late first century BCE, contains a collection of verses on the theme of the last days, drawn from 2 Samuel and the Psalms. 4Q174 offers an interpretation of the selected verses, but even where commentary is absent, the simple juxtaposition of different texts from different parts of the Bible involves illuminating Scripture from Scripture and constitutes in itself a kind of elementary commentary. (Text: García Martínez and Tigchelaar (1997: i. 352–7); tr.: Vermes (1997: 493–6); see further: Brooke (1985); Lim (1997).)

Translation

11. In the Second Temple period the use of Hebrew as a Jewish vernacular steadily declined. Large numbers of Jews in the Greek-speaking Diaspora seem to have had at best a minimal knowledge of the language, and even in Palestine more and more Jews went over to speaking a cognate, but quite distinct language, Aramaic. This created the need for translations of the Bible. The earliest of these was the Septuagint, a Greek version of the Torah, sponsored according to Jewish tradition by the Ptolemy Philadelphus of Egypt (285–246 BCE), who wanted a copy of the Jewish law for his famous library in Alexandria. Aramaic renderings were also produced. Small fragments of an Aramaic translation of Leviticus have been found among the Dead Sea scrolls, as well as substantial remains of an Aramaic version of Job. Aramaic translations, known as Targumim, covering the whole of the HB (with the exception of Ezra, Nehemiah, and Daniel, which are already substantially in Aramaic) are found in medieval Jewish MSS. These Targumim are of various dates, but some at least go back to the Talmudic era and are derived from the translations used then in synagogue simultaneously to render the biblical lections into the vernacular. This practice of rendering the public reading from Scripture simultaneously into Aramaic is well attested in the Talmudic period, but when it originated is still debated. That it goes back in some shape or form to the Second Temple times is probable. Though the extant MSS of the Targumim are all late, many have been shown to contain very early traditions. *Targum Pseudo-Jonathan* to the Pentateuch (so called because it was mistakenly attributed to Jonathan ben 'Uzzi'el the putative author of the 'official' *Targum of the Prophets*), is a case in point (ANTH A.7). (Text: Clarke (1984); tr.: Maher (1992); introduction to the Targumim: P. S. Alexander, in Mulder (1988: 217–53)). In its present form it cannot have been composed earlier than the seventh century CE, yet it contains material dating from Second Temple times. The Targumim are invaluable repositories of early Jewish Bible interpretation, which have been used successfully to illuminate early Christian use of the OT. All translations are interpretations, but the Targumim contain more interpretation than most, since they are often very paraphrastic and incorporate additions reminiscent of the Rewritten Bible type of exegesis. Unlike the Rewritten Bible texts, however, the Targumim, as translations, cannot be selective but must include the whole of the original, and follow the original order.

B. Law. 1. Within the domain of Bible interpretation law constitutes a special case and deserves separate treatment. The canon of Scripture which emerged as authoritative in Second Temple Judaism had at its heart a body of law, the Torah of Moses, which had become universally regarded as the foundation of the Jewish polity. Zealots and other renewal movements and sects exerted unrelenting pressure to maximize the application of this law to everyday Jewish life.

2. One obvious way of applying the law was through the Jewish courts. The legal system in Palestine throughout the Second Temple period was complicated and is not well understood. The Jews there found themselves living under different political regimes. Sometimes they were ruled directly by foreign powers—Persians, Greeks, and Romans. Sometimes they enjoyed independence, or quasi-independence, under their own native rulers—the Hasmoneans, and Herod and his sons. The change in the overall political authority, however, probably did not fundamentally affect the administration of Jewish law or the functioning of the Jewish courts. No state authority had either the political will, the bureaucracy, or the police force to impose a unified legal system throughout its domains. Most seem to have been willing to allow the separate ethnic groups to dispense their own law in their own courts—while reserving for state adjudication the most serious cases, e.g. those involving state security or capital offences. Under Roman rule (and almost certainly earlier), in addition to the Roman tribunals, there existed parallel networks of overlapping ethnic courts administering various systems of ethnic law—Jewish, Nabatean, Greek, and Samaritan.

3. On the face of it the legal system was somewhat chaotic, but, in fact, it probably functioned fairly efficiently. The ethnic courts were basically courts of conciliation which attempted to promote agreement between litigating parties. Any skilled conciliator could play this role, provided both parties to the dispute agreed to submit their case to him and to abide by his decision. There is evidence to suggest that within a given region the various ethnic courts may have influenced each other's practice and, perhaps, even inclined towards the creation of a local common law, so that the justice anyone received in the courts of one ethnic group might not have differed much from what one would have received in the courts of another ethnic group. However, the existence of parallel courts may have tempted people to 'shop around' for justice, and to present their cases in the court which they felt would be most favourable to them. This practice was frowned upon in later rabbinic law, and probably earlier as well. Though the rabbis acknowledged that 'the law of the state is the law', they encouraged Jews to keep their legal disputes within the Jewish community and to submit them to Jewish courts. The Talmud stipulates that 'any place wherein you find court sessions in the market-place, even though their laws are like the laws of Israel, you are not permitted to rely on them' (b. Git. 78b). Thus by exercising communal self-discipline the Jews had the possibility of running a largely autonomous Jewish legal system, whoever was in overall political control.

4. By late Second Temple times there were probably three levels of court within the Jewish legal system in Palestine. The highest court was the Great Sanhedrin. It convened in Jerusalem in the Chamber of Hewn Stone (Lishkat ha-Gazit), which was located somewhere on or near the Temple Mount (ANTH B.I). Functioning both as the supreme court and the supreme legislative assembly of the Jews, it would have reserved to itself cases which were politically sensitive, such as the trial of Jesus. The country was divided, according to Josephus, into eleven regions (J.W. 3.54–5), and the regional capitals probably contained regional courts. Finally, scattered throughout the major rural settlements were local courts which met on Mondays and Thursdays, the two market-days in the week. Much remains deeply obscure about even the most basic features of these arrangements. How the courts functioned, what their respective jurisdictions were, who appointed the judges, what qualifications and training judges were required to have, how the courts were financed, how (if at

all) cases were referred to the higher courts, and what system of enforcement backed the decisions of the courts, are all fundamental questions to which we have few answers. The Mishnah provides some information. It suggests that local sessions required a bench of three judges, regional sessions a bench of twenty-three, and sessions of the Great Sanhedrin a bench of seventy-one, and it attempts to differentiate the jurisdictions of the different courts, but it leaves many points obscure, and it is probably to some extent prescriptive rather than descriptive of actual practice.

5. In principle the Jewish courts would have claimed that they applied the Torah of Moses, but in practice they cannot have done so in any very direct way. For a number of compelling reasons it is highly unlikely that judges in a court would have unrolled a scroll of the Torah, consulted the relevant section and passed their judgement. In the first place the form in which the Torah is cast makes it very inconvenient for everyday legal purposes. It combines strictly legal material (halakah) with large quantities of legally irrelevant narrative (aggadah). It mixes together commandments that fell within the jurisdiction of the courts and were enforceable through them, with commandments that belonged more to the domain of one's conscience and personal relationship with God, and whose enforcement was left 'in the hands of heaven'. Important rulings on the same subject are scattered in different parts of the text, and, when they are compared, they do not always tally. Though, as modern literary analysis has shown, the Pentateuch embodies earlier law-codes, it is not a law-code itself, and its direct usefulness in a court of law would have been severely limited.

6. A second problem with using the Pentateuch as a body of practical law to be applied in the courts is that it is incomplete. Important areas of law—laws of contract, marriage and divorce, and inheritance—are either touched upon only sketchily or not at all. It is thin on evidence and procedure. All this is the very stuff of the law, and the courts, if they functioned at all, must have formulated ways of dealing with these matters. The Torah of Moses, if it constituted the law of the community, must have been heavily supplemented in practice. These supplements would have come from a variety of sources. One source was probably the decisions of the courts themselves, which would have created precedent. Another would have been the custom of the community. Custom (minhag) was recognized by later rabbinic jurisprudence as an important source of law, and there is no reason to think that the same would not have been true in Second Temple times. Indeed, it is possible that there was considerable variation in the detailed application of the law across the country, owing to the force of local custom.

7. All law in practice requires interpretation. This would have been as true of the Pentateuch as of any other legal text, even of those parts which are reasonably full and clear. With the passage of time much of this interpretation would have become traditional: lawyers and judges would have reached a consensus as to how certain terms and clauses were to be understood, though, as we shall see, there was always room for disagreement. Ancient law tended to be conservative: innovation was not encouraged, at least in the practice of the law. There must have been a body of traditional interpretation which stood side by side with the Pentateuch, without which

it could not have been applied. This too, like custom and case law, would have supplemented the Torah and created law.

8. The process of clarifying and extending the law of Moses is well attested in the Second Temple Jewish legal literature that has survived. The texts from Wadi Murabba'at near the Dead Sea illustrate legal documentary forms, such as marriage contracts (*kĕtûbbôt*) and bills of divorce (*gittîn*), which though not given in the Torah itself, would have been necessary for the implementation of the law. We find similar documents embedded in the Mishnah. A case in point is the famous *Prosbul* of Hillel, which, arguably, was not so much intended to implement the biblical law of the sabbatical year as to ameliorate it (or at least one aspect of it) to the point of circumventing it (ANTH B.3). The bill of divorce from Wadi Murabba'at (ANTH B.2; text with Fr. tr.: Benoit, Milik, and de Vaux (1961: 104–9)) is in Aramaic and dates to the early second century CE, but there is every reason to think that its legal forms are much older. And although the Mishnah was not edited till around 200 CE (see MAJ GEN B.11), there are no solid grounds for denying that the legal instrument of the *Prosbul* is accurately attributed to Hillel, the great Pharisaic scholar of the early first century CE.

9. The surviving legal literature also demonstrates a clear tendency towards codification, that is to say, the rearrangement of the biblical laws in a more systematic, user-friendly way. Significantly all the surviving 'codes' combine, to greater or lesser extent, biblical material with interpretation of the Bible, and with custom, in a more or less seamless whole. The move towards codification is seen most clearly in the great *Temple Scroll* from Qumran (text: García Martínez and Tigchelaar (1997: ii. 1228–307); tr.: Vermes (1997: 190–219); commentaries: Yadin (1983); Maier (1985)). Several copies of this Hebrew text seem to have been preserved. The main copy palaeographically dates to the Herodian period, but the text itself was probably composed somewhat earlier, possibly towards the end of the second century BCE. The code, as its name suggests, has largely to do with temple matters, but it also includes sections on procedure, on laws regarding the king (ANTH B.4) and on family law. The text, unlike Deuteronomy, is put in God's mouth and some have suggested, probably wrongly, that it was meant to replace the Torah. The *Temple Scroll* was produced by the Dead Sea sect and represents their view of how the temple and the state should be run. It presents an idealized plan of the temple and its courts that differs fundamentally from the layout of the temple which stood in Jerusalem in the sect's day. It is a plan of the temple that would be erected at the end of history, when the present polluted sanctuary would be destroyed, and its illegitimate priesthood and sacrifices replaced. The *Temple Scroll* has, therefore, an eschatological orientation. It is, none the less, indicative of interest in codification of the law. The Torah of Moses as stated in the Pentateuch needed clarification and supplementation before it could be applied in the messianic age.

10. There is abundant evidence, both from Jewish and non-Jewish sources, that the observance of sabbath was one of the defining practices of Second Temple Judaism. Sabbath is clearly enjoined in the Torah, but the exact laws of sabbath observance are remarkably unclear. The *Damascus Document* from Qumran illustrates one attempt to codify sabbath law (ANTH B.5). Its sabbath code is found in the section of laws which forms the second, major part of this work, and it integrates both Torah and sectarian law. (On the *Damascus Document* see MAJ GEN F.3.)

11. Historically the most important of the early Jewish law codes is the Mishnah. Tradition ascribes the editing of this massive Hebrew work, probably correctly, to Rabbi Judah the Prince, around 200 CE (ANTH B.3, 6; text: Albeck (1952–8); tr.: Danby (1933); introduction: Stemberger (1996: 108–48)). It contains a digest of the debates and discussions on the law which took place within the rabbinic and Pharisaic schools over the previous 150 years. Though it is fuller and more systematic than the Torah, it is not, in fact, a code of decided law. On many issues it gives a range of opinions from competent authorities, together with the arguments deployed to support them. It was cast in this form because it was intended not simply as a cut-and-dried code to be applied in court, but as a manual for training lawyers to think jurisprudentially. The Mishnah became the basic text for study within the rabbinic schools after 200, in Babylonia as well as in Palestine, and two great Aramaic commentaries on it were created—the Jerusalem Talmud (edited *c.*400 CE) and the Babylonian Talmud (edited *c.*500 CE). (The standard edns. of the Jerusalem Talmud (often reprinted) are Krotoshin (1866) and Romm (1922); tr. Neusner (1982–94); the standard edn. of the Babylonian Talmud (often reprinted) is Romm (1880–6); tr. Epstein (1935–52); introduction: Stemberger (1996: 164–224).)

12. The Torah of Moses was applied with greater or lesser rigour in the Jewish courts, and thereby was clarified, modified, and extended. But it was much more than a system of practical law, and was an object of interest to more than the judges and professional lawyers. It was the constitution of Israel and the central religious authority in Judaism. All sects and parties in Judaism cited its support, and claimed to have exclusive insight into its meaning. The Torah formed the battleground in inter-sectarian debates. This function is well illustrated by the so-called *Halakic Letter* (4QMMT) from Qumran. (Text: Qimron and Strugnell (1994); García Martínez and Tigchelaar (1997: ii. 790–805); tr.: Vermes (1997: 220–8); see further Kampen and Bernstein (1996).) Several copies of this intriguing Hebrew document, all dating from the late Hasmonean or Herodian periods, have been identified among the Dead Sea scrolls. Even when all the extant copies are pieced together, the document still remains fragmentary and enigmatic, and, crucially, its opening is missing. However, it has been plausibly suggested that it is the remnants of a letter which was sent by the Teacher of Righteousness, the founder of the Dead Sea sect, to the high priest in Jerusalem, urging him to accept the Essene interpretation of certain moot points of law, rather than the interpretation of the Pharisees (ANTH B.7). The *Halakic Letter* clearly shows that what was at stake in these inter-sectarian disputes was not simply the truth but political power. Whichever party or sect persuaded the powers that be to adopt its view of the meaning of Torah in effect became part of the government, and could claim to be the real rulers of the state.

C. Apocalyptic. **1.** Apocalyptic forms a vital part of the literary legacy of Second Temple Judaism. It was the genre that most directly challenged the closing of the canon by appealing to new, direct, divine revelation. The apocalyptic texts, and the circles that produced them, indelibly stamped their mark not only on Judaism, but, through their influence on Christianity, profoundly affected Western thought as well. The term 'apocalyptic' is modern: it was coined by Christian scholars to designate a collection of texts that resemble the Apocalypse of John (or book of Revelation) in the NT. Works so designated included Daniel (which found its way into the canon of Scripture), *1* and *2 Enoch*, *4 Ezra* (*2 Esdras*), and *2 Apoc. Bar.* The term 'apocalyptic' is doubly useful: not only does it help broadly to define a genre of literature by using the book of Revelation as a yardstick, but it also highlights a fundamental characteristic of that literature: 'apocalypse' comes from the Greek word *apokalypsis*, meaning 'revelation', 'the disclosure of what is hidden'. The apocalypses above all claim to reveal secrets.

2. The secrets which they disclose are varied, but they fall under three general heads: (1) *Theosophy*: apocalyptic explores the mysteries of the deity, or more generally, of the heavenly world. It contains vivid, symbolic descriptions of God's throne, his celestial palace, and his retinue of angels. These descriptions provide the setting for the main revelations that the apocalypse conveys. The fact that these are received before the celestial throne of glory gives them solemnity and guarantees their authenticity. (2) *Cosmology*: apocalyptic is also, in some texts more than in others, concerned with the mysteries of the cosmos, particularly with its basic structure—the seven heavens, the location of the places of reward and punishment for souls after death, the heavenly storehouses in which the natural phenomena are kept, and the motions of the heavenly bodies. This material also tends to be subordinate to the primary concerns of the apocalyptist. Thus it is often incidentally, in the course of his ascent to heaven (whether in the body or in trance), that the hero of the apocalypse discovers the structure of the world. There are, however, cosmological traditions of a more disinterested, scientific character in some apocalypses, notably in *1 Enoch* (see ANTH D.5). (3) *Eschatology*: both theosophy and cosmology are, however, on the whole secondary to apocalyptic's main concern—eschatology, the mysteries of the future. The apocalyptists believed that the present world order will culminate in the coming of the Messiah and in the establishment of the kingdom of God. They tried to discover how and when this would happen. They searched for a pattern or rhythm in history that would enable them to tell when the messianic age would dawn. They were also deeply interested in the fate of souls immediately after death, and in the ultimate destiny of the soul after the last judgement.

3. The style of apocalyptic is highly distinctive. The texts are full of fantastic and arresting images—strange beasts, surreal landscapes, portents, prodigies, and wonders. They have at times a nightmarish quality, and, indeed, are often presented as dream- or trance-visions. They represent the re-emergence within Judaism of a mythological mode of discourse (with links to Canaanite and Near-Eastern mythology) which had been suppressed in earlier times. The apocalyptists frequently interpret their visions for us, and from these interpretations it becomes clear that the fantasy is under tight control. The visions are elaborate allegories: the imagery has symbolic meaning and its details are worked out with great precision and care.

4. There is no standard apocalyptic literary form: the apocalypses combine the basic apocalyptic motifs in a bewildering variety of ways, and apocalyptic material can frequently be found in texts belonging basically to other literary genres such as Bible commentary, wisdom, and liturgy. *2 Enoch*, however, will serve to illustrate one pattern, which is particularly common in later texts. *2 Enoch*, which now survives in its entirety only in old Slavonic, was popular in the Slavonic church and was reworked several times by medieval editors. There are now two major Slavonic versions of it (the long Recension A and the short Recension B). Its textual history is very complicated, but there is general agreement that in some form or other the Slavonic versions go back to a Jewish apocalypse composed originally in Greek, probably in Alexandria, in the first century CE. (Text: Vaillant (1952); tr.: Forbes, *APOT* ii. 425–69; Pennington, in Sparks (1984: 321–62); Andersen, *OTP* i. 91–222; commentary: Charles and Morfill (1896).)

5. The work, which manifestly builds on the traditions of *1 Enoch* (on which see MAJ GEN A.7), falls into six sections. The first of these (chs. 1–2) sets the scene: Enoch is awakened from sleep by two glorious angels who tell him that God has sent them to escort him up to heaven. The second section (chs. 3–21) describe in some detail Enoch's ascent through the seven heavens (so Recension B), or the ten heavens (so Recension A). It tells us what he saw in each heaven: the subjects are partly cosmological, partly concerned with the fate of souls after death and with the angelic hierarchies. The third section (ch. 22) contains the climax of the ascent. Enoch sees God's glorious throne and apparently undergoes physical transformation into an angel (ANTH C.1). The next section (chs. 23–38) records the revelations that Enoch received before God's throne. God commands an archangel to bring the books from the celestial archive and to instruct Enoch in certain mysteries. The secrets imparted to him are largely cosmological and are presented in the form of a loose commentary on the work of the six days of creation in Gen 1. In section five (chs. 39–66) Enoch returns to earth to impart the knowledge he has been given to his sons. The content is once again cosmological, but it passes over into ethical admonition. The last section (ch. 67 + ch. 68, Recension A) forms an appendix to the work and tells of the final translation of Enoch. Enoch is carried by the angels to heaven and set before God's face 'for ever' (Recension B). *2 Enoch* exhibits one of the basic patterns of apocalyptic literature, which contains five elements: (1) trance/dream; (2) ascent to heaven; (3) vision of God's throne and glory; (4) revelation of mysteries; (5) descent to earth and communication of these mysteries. In *2 Enoch*, as we have indicated, the secrets disclosed are mainly cosmological, but they could equally, and indeed more typically, have been eschatological—a vision of the course of history up to the messianic age, or of the fate of souls, or both.

6. Apocalyptic appears to have flourished in early Judaism at two distinct periods. The first of these coincided roughly with the Hellenistic crisis (*c.*180–150 BCE). It is to this period that Daniel and parts of the apocalyptic material in *1 Enoch* and in the *Book of Jubilees* belong. The second period covers the first few decades after the destruction of the temple in 70

CE. It is to this period that the book of Revelation belongs, as well as (probably) the important apocalypses known as 4 Ezra and 2 Apoc. Bar. (ANTH C.6, 9). 4 Ezra is the name commonly given to an apocalypse found in Latin Vulgate Bibles either under the title 4 Esdras (the Gk. form of Ezra), or as chs. 3–14 of 2 Esdras (see 2 ESD). 2 Apoc. Bar. is now extant in a single Syriac manuscript dating from the sixth century CE, but it is widely recognized that it too goes back to a Jewish apocalypse written in Greek probably around 95 CE. (Syriac text: Dedering (1973: 1–50); Gk: Denis (1970: 118–20); trs.: Charles, APOT ii. 470–526, rev. Brockington, in Sparks (1984: 835–97); Klijn, OTP i. 615–52; commentaries: Charles (1896); Bogaert (1969).) It has close affinities in language and ideas to 4 Ezra.

7. The periods 180–150 BCE and 70–100 CE were marked by political and religious turmoil. It is hardly surprising, therefore, that many have interpreted apocalyptic as a literature of crisis, which aims to give consolation to the persecuted and the religiously bemused. The strong emphasis in some apocalyptic texts on proclaiming the imminence of redemption and on justifying God's ways towards Israel tends to support this view. It is interesting to note that there was another outburst of apocalypticism within Judaism coinciding with the period of spiritual and political upheaval engendered by the Islamic invasions of the Near East in the early seventh century CE: it produced the Midrashim of Redemption, such as the Book of Zerubbabel and the Prayer of Rabbi Simeon bar Yohai. But it is important not to link apocalyptic too closely with political crisis. To do so can result in overstressing the eschatological element. Moreover, once launched, apocalyptic ideas became a permanent feature of the Jewish intellectual tradition and attracted interest through good times as well as bad. More often than not what fosters the apocalyptic mood is not objective historical reality, but individual perceptions of reality, which are not necessarily the same thing.

8. Apocalyptic texts share a family likeness and play on the same limited repertory of themes. They belong to a genuine literary tradition. But who was responsible for them? It was once proposed that apocalyptic provided evidence for popular Judaism in late Second Temple times. This is highly implausible. On every page of this literature are traces of immense learning. Apocalyptic is a scholarly literature, and its authors should be sought in the circles of the scribes (the Soferim), whose influence was increasingly felt in late Second Temple Judaism. Apocalyptic cannot be tied to any single Jewish sect. It seems to have arisen before the emergence of the sects, and it influenced all of them, with the possible exception of the Sadducees. Apocalyptic literature was found in abundance among the Dead Sea scrolls, including fragments of hitherto unknown apocalypses. This is hardly surprising, given that the Dead Sea sect believed it was living at 'the end of days'. Just how seriously it took this belief is shown by the War Rule and the Messianic Rule. Though neither of these texts is strictly speaking an apocalypse, both show how committed the community was to apocalyptic teaching about the imminence of the messianic age. The Dead Sea community believed it would play a leading role in the wars at the end of history, and in the War Rule it worked out what tactics it would adopt (ANTH C.7; text: García Martínez and Tigchelaar (1997: i. 112–45); tr.: Vermes (1997: 161–83); commentary: Yadin (1962);

see further Davies (1977)). The War Rule is written in Hebrew and several versions of it are extant, all dated palaeographically to the Herodian era. Another element of the apocalyptic scenario was the messianic banquet. The Dead Sea community believed that it had a major part to play in this event as well. In the Messianic Rule, an appendix to the Cave I version of the Community Rule (on which see MAJ GEN F.2), it sets out how the community was to behave when it sat down with the Messiah at the eschatological feast (ANTH C.8; text: García Martínez and Tigchelaar (1997: i. 98–103); tr.: Vermes (1997: 157–60); see further Schiffman (1989)). It is clear from the NT that apocalyptic decisively influenced early Christianity as well, and Pharisaism too probably felt its impact. The Pharisees certainly believed in the resurrection of the dead, one of the key doctrines of apocalyptic (ANTH C.9). The later Merkabah and Hekalot texts testify to the persistence of apocalyptic ideas and literary forms even in a rabbinic milieu—a fact most simply explained by supposing that the rabbis had inherited apocalyptic traditions from their Second Temple predecessors, the Pharisees.

9. Apocalyptic has roots in earlier traditions to be found not only in the great canonic prophets, but in the wisdom writings as well (on which see MAJ GEN D). Isa 24–7, 40–55, 56–66, and Zech 9–14 provide particularly important antecedents. Yet the dominant impression one gets from reading apocalyptic is of its novelty. It brought together and promoted a number of ideas which were rather new to Judaism—a full-blown doctrine of the Messiah, with elaborate scenarios of the end of history; a belief that history is purposeful and patterned, and moving towards a grand climax; the survival of the soul after death in places of reward and punishment; the bodily resurrection of the dead; and an interest in angels and in the workings of the celestial world. The apocalyptists were concerned with areas of knowledge that were regarded as mysterious; they touched on dangerous subjects. Later rabbinic tradition was to ban public discussion of two of their major themes—the Account of the Chariot (Ma'aseh Merkavah), i.e. the mysteries of the heavenly world, and the Account of Creation (Ma'aseh Bere'shit), i.e. the mysteries of the natural order (m. Hag 2:1).

10. Besides the novelty and daring of their speculations, the apocalyptic texts create in the reader a strong sense of fresh revelation. Time and again the apocalyptists expressly claim that what they write was received directly from God or from his angels. They use prophetic modes of discourse, and describe visions of God as impressive as any granted to the earlier prophets. But there was a problem here. Apocalyptic flourished at a time when it was widely accepted in Judaism that direct prophetic revelation had ceased, and that revelation was to be found only in the prophetic writings from the past. Claims to new revelation would have been looked at askance. This faced the apocalyptists with the problem of how they could justify their novel ideas. Basically they used two strategies. First, they linked them as closely as they could to the canonic texts, presenting them, wherever possible, as an interpretation of Scripture. Thus, as we noted earlier, the cosmological speculations of 2 Enoch 24–33 are set out as a kind of commentary on Gen 1–3, and the story of the fall of the Watchers in 1 Enoch is made to hang on Gen 6:1–5 (ANTH A.4). This element within apocalyptic brings it close to the Rewritten

Bible type of Bible interpretation. It allows the apocalyptists to domesticate their novelties within accepted tradition, and to cover them with that tradition's authority. Secondly, the apocalyptists claimed to be in receipt of teachings passed down secretly from the great sages who lived back in the classic age of prophecy. These teachings, though given then, could not be disclosed till the end of time to which they referred. This claim, expressed with greater or lesser clarity, lies behind many apocalyptic works (see e.g. Dan 12:4). They attributed their work to such great prophetic figures of the past as Enoch, Moses, Elijah, Baruch, and Ezra. The implication is clear: despite appearances, what they are offering is not new fangled; it is, in fact, ancient teaching of unimpeachable authority. Significantly the one apocalypse that breaks with this convention of pseudepigraphy is the book of Revelation in the New Testament. Perhaps because he lived in a community which believed that prophecy had been restored to Israel, John, the author of this work (whoever he was), felt he could put it out under his own name.

D. Wisdom. 1. The ancient scribes were the bearers of an intellectual tradition which they themselves called 'Wisdom'. This wisdom consisted first and foremost in knowing how to behave properly towards one's fellows, particularly social superiors. At the most trivial level it was concerned with etiquette, at the most profound with how to live the life of the sage, honoured by all and influential in society's affairs. The scribes invented an ethical literature which embodied their wisdom on how to live the good life, examples of which have been included in the canon, notably in Proverbs, which is attributed to one of the great patrons of Wisdom, King Solomon. Proverbs illustrates one of the classic forms of Wisdom—the short, gnomic utterance that encapsulates in striking and memorable language a wise saying.

2. This tradition of ethical wisdom flourished throughout the Second Temple period and beyond. A late example of it, still largely in the classic form of a collection of pithy sayings, is found in the *Chapters of the Fathers* (*Pirqei 'Abot*), one of the tractates of the Mishnah (ANTH D.I). '*Abot*, probably the single most influential ethical treatise in the history of Judaism, is anomalous within the Mishnah (on which see MAJ GEN B.II). It is the only non-halakic tractate in the whole corpus, and its inclusion within a law-code raises sharply the question of the relationship between ethics and law. Whoever included '*Abot* within the Mishnah (possibly Judah the Prince, the Mishnah's traditional editor) must surely have felt that its contents were a necessary complement to the legal material contained in the rest of the work. But in what sense does it complement the law? Is there an implication that '*Abot* expresses the universal moral principles that underlie the concrete prescriptions of the halakah? This may well be the intention, though as some rabbinic jurists pointed out, it is hard to find a rational, moral basis for some of the ritual laws of the Torah, such as the prescriptions regarding the red heifer (Num 19:1–13), which nevertheless should be obeyed as divine commandments (*Pesiq. Rab Kah.* 4.7).

3. Given the scribes' basic concern with morals, and their increasing involvement during Second Temple times with Torah, it was inevitable that the relationship between ethics and law should have become an issue for them. There is

evidence of a lively interest in this topic. Philo argued that the Ten Commandments were the basis of all the detailed legislation of the Pentateuch, which he called 'the special laws': each special law is the concrete expression of one of the broad, moral principles of the Decalogue (Philo, *Dec.* 154; cf. *Spec. Leg.* 1.1). This view was also, apparently, acceptable to some rabbinic jurists, though some were worried about over-emphasizing the Decalogue, and banned its separate liturgical use, so that heretics should not say that only the Ten Commandments were important. In the gospels Jesus is challenged to identify the fundamental principle of the law (Mt 22:34–40; Mk 12:28–34). He replies by citing Deut 6:5 and Lev 19:18 (the 'love commandment'). On another occasion he is quoted as saying that the Golden Rule is the sum of the law and the prophets (Mt 7:12; Lk 6:31). Jesus' contemporary, the Pharisaic scholar Hillel, is depicted in rabbinic tradition as giving the same answer to a proselyte (ANTH D.2). A late echo of this debate is found in a remarkable passage in the Babylonian Talmud (*b. Mak.* 23b–24a), which concludes that Hab 2:4, 'the just shall live by his faith', is the essence of the Torah. (On the Talmud see MAJ GEN B.II.)

4. Besides the sayings-collection, another form of ethical literature that has survived from early Judaism is the Testament. This purports to be the last will and testament of some biblical figure who, on his deathbed, at a moment of particular solemnity and insight, passes on to his posterity his accumulated wisdom (cf. Gen 49:1–28). The best-known example of such a work is the *Testaments of the Twelve Patriarchs*. (Gk. text: de Jonge (1978); trs: Charles, *APOT* ii. 282–367; de Jonge, in Sparks (1984: 505–600); Kee, *OTP* i. 775–828; commentary: Charles (1908); see further de Jonge (1953).) Though some maintain that this composition, which survives only in Greek, Armenian, and Slavonic, is Christian in origin, behind it (with its unquestionably Christian elements) probably stands a Jewish text, only minimally Christianized, which may date back to as early as the second century BCE. Certainly such testaments were known in Second Temple Judaism, as the Aramaic fragments of a *Testament of Levi* from Qumran prove. The *Testament of Reuben*, the first of the testaments in the collection, illustrates one of the themes explored in wisdom, namely the nature of woman, her place in society, and how the sage should behave towards her (ANTH D.3). This topic features prominently already in Proverbs, which in its account of 'the woman of valour' paints a picture of the ideal woman, ideal at least from the standpoint of her husband (Prov 31:10–31), though it also notes her less than ideal sisters, the prostitute and the adulteress, and warns against their snares (Prov 2:16–19; 6:24; 7:10–23). *Testament of Reuben* takes an altogether darker view: 'Women are evil, my children, and by reason of their lacking authority or power over man, they scheme treacherously how they might entice him to themselves by means of their looks.' The world of the scholars and sages was an intensely male world, in which women seem to have played no part.

5. Abstract reflection on the wellsprings of ethical behaviour reaches its climax, as far as the surviving literature of Palestinian Judaism is concerned, in the *Instruction on the Two Spirits* from the Qumran *Community Rule* (1QS 3:13–4:26) (ANTH D.4). The discursive, systematic, theological nature of this text is hard to parallel in Hebrew literature before the

Middle Ages. The author sees the world as a battleground between a spirit of good and a spirit of evil. Each individual's behaviour is good or bad according to the extent to which he is dominated by one or other of these spirits. Only those dominated by the spirit of good are fit to join the community. In the providence of God the spirit of good will ultimately triumph over the spirit of evil. The rabbis also, later, reflected on the sources of moral action and identified within the human personality two tendencies—an inclination towards evil (yēṣer hārāʿ) and an inclination towards good (yeṣer haṭṭôb). For the rabbis these two inclinations belong to the human psyche and are essentially under the control of the individual's will: the inclination towards evil can be suppressed and the inclination towards good promoted through the study of Torah and the observance of the commandments. The Qumran theologian's position, however, is less clear. It is possible he is saying little more than this, but some have argued that he holds that each individual's moral character is irrevocably predetermined by cosmic forces beyond his control. The uniqueness of the *Instruction on the Two Spirits* within early Palestinian Judaism favours the view that it has been influenced by Persian dualistic thought about the cosmic conflict between Ahura Mazda (the spirit of good) and Angra Mainyu (the spirit of evil). The *Instruction on the Two Spirits* comes from the preamble to the *Community Rule* (on which see MAJ GEN F.2), which deals with initiation into the community and the definition of its boundaries. It is clearly attested only in the Cave 1 version of the *Rule*, which dates palaeographically to around 100 BCE.

6. Though Wisdom originally may have had to do with morality, the content of the term seems to have been expanded from an early date to include also knowledge of how nature works. Solomon, the great patron of Wisdom, was seen as being expert not only in the principles of correct behaviour but also in the mysteries of nature (cf. 1 Kings 4:29–34). Opinion seems to have been divided in early Wisdom circles on the question of whether nature could be comprehended by the human mind. At the end of Job, a text dating probably to the fifth century BCE which belongs fundamentally to the Wisdom tradition, the view seems to be taken that nature is intrinsically unknowable: it is deeply mysterious and beyond human comprehension, and the only human response possible to it is one of awe and praise of God's power (Job 38:1–6). In Proverbs, however, which dates probably from roughly the same period, a very different position is taken. There it is claimed that Wisdom was used by God as the architect of the universe, and that that same Wisdom is accessible to men (Prov 8:22–33). The implication clearly is that there is a rational order in nature (what the Ionian philosopher Heraclitus, probably a near contemporary of the author of Proverbs, called a *Logos*), and that this rational order could be comprehended by the human mind. To put it in the language of Proverbs: man can attain to Wisdom, and that Wisdom includes an understanding of how nature works. We have here the first glimmerings of Jewish interest in science—the establishment of the necessary preconditions that make the rational investigation of nature possible.

7. This interest in the workings of nature is clearly attested in the earliest layers of *1 Enoch*—the *Book of the Heavenly Luminaries* (ANTH D.5), which probably dates to the Persian period. (On *1 Enoch* see MAJ GEN A.7.) The underlying astronomical ideas of this part of *1 Enoch* are probably Babylonian in origin, though they are almost certainly primitive compared to the best Babylonian astronomy of their time. This Babylonian science came to the author of the *1 Enoch* treatise through the medium of Aramaic, which was the official language of administration and diplomacy in the Persian empire, and which would have been known, of necessity, by Jewish scribes in Jerusalem. This explains why *1 Enoch* is in Aramaic and not in Hebrew. It was probably a group of such scribes, alive to developments in thought beyond the borders of Judah, who introduced this alien wisdom into Israel.

8. According to *1 Enoch* it was the angels who revealed this knowledge to Enoch. The appeal to revelation is standard in early Jewish 'science', and it is for this reason that scientific texts are largely to be found in the apocalypses. This is puzzling to the modern mind. Since the basic premise of the scientific approach is that nature is governed by laws that can be discovered and understood by the human mind, why involve revelation? Surely the author the *Book of the Heavenly Luminaries* knew that the observations of the sun's motions which he has reported went back ultimately to painstaking observation and recording in the great temples of Babylonia. Why then claim that this doctrine was divinely revealed to the antediluvian sage Enoch? Perhaps he felt that this was the only way in which to get a hearing for these ideas. While he himself might have had faith in the power of the unaided human intellect, his compatriots needed the stronger validation of divine revelation. However, it was common throughout antiquity to link scientific discovery to divine revelation. Great new advances in knowledge or technology were routinely traced back to culture-bringers (whether divine or human) who derived their crucial knowledge from the gods.

9. Enoch, then, was acclaimed by the Enochic circles as the patron of the new science—a role that he continued to play within Judaism for many centuries to come. It is interesting that they did not try to appropriate Moses as their patron, or link their doctrine more obviously with the account of creation in Gen 1. This might be because in their day Moses had not yet achieved the position of supreme authority within Judaism. This seems unlikely, since they probably lived after the reforms of Ezra, which, apparently with Persian backing, promulgated the Torah of Moses as the law of the Judean community. It is more probable that by claiming to be heirs of ancient doctrine from well before the time of Moses they were challenging Moses' dominance and proposing an alternative Enochic paradigm for Judaism. Certainly their new knowledge had repercussions in the strictly religious domain. On the basis of their astronomical observations they appear to have advocated a reform of the calendar, which would have involved following a strictly solar calendar rather than the luni-solar calendar that prevailed in Judaism at the time. Certainly, as is evident from the *Book of Jubilees*, the *Book of the Heavenly Luminaries* was later used to support calendrical reform. The Qumran community seems to have adopted the Enochic solar calendar and this was one of the reasons for their split with the Jerusalem establishment which controlled the temple and still followed the old luni-solar calendar.

10. Wisdom also embraced much that we would loosely today regard as falling within the domain of magic. Historians of science have long recognized that it is impossible to distinguish sharply between 'magic' and 'science' in pre-modern times. Magic often shares with science the belief that there are rigorous laws governing natural phenomena, which can be known and manipulated. Pseudo-sciences (such as astrology and alchemy) have contributed much to the growth of real science. The interconnection of religion, magic, and science in early Judaism is seen most clearly in the field of medicine. There was a widespread belief in late Second Temple Judaism that sickness was caused by demons. The demons could be expelled in a variety of ways. The victim could exercise self-help by praying, repenting of his or her sins, and bringing gifts to the temple. An exorcist could be called in to drive out the demon by reciting incantations or performing other magical rituals. Or a doctor could apply medicine in the form of herbs or other *materia medica*. Sometimes a combination of these different methods of healing would be used, as a vivid description by Josephus of an exorcism in the name of Solomon shows (*Ant.* 8.44–9). The arts of healing were seen as belonging to the domain of Wisdom. It is not surprising, therefore, that Solomon was revered also as the great patron of 'magic', and that exorcists and other magicians often claimed to be relying on doctrines and practices that went back to him.

11. That the darker magical arts were also practised is shown by the *Book of Mysteries* (*Sefer ha-Razim*; text: Margalioth (1966); tr. Morgan (1983); see further Alexander (1986)). The framework of this strange Hebrew work, which has been successfully reconstructed from a number of medieval fragments, consists of a chain of tradition showing how it was passed down from the time of Noah, who received it from the angel Raziel, followed by a description of an ascent through the seven heavens, and concluding with a doxology to be recited before the Throne of Glory. Into this framework, which recalls the apocalypses and the Hekalot literature, has been woven a series of incantations for curing sickness, harming enemies, influencing people, and so forth. The *Book of Mysteries* is basically a magician's manual of a type well known in antiquity, from which the magician would have copied out and personalized an incantation for the use of a client. What is so shocking about it is that its magic is almost totally *black*, i.e. it is aimed at causing harm (ANTH D.6). The *Book of Mysteries* cannot be dated in its present form before the late fourth century CE, but the sort of magic it contains is well attested earlier. The fragmentary Qumran text 4Q560, dated palaeographically to the early first century CE, is probably the remnants of a broadly similar book of magical recipes. (Text and tr.: García Martínez and Tigchelaar (1997: ii. 1116–17).)

12. The Dead Sea scrolls indicate that some Jews in Second Temple times were interested in another early 'science'—physiognomy. 4Q186, the key text, dates palaeographically to the Herodian period (text: García Martínez and Tigchelaar (1997: i. 380–3); tr.: Vermes (1997: 358–9); see further Alexander (1996: 385–94).) The language is Hebrew, but it is written in a rather childish code, which suggests that its contents were deemed esoteric within the community (ANTH D.7). Physiognomy is based on the idea that a person's character or the nature of their 'soul' can be deduced from their physical appearance, such as the shape of their limbs. Possibly originating in Babylonia, physiognomy was a respected branch of knowledge in antiquity, with an extensive body of technical literature, including a treatise on the subject by Aristotle. It remained influential in Western thought down to the nineteenth century when it had a late flowering in the pseudo-science of phrenology. At Qumran physiognomical lore was probably the province specifically of the Master (*Maskil*), the sage who was the spiritual mentor of the community. It may have been used for divinatory purposes, to determine who belonged to the Sons of Light, and hence was worthy to enter the exclusive community at Qumran. The Pythagoreans and the later Hekalot Jewish mystics may also have used physiognomy to control entry into their conventicles.

E. Hymns and Prayers. 1. Prayer is one of the elementary forms of religious life and was probably always a feature of the worship of ancient Israel. However, there are grounds for thinking that late Second Temple Judaism witnessed a remarkable flowering of prayer and liturgy, stimulated, perhaps, by the intensification of national and religious life that followed the Hasmonean revolution. A substantial proportion of the surviving literature from the period consists broadly speaking of hymns and prayers. These are found both embedded in literary texts (e.g. in apocalyptic works such as 2 *Apoc. Bar.*: ANTH E.6) and in liturgical collections—prayer-books for various occasions. The most important of these collections is the biblical book of Psalms. While many of the Psalms go back to the pre-exilic period, it has long been suspected that a proportion is post-exilic in origin (some being possibly as late as the Hasmonean period), and that the collection as a whole was not put together till fairly late in Second Temple times. The numerous copies of the Psalter from Qumran show how fluid the collection still was even in the first century BCE. Though the copies are in broad agreement as to content, they differ significantly as to the order and the text of the individual Psalms, and they contain Psalms which are not found in the standard synagogue and church psalters.

2. The Dead Sea scrolls have yielded a particularly rich harvest of prayerbooks. There was a tendency among early researchers to regard these all as sectarian compositions and as reflecting, therefore, the peculiar practices of one, possibly atypical, community. It has become increasingly clear, however, that there is nothing distinctively sectarian about many of these texts and that they probably reflect liturgies in more general use. And even those that contain sectarian language may involve the adaptation of common prayers to sectarian worship.

3. It is far from clear who composed the numerous surviving hymns and prayers, and when, where, and by whom they would have been used. Prayers and hymns of various kinds must have been part of the temple service from time immemorial (cf. Sir 50:18–19). Many of the Psalms presuppose great cultic occasions in the temple and were probably chanted by levitical choirs. The priests in the temple blessed the people, using from time to time the famous Priestly Benediction (Num 6:24–6)—an ancient and influential liturgical text, adaptations and echoes of which can be detected in other prayers (ANTH E.4). And worshippers made confession over the offerings they brought to the temple and may have received words of absolution or encouragement from the priests.

4. Another locus of prayer was the synagogue. The origins of the synagogue are obscure. As an institution it is first attested in Egypt during the reign of Ptolemy III (Euergetes), 247–221 BCE. It may have been a Diaspora invention which was later imported into the Land of Israel. Certainly by the early first century CE there is evidence of synagogues in Palestine, at least in Galilee. From the outset it was recognized that the synagogue was liturgically subordinate to the temple. It could not be a place of sacrifice, since only in Jerusalem could sacrifices be offered to God. It was a place for prayer and the public reading of the Torah. It is no longer possible, however, to reconstruct with any certainty its order of service in the pre-70 period. Some sectarian groups, as the Dead Sea scrolls clearly prove, developed their own elaborate liturgies for their own sectarian assemblies. Finally, there is evidence to suggest that private prayer at fixed times of the day (morning and evening), was becoming an important part of individual piety in late Second Temple times.

5. It is not easy to match the surviving Second Temple prayer-texts to the various life-settings in which prayer may have been offered. The present-day tradition of prayer in the synagogue is rich and varied, and elements of it may go back to the Second Temple period. The Eighteen Benedictions, or Amidah, which, together with the Shema and its blessings, forms the core of the current synagogue liturgy, is very old (ANTH E.1, 5; for texts of the Amidah and the Shema see Singer (1962); on the synagogue liturgy see Idelsohn (1932); Elbogen (1993); Reif (1993)). Its use was already well established when the Mishnah was compiled (c.200 CE), and, although in its current forms it presupposes the destruction of the temple, a version of it may have been in use before 70 CE. Parallels between the Amidah and parts of Ben Sirach have long been noted (cf. Sira 36:1–17; 51:12 i–xvi (Heb.): though the latter passage may not be genuine Ben Sirach, it is probably, nevertheless, a genuine Second Temple period composition). However, the text is inescapably political in content, and calls explicitly and implicitly for the overthrow of the existing political order. It is hard to envisage on what occasion such a prayer could have been publicly recited before 70 in either synagogue or temple.

6. The growth of sectarian liturgies is clearly illustrated by the Dead Sea scrolls. Qumran may have been a forcing-house for the development of liturgy, because its members had withdrawn from worship in the Jerusalem temple, which they regarded as controlled by an illegal priesthood and polluted. Instead the community followed a rigorous regime of prayer and study, reminiscent of later Christian monasticism (ANTH E.2; see further Falk (1998)). Every year the members reaffirmed their commitment to the community. The basic order for this ceremony of the renewal of the covenant is contained in the opening columns of the Community Rule (on which see MAJ GEN F.2). Its use of adapted versions of the Priestly Blessing is noteworthy (ANTH E.3).

7. One of the most interesting hymnic texts from Qumran is the Scroll of Thanksgiving (Hôdayôt) from Cave 1 (ANTH E.4; text: García Martínez and Tigchelaar (1997: i. 146–205); tr.:

Vermes (1997: 243–300); commentary: Mansoor (1961); see further Kittel (1981)). This fine collection of Hebrew hymns strikes a note of intense, personal piety, but it is uncertain whether one or several authors were involved in its composition, or the occasion for which it was composed. It is possible that it was intended for use at the Qumran sect's annual festival for the renewal of the covenant. The large Cave 1 Scroll of the Hôdayôt is palaeographically dated to the late first century BCE. Fragments of other hôdayôt-like hymns have also been found at Qumran.

8. A striking motif, widely attested in Second Temple liturgical texts, is the idea that matching the temple on earth is a temple in heaven, in which the angels worship God. There are, of course, antecedents to this notion in earlier Jewish tradition, notably in Isa 6:1–5, but it seems to have received renewed attention in late Second Temple times. One of the most elaborate expressions of this idea is to be found in the Qumran work known as the Songs of the Sabbath Sacrifice (4Q400–5; 11Q17), the surviving Hebrew texts of which date palaeographically between the mid-first century BCE and the early first century CE (text: García Martínez and Tigchelaar (1997: ii. 806–37, 1212–19); tr.: Vermes (1997: 321–31); see further Newsome (1985)). Though fragmentary, it is possible to see that this text must originally have described the celestial liturgies in considerable detail, though how the author or authors acquired this knowledge, whether by revelation or by deduction from the terrestrial liturgies, is far from clear. The Songs of the Sabbath Sacrifice envisage the praying community on earth joining with the angels in heaven to worship God. There is a marriage of earth and heaven. Terrestrial worship is given an added solemnity because the angels are present in the congregation. This same idea lies behind an old element of the synagogue service known as the Qedushah (ANTH E.5), which describes in exalted language the worship of the angelic choirs. The antiquity of the Qedushah is suggested by the fact that a version of it forms part of the Christian eucharistic service. It was probably taken over from the synagogue service early in the history of the church. Such a direct borrowing at a later date would be most unlikely. Similar ideas about the worship of the angels are found in the Hekalot texts of the Talmudic period, which contain some strong and interesting parallels to the Songs of the Sabbath Sacrifice. It is unlikely that the Hekalot mystics borrowed directly from the Qumran texts: Hekalot mysticism, for all its peculiarities, belongs firmly within the tradition of rabbinic Judaism, whose Second Temple forerunners were the Pharisees, whereas the group that produced the Qumran texts was almost certainly the Pharisees' opponents, the Essenes. Rather, both traditions probably originated in the speculations of priestly circles in the Jerusalem temple in late Second Temple times. These priests were probably attempting to reach a more theological understanding of prayer, and to deepen the spirituality of temple worship. The same general motivation may lie behind the emergence of a sacramental theology of sacrifice which linked the binding of Isaac (ANTH A.6) with the Temple Mount, behind which was the idea that the great temple sacrifices were efficacious to atone for sin because they were a re-enactment of the offering of Isaac.

9. It is hard to identify for certain purely private prayers among the surviving Second Temple period prayer texts.

Unquestionably the Amidah in the second century CE was prayed both as a private prayer and with the congregation. It is also hard to know how to contextualize some of the prayers and hymns embedded in the literary texts. Were these composed purely for literary effect, or were they intended for actual liturgical use, or so used? 2 Bar. Apoc. (on which see MAJ GEN C.6) illustrates the problem. It contains a number of very fine laments for the destruction of the temple (ANTH E.6). Might these, or similar texts, have been used as part of a special litany for the destruction of the temple? There is evidence later in Judaism for groups, known as the Mourners for Zion ('abĕlê siyyôn), who dedicated themselves to special liturgies commemorating the fall of the temple.

F. Rules of Religious Associations. 1. Another feature of late Second Temple Judaism was the growth of private religious associations. The great public religious institutions of Judaism were the temple and the synagogue. Any Jew was free to attend either. The private religious associations, however, imposed restrictions on membership over and above Jewishness. In some cases very strict criteria for membership applied. Participation in the group's activities was only possible after an act of commitment to the group's distinctive world-view. These associations were sectarian in character. Their basic assumption was that the generality of Jews were too lax in their observance of Judaism. The group felt it had to adopt stricter standards, to follow a more demanding spirituality. These associations were linked to renewal movements, which were openly critical of official religion, and which campaigned vigorously to win their fellow Jews to a more rigorous way of life.

2. First-hand evidence as to how one of these groups organized itself comes from the Dead Sea scrolls, among which are a number of Community rule books (known as sĕrākîm: sing, serek), the most important of which is the great Community Rule (Serek hayyaḥad) from Cave I, a work written in distinctive Qumran Hebrew, which dates palaeographically to around 100 BCE (ANTH F.I). (Text: García Martínez and Tigchelaar (1997: i.68–99); tr.: Vermes (1997: 97–117); for the Cave 4 fragments see Alexander and Vermes (1998); commentaries: Wernberg-Møller (1957); Leaney (1966).) From this it is clear that entry into the community was tightly controlled, and involved a novitiate of two or possibly three years. When the novice was finally admitted to full membership his property was merged with that of the community. He then lived a life of prayer (ANTH E.2), study, and probably work under a strict discipline which governed all aspects of his life and behaviour. The community was hierarchical and authoritarian, and was dominated by a priestly élite. The spiritual head of the community bore the title Maskil (or Enlightener). As we have already noted the Qumran community had a very dark, dualistic view of the world (ANTH D.4). They divided humankind into Sons of Light and Sons of Darkness—a division, significantly, which applied to their fellow Jews as well.

3. Another rule book from Qumran is the Damascus Document, a number of copies of which partially survive, including two from the Middle Ages which turned up in a storeroom (genizah) in the Ben Ezra Synagogue in Cairo at the end of the nineteenth century (ANTH F.2; texts: Charlesworth (1995);

García Martínez and Tigchelaar (1997: i. 550–627; ii. 1134–5, 1152–5); tr.: Vermes (1997: 125–56); see further Schiffman (1975); Davies (1982); Campbell (1995); Hempel (1998)). The rule contained in the Damascus Document is less strict than that in the Community Rule, which seems to envisage a celibate, all-male society, largely self-contained, with only limited contact with the outside world. The Damascus Document envisages marriage and procreation, and a wider range of social and commercial contacts. The groups to which it applied seem to have been scattered through the towns of Judea. The relationship of the Community Rule and the Damascus Document has been the subject of lively debate. There is no totally satisfactory solution to this problem, but one plausible suggestion is that the Community Rule and the Damascus Rule relate to two different wings of the same broad religious movement. The 'mother' community was at Qumran, and the Community Rule relates to life there. The Damascus Rule relates to groups of supporters of the Qumran community who lived under a less demanding spiritual regime in various parts of Palestine, and possibly even abroad, but who looked to Qumran for spiritual guidance, and may from time to time have joined the community there in worship, for example at the annual festival of the renewal of the covenant (on which see ANTH E.3). The usefulness of such support groups to the Qumran community is obvious. If the Qumran community was celibate, then it could not have renewed itself by natural means. It would have had to rely on fresh vocations to replace the members who had died or left. The support groups, which did marry, would have provided a natural pool of recruitment. The Damascus Rule is in the same style of Hebrew as the Community Rule. The earliest copy of it found at Qumran seems to date to around the mid-first century BCE, long after the Quman community was founded. This may be purely accidental. However, it might suggest that the marrying wing of the movement developed comparatively late in the movement's history.

4. Another religious community, similar in some respects to the one at Qumran, is described by Philo of Alexandria (on whom see MAJ GEN A.3) in his treatise De Vita Contemplativa (ANTH F.3; text and tr.: Colson and Whitaker (1971: ix. 112–71)). They were known as the Therapeutae, and their communal settlement was located on the shores of the Mareotic Lake outside Alexandria in Egypt. They lived a life of withdrawal from the world and had affinities with pagan communes such as the 'Pythagorean' communities, which sprang up from time to time in the Mediterranean world in antiquity. Philo's account of the Therapeutae is so utopian that some have doubted whether any such group ever actually existed. However, the parallels with Qumran and with the Pythagoreans suggest that there is some historical reality behind his idealized picture. And even if it is not real, it still shows that people were beginning to conceive of the possibility of such closed religious orders, and such an intense, unworldly way of life.

5. Rabbinic sources in the Mishnah and Tosefta have preserved evidence of groups of observant Jews who banded together to form 'associations' (ḥaburôt) in order to observe stringently the laws of tithing, and to prepare and eat their everyday secular food in conditions of ritual purity (ANTH F.4). On the Mishnah see MAJ GEN B.II. The Tosefta is a parallel law-

code to the Mishnah, of roughly the same date (3rd cent. CE) (text: Zuckermandel (1937); tr.: Neusner (1977–86); introduction: Stemberger (1996: 149–63)). Since some of these rabbinic traditions seem to refer to the period before 70 CE, the question arises as to the relationship between these associations and the pre-70 Pharisees. This is a matter of some dispute. It is likely that the associations were Pharisaic institutions. The traditions regarding them have been passed down by the post-70 rabbis, the Pharisees' spiritual heirs, and the associations shared with the Pharisees a distinctive, and socially divisive, concern for tithing and ritual purity. It would probably be wrong to identify the associations totally with the Pharisaic movement. All the members of the associations may have been Pharisees, but not every Pharisee may have belonged to an association. The associations may have represented an inner circle of the particularly observant, within the broader Pharisaic movement. There were degrees of affiliation to an association. A candidate went through a period of initiation and probation in which he progressively took upon himself the duties of an associate (ḥabēr). After the period of probation he entered into full membership by making a solemn declaration before the whole association (or, according to another source, before three of its members) that he would observe the laws of tithing and of ritual purity with regard to secular food. Anyone who broke the rules of the association was expelled. The associations had a rather loose structure. They were not communes. There is no evidence that the associates lived together, or held their property in common (as did the Qumran Essenes and the early Christians). We do not hear of the associations having governing bodies. We do not even have clear evidence that they met for communal meals—though it is a reasonable assumption that there must occasionally have been communal sessions accompanied by a meal. Basically what the associations seem to have been were loose fellowships of people who formally recognized each other as strictly observant in matters of purity and tithing, as Jews with whom even the most scrupulous could share a meal with a good conscience.

6. Religious schools formed another type of religious association in early Judaism. The Qumran community had many of the attributes of a school: certainly study and teaching were among its primary functions. Most schools, however, were smaller and less complex than Qumran and comprised only a teacher and a circle of students. The school did not necessarily have its own buildings, but may have met in public places, such as the porticoes of town market-places. Some teachers were peripatetic and wandered around with their students. During a session of the school the teacher may have sat on a stool while the students sat in a circle on the ground 'at his feet'. The sessions of the school were public and passers-by would have stopped and stood at the back listening to the discussion. Rival teachers might have appeared from time to time and challenged the master to debate, and perhaps have tried to draw some of his students away. The organization was simple. On the teacher's death the students scattered. Some may have attached themselves to other schools, others may have gone back into ordinary life or set themselves up as teachers on their own account. Only in rare cases would the school have survived the teacher's death. A vivid picture of these schools emerges incidentally from rabbinic literature.

The story quoted at ANTH F.5 is typical. It is taken from the fourth-century Hebrew commentary on 'Abot (see MAJ GEN D.2), known as the 'Abot de Rabbi Nathan. Two major recensions (A and B) of this work survive. The story is taken from the A recension (text: Schechter (1979); trs.: Goldin (1955) [Recension A]; Saldarini (1975) [Recension B]; see further Saldarini (1982)).

7. Though primitive, these schools were among the most creative institutions of Second-Temple Judaism. The students were for the most part young adult males who would have had some basic education. They were probably unmarried, and had not yet acquired family responsibilities. Even when they left the school they may have retained links with the teacher and returned to him from time to time for instruction. The schools were fellowships. The students were expected to minister to the teacher and to treat him with respect. Teacher and pupil took their meals together, and seem to have observed distinctive rules of etiquette, and possibly in some cases even of dress, which marked them out from the rest of society. Historically speaking one of the most important of these schools was the Jesus-circle. The followers of Jesus formed a classic sect within Judaism, which managed to survive the violent death of its founding teacher. The organization of the early church fits well into the patterns of religious association found in late Second Temple period Judaism. The closest literary parallels to the Qumran *Community Rule* are to be found in early church orders such as the *Didache*. In fact the organization of the Qumran community in remarkable ways anticipates the organization of two of the major institutions of later Judaism and Christianity—the yeshivah and the monastery.

G. Hagiography. 1. A rudimentary biographical literature begins to develop in Second-Temple Judaism. Initially it focused on the biblical heroes, and filled out their lives with legendary additions. It grew naturally out of the process of retelling and filling the lacunae in the biblical narratives (see ANTH A.6). The Bible story functioned as the national epic of ancient Israel, and was crucial for Jewish national identity, just as the Homeric epics were crucial to Greek national identity. It is not surprising, therefore, that the major figures of the national epic should have become cultural icons and their stories embellished. Moses, the lawgiver of Israel, whose Torah was the foundation of the Jewish polity, became the most revered national hero. Philo wrote an important life of him in Greek, which represented him as the wisest of lawgivers. Josephus recorded extensive legendary material, probably originating among Egyptian Jews, which fills out the obscure period of Moses' life when he was a prince at the court of Pharaoh. He describes a series of successful military campaigns which Moses conducted on Pharaoh's behalf in Ethiopia (*Ant.* 2. 238–53). The exaltation of Moses reached its peak in the *Exagoge* of Ezekiel the Tragedian. This Greek drama, composed probably by a learned Alexandrian Jew in the second century BCE, has survived only in fragmentary quotations in later writers (text, tr., and commentary: Jacobson (1983); tr.: Robertson, *OTP* ii. 803–20). It seems to have retold the story of the Exodus of the Hebrews from Egypt down to about Exod 15. In one crucial passage in which he forsees in a dream the giving of the Torah on Sinai, Moses is apotheosized

(ANTH G.I). Though pre-eminent among the biblical heroes, Moses was by no means the only biblical figure to attract legend. We have already noted the strong interest in some circles in Enoch (see MAJ GEN A.7, C.4–5, D.7–9). The Qumran scrolls also attest a surprisingly deep interest in the figure of Noah.

2. These legends about the biblical saints served two main purposes. They contained an element of pure entertainment. This can be seen clearly in *Joseph and Aseneth* (ANTH G.2). This work, which was probably composed by a Jew in Greek in the first century BCE or the first century CE (though whether in Palestine, Syria, or Egypt is much disputed), is basically a romantic novel which elaborates at length on the passing reference in Gen 41:45 that 'Pharaoh gave Joseph...Asenath daughter of Potiphera [= Pentephres in our text], priest of On, as his wife'. (Text: Philonenko (1968); tr: Cook, in Sparks (1984: 465–504); Burchard, *OTP* ii. 177–248; Kraemer (1998) calls into question the date and origin of *Joseph and Aseneth* proposed above.) *Joseph and Aseneth* and the Esther cycle of stories (both the original Heb. and the Gk. additions) are among the earliest examples that survive from the ancient world of what might be called novels, and it has been argued that Jewish writers made a significant contribution to the development of this genre. However the majority of these tales of the biblical heroes, including *Joseph and Aseneth*, also had a serious purpose and were meant for edification. The biblical figures were put forward as exemplars whose behaviour was to be followed—or occasionally shunned—by the pious.

3. The veneration of the biblical heroes began to develop in late Second-Temple Judaism into a cult of the saints. Herod built a great mausoleum to mark the graves of the patriarchs in Hebron and adorned the tomb of David with a marble memorial (Jos. *Ant.* 16.182). Both these sites may have become centres of pilgrimage. Interest in the tombs of the saints is further shown by the curious work transmitted under the name of the *Lives of the Prophets* (ANTH G.3; text: Torrey (1946); tr.: Hare, *OTP* ii. 379–400; see further Schwemer (1997). Though passed down within the Christian church, and containing in some of its versions Christian additions, the *Lives of the Prophets* is generally agreed to go back to a Jewish text, probably composed in Palestine in Greek in the first half of the first century CE. The text shows a clear interest in memorializing the sites where the biblical prophets lay buried, with a view, presumably, to encouraging people to visit the tombs and venerate their occupants. The cult of the saints which became so powerful and popular a religious movement among Christians throughout the Levant in the Byzantine period, seems to have its roots in a Second Temple period Jewish practice. Indeed, the fact that so many of the legends of the saints contained in the *Lives of the Prophets* are found scattered throughout latter rabbinic literature may indicate that the practice persisted among Jews in the Talmudic period as well. It was certainly widespread among Jews in medieval and modern times.

4. It was not only biblical heroes who were held up as exemplars. Figures from more recent history were treated hagiographically. A martyr literature began to develop, the initial focus of which was the Jews who had embraced death at the time of the Maccabees rather than obey the command of the Greek king to renounce their religion. There was a widely circulated story about a mother who was forced to witness the death of her seven sons before she herself paid the ultimate price. This story was given powerful philosophical treatment in 4 Maccabees (ANTH G.4; text: Rahlfs (n.d: i. 1157–84); trs.: Townshend, *APOT* ii. 653–85; Anderson, *OTP* ii. 531–64; commentary: Hadas (1953); see further van Henten (1997)). The author, provenance, and date of this work, which influenced later Christian martyr literature and iconography, have been much debated. The text is written in a highly cultured Greek by a Jew well-trained in rhetoric and philosophy (its underlying message is the power of reason to control the emotions). It is clearly a Jewish text and was probably composed in Palestine or Syria in the late first or early second century CE. The possibility cannot be ruled out that it originated in Antioch where, in the patristic period, there was a cult of the Maccabean martyrs centred on tombs which were supposed to contain their relics. Though the evidence is far from clear, it is possible that this Antiochian cult of the Holy Maccabees was pre-Christian Jewish in origin.

5. A martyr literature also developed within rabbinic Judaism. This focused not on the Maccabean period, but on the persecutions under Hadrian (132–5 CE), during which a number of leading rabbis lost their lives. A version of the story of the mother and her seven sons circulated among rabbinic Jews, but significantly the setting was transferred to the time of Hadrian. The definitive rabbinic martyrology was the Hebrew *Legend of the Ten Martyrs*. (Text: Reeg (1985); tr.: Gollancz (1908: 118–44).) Though in its present form this work may date no earlier than the early Middle Ages, most of the individual tales of martyrdom which it contains are attested much earlier in rabbinic literature (ANTH G.5), and the genre of martyr-tale, as we have seen, goes back to Second Temple times. A central motif of the martyr literature is resistance to tyranny: this element is particularly strong in 4 Maccabees, and, interestingly, it echoes through the speech which Josephus puts in the mouth of Eleazar, when he exhorts the Sicarii at Masada to kill themselves rather than submit to Roman slavery (*J.W.* 7.323–36). This motif had resonance in the wider non-Jewish world. It brings the Jewish martyr literature into alignment with pagan Greek texts, such as the work called by modern scholars the *Acts of the Alexandrian Martyrs*, which records acts of heroic philosophical opposition to political tyranny. A hero of this pagan philosophical movement was undoubtedly Socrates, the story of whose death, so powerfully told by Plato and Xenophon, seems to have been an inspiration to the philosophical opponents of the Roman empire.

6. Sanctifying the name of God in martyrdom was the supreme example of piety that the great saints could provide. But other exemplary stories were also told about them. Anecdotes about the great teachers circulated within the schools. A particularly rich assortment of these has survived in rabbinic literature. It is natural for students to tell stories (some of which may be far from flattering) about their teachers, but this story-telling served a serious purpose. The teacher was seen as an embodiment of his teaching; he was nothing less than the Torah incarnate (ANTH. G.6, taken from the Babylonian Talmud, on which see MAJ GEN B.II). The student not only listened to what he said but observed his every action. The

imitation of the master was a cardinal principle of rabbinic education. In the absence of explicit teaching by the master on a given subject, a student could cite the master's actions as evidence of his views. Though large numbers of anecdotes about the leading scholars circulated in the rabbinic schools, in some cases constituting all the necessary raw material of a biography, curiously no one ever felt impelled to draw the anecdotes together to form a Life. Had they done so, the resultant text would have looked something like Diogenes Laertius's *Lives of the Philosophers*. The biographical urge was not entirely absent from post-biblical Judaism, as the expansions of the biblical narratives and the anecdotes about the non-biblical saints and scholars clearly prove, but, with the possible exceptions of Philo's *Life of Moses* and the Christian gospels, that biographical urge never reached fruition in anything like a full biography of any individual saint, scholar, or hero.

ANTHOLOGY OF POST-BIBLICAL TEXTS

Note: Round brackets indicate explanatory additions; square brackets supplements of lacunae in MS.

A. Bible Interpretation

1. *Pesher Habakkuk* (1QpHab), 11:2–12:10: The Trials of the Saints Foretold in Scripture (=Hab 2:15–17)

(11:2) *Woe to him who gives his neighbours to drink, pouring out* (3) *his venom till they are drunk, so that he may gaze at their appointed festivals* (Hab 2:15).

(4) Interpreted this concerns the Wicked Priest who (5) pursued after the Teacher of Righteousness so that he might confuse him with his venomous (6) fury in the house of his exile. And at the time appointed for rest on (7) the Day of Atonement, he appeared before them to confuse them, (8) and to make them stumble on a day of fasting, a sabbath set aside for their repose.

You have been sated with (9) *ignominy rather than with glory. Now you drink and stagger!* (10) *The cup in the Lord's right hand will come round to you, and shame will come* (11) *upon your glory* (Hab 2:16).

(12) Interpreted this concerns the priest whose ignominy became greater than his glory. (13) For he did not circumcise the foreskin of his heart, and he walked in the ways of (14) drunkenness, so that he might quench his thirst. But the cup of the venom of (15) God shall confuse him, incre[asing] his [ignominy] and the pain of [(16) his . . .]

[*For the violence done to Lebanon will overwhelm you, and the destruction of the beasts*] (12:1) *will terrify you, because of bloodshed and the violence against the land, the city, and all its inhabitants* (Hab 2:17).

(2) Interpreted this saying concerns the Wicked Priest, who will be repaid (3) the recompense which he himself gave to the Poor. For *Lebanon* is (4) the Council of the Community; and the *beasts* are the simple-hearted of Judah who keep (5) the Torah. God shall condemn him to utter destruction, (6) just as he himself plotted utterly to destroy the poor. And as for what it says, *Because of bloodshed* (7) *in the city and the violence against the land*, its interpretation is that *the city* is Jerusalem (8) where the Wicked Priest committed abominable deeds and defiled (9) the temple of God, and *the violence against the land* refers to the cities of Judah where (10) he robbed the poor of their possessions.

Comment: The Pesharist sees in the words of Habbakuk foreshadowings of precise events in the life of his community, but he refers to these events cryptically. The Teacher of Righteousness was probably the founder of the Community, who was driven out of Jerusalem by the Wicked Priest (one of the Hasmoneans). There is a hint that the community did not observe the Day of Atonement at the same time as the rest of Israel, otherwise the Wicked Priest would have been unable to travel to the Teacher's 'house of exile' (? Qumran) on the most holy day of the Jewish year. 'The Poor' is one of the community's self-designations. The term 'Lebanon', which was widely used in early Jewish writings as a designation of the temple (based on 1 Kings 7:2; cf. Sifre Deut. 6; Num.R. XI 3), is here transferred to the community: they are now the true temple. On Pesher Habakkuk see MAJ GEN A.2.

2. Philo, *On the Creation of the World*, 1–3, 7–9, 16–20: God as the Architect of the Cosmos (= Gen 1)

(1) Some lawgivers have set out nakedly and without adornment what they consider to be just, while others, investing their thoughts with over-abundant amplification, have befuddled the masses by obscuring the truth with mythical inventions. (2) But Moses, rejecting both these courses, the one as inconsiderate, thoughtless, and unphilosophical, the other as mendacious and full of trickery, introduced his laws with a most fine and noble exordium. He refrained, on the one hand, from declaring at once what should or should not be done, or, on the other hand, from himself inventing myths or acquiescing in those composed by others, because he needed to predispose the minds of those who would use his laws to accept them. (3) His exordium, as I have said, is most admirable. It consists of an account of the creation of the world, thus implying that the world is in harmony with the law and the law with the world, and that the man who obeys the law becomes at once a citizen of the world, regulating his actions in accordance with the will of Nature, by which the whole world is itself administered. . . .

(7) Some, admiring the world rather than its Maker, have declared it to be ungenerated and eternal, and, falsely and impiously, have attributed an almost total inactivity to God, whereas they ought, on the contrary, to have marvelled at his powers as Maker and Father, and not to have glorified the world beyond proper measure. (8) But Moses, because he had reached the very summit of philosophy, and been instructed by oracles in the numerous fundamental principles of nature, recognized that all things that exist must be classified either as active Cause or as passive object, and that the active Cause is the pure and unsullied Mind of the universe, transcending virtue, transcending knowledge, transcending the good itself and the beautiful itself, (9) while the passive object is in itself incapable of life and motion, but, once set in motion and shaped and given life by Mind, is transformed into that most perfect work, our world. . . .

(16) God, since he was God, foresaw that a good copy could never be produced without a good pattern, and that no object of sense perception could ever be faultless that was not made in the image of an original discerned only by mind. So when he had determined to create our visible world he first formed the intelligible world, in order that he might have an incorporeal, Godlike pattern to use to produce the material world, which would be the exact replica of the older creation, and contain as many objects of sense perception as the other contained objects perceptible only to mind.

(17) To speak of or imagine that world which consists of ideas as being in some place is impermissible, but we may understand how it exists, if we consider an analogy from our own world. When a city is founded to gratify the great ambition of a king or governor, who, claiming absolute power and harbouring grandiose designs, is eager to display his good fortune, a trained architect comes along who, observing the favourable climate and convenient position of the site, first sketches in his own mind nearly all the parts of the city that is going to be completed—temples, gymnasia, town-halls, market-places, harbours, docks, streets, the position of the walls, and the location of the private and public buildings. (18) Having received in his own soul, as on a wax tablet, the form of each of these buildings, he carries about in his head a picture of a city which is as yet

perceptible only to his mind. Then by his innate power of memory, he recalls the images of the various parts of this city, and imprints their outlines yet more clearly in it. And so, like a good craftsman, he begins to erect the city of stones and timber, keeping his eye upon his pattern, and making the material objects correspond to each of the incorporeal ideas.

(19) We must think about God in the same way. We must suppose that, when he had decided to found the one great city, he conceived beforehand the plans of its parts, and that from these he formed a world discernible only by the mind, and then, using that as a template, he completed the world which our senses perceive. (20) Just as the city which was planned beforehand in the architect's mind had no place in the external world, but had been imprinted on the soul of the artificer, so the universe that consists of ideas could have had no other location than the Divine Reason, which had set them in order.

Comment: If the essence of Torah lies in its commandments ('what should or should not be done'), why does Moses not plunge straight into an enumeration of the laws? Why does he begin with the story of the creation? The answer is that he wishes to make the point that 'the world is in harmony with the law and the law with the world', and, therefore, whoever follows the law is living in conformity to nature. Philo rejects the common philosophical notion that the world, though contingent, is eternal. He was one of the first to assert (incorrectly) that Gen 1 teaches the doctrine of creation out of nothing. In keeping with the Platonic theory of ideas, he implies that Gen 1:1 refers to the conception of the plan of creation in the Divine Reason, in accordance with which the physical world was then created (Gen 1:2–2:2). On Philo see MAJ GEN A.3.

3. *Mekilta of Rabbi Ishmael, Bahodesh*, 6: The Prohibition of Images (= Ex 20:4)

You shall not make for yourself an idol (Ex 20:4).

He may not make for himself one that is engraven, but perhaps he may make one which is solid? But Scripture says, 'Or any likeness' (Ex 20:4). He may not make for himself one that is solid, but perhaps he may plant a sacred tree? But Scripture says, 'You shall not plant any tree as a sacred pole (an Asherah)' (Deut 16:21).

He may not plant a sacred tree, but perhaps he may make an idol of wood? But Scripture says, 'Of any kind of wood' (Deut 16:21). He may not make one of wood, but perhaps he may make one of stone? Scripture says, 'Or place any figured stones' (Lev 26:1). He may not make one of stone, but perhaps he may make one of silver or gold? Scripture says, 'You shall not make any gods of silver alongside me, nor shall you make for yourselves gods of gold' (Ex 20:20). He may not make one of silver or gold, but perhaps he may make one of bronze, iron, or tin? Scripture says, 'Do not turn to idols or make cast images for yourselves' (Lev 19:4).

He may not make for himself an image of any of these, but perhaps he may make an image of a figure? Scripture says, 'So that you may not act corruptly by making an idol for yourselves in the form of any figure' (Deut 4:16). He may not make an image of a figure, but perhaps he may make an image of cattle or fowl? Scripture says, 'The likeness of any beast that is on the earth, the likeness of any winged bird that flies in the air' (Deut 4:17). He may not make an image of any of these, but perhaps he may make an image of fish, locust, unclean animals, or reptiles? Scripture says 'The likeness of anything that creeps on the ground, the likeness of any fish that is in the waters below the earth' (Deut 4:18).

He may not make an image of any of these, but perhaps he may make an image of the sun, the moon, the stars, and the planets? Scripture says, 'And when you look up to the heavens and see the sun and the moon and the stars, all the host of heaven, do not be led astray and bow down to them and worship them' (Deut 4:19).

He may not make an image of any of these, but perhaps he may make an image of the angels, the Cherubim, and the Ofannim (an order of angels)? Scripture says, 'Of anything that is in the heavens above' (Ex 20:4). One might think that 'in the heavens' refers to images of the sun, the moon, the stars, and the planets, but it says, 'of anything that is in the heavens *above*'—not the image of the angels, nor the image of the Cherubim, nor the image of the Ofannim.

He may not make an image of any of these, but perhaps he may make an image of the deeps or the darkness? Scripture says, 'Or in the waters under the earth' (Ex 20:4), which includes reflected images. Thus is the opinion of Rabbi Aqiba. Some say that it includes the *Shabriri* (demons).

Thus Scripture goes out of its way to pursue the evil inclination, in order to leave no room for anyone to find the least excuse to permit [idolatry]!

You shall not bow down to them or worship them (Ex 20:5).

Why is this said? To show, in accordance with the verse, 'And has gone to worship other gods and has bowed down to them' (Deut 17:3), that one is guilty for the act of worshipping by itself and for the act of bowing down by itself. (You might say,) This is your opinion, but perhaps one is not guilty unless he both worships and bows down? However, Scripture says, 'You shall not bow down to them or worship them', thus indicating that one is guilty for the act of worshipping by itself and for the act of bowing down by itself.

Comment: Does Ex 20:4–5 contain one commandment or two? Is the injunction directed against making images *in order to* bow down to them, or against *both* making images *and* bowing down to them? The first interpretation allows the possibility of images for decorative, non-religious purposes; the second precludes all figurative art. The Mekilta takes the latter view. It also treats 'bowing down' and 'worshipping' in v. 5 as two separate offences and draws in all the parallel verses so as to forbid figurative art in any medium, form, or material. A strict interpretation of the law on images seems to have prevailed in Second Temple times, but archaeology suggests that some took a more liberal attitude in the Talmudic period, when figurative art was found even on the mosaic floors of synagogues. On the *Mekilta of Rabbi Ishmael* see MAJ GEN A.4–5.

4. *1 Enoch*, 6:1–6; 7:1–6; 8:1–4: The Fall of the Angels (= Gen 6:1–5)

(6:1) And it came to pass, when the sons of men had multiplied, that in those days handsome and beautiful daughters were born to them. (2) And the angels, the sons of heaven, saw them and desired them; and they said one to another: 'Come, let us choose for ourselves wives from the daughters of the men of earth, and let us beget for ourselves children'. (3) And Shemihazah, who was their leader, said to them: 'I am afraid that you will not want to do this deed, and that I alone will pay the price for a great sin.' (4) And they all answered him and said: 'Let us all swear an oath, and bind one another with curses, that none of us will change this plan till we have fulfilled it and have done this deed.' (5) Then they all swore together and bound one another with curses. (6) And there were two hundred of them who descended in the days of Jared on the summit of Mount Hermon; and they called the mount Hermon, because they swore and bound one another with curses upon it. . . .

(7:1) And they took wives for themselves; each chose for himself a wife; and they began to cohabit with them and to defile themselves with them. And they taught the women charms and spells and showed them the cutting of roots and herbs. (2) And they became pregnant by them and bore great giants, three thousand cubits tall. (3) These devoured the entire fruits of men's labour, so that men were unable to sustain them. (4) Then the giants treated them violently and began to devour mankind; (5) and they began to sin against the birds and the beasts and the reptiles, and the fish, and to devour each other's flesh, and drink their blood. (6) Thereupon the earth complained against the lawless ones.

(8:1) Azael taught men how to make swords and knives and shields and breastplates and every weapon of war; and he showed them the metals of the earth, how to work gold to fashion ornaments, and how to make silver into bracelets for women; and he instructed them about antimony, and eye-shadow, and about all kinds of precious stones and coloured dyes; and the children of men fashioned these things for themselves and for their daughters, and they transgressed and led astray the saints. (2) Much impiety arose upon the earth, and they committed fornication and went astray and corrupted their ways. (3) Shemihazah taught about spells; Hermoni taught about medicines and the loosing of spells; Baraqiel taught about the auguries of lightning; Kokabiel taught about the auguries of the stars; Ziqiel taught about the auguries of meteors; Araqiel taught about the augur of the earth; Shimshiel taught about the auguries of the sun; Sahriel taught about the auguries of the moon. They all began to reveal secrets to their wives and sons. (4) Then the giants began to devour the flesh of men, and men began to be few upon the earth; and as they perished, their cry went up to heaven: 'Bring our cause before the Most High, and our destruction before the Great Glory, before the Lord of Lords in majesty.'

Comment: The 'sons of God' of Gen 6:1 are identified with angels, and the Nephilim of 6:4 with the offspring of the monstrous union of angels and human women. The wickedness which marked those days and led to the Flood is attributed to the forbidden knowledge (about weapons of war, magic, jewellery, and cosmetics) that the angels imparted to humankind. The text, which reflects a view widely held in antiquity that great technological advances depend on extraterrestrial knowledge being brought down (often illicitly) to earth, displays a deep-seated ambivalence towards technological progress. On *1 Enoch* see MAJ GEN A.7.

5. *Jubilees*, 8:10–17; 22–30; 9:14–15: The Division of the World among the Sons of Noah (= Gen 10)

(8:10) And it came to pass at the beginning of the thirty-third jubilee that they divided the earth into three portions, one portion for Shem, one for Ham, and one for Japheth, a patrimony for each, in the first year, in the first week, while one of us, who had been sent to them, was still with them. (11) And Noah called his sons and they came to him, they and their children; and he divided the earth by drawing lots to decide what each of his three sons would possess, and they reached out their hands and took the document from their father Noah's lap.

(12) And the lot of Shem was assigned in his document as the middle of the earth, which he would take as his patrimony and his sons' patrimony for ever. From the middle of the Mountains of Rafa, from the mouth of the river Tina, his portion runs westwards along the middle of this river, and extends (eastwards) as far as the Waters of the Abysses, out of which this river rises. The river empties its waters into the Sea of Me'at, and this flows into the Great Sea: all the land on the northern side belongs to Japheth and all the land on the southern side belongs to Shem. (13) And his portion extends to the vicinity of Karaso, which is in the centre of the tongue that faces south. (14) And his portion goes on in the direction of the Great Sea, and it goes straight on till it reaches the west (? east) of the tongue that faces south (for this sea is called the tongue of the Sea of Egypt). (15) And it turns from here southwards, along the coastline, and it continues westwards, in the direction of the mouth of the Great Sea,

to Afra. It goes on till it reaches the waters of the river Gihon, and (it turns) southwards to the waters of the Gihon, to the banks of this river. (16) And it goes on towards the east till it approaches the Garden of Eden on its south side, the south and east of the whole land of Eden and the whole east. It turns in the east and goes north till it approaches the east of the mountain called Rafa, and it goes down to the bank of the mouth of the river Tina. (17) This portion was assigned by lot to Shem and to his sons as an eternal possession for his descendants for ever....

(22) And to Ham was assigned the second portion—all that lies beyond the Gihon southwards, to the right of the Garden. And his portion extends southwards and goes along the Mountains of Fire; and it goes towards the west to the Sea of Atel, and it continues westwards till it approaches the Sea of Ma'uk, on which nothing sets sail without perishing. (23) And it goes northwards to the vicinity of Gadir. And it goes along the coast, along the edge of the waters of the Great Sea, till it approaches the river Gihon. And it goes along the river Gihon till it reaches the right side of the Garden of Eden. (24) And this is the land that was assigned to Ham, which he was to occupy for ever, he and his sons, generation after generation for ever.

(25) And for Japheth the third portion was assigned—all that lies beyond the river Tina, to the north of the outflow of its waters. And his portion extends towards the north-east to the whole region of Gog and to all the country east of it. And it goes northwards as far as the mountains of Qelt; and it goes to the east (? west) of Gadir as far as the shore of the waters of the sea. (27) And it goes on until it approaches the west of Fereg, and returns towards Afreg; and it continues on eastwards to the waters of the Sea of Me'at. (28) And it goes on alongside the river Tina in a north-easterly direction till it reaches the end of its waters towards Mount Rafa; and then it turns round towards the north. (29) This is the land that fell to Japheth and his sons as the portion of his inheritance, which he was to occupy, himself and his sons, generation after generation for ever—five large islands, and a large tract of land in the north. (30) But it is cold, and Ham's land is hot, but Shem's is neither hot nor cold, but a blend of cold and heat....

(9:14) And Noah's sons divided their lands among their sons in the presence of their father Noah; and he made them all swear an oath, to put a curse on anyone that tried to seize a portion that had not been assigned to him by lot. (15) And they all said, 'So be it! So be it!', for themselves and their sons for ever, in every generation till the day of judgement, when the Lord God will judge them with a sword and with fire on account of all their uncleanness and the wickedness of their misdeeds, which have filled the earth with sin, uncleanness, fornication, and transgression.

Comment: The passage is poorly preserved (the translation above is based to some extent on conjectural restoration), but there emerges from it nevertheless a vivid image of the world, such as an educated Jew would have had in late Second Temple times. It correlates the three sons of Noah with the three continents of the Ionian Greek geographers (Japhet with Europe; Shem with Asia; and Ham with Libya/Africa). Since Noah's sons solemnly agreed to this division of the world after the Flood, it has the force of international law. Elsewhere the author of *Jubilees* exploits this idea to deny the legitimacy of the Greek occupation of the Land of Israel. The Greeks, as sons of Japhet, had their allotted patrimony in Europe. By seizing 'a portion that had not been assigned to them by lot', they had brought upon themselves a curse. He also exploits the same idea to argue that Canaan, a son of Ham, had usurped the so-called Land of Canaan. The true owners of this land were the Jews as sons of Shem. On *Jubilees* see MAJ GEN A.8.

6. Josephus, *Antiquities* 1.222–36: The Binding of Isaac (= Gen 22:1–19)

(222) Now Abraham loved Isaac deeply, because he was his only son, born to him by the gift of God on the threshold of his old age. The child, for his part, earned still more good will and affection from his parents by practising every virtue, fulfilling his obligations to his father and mother and being zealous in his piety towards God. (223) Abraham placed all his own happiness in the hope that, when he died, he would leave his son unharmed. This indeed he achieved in the end by the will of God, but God, wishing to test his piety towards himself, appeared to him and, after enumerating all the blessings he had bestowed on him, (224) how he had made him stronger than his enemies, and how he owed to him his present happiness and his son Isaac, asked him to offer up that son to him as a sacrificial victim. He commanded him to take the child up to Mount Moriah, erect an altar and make a burnt-offering of him: thus he would show his piety towards God, if he put his good pleasure above the preservation of his child.

(225) Abraham judged that nothing could justify disobedience to God but that all should submit to his will, since all living creatures owe their existence to his providence and bounty. So, hiding from his wife God's command and his own resolve to sacrifice the child, indeed, concealing it even from his servants, lest he should be prevented from obeying God, he took Isaac with two servants, loaded an ass with everything needed for the sacrifice and set off for the mountain. (226) For two days the servants accompanied him, but on the third, when the mountain came in sight, he left his companions on the plain and went on with his son alone to the mountain, which later King David fixed as the site of the temple. (227) They brought with them everything needed for the sacrifice except a victim. As Isaac, who was now twenty-five years old, was preparing the altar, he asked his father what he was going to sacrifice, since there was no victim; to which his father answered that God would provide for them, since he was able to make abundant provision for those who had nothing, and to take away the possessions of those who felt assured of them. So God would grant him a victim, if he was pleased to grace the sacrifice with his presence.

(228) But when the altar had been prepared and he had arranged the firewood on it and all was ready, he said to his son: 'My boy, I prayed to God ten thousand prayers to have you as my son, and when you came into the world, I spared no pains on your upbringing. I had no thought of greater happiness than to see you grow up, and to leave you at my death heir of my estate. (229) But, since it was by God's will that I became your father, and now again it pleases him that I should give you up, bear this consecration valiantly, for I yield you to God who now claims from us this honour in return for the favours he has granted me as my supporter and defender. (230) As you were born [contrary to nature, so] quit this life not in the usual way, but sent by your own father to God, the father of all, through the rite of sacrifice. I suppose, he does not reckon it right for you to depart this life by sickness or war or any of the calamities that usually happen to men, (231) but rather would receive your soul with prayers and sacrifice and keep it near himself; and you will be my support and stay in my old age, the very purpose for which I reared you, by giving me God instead of yourself.'

(232) Now Isaac, since the son of such a father could not but be noble-minded, received these words with joy, and said that he was not fit to have been born at all if he rejected the decision of God and his father and did not readily submit to both their wills, seeing that it would be wrong to disobey even if his father alone was so minded. He rushed to the altar to be sacrificed, (233) and the deed would have been done, if God had not intervened, for he called Abraham by name and forbade him kill the boy. It was not, he said, from any desire for human blood that he had commanded him to kill his son,

nor did he wish in such a wicked way to rob him of the son that he himself had given him. Rather, he wanted to test his disposition and see whether he would obey even such a command. (234) Now that he knew his zeal and the depth of his piety, he was pleased with the benefits he had already given him, and would in the future always watch over him and his race with the greatest care. His son would attain to a ripe old age, have a happy life and bequeath to a virtuous and legitimate offspring a great dominion. (235) He also foretold that their race would grow to become many nations, whose wealth would increase and whose founders would be held in perpetual remembrance, that they would subdue Canaan by force of arms and be the envy of everyone.

(236) When God had said this, he produced for them a ram for the sacrifice from a hidden place. So, having been restored to each other beyond all their hopes and having heard promises of such great blessings, they embraced each other, and, when they had offered the sacrifice, they returned home to Sarah and lived happily, God helping them in whatever they desired.

Comment: Josephus fills out the story with speeches and explanations to heighten the drama: his wordy, syntactic, typically Greek style stands in stark contrast to the economy of the Hebrew. He adds little of substance, save for two points: (1) He depicts Isaac as a full-grown man whose co-operation would have been needed (and, indeed, was freely offered), if the sacrifice had taken place. Isaac thus becomes as much a hero as Abraham, and is shown in an equally meritorious light. (2) Mount Moriah is identified as the place 'which later King David fixed as the site of the temple'. This was an old and widespread tradition in early Judaism (cf. 2 Chr 3:1). On the basis of it some seem to have argued that the temple sacrifices were not efficacious in themselves, but only as a re-enactment and recollection of the sacrifice of Isaac. On Josephus see MAJ GEN A.9.

7. *Targum Pseudo-Jonathan* to Gen 4:1–8: The Reason for the World's First Murder

(4:1) *And Adam knew* that *Eve his wife* had conceived from Sammael the angel, *and she became pregnant and gave birth to Cain*, and he was like those on high, not like those below; *and she said, 'I have acquired a man*, the angel of *the Lord.'* (2) *And she went on to bear* from Adam, her husband, his twin sister and *Abel. And Abel was a keeper of sheep, but Cain was* a man *tilling the earth*. (3) *And it came to pass at the end of days*, on the fourteenth of Nisan, that *Cain brought of the produce of the ground*, of the seed of flax, *as an offering* of first-fruits *before the Lord*. (4) *And Abel, for his part, also brought of the firstlings of his flock and of their fat parts, and it was pleasing before the Lord, and the Lord showed favour to Abel and to his offering*: (5) *but to Cain and to his offering he did not show favour. And Cain was very angry, and the* expression *of his face fell*. (6) *And the Lord said to Cain, 'Why are you angry? and why has the expression on your face fallen?* (7) *If you have done* your work *well, your guilt will be forgiven. But if you have not done* your work *well* in this world, your sin will be kept for the great day of judgement. *At the doors* of your heart *sin lies waiting*, but in your hand I have given power over the evil inclination; *towards you will be its desire, but you will have authority over it* either to act righteously or to sin.'

(8) *And Cain said to Abel his brother*, 'Come, let us both go out into the field.' *And it came to pass that when they had* both *gone out into the field*, that Cain answered and said to Abel: 'I see that the world was created with mercy, but that it is not governed according to the fruit of good deeds, and there is partiality in judgement; therefore your offering was accepted with favour, but my offering was not accepted from me with favour.' Abel answered and said: 'The world was indeed

created with mercy, and it is governed by the fruit of good deeds, and there is no partiality in judgement. But because the fruit of my deeds was better than yours and offered prior to yours, so my offering was accepted with favour.' Cain answered and said to Abel: 'There is no judgement and no judge and no other world; there is no good reward to be given to the righteous, and no punishment for the wicked.' Abel answered and said: 'There is a judgement and a judge and another world; there is a good reward to be given to the righteous, and there is punishment for the wicked.' And concerning these matters they fell into a dispute in the open field, (9) *and Cain rose up against Abel his brother*, and drove a stone into his forehead, *and slew him*.

Comment: As in Rewritten Bible the *Targum* fills in the narrative lacunae of the biblical text (which is given here in italics). Thus it explains how Cain killed Abel (with a stone), and why (the world's first murder happened because of a theological argument about whether God governs the world justly). It offers an interpretation of the famous crux in Gen 4:7, where it finds a reference to the rabbinic doctrine of the two inclinations, one towards good, the other towards evil (cf. ANTH D.4). The assertion (v. 1) that Cain was born of the union of Eve and Sammael (a rabbinic name for the Devil) is surprising (cf. the story of the intercourse of angels and humans in ANTH A.4). It explains why Cain was evil: he was an alien, a child of the Devil, who did the Devil's work. On the Targumim see MAJ GEN A.11.

B. Law

1. Mishnah, *Sanhedrin*, 4:3–4: The Great Sanhedrin

(4:3) The Sanhedrin was arranged like half a round threshing-floor so that they might see one another, and two judges' clerks stood in front of them, one to the right and the other to the left, and wrote down the arguments for acquittal and the arguments for conviction. Rabbi Judah said: There were three: one to write down the arguments for acquittal, one to write down the arguments for conviction, and a third to write down the arguments both for acquittal and for conviction.

(4) Three rows of Students of the Sages sat in front of them, and each one knew his place. If they needed to appoint (another judge), they appointed him from the first row, and one from the second row moved up to the first row, and one from the third row moved up to the second; and they selected someone from the assembly and seated him in the third row. He did not sit in the place of the former, but he sat in the place appropriate for him.

Comment: The picture is not entirely clear, nor is its historical accuracy certain. One way of understanding it is to suppose that the actual members of the Sanhedrin, numbering seventy-one according to the Mishnah (*m. Sanh.* 1:6), sat in three, tiered, semi-circular rows. The Students of the Sages sat opposite them in three straight rows. Behind the rows of the Students of the Sages stood a general audience ('the assembly') comprising other scholars and perhaps members of the public and friends of the parties. The action took place in the semi-circular space between the rows of the Students of the Sages and the members of the Sanhedrin. In this space the clerks of the court sat, and perhaps also the two senior judges, whom the Talmud calls the President (*nāśî*') and the Father of the Court (*'āb bêt dîn*). The Students of the Sages were senior scholars who were, in effect, learning how to be judges by observing the Sanhedrin at work. They provided a necessary pool from which to fill temporary or permanent vacancies on the bench. See further MAJ GEN B.4, 11.

2. *Papyrus Murabbaʿat*, 19: An Aramaic Bill of Divorce (*Get*)

(1) On the first of Mareshvan, in the year six, at Masada: (2) 'I divorce and repudiate of my own free will, I, (3) Joseph, son of Naqsan, from [—]ah, resident at Masada, you, (4) Mariam, daughter of Jonathan [f]rom Hanablata, resident (5) at Masada, [you] who were formerly my wife, so that you are (6) free for your part to go and to become the wife of any (7) Jewish man, whom you wish. And let this serve you as a document of repudiation from me (8) and as a bill of divorce. And her[ew]ith I am giving back [to you] the [dow]ry, and for all destroyed or damaged or [—] property I will [re-embu]rse you, as I am obliged to do, (10) and I make fourfold restitution. And whe[never] you ask me, I will provide you with another copy of (11) [this] document, for as long as I live.'
(26) Joseph, son of Naqsan, for himself
(27) Eliezer, [son of] Malkah, witness
(28) Joseph, son of Malkah, witness
(29) Eleazar, son of Hananah, witness.

Comment: The Bill of Divorce is a Torah law, though the wording of the document is not laid down: see Deut 24:1–4 (cf. Mt 5:31; 19:7; Mk 10:4). This document was written in the year 111 CE. Like the marriage contracts of the period, the text is written twice, once on the front and once on the back of the papyrus. Though divorce seems easy, the necessity to repay dowry, with the fourfold restitution for any damaged or destroyed property, must have acted as a powerful restraint on hasty action. See further MAJ GEN B.8.

3. *Mishnah, Sebīʿit*, 10:3–6: The *Prosbul* of Hillel

(10:3) A *Prosbul* is not cancelled [by the Seventh Year]. This is one of the enactments of Hillel the Elder. He saw that people were reluctant to give loans to one another and transgressed what is written in the Torah, 'Be careful that you do not harbour in your heart a mean thought [by saying, The Seventh Year, the year of release, is coming. You view with hostility your poor brother, and lend him nothing; and he cries out to the Lord against you, and you incur guilt]' (Deut 15:9). So Hillel ordained the *Prosbul*.
(4) This is the formula of the *Prosbul*: 'I entrust to you, so-and-so, the judges in such-and-such-a-place, that I may be able to collect any debt due to me [from so-and-so], whenever I wish.' And the judges or the witnesses sign below.
(5) An ante-dated *Prosbul* is valid, but a post-dated one is not valid. Ante-dated bonds are not valid, but post-dated ones are valid. If one borrows from five persons, a *Prosbul* is drawn up for each of them separately. If five persons borrow from one, only one *Prosbul* is drawn up for them all.
(6) A *Prosbul* may be written only for (a loan secured by) immovable property. If the debtor has none, the creditor gives him title to part, however small, of his own land. If the debtor has land held in pledge in the city, a *Prosbul* may be written on its security. Rabbi Huspit says: They may write a *Prosbul* for a husband on the security of his wife's property, or for orphans on the security of their guardians' property.

Comment: Since all debts were cancelled by the sabbatical year (Deut 15:2–3), it became increasingly difficult as the sabbatical year approached to raise loans. Hillel's *Prosbul* allowed debts to be collected after the sabbatical year: the written declaration, signed by the court, made the court ultimately responsible for the collection of the debt, and the court, being a corporate body, was not affected by the law of Deut 15:2–3, which envisages transactions between individuals. It illustrates how clever jurists could ameliorate the law. If the tradition is genuine, then it suggests that the sabbatical year was still being observed in the time of Hillel in the early first century CE. The term *Prosbul* is probably a shortening of the Greek *pros boulē(i) bouleutōn*, 'before the assembly of counsellors'. See further MAJ GEN B.8, 11.

4. The *Temple Scroll* (11 QTemple), 56:12–57:21: Laws Regarding the King

(56:12) When you have come into the land that I am giving to you, and you have taken possession of it, and settled (13) in it, and you say, 'I shall set over myself a king like all the peoples round about me', (14) then set over yourself a king whom I will choose. From your brothers you may set a king over yourselves (15) but you may not place over yourselves a stranger who is not your brother. Even so he may not (16) acquire for himself many horses nor lead the people back to Egypt to make war in order (17) to acquire for himself many horses and much silver and gold, since I have said to you: 'You must never (18) return on that way again.' And he must not acquire for himself many wives, lest they turn his heart away from me. Also silver and gold he must not acquire for himself in great quantity. (20) And when he sits on the throne of his kingdom, they shall write (21) for him this Torah on a scroll in the presence of the priests.

(57:1) And this is the Torah [that they shall write for the king in the presence of the] priests. (2) On the day when they install hi[m] as king [they shall take a ce]nsus of the Israelites from (3) 20 years old to 60 years old, according to their divisions, and he will appoint (4) at their head commanders of thousands, commanders of hundreds, commanders of fifties, (5) and commanders of tens throughout all their cities. And he shall select for himself from them a thousand men (6) from each tribe, so that he shall have with him twelve thousand warriors (7) who will never leave him unattended, so that he can be taken captive by the nations. And all (8) those selected men whom he has chosen shall be honest, God-fearing, (9) disdaining ill-gotten gain, able-bodied warriors. And they shall stay with him constantly, (10) day and night, to guard him from every sin (11) and from foreigners, lest they should take him captive.

Twelve (12) leaders of his people shall be with him, and twelve Priests and (13) twelve Levites. They shall sit in council with him to administer justice (14) and Torah. And he shall not be too proud to listen to them, nor shall he do anything (15) without their advice.

He may not take a wife from any of (16) the daughters of the nations; rather he shall take for himself a wife from his father's house, (17) from his father's family. And he may not take any other woman in addition to her, but (18) she alone shall be with him as long as she lives. And if she dies, he may take (19) for himself another wife from his father's house, from his family.

He must not pervent justice, (20) nor take a bribe to pervert righteous judgement. And he shall not covet (21) any field, vineyard, property, house or anything valuable in Israel so as to steal [it].

Comment: Comparison with the law of the king in Deut 17:14–20 shows that the *Temple Scroll* not only repeats the biblical text more or less verbatim, but also interprets it and supplements it with new laws. 56:12–21 largely reproduces Deuteronomy, the standard text of which is presented in italics above. Note, however, that the *Temple Scroll* systematically recasts the passage in the first person ('the land that *I* am giving you', rather than 'the land that *the* LORD *your God* is giving you', emphases added). 57:1–21 purports to contain the contents of the scroll which Deuteronomy stipulates should be written for the king on his accession to the throne. Its laws regarding the royal bodyguard and the royal council (consisting of equal representation from the three estates—People, Priests, and Levites) are not biblical, nor is its law that the royal consort must be from the king's clan. And its stipulation that the king must have only one wife at a time is a curiously strict interpretation of the Deuteronomic injunction not to 'acquire

for himself many wives' (Deut 17:17). On the *Temple Scroll* see MAJ GEN B.9.

5. *Damascus Document* (CD), 10:14–11:18: Sabbath Laws

(10.14) Concerning the sabbath, how to observe it according to its law.

No man shall (15) work on the sixth day from the moment when the sun's disc is (16) distant from the gate [where it sets] by its full diameter, for this is what Scripture means by saying, 'Observe (17) the sabbath day to sanctify it' (Deut 5:12).

No man shall speak (18) a vain or idle word on the sabbath day.

He shall not make a loan to his neighbour. He shall not take any decision relating to money or profit. (19) He shall say nothing about matters of business or work to be done on the following day.

(20) No man shall walk about in the field to carry out his tasks (21) on the sabbath. He shall not walk more than one thousand cubits beyond his town.

(22) No man shall eat on the sabbath day anything that has not been prepared beforehand. He shall not eat anything lying about (23) in the field. He shall drink only in the camp. (11.1) If he is on a journey and goes down to bathe, he may drink where he stands, but he may not draw water into (2) any vessel.

He shall not send a Gentile to do an errand on the sabbath day.

(3) No man shall put on dirty clothes, or clothes that have been kept in a store, unless (4) they have been washed with water or rubbed with frankincense.

No man shall starve himself (?) voluntarily (5) on the sabbath.

No man shall walk after an animal to pasture it outside his town (6) more than two thousand cubits. He shall not raise his hand to strike it with his fist. If (7) it is stubborn he shall not take it out of his house.

No man shall take anything from his house (8) outside, or bring anything from outside into the house. If he is in a temporary shelter, he shall not take anything out from it (9) nor bring anything in.

He shall not open a sealed jar on the sabbath.

No man shall carry on himself (10) perfumes while going out and coming in on the sabbath.

He shall not lift in his dwelling-house (11) either stone or dust.

No man minding a child shall carry it while going out or coming in on the sabbath.

(12) No man shall scold his male or female slave or his hired servant on the sabbath.

(13) No man shall help an animal to give birth on the sabbath day. And if it should fall into a cistern (14) or pit, he shall not lift it out on the sabbath.

No man should rest in a place close (15) to Gentiles on the sabbath.

No man shall profane the sabbath for the sake of [acquiring] wealth or profit on the sabbath day.

(16) If anyone falls into water or [into a pit], (17) no one should pull him out with the aid of a ladder or rope or any such instrument.

No man shall offer on the altar on the sabbath any offering (18) other than the sabbath burnt-offering, for thus it is written, 'Except your sabbath offerings' (Lev 23:38).

Comment: The laws found in this sectarian document go well beyond the outline sabbath legislation in the Torah. The position taken is strict. Saving of human life on sabbath is permitted, but not if a utensil has to be used! Saving of animal life is not permitted (cf. Mt 12:11; Lk 14:5; Deut 22:4), nor is assistance to an animal giving birth. A child may not be carried between one domain and another, nor may perfumes be worn (presumably in containers such as sachets or phials), since this would constitute 'carrying'—a form of work forbidden on the sabbath. A strict position is also taken on the feeding and watering of animals on the sabbath, which would obviously have been an issue in farming communities (cf. Lk 13:15). One may 'walk after' (the language is precise; one may not 'lead') the animal no more than 2,000 cubits out of the town. Note also the stipulation to 'add' to the sabbath, i.e. begin it early, before the sun has actually set, in order to avoid any risk of profaning it. On the *Damascus Document* see MAJ GEN B.10 and F.3.

6. Mishnah, *Baba Batra*, 2:1–3: On Not Causing an Nuisance to Neighbours

(2:1) No one may dig a cistern (on his own land) close to a cistern of his neighbour; nor may he dig a trench, cave, water-channel, or laundry-pool unless he keeps it at least three handbreadths away from his neighbour's wall, and plasters its sides with lime. He must keep olive-refuse, manure, salt, lime, or stones at least three handbreadths away from his neighbour's wall, and he must plaster it with lime. He must keep seeds and furrows and urine at least three handbreadths away from the wall. Millstones must be kept at least three hand-breadths from the wall measuring from the lower millstone, or four measuring from the upper millstone. An oven must be kept at least three handbreadths from the wall measuring from the belly of the oven, or four measuring from the rim.

(2) No one may set up an oven inside a house unless there is a void of four cubits above it. If he sets it up in an upstairs room there must be a concrete floor at least three handbreadths thick beneath it, or, for a small stove, one handbreadth thick; and if it causes damage (to the floor) the owner of the oven must pay for the damage caused. Rabbi Simeon says: These measurements were stipulated so that if, (having observed them,) damage ensues, he will not be liable to pay.

(3) No one may open a bakery or a dyer's workshop beneath his neighbour's food-store, nor (may he open) a cowshed. In fact, they allowed all these under a wine-store, apart from the cowshed. If someone wants to open a shop within a courtyard, his neighbour may stop him on the grounds that he would not be able to sleep because of the noise of the customers. However, if he is making articles to take out and sell in the market, his neighbour cannot stop him on the grounds that he would be unable to sleep because of the noise of the hammer, or the noise of the millstones. Nor can he protest about the noise of (school) children.

Comment: The matters dealt with here would be regarded today as secular and falling within the remit of municipal planning by-laws. Here no such distinction between 'religious' and 'secular' applies: to create a civil society is a religious duty. The formulation of the law, as throughout the Mishnah, is casuistic, i.e. concrete illustrations are given of a fundamental principle, which is not itself stated. Here the underlying principle (the *kelal*) is clear: no one, even when acting within his own domain, has a right to cause a nuisance to a neighbour. These laws are not found in the Torah, but can be seen as an attempt to work out concretely the commandment to 'love your neighbour as yourself' (Lev 19:18). On the Mishnah see MAJ GEN B.11.

7. The *Halakic Letter* (4QMMT), B.52–62 + C.7–12: Disputes over the Interpretation of the Law

(B.52) [And further]more concerning the deaf who have not heard the statute, the [jud]gement or [the rules of] purity, and have not (53) [he]ard the ordinances of Israel, [we are of the opinion] that he who has not seen and has not heard [these] does not (54) [k]now how to perform [them]. However, they may partake of the pu[r]e food of the Sanctuary.

(55) [And] furthermore, concerning streams of liquid, we are of the opinion that they are not in themselves (56) [p]ure, and furthermore

that streams of liquid do not separate between impure (57) [and] pure liquids, for the poured liquid and the liquid in the receptacle into which it is poured are alike, (58) a single liquid.

And one must not bring dogs into the h[o]ly camp for they (59) may eat some of the [b]ones from the Sanctua[ry] to which meat is still attached. For (60) Jerusalem is the holy camp and the place (61) which God has chosen from all the tribes of Is[rael]. For Jer]usalem is the head of (62) the [c]amps of Israel...

(C.7) [And you know that] we have separated ourselves from the mass of the peo[ple] and from all their impurity, (8) and] from joining with them in these matters, or going along w[ith them] in these things. And you k[now that no] (9) treachery or lie or evil can be found in our hands, for [w]e are paying [close attention] to [these matters].

[And furthermore] (10) we [have written] to you (sing.) so that you should understand the Book of Moses [and] the Book[s of the Pr]ophets and Davi[d and the enactments] of every age. And in the Book is written [———for] (12) you, and the former things [—]. And furthermore it is written that [you would depart] from the w[a]y and that evil would befall [you] (cf. Deut 31:29).

Comment: The text has been patched together out of fragments from different copies of the original work. The 'you' (sing.) of C.10 is probably the high priest of the day, to whom the writer has sent a letter disputing certain interpretations of the law proposed by a third party. The issues may now seem very trivial, but they were of vital interest to priests who had to maintain strict and complex purity laws. If pure water in one vessel is poured into impure water in another, the pure water is contaminated as soon as the stream of pure water touches the impure water. The alternative view presumably was that the pure water remained pure because impurity could not travel upwards against the flow of the stream. The attitude towards the physically challenged is also noteworthy. At Qumran there was a move to exclude anyone with physical impairment from public worship, just as any physically handicapped priest was excluded from public duties. On the *Halakic Letter* see MAJ GEN B.12.

C. Apocalyptic

1. *2 Enoch*, 22:5–23:2: Enoch's Ascent to Heaven

(22:5) And the Lord, with his own mouth, said to me, 'Courage, Enoch, do not fear! Arise and stand before my face forever.' (6) And Michael, the *archistratege* [highest archangel], lifted me up and led me before the face of the Lord. And the Lord said to his servants, testing them, 'Let Enoch ascend and stand before my face forever!' (7) And the Lord's glorious ones bowed down and said, 'Let Enoch ascend in accordance with your will, O Lord!'

(8) And the Lord said to Michael, 'Go and take Enoch out of his earthly garments and anoint him with sweet oil, and put him in the garments of my glory.' (9) And Michael did so, as the Lord had commanded him. He anointed me and clothed me. And the sheen of that oil was brighter than the greatest light, its texture was like sweet dew, its fragrance like myrrh, and its glitter like the sun's rays. (10) And I looked at myself, and I had become like one of his glorious ones, and there was no visible difference.

And the Lord summoned one of his archangels, Vrevoil by name, who was more versed in wisdom than the other archangels, and who records all the Lord's deeds. (11) And the Lord said to Vrevoil, 'Bring out the books from my storehouses, and fetch a reed for speed-writing, and give it to Enoch and dictate to him the books.' And Vrevoil made haste and brought me the books ... and he gave me the reed for speed-writing from his hand. (23:1) And he told me about all that happens in heaven, on earth, and in the sea, about all the elements, their motions and courses, and how thunder thunders, about the sun, the moon, and the stars, their courses and their changes, about the seasons, days, and hours, how clouds are formed and the winds blow, about the number of the angels and the songs of the Armed Host [the angels], about the language of every kind of human song, about rules and regulations and sweet-voiced singing, and about everything that it is permitted to learn.

Comment: This extract, from the longer recension of *2 Enoch*, records the climax of Enoch's ascent through the seven heavens. Even though he has reached the highest heaven he is still in his 'earthly garments' (his terrestrial body). But he cannot remain in that form if he is to stand before the Lord's face forever, for flesh and blood cannot endure heaven: he must be transformed into an angel. His transformation involves not only the divesting of his flesh but the illuminating of his mind. The prominence of cosmology in the instruction that he receives is noteworthy. God's testing of the angels to see if they will oppose Enoch's transformation hints at the idea, widespread in early Judaism, that the angels are jealous when humans intrude into the heavenly realm. On *2 Enoch* see MAJ GEN C.4–5.

2. *1 Enoch*, 14:8–25: God's Celestial Palace

(14:8) And in the vision thus it appeared to me: Behold, clouds called me in the vision, and mists summoned me. Shooting-stars and lightnings urged me on and whirled me along, and in my vision winds gave me wing, and lifted me up and carried me into heaven. (9) And I went in till I came near a wall built of hailstones, with tongues of fire surrounding it; and they began to terrify me. (10) And I went into the tongues of fire and approached a large house built of hailstones; and the walls of the house were like paving stones, all of snow. Its lower floors were of snow; (11) its upper floors were like shooting-stars and lightnings, and in the midst of them were fiery Cherubim, and their heaven was like water. (12) And fire was burning round the walls, and the doors were ablaze with fire. (13) And I entered that house, and it was hot as fire and cold as snow; and there was nothing to sustain life in it. Fear overwhelmed me, and trembling seized me, (14) and, shaking and trembling, I fell down.

And I saw in my vision, (15) and behold, another door lay open before me, and [another] house larger than the former, and it was entirely built of tongues of fire. (16) And it surpassed the other house so totally in glory, splendour, and size that I am unable to describe to you its glory and size. (17) It lower storey was of fire, its upper storey of lightnings and shooting-stars, and its roof of blazing fire. (18) And I looked and saw a lofty throne, and its appearance was like ice-crystals; and there was a wheel like the [disc of] the shining sun, and a choir (?) of Cherubim. (19) And from beneath the throne streams of blazing fire flowed out, and I was unable to look. (20) The Great Glory sat on it, and his garment was brighter than the sun, and whiter than any snow. (21) And no angel was able to enter this house, or look on his face, because of the splendour and glory; and no flesh was able to look at him. (22) A fire blazed round him, and a great fire stood in front of him, and no one approached him. All round ten thousand times ten thousand stood before him, and his every word was a deed. (23) And the most holy angels who were near to him do not leave him by night or by day, nor do they depart from him. (24) As for me, till then I had been prostrate on my face, trembling. And the Lord called me with his own mouth and said to me: 'Come here, Enoch, and hear my word.' (25) And one of the holy angels came to me, raised me up, stood me on my feet and brought me to the door; and I bowed down my face.

Comment: This impressive vision marks Enoch's calling to the prophetic office (cf. Isa 6; Ezek 1). He is commissioned before

God's heavenly throne itself, in the celestial palaces. It is unclear whether he ascends here to heaven physically (as he does in *2 Enoch*: see ANTH C.1), or in spirit, or whether heaven is simply shown to him in a dream, and he dreams of ascending. The heavenly world is a hostile environment for humans, disorientating and paradoxical, and the terrestrial laws of nature do not apply there: ice can exist in the middle of fire, and the larger of the two celestial houses can be located inside the smaller. The idea of heaven as a topsy-turvy world where opposites meet was to be exploited at length later by the Jewish Hekalot mystics of the later Talmudic period. On *1 Enoch* see MAJ GEN A.7.

3. *1 Enoch*, 46:1–4; 48:2–7; 69:26–9: The Heavenly Son of Man

(46:1) And I saw there one who was Ancient of Days [lit. Head of Days], and his head was white like wool, and with him was another whose face had the appearance of a man. His face was full of graciousness, like one of the angels. (2) And I asked one of the angels who accompanied me, and showed me all the secrets, concerning that Son of Man, who he was, whence he had come, and why he was with the Ancient of Days. (3) He answered and said to me: 'This is the Son of Man who possesses righteousness, and with whom righteousness dwells; and all the treasures regarding what is hidden he reveals, for the Lord of Spirits has chosen him, and his destiny is always to be victorious before the Lord of Spirits in uprightness for ever.' ...

(48:2) And at that hour the Son of Man was named in the presence of the Lord of Spirits, and his name was mentioned before the Ancient of Days. (3) Even before the sun and the signs were created, before the stars of heaven were made, his name was named before the Lord of Spirits. (4) He shall be a staff to the righteous, that they may lean on him and not fall, and he shall be a light to the Gentiles, and a hope to those who are troubled in their hearts. (5) All who dwell on earth shall fall down and worship before him, and shall glorify, bless, and celebrate with song the name of the Lord of Spirits. (6) And for this reason he has been chosen and hidden before him from before the creation of the world and for evermore. (7) And the wisdom of the Lord of Spirits has revealed him to the holy and righteous; for he has preserved the portion of the righteous, because they hate and despise this unrighteous world, and hate all its works and ways in the name of the Lord of Spirits: for in his name they will be saved and he will be the vindicator of their lives. ...

(69:26) And they had great joy, and they gave blessing, glory, and praise, because the name of that Son of Man had been revealed to them. (27) And he sat on the throne of his glory, and all judgement was given to the Son of Man, and he will cause sinners to pass away and be destroyed from the face of the earth, and those who have led the world astray (28) shall be bound with chains and imprisoned in the assembly-place of destruction, and their works shall vanish from the face of the earth. (29) And from henceforth there shall be nothing corruptible, for that Son of Man has appeared, and has seated himself on the throne of his glory, and everything evil shall pass away and depart from before his face, and the word of that Son of Man shall prevail before the Lord of Spirits.

Comment: This late stratum of *1 Enoch* offers a reinterpretation of Daniel's vision of the Ancient of Days in Dan 7:9–14. There the Son of Man seems to be Israel's symbolic representative in heaven, who accepts, on Israel's behalf, political dominion over her earthly enemies. Here, however, he appears to be a pre-existent angelic figure, the champion of the righteous, who will be revealed from heaven at the end of history to pass judgement on sinners. The relationship of the

Enochic Son of Man to early Christology, and to the appellation 'son of man' for Jesus in the gospels, is a matter of intense debate. On 1 Enoch see MAJ GEN A.7.

4. 1 Enoch, 22:1–13: A Vision of Hell

(22:1) And he (the angel Uriel) showed me, towards the west, a large and lofty mountain of hard rock, (2) with four hollows in it, deep and wide and very smooth, three of them dark, and one bright, with a spring of water in its midst. And I said: 'How smooth are those hollows, and deep and dark to look at.' (3) Then Raphael, one of the holy angels who was with me, answered and said to me: 'These hollows are there so that the spirits of the souls of the dead should be gathered together into them. For this purpose were they created so that here all the souls of men should be gathered together. (4) And these places were made for their reception, until the day of their judgement and until the appointed time when the great judgement will come upon them.' (5) There I saw the spirit of a dead man making complaint; and his lamentation reached up to heaven as he cried out and complained. (6) Then I asked Raphael, the Watcher and Holy One who was with me, and I said to him: 'Whose is this spirit whose voice thus reaches heaven in complaint?' (7) And he answered me saying: 'This is the spirit that came forth from Abel whom Cain, his brother, slew: and Abel will make complaint against him till his offspring perishes from the face of the earth, and from the offspring of men his offspring is destroyed.'

(8) Then I asked about the hollows, why they are separated one from the other. (9) And he answered me, saying: 'These three (? four) hollows were made so that the spirits of the dead might be separated. That one, in which there is a bright spring of water, was set apart for the spirits of the righteous. (10) That one was created for the spirits of the sinners, when they die and are buried in the earth, but judgement has not been executed upon them during their lives. (11) Here their spirits shall be set apart for this great torment, until the great day of judgement, of scourgings and of torments for those who are eternally accursed, so that retribution may be exacted from their spirits: there he shall bind them forever. (12) That (third hollow) has been set apart for the spirits of those who make complaint, who have information to give regarding their destruction, when they were murdered in the days of the sinners. (13) That (fourth hollow) has been created for the spirits of men who are not righteous but sinners, and who have collaborated with the lawless, but because they have endured suffering here (in this life) their spirits receive a lesser punishment, and retribution shall not be exacted from them on the day of judgement nor shall they be raised from there.'

Comment: The gloomy netherworld (Sheol) of earlier Hebrew thought (the equivalent of the Homeric Hades), into which the spirits of the dead, good and bad alike, descend, is here compartmentalized. In earlier tradition the dead survive only as attentuated, barely sentient ghosts. Here they experience a more vivid life and feel intensely pleasure and pain. The four compartments are assigned respectively to the righteous, to sinners who have died unpunished, to the murdered, and to sinners who have died having been, at least in part, punished while they were alive. These ideas arose after the doctrine of the resurrection of the dead for judgement emerged (see ANTH C.9). To have left the righteous and the wicked in the same, undifferentiated, joyless state between death and final judgement was morally repugnant to some, so they held that the final judgement is anticipated for each individual on the point of death, and each, in accordance with his deeds, has at once a foretaste of his final destiny. We have here the first glimmerings of the 'Tours of Hell' literature which was to

reach its literary climax in Dante's *Inferno*. On 1 Enoch see MAJ GEN A.7.

5. 1 Enoch, 93:3–10; 91:11–17: The Pattern of History

(93:3) Then Enoch took up his discourse and said: I was born the seventh of the First Week, while justice and righteousness still endured. (4) And thereafter in the Second Week great wickedness shall arise, and deceit spring up; and in it (the Second Week) the First End will occur, and in it a man shall be saved. And after it has ended, oppression shall increase, and he shall make a law for sinners. (5) And thereafter, in the Third Week, at its close, a man shall be chosen as a plant of righteous judgement; and his posterity (?) shall emerge as a plant of righteousness for ever. (6) And thereafter, in the Fourth Week, at its close, visions of holy ones and of righteousness shall be revealed, and a Law for all generations, and a Court shall be made for them. (7) And thereafter, in the Fifth Week, at its close, a house of glory and dominion shall be built for ever. (8) And thereafter, in the Sixth Week, all who live then shall be blinded, and the hearts of all of them, forsaking wisdom, shall become godless. And in it a man shall arise; and at its close the house of dominion shall be burnt with fire, and in it the whole race of the Chosen Plant shall be dispersed. (9) And thereafter, in the Seventh Week, an apostate generation shall arise; its misdeeds shall be many and all its doings perverse. (10) And at its close the Elect Ones shall be chosen, as witnesses to righteousness, from the Eternal Plant of righteousness, to whom shall be given sevenfold instruction concerning all his creation. (91:11) And they shall uproot the foundations of oppression, and the works of falsehood therein, in order to execute judgement. (12) And thereafter there shall arise the Eighth Week of righteousness, in which a sword shall be given to all the righteous, to execute a righteous judgement on all the wicked, and they will be given over into their hands. (13) And at its close they shall acquire riches in righteousness, and a Royal House shall be built for the Great King in splendour for ever. (14) And thereafter, in the Ninth Week, righteous judgement shall be revealed to all the children of the whole earth, and the deeds of the wicked shall vanish from the whole earth, and they shall be cast into the eternal pit, and all men shall look to the path of eternal righteousness. (15) And thereafter in the Tenth Week, in the seventh part of it, eternal judgement and the time appointed for the Great Judgement shall be executed upon the Watchers. (16) And in it the first heaven shall pass away, and a new heaven shall appear, and all the powers of heaven shall arise for evermore with a sevenfold light. (17) And thereafter there shall be many Weeks (to all their number there shall be no end for ever) in which they shall perform goodness and righteousness; and sin shall be spoken of no more for ever. (17b?) And the righteous shall awake from their sleep, and they shall arise and walk in the paths of righteousness; and unrighteousness shall totally cease, and the earth shall be at rest from oppression, for all generations for ever.

Comment: Schematizations of history, common in apocalyptic (cf. Dan 9:24–7; Rev 6–11—the seven seals and the seven trumpets), were to influence profoundly the Western imagination by creating a sense that history is moving purposefully towards a grand climax (for the apocalyptists the messianic age and the last judgement). Here history is divided into ten symbolic weeks. The writer probably believed that he was writing towards the end of the seventh week. The previous weeks cover cryptically the biblical history; the following weeks all lie, from his standpoint, in the future. The eighth week is, in effect, the beginning of the messianic redemption: therefore the end of history is imminent. See further MAJ GEN A.7, C.2.

6. *2 Apocalypse of Baruch*, 70:2–71:1; 72:2–73:1: Messianic Woes, Messianic Redemption

(70:2) Behold, days are coming, and when the time of the world has ripened, and the time to harvest whatever of good or evil has been sown has come, then the Mighty One will bring upon the earth and upon its inhabitants and its rulers confusion of spirit and consternation of mind. (3) And they will hate one another, and provoke one another to fight. Obscure men will have dominion over men of repute, and the low-born will be exalted above the nobles. (4) The many will be delivered into the hands of the few, and those who are nothing will lord it over the strong, the poor will have greater abundance than the rich, and the wicked will prevail over the valiant. (5) The wise will be silent, and fools will speak. Neither the designs of ordinary men nor the plans of the powerful will come to anything, nor will the hope of those who hope be fulfilled. (6) And when what has been predicted has come to pass, then confusion will fall upon all men: some of them will fall in battle, some of them will perish in tribulations, and some of them will be destroyed by their own people. (7) Then the Most High will reveal those peoples whom he has prepared beforehand, and they will come and make war with the leaders that then remain. (8) And whoever escapes in the war will die by the earthquake, and whoever escapes the earthquake will be burned by fire, and whoever escapes the fire will perish through famine. (9) And whoever, whether victor or the vanquished, escapes all these things, and emerges safe and sound, will be delivered into the hands of my Servant, the Messiah. (10) For the whole earth will devour its inhabitants. (71:1) But the Holy Land will have mercy on its own, and will protect its inhabitants at that time....

(72:2) After the signs, about which I have spoken to you before, have appeared, when the nations are troubled, and the time of my Messiah has come, he will call all the nations together. Some of them he will spare, but others he will destroy. (3) This is what will happen to the nations spared by him. (4) Every nation that has not conquered Israel nor trampled the race of Jacob underfoot will be spared. (5) And they will be treated thus because, out of all the peoples, they have been submissive to your people. (6) But all those who have exercised dominion over you, or have conquered you, will be given over to the sword. (73:1) And when he has brought the whole world low, and has sat down in peace for ever on the throne of his kingdom, then joy shall be revealed, and rest made manifest.

Comment: There was a widespread belief among apocalyptists that the coming of the Messiah would be preceded by a time of unparalleled tribulation for the righteous, often accompanied by prodigies and wonders in nature. In *2 Apoc. Bar.* the messianic woes are characterized primarily by the overthrow of civil society, though natural disasters (earthquake and famine) also play a part. The onset of the messianic woes is a sure sign of the end, but *2 Apoc. Bar.* describes them in a such a vague way that anyone affected by the apocalyptic mentality could always fancy he could detect them beginning in his own days. The Messiah glimpsed here is a purely political figure— a king who would lead Israel to victory against her political enemies and give her world dominion. On *2 Apoc. Bar.* see MAJ GEN C.6.

7. The *War Scroll* (1QM), 1:1–15: The War to End All Wars

(1:1) *For the M[aster. The Rule of] War. The first engagement of the Sons of Light shall be to attack the company of the Sons of Darkness, the army of Belial—the troops of Edom, Moab, and the Sons of Ammon, the ar[my of the inhabitants]* (2) *of Philistia, and the troops of the Kittim of Assyria, with whom the Covenant-breakers have allied themselves...*

(3) The Sons of Levi, the Sons of Judah and the Sons of Benjamin, the exiles of the wilderness, shall fight against them [———] according to all their troops, when the exiles of the Sons of Light shall return

from the Wilderness of the Nations to encamp in the Wilderness of Jerusalem, and after the battle they shall go up (to Jerusalem) from there. (4) And [the King] of the Kittim [shall enter] into Egypt, and in his time he shall set out in great wrath to wage war against the kings of the north, and in his anger he shall destroy and cut off the horn (5) of [Israel]. That shall be a time of salvation for the people of God, and an appointed time of dominion for all the members of his company, but of everlasting destruction for all the company of Belial. Gr[eat] panic (6) [shall seize] the Sons of Japhet, and Assyria shall fall with none to help her. The dominion of the Kittim shall pass away and iniquity shall be vanquished, leaving no remnant; (7) there shall be no escape [for the Sons of Darkness, (8) [but the Sons of Righteous]ness shall shine to all the ends of the earth; they shall go on shining till all the seasons of darkness are ended and, at God's appointed time, his exalted greatness shall shine (9) et[ernally] for the peace, blessing, glory, joy, and long life of all the Sons of Light.

On the day when the Kittim shall fall, there shall be fighting and terrible carnage before the God (10) of Israel, for that shall be the day appointed from of old for a war of annihilation against the Sons of Darkness. Then the assembly of gods and the congregation of men shall clash with great carnage, (11) the Sons of Light and the Company of Darkness fighting together to (make manifest) God's might, amid the sound of a great tumult and the clamour of gods and men—a day of calamity! It shall be a time of (12) g[reat] tribulation for the people whom God shall redeem; of all their afflictions none shall be like this, from its sudden onset till its end in eternal redemption.

On the day of their battle against the Kittim (13) [they shall set out to wreak] carnage in battle. In three skirmishes the Sons of Light shall prevail and strike down iniquity, and in three skirmishes Belial's host shall rally and repel the Company (14) [of God. And when the detach]ments of foot-soldiers begin to falter, then shall God's might strengthen [the hearts of the Sons of Light]. And during the seventh skirmish the mighty hand of God shall subdue (15) [the army of Belial, and all] the angels of his dominion, and all the members [of his company with an everlasting destruction].

Comment: So seriously did the Qumran sect believe that they would play a role in the eschatological conflict between the forces of good (the Sons of Light) and the forces of evil (the Sons of Darkness) that, like a General Staff, they composed war-books in which they worked out the strategy and tactics that they would adopt. The war would be a real war, involving bloody carnage, but parallel to the human conflict would be a clash of spiritual agencies headed respectively by God, or God's angelic general, Michael, and Belial (the Devil). The political protagonists in the last battle are given biblical code-names. The Kittim are probably the Romans, the Kittim of Assyria the Persians. A global conflict between Rome and Persia would enable Israel (or the elect of Israel) to intervene and to triumph over both these superpowers. On the *War Scroll* see MAJ GEN C.8.

8. The *Messianic Rule* (1QSa), 2:11–22: The Messianic Banquet

(2:11) *[This shall be the ass]embly of the men of renown [called] to the meeting of the Council of the Community.*

When God brings (12) the (royal) Messiah, the priest(ly Messiah) shall come with them [at] the head of the whole congregation of Israel and of all (13) [his brethren, the sons] of Aaron, the priests, [those called] to the assembly, the men of renown; and they shall sit (14) be[fore him, each man] in the order of his dignity. And then [the Mess]iah of Israel shall [enter], and the chiefs of (15) the [clans of Israel] shall sit before him, [each] in the order of his dignity, according to [his place] in their camps and on their manœuvres. (16) And all the heads of [family of the congreg]ation, and their sage[s and scholars], shall sit before them, each in the order of (17) his dignity.

And [when they] shall assemble for the common [tab]le, [to partake of bread and n]ew wine, and the common table is set (18) [for eating and the] new wine (poured) for drink[ing], no man shall reach out his hand to the first fruits of (19) the bread or [the win]e before the priest; for [it is he] who shall bless the first fruits of the bread (20) and the win[e, and shall be the first to reach out] his hand to the bread. Thereaf[ter], the Messiah of Israel [shall rea]ch out his hand (21) to the bread, [and then] all the congregation of the community [shall pronounce a bles]sing, [each man in the order] of his dignity.

And it is according to this statute that [they] shall proceed (22) at every me[al at which] at least ten men are [gat]hered together.

Comment: According to Qumran theology there would be two Messiahs—a priestly (the Messiah of Aaron) and a political (the Messiah of David). The new messianic order would be inaugurated by a great solemn national assembly in which Israel (or rather the surviving elect portion of Israel) would join in a banquet with the two Messiahs to inagurate the messianic age. Significantly all subsequent meals at which at least ten men are present will be held as a memorial of this inaugural feast. On the *Messianic Rule* see MAJ GEN C.8.

9. 2 *Apocalypse of Baruch*, 50:1–4; 51:1–13: The Form of the Resurrection Body

(50:1) And he (God) answered and said to me, Listen, Baruch, to what I say, and engrave on the memory of your heart everything that you learn. (2) The earth will surely give back the dead that it now receives so as to preserve them: without changing their form, it will give them back just as it received them; and as I delivered them to it, so will it raise them again. (3) For it will be necessary then to show to the living that the dead have come back to life again, and that those who have departed have returned. (4) And when those who are acquaintances now have recognized each other, then the judgement proper will begin, and the events spoken of before will come to pass.

(51:1) And after the appointed day is over, the appearance of those who have been condemned and the glory of those who have been justified will be changed. (2) For the appearance of the evildoers will go from bad to worse, as they suffer torment. (3) But the glory of those who have now been justified through their obedience to my law, who have shown understanding during their lives, and who have planted the root of wisdom in their hearts—their splendour will become more glorious as they are transformed, and their features will assume a luminous beauty, so that they may be able to attain and receive the world which does not die, which has been promised to them then. (4) The others who return then will lament greatly because they rejected my law, and stopped up their ears, so that they might not hear wisdom or receive understanding. (5) For they will see those whom they now regard as their inferiors elevated and glorified above them, for both these and those will be transformed, the one into the splendour of angels, and the other into terrible forms and horrible shapes, and they will utterly waste away. (6) For they will see all this first; and afterwards they will depart to be tormented.

(7) But those who have been saved by their works, whose hope has been in the law, who have put their trust in understanding, and their confidence in wisdom, shall see marvels in their time. (8) For they shall see a world which is now invisible to them, and they shall see a time which is now hidden from them, (9) and time shall no longer age them. (10) In the heights of that world shall they dwell, and they shall be like angels, and comparable to stars; and they shall be changed into whatever form they will, from beauty into loveliness, and from light to the splendour of glory. (11) The extent of Paradise will be spread before their eyes, and they shall be shown the majestic

beauty of the Living Creatures that are beneath the Throne, as well as all the armies of the angels, who are now held back by my word lest they should reveal themselves, and are restrained by my command, so that they may keep their stations till the time of their advent comes. (12) Then shall the splendour of the righteous exceed even the splendour of the angels. (13) For the first shall receive the last, for whom they have been waiting, and the last shall receive those whom they have heard had passed away.

Comment: The form of the resurrection body is one of the many problems raised by the doctrine of bodily resurrection. 2 *Apoc. Bar.* here takes the view that the dead will emerge from their graves with recognizably the same bodies with which they were buried. Then, after the final judgement, they will be transformed: the wicked will 'go from bad to worse' (their physical degeneration being hastened by the anguish of seeing the glorification of the righteous), and they will pass into a place of torment; the righteous will become like angels and pass into Paradise, where, in an anticipation of the later doctrine of the beatific vision, they will enjoy direct intercourse with the unseen angelic world. On 2 *Apoc. Bar.* see MAJ GEN C.6.

D. Wisdom

1. The *Chapters of the Fathers* (Pirqei 'Abot), 2:1–6: Miscellaneous Moral Maxims

(2:1) Rabbi said: Which is the straight way that a man should choose? Whatever is an honour to him and gets honour from men. Be as careful to fulfil a light precept as a weighty one, for you do not know what recompense is awarded for each precept. Reckon the loss (incurred) through (fulfilling) a precept against its reward, and the reward (gained) from a transgression against its loss. Consider three things and you will not fall into the hands of transgression: know what is above you—a seeing eye and a hearing ear and all your deeds recorded in a book.

(2) Rabban Gamaliel the son of Rabbi Judah the Prince says: It is excellent to combine the study of the Torah with a worldly occupation, for toiling at both of them puts sin out of mind. But all study of the Torah without worldly labour comes to nothing in the end and brings sin in its train. Let all those who labour with the congregation labour with them for the sake of Heaven, for the merit of their Fathers sustains them and their righteousness endures for ever. And as for you, (God will say,) I count you worthy of great reward as though you yourselves had done everything.

(3) Be heedful of the government for they only bring a man near them for their own ends; they seem to be friends when it is to their advantage, but they do not stand by a man when he is in distress.

(4) He used to say: Do his will as if it was your will so that he may do your will as if it was his will. Negate your will before his will so that he may negate the will of others before your will.

(5) Hillel says: Do not separate yourself from the congregation, and do not put any trust in yourself till the day of your death. Do not judge your fellow till you have been in his situation. Do not suppose that anything (you say) which cannot be understood (at once) will be understood in the end. Do not say, 'When I have leisure I will study.' Perhaps you never will have leisure.

(6) He used to say: A boor does not fear sin, an ignoramus cannot be pious, a shy person cannot learn nor a short-tempered person teach, and whoever engages much in trade cannot become wise. Where there are no men strive to be a man.

Comment: Though clearly within the ancient wisdom tradition of pithy sayings that provide food for thought, the values of *'Abot* are those dear to the rabbis' hearts: the centrality of the study of Torah to a moral life; engaging with the congregation; doing everything 'for the sake of heaven' (i.e. not for financial gain or personal glory); the need to live a balanced life combining study of Torah with a trade or profession, to 'put sin out of mind', and, as is stated elsewhere in 'Abot, to avoid taking payment for teaching the necessary truths of Torah. See further MAJ GEN B.II, D.2.

2. Babylonian Talmud, Šabbat, 31a: Hillel and the Golden Rule

Our rabbis taught: Once a heathen came before Shammai and asked him: 'How many Torahs do you have?' 'Two,' he replied, 'the Written Torah and the Oral Torah.' The heathen said: 'I believe you about the Written Torah, but not about the Oral. Make me a proselyte on condition that you teach me only the Written Torah.' Shammai scolded him and angrily ordered him to get out. When he went before Hillel, he made him a proselyte. On the first day he taught him 'aleph, beth, gimmel, dalet. The following day he reversed the order of the letters. The heathen protested: 'But yesterday you did not teach me thus.' 'Must you not rely upon me in this matter?' Hillel replied. 'Then rely on me with respect also to the Oral Torah.'

On another occasion it happened that a heathen came before Shammai and said to him: 'Make me a proselyte on condition that you teach me the whole Torah while I stand on one foot.' Shammai drove him out with the builder's cubit which was in his hand. When he went before Hillel, he made him a proselyte. He said to him, 'What is hateful to you, do not do to your neighbour. That is the whole Torah. The rest is commentary. Go and learn!'

On another occasion it happened that a heathen was passing behind a school and heard the voice of a teacher reciting. 'And these are the garments which they shall make: a breastplate and an ephod' (Ex 28:4). Said he: 'For whom are these made?' 'For the high priest', said they. The heathen said to himself: 'I will go and become a proselyte, so that I may be appointed a high priest.' So he went before Shammai and said to him: 'Make me a proselyte on condition that you appoint me high priest.' Shammai drove him out with the builder's cubit which was in his hand. When he went before Hillel, he made him a proselyte. Hillel said to him: 'No one is appointed king who does not know the arts of government. Go and study the arts of government!' He went and read. When he came to the words, 'The stranger that comes nigh shall be put to death' (Num 1:51), he asked Hillel: 'To whom does this verse apply?' 'Even to David, king of Israel,' was the answer. Thereupon the proselyte reasoned a fortiori: 'If the words, "The stranger that comes nigh shall be put to death", are applied in Scripture to Israel, who are called sons of the Omnipresent, and whom in his love he designated, "Israel, my firstborn son" (Ex 4:22), how much more do they apply to a mere proselyte, who comes with his staff and his bag!' He went before Shammai and said to him: 'Could I ever have been eligible to be High Priest? Is it not written in the Torah, "The stranger that comes nigh shall be put to death"? He went before Hillel and said to him: 'O gentle Hillel, may blessings rest on your head for bringing me under the wings of the Shekinah [the Divine Presence]!'

Some time later when the three proselytes met in one place, they said: 'Shammai's impatience nearly drove us out of the world, but Hillel's gentleness brought us under the wings of the Shekinah!'

Comment: Hillel exemplifies the patience of the great Sage, in contrast to his irascible contemporary Shammai. His summation of the Torah is, curiously, not a statement from Torah itself, but a commonplace of folk ethics. However, there are grounds for thinking that some rabbis saw the Golden Rule as essentially another formulation of the love-commandment of Lev 19:18, 'You shall love your neighbour as yourself.' Hillel reaches out to the Gentile where he is and quotes him a principle well known in his own society. The ease and speed with which Hillel converts the Gentile, contrary to normal rabbinic procedure, does not seem to have troubled the narrator. It is unlikely that this story is historically accurate since it appears for the first time in the Babylonian Talmud, which was edited around 500 CE, some 500 years after the time of Hillel (see MAJ GEN B.II). However, the debate on what is 'the great principle' that sums up the whole Torah goes back to Second Temple times (see MAJ GEN D.3).

3. Testament of Reuben, 5:1–6:4: The Wiles of Women

(5:1) For women are evil, my children, and since they lack authority or power over a man, they scheme how they might entice him to themselves by means of their physical attractions. (2) And whoever they cannot bewitch by physical appearance they conquer by guile. (3) Indeed, the angel of the Lord told me and taught me that women are more easily overcome by the spirit of promiscuity than are men. They plot in their hearts against men; then by adorning themselves they first lead men's minds astray, then by a glance they implant their venom, and finally by the (sexual) act they take them captive. (4) For a woman is not able to coerce a man openly, but by a harlot's attractions she accomplishes her villainy. (5) Flee, therefore, my children, from sexual promiscuity, and command your wives and your daughters not to adorn their heads and faces to deceive men's minds. For every woman who schemes in this way is destined for eternal punishment.

(6) For it was thus that they allured the Watchers, who were before the Flood. As they gazed continuously at the women, they were filled with desire for them and committed the act in their minds. They changed themselves into the form of human males, and while the women were having intercourse with their husbands they appeared to them. Because the women's minds were filled with lust for these apparitions, they gave birth to giants, for the Watchers appeared to them to reach up to heaven.

(6:1) So guard yourself against sexual promiscuity, and if you want to remain pure in your mind, guard your senses from women. (2) And command the women not to associate with men, so that they too may be (3) pure in mind. For constant meetings, even though the ungodly act itself is not committed, are for these women an incurable disease, and for us they bring Beliar's ruin and eternal disgrace. (4) Because in sexual promiscuity there is neither understanding nor piety, and in the desire for it all forms of jealousy reside.

Comment: The advice is aptly given by Reuben, who succumbed to the charms of Bilhah, his father's concubine, and committed incest with her (Gen 35:22). Women are all essentially harlots, who scheme to dominate men sexually. 5:6 seems to imply that male sexuality is constructed by women, without whom men would be asexual (cf. ANTH G.2). Apparently unconcerned by the need to procreate, the author dubs sexual intercourse 'the ungodly act' (6:3). The reference to the fall of the Watchers (see ANTH A.4) is noteworthy. The author rejects as too problematic the idea that the women could have had physical intercourse with heavenly beings. His alternative explanation relies on the idea that the images in the mind during intercourse can affect the nature of the offspring. On the Testaments of the Twelve Patriarchs see MAJ GEN D.4.

4. Community Rule (1QS), 3:13–4:1, 15–26: Instruction on the Two Spirits

(3:13) For the Master (Maskil), so that he may instruct and teach all the Sons of Light concerning the nature of all the children of men (14) with respect to the kind of spirit which they possess, concerning the signs which they show in their works, and concerning their generations—the times when they are visited for chastisement and (15) the times when they have peace.

From the God of knowledge comes all that is and shall be. Before ever they existed he determined their whole design, (16) and when, at their appointed times, they come into being, it is in accordance with his glorious design that they accomplish their tasks without change. In his hand are (17) the laws of all things, and he provides them with everything they need.

He created man to govern (18) the world, and has appointed for him two spirits in which to walk until the time of his visitation—the spirits of (19) truth and of falsehood. From the source of light truth is born, but from the fountain of darkness falsehood originates. (20) The Prince of Light rules over all the children of righteousness, and they walk in the ways of light, but the Angel of (21) Darkness rules over all children of falsehood, and they walk in the ways of darkness. The Angel of Darkness leads astray (22) all the children of righteousness, and, until his end, all their sins, iniquities, wickedness, and wrongdoings are caused by his dominion, (23) in accordance with the mysteries of God. And all their afflictions and their times of suffering are (the result) of his hostile rule; (24) for all his allotted spirits seek to overthrow the Sons of Light.

But the God of Israel and his Angel of Truth assist all (25) the Sons of Light. For it he who created the spirits of light and of darkness, and founded every action upon them (26) and every deed [upon] their [ways]. And God loves the one, (4:1) world without end, and takes delight in its works forever; but the assembly of the other he loathes and hates its ways eternally...

(15) In these (two spirits) the natures of all the children of men (partake), and in their divisions their hosts have a share, throughout all their generations, and walk in their ways. And all the deeds that they do, (16) for everlasting ages, shall be according to whether each man's portion in their divisions is great or small. For God has established the spirits in equal measure until the final (17) age, and has set eternal enmity between their divisions. Truth loathes the works of falsehood, and falsehood loathes all the ways of truth. And there is fierce (18) dispute about all their judgements, for they do not walk together.

But in the mysteries of his understanding, and in his glorious wisdom, God has ordained an end for falsehood, and at the time of (19) the (final) visitation he will destroy it forever. Then truth shall prevail in the world, for it will have wallowed in the ways of wickedness during the dominion of falsehood till (20) the time appointed for judgement. Then God will purify all the deeds of men through his truth; he will refine for himself the children of men by rooting out all the spirit of falsehood from their physical (21) frame, and by purifying them from all their wicked deeds through a spirit of holiness. He shall shed upon them, like purifying water, the spirit of truth (to cleanse them) from all lying abominations. And they shall be plunged (22) into a purifying spirit, so that the upright in knowledge may be instructed in the knowledge of the Most High and those who are perfect in the way may be enlightened in the wisdom of the sons of heaven. For God has chosen them for an everlasting covenant, (23) and all the glory of Adam shall be theirs, without falsehood, and all the works of deceit shall be put to shame.

Until now the spirits of truth and falsehood struggle in the hearts of men (24) and they walk in both wisdom and folly. According to a man's portion in truth so he hates falsehood, and according to his inheritance in the lot of falsehood so he acts wickedly and (25) hates truth. For God has established the two spirits in equal measure until the foreordained end and until all things are made new, and he knows the deeds that they do for (26) ever[more]. He has apportioned them to the children of men so that they may know good [and evil, and] so that the (final) destinies of all the living may

be assigned in accordance with the spirit that is within [them at the time] of the visitation.

Comment: Though propositional and overtly theological to a degree scarcely paralleled in early Jewish literature, the Instruction on the Two Spirits begs many questions. At first reading it seems to be advocating a rigid, almost Calvinistic, determinism: every man's destiny is foreordained by the portions of good and evil that God has assigned to him. Some at Qumran may actually have understood the text in this way (see ANTH D.7). But it can be read differently. All that has been foreordained is that there should be two principles—good and evil—and that everyone should have a share in both. It is possible to change one's portions in good and evil through submission to 'the truth'. It is clearly envisaged that the residual evil in the righteous will be eradicated at the end of history through the truth. And the statement that one's destiny is determined by the proportions that prevail in one's spirit 'at the time of the visitation', implies that the proportions can be altered, otherwise there is little point in mentioning a census date. The objectification of good and evil into cosmic principles, and their close identification with personal agents (the Prince of Light and the Angel of Darkness) may reflect the influence of Persian thought. See further MAJ GEN D.5, F.2.

5. 1 Enoch, 72:2–37: The Motion of the Sun in the Heavens

(72:2) This is the first law of the luminaries: the light (called) the sun rises in the gates of heaven that are in the east and it sets in the gates of heaven that are in the west.

(3) And I saw six gates from which the sun rises and six gates in which the sun sets. The moon (also) rises and sets in the same gates, as well as the leaders of the stars (the planets and major stars), together with those whom they lead. (There are) six (gates) in the east and six in the west, all arranged in sequence, one beside the other. And there are many windows to the right (= north) and the left (= south) of these gates.

(4) And the greater light called the sun comes out first. Its roundness is like the roundness of heaven, and it is totally filled with fire which gives off light and heat.

(5) The winds blow along the chariot on which it rises. And the sun goes down from heaven and turns northwards in order to reach the east; and it is guided in such a way that it arrives at the (correct) gate and shines (again) in heaven.

(6) In this way the sun rises in the first month from the great gate, the fourth of those gates that are in the east. (7) And in this fourth gate from which the sun rises in the first month there are twelve window-openings from which flames issue when they are opened at their appointed times.

(8) When the sun rises in heaven it emerges from this fourth gate for thirty days, and it sets exactly in the fourth gate in the west of heaven. (9) During this period day increases and night decreases until the thirtieth day. (10) And on the thirtieth day the day is two parts longer than the night, the day being exactly ten parts and the night eight parts. (11) And the sun rises from the fourth gate and sets in the fourth (gate).

The sun returns to the fifth gate in the east for thirty mornings, and rises from it and sets in the fifth gate (in the west). (12) Then the day increases by two parts, till the day amounts to eleven parts, and the night decreases till it amounts to seven parts.

(13) The sun returns to the east and enters the sixth gate, and rises and sets in the sixth gate for thirty-one days, to act as a sign. (14) During this period the day increases over the night (until) the day is

double the night, the day amounting to twelve parts and night decreasing to six parts. (15) Then the sun sets out to shorten the day and lengthen the night.

The sun returns to the east and enters the sixth gate and it rises from it and sets in it for thirty days. (16) And when the thirty days are completed the day has decreased by exactly one part; the day amounts to eleven parts and the night to seven parts.

(17) Then the sun departs by the sixth gate in the west and travels to the east to rise in the fifth gate for thirty days; and it sets in the west again in the fifth gate. (18) And on the thirtieth day the day has decreased by two parts, the day amounting to ten parts and the night to eight parts. (19) And the sun rises from the fifth gate (in the east) and sets in the fifth gate in the west.

Then the sun rises from the fourth gate in the east for thirty-one days, to act as a sign, and it sets (in the fourth gate) in the west. (20) On the thirty-first day the day equals the night and they are the same, the night amounting to nine parts and the day to nine parts. (21) And the sun rises from this (fourth) gate (in the east) and sets (in the fourth gate) in the west.

Then the sun returns to the east and rises from the third gate for thirty days, and it sets in the west in the third gate. (22) During this period the night increases over the day: the nights grow longer and the days grow shorter until the thirtieth day when the night amounts exactly to ten parts and the day to eight parts. (23) And the sun rises from this third gate (in the east) and sets in the third gate in the west.

Then the sun returns to the east and rises for thirty days in the second gate in the east, and likewise it sets in the second gate in the west of heaven. (24) And on the thirtieth day the night amounts to eleven parts and the day to seven parts. (25) And the sun rises from the second gate (in the east), and sets in the second gate in the west.

Then the sun returns to the east and rises from the first gate for thirty-one days and sets in the west in the first gate. (26) On the thirty-first day the night has increased to become twice as long as the day, the night amounting to exactly twelve parts and the day to six parts.

(27) The sun has (thus) completed (all) the stages of its journey, and it now retraces its path along the stages of its journey.

The sun rises from the (first) gate (in the east) for thirty days, and sets in the west opposite it. (28) And on the thirtieth day the night has decreased in length by one part, the night amounting to eleven parts and the day to seven parts.

(29) And the sun returns and enters the second gate in the east for thirty days, rising and setting (in the second gate). (30) And on the thirtieth day the night has decreased in length, the night amounting to ten parts and the day to eight parts. (31) And during this period the sun rises from the second gate (in the east) and sets (in the second gate) in the west.

Then the sun returns to the east and rises in the third gate for thirty-one days and it sets (in the third gate) in the west of heaven. (32) And on the thirty-first day the night has decreased and amounts to nine parts and the day to nine parts, night and day being equal. And the year amounts to exactly 364 days.

(33) And the length and the length of the day and the night, and the shortness of the day and the night, are determined by the path of the sun, (34) because its path becomes longer day after day, and shorter night after night. (35) And this is the law for the path of the sun, and it returns and rises as often as sixty times (in each gate). This greater luminary is called the sun for all eternity. (36) And that which thus rises is the greater luminary, and it is so named in accordance with its appearance, as the Lord commanded. (37) And thus it rises and sets, and it does not decrease (in brightness), nor does it rest, but travels day and night in its chariot. And its light is seven times as bright as the (light of the full) moon, but in size the two are equal.

Note: v. 13, 'to act as a sign'—Four of the months have thirty-one and not thirty days. The extra day is a sign of the two solstices and the two equinoxes.

Comment: The calendar proposed is neatly regular. In effect it divides the year into twelve thirty-day months plus the two solstices and the two equinoxes, the four additional days being added to the months preceding them, giving those months thirty-one days each. The year begins, as in the old Jewish calendar, at the spring equinox. The regularity of the pattern doubtless commended it, and suggested conformity to the divine order of nature. Behind the schema lies genuine scientific observation. From his standpoint in the northern hemisphere the writer notes that the sun rises on the eastern horizon at different points in the year, and that the point of its rising correlates with the length of day and night (which he measures on an eighteen-point scale). The point furthest south is the winter solstice, that furthest north the summer solstice. He divides the distance between these into six gates. Note also his attempt to establish the relative brightness of the sun and the full moon, and the implication that the moon reflects the light of the sun. See further MAJ GEN A.7, D.6.

6. *Book of Mysteries*, 2. 62–72: Incantation for Depriving an Enemy of Sleep

If you wish to deprive your enemy of sleep, take the head of a black dog that has been blind from birth and take a strip of lead from a water-pipe and write upon it (the names of) these angels (listed earlier), and say thus:

I hand over to you, angels of anxiety who stand upon the fourth step, the life, soul and spirit of N son of N, so that you may imprison him with chains of iron and bind him with bars of bronze. Do not grant sleep to his eyelids, nor slumber, nor drowsiness. Let him weep and cry like a woman in travail and do not permit anyone to release him [from this spell].

Write thus and put [the lead strip] in the mouth of the dog's head. Put wax on its mouth and seal it with a ring which has a lion (engraved) upon it. Then go and conceal it behind his house, or in the place where he goes out and in.

If you wish to release him, bring up (the dog's head) from the place where it is concealed, remove its seal, withdraw the text and throw it into a fire. At once he will fall asleep. Do this with humility and you will be successful.

Comment: This is a piece of voodoo of a type widely practised throughout the ancient world. Apart from the reference to the angels, it is devoid of religious content and is totally immoral. This kind of black magic was universally condemned in antiquity by religious and civil authorities. On the *Book of Mysteries* see MAJ GEN D.11.

7. *4Q186*: Fragments of an Astrological Physiognomy

Frag. 1: (2:5) . . . and his thighs are long and slender, and his toes are (6) slender and long. He is of the second column. (7) His spirit has six (parts) in the House of Light and three in the House of (8) Darkness. And this is the sign in which he was born: (9) the foot of the Bull. He will be poor. And his animal is the bull.

(3) . . . (2) and his head . . . [his eyes] are (3) frightening. His teeth are irregular (?). His fingers (4) are fat, and thighs are fat and covered with [h]air . . . (5) His toes are fat and short. His spirit has [e]ight (parts) in the House of [Darkness] and one in the House of Light . . .

Frag. 2: (1) . . . regular. His ey[es] are between black and grey (?) (in colour). His beard (2) is sp[arse] and curly. The sound of his voice is gentle. His teeth (3) are sharp and regular. He is neither (too) tall (4) nor (too) short, but is as he should be (?). His fingers are slender (5) and long. His thighs are smooth, and the soles of his feet are

(6)[...and his toes] are regular. His spirit has eight parts [in the House of Light {of the second Column} and o[ne] in [the House of Darkness. And this is] the sign in which he was born: (9)...his animal is...

Note: The words in braces {} should probably be omitted.

Comment: Fragmentary though it is, it is still possible to see that this text was attempting to deduce from a man's physical characteristics the nature of his spirit, and, presumably, on this basis to decide whether or not he could join the community. Everyone is measured on a nine-point scale, so no one can be evenly balanced between good and evil. The person's spirit was determined by the configuration of the heavens at the time of his birth—the classic claim of astrology. The links between this text and the Instruction on the Two Spirits (ANTH D.4) are clear. 4Q186 seems to represent a deterministic reading of that text. Everyone's character is foreordained. What is needed is some scientific way of distinguishing the Sons of Light from the Sons of Darkness. On the Astrological Physiognomy see MAJ GEN D.12.

E. Hymns and Prayers

1. The Eighteen Benedictions ('Amidah)

1. Blessed are you, O Lord, God of our Fathers, God of Abraham, God of Isaac and God of Jacob, great mighty and fearful God, most high God who created heaven and earth, our shield and the shield of our Fathers, our trust in every generation. *Blessed are you, O Lord, shield of Abraham.*

2. You are mighty, humbling the proud; strong, and judging the violent; you live for ever and raise the dead; you make the wind blow and bring down the dew; you provide for the living and make the dead alive; in an instant you make our salvation to spring forth. *Blessed are you, O Lord, who make the dead alive.*

3. You are holy and your Name is awesome, and beside you there is no God. *Blessed are you, O Lord, the holy God.*

4. Grant us, O our Father, the knowledge [which comes] from you, and the understanding and discernment [which come] from your Torah. *Blessed are you, O Lord, who grant knowledge.*

5. Lead us back, O Lord, to you and we shall repent. Renew our days as of old. *Blessed are you, O Lord, who delight in repentance.*

6. Forgive us, O our Father, for we have sinned against you. Blot out and remove our evil deeds from before your eyes. For your mercies are numerous. *Blessed are you, O Lord, who are ready to forgive.*

7. Look on our misery, champion our cause and redeem us for your Name's sake. *Blessed are you, O Lord, the redeemer of Israel.*

8. Heal us, O Lord our God, from the pain of our hearts; remove from us sorrow and sighing, and raise up healing for our wounds. *Blessed are you, O Lord, who heal the sick of your people Israel.*

9. Bless this year for us, O Lord our God, and make all its produce prosper. Bring swiftly the year of our final redemption; give dew and rain to the land; satisfy the world from the treasuries of your goodness; and bless the work of our hands. *Blessed are you, O Lord, who bless the years.*

10. Proclaim our liberation with the great trumpet and raise a banner to gather together our dispersed. *Blessed are you, O Lord, who gather the dispersed of your people Israel.*

11. Restore our judges as in former times and our counsellors as in the beginning; and reign over us, yourself alone. *Blessed are you, O Lord, who love justice.*

12. For apostates let there be no hope; and may the arrogant kingdom be swiftly uprooted, in our days. May the Nazarenes and the heretics perish quickly; may they be erased from the Book of Life; and not be inscribed with the righteous. *Blessed are you, O Lord, who humble the arrogant.*

13. May your mercies be showered upon righteous proselytes; and grant us a rich reward, together with those who do your good pleasure. *Blessed are you, O Lord, trust of the righteous.*

14. Show mercy, O Lord our God, in your great mercies, to Israel your people and to Jerusalem your city; to Zion, the dwelling-place of your glory; to your temple and your habitation; and to the kingship of the house of David, your righteous Messiah. *Blessed are you, O Lord, God of David, who build Jerusalem.*

15. Hear, O Lord our God, the voice of our prayer, and be merciful to us; for you are a gracious and merciful God. *Blessed are you, O Lord, who hear prayer.*

16. Be pleased, O Lord our God, to dwell in Zion; and may your servants serve you in Jerusalem. *Blessed are you, O Lord, whom we worship in awe.*

17. We praise you, O Lord our God, and the God of our fathers, on account of all the goodness, grace, and mercies which you have granted us, and have done to us and to our fathers before us. And if we say our feet are slipping, your grace, Lord, succours us. *Blessed are you, O Lord, the All-good; you are to be praised.*

18. Bring peace upon Israel, your people, upon your city and upon your inheritance; and bless all of us together. *Blessed are you, O Lord, who make peace.*

Comment: This is known as the Palestinian recension of the Eighteen Benedictions or 'Amidah. The blessings in italics remain relatively unchanged in the various recensions. The Palestinian recension is probably closer to the first-century text than is the standard version found in modern prayer-books. The sense that the temple has been destroyed is less strong in it than in the other versions. It may be implied by Benediction 14, but not necessarily. Benediction 12, the famous 'Blessing of the Heretics' (*Birkat ha-Minim*), was according to the Talmud (*b. Ber.* 28b–29a), composed in the rabbinic school at Yavneh at the end of the first century CE. It was probably directed particularly, though not exclusively, at Jewish Christians, and is the grounds for patristic complaints that Jews curse the Christians in their prayers (Just. *Dial.* 16, Epiph. *Pan.* 29:9; Jerome, *Comm. in Isa.* 5:18–19; 49:7; 52:4). For a similar liturgical cursing of outsiders see ANTH E.3. On the Amidah see MAJ GEN E.5.

2. *Community Rule* (1QS), 9:26–10:16: A Calendar of the Times of Prayer

(9:26) He shall bless him [with the offering] of the lips (10:1) at the times which God has ordained: at the beginning of the dominion of light, and at its turning, when it retires to its appointed place; at the beginning of the (2) watches of darkness when he unlocks its storehouse and spreads it over the earth, and at its turning, when it retires before the light; when the heavenly lights (3) shine out from the abode of holiness, and when they retire to the dwelling of glory; at the commencement of the seasons on the days of the new moon, as well as at their turnings, when (4) one hands over to the other (when the seasons are renewed it is a great day for the Holy of Holies, and a s[ure] sign that the everlasting mercies will be opened at the beginning of the seasons for all time to come):
(5) At the beginning of the months at their appointed times,
and on the holy days established as a memorial at their appointed times,
(6) I will bless him with the offering of the lips
according to the precept engraved for ever;
at the beginning of the years and at the turning of their seasons,
when the statute (7) prescribed for them is fulfilled,
on the day that he has decreed the one (should hand over) to the other,
the season of (grain) harvest to the summer,

the season of sowing to the season of new shoots;
(at) the appointed times of the years, namely their heptads,
(8) and at the beginning of their heptads, the appointed times
of liberty.
As long as I live the engraved precept shall be on my tongue
as the fruit of praise and the portion of my lips.

(9) I will sing with knowledge and all my music shall be to the glory
of God.
I will strike up my lyre in tune with his holy decree,
and I will lift up the pipe of my lips to his right measure.
(10) With the coming of day and night I will enter the Covenant of
God,
and when evening and morning depart I will recite his precepts.
I will place in them (11) my bounds without backsliding.

I will approve his judgement concerning my sins,
and my transgressions shall be before my eyes as an engraved precept.
To God I will say, 'My Righteousness',
(12) and to the Most High, 'Foundation of my Goodness',
'Fountain of Knowledge' and 'Source of Holiness',
'Summit of Glory' and 'Almighty Eternal Majesty'.
I will accept that which (13) he teaches me,
and will delight in his judgement of me.

Before I move my hands and feet I will bless his Name.
Before I go out or in, (14) or sit or rise, or while lying on my bed I
will extol him.
I will bless him with the offering of the utterance of my lips in the ranks,
(15) and before I raise my hands to enjoy the pleasant produce of the
earth.
At the onset of fear and dread,
and in the abode of distress and desolation (16) I will bless him.
When he does wonders I will give thanks;
on his power I will meditate,
and on his mercies I will lean all day long.

Comment: The hymn was sung by the Maskil, the spiritual
leader of the Qumran community, to remind him of his
duties. The times of prayer that it stipulates include not only
the statutory sabbaths and festivals of the Torah, but many
others: the four days that mark the transitions between the
seasons of the year (see ANTH D.5), morning and evening,
before sitting down or standing up, when entering and leaving a house, before eating food and in times of sudden distress
or danger. It is clear from the surviving scrolls and from early
rabbinic literature that benedictions were composed specifically for these occasions. Thus the idea of a life of prayer—a life
of constant dialogue with God—was born. See further MAJ
GEN E.6, F.2.

3. *Community Rule* (1QS), 1:18–2:19: Ceremony for the Re-
newal of the Covenant

(1:18) On entering the Covenant, the Priests (19) and Levites shall
bless the God of salvation and all his true acts; and all (20) those
entering the Covenant shall say after them, 'Amen, Amen!'

(21) Then the Priests shall recite the favours of God (manifested)
in his mighty deeds, (22) and shall declare all his merciful favours
towards Israel, and the Levites shall recount (23) the iniquities of the
Children of Israel, all their guilty rebellions and the sins (that they
have committed) during the dominion of (24) Belial. [And al]l those
entering the Covenant shall make confession after them and say:

We have strayed, (25) we have re[belled], we have sinned and acted
wickedly, we and our fathers before us, by walking (26) [contrary to the
precepts] of truth. But [God is] righteous, [who has executed] his
judgement upon us and upon our fathers. (II 1) And he has bestowed
the mercies of his grace upon us from everlasting to everlasting.

And the Priests shall bless all (2) the men of the lot of God who walk
perfectly in all his ways, saying:
May he bless you with all (3) good,
and preserve you from all evil!
(4) May he enlighten your heart with life-giving wisdom,
and grant you eternal knowledge!
May he lift up his merciful face towards you for everlasting peace!

And the Levites shall curse all the men of (5) the lot of Belial; they
shall answer and say:

Cursed are you on account of all your wicked, guilty deeds!
May God inflict on you (6) torture at the hands of the avengers!
May he visit you with destruction at the hand of those who exact (7)
retribution!
May you be cursed without mercy in keeping with the darkness of
your deeds!
May you be damned (8) in the gloom of everlasting fire!
May God show you no mercy when you call on him,
Nor pardon you by blotting out your sins!
(9) May he lift up his angry face to exact vengeance from you!
And may those who hold faithfully to the fathers not greet you with
words of peace!
(10) And after the blessing and the cursing, all those entering the
Covenant shall say, 'Amen, Amen!'

(11) And the Priests and the Levites shall continue, saying:
Cursed be the man who enters this covenant while walking in the
idols of his heart, (12) and who sets up before himself the stumbling-
block of his sin so that he may backslide! (13) When he hears the
words of this covenant he blesses himself in his heart and says,
'Peace is with me, (14) even though I walk in the stubbornness of my
heart' (Deut 29:18–19). His spirit shall perish from thirst, though
surrounded by abundant water, and shall receive no (15) respite.
God's wrath and his zeal for his precepts shall consume him in
everlasting destruction. All (16) the curses of the covenant shall cling
to him and God will single him out for evil. He shall be cut off from
the midst of all the Sons of Light, and because he has backslidden
(17) from God on account of his idols and the stumbling-block of his
sin, his lot shall be cast among those accursed for ever.
(18) And all those entering the covenant shall answer and say after
them, 'Amen, Amen!'

(19) Thus shall they do, year by year, for as long as the dominion of
Belial endures.

Comment: The festival of the renewal of the Covenant probably took place at Qumran on Shabu'ot (Pentecost), appropriately, since Shabu'ot was the feast of the giving of the Torah at
Sinai. (Shabu'ot falls in the third month of the year and,
according to the Bible, the Israelites first camped at Sinai in
the third month.) However, the Qumran ceremony is deeply
sectarian: it involves a rededication to the group's own distinctive vision of the Covenant. The Priestly Blessing (Num
6:24–6), the most solemn benediction of the liturgy, is
adapted to create a blessing for those within the fold (the
Qumran community), and a curse for those outside it (the
rest of Israel). The marking of the boundaries is emphatic.
Belial is the name given in the scrolls to the evil spirit who,
under God's mysterious providence, controls the world in this
present age. He is the implacable spiritual enemy of the
community. See further MAJ GEN E.6, F.2.

4. The *Thanksgiving Hymns* (1QHᵃ), 10:20–30: A Hymn of
Confidence in Divine Protection

(20) I thank you, O Lord
that you have placed my soul in the bundle of the living,

(21) and that you protect me from all the snares of the pit.

For violent men sought after my life
when I held fast (22) to your covenant.
They, a council of futility and a congregation of Belial,
do not know that it is through you that I stand firm,
(23) and that by your acts of lovingkindness you save me,
because I walk with your help.

It is with your permission that they assail (24) my life,
so that you may be glorified when you judge the wicked,
and manifest your might through me before the sons of (25) men;
for it is by your lovingkindness that I stand firm.

I said, Mighty men have camped against me,
surrounding me with all (26) their weapons of war.
They have shot arrows against which there is no cure,
and the blades of (their) spears are like fire devouring the trees.
(27) Like the roar of mighty waters is the clamour of their shouting,
like a river that bursts its banks and destroys many;
(28) nothingness and futility break out in torrents(?), when their
    waves rise up.
Though my heart melted like water, my soul held fast to your
    Covenant.
(29) The net which they spread for me snares their own foot;
and they themselves have fallen into the traps which they hid to
    catch me.
'But my foot stands firm upon level ground;
(30) (even) from their assembly I will bless your Name' (cf. Ps
    26:12).

Comment: The intimate tone makes it uncertain whether this hymn was intended for public or private use. Even if sung publicly it establishes a close personal relationship to God. The sense of real persecution and danger has led some to suggest that this particular hymn may have been composed by the Teacher of Righteousness, the founder of the Dead Sea sect. On the *Thanksgiving Hymns* see MAJ GEN E.7.

5. The Benediction 'Creator of Light' (*Yoṣer ʾor*)

Blessed are you, O Lord our God, King of the universe, who form light and create darkness, who make peace and create all things. In mercy You give light to the earth and to those who dwell in it, and in your goodness you renew the work of creation each day continually. How numerous are your works, O Lord! In wisdom you have made them all: the earth is full of your possessions. O King, alone exalted from aforetime, praised, glorified, and extolled from days of old, O eternal God, in your abundant mercies have mercy upon us, Lord of our strength, Rock of our refuge, Shield of our salvation, Refuge of ours!

The blessed God, whose knowledge is great, prepared and made the sun's rays: he formed a good which brings glory to his name. He set the heavenly luminaries round about his strength. The chief of his hosts are holy beings who exalt the Almighty, and continually declare the glory of his holiness. Be blessed, O Lord our God, for the excellence of your handiwork, and for the bright luminaries which you have made that they should glorify you.

Qedushah: Be blessed, O our Rock, Our King, Creator of ministering spirits, whose ministers stand one and all in the heights of the universe and proclaim aloud with awe in unison the words of the living God and eternal King. They are all beloved, all pure, all mighty, and they all in dread and awe perform the will of their Master; they all open their mouths in holiness and purity, with song and psalm, while they bless, praise, glorify, and ascribe power, holiness and sovereignty to the Name of God, the great, mighty, dreaded King, holy is He; and they take upon themselves the yoke of the kingdom of heaven one from another, and give sanction one to another to sanctify their Creator. In serenity of spirit, with pure speech and holy melody, they all respond

in unison and exclaim with awe: 'Holy, holy, holy is the Lord of hosts; the whole earth is full of his glory' (Isa 6:3). The Ofannim and the Holy Creatures with great tumult raise themselves up towards the Seraphim; over against them they offer praise and say: 'Blessed be the glory of the Lord from his dwelling place' (Ezek 3:12).

To the blessed God they offer sweet melodies; to the King, the living and everlasting God, they utter hymns and declare their praises; for he alone performs mighty acts, and makes new things. He is the Lord of battles; he sows charitable deeds, causes salvation to spring forth, creates healing remedies, and is revered in praises. He is the Lord of wonders, who in his goodness renews the work of creation each day continually, as it is written: 'Give thanks to him who made great lights, for his kindness endures for ever' (Ps 136:7). Cause a new light to shine upon Zion, and may we all be worthy to enjoy its brightness. Blessed are you, O Lord, Creator of the heavenly luminaries.

Comment: This is the first of the two benedictions that precede the morning recitation of the Shema proper (Deut 6:4–9; 11:13–21; Num 15:37–41). It includes (paras. 3–4) a Qedushah—a prayer describing the liturgy of the angels. A similar Qedushah is inserted into the Amidah after the third benediction. The text given here is taken from a modern, standard Ashkenazi prayerbook, and probably reflects an early medieval rewording of the prayer influenced by the ideas of the Jewish Hekalot mystics. However, that both the *Yoṣer* benediction and the insertion into it of a Qedushah are very ancient is suggested by a passage in the early Christian text known as the *Apostolic Constitutions*, which preserves many old synagogue prayers only superficially Christianized (see *Ap. Con.* 8:12). And there is an obvious thematic link: the heavenly luminaries, whose creation is praised in the *Yoṣer ʾor*, are seen as heavenly beings praising God (cf. Job 38:7). See further MAJ GEN E.5, 8.

6. *2 Apocalypse of Baruch*, 10:5–19: Lament over Zion

(10:5) I, Baruch, returned and sat before the gates of the temple and made this lament over Zion and said:

(6) Happy is the man who was never born,
or the child who has died at birth.
(7) But woe to us who are alive,
for we have seen the sorrows of Zion,
and the fate of Jerusalem.
(8) I will summon the sirens from the sea—
and you, Liliths, come from the desert,
and you demons and jackals from the forests,
awake and gird yourselves for mourning.
Take up with me the funeral dirges,
and make lamentation with me.
(9) You, farmers, do not sow again.
You, earth, why do you yield your crops at harvest?
Keep to yourself your pleasant produce.
(10) And you, vine, why do you still give your wine?
For you will never again be offered in Zion,
nor will your first fruits again be offered.
(11) You, heavens, withhold your dew,
and do not open the storehouses of the rain.
You, sun, withhold the radiance of your rays,
(12) and you, moon, hide the brightness of your light;
for why should daylight rise again
when the light of Zion is darkened?
(13) You, bridegrooms, do not enter the bridal chamber,
and let not the virgins crown themselves with garlands.
You, married women, pray not for children,

(14) for the barren shall greatly rejoice;
those without sons shall be glad,
but those who have sons shall be in anguish.
(15) For why should they bear children in pain,
only to bury them with tears?
(16) Or why, again, should men have sons,
or why should their offspring any longer be given a name,
when this mother [Jerusalem] is desolate,
and her sons are led away into captivity?
(17) Speak no more of beauty,
talk no more of finery.
(18) And you, priests, take the keys of the sanctuary,
And throw them up to the heights of heaven.
Return them to the Lord and say,
'Protect your House yourself,
for we have been found to be false stewards!'
(19) You, virgins, who weave fine linen
and silk with the gold of Ophir,
take the lot in haste and throw them into the fire,
that it may carry them up to him who made them,
that the flame may send them to him who created them,
lest the enemy seize them!

Note: A Lilith (v. 8) is a female demon (masc. Lili), which particularly attacked pregnant women and newborn infants.

Comment: Using the persona of Baruch, the prophet Jeremiah's secretary who witnessed the destruction of the temple in 586 BCE (Jer 36, 45), the poet here mourns the destruction of the temple by the Romans in 70 CE. He manages skilfully to avoid too obvious dependence on the biblical book of Lamentations. Calling on heaven and earth to share in one's grief is a poetic commonplace, but here it hints at the deeper theological idea that the world is sustained by the service of the temple. See further MAJ GEN C.6, E.9.

F. The Rules of Religious Associations

1. *Community Rule* (1QS), 6:24–7:12: The Penal Code of the Qumran Community

(6:24) *These are the laws by which they shall judge at a community court in accordance with the facts.*

If anyone is found among them who has lied (25) deliberately in matters of property, he shall be excluded from the pure meal of the Congregation for one year and shall be fined a quarter of his food.

Whoever answers (26) a fellow-member obstinately, or speaks to him short-temperedly, rebelling against the authority of his colleague by disobeying the order of a fellow-member ranked before him, (27) has taken the law into his own hands. He shall be fined [and excluded from the pure meal] for one year.

If any man swears an oath by the [Most] Venerable Name [he shall be put to death]. (7:1) But if he has blasphemed, either because he has been overcome by distress, or for any other such reason, or while he is reading a scroll or reciting a benediction, he shall be excluded (2) and shall return to the Council of the community no more.

If he has spoken in anger against one of the priests inscribed in the scroll, he shall be fined for one year (3) and shall be excluded for his own good from the pure meal of the Congregation. But if he spoke unwittingly, he shall be fined for six months.

Whoever lies knowingly, (4) shall be fined for six months.

Whoever deliberately insults a fellow-member without good cause shall be fined for one year (5) and shall be excluded.

Whoever deliberately deceives a fellow-member or acts deceitfully towards him shall be fined for six months.

If (6) he acts without due care towards a fellow-member, he shall be fined for three months. If he acts negligently towards community

property and damages it, he shall replace it (7) in full. (8) And if he is unable to replace it, he shall be fined for sixty days.

Whoever bears malice against a fellow-member without good cause shall be fined for six months/one year; (9) and likewise, whoever takes revenge in any matter whatsoever.

Whoever speaks foolishly: three months.

Whoever interrupts a fellow-member while he is speaking: (10) ten days.

Whoever lies down and sleeps during a session of the Congregation: thirty days. And likewise, for whoever goes out during a session of the Congregation (11) without permission. And he who dozes off up to three times at a single session shall be fined for ten days. And if they stand up (12) and he (then) goes out, he shall be fined for thirty days.

Comment: This is the beginning of the Penal Code of the Qumran community, as found in the Cave 1 version of the *Community Rule*. Four forms of punishment are indicated: (1) death, if the restoration of the lacuna is correct; (2) permanent expulsion from the community; (3) exclusion from the 'pure meal of the Congregation', i.e. the communal meal; and (4) fining, which seems to involve being put on short commons and deprived of a quarter of one's food allowance. The rules listed here are not rules of Torah: they are specific rules of the Qumran community, breaches of its communal order (*serekh*), and they are tried in the community's own lawcourt. On the *Community Rule* see MAJ GEN F.2.

2. The *Damascus Rule* (CD), 13: 7–14 + 14: 12–16: The Rule for the Guardian and the Rule for Charity

(13:7) *This is the Rule for the Guardian of the Camp.*

He shall instruct the congregation in the works of (8) God. He shall impart to them understanding of his marvellous miracles, and shall recount to them all the events that are about to take place, together with their interpretations. (9) He shall love them as a father loves his children, and shall watch over them in all their distress like a shepherd his sheep. (10) He shall loosen all the fetters that bind them, so that there may be none that are oppressed or broken in his community.

(11) He shall examine whoever joins his community with regard to his deeds, understanding, ability, strength, and possessions, (12) and shall inscribe him in his proper place according to his portion in the lot of li[ght].

No member of the camp shall have the authority (13) to admit anyone into the community without the permission of the Guardian of the Camp.

(14) None of those who have entered into God's covenant shall give or receive anything from the Sons of the Dawn (15) other than from hand to hand.

No man shall form any association for buying and selling without informing (16) the Guardian of the Camp....

(14:12) *This is the Rule for the Congregation by which they shall provide for all their needs.*

The earnings of at least (13) two days out of every month shall be placed in the hands of the Guardian and the Judges, (14) and from it they shall give to the [fathe]rless, and from it they shall support the poor and the needy, the elder who (15) is [feeb]le, the afflicted, the captive taken by a foreign people, the virgin (16) who has no next of kin, and the you[th for] whom no one cares—all the communal services.

Note: At 13:14 read 'Sons of the Dawn' (*bĕnê haššaḥar*) rather than 'Sons of the Pit' (*bĕnê haššaḥat*). The Sons of the Dawn, who are addressed with words of exhortation by the Maśkîl in 4Q298, cannot be total outsiders, but rather a group linked in some way to the

Damascus Covenanters and the Qumran community. They might be people sympathetic to the movement or in process of joining it but not yet full members, or it is possible that the title designates the Damascus Covenanters themselves and that 'those who have entered into the God's Covenant' here denotes the Qumran community.

Comment: The Guardian (Heb. *mĕbaqqer*) has a role in teaching, in assessing the suitability of new members, and in controlling the relationships between the Congregation and the outside world. His office is not unlike that of a bishop in the later Christian church. Unlike the community in the *Community Rule* (ANTH F.I) the members of the Congregation here retain their earnings for their own use. However, they are required to pay a portion of them into a communal fund to help those unable to support themselves. From a social point of view, the mutual support provided by the religious associations must have been one of their most attractive features. See further MAJ GEN B.IO, F.3.

3. Philo, *De Vita Contemplativa*, 21–25 + 30–31: The Contemplative Order of the Therapeutae

(21) These kind of people (who withdraw from ordinary life) exist in many places in the inhabited world, for it is fitting that Greece and the non-Greek lands should alike share in perfect goodness, but they are numerous in Egypt in each of the so-called nomes and especially around Alexandria. (22) The best of them travel from all quarters to a certain most suitable spot as if they are going to their fatherland. It lies beyond the Mareotic Lake on a rather low-lying hill, well situated both because of its security and its temperate climate. (23) The security is provided by the farms and the villages round about, and the pleasantness of the air by the continuous breezes given off from the lake, which flows into the sea, and from the nearby ocean, the sea breezes being light and the lake breezes heavy, the two combining to produce a most healthy climate.

(24) The houses of this community are very basic and provide protection only against the two most immediate dangers, the heat of the sun and the cold of the air. They are neither close together like houses in towns, since living at close quarters would be troublesome and unpleasant to people earnestly seeking solitude, nor are they placed far apart, because they welcome fellowship, and so that they can come to each other's aid if they are attacked by robbers.

(25) In each house there is a sacred room which is called a sanctuary or solitude (Gk. *monastērion*), and closeted alone in this they perform the mysteries of the sanctified life. They take nothing into it, neither drink nor food nor any thing else necessary for the needs of the body, but only laws and oracles delivered by prophets, and hymns and any other writings by which knowledge and piety are increased and brought to perfection....

(30) For six days each of them seeks wisdom by himself, sitting alone in the solitudes mentioned earlier, never passing through the outer door of the house or even looking at it from afar. But every seventh day they come together as for a general assembly and sit in order according to their age with becoming gravity, keeping their hands inside their robes, the right hand between the breast and the chin and the left stretched out along their sides. (31) Then the eldest of them, and the most versed in their doctrines, comes forward and with steadfast look and steady voice delivers a well-reasoned and prudent discourse.

Comment: There is curiously little in Philo's description of the Therapeutae to identify them as a distinctively Jewish group, and in fact he notes that they conform to a pattern of withdrawal from the world that was practised by both Greeks and non-Greeks. In terms of later Christian monasticism the Therapeutae combine features of both the eremitical and the cenobitical way of life. During the week they live as hermits, scattered in their isolated cells, but on sabbath they come together in a central communal building, to eat, to listen to improving discourses, and to sing hymns and psalms. See further MAJ GEN A.3, F.4.

4. Mishnah *Demai*, 2:2–3 + Tosefta *Demai*, 2:2, 11, 12: The Duties of an Associate (*ḥaber*)

(*m. Dem.* 2:2) He who undertakes to be reliable (*ne'ĕman*) must give tithe from what he eats and from what he sells and buys, and he may not be a guest of an outsider ('*um hā-'āreṣ*). Rabbi Judah says: Even he who is the guest of an outsider may still be deemed reliable. They said to him: If he is not reliable in what concerns himself, how can he be reliable in what concerns others?

(*m. Dem.* 2:3) He who undertakes to be an Associate (*ḥaber*) may not sell to an outsider (foodstuffs that are) wet or dry, or buy from him (foodstuffs that are) wet; and he may not be the guest of an outsider, nor may he receive him as a guest in his own clothes.

(*t. Dem.* 2:2) He who takes upon himself four obligations is accepted as an Associate: not to give heave-offering or tithes to an outsider; not to prepare his pure food in the house of an outsider; and to eat even ordinary food in purity...

(*t. Dem.* 2:11) He is accepted first with regard to 'wings' (cleanness of hands) and after that with regard to pure food. If he takes upon himself only the obligation concerning 'wings' he is accepted; but if he takes upon himself only the obligation concerning pure food, but not concerning 'wings', he is not considered reliable even concerning pure food.

(*t. Dem.* 2:12) How long is it before a man is accepted? The School of Shammai say: For liquids, thirty days; for clothing, twelve months. The School of Hillel say: For either, thirty days.

Comment: The concern here for fully tithing produce and for preserving all foodstuffs in a condition of ritual purity is obvious. It is also clear that there were degrees of affiliation to the association, though what these were, and the stages of acceptance into full membership, are now hard to untangle. The social implications of submitting to this regime were profound. The fully committed *ḥaber* would have found it impossible to eat with non-members (who were called '*ammê hā-'āreṣ*, lit. peoples of the land). He would also have found it difficult to be in physical contact with a non-member (who could convey ritual impurity to his clothes, from which it could be transferred to food), or to trade with him. The '*ammêi hā-'āreṣ* were not Gentiles but fellow Jews. The intensification of religious norms within these associations, and the other religious fellowships of late Second-Temple Judaism, must have been deeply divisive. See further MAJ GEN B.II, F.5.

5. '*Abot de Rabbi Nathan*, A.6: Eliezer Goes to the School of Yoḥanan ben Zakkai

What were the beginnings of Rabbi Eliezer ben Hyrcanus? He was 22 years old and had still not studied Torah. Once he said: 'I am going to study Torah with Rabban Yoḥanan ben Zakkai.' His father Hyrcanus said to him: 'You shall not taste a bite of food till you have ploughed an entire furrow.' He rose early in the morning, ploughed an entire furrow and went off. (Some say: That day was sabbath eve and he dined at his father-in-law's.) But others say: He tasted nothing for six hours before sabbath started till six hours after it ended. As he walked along the road he saw a stone; he picked it up and put it in his mouth. (Some say: It was cattle dung.) He went and spent the night in a hostel. Then he went and sat before Rabban Yoḥanan ben Zakkai in Jerusalem—until his bad breath became noticeable.

Rabban Yoḥanan ben Zakkai asked him: 'Eliezer, my son, have you eaten anything today?' Silence. Again he asked him, and again silence. Rabban Yoḥanan sent for the proprietors of the hostel and asked them: 'Did Eliezer have anything to eat at your place?' They replied: 'Master, we thought that he was eating with you.' He said to them: 'And I thought that he was eating with you! You and I, between us, left Rabbi Eliezer to perish!' Rabban Yoḥanan ben Zakkai said to Rabbi Eliezer: 'Just as the bad breath came forth from your mouth, so shall your fame in Torah spread abroad.'

When Hyrcanus, Rabbi Eliezer's father, heard that he was studying Torah with Yoḥanan ben Zakkai, he declared: 'I shall go and ban my son from all my possessions.' They said: That day Rabban Yoḥanan ben Zakkai sat expounding in Jerusalem with all the important men of Israel sitting before him. When he heard that Hyrcanus was coming he set guards and told them: 'If Hyrcanus comes, don't let him sit down.' Hyrcanus arrived and they would not let him sit down, but he pushed his way up to the front until he found himself beside Ṣiṣit ben ha-Keset, Naqdimon ben Gorion, and Ben Kalba Shabna. He sat among them trembling. They say: On that day Rabban Yoḥanan ben Zakkai fixed his gaze on Rabbi Eliezer and said to him: 'Deliver the exposition!' 'I cannot,' Rabbi Eliezer replied. Rabban Yoḥanan ben Zakkai pressed him to do it, and the other students pressed him as well. So he rose and delivered a discourse on things such as the ear had never heard before. As each word came from his mouth Rabban Yoḥanan ben Zakkai rose to his feet and kissed him on the head and exclaimed: 'Rabbi Eliezer, my master, you have taught me the truth!' Before the session had ended, Hyrcanus, the father, rose to his feet and declared: 'My masters, I came here only in order to ban my son Eliezer from my possessions. Now all my possessions shall be given to Eliezer my son. All his brothers are disinherited and shall have none of them.'

Comment: Though doubtless embellished and obviously self-promoting, the story reflects accurately social and historical realities. The loss of the labour of a full-grown son who wanted to go off to study at yeshivah could well have created tensions within poorer families. And the picture of the school in session is convincing. Immediately in front of the teacher sits a row of local grandees. They are not students, but wealthy supporters of the school, on whose contributions its existence probably depended, since the school is unlikely to have charged fees. Behind the grandees sit the rows of students. Not only the teacher lectures: students could be called upon to expound as well. Though the story comes from a fourth-century source, it purports to speak about the school of Yoḥanan ben Zakkai in Jerusalem before 70 CE. Yoḥanan was a leading Pharisee, who after the destruction of the temple founded the school at Yavneh. His school in Jerusalem was probably bigger than most and had its own dedicated premises. The hostel mentioned may well have been attached to the school and intended specifically to house its students. On the 'Abot de Rabbi Nathan see MAJ GEN F.6–7.

G. Hagiography

1. Ezekiel the Tragedian, *Exagoge*, 68–82: The Apotheosis of Moses

> In a vision I saw a throne on top of Mount Sinai,
> so great in size that it reached the clouds of heaven.
> (70) Upon it sat a noble figure,
> crowned with a crown and holding a mighty sceptre
> in his left hand, while with his right he beckoned me.
> So I approached and stood before the throne.
> He handed the sceptre to me and on the great throne

> (75) he bade me sit; he gave to me the royal
> crown, and he himself quitted the throne.
> I beheld the whole world round about;
> things beneath the earth and above the skies.
> At my feet a multitude of stars
> (80) fell down, and I counted all their number.
> They paraded past me like a troop of soldiers.
> Then in terror I woke from my dream.

Comment: Moses is here telling his father-in-law Jethro about a dream that he has had, which relates to his future receiving of the law on Mount Sinai, an event which lay beyond the scope of Ezekiel's narrative. Ezekiel, like many early Jewish commentators, seems to have held that Moses not merely ascended the mountain, but went up into heaven itself. The noble figure on the throne is God, pictured as the Ancient of Days as in Dan 7 (cf. ANTH C.3). God enthrones Moses, appointing him his viceregent over the world, and Moses receives the homage of the hosts of heaven. On Ezekiel the Tragedian see MAJ GEN G.I.

2. *Joseph and Aseneth*, 7:1–11: Joseph's First Sight of Aseneth

(7:1) Joseph entered Pentephres' house and sat on a seat, and Pentephres washed his feet and set a table before him by itself, because Joseph never ate with the Egyptians, for this was an abomination to him. (2) And looking up, Joseph saw Aseneth leaning through (the window). And Joseph spoke to Pentephres and his whole family, saying, 'Who is that woman standing in the solar by the window? Tell her to leave this house at once.' (3) This was because Joseph was afraid lest she too should pester him, for all the wives and daughters of the noblemen and satraps of the whole land of Egypt used to pester him to sleep with him, (4) and all the wives and daughters of the Egyptians suffered badly when they saw Joseph, because he was so handsome. They used to send their messengers to him with gold and silver and precious gifts, (5) but Joseph sent them back with threats and insults, saying, 'I will not sin before the God of Israel.' (6) And Joseph kept the face of his father Jacob always before his eyes, and remembered his father's commandments. For Jacob used to say to his son Joseph and to his brother, 'My children, guard strongly against associating with a strange woman, for she is ruin and destruction.' (7) Therefore Joseph said, 'Tell that woman to leave this house.'

(8) Pentephres said to him, 'My Lord, that woman you have seen in the upper storey is no stranger but our daughter, a virgin hating every man, and no other man has ever seen her save you alone today. (9) And if you wish, she will come and speak with you, because our daughter is like a sister to you.' (10) And Joseph was overjoyed because Pentephres had said, 'She is a virgin hating every man.' And Joseph said to himself, 'If she is a virgin hating every man, she will certainly not molest me.' (11) And Joseph said to Pentephres and his wife, 'If she is your daughter and a virgin, let her come, because she is my sister, and I love her as my sister from this day.'

Comment: When Joseph, who holds the position of vizier of Egypt, arrives at Potiphar/Pentephres' house with all his retinue, Aseneth coyly runs upstairs to avoid meeting him, but she cannot resist peeping out at the visitor and noticing how handsome he is. Joseph catches a glimpse of her, and demands that she leave the house, lest she seduce him into violating his father's command to keep away from women (cf. ANTH D.3). The reference to Joseph's fatal attractiveness to Egyptian women is based on Gen 39:6–20, where Potiphar/Pentephres' wife attempts to seduce him. Joseph resists, is slandered by the woman, and is thrown into jail. Curiously the author of *Joseph and Aseneth* makes no direct allusion to these events. Perhaps he felt that to introduce Joseph's earlier life as a servant of Potiphar/Pentephres might have confused his story, though it could also have provided him with some interesting dramatic ironies: Joseph, now the second-in-command in Egypt, returns to the house of the master and mistress who had wronged him; having spurned the mother, he falls for the daughter's charms. Instead he generalizes the Potiphar/Pentephres' wife episode into a universal condemnation of the predatory behaviour of Egyptian women. The serious side of the story is seen in its stress on Joseph's piety: he resists the temptations that come from moving in Gentile society. He keeps the dietary laws and rejects the sexual advances of Gentile women. When he does marry a Gentile girl, she is a chaste virgin, and he only takes her after she has converted to Judaism. On *Joseph and Aseneth* see MAJ GEN G.2.

3. *The Lives of the Prophets*, 1:1–13: Isaiah's Spring and Tomb

(1:1) Isaiah, from Jerusalem, was killed by Manasseh by being sawn in two, and he was buried beneath the Oak of Rogel, hard by the ford through the waters which Hezekiah stopped by blocking up their source (cf. 2 Chr 32:3–4). (2) And God worked the miracle of Siloam for the prophet, for, being faint before he died, he prayed for water to drink, and immediately it was sent to him from this source. Hence it is called Siloam, which means 'sent' (cf. Jn 9:7). (3) And in the time of Hezekiah, before he made the pools and cisterns, a little water came out in response to Isaiah's prayer, so that the city might not perish for lack of water, for the people were being besieged by foreigners. (4) For the enemy were asking, 'From where are they drinking?' (5) And, while investing the city, they were encamped at Siloam. (6) If, then, the Jews came, water would flow out, but if the foreigners came, it would not. (7) Therefore to this day it comes out suddenly, in order that the mystery might be made manifest. (8) And since this happened with Isaiah's help, to keep it in mind the people buried him nearby with great care and honour, so that through his prayers, even after his death, they might continue to enjoy the benefit of the water, for an oracle also was given to them about this.

(9) His tomb is hard by the tomb of the kings, behind the tomb of the priests, in the southern quarter. (10) For Solomon made the tombs, following David's design, east of Zion, which has an entrance from Gabaon (Gibeon), some twenty stadia distant from the city. (11) And he made a construction with twisting passages, which to this day is unknown to most of the priests and to all of the people. (12) There the king kept the gold from Ethiopia and the spices. (13) And since Hezekiah had disclosed to the Gentiles the secrets of David and Solomon (cf. 2 Kings 20:12–18), and had defiled the bones of his fathers, God swore that, on account of this, his offspring would be enslaved to his enemies, and God made him impotent from that day.

Note: At v. 11, some sort of souterrain seems to be envisaged.

Comment: The author regards the Pool of Siloam as being fed by a spring which was miraculously created by the intercessions of the prophet Isaiah, and which is maintained by his prayers even after his death. (He seems to be unaware of the fact that it is fed from the Gihon spring through Hezekiah's tunnel.) An important physical feature of the landscape is linked with a saint, who is shown in typical role protecting his devotees. The careful description of the location of the saint's tomb is presumably meant to assist those who wish to visit it. The saint in this case is also a martyr: he was sawn in two during the reign of wicked king Manasseh. The tradition is not biblical but is found also in the *Martyrdom and Ascension of Isaiah*, 5:1–5, and in the Talmud (y. *Sanh.* 10 (28c. 37); b.

Yebam. 49b). It is probably alluded to in Heb 11:37. Hezekiah's desecration of the bones of his ancestors is also not biblical. Appropriately he is punished with impotence as well as exile. Saints were often venerated because they were seen as being able to grant offspring to childless couples. On the *Lives of the Prophets* see MAJ GEN G.3.

4. 4 Maccabees, 9:10–25: The Eldest Son Defies the Greek Tyrant

(9:10) When they had said these things the tyrant was not only indignant at the the youths' disobedience, but even more enraged at their ingratitude. (11) Then, at his command, the guards brought forward the eldest brother, ripped off his tunic, and bound his hands and arms on both sides with thongs. (12) When they had worn themselves out flogging him with whips, without achieving anything, they put him on the wheel. (13) Stretched on this, the noble youth's limbs were all put out of joint, (14) and as each limb was dislocated, he denounced the tyrant, saying, (15) 'Most foul tyrant, enemy of heavenly justice and pitiless, you punish me in this fashion not as a murderer or an impious man but as a defender of the divine law.' (16) And when the guards said to him, 'Consent to eat and you will be released from the tortures,' (17) he answered, 'Your wheel is not so strong, foul lackeys, as to strangle my reason. Cut off my limbs, burn my flesh, twist my joints, (18) and through all these torments I will convince you that the children of the Hebrews alone are invincible defenders of virtue.' (19) While he was saying this they spread fire under him and, stoking it up (?), they turned the wheel still tighter. (20) The wheel was spattered all over with blood, the heap of coals was being quenched by drops of gore, and strips of flesh were turning round the axles of the machine. (21) Although the ligaments joining his bones were already severed, the great-souled youth, true son of Abraham that he was, did not groan, (22) but as though being transformed by fire into incorruptibility, he nobly endured the rackings, saying, (23) 'Imitate me, brothers; never give up my struggle nor foreswear our brotherhood in courage. (24) Fight the sacred and noble fight for true religion, on account of which the just providence that came to our fathers' aid will show mercy to our nation and take vengeance on the accursed tyrant.' (25) And with these words the saintly youth expired.

Comment: Rather than eat 'unclean food' in violation of the Torah, the eldest of the seven brothers is prepared to undergo excruciating torture and finally death. In doing so he obeys a higher, divine authority than that of the tyrant, Antiochus, the limits of whose power he demonstrates. The stress on the gruesome details of the torture are noteworthy. They were to become typical of later martyr literature. They evoke pity and they highlight the triumph of reason over the passions, but they also appeal to a voyeuristic fascination with pain and suffering. The 'gratitude' of the king which the seven brothers spurn (9:10) was his offer that 'if you will renounce the ancestral law of your polity you will receive leading positions of authority over my domains' (8:7). On 4 Maccabees see MAJ GEN G.4, and 4 MACC.

5. Babylonian Talmud, *Berakhot*, 61b: The Martyrdom of Rabbi Aqiva

Our rabbis taught: Once the wicked government issued a decree forbidding the Jews to engage in the study of Torah. Pappus ben Judah came and found Rabbi Aqiva publicly holding meetings and engaging in the study of Torah. He said to him: 'Aqiva, are you not afraid of the government?' He replied: 'I will tell you a parable. A fox was once walking alongside a river, and he saw fish darting in shoals from one place to another. He said to them: "From what do you flee?" They replied: "From the nets which men cast out for us." He said to them: "Would you like to come up on to dry land so that you and I can live together in the way that my ancestors lived with your ancestors?" They replied: "Are you the one men call the cleverest of animals? You're not clever; you are stupid. If we are afraid in the element in which we live, how much more should we be afraid in an element in which we would die!" So it is with us. If we are in our present plight while sitting studying Torah, of which it is written, "It brings you life and longevity" (Deut 30:20), how much worse off would we be if we were to go and neglect it.'

They say that a few days later Rabbi Aqiva was arrested and thrown into prison, and Pappus ben Judah was also arrested and thrown into prison beside him. He said to him: 'Pappus, who brought you here?' He replied: 'Happy are you, Rabbi Aqiva, for you have been arrested for busying yourself with Torah! But alas for Pappus, who has been arrested for busying himself with trivial things!'

When Rabbi Aqiva was taken out for execution, it was the time for the reciting of the Shema. While they combed his flesh with combs of iron, he was taking upon himself the yoke of the kingdom of heaven. His students said to him: 'Our teacher, are you prepared to go this far!' He said to them: 'All my life I have been troubled by the words "With all your soul" (Deut 10:12; 26:16), which I understand to mean "Even if God takes your soul". I said: "When shall I ever have an opportunity of fulfilling this?" Now that I have an opportunity, shall I not fulfil it?' He prolonged the word 'one' and expired while saying it. A heavenly voice went forth and said: 'Happy are you, Rabbi Aqiva, because you expired with the word "one" on your lips!' The ministering angels said before the Holy One, blessed be He, 'Such Torah and such a reward! He should have been "one of those that die by your hand, Lord"' (Ps 17:14). He replied to them, 'Their portion is in life' (Ps 17:14). A heavenly voice went forth and proclaimed, 'Happy are you, Rabbi Aqiva, for you are destined for the life of the world to come.'

Comment: The Babylonian Talmud, from which this version of the martyrdom of Aqiva is taken was edited around 500 CE (MAJ GEN B.II), but it is given as a Tannaitic tradition, which, if correct, would date it to before 200 CE. The 'wicked government' is Rome, and the story purports to come from the time of the Hadrianic persecutions (132–5). The 'combs of iron' are a reference to a Roman instrument of torture known as 'the claws' (Lat. *ungulae*), which was used to flay the victim. The approbation of the martyr, either through a comforting vision or a 'heavenly voice', the dialogue between the martyr and bystanders/friends/pupils, and the comment of the angels became standard motifs of the martyr literature. See further MAJ GEN G.5.

6. Babylonian Talmud, *Berakot*, 62a: The Teacher as Torah Incarnate

It has been taught: Rabbi Aqiva said: 'Once I went in after Rabbi Joshua to a privy, and I learnt from him three things. I learnt that one does not sit east–west but north–south; I learnt that one does not evacuate standing up but sitting down; and I learnt that it is proper to clean oneself with the left hand and not with the right.' Ben ʿAzzai said to him: 'Did you dare to take such liberties with your master?'—He replied: 'It is a matter of Torah, and I needed to learn.'

It has been taught: Ben Azzai said: 'Once I went in after Rabbi Aqiva to a privy, and I learnt from him three things. I learnt that one does not evacuate east–west but north–south. I also learnt that one evacuates sitting down and not standing up. I also learnt that it is proper to clean oneself with the left hand and not with the right.' Rabbi Judah said to him: 'Did you dare to take such liberties with your master?'—He replied: 'It is a matter of Torah, and I needed to learn.'

Rab Kahana once went in and hid under Rav's bed. He heard him chatting [with his wife] and joking and doing what he required. He said to him: 'One would think that Abba's mouth had never sipped the dish before!' He said to him: 'Kahana, are you there? Get out! This is not done (lit. not the way of the world)!' He replied: 'It is a matter of Torah, and I need to learn.'

Note: Abba ('Father') is here used by Kahana as a title of respect for his teacher.

Comment: The examples cited are exaggerated, in typical rabbinic style, and are doubtless meant to bring a smile to the faces of the 'pupils of the Sages', but a deeply serious point is being made. It is that Torah extends into all areas of life, and should govern even etiquette. The teacher embodies the Torah, and his actions should be observed and imitated, for they reveal the truth as much as his words. The same sentiment was later expressed in the modern Hasidic maxim that one goes to the Rebbe not just to hear his teaching but to see how he ties and unties his shoe-laces. See further MAJ GEN B.II, G.6.

REFERENCES

Albeck, C. (1952–8), *Shishah Sidrei Mishnah* (6 vols.; Jerusalem: Mosad Bialik).

Alexander, P. S. (1986), 'Incantations and Books of Magic', in E. Schürer, *The History of the Jewish People in the Age of Jesus Christ*, rev. G. Vermes, F. Millar, and M. Goodman (Edinburgh: T. & T. Clark), iii. 342–79.

—— (1988), 'Jewish Aramaic Translations of Hebrew Scriptures' in M. J. Mulder (ed.) *Mikra: Text, Translation, Reading and Interpretation of the Hebrew Bible in Ancient Judaism & Early Christianity*, Compendia Rerum Iudaicarum ad Novum Testamentum II. 1 (Assen/Maastricht: van Gorcum; Philadelphia: Fortress) 217–54.

—— (1996), 'Physiogmony, Initiation and Rank in the Qumran Community', in P. Schäfer, H. Cancik, and H. Lichtenberger (eds.), *Geschichte—Tradition—Reflexion: Festschrift für Martin Hengel zum 70. Geburtstag* (Tübingen: Mohr [Siebeck]), i. 385–94.

—— (1997), 'Jerusalem as the Omphalos of the World: On the History of a Geographical Concept', *Judaism*, 46: 147–58.

—— and Vermes, G. (1998), *Serekh ha-Yahad and Two Related Texts*, DJD 26 (Oxford: Clarendon).

Benoit, P., Milik, J. T., and de Vaux, R. (1961), *Les Grottes de Murabbaʿat*, DJD 2 (Oxford: Clarendon).

Black, M. (1970), *Apocalypsis Henochi Graece* (Leiden: Brill).

—— (1985), *The Book of Enoch or 1 Enoch* (Leiden: Brill).

Bogaert, P. (1969), *L'Apocalypse syriaque de Baruch* (2 vols; Paris: Éditions du Cerf).

Brooke, G. J. (1985), *Exegesis at Qumran: 4Q Florilegium in its Jewish Context* (Sheffield: JSOT).

Brownlee, W. H. (1979), *The Midrash Pesher of Habakkuk* (Missoula, Mont.: Scholars Press).

Campbell, J. (1995), *The Use of Scripture in the Damascus Document 1–8, 19–20* (Berlin: de Gruyter).

Charles, R. H. (1895), *The Ethiopic Version of the Hebrew Book of Jubilees* (Oxford: Clarendon).

—— (1896), *The Apocalypse of Baruch . . . Edited with Introduction, Notes and Indices* (London: Black).

—— (1902), *The Book of Jubilees or Little Genesis* (London: Black).

—— (1908), *The Testaments of the Twelve Patriarchs . . . with Introduction, Notes and Indices* (London: Black).

—— (1912), *The Book of Enoch* (Oxford: Clarendon).

—— and Morfill, W. R. (1896), *The Book of the Secrets of Enoch* (Oxford: Clarendon).

Charlesworth, J. H. (1995) (ed.), *The Damascus Document, War Scroll, and Related Documents*, Dead Sea Scrolls, 2 (Tübingen: Mohr [Siebeck]).

Clarke, E. G. (1984), *Targum Pseudo-Jonathan of the Pentateuch: Text and Concordance* (Hoboken, NJ: Ktav).

Colson, F. H., and Whitaker, G. H. (1971), *Philo*, LCL (12 vols.; Cambridge, Mass.: Harvard).

Danby, H. (1933), *The Mishnah* (Oxford: Oxford University Press).

Davies, P. R. (1977), *1QM: The War Scroll from Qumran: Its Structure and History* (Rome: Biblical Institute Press (Biblica et Orientalia 32)).

——(1982), *The Damascus Covenant: An Interpretation of the 'Damascus Document'* (Sheffield: JSOT).

Dedering, S. (1973), *Peshitta* (Leiden: Brill), 4/3, pp. 1–50.

de Jonge, M. (1953), *The Testaments of the Twelve Patriarchs: A Study of their Text, Composition, and Origin* (Leiden: Brill).

——(1978), *The Testaments of the Twelve Patriarchs: A Critical Edition of the Greek Text* (Leiden: Brill).

Denis, A.-M. (1970), *Fragmenta Pseudepigraphorum quae supersunt Graeca* (Leiden: Brill).

Elbogen, I. (1993), *Jewish Liturgy: A Comprehensive History*, tr. R. P. Scheindlin (Philadelphia: Jewish Publication Society).

Epstein, I. (1935–52) (ed.), *The Babylonian Talmud Translated into English with Notes, Glossary and Indices* (35 vols.; London: Soncino).

Falk, D. K. (1998), *Daily, Sabbath and Festival Prayers in the Dead Sea Scrolls* (Leiden: Brill).

Feldman, L. H. (1998), *Studies in Josephus' Rewritten Bible* (Leiden: Brill).

García Martínez, F., and Tigchelaar, E. J. C. (1997), *The Dead Sea Scrolls Study Edition* (2 vols.; Leiden: Brill).

Goldin, J. (1955), *The Fathers according to Rabbi Nathan* (New Haven: Yale University Press).

Gollancz, H. (1908), *Translations from Hebrew and Aramaic: The Targum to 'The Song of Songs', the Book of the Apple, the Ten Jewish Martyrs, A Dialogue on the Games of Chance* (London: Luzac).

Hadas, M. (1953), *The Third and Fourth Books of Maccabees* (New York: Harper).

Hempel, C. (1998), *The Laws of the Damascus Document: Sources, Tradition and Redaction* (Leiden: Brill).

Horgan, M. (1979), *Pesharim: Qumran Interpretations of Biblical Books* (Washington: The Catholic Biblical Association).

Jacobson, H. (1983), *The Exagoge of Ezekiel* (Cambridge: Cambridge University Press).

Idelsohn, A. Z. (1932), *Jewish Liturgy and its Development* (New York: Dover).

Kampen, J., and Bernstein, M. J. (1996) (eds.), *Reading 4QMMT: New Perspectives on Qumran Law and History* (Atlanta: Scholars Press).

Kittel, B. (1981), *The Hymns of Qumran* (Chico, Calif.: Scholars Press).

Knibb, M. A. (1978), *The Ethiopic Book of Enoch* (2 vols.; Oxford: Clarendon).

Kraemer, R. S. (1998), *When Asenath Met Joseph* (Oxford: Oxford University Press).

Lauterbach, J. Z. (1933–5), *Mekhilta de Rabbi Ishmael: A Critical Edition on the Basis of the MSS and Early Editions with an English Translation, Introduction and Notes* (3 vols.; Philadelphia: Jewish Publication Society).

Leaney, A. R. C. (1966), *The Rule of Qumran and its Meaning* (London: SCM).

Lim, T. (1997), *Holy Scripture in the Qumran Commentaries and Pauline Letters* (Oxford: Oxford University Press).

Maher, M. (1992), *Targum Pseudo-Jonathan: Genesis, Translated with Introduction and Notes*, Aramaic Bible, 1B (Edinburgh: T. & T. Clark).

Maier, J. (1985), *The Temple Scroll: An Introduction, Translation and Commentary* (JSOTSup 34) (Sheffield: JSOT).

Mansoor, M. (1961), *The Dead Sea Scrolls: A College Textbook and a Study Guide* (Leiden: Brill).

Margalioth, M. (1966), *Sefer Ha-Razim: A Newly Discovered Book of Magic from the Talmudic Period* (Jerusalem: Yediot Acharonot).

Milik, J. T. (1976), *The Books of Enoch: Aramaic Fragments of Qumran Cave 4* (Oxford: Clarendon).

Morgan, M. A. (1983), *Sepher Ha-Razim: The Book of Mysteries* (Chico, Calif.: Scholars Press).

Mulder, M. J. (1988) (ed.), *Mikra*, CRINT 2/1 (Assen: Van Gorcum).

Neusner, J. (1977–86), *The Tosefta: Translated from the Hebrew* (6 vols.; New York: Ktav).

——(1982–94), *The Talmud of the Land of Israel* (35 vols.; Chicago: Chicago University Press).

——(1988), *Mekhilta according to Rabbi Ishmael: An Introduction to Judaism's First Scriptural Encyclopaedia* (Atlanta: Scholars Press).

Newsome, C. (1985), *Songs of the Sabbath Sacrifice* (Atlanta: Scholars Press).

Philonenko, M. (1968), *Joseph et Aséneth: Introduction, texte critique, traduction et notes* (Leiden: Brill).

Qimron, E., and Strugnell, J. (1994), *Miqsat Ma'aseh Ha-torah*, DJD 10 (Oxford: Clarendon).

Reeg, G. (1985), *Die Geschichte von den Zehn Märtyren* (Tübingen: Mohr [Siebeck]).

Rahlfs, A. (n.d.), *Septuaginta*, 6th edn. (Stuttgart: Württembergische Bibelanstalt).

Rajak, T. (1983), *Josephus: The Historian and his Society* (London: Duckworth).

Reif, S. C. (1993), *Judaism and Hebrew Prayer* (Cambridge: Cambridge University Press).

Runia, D. (1990), *Exegesis and Philosophy: Studies on Philo of Alexandria* (Aldershot: Variorum).

Saldarini, A. J. (1975), *The Fathers according to Rabbi Nathan* (Leiden: Brill).

——(1982), *Scholastic Rabbinism: A Literary Study of the Fathers according to R. Nathan* (Chico, Calif.: Scholars Press).

Sandmel, S. (1979), *Philo of Alexandria: An Introduction* (New York: Oxford University Press).

Schechter, S. (1979), *Aboth de Rabbi Nathan: Edited from Manuscripts with an Introduction, Notes and Appendices* (repr. Hildesheim: Olms).

Schiffman, L. H. (1975), *The Halakhah at Qumran* (Leiden: Brill).

——(1989), *The Eschatological Community of the Dead Sea Scrolls: A Study of the Rule of the Congregation* (Atlanta: Scholars Press).

Schwemer, A. M. (1997), *Vitae Prophetarum* (Tübingen: Mohr [Siebeck]).

Siegert, F. (1996), 'Philo of Alexandria', in M. Sæbø (ed.), *Hebrew Bible/Old Testament: The History of its Interpretation*, 1/1 (Göttingen: Vandenhoeck & Ruprecht), 162–89.

Singer, S. (1962), *The Authorized Daily Prayer book* (London: Eyre and Spottiswoode).

Sparks, H. F. D. (1984), (ed.), *The Apocryphal Old Testament* (Oxford: Clarendon).

Stemberger, G. (1996), *Introduction to the Talmud and Midrash*, 2nd edn. (Edinburgh, T. & T. Clark).

Thackeray, H. St., Marcus, R., Wikgren, A., and Feldman, L. H. (1965), *Josephus*, LCL (9 vols.; Cambridge, Mass.: Harvard University Press).

Torrey, C. C. (1946), *The Lives of the Prophets: Greek Text and Translation* (Philadelphia: Society of Biblical Literature & Exegesis).

Vaillant, A. (1952), *Le Livre des secrets d'Hénoch* (Paris: Institut d'Études Slaves).

VanderKam, J. C. (1977), *Textual and Historical Studies in the Book of Jubilees* (Missoula, Mont.: Scholars Press).

van Henten, J. W. (1997), *The Maccabean Martyrs as Saviours of the Jewish People: A Study of 2 and 4 Maccabees* (Leiden: Brill).

Vermes, G. (1997), *The Complete Dead Sea Scrolls in English* (London: Allen Lane).

Wernberg-Møller, P. (1957), *The Manual of Discipline* (Leiden: Brill).

Whiston, William (1737) (tr.), *Josephus*, 1st edn. (repr. n.p.: Hendrickson, 1987).

Yadin, Y. (1962), *The Scroll of the War of the Sons of Light against the Sons of Darkness* (London: Oxford University Press).

——(1983), *The Temple Scroll* (3 vols.; Jerusalem: Israel Exploration Society).

Yonge, C. D. (1993), *The Works of Philo* (n.p.: Hendrickson).

Zuckermandel, M. S. (1937), *Tosefta* (Jerusalem: Wahrmann).

56. Introduction to the New Testament LESLIE HOULDEN

A. Introduction. **1.** This article sets out to 'introduce' the New Testament. But in literature as in life, introductions may be of two kinds. At a formal lecture or public meeting, the speaker is usually introduced with a factual account of career and achievements. We receive in effect the speaker's credentials, flattering him or her and reassuring the audience as it settles to what lies ahead. Such introductions, with their battery of facts, generally bear no close relation to the substance of the ensuing utterance, except that they lead the listener to expect a display of some competence in, say, economics, but none in civil engineering.

2. Introductions at social gatherings are of a different character. When we are introduced to someone, we do not expect a monologue of information about our new acquaintance to flow from the introducer, still less from the person who faces us. No, introduction is a mere beginning. It offers the prospect of conversation where we shall range around for points of contact and explore possible features of character and opinion; so that gradually, but quite unsystematically, we may build up a picture of the one who has been introduced to us. If the introduction leads to sufficient interest, we shall hope that it leads to further meetings, so that our sketchy picture may become fuller and more exact. We shall take steps to ensure that the process continues from this propitious beginning. We shall certainly not expect that the first encounter provides more than a few unrelated bits of information and half-formed impressions. Loose ends will not worry us in the least.

3. This Introduction is of this second kind. At many points, the reader who is new to the subject will wish to question and clarify, and may even be frustrated by the incompleteness of what is provided. The aim, however, is to open subjects rather than to close them. Moreover, though a range of ideas on a particular subject will often be given, to indicate that it is not all plain sailing and where the rocks and shoals lie, this Introduction represents only one among the many possible perspectives on its subject. Further information on many topics comes in the detailed articles that follow, or else in other works of reference, such as Bible dictionaries or encyclopedias or in fuller commentaries on particular NT books. The aim here is to stimulate curiosity, even to incite to discontent, so that the New Testament may continue to fascinate as well as edify its readers.

B. The Idea of the New Testament. **1.** It is natural to suppose that the NT is virtually as old as Christianity itself. It is equally natural to assume that the NT has always been part and parcel of Christianity, integral to its very being. It is refreshing to the mind to recognize that the truth is not so simple. We shall list some of the facts that cast doubt on those assumptions about the NT.

2. But first we should identify what we have in mind when we think of 'the NT'. Most people will visualize a slim volume containing twenty-seven writings from early Christianity, or else think of the second part of the Christian Bible, most of it

occupied by the OT. These writings vary in type (though most are either gospels or letters) and in length (from the 28 chapters of Matthew's gospel and Acts to the few lines of the 2nd and 3rd Letters of John). Though there are connections between some of them, by way of authorship (e.g. the letters of Paul) or in a literary way (dependence among the first three gospels and common material in Colossians and Ephesians), each is in origin a separate work, composed in its own time and place for its own particular purpose.

3. These writings differ also in accessibility: we are likely to feel most at home with the gospels and Acts, with their strong story-line, much less at home with some of the letters and the Revelation of John; and when we survey the list, there may be some titles that we have scarcely heard of. It is interesting then how rapidly diversity among these writings forces itself on our attention, even though we are attending to the NT as a single entity. Clearly this is not a single entity at all in some senses of that term, either in itself or in our awareness of its contents.

4. The NT we think of is probably in the English language. But every bit of it began in the Greek language of the first century of our era (apart from a handful of words taken over from Hebrew, Aramaic, or Latin); so what we have is a translation, never a simple operation and always involving decisions that amount to interpretation. Until fairly recently, it would have been overwhelmingly likely that the NT in our hand or in our memory was the translation issued in England in 1611, usually known simply (and confidently) as 'The Authorised Version', or sometimes as the King James Version, after James I in whose reign and by whose authority the work was done.

5. In the last fifty years, however, a plethora of different translations has appeared, each attempting the task in a particular way or even looking at the NT from a particular doctrinal standpoint. Most aim to give a more modern English version than that of 1611: old words have changed sense or gone out of use, new ways of putting things have come in. Some recent versions do their modernizing in a way that stays close to the old version (e.g. the RS Version), others break right away from it (e.g. the NEB and the GNB). In a determination to make the NT speak today, they may go so far as to amend the strong masculine assumptions of former times, embodied in the Bible, by producing gender-neutral renderings simply absent from the original. Churches, using the NT in worship or for study by their members, take varying views about new versions, some favouring the resonance and familiarity of traditional language, others seeing it as an obstacle to the use of the NT by modern people.

6. It is not just a question of modernizing the English or not, though often the subject is discussed as if it were. There are also issues of accuracy. For one thing, because of the discovery since the seventeenth century of numerous very old manuscripts of the NT, some going back to within a hundred years or so of the original writing, we have a better idea of the NT authors' precise wording than was available to our ancestors (Metzger 1964; Birdsall 1970). (Never lose sight of it: until the invention of printing, every copy of the NT was made by hand, with all the inevitable slips and blunders, and even the alteration of the text to bring it into line with what the copyist believed the scriptural writer 'must' or 'should' have put.) Despite this opportunity for a better informed judgement about the text itself, however, there remain numerous places of disagreement; and translations differ as they reflect differences of judgement in what are often nicely balanced decisions. All this is in addition to unavoidable variations of style and emphasis as translators view the text before them. Again, the NT is far from the stable entity that it appears at first sight.

7. And there is more to come. Look at the NT historically. Only gradually did these writings come to be accepted in the Christian churches in such a way that they could begin to be seen as a single book with a name of its own. This is not the place to go into details of the process whereby this came about (von Campenhausen 1972; Metzger 1987). Suffice it to say that a collection of Paul's letters was probably made before the end of the first century; that the idea of Christians needing both a gospel (i.e. the story of Jesus) and Paul's letters caught on soon after; that the end of the second century saw the acceptance in a number of major Christian centres (e.g. Rome, Alexandria) of something close to the present collection (four gospels, Acts, Paul's and other letters; but that it was four centuries before most churches accepted more or less the set of writings that have remained to this day as those authorized for official use—it is a list that has survived (despite occasional marginal hesitations) all the great divisions of the church, the same for all. The negative corollary of this progressivist way of putting things is of course that the church, viewed as a whole, managed for four centuries or so without the NT as we know it.

8. Again it cannot be our concern here, but it is worth recognizing that there was no discernible inner drive towards the production of such a thing as the NT: that makes it sound much too purposive. Historically speaking, it was all more haphazard. It is more realistic to look at it this way: the Christian communities, widely scattered around the Mediterranean within a few decades of Jesus' lifetime, had certain needs that had to be met if their life and mission were to flourish and if they were to have any coherence as (despite their plurality) a single phenomenon—the Christian church, or even 'Christianity'. They needed first to communicate with each other and to profit from one another's experience and wisdom, not to speak of bringing one another into line. Hence the early importance of letters. Even if these originally addressed passing situations and had no eye on the long term, they might profitably be preserved against future crises or simply for encouragement and edification. Inevitably, they would be circulated and acquire authority, both forming and buttressing church leaders in their work.

9. The Christian communities also needed to have ways of recalling Jesus, both in his time on earth and in terms of present relationship with his heavenly reality. The content of the letters (e.g. of Paul) might often help with the second, as did the eucharistic worship and prayers of the church; the gospels were essential for the first. There is a question about how early this need came to be strongly felt; but soon the gospels were used as tools for teaching and, from at least the

middle of the second century but probably earlier, as an element in the Christian gatherings for worship, where extracts were read to the community and were no doubt the subject of preaching. In this way, the parts of the NT were prior to the whole—that is, in the church's use of these writings. The more one looks at the matter from the point of view of use, the more the final production of a single entity, 'the NT', appears to be an afterthought, a tidying up.

10. That it was more than this is to do with the fact that an element of selection entered into the matter. The NT is far from containing the whole of early Christian literature (Schneemelcher (ed.) 1991, 1992; Staniforth and Louth (eds.) 1987). We know there were numerous other writings, from the second century if not from the first, because copies of them have survived, often in fragments and extracts. Some of them indeed are as old as at least the later of the writings included in the NT itself. It is apparent then that the authorized collection did not come together simply on the basis of antiquity—it was not just the early church's archives. It looks as if a number of factors played a part: simply, popularity and usefulness on a sufficiently wide scale; but also the attachment of an apostolic name, that is the name of one of the earliest Christian leaders, increasingly venerated as authorities, perhaps as martyrs, certainly as close to Jesus. These two factors were not wholly distinct: indeed it looks as if a bid could be made for the authoritativeness of a writing by attaching to it an apostle's name, whether Paul or Peter or John. It is not clear how far this was done in what we should regard as a deliberately fraudulent way and how far it was a matter of claiming the revered figure's patronage—this is what he would have written if he had been in our shoes. Both strategies can be paralleled in the relevant parts of the ancient world. It is not even wholly clear whether it is legitimate to draw a sharp distinction between them ('Pseudonymity', in ABD 5). However that may be (and modern literary ethics are surely inappropriate), there was a Christian literature far larger than the NT itself that failed to win general endorsement.

11. In any case, it is evident that the NT grew piecemeal, both in its parts and as a whole. Evident too that it is an instrument of the church, which for all the authority that, in whole and in parts, it came to have in the church, came into being within the already existing life and work of the Christian communities. In so far as the church had a Bible from the start, it consisted of the Jewish Scriptures, eventually designated by Christians 'the Old Testament', which it interpreted in the light of the career and person of Jesus, seen as its fulfilment. More will be said about this at the end of this section.

12. If the church managed without a fully formed and authorized NT for its first few centuries, it is equally true that, in a contrary movement, the NT has undergone a disintegrative process in the last three or four centuries. This has not occurred primarily (often scarcely at all) in the official life of the churches, but in the realm of scholarship, itself church sponsored (especially in mainstream Protestantism) if not church endorsed in many of its results (Houlden 1986; Carroll 1991). During that period, the NT writings have been subjected to all kinds of analytical procedures. Almost all of these have involved treating them as separate units, often

indeed identifying possible sources behind them (notably in the case of the gospels) or possible earlier units that have gone to form them as composite wholes (some of the letters, e.g. 2 Cor). Mostly, it has been a matter of attempting to suggest the original form, setting, and intention of each of the writings by the use of informed historical imagination and literary observation. Nearly always the effect has been to break down in the reader's mind the the sense of NT as a whole, which was so laboriously built up in the early centuries. The NT comes to be seen very much as a collection of independent, or semi-independent, works, each to be examined in its own right as well as in relevant wider contexts.

13. The upshot is that, in the strict sense, the heyday of the NT as a compact entity (the book within the covers) was in the middle millennium of the church's 2,000-year history; even then, its most characteristic use, the form in which it was mainly experienced, was in bits—sometimes as little as a few words, that would support a doctrinal or ethical point, more often a longer section recited in liturgy or, especially in the later part of the period, used in private meditative prayer. It is interesting to note that for much of that middle period, Christian imagination was filled not only with material derived from Scripture but with legendary stories that the church had specifically rejected from the authorized canon. In for example, the sequence of windows at Chartres Cathedral, details of Jesus' family, birth, and childhood drawn from the Protevangelium of James (2 cent.) figure alongside those drawn from the gospels.

14. At the same time, in whole or in substantial parts, 'the NT' played a recognized part in Christian life. The NT as a volume came in medieval times to carry the sacred weight of an icon, as did the gospels, bound separately—to be reverenced, viewed with awe, even feared, as charged with numinous power. The ceremonial carrying of the book of the gospels in Eastern Orthodoxy and (much less often now) in the Western eucharistic liturgy retains this sense. So, at a more mundane level, still sometimes tinged with superstition, does the use of the NT in courts of law in some countries for the swearing of oaths. More grandly, the British coronation ritual includes the monarch's oath-taking on the fifth-century NT manuscript (actually far from complete), the Codex Bezae. In these residual uses, 'the NT' survives in a way that our medieval ancestors saw as wholly normal: and notice, this use of it did not necessitate its being opened or read at all. Of course, for the many Christians who remain immune to the analytical endeavours of scholarship, the NT, in whole and in parts, retains its verbal authority, speaking to the reader as God's very utterance, with Paul and his fellow-writers as no more than instruments. There are of course many intermediate stages between such literalism and the recognition of variety within the NT, understood in the light of the diverse settings of the various writings (Houlden (ed.) 1995).

15. This brings us to the final recognition that tends towards the breaking up of the NT as we may now read it. Once we attend to the likely origins of the various writings, we find that they do not all sing the same tune. Certainly, we must abandon any idea that they were the result of some kind of collaborative exercise—an impression that the single, tightly bound volume easily creates. It may be retorted that divine inspiration—the idea that, through the various human agents, the one divine 'pen' is at work—implies a transcending singleness of mind. But it is not wholly transparent that, even on such a strong view of inspiration, God necessarily favours singleness of statement at the expense of (for example) the emergence of truth by way of dialogue or controversy, even in early Christianity whose memorial the NT is. At all events, a candid historical view of the NT writings, while recognizing their overall unity of purpose and interest, is bound to recognize that they represent different viewpoints in the early church, and even that some of them look as if they were written to correct and refute others. For instance, it is likely that the Gospels of Matthew and Luke were designed, not simply to amplify but rather to improve on the Gospel of Mark, eradicating what were seen as its inadequacies. The formal opening of Luke, the first four verses, seems to suggest as much. And the Pastoral Epistles (1 and 2 Tim, Titus) and perhaps Ephesians (as well as the latter half of Acts) were probably designed to put Paul in a different light from that in which his letters had come to place him: they smooth out the sense of him as a strident and pugnacious figure, ready to take on esteemed church leaders when in his view the gospel dictated it. The Letter of James seems to subvert one of the crucial emphases of Paul's teaching. The NT does not support the view that the early church enjoyed harmonious unanimity of opinion or homogeneity of teaching. Their disputes may often have related to issues long since dead, so that we tend to discount them, but the battles were real enough in their day, sometimes have modern counterparts, and in any case caution us against over-ready adoption of a particular idea or teaching as *the* NT view of the subject in question. On almost every topic of importance, there was diversity and conflict.

16. There is one more important point. Throughout this section we have had in mind the NT as a self-contained work, bound in its own covers, albeit a collection of twenty-seven distinct writings. But more often that not, we encounter the NT as the second (and much the smaller) part of the Bible: in sheer prominence, it can even look like a sort of adjunct to the OT. From the fourth century, Bibles have been produced by Christians consisting of these two parts, and both parts have been in constant use in Christian worship and Christian study. This combination of the NT with the OT compels us to consider the relation between the two. It is impossible here to detail the many different ways in which that relation has been seen. But, despite the comparative brevity of the NT, Christians have always seen it as the climax and goal of the Bible as a whole. Most commonly (as was hinted earlier), they have seen the NT as fulfilling the OT; or, more precisely, Jesus as fulfilling the old Scriptures and the NT as commenting on the manner of that fulfilment. In the NT's own terms, the fulfilment was expressed by way of OT images and themes which were taken up and applied to him (e.g. king of Israel, son of God, lamb), often with startling paradox and originality; also by way of statements in the OT which were read through fresh eyes and seen as relevant to some aspect or detail of Jesus' life or teaching. Most NT books, most obviously the Gospels of Matthew (e.g. 1–2) and John, contain many such applications of OT quotations to Jesus (Lindars 1961). The modern reader who looks up the original OT context will often see audacity (or even fraudulence) in many of these applications—a difficulty removed or at least alleviated once it is understood that the NT writers are using techniques of scriptural interpretation current in Judaism at the time, and applying them creatively to their own subject-matter. Again from a modern point of view, it is necessary to recognize that they were reading Scripture as sheer words, God-given, with only a minimal sense of historical context such as modern scholarship has so vigorously pursued. So words that originally related to the birth of a child in the royal house in Jerusalem in the late eighth century BCE (Isa 7:14) are applied to the birth of Jesus many centuries later and taken to illuminate its character (Mt 1:23; Brown 1993).

C. The Background of the New Testament. 1. So far we have considered the *idea* of the NT. In terms of introduction, this has been the stage of sizing up the new acquaintance. Another important aspect of introduction lies a little behind the scenes and is often slow to emerge. It concerns the world and the culture from which the new acquaintance comes. Only if we find out about that will the introduction progress and lead to understanding.

2. As we face this matter, we immediately encounter what can seem a puzzling fact. All the NT books were written in Greek (though just possibly Hebrew sources lie somewhere behind one or two of them), but their culture is chiefly Jewish. There are in these writings only occasional instances of Hebrew or Aramaic (the Semitic vernacular of the area), the words of Jesus from the cross in Mk 15:34 (Aramaic = Mt 27:46 Hebrew) being much the most extensive. In one way this creates an obstacle—when for example we hope to read the very words of Jesus. While (as we shall see) there is a chance that Jesus knew some Greek, the overwhelming probability is that the main vehicle of his teaching was Aramaic. Therefore, at best (i.e. even if no other factors are involved) we have in the gospels renderings of Jesus' words into a foreign tongue—with the distortions that translation cannot but entail.

3. It is worth noting at this point that, apart from a few words and references to a few military or legal institutions, Latin culture has left little mark on the NT: these writings reflect life in the eastern half of the Mediterranean world, parts of the Roman empire with their own strong and often mixed cultures, with Greek as the dominant force in many areas of life. True, descendants of Roman army veterans with Latin names (e.g. Tertius, Rom 16:22) appear in the church at Corinth; Roman officials are not inconspicuous in Acts, Pilate is a key figure in the gospel story, and the empire sometimes broods over the scene, as in Revelation, or is an acknowledged presence, as in 1 Peter and Philippians; but even so, Roman cultural penetration is not deep in the circles from which the NT comes.

4. Yet the obstacle referred to above is modified once we realize that in the first century there was no impenetrable wall between Greek language and Jewishness, or indeed between Jewish and Greek cultures. It is only fair to say that some aspects of the first-century situation, even quite important ones, remain obscure and contentious. But two major facts are clear. First, Palestine, at least as far as the towns were concerned, had become deeply affected by Greek culture during the three centuries before the time of Jesus. It showed itself in public matters such as civic architecture (e.g. Herod's

Temple in Jerusalem, built just before Jesus' time), leisure provision (amphitheatres, games), commerce and language (Greek inscriptions on buildings and burial urns); in matters of the mind, so that for example the old Jewish tradition of wisdom writing (classically represented in Proverbs) seems to have absorbed elements of Greek thought (e.g. in Job and Ecclesiasticus). While politically the area that would later be called Syria Palestina was, in Jesus' day, part of the Roman empire, its Herodian rulers and many aspects of the Jewish life over which they presided were in practice deeply affected by Hellenistic culture especially in the upper reaches of Jewish society. It is much less clear how far the countryside was affected: throughout the Mediterranean world, old indigenous cultures tended to survive intact outside the limits of the towns and cities. The town of Sepphoris, only a few miles from Nazareth, was being rebuilt along Hellenistic lines in the years of Jesus' youth, but it is impossible to be sure how far such a place would radiate its influence and in exactly what respects. Certainly it is never referred to in the gospels. We shall discuss the setting of Jesus' own life later: suffice it to say here that the extent of his exposure to things Greek *may* have been minimal.

5. Secondly, in the Diaspora (i.e. among the Jews living in the cities of the Mediterranean world), Greek was the predominant medium—even the Scriptures had been translated (the Septuagint); and it is this more firmly Hellenized Judaism that forms the background for most, perhaps all, the NT writers and their books. That does not imply total cultural homogeneity: there were many styles and grades of the conditioning of Judaism by Hellenistic thought and Greek language, and the early Christians whose outlook is encountered through the books of the NT differ a good deal along these lines. None of them displays more than a perfunctory acquaintance with Greek literature (Acts 17:28; 1 Cor 15:33): overwhelmingly their literary formation comes from the Jewish Scriptures, mostly in their Greek form, and often with emphasis on some parts more than others—depending perhaps on the availability of expensive and cumbersome scrolls.

On the other hand, some of them show knowledge of Greek literary forms. Thus, there is a good case for saying that the gospels have affinities with Roman and Greek lives of celebrated figures (Burridge 1992). To judge from books of the period, Luke's preface (1:1–4) indicates that he saw himself as providing a kind of handbook about Jesus, whether for the Christian community or for a wider public (Alexander 1993). Mark shows signs of a degree of training in rhetoric as taught in the Greek schools of the period (Beavis 1989), and the same may be true of Paul (Betz 1979). These writers, for all the Jewishness of their thought and culture, were dependent also on the Greek culture of the setting in which they had been formed—and unselfconsciously so. In their very different ways—and the same variety is found among Jewish writers of the period—they drew upon Greek models. They were part and parcel of their habitat. Partly because of this close interweaving of Judaism and Hellenism by this time, it is not always easy to assign a given feature of a NT book to Jewish or Greek influence. It can still be discussed, for example, whether the prologue of the Gospel of John owes more to the Jewish tradition of 'wisdom' writing or to Greek philosophical discourse of a Platonist kind; and though current opinion tends to the former opinion, the matter is immediately complicated by the understanding that the wisdom tradition itself had already been open to strands of Platonist thinking (Hengel 1974; Meyers and Strange 1981).

6. Attempts to produce more exotic sources for central early Christian ways of thinking or behaving have failed to earn a permanent place in our picture of the time. The suggestion is made that Paul's ideas on baptism, seeing it in terms of dying and rising with Christ (Rom 6:3–11), and perhaps John's on the eucharist, in terms of eating and drinking Christ's flesh and blood (6: 51–8), have links to supposed beliefs of mystery cults or other esoteric sects, but the chronological difficulties in making some of these connections (especially if gnostic links are introduced) can scarcely be removed and the match of mental worlds is a long way from being exact (Wagner 1967; Wedderburn 1987). At points like these, there must be space for real Christian originality. On any showing, Paul and John were figures of great creativity. Equally, whatever the roots and affinities of his teaching, the impact of Jesus and his followers in the years following his lifetime was so great and so novel that it is vain to hope that every aspect of thought about him, every item of Christian observance, can be shown to be derived easily and directly from phenomena already present in one circle or another in the vastly diverse religious scene of the first-century Mediterranean world. Jesus, the new, unique factor, produced new patterns, new ways of looking at the world. In the gospel's own words, it really was a case of new wine even when there might be old bottles to contain it.

7. Let us look a little more closely at some of the varieties of Hellenized Jewishness, now Christianized, that are visible to us in the NT. With the possible exception of the author of Luke–Acts (and even he was imbued with Jewish lore and culture), every one of the main NT writers was almost certainly Jewish in birth and upbringing. But they exhibit a variety of styles of Jewishness as currently found in various parts of the Jewish world. None of them matches the sophisticated Platonized mentality that Philo of Alexandria was bringing to bear on traditional Jewish themes and biblical texts at precisely the time of Christianity's birth. But Matthew's gospel, for example, with its many scriptural quotations, is the work of someone skilled in the contemporary scribal techniques of biblical interpretation, as abundant examples in the Dead Sea scrolls have demonstrated (Stendahl 1968; Goulder 1974). The kind of training to which they testify, in a work written in Greek, comes most naturally from a Syrian context, affected by the methods elaborated in nearby Palestine and by issues (of law observance) that were hotly debated in the sectarian life of the Jewish heartland in the period (Sanders 1992). Paul and John show similar expertise in the handling of scriptural texts, and the former tells of his background in Pharisaism (Phil 3:5), which operated in a thought-world of such interpretation. John's gospel can be seen as a thoroughgoing reworking of scriptural themes and symbols (light, life, bread, shepherd, lamb), applying them to the determinative figure of Jesus.

8. Luke's reliance on the traditional Scriptures comes out in an ability to write in a Septuagintal style where the context demands it. So, while the stories of the birth of John Baptist and Jesus (1–2) contain no biblical quotations, their language

is biblical from end to end, and the characters they depict evoke familiar scriptural figures, most obviously Hannah (1 Sam 2) in the case of Mary, but also couples such as Abraham and Sarah and Manoah and his wife (Jdt 13), who serve to create an ethos of profound biblical piety and solid embeddedness in history for the life of Jesus which follows. Luke is deeply imbued with biblical language and the biblical story.

9. The latter comes out in passages such as Stephen's speech (Acts 7), with its survey of Jewish history presented in a manner reminiscent of numerous Jewish writings (most notably and extensively the contemporary historian Josephus), including its mixture of example and warning. In the NT, the same feature appears in Hebrews, most explicitly in ch. 11.

10. In the NT it is plain that we are reading the work of people soaked in the stories, images, themes and language of the Jewish Scriptures (chiefly in their Greek translation). This sense of thorough permeation comes across nowhere more strongly than in the Revelation of John, where there are no quotations yet almost everything is owed to a disciplined reflection on the books of Ezekiel, Zechariah, and Daniel in their own symbolic and linguistic terms. To call it pastiche would be to undervalue the degree of ingenuity and visionary creativity displayed in this reminting of old motifs in the light of Jesus and beliefs about his person and significance (Farrer 1949; Sweet 1979).

11. The Jewish background of the NT writings comes out as clearly and distinctively as anywhere in the cosmic framework within which their reflection on Jesus and his achievement is set. It is true that much Jewish religious energy went into the minutiae of the application of the Law to daily living, both in spheres that we should call secular and in matters of plain religious observance: Judaism drew no line between the two as far as the applicability of the Law was concerned. In other words, Judaism was (and is) a faith and a lifestyle that viewed the present with intense seriousness and subjected daily conduct to the closest scrutiny (Sanders 1985, 1992).

12. But alongside this concern with the details of present living, and to our eyes perhaps at variance with it, we find, sometimes (as at Qumran) in the same circles, an equally intense interest in the future destiny of the individual, of Israel, and indeed of the world as a whole. This concern with the future and with the cosmic dimension is part and parcel of the Jewish mentality which the first Christians inherited, and both in many of its characteristics and in its strength it differentiated Judaism from other speculative systems and 'end-expectations' of the time. This strength is generally thought to be closely related to the cohesiveness of the Jewish people (despite geographical dispersion) and to the many national catastrophes and disappointments they had endured. These pressures gave rise to extravagant and even desperate hopes of divine intervention and the restoration of Israel. But the power and grandeur of this understanding was enhanced by the strong underlying tradition of monotheism. It was the one God of the universe whose purpose would soon be fulfilled (Rowland 1982).

13. Christian expressions of this world-outlook, centring on the figure of Jesus as God's agent in the hoped-for intervention, are to be found in one form or another in most of the NT books, most notably in the Revelation, a work that is (apart from the letters in chs. 2–3) wholly couched in the idiom of apocalyptic, focused on the heavenly realities and the consummation about to be revealed.

14. But this perspective is by no means confined to Revelation. Jesus himself is depicted as imbued with it in all the gospels, but especially in the first three (Mk 13; Mt 24; Lk 17, 21; but also Jn 5:24–7). Not only does it therefore carry his authority, but its presence as an important constituent in these works lends to each of them as a whole an apocalyptic character: if the modern reader is inclined to skip over these passages, that is simply a symptom of the gap between then and now. Moreover, the actual expression of this feature goes well beyond the chapters that are formally labelled 'apocalyptic', extending, for example, to parables which look forward to cosmic judgement (eg Mt 13:36–43; 25:1–46; Lk 12:35–40). This placing of apocalyptic material cheek by jowl with narrative is already found in Jewish models such as Daniel and serves to place the story as a whole against a cosmic backcloth: we may seem to be reading about events in Galilean villages, but in fact the story is set in the context of the whole universe, heaven and earth and Hades. What is being described has a meaning far beyond that of earthly events and words, however impressive or profound. Further, while the Gospel of John has little explicit apocalyptic material in a formal sense, and its precise literary background is not easily defined, there is a good case for saying that in this work Jesus is seen in his entire career as a manifestation of the divine from heaven—with the consummation of God's purposes both embodied and so concretely anticipated in his life and death. It is a revelatory work *pur excellence* (Meeks in Ashton (ed.) 1986; Ashton 1991).

15. Paul too clearly works within an eschatological framework that is apocalyptic or revelatory in character, that is, he sees history, under God's energetic providence, moving rapidly to a climax of judgement and of renewal for his people; and in expressing this conviction he uses the revelatory imagery familiar, in various forms and combinations, in Judaism. There will be judgement according to moral deserts (2 Cor 5:10; Rom 2:16); there will be a resurrection seen as the transformation of God's faithful ones into the form of spiritual bodies (1 Cor 15:35–56); there will even be what amounts to a new creation (2 Cor 5:17; Gal 6:15).

16. For both Paul and John, especially, this picture is linked strikingly to the coming of Jesus and in effect given a new shape as a result of the conviction that the fulfilment of God's purpose centres on him. This conviction necessitates an intensifying of the apocalyptic sense and a shift in its temporal framework. If Jesus is the decisive revelation of God and agent of his purpose, then the process of cosmic consummation is already under way and those who adhere to him embody the fulfilment of Israel's hope. Here is the essential (and radical) amendment to the Jewish picture of things that makes for Christian distinctiveness. It may have taken some decades to be widely manifest and institutionally plain, but from our earliest source (the letters of Paul) the Christian movement was on its own new path. From a Jewish point of view, this was a fatal distortion of the heritage—especially when, already for Paul, it involved the free inclusion of Gentiles within the new people of God. From the Christian side, it is the goal to which all has tended. No wonder Christians immediately had to set

about the appropriation of the old Scriptures—the agreed data—to their picture of things; no wonder the Scriptures were the battleground in the struggle to decide whose right it was to inherit the mantle of Israel's history and God-given privileges.

17. The attaching of a hitherto future hope to the career of Jesus, now past, and to the life of the church, the people that stemmed from him, was a decisive shift; all the more so when (as we shall see) that career was by no means the obvious match to the terms of that hope. In order to accomplish the shift, the apparatus or imagery of apocalyptic was the most readily available tool. So: Jesus was cast (and had perhaps cast himself) in the role of instigator of the fulfilment of God's purpose; the resurrection process began in his own rising on the third day; the Spirit of God, whose outpouring in a new God-given vitality was associated with the coming consummation, was already experienced in the Christian groups (1 Cor 12:1–13; Rom 8); judgement could be seen as linked to the act of adherence to Jesus or the refusal to make that act—to accept the shelter of his gift of overwhelming grace was to come safely to the far side of judgement and into a state of reconciliation with God (Rom 5:1–11; 2 Cor 5:17–21; Jn 5:24). It made a breathtaking offer and no wonder it was put in the most audacious terms.

18. Paul and John saw the implications of this reworking of old categories more clearly than others: it is certainly carried through in their work more thoroughly than in any other of the NT writings. For both of them, concentration on the decisiveness of Jesus is combined with a sense of driving on towards an assured end. The Jewish framework of the one God of the universe, the achieving of whose purpose of salvation will assuredly be realized, is preserved intact. What is new is, first, that it centres on Jesus and is seen as visibly guaranteed by his life, death, and resurrection (and that very attachment to an actual human career, capable inevitably of numerous assessments, opened the door immediately to controversy); and, second, that the fulfilment now has both an urgency and an institutional frame (the church). Only the Qumran sect could rival it in Judaism in this sense of urgency and expectancy, and that group lacked universality of vision and missionary drive, so that its failure to survive the Jewish rebellion of 66–73 CE is in no way surprising. By that time, the followers of Jesus, with their openness to all-comers, Jew and Gentile alike, were well established in the main towns and cities of the Mediterranean world.

19. Only in some of the later books of the NT (1 and 2 Tim, Titus, 2 Pet) do we begin to get a sense of the slackening of the kind of dynamism we have been noticing, a loss of the creative theological vision which had set the people of Jesus on their own distinctive path. The church is here just beginning to be the defender of a system, of both thought and organization, rather than the originator of a novel response to God's action in the world. Sociology teaches us to see such a development as inevitable (von Campenhausen 1969; Holmberg 1990). It is a remarkable fact about the Gospel of John that, in these same last years of the first century, it is able to produce a more thoroughly creative reworking of the traditional Jewish pattern of history, in the light of Jesus, than any other early Christian writing. Anyone inclined to think in terms of single-track, linear development should reflect that, with regard to the basic perspectives that we have been discussing, we find an essential community of mind between Paul, the first Christian writer of all, and John, writing towards the end of the period.

20. Anyone who knows about the ancient world will wish to raise questions about this account of the NT's cultural milieu. The pervasive Hellenizing of the life of the societies around the Mediterranean, especially in the East, must surely point to certain influences on which nothing has been said. Was this not a world in which the great philosophical achievements of Plato and Aristotle, not to speak of Stoics, Cynics, and Pythagoreans, were currents in the prevailing air? It has to be said that the great philosophies have left little trace in these writings. This is not wholly explained by their dominant Jewishness, for, as the case of Philo shows, Judaism was not in itself inimical to the Platonist idiom of thought. It is more a matter of the social strata from which the NT writers came. They were, by definition, not illiterate, but either their education was scriptural or scribal in content and manner or it stopped at a stage on the ladder below that where serious philosophical teaching would have occurred. All we get then is perhaps a few scraps of Stoicism, possibly affecting Paul's teaching on 'nature' in Rom 1 and 2:14–15, and showing itself in the discussion of the divine in Acts 17:22–31, and in a few other features; and, a subject of much current discussion, Cynic moral wisdom as a factor behind some aspects of Jesus' teaching. It is a disputed question, not so much whether parallels can be identified, as whether, in the circumstances of Jesus' Galilee (or indeed of the evangelists), Cynic influence is at all probable. The day was not far distant, however, when philosophy (chiefly Platonist and Stoic) was to provide a framework of thought in which Christian thinkers sought to operate. Within a few years of the writing of the last books to find a place in the NT (120 CE?), such attempts were beginning to get into their stride.

D. The Church of the New Testament. 1. The Christian church is both depicted in most of the books of the NT and presupposed by all of them. Every one of them is the product of one setting or another in the early Christian communities. Sometimes the location of that setting is actually stated; in other cases it is not hard to see a good deal about its character. Though most of the books bear the name of a single author, there is good reason to think that, even if those ascriptions were in fact accurate (and most of them probably are not), we ought to see these writings partly as productions of the church. While they reflect the thought of some single mind—a genuine author—they were not written in isolation in some equivalent of a modern author's secluded retreat, but from the midst of a particular group of Christians with whom the author was in close interaction. Even the author of Revelation, shut away on Patmos, has his mind on the fellow-Christians from whom he is separated.

2. But, as we saw earlier, churches were not all of one kind or, in many matters, of a single mind. They differed in geographical location; in exposure to some of the cultural features that have been described; in their relation to Jewish observances and the local Jewish community; in attitudes to leading Christian figures such as Peter and Paul; in social composition (Jews, Gentiles, rich, poor); in the handling of moral problems, such as divorce and the scope of generosity. While the Christian churches were a far closer network than any other organization of the time that is at all comparable (and this is surely a major factor in their success, both now and later), held together by visits, letters, and a measure of supervisory responsibility felt by founders and leaders and by one church for another, they were nevertheless often strung out across great distances and surely were compelled to engage in much independent decision-making. As letters such as Galatians and 1 Corinthians show very well, the independence and the supervision could find themselves on a collision course. Many of the NT writings were indeed both an instrument of cohesion (as in due course they recommended themselves to a variety of communities) and a product of difference (in so far as they were designed to meet local and transient needs, or to counter or correct lines taken in other writings and places).

3. If our interest is in the churches within or for whom the NT books were produced, then the most obvious place to begin—and the place where we shall get the most direct results—is the corpus of genuine letters by the apostle Paul. Here is the most transparent (or at any rate the least opaque) window available to us as we seek to look at the life of early Christian communities. That immediately creates narrowness, for they cover only a limited range of churches—in Greece and Macedonia (1 and 2 Cor, 1 and 2 Thess, Phil), Asia Minor (Gal, Col, Philem), and Italy (Rom). (Other letters are of uncertain Pauline authorship or unclear geographical destination: Eph, 1 and 2 Tim, Titus.) Moreover, they vary a great deal in the degree to which they illuminate for us the lives of those to whom they are addressed—as distinct from the thought and interests of Paul who addresses them. Clearest of all is the church in Corinth, where we have the two NT letters (the first of them directly concerned with a welter of practical problems) and personal information from Rom 16, written at Corinth and including greetings from members of the Corinthian church. And Acts 18 gives an account of Paul's initial mission in the city. There is also archaeological and literary material shedding light on the Corinthian background (Theissen 1982; Meeks 1983; Murphy-O'Connor 1983).

4. What is perhaps most surprising about this community, established in the early 50s, is the small degree to which its manifold problems appear to reflect difficulties that are related to Christianity's Jewish origins. There were, it appears, some Jewish members, but what one might expect to be their concerns (Law observance, relations to Gentile members, and scriptural interpretation) scarcely figure. This was, already, largely a Gentile community, and most of its problems sprang from overexuberant and élitist religiosity on the part of the most articulate and wealthy members. More clearly than any other NT writings, these letters give evidence of a church whose cohesion was made precarious by the dominance of these religious 'experts'. Precarious, that is, in the eyes of Paul, who insists that all-embracing dependence on Christ implies the transcending of social and racial divisions (1 Cor 1–4; 12:13) and the giving of full honour and consideration to the simpler and poorer members (11:17–34; 12:1–13). In Paul's perception, the Lord's supper was to be the outward manifestation of this basic equality of generous love, rather than the focus of social division that it had become in Corinthian practice. They were simply continuing to run their meetings along the hierarchical lines taken for granted in a place such as Corinth in households and in guilds and associations of various kinds.

5. Galatians gives evidence of a different situation. Here it is indeed the implications of Christ for the adherence of his followers to Jewish observance that is in question, in particular the traditional Jewish identity-markers of circumcision, sabbath, and food rules. This letter gives a vivid picture of the bitterness caused by this issue (1–2 especially). Whether or not Paul was the first to see adherence to Christ as transcending this observance, and so as eliminating it at least as far as Gentile Christians were concerned (and therefore in effect dethroning it for all Christians), he it was who gave a rationale, scripturally based at that, for resistance to the imposition of the old Jewish marks of valid membership of God's people (3–4; see also Rom 4).

6. Some writings point to there being groupings of churches, whether on a geographical basis, or in relation to a shared missionary-founder. There would often be a shared language—a particular idiom or set of ideas in which to express Christian belief. This is most easily seen in the case of the communities visible in the Johannine Epistles. Here we have evidence of a number of Christian groups (it is unclear how many), where there is a limited degree of common acquaintance (3 Jn) and so perhaps a fairly wide geographical spread, but all sharing some sort of organizational unity (2 Jn 1)—and having to struggle to maintain it (3 Jn). The basis of this unity, fragile as it was, was the form of Christian belief whose classic expression was in the Gospel of John, with its distinctive, finely tuned vocabulary of key words (light, life, truth, word), endlessly rewoven like elements in a complex fugue. But it is plain that there was no machinery for the exerting of rigid discipline among these Johannine Christians: the occasion for the first two letters is the emergence of division about the interpretation of their manner of belief concerning the person of Jesus. It is also plain that, even in the short time that must have elapsed between the writing of the gospel and the letters, some of the key words changed subtly in sense, in response to the quarrels. 'Love', for example, becomes a duty confined to the like-minded (Brown 1979).

7. The Revelation of John, with its letters to seven churches in Asia Minor (chs. 2–3), may again testify to some kind of group consciousness among a set of congregations, though it is unclear whether the admonitory role adopted by the seer is self-appointed or represents a formal acceptance by these churches of a special relationship. That such groupings might not be tight or exclusive is suggested by the fact that the church in the major centre of Ephesus appears in three different sets: the seven churches of Revelation, the largely different seven churches who received letters from Ignatius of Antioch (c.110 CE), and the Pauline foundations (Acts 19). The speed with which the main NT writings seem to have circulated itself suggests the effectiveness of at least informal ties among the churches, as does such a project as the collecting of Paul's letters, presumably from the churches which had initially received them, a process perhaps concluded by the end of the first century.

8. What has been said so far about the early Christian communities may seem to point to virtual simultaneity among the situations depicted; and it may seem that as, at the outside, the time-span of their composition was no more than seventy years (say, 50–120 CE), and as the period is so distant and obscure, there is little scope for attempts to refine that approach. But we are not entirely without the possibility of identifying developments even within that relatively short period, though certainty very often eludes us.

9. The first development was the shift in the character of the Christian movement from the period of Jesus' ministry to the subsequent mission and the living of the Christian life. Our written sources in the NT itself, the gospels and Acts, present it as the smoothest of transitions. At first there was, it seems, a brief time of Galilean ministry by Jesus and a small group of adherents, supported from time to time by transient and anonymous crowds. It was marked by constant movement, and a few references to Jesus' home (Mk 2:1, 15) scarcely modify this picture of endless mobility. The fact that the dominant mode of Christian life soon came to be settled and static speaks for the accuracy of this picture: any temptation to redescribe Jesus' circumstances in the light of later times has been resisted.

10. This time was also marked by the rural character of its setting: the big urban centres of Galilee in Jesus' day, notably Sepphoris and Tiberias, are conspicuous by their absence, even though the former was only a few miles from Nazareth where Jesus was brought up. There are of course numerous references to 'cities', in general and by name, but none of them is much more than a village or small town in modern terms. They were small settlements in an overwhelmingly peasant-dominated and agriculture-centred world. We have already seen that, in congruity with this mode of life, this was a setting where Aramaic was the dominant language and where literacy and a wider culture were almost certainly rare. While, like the wandering character of Jesus' ministry, the rural setting has amply survived any attempt the evangelists might have been expected to make to conform their account of Jesus' activities to the urban setting of the churches of their own experience, the Semitic speech has been almost totally obliterated (Mk 5:41; 7:34; 14:36—all dropped by Matthew and Luke in their parallel passages), and Jesus is depicted as possessing both scriptural knowledge and technical interpretative skill, including the ability to read (Lk 4:17), and even perhaps some acquaintance with current popular moral teaching with Cynic affinities. The question attributed to the people in the synagogue (Mk 6:2), 'Where did this man get all this?' has never been satisfactorily answered, except in the terms of supernatural endowment—which the evangelist is no doubt content for us to entertain. However, it has to be said that evidence about synagogues in Galilee in this precise period (as distinct from a little later) and about educational opportunities at village level is practically non-existent and intelligent guesses vary, some more optimistic than the tone adopted here (Freyne 1988).

11. Leaving these matters aside, we do not have to look for the reason behind the original organizational simplicity, even indifference, of the movement that centred on Jesus. It lay surely in the vivid sense of God's imminent fulfilment of his saving purpose—to which, as we have seen, the gospels (not to speak of Paul and most other early Christian writers) bear witness. True, in the Qumran sect we have a Jewish group that combined such a sense (despite their existence for two centuries without its realization) with the most meticulous rules and observance covering every aspect of the common life. But in the case of both John Baptist and Jesus, the policy is different: open not secluded, of mass appeal not separatist, personal not immediately communal in its effects. There is not much sign in the gospels (and again the resistance of inevitable pressure to conform the story to later situations is impressive) of any attempt by either of these charismatic figures to ensure the survival and stability of a movement, with the structural provision which that requires. What there is, for example the commission to Peter (Mt 16:17–19), has all the marks of coming from later times: in this example, the words are added by Matthew to Mark's narrative, reducing it to confusion when we read on to 'Get behind me, Satan', addressed now to one just assured of the most crucial role in the church. Even when such material is taken into account, it does not amount to a blueprint: in the later first century, when the gospels were written, the church had still not reached a Qumran-like point, where every detail of life should be provided for by rule. The strong eschatological impulse from Jesus had not exhausted itself, despite the great changes which had nevertheless occurred.

12. Those changes were indeed momentous. Almost all the features of Jesus' ministry that have been described were replaced by their contraries. Mesmerized by the smoothness of the transition as described by Luke, as we move from his gospel to the beginning of Acts, readers have been reluctant to grasp how incongruous are the 'before' and the 'after'. Much attention has long been given to the question of how and why the Christian movement survived the death of its founder and the seeming failure of all his hopes and promises; and in answering that question, attention has focused chiefly on the resurrection of Jesus as offering, somehow, the key to the problem's solution. But there is the at least equally fascinating institutional problem. Evidence to shed light on it is almost non-existent, and Luke has thrown us off any scent there might be, encouraging us to see the move as the most natural thing you could imagine: of course, Jesus' followers simply established themselves in Jerusalem, where they happened to be, and started preaching.

13. In fact it was remarkable that, in institutional terms, the Christian movement survived the crisis. It was done at the cost of severe changes to some of its central attributes and perspectives. Most obviously, there was a shift from rural to urban settings, probably first in Jerusalem, as Acts says, but soon in other major cities—Antioch (one of the largest cities of the ancient world) and then, in due course, in Asia Minor, Greece, and Rome, in the 40s and 50s. The world of Galilee was left behind. Indeed, with the exception of a single allusion in Acts 9:31, we have no clear evidence of Christian activity there after Jesus left for Jerusalem. For all we can tell, his work there was without trace—a passing whirlwind. (References to appearances of the risen Jesus there, in Mt 28 and Jn 21, are of uncertain value in this regard and nothing visible follows from them.)

14. There was a shift too (and necessarily, given the urban locations) from itinerant to settled life, with missions undertaken from permanent urban centres. The result of this shift was that tensions arose between the more mobile missioners and the members of Christian congregations who did not normally reckon to leave their city boundaries and whose Christian life soon expressed also a change from a movement of unorganized individual adherents, many of them perhaps transiently impressed by the preaching of Jesus (the 'crowds' of the gospels), to one of tightly knit congregations, many of their members belonging probably to a small number of households in a given place and living quite circumscribed lives, marked in all kinds of ways by their Christian allegiance. We have seen that the letters of Paul testify amply to some of the problems resulting from this new allegiance, working its way within the social framework of such cities of the Graeco-Roman world as Corinth and Thessalonica.

15. We said that the strong sense of an imminent manifestation of God's power, to judge and then to save his own, survived the lifetime of Jesus—it is the framework of Paul's faith—and the shift to a more organized mode of existence. But certain of its concomitants in the earlier phase are no longer prominent. It was not practicable in the circumstances of an urban institution to follow the pattern of abandonment of family and property which is so strong in the preaching of Jesus. No doubt, with the exception of Jesus' immediate circle of itinerant preachers, there was always a measure of metaphor in the interpretation of this theme: Peter was married when he 'forsook all and followed' Jesus (Mk 1:16–20, 29–31), and remained so (1 Cor 9:5), and indeed Mark studiously omits wives from the list of relations to be left behind (10:29–31; cf. the prohibition of divorce in 10:1–12)—though Luke (looking back through ascetic rose-tinted spectacles?) does not (18:29). The message might be interiorized into attitudes of single-mindedness and self-abnegation, or modified to spur Christians into generosity (forsaking not all wealth but certainly some), whether to the needy of the Christian group or to outsiders (Lk 10:25–37). There is astonishingly little on these themes in the ethical sections of the letters of Paul (Rom 12:13; 16:1–2 on giving; and 1 Cor 7:12–16 on marital problems in relation to conversion); though it is hard to believe that passages such as Mk 1:16–20 did not resonate with people whose Christian decision cost them dear in terms of family relationships and inheritance (cf. Jn 9).

16. Christian family life, with its development of injunction and advice for its regulation, was not long in becoming a primary concern in the urban congregations. It had soon become an institution in its own right, and it figures in one form or another in many of the NT letters (1 Cor 7; Col 3:18–4:1; Eph 5:21–6:9; 1 Pet 2:18–3:7), in terms much like those found in both Jewish and Greek compendia dealing with the same themes. The church had become domesticated. The note of abandonment, as a constant sound in the Christian ear, was muted, as emphasis shifted to the maintenance of church life.

17. It has become common to give more attention to a second transition in church life during the period in which the NT books were written, and sometimes it has been exaggerated or misleadingly described, perhaps in surrender to the impulse to contrast an early golden age with subsequent decline. This is the development in the later years of the first century and the earlier years of the second, of a greater concern to formalize and legitimate Christian institutions of many kinds. The first moves towards an authorized body of

Christian writings probably belong to this time and are one mark of this trend. Others include the final replacement of itinerant missionaries (such as Paul and his associates) by the leaders of local churches, so that the churches now bear the weight of Christian organization and authority: there is no outside body to turn to, except other churches comparable to one's own. Despite the emergence of networks and groupings, local leaders became more prominent, and in more and more places, a single 'supervisor' (*episkopos*, later acquiring the status of a Christian technical term, 'bishop') came into being as the chief officer of the Christian community. As a matter of history, he probably arose from among the natural leaders of household-churches in a given place, but some bishops at least soon came to see their role in much more lofty terms: as representatives of God the Father and vehicles of the Spirit's utterance. The letters of Ignatius of Antioch (*c*.110 CE; Staniforth and Louth 1987) show us a man whose high sense of his place in the Christian scheme of things makes Paul's idea of an apostle pale by comparison (Campbell 1994).

18. There is little surviving evidence, but it is likely that forms of worship came to be formulated in the same period. The Didache (not in the NT and unknown until a single manuscript came to light in 1873) contains forms of eucharistic prayer from Syria, probably from the late first century. There are signs too of an increasing concern with conformity to whatever in a particular place was seen as orthodoxy: both the Johannine and the Pastoral Epistles show this trait, and in the latter case, there is more interest in urging such conformity than in elaborating on the beliefs actually involved. These pseudonymously Pauline letters are also insistent on the need for respectable behaviour, acceptable to society at large, and on the sober qualities required in church leaders (1 Tim 2:1–4; 3:1–11). It is all a far cry from the exuberance and brave independence of mind that mark the mission of Paul half a century before.

19. All the same, it does not do to paint too sharp a contrast between the solid and perhaps unexciting interests visible in some of the late NT writings and the enthusiasm and innovation of earlier days. If Paul is aware of the inspirational force of the Spirit in himself and among his converts, Ignatius shows comparable assurance, speaking with the voice of God. He is no mere ecclesiastical official, basing his position on human legitimation and just, as it were, doing a job for the church. On the other hand, Paul himself is far from being uninterested in due order in his Christian communities. It may sometimes have been hard to achieve or, as in Corinth, power had come to be concentrated in persons he disapproved of—even if they were themselves, it appears, claiming charismatic inspiration. But the whole tone of his correspondence shows an acute concern for properly accredited leadership, as 1 Cor 16:15–17 tactfully indicates. He was no lover of spiritual anarchy (Holmberg 1978).

20. However the matter is analysed in detail—and there is room for difference of opinion—it is evident that the churches underwent considerable changes, even within the relatively brief period to which the NT testifies and even to the extent of producing contradictory opinions and policies (for example on ethical questions such as the continuing role of the Jewish Law in daily life, Houlden 1973).

21. It is to be noted that all this took place among a still obscure body of people—spreading rapidly across the Mediterranean map and growing in numbers right through the century, but, in the writings available to us, showing little awareness of the world of the history textbook. There are, however, some marks of that world: the author of Revelation has his eyes on the fate of the Roman Empire and is aware of the rise and fall of emperors; Luke knows about Roman governors and other officials in the territories he describes, as well as something of the system they operate (Sherwin-White 1963; Lentz 1993). Yet the events that might be expected to have made an impact on the late first-century writings of a religious group with Jewish antecedents—the Jewish rebellion in Judea, the destruction of the Jerusalem Temple at Roman hands, and the mass suicide at Masada—have left only oblique traces, such as elements in a parable (Mt 22:7) and symbol-laden prophecies on Jesus' lips (Lk 21:20–4). On the face of it, this is astonishing, so much so that some critics have been led (in the teeth of all other considerations) to date the NT books well before those happenings of 66–73 CE (Robinson 1976). It may be better to see this silence as evidence of the degree to which the Christian communities responsible for these books had by the time of writing abandoned their Palestinian and, in many cases, their Jewish roots, at least in social and institutional terms. These events impinged, on people whose loyalties and interests now lay elsewhere and who were removed from the immediate scene, less than seems to modern people to be credible.

22. Finally, part of the explanation lies also in the high concentration that marked the self-understanding of the Christian communities: they had strongly formed beliefs not just about God and Jesus, but also about the church itself. In other words, the detached and analytical terms in which the church has been discussed in this article would have been wholly alien to them. In Jesus' own preaching, there can be little doubt that, even if he did not establish 'cells' of followers in the Galilean countryside and villages (and there is no sign of such groups), his preaching of the dawn of God's kingdom, his visible and effective sovereignty, involved communal assumptions. What was to emerge was a purified and rejuvenated 'people of God'—some sort of 'Israel'.

23. The urbanizing of Christianity, visible in Paul and elsewhere, brought no break in this 'Israel-consciousness'. Above all in Rom 9–11, Paul produced a complex and ingenious theory to demonstrate the continuity between the Israel of the Scriptures and the Christian community, made up of Jews and Gentiles on equal terms (at least in Paul's determined view). But Paul also saw the church in a quite different perspective, one that was in tension, if not contradiction, with the idea of continuity which his Jewish roots and his sense of the one God of history would not allow him to forgo. This other perspective, for which he also argued with great skill and passion, centred on Christ and the sheer novelty that had come on the scene with him. It was nothing less than a new creation (2 Cor 5:17), with Jesus as a new Adam, starting the human journey off all over again (Rom 5:12–21; 1 Cor 15:22). In him, the human race was created afresh. Paul's highly concentrated image of the church as Christ's body encapsulates this consciousness, in which the Jew–Gentile divide is not so much overcome as undermined and rendered irrelevant (1 Cor 12; Rom 12; Gal 3:28). By clever scriptural arguments, chiefly involving the figure of Abraham (Gal 3; Rom 4), Paul sought to reconcile these two perspectives. They did not convince Jews, and while Christians mostly maintained that they were the true heirs of the old Israel, it was the idea of their membership 'in Christ', expressed in baptism and eucharist, and worked out in following his teaching as found in the gospels, that chiefly occupied their practical consciousness. John's gospel systematically shows Jesus, and then those attached to him as branches to vine and as sheep to shepherd (15; 10), as embodying and absorbing all the great attributes and properties that had belonged to Judaism and the people of Israel. They belonged now to the people of Jesus.

E. Jesus and the New Testament. 1. It might be expected that an introduction to the NT would open with an account of Jesus rather than delay the subject to the end. After all, directly or obliquely, Jesus is the subject of most of the NT books, and is the most significant factor in their ever having been written at all. There are, however, good reasons for the roundabout approach to the heart of the matter. For, despite all his prominence, Jesus is in the NT a figure to be approached with caution. For one thing, much depends on the reader's interest: whether, for example, you are keen to find out about the facts and circumstances of Jesus' life, personality, and teaching, or about the origins and terms of faith in him. There is a well-grounded distinction between Jesus as a figure of early first-century Jewish history and Jesus as the object of devotion and faith, presupposed by all the NT writers; with the resurrection (that most difficult of phenomena to pin down) as the hinge between the two.

2. It is a basic truth that, whatever the claims and the appearances, Jesus is never encountered 'neat' in the NT. Apart from the fact that the gospels are unlikely to be the work of stenographers who hung on Jesus' every word and of adherents who witnessed his every act, those brief books have all the inevitable distortion that goes with selectivity; moreover, it is apparent that the selectivity was not unprincipled or merely random. It worked by way of filters, some obvious, others more hypothetical, by which material was affected on its way into the gospels we read. We have already referred to the frequently ignored filter of translation of speech from Aramaic into Greek. It is accompanied by the equally frequently ignored filter by which the material moves from an originally uneducated Galilean and rural setting to more sophisticated urban settings, in Syria, Asia Minor, or elsewhere, where much vital original colouring must have been invisible. Sometimes the provision of new colouring is obvious enough: the well-known example of the tile-roofed Hellenistic town house described in Luke's version of the healing of the paralytic (5:19; contrast the Palestinian house in Mk 2:4). For all we know, there are many details, large and small, in the gospels that are both harder to spot and more significant for the general picture than that.

3. Equally important as a distorting factor is the effect of developing convictions and attitudes in the church in the years following Jesus' lifetime. Some instances have proved devastating in their results, above all the way the gospels (increasingly as one succeeds another) place responsibility for Jesus' death on Jewish heads (on *all* Jewish heads, Mt 27:25), with Pontius Pilate as their pliable but scarcely guilty accomplice (Mt 27:24; Lk 23:22). There is good reason to suppose that this is unlikely to represent the truth of the matter and that it reflects instead the increasing tension between Christians and (other) Jews, as the former were virtually compelled to define themselves over against the latter. Historically, the probability is that, at a time of governmental nervousness in a Jerusalem crowded for Passover, the Roman authorities combined with the Jewish priestly aristocracy who administered the Temple to remove one whom they perceived to be a possible occasion of civil disorder. His execution was, after all, by the Roman method in such cases, that is crucifixion (Rivkin 1984; Brown 1994).

4. But this is only the most spectacular instance of a pervasive principle, often hard to identify with assurance. Take, for example, the matter of Jesus' attitude to the Jewish Law. Did he simply take it for granted as the air he breathed, perhaps taking one side or another on subjects of current dispute, but not stepping outside the limits, as currently seen, of legitimate debate? His society did not, it seems, operate under a rigid orthodoxy and there was much diversity of interpretation about such matters as sabbath observance and tithing of produce. Or did he go beyond such bounds, offering a radical critique of the Law's very foundations? If so, it is puzzling that none of the gospels offers this as the reason for his final condemnation (though he is attacked for it in the course of the story, e.g. Mk 3:1–6). But the gospels differ in their presentation of Jesus' teaching on this subject in the course of his ministry.

5. In brief, Mark depicts him as radical, marginalizing food taboos and the priority of sabbath observance (7:19; 2:23–3:6) and down-playing the sacrificial system in favour of an ethic of active love (12:28–34); while John shows him superseding the Law in his own person as the medium of God's disclosure to his people (1:17; 2:21; 7:37–8). Matthew, by contrast, has Jesus endorse and intensify the requirements of the Law (5:17–20; 23:23), while he takes a humane view on certain currently disputed issues (12:1–14; 19:1–9; adapting Mark). And Luke places his attitude somewhere between Mark and Matthew, rather in the spirit of the compromise he shows the Jerusalem church arriving at later in the light of substantial Gentile conversions to the church (Acts 15). It is hard to avoid the conclusion that all these presentations have been affected by the diverse resolutions of this problem, both pressing and practical in the first decades of the Christian movement, that were adopted in various different quarters of the church.

6. Moreover, all the evangelists were writing after the shock of Paul's strong stand on this very matter, releasing Gentile converts from the adoption of the key marks of Jewish identity—sabbath observance, food laws, and circumcision—and thereby implicitly placing allegiance to Christ as the sole identity marker for all Christians. It appears that the whole subject remained contentious for some time, with a variety of positions being taken (though it remains a puzzle that neither radical nor conservative presentations in the gospels refer to the matter of circumcision on whose irrelevance Paul was so insistent, as Galatians in particular demonstrates). The upshot of all this is that we really cannot tell with certainty exactly what Jesus himself taught or practised, and scholarly opinion remains divided. Careful analyses of crucial sayings, fitting them plausibly into the setting of his time and place, always remain open to alternative interpretations which see them as reflections of the particular evangelists' views (Harvey 1982; Sanders 1993).

7. Jesus is obscured too by the fact that, by the time the gospels were written, interest in the sheer preservation of his words and ideas was overshadowed by his being the object of faith—and by the consequent need to make a case for that faith, which saw him not simply as a figure of the past who had once revealed God and his saving purposes and whose death and resurrection had given new insight into those purposes or marked their realization; but as the present heavenly Lord who enjoyed supreme triumph as God's co-regent and would soon return in the public display of that reality.

8. The scriptural text that seemed best to epitomize that faith was 'The Lord said unto my Lord, Sit at my right hand, till I make your enemies your footstool' (Ps 110:1). This text is quoted more widely across the gamut of NT authors than any other—closely followed by 'Thou art my son, this day I have begotten thee' (Ps 2:7), less precise but not dissimilar in import. It is impossible to believe that this faith failed to colour the memory of Jesus' earthly life, even if there had been in the churches a strongly archival sense, or, more likely, a reverence for Jesus' words and the stories of his deeds, which could stand alongside that faith: argument ranges back and forth on the balance of effect of these various aspects of the situation (Gerhardsson 1961; Stanton 1974; Meier 1991).

9. The faith in Jesus which prevents the gospels being neutral records (whatever that might mean) was largely articulated by means of material drawn from Judaism, and especially from the old Scriptures. This was partly for purposes of Christian self-understanding (to what other medium could the first Christians practically turn?) and partly for purposes of self-definition in relation to (other) Jews who did not share their assessment of Jesus and adherence to him. But this appeal to Scripture, which pervades the gospels, makes yet another screen between us and the realities of Jesus' historical life. It is an interpretative tool that was certainly used, in one form or another, by all schools of thought in the early church, but, when it comes to the gospels, we are faced with the question of whether Jesus himself initiated the process—as in the depiction that is before us. Did he not, inevitably, interpret his own mission and person in scriptural terms? If so, to which models did he appeal? And to what extent did the amplifying of this mode of thought in the church, as evidenced in the gospels and elsewhere, merely build upon his foundations and continue along lines he laid down, as distinct from moving along altogether more ambitious paths? For example, when the Gospel of John views Jesus under the image of God's pre-existent Word, his co-partner in the work of creation itself (1:1–18), thus drawing on a symbol current in Judaism (e.g. Ps 33:6; Wis 9:1), there is nothing to suggest that Jesus himself made use of that category of thought. It is quite otherwise with Jewish terms such as Messiah, son of God, or son of man. These appear on his lips or are inseparable from the tradition about him. None of them is easy to interpret, and if Jesus used them, it is as likely that they received, by the very fact of their application to him if not from his explicit teaching, twists of sense, perhaps to the extent of sheer paradox, that were novel. Jesus was, after all, on

any showing a most un-messianic Messiah, given the nationalistic associations of the term—if indeed he did make any such claim. And the same would be true even if in reality the claim derives from his followers after his lifetime rather than from himself.

10. None of this caution, this indirectness, is designed to say that the gospels merely obscure the figure of Jesus or tell us nothing of value about him. There are certain features of his life and teaching that not only come across loud and clear but were less than wholly welcome in the early church—and would not therefore have survived if the church, like a traumatized individual, simply eliminated that which it no longer approved of or no longer served its purposes. We have seen that the renunciatory teachings of Jesus the Galilean charismatic preacher were toned down or repackaged quite rapidly in the more settled life of the urban churches. Yet we see them prominently displayed in the first three gospels. Much has been made (Hengel 1981) of the saying in Mt 8:22 ('Follow me, and let the dead bury their own dead'), advocating, in the name of the extreme urgency of God's call and of his kingdom, a stance of provocative immorality by the standards of virtually any culture and soon abandoned in the family ethic of the church, as Eph 6:4 demonstrates. It is these harder, more uncomfortable elements in the story of Jesus which, however they may sometimes visibly as one evangelist modifies another, have been modified by the church, speak most powerfully for the tenacity and authority of Jesus' vision, simply because it was his (Harvey 1990).

11. A promising line of enquiry begins by bypassing the gospels altogether. We know when and where Jesus lived: what then can we learn from a knowledge of the times derived from other sources, such as archaeology and histories of the period? We have already made reference to evidence of this kind: the Qumran sect and the Dead Sea scrolls left by them (Vermes 1977, 1995); the probabilities about the circumstances of Jesus' death; the mixed culture of Galilee with its peasant countryside and Hellenistic cities. But can this approach bring us nearer to a realistic view of Jesus himself, at any rate to a view of his role in the society of his time—what sort of part he played, how he may have fitted into its structure and been perceived (Finegan 1992; Stanton 1995)?

12. This more detached and wider-ranging approach does not yield unquestioned results, but many would agree that it places Jesus in a category of persons recognizable in the period (Vermes 1973). In traditional terms, such persons have affinities with the prophets of former centuries, men who stood out from the prevailing religious culture and social system, declaring the will of God and the imminence of his judgement. More sociologically, we can refer to them as charismatics, that is people whose message threatens to turn the world upside down, challenging conventional values—even those whose morality seems unimpeachable—and looking towards an order of things where life is lived at a new level of righteousness and God is all in all. Such people rarely get much of a hearing: often their day is brief or they are snuffed out by authorities who feel endangered by them. First-century Galilee, somewhat removed from the centre of power in Jerusalem and probably unstable in its rural economy, spawned several such figures, most of them leaving practically no trace. John Baptist had more identifiable effects: he comes into the

story of Jesus, and the late first-century Jewish historian Jose-phus (like Mark and Matthew but in somewhat different terms) tells of his execution for his righteous meddling in the affairs of the great ones in the land—a classic prophet's predicament. Moreover (and somewhat mysteriously), like Jesus, he gave rise to a group of followers who, according to Acts 18:24–19:6, had spread to Ephesus in the later years of the century—thereafter they fade from view.

13. Much of the broad picture of Jesus in the gospels coheres with this identification of his social role: the radical, shocking teaching about ties to family and property; the call to 'follow' that brooks no delay, no appeal to prudence; the ready challenge to established religious groups, even the most pious, for their routines and their self-satisfaction; the chal-lenge to central authority—if that is how we are to construe the incident in the Temple (Mk 11:15–17) which probably pre-cipitated the perception of Jesus as a breacher of the peace and his speedy elimination; above all, the sense of the imminent realization of God's rule.

14. However, other readings are possible and win some support, even within the method we have been describing. The picture of Jesus as charismatic leader or prophet, once put forward, seems obvious: it makes best sense of the most basic recognition of modern scholarship—that Jesus was a Jew of his time. It brings it into sharp focus and takes us behind some of the other characterizations of Jesus (for example, as the heavenly one come to earth) that soon came to dominate Christian accounts of him (Rom 1:3; Gal 4:4). But it does less than justice to certain other aspects of the gospel material: such as the teaching about there being no need for anxiety, no need for complexity of lifestyle (Mt 6:25–34); or the picture of Jesus and his followers as a band of brothers espousing free-dom and simplicity of life under God's heaven, somewhat after the manner of modern opters-out from society. Jesus' common meals with his followers (specially emphasized in Luke) were then the central symbol of this lifestyle, focused on the present.

15. This is a distinctly non-apocalyptic picture of Jesus and, in terms of Jewish heritage, seems to owe more to some facets of Jewish 'wisdom' tradition, with its provision for moral life here and now. But its associations and provenance may lie more in the teaching of Cynic philosophers who adopted values of this kind and whose influence had perhaps penetrated into northern Palestine. The straightforward view is of course, that Jesus himself sensed a directness and simplicity of filial relationship with God—it was his stance in daily life ('father' e.g. Mt 6:7–14). Alternatively, this picture may represent one style among others of church reflection on Jesus, as the tradition about him was exposed to the variegated culture of the Graeco-Roman world (Crossan 1991; 1994).

16. This discussion started, somewhat negatively, under the injunction to approach the figure of Jesus with caution: the nature of our evidence, literary and circumstantial, dictates it. But (to repeat) it would be a mistake to let caution lead to the conclusion that Jesus is a mere enigma, lost in the mists of time or a welter of church obfuscation of whatever clarity there might otherwise have been. As we have seen, some features are unmistakable and their strength shines through. But the equally unmistakable effects of church interpretation

of various kinds are there in the gospels, and they lead us to our final topic: Jesus as the object of faith.

17. If we had only the letters of Paul, we should think that all that really mattered about Jesus' career was his death and resurrection: that is, its importance centred almost wholly on a period of some forty-eight hours—and if more than that, then what followed it (his heavenly rule and presence in his adherents) was more notable than what preceded it. That is the earliest Christian perspective of which we have evidence.

18. How different it is from the picture we get from the gospels. There, though the death and resurrection are plainly the climax of the narrative and occupy a disproportionate place from a purely biographical point of view, these elements are nevertheless parts of a much greater whole. To put it more succinctly, they form the end of a story, where in Paul they acted much more as the inauguration of a continuing state of affairs. It is not wholly satisfying simply to point out that these are different genres of writing and so naturally differ in their perspective. After all, none of these writers was compelled to write as he did, and each wrote in a particular way because, presumably, it reflected the 'shape' of his convictions about Jesus.

19. The two perspectives meet, however, precisely in the death and resurrection, and the latter in particular may be seen as the junction between them (Evans 1970; Marxsen 1970). Luke's two-volume work (Gospel and Acts) comes nearest to meeting the need to unite Jesus' life before the resurrection and the life of the church after it—though even this narrative probably ends before the time of writing, and so, like the gospels, looks back from the Christian present to an (albeit longer) normative history. On the other hand, though the gospels do indeed describe a past that culminates in Jesus' death and resurrection, they are nevertheless imbued with a present faith in the living Christ who, in his heavenly rule, may still be said to inspire his people and even to dwell in and among them: perhaps especially in Mark and John, the back-drop is that of Jesus' past life but he addresses the present of the gospels' readers. So much is this the case that, as we have seen, we must be alert to the effects of this factor as we read the gospels with a view to discovering simply what happened and how things were in Jesus' lifetime.

20. To take a small example, but significant for that very reason (and capable of being paralleled almost limitlessly): Mk 9:40 ('Whoever is not against us is for us') suggests that Jesus urged on his followers an open, expansive attitude to possible supporters and deflects them from any narrowness or the erection of barriers and the application of tests. This is, in the words of the church poster, a case of 'All welcome'. But Mt 12:30 ('He who is not with me is against me') reflects the precise opposite. Jesus makes stringent demands on potential followers and there is no easy entry to their company: adher-ing is sharply distinguished from remaining outside. The boundary wall is high. Must we not see here the effects of two different outlooks in different parts of the early church, both equally comprehensible, but contrasting in their pol-icies—and far-reaching in their twin visions of Christian life? It does not take much imagination to see that the two statements betoken two very different ways of believing in Jesus' significance and the scope of his work, as they also may be seen as the founts of two different traditions in Christian life down to our own day. The gospels, accounts of the pre-resurrection life of Jesus, then reflect the faith of the post-resurrection church, in small ways as in great. These considerations go some way to mitigate the contrast that we drew between the perspectives of Paul and the gospels.

21. From another point of view, we may indeed say that these writings—and indeed almost all the NT books (the Letter of James is a strange exception)—testify to a remarkably homogeneous faith in the centrality of Jesus as the agent of God's saving purpose. True, they differ in certain respects, in emphasis and terminology, but the unanimity is striking. To return to the obvious: it is this common conviction about Jesus as the one who 'makes all the difference' that holds together the early Christian movement, and so the NT as its literary deposit—whatever other factors loomed large in its life and whatever the problems to which it had to attend.

22. Yet we may observe interesting variations of resonance even in the use of certain terms to express this conviction about Jesus. For example, many early Christian writers speak of him as 'son of God'. But what associations did this expression have for them? It is not, after all, an expression that simply comes out of the blue: it has numerous antecedents in Judaism, and without recognizable resonances it could scarcely have been used at all in its new context. In Paul, the earliest writer to use it, it is not altogether clear what is in mind, for he gives it multiple applications. In Rom 9:4, it receives one of its traditional applications, to Israel as a people (cf. Ex 4:22; Hos 11:1); in Gal 3:26 and Rom 8:14, it denotes Christian believers—a usage paralleled in Jewish wisdom writing (Wis 2:18), where it is applied to righteous servants of God. Yet clearly, for Paul, this application to Christians is now closely related (but exactly how?) to its central use for Jesus himself; just as God's 'fatherhood' of Jesus is related to their right to claim that same fatherhood (Gal 4:4–6; Rom 8:14–17). Paul perhaps comes nearest to showing his mind in Rom 8:32, where he appeals to the giving by Abraham of his son Isaac to death (narrowly averted, Gen 22) as a parallel to God's giving of Jesus: 'God did not spare his only son' (cf. Gen 22:16). That model of sonship splendidly and appropriately illuminates the death of Jesus and is an important ingredient in the quest for scriptural texts that could put that otherwise catastrophic event, as far as the hopes of Jesus' followers were concerned, in a positive light. Here was a case where the giving of a son by a father was the seed of total good—the establishing of the people of Israel (Byrne 1979).

23. The same model may play a part in the Markan story of Jesus' baptism, where his sonship is announced by God himself: the word 'beloved' in 1:11 is the Septuagint's repeated adjective for Isaac in Gen 22. But here, in what is for Mark the crucial opening scene, establishing Jesus' identity, it is joined with the words of Ps 2:7, 'Thou art my son', probably seen as messianic in import in the Jewish background upon which Mark draws.

24. In Matthew and Luke, Jesus' sonship is for the first time linked to his conception and birth, but even here the focus is not on physiology but on scriptural texts and models which are seen to foreshadow Jesus and to authenticate his role. In Matthew, for example, Isa 7:14 plays a crucial role (cf. 1:23). In Luke, the whole narrative of chs. 1 and 2 is couched in lan-guage that echoes the old stories of providential births, such as those of Isaac, Samson or Samuel.

25. In John, the sonship of Jesus in relation to God is taken further still. Partly by way of its associations with other terms and models, it now describes a relationship that does not begin at Jesus' baptism or conception, but exists from all eternity. Jesus' relationship with God, as Father, is, for the Gospel of John, anchored at that most fundamental level. From the vantage point of this climax in the development of the model (soon to be taken up in a more philosophical idiom), we can see how Jesus' representation of God comes to be seen in more and more extensive terms, until it operates on the scale of the cosmos itself.

26. This example of development and of many-sidedness could be paralleled for other expressions and ideas in which the Christians of the NT period clothed their belief in Jesus. Typically, it is based on a variety of scriptural passages, each pointing to its own associations and concepts. Typically too, even within the narrow temporal confines of the NT period, it is neither static nor universal. It is symptomatic of the explosion of symbolic energy which so imaginatively produced the new devotion that saw in Jesus the key to every-thing.

REFERENCES

Alexander, L. (1993), *The Preface to Luke's Gospel: Literary Convention and Social Context in Luke 1:1–4 and Acts 1:1* (Cambridge: Cambridge University Press).

Ashton, J. (1991), *Understanding the Fourth Gospel* (Oxford: Clarendon).

Beavis, M. A. (1989), *Mark's Audience: The Literary and Social Setting of Mark 4:1–12* (Sheffield, JSOT).

Betz, H. D. (1979), *Galatians*, Hermeneia (Philadelphia: Fortress).

Birdsall, J. N. (1970), 'The New Testament Text', in P. R. Ackroyd and C. F. Evans (eds.), *Cambridge History of the Bible* (Cambridge: Cambridge University Press), i. 308–77.

Brown, R. E. (1979), *The Community of the Beloved Disciple: The Life, Loves and Hates of an Individual Church in New Testament Times* (London: Geoffrey Chapman).

—— (1993), *The Birth of the Messiah: A Commentary on the Infancy Narratives in the Gospels of Matthew and Luke* (London: Geoffrey Chapman).

—— (1994), *The Death of the Messiah: A Commentary on the Passion Narratives* (London: Geoffrey Chapman).

Burridge, R. A. (1992), *What Are the Gospels? A Comparison with Graeco-Roman Biography* (Cambridge: Cambridge University Press).

Byrne, B. (1979), *'Sons of God'—'Seed of Abraham': A Study of the Idea of the Sonship of God of All Christians in Paul against the Jewish Background* (Rome: Biblical Institute Press).

Campbell, R. A. (1994), *The Elders: Seniority within Earliest Christianity* (Edinburgh, T. & T. Clark), 1994.

Campenhausen, H. von (1969), *Ecclesiastical Authority and Spiritual Power in the Church of the First Three Centuries* (London: A. & C. Black).

—— (1972), *The Formation of the Christian Bible* (London: A. & C. Black).

Carroll, R. P. (1991), *Wolf in the Sheepfold: The Bible as a Problem for Christianity* (London: SPCK).

Crossan, J. D. (1991), *The Historical Jesus: The Life of a Mediterranean Jewish Peasant* (Edinburgh: T. & T. Clark).

—— (1994), *Jesus: A Revolutionary Biography* (London: HarperCollins).

Evans, C. F. (1970), *Resurrection and the New Testament* (London: SCM).

Farrer, A. M. (1949), *A Rebirth of Images: The Making of St John's Apocalypse* (Westminster: Dacre).

Finegan, J. (1992), *The Archeology of the New Testament: The Life of Jesus and the Beginning of the Early Church* (Princeton, NJ: Princeton University Press).

Freyne, S. (1988), *Galilee, Jesus and the Gospels: Literary Approaches and Historical Investigations* (Dublin: Gill & Macmillan).

Gerhardsson, B. (1961), *Memory and Manuscript: Oral Tradition and Written Transmission in Rabbinic Judaism and Early Christianity* (Lund: Gleerup).

Goulder, M. D. (1974), *Midrash and Lection in Matthew* (London: SPCK).

Harvey, A. E. (1982), *Jesus and the Constraints of History* (London: Duckworth).

—— (1990), *Strenuous Commands: The Ethics of Jesus* (London: SCM).

Hengel, M. (1974), *Judaism and Hellenism* (London: SCM).

—— (1981), *The Charismatic Leader and his Followers* (Edinburgh: T. & T. Clark).

Holmberg, B. (1978), *Paul and Power: The Structure of Authority in the Primitive Church as Reflected in the Pauline Epistles* (Lund: Gleerup).

—— (1990), *Sociology and the New Testament: An Appraisal* (Minneapolis: Fortress).

Houlden, J. L. (1973), *Ethics and the New Testament* (Edinburgh: T. & T. Clark).

—— (1986), *Connections* (London: SCM).

—— (ed.) (1995), *The Interpretation of the Bible in the Church* (London: SCM).

Lentz, J. C. (1993), *Luke's Portrait of Paul* (Cambridge: Cambridge University Press).

Lindars, B. (1961), *New Testament Apologetic: The Doctrinal Significance of the Old Testament Quotations* (London: SCM).

Marxsen, W. (1970), *The Resurrection of Jesus of Nazareth* (London: SCM).

Meeks, W. A. (1983), *The First Urban Christians: The Social World of the Apostle Paul* (New Haven: Yale University Press).

—— (1986), 'The Man from Heaven in Johannine Sectarianism', in J. Ashton (ed.), *The Interpretation of John* (London: SPCK), 141–73.

Meier, J. P. (1991), *A Marginal Jew: Rethinking the Historical Jesus* (New York: Doubleday).

Metzger, B. M. (1964), *The Text of the New Testament: Its Transmission, Corruption, and Restoration* (Oxford: Clarendon).

—— (1987), *The Canon of the New Testament: Its Origin, Development, and Significance* (Oxford: Clarendon).

Meyers, E. M., and Strange, J. F. (1981), *Archaeology, the Rabbis and Early Christianity* (London: SCM).

Murphy-O'Connor, J. (1983), *St Paul's Corinth: Texts and Archaeology* (Wilmington, Del.: Michael Glazier).

Rivkin, E. (1984), *What Crucified Jesus* (London: SCM).

Robinson, J. A. T. (1976), *Redating the New Testament* (London: SCM).

Rowland, C. C. (1982), *The Open Heaven: A Study of Apocalyptic in Judaism and Early Christianity* (London: SPCK).

Sanders, E. P. (1985), *Jesus and Judaism* (London: SCM).

—— (1992), *Judaism, Practice and Belief, 63BCE–66CE* (London: SCM).

—— (1993), *The Historical Figure of Jesus* (London: Allen Lane, Penguin).

Schneemelcher, W. (ed.), (1991; 1992), *New Testament Apocrypha* (Cambridge: James Clarke), i and ii.

Sherwin-White, A. N. (1963), *Roman Society and Roman Law in the New Testament* (Oxford: Clarendon).

Staniforth, M., and Louth, A. (eds.) (1987), *Early Christian Writings* (Harmondsworth: Penguin).

Stanton, G. N. (1974), *Jesus of Nazareth in New Testament Preaching* (Cambridge: Cambridge University Press).

—— (1995), *Gospel Truth? New Light on Jesus and the Gospels* (London: HarperCollins).

Stendahl, K. (1968), *The School of St Matthew and its Use of the Old Testament* (Philadelphia: Fortress).

Sweet, J. P. M. (1979), *Revelation* (London: SCM).

Theissen, G. (1982), *The Social Context of Pauline Christianity* (Edinburgh: T. & T. Clark).

Vermes, G. (1973), *Jesus the Jew: A Historian's Reading of the Gospels* (London: Collins).

—— (1977), *The Dead Sea Scrolls: Qumran in Perspective* (London: Collins).

—— (1995), *The Dead Sea Scrolls in English*, 4th edn. (Harmondsworth: Penguin).

Wagner, G. (1967), *Pauline Baptism and the Pagan Mysteries* (Edinburgh: T. & T. Clark).

Wedderburn, A. J. M. (1987), *Baptism and Resurrection* (Tübingen: Mohr).

57. Matthew

DALE C. ALLISON, JR.

INTRODUCTION

A. Authorship. 1. Eusebius, *Hist. Eccl.* 3.39, attributes to Papias, a second-century Bishop of Hierapolis in Asia Minor, the earliest testimony to Matthew's authorship: 'Now Matthew made an ordered arrangement of the oracles in the Hebrew [or: Aramaic] language, and each one translated [or: interpreted] it as he was able.' These words and the traditional title, 'According to Matthew', show that not long after it was written people attributed our gospel to the disciple named in Mt 9:9; 10:3. Because the tradition is so early, and because the apostle Matthew is a relatively unimportant figure in early Christian literature, the traditional attestation still has its defenders; see e.g. Gundry (1982).

2. Most, however, now doubt the tradition. For (1) from Papias on, Christian tradition consistently associated Mat-

thean authorship with a Semitic original; but this gospel is unlikely to be the work of a translator. (2) It is improbable that a Semitic document, such as Papias speaks of, would have incorporated a Greek document (Mark) almost in its entirety. (3) Would an apostle who accompanied Jesus have used so little personal reminiscence but rather have followed Mark so closely? (4) Papias' tradition might have originally referred to an early version of lost sayings (source known as Q) and then, when Q disappeared, have been connected with Matthew. It was common enough for a document to carry the name of the author of one of its sources (cf. the evolution of Isaiah).

3. These points are sufficiently strong that in the present commentary 'Matthew' will be used of the author without any claim to his apostolic identity. On one point, however, the tradition appears quite correct: the author was a Jew. The gospel has numerous Jewish features which cannot be attributed to the tradition—e.g. *gematria* (see MT 1:2–17), OT texts seemingly translated from the Hebrew specifically for this gospel (e.g. 2:18, 23; 8:17; 23:18–21), concentrated focus on the synagogue (e.g. 6:1–18; 23:1–39), and affirmation of the abiding force of the Mosaic law (5:17–20). Matthew, moreover, records Jesus' prohibitions against mission outside Israel (10:5; 15:24) and shows concern that eschatological flight not occur on a sabbath (24:20). These and other Jewish features have not been sprinkled here and there for good effect: they are an organic part of the whole and imply a Jewish-Christian author and audience.

B. Date and Place of Origin. 1. Although there has recently been a slight tendency to date Matthew before 70 CE, the majority opinion rightly holds that Matthew was written in the last quarter of the first century CE. (1) Ignatius of Antioch, the *Didache*, and Papias—all from the first part of the second century—show knowledge of Matthew, which accordingly must have been composed before 100 CE. (See e.g. Ign., *Smyrn.* 1; *Did.* 8.2.) (2) 22:7 (a seeming allusion to the fall of Jerusalem) and the dependence upon Mark (written c.60–70 CE) indicate a date after 70 CE. (3) Matthew reveals points of contact with early rabbinic Judaism as it struggled to consolidate itself after the Jewish war; see esp. Davies (1964).

2. Many have urged that Matthew originated in Antioch in Syria. Peter's prominence harmonizes well with his undoubted status there (cf. Gal 2:11), and the mixture of Jew and Gentile in a large urban area is consistent with composition in Antioch. Further, Ignatius may be the earliest witness to Matthew, and he was bishop of Antioch. But these and additional considerations do not add up to proof, and patristic tradition places neither this gospel nor the apostle Matthew in Antioch. So other suggestions have been made—Jerusalem, Galilee, Alexandria, Caesarea Maritima, Phoenicia, or, more generally, east of the Jordan (on the basis of 4:25 and 19:1, which may view Palestine as being on the other side of the Jordan).

C. Matthew's Purpose and its Setting in Judaism. 1. Following the revolt of 70 CE the Pharisees emerged dominant. They set in motion a process which was to allow Judaism to continue and even thrive after defeat. To the early stages of this process the rabbinic sources apply the term 'Jamnia', after the place where, according to tradition, Pharisaic sages congregated after the war. These sages were concerned with the disunity of the Jewish people and with the attraction of movements from without, including Christianity. They accordingly promoted unity, began the process of collecting their oral laws, sought to establish a standard calendar for the religious year, and tried to transfer to the synagogue rites previously performed in the temple itself. So in Matthew's time a highly self-conscious and probably aggressive Pharisaism was asserting itself to reunite Israel; and this involved defining itself in opposition to others, including Christians. It probably also involved activities Christians interpreted as persecution. Tolerance comes in times of self-confidence;

but the period after the destruction was not such a time for formative Judaism.

2. Matthew's mainly Jewish community had to come to terms with such a Judaism—a fact which helps explain the great interest in the scribes and Pharisees. That community seems, on the one hand, to have demanded its own inclusion within Judaism, whose faith it thought to share, and, on the other, to have sought the expansion of Judaism beyond strictly Jewish confines by challenging that faith to shed its tendency to ethnic privacy. But scholars disagree whether Matthew's community was still—as 23.3 so strongly implies—within Judaism or whether it had recently declared itself independent of its parent faith so that it had become a sect outside Judaism or, again, whether, having long been regarded as deviant by the Jewish community, it was in the process of deciding if it should leave while yet remaining under the authority of the local synagogue.

3. Whatever the exact status of Matthew's community in relation to Judaism, his writing points to a process of differentiation which took place between his community and 'their synagogue'. Believers in Jesus may have preferred to refer to their own gatherings not as 'synagogue'—in Matthew the expression is 'their synagogue'—but as 'church'. Again, Christian leaders were not to be called 'rabbi', a term which was, in the Jamnian Judaism of Matthew's day, becoming an official title (23:7–8). Along with the differentiation went outright, polemical criticism, especially of the Pharisees. The cohesion of the believers in Jesus was no doubt strengthened by such criticism: a common enemy unites the divided and insecure.

4. The establishment of group identity also involved legitimizing belief in Jesus over against Jewish criticism. Explicit about the existence of such criticism is (28:15), which no doubt helps account for the formula quotations, the parallels between Jesus and Moses, and Jesus' endorsement of the Torah. One detects in all this a sort of apologetics. Christians claimed to be vindicated by antiquity, to have a lawgiver like Moses, and to keep Torah.

5. The need for group identity made the need for unity a paramount concern. This illuminates the emphasis in both the Sermon on the Mount and ch. 18 on forgiveness and reconciliation. Forgiveness up to seven times is advised in Luke, but 'seventy times (and) seven' in Mt 18:22. Despite its often violent polemics, perhaps no other ancient document shows more sensitivity to the desperate need for love and peace rather than hate and vengeance than does Matthew. The tendency towards reconciliation appears also in Matthew's desire not to give away too much of his Jewish heritage but to bridge as sensitively as possible the gulf between Jewish and Gentile believers. He tried to preserve both the old and the new (8:17; 13:52). While he called for a mission to Gentiles, he also recognized Israel's special place (10:5–6; 15:21–8) and insisted on the demands for a righteousness even higher than that of the Pharisees. The proof of Matthew's ecumenical character is that both Jewish and Gentile Christians welcomed it as their own: it became the chief gospel of both groups.

6. Despite both the polemic and the ecclesiastical tactics, the gospel remains eloquent testimony to the faith that inspired Matthew. Further, we cannot doubt that while he had one eye on his own social setting, he also envisaged a broader readership. For it is only through a studied neglect of the obvious that one can miss that a major and perhaps the primary impulse behind the First Gospel was the natural desire to record what Jesus said and did and to preserve that memory for posterity. Matthew was composed so that the story of Jesus, rightly interpreted, might continue to be heard beyond as well as in his own time and place.

D. Theology. 1. Although there are aspects of a theology in Matthew they do not present themselves as a coherent or abstract edifice; there is no systematically developed body of thought. Despite the book's theocentricity, a theology of Matthew, in our sense of the term, is not really possible. Like the rabbinic corpus Matthew contains much implicit theology but is primarily concerned not with correctness of belief but with obedience.

2. Matthew did not offer a theological system as an expression of his faith in Jesus. Rather he drew upon and applied texts he had reflected upon—the OT, Mark, Q, M. As pastor he was above all an exegete and commentator. That is, he was primarily concerned to pass on the traditions handed to him. His gospel is less a statement of personal opinions than the expression of a traditional faith. He told a story more than he authored it, or rather he retold his community's story to which he added commentary.

3. Matthew's genius was not that of theological invention. He was not a Paul or an Origen. To judge from his gospel the evangelist's religious convictions were traditional. Along with all the NT authors his God was the God of the OT, that is, the God of Israel. In other words his theology, in the proper sense of that word, was Jewish theology as transmitted to him by his Jewish education and the church. There was also nothing much original about his Christology. All the Christological titles found in his gospel appear in other early Christian texts; and even his story of a virgin birth has its parallel in Luke. Matthew also contributed nothing new to soteriology. The gospel says only that Jesus gave his life as a ransom for many and saved his people from their sins—convictions common enough in primitive Christianity.

4. One could, if the non-Markan material in 16:13–20 were thought redactional, make a case for a novel contribution to ecclesiology. But here the evidence again points to tradition. It is the same with Matthew's Deuteronomistic view of history and his eschatology. The former reminds one of Q, and regarding the latter, while certain themes receive special accent, one can easily find parallels to every strand of Matthean eschatology—to Matthew's hope for a near end, to his realized eschatology, and to his use of apocalyptic expectation to tender encouragement, offer paraenesis, and explicate Christology. Also in Matthew's moral teaching we find, first of all, tradition. The demand to love, the call to non-retaliation, and the imperative to imitate Christ were standard in the early church.

5. Even with regard to the law Matthew was no innovator. In some ways indeed he was on this matter at one with Paul: Gentiles did not have to become Jews in order to be saved; that is, they did not have to become circumcised and obey Moses. If it had been otherwise, Matthew could not have enthusiastically endorsed the Gentile mission in his conclusion, for by his time that mission was in most areas presumably free of the demand for circumcision. At the same time—here the relationship with Paul is more difficult to assess—Matthew believed that the Mosaic law was still in effect. This can only have meant that Matthew expected Jewish Christians to keep it. But this was also the position of Luke, who had no trouble passing on stories in which even the apostle to the Gentiles keeps the law. Moreover, the idea that Jewish Christians should observe the precepts of the Torah from which Gentiles Christians were free, was not unknown. So much is clear from the decree reproduced in Acts 15 (see ACTS 15:29). Whatever its precise origin, that decree was not Luke's invention, and it assumes that while Jewish Christians will observe the law, Gentiles need only follow a few general proscriptions. This position was probably the dominant one in first-century Christianity. Here too then, Matthew swims in the mainstream.

E. Story, Structure, and Plot. 1. Mt 1–4 opens with the title (1:1) and Jesus' genealogy (1:2–17). There follow infancy stories (1:18–25; 2:1–11, 12–23), the section on John the Baptist (3:1–17), and three additional pericopae that directly prepare for the ministry (4:1–11, 12–17, 18–22). All this material constitutes an extended introduction. We are told *who* Jesus was (1:1–18; 2:1, 4; 3:11, 17; 4:3, 6), *where* he was from (2:6), *how* he came into the world (1:18–25), *why* he came into the world (1:21; 2:6), *when* he came into the world (1:17; 2:1), and *what* he proclaimed (4:17).

2. The Sermon on the Mount, the first major discourse, opens with a short narrative introduction (4:23–5:2) and closes with a short narrative conclusion (7:28–8:1). The discourse proper, 5:3–7:27, is also symmetrically centred: blessings (5:3–12) are at the beginning, warnings (7:13–27) at the end. In between there are three major sections, each one primarily a compilation of imperatives: Jesus and the law (5:17–48), Jesus on the cult (6:1–18), Jesus and social issues (6:19–7:12). The sermon contains Jesus' demands for Israel.

3. If the Sermon on the Mount presents us with Jesus' words, Mt 8 and 9 recount his deeds. The chapters are largely a record of Jesus' acts, particularly his compassionate miracles, which fall neatly into three sets of three: 8:1–4, 5–13, 14–15 + 8:23–7, 28–34; 9:1–8 + 9:18–26, 27–31, 32–4. Jesus also speaks in this section, but the emphasis is upon his actions, what he does in and for Israel (cf. 8:16–17).

4. Having been informed of what Jesus said and did, we next learn, in Mt 10, the second major discourse, what Jesus instructed his disciples, as extensions of himself, to say and do. The theme of imitation is prominent. The disciples are to proclaim what Jesus proclaimed (cf. 10:7 with 4:17) and do what Jesus did (cf. 10:8 with Mt 8–9 and 11:2–6). The disciple is like the teacher, the servant like the master (10:24–5). In Matthew Jesus is the first Christian missionary who calls others to his example.

5. The chapters on the words and deeds of Jesus and the words and deeds of the disciples are followed by chs. 11–12. These record the response of 'this generation' to John and Jesus and the twelve. This is what the material on the Baptist (11:2–6, 7–15, 16–19) is all about, as well as the woes on Galilee (11:20–4) and the conflict stories in Mt 12 (1–8, 9–14, 22–37, 38–45). It all adds up to an indictment of corporate Israel: the Messiah has been rejected. But this is unexpected. In Jewish eschatology God saves Israel in the latter days. One hardly expects the Messiah to meet opposition from his own people—which explains Paul's agonizing in Rom 9–11. Mt 13, the parable chapter, the third great discourse, is Matthew's attempt to tackle this problem. That is, Mt 13 offers various explanations for the mixed response to the Messiah: there can be different responses to one message (13:1–23), the devil works in human hearts (13:24–30), and, if things are not right now, all will be made well in the end (13:31–3, 36–43, 47–50).

6. The fourth major narrative section, chs. 14–17, follows the parable chapter. The most memorable pericope is 16:13–20, where Jesus founds his church. This suits so well the larger context because after corporate Israel has, at least for the time being, forfeited her role in salvation-history, God must raise up a new people. That this is indeed the dominant theme of the section is hinted at not only by the ever-increasing focus upon the disciples as opposed to the crowds but also by Peter's being the rock upon which the church is built. For it is precisely in this section that he comes to the fore; see 14:28–33; 15:15; 16:13–20; and 17:24–7—all insertions into Mark. Peter's emerging pre-eminence correlates with the emergence of the church.

7. All this is confirmed by Mt 18, the fourth major discourse. Usually styled the 'community' or 'ecclesiological' discourse, this chapter is especially addressed to the topic of Christian fraternal relations. How often should one forgive a brother? What is the procedure for excommunicating someone? These ecclesiastical questions are appropriate precisely at this point because Jesus has just established his church.

8. Having founded the new community and given her teaching, it remains for Jesus to go to Jerusalem, which is what happens in the next narrative section, chs. 19–23. The material is mostly from Mark, with the woes of ch. 23 added. The bankruptcy of the Jewish leadership and the rejection of the Messiah are to the fore.

9. Before the passion narrative proper, however, Jesus, in chs. 24–5, speaks of the future, that is, the future of Israel and of the church. Here, in the fifth and last major discourse, we are taken beyond chs. 26–8 into the time beyond the narrative. The discourse foretells judgement upon Jerusalem and salvation through difficulty for the church.

10. Following chronological order, Matthew closes as does Mark (and Luke and John for that matter). The passion and resurrection constitute the conclusion.

11. The primary structure of the gospel is narrative (N) + discourse (D) + narrative (N) + discourse (D), etc., and the plot is determined by the major theme of each narrative section and each discourse. Pictorially, and in minimum compass:

1–4	N	the main character introduced
5–7	D	Jesus' demands upon Israel
8–9	N	Jesus' deeds within and for Israel
10	D	extension of ministry through words and deeds of others
11–12	N	negative response
13	D	explanation of negative response
14–17	N	founding of new community
18	D	instructions to the new community
19–23	N	commencement of the passion
24–5	D	the future: judgement and salvation
26–8	N	conclusion: the passion and resurrection.

F. The Nature of the Text. 1. Much of Matthew's meaning remains implicit, even much of importance. We know this after only the first few verses, for the insertion of four women into the genealogy, a fact that cannot be ignored, must mean something. But the meaning is not made explicit. And so it is throughout: Matthew is a discourse full of tacit references; it is densely allusive. The ubiquitous scriptural citations and allusions—which are anything but detachable ornamentation—direct the informed reader to other books and so teach that Matthew is not a self-contained entity: much is missing. The gospel, in other words, stipulates that it be interpreted in the context of other texts; it evokes tradition through the device of allusion. This means that it is, in a fundamental sense, an incomplete utterance, a book full of holes. Readers must make present what is absent; they must bring to the gospel knowledge of what it presupposes, i.e. a pre-existing collection of interacting texts, the Jewish Bible (the main source for our knowledge about the four women in the genealogy). The First Gospel, like so much ancient Jewish literature, is partly a mnemonic device, designed to trigger intertextual exchanges which depend upon informed and imaginative reading. It is a catena of allusions.

2. If Matthew constantly alludes to the Jewish Bible and the traditions parasitic upon it, it also often alludes to itself. Our text was almost certainly composed with some sort of liturgical (and perhaps also some sort of catechetical) end in view, which means that it was designed to be heard again and again. In line with this the text assumes that listeners will appreciate not only intertextual allusions but intratextual allusions. For instance, 5:38–42 alludes to Isaiah, but also, plainly, to Matthew's own passion narrative; and if 17:1–8 develops a Moses typology, it also foreshadows the crucifixion and perhaps Gethsemane. Our gospel was not composed for bad or casual readers. It was rather written for good and attentive *listeners* accustomed, because of their devotion and relatively small literary canon, to polysemous and heavily connotative religious speech; and such listeners, who heard Matthew repeatedly, would be expected to relate the gospel to itself.

G. Genre and Moral Instruction. 1. Prior to our century Matthew was, despite its many gaps and relative brevity, often referred to as a biography. Most twentieth-century scholars, however, have rejected this view: the canonical gospels are not historical retrospectives but rather expressions of the earliest Christian proclamation. Yet recently there has been a change in the minds of at least some scholars, a reversion to the older view, to the idea that the gospels are biographies—*if* the term is used not in its modern sense but in accord with ancient usage. The canonical gospels then qualify as a subtype of Graeco-Roman biography.

2. The truth is that Matthew is an omnibus of genres: apocalypse, community rule, catechism, cult aetiology, etc. Like the book of Job it is several things at once, a mix of genres, including biography. There are indeed significant resemblances between the First Gospel and certain Hellenistic biographies; and despite its incompleteness as a biography in the modern sense, it is none the less the partial record of a man's life.

3. The content of Matthew's faith partly explains why the First Gospel is biographical. The distinctiveness of Matthew's thinking over against that of his non-Christian Jewish contemporaries was the acceptance of Jesus as the centre of his religion: it was around him as a person that his theological thinking revolved. For Matthew, revelation belonged supremely to the life of the Son of God. The significance of this can be measured when Matthew's comparatively brief gospel is set over against the literature of rabbinic Judaism. In rabbinic sources there are stories about rabbis but no sustained lives such as we find in the Gospel of Matthew, report upon report of what Rabbi X or Rabbi Y purportedly said, but no biographies. Particular sages are seldom an organizing category or principle in rabbinic literature. So whereas rabbinic Judaism, with its subordination of the individual to the community and its focus upon the Torah instead of a particular human being, produced no religious biographies, the substance of Matthew's faith was neither a dogmatic system nor a legal code but a human being whose life was, in outline and in detail, uniquely significant and therefore demanding of record.

4. Matthew's biographical impulse also owes much to the circumstance that whenever social crisis results in fragmentation (as happened at the beginning of Christianity), so that the questioning of previous beliefs issues in the formation of a new social unit, new norms and authorities are inevitably generated, which are always most persuasively presented when embodied in examples: new fashions must first be modelled. In Matthew, Jesus is the new exemplar. There is a multitude of obvious connections between Jesus' words and his deeds. If Jesus indirectly exhorts others to be meek (5:5), he himself is such (11:29; cf. 21:5). If he enjoins mercy (5:7), he himself is merciful (9:27; 15:22; 20:30). If he congratulates those oppressed for God's cause (5:10), he himself suffers and dies innocently (27:23). Jesus further demands faithfulness to the law of Moses (5:17–20) and faithfully keeps that law during his ministry (8:4; 12:1–8, 9–14; 15:1–20). He recommends self-denial in the face of evil (5:39) and does not resist the evils done to him (26:67; 27:30). He calls for private prayer (6:6) and subsequently withdraws to a mountain to pray alone (14:23). Moreover, Jesus advises his followers to use certain words in prayer ('your will be done', 6:10; 'do not bring us to the time of trial', 6:13) and he uses those words in Gethsemane (26:41–2). He rejects the service of mammon (6:19), and he lives without concern for money (8:20). He commands believers to carry crosses (16:24), and he does so himself, both figuratively and literally.

5. The evangelist's moral interest, apparent above all in the Sermon on the Mount, was well served by a story in which the crucial moral imperatives are imaginatively and convincingly incarnated. This the First Gospel supplies. To quote Clement of Alexandria, Matthew offers two types of teaching, 'that which assumes the form of counselling to obedience, and that which is presented in the form of example' (*Ped.* 1.1). Jesus embodies his speech; he lives as he speaks and speaks as he lives.

COMMENTARY

Jesus Introduced (1:1–4:17)

(1:1) The second word of this verse (*genesis*) may be translated 'genealogy' and so made the heading for 1:2–17. But the word can also mean 'birth' (as in 1:18), 'origin', or 'beginning' and be taken as the introduction to 1:2–25 or 1:2–2:23 or 1:2–4:16. Yet another suggestion is that 1:1 is Matthew's title: 'Book of the New Creation wrought by Jesus Christ'. In accord with this last option, Matthew's very first word, *biblos* (NRSV 'account') literally means 'book', and Matthew's opening phrase, *biblos geneseōs*, is not a usual title for genealogies. Moreover, in Gen 2:4 and 5:1, the only two places in the LXX to use Matthew's expression, it is associated with more than genealogical materials. Finally, other Jewish books open with an independent titular sentence announcing the content of the whole (e.g. Nah 1:1; Tob 1:1; Bar 1:1; *T. Job* 1:1; *Apoc. Abr.* title; 2 Esdr 1:1–3). Whatever the reach of 1:1, the first book of the Bible was already known by the title 'Genesis' before Matthew's time, so to open a book with *biblos geneseōs* would inevitably have recalled the first book of Moses. John's prologue, which introduces Jesus by recalling the creation story ('in the beginning'), supplies a parallel.

'Jesus Christ' combines a personal name (one quite popular among Jews before 70 CE) with a title (cf. 2:4; 16:16, etc.). 'Son of David' prepares for the following genealogy, in which David is the key figure. It also explicates 'Christ': the anointed one fulfils the promises made to David (2 Sam 7:12–16; Isa 11:10; Zech 3:8; etc.). Jesus himself later acknowledges that he is 'the Christ' (16:13–20), and the title plays an important part in his trial (26:57–68).

'Son of Abraham' was not a messianic title but rather an expression used to refer either to a descendant of the patriarch or one worthy of him. Here both meanings may be present. Further, the phrase probably foreshadows the salvation Jesus brings to Gentiles. For Abraham was himself a Gentile by birth, and Gen 17:5 promises that all the nations will be blessed in him. It is fitting that soon after his birth Jesus is honoured by Gentile representatives, the magi (2:1–12).

The three personal names of 1:1 reappear in reverse order in 1:2–16: Jesus Christ—David—Abraham ‖ Abraham (1:2)—David (1:6)—Jesus Christ (1:16). So Matthew opens with a triad (one of his favourite literary devices) and a chiasmus.

(1:2–17) The genealogy first offers evidence for the title: it shows that Jesus is indeed a descendant of the royal Davidic line. Secondly, it makes Israel's history culminate in Jesus Christ: the Messiah is the goal of the biblical story. Thirdly, the genealogy helps to give the church its identity: the community, by virtue of its union with Jesus, shares his heritage.

The outstanding formal feature of this passage is its triadic structure: there are fourteen generations from Abraham to David, fourteen from David to the captivity, and fourteen from the captivity to Jesus (v. 17). The scheme is artificial. Not only have several names been omitted from the monarchial period, but there are only thirteen generations in the third series. (But cf. *v.l.* at v. 11.) Probably the key to understanding the composition is the device known as *gematria*, by which names are given numerical value (cf. Rev 13:18). In Hebrew David's name has three consonants, the numerical value of which amounts to fourteen: $d + w + d = 4 + 6 + 4$. When it is added that David's name is fourteenth on the list, that he is given the title, 'king', and that 'David' occurs both before and after the genealogy, we may infer that 'David' is the structural key to vv. 2–17.

Women are not usually named in Jewish genealogies, so the mention of Tamar, Rahab, Ruth, and the wife of Uriah must betray a special interest. Some have suggested that the reader should remember that the women were sinners, or that their marital unions were irregular, the lesson being either that God saves his people from their sins, or that providence can turn scandal into blessing (as in Matthew's story of Mary). But the best guess is that the four women are named because they were Gentiles: their presence in vv. 2–17 foreshadows the inclusion of non-Jews in the people of God.

(1:18–25) The story of Jesus' miraculous conception, like 1:1 and 1:2–17, continues to clarify Jesus' identity. He is conceived of the Holy Spirit. He will save his people from their sins. And he fulfils biblical prophecy (Isa 7:14). The passage also tells how Jesus can be a descendant of David and yet have a supernatural origin: although not literally Jesus' father, Joseph makes Jesus legally a Davidid by acknowledging him as his own. This passage (like the stories in Lk 1) is modelled upon older birth stories and so adds a hallowed cast to the narrative. Gen 16 (Ishmael) and Judg 13 (Samson), for example, also recount (1) introductory circumstances; (2) the appearance of the angel of the Lord; (3) an angelic prophecy of birth, including the child's future deeds; and (4) the issue of things. But Matthew's paragraph also resembles 2.13–15 and 19–21, the other two angelic appearances to Joseph. All three have this outline: (1) note of circumstance; (2) appearance of the angel of the Lord in a dream; (3) command of angel to Joseph; (4) explanation of command; (5) Joseph rises and obediently responds.

The story opens with Mary betrothed to Joseph; they do not yet live together as man and wife. But Mary is with child 'of the Holy Spirit'. One might think of a new creation (cf. MT 1:1), for creation was the work of the Spirit (Gen 1:2), or perhaps of the traditional link between the Spirit and messianic times (e.g. Isa 44:3–4). But the main point is that Jesus has his origin in God, in fulfilment of a prophecy, Isa 7:14. It is true that the Hebrew text says only that a 'young girl' will conceive, and that the LXX, which does indeed use 'virgin', seems only to mean that one who is now a virgin will later give birth; no miracle is envisaged. In Matthew, however, the text has been interpreted in the light of the story of the virgin birth, and it refers to the supernatural conception of Jesus.

Isa 7:14 speaks not only of a virgin birth but of 'Emmanuel', which means 'with us is God'. This does not entail that Jesus is God in the sense proclaimed at Nicea; Matthew's Christology is not that elevated. The idea here is rather that Jesus is the one through whom divine favour and blessing show themselves. At the same time, in 18:20; 25:31–46; and 28:20 (which makes an *inclusio* with v. 23) the presence of Jesus with his people is more than that: the divine presence is (as in Paul) conceived of as the presence of Christ.

When Joseph learns of his wife's state, he resolves, in accord with Jewish law, and because he thinks her guilty of adultery, to divorce her. This action is introduced with the observation that Joseph is 'just'. This matters for the interpretation of 5:31–2 and 19:3–12, where Jesus prohibits divorce except on the ground of *porneia*. There has been much debate over the Greek word, but if it does not mean unchastity within marriage, then the narrator would not be able to call Joseph 'just' for the course he purposes.

(2:1–12) The story of the mysterious magi, which overturns the traditional motif of the superiority of Jewish hero to foreign wise man, continues the theme of Davidic kingship. Jesus is born in Bethlehem, where David was brought up and anointed, and Mic 5:1, 3, which is here quoted as fulfilled in Jesus, is, in its original context, about a promised Davidic king. The central theme, however, is the homage of Gentiles. The magi, whose country of origin is unspecified—Persia, Babylon, and Arabia are the usual guesses—represent the best wisdom of the Gentile world, its spiritual élite. Perhaps Isa 60:3–6 is in the background. Num 23:7 LXX, according to which Balaam is 'from the east', almost certainly is. Jewish tradition made Balaam a magus and the father of magi; and, according to the OT, when the evil king Balak tried to enlist Balaam in the cause against Israel, the seer instead prophesied the nation's future greatness and the coming of a great ruler. This is close to Matthew, where the cruel Herod, attempting to destroy Israel's king, employs foreign magi who in the event bring only honour to the king's rival. Matthew's magi are Balaam's successors.

The 'star' goes before the magi and comes to rest 'over the place where the child' is. This is no ordinary star, and attempts to identify it with a planetary conjunction, comet, or supernova are futile. The *Protevangelium of James* (21.3), Ephrem the Syrian in his commentary on the *Diatessaron*, and Chrysostom in his commentary on Matthew all rightly recognize that the so-called star does not stay on high but moves as a guide and indeed comes to rest very near the infant Jesus. Matters become clear when we recall that the ancients generally believed stars to be animate beings, and Jews in particular identified them with angels (cf. Job 38:7). The *Arabic Gospel of the Infancy*, 7, and Theophylact must be right in identifying the magi's star with an angel, and one may compare the angelic guide of the Exodus (Ex 23:20, 23; 32:34).

Justin Martyr, *Dial.* 106, and other commentators have found the scriptural key to v. 2 in Num 24:17, where Balaam prophesies that a star will come out of Jacob, and a sceptre will rise out of Israel. This text was given messianic sense by ancient Jews (as in the targums); sometimes they identified the star with a messianic figure (CD 7:18–26), sometimes with a star heralding the Messiah (*T. Levi* 18:3). Matthew recounts the fulfilment of Balaam's prophecy.

The passage contains several elements which anticipate the story's end. Here as there the issue is Jesus' status as 'king of the Jews' (v. 2; 27:11, 29, 37). Here as there the Jewish leaders gather against him (vv. 3–4; 26:3–4, 57). Here as there plans are laid in secret (v. 7; 26:4–5). And here as there Jesus' death is sought (vv. 13, 16; 26:4). So the end is foreshadowed in the beginning. But there are also artistic contrasts. Here a light in the night sky proclaims the Messiah's advent; there darkness during the day announces his death (v. 2; 27:45). Here Jesus is worshipped; there he is mocked (26:67–8; 27:27–31, 39–44). Here it is prophesied that Jesus will shepherd his people Israel; there it is foretold that Jesus the shepherd will be struck and his sheep scattered (26:31). Here there is great rejoicing; there we find mourning and grief (26:75; 27:46).

(2:13–23) With 2:1–12 we move from a scene of gift-giving to one of murder and flight. The extremes of response to Jesus are here writ large. The quotation of Hos 11:1 in v. 15 evokes thought of the Exodus, for in its original context 'Out of Egypt I have called my son' concerns Israel. Our text accordingly offers a typological interpretation of Jesus' story. By going down to Egypt and then returning to the land of Israel Jesus recapitulates the experience of Israel. But there is, more particularly, a Moses typology here. vv. 19–21 borrows the language of Ex 4:19–20: just as Moses, after being told to go back to Egypt because all those seeking his life have died, takes his wife and children and returns to the land of his birth, so too with Jesus: Joseph, after being told to go back to Israel because all those seeking the life of his son have died, takes his wife and child and returns to the land of his son's birth.

A Moses typology in fact runs throughout Matthew's infancy narrative. Joseph's contemplation of what to do about Mary and the angel which bids him not to fear and then prophesies his son's future greatness recalls the story of Amram in Josephus, *Ant.* 2.210–16. In Josephus Moses' father, ill at ease over what to do about his wife's pregnancy, has a dream in which God exhorts him not to despair and prophesies his son's future greatness. 'You are to name him Jesus, for he will save his people from their sins' (1:21) reminds one of Moses' status as saviour of his people (Jos. *Ant.* 2.228; *b. Sot.a* 12b). Herod's order to do away with the male infants of Bethlehem (vv. 16–18) is like Pharaoh's order to do away with every male Hebrew child (Ex 1). And if Herod orders the slaughter of infants because he has learned of the birth of Israel's liberator (2:2–18), in Jewish tradition Pharaoh slaughters the children because he has learned of the birth of Israel's liberator (Jos. *Ant.* 2.205–9; *Tg. Ps.-J.* on Ex 1:15). Further, whereas Herod learns of the coming liberator from chief priests, scribes, and magi (2:1–12), Josephus, *Ant.* 2.205, 234, has Pharaoh learn of Moses from scribes, and the *Jerusalem Targum* on Ex 1:15 says that Pharaoh's chief magicians (Jannes and Jambres, the sons of Balaam) were the sources of his information. For further parallels see Allison (1993: 137–65), where the possibility of a tradition about Moses' virgin birth is raised.

The most difficult verse in the passage is the very last, v. 23. 'He will be called a Nazorean' does not appear in the OT. Yet Matthew refers to 'the prophets' being fulfilled. Many explanations have been put forward—the biblical text is Isa 11:1 (the branch [*nēṣer*] from Jesse) or 42:6 or 49:6 or Jer 31:6–7 or Gen 49:26, or we should think of Nazareth as a humble place and so connect it with the contempt for Isaiah's suffering servant. It is more likely, however, that Matthew contains an involved wordplay. The LXX interchanges 'holy one of God'—an early Christian title for Jesus (Mk 1:24; Lk 4:34; Jn 6:69)—and 'nazarite' (cf. Judg 13:7; 16:17). This matters because if we make that substitution in Isa 4:3 MT ('will be called holy'), the result is very near v. 23. Further, in Acts 24:5 Christians are 'the sect of the Nazarenes' (an appellation also attested in Tertullian, *Adv. Marc.* 4.8), and in rabbinic writings Christians are *nôṣrîm*. Given the striking links between Matthean Christianity and Nazorean Christianity as known through the fathers, as well as the fact that Syrian Christians called themselves *nāṣrāyā*, it is likely that members of the Matthean community referred to themselves not as 'Christians' (a term missing from this gospel) but as 'Nazoreans'. Certainly

that would have given v. 23 an even greater impact: Jesus' followers bear the name that he bore.

(3:1–6) Matthew passes from its hero's infancy to his adulthood and so jumps over many years (cf. Ex 2:11). The intervening period does not even merit allusion; and when readers move from Nazareth to the Jordan and far forward in time, they first meet not Jesus but John the Baptist. Throughout Matthew John has two distinguishing characteristics. First, he prepares Israel for Jesus' coming; that is, he is the eschatological Elijah (11:14; 17:11–13; here in v. 4 John even dresses like Elijah; see 2 Kings 1:8 LXX). He baptizes and preaches repentance in order to make the people ready to receive the person and work of Jesus. Secondly, John is Jesus' typological forerunner: his life parallels and so foreshadows that of Jesus. Both say similar things (cf. 3:2, 7, 10; 4:17; 7:19; 12:34; 23:33). Both attack the Sadducees and Pharisees (3:7–10; 12:1–14, 34; etc.). Both appeal to the same generation to repent (11:16–19). Both act by the same authority (21:23–32). Both are thought of as prophets (11:9; 14:5; 21:11, 26, 46) and feared by their enemies because of the people (14:5; 21:46). Both are seized and bound (14:3; 21:46; 27:1). Both are sentenced by reluctant authorities (14:6–11; 27:11–26). Both are executed as criminals (14:1–12; 26–7). And both are buried by their own disciples (14:12; 27:57–61).

John's ministry is the fulfilment of Isa 40:3 LXX, cited in v. 3. In the OT the prophecy is comfort for the exiles in Babylon: a new exodus and return to the land lie ahead. In Matthew the words no longer have to do with a literal restoration to Palestine. But the theme of new exodus remains in so far as the story of Jesus, who is so much like Moses, is a sort of replay of Israel's formative history. After the story of the birth of Israel's saviour and the wicked king's slaughter of innocent Jewish children Jesus passes through the waters of baptism—other texts compare baptism with passing through the Red Sea (1 Cor 10:1–5; *Sipre Num.* §108)—and then enters the desert, where he faces the temptations once faced by Israel and then goes up a mountain to give his commandments. The new Moses recapitulates Israel's Exodus.

(3:7–12) John preaches to the Pharisees and Sadducees. The two groups also appear together in 16:1–12. The former are Jesus' chief opponents and, with the scribes, come under withering attack in ch. 23. Matthew evinces a special, lively preoccupation with the Pharisees, and one infers that his own Jewish opponents considered themselves heirs of the Pharisees.

The Baptist divides his hearers into two categories—the fruitful and unfruitful, the wheat and the chaff. This sort of dualism runs throughout Matthew: things are usually black and white. There are those who do Jesus' words and those who do not (7:24–7); there are good and bad fish (13:47–50), sheep and goats (25:31–46). This division of humanity, which also characterizes the Dead Sea scrolls and Jewish apocalyptic literature, reflects the nearness of the eschatological judgement, at which only two sentences—salvation and damnation—will be passed.

John threatens that God can raise up or cause to be born children to Abraham from 'these stones'. As Chrysostom has observed, Isa 51:1–2 (where Abraham is the rock from which

Israel was hewn) is in the background. If God once brought forth from the lifeless Abraham descendants as numerous as the stars of heaven, so can he raise up a new people. The threat is aimed at what has been called 'covenantal nomism'. Many Jews no doubt assumed that to be a descendant of Abraham meant, if one did not commit apostasy, having a place in the world to come (cf. *m. Sanh.* 10.1). But in Matthew salvation is linked solely to Christology: one's decision for or against Jesus decides one's fate (cf. 10:32–3). This is why John denies the efficacy of Abrahamic descent and instead prophesies the coming one.

The prophecy of baptism in Holy Spirit and fire has traditionally been taken in two ways: either fire means the same thing as Spirit (cf. Acts 2), in which case there is only one baptism, or it refers to eschatological judgement, in which case there are two baptisms, one in the present and one in the future. Because Matthew elsewhere associates fire not with the Spirit but with judgement, the second interpretation is to be preferred.

(3:13–17) Matthew focuses not upon the baptism itself but a prefatory episode—John's protest of Jesus' desire for baptism—and subsequent events. Although Jesus' sinlessness is not taught in Matthew, it is probably assumed (cf. Jn 8:46; 2 Cor 5:21; Heb 7:26). And because John's baptism involves the confession of sins (3:6), Jesus' submission to it is awkward. But Matthew's Jesus declares that the act fulfils all righteousness. Here fulfilment is probably, as elsewhere, a reference to biblical prophecy. In line with this, v. 17 draws upon both Ps 2:7 and Isa 42:1. Jesus, knowing the messianic prophecies, obediently fulfils them and thereby fulfils all righteousness. Because prophecy declares God's will, to fulfil prophecy is to fulfil righteousness.

The appearance of the symbolic dove has occasioned much speculation. Since Tertullian it has often been connected with Noah's dove: the former dove announced deliverance from the flood, the latter dove deliverance from sins (cf. Theophylact and 1 Pet 3:20–1). It is also possible to associate the dove with the new-exodus motif, for in the *Mekilta* the Holy Spirit rests upon Israel as she crosses the Red Sea and the people are compared to a dove (cf. Ps.-Philo, *LAB* 21:6) and granted a vision. But the best guess relates the text to Gen 1:2, which involves the Spirit of God, water, and the imagery of a bird hovering. Further, in *b. Ḥag.* 15a the hovering of the Spirit over the face of the waters is represented more precisely as the hovering of a dove. The meaning is then once again that the last things are as the first: Jesus inaugurates a new creation. The correctness of this interpretation is confirmed by a Dead Sea scroll fragment, 4Q521. In line 6 ('his Spirit will hover over the poor') the language of Gen 1:2 characterizes the eschatological redemption: just as the Spirit once hovered over the face of the waters, so too, at the end, will the Spirit hover over the saints and strengthen them. This pre-Christian application of Gen 1:2 to the eschatological future has the Spirit hovering over human beings as opposed to lifeless material. The striking parallel with Matthew evidences a similar creative application of Gen 1:2.

The divine voice of v. 17, which anticipates 17:5, conflates two scriptural texts, Ps 2:7 and Isa 42:1 (which is formally quoted in 12:8). The result is that Jesus is revealed to the Baptist and to those standing by as the Son of God (cf. Ps 2:7) and the suffering servant of Isaiah (Isa 42:1; cf. 8:17; 12:18–21; 20:28; 26:28). Here 'Son of God' refers first to Jesus' special relationship to God the Father (cf. 11:25–30). But one cannot give a simple or single definition to the title; its connotations vary. In 4:1–11, as in 2:15, it is associated with an Israel typology; and in 16:13–20 and 26:59–68 it is linked with Jesus' status as Davidic Messiah (cf. 2 Sam 7:14; perhaps this is so also in 3:17, for Ps 2 is a royal psalm).

(4:1–11) This pericope has most commonly been given either a paraenetic interpretation according to which Jesus is the model disciple or a Christological interpretation according to which Jesus rejects a false understanding of political messiahship. Neither interpretation can be discounted; but Jesus' obedience as Son of God in the face of temptation is first of all a statement about salvation history: the Son of God now recapitulates the experience of Israel in the desert (cf. esp. Deut 8:2–3); the end resembles the beginning. Like Israel Jesus is tempted by hunger (Ex 16:2–8), tempted to put God to the test (Ex 17:1–4; cf. Deut 6:16), and tempted to idolatry (Ex 32). On each occasion he quotes from Deuteronomy— from Deut 8:3 in v. 4, from Deut 6:16 in v. 7, and from Deut 6:13 in v. 10. Unlike Israel, Jesus neither murmurs nor gives in to temptation.

Although the forty days of temptation are the typological equivalent of Israel's forty years of wandering, they also have rightly reminded Irenaeus, Augustine, Calvin, and many others of Moses' fast of forty days and forty nights (Ex 24:18). As in Mt 2, so also here: the Israel typology exists beside the Moses typology. In line with this, when the devil takes Jesus to a very high mountain to show him all the kingdoms of the world (v. 8), one may think of Moses on the top of Pisgah, for, among other things, not only does v. 8 use the language of Deut 34:1, 4 LXX, but Jewish tradition expands Moses' vision so that it is of all the world. See further Allison (1993: 165–72).

The three temptations contain a spatial progression: we move from a low place in the desert to a pinnacle in the temple to a mountain from which all the world can be seen. This progression corresponds to the dramatic tension which comes to a climax in the third temptation. The mountain here forms an *inclusio* with the mountain of 28:16–20. On the first mountain the devil offers to give Jesus all the kingdoms of the world and their glory on the condition that he worship him. On the last mountain, where Jesus is worshipped by others, Jesus declares that he has been given all authority in heaven and earth. The two texts mark the beginning and end of Jesus' labours: he rejects the devil's temptations, choosing instead to travel the hard road of obedient sonship which in the end brings exaltation.

The devil is the same as Satan (v. 10; 12:26; 16:23) and Beelzebul (10:25; 12:24, 27). He is 'the enemy' (13:39) who, in tempting Jesus, only acts as he does towards all (cf. 6:13; 26:41). But throughout Matthew he and his evil underlings (4:23; 8:16, 28; 9:32; 12:22; 23:39; 15:22; 17:18) always wear faces of defeat. The devil's failure with Jesus in the temptation narrative is paradigmatic: he nowhere wins. Jesus, for instance, easily casts out demons. So there is in Matthew a recognition of the limitations of the powers of iniquity. These are strictly circumscribed.

(4:12–17) On the literary level these verses signal the beginning of the public ministry, move Jesus from Nazareth to Capernaum, and introduce in summary fashion the content of Jesus' proclamation. On the theological level, they underline three recurring themes—the fulfilment of Scripture (vv. 14–16), the salvation of the Gentiles (v. 15), and the announcement of the kingdom of God (v. 17). This last calls the most attention to itself; for it not only repeats words of the Baptist (3:2), but the ingressive aorist (*ērxato*) connotes repetition: Jesus evidently utters the words again and again. So just as 1:1 stands over the whole gospel, so does v. 17 stand over the entire public ministry.

Jesus, like the Baptist, proclaims the nearness of the kingdom of God (or heaven; the expressions are, *pace* some scholars, equivalent). In Matthew this kingdom is God's eschatological rule which is even now establishing itself. In fact, it is entering the world through a complex of events, some of which have taken place (e.g. the Messiah's first advent; cf. 11:12: 12:28), some of which are taking place (e.g. 10:16–23), and some of which will take place in the near future (e.g. much of chs. 24, 25).

(4:18–22) The structure of the two short passages in this paragraph—(1) appearance of Jesus; (2) disciples at work; (3) call to discipleship; (4) obedient response—reappears in 9:9. The source of the common arrangement is 1 Kings 19:19–21, Elijah's call of Elisha. There Elijah appears and finds Elisha at work, after which the former puts his mantle upon the latter, that is, calls him to share his prophetic office. The story ends with Elisha following Elijah. The difference between Kings and the NT accounts is that whereas Elisha asks if he may first kiss his parents and perform a sacrifice and then is (in the LXX and Josephus' retelling) given permission so to act, in the NT Jesus permits no tarrying. His radical demand leaves no time even for saying farewell (cf. 8:21–2; 10:35–7). See further Hengel (1981). Within their broader context, vv. 18–22 illustrate the nature of Christian discipleship. They offer an example of wholehearted obedience to the call of Christ, an obedience which is expected of all, even to the point of great personal sacrifice. (Cf. further FGS F.)

(4:23–5:2) This is the first of many editorial summaries (of which there at least two between each major discourse). They do not just summarize what comes before or after, but also supply narrative continuity, lengthen narrative time, expand the geographical range, create a picture of movement (Jesus goes from here to there), highlight central themes, and tell us that Matthew's material is only a selection: Jesus did much more.

Between 4:23 and 9:35, which together create an *inclusio*, Jesus first teaches (the Sermon on the Mount—hereafter SM) and then secondly acts (chs. 8–9). Afterwards, in ch. 10, where he instructs and sends out the disciples for mission, he tells them to do and say what he has said and done. This circumstance means that Jesus is the model missionary, and it explains the parallelism not only between 4:23 and 9:35 but also between 4:17 and 10:6 and 4:24 and 10:1.

It is common to view the mountain of 5:1 as a counterpart to Sinai. As Matthew Henry had it, 'Christ preached this sermon, which is an exposition of the law, upon a mountain, because upon a mountain the law was given.' Matthew's

Greek (*anebē eis to oros*: he went up the mountain) does recall pentateuchal passages having to do with Moses (e.g. Ex 19:3, 12, 13). And Jewish tradition spoke of Moses *sitting* on Sinai (so already the *Exagogue* of Ezekiel; cf. *b. Meg.* 21a). Furthermore, other Moses typologies from antiquity have their Mosaic heroes sitting on a mountain (e.g. 2 Esdras 14); *Mekilta* on Ex 19:11 and 29:18 and other sources claim that Israel was healed at the foot of Sinai (cf. 4:23); and 8:1, the conclusion of the SM, is identical with Ex 34:29 LXX A, which recounts Moses' descent from Sinai.

In its entirety, this passage, which gives us a brief overview of Jesus' ministry to Israel, introduces the SM. It makes the crowds as well as the disciples hear Jesus, who heals them. So before the demands there is healing. The crowds, having done nothing, are benefited. Grace comes before task.

Jesus' Demands upon Israel (5:3–7:27)

4:23–5:2, which opens the SM, and 7:28–8:1, which concludes it, share several words and phrases—'great crowds followed him', 'the mountain', 'going up/down', 'teaching'. The correlations mark the intervening material in 5:3–7:27 as a distinct literary unit with its own beginning and end. Within that literary unit the eschatological blessings of the faithful in 5:3–12 are balanced by the eschatological warnings of 7:13–27.

The beatitudes are followed by 5:13–16 (salt and light), a section which supplies a general heading for the detailed paraenesis that follows. It is a transitional passage which moves from the life of the blessed future to the demands of life in the present, in which the theme switches from gift to task, and in which those who live as 5:17–7:12 directs are summarily characterized.

5:17–7:12 in turns divides itself into three major sections. There is first of all 5:17–48, on Jesus and Torah. Then there is the 'cult-didache' (Betz 1985) in 6:1–18. It covers properly ecclesiastical issues—almsgiving, prayer, fasting. Thirdly there is 6:19–7:12, the first half of which has to do with worldly goods and cares (6:19–34), the second with, primarily, attitude towards others (7:1–12). So the section in its entirety covers social issues. One suspects that the very structure of the SM reflects the famous maxim attributed to Simeon the Just, according to which the world stands on three things—Torah, temple service, and pious social acts (*m. 'Abot* 1.2). The period after 70 CE evidently saw discussion of the traditional pillars because the second, after the destruction of the temple, became problematic (cf. '*Abot R. Nat.* 4). Was the SM a Christian answer to the old Jewish question, What does the world stand upon?

Valid interpretation of the SM must keep several things in view. First, the SM is not an adequate or complete summation of anybody's religion (contrast Betz 1985; Betz interprets the SM as an epitome). It was never intended to stand by itself; it is rather part of a larger whole. The SM's demands are perverted when isolated from the grace and Christology which appear from Matthew in its entirety. The SM is in the middle of a story about God's gracious overture to his people through his Son. Read in its entirety it brings together gift and task, grace and law, benefit and demand. Secondly, the SM presupposes the existence of the Christian community. This is why God is 'our Father'. The church is the surrogate family which lightens the Messiah's Torah: tasks jointly undertaken become easier. In addition, the church belongs to salvation history; its story is the story of Israel and the story of Jesus, and these stories, it is assumed, have altered human existence and changed the historical possibilities. Thirdly, the SM must be associated with the Kingdom of God. The SM does not speak to ordinary people in ordinary circumstances. It instead addresses itself to those overtaken by an overwhelming reality. This reality can remake the individual and beget a new life. Beyond that, the SM sees all through the eyes of eternity. It does not so much look forward, from the present to the consummation, as back from the consummation to the present. Mt 5–7 presents the unadulterated will of God because it proclaims the will of God as it will be lived when the kingdom comes in its fullness. This is why the SM is so radical, so heedless of all earthly contingencies, why it always blasts complacency and shallow moralism and disturbs every good conscience.

Finally, the SM is a Christological document. Not only do the beatitudes imply that Jesus is the eschatological herald of Isa 61, but the qualities they praise—e.g. meekness and mercy—are manifested throughout the ministry (cf. 9:27–31; 11:29: 20:29–34; 21:5). Again, the paragraph about turning the other cheek (5:38–42) has been moulded so as to foreshadow events from the last days of Jesus, and the Lord's Prayer is echoed in Jesus' own prayer (see 26:42). The SM then is partly a summary of its speaker's deeds; or, put differently, Jesus illustrates his demands. In Matthew Jesus is a moral model, and the SM proclaims likeness to the God of Israel (5:48) through the virtues of Jesus Christ.

(5:3–12) The beatitudes do not exhibit any obvious structure; but it may be significant that the triad is the structural key to the SM and that there are nine (= 3 × 3) beatitudes (cf. Epiphanius, *Apophthegmatu Putrum*, 13, where the number of the beatitudes is reckoned as three times the Trinity). However that may be, vv. 3–12 contain first of all eschatological blessings; that is, the beatitudes are first of all promise and consolation. The first half of each beatitude depicts the community's present; the second half foretells the community's future; and the juxtaposition of the two radically different situations permits the trials of everyday life to be muted by contemplation of the world to come. This hardly excludes the implicit moral demand: one is certainly called to become what the beatitudes praise (cf. the beatitudes in Sir 25:7–10; 4Q525 2). But Matthew's beatitudes are not formally imperatives. Like the eschatological blessings in 13:16 and Rev 19:9 and 22:14, they offer hope and indeed function as a practical theodicy. Although there is no explanation of evil, the imagination, through contemplation of God's future, engenders hope and makes the present tolerable.

Because Isa 61:1, 2, and 7 speak of good news for the poor (cf. Mt 5:3), comforting all who mourn (cf. Mt 5:4), and of inheriting the earth or land (cf. Mt 5:5), Matthew's beatitudes make an implicit Christological claim: they are uttered by the anointed one of Isa 61. The Spirit of the Lord is upon Jesus (3:16); he has been anointed to bring good tidings to the poor, to bind up the brokenhearted, to proclaim liberty to the captives, to comfort those who mourn (cf. Lk 4:18–19 and the messianic application of Isa 61 in 4Q521).

There is nothing formally remarkable about Matthew's beatitudes. The form, 'blessed' (*makarios*) + subject + 'that'

(*hoti*) clause, is attested elsewhere (cf. Gen 30:13; Tob 13:16), as are the eschatological orientation (cf. Dan 12:12; 1 *Enoch* 58:2–3), the grouping together of several beatitudes (cf. 4Q525 2; 2 *Enoch* 52:1–14), and the third person plural address (cf. *Pss. Sol.* 17:44; Tob 13:14).

'Blessed are the poor in spirit' (cf. 1QM 14:7) means much the same as 'blessed are the meek', and 'for theirs is the kingdom of heaven' is another way of saying 'they will inherit the earth' (cf. Ps 37:11). Both beatitudes are about eschatological reversal. Those who are without power or status and who depend upon God will be given the kingdom of heaven and inherit the earth when things are turned upside down at the last judgement. As it says in *b. Pesah.*. 50a, 'those who are on top here are at the bottom there, and those who are at the bottom here are on the top there'.

'Those who mourn' (v. 4) are not, against Augustine, sorry for their sins so much as they are aggrieved that while now the wicked prosper, the saints do not, and God has not yet righted the situation. The 'righteousness' that the saints hunger and thirst for (v. 6) is neither justification nor eschatological vindication but the right conduct that God requires (cf. v. 10). Seemingly implied is the notion that the saints are not as a matter of fact righteous; rather, righteousness is always the goal which lies ahead: it must ever be sought. To be 'pure in heart' (v. 8; cf. Ps 24:3–4) means harmony between inward thought and outward deed; it involves a singleness of intention, that intention being the doing of God's will. To 'see God' (v. 8) has been understood as a literal vision of God's body (cf. *Ps. Clem. Hom.* 17:7), a literal vision of the glorified Christ (cf. 17:1–8; Cor 15:3–11; so Philoxenus), a spiritual or mental apprehension (cf. 'I see the point'; see Origen, *C. Cels.* 7.33–4), an indirect perception through unspecified effects of God (cf. Irenaeus, *Adv. haer.* 4.20.6), or an apprehension of the image of God in the perfected saints (so Gregory of Nyssa and much Eastern Orthodox tradition). The text unfortunately does not decide the point. But one thing is obvious: the vision of God is here eschatological. Nothing is said of the possibility of seeing God in the present life. One day the saints will enjoy what the angels, according to 18:10, even now experience (cf. Augustine, *De civ. dei* 22.29). (Cf. further FGS G.)

The last two beatitudes (vv. 10–12) envisage the most difficult aspects of discipleship—persecution and ridicule. They offer consolation not only by promising reward in heaven but also by observing the similar ill-treatment of 'the prophets'. The effect is to draw into Israel's sacred history the community of readers who find themselves in Matthew's text.

(5:13–16) The parables about salt, light, and lamp are the general heading for 5:17–7:12. They together offer a summary description of those who live the SM. It is no longer the Torah or the temple or Jerusalem or Israel that is the salt or light of the world (cf. Isa 60:1–3; Bar 4:2; *b. Ber.* 28b) but the church. Moreover, Jesus' followers are not the salt or light of Israel (contrast *T. Levi* 14:3) but of the whole world (the Gentile mission is presupposed). 'What the soul is in a body, this the Christians are in the world' (*Ep. Diogn.* 6.1).

(5:17–20) In denying the suspicion that Jesus abolishes the Torah, these verses look forwards, not backwards, for no such suspicion could arise from what has gone before. They introduce 5:21–48 and declare that the so-called 'antitheses' are not antitheses: Matthew's Jesus does not overturn Moses or set believers free from the law. (Alternative interpretations of this passage are often motivated by a desire to bring Matthew closer to Paul; but the NT appears to have more than one judgement on the status of the Torah, and we should read Matthew on its own terms.)

These verses not only rebut in advance a wrong interpretation of 5:21–48 but also supply a clue for the right interpretation. In announcing that the righteousness of disciples must exceed that of the Jewish leaders, v. 20 anticipates that Jesus' words in the subsequent paragraphs will require even more than the Torah itself requires. The tension between Jesus' teaching and the Mosaic law is not that those who accept the former will transgress the latter; rather it is that they will achieve far more than they would if the Torah were their only guide.

(5:21–48) This section, which falls into two triads— 5:21–6 + 27–30 + 31–2 ‖ 5:33–7 + 38–42 + 43–8—has generated many conflicting interpretations, but four propositions seem more probable than not. First, 5:21–48 does not set Jesus' words over against Jewish interpretations of the Mosaic law; rather there is contrast with the Bible itself. 'You have heard that it was said to those of ancient times' refers to Sinai. Secondly, although Jesus' words are contrasted with the Torah, the two are not contradictory (cf. 5:17–20). Certainly those who obey vv. 21–48 will not find themselves breaking any Jewish law. Thirdly, 5:21–48 is not Jesus' interpretation of the law. The declaration that remarriage is adultery, for example, is set forth as a new teaching grounded not in exegesis but Jesus' authority. Fourthly, the six paragraphs illustrate, through concrete examples, what sort of attitude and behaviour Jesus requires and how his demands surpass those of the Torah without contradicting the Torah.

Many have complained that the teaching of vv. 21–48 is impractical. As Dostoevsky's Grand Inquisitor says, Jesus 'judged humanity too highly', for 'it was created weaker and lower than Christ thought'. But the SM, which is so poetical, dramatic, and pictorial, offers not a set of rules—the ruling on divorce is the exception—but rather seeks to instil a moral vision. Literal (mis)interpretation accordingly leads to absurdities. The text, which implies that God demands a radical obedience which cannot be casuistically formulated, functions more like a story than a legal code. Its primary purpose is to instil principles and qualities through a vivid inspiration of the moral imagination. What one comes away with is not an incomplete set of statutes but an unjaded impression of a challenging moral ideal. That ideal may ever be beyond grasp, but that is what enables it ever to beckon its adherents forward.

(5:21–6) Moses prescribes punishment for murder (cf. Ex 21:12; etc.), Jesus punishment for anger and insulting speech. The hyperbolic equation of murder with anger (also found in Jewish tradition) shifts attention from the outward act to the inward state (cf. 5:27–30) and makes anger and harsh words grievous sins to be exorcized at all costs. In contrast to later Christian interpretation, Jesus makes no allowance for justified anger (such as anger towards the devil). This seems to take us beyond the wisdom tradition, which permits, even

encourages, appropriate hatred and anger (cf. Sir 1:22; Eph 4:26).

(5:27–30) Jesus' prohibition of lust and its equation with adultery (cf. T. Iss. 7:2) do not contradict the biblical injunction against adultery (Ex 20:14; Deut 5:18), for Jesus himself speaks against this sin (5:32; 15:19; 19:9). Rather does he pass beyond the Decalogue to require more: vv. 27–30 at once uphold and supplement the law. While the verses assume that the external act is evil, no less evil is the intention that brings it forth, and 'it is each one's intention that is examined' (Ps.-Phoc. 52; cf. Ep. Arist. 133; in holding that intention is to be judged as deed—as also in 5:21–6—Jesus is closer to the rabbis associated with the House of Shammai than those associated with Hillel; see b. Qidd. 43a). Matthew's construction (pros to epithumēsai, 'to lust') implies that the sin lies not in the entrance of a thought but in letting it incite to wrongful passion.

The vivid demands for personal sacrifice in vv. 29–30 (which reappear in 18:8–9) are hyperbolic: they underscore the seriousness of the sin. Literal amputation is hardly envisaged, for the problem is not the body as such but the sin that dwells in it (cf. Rom 7:17, 20). Nor should we (despite Jn 20:20, 25) visualize a mutilated resurrected body. The bizarre images, which arouse the imagination and enhance memory, instead underline that one cannot disclaim responsibility by blaming the body. Actions are psychosomatic, and body and soul, being united, are judged as one accountable individual.

(5:31–2) If lust is like adultery, so too is divorce. Jesus summarizes Deut 24:1–4, where allowance is made for remarriage, and then goes on to say that (for a man) to divorce (a woman) except for porneia causes her (because she will remarry) to commit adultery. As it stands no explanation is offered; but 19:3–9 will provide such. The assumption is that monogamy must be upheld.

Erasmus and most Protestants have thought Matthew allows the innocent party to divorce and remarry in the event of porneia. But according to the almost universal patristic as well as Roman Catholic opinion, separation but not remarriage is permitted. Unfortunately the text does not admit of a definitive interpretation.

The meaning of porneia has been disputed. Most take it to mean either sexual unfaithfulness within marriage or incest. In favour of the latter, we can envisage a situation in which Gentiles entering the community were found to be, because of marriages made before conversion, in violation of the levitical laws of incest (see Lev 17). But there is no patristic support for the equation of porneia with adultery, and in 1:18–25 Joseph, who determines to divorce his wife because of suspected adultery, is 'just'—an odd comment if Jesus' ruling does not cover his case.

(5:33–7) The OT permits oaths in everyday speech—provided they are neither false nor irreverent. But for Jesus oaths are not needed (cf. Jas 5:12); for the presupposition behind the oath is that there are two types of statements, one of which demands commitment (the oath), one of which does not (the statement without an oath). But Jesus enjoins invariable commitment to every statement so that the oath becomes superfluous.

The paragraph opens by summarizing the teaching found in Ex 20:7; Lev 19:12; Num 30:3–15, and elsewhere. Perhaps Ps 50:14 in particular is in mind. Despite the reservation shown to oaths in some Jewish sources (e.g. Sir 23:9; *m. Dem.* 2:3), one wonders whether Jesus' command is to be understood literally as forbidding all oaths. (Tolstoy went so far as to affirm that Jesus' words require the abolition of courts.) Perhaps indeed the situation envisaged is not swearing in court but swearing in everyday speech. However that may be, early Christian literature does not show much aversion to swearing (e.g. Gal 1:20; Rev 10:6; *Prot. Jas.* 4:1), and Matthew itself seems to presuppose the validity of certain oaths (23:16–22). Further, the reduction of speech to 'yes, yes' and 'no, no' is obviously hyperbole. (The meaning of this last appears to be: let your yes be true and your no be true; or perhaps: let your yes be only yes—not yes and an oath—and let your no be no—not no and an oath.)

In the Mishnah oaths by heaven, by earth, and by one's own head are all viewed as not binding by at least some authorities (e.g. *m. Ned.* 1.3). This may explain their appearance here. If it was claimed by some that oaths by heaven or earth or Jerusalem or one's head were, because not binding, not covered by Jesus' prohibition, vv. 34–5 counters by linking heaven and earth and Jerusalem to God, thereby making all oaths binding and so nullifying any casuistic attempt to circumvent v. 34a.

(5:38–42) Following the citation of the law of reciprocation in v. 38 (cf. Ex 21:24; Lev 24:20; Deut 19:21) Jesus goes on to offer a general principle in v. 39 which has four illustrations: the disciple is (1) personally insulted then (2) taken to court then (3) impressed to do a soldier's bidding then (4) asked to help one in need of funds. The brief scenes vividly represent the demand for an unselfish temperament, for naked humility and a willingness to suffer the loss of one's personal rights: evil should be requited with good. There is no room for vengeance on a personal level (cf. Rom 12:19).

These verses are not a repudiation of Moses. While in the Pentateuch the *lex talionis* belongs to the judiciary process, this is not the sphere of application in Matthew. Jesus does not overthrow the principle of equivalent compensation on an institutional level—that question is just not addressed—but declares it illegitimate for his followers to apply it to their private disputes.

This passage shares language with Isa 50:4–9 LXX. There are also thematic parallels—both this and Isa 50:4–11 depict the unjust treatment of an innocent individual and use the terminology of the lawcourt. Clearly Matthew alludes to the third Servant Song; the allusion does more than inject a vague scriptural aura, rather do we see the truth when we observe that Isa 50:4–9 is again alluded to in the passion narrative, in 26:67 (cf. 27:30): the scriptural text associated with turning the other cheek is also associated with the passion of Jesus. Furthermore, of the seven words shared by this passage and Isa 50:4–9, two appear again in the passion narrative—'strike' (*rapizō*) (26:67) and 'cloak/clothes' (27:31, 35). Indeed, 'strike' appears only twice in the First Gospel, here in v. 39 and in 26:67; and in both places an innocent person is struck—just as in v. 40 and 27:31, 35, an innocent person's clothes are taken. So the allusions to Isa 50:4–9 are in effect allusions to the passion of Jesus. Put otherwise, this passage superimposes three images: the suffering Christian, the suffering Christ, and the suffering servant. Jesus' own story offers an illustration of his imperative. If he speaks of eschewing violence and not resisting evil, of being slapped, of having one's clothes taken, and of being compelled to serve the Romans, the conclusion to his own life makes his words concrete: he eschews violence (26:51–4); he does not resist evil (26:36–56; 27:12–14); he is struck (26:67); he has his garments taken (27:28, 35); and his cross is carried by one requisitioned by Roman order (27:32). Here then we meet two themes found throughout Matthew: the congruence between word and deed, speech and action—an idea so important for Hellenistic philosophy—and Jesus' status as moral exemplar, which requires an imitation of Christ.

(5:43–8) The material on love of one's enemy, as the last of the six paragraphs introduced by 5:17–20, is climactic, and it contains the most important and most difficult commands. Jesus begins by quoting Lev 19:18 ('Love your neighbour'), which he will again quote—and uphold—in 19:19 and 22:39. But 'hate your enemy' is not found in the OT, although similar sentiments appear (e.g. Deut 7:2; the closest parallels occur in the Dead Sea scrolls, where the sons of light hate the sons of darkness). Jesus does not contradict Lev 19:18 but goes beyond it. For the Pentateuch understands 'neighbour' as fellow Israelite, and this allows one to confine love to one's own kind, or even to define 'neighbour' in opposition to 'enemy'. These verses, however, give 'neighbour' its broadest definition (cf. Lk 10:29–37). If one loves even one's enemies, who will not be loved?

The context equates enemies with those who persecute the faithful. This means those enemies are not just one's personal opponents but God's opponents. Further, 'love' is clarified by what follows: one must pray for enemies, do good to them, and greet them. Jesus is speaking of actions which benefit others. In this the disciple is only imitating God, who causes the sun to shine and the rain to fall upon all, not just the righteous.

v. 48 belongs first to the unit that begins in v. 43. Certainly the motif of imitating God takes one back to v. 45. At the same time v. 48 is the fitting culmination of all of 5:21 ff., for throughout the section Jesus asks for 'perfection', for something that cannot be surpassed. What more can be done about lust if it has been driven from one's heart? And who else is left to love after one has loved the enemy? 'Be perfect' is not a call to sinlessness; nor does the imperative posit two sorts of believers, the merely good on the one hand and the perfect on the other. Jesus' call to perfection is a call to completeness.

(6:1–18) While the subject of 5:21–48 is Jesus and the Torah, in vv. 1–18 the cult becomes the subject. The former has mostly to do with actions, the latter with intentions. That is, this passage is a sort of commentary on 5:21–48: having been told *what* to do, one now learns *how* to do it.

The little cult-didache opens with a general statement of principle. Righteousness is not to be done in order to be seen by others (cf. Rom 2:28–9); right deeds must come from right intention, which involves humility and self-forgetfulness (v. 1). The idea is elaborated upon in the three subsequent paragraphs. The first is on almsgiving, the second on prayer, the third on fasting. Each opens with a declaration of subject (vv. 2*a*, 5*a*, 16*a*), follows with a prohibition of wrong practice (vv. 2*b*, 5*b*, 16*b*), and gives instruction on proper practice (vv. 3–4, 6, 17–18).

vv. 2–4 concern not whether one gives alms but how. The teaching is akin to *b. B. Bat.* 9b: 'One who gives charity in secret is greater than Moses.' The blowing of a trumpet is probably just a picturesque way of indicating the making of an announcement or the calling of attention to oneself. But trumpets may sometimes have been blown when alms were asked for (cf. *b. Ber.* 6b), so it is just possible that some unknown custom is being protested. There may also be a pun on the shofar chests that were set up in the temple and in the provinces. If the trumpet-shaped receptacles for alms could be made to resound when coins were thrown into them, perhaps our verse was originally a polemical barb at the practice.

The section on prayer, vv. 5–15, rejects praying in public places with the intent to be seen by others and then goes on to spurn long-winded or repetitious prayer (cf. Eccles 5:2; Matthew's 'do not heap up empty phrases as the Gentiles do' is consistent with his audience being largely Jewish Christians). There follows the Lord's prayer, a model of brevity. Although Christian tradition has usually understood the prayer as having to do with everyday needs, much is to be said for interpreting it as an eschatological prayer. 'Hallowed be your name', 'your kingdom come', and 'your will be done' may ask God to usher in his everlasting reign. The request for 'bread of the morrow' (NRSV marg.) may be a prayer for the bread of life or heavenly manna of the latter days. 'Forgive us our debts' may envisage the coming judgement. And 'do not bring us to the time of trial' may refer to the messianic woes (cf. Rev 3:10), (see further Lk 11:1–13).

The Lord's prayer is followed by two verses on forgiveness. A similar sequence appears in Mt 11:23–5 and Lk 17:3–6. There appears to have been a traditional connection between prayer and forgiveness: prayer is not efficacious unless the members of the community are reconciled to each other.

(6:19–34) The four paragraphs which make up this passage have to do with earthly treasure—vv. 19–21 with not storing it up, vv. 22–3 with being generous, v. 24 with serving God instead of mammon, and vv. 25–34 with not being anxious about food and clothing.

The passage contains three antitheses—earth/heaven (vv. 19–21), darkness/light (vv. 22–3), wealth (= mammon)/God (v. 24). The focus of the first is the heart, the second the eye, the third service. The determination of the heart to store up treasure in heaven or on earth creates either inner light or darkness while the resultant state of one's 'eye' (intent) moves one to serve either God or mammon. So one's treasure tells the tale of one's heart.

vv. 22–3 do not liken the eyes to a window but to a lamp (cf. Dan 10:6; Zech 4; *b. Šabb.* 151b). The picture is not of light going in but of light going out. This accords with the common pre-modern understanding of vision, according to which the eyes have their own light (so e.g. Plato and Augustine). To say that when one's eye is 'healthy' (generous, cf. Prov 22:9; *m. 'Abot* 2.19) one is full of light means that generosity is proof of the light within—just as to say that when one's eye is 'un-

healthy' (ungenerous, cf. 20:15) one is full of darkness means that covetousness is a sign of inner darkness. vv. 24–34 follow 19–23 as encouragement follows demand. The commands to serve God instead of mammon, especially when interpreted in the light of the rest of the gospel (e.g. 5:39–42; 19:16–30), are difficult, and their observance will bring insecurity. So vv. 24–34 are the pastor's addendum: they are respite from the storm that is the SM. Those who undertake the hard demands of the gospel have a Father in heaven who gives good gifts to his children.

(7:1–12) Matthew now turns from one social issue, what to do with and about mammon (6:19–34), to another, how to treat one's neighbour. The new subject opens with the imperative not to judge or condemn. This is not a prohibition of simple ethical judgements but rather a way of calling for mercy, humility, and tolerance. The verses about the 'speck' and the 'log' (vv. 3–5) continue the theme of vv. 1–2 but focus on hypocrisy (cf. Jn 7:53–8:11; Rom 2:1). But v. 6 is difficult. Some have even thought it without meaning in its present context. The point, however, is that if there must not be too much severity (vv. 1–5), there must at the same time not be too much laxity (v. 6). While this much is plain, one does not know whether 'your pearls' stands for any particular thing. Should we think of the gospel itself (cf. 13:45–6) or of esoteric teachings or practices? vv. 7–11 follow. They are the twin of 6:24–34. Both follow an exhortation (6:19–21; 7:1–2), a parable on the eye (6:22–3; 7:3–5), and a second parable (6:24; 7:6), and both refer to the heavenly Father's care for his own. Both also argue from the lesser to the greater and offer encouragement for those bombarded by the hard instruction in the rest of the SM.

The Golden Rule (which was well known to pre-Christian Jewish tradition) brings to a climax the central section of the SM (5:17–7:11). Mention of 'the law and the prophets' creates an *inclusio* within which Matthew has treated the law, the cult, and social issues. v. 12 is then, in rabbinic fashion, a general rule which is not only the quintessence of the law and the prophets but also of the SM. Interpreted within this gospel as a whole it is certainly not an expression of 'naive egoism' (Bultmann 1963: 103); nor is it even an expression of 'common sense' or 'natural law' (Theophylact). Rather, as Luz (1985: 430) has it, the Golden Rule is 'radicalized' by the SM: 'everything, without exception, which is demanded by love and the commandments of Jesus you should do for other people'.

(7:13–29) The SM winds down with warnings. There is first the declaration about the two ways (vv. 13–14), then the warnings about false prophets (vv. 15–23), then the parable of the two builders (vv. 24–7). All this balances the blessings which open the SM.

v. 14 is not a dogmatic calculation that most human beings will go to hell. Not only does this interpretation clash with the use of 'many' in 8:11 and 20:28, but hyperbolic declarations are common in Jewish hortative material (cf. *m. Qidd.* 1.10: 'If one performs a single commandment it will be well with him and he shall have length of days and shall inherit the land; but if he neglects a single commandment it shall be ill with him and he shall not have length of days and shall not inherit the land'). It probably means that one should act *as if* only a very few will enter Paradise.

editor@salvationhistory.com

Katy —
503 690 8619

Mt 6:21

" For wherever your
treasure is, there your
heart will be also."

The identity of the false prophets in vv. 15-23 is unknown, although suggestions abound (e.g. Pharisees, antinomians, enthusiasts). We can say no more than that they were Christians (cf. 7:21) whom Matthew wished to attack (cf. 24:23-8).

The memorable concluding parable in 7:24-7 stresses the gravity of Jesus' imperatives by taking a dualistic point of view: there are really only two responses, obedience and disobedience, and only two human fates, salvation and destruction. Shades of grey do not have much place in Matthew's moral exhortation. Many take the storm that strikes the two houses to stand for the calamities and afflictions of everyday life, but in the OT God's judgement can come in a storm (as with Noah's flood); and in later Jewish literature the trials of the latter days are sometimes pictured as terrible tempests (e.g. 2 Apoc. Bar. 53:7-12). Maybe our parable should conjure up in the mind the storm of the eschatological ordeal.

vv. 28-9, which conclude the SM, should not be quickly passed over. First, the items it shares with 4:23-52 make the beginning and end of the SM mirror each other. Secondly, the line is similar to others which close chs. 10, 13, 18, and 24-5 and helps clarify the outline of the entire book (see MT E.11). Thirdly, one is put in mind of a formula used in Deut 31:1, 24 and 32:45. It seems likely enough, given the clear allusions to Moses in 5:1-2 and 8:1 (cf. Ex 34:29 LXX), that vv. 28-9 are one more piece of Matthew's Moses typology.

Jesus' Deeds within and for Israel (8:1-9:34)

Following the challenge of Jesus' difficult speech in the SM, this passage gives us the challenge of his merciful deeds, which are performed for people from the margins of Jewish society or without status—a leper, a Roman's servant, Peter's mother-in-law, two demoniacs, etc.—and are grouped into three triads; see MT E.3.

(8:1-4) The story of Jesus cleansing a leper—the disease is probably not what we know as leprosy but may be any one of several skin diseases—echoes both Num 12 (Moses heals Miriam) and 2 Kings 5:1-14 (Elisha heals Nathan). It comes appropriately here as illustration of one of the central themes of the SM: Jesus, who sends the healed man to a priest, observes the law of Moses (cf. Lev 13:49). But the story also links up with what follows. 11:5 makes the cleansing of lepers an item of eschatological expectation; so these verses stand as fulfilment to prophecy. Further, 10:8 instructs missionaries to heal lepers and so extends the notion of the imitation of Christ.

(8:5-13) A nameless Roman centurion, an exemplar of faith, asks help from Jesus the Jew: a Roman commander becomes a suppliant. The request is for the man's 'son' or 'servant' (the Gk. is ambiguous). Jesus' response is apparently a question: 'Should I come and cure him?' (my tr.). Jesus hesitates to help a Gentile (cf. 15:24). But the soldier wins him over by a declaration of faith: Jesus, whose spiritual authority is analogous to the centurion's military authority, needs only speak a word. Jesus' response is threefold: (1) he declares that no one in Israel has such faith; (2) he makes a prophetic threat using the language of Ps 107:3—'the heirs of the kingdom' (which cannot mean all Jews) will suffer eschatological rejection while many from east and west (Gentiles or diaspora Jews)

will enjoy eschatological salvation—and (3) he heals the boy. (Cf. further FGS H.)

(8:14-17) Following the simple short story of the healing of Peter's mother-in-law there is a brief summary (cf. 4:23-5; 9:35) which offers the NT's only explicit citation of Isa 53. (But Matthew alludes to the chapter in 20:28; 27:12; 26:28.) The quotation attributes Jesus' healings to his spirit of self-sacrifice.

(8:18-22) Before the next three miracle stories there are two encounters which emphasize the hardships of discipleship. The encounters belong here because they illustrate the moral of the stilling of the storm, which is a symbolic illustration of what it means to follow Jesus. The first, vv. 19-20, in which a scribe addresses Jesus as 'teacher' (not 'Lord') and is not asked to follow, may offer a negative illustration, whereas the second, vv. 21-2, in which Jesus is called 'Lord' and issues the call, 'Follow me', may offer a positive illustration. v. 20 could allude to Ps 8: 'the Son of Man', who has nowhere to lay his head, in truth has all things under his feet, including the birds of the air. v. 22, which many have thought in tension with the commandment to honour father and mother, demands that 'the [spiritually] dead' take care of burial: Jesus must be followed now. The shocking saying should not be explained away as a mistranslation of a hypothetical Aramaic original or in terms of secondary burial or rites of mourning. Only a little more plausible is the attempt to find here an idiom expressing the duty of caring for one's aged parents until they are dead. More likely we should find here a prophetic consciousness which can, 'according to the need of the hour' (b. Yebam. 90b), flout custom and law (cf. Jer 16:1-9; Ezek 24). In any case early Christian texts follow Jewish tradition in making burial an act of lovingkindness (27:57-61, etc.).

(8:23-7) The stilling of the storm is 'a kerygmatic paradigm of the danger and glory of discipleship' (Bornkamm 1963: 57). The sea and its storm symbolize the world and its difficulties (cf. Ps 65:5; 69:1-2), and the ship is, as in patristic exegesis, the church. So the main point is that discipleship requires faith in Jesus in the midst of trial. But there is also a Christological message. Jesus is a prophet greater than Jonah. (The parallels with Jonah are obvious; cf. esp. v. 24 with Jon 1:4 MT.) Unlike Jonah, Jesus does not pray to God but directly addresses the storm; and in stilling the cosmic forces of evil that threaten the created order (cf. Ps 46; Rev 13:1; 21:1), he exercises the power of YHWH himself (cf. Ps 65:7; Isa 51:9-10).

(8:28-34) This narrative continues the theme of Jesus' authority. It may depict the healing of Gentiles (cf. 8:5-13). Such is suggested by the location in the Decapolis and the fact that swine are being raised nearby. On the other hand, the population along the east coast of the Sea of Galilee was mixed, and in the other cases where Jesus bends his rule of confining his mission to the lost sheep of the house of Israel this is made plain (8:5-13; 15:21-8). In either event Jesus sends the demons into the water—apparently a punishment as they were thought to prefer dry places (cf. 12:43). But this success does not garner support for Jesus' cause. As elsewhere his service for others generates hostility: good is repaid with evil.

(9:1–8) In the story of the man sick with palsy Jesus—now home in Capernaum (cf. 4:13)—sees and responds to the faith of those who bring a paralytic: he forgives the man's sins. The story presupposes that the infirmity has a spiritual cause (cf. Ex 20:5; 1 Cor 11:29–30; Jas 5:14–15; in 9:32–4 a demon makes a man deaf and dumb). So by forgiving sins Jesus uproots the cause of the paralysis. Although 4QPrNab proves that at least some Jews could think of one person forgiving another's sins (with healing as the result), in Matthew the scribes object that Jesus has spoken evil ('blaspheming') because he has done what only God can do. Jesus, however, urges that it is easier to pronounce the forgiveness of sins than to command someone to walk, this because only the latter can be objectively verified. Further, because Jesus, in the event, can in fact make the paralytic walk and so do the harder thing, others must wonder whether he cannot also forgive sins.

(9:9–13) The first verse is an extraordinarily brief call story with the same structure as the two stories in 4:18–22; see above. The arrangement depends upon 1 Kings 19:19–21. In the objection story in vv. 10–13, which may be set in Peter's house, Pharisees denigrate Jesus by asking how he can eat with tax collectors and sinners, that is, those who through apostasy have removed themselves from the covenant. Jesus responds with a proverb (the sick need a physician), a scripture (Hos 6:6), and a declaration about his mission (in which the 'righteous' are apparently the '(self-)righteous'). The scripture, again quoted in 12:7, was probably an important text for Johannan ben Zakkai in the period after 70 CE: it helped people come to terms with the destruction of the temple. Perhaps then Matthew's use of Hos 6:6 was polemical: Jesus, not the rabbis, properly applies the prophet's words.

(9:14–17) John the Baptist's disciples (cf. 14:12) ask why the disciples of Jesus, the preacher of repentance, do not fast, that is, display acts of repentance. The question is not why they do not fast at all. For 5:17–20 implies that they at least keep the fast for the day of atonement (cf. Lev 16:1–34), and Jesus himself fasts in 4:1–11. Rather the issue is probably why they do not follow the custom (which the Pharisees followed) of fasting on Mondays and Thursdays. Jesus declares that guests do not fast during wedding celebrations and implies that the time of the Messiah's presence is in this particular akin to a wedding celebration. But this in turn means that when the Messiah has gone such fasting will be appropriate. Jesus then adds the parables about the patch and wineskins. These too offer paradoxical combinations. Putting new cloth on an old garment and new wine into old wineskins are as improbable as wedding guests fasting. The implicit subject continues to be the discontinuity between old and new. But there is also continuity: 'so both are preserved'. Jesus' message and the kingdom of God not only bring the new but fulfil Judaism: the past is not abandoned but fulfilled.

(9:18–26) Here Jesus raises from the dead the daughter of a synagogue director (this justifies 11:5: 'and the dead are raised') and heals a woman with a uterine haemorrhage. The former he sets his hand upon (cf. the OT's 'hand of God'), the latter puts her hand upon him (or rather his 'fringe', that is, 'tassel', cf. 23:5). Because Jesus can read the thoughts of the woman with a haemorrhage, vv. 20–2 are really a sort of conversation. Their theme is faith—which in 9:28 is clarified

as faith in Jesus as the embodiment and channel of God's power and grace.

(9:27–31) This colourless healing story closely resembles 20:29–34, of which it may be a redactional doublet. It prepares for 11:5, which cites Isaiah's prophecy of the healing of the blind. Blindness for an ancient Jew could involve not only poverty and hardship (cf. Mk 10:46) but also religious alienation (cf. Lev 21:20; 11QTemple 45:12–14). But the Torah makes some humanitarian provisions for the blind (e.g. Lev 19:14), and Jesus' ministry to the blind may be interpreted as an extension of such concern. The blind men call Jesus 'Son of David'. This is a messianic title (1:1); but Jesus also heals as Son of David in 12:23; 15:22; and 20:30–1. This matters because, with one exception, 'son of David' is, in the OT, used of Solomon, who was later renowned as a mighty healer and exorcist (cf. T. Sol. 1:7; 5:10; 20:1; 26:9). Perhaps then Matthew offers a Solomon typology.

(9:32–4) The healing of a demoniac who is deaf and dumb—the Greek word, kōphon, here means both—appropriately closes Matthew's third miracle triad. Not only does it prepare for 11:5 ('the deaf hear'), but the crowd's declaration that Jesus' ministry is like nothing in Israel's history (cf. Judg 19:30) is climactic. Moreover, v. 34 records the negative reaction of the Pharisees to the crowd's wonder and so anticipates the theme of opposition in the missionary discourse (cf. esp. 10:25).

(9:35–10:4) This unit, like 8:16–22, concludes a miracle triad, contains summary statements about Jesus' healing ministry, and uses Scripture ('sheep without a shepherd' appears in Num 27:17; 2 Chr 18:16; Jdt 11:19). It also closes off one section and opens another, concluding chs. 8–9 and introducing the missionary discourse by equating the work of the disciples with the compassionate work of Jesus (cf. 9:35 with 10:1). They do what he does and work in the eschatological harvest. By harking back to 4:23 and so forming an *inclusio* with the introduction to the SM, the passage makes Jesus' words (chs. 5–7) and deeds (chs. 8–9) the fundamental context for understanding 10:1–42. The twelve are to preach to Israel about the kingdom of God and to heal the sick (10:1, 7–8) and so imitate Jesus. Moreover, as 5:1–7:27 gives content to the command to preach the gospel (10:7), and as 8:1–9:34 gives content to the command to heal the sick, raise the dead, cleanse lepers, cast out demons (10:8), Jesus' words and deeds are for the missionary example and precedent.

The Disciples' Ministry of Words and Deeds (10:1–42)

10:1–4 opens with an implicit call to imitate Jesus the missionary. By casting out 'unclean spirits' (cf. 12:43) and healing the sick (cf. 4:23) the twelve, who have been in the background until now, repeat his deeds. Unlike a genealogy, in which the names outline a pre-history (cf. 1:2–17), a list of students (cf. m. 'Abot 2.8) indicates a post-history—here the church under Peter's head. Peter is 'first', by which is meant not just first on the list but of privileged status. Judas, the most dishonoured, is last.

(10:5–25) Following the instructions in vv. 5–15 there comes first a list of hardships (vv. 16–23) and then a warning that the twelve—their number corresponds to the tribes of Israel—will be treated as Jesus was treated (vv. 24–5). Altogether the picture is bleak: the future is full of tribulation. Thus the scene is set for 10:26–31, which (in a way reminiscent of 6:25–34 and 7:7–11) offers consolation.

Jesus opens with a prohibition—given prominence by its initial position—not to go to Gentiles or Samaritans (v. 5; in Matthew Jesus never visits Samaria). Jesus is sent only to the lost sheep (cf. 9:36) of the house of Israel. It is not until the turning-point marked by his death and resurrection that there will be a Gentile mission (28:19). The Messiah is, in accordance with the Scriptures, sent to Israel.

vv. 11–15 concern the reception and rejection of missionaries in 'town or village' (cf. 9:35) and their response to such. The gift of peace is not just a social convention. Given the prophecies of peace for the eschatological age (e.g. Isa 52:7) and the eschatological content of the disciples' mission, the apostolic greeting should be understood as a sign of the inbreaking of the kingdom: God is bringing šālôm. But when a place does not receive the good news, the Messiah's emissaries will wipe their feet or shake the dust off themselves as they leave it. Such action is a public demonstration of the breaking of communion and the repudiation of responsibility (cf. 27:24); and it intimates a fate worse than that which came to Sodom and Gomorrah, two cities remembered as so wicked that God made them a burned-out waste (Gen 18:16–19:29). Obviously it is unprecedented honour to hear the disciples' proclamation and unprecedented failure to reject it.

The prophecies of affliction in 10:16–23 go beyond the pre-Easter period to include later missionaries. So we pass from past to present without notice (cf. the situation in Jn 3). The transition reflects Matthew's typification of the twelve: they stand for the Christians of later times. Further, the eschatological character of the sufferings, reinforced by the parallels in 24:9–14 as well as in Jewish apocalyptic literature, imply that the post- and pre-Easter periods both belong to the messianic woes and will only be ended when the Son of Man comes on the clouds of heaven. (So 10:23; the verse is not a reference to the resurrection, Pentecost, or the destruction of Jerusalem.) The missionary endeavour takes place in the latter days, and the suffering of missionaries is a manifestation of the birth-pangs which herald the advent of God's new world.

The passion narrative has left more than traces in vv. 16–23. The fate the disciples face is analogous to what Jesus suffers in later chapters. Jesus too is handed over (26:45). He appears before a sanhedrin (26:59). He is whipped (20:19; cf. 27:26). He is led before a governor (27:1–26). He bears testimony before government officials (26:57–69; 27:11–26). He is betrayed by a member of the group closest to him (26:47–56). And he is killed. The reader recalls all this not only because ch. 10 is permeated by the implicit notion of Jesus Christ as model missionary but also because 10:24–5 explicitly sets the mistreatment of Jesus beside the mistreatment of the disciples. So we have in vv. 17–23 what we also meet in 5:38–42: Jesus in his passion is the exemplar of suffering discipleship.

The theme of the imitation of Christ, already strongly implicit, becomes explicit in vv. 24–5. The verses (cf. Jn 13:16) declare that suffering will come to those who are like Jesus. The implicit subject of 'call' and 'malign' may be the Pharisees (cf. 9:34). Beelzebul is Satan, the prince of demons (12:24–6).

(10:26–31) Three negative injunctions (vv. 26a, 28a, 31a) mark three different points. vv. 26–7, with their antitheses between covered and revealed, hidden and made known, darkness and light, whispering and proclamation, speak of the eschatological revelation of God's truth in which the inspired imagination can even now find solace. v. 28 unfolds the real meaning of death. And vv. 29–31 declare God's sovereignty over the present. In its entirety the section is a sort of theodicy that offers consolation. It declares that the eschatological future will reverse the present (v. 26) and that what happens after death matters above all (v. 28). But lest one suppose that only the future will see God's will done, v. 29 asserts God's present sovereignty. This of course leaves unanswered the problem of how God can be sovereign in a world where his saints suffer so. v. 30 responds with the lesson of Job: God knows what we do not (the verse is not a promise of God's protection—that is contradicted by the context—but a proverb which contrasts God's omniscience with human ignorance; cf. Job 38:37; Sir 1:2; Apoc. Sed. 8.6).

(10:32–42) This section on confession (vv. 32–3), conflict (vv. 34–9), and consolation (vv. 40–2) is partly repetitious: public confession, familial division, eschatological trial, endurance in suffering, and the reception of missionaries have already been treated. The repetition, however, adds emphasis: suffering is indeed inevitable. But there is more than repetition. Whereas 10:5–25 is largely specialized instruction for missionaries, vv. 32 ff. could be heeded equally by every believer. While the non-missionary might find much of vv. 5–25 beside the point, the last portion of the discourse imposes itself upon all.

The prophecy of family strife is based upon Mic 7:6, which was thought to describe the discord of the latter days (cf. m. Sota 9:15); and the conviction that the great tribulation would turn those of the same household against one another was widespread (cf. Jub. 23:16). So v. 35 comprehends the ministry of Jesus and the time of the church—literal and figurative crucifixion characterizes and so unifies both periods (v. 38) in terms of the eschatological woes (cf. Rev 6:4).

The missionary discourse winds down with promissory words in which the disciples are not active but passive: they are received and served (vv. 40–2). The main theme is compensation: those who welcome the eschatological messengers of Jesus welcome Jesus himself and so gain eschatological reward. The 'little ones' are Christian missionaries; so v. 42 is a word not for them but for others—those who, although not itinerants, can share in the Christian mission.

The Response of Israel (11:1–12:50)

(11:1–12:46) Chs. 11–12 recount the failure of 'this generation' to accept God's eschatological messengers and recognize 'the deeds of the Messiah' (11:2, my tr.; the term is a comprehensive reference to Jesus' ministry in Israel). But the focus on rejection is punctuated by the invitations and hope found in 11:25–30; 12:15–21; and 12:46–50. Not all is bleak. There is a remnant.

(11:1–19) Following a transitional sentence (see MT 7:28–9), we have the Christological question of John the Baptist. It is rather surprising in view of John's recognition of Jesus in ch. 3. It is also surprising that the upshot of the disciples' mission is not recorded: while they are commanded to go out, they are never said to return. Perhaps the odd circumstance not only prevents 10:23 from being viewed as a false prophecy but also implies that the Jewish mission is still continuing.

Jesus' answer to John conflates the language of Isa 26:19; 29:18; 35:5–6; 42:7, 18; and 61:1. All the items listed—which might remind one of Elijah—refer to things that have already happened, so that the reader sees in Jesus the fulfilment of Isaiah's eschatological prophecies. (Cf. the list of eschatological events listed in 4Q521; this includes giving sight to the blind, raising the dead, and preaching good news to the poor.)

In vv. 7–15 Jesus ceases to speak of himself and instead speaks of John. He makes five points. John is a prophet and more than a prophet (v. 9). He is the figure foretold by Mal 3:1 (so v. 10; cf. Ex 23:20). He is the greatest of those born among women (v. 11—although the least in the coming kingdom will be greater than he). He is the turning point in salvation history (vv. 12–13; the suffering of John and the saints after him belong to the time when the kingdom is attacked by violent men). And he is Elijah (v. 14; cf. Mal 4:5–6 and John's resemblance to Elijah in Mt 3:4; the issue will come up again in 17:9–13).

Having spoken about himself (vv. 2–6) and about John (vv. 7–15), Jesus next speaks about the response of 'this generation' to both (vv. 16–19). Most commentators identify the children of v. 16 with Jesus and John: the former's invitation to rejoice and the latter's call for the mourning of repentance have fallen upon hostile ears. But the text literally identifies 'this generation' with the piping and wailing children, and it may be better to think that the Baptist, who sternly demanded repentance, met with those who wanted rather to make merry ('we played the flute for you, and you did not dance'), and that Jesus, who preached good news and likened the present to a wedding celebration, was thought to be insufficiently sombre ('we wailed, and you did not mourn', cf. 9:14–17). In any case the deeds of Jesus are the deeds of Wisdom, and they exonerate him (v. 19).

(11:20–4) The two eschatological woes, whose form—address, indictment, verdict—recalls OT oracles (e.g. Isa 5:11–17), carry forward the disappointment registered at the end of 11:16–19—although nothing has prepared for the mention of Chorazin or Bethsaida. But we have read of scribes and Pharisees in Capernaum opposing Jesus (9:3, 11) and of a crowd in Capernaum laughing at him (9:24). The passage serves notice that Jesus' mission to Israel has not summoned corporate repentance and that the consequences will be devastating.

(11:25–30) The theme of rejection (11:2–24) now recedes as we read of those—the 'infants' (cf. 10:42)—who respond rightly to the deeds of the Messiah (11:2). vv. 25–6 (instead of making justified complaint) offer thanksgiving; v. 27 reveals that Jesus is the revealer; and vv. 28–30 are an invitation. The whole has a Mosaic colour. The declaration about Father and Son knowing each other depends upon Ex 33:12–13, in which Moses says that God knows him and in which Moses prays that he might know God; and the promise of rest (cf. the realized eschatology in Heb 4:1–13) is modelled upon Ex 33:14. Jesus moreover is like Moses in that he is 'meek' (Num 12:3), full of revelation (Jewish tradition made Moses all but omniscient; cf. *Jub.* 1:4; *Sipre Deut.* §357), and has a 'yoke' (a word often applied to the Mosaic law). All this accords with Jesus' status as the new Moses of the new covenant.

(12:1–8) Although Jews certainly recognized that exceptional circumstances sometimes allowed the non-observance of Torah (cf. 1 Macc 2:39–41), the Pharisees object that the disciples, by plucking and eating grain on the sabbath, are acting unlawfully (cf. Ex 34:21). But Jesus answers by appealing to an unlawful act—which some late rabbinic sources place on a sabbath—of his royal ancestor David, an act motivated by hunger: the king and those with him ate the bread of the Presence (1 Sam 21). Only the priests were allowed to eat such bread (Lev 24:9). The force of Jesus' appeal is debated, but the following suggestions (which are not contradictory) should be considered: (1) because Scripture does not condemn David for his action, the Pharisees' rigidity is unacceptable; (2) one can observe one commandment at the expense of another (cf. vv. 5–6), and here Jesus puts mercy first (cf. 12:7, 9–14); (3) if David could break the Torah, so can the Messiah (cf. vv. 6, 8). vv. 5–6 then add that if the priests in the temple could violate the sabbath for a higher good, how much more he who is greater than the temple? The argument concludes with (1) an appeal to Hos 6:6 (already cited in 9:13) which shows Scripture's overriding demand for mercy; and (2) a clarifying addition: Jesus' ministry stands above the sabbath. Nothing in the pericope outlaws sabbath observance. Such observance is indeed presupposed by 24:20. Jesus is not setting aside the law but, in traditional Jewish fashion, placing one divine imperative over another for the moment.

(12:9–14) Jesus does a second controversial thing on the sabbath: he heals a paralysed or withered hand. Probably many but not most Jewish teachers of Jesus' day would have thought it wrong, unless a life were at risk, to heal on a sabbath. In defence Jesus (who here does nothing but speak) appeals not to scriptural precept or example (contrast 12:1–8) but to the human sentiment of his hearers. He assumes that their common practice is to help animals on a sabbath (contrast CD 11:23–14). He then makes the inference from the lesser to the greater: if it is lawful to do good to an animal on a sabbath, surely it is lawful to do good to a human on a sabbath.

(12:15–21) As in 8:16–17, we have a summary of Jesus' healing activity followed by a formula quotation from Isaiah. The text is Isa 42:1–4, 9, the longest OT quotation in Matthew. Jesus is the chosen servant, the beloved with whom God is well pleased, and the Spirit (cf. the following paragraph) is upon him—all of which recalls the baptism. The mention of Gentiles harks back to 4:15 and anticipates 28:19. The voice not heard in the streets relates itself naturally to v. 16 and Jesus' lack of self-publicity. The 'bruised reed' and 'smouldering wick' probably represent Jesus' compassion for those at society's margin.

(12:22–50) As in 12:1–21 two controversies with the Pharisees (vv. 22–37 and 38–45) are followed by a paragraph which focuses on those who accept Jesus. 11:1–30 has a similar structure: after the section which ends with the rejection of John and Jesus by 'this generation' (11:16–19) and the woes upon Galilee there follows the invitation in 11:25–30.

(12:22–37) This drawn-out objection story consists of (1) an exorcism (v. 22); (2) the positive (if inadequate) response of the crowd (v. 23); (3) the dissenting and polemical reaction of the Pharisees to the crowd (v. 24); and (4) Jesus' extended response. This last consists of three rebuttals and a warning (vv. 25–30), teaching on the unforgivable sin (vv. 31–2), and a unit on fruits and words (vv. 33–7).

Jesus first responds by appeal to common sense (vv. 25–6). But vv. 27–8 are difficult. If v. 27 urges that two similar activities (exorcisms of Jesus, exorcisms of others) should not be assigned to radically dissimilar sources (Beelzebul, God), v. 28 goes on to make a claim whose logic has seemed to many unclear. Why should Jesus' exorcisms signal the coming of the kingdom? By his own reasoning should not the same be signalled by the exorcisms of others? But the questions miss the implicit Christological claim. Jesus accepts the miracles of others but holds his own to be of different import because of his identity as the Messiah. What matters is not the exorcisms but the exorcist ('if *I* cast out demons'). The Messiah has come as victor over evil forces, so the kingdom is already establishing itself.

In vv. 31–2 Jesus drops his defensive posture and takes up the offensive. His words are warnings to those who have not accepted what has just been said. v. 31 simply declares that although God is ready and willing to forgive, those who oppose the eschatological work of God's Spirit in the ministry of Jesus push God's inclination to forgive past its limit. (Cf. 4Q270 ii 12–15, where we read of those who curse or speak against 'those anointed with His Holy Spirit'.) Despite the common tradition of associating the sin against the Holy Spirit with 1 Jn 5:16, nothing is here taught about post-baptismal relapse. The meaning of v. 32, however, remains obscure. For speaking a word against the Son of Man seems in context to be the same as blasphemy against the Holy Spirit—the one is forgivable, the other is not. A truly satisfying interpretation has yet to be offered. vv. 33–7 conclude the unit by opposing the possible supposition that blasphemy cannot really have eternal consequence because it consists of nothing but words with the assertion that to speak evil is to be evil: words reflect the true self and so can be the criterion of divine judgement. (Cf. further FGS I.)

(12:38–45) After being asked for a sign Jesus speaks of the one sign to be given to 'this generation', refers to the eschatological judgement of 'this generation', and utters a parable about 'this generation'. The scribes and Pharisees want from Jesus not words but a stupendous miracle. The irony is that Jesus has already worked enough miracles to persuade an open mind. So he brands the request as coming from 'an evil and adulterous [i.e. faithless] generation', an expression which recalls Deut 1:35 and 32:5. Jesus' contemporaries are like those who grumbled in the wilderness, those whom God punished by not letting them see the land of promise. None the less, a stupendous sign still will be given—Jesus' resurrection from the dead. ('Three days and three nights' is from Jon 2:1 LXX and, in view of Matthew's chronology, can hardly be taken literally.)

Following the mention of Jonah we read that the Ninevites who repented at or because of the prophet's preaching (cf. Jon 3:2) and the queen of the South (i.e. Sheba) who visited Solomon (cf. 1 Kings 10:1–10; 2 Chr 9:1–9) will be raised at the last judgement and be the standards by which 'this generation' will be condemned. The Ninevites and the queen responded rightly to Jonah and Solomon; but to the one greater than Jonah and Solomon, namely, Jesus (cf. 12:6), 'this generation' has not rightly responded. This then leads to a parable about exorcism, in which the last things are worse than the first. This illustrates the situation with those who have rejected the proclamation of Jesus and the church: they would be better off at the final assize if they had never heard the gospel.

(12:46–50) 4:21–2; 8:22; and 10:34–7 entail at best a loosening of family ties, at worst renunciation of one's parents and siblings. But Jesus offers consolation when he declares that his disciples are his family, and that all who do the will of his Father belong to that family. The obedient disciple is not left alone, without a family; for the church is the household of faith in which there is a father (God) and in which there are brothers and sisters (23:8). Jesus' demand to forsake family is not a call to solitary existence but an invitation to join a new spiritual community.

Explaining Israel's Response (13:1–52)

This discourse is a sort of theodicy—not a solution to the problem of evil in general but a solution to the rejection of Jesus in particular. See MT E.5.

(13:1–23) The parable of the sower (vv. 1–9) comes with an allegorical explanation (vv. 18–23) which makes matters plain: the effects of Jesus' proclamation in Israel are varied because of various factors (including the devil's activity, lack of character under trial, and inappropriate love for the world). vv. 10–17 are more difficult. The disciples want to know why Jesus speaks in parables. He answers that the parables reveal and (in accordance with Isa 6:9–10) hide at the same time, for their effect depends upon the moral status of the hearer. So parables uphold the concept of a closed group in Matthew's thinking (cf. 7:6). Things that should not be revealed to unbelief are not. Only those who do the will of the Father in heaven and so belong to Jesus' family will understand Jesus' parables (cf. 11:25–30; 12:46–50). Those who do not do the will of the Father will not understand. Knowledge has a moral dimension. While the mysteries of the presence of the eschatological kingdom are given by grace through his parables, such teaching falls upon closed as well as open ears. As in the parable of the sower, so too in vv. 10–17: the divine message begets different responses.

(13:24–43) Here Jesus utters three parables (vv. 24–30, 31–2, 33), makes another general statement about parables (vv. 34–5), and offers an interpretation of vv. 24–30 (vv. 36–43). The structure is reminiscent of 13:1–23, the only difference being that instead of one parable there are three:

Parable of sower	Parable of the tares
	Parable of the mustard seed
	Parable of the leaven
Discussion of parables	Discussion of parables
Interpretation of sower	Interpretation of tares

The parable of the tares employs motifs from 13:1–23—sowing, seeds, soil, kingdom, obstacles to growth, the devil—and there is a common message: while the victory of God's kingdom is sure, the progress of the gospel is hampered by unbelief and its effects. But while the sower focuses on human responsibility (the devil being only one factor among others), the tares concentrates on the devil, who imitates Jesus (the sower of 13:1–9) by sowing his own seed. Satan shares responsibility for human sin; those without faith are 'sons of the evil one'. Many commentators have thought the parable reflects concern over the character of some members of Matthew's church and teaches tolerance, but vv. 24–30 do not clearly address a situation in the Christian community. Augustine used this parable to argue against the Donatists, who wanted to exclude the lapsed from church. 13:36–43, however, quite plainly identifies the field with the world, not the church. Moreover, the broader context is not ecclesiological affairs but failure to believe in Israel's Messiah, and 18:15–20 shows us that Matthew had no qualms about pulling up Christian weeds when necessary.

The parable of the mustard seed (a proverbially small seed: cf. 17:20) in vv. 31–2 teaches that a humble beginning is not inconsistent with a great and glorious destiny. The juxtaposition of two seemingly incongruent facts—the tiny seed and a tree for birds—illustrates the contrast between the experience of Jesus and his followers in the present and their expectations of the future. Our parable implicitly sets reality and hope side by side and offers that the grand end is in the mundane beginning. Just as the seed produces the tree, so that which is inconspicuously present in Jesus' ministry will become the universal reign of God.

The introduction to the parable of the leaven (v. 33) resembles the introduction to the parable of the mustard seed, and both parables tell of a small, hidden thing that becomes large through an organic process. These similarities signal an identity of theme. Both teach that the coming of the kingdom begins not with a grand spectacle but a hidden presence. In this way the character and nature of Jesus' ministry, including its failure in Israel, can be better understood.

vv. 34–5 is a formula quotation about Jesus' use of parables. The quotation from Ps 78:2 grounds Jesus' parabolic manner of speaking in prophecy: the OT prophesies the Messiah's use of revelatory parables. These verses also serve as a transition from one audience to another: Jesus turns from those who do not understand to those who do (cf. 13:10–17).

vv. 24–30 tell a parabolic story. vv. 37–9, in response to the disciples' request for its interpretation (cf. 13:10), supply a sort of lexicon which explains the allegorical meanings of seven figures in that story. vv. 40–3 then take those meanings and with them constructs a second narrative about the last judgement. The result is two stories—vv. 24–30 and 40–3—with one meaning. Together they put things in eschatological perspective. If the sun now shines on the just and unjust, it shall not always be so. The tares will eventually be plucked up, the wheat gathered. History's end will give the answers to the difficult questions that history, including the history of Jesus, raises.

(13:44–52) The three parables (cf. 13:24–33) of the treasure, pearl, and net are followed by an interpretation of the latter (cf. 13:18–23, 13:36–43) and a general discussion of parables (cf. 13:10–17, 34–5) which concludes the discourse. The first two parables (vv. 44–6) concern finding the kingdom (represented by the treasure and the pearl) and doing everything to obtain it. The focus is on the present, not the future, and on the

actions of believers, not unbelievers. The point is that although the kingdom is hidden (cf. 13:31–3) it can be found; and when it is, one should make whatever sacrifice is necessary to obtain it. 'Anyone who counts the cost of discipleship has completely failed to grasp the greatness of the reward' (Beare 1981: 315).

The parables of the treasure and pearl appropriately succeed 13:1–43 by offering paraenesis—buy, sell, seek. Granted the kingdom's value and its sure triumph, one must strive to overcome every obstacle in the way of obtaining it. One must not respond as the people denounced in chs. 11–12 or be like the unfruitful seeds of 13:1–23. The necessity for such action is, in turn, underlined by vv. 47–50, which return to the last assize (cf. 13:36–43): judgement will come upon those who reject the kingdom. There is, accordingly, a shift of emphasis between 13:1–43 and vv. 44–50. Whereas the former is more descriptive, the latter is more hortative.

The discourse ends with vv. 51–2, a comparative proverb. The major point is that the disciples have indeed understood Jesus' discourse and so qualify as scribes instructed in the truths of the kingdom of heaven. Perhaps a Christian counterpart to the Jewish rabbinate is envisaged. It is altogether probable that Matthew belonged to a 'school' of Christian scribes. In this case the verse would be a sort of self-portrait. What exactly is meant by 'new' and 'old' is unclear. Should we think of the new revelation in Jesus and old revelation in the Torah, or of Christian tradition and Jewish tradition, or of the teaching of Christians and Jesus' teaching, or of Matthew's interpretations of Jesus' parables and those parables themselves?

The Birth of the Church (13:53–17:27)

(13:53–8) This pericope, which supplies a concrete example of people hearing but not hearing and seeing but not seeing (cf. 13:13), illustrates that the failure to understand leads not to indifference but to hostility, and further that unbelief does not correspond to any geographical pattern: Jesus' words and deeds are rejected in the north (here Nazareth) as well as the south, in his home town as well as the capital. There is no sacred space uncontaminated by hostility. The lesson complements 12:46–50, which immediately precedes 13:1–52. For if in vv. 53–8 one learns that geographical and social ties do not really matter, in 12:46–50 it is taught that family ties may be relaxed by commitment to Jesus. So the great parable discourse is framed by two texts which relativize the significance of earthly ties.

vv. 53–8 link up not only with what precedes but also with what follows. In v. 57 Jesus implicitly proclaims himself a prophet, and in 14:5 the people hold John to be a prophet. The upshot is clear. John's fate, which is recounted in 14:1–12, is that of a prophet, and a similar fate must also lie ahead for Jesus. To be a prophet means to suffer rejection and ultimately death (cf. 23:29–39).

On the concluding formula in v. 53 see MT 7:28–9. In v. 55 the crowd attempts to explain away the extraordinary by associating it with the familiar. Their unbelief, which moves Jesus to restrict his effort on their behalf, is not explained. But 13:1–30 has already supplied the answers.

(14:1–12) Having in the parable discourse examined the roots of unbelief, Matthew now shows us how the failure to gain faith can manifest itself. In this passage (cf. the rather different account in Josephus, *Ant.* 18 §§ 117–19) unbelief begets not only misunderstanding (vv. 1–2—Jesus is mistaken for John raised from the dead) but violent opposition (vv. 3–12; cf. 13:53–8). Moreover, the passage portends in some detail the passion narrative, for there are many parallels between Jesus and John. Both are seized (v. 3; 21:46) and bound (v. 3; 27:2) and suffer the shameful deaths of criminals. Both are executed at the command of a government official (Herod, Pilate) who acts reluctantly at the request of others (vv. 6–11; 27:11–26). Both are buried by their disciples (v. 12; 27:57–61), and in each case opponents fear what the crowds might do because they hold John and Jesus to be prophets (v. 5; 21:46). As in 2:1–23 (where the opponent is Herod the Great, Herod the tetrarch's father); 5:38–42; and 10:17–23, the end is foreshadowed. So John's martyrdom is not an interesting aside, a slack moment in the narrative during which someone other than Jesus is the focus, but rather a Christological parable: the fate of the fore-runner is that of the coming one (cf. 17:12).

Because John is elsewhere identified with Elijah (11:14), and because in 1 Kings 17–19 the prophet Elijah accuses King Ahab of misdeeds while the evil Queen Jezebel seeks the prophet's life, one may liken Herod to king Ahab and Hero-dias to Jezebel. It is suggestive that in the very next pericope Jesus acts like Elisha, Elijah's successor (see 2 Kings 4:42–4).

(14:13–21) The feeding of the five thousand is above all about the compassionate (cf. v. 14) Jesus and his supernatural ability to satisfy those in physical need—a theme that runs throughout the gospel. Here, as in the similar stories in 1 Kings 17:8–16; 2 Kings 4:42–4; and Jn 21:4–8, the miracle, itself undescribed, comes not in response to a request but flows from the spontaneous goodness of the miracle worker. (Despite the opinions of many, it is not clear that the numbers—five loaves, two fishes, twelve baskets, 5,000 men—have symbolic significance.)

The verbal parallels with 26:20–9 make the present episode foreshadow the eucharist, and this episode may even be a sort of allegory of the church's eucharistic celebration. But there is more. Like the last supper, the feeding of the five thousand anticipates the messianic banquet. It also strongly recalls 2 Kings 4:42–4, where (1) Elisha takes bread and (2) commands, 'Give to the people, and let them eat', whereupon (3) a question is raised as to how so many can be fed by so little; but (4) the people eat anyway and (5) food is left over. The parallelism implies that Jesus is an eschatological prophet like Elisha. Finally, Jesus' miracle in a deserted (*erēmon*) place in the evening after crossing water recalls the miraculous evening fall of manna in the wilderness (*erēmos*) under Moses after passage through the Red Sea (Ex 16; Num 11). *Sipre* on Num 11:22 records that the Israelites ate fish in their desert wanderings (cf. Wis 19:12), and the manna in the wilderness was spoken of as a sort of 'bread' (e.g. Deut 8:3). Matthew's Moses typology is, as patristic exegesis saw, again present (cf. Jn 6:25 ff.). In sum, the miraculous feeding looks to the past and to the future—it anticipates the Lord's supper and the messianic banquet and it looks back to OT miracles of Moses and Elisha.

(14:22–36) This passage, which is rich in both its Christo-logical implications and its instruction on discipleship, is a epiphany which brings rescue. Jesus orders the disciples to cross without him—a circumstance which may be intended to teach that if obedience to Christ puts one in dire need then Christ himself will offer help. Jesus, illustrating 6:6, then goes by himself up a mountain to pray (cf. the circumstance that Moses prayed alone on Sinai, e.g. Ex 32:30–4). But when the disciples suffer distress during the last watch of night, Jesus walks on the sea towards them and, to calm a terror born not only from the wind but also from fear of a ghost, commands them not to be afraid. By walking on the sea, Jesus, like the omnipotent creator of the OT, overcomes the powers of chaos (cf. Job 9:8), and by crossing the sea so that his disciples may in turn cross safely he is again like YHWH, who prepared the way for the Israelites to pass through the Red Sea (Ps 77:19). Clearly the powers of the deity are incarnate in God's Son, who can here borrow the theophanic 'I am' (*egō eimi*, v. 27; cf. Ex 3:14). (Cf. further FGS J.)

vv. 28–31 constitute a story within a story. Peter rightly wishes to imitate his Lord, who can share his authority and power with his followers. But Peter begins to sink because of his little faith (cf. 6:30; 8:26) and so must cry for help (cf. Ps 69:1–3). Jesus, however, is there to answer his call despite inadequate faith. What counts is not strength of will or courage but Jesus' saving presence.

(15:1–20) Jesus speaks with the scribes and Pharisees (vv. 1–9), then with the crowd (vv. 10–11), then with the disciples (vv. 12–20). The theme of the first conversation is the Pharisaic tradition: that tradition does not have the same authority as Scripture, and where it goes against Scripture it must be condemned. (23:2–3, 23 imply that the tradition is not rejected completely.) Then in vv. 10–11, 15–20, Jesus teaches the truth about purity: the serious defilement is that created by the heart. vv. 12–14 attack the Pharisees themselves: their lives exhibit hypocrisy and they cannot be followed (cf. 16:5–12). There is no obvious thematic link with the surrounding material.

The legal question of why the disciples do not ritually wash their hands before eating is for us a dim one. Not only do we no longer think in terms of ritual purity, but we have no detailed sources on the subject of handwashing from the first century. 7:3, according to which no Jew would eat with unwashed hands, is usually said to be exaggeration. But Jn 2:6, which refers to stone jars of water for purification at a wedding, is perhaps some evidence that ritual handwashing was widely practised before 70 CE.

Jesus does not directly answer the Pharisees but rather accuses them of hypocrisy: they keep their own tradition at the expense of violating Torah, specifically the commandment to honour one's parents (Ex 20:12; Deut 5:16)—a commandment whose importance is shown by Ex 21:17, which prescribes death for speaking evil of father or mother. The Pharisees teach that one can pronounce a *qorbān* vow—a vow which withdraws something from profane use and makes it as though it were dedicated to the temple—for the purpose of not sharing property, even with one's parents (cf. *m. Ned.* 5:6; contrast 4:7–8). But this is hypocrisy, which can be illustrated by the quotation from Isa 29:13.

Nothing so far said annuls any OT law. On the contrary, Jesus is presented as upholding Torah (cf. 5:17–20). Even the declaration in v. 11 (cf. Rom 14:14) does not abolish Moses. It is not halakah but a moral pronouncement. We have here the Semitic idiom of relative negation in which all the emphasis lies on the second half of the saying. Food cannot defile because true defilement is a function of morality. What matters is not the belly (v. 17) but the heart (cf. 5:21–8; 23:16–26; also the interesting parallel in 2 Chr 30:18–20). The 'parable' (v. 15) may relativize the ritual law but it does not set it aside. Compare the teaching in *Num. Rab.* 19:8: 'It is not the dead that defiles nor the water that purifies. The Holy One, blessed be He, merely says:"I have laid down a statute, I have issued a decree. You are not allowed to transgress my decree."' As Maimonides later said, defilement 'is a matter of scriptural decree and dependent on the intention of the heart'. v. 11 could be formulated as is 5:27–8: 'You have heard that it was said, "One is defiled by what goes into the mouth." But I say to you: what comes out of one is what defiles one.' Just as the condemnation of lust does not mean indifference to adultery, so too the identification of the heart as the source of defilement does not mean the dismissal of levitical law.

The unit concludes with a list of vices (v. 19; cf. the Decalogue) which tell the tale of the defiled heart and then a summary conclusion (v. 20). This last makes plain that the whole discussion turns on the question of Pharisaic tradition, not the written law, for the washing of hands before meals is only enjoined in the former.

(15:21–8) When Jesus goes to the region of Tyre and Sidon (v. 21)—two cites with evil reputations (cf. Ezek 28)—he meets a Canaanite woman. 'Canaanite' adds to the negative connotations of 'Tyre and Sidon'. As Chrysostom rightly had it, 'the evangelist speaks against the woman, that he may show forth her marvellous act, and celebrate her praise the more. For when you hear of a Canaanite woman, you should call to mind those wicked nations which overturned from their foundations the very laws of nature and, being reminded of these, consider also the power of Christ's advent.'

The woman surprisingly addresses Jesus as Lord and Son of David and asks for mercy for her daughter, who suffers from a demon. Jesus' response is silence—he is either turning her down or trying her faith. The disciples then want her dismissed (cf. 14:15). Jesus, in accordance with 10:6, declares his commitment to Israel, the nation which is by and large lost for lack of leadership. He thus promotes a biblical doctrine of election. Israel is God's chosen people, and to them the Messiah goes first of all. Even in the face of opposition and disbelief Jesus, the mirror of God's faithfulness, continues to direct his mission to the leaderless sheep of Israel. Instead of taking Jesus' theological pronouncement for the last word the woman again asks for help. Jesus responds with seemingly cruel words (which may reproduce a proverb): it is not good to take the bread of the children (that is, what Jesus has to offer Israel) and to give it to dogs (Gentiles). The woman then offers an unexpected riposte: the dogs eat the scraps that fall from their masters' tables. This recognizes Israel's privileges yet simultaneously implies that others can be benefited. Jesus acknowledges the clever reply as the product of great faith and so grants the daughter's healing.

The parallelism with 8:5–13 is striking. Both passages are about Jesus encountering a Gentile who wants him to heal a child. In both, the supplicants call Jesus 'Lord'. In both, the focus is not on the healing itself but the preceding conversation, which in each instance contains a general statement by Jesus about Israel. In addition, both record initial hesitation on the part of Jesus, relate how the Gentile wins Jesus over by clever words which illustrate great faith, and have the healings, which are accomplished at a distance, transpire 'from that hour'. The assimilation of the two episodes is part of our author's wider habit of assimilating like to like. But the repetition also reinforces the common themes, above all the theme that salvation comes to those outside Israel in response to their faith in Jesus.

(15:29–39) The feeding of the four thousand is very much like the feeding of the five thousand (14:13–21), and so the meaning of the two stories is much the same: again the repetition makes for emphasis. (And again it is dubious to find symbolic significance in the various numbers.) There is indeed an old tradition that the five thousand were Jews, the four thousand Gentiles; but nothing substantial in Matthew supports this interpretation, and 15:21–8 seemingly contradicts it. There is, however, one major way in which vv. 29–39 add to the narrative. The gathering of the crowds, the healing of the sick (cf. 11:5), the allusion to Isa 35:5–6 (vv. 30–1), the compassionate feeding of many, and the mountain setting together recall OT prophecies about Mount Zion (see Donaldson 1985). So the second feeding shows us that the eschatological expectations associated with Zion have come to fulfilment in Jesus.

(16:1–4) Despite everything Jesus has said and done, the Pharisees and Sadducees—an unlikely alliance—remain unconvinced; and because they find Jesus a threat to themselves, they seek to trip him up by making a request they think he cannot fulfil. They profess to want a spectacular sign in or from the heavens but refuse to see the many proofs right before their eyes (cf. 12:38). They can read the signs of the weather but are blind to the signs of the last times set by God. Jesus, who here makes no vain attempt to persuade, does not grant their request—we assume that he could (cf. 26:53)—but offers them only the sign of Jonah, that is, his resurrection (cf. 12:40; the Sadducees dogmatically denied the general resurrection). The chief point is that seeing is not believing. Rather, one does not see until one believes. For the faith that holds the soul also rules one's perception. It is vain to expect hardened hearts to be melted by demonstrations of power. This is why, in this gospel, miracles, while certainly pointers to God's presence in Jesus, are always therapeutic or salvific; their object is not the convincing of sceptics (cf. 13:56).

(16:5–12) The emphasis is not upon Jesus' ability to meet physical needs or his pedagogical skills, although both themes are present; the focus is the admonition about the Pharisees and Sadducees. The warning to beware of their 'leaven', repeated twice, frames the discourse, and is interpreted in the conclusion (v. 12: 'leaven' means teaching). It is clearly the main point. Perhaps among early readers of this gospel there were still some who attended Jewish synagogue. To them the warning would be most appropriate. The tension with 23:2–3, where Jesus tells disciples to observe what the scribes and Pharisees say, is more apparent than real; vv. 5 and

11 do not imply that everything taught by the Jewish leaders is false, just as 23:2–3 can scarcely mean that everything they say is true. And whereas the latter is about what followers of Jesus and Jewish teachers have in common, the former is about what divides the two groups. It follows that believers should listen to the synagogue leaders in so far as the leaders' speech is grounded in the authoritative oracles of the OT and so true; at the same time, believers must also take heed, for the leaders' opposition to Jesus means that much of what they teach must be false.

(16:13–20) The primary function of this passage is to record the establishment of a new community, one which will acknowledge Jesus' true identity and thereby become the focus of God's activity in history. The event has been occasioned by the rejection of Jesus by so many in Israel, including Israel's leaders, a rejection chronicled in the previous chapters.

The major themes have their collective root in Davidic messianism, above all in Nathan's famous oracle to David, preserved in 2 Sam 7:4–16 || 1 Chr 17:3–15. Jesus is confessed as both Christ and Son of God; he builds a church or temple; and he gives to Peter the keys to the kingdom of heaven. These are all Davidic motifs. In 2 Sam 7 and 1 Chr 17 it is promised that one of David's descendants will rule Israel as king (and therefore as anointed one), that he will be God's son ('I will be his father, and he will be my son'), that he will build a temple, and that his kingdom will be forever. This oracle was, before Matthew's time, understood to refer not just to Solomon but to Israel's eschatological king (cf. 4QFlor). Matthew asserts its fulfilment in Jesus. Moreover, the giving of the keys of the kingdom of heaven to Peter has its closest OT parallel in Isa 22:22, where God will place on Eliakim's shoulder 'the key' of 'the house of David' (a term with messianic associations; cf. Zech 12:7–13:1; Lk 1:27); with it he will open and none will shut, and he will shut and none will open. This text, which is applied to Jesus in Rev 3:7 and here lies behind Jesus' promise to Peter, is about the activity of a man second only to the king. In sum, vv. 13–20 record the eschatological realization of the promises made to David.

When Jesus gets to Caesarea Philippi, a Gentile town 20 miles north of the Sea of Galilee, he asks his disciples what others think of him. The consensus is that Jesus is a prophet. People identify him with John the Baptist (so Herod, 14:2) or Elijah (in 4:18–22 Jesus acts like Elijah) or Jeremiah (a prophet like Moses who spoke against the temple, suffered, and was remembered as a martyr) or more generally 'one of the prophets'. But when Peter confesses that Jesus is more than a prophet, that he is the Christ, the Son of the living God, Jesus pronounces over him (not the disciples as a group) a beatitude. Jesus goes on to utter three sentences, each of which consists of three parts—a statement of theme plus an antithetical couplet. The first sentence, v. 17, interprets the confession as an eschatological secret revealed through divine agency.

The second sentence, v. 18, concerns Peter and the *ekklēsia*, the end-time community, the counterpart of the Sinai congregation (which in Deuteronomy is called the *ekklēsia*). The verse is among the most controversial in all Scripture. 'You are Peter' matches 'you are the Messiah', and Jesus, like Peter, also utters revelation. The most natural reading is that 'this rock' (*petra*—we have a wordplay) refers to Peter, the foundation stone of the new temple which Jesus builds. This does not mean Peter is the first holder of an office others will someday hold, as Roman Catholic tradition has it. But he is surely more than a representative disciple, as so many Protestants have anxiously maintained. Rather, he is a man with a unique role in salvation history. His person marks a change in the times. His significance is akin to that of Abraham: his faith is the means by which God brings a new people into being. In fact, one should perhaps think of Gen 17. There too we witness the birth of the people of God through an individual whose name is changed to signify his crucial function (Abram becomes Abraham, 'father of a multitude'). Moreover, Abraham is, in Isa 51:1–2 (cf. the comments on 3:9), a rock from which the people of God are quarried. Is not Peter the patriarch of the church?

That the gates of Hades will not prevail against the church is not an allusion to Jesus' death and resurrection, nor to the general resurrection, nor to Christ's descent into hell (a thing otherwise unattested in this gospel). The most plausible interpretation is that the gates of Hades are the ungodly powers of the underworld who will assail the church in the latter days: the church will emerge triumphant from the eschatological assaults of evil. In the background is the end-time scenario of powers which, unleashed from below, rage against the saints (cf. *1 Enoch* 56:8; Rev 11:7; 17:8). One may compare Rev 9:1–11, where the demonic hosts, under their king, Abaddon, come up from the bottomless pit to torment humanity. They prevail against all except those with the seal of God.

In v. 19 Peter is given the keys to the kingdom, which is explicated to mean that he has the authority to bind and loose (cf. 18:18). This is not a statement about exorcism or the forgiveness of sins (cf. Jn 20:23). Rather, Peter, as a sort of supreme rabbi of the kingdom, is given teaching authority. His decisions stand.

(16:21–3) Once it is evident that Israel as a corporate body is not going to welcome Jesus as the Messiah, two things remain to be done. First, Jesus must found a new community. Secondly, he must give his life as a ransom for many. Having just begun the first task in the previous paragraph, he now turns his eyes towards the second. His prophetic foresight is such that he can see the future, including his own death. But Peter, who here goes from the heights to the depths and functions not as the rock on which the church is built but as a stone of stumbling (Isa 8:14), behaves like a fool and does not recognize the necessity of messianic suffering. Jesus rebukes him in the strongest possible terms—and shows that the Messiah goes to his death as a free man: he chooses his own destiny.

(16:24–8) After the brief narrative setting (v. 24a) there are sayings on discipleship (vv. 24b–26) and the eschatological future, which will come sooner rather than later (vv. 27–8). The logic is clear: thought of the future should encourage acts of discipleship in the present, for only the final state matters (cf. v. 26). But discipleship is not easy of achievement. Jesus is not a substitute but a leader who must be followed (v. 24; cf. 4:18–22; 8:18–22; 9:9), and his life ends in suffering and crucifixion (vv. 21–3). Further, Jesus calls for a surrender or denial of self no matter what the cost or dangers (v. 25). This means above all obedience to another's will (cf. Gethsemane).

Anything more difficult could hardly be asked of human beings. Faith is obedience, and obedience is the grave of the will.

(17:1–8) The major theme of this epiphany is Jesus' status as a new Moses. 'Six days later' (v. 1, an ambiguous reference, but cf. Ex 24:16) Jesus' face shines like the sun (v. 2) as does Moses' face in Ex 34:29–35 (cf. Philo, *vit. Mos.* 170; Ps.-Philo, *LAB* 12:1). As in Ex 24:15–18; 34:5 a bright cloud appears, and a voice speaks from it (so too Ex 24:16). The onlookers—a special group of three (v. 1; cf. Ex 24:1)—are afraid (v. 6; cf. Ex 34:29–30). And all this takes place on a mountain (v. 1; cf. Ex 24:12, 15–18; 34:3). Moreover, Moses and Elijah, who converse with the transfigured Jesus, are the only figures in the OT who speak with God on Mount Sinai, so their presence together makes us think of that mountain. Jesus is the prophet like Moses of Deut 18:15, 18.

The transfiguration relates itself to the immediately preceding narrative. It illustrates 16:24–8 first by showing forth the glory of the parousia foretold in vv. 27–9 (cf. 2 Pet 1:16–18) and secondly by making concrete the resurrection hope of those who follow the hard commands of Jesus issued in vv. 24–6. (In 13:43 the resurrected saints shine like the sun.) As for the prophecy of passion and resurrection in 16:21–3, the transfiguration anticipates Jesus' exaltation. Further, through the allusion of the voice to Isa 42:1 ('with him I am well pleased') Jesus is made out to be the suffering servant of Isaiah. Going back even further, to 16:13–20, the divine confession of Jesus as the Son of God confirms and underlines Peter's confession.

The transfiguration not only resembles the baptism but also has a twin of sorts in 27:32–54. 17:1–8 records a private epiphany in which an exalted Jesus, with garments glistening, stands on a high mountain and is flanked by two religious giants from the past. All is light. But 27:32–54 relates a public spectacle in which a humiliated Jesus, whose clothes have been taken from him and divided, is lifted upon a cross and flanked by two criminals. All is darkness. In both accounts there are three named onlookers (17:1; 27:56), Jesus is confessed as Son of God (17:6; 27:54), and people are afraid (17:6; 27:54: 'and were overcome with fear'; the Greek is the same in both places although this does not appear from the NRSV). And whereas Elijah is present in one place (17:3), in the other he fails to appear (27:46–9). We have in all this pictorial antithetical parallelism, a diptych in which the two plates have similar lines but different colours. As God's Son Jesus participates in the whole gamut of human possibilities; the eschatological prophecies of doom and vindication play themselves out in his life. Jesus is humiliated and exalted, surrounded by saints and ringed by sinners, clothed with light and wrapped in a mantle of darkness.

(17:9–13) Just as Peter's confession of Jesus as the Son of God is immediately followed by a passion prediction (16:13–23), so now is the transfiguration immediately followed by another prophecy of the suffering of the Son of Man. The verses deprive Jewish criticism of Christian claims of one forceful objection, namely, since Elijah has not yet come (cf. Mal 4:5), the eschatological scenario cannot be unfolding. Jesus counters that Elijah, in the person of the Baptist, has indeed come (v. 12). Beyond that the passage emphasizes yet once more the parallels between Jesus and John: both suffer similar fates.

Lastly, the command to keep silent until Jesus has risen from the dead (v. 9) not only stresses the impossibility of preaching the whole truth about Jesus until he has completed his mission—this underlines the centrality of the cross—but also makes Peter, James, and John authoritative bearers of the Jesus tradition.

(17:14–21) Jesus' exorcism of a demon who is causing self-destructive behaviour (v. 15) is told primarily for the sake of Jesus' provocative declaration in v. 20. The focus is not on Jesus as healer but on discipleship and faith. The lesson is not what Jesus can do but what his followers should do. Despite 10:1 the disciples have been unable to cast out the demon. They, by their 'little faith' (v. 20), have retrogressed to the spiritual level of the multitude (v. 17). But this is needless. So after expressing prophetic exasperation and healing the boy himself, Jesus informs them that any faith at all can move mountains, that is, work wonders. This seemingly stands in tension with his diagnosis of 'little faith'. That is, v. 20 affirms that the disciples have at least some faith, whereas v. 21 (NRSV marg.) suggests that only a little faith will do miracles (cf. 1 Cor 13:2). Although the way the two ideas should be harmonized is unclear, the main point stands: faith enables; its lack cripples. Faith, which is not belief but trust and hope in God in Christ, is the precondition which God has set for many of his actions in the world (cf. 13:58).

(17:22–3) Jesus, without adding any additional details, again plainly prophesies his end. The repetition not only emphasizes Jesus' prophetic powers and makes plain the voluntary nature of his suffering but also pushes the reader forward in anticipation: the key to everything must be in the end. If in 28:18 Jesus declares that all authority has been delivered to him (by God), here he speaks of being delivered into the hands, that is, authority, of sinful people. The poles of experience represented by the two texts are worlds apart. This adds pathos. God gives the Son of Man into the hands of others, and God gives the Son of Man universal authority. It is the burden of the gospel to demonstrate that these two opposing acts, far from being contradictory, are, in God's hidden but sovereign will, the two complementary halves of the same divine purpose.

(17:24–7) After Peter tells tax collectors that Jesus pays the tax for support of the sacrificial system in Jerusalem, the apostle goes to Jesus for instructions about that tax. Jesus says that the relationship between God and Israel is like that between a king and his family. Just as a king does not tax his own family, so God does not tax his people. The point is not that Jesus rejects the temple cult. He rather rejects the idea that theocratic taxation is the appropriate means of maintaining that cult. But with the miracle—not actually narrated—of the coin in the fish (which sounds like a piece of folklore), Jesus makes arrangements for payment. He thereby avoids offending the devout people who, in collecting the money, think themselves to be serving God. Personal freedom must be delimited because it must be responsibly exercised, which means it must take into account the effect upon others (cf. 1 Cor 8:13). At the same time, by not giving his own money but only a lost coin, Jesus does not acknowledge the legitimacy of a mandatory tax. One may compare Paul's collection for the poor in Jerusalem (which was seemingly modelled on the collection of the temple tax). The apostle stressed that payment was purely voluntary: he was not collecting a tax (Rom 15:25–7).

Instructions for the Church (18:1–35)

This, the fourth major speech, is the ecclesiastical discourse; see MT E.7. vv. 1–5 focus on the theme of imitating and receiving children; vv. 6–9 warn about causing others or oneself to stumble; vv. 10–14 speak of God's love for the lost. All three paragraphs refer to 'children' or 'little ones'. But with 18:15 ff. the key word becomes 'brother' (which the NRSV translates 'member of the church'). In this second half there are instructions for communal discipline (vv. 15–20), teaching on forgiveness (vv. 21–2), and a long parable (vv. 23–35). It may be that the three paragraphs before vv. 15–20 and the two after are buffers of a sort; that is, they emphasize the qualities required if one is going to be so bold as to carry out the difficult directions on discipline. Before talking about reproof Jesus goes on at length about humility, not offending others, and God's love. And as soon as he finishes the subject of disciplinary measures he talks about reconciliation and forgiveness. The pastoral effect is to strike a balance. Just as 7:6 joins a logion about discernment to injunctions prohibiting condemnation of others (7:1–5), so ch. 18 surrounds the material on fraternal correction with calls for generosity, humility, and forgiveness.

(18:1–14) This block of moral teaching, which presupposes a communal setting, begins by referring to literal children (v. 2), but by vv. 10–14 'little ones' designates believers (cf. 10:42). The transition from one thing to the other is probably marked by the change in vocabulary: *paidion* is the key word in vv. 1–5, *mikros* in vv. 6–14; i.e. vv. 1–5 concern literal children, vv. 6–14 believers. The former teaches that one should become like little children, for only by this will one enter the kingdom (v. 3). One should humble oneself as a child, for in the kingdom the humble will be great (v. 4; cf. 23:12). The point is not that children are self-consciously humble but that they are, within society, without much status or position. One also should— perhaps this is an illustration of humility—welcome children in 'my name', for to receive such a one is to receive Jesus himself (v. 5; Jesus' own action in 19:13–15 illustrates his words here). The sequence is: entrance into the kingdom (v. 3), greatness in the kingdom (v. 4), service in the world (v. 5).

With v. 6 the tone is no longer one of promise but warning. To cause a believer to be misled or perverted morally brings a fate worse than being thrown into the dark, eternal grave of the sea with a donkey millstone around one's neck (cf. Rev 18:21). God sees to it that one cannot harm others without harming oneself. It is indeed true that *skandala*, 'stumbling blocks', are necessary, for evil must flourish in the latter days (24:6); but this does not entail that any one individual must commit them (v. 7). The self is in fact called to rid itself of whatever in it leads to sin (vv. 8–9; the references to hand and eye do not, in Pauline fashion, represent members of the church; they are rather hyperbolic illustrations, as in 5:29–30). The underlying logic seems to be that in order to avoid offending others (v. 7) one must also take care of oneself (vv. 8–9). The self must suffer a 'life-giving mortification' (Symeon the New Theologian).

The warning against harming 'little ones' is reinforced by the parable in 18:10–14. The shepherd recovering his lost sheep stands for God's work in Christ and so illustrates God's concern for the faithful who go astray. His concern for such— represented by his appointment of guardian angels for them (v. 10)—is the paradigm and illustration for a similar human concern (cf. v. 14; cf. 5:45–8). To harm them would be to set oneself against God.

(18:15–35) If one Christian sins against another, the offended party, imitating the shepherd who goes after the lost sheep, should first seek reconciliation in private by bringing up the fault (cf. Lev 19:17, alluded to in v. 15). If this attempt fails, the offended should next seek the aid of another, maybe two (cf. Deut 19:15; 2 Cor 13:1; 1 Tim 5:19), and try again. If that likewise does not produce results, the matter is to be brought to the whole community. If, after that, a sinner remains recalcitrant, he or she must be regarded as outside the community (excommunication). The community's decision then has the authority of heaven itself (vv. 18–20), for its prayer is in effect Jesus' prayer, and his prayer cannot but be answered (v. 20). (This verse may revise the rabbinic notion that the *shekinah* or divine effulgence is present when two or more gather to study Torah; cf. m. 'Abot 3.2, 3, 6. As in the Mishnah, so in Matthew: holy space is determined not by geography but activity. The difference is that in the gospel space is made holy by the presence of Christ and entered into by gathering in his name.)

The instructions to correct another have a long history in Jewish literature. The key text is Lev 19:15–18, which enjoins not hating others but reproving them (cf. Sir 19:13–20:2). In the Dead Sea scrolls Lev 19:15–18 is behind a formal procedure: one first takes a complaint to the individual against whom it is directed; if this does not have the intended effect, one then goes before the community. Also close to Matthew is T. Gad 6:3–5, where, on the basis of Lev 19:15–18, one is to speak in love to an offender, forgive if repentance is made, and do all this in secret.

Following the hard instructions on excommunication is teaching on forgiveness which functions as a hedge against rigidity and absolutism (vv. 21–2). To Peter's question whether he should forgive seven times, Jesus says that he should forgive seventy-seven or (the Greek is ambiguous) seventy times seven times. This makes explicit the attitude required if one is to correct another. Forgiveness, like love, must be limitless. Without such forgiveness the community cannot correct the wayward, pray as a united front, and have Christ in its midst.

Although many have felt tension between vv. 21–2 and 15– 20, Lev 19:17 joins reproof and love, and so in Judaism the two belong together. Further, membership in the Matthean community disallows certain acts; the church would cease to be itself if it did not insist that its members acknowledge Christ's standard of behaviour. The spirit of forgiveness is not indifference to sin. So we may suppose that when the offended goes to the offender, there has already been forgiveness; the reproof is for the sake of the other.

The chapter ends with the parable of the unforgiving servant (18:23–35). It does not merely illustrate vv. 21–2, which are a call for repeated forgiveness. Rather vv. 23–35 make the additional points that failure to forgive (1) is failure to act as

God—represented by the king who remits the incredible sum of 10,000 talents—and (2) will merit eschatological punishment (cf. 6:15).

Commencement of the Passion (19:1–25:46)

(19:1–12) Ch. 18 has to do with ecclesiastical issues, ch. 19 with everyday existence: marriage and divorce (vv. 1–9), celibacy (vv. 10–12), children (vv. 13–15), and money (19:16–20:16)—all key social concerns. There is in all this a certain parallelism (reflective of a catechetical order?) with 6:1–7:12, where Jesus first discusses cultic issues (6:1–18) and next speaks to social issues (6:19–7:12).

The extended dialogue in 19:1–12, in which Jesus three times responds to a challenge or question, covers a topic already considered in the SM (5:31–2); but the declaration there made, without explanation, is now elucidated. The subject of celibacy, on the other hand, has not previously appeared (although in 1:24–5 Joseph refrains from 'knowing' Mary for a time).

The Pharisees, who want Jesus to contradict Moses, challenge their opponent to interpret the *erwat dābār* of Deut 24:1, a phrase given different interpretations by the schools of Hillel and Shammai. Matthew's 'for any cause' reflects knowledge of the more liberal and presumably dominant Hillelite position, according to which many things constitute grounds for divorce. The question then is whether Jesus agrees or, on the contrary, holds a less liberal position. Jesus directs his opponents to Gen 1:27 and Gen 2:24 and so responds by raising the issue of the permanence of marriage. 'Have you not read?' invites reconsideration of the implications of Genesis: has God not established lifelong partnership? CD 4:19–21 shows that before Jesus' time Gen 1:27 was brought into connection with the subject of marriage and used to endorse its permanence. (Cf. perhaps Mal 2:15; in Gal 3:28 the allusion to Gen 1:27 LXX upholds the theme of reunification.)

Jesus' position requires him to elucidate Deut 24:1, where God permits divorce. The main point is not that the teaching of Genesis is from God, that in Deuteronomy from Moses. Rather, the instructions in Deut 24:1 are a concession to the moral petrification of the post-fallen state. Jesus does not undo Deut 24:1 but rather distinguishes the perfect will of God from the commandments which reflect human sinfulness (cf. the legislation for kingship, an institution due to divine concession). With this distinction in mind Jesus can demand conformity to the will of God as it was expressed in the beginning. Probably in the background is the equation of beginning and end: the coming of the kingdom is the restoration of paradise and so the realization of what God intended from the beginning. In any case the only command in Deut 24:1–4 is that 'her first husband, who sent her away, is not permitted to take her again to be his wife'. This matters because whereas in v. 7 the Pharisees ask why Moses 'commanded' a certificate of divorce to be given, in v. 8 Jesus speaks of Moses giving permission. Here then there is a correction: Moses did not command divorce; he only allowed it—seemingly as the lesser of two evils in some circumstances.

The problem of whether v. 9 allows remarriage for the innocent party (so traditionally most Protestants) cannot finally be answered. Does 'except for unchastity' qualify only the first verb ('divorces') or both verbs (also 'marries')? Patristic opinion, burdened by a less than enthusiastic view of marriage, disallowed remarriage and so understood our text accordingly. The link with vv. 10–12, which have to do with sexual abstinence, has been taken to uphold this view: the eunuchs for the kingdom are those who separate from their spouses because of 'adultery' and do not remarry. Yet the saying about eunuchs is not a command but a qualified recommendation: not all are given the gift. So if vv. 10–12 are closely associated with v. 9, it might appear that some *can* remarry. One also wonders whether something like the later distinction between separation and divorce would have made sense in Matthew's environment. The Jewish divorce bill contained the clause, 'You are free to marry again.' To obtain a divorce was to obtain permission to remarry (5:32 simply assumes that divorce leads to remarriage: to divorce a wife is to make her commit adultery—because she will take another spouse).

The disciples' response to Jesus' teaching is unexpected. Just as they wrongly rebuke people for bringing a child to Jesus in the next paragraph, and just as they will wonder, 'Then who can be saved?' in the paragraph after that, so here too: they misunderstand. The correct inference from Jesus' exaltation of lifelong marriage is not the promulgation of celibacy. But the disciples, holding a view of marriage and divorce akin to that in Sir 25:16–26, and reasoning that a lifetime of commitment to one woman is more burdensome than no involvement at all, conclude that it is better not to marry.

The crux of v. 11 is 'this teaching'. Does it refer to vv. 3–9 or to v. 9 (Jesus' teaching on divorce) or to v. 10 (the disciples' inference from Jesus' teaching) or does it anticipate or introduce v. 12 (the saying about eunuchs)? Or can no sense be made of the passage because disparate traditions have been merged? A reference to vv. 3–9 or 9 is unlikely. It would make v. 12 address those who have separated from their wives and enjoin them to remain single. But v. 9 does not clearly exclude the prospect of remarriage if there has been divorce for adultery. Further, the gift of celibacy is something exceptional, something that cannot be accepted by everyone, whereas surely Jesus' teaching on divorce is for all. Finally, one could not in any case speak of a *command* not to remarry: vv. 11–12 contain only a recommendation.

Does 'this teaching' then point forward to v. 12? This is possible. But a connection with v. 10 is more likely. The disciples' remark in v. 10 is a transitional sentence. They have drawn an inference about celibacy from Jesus' teaching on marriage. Jesus does not go back to the subject of marriage but takes up the question of celibacy ('this teaching'). His main thrust may be seen in the contrast between the disciples' unqualified generalization and his own denial of universal applicability. Note how the qualifications are piled up: 'not everyone', 'those to whom it is given', 'let anyone accept this who can'. Bengel rightly wrote: 'Jesus opposes these words [vv. 11–12] to the universal proposition of his disciples.' Matthew does use the saying on eunuchs to confirm celibacy as a calling; but his emphasis—in contradiction to the disciples—is upon its special character. Perhaps the evangelist felt a need to combat a perceived excess in his own community. There was certainly a growing fondness for asceticism and so for celibacy in the Hellenistic world.

According to the rabbis there were two sorts of eunuchs, those of human device and those of nature's making (cf. *m. Zab.* 2:1). The first, the 'eunuch of man', was a male who had either been literally castrated or who had, sometime after birth, lost the power to reproduce. The second was the 'eunuch of the sun', that is, from the first seeing of the sun—one born with defective male organs (cf. *b. Yebam.* 79b). While the rabbinic sources are late, 19:12 shows that in this regard they preserve an old way of speaking. Jesus takes up the traditional categories and to them adds a third—men who are unmarried not because they cannot take a wife but rather because they will not, because the duty placed upon them is such that it is best discharged outside marriage. For these people, the good and valuable thing that marriage undoubtedly is must be sacrificed in view of the demand made upon them by something greater.

(19:13–15) This stark narrative consists of narrative introduction (v. 13) + dominical word (v. 14) + narrative conclusion (v. 15). The introduction sets the scene: some (unspecified) want Jesus to bless children (infants?); the disciples, for reasons unknown, protest. Once the opposition is generated, Jesus reveals with whom he sides—first by word, then by deed. Both acts of communication implicitly rebuke the disciples while an *inclusio* (the laying on of hands appears in both vv. 13 and 15) confirms the instincts of those who bring the children for blessing. Thus the pericope reinforces the sympathy one feels for children elsewhere in this gospel (14:13–21; 15:21–8, 29–39; 18:3; 21:15).

After the discussion of marriage and celibacy, children are now the subject. The order is natural and occurs elsewhere, as in Philo, *De fug.* 1.3; Eph 5:21–6:4; Josephus, *Ag. Ap.* 2. 199–204; *Ps.-Phoc.* 175–217. Children should be received 'for it is to such as these [those in the situation of children] that the kingdom of heaven belongs' (cf. 5:3, 10; Ps 8:1–2; *b. Sanh.* 110b). Interpreted in the light of 18:3, this teaches humility, by which is meant lack of concern for worldly status. To be childlike is to be without power or position. So there are two lessons: be kind to children, embody humility.

If in 19:10 the disciples assert that it is better not to marry, in v. 13 they belittle children. Both judgements are consistent with a negative view of family life—and in both cases Jesus offers correction. In 19:11–12 he makes it plain that celibacy is not for everyone, and in vv. 13–15 he affirms that children are to be welcomed. So vv. 13–15, in their present context, reinforce 19:11–12 and so confirm the high view of marriage put forward in 19:1–9.

This passage has been used to justify infant baptism; but there is hardly evidence for thinking that this was an issue for the synoptic evangelists. On the other hand, perhaps the practice of blessing children in church was already a matter for discussion in the first century.

(19:16–30) The subject of domestic affairs continues with a section on wealth and the kingdom. The topic has already been extensively treated in the SM. Indeed, the saying about the impossibility of serving both God and mammon (6:24) is here concretely demonstrated. The subjects of treasure in heaven (6:19–21), generosity (6:22–3),

eschatological reversal (5:3–12), and perfection (5:48) also resurface here.

This passage also reinforces and illustrates the SM's teaching on Torah. Jesus' words to the rich man and the disciples do not abolish the law. On the contrary, they enjoin the commandments. Indeed, because the two texts cited—the Decalogue and Lev 19.18—were understood as summaries of, or headings for, the law (see below), their endorsement perhaps even implies the validity of 'the least of these commandments'. In any event two of the OT verses cited in 5:21–48 (Ex 20:13, 14 || Deut 5:17, 18) are here quoted by Jesus, and without any qualification. The Decalogue is plainly still in force. Both the SM and vv. 16–30 affirm the Torah and at the same time demand more.

vv. 16–22 recount a call to discipleship. To the question about eternal life, Jesus responds with a question, a theological assertion, and an imperative. This last changes the metaphor from market to road: Jesus demands not a purchase but a pilgrimage. He also rejects the implication that in some way the OT is inadequate. Pilgrimage means keeping the second table of the Decalogue (the table on social relations: Ex 20:12–16; Deut 5:16–20) and, in accord with Leviticus, loving one's neighbour as oneself. The omission of the first table is perhaps surprising; but the issue at hand will prove to be social, and certainly Calvin was correct to observe that right action (as depicted by the second table) is proof of right religion (as outlined by the first table; *Inst.* 2.8.52–3).

The question, 'Which ones?' (v. 18), might imply the unimportance of parts of the Torah: only some commandments are required for salvation. Jesus' response dispels that notion. He quotes the Decalogue and Lev 19:18. The former was thought of as a summary of, or heading for, the whole law (cf. Philo, *Spec. leg.* 1.1) whereas the latter (or the chapter to which it belonged) was sometimes said to contain the Torah *in nuce* (*Sipra Lev.* on 19:1–4). So v. 19 directs attention not to isolated texts but to parts that stand for the whole.

In v. 21 Jesus demands not merely alms but everything. This is not an imperative of the Decalogue or the OT but something new, a novel charge engendered by the nature of discipleship and the greater righteousness announced by 5:20. But what is meant by being 'perfect'? There has always been a tendency to sort Christians into two grades, one more advanced than the other, e.g. in monasticism. But v. 21 does not mean that Christians who sell all will be 'perfect' while others will be stuck with 'a second degree of virtue' (Jerome). Calvin was right: 'Our Lord is not proclaiming a general statement that is applicable to everyone, but only to the person with whom He is speaking.' This passage is a call story, like those in 4:18–20; 8:18–22; and 9:9. The rich man is being invited to follow Jesus in a specific situation. This circumstance determines what is asked of him. One can no more generalize v. 21 than turn 8:22 ('leave the dead to bury their own dead') into a general order to neglect the deceased. Moreover, the continuation in 19:22–6 shows that the rich man loses not perfection but salvation.

What then is meant by 'perfect'? It can hardly be a reference to sinlessness, although such an idea would not have been foreign to ancient Jews. In 5:48 the connotation of completeness is foremost, but whereas there it is the completeness of love, here it is the completeness of obedience: perfection is perfect obedience. The rich man would be perfect if he exhibited wholehearted obedience to Jesus Christ.

In vv. 23–6 Jesus turns from the rich man to his disciples and gives commentary on what has just happened. His point is that God's kingdom is hard to reach if one is rich, for the rich inevitably trust in the security of wealth rather than in God alone. Indeed, in the absurd juxtaposition of the largest native beast in Palestine with a well-known example of a very small opening in v. 24, Jesus speaks about the impossible: 'one impossibility is compared with another' (Jerome).

The disciples' subsequent question, which uncritically presupposes (against the rest of Matthew) that wealth is a sign of divine favour, implies that if not even the rich man, blessed as he is by God, can enter the kingdom, who can? The answer lies in God's omnipotence, which is antithetical to human impotence: regarding salvation only God has strength—just as, with regard to goodness, God and human beings belong to different categories (cf. v. 17). But note that v. 26 speaks only of the possible, not the probable. God's omnipotence does not guarantee anyone's salvation. v. 26 is not comfort for the rich; it does not cancel vv. 23–4.

In vv. 27–30 Peter asks how things stand with itinerants such as himself who have, in contrast with the rich man, forsaken all. Jesus responds first by offering congratulations and promising future reward. But the happy words are soon balanced with the caution of 20:1–16: if the twelve are examples of the last becoming first, they need beware, lest they likewise become examples of the first becoming last.

The crucial v. 28, which alludes to Dan 7:9–27, refers not to a one-time judgement but to lordship. The text is not about Israel's condemnation at the consummation but the disciples' exercise of authority in the future (cf. 20:20–1). As the twelve phylarchs once directed the twelve tribes under Moses, and as Israel was once ruled by judges, so shall it be at the end. Compare the Jewish prayer in the *Shemoneh 'Esreh*: 'Restore our judges as in former times.'

(20:1–16) The parable, which recounts the events of a single day, falls into two parts. vv. 1–7 (which open with sunrise) describe the hiring of labourers, and vv. 8–16 (which are set in the evening) then recount the story of payment. The point is not to contrast Jews and Gentiles (or Jewish Christians and Gentile Christians); nor is the passage an allegory of human life (childhood, adolescence, etc.) or of world history, or salvation history, or spiritual progress; neither is it a pictorial representation of 21:31—the toll-collectors and prostitutes (i.e. the last) go into the kingdom of God before the Pharisees (i.e. the first). It is also not a supplement to 19:16–30, illustrating how the last (cf. the disciples and those who come at the eleventh hour) become first and how the first (cf. the rich man and those hired at the first hour) become last. The text is rather a parable of the last judgement which functions as a warning against boasting or presuming oneself to be among the first. vv. 1–15 are framed by 19:20 and 20:16, which teach eschatological reversal. So vv. 1–15 mean above all that the promise of reward (cf. the previous paragraph) should not become ground upon which to stand. The last can become first.

Beyond this the parable teaches that God rewards human beings according to an unexpected goodness—although this teaching functions not as encouragement but as warning (cf. 19:30). God's kindness, in this regard analogous to Jesus' moral imperatives, satisfies justice and then goes further. So the less deserving may receive as much as the more deserving. Like the Spirit, the divine grace blows where it wills. That destroys all human reckoning and therefore all presumption. It is a truth that must be absorbed after the heady promises of 19:28–9: hope should never become self-satisfaction.

One might suppose that in 19:16–30 salvation is according to works: one must obey the Torah and Jesus Christ. But vv. 1–15 disallow this simplistic interpretation, for they clearly teach, albeit in a picture, that there is no necessary proportion between human work and divine reward; or, as Isaac the Syrian provocatively put it, 'How can you call God just when you come across the Scriptural passage on the wage given to the workers?' (*Ascetical Homilies*, 51). Many have even found a Pauline doctrine of grace here.

(20:17–19) This detailed passion prediction summarizes the major events subsequent to Gethsemane. Their order is that of the passion narrative, except in the latter the scourging comes before the mocking. vv. 17–19 move the story forward by taking Jesus closer to Jerusalem and by forecasting for a third time and so emphasizing upcoming events. As compared with the earlier passion predictions (16:21; 17:22–3), the condemnation to death, deliverance to Gentiles, mocking, scourging, and crucifixion are new. As Jesus nears his end, its shape becomes plainer. Also plainer is Jesus' foreknowledge, which is not vague but exact.

This passage is surrounded by two sizeable paragraphs having to do with eschatological rewards. But vv. 17–19 are not a disruptive foreign body; they illustrate 19:30–20:16 in that Jesus is the last (in his sufferings and death) who will be the first (when God exalts him). As for the link with 20:20–3, the passion prediction illumines exactly what 'the cup' there spoken of is. Further, the tragic solemnity of vv. 17–19 is a perfect foil for v. 20: following Jesus' announcement of suffering we do not next read that his disciples showed concern for him—only that some people were preoccupied with their self-centred hopes. The loneliness of the passion narrative is already felt here.

(20:20–8) The two scenes—vv. 20–3 (on false ambition) and vv. 24–8 (on true service)—exhibit parallelism (cf. v. 21 with 23, v. 22 with 23, v. 25*b* with *c*, v. 26 with 27) and continue the theme of the third passion prediction, namely, Jesus' death (vv. 17–19). It is not the sons themselves who make the request but their mother. Perhaps the reader should recall 1 Kings 1:15–21, where Bathsheba appears before King David. The king enquires, 'What do you wish?' She in turn asks the throne for Solomon. The LXX uses *prosekunēsen* of the mother (v. 16; cf. v. 31) and *kathēsetai* of the son (vv. 17, 20; cf. v. 30). One can also think of the one other place in the gospel where a mother appeals to Jesus on behalf of a child: 15:21–8, the story of the Canaanite woman. Of that woman too *prosekunei* is used (v. 25). Is the similarity of the two texts designed to stimulate reflection on the differences between the two supplicants and so instruct one in what sorts of petitions are proper and which not?

The mother's question, which is about eschatological rule and places of honour, recognizes Jesus' destiny and correctly assumes his great authority. But the request is misdirected and takes no account of what has just been predicted. Although crowds will soon hail Jesus as the Davidic Messiah, Jerusalem will see him mount not a throne but a cross—and those at his right and left will be not glorified apostles but crucified criminals (27:38). That Matthew indeed intended an ironic allusion to this last scene seems probable: in both places the Greek wording is the same.

Neither for Jesus nor for Matthew should the 'cup' be equated with 'temptations' or (with reference to 26:27) given a sacramental interpretation; nor can there be any real connection with the drink given to Jesus on the cross (27:34, 48). It is also improbable that 'cup' refers simply to death (although the targums do know the expression, 'taste the cup of death') or martyrdom (as in later Christian texts). In the OT and intertestamental literature 'cup' is often used figuratively in texts about suffering, especially suffering God's wrath or judgement; and that illumines the usage here. The cup that Jesus will drink (cf. 26:39) is the cup of eschatological sorrow, which will be first poured out upon the people of God (cf. Jer 25:15–29). Jesus will face God's judgement.

v. 28, which probably alludes to both Dan 7:13–14 and Isa 53:10–12, is the climax to vv. 20–8. It is the last word Jesus speaks before going up to Jerusalem and shows him to be the Son of Man in whom word and deed are one, the true king whose one aim is to benefit his subjects. The word traditionally translated 'ransom' means deliverance by payment. In the LXX it invariably means 'ransom-price' and appears in various contexts—of the half-shekel poll tax, of payment to save one's life after one has killed another, of buying back mortgaged property, of buying an enslaved relation, and of the redemption of the firstborn. In the present instance the principle of 'life for life' (Ex 21:23) is operative. Like the death of the martyrs in 4 Macc 1:11; 6:28–9; and 17:20–2, Jesus' death has a beneficial effect upon others—here 'the many', by which is meant 'all' (cf. Rom 5:15, 19; 1 Tim 2:6).

If v. 28, as appears, combines Dan 7 and Isa 53, there is an interesting parallel in Mt 8:20. In both the Son of Man is subject, in both he is humbled, and in both Scripture is seemingly alluded to ironically: the Son of Man, against Dan 7, has come not to be served but to serve; and the Son of Man, against Ps 8, does not have dominion, glory, and honour but rather no place to lay his head.

v. 28 is a particularly apt conclusion to 20:20–7. When the mother of the sons of Zebedee envisages James and John sitting on the right and left of Jesus in the kingdom, the reader is reminded of 19:28, where the twelve are promised thrones beside the Son of Man. It is hence fitting that the paragraph culminates in a declaration about the Son of Man. But here, as opposed to 19:28, the subject is not the Son of Man's glory but his service unto death. As in vv. 20–3, visions of grandeur (cf. Dan 7:13–14) give way to forecasts of suffering and death (cf. Isa 53; Dan 7:21–5), for the king cannot sit on his throne until he has, through self-sacrifice, rescued his people.

(20:29–34) Carter (1994: 203) has observed that if chs. 19–20 outline a difficult way of life at odds with 'dominant hierarchical household patterns', a way of 'life that is opposed and misunderstood', our story appropriately follows: 'after the uncompromising demand of chs. 19–20 . . . this pericope underlines that God's compassionate mercy and power are available for all disciples who, in the midst of difficult circumstances, recognize their inadequacy and call for God's help'.

This passage is remarkably reminiscent of 9:27–30. In both Jesus is being followed, two blind men appear, the blind men cry out and say, 'Have mercy on us, Son of David', Jesus touches their eyes, and they see again. There are also striking verbal links (cf. e.g. 20:29, 30, with 9:27). These parallels form a sort of *inclusio*. The first restoration of sight occurs towards the beginning of the ministry, the second near the end. This gives an artistic unity to the whole gospel. Furthermore, the first takes place before corporate Israel has rejected Jesus, the second after that rejection has become manifest. So despite being rejected, Jesus' charity remains the same throughout. His difficulties do not cancel his compassion.

Is there a lesson in the juxtaposition of 20:20–8 and vv. 29–34? In the former, two privileged insiders (James and John) make a request through a third party (their mother). The request is prefaced by no title of respect or majesty, it concerns the eschatological future, and it involves personal exaltation (to sit at the right and left of the Messiah). In the latter, two outsiders (the blind men) make a request that a third party (the crowd) tries to stifle. That request is prefaced by titles of respect and majesty, concerns the present, and is for something necessary that is taken for granted by most (sight). One might infer that petitions are more likely to be heard when addressed directly, with respect, and for things truly needful.

(21:1–11) This story, which reminds one of 1 Sam 10:1–9 (the finding of donkeys for Saul), pulls forward several threads from the previous chapters—the theme of prophetic fulfilment (cf. 1:22–3, etc.), Jesus' trek to Jerusalem (cf. 16:21; 20:17), his 'meekness' (cf. 11:29), his status as 'king' (cf. 2:1–12), 'Son of David' (cf. 1:1–18), 'the coming one' (cf. 3:11; 11:3), and 'prophet' (cf. 13:57). But vv. 1–11 also offer two firsts—(1) Jesus' public claim (albeit indirect) to messianic kingship, and (2) recognition by 'the crowds' of that kingship (contrast 16:13–14). Together these two firsts challenge Jerusalem to make a decision: who is this Jesus (cf. v. 10)? What follows depends upon the city's answer to that question.

Other texts recount the triumphal arrival (*parousia*) of a ruler or military hero and contain a standard cluster of motifs: approach of the king, public acclamation/celebration (sometimes with song), entrance into city, cultic activity (including the cleansing of cultic pollution); see e.g. 1 Kings 1:32–40; Zech 9:9; 1 Macc 5:45–54; 2 Macc 4:21–2; Jos. *Ant.* 11.325–39. 1 Macc 13:49–53, like v. 8, even refers to palm branches. But Jesus' entry is not a military triumph. On the contrary, the Son of David is 'meek' and has not conquered anything. Further, Jesus does not sacrifice in the temple but rebukes the cult. It does not legitimate him; he stands above it (12:6).

(21:12–17) Having entered the capital as king, Jesus next enters the temple, the symbol of national identity, and there, through prophetic deed and scriptural word, declares divine disfavour. The disfavour is not directed against the temple as such but against those who have corrupted it. In the temple the meek king heals those without status (the blind and the lame) and is praised by those without power (children). Opposed to him are men of authority, prestige, and influence. But in truth those who appear to be in charge are not, and judgement will soon overtake them.

(21:18–22) For the third time in three paragraphs Jesus performs a symbolic act. Here that act and its effect are prophetic. The visual parable inaugurates judgement against that for which it stands. That the fig tree 'near the road'—we should envisage a wild fig tree: Jesus does not curse another's property—withers is a symbol of judgement (cf. Isa 34:4; Jer 8:13; Hos 2:12). The judgement is not against Israel as a whole but Jerusalem and/or those in charge of the temple. vv. 18–22 are located between two paragraphs having to do with the temple, in the first of which Jesus protests, in the second of which the priests protest against Jesus. So in context this passage shows that the divine wrath has begun to manifest itself against the temple establishment. Beyond this, if 21:13 refers to the temple as 'a house of prayer', it is not coincidence that our pericope concerns petition. In Matthew the old temple has been replaced by the church. So the sequence in 21:12–22—judgement of the old place of prayer, promise of prayer's efficacy within the church—reflects the course of salvation history as well as the deterritorialization of Matthean religion: portable community (cf. 18:20) substitutes for fixed holy space.

(21:23–7) These verses both add to the dramatic tension between Jesus and his opponents and demonstrate the character of the latter. And trailing upon the protest in the temple and the cursing of the fig tree they illustrate why the temple is doomed: the leaders have become deaf to God's messengers.

This section is less about Jesus—it is certainly not about his debating skills—or the Baptist than it is about the chief priests and elders. Here they enquire of Jesus 'without reason or respect, a thing that was plain to all' (Calvin). Further, out of cowardly expediency, they respond to his questions with a lie ('we do not know'). As if that were not enough, they show themselves to be spiritually less perceptive than those over whom they preside, for the multitudes recognize John's prophetic status. The effect of all this is to set the passion of Jesus within a moral context. Jesus' death is not the upshot of an unfortunate misunderstanding by uninformed authorities; instead is it brought about by the plotting of self-serving men of ill will. The passion narrative depicts a struggle between good and evil.

(21:28–32) The polemical parable is allegorically interpreted in vv. 31–2: the father represents God; the first son represents toll collectors and prostitutes, those who were lax in the law but came to obey God through John's ministry; the second son represents the chief priests and the elders, those who, despite their religious profession, disobeyed God by not believing in John. The main function is to characterize Jesus' opponents. Chrysostom urged that the two children represent Jews and Gentiles: the former, having heard the law and promised obedience, were disobedient, while the latter, not having

heard the law, became obedient in Christ. This interpretation in terms of salvation history has dominated exegetical history. Recent exegetes, however, have rightly begun to question it. Nothing so far in 19:1 ff. has directly addressed Jewish–Gentile relations. Indeed, the section has encouraged us rather to think in terms of believing and unbelieving Israel. In addition, the parable is explicitly about different responses to John the Baptist, not Jesus or the Christian kerygma. The most natural interpretation, then, is that which finds in this pericope (1) depiction of a divided Israel; (2) characterization of Jesus' opponents as hypocrites; and (3) illustration of the first (the chief priests and elders) becoming last and the last (toll collectors and prostitutes) becoming first. In 21:23–5 Jesus asks his opponents several questions. Their answers are: 'we do not know' (21:27), 'the first' (v. 31), 'he will put those wretches to a miserable death, and lease the vineyard to other tenants who will give him the produce at the harvest time' (21:41), 'Caesar's' (22:21), 'the Son of David' (22:42), and, finally, silence (22:45). These answers, brief and colourless, are always dictated by the question and empty of insight. Further, two answers confess ignorance (21:27; 22:45) and two are self-incriminating (21:27, 41). Jesus' opponents are adept at laying traps, but they are also good at falling into them. Jesus' answers, on the other hand, are uniformly creative, clever, and memorable; and they avoid entanglement either by turning a question back on others or moving the discussion to another level. Jesus' spiritual authority gives him a rhetorical sovereignty.

(21:33–46) This parable is an allegory about faithlessness and judgement. Its character as an allegory does not mean that it is not true to life—it largely seems to be—or that every element has a symbolic meaning, only that equations for the main elements can be given: the vineyard stands for Israel; the householder stands for God; the tenant farmers stand for leaders of Israel; the fruit stands for what is owed to God; the rejection of servants stands for rejection of prophets; the sending and rejection of the son stand for the sending and rejection of Jesus; the punishment of tenants stands for Jerusalem's destruction; the new tenants stand for the church.

Our parable and its interpretation combine the traditional motif of the rejection and even murder of the prophets with the traditional metaphor of Israel as God's vineyard (cf. Isa 5:2). What is new is the joining of the two themes in the service of Christology: the rejection of Jesus is the climax in the story of rebellion against Israel's God.

This passage is not about God's rejection of the Jews and the Gentiles' acceptance of Jesus. The parable identifies the tenants not with the Jews in general but with the Jewish leaders in particular. Further, the context is conflict between Jesus and Israel's leaders, not Jesus and Judaism; and it is not the vineyard (i.e. Israel) that suffers judgement but those in charge. So the kingdom is taken from the Jewish leaders and given to the church of Jew and Gentile.

(22:1–14) The passage consists of introduction (v. 1), parable (vv. 2–13b), commentary (vv. 13c–14). The parable (perhaps based upon a traditional story; cf. *y. Sanh.* 6:23c) contains two parallel sequences. Each recounts three actions of the king.

2–3a   action of king (invitation)
3b   response (rejection)
4   reaction of king (invitation)
5–6   response (rejection and violence)
7   reaction of king (punishment: death and destruc-
            tion)
8–9   action of king (invitation)
10   response (acceptance)
11–12b   reaction of king (entrance and question)
12c   response (silence)
13b   reaction of king (punishment: binding and casting
            out)

The whole sequence is dominated by the speech of the king: no one else says anything. Everything revolves around his words.

vv. 1–10 are an allegory much influenced by 21:33–41. The king stands for God; his son represents Jesus (cf. 21:37–8); the royal wedding feast symbolizes the eschatological banquet. The dual sending of the servants is, as in the preceding parable, the sending of God's messengers; the murder of the servants represents the murder of the prophets and Jesus (cf. 21:35–9). v. 7 alludes to the destruction of Jerusalem in 70 CE. The third sending of servants is the mission of the church, in which good and evil stand side by side until the end. The man without a garment, who stands for a whole class at the last judgement, lacks either good works (cf. Rev 19:8) or a glorious resurrected body (cf. 13:43). His punishment may reflect a tradition about Azazel. According to 1 Enoch 10:4–5, God instructed the angel Raphael to bind Azazel 'hand and foot and throw him into the darkness'. And according to Apoc. Abr. 13:14, the fallen Azazel lost his heavenly garment, which will be given to Abraham. All this is strikingly close to our text. Perhaps we should think of the man's fate as akin to that of Azazel. Just as the righteous will wear garments of glory and so be like the heavenly angels, so will the wicked be unclothed and suffer like the fallen angels.

vv. 11–14 turn attention from outsiders to insiders, from opponents to the church. The evangelist as pastor was all too aware that criticism of others as well as the doctrine of election (cf. v. 14) are both fraught with moral peril; for the former tends to nourish complacency—censure of our enemies always makes us feel better about ourselves—while the latter can beget feelings of superiority. Matthew, however, understood that while censure has its place in moral instruction, and while election is of the essence of Judaism, the two things can foster illusions; and they are no substitute for self-examination and personal effort. So it is that Christian readers of vv. 11–14, who necessarily identify with those at the king's banquet, cannot read the text and feel self-satisfaction. They must instead ask whether they are like the man improperly clothed, whether they are among 'the many' despite profession to be among 'the few'. God's judgement comes upon all, including those within the ecclesia.

(22:15–22) Here begins a series of discussions that runs through the rest of ch. 22. The first pits Jesus against Pharisees and Herodians (vv. 15–22), the second against the Sadducees (22:23–33), the third against a Pharisaic lawyer (22:34–40), and the fourth against the Pharisees (22:41–6). Taken together the four passages add to the negative characteriza-

tion of the Jerusalem leaders. The first question for Jesus is whether God would have one contribute to the Roman *census*, a tax upon agricultural yield and personal property, collected through census or registration (Lk 2:1–5; Acts 5:37) and probably amounting to one denarius a year. Although Jewish authorities (including the Sanhedrin) helped farm the tax, many resented it and objected on religious grounds. Indeed, although Roman taxation had been a reality since 63 BCE, the census of 6 or 7 CE, when Judea came under direct Roman control, encouraged a revolt; and resentment of taxation also contributed to the unrest that culminated in the revolt of 70 CE.

Although the story would be coherent without vv. 19–21a, the use of a visual aid adds drama, while the coin being in the possession of Jesus' opponents highlights their insincerity: they have no qualms about using pagan money—and even bring a coin with the emperor's image and blasphemous inscription into the holy precincts of the temple.

Instead of trapping Jesus, the Pharisees and Herodians are trapped by him. Jesus' words distance him from those who oppose supporting Rome. At the same time, the inclusion of giving to God what is his relativizes the political obligation. There is here no firm principle of loyal submission to the state. Implied rather is a reservation regarding the state, a lack of reservation regarding God. While obedience to God can, as in the current instance, coexist with doing what the state requires, obligation to the former overshadows obligation to the latter. So there is no simple or straightforward rule, but the imperative to weigh the demands of two (very unequal) authorities. When those demands are not at odds (as here), obligations to both can be met (cf. Rom 13:1–7; 1 Pet 2:17). In cases of conflict, however, it is manifest which authority requires allegiance. Our text has rightly been cited to curb the powers of the state (e.g. John of Damascus, *De Imaginibus* 2.12). God, who after all determines what is Caesar's and what is not, is sovereign over the state, albeit in a non-theocratic fashion. In the end, no one can serve two masters (6:24), and all that truly matters is obedience to God. (Beginning with Tertullian, many have identified 'the things that are God's' with human beings. If coins with Caesar's image and inscription belong to Caesar, then human beings created in God's image (Gen 1:26) belong to God.)

(22:23–33) If the Pharisees raise a political issue, the Sadducees (who presumably believe only in the OT's shadowy Sheol) now pose a theological riddle which combines the teaching of the levirate law in Deut 25:5 with the concrete example in Gen 38:8. Although the two parties disagree regarding resurrection, they are one in opposing Jesus.

In 22:15–22 no one cites Scripture. Here, however, Scripture is at the centre, as also in 22:34–40, 41–6. The effect is to uphold Jesus' harmony with the Torah and to display his skill in its interpretation.

The Sadducees' question, which assumes that polyandry is unacceptable and implies that the resurrection is foreign to the Pentateuch, is rejected by Jesus as the product of culpable ignorance and bad theology. The Sadducees deny the resurrection because they imagine the eschatological future others profess to be mundane and terrestrial. But their materialistic view is not the view of Jesus, according to whom Israel's God is the omnipotent who can transform the saints. 'Neither marry nor are given in marriage' means 'Neither do (men) marry nor are (women) given in marriage.' 'In the resurrection' means not 'at the resurrection' but 'in the resurrected condition (of the just)'. The argument moves from the general to the particular. If in general people will be like angels (then a common belief), then the marital bond in particular will be transcended, for angels (who are immortal) live without marriage (not because they are sexless or androgynous— they were typically thought of as male—but because they refrain; cf. 2 Apoc. Bar. 56:14).

In passing, in v. 31, from the *manner* of the resurrection to its *fact*, Jesus does not cite Dan 12:1–3 (or other possible biblical proof-texts for the resurrection) but a Pentateuchal text. He accordingly meets the Sadducees (who recognized only the authority of Moses) on their own ground. He cites Ex 3:6. The point seems to be this: God does not say, 'I was the God of Abraham, etc.' but 'I *am* the God of Abraham, etc.'— even though Abraham and the others are dead at the time of the pronouncement. They therefore cannot have ceased to be.

(22:34–40) A representative of the Pharisees continues the series of hostile challenges begun in 21:23. Again the issue regards Torah, and again Jesus speaks truth without becoming ensnared. His summary of the law and the prophets, which recapitulates the unifying theme of his own words and deeds, simply joins, against all possible complaint, two traditional Jewish summaries, the commandment to love God (part of the Shema, Judaism's closest thing to a creed) and the commandment to love neighbour (which Akiba reportedly called 'the greatest principle in the law', Sipre Lev. 19:18; cf. Gal 5:14; Rom 13:8–10). Together they summarize the Decalogue (cf. Philo, Dec. 19–20, 50–1, 106–10, 121, 154). Jesus, although asked for the greatest commandment, answers with two which are inextricable. ('A second is like it' is purely numerical; the second commandment equals in importance the first.) But Matthew does not clarify how the two commandments to love relate to one another. Evagrius Ponticus argued that love of neighbour is love of God because it is love of the image of God. Theodoret of Cyrrhus urged that, as contemplation is to action, so love of God is to love of neighbour: the one is the foundation of and inspiration for the other. We imitate what we love; so to love God is to imitate the One whose love is catholic (5:43–8). Ailred of Rievaux contended that 'love of neighbour precedes love of God': the latter grows out of the former. Luther argued that while our neighbour is needy, God needs nothing, so true service of God must always be for the sake of the neighbour. Harnack thought that the gospel places love of neighbour beside love of God because 'the love of one's neighbour is the only practical proof on earth of that love of God which is strong in humanity'. While there may be an element of truth in the other proposals, Evagrius' claim resonates most with the rest of Matthew. For there is some sense in which, according to Matthew, God is in others. Especially striking is 25:31–46. In this, Jesus, the functional presence of God (cf. 1:23; 18:20; 28:20), is the direct recipient of acts of love done to others: 'as you did it to one of the least of these . . .' Service of neighbour is service of Christ, which means service of God. Chrysostom was right: 'to love God is

to love one's neighbour'. As the agraphon has it: 'You have seen your brother; you have seen God.'

Often cited as a parallel to our verse is b. Šabb. 31a, where Hillel, in response to a request to teach the Torah while standing on one foot, answered with this: 'What you hate for yourself, do not do to your neighbour. This is the whole law. The rest is commentary.' This is even closer to Matthew than the commentaries indicate; for in Jewish tradition, as in Christian, the Golden Rule (or its negative form) was thought synonymous with Lev 19:18, cited here (cf. Tg. Yer. I on 19.18; Sipre Lev. on 19:18).

Lev 19:18 is quoted three times in this gospel, more than any other OT text: at 5:43; 19:19; 22:39. The first citation expands the meaning of neighbour to make it universal: even the enemy is to be loved. The second citation reveals Lev 19:18's status as a fundamental summary of the moral demands of the Decalogue. The third brings the love of neighbour into intimate connection with the commandment to love God and thus, in typically Matthean fashion, fuses religion and ethics.

(22:41–6) Following the narrative introduction (v. 41), Jesus abandons his defensive posture and takes the offensive. He asks the Pharisees two questions (v. 42a). After they return their expected, two-word answer (v. 42b), Jesus asks two more questions, this time quoting Scripture (vv. 43–5). In the narrative conclusion (v. 46) the opponents are unable to respond. This effectively closes off 21:23–22:46, throughout which Jesus has been asked question after question.

Jesus' questions, unlike those of his opponents, go to the heart of things, for they concern Christology. The first question, 'What do you think of the Messiah?' is completed by the second, so that the meaning is: 'Whose son is the Messiah?' The answer of the Pharisees, 'David's', is only half the truth. The other half, unpronounced by Jesus but clear from the rest of the narrative, is: 'God's'. Jesus' argument makes two assumptions: (1) in accordance with Jewish tradition, David composed Ps 110 (cf. the superscription) and (2) Ps 110 is messianic (cf. 23:39). It follows that David wrote about 'the Lord' (i.e. God) speaking to 'my Lord', and that the latter must be the messianic Son of David (cf. v. 42). We have here an apparent contradiction. For how can one standing at the right hand of God and addressed as 'Lord' be David's 'son'? A son may address his father as 'Lord' (cf. 21:29), but a father does not so speak to his son. The Pharisees' silence shows that they have no solution to the riddle, even though it is superficial for the Christian reader, who knows that although the Messiah is of the lineage of David, he is also exalted to God's right hand and reigns as 'Lord'. The 'Son of David'—neither the title nor its content is rejected or denigrated—is a descendant of King David, and his destiny surpasses that of his forebear.

(23:1–39) Ch. 23 does not criticize isolated beliefs or activities; rather its charges amount to a rejection of Pharisaism itself. Surprisingly, however, Mt 23 does not censor the scribes and Pharisees for failure to believe in Messiah Jesus. Instead it convicts them by their own standards. No scribe or Pharisee would have defended hypocrisy, or commended the slaying of God's prophets, or affirmed that preoccupation with the lesser matters of the law should be at the expense of the greater. So the text presupposes that the scribes and Pharisees actually know better: they are hypocrites in the full sense of the word. The presupposition is possible because the scribes and Pharisees, like those in Matthew's community, were heirs to the Jewish tradition. Matthew's Jesus accordingly argues as a Jew with Jews: the leaders have been unfaithful to their own tradition.

Matthew's Jesus here passes from woe to woe; his polemic depicts the scribes and Pharisees as more than hard-hearted: they are already suffering spiritual rigor mortis. Yet surely the best of them were admirable men who faithfully practised their religion and honestly doubted that the Messiah had come. Without either excusing the harsh language or minimizing its historical misuses, one may emphasize the conventional nature of the chapter's polemical rhetoric. Josephus depicted the Zealots or Sicarii as murderers, transgressors of the laws of God and nature, impostors, madmen, hard-hearted wretches, 'bastards' and 'scum' more wicked than Sodom, as men guilty of 'barbarity...avarice...impudent undertakings...wicked practices, impiety...tyranny over others...the greatest madness ...wild and brutish disposition' (J.W. 4.377–8; 5.401–19, 442–5; 7.252–74). Those who wrote the Dead Sea scrolls laid every sort of pejorative adjective upon 'the sons of darkness', whom they cursed in their rituals. The thoroughly traditional nature of Matthew's polemic is demonstrated by the many Jewish sources in which opponents are hypocrites (1QS 4:14), blind (cf. Wis 2:21), guilty of economic sins (cf. As. Mos. 5.5), unclean (cf. Jos. J.W. 4.382), persecutors of the righteous (cf. Philo, Leg. ad Gaium, 18.120 ff.), like sinful generations of the past (cf. T. Levi, 14:6), like snakes (cf. 4Q525 5:1–4), destined for eschatological destruction (cf. m. Sanh. 10:1), and the cause of God forsaking his temple (cf. Jos. J.W. 2.539). In Matthew's world one's opponents were, as a rule, these things and much else besides. The language of vilification was as stereotyped as the language of praise. Accordingly we have here no more a fair account of Pharisaic Judaism than we have such an account of Christianity in later pagan polemic. Moreover, the ferocity of rhetoric in Jewish texts shows Matthew's polemic need not signal a break with Judaism. It is no more 'anti-Semitic' than the Dead Sea scrolls.

(23:1–12) These verses condemn hypocrisy (v. 3), religious show (vv. 4–6), and self-exaltation (v. 7). They commend obedience to the truth (v. 3), equality (v. 8), and humility (vv. 11–12). The same vices and virtues have been assailed and praised before, especially in the SM and ch. 18.

'Moses' seat' (v. 2) is ambiguous. It may either refer to a literal chair for synagogue authorities or be a metaphor for teaching authority (cf. the professor's 'chair'). In any case only here are the Jewish leaders presented in a positive light: they should be obeyed. Some have suggested we have here a pre-Matthean tradition out of harmony with the rest of the gospel, others that the command belongs only to the pre-Easter period, still others that it is ironic. It is also possible to regard the 'all' as hyperbole. The sentence indicts the scribes and the Pharisees by parading their inconsistencies. 'Do whatever they teach' is then less practical imperative than proof of a bad character which cannot be excused by ignorance. The focus is not upon Christian obedience but upon the opponents' knowledge, which condemns them. Yet another pos-

sibility is that 'whatever they teach you' refers to their reading of Scripture, 'they do' to Pharisaic doctrine and practice.

'Phylacteries' (v. 5) are the two black leather boxes containing parchment Scriptures that, since at least the second century BCE, have been commonly worn on the upper left arm and forehead following the literal understanding of Ex 13:9, 16; Deut 6:8; 11:18. Their ostentatious and superstitious use can be documented (cf. Christian use of medallions and crosses). 'Fringes' (which Jesus himself wears: 9:20; 14:36) consist of blue and/or white threads worn on the four corners of the rectangular outer garment (cf. Num 15:38–9; Deut 22:12). The presumption is that the scribes and Pharisees who make their tassels long (cf. Sipre Num. 15:37–41) do so to gain attention. The attack is not against a scriptural ordinance but its observance for self-glorification.

Unlike the scribes and Pharisees (v. 7) Christian authorities are to shun titles. Such titles are inconsistent with the demand for humility and mutuality and the need to restrict certain appellations to God and Christ. It is implied that the scribes and Pharisees enjoy wrongful flattery and think in hierarchical terms.

(23:13–33) The seven woes, in which the judge of the last day humbles the exalted in illustration of v. 12, draws a firm line between two groups by criticizing one. The scribes and Pharisees, here representatives of emergent rabbinic Judaism, are depicted as hopelessly corrupt. The upshot is edification and self-definition, for the debasement of the church's antagonists both indirectly vindicates the faithful and exhibits, through counter-examples, what the church should not be.

The woes, which commence with halakic disagreements and culminate in the murder of God's messengers, mirror the plot of the whole gospel, in which religious disputes lead to Jesus' death. Further, although ch. 23 strikes the reader as distinctive, this is not because its content is new: the woes constitute a climax, not a novum. All of the major accusations and assertions have already been made (cf. e.g. vv. 13, 15, with 11:21 and 18:7, vv. 13, 15, 25–8 with 15:7 and 22:18, and v. 13 with 5:20). Even the polemical harshness of 23:13–33 is not unique (cf. 22:1 ff.). New is its concentrated repetition alone.

The first woe (v. 13) appropriately prefaces the series as a sort of summary: the scribes and Pharisees, despite their religious efforts, neither enter the kingdom nor allow others to. The second woe (v. 14) indicts the scribes and Pharisees not because they are missionaries, but because their missionary activity, which makes others like themselves, has tragic effects. The problem is not conversion to Judaism but conversion to Judaism without the Messiah.

The third woe (vv. 16–22), which turns to specific halakah, argues first against the distinction between binding and non-binding oaths (vv. 16–19) and secondly asserts that all oaths are binding because all oaths relate themselves to God (vv. 20–22). In 5:33–7 oaths are attacked. Here their use is assumed. Common to both passages, however, is the idea that to swear by one thing is to swear by another. Indeed, both assert that to swear by heaven is to swear by God's throne. Evidently vv. 16–22 presuppose Jesus' criticism of oaths (understood as hyperbole, not halakah?) and present additional criticism of non-binding oaths.

The fourth woe (vv. 23–4) condemns not tithing but a lack of justice, mercy, and faith. The lesser things, however useful or needful, must never eclipse the greater. 'Strain out a gnat' refers to straining wine, as in Am 6:6. According to Lev 11:41, 'all creatures that swarm upon the earth are detestable; they shall not be eaten'. This verse was understood to require the straining of wine so as to keep out small insects. When it is added that the camel, like the gnat, was reckoned unclean (Lev 11:4), the point of v. 24 becomes plain: while the scribes and Pharisees strain their wine and so do not swallow the tiniest bugs that defile—a practice not here obviously rejected—they overlook the large things that defile, that is, they swallow the camel (a proverbially large beast: 19:24).

The fifth woe (vv. 25–6) adds to the charge that the scribes and Pharisees do the less important thing to the neglect of the more important. They cleanse the outside of the cup and plate but neglect the inside. They appear to be righteous (cf. 23:2–7, 23a) but inside are full of extortion and intemperance. (vv. 25–6 are about neither the purity of vessels nor legal matters, nor is v. 25 to be understood literally, v. 26 figuratively. Both verses rather speak metaphorically: the leaders are dirty cups and dishes. That is, they are clean on the outside (they have a righteous appearance) but impure on the inside (cf. vv. 27–8).)

The sixth woe (vv. 27–8) likens the scribes and Pharisees to tombs, which they regarded as unclean. The phrase translated 'whitewashed tombs' may refer to monuments or tombstones that were plastered. Porous limestone structures were often plastered with lime to smooth surfaces and add a sheen. One may picture beautiful monuments and their finished splendour.

The seventh woe (vv. 29–33) is the most serious and so climactic. Because v. 33 recalls the Baptist's words to the Pharisees and Sadducees in 3:7 (cf. also 12:34), Jesus again speaks like John, and his message is that of his forerunner: the Pharisees cannot escape eschatological wrath (cf. Rev 6:15–17). It follows that the character of the Pharisees has not changed, that the ministries of John and Jesus have been in one important way without effect.

(23:34–9) These verses, which record a definite rejection of Jerusalem and Israel's leaders, outline Jerusalem's history: (1) a time of overture and rejection, when the city was sent prophets who were murdered (the past, v. 37); (2) a time of abandonment, from the Son of Man's departure to the parousia (the present, v. 38); (3) the time of repentance and reconciliation, in which the Messiah is welcomed (the future, v. 39).

'Zechariah, son of Barachiah' (v. 35) is difficult. Zech 1:1 refers to its author as 'Zechariah, son of berekyâ'. There is, however, no biblical evidence of his death as a martyr; and, as Jerome observed, the temple was in ruins in his time. The one biblical martyr named Zechariah is the son of Jehoiada, a priest whose story appears near the end of Chronicles. Jewish tradition, however, conflated the prophet Zechariah with the son of Jehoiada, and given that the death of the latter became the popular subject of legends, we may assume the same identification is made in our text. The passage refers to the murders of the righteous from Gen 4 (the first murder in the HB) to 2 Chr 24 (the last murder in the HB).

Ch. 23 concludes by referring to two events that are closely related in the next chapter, the destruction of Jerusalem (v. 38) and the Parousia of the Son of Man (v. 39). 'Until you say' probably signals a conditional sentence. The meaning is that when his people bless him the Messiah will come. While Israel's redemption may be, on the basis of the OT and 19:28, a firm hope, its date is contingent upon Israel's acceptance of Jesus.

vv. 37–9 temper what has gone before. Without these verses the Jesus of ch. 23 issues nothing but judgements, with no tinge of regret. But the the conclusion discloses that the woes are uttered in sadness, that the indignation is righteous. When the threats give way to the image of Jesus as a mother hen lamenting her loss, the reader is reminded of the compassionate Son of 11:28–30. In this way the prophetic judgements are mingled with affection and Jesus becomes, like Jeremiah, a reluctant prophet.

(24:1–35) The introductory scene in which Jesus predicts the temple's destruction (vv. 1–2) provokes a query concerning the timing of things to come, to which Jesus first responds with warnings and predictions about eschatological tribulation: the beginning of the woes in the world at large (vv. 3–8), the intensification of the woes in the church (vv. 9–14), the climax of the woes in Judea (vv. 15–28).

Much of the traditional end-time scenario is untouched. There is, for example, no account of either the resurrection or the eternal state. Mt 24 is not a detailed blueprint (cf. the chronological imprecision). Interest is elsewhere—(1) in supplying the true ending of the Messiah's story so that the whole can be rightly grasped; (2) in foretelling and therefore making bearable Christian suffering; (3) in nurturing hope by showing how a good future can issue from an evil present; and (4) in encouraging battle against moral languor. Concerning this last, imperatives appear in vv. 4, 6, 16–18, 20, 23, 26, and 32. So eschatology does not simply console: it also demands discernment and adherence to Jesus' commands. The eschatological imagination does not displace practical moral concern.

Beyond these generalities the reference of the whole is disputed (a situation largely due to the lack of any direct answer to the question in v. 3). One approach holds that much or most of Mt 24 is fulfilled prophecy—that vv. 3–32 or 35 have to do with the events surrounding the destruction of Jerusalem in 70 CE within Jesus' 'generation', vv. 36–44 with the parousia, whose date is unknown. A second opinion, which holds that ch. 24 is purely eschatological, is favoured by the 'immediately' of v. 29; for if Matthew wrote much after 70 CE, he could not have thought the parousia would follow immediately upon the destruction of the temple, which in turn makes it unlikely that vv. 15–22 depict that destruction. A third option urges that our text refers to both the destruction of Jerusalem and the parousia and holds them in close chronological sequence (which would imply a date for Matthew c.70 CE). A fourth approach also thinks of both 70 CE and the end. Unlike the third, however, it finds not a chronological sequence—the destruction of the temple, then (soon) the end—but a single prophecy with two fulfilments.

It seems best to hold that vv. 4–28 are a depiction of the entire post-Easter period, interpreted in terms of the messianic woes. The discourse concerns the past, the present, and the future. What has happened will continue to happen and indeed worsen (cf. 2 Thess 2:7). Whether the fall of Jerusalem in 70 CE is directly referred to in vv. 15–22 or is instead indirectly included in the tribulations of that section remains unclear. But if the former, 70 CE does not exhaust the significance of vv. 5–22, which plainly envisage eschatological events to come. So the answer to the disciples' two-part question in v. 3 is this: the temple will be destroyed during the tribulation of the latter days, which runs from the first advent to the second; and after that tribulation the end—whose date cannot be known—will come.

Ch. 24 interprets the interim between the two advents as the time of messianic woe, when Jesus is absent. But 28:16–20—which recalls this discourse in that it also features a mountain, refers to 'the end of the age', alludes to Dan 7:13, and proclaims the Gentile mission—depicts the age of the church as one of Jesus' consoling and all-powerful presence. The two different perspectives on the same period reflect Christian experience. Jesus is even now the present Lord who rules heaven and earth. But he is also the absent master whose delay permits evil to inflict tribulation.

While it alludes to many OT texts, Mt 24 draws especially upon Daniel: cf. v. 3 with Dan 9:26; 12:6–7, v. 6 with Dan 9:26; 11:44, vv. 9–11 with Dan 7:25; 11:33, v. 15 with Dan 8:13; 9:27; 11:31; 12:11, v. 21 with Dan 12:1, and v. 30 with Dan 7:13. These clear allusions and the explicit citation of 'the prophet Daniel' (v. 15) are proof that, in Matthew, the end-time scenario fulfils the words of Daniel and Jesus simultaneously.

v. 2 prophesies the end of the temple (cf. 26:61; 27:40). This is usually thought of as a fulfilled prophecy for the reader, who knows the events of 70 CE. The declaration does not of itself question the legitimacy of the cult. Other Jewish prophets foretold doom without attacking the Pentateuch. What we have here is a tragic forecast of a disaster fostered by human sin. The destruction of the temple is God's verdict upon the capital.

Regarding vv. 4–5, the first century saw several famous false prophets who made eschatological claims. That any of them (before Bar Kochba) said, in so many words, 'I am Messiah' is not documented. But several of them did identify themselves as the eschatological prophet like Moses, a figure Matthew equated with Messiah. So for him the two things were one. This verse is then about Jewish messianic deceivers.

The climax of the woes concerns three subjects: the abomination which marks the time for flight (vv. 15–20), the shortening of the tribulation (vv. 21–2), and false Christs and prophets (vv. 23–8). 'The desolating sacrilege' (v. 15) is from the prophet Daniel, where it refers to the pagan altar and/or image of Olympian Zeus set up in the Jerusalem temple by Antiochus IV Epiphanes in 167 BCE. Here it could refer to the destruction of the temple in 70 CE, or some future, eschatological defilement and destruction, and perhaps even activities of an antichrist (cf. 2 Thess 2:3–4). In any case the sacrilege sets off a series of frightful events which one should flee. As in 10:23, eschatological flight will be interrupted by the return of the Son of Man (v. 29). Whether one is fleeing from evil or fleeing because God, in response to the abomination, is about to let loose his wrath (cf. Gen 19), is not stated. It is also not stated why one should pray that flight not come on a sabbath. But it is probably because members of

Matthew's community still observed the sabbath; and, given the traditional travel restrictions, they would be both hesitant and unprepared for flight on the day of rest.

vv. 24–5 makes three points: (1) Jesus himself has made it plain that signs and wonders are not of themselves guarantees of God's activity: incredulity has its place (cf. 7:21–3); (2) tribulation can be no surprise for it has been predicted and so it must be endured; (3) unlike the false prophets, Jesus' prophecy is true.

v. 28, which ends the review of tribulation, was an old proverb (cf. Job 9:26; Seneca, *Ep.* 95. 43). Here its meaning may be that the coming of the Son of Man will be as public and obvious as eagles or vultures circling over carrion. Less likely is the thought that the eschatological tribulation will be concluded by vultures devouring the flesh of the wicked dead, as in Ezek 39:17.

The paragraph in vv. 29–31 ends the tribulation and narrates the parousia in the traditional language of the OT theophany so that Jesus' coming is the arrival of God's glory. Having, in v. 28, moved the mind's eye from earth to sky, the text now directs our gaze even higher. This imaginative raising of vision leaves distress behind and prepares for envisaging the good help that comes from heaven (v. 30).

The supernatural darkness of the consummation (v. 29) is richly symbolic. Not only does it belong to the correlation of beginning and end (cf. Gen 1:2), but it is a sign of both divine judgement (Am 5:18, 20) and mourning (Jer 4:27–8) and becomes the velvet background for the Son of Man's splendour (24:27, 30). Moreover, on the literary level it foreshadows the darkness of Jesus' death (27:45) while that darkness in turn presages the world's assize.

vv. 31–2 are the dramatic zenith of ch. 24. The coming of the Son of Man—which takes place neither in desert nor inner room but is universally witnessed—is what 24:3–28 introduce and that for which vv. 32–44 call one to look. 'The sign of the Son of Man' (an unparalleled expression) might be the sign which is the Son of Man himself, or rather his coming. More likely 'sign' means the same as the Hebrew *nēs*, 'ensign': the Son of Man will signal the eschatological battle by raising an eschatological sign. In Israel a ram's horn was blown to rally the tribes for war. This act was accompanied by the raising of a standard upon a hill. The standard consisted of a wooden pole upon whose top crosspiece was an insignia, most often an animal. In Isaiah the old custom is put to prophetic use: the Lord himself will raise a standard and call for war (Isa 13:2–4), or the root of Jesse will 'stand as a signal to the peoples' (Isa 11:10). The old tradition that the cross will accompany Jesus at his parousia has a straightforward explanation if 'sign' means *nēs*, for the *nēs* had a crossbar and would naturally have encouraged Christians to think of a cross.

vv. 34–6 recall v. 3. But the reference to 'generation' has seemed problematic because unfulfilled. Some have referred 'all these things' to 70 CE. But it seems best to think of the eschatological signs as outlined in vv. 4–29: the parousia will come to pass before Jesus' 'generation' has gone. In favour of this is the imminent eschatological expectation of many early Christians (cf. 10:23) as well as Jn 21:20–3, which reflects the belief that Jesus would come before all his disciples had died.

Matthew's last major discourse is the only one to treat eschatology exclusively. But the other four end by turning to the last things. So the pattern of the individual discourses is the pattern of the five taken together: the conclusion is always eschatology. The meaning of Matthew's story is determined not only by its literary ending but by the ending of history itself: if history's conclusion is not Christological, then Christology itself becomes a question.

(24:36–25:30) The declaration of ignorance in v. 36 grounds the entire section: one must be ever prepared for what may come at any time. There follow as illustrations (1) a simile: as it was in the days of Noah, when unexpected judgement suddenly fell, so shall it be at the Son of Man's parousia (vv. 37–9); (2) a description of the division caused by the coming of the Son of Man plus an imperative: one will be taken, one left, so watch (vv. 40–2); and (3) a parable and its application: the Son of Man will come as unexpectedly as a thief, so be ready (vv. 43–4). These sayings and similes preface three long parables—the faithful and wise servant (24:45–51), the wise and foolish virgins (25:1–13), the talents (25:14–30). All three concern the delay of the parousia, preparedness for the end, and recompense at the great assize.

If 24:4–36 should quell uninformed eschatological enthusiasm, the intended effect is not apathy. This is why 24:37–44 seeks to foster an appropriate eschatological vigilance. Ignorance concerning the date of the end (24:36), although necessary, is dangerous, for it can lead to spiritual lethargy. But in Matthew it leads instead to moral preparation. For the parousia (like death) may come at any time. So one must be ever prepared to give an account before the divine justice, from which there is no escape (25:31–46).

24:37–51 conjures up scenes from everyday life—people eating and drinking, marrying and giving in marriage, two men in a field, two women at a mill, a man asleep in his house, a slave doing his duty, a slave not doing his duty. These images of day-to-day existence stand in stark contrast to the unusual, even surrealistic events depicted in 24:4–31—wars, famines, earthquakes, flights, darkened luminaries, a sign in the firmament, the Son of Man on the clouds of heaven. But the transition from the extraordinary to the ordinary serves Matthew's purpose. Those whose imaginations hold the terrors and hope of things to come still live in the mundane present; they must still work in the field and grind at the mill.

24:36 invites the vigilance of eschatological agnosticism. Irenaeus could take the declaration of Jesus' ignorance at face value. But Luke omits the saying, as did certain copyists of Matthew and Mark. Origen wondered whether Jesus was referring to the church of which he is the head. Ambrose attributed 'nor the Son' to Arian interpolation. Athanasius suggested that Jesus only feigned ignorance. But modern theology, emphasizing with the creeds that Jesus was 'truly man', has come to terms with the saying as an expression of kenosis, or the self-emptying of the Son of God.

In 24:40–1 one is taken and one is left. But are the righteous taken to meet the Lord in the air? Or are the wicked removed by angels and cast into fire? The former is more likely: the picture of angels taking the saints to meet the Son of Man was probably common in early Christianity (cf. Mk 13:27). ·

The parable of the servant (24:45–51) is congruent with an agraphon preserved in Justin, Dial. 47: 'In whatsoever I find you, in this will I also judge you.' But 24:45–51 may be espe-

cially for community leaders, for the 'servant' is set over 'fellow servants' to give them their food at the proper time. Such a reading has been popular from the the early church to today.

The parable of the wise and foolish virgins (25:1–13) is an allegory of the parousia of Christ, the heavenly bridegroom: the virgins represent the Christian community, the delay of the bridegroom is the delay of the Son of Man's return, the sudden coming is the unexpected arrival of his parousia, and the spurning of the foolish virgins is the great assize. The parable teaches three lessons: (1) the bridegroom delays and comes at an unforeseen time; this means yet again that no one knows the date of the Son of Man's parousia; (2) the wise virgins, who stand for the faithful, reveal that religious prudence will gain eschatological reward; (3) the foolish virgins, who stand for unfaithful disciples, reveal that those unprepared at the end will suffer eschatological punishment.

Whether or not one uses the word 'allegory', 25:14–30 is filled with obvious symbols. The master stands for Jesus, his slaves for the church, whose members have received various responsibilities. The master's departure represents the departure of the earthly Jesus, and his long absence is the age of the church. His return is the return of the Son of Man. The rewards given to the good slaves stand for heavenly rewards given to the faithful at the great assize, and their joy is that of the messianic banquet. The punishment of the evil slave represents those within the church who, through their sins of omission, condemn themselves to eschatological darkness. Most of this is familiar, but the passage is not otiose. Repetition makes for emphasis. Moreover, new are the notions that Christians have received gifts according to their ability (v. 15) and that it is what they make of those gifts which counts in the end.

(25:31–46) Although reminiscent of earlier parables of separation (13:24–30, 36–43, 47–50), this, the poetic and dramatic climax of the final major discourse, is not a parable but a 'word-picture of the Last Judgement' (Manson 1949: 249). The previous pericopae have enjoined readers to be faithful, to be prepared, and to invest talents. But exactly what these things entail has not been explicit. This passage makes all clear and so culminates Matthew's eschatologically grounded paraenesis. One prepares for the parousia by living the imperative to love one's neighbours, especially the marginalized. By this will all be judged on the far side of history.

The identity of those gathered (panta ta ethnē) is disputed, but they are probably all humanity. For the passage belongs to a long section which is full of paraenesis for believers, and one expects here a solemn appeal to those within the church. It also seems best to identify 'the least of these my brethren' in v. 40 (cf. v. 45) with the needy in general (and not with all Christians or Christian missionaries or leaders). This identification is consistent with the command to ignore distinctions between insiders and outsiders and with Jesus' injunction to love even enemies.

The concept of service to Jesus through service to others goes back to Prov 19:17: 'Whoever is kind to the poor lends to the Lord, and will be repaid in full.' What is new in Matthew is the Son of Man's identification with the needy. This novelty is, however, not explained. Do we have here the real personal presence of the Son of Man in the poor? Or what one scholar has called 'juridical mysticism'? Or the identification of the world's king with his people?

Feeding the hungry, welcoming strangers, and visiting the sick are mundane acts. In this sense 'virtue is not far from us, nor is it without ourselves, but it is within us, and is easy if only we are willing' (Anthony the Great). The Son of Man does not demand supernatural feats but simple, unobtrusive charity. The former but not the latter can easily be counterfeited (24:24). Charity is accordingly the true test of faith.

The Passion and the Resurrection (26:1–28:20)

(26:1–5) vv. 1–2 + 3–4 together constitute the prologue to the passion narrative. They are parallel in structure but antithetical in content. In the first Jesus prophesies his black future. In the second the chief priests and elders conspire against him (cf. Ps 2:2). (The absence of the Pharisees here and hereafter—except only 27:62—surprises; but historically no doubt Jesus' opponents at the end were the temple aristocracy. This also explains why the scribes henceforth appear only in 26:57 and 27:41.)

'After two days' (v. 2) may allude to the Isaac traditions. Gen 22:4 puts the sacrifice of Isaac on the third day, and in *Jubilees* it is during Passover (17:15; 18:3), while in Ps.-Philo, *LAB* 32:1–4 Isaac voluntarily offers himself (cf. 4 Macc 16:20). Further, a parallel between Jesus and Isaac is explicit in *Barn.* 7.2 (cf. already Rom 8:32?), and Mt 26:36 could allude to Gen 22:2–5.

(26:6–13) While Jesus is at the home of Simon 'the leper'— yet another befriended outcast—a woman, with motives unknown, performs an extravagant act which inevitably suggests Jesus' messianic status: he is the anointed one. (Cf. Dodd 1963: 173: 'the idea of an anointing, as of a king or priest, which is also an embalming of the dead', means that Jesus is 'the messianic King whose throne is a cross'.) Because anointing was evidently customary at feasts (cf. Ps 23:5), one may think the woman affectionately anoints Jesus as part of a celebration (cf. Ps 45:7). The use of 'head', however, makes one think of the OT narratives in which kings are anointed. The disciples' pious denigration is not about the act itself but the luxurious waste. Jesus' different opinion rejects utilitarian calculation. He praises the woman's deed as above almsgiving because it shows her 'personal commitment of love for the specific person of Jesus at a time of urgent need rather than an impersonal giving to the general group of the poor always in need' (Heil 1991: 26; cf. Deut 15:11). The situation is akin to 8:21–2, where allegiance to Jesus also means leaving a good deed undone. Here such allegiance means not being prudent with resources, even when they could benefit the poor.

(26:14–16) In contrast with the woman who anoints Jesus, Judas (cf. 10:4) acts treacherously. While she unselfishly gives what she has, Judas seeks his own gain; and whereas her sacrifice is costly, Judas strikes his bargain for a relatively paltry sum. In complete antithesis to everything Jesus has taught, Judas wants money (cf. 1 Tim 6:10). None the less Judas later returns the silver, so his avarice is not unbounded.

v. 15, which anticipates 27:9, stands under the influence of Zech 11:12: 'So they weighed out as my wages thirty shekels of silver.' This text shows that the betrayal is in accord with what God has foreseen. Indeed, the apparent triumph of evil is mysteriously also the work of God—as in Gen 50:20: 'Even though you intended to do harm to me, God intended it for good.' There might also be an allusion to Ex 21:32: Judas reckons Jesus worth no more than a slave. Whether that is so or not the amount is surely intended to be trifling; and his action likens him to the guards at the tomb, whose cowardice leads them to lie: they also take silver from the authorities (28:11–15).

When Judas strikes his bargain Jesus' freedom to speak and act is almost gone. This lends emphasis to what follows, for what Jesus does with time running out has special meaning. In other words, vv. 14–16 not only make the time before the arrest tense with anticipation, they also indicate that the narrative is about to depict Jesus' final free acts and in this way enlarge the significance of those acts.

(26:17–29) Jesus, as a law-observant Jew, celebrates the Passover within Jerusalem. vv. 26–9, which record the foundation of the Lord's supper, interpret the tragedy revealed in vv. 20–5 as redemptive: the betrayed Jesus is a sacrifice whose blood is poured out 'for many'. The passage is enriched by its links with other texts. vv. 26a and 27a strongly recall the two feeding stories of chs. 14 and 15: the last supper has been foreshadowed by the miraculous multiplications. Our passage has also often been connected with the bread of the Lord's prayer, while 'this is the blood of the covenant' takes up Ex 24:8 and makes the act of Jesus resemble an act of Moses. The reference to 'covenant' might also allude to Jer 31:31. 'For many' and 'poured out' probably advert to Isa 53:12 and so imply that Jesus in his death is the suffering servant of Isaiah.

The connections with Ex 24:8 are perhaps particularly important. Mark and Luke make Jesus' last supper a Passover Seder. Jn 6 links the bread of the eucharist with the manna given to Israel during the Exodus. In 1 Cor 10:1–4 participation in the Lord's supper is likened to drinking from the rock which followed Israel in the desert. And Heb 9:15–22 uses eucharistic language in retelling the story of Moses' covenantal sacrifice. Clearly it was conventional to view the last supper as part of a new exodus. And so it is in Matthew. The last supper is foreshadowed by stories in which Jesus is like Moses and contains parallels with the Exodus narrative: Jesus celebrates the Passover, vv. 17–18 (cf. Ex 12); the disciples do as Jesus directs them, v. 19 (cf. Ex 12:28); and the blood of the covenant is poured out for the forgiveness of sins, v. 28 (cf. Ex 24:8 and the targums on this). The last redeemer is as the first.

The command to eat, followed by 'this is my body', implies participation in the death of Jesus or its effects: just as those who partake of Passover share in the redemption from Egypt, so too those who take and eat share in the benefits of Jesus' atoning death. While so much is clear, bitter debate has centred upon Jesus' words. There is a natural tendency to think of 'blood' and 'body' as correlative: together they are the elements of sacrifice, or the two elements making up a person. But in Luke and Paul the two elements are separated by a meal. Moreover, the Greek 'body' (*sōma*) can mean simply 'self'.

The identification of the elements with the body and blood of Jesus Christ has made much of the verb, *estin* ('is'), and taken it literally. But others have found here only figurative representation: the bread symbolizes Jesus or what will happen to him. This accords with the use of 'is' in 13:19–23, 37–9 ('this is that' means 'this represents that'). The truth is that *estin* has a range of uses and is in itself ambiguous. Moreover, we cannot determine what Matthew believed about the elements—whether, for example, we should think of him as being closer to Luther than to Zwingli—or whether the categories from later theological debates would even be relevant.

The prophecy of abstinence in v. 29 is another passion prediction: it foretells imminent death as well as eschatological victory. So the Lord's supper is not just commemorative but prophetic. One wonders whether the sequence in Ex 24:8–11 underlies vv. 28–9. In Exodus the establishing of the covenant through blood is followed by eating and drinking and seeing God. In Matthew the proclamation of the eschatological covenant through blood prefaces the promise of the eschatological banquet. Already Isa 24:23–25:8 takes up the language of Ex 24:8–11 to prophesy the future and the eschatological feast.

(26:30–5) From this gloomy prophecy of impending events, which is almost an outline of the remainder of the gospel, we learn the future (1) of the disciples—they will all fall away and be scattered but later gathered in Galilee to see Jesus; (2) of Peter—he will deny his Lord three times before the cock crows; and (3) of Jesus—he will be killed but then raised and appear to his disciples in Galilee. Because the last supper is a Passover meal, many have referred 'sung the hymn' to the custom of singing at Passover the second half of the great Hallel (Ps 114–18). But first-century Christian readers may also or instead have thought of hymns sung with or after the eucharist. v. 30 (cf. 21:1; 24:3) alludes to 2 Sam 15:30 where David, who has been plotted against by his trusted royal counsellor, Ahithophel, leaves Jerusalem and goes up 'the ascent of the Mount of Olives'. There the king weeps and prays for deliverance (cf. Gethsemane). That Matthew intends the parallelism follows from 27:3–10, where Judas is modelled upon Ahithophel. Perhaps then it is more than coincidence that Ahithophel wants to overtake David at night (2 Sam 17:1; cf. Mt 26:31) with 12,000 men (17:1; cf. Mt 26:53) so that he can strike (*pataxō*, 17:2; cf. Mt 26:31) the king and cause all the people with him (*meta autou*, 17:2; cf. Mt 26:18, 20, 38, 40, 51, 69, 71) to flee (*pheuxetai pas*, 17:2; cf. Mt 26:56).

v. 31 quotes Zech 13:7. Zechariah's imperative 'smite' becomes in the NT 'I will smite' (cf. Ex 12:13; 2 Sam 17:2, both LXX). This emphasizes God's activity. The promise of restoration in v. 32 (fulfilled in 28:16–20; cf. 28:7, 10), which offers forgiveness in advance, reverses the scattering and so softens the disciples' failure. It alone is not disputed by Peter.

(26:36–46) One can embrace death because one hopes it a good (so Plato's Socrates) or one can resist it because one thinks it an evil (as in Jewish legends about Abraham and Moses). Jesus does neither. Although he recoils from death, or at least crucifixion, his course is fixed by the will of God, and this overrides whatever beliefs or feelings he has about death. For Jesus the issue is not death but submission to the divine will: 'Thy will be done.' (This phrase comes from the Lord's prayer; cf. the address, 'my Father' in v. 39 and 'that you may not come into the time of trial' in v. 41.)

There are three sources of pathos in this passage. First there is the innocence of the one who suffers: like Job, he is not guilty. Secondly, Jesus, although he has plainly prophesied crucifixion for himself, here contemplates a route around suffering. Obviously he is at war with himself. Thirdly, there is Jesus' isolation. Although he comes with his disciples he soon separates himself from them and casts his face to the ground. The physical circumstances are symbolic: Jesus is alone. Despite the threefold *meta* ('with') linking him to others, his followers, as though indifferent, abandon him for sleep. Moreover, we likewise hear nothing from heaven. It is as if Jesus' prayers go unanswered.

Jesus goes to *Gat-šemānî* ('oil-press' Heb.), an olive orchard on the Mount of Olives. Following the exposition (vv. 36–8) is an alternating series of triads—three prayers of Jesus and three encounters between Jesus and the sleeping disciples. The three prayers (vv. 39, 42, 44) display much parallelism, as do the scenes in which Jesus speaks with his disciples. The whole is dominated by Jesus' speech. Four times he speaks to his disciples and three times he prays. (Asking for something three times expresses earnestness; cf. 2 Cor 12:8.) The three parallel prayers exhibit a literary technique found elsewhere (cf. Josh 6:12–14). While Jesus' first and second prayers are quoted, his third is just summarized ('saying the same words'). This recalls 20:1–16, wherein we hear the instructions given to the labourers hired at the early hour and the third hour but not the instructions given to those hired at the sixth and ninth hours. Of these last we are simply told: 'he [the householder] did the same'. Similar is 27:39–44, which quotes the mockery of two groups but says of a third: they 'also taunted him in the same way'.

The adverbial use of *autou* ('here') in v. 36 appears only here in Matthew. Does it allude to Gen 22:5 LXX? In the story of the binding of Isaac Abraham says to his servants: 'Stay here . . . the boy and I will go over there . . .' Is there a parallel between Abraham's faith and Jesus' faith? or between Isaac's sacrifice and Jesus' sacrifice? In addition to the parallels of wording and content just noted both Abraham and Jesus take along three people, Abraham and Isaac separate themselves from others for worship or prayer, both episodes are set on a mountain, and each involves 'trial' (*peirasmon*; Gen 22:1 LXX: *epeiraxen*).

The words which convey that Jesus' sorrow is so great as to feel fatal (v. 38) conflate Ps 41:6, 12 ‖ 42:5 LXX with Jon 4:9. His grief, enhanced by his companions' failure to give him companionship and solace, is such that he prays for 'this cup' to pass. In *T. Abr.* 16:11 the angel of death calls himself 'the bitter cup of death' (cf. 1:3). But in the OT, intertestamental literature, and the Apocalypse, 'cup' is most often used figuratively in texts about suffering, especially suffering God's wrath or judgement (e.g. Ps 11:6; 116:13). And in 20:22 the cup Jesus must drink is neither temptation nor death nor martyrdom but rather eschatological sorrow, which will be first poured out upon the people of God (cf. Jer 25:15–29). It is the same here: the crucifixion belongs to the messianic woes. (Cf. further on this passage FGS K.)

(26:47–56) The busy story of Jesus' arrest, which is unusually full of characters, pulls together several strands from earlier sections. The setting at night matches the intention of the

Jewish leaders to take Jesus 'by stealth' and avoid a riot (v. 4; cf. v. 16). Judas' presence vindicates Jesus' foresight in vv. 21, 25, and 45. That the crowd is 'from the chief priests and the elders of the people' takes one back to vv. 3–5 and 14–16 and likewise to Jesus' passion predictions. Judas' use of 'rabbi' recalls v. 25 and here as there tells us he is no authentic disciple of Jesus. 'They came and laid hands on Jesus' (v. 50) makes for a literal fulfilment of 17:22. Jesus' passivity and non-resistance harmonize with his decision in Gethsemane and his earlier moral instruction (cf. the SM). The two references to Scripture (vv. 54, 56) resonate with the entirety of Matthew. And the disciples' flight shows Jesus, not his disciples, to be the true prophet (cf. vv. 31–5).

The narrative conveys sorrow through irony. Judas is no stranger but 'one of the twelve' (v. 47). The crowd has swords and clubs (v. 47) while the man they seek does not resist evil. Judas, the betrayer, kisses Jesus and greets him (v. 49). And Jesus' own disciples, instead of standing by him, forsake him and flee (v. 56). At the same time, the sorrow is balanced by Jesus' authority and the motif of fulfilment. The Messiah's fate is his own will: he decides not to ask for legions of angels (v. 53; cf. 4:6–7). Moreover, his resolution is determined by the voice of the prophets (vv. 54, 56), which is to say: Jesus' will is God's will.

(26:57–68) Jesus is neither the victim of tragic, impersonal circumstances nor the casualty of the ordinary machinery of justice. He is rather assailed by wicked people. Jesus' adversaries speak falsehoods (vv. 59–60), accuse him of blasphemy (v. 65), condemn him to death (v. 66), and viciously hit and mock him (vv. 67–8). In the midst of this sinful folly Jesus' identity becomes fully visible. He is the Son of God and Messiah who, in accordance with 2 Sam 7:14, builds the temple. He is the king of Ps 110:1 who sits at God's right hand. He is the suffering servant of Isa 50:6 whose face is spat upon. And he is the Son of Man of Dan 7:14 who will come on the clouds of heaven. The passage is, like 16:13–20, a climactic confluence of the main Christological streams which run throughout the text.

The chief literary feature of 26:57–68 is its irony (cf. the irony of 26:47–56). The authorities pass judgement on the one who will some day pass judgement on them. They, by seeking false witnesses, and the high priest, by rending his robe, disobey Moses (cf. Lev 21:10) whereas Jesus, by refusing an oath, lives by his messianic Torah. The authorities mock Jesus' claim to be the Davidic Messiah, the fulfilment of OT hopes, while their very actions bring to pass in Jesus OT prophesies. They accuse Jesus of blasphemy and yet it is they who blaspheme the Son of God. Lastly, those who accuse Jesus of saying that he will destroy the temple of God and in three days build another themselves help fulfil that prophecy; for by sentencing him to death they are creating the circumstance that makes it possible for the temple of his body to be raised in three days. So the Sanhedrin has everything backwards and it ironically acts against its own true interests. This is crystal clear to the reader. It will not, however, be evident to Jesus' persecutors until the parousia.

The Sanhedrin violates Torah (cf. Ex 20:16; Deut 5:20) and does not seek the truth. It rather wants only testimony that will incriminate Jesus. But it does fulfil the requirement of Deut 19:15 by getting two witnesses, and so despite itself the Sanhedrin hears true testimony. The words about the temple should be interpreted neither as an ecclesiological statement—Jesus will raise up the church—nor an apocalyptic prophecy about the destruction and rebuilding of Jerusalem's temple but as a passion prediction: 'I am able to destroy the temple of God' means 'I am able to lay down my life', and 'to build it in three days' means 'to rise from the dead in three days'. This is how the prophecy is interpreted in Jn 2:21, and 'in three days' inevitably recalls Jesus' other prophecies of resurrection. Paul, moreover, shows us the possibility of speaking of the individual as a temple (1 Cor 3:16; 6:19; 2 Cor 5:1).

When the high priest stands—which is what wicked accusers do in Ps 27:12 and 35:11—he asks the fundamental question of the pericope. Jesus' silence probably alludes to Isa 53:7 (quoted in Acts 8:32), for the language of 26:67 in several respects recalls Isa 50:6. But what explains the transition from the temple saying to Christology? Zech 6:12 predicts that 'the Branch' will 'build the temple of the Lord'. And 2 Sam 7:13–14—given messianic sense in both the Dead Sea scrolls and the NT—foretells a royal figure who will build for God a house and be God's 'son'.

Jesus speaks for the last time of the Son of Man and makes a dramatic public confession. He goes beyond the high priest's question and in effect answers the question left unanswered in 22:45. 'You have said so' has affirmative sense (cf. v. 25; 27:11). Why then the indirect response? First, the wording assimilates the trial before the high priest to the trial before Pilate. Secondly, the use of 'you' puts responsibility upon Caiaphas, who knows the truth: he must live with the consequences of knowing the truth. Thirdly, given his teaching on oaths (5:33–7) Jesus may wish to distance himself from the high priest's language.

Jesus' public confession combines Ps 110:1 and Dan 7:13–14. But 'from now on' is not from the OT. The words are enigmatic because a prediction beginning 'from now on' should introduce a continuous state. Some have thought the expression stresses that Jesus' trial marks the moment of God's rejection of the Jewish people, or that the emphasis is upon the contrast between Jesus' humiliation in the present and his vindication in the near future. It is certainly intriguing that 28:18 implies the fulfilment or proleptic realization of Dan 7:14. On the other hand, 28:11–15 does not imply that the authorities are in any way changed by subsequent events; in no sense can it be said that they 'see' the Son of Man. So then maybe the Greek means in effect 'in the future'. Jesus will no longer be seen as he is now; rather will he be seen when he comes in glory, seated on a throne and riding the clouds. In line with this the verse has to do with public revelation ('you will see', 'clouds').

The scene ends with Jesus passively enduring violence and a ritual of dishonour. This makes him the exemplar of the teaching in 5:38–42. For there Jesus exhorts disciples to eschew violence and not resist evil, and several illustrations follow which borrow language from Isa 50:4–9 LXX, which, as already noted, is again alluded to in the present verse (cf. 27:30). So the OT text associated with turning the other cheek is also associated with the passion of Jesus.

(26:69–75) Earlier in this chapter Judas defects. Later the other disciples flee. Now Peter, retreating from his promise (v. 35), denies his Lord. This is the climax of the disciples' failure. The first to be called is now the last to fall away.

The first accusation is spoken to Peter by a maid, the second to bystanders by another maid, and the third to Peter by bystanders: things become more and more public. Further, the intensity of Peter's denials increases with the accusations: he first denies that he knows what is being said, then he denies with an oath that he knows Jesus, then he denies Jesus with both an oath and a curse (probably of Jesus). Peter's movements, which take him further and further away from Jesus, also add drama: he is in the courtyard, then he goes to the gateway, then he leaves altogether.

In its present context this passage supplies irony by balancing v. 74, where Jesus' prophetic powers are mocked. Although Jesus makes no appearance in our story, it shows that, so far from being a false prophet, he has predicted the events of the evening in detail. 'Before the cock crows, you will deny me three times' (v. 34) comes to literal fulfilment precisely while Jesus is being reviled with 'Prophesy to us, you Messiah!' (v. 68).

Our story also balances the trial, where Jesus, like Peter, who is not far away, faces three sets of accusers (false witnesses, v. 60, the two true witnesses, vv. 61–2, Caiaphas, vv. 63–6). There Jesus is asked whether he is the Messiah, the Son of God. He, although heretofore reticent about his identity, fearlessly confesses that he is. But Peter, who earlier confessed Jesus to be the Christ, the Son of God, no longer acknowledges his Lord: when confronted he becomes a coward. Jesus illustrates the good confession of 10:32, Peter the damning denial of 10:33.

The 'sitting' of v. 69 (cf. v. 58) interests because the disciples sit in Gethsemane (v. 36), the guards (and evidently the high priest) sit at the trial (cf. vv. 58, 62), Pilate sits when interrogating Jesus (27.19), and the soldiers at the cross likewise sit (27:36). All this contrasts with earlier chapters, in which it is Jesus who sits, that is, takes the position of authority and rest (5:1; 13:2; 15:29; 21:7; 24:3; 25:31). But after the last supper he no longer sits or reclines. He instead stands (27:11), falls to ground (26:39), and hangs from a cross (27:35). His posture during the passion reflects his temporary renunciation of authority (cf. 26:53) and the lack of all comfort.

Matthew's gospel does not idealize Peter and the other disciples. Rather does it present them as completely human, as complex and inconstant creatures who resist easy caricature. While on the one hand they leave all to follow Jesus, on the other they forsake and deny him. And Peter, who confesses Jesus to be the Christ, the Son of the living God, in the end denies that he knows him. Such contradictory behaviour should not surprise. The Bible of the Matthean community, the OT, does not free Noah, or David, or Solomon from their sins. Even Moses is said to have disobeyed God when he struck the rock twice. We may assume that Matthew's readers interpreted the disciples' failures as they did the failures of OT heroes: God can use ordinary people for his extraordinary purposes and, when they fall into sin, he can grant them forgiveness. As Peter says in the *Acts of Peter* 7:20: 'He who defended me also when I sinned and strengthened me with his greatness will also comfort you that you may love

him.' Calvin had it right: 'Peter's fall . . . brilliantly mirrors our own infirmity. His repentance in turn is a memorable demonstration for us of God's goodness and mercy. The story of one man contains teaching of general, and indeed prime, benefit for the whole Church; it teaches those who stand to take care and caution; it encourages the fallen to trust in pardon.'

(27:1–2) In fulfilment of the prophetic 20:18–19, the Jewish leaders deliver Jesus to the prefect of Judea. The unexplained act probably assumes that the Jews usually did not have the authority to execute criminals (Jn 18:31): such was the responsibility of the Romans. However that may be, throughout 26:1–56 Jesus has been the active protagonist, and one has the impression that he is in charge of his own destiny. Now this changes: he becomes the passive victim, and the text fixes upon those who act against him.

Tradition, impelled to turn Pilate into either a saint or a devil, has offered two contrasting pictures. In one (mostly Egyptian and Syrian) Pilate is, at the expense of the Jews, presented as an unwilling participant in the death of Jesus: he is innocent of Jesus' blood. Tertullian, *Apol.* 21, even makes him 'a Christian in his own convictions', and the Coptic church has canonized him. In the other (mostly Western) picture Pilate bears full responsibility for the death of Jesus and is presented as 'an unjust judge'—weak-willed at best, evil at worst. In the *Mors Pilati* he commits suicide, and his corpse becomes a home for demons. Matthew is closer to this second picture. Pilate's wife, after her dream, warns her husband not to have anything to do with Jesus—but Pilate disregards her; and after Jesus is dead Pilate co-operates with the Jewish authorities to appoint a guard for the tomb. So the declaration of innocence in v. 24 is ironic: despite his words Pilate is responsible. Washing his hands does not make them clean.

(27:3–10) The most obvious formal feature of this interruption is the parallelism between the scriptural quotation (cf. Zech 11:13) and the narrative, a parallelism that underlines fulfilment:

The narrative:	The quotation:
'taking' (6)	'they took' (9)
'thirty pieces of silver' (3,5,6)	'thirty pieces of silver' (9)
'money' (*timē*) (6)	'price' (*timēn*) (9)
'the potter's field' (7,8)	'the potter's field' (10)

There are three other early Christian accounts of Judas' death—Acts 1:16–20 and two fragments assigned to Papias *apud* Apollinarius (of Laodicea) and preserved in catenas to Mt 27 (a short account) and Acts 1 (a long account). Although very different from Matthew and each other, there are common items: (1) money from Judas purchases a property near Jerusalem (Matthew: the chief priests use the money of betrayal; Luke: Judas himself acquires the land); (2) that property was known as 'the Field of Blood' (but whereas in Matthew the name is associated with the innocent blood of Jesus, in Acts it derives from Judas' gruesome end); (3) the fate of Judas fulfils Scripture (Matthew and Luke cite different OT texts); (4) Judas comes to a bad end (Matthew: he hangs himself; Acts: he bursts open; Papias' short version: a wagon runs over him).

What does 'he repented' (v. 3) mean? The accounts in Acts and Papias have Judas die by the hand of heaven: there is no room for authentic repentance. This, and the depiction of Judas throughout much of church history as infamy embodied, have led most to see in Matthew's Judas an everlasting failure doomed for destruction. This accords with 26:24. On the other hand, the verb translated here by 'he repented' is used in Mt 22:29 and 32 of authentic repentance. Further, there are no biblical condemnations or prohibitions of suicide. Indeed, Jewish tradition excuses or justifies the suicides of Saul, Samson, Zimri, and the Roman soldier who killed himself after talking to R. Gamaliel (b. Ta'an. 29a); and Josephus, in telling the story of Masada, refers to the participants' 'free choice of a noble death' (J.W. 7. 320–401). Moreover, if 4 Macc 17:21 states that the deaths of a mother and her seven sons became 'a ransom for the sin of our nation', 12:19 and 17:1 inform us that the deaths of that mother and of one of her sons were self-inflicted: 'he threw himself into the braziers and so gave up his life'; 'she threw herself into the fire so that no one would touch her body'. Are we to think that Judas' suicide atones for his sin (cf. Gen. Rab. on 27:27)?

There is a parallel of v. 4 in 27:24. Pilate, as he washes his hands, declares, 'I am innocent of this man's blood; see to it yourselves.' But the similarities are really differences. Whereas Judas declares his guilt for innocent blood, Pilate denies his; and while Pilate, seeking to avoid responsibility, tells others to 'see to it yourselves', this is what Judas, who acknowledges his responsibility, is told to do by others.

The story of Ahithophel is recalled by v. 5 (cf. 2 Sam 17:23) making Judas akin to the famous betrayer of David. The correlation between Judas and Ahithophel was traditional. Cf. 2 Sam 15:23 with Jn 18:1; 2 Sam 15:31 with Mt 26:36–46 and par., also Ps 41:5 and 11 (which tradition refers to the incident with Absalom and Ahithophel); 2 Sam 17:1–2 with Mt 26:47–56 and par.; Ps 41:9 (attributed to David; cf. b. Sanh. 106b) with Mt 14:18 and Jn 13:18; and 2 Sam 18:28 with Jn 13:18.

To the allusion to Zech 11:12 made with reference to Judas in 26:15, 27:9–10 adds a formal citation of Zech 11:13, which has been prepared for by allusions in vv. 3–8. 'Jeremiah' may be due to textual corruption, or perhaps it is a reference to the entire prophetic corpus, which Jeremiah heads in some old lists, or perhaps the evangelist simply had a mental lapse, or perhaps the text comes from an apocryphon. But the best guess is that the quotation is mixed: words from Jeremiah and Zechariah have been combined. (Mk 1:2 attributes Mal 3:1 + Isa 40:3 to Isaiah, and Rom 9:27 assigns Hos 2:1 + Isa 10:22 to the same prophet.) Jer 18–19 concerns a potter (18:2–6; 19:1), a purchase (19:1), the Valley of Hinnom (where the Field of Blood is traditionally located) (19:2), 'blood of the innocent' (19:4), and the renaming of a place for burial (19:6, 11). Further, Jer 32:6–15 tells of the purchase of a field with silver.

(27:11–26) This passage, which returns to 27:1–2, is crowded with characters—Jesus, Pilate, the chief priests, the elders, Barabbas, Pilate's wife, a crowd. If the subject is the Roman trial of Jesus, which 'sounds less like a formal judicial hearing than a macabre example of oriental bargaining' (France 1985: 388), the focal issue is culpability for Jesus' execution. The main character, the governor, instead of conducting an objective inquiry and justly acting upon the outcome, rather gives cowardly heed to the hostile Jewish leaders and the crowd they have agitated. The effect is to highlight not just the innocence of Jesus but also the fault of Rome's representative and especially the guilt of the chief priests and elders, who manipulate Pilate and stir up the crowd against the Messiah.

The interrogation is in many respects reminiscent of the Jewish trial. The chief priest(s) and elders are present both times (26:57; vv. 12, 20). On both occasions Jesus is called by others 'the Messiah' (26:63; vv. 17, 22). In both Jesus is silent (26:62–3; vv. 11–14). In both he none the less says to his interrogator, 'You have said so' (26:64; v. 11). Both trials deem Jesus worthy of death (26:66; vv. 24–6). And both are followed by scenes of mockery (26:67; vv. 27–31). The correlations convey futility: the new trial corrects nothing of the first. Roman justice does no better than the Sanhedrin.

When Pilate washes his hands (v. 24) he is more concerned with his own innocence than with justice and the innocence of Jesus. His act is hypocritical; he is not free of responsibility. Pilate's declaration against the facts contrasts with the dramatic cry of 'the people as a whole'. 'His blood be on us and on our children!' is not a self-curse but a declaration of responsibility—in effect: we acknowledge our involvement if the governor will not. The words are an ironic prophecy (cf. Jn 11:50); for surely Matthew, like so many after him, related the cry to the fall of Jerusalem in 70 CE (cf. 23:35). This accords with the Jewish habit of associating disaster with sin—even (despite Jer 31:29–30) the disaster of one generation for the sin of another. 'And our children' accordingly carries literal sense. We have here an aetiology, an explanation in terms of collective guilt for the destruction of the capital. (The exegete must distinguish between the original intention of verses and their effects, especially here; v. 25 does not refer to all Israel— neither Jewish Christians nor the Jewish diaspora are represented by the crowd—nor should we find here a curse for all time. Nor does the verse explain God's supposed abandonment of Jews or of the end of the Jewish mission.)

Concerning v. 26, 10:17 prophesies that missionaries will be flogged; so once more the story of Jesus, the exemplar in suffering, makes his speech come to life. The 'flogging', perhaps intended to recall Isa 53:5, is not described but only referred to. The Roman act of flagellum, of tying non-Romans and slaves to a post and then whipping them with knotted leather straps (which sometimes held pieces of metal and/or bone), often preceded crucifixion, and sometimes prisoners were whipped on the way to crucifixion. The horrendous punishment (not humanely limited to forty stripes, cf. Jewish law) was so severe that it could expose bone and by itself be fatal.

If the main theological theme of this passage is responsibility, the literary method is irony. Things are upside down, and words have unintended meaning. The judge of the world, instead of sitting upon his judgement seat, stands before the bēma of a lesser. The governor does not govern. While the religious leaders of Judaism rail against God's anointed, the truth is revealed to a pagan. The crowds prefer to free a criminal instead of a just man they once acclaimed. The criminal is named 'Jesus, Son of the Father'. Pilate declares his lack of responsibility in word and deed when he is in fact in charge of the proceedings and their outcome. And the crowd willingly accepts responsibility in words which unwittingly prophesy tragedy. As throughout the gospel things are not what they seem, and God's will works itself out in unexpected circumstances.

(27:27–31) This passage (cf. Philo, *In Flac.* 6.36–40), uncharacteristically full of vivid details, partially fulfils the third passion prediction: 'hand him over to the Gentiles to be mocked and flogged' (20:19) as well as Isa 50:6. It also in several particulars repeats the conclusion of the trial before Caiaphas (see esp. 26:67).

Kings are proclaimed by their soldiers. But when the Roman soldiers give Jesus a robe, a sceptre, and a crown—whose thorns may simulate the light rays supposed to emanate from the heads of divinities—and then hail him king they are making fun of him for their own amusement. Their homage is pretended. Yet in truth the seemingly hapless criminal before them—here Jesus is an utterly passive object—is indeed a king who shall shortly wield all authority in heaven and earth (28:18). In this way the irony of the Roman burlesque is turned on itself, and the scene continues the message of 27:11–26: things are the opposite of what they seem to be.

(27:32–56) This haunting passage depicts Jesus as the suffering righteous one akin to the figures in Ps 22, Isa 53, and Wis 2; and perhaps its outstanding feature is its scriptural language. Although the OT is never once formally introduced, its presence is everywhere:

34, wine mingled with gall: allusion to Ps 69:21
35, division of garments: borrowing from Ps 22:18
38, death between robbers: possible allusion to Isa 53:12
39, passersby wag their heads: cf. Ps 22:7; Lam 2:15
39–40, mockery: borrowing from Ps 22:7 (cf. 109:25)
43, mockery: borrowing from Ps 22:9
44, mockery: possible borrowing from Ps 22:7 or 69:9
45, darkness at noon: allusion to Am 8:9
46, cry from the cross: borrowing from Ps 22:1
48, vinegar to drink: allusion to Ps 69:21
51–3, earthquake and resurrection: use of Ezek 37; Zech 14:4–5

Matthew does not recount the glorious death of a martyr. Of Jesus' heroic valour and faith we hear nothing. vv. 32–50 do not encourage or inspire but rather depict human sin and its frightening freedom in the unfathomable divine silence. There is terror in this text. The mocking and torture of the innocent and righteous Son of God are not intended to make but to shatter sense, to portray the depths of irrational human depravity. And the patient endurance of God, which is so overdone that the Son himself screams out feelings of abandonment, powerfully conveys the frightening mystery of God's seeming inactivity in the world. vv. 32–50 are the divine absence, a sort of deistic interlude, a portrait (in Luther's phrase) of *Deus absconditus in passionibus*. They are akin to portions of Job, and like the speech out of the whirlwind they can evoke what Rudolf Otto called the *mysterium tremendum*. 'Truly, you are a God who hides himself, O God of Israel, the Saviour' (Isa 45:15).

While vv. 32–50 are seemingly devoid of supernatural activity, vv. 51–4 offer an explosion of the supernatural. One cannot but recall the habit of world mythology and literature to encircle the ends of great figures with extraordinary events.

Trees bloomed out of season and powder fell from the sky when Buddha slipped away. The heavens shook when Moses was taken to God (2 *Apoc. Bar.* 59:3). As Francis of Assisi left the body, larks, otherwise only heralds of dawn, sang at night. vv. 51–4 are in one important respect conventional. At the same time, the Matthean signs have their own special meaning. First, most of them—darkness, end of the temple, resurrection, conversion of Gentiles—are eschatological. It follows that the day of the Lord dawns on Golgotha: the divine judgement descends, and the first fruits of the resurrection are gathered. The end of Jesus is the end of the world in miniature.

Secondly, the miracles come only *after* Jesus dies. Before then the Son's passivity is matched by God's passivity—so much so that the bystanders can jeer and proclaim God's indifference. But the preternatural events which follow death refute the mockers: their calls for a sign are more than answered. God does indeed fight for the one who has not fought for himself. The mystery is only why God is tardy, why torment and death must come first. Whatever the answer to that eternal question might be, the sequence itself cannot surprise. For the same pattern appears in Jesus' own preaching, in which tribulation and suffering precede vindication and victory (e.g. 5:10–12; 10:17–23; 24:4–34).

There is resemblance between vv. 51–5 and 28:1–11:

The Death of Jesus	The Resurrection of Jesus
An earthquake	An earthquake
Opening of tombs	Opening of tombs
A resurrection	A resurrection
The guards fear	The guards fear
Witnesses to the events (the resurrected saints) go to the holy city	Witnesses to the events (the Roman guards) go to the city
There are women witnesses (including Mary Magdalene and another Mary)	There are women witnesses (Mary Magdalene and another Mary)

Clearly the resurrection of the saints foreshadows the resurrection of Jesus.

(27:57–66) The stories about the burial and the guard set the stage for 28:15. The tomb that is filled here (in accord with Deut 21:23, before sundown) is emptied there. The stone that is here rolled across the door of the tomb is there rolled back. The guard that here secures the sepulchre there proves ineffective. The leaders who here worry that the disciples will come and steal Jesus' body there put out the lie that just such a thing happened. And the women who here see all become witnesses there to the empty tomb and risen Lord.

A corpse can be either disposed of dishonourably or given an honourable burial. In view of how Jesus has been treated throughout the passion narrative one would anticipate for him the former. But thanks to Joseph of Arimathea's unexpected and reverent intervention, Jesus receives a worthy entombment. Further, like the kings of Israel, he is buried beside Jerusalem (1 Kings 15:8, 24, etc.).

The apologetic tale of the guard at the tomb (vv. 62–6) refutes the criticism of 28:15, that is, rebuts Jewish slander against the disciples by showing that they could not have stolen Jesus' body—there was a guard and in any case they were nowhere around—and reinforces belief in Jesus' resurrection: given the guard the empty tomb is a very suggestive sign. One can imagine an exchange between Matthew and critical Jews. Matthew: Jesus rose from the dead and his tomb was empty (28:6). Opponent: did Jesus really die? Matthew: a Roman guard kept watch over him; surely he was dead before his body was released (27:36). Opponent: was there a mix-up in tombs? Matthew: the women saw where Jesus was buried (v. 61). Opponent: the disciples, seeking to confirm Jesus' prophecy of his resurrection after three days, stole the body. Matthew: the disciples had fled, they were nowhere near (26:56). Opponent: then someone else stole the body. Matthew: a large stone was rolled before the tomb; it was sealed; and Roman soldiers kept watch (28:62–6). Opponent: the soldiers fell asleep. Matthew: they were bribed to say that (28:12–15).

Ps 2:1 asks, 'Why do the nations conspire, and the peoples plot in vain?' The theme of human impotence versus divine power runs throughout the Bible, and it is part and parcel of vv. 62–6. Jesus' opponents take every precaution to prevent proclamation of the resurrection: they seal the stone and set a guard. But their efforts are futile: 'he who sits in the heavens laughs'. Human beings cannot oppose earthquakes and angels and the power of God.

(28:1–15) The resurrection is the necessary end to Jesus' story. Without it his words are vacant and his opponents exonerated. With it, Jesus is vindicated, his cause and authority confirmed, and his—and so Matthew's—opponents disgraced.

Matthew's account opens with an angelophany (cf. Dan 10:2–14; 2 Enoch 1:3–10) with eschatological motifs (earthquake, resurrection) (vv. 1–8); this is followed by an appearance of the risen Jesus (vv. 9–10) and a story of how unbelievers treated the facts (vv. 11–15). The verbal repetition between vv. 5–7 and 10 makes for emphasis while an additional unifying feature is the artistic correlation between the women and the guards. Both groups gather at Jesus' tomb (vv. 1, 4). Both see an angel (vv. 2–5). Both feel fear (vv. 4, 8). Both leave the tomb in order to tell others what has happened (vv. 8, 11). And both are told by others what they should say (vv. 7, 10, 13–14). The difference lies in this, that while (we assume) the women tell the truth to the disciples, the ineffectual guards (cf. Dan 3:19–23; Acts 5:17–26)—the last nameless walk-ons—lie about the disciples.

The women (cf. 27:55, 61), having observed the sabbath and waited until the following dawn, set forth to visit the tomb on the first day of the week. They become witnesses to Jesus' resurrection as well as to his death and burial. Although 'to see the tomb' is unexplained, visitation of the newly entombed was probably an established burial custom. Ṣem. 8:1 records the habit of visiting graves 'until the third day' (cf. Jn 11:17, 39) as a precaution against burying someone alive (examples of which are given in Ṣem.). If this is the premise of Mt 28:1, then the women who go to confirm Jesus' death become instead the first witnesses of his new life. It is not Jesus who is dead but (at least figuratively) the guards ('became as dead men').

vv. 11–15 take up 27:62–6 and 28:2–4 and like them are apologetic. Evidently the Jewish opponents of Matthean Christianity (like Reimarus centuries later) did not dispute the historicity of the empty tomb but rather assigned its cause

to theft in the cause of piety. Our story answers that slander in kind: the rumour of theft was a self-serving lie fortified by money. Clearly Matthew's Christian community knew and cared about what the synagogue across the street was saying.

(28:16–20) Matthew's conclusion has the same broad outline as Mk 16:14–20; Lk 24:36–49; and Jn 20:19–23. All four texts presumably go back to the same primitive proto-commissioning.

The resurrection marks the end of Jesus' earthly time and inaugurates the time of the post-Easter church. Accordingly this pericope both looks back to summarize Jesus' ministry as a whole ('all I have commanded you') and looks forward to the time of the church to outline a programme. So the passage functions to relate two periods which, although different, have the same Lord and so the same mission.

In addition to the allusion to Dan 7:13–14 in v. 18, some have also found dependence upon 2 Chr 36:23 (the final sentence in the Former Prophets). This is improbable. More persistent has been the proposal, usually tentative and muted, that the passage evokes Moses. The mountain itself, given its Mosaic associations throughout Matthew, is suggestive, as is the circumstance that Moses ended his earthly course on a mountain. Further, the narrative has close parallels in Deut 31:14–15, 23; and Josh 1:1–9, which are all about God, or God through Moses, commissioning Joshua. Josh 1:2 tells Joshua to 'go' (v. 9) and cross the Jordan. Josh 1:7 enjoins Joshua to 'act in accordance with all the law that my servant Moses commanded you'. And Josh 1:9 (the pericope's conclusion) promises God's presence: 'for the Lord your God is with you wherever you go'. Given the undeniable presence of a strong Moses typology elsewhere in Matthew, one infers that this passage, like the commissioning stories in 1 Chr 22:1–16 and Jer 1:1–10, deliberately borrows from the traditions about Moses. Just as Moses, at the close of his life, commissioned Joshua both to go into the land peopled by foreign nations and to observe all the commandments in the law, and then further promised his successor God's abiding presence, so similarly Jesus: at the end of his earthly ministry he tells his disciples to go into all the world and to teach the observance of all the commandments of the new Moses, and then further promises his assisting presence.

Jesus is interpreted by v. 20 as the authoritative bringer of revelation, and 'all that I have commanded you' refers not to one command or to the SM but to the whole of Jesus' teaching—not just imperatives but also proverbs, blessings, parables, and prophecies. But more than verbal revelation is involved, for such revelation cannot be separated from Jesus' life, which is itself a command. Jesus' final words accordingly unify word and deed and envisage the entire book. The ministry as a whole is an imperative.

This section satisfyingly completes the gospel in part because it is almost a compendium of Matthean theology: 'Galilee' fulfils the prophecies in 26:32 and 28:7 and creates a literary arch with 4:12 that spans the gospel; 'mountain' recalls other mountain scenes, especially 4:8. 'They worshipped him; but some doubted' has been foreshadowed by 14:31–3. 'All authority in heaven and on earth has been given to me' echoes 11:27 as well as Dan 7:13–14, which Jesus has elsewhere applied to himself (24:30; 26:64); it further brings to completion the theme of Jesus' kingship (1:1, etc.). 'Make disciples' reminds one of 13:52 (cf. 27:57); 'all nations' terminates the prohibition of 10:5–6 (cf. 15:24); 'of the Father and of the Son and of the Holy Spirit' in connection with baptism reminds one of ch. 3, where the Son is baptized, the Father speaks, and the Spirit descends. 'Teaching' recapitulates a central theme and gives the disciples a task heretofore reserved for Jesus; 'everything that I have commanded you' envisages all Jesus has said and done; 'I am with you always' forms an *inclusio* with 1:23 and is similar to 18:20; 'the end of the age' recurs in 13:39, 40, 49; 24:3, and puts one in mind of Jesus' teachings about the end. The allusions to Moses reactivate the Moses typology.

The climax and crown of Matthew's gospel is profoundly apt in that it invites the reader to enter the story: 28:16–20 is an open-ended ending. Not only does v. 20*a* underline that the particular man, Jesus, has universal significance, but 'I am with you always' reveals that he is always with his people. The result is that the believing audience and the ever-living Son of God become intimate. The Jesus who commands difficult obedience is at the same time the ever-graceful divine presence.

REFERENCES

Allison, D. C. (1993), *The New Moses: A Matthean Typology* (Minneapolis: Fortress).

Beare, F. W. (1981), *The Gospel According to St. Matthew* (London: Harper & Row).

Betz, H. D. (1985), *The Sermon on the Mount*, Hermeneia (Minneapolis: Fortress).

Bornkamm, G. (1963), 'The Stilling of the Storm in Matthew', in G. Bornkamm, G. Barth, and H. J. Held, *Tradition and Interpretation in Matthew* (London: SCM).

Bultmann, R. (1963), *History of the Synoptic Tradition* (Oxford: Basil Blackwell).

Carter, W. (1994), *Households and Discipleship*, JSNTSSup 103 (Sheffield: JSOT).

Davies, W. D. (1964), *The Setting of the Sermon on the Mount* (Cambridge: Cambridge University Press).

Dodd, C. H. (1963), *Historical Tradition in the Fourth Gospel* (Cambridge: Cambridge University Press).

Donaldson, T. L. (1985), *Jesus on the Mountain: A Study in Matthean Theology*, JSNTSSup 8 (Sheffield: JSOT).

France, R. T. (1985), *Matthew* (Leicester: Inter-Varsity).

Gundry, R. H. (1982), *Matthew: A Commentary on his Literary and Theological Art* (Grand Rapids, Mich.: Eerdmans).

Heil, J. P. (1991), *The Death and Resurrection of Jesus* (Minneapolis: Fortress).

Hengel, M. (1981), *The Charismatic Leader and His Followers* (Edinburgh: T. & T. Clark).

Luz, U. (1985, 1990), *Das Evangelium nach Matthäus*, EKKNT 1/1, 2, 2 vols. (Zürich and Neukirchen-Vluyn: Benziger and Neukirchener).

Manson, T. W. (1949), *The Sayings of Jesus* (London: SCM).

58. Mark

C. M. TUCKETT

INTRODUCTION

A. The Earliest Gospel. The Gospel of Mark is probably the earliest of the three synoptic gospels to be written. Although it is disputed by some, the most widely held solution today to the Synoptic Problem, the problem of the relationship between the three synoptic gospels, is that Mark's gospel was written first and was then used as a source by Matthew and Luke. That theory will not be discussed in detail here but will be assumed in what follows. (On this, see discussions on the Synoptic Problem in ch. 61, below and e.g. Tuckett 1992.)

B. Author. 1. About the author of the gospel we probably know very little. Ancient tradition calls him Mark, almost certainly intending to identify him as the John Mark mentioned elsewhere in the NT, a member of the primitive Jerusalem church. A tradition going back at least as early as the second-century Church Father Papias also connects Mark with the apostle Peter, so that the gospel is sometimes regarded as in some sense Peter's memoirs. The link with Peter has then also led to Mark's gospel being associated with the city of Rome, perhaps reflecting a situation of extreme suffering by the Christian community there in the persecutions instigated by Nero in the 60s after the great fire of Rome.

2. None of this, however, is certain. It seems very unlikely, for example, that the author of the gospel was a Palestinian Jew. He appears to be rather ignorant about local geography (see MK 5:1; 7:31), as well as about Jewish customs or laws (see MK 7:3–4; 10:11–12). He may well have been called Mark, but the name was a very common one in the Roman empire and we cannot simply equate all the Marks we know!

Any link between our gospel and Peter is also hard to establish. It is true that Peter is regularly one of an inner group of disciples (cf. 1:29–31; 9:2–13; 13), and Peter is regularly belittled (cf. 8:33), a fact which some argue is only explicable if Peter had given explicit sanction to the gospel. However, Peter is not unique in all this, and the negative picture is shared with all the disciples; in fact Matthew and Luke have more traditions specifically about Peter (Mt 16:17–19; Lk 5:1–11). The link alleged between Mark's gospel and Peter is probably part of a second-century attempt to give the gospel more status by linking it with the leading apostle.

C. Date. The date of the gospel is also uncertain. The traditional view is, as we have seen, that Mark dates from the 60s. Much depends on the interpretation of ch. 13, where Mark's Jesus looks into the future to what is to come, though for Mark no doubt some of what is predicted has already happened. The language there is at times cryptic, and perhaps deliberately so. The view adopted in this commentary is that Mark is looking back to the fall of Jerusalem in 70 CE as an event in his past: hence Mark is to be dated after 70 CE (though probably not long after). For discussion of this, see MK 13, especially 13:14–20.

D. Place. By tradition, Mark is to be located in Rome. In support of this one can point to the fact that Mark uses Latin loanwords (e.g. for 'centurion' in 15:39) and seems to think in terms of Roman coinage (see 12:42) and the Roman divisions of time (see 13:35). However, although a Roman origin would fit with this evidence, it is not the only possibility. Latin loanwords and Roman coinage would have been influential in other places than Rome in the empire.

The stress on suffering in Mark's gospel (see below) has also been thought to fit a Roman origin. However, it is not absolutely clear that Mark's stress on suffering is necessarily reflecting the situation of his community: it might just as well be due to his wishing to speak *to* his community about possibilities and dangers which they were not yet facing. See MK 8:34–9:1. Further, a date after 70 for the gospel would mean that it could not be situated directly in the Neronian persecutions. In the end we probably have to be agnostic and say we do not know precisely where Mark comes from or what community he is writing for.

E. Genre. What kind of a text is Mark's gospel? To what genre does it belong? Ever since the second century the book has been known as a 'gospel'. Yet that is a very unusual term for a literary text, let alone an account of the life and ministry of Jesus (see MK 1:1). Older studies had claimed that the gospels were in some sense 'biographies', comparable to works such as those about Socrates (by Plato) or Epictetus (by Arrian). However, early in the twentieth century form critics (Bultmann, Dibelius) argued that the gospels were really folk literature, not to be compared with literary works. The evangelists were simply popular story-tellers who did not impose their own ideas on the material. In particular a text such as Mark displayed none of the characteristic features of biography (nothing on Jesus' personality, psychological development, origins, or education). The gospels were thus without analogy and were *sui generis*.

Such a claim is very odd in literary terms. Some understanding of the genre of a text is essential if it is to be understood at all. Further, this rather low view of a writer such as Mark has been radically questioned in more recent study. Thus, whilst it remains true that close parallels to Mark are hard to find, in either the Jewish or Hellenistic world of the period, many have swung back to the view that Mark may be seen as in some sense a biography, although not in the modern sense of the word. There is indeed very little on Jesus' background or personality in Mark. Yet equally, ancient writing claiming to give the lives (Gk. *bioi*) of individuals often lacked some of these features. Thus if one takes a relatively broad spread of ancient 'lives' of individuals, Mark's gospel can be shown to lie within those parameters. (See Burridge 1992.)

Yet this does not determine exactly how the text should be read. It does not, for example, necessarily imply that the text is *ipso facto* historically reliable. Many other 'biographies' were written with an author's own axe to grind. In this Mark is no exception. Certainly Mark presents us with a highly distinctive account of Jesus' life and some of its implications.

F. Key Themes. 1. As already noted, a key theme of the gospel is suffering: Jesus is the one who supremely fulfils his destiny as the one who suffers and dies, and any disciple of Jesus is called to follow in the same way (see 8:34–10:52). Jesus is also the great miracle worker, though one suspects that Mark would not see this as the most important part of Jesus' ministry. Jesus *is* indeed the great miracle worker, but miracles must, for Mark, be seen in their proper context: they can never be the basis for faith, indeed without an existing context of

faith they cannot take place (see 6:5); further, the one who performs all these mighty works is the one who will end up on the cross.

2. Above all the centre of the story for Mark is the person of Jesus. What is crucial for Mark is the question of Christology. At one level this statement is trite since, for all the evangelists, Jesus is the centre of attention in the story. Nevertheless, for Mark it is above all the question of *who* Jesus is that is paramount. Further, for Mark, it seems that this cannot be answered simply in words or titles. There is an element of secrecy in the story, so that characters in the narrative do not grasp who Jesus is. The reader is told right at the start what are the most appropriate terms in which to understand Jesus (see MK 1:1), but even then, Mark has more to say: indeed that is presumably why he writes his *story*, to show what any words of title mean in concrete terms. For Mark, Jesus is supremely 'Son of God', but what Mark understands by this is not fully clarified, even for the reader, until the cross (cf. 15:39). Mark gives us what can be described as a narrative Christology. It is the narrative which, in the end, tells the reader how Mark wishes Jesus to be understood.

3. A theme almost as important for Mark as Christology is that of discipleship. What does it mean to be a follower of the one who is the Son of God in this Markan sense? As already noted, Mark's Jesus gives an extended block of teaching on discipleship as entailing following Jesus in the same way of suffering and death, the way of the cross (see 8:34–10:52). So too the characters of the disciples play a key role in Mark's story. For Mark it is a matter of concern to show something of what is, or should be, involved in being a follower of Jesus within the Christian church.

G. Purpose. 1. Why then has Mark presented his story in the way he has? There is almost certainly no single answer. Mark writes for a variety of reasons and it would be wrong to pin him down to one single purpose. Some quite general factors are no doubt possible: for example, with the spread of the Christian church geographically, and with the passing of time, Christians no doubt needed information about Jesus and his teaching.

2. Nevertheless, Mark's distinctive presentation remains unexplained by such general considerations. As already noted in passing, the traditional view is that Mark writes for a suffering community (perhaps in Rome) to strengthen their faith in a time of intense persecution. This too is possible, though it is noteworthy that, whilst Mark's Jesus has a lot to say about the necessity of suffering, there is very little in the gospel about any positive significance in such suffering. It is just as likely that Mark's very distinctive account, with the cross so central, is making a positive point *to* his readers quite as much as reflecting the current experiences of his community. The most extreme form of such a theory is that of Weeden (1971) who argues that Mark is involved in intense Christological debates with a group of people he regards as heretics in his community: they advocate a view of Jesus as a divine man, a super-hero characterized by miracles, glory, and power; Mark opposes them with his view of Jesus characterized by weakness, service, and suffering. Weeden also advocates that, in the story, Mark's point of view is represented by Jesus, that of the heretics by the disciples.

3. Weeden's theory is probably too extreme. His view of the role of the disciples in the story is questionable (see Tannehill 1977 and MK 1:16–20), and the language of 'heresy' in a context such as Mark's is probably anachronistic. Nevertheless, the overall theory may have an element of truth in it. Mark's portrait of Jesus may be intended to modify or correct the views of the readers of the gospel (even if talk of 'opponents' is too extreme). Mark clearly wants to present Jesus in one light and *not* another (cf. e.g. 10:45: Jesus as Son of Man came *not* to be served but to serve). Similarly, Mark may be wanting to mould, perhaps change, his readers' views about the nature of Christian discipleship.

4. With his stress on the centrality of the cross, Mark is very like Paul in his views about Jesus and the nature of Christian discipleship. Yet we should not take this for granted, as if Mark could be no different and all first-century Christians were the same. We know from Paul's letters that his own views were frequently controversial and disputed by other Christians within his communities. It may be similar with Mark, whose presentation of Jesus in his gospel is, among other things, a call to his readers to re-evaluate their views about both Jesus and themselves (see also MK 16:8). How we read the gospel may be in part determined by how we respond to such a challenge.

COMMENTARY

(1:1–13) Introduction There is widespread agreement that the opening verses of Mark form an introduction to the book as a whole. As such they set the scene for the detailed story that is to come. Moreover, in many respects they identify the characters of the story and define the terms in which Mark intends it to be read. As we shall see, the motif of secrecy is an important theme in Mark's narrative: on several occasions characters in the story fail to understand who Jesus is or what his ministry is about. Yet for the reader of the gospel there is no secrecy at all: Jesus' identity is disclosed right from the start. On the other hand, not everything is revealed, otherwise Mark's story would be redundant. Thus Jesus is identified as Son of God in these introductory verses; but the full significance of what it means to be a/the true Son of God is maybe only shown by the ensuing narrative. Older editions of the text, and older commentaries, suggested that the introduction comprised vv. 1–8. However, it is now widely accepted that the introduction goes at least as far as v. 13, if not v. 15. Certainly vv. 1–8 are incomplete without the sequel in vv. 9–13 which serve to identify the person of Jesus.

Almost every aspect of v. 1 is debated. The words 'the Son of God' are missing from some Greek manuscripts, but probably do represent the original text of Mark: the importance of the term for Mark's Christology, and the key place of this opening verse to announce the terms of the story to come, make this highly probable. The 'good news' is in Greek *euaggelion*, or 'gospel'. Elsewhere in the NT, the gospel is the Christian message which is preached; it is not a literary product which is written or read. The same is probably true here, though this verse may have contributed to the process whereby 'gospel' became the term to refer to a written account of the life of Jesus. It is not clear how this gospel is the gospel 'of Jesus

Christ'. Is it the good news *about* Jesus, or the good news preached *by* Jesus? v. 14 (where Jesus proclaims the good news) suggests that the latter is in mind, though it is not impossible that both are intended. The force of the reference to the 'beginning' is also uncertain. Does this mean that v. 1 refers only to the introductory verses (so that the full 'gospel' then follows)? Or is there a sense in which the whole of Mark's story is only a 'beginning', and it is up to each reader to carry on where the story leaves off to find the complete gospel? The nature of the ending of Mark's story, with its startling abruptness (see MK 16:8), makes the latter possibility an attractive option. But in any case the opening verse makes it crystal clear to the reader who is the subject of the story to come: it is Jesus who is the Messiah and Son of God. Yet what these terms mean is not yet made clear.

vv. 2–8 serve to set the scene in a wider context. They first bring on to the stage not Jesus himself but the figure of John the Baptist, and in turn John is introduced by a (mixed) OT citation. (v. 2 is a mixture of Ex 23:20 and Mal 3:1; v. 3 is from Isa 40:3. The reference to Isaiah in the introductory words in v. 2 is probably a mistake.) Yet John has little significance of his own in Mark's narrative. Mark tells us nothing of John's own eschatological preaching (as in Mt 3:7–10 and par.), nor of any of his ethical teaching (cf. Lk 3:11–14). The only words John speaks point forward to Jesus (vv. 7–8). Similarly the OT citation (one of the very few explicit citations in Mark) is only brought in to point forward to John. vv. 2–8 are really therefore constructed from the end backwards, where each element points forward to the next. The citation of the OT identifies the time as one of the fulfilment of Jewish eschatological hopes. Moreover, the note in v. 6 of John's clothing may be intended to evoke the clothing of Elijah (2 Kgs 1:8): hence John is cast in the role of an Elijah-figure, and Elijah was the prophet expected to come before the final day of the Lord (cf. Mal 4:5–6). So too the 'wilderness', as the place of John's baptizing activity, was the place from where many Jews expected the final eschatological deliverance to appear. Thus the details of Mark's account serve to place the events to come within a context of the fulfilment of Jewish eschatological hopes. How far all these expectations relate to the historical person of John himself is hard to say. It is not easy to ascribe the words of the saying in vv. 7–8 to the historical John: John may have been expecting the coming of God Himself. Nevertheless, for Mark, the saying now refers to Jesus.

This is made clear in v. 9: the one announced by John is Jesus from Nazareth. Further, Jesus is now baptized by John. Historically it seems very likely that this reflects a real event in the life of Jesus. (Later writers are clearly embarrassed by it: why should Jesus, the sinless Son of God, be baptized for the forgiveness of his sins? However, Mark shows no such embarrassment.) But what the event might have meant in Jesus' psyche we just do not know. The most we can say is that it probably signified Jesus' commitment to John's cause and expressed his agreement with his message. For Mark, the significance of the event is that this is the moment when Jesus' identity is given the absolute seal of divine approval: God himself declares Jesus to be His Son. The reader is now in no doubt: the story to come is the story of the Son of God. The precise meaning of 'Son of God' in Mark is much debated. The words of the voice from heaven here conflate two OT verses in addressing Jesus as 'Son': Ps 2:7 (suggesting a royal figure) and Isa 42:1 (implying an idea of Jesus as the servant); in addition the words 'the beloved' may recall the words of Abraham about Isaac (cf. Gen 22:2). The phrase 'Son of God' can have a wide range of meanings. Later it came to signify Jesus' full divinity as a member of a divine Trinity. But in the first century the term had no necessary overtones of divinity: it could refer to a royal figure (cf. Ps 2:7), or to the nation Israel (cf. Hos 11:1) or to a righteous sufferer (cf. Wis 2:17). Perhaps it would be wrong to press Mark into too rigid a mould here: Jesus *is* a royal figure (as will be stressed particularly in ch. 15); but as Son of God he is supremely one who will suffer and die. Indeed it may be Mark's intention precisely to spell out in his story the way in which true divine sonship should be seen. The reference to the heavens being 'torn apart' indicates a theophany (cf. Isa 64:1); and the coming of the Spirit again implies the fulfilment of Jewish eschatological hopes (cf. Joel 2:28–31 cited in Acts 2:17–21). The significance of the Spirit being symbolized as a 'dove' is uncertain, but may allude to the creation story in Gen 1:2 where some Jewish exegetes interpreted the words there as referring to the Spirit 'hovering' like a dove. In that case, the story here may again be indicating the start of a *new* creation.

vv. 12–13 recount the so-called 'temptation' of Jesus ('testing' would be a better description.) The story is much shorter than the threefold temptation story of Jesus in Matthew and Luke. Jesus is in the wilderness for 'forty days' (a time with many OT resonances: cf. Moses in Ex 34:28; Elijah in 1 Kgs 19:8). The 'testing' by Satan is probably to be thought of as a titanic struggle with the powers of evil. The exact details are uncertain (e.g. does the struggle last for forty days? Do the angels minister during, or after, the struggle? What do the wild beasts signify?). But the general thrust of the narrative seems to be that Jesus is victorious in the battle against Satan. Mark probably intends the story to act as the interpretative key for at least part of the narrative to come. Exorcisms and battles with unclean spirits will occupy a significant part of Jesus' ministry. The temptation narrative shows that these are part of a broader eschatological battle with the powers of evil; and also that Jesus is victorious in that battle, as 3:22–30 will show.

(1:14–15) Jesus' Preaching This is something of a transition, in which Mark gives what is probably intended as a summary of Jesus' preaching. John is almost forgotten (his arrest is mentioned only in passing, and no reason for it is given): all attention is focused on the person of Jesus. Yet Jesus' preaching does not focus on himself, but on God. It is the time of the fulfilment of Jewish eschatological hopes ('the time is fulfilled'), and Jesus proclaims the imminence of the kingdom of God. (The verb 'has come near' represents a Greek word which probably implies that the kingdom is very close, but not yet present.) Reflected here are Jewish eschatological hopes for the intervention of God in the affairs of the world to establish himself as king and for his kingly rule to be acknowledged by all. (The 'kingdom of God' is probably meant in an active sense of God ruling as king, rather than as a spatial area over which he rules.) The time is thus one of the imminent fulfilment of eschatological hopes. In the face of this imminent event, people must 'repent', i.e. change their lifestyle in preparation for what is to come, and 'believe in the good news'. It is worth noting that here, as throughout the synoptic gospels generally, the object of faith is not Jesus himself. Here it is the gospel, the good news, which must be 'believed'. Jesus becomes the object of faith after Easter. Thus Mark seems to reflect the pre-Easter situation quite well in that Jesus does not refer to himself explicitly as the focus of the belief of others.

What is announced here is that the kingdom in its fullness is still to come. However, there is a sense in which the events of Jesus' ministry represent the fulfilment of eschatological hopes, so that the kingdom is in part already present in the work and preaching of Jesus. Thus the eschatological claims in Mark have a characteristic dual element: the eschatological events are proclaimed as due to come—and to come soon—but also they have already partly arrived in the person of Jesus.

After the summary statement of Jesus' preaching the story moves on to a different level with the more historical account of Jesus' ministry in Galilee.

(1:16–20) Call of Four Disciples The first event narrated by Mark is the call, and response, of the first four disciples of Jesus. The story is told in an extremely compressed way. No unnecessary detail of information is supplied. It is thus quite pointless to speculate, for example, on why the disciples responded without demur, or whether Jesus had met them beforehand. Mark is not interested in the psychology of the disciples or of their response. Rather, for him the centre of the action is once again the person of Jesus: Jesus is the one who calls and summons others to be his followers with the single authoritative word 'Follow me!'; and those who are summoned in this way obey him without any hesitation. Yet whilst it is the case that Jesus is the central character in the story, it remains the case that the disciples will also occupy a key role in the narrative to come. Much has been written on the role played by the disciples in Mark's story, focusing in particular on the very bad press they get later, when they fail to understand Jesus (cf. 8:17–21) and finally desert him completely (cf. 14:50). (See Weeden 1971; Tannehill 1977.) Here it must be said that the portrait of the disciples is entirely positive: Jesus calls them and they obey him instantly and without reserve. The effect of the story is thus to place the disciples in a good light so that the reader responds to them thoroughly positively. Any negative portrayal of the disciples later in the story will have to be balanced against this initial picture.

The phrase 'fish for people' (lit. 'fishers of men/people') is highly unusual, despite its later popularity in Christian hymns and songs: the phrase suggests a somewhat harsh and negative activity of ensnaring for judgement (cf. Jer 16:16; Ezek 29:4–5). Mark refers to 'Simon' here, and only later (after 3:16) does he use the name 'Peter'. All four men called are fishermen; as such they were certainly not destitute in economic terms, apparently owning boats and probably making a reasonable living (cf. 10:28). Jesus' call to others to 'follow' him by joining him physically in his itinerant ministry is quite unlike that of a Jewish teacher having pupils who study the law under him. It is thus difficult to find any close analogies in the immediate Jewish background for the phenomenon of discipleship in the sense envisaged in the gospels. The theme of the authority of Jesus, which is clearly central for Mark, is continued and developed in the next story.

(1:21–8) An Exorcism in Capernaum The action takes place on the sabbath (though no question of a possible breach of sabbath law is raised here). The pericope consists of the account of the exorcism, which Mark appears to have framed between two notes about Jesus' teaching (vv. 21–2, 27). Such a sandwiching technique is very typical of Mark, who seems to use the resultant structure to allow one part of the sandwich to provide an interpretative key for the other part. The story of the exorcism itself may well be traditional. There seems to be a note of secrecy here, and secrecy is a characteristic Markan motif; but in fact it is really only apparent. The unclean spirit tries to utter Jesus' name (v. 24). The motif can be paralleled in other similar exorcism stories: uttering the other person's name was thought to be a means of overpowering your opponent. Jesus thus silences the demon (v. 25), not to impose secrecy, but in order to stop the demon naming him: the act of silencing is itself the action which gains mastery over the demon. However, as we shall see, Mark develops this motif in a peculiar way later (see 1:34; 3:12). Jesus' activity as an exorcist is well attested. Jesus was by no means unique in claiming the power to exorcize (cf. Lk 11:19), though in the Christian tradition, Jesus' exorcisms are claimed to be the manifestation of the arrival of the kingdom of God (Lk 11:20, cf. Mk 3:22–30). For Mark the emphasis clearly lies on the authority and power shown by Jesus in exorcizing. This is shown in part by the way in which Mark inserts the exorcism story into two notes about Jesus' 'teaching' with 'authority' (vv. 22, 27). The fact that the story itself is not about Jesus' teaching at all suggests that these framing references are secondary; moreover the fact that, so far in Mark's story, Jesus has given virtually no explicit teaching suggests that Mark is at this stage more interested in the fact that Jesus' teaching is authoritative than he is in the contents of that teaching. (The contents will come later, e.g. in ch. 4.)

One other detail should be noted here. Jesus' authority *qua* teacher is said to be 'not as the scribes' (v. 22). (The scribes were the legislators in Judaism, those who decided how the law should be applied in new situations, and made decisions when different laws clashed; but it is not apparent that Mark knows clearly the differences between the Jewish groups he mentions.) The reference here is left hanging, but the scribes reappear soon, i.e. in 2:6, where they are again opponents of Jesus. This is the first hint of a theme that will dominate the whole gospel: Jesus as the authoritative figure who teaches and exorcizes is the one who as such will clash with the Jewish authorities, and that clash will ultimately lead to the cross. The theme is only hinted at here, but will be developed significantly in the next chapter.

(1:29–31) The Healing of Peter's Mother-in-Law As in previous stories, the extraneous detail is kept to an absolute minimum. Some have suggested that the story may be due to Peter's own recollections: this is possible, but scarcely provable one way or the other. For Mark the story no doubt shows Jesus' continuing authority, here extending to an ability to heal physical illness as well as to exorcize. The story is told in the form of a classic healing story: the description of the illness with a request for healing, the healing itself, followed by a demonstration of the cure or an acclamation. The final phrase ('she began to serve them') might be intended as just a piece of evidence that she really had been cured; alternatively, and more probably, it also shows Peter's mother-in-law performing what is, for Mark, the supreme Christian action of 'serving' others (cf. 10:44–5). In Mark's gospel it is striking how often the women characters are presented in a far better light than the male disciples. Here Peter's mother-in-law does what every Christian is called to do, namely to serve others.

(1:32–4) General Healings and Exorcisms The note about 'evening' (v. 32) indicates that the sabbath (cf. v. 21) is over, and so people are allowed to carry the sick to Jesus. The account is general and the details rather hyperbolic ('*all* who were sick', v. 32, 'the *whole* city', v. 33). Mark thinks that this reflects Jesus' usual activity, and it shows the importance Mark places on Jesus' miracles. There is thus no real place for any theory that Mark positively disapproved of this aspect of Jesus' ministry, as some have argued (cf. Weeden 1971); however, as we shall see, there may be a sense in which Mark shows an element of reserve about whether this is the most significant aspect of Jesus' life and work. A characteristic Markan note comes for the first time in v. 34, where Jesus commands the demons to be silent. The motif was present in Mark's tradition (cf. v. 24), but Mark seems to develop it in a peculiar way: now the demons know Jesus' identity and are forbidden by Jesus to make this knowledge public (cf. too 3:12) so that others remain in ignorance. This is then the first appearance of the so-called 'messianic secret' in Mark. In many respects it is somewhat artificial and probably represents Mark's own interpretation of his tradition. (Certainly v. 34 alongside v. 24 indicates that the secrecy motif has been imposed secondarily as a development of the earlier tradition.) The significance of the secret in Mark is debated (see the survey of views in Tuckett 1983). Perhaps the best solution is that, via the secrecy charges, Mark indicates to the reader (for whom there is no secret at all! cf. 1:1) that Jesus' identity must remain a secret to human characters in the story—at least prior to the cross. Jesus' identity is finally recognized by a human being at the cross (cf. 15:39), but not before. Mark may thereby wish to indicate that Jesus' identity *can* only be truly perceived in the light of the cross. Hence, in the story-world created by Mark, before one gets to the cross, Jesus keeps his identity secret. (See Räisänen 1990.)

(1:35–9) Extension of the Ministry These verses portray a slight interlude in the narrative. Not all the details are entirely clear. Jesus withdraws to a private place to pray (v. 35): perhaps the note underlines the fact that Jesus is ultimately dependent on God for all that he does. Does the withdrawal indicate also an element of reserve on Mark's part about the importance of the miracles? This is possible (cf. too 8:27–30), though in v. 29 Jesus goes out and about not only preaching but also 'casting out demons'. The disciples are said to 'hunt' for Jesus (v. 30). The verb used is rather unusual, indicating perhaps some kind of hostile pursuit. It is possible that this is the first indication in the narrative of the motif which will be considerably developed later whereby the disciples fail to respond properly to Jesus (ctr. MK 1:16–20). Perhaps then the story hints here at what will come more fully later. The disciples have, it is true, followed Jesus in one sense: but the true following will be shown later to be rather different (cf. 8:34; 10:52). Jesus' response is to go 'throughout Galilee'. Again we have a summarizing statement from Mark, showing Jesus' universal activity in preaching and healing. The reference to 'their' synagogues in v. 39 may be revealing: does this show that for Mark, the Christian community had separated from the Jewish community? Certainly it is likely that Mark was writing for a Gentile audience and this may be one piece of evidence for this.

(1:40–5) A Leper Healed The next story, only loosely connected with its context, shows Jesus healing a leper. (The condition referred to as 'leprosy' in the Bible probably covers a wide range of illnesses.) A number of details in the story are obscure. Jesus' action is said in v. 41 to be due to his 'pity', or compassion; however, some Greek manuscripts say here that Jesus was 'moved with anger'. In view of the fact that it is hard to see why 'pity' might have been changed to 'anger' by a scribe, but very easy to see how the reverse change might take place, some have argued that the reference to 'anger' here may be original. Matthew and Luke also both omit the phrase, which would also be easier to explain if the original reference here was to Jesus' anger. References to pity, or compassion, as the motive for Jesus' miracles in the gospels are rare. However, the reason for any 'anger' here is not clear (cf. also below on v. 43). Touching the leper would render Jesus unclean according to Jewish purity laws. Jesus' action here may thus show him seeking to break down the barriers created within human society by such purity laws. (Cf. further MK 5:21–43.) The reference to Jesus 'sternly warning' the man (v. 43) is also difficult. The verb used is a rare one, usually expressing intense anger. But who or what is Jesus angry with? The man? The leprosy? Evil spirits thought to be behind the illness? Perhaps Mark simply understands the note as referring to Jesus' urgency in sending the man to the priests; but in an earlier version of the story, Jesus' anger might have been thought to be directed against evil spirits.

Jesus commands secrecy in v. 44: the man is to say nothing but to go to the priests to have his cure certified (as required by the law in Lev 14: at this point there seems to be no critique of the law at all). Although these secrecy commands after miracles have sometimes been linked with the messianic secret, they should probably not be so interpreted. Here the secrecy commanded in v. 44 is limited, since the man *is* to make his cure known to the priests. But in any case v. 45 shows that secrecy is not in fact maintained: the man goes out and proclaims openly what has happened. Perhaps this is one way in which Mark's narrative emphasizes the success of Jesus' activity as a healer: despite Jesus' own attempts to keep things quiet, the news spreads like wildfire! This then is rather different from the secrecy of 1:34 where other people in the story do *not* come to share the knowledge about Jesus that the demons had. Thus it is probably right to distinguish between a 'messianic secret' which is kept (as in 1:34) and a 'miracle "secret"' which is immediately broken (as here). (See Luz 1983.) The story thus ends on a note of Jesus' great popularity. The very next story will show that such popularity is *not* universal.

(2:1–3:6) The next section of the gospel comprises five stories showing Jesus in a series of controversies with the Jewish authorities, and this series reaches its climax in the plot to have him killed (3:6). Although it is sometimes argued that the collection is pre-Markan, partly because the plot to kill Jesus seems to come very early, such a theory is unnecessary. The note in 3:6 is not isolated: as we shall see there are a number of details pointing the reader forward to the passion to come (see MK 2:7, 20, as well as the references to Jesus as Son of Man). This series may in fact be Mark's way of indicating very early in his story the course which the ensuing narrative will take. For Mark Jesus is supremely the one who will suffer and die, and this theme dominates the account. The collection here, with all its forward-looking references to the passion, may well be Mark's own composition.

(2:1–12) The Healing of the Paralytic The story in its present form is probably composite: a straight healing story (vv. 1–5, 11–12) has been disrupted by the insertion of a debate between Jesus and the scribes about his authority (vv. 6–10). The healing story itself is fairly straightforward, but it is important to note the reference to 'faith' in v. 5: miracles in Mark generally only occur, and can only occur, in a context of faith (cf. 6:5). Yet it should also be noted that this faith is not necessarily faith 'in Jesus', but rather in God who works through Jesus; moreover, the faith here is *not* that of the paralysed man himself, but of his friends. This is then not quite the same as some present-day kinds of 'faith-healing' that emphasize the faith of the sick person. The connection between illness and sin is here assumed and not discussed (cf. Jn 9:2–3); though whether this element was present in the original healing narrative is uncertain. Perhaps it was added as simply the motif to generate the following controversy about Jesus' authority.

The debate in vv. 6–10 focuses on Jesus' authority (cf. 1:22), an authority which is questioned by the scribes (again reminiscent of 1:22: thus the implicit opposition between Jesus and the scribes now becomes explicit). The scribes accuse Jesus of 'blasphemy' (v. 7), which is precisely the charge on which Jesus will be condemned to death at his trial (14:64). The historical problems are acute as Jesus has not technically committed blasphemy, an offence which involved uttering the divine name (*m. Sanh.* 7.5: see MK 14:64). It is possible that, *if* the account here is at all historical, the scribes may have meant that Jesus was guilty of blasphemy in a looser sense than that defined by Jewish law. However, Mark may not have been aware of such details. For him, what is important is to show that the conflict between Jesus and the scribes here is literally a life-and-death struggle.

The debate is about Jesus' authority, and his authority to forgive. By implication, the story claims that Jesus does have this authority, which is usually the prerogative of God alone (though strictly Jesus does no more than declare God's forgiveness). At this point, Jesus' authority is said to be signalled in part by reference to him as Son of Man. This enigmatic phrase has generated enormous discussion. It is possible that the phrase alone (in Aramaic) simply means 'a man', or 'someone'. Yet this scarcely fits the present context where the issue is the authority of *Jesus*, not of any human being. Elsewhere in Mark, 'Son of Man' is a term used to refer to Jesus' suffering (cf. 8:31 etc.) and future vindication (14:62 etc.). Although disputed, one very plausible background for the term, certainly at the level of Mark's understanding, is that of Dan

7:13, where a figure described as 'one like a son of man' appears as a symbol for the vindicated people of God in the heavenly court; and since the people concerned in Daniel are presently suffering violent persecution (probably under Antiochus Epiphanes), the figure of Dan 7 may be associated with suffering as well as vindication. (This last point is more disputed.) If so, then the term 'Son of Man' as applied to Jesus by Mark may be intended to evoke this twin idea of suffering and vindication as the role which lies ahead for Jesus.

The present reference to Jesus as Son of Man may seem out of place in such a schema. In fact it is probably thoroughly appropriate. The wider context in Mark is the series of controversies leading to Jesus' death; so here then, Mark may also be indicating allusively (as in v. 7) that the controversy is one which will lead to death: the one with authority is the 'Son of Man', i.e. the one who must suffer and die. Since the reference to 'Son of Man' here makes excellent sense in Mark's literary scheme, and really makes sense only there, it is probably due to Mark himself, though the substance of the saying, without Jesus' explicit self-reference as Son of Man, may be pre-Markan.

(2:13–17) Jesus and Social Outcasts The second of the five controversy stories concerns Jesus' relationship with tax-collectors and sinners. In what may originally have been a separate story, Mark tells of the call of Levi in vv. 13–14. The story, with its stark simplicity and lack of any extraneous detail, is similar in form to the call stories of 1:16–20. Levi appears nowhere else in this gospel (though Matthew evidently identified Levi with 'Matthew', one of the twelve: cf. Mt 9:9; 10:3). Levi is said to be a 'tax-collector': what is probably meant is not someone who collected taxes for the Romans directly, but an employee of Herod responsible for collecting some of the local tolls. Such people had a uniformly bad name amongst Jews, primarily for their unscrupulousness and dishonesty.

Levi's response to the call is to invite Jesus to his house (v. 15: it is *possible* that the house actually belongs to Jesus—the Greek is ambiguous, speaking only of 'his' house—but this seems unlikely). Again Jesus comes into conflict with the authorities, here 'the scribes of the Pharisees'. The exact nature of the Pharisaic party is debated. They seem to have been an influential group of lay people, deeply concerned to apply the law to ever new situations, if necessary by legislating afresh, and also concerned to maintain a higher than normal level of purity in their everyday lives. Here they accuse Jesus of eating with tax-collectors and sinners. Eating with such people may have signified an offer to associate with them without condemning their faults, and this may have offended a strict law-abiding group such as the Pharisees. The identity of the 'sinners' is even more uncertain. The term might refer to those who did not maintain a Pharisaic interpretation of the law; or it may refer to those who deliberately flouted the law. The former is perhaps more likely: the term is often used in polemical contexts to refer to those who do not belong to the speaker's own in-group; it is then a way of castigating outsiders. If so it may indicate that the Pharisees expected Jesus not to consort with those outside their group, and hence may suggest that in fact Jesus had quite close links with the Pharisees. If that were the case, it might explain better why the

Pharisees so bitterly opposed Jesus. For Mark, however, the Pharisees seem to be no longer very relevant for his own community: e.g. in 7:3–4 he has to explain some of their customs for his readers.

Jesus' final reply in v. 17 is enigmatic. Does it imply that there are righteous people who need no call? It is perhaps better taken as ironic. The righteous need no call—but by implication those who think that they are righteous are perhaps thereby showing they are not righteous. Certainly the saying links with the previous story in showing both Jesus' concern with sinners and sin and his unique authority.

(2:18–22) Old and New The next story concerns the issue of fasting. Again the story is probably composite, with vv. 19b–20 representing a secondary allegorizing of an original tradition.

John's disciples and Pharisees are said to be fasting, and Jesus is asked why his own disciples do not. Fasting was required of all Jews at times, though the story here, by singling out the Pharisees and John for mention, suggests that the fasting in question was an extra obligation taken on freely. The very fact that Jesus is asked why his disciples do not join in is a further indication that Jesus may once have had close links with the Pharisees and hence his failure to follow their practices was a matter of surprise to them. Jesus' reply is to refer, in a variety of metaphors, to the totally new situation that now obtains and its incompatibility with the old: it is like a wedding when fasting is simply inappropriate; similarly, the old and the new will not mix, just as one cannot mend a cloak with unshrunk material, or use old wineskins for new wine. By implication, the 'new' is the presence of Jesus in his ministry: as such it is incompatible with the old ways. The new life of the kingdom is one of joy and celebration and renders fasting obsolete. The implicit claim by Jesus is startling in its scope.

vv. 19b–20 probably represent a secondary allegorizing of the tradition, looking ahead (in the story's terms) to the time when the bridegroom (i.e. Jesus) will be 'taken away' (i.e. die). Fasting will then be reintroduced (as we know it was in the early church). These verses may then be looking ahead to the time of the church, and justifying current church practice; but they also draw the reader's attention forward to the moment of the taking away of the bridegroom, i.e. to the death of Jesus. Like the hints in v. 7 and perhaps v. 10, the reader's gaze is directed to the cross which, for Mark, is never far away in the story.

(2:23–8) Jesus and the Sabbath: The Cornfields The final two controversy stories involve sabbath law, the command that one shall do no 'work'. In the first of these stories, Jesus and his disciples go through the cornfields, plucking corn as they go (v. 23). Such action was not in itself illegal, but interpreters of the sabbath legislation decided that reaping and threshing should count as work and hence were not allowed on the sabbath. The presence of Pharisees, apparently spying in a cornfield on the sabbath, strains credulity and is unlikely to be historical. Possibly we have here then a reflection of a debate in the early church about how far sabbath law should be obeyed by Christians (note it is the *disciples*, not Jesus, who perform the questionable activity); yet it seems equally likely that Jesus himself was engaged in similar debates.

Jesus' first reply (vv. 25–6) refers to the example of David breaking the law by eating the shewbread when he was hungry (1 Sam 21: the reference to Abiathar being high priest at the time is wrong, and Matthew and Luke both omit the note). The example provides some precedent for acting illegally, but scarcely provides a strong argument for breaking such an important law as the sabbath law. The repeated introductions in v. 25 and v. 27 may indicate a seam in the tradition, and v. 27 is more likely to be the original conclusion to the story. The lack of appositeness in vv. 25–6 may betray the secondary origin of this tradition.

Jesus' second reply is far more devastating. v. 27 seems to relativize the whole sabbath law, so that any human need would legitimize not keeping the sabbath. (Jews at the time certainly allowed work on the sabbath if life was in danger, but this verse seems to go much further.) The implication of this saying in relation to the law is very radical. (Matthew and Luke, perhaps because they realize this, both omit the verse.) v. 28 may represent a slight backing away from the radicalness of v. 27: *Jesus* (as Son of Man) is lord of the sabbath. Does this imply that *Jesus* can abrogate sabbath law, but not anyone else? (If we took 'Son of Man' as meaning 'a man', then v. 28 would say the same as v. 27: human need would override the sabbath; but this seems impossible for Mark—for him the Son of Man is Jesus and Jesus alone.) Certainly in Mark's eyes it would seem that the one with the unique authority to dispense sabbath law is Jesus alone. Why then is he referred to as Son of Man? Perhaps again, as in v. 10, it is Mark's way of pointing forward to what is to come: the one who claims this authority inevitably clashes with other authority figures, a clash which will lead to suffering and death, the appointed lot of the one who is 'Son of Man'.

(3:1–6) Jesus and the Sabbath: The Man with the Withered Hand In the last of the five controversy stories here, Jesus is again in dispute over sabbath observance. The occasion is a miracle, Jesus healing a man with a withered hand. But in form-critical terms, the story is not a 'miracle story': the focus of attention is not the miracle for its own sake, but the controversy between Jesus and the authorities about his right to heal the man on the sabbath. There is debate about whether Jesus' actions here do in fact constitute 'work' and thus breach sabbath law. Strictly speaking, Jesus is recorded as doing nothing that could be deemed to be work. However, in its present form, all the parties concerned in the debate presuppose that Jesus has worked. Jesus' justification for his action would scarcely satisfy a Jewish opponent. The principle of working on the sabbath to save life was accepted by all; but a man with a withered hand was not in danger of losing his life. Jesus' rhetorical double question in v. 4 would have had a clear answer from Jews: one must of course save life on the sabbath; otherwise one 'does good', which means obeying God's law and *not* working. Jesus' saying here seems to presuppose a significant extension of the meaning of saving life: his own ministry is an activity of saving life in a radical sense, and hence justifies relativizing the sabbath law. Yet it is hard to avoid the impression that the story here shows Jesus acting in a rather provocative way in relation to his Jewish contemporaries and their sensibilities regarding what was acknowledged as one of the most important parts of the whole Jewish law.

The conclusion to the story—and to the series of five stories—is a plot to kill Jesus (v. 6). The alliance of Pharisees and 'Herodians' seems implausible historically. The Herodians were not a party, but may have been the supporters of Herod Antipas: as such they would normally have been opposed by the Pharisees. It is notable too that the Pharisees rarely make any appearance in the passion narratives themselves. Perhaps the mention of the two groups here is intended by Mark simply to indicate the combined forces of religious and secular power in general. The key point is the note that the authorities plot to have Jesus killed. The controversies are so deep-seated that they will lead to Jesus' death. For the reader, the cross is now clearly in view. Jesus' life and ministry inevitably lead to conflict, suffering, and death. The cross for Mark is an inalienable part of what it means for Jesus to be God's Son.

(3:7–12) General Healings Mark now gives another summary statement about Jesus' activity as a healer and an exorcist, similar to 1:32–4. Jesus' popularity and success are again emphasized. As in 1:34, however, a typically Markan motif recurs in v. 12: Jesus commands the demons not to make known his identity (here as Son of God): other human beings in the story are not allowed to know who Jesus is at this stage. Once again Mark seems to be taking up a traditional motif from exorcism stories (the exorcist silences the demon) and giving it his own peculiar interpretation. As before, for Mark the true nature of Jesus' divine sonship cannot yet be revealed: such knowledge will only come at the cross.

(3:13–19) The Call of the Twelve The appointment of an inner group of twelve disciples is well attested in the earliest Christian tradition (cf. 1 Cor 15:5). Mark does not make a lot of this. The number twelve is probably deliberately intended to evoke the number of the tribes of Israel: the new body round Jesus is the nucleus of a new people of God. The fact that the number is twelve, not eleven, so that Jesus himself is not one of the number, implies an even more privileged place for Jesus. He is the creator and inaugurator of the new Israel. The twelve are said to be 'apostles' here (though the phrase is absent from some Greek manuscripts). Mark uses the term elsewhere only at 6:30. The use of the word may be anachronistic here and reflect post-resurrection usage: it was used in the later Christian church to refer to special authority figures in the movement, but it is doubtful if Jesus himself used the term. The names of the twelve are mainly traditional, and nothing is known of most of them. The extra name of Peter given to Simon is not explained (cf. Mt 16:18); the name 'Boanerges' given to James and John is peculiar to Mark here. Some discussion has taken place over the penultimate name 'Simon the Cananaean' (NRSV). The word for 'Cananaean' has been interpreted as 'Zealot', with conclusions drawn about the possible presence in Jesus' immediate circle of a member of the Zealot party, the political group later very influential in fomenting armed rebellion against the Romans. However, it is almost certain that such a party did not exist prior to the time of the Jewish War in *c.*66 CE. Hence no conclusions can be drawn about Jesus' possible involvement with the activity of such a group, which is in any case extremely unlikely. The word here may simply imply that Simon was a very zealous character.

The reference to Judas Iscariot once again reminds the reader of the story to come: even at this moment, betrayal and its consequences are not far away.

(3:20–35) Further Controversy This section represents another example of Mark's sandwiching technique: the story of the Beelzebul controversy with the scribes (vv. 22–30) comes between the two halves of the story of the dispute between Jesus and his family (vv. 20–1, 31–5). Mark thereby shows the increasing hostility and alienation experienced by Jesus: the failure of his family to accept him is shown to be akin to the hostility of the scribes. Throughout the gospel, Jesus becomes more and more isolated, as one group after another—steadily getting closer to home—deserts him. The Beelzebul controversy demonstrates the increasing intensity of the hostility from the 'scribes' (cf. 1:22; 2:6). Here they are said to be 'from Jerusalem', one of the first indicators in Mark of what will be a strong distinction between Galilee and Jerusalem, with Jerusalem as the place of hostility and, finally, death. The issue is again about Jesus' authority and power, the scribes accusing him of using demonic power. ('Beelzebul'—the name varies in different manuscripts—was probably originally the name of a minor demon: this period was a time of great flux in beliefs about demonic figures, with no standardized model of a monolithic Devil figure universally established. However, Mark himself does seem to presuppose such a model and evidently regards the two names as referring to the same figure.) Jesus replies at first in a series of images (literally 'parables', v. 23), but all based on the same theme: a power fighting against itself would collapse immediately. By implication, Satan's kingdom is thought of as still standing: hence it cannot be opposed by its own forces—Jesus' power must have other roots.

The saying in v. 27 may have had a separate origin. The presuppositions now seem to be different: Satan is the strong man who has now been bound and his property is being plundered, i.e. by Jesus. The image derives from Jewish eschatology (cf. Rev 20:2): the binding of Satan is a feature of the eschatological end-time. The claim being made here is then that the end-time has arrived: Jesus' exorcisms are not just everyday events, but the final overthrow of the power of Satan. Moreover, Mark's arrangement of the material, with v. 27 following vv. 24–6, suggests that he regards v. 27 as providing the hermeneutical key for the previous verses. Thus, whatever these sayings may have implied earlier in the tradition, Mark regards Jesus' argument in vv. 24–7 as claiming to have won the final victory over Satan. The saying in vv. 28–9 reverts to the issue of Jesus' authority. The Markan version is probably more original than the parallel in Q (cf. Lk 12:10) which speaks of blasphemy against the Son of Man being forgivable. Here all sins are said to be forgivable, except blasphemy against the Holy Spirit. In context the meaning is clear: blasphemy against the Holy Spirit is a denial of the power of Jesus in his exorcisms. By implication, therefore, Jesus exorcizes by the power of the Holy Spirit (cf. 1:12–13), and a refusal to accept this by the scribes is the unforgivable sin. Yet again Mark focuses all attention on the person of Jesus and the authority by which he acts. For Mark the centre of attention is supremely the Christological question of who Jesus is.

(4:1–34) Parables At this point, Mark gives the first extended block of teaching by Jesus. Up to now, Jesus' teaching has been important as illustrating his authority (cf. 1:22); here, for the first time, some content is given. The content here consists mostly of parables. The parables are widely thought to be the most characteristic part of Jesus' teaching, though Mark does not give many examples. Christians very soon interpreted Jesus' parables as allegories, finding significance in each detail of the story, and we can see that process starting as early as Mark himself (see vv. 14–20). The recognition that Jesus' parables were not originally allegories in which every detail of the story has significance is now well accepted in modern scholarship. Some though have taken this to the other extreme, arguing that they have only one single meaning. This is probably too rigid: the parables may have been intended to make more than one point, even if a detailed allegorical interpretation by Jesus is unlikely. It is generally thought that Jesus used parables in order to enhance his teaching and to get his message across. As we shall see, this makes Mark's account of Jesus' speaking about his own parables in vv. 11–12 here extremely difficult to accept as historical.

This section in Mark is almost certainly composite. The large number of (often unnecessary) introductions (cf. vv. 2, 10, 13, 21, 24, 26, 30), as well as the inconsistency in the settings (Jesus speaks to the crowd in v. 2, withdraws to an inner group in v. 10, but still seems to be speaking to the crowd in v. 33) suggest that originally separate traditions have been combined here. For example, some have argued that Mark has taken over a prior collection of three 'seed' parables. Whether there is such a pre-Markan collection here is uncertain. Much depends on one's interpretation of the difficult vv. 10–13 (see below), and whether one judges the ideas there to be non-Markan and hence pre-Markan.

(4:1–9) The Parable of the Sower It is generally assumed that Jesus' parables are true to life and not artificially constructed, unrealistic stories. (Such a broad generalization is unlikely to be true always: sometimes they make their point precisely because what they describe is *un*expected and *extra*ordinary.) Much discussion has taken place about whether the details of the parable of the sower are true to life: is the action of sowing seed 'on the path' (v. 4) normal practice? Are the yields of the good seed (v. 8: 'thirty and sixty and a hundred fold') normal or abnormal? Perhaps the issue, at least in relation to the first point, is not too important: this is *not* a story inculcating good horticultural practice! It is a story about how preaching is received. The story is thus almost inherently allegorical—at least to a certain extent, if not down to the smallest detail. The yields in v. 8 *are* probably extraordinary: the result of the seed falling on good earth is not just what 'normally' happens, but a divine miracle.

The overall interpretation of the parable can be taken in two quite different ways: it can be assurance to those who receive the 'seed' that all in the end will be well—the harvest *will* come; or it can be a warning to those who hear the message to ensure that they receive it properly and not be like the three types of unproductive soil. The first interpretation has in its favour the fact that the other two parables in this chapter probably have a similar message. However, there is no reason why all three parables should be saying the same thing; and the fact that all three are included suggests that maybe Mark at least thought they were not simply repetitions of each other in slightly different wording. Further, the considerable detail given to the first three kinds of soil suggests that these are of interest in themselves, and are not simply negative foils to the good soil which is alone the point of the story. Thus it seems likely that the parable is in some sense a warning to people to take care how they receive the preaching of Jesus. It is not just encouragement to the 'good' that all will be well in the end; it is as much a warning to those who listen to make sure that they are 'good soil'. Mark's own interests may come to the fore in his description of the second type of soil (vv. 5–6). The description here is longer than the other three and may have been expanded by Mark: for Mark, 'rootless' Christians are perhaps the cause for most concern. What this might mean in practice is spelt out later (see on v. 17).

(4:10–13) The Theory of Parables These verses are, by almost universal consent, among the hardest in the whole gospel to interpret. vv. 11–12 seem to ascribe to Jesus the view that he teaches in parables precisely in order to hide his meaning and to prevent other people (the crowds) from understanding him. This is what Mark's Greek clearly means, and it is thus virtually impossible to see this as coming from Jesus himself, who (it is usually assumed) used parables to enable understanding, not prevent it. Hence the saying in its present form is almost certainly the product of someone writing later than Jesus. v. 12 uses the words from Isa 6:9 to say that the failure of people to understand Jesus' message is due to divine predestination. Attempts are sometimes made to rescue the saying for the historical Jesus by claiming that the words 'in parables' in v. 11 originally (in Aramaic) meant 'in riddles', and were unrelated to Jesus' using stories ('parables') to enhance his message. Hence Jesus was simply reflecting on the fact that people had not accepted his message (so Jeremias 1963). However, this scarcely solves the problem of what the saying now means in Mark's Greek: at this level it clearly relates to Jesus' use of 'parables', i.e. stories.

The verses suggest a rigid division between a privileged in-group and a condemned out-group. The latter fail to understand the message as a result of a divinely predetermined decision (v. 12). The text cited (Isa 6:9–10) is one of the classic texts used by Christians to seek to explain the failure by others to respond positively to the Christian message (cf. Jn 12:40; Rom 11:8). In the light of hostility experienced, Christians sought to come to terms with apparent failure by 'explaining' their lack of success as due to predetermined action by God. What we see here, therefore, is probably not any reflection of a conscious decision by Jesus, but an attempt at rationalization by a later Christian group in the light of bitter experience of rejection, but struggling to maintain an overall theistic world-view. The sentiments here may be unattractive in one way; but the struggle to reconcile belief in God with apparent failure in the world's terms is a perennial problem for many.

The in-group are said to be those who have received the 'secret' (NRSV, lit. mystery) of the kingdom. The benefits enjoyed by this in-group of disciples are often read out of v. 12 by reversing what is said there: the disciples must 'understand'. Perhaps too, taking into account v. 34, the disciples have been privileged to receive 'interpretation' of the parables which is denied to the crowds. This is sometimes then contrasted with the picture elsewhere in Mark (e.g. 8:17–21), and

also in v. 13 here, where ... understand: hence, it is argued, perhaps ... Markan tradition which Mark has radicalized by making even the disciples fail to understand.

This however makes Mark into something of an authorial idiot, including verses with which he apparently patently disagreed and which he immediately had to correct. In fact it is not said in v. 11 (or indeed in v. 34) that the disciples actually understand Jesus. In one sense of course they do, as indeed do the crowds: they 'understand' *parables* (cf. 3:23; 12:9) in that the latter are not unintelligible nonsense. Nevertheless, they do not lead everyone to faith: in that sense they do not lead to (deeper) 'understanding'. The disciples are in a different position, which is somewhat ambivalent. They do not yet fully 'understand', indeed perhaps they cannot (in the story-world) yet understand—prior to the cross. Yet they are in a uniquely privileged position. They have been given the 'mystery' of the kingdom. Unlike Matthew and Luke, who both talk of 'knowing mysteries' (plur.) here, Mark talks only of a single mystery. Perhaps the reference is primarily Christological: Jesus himself is the mystery, and the disciples are privileged by being called by Jesus to be 'with him' (cf. 3:14). Their understanding can only—but will—come later.

There is thus no need to drive a wedge between vv. 11–12 and the rest of Mark, even though Mark is maybe trying to say more than one thing here. The crowds' failure to understand—a mirror of the rejection experienced by later Christians—is the result of God's will. The disciples' privileged position is also the result of the same will; yet their failure to understand at this stage in the story is not minimized.

(4:14–20) Interpretation of the Parable of the Sower Mark now gives a detailed, allegorical interpretation of the parable of the sower. Jeremias (1963) has shown that the vocabulary here is almost exclusively language characteristic of the early church, not of Jesus. Hence the interpretation is unlikely to be dominical, even though, as argued above, it is likely that the parable did have an inalienable 'allegorical' slant originally, with the different soils all having significance. Some have tried to correlate the different descriptions with characters in the story (Tolbert 1989: e.g. the first group are the Jewish opponents; the rocky ground represents the disciples, etc.). This may, however, read too much into the details; in any case, the warnings implied in the descriptions of the different soils seem to be more directly related to Mark's Christian readers who could only with some difficulty identify with, say, the Jewish opponents in Mark's story. The longest description of the poor soil concerns the rocky ground and those who have 'no root' (vv. 16–17, corresponding to the longest description in Mark's version of the parable itself: vv. 5–6). Perhaps this is the danger Mark feels most acutely: the detailed explanation refers to 'trouble *or persecution*' threatening initial commitment. It is possible that one sees here a reflection of (part of) Mark's own situation of a community facing the threat of persecution and leading to some followers giving up their Christian commitment. Perhaps too the warning against 'the cares of the world and the delight in riches' reflects other problems within Mark's community (cf. 10:17–22). In this interpretation of the parable in Mark, relatively little space is given to the description of the good soil (v. 20): the aim of the

...tion is thus not so much to give assurance that all will in the end be well, but to warn people of the dangers of the present. As noted on the parable itself, the aim is more that of warning than encouragement.

(4:21–5) Collected Sayings Mark now collects together a series of what originally were almost certainly isolated sayings in the tradition. (They appear scattered in widely different contexts in Matthew and Luke.) vv. 21–2 continue the theme of secrecy and openness. The opening of v. 21 is in Greek literally 'Does the lamp come . . . ?' The unusual personification of the lamp, and the significant way in which, for Mark, Jesus has 'come' (cf. 1:38), suggests that Mark sees Jesus himself as the lamp. The aim of Jesus' coming is not in the end permanent secrecy or hiddenness. Rather, any secrecy will in the end result in openness. Exactly when this will happen is not specified precisely here; but the purpose of the sayings seems to stress the inevitable end of any secrecy surrounding Jesus and his person. vv. 24–5 strike a rather different note, with warnings as well as encouragement. Human response is also required in full measure. Perhaps what is in mind is the preaching of the gospel by later Christians. Those who respond positively will be rewarded abundantly; those who do not will forfeit even what they have.

The section as a whole thus combines assurance and exhortation with warning. As with the previous parable of the sower and its interpretation combined with vv. 10–13, there are both encouraging and warning elements in the Christian gospel. But if the warning side has been stressed so far, the encouragement is not forgotten, as the next two parables show.

(4:26–32) Two Seed Parables Mark gives two parables, very closely related to each other and probably (in his view) with very similar meanings. The first, the parable of the seed growing secretly (vv. 26–9), is peculiar to Mark; the second, the parable of the mustard seed (vv. 30–2) is shared with Matthew and Luke who probably also know a Q version of the parable (cf. Lk 13:18–19). Both parables are said to be parables illustrating the reality of the 'kingdom of God'. Both imply that the kingdom is present in minute, hidden form as a 'seed', but that it will be shown in its full glory in the future. The parable of the seed growing secretly (vv. 26–9) uses the image of the harvest, perhaps alluding to the final judgement (cf. Joel 3:13). The parable of the mustard seed (vv. 30–2) uses the image of the birds flocking to nest in the branches of the tree, perhaps alluding to the Gentiles coming into the kingdom (cf. Dan 4:12; Ezek 31:6). The stress in both parables is on the divine miracle and lack of human influence in the process of growth. There is no hint of any long period of time, nor of any idea of the kingdom 'growing in the hearts of men and women', an idea popular in nineteenth-century liberal theology. Rather, all the emphasis is on the divine initiative and the assurance of the end result.

This might be thought to contradict the emphasis in the earlier part of the chapter on human responsibility and involvement. In one sense, this is true. But perhaps Mark is emphasizing the other side of the coin here: the kingdom *will* come in its fullness, and of this the followers of Jesus can be assured. Moreover, the kingdom is something which is present already in hidden form (as a seed) now. The reference

may again be to the person of Jesus himself: Jesus in his ministry brings God's kingly rule into the present as a reality now. As noted before, eschatology for Mark is both futurist and realized. However, the idea of the presence of the kingdom in an institution such as the church, after Jesus and before the Eschaton, seems foreign to Mark.

(4:33–4) Jesus' Use of Parables The conclusion of the discourse takes up the division outlined in vv. 11–12. v. 33 is often taken as the tradition used by Mark, apparently implying that parables were used to be understood; this was then glossed by Mark in v. 34, suggesting that only the privileged in-group of disciples are allowed to receive the interpretation of the parables, so that everything remains enigmatic to outsiders. As we saw in vv. 11–12, there is a division between disciples and others, Mark in part reflecting on the mixed responses to the Christian message which have been experienced. And the disciples are in a privileged position. But the division is not clearly one of understanding: even though the disciples have had Jesus explain 'everything' to them, they still fail to understand at a deep level who he is and what he is about. The next story will illustrate this. In the narrative, the time for openness is not yet.

(4:35–5:43) Nature Miracles Mark now gives a series of three stories of Jesus' miracles, showing his power over the forces of nature as well as his ability to heal and to exorcize. Although modern interpreters might wish to distinguish between healing/exorcistic powers and claims to be able to change the course of nature, such a distinction would be foreign to a first-century reader or writer. Both alike show the divine power at work in Jesus. But equally, it is clear from these stories that miracles alone have little evidential value: they cannot create faith where none is present.

(4:35–41) The Stilling of the Storm The story is somewhat artificial: fishermen used to the lake and its ways are terrified by a sudden storm, a storm so severe that they panic, and yet through which Jesus sleeps. But Mark is not interested in such niceties; for him, the story shows Jesus' ability to deal with the primeval forces of chaos. The 'sea' in the OT sometimes stands for the primal chaos which God alone can order and calm (cf. Ps 65:7; 74:13), as well as being used often as a symbol for the sufferings endured by human beings (cf. Ps 107:23–32). Mark's verb in v. 39, referring to Jesus 'rebuking' the wind, is the same as that used in 1:25 where Jesus 'rebukes' a demon. Perhaps it is implied that the ability to control the storm shows a victory over the demonic powers of chaos and evil.

The disciples' reaction is not presented positively. Their question in v. 38 ('do you not care that we are perishing?') suggests a harsh accusation against Jesus. Jesus' reply is to still the storm and then address them with the rhetorical questions 'Why are you afraid? Have you still no faith?' By implication they do not. They are as yet blind. They ask 'Who then is this?' (v. 41) and cannot provide an answer. They have not yet reached any insight into who Jesus is, despite their privileged position. The negative portrait of the disciples in the story is thus developed a stage further; and even a stupendous miracle such as this has not created any 'faith'.

The note about the 'cushion' in v. 38 has sometimes been seen as a vivid life-like feature, perhaps indicating an eyewitness account. This seems difficult to prove one way or the other: but the detail could just as easily be invented precisely in order to create a vivid narrative and to make it seem life-like.

(5:1–20) The Gerasene Demoniac Mark follows with a story of a further exorcism by Jesus. The story is told with a wealth of circumstantial detail, designed above all to show Jesus' great power in overcoming such massive opposition in the forces of evil. However, a number of details and inconsistencies within the present narrative suggest that Mark may be combining more than one tradition here into a single story. (v. 6 is awkward after v. 2; v. 8 seems an awkward interruption; v. 15 seems odd after v. 14, since the latter presupposes a considerable time lapse.) But whatever the prehistory of the story in its present form, Mark's narrative serves to highlight the terrible initial state of the man, and hence to magnify the significance of the cure effected.

Some details of the passage remain obscure. v. 1 states that the action takes place as Jesus crosses the Sea of Galilee to the country of the 'Gerasenes' (so most MSS), although Gerasa is c.30 miles south-east of the Sea of Galilee: perhaps this simply indicates Mark's lack of detailed knowledge of Galilean geography. Probably Mark does intend that the incident take place in the partly Gentile territory of the Decapolis.

The battle about the names of the protagonists is similar to that seen before (cf. MK 1:22–7). The name given to Jesus by the demon ('Son of the Most High God') uses a description of God often used by, or in relation to, non-Jews (cf. Gen 14:18; Dan 3:26; 4:2). Jesus does not here explicitly silence the demon, perhaps because in the story there are no bystanders at this point. The significance of the name of the demon as 'Legion' is not quite clear: it is possible that this is an attempt to evade giving a name. However, for Mark, such niceties are probably lost: for him, the giving of the name may simply show that the demon cannot resist Jesus' demand for a name, and the name itself indicates the huge power of the demon, equivalent to a Roman legion in number, i.e. 6,000 men. The details of the pigs and their destruction grates on some modern sensibilities in relation to animal welfare, though in a Jewish context pigs were regarded as unclean animals. Their destruction would therefore be seen as appropriate. Trying to discover possible natural causes for the pigs' sudden flight is probably a fruitless exercise.

The story ends with Jesus' refusal to accept the man as an immediate follower (v. 18): Jesus' authority here is absolute. Jesus commands him to tell his friends what has happened (v. 19). It is not quite clear if this is intended as implying an element of secrecy (i.e. tell your friends and no one else). Certainly the sequel suggests otherwise: there is no adversative in v. 20, and it implies that the man obeys Jesus in proclaiming publicly what has happened. (Alternatively, one could interpret v. 20 as implying that the man disobeyed Jesus, as in 1:45.) Either way the net result is the same: Jesus' power as an exorcist is publicized freely and everyone is amazed. There is then no hint of any critique of Jesus' activity in this respect.

(5:21–43) The Haemorrhaging Woman and Jairus' Daughter The final unit in this section comprises two miracles: the healing of the woman with the haemorrhage and the raising of Jairus' daughter. The former is sandwiched in between the two parts of the latter story, a Markan technique already noted. Mark clearly wants the two stories to interpret each other. Both focus on the theme of faith as the important precondition for any miracle to occur (vv. 34, 36), as well as being linked to the number twelve (vv. 25, 42; though whether there is any significance in this is not clear).

The condition of the woman with the haemorrhage is described in terms very similar to Lev 15:25 LXX. The woman's condition rendered her unclean, and also anything or anyone she touched would be unclean. Her action in explicitly touching Jesus' clothes thus brings Jesus into the realm of the unclean. Quite as much as dealing wiht the disease itself, the miracle thus serves to break down the social and religious barriers created by the purity laws (cf. MK 1:40–5). In an aside, the disciples are shown to be somewhat lacking in insight (v. 31, cf. MK 4:38). By contrast, the woman comes forward and confesses publicly what she has done. Jesus' reply is to commend her 'faith', which is the necessary prerequisite for the miracle to happen. The miracle does not generate faith; rather, faith must be present for the miracle to occur.

A similar point is made in the story of Jairus' daughter: news of the death of the child (v. 35) leads Jesus to address Jairus and exhort him to 'believe', have faith (v. 36). Jesus tells the crowd that the girl is not dead but sleeping, a statement which produce mocking laughter (v. 40). They show no faith. Perhaps this can then explain the strange feature of the story which follows, i.e. the otherwise inexplicable secrecy command in v. 43: Jesus takes a small group of his disciples together with the girl's parents with him, and raises the child to life; but then he commands secrecy about what has happened! For many such a command is impossible historically (how could such an event be kept secret?), but also difficult to fit into any consistent Markan pattern: elsewhere in Mark commands for secrecy after miracles are regularly broken (1:45; 7:36). Should one assume the same here and see the motif as highlighting by implication Jesus' success (cf. 1:45: so Luz 1983)? But this is not what Mark says. Perhaps the point is that the crowds outside have shown no faith at all in their mocking laughter (v. 40). By implication they already have a very superficial explanation of what will inevitably be the public knowledge of the girl's health: she was simply asleep and not really dead at all. The true nature of the action of Jesus, in rescuing the girl from death itself, is only open to the eye of faith and publicizing it in a context of unbelief will not by itself create faith.

Jesus' words to the girl are given in v. 41. Mark uses the Aramaic words *talitha cum*, even though he is writing in Greek. Some non-biblical healing stories do use 'magical' formulae, often a jumble of unintelligible words. Here, however, the works are not unintelligible but simply in a foreign language and Mark does translate them. Cf. too 7:34.

(6:1–6a) Jesus Rejected in his Home Town The themes of faith, and the growing opposition faced by Jesus, are continued in the story of the rejection of Jesus in his home town. Jesus has come into conflict with the authorities (2:1–3:6) and with his own family (3:21–35). Now the opposition seems to spread to his own home town (not explicitly stated here to be Nazareth, though cf. 1:9). As in 1:22–3, the occasion is Jesus' teaching (v. 2), and again Mark seems more interested in the negative reaction this provokes than in the actual contents of the teaching. This reaction is articulated in the rhetorical questions about Jesus' origins and his family (v. 3). At one level, all that is said is that Jesus' origins imply that he is a very ordinary person. Whether anything more is implied is not clear. It was very unusual to refer to a Jewish man as the son of his mother, rather than his father. Various possible interpretations of this have been suggested: is this a hint of doubts about the legitimacy of Jesus' birth (Joseph was not really his father)? Is this a hint that Jesus has no human father because he is the Son of God? It is doubtful though if Mark sees any great significance in the words here: any hints of the type suggested are at most extremely allusive. Likewise the mention of Jesus' brothers and sisters (v. 3) is probably to be taken at face value and can only with difficulty be interpreted as referring to, say, half-brothers and half-sisters. The notion of the perpetual virginity of Mary comes from a much later period of Christian history, and Mark shows no awareness of it. Jesus' reply in v. 4 implicitly compares his own position with that of a prophet. The saying may be traditional: Mark nowhere else makes much of the idea of Jesus as a prophet. If anything, the saying is more at home on the lips of the historical Jesus.

The story concludes with the note about Jesus' inability to do any miracle because of the unbelief of the people. (The apparent reference to Jesus' impotence here is toned down by Matthew.) This is the negative side of the positive correlation between faith and miracles seen already in Mark: miracles can and do take place in a context of faith (cf. 2:4; 5:43, 36); conversely, where there is no faith, miracles cannot occur.

(6:6b–13) The Mission of the Twelve Mark records the tradition (probably also found in Q: cf. Lk 10:1–16) of Jesus giving instructions for a 'mission' by the disciples, commanding them to take only the barest minimum by way of clothing or supplies, and with instructions about what to do when they are not accepted. The widespread nature of the tradition suggests that it is old (i.e. pre-Markan), though whether it goes back to Jesus himself is not certain. It seems likely that some Christians did take these instructions to the letter (cf. G. Theissen's suggestions about the existence of 'wandering charismatics' in the early church: Theissen 1978). However, Mark does not make much of it. For him, the story further develops the mixed portrait of the disciples in his story. We have already seen the beginnings of the negative picture that will come more strongly from now on (cf. 1:36; 4:38). But this negative picture is always the counterfoil of a positive side which should not be forgotten (cf. 1:16–20; 3:13): here too the disciples are instructed by Jesus, and they obey his instructions fully and without demur.

Some details remain obscure. Mark allows the disciples to wear sandals (v. 9: Q does not: cf. Lk 10:4). Perhaps Mark is easing an almost impossibly ascetic earlier version to make it more practicable. The significance of shaking the dust off one's feet against unresponsive places (v. 11) may allude to the practice of Jews shaking the dust off their feet when they entered the land of Israel to avoid contaminating the holy land. Does this gesture then imply rejection from the (new) people of God by the disciples? This may have been the case in

the tradition. However, Mark seems to know virtually nothing of what may actually have happened on the mission except in the most general terms, and the gesture is not expanded here. So too it seems that Mark envisages the mission as taking place in Jesus' lifetime, and he gives no indication that these instructions are to apply to Christian missionaries in his own situation.

(6:14–29) Herod and the Death of John the Baptist Between the sending out of the twelve on mission and their return (v. 30), Mark inserts the note about Herod's views on Jesus, which leads into a retrospective account of the death of John the Baptist. In literary terms, the insertion serves to fill a gap in the story of the mission (about which Mark seems to have had very little information); but it also serves to intensify the general theme of the fate that awaits Jesus. John is the forerunner of Jesus, and here his violent death is recalled. The reader cannot fail to be reminded of the similar fate that awaits the one to whom John has pointed (cf. too 9:12–13).

The opinions about Jesus echoed in vv. 14–16 may reflect views held by some at the time, though it is unclear whether anyone would have seriously thought that Jesus could be an executed John brought back to life. The structure of the story in the overall narrative (as in 8:28 where very similar opinions are also recorded) suggests that Mark thinks that these opinions are at best inadequate (Jesus is 'one of the prophets'), at worst quite clearly wrong (Jesus is John returned).

The story of John's death itself has a number of bizarre features and is quite unlike Josephus' account of John's death, where John is executed because Herod fears an insurrection. Mark has probably confused personnel in identifying Philip as the (first) husband of Herodias: Philip was in fact Herodias' son-in-law. However, the relationships of the Herod family were so incestuous and tortuous that anyone could be forgiven for being somewhat confused! The picture in Mark's story of Herod as full of respect for John, but feeling morally bound to agree to honour a 'blank cheque' offered to his/Herodias' daughter, strains credulity. The account in Josephus seems far more plausible. For Mark though, the function of the story is to point to the similar fate awaiting Jesus. Thus the note about the burial of John at the end of the story (v. 29) is reminiscent of the note of the burial of Jesus (15:45–6). Even in the midst of the apparent success of the mission, the shadow of the cross falls.

(6:31–44) The Feeding of the 5,000 This feeding story has a doublet in the account of the feeding of the 4,000 in ch. 8. Several commentators have pointed to a possible parallel structure in the two sequences of events in 6:31–7:37 and 8:1–26: a feeding story (6:35–44; 8:1–10) is followed by a journey across the lake (6:45–52; 8:10), a dispute with Pharisees (7:1–23; 8:11–13), a discussion about bread (7:24–30; 8:14–21) and a healing involving some kind of 'magical' techniques (7:31–7; 8:22–6). However, too much should probably not be made of this. Mark is certainly aware of the duplication in the feeding narratives (cf. 8:17–21), but not of the other parallels which in any case are at times rather weak (there is no miracle in the crossing of 8:10, unlike 6:45–52; the dispute with the Pharisees in 8:11–13 does not concern the law as in 7:1–23). The sequence may be in part traditional (cf. Jn 6, where the feeding story is also followed by the walking on the water: unless one posits John's dependence on Mark, the parallel structure indicates a common tradition available to both evangelists). For the possible significance of the doublet in the feeding story, see MK 8:1–10.

What actually happened is probably impossible to say, though many have tried to do so. The famous 'lunch-box' theory—everyone had brought their own supplies and were encouraged to share what they had brought—can gain a little support from the fact that there is no report of an acclamation from the crowd that a great miracle has occurred. Nevertheless, it is quite clear that Mark himself regarded the event as a miracle. It is probably more fruitful to ask what the evangelist made of the story.

The account is full of many reminiscences, from both Jewish and Christian tradition. The story recalls the giving of manna in the desert, and perhaps the miraculous feeding by the prophet Elisha in 2 Kings 4:42–4. Likewise the note about 'sheep without a shepherd' (v. 34) reminds one of David as the shepherd and the people of Israel as the sheep; since too by implication, Jesus fills the role of the missing shepherd, one recalls various OT passages which speak of the future Davidic leader as a shepherd (Jer 23:1–6; Ezek 34:23).

But the strongest parallel for Mark is probably the Christian tradition of the eucharist: Jesus' actions in v. 41 of blessing, breaking, and giving bread are the same as at the Last Supper (14:22), and bread and fish very soon became eucharistic symbols. Jesus' feeding the crowds here is no doubt seen by Mark as a symbol of the feeding of the new people of God through the Christian eucharist in his own day in his community's worship. This is probably also the relevance of the note about the grass being 'green' (v. 39). This is sometimes taken as an indication of an eyewitness account (and is of course by no means trivial: grass in Palestine would not often be green, but very quickly became scorched and brown in the heat). It may though be a symbolic hint: grass is green in the spring, and for a Christian reader this evokes ideas of Jewish Passover, Christian Easter, and everything associated with them, including (for Mark's readers) the institution of the eucharist. Hence the greenness of the grass may be a further subtle allusion to the eucharistic symbolism and significance of the story.

The gathering of the fragments (in itself a miracle, since more is collected than distributed) no doubt had symbolic significance for John (cf. Jn 6:12), though Mark makes nothing of it. For the possible significance of the numbers involved, see on 8:1–10.

(6:45–52) The Walking on the Water This story was probably already connected with the feeding story in Mark's tradition (see MK 6:31–44). The historical basis for the account, as with the feeding miracle, is probably irrecoverable, though some have again sought to solve the problem of the miracle by a natural explanation (e.g. Jesus was on solid ground in very shallow water and the disciples thought he was actually walking on water). As before, this is certainly not the view of Mark, who doubtless regarded the story as a genuine miracle. God's power to subdue the sea and its forces (see MK 4:35–41) is well attested in the OT, and sometimes described in terms of walking on or through the sea (Job 9:8); so too the miracle

of passing through the Red Sea at the Exodus attests to YHWH's power (Ps 77:19; Isa 43:16). The latter motif may provide some link with the feeding story in so far as the latter is redolent of the manna incident: both stories may then show Jesus as a latter-day Moses, feeding people miraculously and passing on/over the sea. This is however more likely to be characteristic of the pre-Markan tradition than of Mark himself who does not generally make much of Jesus as a Moses figure (such a typology is more prominent in Matthew). For Mark, the story may simply illustrate Jesus' power over the forces of nature once more.

Jesus' words to the disciples in v. 51 (NRSV 'it is I') are literally 'I am' (Gk. *egō eimi*). It is just possible that this is an allusion to the divine name of YHWH himself (the Greek LXX renders the divine name 'YHWH' as *egō eimi*). However, the Greek is ambiguous (NRSV's translation is perfectly possible) and Mark does not clearly take it as a claim to divinity as such.

A typically Markan motif comes at the end in v. 52. After the general note of astonishment in v. 51 (the expected end of a miracle story), Mark records the inability of the disciples to understand 'about the loaves'. In general terms this portrays the now increasingly negative portrait of the disciples in the narrative: they fail to understand almost everything about Jesus from now on. With 'their hearts . . . hardened', they are almost in as bad a position as the Pharisees of 3:5 (but see further on 8:17–21). What it is about the loaves which they should have understood here is not spelt out explicitly. Clearly Mark sees the two stories as closely linked: both show Jesus' power and authority to act in sovereign freedom and in the power of God.

(6:53–6) General Healings The same power and authority are exhibited in the summary statement which now follows, Mark recording general healings by Jesus in the area. Again there is no hint of a critique by Mark of the miracles performed by Jesus.

(7:1–23) Dispute about Purity Mark now gives a long section of Jesus' teaching, delivered apparently in relation to a dispute raised by Pharisees and some scribes. The section is almost certainly composite: the repeated introductory phrases (vv. 9, 14, 18, 20) and changes of venue or audience (vv. 14, 17) suggest that different traditions are being brought together, a view supported by the fact that some of the traditions do not cohere very well with the wider context in which they have been placed here by Mark.

The initial issue raised is why Jesus' disciples eat with unwashed hands. The 'washing' refers here to ritual purity, not to simple hygiene. Mark then seeks to explain the practice of hand-washing for his (almost certainly Gentile) audience in vv. 3–4. Unfortunately, his explanation is, by universal consent, confused and erroneous: Mark says that hand-washing was incumbent upon 'all Jews', whereas we know that such ritual cleansing was only required of priests at this time. (Such hand-washing was practised by all Jews at a later period, after 100 CE.) Clearly Mark is unaware of some of the details of Jewish Torah observance. There is though the question of why this practice should be expected of Jesus' disciples. It is possible that the story is wholly artificial; alternatively, the implicit assumption made here—that Jesus' disciples would obey such rules—may indicate that Jesus and his disciples were closely connected with the Pharisaic movement and hence were expected, at least by other Pharisees, to adopt the Pharisaic way of life which may well have involved the voluntary taking on of such extra purity requirements. Cf. MK 2:16, 18.

Jesus' first reply in Mark comes in vv. 6–8. He cites Isa 29:13 to reject the Pharisees' complaint, claiming that their human tradition is jeopardizing the obeying of the Torah itself. The 'reply' is scarcely apposite. It is not said, for example, how the practice of hand-washing has actually led to any abandonment of the written law. Moreover, it is not clear how the Pharisees' behaviour justifies the charge of their being 'hypocrites' (v. 6: generally this refers to saying one thing and doing another, but it is not said that the Pharisees themselves have not washed their hands.) Further, the version of Isa 29:13 cited here is that of the LXX, which differs markedly from the Hebrew text, and which can only make the relevant point (about the human, as opposed to divine, origins of the commands) precisely at the points where the LXX differs from the Hebrew. The saying can thus scarcely go back to the historical Jesus, and the connection with the present context is very artificial. Nor are the sentiments expressed here (maintaining the written law and simply rejecting the later tradition) Mark's last word on the topic. Perhaps Mark simply uses this tradition to castigate Jesus' opponents.

The second reply is even harder to integrate into the context. Jesus refers to the apparent practice of people evading their responsibilities to parents as set out in the Decalogue by appealing to the inviolable nature of an oath which dedicates an offering to the service of the temple. Such practice is condemned here in forthright terms. But other Jews would be equally forthright and would have—and did—stress the primacy of filial obligations. Further, it is not at all clear how this relates to any antithesis between written law and human tradition, since the inviolability of oaths was also part of the written law (Num 30:2). Once again, a separate tradition seems to be incorporated here, somewhat clumsily. For Mark, the prime point again seems to be the polemic against the opponents of Jesus.

Jesus' positive reply to the initial charge, at least in Mark's story, comes in v. 15. However, the extra introduction in v. 14, and the summoning of the crowd, may indicate a further seam in the tradition. Moreover, the question of hand-washing seems now to have been left far behind and the issue is now one of the purity of food on its own. Jesus' saying in v. 15 has been extensively discussed, above all because of its possible implications for determining Jesus' attitude to the law. At first sight, the saying appears to deny that any food in and of itself can be unclean, and hence calls into question all the food laws of Leviticus. Those who see the saying as authentic, but find such a radical claim hard to credit to Jesus, have argued that perhaps the negative statement in the first half of the saying is not to be taken too literally but only comparatively: the antithesis (not A but B) means that one thing (B) is much more important than the other (A), not that the other (A) itself is to be rejected. This is possible, though it is not what Mark's Greek says, and Mark himself clearly understands the saying as implying that Jesus *has* abrogated the food laws of the OT (cf. v. 19). Others accept this meaning of the saying, but then deny that Jesus could ever have said it,

claiming in part that the subsequent controversies in the early church on the food laws are unintelligible if Jesus had ever said anything as clear as this (Räisänen 1982). It seems hard to deny that in some ways Jesus did play free with the law and claimed the right to do so. As such, it may explain part of the opposition and hostility he clearly aroused in the Jewish establishment and also amongst the Pharisees. It may be therefore that Mark's understanding of the saying is not so far removed from Jesus as some have claimed.

But whatever the meaning of the saying on the lips of Jesus, Mark is in no doubt: his explanatory gloss in v. 19 says explicitly that Jesus' saying, backed up by an explanation in v. 18 (which is in fact little more than a restatement of the saying) has 'made all foods clean'. Certainly by now Mark has gone far beyond the claims of vv. 6–8 or 9–13, that the issue is simply one of human tradition over against a valid written law. The written law itself is now questioned.

The positive side of what is required of men and women is spelt out in vv. 21–2. This list of inner thoughts and actions is typical of many Hellenistic ethical instructions. The ethic propounded here would thus be at home in the wider Hellenistic world. But *en route* to this, parts of the Jewish legal system, especially the purity laws and the social and religious barriers they create, are radically called into question by Mark's Jesus by the end of this section.

(7:24–30) The Syro-Phoenician Woman It is surely no coincidence that Mark follows the controversy with the Pharisees, where Jesus has implicitly claimed to pull down the barriers separating Jews and Gentiles, by showing Jesus explicitly crossing those barriers himself. Jesus goes to the region of Tyre, i.e. to an area which was at least partly non-Jewish. There he meets a Syro-Phoenician woman who is explicitly said to be a Gentile (lit. 'Greek', v. 26). The woman begs Jesus to heal her daughter. The ensuing dialogue creates many difficulties. Jesus' first statement (v. 27) seems rude and offensive, apparently refusing to help and referring somewhat abusively to the woman and (by implication) other non-Jews as 'dogs'. It seems highly likely that in fact Jesus himself did restrict his ministry almost exclusively to Jews and saw himself as primarily involved in addressing, and restoring, Israel. A saying such as v. 27 is not impossible in general terms on the lips of Jesus. (How offensive the reference to 'dogs' is is not certain: it is possible that the dogs concerned are pets and not thought of as distasteful.) Or perhaps the saying is intended to try to evoke a response from the woman.

No doubt for Mark, the woman simply exhibits the necessary response of faith and trust in Jesus. Her initial address of Jesus is in Greek *kyrie*—which can be translated as simply a polite form (NRSV, 'Sir!'), or as 'Lord!', expressing a much higher Christology. Mark does not elsewhere make much of the idea (common in Hellenistic Christianity) of Jesus as 'Lord', but it may be alluded to here. Thus the woman makes an exemplary response. Again it is noteworthy that a woman responds in a way that the male disciples have failed to do (see MK 1:31). Moreover, despite any apparent initial reluctance by Jesus to act, the woman's response does create the necessary preconditions for a miracle to occur: hence the girl is healed, and Mark's Jesus has put into practice what was implicit in his teaching about purity immediately prior to this story.

(7:31–7) The Deaf Man Cured There is uncertainty as to whether Mark thinks that the next story, the healing of the deaf mute, concerns a Gentile or not. The route taken by Jesus according to v. 31 (from Tyre through Sidon to the Sea of Galilee) is very circuitous: Sidon is well to the north of Tyre, which in turn is north of the Sea of Galilee. Perhaps Mark does not know very much about Galilean geography (cf. MK 5:1). It is also not clear if Mark realizes that the region of the Decapolis, where the story is sited, is well away from the Sea of Galilee and also predominantly Gentile. Mark's story seems to suggest a return *from* Gentile territory. Certainly little in the story itself suggests a Gentile milieu.

The description of the man's condition, having 'an impediment in his speech' (v. 35), uses a very rare Greek word *mogilalos*. This occurs only once in the LXX, in Isa 35:6. The allusion then seems to be clear: Jesus' action in healing the man is the fulfilment of Jewish eschatological hopes as articulated in such passages as Isa 35. The word Jesus speaks to the man here is given by Mark in Aramaic, as in 5:41. But as in the other context, there is no idea that this word can act as a quasimagical formula. There is an element of secrecy about the healing: Jesus takes the man aside privately (v. 33) and orders him to be quiet afterwards (v. 36). But this results in even more publicity (v. 37). Rather than trying to impose any real secrecy, the motif here probably simply serves as a means of highlighting the success and popularity enjoyed by Jesus as a result of the cure. (See MK 1:44–5.) We should probably distinguish between a 'miracle secret' and the messianic secret proper, and see here only an example of the former.

Jesus here uses a technique which could be conceived of as magical (using spittle). Mark shows no embarrassment about this, but it may be the reason why Matthew and Luke both omit the story.

(8:1–10) The Feeding of the 4,000 The story is clearly a duplicate of the earlier story of the feeding of the 5,000. A few details disappear here, but the overall structures of the two accounts are so similar that one is forced to conclude that both reflect the same original tradition. Why then does Mark include both accounts?

Much has been made of the possible symbolism in the numbers involved in the two stories, whereby the story of the 5,000 may reflect the gospel going to the Jews, that of the 4,000 reflecting the gospel going to the Gentiles. Thus, 5,000 and twelve baskets may allude to the five books of the Pentateuch and the twelve tribes of Israel; 4,000 may reflect the four corners of the earth, and the seven baskets the seventy nations of the world. Possibly too the different Greek words for the 'baskets' used to collect the fragments in the two stories may be relevant: it is sometimes said that the word used in the story of the 5,000 implies a more Jewish kind of basket, that in the 4,000 a more common Hellenistic basket. However, the most one can say is that this is possible but by no means certain. The symbolism makes at times for a bizarre set of parallelisms. (Surely 'twelve' would be better as parallel to the number of people, and 'five' to what they are fed with, if the above symbolism were in mind.) Moreover it is not at all clear that Mark thinks that Jesus is among Gentiles (see MK 7:31). There is nothing in the story itself to indicate that the crowd here is Gentile.

More directly, the story serves in Mark to underline the obtuseness of the disciples. The very fact that the two stories occur so close together in the gospel, and the accounts are so closely parallel, makes the disciples' initial reaction here all the more pointed. They have just witnessed Jesus feed 5,000 people miraculously; exactly the same situation recurs and yet the disciples again ask 'How can one feed these people with bread in the desert?' (v. 4). What they have just experienced should surely tell them how! The duplication in the story thus serves to highlight the growing incomprehension of the disciples. (See Fowler 1981.)

(8:11–13) Request for a Sign The story highlighting the obtuseness of the disciples is followed by a short incident showing the total blindness of the Pharisees. Immediately after Jesus has performed a clear sign of his credentials, the Pharisees come and ask for a sign from heaven! In the present Markan context, the very existence of the request shows the failure of the Pharisees to grasp anything at all about Jesus. Jesus' blanket refusal to give a sign inevitably follows.

Matthew and Luke (and hence probably Q) have a different version of the incident: here Jesus' refusal is qualified by the phrase 'except the sign of Jonah'. Mark may have omitted this (perhaps because it was unintelligible to his audience); but the Markan account is almost certainly pre-Markan: the words of Jesus' refusal are literally: 'if a sign shall be given', reflecting a Semitic oath formula 'May I be cursed if God gives a sign', a feature which Mark is very unlikely to have created himself. Hence Mark's version is not simply due to Mark's own redaction of the Q version. In any case it is likely that the Markan and Q versions mean similar things: both deny, more or less implicitly, that any sign will be given beyond Jesus' own present activity. Once again in Mark, the story shows that miracles cannot engender a positive response to Jesus if no such response is already present.

(8:14–21) Discussion about Bread The section brings to a climax the theme of the disciples' growing obtuseness. They are in a boat with Jesus and worried about lack of food. In general terms the story is clear: they obviously should have realized what Jesus can do by way of feeding large masses, and yet once again they show their lack of trust and faith (vv. 14–16). Some details are, however, not quite so clear. The significance of the 'one' loaf the disciples do have with them (v. 14) is disputed. Some have seen this as a eucharistic allusion to Jesus as the one bread, others more generally as a Christological allusion to the person of Jesus, others to the one bread sufficient for Jews and Gentiles. Mark, however, gives no direct hint. It may simply be another way of highlighting the disciples' obtuseness: they do have one loaf with them and so, since Jesus has fed 5,000 people with twelve loaves, feeding twelve people with one loaf should be relatively easy; the fact that they still worry brings out their total lack of faith.

The warning of Jesus against the 'leaven' of the Pharisees and of Herod (v. 15) seems at first sight out of place. It is not picked up in the ensuing dialogue which focuses only on the issue of lack of food. Again many possible interpretations have been suggested as to what the leaven symbolizes here. Luke takes it as hypocrisy (Lk 12:1), Matthew as teaching (Mt 16:14). Leaven in Jewish tradition symbolizes evil (1 Cor 5:6–8; Gal 5:9). The saying may not, however, be out of place in Mark.

The Pharisees and Herod have been shown to fail to recognize who Jesus is on the basis of what he has done (6:14–16; 8:11–12); moreover, supporters of Herod have joined with the Pharisees in plotting to kill Jesus (3:6). The 'leaven' of Herod and the Pharisees is thus probably the unbelief that refuses to recognize Jesus and hence rejects him.

Jesus' reply to the disciples in vv. 17–21 highlights all the details (right down to the numbers of baskets and the Greek words used in the two accounts) of the feeding stories. The disciples have failed to understand; as a result they show themselves to have hardened hearts, eyes which do not see, and ears which do not hear. By implication, they are similar to the outsiders of 4:12 to whom Isa 6:9–10 is applied. (The language is very similar here, though the allusion is in fact closer to Jer 5:21.) Yet the situation of the disciples is not quite the same as that of the crowds. Jesus gives only a series of rhetorical questions, rather than any blanket statements of their rejection; and the warning of v. 15 remains as a warning: they are not yet in the position of Herod and the Pharisees. This ambivalent position of the disciples comes to the fore in the next two stories.

(8:22–6) The Blind Man at Bethsaida Jesus' cure of the blind man here has some affinities with the story of 7:32–7 in that both involve use of a 'magical' technique (use of spittle). However, the closer parallel is probably with the story of the cure of Bartimaeus (10:46–52). The two stories of healing blindness form an *inclusio* round a long section of Jesus' teaching devoted to the meaning of discipleship (8:31–10:45). Probably then Mark intends both stories to illuminate and illustrate Christian discipleship so that the coming to sight of the two men symbolizes the new life and salvation that is available to those who follow Jesus. It is widely agreed that the story here is integrally related in Mark's narrative to the next story of Peter's confession: the man receiving his sight serves as an acted parable for the disciples' coming to insight about who Jesus is. One notable feature of the story is the fact that the man needs two stages in which to be healed. For the possible significance, see MK 8:27–30. The text at the end of the story is uncertain: many MSS add an explicit command to secrecy, though even the shorter text (implied in the NRSV's translation) suggests an element of secrecy. The explicit command in 8:30, and the close parallelism between the story of the blind man and Peter's confession, suggests that a secrecy charge *is* intended by Mark at v. 26; however, it almost certainly gains all its meaning from 8:27–30, the story that it introduces and that provides for Mark its true significance.

(8:27–30) Peter's Confession This section is often seen as a watershed in Mark's narrative. Whether it is a watershed in the ministry of Jesus himself is quite another matter. The work of the form critics suggests that we can place little if any reliance on the chronological sequence of the stories in the gospels: rather, the arrangement of the individual stories is due to later editors. Hence we cannot know where, if anywhere, this story might be placed within the life of Jesus himself. In fact the historicity of the whole story must be somewhat questionable. There may be an underlying tradition: e.g. the reference to Caesarea Philippi, a town well to the north of Galilee, is unlikely to have been invented *de novo*.

However, the present story, focusing as it does explicitly on Jesus' identity, with Jesus himself provoking the question of who he is, seems very strange in the life of Jesus: elsewhere Jesus points away from himself to God as the principal actor and focus of concern. The exclusive focus on the explicit Christological question looks more characteristic of Mark than of Jesus.

At the level of Mark, the proper interpretation of the story is much debated. Especially the significance of the secrecy charge in v. 30 is disputed. Does it indicate that, in Mark's eyes, Peter's confession is right, or wrong, or half right and half wrong? Some have argued that the secrecy charge, together with the following remonstration by Jesus against Peter, indicates that, for Mark, Peter is quite wrong: Peter confesses Jesus as the Messiah on the basis of the stupendous miracles that have happened so far in the story—hence for Peter Jesus *qua* Messiah is the wonder worker; Mark's Jesus then rejects such a view by putting forward his own view of himself as the suffering Son of Man (so Weeden 1971). Others, however, have pointed to the positive way Mark uses the term 'Messiah'/Christ elsewhere, including the title to the gospel (1:1): hence Peter's confession must be viewed by Mark positively.

There is strength in the latter argument. Mark nowhere else indicates any reserve about the term 'Messiah', and indeed uses it quite positively in 1:1. There is moreover little indication that Mark positively disapproves of Jesus' miracle-working activity. Indeed verses such as 8:17–21 suggest precisely the opposite. Further, the structure of the present story would seem to support the view that Peter's confession is certainly not regarded by Mark as wholly wrong: Peter's confession is set in clear contrast to the views of other people, which the disciples report in v. 28 (and which in turn echo the views expressed in 6:14–15); by implication these views are wrong and Peter's view is therefore not mistaken.

However, there may be a real sense in which Peter's view is not regarded by Mark as expressing the deepest truth about Jesus. At the level of nomenclature, it may be significant that Mark does not have Peter use the term 'Son of God' here, and for Mark it is that term that expresses the most fundamental truth about Jesus (cf. 1:1; 1:11; 9:7; 15:39). Further, whatever words, or title, Peter uses to describe Jesus, the sequel does make it clear that Peter has not understood the most important thing about Jesus—that he must suffer and die. There is much therefore to be said for the view that, in Mark's eyes, Peter gets things only half right here. Peter is thus perhaps in the intermediate state of the blind man of 8:22–6. He has come to some insight about Jesus, and it is a genuine and valuable insight. Unlike some with mistaken views, he recognizes Jesus as Messiah. But whatever Mark thinks of the title itself, words are not enough. Peter evidently does not yet appreciate the proper significance of who Jesus is and what his role in life (and death) is to be. Thus to reach the deepest insight about Jesus, Peter has to be led further: a need which is met by Jesus' further teaching in vv. 31–8.

This then may also be the significance of the secrecy charge in v. 30. For Mark secrecy is imposed not because others without Peter's faith are not to identify Jesus. Rather, in Mark's story, people cannot come to the full realization of who Jesus is until the story is complete and Jesus' full role as the one who dies on the cross has been finally disclosed (see MK 1:34). Quite irrespective of the correctness of any words or titles used, Peter has not yet come to the deepest insight and understanding, and indeed prior to the cross he cannot. Hence Jesus' identity cannot be divulged—yet. If it is, it will be misunderstood, and precisely such misunderstanding is immediately shown by Peter.

(8:31–3) The First Passion Prediction More details about Jesus' future role are now spelt out by Jesus in the prediction of the coming passion. This prediction is the first element in an extended section of the gospel (8:31–10:45) where Jesus predicts his passion and elaborates on the implications of that suffering not only for himself but also for any would-be followers. The passion itself is predicted three times in Mark's story in relatively quick succession (8:31; 9:31; 10:33–4), which gives added emphasis to the motif; and on each occasion, Jesus follows this up with further teaching on the relevance of this for discipleship. Correspondingly, in this part of the gospel, the stress on Jesus' miracles is reduced and more weight is now placed explicitly on the cross and its significance.

The passion predictions themselves probably owe a lot to later Christian creativity. It is unlikely that Jesus predicted his own trial and death with quite such accurate detail as is recorded here: if he did, the apparently total confusion of the disciples when the events occurred is harder to explain. Jesus may have foreseen in a more general way the opposition his ministry was provoking, and may have realized—and said—that this could lead to violence and even death. Nevertheless, the detail of the predictions, corresponding so precisely to the later passion narrative, is less likely to be genuine.

The passion predictions are all predicated of Jesus *qua* Son of Man. The stress on the necessity of the suffering of the Son of Man is thoroughly characteristic of Mark. The background of the use of 'Son of Man' in the gospels is much disputed, but if one accepts that it lies in Dan 7, with its twin foci of suffering and vindication, there is no need to see any artificiality in the use of the term here in Mark: Jesus quite appropriately talks of his coming destiny involving suffering *and* vindication (the predictions are all of suffering *and* resurrection) in terms of his role as Son of Man (see MK 2:10).

Peter's rebuke, and Jesus' stern counter in v. 33, are widely regarded as based on firm tradition. (It is unlikely that such a negative view of Peter would be invented by later Christians.) Nevertheless, the picture closely matches Mark's progressive story as well: Jesus' role involves suffering, and denial of that is effectively denial of God and of God's chosen way—hence it is demonic. Whoever opposes God is Satanic, whoever that person may be.

(8:34–9:1) The Cost of Discipleship Mark follows Peter's rebuke with teaching by Jesus about the implications of his suffering for any who would join his cause and 'follow' him. Mark is probably using a variety of sayings which come from various origins: certainly the parallels in Matthew and Luke appear in scattered contexts—almost certainly many of the sayings belonged to Q as well, and were preserved in different contexts. The present arrangement of the sayings is thus probably due to Mark himself. The kernel of the collection concerns the physical dangers which will face any would-be

follower of Jesus. Just as Jesus' destiny is to suffer and to die, so any disciple of Jesus must be prepared to do the same. The fact that Mark has this teaching addressed to the 'crowd' (v. 34) as well as the disciples may suggest that Mark deliberately intends this message to be taken to apply to a wider audience than just the twelve as contemporaries of Jesus. The same may be implied by the reference to the 'gospel' in v. 35 (in a phrase omitted by Matthew and Luke, and probably due to Mark). The 'gospel' here is parallel to Jesus himself, so that suffering for the sake of the gospel and for the sake of Jesus are virtually synonymous. Mark has in mind the later Christian community preaching the gospel, warning them that they too must be prepared to suffer.

The saying about cross-bearing (v. 34) has been much discussed. It is very hard to locate this saying with such vocabulary in the ministry of the pre-Easter Jesus. Crucifixion was a punishment administered by the Roman authorities for political rebels. It is very unlikely that Jesus could have foreseen his own *crucifixion*, even if he might have realized that his conflicts with the Jewish authorities would lead to death. It is even more improbable that Jesus foresaw crucifixion as being a real possibility for his followers. It is more likely that the detailed imagery is the language of the post-Easter community, looking back on the manner of Jesus' death and claiming that would-be disciples must be prepared to follow in his footsteps. How literally the saying is meant is also not clear. The very finality of death suggests that some metaphorical element is present: if every disciple literally took up his or her cross and was crucified, the movement would die out immediately! Probably what is intended is a vivid and stark metaphor of the call to give up all security and claims to look after one's own interests, even, if necessary, to the point of death itself.

What these sayings tell us about the situation of Mark's own community is not clear. It is often assumed that sayings such as this imply that it was suffering violence and persecution, with martyrdoms taking place (possibly in Rome under Nero). On the other hand, there is little here that seems to address such a situation with any note of comfort or help. These sayings give little if anything by way of explanation or interpretation for any suffering. Rather, there is only the somewhat bleak and stark call to be prepared to suffer. It may therefore make more sense if Mark's community were in a situation of relative peace and security, and Mark feels that it needs to be roused out of possible complacency and warned of the dangers that can befall any who claim to be followers of the crucified one.

The saying in v. 38 is couched in wholly negative terms as a warning. (The Q parallel has both a positive and a negative element: cf. Lk 12:8–9.) The Son of Man here is a figure exercising a key role in eschatological judgement. This saying and its Q parallel have provided the strongest evidence for the theory that Jesus looked forward to the coming of a Son of Man figure other than himself. However, Mark clearly regarded the two as identical and saw no difficulty in taking Jesus' reference to the Son of Man in the third person here as a self-reference. The eschatological role of the Son of Man may be the other pole in the twin theme of suffering and vindication as in Dan 7: Jesus *qua* Son of Man is a suffering figure in

v. 31; here Jesus *qua* Son of Man is the one who will exercise judgement (cf. Dan 7:14).

The final saying in this section, in 9:1, is also much debated. It seems to suggest that the final consummation of all things, and the arrival of the eschatological kingdom of God in power, will come within the lifetime of the bystanders of Jesus. If that is what is meant, the promise has clearly failed to materialize. Precisely for that reason, many have seen here a genuine saying of Jesus, on the grounds that such an unfulfilled prophecy would not be invented by later Christians. Attempts to explain the saying away (e.g. by referring it to the cross, or even the transfiguration story immediately following) seem unconvincing. So too C. H. Dodd's famous attempt to interpret the saying as one of realized eschatology (people will realize that the kingdom has *already* come, i.e. in the ministry of Jesus) has also failed to convince others. As far as detailed time-scales are concerned, the saying has indeed been an unfulfilled prophecy. Yet Mark himself (and probably Jesus too) is not concerned with detailed time-scales (cf. 13:32). Quite as much as expressing a time limit, the saying also expresses the ultimate certainty of the establishment of God's kingly rule. It is that belief and that faith which is perhaps in the end more important than any detailed chronologies.

(9:2–8) The Transfiguration The possible historical origins of this story are probably irretrievably lost. Whether anything like this might have happened we simply do not and cannot know. Attempts have often been made to see this as a misplaced, or displaced, resurrection appearance story; however, the differences between this and the gospel resurrection appearances are considerable. Mark's understanding of the story is not much easier to determine. In one way it is clear that the account gives a proleptic anticipation of Jesus' future glory, and thereby serves to give the reader assurance of the claim made in 9:1. So too the heavenly voice's declaration of Jesus as God's Son serves to reinforce the true nature of Jesus' identity, the issue explicitly raised in 8:27–30. In one way, the heavenly voice confirms the truth of Peter's confession, since Messiah and Son of God can be, and are, used in parallel in Mark (1:1; 14:62); and indeed the words of the heavenly voice simply repeat (though in a third-person statement rather than in a second-person address) the words of the voice from heaven at Jesus' baptism (1:11). But perhaps the use of 'Son of God' here also serves to deepen the meaning of Peter's confession of Jesus as (just?) Messiah. For Mark, Jesus' sonship is seen supremely in his obedience which leads to death (cf. 15:39); thus the declaration of Jesus as Son of God here serves to reinforce the passion prediction of 8:31 which has just been given.

The precise significance of Moses and Elijah in the story is not certain, and it is noteworthy that Elijah here precedes Moses. (Matthew and Luke both revert to the more 'natural', or certainly chronological, order of Moses followed by Elijah.) Perhaps both appear here as witnesses to Jesus: Elijah as the anticipated forerunner of the Messiah, Moses as the representative of Scripture.

There may also be an element of mild polemic in the story, seeking to counter any claims that Jesus is on a par with Moses and Elijah. This may be the thrust of the implied rebuke of Peter's suggestion that he build three 'booths' for Jesus, Moses, and Elijah. In one way this is another feature of the general incomprehension of the disciples, but it may be implied more specifically that what Peter has failed to understand is that Jesus is so much greater than Moses or Elijah (perhaps reflected too in Peter's address of Jesus as just 'Rabbi' in v. 5: Jesus for Mark is far more than just a Jewish teacher). Elijah was also famous for not having died; and some Jewish tradition also claimed the same for Moses: in such a tradition, both figures were thus translated to heaven without experiencing death. Jesus' path to heavenly glory is, however, via a different route: he must suffer and die first, and the supreme title or term expressing this is his identity as Son of God. By treading this road, he is so much greater. But equally, any follower of his must tread the same road: hence the command of the heavenly voice to 'listen to him' (v. 7), especially to the teaching which he has just given in 8:34–9:1 on the meaning of discipleship.

(9:9–13) Coming Down from the Mountain These enigmatic verses contain a number of exegetical problems. The section is probably composite: vv. 9–10 deal with the theme of secrecy and resurrection, vv. 11–13 with Elijah. v. 9 is the clearest statement in the gospel that the secrecy surrounding the person of Jesus has a temporal limit, and provides the strongest support for the interpretation of the messianic secret adopted here: until the cross, Jesus' identity remains a secret, but after that all will be revealed, for then its true nature will be clear. (Mark probably conceives of the cross and resurrection as a single point in time for these purposes.) The disciples' response in v. 10 seems to imply that they do not understand what resurrection in general means. This seems incredible in historical terms: resurrection was a well-known idea in Judaism of the period. v. 10 is thus either a highly artificial note by Mark to bolster his motif of the disciples' lack of understanding, or it refers specifically to the resurrection of the Son of Man: resurrection was generally thought to be a corporate affair (of all, or of all the righteous): an individual resurrection prior to the End is not so easy to parallel in Jewish thought of the time.

vv. 11–13 focus on the person of Elijah. What seems to be reflected is the expectation that Elijah would reappear at the End (cf. Mal 4:5–6). In Malachi, Elijah appears before the Day of the Lord itself; Christian tradition appears to have taken this schema over and modified it so that Elijah appears as the forerunner of the Messiah, Jesus, though such a twofold expectation cannot be found in non-Christian Judaism of this period. In this Christian modification, Elijah is identified as John the Baptist. The full schema is clearly present in Matthew's parallel to this passage; it is probably present in Mark here as well, though the language is more cryptic. John the Baptist, for example, is not mentioned explicitly, though the allusion seems clear. Whatever the precise background, Mark uses the verses to focus again on the coming passion of Jesus. Elijah's role as a forerunner is made more specific by the claim that 'Elijah' has suffered. In terms of the implied identification of Elijah with John, this suffering has led to violent death: hence a similar fate awaits Jesus. (That such a fate was predicted of the returning Elijah in Scripture (cf. v. 13b) is otherwise unattested. In mind may simply be the suffering the first Elijah endured: cf. 1 Kings 19:2–3.)

(9:14–29) The Epileptic Child This very long story in Mark may represent the coming together of two stories, or of two versions of the same story: cf. the double description of the child's illness (vv. 17–18, 22), and the apparent assembling of the crowd in v. 25, even though the crowd is already assembled in v. 14. The first half of the present story focuses on the failure of the disciples, the second on the faith of the boy's father. Yet fundamental to both parts of the story is the importance of faith—faith not shown by the disciples (v. 19) and the stuttering faith of the father elicited by Jesus (v. 24).

The story has some features of a 'miracle story' in form-critical terms, though the cry of astonishment does not come at the end but at the start of the story (v. 15, in response to the crowd seeing Jesus, perhaps implying that some vestige of his transfigured form still remains). The stress is not so much on the power of Jesus the miracle worker as on the response of the disciples in the story and hence of any would-be disciple in the Christian community. The disciples have been unable to perform the miracle, and their failure leads to Jesus' cry about them and the crowd as a 'faithless generation'. Miracles in Mark can only take place in a context of faith (cf. 2:4; 5:43; 6:5).

The second half of the story focuses on the man's father. The plea to Jesus evokes an almost contemptuous response by Jesus (v. 23) about his ability. It is, however, not quite clear who 'the one who believes' in v. 23 is meant to be. It appears to be Jesus, and yet Jesus is never portrayed elsewhere in Mark as having 'faith', and the sequel focuses on the father's faith. Perhaps it is impossible to be precise and the ambiguity is intentional. 'Faith' in relation to miracles in Mark is not necessarily the faith of the recipient, nor necessarily the faith of the would-be healer alone. Rather, it is a description of the total human context in which a potential miracle might take place. The man's famous reply (v. 24) shows that faith is both a human response and a gift from outside. Cf. 4:11. Human response is essential, but in the end, for Mark, such response is itself a matter of divine grace.

The final two verses are sometimes thought to be an appendix, not closely related to the rest of the story in that they focus on prayer, rather than faith. However, the motif of Jesus explaining privately to his disciples in a 'house' the deeper significance of what has just happened is typically Markan (cf. 4:10; 7:17; 10:10). Moreover, the difference between prayer and faith as the principal focus can be overstressed: faith for Mark is the absolute trust and dependence on God which can be and is reflected precisely in the activity of prayer.

Mark's vocabulary in vv. 26–7, where the boy appears to be dead and Jesus 'raised him' and he 'arose', is similar to other language in the NT used of resurrection. The words can be used quite naturally here, but Christian readers probably saw deeper significance in them: Jesus' action foreshadows the new resurrection life that is available through Jesus to believers in the new age.

(9:30–2) The Second Passion Prediction This is the least detailed of the three passion predictions in Mark, and has the greatest claims to historicity: certainly the very general language has been least explicitly influenced by the details of the passion narrative. However, the key element of the fact that it is as Son of Man that Jesus will suffer and be vindicated remains constant through the three predictions. In v. 32 Mark once again emphasizes the disciples' failure to understand what is said.

(9:33–50) Further Teaching As after the first passion prediction in 8:31, Mark follows the second prediction with more teaching about discipleship, much of it somewhat disparate and linked by catchword connections. The first unit, in vv. 33–7, concerns the importance of humility and the meaning of true greatness. As in ch. 8, the teaching is provoked by a brief note indicating the disciples' failure to grasp the true significance of what it means to be a follower of the crucified one (vv. 33–4, cf. 8:33). This motif may well reflect Mark's own concerns in developing the negative portrait of the disciples, though the reference to Capernaum in v. 33, which scarcely fits the wider context in Mark of Jesus passing through Galilee to Judea (9:30; 10:1), may imply the presence of a tradition here. The kernel of the section is the saying on the first and the last and the supreme importance of becoming a servant of all (v. 35). The saying is a popular one and recurs elsewhere in the tradition (Mk 10:43–4; Mt 23:11; Lk 22:26). For Mark, its significance is further developed in 10:41–5. The word for 'servant' here is perhaps better translated as 'slave'. The saying thus advocates a total reversal of the values of contemporary society: all that is regarded as valuable and honoured in human society is here called into question, and the Christian must adopt the role of the lowest and most despised member of the social community.

This is then illustrated by the saying about the child (vv. 36–7). The saying here is a doublet of the similar saying in 10:15. The interpretation is disputed. Matthew clearly takes the child as an example to be imitated, in particular as an example of humility (cf. Mt 18:3). This suffers from some problems: children are not necessarily always humble; further, children in the ancient world were not necessarily as highly valued as they have become in contemporary Western society. Rather, children were considered to be of very low status and of little value. Hence it is more likely that v. 36 sets up the child as an example of the *object* of the disciples' action: in their role as servants, they are to be slaves of *all*, even to the most lowly and least esteemed members of society, i.e. children. In so doing they will be serving Jesus, and by implication, God Himself (v. 37). The last saying is developed elsewhere in relation to Christian missionaries (cf. Lk 10:16; Mt 10:40–2, and perhaps Mt 25:31–46), but the idea that in helping the poor, one is helping God is well rooted in Jewish tradition (cf. Prov 19:17).

The small pericope about the strange exorcist follows (vv. 38–40). The story may well reflect problems experienced in the later Christian church (cf. Acts 19:13–17). The reaction of Jesus portrayed here is surprisingly open, and diametrically opposed to its Q parallel (cf. Lk 11:23) in its attitude to the neutral and those not explicitly committed to the Christian cause: here anyone who is not an active opponent is regarded as 'one of us'; in the Q version, neutrality is condemned fiercely. The story condemns any factionalism or triumphalism within the body of those who would be followers of Jesus. Just as faith is ultimately a gift and not an achievement (cf. 9:24), so what in the end matters is not church allegiance but allegiance to Jesus: the exorcist still carries out his exorcisms in the name of Jesus. Mark thus has a much more open-ended ecclesiology than, say, Matthew does. For Mark, what is crucial is the issue of Christology, the person of Jesus. Everything else is subordinate to that.

The story is followed by a series of sayings, at times only loosely connected by means of catchwords. The first saying (v. 41) may have continued after v. 37 originally, though there is also a catchword link with vv. 38–40 via the use of the word 'name'. But the saying here does represent a shift from v. 37 in that the recipient of the action is no longer the child but the Christian disciple or missionary (as in the parallels to v. 37). The word 'Christ' here seems to be used as virtually a proper name, with all idea of its titular sense (cf. 1:1) forgotten. In its present form, therefore, the saying must reflect the vocabulary and thought of early Christians and not Jesus. For Mark, the saying perhaps continues the thought of vv. 38–40: *any* positive service, however small and insignificant, will be rewarded. Plaudits cannot be reserved for an in-group of privileged 'church' members.

The reverse side of the idea of reward is that of punishment and this is developed in the series of sayings in vv. 42–8, linked by the common use of the verb 'cause to stumble' (Greek *skandalizo*). The first saying (v. 42) picks up from v. 41 the motif of treatment given to Christian disciples: the 'child' from before has become a 'little one who believes', clearly a Christian disciple. (Some, but not all, MSS have 'believe in me' here: this would then be one of the very rare occasions in the synoptics, and the only instance in Mark, where Jesus is the object of faith. More typically for Mark, Jesus points away from himself to God as the important object of faith.) Here the threat of judgement is probably directed at other Christian disciples (rather than, as some have suggested, persecutors of the Christian movement): the saying is a warning to followers of Jesus, not comfort for disciples threatened by opponents. In vv. 43–8 the attention shifts from the danger of causing others to stumble to the dangers of causing oneself to stumble (i.e. to threaten one's Christian commitment). In a series of vivid metaphors (which are only metaphors!), Mark's Jesus stresses the extreme nature of the self-sacrifice to which the would-be disciple is called. The thought is in general similar to 8:34–7: the true 'life' of the Christian is far greater than the old life, or even physical life itself, and can call for the ultimate in self-sacrifice at the physical level. The alternative is to be 'thrown into Gehenna' (vv. 43, 45, 47), a valley near Jerusalem used as a rubbish dump which became a symbol for the place of the future destruction of the wicked. The unquenchable fire of v. 48 (several MSS repeat v. 48 in vv. 44, 46) is probably that which destroys: there is no idea of eternal torment and punishment.

The last two verses of the complex (vv. 49–50) are obscure and the connection of thought (beyond the catchwords 'fire' and 'salt') not clear. The image of v. 49 ('salted with fire') is notoriously uncertain. It is possible that both fire and salt are seen as images of purification. Elsewhere in the NT, fire is seen as a process which can be destructive but also purifying (cf. 1 Pet 1:7). The same may be implied here: the physical dangers to which the Christian disciple is exposed can also act as a purifying agent. The appended sayings about salt in v. 50 defy clear exegesis. The general thought may be that Christian disciples must continually show their true nature as followers of Jesus, otherwise they will be rejected. The final exhortation to live at peace with each other recalls the original

occasion of the whole complex: disputes about relative superiority within the community are no part of the life of followers of Jesus who must live harmoniously ('at peace') with one another.

(10:1–12) Divorce The next section is somewhat loosely appended and might appear a little out of place in a wider context dealing with specifically Christian discipleship. Some have even suggested that 10:1–31 constitutes a small preformed household code on the themes of marriage, children, and possessions (cf. Col 3:18–4:1; Eph 5:21–6:9). However, this is not necessary: what is presented here is in some ways the ideal for the Christian disciple and the section is not out of place within the broader context of 8:34–10:45.

Jesus is asked about the legitimacy of divorce. The question is in many ways an artificial one coming from Pharisees, since Jewish law clearly assumed that divorce was legitimate, the only discussion being what were the proper grounds for divorce. (The divorce legislation in Deut 24:1–2 is very vague as to the grounds for divorce and deals more with the procedures of the divorce itself.) Yet if, as seems likely, Jesus did express himself very negatively about the whole principle of divorce (it is very deeply embedded in the tradition: see 1 Cor 7:10, as well as what is probably a Q tradition in Lk 16:18/Mt 5:32), some such question must have arisen in Jesus' own ministry. Jesus' reply goes behind the divorce legislation of Deut 24 to the principle of creation itself. He claims that divorce was only instituted as a concession to human failure and that the ideal is life-long, monogamous marriage. Although this could be interpreted as an attack on the law, it is not presented as such here. Nor is it necessarily an attack to demand greater strictness than the law technically presupposes. (Further, some of the Qumran texts adopt a position very similar to that of Jesus here, and no one could accuse the Qumran sectarians of playing loose with the law!) Nevertheless, an important part of the law is here relativized, and this shows the great authority implicitly claimed by Jesus. Yet it is important too to note what is proposed. Jesus' saying is not necessarily a legal ruling which brooks no exception (as it has frequently been taken). Rather, it sets up an ideal, and puts forward the divine purpose in marriage. It is an ideal for the Eschaton. (In Jewish thought the end-time was often conceived as representing a return to the primeval conditions of the creation period.) But in a fallen world, that ideal is frequently not met. To apply Jesus' sayings to this situation as a legal ruling forbidding divorce under all circumstances is probably the worst kind of legalism: in the teaching of Jesus, any ideals of the eschatological kingdom would always have to be tempered by the overriding concerns of compassion and love.

In an 'appendix', Mark's Jesus spells out to the disciples further implications of what he has said. In one way the teaching here is strange, since the issue no longer seems to be that of divorce as such, but of remarriage after divorce. Here any such remarriage is branded as adultery. (Further, the parallel formulation in v. 12, placing a woman's action in divorcing her husband alongside a man divorcing his wife, presupposes the conditions of Roman law: in Jewish law a woman had no such right to institute divorce proceedings.) We may have here a saying of the early church, seeking to interpret the Jesus tradition in relation to the concrete problems faced by Christians in the world. The NT generally does appear to ban remarriage after divorce (cf. Lk 16:18; Mt 5:32). Again, whether that should be taken as rigid and eternal legislation for a fallen world seems rather doubtful.

(10:13–16) The Children This small section is often taken as composite: vv. 14c + 15 seem to interrupt a story about the importance of *receiving* children with a saying requiring being *like* children. This pericope was also used later in the early church to justify the practice of infant baptism. Such an application in a later situation is quite natural, but is not hinted at explicitly by Mark, and would clearly be totally anachronistic at the level of Jesus. The saying in v. 15 forms a doublet with 9:37 and many have regarded the latter context as more appropriate. As noted there, the idea of a child as an example to imitate is not easy to interpret. Children in the ancient world were of the lowest status in society (see MK 9:36–7). Perhaps though this is precisely what Mark (unlike Matthew) has in mind. The Kingdom is for those who are like children in the ancient world, i.e. the poor, the hungry, the dispossessed, those without rights and without any esteem amongst their contemporaries. Followers of Jesus can only receive the kingdom, i.e. accept God's rule as king, if they too become like this: they too must recognize their radical dependence on God for all that they have and all that they are, and they must give up all claims to rights over others in the world, a theme which will be developed further in vv. 35–45. Taken in this way, the saying in v. 15 is not so out of place within vv. 13–16: only if disciples become like children in this sense can they be 'received' by Jesus, i.e. become true followers of the crucified one. As such, the pericope is also firmly in place within the broader context of the general teaching on discipleship in 8:34–10:45.

(10:17–31) Riches and Possessions The section is again composite. The story of the rich young man (vv. 17–22) has been expanded by further sayings about wealth and/or the difficulty of entering the kingdom (vv. 23–7), followed by promises about the rewards due to disciples (vv. 28–31). However, the sayings are so closely related in one way (though significantly different in another) that it is hard to envisage totally independent traditions being used here: more probably, Mark has expanded the earlier tradition in his own way to develop the themes of particular concern to him.

The kernel of the section is the story of the rich young man. The evident embarrassment caused to later Christians (e.g. Matthew!) by the story in which Jesus appears implicitly to reject the notion that he himself is 'good' suggests that we have here a genuine tradition. (Matthew, for example, rewrites the story to have the man ask Jesus 'what good thing must I do?') The man asks about how to 'inherit eternal life', probably meaning the same as to enter the kingdom. (The vocabulary of 'eternal life', or life of the age to come, is rare in the synoptics, though it is greatly developed in the fourth gospel.) Jesus' first reply cites the second half of the Decalogue (but replacing 'Do not covet' with 'Do not defraud'), focusing on those commandments which concern human relationships. The young man's reply indicates that he realizes that obeying the letter of the law is not enough, but his further question ('What more must I do?') perhaps suggests that he is still thinking in terms of a measurable human achievement. Jesus' reply indicates that

no such measuring is appropriate: the demand of discipleship is total and absolute.

In the case of the young man, the barrier to his total commitment is evidently his wealth. However, the further development in the teaching now extends the difficulty experienced by rich people in responding to Jesus' call to the difficulty experienced by all. Hence v. 24 says how hard it is for anyone to enter the kingdom. This is then illustrated by the hyperbolic (and perhaps partly humorous) image of the camel and the eye of the needle—though now reverting to the question of riches again. (The slight confusion—is it hard for the rich, or for all, to enter the kingdom?—is what has probably led to some scribes adding a phrase in v. 24 to make it apply only to those 'who trust in riches'.) Entry into new life is thus ultimately not a matter of any human achievement or merit at all. It is in one way impossible for anyone with their own resources to enter the kingdom. In the end, it is all a matter of divine grace (v. 27).

Yet the consequences of the commitment required of the disciple are not lost. Those who give up everything will be rewarded. And indeed Mark's Jesus here implies that there will be reward both in this life and in the age to come. The reference to the rewards in this life indicate that, even though Christians have given up family and possessions now, they will experience a new family and a new social community, i.e. in the church. Mark thus paints a rather different picture from the Q tradition where (at least some) Christians appear to give up all social ties and adopt a wandering life-style with no settled community existence (the so-called 'wandering charismatics': cf. the mission charge in Matthew and Luke). In Mark, Christians are assured of a place in a new social community. However, two features of this new existence are notable. The list in v. 30 of people/things which will be repaid to the disciple largely repeats the list in v. 29 of things surrendered; but (a) no 'father' reappears in v. 30, presumably because God is Father and cannot be duplicated; (b) v. 30 adds a reference to 'persecutions'. This may reflect the situation *of* Mark's community; alternatively, it may be a warning *to* them of things that may come. The final promise of 'eternal life' provides an *inclusio* with the start of this whole complex in v. 17 and the question of the young man about what he should do to obtain eternal life.

(10:32–4) The Third Passion Prediction This is the most detailed of all the predictions and seems to have been written in the light of the details of the passion narrative (a Jewish trial preceding a Roman trial, followed by a mockery involving spitting etc.). As before, the 'Son of Man' reference, and the inclusion of a prediction of 'resurrection', remain constant. v. 32 is a little obscure: how are the amazement and the fear related? And are there two groups of people intended here, or one? Jesus is 'on the way', 'going ahead' of his disciples. In one sense he is simply on a road, but in a deeper sense he is also on the 'way' that leads to Jerusalem which for Mark is the place of suffering and death. Jesus is thus on the way of the cross, and this perhaps is part of the reason why those who 'follow' in this way where Jesus 'goes ahead' are 'afraid'.

(10:35–45) True Service Once again the passion prediction is followed by a feature showing the failure of the disciples to understand the full implications of Jesus' teaching about his future suffering (cf. 8:32; 9:33). Here it is a more extended pericope, the story of the request of James and John for the chief seats in the coming kingdom. The two disciples ask for positions of glory. Jesus' reply is at first a question, asking if they can share his cup and baptism. The image is not explicit but probably refers to intense suffering and death. The 'cup' is used in the OT to refer to divine punishment (cf. Ps 75:8), though such ideas are probably too specific here, and the image may simply refer to great suffering (cf. 14:36). The verb 'baptize' can refer to being overwhelmed or flooded with catastrophes (cf. Ps 42:7; Isa 43:2 for a similar idea, if not the word). James and John's first reply is 'we can', perhaps an indication for Mark's readers of their (past?) martyrdoms. (James was killed very early: cf. Acts 12:2; John's fate is less certain and the traditions vary, some having him live to an old age, other having him martyred, though the latter are admittedly very late.) However, Jesus' reply to them puts their apparent acknowledgement into another light. They perhaps have accepted suffering as simply a temporary prelude to more assured glory. Jesus tells them that suffering will indeed await them, but future glory is not, and cannot, be assured: it is a matter of God's grace. There may indeed be an element of savage irony here too: James and John have asked to be at Jesus' 'right' and 'left'—for Mark's readers there is perhaps an echo of the two robbers, one on Jesus' right and one on his left, on their crosses. That in some sense *is* Jesus' glory. (Cf. the fourth gospel where this is more explicit.) Perhaps then they really 'do not know what [they] are asking' when they make their request!

As before, the motif of the disciples' failure to understand leads on to further teaching by Jesus. Here it is on the significance of service. True greatness lies not in having a position of authority over others, but in being the slave of all, a theme that has dominated all Jesus' teaching about discipleship in this section of the gospel. And as a final clinching argument, Jesus adduces himself as an example in his role as Son of Man: the Son of Man himself came not to be served but to serve. By implication, any follower of the Son of Man can do no less.

The final half-verse (10:45*b*) comprises the famous ransom saying and has given rise to intense debate. It is one of the very few verses in the synoptics where Jesus gives any kind of interpretation of his death. Its authenticity is much disputed, as is the precise meaning of virtually every word in the saying. The saying is almost certainly pre-Markan: it assumes that Jesus' death is unique, and yet Mark uses it in a context where Jesus sets himself up as an example to be imitated by others. The background is often taken to be Isa 53, with Jesus here setting himself up as the suffering servant of this Servant Song, offering his life as a sin offering for others. This is, however, unconvincing. The linguistic parallels between this verse and Isa 53 are virtually non-existent. Jesus is not here called 'servant'; nor is the language of 'ransom' the same semantically as that of 'sin offering'. The present verse does not even mention 'sin' as such. The word 'ransom' (Gk. *lutron*) is in fact used very widely, sometimes in relation to prices being paid, e.g. as the price paid to compensate for a crime, as the money equivalent to the sacrifice of the first-born child, as the money paid to buy back prisoners of war. Hence the idea in later Christian theology of Jesus' death as some kind of price that is paid (e.g. for sin). But the word is also used without any idea of a specific price paid: thus God's deliverance of his people in the Exodus is frequently referred to as his 'ransoming' or 'redeeming' the people of God, with no idea of any price being paid. This may be the underlying idea here: Jesus' death is presented as in some way the rescue, or redemption, of the new people of God. Why this needs a *death* is not spelt out. Strictly speaking, the preposition translated in the NRSV as 'for' (Greek *anti*) means 'instead of': hence ideas of substitutionary atonement which have been read into, or out of, this verse. But this is by no means necessary. The word may simply mean 'on behalf of', 'for the benefit of' (like the Greek preposition *huper*, which is the most commonly used NT word in this context). Jesus' saying here thus evokes the idea of a new people of God to be created and formed as a result of his life and death. Further, it is by virtue of his role as Son of Man, as the one who must suffer but who will then be vindicated, that this will be achieved. The saying coheres well with a number of other elements which are firmly embedded in the tradition (e.g. Jesus' choice of exactly twelve disciples, perhaps symbolizing the new Israel), and hence may well be genuine.

(10:46–5) Blind Bartimaeus Mark finishes this long section of teaching about discipleship as it started, with a story about the healing of a blind person. As with 8:22–6, this story here almost certainly represents an acted parable: the granting of physical sight to Bartimaeus symbolizes the true 'insight' which is necessary for any disciple of Jesus. Thus the consequence of the miracle is presented in language that is almost certainly deliberately evocative: the miracle is due to Bartimaeus' 'faith' which is said to have 'saved' him, i.e. not only healed him physically but also brought a much deeper and more profound 'salvation'; and Bartimaeus then 'follows' Jesus 'on the way': this is the language of discipleship, and Mark's wording is almost certainly meant to suggest that Bartimaeus becomes a full disciple, 'following' Jesus on the way which Jesus treads, i.e. the way of the cross. It may also be significant that, before he is healed, Bartimaeus calls out to Jesus as 'Son of David' (v. 47). This is a rare term in Mark (used elsewhere only in 12:35–7, and there somewhat negatively), and may be intended to be synonymous with Messiah. The latter is the term Peter uses in 8:29, and Mark may by his story indicate that this is partly correct, but does not express the fullest truth about Jesus. (See MK 8:29.) Similarly here, Bartimaeus when blind addresses Jesus as Son of David. As such he is partly correct, and certainly shows a sufficient degree of faith to enable Jesus' miracle to take place. But the fuller sight—and the deeper insight into who Jesus really is—follows as a divine gift. Only then does Bartimaeus become a full disciple, 'following' Jesus 'on the way'.

Ministry in Jerusalem

The Passion narrative in Mark is usually adjudged to start at ch. 14, but there is a real sense in which it can be said to start here at the start of ch. 11. Jesus now arrives in the city of Jerusalem, the goal of his journey 'on the way', and for Mark, Jerusalem is supremely the place of opposition and hostility, culminating in Jesus' death. The cross thus now dominates the story. In Mark's account, Jesus' time in Jerusalem occupies apparently one hectic week only (giving rise to the Christian liturgical celebration of Holy Week). In fact it seems very likely that Mark has telescoped things: Jesus seems to be well known in the city (cf. 14:3) and says that he has been teaching continuously in the Temple ('day after day' 14:49). John's gospel implies a much longer stay in the city and this seems historically much more plausible. The same may also be implied in some details of the story that now follows.

(11:1–11) The Triumphal Entry Jesus enters the city in a deliberately unusual way—on a donkey. The later evangelists clearly regard the event as an explicit messianic claim by Jesus, fulfilling the prophecy of Zech 9:9. Mark's understanding of the event is not quite so certain. Any reference to Zech 9 is at best implicit, as the verse is not cited here. Mark probably regarded the crowds' acclamation of Jesus as implying an acclamation of him as Messiah, but again it is not quite explicit: they welcome the 'one who comes in the name of the Lord', and also the coming kingdom of David, which is almost, but not quite, the same as the coming king. (Matthew and Luke make things more explicit here.) Mark probably does understand Jesus' action as implying a royal status, but as with the messianic secret generally, the true nature of Jesus' kingship has yet to be revealed: it will become far more explicit as the cross approaches (see esp. ch. 15).

The earlier details of the story are also ambiguous. The incident about finding the ass may imply a miracle, though this is again rather cryptic here. The words of the disciples (NRSV 'the Lord needs it') are also ambiguous. The Greek word for NRSV's 'Lord' is *kyrios*, which can be translated as simply 'master' or 'owner'. Nowhere else does Mark clearly refer to Jesus as 'Lord' in a Christologically significant way (though see MK 7:28), so the word here may simply mean 'our master', or 'its [the ass's] owner'.

As far as historicity is concerned, the story is clearly deeply embedded in the tradition, being present in all four gospels. Some kind of (veiled) messianic claim seems to be implied: coming into the city on an ass (rather than walking) was highly unusual, and riding on an ass was a royal prerogative. On the other hand, it is odd that the incident is never referred to in the trial narratives, where the issue is explicitly that of the possible messianic/royal status of Jesus. Further, the incident seems to have provoked no reaction at all from the Roman authorities, despite the charged atmosphere of the Passover season. It has, however, often been noted that the actions of the crowds (waving palm branches, and using words from one of the so-called Hallel psalms, Ps 118) is reminiscent of actions prescribed for the Feast of either Tabernacles (in the autumn) or Dedication (in the winter). It may therefore be that, if the incident is historical, it took place rather earlier than Mark's chronology implies. Hence Jesus may have arrived in Jerusalem much earlier than the one week prior to his death as suggested by Mark (cf. also above) and by later Christian tradition.

The crowds cry 'Hosanna', literally 'Save now!' Such a meaning appears to have been lost to Mark (and to later Christian liturgy) where the phrase 'Hosanna in the Highest', virtually meaningless if translated literally, becomes simply a general cry of jubilation.

(11:12–26) The Temple and the Fig-Tree The two incidents which now follow, the cleansing of the temple and the cursing of the fig-tree, constitute the most famous example of Mark's 'sandwiching' technique: the story of the incident in the temple is sandwiched between the two halves of the story of the fig-tree. By this device, Mark clearly wants the one story to interpret the other. Hence the fig tree incident provides the hermeneutical key for the temple account, at least as far as Mark is concerned. Thus for Mark, Jesus' action in the temple is probably not a cleansing (as it is traditionally described), but a 'cursing', a final and definitive act of judgement against the temple and, perhaps, Israel.

The fig-tree incident has always caused problems in relation to questions of historicity. Jesus' action here seems highly arbitrary, and a pointless act of gratuitous destruction. It is even compounded by the fact that the tree has no figs and yet it is not even the season for figs (v. 13)! Given all these problems, it is very hard to trace any such incident back to Jesus' own ministry. Probably we have here a symbolic narrative, acting as some kind of acted parable, the historical roots of which are lost completely. What lies behind it may be passages in the OT which speak of God looking for figs from his fig-tree, a metaphor used to refer to Israel and her proper response to God (cf. Jer 8:13); also the image of the fig-tree in fruit is used to represent Israel in the messianic age. The fruitless tree thus represents Israel who should have welcomed her Messiah, Jesus; yet when Jesus comes to the heart of Israel, Jerusalem and the temple, he is rejected, and the tree has no fruit: the result is inevitably judgement.

The temple incident is thus, for Mark, to be taken in the same way as a symbolic judgement on the temple and on Israel. The national dimension is then clearly highlighted in the version of the words placed on Jesus' lips: quoting Isa 56:7 he says that the temple should have been a house of prayer *for all the nations*. (Matthew and Luke both omit the last phrase.) Set in these terms, the action of Jesus places him on a collision course with Israel herself, and so it is not surprising that the outcome is the renewal of the plot to kill Jesus by the chief priests and scribes (v. 18, cf. 3:6).

Exactly what lay behind this for Jesus is less certain. Some have argued that he had in mind only the renewal of the temple in the new age: his action is thus simply a prophetic sign claiming that the new age had all but arrived (Sanders 1985). This, however, does not really explain why such an action would have been offensive to the authorities (if indeed it was) and why then it led to the plot to have Jesus killed. Others have sought to argue that Jesus was attacking the exploitation and oppression of the poor which the temple system engendered. The issue is debated, but there does seem to be some evidence to suggest that the temple authorities, and the whole system, did lead in many cases to the poor being exploited, poor priests being robbed by richer ones, etc. Hence Jesus' protest may have been against the priestly aristocracy, rather than against the whole Jewish nation. In that case, the move by the authorities against Jesus might become rather more plausible: Jesus and his teaching, especially if it was engendering popular support among the masses, may have been seen as a threat by the upper social classes to the status quo which enabled them to enjoy their position.

The fig tree 'incident' provides the occasion for further teaching on the importance, and power, of faith and prayer. The saying about moving mountains (v. 23) is proverbial and appears elsewhere in the tradition, as does the saying about the unlimited power of prayer (v. 24, cf. Lk 11:9–10; Jn 14:13). Yet such prayer can only be effective in a context of faith, which perhaps rules out such petitionary prayer being a licence for anything. The saying in v. 25 on forgiveness is very close to Mt 6:14 (as well as the petition for forgiveness in the Lord's Prayer), and this may have led some scribes to add v. 26 in some MSS, which is virtually identical to Mt 6:15.

(11:27–33) Jesus' Authority Mark follows the incident in the temple with a series of controversy stories, similar to 2:1–3:6, showing Jesus debating with the various groups of Judaism, though unlike the earlier series, the issue now is mostly Jesus' teaching rather than his actions. The first story brings all the Jewish leaders on to the stage, asking about the source of his authority in doing 'these things' (v. 28; in Mark's context this probably refers to the temple incident, though it may have had a much wider reference earlier in the tradition, referring to Jesus' teaching and other activity in general). Jesus replies with a counter-question (a feature typical of many debates among Jewish teachers), throwing the issue back and asking his questioners what they thought about John the Baptist. This is somewhat surprising: in Mark's narrative John scarcely figures as a person in his own right with his own 'ministry' amongst the Jews of the time: rather, he simply comes on to the stage to point forward to Jesus (see MK 1:3–8). Similarly his fate prefigures Jesus' coming fate (see MK 9:11–13). Perhaps we have here a reflection of Jesus' own strong belief that his work was very closely tied to that of John (as probably his decision to be baptized by John also indicates). The Jews' musings indicate John's great popularity among the masses (cf. Mk 1:5). Jesus' final statement is thoroughly in line with the whole of Mark's presentation so far. Just as there are no authenticating signs (cf. 8:11–12), so too there are no verifiable claims or assertions to back Jesus up. Within a context of faith, Jesus' claims can be accepted; without such a context, such claims would be fruitless—hence Jesus' refusal to speak.

(12:1–12) The Wicked Husbandmen The sense of hostile debate continues, though here Jesus takes the initiative by telling a parable, the parable of the wicked husbandmen. Clearly it illustrates the rejection by Israel of God and his messengers down the ages. As it now stands in Mark, the parable is a clear allegory. The language of the opening description of the vineyard clearly echoes the language of Isa 5:1–2 which itself is an allegory of Israel and her dealings with YHWH. The first messengers represent the prophets sent by God, all of whom suffer rejection and violence. Finally the last messenger is the Son, clearly for Mark Jesus as the Son of God, and the killing of the Son prefigures Jesus' own death. The parable thus expresses divine judgement against Israel for her rejection of God's Son. The story seems so heavily allegorized—and Christianized—that many have regarded it as a creation of the early church *in toto*. However, the story does fit well into the social situation of Galilee at the time of Jesus, when many

tenant farmers suffered at the hands of absentee landlords who demanded crippling returns from the land by way of rent. The resentment and anger of the tenants in the story reflects this situation well. It is thus possible that the parable goes back to Jesus. Whether the implied identification of Jesus as the 'son' is also genuine is less easy to guage. The idea of God as Father is deeply embedded in the Jesus tradition; but how Christologically significant this is at the level of Jesus is harder to assess: so much of the Jesus tradition assumes that others also share, or can share, Jesus' relation to God as son to Father (cf. the Lord's Prayer, Lk 11:2). For Mark, however, Jesus *qua* Son is unique, and Jesus' sonship is seen most clearly in his suffering and death (cf. 15:39).

An appended saying in vv. 10–11 cites Ps 117:22–3 LXX. The text is cited elsewhere in the NT (cf. Acts 4:11; 1 Pet 2:7), and the image of the stone applied to Jesus (using Isa 8:14; 28:16) is also attested (Rom 9:32; 1 Pet 2:6–8). The presence of the saying here is almost certainly due to the early church, if not Mark himself, adding a note predicting the resurrection as well as Jesus' death: the rejected stone becomes the chief cornerstone (it is not clear if this is the main stone in the foundations or the stone at the apex of the arch).

The reaction of the audience is intelligible, but also noteworthy here: whatever 4:11–12 implies, it cannot mean that parables for outsiders are totally unintelligible gibberish! The audience here 'understand' at one level all too well what, or perhaps better who, the parable is getting at. 4:11–12 must then mean that such people do not in a deeper sense 'see' or 'hear', i.e. they do not respond in faith to the challenge posed by Jesus. Instead they persist in their hardness of heart by further resolving to try and arrest him.

(12:13–17) A Question about Tax The story of mounting hostility continues with a series of incidents where Jesus deals with questions on specific topics posed by various different groups. The first concerns the payment of tax to the Roman authorities and is posed by an alliance of 'Pharisees and Herodians', a grouping recalling the earlier death plot in 3:6 and perhaps thereby indicating for Mark the (literally) mortal nature of the controversy and conflict that is taking place (cf. too 11:18). The question of the legitimacy of paying taxes to the Roman authorities was a very pressing one. The tax concerned was a poll tax imposed on all those in Judea, Samaria, and Idumea in 6 CE when these areas became a Roman province ruled by a procurator. It was deeply resented by the Jews, symbolizing as it did foreign interference in Jewish affairs. It led to active revolt in 6 CE under Judas the Galilean (cf. Acts 5:37), an event which, according to Josephus, led to the rise of the Zealot party in Judaism which was responsible for the Jewish revolt in 66–70 CE. (In fact it is unlikely that such a party existed in any organized form prior to the Jewish revolt; however, it is likely that the simmering resentment which led ultimately to the revolt remained throughout this period.)

The question is, according to Mark, clearly intended to trap Jesus. If he opposes paying the tax, the Roman authorities will arrest him; if he accepts it, he will lose popular support. The precise meaning of Jesus' answer has been much debated. As it stands, it is ambiguous. It enjoins paying Caesar what is Caesar's, and God what is God's, but does not clarify what is Caesar's and what is God's. Certainly it does not specify whose the Roman poll tax is! The saying has sometimes been interpreted as implying a doctrine of two kingdoms—a secular and a religious realm, each with its own sphere of influence. This, however, seems unlikely, especially in a first-century Jewish context. More plausible is the interpretation that takes the second half of the saying as interpreting and radically qualifying the first half: Caesar is to be paid what is his, but this is only under the more universal presupposition and rubric that God as the all-mighty and all-powerful is owed supreme allegiance. If the claims of Caesar and God clash, then the claims of God must always take precedence. The saying thus does not give *carte blanche* to any claims of the state; but nor does it deny all claims of the state. Rather, it challenges the listener to work out how competing claims of state and God have to be resolved in practice under the general rubric implicit in a monotheistic faith that God in the end must be supreme.

(12:18–27) Resurrection The second question comes from Sadducees and concerns the issue of resurrection. The precise delineation of a 'party' of Sadducees in the first century is not entirely clear. They seem to have been primarily members of the aristocratic, priestly families, and generally conservative in their views. Thus they adhered to the written law only, refusing to countenance innovation in later traditions (as espoused by the Pharisees); in particular, according to Josephus, they did not believe in a resurrection, perhaps because it was not mentioned in the law itself. (Belief in a resurrection developed relatively late in Jewish history, appearing in the latest parts of the OT: cf. Dan 12:2.) Jesus' reply in Mark clearly sides with the Pharisaic viewpoint. (Cf. MK 2:16, 18; 7:3–4.)

How far the story is historical is not clear. This is the only occasion in the synoptic tradition where Jesus debates with Sadducees. It would no doubt have been useful for later Christian claims about the resurrection of Jesus to be able to appeal to Jesus' own support for at least the principle of resurrection in general. The story in its present form shows some signs of internal dislocation: Jesus' first reply (v. 25) seems to focus on the manner of resurrection life, whereas the second reply (vv. 26–7, slightly awkwardly appended with an extra introduction in v. 26) focuses on the fact of the resurrection. At the very least, an earlier tradition has probably been expanded in the Christian tradition history. Since the real question is the fact of the resurrection, it may be that the reply about the manner of resurrection life in v. 25 is a secondary expansion.

The question posed by the Sadducees is in some ways an absurd one. The issue is the institution of levirate marriage (cf. Deut 25:5–10) which was designed to ensure that a man's name would be preserved and his property inherited. It is uncertain whether such a practice was still current at this period. Jesus' first reply simply states that resurrection life is qualitatively different from present life, 'like angels in heaven'. (For such a difference between present life and resurrection life, cf. 1 Cor 15:35–50; also 1 Enoch 104:4; 2 Apoc. Bar. 51:10.) The answer seems to be more at home in debates (possibly among Pharisees and/or Christians) about the precise nature of resurrection life, and does not seem to recog-

nize the (deliberately) absurd nature of the situation posed by the question.

Jesus' second reply tackles more directly the real question of the Sadducees about the very possibility of resurrection itself. The argument appeals to the words of the OT (Ex 3:6) and claims that since God says he is the God of the patriarchs, and that he is the God of the living not the dead, the patriarchs must still be alive. The claim is somewhat artificial to modern ears, but would have been far less so in a first-century context. So too the argument itself is unrelated to the specific issue of resurrection as such (it could equally well justify a belief in the immortality of the soul: though for many Jews, full existence was assumed to require a body as well as any immaterial 'soul'). Nevertheless the force of the argument is not lost completely and is not unrelated to the previous pericope, focusing as it does on God alone: if God is truly God, then as the God of the living he will not allow his care and concern for human beings to be destroyed by death.

(12:28–34) The Greatest Commandments The third question posed to Jesus is unlike the previous two in that the questioner appears not to be hostile. The person is a 'scribe', and unlike the scribes elsewhere in Mark, he is presented as friendly. This unusual picture indicates that we have a pre-Markan tradition here, a fact also suggested by the existence of what is probably an independent version of this tradition in Lk 10:25–8. (Matthew may know both versions; there are a number of [relatively small] agreements between Matthew and Luke, hence the Lukan version may have belonged to Q.) Notably, in the other two gospels, the scribe is more hostile ('testing' Jesus: cf. Mt 22:35; Lk 10:25).

The question concerns the 'greatest' commandment in the law. Such a question was not foreign to Judaism of the period and several sought to give one command which formed the basis for the whole law and from which the rest of the law could be derived. (Cf. Hillel in b. Šabb. 31a focusing on the Golden Rule of not doing to others what you would not want done to you, or T. Iss. 5:2; T. Dan. 5:3, as here, focusing on the love commands.)

In the synoptic gospels, Jesus' reply articulates the double love command—to love God and to love one's neighbour. These are not peculiar to Jesus: both are taken from the OT law itself (Deut 6:5; Lev 19:18). However, each evangelist deals with the tradition in his own way. In Mark (unlike Matthew and Luke) the love commands are preceded by the words of the Shema (Deut 6:4), the great monotheistic confession of God's uniqueness; also Mark follows Jesus' words by a response from the scribe which echoes, but also interprets, them by focusing on specific aspects of what Jesus has said. It looks then as if Mark's version intends the scribe's response to provide the hermeneutical key for the love commands. Here the words of the Shema are repeated (v. 32): clearly these words are not just seen as an introduction to the command to love God; rather, they evidently articulate for Mark a profound truth about the uniqueness of God, and this may reflect the way in which the tradition was being used in a more Hellenistic environment where polytheism was more of a live issue than in Jewish Israel. The scribe also takes up the love commands themselves, summarizing Jesus' words, but then adding that 'this is much more important than all whole burnt-offerings and sacrifices' (v. 33). The love commands are thus taken as ethical commands which far outweigh any cultic rites. Such an attitude is quite characteristic of Hellenistic Judaism of the period.

(Mark's version is thus rather different from Matthew's, where the love command is taken as the basis from which the whole of the rest of the law can be derived, cf. Mt 22:40; it also differs from Luke's version, where all attention is on the command to love one's neighbour which is interpreted by the following parable of the Good Samaritan as referring to practical action to help all people, cf. Lk 10:29–37.)

Such an attitude to the cult is of course not foreign to the OT (cf. Hos 6:6) and is at home in Judaism; yet the way in which this story in Mark follows closely on the story of the incident in the temple (11:15–19) suggests that the negative attitude to the cult expressed here is part of a broader polemic and negative attitude to the temple.

The authenticity of the tradition is debated. Some have argued that the Jewish parallels to Jesus' sayings here suggest that the tradition originated in Hellenistic Jewish Christian circles. However, the fact that Jesus' teaching here is not unprecedented within Judaism by no means implies that it is thereby not genuine. Certainly the general attitude of enjoining exclusive focus on God alone, coupled with care and concern for one's fellow human beings is thoroughly consistent with the rest of the Jesus tradition. Nevertheless, the radically different ways in which the double love command is interpreted in the three synoptic gospels should warn us against deducing too much too quickly about what this might imply about Jesus' attitude to the rest of the Jewish law.

(12:35–7) The Messiah and David In the fourth of the mini-controversy scenes, Jesus himself takes the initiative and poses the question about whether the Messiah can be, or must be, a 'son of David'. The dialogue appears somewhat cryptic: on the surface it is a theoretical discussion about 'the Messiah' without ever identifying who the Messiah might be—though no doubt Mark sees it as referring to Jesus! Such theoretical questioning about Jesus' own person seems alien to his ministry and more in place at the level of Mark for whom the issue of Jesus' identity is crucial (cf. 8:29). Also the messianic use of Ps 110 was widespread in early Christianity, but the existence of such use of Ps 110 in pre-Christian Judaism is difficult to establish. Thus the argument almost certainly reflects a post-Easter composition.

Precisely what is implied here is not clear. Jesus raises the question whether the Messiah can be the son of David, and responds by citing Ps 110:1 where David (the assumed author) seems to refer to someone else as his 'lord'. This someone else is taken as 'the Messiah', and the (rhetorical?) question is raised: if he is David's 'lord', how can he be David's son? It seems that 'son' and 'lord' are taken as incompatible. This might then reflect Christian attempts to defend the messiahship of Jesus in the face of objections that Jesus was not of Davidic descent. On the other hand, the notion that Jesus was a 'son of David' is attested elsewhere (albeit not strongly, cf. Mt 1; Lk 3:23–8; Rom 1:3–4) and is nowhere a matter of dispute. So too Mark records Jesus being addressed as 'Son of David' without any hint of critique (10:47). It may therefore be that physical descent as such is not the issue: what is at stake is not

Jesus' genealogical credentials, but his authority: Jesus *qua* Messiah is not subservient to David, but is David's lord. If so, the scene fits well into the present Markan story-line where the context is one of Jesus' authority being constantly challenged in a situation of mounting hostility and rejection.

(12:38–44) Warnings against Scribes Mark concludes this series of controversies with a brief tirade by Jesus against the scribes (vv. 38–40). Mark either does not know, or chooses to ignore, the longer series of woes against scribes and Pharisees which appears in Mt 23 and Lk 11 (and which hence probably derives from Q). Here there is just a single woe, though covering at least two aspects: the scribes are accused of parading their status to curry human favour by wearing special clothes and claiming special seats in public places (vv. 38–9); they are also accused of exploiting widows financially (v. 40). The first accusation is the language of polemic and no doubt reflects as much the bitter divisions between Christians and Jewish leaders in the early Christian church. The charge of financial impropriety is hard to assess. The care of widows (and orphans) in Jewish society was of paramount concern, so the charge here is a serious one. How far it was ever justified, or indeed why scribes as such should be singled out for mention, is not at all clear. (It has been suggested that perhaps some scribes acted as guardians or trustees of estates and took more than their fair share of profits.)

Mark, however, vividly contrasts the behaviour of the scribes with that of a widow who gives a gift for the temple (vv. 41–4). As noted already, women in Mark often function as role models, in contrast to men, for how true disciples should behave (cf. 1:29–31). Here the woman's gift is minute in monetary terms (it has been estimated to be about one sixty-fourth of a denarius, a day's wage for a poorly paid labourer); but it is all she has and hence its value in God's eyes is far greater than the value of anything put in by other, well-off people. Perhaps we are to see here both a negative and a positive example of the love command in practice: the scribes' behaviour indicates that their 'service' to God is sham, and they seek only to profit themselves: they love neither God nor their neighbours. The widow gives her little which is her all: she is the one who is seen truly to love God.

We should perhaps also note another possible interpretation of this story, i.e. that it is an implied critique of the social situation (and of the socially powerful who exploit the situation) which compels a poor widow to give all that she has and impoverish herself. However, the final saying of Jesus implies no such critique by referring to the compulsion the widow is under: rather it seems to refer to her act as a free act of generosity which as such is commended.

The Apocalyptic Discourse

In ch. 13 Mark records an extended block of teaching by Jesus, the so-called Markan Apocalypse, where Jesus looks to the future and predicts what is in store for his followers. Such predictions are a standard feature of much so-called 'apocalyptic' writing. For the authors of such texts, the predictions are placed on the lips of a figure in the past so that what is ostensibly a prediction of what is to come in the future is in fact for the reader often partly a reference to what has already happened. The same is probably the case here: Mark's Jesus looks forward; but for Mark and his readers, part at least of what is predicted has already happened. This serves to confirm the conviction that what is still future for Mark and his readers will indeed happen. Part of the problem of the chapter is to know exactly where the speech switches from Mark's past or present to his future.

Another stock problem of the interpretation of the chapter is to know what general message Mark is trying to convey. Jesus' predictions take the form not just of exhortations to be vigilant because the End may come at any time (cf. vv. 33–7), but also warnings not to get too excited and think that the End is imminent when certain events take place (this is the thrust of at least vv. 5–8, 9–13, 21–3). This then creates considerable tension in interpreting the discourse as a whole. Is Mark's Jesus trying to encourage eschatological awareness and enthusiasm, or is he trying to dampen it down? The line taken in this commentary will be that the latter is the dominant motif (it certainly occupies more space). But maybe precisely by dampening down some sorts of enthusiasm, in particular by pointing away from the likelihood of any preliminary signs to the coming of the End, and by pointing to the suddenness of the End when it comes, the exhortation to constant readiness and vigilance (vv. 33–7) can be asserted.

(13:1–4) The Occasion of the Discourse The discourse is set in the context of the temple and, at least in part, is presented as an answer to the question about the timing of the destruction of the temple. The disciples' comment about the magnificence of the temple building (v. 1) is entirely apposite: the temple was a colossal building, with enormous stones, and represented a triumph in engineering and construction. Jesus here predicts that the temple will be destroyed, an event which of course happened in 70 CE. Such a prediction is deeply embedded in the tradition (cf. 14:57–8; 15:29; Jn 2:19; cf. Acts 6:14), and is almost certainly historical. For Mark, no doubt, the destruction of the temple reflected divine punishment for Israel's failure to respond.

In a further, somewhat artificial, development, Jesus is now asked by the inner group of four disciples to explain what he has just said, and in particular to say when this will happen. It is unclear as it stands whether the questions in v. 4 are asking about the time of one event (i.e. the destruction of the temple), the one question being effectively repeated by the other, or whether v. 4 constitutes two genuinely separate questions, asking about two events, the destruction of the temple and the end of the present world order. It seems likely that vv. 14–20 refer to the destruction of the temple (see below); since this does not cover the whole discourse, it may be that the rest of the chapter, referring to the end of the present world order, is an answer to what is a different question in v. 4b. Hence v. 4 should be taken as asking two different questions.

(13:5–8) The Start of the Troubles The main thrust of these verses seems clear in general: the disciples are not to be led astray by various events into thinking that the End is about to come. The section is thus a warning against overenthusiasm: such events must take place first, but they do not indicate that the present world order is about to end.

Despite the clear nature of the section in general, the details are highly obscure, especially the reference in v. 6 to people coming 'in my name' saying 'I am he!' (literally in Greek 'I am'). As Jesus is the speaker, it is not at all clear what such people might be claiming in saying 'I am he!'. Are they claiming to be Jesus himself returning (perhaps from the dead)? Are their words meant to echo the divine name itself ('I am') so that they are claiming to be quasi-divine beings? Are they coming in the 'name' of Jesus as Messiah and claiming to be the (true?) Messiah? Or are they coming as the Messiah's true agents or representatives? Certainty is simply impossible, except to say that the verse is extremely obscure! A similar warning appears in vv. 21–3, though there it is clearly a reference to messianic claimants other than Jesus. That *may* be so here as well, in which case the repetition of the warning shows its importance for Mark and may indicate that the presence of such false claimants was felt as a real threat in Mark's own day. Mark may have been faced with competing messianic figures and anxious to identify the true Messiah as Jesus: hence his constant stress on the Christological question throughout his gospel.

The prediction of wars and natural disasters (vv. 7–8) has been used by some to try to date the Markan apocalypse more precisely by when such events occurred. Thus it has been argued that perhaps these verses reflect the events of the years c.68–9 CE quite precisely, when there was great civil unrest in many parts of the empire as well as reports of earthquakes (Hengel 1985). However, the prediction of such events is a standard feature of apocalyptic literature (cf. Isa 13:13; 1 *Enoch* 1:6–7 (earthquakes); Isa 14:30; 2 *Bar.* 27:6 (famines); 2 Esd 9:34; 13:31 (wars)), so one need not necessarily see any specific events reflected. In any case the general message is clear: such events constitute only preliminary stages to the End: 'the end is still to come' (v. 7).

(13:9–13) Persecution The same applies to the phenomenon of persecution. Probably we see here a reflection of the experiences of various Christians: they have experienced persecution (though the persecution referred to here clearly covers a wide range—in Jewish synagogues and before non-Jewish rulers), though how far this has affected Mark's own community directly is not so clear (cf. 8:34–8). But such persecution, like wars and natural disasters, is not to be taken as a sign of the End.

Similarly, the gospel must be preached world-wide before the End will come (v. 10). Persecution then seems to be set in a context of missionary preaching: it is evangelization itself which has led to persecution; but such persecution will not stop, and the End will not come, until the gospel has been preached to the whole Gentile world ('all the nations'). Once again the thrust of the section is to dampen down at least some kinds of eschatological enthusiasm, namely the view that regarded persecution as a sign of the End.

(13:14–20) The Desolating Sacrilege With vv. 14–20 the emphasis shifts somewhat. In the two earlier sections, the stress had been on steadfastly waiting and not expecting things to happen. Now the stress is on firm action: 'When you see ... then flee!' However, the action concerned makes it very clear that the event concerned cannot be the end of the world and the final judgement; for then any flight would be impossible.

The event itself is described in deliberately cryptic language, using words from the book of Daniel ('the desolating sacrilege' cf. Dan 9:27; 12:11), and Mark himself indicates their cryptic nature by his aside 'let the reader understand'. The desolating sacrilege is 'set up where it ought not to be'. (Grammatically the participle here is masculine in Greek, qualifying a neuter noun: hence the 'thing' concerned is clearly personified in some way.) In Daniel the reference is to the pagan altar set up in the Jerusalem temple by Antiochus Epiphanes (1 Macc 1:54–9). Presumably a similar desecration of the temple is in mind here. Although many have argued that what is reflected here is the threat of Caligula to set up his own statue in the temple in 40 CE (Theissen 1992), it is unclear why people should then 'flee' (certainly no one did). Perhaps more likely is the view that this reflects the destruction of the temple at the end of the Jewish revolt in 70 CE, when Titus' soldiers set up their standards in the temple and offered sacrifices. If so then Mark must have been written after 70 CE and this verse may be the strongest evidence for such a theory. It is sometimes argued against this view that, during the siege of Jerusalem, the city was surrounded and no one could have fled to the hills. But Mark may not have known all the details of what happened in Jerusalem itself at this time, so the lack of precise correspondence between these verses and what actually happened is no bar to the view that Mark is writing after 70 CE. If so, then these verses are part of the answer to the first of the disciples' questions in v. 4.

Certainly the action urged is decisive and quick: all must get away as soon as possible for the suffering will be intense. However, within the broader context it is again clear that this event, however painful and catastrophic, is not a sign of the arrival of the End itself.

(13:21–3) False Messiahs and Prophets The same is implied in the next section which *may* (cf. above) repeat the warnings of v. 7 of false Messiahs and false prophets. Such people will even produce 'signs and wonders': Josephus records various such prophetic and/or messianic claimants at this period who claimed to be able to perform various miracles. It seems then that we are still in the realms of past or present for Mark.

(13:24–7) The Coming of the Son of Man With the next verse, the scene changes dramatically and quite clearly to the future. Now we have a description of the End itself, and the accompanying signs are described in such a way as to show that (*a*) they are completely unmistakable as presaging the End, and (*b*) they are not really preliminary at all: they are part of the End itself. The 'signs' are in fact the total break-up of the present cosmic order: sun and moon failing, and the whole universe collapsing. The description is traditional (cf. Isa 13:10; 34:4) and no doubt is intended as a mixture of 'myth' and reality. The climax is the description of the coming of the Son of Man figure, coming with 'clouds' and 'great power and glory', gathering the elect from the four corners of the earth. The language is clearly inspired by the vision of Dan 7:13–14, though here the Son of Man is now coming from heaven to earth (in Daniel he goes *to* heaven, to the throne of the Ancient of Days); and his mission is now to collect the faithful (cf. Isa 11:11), presumably to bring them together as the new people of God.

This description, strictly, brings to an end the apocalyptic prediction of the discourse. What follows are various exhortations and comments to the listeners on how they should behave or react to this vista of the future that is held out for them.

(13:28–32) Various Sayings This may have been a collection of originally isolated sayings, only placed here secondarily. Jesus puts forward a mini-'parable' about a fig-tree coming into leaf as a sign of the imminent summer; this is then said to be an image of 'these things' which are a sign of the imminent End. Clearly the reference cannot be to the coming of the Son of Man (vv. 26–7) since this is the End itself; it may therefore be the cosmic signs of vv. 24–5 that herald the coming of the Son of Man (though they are almost part of the same event). The point may then be that these signs are so unmistakable that only when one sees them can one deduce that the End is about to come. Other alleged preliminary signs are misleading.

If that is so, the tone shifts markedly in v. 30—from warning against over-enthusiasm to encouraging eschatological awareness: the End will come within the lifetime of the present generation. Certainly then for Mark, a false enthusiasm based on potentially misleading signs does not preclude a genuine and proper expectation that the End *will* come—and soon.

v. 31 is yet another independent saying, stressing the abiding validity of Jesus' teaching. Clearly, if it is genuine, it is a massive claim to authority. In its present context, the saying serves to buttress the validity of the claims made by Jesus in the preceding discourse, and to give added assurance to Mark's readers of the truth of his prediction of what is for them still in the future. Yet despite any claims about Jesus' authority, the next verse (v. 32) expresses the limited nature of Jesus' knowledge about any detailed timings. In its present form, the saying is highly unusual in that Jesus refers to himself as the Son in absolute terms, a feature very rare elsewhere in the synoptics, and hence raising the suspicion that this is a Christian post-Easter creation. On the other hand, it seems very unlikely that later Christians would invent a saying in which Jesus confesses such ignorance. Perhaps a genuine saying of Jesus has been glossed by later Christians so that Jesus now refers to himself as the Son. For Mark the saying no doubt serves to assure Mark's readers about their own ignorance: if they do not know exactly when the End will come, they can be assured that neither did Jesus himself.

(13:33–7) The Returning Master As a result Mark's Jesus issues his final call to be continually ready and vigilant. The call is in the form of a parable (vv. 34–6). The parable has various synoptic parallels (cf. Lk 12:35–8, 42–6; 19:11–27), though Mark's story here seems to confuse two images: a man going on a long journey and entrusting servants with various tasks, and a man going out for an evening and expecting servants to await his return. At least two stories seem to be conflated here. The points of time mentioned in v. 35 (evening, midnight, cock-crow, morning) correspond to the four watches of the night on the Roman reckoning and this may indicate Mark's own *Sitz im Leben*. The message of the section is spelt out in the final verse, which in turn is explicitly said to apply not only to the four disciples of the story-world, but to 'all', i.e. all Mark's readers: 'keep awake', be ready for the End which may come at any time.

This then is the final word of Jesus before the story of his passion and death.

Passion Narrative

Ch. 14 is often thought to be the start of the passion narrative proper. It is sometimes held that the passion narrative as a connected whole was put together very early and that this version reflects an earlier, pre-Markan account. Mark's story may well be traditional—and certainly a number of unevennesses in the present account are probably due to separate traditions being secondarily put together. On the other hand, it is also clear that Mark's present narrative is an integral part of the broader narrative in his gospel and in many ways it forms the climax of what has gone before.

Mark's account is very stark and unadorned. Yet the passion of Jesus was for Christians never a matter of simply 'plain fact' about Jesus' death. Christians believed that Jesus' death was in some sense 'according to the scriptures', i.e. part of a divine plan and somehow 'fulfilling' the OT. Exactly how this 'fulfilment' took place was conceived in different ways by different writers and different parts of the OT are referred to in this context. For Mark, some of the Psalms describing a righteous sufferer are clearly very important, so Mark writes up some aspects of the account of Jesus' passion in the words of these Psalms, especially Ps 22. Perhaps surprisingly, the evangelists do not make much, if anything, of any parallels between Jesus' death and the suffering ascribed to the servant figure of Isa 53. Generally speaking, the gospels are very reticent about ascribing *atoning* significance to Jesus' death: the story only occasionally implies that Jesus dies 'for us' or 'for our sins'.

(14:1–2) The Plot These verses set the following scene into a chronological framework in relation to the feast of Passover. The chronological details are potentially very significant (was the Last Supper a Passover meal? Did Jesus' trial take place on the feast of Passover itself?). But the exact details are tantalizingly obscure and Mark himself may have been confused.

v. 1 dates the events two days before the feast of Passover, which was at this time the same as the first day of the (sevenday) Feast of Unleavened Bread. Since Jewish days started at sunset, and Jesus was crucified on a Friday, Mark here probably refers to the Wednesday before. The Jews plot to arrest Jesus but say they will not act during the festival for fear of disturbance (v. 2). Yet the story shows them doing precisely that! Could it be that Judas' action (in betraying whatever he did betray) led them to change their minds? Alternatively, this could be an indication that the events concerned took place in a chronology which was rather different from the one presupposed by (some) later parts of Mark's narrative, so that Jesus died *before* the Passover, as indeed John's gospel implies (cf. Jn 19:31). See further MK 14:12–16.

(14:3–9) The Anointing at Bethany The story may originally have been independent of the passion narrative: Luke, for example, places a similar story much earlier in Jesus' ministry (Lk 7:36–50). For Mark, the story highlights at least three points:

1. It shows an act of true generosity by the woman, in contrast to the penny-pinching objections of the bystanders (vv. 4–5). The woman uses up a huge amount of oil, at least in monetary terms (300 denarii was almost a year's wages for a labourer). Yet Jesus praises such extravagance: his own temporary presence is more important than the constant needs of the poor (v. 7). The Christological significance is obvious, though how much such sentiments might translate into a contemporary Christian social ethic is by no means so clear!

2. The woman 'anoints' Jesus' head. This is explicitly said to anticipate Jesus' burial (v. 8): this action is the start of the sequence of events that will lead to Jesus' death. What may also be in mind is the fact that Jesus' body was not later anointed: the women went to the tomb to do this on the first Easter Day, but found the tomb empty. Hence Jesus' body was never anointed after his death: the woman's action here therefore anticipates his death by the prior anointing of his body.

3. There is probably further significance for Mark in the story. As we shall see, much of the passion narrative is dominated by the idea that Jesus is a king: he will be mocked as a king, and crucified as a royal pretender. So too he has entered Jerusalem in royal fashion (see MK 11:1–10). Anointing is also an act associated with a king: Jesus then is portrayed here as the anointed royal figure who as such, goes to his death.

(14:10–12) Judas' Betrayal The account of Judas' betrayal of Jesus is told starkly and briefly here. (It is elaborated considerably in the other gospels.) No details are given and one can only speculate about possible answers to questions such as: what were Judas' motives? What exactly did he betray to the authorities? (Jesus' whereabouts? Aspects of his message?) However, the incident as a whole is scarcely likely to have been invented by later Christians.

Judas' action is described as 'betraying', or 'handing over', Jesus. The same Greek verb is used in the passion predictions (9:31; 10:33; cf. 14:41), where it is implied that God is the subject of the action. Perhaps there is a hint here then that even in Judas' act of treachery, God's plan is actively being fulfilled.

(14:12–16) Preparations for the Passover This is the only story in Mark which serves to identify the Last Supper as a Passover meal. The account of the Supper itself makes no explicit reference to its being a Passover meal; and although some details of the meal are consistent with its being a Passover celebration (the meal is eaten at night, wine is drunk, those taking part recline, Jesus interprets some elements of the meal, a hymn is sung at the end), other essential elements of the Passover celebration are notorious by their absence in the narrative (no mention of the bitter herbs, the passover lamb, the explanation of the ritual in relation to the events of the Exodus from Egypt). There are also chronological difficulties raised by Mark's account in relation to the Sanhedrin trial: capital trials were not allowed on a feast-day, nor indeed on the eve of a feast-day, since a second session was required the following day to confirm the sentence (cf. *m. Sanh.* 4:1). Hence, if Mark's chronology here is correct, the Jewish authorities must have acted in a highly irregular or illegal way. (See further MK 14:53–65.)

Such difficulties have thus led many to conclude that this section in Mark is a post-Easter insertion (whether by Mark or an earlier tradition) identifying the Last Supper as a Passover meal. The secondary nature of the pericope may also be indicated by the reference to Jesus coming to the room with 'the twelve' in v. 17—even though according to vv. 12–16 two of them have gone ahead to make the preparations. The chronology implied by John's gospel is, of course, different: there

Jesus dies as the Passover lambs are being killed, i.e. on the *eve* of Passover, so that Jesus' last meal cannot be the Passover meal itself. The Johannine chronology may well be theologically determined (Jesus' death coincides with that of the Passover lambs, so that Jesus is the true 'lamb', cf. Jn 1:26); but the Markan chronology may be equally theologically determined, though via a different scheme (the Last Supper is the true Christian 'Passover'). Thus while the Johannine chronology is not necessarily accurate in absolute terms, it may be more accurate than Mark's in dating Jesus' death as *prior* to Passover itself (and indeed this may be hinted at in Mark's own account: cf. MK 14:2).

Some confusion is evident on Mark's part in the opening time reference in v. 12: the first day of the Feast of Unleavened Bread would *not* have been when the passover lambs were sacrificed, but would have started in the evening when the feast of Passover itself began.

The events described here are very similar to the events prior to the triumphal entry into Jerusalem (11:1–6). At the very least, Mark has probably written up both accounts to reflect each other. Speculations about whether Jesus might have made prior arrangements are probably quite beside the point as far as Mark is concerned. For him, the story shows clearly that Jesus is fully aware, and in command, of the situation. It thus illustrates Jesus' full authority.

(14:17–21) Prediction of the Betrayal This may also be secondary in relation to vv. 22–5 (the reference to 'while they were eating' in v. 22 seems to repeat v. 18*a*); the account is also rather artificial in that, in response to the prediction that one of the disciples will betray him, they ask not who the betrayer is, but only 'Is it I?' In its present form, the story serves to highlight again Jesus' full foreknowledge of what is coming and also his obedience to God's will. Jesus' words in v. 20 echo the words of Ps 41:9 (cited explicitly in this context in Jn 13:18), and show the events taking place 'in accordance with' Scripture. The Son of Man saying in v. 21 again emphasizes the divinely ordained nature of the course of events to come (cf. 8:31): it is as Son of Man that Jesus is to suffer and die, and this is ordained in Scripture ('as it is written of him'). The reference is probably to Dan 7. As in v. 11, Jesus is to be 'betrayed', or 'handed over', a verb implying not only human treachery but also divine intention.

(14:22–5) The Last Supper Mark's account is brief and to the point. As already noted (see on 14:12–16), there are no references to the Passover ritual; almost certainly Mark's narrative has been affected by the celebration of the Christian eucharist in his own community.

The development of the history of the tradition about the events of the Last Supper, and especially Jesus' 'words of institution' over the bread and the wine, is not totally clear and the evidence is complex. There are probably two quite independent accounts of the tradition: Mark's narrative here and Paul's citation of his tradition in 1 Cor 11:23–6. (Matthew's gospel here is probably dependent solely on Mark; Luke's may reflect a conflation of the Markan and Pauline traditions.) Probably neither Mark nor Paul consistently represents the earlier form of the tradition. The saying over the bread ('this is my body') is very brief in Mark. (The Pauline version adds 'which is for you', perhaps assimilating it to the saying over

the cup, and also an explicit command to repeat the rite: the latter is probably not original, since it is far easier to envisage such a command being added secondarily than deleted, though Mark may have assumed that such a command was self-evident anyway.) The word for 'body' (Gk. *sōma*) can mean physical body, but also 'person' or 'self'. The original Aramaic would certainly have had no word corresponding to the Greek verb for 'is'. It is then unlikely that any clear ontological identification between the bread and Jesus' physical body is intended. More likely, what is in mind is that the act of sharing the common bread serves to unite the disciples with Jesus and his cause so that the eating of the bread is some kind of prophetic sign, simultaneously enacting what it signifies, which enables the disciples to be one with Jesus and his cause. For Mark, no doubt, the eating of the bread enables the presence of the risen Lord to be shared and experienced by post-Easter Christians. For Jesus himself, perhaps the act was one whereby he sought to unite his followers with himself in the coming events of the passion. Part of his subsequent desolation may then be due to their failure to stick with him and his having to face his fate in total isolation.

The saying over the cup is longer and the differences between the Markan and Pauline versions are greater. The Markan version seems to equate the cup (or its contents) with Jesus' blood ('this is my blood of the covenant'), whereas the Pauline tradition relates the cup directly to the covenant ('this cup is the new covenant in my blood'), though both clearly agree on the centrality of the covenant idea. The relative age of the two traditions is disputed, but it seems likely that Mark's tradition is in some ways more developed and less original than Paul's: the idea of drinking blood would be abhorrent in a Jewish context; it is easier to see a development from the Pauline version to the Markan, bringing the two sayings into parallel form, than vice versa; also the Markan version as it stands is all but impossible to translate into Aramaic. Hence it is likely that the original form of the saying focused on the covenant established by Jesus' 'blood', rather than on the blood itself (though in any case such an idea is firmly present in Mark as well). Fundamental therefore is the idea of the covenant established by Jesus: the surrender of his life in death (his 'blood') is the means by which a new covenant relationship is established. Further, since in Jewish tradition the covenant is integrally connected with the establishment of Israel as the people of God, the claim about the new covenant here implies the establishment of a new people of God. The final phrase in Mark ('poured out for many') is a clear indicator that Jesus' death is being seen in sacrificial terms. However, Jewish sacrifice was very varied and by no means monochrome. What is *not* said here is that Jesus' death is a sin offering or a means of dealing with individual sins or sinfulness (Matthew adds 'for the forgiveness of sins' here, but this is clearly secondary). Rather, Jesus' death is interpreted here as a *covenant* sacrifice, the means by which a new *community* is created by God's own initiative (see too on 10:45); by drinking the cup, the disciples share in all the benefits established by Jesus' sacrifice, i.e. they take their places as members of the new people of God, the new covenant community.

The final verse here (v. 25) looks ahead to the eschatological future, a feature shared (in general terms) by both Mark and

Paul (cf. 1 Cor 11:26). For Mark, Jesus' 'words of institution' look to the present and/or the past. Here the reference is to the future: the special meal is an anticipation of the time of the kingdom. What is probably in mind is the messianic banquet (cf. Isa 25:6), symbolizing the joy of the new age. This may well be the most primitive aspect of the traditions of the eucharist, connected too with the evidently special nature of the meals held by Jesus during his lifetime: the special meal is a foretaste and anticipation of what is to come in its fullness in the future.

(14:26–31) Predictions of Denial Just as Jesus has earlier predicted Judas' betrayal, so now he predicts the defection of all the disciples, especially that of Peter. The story as it stands is probably composite: the citation of Zech 13:7 in v. 27b and the prediction about Galilee in v. 28 seem to intrude before Peter's protestation in v. 29 which would follow much more naturally after v. 27a. Hence vv. 27b–28 are probably an insertion which, in view of the similarity between v. 28 and 16:7, may be due to Mark himself.

The story as a whole serves to highlight again Jesus' full knowledge of what is to come. Further, Jesus is shown here to be a thoroughly reliable predictor of the future: he foresees and predicts Peter's denial right down to the smallest details ('three times', 'before the cock crows *twice*', cf. v. 72). In turn this serves to establish the reliability of Jesus' other predictions whose outcomes are not recorded in Mark's story. Some of these are no doubt past for Mark (cf. v. 28), some are still to come (cf. 14:62). Peter's denial is in one sense the climax of the story of the deepening and radical failure of the disciples to understand Jesus. Yet v. 28 indicates that this is by no means the end of the story. (See further on the Ending of Mark.)

Zech 13:7 is a verse which may well have been used by Christians originally to 'explain' Jesus' death as in some way in accordance with Scripture. In its present context, however, the stress is as much on the sheep (i.e. the disciples) as on the shepherd who is smitten (i.e. Jesus): the defection of the disciples is as much part of the divine plan as is Jesus' death itself. The text form used here is also unusual: contrary to both the Hebrew and LXX texts, the version here has 'I will strike' in place of the imperative 'Strike!'. Clearly God is now the one who strikes. Thus again, the events to come are shown to be not only the result of human failings and sinfulness: they are also the actions of God himself and part of the divine plan.

(14:32–42) Gethsemane The account of Jesus' agony in Gethsemane is one of the most powerful and poignant stories in the whole of the gospel tradition. Its historicity has been questioned (how could the disciples have known what happened if they were all asleep at the time?). However, it is deeply embedded in the tradition (cf. the echoes of the story in Jn 12:27; 18:11; also Heb 5:7–8, as well as the parallels in Matthew and Luke); further, the picture of Jesus apparently doubting his willingness to face the future is unlikely to have been invented by later Christians. Hence it is very probable that the story has firm roots in the tradition. Perhaps Jesus believed that his mission was now a failure; perhaps too he had expected, or hoped, that his disciples would stay with him and share his lot (cf. 10:39; 14:22), but he now found himself totally alone. For Mark, the story is part of the growing isol-

ation of Jesus whereby he is deserted by his friends and, in the end, feels deserted by God himself (cf. 15:34).

If, however, the story may have firm historical roots, this does not mean that every detail is historically accurate. In its present Markan form the account has some redundancies and repetitions (cf. the way in which Jesus goes away twice and comes back three times), suggesting at least some secondary developments of the story. In particular, the words of Jesus' prayer to God in v. 36 may reflect as much what Christians thought Jesus would have said on such an occasion as anything he did actually say on this particular occasion.

Jesus' words echo the Lord's Prayer (the address to God as Father, 'your will be done'). Jesus' address of God as 'Abba', Father, is noteworthy. Too much has probably been made in the past of 'Abba as a child's address to its father. Nevertheless, the word is distinctive as showing close intimacy, and the fact that the Aramaic word 'Abba is preserved here suggests that this was remembered as characteristic of Jesus. However, it is not at all clear how unique this makes Jesus: Jesus himself gave others the same right/privilege (cf. the Lord's Prayer, Lk 11:2), and other Christians certainly followed suit (Cf. Gal 4:6; Rom 8:15). Rather than reflecting any self-awareness by Jesus of himself as a unique Son of God, the use of 'Abba shows Jesus' close relationship with God which he *shared* with, and offered to, others. Here it is part of a general picture of sonship as denoting obedience and subservience: Jesus as the implied son is the one who submits to God's will, not his own. The reference to the 'cup' here is probably simply an image of intense suffering (cf. 10:38–9), not of any divine punishment (e.g. for the sins of others): such ideas are foreign to Mark.

As well as showing Jesus' own submission to God's will, the story highlights the failure of the disciples. The Greek word here for 'keep awake' (vv. 34, 37, 38) is the same as that used in the commands to watch in 13:34, 35, 37. By sleeping and failing to stay awake, the disciples are failing to obey the command of Jesus given to all his followers (cf. 13:37). Jesus' willing submission in the end to God's will thus contrasts dramatically with the human failings of his followers.

(14:43–52) The Arrest The story of Jesus' arrest may represent the start of an early account of Jesus' passion: from here the synoptic and Johannine accounts of the passion run closely parallel with each other, and the redundant (i.e. for Mark) reference to Judas as 'one of the twelve' in v. 43 may indicate that Mark is using an earlier tradition here. The account suggests more of a disorganized mob than an official party (cf. the reference to 'swords and clubs'). Judas' action in kissing Jesus *may* have been intended to identify who Jesus was (though why this should have been necessary is not clear); but in its present form it highlights Judas' treachery: an act of respect and/or affection is used as an act of betrayal. The reaction of one of the bystanders in cutting off the ear of the high priest's slave is told here very briefly. The story is elaborated in the later gospels (it is an action of Peter, the victim is named, Jesus responds to the action), but here it is left in isolation. Jesus' response focuses on the violence of his opponents. The words of v. 49a, referring to Jesus' continued presence in the temple, conflict with Mark's general chronology, since they seem to imply that Jesus had been in Jerusalem much longer than the one hectic week implied by Mark. This in turn gives some added support to the theory that Jesus arrived in Jerusalem much earlier than Mark suggests (see MK 11:1–10). Jesus' final words (v. 49*b*) emphasize once again that everything takes place in accordance with Scripture and hence with God's will. The final note in v. 50 about all the disciples fleeing also confirms that everything happens as Jesus himself has predicted (cf. v. 27).

The small story about the young man running away naked has led to much speculation. Some have seen here a cryptic autobiographical note by Mark himself; however, it is unlikely that Mark was a Palestinian Jew. Possibly the story has been influenced by Amos 2:16. Attempts to see deeper significance in the 'linen cloth' work by the man (e.g. is this a reference to baptismal clothes 'taken off'?) are probably fanciful.

(14:53–65) The Sanhedrin Trial The account of Jesus' trial before the Jewish authorities is one where the historical questions of what actually happened are most acute, and almost intractable. The story as it stands gives rise to innumerable historical difficulties. Above all, there is the fact that Mark seems to think of the events described as some kind of formal 'trial', resulting in a death sentence, and yet the authorities seem to have broken a large number of their own rules in conducting a capital trial in the way described. Our evidence for such rules—mostly from the Mishnah—is admittedly from a later time, but infringements implied here include holding a trial on a feast-day, not having a statutory second session on the following day to confirm the sentence, Jesus being condemned to death for blasphemy yet technically he has not blasphemed (see MK 14:64). Some of these problems are resolved if one takes the event as less of a formal trial and more of an informal hearing, as is implied by Luke's account (which may be independent of Mark here) and also by John's (though there are the perennial problems of the historical reliability of John), and if one jettisons the Markan chronology which implies that all this happened on Passover itself (cf. MK 14:12–16).

The Markan account has been somewhat embroidered and one certainly cannot simply read it as a straight transcript of what actually happened. How much Mark himself was aware of this is not certain: did Mark deliberately set out to portray the Jewish authorities as breaking all their rules in order to get Jesus killed? Or was he simply ignorant of the finer points of Jewish legal procedure and unaware of the problems his account would cause for later interpreters? In view of the lack of any explicit hints of irregularities in procedure here, the latter possibility seems more likely.

In terms of historicity, there is also the problem of how later Christians would have had access to any reliable information about what actually happened during the hearing. Maybe some general information was available, but the details must have remained unknown. Perhaps part of the difficulties raised by the accounts is due to some information which may have been available being coupled with a general belief on the part of later Christians that Jesus was fundamentally innocent of any 'charge' brought against him.

Jesus is questioned first about an alleged claim to destroy the temple. As it stands, the account is highly implausible: Jesus is accused by false witnesses who cannot agree—but such testimony should then be rejected. Yet for Mark there is a constant theme of dramatic irony running through this account of the passion: what is at one level false is also at a deeper level an expression of profound truth. The 'falsity' may partly derive from the general belief that Jesus was innocent of any charge (cf. above); it may also be partly due to the fact that the falsity applies not so much to the truth of what is said as to the people making the claims. Jesus' prediction of the destruction of the temple is, as we have seen, deeply embedded in the tradition (see MK 13:2). Here such a prediction is expanded by a contrast between the physical temple, which will be destroyed, and a temple 'not made with hands' which will replace it 'in three days'. For Mark and his Christian readers, the reference is certainly to the spiritual temple of the church, established by Jesus in the resurrection (after 'three days'). For many, such an idea is best explained as a Christian development in the light of the resurrection. However, we now know from some Qumran texts that the Jews at Qumran had a similar interpretation of the 'temple' as the community; moreover, in some of these texts, building this new/metaphorical temple was conceived of as the task of an expected Davidic messianic figure (cf. 4QFlor). Thus Jesus could have conceived his own role as that of a messianic figure whose primary task was to establish a new community as the new people of God, a new 'temple'. With this background of thought, the transition to the next question about Jesus' messiahship, often felt to be difficult to explain, becomes more comprehensible and may thus reflect historical fact rather better than is sometimes claimed.

Jesus' refusal to answer (which could then be taken as a refusal to deny the 'accusation') leads on to the specific messianic question of Jesus' own identity. Jesus is asked explicitly if he is the Messiah, the Son of the Blessed. (The high priest's words avoid uttering the divine name of God.) For the first time in Mark's narrative, Jesus now openly acknowledges his identity. Secrecy is no longer commanded. The reason for Mark may be that the context provides the true hermeneutical key: the one who is Messiah and Son of God is the one who stands as prisoner in the dock and is about to be condemned to death. True messiahship, true divine sonship, for Mark means obedience, suffering, and death. When that is made clear, no secrecy is necessary. Yet, as in ch. 8 when Jesus was alone with his disciples, talk about messiahship is immediately qualified by reference to himself as Son of Man (cf. Mk 8:27–33). For Mark it is the idea of Son of Man that provides the proper key to any talk of Jesus as Messiah. As we have seen on several occasions, 'Son of Man' implies obedience, suffering, and subsequent vindication. Here the stress in on the last of these (cf. too 13:26). The one who is obedient to the cross will ultimately be vindicated by God. Further, the predictions of Jesus which have been fulfilled in the passion itself serve to buttress the validity of this prediction which for Mark awaits fulfilment in the future.

The story in vv. 61–2 clearly reflects key elements in Mark's narrative. How far they are also historical is much harder to say. As we have seen, the sequence from the temple saying to the question of messiahship is plausible. Further, it is almost certain that Jesus *was* crucified as a messianic claimant (cf. the titulus over the cross). Open messianic claims by Jesus are however very rare in the gospels, and their historicity is suspect. Perhaps the most one can say is that Jesus must have been confronted by such claims at his trial and at the very least refused to deny them (perhaps because they reflected at least some of his positive aspirations, e.g. his wanting to rebuild a new Israel, even if other aspects of messiahship, such as political nationalism, were less appealing).

The high priest claims that Jesus has blasphemed (v. 64). Strictly speaking, Jesus has not, since blasphemy technically involved uttering the divine name (see *m. Sanh.* 7:5) and this Jesus has scrupulously avoided doing. In terms of history, it may be that Jesus was regarded as having made 'blasphemous' claims or assertions in a loose way, though not necessarily uttering the divine name, and it was this that led the authorities to want him killed, even if they may not have been legally empowered to execute him themselves—hence their decision to involve the Roman authorities. (The whole question of Jewish legal powers to execute at this period is a very vexed one: see the survey in Brown 1994: 363–72.) But for Mark, such legal niceties were probably irrelevant. Perhaps he knew that the question of Jesus' identity as Messiah was a key one in the 'trial', and he clearly believed that the Jews did condemn Jesus to death for what they regarded as blasphemy.

The mockery of Jesus which now ensues involves deep irony. Jesus is mocked as a prophet: yet he has just been shown to be a true prophet in predicting the flight of the disciples; Mark's story is about to show his prediction of Peter's denial being fulfilled very literally; and Jesus has just predicted his own vindication as Son of Man. Mocked as a false prophet (by implication), Mark's narrative shows Jesus to be a true prophet, and his apparent demise is in fact the true and only path that will lead to ultimate vindication by God.

(14:66–72) Peter's Denial The story of Peter's threefold denial spans the account of Jesus' trial. (Mark starts the story about Peter in v. 54, but then adds the trial scene to create a typical sandwich structure.) The net effect is to highlight the contrast between Jesus who stands firm and Peter who capitulates to pressure. Mark goes out of his way to show that the events fulfil Jesus' prediction precisely, even down to the cock crowing twice (cf. v. 30). The final sentence is obscure: the verb translated 'broke down' (NRSV) is totally unclear as to its precise meaning. If we are to see in Peter's tears remorse and contrition, any sequel is left unspoken: this is the last appearance of Peter in the gospel (though cf. 16:7).

(15:1–15) Trial before Pilate The story of the hearing before Pilate raises almost as many historical problems as the account of the Sanhedrin trial. That there was some Roman involvement in the trial and death of Jesus seems undeniable: at the very least we have to explain the fact that Jesus was crucified, and crucifixion was a Roman punishment, reserved primarily for political rebels. The tendency in the Christian tradition, however, is to take the blame away from the Romans and put it on to the shoulders of the Jewish authorities. Undoubtedly we see this process happening here. The scene starts with Pilate abruptly asking Jesus 'Are you the King of the Jews?', and, when met with silence from Jesus, seeking desperately to release him. The picture is quite implausible, both in general and in detail. The picture of Pilate here as weak and vacillating, anxiously trying to please the Jews, in no way squares with what we know from elsewhere of the man,

viz., a cruel tyrant who would have not had the slightest compunction in executing an odd Jew or two to keep the peace. So too the Barabbas incident defies explanation: no such custom of releasing a prisoner on a regular basis is known, nor is it really credible. Most likely the account here has been influenced by the tendency to shift the blame away from the Romans and on to the Jewish authorities.

The question of Jesus' kingship, raised here by Pilate, is the one that will now dominate the chapter (cf. vv. 9, 12, 18, 26, 32). The charge of being king of the Jews was almost certainly the charge on which Jesus was crucified by the Romans (cf. the titulus, v. 26): it was in any case a political charge (which would naturally lead to the punishment of crucifixion: cf. above), and moreover it was a charge on which someone like Pilate would feel obliged to act: a royal pretender would clearly pose a threat to political power which Pilate could not ignore. Hence some aspects of the story here are very plausible. However, it is much more likely that Pilate simply ordered Jesus' crucifixion without any compunction at all. For Mark, the issue is no doubt one of Jesus' kingship—yet not so much Jesus' identity as king as the nature of that kingship and of the royal power he exercises.

(15:16–20) The Mockery This is brought out in the mockery scene which now follows, a scene impregnated with almost savage irony. Jesus is clothed by the soldiers in royal clothes—a purple cloak and a 'crown' that is an instrument of torture. The soldiers then do mock homage to him and hail him—for them ironically—as 'king of the Jews'. But the real irony goes one stage further because, for Mark, what is said here in mocking jest *is* in fact profound truth. Jesus *is* the king of the Jews. What the soldiers say in jest expresses for Mark the deepest reality.

(15:21–32) Crucifixion Jesus' cross is carried, under pressure, by one Simon of Cyrene: we know nothing of him (though his sons 'Alexander and Rufus' may have been known in Mark's community—hence their mention here). Jesus is then crucified and given a drugged drink. Possibly the story has been influenced by Ps 69:21 (certainly Matthew, who changes Mark's 'myrrh' to 'gall', makes the allusion clearer). Jesus however refuses. The next verse (v. 24), with its reference to casting lots for Jesus' clothes clearly echoes Ps 22:18, just as the note in v. 29 of the bystanders 'shaking their heads' echoes Ps 22:7. Ps 22 has had a powerful (if unstated) influence on the Markan narrative.

The mockery of the bystanders again employs the motif of irony. The charge about the temple is brought up again, including the note about rebuilding a new temple, and the people call on Jesus to save himself and come down from the cross. But the new temple is the new covenant community, brought into being by Jesus' own death so that Jesus cannot save himself if the prediction of the new temple is to be fulfilled. Similarly, the words of the Jewish leaders, 'He saved others; he cannot save himself' (v. 31) are, like the soldiers' mockery in vv. 16–20, both a taunt and simultaneously at a deeper level a profound truth: Jesus is saving others precisely by being where he is and by not saving himself—he cannot save himself if he is indeed to be the saviour of the world.

A final bitter irony comes with the claim that if Jesus, as Messiah and king, could come down from the cross, they would then 'see and believe'. Yet Mark and Mark's readers know that such 'seeing' is not available, nor does it lead to the right sort of 'belief'. Faith for Mark can never be based on miracles: miracles can only occur in the context of already existing faith and commitment (cf. 8:11–12).

(15:33–9) Jesus' Death The same note of mockery, and possible irony, may continue as the story moves to its climax in Jesus' death. Darkness falls, an event which is clearly understood as a divine miracle. (An eclipse of the sun would have been impossible at the time of Passover which would have been a full moon.) Jesus then utters his only words from the cross in Mark, the opening words from Ps 22:1. Some have argued that this 'cry of dereliction' should not be taken too negatively: the citation of the opening words of Ps 22 imply that the later part of the psalm (expressing great hope) is also in mind. This seems unlikely. Mark's account has shown a progressive increase in Jesus' isolation and abandonment by others. He has been abandoned by all his friends, condemned by all human agencies, and now he feels himself abandoned even by God himself. Any reading of the text should not water down or dilute the starkness and harshness of the narrative Mark presents.

Jesus' citation of Ps 22:1 (in Aramaic) is taken as a call to Elijah (why this should be so is not clear: such confusion could only occur if Jesus had spoken in Hebrew—as indeed Matthew claims—not in Aramaic). Perhaps what is in mind is the notion, evidenced in some later Jewish traditions, that Elijah, as the one who did not die, would help the righteous in times of trouble. This, however, seems to have been confused with another tradition of a bystander giving Jesus a drink (cf. Ps 69:21 again), either a drug to ease the pain, or vinegar to aggravate thirst—hence a mocking 'help'. The idea of Elijah as possibly coming to help may also be ironic since, for Mark's Jesus, Elijah had already come, been rejected and killed (cf. 9:11–13).

Jesus' death comes—mercifully quickly in the end for a crucifixion. The events which follow are undoubtedly Mark's own theological interpretation of what has happened. The veil of the temple is torn in two, and the centurion confesses Jesus as Son of God. (The words of the centurion could be translated as saying simply that Jesus was a son of a god. However, for Mark, it seems certain that he intends the centurion to make the ultimate Christological confession: Jesus is *the* Son (capital S) of God. For what this means, see below.)

The precise identification of the 'veil' of the temple is uncertain. Two possible curtains could be intended: that which stood at the entrance to the temple building, or that which stood at the entry to the Holy of Holies, symbolically preventing God from being seen by human beings. This Markan verse is often taken as referring to the temple as a whole, and the tearing of the veil as a symbol of the destruction of the temple and the end of the Jewish cult (cf. 11:16–19; 13:2; 14:58). This is possible, though it seems just as likely that v. 38 should be taken as integral with v. 39 as well: the tearing of the veil enables one to *see* now: and in particular it enables the centurion to *see who Jesus is*: for the first time in Mark's story, a human being now comes to the realization that Jesus is truly 'Son of God'. But what does this mean? At one level the interpretation may be provided by v. 38: the 'curtain'

may rather be the one veiling the Holy of Holies, so that, when this is torn in two, the barrier separating God from men and women is ripped apart: God himself is seen. Mark's scene here may thus be vividly and dramatically presenting Jesus *qua* Son of God as the very representation of God himself.

There is, however, a vital corollary. For the context for the confession of v. 39 is not only v. 38 but the whole scene itself, including v. 37. The centurion sees—a dead man hanging on a shameful cross, and says that *this* man is the Son of God. If Mark intends by v. 38 to claim that Jesus *qua* Son of God represents God, then his story also vividly and violently not only says something about what it means to be a Son, it also says something about God. It is not only about Christology, it is also about theology. God is to be seen most clearly and starkly in the abandonment, the weakness, and the powerlessness of the crucified one.

The identity of Jesus has been no secret for the reader from the very start of the story (cf. 1:1). However, the nature and significance of what it means to be Son of God—not only Son but also Son *of God*—are now spelt out in Mark's narrative. The scene is at one level the climax to which the whole of Mark's story has been leading.

(15:40–7) Burial The note about the women watching from afar (vv. 40–1) prepares for the account of the women coming to the tomb on the first day of the week. As we have noted already, in Mark women often do what the male disciples have failed to do. At least these women have not deserted Jesus completely. The account of the burial of Jesus follows, told simply and with little adornment except for the extra conversation between Pilate and the soldiers which simply confirms the reality of Jesus' death.

(16:1–8) The Empty Tomb The sequel to the story of Jesus' death and burial is in Mark's gospel terse and compressed. By universal consent, the sequel as we have it comprises only vv. 1–8 of this chapter. Continuations of the narrative, either in a short ending or in a longer ending (printed as vv. 9–20 in some English Bibles) appear in some MSS of Mark; but these are clearly not by the author of the text of the rest of the gospel and represent attempts to complete the narrative. Thus the final section we have of Mark's story contains only an account of the discovery of the empty tomb by the women with no actual appearance of the risen Jesus.

The story of the women coming to the tomb to anoint Jesus' body raises a number of well-known historical problems: e.g. if the women had no idea how the stone over the entrance to the tomb could be removed (cf. v. 3), why did they come at all? For Mark, however, such questions are beside the point: the narrative rather shows the miracle of the empty tomb which surpasses all human expectations and thus leads to astonishment on the part of the women.

The 'young man' encountered by the women is 'dressed in a white robe', probably indicating that he is to be thought of as an angel. He tells the women what the empty tomb implies: 'He has been raised; he is not here.' The order of the clauses is striking. The resurrection is almost assumed without question, and the empty tomb interprets it by the (self-evident) fact that Jesus is 'not here'. He is *not* present. There is thus no sense in which for Mark the empty tomb guarantees the reality of the resurrection or assures the presence of the risen

Jesus. Almost the reverse is the case: the empty tomb is an *empty* tomb: Jesus is *not* here to be experienced as a tangible objective proof of anything. If then he is not here, where is he to be found? The next verses provide an answer—albeit enigmatically.

In v. 7, the young man gives a message to the women for the disciples and Peter: Jesus is 'going ahead' of them to Galilee, and they will see him there. The specific reference to Peter makes it highly likely that the 'seeing' involves a resurrection appearance, with the mention of Peter perhaps referring to a special appearance to Peter (cf. 1 Cor 15:3; Lk 24:34). (Hence the reference is not, as some have argued, to the parousia: cf. Marxsen 1969.) Further, the young man's last words ('as he told you') clearly recall Jesus' prediction in 14:28. The reference is thus to a meeting between the risen Jesus and the disciples when the latter will be forgiven and restored; their relationship with Jesus, broken by their failure to stick with him, will be renewed. Once again they will become disciples, with Jesus 'going ahead' of them, just as he did before (cf. 10:32).

The women's reaction is, however, to ignore what they have been told. They are seized with 'terror and amazement'; they flee away, and say 'nothing to anyone, for they were afraid'. It seems highly likely that, from Mark's point of view, the women's reaction is to be regarded negatively. Although amazement and awe in the presence of the numinous (e.g. an angel) is in one sense entirely appropriate, the 'fear' shown by the women here seems to be wholly bad. 'Fear' elsewhere in Mark is the reaction which contrasts with faith (cf. 4:40); and the women here fail to do what they have been explicitly told to do. There is an almost ironical reversal of the situation earlier in the gospel. Earlier, people were regularly told to be silent about Jesus (and often disobeyed); here, the women are told to speak out openly—indeed the earlier secrecy charge in 9:9 had indicated that the time after the resurrection would be the time for openness; yet they are silent! There seems to be then an underlying pattern of divine command and human failing, which does not stop even here in the story with the resurrection. So too, however much the women in Mark act as correctives to the behaviour of male disciples, in the end they too are shown as failing. Human weakness and failing is thus shown to be universal. But is this Mark's last word? We must consider the problem of the ending.

The Ending

As already noted, Mark's text as we have it ends at 16:8. Other endings found in some MSS of the gospel are clearly (on stylistic grounds) secondary additions, mostly being compressed conflations of the resurrection appearance stories in the other gospels. Did then Mark intend to end at 16:8? Many have felt that an ending at this point is unsatisfactory and extremely difficult to conceive. Grammatically, 16:8 ends very abruptly and clumsily in Greek (with a conjunction). More important perhaps is the question of substance. The very existence of the alternative endings in some MSS testifies to a feeling by later scribes that the gospel was incomplete; and even Matthew and Luke, in some sense Mark's first interpreters, both clearly believed that Mark's gospel needed completion by the addition of accounts of resurrection appearances. Many modern scholars have felt the same, and hence have argued that Mark's gospel was not intended to end

where it does: It must be that either Mark continued with accounts of resurrection appearances and the ending has been lost (by accident or deliberate suppression), or he was prevented from finishing his work (e.g. by illness, or by being arrested).

Neither of these theories is entirely satisfactory: one would expect a lost ending to be restored, and theories about Mark's personal circumstances are entirely speculative. In any case such theories depend heavily on preconceived ideas about what a gospel narrative, in particular the conclusion to such a narrative, 'must' contain. Without such preconceptions, the onus is probably on the reader to try to make sense of the narrative as it stands and to take seriously the possibility that 16:8 is indeed the intended ending.

It seems clear that the end of the narrative is *not* the end of the line of events which start in the narrative itself. For example, the prediction of 16:7 of a renewal of the relationship between Jesus and the disciples must, for Mark, have been fulfilled. Throughout Mark's passion narrative, Jesus has been shown to be a reliable prophet, predicting events to come with great accuracy (cf. on Peter's denial). The whole literary plot of the narrative therefore demands that Jesus' predictions are fulfilled, including those not explicitly covered by the narrative itself. Thus the narrative structure created by Mark compels us to believe that the continuation of Mark's story-world into Mark's real world has led to the meeting implied in 16:7 having taken place.

Hence too the women's silence in v. 8 cannot have been absolute and everlasting. Despite it, the message to the disciples must eventually have got through to them so that they met up with the risen Jesus in Galilee. In any case, Mark's own Christian community must have known of the resurrection of Jesus (cf. the passion predictions which all include predictions of the resurrection as well: again Mark must have believed that they were fulfilled), and this must presume that the message of the young man did (eventually) reach its goal.

Perhaps though the message to the disciples has more significance for Mark than just its surface meaning. They are to meet up with Jesus in 'Galilee' where Jesus is 'going ahead' of them. For Mark, however, Galilee is the place where discipleship starts, and the path of discipleship is one which leads from Galilee to Jerusalem, which for Mark is the place of suffering and death. Similarly, 10:32 makes it clear that Jesus' 'going ahead' means going ahead on the road that leads to Jerusalem, the place of suffering. The way of discipleship for Mark is the way of the cross (cf. 8:34 etc.). If the disciples are to meet with Jesus in Galilee, then this is not necessarily some glorious panacea that will enable them to forget about the preceding events and mean a glorious, trouble-free existence. It is rather *suffering* discipleship to which they are called, as indeed ch. 13 has made clear.

Moreover, it is an existence that is perhaps permanently characterized by human failure. Just as the disciples have failed during Jesus' lifetime, the women have failed even during the apparent success of the era of resurrection; so the Christian readers of Mark may assume that failure will be a constant feature of Christian discipleship. But equally, as Mark's story implies (but does *not* state explicitly), failure can be and is overcome. The power of forgiveness and restoration is in the end greater than human failure and its consequences.

Mark's abrupt ending violently shifts attention away from what some of his readers may have expected (and from what some of his later readers such as Matthew and Luke evidently did expect). The era of the Christian church for Mark is not one of power and glory which nullifies the previous suffering and death. Stories of appearances of the risen Jesus might give that impression, and Mark does *not* recount these. As with the messianic secret in the earlier story, Jesus' true identity is to be seen as the crucified one; Jesus' divine sonship is seen most clearly and starkly when he *dies* (cf. 15:39). If Jesus is risen, he is risen as the crucified one. The gospel for Mark is thus the good news about Jesus—but it is *Mark's* Jesus that Mark's gospel is about, and for Mark, Jesus is supremely the Son of God seen most clearly in his suffering and death. Further, Mark's narrative may be only the beginning of the gospel (see 1:1). The rest of the gospel is to be completed by the reader, but the reader can only complete the story by following as a disciple of Mark's Jesus, and that means going to Galilee, being prepared to follow in the way of discipleship as spelt out by him, i.e. the way of the cross. There, and only there, will Jesus be 'seen' and experienced. There is then no happy ending to the gospel. There is certainly no objective account of the reality that informs Christian existence for Mark, namely the presence of the risen Jesus with his people: such would be inappropriate for Mark. Maybe Mark's gospel is indeed unfinished. But perhaps that is deliberate. It is up to the reader to supply the ending—and that is the perennial challenge of this gospel to all its readers today.

REFERENCES

Brown, R. E. (1994), *The Death of the Messiah* (New York: Doubleday).

Burridge, R. A. (1992), *What are the Gospels?* (Cambridge: Cambridge University Press).

Fowler, R. M. (1981), *Loaves and Fishes* (Chico, Calif.: Scholars Press).

Hengel, M. (1985), *Studies in the Gospel of Mark*, ET (London: SCM).

Jeremias, J. (1963), *The Parables of Jesus*, ET (London: SCM).

Luz, U. (1983), 'The Secrecy Motif and the Marcan Christology', ET in Tuckett (1983), 75–96. German original, 1965.

Marxsen, W. (1969), *Mark the Evangelist*, ET (Nashville: Abingdon).

Räisänen, H. (1982), 'Jesus and the Food Laws: Reflections on Mark 7.15', *JSNT* 16: 79–100, repr. in Räisänen, *Jesus, Paul and Torah: Collected Essays* (Sheffield: Sheffield Academic Press, 1992), 127–48.

—— (1990), *The 'Messianic Secret' in Mark's Gospel* (Edinburgh: T. & T. Clark).

Sanders, E. P. (1985), *Jesus and Judaism* (London: SCM).

Tannehill, R. C. (1977), 'The Disciples in Mark: The Function of a Narrative Role', *JR* 57: 386–405, repr. in W. R. Telford (ed.), *The Interpretation of Mark*, 2nd edn. (Edinburgh: T. & T. Clark, 1995), 169–95.

Theissen, G. (1978), *The First Followers of Jesus: A Sociological Analysis of the Earliest Christianity*, ET (London: SCM).

—— (1992), *The Gospels in Context: Social and Political History in the Synoptic Tradition*, ET (Edinburgh: T. & T. Clark).

Tolbert, M. A. (1989), *Sowing the Gospel: Mark's World in Literary-Historical Perspective* (Minneapolis: Fortress).

Tuckett, C. M. (1983), *The Messianic Secret* (London: SPCK).

—— (1992), 'Synoptic Problem', *ABD* vi. 263–70.

Weeden, T. J. (1971), *Mark: Traditions in Conflict* (Philadelphia: Fortress).

59. Luke

ERIC FRANKLIN

INTRODUCTION

A. Luke among the Synoptic Gospels. 1. As one of the three Synoptic Gospels, Luke's story of Jesus has much in common with those of Matthew and Mark. Based on the same outline of his ministry, it includes a large number of episodes common to all three and puts emphasis upon many of the same things. It shares with the other two the same overall perspective from which Jesus' life is described and its significance assessed. Jesus is presented as the one who announces the arrival of the kingdom of God, his exorcisms and miracles are interpreted as witnessing to its presence in him and his teaching, often given by way of parables, explains its implications for those who would receive it.

2. Within this common framework, however, Luke's gospel includes many episodes which are peculiar to it and a significant number which, paralleled in one or both of Matthew and Mark, appear in his gospel in a different form and give a particular distinctiveness to his narrative. Among the most important of these are:

(*a*) Luke's infancy narratives, though agreeing with Matthew's on a number of important points, are, in the story they tell, quite other than his. Preparations for the birth of John the Baptist form a prelude to those of Jesus which they closely parallel—though in a less dramatic way—and with which they are interwoven. Jesus is linked firmly to Israel's prophetic line whose mission he fulfils. Born while all the world is on the move, he is ignored except by a number of Jewish outcasts who alone receive the divine announcement of his birth. Taken to the temple, however, he is recognized by true representatives of its piety who acknowledge that he will cause divisions in Israel but will become a light to the Gentiles, whose response will rebound to Israel's glory.

(*b*) Luke's narrative introduces Jesus' Galilean ministry with an account of a rejection at Nazareth which Matthew and Mark have much later in their gospels where it becomes Jesus' last visit to a synagogue. Luke's story includes a sermon in which Jesus proclaims himself as the fulfilment of Isaiah's hopes for Israel. He virtually compels his rejection but justifies it on the grounds that no prophet is acceptable to his own. His lack of works at home is defended by pointing out that both Elijah and Elisha gave attention to foreigners. When the townsfolk rise up against him, their attempt to kill him is thwarted and leads only to a furthering of his progress towards his goal.

(*c*) All three Synoptic Gospels tell of Jesus' one, determined journey to Jerusalem to fulfil God's purposes for him.

Whereas Matthew covers it in two chapters and Mark in only one, Luke devotes some ten chapters to it. Its beginning is marked by a verse of exceptional solemnity (9:51) and frequent references to it remind the reader of its importance. The concept of a journey is obviously significant for Luke. The great majority of its episodes are peculiar to him whilst its contents as a whole offer different aspects of his own particular understanding of Jesus.

(d) Whilst Luke's account of Jesus' teaching in Jerusalem and of his conflicts with the religious authorities there are paralleled in Matthew and Mark, once the passion narrative proper begins with the account of Jesus' last supper, the distinctiveness of his story is apparent. His account of Jesus' actions at the supper is not easily accommodated to theirs and he includes a significant discussion with the twelve which they lack. The agony in the garden and the arrest resemble theirs (though with significant differences) but his story does not have their account of the night examination of Jesus by the Jews. He has but one single session of the council in the morning. No actual condemnation of him to death is made but all is rather regarded as a preparation for the accusations they are to make against him before Pilate, whose unwillingness to accede to their demands is emphasized by a threefold declaration of his innocence. Pilate's favourable judgment is supported by Herod who in Luke alone is given a role in the drama at this point. Eventually, Pilate delivers up Jesus 'to their will' and the Jews take a leading part in bringing him to the cross. His crucifixion scene presents a different picture from that found in Matthew and Mark. Their starkness is mellowed and Luke's, though having the same general contours as theirs, is given in colours that in many ways come closer to those used in John. The cry of desolation is not included and Jesus is serene throughout. He forgives his persecutors, receives the acknowledgment of the penitent thief and promises him a place in paradise, and commends himself into his Father's hands. The picture is of a death which reveals the characteristics that determined the life. What follows can only be a completion of what is now happening. Jesus' *exodos*, to which 9:31 pointed and which was to be accomplished at Jerusalem, is in the process of being realized.

(e) Whereas Mark expects Jesus' resurrected appearances in Galilee, and Matthew describes his final scene there, Luke's narrative leaves no room for such episodes. At the empty tomb, instead of Mark's promise of a future Galilean happening., Luke has a reference to a past event. All the appearances of the risen Jesus take place in or around Jerusalem. The theologically charged story of the journey to Emmaus is followed by the most materialistic of all the NT resurrection stories. What sets out to show that Jesus really is raised from the tomb becomes the setting for his farewell discourse, which justifies the events as those expected of the Messiah. It grounds in the Scriptures the universal mission that it enjoins. It sees its success as reason for believing in Jesus and as proof of the Spirit's presence in the community. Luke alone has a separate ascension event which both brings the resurrection appearances to a close and also accomplishes Jesus' glorification.

B. Luke's Narrative. 1. Whilst these distinctive episodes serve as a valuable tool in the quest for determining the nature of Luke's work and his purpose in writing, what can be learned from them has to be supplemented, and in part determined, by what the author himself says in his preface (see LK 1:1–4). This is unique in the gospels and in it Luke sets out his aims. His work is offered as an addition to an unspecified number of 'narratives' which have purported to give a basis for an adequate understanding of Jesus. His careful research into the traditions (probably both oral and written) that were available to him results in an 'orderly account' that deepens and maybe even corrects theirs at points. Just what claim he is making for his 'orderly account' is not clear. It is certainly one of providing a firm basis in hard events for the response of faith that Luke hopes to evoke. Luke believes his narrative to be grounded in real history.

2. The gospel's presentation of events, however, is not controlled by historical objectivity. Luke's story of the rejection at Nazareth owes it place at that point in the narrative less to a historical concern than to a desire to make it an introduction to the ministry as a whole. The details of Luke's crucifixion scene suggest that he wants to make it conform to what the gospel says about Jesus' stance during his life. The death sums up the life and reflects what happened in it. Resurrection appearances were all placed in the neighbourhood of Jerusalem because, in the events that happened there, the eschatological hopes of Israel were seen as actually being realized. The mission to the nations of the world had to reach out from there and start with the remaking of the Jewish people (Acts 2:1–13). Luke's desire to present an account of 'the things that have been fulfilled among us' could be achieved only by bathing the events themselves in a light that enabled their full reality, as the author understood it, to be seen. The 'order' of his account was determined less by a concern that asked 'What actually happened next?' than by a desire to unfold and justify the overall movement in Jesus' life that effected the achievement of his status. Luke's gospel becomes the step by step unfolding of his thesis that Jesus is both 'Lord and Christ' and that it is through him that God has fulfilled the promises of redemption that he had made to Israel and, through her, to the world.

3. The Graeco-Roman outlook to which the preface links its author, and the biblical mould in which he casts his work, come together to make his narrative the expression of a faith that itself determines not only the perspective from which the events are described, but also the way they are actually perceived to have happened. Luke's preface makes claims that are both more convoluted and at the same time more profound than one to historical exactitude.

C. The Question of Sources. 1. The gospel's preface speaks of its author's search for traditions and of his knowledge of other narratives with which he could compare his own. All these contributed in some way to the work, though commentators are by no means agreed upon either their number or the extent of their influence upon the gospel's final form. Conclusions reached are to a considerable extent determined by their advocate's study of the gospels as a whole and what this suggests about the freedom with which their authors handled the material at their disposal.

2. The majority view is that Mark is the primary source of Luke's work. The actual manner of its use, however, remains something of an open question. Many of Luke's episodes differ in varying degrees from their parallels in Mark. At what point the differences are such as to make the move from Mark to another source a distinct probability is a matter of fine judgement. Some commentators are so impressed by the unity of the final work that they will maximize Luke's creativity. Others, impressed by what they regard as foreign elements in the gospel (e.g. LK 1:67; 4:23; 11:49), see these as strong evidence for sources. If the latter look to Luke's preface for support, the former regard Luke's creativity as largely determined by his concern to write up his narrative in a biblical mould.

3. The position espoused by this commentary is that Luke most probably used Mark as his primary source and that, where they have parallel episodes, his are the result of a relatively free handling of what is found there. The use of supplementary sources to influence the final shape of Luke's episodes cannot be ruled out. So his reporting of Jesus' rejection at Nazareth is seen as determined by the basic pattern of Mark's episode. Its ending is written up as a commentary on Mark's scene which enables it to further the thrust of Luke's gospel. The speech expresses an understanding of Jesus which makes him the fulfilment of OT expectations and justifies his career on the basis of earlier OT prophetic activity. That Luke is here using a source to supplement Mark must be acknowledged as a possibility, but its function as the expression of ideas which are fundamental to Luke's narrative as a whole makes it more likely to have been the evangelist's own composition. The whole episode, shaped and in part created by him, is put at the beginning of the ministry to serve as its statement and the justification of its course as Luke describes it.

4. Apart from this material parallel to Mark, Luke has some 200 verses, mainly of Jesus' sayings, that, in varying degrees of closeness, are found also in Matthew. The majority of commentators assign this to a source, usually designated Q, which was used independently by the two evangelists (see FGS). Those who take this view tend to believe that Luke has introduced it into his gospel in a relatively unrevised form. That he handled what is accepted as a secondary source with such restraint, however, is unlikely if he used Mark, his primary source, freely. Some, impressed by this argument, therefore accept some form of the Proto-Luke hypothesis which, less favoured than it was, holds that the basis of Luke's work is not Mark but a blend of Q and some other sources into which he fitted a number of episodes which he took from Mark (Caird 1963). This, however, would seem to do less than justice to the unity of the final work. A minority of commentators, impressed by this unity, would actually doubt the existence of Q and would account for the material common to Luke and Matthew by suggesting that Luke knew that gospel and actually made use of it in the composition of his work (Goulder 1989). This suggestion would make Luke an extremely free handler of his sources and would emphasize his creativity to an extent that most interpreters of his gospel would be unwilling to allow.

5. Questions about Luke's sources must remain unresolved. Any serious student of his gospel will regard a synopsis as an indispensable tool, for comparison of his episodes with their parallel forms in Matthew and Mark allows the contours of Luke's stories to be clearly seen; understanding of his stance is helped. Firm conclusions based upon any particular theory of how the gospels are related must, however, be avoided. Though these may make for a sharpened approach, their hypothetical nature must be recognized. To build too much upon them is to construct an edifice upon shifting sand.

D. Luke the Evangelist. 1. Luke's preface suggests that the evangelist writes himself firmly into his narrative. Other gospels do not point to their authors in this way and, though perhaps each leaves a hint of his presence, search for the gospel's setting and the reasons for its production focus primarily upon the community with which it is related. Though some interpreters have approached our gospel in this way, reading it as something of a mirror-image of the community with which it is thought to be associated, the gospel itself does not obviously suggest this approach (though see Esler 1987). It must, of course, make contact with a community of some sort, but it is addressed to it and is the author's response to a situation which is perceived through his own eyes rather than through those of the community itself. Luke's is a personal offering and the address to a person, whatever that may mean (see LK 1:4), suggests that it is the person of the author which determines what is included and the stance which is adopted. His gospel has something of the character of an epistle.

2. The author does not give his name but, from the second century, our gospel has been attributed to Luke who, in Philem 24, is called Paul's 'fellow-worker' and in Col 4:14 is described as 'the beloved physician'. The author of the gospel also wrote Acts and the most obvious reading of his use of the first person plural at various points in the second half of that volume (16:10–17; 20:5–15; 21:1–18; 27:1–28:16) would seem to be that on these occasions he was a companion of Paul.

3. Recent years, however, have seen a widespread questioning of this relationship (Vielhauer 1968). The picture of Paul in Acts differs appreciably from what Paul says about himself. Not only is it hard to fit Acts' biographical details into what Paul maintains, but it suggests a different approach to some of the issues that were at the heart of Paul's beliefs. The author's obvious enthusiasm for Paul is not felt to be equalled by his understanding of him.

4. Luke's description of Paul in Acts has sometimes been defended on the grounds that the apostle's was not always such a rigorous position as his more polemical utterances suggest (Marshall 1980). It is hard, however, to resist the conclusion that it is an interpretation of Paul's own outlook (Wilson 1973). The question is whether it is an illegitimate interpretation or whether it represents a legitimate one by someone who knew Paul, who had learned from his deepest insights, but who did not fully share the implications Paul himself drew from these. He presents Paul as he himself had learned from him, and writes his gospel to reflect this understanding (Franklin 1994).

5. From Paul, Luke learned of God's wide outreach in Jesus, and he received from him his wonder at the gracious inclusion of Gentile outsiders within the people of God. Whereas

Paul, however, emphasized the newness of God's act in Christ and saw its otherness from his earlier dealings with both Jews and Gentiles, Luke saw it as continuous with his earlier and, indeed, his wider actions. Luke himself was almost certainly a Gentile and was most probably one of that group of Gentiles—the Godfearers—who, though greatly honouring the Jewish faith, shrank from circumcision and therefore remained excluded from the covenantal people of God. In Christ he found that inclusiveness which had previously been denied him, and it was this that determined his own picture of God's redemption in Jesus. A student of the Scriptures, he presented Jesus as the fulfilment of their promises.

6. Luke probably wrote his gospel around 80–5 CE, not far from the time Matthew produced his work. They responded to a common situation when the vast majority of the Jewish people had rejected the gospel and when its future seemed to lie with the Gentiles. Jewish refusal raised real problems for anyone who saw Jesus as the fulfilment of the promises contained in the Scriptures. These were probably compounded by the continuing hiddenness of Jesus and the indifference, issuing in occasional hostility, on the part of the Roman power. It was this situation, and probably also some local tensions which are now beyond our ability to describe, that caused Luke to put pen to paper. But his gospel transcends these immediate issues to present to his fellow-Christians a proclamation of God's strange work in Jesus which is set to raise their sights and justify a faith in him as both Christ and Lord (Maddox 1982).

7. Tradition associates Luke with Antioch, and Acts at any rate could suggest connections with that city. He might have written there under the patronage of Theophilus who could as a private person have been impressed by him and have commissioned his work. On the other hand, he could have written, perhaps to that city, from Rome. Luke's work is best understood as written from faith to faith. Directed in the first place at those who were already Christians, it addressed outsiders only indirectly. It set out to give his fellow-Christians a firm foundation for the hope that was in them.

E. Luke's Story. 1. Luke's presentation of the redemptive work of God accomplished through Jesus is controlled by his understanding of its gracious outreach and wide embrace. Jesus' work is one of redemption, of release, of the overthrow of all that holds people in the clutches of powers that restrict the fullness of life that God wills for them (4:18–21; 1:68–79; 6:20–3; 8:26–39; 13:10–17). His God is above all merciful (6:36), reaching out to people in an acceptance that is creative (7:36–50; 19:1–10). The initiative of grace itself creates a response which can, though it is not guaranteed, issue in repentance (15:1–32) and a newness of life that is born out of the disclosure that God's outreach makes possible (8:42–8; 17:11–19; 23:39–43). The Jesus of Luke's gospel is presented as having a special concern for those who are on the fringes of society and of religious respectability. Jesus is said to have made a habit of eating and drinking with tax-collectors and sinners (5:29–32; 7:34; 15:1–2; 19:1–10). Women have an important role. They accompany Jesus and his disciples on the way and provide for them out of their means (8:1–3). They are representative disciples (10:38–42). They are present at the cross, watch at the burial, and are the first believers in the

resurrection, for, in contrast to the unbelief of the men, they accept the witness of the two angelic messengers at the tomb (24:1–12). Luke's is the only one of the Synoptic Gospels to mention Samaritans and to present them in a favourable light (10:25–37; 17:11–19). The poor are blessed and, though Luke uses the term as a designation for the disciples as a whole, the sociologically poor are the special objects of God's redemption (1:46–55; 4:18–19; 6:20–1). Their situation demands God's concern and is seen as making them potentially responsive to his outreach. Conversely, riches are for Luke a burden for they encourage an attitude of self-sufficiency, self-satisfaction, and manipulation of others (16:1–8, 19–31). Mammon is tainted (12:13–34; 16:9–15), its possession is a hindrance to a response to God's call. On the other hand, the rich man, though he resists Jesus' command to follow, is not simply dismissed (18:18–27). The tax-collectors must use their money in the service of others; it is not said that they have to become paupers (5:27–32). Discipleship, however, is not easy. Disciples are to take up their cross daily, to be alert, to be open to the demands of the hour, and to use their gifts in the service of their Lord (9:23–7; 12:35–59; 16:1–9; 17:20–18:8; 19:11–27).

2. Luke's understanding of God's redemption as bringing a reversal of fortunes means that the rich, the religiously secure, the proud, and the exclusive will face judgement (1:46–55; 6:24–6; 18:9–14). All these groups are essentially satisfied with where they are, and so remain closed to the opportunities and challenges that Christ brings. They are not open to his radical message of the grace and outreach of God. This is especially true of the leaders of the Jewish people whose rejection of Jesus was for Luke the ultimate tragedy (20:41–4). He can present Jesus as harsh towards the Pharisees (11:37–54) and in his parables Jesus is highly critical of them and of the religious system of which they are a part (10:25–37; 15:1–32; 18:9–14). Yet he remains in dialogue with them and explains their perversity and that of the Jewish nation at large (4:16–30; 14:15–24). His crucifixion is brought about by the religious/political leaders of Jerusalem with little support from them. Yet the rejection of Jesus by the Jews forwards the purposes of God and results in a wider mission (24:46–9). Caught up in God's plans for the world, it can even be seen to have a positive function. In spite of the critical situation, the Jewish nation is not finally rejected by God, and Gentiles have not taken over the place of the Jews in his covenantal people (4:16–30; 13:34–5; 21:14; 23:34; 24:47). The promises of the infancy narratives will not be brought to nothing, for the inclusion of the Gentiles will ultimately rebound to the 'glory of Israel' (2:32, 38).

3. For Jesus stands as the climax of God's redemptive work in Israel. He is the culmination of her servants of God, one with them and the fulfilment of their hopes. Luke pictures him in terms of the OT categories, as eschatological prophet, Messiah, at one with Moses, Elijah, the Servant of Deutero-Isaiah, and John. Like them, he is Spirit-endowed (1:26–38) though, being more than them, is wholly possessed by the Spirit. Jesus is the agent of God, the climax of the old order of servants but, by reason of his complete obedience, exalted by way of death to be at God's right hand and to exercise that Lordship to which the psalmist pointed (20:39–44; Acts 2:32–6). The kingdom of God is now a reality in heaven, and the community on earth lives out of its power (11:1–13) and in the

hope of its future revelation (21:29–30). Luke does not expect that revelation to be long delayed. (For a development of these themes, see Franklin 1975.)

COMMENTARY

Preface (1:1–4)

This highly-stylized sentence places Luke's writings firmly in the Graeco-Roman world. Just what genre it suggests, however, is not easily determined. Biographies did not often have prefaces and those of historical writings were usually much longer. It has been suggested (Alexander 1993) that it is like those that introduced semi-popular scientific and technical treatises and which were largely designed to hand on the traditions of their particular disciplines. Others ('many' may be for stylistic effect) have written 'narratives', that is purposefully ordered accounts, and Luke joins his own to theirs, not without a hint that he is offering an improvement. The subject of these narratives is 'the events that have been fulfilled among us'. They are not disinterested accounts but their contents are viewed as the outcome of God's purposes and, probably, as the fulfilment of earlier expectations. The sources for these narratives were 'eyewitnesses and servants of the word', most probably a single group who handed down their witness in the service of the gospel. Luke is not claiming to have been their contemporary: his own 'orderly account' rests rather on careful research.

Theophilus ('lover of God') to whom Luke addresses his work is most likely to have been a real person of some standing and may have been Luke's literary patron. It has sometimes been suggested that he was a Roman official, that he was not a Christian, and that Luke was writing to make a case for Christianity and its political innocuousness. If so, the 'instruction' he had received was false, or at least biased, and Luke was seeking to give him the true picture. Luke–Acts as a whole, however, does not suggest that it was written for non-Christians: it contains too much Christian reflection for that and its stories of the trials of Jesus and Paul express little confidence in Roman justice. Theophilus is more likely to have been one who was knowledgeable about the Christian faith (Acts 18:25) and who was in fact already a Christian. In giving him 'the truth', Luke was seeking to offer him a firm foundation for his beliefs, to confirm them, and perhaps even to strengthen them when they were undergoing some trials. Luke's work is, of course, meant for public consumption and, through Theophilus, he is addressing every reader.

Infancy Narratives (1:5–2:52)

The narratives of the infancy stand in some tension with those of the rest of the gospel. Jesus is accorded a dignity otherwise not bestowed on him before the ascension, the Spirit is active in people in a way which in the narrative proper does not happen until after Pentecost, and Jesus and John are brought together in the closest possible manner which seems to belie their sharp separation later. These differences led possibly the greatest interpreter of Lucan theology of the twentieth century to leave them out from his exposition (Conzelmann 1960). This was undoubtedly a mistake though it remains likely that they were added at the conclusion, if not of the two volumes, then at least of the gospel. They are best understood as the prologue to Luke's whole work, summing up its message, proclaiming it, and giving it a firm basis in Israel's story. To pass from Luke's preface to his infancy narratives is to move into another world. The tight, carefully constructed sentence is followed by a piece where the expansive craft of the storyteller is supreme. Graeco-Roman literary sophistication gives place to a biblical style that makes a fitting vehicle for episodes that in their outlook and atmosphere are one with some of the most characteristic of the OT accounts of God's approach to humankind. They are a pastiche of OT words, sentences, images, and ideas and are formed by a conscious imitation of incidents taken from various parts of Israel's story. The coming of Jesus into the world is the fulfilment of—and of one kind with—that which was begun in God's earlier activity. The narratives exude the spirit of joy, of wonder, and of worship—though also of a certain puzzlement. God's final redemptive work has been brought about through the life, death, and resurrection of the child whose birth these stories celebrate. That is the faith they express.

(1:5–25) **The Annunciation to Zechariah** The infancy narratives begin in the temple with the promise of the wondrous birth of John the Baptist who was in Luke's eyes the last and greatest of the Hebrew prophets and the immediate herald of the Messiah. His parents are both of priestly stock and represent all that is good in the temple and its piety. Following all the commands of the moral and ritual law, they were 'righteous before God', accepted and acknowledged by him. Law, temple, and prophecy together were to produce John who, while yet in the womb, would acknowledge his Lord and witness to him (1:44). Zechariah was a member of one of the twenty-four orders of priests who twice a year for a week officiated at the temple services. On this occasion he was within the sanctuary itself where the altar of incense stood immediately before the holy of holies. At this holy place, the angel of God appeared to announce a new climactic stage in God's redeeming work. The main emphasis is upon the task assigned to John. OT tradition looked for Elijah to return to restore a people within Israel who would be acceptable to God when he came to establish his righteousness among them (Mal 4:5–6; Sir 48:10). John, having been made a nazirite (Num 6:3) from the womb to show his permanent dedication to God, will do this 'in the spirit and power of Elijah'. Both Matthew and Mark picture John as Elijah returned (Mt 7:12; Mk 1:6). Luke actually avoids saying this. John, as Elisha before him (2 Kings 2:15) would be like Elijah rather than a new Elijah. This is probably because Luke saw Jesus himself in terms of Elijah and did not wish the Elijah typology to be exhausted in John (4:25; 7:15; 9:57–62).

Agents of God in the OT were often said to have been empowered by the Spirit in order to do their work (Judg 6:34; 1 Sam 11:6; Isa 61:1). As the climax of God's agents in Israel, John would be 'filled with the Holy Spirit from the womb'. His was no temporary commission; it was a full endowment to be exceeded only by that of Jesus who would actually be conceived by the Spirit. Yet Zechariah demurs. Even for a faithful servant of the covenant, going forward into its climax in Jesus is not easy and he had to receive a demonstration of its truth which was at the same time a judgement on his lack of trust. Elizabeth conceives but remains hidden for five months, rejoicing alone at the sign of God's favour. The note of time binds her part into that of Mary and means that when Mary comes to visit her, the babe is formed enough to acknowledge the one who is carrying his Lord.

(1:26–38) The Annunciation to Mary By placing it 'in the sixth month' Luke binds the annunciation to Mary into that to Zechariah. The parallelism of the two accounts serves not only to join the events together, as part of God's final coming to his people, but also to put the climax on that to Mary for which the angel's visit to Zechariah is but a prelude. The fulfilment of its promise guarantees that those to Mary will not fail. The annunciation scene to Mary outstrips that to Zechariah in the wonder of the birth, the status of the child, the nature of his work, and the response of the one addressed.

Luke is emphatic that Mary, though betrothed to Joseph, was a virgin. Betrothal meant the entering into the legal contract of marriage though consummation did not normally occur until the time when, probably around a year later, the bride left her father's house to join her husband's. The angel's greeting, 'Rejoice', may have overtones of Zeph 3:14–17 and Zech 9:9 where God announces redemption to Jerusalem and her people. Mary is 'the favoured one' in that her life has revealed a response to God that suggests that she will respond faithfully to his further approach to her. She will conceive and bear a son whom she must name 'Jesus' ('the Lord saves').

The declaration of Jesus' status is unfolded in two stages. Gabriel's initial announcement is made in terms of a reading of the OT account of God's promises to David (2 Sam 7:11–16; Ps 132:11–18). Though these passages said that the promise was to be fulfilled in an ongoing line rather than in a single person, the Psalms tended to apply it to an individual king (Ps 2:7; 110:4) and these were later read as referring to a messianic figure. Jesus is to be the recipient of the promises for he will inherit David's throne, will reign over Israel ('the house of Jacob') for ever, 'and of his kingdom there will be no end'. This last part of the promise suggests a rule wider than over Israel alone. 'Son of the Most High', though found in the Graeco-Roman world, reflects biblical usage where God is addressed as 'Lord of Hosts' (Isa 6:3). Luke uses it more than any other NT writer (1:35, 76; 6:35; Acts 7:48). 'Son of God' could be applied to angels (Job 1:6), to the Davidic king (Ps 2:7), to the individual faithful Israelite (Wis 2:12–18), and, later, to a messianic figure (Dead Sea scrolls). It meant that the one addressed was thought of as having a special relationship with God. Just what the nature of that relationship was, however, it did not specify.

Mary demurs, not like Zechariah demanding some sign to back up the promise, but rather questioning its possibility. This enables a further declaration of Jesus' status which actually strengthens Gabriel's initial statement. God will be wholly operative in Jesus' conception. Whereas earlier agents of God's activity had been possessed by the Spirit to perform a particular task and John had been filled by the Holy Spirit from the womb, Jesus, whose status far exceeded that of

John's, was actually to be conceived through the Spirit. His whole creation, his very being, was itself the work of the Spirit. For Luke, the Spirit is essentially the agent and sign of God's eschatological redemptive activity (Acts 2:17–21, 10:44). Jesus, as the one to realize that, is wholly one with the Spirit. The Spirit is associated with God's power (Acts 1:8) which is here said to 'overshadow' Mary.

This total endowment with the Spirit marks Jesus as unique. He is 'holy', that is embraced within God's outreach and reflecting him (Lev 19:2), and 'Son of God'. Though 'Son of God' means the same as 'Son of the Most High', its climactic place here in Gabriel's message suggests that it pushes out beyond the boundaries of the OT imagery. Luke appears to see Son of God as more than a messianic title and endows it with something like Paul's declaration in Rom 1:4 (22:70; Acts 9:20).

In this passage, Luke uses the narrative to present a careful declaration of the nature of Jesus and his work. At the same time, through his presentation of Mary and the relation this has to that of Zechariah in the previous episode, he is able to show the ideal response of the faithful in Israel and to give some picture of discipleship.

Luke insists that Mary is a virgin, and it is this belief that enables the narrative to move to a climax. The declaration of Jesus' sonship does not, however, rest upon that but depends rather upon his total possession of the Spirit which unites him to God. The virginal conception witnesses to his possession of the Spirit rather than being the cause of it. Though Luke's narrative expresses a firm belief in the virginal conception, it is unlikely to present the basis in history for that belief. To focus a young betrothed girl's consternation on child-bearing rather than upon the wondrous nature of the child she is called upon to bear suggests literary and theological concerns rather than strictly historical ones.

Justification of Mary's response on the grounds either that she mistook the announcement for one of an immediate conception or that she had already entered upon a vow of virginity is to import external considerations into the story (Brown 1977). Rather, in it we have Luke's response to the tradition that he shared with Matthew. Luke gives us little help in assessing the historical basis for the tradition. What he has done is, in the light of the traditions he received and of his belief in the OT's witness to Christ, to present in narrative form his proclamation of the significance of Jesus and to see it summed up in his birth.

(1:39–56) Mary Visits Elizabeth Luke binds the lives of John and Jesus together in this episode which enables the child in Elizabeth's womb to acknowledge the status of the one in Mary's, allows Elizabeth to greet Mary, and makes a setting for Mary's song. Mary remains the ideal disciple even as she is acknowledged as 'the mother of my Lord'. 'Lord' is Luke's most characteristic title for Jesus and his favourite address to him. Breaking out of the nationalistic overtones of Messiah ('Christ') it points to the universality of Jesus' sway (Acts 10:36). Since God is also called 'Lord' (2:45, 46), it points to Jesus' close relationship to him though, because its main influence in Luke's usage is provided by Ps 110:1 (Acts 2:34), it retains that subordination and instrumentality that is so characteristic of Luke's Christology.

Luke brings the episode to its climax with the song of Mary. This has much in common with that of Zechariah which follows closely upon it and a number of commentators would see both (together, perhaps, with that of Simeon in 2:29–32) as incorporated by Luke from some source. It is pointed out that they sit only loosely to their contexts, that this is emphasized by a few MSS attributing Mary's song to Elizabeth, that they are not wholly appropriate for their respective singers, and that they are not particularly closely related either to Luke's theology or his vocabulary. However, though full value must be given to these opinions, it remains more likely that Luke himself was responsible for them. They are in fact an appropriate expression of Luke's outlook. Mary's song is strongly influenced by that of Hannah in 1 Sam 2:1–10 which, celebrating the birth of the young Samuel, sees the wonder of God's action in this event as an illustration of the nature of his whole work for his people. Hannah's piety makes her a fitting forerunner of Mary, and Samuel's role as prophet and leader under God in Israel makes his work a type of that of Jesus. In choosing Mary as the mother of his son, God has rewarded her 'lowliness' and lifted her high. His dealings with her become a paradigm of the redemption that he effects through Jesus. The militaristic imagery of vv. 49, 51, and 52 is taken over from Hannah's song and is used by Luke, either of God or of Jesus in 24:19; Acts 13:17; 19:20. It is not out of place in a psalm-like canticle that celebrates God's powerful act of redemption through Jesus in biblical terms. The theme of reversal, taken over here from 1 Samuel, is particularly amenable to Luke who has already, in his two annunciation narratives, focused God's work in Jesus upon his approach to those who, out of a piety which looks to God for fulfilment and hope, are open to receive his redemption. As in the Lukan form of the Beatitudes (see LK 6:20–6) this redemption is centred upon the sociologically marginalized for, in accordance with the biblical tradition (Ps 34:6; 72:12), it is they who are thought likely to exhibit this outlook. The reverse side of the coin is that those who are 'proud', 'powerful', and 'rich', and who therefore maintain and exploit their self-sufficiency, are unlikely to be open to God's future. In Jesus, that self-sufficiency has been shown to be foolish and blameworthy (12:13–21; 16:19–31). Luke knows that it is those who are dissatisfied with the present who have responded to the gospel whilst those who have felt already fulfilled have missed out on its challenge and therefore on its redemption.

The use of the past tense in the hymn's proclamation of redemption has sometimes been felt inappropriate at this point in the story and so has been seen as evidence for Luke's having taken the hymn from a source. This, however, is to forget the function of the infancy narratives as the prologue rather than the first chapter of Luke's story. They sum up the whole event of Jesus and look at its beginnings in terms of its end. Mary's song is less one that would have been appropriate for her at that point in time than a hymn of praise which, through her, expresses the response of the ideal Israelite who had become a Christian disciple to God's whole work in Jesus.

(1:59–80) The Naming of John The circumcision of Jewish male children on the eighth day marked their incorporation into the people of God (Gen 17:11–12; Lev 12:3). It is not clear that naming necessarily occurred at the same time. Though

Luke records a similar pattern of events for Jesus, he is not wholly reliable in his information about Jewish customs as they were practised in Israel itself. The story furthers Luke's interest in the fulfilment of prophecy and adds to the wonders surrounding the child. In challenging what Luke regards as the usual practice about names, it points to the new demands of Jesus; there is not an easy progression from the old to the new. The publicity surrounding John contrasts with the total obscurity that marked Jesus' birth. John will later question Jesus and will wonder whether his ministry measures up to what he expected of the figure for whom his own ministry was a preparation (7:19). In the light of these later events, Zechariah's witness in his song takes on an added significance.

Zechariah's song is essentially a witness to God's action in his Messiah, and the preparatory role of John is emphasized. Like the song of Mary, it comments upon the scene in which it is set only to transcend it and to view the actions of which it is a part in the light of the whole event of Jesus on which Luke looks back. It serves to sum up the significance of Jesus within the setting of God's actions in Israel. vv. 68–75 proclaim these as the fulfilment of God's promises to Israel. Through Jesus and the events surrounding him, God comes to establish his presence with his people and to confirm his covenantal promises. He has 'visited and redeemed his people' and has raised up a 'horn of salvation'. 'Horn' is a symbol of strength. Ps 132:17 talks of a horn sprouting up for David, and the song sees this fulfilled in Jesus who is presented as the consummation of God's promises to Abraham, the ancestor of the whole Jewish people and the receiver of God's unconditional commitment to her. As 'prophet of the Most High' John becomes the preparer for him who is Son. He will 'go before the Lord' who here is really both God and Jesus. Through 'bringing forgiveness of their sins' to the people, he will prepare them to receive what is essentially God's redemption in Jesus who is 'the dawn from on high' who will bring 'light', 'life', and 'peace'. So, in the narrative proper, John will be pictured, both through his baptism and his firm religious and ethical teaching, as preparing the way for Jesus' proclamation of the visitation of God in himself and in redemption.

The proclamation of redemption completed, and the ground prepared for the birth of the saviour, John awaits his proper time and the spotlight now falls on Jesus alone.

(2:1–7) The Birth of Jesus As at the beginning of chs. 1 and 3, Luke is anxious to set the events of God's salvation through Jesus within the context of secular history. Though this has caused some to criticize him for reducing the eschatological dimension of Christianity and for making it into an event within world history (Conzelmann 1960), this relating of the gospel to the world in which it is acted out, and the more positive approach to that world which this displays, is a fundamental instinct that underlies Luke's understanding of Jesus and his work. Unfortunately, the effectiveness of his sortie into world history at this point does not measure up to his reasons for making it. Luke's notice of the census raises many virtually insurmountable problems. We have no evidence for an empire-wide census under Augustus and the likelihood of this including the land of a client king such as was Herod the

Great is remote. Indeed, the census held when his son was deposed and Judea was incorporated into the Roman system was seen as such a novelty that it provoked a rebellion (Acts 5:37). Though there is some evidence from Roman sources in Egypt that participants were required to register in their own homes, this meant their present rather than their ancestral abodes. Herod died in 4 BCE and Quirinius was not governor of Syria until 6–7 CE. (See the balanced discussion of the evidence in Evans 1990.) Attempts to reconcile the differences have not met with widespread endorsement. A suggestion that Quirinius served an earlier term as an official in our area and that he was then involved in the census lacks real evidence. Perhaps the best attempt at harmonization is that which suggests that the Greek can be translated to read, 'This registration happened before Quirinius became governor of Syria' (Nolland 1989–93). It is not, however, a natural reading of the Greek and has about it something of the air of desperation (Fitzmyer 1981).

Luke, in contrast to Mt 2:21–3, has Nazareth as the home of Joseph and Mary. The census is used by him as the means of enabling Jesus to be born at Bethlehem where the tradition on which he bases his proclamation places the birth. That, however, does not exhaust the significance he sees in it. The census is of 'all the world'. Jesus is born at the time when all the world is on the move at the behest of one who, given a divine name, allowed himself to be addressed as Son of God and was regarded as having brought security to the world. Jesus, rather than the Roman power, however, is the real means of salvation from external oppression and the guarantee of unity to mankind. The timing of Jesus' birth proclaims his universal significance. The Roman power which, by the time Luke wrote, was uncomprehending of Christianity, often suspicious, sometimes hostile, and always threatening, unwittingly enabled Jesus to be born in Bethlehem, the place of David. The final power belonged, not to it, but to God.

Jesus' birth was nevertheless hidden, ignored by the world in its quest for security. Jesus, cared for by his mother, is placed in a 'manger', which could be either a feeding trough or a cattle stall, because 'there was no room in the inn'. Luke uses the same word at 22:11 for the 'guest chamber' where the company is to eat the last supper. Jer 14:8 (LXX) uses the word when it laments that God is a stranger, like one who stays in a guest chamber for but a night. For Jesus, there is not room even in the guest-place; his birth points forward to the life of one who has nowhere to lay his head (9:58). No doubt the scene is infused with ideas taken from Isa 1:3.

(2:8–21) The Shepherds At the heart of Luke's understanding of the redemption wrought by Jesus was his knowledge that in him the excluded had been included; the outsider had been brought within the people of God. His story will tell of the inclusion of tax-collectors and sinners, of women, of the poor, of the marginalized, and, ultimately, of the Gentiles. So it is right that his infancy narrative should tell of the message of angels to shepherds and that it should be they, rather than the Gentile sages of Matthew's gospel, who should visit the infant Jesus. David was called to Bethlehem from minding the sheep in order to receive anointing at the hands of Samuel (1 Sam

16:11), and later tradition emphasized the graciousness of the action (2 Sam 7:8). After the Exile, the shepherd's task became devalued and, outside the biblical period, was despised. Luke's story does not reflect that belittling, but it does picture them as outsiders, apart from the general ordering of society that was taking place at the time of the census. It is to them that the announcement of Jesus' birth is made.

Jesus is revealed as 'Saviour', Messiah', and 'Lord', three terms that sum up what the infancy narratives have said about Jesus and what the gospel as a whole will unfold and justify. The OT spoke frequently of God himself as saviour of his people, the one who would rescue them from their enemies and restore them to a relationship with himself (Ps 106:21; Isa 43:3; 60:16). Occasionally it spoke of his giving a saviour to his people (Judg 3:9; 6:14; 2 Kings 13:5). Jesus now brings the salvation of God himself (1:69). For Luke, it is all-important that Jesus is the Messiah of Israel and that he fulfils OT expectations of him (24:26, 45). 'Lord' is his most characteristic term for Jesus, which sums up his exalted status, his universality, and the devotion he receives from his followers. Proclaimed at the birth, these three terms express the Christian response to Jesus which his career and exaltation will evoke (Acts 2:36; 13:23). The song of the angels recalls that of Isaiah in the temple (Isa 6:3) though now it is Jesus rather than the temple that realizes God's glory and enables it to be reflected on earth. As people on earth receive his 'good pleasure', they share in a 'peace' which, much more than an absence of strife, is a wholeness of person and unity with others. (This represents the reading of the majority of the Gk. MSS. Some have 'peace, goodwill among people'. This reading however destroys the parallelism of the song and tends to make 'goodwill' a human response rather than one derived from a relationship with God. The whole outlook of the infancy narratives centres upon God's outreach to his people and the new possibilities he brings them.)

v. 19 (cf. v. 51) has sometimes been used to support the view that these parts of the infancy narratives rest upon reminiscences of Mary. There is in fact little to support this for we have seen that the annunciation story is shaped by literary rather than strictly historical influences. Mary is vitally important for Luke for she represents the ideal Israelite who becomes a disciple. Mary treasures the shepherd's witness and 'pondered it in her heart'. This last expression has sometimes been interpreted as coming to a right understanding of its significance. More likely, however, in Luke's narrative it retains the idea of puzzlement. Here and in the episode in the temple, Mary has not yet come to a complete understanding of the significance of Jesus. Her greatness was to accept in obedience of faith the divine call, the full implications of which she had yet to enter into.

(2:22–40) Jesus Presented in the Temple This episode allows Jesus to be seen as acknowledging the Jewish religious tradition which was focused in the temple and which ultimately made possible God's final redemption in him. It also enables the temple to make its witness to him. Once more, Luke's purpose in recounting the story controls the way in which he tells it. Here, it has resulted in a slight confusion about the

Jewish practices it describes. Three ceremonies are included, those of the purification of the mother, the redemption of the firstborn, and the presentation of a child to the service of God. 'Their purification' is a misnomer, for the ceremony involved the mother alone. After forty days the mother of a male child offered sacrifice as an act of cleansing. Mary makes the offering of the poor (Lev 12:6–8). The redemption of the firstborn is a separate ritual (Ex 13:2, 12–13) though there is nothing to suggest that it could not have happened in the temple and at the same time. Five shekels were paid to the priest. The third element is that of the dedication of the child to God. This was closely related to the redemption of the firstborn, though Luke gives it an emphasis which is no doubt determined both by his understanding of Jesus' significance and by the account of the dedication of Samuel (1 Sam 1:21–8) whose mother's song has already been used as a pattern for Mary's.

It is in the temple that Simeon, who is presented not merely as the ideal observer of the Jewish covenantal obligations, but also as one who is led by them to look for God's further action, comes and acknowledges Jesus as Christ. In the final song of the infancy narratives he makes what for Luke's gospel is the climactic declaration of the wide embrace of the redemption to be worked through Jesus. In words that reflect the Servant Song of Isaiah 49:5–6, Jesus is proclaimed as having a significance for 'all peoples'. He is a 'light' to reveal God to the nations. God's glory which is to be made known to them is to be seen in the child he holds in his arms whose birth in a manger causes the expectations of the earlier songs to be realized in an unexpected way. The salvation of God is to be achieved, not through naked power, but in the surrender of his Son. That salvation will make for the 'glory' of Israel. Her glory will be real but it will come about only as her expectations are confronted and re-formed. Jesus will cause the 'falling and rising of many in Israel' as he challenges their security and questions their confidence. Many will oppose him, but that will reveal the limited nature of their response to the God who has made them his people. Even Mary, the true Israelite, will be pierced by the sword, not only of suffering, but also of judgement as she herself is called to move into a deeper understanding of the implications of Jesus. To be real, the grounds of the confidence expressed in her song have to be reviewed in the light of the babe who confirms it and makes it possible. Finally, Anna makes her witness to 'all those who were looking for the redemption of Jerusalem'. Jesus is the one through whom it will be accomplished, though again not in the manner that they will be expecting. Jerusalem will reject him and will instead follow a way that will lead to disaster (19:41–4). They will seem forsaken by God, but Anna is a reminder that the disaster is not God's last word: Jesus remains for Jerusalem a sign of hope.

(2:41–52) **Jesus at Age 12** The last episode in the infancy narratives stands rather apart from the rest and forms something of an anticlimax. It fits Luke's intention to write a narrative, however, and seems to be influenced by the episode of the child Samuel, which also forms a bridge between his dedication and the ministry he is to exercise (1 Sam 3:1–14). It has the character of a legend but is used by Luke to point to Jesus' natural authority and home in the temple, a point that he makes in his account of Jesus' final visit to Jerusalem

(19:45–6). Though the teachers in the temple were 'amazed at his understanding and his answers', their wonder has the potential to turn into hostility. For his parents, too, it represents a learning situation. Jesus rebukes them, though the significance of the rebuke is not entirely clear. NRSV margin suggests the most literal meaning, 'Did you not know that I must be about the things of my Father?' 'In the things of' can mean 'in the house of'. Either way, it represents a challenge to acknowledge him for what he is—son of 'my Father'—and to accept that he is not bound to them or bounded by their expectations. Faithful Israelites are challenged by Jesus to raise their sights and to acknowledge that he cannot be constrained by their own preconceived understandings. He must be allowed to transcend these and move out to the Gentiles. Luke is perhaps here thinking of the conflicts in the early church which had difficulty in coming to terms with the Gentile mission. Like Mary and Joseph, the Jewish-Christian community had to learn not to constrict the freedom of the outreach which God's action in Jesus demanded. This freedom did not, however, mean a lessening of ties with the Jewish people. Jesus lived with his parents at Nazareth 'and was obedient to them'.

Jesus in Galilee (3:1–9:50)

In this section of the gospel Luke's narrative takes on a shape and outlook which, in spite of its distinctive aspects, are closely aligned to those of Matthew and Mark. Luke shares with them a common understanding of Jesus' time in Galilee. After his baptism by John and the Baptist's forced removal from the scene, he begins a ministry that proclaims the advent of the kingdom of God and reveals this in exorcisms and miracles. His understanding of this new approach of God to Israel brings him into conflict with religious leaders, though crowds follow him; in the main, however, without having a real understanding of him. He gathers a band of disciples and out of them chooses twelve apostles. These come to appreciate his messianic role without as yet, however, perceiving that it is focused upon a way of suffering that is to climax in a cross.

(3:1–20) **The Ministry of John the Baptist** Once again, Luke sets God's saving work within the context of world history. Though its details are not easily unravelled, its general impact is clear—Jesus' ministry was a real event which brought God's redemption into both the Jewish and the wider world. 'The fifteenth year of...Tiberius' would be 28–29 CE. Pontius Pilate was governor of Judea 26–36 CE, being in the succession of Roman prefects who were appointed to rule Judea after Archelaus was deposed in 6 CE. Herod Antipas, son of Herod the Great, ruled Galilee until 39 CE. 'His brother Philip' was tetrarch (ruler of one of the four parts into which Herod the Great's kingdom had been divided) of the region to the north and east of Galilee into which Jesus made an occasional sortie. Abilene was an area near Damascus. It does not serve as a setting for any part of the gospel story. 'The high-priesthood of Annas and Caiaphas' is more difficult. Joint office was not permitted. Annas was high priest from 6 CE until he was deposed by the Romans, 15 CE. Caiaphas was in office 18–36 CE. Annas appears only in the Lukan and Johannine writings (Acts 4:18; Jn 18:24).

This historical reference firmly includes John within the action of God to which its sonorous tones point. 'The word of God came to John' uses recognized biblical language to enhance its affect (1 Kings 16:1; 18:1). As far as Luke is concerned, the adult John has as important a part to play as the infancy narratives have already suggested. John proclaims and administers a 'baptism of repentance which issues in the forgiveness of sins'. John himself points to the difference between the effects of his baptism and those brought about through the 'one more powerful than I'. Nevertheless, though Luke is quite clear that his has a preparatory role, the importance of that preparation could hardly be greater. Luke alone of the evangelists includes an account of John's ethical teaching. The crowds who come for baptism are to 'bear fruits worthy of repentance' and specific teaching is given to a number of particular groups. Seemingly rather haphazard in their selection, they nevertheless reflect important ethical requirements of groups of people who were particularly open to exploiting their fellow human beings. Those well provided for are to share their resources, tax-collectors are not to abuse their legitimate authority, soldiers are not to exploit their powers. Contentment with their wages means that the land in which they serve will not be further denuded of its produce for their benefit. John is here made to share that strong social concern which is so evident in Luke's gospel. His further importance is that, by putting forward these demands, he gives a place to ethical obligations which might seem to be overlooked in the free acceptance by Jesus of those whose lives are not always put under scrutiny. John here really acts as a forerunner for Jesus and becomes an important part of God's action in him. He fulfils Zechariah's expectation that he would 'turn the hearts of the disobedient to the wisdom of the righteous, to make ready a people prepared for the Lord' (1:17).

(3:21–4:13) The Baptism and Temptation of Jesus Luke's mention—for it cannot be called an account—of Jesus' baptism is surprising and parts company with those of Matthew and Mark whilst sharing some similarity with John (which is also a mention rather than an account). The story of Jesus' having undergone a 'baptism of repentance with a view to remission of sins' obviously caused some embarrassment to the early church (see MT 3:14–15). Yet Luke's reason for his surprising treatment of the story goes deeper than embarrassment for he does not attempt to deny the fact. Jesus is baptised 'when all the people were baptised'. 'The people' is a loaded term for Luke and is used as shorthand for 'God's true people'. Those who underwent John's baptism are identified as God's own people awaiting his redemption; they have been marked out as his. Jesus identifies himself with them: he unites himself to them so that he can incorporate them into the age of the Spirit.

Conzelmann (1960) saw Luke's handling of the baptism as evidence that he was separating out John and Jesus, identifying John with the age of Israel that was now passing away as Jesus brought a new period of God's action into being. Such an explanation, however, ignores not only the infancy narratives but also Luke's account of John's own ministry. John and Jesus are brought together in the closest possible way and as two players, though in no way equal in God's final act of redemption. The reason for this separation of John and Jesus

at this point is rather to serve Luke's Christology. As he does so often, Luke sets significant points of Jesus' career within the context of his prayer. After he is baptized, Jesus prays in an act of surrender and dedication to what his baptism has signified. It is his response to what he has recognized as God's call. The descent of the Spirit and the divine voice of approval come in response to his response. Luke's Christology is one which, emphasizing the divine initiative, points to Jesus' response which is then sealed with God's approval. What is set in motion now will climax in the death and resurrection (Acts 13:34). So the Holy Spirit descends upon him 'in bodily form', that is fully, actively and powerfully. The symbolism of the dove 'remains baffling' (Evans 1955). Most probably it is connected with Gen 1 where the Spirit of God broods over the waters and Gen 8:11 where the dove becomes the harbinger of the covenant God makes with Noah. But these may be guesses born of exasperation. The voice from heaven bestows the divine approval of the course he has entered upon. It probably reflects ideas of Ps 2:7, Isa 42:1–4, and, perhaps, Gen 22:2, 16. A number of MSS of Luke have instead the whole of Ps 2:7. Though the genealogy which follows and which traces Jesus back to Adam may suggest the appropriateness of this reading, Luke elsewhere quotes Ps 2:7 in relation to the resurrection of Jesus (Acts 13:33). It is therefore likely that he himself did not use it of the baptism. Nolland (1989–93) notes that 1:35 would make its idea of a begetting or adoption into sonship inappropriate for this point in time.

It is at this point that Luke includes the genealogy which, in view of the biblical attitude to genealogies and its differences from Matthew's, was designed to be of theological rather than factual significance. Matthew's three groups of fourteen generations is obviously meant to point to a climax in Jesus (Mt 1:17). Luke's does so less obviously. Seventy-seven generations represent eleven weeks, one week short of the twelve which marks finality. Of more significance is the way Luke traces the genealogy back from Jesus via David and Abraham to Adam who is, somewhat surprisingly, designated 'son of God'. Jesus is effecting something for David—the restoration of the people of Israel; for Abraham—the fulfilment of God's promise to him of a wider salvation (Gen 12:3); and for Adam—the restoration of universal sonship which was lost at the Fall. Luke here pictures Jesus as the Second Adam, the restorer of the human race, the means of re-establishing the relationship with God that Adam lost, and the remover of the shackles that had afflicted creation since then (1 Cor 15:20–5; Phil 2:5–11).

Matthew and Mark both have stories of the testing of Jesus by the devil, Mark picturing something of a battle between them, and Matthew telling of a testing of Jesus' Sonship. Luke is closer to Matthew though, like Mark, he has a testing that extends over forty days. The earlier voice from heaven had approved of Jesus' response to his baptism and had proclaimed his Sonship. Now, however, he has that initial reponse tested. He must make a determined entry upon a way that will really establish his Sonship and enable the restoration of the image of God in people which Adam's disobedience had lost. Our usual understanding of the event is made by following the order of temptations found in Matthew. Luke's account, however, has a different order and climaxes in one to jump down from the pinnacle of the temple. The three temptations tempt Jesus to leave the way of the servant on which he has determined, and which the divine voice has approved, and to assert his Sonship in a different way. That to command a stone to become a loaf of bread is to assert his authority and make use of his status, that to worship the devil is to follow the way of the world and exercise his power, that to jump off the temple's pinnacle is to force God's hand, to leave the way of service and humble obedience and go instead for a dramatic demonstration that would compel recognition of his status. All three temptations would have meant his following in the way of Adam for they would all have involved an exercise in self-assertion. The climax for Luke was that to jump from the temple. It was the complete contrast to the course of action which God's call placed upon him—a way of humble obedience and service leading to a cross which was the necessary prelude to exaltation. The third temptation points to the end of Luke's gospel and its account of Jesus' exaltation which installed him in the Sonship which was his. To have succumbed to the third temptation would have destroyed his Sonship; victory over it set him off on the way that established it. Matthew and Mark both record how angels came to minister to Jesus after his defeat of Satan. Luke does not, for the victory is only beginning to be won. He tells how the devil departs from him 'until an opportune time'. That time will be Gethsemane.

(4:16–30) Rejection at Nazareth Luke's story of Jesus' ministry begins with his distinctive account of the rejection at Nazareth, which all commentators on his gospel agree plays a programmatic role for him (cf. Mt 13:53–8; Mk 6:1–6). The infancy narratives have already hinted at the divisions Jesus' ministry would cause in Israel and, by the time Luke wrote, the people of Israel as a whole had rejected not only Jesus, but also the proclamation of the gospel. The problem this caused for the early church is reflected in the NT as a whole but perhaps nowhere with more urgency than in Luke's writings. For him, that rejection was a tragedy but it raised the questions, not merely of why it happened, but also of the nature of God's response. Did the Jewish rejection of God's Son mean a rejection of them by God? Was it even determined by God and did it come about as a result of God's decision to abandon his ancient people in the making of a new people? Was he establishing a new covenant that brought about the end of the old? Luke's writings certainly wrestle with these questions, though they are seen in their full intensity in his story in Acts. They come to the surface from time to time in his gospel and nowhere more obviously so than in this episode which is written up as a commentary upon the event that is recorded in Matthew and Mark (not however without their own different interpretations of the reasons behind the rejection). Luke shapes this story in the light of the events that have happened down to his own time. It expresses his own understanding of the tragedy. However, though commentators on Luke are all agreed on the importance of this episode, there is a wide variety of opinion on what he was actually saying through it. (For an interpretation which is quite different from the one given here, see J. T. Sanders 1987.)

Jesus, in the synagogue on the sabbath day, uses an OT passage to explain both himself and the nature of the salvation that God is bringing through him. The passage is actually a composite one, taken from the LXX version of Isa 61:1–2 into which is fitted a clause, 'to let the oppressed go free', from Isa 58:6. Luke's Jesus presents himself as the fulfilment of Isaiah's Spirit-filled prophetic figure who proclaimed God's eschatological redemption. What Isaiah's prophet anticipated, Jesus brings into being for, not only is he the final proclaimer of the saving act of God, he is actually realizing it in his own preaching and actions: 'Today, this scripture has been fulfilled in your own hearing.' He proclaims 'good news to the poor', that is to those who, marginalized in the present, are looking for God's redemption (see LK 6:20–6). The 'year of the Lord's favour' is here. What was anticipated in the year of Jubilee, which took place (at least in theory) every fifty years, when 'you shall proclaim liberty throughout the land to all its inhabitants' (Lev 25:10), is now becoming a reality. The bonds that oppressed God's people are being broken. It is noteworthy that Luke has Jesus leave Isaiah in the middle of a sentence without including 'the day of vengeance of our God'. As in the infancy narratives, Luke understands Jesus' work primarily as one of redemption.

The people of Nazareth respond favourably; his 'gracious words' impress them. 'Is not this Joseph's son?' expresses approval and local pride. Yet it has within it the seeds of misunderstanding and it is but a limited response. So Jesus quotes a proverb (rather more emphatically than the version found in Matthew and Mark) that points to the inevitability of a city's rejecting the prophetic message of one who is its own (v. 24). Familiarity limits expectations and resents challenge. It presumes upon the relationship and assumes that any message of good news must include natural associates within its sphere (v. 23). It fails to recognize the strength of the challenge that is actually being made. Jesus elaborates on the situation and, in doing so, hardens his stance.

Having spoken of the inevitability of rejection by his own, and therefore of his own inability to perform deeds for them, he uses the instances of Elijah's dealings with the widow of Zarephath (1 Kings 17) and of Elisha's with Naaman (2 Kings 5) to show that earlier prophets worked among outsiders even to the seeming neglect of their own. This elaboration has often been seen as a rejection of his own people in favour of a movement out into the Gentile world. It has been understood as an expression of Luke's belief that the ministry of Jesus meant a new action of God which virtually drew a line under his covenantal dealings with the Jewish people. He was establishing a new Israel that now inherited the earlier promises made to the Jews.

Another reading of the significance Luke saw in the references to Elijah and Elisha is, however, possible and is one which does not make such a sharp departure from the positive attitude to the Jewish people expressed in the infancy narratives: the proverb of v. 24 explains the inevitability of the rejection and, indeed almost justifies it; regrettable though it is, it is an understandable response. The OT incidents are used, not to support a rejection of the local people, but to show that prophets of Israel worked outside her borders, that they were often unsuccessful at home and that their lack of success denied neither their calling nor their continuing commitment to Israel. Jesus had not turned aside from Israel, any more than had Elijah and Elisha. The nation's rejection of him had not resulted in its own rejection—either by him or by the God who stood behind him.

Whatever the implications, the sermon provoked a furious response on the part of the listeners who set out to kill Jesus. His challenge to established certainties made them determined to stone him as a false prophet (Deut 13:1) (v. 29). They were unable to destroy him, however, but he, 'passing throught the midst of them, went on his way'. Here, Luke uses a favourite verb to express Jesus' movement to his goal (9:51; 13:53). The rejection by his own, so far from destroying him, furthers God's purposes.

(4:31–44) A Preliminary Ministry Luke here seems to be following Mark who begins his story of Jesus' ministry with a quick survey of what has been called 'a typical day'. Mark has described the temptation of Jesus in terms of a battle with Satan and this 'typical day' presents him as throwing back the power of the demonic world (Mk 1:21–2:12). Having at Nazareth presented Jesus' work in terms of bringing freedom from oppressive powers, Luke now takes over some of these healings and exorcisms. They show the presence of God's kingdom in Jesus. In the synagogue at Capernaum 'his word is with authority' and this is substantiated by his power over an unclean spirit. The confrontation is real; the demon (or demons, for v. 34 has the plural) uses Jesus' name and mentions his status in a real effort to unmask him and so constrain his power. But Jesus' authority—that of the 'Holy One of God'—overwhelms him. Luke alone adds, 'having done him no harm', for the freeing power of God really is redemptive. The witnesses recognize the marvel and ask, 'What kind of word is this?' 'The word' is a favourite term with Luke, which he uses, as here (vv. 32, 36), to point to the effective power of the gospel.

The healing of Peter's mother-in-law follows and leads into a general ministry of healing and casting out of demons. Luke once more emphasizes that the demons recognize his divine Sonship and acknowledge his power. Jesus, however, would not allow them to speak 'because they knew that he was the Christ' (v. 41). This presents more than an exercise of power; it forbids them from giving a false impression of him. What makes him 'Christ' for people will be an acceptance of his way of the cross. Without that acceptance, any ascription of messiahship would be useless.

At daybreak Jesus leaves that place to go on his way. Crowds try to stop him. They act virtually as the continuation of the temptation. Jesus resists. His exorcisms have to be set in a wider context, that of proclaiming and therefore enabling 'the kingdom of God' (v. 43). The freeing activity of Jesus which this preliminary work has revealed should be seen in the light of his teaching about the nature of the God who does this and of his relationship with humankind. Only then does it reveal the life of the Kingdom. Jesus must go forward and proclaim the Kingdom even if, by living it himself, it leads him to a cross. It was for this reason that he was sent. So, says Luke, 'he continued proclaiming the message in the synagogues of Judea'. The latter word here is to be taken as meaning the 'land of the Jews' as in 1:5; 6:17. It does not suggest an extended ministry in Judea proper.

(5:1–11) Call of the First Disciples Luke postpones the call of the first disciples, which Matthew and Mark describe as the first act of Jesus' ministry, to this point, that is until after Jesus

has had some dealings at least with Peter. He describes it in a scene which has close links with a post-resurrection episode in Jn 21:4–8. The 'lake of Gennesaret' is the sea of Galilee, Gennesaret being the district to the south of Capernaum. The episode centres upon Peter and is really an account of a marvel which becomes for him a moment of disclosure. The unexpected catch of fish points to the nature of the one who made it possible. He discerns the presence of God in Jesus and is moved to make a response that equals that of the prophet Isaiah when in the temple he had his vision of God (Isa 6:5). James and John share in the amazement of those who saw the marvel, though it is not said that they share Peter's discernment. Though the episode, like that in Matthew and Mark (cf. FGS F), describes the call of the inner group of disciples, Luke's narrative focuses upon Peter. For him, Peter has a very special role which is determined, not merely by that which he is given in the general gospel tradition, but also by the part he plays both in the Acts account of the incorporation of Gentiles into the new community and also in the maintenance of its unity (Acts 10–11; 15). Luke claims Peter as the protagonist of his own understanding of the significance of the event of Jesus. He is aware of Peter's weakness but he minimizes it. Jesus does not accept Peter's declaration of messiahship (9:20) but, in the third gospel, Peter does not try to deflect him from his path of suffering. At the last supper, Jesus tells how he has kept Peter from Satan's clutches and that he will be the one to restore his fallen brethren (22:31–4). Luke therefore softens both the failure of the disciples at Gethsemene and the denial of Peter (22:39–46, 54–62). It is to Peter that Jesus appears first after the resurrection (24:34). The original theophany that Peter experiences makes an impression upon him that, in spite of his failings, never leaves him. It enables him to play the leading role which Luke will later ascribe to him.

(5:12–16) Healing of a Leper The next few episodes where Luke is very close to Mark point to the growing tension between Jesus and the religious leaders in the persons of the Pharisees and teachers of the law. The story of the cleansing of the leper emphasizes Jesus' willingness to perform the cure in the face of the leper's own doubt about it. Jesus is bringing precisely that release which the Nazareth sermon promised. It was necessary for a priest to pronounce him free from leprosy before he could take his place again within the community. Lev 13–14 described the sacrificial ritual that effected the restoration. Whatever is meant by 'a testimony to them', Jesus is calling attention to himself. The episode's place at the beginning of a section that points to a growing hostility climaxing at 6:11 suggests that Luke understands Jesus to be already challenging the finality of the Jewish religious institutions. He points the leper into the way of observing the law but from the position of one who already transcends it.

(5:17–26) The Healing of the Paralysed Man In this episode 'the power of the Lord [which] was with him to heal' (a distinctively Lucan phrase) is to face its first real challenge: 'Who can forgive sins but God alone?' The story raises some difficulties. In the first place, it seems to associate a person's sickness with his or her sin, a position which the OT itself, in such writings as the book of Job, questions. Secondly, Jesus seems to be appealing to his ability to cure sickness as proof of his greater claims (v. 24). Finally, v. 24 itself reads badly and suggests some haste—perhaps even, as some have suggested, a joining up of two sources. Why, when asked to heal, does Jesus say, 'Your sins are forgiven'? The most likely explanation seems to be that he was encouraging those who were requesting his help to raise their sights and to put the physical need within the wider context of their whole relationship with God. Jesus had earlier left the crowds when they threatened to overwhelm him and confine his mission (4:42–4). Here, he was meeting the need but was setting it in a larger framework. He proclaimed a restoration of a relationship with God that included physical redemption but was not exhausted by it. Physical healing came from the restoration of the kingdom of God. The physical ills of the world pointed to the restriction of God's sway. The prophet Isaiah looked forward to the day when wholeness and harmony would be restored (Isa 35:3–10).

The scribes and the Pharisees recognize Jesus' action and his interpretation of it as a claim to be acting on behalf of God. Strictly, of course, he was saying that God was forgiving the man, but the point was that he was acting with the authority of one who had the mind of God and could speak for him. Jesus is here for the first time called 'Son of Man', his favourite self-designation. Just what he meant by it, however, has produced a lively and still inconclusive debate. Discussion of it would take us far outside the confines of this commentary. More important for our purpose is the Synoptic Gospels' own understanding of it in which Luke shares. Probably influenced by Dan 7:13, it sees Jesus as an earthly figure, authoritative yet unacknowledged, suffering, vindicated, and exalted to heaven from where he will return in glory. Luke emphasizes the amazement of the bystanders, their 'glorifying God', and their awe. For him, the story makes a true witness to the person of Jesus.

(5:27–32) Jesus and Levi Jesus now calls Levi to join his inner group of disciples. He is 'a tax-collector', that is, one of a group of minor officials who were employed to collect indirect taxes, mainly tolls. Working for an alien power and widely extortionate, they were regarded with hostility and were marginalized. Luke has Jesus take a special interest in this group. Levi gives a great banquet for Jesus in his house even after Luke has emphasized that he had 'left everything'. The Pharisees and their scribes complain, for tax-collectors and sinners were those who had opted out of the covenantal people of God; by living outside the Mosaic law, they had excluded themselves from any share in God's future rule. A meal, of course, had sacral significance and Luke sees its function as an anticipation of meals in the kingdom of God. In this perception, he was probably correctly interpreting Jesus' own understanding of his actions. Here, Jesus points to his particular concern to call those whose lives are judged unhealthy by current religious requirements. Luke alone adds 'to repentance'. Though his gospel is one which emphasizes the divine initiative in Jesus and the outreach of God's grace, he is aware that this outlook could lead to an abandoning of ethical principles and play down the need for a response. He therefore points out that Jesus' outreach did lead to repentance (cf. 15:7, 10).

(5:33–9) New and Old Having shown God's new approach in Jesus and the challenge this made to the Jewish religious tradition, this section emphasizes the move forward that was required if it was to be accepted. New material could not be made to fit in with the old: to use it as a patch to complete the old would not work, for not only would it tear the new garment and in effect destroy it, but it would also not match the old. Likewise, new wine needed new bottles. For all his understanding of God's approach in Jesus as the climax of what he had done in Israel, Luke was aware of its radicality and of the jump that was required if members of the covenantal people were to receive it. v. 39, which is peculiar to him, gives his reason for the Jewish failure to respond to Jesus' new challenge.

(6:1–11) Sabbath Controversy Luke writes up these two stories, to be found also in Mark and Matthew, in a way that, though having Jesus less critical of the sabbath than he is in Mk 2:27, nevertheless presents him firmly as the sabbath's Lord. Jesus' disciples break the sabbath law, not only by reaping, but also (in Luke only) by threshing. When 'some' (a Lucan addition that mellows the story's opposition to the Pharisees) object, Jesus reminds them that David himself broke the law (though not the sabbath law) when his followers as well as he were hungry. Luke (unlike Matthew and Mark) adds nothing else but goes straight to what was for him the significance of the story: 'The Son of Man is Lord of the Sabbath'. David showed his superiority to the law: the son of David who is Son of Man, being greater, has an even greater superiority. A further story strengthens the point. Jesus on a sabbath teaches in the synagogue when a man with a withered hand is present. In the light of the previous story, scribes and Pharisees watch to see whether he will compound his refusal to be bound by the law's requirements. He refuses to be intimidated by them. His action raises one further dimension of his attitude to the law. Was the sabbath designed for the benefit of humankind or for its oppression? Admittedly, his question, 'to save life or to destroy...?' (v. 9), puts the alternatives over-sharply and in a way that goes beyond the particular issue. Nevertheless, it makes the point clear and, though maintaining Jesus' freedom concerning the sabbath, makes his action one neither of blatant disregard nor of naked power. The result, however, is their fury and a determination to confront Jesus.

(6:12–49) Jesus' Sermon It is at this point, when opposition is forming and confrontation becomes a certainty, that Luke places his account of Jesus' call of the twelve and follows it immediately with his sermon given to 'a great crowd of disciples' in the presence of a 'great multitude of people' from all over the area. As on other important occasions, Jesus spends the night in prayer. From his disciples, he chooses twelve. Luke's list differs from those of Matthew and Mark in that he has 'Judas son of James' in place of Thaddeus and describes Simon the Cananaean as 'the Zealot'. This term probably refers to a religious rather than a political zeal. Whereas Matthew and Mark say that Jesus chose the twelve in order to send them out to preach and heal, Luke records no reason for the choice. Instead he simply says, 'He chose twelve of them, whom he also named apostles'. For Luke, the Twelve are not merely a distinct group as in Matthew and Mark, their distinctiveness is found in their being 'apostles', a title which he limits to them. Their importance lies not in what they do but in what they are, namely the foundation pillars of the restored, eschatological Israel that Jesus is bringing into being. So, like Moses before him (Ex 24:1, 3, 12–14), Jesus goes to the mountain, takes with him the leaders of Israel, and comes down to form the people of God. The twelve stand alongside him, witnessing to the nature of the community that is being brought into being as he delivers a sermon that defines its essence. The sermon as Luke gives it has long suffered in comparison with Matthew's (vv. 5–7). The Sermon on the Mount presents a demand for an ethical righteousness the radical nature of which far exceeds that of the law. The demands of Luke's sermon are equally radical but are more focused. They home in upon the need to recognize the nature of the community that Jesus is calling into being and therefore upon the necessity for members of it to respond with mutual love, toleration, and acceptance. The radical demands are seen, not in a high moral tone, but in the overriding concern for love (vv. 27–36), a non-judgemental attitude (vv. 37–42), a life of integrity (vv. 43–5), and a total response to Jesus' call (vv. 46–9).

The Beatitudes which introduce it therefore have a different stance from those found in Matthew (cf. FGS G). Whereas his provide a standard after which members of his community can strive, Luke's state the nature of the new community. They address the disciples directly (NB the second person) as the poor, the hungry, the weepers, and the excluded. Not all are in fact these, though many within the community are. All however are to share in the attitude that characterizes these groups—their looking for God's future and their lack of satisfaction with the present. They look for the Kingdom to redress the inequalities of the present. In the OT the poor are seen as the special concern of God, and the authors of the Psalms of lament can picture themselves as poor in attitude and so as looking for God's vindication (40:17; 86:1). People like these are to be deemed 'blessed' for God can and will vindicate them.

The converse of this is that the rich, the full, the satisfied, and the easily accepted are challenged and made to face the consequences of their lot. This leads to a self-satisfaction and self-sufficiency which is not merely in grave danger of shutting them off from the grace of God but which also encourages a manipulation of their fellow human beings. At a number of points in his gospel, Luke will reveal his strong suspicion of riches and the challenge he believes they present to would-be disciples (14:33; 16:1–15, 19–31; 18:18–30).

Luke's version of Jesus' foundation sermon, then, challenges the community he is bringing into being to be one which, seeing itself as the eschatological people of God, lives out of grace and in hope of God's redemption. It is to be a sign of that hope. Whereas Leviticus called upon Israel to reflect God's holiness which it saw as the defining character of God (Lev 19:2), and Matthew called his community to a perfection which reflected God's own (Mt 5:48), Luke's Jesus calls rather for mercy because it is that which for him lies at the heart of God. The sermon does not judge a section of the community as does Matthew's (Mt 7:21) but rather somewhat wistfully has Jesus exclaim to all: 'Why do you call me "Lord, Lord", and not do what I say?' Luke does not share Matthew's concern to relate the ethical standards required by Jesus to those demanded by the Law (see MT 5–7). He pictures a community formed by a response to the grace of God revealed in Jesus and

one which lives out of the life of the Kingdom which Jesus established and which the community's life itself anticipates. The sermon's demands are therefore radical. The disciples are to become like their master (v. 40): they are not to try to outdo his non-judgemental attitude. Their good fruit must reflect a 'good treasure of the heart'. The true disciple of the Lord hears his call and acts upon it (cf. 8:15).

(7:1–10) The Centurion's Slave This episode, not in Mark, is found also in Mt 8:5–13 (cf. FGS H). Comparison of the two accounts brings out Luke's particular perspective. In his gospel the centurion does not meet Jesus but instead sends elders of the Jews to intercede on his behalf. Their plea for him is based on the fact that he was favourably disposed to the Jewish people and that he was instrumental in the building of this group's synagogue. He was a Gentile, perhaps a Roman officer who, in Galilee, would be in the service of Herod Antipas. He was probably a God-fearer who, though linking himself to the Jewish community and joining in some part of its life, being uncircumcized remained an alien and outside the covenantal people. Jesus accedes to the Jews' request and begins to go with them to the centurion's house. On their way, however, the centurion sends friends to Jesus to make two points on his behalf. The centurion can make no claims on Jesus; that is why he would not presume even to approach him. Even now, he cannot expect him to enter his house. But, secondly, as a man both under authority and also exercising authority, he recognizes the nature of the authority that belongs to Jesus. A word from him is all that is required. That is all he dare ask, but it is enough. Jesus marvels at his faith and says for all to hear, 'Not even in Israel have I found such faith.' The difference from Matthew's version of Jesus' wonder makes clear the significance Luke sees in the story. Mt 8:10, 'in no one in Israel have I found such faith', can be heard as pointing to a lack of faith in Israel, whereas Luke's version rather emphasizes the exceptional nature of the centurion's. The centurion's slave is healed as a result of Jewish faith which has actually made the centurion's own faith possible. In the end, however, that of the centurion outstrips the faith shown by the Jews. His lack of all claims enables the wonder of Jesus' full redemptive power to be freed. The healing takes place from a distance.

(7:11–17) The Raising of a Widow's Son Only in Luke, this story seems to owe its position here to Jesus' appeal in 7:22 to his raising of the dead. The story has strong overtones of Elijah's raising of the widow's son in 1 Kings 17:17–24 and has echoes in Peter's raising of Tabitha in Acts 9:36–42. For Luke, Jesus, like John before him, is foreshadowed by Elijah, the archetype of OT prophecy, as he is by Moses. Luke uses 'The Lord' frequently in his references to Jesus when they, as here, point to his role as Christians understand it. Whilst acting in the past, he is revealed as the community's source and strength, and the one who is the object of its devotion. As Lord, Jesus brings the weeping of the woman to an end (6:21). 'Fear' is the response of awe in the presence of the numinous. They 'glorify God', a phrase that Luke uses to introduce significant responses to the actions of Jesus (2:20; 13:13; 23:47). Jesus for Luke is 'a great prophet', indeed the eschatological prophet. In him, 'God has looked favourably on his people'. The same verb is used in Zechariah's song (1:68) to speak of

God's redemption of his people. The true in Israel recognize him.

(7:18–35) Jesus and John Luke's infancy narratives have brought Jesus and John together in the closest possible relationship but have, at the same time, shown how the redemption Jesus brings is in some tension with the OT expectations that John expresses. Baptized by John, Jesus sets out on a course of action that is less obvious than John might have expected. He has embraced a way of surrender and, in his sitting loose to the law, has reached out in a manner that appears to do less than justice to John's prophecy of one with a 'winnowing-fork in his hand' (3:17). John therefore sends two of his disciples to ask whether Jesus really is the one who fulfils the OT hopes and whether in him the final action of God is being realized. In v. 21 Luke points out the wonders that Jesus 'at that time' had been doing. The basis for his response to John is secure. So Jesus appeals to his actions in a list that freely quotes from Isa 35:5–6 and 61:1. For those who have eyes to see, they make his case. v. 23 contains a challenge to, and perhaps a criticism of John. The presence of Jesus demands a willingness to have established beliefs questioned.

Jesus now talks to the crowds about John and his relationship to himself. He begins with a compliment. When they went to hear John, they knew he was not one who would bend with the wind or be ensnared by the power or luxuries of the court. Luke has already told his readers that John had been wrongly put in prison by Herod because he had rebuked him for the evil he was doing (3:18–20). Had they gone out to see a prophet? Jesus gives John a higher status in God's plans than that. He applies to him a mixed OT quotation from Ex 23:20 and Mal 3:1 which, by a slight adaptation of pronouns, makes John the immediate forerunner of himself. He brings this to a climax with a further compliment which is, nevertheless, something of a backhanded one. No one in the world has arisen greater than John, 'yet the least in the kingdom of God is greater than he'. As it stands, this says that John is as yet outside the Kingdom. He still works from within the old expectations. He has not yet come to appreciate the radical challenge Jesus brings to these and the new perspectives from which they have to be viewed. However, this interpretation has been challenged ever since the time of Tertullian. Because the Greek in v. 28 uses comparatives ('lesser', 'greater'), the saying has been taken to refer only to Jesus and John and to their places in the Kingdom. Jesus is younger than John, perhaps originally a disciple of John, perhaps even a servant figure unlike John. He is nevertheless the greater in the Kingdom, though this interpretation would not suggest that John himself was not yet in the Kingdom. This, however, is not the most likely interpretation of the usual NT usage. John has not embraced the outlook of the Kingdom and as yet remains outside it. Those who have acknowledged it are already living within its embrace, out of its grace. They await its future revelation. For John, that embrace awaits the future (13:28).

The part of John in God's redemptive act, however, is emphasized in Luke's comment (vv. 29–30). 'All the people', that is those true Jews who had come to respond to Jesus and so be included within God's redeeming action, 'acknowledged the justice of God', his work of redemption that began through

John's baptism that prepared them for their acceptance of Jesus. Those who were to reject Jesus were also the ones who rejected John.

Jesus acknowledges John's part by comparing his contemporaries to children at play. They are like those who fail to respond to all efforts to entice them to take part, whether it be a call to mourn or dance. John challenged them with the demands of God and they accused him of misanthropy. Jesus, on the other hand, presented them with the freeing grace of God and they cast him as a libertine. They will not respond to the challenge found in either proclamation. The section finishes with v. 35 which acts as a counterbalance to the rejection of which vv. 31–4 speak. 'Wisdom' in the OT came (alongside Spirit and Word) to be personified as the expression of God's outreach to humankind in which he made himself known and united them to himself (Prov 8; Wis 7). This verse takes up this thought. God's way is 'vindicated' (the same Gk. verb is used in v. 29), that is acknowledged and praised by all those who through the ministries of John and Jesus have experienced God's embrace and so have recognized his work both in them and in themselves.

(7:36–50) Jesus and the Woman who was a Sinner All four gospels tell of Jesus' anointing by a woman (Mt 26:6–13; Mk 14:3–9; Jn 12:1–8) though all three others link the anointing to Jesus' passion and record a complaint about the waste of money. Whereas Matthew and Mark have an anointing of Jesus' head, Luke, like John, tells of the anointing of his feet. Only Luke speaks of the woman as a 'sinner'. The significance Luke sees in the story depends on the actual meaning of a number of verses which are not easily interpreted. Simon, a Pharisee, invites Jesus to a meal; a woman comes into the room, as was possible on semi-public occasions, bathes his feet with her tears and dries them with her hair. She publicly kisses his feet and anoints them with ointment in an extravagant display of affection. Simon feels that Jesus' acceptance of such affection from one who was a sinner was not consistent with a prophet come from God. Jesus replies by telling a parable of two debtors which makes the point that one who is forgiven much is likely to respond more warmly than one who is forgiven little. So much is clear. The difficulty is in determining how it applies to the two characters. The woman is demonstrating her love. Is this because she has already been forgiven which is what the parable would imply? 'The woman's actions can only be accounted for by reference to something the story does not itself contain' (Evans 1990). On the other hand, v. 47, on a first reading at any rate, does not appear to support this but rather suggests that she has been forgiven because of her love. This is how RSV translates the verse. More recent translations, assuming a consistency in the story as a whole, take the Greek *hoti* to mean, not 'because' but 'with the result that'. So, REB translates, 'Her great love proves that her many sins have been forgiven.' v. 48 then proclaims her forgiveness which such a translation assumes has already been pronounced to her.

Perhaps however we are trying to force into a time sequence something that cannot be so easily ordered. The woman hears of Jesus and of his proclamation of the outreaching redemption of God. God's recreating acknowledgement of the outsiders is being enacted in him, the one who accepts the title of 'the friend of tax-collectors and sinners'. She responds with love and a warmth which is accepted. The story says nothing about her penitence in any formal sense and to assume this is to assume too much. What she brings is rather a response to a lack of condemnation, to an outreach, to a recognition. It is that response of love that Jesus acknowledges, accepts, and meets with a declaration that God has forgiven her. 'The woman does not love because she has been forgiven, but vice versa' (Lampe 1962). She loves, because in Jesus she meets with acceptance. In turn, her love receives the forgiveness for which he stands.

The parable is addressed to Simon and is looking at them both from Jesus' own point of view whilst engaging with Simon's own stance. It is a condemnation of his judgemental attitude and of his lack of openness. Is it suggesting more and saying that he was discourteous to Jesus? On the whole, this is unlikely. Though the lack of provision for the washing of feet is 'surprising' (Evans 1990) the other omissions would seem to be additional courtesies rather than requirements of the host. The story does not suggest that Jesus was singled out from the other guests; that would have meant a hostility that Simon's address to Jesus (v. 40) does not imply. The contrasts are caused by the woman's actions rather than by Simon's discourtesies. What the contrast emphasizes is Simon's lack of response to Jesus and his message of the gracious approach of God. Simon feels no great need but is rather, if not content, then at least comfortable with the position at which he has arrived. Comparatively, he does need to be forgiven little, but it is that little need that has made him miss out on Jesus' message. He actually needs to learn from the incident.

(8:1–21) Proclaiming the Good News After a fairly static period, Jesus now resumes his itinerant role of proclaiming the good news of the kingdom of God (cf. 4:43; 9:6). The Twelve are with him and some women 'who had been cured of evil spirits and infirmities'. They had been psychologically and physically distressed. Mk 15:41 mentions a group of women who had come to Jerusalem from Galilee with Jesus. Luke brings the mention forward to this point so as to link them with the Twelve in their accompanying Jesus. Mary Magdalene is mentioned first, probably because of her role at the tomb which is noticed in all four gospels. Jesus had cast out 'seven demons' from her—a witness to the severe nature of her illness, though not a pointer to any immorality; she is not to be brought into connection with the woman of the previous episode. Joanna the wife of Herod's steward Chuza, a woman of some social standing, is also mentioned at the tomb. Susanna is not found elsewhere. With other women, they provided for Jesus and the Twelve out of their resources. Women of means are found frequently in Acts. The most significant instance is the mention of Lydia who in Acts 16:15 acted as host for Paul and his companions at Philippi in the first of the 'we' passages in Acts. It is not beyond the bounds of possibility that Luke himself lodged there and perhaps even stayed there after the rest of the party had left (Acts 20:6). Luke may have been looking at the part women played in the ministry of Jesus in terms of his own later experience. He is anxious to point to their presence at the cross (23:49), the burial (23:55), the empty tomb (24:10), and when the community waits for the gift of the Spirit (Acts 1:14). He has no appearance of the risen Jesus to them as does Mt 27:9 and Jn 20:18, but this would seem to be because of his concern to have Peter be the first witness of the risen Lord (24:34).

It is in this setting of Jesus' preaching ministry that Luke places the parable of the sower which for him, as for the other synoptic evangelists, becomes an image of the varied success of the preaching, not only of Jesus, but also of the early church. Jesus tells a parable about a sower and his method of sowing which actually appears to sow seed where there can be no hope of a harvest. A waste of much seed becomes inevitable because of the nature of the ground on which it is allowed to fall. The distinctive feature of Luke's parable when it is compared with the versions given in Mt 13:3–9 and Mk 4:3–9 is his statement that all the good seed yielded 'a hundred fold'. All his good seed produces, if not a spectacular harvest, then at least a bumper one. The reason for this becomes clear in his version of the allegorical interpretation. Before that, however, he includes, as do the other evangelists, a statement in which Jesus is heard giving his reason for the use of parables. It is 'so that looking they may not perceive, and listening they may not understand'. Though this softens Mark's parallel statement (Mk 4:11–12), it shares something of his belief that Jesus' parables were meant to discriminate, to cause discernment in some and to harden others. Jesus' parables were not easy (to imagine they are rather helpful teaching aids is to do them total disservice), and the early church tended to find their challenge difficult to comprehend. This led them to think that they were deliberately obscure and that the key which they used to unlock them was meant for only the chosen few. It is usually accepted that the interpretation of the parable of the sower that follows (vv. 11–15) owes more to the early church than to Jesus himself. Whereas the parable itself is about a sower, the interpretation concentrates not upon him (for he is not even mentioned) but upon the seeds, or rather upon the soils into which the seeds fall. The soils become the hearers, and their attitudes that are described are used to account for the success or failure of the seeds. Most of the seeds are destroyed by the various deficiencies of the soils. Yet the seeds as a whole do not fail. The good soil becomes a symbol for those who exhibit the qualities that the Gentile Luke can appreciate (v. 15). These bear fruit a hundredfold. Luke, in Acts, will go on to show how 'the word of the Lord grew mightily and prevailed' (Acts 19:20). vv. 16 and 17 promise that future. v. 18 warns of the need to hear 'with patient endurance' and discrimination.

The final episode in the section introduces Jesus' mother and brothers. They come seeking him. When Jesus is told of their presence he answers in a way that, unlike Mk 3:31–5, does not exclude them from the relationship but extends it. All those who 'hear the word of God and do it' are to be accounted Jesus' mother and brothers. Translations of the saying that make Jesus claim that his natural relations are the ones who are already doing this depend upon a somewhat forced reading of the Greek (Fitzmyer 1989). Mary and Jesus' brothers are, however, in Acts (1:14) among the earliest disciples waiting for the gift of the Spirit. The last episode in the infancy narratives suggests that Mary too had to face a learning experience. This was realized in her response to the life, death, and resurrection of her son. In this way she lived up to the infancy narratives' picture of her as the ideal disciple.

(8:22–56) Redeeming Works All three Synoptics tell of Jesus stilling the storm (Mt 8:23–7; Mk 4:35–41). It is the sign of Jesus' power over 'the deep', which was for them the ultimate symbol of chaos and the home of forces alien to God. Gen 1:2 told how the Spirit of God tamed the waters at creation, whilst Ps 89:10 made use of the old myth that saw the sea as the abode of the monster of chaos, Rahab. Isa 51:9 associates the same myth with God's victory over the sea at the Exodus. Moses and Elijah were associated with command over seas and rivers (Ex 14; 2 Kings 2:8). Jesus, as God's final act of redemption, now reveals his total power over the deep. All three evangelists regard the action as a point of disclosure to the disciples. In Mark, they awake Jesus with rough words; in Matthew they treat him with great respect. Luke takes something of a middle position; Jesus' rebuke is delivered after he stills the storm and their response is made in its light.

Jesus now arrives 'at the country of the Gerasenes' on the other side of the lake from Galilee. The actual name of the place varies in different MSS and all present problems. The really important thing is that the event takes place in Gentile territory. For Luke, who usually avoids having Jesus make contact with Gentiles, it provides a concrete example of an anticipation of the Gentile mission at which he has hinted so strongly and which he will go on to record in Acts. The story should not be pressed for answers to modern questions that were outside the concerns of its tellers who recount it in terms of symbols that were highly significant for them. The tormented man calls Jesus 'Son of the Most High God', a pagan title that is also used by a spirit-possessed slave girl at Philippi (Acts 16:17). Jesus exercises a power over the demon that makes him reveal his name, 'Legion'. A legion was a unit in the Roman army of something around 6,000 men. The use of the term witnesses to the severity of the possession. The state of the man, his being held in chains and shackles, may well suggest something of the burden of the Roman occupation. The story may have been handed down with the intention of associating Jesus' throwing out of demonic powers with the expectation of the overthrow of the equally oppressive political authorities. The local citizens may well have been understood by Luke as asking Jesus to leave their area because they regarded him as a threat to stability. This would be seen by Luke as one with the situation that he describes frequently in Acts (16:39; 17:14; 20:1).

Jews regarded pigs as unclean, so the request of the demons to be allowed to enter them was one of self-preservation. However, their plea, though accepted, was of little use. The pigs rush down to the sea and the demons are pushed back into the abyss. The previous episode showed that this was not outside the control of Jesus. Jesus does not allow the healed man to go with him. In contrast to his not infrequent commands to silence, Jesus tells him to return and spread 'how much God has done for you'. It was not the 'Most High God' whom Jesus served but the God of the Jews. The Gentile mission had in effect begun.

This healing of a Gentile is quickly followed by an even greater wonder performed for a Jew, 'a leader of the syna-gogue'. Within that story, however, Luke, as Matthew and Mark, inserts the episode of the healing of the woman with a haemorrhage. Lev 15:25–30 tells how such a tribulation was not merely a physical misfortune, but that it virtually excluded her from her place within the people of God. Anyone touched by such a person was regarded as unclean. Jesus notices that 'power had gone out from me'. This has sometimes suggested to commentators that Luke still worked within the idea of Hellenistic magic that regarded Jesus as possessing a kind of impersonal force that was not entirely under his control (Hull 1974) (cf. 5:17). It should perhaps rather be seen as his oneness with God that becomes a channel of God's outreach to people. Whereas in the OT what was conveyed was the holiness of God that overwhelmed those with whom it made contact (2 Sam 6:6–11), it was the redeeming outreach of God that was bestowed. Luke is perhaps less influenced here by Hellenistic magic than by the admittedly impersonal ideas of God and the Spirit that play a large part in the OT. Jesus' word to the woman raises the impersonal to the level of faith, and the Greek shows that the wholeness that is given, 'made you well', is interpreted at the deeper level of salvation, 'has saved you' (cf. 17:19).

Before he gets to the house, news is brought that the child had died but, when he arrives, he says, 'She is not dead, but sleeping.' Though sleep is a familiar biblical expression for death, so that this passage can be used as a pointer to a Christian understanding of death in much the way that the Johannine story of the raising of Lazarus can be so used (Jn 11), Jesus' words are recounted, not for this, but to point to the nature of the miracle he works. It is a restoration of the girl to life from death. To make this clear, Luke adds the reason for their laughter at him: 'knowing that she was dead'. Whether v. 55, 'Her spirit returned, and she got up at once', reflects the idea of the survival of the soul or spirit through death, or whether it does no more than use 1 Kings 17:22 is not easy to say. Perhaps, in view of 23:43, it is the former. Luke, any more than the rest of the NT, has no clearly worked out pattern of belief about the afterlife. The message of the story is that Jesus brings life from death.

(9:1–50) Climax in Galilee The climax of Jesus' time in Galilee begins with the sending out of the Twelve which, though close to Mark's account (6:7–13), differs at significant points. Luke, unlike Mark but like Mt 10:10, has Jesus refuse them the use of staff or sandals (22:35). All three evangelists record Jesus' command to extreme simplicity, which goes beyond both the normal requirements of a journey and the dress of the cynic wandering preachers which the evangelists would have encountered in the cities of the Roman empire. Whether Jesus saw both himself and his travelling disciples in terms of these cynic preachers (Crossan 1991) is disputed. The extreme simplicity is most likely a contrast even with them and reflects rather his belief in the challenge and nearness of the kingdom of God. Luke differs more significantly from Mark over the contents of the mission. For Mark, they proclaim that all should repent, and therefore repeat what he understands to be at the heart of Jesus' own preaching (1:15). Luke, who does not have this summary, tells rather of Jesus' proclaiming the good news of the kingdom of God (4:43; 8:1; 9:11), and it is this that the disciples also preach. Repentance, though important for Luke (4:32; 15:7), seems to arise out of redemption rather than being understood as a condition of it (7:47). He does not have Mark's statement that Jesus sent them out two by two (6:7), but keeps that for the mission of the seventy (10:1). This seems to be because, unlike Matthew and Mark, he does not see the mission of the Twelve as a pattern for later work which he reserves rather for his account of the seventy. For Luke, the twelve are a distinct group whose work is not extended into that of later disciples.

Mark at this point has an extended account of the death of John the Baptist which Luke does not take over. Luke will later omit an account of Paul's death and, though he will tell of Stephen's, he will emphasize, not that, but the preaching which is his primary witness (Acts 7:55). He will not isolate the death of Jesus as the moment of redemption (see LK 23:32–48). He records Herod's perplexity, however, for it makes a fitting prelude to vv. 18–20. Herod himself (unlike Mk 6:16), is not said to believe that Jesus is John risen from the dead. He rather contrasts Jesus with John and wishes to see him (cf. 23:8 and see also Acts 26:27–32).

The return of the disciples, as in Mark, leads into the story of the feeding of the five thousand. Moses had fed the Israelites in the desert (Ex 16; Num 10) and Elisha had fed 'the people' enabling them to have more than they required (2 Kings 4:42–4). Jesus as the fulfilment of both these prophets would perform a feeding the wonder of which would exceed theirs. At the heart of the story is the dialogue between him and the Twelve. Their perplexity at Jesus' command, 'You give them something to eat', shows that they have not yet come to appreciate his real nature. Luke uses the miracle as a point of disclosure for the disciples. For him, it is the event that enables their growing perception of Jesus to be realized and brought to the level where Peter can make his declaration of Jesus' messiahship (9:20). It becomes an anticipation of the messianic banquet. Like all the evangelists, he seems to be viewing Jesus' actions as having eucharistic overtones though the verbs he uses to describe Jesus, words over the bread and fish do not make this explicit.

Luke's story of the five thousand, unlike those of the other evangelists, leads immediately into Peter's acknowledgment of Jesus as Messiah. For him, there is a strong connection between the two events. Mark has a whole series of stories, including another feeding miracle, between the two and in this he is followed by Matthew. Luke, if as seems most likely he is using Mark as his primary source, has chosen to leave them out. They show a Gentile concern which he will not pursue until his second volume, deal with a question of eating meats which he will resolve in Acts 15, and reveal the disciples in a light less favourable than his own. Once more, as on important occasions, Jesus is at prayer. Mark names the place as Caesarea-Philippi. Luke omits this for he would not have regarded Gentile territory as a suitable context for what was in the first instance a necessary and essentially Jewish recognition. The responses of the crowds are inadequate for, in defining Jesus in terms of a return of John, Elijah, or one other of the prophets, they are not merely undervaluing him but are seeking to keep him and the work of God through him within the terms of their own expectations. Though a less hostile response than that of the religious leaders, it ultimately amounts to the same thing (11:14) and shows an equal

failure to move forward into the new outlook that Jesus is bringing. Jesus then asks the disciples to express their own perception of him and their level of commitment. Peter responds, 'The Christ of God.' All three evangelists report Peter's response in terms that express either their own understanding or that of their church (Mt 16:16; Mk 8:29). Luke's form expresses his own belief that Jesus' messiahship fulfils OT expectations when these are rightly understood (24:25), and emphasizes his function as the agent of God. Jesus issues a stern command to silence for, though the confession is right as far as it goes, the content of Jesus' messiahship has to be filled with suffering. It is that alone that is to make it a reality.

There now follows (vv. 21–7) the first of three predictions of the passion (9:43–5; 18:31–4). Jesus says that the Son of Man must be rejected, killed, and 'on the third day be raised'. He must get the disciples to understand the necessity for his death, and to believe that this will lead to his vindication by God. This prediction is of supreme importance for all the evangelists and reflects a belief that was fundamental to the early church (1 Cor 15:3–4). The cross made the resurrection possible and was therefore seen as part of the determined plan of God. It was early given saving significance. How far Jesus himself was actually conscious of the necessity of his death is disputed. The Gethsemane scene suggests that he was not necessarily certain of its inevitability. That he was aware from the beginning that his task was very different from what was expected of a messianic figure, and that his understanding of God's redemption made a clash with Jewish religious susceptibilities inevitable, meant that his rejection and death were a real possibility. But that he went up to Jerusalem deliberately in order to die is much less certain (Moule 1977). The gospels say that the empty tomb did not quickly lead to an understanding that Jesus was raised, and this suggests that his prophecy of a resurrection was far less unambiguous than these passages maintain. These passion predictions have certainly been shaped by the early church, and it is hard to know just how far that shaping extends.

Jesus' revelation of the path of suffering for himself is followed immediately by a call to his disciples to follow the same way. They are to 'deny themselves', the word used of Peter's denial of Jesus, and to take up the cross 'daily'. The last word is a Lukan addition and is sometimes thought to play down the absolute demand that the challenge might otherwise make. Luke demands a daily pursuit of the way that led Jesus to the cross rather than a once for all abandoning of the world. It reflects his more positive approach to the world and also his refusal to make Jesus' own cross into a point of atonement. For him, it is rather one with, though the climax of, his whole life which led to it and which thereby becomes not merely the means of resurrection, but also the means of God's redemption. Luke's version of the command is not a watering down of its absoluteness; it is rather a demand to be remade daily in the image of Christ. It reflects just that concern for daily life that his addition of the same phrase to the bread petition of the Lord's prayer makes obvious (11:2).

The strong demand is justified by an eschatological urgency. Those who refuse to line up with Jesus and his words will find themselves refused by him 'when he comes in his glory'. This verse can hardly refer to anything other than the parousia for it points to the revelation of a glory that had previously been established at his exaltation (24:26). v. 27 brings this urgency to a climax. Unfortunately, the meaning of that climax is not entirely clear. Mk 9:1 speaks of the Kingdom's coming 'with power' and Mt 16:28 suggests that he read this as a reference to the parousia. Luke's omission of 'with power' has sometimes been taken as suggesting that he changed the reference to make it apply, not to the parousia, but to the gift of the Spirit or the growth of the church. However, this is unlikely. Luke expressly associates the Spirit and the mission he enables with 'power' (24:49), and it is precisely this powerful reality of the present Kingdom that makes Luke drop 'with power' from his reference to the return of Jesus. The Kingdom in power does not await the parousia for its establishment. Already established in heaven, the return of Jesus will reveal its reality on earth (see LK 17:21). Luke, in common with the vast majority of early Christians, anticipated the speedy return of Jesus. Whether this represents a misunderstanding of Jesus' own outlook is a matter that takes us beyond the limitations of this commentary (see Borg 1994; Allison, 1998).

Luke (like Matthew and Mark) links these sayings to the transfiguration by a time reference that is unique in the gospels outside the passion narrative. Some have suggested that this is because the evangelists believed that the promise of v. 27 is fulfilled in its mysterious happening. This, however, is wholly unlikely. Luke presents the transfiguration not as the fulfilment of a promise, but as the anticipation of something greater. The time link is to relate it firmly both to the warning of imminent suffering and to the promise that out of it will come a future glory. The transfiguration becomes a guarantee of that. Luke has 'about eight days after these sayings' in place of Mark's 'after six days'. This may mean little more than a different way of calculating time and like Mark would seem to have Ex 24:15–18 in mind. It may also be mindful of Lev 9:1, a passage that, also concerned with the glory of God, speaks of that glory appearing to Aaron. Luke emphasizes the impact the event has upon the disciples. They 'saw his glory' (v. 32, cf. Lev 9:6) and actually 'entered the cloud' (v. 34). Peter's response, though not a valid one, is regarded as less arbitrary than it is said to be in Mark. His attempt to perpetuate the vision, which is what his request to make 'dwellings' suggests, is less derided than in Mark.

Luke puts emphasis upon the appearance of Moses and Elijah. They also (only in Luke) appear 'in glory'. These two have a strong typological significance for him because, not only were they prophets who suffered greatly in bringing God's redemption to Israel, but Jewish tradition said that both were taken up into heaven. They therefore speak of Jesus' 'departure' (Gk. *exodos*) which he was 'about to accomplish at Jerusalem'. From the beginning of the ministry, Luke has pointed the narrative towards Jerusalem where its purpose is to be achieved (4:9, 30). From the end of the time in Galilee, this movement will become even clearer. At Jerusalem will occur the events that will accomplish not only Jesus' glorification but also the redemption that God wills for his people.

At the conclusion of the visionary appearance, the voice that earlier came to Jesus (3:22) now addresses the disciples. It expresses the divine approval of Jesus and, in words that

follow Deut 18:15, enjoins them to give him their trust and obedience. The three disciples are given a glimpse of the glory that is rightly Jesus' and are themselves therefore strengthened to follow him on the way to his cross and glorification. What they have now seen anticipates both the empty tomb and the ascension, where two men in white will again interpret the events they witness (24:4; Acts 1:11). In Mk 9 and Mt 17, as they come down from the mountain, Jesus commands them to silence about what they had seen until after the resurrection. This is absent from Luke as befits his telling of the story in a way that brings out its divine witness to them. They did, however, keep silence 'in those days'. Perhaps Luke implies that they will use it at an appropriate time which will be—not as in Mark after the resurrection—but at the passion.

The incidents following the transfiguration show, however, just how much these three, along with the rest of the disciples, have to learn. Luke, unlike Mark (cf. Mk 9:14), places the story of the disciples' inability to expel a demon on the following day and thus does not exclude the three from its failure (v. 37). Again, their failure to understand Jesus' prediction of his suffering and their refusal to ask him about it shows how little they have learned (v. 45). The contrast between what Jesus is saying and their inability to enter into it is further strengthened by their discussion about their relative greatness (vv. 46–8) and by the attempt of John, one of the witnesses of the transfiguration, to remain exclusive (vv. 49–50). It is possible, of course, that the exorcist was using Jesus' name in a magical way rather than expressing a genuine response to Jesus. This appears to be the import of a similar situation in Acts 8:14–24. Here, however, in this particular context it seems that Luke is thinking not so much of an opportunist as of one who was not 'following with us', namely a disciple from that wider group that did not travel with them on the road but was influenced and moved by Jesus. Jesus' answer looks for a greater openness and is a rebuke of all exclusiveness. The disciples clearly have much to learn as they follow Jesus on the road.

The Journey to Jerusalem (9:51–19:27)

With 9:51, a verse of exceptional solemnity and loaded with biblical imagery, we enter upon a new section of the gospel that takes Jesus to the very gates of Jerusalem. Though the sense of movement is not always obvious, references to his progress occur from time to time (13:22, 33–4; 17:11; 18:31; 19:11) and show that it is the journey motif which holds this long section together. Geographically, these notices make little sense and together point to a meandering which appears to make little headway. For Luke, their significance is theological rather than factual. They keep Jerusalem as a goal in the reader's mind and point to that city as the climax and focal point of Jesus' ministry. In the light of the infancy narratives, they seek to present that ministry as the climax of God's workings in Israel. With Jesus' movement to Jerusalem, the whole of Israel's history is caught up and brought to a climax in him. In what happens there, Israel is reconstituted and the gift of the Spirit, which his exaltation makes possible, proclaims her eschatological renewal.

Recognizing the importance of this section for Luke, commentators have sought to discover an overarching scheme which gives some coherence and unity to a collection of material that does not easily reveal either a logical development or an easy progression of thought. Schemes which put forward some form of chiastic structure have not been able to account for the order of all the material in the section. The suggestion that Deuteronomy provided the pattern, though attractive, again falls short of clear demonstration (see Nolland 1989–93; Evans 1990). There are, however, clear links with that book and these are such as to suggest that it is Deuteronomy that gives an insight into the way the material in this section is to be read. Luke has already presented Jesus in terms of the prophet Moses. Clearly visible at the transfiguration as an influence upon Jesus, his experience on Mount Sinai has already been used to shape the events around the choice of the twelve and the delivery of the inaugural sermon (6:12–49). In Deuteronomy, Moses addressed Israel on the way to his 'departure' (which in Jewish tradition became an assumption into heaven) and their movement into the promised land. Deuteronomy was seen as his farewell address, which became a contemporary exhortation to every future generation. It spoke about the nature of their God, his own withdrawal, their life in the future, and their attitude as they faced disobedience within Israel and temptations from without. What Deuteronomy does for Moses and historical Israel, the journey to Jerusalem does for Jesus and the community of eschatological Israel that he calls into being. Whilst in this section, Luke tells of a past movement and of the learning situation of those who journeyed with Jesus to Jerusalem, he enables him to speak now as the exalted Lord to those who would travel with him in the present (Moessner 1989).

(9:51–62) Eschatological Urgency 'When the days drew near' does little to convey the true awesomeness of the Greek, which is better rendered, 'As the days were being accomplished'. The wheel is turning full circle and coming to its appointed fulfilment. Jesus' being 'taken up' is achieved not merely by the ascension but also by the resurrection and passion—and indeed by the movement to Jerusalem. All is included within the embrace of this eschatological perspective. Jesus is already being seen in the light of that exaltation. To 'set his face' is often used in LXX of a threatening action. Luke however does not follow it with 'against' but rather with an infinitive of purpose. The servant in Isa 50:7 'sets his face like a solid rock' in obedience to the Lord's will and it is this imagery that is uppermost in Luke's mind.

Samaritans refuse him precisely because his goal is Jerusalem and her people. The time of the Samaritans will come, but it will not be until Acts 8:4 when it will happen as a result both of the renewal of Israel and of the disobedience of many of her people. Jesus, unlike Elijah in 2 Kings 1, has no need of the vindication of a miraculous sign. James and John, in wishing to follow in the way of Elijah, reveal just how much they have still to learn.

The new stage of God's action in Jesus, and its contrast with the preparatory nature of all that went before, is shown in Jesus' refusal to allow would-be disciples to act in accordance with the outlook of that earlier age (9:57–62). Discipleship now meant journeying with the Son of Man who had nowhere to lay his head. His call required a response that cut across the law's demand for care of parents. If it refers to more than fulfilling long-term obligations and is to be taken literally, then it demanded the neglect of what was regarded as the most solemn of all obligations. Luke sees that on which Jesus was now engaged as the climactic point of God's redeeming activity, which, in the benefits it brings, overrides all other acts of piety and natural ties. Less stark, the final call contrasts the present time with that of Elijah and Elisha (1 Kings 19:20).

(10:1–24) The Mission of the Seventy Luke alone has the mission of the seventy—or is it seventy-two? The MS evidence is fairly divided and it is not easy to conclude what Luke actually wrote. Both numbers are linked to the two OT episodes that might be reflected in Luke's story. Gen 10 has a list of seventy nations of the world, though LXX has seventy-two. Num 11 speaks of Moses choosing seventy elders upon whom a portion of the spirit that was upon him would rest, but since two others shared the gift, this could be taken as seventy-two. Which of these two episodes influenced Luke's telling of the story is not certain. That they were sent 'before Jesus to every town and place where he himself intended to go' suggests the situation of the world-wide church as it preached and witnessed in anticipation of the return of Christ. On the other hand, the woes against the Galilean towns of vv. 13–15 point to Jewish perversity which was not wholly other than that which caused Moses' appointment of the seventy elders. The episode is certainly related to the continuing mission to Israel and the varied response that this caused. Luke probably sees it as a pointer to the missionary experiences of his contemporaries as they challenged both Jews and Gentiles.

The message they are to preach is that 'the kingdom . . . has come near', though its embrace ('near to you', v. 9 but not in v. 11) is limited to those who respond favourably to them. This latter fact suggests that the Kingdom is a present reality and that its nearness is likely to be spatial rather than temporal. Yet it hovers over them rather than actually including them; there is an apartness about it, an otherness which means that their relationship to it is as yet tangential; they are not yet actually within its circle. When the missionaries return (v. 17), and rejoice that they have had power over the demons, the Lord bids them to raise their sights and to see that what has happened on earth is a reflection of, and a pointer to, something even more sublime in heaven; 'I watched Satan falling like lightning from heaven.' What is ultimately real and final takes place in heaven and it is this, as it is reflected on earth, that enables the world to be more open to God's rule. Luke has a strong sense of the transcendence of God's kingdom. It is the victory in that sphere that enables Jesus to bring about God's redemption on earth. They are to rejoice that their names are written in heaven (v. 20).

The success of the mission and Jesus' vision of triumph in heaven cause him to 'rejoice in the Holy Spirit' (some MSS have simply 'in spirit' and so point rather to his ecstatic state), and to make a thanksgiving to his Father who has brought about this success. In keeping with the Jewish understanding of revelation which thinks in terms of hiding as well as revealing, he points to God's hiding these things from the wise and revealing them to those who are open to receive ('babes'). God's redemption passes by the self-sufficient but is grasped by those who are looking for it. Now follows (v. 22) a saying in which Jesus reveals himself in terms that, going beyond what is usually found in the Synoptic Gospels, comes close to his self-revelation in John. The Father has 'handed over all things' to the Son to give him an authority that is close to his own. That authority is centred on the act of redemption. The Father alone is the one who really knows the Son. Equally, it is the Son alone who really knows the Father. Such is his knowledge of the Father that he is able to make him known to anyone he chooses. Revelation of God through Jesus is not an idea that is elsewhere embraced in Luke. The section ends by pointing out how blessed the disciples are to have shared in this revelatory moment. The whole section has emphasized the reality of the heavenly Kingdom and its influence upon and future presence in the world.

(10:23–37) The Parable of the Good Samaritan At this point we meet the first of the many parables which are such a feature of the central section of this gospel (Bailey 1976; 1980). Luke links the episode firmly to Jesus' revelation of himself (v. 25). A lawyer who would no doubt have claimed that he 'saw', seeks to 'test Jesus', to determine his credentials. Matthew and Mark have a similar confrontation (where Matthew also has 'test') during Jesus' last visit to Jerusalem (Mt 22:34–40; Mk 12:28–31). Luke does not have that episode for, in some way, he sees its purpose satisfied here. Some interpreters believe that he has taken it over as a setting for the parable for which the original context in the life of Jesus was forgotten. This they believe would account for the twist that occurs between the lawyer's question and Jesus' reshaping of it; the parable itself does not follow on from the lawyer's question. On the whole, it is likely that this exhibits undue scepticism. That Jesus was only tested once in this way is not a necessary assumption. The twist between the lawyer's question and Jesus' answer is entirely in keeping with Jesus' radical stance: he was making the lawyer rethink his presuppositions and telling him that the assumptions with which he started out and which determined his question—'What bounds do I draw around my acceptance of others as my neighbour?'—had to be revised in a radical way. Neighbourliness knows no bounds and must proceed from an attitude of spontaneity and self-forgetfulness. The parable was remembered in its setting which actually gave depth and direction to it.

This, of course, does not mean that Luke has not shaped the episode as we now have it. That the commands to love God (Deut 6:5) and neighbour (Lev 18:5) were joined in this way before Jesus is disputed. Luke's concern to point to the strengths of the Jewish faith may have made him put into the lawyer's mouth a belief that originally was said to have been expressed by Jesus himself. It would then have made a way for his statement that the lawyer attempted to 'justify himself', an attitude that for Luke was largely responsible for the tragedy of the Jewish rejection of Jesus. As Luke sees it, the parable overturns the lawyer's stance and puts before him the challenge of emulating that of a Samaritan who was prepared to go to the aid of one who despised him. The parable in its setting calls for an abandonment of all status, privilege, and exclusiveness, that is, of just those things which for Luke stopped the Jewish people from responding to the outreach of Jesus.

For Luke, the parable is an indictment of the lawyer's attitude. Some have seen this as evidence of his alleged anti-Semitism (J. T. Sanders 1987). It reflects criticism, however, rather than hostility. It challenges rather than condemns. The Jewish religious leaders, the priest and the Levite, are there not as objects of attack but as examples of the deficiencies of the best in Judaism. Their proper consideration of the purity requirements of the law (for contact with a possible dead body would have prevented them from functioning in their proper tasks) led them to make a decision which the action of the Samaritan showed to be wrong. As with the lawyer and his question, the attitude inculcated by the law in the end hindered the exercise of that love which it so clearly enjoined. In his infancy narratives, Luke has already shown just what a leap forward was required if the priest was to move into the new outreach of God. Nevertheless, it was in the temple that that outreach began (1:5–20).

(10:38–42) Martha and Mary The Jewish lawyer had to learn to listen to the law which on his own understanding was meant to foster the love of God and humankind. It required a spontaneity of action that went beyond that which could be finely calculated and be seen to be under his own control. Earlier, as the journey was about to begin, the disciples had had to learn to give up status and become like children, to accept outsiders, and to eschew quick retaliation (9:46–56). Now, the fundamental requirement of discipleship is illustrated through the story of Martha and Mary. Two sisters welcome Jesus into their home, the one distracted by the burden of hospitality whilst the other, almost oblivious to its demands, sits listening at Jesus' feet. When Martha complains, Jesus rebukes her and, in the most likely reading, says, 'only one thing is necessary', namely, 'the better part' which Mary has chosen and which will not be taken away from her. Though the 'one thing' has sometimes been taken as suggesting that Martha is overdoing the hospitality, it rather refers to Mary's role of listening to Jesus. This is what had been commanded by the voice at the transfiguration (9:35) and the disciples had already shown how hard it was to do this. Martha, like them and the lawyer before her, wanted to be in control. The whole journey section of the gospel emphasizes the need for listening to the Lord. Only so will disciples be able to follow him on the way.

It is hard not to have sympathy with Martha, for Jesus' rebuke is certainly stern. Some recent readings have pictured Martha's as a leadership role which has been questioned in the story, as it was told by the early church, in favour of a more passive one such as is exercised by Mary (Schüssler Fiorenza 1983). Luke would almost certainly not have taken it in this way. For him, it expresses the absolute necessity of the priority of obedience to the call of Christ which is itself understood as a radical challenge to that self-sufficiency that characterized the outlook of those who refused Jesus or who were not easily open to his call.

(11:1–13) Teaching on Prayer Following a statement of Jesus' own prayer (v. 1) and the commendation of Mary's listening to him, it is an appropriate place for Luke to include teaching about prayer. The disciples' request for such teaching becomes the opportunity for including the Lord's prayer. Its

Lukan form is shorter than Matthew's (6:9–13) and interpreters are by no means united in determining the relationship between the two. Matthew's shows clear signs of use within the Christian community and is most probably the form that was prayed in his church. Luke's is also sometimes thought of as that of his church. This, however, is less likely for it certainly shows his hand and reflects his own theological understanding. It expresses a response to Jesus' teaching that brings out what Luke believes are the essential features of it. 'When you pray, say:' allows for no flexibility. It lays down a standard that must be expressed in all prayer: it says what prayer is about. 'Father' is the direct, confident approach to God that Luke sees as characteristic of Jesus' own prayer (22:42; 23:34, 46) and which his exaltation made possible for those who would follow him (Rom 8:15; Gal 4:6). God's 'name', in accordance with OT imagery, is his very nature which is expressed especially in his merciful outreach to humanity (Ex 33:17–19). To pray for its hallowing, therefore, is to pray that his true nature may be acknowledged by them and his redeeming activity be effective in the world. To pray for the coming of God's kingdom, which for Luke is already a reality in heaven (10:11), is to pray that it may be realized in the world. That for Luke will be at the parousia when what is real in heaven will be revealed to the world and will embrace it (17:24; 8:8). The request for bread (Luke adds 'each day'), which on the surface seems to be the most obvious and immediate of the petitions, is not easily understood. The meaning of the Greek word translated 'daily' is wholly uncertain. The claim that it appeared in a text with the meaning 'daily rations' is not open to verification and therefore can carry little weight. It might mean 'essential', though whether it is then to be understood in a physical or spiritual sense is not clear. It might mean 'bread for the coming day' and have some pointer back to the Israelites in the wilderness and their gathering of the daily manna (Ex 16:4). In the light of the eschatological nature of the prayer as a whole, and following on from the plea for the coming of the Kingdom, many would see it as a prayer for a taste in the present of the eschatological bread of the future Kingdom. May we live daily out of the power of the Kingdom. On the other hand, the following petition about forgiveness and forgiving is wholly about the present. Luke's hand is visible here, for its plea for forgiveness of 'sins' breaks the parallelism of our forgiving of 'debts'. Matthew has 'debts' in both parts of the petition and, because Jesus elsewhere talks of sin as 'debts' (7:41), it is likely that Luke has rephrased it here to make it more intelligible to his non-Jewish readers. The conditionality of the clause seems to owe its severity to Jesus himself and would fit the emphasis of the evangelist's version of Jesus' foundation sermon (6:20–49). Luke's version of the prayer ends with the petition, 'Do not bring us to the time of trial' (*peirasmos*). This translation would certainly represent Luke's own understanding of the petition's significance and does more justice to its meaning than the weaker 'temptation'. For him, the 'time of trial' was that point when a person is open to the ultimate of Satan's onslaughts such as was expected before the final revelation of the Kingdom. Whereas at Gethsemane, Matthew and Mark see the disciples open to the *peirasmos* when they fall asleep, Luke regards it as a future fall when they would abandon Jesus and enter into the grip of Satan (22:46; cf. Mk 14:41). Since it

would not allow a hope of deliverance but would rather witness to Satan's triumph, any petition for deliverance from his power would be superfluous.

For Luke, the prayer has a strong eschatological orientation. It is one for the open manifestation of the Kingdom and a plea that, meanwhile, the disciples should live under its shadow and out of its strength. So the parable, which talks of the need for urgent and insistent prayer, pictures this under the guise of a determined petition for bread. The parable talks of contrasts. God, who wills to answer the disciples' petitions, is contrasted with an earthly person who is indifferent to his friend's pleas, and a request for physical bread is contrasted with the pleas for the Kingdom's food. If the plea for earthly benefit produces a response, how much more will God respond to those requests for things that are in accordance with his will. The parable says that God is not indifferent, and any suggestion that he is arises out of a misreading of the signs of the times.

The section therefore ends with a further contrast, yet one that this time depends on what actually links God and the best of family life. Earthly parents for all their imperfections ('being evil' is a typical Semitic exaggeration which is used to make the point) give good gifts to their children. How much more will God give the 'Holy Spirit' to those who ask him. For Luke, the Holy Spirit is God's power and strength which enables a response to him and a witness to his Kingdom (Acts 6:10; 9:17, 31). His presence is a sign of incorporation into the eschatological people of God and a guarantee of inclusion in his Kingdom which is to be revealed (Acts 1:8, 11). Though it remains most likely that Luke himself wrote the petition for the Kingdom at 11:2, the few MSS that read, 'May your Holy Spirit come upon us and cleanse us' would not be out of keeping with his thoughts.

(11:14–36) The Beelzebul Controversy Exorcism played a large part in the ministry of Jesus and, indeed, in that of the early church. Demon possession was widely believed in at that time and, as this episode makes clear, Jesus was by no means the only exorcist around. His opponents do not attack him for performing exorcisms, but rather question his motivation and the power by which he was able to do them: he was accused of casting out demons 'by Beelzebul, the ruler of the demons'. Beelzebul appears in some ancient Canaanite texts as 'Baal, Lord of the Heavenly House', a local or Syrian deity who was treated by Hebrew thought as an alien power, hostile to YHWH. 'Beelzebub', which appears in some texts, is a corruption of this, meaning 'Lord of the flies'. With a growing appreciation of the power of YHWH, these other gods were undeified and then treated as hostile agents of Satan. Jesus, therefore, is here accused of being an agent of Satan. On what grounds would they make this charge? Unlike any comparable Jewish exorcists, he did not use prayer or claim to draw on the strength of the Jewish tradition. He acted on his own authority and outside the covenant. Moreover, in his sitting loose to the law and its demands, he could be seen to be despising the covenant itself. All this could make him open to the charge of being a godless person.

He points to the basic nonsense of the charge, for Satan was unlikely to be wishing to destroy his supporters. And were their associates also to be charged with being agents of Satan?

This is basically a *non sequitur* for, though their activities might look no different from those of Jesus, they themselves presumably still worked within the law and so were not subject to the complaints that were being made against him. More important is his understanding of the significance of his exorcisms. 'The finger of God' is a phrase used in Ex 8:19 by the men of Pharoah to describe Moses' wonders in Egypt; they were worked by God. If Jesus was doing his works by the finger of God—if he could be acknowledged as a man of God, reflecting his character and his goodness—then his exorcisms, far from witnessing to his service of Satan, witness rather to his being the agent of the kingdom of God. They show that, through him, 'the kingdom of God has come to you'. The translation of REB reads 'has already come upon you' and by allowing for the Greek preposition, *epi*, does more justice to it. The Kingdom has 'come upon' us, that is arrived to hover over us, to cast its glow over us, to be an effective power out of which we can now live. It is not yet here in its fullness, though we are already living within its embrace. (Cf. further FGS I.)

If this verse serves as an important witness to Jesus' understanding of the Kingdom, it is equally important as a witness to his understanding of the significance of his exorcisms. They do not prove him, they do not even authenticate him. It is rather he who authenticates them and can enable them to be seen as signs of the presence of the Kingdom. So Jesus sees himself as overpowering Satan. The urgency of the contest is such that a saying (v. 23) is used in a manner that reverses its meaning at 9:50. The same sense of urgency controls the interpretation of vv. 24–6. If it is to endure, Jesus' saving work demands a positive response from those who receive it. So, when a woman in the crowd extols him by way of his mother, Jesus replies by declaring the blessedness of those who not only hear God's word, but actually obey it. If it is to achieve its pupose, grace must be met with a response.

Those who accused him of being in the pay of Beelzebul would not acknowledge what was before their eyes. Jesus himself now accuses those who demand a sign, that is an irrefutable demonstration of proof of his status. Instead, they are offered only the sign of Jonah when he preached to Nineveh (Jon 3–4). The people of Nineveh recognized the force of Jonah's preaching and the justice of his challenge to them. The queen of Sheba recognized the wisdom of Solomon and acted (1 Kings 10). Jesus' contemporaries are able neither to discern nor to respond. The final part of the section uses a saying about a lamp, not this time to talk about a future revelation of what is now hidden (8:16), but to warn that light must be allowed to do its work. It can easily be reduced to ineffectiveness.

(11:37–12:12) Jesus and the Pharisees Jesus in this central section of the gospel is often at meals which for Luke, as probably for Jesus himself, are seen as anticipations of the Kingdom of God. By his teaching, Jesus shows how they reflect or fail to reflect the Kingdom. This passage contains his harshest criticisms of the Pharisees. Much of its criticism is found also in Mt 23 where it is actually heightened and, addressed to crowds and the disciples about the Pharisees, becomes a climactic attack upon them. In Luke, since his criticisms are made at a meal and are given face to face, they

do not mark the end of any relationship with them. There is still a dialogue. Jesus' dealings with the Pharisees were often confrontational, for his approach to purity, which was a major concern of theirs, was quite different from their own. Here, when Jesus is invited to dine with a Pharisee, he does not use the water provided to join in the ritual washing that would have been expected of those who were guests. He meets his host's disapproval with a determined attack upon his group. Their inner attitude does not measure up to their concern for externals. Tithing laws were complicated but Luke's point is that the Pharisees expended too much energy on little things such as tithing herbs which would have been better spent on more important commandments such as justice and love. They are like unmarked graves which actually defile people who come into contact with them.

A 'lawyer', who is a professional exegete of the law of Moses and who, by addressing Jesus as 'teacher' appears to acknowledge an affinity with him, resents these attacks but is in turn himself accused. The Pharisees' interpretation of the law puts undue burdens upon people. It is hard to see how their building tombs for the prophets actually continues their predecessors' persecution of them. It would seem to suggest the reverse. Their actions, however, do not really amount to a dissociation of themselves from the outlooks of their ancestors. They are seen rather as hypocritical. The attack is used as an entry into the final charge (11:49) that 'this generation' (which includes those who are contemporary with Luke) will bring to a climax their predecessors' harassment of God's servants by persecuting and killing Christian prophets and apostles. 'The Wisdom of God said' (11:64) is an unusual expression and, if it means more than 'God in his wisdom', reflects a saying of the early church. Abel was the first victim of jealousy (Gen 4:8). Zechariah is usually identified with the priest who was stoned by the people (2 Chr 24:20–2).

This passage, like that in Mt 23, has caused considerable disquiet for interpreters of the NT because it serves as a basis for that understanding of Pharisaism which, by presenting it as hypocritical in the extreme, is wholly unjust to that religious movement within Judaism to which in many ways Jesus was most closely related. In spite of some claims to the contrary (E. P. Sanders 1985) it is likely that Jesus did engage in disputes with them, but the stories of these conflicts have come down to us by way of the early church and reflect the growing hostility that later history encouraged. By the time Luke wrote, Pharisaism and the young church were engaged in a battle for the soul of Judaism. Our gospels reflect the heat this engendered and present a picture of Jesus' dealings with them which is coloured by these experiences.

The final component in this section takes up the earlier attack upon the Pharisees to characterize their basic outlook as 'hypocrisy'. 'Leaven' in the Bible is frequently used as a symbol for a hidden but pervasive corrupting influence (1 Cor 5:6–8). Pharisaic hypocrisy will, however, be uncovered. Meanwhile, the disciples must not fear those who persecute them. Everyone who acknowledges Jesus before human beings will be acknowledged by Jesus as Son of Man before the heavenly host (cf. Acts 7:56). Denial, on the other hand, will bring denial; 12:10 seems best understood as underlining this warning. Everyone who speaks against Jesus is open to forgiveness (cf. Jesus' first word from the cross, 23:34). Blasphemy 'against the Holy Spirit', however, is Christian denial of the truths revealed to them by their possession of the Spirit. Seen supremely as apostasy, it is extended to include a denial of the community brought into being through the Spirit (Acts 5:3). People are not to worry about what to say when they are brought to trial for being Christians. The Holy Spirit will himself direct their witness at this point (Acts 4:8; 6:10).

(12:13–53) Alert for the Kingdom Whilst a large number of interpreters have suggested that Luke no longer believed in the imminence of Jesus' return (Conzelmann 1960), there are a number of sections that suggest otherwise, and here we meet the first of them (cf. 17:21). It begins with a request for Jesus to take sides in a dispute over a family inheritance, and this enables Luke to include some teaching about the dangers of riches and of the attitude that concern for material things can encourage. To illustrate the point that one's life 'does not consist in the abundance of possessions' he includes the parable of the rich fool whose concern for material things and his confidence in them made him forget both the fragility of life and its deeper obligations, 'rich towards God'.

Jesus then turns from this more general teaching to address the disciples. They are 'not to worry about' their life (v. 22) Whilst this might mean 'put no effort into' and thus commend an eschatological detachment from the world, more likely in Luke's context it means 'do not be unduly concerned about'. The parable has pointed out that one has but limited control over one's future, and the teaching which follows stresses God's care. Undue striving for the things of this life actually leads one into the way of the 'nations of the world' which becomes a forgetfulness of God and of the things of the Kingdom. As Evans (1990) expresses it, 'The question then at issue is when a proper concern has become an improper anxiety'. Modern life would suggest the importance of the question, though the ongoing existence of the world and its responsibilities might place the move from one to another at a different point from Luke. Luke sees undue concern for the things of the body and of 'life', that is the business of living in the world, as a definite hindrance to striving for God's Kingdom. Though it is God's 'good pleasure' to give the Kingdom, entry into its sphere demands considerable effort on the part of men and women. It certainly does not allow for one's primary drive to be in the direction of the things of this world. Luke sees a definite either/or, though his challenge to exclusiveness is undermined by his inclusion of Jesus' promise that striving for the Kingdom will bring with it the bonus of these material benefits 'as well'. v. 34 gives the rationale of the antithesis which dominates the whole passage.

Jesus now (v. 35) warns the 'little flock' to be alert and ready for their master when he returns from the wedding banquet. 'The wedding banquet' would seem to be a symbol here for Jesus' enthronement in heaven and points to his return at the parousia. The whole passage carries two convictions. First, the disciples must be ready for a return of Jesus at any moment (v. 40). Secondly, they must allow for a delay that must neither reduce their expectancy nor impede their preparedness (v. 38). Peter's question at v. 41 makes it clear that 'the Lord', that is Jesus as he is worshipped and believed in by those whom Luke addresses, is speaking directly to Luke's contemporaries. The warning is directed to them, in the light of the belief, however

(v. 32), that God is anxious to give the Kingdom to them. The urgency of the response demanded is controlled by the greatness of the gift that they are promised. The promise is real, and this suggests that it will not be long delayed. The element of delay points not to the future but to the past. Time has gone on. Luke's readers are in danger of losing hope and that preparedness that characterized the earliest Christians (1 Thess 4:13–18).

So, in vv. 49–53, Luke includes a passage that points to the need for disciples to respond to the urgency of the times even at the expense of causing divisions within their own families. vv. 49 and 50 contain singularly difficult sayings of Jesus. Set in the context of a particular stage of his ministry, they nevertheless are directed to Luke's contemporaries. What is the fire that Jesus came to bring? In the prophets, fire can be a symbol of purification (Isa 4:4) and, more frequently, of judgement (Am 1:4). Jesus here seems to be referring to the work of the Spirit (Acts 2:19) especially through baptism into the Christian community (3:16). That activity will come about as a result of his own 'baptism' which would be achieved by way of his death and exaltation. A saying at Mk 10:38 understands Jesus' death in this way and links it to the suffering of the disciples. Luke is probably using the same ideas, though, in keeping with his refusal to isolate the deaths either of Jesus or the disciples, he extends its meaning to embrace Jesus' whole way of life which makes his exaltation possible. Luke's readers must be prepared for difficult times.

(12:54–13:35) Jewish Refusal of the Signs of the Times In Palestine, rain clouds come from the west, the Mediterranean, and dry winds from the south or east. People, adept at reading these signs, remain totally insensitive to other signs that are around them. Crises in their lives are settled speedily and before they bring irreversible disasters, yet the greatest crisis of the present is ignored. Luke uses two otherwise unknown episodes to point to the reality of the crisis facing them. Some Galileans were killed by Pilate's men in the temple and some other people, staying in Jerusalem, died when a tower in the city walls collapsed. They were no worse than the people Jesus is addressing who face an equal fate if they do not repent (see LK 21:20–4). It is now the climactic hour. In a parable, Jesus talks of the last, desperate measures to produce fruit from an unfruitful tree and of the severity of the response that a further failure to produce will bring. 'If it bears fruit next year, well and good; if not, you can cut it down.'

The nature of the problem with the Jewish nation is illustrated by an incident in the synagogue. Jesus, on the sabbath, heals a woman who for eighteen years had been crippled with some spinal injury. The one who had general responsibility for ordering the life of the synagogue objects on the grounds that, since the illness was not life-threatening, the people, who presumably were understood as encouraging Jesus to respond to the need, might seek such healings at times other than the sabbath. In reply, Jesus points out how this attitude denies the rational approach which they in fact exercise in relation to the sabbath law. More seriously, it fails to acknowledge just what is happening in Jesus' ministry. It does not recognize that what is taking place here is nothing less than the defeat of Satan and the establishment of God's rule (13:16). Two further parables make this point. The Kingdom to which the miracle witnesses is like a mustard plant. In its beginnings, it is small and insignificant; when it is grown, however, it becomes a tree that, like that of Dan 4:21, is strong and embraces the nations of the earth. The parable of the yeast makes the same point. What begins as insignificant and virtually unseen, permeates three measures of flour. Gen 18:16 connects such an amount with Sarah's feeding of her godlike visitors. It has been suggested that in ordinary circumstances, the amount would feed more that one hundred people. In any case, the point here is the power of that which seems to have but little beginnings, and the contrast between the beginning and the end. Something strange and not easily comprehended is happening in Jesus' ministry.

So, Luke reminds his readers of Jesus' journey (13:22), of the urgency it proclaims, and the response it demands. The message of the section is summed up in a further parable where people, invited to enter but failing to respond, will not discern the reality of the situation until it is too late (13:25–30). Their pleas of affinity will carry no weight. Jesus' contemporaries will see the patriarchs and the prophets included but they themselves left outside. Their founding fathers will be joined, not by themselves, but by those from the nations. Those who consider themselves first will in actuality be last. Such is the challenge of Jesus.

The first half of the journey comes to a climax (13:31–5) with a challenge to Jerusalem that actually prefigures the events of Palm Sunday (19:29–44). Some friendly Pharisees warn Jesus of his danger. Jesus' reply in 13:32, 33 allows Luke to give his understanding of the significance of the journey and its conclusion. They carry forward what he has already expressed at 9:31, 51. Jesus in his exorcisms and healings is already sowing the seed of the Kingdom. That will happen 'today and tomorrow' and will lead into 'the third day' when Jesus will 'finish his work'. In the light of 9:31, 51, what completes his work is the cycle of events in Jerusalem—the passion, resurrection, and ascension—which will enable both his exaltation and the gift of the Spirit on his people. That may well involve his death, but there is the divine necessity about it. The actual words of 13:32 are 'I am being perfected', which uses the divine passive and means 'God is perfecting me'. Jesus, for Luke, is the eschatological prophet of whom Moses spoke (Deut 18:15) and, since he is the agent of God's renewal of Israel, he must like so many of the prophets suffer, and that nowhere other than in Jerusalem. Luke's gospel begins and ends in that city.

Jesus now (13:34) laments over the city, as he will do when he enters it (19:41–4), for he sees her rushing onwards to complete her history of refusal of God's agents. She will choose instead to follow a path that will lead to her own destruction. Jesus is often understood here as speaking as God's wisdom who reaches out to Israel with a tenderness that expresses her feminine concern (e.g. Wis 6:12–20). He reflects her gentleness and desire to draw humanity into relationship with God. Jerusalem rejects him. When he enters the holy city, only his disciples, and not her people, will acknowledge him (19:37–40). Her acknowledgement must await another day.

(14:1–24) A Sabbath Meal with a Pharisee Jesus, at a meal with a Pharisee, is again critical of the assembly, though this time with far less severity than his prevous attack (11:37–53). Here, they watch him not with hostility as in 6:6, but with an interest that rises above mere suspicion. To Jesus' question, 'Is it lawful to cure on the sabbath or not?' their silence, though not assent, acknowledges the correctness of Jesus' stance. His further question (v. 5) would seem to recognize that. Sabbath meals in particular take on the character of anticipations of those in the Kingdom. Jesus now gives reasons why their meals fail in this respect. They reflect pride rather than humility (he records the same deficiency on the part of the disciples at the last supper (22:24–7)). They are exclusive rather than outreaching (vv. 12–14). At this point, a guest proclaims the blessedness of those who will share in the banquet of the Kingdom. He no doubt assumes that he will be one of those, and it is to this attitude that Luke directs Jesus' parable of the rejected invitation which is found, in a different setting and with significantly different details, in Mt 22:1–14. The meaning Luke sees in the parable depends upon the view taken of the 'excuses' which almost certainly express his own ideas. What is suggested of the attitude of those who make them? Do they regard them as legitimate reasons for their non-attendance or are they put forward as excuses born of indifference? Commentators who accept them as reasons suggest that the business deals needed to be completed before the end of day and that inspection of the merchandise could take place after the deal itself had been agreed. The excuses reflect those of Deut 20:5–7 that allow reasons for not answering the call to take part in a holy war. However, though this might be suggested of the third excuse, it bears little relation to the first two. The parable itself would appear to take them as excuses rather than reasons. Yet the first two are given politely and point to the necessity of the tasks they go to perform. The third, though sometimes seen as less polite, is not really so but, relating to Deuteronomy, assumes its validity. It seems that the excuses appear valid to those who make them. They assume that they will be acceptable to the host. His reaction, which is severe, no doubt caught them by surprise. Where did they go wrong? Their mistake was to presume upon the relationship that demanded more response from them than they realized. They failed to acknowledge the urgency of the summons.

The giver of the banquet reacted fiercely. The invitation was issued to the outsiders of the city and then to those who inhabited the country, to those who rested along the lanes. This double invitation reflects Luke's interest in both the Jewish and the Gentile missions of the church. 'Compel' expresses the urgency of the task. As in 13:22–30, those originally invited will be excluded. Their attitude makes it a self-exclusion. The Jews, the people of God, were failing to see either the truth in Jesus or the urgency of his call. As was suggested in the Nazareth sermon (4:23–4), their confidence in their relationship with God was misplaced.

(14:25–35) The Cost of Discipleship Discipleship may be a response to grace, as Luke's story of Jesus emphasizes, but it makes demands which mean that it should not be entered upon lightly. The requirement to 'hate' is Semitic exaggeration and may reflect an idiom which means 'love less than' as Mt 10:37 correctly interprets it. Luke is certainly emphatic, and the references to 'wife' and 'life itself' may be due to him.

Disciples are to 'carry the cross' in a manner of life which reflects that of Jesus and in a discipleship that goes with him all the way to Jerusalem. They are to recognize the true cost of discipleship and are not to enter upon something that they do not have the resources to pursue. Otherwise, they are in danger of being in the ridiculous position of one who sets out to build a watch-tower—which may be either for the protection of personal property or, more grandly, part of a city's defence—and does not have the resources to complete the operation. A king will not go to war without first realistically assessing both the demands of the task and the resources he needs to meet it. v. 33, like 12:33, expresses the Lucan emphasis upon the complete renunciation of possessions (though see LK 16:9–13). Salt is 'good' in biblical thought for giving taste where there is none (Job 6:6) and for preserving what otherwise would perish (Num 18:19). Whether salt can lose its flavour has been much debated. The point here of course is the contrast in this respect between salt and discipleship. What is difficult if not impossible for one, is relatively easy for the other. Discipleship which loses its commitment is worse than useless.

(15:1–32) At Meals with Tax-Collectors and Sinners Jesus has already been shown at a meal with tax-collectors and sinners (5:30), and 7:34 has called him their friend. Tax-collectors (rather, 'toll-collectors') and sinners were those who, by their lifestyle, had deliberately opted out of membership of the covenantal people of Israel. They were outsiders. Now, the Pharisees and scribes complain that he not only receives them, but is in the habit of eating with them. They acknowledge that, by this action, Jesus is anticipating their inclusion within the kingdom of God. Not only is Jesus claiming to have God's authority to do this but, in his easy acceptance of them, he is from their point of view belittling the holiness of God. In bypassing the law and its standards in this way, he is in danger of denying the righteousness of God and the very outlook on which the Mosaic covenant was grounded. Luke was very conscious of this complaint, that was addressed not only to Jesus but, later, to the early church and that was in fact a subject of disagreement within the young church. In reply, he brings together three parables of Jesus which may or may not originally have been directed specifically to this issue.

Compared with Matthew's version of the parable of the lost sheep (Mt 18:12–14), Luke emphasizes the shepherd's responsibility for the loss (v. 3), the unconditional nature of the search, and the fact that the joy was brought about by the sinner's repentance. Repentance is emphasized in Luke's gospel (5:32; 7:47) but in this parable, as at 7:36–50, it is the outreach of God that is primary. It is his searching and finding which bring about repentance. The move to restore the relationship enables the repentance even though it cannot compel it. The initiative of God and his part in bringing about restoration is further emphasized in the parable of the lost coin. Again, talk of 'repentance' does not quite fit the stance of the parable. It appears to have been introduced, not because the movement of the parable itself required it, but because Luke was sensitive to the charge that emphasis upon the gracious outreach of God could underplay the necessity for response on the part of those it met.

So these shorter parables lead into that of the prodigal son. Its significance has been variously assessed, depending upon which character is thought to be the central means of giving expression to it. This in turn depends upon how those characters are perceived and how their various actions are understood. Recent interpreters have emphasized the outrageous conduct of the younger son. His initial request of the father has been seen as one which totally disregards the fifth commandment (Ex 20:12), his realizing of his assets as giving little heed to the Jewish belief in the land as God's gift to his people (1 Kings 21:3), his squandering of his money as a sign of his loose living, and his hiring of himself to a Gentile as a witness to his contempt for the covenantal people. This assessment would not appear too negative. The story builds up his offences in a spectacular way to make him a strong foil to the actions of the father which demand some evaluation and on which the point of the story depends. More open to question is the motive which brought about the prodigal's decision to return. v. 17a has sometimes been claimed as a Semitism which carries the meaning 'to repent'. This, however, is by no means clear. The Greek can rather mean 'starting to think straight', that is to stop being in despair and to be logical. v. 17b bases his rethinking on self-centred considerations, and it is these that determine the words of his approach to the father which could as easily give expression to calculation as to genuine penitence. Some interpreters would see a change of heart at v. 21 and think that this is brought about by the father's initiative. This appears to be more in keeping with the story as a whole, though a genuine repentance remains a possibility rather than a certainty.

If this is the reading of the younger son which the story demands, it has implications for an assessment of the father's actions. It is generally agreed that the father's act of running to meet his son and the manner of his embrace would be regarded as demeaning for a Near-Eastern parent. A Jewish parable, often compared with that of the prodigal son, portrays a father who, though equally concerned for his son and anxious for his return, takes an initiative which is nevertheless consistent with his own honour (quoted in Young 1998: 149–50). The father of our parable seems peculiarly indifferent to it. It is not at all clear that those who later join the festivities would have approved of his actions and would not have thought that these were going wholly over the top. It is in the light of this that his earlier dealings with this son have been examined. Jewish law made provision for his actions in dividing his 'living' (the Gk. in 12b is a stronger term that that used in 12a and really suggests 'his means of living'), though Sir 33:19–23 warns against it. A safeguard was possible which, by the use of the phrase, 'From today and after my death', guaranteed the future gift but allowed no use of it until then (see the discussion of the parable in Scott 1989). The father ignores this safeguard. He has acted generously, even foolishly, towards his son's demands.

Luke's use of the parable as the climax of Jesus' reply to the Pharisees places the emphasis upon its last part. Whilst this has sometimes been seen as a Lucan addition—for it certainly serves as a true expression of his understanding of God's relationship with the Jewish people—there seems little reason to demand this. The story of the elder brother serves as the climax of the parable which loses its cutting edge without it. It is this which encapsulates what would seem to be Jesus' own challenge to those who opposed his stance. But how is the elder brother to be assessed? He has often been seen as hard, dutiful but unloving, ungenerous in his actions and dismissive in his judgements both of the brother and his father. vv. 29–30 certainly portray anger, fury even, and resentment. Whilst not meant to present him in a good light, it should not be assumed, however, that they express an outlook that merits instant condemnation. No doubt already critical of his brother, and, indeed, of his father's indulgence of him, he hears of the latest happenings from a servant after a day's work in the fields. Festivities are happening because of events that concern him fundamentally, and he is left to discover them for himself. The father's indulgence of one son amounts to a seeming indifference to the other. But appearances are wrong. The father is as concerned for him as for the other, and all that he has is his (v. 31). He is faced nevertheless with a radical challenge. If he does go in, the learning experience for him will be almost as great as it must be for the younger brother. He will have to see himself and his relationships with both his father and his brother in a wholly new way.

(16:1–13) The Dishonest Steward Ch. 15 has revealed a clear standpoint which is developed in a unified manner. Ch. 16 is very different. Though not as disconnected as is sometimes suggested, the overriding concern with riches does not permeate the whole chapter, and the parable of Dives and Lazarus (vv. 19–31) is not wholly exhausted by this one theme. If the final parable in ch. 15 is one of those with obvious relevance, the first in ch. 16 is noteworthy for its obscurity. It is not evident that Luke himself does justice to it.

Commentators are uncertain of the extent of the parable, for a number of injunctions about the use of money have been appended to it. Because they relate in different ways to the events in the parable itself, they are likely to come from various occasions in Jesus' ministry and to have been brought together by Luke in a somewhat artificial manner. vv. 7, 8a, 8b, and 9 have all been suggested as endings of the original parable. That v. 9 is part of the parable is unlikely. It uses the same Greek word, translated 'dishonest' in NRSV in both instances, in a way that is different from its use in v. 8. The servant is 'dishonest' in our understanding of the term. All mammon (NRSV wealth), however, is called 'dishonest' in the sense that it is material possessions understood as the things in which one puts one's trust and that therefore encourage an acquisitive attitude and a self-reliance; it separates one from God (hence 'unrighteous' is probably a better term). 'The meaning is worldly wealth as opposed to heavenly treasure' (Marshall 1978). If v. 9 were part of the parable, it would be encouraging us to use our wealth gained dishonestly in a way that brought us some benefits: it would be virtually condoning dishonesty! On the other hand, it is unlikely that the parable stops at the end of v. 7. The reason this is sometimes suggested is because of the problem of v. 8. Why would 'his master' commend one who had actually defrauded him even if he had acted shrewdly? The Greek of v. 8 has simply 'the lord' and, since this is the term that Luke uses frequently in the journey narrative to refer to Jesus, the verse is then accepted as a comment by him on the parable. Such a view, however, leaves the parable too open-ended and avoids the

shock that is at the heart of so many of Jesus' parables. The real challenge is the master's commendation of the steward. What does this say, not only about the steward but also about the master?

It is sometimes maintained that the master's commendation of the steward does not present a problem. In order to bypass the biblical prohibition of usury, when a loan was made the interest was often added to the capital as a single figure. It is this final figure, that would have included not merely the master's interest but also the steward's legitimate commission, which was being reduced. The master was not being harmed but was actually being made to appear generous to the debtors. Ingenious though this explanation is, it does not account for the parable's description of the steward as 'dishonest'. Moreover, it does not allow for the fact that Jesus' parables are not simple, realistic stories, but rather tales of unusual situations which challenge so much of the accepted and natural order of things.

It seems then that the parable proper ends at v. 8a with 8b being Jesus' own comment on the story. v. 9, 'And I tell you', marks Luke's introduction to the further, but not necessarily related, sayings of Jesus. Read thus, the parable tells a story of an inefficient (v. 1) steward who, facing dismissal for his indolence, meets the crisis with uncharacteristic vigour and ingenuity. The master, though defrauded, recognizes the initiative and, himself working fom the perspective of 'unrighteous mammon', actually commends the steward's shrewdness. There is nothing to say that he reinstates him, but sharing in his worldly stance, he can appreciate a sensible move, indeed an ingenious one, when he sees it. 'If only', says the parable, 'the sons of light had the same appreciation of the crisis confonting them in the drawing near of the Kingdom, and the same energy in meeting it.' It is a parable on a par with those of ch. 12.

Luke has the parable addressed to disciples. In its context, they would include those whom Jesus' table-sharing was receiving into the Kingdom, the tax-collectors and sinners. Their reception needed a response and this parable confronts them. v. 9 tells them to 'make friends' by a right use of 'unrighteous mammon'. These friends may be the poor who will inherit the Kingdom; more likely, it is the heavenly court who will then receive them when the things of this world come to an end. Faithfulness with 'unrighteous mammon' means using it in the service of the poor (v. 11). They must free themselves from its shackles. They cannot be slaves to God and to mammon. Luke's use of the parable has reduced some of the eschatological urgency of the original. It shows how parables can be used outside their original context, but it shows too that such a use can all too easily evacuate the parable of some of its shock and challenge.

(16:14–31) Reply to the Pharisees Pharisees ridicule Jesus' challenge to the tax-collectors; they obviously do not expect them to give up attitudes of a lifetime. Luke calls them 'lovers of money' but this charge should not be seen as a considered historical evaluation of them. It is determined more by the demands of the narrative than by historical fact. They are seen as self-reliant, self-satisfied, and, therefore, as dismissive of others. Jesus, however, justifies his call to the tax-collectors. It is true that his coming marks a new age when the grace of the

Kingdom is proclaimed and people are rushing into it (v. 16). But that does not mean the end of the law's demands (v. 17). The tax-collectors must adopt a new attitude to the things of this world. Jesus was also criticized for receiving the sinners too freely. Again, however, that does not mean an end of the righteous requirements of the law. At the heart of its commandments about sexual morality was its high standard concerning marriage and divorce. Jesus said little about sexual attitudes, but he did talk about marriage. Luke therefore includes this saying where he actually intensifies the law's demands. His free acceptance of sinners did not mean an indifferent acquiescence in their standards. Grace exposed and recreated those who responded to its gentle outreach.

Luke includes the parable of Dives and Lazarus, for it continues the theme of the dangers of riches and the self-centredness they encourage. It makes its point by taking over a tale that was widely disseminated in the ancient world. Luke himself possibly found it in the source from which he has taken the parable of the dishonest steward. Proclaiming the reversal of fortunes in the future age, it judges those who neglect the poor. Luke has Jesus direct it to the Pharisees, and it may be this parable that has encouraged him to call them 'lovers of money'. Its final verse (31), which is an address of Abraham to Dives, would seem to contain Christian thoughts about the resurrection of Jesus. This widens out the meaning of the parable beyond its concern with money. It becomes a comment on the Pharisees who fail to respond, not only to Jesus himself, but also to the Christian proclamation about him. If they had really understood Moses and the prophets, they would, like the loyally devout Jews of the infancy narratives, have responded to him. As far as Luke is concerned (as he will make abundantly clear through his picture of Paul in Acts), Christianity is the fulfilment of the Jewish faith. A responsive Jew will embrace Jesus as Christ (Acts 26:22–3). At 16:31 a section of the journey narrative which began with 14:1 and which is largely concerned with the tragedy of the Pharisees' rejection of Jesus is completed.

(17:1–10) Teaching for the Disciples Ch. 17 begins the last section of the journey narrative. As befits a journey that ends with the disciples greeting Jesus as he enters Jerusalem (19:37–8), the teaching of this last section is aimed at them. Other characters and incidents are included, but the lessons to be learned from them are directed primarily to the disciples who are travelling on the road to Jerusalem with Jesus and who will, in relation to the twelve, become the nucleus of the renewed people of God.

The section begins with four disparate sayings which talk about life in that community. 'The little ones', that is, its vulnerable members, will inevitably be caused to stumble by the actions of some of their fellow-Christians. They will even be made to lose their faith. The punishment of the one who is responsible for this will be great. The sinner within the community must be rebuked, but forgiveness must follow repentance. Individuals must be constant in their forgiveness of those who ask it of them. They must strive after faith, but must avoid all sense of superiority that arises out of the attitude that God is obligated to them.

(17:11–19) The Ten Lepers v. 11 points to Jesus' continuing journey to Jerusalem in terms that have caused considerable

difficulty. The Greek text has a number of variations in attempts to have it make better geographical sense. It may be that Luke's knowledge of the geography of Palestine was hazy; certainly, he was controlled more by literary than by geographical concerns. The odd geographical reference is determined by the need to have a Samaritan leper and Jewish lepers together meet Jesus as he journeyed to Jerusalem. All ten were cleansed, but it is only the one who returns to give thanks who is 'saved' (the Gk. has this significance for Lk 8:12, 36, 50). He is a Samaritan. Like Luke's characterization of the disciples as 'the poor' (6:20), he is an outsider who has been brought in. Christians must retain that sense, and the thankfulness that should go with it, if they are not to become like the Pharisees and cease to act as those who live out of grace.

(17:20–18:8) Eschatological Urgency The passage 12:32–53 had warned the disciples to be alert for the return of Christ. This section takes up this theme and expands upon it, this time, however, climaxing not so much in the warning as in a pointing to the event as an object of hope.

Some Pharisees ask Jesus 'when the kingdom of God was coming'. There is not a straight fit between their question and Jesus' answer for, whereas the former is concerned with the timing of the Kingdom, the reply talks rather about its nature. What is meant by the reply is not easily determined, however, for, as the translations make clear, the meaning in the Greek of its crucial term *entos humōn* is not unambiguous. Most naturally, it means 'within you' and would seem to suggest that the Kingdom is an inner disposition, attitude, and quality. This however would give to the Kingdom a meaning which would be unique in the NT. Elsewhere, the Kingdom is understood as corporate, an activity of God, something which is being established either on the earth or in heaven and which embraces the whole person. Whilst an inner disposition might do justice to the thought of 'receiving the Kingdom', it does not express the idea of 'entering it' or of its visible manifestion in power. The term should therefore rather be understood as 'in the midst of you'. Jesus' refusal of 'things that can be observed' refers to unambiguous signs that enable the coming of the Kingom to be deduced, calculated, and guaranteed. 'Look, here it is', or 'There it is', are responses to observable facts that give irrefutable witness to its coming. They guarantee its certainty. Jesus denies this possibility but says that, even if they cannot see it, the Kingdom is already present 'in your midst'. As with 7:22, 11:20, and 16:16, it has to be acknowledged in situations in which it can be discerned but which nevertheless remain less than irrefutable demonstrations of its presence. Jesus answers the Pharisees' question which, though its underlying outlook is quite different, has presuppositions that are not far removed from those of the disciples at 21:7. The different answers meet the different stances of the questioners. Pharisaic scepticism has to be countered in a way that is different from the quieting of disciples' understandable fears.

It is those fears, however, that Jesus now addresses. The disciples will long to see 'one of the days of the Son of Man' and will not see it (v. 22). The use of the plural here is strange. It is used again at v. 26, though there it may simply be occasioned by the use of 'the days of Noah'. Elsewhere in the passage, the single 'day' is used (vv. 24, 30) and this suggests that the plural may have no special significance but simply refers to the period after the initial revelation of the Son of Man in glory. On the other hand, it is possible that it has more significance. If this is so, Luke may be using it to refer to those occasions when, in the ongoing life of the community, a glimpse of the Son of Man is allowed. Luke tells how Stephen has a vision of the Son of Man in glory (Acts 7:56), and it may be that he is thinking of moments like this.

The disciples will long for the revelation of the Son of Man in glory and, in their urgency, may be tempted to fix their hopes on false substitutes. By the time Luke wrote, some disciples were saying that the parousia could be accepted as a present inner experience which had already taken place and which gave them an esoteric understanding and a licence to behave in a way that was unconstrained by the ethical stand- ards of the present order. Paul, in 1 Corinthians, may be combating such an outlook. Luke here has Jesus warn against these untrue, but alluring, substitutes. Disciples must not be led into the false sense of security that they promised and must not enter upon a life of self-indulgence that was based upon nothing other than delusion. Just as Jesus had to suffer and be rejected, those who are his must follow the same path which cannot be avoided (v. 25). The day of the Son of Man will be devastatingly obvious to all and will result in a judgement as severe as that which befell the inhabitants of the earth at the time of the flood and of Sodom at the time of Lot (Gen 19:24– 6). The disciples' final question, 'Where, Lord?' (v. 36) seems still lacking in understanding. Its purpose would seem to be to allow the warnings to come to a climax with the proverbial saying of v. 37. Its cryptic but vivid imagery, as anyone who has thrown a piece of bread to gulls on the seashore knows, points to the suddenness of an appearance, the tumult it occasions, the fierceness of the event, and the inescapable certainty that something has happened.

Warning gives way to hope, for it is that which, for Luke, expresses the main significance of the parousia. The parable of the importunate widow (18:1–8) teaches that the disciples should pray for its coming and that they should not lose heart. If even an unjust judge is moved to respond to a widow's cry for vindication, how much more will the just God vindicate those who set their hopes on him? He hears their cries and will vindicate them 'speedily'. v. 8a has sometimes been translated 'suddenly' in support of the theory that Luke did not expect an early paraousia, but the use of the term at Acts 12:2, 25:4, as well as the sense of the parable itself, is against this. The verse promises a speedy vindication of those who long for it, and the sense of the passage as a whole means that this cannot refer to anything other than the parousia. v. 8b, of course, does allow enough time for a loss of faith but, as at 12:35–48, this is already happening. One of Luke's purposes in writing was to combat this.

(18:9–17) Parable of a Pharisee and a Tax-collector and the Incident of the Children Luke has Jesus tell the parable to some who 'trusted in themselves that they were righteous and regarded others with contempt'. 'The ones who trusted in themselves' are those who, when they engaged in self- examination, concluded that they were overall acceptable to God; they had a basic confidence that God would look favourably upon them. To suggest that it expresses a trust in

oneself rather than in God would be overstretching the mean- ing, for this is not what is suggested of the Pharisee in the parable and it is unlikely that Luke read it in this way. The phrase serves as a foil to the 'despising' of others. This, for Luke, is a very strong term and is used by him of Herod's mockery of Jesus (23:11). An attitude that expresses disdain is every bit as bad as open physical mockery. Who, though, are the ones whom Luke sees as addressed by the parable? It is certainly not limited to the Pharisees, but are they included within the addressees? This is, in the end, unlikely. To address it directly to a group that included Pharisees would seem gratuitously offensive and would be in danger of encouraging its other hearers to regard them with something of the outlook that the parable itself condemns. It would not have fitted a Jesus who was often at meals with them. Jesus, rather, uses this parable to address the crowd of disciples, and the incident of the children which follows it actually illustrates the need. Disciples were themselves in danger of becoming as exclud- ing in their way as the Pharisees were in theirs (cf. 9:59–60).

The Pharisee stands apart, 'by himself'. This seems the most likely translation, though the Greek is again ambiguous and could mean 'prayed to himself'. This would then mean that he prayed silently; again, however, it should not be pressed to suggest that his prayer stayed with him and did not ascend to God. The grounds of his confidence are his keeping the rules of his group which, going beyond the re- quirements of the law which did not require regular fasting, sought to express a purity which exceeded that of most people. He also tithed beyond the requirements of the law. These actions are not condemned. Disciples of John fasted and Luke reports how Jesus accepted the practice for members of the Christian community (5:35). It was the attitude of this particular Pharisee (and it is not suggested that he was typical of all Pharisees any more than it maintains that the one in the parable stood for all tax-collectors) that let him down. His thanksgiving was genuine and was certainly not portrayed as hypocritical. It is an extension of that outlook that is found in the Psalms and expresses a genuine piety (119:65–72). But it has its dangers. Here, the primary one is the separation from humanity as a whole which, in the thanksgiving for one's own acknowledgement by God, denies it to others. So, the tax-collector went away 'justified rather than the other'. His acknowledgment of his sin and his call for mercy make for a bridge between himself and God that the other's attitude did not allow. He was justified, that is, acknowledged by God and open to his reconciling power. Whether his prayer can be counted as penitence is more doubtful, for there is no sugges- tion that he was turning aside from his actual way of life (cf. the response of Zacchaeus, 19:8). Yet it is precisely this that gives the parable its starkness. He, whilst remaining a sinner, was actually more open to God than was the Pharisee. 'Justi- fied rather than the other' should probably be read as 'more than'. This is how Luke uses the phrase at 13:2, 4, and it makes the startling contrast without either denying entirely the prayer of the Pharisee or approving completely the lifestyle of the tax-collector.

Luke follows the parable with the episode of the disciples and the children. By not having the Markan reference to Jesus' blessing of them (Mk 10:16), he makes the whole point of the story focus upon the rebuke of the disciples. It is to 'such as these that the Kingdom belongs'. It is to those without status and without self-sufficiency that the Kingdom is offered and, indeed, given. It is pure gift and therefore cannot be received unless one takes on the stance of a little child. This should not be seen as simplicity, or innocence, or some other idealistic outlook. It is something much more demanding, namely a consciousness of need, of a total lack of self-sufficiency, and a recognition of one's dependence upon others and so upon God. It is an abandoning of all concern with status. The Kingdom is something that in the end can only be received. Any striving for the Kingdom that is enjoined (12:31) must be exercised only as a conscious response to grace.

(18:18–30) The Very Rich Ruler Luke's is a sympathetic version of the story that is found also in Matthew and Mark. At Mk 10:22 the man is so shocked by Jesus' call to dispose of his goods and follow him that he goes away grieving. Jesus' comments about the snare of riches are addressed to the disciples. In Luke, he is saddened by Jesus' reply for, since he was 'very rich', the demands being made upon him are severe. But he does not immediately go away. Jesus 'looks at him' and tells him about the difficulties that face the rich man's entry into the Kingdom. Luke's version of the story presents a continuing challenge to the ruler. It does not underplay the snares of riches, but, in keeping with what Luke's narrative has said earlier about the tax-collectors (16:1–13) (and with its reporting of the Zacchaeus incident, 19:1–10), it does not rule out the ruler's future response. The suggestion of its impossibility is countered by Jesus (vv. 26–7). Peter's assertion that they have done what the ruler seems unwilling to do is met by the promise of compensation in this age and eternal life in the age to come. They serve as contrasts to the ruler's refusal. That they have not yet perceived the real nature of the demand, however, is made clear by the stark contrast between Peter's outlook and that of Jesus as this is revealed in the following episode.

(18:31–4) The Third Passion Prediction In Matthew and Mark, this prediction occurs at the beginning of the journey to Jerusalem. Luke has now resumed an order of events that is close to theirs, but, because of his long central narrative, this prediction occurs near journey's end. A number of things are significant in Luke's version and show clear evidence of his hand. The events that are to take place are in 'accomplishment' of all the prophetic witness to the Son of Man (the same verb that is used of Jesus' time in Jerusalem at 13:32). Nothing is said (as at 22:66–71) of his condemnation by the Jews. At the conclusion of Jesus' disclosure, Luke alone points to the twelve's total lack of understanding (cf. 9:45). Luke could hardly have given this a greater emphasis. They still have much to learn. Even though he treats them less harshly than Mark (e.g. he does not have the incident found next in Mk 10:35–45), he continues to show how much understanding they lack (cf. 22:24–7).

(18:35–43) The Blind Man of Jericho In order to accommodate the story of Zacchaeus that Luke uses as a climax, he puts this episode at the approach to Jericho rather than at its exit as the other evangelists suggest. Those who rebuke the blind man are disciples who are at the front of the procession and it is these therefore who are themselves rebuked by Jesus' action in stopping his progress in order to respond to the pleas of the blind man and heal him. The blind man follows Jesus 'glorifying God', a response that is used by Luke on occasions he deems significant (2:20; 7:16; 23:47).

(19:1–10) Zacchaeus 'Chief tax-collector' is not found elsewhere in the NT and probably not outside it. It seems coined by Luke to make this episode climactic in Jesus' dealings with the tax-collectors. For the same reason, he describes Zacchaeus as 'rich'. The cards are stacked against him but his response to Jesus is met by a request, not merely to eat with him, but actually to stay with him. Those who hear it 'grumble', the same response that the Pharisees have earlier made (15:2). Now, it is made by 'all', which must include the disciples who are accompanying Jesus. They complain that Jesus has gone in to be 'the guest of a sinner'. Zacchaeus's words in v. 8 are sometimes understood as descriptions of his present actions: they report his current lifestyle, and Jesus' reply is then taken as an acknowledgement of this. Such an interpretation, however, fails to do justice to Luke's previous stories of Jesus' dealings with tax-collectors. Zacchaeus's response is rather a declaration of intent. Jesus proclaims that it makes him a true son of Abraham and means that he is included within God's saving act which fulfils his promises to the patriarch (1:55, 73).

(19:11–27) Parable of the Pounds Luke says that Jesus told the parable in order to combat the belief of some that his arrival in the city would trigger the appearance of the Kingdom. Just what is meant by that, however, is not easily determined for, as the parable stands, it does not point to a delay. The introduction therefore suggests that Luke himself saw the parable as a means of meeting the disappointment caused to some of his contemporaries by the delay of the parousia; Jesus himself did not expect it to be immediate. The parable as Luke tells it is likely to have developed from the one which is included at Mt 25:14–30 where it is also given an eschatological setting. Luke replaces talents with pounds which were coins of much smaller value; he does not differentiate between the disciples' gifts of grace (cf. 8:8), and the ten stand for everybody. He nevertheless deals with only three of the servants. Luke's version of the parable is made more complicated by the addition of a subplot in which the nobleman goes away to receive a kingdom and, on his return, acts as a monarch. Though it is usually read as an allegory of Jesus' ascension and parousia, this is not really obvious, for it is unlikely that Luke would have presented Jesus as a claimant to his throne. He sees his kingship rather as bestowed on him by God because of his obedience and surrender; Jesus certainly does not claim it (3:9–12). The story-line owes much to the events of 4 BCE, when Archelaus went to Rome to claim his father's throne and encountered strong resistance. To picture Jesus in terms of such an incident would be extremely odd. That the nobleman-become-king stands for Jesus is made more unlikely by the third servant's wholly unflattering description of him (v. 21) as rapacious and a fraudster, an assessment that the king does not deny (v. 22). If his reply were to be taken as an accommodation to the servant's assessment of him, that in itself would seem to confirm the judgement. It is more likely, however, that he is described as acknowledging the truth of the servant's description. The king is not a pleasant character.

The parable therefore is unlikely to be an allegory, but is rather, in the words of Evans (1990), 'another of the risqué parables . . . in which the central figure is a reprehensible character'. In pointing to the demands made by the manner of the Kingdom's appearing in Jesus, Luke has used this device, not only in the parable of the dishonest steward (16:1–9), but also, and with a close parallel, in that of the importunate widow (18:1–8), where one is encouraged to pray for its coming, and the friend at midnight (11:5–8) where one is told to ask to live out of its power. All these use unlikely characters to point to the crisis which the coming of the Kingdom brings to those who would be ready to receive it. Their use emphasizes the radicality of its demands. This does not mean, however, that the third servant is to be admired as someone who refuses to play by the lord's corrupt rules (Herzog 1994). He made a wrong response to the demands of one whose character he had rightly assessed and whose service he had entered into. His lord required of him a commitment and a willingness to venture all which he was not able to meet. Fear and self-protection held him back. For him there might be some excuse. There is none, says the parable, for those who have willingly committed themselves to discipleship in the service of him who is not to be feared but loved and whose treasures do not consist of unrighteous mammon but of the life of the Kingdom itself. Disciples must risk all for the Kingdom and not let its gifts come to nothing either by acquiescing in the present or by despairing of its future (17:22–18:8).

Jesus in Jerusalem (19:28–24:53)

(19:28–44) The Entry into Jerusalem All four gospels tell of Jesus' entry into Jerusalem. Luke's narrative has a number of distinctive features. He emphasizes the connection of the event with the Mount of Olives which stands some 2 miles east of Jerusalem. Like Matthew and Mark, the story begins on the approach to the mount (v. 29) but, unlike them, he has the acknowledgement of Jesus take place on the top of the mount itself, just as Jerusalem is coming into view (vv. 37–8). In Acts the ascension takes place there and, in view of Acts 1:11, this is where Luke expects the return of Jesus (cf. Zech 14:4). In keeping with the last section of the journey narrative, Jesus is acknowledged by the disciples alone (vv. 36, 37). Jesus' reply to the Pharisees (v. 40) suggests that Jerusalem's inhabitants are silent. The disciples stand for her true people and, if they had kept quiet, the stones of the city would have had to respond to Jesus because Jerusalem herself could not have allowed him to enter her unacknowledged. The response, as Luke tells it, addresses Jesus as king but does not have Mark's reference to the coming Kingdom. It stresses Jesus' messianic entry into his inheritance (Zech 9:9) but, in a revised version of the angels' song (2:14), emphasizes that this is first realized in the heavenly realm which is all-important for Luke. What is to happen on earth follows from what happens there (cf. 10:18).

Luke alone tells how Jesus weeps over the city (vv. 41–4). This is the time of her 'visitation', a term which, though in the OT can be one of either judgement or redemption, in the light of 1:68, 7:16, is here to be understood in the latter sense. Because Jerusalem rejects this and follows her own determined path, her destruction is inevitable. Though this is described in terms which are taken from the OT, it suggests knowledge of the Roman destruction of Jerusalem in 70 CE. Jewish rejection of Jesus and his way of peace leads them into confrontation with Rome with its inevitably disastrous results. Though the biblical language catches these up into the purposes of God, the description as a whole does not suggest that the events are understood by Luke as actually determined by him. Israel is the cause of her own ruin.

(19:45–8) Jesus and the Temple In Mark, what is usually described as Jesus' 'cleansing' of the temple is pictured as its rejection and, at his trial before the Sanhedrin, false witnesses accuse him of saying that he would destroy it. In Matthew Jesus takes possession of it and it is there that his messiahship is acknowledged; at the trial, false witnesses say rather that he claimed to be able to destroy it. Luke's episode is much shorter. Jesus drives out the money-changers and complains about the temple's misuse. There is no reference at the trial to any threat against it. In the light of the way Luke has reported Jesus' lament over Jerusalem, it seems that he wishes to dissociate Jesus from the destruction of the temple which he knows has already happened by the time he writes. He does, however, share Matthew's picture of Jesus' taking over the temple. It witnessed to him at his infancy and, as a boy, he was already showing his authority there (2:25–51). Now, he reasserts that authority and teaches daily in it. From there the leaders of the nation seek a way to kill him but are as yet helpless because 'the people' (a favourite Lukan term denoting God's covenantal community) were 'spellbound' by what they heard. The temple acknowledges him, the leaders reject him; the people are spellbound by him. At Nazareth earlier, when their expectations were not realized, their wonder soon turned to hostility (4:21–30). Luke's narrative begins to unfold the inevitable progression to the cross.

(20: 1–47) Controversies in the Temple In common with Matthew and Mark, Luke now has a number of incidents in the temple where Jesus is in conflict with the leaders of the Jerusalem community. Unlike them, however, he does not include Pharisees in these hostile incidents and he also has Jesus continuing to teach 'the people' who are still presented as favourably disposed to him. As they now stand, these incidents reflect the experiences of the early church and the attitudes these engendered. The first controversy story (20:1–8) concerns the authority of Jesus. Elsewhere, when Jesus is questioned, and even when the question is motivated by hostility, he deals with it seriously (10:25; 17:20). Here, he engages in a form of one-upmanship that would seem to be shaped by later Jewish–Christian debates. The logic behind the appeal to the Baptist is not obvious though the general Christian acceptance of him as a new Elijah (in which however Luke does not share, see LK 1:5–25) might mean that Mal 3:1 forms a link.

The parable of the wicked tenants (20:9–19) is the only parable to appear in all three Synoptic Gospels in the same setting. Comparisons of the three versions, however, show that it has been strongly shaped by the beliefs of the three evangelists as well as by the oral traditions which lay behind their gospels. Much of that shaping has taken the form of a more thorough allegorization to enable it fully to reflect both the life of Jesus and the history of Israel. Added allegorization, however, has only carried on what was latent in its beginnings. Jesus told a parable that spoke of his place in God's dealings with Israel and which reflected his understanding of his relationship with her. Luke, like Mark, has the vineyard owner send one servant after another in a generous, but ultimately unrealistic, attempt to bring the tenants to a recognition of their responsibilities. In Luke, however, they do not kill any of the servants. This, rather than Matthew's confrontational groups of servants, is at one with the action of sending the son in a last, desperate attempt to bring them to their senses. v. 13 recognizes the wishful thinking that this involves but which is made inevitable by the father's desire to commend rather than impose his authority. Recent interpreters have pointed to the father's change of outlook that is brought about by the killing of the son, and have wondered how far this reflects early church elaboration since it appears scarcely consistent with one who before was unwilling to take revenge. It almost suggests that the father regarded the servants as expendable in a way that the son was not. Certainly, the three evangelists present the father's reactions in different ways. Luke's inclusion of the people's 'God forbid' (v. 16) to the threatened destruction may point to his belief that it was not inevitable. v. 17 with its quote from Ps 118:22 pictures the vindication of Jesus as the climax and he could have seen this fulfilled at the resurrection and ascension. Luke has a reference (v. 18) to Isa 8:14 which is also found joined to the quotation from Ps 118 at 1 Pet 2:8 and occurs again in some versions of Mt 21:42. Individuals who are opposed to Jesus or who merit his wrath will be dealt with firmly. Acts shows how Luke sees this happening (Acts 1:18; 5:6; 12:23).

Jesus' message about the coming of the Kingdom may not have been overtly political (though this is disputed), but it certainly had strong political and social implications. The question about the legitimacy of paying taxes to Caesar (vv. 20–6) recognizes this and is asked in an attempt to discredit him in the eyes either of those who looked for the overthrow of Rome or of the civil authorities who were quick to act against political agitators. Mark's statement that it represents a combined attack of Pharisees and Herodians suggests a fairly even-handed approach. Luke's introduction, on the other hand, shows that he regards it as a deliberate attempt by the Jewish authorities to make Jesus espouse a stance that would enable them to denounce him to the Romans as a threat to the state. This is precisely what they will do later (23:2) when they hand him over to Pilate. Luke sees Jesus' answer as a slick side-stepping of the trap. It gives them no grounds for their later charge which is exposed as perverse and fraudulent. Recognition of this has often led interpreters of Luke's work to suggest that it was written with the aim of rebutting the charge that Christianity was a threat to Rome; claims that it was are seen to arise out of Jewish hostility. Whilst this is true in so far as no Roman official in Acts ever condemns Paul, Christianity is often regarded by them as a threat to Roman stability, and both Jesus and Paul are judicially executed by the Roman power. Luke knows that Rome was perplexed by Christian claims and was always in danger of acting against them. Christians are those who 'turn the world upside down'

(Acts 17:6). Jesus' reply (v. 25), though not unambiguous, left room for a conflict of interests for it said that both God and the state had legitimate claims on the coin and what it stood for. This made for an inevitable tension which could be resolved only by denying the legitimate sphere of one party or by compartmentalizing their claims in a way that did less than justice to the overarching concerns of God.

The Sadducees then put something of a trick question to Jesus (vv. 27–40). Members of the religious and political establishment in Jerusalem, they were conservative in both areas. Using the Mosaic rule of levirate marriage (Deut 25:5) to make their point, they question the sense in which life after death can be meaningful. Jesus' reply points to the newness of God's eschatological, recreative act. It is not simply the continuation of what now is. vv. 35–6 give to Luke's reporting of Jesus' answer a deeper dimension than that found in the other gospels as he struggles to express what he sees as its meaning. This is true also of his handling of the use of Ex 3:6 ('the story about the bush') where he adds v. 38b to what is presented as a typical piece of scribal reasoning which ignores the original meaning of the quotation. The scribes, however, are impressed by this exegetical *tour de force*. Jesus has outwitted his opponents.

In the light of this victory, Jesus, using the same scribal methods, himself goes on the attack. Psalm 110:1 plays a large part in NT apologetic (Mk 14:62; Rom 8:34; Eph 1:20; Heb 1:3; 1 Pet 3:22). It gives biblical justification for believing in the exalted nature of Jesus. For Luke, the passage exercises a great deal of control over his presentation of Jesus, as Acts 2:34 makes clear. 'Lord' is perhaps his most fundamental title for describing Jesus' relationship to both God and his disciples. Its basis in Ps 110:1 means that he can retain Jesus' subordination to the Father as he describes his role in terms that remain largely functional. Though the passage reflects the usage of the early church, this does not necessarily mean that it was not used by Jesus of himself in an attempt to enlarge his contemporaries' limited expectations about the nature of messiahship. Whether it is believed to reflect his use, however, is ultimately determined by the wider question of whether Jesus himself thought in terms of his own messiahship. On this, there is little scholarly consensus. As though himself dissatisfied with the pedestrian nature of this reasoning, Jesus is said to have gone on to attack the scribes who were responsible for its use (vv. 45–7).

(21:1–38) **Jesus' Apocalyptic Discourse** All three Synoptic Gospels present this extended discourse as the conclusion of Jesus' ministry and the immediate introduction to the passion narrative. On the one hand, it brings to a climax Jesus' teaching about the Kingdom, the hostility this provokes, and the challenge it makes to the disciples, and, on the other, it acts as the backcloth against which the passion and resurrection of Jesus is to be viewed. It brings all these happenings into relation with the future experiences of the disciples as they face the problems of maintaining faith in the midst of a hostile world. Past and present will together issue in the open revelation of God's kingdom which the appearance of Jesus as Son of Man in glory will establish. The life, death, and resurrection of Jesus have revealed his ultimacy. In the light of this faith, the present of Luke's readers can be seen as contributing to the final revelation of him and of the Kingdom that he guarantees.

Three interwoven strands run through the chapter and determine its structure. These talk about persecutions which the disciples will face in the world and in which they must maintain their witness, historical events whose turmoil will bring a perplexity which is, nevertheless, not devoid of hope, and the expectation of the coming of the Son of Man in glory. History, myth, belief, and imagery come together to create a vision the strength of which is not in its details but in the overall impression it conveys as it takes up the whole event of Jesus and views it from the perspective of the finality and ultimacy that it believes it to be.

Luke's introduction (vv. 5–7) differs substantially from those of Matthew and Mark in that, whereas they have the discourse delivered away from the temple and in some sense over and against it, Luke has Jesus give it in the temple itself and as part of his general teaching to the people (v. 38). He has Jesus pay more attention to the destruction of the temple for its own sake and does not see it as the inevitable prelude to the end of the age (v. 7, cf. Mt 24:3; Mk 13:4). The historical events have an importance in their own right and are not to be seen purely as signs of his coming (v. 8), for the end is not an immediate event (v. 9). Nevertheless, political catastrophes will be preludes to natural ones (v. 11). vv. 12–19, however, break this interconnectedness to concentrate upon the witness of the disciples when they are persecuted and brought to trial because of their allegiance to Jesus and his saving work ('my Name', cf. Ex 33:17–19). These are not merely a prelude to his future revelation but are an inevitable part of their discipleship. Though he may seem absent, Jesus himself is actually present then, seeking to inspire their witness (v. 15) (cf. Acts 7:55). Whereas 13:13 points to their vindication at the parousia, Luke places it in 'the gaining of their souls' (v. 19), that is, in a heavenly life into which the present leads (20:38; 23:43). It is in this sense that the promise of security in v. 18 is to be understood; no part of their real being will be lost or be brought to nothing. Once more we see how the heavenly dimension is very real to Luke and how the ascension of Jesus enables those who follow him to enter into it.

At v. 20 Luke, in line with Matthew and Mark, brings the destruction of Jerusalem, which by the time he writes will have already occurred, into relation with the programme of the last things. Unlike them, however, he does not invest it with the dimension of apocalyptic mystery (Mk 13:14). For him it remains an event that is important in its own right. As with 19:41–4, he describes the historical events of its fall in biblical terms which present them as the fulfilment of prophetic expectations (v. 22). This verse is his closest approach to expressing a belief that God was involved in its destruction; Luke generally does not make this assertion (23:31). The fall of the city begins 'the time of the Gentiles' which is to go on until the point at which its purpose is completed. This suggests an end to Jerusalem's captivity and a restoration of her by God. He has not turned his back upon her but has used even her destruction to further his purposes which will rebound to her ultimate good (2:32). The period of her desolation (which is not necessarily short) will lead into the time of the imminent end when cosmic disasters will occur that will climax with the ' "Son of Man coming in a cloud" with power and great glory'.

This quotation from Dan 7:13 has been altered by Luke so that the 'cloud' in the singular may bear reference to the ascension of Jesus (Acts 1:9, 11) which for him is both a pointer to, and guarantee of, the parousia. He has no mention of the gathering together of the elect at the parousia (Mk 13:27) for he does not emphasize it as a time of negative judgement upon the world. For him, it is the time of 'redemption' (v. 28) and, since the people are not excluded from Jesus' audience, the hope that this offers is not denied to them. v. 31 (peculiar to Luke in its particular emphasis) sets 'these things'—including the trials and the fall of Jerusalem—against the backcloth of the reality of the Kingdom that has been established through Jesus. Though this present heavenly reality must be their primary compass point for determining their attitude to all that happens, it does not do away with a lively expectation of the appearing of the Son of Man. v. 32 includes that within the events expected in 'this generation'. Luke stretches that to include the period of his own contemporaries, but there is nothing to suggest that it could be extended much further. Meanwhile, they must pray for a faithfulness that will enable them to face his return with confidence (v. 36) (cf. 18:8).

Luke's is a free handling of the tradition which he most probably took over from Mark. Though it is often maintained that he reduces the expectation of an early parousia, there is little in this chapter to suggest it. What he does is to separate out a number of events that Mark sees as leading directly into it. The fall of Jerusalem will have happened by the time Luke wrote and he could look back on times of persecution. The parousia remained his ultimate hope, however, and this continued to impinge directly upon the present. The confidence with which he could proclaim it came from his belief that Jesus, now exalted to the right hand of God, guaranteed the Kingdom as a present reality. Its very nearness in spatial terms meant that its open revelation would not be long delayed in time.

The confidence of the early church that emphasized the hope of the imminence of the parousia was doomed to disappointment (2 Pet 3:8–10). The beliefs that determined the apocalyptic images in which those hopes were expressed had to be reassessed as the full significance of God's action in Jesus came gradually to be understood. How far Jesus himself used that imagery, what he meant by it if he did, and how much its use in the Bible depends not on him but on the outlook of the early church, remain important, though hotly disputed, questions. All a commentary on this one gospel can say is that Luke's handling of it shows that he was aware that he was dealing with images that could be reshaped to express new outlooks. Nevertheless, as a first-century man, he did not evacuate them of all historical content or undervalue the radical nature of what they were proclaiming. Luke still looked for a direct and powerful intervention of God in the world and he did not expect it to be long delayed.

(22:1–38) The Last Supper The apocalyptic discourse that bases all its thought upon the reality of the Kingdom leads directly into the passion narrative that shows how it was established. Luke alone of the synoptic writers (22:3, 31–4, 43, cf. Jn 13:2) sets the earthly events of the passion in the context of an eschatological battle with Satan. He emphasizes that it is the passover meal that Jesus shares with the apostles

(22:1, 7, 8, 13). This obviously has some important significance for him (9:31).

Discovering the meaning he gives to it, however, is complicated by the fact that Jesus' interpretative words over the bread and cup(s) are given in two versions with the shorter of them ending at 19a, 'this is my body'. After a period of near-universal espousal of this shorter text, interpreters have moved decisively in favour of the belief that Luke himself wrote the longer text that ends with v. 20 and that one manuscript tradition shortened it (though cf. REB and Evans 1990). In spite of this growing consensus, however, and the weight of manuscript evidence in its favour, there is much to be said for the view that Luke himself wrote the shorter text. The longer version bears all the marks of a hybrid resulting from the contributions of many hands to bring Luke into some sort of conformity with the general eucharistic traditions of the early church. The shorter text is the more distinctive and, indeed, more difficult reading and, if Luke himself is not responsible for it, it is hard to see why anyone should have shortened what he wrote to arrive at this unusual and not easily explained interpretation of Jesus' actions. Its ending reflects the Markan 'bread' word which Luke appears to be following at this point. His earlier description of the beginnings of a passover meal (vv. 15–18) has been influenced by Mark's version of Jesus' eschatological statement that forms the climax of his account (Mk 14:25). The passover meal itself already gave expression to this dimension, and it is this eschatological emphasis that Luke sets at the heart of his narrative. Whether Jesus eats and drinks or abstains (the former being more likely)—for the text is again doubtful—he brings the meal into close relation with his entry into the Kingdom which will be established by his exaltation (vv. 16, 18, cf. 22:69). Luke has one cup (v. 18) to which he gives this eschatological significance. It binds together those who share the meal in an anticipation of their part in the Kingdom. He distributes the bread to 'the apostles' (v. 14, cf. Acts 1:3) and calls it 'my body', 'me', not broken in death, but his living presence that enables them to live out of his life. Luke does not give sacrificial significance to either the bread or the wine, for he does not understand Jesus' death as itself the point of atonement. His narrative of the crucifixion will present it otherwise. In Acts, the eucharist is the 'breaking of bread' (2:42), and the Emmaus episode shows that Luke finds its significance in the way it enables those who participate to share with Jesus in the life of the Kingdom.

Judas breaks this eschatological unity and is wholly condemned. The disciples are in danger of doing so by reason of their seeking after positions of glory (vv. 24–7). Luke gave no place to an earlier instance of this outlook which the tradition contained (Mk 10:35–45), presumably not to spare their blushes but to save it for this dramatic context. In place of that tradition's reference to Jesus' death as a ransom (Mk 10:45), Luke sees his saving work accomplished through his service, climaxing in the cross and controlled by it but, nevertheless, not actually isolated in it. From such a perspective, Jesus can bestow upon the apostles a share in the Kingdom which his father has conferred upon him (vv. 28–30). They will judge Israel and those who are associated with her when she is restored, that is when Jesus' Kingdom is revealed.

Before Jesus can enter his Kingdom, however, he must undergo his final act of surrender and make his climactic response to the way of obedience upon which he embarked when he rejected the blandishments of Satan (4:1–13). Satan is decisively active at this point and is about to release his power against the apostles. Jesus has interceded for Peter (vv. 31–4) and, though he will slip, his faith will not desert him. When he has recovered, he is to strengthen his brethren. Luke will present Peter as the first witness of the resurrection (24:34) and will portray him in Acts positively as the one who will lead the church into its universal witness. Now is the eschatological hour, the time of crisis which calls for a different stance from that which characterized their earlier work for Jesus (9:1–6; 10:1–12). The episode of the two swords (vv. 36–8) is peculiar. Luke is aware of the tradition (which he uses) of some violence at the arrest (22:5) and he is emphatic in his presentation of Jesus as crucified in the midst of evildoers (23:32). He presents Jesus as the fulfilment of Isaiah's suffering servant (Isa 52:13–53:12). v. 37 contains Jesus' only direct quote from there, and the disciples' possession of swords is seen as a part of that passage's witness to him.

(22:39–53) On the Mount of Olives Luke's story of the agony in the garden is shorter than those given elsewhere, not, it seems, in order to reduce Jesus' distress, but to play down the ineptitude of the disciples. Peter, James, and John are not singled out, and Jesus finds them asleep only once and 'because of grief' (v. 45). 'The trial' that they are to pray not to enter becomes, not their time in the garden, but rather what is yet to happen (v. 46). It is a time when Satan is wholly rampant and they are unable to escape his clutches (cf. 11:4). The result of this shortening is to throw all the emphasis on Jesus' prayer that his will may be aligned to the Father's. The prayer itself expresses confidence in his own constancy. vv. 43–4 are absent from many MSS though they are found in some early writings. Recent interpreters have tended to regard them as additions to what Luke wrote (Nolland 1993). Though doctrinal considerations could have been responsible for either their inclusion or omission, the latter is more likely and they are not out of keeping with Luke's belief that this incident represents the focal point and climax of Jesus' obedient surrender to his calling. Their mention of an angel now brings to mind the absence of angelic succour from Luke's temptation narrative, and his expectation of a renewed struggle with Satan (4:13). This emphasizes the 'stress' that Jesus expected to accompany his 'baptism' (12:49) and, if it fulfilled it, would account for the move into that quiet confidence that characterizes Luke's account of the arrest and trial, and the crucifixion itself.

The time of the disciples' trial begins, even while Jesus is still speaking (v. 47). It is at this point that the atmosphere of Luke's narrative moves away from Matthew's and even more from Mark's in the direction of John's (cf. FGS K). Jesus is more in control, not obviously as in John, but with a gentle confidence of one who has had his struggles and now moves serenely to complete what has been given him to do. Jesus addresses Judas before he kisses him, stops any resistance, heals the harm done, and sets the actions of those who have come to take him—who in Luke include the chief priests and elders themselves and not merely their officers—within the context of eschatological evil (v. 53). What is happening is invested with cosmic significance. Jesus is fully aware of the shift in aeons that is taking place. Everything he has done has led up to this moment. There is no mention of the disciples' flight (Mk 14:50).

(22:54–65) The Evening Wait Luke has no night session of the council (Mt 26:57–68; Mk 14:53–65) which does not meet, either formally or informally, until the morning. This has the result of removing the mockery of Jesus, which took place during the night, from the members of the council and also of lessening the contrast between Peter's weakness and Jesus' steadfastness. The failure of Peter is made less drastic in both Matthew and Luke by the inclusion of only one cock-crow. The reference to Peter's 'going out and weeping bitterly' (v. 62) is absent from at least one MS. Whilst later hands may have added it to Luke's narrative, it is more likely to be his own conclusion to his dramatic mention of Jesus' glance (v. 61). It marks the beginning of the Lord's rescue of Peter and the preparation for his strengthening of the others (vv. 31–2).

Members of the council are spared the indignity of being involved in the horseplay with Jesus. The cry of mockery, 'Prophesy! Who is it that struck you?' is often pointed to as one of the most important agreements of Matthew and Luke against Mark (Goulder 1989). It has been accounted strong evidence for the belief that Luke knew Matthew and used him in the composition of his gospel. On the other hand, it has been used by others to support the theory that Q contained a passion narrative. Its taunt is appropriate for the Lukan assertion that it was made by the guards who were holding Jesus. Mt 26:68, on the other hand, has it made by the council to a Jesus who is not blindfolded.

(22:66–71) Jesus Before the Council In Luke's gospel, the council meets formally in the morning when the examination of Jesus takes place. It has less characteristics of a trial than have Matthew's and Mark's night session, however, for there are no witnesses, no formal accusations, and no condemnation of Jesus. Whilst this might reflect a greater historical awareness, little can actually be built on it for the differences may simply be the result of theological rather than historical concerns. Luke's gospel gives little basis for any suggestion that Jesus was hostile to the temple which rather acknowledges him as its lord. On the principle of there being no smoke without fire, therefore, he would not want suggestions of Jesus' hostility to the temple to be recorded (cf. Acts 6:13–14). The council rather addresses directly the question of Jesus' status: 'If you are the Christ, tell us'. Jesus' reply has two parts. vv. 67b–8 point to their total perversity. They will neither believe, nor even acknowledge, the truth. They will not accept him as Christ in the manner that they should, but they would like to hear from him a declaration of messiahship which could be reported to Pilate as subversive. Jesus refuses to fall into their trap but answers in a way that defines his status in terms which transcend their categories. From this point in time (emphatic in Luke), he will be exalted to the right hand of God. As opposed to Mark's version of his reply, Luke makes no mention of a future, visible coming (Mk 14:62). Jesus' exaltation will be for the eyes of faith alone. It is that event which forms the contents of both his claims and the disciples' belief. The council acknowledges the significance of the declaration, however, and 'all of them' ask, 'Are you therefore the Son of God?' This for Luke has a deeper significance

than 'Christ'. It recalls the second part of the angel's declaration to Mary (1:35) and foreshadows the preaching in Acts (9:20; 13:33). In the light of Mt 26:64, Jesus' reply seems to be an acceptance of the implications of the question and a witness to their recognition of them. Their perversity however makes them disown him and refuse their own insights. Their accusations before Pilate reveal just how great that perversity is (23:2).

(23:1–25) Before Pilate Luke's version of this episode emphasizes Pilate's reluctance to act against Jesus, brings out, therefore, the Jewish initiative in the crucifixion of Jesus, and introduces an appearance of him before Herod. Luke alone has Jesus appear before Herod (vv. 6–12). As an event in history, it makes strange reading for, though it is possible that Roman justice could allow a man to be tried in the place where he lived (Acts 23:34), to hand over responsibility to a non-Roman would be unusual. Pilate, however, seems to be associating Herod with his own involvement rather than handing over the case to him. The purpose of this remains entirely obscure and the incident is therefore best interpreted as a Lukan story occasioned partly by the influence of Ps 2:1–2 which is quoted at Acts 4:25–6 where it is seen as fulfilled in the actions of Pilate and Herod, partly by the appearance of Paul before another Herod (Acts 25–6), and partly by Luke's earlier references to Herod's interest in Jesus. At 9:7–9, Herod is both perplexed by and interested in Jesus, and at 13:31 is reported as being hostile to him. By including him, Luke (since he leaves Pharisees out of the hostile actions in Jerusalem itself), is able to present what is happening as the outcome of the whole career of Jesus and, at the same time, to emphasize the perversity of the Jerusalem authorities whose insistence brings about his death, not, however, without their contributing to the divine plan. The Roman power unwittingly enables God's plan to be fulfilled at the death of Jesus just as it did at his birth. Herod does not even have that dignity. He himself joins in the mockery of Jesus. Yet his encounter does not leave even him unaffected (v. 12).

When Pilate asks him if he is 'the Messiah, the king of the Jews', Jesus' reply is probably meant by Luke to be taken in the affirmative, for it is as such that he is crucified (23:38). Pilate, like the Jewish leaders, has completely misunderstood the implications of what he mouths. Yet he three times declares Jesus innocent (vv. 4, 15, 22) of the charges they bring against him, for Luke is at pains to show that Jesus' role was not a political one. All is to be kept on the level of the religious. Pilate succumbs to the Jewish pressure but his surface acceptance of their charge (v. 38) shows the incredibility of it and, unwittingly, witnesses to the truth.

v. 13 reintroduces 'the people' who have been absent since 21:38 where they were presented as favourable to Jesus. Now, however, their mood changes and they are included among those whose 'voices prevailed' (v. 23). The people share in the perversity of their leaders but they remain dignified with that term and, even as they contribute to the fulfilment of the divine plan (Acts 4:27–8), they avoid the excesses of their leaders (23:35) and remain dissociated from their more grotesque actions (23:27, 48).

v. 25 brings the scene to an end with a Lukan comment on the magnitude of the tragedy. The Jews as a whole (v. 18) asked for a murderer to be released and to be given Jesus to do with 'as they wished'. It is they who crucified him (Acts 3:13–15); the representatives of the political power do not come to the surface again until 23:36 when they join in mindless mockery (cf. 22:63–4; 23:11).

(23:26–49) The Crucifixion Luke alone of the evangelists has a Jewish crowd accompany Jesus to his execution. 'A great number of the people' follow him, including some women who, perhaps taking on a role that was not uncommon on such occasions and which may originally have had some quasi-religious significance, lament on behalf of the one who was going to his death. Addressing them as 'daughters of Jerusalem', he speaks to them as representatives of the true among the people of that city. They are to lament the future, for a time of great distress is coming (Hos 10:8). What that occasion is can be determined only from the cryptic saying of v. 31. If it is to be given a specific reference, that is most likely to the destruction of Jerusalem in 70 CE. Compared with Jesus, Jerusalem and her people take on the characteristics of a dead tree. 'They' who will treat her harshly will be the Romans or, perhaps more likely, a combination of the powers who together brought Jesus to his cross. Luke has earlier twice brought the suffering of Jerusalem in relation to both Jesus' own and those of the disciples (19:41–4; 21:20–4). Jesus himself remains the true son of Jerusalem.

Luke's crucifixion scene is distinctive. Whilst this might be the result of his use of special sources, the overall unity of outlook between this scene and the gospel as a whole suggests that any sources that he did use were handled freely so as to become effective vehicles for the expression of his own particular insights. What happens at the cross, as Luke tells its story, is completely at one with his gospel's presentation of Jesus as he moved determinedly towards it.

Jesus' plea for the forgiveness of his persecutors (v. 34) is textually doubtful and, on the textual evidence alone, would most likely have to be regarded as an addition to what Luke himself wrote. It would then be seen as either included because of the availability of a tradition unknown to Luke, or added as appropriate in the light of Stephen's response to his persecutors as this is found at Acts 7:60. It is just that response, however, that makes it most likely that Luke himself included Jesus' prayer. He describes Stephen's martyrdom in terms of Jesus' own, and it is wholly unlikely that he would have had him outstrip Jesus in that merciful outlook that he has earlier declared to be of the essence of God himself (6:36). Acts 3:17 also suggests ignorance as a mitigating factor for the Jews and, since Jesus' prayer is in Luke made primarily on their behalf, Peter is there again drawing on Jesus' example. The plea is virtually demanded by Luke's overall presentation of Jesus.

The story of Jesus and the criminal (vv. 39–43), which Luke alone has, is again wholly at one with Luke's total picture. To call the criminal 'penitent' goes further than the story itself suggests. His plea is rather a recognition of that which in Jesus has drawn the outsider to him in a response of hope which, in turn, was always acknowledged and included in a greater work (7:36–50; 8:43–8; 17:11–19). This episode is entirely in keeping with those earlier stories of Jesus' open acceptance of the outsider. The new dimension in Jesus'

promise is determined by the difference in the shared circumstances of the one to whom it is made and of the one who makes it. To suggest that it points to a new situation brought about by the saving cross (Fitzmyer 1985) does less than justice to Luke's distinctive understanding of the place of the cross in the redeeming work of Jesus. For him, the cross is the climax and determining fact of Jesus' whole ministry which, taken up at the ascension, becomes God's outreaching redemptive act. He does not isolate the cross to make it the point of atonement or to suggest that something is achieved by it in itself. As earlier (16:19–31; 8:55; 20:38; 21:19), Luke seems to allow for the continuity of life through death. 'Paradise', originally meaning a park or garden, came to be regarded as a perhaps temporary abode of the righteous departed after death. For Luke this is appropriate, for he regards the ascension as the point of Jesus's entry into his kingdom.

With v. 44, Luke (as Mark) moves into the final stages of Jesus' crucifixion. However, there are big differences at this point. Like Mark, he has the three hours of darkness which signifies the awesomeness of what is taking place. He places the tearing of the temple's curtain before Jesus' last cry rather than at his death (Mk 15:38). The temple's holy of holies gives place to Jesus' whole life rather than to what is achieved through death alone, for it is that life as a whole which becomes the place where God is known. Jesus' crying 'with a loud voice' (v. 46) is not, as in Mark, one of desolation (see MK 13:33–6), but of confidence. Jesus quotes, not Ps 22:1, but Ps 31:5. The agony, which is real, is caught up into the obedience that enables a secure confidence. The compulsion that has driven Jesus has allowed him to maintain the certainty of God's vindication. His last cry expresses the surrender born of the knowledge of a course well run. Like Mark, Luke has Jesus 'breathe his last'. He records a real outpouring, a complete emptying of himself.

In Luke, unlike Mark, where his response is to the death of Jesus (Mk 15:39), the centurion witnesses to 'what had taken place', that is to the whole demeanour of Jesus as he hung on the cross. By his response, he 'glorifies God', that is he makes what Luke regards as an appropriate witness to the significance of the event which causes it (7:16; 18:43). NRSV and REB both give his witness as 'This man was innocent'. This is without doubt a translation that does less than justice to Luke's meaning (Doble 1996). The Greek is *dikaios*, a word that Luke has used earlier to describe the status of the true in Israel who, being open to God's ways, acknowledged Jesus as the redeemer of his people (1:6; 2:25). The word as used by Luke witnesses to a religious rather than a judicial status. It is a word with strong LXX influence. Used in the Psalms of the righteous person who is the taunt of enemies but who is vindicated by God (Ps 37, cf. 5:12; 34:19; 55:22; 118:20), it is developed in Wis 1–6 to give a picture of the persecuted righteous one who is vindicated by God, lives through death, and will witness the discomfiture of his enemies (2:12–20; 3:1–9; 5:15–20). Closely aligned with this picture in both Psalms and Wisdom is that of the suffering servant of Isa 53 who is called *dikaios* and is said to be both justified by God and the one who serves many well (LXX). Luke's picture of Jesus on the cross recalls that of the servant in that he is clearly set with the transgressors, makes intercession for his captors, serves those who are crucified with him, and awaits God's vindication which will make him the vindicator of others. Luke does not take over the idea of the servant as sinbearing nor that of his death as vicarious, but the close links with that picture make Jesus more than an example. He will actually make many like him.

Luke pictures Jesus as more than the first martyr and as more than an example. He is the redeemer who in Acts, through his name and through the Spirit, reproduces his likeness in those who follow him.

Luke's narrative ends more positively than Mark's in that the crowds 'beat their breasts' and Mark's women are joined in their witness of the events by 'all his acquaintances'. Using the language of Ps 38:11, this is probably intended to include the apostles who are not reported as fleeing at the arrest and who at Acts 1:21 are said to have been constantly with him.

(23:50–24:12) The Tomb Luke's account of the events at the tomb is closer to Mark than to either Matthew or John. Joseph is described as a member of the council rather than as a Christian. He lays Jesus in the tomb, the women watch what is happening and then go away to prepare spices so that they might anoint him after the sabbath rest is over. Whereas Mark says that the women watch 'where' Jesus is laid, for it must not be thought that they later were to go to the wrong tomb, Luke, though sharing this concern, says 'how' he was laid, that is, unanointed. Anointing of the corpse was necessary to hinder the process of decomposition which would almost certainly have begun before the delayed anointing by the women. Luke does not name the women at this point. They have watched Jesus on the cross, seen the burial, prepared the spices, will witness the empty tomb and receive the message of the two men. In Luke, the women are the faithful witnesses. The 'two men' are angelic beings who also appear at the ascension (Acts 1:10). The message of the angels is for the women, rather than given to them in order to be passed on to the disciples (Mk 16:7). There is no command to go to Galilee, for Luke insists that all must happen within the environs of Jerusalem (24:49). The women respond to the message and 'remember'. They acknowledge its truth and their names are now given. The apostles, however, do not believe them. v. 12 is textually doubtful and it could be taken over from John; its 'linen cloths' are in his account and were not used earlier by Luke (23:53). On the other hand, its thought is entirely at one with Luke's picture of Peter who was to be kept from Satan's clutches (22:31–3). He does not share the scepticism of the others which represents the nadir of their discipleship. The women are the first witnesses to the resurrection; Peter is ready to be the first witness of the risen Lord (24:34). In Luke, the women play the part which, in the Fourth Gospel, is reserved for the beloved disciple (20:8).

(24:13–49) Resurrection Appearances Luke's resurrection narratives are quite distinctive and reflect his own particular concerns. The form in which he narrates them is determined by the fact that he alone of the evangelists witnesses to an ascension event which is separated out from the resurrection, brings the resurrection appearances to an end, and takes up the physical body of Jesus into heaven. The ascension becomes the point at which it is deemed appropriate to 'worship' him (24:52). Until then, his followers neither recognize the

significance of the resurrection, nor appreciate the full import of his life. The resurrection appearances become points of teaching and convincing. In themselves, they are 'something of a half-way house' (Evans 1970).

The Emmaus story (24:13–27) tells of Jesus' appearance to two otherwise unknown disciples who, somewhat apart from the rest, are making a 7-mile journey from Jerusalem. It plays the part in the resurrection narratives that the mission of the seventy plays in the body of the gospel (10:1–24). Like that episode, it roots actions which will be at the heart of the life of the Christian community in the life of Jesus. To ask how two people could walk 7 miles without recognizing someone who was not only familiar to them but was also at that time in the forefront of their concerns, is to misread the nature of Luke's story, which is told, not so much as to describe a past encounter, as to show how the eucharistic meals of his church unite them to the living presence of the risen Lord. Acts will put the 'breaking of bread' at the heart of the life of the young community (2:42). That formed the climax of the action of Jesus at the last supper as Luke tells of it (22:19a), and it is that action that realizes and discloses his presence after the resurrection (24:35). The story, both in its characters and its significance, stands somewhat apart from the gradual development that marks Luke's narrative as a whole. It really conveys the actions of one who is already ascended and contemporary with Luke's community. Jesus' witness to himself which he gives within the story speaks of him as being already 'glorified' (v. 26). This, however, does not suggest a different source which is not fully in line with Luke's own outlook, nor does it put a question mark against the ascension as the point of glorification. The story reflects the times and outlook of the life of the community as Luke would have it be after the ascension. His own understanding made the time between the resurrection and the ascension a period of teaching and convincing. He had to place it then. But, unlike the rest of the stories, it speaks not of a past event but of one that is contemporary with every age. Jesus, unrecognized, travels with his church on its pilgrimage and in its perplexity. Its heart is warmed as it hears the Scriptures (v. 32), but Jesus himself is discerned in 'the breaking of the bread'.

Jesus now appears in what is in fact the most unashamedly materialistic of all the resurrection narratives. Lacking the unwillingness of Thomas actually to put the witness of Jesus to the test (Jn 20:26–8), the story tells how Jesus himself answers their doubts by eating in front of them. If it is accepted that the Emmaus story reflects Luke's thoughts about the later church and her relationship with her Lord, this story, which leads straight into the ascension, reveals Luke's emphasis upon the actual physicality of the Lord's body in a way that outstrips the thinking of the other NT writers. Everything in Luke depends upon the certainty of the resurrection. Whilst this story may be composed in the service of combating Gnosticism (Talbert 1966), it is more likely described in this way in order to maintain the reality of the eyewitness testimony. The women beheld his death, burial, and the empty tomb. Disciples do not believe their testimony for they need more certain evidence. When Jesus does appear to them—even after his appearance to Peter—they still need convincing. Others had been summoned from the dead (1 Sam 28:13). Jesus, however, was no ghost but was the very person with whom they had walked, lived, and engaged from those early days in Galilee. They have to become convinced and reliable witnesses to the resurrection (Acts 1:22). Jesus now 'open[s] their minds to understand the scriptures'. For Luke, it is fundamental that Jesus' whole career fulfilled the Scriptures—but it needed the risen Jesus to make the real connection, for they do not obviously find their fulfilment in his life. They do so only when they are read with the prior conviction that Jesus is the Messiah, and, even then, there is more tension between the promise and the fulfilment than Luke allows. Jewish ignorance of that connection was not necessarily blameworthy (Acts 13:27). Jesus commands the disciples to remain in Jerusalem until after the gift of the Spirit, for that event will accomplish the eschatological renewal of Israel which, from Luke's point of view, must take place before the universal witness can be begun. They will be clothed with 'power from on high', for the Spirit will empower their witness and move it out until it becomes world-wide (Acts 6:10; 9:17; 10:47; 19:21).

(24:50–3) The Ascension It is not certain that this passage describes an ascension of Jesus, for the two crucial clauses that would make it so are omitted from some MSS. That Jesus 'was carried up into heaven' and that the disciples 'worshipped him' are not included in a number of versions. After a long period when they were described as additions, introduced to bring the gospel to a firm conclusion, the majority of commentators now opt for their integrity. They believe that the two clauses were omitted because, with their inclusion, the gospel passage seemed to be at variance with the more obvious description of the ascension with which Luke begins Acts. It is just that contradiction, however, that makes it difficult to accept the ending of Luke as another account of the one event. The real problem is that, whereas Acts talks of Jesus' period of teaching and confirming as lasting forty days (Acts 1:3), Lk 24 has this final scene on Easter day itself. This time difference should not, however, be pressed. We have already seen that the Emmaus story stands somewhat outside the sequence of events, and it is this that actually sets the timing whilst itself causing difficulties for including everything within the one day. Time is subservient to what Luke was certain had to be done between the resurrection and the ascension. The forty days of Acts 1:3 witnesses to this same emphasis and should no more be pressed than the time sequence in Lk 24. Other differences between the two accounts are minimal. The cloud is emphasized in Acts because it not only receives Jesus, but also veils him from the disciples. It is their perplexity that dominates the Acts story and that is countered by the gift of the Spirit and the success of the mission. In the gospel, Jesus has already demonstrated his credibility. The ascension sets the seal on that. It represents in story form the fundamental belief that Jesus is Lord. What the infancy narratives proclaimed, what the voice which accepted his response to his baptism acknowledged (3:22), what Moses and Elijah at the transfiguration discussed in glory (9:31), and what everything from 9:51 has moved towards is now completed. The whole of that life is now caught up into God's presence. Jesus blesses

his community and that blessing is brought into the present. Acts will show just how effective that has been. The disciples worship. The gospel ends as it began, with the praise of God in the temple.

REFERENCES

Alexander, L. (1993), *The Preface to Luke's Gospel*, SNTSMS 78 (Cambridge: Cambridge University Press).

Allison, D. C. (1998), *Jesus of Nazareth* (Minneapolis: Fortress).

Bailey, K. E. (1976), *Poet and Peasant* (Grand Rapids: Eerdmans).

—— (1980), *Through Peasant Eyes* (Grand Rapids: Eerdmans).

Borg, M. J. (1994), *Jesus in Contemporary Scholarship* (Valley Forge: Trinity).

Brown, R. E. (1977), *The Birth of the Messiah* (London: Geoffrey Chapman).

Caird, G. B. (1963), *Saint Luke* (London: Penguin Books).

Conzelmann, H. (1960), *The Theology of St Luke* (London: Faber & Faber).

Crossan, J. D. (1991), *The Historical Jesus* (San Francisco: Harper).

Doble, P. (1996), *The Paradox of Salvation*, SNTSMS 87 (Cambridge: Cambridge University Press).

Esler, P. F. (1987), *Community and Gospel in Luke-Acts* SNTSMS 57 (Cambridge: Cambridge University Press).

Evans, C. F. (1955), 'The Central Section of St Luke's Gospel', in D. Nineham (ed.), *Studies in the Gospels* (Oxford: Blackwell).

—— (1970), *Resurrection and the New Testament* (London: SCM).

—— *Saint Luke* (1990), TPI NT Commentaries (London: SCM).

Fitzmyer, J. A. (1981; 1985), *The Gospel According to Luke*, AB (New York: Doubleday).

—— (1989), *Luke the Theologian* (New York: Paulist Press).

Franklin, E. (1975), *Christ the Lord* (London: SPCK).

—— (1994), *Luke: Interpreter of Paul, Critic of Matthew*, JSNTSup 92 (Sheffield: JSOT).

Goulder, M. D. (1989), *Luke: A New Paradigm*, JSNTSup 20 (Sheffield: JSOT).

Herzog, W. R. II (1994), *Parables as Subversive Speech* (Louisville, Ky.: Westminster/John Knox).

Hull, J. M. (1974), *Hellenistic Magic and the Synoptic Tradition* (London: SCM).

Lampe, G. W. H. (1962), 'Luke', in *Peake's Commentary on the Bible*, ed. M Black and H. H. Rowley (London: Nelson).

Maddox, R. (1982), *The Purpose of Luke–Acts* (Edinburgh: T. & T. Clark).

Marshall, I. H. (1978), *The Gospel of Luke* (Grand Rapids: Eerdmans).

—— (1980), *The Acts of the Apostles*, Tyndale NT Commentaries (Leicester: Inter-Varsity Press).

Moessner, D. P. (1989), *Lord of the Banquet* (Minneapolis: Fortress).

Moule, C. F. D. (1977), *The Origin of Christology* (Cambridge: Cambridge University Press).

Nolland, J. (1989–93), *Luke*, WBC (Dallas: Word).

Sanders, E. P. (1985), *Jesus and Judaism* (London: SCM).

Sanders, J. T. (1987), *The Jews in Luke–Acts* (London: SCM).

Schüssler Fiorenza, E. (1983), *In Memory of Her* (New York: Crossroad).

Scott, B. B. (1989), *Hear Then the Parable* (Minneapolis: Fortress).

Talbert, C. H. (1966), *Luke and the Gnostics* (Nashville: Abingdon).

Vielhauer, P. (1968), 'On the "Paulinism" of Acts', in L. E. Keck and J. L. Martyn (eds.), *Studies in Luke–Acts* (London: SPCK).

Wilson, S. G. (1973), *The Gentiles and the Gentile Mission in Luke–Acts*, SNTSMS 50 (Cambridge: Cambridge University Press).

Young, B. H. (1998), *The Parables* (Peabody: Hendrickson).

60. John

RENÉ KIEFFER

INTRODUCTION

A. Special Features of the Gospel of John. 1. In comparison with the Synoptics, John's gospel is much more unified in content and style. It has sometimes been called 'seamless, woven in one piece' (cf. Jn 19:23). The differences between John and the Synoptics have been used in both positive and negative ways, especially concerning their reliability. But one should not forget all that unites John with the other gospels: it is about Jesus' public life, death, and resurrection, with concrete biographical indications that may not always satisfy a modern historian.

2. My view is that John in his structure and in many details has been inspired by Mark, perhaps even by Luke (or common traditions behind Luke and John). But John also has his own information, which allows him to treat his material in a sovereign way (Kieffer 1987–8; 1992). He wants primarily to show that Jesus really is the Messiah and the Son of God (cf. Jn 20:31). Matthew has already dared to group Jesus' preaching into five or six longer discourses in order to favour his own theological purpose; John is even bolder when he freely organizes his material according to his theological views, making no stylistic difference between what Jesus, the Baptist, or he himself has to say.

3. The Johannine presentation is permeated with contrasts between light and darkness, life and death, truth and falsehood, heaven above and the earth below. Ambiguous expressions are used to create a kind of suspense. Subtle ironic devices suppose that the reader is shrewder than those who meet Jesus without understanding. The Master who stands in the centre of the text is described with the help of lively metaphors. His encounters, his words, and his miracles often have both a concrete and a metaphorical meaning. One could speak of a kind of progressive 'metaphorization' of words and deeds in the Johannine text (Kieffer 1989). Sayings of Jesus in the Synoptics, and even in the *Gospel of Thomas*, are stamped by simple images and parables. In John these give way to long and complicated monologues and dialogues, with a rather limited vocabulary used very skilfully.

4. In the Prologue Jesus Christ is identified with the Word of God. Already in the beginning of his activity he cleanses the temple, a symbolic action that, like the miracle at Cana in ch. 2, announces that the new cult around the risen Christ will replace Jewish feasts and ceremonies. In chs. 3–4 the discussions with Nicodemus and the Samaritan woman show that the Son of Man, who comes from above and will be elevated on a cross, will give his Spirit, independently of Jewish and Samaritan places of worship. In chs. 5–6 the reader is informed about Jesus' life-giving power. The polemic with the Jews in chs. 7–8 and the healing of the blind man in ch. 9 concern Jesus' identity, a subject that continues throughout chs. 10–12. In the farewell discourses in chs. 13–17 Jesus finally reveals for his disciples his deep connection with his Father and the Spirit whom he will send after his death and resurrection (chs. 20–1). Despite his main theological purpose, the evangelist shows a vivid interest in geographical and historical details, which makes his gospel sometimes a better source of historical information than the Synoptics.

B. The Gospel of John in a Historical Perspective. 1. The unity of the gospel is sometimes marred by contradictions: twice Jesus brings his activity to an end (10:40–2 and 12:37–43). Jesus' first sign in Cana is followed by different signs in Jerusalem, but in 4:54 a miracle in Galilee is called the second one. In 7:3–5 Jesus' brothers speak as if the Master had not done any signs in Jerusalem, despite 2:23 and ch. 5. In 16:5 Jesus seems to ignore the questions Peter and Thomas had already put in 13:36 and 14:5. In 14:31 Jesus says, 'Rise, let us be on our way', yet he continues his farewell discourse. In 20:30–1 the reader is given a conclusion but the book continues in ch. 21. Some of the contradictions are not very important, but it is impossible to ignore the question of an evolution behind our present gospel.

2. Different theories have been proposed: (1) Rearrangements: the best known hypothesis is that originally ch. 6 was placed before ch. 5. Bultmann (1971) proposes many other rearrangements, which are hardly acceptable. (2) Sources: in his commentary Bultmann also proposes three different sources behind our gospel: a sign-source, a Gnostic source, and a passion narrative source. Moreover he thinks that a later redactor has reworked the gospel, adding to it sacramental and traditional eschatological material (for other source analyses, see Fortna 1970; 1988; Boismard 1977). I am sceptical about the possibilities of reconstructing different sources behind the Gospel of John. (3) Different editions: with other exegetes such as Lindars (1972), my belief is that parts of the gospel have been added in a second edition, e.g. chs. 6; 15–17; 21. Probably the evangelist himself reworked his gospel in a process of 're-reading' to which others also have contributed. (4) The history of the Johannine community: in Brown (1979) we find a reconstruction of the history of the Johannine community. Between 50 and 90 there were two groups, one centred around a man who had known Jesus and would become the 'beloved disciple'; this group accepted Jesus as a Davidic Messiah. Another group was critical about the temple cult and understood Jesus against a Mosaic background. The fusion of these two groups was the catalyst for the development of a high Christology, which was expressed in a first version of the gospel. About 90 CE the community became more anti-Jewish under the influence of converted pagans. This was reflected in a new version of the gospel. Around 100 CE a faction gathered around the author of the Johannine letters and fought against the Docetists who overinterpreted the divine aspect in the gospel and neglected Jesus' humanity. Such reconstructions are interesting but are difficult to prove. They simply project contradictions in the Johannine literature onto a historical axis.

3. My own view is that the main author, whom I call 'the evangelist', tries to unite his community by transmitting the testimony of the beloved disciple. This person is presented in such a way that the reader who knows the synoptic tradition can identify him with John the son of Zebedee. Historically it is possible that somebody other than the apostle John was the mediator, but the evangelist wants us to identify the beloved disciple with the apostle. This is quite in agreement with an old tradition we find in Irenaeus (*Adv. haer.* 2.22.5; 3.1.1; cf. Eusebius, *Hist. eccl.* 5.20. 4–8). The final version of the gospel was probably produced about 90–100 in Ephesus (see details in Hengel 1993).

C. Structure. 1. The first part (1:19–12:50), now often called 'the book of signs', is regularly distinguished from a second one called 'the book of glory' (13:1–20:31; see Brown 1966). In that outline ch. 21 is usually considered as an appendix written by a member of the Johannine school (and 7:53–8:11 as a non-Johannine text; see JN APP). It is difficult to come to a consensus concerning the first part. One can state that it is punctuated by seven miracles (two at Cana and Capernaum, two near the Sea of Galilee, two in Jerusalem and one at Bethany near Jerusalem), and by different tableaux and discussions (the meetings with the Baptist and his disciples, with Nicodemus and with the Samaritans, the temple cleansing in Jerusalem, the disputes in Jerusalem, the acclamation near Jerusalem, the anointing at Bethany). One can often find chiastic and concentric schemes in the text, but it is difficult to establish the author's plan with their help alone.

2. The whole book may be considered as a unity. If the geographical indications are studied, four cycles become apparent. A first grouping (1:19–3:21) leads from the region across the Jordan (1:28) to Cana (2:1, 11) and Capernaum in Galilee (2:12), and finally to Jerusalem (2:13, 23). A second grouping (3:22–5:47) starts in Judea, probably across the Jordan (3:26), and takes the reader through Samaria (4:4) to the second stay at Cana in Galilee (4:46) and finally to Jerusalem (5:1). A third grouping (6:1–10:39) starts on 'the other side' of the Sea of Galilee (6:1–16; cf. 6:17, 22, 25) and leads again to Jerusalem in Judea. The last grouping (10:40–21:23) carries one from the region across the Jordan (10:40) to Jerusalem (12:12), through Bethany (11:1), and finally back to the Sea of Tiberias in Galilee (see Gyllenberg 1960; 1980; Kieffer 1985). The regions across the Jordan and on the other side of Galilee are somehow starting-points. Galilee and Samaria are, with the exception of the end of ch. 6, regions where Jesus is well received, whereas in Judea violent discussions during Jewish feasts lead to various threats to kill him (5:18; 7:1, 19–25; 8:37, 40; 10:31–9; 11:53).

3. If one considers more closely the Christological aspects in the Fourth Gospel, one can observe a dramatic progression from Jesus' initial signs and encounters (2:1–4:54), his works and discussions at Jewish feasts in Jerusalem (5:1–10:39), the climactic sign of raising Lazarus and the bridge section on the coming of Jesus' hour (11:1–12:50), to Jesus' farewell at the Last Supper (13:1–17:26), and finally his hour of passion, death, and resurrection (18:1–21:23). The Prologue and the encounter with the Baptist can be considered as two Christological introductions, and both 20:30–1 and 21:24–5 as two conclusions (see a slightly different version in Mlakuzhyil 1987).

4. In presenting the material I shall draw attention to these different geographical and dramatic groupings without putting them into the centre of the commentary; proper analysis of the structure and development of each single scene is more important.

D. Suggested Outline.

Prologue: The Word became Flesh and Revealed the Father (1:1–18)

First Book: Jesus Reveals his Glory to this World (1:19–12:50)

1:19–3:21: First geographical grouping:
  The Baptist's Testimony (1:19–34)
  Jesus' First Disciples (1:35–51)
  The First Sign at the Wedding in Cana (2:1–12)
  Temple Cleansing in Jerusalem (2:13–25)
  Dialogue with Nicodemus (3:1–21)

3:22–5:47: Second geographical grouping:
  The Baptist's Last Testimony (3:22–30)
  Jesus Comes from Above (3:31–6)
  Jesus' Work in Samaria (4:1–42)
  The Second Sign at Cana: The Healing of the Royal Official's Son (4:43–54)
  Jesus Heals a Lame Man: He Gives Life to Whom he Wishes (5:1–47)

6:1–10:39: Third geographical grouping:
  Jesus Feeds 5,000 and Walks on the Sea: He is the Bread of Life (6:1–71)
  Jesus at the Festival of Booths (7:1–8:59)
  Jesus Restores Sight to the Blind Man (9:1–41)
  Jesus is the Door and the Good Shepherd (10:1–21)
  Jesus at the Festival of Dedication (10:22–39)

10:40–21:25: Fourth geographical grouping:
  Back across the Jordan (10:40–2)
  Jesus who Raises Lazarus Must Himself Die (11:1–54)
  Jesus is Anointed and Acclaimed before his Death (11:55–12:36)
  Faith and Unbelief (12:37–50)

Second Book: Jesus Reveals the Glory of his Death and Resurrection to the Disciples (13:1–21:25)

Jesus Washes the Feet of his Disciples and Points out the Traitor (13:1–30)
The First Part of the Farewell Discourse (13:31–14:31)
The Second Part of the Farewell Discourse (15:1–16:4*a*)
The Third Part of the Farewell Discourse (16:4*b*–33)
Jesus' Prayer to his Father (17:1–26)
Jesus' Passion, Death, and Burial (18:1–19:42)
The Risen Christ (20:1–21:25)

COMMENTARY

Prologue: The Word became Flesh and Revealed the Father (1:1–18)

In a kind of overture the narrator gives his readers the impression that his story will be told 'from a transcendent and eternal vantage point' (Stibbe 1993: 22–3). The author uses subtle imagery to sum up main themes in the following work. As elsewhere in the Jewish tradition, light, life, and darkness, which are elements of the creation, are meant to symbolize spiritual realities. Life and light which were created in the beginning by the word of God (Gen 1) are manifested in the Word both before and after creation. The theme of light leads to that of the visible glory of the Word (v. 14) whereas the theme of life gives birth to that of the fullness from which believers receive (v. 16). The prologue begins with what appeals to the ear, the Word, and finishes with what the eye cannot see, God (v. 18). Through the Word, who is both light and life, the invisible and unheard God is revealed.

There has been much discussion about a pre-Christian or Christian hymn which the author may have used and adapted to fit his purpose. On these hypotheses, vv. 6–8 and 15, on the Baptist, are generally considered as later additions (see different reconstructions in Rochais 1985; cf. Schnackenburg 1977–9: i). But these views are open to objection; the whole prologue may have been written by the same author in a kind of solemn prose, with chiastic phrases which are developed by amplifications and contrasts. Moreover there is a kind of concentric construction with a centre in vv. 12–13 and different sentences that correspond to each other around this centre. This is especially clear for vv. 6–8 and 15 on the Baptist, but also for the beginning in vv. 1–3 and the end in vv. 17–18 (cf. Culpepper 1979–80).

The evangelist may have had in mind the gospel of Mark: 'The beginning of the good news of Jesus Christ, the Son of God' (Mk 1:1). He wanted to prolong this 'beginning' by going back to God and the creation. In his prologue he mentions John the Baptist who in Mark opens the gospel proper. But, like Mark, he gives the reader a key to interpret his book: it will be about the revelation of Jesus who is both Christ and the Son of God, Jn 1:18 (see the purpose of John's book in 20:30–1; cf. Hooker 1974–5).

(1:1–11) The evangelist shows first how the Word which was with God came to what was his own. vv. 1–2, the author alludes to Gen 1:1, but describes what was *before* the creation. If he has Mk 1:1 in mind, he wants to show that the gospel begins with the Word which was with God. God's Wisdom is created at the beginning (Prov 8:22), but John tells us about the uncreated Word. John usually uses *pros* with an implication of movement and one might therefore translate 'the Word was turned towards God' (so the Fr. TOB). This could be paralleled by an alternative translation of *eis* in v. 18: 'the only Son, who turns *towards* the Father's bosom'. Such a translation could fit the gospel's description of the Son's orientation towards the Father. But the preposition *eis* in v. 18 is probably used in place of *en*. The parallelism between vv. 1 and 18 favours therefore the usual translation of v. 1, 'was with God'. The Greek verb *ēn* has three different meanings in v. 1: an existential (the Word was), a relational (was with God), and an identificational (the Word was God). *Theos*, 'God', is used without the article, which is normal in a predicate, but the author could have used it if he had wanted to underline a complete identification of the Word with God. Jesus is God (1:1, 18; 20:28), but normally it is his Father who is *theos* with a precedent article in Greek. v. 3, the expression *ho gegonen*, 'what has come into being' at the end of v. 3 probably must be taken together with v. 4, which was the normal interpretation among the Church Fathers before the heretics of the fourth century used it to

prove Jesus' inferiority. Moreover, the joining of 'what has come into being' to v. 3 would yield a strange Greek sentence, which would be correct only if the expression were changed to *hōn gegonen*. There is a parallel text in 1QS 11:11: 'without Him not a thing is done'. The author now describes the Word's function in creation, as either the instrument by which God created, or as the fountain-head which made creation possible. The whole creation is marked by God's Word and reveals God, in opposition to later Gnostic speculations where the world is created by an evil demiurge. The Word in John is both an instrument and a model, similar to Col 1:16, 'all things have been created through him'. But in this text creation is also 'for him', whereas in John the goal of creation is the Father. vv. 4–5, 'What has come into being in him was life.' One could also translate: 'In what has come into being, there was life'; 'In what has come into being, he was life'; or 'What has come into being, was life (alive) in him'. But the NRSV translation best fits the context. Life and light have in these verses soteriological connotations: the creating Word of God is the fountainhead of spiritual life and light for all people. The author is specially interested in a moral choice between light and darkness. The image of a cosmic battle corresponds to humankind's spiritual struggle, and therefore the translation 'did not overcome it' fits the context better than 'did not understand it' or 'did not accept it'. vv. 6–8, these verses interrupt the cosmic viewpoint and introduce the description of the Word's incarnation. In a similar way Luke introduces Jesus' birth by the preparatory birth of John the Baptist (Lk 1–2). The expression *para theou* in v. 6 can mean, as in classical Greek, 'from God' or, as in later Greek, 'by God'. John the Baptist is only a witness to the light of the Word, whereas Jesus himself is the light (Jn 3:19; 8:12; 9:5; 12:35–6). Jesus' testimony is greater than the Baptist's (5:36). This is probably an attack against disciples of the Baptist who considered him as a messianic figure (see also John's negative utterances about himself in 1:20–7). vv. 9–11 could be translated, 'There was the true light that enlightens everyone who is coming into the world,' but in that case 'everyone who is coming into the world' would be redundant. Another translation could take the remote 'Word' as the grammatical subject of the sentence (as in vv. 10–11), but NRSV is probably right when it considers the just-mentioned 'light' as the subject of a periphrastic construction. Theologically it is the light of the Word who comes to a world created through him. Therefore one can say that he comes to what is his own (v. 11). Some exegetes think that vv. 9–11 describe the presence of the Word in Israel during the OT period and that v. 12 alludes to the faithful remnant of Israel. But the concentric structure of the prologue makes it more probable that vv. 9–11 describe the time of Jesus' activity, since they correspond to v. 14 about the Word who became flesh. John's testimony in vv. 6–8 introduces vv. 9–11 and his testimony in v. 15 confirms v. 14. Moreover, in the rest of the gospel those who reject Jesus' witness can easily be identified with his own people who did not accept him. What v. 5 describes as a cosmic conflict is in vv. 9–11 applied to the human world, which does not recognize or accept Jesus.

(1:12–13) All that was said about the Word before vv. 12–13 and that which follows after has its centre in those who received the Word and became children of God. This agrees with the aim of the entire gospel that 'through believing you may have life in his name' (20:31). The contrast between those who receive him in v. 12 and those who do not accept him in v. 11 is fundamental throughout the gospel. In 1:19–12:50 different attitudes in relation to Jesus are described, in 13:1–17:26 everything is concentrated on the disciples, 'his own', whom Jesus has loved to the end (13:1). Those who become disciples are allowed to be called 'children of God' and are in relationship with the only one who in the Fourth Gospel is called 'God's Son'. v. 13, children of God cannot be born in a carnal way. The Greek has 'blood' in the plural, which might allude to the rabbinic doctrine (derived ultimately from Aristotle), that man's seed, considered as 'blood', is in the act of conception mixed with woman's blood. The mention of 'the will of man' reflects the prevailing idea that the male was the only active party in procreation. Some MSS have changed the plural 'bloods' into the singular in order to allude to the virgin birth of Jesus.

(1:14–18) The evangelist finally shows how the Word become flesh has revealed the Father. v. 14, in contrast to what is said in v. 13 about the 'carnal will', the Word that was with God becomes flesh. The author repeats *logos*, 'the Word', that he mentioned in v. 1, but has had in mind all the time. The concrete word *sarx*, 'flesh', is used probably in order to refute Docetic views similar to those we meet in John's letters (1 Jn 1:2–3; 4:2; 2 Jn 7). 'Lived among us', or literally 'put up his tent among us' is used of Wisdom in Sir 24:10. The temple in Jerusalem replaced the tabernacle in the desert as a dwelling-place for God. God's Wisdom is thus present in Israel and in its temple, but the presence of the Word in the flesh is physical. 'Among us' and 'we have seen' underline the Johannine witness to God's initiative. The Word's glory is dependent on the Father's presence in his only Son (cf. 17:5). *Monogenēs* can mean 'only', 'unique', 'precious' (cf. Heb 11:17 about Isaac), or 'born from the one'. It is used four times in John (1:14, 18; 3:16, 18), and once in 1 Jn 4:9. It seems to sum up the very special relationship between Jesus and his Father. 'Full of grace and truth' is best connected with 'only son', rather than with 'glory'. The expression reflects God's revelation to Moses as 'merciful and gracious' (Ex 34:6), i.e. 'full of loving initiative and of fidelity'. In the Word made flesh humanity can meet God's glory. v. 15, in vv. 6–8 John testified to the light, but now he attests that the one who came after him in fact ranks ahead of him because he precedes him in time as God's Word. This anticipates v. 30. v. 16, the verse resumes what was said in v. 14, but concentrates on the word *charis*, 'grace'. Even if the preposition *anti* normally means 'instead of', the context favours NRSV 'upon' (cf. Philo, *De posteritate Caini*, 145). The word *plērōma*, 'fullness', does not yet have the later Gnostic meaning of the pantheon of deities, but the normal one (as in e.g. LXX Ps 23(24):1). 'We' are all those who in v. 12 become children of God, in contrast to v. 11, 'his own people'. v. 17, what was given by Moses is not depreciated (as it often is in Paul), but 'grace and truth', already mentioned in v. 14, are considered as of higher dignity and fulfil the former revelation. The prologue now makes it explicit that the Word is identical with Jesus, the Messiah. v. 18, in contrast to Moses, who could not see God without dying (Ex 33:20), Jesus is said to be in the Father's bosom and is himself 'God' (probably the

original reading, attested already in P66 and P75). The 'bosom' expresses the intimacy Jesus shares with his Father (see 13:25 on the beloved disciple), in his pre-existence, his mission on earth, and his return to the Father (cf. 17:5). He is therefore the proper revealer of God. Those who adhere to Jesus can in their turn see God (14:8–9).

First Book: Jesus Reveals his Glory to this World (1:19–12:50)

(1:19–3:21) First Geographical Grouping

(1:19–34) The Baptist's Testimony In 1:19–51 the evangelist develops some aspects of the prologue by means of a more concrete introduction to Jesus' activity. The testimony of the Baptist and the first disciples' discovery of Jesus introduce the reader to different features of the gospel's Christology. In contrast to the Synoptics the Gospel of John does not mention the events that surround the Baptist's activity and does not describe how Jesus was baptized by him. The evangelist wants the reader to see the decisive difference between the Baptist and Jesus, with the help of the former's testimony concerning himself (vv. 19–28) and concerning Jesus (vv. 29–34).

(1:19–28) The evangelist first lets the Baptist testify that he is not the Messiah, the prophet, or Elijah. v. 19, 'the Jews' in the Fourth Gospel is often used negatively for the authorities who are opposed to Jesus, especially the Pharisees and high priests, but sometimes also for ordinary people (6:41, 52). The expression can be treated in a neutral way (e.g. 5:1) or even have a positive connotation (4:22). The Jews are sent from Jerusalem, the centre of resistance to Jesus' message. They are associated with two religious factions, priests and Levites, probably as specialists on Jewish purifications which are so important in chs. 1–2. In v. 24 a second group is that of the Pharisees. vv. 20–1, just as in vv. 6–8 the Baptist underlines what he is not; there he was not the light, here he is not the Messiah, Elijah, or the prophet. The Hebrew *māšîah* and the Aramaic *mešicha*', which in 1:41 and 4:25 are transcribed in Greek, mean 'the anointed one', a word derived from the anointing of kings. In Dan 9:25 a future anointed agent of God is expected and in the Dead Sea scrolls two such messianic figures are looked forward to, 'one of Aaron and one of Israel', i.e. a priestly Messiah and a kingly Messiah, who would be a descendant of David (see 1QS 9:11). In Lk 3:15 people also wonder if the Baptist is the expected Messiah. According to Mal 3:1 and 4:5 (HB 3:23), Elijah would be sent as a messenger to prepare the way of the day of the Lord. In the Synoptics the Baptist is normally identified with Elijah as the forerunner of Jesus the Messiah (Mk 9:13 par. and Lk 1:17; 7:27). In the Fourth Gospel Jesus himself seems to be a figure like Elijah (see Jn 1:27), as he is in some Lukan texts (Lk 4:24–6; 9:51; Acts 1:2, 9–11). The expectation of the prophet is derived from Deut 18:18 and is also present in 1QS 9:11 ('until the coming of a prophet'). It plays an important role especially in Jn 4 and in Samaritan theology. vv. 22–3, in his self-presentation the Baptist quotes only Isa 40:3 and not Mal 3:1, unlike the Synoptics which identify him with Elijah. The evangelist adapts the citation to the only role the Baptist may assume, that of a voice preparing the way of the Lord. vv. 24–5, 'Now they had been sent', the Greek text can also be translated: 'Also *some* Pharisees had been sent', as a partitive. Some MSS have added the article *hoi* in the beginning of the sentence: 'Those who were sent were Pharisees'. In any case, the author does not describe the situation during Jesus' time when the Pharisees often were opposed to the priests and the Levites. After 70 CE the Pharisees could more easily be identified with 'the Jews'. The new question put to the Baptist supposes that in order to be allowed to baptize he must be a kind of messianic figure. It may reflect discussions between Christians and the followers of the Baptist (see also 3:22–3; 4:1–2). vv. 26–7, just as in the Synoptics, the Baptist underlines that he baptizes only with water. Instead of mentioning Jesus' baptism with fire, however, here he points out their inability to recognize the one who stands among them. In a way similar to the synoptic tradition he stresses his unworthiness in comparison to Jesus, but with different words (Mk 1:7–8 par.). v. 28, Bethany across the Jordan is difficult to locate and has therefore been changed to Beth-barah (see Judg 7:24) by Origen and in some MSS after him.

(1:29–34) Now the evangelist refers to the Baptist's testimony about Jesus. In vv. 29–31, different days in Jesus' first week are mentioned: 'the next day' in 1:29, 35, 43, and 'on the third day' in 2:1. There will also be a last week before Jesus' death (12:1–19:31), and a week of appearances after the resurrection (20:1, 19). The evangelist replaces the synoptic baptism of Jesus (Mk 1:11 par.) by the Baptist's double testimony before the people of Israel: about Jesus as the Lamb of God (Jn 1:29–31), and about Jesus on whom he has seen the Spirit descend (vv. 32–4; Richter 1974). The image of the lamb has, in the tradition behind the gospel, a double connotation: both the Suffering Servant (see 12:38), who is like a lamb led to the slaughter (Isa 53:7), who bears our infirmities, and is crushed for our iniquities (Isa 53:4–5)—both 'bear' and 'take away' are possible translations of the Hebrew word *nāsā'* in Isa 53:4, 12—and the passover lamb, alluded to at the death of Jesus (Jn 19:31, 34). Even if the passover lamb has no atonement function in Judaism, it receives this in the Christian tradition by its association with the death of Jesus and of the Suffering Servant (cf. 1 Cor 5:7 and 1 Jn 3:5). v. 30 resumes the same thought that was expressed in the prologue (v. 15). If the expression 'after me comes a man' alludes to Elijah, Jesus is considered as the hidden Elijah, who already existed before the Baptist. But the latter also underlines Jesus' pre-existence (cf. 8:58), and, in contrast, his own ignorance (v. 31). vv. 32–4, in the Synoptics the Baptist testifies to the baptism with the Holy Spirit before his encounter with Jesus. In the Fourth Gospel both the descent of the Spirit on Jesus and the baptism with the Holy Spirit are described as the object of the Baptist's witness. The scene culminates with the confession that Jesus is the 'Son of God', a reading already present in P[66] and P[75], which probably is better than 'the Elect of God' we find in other MSS. As in the Synoptics the dove is a symbol for the Spirit; John adds that the Spirit remains over Jesus. In contrast to the Baptist's mission as a mere witness, Jesus is sent by his Father with a unique task and message.

(1:35–51) Jesus' First Disciples The text tries to link together two traditions, one on the Baptist's own activity and one concerning his meeting with Jesus, which in its turn results in the first disciples' encounter with Jesus. Two days are described: one when Jesus meets two of the Baptist's disciples and Andrew's brother Simon, vv. 35–42, and another when he encounters Philip and Nathanael, vv. 43–51. In both episodes a disciple expresses his joy to have found the expected Messiah (vv. 41, 45). Jesus invites some of them to 'come and see' (v. 39) or to 'follow' him (v. 43). The whole text underlines the concrete and the symbolic meaning of different ways of 'seeing' Jesus or of 'being seen' by him, of 'coming' to him and of 'finding' him.

(1:35–42) Jesus first meets two disciples of the Baptist, and then Simon. vv. 35–7, in vv. 29–34 the Baptist testified before a larger crowd, whereas in vv. 35–7 his witness is directed towards the two disciples who leave him for Jesus. v. 38, the address 'Rabbi', usual in Matthew and Luke, is explained in Greek (*didaskale*, teacher). In Jn 3:26 the Baptist is also addressed as 'Rabbi', but elsewhere in the Fourth Gospel the title is reserved for Jesus. v. 39, 'Come and see' is usual in rabbinic literature, but gets a special meaning here by the double sense of *menein*, 'to stay' and 'to remain' with Jesus, and by an exact indication of time ('the tenth hour'). vv. 40–2, as the evangelist is probably acquainted with the Gospel of Mark the anonymous disciple is best identified with one of the sons of Zebedee (see Jn 21:2), and presumably with the apostle John, since James had already died in 44 CE. Andrew confesses that Jesus is the 'Messiah'; as in 4:25 the reader is given the Greek equivalent, *christos*. Simon Peter is the son of John, as in 21:15–17 (contrast Mt 16:17, in Aramaic *bar-yōnâ*). Jesus calls Simon 'Cephas', which is explained by the Greek *petra*, 'rock', as in Mt 16:16–18. But the Fourth Gospel puts the renaming of Peter early, after his brother's confession rather than his own. Matthew seems to have combined Simon's confession at Caesarea Philippi with the change of name in order to emphasize his importance in the church.

(1:43–51) Jesus now meets Philip and Nathanael. vv. 43–4, according to Mk 1:29 Simon and Andrew lived in Capernaum, but the Fourth Gospel seems to correct this by locating them at Bethsaida across the Jordan, which according to Jn 12:21 is in Galilee (more properly Gaulanitis). As in the synoptic tradition, Jesus explicitly calls a disciple to follow him (cf. Mk 2:14 par.). Philip is one of the twelve (Mk 3:18 par.) but probably not identical with the evangelist Philip (Acts 6:5; 8:4–8, 26–40; 21:8). v. 45, the Hebrew name Nathanael means 'God gives'. Some have tried to identify him with Matthew or Bartholomew, but he rather represents all Jews who understand the great gift of God. The particular man Jesus from Nazareth is seen as a messianic figure announced by Moses and the prophets (cf. Lk 24:37). But there may also be an allusion to a prophet like Moses in Deut 18:15–18. Jesus is the son of Joseph (as in Lk 3:23 and 4:22, but in contrast to Mk 6:3 where he is the son of Mary). v. 46, a typical Johannine irony makes Nathanael admit in the following discussion that something good comes from Nazareth (see Jn 1:49). v. 47, truly (*alēthōs*) underlines the signification of 'Israelite', perhaps as 'one who can see God', *horōn ton theon* (e.g. Philo, *De mutatione nominum*, 81). v. 48, the fig tree symbolizes in rabbinic literature the place where one studies the Torah (see *Eccles. Rab.* 5:11). That Jesus knows 'under' which 'tree' Nathanael was can also be compared with Daniel's prophetic knowledge (Sus 54, 58). v. 49, the title 'Son of God' has in the

Fourth Gospel a much profounder meaning than in the Jewish tradition, where it can be applied to an angel, a king, Israel, a judge, or a just man. Also the title 'King of Israel' fulfils an important purpose as will be shown in the discussion with Pilate (Jn 18:33–8a) and in the inscription on the cross: 'King of the Jews' (19:19–22). vv. 50–1, the reader is invited to expect greater things, that Jesus will soon reveal his glory (2:11), a beginning that will be concluded with the glorification on the cross. The final words of Jesus are still addressed to Nathanael, but also include all encounters with Jesus. By interpreting the gospel, the reader will see heaven opened. The angels of God ascend and descend not upon a ladder as in the dream of Jacob/Israel (Gen 28:12), but upon the Son of Man, who is the link between the Father and the world of humankind. The believing community will be able to see the unique revelation of the Son of Man (Neyrey 1982).

(2:1–12) The First Sign at the Wedding in Cana In 2:1–4:54, which leads the reader from Cana back to Cana, the reader is confronted with Jesus' initial signs and works in Galilee, Jerusalem, and Samaria. In 2:11 the narrator draws attention to the account of the miracle in Cana by calling it the first of Jesus' signs. The healing of the official's son is considered as the second sign (4:53). In 20:30 the evangelist indicates that he has chosen only a few signs of Jesus. There have been learned and rather contradictory hypotheses about a 'signs-source' which the evangelist might have used (Fortna 1970; 1988). The actual gospel invites the reader to count the different miracle-stories that are reported. One can easily come to the number seven before Jesus' death and resurrection: after the first two signs we have the healing of a lame man in 5:1–9; the feeding of the five thousand in 6:1–13; the walking on water in 6:16–21; the healing of a man born blind in 9:1–12; and as a climax the raising of Lazarus in 11:1–44, which anticipates Jesus' own death and resurrection. The main point of the wedding in Cana is therefore Christological and not to underline the sacramental aspects of water, wine, or wedding, or to show how important Jesus' mother is. The messianic time is inaugurated when Jewish purifications give way to the revelation of Jesus' glory (Olsson 1974). The miracle has been compared with stories about Dionysus, but OT models, such as the feeding miracles of Elijah and Elisha (1 Kings 17:1–16; 2 Kings 4:1–7, 42–4), are closer to it.

(2:1–2) It is difficult to know whether the author already has the Twelve in mind or only the disciples named in ch. 1. Their invitation is mentioned after that of the mother of Jesus who has a special connection with Galilee (cf. 1:46). She is never called Mary in the Fourth Gospel, perhaps in order not to confuse her with other Marys (11:1; 19:25). The third day may be an allusion to the day of resurrection, but it also completes Jesus' first week. vv. 3–5, in preparation of the miracle Jesus' mother takes the initiative, both before and after her son's answer. Jesus addresses his mother with 'woman', which has no derogatory significance (see also 19:26). By his apparent rebuke ('what concern is that to you and to me?'), Jesus wants her to understand that a miracle in Cana will lead to the hour of glorification on the cross. vv. 6–8, the water jars are made of stone because they are used for purifications. The quantity of water is enormous for a private person, 120–80 gallons, but the miracle of the wine has rather an illustrative function. The

number 'six' may symbolically express incompleteness, and the jars filled to the brim completeness. The second injunction of Jesus in v. 8 indicates indirectly that the miracle has taken place. vv. 9–10, we do not get the reaction of the guests, but the steward expresses their astonishment. Ironically enough the one who is normally responsible for the meal does not know where the wine has come from, whereas his servants know. There is a comic aspect to the story in the allusion to the guests' drunkenness. The bridegroom appears in the story only here, but soon the Baptist will speak of Jesus himself as the bridegroom (3:29). The wine's quantity and quality hint at the time of the messianic wedding (cf. Am 9:13–14; Isa 25:6; 54:4–8; 62:4–5). vv. 11–12, the reader is given the narrator's viewpoint on the miracle, and an echo from vv. 1–2, with the happy conclusion that the disciples believed in Jesus. The 'brothers' make an appearance here, accompanying Jesus to Capernaum. In 7:3–5 they will show a rather sceptical attitude towards him.

(2:13–25) Temple Cleansing in Jerusalem v. 13 is a rather abrupt transition from the sign in Galilee to the cleansing of the temple in Jerusalem, whereas vv. 23–5 describe the narrator's understanding of the people's reactions and forms a bridge to the following discussion with Nicodemus. The narrator's point of view is 'an enlightened, post-resurrection one' (Stibbe 1993: 51), which is especially apparent in vv. 17 and 22. In the synoptic tradition the cleansing of the temple is the main cause of Jesus' arrest, whereas in the Fourth Gospel the raising of Lazarus has that function. Therefore the temple scene is placed much earlier as an illustration of how Jewish institutions (as already seen in the case of Cana), are meant to be replaced by Jesus. The actual scene is described in a way which differs markedly from the synoptic account. Through the reactions of the Jews and the disciples the purification of the temple becomes a sign of the destruction and raising of another temple, Jesus' body. The metaphors go in two directions: from Jesus' zeal for the house of God to his body, and from his risen body to the cleansing of the temple.

v. 13, the Passover is mentioned also in 6:4 and 11:55. Here it introduces Jesus' allusions to his last Passover when he will die and rise from the dead. vv. 14–16, in the Fourth Gospel people sell not only doves as in the synoptic tradition, but also cattle and sheep, which was quite possible to do in the outer area of the temple (*hieron*) at the time of Caiaphas. The whip of cords, not mentioned in the synoptic tradition, is probably only meant for cattle and sheep. The money-changers are named *kermatistai* in v. 14, but in v. 15 *kollubistai* as in the synoptic tradition. They exchanged Roman and Greek coins, with the image of the emperor (cf. Mk 12:16) or of gods, for Tyrian money which was allowed in the temple area. Unlike the synoptic account, in John Jesus does not cite Scripture (Isa 56:7; Jer 7:11) but speaks with authority about his own Father's house (cf. Lk 2:49). vv. 17–18, the evangelist contrasts the disciples' understanding of Jesus' messianic action (in the light of Ps 69:10 where the present tense is replaced by the future) and the negative attitude of the Jews who ask him to legitimate his behaviour by signs. This request for 'signs' here and in Jn 6:30 is similar to the synoptic one (cf. Mk 8:11–12 par.). vv. 19–22, in contrast to vv. 14–15 Jesus speaks now of destroying the inner temple area (*naos*). The eschatological catastrophe for Jerusalem and its temple became an important item in the lawsuit against Jesus (cf. Mk 13:2 par.). Perhaps he was also charged for his prophecy about its reconstruction. 'The third day' may be inspired by Hos 6:2. By a typical Johannine misunderstanding the Jews continue to think of the forty-six years of rebuilding the temple. According to Josephus (Ant. 15.380) Herod started it about 20/19 BC. The scene would then take place about 27/8 CE, a satisfactory Johannine chronology to fit Jesus' death on the 14 Nisan in the year 30. vv. 23–5, the reference to Passover and Jerusalem resumes what was said in v. 13. The author has mentioned only one sign in Jerusalem, but he probably includes what has happened in Cana. By his close relation to the Father Jesus has a profound knowledge of people and therefore cannot trust their rather superficial faith.

(3:1–21) Dialogue with Nicodemus This scene contrasts Nicodemus' earth-bound understanding with Jesus' wide perspective on God and the Spirit. The mysterious origin and direction of the wind prepares the reader for the heavenly things that Jesus is about to reveal. The Son of Man will be lifted up on the cross as a link between heaven and earth, and as a sign of God's love. The text moves from the night in the beginning of the dialogue to the light which those who do what is true will receive. Three short questions of Nicodemus receive three answers which progessively become longer and in vv. 16–21 end up in a kind of commentary (by Jesus or by the evangelist). Nicodemus in this chapter still hesitates before Jesus' claims. In 7:50–1 and 19:39 he will spiritually evolve and become a secret disciple of Jesus.

vv. 1–2a, Nicodemus, a Pharisee, a teacher, and a 'leader of the Jews' (cf. 7:26, 48, 50–1), is presumably a member of the *synedrion*, a legal assembly which may at this time have comprised *c*.70 members representing three groups: the chief priests, the elders, and the scribes, of whom some were Pharisees. He encounters the personification of a higher wisdom. In Lk 18:18 a certain ruler also questions Jesus, but in the Fourth Gospel the discussion with an important representative of the Jewish faith takes place at the beginning. 2b–3, Nicodemus, like the people in Jerusalem, is probably impressed by the Jesus' signs (Jn 2:23), but he still has to learn in what sense Jesus 'has come from God'. Jesus answers him with a solemn double 'Amen', a revelation formula characteristic of the Fourth Gospel. He does so indirectly by speaking of how one is able to 'see' (in v. 5 to 'enter') the kingdom of God. Only in these two verses does the Fourth Gospel mention the synoptic theme of the kingdom of God, but in 18:36 Jesus answers Pilate that he is king in a kingdom which is not from this world. According to the ideas of that time a child was conceived by his father. In a similar way a child must be born from above (cf. 1:12–13 and 1 Jn 3:9). But the answer of Nicodemus shows that the evangelist also considers the mother's contribution to birth. The Johannine sayings are similar to the synoptic theme of becoming like a child in order to enter the kingdom (Mt 18:3 par.). vv. 4–8, the Greek expression *anōthen* in the Fourth Gospel generally means 'from above' (Jn 3:31; 19:11, 23), but Nicodemus interprets it as 'again', which is quite possible in Greek. Moreover, the evangelist lets him imagine the irony of an old person entering his mother's

womb. Jesus alludes to Christian baptism, which the Baptist has already predicted in 1:33 (cf. also 7:38–9). There is no textual evidence supporting Bultmann's hypothesis that 'and water' has been added by a redactor (Bultmann 1971: 138). In order to explain the difference between natural birth and birth as a child of God (cf. 1:12–13) Jesus opposes flesh and spirit. The short parable on the 'wind' (the same word as 'Spirit' in both Hebrew, *rûaḥ*, and Greek, *pneuma*) prepares the reader for the mysterious origin and destination of the Son of Man which will be revealed in the following verses. vv. 9–15, the third question of Nicodemus in v. 9 is short and gives Jesus an occasion to reveal who he is and how he will influence humankind's rebirth. But before that Jesus rebukes the teacher of Israel for his lack of understanding (vv. 10–11), an indirect attack on the Jewish contemporaries of the evangelist who do not accept the Christian testimony. As Son of Man Jesus is pre-existent and will ascend to heaven (v. 13), which is far more difficult to understand than the more earthly matter of baptism Jesus was speaking about (v. 12). At the end of v. 13 most MSS, of different text types, add 'who is in heaven'. This difficult reading may be original and have been suppressed in important Alexandrian witnesses (among them P[66], P[75], and B). It underlines that even during his life on earth Jesus still has direct contact with heaven and can therefore testify to what he has seen (v. 11). The 'we know' in v. 11 contrasts with the 'we know' in v. 2. Nicodemus' solemn declaration about what he knows as a representative Jew is insignificant in comparison with Jesus' personal knowledge of God. Nicodemus can now disappear and let Jesus reveal heavenly things about the Son of Man (vv. 13–15) and about the Son of God (vv. 16–18). Jesus is the light that attracts all believers (vv. 19–21). In the Jewish tradition we have different heroes who have seen heavenly visions (e.g. Enoch, Isaiah, Daniel), but only Wisdom, the Word, or the Spirit are presented as coming from God. The perspective of crucifixion (v. 14) in the gospel tradition is a common way of introducing the theme of the Son of Man. In Num 21:9 the serpent is placed upon a pole, but already in the targums the serpent is put in an elevated place (see *Neofiti 1* and *Pseudo-Jonathan*; cf. Wis 16:6–7). That the Servant of God is exalted and lifted up in Isa 52:13 may also have contributed to the interpretation of the crucifixion as an elevation and a glorification. To see or enter the kingdom of God (Jn 3:3, 5) is reformulated in v. 15 as having eternal life. vv. 16–21, after the prologue this is the first time the evangelist speaks of God's initiative. It is also the first time the theme of 'loving' is introduced, which will play an important role in the rest of the gospel. In v. 16 we have a kind of gospel in miniature, where Jesus' death is combined with God's love for humanity, in order to give it eternal life. v. 17 develops what is hinted at in v. 16a, whereas v. 18 gives some precision on the importance of faith which was mentioned in v. 16b. The idea of a judgement, which was implicit in v. 18, is developed in vv. 19–21 with the help of the sharp contrast between light and darkness. The whole section is concentrated on the sending of the Son and the double way people respond to it. In 12:46–8 the evangelist will evoke the last judgement, whereas here the judgement is already present in this life. In 3:16, 18 Jesus himself reaffirms what was said about God's only Son in the prologue (1:14, 18). In the rest of the gospel Jesus often speaks of himself simply as the Son. In the beginning of the dialogue with Nicodemus baptism was evoked (cf. Mk 16:16), in the end all is concentrated on faith.

(3:22–5:47) Second Geographical Grouping

(3:22–30) The Baptist's Last Testimony In the beginning of this scene different rites of purification with water are mentioned: the Baptist's, the Jews', and Jesus'. They serve to introduce the Baptist's second testimony about Jesus the Messiah. vv. 22–4, the evangelist does not indicate precisely where in the Judean countryside Jesus is baptizing. The discussion in v. 26 alludes to Jesus' meeting with the Baptist across the Jordan. Perhaps the evangelist supposes that Jesus is now baptizing there, a normal starting-point for his ministry. He will return there in 10:40–1. The Baptist has gone to 'Aenon near Salim', probably near Scythopolis (Lagrange 1936: 92–3). His move permits Jesus to take his own initiative, though this is partly corrected in 4:2. Contrary to the Synoptics, the Fourth Gospel does not describe the Baptist's imprisonment and death. vv. 25–6, the evangelist only mentions different kinds of baptisms, without indicating their differences. He also alludes to conflicts between disciples of John and disciples of Jesus. He lets the Baptist himself solve the conflict. vv. 27–30, the Baptist does not directly answer the question put to him, but he simply describes his own function as subordinate to that of Jesus. The evangelist reworks here the synoptic tradition where Jesus calls himself the bridegroom (Mk 2:18–22 par.), and makes this the object of the Baptist's testimony. In Jn 1:20 the Baptist denied that he was the Messiah or Elijah, but now he seems to allude to Mal 3:1 and consider himself as Elijah who is sent ahead of the Messiah (cf. Mk 1:2 par.). The Baptist, in Jn 1:23, was presented as a *voice* crying in the wilderness. He decreases now to the degree that his joy is fulfilled by listening to the bridegroom's *voice*. The 'friend of the bridegroom' corresponds to the *šôšebîn* mentioned in the Mishnah (*m. Sanh.* 3:5). According to 1 Macc 9:39 there was more than one such friend.

(3:31–6) Jesus Comes from Above The Johannine style marks the whole gospel and makes it difficult to decide whether vv. 31–6 belonged originally to the dialogue with Nicodemus, or are a continuation of the Baptist's testimony, or finally are the evangelist's personal summary of 3:1–30 (which is most likely; a similar difficulty occurs at Jn 2:16–21). The contrast between earthly things and heaven is the point of departure for a meditation about the difficulties of accepting the Son's own testimony. v. 31, this verse reflects the contrast between 'earthly things' and 'heavenly things' in v. 12. It also makes clear that vv. 3 and 7 are fulfilled in Jesus who is the one 'who comes from above' and 'is above all'. vv. 32–3, as in the prologue, the evangelist underlines the testimony which comes from spiritual insight and hearing. This witness is not accepted by all (cf. v. 11), but those who receive it set a seal on it, which means they recognize that God speaks the truth through the testimony of Jesus. v. 34, by accepting the testimony of the one who has been sent, the believer can verify that he speaks the words of God. The Spirit was mentioned in vv. 5–8. In our verse it is not clear who is meant by 'he' who gives the Spirit, but in the context it is more likely that it is God than Jesus. The expression *ou gar ek metrou* is not good Greek, but probably means that God lets his Spirit remain over Jesus

(cf. 1:32). This sense is also specified by the following verse. vv. 35–6, for the first time the Father's love for the Son is mentioned (cf. 5:20; 10:17; 15:9–10; 17:23–4, 26). In the expression 'has placed all things in his hands' (cf. 10:28–9; 13:3) the Greek *en* does not mean 'by means of his hand' but is used for *eis*. In the gospel different powers are given to the Son by his Father: to judge (5:22, 27), to have life in himself (5:26), to have disciples (6:37; 17:6), to speak God's words (12:49; 17:8), to receive the name and the glory from God (17:11–12, 22), to have authority over all people (17:2). Here what is given into his hand is the message pertaining to different responses to the Son. Therefore humankind is divided into two groups. The power of Jesus' hand protects those who believe and gives them eternal life (cf. vv. 15–16), but becomes implicitly also God's hand that punishes those who do not believe.

(4:1–42) Jesus' Work in Samaria The theme of the new cult that Jesus inaugurates is now further developed by his encounter with Samaritans, who stand outside normal Jewish faith. The dialogue with the Samaritan woman gives the reader more profound instruction on the living water (vv. 7–14) which Jesus the Messiah and true teacher can give (vv. 16–26). After the woman's testimony (vv. 27–30) and the dialogue with the disciples on spiritual food and the mission's result (vv. 31–8), Jesus meets the Samaritans who come to believe in him (vv. 39–43). Jacob's well, the woman's many husbands, the food that the disciples bring to Jesus, the time of harvest, are concrete starting-points for discussions about spiritual matters. With the exception of vv. 1–3 there is no reason to consider this narrative as composite (as e.g. Bultmann 1971: 176 ff. does; for arguments against him, see Olsson 1974).

(4:1–3) These three verses try to explain Jesus' return to Galilee, where he fulfils his second miracle. His departure seems to be the consequence of the Pharisees' negative reaction to his success in Judea, but that reason remains unsatisfactory, because the Pharisees also had some influence in Galilee. Perhaps the author (or a redactor?) wants the reader to understand that just as the Baptist left Bethany for Aenon, so Jesus has to leave Judea because of the Pharisees, who are the controlling authorities in Jerusalem (cf. 1:24). The author also corrects 3:22, 26 by noting that Jesus did not baptize himself. In the rest of the gospel neither Jesus nor his disciples baptize. Many good MSS have in v. 1 *kyrios*, 'the Lord' in place of 'Jesus', but this is probably a correction in order to improve the text where Jesus is twice the subject.

(4:4–15) These verses describe Jesus' first dialogue with the Samaritan woman. vv. 4–5, in the Fourth Gospel the Greek *(e)dei*, 'must', often indicates a work or an operation according to God's will (see 3:14, 30; 9:4; 10:16; 12:34; 20:9). Jesus has come to Samaria in order to do God's work. Sychar is not mentioned in the OT, but is probably *Sôker* which is in the Mishnah and the Talmud. One can identify it with the modern 'Askar, about 1.5 km. from Jacob's well. The evangelist alludes also to Sikem, today Tell Balata, when he mentions 'the plot of ground' given to Joseph (cf. Gen 33:19; 48:22; Josh 24:32). v. 6, 'about noon', literally 'at the sixth hour', as in 19:14, a rather unusual time to travel. The Greek word *pēgē* in vv. 6, 14, seems to indicate that the well is supplied by a living source of water. It is probably covered with a stone, so Jesus can sit on it (Gk.

epi, 'upon'). Although there are many wells in Genesis, not one is directly called 'Jacob's well'; however, Jacob meets Rachel at a well (Gen 29:1–12). In 1:51 the evangelist has already alluded to Jacob/Israel. vv. 7–15, Jesus' words, 'Give me a drink', and the mention of Jacob's well, are probably meant as an allusion to two scenes in the OT: the demand for water in the desert (Ex 17:2) and the gift of water at Beer (Num 21:16), which is celebrated by a famous song: 'Spring up, O well! Sing to it' (Num 21:17). In the LXX and in the targums 'Beer' is considered as a 'well' and not as a place. In the targums the place Mattanah is interpreted as 'gift'. Therefore the targum *Pseudo-Jonathan* considers the well as God's gift. In the Dead Sea scrolls the well is a symbol of the law given to Israel (CD 6:4–11), whereas Philo considers it as an image of wisdom (*De ebrietate*, 112–13; *De somniis*, 2.267–71). This is more or less the background of Jesus' first dialogue with the Samaritan woman. Jesus' demand for water is only an introduction to the counter demand of the woman for living water (v. 15). The water Jesus can give is a 'gift of God' (v. 10). Those who drink of it will never be thirsty (v. 13). Jesus is greater than the ancestor Jacob, because his teaching will replace the law or wisdom that the Jews or the Samaritans regard as God's gifts. The fullness of grace that was mentioned in the prologue (1:16) becomes very concrete in the image of the living water, which becomes a spring gushing up to eternal life (v. 14). In a similar way Paul alludes to the spiritual drink from the spiritual rock that followed the people in the desert (1 Cor 10:4). The theme of living water appears often in the OT as an image of salvation (e.g. Isa 12:3; 55:1; Ezek 47:1–12; Zech 14:8; Sir 24:21). What is new in the Fourth Gospel is not only that the faithful are thirsty but that the spring of water (a symbol of Jesus' teaching and of his Spirit) is now in them as God's gift. Some ancient authorities omit the remark in v. 9 on the Jews and the Samaritans, but there are good attestations for it in different textual traditions. The observation is very similar to others in John.

(4:16–26) The evangelist now describes Jesus' second dialogue with the Samaritan woman. vv. 16–18, that the woman has had six men is strange; it reflects the Jews' negative attitude towards Samaritans who are thought to remarry more often than is normally allowed to a woman (two or three times). On this natural level the purpose of the text is to show Jesus' prophetic knowledge. But the distinction Jesus makes between the five husbands and the last one who is not her husband can also favour a symbolic interpretation of the text. The woman represents the Samaritan people, just as Nicodemus in ch. 3 represents the leaders of the Jews. According to Josephus (*Ant.* 9.288) the Samaritans were composed of five different nations, each one having its special god. The woman's five husbands could symbolize these five gods whom the Samaritans had formerly worshipped, and the one who is not the husband could be YHWH whom the Samaritans are only partly linked to, because they worship him at a different place from that of the Jews (see v. 22). A minor problem with this interpretation is that 2 Kings 17:24–34, on which Josephus' story is built, tells us of five nations two of whom had two gods each (making seven altogether). vv. 19–20, the woman identifies Jesus with the coming prophet (Deut 18:15–18), who will vindicate the place of worship on Mt.

Gerizim, the mount of blessings (Deut 11:29) where the Samaritans thought Jacob had his heavenly vision (Gen 28:11–17). The Samaritans call him *tāhēv* ('the one who will come again') and consider him as a teacher and political leader rather than as a kingly Messiah. vv. 21–2, the evangelist underlines that Jesus himself is a Jew (cf. v. 9) and that salvation comes to the nations through the Jews (cf. Isa 40:1–31 and the synoptic tradition). But at the same time Jesus questions the two places of worship, Mt. Gerizim and Jerusalem. vv. 23–4, 'in spirit and truth' is a double phrase with a single sense, similar to 'Spirit of truth' in 14:17; 15:26; 16:13. It means an openness towards the Spirit whom Jesus gives (3:6; 4:14) and the truth that he reveals (1:14, 17; 14:6). 'God is spirit' has nothing to do with the Enlightenment description of the nature of God, but underlines that God will give his Spirit through his Messiah. The new cult revealed by Jesus will supplant Jewish and Samaritan worship, as much as it replaces Jewish purification rites (1:33; 2:6–11; 3:25–30) and the temple cult in Jerusalem (2:13–22). vv. 25–6, when speaking of the Messiah the woman goes beyond normal Samaritan expectations. The purpose of the dialogue is to have her recognize Jesus not only as the expected prophet but also as the Jews' Messiah. In 1:41 Andrew asserted that he had encountered him; in 1:19–23 and 3:28–30 the Baptist admitted that he himself was not the Messiah. To the Samaritan woman Jesus explicitly reveals that he is the Messiah. When he answers *egō eimi*, one cannot avoid seeing a link with the absolute use of the revelation formula in 8:24, 28 and 13:19.

(4:27–38) The evangelist portrays Jesus' dialogue with the disciples. vv. 27–30, the woman's missionary activity among her people makes it possible for them to be 'on their way' to Jesus. In the meantime Jesus is engaged in a dialogue with his disciples. That the woman leaves her jar has been interpreted in various ways (readiness to leave everything; desire to forget her past actions; wish to come back; readiness to go to her people). The best explanation is probably that she now relies on Jesus' promise in v. 14. vv. 31–4, unlike the dialogue with the Samaritan woman, Jesus here is not the initiator, but the misunderstanding concerning the food to be eaten is similar to that of the water to be drunk. Whereas Jewish traditions could regard Wisdom as the substance of a meal (e.g. Prov 9:5; Sir 24:21), Jesus considers the will of God (cf. 5:30; 6:38) to be his food. The will of the Father is that the one he has sent (i.e. his 'apostle') completes his messianic work (cf. 5:36; 17:4). In the Fourth Gospel all missionary activity starts with the Father and leads back to him. vv. 35–8, the harvest is mentioned in the synoptic parables on the growth of the kingdom of God (Mk 4 par.). The Fourth Gospel adapts Jesus' words to the actual situation in Samaria. He uses two proverbs, one on the interval between sowing and harvesting (v. 35a), and one on the difference between the sower and the reaper (v. 37). Concerning the first proverb Jesus says that a miraculous event has occurred, as he has just sown the Father's message in Samaria and can already gather a harvest. That this proverb forms an iambic trimeter is probably accidental. The other proverb is often used in a negative way in the OT (e.g. Deut 20:6; 28:30; Job 31:8; Mt 25:24), but Jesus gives it a positive meaning in Jn 4:38: both sower and reaper can rejoice together (v. 36). Who are the others who have laboured? Several answers have been given: the prophets in the OT; the Baptist and his disciples; Philip in Samaria (Acts 8:4–8). But the most natural interpretation in the context is to consider Jesus and his Father as those who have laboured, and the disciples as those who after Jesus' exaltation on the cross (cf. 12:32) will harvest what they have not sown. In this sense what is told in Acts 8 is only the result of the work Jesus has done in Samaria as the Father's 'apostle'. In a similar way the mission to the pagans in 12:20–1 is related to Jesus' work (cf. 7:35).

(4:39–42) Finally we get information concerning the Samaritans' meeting with Jesus. The evangelist has skilfully let the woman inform her people while the disciples had the discussion with their master. Now the Samaritans themselves meet the prophet and Messiah, and can, during two days as eyewitnesses, confirm the testimony of the woman. The evangelist is much concerned about how people come to faith by the testimony of the disciples (cf. 17:20), and about those who believe without having seen (20:29). There are now many more who come to a personal faith in Jesus as the Saviour of the world (cf. 3:16–18). In this way the schismatic Samaritans manifest a deeper understanding than the Jews in Jerusalem (2:23–5). The title 'Saviour', *Sōtēr*, is used for Jesus especially in later NT writings, as it could be associated with the cult of the emperor. Naturally for the evangelist Jesus is a Saviour in a more profound sense than the emperor, since the world has been created in and by him, the *Logos* (1:3–14).

(4:43–54) The Second Sign at Cana: The Healing of the Royal Official's Son Twice the narrator recalls the first sign at Cana (4:46, 54). The two miracles take place when Jesus comes to Galilee and in both the reader is reminded of that location (2:1, 11 and 4:43–7, 54). The narrative model is similar: Jesus' mother and the royal official ask the Master to interfere but his attitude is at first negative (2:4; 4:48). When both insist Jesus finally decides to intervene (cf. 2:5, 7–8 with 4:49–50). The miracle is described through the people's reactions (cf. 2:9–10 with 4:51–3) who come to believe in Jesus (2:11; 4:53). In contrast to the following miracles in John there is no sceptical discussion before or after the intervention. Thus the narrator suggests that Jesus was successful in Galilee, in contrast to what happened in Judea. If the royal official is a pagan we can observe that faith now spreads not only to the schismatic Samaritans but also to the Gentiles. The miracle illustrates how Jesus is a source of life, a theme which was important in 3:1–4:14, and will be continued in chs. 5–6.

There are strong links between the Johannine scene and the account of the healing of the centurion's son or servant in Matthew and Luke (Mt 8:5–13; Lk 7:1–10; see Neirynck 1984a), but the evangelist has also other information. He seems to have reworked his material with the help of the narrative of the healing of a Gentile woman's daughter in Mk 7:24–30 (cf. Mt 15:21–8).

(4:43–5) These verses have been composed either by a redactor or by the evangelist in a later edition of his gospel. He seems to have a direct knowledge of Mk 6:1–6 (both, alone in the NT, have the expression *exēlthen ekeithen*, 'he left that place'). He reworks the tradition of Mk 6:1–6 par. and has the prophet's 'own country' allude not to Nazareth but to Judea or perhaps more precisely to Jerusalem. The contrast in vv. 43–5 gives a positive description of Galilee and a negative one

of Judea. Only after the miracle of the bread are there negative reactions also in Galilee, but Jesus is never threatened with death as he is in Judea. According to 7:42 the Messiah comes from Bethlehem in Judea. So it is in Judea that Jesus as prophet and Messiah has no honour. vv. 46–7, 54, the Greek word *basilikos* (a 'royal') could designate a person of kingly dignity, but in the context it is probably a person who serves the king as a soldier or in his household. If he is a soldier he is a pagan like the synoptic centurion. A new introduction to the miracle indicates its link with the first sign. Like the centurion in Mt 8:5, but unlike the one in Lk 7:3–10, the royal official begs Jesus himself and not through intermediaries. vv. 48–50, in Matthew and Luke the centurion's words provoke Jesus' admiration and willingness to heal the son. In John the royal official is first criticized like all the others who are eager to see signs and wonders. The evangelist wants the reader to come to faith without seeing miracles (20:29, 31), but he also knows that Jesus revealed his glory by accomplishing his work. vv. 51–3, the royal official gets a confirmation of the miracle by his slaves on his way home. Perhaps the evangelist is aware directly or indirectly of Luke's different delegations from the centurion. For the reader it is important to have the miracle controlled by the father so that the glory of Jesus becomes manifest to all, including the official's household (cf. Acts 10:2; 11:14; etc.). The faith that the official had in Jesus' word is now strengthened.

(5:1–47) Jesus Heals a Lame Man: He Gives Life to Whom he Wishes Chs. 5:1–10:39 describe Jesus' confrontation with the Jews, both in Jerusalem and in Galilee. In Jerusalem the hostility leads to different threats to kill him (5:18; 7:1, 19–25; 8:37, 40; 10:31–9). His activity is presented in the framework of Jewish feasts which Jesus replaces by his own person. The exegetes who place ch. 5 after ch. 6 have not been able to give decisive arguments for their hypothesis; but it is possible that ch. 6 has been added in a second edition of the gospel, causing some tensions in the presentation of the material.

The evangelist has created a subtle contrast between the healing of the man at the pool Beth-zatha in ch. 5 and that of the blind man at the pool of Siloam in ch. 9. The former is merely a passive object of Jesus' work, whereas the latter illustrates the active response of a man with a growing faith. The special technique of the evangelist transforms the healing at the pool Beth-zatha into a kind of illustration of the transformation from death to life. The sick man is healed (vv. 9, 15) but Jesus himself is threatened by imminent death (v. 18). Nevertheless, this threat is ineffective, because the Father raises the dead, and the Son can give life to whom he wants (v. 21). This theme introduces the consideration regarding the dead who come out of their graves (vv. 28–9). The negative judgement on those who do not believe is evoked (vv. 29, 45–7). The opposite theme is that of the Father's love for his Son (v. 20), and the joint life-work of the Father and the Son (vv. 17, 21, 26). Jesus is described as the life-giving Son who is not obliged to observe the sabbath laws.

(5:1–9a) The evangelist describes first the healing, which has some similarities with that of a paralysed man at Capernaum in Mk 2:1–12 par. v. 1, 'a festival', without definite article before *heortē*, is probably the original reading and vaguely indicates one of the Jewish feasts. In v. 9 it is considered a sabbath, which makes it unnecessary to identify it with Passover or Pentecost. v. 2, the Copper Scroll (3Q15 11:12–13) refers to *Bethesdatayin* and its water basin, which seems to confirm *Bēthesda*, but Beth-zatha (NRSV) seems to be more satisfactory, as Bethesda may have been substituted because of its meaning, 'house of mercy'. Even less satisfactory are the variants *Bēthsaida, Bēzatha, Belzetha*. Near the temple area and St Anna's church archaeologists have found two connected pools, but the five porticoes are missing. At the time of Hadrian there was a cult devoted to the healing god Asklepios. v. 3, the Greek *xēroi* designates those who have malformed limbs, or who are 'paralysed', whereas *chōloi* are those who are lame (in one foot or both feet). The addition in vv. 3b–4 concerning the angel who stirs the waters is old but not original. It may go back to a local tradition and is inspired by v. 7. vv. 5–7, Jesus takes the initiative to heal the sick man, who in a naïve way describes his situation. Contrary to the Synoptic Gospels, Jesus does not require him to believe but asks only if he wants to be made well. The stirred water may be due to a system of pipes conducting the water from one pool to the other, or is a confusion with movement of water at the pool of Siloam. The addition in v. 4 attributes it to an angel. v. 8, Jesus' admonition is nearly identical with that of Mk 2:9, 11, one of the many indications that the author of the Fourth Gospel had a direct knowledge of Mark (Kieffer 1992). v. 9a, in a similar way the evangelist mentions the sabbath rather late in the narrative on the healing of the blind man (9:14). From 2:13 onwards the Jewish feasts play an important role in Jesus' stay in Jerusalem. By walking the man shows that he is healed, as in Mk 2:12, but there the mat he carries has a natural function. Contrary to the two first miracles the healing does not lead to faith in Jesus, but to violent discussions in vv. 9b–18.

(5:9b–18) The fact that Jesus healed on a sabbath leads to difficulties with the Jews. vv. 10–11, as early as Jer 17:21 and Neh 13:19 it was not permitted to carry a burden on a sabbath (cf. also the Mishnah, *Šabb.* 7:2). The healed man refers to Jesus' authority in response to the prohibition. vv. 12–14, Jesus disappears for a while in order to allow a discussion to be raised with the man who was healed (cf. a similar device in ch. 9). When he meets him in the temple, Jesus seems to establish a link between sickness and sin, just as in the synoptic tradition (Mk 2:5–12 par.), but contrary to Jn 9:2–3. The sick man is depicted in a rather negative way, in contrast to the blind man in ch. 9, who is an example of how to believe in Christ. vv. 15–18, thanks to the healed man identifying Jesus, the evangelist can introduce his main theme of the Jews' persecutions. Jesus' provocative statement is reinforced when he compares his activity with God's creative work even on a sabbath. For the first time the Jews want to kill him as a blasphemer. This will be stated even more clearly in 10:33.

(5:19–47) Jesus Gives the Jews a Thorough Answer

(5:19–30) In the first part of his long answer Jesus elucidates v. 17 on the joint work of the Father and the Son. It anticipates the sign of Lazarus' resuscitation and Jesus' own resurrection. vv. 19–20a, just as in 1:51; 3:3, 5, 11, the formula 'very truly' (in the text a double *amen*) introduces here and in vv. 24–5 a solemn revelation. At that time a son learned much from his father; the work of the Son is presented as entirely dependent

on that of the Father. This goes beyond what is said of Moses in Num 16:28. The evangelist uses here the word *phileō* for the Father's love for the Son, but elsewhere *agapaō* (3:35; 10:17; 15:9; 17:23–6). vv. 20b–23, the 'greater works' are those mentioned in vv. 21–2: to give life and to possess the power to judge now (v. 22; cf. 3:31–6). This is intended to anticipate what will happen at the end of the world (vv. 28–9). As the agent of God Jesus is worthy of the same honour as the Father (v. 23; cf. 15:23). vv. 24–5, in 3:15 it was faith in the Son of Man that led to eternal life, now it is belief that the Father has sent the Son. In both cases the believer accepts the one who has been sent. As in 4:23, the link between the future and the present is underlined. The evangelist describes the present situation with the help of eschatological expressions. Later Gnostic speculations reinterpreted this passing from death to life in the framework of the soul's delivery from its imprisonment in the body (e.g. *Ap. John*, 30:33–31:25). vv. 26–7, v. 26 reformulates v. 21 with the help of creational terminology (cf. the prologue). Just as in the Greek translation of Dan 7:13–14, there is no definite article before Son of Man; so one could translate 'a son of man', but the context shows that the evangelist refers to the early Christian tradition of Jesus' coming as eschatological judge. This is an exception in the Fourth Gospel, where the theme of the Son of Man is normally connected with Jesus' pre-existence, incarnation, death, and resurrection (cf. 1:51; 3:13–15; 6:27, 53, 62; 8:28; 12:23, 34; 13:31). vv. 28–30, without sufficient reason vv. 28–9 have been considered as redactional (e.g. Bultmann 1971: 261). On the contrary, the entire passage in 5:19–30 shows the connection between future and present judgement. There is a subtle correspondence between vv. 19 and 30, 20 and 28–9, 21–3 and 26–7, 24 and 25. The evangelist wants to show that the traditional last judgement already begins in this life. The resurrection of life is for those who have done good (v. 29) and believe in Jesus and his Father (v. 24). The resurrection of condemnation is for those who have done evil (v. 30; cf. 3:18). We meet this double resurrection also in Acts 24:15 (cf. Dan 12:2), whereas other Jewish traditions let the unrighteous remain in their graves. According to John the resurrection will take place at the voice of the Son of Man, whereas in 1 Thess 4:16 Paul uses Jewish apocalyptic imagery: the commandment from God, the archangel's call, and the sound of God's trumpet. In John Jesus' judgement follows the Father's decrees (cf. v. 30).

(5:31–47) In the second part of his answer Jesus is concerned about the fourfold testimony that justifies the great claim he makes to judge and to give life, as his Father does. vv. 31–2, an implicit objection to what Jesus has hitherto said could be: 'You consider yourself as judge, but we judge your testimony as not valid' (cf. 8:13). Therefore Jesus relies upon the supreme testimony of his Father. At the same time the evangelist perceives that the Son's testimony has great value, because Jesus knows where he has come from and where he is going (cf. 8:14). vv. 33–6, the Baptist's testimony to truth in 1:19–36 was only a human testimony and cannot therefore be compared to the greater one of the Father, which leads to the third testimony, the Son's works (cf. 10:25; 14:10–11). The Baptist is again presented as inferior to Jesus: only a shining lamp, but not the light (cf. 1:7–8). In v. 35 the audience is implicitly criticized for not having understood the Baptist's witness

(v. 33). This could also imply that the Baptist is now dead. vv. 37–8, the evangelist continues to move in a kind of circular demonstration: only a positive relation to the Son who has been sent can enable you to grasp the testimony of the Father! Those who have not heard the voice of God or seen him are implicitly contrasted to Jesus who has both seen and heard the Father (cf. 1:18; 5:19, 30; 6:46). Those who believe in Jesus see how the Father's testimony is present in the Son. vv. 39–40, 'to search' is a technical expression (Heb. *dāraš*). One could also translate *ereunate* as an imperative (so Origen, Tertullian, and probably the Egerton Papyrus 2 from the second century). But the indicative goes better with 'because you think'. The fourth testimony is that of Scripture, but the Johannine community knows by experience that many Jews cannot discern its testimony. vv. 41–4, one of the reasons for their shortcomings before the different testimonies is a lack of love for God and for his glory (cf. 12:43). Jesus underlines his own contempt for human glory, a theme that we also find among philosophers who prefer to speak the truth than to earn human glory (e.g. Dio Chrysostom, *Or.* 32:11). But the evangelist is moreover especially interested in the Son's and the Father's glory (Gk. *doxa*; cf. 1:14; 2:11; 7:18; 8:50, 54; 9:24; 11:4, 40; 12:41, 43; 17:5, 22, 24). Jesus also contrasts his own coming from the Father with those who come in their own name, perhaps an allusion to antichrists (cf. 1 Jn 2:18). At Jn 5:44 MSS as early as P75 and P66 leave out *theou*, 'God', but this is probably due to the copyists' error, and overlooked because its abbreviated form resembled too much the final vowels in the preceding word *monou* ('alone'). vv. 45–7, in Jewish tradition Moses is often depicted as Israel's intercessor or advocate before God (cf. Ex 32–4; Deut 9–10; Aurelius 1988). In John he is turned into the accuser of those who do not believe in Jesus, because they do not really read what Moses has written. The evangelist either alludes to the coming Prophet (Deut 18:15; see Jn 1:21; 4:18; 7:40), or more generally to the books of Moses, as in 5:39. The audience reads the Scriptures in a superficial way and does not see how the Father's testimony becomes evident in Jesus' mission and work, to which even Moses testifies.

(6:1–10:39) Third Geographical Grouping

(6:1–71) Jesus Feeds 5,000 and Walks on the Sea: He is the Bread of Life Ch. 6 is a well-defined unit about Jesus as the bread of life. Even vv. 51–9 belong originally to this unit (against Bultmann's redactional hypothesis, see Kieffer (1968: 152–4)). Possibly ch. 6 has been inserted between ch. 5 and ch. 7 after a first sketch of the gospel, or in a second edition, causing an interruption of the discussion in Jerusalem from ch. 5 to ch. 10. Nevertheless, chs. 2–4 have prepared the reader for Jesus' travels to Galilee. The whole of ch. 6 can also be considered as a concrete example of how Moses wrote about Jesus (5:46).

The approach of Passover in ch. 6 anticipates the last Passover in chs. 13–17, where the evangelist replaces the words spoken over the bread and the wine with the washing of the disciples' feet. As in ch. 5, a miracle is the occasion of a long discussion. The stage-setting begins with Jesus' stay on a mountain and the contrast between the five barley loaves and two fish on one side, and on the other the superabundant food for the five thousand people (vv. 1–15). The greatness of Jesus is also expressed by his walk on the sea during a storm and his leading of the disciples to the land (vv. 16–21). The following discussion (vv. 25–59) is introduced by vv. 22–4, and because of the contents and the different protagonists can be divided into four parts (vv. 25–7, 28–40, 41–51, 52–9). Jesus opposes the perishable food to that which endures for eternal life. Even the bread that Moses gave in the desert is contrasted to the bread of life that the Father gives from heaven. The concrete allusions to Jesus' flesh and blood (vv. 52–9) give rise to sharp reactions from the crowd and the disciples. Peter's confession contrasts with Judas' future betrayal (vv. 60–71).

Ch. 6 has much in common with the two miracles in Mk 6:30–52 par., and even with Mk 8:11–13 (the sign requested), Mk 8:14–21 (discussion on bread), Mk 8:27–30 (Peter's confession), Mk 8:31–3 (the Son of Man's rejection). The evangelist seems to follow Mk 6:30–52 and 8:11–33, omitting the duplicate feeding miracle in Mk 8:1–10 par., but adding his own material and his personal theology.

(6:1–15) The evangelist describes the feeding of the five thousand. vv. 1–4, only the Fourth Gospel underlines in this context the crowd's interest in Jesus' signs. That prepares the reader for Jesus' criticism in vv. 26–7. The location of the miracle is more vague than in the Synoptic Gospels. The starting-point of Jesus' journey seems to be Capernaum, mentioned in 2:12 and 4:46. If John follows Mark, the 'other side of the Sea of Tiberias' is not too far away from Capernaum, so that people can arrive on foot ahead of Jesus (Mk 6:33). But in Jn 6:23 one gets the impression that the place is also near Tiberias (mentioned only in John). Still, most important is the location on 'the other side', perhaps the pagan area of Decapolis or Bethsaida (cf. 1:44; 12:21). The 'mountain' has a symbolic meaning of proximity to God's authority, as in Mt 5:1 and 28:16. That Jesus sits down with his disciples (probably the twelve mentioned in 6:71) possibly underlines his special function as a teacher (cf. Mk 4:1; 9:35; Mt 5:1). The miracle takes place shortly before Passover, an indication that is absent in the Synoptic Gospels. It is possible that parts of the Johannine text were used in a Christian Passover feast where the eucharist was celebrated. Therefore Jesus' words are reformulated as a kind of homily on readings from the Jewish synagogue. vv. 5–9, in the first synoptic feeding miracle (Mk 6:30–44 par.) the disciples take the initiative, whereas here and in the second feeding (Mk 8:1–10 par.) it is Jesus who does so. In John the Master does not ask collectively all the disciples but only Philip. Andrew also intervenes and mentions the boy with the five loaves and two fish, whereas in the first synoptic account the disciples themselves had the five loaves and the two fish (in the second, seven loaves and some fish). It is clear that the author of the Fourth Gospel has made the stage-setting more dramatic by indicating Jesus' test. He also underlines Jesus' sovereign attitude and knowledge. v. 10, if John follows Mark, he replaces the finer word *anaklinomai* ('sit down') with the more common *anapiptō* found in Mk 6:40 and 8:6. The grass is also mentioned in the first miracle of Mark and Matthew; in Mk 6:39 it is even 'green', which suits the Passover in John. v. 11, as in most synoptic accounts of the feeding of the people, the evangelist uses words that recall the eucharist during Jesus' last meal. John underlines the thanksgiving in connection with the bread (cf. Lk 22:19; 1 Cor 11:24), whereas the fish play a minor role. Strangely enough he does not mention that Jesus broke the loaves, a detail we find in all other descriptions of the feeding miracles and of Jesus' eucharistic meal. vv. 12–13, as in all feeding miracles the evangelist emphasizes that the people were satisfied and that there was much left over. In the first synoptic feeding miracle there were twelve baskets of fragments of bread and fish, in the second only seven. In John Jesus himself orders the people to gather what is left. Again the evangelist is only interested in the bread. vv. 14–15, after the miracle the people think that Jesus is the expected prophet according to Deut 18:15–18 (cf. Jn 1:21; 4:19; 7:40). Only the Fourth Gospel mentions that the people want to make him a king, which Jesus refuses because he is 'king' in a quite different sense (cf. 18:33–4).

(6:16–21) Jesus Walks on Water. In Mk 6:48 Jesus comes to the disciples in the morning, in John when it is dark (Jn 6:16). The disciples have rowed 'twenty-five to thirty stadia' (v. 19, lit. tr.), about 5 or 6 km.; that means that they are in the middle of the sea. The stage-setting separates Jesus from the crowd and prepares the disciples for the following heated discussions where they have to decide about their own relationship to their master (vv. 60–71). We can compare two kinds of synoptic texts: Jesus walking on the sea (Mk 6:45–52 par.) and Jesus stilling the storm (Mk 4:35–41 par.). In both cases there is a strong wind blowing which Jesus calms, but in the first case Jesus is apart from the disciples whereas in the second case he is with them, sleeping in the boat. It is possible that both stories go back to the same event. In Mk 6:45–52 the evangelist shows that the disciples do not really recognize the saving epiphany of Christ, whereas in Mt 14:22–33 the scene is concluded with the disciples' confession: 'Truly you are the Son of God'. In John the epiphany is in the foreground, with the formula 'it is I', *egō eimi*. This sentence is used in John either with a complement, or without, as here. In three cases, in 8:24, 28, and 13:19, the absence of a complement makes the expression allude to *ănî hû* which designates YHWH in Deut 32:39; Isa 43:10; 52:6. It is possible that even in Jn 6:20; 18:5–6, 8, there is more than a simple statement 'it is I'. The miraculous landing during a storm is similar to that which is attributed to YHWH in Ps 107:23–30. There may also be an allusion to Jewish passover readings on the crossing of the Red Sea under Moses' guidance (Giblin 1983).

(6:22–4) The introduction to the discussion is awkward and may reflect a redactor's work (cf. JN 4:1–3; 4:43–5). The diminutive *ploiarion* ('a little boat') is used three times instead of the former *ploion* (in vv. 17, 19, 21–2). The words 'after the Lord had given thanks' in v. 23 are found in different old textual traditions and are probably original, but the designation *kyrios* reflects a Christology of the Lord which the evangelist normally reserves for the texts after the resurrection. The discussion with the people can take place only if they come to Capernaum where Jesus and the disciples have landed. But the author also wants the crowd to discover that Jesus had not used the disciples' boat (v. 22). The boats which come from Tiberias (v. 23) are meant to create a link between the unspecified place where Jesus fed the people and the locality of the discourse. The textual tradition in v. 23 is rather confused.

(6:25–7) These verses introduce a discussion on seeking Jesus in a wrong way (cf. 7:34–6), instead of looking for the eternal life he can give. In vv. 14–15 the people considered Jesus as the Prophet and wanted to make him a king, but now they address him as a teacher. In the following discussion he will speak as a revealer of wisdom. The reader already knows the extraordinary way in which Jesus came to Capernaum, but the Master rebukes the people for seeking him because of the signs and the food. The food he wants to give is salvation offered by God in the Son of Man. The allusion to the eucharist will come later in Jesus' discourse. In Isa 54:9–55:5 the Lord invites his people to be fed by his word. In a similar way Jesus speaks of a spiritual hunger. In v. 27 the seal which the Father has set (cf. 3:33) consists in his attestation of the Son's role, perhaps an allusion to 1:32.

(6:28–40) In this passage Jesus speaks about God's work and the bread of heaven. The citation in v. 31 is decisive for the whole discourse up to v. 59. vv. 28–9, as often in the Fourth Gospel the discussion is carried on with the help of a catchword, in this case 'the work of God', in v. 28 in the plural and in v. 29 in the singular. The people have not understood that the point is not to achieve many things but to let God do his unique work through a living faith in the Son he has sent. vv. 30–1, even if Jesus has already given a sign by feeding the crowds, they want a further sign from heaven, as requested in Mk 8:11–13. They express their solidarity with the Patriarchs, and especially with Moses and his signs (cf. Ex 16:4–5). vv. 32–3, in v. 31 the people had quoted Ps 78:24 (combined with Ex 16:4, 15): 'He gave them bread from heaven to eat.' In a typically rabbinic way Jesus underlines that 'he' alludes to the Father and not to Moses; one ought to say 'gives' and not 'gave', as the consonants *n-th-n* in Hebrew can be read both as *nāthan* ('he gave') and *nôthen* ('he is giving'). So God is the origin of both the manna and the true bread which gives life to the world. The God of the OT is called 'my Father'. Jesus' mention of 'true bread', as opposed to both manna and ordinary bread, is reminiscent of the Lord's prayer, addressed to the Father for bread for tomorrow (Mt 6:9–13). In v. 33 the Greek definite article *ho* may refer to Jesus ('he who comes down') or better, as in NRSV, to the bread ('that which comes down'; cf. v. 34). v. 34, just as the Samaritan woman had a very limited understanding when she said 'give me this water' (Jn 4:15), so the people's simple demand 'give us this bread always' is only a starting-point for Jesus' fuller revelation in the following verses. v. 35, in Greek *egō eimi* can be used in different contexts. It can answer the questions: 'Who are you?', 'What are you?', and 'Of whom are we speaking?'. In the first case it underlines a person's identity, in the second his or her qualifications, and in the third that one recognizes him or her. In vv. 35, 41, 48, 51, we have to do above all with this third kind of understanding: it is Jesus who is the bread of which we are speaking (cf. also 8:12; 10:7, 9, 11, 14; 15:1). 'The bread of life' means the bread which gives eternal life (cf. v. 27: 'the food that endures for eternal life') and is synonymous with 'the living bread' in v. 51. Similar expressions are found in Isa 55:1–2 (to thirst and be hungry for the word of God). Perhaps there is even a subtle allusion to the contrary statement in Sir 24:21: 'Those who eat of me will hunger more, and those who drink of me will thirst more.' In vv. 31–5 the author has passed from the OT 'bread from heaven' to 'bread of God' and finally to 'bread of life' (cf. *Joseph and Asenath* 16.8–9). v. 36, this critique is similar to that in v. 26. It interrupts Jesus' self-revelation, which will be continued in the following verses. Since this corresponds to a typical Johannine technique there is no reason to displace the verse, as Bultmann (1971) and Brown (1966) do. vv. 37–40, in these verses v. 38 is in the centre of a composition where v. 36 is the opposite of v. 40 and vv. 37 and 39 express a similar idea. v. 37 introduces the main theme: the Father gives the believers to Jesus. The three other verses describe the connection between the Father and the Son (v. 38; cf. 5:30), and the relationship of the believers to the Father and to the Son. Even if there is no direct link between vv. 36–40 and the theme of the bread of life from heaven in vv. 35 and 41, these verses give information on connected themes about Jesus being sent from heaven and the difficulty of believing in his self-revelation. 'Everything' in v. 37 corresponds to Aramaic *kol dĕ*. The evangelist likes to consider believers as the totality of people who have been given to Jesus by the Father (cf. 6:39; 17:2, 24). In Mt 18:14 it is the Father's will that not one of these little ones should be lost, whereas in Jn 6:39 it is the will of the Son. The Father's will is that believers should have eternal life, but it is the Son who will raise them on the last day (cf. v. 44), a rather unique affirmation in the NT. Contrary to 5:28–9 here the evangelist mentions only the believers' resurrection. In v. 40 to see the Son is nearly synonymous with believing in him.

(6:41–51) repeats certain affirmations made in vv. 28–40, but at the same time prepares the reader for the identification of the bread with Jesus' flesh in vv. 51–8. vv. 41–2, the evangelist replaces the crowds by the 'Jews' who murmur (*egoggyzon*; cf. vv. 43, 61), as did the people in the desert (Ex 16:2, 7–12). He probably thinks of Galileans who know Jesus' family and therefore challenge his heavenly origin. They resist Jesus, but without threatening him with death as the Jews in Judea do. They call him 'the son of Joseph', as in 1:45 and Lk 4:22, whereas in Mk 6:3 par. Jesus is 'the son of Mary'. Jesus' mother has been already mentioned in 2:1–12 and will be present at the crucifixion in 19:25–7. vv. 43–7, Jesus answers in an indirect way by speaking of his heavenly Father's work in those who believe (cf. vv. 37–40). In v. 44 the Father draws the believers to Jesus, whereas in 12:32 it is the elevated Jesus on the cross who draws all people to himself. Probably the evangelist is alluding to love's power to attract (cf. Hos 11:4; Song 1:4; Jer 31:3 (= 38:3 LXX)). As in v. 40 Jesus himself will raise the dead. The quotation in v. 45 from Isa 54:12–13 LXX is very free (perhaps with the help of Jer 31:34). Just as in the prologue, the evangelist in vv. 46–7 encourages the reader to rely on the Father and on the Son who alone has seen him. Once again the believer is said to have eternal life (cf. 3:15–16, 36; 5:24; 6:40). vv. 48–51, in v. 31 Jesus had emphasized that it was God and not Moses who gave the manna. Now he underlines that the manna, in contrast to the bread from heaven, could not prevent the ancestors from dying. In v. 49 Jesus says 'your ancestors' as if he himself were not a Jew. The evangelist writes from a later perspective when Jews and Christians were already separated (cf. 7:19; 8:17; 10:34). To eat of the bread in v. 50 prepares for the eating of Jesus' flesh in v. 51. The Greek word *sarx* ('flesh'), like *sōma* ('body') in the other eucharistic texts, is a translation of the Aramaic *besār*. Possibly the evangelist chose *sarx* in order to underline that the Word really became flesh and

blood (cf. 1:14). Implicitly Jesus alludes to his own death which gives life. In vv. 35 and 48 Jesus spoke of 'the bread of life', in v. 51 he speaks of the 'living bread', just as in 4:10 he mentioned the 'living water'. These metaphors describe Jesus as the Saviour of the world (cf. 4:42). The discussion has moved from the scriptural texts on the manna to the Son who has been sent from heaven in order to give life to believers.

(6:52–9) This explicit statement on the eucharist is the climax of the whole discussion and leads to strong reactions in vv. 60–6. v. 52, the Jews' negative reaction at the content of v. 51 is the starting-point of Jesus' even clearer statements in the following verses. vv. 53–4, in contrast to v. 51 Jesus also emphasizes the importance of drinking the Son of Man's blood, which is even more provocative (cf. v. 35). He uses both a negative and a positive formulation to characterize those who do or do not partake of the Son of Man's life. In v. 40 the importance of faith was underlined for those who will be raised by Jesus, whereas here it is the importance of the eucharist. v. 55, the reading *alēthōs* (adv. 'truly') is probably original, since it is attested in different textual traditions, in contrast to *alēthēs* (adj. 'true', NRSV), which probably arises from an early alteration in the Alexandrian traditions. The use of *alēthōs* as specifying the predicate is typically Johannine (cf. 1:42; 4:42; 6:14; etc.; Kieffer 1968: 152 ff.). 'Flesh' and 'blood' underline again Jesus' real humanity. vv. 56–7, just as he will in the image of the vine and the branches (15:1–11), Jesus stresses the mutual abiding of the believer and himself. The expression 'the living Father' is rare (cf. *Gos. Thom.* 3), but may have been coined in parallel with 'living bread' in v. 51. The Greek preposition *dia* with accusative normally means 'for the purpose of', but in our context it has nearly the meaning of 'by', 'through' (cf. 1 Jn 4:9). There is a link between the sending of the Son and the fact that the believer can live through the Son (who himself lives through the Father, cf. 5:26). In vv. 55 and 57 the future life is mentioned, whereas in v. 56 the present relationship is in view. v. 58, the evangelist sums up what has been said hitherto. The shortest reading 'the ancestors ate' is probably original, as the copyists were tempted to add words borrowed from v. 49 ('the manna' and 'in the wilderness'). v. 59, because of the absence of an article in *en synagōgēi* one could translate 'in an assembly', but since John probably knows Mk 1:21–8 he is thinking of the synagogue at Capernaum.

(6:60–71) After the mention of the Jews' repeated complaints we now get the disciples' reactions. The miracles at Cana resulted in faith (2:11; 4:53), whereas the healing of the lame man in Jerusalem provokes the Jews to such a degree that they seek to kill Jesus (5:18). The miracle of the bread and the following discussion meet both positive and negative responses, but this time even some of Jesus' disciples leave him. v. 60, 'many of his disciples' will leave Jesus in v. 66 and are distinct from the twelve in vv. 67–71. One can also translate: 'who can *listen to him*?' (the Greek *autou* can refer either to 'his teaching' or to Jesus). v. 61, the evangelist often stresses that Jesus knows what people are thinking or doing (e.g. 1:47–8; 2:25; 6:64). v. 62, there is no main clause in the conditional sentence, therefore different ways have been proposed to complete it: 'then the offence will be even greater'; 'then the offence will be diminished'; 'then the offence will be both greater and diminished'. This last suggestion fits the context best, because the ascension of the Son of Man will be as mysterious as his descent from heaven and the consumption of his flesh and blood. In this interpretation v. 62 corresponds not only to v. 61, vv. 48–50, or 51–8, but to the whole foregoing discussion. v. 63, the flesh and blood of the Son of Man must be understood in the light of Jesus' connection with the living Spirit of God (cf. 3:5–8; 4:24; 7:38–9). Jesus lives through the Father (v. 57) and after the resurrection will transmit this life through the eucharist. v. 64, the remark on Jesus' knowledge refutes possible objections concerning the choice of Judas. v. 65, the Father's action is mentioned in v. 44 (cf. also 6:37; 8:47). v. 66, The strange Greek expression *apēlthon eis ta opisō* is also used in 18:6 and means literally 'they went away, backwards'. In Isa 1:4 and 50:5 a similar Hebrew expression means 'to leave'. v. 67, the twelve are mentioned here and in vv. 70–1 for the first time and will appear also in 20:24. It is possible that they already are understood to be with Jesus in 6:3. The narrator assumes that the reader knows them as a chosen group, but (in 1:35–51) he describes the call of five disciples only. The question with *mē* (not: lit. 'Not also you wish to go?') introduces here not the expected negative answer but an indecisive one. vv. 68–9, Peter answers in the name of the twelve. He says rhetorically, 'to whom can we go?'; he accepts what Jesus has said in v. 63; he makes a solemn declaration about Jesus, similar to that at Caesarea Philippi in Mk 8:29 par. 'The Holy One of God' is the best reading, whereas many MSS have changed the text under the influence of Mk 8:29; Mt 16:16; and Jn 11:27. As the evangelist has already shown that Jesus is the Messiah, he stresses here another aspect of Jesus. vv. 70–1, the evangelist knows that according to the Synoptics Jesus chose the twelve (cf. 13:18; 15:16), even if he does not describe the circumstances of their call (cf. Mk 3:14 par.). The devil is named Satan in 8:44 and 13:2. Judas betrays Jesus under the influence of Satan (cf. 13:2). In the Synoptics and in Jn 12:4 and 14:22 Judas is called Iscariot, whereas here and in 13:2, 26 this is his father Simon's surname. Perhaps the original name was *Scariōth* (Codex Bezae; cf. Kieffer 1968: 201–4).

(7:1–8:59) Jesus at the Festival of Booths With the exception of 7:53–8:11, which originally did not belong to the Fourth Gospel (see JN APP), these verses form a narrative unity devoted to Jesus' stay in Jerusalem during the festival of Booths (or Tabernacles). Some verses describe how Jesus the Messiah replaces the Jewish rites at Tabernacles, both the ceremony with water (7:37–9) and the celebration of light (8:12). At the same time the conflict with the Jews in Jerusalem is increasing: they do not understand Jesus' identity and therefore discuss in a polemical way the Messiah, the son of David, the law of Moses, their kinship with Abraham. In 7:32 and 7:45 the reader is for the first time informed that the Pharisees and the chief priests try to arrest Jesus but do not succeed. This anticipates their new initiatives in chs. 9–12 where they finally achieve their plans. In 7:15–24 the discussion in ch. 5 is continued, just as 7:37–9 extends the theme of water in chs. 1–4. The theme of the light in 8:12 will be in the centre in ch. 9, and the relation of Jesus to God, discussed in chs. 7–8, will be treated extensively in chs. 13–17.

The chronological indicators, the content of the discussion, and the people's different interventions can help us to divide the text into seven sections: (1) Jesus hesitates to go up to Jerusalem at the festival of Booths (7:1–13). (2) Jesus' teaching and Moses' law (7:14–24). (3) The mysterious origin of Jesus (7:25–36). (4) Jesus, Messiah and prophet (7:37–52). (5) The Father's testimony to Jesus (8:12–20). (6) Jesus' return to his Father (8:21–30). (7) Jesus and Abraham (8:31–59). These sections are organized into three scenes. About the middle of the festival Jesus suddenly appears at the temple (sect. 2–3). The next scene is on the last day of the festival (sect. 4). The third scene is introduced in 8:12 with a vague indication, 'again', and takes place in the treasury of the temple (cf. 8:20; sects. 5–7). The three scenes are linked together with the help of three main actors: Jesus, the people, and the official authorities (see among others Rochais 1993).

(7:1–13) Jesus hesitates to go up to Jerusalem at the festival of Booths. His secret journey from Galilee to Jerusalem and its temple is only a reflection of his even more mysterious journey from the Father to this world and back to him (cf. vv. 25–36 and 8:21–30). But what Jesus expresses clearly is not understood by the Jews, who know only his human origin and instead of seeking God rely upon their law (cf. 7:14–15). v. 1, 'After this' (Gk. *meta tauta*) is a typical Johannine transition (cf. 5:1, 14; 6:1; 19:38; 21:1). Sometimes it is changed to *meta touto* (2:12; 11:7, 11; 19:28). The variant reading 'was not at liberty' is probably not original, since it is less well attested in different textual traditions than NRSV's 'he did not wish'. Jesus' hesitation is due to the threat in 5:18. vv. 2–5, between the Passover in ch. 6 and the festival of Booths in chs. 7–8 is a time-span of about six months. Jesus' brothers have already been mentioned in 2:12. In the Synoptics they are named: James, Joses, Judas, and Simon (Mk 6:3; Mt 13:55). A comparison with Jn 19:25 makes it probable that in the Fourth Gospel they are half-brothers or cousins. In Mk 3:21, 31–2 Jesus' relatives fail to understand his mission. In a similar way the brothers in John are incredulous, in contrast to the beloved disciple. The disciples may be either those named in 2:23 and 4:1, or (better) those who left him in 6:66 and want to see a spectacular sign in Jerusalem (cf. 6:14–15). The sceptical brothers seem to reformulate a sentence of Jesus that we find in the Synoptics (Mk 4:22 par.). The evangelist knows that Jesus will in fact show himself to the world (cf. 18:20). vv. 6–9, as in 2:1–11 Jesus wants to keep the initiative. He knows that when the time of his clear manifestation will come, it will provoke hatred from the world, a theme developed in 15:18–25. Only here does the evangelist use the word *kairos* ('time') and not his usual *hōra* ('hour'), perhaps under the influence of Mk 1:15 par. In v. 8 P66, P75, and B have *oupō* ('not yet') in place of *ouk* ('not'), but that seems to be an early correction in order to avoid a contradiction between what Jesus says in vv. 6–8 and what he finally does. vv. 10–13, in v. 10 the NRSV's 'as it were' renders *hōs* which we find in many important MSS, but which is missing in others. It might have been added very early in order to soften the meaning. The Jews in v. 11 probably represent the official authorities, as in v. 13. They want to seize Jesus (cf. vv. 32 and 45). They are not identical with the crowds in v. 12 or the people of Jerusalem in v. 25 who react in quite different ways. The 'complaining' in

v. 12 is probably a 'muttering' as in v. 32, unlike the stronger complaining recorded in 6:41, 43, 61. Very early the Jews accused Jesus of deceiving the crowds (cf. v. 47 and Mt 27:63–4; in Lk 23:2, 5 this even becomes a legal charge). Later Jewish and Christian sources refer to Jesus as a magician who has seduced Israel (b. Sanh. 43a; 107b; Justin, Dial. 69; 108). John answers those accusations. Jesus himself warned against those who would lead the disciples astray (Mk 13:5–6).

(7:14–24) These verses compare Jesus' teaching with Moses' law. In 2:13–22 Jesus had cleansed the temple and spoken of his risen body as the new temple. In chs. 7–8 he is showing how he replaces the law of Moses and the Jewish festival of Booths. v. 14, the evangelist distinguishes between the beginning of the festival which Jesus does not want to attend (v. 9), the middle when he is teaching (v. 14), and the last day (v. 37) when he cries out his solemn message. It is impossible to know which day is meant in v. 14 (the third, the fourth, the fifth?), but perhaps it is on a sabbath (cf. vv. 22–3). Jesus' teaching in the temple of Jerusalem is given greater esteem than that in the synagogue at Capernaum in 6:59. v. 15, as the word grammata (learning) also appears in 5:47 some exegetes want to insert vv. 15–24 immediately after 5:47 (see Bultmann 1971: 268 ff.). But in 5:47 the word means what Moses has written, his 'teaching', and in 7:15 the instruction in the Scriptures, the 'learning'. vv. 16–18, Jesus' self-defence is similar to that in 5:19, 30, 41, 44: he does not speak on his own, he does not do his own will, or seek his own glory. Only in the Fourth Gospel is Jesus' teaching directly attributed to God who has sent him. To do the will of God is the necessary presupposition for recognizing that Jesus seeks only God's glory. He is true, as God himself is true in 3:33 and 8:26. This implies also the negative statement that there is no falsehood (adikia) in him. This word is not found elsewhere in John, but we have it in 1 Jn 1:9 and 5:17. v. 19, Jesus speaks as if he himself was not a Jew (cf. 8:17; 10:34). The text is written from a later perspective when Jews and Christians had parted their ways. To keep the law is to do God's will. Therefore the Jews go against his will when they want to kill the one whose teaching comes from God. Possibly there is also the reflection of a later polemic against Jews who are proud of their law but circumcise on a sabbath (v. 22). v. 20, the crowd is divided concerning Jesus (v. 12), and therefore, unlike the authorities, does not make plans to kill him. But they think he is possessed, an assertion we find in Mk 3:20–2, and which Jesus will refute in Jn 8:48–52; 10:20–1. vv. 21–3, Jesus defends his healing of the lame man on a sabbath (5:1–9) by citing the circumcision the Jews themselves practise on a sabbath (cf. the Mishnah, Ned. 3:11; Šabb. 18:3; 19:2). He uses a rabbinic argument, qal waḥômer, which proceeds from a lesser case (circumcision of a man's foreskin) to a greater one (the healing of a man's whole body). A similar argument is found in b. Yoma 85b and t. Šabb. 15:16. The remark concerning the patriarchs can reflect a later Christian polemic against Jews who attributed circumcision to Moses' law, whereas it originated in the time of Abraham (Gen 17:10; 21:4; see also Paul's argumentation in Gal 3 and Rom 4). v. 24, if the aorist krinate is the original reading, one ought to translate, 'Cease judging by appearances'. In 8:16 Jesus will speak of his own judgement as a valid one, because it is entirely dependent on his Father's judgement.

(7:25–36) The discussion turns towards the question of Jesus' origin. vv. 25–7, the people of Jerusalem (Hierosolymeitai) are in the NT named only here and in Mk 1:5. In contrast to the people who have come to Jerusalem for the festival they are informed about the authorities' plans to kill Jesus (5:18; 7:19). As they let Jesus speak openly they seem to accept him as the Messiah. Ironically the evangelist notices that the people of Jerusalem both know and do not know where Jesus comes from. Their expectation of a hidden Messiah corresponds to elements of Jewish literature, as attested by Justin (Dial. 8:4; 110:1; cf. 1 Enoch, 48:6; 4 Ezra 13:52). vv. 28–9, Jesus' answer is introduced by a solemn 'cried out' (ekraxen; a verb used for Jesus in 7:37 and 12:44, and for the Baptist in 1:15). The audience knows only Jesus' human origin and not that he comes from God, who alone is true (cf. 17:3; 1 Jn 5:20). In 5:46 Jesus said that if they really believed in Moses they would also believe in him. Now he is contrasting his own knowledge of God and of his origin in God with their lack of knowledge. vv. 30–2, those who try to arrest him are probably inhabitants of Jerusalem. They do not succeed because the 'hour' has not yet come, just as the official actions from the authorities in vv. 32 and 45 are without result. But some of those who came up to Jerusalem have a more positive attitude towards the signs of Jesus. Here the evangelist reflects the Christian conception that by his miracles Jesus proved himself to be the Messiah, which corresponds to Jewish expectations according to Josephus (Ant. 18.85 ff.; 20.168 ff.). The favourable attitude of the crowd provokes the Pharisees and the chief priests to send the police which are at the disposal of the official council (cf. 18:3). v. 33, for the first time Jesus describes his death as a departure in order to go to God (cf. 8:14, 21–2; 13:3, 33, 36; 14:4–5, 28; 16:5, 10, 17). The theme of the 'little while' before the death will reappear in 12:35 and 13:33. In 14:19 and 16:16–20 it is transformed into the 'little while' the disciples will not see Jesus and then see him again. All these passages express Jesus' sovereign power over human time, which is short in comparison with the time before his incarnation and after his return to his Father. v. 34, hitherto the Jews have sought Jesus in a negative way, in order to arrest him (7:11, 19–20, 25, 30). Now seeking has a positive quality but is frustrating when one cannot find Jesus (cf. Gos. Thom. 38). Perhaps the evangelist alludes in an ironic way to the synoptic saying, 'search, and you will find' (Mt 7:7; Lk 11:9). The Jews will not find Jesus if they refuse to recognize his divine origin. In a similar way Wisdom says: 'They will seek me diligently, but will not find me' (Prov 1:28). There is no need to understand hopou eimi egō ('where I am') in connection with the formula egō eimi we have encountered before. The present tense stands probably for a future, 'where I shall be' (after my departure). vv. 35–6, the Dispersion among the Greeks may designate the area of the Decapolis. The evangelist is interested in those outside Judaism who believe in Jesus (e.g. the Greeks in 12:20–2; other people in 10:16; 11:52; 17:20–4). The Jews' naïve interpretation of the words of Jesus contains an ounce of truth: they prophesy that the teaching of Jesus will be spread among the Greeks.

(7:37–52) Jesus is both the Messiah and the prophet. Even if this part of the discussion takes place on a day other than that of vv. 14–36 we meet the same three aspects: Jesus' teaching

(vv. 37–9), the people wondering about who Jesus is (vv. 40–4), and the authorities' project to arrest Jesus (vv. 45–52). v. 37, NRSV, JB, and TOB link 'and let drink' (*kai pinetō*) in v. 37*b* with 'who believes' in v. 38; others, such as many Greek Fathers and P[66], prefer to relate it to v. 37*a*: 'come to me and drink'. In the first interpretation one can connect 'out of the heart' (lit. belly) in v. 38 with Jesus or the believer, in the second it is more natural to connect it with the believer. Because of v. 39 and the witness of P[66] we prefer this second reading. The last day is either the seventh or the eighth. On the seventh day there was a procession with water from Siloam to the temple, and a ceremony of light in the women's court (cf. *Sukk.* 3–5). These ceremonies were missing on the eighth day, but people could still mentally associate them with Jesus' teaching (see vv. 37–9; 8:12), just as in chs. 4 and 6 one can see the connection with Isa 55:1, 'Everyone who thirsts, come to the waters'. During the water ceremony people sang, 'With joy you will draw water from the wells of salvation' (Isa 12:3; *b. Sukk.* 48b). The water was not drunk but was taken up to the temple. The combination of these two passages of Isaiah shows that the believer can now drink the water of salvation from Jesus. vv. 38–9 Bultmann (1971), Brown (1966), and Schnackenburg (1977–9: ii) think that the waters flow from Jesus; NRSV, Barrett (1978), and Lindars (1972), from the believer. The comment on the Spirit in v. 39 favours the second interpretation. The believer who receives the living water from Jesus has it in his heart (lit. his belly) through the influence of the Spirit. The water becomes in the believer 'a spring of water gushing up to eternal life' (4:14). Those who favour a Christological interpretation often establish a link with 19:34, but there blood and water come from Jesus' side (*pleura*) and not from his belly (*koilia*). These exegetes are obliged to consider v. 39 on the Spirit as secondary. It is difficult to know which passages of Scripture the evangelist is alluding to in v. 38, perhaps such texts as Prov 18:4; Isa 58:11; Sir 24:30–4. In a Jewish environment it is usual to compare the Spirit with water (e.g. 1QS 4:18–21). In the later *Midrash, Gen. Rab.* 70:8, the water at the festival of Booths symbolizes the Spirit. In the early Christian tradition the Spirit is linked with the water of baptism (Jn 1:35; 3:5). Paul makes explicit the connection between drinking water and being baptized in water (1 Cor 12:13). There may therefore be an implicit allusion to Christian baptism even in Jn 7:39. In the Fourth Gospel the Spirit is given after Jesus' death and resurrection (cf. 14:16, 26; 15:26; 20:22). vv. 40–4, the discussion on Jesus' messianic origin, which began in vv. 25–31, is now continued. Some people think that Jesus is the prophet like Moses (Deut 18:15; cf. Jn 4:19–29; 6:14). The evangelist wants to show that he is both the prophet and the Messiah. He also implicitly accepts that Jesus comes both from Galilee (cf. Isa 9) and from Bethlehem (v. 42). He seems to be informed about Jesus' birth at Bethlehem but wants to underline that his divine origin is much more important (cf. vv. 25–31 and 8:14–19). Those who want to arrest him could be the men whom the Pharisees and the chief priests had sent out in v. 32 (cf. also vv. 45–9). vv. 45–52, there is some irony in the statement that the temple police could not arrest Jesus, because they were impressed by his teaching. The Pharisees therefore stress that the authorities, in contrast to the vulgar crowd, do not believe in Jesus. Nicodemus is a Pharisee who probably belongs to the *synedrion* (cf.

Jn 3:1). His prudent advice, which may be based on Lev 19:15 and Deut 1:16–17 is rejected by his colleagues, because Jesus comes from Galilee, contrary to messianic prophecies (see Jn 7:40–4). Despite the fact that the prophet Jonah came from Galilee, the Jews can assert v. 52, that the Scripture nowhere affirms that a prophet *will arise* from Galilee. Moreover Galileans are often considered as unclean by the inhabitants of Jerusalem because they live in close proximity to pagans.

(7:53–8:11) see JN APP.

(8:12–20) In 7:25–52 the Jews discussed the qualifications of the Messiah and the prophet, whereas Jesus underlined his own divine origin. Here Jesus speaks of his Father's testimony, a subject he has already treated in 5:31–8. In 8:21–30 he will allude to his going back to his Father, and in 8:31–59 he will invite the audience to become his disciples. v. 12, this solemn declaration is similar to Wisdom's disclosure (e.g. Prov 8–9). In Wis 7:26 wisdom is described as a reflection of God's eternal light. Light in the Jewish tradition is often an image of salvation (e.g. Isa 9:2; 42:6; 60:19). The people have to choose between two ways, between light and darkness (e.g. Jer 21:8; Deut 30:15; 1QS 3:3). In the Synoptics Jesus fulfils the prophecies concerning the future light (e.g. Mt 4:16; Lk 1:78–9; 2:32), and his disciples are in their turn 'the light of the world' (Mt 5:14). Even if we have there a similar formulation to v. 12, Jesus' self-revelation is of a higher order: in him the world meets the fountainhead of light (cf. Jn 1:5, 9; 9:5; 11:9–10). There is also an implicit allusion to the festival of Booths with its ceremony of light in the women's court (see above). Jesus fulfils the deeper meaning of the feast. vv. 13–15, contrary to the Pharisees' objections against his own witness (cf. 5:31), Jesus argues first that they judge by human standards, knowing neither where he comes from nor where he is going. vv. 16–18, the reading *alēthinē* ('right') attested in v. 16 by among others P[75], B, D, and W is probably original, since it is different from the nearby occurrences of *alēthēs* ('valid', NRSV) in vv. 13–14, 17. Jesus' second argument is that he is not alone when he judges or gives his testimony. So there are two witnesses, as the Jewish law prescribes (cf. Num 35:30; Deut 17:6; 19:15). But in fact it is through Jesus that the audience is given information on the Father's testimony. Just as in 5:31–47, the arguments are circular: only those who accept Jesus' divine origin can understand both his and his Father's witness, and conversely those who accept the witness of each can see in Jesus the Son whom the Father has sent. It is possible that the sentence, 'I judge no one' (cf. 3:17) encouraged an editor to insert the pericope on the adulteress in this Johannine context. vv. 19–20, the audience has hitherto not really understood the relation between Jesus and his Father. The reason is that they know neither Jesus nor his Father. This time the discussion is *near* the treasury of the temple (the Greek preposition *en* is scarcely used here in the sense of 'inside'). The treasury is probably the room for the people's gifts, near the women's court (cf. Mk 12:41).

(8:21–30) Jesus' return to his Father is unique. v. 21, the discussion continues with a vague 'again he said to them', as before, in v. 12. A new aspect in comparison with 7:32–6 is that the audience will die in their sins, because they do not believe (cf. v. 24). v. 22, according to vv. 30–1 many of the Jews believed in Jesus. But others do not understand what Jesus is saying about his return to the Father. In 7:35 they thought he would go to the Greeks, now that he intends to commit suicide. But Jesus will freely give up his life without committing suicide (10:11, 17–18). v. 23, in Jewish apocalyptic literature there is a contrast between this world and that to come. In the Fourth Gospel God and the world from above replace the world to come. The Johannine dualism between two worlds is different from later Gnostic systems because it is moral (Jesus' message from above is rejected) and not cosmic (even this world was created by God). v. 24, the *egō eimi* has no complement (see JN 6:16–21). It is possible that this 'I am he', spoken as it is during the festival of Booths, is also an allusion to YHWH (cf. *Sukk.* 4:5). v. 25, the words *tēn archēn* can mean 'at all' (NRSV) and be an expression of exasperation. But since *archē* is important in the theology of the Fourth Gospel (1:1–2; 2:11; 6:64; 8:44; 15:27; 16:4) the literal translation 'at the beginning, which is what I tell you' might be better, with the force, 'I am the One at the beginning, which is what I keep telling you' (see Miller 1980). vv. 26–9, the judgement of condemnation supplements the promise of salvation in 3:17 and 12:32, 34. It will be more explicit with the sending of the Helper in 16:8. Jesus once again underlines his close link with the Father: he says what he has heard from him, he is not left alone, and he does what pleases the Father (see 5:19–47). But the *egō eimi* in v. 28 concerning the uplifted Son of Man, which extends the thought of v. 24, adds a new dimension to the question of Jesus' identity. Only believers will be able to recognize the divine 'I am' revelation on the cross. v. 30, the Jews who believe in Jesus still need further teaching, as is shown by vv. 31–59.

(8:31–59) The question of truth in vv. 32, 40, 44–6 gives rise to a discussion about Jesus and Abraham. vv. 31–2, in 5:31 Jesus criticized the audience for not having God's word abiding in them. Now he admonishes the Jews who believe in him to abide in his word (cf. also v. 51), if they want to be truly his disciples. This anticipates the teaching Jesus will give his disciples after his last supper (chs. 15–17). There are different ways to believe in Jesus, the superficial way as in 2:23–5 and 6:14–15, 26, and the deeper way of real discipleship that is described here and in 13:35; 15:8–9. The truth that makes the disciples free is not obtained by their own investigations but is revealed from above. v. 33, the Jews often boasted of being the descendants of Abraham, which Paul criticizes by showing that the pagans are also included in Abraham's faith (cf. Galatians and Romans). But already the Baptist (Mt 3:9; Lk 3:8) had attacked the Jews' superficial attitude when he noted that God can raise up new children to Abraham (cf. also Jesus' critique in Mt 8:11–12; Lk 13:28–9). The Jews have often been politically dependent on foreigners but they have kept their own religion. vv. 34–8, the Jews cannot be free if they sin by wanting to kill Jesus, who declares what he has seen in the Father's presence. There is a sharp contrast between the disciples who share all the rights of the Son, and the slaves of sin who have no rights. In a similar way Paul opposes the son of the free woman, Sarah, and the son of the slave woman, Hagar (Gal 4:21–31; cf. also Heb 3:5–6). In v. 38 NRSV understands *poieite* as an imperative: 'you should do what you have heard from the Father'. Because their father in v. 44 is identified with the devil, it is probably better to take *poieite* as a present indicative and translate: 'you do what you have heard from

your father'. vv. 39–40, since the explicit identification of their father with the devil has not yet been made, the Jews continue to consider Abraham as their father. This causes Jesus to reply that they should then do the good deeds that were connected with his faith (cf. Jas 2:22). Abraham believed in God and relied on God's truth, which is contrary to their intention to kill the one who tells them the truth from God. In my opinion both *este* (you are) and *epoieite* ('you would do') in v. 39 are original. Different MSS have tried to improve the poor Greek of this sentence. vv. 41–5, Jesus still does not explicitly say who their father is. The Jews insist on their legitimate claims to be the children of God, probably in contrast to all Gentiles (cf. 1 Thess 4:3, 5). There might be an implicit accusation that in this respect they are different from Jesus whose father is unknown (cf. the accusations of Celsus in Origen, *Contra Celsum*, 1:28, and later Jewish literature). But this point remains uncertain. If God were their Father they would accept Jesus who comes from him (cf. 5:43). Jesus now gives the explicit reason for their resistance: their father is the devil (cf. 1 Jn 3:8), who is the father of lies and a murderer from the beginning. Probably the evangelist alludes to Cain who was from the evil one and killed his brother (1 Jn 3:11–12). The strong contrast between truth and falsehood resembles the one we find in the Dead Sea scrolls between the spirit of truth and the spirit of deceit (e.g. 1QS 3:18ff.; cf. also the Man of Lies in 1QpHab 2:2; 5:11). vv. 46–47, since Jesus does not sin when he speaks the truth about God, those who do not believe in him cannot have God as their Father. vv. 48–51, the Samaritans were considered by the Jews to be an unclean people (cf. Jn 4:9). They could be considered as 'illegitimate children' (8:41), but also as possessed by a demon. The evangelist, unlike the Synoptics, does not explicitly present Jesus as an exorcist, but it is possible that he is here alluding to the scribes' accusations that Jesus drives out demons with the help of Beelzebul (Mk 3:22–30 par.). Jesus refutes the Jews by stressing his own interest in God's glory (cf. 5:44) and appeals to God's judgement. vv. 52–3, just as in the discourse on the bread of life, Jesus promises eternal life to his disciples. Without knowing it the Jews indirectly speak the truth: Jesus is greater than Abraham who died, just as he is greater than Jacob (4:12). vv. 54–6, Jesus once again affirms that his glory comes from his Father and that he keeps his Father's word. The Jews' question in v. 53 allows him to affirm that in fact he is greater than Abraham, since the latter rejoiced that he could see Jesus' day. Perhaps the evangelist is thinking of Gen 17:17 when Abraham laughed at the promise of a child. The comparison with Gal 3:16 shows that in Isaac Abraham could greet his descendant, the Christ. There are also texts that underline Abraham's prophetic knowledge of the future (cf. Heb 11:13 and the Jewish texts quoted in Str-B ii. 525–6). vv. 57–9, the evangelist is interested in chronology, but 'fifty years' is a conventional indication. Some MSS have transformed it into forty years in order to fit Lk 3:23. Since Abraham is the most important figure for the Jews, they now ask how Jesus can have met him. Jesus answers with an *egō eimi* formula different from that in vv. 24 and 28, because it is part of a normal sentence. He contrasts Abraham's birth with his own sovereign being that transcends time. One might compare Ps 90:2, 'Before the mountains were brought forth . . . you are God.' Jesus has been able to see Abraham because he was before him. This assertion is considered as a blasphemy and therefore the Jews want to stone him (Lev 24:16). Jesus escapes from them in the same way as before (7:30, 32, 45).

(9:1–41) Jesus Restores Sight to the Blind Man As in ch. 5, a miracle takes place in a pool on a sabbath day, and provokes violent debates. But whereas in ch. 5 Jesus was directly the revealer, the progressive insight of the blind man is in the centre of the controversies in ch. 9. The motif of his blindness from birth is enriched by the themes of night and sinfulness. In contrast to that, Jesus is the light of the world. His divine work among humankind is symbolized by the mud he makes with his saliva (cf. Gen 2:7). The blind man must wash his eyes in the pool of Siloam. At the festival of Booths the water of salvation was fetched from Siloam (see JN 7:37–9). The evangelist underlines that Siloam means 'Sent' (v. 6), so that Jesus who has been sent by his Father (v. 4) is also present in this water. There may be a hint at the importance of water in Christian baptism. The blind man comes to a complete faith in Jesus. In contrast to him some of the Pharisees remain in their sin. Certain aspects of the story recall synoptic miracles on blind people (Mk 8:22–6; 10:46–52 par.; Mt 9:27–31; 12:22–3 par.), but on the whole the evangelist seems to rely on his own information.

The scene is well organized: a discussion between Jesus and his disciples (vv. 1–5) introduces the proper miracle (vv. 6–7). The man blind from birth is interrogated on different occasions, first by his neighbours and those who have met him (vv. 8–12), then by the Pharisees (vv. 13–17), and after the enquiry from his parents (vv. 18–23), a second time by the Jewish authorities (vv. 24–34). After all these interrogations he finally meets Jesus himself who is revealed to him as the object of faith, and who criticizes the Pharisees (vv. 35–41).

(9:1–5) From the information in v. 8 one can guess that the blind man was sitting as a beggar at the entrance to the temple. The discussion between Jesus and the disciples gives the meaning of the miracle story in advance; it replaces the synoptic description of how blind people ask to be cured (Mk 10:47–8 par.; Mt 9:27–8). Jesus' answer to the problem of suffering is similar to that in Lk 13:2, but different from Jn 5:14. Jesus does not accept rabbinic discussions concerning who has sinned (see the examples in Str-B ii. 527–9), but stresses God's ability to transform difficult situations. Jesus has to do the work of his Father before he himself will be condemned to death. The NRSV is probably right when it chooses as original the apparently contradictory 'we' and 'me' in v. 4. vv. 6–7, in the first two miracles Jesus' mother and the royal official took the initiative (2:3; 4:47). At the pool of Beth-zatha and here it is Jesus who initiates the miracle. In 5:6 Jesus asked, 'Do you want to be made well?' Here he simply accomplishes the miracle as part of God's plan.

(9:6–12) The evangelist combines two kinds of synoptic miracles, those by contact (the mud on the eyes in v. 6), and those by distance (the healing at the pool in v. 7). In Mk 7:33 and 8:23 Jesus heals with the help of saliva, which at that time was considered as a remedy (cf. Tacitus, *Hist.* 4.81 and Suetonius, *Vesp.* 7). But in John Jesus makes mud with the dust of the earth, which might symbolize his creative power (cf. Gen 2:6–7.; Job 10:9; Irenaeus, *Adv. haer.* 5.15.2). The blind man seems to represent the Christians who by their baptism (cf.

3:5) are able to 'see' the one who has been sent by the Father. vv. 8–12, just as in the miracle at Beth-zatha, and in contrast to the two first miracles in Galilee, there are at first negative reactions to Jesus' action. But in the end the healed one will come to an explicit faith. In contrast to all those who hesitate concerning his identity, the once-blind man confesses what Jesus has done for him. He does not mention that the mud was made with the help of saliva. He only knows that the healer is called Jesus, but does not know where he is. This prepares the reader for his arrival in v. 35. In v. 11 the Greek word *aneblepsa*, which properly means 'I saw again', is used of the one who was born blind (cf. Dittenberg., *SIG* 1173. 15–18).

(9:13–17) By the information in 1:24; 3:1 and especially in chs. 7–8 the reader is accustomed to consider the Pharisees as Jewish authorities who sometimes are also simply called 'the Jews' (see 9:18, 22). The evangelist seems to describe the judicial capacity of the Pharisees in the light of their importance in the *bêt dîn* after 70 CE. Their power in the Sanhedrin before 70 was rather limited. The healing and the making of mud by Jesus could be interpreted as works that were forbidden on a sabbath (cf. *Šabb.* 7:2). The Pharisees who doubt Jesus' origin from God go against what Nicodemus formerly had admitted (3:2). The healed man considers Jesus as a prophet, just as some in the audience will do in v. 31. But both in the OT and the NT a sinner can also perform miracles which lead people astray.

(9:18–23) The parents of the man witness that their son was born blind, but prefer to let him speak of the miracle on his own behalf. They represent the Christians who after 70 CE hesitate to confess Jesus as the Messiah, because they might be put out of the synagogue. Later Jewish documents distinguish between three forms of exclusion, two temporary ones, for a week or for at least thirty days, and a more decisive one, the 'ban' (*ḥērem*). It is possible that such a definitive exclusion was first introduced about 80–90 with the *birkat hamminim*, a prayer of 'benediction' (= 'malediction') against pagans, perhaps even against Christians. The *aposynagōgos* in 9:22; 12:42; 16:2 might refer to this severe exclusion from the Jewish community (cf. Forkman 1972: 87–114), even if some scholars today contest this interpretation.

(9:24–34) 'Give glory to God' in v. 24 means simply to speak the truth (cf. Josh 7:19; *Sanh.* 6:2). The authorities now accuse Jesus of being a sinner, just as some of the Pharisees had already done in 9:16. The once-blind man, on the contrary, is of the same opinion as the other Pharisees in v. 16. He implicitly opposes Jesus' authority to that of the law (cf. 5:17). Ironically he remarks in v. 27 that they perhaps want to be Jesus' disciples. They naturally reaffirm their own fidelity to Moses (cf. Mt 23:2: 'the Pharisees sit on Moses' seat'). They claim that Moses has spoken to God, whereas Jesus' origin is obscure to them, despite all that has been said in chs. 7–8. The evangelist reflects here the conflict which took place in his time between disciples of Jesus and those of Moses (cf. 5:45–7). The man becomes more adamant and explicitly states that Jesus comes from God (vv. 30–3; cf. 3:2), reaffirming what Jesus himself had maintained after the miracle at Beth-zatha (5:19–24). The audience refuses to be taught by a man born in sin, but Jesus has already denied this interpretation in vv. 2–3 and he will affirm in v. 41 that on the contrary it is the unbelieving audience which is sinning.

(9:35–41) During the whole controversy Jesus was absent, but his miracle was the main subject of discussion. The healed man has progressively become more confident about Jesus' origin from God. He is now prepared to confess his faith in him who reveals himself as Son of Man. A few MSS such as P75 and Sinaiticus omit the whole of v. 38 and the beginning of v. 39. Contrary to Brown's hypothesis on a liturgical addition (Brown 1966) the text is original since it is well attested in different textual traditions. Jesus' revelation to the blind man is similar to his self-disclosure as Messiah to the Samaritan woman (4:26). The healing of the blind man concludes with an emphasis on the sign of faith. Jesus speaks of the actual judgement which will also be the Son of Man's final judgement (cf. 3:17–21 and 5:27–30). He alludes to Isa 6:9–10, a text that the Synoptics apply to the reception of God's rule (Mk 4:12 par.). In the early Christian communities this text was also used against Jews who did not believe in Jesus (cf. Acts 28:25–8 and Jn 12:39–40). Jesus employs the word 'blind' in two ways: inability to see, and unwillingness to understand. The Pharisees who do not want to understand are immersed in a deeper moral and spiritual blindness than those who are physically blind from birth.

(10:1–21) Jesus is the Door and the Good Shepherd The shepherd's care for his sheep is a frequent theme in the synoptic tradition: Jesus has compassion for the crowds who are like sheep without a shepherd (Mk 6:34; Mt 9:36), or are sent into the midst of wolves (Mt 10:16; Lk 10:3). There may be ravenous wolves who come in sheep's clothing (Mt 7:15). In the parable of the lost sheep according to Mt 18:12–14 Jesus describes God's care for all those who might get lost. In Lk 15:3–7 the same parable, directed against the Pharisees and the scribes, is applied to a sinner who repents from his sins. The little group of disciples is addressed by their master as a flock to whom the Father is giving the kingdom (Lk 12:32; cf. Mt 25:32–4). Finally Jesus alludes to his death with the help of Zech 13:7: 'I will strike the shepherd and the sheep will be scattered' (Mk 14:27; Mt 26:31), a situation which is also described in Jn 16:32.

In these verses two main lines from the synoptic tradition are developed: Jesus is identified with the shepherd as in Mk 14:27 par. He takes active care of his sheep as in Matthew and Luke. But the perspective is different: Jesus speaks of the shepherds who do not fulfil their vocation, and alludes to the OT expectation of God becoming Israel's true shepherd in the future (cf. Isa 40:11; Jer 31:10; Ezek 34:11–16). This prospect could also be applied to David who shepherded the people of Israel (2 Sam 7:7) and became the figure of the predicted Messiah (cf. Jer 23:4–8; Ezek 34:23–4; 37:24). But in Jn 10 Jesus is less a messianic figure than one sent by the Father who loves him. In Jn 21:15–17 Jesus' function as a shepherd will be transmitted to Peter if he loves his master (cf. Acts 20:28–30 on Paul).

In Jn 10 the shepherd does not seek what was lost but keeps his sheep from all dangers. He is even willing to give his life for them, struck as the shepherd is in Zech 13:7. More clearly than in the Synoptics Jesus himself takes the initiative to give his life (cf. Isa 53:5–8 and 1 Pet 2:24–5).

A special feature in John is that even the gate through which the sheep pass becomes important, giving rise to another parable on thieves and bandits. Contrary to Bultmann's (1971) opinion, there is insufficient reason to think that this theme derives from Mandean literature.

(10:1–3a) The solemn 'very truly' introduces a narrative which in v. 6 is called a 'figure of speech' (*paroimia*), and which corresponds to a synoptic parable, something always difficult to understand (Mk 4:11–13 par.; cf. Jn 16:25, 29). Both words translate the Hebrew *māšal*, with the difference that the Johannine *paroimia* prepares for Jesus' self-revelation in 10:7–18. The first parable in vv. 1–3a contrasts the man who enters by the gate, and the thief or the bandit who climbs in by another way. The normal image in this type of parable would be the burglary of a house or a palace (cf. Lk 12:39), but the evangelist has obscured this by speaking from the beginning of a sheepfold and a shepherd. One can associate this in the Synoptics with the narrow gate that leads to life (Mt 7:13–14; Lk 13:24–5). The evangelist possibly thinks of a sheepfold close to a house and of the shepherd's own sheep in contrast to others (vv. 3–4).

(10:3b–6) The second parable is about a shepherd who knows his own sheep by name and can therefore lead them out of the sheepfold, in contrast to the stranger whom they do not follow. Comparison should be made with Ezek 34:11–16, where God in the future will be the shepherd of his people. Since in both parables the gate and the shepherd remain unidentified the audience (i.e. the Pharisees of 9:40 and others) at first does not understand.

(10:7–10) The obscure figure of speech is partly explained by Jesus' self-identification with the gate. But he avoids a total allegorization of the first parable by not elucidating who the gatekeeper, the thief, and the bandit are. Jesus is the gate in two ways: first, in vv. 7–8 he is the gate through which the shepherds have to go to reach the sheep. The thieves and the bandits (possibly identified with the Pharisees and all the false prophets who have preceded them), do not want this. Secondly, in vv. 9–10 he is the gate through which one can come in and go out to find pasture. Here it is not the shepherd who goes through the gate but the sheep. This is similar to the synoptic narrow gate which leads to life, and Jesus' saying: 'I am the way, and the truth, and the life. No one comes to the Father except through me' (Jn 14:6–7; cf. also Ps 118:20). In order to understand how the gate leads to pasture one has to consider the function of Jesus as shepherd. He guides his sheep to life just as he earlier promised living water and bread from heaven. In opposition to this the thief comes only to kill and destroy (v. 10).

(10:11–18) vv. 11–13 form a short parable, in addition to what had been said in vv. 1–5. There the shepherd was opposed first to the thief and the bandit, then to the stranger. Now a second theme is developed: the hired hand runs away, vv. 12–13. New aspects are introduced: the wolf who attacks the sheep and scatters them takes over the negative function of the thief and the bandit. Jesus identifies himself with the good shepherd, in contrast to all those who in Israel did not behave as such (cf. Ezek 34; Zech 11:4–9; CD 13:9–10). In a similar way, in 6:32–40 he was the true bread from heaven and in 15:1 will be the true vine. In contrast to the hired hand he is willing to give his life for his sheep, as there is a deep solidarity between him and them. This is expressed with the help of reciprocal knowledge, which had been foreshadowed in vv. 3–4 and will be described in 15:1–11 as a reciprocal abiding in love. In 10:16 suddenly the perspective is widened with the reference to 'other sheep', probably an allusion to pagans (cf. 7:35; 11:52; 12:20–2). It is not clear whether the one flock will also be in one sheepfold. In vv. 15, 17, and 18 Jesus' leadership is anchored in the plan and love of his Father. In v. 18 there is even an allusion to Jesus' initiative in his future resurrection.

(10:19–21) Just as the Pharisees had different opinions concerning the miracle in ch. 9, the Jews (who include the Pharisees of 9:40) are now divided into two groups. As in chs. 7–8 some believe that Jesus has a demon, which in vv. 22–39 will lead to even sharper accusations. Those who defend Jesus do so by referring to his healings of the blind.

(10:22–39) Jesus at the Festival of Dedication During the festival of Dedication (Gk. *ta egkainia*, Heb. *ḥănukkâ*) Jesus is surrounded by Jews who are not his sheep, and therefore cannot understand either his unity with the Father or his identity as Messiah and God's Son. In contrast to those who hear Jesus' voice they try to stone him for blasphemy. Jesus is strong by virtue of all his links with the Father and therefore nobody can snatch his sheep out of his hand. He is simply doing his Father's work, being the Messiah (vv. 22–30), and God's Son (vv. 31–9).

(10:22–30) Jesus is truly the Messiah. vv. 22–3, the Festival of Dedication took place three months after the Festival of Booths, with similar ceremonies (cf. 1 Macc 4:47–59; 2 Macc 10:6–8). Winter in the Near East is particularly the month of December. Jesus comes back to the temple which he left after the Jews had attempted to stone him in 8:59. According to Acts 3:11 and 5:12 the portico of Solomon was a gathering place for the first Christians. Josephus records that it ran along the east side of the temple (*Ant.* 15. 396–401; *J. W.* 5. 184–5). v. 24, since in 12:13 a verse from Ps 118 is quoted, and in 10:9–10 another verse seems to be alluded to, 'gathered around' may be due to Ps 118:10–12 where the word occurs three times. In the discussion in chs. 7–8 the audience was divided concerning Jesus as Messiah, despite the demand from the brothers of Jesus that he should make himself more widely known (7:4: *en parrhēsiai einai*). Therefore the audience in 10:25 wants him to tell them plainly (*parrhēsiai*) if he is the Messiah. vv. 25–8, Jesus has already explicitly said to the Samaritan woman in 4:26 that he is the Messiah, and to the blind man in 9:35 that he is the Son of Man. His teaching has been so clear that Peter could confess him as 'the Holy One of God' (6:69). Moreover, during the festival of Booths some people were able to understand that he was the Messiah (chs. 7–8). But the audience in ch. 10 does not want to come to faith (cf. Lk 22:67); it wishes only to accuse Jesus, because it has no positive relation to him. Some exegetes would like to connect vv. 27–30 about the sheep with v. 15*a*, but the evangelist may have consciously wanted to link together chs. 7–10 with the help of two themes: seeing (ch. 9) and listening (ch. 10). For those who are able to understand, Jesus the good shepherd replaces both festivals. Those who refuse to understand are blind (ch. 9), and do not belong among his sheep (vv. 26–7). According to v. 28 Jesus gives his sheep eternal life (cf. v. 10), and he can protect them

against those who want to snatch them away, such as the wolf in v. 12. vv. 29–30, according to the translation in NRSV the things the Father has given Jesus are greater than all; according to JB and TOB it is the Father who is greater than all. If in the original reading the definitive article had been the masculine *hos* there would probably not have been any problem. Therefore the neuter *ho* in our MSS is original and at the same time the masculine *meizōn* is also original: *ho patēr mou ho dedōken moi pantōn meizōn estin* (cf. Birdsall 1960; Lindars 1972: 369–70; Schnackenburg 1977–9: ii. 385–6). The literal translation is 'The Father is, as to what he has given me, greater than all'. 'What he has given' is a typical Johannine expression (6:39; 17:2, 24), which underlines the Father's initiative. Jesus' strength comes from his Father who is greater than all. There is a profound unity between both (cf. 5:19–20; 7:16–18), which in 17:11 will also include believers.

(10:31–9) The evangelist continues to stress that Jesus is God's Son. vv. 31–3, first in v. 33 the Jews indicate blasphemy as the reason why they want to stone Jesus (cf. Lev 24:16). As in 8:59 it is an attempt to kill him without official trial. In the synoptic tradition Jesus is accused of blasphemy when he forgives sins (Mk 2:5–7 par.), and when he speaks of the coming Son of Man seated at the right hand of the Power (Mk 14:62–4 par.). Probably all propositions that questioned God's uniqueness were considered as blasphemy in Jesus' time (cf. 5:18). Ironically the Jews speak the truth: for the evangelist Jesus is in a certain sense 'God'. 'Good' is used in 2:10 of the wine, and in 10:11, 14 in reference to the shepherd. The good shepherd is sent by the Father, and therefore his work exhibits the Father's goodness (cf. v. 25). vv. 34–6, Jesus uses an argument *a fortiori*: if the Scripture refers to those who received the word of God as 'gods', the one whom God has sanctified cannot blaspheme when he says that he is God's Son. The argument holds only if you accept that the one sent by God is of a higher standing. Just as in 7:19 and 8:17 Jesus speaks of 'your' law, as if he himself were not a Jew. The 'law' here is synonymous with Scripture (cf. 12:34; 15:25). Jesus quotes Ps 82(81):6*a* LXX. In the psalm the subordination of the pagan gods to Israel's God is described, but Jesus' point is that 'god' can also be applied to those other than Israel's God. In Ps 82:6*b* 'the sons of the Most High' may have facilitated the transition from 'gods' to 'God's son'. Perhaps the word 'sanctified' is used in v. 36 to fit in with the festival of Dedication during which Num 7:1–89 was read (cf. *Meg.* 3:6). In Jn 17:18–19 Jesus sanctifies himself for the disciples' sake so that they may be sanctified in truth. vv. 37–9, Jesus resumes the question of his works, first in a negative formulation (v. 37), then in a positive one (v. 38). The latter is surprising because it invites the Jews to believe at least in Jesus' works even if they do not believe in him. There may be a hint here of the evangelist's fatigue in finding new arguments for his contemporaries in favour of faith in Jesus. In fact, it is not easy to understand the deep unity between Jesus and his Father (v. 30), or the mutual 'indwelling' (cf. 14:10–11; 17:21). As in 7:30 and 8:20, 59 Jesus is able to escape from their hands, but his inability to engage with the Jews will lead to the final plan to put him to death (11:53, 57).

(10:40–21:25) Fourth Geographical Grouping

(10:40–2) Back across the Jordan In comparison with what happens in Jerusalem the events across the Jordan are positive. Even across the Sea of Galilee Jesus is not threatened with death. We have seen a positive attitude towards him both in Galilee and Samaria. After the dramatic episodes at the two festivals in Jerusalem Jesus must retire to the 'friendly' place where John first baptized. To Galilee, which he left after ch. 6, he will return only after his resurrection (ch. 21). By mentioning the place across the Jordan the evangelist can make a final comparison between Jesus and the Baptist. The latter has not done any miracles and therefore could not be the Messiah. The number of people who come to Jesus and believe in him in the place where he had called his first disciples verifies that the testimony of the Baptist was true. This is an invitation to the reader to believe in Jesus, the crucified and risen one.

(11:1–54) Jesus Who Raises Lazarus Must Himself Die The raising of Lazarus is the seventh and most important sign, since it directly foreshadows Jesus' own death and resurrection. Lazarus' illness both does and does not lead to death. Therefore Jesus can successively say that his friend has fallen asleep and that he is dead (vv. 11, 14). The reason is that Jesus has his own view on what real life is about. The passage from death to life corresponds to the transition from unbelief to faith. This is clear when, despite her brother's death, Martha confesses her faith in the Lord. Lazarus in his tomb embodies the power of death. When he comes out of the tomb and is unbound (vv. 43–4) he is an illustration of the capacity of faith. Jesus accomplishes the work of light among humanity: those who walk with him do not stumble (cf. vv. 9–10) in the dark.

But the death and raising of Lazarus also suggest beforehand what will happen to Jesus who goes to Judea in order to die and be raised from the dead (cf. vv. 7–16). People think that Mary goes to the tomb to weep there, but she meets Jesus (vv. 31–2). She prefigures Mary of Magdala who weeps at the tomb where the risen Jesus is revealed to her (20:11–16). Like her sister Martha she knows that if Jesus who is the resurrection and life (v. 25) had been there, her brother would not have died (v. 32). Jesus weeps and is deeply moved by Lazarus' death, which forecasts his own departure (vv. 35–8).

But there are also contrasts between the deaths of Lazarus and Jesus: Lazarus has been dead for four days (v. 39) but Jesus will rise on the third day (cf. 2:19–22). The reader is invited to join those who believe that the risen Lord will give them eternal life. Through his death and resurrection he will gather into one all the dispersed children of God (v. 52).

The scene is well composed: after a delay (vv. 1–16) Jesus goes to Bethany and meets Martha (vv. 17–27), and Mary (vv. 28–32) separately. He then goes to the tomb (vv. 33–41a), and raises his friend (vv. 41b–44). In vv. 45–54 the evangelist describes the consequences of Jesus' ultimate sign.

(11:1–16) Jesus delays his intervention in Bethany because it is linked to his own death. In the Synoptics Jesus restores to life two persons who have just died, Jairus' daughter and the son of a widow at Nain (Mk 5:21–43 par.; Lk 7:11–17). In John Lazarus dies while Jesus is absent, but has been buried for four days before Jesus arrives and raises him. The revival is therefore more dramatic. vv. 1–2, in Lk 16:19–31 another story

is told about a poor man, Lazarus, who dies and is honoured in heaven in contrast to the rich man who before his death had no pity for him. In Lk 10:38–42 Mary and Martha are also named in another context. John alone speaks of their brother Lazarus, and he identifies Mary with the anonymous woman, who according to Mk 14:3–9 and Mt 26:6–13 anointed Jesus in the house of Simon the leper at Bethany (in Lk 7:36–50 the woman is a sinner). vv. 3–6, because the sisters speak of 'whom you love' (*hon phileis*) some exegetes want to identify Lazarus with the beloved disciple, but for him the evangelist uses (with one exception) the verb *agapaō*. Jesus knows that Lazarus will die but it will not be a definitive death. It will reveal God's glory in his Son. The two days of delay are necessary to prepare the statement in v. 17 that Lazarus had been in the tomb four days. vv. 7–10, the decision to go to Judea establishes a link between Lazarus' death and Jesus' imminent condemnation. In 9:4 Jesus declared explicitly that he was the light of the world. Now he states it indirectly by calling the sun the light of the world. According to ancient physics the light was in the human eye (cf. Mt 6:22–3; Lk 11:34–5). There is therefore an interplay between the sun or Jesus and the human eye. One can compare *Gos. Thom.* 24: 'There is light within a man of light.' vv. 11–14, as in other languages, in Greek one can use the euphemism 'to sleep' for 'to die' (cf. Mt 27:52; 1 Thess 4:13–15; 1 Cor 15:18, 20). But the evangelist likes to play on words (see JN 3:4). This permits him to allude to the raising of the dead while using the word 'awaken'. Jesus finally tells them plainly that Lazarus is dead. vv. 15–16, the evangelist presupposes that Jesus' presence would have prevented Lazarus from dying (cf. v. 21) and thus from being raised. Thomas (which in Aramaic means 'twin') plays an important role in the Fourth Gospel (cf. 14:5; 20:24–9; 21:2) and in the *Gospel* and the *Acts of Thomas*. An old Syriac tradition which is scarcely reliable considered him as Jesus' twin and identified him with Judas, a brother of Jesus according to Mk 3:18. On the spiritual level Thomas is right that the believer dies with Christ (e.g. Rom 6) but he has not yet understood what Jesus meant in vv. 9–11. Perhaps the evangelist is suggesting that for Thomas there is nothing beyond Jesus' death (cf. 20:24–9).

(11:17–27) In Bethany Jesus first meets Martha. v. 17, the four days Lazarus has been in the tomb prove according to Jewish conceptions that the soul has definitively left the body (cf. Str-B ii. 544–5). In v. 38 it becomes clear that the tomb is a cavity, either in the soil or, more probably, in the rock, with a stone in front of it (cf. 20:1). vv. 18–19, the evangelist clearly distinguishes between two places, the Bethany across the Jordan, where the Baptist first baptized (1:28), and the Bethany near Jerusalem, generally identified with today's Eizariya. This second Bethany is named in the Synoptics in relation to Jesus' entry into Jerusalem (Mk 11:1 par.) and the anonymous woman in Simon's house (Mk 14:3 par.). In Lk 24:50 Bethany is also the place from which Jesus is carried up to heaven. Thirty days of mourning was usual for women. To console them was one of the important Jewish duties (cf. Str-B ii. 592–607). vv. 20–2, Mary stays at home, probably in order to take care of the guests. In v. 29 we learn that she did not know that Jesus had arrived. As in Lk 10:38–42 Martha is the one who takes the initiative. She expresses her confidence in the power of Jesus. vv. 23–6, the dialogue between Jesus and Martha is built on a major misunderstanding: Martha thinks that Jesus is speaking about the resurrection at the end of time, but Jesus asserts that he himself is the resurrection and life, so that soon Lazarus will be raised. Those who believe in Jesus will be able to overcome their own physical death. v. 27, Martha expresses a complete faith in Jesus, the faith which the evangelist himself wants to promote (cf. 20:31).

(11:28–32) In ch. 4 the meeting with the disciples followed the dialogue with the Samaritan woman and prepared for the meeting with the Samaritans. In a similar manner the dialogue with Martha gives way to a short meeting with Mary, in order to introduce Jesus' visit to the tomb (vv. 33–41a). Martha calls Jesus 'the Teacher'. In 1:38 the Greek *didaskalos* translates the Hebrew *rabbi* and in 20:16 the more solemn *rabbouni*. Jesus is also called 'teacher' in 3:2 and 13:13–14, and 'rabbi' in 1:49; 4:31; 9:2. More often he is addressed as *kyrios*, 'Lord' (11:21, 32). Mary weeps—and suddenly sees Jesus, anticipating what Mary of Magdala will do at the Lord's tomb. Like her sister, she affirms that Jesus could have healed her brother, but the dialogue does not continue.

(11:33–41a) Jesus comes to the tomb. vv. 33–5, the transition from the scene with Mary to the next scene is smooth. The Jews who followed Mary come to Jesus and are weeping with her. The NRSV 'was greatly disturbed' translates the Greek *enebrimēsato*, which implies anger. The hypotheses that have been produced about a possible Aramaic or Syriac background (cf. Black 1967: 240–3) do not sufficiently explain our actual text. Probably Jesus' anger is not so much directed against the lack of faith of those who are weeping (so Bultmann 1971: 407) as against the power of death he is now confronted with (cf. 12:27; 13:21). Jesus' own sorrow is real (cf. v. 35), but at the same time he envisions his fight against Satan, the ruler of this world (cf. 13:27, 30; 14:30). vv. 36–7, as with all that Jesus says and does, his weeping can be interpreted in opposite ways. The negative interpretation of Jesus' tears leads us back to the polemical situation after the miracle with the blind man (chs. 9–10). vv. 38–41a, the preparation for the miracle underlines the contrast between the real death of Lazarus and the glory of God revealed to those who believe, but only the disciples have formerly heard about this (v. 4). Martha's statement concerning the decay of her brother's corpse can be interpreted as a friendly warning, because Jesus has not yet told her explicitly what he plans to do.

(11:41b–44) In 2:7–8; 4:50, and 6:10 we have already encountered Jesus' orders in preparation for the miracle. Here he commands people to take away the stone, and Lazarus to come out. The loud voice reminds us of what was said in 5:28–9. Jesus looks upwards (cf. 17:1; Mk 6:41; Lk 18:13) in an attitude of prayer to his Father, in agreement with his practice in some miracles in the synoptic tradition (cf. Mk 6:41 par.; Lk 3:21; 9:28). Still here as in Jn 9:31 the miracle is presented as God's answer to Jesus' prayer. In Mk 14:36 Jesus addresses God with *'abba*, an Aramaic expression that corresponds to the simple *patēr* in Jn 11:41 (cf. Lk 11:2). In place of asking God's help Jesus expresses his profound link with the Father (cf. 12:27–30; ch. 17), who glorifies his Son and is

glorified by him. Just as the voice from heaven in 12:20 is for the people's sake, so is the mention of his prayer. The strips of cloth in v. 44 may correspond to the *othonia* in 19:40 and 20:5–7, and the *soudarion* (head cloth) to the one mentioned in 20:7. The evangelist does not concern himself with how Lazarus can come out of his tomb before the strips of cloth were unwound.

(11:45–54) The raising of Lazarus provokes opposing reactions. vv. 45–6, the faith of many Jews is counterbalanced by the unbelief of those who denounce Jesus to the Pharisees. vv. 47–8, John simplifies by associating the chief priests of the Sanhedrin with the Pharisees alone. The main concern of the council is to avoid the destruction of the holy place (which at the time the evangelist wrote had already happened). In Mk 14:1–2 the plot of the chief priests and the scribes to arrest Jesus precedes the anointing at Bethany and the eucharistic meal, but the official hearing comes later (Mk 14:53–65 par.). John on the contrary places an official meeting of the council before the anointing at Bethany. Later there will be different hearings but no formal verdict. In this way Jesus is sentenced to death in his absence, whereas in the hearings he sovereignly answers the questions of his judges (cf. Jn 18:19–38). vv. 49–53, according to Josephus (*Ant.* 18.35, 95) Caiaphas was chief priest from 18 to 36 CE, and naturally not only in the year Jesus was crucified. Ironically Caiaphas prophesies the truth, but the evangelist adds that Jesus will die not only for the Jewish nation but also for all the dispersed children of God (cf. 10:16). There may be a conscious contrast between Jesus' gathering of the children, and the council's gathering in v. 47. Jesus' death is implicitly a propitiating sacrifice (cf. 1:29; 19:14, 36), but the evangelist especially underlines his obedience to the Father (cf. 10:17; 13:1–33; 19:30). v. 54, according to 7:51 the council's death sentence is illegal (cf. 7:51). Just as Jesus in 10:40 retired across the Jordan, so he leaves Bethany for Ephraim, perhaps the modern Et-Taiyibeh, about 20 km. north of Jerusalem. Thus these two quiet places enclose the supreme sign of the raising of Lazarus.

(11:55–12:36) **Jesus is Anointed and Acclaimed before his Death** It is not easy to know how the evangelist organizes the material between the raising of Lazarus and the last supper discourses. In 12:37–50 he seems to comment on the whole first part of his work. In 11:55–12:36 he relates what happened shortly before Jesus' last supper. After the festival of Dedication in 10:22–44 we encounter in 11:55 and 12:1 the mention of Passover, which is resumed in 13:1. It will also be named in the interrogation before Pilate in 18:28, 39; 19:14. vv. 11:55–12:36 seem to be a kind of summary of what happened when Jesus' last Passover was near.

Three distinct scenes prepare the reader for what soon will happen to Jesus:

1. The anointing at Bethany in 11:55–12:11 shows that Jesus' future burial will not be accidental but is already prepared for by Mary's pious action.

2. In connection with the anointing, the solemn acclamation near Jerusalem in 12:12–19 points Jesus out as Israel's king in a deeper way than the crowds can grasp.

3. The discourse with the Greeks and the people in 12:20–36 gives a final meaning to Jesus' imminent death. It shows how death leads to life (vv. 20–6), how Jesus goes through

a kind of 'Gethsemane' (vv. 27–30), and how a struggle between light and darkness is now going on (vv. 31–6).

In different ways these three scenes attempt to illuminate the two aspects of death and life that are revealed in Jesus' last Passover. The meal in the presence of the raised Lazarus is the context for Jesus' revelation of his approaching burial. The acclamation near Jerusalem allows a big crowd to meet the one who has raised Lazarus. The Greeks and the people witness Jesus' distress before his death but also his acceptance of the decisive hour.

In ch. 11 Lazarus was in a certain sense in the foreground, now on the contrary it is Jesus himself who occupies centre-stage. He is anointed and acclaimed, and he takes the initiative to obtain and ride a young donkey. In contrast to Mary's affectionate attitude we encounter Judas's mean remarks, which anticipate his future betrayal. The crowds who praise Jesus behave in a way quite different from the caustic Pharisees and the high priests who plan to put Lazarus to death. Many want to see Jesus, who informs them that a grain of wheat must die in order to bear fruit.

(11:55–12:11) In Mk 14:3–9 and Mt 26:6–13 the anointing at Bethany comes after the acclamation in Jerusalem and is dated differently from John: two days before Passover, when the high priests and the scribes have already decided to kill Jesus. In Lk 7:36–50 a sinner in Galilee anoints Jesus, but there is no connection with Jesus' burial. vv. 55–7, since Jesus had left Bethany for Ephraim after the raising of Lazarus, these verses introduce a new scene at Bethany. As early as 2:13 and 6:4 we met the formula that the Passover of the Jews was near, so that Jesus' official life in John comprises at least two or three years. According to some estimates about 100,000 pilgrims came every year to Jerusalem. Josephus evidently exaggerates when he writes that in the 60s 2,700,000 people were sanctified by 256,500 sacrifices (J.W. 6. 422–5). The purifications could start a week before Passover, and were accomplished according to Ex 19:10 and Num 9:6–12 (cf. also Pesaḥ. 9:1 ff.). Contrary to 7:11 the people are looking for Jesus in a positive way, but the authorities have already decided to kill him (vv. 53, 57). Still they will wait until Judas has betrayed him (13:18–30; 18:2–3). 12:1, the six days before Passover indicate that the anointing at Bethany is connected with Jesus' last Passover, just as the death and raising of Lazarus is. 12:2–3, as in Lk 10:38 42 Martha serves Jesus, and Mary is sitting at the Lord's feet, but now in order to anoint them and wipe them with her hair, just as the sinner in Lk 7:38 (who moreover bathes them with her tears and kisses them). In Mk 14:3 and Mt 26:7 an anonymous woman pours the ointment on Jesus' head. In John the scene seems to have different functions: Mary's action anticipates Nicodemus' kingly burial of Jesus in 19:39. It introduces the acclamation of Jesus as anointed king of Israel (even if the anointing is done to the feet and not the head). Jesus himself interprets the anointing in v. 7 in connection with his future burial, but since the tomb is the place from which he will rise it is also a preparation for his glory. Mary who anoints and wipes Jesus' feet anticipates also the scene where Jesus will wash and wipe his disciples' feet. Judas has a similar negative function in both scenes (12:4–7; 13:2, 21–30). The fragrance of the perfume may symbolize the fame of Mary's good action and

correspond to Mk 14:9 and Mt 26:13, 'what she has done will be told in remembrance of her'. The rare word pistikos found in both Mk 14:3 and Jn 12:3 probably means 'pure'. Only John indicates a measure of one litra, 327 grams, which is an enormous quantity, corresponding to the kingly amount of myrrh and aloes in 19:39. 12:4–6, the MSS do not agree on whether Judas or his father Simon is called Iscariot (see JN 6:71). v. 5 probably depends on Mk 14:4–5, but there 'some' criticize the waste of ointment (in Mt 26:8 'the disciples'). Judas keeps the common purse as in 13:29, but moreover steals from it, an information we do not have in the Synoptics. Perhaps the thief and bandit in the parable of the shepherd in 10:1–5 has influenced the story here. 12:7–8, one can translate v. 7, aphes autēn, hina eis tēn hēmeran tou entaphiasmou teresēi auto, as NRSV does (adding 'she bought it'), but perhaps better 'leave her alone, so that she might perform this for the day of my burial'. In Mk 14:8 it is clear that the woman has anointed Jesus beforehand because neither at his burial nor on the day of resurrection could the women do it. But since in Jn 19:38–40 Nicodemus comes with a mixture of myrrh and aloes, it is best to understand Mary's anointing in John as a symbolic precedent that Nicodemus will complete later on. The whole of v. 8 is found in Mt 26:11, whereas Mk 14:7 adds 'and you can show kindness to them whenever you wish'. Perhaps it is only a coincidence that Matthew and John omit the same words. 12:9–11, these rather ironical verses underline the link between the two scenes at Bethany, and between what happened to Lazarus and will happen to Jesus. To kill Lazarus, the living sign of Jesus' future resurrection, is to extend the decision taken in 11:47–53. Nothing is said about the authorities' success in their new plans.

(12:12–19) In all four gospels Jesus' last days are introduced by the people's acclamation. In the Synoptics the messianic homage is directly linked to the following temple cleansing, which shows Jesus' zeal for God's house (cf. Mark 11:1–19 par.). In Mark and Matthew moreover the Master curses a fig-tree, a symbolic action against those in Israel who are unfaithful. All this leads to the trial against him. Since John has put the symbolic cleansing of the temple at the beginning of Jesus' official activity, the raising of Lazarus becomes the chief reason for arresting Jesus. In the Synoptics there are two stages in the scene of acclamation: first Jesus sends out two disciples to bring a donkey or a colt to him, and then he rides on it and is acclaimed. In John we have first an acclamation outside Jerusalem, and then Jesus finds himself a young donkey to sit upon (vv. 12–15). v. 12, 'The next day' is counted from the time reference at 12:1, i.e. Sunday before Passover. Two groups are present, those who had come to the festival, and those who had witnessed the raising of Lazarus (cf. vv. 17–18). v. 13, the branches of palm trees are probably conceived as a lûlāb, used at the festivals of Booths and of Dedication. 'Hosanna' means 'save!', a prayer used in Ps 118:25–6, particularly at the festival of Booths. In Luke Jesus is acclaimed as 'the king', in John as 'the King of Israel' (cf. Jn 1:49). In contrast to Mk 11:10 and Mt 21:9 neither David nor his son are mentioned. Thus John underlines Jesus' royal function without linking it to David's dynasty (cf. 18:33–8). vv. 14–15, due to different interpretations of the Hebrew and the Greek text of Zech 9:9, the young donkey (onarion) in v. 14 and the donkey's colt (*pōlos onou*) in v. 15 are in Mk 11:2 and Lk 19:30 a colt (*pōlos*), in Mt 21:2, 7 both a donkey and a colt (*onos* and *pōlos*). The word 'comes' is used in both Ps 118:26 and Zech 9:9, and may explain the link between both quotations. v. 16, the disciples understand the events better after Jesus' resurrection, as in 2:17, 22. vv. 17–19, these verses attempt to link the acclamation with the raising of Lazarus. In contrast to the positive attitude of the crowds, we have in v. 19 the Pharisees' impotence. 'The world' (*ho kosmos*) corresponds to Hebrew *kol hā'ôlām* and means 'all people'. But perhaps there is also an allusion to the theological theme of Jesus' coming to this world (1:9–10; 3:16–17). Ironically the Pharisees anticipate Jesus' own prophecy that he will draw all people to himself (12:32).

(12:20–36) Jesus Speaks about his Imminent Death Some Greeks ask to see Jesus through the mediation of the disciples (cf. 1:44–5). Jesus reveals the mystery of his imminent death to them and to the rest of the audience. The grain of wheat that dies in the earth symbolizes the rich future harvest. The voice from heaven is a sign addressed to the audience, so they will understand that the Son of Man who will be lifted up is really the light present among them. vv. 20–6, these verses show how Jesus' death will lead to life. The Greeks are either proselytes or God-fearers like Cornelius in Acts 10–11. Already in 7:35 the evangelist alluded to the mission among the Greeks. The intermediaries Philip and Andrew both have Greek names. The hour which formerly had not yet come (2:4 and 7:6, 8; cf. 7:30; 8:20) is now at hand. It is not only the hour when Jesus will be arrested, but also the hour of his glorification (cf. 13:1–32). From now onwards the crucifixion will be seen in the light of Jesus' future resurrection and glorification. Paul uses the simile of the grain to illustrate humankind's future resurrection (1 Cor 15:37–58), whereas in John it has to do with the missionary harvest (cf. Mk 4:1–9). The Christian community will not 'remain alone' (lit. tr.) after Jesus' death but will be united in the same faith. The logion on loving or hating one's life is in the Synoptics expressed in at least three different ways: Mk 8:35 and Lk 9:24; Mt 10:39; Lk 17:33. The Johannine formulation 'love' and 'hate' may be more original than the synoptic 'save' and 'lose', but the evangelist has probably added 'in this world' and 'eternal life'. The other logion in v. 26 also has parallels, in the synoptic theme of 'serving' and 'following' (Mk 8:34 par. and 10:43–5 par.), but John stresses the importance of serving Jesus (and not only humankind) and of being honoured by the Father (cf. 14:23; 16:27, where the believers are loved by the Father). vv. 27–30, these verses correspond in some respects to the synoptic scene at Gethsemane (Mk 14:34–6 par.). The evangelist probably knew Mark's text: he alludes to a garden across the Kidron (18:1), he names the cup (18:11), and is inspired by Mark's mention of the hour (Mk 14:35). v. 27, in John the Lord's trouble before his imminent death has already been expressed in Jn 11:33, 38. But typically enough, the Johannine Jesus does not hesitate to accept the hour which is approaching. v. 28, the glorification of the Father's name seems to allude to the first part of the Lord's prayer (Mt 6:9; Lk 11:2). The voice from heaven reminds us of the voice at Jesus' baptism and transfiguration (Mk 1:11 par.; 9:7 par.), but the message is typically Johannine: God is glorified by Jesus' work on earth (cf. 17:4)

and he will be glorified by Jesus' acceptance of the hour (cf. 17:5). vv. 29–30, thunder in the OT is often a manifestation of God's voice (e.g. in Ps 29:3; Job 37:4). The angel can remind us of Luke 22:43, but in John he appears for the benefit of the audience and not in order to comfort Jesus. The crowd needs Jesus' interpretation to understand what is going on. Thus Jesus' private agony is transformed into a public confession of his obedience to his Father's will. vv. 31–6, the ruler of 'this world', understood here in a negative way, will be judged by Jesus' death (v. 31). vv. 32–3, Jesus is lifted up on the cross from which he exercises his Lordship by attracting all people, a thought already adumbrated in v. 19. This attraction is dependent on the Father's will (cf. 6:44). vv. 34–5, the audience ironically speaks the truth when it stresses the common expectation that the Messiah remains forever (e.g. *T. Levi*, 18:8; cf. de Jonge 1972–3). Jesus, the Son of Man, will indeed remain forever with the Father, but as light in the world his time is limited. v. 36, the audience has a unique opportunity to become children of light (cf. 'children of God' in 1:12). Jesus' sudden departure expresses symbolically that the period in which he instructed the people is now finished. It is also a transition to the next section, concerning unbelievers whose eyes are blinded.

(12:37–50) Faith and Unbelief In 3:31–6 we saw a passage that could be understood as words of Jesus, or of the Baptist, or that could simply be the evangelist's commentary on the foregoing discussion. In vv. 37–50 it is even clearer that the author speaks on his own behalf, quoting what Jesus had said, in order to conclude the first part of his gospel. We meet a faint echo from the Prologue: the light that has come to the world, the words that come from the Father, Jesus' glory, the importance of faith. The text is divided into two parts: the people's faith and unbelief, with a quotation from Isaiah as the starting-point (vv. 37–43; cf. Rom 10:16); different sayings of Jesus on faith and unbelief (vv. 44–50). Many commentators underline the repetitive character of these verses, and some attribute them to a less gifted redactor. As the audience is not named some have also proposed displacing the passage. But in my opinion all these theories neglect an important feature of Johannine technique, where repetition is used to stress the implied author's point of view.

(12:37–43) The many signs do not lead to faith, contrary to the other mention of signs in 20:30–1. vv. 38–40, two quotations from Isaiah are combined: 53:1 and 6:10. The first is taken straight from the LXX, while the second one follows neither MT, nor the LXX, nor the Aramaic targum. It does, however, coincide with the LXX in the three last words: 'and I shall heal them'. John omits the reference to the hearing ears, and reverses the order, starting with 'he has blinded their eyes' before the hardened heart. He has different words from the LXX for 'he has blinded', 'he has hardened', 'understand', 'turn' and even 'so that'. Moreover God is the subject ('he has blinded'), whereas in the LXX it is the people. In Acts 28:26–8 the quotation of Isa 6:9–10 is linked to the unbelief of the Jews and the acceptance of the Gentiles. vv. 41–3, it is possible that John, like Isaiah, alludes to a proclamation among Gentiles (cf. v. 20), with the regret that so many Jews (and probably even Christians) do not dare to confess Jesus because of both fear of the authorities (cf. a similar remark in

9:22), and vain human glory (cf. 5:44). In v. 41 John has a wording that recalls the targum on Isa 6:1–5, where it is said that the prophet saw only 'the glory in the *shekina* of the King of the *aeons*'. The glory of God in v. 41 may be either that of the pre-existent Christ, or better, an anticipation of the glory that Jesus has come to reveal (cf. Abraham's joy to see Jesus' day in 8:56). vv. 44–50, without indication of time and place Jesus suddenly cries aloud as in 7:28, 37. These verses could have come as part of the scene described in 12:20–36, but they are here integrated into the author's general commentary on the first part of his work. In connection with the two quotations from Isaiah Jesus speaks of faith and unbelief. vv. 44–6, Jesus sums up what he has said earlier on his being sent as the light into this world (cf. 1:5; 8:12; 12:35–6). A new theme in v. 45 is the link established between seeing Jesus and seeing the Father (also in 14:9 and cf. 13:20). In v. 46 those who believe in Jesus are now assured that they will not remain in the darkness. vv. 47–8, those who do not believe are said to be judged not by Jesus but by his words at the last judgement (cf. 3:18; 5:24). vv. 49–50, Jesus stresses once more that what he says comes from the Father (cf. 5:30; 7:16–17). This could be compared with what is said about the 'prophet like [Moses]': 'I will put my words in the mouth of the prophet, who shall speak to them everything that I command' (Deut 18:18). 'Eternal life' is the goal of believers, as in 5:24 and 6:54.

Second Book: Jesus Reveals the Glory of his Death and Resurrection to the Disciples (13:19–21:25)

(13:1–30) Jesus Washes the Feet of his Disciples and Points out the Traitor A kind of rereading of 13:1–14:31 seems to have been at the origin of the new well-composed unity of 13.1–17:26. One can distinguish five subdivisions (see, among others, Schnackenburg 1977–9: ii): Jesus' last meal (13:1–30), the first part of his discourse (13:31–14:31), the second part of his discourse (15:1–16:4*a*), the third part of his discourse (16:4*b*–33), and finally his prayer to the Father (17:1–26). The first and the second part correspond respectively to the fifth and the fourth, with the third at the centre of the whole concentric structure. The passage on the last meal can in turn be divided into five items: the introduction (vv. 1–5), the dialogue between Jesus and Peter (vv. 6–11), the footwashing as an example (vv. 12–17), Jesus' words about the disciples (vv. 18–20), Jesus' designation of the traitor (vv. 21–30). In the Synoptics the last supper is a passover and eucharistic meal, without footwashing and without longer discourses (with the exception of Lk 22:25–38). It is possible that the concentration on the footwashing made it difficult for John also to have a eucharistic meal. He does not agree with the Synoptics on the date of the Passover, since in his gospel Jesus' death takes place on the day of Preparation, when the Passover lambs are slaughtered (cf. Jn 19:31, 36; cf. Ex 12:21, 46). In ch. 6 he has inserted his own conception of the eucharist, possibly in a second edition of the gospel.

The footwashing in John is not a symbol for the institution of the eucharist, but it is similarly linked with Jesus' sacrificial death. A cosmic drama is described in connection with the festival of the Passover: Jesus who has come from the Father and will return to him has loved his disciples to the end, as is

shown by the symbolic action of the footwashing. But Judas leaves the circle of disciples in order to betray his master (cf. Richter 1967).

(13:1–5) In a skilful way the evangelist combines the introduction to the second book (v. 1) with the introduction to the footwashing (vv. 2–3). In the Greek text vv. 1–4 can be taken as a single long sentence, in view of the double *eidōs* ('knowing') in vv. 1 and 3. It is in the light of Jesus' close knowledge of his Father's purpose that we have to consider the meaning of the footwashing. The Son's Passover is 'to pass over' from this world to the Father from whom he came. The footwashing has therefore a soteriological aspect. vv. 1–3, v. 1 points forwards to the cross, whereas v. 2 underlines how Jesus' love for his disciples is really *eis telos*, which means both 'to the end' and 'perfect'. This is realized both in the footwashing and in the acceptance of imminent death. In v. 2 the aorist *genomenou* is a variant reading for the present *ginomenou*. It is the more difficult reading, but can be translated '[as the meal] had already begun'. The link between the footwashing and Jesus' death is stressed by the mention of Judas's betrayal. The Father has given all things into Jesus' hands because he loves him (3:35). Nobody can snatch them out of his or his Father's hands (10:28–9). vv. 4–5, after the first three theological verses the evangelist describes what Jesus actually did. That he takes off (Gk. *tithesin*) his outer robe may be an allusion to the good shepherd who lays down (*tithesin*) his life for the sheep (10:11). Footwashing was a sign of hospitality (cf. Lk 7:44), but normally it was the servants who performed the act and not their master (cf. *Jos. Asen* 7.1).

(13:6–11) In a dialogue with Peter we get a first approach to the meaning of the footwashing. Peter, disciple from the beginning (1:40–4), confesses that Jesus is the Holy One (6:67–8.). In chs. 18–21 he has a prominent place, but his insight is sometimes deficient compared with that of the disciple whom Jesus loves. In ch. 13 we have a similar lack of understanding. The dialogue with Jesus prepares for the prophecy of Peter's defection in 13:36–8. vv. 6–8, in 2:22 and 12:16 the evangelist underlined that the disciples would understand after Jesus' resurrection. Now the Lord seems to say that even his explanation in 13:12–20 will later on require a deeper understanding. Since Jesus in 14:3 refers to the place he will prepare for them, the 'share' (Gk. *meros*) might allude to that which Peter will have with the Father (cf. 17:24). vv. 9–11, because Peter does not understand the deeper meaning of the footwashing he asks for more washing, a misunderstanding similar to those we have met in chs. 3 and 4. In v. 10 JB and TOB omit, with some ancient authorities, 'except for the feet'. But the longer reading accepted in NRSV is probably original, since the difficult text invited copyists to omit the words. How ought one to understand 'one who has bathed'? In my opinion it is primarily an allusion to the Jewish bath before the festival of the Passover (cf. 11:55 and 13:1). Those who have already purified themselves by a bath need now only a footwashing, as is normal when one is received at a Jewish home. By association Jesus passes from bodily to moral cleanness, which allows him to implicate Judas. The sharing with Jesus mentioned in v. 8 and the explanation given in vv. 12–15 invite the reader also to associate the footwashing with Christian baptism.

(13:12–17) Jesus gives a fuller explanation of the footwashing as an expression of his own love (cf. vv. 1–3), and as an example for later disciples. In these verses there are several contacts with synoptic sayings (Mk 10:42–5; Lk 6:40; 22:27; Mt 10:24). vv. 12–14, in John *kyrios*, 'Lord', is often nearly synonymous with 'teacher'. But in the passages after the resurrection and in 6:23 and 11:2 it designates the risen Lord. Jesus uses a typical argument *a fortiori*: what the person of higher status has done must also be practised by the one of lower status. v. 15, this is the only time Jesus calls one of his actions an 'example' to follow. In the changed social circumstances of the church, footwashing was practised only sporadically. It seems therefore to have been understood more as a spiritual example. vv. 16–17, John uses the word 'messenger' (*apostolos*) only here, but he has a developed theology of mission: Jesus who has been sent by his Father sends his disciples into the world in order to lead the believers to the Father (Dewailly 1969). 'If you know these things' is probably a commentary not only on v. 16 but on the meaning of the footwashing.

(13:18–20) Jesus speaks of both the traitor and the sending of his disciples. vv. 18–19, the treason of Judas preoccupies the evangelist (see vv. 2 and 10; cf. 6:70). He indicates two motives why Jesus chose him: the first is that the Scripture must be fulfilled, the second is that Jesus' prophetic knowledge about Judas will help the disciples to believe. The quotation of Ps 41:10 belongs to the passion narrative (Mk 14:18), but is here adapted to the context, differing both from MT and LXX. For the formula 'I am', see JN 8:24. v. 20, this verse continues the reflection in v. 16. The evangelist has often expressed the intimate connection between the Father and the Son, e.g. in 5:17–30; 7:17–18 and 12:44–50. It is therefore not surprising that whoever receives Jesus receives the Father. In 14:9 the same idea is expressed with other words: to see the Son is to see the Father.

(13:21–30) Jesus points out the traitor, who in turn leaves the group of disciples. vv. 21–2, the solemn announcement of the betrayal is similar to that in the Synoptics (Mk 14:18 par.), but John introduces the whole scene by indicating for the third time how Jesus is troubled before his passion (cf. 11:33; 12:27). vv. 23–5, the beloved disciple, who is explicitly introduced here for the first time (cf. 19:26; 20:2; 21:7), is asked to mediate Simon's question to Jesus, whereas in Mk 14:19 and Mt 26:22 each disciple asks Jesus directly. vv. 26–7, Mk 14:20 par. probably describes the special passover ceremony of dipping into the same bowl of spices, whereas in John it is the eating of an ordinary piece of bread (cf. v. 18), which in this gospel alone Jesus hands over to Judas. The Hebrew *sāṭān* ('the adversary'; cf. Job 1–2) is elsewhere in John replaced by the Greek *diabolos* ('devil', in 6:70; 8:44; 13:2), or by 'the ruler of this world' (12:31; 14:30; 16:11). vv. 28–9, as some disciples misunderstand Jesus' words in v. 27 ('do quickly what you are going to do'), the drama increases. v. 30, because Jesus is often described in John as the light of this world, Judas's departure during the night has probably a symbolic meaning.

(13:31–14:31) The First Part of the Farewell Discourse Both in Greek and Jewish literature there is a special genre called 'testaments' (see e.g. Plato's *Phaedo*, Paul's speech in Acts 20:17–35, the *Testaments of the Twelve Patriarchs*). Before his death the hero foresees his friends' sorrow but encourages them to be united in love and to keep his message. In 13:33 we have a main outline of the first discourse: the disciples cannot follow now, which is shown in 13:36–8; in 14:1–14 Jesus announces that he is going to the Father; in 14:15–24 he indicates how the Holy Spirit, the risen Christ, and the Father will later on be with the disciples. The whole discourse is introduced by Jesus' announcement of his departure, and is concluded by different logia on the Spirit and on peace. The text is wrestling with the difficult question of God's presence with the disciples after Jesus' departure. In contrast to the reciprocal love between the Father, the Son, and the disciples, the text describes the powerless hostility of the ruler of this world (see JN 14:30–1). The discourse is interrupted by different interventions of Peter, Thomas, Philip, and Judas (not Iscariot).

(13:31–8) Jesus Announces his Departure and Peter's Future Defection vv. 31–2, the aorists in these verses make Jesus speak retrospectively at the time of fulfilment. The omission of v. 32*a* in important MSS is probably due to the similar endings *en autō*. The evangelist wants to impress his reader through repetitions of the same theme. In 11:4 he underlined how the Son of God was glorified through the illness of Lazarus. In 12:23, 27–8 Jesus spoke to the crowds about the arrival of his hour of glorification. Now, when Judas has left, he says the same thing to his disciples. In 17:1–5, in his prayer to the Father, he will be much more explicit: the Father has given him authority over all people through the glorification on the cross; the Father is glorified by the work the Son has accomplished, and he will glorify his Son with the glory he had before the world existed. In 13:31–2 part of this is expressed only briefly. In the Johannine use of *doxazō* ('glorify') there is a subtle combination of the Greek *doxa*, 'honour', and the Hebrew *kābôd* ('glory'). Through his resurrection Jesus elevated on the cross is both honoured and glorified with his Father. v. 33, 'Little children' is not employed elsewhere in the gospel, but is usual in 1 John. This affectionate designation prepares the personal message on love in vv. 34–5. Jesus' time on earth can be called short in comparison with his eternal stay with the Father (cf. 7:33; 14:19; 16:16–19). The words to the Jews to which Jesus refers (7:33 and 8:21–30) function differently for the disciples, because the latter will be able to follow him later on (14:3). vv. 34–5, the departure makes Jesus think of the task the disciples will have in the world (see JN 13:6–11 on the meaning of the footwashing). In John the 'commandment' (Gk. *entolē*) in the singular is used for the mission Jesus received from his Father (10:18; 12:49–50), or for his assignment to the disciples (13:34; 15:12). In the plural it specifies Jesus' or his Father's prescriptions (14:15, 21; 15:10). The love commandment is 'new' in that the reciprocal love is founded on Jesus' own love (13:1–4; cf. 1 Jn 2:8; 2 Jn 5). In 15:9–12 it will even be based on the love of the Father for Jesus. In our text the reciprocal 'glorification' of the Father and the Son is the background for the love between the disciples. John has nothing to say about the love of one's enemies (Mt 5:43–8; Lk 6:27–8). It is possible that the word 'new' also alludes to the new covenant mentioned in Lk 22:20 and 1 Cor 11:25, with its OT link to Jer 31:31–4. For the Jews a commandment is normally associated with a covenant. Jesus' love unto death is in that sense the starting-point of a renewed covenant. vv. 36–8, Peter takes up what Jesus said in v. 33. This gives the Master an opportunity to touch upon the theme 'to follow'. In the first instance Peter will not lay down his life for his master but deny him three times (cf. 18:17; 25–7). According to 16:32 *all* the disciples will abandon Jesus. But afterwards Peter will follow him unto death (21:18–19). Jesus' prediction is part of the synoptic tradition (Mk 14:29 par.), but John alone alludes to Peter's future perfect discipleship.

(14:1–14) Jesus is Going to his Father v. 1, as the imperative is used in 1a, both occurrences of *pisteuete* in 1b are probably to be taken as in the imperative (as NRSV) rather than the present indicative, just as in v. 11. v. 2, the 'many dwelling places' (Gk. *monai pollai*) resemble those found in 1 Enoch 39:4; 45:3; 2 Enoch 61:1 ff., and other Jewish texts, but distinctively the evangelist does not insist on the different kinds of dwellings in heaven. The main point for Jesus is 'abiding' (Gk. *menō*) in his Father's house (cf. 2:16). In v. 2a one can translate the Greek *hoti* with 'for': 'if it were not so, I would have told you; *for* I go', or better as NRSV with 'that' ('if it were not so would I have told you *that* I go . . . ?'). Jesus then alludes to what he has already said about his special way to the Father (cf. also 12:26), a theme he will develop in vv. 4–12. v. 3, the first Christians expected Jesus to return at the end of time. The evangelist anticipates this return in the spiritual presence of the risen Lord among his disciples (cf. vv. 15–23). There are some points of contact between this verse and 1 Thess 4:16–17 where Jesus will descend from heaven to meet the faithful, and all finally 'will be with the Lord for ever'. Perhaps John suggests that Jesus' return takes place in a sense when disciples die. vv. 4–5, Jesus describes the way to the goal he has proposed in vv. 1–3. Thomas, who in 11:16 did not fully understand Jesus' purpose, even now hesitates about the goal and the way of which Jesus speaks. v. 6, this verse does not mark out Jesus' identity, but it describes who he ought to be for the faithful disciples: a leader on the way which leads to eternal life with the Father, because Jesus himself has revealed the truth he has learned from him. v. 7, most MSS have pluperfect in both verbs of 7a, indicating a condition contrary to the facts: 'If you had known me, you would have known . . .'. This variant, which is accepted in TOB, seems to have arisen under the influence of 8:19. Therefore the reading adopted in NRSV, with a perfect and a future tense ('if you know me, you will know . . .'), seems to be preferable, even if there are fewer witnesses in its favour. Those who see Jesus by faith can see the Father who has sent him (cf. 6:40; 12:45). v. 8, Philip is naïve when he thinks that he can already see God's glory (cf. the similar demand of Moses in Ex 33:18). vv. 9–11, Jesus once again explains the special relationship between himself and the Father: to see or to hear Jesus is to see or to hear the Father. In a more onto-logical meaning Jesus is in the Father and the Father in him. Even his works manifest his deep link with the Father. In short, his whole person is a revelation from the Father (cf. 3:34; 7:17–18; 8:28; 12:45, 49). vv. 12–14, the works of the disciples presuppose Jesus' missionary activity (cf. ch. 4 and 12:20–6) and his glorification with the Father. They are 'greater' only because they are done in the name of Jesus. Several ancient versions and some MSS omit v. 14, either by

accident or because it was considered as a repetition of v. 13. Moreover it could be thought to contradict 16:23. In the different farewell discourses the words 'in my name' are used five out of seven times in connection with prayer. On three occasions Jesus speaks of prayer in his name: here, in 15:16, and in 16:23–6. In this text Jesus underlines the importance of faith and of his departure to the Father. In the second text he speaks of the missionary work of the disciples, and in the third of their prayer after his resurrection. Here Jesus is the one who hears the prayer, in the two other texts it is the Father. In his own prayer Jesus replaces the formula 'in my name' with 'in your name' (17:11–12, cf. 17:6, 26). There is therefore a close link between the names of Jesus and of his Father, just as there is a reciprocal relationship between the Son and the Father. In the synoptic material we have only one explicit text about prayer in the name of Jesus (Mt 18:19–20), but in Acts the disciples baptize and do miracles 'in his name'.

(14:15–24) The Holy Spirit, the Risen Christ, and the Father will be with the Disciples Soon After Jesus' Glorification v. 15, the imperative *tērēsate* ('keep!') is well attested in the MSS but fits the context less well than the future *tērēsete* ('you will keep'), accepted by NRSV from several important witnesses. Jesus underlines that to keep his commandments is to remain in his love. On 'commandment' (*entolē*) in the plural, see JN 13:34. vv. 16–17, one can distinguish five passages on the Helper: here, 14:26; 15:26–7; 16:7–11; 16:13–17, all well integrated in their context. The word *paraklētos* is a verbal adjective, often used of one called to help in a lawcourt. In the Jewish tradition the word was transcribed with Hebrew letters and used for angels, prophets, and the just as advocates before God's court. The word also acquired the meaning of 'one who consoles' (cf. Job 16:2, Theodotion's and Aquila's translations; the LXX has the correct word *paraklētores*). It is probably wrong to explain the Johannine *paraklētos* on the basis of only one religious background. The word is filled with a complex meaning: the Spirit replaces Jesus, is an advocate and a witness, but also consoles the disciples. He encourages them to remember Jesus' work and leads them into the whole truth. He has his own personality (see Johansson 1940; Betz 1963; Franck 1985). In this text the Spirit of truth is considered as 'another Advocate' (or better, 'Helper'), with an allusion to Johannine traditions where Jesus himself is the first advocate with his Father (1 Jn 2:1). The Helper is a Spirit of truth, as in 16:13. In 1 Jn 5:6 the Spirit is simply identified with truth, because he is a witness (cf. Jn 15:26). He is naturally dependent on Jesus who is the truth (14:6), i.e. the revelation from the Father. The Spirit of truth in John has often been compared with the same phrase used in Qumran texts (1QS 3:18; 4:23). But there he is a spiritual force who influences man's moral dispositions, whereas in John the Spirit mediates truth. Still the fight of Beliar against the angelic figure of truth in 1QS 3:18–4:26 is similar to that of the 'world' which refuses to accept the revelation of God's truth in Jesus. In ch. 14 it is the Father who gives the Spirit at the demand of Jesus (vv. 16 and 24), whereas in chs. 15 and 16 Jesus himself sends the Spirit (15:26; 16:7). But as the Father sends the Spirit in Jesus' name (14:26) one can say that even in ch. 14 the Spirit is implicitly sent by Jesus. After the Master's departure the Helper will be permanently with the disciples. vv. 18–21, Jesus comments on the 'little while' (13:33) when the world will no longer see him. The disciples will in the near future see the risen Christ and understand their reciprocal indwelling and love, but also the love from the Father. There is a parallelism between vv. 15–17 on the Helper and vv. 18–21 on Jesus: the world cannot receive the Spirit (v. 17a) and cannot see Jesus (v. 19a). The disciples on the contrary know the Spirit who abides in them (v. 17b), just as they have their life in Jesus (v. 19b). Those who love Jesus keep his commandments (v. 15), and conversely those who keep his commandments love him (v. 21a). The evangelist is convinced that the Spirit is given after Jesus' glorification. In a certain sense Jesus himself returns with the Helper. But the disciples will also have the joy of meeting him as the risen Christ. The Father's and Jesus' love to which they will respond by their own love will be a new presence of Jesus. It is possible that the evangelist even has the definitive return of Christ in mind (cf. JN 14:1–3). Augustine expresses this paradox nicely: 'Now we love when we are believing in what we shall see; but then we shall love when we see what we have believed in' (In Johannem, 75:4). vv. 22–4, Judas seems to misunderstand the word 'reveal' and thinks that Jesus is speaking of a public manifestation. Perhaps the evangelist is reflecting the problem of why the risen Christ was seen only by the disciples (cf. Acts 10:40–2). Jesus answers indirectly by repeating what he has said on love in vv. 15 and 21, but now he adds that the Father will also be with them. Since 'the Word became flesh and lived among us' (1:14) the Father and the Son are both present with those who receive the revelation in faith and love. They worship God in spirit and truth (4:24). But those who do not love Jesus and his commandments also reject the Father who has sent him.

(14:25–31) These verses round off the first farewell discourse by adding new material. v. 25, 'I have said these things to you' occurs six other times: in 15:11; 16:1, 4, 6, 25, 33. Normally the formula concludes a passage, either directly as in 16:4, 33, or indirectly by introducing a summary of what has been said (here; in 15:11; 16:1, 25). In 16:1–4 and 25–33 the formula is repeated in order to frame a passage. v. 26, the 'Holy Spirit' is mentioned in 1:33 and 20:22, but only here is he identified with the Helper. As a teacher the Helper is entirely dependent on what Jesus has said (cf. 16:13). v. 27, in the OT friends who are parting wish each other peace (e.g. 1 Sam 20:42; 29:6–7). Jacob blesses his sons at the end of his farewell speech (Gen 49:28). The peace that Jesus gives to his disciples is a kind of blessing, anticipating the peace he will give after his resurrection (20:19, 21, 26), when the disciples will receive the Holy Spirit (20:22). In this way the evangelist stresses the spiritual presence of Jesus and his Spirit among his disciples. This prevents their hearts from being troubled, something the *Pax Romana* was not able to do. vv. 28–9, a new aspect in this summary is that the disciples ought to rejoice at Jesus' departure, because the Father is greater (cf. 10:29). This caused problems when the patristic writers discussed the relationship between Jesus and his Father. John often stresses that the Father and the Son have everything in common and love each other, but still the Father is the origin of the Son's sending and is also the goal of his mission. vv. 30–1, as in 12:31 the ruler of this world is mentioned, but Jesus underlines that he is powerless before the Son's loving obedience to his Father.

The final words indicate that the (first) discourse is concluded.

(15:1–16:4a) The Second Part of the Farewell Discourse The actual farewell situation that has dominated 13:31–14:31 is suddenly interrupted in ch. 15, where the timeless union between the Master and his disciples is in the foreground. Perhaps this is a later insertion, added when the community reflected on its union with Christ. There was in ch. 6 (which might also have been added later) a subtle allusion to the eucharist. The parable concerning the vine leads the thought in the same direction. In Mk 14:25 par. Jesus says: 'Truly I tell you, I will never again drink of the fruit of the vine until that day when I drink it new in the kingdom.' John seems to have meditated on this text and the significance of the eucharist. The believer has to eat the bread from heaven in order to live for ever (6:58–9). In a similar way he has to abide in Jesus the true vine, if he wants to bear fruit. But still there is no precise indication here of the eucharist itself. The text in 15:1–16:4 has been subtly adapted to the context. The commandment to love in 15:11–17 has been touched upon in 13:34 and 14:15, 20–1. The answering of prayer in 15:7, 16 has its counterpart in 14:13–14, while the complete joy in 15:11 will be referred to again in 16:24. The world's hatred mentioned in 15:18–16:4 has been touched on in 14:17–27 and will be taken up again in Jesus' prayer in 17:14–16. What is said about the Helper in 15:26–7 naturally has connections with the other four mentions of him (14:16–17, 26; 16:7–11, 13–15). This shows that the text has been reworked to fit into the larger arrangement of chs. 13–17. Above I have suggested that it is in the centre of the whole composition, which would not be surprising if it echoes a profound reflection on the meaning of the eucharist. The text is well structured: the first part on love (15:1–17) starts with the short parable of the vine and its explication in vv. 1–10, which is further developed in vv. 11–17. The second part on hatred (15:18–16:4a) describes the world's hatred (vv. 18–25) and the Helper's testimony (vv. 26–7), and concludes in 16:1–4a. There are many similar texts in the Synoptics: on the vine (Mk 12:1–12 par.; Mt 20:1–16; 21:28–32; Lk 13:6–9) and a number of logia: the hatred of the world (Mk 13:13 par.); the servant and his master (Mt 10:24); the Spirit who witnesses (Mk 13:11 par.); the disciples who witness (Mk 13:9 par.); the disciples who are killed (Mk 13:12 par.).

(15:1–10) The Parable on the True Vine Explained by the Master In ch. 10 we saw how Jesus in the parable of the sheepfold identified himself with both the gate and the good shepherd. In the parable of the vine we meet the same technique, but this time the identification in vv. 1 and 5a frames the parable. Unlike the synoptic tradition the Johannine parable (Heb. *māšāl*) mixes up the explanation with the narration. vv. 1–5a, whereas Jesus in v. 1 presents himself as the true vine and his Father as the vinegrower, in v. 5a he underlines the link between himself, the vine, and his disciples who are the branches. Subtly Jesus moves from the cleansing of the branches by his Father (vv. 1–2) and by his own proclamation (v. 3) to their abiding in him (v. 4). There is in the Greek a wordplay between 'he removes' (*airei*), 'he prunes' (*kathairei*) and 'you have been cleansed' (*katharoi este*). In spite of the use of the designation of Israel as the true vine in Jer 2:21 (LXX) it is more probable that the evangelist wants in v. 1 to contrast

Jesus as the true vine to Israel which has been deceitful (cf. Isa 5:1–7; Borig 1967). In v. 4 the reciprocal indwelling of Jesus and his disciples leads to the description of the negative consequence if they live apart from him. vv. 5b–10, in v. 5b Jesus reformulates what he said in v. 4. In v. 6 we get the negative picture of one who does not abide in Jesus: he is thrown away, withers, and is burnt, probably an allusion to the last judgement (cf. Mk 9:43–7 par.). In vv. 7–8 the abiding of the disciples in Jesus leads to two positive consequences: the efficacy of their prayer and the glorification of the Father. In vv. 9–10 the theocentric aspect of the parable is stressed: the disciples' love is rooted in the reciprocal love of the Son and his Father. Thus the parable of the vine visualizes different subjects and objects of love (from the Father to the Son, from the Son to the disciples, from the disciples to the Son and the Father) which have already been touched upon.

(15:11–17) These verses underline the commandment of love, in connection with the parable of the vine. The evangelist seems to have taken vv. 7–10 as his model, but in reverse direction: vv. 12 and 14 take up the link between love and obedience to Jesus' commandments, as in v. 10. In v. 15 the Father and Jesus' love for his disciples are mentioned, as in v. 9. In v. 16 we have the combination of prayer and bearing fruit as in vv. 7–8. v. 11 seems to be at the centre of the whole passage (i.e. vv. 1–17), with the mention of joy in connection with reciprocal love (cf. above 14:28). But at the same time the formula, 'I have said these things' separates vv. 12–17 from vv. 1–10. Twice Jesus speaks of his commandment to love one another (vv. 12, 17). In v. 12 Jesus' love is indicated as model and ground ('as I have loved you'). v. 13 describes Jesus' own sacrificial attitude (cf. 13:1), an example for his friends (v. 14). In vv. 15–16 the Master stresses his sovereign choice of disciples (cf. 6:70; 13:18), whom he calls his 'friends'. In the OT Abraham and Moses are God's friends (Isa 41:8; Ex 33:11). Philo calls wise men 'friends of God' and not his slaves (De Migr. Abr. 45; Leg. All. 3:1). Jesus' gift implies an obligation on the disciples to bear fruit. Just as in vv. 12–17, the reciprocal love between disciples in 1 John is seen as a consequence of God's love (e.g. 1 Jn 2:29; 3:7, 11, 18, 22–3; 5:2–4).

(15:18–16:4a) The Disciples are Warned against the World's Hatred; but are at the same time encouraged by the Helper's testimony and Jesus' words. 15:18–25, the 'world' has different meanings in John: it is created by God's Word (1:10) and is the object of his love (3:16–17; 17:18); it needs Jesus as its Saviour (4:42). But when it refuses God's revelation it is considered as hostile. The evangelist underlines the relationship between Jesus and the disciples in a future missionary situation. They must then remember that they are meeting the same hatred that Jesus and his Father have met (vv. 18–19). Though they have just been called 'friends' (v. 15) they are still servants who must share their master's lot (v. 20; cf. 13:16). There is perhaps a slight irony in v. 20b: they will keep your words as well (and as badly) as they kept my words. Already in the synoptic tradition the logion on the master and his servants is linked to a situation of persecution (Mk 13:13 par.), but John adds to it his specific theme about the world's ignorance (v. 21). In vv. 22–5 Jesus sums up the confrontation he had had on the festival of Booths (chs. 7–8). Behind these verses one can imagine the harsh discussions which the Christians had with the 'Jews' who excluded them from their synagogues (cf. 16:1–4). The disciples are to be encouraged by the fact that they will meet the same difficulties as their master. In v. 24 the accusative object of 'they have seen' is probably the 'works' (not 'me and my Father'). In v. 25 Jesus uses the word 'law' for the scriptures, and moreover keeps his distance by calling it 'your' law (cf. 8:17; 10:34). The 'fulfilment' quotation is probably taken from Ps 69:5 (= Ps 35:19), since this psalm is alluded to also in Jn 2:17 and 19:28. 15:26–7, unlike the two first logia on the Helper, this logion seems to interrupt the flow of thought. The remark on the exclusion from the synagogues in 16:1–4 would be a natural continuation of 15:22–5. Nevertheless one should remember that the Helper comes in order to remind the disciples of Jesus. Here his witness confirms the words and works mentioned in vv. 22–5. John's gospel gave rise to a dogmatic dispute concerning the introduction in the west of the *filioque* in the Nicene Creed. The eastern church insisted on the fact that in v. 26 the Spirit of truth 'comes from' (*ekporeuetai*) the Father, whereas the western church underlined that both the Father (14:16, 26) and the Son (15:26; 16:7) 'send' (*pempō*) the Helper. In v. 27 the evangelist stresses the importance of the disciples' witness in connection with that of the Spirit. 16:1–4a, the future exclusion from the synagogue was alluded to in 9:22 and 12:42, but now it is Jesus himself who foretells it in order to help his disciples. We have met a similar positive motive concerning Jesus' predictions in 13:19 and 14:29. In the synoptic tradition Jesus prophesies that his disciples will be persecuted (see Mk 13:3–13 par; Mt 10:16–42). But there the disciples will be brought to trial and will be beaten in synagogues, whereas in John they will be *excluded* from the synagogue, which probably marks a later time (see also above on 9:18–23). The 'Jews' think that they are worshipping God by killing the disciples (v. 2), but ironically enough it is the disciples who will worship him. The reason for the persecutors' shortcomings is their lack of knowledge of God and of Jesus. In v. 4a 'their', which is found in many MSS and is accepted in TOB and NRSV, is probably original; it has been omitted in some MSS because of another 'their' in v. 4b. The expression 'their time' is similar to 'your hour' in Lk 22:53.

(16:4b–33) The Third Part of the Farewell Discourse In 16:4b–33 the reader is called back to the farewell perspective of 13:31–14:31, but he is also reminded of the hostile world which was condemned in 15:18–27. Before his departure Jesus tries to console his disciples by speaking of the joy that they will receive from the Helper. The difficult time they have to go through can be compared with a woman's labour, but when the child is born, the feeling of joy entirely dominates. This section repeats things that have been treated in ch. 14, but adds some new aspects. The Helper now has a clear forensic function that he did not have before. The short time mentioned in 14:19 is developed in 16:16 into two different periods. The author also recalls the world's hatred that was discussed in 15:18–25. Since the dominant aspect of this section is consolation, one can rightly call it a 'speech of consolation before Jesus' departure'. For the community after Easter it is also an important encouragement in their missionary work (see Painter 1980–1).

One can distinguish four parts: (1) In vv. 4b–11 the same question is dealt with as in 14:1–12, but as if it had not been spoken of before. Concerning sin, righteousness, and judgement the Helper will have a threefold indictment against the world. (2) In vv. 12–15 we meet the same encouragement about the Spirit of truth as in 14:25–6. (3) In vv. 16–24 the short time mentioned in 14:18–21 is developed with more details. It is concluded with a logion on prayer that reminds us of 14:13–14 (4) vv. 25–33 are framed by the words, 'I have said these things [or this] to you'. We get a clear conclusion here both for vv. 4b–24 and for the two first parts of the farewell discourse. Logia on prayer and on peace, which have already occurred in ch. 14, are added and prepare the reader for the Son's prayer in ch. 17.

(16:4b–11) Jesus' Departure and the Helper's Mission v. 4b, by retaining 'from the beginning' from 15:27 and by changing 'you have been with me' to 'I was with you', the author (or a redactor) links the second and third parts together. vv. 5–6, the new discourse seems to ignore that in 13:26–14:11 Peter, Thomas, and Philip have already put questions to Jesus. In v. 6 the word *lypē*, 'sorrow', is introduced for the first time in John and will be taken up in 16:20–2, where the theme of joy is also developed. The main purpose of the new speech is to console the disciples in their sorrow. vv. 7–11, the Helper comes to replace Jesus who goes to his Father. As in 14:27–8 the disciples are asked to rejoice in Jesus' departure (v. 7). A special reason for this might be that the Spirit will first be given after Jesus' resurrection (7:39; cf. 20:17, 22). vv. 8–11, the Helper is an advocate for the disciples whom he consoles, but an accuser and a judge in a trial against the world. In 15:26–7 the logion about the Helper interrupted the development on the world's hatred. In 16:8–11 the Helper is more specifically the one who accuses the world. The Greek word *elengchō* in v. 8 has a general meaning of 'to show' or 'to prove'. The Helper will accuse the world of unbelief (v. 9), a sin already highlighted on many occasions (e.g. 1:11; 3:19, 36; 8:24; 10:37–8; 15:22–5). The Master's righteousness will be proved by his glorification (v. 10; cf. 5:30), and his victory is a judgement on the prince of this world (v. 11; cf. 12:31; 14:30; 16:33). We encounter here a cosmic trial against sin and evil. What takes place at the end of the world in the Synoptics is anticipated already by the action of the Helper in the Fourth Gospel.

(16:12–15) The Spirit as the Disciples' Guide v. 12, The sentence, 'I have many things to say you,' separates the following logia on the 'Spirit of truth' from those on the 'Helper' in vv. 7–11. Since Jesus has not yet been glorified, his disciples cannot bear all he would like to say. vv. 13–15, in vv. 7–11 the 'Helper' was presented as the accuser of the world, now the 'Spirit of truth' is seen in his function of transmitting Jesus' teaching to the disciples. As at 14:26 the Spirit is dependent on what Jesus has said, but now he also will glorify the Son (just as the Father glorifies him). A strong link is established between the Father, the Son, and the Spirit of truth. For the evangelist the 'truth' is that which Jesus has received from his Father (see 14:6). Therefore the 'Spirit of truth' acts in relation to Jesus just as the Father does. The Son has been charged to accomplish the Father's work, but after Jesus' departure the Spirit makes his work present among the disciples, because it is 'the

spirit that gives life' (6:63; cf. 1 Jn 3:24; 4:13). But he does not add new revelations to those of Jesus.

(16:16–24) 'The little while' Before and After Jesus' Death In 7:33; 12:35, and 13:33 Jesus has already spoken of the little while he was spending among humankind. According to 14:19 the world, unlike the disciples, would no longer see Jesus. It is developed in a new way here. v. 16, Jesus speaks of two different periods, one before and one after his death. vv. 17–18, with the help of rhetorical repetitions, the evangelist underlines the puzzle of Jesus' saying. vv. 19–22, in a sovereign way Jesus knows what the disciples are discussing. His answer in v. 19 resumes what he already said in v. 16. After a solemn introduction ('very truly') he proclaims that there will be a first period of sorrow for the disciples and of rejoicing for the world, but afterwards a second period when their pain will be changed into permanent joy. In order to illustrate what will happen at his own hour, Jesus alludes to the hour of a woman's labour, an image used in the Synoptics to picture the eschatological afflictions (Mk 13:17 par.; cf. also Isa 66:7–10).

(16:25–33) Conclusion on Love, Prayer and Peace v. 25, 'I have said these things to you' introduces the end of the third part of the discourse, just as it did in 14:25 for the first part. The Greek word *paroimia*, 'proverb' or 'figure', was used in 10:6 without further explanation. In 16:26, 29 it is contrasted to 'plainly' (*parrhēsiai*), which gives *paroimia* a meaning of 'enigmatic speech'. The Hebrew *māšāl*, which lies behind the synoptic word 'parable', is probably also the background of the Johannine 'figures of speech'. What Jesus has said in enigmatic language will later on be clearer thanks to the gift of the Spirit. vv. 26–7, in 14:13–14; 15:7, 16; 16:23–4 there were similar logia about how the Father or the Son hears the disciples' prayer. Now it is added that the Father himself loves them, just as they love Jesus and believe in him. But even their faith and love are divine gifts. Instead of 'from God' some important MSS read 'from the Father', probably by assimilation to the following verse. v. 28, Jesus sums up what he has already said on different occasions about his coming from the Father and going back to him (see especially the Prologue and chs. 3; 7; 8). vv. 29–30, the disciples misunderstand Jesus' plain speech; thinking that they understand his divine origin, they nevertheless will not accept his painful way back to his Father. Their self-confidence is as exaggerated as that of Peter in 13:36–7. vv. 31–2, Jesus perceives in advance that the disciples will 'be scattered', an allusion to Zech 13:7 ('Strike the shepherd, that the sheep may be scattered'), which has already occurred in Jn 10:12. The evangelist seems to know Mk 14:27 par., but forgets that according to his own account the beloved disciple is not 'scattered' with the others (cf. Jn 19:26–7). v. 33, Jesus' prophecy will later on be a consolation for the disciples who abandoned him. As in 14:27 Jesus assures them of his peace despite all the persecutions they will meet. The farewell discourse is concluded with the main motive of consolation for the disciples: their master's victory over the world (cf. 16:11).

(17:1–26) Jesus' Prayer to his Father In the sixteenth century this chapter was for the first time explicitly called *precatio summi sacerdotis*, 'the prayer of the high priest', by D. Chytraeus, but some Church Fathers had already used similar expressions. Yet in John Jesus is not really a high priest as he is in Hebrews, even if his death according to Jn 17:19 is a kind of sacrifice. One can compare Jesus' prayer to Jacob's benediction in Gen 49, to Moses' prayer in Deut 32–3, or to similar prayers in Jewish intertestamental literature (e.g. *Jub.* 1:19–20; 20–2). But in a certain sense Jesus' prayer is unique, since he has already left the world and is coming to his Father (see Jn 17:11); the prayer has a kind of timeless aspect. Bultmann's (1971) proposal to insert it between 13:1 and 13:30 and other hypotheses of displacement have not been successful.

In the farewell discourse we have on different occasions encountered Jesus' encouragement to his disciples to pray in his name (14:13–14; 15:16; 16:23–6). Jesus' last prayer is directly addressed to the Father and the formula 'in my name' is replaced by 'in your name' (vv. 11–12). It is also the name of the Father that Jesus has made known according to vv. 6, 26. The link between Jesus' name and the Father's name is reinforced, when Jesus in his prayer expresses the reciprocal relationship between himself and his Father.

The words, 'Father, glorify your name', which in 12:27–9 resemble the first demand in the Lord's prayer in Mt 6:9 and Lk 11:2, are further developed here (vv. 1, 6, 11–12, 26). The two last demands of the Lord's prayer are also alluded to in vv. 11 and 15: 'do not bring us into temptation' and 'rescue us from the evil' (or 'the evil one', Mt 6:13; cf. Lk 11:4). Even doing the will of God is hinted at in v. 4 (cf. Walker 1982). Just as in both 11:41–2 and 12:27–9, Jesus expresses in this chapter his profound unity with the Father and his dedication to his mission. In Jesus' prayer we meet the same sovereign attitude as in 13:1–30, with references to what has been said in the farewell discourse. Different literary forms are combined: demands (vv. 1*b*, 5, 11*b*, 17, 24), commentaries on prayer (vv. 9–11*a*, 15–16, 20–1), indications on the presuppositions of prayer (vv. 2, 13, 18–19), a confession of faith (v. 3), summaries on the work Jesus has accomplished on earth (vv. 4, 6–8, 12, 14, 22–3, 25–6*a*).

There have been many discussions on the structure of Jesus' last prayer (see Schnackenburg 1977–9: iii; Malatesta 1971; Segalla 1983). I am not convinced by the arguments of those who consider some verses as redactional. Segalla is probably right in stressing the missionary aspect in vv. 17–19, but I am sceptical about his rather artificial concentric construction. Therefore I propose the following structure:

1. Jesus asks the Father to be glorified (vv. 1–5).
2. Jesus prays for the disciples (vv. 6–19).
    a. The disciples have been chosen (vv. 6–11*a*).
    b. The disciples are protected (vv. 11*b*–16).
    c. The disciples are sanctified (vv. 17–19).
3. Jesus prays for the unity of all the believers (vv. 20–3).
4. Jesus prays for the disciples' love (vv. 24–6).

(17:1–5) Jesus Asks the Father to be Glorified Two themes are interwoven: 'glorification' in vv. 1, 4–5 and 'eternal life' in vv. 2–3. v. 1*a*, the short introduction establishes a link between Jesus' farewell discourse and his last prayer. Probably the whole of ch. 17 was conceived when chs. 15–16 were added to the first part of the farewell discourse. To look up to heaven is a common posture of prayer both in the Jewish and the Graeco-Roman world (cf. also 11:41). v. 1*b*, the address 'Father'

is the same as that in Jesus' prayers in the Synoptics. It will be repeated in vv. 5, 21, 24. In v. 11 the evangelist adds 'holy' and in v. 25 'righteous'. As in 12:23 and 13:1, the 'hour' has come, contrary to what was the case in 2:4; 7:30; 8:20. It is the hour of Jesus' crucifixion and glorification. In 17:1 the Son glorifies the Father as a consequence of being himself glorified, whereas in 13:31 it seems to be the reverse. But the difference is only apparent, as in both passages the accomplishment of Jesus' work is presupposed. It is difficult to decide whether *sou* ('your') after the second *hyios* ('Son') is original or not. v. 2, since v. 5 speaks of Jesus' glory before the world existed, the authority over all people (lit. all flesh) could be from the creation or from his incarnation (cf. 1:1–3, 14). But in the context of the 'hour', it is more normal to think of the crucifixion and the resurrection (11:51–2; 12:32; cf. also 5:20–7). The Greek *pan ho*, 'all that', corresponds to Hebrew *kol ăšer*, and denotes 'humankind' that has been given to Jesus. The evangelist often underlines that it is the Father who is the origin of all gifts to Jesus (cf. 3:35; 5:22–7; 6:37; 12:49; 17:6, 8, 11–12, 22). v. 3, on 'eternal life', see JN 3:15. Because this verse is a kind of confession of faith, many commentators consider it a later addition, but the style is typically Johannine and the verse fits well into the context. In 5:44 Jesus confessed his Jewish faith in 'the one who alone is God' (cf. Isa 37:20). Despite its very high Christology, the Fourth Gospel remains in the framework of monotheism (Hartman 1987). vv. 4–5, whereas vv. 2–3 describe the importance of Jesus' work for humanity, vv. 1, 4–5 deal with different aspects of Jesus' and his Father's glorification. v. 4 redefines Jesus' work on earth as a glorification of his Father; v. 5 resumes the perspective of divine pre-existence in the Prologue (cf. 1:1–3).

(17:6–11*a*) The disciples have been Chosen All those whom the Son has received from his Father (see vv. 2–3) are in vv. 6–19 described as disciples, and in vv. 20–3 as future believers. v. 6, probably there is an allusion to the Lord's prayer, 'hallowed be your name'. In v. 26 the same idea is expressed with 'I made your name known'. In the OT the Lord's name remains enigmatic (e.g. Ex 3:14), but Isa 52:6 promises that 'my people shall know my name'. According to 1:18 no one has ever seen God, but the Son has made the Father known. Likewise in 1:11–12 there is a sharp contrast between the world and those who belong to Jesus. vv. 7–9, before the explicit demand in vv. 11*b*–19, Jesus summarizes in vv. 6–11*a* his work among the disciples. They have been given to him by his Father (vv. 6, 9) and, quite differently from the audiences in 8:21–9 and 10:22–39, they have believed that he and his words came from God. This positive description, which contradicts 16:32, presupposes a post-resurrection perspective. It is also after Jesus' departure that the disciples will meet difficulties in their mission in the world in which they remain. vv. 10–11*a*, as in 16:15 and in ch. 10 Jesus stresses his strong links with the Father to whom he soon will return.

(17:11*b*–16) The Disciples are Protected Two verbs in the imperative punctuate Jesus' prayer for the disciples: 'protect' (v. 11*b*) and 'sanctify' (v. 17). They will be continued by the demand for all believers 'to be one' (v. 21). The three expressions are close to one another and encourage the readers to keep together communities that are threatened from the outside (cf. 1 Jn 2:24; 3:11–24). v. 11*b*, the adjective 'holy' is used only here for the Father (otherwise for the Spirit). It prepares the reader for what in vv. 17–19 will be said about the sanctification of Jesus and the disciples. In the Greek text the sing. *hōi* ('the name that you have given me') is probably original. The reading pl. *hous* ('the disciples that you have given me') is probably due to the influence of v. 6. As Jesus has revealed the Father's name, one can also say that this has been given to the Son. In other texts Jesus' (13:34–5; 15:12) or the Father's (15:9) love has been presented as the origin and model of human love. Now the unity between the Father and the Son is the fountain-head of the unity among the disciples, as it was in the parable of the vine in ch. 15 (cf. also 17:20–3). v. 12, here also it is the name that has been given, not the disciples. The future protection is similar to that which Jesus himself gave to his disciples. That nevertheless the unnamed disciple could betray his master is explained by a reference to 'the scripture'; this is reminiscent of Ps 41:10 which was quoted in 13:18. The Greek expression *ho hyios tou apōleias*, 'son of perdition', is Semitic (cf. 2 Thess 2:3) and suggests perhaps that Satan had an influence on him (cf. 6:70; 13:2, 27). It is even possible that the Johannine community considered Judas as a kind of prototype of the antichrist (cf. 1 Jn 2:18–22; 4:3). vv. 13–16, as in the farewell discourse, Jesus speaks both of the joy he has transmitted to his disciples and of the world's hatred. In the same way as in the last petition of the Lord's prayer, there is an ambiguity as to whether the Greek *ek tou ponērou* in v. 15 means from 'the evil' or 'the evil one', Satan. Since 'the ruler of this world' occurs several times (12:31; 14:30; 16:33), it is probable that it is he who is referred to. vv. 14 and 16 underline that the disciples share their master's fate in their relationship to the world.

(17:17–19) The Disciples are Sanctified The truth that comes from the Father through the Son will be their weapon in missionary work. vv. 17–18, in vv. 14–15 the word of God protected the disciples, but now 'the word of truth' sanctifies them. The meaning of 'sanctify' is determined by the fact that the Father has sent his Son (cf. 10:36). v. 19, the preposition *hyper* ('on behalf of', 'for') and the reflexive *emauton* ('myself') give the word 'sanctify' a meaning other than in v. 17. It now implies a 'sacrifice' for their sake (cf. also 10:11, 15; 15:13). We should remember that the death on the cross will coincide with the sacrifice of the paschal lambs (19:31, 36; cf. 1:29, 36). vv. 20–3, not only the disciples' protection (v. 11), but also the future believers' unity (cf. also 10:16) is important. One can guess that difficulties similar to those described in the Johannine letters are important obstacles to the missionary activity of the church. By showing Jesus at prayer for the future church, the evangelist invites today's reader to apply this prayer to a fragmented church struggling to unite; a kind of fusion takes place between the times of Jesus, the evangelist, and the reader. vv. 20–1 can more easily be applied to future believers than can vv. 22–3. Even in Moses' farewell speech in Deut 29:14–15 there is a distinction between those present and others: 'I am making this covenant, sworn by an oath, not only with you . . . but also with those who are not here with us today.' vv. 22–3, vv. 22b and 23 repeat with some modifications what was said in v. 21. The glorification and the perfect unity are destined for the disciples who will soon gather round the risen Lord. Their unity has its fountain-head in the Father and the Son; as their union is a prototype of later communities, these are also included in the prayer.

(17:24–6) Jesus Prays for the Disciples' Love v. 24, Jesus wants his disciples to share his eternal glory (cf. 14:2–3). A new point is that the Father loved the Son before the creation of the world (cf. also v. 5). The same mystery of Jesus' pre-existence is hinted at in the Prologue. In 1 Jn 4:8 'God is love'. The reading *ho*, 'that [which you have given me]' is more difficult and attested in several ancient traditions. It is therefore probably original and has been changed into the easier reading *hous* ('those [whom you have given me]'). But the meaning is nearly the same. vv. 25–6, Jesus returns to the concrete situation in which the disciples are still living. The Father is called righteous, because on the one hand the world already is judged (cf. 16:10–11), and because on the other hand the Father loves the disciples who believe in Jesus' words. The Master sums up what he has already said in vv. 6, 8, 11–12, 23. 'I will make it known' probably alludes to the Helper who comes in Jesus' place (cf. 14:26–7; 16:13–14). In v. 23 the Father's love for Jesus and the disciples was mentioned; in v. 26 the same thing is said in a more expressive way, concluding chs. 13–17. These chapters started with the expression of love in the footwashing, found their centre in ch. 15 around reciprocal love illustrated by the parable of the vine, and are concluded with a prayer for love before the sacrifice of the passion narrative takes place.

(18:1–19:42) Jesus' Passion, Death, and Burial In the four gospels the passion narratives follow a similar structure: arrest, trial before the Jewish and Roman authorities, condemnation, crucifixion, and burial. The four evangelists record the disciples' deceitful behaviour, and specially Judas's treason and Peter's three denials. The Jewish and the Roman officials threaten Jesus, the soldiers mock him as a Jewish king, whip and torment him. But with the help of quotations from the Scriptures, the evangelists underline how Jesus' humiliation fulfils a divine plan. They know that his death will lead to victory on the day of his resurrection. They are believers who transform the cruel story into an edifying narration for the reader. He or she is reminded of the difficulties the disciples meet after their decision to follow Jesus. Judas's treason and Peter's denial are warning examples. That the crowd wants Jesus crucified and the criminal Barabbas released is a tragic fact. But there are also positive roles which the reader can meditate upon: the women who are present during the crucifixion (in John also Jesus' mother and the beloved disciple); the disciples who bury Jesus with piety; in the Synoptics Simon of Cyrene who bears Jesus' cross, and the centurion who confesses that Jesus was innocent (Luke) or God's Son (Mark–Matthew). The passion narrative is therefore not an ordinary historical account of what happened, even if there are many aspects which can be related to contemporary Roman and Jewish legal proceedings and to the punishments they inflicted (see Brown 1994).

In the Fourth Gospel the crucifixion coincides with the hour of Jesus' glorification (cf. 3:14; 8:28; 12:32–3): by his death Jesus will be glorified with his Father (13:31–2; 17:1–5). Therefore the evangelist stresses the majesty of Jesus despite his humiliation. Already when he is arrested, the repeated 'I am he' causes the soldiers to step back and fall to the ground.

The interrogations before the high priest and before Pilate are occasions where Jesus continues his public teaching. On the cross Jesus makes arrangements for his mother and the beloved disciple (19:25-7). He fulfils the scriptures by saying 'I am thirsty' (19:28) and comments upon his own work on earth by saying 'It is finished' (19:30). The burial is that of a 'king'.

A comparison between the gospels shows that Matthew follows Mark but adds his own material in order to augment the dramatic effect of the narrative. Luke is less dependent on Mark than Matthew because he has his own information. He underlines more than Matthew and Mark that Pilate considered Jesus to be innocent. The author of the Fourth Gospel probably knows Mark's account (*contra* Brown 1994), but he has much material of his own which he applies in a very free way. He has already used certain aspects of Mark's passion narrative earlier in his gospel; others do not fit his own main theological purpose. He tries to show that Jesus was sentenced to death as the king of the Jews and not as a bandit. Like Luke he emphasizes Pilate's knowledge of Jesus' innocence. He underlines the responsibility of the Jewish authorities, but tries to diminish that of Pilate, even if he also criticizes him for his lack of integrity. He eliminates Jesus' desperate cry and stresses the Master's regal character in the face of death. In place of groups who mock Jesus he recounts the affectionate scene between Jesus' mother and the beloved disciple.

That John omits that the curtain of the temple was torn in two and the darkness at the moment of Jesus' death has been used as an argument against his dependence on synoptic texts. But such a mention was unnecessary since he had a theological equivalent in the temple cleansing in Jn 2:13-22 and in his descriptions of the battle between darkness and light. The symbols of water and blood flowing from Jesus' side were more suitable to his own purpose of describing Jesus' death as a glorification.

It is impossible to reconstruct with certainty the documents that Mark used. If John knew Mark, it is remarkable that he dared to correct him, just as Luke does in his own way. In many regards John's account is more satisfactory than Mark's with its meeting of the Sanhedrin at night. In John the meeting before Annas during the night is only a preparatory inquisition. The evangelist seems to be better informed than the Synoptics when he has Jesus die on 14 Nisan, when the paschal lambs were slaughtered to be eaten that evening (i.e. the beginning of 15 Nisan).

Some Jewish and Christian scholars have tried to transfer the whole responsibility of Jesus' death to the Romans. They are right when they criticize Luke's and John's apologetic motives in connection with Pilate's sentence, but still the Jewish authorities probably had their own share in the arrest of Jesus. It is historically doubtful whether there was ever an official gathering of the Sanhedrin before Pilate's judgement. In any event, Christians ought to combat all anti-Semitic feelings in connection with the trial against Jesus.

The Johannine passion narrative is well organized: (1) Jesus is arrested (18:1-11) and Annas interrogates Jesus while Peter denies him (18:12-27). (2) The trial before Pilate (18:28–19:16*a*) is divided into seven scenes by the alternation between what is happening outside or inside Pilate's headquarters. (3)

Jesus is crucified and dies (19:16*b*-30), which gives the author the chance to provide a theological commentary (19:31-7) and describe Jesus' burial (19:38-42).

(18:1-11) The arrest of Jesus is linked in different ways to the interrogation before Annas in 18:12-27. In both scenes Peter is active: in the first scene as an over-courageous defender of his master, in the second as a coward who denies him. In the first scene the question of Jesus' identity is raised, in the second that of his teaching; the two aspects are complementary. By introducing the passion narrative with the arrest and not with the spiritual fight at Gethsemane, John can show Jesus' majesty in the face of his adversaries. vv. 1-3, in a first edition of the gospel v. 1 probably followed immediately after 14:31. The references 'across the Kidron' and 'garden' can be fitted in with the synoptic topography: 'to the Mount of Olives' (Lk 22:39) and 'a place called Gethsemane' (Mk 14:32; Mt 26:36). The Johannine garden is then simply a plantation of olive trees. Whereas the synoptic Judas points Jesus out by a kiss, in John he only indicates the place, which, since the Johannine Jesus had been in Jerusalem several times, was known to Judas. A *speira* ('detachment') is composed of 600 soldiers. Their presence is strange, since Pilate in 18:29-30 does not seem to be informed about it. Perhaps the evangelist only wanted to show symbolically how Jewish police and Roman soldiers collaborated in their actions against Jesus. vv. 4-8*a*, the evangelist often underlines that Jesus knows everything in advance (cf. 1:47-8; 6:6, 61, 64; 13:1). In contrast to the Synoptics Jesus in John takes the initiative himself to go to Judas and to the others. Jesus is also called 'of Nazareth' in the inscription in 19:19. Since John with the help of *egō eimi* sometimes suggests Jesus' divinity (see JN 8:24, 28; 13:19), there may be here more than a simple statement 'I am he'. This is at least suggested in v. 6 when all fall to the ground because of the revelation of Jesus' identity. Judas is stereotypically called in vv. 2 and 5 the one 'who betrayed Jesus'. The Jews take over his role when they hand Jesus over to Pilate (18:30, 35). Pilate in his turn will hand him to the Jewish authorities (19:16). vv. 8*b*-9, Jesus indirectly accepts becoming their prisoner when he asks that the disciples be allowed to go. This time it is not Scripture but Jesus' own words that are fulfilled. The quotation is not exact, but one can refer to 6:39; 10:27-8; 17:12. Still there is a change of perspective, since these three texts are concerned with eternal life, whereas the concern here is with the disciples' escape from actual dangers. vv. 10-11, unlike the Synoptics John indicates the disciple's identity (Simon Peter) and that of the slave (Malchus). In a subtle way the evangelist alludes to the Gethsemane scene by referring to the cup that the Father has given him to drink (cf. esp. Mt 26:42).

(18:12-27) Jesus' questioning before the high priest Annas is organically linked with Peter's three denials, in order to augment its dramatic aspect (Fortna 1977-8). Since a kind of trial by the Sanhedrin has already taken place in 11:47-50, the evangelist alludes only to a gathering before the present high priest Caiaphas (see vv. 24, 28) but fills it out by mentioning a more private questioning before Annas, the former high priest. vv. 12-14, the Roman soldiers and the Jewish police work together (cf. vv. 1-3). The evangelist is well informed about the relationship between the two high priests. Annas was high priest 6–15 CE and in normal fashion retained his title. He was influential even later, since his five sons became high priests (Josephus, *Ant.* 18.26, 34; 20.198). The evangelist probably knows that Caiaphas was not functioning as high priest only for that year (according to Josephus, *Ant.* 18.34–5, 95, he held office from about 18–37 CE). Caiaphas's prophecy in 11:50 and 18:14 seems in 18:8–9 to be applied to the disciples: they can escape because Jesus gives his life for them. vv. 15–18, even if the reading 'another disciple', without the definite article, is original, the evangelist is probably thinking of the beloved disciple whom he introduced in 13:23 and who will reappear in 19:26. If he is identical with John, the son of Zebedee, as chs. 1 and 21 suggest, one wonders how a simple fisherman came to be known to the high priest. But the evangelist has his own reasons to present the things in this way. Whereas this disciple follows Jesus into Annas's courtyard, Peter, whom he introduces there, becomes a renegade. The reference to the woman who interrogates Peter occurs also in Mk 14:66 par., but uniquely in John she guards the gate. Only John indicates that it was cold and that the fire was made of charcoal. vv. 19–21, the high priest Annas tries to show that Jesus is a false prophet (cf. 7:45–52). Ironically enough he asks Jesus about his disciples, at the very moment when Peter is denying him. Jesus answers only the question about his teaching, which has been quite open (cf. 7:4; 11:14). One would expect Annas also to interrogate those who had heard Jesus' teaching but he seems not to be interested in the truth. vv. 22–4, in Mk 14:65 members of the Sanhedrin spit on Jesus and the guards beat him. In Lk 22:63 only the guards insult Jesus. Jn 18:22 is a kind of combination of both: only one of the police strikes Jesus. In John alone Jesus insists that he has not offended the high priest (cf. Ex 22:27 and Acts 23:5). vv. 25–7, Peter is still in the courtyard just as he is in Lk 22:55–62, whereas in Mk 14:68 he goes out into the forecourt and in Mt 26:71 he proceeds to the porch. That one of the slaves was a relative of Malchus intensifies Peter's denial in the Fourth Gospel. The cock crows once, as in Matthew and Luke, whereas in Mk 14:72 he crows twice, in accordance with Jesus' prophecy at Mk 14:30. Contrary to the Synoptics John does not report anything about Peter's reaction after the third denial, but in Jn 21:15–17 Jesus will ask Peter three times if he loves him. The third time Peter feels hurt.

(18:28–19:16a) In a subtle way the trial before Pilate moves from a first accusation that Jesus is a criminal (18:30) to the charge that he made himself 'Son of God' (19:7), and finally that he claims to be a 'king', which is a revolt against the emperor (19:12). Three times Pilate declares Jesus innocent (18:38; 19:4, 6), but the Jewish accusers try by every means to have him condemned to death. The alternation of the seven scenes is highly dramatic: the accusers are outside Pilate's headquarters and Jesus is inside but comes out in the end as the mocked king of the Jews.

1. 18:28–32. Ironically enough, the Jews want to be able to eat the Passover without ritual defilement, but they are actively pursuing the death of Jesus, who is the real paschal lamb (cf. 1:29, 36; 19:31, 33). As they accuse Jesus of being a criminal, Pilate asks them to judge him according to their own laws. The Jews are therefore obliged to make a precise request for the death sentence, which only the Romans could

grant. In his discussions with the Jews Jesus has already stated that when they seek to kill him, they are acting against their own law (7:51; 8:37–47). The evangelist stresses that Jesus knew he would be lifted up on the cross (3:14; 8:28; 12:32–3), the normal Roman punishment. Pilate, who was governor in Judea from 26 to 36 CE, had his headquarters (*praitōrion*) probably at Herod's palace near the Joppa Gate, and not at Antonia, the Hasmonean palace (Benoit 1961: 332–3).

2. 18:33–8a. The question in v. 33 and Jesus' answer in v. 37 are similar to Mk 15:2 par., but the rest of the dialogue is typically Johannine. The Greek substantive *basileia*, normally translated 'kingdom' or 'kingly rule', seems in these verses to mean 'royal dignity'. The Jews have informed Pilate about Jesus' claims to be the Messiah with royal dignity. Jesus accepts the title King of the Jews (cf. 1:49) with a quite special meaning: his royal dignity comes from his Father who has sent him to testify to the truth (cf. 8:32–47). His royal dignity is similar to that of a shepherd to whom the sheep listen (10:16, 27). But Pilate does not belong to them and is therefore sceptical about truth.

3. 18:38b–40. Pilate seems to conclude that he has to do with typical Jewish questions and that Jesus therefore is innocent. In the Synoptics the bandit Barabbas is likewise released and Jesus condemned to death (Mk 15:11 par.). The custom of an amnesty at Passover is also mentioned in Mk 15:6 and Mt 27:15, but uniquely in John it is Pilate himself who refers to the custom. Contrary to the Synoptics, John postpones the Jews' shouting 'crucify him' in order to increase its dramatic effect (cf. Jn 19:6).

4. 19:1–3. The four gospels agree on two humiliations: one before Caiaphas or Annas (Jn 18:22–3), and one before Pilate (in Luke before Herod). The Roman soldiers dress him as a king with a crown of thorns. In Mt 27:28–9 they even put a reed in his right hand, mocking his royal power. In John they strike Jesus on the face, in Mk 15:19 and Mt 27:29–31 they strike his head with a reed, spit upon him, and kneel down in homage to him. In all three gospels the soldiers say ironically, 'Hail, King of the Jews!' Matthew and John seem both to depend on Mark whom they dramatize in different ways. John leaves out the spitting and the ironical kneeling which he probably considers offensive. Since Pilate continues to consider Jesus innocent, the flogging is only a kind of warning.

5. 19:4–7. As in Lk 23:14, 20–3 Jesus' innocence is underlined, but only in John does Pilate come out of his headquarters with the mocked royal Jesus. The words 'here is the man!' may be an allusion to 'Son of Man', which in Aramaic means precisely 'a man'. But John has given the expression a deeper meaning, with Dan 7:14 as a model (see esp. 5:27). In fact, during the trial in the Synoptics Jesus alludes to the coming of the Son of Man (Mk 14:61–2. par.). That the simple word 'man' can hint at 'Son of Man' becomes even clearer in the following scene, where Jesus is accused of having claimed to be the 'Son of God' (Jn 19:7). A first climax is reached with the authorities' double 'Crucify him!' It is now clear that the accusation against Jesus is religious, but in the further trial it will be given a political character (vv. 12–16a).

6. 19:8–11. 'Son of God' is a worrying expression to Pilate, who wants to know more about Jesus' origin. Jesus' silence is

also a motif in Mk 15:3–5 par., where it concerns a refusal to respond to the authorities' accusations. In v. 9 Pilate's lack of sincere enquiry deserves only silence in reply. He therefore reformulates his question as one about power. Jesus discloses a paradox: Pilate who has his power from above thinks that he can exercise it over the one who comes from God! Jesus thus reveals that he fully accepts God's will. Once again Pilate's guilt is diminished in comparison with that of Judas and of the Jewish authorities.

7. 19:12–16a. The seventh scene is decisive for Jesus' crucifixion. vv. 12–13, 'friend of the emperor' (Gk. *philokaisar*) was in fact an honorific title given to Herod Agrippa I. Contrary to what Jesus said to Pilate about his royal dignity, the Jews now present him as a man with political ambitions that go against the emperor's interests. In the Greek text it is unclear whether Pilate or Jesus sat on the judge's bench. But since Pilate is afraid of Jesus' power (v. 8), it is unlikely that he would mock him. In any case, Pilate's judgement is not a formal one. The Aramaic *Gabbatha* in v. 13 ('bald head'? 'eminence'?) does not really correspond to the Greek *Lithostrōton* (Stone Pavement). It was usual to have stone pavements inside palaces and outside in the courtyards. vv. 14–16a, normally the word *paraskeuē* means the preparation day for the sabbath (cf. vv. 31 and 42). But in v. 14 it seems to be the preparation day for the Passover, that means 14 Nisan (cf. 18:28). It coincides in John with the preparation day for the sabbath. When Pilate in v. 5 said 'Here is the man', the Jewish authorities replied with a double 'Crucify him!' When in v. 14 he presents the mocked royal Jesus with the words, 'Here is your King!', they cry out twice, 'Away with him!' and add, 'Crucify him!' The Johannine irony comes to a climax when the Jewish authorities seem to forget all their own messianic expectations in favour of their loyalty towards the Roman emperor.

(19:16b–42) Jesus' Crucifixion, Death, and Burial

(19:16b–30) We can distinguish five moments in this part: in vv. 16b–18 Jesus carries his cross; in vv. 19–22 Pilate has an inscription written; in vv. 23–5a the soldiers divide Jesus' clothes; in vv. 25b–27 the women and the beloved disciple are standing near the cross; in vv. 28–30 Jesus finally dies. The different scenes are separated by repeated words in the beginning and at the end of each scene: 'Jesus' in vv. 16b–18; 'write' in vv. 19–22; 'soldiers' and 'clothes' in vv. 23–5a; 'mother' in vv. 25b–7; 'finished' in vv. 28–30. vv. 16b–18, the Jewish authorities to whom Pilate hands Jesus over in v. 16a have not themselves the right to crucify him but let the Roman soldiers do it (cf. v. 23). John underlines that Jesus carries the cross by himself, without the help of Simon of Cyrene (Mk 15:21 par.). Some exegetes think that the evangelist alludes to Isaac who carries the wood of the burnt offering (Gen 22:6). In the normal way, Jesus would have carried only the crossbeam (*patibulum*), on which he will be nailed at Golgotha and elevated on the pole which already stands there. The Greek *cranion*, 'skull', is a correct translation of the Aramaic Golgotha and probably denotes a hillock. Only John emphasizes the fact that Jesus is in the middle between the two others. v. 19–22, the Fourth Gospel alone stresses that the inscription (cf. Mk 15:26 par.) had a universal character by being

written in three languages, and that Pilate himself had ordered it. John adds here 'of Nazareth' (cf. 18:5) in order to stress the origin of the 'King of the Jews', but in v. 21 he has the shorter formula of Mk 15:26. The evangelist considers Pilate's initiative as prophetic. Since the charge in Mt 27:37 and Lk 23:38 is placed over Jesus' head, the tradition has not represented the cross as *crux commissa*, in the form of a T, but as *crux immissa*. vv. 23–5a, the Greek *himation* normally designates a robe in the singular (cf. vv. 2, 5), and all kinds of clothes in the plural. But since the *chitōn* in v. 23 is a tunic under the robe, *himatia* seems to be a robe just as in 13:4. In Mk 15:24 par. there is only an allusion to Ps 22(21):18, whereas John quotes the Psalm according to the LXX. He distinguishes between the 'clothes' (the robe) and the 'clothing' (the tunic), whereas the psalmist only used parallel expressions to designate the same object. In order to underline God's protection the tunic is not divided, which probably has a symbolic meaning of unity similar to that in 21:11. vv. 25b–27, in Mk 15:40–1 par. the women are at a distance, which is more probable during a crucifixion. But in John they stand near the cross to hear Jesus' words. The name of Jesus' mother is not indicated, as in Jn 2:1–12 and 6:42, probably in order not to confuse her with the three other Marys: Lazarus' sister (ch. 11) and the two Marys named here. In the Greek text 'Mary the wife of Clopas' could be in apposition to 'his mother's sister', but as the women are contrasted to the four soldiers, it is more likely that they also are four. In Mk 15:40 par. the mother of Jesus is not named at all. Mary Magdelene appears in all four gospels. Commentators who want to harmonize John with the Synoptics identify 'the wife of Clopas' with the synoptic 'Mary, the mother of James and of Joses'; 'his mother's sister' in John is then identical with Salome (Mk 15:40) and the mother of the sons of Zebedee (Mt 27:56). In that case Jesus' aunt Salome would be the mother of James and John. The scene where Jesus entrusts the beloved disciple to his mother would have a basis in a family relationship if this disciple were John, the son of Zebedee. But these are guesses, which do not fit Lk 8:3 and 24:10 (cf. also our remark above on 7:3). There is no textual reason to see in Jesus' mother and in the beloved disciple representatives of two different communities, the Jewish-Christian and the Gentile-Christian (as Bultmann 1971: 673). Mary is not yet the 'mother of the Church' of later Catholic tradition. According to chs. 14–16 the Helper would lead the disciples into the whole truth. In a similar way the mother of Jesus and the beloved disciple transmit Jesus' message: they are together ideal representatives of the Christian faith (cf. also 19:35 and 21:24). vv. 28–30, once again the evangelist stresses Jesus' sovereign will in fulfilling the Scripture, alluding probably to Ps 69:22 ('for my thirst they gave me vinegar to drink', cf. Mk 15:36 par.). Only John underlines that Jesus is thirsty, which is said only indirectly in the Psalm. In Mk 15:36 the sponge is put on a stick, but in John it is on a branch of hyssop, an allusion to the paschal meal (cf. Ex 12:22). Even the words 'it is finished' have in Greek a meaning of fulfilment: probably the work of his Father (cf. 14:31; 17:4). Jesus willingly (cf. 10:18) gives up the spirit which remained upon him in 1:32. He accomplishes for the first time his promise in 7:37–9, giving the Spirit to the faithful around his cross. In 20:22 the risen Christ will be more explicit about the gift of his Spirit.

(19:31–7) There have been many discussions on the composition of this theological commentary. Some believe that vv. 34*b*–35 on blood and water are later additions to the soldiers' action in vv. 31–4*a* and to the fulfilment of the scripture in vv. 36–7. Others think that even vv. 34*a* and 37 are additions. All these reconstructions are merely hypothetical. The evangelist himself distinguishes between two actions: the breaking of the legs in vv. 31–3 and the piercing of the side in v. 34. In vv. 35–7 he comments on both actions. vv. 31–3, the sabbath coincides with 15 Nisan (cf. v. 14). According to Deut 21:23 a corpse hanged on a tree must be buried before nightfall. For purity reasons this is especially important before Passover. Only John has the breaking of legs (*crurifragium*), which was used either as punishment, or as here in order to hasten suffocation. v. 34, Jesus' pierced side is also mentioned at the resurrection in 20:20–7. The soldier determines if Jesus is dead. Immediately after death, blood and a watery substance from the lungs, can emerge. The evangelist stresses the paradox that two important components of life appear in Jesus' dead body. If the evangelist is informed about 'mixed blood' that was thrown at the altar on Passover (cf. Mishnah, *Ohol.* 3:5; *ḥul.* 2:6; *Pesaḥ.* 5:8), we would have here a further allusion to Passover. But probably it is better to compare 1 Jn 5:6–8, where Jesus Christ is said to have come by water and blood, which means by his baptism and his death. According to Jn 6:53–6 blood is connected with the eucharist, and according to 3:1–15 water with baptism. The evangelist may be alluding these two sacraments. The Spirit who is mentioned in 1 Jn 5:6–8 is also present at Jesus' death in Jn 19:30. The Church Fathers thought that even the church was born out of Jesus' side, but in contrast to Paul the evangelist does not develop the theme of Jesus as a new Adam. v. 35, similarly to 21:24 we have one who testifies, the beloved disciple (cf. 18:15–16 and 19:25–6), and another who states that his testimony is true, probably the Johannine community. It is unclear whether 'he knows that he tells the truth' is said of the Johannine group, the beloved disciple (preferable), Jesus or God (less probable). vv. 36–7, the quotation in v. 36 alludes to Ex 12:46 and is at the same time dependent on Ps 34(35) LXX. Jesus dies as the passover lamb whose legs are not broken (cf. Jn 1:29, 34), but also as the righteous man of Ps 34 (cf. Lk 23:47). It is more difficult to see how the soldier who pierced Jesus' side fulfils the scripture. In v. 37 there is a quotation of Zech 12:10*b* (Heb. text), similar to that of Rev 1:6. Possibly the first Christians utilized Zech 12:10*b* to point out Jesus whose hands had been pierced with nails. John applies the quotation to the pierced side.

(19:38–42) The narrative concerning Jesus' burial was important for the first Christians, because of the connection between the empty tomb and the resurrection (perhaps implicit in 1 Cor 15:4). In the four gospels we have a similar main narration: Joseph of Arimathea asks Pilate for permission to bury Jesus. John, however, adds the figure of Nicodemus and other details. vv. 38–9, according to Mk 15:43 and Lk 23:50–1 Joseph is a respected member of the council who is waiting expectantly for the kingdom of God. In Mt 27:57 he is a rich man who had become a disciple of Jesus. John's Joseph is similar to Matthew's, but his Nicodemus resembles Joseph in Mark and Luke. The evangelist does not clearly say that Nico-

demus had become a disciple of Jesus, but his sympathy for Jesus has developed since 3:1–21 and 7:50–2. Fragrant spices weighing 100 lb. are just as impressive as 1 lb. of costly perfume used by Mary to anoint Jesus in 12:3–8. vv. 40–2, Nicodemus fulfils what Mary has done in advance: Jesus gets a kingly burial. One can compare the quantity of spices used at the death of Herod (Jos. *Ant.* 17.199; cf. also Jer 34:5). The linen cloths (Gk. *othonia*) are also mentioned in Jn 20:6–7, whereas in 11:44 they are called *keiriai*, 'strips of cloth', different from the cloth round the face. In Mk 15:46 par. it is a single linen cloth (Gk. *syndōn*). Some have tried to combine John and the Synoptics: the synoptic *syndōn* could be the material out of which the Johannine cloths are made, or the Johannine cloths in fact only one single piece. Others think that a *syndōn* was fixed with the help of strips of cloth. Historically it is more probable that the spices were carried to the tomb at the burial than on the day of the resurrection (Mk 16:1–2 par.). John alone indicates that the tomb was near the place of crucifixion. The next reference to the garden will be at 20:1.

(20:1–21:25) The Risen Christ In the canonical gospels Jesus' resurrection is both the object of faith and a concrete event. Unlike the apocryphal *Gospel of Peter* (39–44) the gospels do not describe exactly how Jesus rose from the dead, but they insist on two aspects: the empty tomb and the appearances to the disciples. John reflects more than the Synoptics on how all certainty about Jesus' resurrection is linked to faith (cf. 20:27, 29). The two conclusions in 20:30–1 and 21:24–5, for example, summarize the relation between the witness of faith to the signs performed by Jesus and belief in him as Messiah and God's Son.

In recent commentaries it has been usual to consider ch. 21 as a later addition by a redactor, because 20:30–1 seems to be a natural conclusion of the whole gospel. Since the 'we' in 21:24–5 is distinguished from the beloved disciple, it has been suggested that a later redactor is responsible for ch. 21, and even for other additions in the gospel. But there are objections to this position: the narrative technique in ch. 21 is very similar to that in chs. 1–20, and the style is nearly the same. Just as themes in chs. 13–14 are completed or replaced in chs. 15–17, so ch. 21 develops aspects that have been adumbrated (e.g. the theme of following Jesus) or introduces new material. The main author ('the evangelist') may have reworked his first sketch of the gospel and added new material to it (e.g. chs. 6; 15–17; 21). He has kept 20:30–1 as commentary on the revelations in Jerusalem, but he wanted to complete these with an appearance by the lake of Tiberias. This gave him the opportunity to inform the reader about the disciples' activity in Galilee that we find in the Synoptics. A redactor may then have reworked this chapter, especially the new conclusion in vv. 24–5.

The whole gospel is given a kind of unity by the alternation of different places where Jesus is present: Galilee, Judea, and 'the other side'. Three times we pass from Galilee to Jerusalem, and in the end once from Jerusalem (12:12–20:31) to Galilee (ch. 21). The week of Jesus' resurrection in chs. 20– corresponds to the first week in 1:19–2:11 and to the last week in Jesus' life in 12:1–19:42. In ch. 20 Jesus appears to his disciples in Jerusalem as in Lk 24; in ch. 21 he appears in

Galilee as it is hinted at in Mk 16:7 and Mt 28:7, 10, and described in Mt 28:16–20.

The following seven sections can be distinguished: (1) Mary and two disciples at the tomb (20:1–10); (2) Mary sees the Lord (20:11–18); (3) the disciples see the Lord (20:19–23); (4) Thomas sees the Lord (20:24–9); (5) first conclusion of the book (20:30–1); (6) Jesus shows himself to the disciples by the Sea of Tiberias: (a) the miraculous catch of fish and the meal; (b) Peter and the beloved disciple (21:15–23); (7) second conclusion of the book (21:24–5). The relationship between chs. 20–1 and the synoptic texts is very complicated (see Neirynck 1984b; 1990).

(20:1–10) Mary and Two Disciples at the Tomb The evangelist wants to frame the running of the two disciples to the tomb with two narratives on Mary Magdalene. She reports first on the empty tomb, then (in vv. 11–18) on Jesus' resurrection. Inconsistencies in ch. 20 are due to the author's many references to synoptic material that he supplements with his own information (cf. Neirynck 1984b). vv. 1–2, Mary Magdalene was first introduced near the cross in 19:25. In Mk 16:1 there are three women at the tomb, in Mt 28:1 two, and in Lk 23:55–24:10 more than three. In Mark and Luke they come with spices to anoint Jesus, but in the Fourth Gospel this has already been done. Possibly the evangelist has special information concerning Jesus' first appearance to Mary alone (cf. Mk 16:9). The stone was not mentioned at the burial, in contrast to Mk 15:46 and Mt 27:60, 66. In Mk 16:4 par. it was rolled away (in Mt 28:2 by an angel). John probably refers to the angel's message in Mk 16:7 when he has Mary inform Peter and the other disciple. The Johannine Mary thinks that grave-robbers or the authorities have stolen the body, whereas Mt 28:11–15 mentions the allegation by the Jews that the disciples stole the body. The 'we do not know' is an inconsistency deriving from the synoptic account about several women at the tomb. vv. 3–8, we find a similar tradition in Luke: in Lk 24:12 (which is original despite the lack of attestation in the Western tradition) Peter goes to the tomb, while in Lk 24:24 it is 'some disciples'. The 'other disciple' in John is presumably the beloved disciple (see JN 13:23; 18:15). He has more insight than Peter (cf. 13:23–5; 19:26–7), whom he outruns, but still he respects Peter's privilege to go in first. The linen wrappings which are left and the cloth rolled up by itself indicate that the body was not stolen but rather rose miraculously. Whereas Peter only looks at them, the other disciple can decipher the signs by faith. vv. 9–10, as in 1 Cor 15:4 the resurrection fulfils the Scripture, but no precise passage is referred to. There is an apparent inconsistency when even the other disciple, who believes, does not understand Scripture (cf. 2:22; 12:16). Perhaps the evangelist wanted to point out that even he had to increase in understanding. The two disciples go home and allow Mary to meet Jesus alone (vv. 11–18).

(20:11–18) Mary Sees the Lord This narrative is close to the synoptic account, where several women see God's angels, and even Jesus himself, on their way to the disciples in Mt 28:9–10. John seems to have fused together two different scenes from Mt 28:1–10: Mary sees first two angels (Jn 20:12–13), then the Lord himself (vv. 14–16). vv. 11–13, it is possible that exō, 'outside', has been added to improve the text. Mary re-

mains outside the tomb, unlike the disciples in vv. 7–8 and the women in Mk 16:5 and Lk 24:3. She bends over to look in as the beloved disciple does in Jn 20:5, but instead of the linen wrappings she sees two angels. They are witnesses of Mary's desolation, but unlike the synoptic accounts they have no message for the disciples; Jesus himself will provide it in v. 17. Only John indicates that the angels are sitting where Jesus' head and feet had been located. This supposes a tomb of the *arcosolium* type, where there is more room for the corpse than in the *kôkîm* type, where the body is put into a wall cavity. vv. 14–16, Mary thinks that Jesus is the gardener who has taken away the body. Jesus addresses her in the same words as did the angels in v. 13, but adds 'For whom are you looking?' When he calls her by her name, she recognizes him as her teacher, in a way similar to sheep recognizing the voice of their shepherd (10:3–4). The Aramaic *rabbouni* (cf. Mk 10:51) is by its length more solemn than the simple *rabbi* (see JN 1:38). v. 17, the present imperative *mē mou haptou* can be translated either 'do not continue to touch me' or 'do not touch me'. The evangelist seems to be commenting on Mt 28:9 where the women take hold of Jesus' feet in a gesture of worship. The reason why Mary ought not to hold on Jesus is that he is on his way to the Father. In the Fourth Gospel the resurrection and the ascension seem to coincide. Therefore Mary needs to hear that after Jesus' appearances, faith, in the absence of physical contact, is the only important thing (see the scene with Thomas in vv. 24–9 and cf. 14:22–3). Jesus calls the disciples 'brothers' in a different sense from that of his sceptical natural family at 7:4 (cf. Mt 28:10). The risen Christ associates the disciples in his community with God the Father, but also marks a difference by referring to him with the pronouns 'my' and 'your'. v. 18, in Mk 16:7 and Mt 28:7 the angel(s) give the women the mission to inform the disciples concerning Jesus' later appearance in Galilee. In Lk 24:33 the two disciples from Emmaus return to Jerusalem to meet the eleven. But in John, Mary reports both on her meeting with Jesus and on his message.

(20:19–23) The Disciples See the Lord In the Christian tradition it remains unclear how often the risen Christ manifested himself to his disciples. Paul names five appearances: to the twelve, to more than five hundred brothers and sisters, to James, to the apostles, and last of all to himself (1 Cor 15:5–7). According to Mk 16:7 Peter and the other disciples would meet Jesus in Galilee; in Mt 28:16–20 this is described as a farewell scene where the eleven disciples are sent out to the whole world (cf. also Mk 16:14–18). In Lk 24:36–49 Jesus appears to them in Jerusalem, wishes them peace, shows them his hands and feet, and eats the fish they give him. He gives them a mission to all people and promises them the gift of the Holy Spirit. Jn 20:19–23 and 21:13 resemble the Lucan narrative in many respects. v. 19, just as in Lk 24:29, 36–53, Jesus appears in Jerusalem in the evening of the day he rose again. John alone mentions that the door was locked, perhaps in order to underline that the risen Christ is no longer bound by normal space conditions. The peace greeting prolongs what Jesus had said in his farewell discourse (Jn 14:27; 16:33). v. 20, the hands and the side are also mentioned in vv. 25 and 27, whereas in Lk 24:39 Jesus shows his hands and feet. vv. 21–2, the missionary work of the disciples depends on the mission of the Son and on the gift of the Holy Spirit. In his farewell discourse Jesus had promised that he would send the Helper. A first gift of the Spirit was already described in 19:30, but now the disciples are so to speak 'baptized' by the risen Christ's Spirit. v. 23, as Lk 24:47–49, the forgiveness of sins is linked to the gift of the Spirit and the disciples' missionary work. But John transforms the Lukan understanding of forgiveness with the help of material similar to Mt 16:19 and 18:18. Matthew stresses Peter's and the other disciples' power to 'bind' and 'loose' certain rules in the assembly, whereas John speaks of retaining (binding) sins or forgiving them. Despite the present and the future tenses in many MSS, the variant *apheōntai* (perfect passive, 'they are forgiven') is probably original. The Christian tradition early linked together Matthew and John in its understanding of penance.

(20:24–9) Thomas Sees the Lord Thomas' encounter with Jesus is modelled on the previous scene. His experience is meant to help all future believers who have not seen the risen Christ. vv. 24–5, the same expression, 'one of the twelve', is applied to Judas in 6:71. The Greek *didymos* means both 'twin' and 'double' or 'twofold'. In 11:16 and 14:5 Thomas had difficulties understanding Jesus, now he hesitates when confronted by his resurrection. The disciples relate their vision of the Lord, as Mary did in v. 18. In the original Greek text the 'mark' of the nails is first *typos*, and then probably *topos* ('place'). The MSS have muddled the two words. The palpable marks have an apologetic function for the reader. vv. 26–7, the week following the resurrection corresponds probably to the first week in 1:19–2:1 and to the last week in Jesus' life in 12:1–19:31. Just as in the previous appearance to the disciples, Jesus enters despite the shut doors. Jesus accepts Thomas' daring demand, but tactfully the evangelist does not describe its fulfilment. v. 28, Thomas' doubts give way to a climax in Johannine Christology. In 13:13–14 Jesus used 'teacher' and 'lord' as synonyms, but now 'my Lord' designates the risen Christ. 'My God' resumes the description of Jesus in the Prologue as 'God' (1:1, 18). In the OT Lord and God are associated terms (e.g. Ps 7:2–3; 30:3). This is more likely to be the background than the pagan acclamation of the emperor as Lord and God (but see Suetonius, *Dom.* 13: 'dominus et deus noster'). v. 29, besides 13:17, this is the only formula using 'blessed' in John. It concerns the future believers (cf. 17:20–4) who have not seen Jesus. Thomas should have believed without seeing the marks. Still his clear confession is an act of faith, as was that of the hesitant Nathanael at the beginning of the gospel (1:43–51).

(20:30–1) The author suddenly expresses himself in a first epilogue to what he calls this book. v. 30, the word 'sign' is a key for the reader to understand both the risen Christ's appearances and their link with the 'signs' during his public life. Those who presuppose a sign-source behind this gospel consider vv. 30–1 as its natural conclusion. But we have seen that the Fourth Gospel forms a unity despite its redactional problems. In this case the 'signs' are not only the seven miracles we have enumerated, but also other scenes and words of Jesus. These signs are no riddles, since the reader is from the beginning informed about the Word, Jesus Christ. But the

reader has to penetrate the mystery of Jesus' revelation of his divine glory. v. 31, it is difficult to decide whether the original subjunctive was an aorist *pisteusēte* or a present *pisteuēte*. In the first case one could translate as NRSV, 'that you may come to faith', in the second case, 'that you may continue to believe'. In 19:35 the variant that has the aorist tense seems to be preferable, but in our verse both variants are well attested. It is not certain that the evangelist himself would in this case make a clear distinction between the two tenses. In any event, he seems to address Christian readers, whom he wants to gain life in Christ by deepening their faith in Jesus as Messiah and Son of God.

(21:1–23) In this chapter Jesus reveals himself a third time to the disciples, but now by the Sea of Tiberias. The evangelist wants to complete the appearances in Jerusalem with the data of Mk 16:7 and Mt 28:7, 10, 16–20. He also completes Jn 1:35–42 with the help of what we know about the occupation of the disciples from Mk 1:16–20 par. The evangelist has read either a source similar to Lk 5:1–11 or that text itself. There a miraculous draught of fish is combined with the disciples' call. Our passage has a similar relationship to Lk 24:41–3 where the risen Christ eats a piece of the fish.

The author has used different kinds of material but has put them together into a well-organized unity. In a first scene we meet seven disciples who on the word of the Lord catch many fish. In the second scene the risen Christ gives Peter a special mission and speaks about the beloved disciple's destiny. The first scene describes different actions, whereas the second consists of a dialogue between Jesus and Peter. The two scenes are linked together through the different relationships between the risen Lord and the two main disciples.

(21:1–14) The miraculous catch of fish and the following meal are closely interrelated. v. 1 the typical Johannine 'after these things' does not indicate a chronological but a thematic progression (cf. 6:1). The same formula 'to show oneself' as in 7:4 is now used in reference to the risen Christ (in 21:14 in the passive form). Strangely enough the word 'disciples' occurs seven times in vv. 1–14, matching the seven disciples named in v. 2. In 6:1 the Sea of Tiberias is mentioned as a synonym for the Sea of Galilee. v. 2, the use of 'together' (Gk. *homou*) is different from that at 4:36 and 20:4, but similar to Luke's in Acts. Three of the seven disciples occur in Lk 5:1–11: Peter, James, and John. Peter and Thomas have been important in the appearances in Jn 20. Nathanael who is mentioned in 1:45–51 is now presented as coming from Cana in Galilee, perhaps under the influence of the wedding in ch. 2. In the synoptic tradition James and John are often presented as sons of Zebedee (Mk 1:19–20 par.; 3:17 par.; 10:35 par.). With Simon and Andrew, who were named in Jn 1:35–42, they form a special group. We have seen that the anonymous disciple in 1:40–2 is best identified with John, one of the sons of Zebedee. He will be called the other disciple, or the one whom Jesus loved, in the rest of ch. 21. The two other disciples in 21:2 could then be Andrew and Philip (see 1:40–4; 6:7–8; 12:22). vv. 3–4, as in Lk 5:5 they have fished during the night. Why they do this after the appearances in Jerusalem has no importance for the author. Despite Greek *epi*, 'on' (the beach) in many MSS, *eis* is probably original, but has here the same meaning as *en* or *epi*.

In contrast to v. 12 the disciples at first do not recognize Jesus, though he has already revealed himself to them in Jerusalem. But in this case ch. 21 is not concerned to be consistent with ch. 20. vv. 5–6, Jesus addresses the disciples with tenderness, by using a diminutive form *paidia* (cf. 1 Jn 2:14, 18), similar to *teknia* in Jn 13:33 (and 1 Jn). The right side signifies blessing, prosperity. In Lk 5:4 Jesus says: 'Put out into the deep water'. Since the miraculous catch has missionary aspects both in Lk 5:10 and in Jn 21:15–17 'to haul in the fish' may allude to this symbolic meaning. In Lk 5:6–7 the partners in the other boat have to come and help. vv. 7–8, as in ch. 20 the beloved disciple understands more quickly than Peter. Respect for the Lord makes Peter do contradictory things: he puts on some clothes before he jumps into the water, probably in order to reach Jesus first (cf. Mt 14:28). The other disciples are only secondary characters, who go with Peter (v. 3) and drag the net (v. 8); vv. 9–10, in a subtle way the story of the catch moves into one of a meal, resembling Lk 24:41–3. But John does not explicitly say that the risen Lord himself ate: he only prepares the fish and the bread (v. 9) and gives them to the disciples (v. 13). v. 11, in the Greek text (*anebē*, 'went up') it is not clear whether Peter went back to the boat (NRSV; TOB; JB) or went up on the shore (Bultmann 1971). The 153 fish have been interpreted as the totality of the kinds of fish known at that time (Jerome, *In Ezekiel* 14. 47.9–12). A better explanation is to see 153 as the sum of all the numbers up to 17. Moreover there were 12 baskets filled with the fragments of the 5 loaves in 6:13, and that makes a total of 17 (cf. Lindars 1972). Other exegetes have proposed calculations based on *gematria*, the value of Greek or Hebrew letters, but this leads to arbitrary hypotheses. In any case, the evangelist symbolically suggests a totality of people recruited through missionary work. vv. 12–13, the author describes in concrete terms how the risen Lord gives the true bread from heaven that was mentioned in ch. 6 (see Hartman 1984). That the disciples do not dare ask Jesus contrasts with Thomas's behaviour in 20:24–9. v. 14, the evangelist frames vv. 2–13 by resuming v. 1 and adding that this revelation was the third one to the disciples (taking into account 20:19–23, 24–9). It is impossible to make this agree with Mk 16:7 and Mt 28:16–20, where the appearance in Galilee is the first one to the disciples (cf. Mk 16:14).

(21:15–23) The comparison between Peter and the beloved disciple which was hinted at in the first scene becomes explicit in the second one. vv. 15–17, the Greek sentence in v. 15 can be understood in three different ways: 'Do you love me more than you love these things?' (*toutōn* is then understood as a neuter pronoun); 'do you love me more than you love those (persons)?'; 'do you love me more than those do?' (this is best in the context). The three questions and the three answers are formulated differently and lead to a climax where Peter feels personally hurt. In a certain sense he makes up for his three-fold denial in 18:15–27. Jesus addresses Peter three times as 'son of John', just as he did in his first call (1:42). At that time Peter loved his master whom he was willing to follow (cf. also 13:36–8). There Jesus called him Cephas or Peter, 'rock' (from Aram. *kêfā'* and Gk. *Petra*). After the three denials Peter must three times confess his love if he is to be the shepherd of Jesus' flock. vv. 18–19, now Peter is ready to follow Jesus: as the

pastor of Jesus' sheep he will give his life, just as the Master himself laid down his life for them (cf. 10:15, 17–18). In v. 19 the author explains what Jesus prophetically formulates in v. 18: Peter will die on a cross (on Peter's death as martyr under Nero, see 1 *Clem.* 5:4). vv. 20–3, in a natural way Peter asks about the destiny of the beloved disciple, who was first explicitly mentioned as such in 13:23. The answer is even more mysterious than that concerning Peter: he will remain until Jesus comes. In his comment in vv. 23–4 the writer (probably a redactor) suggests that the beloved disciple will finally die, but that he will remain until Jesus comes. This has a symbolic meaning: his message will remain.

(21:24–5) Probably a redactor, who had already reworked the preceding verses, is responsible for this second conclusion to the gospel and perhaps also for 19:35 to which he alludes. By speaking of 'we' he designates the group who has approved the testimony of the beloved disciple, reflected in the gospel. The evangelist has transmitted the message and testimony of the beloved disciple, whom he wants the reader to identify with John, the son of Zebedee. As Christians must still wait for Jesus' return, the witness of the beloved disciple helps them even after his death and completes Peter's pastoral function. The words 'many other things' amplify what was said in the first conclusion in 20:30.

Appendix: 7:53–8:11

This passage, though canonical, does not properly belong to the Gospel of John, since it is missing in the oldest textual witnesses (e.g. P[66], P[75], Sinaiticus, Vaticanus, old translations). Most MSS that have the text put it after Jn 7:52, probably because of the words 'neither do I condemn you' in 8:11, which can be compared with 8:15. Some MSS, however, place it after 7:36, 7:44, or 21:25; the Ferrar group after Lk 21:38. Several witnesses mark the text as doubtful.

Papias seems to allude to it in *c*.130 CE, if we can trust Eusebius, *H.E* 3.39.17. In the fourth century we find it in a simpler form in the Syrian *Didascalia Apostolorum*, 8.2, and in Didymus' commentary on Eccl 7:21–2. The style reminds us of Luke and the story may be compared with Lk 7:36–50. It could be called a biographical apophthegm, in which a saying of Jesus has been developed into the story of a woman caught in adultery. Just as in the Synoptic Gospels, here Jesus does not reject the law directly but criticizes those who apply it mechanically. The law must be interpreted in the light of God's mercy for sinners.

(7:53–8:11) Jesus teaches in the temple as he does every day in Luke (Lk 19:47; 20:1; 21:37). He goes to the Mount of Olives as in Lk 21:37. Just as in the synoptic tradition, the scribes and the Pharisees suddenly come to test the Master. The woman seems to be married, as the text emphasizes that she had committed adultery. 8:3b–6, the legal basis of the accusers' action is not specified, but it may refer to Lev 20:10 and Deut 22:21. According to the Mishnah (*Sanh.* 7:4; 11:1), an adulterous betrothed girl should be stoned and a married woman strangled, but this legislation is later than the time of our text.

Jesus' silence makes the story more lively. Perhaps what he was writing referred to Jer 17:13: 'Those who turn away from me shall be written on the earth'. The accusers are not the appropriate persons to be judges. vv. 7–8, 'without sin' does not imply only sexual sins. Jesus' saying is in harmony with Mt 7:1: 'Do not judge, so that you may not be judged' (cf. Lk 6:37). The accusers have to face God's judgement upon their own sins. According to Deut 13:9 the witness should be the first to throw a stone. vv. 9–11, as the elders in the Sanhedrin have not been mentioned before, *presbyteroi* designates probably the oldest men. Perhaps there is even an allusion to the elders of Sus 28 and 41. With much skill the author has delayed the dialogue with the accused woman to the end of his story. In the synoptic tradition Jesus can forgive sins (cf. Mk 2:5; Lk 7:46). Something similar is suggested here, when Jesus says: 'from now on do not sin again' (cf. Jn 5:14), which supposes her contrition.

REFERENCES

Aurelius, E. (1988), *Der Fürbitter Israels: Eine Studie zum Mosebild im Alten Testament*, CBOTS 27 (Stockholm: Almqvist-Wiksell).

Barrett, C. K. (1978), *St John: An Introduction with Commentary and Notes on the Greek Text*. 2nd edn. (London: SPCK).

Benoit, P. (1961), *Exégèse et Théologie* (Paris: Cerf), i.

Betz, O. (1963), *Der Paraklet* (Leiden: Brill).

Birdsall, J. N. (1960), 'John X.29', *JTS* 11:342–4.

Black, M. (1967), *An Aramaic Approach to the Gospels and Acts*, 3rd edn. (Oxford: Clarendon).

Boismard, M. E., and Lamouille, A. (1977), *L'Évangile de Jean* (Paris: Cerf).

Borig, R. (1967), *Der wahre Weinstock*, SANT 16 (Munich: Kösel).

Brown, R. E. (1966), *The Gospel According to John, I–XII* (Garden City, NY: Doubleday).

—— (1970), *The Gospel According to John, XIII–XXI* (Garden City, NY: Doubleday).

—— (1979), *The Community of the Beloved Disciple* (New York: Paulist).

—— (1994), *The Death of the Messiah: From Gethsemane to the Grave: A Commentary on the Passion Narratives in the Four Gospels* (2 vols.; New York: Doubleday).

Bultmann, R. (1971), *The Gospel of John*, German original (Göttingen: Vandenhoeck & Ruprecht, 1941).

Culpepper, R. A. (1979–80), 'The Pivot of John's Prologue', *NTS* 27: 1–31.

de Jonge, M. (1972–3), 'Jewish Expectations about the Messiah according to the Fourth Gospel', *NTS* 19: 246–70.

Dewailly, L. M. (1969), *Jésus-Christ, Parole de Dieu*, 2nd edn. (Paris: Cerf).

Forkman, G. (1972), *The Limits of the Religious Community* (Lund: Gleerup).

Fortna, R. T. (1970), *The Gospel of Signs: A Reconstruction of the Narrative Source Underlying the Fourth Gospel* (Cambridge: Cambridge University Press).

—— (1977–8), 'Jesus and Peter at the High Priest's House: A Test Case for the Question between Mark's and John's Gospels', *NTS* 24: 371–83.

—— (1988), *The Fourth Gospel and Its Predecessor: From Narrative Source to Present Gospel* (Philadelphia: Fortress).

Franck, E. (1985), *Revelation Taught: The Paraclete in the Gospel of John* (Uppsala: Gleerup).

Giblin (1983), 'The Miraculous Crossing of the Sea (John 6, 16–21)', *NTS* 29: 96–103.

Gyllenberg, R. (1960), 'Cykliska element i Johannesevangeliets uppbyggnad', *TT* 65: 309–15.

Gyllenberg, R. (1980), *RBI:s Studiebibel, Nya testamentet* (Stockholm: Verbum), 177–9.

Hartman, L. (1984), 'An Attempt at a Text-Centered Exegesis of John 21', *ST* 38: 29–45.

—— (1987) 'Johannine Jesus-Belief and Monotheism', L. Hartman-B. Olsson, *Aspects on the Johannine Literature*, CBNTS 18, (Uppsala: Almqvist-Wiksell), 85–99.

Hengel, M. (1993), *Die johanneische Frage: Ein Lösungsversuch* (Tübingen: Mohr). ET, *The Johannine Question* (London: SCM, 1989).

Hooker, M. D. (1974–5), 'The Johannine Prologue and the Messianic Secret', *NTS* 21: 40–58.

Johansson, N. (1940), *Parakletoi: Vorstellungen von Fürsprechern für die Menschen vor Gott in der alttestamentlichen Religion, im Spätjudentum und Urchristentum* (Lund: Gleerup).

Kieffer, R. (1968), Au delà des recensions? L'Évolution de la tradition textuelle dans Jean VI, 52–71', CBNTS 3 (Lund: Gleerup).

—— (1985), 'L'Espace et le temps dans l'évangile de Jean', *NTS* 31: 393–409.

—— (1987–8), *Johannesevangeliet* (2 vols.; Uppsala: EFS).

—— (1989), *Le Monde symbolique de S. Jean*, Lectio divina, 137 (Paris: Cerf).

—— (1992), 'Jean et Marc: Convergences dans la structure et dans les détails', in A. Denaux (ed.), *John and the Synoptics*. BETL 101 (Leuven: Leuven University Press), 109–25.

Lagrange, M.-J. (1936), *Evangile selon saint Jean*, 6th edn. (Paris: Gabalda).

Lindars B. (1972), *The Gospel of John* (London: Oliphants).

Malatesta, E. (1971), 'The Literary Structure of John 17', *Bib.* 52: 190–214.

Miller, E. L. (1980), 'The Christology of John 8:25', *TZ* 36: 257–65.

Mlakuzhyil, G. (1987), *The Christocentric Literary Structure of the Fourth Gospel*, AnBib 117 (Rome: Pontifical Institute).

Neirynck, F. (1984a), 'John 4, 46–54: Sign Source and/or Synoptic Gospels?', *ETL* 60: 367–75.

—— (1984b), 'John and the Synoptics: The Empty Tomb Stories', *NTS* 30: 161–84.

—— (1990), 'John 21', *NTS* 36: 321–36.

Neyrey, J. (1982), 'The Jacob Allusions in John 1:51', *CBQ* 44: 586–605.

Olsson, B. (1974), *Structure and Meaning in the Fourth Gospel: A Text-Linguistic Analysis of John 2:1–11 and 4:1–42* (Lund: Gleerup).

Painter, J. (1980–1), 'The Farewell Discourses and the History of Johannine Christianity', *NTS* 27: 525–43.

Richter, G. (1967), *Die Fusswaschung im Johannesevangelium* (Regensburg: Pustet).

—— (1974), 'Zu den Tauferzählungen Mk 1:9–11 und Joh 1:32–34', *ZNW* 65: 43–54.

Rochais, G. (1985), 'La Formation du prologue (Jn 1, 1–18)', *ScEs* 37: 5–44, 161–87.

—— (1993), 'Jean 7: Une confrontation littéraire dramatique, à la manière d'un scénario', *NTS* 39: 355–78.

Schnackenburg R. (1977–9), *Das Johannesevangelium* (Fribourg), i–iii (i, 4th edn.; ii, 2nd edn.; iii, 3rd edn.). ET, *The Gospel According to St John* (3 vols.; New York: 1968–82).

Segalla, G. (1983), *La preghiera di Gesu al Padre (Giov. 17): Un addio missionario* Studi Biblici, 63 (Brescia: Paideia).

Stibbe, M. W. G. (1993), *John* (Sheffield: JSOT).

Walker, W. O. (1982), 'The Lord's Prayer in Matthew and John', *NTS* 28: 237–56.

61. The Four Gospels in Synopsis Henry Wansbrough

Outline

A. Gospel as a Literary Genre. 1. Mark opens with the words, 'The beginning of the gospel of Jesus Christ' (Mk 1:1). A modern reader would unhesitatingly see the writing that follows as the gospel of Jesus Christ. In fact the concept of 'gospel' is not without its problems. We shall begin with the name 'gospel' before going on to examine the use of the term.

The English word 'gospel' (originally 'godspell' or 'good tidings') is the translation of the Greek *euaggelion*, but it is not obvious that the writers of the four documents applied this term to their writings. Luke at any rate never uses the noun (except in Acts), though he frequently uses the corresponding verb for the activity of spreading the good news (e.g. 1:19; 4:18). He seems to consider his work rather in terms of a narrative (*diēgēsis*) or an orderly account (1:1–3). Both noun and verb are used frequently by Paul, who may rely on one or both of two backgrounds. In the religious cult of the emperors the term was used of a piece of imperial good news of salvation, such as a victory or the birth of an heir, which was flashed round the empire, and to which the various provinces, city-states, and other political units were expected to respond with congratulatory gifts. The elements of novelty, salvation, joy, and response, as well as the religious connotations, would have made the term a suitable one for Paul to use for 'my gospel' (Rom 16:25; Gal 1:11). Paul may also, however, be drawing on the use of the word in Isa 61:1, 'the Lord has anointed me to bring *good tidings* to the afflicted'. This usage may go back to the proclamation of Jesus himself; it certainly occurs on his lips in Mt 11:5 and Lk 4:18 (see Stuhlmacher 1983).

Neither Luke nor John uses the noun, and when it began to be used as a title of the four writings is disputed. Koester (1989: 380) holds that the term was 'always and everywhere understood as the proclamation of the saving message about Christ or the coming of the kingdom' until Marcion in the mid-second century applied it to the written works. In his six usages apart from the heading, Mark certainly uses the term for the proclamation of the saving message, so that in his first verse also it is reasonable to take it in this sense rather than as 'The beginning of the *written record*' (see MK 1:1–13). In Matthew the word is used twice for Jesus' own proclamation of the kingdom (4:23; 9:35) and twice with the addition of '*this* gospel' (24:14; 26:13); in the former case the whole gospel message seems to be meant, and in the latter Matthew may possibly intend to restrict Mark's meaning to the particular incident of the gospel message, the anointing at Bethany. Stanton (1992a), on the other hand, argues persuasively that usages of the term as early as the *Didache*, 8:2; 11:3; 15:3–4, seem to refer to our written gospel texts, and argues further that as soon as more than one of them existed they must have been known as something!

Finally it is important to realize that none of the four gospels originally included an attribution to an author. All were anonymous, and it is only from the fragmentary and enigmatic and—according to Eusebius, from whom we derive the quotation—unreliable evidence of Papias in 120/130 CE that we can begin to piece together any external evidence about the names of their authors and their compilers. This evidence is so difficult to interpret that most modern scholars form their opinions from the content of the gospels themselves, and only then appeal selectively to the external evidence for confirmation of their findings.

2. As recently as 1970 the type of writing now called 'gospel' was considered to be without parallel in the ancient world. Norman Perrin (1970–1: 4) could write assertively that it was 'the unique literary creation of early Christianity. This is a statement I would make with confidence... If we are to come to terms with this genre we must concentrate our attention upon the Gospel of Mark'. Perrin sees a gospel as being a narrative of an event from the past, in which interest and concerns of the past, present, and future have flowed together, since the events of Jesus' ministry are interpreted in the light of the writer's own time and of things expected of Jesus' future coming.

In 1987 Christopher Tuckett could, with misgivings, still give as the majority opinion the view that there was no close parallel to the genre of the gospels. In the last decade, however, it has become clear that the literary genre of 'gospel' can no longer be considered as completely unique. To enable a reader or listener to understand a document it must be possible to a certain extent to categorize it into a known type. Tuckett (1987: 75) wittily gives the example of 'Vicar gives directions to Queen? Just the opposite', to be understood as a newspaper headline or as a crossword puzzle clue for REV-ER-SE. The features of a particular genre of literature form a conventional set of expectations, a sort of implied contract with the reader that enables the reader to categorize the document. The expectations are not necessarily always identical in all respects with what the reader finds, but at least provide a family resemblance. Burridge (1992) has shown that the gospels fall within the varied and well-attested Graeco-Roman concept of biography. Of this genre there are many subdivisions, inevitably including cross-border borrowing with other genres, such as political propaganda, encomium, moralistic encouragement, and travelogue. Even religious biographies in the broad sense were not unknown. The respectful atmosphere found in the gospels, 'tinged with praise and worship' (ibid. 211) occurs also in such works as Tacitus' *Agricola* and Philo's *De vita Mosis*. What is, however, unique to the gospels, and constitutes them as an unprecedented subgroup, is the importance and salvific claim of their message, expressed most clearly by Jn 20:31, 'these things are written that you may believe . . . and that believing you may have life'. It is not, then, an unprecedented type of writing, so much as the conviction of the writers that their subject and message had the power to change the world for those who accepted them, that is unique. But this does not exclude the gospels from the broad category of Graeco-Roman biography.

B. The Basic Interrelationship of the Gospels. The three gospels of Matthew, Mark, and Luke are clearly related very closely to one another, much more closely than John is related to any of them. They share the same basic outline, roughly the same order of events, the same way of telling stories and relating sayings, and even the basically same portrait of the good news of the kingdom and its preaching by Jesus.

This similarity among the first three gospels is best seen by contrast to John. The geographical outline is different: in the first three gospels Jesus goes to Jerusalem only once during his ministry, for the final week, whereas in John he pays several visits to Jerusalem. The order of events is different, for example the cleansing of the temple comes early in John, introducing Jesus' ministry (Jn 2:13–22), whereas in the other three gospels it forms the climax (Mk 11:15–19). John relates many fewer miracles, but almost invariably these are developed by means of a subsequent long discourse of Jesus or by a controversy that brings out the sense and meaning of the event (for example the cure at the Pool of Bethesda continues into a discourse on the works of the Son, Jn 5; the multiplication of loaves flowers into the bread of life discourse, Jn 6:1–15, 22–66). While the Jesus of the first three gospels turns attention away from himself to the kingship of God, in John the kingship of God is mentioned only in 3:3–5; the Johannine Jesus teaches about *his* kingship only in 18:6, and otherwise concentrates rather on his gift of eternal life. In the first three gospels story-parables are an important vehicle of teaching, whereas the fourth gospel barely uses them, preferring instead extended images such as that of the Good Shepherd (Jn 10:1–18).

The similarity between the first three gospels may be roughly described in terms of the number of verses shared. Of Mark's 661 verses, some 80 per cent feature in Matthew and 60 per cent in Luke. Conversely, only three pericopes of Mark (the seed growing secretly, Mk 4:26–9, the healing of the deaf-mute, Mk 7:31–7, and the blind man of Bethsaida, Mk 8:22–6) have no equivalent in either Matthew or Luke. Time and again such long stretches show almost *verbatim* agreement between Matthew and Mark or Mark and Luke that some literary relationship at the textual level must be postulated between them. Similarly Matthew and Luke have some 220 verses in common, mostly of sayings-material, so that some literary relationship between these two is undeniable. The possibility of viewing these three gospels together has led to the appellation Synoptic Gospels, and the difficulty of

reaching an agreed solution to account for their interrelationship has been dubbed the 'synoptic problem'. The issue is so complicated that some scholars regard it as little more than an intellectual game. Brown (1997: 111) opines that 'most readers of the NT find the issue complex, irrelevant to their interests, and boring'.

Three proposed solutions to the synoptic problem will be outlined (C), which will be tested in a discussion of six pericopes (F–K).

C. Proposed Solutions to the Synoptic Problem. 1. The Griesbach Hypothesis. Truly scientific study of this problem did not begin until in 1776 J. J. Griesbach produced a critical edition of a Synopsis of the Gospels, printing the gospels in parallel columns and thus enabling the reader to see in detail the similarities and differences between them. His conclusion, published in 1789, was that Mark was nothing but a combination of Matthew and Luke. The same conclusion had been reached slightly earlier by the little-known Oxford scholar Henry Owen in 1764, so that this view is sometimes called the Owen–Griesbach hypothesis. It later fell into obscurity, but has been revived by William R. Farmer in 1964, and has since become known strictly as the Two-Gospel Hypothesis. For brevity and to avoid confusion it will here be named the Griesbach theory.

The theory is that the first gospel to be written was that of Matthew, the most Semitic of the gospels, written for Christians of Jewish extraction. Next, for Christians of Gentile origin, but still before the destruction of Jerusalem, Luke was written. Finally Mark combined the two. The fundamental argument for this hypothesis, both for Griesbach and for Farmer, lies in the order of pericopes. Wherever Mark departs from Matthew's order, he supports Luke's; if there is a difference between the order of Matthew and Luke, Mark zigzags between the two, following first one, then the other. In addition, the supporters observe, Mark always proceeds forward, never turning back in the order established by Matthew and Luke. These observations are correct, but are not enough to prove the point that Mark combines Matthew and Luke, for in the same way the order of Matthew and Luke can be explained at least as well (see C.2) if Mark is taken as the starting-point.

Support for the theory is claimed also from the material within pericopes. Mark has many double expressions, of which half occur in Matthew and half in Luke. The paradigm case is Mk 1:32, 'That evening, at sunset', where Matthew has in the corresponding passage (8:16) 'That evening', and Luke (4:40) 'when the sun was setting'. The explanation given by the Griesbach theory is that Mark takes one phrase from each of the other gospels and combines them. There is a number of instances of this phenomenon (e.g. Mk 1:42, 'the leprosy left him, and he was made clean'; Mk 8:3, 'his leprosy was made clean'; Lk 5:13, 'the leprosy left him'; similarly at Mk 10:29, 'for my sake and for the sake of the good news').

The Griesbachian explanation, however, is not compelling. Opponents claim, with good evidence, that duality of this kind is a feature of Mark's own style, specifically a feature of his oral style, in which a certain repetitiveness aids the hearer (see E.1). Rather than Mark combining his predecessors, he serves as a quarry for his successors; the phenomenon noted could equally well be the result of Matthew taking one of Mark's two elements and Luke taking the other. It might seem that here again the argument may run either way, except for another observation. On many occasions Matthew keeps both Mark's elements while Luke has only one (Mk 4:5, 'other seed fell on rocky ground where it did not have much soil'; Mt 13:5 has both elements; Lk 8:6 has only 'some fell on the rock'); on many occasions Luke keeps both elements while Matthew has only one (Mk 4:39, 'the wind ceased and there was a dead calm'; Luke, 'they ceased and there was a calm'; Mt 8:26 has only 'and there was a dead calm'; similarly at Mk 6:36); on many occasions Matthew and Luke choose the same half of the double expression (Mk 2:25, 'were hungry and in need of food'; Mt 12:3 and Lk 6:3, 'were hungry'; similarly at Mk 3:26; 12:23). Double expressions occur also in Mark even in those few passages where there is no parallel in Matthew or Luke (Mk 4:28, the double 'head'; Mk 8:24, 25, the double 'looked' in each verse). How widespread a feature it is of Mark's own style has been fully documented by Neirynck (1988). There is therefore no need to postulate that it derives from the combination by Mark of Matthew and Luke.

The greatest difficulty for the Griesbach theory is, however, why Mark should have written a gospel (and why the church should have accepted it) in which he deliberately omitted so much that is valuable: the infancy stories, the beatitudes, the Lord's prayer, the resurrection appearances, and many other important and favourite passages which had already been included in Matthew and Luke.

2. The Two-Source Theory. Since it was extensively proposed by C. Lachmann in 1835, seconded by C. G. Wilke and H. Weisse in 1838, the Two-Source theory has won overwhelming acceptance, at least as a working hypothesis. It still holds the dominant position in NT scholarship. The theory is that Mark is the first gospel, and was used independently by Matthew and Luke, neither of whom knew each other's texts. The large quantity of material shared by Matthew and Luke (but not by Mark), mostly sayings material, derives from a common source. Since an article by J. Weiss in 1890 this common source has been known as 'Q' (Neirynck 1978; 1979). The acceptance of this common source has been greatly assisted by the mention by the early second-century Bishop Papias (quoted by Eusebius) of a collection of Sayings of the Lord in Aramaic made or used by Matthew. Although few scholars accept all Papias' evidence, his mention of the collection of sayings has been widely taken to support this theory.

Despite the hypothetical nature of the very existence of Q, studies have progressed which have established what this document would have been like, e.g. Piper (1995), magisterially summed up by Kloppenborg (2000). It was caricatured by Meier (1994: 181) as a 'grab bag', without any coherent theology or genre. Its most striking feature was, however, that it contained no account of the Passion and Resurrection of Jesus, and indeed showed no interest in these events, containing no hints that they were to occur. Kloppenborg suggests that Paul's stress on these events could be a deliberate corrective to their neglect in this very early document. The most important stress is on the threat of the coming judgement; this frames the whole document (Luke 3:7–9, 16–17 and 19:12–27; 22:28–30), as well as many of the fourteen sub-units isolated by Kloppenborg. Combined with this is a 'deuteronomic' criticism of the continual rejection of the prophets (Luke 6:23; 11:47–51; 13:34–5), and a promise of fulfilment through 'the one who is to come' (Luke 7:18–23; 13:35). Many of the sections isolated show a common structure, beginning with programmatic sayings, introducing a series of imperatives and concluding with affirmations of the importance of its message (Luke 6:21–49; 9:57–10:24). Kloppenborg (2000: 187) likens it to the 'widely attested genre in Near Eastern literature', the instruction or sapiential discourse. According to some scholars (e.g. Burton Mack) the principal function of its authors is social critique and the destabilization of a corrupt society, after the manner of itinerant Cynic teachers. There is reference to the rule of God, but—by contrast to the canonical gospels—there is no interest in exegesis of the Torah. This carefully elaborated characterization is, however, obviously secondary to proof of the existence of Q. The strongest arguments for this theory are the order of pericopes, the detailed editing, and the mutual independence of Matthew and Luke.

With Mark as starting-point it is possible to explain the order of pericopes in Matthew and Luke. However the crucial point here (by contrast to the Griesbachian zigzag claim, see B) is that whenever they diverge from Mark's order it is possible to give clear and plausible reasons for this divergence. Matthew follows Mark's order of pericopes strictly except when he is composing two series, the collection of miracles in Mt 8–9 and the discourse on mission in Mt 10. For these two collections he takes material that occurs later in Mark (Mk 1:40–5; 3:9–13; 3:13–19; 4:35–5:43; 13:9–13). It is quite clear that Matthew is a careful and orderly teacher who likes to assemble into complete collections all the material on one subject. Thus all the changes in Matthew's order are explained as anticipations in accordance with his teaching methods. Luke's changes of the Markan order are not to be explained so simply and schematically, for Luke is far more creative in his writing and independent of his sources than is Matthew. So he puts the rejection of Jesus at Nazareth (Mk 6:1–6) earlier and builds it up into the programmatic opening speech with which Jesus begins his ministry at Nazareth (Lk 4:16–30). On the other hand Luke postpones until 5:1–11 the call of the first disciples (Mk 1:16–20) and builds it into an important lesson in discipleship (see F). Luke's most far-reaching change in order is the construction of the great journey to Jerusalem (9:51–18:14), by which he locates much of Jesus' teaching on the final journey to his death at Jerusalem. All other distracting geographical names are there suppressed, to subserve the typical Lukan concentration on Jerusalem, where Jesus will die as a prophet and from where the gospel will spread to the ends of the earth. Luke's order varies so widely and imaginatively from that of his predecessors that Luke's supposed rearrangement of Q's order was mocked in 1924 by B. H. Streeter as that of a 'crank', a charge disputed by Goulder (1984). An alternative explanation of Luke's order is given in the same volume by H. B. Green (1984). A full explanation of the changes in order by Matthew and Luke, on the hypothesis of Markan priority, is given by Tuckett (1984a).

The argument from the detailed editing can hardly be briefly summarized. Some impression of it will be given by the pericopes discussed below (F–K). The outlines, however, are:

(a) There are numerous occasions when both Matthew and Luke improve the grammar and style of Mark's unsophisticated Greek; it seems perverse to argue in the opposite direction that Mark deliberately roughens a more cultured presentation.

(b) Some features of Markan style and composition appear also in Matthew and Luke where and only where Mark uses them. It is more reasonable to suppose that Matthew and Luke derived them from Mark than that Mark adopted *all* the instances from both Matthew and Luke. One example of this is the Markan afterthought-explanation with a past tense of *eimi* and *gar* ('for they were fishermen'); this is a feature of Markan style which occurs in Matthew and Luke only in passages parallel to those of Mark: in Mk 2:15; 5:42; 16:4 the construction occurs only in Mark; in Mk 1:16, 22; 6:48; 14:40 it is paralleled in Matthew, in Mk 10:22 it is paralleled in both Matthew and Luke.

(c) There are several theological differences between Mark, Matthew, and Luke which may perhaps point (though uncertainly) in the direction of a development from Mark to Matthew and Luke rather than in the opposite direction. Thus Matthew and Luke show a distinctly more explicit Christology than Mark. Again, Mark is highly, even shockingly, critical of the disciples' lack of faith and understanding; Matthew and Luke both weaken this criticism, in a way that might be expected to have occurred at a time when reverence for the first leaders of Christianity was increasing.

The mutual independence of Matthew and Luke is a point crucial for establishing the extent and indeed the existence of Q. If Luke knew Matthew (or vice versa), the links between Matthew and Luke can be accounted for without the intervention of any Q. The large number of minor agreements (some calculate there are as many as 1,000) between Matthew and Luke against Mark demands some explanation in the sources. It may, however, be approached at various levels:

1. The minor agreements. In texts of this length it is quite possible that many agreements may occur where Matthew and Luke make the same change to their version of Mark by sheer coincidence. This will especially be the case where they share the same principles, either linguistic (objection to Mark's primitive historic present and wearisomely repetitive conjunction *kai/kai euthus* = 'and/and immediately') or theological (increasingly explicit Christology or reverence for the disciples). It cannot be considered surprising that two Christian writers sometimes share the same reaction to a primitive Christian text. It requires explanation only if the identical expression of this becomes remarkable by its frequency or its extent. There can be no verdict on the likely frequency of such similarity, and little agreement on the significance of individual cases. The most striking single case is Mt 26:68 ∥ Mk 14:65 ∥ Lk 22:64, where both Matthew and Luke have 'Who is it that struck you?', lacking in Mark. So difficult is this of explanation that determined advocates of the theory that Matthew and Luke are totally independent of each other sometimes turn to the desperate expedient of declaring all the MSS corrupt. There are, however, scholars who are prepared to rebut the claim for each passage that Luke knew Matthew, e.g. Tuckett (1984b). Another significant minor agreement is in the order of pericopes: an important support for the Q-theory is the claim that the Q-material always occurs in different places in Matthew and Luke. But in three instances both these gospels have material in the same sequence: the Baptist's preaching of repentance (Mt 3:7–10; Lk 3:7–9) comes between the same triple-tradition pericopes; the testing in the desert (Mt 4:1–11; Lk 4:1–13) occurs in both between the baptism and the first proclamation in Galilee; the parable of the leaven (Mt 13:33; Lk 13:20–1) in both follows the parable of the mustard seed.

2. Clusters of agreement between Matthew and Luke occur in a limited number of pericopes. Since B. H. Streeter it has been accepted that there are passages where the agreements between Matthew and Luke against Mark are so pronounced that there must be literary contact between them apart from Mark, either directly or at least through Q; these are known as 'Mark–Q overlaps'. Streeter listed five major passages (John's preaching, the temptation, the mustard seed, collusion with Satan, and commissioning the twelve) and eleven others where this Mark–Q overlap occurs. In all these passages put together there is a total of 50 verses in which Streeter finds *verbatim* agreement between Mark and Q. This causes two major difficulties:

(a) The source-question is therefore in fact simply pushed one stage further back: what is the literary relationship between Mark and Q? This widespread agreement must be explained; *verbatim* agreement in 50 verses must presuppose some literary connection. If Mark used Q for some passages, why did he not use Q more widely, especially to include some of those precious passages mentioned in c.1? Was only a partial edition of Q available to him? The number of unknown documents begins to proliferate, for example by different editions of Q. Alternatively, if the whole of Q was available to Mark, why did he omit so much?

(b) While it is accepted that on many occasions both Matthew and Luke show major inventiveness, editing their sources with imagination and steady theological purpose, on these occasions their inventiveness is assumed to have deserted them. For instance, in the case of the mustard seed, they have carefully stitched together the versions of Mark and Q simply for the sake of using both versions without any large theological advantage.

3. Recourse to other editions of Mark is a possible expedient to account for a number of agreements, both positive and negative, between Matthew and Luke against Mark. If both Matthew and Luke include a phrase absent from Mark (a positive minor agreement), it may be that they had an earlier text of Mark that included this phrase. There was therefore an earlier version of Mark (Proto-Mark) on which both Matthew and Mark drew.

Conversely, if Matthew and Luke both lack a phrase, it may be that the phrase was added to Mark after they used that gospel. Sanders (1969) offers a list of such suggested additions to Mark after it had been used by Matthew and Luke, e.g. 'and Andrew with James and John' in Mk 1:29; or 'carried by four of them' in Mk 2:3; or 'and there he prayed' in Mk 1:35, a phrase that would have fitted Luke's emphasis on prayer, but is lacking in Luke's parallel passage; or Mk 2:27. This 'Deutero-Mark' theory will explain many negative minor agreements (that is, where Matthew and Luke agree on omitting a Markan phrase), and the lack of phrases in Matthew or Luke that might be expected to appeal to the particular evangelist. The suggestion is that Mark is the first evangelist, but these phrases were simply not contained in the edition of Mark used by the later two. The difficulty about this theory is that many of the phrases are consistent with the style and methods widespread in and characteristic of the main part of the gospel. If they are consistent with the author's style, it seems unjustified to attribute them to a second editor. Deutero-Mark is, however, a possible way to evade some of the difficulties of the minor agreements.

The suggestion that a Matthean form (Proto-Matthew) existed before Mark is, however, attractive as a solution to some passages where Matthew seems more correct (or more faithful to the Jewish background) than Mark. For instance, in the pericope on plucking corn on the sabbath, Matthew's version makes far more sense than Mark's. In Mark's version (2:23) the disciples simply tear up the corn to make a path; this leads to a badly focused legal dispute. In Matthew's version (12:1) they pluck ears of corn to assuage their hunger as they pass through the field, in accordance with Deut 23:26; this gives rise to a good legal dispute about threshing on the sabbath. On the Proto-Mark theory Matthew would be drawing on an earlier version of Mark, which was later misunderstood and simplified by an author unfamiliar with niceties of Jewish law; finally Matthew would have simplified the legal issues and adopted some expressions from the final edition of Mark. The question is whether it is more economical to postulate this earlier version of the gospel, or to suppose that Matthew used Mark, but correctly spelt out and narrated the legal situation that alone makes sense of Mark's story. (However, Casey (1998) maintains that Mk 2:23–3:6 is itself the translation of a very ancient Aramaic document.)

Similarly, in the story of the empty tomb, the women's motive in Mt 28:1 (to pay a pious visit to the tomb) accords with Jewish custom, and with good sense, better than the motive in Mk 16:1 (to anoint an already decaying body, blocked off by a great stone). Has Matthew made better sense out of Mark's version, or has Mark misunderstood and simplified the story from an earlier version used by Matthew?

3. The Multiple-Level Hypothesis. This theory, put forward by M.-E. Boismard and other distinguished members of the French Biblical School in Jerusalem, goes a step (or several steps) beyond the theories of Proto-Mark and Deutero-Mark just outlined. It is little known beyond the French-speaking world, but is nevertheless important. The basis of the theory is that all the hypotheses hitherto put forward are too simplistic. There were several basic versions of the gospel material, which have interacted on one another at more than one stage of the development of the tradition to its final form. Traces of such development may also be garnered from divergent, non-standard quotations of the gospels in very early church fathers. These are often attributed to faulty citations by the fathers from memory, but in this theory it is suggested that they are genuine relics of earlier versions of the gospels.

Boismard (1972) holds that there are four documents at the basis of the tradition. One (A) is a Palestinian version, stemming from Judeo-Christian circles. The second (B) is a Hellenistic reinterpretation for use in the non-Jewish Christian circles. The third (C) is less well defined, an independent version, probably of Palestinian origin. Document A gave

rise to an intermediate version of Matthew, into which fed also Q (possibly not a single document itself). This Intermediate-Matthew had no contact with B, C, or the Markan tradition. It was only subsequently that large sections of this tradition were replaced by sections drawn from an intermediate version of Mark, and further editorial changes were made by an editor whose style is in some ways remarkably similar to Luke. Such 'criss-crossing' is shown by the appearance in one gospel of expressions characteristic of another. It may well be attributed to the influence of each gospel on the others at a late stage of the tradition.

Boismard's method is to look for a pure and simple form of a story, eliminating the least illogicality or unevenness. He attributes any illogicality or development to a written source, until the characteristics of the final authors are reached. One example of this method may be seen in his treatment of the return of the apostles (Mk 6:30–4 and par.). Mt 14:13 has the same pattern as Mt 12:15 and 19:1–2, which shows that it stems originally from an earlier version of Matthew, and has received further Markan vocabulary at a later stage. According to one version (mostly vv. 32–3) Jesus goes away to a deserted place, where the local people recognize him and hurry to meet him; this comes from Document A. According to another version (mostly vv. 31–2) the crowd is already present and sees Jesus and the apostles depart in a boat; this version is from Document B. It is, of course, no longer possible to separate out the two versions completely now that they have been combined.

This particular case (which Boismard claims is a strong one for his schema) presents difficulties for the Two-Source Theory, since there are three positive minor agreements in two verses of Matthew and Luke against Mark: 'withdrew', 'the crowds followed him', and the mention of healing; Matthew and Luke also agree in three omissions against Mark. It does therefore seem likely that there is some direct relationship between Matthew and Luke. But there is no need at the documentary stage for the complications suggested by Boismard. Such a criss-crossing process may well have occurred at the stage of oral tradition. It fits better the more fluid consistency of a body of oral tradition, passing backwards and forwards between many witnesses.

4. Mark as the Single Source. This final theory is that of Goulder (1974; 1989), a revival and elaboration of a position put forward by Austin Farrer in 1955, 'On Dispensing with Q'. Goulder holds that Mark is the first gospel. Matthew's only written source was Mark, which he edited and developed through his own theological resources. The material in Matthew which is not drawn from Mark shows a consistency of method and approach that can only be the stamp of one mind. This approach extends to the material taken over from Mark, to the material shared with Luke, and to the material proper to Matthew alone. The elements said to be characteristic of Q (a concern for eschatology, the threat of judgement, the need to bring forth good fruit, the importance of the Christian community) are in fact characteristic of Matthew, and expressed in Matthean language, so that there is no need to postulate (let alone reconstruct) any such hypothetical source. Two reservations about the original statement of Goulder's theory have been repeatedly and strongly expressed: Matthew should not be tied to any theoretical arrangement of a lectionary, which is too nebulous. Nor should Matthew's process of elaborating Mark be termed 'midrash', for midrash can be done only on a sacred text, and Mark has not yet this status. Neither of these reservations affects the main thrust of the theory, though it would certainly strengthen it if it could be shown that Matthew was doing only what many other midrashists had done.

In order to show the uniformity of Matthew's style and theology Goulder 'finger-prints' Matthew not only by means of vocabulary, but principally by means of the consistent use of imagery and patterns of speech (e.g. pairs or double pairs of images, pairs of parables, consistent use of contrast in parables; such contrast is a feature of all Matthew's own story-parables, and is also introduced into parables taken over from Mark), see E.2.

The same finger-printing technique is applied to Luke. The new material in Luke is largely parables and other stories, and in these not only a characteristic vocabulary but also a characteristic method of storytelling can be charted (entries and exits, conversation, soliloquies of the chief character, varied, lively, and often disreputable personalities). Vocabulary, techniques of storytelling, and recognizable theological interests (concern for the poor and underprivileged, stress on the need for repentance) are discernible throughout, not only in passages proper to Luke but also in Luke's treatment of passages shared with Mark and Matthew. Once Q has been set aside, the way lies open to explain the many agreements between Matthew and Luke, which remain such a bugbear for the Two-Source Theory, by Luke's knowledge and use of Matthew.

Three major difficulties remain with this theory. The first is the different position of much of the teaching material in Luke from that of Matthew. The Sermon on the Mount becomes the Sermon on the Plain. Matthew's long, carefully structured discourses are cut up and cut down. Goulder explains this by Luke's theory that only a limited amount of teaching can be digested at one time; Luke therefore discards some material and redistributes other. Luke, in any case, shows no hesitation in relocating material (the rejection at Nazareth, the call of the disciples) if it suits his purpose. The second difficulty is that the theory attributes considerable freedom of inventiveness to both Matthew and Luke. This is particularly true in the parables, where both evangelists would have introduced whole stories which they did not receive from the Jesus-tradition. However, Goulder shows convincingly how Luke consistently builds his own stories out of existing hints. For example, Luke's parable of the prodigal son (Lk 15:11–32) is a characteristically Lukan version of Matthew's parable of the two sons (Mt 21:28–30). Luke's infancy stories could be his own retelling, according to his own theology, interests, and style, of minimal data derived from Matthew's. Similarly Luke's story of the ten lepers (Lk 17:11–19) could well be Luke's own remoulding, according to his own techniques and theology, of the healing of the leper in Mk 1:40–5. The third difficulty, somewhat intangible, is the doubt whether such a careful, modern, scissors-and-paste method of editing two previous texts may be postulated of an ancient author. This difficulty is, however, common to almost all explanations of the interrelationships of the gospels. It may be less extreme if the texts on which the later evangelists worked are regarded

not as written documents but as texts held firmly and word for word in the memory, and thus allowing greater flexibility. However, proponents of the Two-Source Theory point out that the first two of these (the Baptist's preaching of repentance, and the testing in the desert) could scarcely occur anywhere else, leaving only the third case to be explained as a partial coincidence.

The attack on Goulder's theory has increased in intensity during the last decade. A particularly strong attack is mounted by Tuckett (1995: 31–45). Principally, Goulder's answer to Streeter's argument has been exploded. Streeter argued that it would be 'the order of a crank' if Luke meticulously followed Mark's order but changed the order of almost every pericope which he took from Matthew. Luke seems carefully to have scraped off every Matthean addition to Mark and then inserted many of them (but not all, e.g. Mt 12:5–7; 16:16–19; 27:19, 24, and why not?) elsewhere. Goulder's explanation of Luke's break-up of the long Matthean discourses—that Luke considered they provided too much richness to be digested at a single gulp—flies in the face of the long speeches in Luke 21, Acts 7 and elsewhere. Goodacre (1996) also casts doubt on Goulder's central vocabulary argument: are the 'Matthean' words which Luke is claimed to have adopted indeed specifically Matthean? In a number of cases it can be argued equally well that the borrowing is in the opposite direction.

D. John and the Synoptic Gospels. 1. The basic differences between John and the Synoptic Gospels have been outlined at the beginning of this article. The relationship between them continues, however, to be highly disputed, several different opinions being put forward. In 1974 Norman Perrin held that John must have known the Gospel of Mark directly. In Denaux (1992) Rene Kieffer held that John knew Mark or a source very similar to Mark, while Frans Neirynck argues for the direct textual dependence of Jn 5:1–18 on Mark. On the other hand in the same work Peder Borgen maintains that John is not using the actual text of the Synoptics, but rather an underlying oral tradition which they have in common; he compares John's use of the synoptic tradition in several passages to Paul's use in 1 Cor 11:23–34 of the tradition of the institution of the eucharist reflected also in Mk 14:22–5.

In detail the links between John and the synoptics are diverse.

(*a*) Some stories are closely similar in both John and the Synoptics, including verbal and structural similarities, though reworked to express the special theology of each author (e.g. the multiplication of loaves and the walking on the waters, see J.1–3).

(*b*) In other cases Johannine miracle-stories are based on stories of the same type as the synoptic stories: controversial healings on the sabbath, Jn 5 and 9, a dead person, Lazarus, is raised to life, as Jairus' daughter or the son of the widow of Nain are in the Synoptics. It may be argued that in John the raising of Lazarus is so crucial to the decision to get rid of Jesus that, had it been known to the synoptic tradition, it could not have been omitted.

(*c*) There are sayings so close that they may simply be different translations of the same original (e.g. Jn 1:26–7; 2:19 compared to Mt 3:11 and Mk 14:58 respectively). In such cases the very form of the saying may be affected by the theology of the writer, and its positioning and use can certainly impart to it a different force.

(*d*) Some sayings in John appear in the form of stories in the Synoptics (e.g. Jn 12:27 and the prayer of Jesus in the Garden, see K.5). The saying of Jn 3:3, 5, is very similar to Mt 18:3; it is the only mention of 'the kingdom' in John, and makes the same point as the Matthew-saying. In the passion narrative John has no scene corresponding to the decision of the Sanhedrin in Mark/Matthew to deliver Jesus to Pilate, but there may be traces of the same discussion and decision in the meeting of the chief priests and Pharisees related in Jn 11:47–53.

A special link between Luke and John is apparent. Luke and John share several omissions from the Mark–Matthew tradition (e.g. the mention of the Baptist baptizing Jesus). Some passages show a close relationship between Luke and John (the call of the disciples in Lk 5:1–11 and Jn 21, see F.5; the anointing in Lk 7:36–50). The link between John and Luke is clearest in the passion and resurrection narrative. Normally it is assumed that, if there is any direct dependence, it is John who is dependent on Luke. It has also, however, been argued by Lamar Cribbs (1971) that dependence goes in quite the opposite direction, and that Luke depends on John. There is a remarkable series of 20 passages where Luke departs from the Mark–Matthew tradition precisely to agree with John. It remains, however, most probable that John's link with Luke, as with Mark and Matthew, remains at the oral level (see J.1).

E. The Features of the Several Gospels Compared. In recent years scholars have devoted considerable attention to discerning the features proper to each evangelist, both in style and in theology. Such study cannot be divorced from the synoptic problem, that is, from the question of the order in which the gospels were written. Obviously features verbal, linguistic, and theological, present in both Matthew and Mark, will owe their origin to whichever of the two has been found to be the earlier, being borrowed thence by the later writer.

Word-lists have long been published, such as those of Hawkins (1909). His criterion for a word characteristic of Matthew and Luke is that the word occur at least four times in that gospel (three times in the case of Mark) and at least twice as often (in the case of Mark, more often) than in the other two Synoptic Gospels together. It has, however, been objected that mere frequency is no indication of origin, for a particular word found in a gospel may take another author's fancy, in which case the derivative author may use frequently a word originally derived from another evangelist, who uses the word only once or twice. Frequency of usage on its own is therefore no criterion of origin, particularly since Matthew and Luke are roughly twice as long as Mark. More progress may be made by means of particular usages of words, such as Mark's repeated transitional phrases, 'and immediately' and 'again'. It has proved possible to establish clusters of linguistic usage associated with such phrases by which Mark structures his stories. So, starting from Mark's highly characteristic and unusual use of 'again' to refer back to a previous incident, Peabody (1987) established that the same hand is responsible for the composition of the whole of Mk 1:16–4:1.

1. Mark. *Narrative Style.* A whole series of features in Mark may be connected to his distinctively oral style of storytelling.

On the grammatical level these include parataxis instead of syntaxis (a series of parallel short sentences, where a more literary writer might use subordinate clauses) and the frequent historical present (which often disappears in translation, and is often 'corrected' by Matthew and Luke). On a more stylistic level Markan duality has been thoroughly documented: Mark's thought often proceeds by two steps, the second frequently defining and focusing the first, 'That evening, at sundown' (1:32), 'in the morning, a great while before day' (1:35), 'the leprosy left him and he was made clean' (1:42). This duality shows also in the frequent double questions ('Do you not yet perceive or understand?, 8:17) and double commands ('Peace! Be still!', 4:39, or 'Take heed, beware!', 8:15). Another frequent oral technique is the afterthought explanation with 'for': 'for it was very large' (16:4), 'for they were afraid' (16:8). These are means by which the oral storyteller imparts his information gradually, at a pace at which it can be absorbed.

Two other oral techniques deserve mention, the frequent triple repetition to stress important points (the three great prophecies of the passion, Jesus' triple return to the sleeping disciples in Gethsemane, the triple accusation of Jesus before the high priest, Peter's triple denial, Pilate's triple appeal to the people in his attempt to set Jesus free), and Mark's knack of focusing his audience's attention on one object easily visualized: Jesus in the boat 'asleep on the cushion' (4:38) or John's 'head on a platter' (6:28). It is these techniques that make Mark such a superb and memorable storyteller.

Mark's Irony. Perhaps the most important feature of Mark's style of writing from the theological point of view is his consistent use of irony. His storytelling operates on two levels, so that events have for the informed reader a sense which the actors in the drama do not comprehend. From the beginning the reader knows the identity of Jesus (1:1; and the voice from heaven at the baptism, in Mark addressed to Jesus, not the onlookers, 1:11), while the actors in the story discover it only gradually. Ironically, it is the blind men at Bethsaida (8:25) and Jericho (10:47) who see clearly who Jesus is, while even in his confession at Caesarea Philippi Peter earns a rebuke for his lack of understanding (8:33). In the passion story this irony reaches a climax, as Jesus is repeatedly mocked for falsely claiming to be what he in fact is: a prophet (14:65) even while his prophecy of Peter's denial is being fulfilled, king (15:18), and saviour (15:31). Such irony serves both to drive home the lessons of the story and to bring readers to examine their own positions and commitment.

Education Levels. Despite, therefore, Mark's often inelegant and popular language, the artistry of composition and arrangement shown by his work is evidence of a considerable degree of education. In the first century primary education was widespread, and at this level, or at any rate before embarking on higher education in rhetoric, children were taught to expand, contract, reform, and refute passages handed to them. It can no longer be considered acceptable to categorize the earliest Christians as exclusively uneducated riff-raff of the slave classes. Luke (especially in Acts) is perhaps overanxious to emphasize the respectable status of those who listened to and were attracted by Paul's message, but the evidence of Paul's letters shows that the community had considerable resources. They were able to travel, own slaves, eat meat, offer their houses for meetings, behave arrogantly and unfeelingly towards less wealthy members. Meeks (1983) opines that the most active and prominent members of Paul's circle were upwardly mobile. There is no reason to suppose that such a group would have selected a primitive ignoramus to write the gospel, or would have accepted it if one had done so.

The Failure of the Disciples. One of the most notable features of Mark's gospel is its criticism of the disciples. They initially respond with unhesitating obedience (1:16–20), and are congratulated as the grain giving a good yield (4:8) and for their first mission (6:30–1), but they continually fail to understand. They fail to rely on Jesus (4:38–40). They are sarcastic towards him (6:37). Time after time he rebukes their lack of understanding (7:18; 8:17; 8:29–33). In the first half of the gospel they are thrice rebuked on the lake for their lack of faith or understanding; in the second half of the gospel, at each of the three great prophecies of the passion they fail to understand that Jesus must suffer and that the disciple must share the lot of the Master. Finally when it comes to the passion they all desert Jesus. They have left all to follow Jesus; now the young man in the garden leaves all, even his makeshift clothing, to escape (14:52). Despite his earlier protestations of loyalty Peter thrice denies his Master, just as Jesus thrice stands up to his accusers. That these instances of failure are not mere historical reportage but bear Mark's emphasis is shown by the fact that they are all shot through with the colouring of his personal style such as dualism and triple repetition.

Various explanations have been offered for Mark's insistence on the disciples' failure. Weeden (1968) suggested that Mark was concerned to correct a group of Christians who saw Jesus only as a miracle-worker and undervalued the importance of his passion. Best (1986) saw a pedagogical element, Mark hinting how hard it was to assimilate the full message of Jesus. A feature of the gospel possibly related to, and contrasting with, the failure of the disciples is the success and praise of those who take the initiative in approaching Jesus: the Syro-Phoenician woman (7:25–30), the father of the epileptic boy (9:18), Bartimaeus (10:46–52), the woman at Bethany (14:9). Mark may be pointing the lesson that a first approach to Jesus is easy enough, but that enduring commitment brings its own difficulties. At any rate the gospel must be reacting to a testing situation of the persecution of Christians in which some (perhaps even some of the leaders of the community) have failed to understand that suffering for the sake of the gospel is an integral part of discipleship.

The Kingship of God. The focus of Jesus' proclamation of the Good News in Mark is, however, the kingdom, or rather kingship, of God. This is the object of his first proclamation, the conclusion of the Markan introduction (1:15). The proclamation is closely followed by Jesus' first miracle, the expulsion of an unclean spirit (1:21–8). As Jesus interprets his power over evil spirits as being a sign of the triumph of the kingdom of God over the kingdom of Satan (3:23–4) his miracles of healing may also be understood as a sign of the advent of God's kingship and rule, the triumph of God over evil, so long awaited in Judaism. From the first teaching of John the Baptist

(1:3) Mark has made clear that acceptance of this sovereignty of God will require a conversion and reorientation of life, though he is far less explicit than Matthew (e.g. the Sermon on the Mount) about the details of conduct required. There is a certain tension between two aspects, whether the kingship of God is already activated or is still to come. As Jesus' passion and resurrection approach, Mark gives a series of sayings that suggest that in some sense these events will bring the kingdom in power (9:1; 14:25, 62). At the same time the eschatological discourse leaves no doubt that all is not yet accomplished, and there is still to occur an overwhelming 'coming of the Son of Man in power' (13:26), preceded by a final great persecution of the disciples as they proclaim the Good News to all the nations (13:10).

The Person of Jesus. Reliance on the person of Jesus is the central condition for acceptance of God's sovereignty. The story Mark tells may be seen as an unveiling of the mystery of who Jesus is. The reader is told succinctly at the start that he is Messiah and Son of God (1:1). Through Markan irony (see above) the actors in the drama discover only painfully and slowly who Jesus is. But the believing reader, already enjoying knowledge of the resurrection, also shares in this discovery, learning as Mark's story unfolds what these titles mean. The reader benefits from the recognition of Jesus by the voice from heaven at the baptism (1:11) and the transfiguration (9:7) and by the unclean spirits as they are expelled (acknowledgements seemingly unnoticed by those present, 3:11; 5:7), but this knowledge is still denied to those who encounter Jesus. No human witness of Jesus reaches full acknowledgement of him as Son of God until the centurion at the cross. The quest pervades the gospel, as those who encounter Jesus attempt to puzzle out who he is (2:7; 4:41; 8:21, 29; 11:28; 14:61). It is made more laborious by Jesus' repeated order to 'tell no one about what they had seen until the Son of Man had risen from the dead' (9:9), the so-called 'messianic secret' (see MK 1:32–4).

The dominant impression of Jesus is one of authority. When he calls the disciples they follow unhesitatingly (1:16–20). He teaches and heals with authority (1:22, 27). The wind and the sea obey him (4:41). Even his unexplained commands are obeyed without question (11:1–6; 14:13–16). Amazement and astonishment follow him everywhere (2:12; 5:20; 6:51; 7:37). A challenge to his authority is easily defeated (11:27–33), until 'no one dared question him any more' (12:34). He acts like the prophets of old (6:15; 8:28), even providing bread in the desert for his followers as Moses did (6:35–44; 8:1–9). He arrogates to himself powers that only God possesses, forgiving sin (2:1–12), claiming to be lord of the sabbath (2:28), rebuking the storm (4:39; cf. Ps 107:23–9), walking on the sea (6:48; cf. Job 9:8). The final blasphemy—again Markan irony—is when he proclaims that the high priest will see him ' "seated at the right hand of the Power" and "coming on the clouds of heaven" ' (14:62), a claim to share the very throne of God (see Donahue 1973). It is against this background that the titles given to Jesus, such as 'Son of Man' (see MK 2:1–12) must be understood.

2. Matthew. *Narrative Style.* Mark and Matthew differ in two major respects. While Mark is concerned primarily to present a picture of the wonder of Jesus' personality Matthew concentrates on the teaching of Jesus. It has been calculated that

Mark contains 240 verses of teaching, and Matthew 620. Invariably Matthew expands the Markan teaching, just as he contracts the miracle stories. The guidance for the Christian life provided by Matthew is certainly one of the reasons why his early became the most popular and widespread of the gospels. Another reason—and this is surely at the heart of Matthew's popularity—is the poetic, rhythmic, and linguistic skill shown in Matthew's teaching sections, making the teaching attractive to remember and to quote.

Matthew tends to think in simple contrasts, using contrasting images, rock and sand (7:24), broad and narrow road (7:14), sun and rain (5:45), as well as many other pairs of images, birds and lilies (6:26–9), speck and log (7:4), moth and rust (6:19–20), and sometimes pairs of pairs, grapes, thorns, figs, thistles (7:16), stone, bread, snake, fish (7:9–10). His parables similarly point contrasts. Goulder (1974: 54) describes all Matthew's thirteen long parables as 'black and white caricature contrasts'. All of them contrast personalities (normally stock contrasting personalities, devoid of human interest or subtlety, the two builders (7:24–7), the two sons (21:28–31), the two servants (18:23–35), the wise and foolish wedding-attendants (25:1–13), and are themselves often in pairs (the mustard-seed and the leaven, 13:31–3, the treasure and the pearl, 13:44–6, the watchful householder and the faithful servant, 24:43–7; the talents and the sheep and goats, 25:14–46).

Nor is it only the liveliness of the imagery that attracts. Matthew has also a balanced rhythm which is far more frequent in his sayings than in the other Synoptics; one of the most frequent forms is described by Goulder (1974: 71) as a 'four point antithesis which has a paradoxical element'. Of these Goulder counts forty-four in Matthew, e.g. 6:3; 7:16; 9:37; 10:16. Where they are shared by Mark and Luke the form given by Matthew is often sharper and more succinct (e.g. Mt 16:26 compared with both Mark's and Luke's versions, or Mt 10:26 with Mk 4:22, or Mt 20:16 with Lk 13:30). Two special types of these four-point sayings may be mentioned, one in which two of the four terms are the same ('You received *without payment*, give *without payment*, Mt 10:8, my itals.), and the other in which the four terms fall into pairs ('with the *judgement* you make you will be *judged*, and *the measure* you give will be *the measure* you get, Mt 7:2 (my itals.)—much more succinct—12 words only—in Matthew's Greek, and quite lost in Lk 6:37–8). If Mark was chosen to relate the Good News for his skill in storytelling, it could well be that Matthew was selected to write a gospel because of the memorably poetic quality of his oral version of the teaching of Jesus.

Matthew's Jewishness. The other feature that contrasts Matthew's style with that of Mark is its Jewishness, and more precisely its rabbinic quality. It is not simply that Matthew leaves Semitic words unexplained (e.g. *rāqā* in 5:22), or that he shows constant interest in Jewish matters, such as the three classic good works of Judaism (almsgiving, prayer, and fasting) or tithes, phylacteries, and the law. Nor yet that he several times demurs from Mark's cavalier treatment of legal observance (e.g. he omits Mk 7:19*c*, 'Thus he declared all foods clean') and in Mt 12:1–8 is careful to justify the disciples' plucking ears of grain on the sabbath with more arguments than

Mark, omitting the sweeping liberalism of Mk 2:27. More positively he frequently uses rabbinic methods of argument, a heading followed by examples (in rabbinic writing known as *āb wĕtōlĕdôt*) in Mt 5:17 before the six great completions of the law in 5:21–48 and in 6:1 before the classic good works, the 'light and heavy' argument (Heb. *qal wāhōmer*, Lat. *a minori ad majus*) in 12:12, and *kĕlāl* or 'summing up' in 7:12.

It is notable that of all NT writers Matthew's formulas to introduce scriptural quotations are closest to those used at Qumran (cf. Fitzmyer 1970–1). His use of Scripture, linked to the word rather than the meaning of texts, is similarly often characteristic of Jewish exegesis of the time (cf. Barthélemy 1963). This reaches its extreme when Jesus is represented as mounted on both the ass and the colt in Mt 21:7, in order to fulfil Zech 9:9 literally.

Most significant on this topic is Matthew's treatment of scribes. Mark shows little interest in the scribes, and has few good words to say for them. Matthew, on the other hand, is careful in his treatment of them, systematically removing them from passages where they could, in Mark's narrative, seem to have a part in the death of Jesus (passages corresponding to Mt 21:23; 26:3, 47; 27:1). On other occasions Matthew makes it clear that particular hostile scribes belong to the Pharisee party (7:28–9; 22:34–40) or he simply substitutes 'Pharisees' for 'scribes' (9:11; 12:24). More positively, scribes are joined to prophets and wise men as those who are to be sent out as messengers in 23:34—Luke, in his corresponding passage, joins them together as 'prophets and apostles'—so that with good reason the approving sketch of the 'scribe who has been trained for the kingdom of heaven' is seen as Matthew's own self-portrait (13:52). Some scholars conclude that Matthew was writing for a community of Christian Jews, possibly at Antioch (Meier 1982; Sim 1998).

Matthew's Christology. In accord with this Jewishness Matthew sees the message of Jesus as bringing the teaching of Judaism to completion. Thus on twelve occasions he shows Jesus acting 'in order to fulfil' the scripture (1:23; 2:6; 15, 18, 23; 4:15–16; 8:17; 12:18–21; 13:35; 21:5; 26:56; 27:9–10) as though with no other motive for action. He sees the miracles of Jesus as the fulfilment of Isa 61 (Mt 8:17; 11:5–6) and the resurrection of Jesus as the sign of Jonah (Mt 12:39; 16:4, whereas Mk 8:12 misses this significance, saying that no sign will be given). He sees Jesus as the new Moses, reflecting Moses' career in his infancy (this is the chief theme of Mt 2), in his lawgiving (Mt 5:1), and in his final charge on the mountain (Mt 28:16). Consequentially, the people of Jesus forms the new Israel, replacing the old. In Mt 16:18 'my church' (or more exactly 'my community/congregation') mirrors the people whom God called to himself in the desert, and they are the nation to which the kingdom will be given when it is taken away from the unresponsive tenants (22:43). The repeated promise of his presence among them (1:18; 18:20; 28:20) corresponds to the presence of God among the people of Israel.

Not unexpectedly, therefore, Matthew's Jesus is a more dignified and hieratic figure than Mark's, almost as though he were already the risen Christ. Many of the human touches of emotion found in Mark are missing in Matthew (e.g. Mk 1:43; 3:5). The thronging crowd scenes of the Markan miracles of healing give way to a solemn lone confrontation between the Healer and the beneficiary (cf. Mt 8:14–15 and 9:20–2 with their Markan equivalents). If Jesus worked no miracles at Nazareth because of their unbelief, it was not that he *could* not (Mk 6:5) but simply that he *did* not (Mt 13:58).

While in Mark the disciples consistently fail to understand Jesus and his message, in Matthew this is no longer possible (cf. Mk 6:52, 8:21 with Mt 14:33, 16:12). Whereas in Mark Jesus is commonly called 'teacher' by friend and foe alike, and 'Lord' only by sapient unclean spirits and the cured, in Matthew the disciples address him as 'Lord'. Only outsiders call him 'teacher', and—Judas at the moment of betrayal (26:25, 49)— 'Rabbi'. This dignity of Jesus is naturally expressed by Matthew primarily in terms of the fulfilment of Judaism. He is greater than the temple, Jonah, or Solomon (12:6, 41, 42). He is the son of David (a title used by Mark only twice, by Matthew six more times, and the adoption of Jesus into the House of David is the principal theme of Mt 1). Above all, he is the new Moses, succeeding in the desert where Israel had fallen to the testing (Mt 4:1–11). As the new Israel he is also God's son, frequently calling God 'Father'. This unique relationship is mysteriously portrayed in the virginal conception and the comparison to God's son in Egypt (2:15). It becomes the central assertion of Peter's two confessions of faith, as the climax of the scene of the walking on the water (14:33) and of the confession of Caesarea Philippi (16:16). Finally it becomes the central object of the ironical mockery of Jesus on the cross (27:40, 43).

3. Luke. It is impossible to discuss the gospel of Luke in isolation from the Acts of the Apostles, with which it shares so many characteristics that few serious scholars have ever disputed the joint authorship of the two volumes. Luke stands out from the other evangelists by his degree of sophistication. This is apparent first of all in his style of writing, on the level both of linguistic and of narrative style. His vocabulary is far more elevated than that of the other evangelists; he uses many compound words, constructions, and grammatical forms (he is the only evangelist to use the optative mood) which are more at home in literary Hellenistic Greek than is the homely language of Matthew and Mark. Luke is familiar with the conventions of Greek historiography: just as in the Acts he uses speeches as a way of conveying editorial comment, so in the gospel he follows the Greek convention of using meals as occasions of teaching (7:36–50; 22:24–38). Two particular points which would have caught the attention of a more sophisticated audience deserve mention: first, both gospel and Acts open with a formal Hellenistic preface (each related to the other), which places the work in the literary category of scientific treatise or monograph (see ACTS 1:1–4); it is intended to be a factual, well-ordered account. Secondly, many of the concepts involved would appeal to a Hellenistic audience, for example 'salvation', a term familiar to those acquainted with the 'salvation' offered by Hellenistic mystery-religions: Luke alone of the gospel-writers (apart from Jn 4:22, 42) uses the term or calls Jesus 'Saviour'; correspondingly, the beneficiaries of Jesus' miracles are described as 'saved' in a way that suggests that their cures bring more than merely physical salvation (8:36, 50; 17:19).

Luke's narrative skill is particularly distinctive. His scenes are carefully crafted, often like dramatic scenes with 'stage-directions' of entrances and exits and liberal use of direct speech and dialogue, for example the little scenes of the infancy stories in Lk 1–2, or Martha and Mary (10:38–42), the ten lepers (17:11–19) or the journey to Emmaus (24:13–32). Luke's skill in presenting theology by means of such dramatic scenes is thrown into relief by similar scenes in the Acts, for example the baptism of the Ethiopian (Acts 8:26–40) or Saul's conversion (Acts 9:1–9). Luke's characters are colourful and varied; contrast the warm family atmosphere and joy of Luke's infancy stories with Matthew's, in which no human being speaks to any other, or the three main characters of Luke's parable of the prodigal son (15:11–32) with Matthew's skeletal and wooden characters in the parable of the two sons (Mt 21:28–32). A special feature is Luke's mixed characters, the blackguard Zacchaeus who makes good (19:1–10), the characters who do the right thing for the wrong reason (the friend at midnight, the crafty steward, the unjust judge).

Luke frequently uses patterns and parallels to convey his message. In the infancy stories the similarity and contrast between John the Baptist and Jesus, and between their parents, is carefully painted. The parallel between the gospel and the Acts shows the continuity between the ministry of Jesus and that of the Spirit (for example, the descent of the Spirit at Jesus' baptism followed by his programmatic speech at Nazareth is paralleled in the Acts by the descent of the Spirit at Pentecost and Peter's speech thereafter; the healings worked by the apostles in the power of the Spirit parallel those worked by Jesus himself). The four Beatitudes are balanced by four Woes (6:20–6). Luke is particularly enamoured of lists of four items (6:37–8; 14:12–13; 17:27). The infancy stories are bracketed by balancing scenes in Jerusalem (1:5–22; 2:41–50), and the Jerusalem ministry itself by prophecies about the fate of the city as Jesus reaches and leaves the city (19:41–4; 23:26–31).

The geographical framework, and especially Jerusalem, have marked significance for Luke. This is not unexpected, in view of the importance of journeying in the Acts, the whole of the second half of which is devoted to Paul's missionary journeys. If the author was indeed a travelling-companion of Paul, journeying was a normal part of his way of life. Many of Luke's greatest stories occur in the framework of a journey (the journey to Emmaus, the conversion of the Ethiopian and of Saul himself). A major section of the gospel consists of the journey to Jerusalem (9:51–19:27).

In the gospels it is chiefly from Luke that we can glimpse the importance of Jerusalem. At every level it held an important position in Jewish hearts. As the city of David it was the city of God's promises. As the city of the temple it was the place of God's presence, the centre of pilgrimage for all Jews. Even by the Gentile Pliny it was described as 'by far the most distinguished city of the East' because of Herod's magnificent construction. For Luke it is the hinge-city of salvation. The gospel begins and ends there, the annunciation to Zechariah being located in the temple itself, and the resurrection appearances being confined to Jerusalem and its surroundings. While in Mark and Matthew the prophetic action of Jesus in the temple is construed as a demonstration of the barrenness of Judaism, Luke removes the image of the barren fig-tree of Israel and makes the action a cleansing of the temple, so that Jesus continues to use it 'daily' (19:47; 21:37) as his pulpit for teaching. When the chief priests challenge his authority, it is not, as in Mark and Matthew his authority to signal the destruction of the temple, but his authority to use it for teaching (20:1–2). The affection of Jesus himself for the holy city is underlined by the repeated expression of his sadness at its failure to respond and to recognize 'the way to peace' (19:42); this marks the mid-point of his final journey up to Jerusalem (13:34–5), and brackets the Jerusalem ministry itself, culminating in the tragic prophetic pronouncement on the way to Calvary (23:28–32). In the Acts Jerusalem is first the birthplace of the church, the home of the ideal community of the followers of Jesus, where they live together in harmony, prayer, and community of goods, and undergo their first persecutions. Then it is the centre from which the message spreads to the ends of the earth (Acts 1:8), to which Paul returns regularly to ensure the unity of the church.

The fate of Israel is for Luke a related preoccupation. The atmosphere of OT piety which pervades the infancy stories, and the deliberate cultivation of biblical language in the style of narration there used, shows that Jesus is born into the bosom of Israel as the fulfilment of God's promises to Israel, the fulfilment also of their longing for the promised deliverance (1:68–75; 2:25, 38). But Luke, like Paul in Rom 9–11, must also face the problem that Israel largely rejected its Messiah. Luke's solution is strikingly different from Matthew's. For all his Jewishness (see E.2), Matthew leaves no doubt that Israel's rejection of Jesus brings on itself its own rejection. From the beginning there is a sharp contrast between the murderous rejection of Jesus by Herod the Jew and the reverence paid him by the Gentile magi. So to the parable of the wicked tenants Matthew deliberately adds, 'the kingdom of God will be taken away from you and given to a people who will produce its fruit' (Mt 21:43). In the parable of the wedding feast the guests originally invited refuse to come, with the result that their city is burnt (Mt 22:7—on the natural level a typical Matthean overreaction). Finally, at the trial before Pilate the people as a whole cry out, 'Let his blood be on us and on our children' (27:25). Does Matthew consider them as representatives of the people as a whole, or only of those who reject Jesus?

By contrast Luke insists that at least part of Israel accepted the promised Messiah. He makes a sharp distinction between the people and their leaders. The people are continually favourable to Jesus, and Luke carefully uses for them the word *laos*, as a technical, biblical term for the people of God (1:10; 3:15; 6:10; 23:27, etc.). At 7:9 where Matthew has '*In no one* in Israel have I found such faith' Luke reads '*Not even* in Israel . . .' (my itals.), implying the presence of some response in faith among at least a part of Israel. In the final scenes the leaders are hostile to Jesus, stir up the people, and jeer at the crucified Messiah, while the people stand watching and return home beating their breasts, the first sign of turning to discipleship (23:35–48). The same pattern continues in the Acts, where the response of the people is enthusiastic (Acts 2:41, 47; 6:1, 7, etc.), while the authorities are again uniformly and bitterly hostile. Paul does indeed three times solemnly turn from the Jews to the Gentiles with a biblical gesture of rejection (in Asia, Acts 13:46–51; in Greece, 18:6; in Rome, 28:25–8), but in each case only after numbers of the Jews had been drawn to Christianity.

The prophet to Israel is, accordingly, one of the chief ways in which Luke represents Jesus. Like the biblical prophets, Jesus is 'filled with the Spirit', 'led by the Spirit' (4:1, 14, 18). Indeed, the scene at the Jordan is, in Luke's case, better described as 'the descent of the Spirit on the occasion of the baptism' rather than 'the baptism of Jesus'. From the beginning the biblical prophetic atmosphere is strong. Zechariah points out the child John as a prophet (1:79), but Jesus will be 'a light for revelation to the Gentiles and for glory to your people Israel' (2:32). Jesus already shows his prophetic qualities in dialogue with the teachers in the temple (2:47). In the crucial 'Nazareth manifesto' (one of Luke's most carefully composed historico-theological scenes, see E.3) Jesus likens his mission to that of Elijah and Elisha (4:24–7); like a prophet, he is not accepted in his own country. After the raising of the widow's son he is publicly hailed as a prophet (7:16). His death at Jerusalem is shown with increasing intensity to be the death of a prophet, firstly by the conversation at the beginning of the journey with the two great prophetic figures of the OT about his *exodos* at Jerusalem (9:31), secondly by the interpretation of the great journey as a journey of destiny to die as a prophet at Jerusalem (13:33), but most of all by the constant prophetic activity on that journey. On the road to Emmaus the disciples sum up Jesus' activity as that of a prophet, and he himself acts as a prophet in interpreting the Scriptures. Finally the ascension shows the likeness of Jesus to the prophet Elijah, taken up to heaven in a fiery chariot (2 Kings 2:11).

That Jesus is more than a prophet is shown by Luke in many ways, particularly by his use of the title 'Son of God'. In Mark this is already used significantly (see E.1, *Person of Jesus*); Luke enlarges this use, so that it is 'moving beyond a functional understanding of Jesus' sonship' (J. B. Green 1995). The significance of the mysterious conception of the Son of the Most High through the Spirit of God without Mary having sexual intercourse (1:35) is confirmed by Jesus' saying about really belonging in his Father's house (2:49). The declaration of the voice at the baptism is given further prominence by the genealogy that follows immediately, linking Jesus 'son, as it was thought, of Joseph' directly to Adam 'son of God' (3:23, 38). The frequent expressions of intimacy between Jesus and his Father (10:21–2; 22:43) reach their climax in Jesus' last words of trust on the cross (23:46). They are reinforced by Luke's stress on Jesus' constant practice of prayer (5:16), and his being found at prayer at all the decisive moments of his ministry (baptism, choice of the twelve, transfiguration, teaching of the Lord's prayer, agony in the garden).

Furthermore, Luke's use of the title *kyrios* of Jesus with the article ('the Lord') hints at a divine status for Jesus, for in contemporary documents the Hebrew and Aramaic equivalents are used of God. Mark uses this title of Jesus only in the vocative (except in the enigmatic Mk 11:3), in which usage it may mean no more than 'Sir!' The title is used overwhelmingly by Luke in narrative sections (e.g. 10:1; 11:39; 17:5), so that Fitzmyer (1979: 203), notes, 'In using *kyrios* of both Yahweh and Jesus in his writings Luke continues the sense of the title already being used in the early Christian communities, which in some sense regarded Jesus as on a level with Yahweh.' The same status is also hinted by such passages as 8:39, where the beneficiary of the miracle is told to 'report all that God has done for you' and in fact 'proclaimed throughout the city all that Jesus had done for him'.

Luke has been described as 'the gospel of the underprivileged' from the emphasis that Luke places on Jesus' invitation to several neglected classes. Foremost among these are women. Luke alone mentions the women who accompany Jesus and minister to him (8:1–3). He habitually pairs women with men as recipients of salvation: Zechariah and Mary (1:11–38, and in their balancing songs of praise, 1:46–55, 68–79), Simeon and Anna (2:22–38), the widow of Zarephath and Naaman (4:26–7), the daughter of Jairus and the son of the widow (7:11–15 and 8:41–56, a double crossover of the sexes), a man searching for a lost sheep and a woman searching for a lost coin (15:4–10). In the same vein, by contrast to Mk 3:31–5, he represents Mary, the mother of Jesus, as the first of the disciples and as their model in her response to God's word (1:38, 46–55; 8:21; 11:27–8).

From the infancy narratives onwards it is clear that Jesus has come to bring comfort to the poor. In Mary's canticle God has 'filled the starving with good things' (1:53). In this Luke echoes the theme, so prominent in the post-exilic writings of Judaism, of God's blessing on the poor and unfortunate who put their trust in him. No house can be found for Jesus to be born in, and he is welcomed by hireling shepherds, themselves inspired by the joyful song of the angels. The text for Jesus' opening proclamation at Nazareth is 'he has anointed me to bring good news to the afflicted' (4:18, quoting Isa 61:1–2). In the Lukan Beatitudes the blessings are not (as in Matthew) on the 'poor in spirit' but on those who are actually 'poor now, hungry now, weeping now' (6:20–1); they concern a social rather than a religious class. This is complemented by Luke's frequent warnings about the dangers of wealth and possessions (the terrible parable of the rich fool, 12:16–21; the excuses of the invited guests, 14:18–19; the parable of the rich man and Lazarus, 16:19–31; Luke's severity towards the rich ruler, 18:18–30). This is all the more striking since Luke's own background and circumstances seem to be reasonably comfortable: his style and language are possibly the most sophisticated of all the NT writers; his images drawn from economics (banking, interest-rates, loans, the sums of money mentioned) bespeak a certain familiarity with finance; in his world the status given by special places at table is important (14:7–14); his anxiety to show that reputable and even high-class persons accepted Christianity, and his horror of shame and humiliation (16:3; 18:5), all suggest a background of middle-class values.

Luke shows Jesus' special care not only for the poor and for women, but also for other classes despised in Judaism, sinners and Gentiles. That Jesus came to call sinners was always at the heart of the gospel, but Luke places additional emphasis on this aspect. Story after story in Luke illustrates Jesus' welcome to sinners and the joy in heaven at repentance: the woman who was a sinner, the lost sheep, the lost coin, the prodigal son, Zacchaeus, the good thief. To be a sinner and to recognize one's state of sinfulness is almost a precondition of being called by Jesus (5:8; 15:2, contrast the spite of the dutiful elder son in 15:25–30 or the arrogance of the observant Pharisee in 18:9–14).

In the gospel of Mark Jesus has contact with Gentiles only in the person of the Syro-Phoenician whose daughter he heals. This contact is seen as exceptional, and the mission of Jesus is limited to his own countrymen. The future mission of the church to the Gentiles is hinted only by the recognition of Jesus as Son of God by the Gentile centurion at the foot of the cross. By contrast to Mark, Luke is concerned, even in the gospel, to show that the good news of Jesus extends also to those beyond Judaism. He is thus preparing for the mission to the world that will take place in his second volume, the Acts. Already Simeon proclaims the child as a 'light to the Gentiles'. In his opening proclamation at Nazareth Jesus announces that he will follow the example of the prophets Elijah and Elisha in bringing his message to those beyond the borders of Israel. This is fulfilled in the cure of the centurion's boy, during which the centurion's merits are warmly praised (7:1–10). Luke's special interest in the salvation of the Gentiles is shown by his rare allegorization of the parable of the great supper (14:16–24): after the messengers have brought in the crippled and beggars of the city (representing the outcasts of the Chosen People), they are sent out a second time into the highways and byways beyond the city, to gather in the Gentiles. A special interest is shown in the Samaritans, the neighbours of Judea to the north, and often especially hated and despised by the Jews. In the parable of the good Samaritan (10:29–37) and the cure of the ten lepers (17:11–19)—both arguably Lukan compositions—the Samaritans are presented mainly in an attractive light which contrasts favourably with Jews.

Running through the whole gospel as an undercurrent is teaching on discipleship. Luke presents Jesus as a model for his disciples. The early followers of Jesus in fact are shown in the Acts to be providing a mirror-image of his preaching, his miracles, his perseverance under persecution, and his witness unto death. Luke stresses the need for constant imitation of Christ. Disciples must take up their cross *daily* and follow him (9:23), just as Simon of Cyrene carries the cross behind Jesus (23:26). Jesus teaches his disciples to pray in imitation of his own prayer (11:1), and gives the whole scene of the agony in the garden as a lesson in prayer in time of temptation (22:40, 46). Beside the imitation of Jesus, the most striking factor in Luke's teaching on discipleship is that it involves a total reversal of current practice and values. This is in line with Luke's stress on the need for conversion at all levels (3:3, 8). The great journey to Jerusalem and the last supper are for Luke valuable occasions for teaching on discipleship, and it is this instruction that comes back again and again. Disciples must first of all recognize their sinfulness, and then leave not merely their possessions but *everything* (5:28; 14:33; 18:22). Luke's social world was built on a network of mutual relationships of patron and client, in which patron expected service from client and client protection from patron. In the community of Jesus' disciples there is to be no such *quid pro quo*. All are to give without hope of return (6:36–8; 12:33–4) and the great are to be servants of all (22:24–7). In this way Luke looks ahead to the life of the Christian community after the resurrection.

5. The Historicity of John. Despite the similarity of tradition behind the Fourth and the Synoptic Gospels, the pattern of John is very different from both a literary and a theological point of view. Gone are the days when it was scholarly orthodoxy to maintain that John was the least reliable of the gospels historically. From Dodd (1955–6) to Dunn (1983; 1991) it has become accepted that John contains sayings that are as primitive as or more primitive than their versions in the synoptic tradition. Similarly John often shows local knowledge superior to that of the Synoptics, especially in the Jerusalem and passion sequences (Siloam, Bethzatha, Kidron, Golgotha). In a number of incidents John seems to be building on parallel historical traditions. Especially in the account of the passion his alternatives to the agony in the garden (Jn 12:27–9) and the meeting of the Jewish authorities (11:47–53) are serious rivals.

The Composition of John. From a literary point of view the Synoptic Gospels are composed, as it has been classically described, like beads on a string, from short, independent episodes and sayings joined together by the several evangelists to form a pattern. The fourth gospel has fewer, longer incidents and far fewer isolated sayings. Both miracles and sayings tend to be prolonged into dialogues and often monologues which bring out the meaning of these signs. Thus the healing of the sick man at the Pool of Bethzatha develops first into a series of dialogues about the miracle and then into a monologue by Jesus on judgement (5:1–9, 10–18, 19–47 respectively).

John's Christology. With this is allied the greatest difference of all: in the Synoptic Gospels the subject of revelation is the kingship or reign of God, of which Jesus is the messenger. In John the primary object of revelation is Jesus himself and his glory, or rather the revelation of God's glory in him, climaxing in the hour of the exaltation and glorification of Jesus, the cross and resurrection. The crucifixion is no longer a shameful humiliation which has to be explained as the will of God expressed in Scripture; it is a royal progress which enables the divinity of Jesus to shine through, and leaves Jesus reigning from the cross until he himself triumphantly signifies that all is fulfilled.

Nevertheless, it is a secret Jesus who is being revealed, and the theme of seeking Jesus runs through the gospel from 1:38 'What do you seek?' to 20:15 'Whom do you seek?' One feature of this is the series of puzzled questions by which the dialogues are advanced (e.g. 3:4, 9; 4:9, 11, 29, 33; 6:9, 28, 42, 52, etc.). Another is the irony that runs through the gospel. This is principally in the mouth of the opponents of Jesus, who make exaggerated and self-important claims about their knowledge, just where they are most ignorant (4:12, 7, 27; 8:41, 47). Such irony becomes all-embracing in such incidents as the cure of the man born blind, when the Pharisees think they see but in fact are blind, and by their insistent refusal to accept the evidence gradually nudge the cured man towards full faith in Jesus; and the incident of the trial before Pilate, when in fact Jesus presides over the self-condemnation of those who think they are condemning him. But the disciples too can be ironical, often through bewilderment and overconfidence (1:46; 11:16; 16:29), as can Jesus himself, often with unanswered questions (3:10; 7:23, 28; 10:32). *Double entendre* is fundamental to all John's language. Just as Nicodemus quite legitimately misunderstands the Greek *anōthen* as 'again' when Jesus means 'from above' (3:3–7), so also the Son of Man 'lifted up' (3:14; 8:28; 12:32–4) means on one level 'lifted onto the cross' but on another level has a far more profound sense. At the same time it is a striking feature of John's language that he thinks in a series of contrasts—'John has dualism in his bones', writes Ashton (1991: 237)—expressed in the bipolarity

of life and death, truth and falsehood, slavery and freedom, light and darkness, worldly and heavenly, openly and in secret, and other countless little contrasts.

John's portrait of Jesus can at last be described as 'incarnational', for this gospel both contains the two unambiguous assertions in the gospels of the divinity of Jesus, bracketing and so setting the tone for the whole gospel, 'the Word was God' (1:1) and 'My Lord and my God!' (20:28), and shows a Jesus subject to human exhaustion (4:6), loneliness (6:67), grief for a friend (11:35), and shrinking from death (12:27). What this means is shown principally in two ways. The first is more obviously dependent on Judaism. In the prologue the Word is shown to be the culmination and fulfilment of the tradition of a personified, life-giving Wisdom, who is both God at work in the world and yet not simply identical with God. The Word is also the culmination of the revelation of God, greater than that made to Moses (1:17), explicable only as the revelation of the awesome glory of God (Ex 33:17–23; Isa 6:1–5). This revelation takes place throughout the ministry of Jesus, but reaches its climax in the exaltation or glorification of the cross (8:28; 12:32–4; 13:32; 14:13).

The Johannine Jesus also takes over for himself the allusive divine title of Deutero-Isaiah, 'I am he'. This is used both absolutely and with a predicate. Used absolutely it is a self-identification, with scarcely veiled divine overtones. Thanks to the ambiguity of Johannine language it is impossible to exclude this awesome connotation when Jesus comes walking on the water (6:20), and it is certainly intended when the detachment, arriving to arrest Jesus, reacts to it by falling to the ground (18:5–8—the biblical reaction to the divine). It is so understood even more obviously by the Jews in 5:28, 58. Used as a predicate it attributes to Jesus awesome manifestations of the divine from within Judaism, which reach their full reality in him, 'I am the bread of life' (6:35), 'the light of the world' (8:12), 'the good shepherd' (10:11), 'resurrection and life' (11:25), 'the true vine' (15:1).

The second way in which the divine quality of Jesus is shown is by his relationship to the Father. The title 'Son of Man' is used frequently by Jesus in all the gospels, the simple title 'the Son', however, only on three occasions in the Synoptics but 20 times by the Johannine Jesus, denoting a close and simple relationship to the Father. There is an intimacy in this language that has no parallel elsewhere. The Son is sent by the Father—'the Father, the one who sent me' is a formula that occurs 21 times in John—and the relationship has been analysed in terms of the Jewish institution of the *shāliāḥ*, an envoy sent out with the same powers as his principal to do the same work, to receive the same honour and to report back to the principal. Whereas the modern, Hellenized mind may define equality in the static terms of being, the Semitic mind, nowhere more clearly than Jn 5:19–30, defines the relationship in the dynamic terms of equality of action and authority, unity of purpose and of honour received. The central importance of this revelation of Jesus determines many other orientations of the gospel.

In John the ethical requirements of the Kingdom, so fully set out in the teaching sections of Matthew and Luke (the Sermon on the Mount and on the Plain, etc.), become simplified into the basic requirement of belief in Jesus 'that you may have life in his name' (12:44–50; 20:31). The only response demanded is love (17:36), an echo of the love that is shared by the Father and the Son, reaches its climax on the cross, and is granted also by Jesus to his followers (13:1; 14:21–31; 17:23–4). The poor, so prominent especially in Luke, are barely mentioned. Indeed there is little of the Galilean peasant feel about this gospel: the action is more frequently in Jerusalem, and many of the people encountered (Nicodemus, the royal official at Capernaum) have a certain grandeur.

Eschatology. The perspective on the future is different. In the Synoptic Gospels there is a constant tension between the present and the future: the kingship of God is in some ways already a present reality, and yet it is still to be brought to reality in the future. There is a vivid expectation of the coming of the kingship in power when the Son of Man comes in his glory with the holy angels (Mk 9:1; 14:25, 62; Mt 24:30–1; 25:31). In John the concept of the kingship of God has virtually vanished—it is mentioned only Jn 3:3, 5—and has been replaced by that of 'eternal life' which is a present reality in Jesus (1:4; 6:35, 63; 11:25) already possessed by believers (5:24; 6:47; 10:28). Since the perspective of the gospel is already resurrectional, Jesus can say already 'the hour is coming and now is when true worshippers will worship the Father in spirit and in truth (4:23)', or 'when the dead will hear the voice of the Son of God' (5:25). This perspective of John has classically been designated 'realized eschatology'. This is not to say that all expectation of the future has vanished, for those who have done good will still 'come forth to the resurrection of life' (5:29). But the decisive moment has already come in the 'hour' of Jesus which reaches its climax in the death and resurrection of Jesus.

Judgement. As far as the individual is concerned one is reminded that throughout the gospel the decisive moment is that of encounter with Jesus. Judgement is not, as in the Synoptics, a 'day of the Lord' in the future, rather the coming of Jesus is a moment of *krisis* or judgement, and the whole gospel is in a sense a great judgement-scene. To 'judge' or 'condemn' (the same word in Gk.) occurs 4 times in Matthew, 5 times in Luke, 19 times in John. The Father has given all judgement to the Son (5:22) but it is not the Son who executes judgement; rather each individual exercises judgement by a personal reaction of faith or unbelief in Jesus (3:17–18). Thus the gospel represents a series of judgements: the disciples at Cana believe and see his glory; 'the Jews' refuse belief at the cleansing of the temple; Nicodemus shows goodwill but not yet belief, and so on until finally 'the Jews' tragically judge themselves before Pilate by rejecting God as king: 'we have no king but Caesar' (19:15)—if God is not king, then Judaism has no reason to exist. Forensic terminology is ubiquitous in the gospel: 'to bear witness' (once each in Matthew and Luke, 32 times in John), 'witness' (Mark thrice and Luke once, both at Jesus' trial, but 15 times in John). The witnesses to Jesus are the Baptist, Moses, his works, the crowds, the Paraclete, and above all his Father. Supporting these are terms like 'testimony', 'accuse', 'condemnation'.

John and Judaism. The side-lining of Judaism comes to expression in the way Jesus in his own person, one after another, supersedes the institutions of Judaism. Already at Cana Jesus provides the wine of the marriage-feast to replace the water of the law. Immediately afterwards his own body is seen to replace the temple (2:21). In 5:1–18 he takes possession of the sabbath, claiming that as God has the right to work on the sabbath, so has he. At the Feast of Tabernacles, Jesus claims to provide the living water which was such an important feature of the feast, symbolizing the blessings of the messianic age (7:37–9). In giving sight to the blind and claiming to be the light of the world (8:12, cf. 1:9; 3:19–21; 12:35, 36, 46) he again usurps the function of the law. Finally his death, at the time of the slaughter of the paschal lambs (19:24), replaces the passover sacrifice. But there is more to John's treatment of Judaism than this. Although at some levels of the gospel it can be acknowledged that 'salvation is from the Jews' (4:22, presumably in the sense of origin), on the whole the term is used to distinguish rites and festivals from the Christian way (2:6, 'the Jewish rites of purification'; 11:55, 'the Passover of the Jews'; 7:2, 'the Jewish festival of Booths'). More hostilely it designates those who will not accept Jesus and are responsible for his death, replacing in this respect not only the Pharisees and the authorities of the Synoptic Gospels, but also the crowds of Jerusalem. Significant of the evangelist's own attitude may be 9:18–23, where 'the Jews' is used as a term for those designated in what may have been an earlier version of the story as 'the Pharisees', and attempts have been made to show that 'the Jews' is used in this hostile sense only in one layer of the gospel (von Wahlde 1989). The fear of the blind man's parents that they will be 'put out of the synagogue' for confessing Jesus may well reflect the hostility between Judaism and Christianity towards the end of the century. In the farewell discourses (perhaps representing a different layer) the same opponents seem to be designated by 'the world' (which can elsewhere be used in a positive sense, 1:9; 3:16–19; 12:46), but their identity is made clear by the phrase 'their law' (15:25) and the similar threat to put you 'out of the synagogue', 16:2.

The Spirit in John. The centrality of Jesus is not compromised but rather enhanced by the importance of the Spirit. There is a sense throughout the gospel that the Spirit is necessary to complete the work of Jesus. The descent of the Spirit at the baptism will enable Jesus to baptize in the Spirit, which is represented to Nicodemus as the means to rebirth and life (3:5–8). The Samaritan woman is taught that worship in the Spirit is the sole true worship (4:23–4). In the bread of life discourse the Spirit is the means of life (6:13). But the Spirit will not be given until after Jesus has been glorified (7:39), and the sense that all these passages envisage the life of the future community is strengthened by the dual reference during Jesus' 'hour'. On the cross his final act is 'he bowed his head and *handed over* [my tr.] the Spirit' (19:30—is it to this that the climactic 'It is *completed*' refers?). The purpose of the first resurrectional appearance to the disciples is expressed as 'Receive the Holy Spirit' (20:22). The role and function of the Spirit are made clear principally in the five Paraclete or Counsellor sayings in the farewell discourses, when Jesus is laying out the future constitution of his community (14:15–17, 25–6; 15:16; 16:7–11, 13–15, see JN 14:16–17). It is to continue and further the presence and work of Jesus after his departure.

Sections F–K give six trial pericopes in which the theological outlook of the different evangelists may be seen, and the arguments in favour of the different solutions to the synoptic problem assessed. Apart from section 1, different pericopes have been chosen than those discussed by Sanders and Davies (1989).

In these examples I frequently use my own translation, in order to reflect more exactly the detailed similarities and differences between the Greek texts of the several gospels.

F. 1. The Call of the First Disciples (Mt 4:18–22 || Mk 1:16–20 || Lk 5:1–11, cf. Jn 1:35–50)

Mt 4:18–22

[18] As he walked by the sea of Galilee, he saw two brothers, Simon, who is called Peter and Andrew his brother, casting a net into the sea, for they were fishermen. [19] And he said to them, 'Follow me, and I will make you fishers of men.' [20] Immediately they left their nets and followed him. [21] And going on from there he saw two other brothers, James son of Zebedee and John his brother, in the boat with Zebedee their father, mending their nets, and he called them. [22] But they immediately left the boat and their father and followed him.

Mk 1:16–20

[16] And passing along by the sea of Galilee, he saw Simon and Andrew the brother of Simon casting a net into the sea, for they were fishermen. [17] And Jesus said to them, 'Follow me and I will make you become fishers of men.' [18] And immediately they left their nets and followed him. [19] As going on a little he saw James son of Zebedee and John his brother, who were in the boat mending their nets, [20] and immediately he called them, and they left their father Zebedee in the boat with the hired men and followed him.

Lk 5:1–11

[1] Once while Jesus was standing beside the lake of Gennesaret, and the crowd was pressing in on him to hear the word of God, [2] he saw two boats there at the shore of the lake; the fishermen had gone out of them and were washing their nets. [3] He got into one of the boats, the one belonging to Simon, and asked him to put out a little way from the shore. Then he sat down and taught the crowds from the boat. [4] When he had finished speaking, he said to Simon, 'Put out into the deep water and let down your nets for a catch.' [5] Simon answered, 'Master, we have worked all night long but have caught nothing. Yet if you say so, I will let down the nets.' [6] When they had done this, they caught so many fish that their nets were beginning to break. [7] So they signalled to their partners in the other boat to come and help them. And they came and filled both boats, so that they began to sink. [8] But when Simon Peter saw it, he fell down at Jesus' knees, saying, 'Go away from me, Lord, for I am a sinful man!' [9] For he and all who were with him were amazed at the catch of fish that they had taken; [10] and so also were James and John, sons of Zebedee, who were partners with Simon. Then Jesus said to Simon, 'Do not be afraid; from now on you will be catching people.' [11] When they had brought their boats to shore, they left everything and followed him.

According to three of the four gospels the first action of Jesus in his ministry is to gather a group of disciples, thus already forming his community. Through the number of the twelve corresponding to the twelve tribes of Israel, they will constitute his new Israel. The accounts of Mark and Matthew are closely related. Luke postpones the first call of disciples. He keeps it geographically similar, but integrates it into a tradition placed by Jn 21 after the resurrection. John himself attaches the call of the first disciples to the ministry of the Baptist, thus implying a location by the Jordan.

2. In Mark's account the stories of the call of the two pairs of disciples are closely similar to each other. The style of the whole incident is significantly Markan and shows that Mark's

is the original account: the Markan phrase 'and immediately' occurs in vv. 18, 20; Mark's introductory 'and' + participle occurs in vv. 16, 18, 19, 20*b*; the duplication of 'Simon and Simon's brother' in v. 16 is typical of Mark's oral style.

By contrast to many biblical calls by the Lord, which begin with some such double vocative and answer as 'Abraham, Abraham!'—'Here I am!', the call of each pair is modelled on the call of Elisha by Elijah in 1 Kings 19:19–21:

1. The prophet sees the disciple, son of X.
2. The disciple was working at his trade.
3. The prophet calls him.
4. The disciple leaves his trade and family and follows.

The call of the second pair is perhaps marginally more closely modelled on Elisha's call. The second pair leave their father without hesitation, in deliberate contrast to Elisha, who asks permission to take leave of his father. On the other hand, the first pair's desertion of their nets, their means of livelihood, links to Elisha's destruction of his yoke and oxen. Each of these factors underlines the immediacy of their response to the uncompromising call. Even if some preparation for or explanation of the call occurred in fact, Mark deliberately omits any mention of it, and thereby lays more stress on the astounding authority of Jesus. Two other slight touches in the call of the second pair also relate to Elisha's call: 'and they in the boat' (v. 10) corresponds to 'and he with the twelfth (1 Kings 19:19). The final 'followed *behind him*' also echoes 1 Kings 19:20. If the call of the second pair is the original narrative, the call of the first pair is inserted before it because it is fitting that Simon should be called first of all. It is also to the first pair that the function to 'fish for people' is given; they are not only disciples but also apostles.

3. Matthew follows Mark's account very closely, with only minor adjustments, mostly literary. Matthew is a careful teacher, even sometimes pedantic. He superfluously (perhaps fussily) inserts the mention that both pairs were two brothers. With similar meticulousness he tells us, before they leave him, that Zebedee was present, whereas in Mark their leaving Zebedee is the first indication of his presence on the scene. Matthew also adds two theological clarifications. First he explains that Simon 'is called Peter'. Consonantly with his concern for the community throughout his gospel, Matthew draws attention right from the start to the office which will be his (Mt 16:16–19). He frequently stresses Peter's prominence, especially by use of this title, though significantly he omits it when Peter fails his Master in Gethsemane (Mk 14:37)! Secondly Matthew mentions explicitly that the second pair leave the boat as well as their father, perhaps to suggest their total renunciation.

4. The Lukan narrative is basically quite different: it concerns primarily Simon Peter and his apostolate. It is perhaps for this reason that Luke transfers the call till later, when they have already witnessed some of Jesus' teaching and miracles. Simon's partners remain faceless until the last two verses, when their names are awkwardly tacked on with 'and so also were...'; it is really a bit late to tell us that the sons of Zebedee were his partners when we have already known about his partners for some time!

Some relationship of the story in Lk 5:1–11 to Jn 21 is undeniable, perhaps at the oral level: there is the night-long unsuccessful toil, the word of Jesus leading to the almost breaking net, and finally the authorization of Peter. It is difficult to be sure which was the original setting of the story. Simon's humble confession of his sinfulness fits Jn 21 better, after his triple denial at the time of the passion. Perhaps also the suggestions of the divine ('Lord', 'Do not be afraid') fit better a resurrection setting, though they do not demand it. Much the same reaction occurs when the disciples see Jesus walking on the water, see J.1. Two typical Lukan touches are the insistence that Peter must confess his sins before he is called to be a disciple (as Zacchaeus repents, and as is stressed in the mass conversions of Acts. Secondly, when they accept the call they leave 'everything', a total renunciation often stressed by Luke (14:33): Levi at his call leaves all (5:28), and the very rich young ruler is advised to sell everything he has (18:23).

5. John's account of the call of the first disciples is significantly different:

(*a*) Again there are two pairs of disciples, to the first pair of whom Simon Peter is attached. The identity of the first disciples is, however, different. The first pair consists of Andrew and an anonymous disciple, the second of Philip and Nathanael. There is no explicit sign of the sons of Zebedee, who feature in Mark's and Matthew's accounts.

(*b*) The location is different. For the first three disciples there is no suggestion of the Lake of Galilee, though Jn 1:44 does note that Philip, Andrew, and Simon were 'from Bethsaida' on the shore of the lake, and the call of Philip and Nathanael takes place after Jesus' decision to go to Galilee (Jn 1:43). The association of the first pair with the Baptist and his activity 'in Bethany across the Jordan' (Jn 1:18) suggests a fair distance from the Markan location at the north end of the lake. This suggests that the rapid succession of days ('the next day' in Jn 1:29, 35, 43) may be an artificial schema, uniting disparate material to form a first week of Jesus' ministry (see JN 1:29–31).

(*c*) The theological emphasis is different. Instead of the magisterial call by Jesus the keynote of the first meeting is on the initiative of the disciples themselves in seeking and finding Jesus as teacher, Messiah, king of Israel, and Son of God. To this search Jesus responds by inviting the disciples to stay with him (1:38–9). On the second occasion the initiative lies with Philip, who leads Nathanael to Jesus.

(*d*) Simon is the third, not the first to become a disciple. However, his special position is indicated by Jesus' imposition of a name, Peter, described much later by Mt 16:16–18.

5. The most interesting feature of all is that the first two disciples are nudged towards Jesus by John the Baptist. Especially since the discovery of the Qumran literature it has been suggested that Jesus himself was originally a disciple of John, and this strengthens the link between them.

G. The Beatitudes (Mt 5:3–12; Lk 6:20–3, 24–6)

Mt 5:3–12	Lk 6:20–6
3 Blessed are the poor in spirit, for theirs is the kingdom of heaven, 4 Blessed are those who mourn, for they will be comforted. 5 Blessed are the meek, for they will inherit the earth.	20 Blessed are you who are poor, for yours is the kingdom of God.

6 Blessed are those who hunger and
thirst for righteousness,
for they will be filled
7 Blessed are the merciful,
for they will receive mercy.
8 Blessed are the pure in heart,
for they will see God.
9 Blessed are the peacemakers,
for they will be called children of God.
10 Blessed are those who are persecuted
for righteousness' sake,
for theirs is the kingdom of heaven.
11 Blessed are you when people revile
you and persecute you and utter all kinds
of evil against you falsely on my account.
12 Rejoice and be glad
for   your reward is great in heaven,
for thus they persecuted the prophets before you.

21 Blessed are you who are hungry now,

for you will be filled.

Blessed are you who weep now,

for you will laugh.
22 Blessed are you when people hate you,
and when they exclude you, revile you and
defame you on account of the son of man.
23 Rejoice in that day and leap for joy,
for surely your reward is great in heaven,
for that is what their ancestors did to the
prophets.
24 But woe to you who are rich,
for you have received your consolation.
25 Woe to you who are full now,
for you will be hungry.
Woe to you who are laughing now,
for you will mourn and weep.
26 Woe to you when all speak well of you,
for that is what their ancestors did to the
false prophets.

The form of a beatitude, announcement of a blessing on certain classes of people, is common in the Bible (see MT 5:3–12) and frequently occurs in such groups as the present collections. It is perhaps to be noted that collections of eight occur also in Sir 14:20–7 (with a ninth added as an explanation, just as the ninth in Mt 5:11 provides a transition to the rest of the Sermon on the Mount). In both Matthew and Luke there are clear eschatological overtones, dependent on Isa 61:1. This text is used elsewhere by both evangelists, especially in Mt 11:5–6; Lk 4:17–21; 7:22–3. The same eschatological fulfilment of Isa 61:1 featured prominently in the messianic expectation of the Qumran community, 11QMelch 16–18 and 4Q521.

The source of the beatitudes has been much debated. Matthew has eight as opposed to Luke's four beatitudes, but Luke has four 'woes' corresponding to his four beatitudes. It has become scholarly orthodoxy to hold that at least the material shared by the two evangelists is drawn from Q, though perhaps from slightly different versions of Q. For many this seems the most important test-case of all. In many of the cases the arguments are evenly balanced, so that it must be admitted that several explanations are possible, though one explanation may be much more appealing than another, and make better sense. If it is possible to show that Matthew's beatitudes form such a carefully composed and engineered whole that they cannot constitute an edition of any previous document, the existence of a Q for this pericope is not merely less likely, but is positively excluded.

If both Matthew and Luke are dependent on Q, Matthew has expanded the original four beatitudes and Luke has added the four 'woes'. In favour of this position it is obvious that

Matthew is more interested in the spiritual dispositions demanded (Matthew has 'in spirit', 5:1) and brackets the whole with his characteristic 'kingdom of heaven' (vv. 3, 10), instead of the more commonly found expression 'kingdom of God' used by Luke. On the other hand the 'woes' show clear linguistic signs of Lukan editing in the repeated 'now' and other features which disappear in translation (oi anthrōpoi, kata ta auta), as well as the more obvious Lukan interest in the real poor and hungry, characteristic of his general concern for outcasts, and his repeated warnings of the dangers of wealth and comfort.

It has been suggested that a document underlies them both, to which Luke is the closer (Tuckett 1983). In order to exclude the possibility of Luke being dependent on Matthew, Tuckett considers two alternatives, either that Luke uses Matthew only or that he uses Matthew and another source (for the 'woes'). The parallelism between the woes and the beatitudes is so close that these woes could have had no independent existence, which excludes the latter alternative. The former alternative is excluded—according to Tuckett—by the Lukan use of the word 'laugh' (Lk 6:21, 25) which does not occur in Matthew's beatitudes and is not a Lukan word, so must be derived from another, non-Matthean source. To this Goulder replies by refusing to attribute to a source all words used only once by Luke. On the contrary, Luke has a large and inventive vocabulary, and in the section Lk 4:31–6:19 (where he is overwriting Mark) among the 606 non-Markan words, 13 are not used elsewhere by Luke. In any case 'laugh' is a reasonably common word, and is introduced by Luke as an exact contrast to 'weep', as in Eccl 3:4. That 'weep' in Lk 6:21 is a Lukan version of Matthew's 'mourn' is clear from the clumsiness with which Luke feels compelled to retain both words in v. 25. Thus Luke's version can, after all, be explained on the basis of Matthew's.

Matthew's beatitudes form a coherent whole which must have been composed at one draft in Greek (Puéch 1993). The question is whether this composition can be a Matthean elaboration of Q. The careful structure of the composition is unmistakable, the principal points being:

1. It is bracketed at beginning and end by the identical phrase 'for theirs is the kingdom of heaven'.

2. The word-count of the four pairs of beatitudes is symmetrical: 20–16–16–20. This must be deliberate, for it is achieved not without difficulty; for example the word-count must have dictated the inclusion of the definite article with 'righteousness' in v. 6, and its omission in the corresponding v. 10.

3. In the first four beatitudes those blessed all begin (in Greek) with the letter 'p'.

4. The blessings correspond symmetrically: 1 and 8 'for theirs is the kingdom of heaven'; 2 and 7 use the same Greek word klēthēsontai; 3 and 6 future active, 'will inherit', 'will see'; 4 and 5 future passive, 'will be filled', 'will be pitied'.

Such careful structure with exact word-count is characteristic of beatitude-collections, as is seen in the Hebrew collections of Sir 14:20–7 and 1QH 6.13–16 and 4Q525. Other features such as the eschatological overtones, the extra, final, transitional beatitude, biblical and Qumranic phrases such as 'poor in spirit' (cf. 1QH 6.14; 1QM 14.7; 4Q491.8–10) show that Matthew's composition fits exactly into a familiar pattern. It is difficult to accept that Matthew could have elaborated this complicated structure on the basis of any existing document that also served as a basis for Luke's beatitudes. It would also be a strange coincidence that both these writers should have independently chosen the beatitudes to head their great sermons. Luke's beatitudes and woes may therefore be explained as Luke's own edition of Matthew, rather than as similarly derived from Q. In outline the process would have been: if Luke is dependent on Matthew, it must be held that he cut the eight to four, a favourite number of his, omitting elements concerned with spiritual dispositions ('the meek') because he wished to concentrate on the aspect of discipleship and its demands, the Christian vocation to poverty and persecution. Luke elsewhere stresses that disciples must leave 'all', so that they are bound to be poor and destitute. Luke likes polar oppositions, so sharpened the reversal of situations to 'hungry' and 'filled', 'weeping' and 'laughing', in place of Matthew's 'hunger and thirst for justice' and his 'merciful' and 'receive mercy'.

The woes do show significant echoes of Matthew, despite being verbally unmistakably Lukan (plen = 'but', Lk 6.24, used by Matthew 5 times, Mark once, Luke 15 times, and Acts 14 times; 'woe to' with dative plural, none in Matthew or Mark, 5 times in Luke; 'rich', 3 times in Matthew, twice in Mark, 10 times in Luke; pleonastic 'all', as Lk 6:26, frequent in Luke). The form of a series of threatened woes could be taken from Mt 23. But whereas Matthew reserves the contrast with the beatitudes of the Sermon on the Mount until his final discourse, Luke makes the contrast more immediate. There are other traces of dependence of Luke on Matthew in the beatitudes. Lk 6:21 substitutes 'weep' for Matthew's 'mourn', but in the woes Lk 6:25 includes both verbs. Similarly in Lk 6:26 'speak well' corresponds to Mt 5:11 'speak evil' rather than to Lk 6:22 'revile'. Luke's formula in the second person plural (Matthew's eight beatitudes are in the third person) is less consonant with the background formula than Matthew's. It is, however, typical of Luke's immediacy of style (as Lk 6:2; 7:34 compared with their parallels).

In this instance, therefore, it is possible to argue either way, and the solution of the problem must be dependent on the overall solution of the synoptic problem.

H. 1. The Second Sign at Cana or Capernaum (Mt 8:5–13; Lk 7:1–10; Jn 4:46–53)

Mt 8:5–13	Lk 7:1–10	Jn 4:46–53
[5] When he entered Capernaum, a centurion came to him appealing to him [6] and saying, 'Lord, my servant is lying at home paralyzed, in terrible distress.'	[1] After Jesus had finished all his sayings in the hearing of the people, he entered Capernaum. [2] A centurion there had a slave whom he valued highly, and who was ill and close to death. [3] When he heard about Jesus, he sent some Jewish elders to him, asking him to heal his slave. [4] When they came to Jesus, they appealed to him earnestly, saying, 'He is worthy to have you do this for him, [5] for he loves our people, and it is he who built our synagogue for us'	[46] Then he came again to Cana in Galilee where he had changed the water into wine. Now there was a royal official whose son lay ill in Capernaum. [47] When he heard that Jesus had come from Judea to Galilee, he went and begged him to come down and heal his son, for he was on the point of death. [48] Then Jesus said to him, 'Unless you see signs and wonders you will not believe.' [49] The official said to him, 'Sir, come down before my little boy dies.' [50] Jesus said to him, 'Go, your son will live.' The man believed the word that Jesus spoke to him and started on his way.
[7] And he said to him, 'I will come and cure him.' the centurion answered, 'Lord, I am not worthy to have you come under my roof; but only speak	[6] And Jesus went with them, but when he was not far from the house, the centurion sent friends to say to him, 'Lord, I am not worthy to have you come under my roof; [7] therefore I did not presume to come to you. But only speak	

the word, and my servant will be healed. ⁹For I also am a man under authority, with soldiers under me, and I say
to one, "Go", and he goes, and to another, "Come", and he comes, and to
my slave, "Do this", and the slave
does it.' ¹⁰When Jesus heard him, he
was amazed and said to those who
          followed him, 'Truly I tell you
in no one in Israel have I found such
faith.'
¹¹I tell you, many will come from east
and west and will eat with
Abraham and Isaac and Jacob
          in the kingdom of heaven,
¹²while the heirs of the kingdom will
be thrown into the outer darkness,
where there will be weeping and
gnashing of teeth.'
¹³And to the centurion Jesus said,
'Go, let it be done for you according
to your faith.' And the servant was
healed in that hour.

the word, and my servant will be healed. ⁸For I also am a man under authority, with soldiers under me; and I say
to one, "Go", and he goes, and to another, "Come", and he comes, and to
my slave, "Do this", and the slave
does it.' ⁹When Jesus heard this, he
was amazed at him, and turning to the
crowd that followed him,   'I tell you
not even   in Israel have I found such
faith.'
Lk 13:28–29 ²⁸*There will be weeping
and gnashing of teeth when you see
Abraham and Isaac and Jacob and all
the prophets in the kingdom of God,
and you yourselves thrown out.* ²⁹*Then
people will come from east and west,
from north and south, and will eat in
the kingdom of God.*

¹⁰When those who had been sent returned to the house, they found the
slave in good health.

⁵¹As he was going down, his slaves
met him and told him that his child was
alive. ⁵²So he asked them the hour when
he began to recover, and they said to
him, 'Yesterday at one in the afternoon
the fever left him.' ⁵³The father realized
that this was the hour when Jesus had
said to him, 'Your son will live.' So he
himself believed, along with his whole
household.

The relationship between the three accounts of the miraculous cure of the official's boy at Capernaum poses unusual
problems. It is the only healing story shared by John and the
Synoptic Gospels, and the only miracle story in the material
normally assigned to Q (i.e. double tradition of Matthew and
Luke without Mark). There are also unmistakable similarities
with two other stories, one the story of the Syro-Phoenician
woman's daughter (similarly healed at a distance) and the
other a miracle-story about Rabbi Hanina ben Dosa.

2. First the link with the Markan tradition of the cure of the
Syro-Phoenician's daughter (Mk 7:25–30||Mt 15:22–8) should
be outlined:

1. In each gospel this is the only miracle worked for a
Gentile.
2. The parent comes to Jesus asking for the healing.
3. The dialogue between Jesus and the suppliant is reported.
4. The faith of the Gentile is contrasted with that of the
Jews.
5. Jesus praises the parent's faith.
6. The cure is effected at a distance.

Such detailed similarity cannot be wholly coincidental. One
explanation is that there was an outline story in the oral
tradition which took on the two or three slightly different
forms in the tradition expressed by Mark, Matthew/Luke,
and John.

Hanina ben Dosa was a well-known rabbi in Palestine in the
generation after Jesus. Of him several wonders are related,
among them this story:

Once Rabban Gamliel's son fell ill. He sent two learned men to
R. Hanina ben Dosa to beg God's mercy for him. R. Hanina saw
them coming and went to an upstairs room and asked God's mercy
for the boy. When he came down he said to them, 'Go! The fever has
left him.' They asked him, 'Are you a prophet?' He replied, 'I am not
a prophet or the son of a prophet. But this I have received from
tradition: if my prayer of intercession flows unhesitatingly from my
mouth, I know it will be answered; if not, I know it will be rejected.'
They sat down and wrote and noted the exact moment at which he
said this. When they got back to Rabban Gamliel he said to them,
'By the Temple Service, you are neither too early nor too late but this
is what happened: in that moment the fever left him and he asked
for water.'

This story teaches the lesson that R. Hanina, though not a
prophet (despite the allusions to 1 Kings 17:19; Am 7:14), had
the healing gift and intercessory power of a prophet. It shares
with the gospel story the following elements:

1. Cure of a child at a distance.
2. Messengers sent by the father to ask for divine help.
3. Stress on simultaneity of the statement and the cure.

The story of R. Hanina also has the added wonder that he goes
to pray without needing to be told. In the Jesus story his
prophetic quality is not stressed—as it is stressed in Jesus'
similar healing of the widow of Nain's son (Lk 7:16). Emphasis
falls on the faith of the recipient rather than on the charisma
of the miracle-worker.

3. In the Matthew–Luke story of the Capernaum cure there
are significant differences between the two evangelists.
Firstly, Matthew has assimilated the Capernaum story to

that of the Syro-Phoenician, including in each three features which are not in the Markan version of the Syro-Phoenician cure:

1. The sick child's parent comes to Jesus, asking for the cure in direct speech, to which Jesus replies.

2. The longer speech by the suppliant, the full expression of faith that earns the cure, is therefore the suppliant's second statement.

3. Jesus' final statement to the suppliant, and the announcement of the cure, are almost identical in the two cases: 8:13: ' "Let it be done for you as your faith demands". And the servant was cured at that moment'; 15:28: ' "Let it be done for you as you desire." And her daughter was cured from that moment.'

On the whole Matthew shortens rather than lengthens Mark's miracle-stories. The purpose of each of these additions is to underline the faith of the suppliant and its reward. But Matthew's most significant addition to the centurion story is of 8:11–12, Jesus' saying that points the contrast between the faith of the Gentile and the disbelief of Israel; this is full of Matthean expressions and vocabulary. Such a contrast is stressed often by Matthew (the magi contrasting with Herod, 2:1–17; the vineyard taken from its custodians and given to others, 21:43; the guests at the marriage feast, 22:1–10).

4. The absence from Luke's version both of this couplet, and of all the Matthean assimilations of this story to the cure of the Canaanite girl, has frequently been used as an argument that Luke presents the more primitive version: he follows the order and content of Q, which has been changed by Matthew. But traces of Lukan editing are also clear. Most recently Franklin (1994: 283), says, 'It is hard to see how the creative hand of Luke could be denied at this point.' Luke likes to show that the history and miracles of the early church continue and mirror those of Jesus. So he assimilates this centurion to the centurion of Ac 10, who

1. is the first Gentile in the book to come to the faith;

2. sends messengers to Peter, as this centurion to Jesus;

3. is similarly praised by the messengers as helpful to the Jewish nation.

In order to prevent the centurion actually meeting Jesus (which would make the first embassy rather pointless) Luke is compelled awkwardly to put his speech of unworthiness (7:6–8), with all its circumstantial detail, into the mouths of the second set of envoys. The emphasis on his own unworthiness (in Luke it comes twice, by contrast to Matthew's once) compares to Simon Peter's protestations of sinfulness in Lk 5:8 and those of Zacchaeus in Lk 19:8. Luke always insists that at least some in Israel were converted (several groups are converted during the crucifixion, a large number at Pentecost, and some in each of the towns visited by Paul). So here Luke avoids the sharp contrast between Gentile and Jew seen in Matthew. If, as in the Goulder theory, Luke is dependent on Matthew, he alters Jesus' statement by the change of two letters, 'in no one in Israel have I found such great faith' (Mt 8:10) to 'not even in Israel have I found such great faith' (Lk 7:9). This leaves room in Israel for at least some faith. A softening of the polemic against Israel could also be the reason for omitting Mt's 8:11–12. When he does use this saying in Lk 12:28–9, he gives it in a less absolute version: others will indeed come from east and west, but at least 'the sons of the kingdom' will not be 'thrown out into exterior darkness', as in Matthew.

Especially a small verbal indication may show that Luke is dependent on Matthew rather than on any Q-version. This would solve the anomaly of a miracle-story in Q, the collection of Sayings of the Lord (if it existed), but would also show a significant dependence of Luke on Matthew. Luke uses a number of words that are favourites of his, but are not in Matthew's narrative. But significantly Luke starts and ends the story (7:2–3, 10) with a 'slave' of the centurion (adding with typical tenderness that this slave was valuable to him); the Greek word used by Matthew, 'boy', may, in Greek as in English, also mean a servant. But in 7:7 Luke once slips into the Greek word, 'boy', used by Matthew. This is described by Goulder as editor's 'fatigue', and taken as evidence that Luke was editing Matthew's story. The same phenomenon occurs in the words used for 'bed' in Lk 5:18–24 || Mt 9:2–7.

5. The story of the healing of the son of the royal official at Capernaum in Jn 4:46–54 is unusual in John, being the only healing-story which does not extend after the healing into a discussion or discourse of Jesus. It has obvious similarities to the synoptic stories just considered:

1. Capernaum enters into the story.

2. An official appeals to Jesus for the cure of his son, who is at the point of death (this is clear in Luke, less clear in Matthew; John is often closer to Luke than to the other Synoptics).

3. Jesus cures the child at a distance.

4. An intermediate group comes from the sickbed with a new message (another link to Luke rather than to Matthew).

5. The emphasis of the story is on the faith of the official.

There are also, of course, significant differences. As often, John's historical detail is persuasive: it is more likely that a royal official of Herod should be at Capernaum (which was a border town in Herod's territory, and not under direct Roman rule) than that a Roman centurion should be stationed there. Some of the differences are characteristic of John, and may well have been introduced by him for theological reasons:

1. The structure of the story is similar to that of the first miracle at Cana. These are the only two occasions on which Jesus at first demurs.

2. The reproach to faith that requires miracles (v. 48, as Jn 2:23–4; 20:29). In fact the two vv. 48–9 may well have been added to the original story. They can be cut out without spoiling the story, and only here is the victim called 'little boy'; elsewhere he is 'son'.

3. In Matthew and Luke the father's faith is praised before the cure. In John it comes at any rate to its full flowering only at the attestation of the cure 'at that hour' (4.58), as in the first sign at Cana the disciples find faith only when they see his glory at the end of the story (2:11).

There are comparatively few exact verbal similarities with the synoptic accounts, though some are notable (the healing occurs 'at that hour', Mt 8:13; Jn 4:53). But the similarity is more at the level of events and circumstances. The link between John and the two Synoptics may therefore be grounded on oral tradition rather than any written text.

I. The Controversy over Beelzebul (Mt 12:24–32; Mk 3:22–30; Lk 11:15–23 + 12:10)

Mt 12:24–32	Mk 3:22–30	Lk 11:15–23
24 They said, 'It is only by Beelzebul, the ruler of demons, that this fellow casts out demons.' 25 He knew what they were thinking and said to them, 'Every kingdom divided against itself becomes a desert, and no city or house divided against itself will stand. 26 If Satan casts out Satan, he is divided against himself, how then will his kingdom stand?	22 And the scribes who came down from Jerusalem said, 'He has Beelzebul, and by the ruler of demons he casts out demons.' 23 And he called them to him and spoke to them in parables, 'How can Satan cast out Satan? 24 If a kingdom is divided against itself, that kingdom cannot stand. 25 And if a house is divided against itself, that house will not be able to stand. 26 And if Satan has risen up against himself and is divided, he cannot stand, but his end has come.	15 He casts out demons by Beelzebul, the ruler of demons.' ... 17 But he knew what they were thinking and said to them, 'Every kingdom divided against itself becomes a desert, and house falls on house. 18 If Satan also is divided against himself, how will his kingdom stand?—for you say that I cast out demons by Beelzebul.
27 If I cast out demons by Beelzebul, by whom do your own exorcists cast them out? Therefore they will be your judges. 28 But if it is by the Spirit of God that I cast out demons, then the kingdom of God has come to you. 29 Or how can one enter a strong man's house and plunder his property without first tying up the strong man? Then indeed he may plunder his house.	27 But no one can enter a strong man's house and plunder his property without first tying up the strong man. Then indeed he may plunder his house.	19 Now if I cast out demons by Beelzebul, by whom do your own exorcists cast them out? Therefore they will be your judges. 20 But if it is by the finger of God that I cast out demons, then the kingdom of God has come to you. 21 When a strong man, fully armed, guards his castle, his property is in safe, 22 but when one stronger than he attacks him and overcomes him, he takes away his armour in which he trusted, and divides his plunder. 23 Whoever is not with me is against me, and whoever does not gather with me scatters.
30 Whoever is not with me is against me, and whoever does not gather with me scatters. 31 Therefore I tell you, people will be forgiven every sin and blasphemy but blasphemy against the Spirit will not be forgiven 32 Whoever speaks a word against the Son of Man will be forgiven but whoever speaks against the holy Spirit will not be forgiven, either in this age or in the age to come.'	28 'Truly I tell you, people will be forgiven their sins and whatever blasphemies they utter; 29 but whoever blasphemes against the holy Spirit can never have forgiveness, but is guilty of an eternal sin' — 30 for they said, 'He has an unclean spirit.'	12 10 And everyone who speaks a word against the Son of Man will be forgiven, everyone who blasphemes against the holy Spirit will not be forgiven.'

One of the most critical passages in the Synoptic Gospels is the Beelzebul controversy. The prominence in the gospel tradition of the accusation that Jesus casts out evil spirits by being in league with Beelzebul, the prince of evil spirits, suggests that it was one of the major ways of discounting Jesus' miracles used by his opponents. Moreover there are also parallels in John to the synoptic tradition, since there also Jesus is accused of having an evil spirit (Jn 7:20); on another occasion Jesus cites his power to work miracles in reply to such an accusation (Jn 10:20–1). The parallels are, however, sufficiently loose to be explained as dependent on oral rather than written tradition; the common point may be merely the memory that Jesus was accused of having an evil spirit. In John the accusation is made twice that Jesus 'has an evil spirit', and on the second occasion this is backed up with the question, 'Can an evil spirit open the eyes of the blind?' The circumstances of the accusation in the Synoptics and in John are entirely different. In the Synoptics the starting-point of the discussion is expulsion of evil spirits; it is more specific than in John: 'They said that he has Beelzebul and casts out evil spirits through the leader of evil spirits.' It then leads on to a full-blown controversy.

The use of this particular tradition is different in each of the gospels. In Mark it is the centrepiece of a typically Markan 'sandwich', showing how Jesus was misunderstood by different groups of people. This then leads on to the recourse to parables in Mk 4. It is, then, part of Mark's demonstration of Jesus turning away from the crowds to instruct his special disciples, an important hinge in the structure of the first part of Mark's gospel. In Matthew the passage provides a commentary on the important quotation in Mt 12:18–21 of Isa 42:1–4, including, 'I shall place my Spirit upon him'; its message is, therefore, the contrast between the Spirit of Jesus and the spirit of Beelzebul. Not dissimilarly, in Luke the main part of the passage comes in the section on discipleship after the Lord's prayer and the promise (11:13) that the heavenly Father will give the Holy Spirit to those who ask him. It serves to contrast the spirit of the disciples with that of Jesus' opponents. Finally in John, the passages are part of the confrontation between Jesus and the temple authorities in Jerusalem, as part of the judgement theme that is so important in John.

From the point of view of the synoptic problem this passage has an importance all its own. Any solution to the problem must, of course, be shown to be valid for all the pericopes of the synoptic tradition. Nevertheless each theory has its special pericopes for which the proponents of the theory claim that their solution is obviously the best, while there are other pericopes where this solution is less obviously the best, and *prima facie* another solution would fit the facts equally well or perhaps even more easily. In the case of this pericope, however, it is claimed as primary evidence for their own theory by proponents of each of the principal solutions to the synoptic problem. The relationships between the synoptic passages have been claimed as evidence by proponents of the Griesbach theory, as evidence of Mark-Q overlap (in which Luke is closer than Matthew to Q) by proponents of the Two-Source theory, and by single-source theorists as evidence of editing of Mark by Matthew and Luke successively.

The basic relationship between the three synoptic texts is shown in Table 1.

One of the chief arguments of proponents of the Griesbach theory is the claim that Mark combines Matthew and Luke by zigzagging between them: when Mark departs from the order they share, Mark follows first one and then the other (see c.1). This is claimed to be exemplified here. So, it is dubiously claimed, Mk 3:22*b* agrees with the order of words in Luke against Matthew. Then Mk 3:25 agrees with Matthew (there is nothing corresponding in Luke). Mk 3:26 agrees with both. Still, after a gap, Mk 3:27–8 agrees with Matthew. Finally, Mk 3:29 corresponds to Lk 12:10*b* (the aorist of the verb *blasphēmeō, eis to pneuma to agion*). The zigzag is, however, in this case hard to sustain. In fact Mark shares overwhelmingly with Matthew, never in this passage with Luke, though there are

occasional elements in the triple-tradition verses where Mark is closer to Luke than to Matthew. In Mk 3:22*b* the phrases are indeed in the Lukan order (Beelzebul first, not second as in Matthew), but the relationship between the verses is more easily explained as independent improvement by Matthew and Luke of Mark's clumsy double-phrase. In Mk 3:29 there are equally strong correspondences with Matthew. The argument is perhaps plausible, but by no means compelling.

On the Two-Source theory it is considered a passage of Mark-Q overlap. It is one of the five principal passages accepted as such by Streeter (along with the preaching of John the Baptist, the temptations, the mustard seed, and the commissioning of the disciples, see c.2). Matthew and Luke share $6^{1}/_{2}$ verses absent from Mark, and in the triple-tradition verses there is persistent minor agreement between them against Mark. Some explanation must be given of these agreements, and if the Mark-Q overlap theory makes sense at all, it is a possible candidate as the explanation. Therefore a three-stage process is postulated: first comes Mark, then Q develops this tradition, then Matthew and Luke independently combine this Q tradition with their version of Mark.

In order to show, however, that at least in this case Mark-Q overlap is the most economical explanation it is necessary to show that Luke's version is the more primitive, and Mark has subsequently been edited by Matthew. So advocates of the Mark-Q overlap claim that Matthew has taken verses from various places in Q (the elements occur in three different sections of Luke) to make a skilfully unified composition, but that the elements of this composition are still visible in their original form in Luke. Advocates of this theory are posed the formidable task of showing that underlying Luke and/or Matthew is a unified theology or style that is distinct from that of the final authors, and can be considered characteristic of Q. So Kloppenborg (1987: 121–7) argues vigorously that Luke is the more primitive version, more coherent than Matthew's form. Luke's parable of the stronger man in 11:21–2 evokes warfare, which better fits the mention of 'kingdom' in the previous verses than does Matthew's household burglary. Matthew would then have adopted the earlier verses from Q, but reverted slavishly to Mark for the burglary. After the little Q-saying of Luke 11:23, Luke would have added another passage (originally separate in Q, and used by Matthew at 12:43–5) to stress that mere expulsion of the evil spirit is not enough without a further positive response to the kingdom. For Kloppenborg both Mark and Q versions have the same origin: 'the starting-point for this complex of Q-sayings is the traditional Beelzebul accusation and its refutation in Mark 3:20–6' (ibid. 127). But Q has enlarged the scene in two ways, first by attributing the accusation not (as does Mark) to the scribes from Jerusalem but to 'your sons' in general, and secondly by applying Jesus' threat not only (as Mark) to those who accuse Jesus of complicity with Beelzebul, but to all who oppose Jesus (Lk 11:23–6).

Opponents of the Mark-Q overlap must show that the Matthean passage is so typical of Matthew that there is no trace of any written source other than Mark. So Goulder (1974: 332) maintains that the changes are best explained as introduced first by Matthew. He points out that in Mt 12:25 the balance of two similarly shaped phrases is a typically elegant

TABLE 1. *Relationship between synoptic texts*

Mt 12:24*b* =	Mk 3:22*b* =	Lk 11:15	(complex relationship)
25*a*	24	17	(6 minor agreements Matthew/Luke against Mark)
25*c*	25	–	
26	26	18	(6 minor agreements Matthew/Luke against Mark)
27	–	19	(1 minor disagreement Matthew/Luke)
28	–	20	(one important difference)
29	27	21–2	(Luke's wording very different)
30	–	23	(identical)
31	28	–	(several small differences)
32*a*	–	12.10*a*	(one characteristic difference Matthew/Luke)
32*b*	29	10*b*	(one minor agreement of Matthew/Luke against Mark)
–	30	–	(typical Markan dualism, not in Matthew/Luke)

Matthean improvement on Mark's rough phrase. Goulder then argues phrase by phrase that the expansions of Mark are so characteristic of Matthew that it would be a mistake to postulate any Q. Particularly the rhythm of vv. 31, 33, 35 is typical of Matthean formations, and such antitheses as 'gather/scatter', 'good/bad'. It is then necessary to argue that Luke can best be explained as derived from Matthew. To begin with, it is pointed out that Luke often breaks up longer Matthean sections, and that the method of so doing is in this case typical of Luke (see c.4).

On the other side it is argued that Luke, with his stress on the Spirit, would never have substituted 'finger of God' (Lk 11:20) for Matthew's 'Spirit of God' if he had been following Matthew. This is taken as an indication that 'finger of God' must have been the original form in Q (e.g. Stanton 1992a: 177 n.3); to which Goulder (1989: 504) replies that this allusion to Moses' miracles in Ex 8:15 is typical of Luke, and that 'Spirit' occurs only twice in Luke's accounts of Jesus' teaching.

In this particular case it is unlikely that either side will finally convince the other. The particular question must be judged in function of the more general question whether a Mark-Q overlap makes sense, and particularly whether this overlapping Q is so close to Mark that some literary dependence of Mark on Q would need to be postulated. This in turn would raise the question of why Mark omitted so much of Q.

J. 1. The Walking on the Water (Mt 14:22–33 || Mk 6:45–52 || Jn 6:16–21)

Mt 14:22–33

22 Immediately he made the disciples get into the boat and go on ahead to the other side   while he dismissed the crowds. 23 And after he had dismissed the crowds, he went up the mountain by himself to pray. When evening came, he was there alone, 24 but by this time the boat, strained by the waves, was far from the land, for the wind was against them. 25 And early in the morning he came to them walking on the lake.   26 but when the disciples saw him walking on the lake, they were terrified, saying it was a ghost, and they cried out in fear. 27 But immediately Jesus spoke to them and said, 'Take heart, it is I; do not be afraid.' 28 Peter answered him, 'Lord, if it is you, command me to come to you on the water. 29 He said, 'Come.' So Peter got out of the boat, started walking on the water, and came toward Jesus. 30 But when he noticed the strong wind he became frightened and, beginning to sink, he cried out, 'Lord, save me!' 31 Jesus immediately reached out his hand and caught him, saying to him, 'You of little faith, why did you doubt?' 32 When they got into the boat   the wind ceased, and those in the boat worshipped him, saying, 'Truly you are the Son of God.'

Mk 6:45–52

45 Immediately he made his disciples get into the boat and go on ahead to the other side to Bethsaida while he dismissed the crowd. 46 After saying farewell to them he went up the mountain to pray. 47 When evening came, the boat was out on the lake, and he was alone on the land. 48 When he saw that they were straining at the oars,   for the wind was against them.   early in the morning he came to them walking on the lake. He intended to pass them by, 49 but when they   saw him walking on the lake they thought   it was a ghost and cried out. 50 For they all saw him and were terrified. But immediately he spoke to them and said to them, 'Take heart, it is I; do not be afraid.'

51 Then he got into the boat with them and the wind ceased and they were utterly astounded, 52 for they did not understand about the loaves, but their hearts were hardened.

Jn 6:16–21

16 When evening came, his disciples went down to the lake 17 got into a boat, and started across the lake to Capernaum. It was now dark and Jesus had not yet come to them

18 The lake became rough because a strong wind was blowing. 19 When they had rowed about three or four miles, they saw Jesus walking on the lake and coming near the boat and they were terrified.

20 But he said to them, 'It is I; do not be afraid.'

21 Then they wanted to take him into the boat with them, and immediately the boat reached the land towards which they were going.

The three evangelists who narrate this incident all use it to express their own theology. It is arguable that John's account is the closest to the oral tradition that lies behind them. Luke omits the story, perhaps because, along with other pericopes in the central section of Mark's gospel, he considers them unnecessary duplication. Before the content of the passage is discussed two preliminary problems must be aired.

The position of the incident is significant. It is rare that John and the Synoptics share any sequence of incidents, but in this case in both traditions the episode follows the miraculous feeding. In the case of John this is decidedly awkward, in that it splits the feeding (Jn 6:1–14) from the bread of life discourse (6:22–71); normally the related discourse in John follows immediately the miracle on which it comments. This suggests that the juxtaposition of the two incidents was considered significant in the previous oral tradition. This juxtaposition may have paschal overtones. Jn 6:4 mentions that the Passover was near, and in both the original Exodus incident and its liturgical commemoration the gift of manna and the crossing of the sea are associated. The OT typology is only slightly altered in the gospel accounts: the order of events is reversed, with the manna coming before the crossing, and Jesus does not cross the sea from one side to the other, but walks towards his distressed disciples in the middle of the sea.

The similarity between the accounts of John and Mark is notable especially in the order of the narration:

1. The disciples start off across the sea;
2. it is evening;
3. the disciples are in difficulty with the wind;
4. the distance covered (John) and time passed (Mark) is mentioned;
5. they see Jesus walking on the sea and are terrified;
6. Jesus says, 'It is I; do not be afraid';
7. they want to take him (John), actually take him (Mark), into the boat and all is well.

The exact verbal similarity is also striking, not all of it dictated by a scene of rowing on the sea. Matthew has an addition link with John in the description of the distance in stades (NRSV miles).

It has been commented that in John Jesus is walking *epi* the sea, which could be translated merely 'at' or 'beside' rather than 'on'. In this case there would not necessarily be any miracle involved, and the original lesson would be that without Jesus the disciples are helpless and distressed (John symbolizes their distress by 'it was now dark', 6:17, as in 8:12; 12:46, cf. 13:30). This would accord with their reaching land 'immediately', before they succeed in their intention of taking Jesus into the boat. But it would be difficult to account for the terror of the disciples, unless it is at the theophanic appearance of Jesus. The significance of Jesus walking on the sea comes from its scriptural echoes (see MT 14:23–36). In Israel the sea was always regarded as a frightening evil power, controlled and dominated only by the Lord (see also MK 6:45–62). Jesus' self-identification is made in the words *egō eimi*, which, at least for John, have the special significance of the divine name (see JN 6:16–21).

2. Despite sharing oral tradition and a number of similar words with John, Mark's narrative is unmistakably written by him. The style includes many of his typical features (see E.I): the characteristic 'immediately' (vv. 45, 50), the afterthought explanation with *gar* (vv. 48, 50, 52), double expressions (v. 45,

'to the other side, to Bethsaida'; v. 50, 'spoke to them and said'; 'take heart, do not be afraid'; v. 52 'they did not understand, their hearts were hardened'), and others invisible in translation. It is reasonable to assume that he himself composed the narrative from oral tradition. Boismard maintains that the narrative existed in different versions in Document A and Document B (see C.3) on the grounds that, if Jesus was alone on the shore 'when evening came' (from the supposed Document B), he could not be said to wait to come to them till 'early in the morning' (from the supposed Document A). John lacks the latter element, so used only Document B. In fact, however, John has traces of the disciples' prolonged wait in the form of the 3 or 4 miles' rowing.

With typical Markan irony (see E.I and cf. Camery-Hoggatt 1992: 147) the climax of the story is the failure of the disciples to understand about the loaves. Mark many times stresses the incomprehension of the disciples. On this occasion, despite their utter astonishment, he links it to the miracle of the loaves, which included (6:37) one of the worst examples of their sarcasm to Jesus. Just as, in the second half of the gospel, they thrice fail to understand the formal prophecies of the passion, so in this first half their failure to understand is three times noted on the lake (also 5:41; 8:17–21).

3. Matthew makes some minor adjustments, though he does not file the story down as much as he does many of the healing miracles. He omits Mark's v. 48c, perhaps because it suggests the unworthy thought that Jesus intended to neglect his followers (who no doubt, as in the calming of the storm, see Mt 8:23–7, stand for the Christian community), and that he changed his mind. He omits also Mark's v. 50a because he dislikes such afterthought explanations. Matthew's most important change, however, is the introduction of Peter's walking on the water. Typically for Matthew, Peter starts well and then comes a cropper (as at Caesarea Philippi and at the trial-scene), but at least his enthusiastic leadership comes to view, and his trust in Jesus merits a controlled compliment from the Lord. As in Mark, the disciples may stand for the community who have difficulty in accepting the full message of Jesus, especially with its implications of persecution, perhaps in Matthew Peter stands for the community, enthusiastic but still too hesitant and repeatedly failing. But the disciples' final confession—so much at variance with Mark's conclusion—leaves little to be desired: it is already at least as full as that of the centurion at the foot of the cross in Mark. The repeated 'Lord' (vv. 28, 30) and 'worshipped him' are also hints of the reaction proper to the divine.

K. 1. Jesus' Prayer in the Garden (Mt 26:36–46 ‖ Mk 14:32–42 ‖ Lk 22:39–46)

Mt 26:36–46	Mk 14:32–42	Lk 22:39–46
36 Then Jesus went with them to a place called Gethsemane,	32 They went to a place called Gethsemane,	39 He came out and went, as was his custom, to the Mount of Olives; and the disciples followed him. 40 When he reached the place, he said to them, 'Pray that you may not come into the time of trial.'
and he said to his disciples, 'Sit here while I go over there and pray.' 37 He took with him Peter and the two sons of Zebedee, and began to be grieved and agitated. 38 Then he said to	and he said to his disciples, 'Sit here while I go over there and pray.' 33 He took with him Peter and James and John, and began to be distressed and agitated. 34 And he said to	

them, 'I am deeply grieved, even to death; remain here and stay awake with me.' [39] And going a little farther he threw himself on the ground and prayed

'My Father, if it is possible let this cup pass from me; yet not what I want but what you want.'

[40] Then he came to the disciples and found them sleeping and he said to Peter, 'So, could you not stay awake with me one hour? [41] Stay awake and pray that you may not come into the time of trial; the spirit indeed is willing, but the flesh is weak.' [42] Again he went away for a second time and prayed, 'My Father, if this cannot pass unless I drink it, your will be done.' [43] Again he came and found them sleeping, for their eyes were heavy.

[44] So leaving them again, he went and prayed for the third time, saying the same words. [45] Then he came to the disciples and said to them, 'Are you still sleeping and taking your rest? See the hour is at hand, and the Son of Man is betrayed into the hands of sinners. [46] Get up, let us be going. See, my betrayer is at hand.'

them, 'I am deeply grieved, even to death; remain here and keep awake.' [35] And going a little farther he threw himself on the ground and prayed that, if possible the hour might pass from him. [36] He said, 'Abba, Father, for you all things are possible; remove this cup from me; yet, not what I want, but what you want.'

[37] He came and found them sleeping; and he said to Peter, 'Simon, are you asleep? Could you not keep awake one hour? [38] Keep awake and pray that you may not come into the time of trial; the spirit indeed is willing, but the flesh is weak.' [39] And again he went away and prayed, saying the same words.

[40] And once more he came and found them sleeping, for their eyes were very heavy; and they did not know what to say to him.

[41] He came a third time and said to them, 'Are you still sleeping and taking your rest? Enough! The hour has come; the Son of Man is betrayed into the hands of sinners.' [42] Get up, let us be going. See, my betrayer is at hand.'

[41] Then he withdrew from them about a stone's throw, knelt down, and prayed,

[42] 'Father, if you are willing, remove this cup from me, yet not my will but yours be done.' [[43] Then an angel from heaven appeared to him and gave him strength. [44] In his anguish he prayed more earnestly, and his sweat became like great drops of blood falling down on the ground.] [45] When he got up from prayer he came to the disciples and found them sleeping because of grief, [46] and he said to them, 'Why are you sleeping? Get up and pray that you may not come into the time of trial.'

Jn 12:27–9

[27] 'Now my soul is troubled. And what should I say— "Father, save me from this hour"? No, it is for this reason that I have come to this hour. [28] Father, glorify your name.' Then a voice came from heaven, 'I have glorified it, and I will glorify it again.' [29] The crowd standing there heard it and said that it was thunder. Other said, 'An angel has spoken to him.'

Jn 18:11

Jesus said to Peter, 'Put your sword back into its sheath. Am I not to drink the cup that the Father has given me?'

2. The account of Jesus' prayer before his passion is a particularly rich example of how the several synoptic evangelists have adapted the tradition they received in order to express their own theology. There are also interesting links to the Fourth Gospel which most probably reflect an oral tradition about the prayer of Jesus at the pre-gospel stage. As a working hypothesis in the discussion of this pericope it will be assumed that Mark is the first of the Synoptic Gospels, used by both the other two.

A long series of scholars has suggested that Mark is here combining two accounts, e.g. one source is 14:32, 35, 40, 41, the other is 14:33–4, 36–8. More probable is the view that Mark is spinning out a minimum of material to convey his own message according to his own manner. It is shot through with elements of Mark's own style. As throughout the passion narrative, a principal motif is to make sense of the stunning events by showing that what happens fulfils the scripture. A little hint of this is the allusion to Abraham's sacrifice of Isaac in 'going a little further' (14:35, as Gen 22:5). But especially marked is the reminiscence in Jesus' words of the laments of the persecuted just man in the Psalms (Ps 41:6 in Mk 14:34, etc.). The accent is on two factors, the obedience of Jesus to his Father's will and—by contrast—the failure of the disciples. Thus, with typical Markan duplication, the prayer of Jesus is given first indirectly (v. 35), then directly (v. 36).

Probably for the prayer itself Mark is using or imitating already the formulae of early Christian prayer, with the Aramaic *abba* immediately followed by its Greek translation (*ho patēr*). This double formula of a particular Aramaic word, regarded almost as a talisman, occurs elsewhere in the NT (1 Cor 16:22; Rev 1:7). Jesus' consciousness that God was his Father was treasured by the early community; this usage, stemming from Jesus himself, was greatly extended, especially in John. However, the use of *abba* for God is not, as Jeremias (1978) contended, unique to Jesus, indicating the affectionate relationship of childhood; children called their father *abi* rather than *abba*, and *abba* does occur occasionally in Jewish prayers. As elsewhere, Mark emphasizes the intensity of Jesus' prayer by the triple repetition beloved of popular story telling (see E.1). But, as in Peter's triple denial, he has barely enough material to trick out the full triad: the prayer is given fully the first time; for the second time the prayer is merely 'the same word', and on the third occasion it is only the return of Jesus rather than his prayer that is mentioned.

Thus the chief emphasis is on the failure of the disciples to take their share in their Master's final trial. Throughout the gospel they have repeatedly failed to grasp the message of suffering; now they are thrice found asleep while their Master prays, and their definite desertion at the arrest will be confirmed by Peter's triple denial at the moment when Jesus thrice faces his accusers. The bitterness of this occasion is underlined by the special involvement of precisely those three disciples who had been favoured with special revelation at the transfiguration (the link is stressed: again in their abashed confusion: they 'knew not what to answer'). James and John had also stoutly protested that they could share Jesus' cup (Mk 10:39).

3. In Matthew's account, besides many little characteristic verbal changes of style, three changes of emphasis are visible. Firstly, Matthew tones down the lurid colours in which Mark paints Jesus' agony of mind: for Mark's word for Jesus' almost stunned distress, Matthew has the more seemly 'grieved'. Instead of Mark's uncontrollable 'falling [repeatedly, if the imperfect is taken seriously, as though Jesus were simply stumbling] to the ground', the biblical attitude of reverent prayer is indicated by 'fell face to the ground in prayer' (26:39, my tr.). This is in accord with Matthew's generally more dignified, and even hieratic, presentation of Jesus.

Secondly Matthew fills out the second prayer of Jesus. After the Jewish manner of respect for the Lord, both prayers are impersonal: 'let this cup pass from me', instead of Mark's direct request, 'remove this cup from me'. Matthew gives content to the prayer by using the Lord's prayer, which he has set down at the very centre of the Sermon on the Mount, 'Your will be done' (26:42; 6:10). It may be presumed that, since Jesus is the model for his disciples, he will pray the same phrases as he taught them to pray. The intimacy of both first and second prayers is stressed by the affectionate address, 'My Father' (26:39, 42); this perhaps indicates both similarity and distinction between Jesus and his disciples, who are instructed to pray with the plural '*Our* Father' (6:9). At the same time, a certain hesitancy is shown—perhaps the hesitancy of respect—by the repeated '*if* it is possible' (26:39), '*if* it is not possible' (26:42), instead of Mark's confident 'for you all things are possible' (14:36). After this elaboration of the second prayer, Matthew can transfer to the third prayer Mark's minimal account of the second, 'saying the same words' (Mk 14:39; Mt 26:44).

Matthew's third concern is to underline the solidarity that should exist between Jesus and his disciples. As always he tones down their failure, here by omitting Mark's critical 'they did not know what to say to him' (Mk 14:40). He also takes the spotlight off Peter by removing Jesus' intimate and disappointed question to him, 'Simon, are you asleep?' (Mk 14:37), and by putting into the plural the criticism, 'could you not stay awake with me one hour?' (Mt 26:40). This now concerns not only Peter but all the disciples. Twice he adds 'with me' to 'stay awake' (26:38, 40); they should share in his passion, just as frequently in Matthew Jesus' community will benefit from his permanent presence (1:23; 18:20; 28:18–20) and will share in his ministry of forgiveness (9:8; 18:18).

4. Luke's version of the scene on the Mount of Olives (there is no mention of 'Gethsemane'; he often omits odd-sounding place-names, and has little interest in the topography of Jerusalem) is drastically shortened and unified. There is only one prayer and one return to the disciples. It is bracketed at beginning and end by the command, 'Pray that you may not come into temptation' (22:40, 46), exemplifying once more the Lukan theme of prayer, and more especially of the disciple praying after the model of the Master. In their persecutions and martyrdom, as in their working of miracles, the Acts of the Apostles will show the disciples mirroring exactly and continuing the life of Jesus into the era of the church. In the passion narrative too this carefully painted imitation comes to view in such details as Simon of Cyrene carrying the cross 'behind Jesus' (23:26). All stress has been taken off the failure of the disciples, both by eradication of the triple repetition and by a couple of subtle changes in 22:45: instead of 'sleeping' they are now (despite NRSV) 'lying down from grief', that is, their sympathy with Jesus is so intense that they could not stay on their feet. Nevertheless, when he firmly 'stands erect' after his prayer he comes to them and tells them too to join him in this posture (22:45, 46).

The most notable difference in Luke is the account of Jesus himself. Quite definitely, though not yet so emphatically as in John, Jesus is in control of his passion and death: he will be arrested only when he has exercised his healing ministry (22:51) and given the arresting party his consent, 'This is your hour' (22:53), and dies only when he has commended his spirit into his Father's hands (23:46). So now, Jesus does not collapse onto the ground, but 'knelt down', as Christians later do in prayer (Acts 7:60; 9:40; 20:36; 21:5). There is no sign of distress: his single prayer is calm and resigned, with the same resignation shown later by Christians (Acts 21:14). But there is nothing lacking to the intensity of his prayer.

The verses 22:43–4 are missing in some MSS, but are widely quoted in the second century. If they are considered part of Luke's gospel they contain two features, showing the preparation of Jesus for his passion. Both have analogies in the books of Maccabees to which the genre of Luke–Acts is so similar. First, Jesus is represented as an athlete about to enter a contest, with his adrenalin up, rather than terrified and horror-struck as in Mark. There is no question of sweating blood; it is merely that his sweat flowed like blood. This is the physical condition of those preparing for martyrdom in the books of Maccabees (2 Macc 3:16; 15:19; 4 Macc 6:6, 11). Secondly, an angel appears to show that Jesus' prayer is regarded, just as in Mk 1:13 at the earlier testing in the desert, and as two angels came to strengthen Eleazar at his martyrdom (4 Macc 6:18). After his prayer Jesus stands confidently upright, and comes to tell his followers to do the same in their prayer during temptation.

5. John has no equivalent scene of the prayer in the garden, but there are clear echoes of the same tradition. Similarly, he has no scene of the trial before the Sanhedrin (Mk 14:53–64), but an echo of this scene appears earlier in the Pharisees' decision to kill him in Jn 11:57. John portrays the passion of Jesus not as the moment of his humiliation but as the hour of his exaltation and glorification (see JN 18:1–19:24). John's Jesus is nevertheless fully human, so that his soul is troubled by the approaching trial (12:27a). However, since it is the moment of his glorification and that of his Father (12:28), to which he has looked forward (2:4; 7:30; 8:20) and will look forward (13:1; 16:32), he thrusts aside the thought of praying to be delivered from it. The image of the cup of suffering seen in the synoptic accounts of the prayer in the garden is also present at his arrest in the garden (18:11). Here it is explicit that Jesus accepts the cup in an atmosphere of triumph, for it comes at the conclusion of the arrest scene. During this scene his divinity has shone through by his use of the mysterious divine 'I am he' (18:5, 6, 8) and the awestruck reaction of the arresting party in falling to the ground. He can be arrested only after he has given this consent. There are further echoes of the tradition in the Letter to the Hebrews, in the mention that 'Jesus offered up prayers and supplications, with loud cries and tears, to the one who was able to save him from death' (Heb 5:7). The echoes of the prayers of the persecuted just man in the psalms are evident here. As already in the wording of the prayer in Mark, Brown (1994: 229) suggests that this prayer 'came from an early Christian hymn of praise constructed of a mosaic of psalm-motifs'. Behind it would be the same tradition as that of the synoptic and Johannine prayer in the garden.

REFERENCES

Ashton, J. (1991), *Understanding the Fourth Gospel* (Oxford: Clarendon).

Barthélemy, D. (1963), *Les Dévanciers d'Aquila* (Leiden: Brill).

Best, E. (1986), *Disciples and Discipleship* (Edinburgh: T. & T. Clark).

Boismard, M. (1972), *Synopse des quatre Évangiles* (Paris: Éditions du Cerf).

Brown, Raymond (1994), *The Death of the Messiah* (London: Geoffrey Chapman).

—— (1997), *An Introduction to the New Testament* (New York: Doubleday).

Burridge, R. (1992), *What are the Gospels?* (Cambridge: Cambridge University Press).

Camery-Hoggatt, J. (1992), *Irony in Mark's Gospel* (Cambridge: Cambridge University Press).

Casey, C. (1998), *Aramaic Sources of Mark's Gospel* (Cambridge: Cambridge University Press).

Denaux, A. (1992) (ed.), *John and the Synoptics* (Leuven: Leuven University Press).

Dodd, C. H. (1955–6), 'Some Johannine "Herrenworte" with Parallels in the Synoptic Gospels', *NTS* 2.

Donahue, J. (1973), *Are You the Christ? The Trial Narrative in the Gospel of Mark* (Missoula: Scholars Press).

Dunn, J. (1983), 'Let John be John', in P. Stuhlmacher (ed.), *Das Evangelium und die Evangelien* (Tübingen: Mohr).

—— (1991), 'John and the Oral Gospel Tradition', in H. Wansbrough (ed.), *Jesus and the Oral Gospel Tradition* (Sheffield: Sheffield Academic Press).

Fitzmyer, J. (1970–1) 'The Use of Explicit Old Testament Quotations in Qumran Literature and in the New Testament', *NTS* 7.

—— (1979), *The Gospel According to Luke* (New York: Doubleday).

Franklin, E. (1994), *Luke, Interpreter of Paul, Critic of Matthew* (Sheffield: Sheffield Academic Press).

Goodacre, M. (1996), *Goulder on the Gospels* (Sheffield: Sheffield Academic Press).

Goulder, M. (1974), *Midrash and Lection in Matthew* (London: SPCK).

—— (1984), 'The Order of a Crank', in Tuckett (1984a).

—— (1989), *Luke—A New Paradigm* (Sheffield: Sheffield Academic Press).

Green, H. Benedict, (1984), 'The Credibility of Luke's Transformation of Matthew', in Tuckett (1984a).

Green, Joel B. (1995), *The Theology of the Gospel of Luke* (Cambridge: Cambridge University Press).

Hawkins, Sir J. (1909), *Horae Synopticae* (Oxford: Clarendon).

Jeremias, J. (1978) *The Prayers of Jesus* (Philadelphia: Fortress).

Kloppenborg, J. (1987), *The Formation of Q* (Philadelphia: Fortress).

Kloppenborg Verdin J. (2000), *Excavating Q* (Edinburgh: T. & T. Clark).

Koester, H. (1989), 'From Kerygma-Gospel to Written Gospel', *NTS* 35.

Lamar Cribbs, F. (1971), 'St Luke and the Johannine Tradition', *JBL* 90.

Meeks, W. (1983), *The First Urban Christians* (New Haven: Yale University Press).

Meier, J. (1982), 'Antioch', in R. Brown and J. Meier, *Antioch and Rome* (London: Chapman).

Meier, J. P. (1994), *A Marginal Jew*, ii (New York: Doubleday).

Neirynck, F. (1978), 'The Symbol Q' *ETL* 54: 119–25.

—— (1979), 'Once More the Symbol Q', *ETL* 55: 382–3.

—— (1988), *Duality in Mark* (Leuven: Leuven University Press).

Peabody, D. (1987), *Mark as Composer* (Macon: Mercer University Press).

Perrin, N. (1970–1), *Expo Times*, 82.

Piper, R. A. (1995), *The Gospel behind the Gospels*, supplement to *Novum Testamentum*, vol. 75 (Leiden: Brill).

Puéch, E. (1993), 'The Collection of Beatitudes in Hebrew and Greek (4Q525. 1–4 and Matt 5, 3–12)', in F. Manns and E. Alliata (eds.), *Early Christianity in Context* (Jerusalem: Franciscan Press), 353–68.

Sanders, E. (1969), *The Tendencies of the Synoptic Tradition* (Cambridge: Cambridge University Press), 290–3.

Sanders, E. and Davies, M. (1989), *Studying the Synoptic Gospels* (London: SCM).

Sim, D. (1998), *The Gospel of Matthew and Christian Judaism* (Edinburgh: T. & T. Clark).

Stanton, G. (1992a), *A Gospel for a New People* (Edinburgh: T. & T. Clark).

—— (1992b), Βίβλος, εὐαγγέλιον or βίος?', in F. van Segbroeck et al. (eds.), *The Four Gospels* (Leuven: Leuven University Press).

Stuhlmacher, P. (1983), *Das Evangelium und die Evangelien* (Tübingen: Mohr).

Tuckett, C. (1983), 'The Beatitudes: A Source-Critical Study, with a Reply by M. D. Goulder', *NT* 25.

—— (1984a), 'Arguments from Order' in C. M. Tuckett, *Synoptic Studies* (Sheffield: Sheffield Academic Press).

—— (1984b), 'On the Relationship between Matthew and Luke', *NTS* 30.

—— (1987), *Reading the New Testament* (Philadelphia: Fortress).

—— (1995), 'The Existence of Q' in R. A. Piper, *The Gospel behind the Gospels*, supplement to *Novum Testamentum*, 75 (Leiden: Brill), 19–48.

von Wahlde, U. (1989), *The Earliest Version of John's Gospel* (Wilmington, Del.: Glazier).

Weeden, T. (1968), 'The Heresy that Necessitated Mark's Gospel', *ZNW* 59.

62. Acts

LOVEDAY ALEXANDER

INTRODUCTION

The book of Acts occupies a unique position in the NT, forming a bridge between the gospels and the epistles. It provides a narrative (the only one we have) of the steps by which the Christian message made the transition from the rural, Palestinian world of Jesus to the largely urban world of Paul and the later epistles, based in the Greek cities of the Roman empire. Whereas the gospels focus on Jesus, Acts focuses on people talking about Jesus, the apostles and others who spread his gospel across the Graeco-Roman world. While the Gospels are set almost exclusively in Galilee and Judea, Acts moves purposefully out from Jerusalem to the wider world of the empire, and its final scene is set in Rome. And while the gospels are located within the world of Palestinian Judaism, Acts moves out into the diaspora, where 'the Jews' are one vocal minority group among others seeking to maintain their identity within the multicultural civic communities of the empire.

A. Authorship. The book of Acts is anonymous: its opening verse (as was common in ancient literature) gives the name of its dedicatee, Theophilus, but not the name of the author. However, this dedication makes it easy to deduce that the author of Acts is the same as the author of Luke's gospel (cf. LK D), and there is sufficient continuity of language, style, and theological interests to make this one of the few virtually unchallenged conclusions of NT scholarship. Since Luke and Acts together account for a quarter of the NT, this makes this anonymous author (whom we shall call 'Luke' for convenience) one of the most important in the NT canon. The other possible indicator of authorship within Acts is the so-called 'we-passages' (see LK D; ACTS 15:36–18:28), which imply that the narrator was a companion of Paul on some of his voyages. Early church tradition identified him with the 'Luke, the beloved physician' of Col 4:14, a co-worker of Paul's (Philem 23) who was with Paul in prison, but this tradition has been questioned by scholars on the grounds that the author of Acts does not show the kind of knowledge we would expect of a close associate of Paul's (see LK D for a summary of the arguments). Since all the evidence on both sides lies within the book itself, it is difficult to resolve the question in advance of reading the text. I have tried to draw attention within the commentary to the passages which have a bearing on this question without prejudging the issue; but on balance I would agree with Fitzmyer and Barrett that it is difficult to find any alternative which makes more sense of all the data than the traditional ascription. See further Fitzmyer (1998: 49–51) and Barrett (1994–9: i. 30–48) (with full survey of all the ancient evidence); ii. pp. xlii–xlv.

B. Date. The question of date is no easier to resolve than the question of authorship, with which it is inextricably bound up. The book ends with Paul in prison in Rome, waiting for his appeal to Caesar to be heard: according to the book's internal chronology he was sent to Rome soon after the accession of Festus (25:1), who was procurator of Judea c.60–2 CE. Acts therefore cannot be earlier than c. 62; and the puzzling failure to narrate the outcome of Paul's trial has been taken as evidence that the book itself was written during the two-year period of imprisonment in Rome (28:30), before the persecution under Nero (64 CE) in which Paul traditionally lost his life. But this is again conjecture, and there are reasons for seeing the work as a more mature reflection on the significance of the Pauline mission, written after the apostle's death (which seems to be presupposed by the valedictory tone of 20:18–38, esp. 25). It must also come after the composition of the gospel, which is referred to in the opening verse (1:1), and therefore probably after the destruction of Jerusalem in 70 CE (Lk 21:20). The gospel preface implies that Luke sees himself as a second-generation Christian, one who has 'followed' the tradition 'handed down by the original eyewitnesses' (Lk 1:2). Thus a date in the 80s (LK D) would make sense, even if the author had earlier been a companion of Paul, and might help to account for some of the mistiness that seems to have grown up around the character and theology of Paul and the details of his travels (cf. Barrett 1994–9: ii. pp. xl–xli). Nevertheless, despite this mistiness in detail, Acts shows remarkable knowledge of the general conditions of life in the eastern Mediterranean at the time of Paul, and belongs unmistakably to the first century.

C. Audience. Despite the address to Theophilus in the opening sentence (1:1), Acts is not a letter or a speech addressing a single reader. The address is properly considered a dedication (not unlike the dedications of published books today), which allows the author to single out and honour one particular reader while implying a wider distribution. Such a dedicatee, within the conventions of ancient literature, would normally be a real person known to the author, a friend or patron, and often (but not necessarily) represents the same kind of reader as the implied readers of the text. If this is the case here, the readers, like Theophilus, will be people who have already had some instruction in the faith and need to be assured of its 'reliability' (Lk 1:4). This seems to imply a both a predominantly Christian readership and one that will appreciate the neutral, academic tones of the preface. But it is also important to take account of the dramatic audiences Luke invokes within the text itself: see ACTS E.

D. Acts and the Gospel Story. Ancient readers of Acts would recognize immediately from the first verse that this is the second volume of a multi-volume work, and a proper estimation of its narrative construction must take this into account. Acts assumes its readers have a basic knowledge of the characters and framework of the gospel story; it also contains a number of explicit summaries of the story of Jesus from the lips of the apostles who are now charged with passing on the tradition (Lk 1:2) to a wider audience (cf. ACTS 2:14–36). There are significant differences between the two volumes, not only in subject-matter but in style, and these may reflect the different sources Luke had at his disposal. Luke's style in the gospel is very largely determined by his synoptic sources, and as a result, it is marginally closer in language to Matthew and Mark than it is to Acts. But there are also striking similarities between the two volumes. Acts shares with Luke's gospel a common interest in rooting the story in the Jewish Scriptures; extensive parallelism between the words and deeds of Jesus in the gospel and those of the apostles and Paul in Acts; an interest in female characters; and similar patterns of narrative construction, especially a tendency to group material topically rather than chronologically and a fondness for 'type-scenes' which encapsulate the whole character of a phase of mission in one dramatic and detailed scene (cf. LK B). There is also a tendency to hold over certain narrative details from the gospel to Acts which suggests that Luke already had Acts in view when he was writing the gospel (cf. esp. ACTS 28:23–31). In particular, major themes introduced in the narrative prologue to the gospel (Lk chs. 1–4) reappear in clearer definition in the narrative epilogue to Acts (Acts 27–8). For a reader who did not know the story in advance, it would not be possible to predict the ending of Acts from the beginning of the gospel. Readers who make it to the end of Acts, however, will be sent back to reread the beginning of the gospel with new eyes, and will have a new appreciation of the prophetic significance of the Nazareth episode (LK 4:16–30) and of Simeon's 'light to the Gentiles' (cf. LK E, ACTS 28:23–31).

E. Genre. 1. The literary genre of Luke's gospel, like its language, is effectively determined by its subject-matter and sources: it is a 'gospel', modelled closely on Mark's (LK A). Acts is a very different proposition, and even though it forms a narrative continuation to the gospel, it is widely accepted that we may need to look further afield for literary models for Acts. Most scholars believe that the title (The Acts of the Apostles) which is first attested in the *Anti-Marcionite Prologue* in the second century is not original. It is a rather misleading description of the book's content given that there are no 'acts' recounted for many of the twelve Apostles and Paul (to whom well over half the book is dedicated) does not rank as an apostle in Luke's eyes. Of the three principal forms of prose narrative in the literature of the Graeco-Roman world (history, biography, novel), Acts is possibly unique in having been ascribed to all three (Powell 1991: 9). Further on the question of genre, cf. esp. Powell (ibid. ch. 1); Winter and Clarke (1993).

2. Greek History. Acts is commonly described as a history of the early church, and in a very broad sense that is what it is. But it is important to appreciate that Acts does not sit easily within the confines of the literary genre of 'history' as it was understood by Greek and Roman readers in the ancient world. In his formal prefaces and dedications, Luke echoes the language and conventions found in other secular prefaces of the time, prefaces to scientific or technical manuals or to academic treatises on ethnography or geography. Historians (who tend to avoid dedication) use this style sometimes in their more academic or antiquarian sections, but it is a far cry from the high-flown rhetoric that was expected of historical writers. Acts does not match the pretensions of contemporary historiography either in style or in subject-matter: history tended to concern itself with great men and public events,

and was expected to express itself in language far removed from the everyday Greek of the streets. Within the broad realm of Greek historiography, Acts could perhaps most convincingly be classified as an antiquarian monograph dealing with institutional history; but this label does not seem to capture the real flavour of the book.

3. Biblical History. It is far easier and more convincing to range Acts alongside other Greek narratives from Jewish writers seeking to place events of their own day within the broader framework of biblical history. Luke has an extensive knowledge of the Greek Bible (that is the Gk. translations of the HB used by diaspora Jews, principally but not exclusively the Septuagint or LXX) and assumes considerable knowledge of these texts in his readers. Quotations from the Bible form an important subplot of Acts, in the series of speeches that cumulatively presents the major scriptural testimonies used in early Christian hermeneutic. Some of these *testimonia* seem to reflect a very archaic stage of Christian hermeneutic and may go back to an early *Florilegium* such as those found at Qumran, an anthology of key scriptural texts arranged to support the sect's hermeneutic (cf. Brooke 2000: i. 297–8; Steudel 2000: ii. 936–8). Luke also draws on the Greek Bible for a rich fund of allusion, narrative typology, vocabulary, and style, all of which give his story a strongly 'biblical' flavour (Fitzmyer 1998: 90–5; 1981: 107–27). It is not surprising, then, that Luke's work should resemble biblical historiography much more than Greek: this is evident especially in its biographical structure (concentration on a succession of single characters) and in its overtly theological framework (Greek historians typically distance themselves from religious interpretations of events).

4. Biography. Greek and Roman biography (an increasingly popular genre in the late 1st cent.) in many ways provides a better parallel to the scope and scale of Luke's work, especially the biography of philosophers: Luke's description of the gospel in Acts 1:1 would most readily suggest a philosophical biography to ancient readers. Philosophical biography is so far the most convincing genre that has been suggested for Luke's two-volume work, following the pattern found in Diogenes Laertius of the life of the founder of a philosophical movement plus shorter biographical notes on his followers. Extant examples of this genre seem to lack the religious intensity of Luke's work, but late first-century philosophical literature shows that there was a real interest in presenting the lives of philosophers as templates for living the philosophical life, especially the life (and even more the death) of the martyr-philosopher Socrates. A number of details in Acts would recall this paradigm for Greek-educated readers: cf. esp. ACTS 17:16–21; 21:1–16; 25:1–12.

5. Novel. The late first century also sees the growth in popularity of a less pretentious narrative genre, the Greek novel, and it has been suggested that Acts is a form of novel. Certainly many readers unaccustomed to biblical narrative might take the book as a novel, with its exotic settings, adventurous plot, framework of travel, and explicit religious ideology. Luke shows some inclination to novelistic narrative techniques in the elaboration of his more dramatic scenes (cf. e.g. ACTS 12:6–11), and the novel throws valuable light on Luke's narrative structure and textures. But there are also many differences, not least the lack of a love-interest, the lack of emotion (*pathos*), and the political realism of Luke's narrative: the heroes and heroines of the novels tend to move in a fantasy landscape which is only superficially parallel to Luke's pragmatic locations.

6. Apologetic. Acts has frequently been described as an apologetic work, presenting the 'speech for the defence' for Paul, or for the church, or for Christianity, before a hostile world. The wide variety of constructions that have been put on this reading demonstrates its weakness: it is not easy to press the wide-ranging narrative of Acts into the service of a single apologetic purpose. It would be more correct to say that Acts contains a high proportion of apologetic speeches (some explicitly so described, e.g. 26:2), and that these must be taken into account when assessing the book's overall purpose and audience. Acts often shows Paul defending himself before a Roman tribunal, and takes pains to show that Roman magistrates believed him to be innocent of any offence against Roman law (e.g. 18:15; 25:8; 26:31), and this has often been taken to be the book's underlying purpose. But it is also noticeable that many of the damaging charges brought against Paul are left unanswered (e.g. 16:20–1; 17:6–7), and that Paul rarely gets the chance to speak in his own defence in these scenes (cf. 18:14; 19:32). The dominant social location addressed by the apologetic speeches in Acts is the Jewish community, both in Jerusalem (chs. 2, 4, 5, 7, 22) and in the diaspora (chs. 13, 28). Even where Paul is speaking before a Roman tribunal, he is addressing a Jewish audience and Jewish charges (chs. 24, 26). Despite Luke's interest in the Gentile mission, it is the relationship of the Christian 'sect' (28:22) to its Jewish parent that dominates his presentation; and this must be taken into account when assessing his audience and purpose.

F. Text. The so-called Western Text of Acts, represented by a number of MSS of which the most famous is Codex Bezae (D), has substantially longer readings at certain points in the text, and the most significant of these are reproduced in the NRSV marginal readings (NRSV marg.). It has been argued that the longer text is original, but on the whole it is easier to explain the longer text as an expansion and clarification of a shorter original. See further Fitzmyer (1998: 66–79); Barrett (1994–9: i. 2–29).

G. Structure. Like much biblical narrative (including the gospels), Acts is an episodic narrative with minimal authorial comment and simplistic chronology. It is not easy to analyse in modern terms. Ancient narrators do not think in terms of chapters or sections but create a seamless flow; Luke often uses summaries to mark the transition from one scene to next, and interleaves characters and themes (e.g. the introduction of Saul at 7:58). But the alternation of 'summary' and 'scene' (typically a significant event followed by diverse reactions and interpretative speech) suggests that we may usefully analyse Acts, like many of the Greek novels, in dramatic terms, as a drama with four major acts, each with several scenes. But it must be stressed that this is a modern, not an ancient, division.

H. Outline.

Prelude (1:1–26)
    Introduction; Ascension; Election of Matthias

Act I: The Church in Jerusalem (2:1–7:60)

    Scene 1: The Day of Pentecost (2:1–47)
    Scene 2: Healing at the Temple Gate (3:1–4:22)
    Interlude: The Spirit-Filled Life (4:23–5:16)
    Scene 3: Apostles on Trial (5:17–42)
    Scene 4: The First Christian Martyr (6:1–7:60)

Act II: The Scattered Church: Samaria to Antioch (8:1–12:25)

    Scene 1: Samaria and Gaza (8:1–40)
    Scene 2: Damascus (9:1–31)
    Scene 3: Caesarea (9:32–11:18)
    Scene 4: Antioch and Jerusalem (11:19–12:25)

Act III: Paul the Missionary (13:1–21:16)

    Scene 1: Paul's First Missionary Journey (13:1–14:28)
    Scene 2: The Apostolic Council (15:1–35)
    Scene 3: Paul's Second Missionary Journey (15:36–18:23)
    Scene 4: Paul's Third Missionary Journey (18:24–21:16)

Act IV: Paul the Prisoner (21:17–28:31)

    Scene 1: Paul on Trial: Jerusalem (21:17–23:30)
    Scene 2: Paul on Trial: Caesarea (23:31–26:42)
    Interlude: Storm and Shipwreck (27:1–28:10)
    Scene 3: Paul in Rome (28:11–31)

COMMENTARY

Prelude (1:1–26)

Before the main action can begin, a narrative prelude smooths the transition from the first volume (1:1–5) by repeating the scene of the ascension in greater detail (1:6–11), and making up the numbers of the apostolic group (1:12–26).

(1:1) Authorial Introduction Luke begins his second volume with a conventional opening sentence in which he repeats the name of his addressee, Theophilus, and reminds his readers briefly of the contents of the first volume. Here the author slips out of the role of narrator and speaks in his own voice directly to the reader, as if to remind Theophilus (and all other readers) of the existence of the person who collected all the information behind the two books, the one who 'investigated everything carefully from the very first' and 'wrote it all up in an orderly fashion' (Lk 1:3) so as to reassure Theophilus of the reliability of the instruction he had received (Lk 1:4). This brief summary is a valuable indication of the way ancient readers would have seen the genre of Luke's first volume. The gospel was about 'all that Jesus did and taught': that is, it was a book focused on an individual (biography), and that individual was a teacher. Outside the world of the Bible, the most obvious niche to fit this kind of story into is philosophical biography, in which anecdotes of great teachers of the past were collected to provide images and examples for successive disciples to follow.

(1:2–5) The Story So Far The detached, academic tone of the preface does not last very long. Luke forgets to tell his readers what the second volume is going to contain. Instead, he takes us back to the closing scenes of the first volume, spinning rapidly back from the ascension to Jesus' final command (v. 2) to the forty-day period of resurrection appearances (v. 3). By the time we reach v. 5 (still within the opening sentence in the original), we have slipped a further notch into direct speech (the 'he said' of v. 4 is not in the Gk.), as if we were standing beside the apostles being addressed directly by Jesus himself. Jesus' words in this section recall the opening scenes of the gospel: the gift of the Spirit, which has marked out Jesus' special status during the period of his earthly ministry (Lk 3:16, 22) is about to be extended to his followers, and Luke's second volume is going to spell out what this promise means. This summary recapitulates the final scenes of the gospel (Lk 24), but with certain small differences. Earlier commentators have speculated that the differences might result from clumsy editing when Luke's work was split into two volumes: but each volume as we have it fits the standard length of a papyrus roll, and it is more likely that the bridge is original. Elsewhere, when he retells a story he has already told, Luke shows that he is not averse to varying the details of the story, perhaps because ancient educational practice placed high value on the ability to introduce variety into the retelling of well-known stories.

(1:6–12) Ascension The narrative of Acts proper begins with the apostles 'gathered together' (v. 6) to question Jesus for the last time. The question about the kingdom takes us back to the gospel (cf. Lk 4:43). Although Luke lacks the eschatological immediacy of Mark, the preaching of the kingdom remains an essential element of the gospel in Luke's two volumes. Jesus' answer redefines the future horizon: the eschatological future of apocalyptic expectation is not ruled out, but the apostles' attention is redirected to a closer and more immediate future. The imminent coming of the Spirit (v. 5) will mean their own empowerment for the task of acting as 'witnesses' to Jesus (v. 8). The primary semantic location for the activity of 'witnessing' is forensic, and indeed much of the action within Acts will take place (as Jesus had foretold, Lk 12:11–12) in a variety of trial situations. v. 8 can be read as a geographical programme for the whole book, with the first 7 chapters set in Jerusalem, 8–11 charting the spread of the gospel to the surrounding areas within Syria-Palestine ('Judea and Samaria'), and v. 13 onwards following Paul's mission ever further afield.

Luke alone of the evangelists closes the story of Jesus with a definite point of departure marking the end of the resurrection appearances. But the ascension is no afterthought: narrative clues to this denouement are laid as early as Lk 9:51, and the story is prefigured in the narrative of the transfiguration (Lk 9:28–36: parallels include the mountain, the cloud, and the two 'men'). Luke's description of the Mount of Olives as 'a sabbath day's journey from Jerusalem' (v. 12) highlights the scene of the ascension as a distinct location, the only narrative setting dignified as a 'mountain' in Acts. This is a story that moves not only outwards from Jerusalem but also downwards from the mountain. The story of Acts starts in a place where Jesus is visible, angels speak clearly, and the cloud between earth and heaven is momentarily thinned. From this point onwards, discerning and understanding God's purpose will become progressively harder.

(1:13–26) Election of Matthias There is one more task to be completed before the action proper begins. The disciples wait obediently in Jerusalem for the promised coming of the Spirit (for the 'upper room' cf. Lk 22:12). 'Devoted themselves . . . to prayer' (v. 14) suggests the virtue of dogged perseverance (cf. Rom 12:12; Col 4:2). 'With one accord' (v. 14) underlines the unity of the group, which here includes women and Jesus' mother and brothers, a surprising (cf. Lk 8:19–21) though unemphasized detail. Luke's list of the names of the apostles acts as a bridge with the first volume (cf. Lk 6:14–16). But it

also highlights the fact that there is now a gap: Judas, the last in the list in Lk 6:16, is no longer one of the group. The story of Judas' treachery (which Luke assumes his readers will know) was described in Lk 22:3–6, 47–53, but Luke has not yet (unlike Matthew, who appears to know a different story: Mt 27:3–10) told his readers anything about the traitor's fate, and this episode gives him an excuse to do so. But the defection of Judas also creates a theological problem, not only because of the symbolic significance of the number 12 (Lk 22:30), but also because of the high value Luke places on the apostolic office. He has already stressed that the apostles were 'chosen' by Jesus and taught by him 'through the Holy Spirit' (v. 2). Judas' treachery shows that neither fact constitutes an automatic guarantee of fidelity. For Luke, acts of treachery against the Spirit (especially if there is a financial motive) are punished by God: cf. Acts 5:1–11.

Peter's call for a replacement for Judas, based (as so often in Acts) on an appeal to Scripture (v. 20), reinforces the identity of the group at this crisis point in its existence, and also constitutes a *de facto* recognition of his own authority in the group. In this interim period between the departure of Jesus and the arrival of the Spirit, the only resource is to ask God to indicate his 'choice' of a replacement (v. 24, cf. 1:2) by means of casting lots (v. 26), a means of ascertaining the divine purpose familiar both in the Graeco-Roman world and in the Bible.

Act One: The Church in Jerusalem (2:1–7:60)

Act I Scene 1: The Day of Pentecost (2:1–47).

As so often in Acts, the first big scene of the book is structured around a major theophanic event, the coming of the Spirit (vv. 1–4), followed by crowd reactions (vv. 5–13). Luke then gives us a theological interpretation of the event in Peter's speech (vv. 14–36). But the speech is also an event in its own right which triggers its own reactions and results (vv. 37–42). This opening section closes with a transitional summary passage describing the growth of the church (vv. 43–7).

(2:1–4) The Coming of the Spirit Like the departure of Jesus, the coming of the Spirit for Luke is a definite event, located in a particular time and place and describable in empirical terms. The 'day of Pentecost' (v. 1) ties the story into a Jewish liturgical time-frame which began with the festival of Passover (Lk 22:1), and which in its turn was to determine the liturgical shape of the Christian year, limiting the passion and resurrection events to a period of fifty days (and incidentally explaining the continuing presence of large pilgrim crowds in the city: vv. 9–11). But Luke's solemn dating formula ('fulfilled': v. 1) suggests that he may also see a symbolic 'fit' between the outpouring of the Spirit and the festival which in first-century Judaism was a major celebration of the Sinai theophany and the giving of the Law to Israel. 'All together in one place' emphasizes the spiritual unity of the group whose constitution has been so carefully described in ch. 1.

The event itself is both an auditory (v. 2) and a visual experience (v. 3): as so often in biblical theophany, the stress is on comparison rather than direct description (cf. Ezek 1:13). Both wind and fire are associated with God's self-revelation in the HB: cf. Ex 19:16–19; 1 Kings 19:11–12; Isa 6:6. But the choice of these two images is particularly apt for the coming of the Spirit. 'Wind', both in Hebrew and in Greek, is closely associated with 'spirit'. The image of fire links with the Spirit's work of judgement (Lk 3:16–17). And the metaphor of 'tongues' (v. 3) links with the fact that the result of this manifestation of divine power is inspired speech (v. 4).

(2:5–13) Varied Reactions The essentially private experience in the 'house' immediately becomes public: a crowd gathers at the sound (v. 5) of a multiplicity of voices speaking in a cosmopolitan variety of languages. This first proclamation is not the result of a conscious mission plan, but a divinely inspired event which draws a curious audience. Luke heightens the dramatic effect of the Pentecost event by shifting his narrative perspective from the house to the streets outside: the crowd displays all the standard reactions to divine action (vv. 6, 7, 12). But while some hear only a confused babble of ecstatic (or drunken?) voices (v. 13), others hear 'each in their own dialect' a proclamation of God's 'great deeds' (v. 11). This is a miracle of hearing, a reversal of the confusion of tongues at the tower of Babel. Some have speculated that Luke has misunderstood the phenomenon of glossolalia; but among groups that practise speaking in tongues today, there are reports of intelligible speech which is heard as a real language unknown to the speaker.

The crowd itself is carefully characterized. The elaborate list of vv. 9–11 evokes the world-wide Jewish diaspora, nonchalantly straddling the borders of the Roman empire, and firmly centered on Jerusalem (Scott 1994: 561). Rome, on this mental map, is peripheral, the westernmost point imaginable in a sequence that looks to points east, north, south, and west before coming back to the centre. The list of exotic place-names is a foretaste of the geographical explosion that will come to dominate the narrative of Acts; but it is also a reminder that there are many potential journeys that will remain unnarrated, just as there are many more apostles and evangelists than those whose stories Luke will tell.

(2:14–36) Peter's Speech Peter acts as spokesman for the apostles (v. 14). As so often in Acts, Luke leaves it to his characters to provide the theological insights that explain the raw data of experience. This speech, the first major rhetorical composition of the book, is carefully signalled as a formal act of speaking (v. 14), with speakers and audience precisely defined. It introduces two key passages in the early Christian armoury of scriptural proof-texts: both show signs of intensive exegetical labour, and they may well have come down to Luke via an oral (or possibly even written) testimonia-tradition (cf. ACTS E. 2).

The first part of the speech (vv. 14–21) answers the question 'What does this mean?' (v. 12). The group cannot be drunk, Peter explains, because it is only breakfast-time (v. 15). On the contrary, this is something predicted in Scripture. The extended quotation from Joel 2:28–32 (LXX) clarifies a number of points about the apostolic proclamation. (1) The phenomenon of ecstatic speech is identified with the biblical gift of prophecy, and is the work of the same Spirit of God. (2) This is a phenomenon of 'the last days' (v. 17: Luke heightens the eschatological dimension of the original), but belongs to a stage before the final 'day of the Lord' (v. 20): for Luke, the coming of Jesus heralded the beginning of the end-time, but

the final end is still to come (cf. Lk 21:9). (3) The promise is inclusive of age, gender, and social class (vv. 17–18); the Spirit is poured out on 'all flesh' (v. 17), and salvation is offered to 'whoever calls on the name of the Lord' (v. 21).

In v. 22 Peter turns to the implied underlying question, Who was Jesus? However dramatic the events surrounding the apostles, they cannot be understood without reference to Jesus. Peter's message here falls into a distinctive pattern analysed in Dodd's (1936) classic study of the apostolic preaching. This pattern is distinct from the Pauline gospel and may well have come to Luke via some form of primitive Christian tradition. The miracles performed by Jesus function as a form of divine attestation of his ministry, but this is a man through whom God was working in the midst of his people (v. 22). Responsibility for his death is threefold: the immediate agency ('lawless men'); the proximate motive force (the local audience which had witnessed Jesus' ministry, vv. 22–3); and behind both, the divine plan (v. 24). Once again, it is Scripture that provides the explanatory key to all this (vv. 25–8, citing Ps 16:8–11). The hope David entertained (v. 26), Peter says, proved false, if it was for himself: David died and his body was disposed of in the normal way (v. 29). Therefore the psalm must be interpreted as a prophetic oracle referring to the Messiah. Only after this scriptural testimony (which establishes the divine necessity of what happened to Jesus) does Peter introduce the personal witness of the apostles to the resurrection (v. 32).

The final section of the speech brings the focus back to the the visible and audible events of Pentecost (v. 33): the gift of the Spirit is the direct result (and thus also the proof) of Jesus' exaltation to heaven. Luke shares a conviction (expressed in different ways in Jn 16:7 and in Eph 4:8–12) that the departure of Jesus was a precondition for the coming of the Spirit. Here the ascension is not described as a separate event, but is implicit in the resurrection, and this is the point at which Jesus achieves the title of 'Lord and Christ' (v. 36, cf. Rom 1:4). The Christological use of Ps 110 (v. 34) is widespread in early Christian hermeneutic, linked to the final phrase of Ps 16:11 by the reference to God's 'right hand' (Lindars 1961: 38–45).

(2:37–41) Reactions and Results The crowd reacts dramatically (v. 37): 'What shall we do?' Peter's prescription encapsulates the basic Christian message in four points: repentance, baptism, forgiveness, the gift of the Spirit (v. 38). Israel has to repent (5:31), but so too does the pagan world (17:30). The double package 'repentance and baptism' is associated with the forgiveness of sins (cf. Lk 3:3); but exactly how the association works is not clearly defined. Baptism is now 'in the name of Jesus Christ', and will be followed (or accompanied) by the gift of the Holy Spirit. This is the 'promise' that has dominated Peter's speech. It is not restricted to an apostolic élite: it is as universal as the need for repentance (v. 39). The final line of the Joel quotation (Joel 2:32), embellished and cross-referenced to Isa 57:19, highlights the universality of God's promise to the polyglot Jerusalem crowd. The final verse of the scene dramatically highlights the sermon's positive results (v. 41) and marks the first stage of the church's exponential growth from the small, inward-looking group described in ch. 1 to a significant movement making a world-wide impact (26:26).

(2:42–7) The Church Grows The first big scene of the drama concludes with a summary passage describing the ongoing life of the fledgling community. Luke does not on the whole show much interest in the regular, established patterns of church life, either in Jerusalem or in the Pauline mission: we are left to assume that the activities sketched here in outline continue to form the unstated backdrop to the more dramatic events highlighted in the narrative. Three new elements (teaching, fellowship, and the breaking of bread) have now been added to the prayer that forms the backbone of the group's regular activities (cf. 1:15). 'The breaking of bread' (vv. 42, 46) seems to be distinct from the mere taking of food (v. 46); it is virtually a technical term in the NT (outside Acts it is used only of the last supper and of Jesus' feeding miracles), and at the time Luke is writing can hardly mean anything other than the ritual meal already known to Paul (1 Cor 10:16; 11:24). 'The fellowship' is the only item on the list to be expanded: the group's unity finds practical expression in the common ownership of property (vv. 44–5). v. 47 sums up this first stage of the church's existence as an idyllic state in which the group is in harmony with its parent community ('the whole people': *laos* in Luke normally refers to the people of Israel) and with God: it is a paradise garden where praise and growth are both spontaneous.

Act I Scene 2: Healing at the Temple Gate (3:1–4:22)

The next major scene opens with the healing of a lame beggar at the temple gate (3:1–10). The miracle is given a theological interpretation through a lengthy speech by Peter (3:11–26), which in turn provokes its own reactions (4:1–4). But this time there is a new twist to the plot. Peter's action attracts the attention of the temple authorities, and the apostles are arrested and put on trial (4:5–12). This is the first of a series of trial scenes that will dominate Acts, bringing out the full forensic implications of the apostles' calling to act as Jesus' 'witnesses' (1:8), and expanding the circle of characters used by Luke to explore the theological implications of the unfolding narrative (4:13–22).

(3:1–10) A Lame Man Healed Luke has already told us that the apostolic band has the power to work miracles (2:43). Now he gives us a detailed account of one paradigmatic healing miracle, precisely timed and located, but with nothing about it at first sight to warn of the controversial situation it will provoke. Luke selects his actors from within a larger group: of all the apostles named in ch. 1, only Peter and John have scenes in their own right, and even John is very much a supporting character here (v. 4). Peter's lack of 'silver and gold' (v. 6: perhaps due to the community's policy on property, 2:44) highlights both the unexpected character of the miracle (the beggar is looking for money, not healing, v. 5) and the apostles' own dependence: only 'in the name of Jesus Christ of Nazareth' can healing take place. There is a deliberate patterning on gospel healing stories here (cf. Lk 5:23), and in both cases the play on words is almost certainly deliberate: Peter 'raised' (*ēgeiren*, v. 7) the beggar to a new way of life as well as to new mobility. The crowd reaction (v. 10) heightens the emotional impact of the miracle as well as its solid attestation: here is a whole crowd of witnesses to whom the lame beggar was well known (cf. 3:16; 4:22).

(3:11–26) 'No Other Name' Peter's second speech essentially answers the same two questions as his first: 'What does this mean?' (cf. 2:12) and 'What shall we do?' (cf. 2:37). This time the focus is on the origin of the power that has healed the lame beggar. The question was just as important for Greek readers as for Jewish: was it their own exceptional piety that had given the apostles this divine power (v. 12)? The answer is No: the healing, as the beggar had correctly surmised (vv. 9–10; 13), was the work of God; but God's agent (just as in 2:22) was Jesus, the one chosen by God but denied and destroyed by this very Jerusalem crowd. Peter's words here forge a damning chain of indictment against his audience. Jesus is described in v. 13 as God's 'servant' or 'child': the word is *pais* (boy), not *huios* (son), and probably echoes the prophetic 'Servant of God' in LXX Isa 52–3 (the word may reflect an early Christology; cf. also Acts 8:32–5). He is the 'holy and righteous one' (v.14) and the 'author [or pioneer] of life' (v. 15, cf. Acts 5:31; Heb 2:10), the one whom God 'glorified' (v. 13; cf. Isa 52:13) and raised from the dead (v. 15). In each case the rhetorical effect is heightened by the contrast between Jesus' status in the eyes of God and his systematic dishonouring and rejection by the people ('whom you delivered up . . . you denied . . . you killed'). As for the apostles, their only claim to fame is to act as Jesus' witnesses (v. 15) and to exercise the faith in his name which brings about wholeness (v. 16).

There are, however, a number of mitigating factors. Both the crowd (whom Peter addresses as 'brothers') and their leaders acted 'in ignorance' (v. 17; cf. 13:27). Jesus' death was also part of the divine plan (v. 18): the suffering of the Messiah is something foretold by 'all the prophets'. This is an important theme for Luke, who has already had Jesus explain it to his disciples after the resurrection (Lk 24:26, 46), but he has not yet revealed precisely which prophetic texts can be interpreted in this way. The type of the 'prophet like Moses' in vv. 22–3 (based on Deut 18:19, linked with Lev 23:29) hints at a biblical typology that will allow Luke to find a scriptural prototype for the rejection of God's messenger (this theme is more fully developed in ch. 7). Here, however, the emphasis (v. 19) is on the appeal for repentance, seen as a precondition for 'times of refreshing' (v. 20) and the 'restoration of all things' (v. 21). These puzzling phrases are not easy to parallel elsewhere: they may be relics of a pre-Lukan eschatology, but both underline the fact that even for Luke the period of apostolic mission marks only a temporary postponement, not a replacement, of the final consummation. The speech closes on a positive note: what is on offer to the Jerusalem crowd is a fulfilment of their heritage, both as 'sons of the prophets' (v. 25, cf. 2:39) and as 'sons of the covenant' (v. 25). There is a Pauline ring about Peter's 'to you first' in verse 26 (cf. Rom 1:16): God's offer of blessing is universal, but it is being offered first to Israel.

(4:1–4) Conflicting Reactions The speech is dramatically interrupted by an intervention from authority. This is the first of many in Acts; here (since the healing took place in the temple precincts), it is appropriately the temple authorities who come to silence the apostles. The Sadducees were an aristocratic party linked closely with the priestly hierarchy. Luke ascribes to them an appropriate motive for the arrest (v. 2), since he has already identified the Sadducees as the party within Judaism who 'say that there is no resurrection' (Lk 20:27); Paul will later exploit this to good effect (Acts 23:6–9). This may explain why Luke picks out the resurrection (which has not been especially prominent) as the particularly offensive aspect of Peter's speech. The circumstantial detail that it was 'evening' (v. 3) ties the episode in with 3:1: we are still within the same dramatic scene. Meanwhile, behind the scenes, the church continues to grow (v. 4): many of 'the people' (v. 1) react positively to 'the word' (a favourite Lukan expression for the preaching of the gospel, cf. Lk 1:2), and the total number of believers now reaches 'about five thousand'.

(4:5–12) **Arrest and Trial** After a night in jail, the apostles are brought before a full session of the Sanhedrin (v. 15), the ruling council of Judea: the titles listed here enumerate all the groups from which the council was made up (cf. Lk 9:22; 20:1). Annas had been deposed as high priest in 15 CE, but continued to wield influence behind the scenes during the term of his son-in-law Caiaphas (18–36 CE: cf. Lk 3:2). The trial scenes so prominent in Acts highlight the forensic dimension of the apostolic call to bear witness (1:8, cf. Lk 21:13–15). In Luke's dramatic presentation it is not easy to distinguish forensic testimony from preaching: Peter's reply to the Council's question (v. 7) picks up more or less where his sermon left off. The key point (as in 3:16) concerns the origin of the power responsible for the healing miracle: by identifying this power with Jesus (v. 10) Peter once again faces the ruling authorities with the possibility that their treatment of Jesus was a terrible misjudgement. The point is rammed home with a new scriptural text (v. 11): the paradox of the rejected stone (Ps 118:22) was a favourite in early Christian reflection on the foreshadowing of Jesus in the Scriptures (Lk 20:17, cf. further 1 Pet 2:7; Lindars 1961: 169–74). Peter's final sentence goes further than anything he has yet said: Christ is the only means of salvation. The Greek word used of the beggar's healing is 'saved', a word used routinely of physical health and well-being (cf. Lk 8:48), and this allows Peter to answer the question in terms of the broader eschatological concept of 'salvation' already evoked in 2:40 and 2:21. Joel 2:32 promises 'salvation' from the tribulations of the last days to 'all who call on the name of the Lord', and this was almost certainly interpreted by the early Christians as a reference to the name of Christ.

(4:13–22) **Deliberations of the Council** Luke uses the privileged position of the narrator to give us an insight into the inner workings of the Sanhedrin. Readers do not need to know much about the politics of first-century Jerusalem to pick up the élitist perspective here (we do not need to assume that the apostles were totally illiterate, just that they had not attained the professional educational levels of the 'elders and scribes'). This élitist perspective is reinforced by the Council's 'us' and 'them' attitude to 'the people' (vv. 16, 17, 21)—an attitude which, Luke implies, is reciprocal (v. 21). 'Boldness' (*parrhēsia* v. 13) is not physical courage so much as 'frankness' or 'freedom of speech', a philosophical virtue particularly admired by the Greeks. The apostles' refusal to be silenced (v. 19) is a classic statement of philosophical *parrhēsia*. Finally, the Council's perspective is characterized by 'wonder' (v. 13): the supernatural is never very far away in this narrative, and Luke makes it clear that the fact of the beggar's healing (v. 14)

is impossible to gainsay, even for hostile observers (v. 22). Thus the 'signs' given by God (v. 22; cf. 2:19) are in their own right an important part of the apostolic testimony (cf. 14:3).

Act I Interlude: The Spirit-Filled Life (4:23–5:16)

Most commentators are agreed that the story of Ananias and Sapphira (5:1–11) is in some way an isolated relic of tradition relating to a bygone phase of the Jerusalem church. Luke has bracketed this with two summary passages about the community of goods (4:32–7) and the progress of the church (5:12–16), and prefaces the whole section with a glimpse of the apostolic circle at prayer (4:23–31). The effect is of an interlude in the drama, underlining the power of the Spirit at work in the church, and the authority of the apostles, especially Peter.

(4:23–31) **A Prophetic Prayer** Like other biblical writers, Luke uses prayer to provide ongoing comment on the storyline. The authorities have just imposed a total ban on speaking or teaching in Jesus' name (4:18), and the new situation has to be reported and evaluated. Peter's 'you must judge' (4:19) is in a sense addressed to the reader as well as to the Sanhedrin: what *is* the correct Christian attitude in the face of such a prohibition, imposed by the legitimate civic authorities? The apostles themselves are in no doubt that the situation calls for the legitimate exercise of free speech in the face of a tyrannical abuse of authority (v. 29). Their prayer creates a theological framework for this stance, first by evoking the sovereignty of God (v. 24), as the ultimate authority that relativizes all human seats of power, and second by locating the present situation in Scripture. Ps 2 (quoted in vv. 25–6) exerted a powerful influence on the Christology of the early church: the word translated Messiah in v. 26 is *christos*, which makes it easy to read the psalm as a direct prophecy of those involved in the trial of Jesus (v. 27). The implication is that the hostility experienced by his followers simply makes them part of the same predetermined pattern (v. 28). Only Luke includes Herod in the passion narrative (Lk 22:6–12). The renewed visitation of the Spirit (almost a second Pentecost, v. 31) serves as a confirmation that the apostles' reading of the situation is the right one.

(4:32–7) **The Common Life** This summary is a slightly fuller repetition of 2:44–5. The added detail that the money raised from the sale of property was channelled through the apostles (v. 35) heightens the sense of centralized authority. There is no sense that Luke envisaged the Jerusalem community establishing a genuine coenobitic life (presumably any Jerusalem residents who joined the church continued to live in their own homes: cf. 2:46; 5:42). The emphasis is on the sale of disposable property by those who could afford it, in order to create a surplus for charitable distribution (v. 34, echoing Deut 15:4). This emphasis ties in with Luke's own interest in the proper use of surplus wealth (cf. Lk 6:20, 24), and it is conceivable that he has simply misunderstood an early tradition that may have reflected something more like the Essene lifestyle. (Sterling 2000). The mention of Barnabas (vv. 36–7) provides a positive example of this ideal use of wealth; it also (with typically Lukan economy) introduces a character, in good standing with the apostles, who will prove important at a later stage in the plot (cf. ACTS 9:26–30).

(5:1–11) Ananias and Sapphira As it stands, this story does not quite fit the background information Luke has given us. v. 4 seems to conflict with 2:44 and 4:32 (unless 'all' is just Lucan hyperbole), and raises questions about the severity of the punishment: if the community of goods could be partial, and was purely voluntary, why is Ananias treated so harshly? The difficulties of understanding the story as it stands make it more rather than less likely that Luke has taken it over from tradition, and perhaps imperfectly understood it. The parallel with Qumran (Fitzmyer 1998: 318) makes it clear that it is the couple's conspiracy to deceive, rather than the absolute monetary value of the sale, that constitutes the heart of their sin against *koinōnia*: the failure to share money is simply a symptom of a more serious failure to be 'of one mind' within the community (cf. Eph 4:25; Col 3:9). Lying to the community is 'lying to God' (v. 4) and 'tempting the Holy Spirit' (v. 9; cf. Phil 2:1–2 and 2 Cor 13:14 for a connection between the Spirit and *koinōnia*). In Luke's narrative, the story also serves to highlight the authority of the church (*ekklēsia*: v. 11 is Luke's first use of this term) as the locus of God's Spirit, and especially to underline the supernatural insight and authority of Peter, who sees through the deception (vv. 3–5, 8–9). It is another of the 'signs' God sends to confirm the church's spiritual authority, and, like the healing miracles, induces 'great fear' (vv. 5, 11).

(5:12–16) Signs and Wonders The interlude concludes with a summary passage describing the ongoing healing ministry of the apostles. The note on 'Solomon's Portico' (v. 12) is a realistic reflection of the group's actual size: the only place such a large group could now be 'all together' is in a large public space. For the *stoa* of Solomon (the site of Peter's impromptu sermon in 3:11), see Jos. *J.W.* 5:185; Jn 10:22. Luke stresses again the high reputation of the Christian group among 'the people' (v. 13). v. 15 implies that the bringing out of the sick for healing is a manifestation of 'belief', and there may be a contrast between this secret form of believing and the public commitment that would be implied by openly 'joining' the crowd in the portico (v. 13); the mention of 'women' (who might not join a public teaching session) may support this view. The scope and popularity of this healing ministry are described in terms that rival that of Jesus (cf. Lk 4:40–1, 6:18–19). The healing power emanating from Peter is so great that there is no need even to touch him (v. 15: cf. Lk 7:1–10; 8:43).

Act I Scene 3: Apostles on Trial (5:17–42)

At the end of the trial in ch. 4, the apostles are issued with a blanket prohibition on teaching in the name of Jesus. Their disdainful reply (4:19) leaves the reader in little doubt that the authorities will soon have cause to arrest them again: and so it proves. But this time things are stacked against the forces of officialdom. Arrest is followed immediately by miraculous release (5:17–26); official reprimand meets only defiance (5:27–32); and at least one respected member of the Council begins to doubt the wisdom of pursuing the case (5:33–40). The scene closes with a brief summary (5:41–2) describing the gospel's triumphant progress.

(5:17–26) Arrest and Escape This time it is the whole apostolic group that finds itself in jail (v. 18). Like his contemporary Josephus, Luke is happy to use the Greek term *hairesis*

(sect, v. 17) to give a more nuanced description of the political groupings of first-century Palestine: the term is appropriately used elsewhere both of the Pharisees (15:5; 26:5) and of the Christians (24:5, 14; 28:22). 'Jealousy' (v. 17) may not be the best description of their motive, however: *zēlos* also means 'zeal', and in Acts may often be better seen in terms of a praiseworthy, if misguided, religious zeal (Paul uses it of himself in Gal 1:14, Phil 3:6, and cf. Rom 10:2). The conundrum posed by Peter in 4:19, if the reader still has any doubts, is dramatically resolved here as the apostles are miraculously released and instructed by no less than 'an angel of the Lord' to continue with their preaching mission in the temple (vv. 19–21). The miracle provides divine sanction for the apostles' civil disobedience, and leaves the priestly authorities in an embarassing and farcical position (recounted by Luke with a touch of dramatic irony, vv. 21–5). The apostles' popularity with 'the people' is again a factor in their treatment by the ruling authorities (v. 26).

(5:27–32) The Trial This second trial is essentially a reprise of the first, with the difference that the charge now is direct disobedience of an explicit instruction (v. 28). Peter's reply (v. 29) is equally unequivocal: like the philosopher Socrates or the prophet Daniel, the apostles take their orders from a higher authority, and cannot consider themselves bound by any human court. The charge that they intend 'to bring this man's blood on us' should be read within the precise sociopolitical context that Luke has taken care to define: 'us' here means the ruling authorities, and stands in contrast to 'the people' who support the apostles. Peter's speech summarizes the essential points made in the previous sermons: Jesus has been raised and exalted by God; his present position at God's right hand is a precondition for the outpouring of gifts (vv. 31–2). A new element is the description of Jesus' death as 'hanging him on a tree' (v. 30), using language derived from Deut 21:22–3 (cf. 10:39); the connection with crucifixion had already been made by exegetes at Qumran (Fitzmyer 1998: 337), and is also made by Paul (Gal 3:13). The primary result of Jesus' exaltation is that the gift of 'repentance and forgiveness of sins' is now offered to Israel (v. 31).

(5:33–9) The Advice of Gamaliel Luke again adopts the privileged position of an omniscient narrator to report a private debate from within the ranks of the Sanhedrin (v. 34). Gamaliel's intervention introduces an ironic commentary on the unfolding plot, posing a question that the reader will be able to answer (Luke makes sure of that) even if the council members cannot (vv. 38–9). In fact Gamaliel's question will prove to be a key issue for the whole narrative: it is not only those outside the church who sometimes fail to recognize where God is at work. The role attributed to the historical figure of Gamaliel at this point in the narrative is not in itself implausible: this is Rabban Gamaliel the Elder, one of the great Pharisaic teachers of the first century, who flourished *c.*25–50 CE and is later said to have been the teacher of Paul (22:3). There is however a historical problem about the examples he cites. Theudas and Judas are both mentioned (in the same order) by Josephus at *Ant.* 20. 97–8, 102; but the mention of Judas is a flashback to the period of the first Roman census of Judea (cf. Lk 2:1–2). Theudas, on the other hand, is dated by Josephus to the procuratorship of Fadus (44–6 CE). This is well after the dramatic date of Luke's story, which must be before the death of Herod in 44 (Acts 12:20–3). Either Luke has made a mistake (possibly due to faulty memory of a source similar to that used by Josephus); or Josephus has; or there was another, earlier Theudas: all these options have been argued by commentators.

(5:40–2) Summary and Transition The Sanhedrin's decision to treat the apostles with caution does not prevent their being flogged (v. 40), a routine treatment in ancient courts used for eliciting the truth from witnesses as well as for punishment. The apostles' 'joy' (v. 41) establishes their credentials as martyrs: 'worthy to be dishonoured for the Name' is a highly paradoxical statement that expresses the Christian theology of martyrdom very well, and illustrates the importance attached to honour and shame in the first-century Mediterranean world. The section closes with an assurance that the apostles' *parrhēsia* is undaunted (v. 42): the gospel message is assiduously proclaimed, not only in the temple but 'from house to house'.

Act I Scene 4: The First Christian Martyr (6:1–7:60)

The Jerusalem section of Luke's narrative closes with an extended trial scene incorporating the longest speech in the book (7:2–53). This scene introduces a new character, Stephen, and his story is prefaced with a piece of church 'business' which provides the necessary background to his appointment (6:1–7) and to the controversy that brought him to trial (6:8–7:1).

(6:1–7) Appointment of the Seven Luke gives us a tantalizingly brief glimpse into the inner workings of the church, bracketed with two summary verses (5:42; 6:7). The terms 'Hellenists' and 'Hebrews' (v. 1) almost certainly refer to a language-based distinction between the two major groupings of converts in the Jerusalem church. The Hellenists are Jews whose major language is Greek (the international language of the eastern Mediterranean), and the Hebrews are Jews whose major language is Hebrew or Aramaic. The fact that all the seven have Greek names (v. 5), and that Stephen immediately gets into dispute with members of a group of diaspora synagogues (v. 9), suggests a diaspora connection, even though it is true that many Palestinian Jews also spoke Greek. The choice of candidates for this extension (or better, division) of the ministry is taken very seriously: the 'body of disciples' (v. 2) is treated like the assembly of a Greek city, who approve the apostles' proposal (v. 5) and 'choose' their representatives with care (v. 5: cf. 1:2, 24). The candidates are already marked out as 'full of the Spirit' (vv. 3, 5), but the transmission of authority from the apostles is very deliberately assured through prayer and the laying on of hands (v. 6).

(6:8–7:1) Stephen on Trial The atmosphere of controversy which has been building up since ch. 4 now enters a new phase. Stephen's opponents are not the temple hierarchy but members of diaspora communities settled in Jerusalem (6:9). The Latin title *libertini* ('Freedmen') indicates a group of Jews of Italian origin who were now settled in Jerusalem: the term is known from Latin sources, cf. e.g. Tacitus, *Annals*, 2:85. Although the synagogue is essentially a diaspora institution (worship in Jerusalem was focused on the temple), rabbinic

sources refer to synagogues in the city, and the Theodotus inscription makes it reasonably certain that there was at least one Greek-speaking synagogue in Jerusalem in the first century (Fitzmyer 1998: 356–8; Riesner 1995: 179–210; text in Falk 1995: 281). The charges against Stephen echo those brought against Jesus in the gospels (for 'blasphemy,' cf. Lk 22:71; and for threatening the temple, cf. Mk 14:56–8). The charge of subverting the law (v. 14) is new, and will reappear in the charges against Paul (cf. esp. 21:28). The law had a peculiar importance in the diaspora as a marker of identity: interestingly, Theodotus declares that his *synagōgē* or 'meeting-house' is set up 'for the reading of the Law and instruction in the commandments'.

(7:2–53) Stephen's Speech Stephen's speech seems on the surface to have little to do with the charges against him. Like most of the apologetic speeches in Acts, it is part of a larger polemical discourse, building on and developing the arguments already put forward in the sermons and trial speeches of the apostles. Nevertheless, this particular speech does have a distinctive ethos, which has led some commentators to suppose an underlying Hellenist or Antiochene source. In genre, the speech is quite different from the speeches of Peter. It falls into the category of 'rewritten Bible', a selective retelling of biblical history from a particular theological standpoint, of which we have several examples in intertestamental literature (cf. PBJL A5; A6); the form occurs already in the Bible itself, cf. e.g. Ps 105. Like other Jewish groups in the Second Temple period, the Christians used the biblical past to define their own identity.

(7:2–8) The Call of God Abraham is recognized throughout the NT as the spiritual ancestor of Jewish and Gentile believers alike. But the main actor in this national epic is God, who commands (v. 3), removes (v. 4), gives (vv. 5, 8), and promises (v. 5). Human achievement is defined in terms of being receptive to the vision of God (v. 2) and obedient to his word (vv. 4, 8). Like the author of Hebrews (11:8–10), Luke stresses Abraham's reliance on God's promise (v. 5) and highlights the experience of alienation rather than the inheritance of the land (v. 6). And by a careful selection of texts from Gen 15 and Ex 2–3 Luke subtly redefines the promise itself to focus on the creation of a worshipping community rather than on the acquisition of land (*latreuein*, 'worship' in v. 7 echoes Lk 1:74, and both pick up Ex 3:12, which refers to Sinai, not Canaan).

(7:9–16) Conflict in the Family Bypassing other episodes in the patriarchal narratives, Stephen moves on to the story of Joseph and Jacob's migration to Egypt, an episode that prepares the ground for the nation's exile in Egypt. This selection allows him to highlight the history of fraternal conflict within Israel, a conflict sparked by *zēlos* (which here does mean 'envy': v. 9, cf. Philo, *De Josepho*, 5). Joseph (like Daniel and Esther) was significant for diaspora Jews as a patriarch who, though forcibly separated from the land of promise, learns to live (and even flourish) in a pagan environment without compromising his faith: the key to Joseph's story is that even in Egypt, 'God was with him' (v. 9). For Christians, there is an additional typology: like Jesus, Joseph is rejected by his brothers, falls into 'afflictions', and is rescued by God (v. 10) in such a way that he in turn is able to save his people. For the number 75 (v. 14), cf. Gen 46:27, where LXX and some Qumran traditions read 75. v. 15 is a highly compressed form of the Genesis account of Jacob's visits to Egypt (Gen 45, 47, 49); and the burial place of Jacob (v. 16) is confused with that of Joseph (cf. Gen 23:16–20; 33:19; 50:13; Josh 24:32).

(7:17–22) The Birth of a Saviour Stephen now picks up the theme of promise (v. 17), identifying the key promise to Abraham (cf. Lk 1:73) as that of Gen 15:13–14, fulfilled in the Exodus (Ex 2:24; 3:12) rather than in the Conquest (which is of only passing interest to Stephen, cf. 7:45). The exposure of newborn infants (v. 22) was routine in the Gentile world—though in that context it would be more normal to expose the females and rear the males (cf. Philo, *Vit. Mos.* 1.10). It was at this precise moment of crisis and potential disaster that Moses was born (v. 20). 'Beautiful' (*asteios*) echoes LXX Ex 2:2, and is highlighted here by the addition of 'before God': cf. Philo's 'more than ordinary goodliness'. The child is 'picked up' by Pharoah's daughter (the technical term used for acknowledging a newborn child and agreeing to rear it). As in Philo, Moses' education in the palace is seen in terms of gaining (and excelling in) the best that the pagan world could offer (cf. Philo, *Vit. Mos.* 1.20–4).

(7:23–9) Moses Rejected Given this auspicious start in life, it is all the more ironic that Moses' first attempt to help his own people results in humiliation and rejection. Unlike the Exodus story (Ex 2:11–15), this retelling presupposes that Moses himself already understands that it is his destiny to act as God's agent of 'salvation' for his people (*sōtēria*, v. 25: NRSV, rescuing), and that the people themselves should have recognized the fact. Neither Philo nor Josephus makes this particular point out of this episode: Josephus ignores it, and Philo mentions it simply as a 'righteous act' on the part of Moses that incurs the wrath of the king and puts Moses' life in danger (*Vit. Mos.* 1.40–6). It is a peculiarly Christian typology, and one well adapted to the dramatic scenario of Stephen's speech, which understands Moses as the prototype of Jesus, sent by God as saviour of his people but rejected by those he came to save.

(7:30–8) Moses Selected Moses' rejection by his own people is placed in stark juxtaposition with his call by God. vv. 30–4 extract the key statements from the much longer narrative of Ex 3, 4. The assimilation of Horeb and Sinai (cf. v. 30 with Ex 3:1) was well established by Luke's day: the 'mountain of God' (Ex 3:1 was pre-eminently Sinai, and it is clearly Sinai to which Ex 3:12 refers. As with Abraham, this is a moment of angelic vision (v. 30) and divine voice (v. 31): Moses' contribution is limited to amazement (v. 31) and trembling (v. 33). Deliverance, too, is all God's work: 'I have seen . . . I have heard . . . I have come down to deliver . . . I will send' (v. 34). But it is 'this Moses' (v. 35), the rejected one, who is chosen by God as the privileged recipient of the divine vision, and the one whom God sends as both 'ruler and deliverer'. The paradox recalls Peter's words at 2:13, 4:10, and it is underlined by the repeated *houtos* ('this one') in vv. 36–8. Like Peter (3:22), Stephen picks out Moses' prediction of the prophet (Deut 18:15 LXX) as a prediction of Christ (v. 37): the typology will be made more explicit in v. 52. And it was this same Moses who received the 'living oracles' of the

law to pass on to the *ekklēsia* ('congregation') of God's people ('to us', v. 38).

(7:39–43) Apostasy in the Wilderness At this point the syntactical focus shifts from Moses to 'our fathers', who become the subject of all the verbs in vv. 39–41. These are verbs of disobedience and apostasy: the message could not be clearer that Stephen's problem lies not with Moses or his teachings (6:11, 14) but with those who have consistently refused to obey them. The request for the golden calf (v. 40) is couched explicitly in terms that reflect the standard biblical denunciation of pagan idolatry (v. 41: Ps 97:7; Isa 48:5; Ps 135:15; Ps 115:4). Stephen uses an extensive quotation from Am 5:25–7 to reinforce his point: the rhetorical question of the opening is interpreted here as evidence that Israel's apostasy can be traced back to the wilderness period.

The passage from Amos is a notorious crux in the Hebrew, and Luke is drawing here on a long tradition of exegetical reflection. In v. 43 Luke follows LXX, which vocalizes the Hebrew *sikkut* (Am 5:26: the name of an Assyrian god) as *sukkat* (tabernacle, 'tent', NRSV), and 'king' (*melech*) as Moloch. The Hebrew 'Kaiwan your star-god' becomes 'the star of your god Raiphan': there are several MS variants for the last name, whose origin is obscure. Luke's only real change to the Amos text is to substitute 'Babylon' for the original 'Damascus', conflating Amos's vision of exile under the Assyrian empire with the later and more paradigmatic experience of exile in Babylon.

(7:44–53) Tabernacle and Temple It can hardly be a coincidence that Stephen moves directly from the 'tent of Moloch' to the 'tent of testimony', i.e. the tabernacle, though the logic of the transition is not entirely clear. Stephen's point seems to be that the wilderness tabernacle, which Moses made in obedience to the 'pattern' given by God (v. 44), was closer to God's will than King Solomon's temple, despite the fact that David had sought God's leave to build the temple (v. 46; cf. 2 Sam 7:1–16). It is of course Solomon himself who recognizes the futility of trying to build a house for God (v. 48; cf. 1 Kings 8:27): Stephen is exploiting an ambivalence about the temple that may be particularly felt in diaspora circles, but is already deeply rooted in the Hebrew Scriptures, as the following quotation from Isa 66:1–2 shows (vv. 9–50). 'Stiff-necked' (v. 51) takes us back to the wilderness generation: cf. Ex 33:3. The charge of 'resisting the Holy Spirit' that forms Stephen's peroration (v. 51) is also based on Scripture, cf. Isa 63:10: from here it is a logical step to the charge of persecuting the prophets who are inspired by the Spirit (v. 52; cf. Heb 11:32–8). This was a widespread tradition in early Judaism (cf. Fitzmyer 1998: 385), particularly highlighted by Luke (e.g. Lk 13:34); here it is linked implicitly with Moses' prophecy (v. 37), and explicitly with the chief role of the prophets for Christians, that of predicting the Messiah. Stephen's speech thus ends up with the same accusation as Peter's (v. 52); the long history of apostasy and rebellion is simply a way of identifying the scriptural patterns that underlie the crisis of rejection in the present generation.

(7:54–60) Stephen's Death Audience reactions to this speech are described in highly dramatic tones (v. 54), heightened even further by the description of Stephen's vision (vv. 55–6). Stephen's vision of the glory of God highlights his continuity with Abraham (7:2) and Moses (cf. Ex 33:18–23); but now the open heaven (v. 56) also contains the figure of Jesus himself. Jesus' position 'at the right hand of God' (v. 55) denotes the highest place of honour: the vision fully confirms Stephen's claim that the rejected saviour is in fact God's 'Righteous One'. Many different explanations of the fact that the Son of Man is 'standing' have been suggested (cf. Fitzmyer 1998: 392–3 and Johnson 1992: 139). Despite the differing circumstances, there are a number of literary parallels with Luke's description of the death of Jesus. Stephen commits his spirit to God and cries out 'in a loud voice' (vv. 59–60; cf. Lk 23:46). The prayer for forgiveness (v. 60) echoes in thought the prayer of Lk 23:34 (omitted in some MSS), though the wording is entirely different. The most dramatic difference is that when Stephen, the prototype for Christian martyrdom, dies 'calling on the name of the Lord' (v. 59), it is the exalted Jesus whom he expects to receive his spirit.

Act Two: The Scattered Church: Samaria to Antioch (8:1–12:25)

Act II Scene 1: Samaria and Gaza (8:1–40)

Stephen's death is the trigger for a 'severe persecution' (8:1) which ushers in a new stage in the church's existence. From now on, the gospel is not confined to Jerusalem, but moves steadily outwards, carried by anonymous Christians (8:4). It will be increasingly hard for Luke to marshal the scattered pieces of information he has about the new foci of the church's life, and this central section reflects that difficulty: there is a less precise geographical structure here, and Luke seems to have few indications as to chronology. But this section forms a vital bridge between the stationary church of the Jerusalem narrative (chs. 1–7) and the evangelistic journeys of the Pauline mission (chs. 13–28). It also includes the two key moments of theophany around which the whole narrative spirals, Paul's conversion (ch. 9) and Peter's vision (chs. 10–11).

(8:1–4) The Church Scattered Geographically, the new stage is focused around two poles. The apostles stay on in Jerusalem (vv. 1, 14); and Jerusalem remains a narrative focus through to ch. 12. But the rest of the church is 'scattered throughout the countryside of Judea and Samaria' (v. 1). We are moving on to the middle stage of the apostolic commission in 1:8, but it is not just the apostles who do the preaching: unnamed disciples exploit their 'scattered' condition (v. 4) to spread the gospel. Interwoven with this story of expansion is the darker theme of persecution: Stephen is buried (v. 2), and Saul, slyly introduced as a bystander in 7:58, is painted in vivid and dramatic language as a zealous instigator of the persecution. How broad the persecution was (or how long it lasted) is not entirely clear. By 9:26 there is a group of 'disciples' back in Jerusalem alongside the apostles; it is possible that the community most affected was the one to which both Stephen and Saul belonged, the believers who belonged to synagogues of diaspora origin.

(8:5–13) Philip's Mission in Samaria Philip is not an apostle but one of the seven (6:5). We shall meet him again at 21:8, still characterized as 'the evangelist' but now settled in Caesarea with four daughters: the connection with a 'we-passage'

suggests an obvious source from which Luke (directly or indirectly) could have obtained this story. 'Samaria' (v. 5) may be either the region (as in RSV) or the name of its capital city (as in NRSV), which was rebuilt under Herod the Great. Philip's preaching is presented as a highly successful piece of evangelism, accompanied by miraculous healings which impress the city's population (vv. 6, 8). It is only in v. 9 that Luke reveals that Philip has a competitor in Samaria: Simon was used to commanding the same focused attention from the Samaritans (vv. 9, 10). Simon's popular title (v. 10) may reflect local divine names. Justin Martyr (possibly drawing on local knowledge) identifies him as a Samaritan magician, later honoured in Rome as a god (Justin, 1 Apol. 26; 56; Dial. 20.6). Luke, however, labels his activity as 'magic' (vv. 9, 11), always a pejorative term in Acts: the magician's powers may be real, but they fade into insignificance beside the powers of the gospel. The preaching of the word brings about not just a nine days' wonder, but belief and baptism, i.e. intellectual conviction and entry into a new community. The fact that the magician himself is impressed by Philip (v. 13) simply serves to highlight the gospel's power: there is nothing in this verse to suggest that Simon's conversion was any less real than those of his auditors.

(8:14–25) The Coming of the Spirit: Samaria The enigmatic character of Simon Magus fascinated later Christians. Irenaeus identifies him as the founder of the 'Simonian' Gnostics (Adv. haer. 1.23). For Luke, however, the issue is not heresy but the illegitimate appropriation of divine power, and money (as so often) is a symptom of a deeper corruption. Simon's request implies that he thought he could enter into some kind of contractual arrangement with the apostles that would enable him to confer the Spirit at will (vv. 18–19). But the Spirit is God's gift (v. 20), and cannot be bought for cash. The sin of 'simony' (defined as 'the purchase and sale of spiritual things': ODCC s.v.) takes its name from this story.

The story also highlights two related issues of church order. (1) The role of the apostles. Luke's structuring of this episode implies a supervisory role for the Jerusalem church, concerned to keep an eye on new developments. The fact that Samaria has received God's word merits an apostolic visitation (v. 14). Luke is able to assure his readers that each significant new step in the expansion of the gospel has been tested and approved by the apostles. (2) Baptism and the Spirit. The sequence of events in this episode seems to imply (a) that baptism in the name of Jesus (v. 12) and the reception of the Spirit (v. 15) were two distinct events for the Samaritans and (b) that the latter could not happen without the laying on of hands by the apostles (v. 17). The passage has therefore been used in some churches to justify the practice of confirmation as a separate rite from baptism, and in others to argue that a distinct experience of the Spirit is necessary as a supplement to baptism. The problem with both these arguments is that although the sequence is clear in this passage, it is by no means universal, even in Acts (let alone in the rest of the NT): elsewhere the Spirit is bestowed before baptism (e.g. 10:44–8), or is not recorded at all (e.g. 8:38). Luke was not writing Acts as a manual of church discipline and is manifestly unconcerned to define the exact order in which the four elements involved in conversion occur (see above on 2:38).

The crucial point here in terms of plot is that the apostles' visit brings about a Samaritan Pentecost which demonstrates conclusively that this new step in the mission of the church has received the seal of the Spirit. The apostles, far from being against this development, are actively promoting it by conducting further evangelistic activity in Samaritan territory (v. 5).

(8:26–40) Philip and the Ethiopian Philip has another significant evangelistic task to perform before he disappears from the stage again. This episode shows Philip to be open and obedient to divine guidance. Luke shows little interest in ontological questions about spiritual phenomena: both angel (v. 26) and Spirit (vv. 29, 39) originate in God, and their effect on the observer is hard to distinguish (cf. 23:8–9). Luke's geography, however, is more exact than many commentators have given him credit for: Philip's route due south from Samaria intersects at Eleutheropolis with the Jerusalem–Gaza road (v. 26: *epi* means 'down to' or 'to meet'). Even the timing of this journey is miraculous: just at that moment (*kai idou*, lit. and behold, 27), Philip's path crosses the route of the Ethiopian pilgrim, heading west to strike the coast road towards Egypt.

What is the significance of this figure? Later tradition identified the eunuch as the first Gentile convert, and the founder of the Ethiopian church (Eusebius, *Hist. Eccl.* 2.1.13), but this does not seem quite to fit Luke's plot, with its elaborate build-up to the conversion of Cornelius in ch. 10. Luke lays more stress on the eunuch's links with Judaism: this is a man who has been to worship in the Jerusalem temple (v. 27) and is reading the prophet Isaiah (v. 28). Given the existence of a well-documented Jewish community at Elephantine (Aswan), Jewish influence south of Egypt is not implausible. Ancient readers would certainly imagine this character as an African: Ethiopia, in ancient geography, was the equivalent of Nubia, today's Sudan, rather than the modern Ethiopia. Readers who knew their Bibles might also pick up prophetic resonances, in which the Ethiopians (Heb. 'Cushites') figure among the most distant peoples from whom God will gather a remnant to worship in Jerusalem (e.g. Isa 11:11, Zeph 3:9–10).

The detail Luke lavishes on this story foregrounds the vital importance the early Christians attached to the correct interpretation of scripture (vv. 30–1): this was an integral part of the apostolic witness (Lk 24:44–9). The eunuch's question (v. 34) is still debated by OT scholars. As so often, a genuine difficulty within the Hebrew text provides a hook for Christological exegesis; but the real value of this passage for Christians lay in providing prophetic warrant for the ignominious death that Jesus had in fact suffered (Lindars 1961: 77–88). According to the Western text, Philip asks for and receives a declaration of faith before proceeding with the baptism, and the eunuch then receives the Spirit; Luke, as noted above, seems distressingly unconcerned to establish uniform practice in the apostolic period, and this reading looks like an attempt to iron out anomalies. The scene ends as abruptly as it began (v. 39): unlike the Cornelius episode, it is pure encounter, with no ongoing implications for the church. When the travellers reach the coast road, the Ethiopian turns south towards Gaza, while Philip (v. 40) turns north towards Azotus; as a character, he is now tidied away to Caesarea (to reappear

briefly at 21:8), but his evangelistic activity en route provides some preparation for Peter's activities in the coastal areas in 9:32–43.

Act II Scene 2: Damascus (9:1–31)

The scene now shifts to back to Jerusalem. The apparently minor character of Saul (7:58; 8:1–3) undergoes a dramatic conversion from persecutor to preacher. This episode, retold twice in Acts (22:4–21; 26:9–18), is one of the most important episodes in the drama, both in its own right and because it introduces and legitimates the man who is to become the central character of the second half of Acts.

(9:1–9) On the Damascus Road The term 'conversion' is anachronistic and misleading if we think of it in terms of a change from one religion to another. Christianity was not at this stage a distinct religion in the modern sense but a sect within Second Temple Judaism, promoting one among a number of contested Jewish identities (ACTS 24:14). It is a 'conversion' in the strict biblical sense, that is a complete change of direction; Luke's use of the term 'the Way' (v. 2; cf. v. 17, 'on the road [= way]') plays up this aspect of the story. Paul himself refers to his experience both as a prophetic call (Gal 1:15) and as an experience of the risen Christ (Gal 1:16; 1 Cor 15:8), and there is a strong element of both these in Luke's account (though Luke does not use the experience to justify giving Paul the rank of apostle).

The dramatic conversion of a persecutor or scoffer was a topos familiar both to Jewish and to Greek readers (cf. Dan 1–6; 2 Macc 3:13–40), and the vivid detail of Luke's story highlights the completeness of the reversal. Saul's threatening and purposeful journey (v. 1) comes to an abrupt halt (v. 3); the heavenly light deprives him of sight (v. 8); the heavenly voice leaves Saul's retinue speechless (v. 7); the instigator of punitive action has to be 'told what to do' (v. 6) and 'led by the hand' (v. 8). As in 2 Macc 3:28, it is a story of reversal which demonstrates clearly 'the sovereign power of God'. But what is particularly terrifying for Saul is that the voice that speaks from the midst of the theophanic light is the voice of 'Jesus, whom you are persecuting' (v. 5)—confirmation that Stephen's vision (7:56) was not total delusion.

(9:10–19a) Ananias's Vision Saul's story (like Cornelius': Barrett 1994–9: i. 453) is in fact the story of two visions, each confirming the other. We are told nothing of Ananias's past history, or of how he came to be a disciple (v. 10), but v. 13 implies that he was a Damascus resident. Ananias is given precise directions as to Saul's address (v. 11: the 'street called Straight' is still shown in the Old City of Damascus). Like many OT characters (e.g. Moses in Ex 3:11–4:17), Ananias does not hesitate to argue with 'the Lord'. The effect of his reluctance is to highlight the dramatic change between Saul's terrifying reputation and his present chastened state ('he is praying', v. 11). It also elicits a divine commission which highlights (in distinctly Pauline language) the contrast between Saul's sorry past and God's elective grace (v. 15: cf. 1 Cor 15:9–10; Rom 9:23). Saul's future career is prophetically outlined in vv. 15–16, which may be taken as a supplementary narrative plan to 1:8; precisely what this implies will be revealed as the narrative unfolds. Ananias's response, however reluctant, is generous (v. 17): laying-on of hands (here primarily for healing) is followed by baptism (v. 18). The gift of the Spirit (here at the hands of one who is not an apostle and has no known connection with Jerusalem) is implied (in intent, v. 17) but not stated—another instance of Luke's lack of concern for precise ritual patterns.

(9:19b–25) Saul in Damascus The dramatic effect of Saul's conversion is immediately apparent: in characteristic style, Luke records a reaction of universal amazement (v. 21). The relationship between Luke's narrative here and Paul's own account of his conversion in Gal 1 is contested. Paul does not mention anywhere that his call took place in Damascus, and does not mention an extended stay. According to Gal 1:17 he goes away immediately after his call to Arabia: but the fact that he then says 'I returned to Damascus' does seem to imply that the call took place there. The only other mention of Damascus in Paul's letters is at 2 Cor 11:32, where he describes being let down over the walls in a basket as an example of the humiliating position an apostle might find himself in. This must refer to the same episode (it could hardly have happened twice), but the details are different: in Paul's account, it is not 'the Jews' but the ethnarch (local commissioner) of Aretas who watches the gates to prevent his escape. Aretas was king of the Arabian kingdom of Nabatea, and since there are only a few years when he could have had any kind of judicial authority in Damascus, this dates the episode to 37–9 CE. Given Luke's general interest in local rulers (cf. Lk 3:1–2), it seems unlikely that he would have omitted this detail had he known 2 Corinthians; he must have had independent access to this piece of Pauline tradition, but has heard (or reconstructs) the details rather differently.

(9:26–30) Saul Returns to Jerusalem A more serious difficulty arises with Luke's account of Paul's return to Jerusalem. Compared with Paul's own account in Gal 1, Luke appears to imply a shorter interval before Paul's first Jerusalem visit (v. 19b), a longer stay in Jerusalem, and a meeting with more than one apostle (v. 27). Though Luke's chronology is notoriously vague, it is hard to reconcile the timing of these two accounts: Barrett's (1994–9: i. 462) conclusion is that 'Luke is correct in saying that Paul travelled from Damascus to Jerusalem, wrong in his dating of the event'. But in other respects the two accounts can be read as different perspectives on the same event: nothing in the Acts account suggests that Paul stayed a long time in Jerusalem, or had many meetings with the apostles, or (the point Paul himself is most keen to deny) that he had extensive instruction in the gospel from the Jerusalem church. Luke in fact highlights the suspicion with which the former persecutor was received by the Jerusalem church (vv. 26–7), and, like Paul, stresses the relative independence of Paul's gospel from apostolic control. So this short summary passage brings the narrative circle back to its point of departure in ch. 6: Saul, the zealous young man who approved of the killing of Stephen, comes back to Jerusalem to finish the argument with the Hellenists that Stephen had started, and arouses the same violent response. The 'brothers', it is implied, are in no way in control of this situation, but recognize its potential danger: Saul is packed off hurriedly to his home town of Tarsus (v. 30; cf. Gal 1:21), still unknown by sight to most members of the Judean churches (Gal 1:22).

9:31 Summary and Transition A final summary verse signals a return to the main narrative thread. Luke reminds us that much is happening of which his narrative only gives us tantalizing glimpses. He has shown us scattered groups of 'brothers' or 'disciples' (both men and women), and allowed us to see some of the individual encounters which they used, under the guidance of the Spirit, to spread their faith. But behind this diversity is a larger unity, something called 'the church' (in the singular) which is growing and 'being built up' throughout the region. Luke's focus on individuals has given us dramatic scenes of conversion and conflict, mostly in the cities: Jerusalem (chs. 1–7), Samaria (ch. 8), and Damascus (ch. 9), as well as one encounter on the desert road (ch. 8). What he does not describe, except in these brief summaries, is the steady consolidation that is going on behind the scenes and in the country regions: Samaria (cf. 8:25), Judea and Galilee, and (as we shall shortly be reminded), all along the coastal plain (cf. 8:40).

Act II Scene 3: Caesarea (9:32–11:18)

Saul, the future apostle to the Gentiles, has heard the call of God, but remains in the wings until Luke is ready to bring him back centre-stage. Before that happens, the mission to the Gentiles (only hinted at in 1:8 and 9:15) must be more fully prepared for through an extraordinary sequence of visions and encounters in Caesarea. Luke makes it quite clear that this crucial development in the history of the church comes about in response to God's initiative; and it is not Paul but Peter, the central figure of the apostolic team in Jerusalem, who is given the responsibility of grasping the vision (told three times over, like that of Paul) and passing it on to the church.

9:32–5 Peter and Aeneas The summary of v. 31 has swung the narrative back to the centre, and we now return to the Jerusalem church and to Peter as its chief figurehead. Going 'here and there among the believers' (v. 32) suggests one of the mechanisms by which the church was 'built up' (v. 31): it implies that Peter has some kind of pastoral oversight over the whole church ('all'), which by now includes believers in the towns of the coastal plain. How these communities may have been founded is suggested at 8:40: Lydda is the modern Lod, and Sharon is the region of Sarona, northwards along the coast towards Caesarea. These two brief miracle stories remind the reader of Peter's power as a healer. There are strong echoes here of the healing miracles of Jesus, though Luke is careful to stress that Peter heals in Jesus' name, not his own (v. 34). A characteristically Lukan 'all' (v. 35) underlines the evangelistic force of these miracles.

9:36–43 The Healing of Tabitha The fledgling community at the port of Joppa (Jaffa) comes across with a little more detail: it includes both men and women, and Luke uses the unusual term *mathētria* for a woman disciple (outside the church, women would not often be characterized as 'students'). Tabitha (Gk. 'Dorcas': both names mean 'gazelle') has developed a charitable ministry among the women of the town, especially (v. 39) the widows who, in a system with no social security, could find themselves in severe financial straits. Tabitha's clothing club is a prototype for the extensive practical aid programmes that grew up in the later churches. The 'upper room' (v. 39) and Peter's prayer (v. 40) recall healings of

Elijah and Elisha at 1 Kings 17:17–24; 2 Kings 4:33 (cf. Lk 4:26, 27); but the closest parallels are with the gospel story of Jesus' healing of Jairus' daughter (Mk 5:22–4, 35–43 par.). It is intriguing that only Mark records the Aramaic form of Jesus' words to the child, *talitha cum* (Mk 5:41); this is so close to Peter's words here (though in the gospel story *talitha* is not a name) that it is tempting to think Luke has either held over this detail deliberately from the gospel to Acts, or has received a parallel healing tradition that transposes the miracle to Peter and to a non-Galilean location.

(10:1–8) Cornelius' Vision Like the conversion of Saul, this is really a story of two visionary experiences, each confirming the other. Luke leaves his main protagonist temporarily immobile (9:43) and takes the reader to Caesarea, 32 miles north up the coast. Here we are introduced to a man with the good Roman name of Cornelius, belonging to the non-commissioned officer class who were the backbone of the Roman army (10:1). The 'Italian Cohort' is known from inscriptional evidence to have been in Syria before 69, though we do not have precise details about its stationing. Cornelius is characterized as a pious man with a godfearing household (vv. 2, 7), and his piety is borne out by actions both charitable and religious (10:2). The term 'devout' (*eusebēs*) is one of a group of words Luke uses rather loosely, apparently to characterize Gentiles who were attracted to the religious practice of Judaism but shrank from the rigours of full conversion (generally called Godfearers to distinguish them from Gentile proselytes who had converted fully to Judaism). This may never have been a formal category, and its existence has been disputed in recent years; but the probability that some such group existed now seems to have been confirmed, at least for some diaspora cities, by the discovery of an inscription in Aphrodisias which includes a category of *theosebeis* among a list of charitable donors to a synagogue (Levinskaya 1996: 51–82: Barrett 1994–9: i. 500–1).

(10:9–16) Peter's Vision Cornelius' vision establishes not only his own piety but the much more important fact that God is taking the initiative in reaching out to the Gentiles. The interleaved timing, with the visitors moving purposefully on to meet a man who does not yet know of their existence (10:8–9) reinforces the point: everything about this sequence is miraculous, even Peter's noontime siesta with its combination of prayer and (albeit enforced) fasting (10:10). 'Trance' (*ekstasis*) is a strong word that strengthens the sense of an awe-inspiring revelation (cf. Mk 16:8; Lk 5:26; Lk 3:10; 22:17). The opening of heaven (10:11) is a standard feature of theophanic vision (cf. 7:55), but the rather bizarre details of Peter's vision are not: the container (*skeuos*) 'like a large sheet' sounds like a ship's sail, and fits the maritime setting of Peter's vision (cf. 10:5). The immediate focus of the vision, however, is on food. The list of 'four-footed creatures and reptiles and birds of the air' (v. 12) echoes the creation narrative of Gen 1, and is deliberately inclusive: the heavenly voice prohibits the classification of foods into 'clean' and 'unclean' that was fundamental to the Jewish food laws (cf. e.g. Lev 11:47). The use of *koinos* ('profane', v. 15, lit. common) as a gloss for 'unclean' is paralleled in the discussion of food laws in Mk 7:1–23 (par. Mt 15:1–20) and in Rom 14:14. Interestingly, however, the heavenly voice in Peter's vision does not make Paul's rather general

philosophical point that 'nothing is unclean in itself' but assigns a more active role to God: the whole range of created food is clean not simply because God made it but because God has 'cleansed' it (v. 15).

10:17–23a Peter Summoned to Caesarea The significance of the vision is only unpacked slowly (though the reader, having had privileged access to Cornelius' vision, has clues that Peter does not). We are still with Peter up on the roof-top, puzzling over its meaning (10:17, 19), when Cornelius' emissaries knock at the door downstairs. It takes a further direct intervention from the Spirit (v. 19) to make Peter go down to meet them: Peter now shares the readers' knowledge that these visitors have been sent by God (v. 20), but their connection with the vision is not yet explicit. Peter is instructed to go with them *mēden diakrinomenos* (v. 20), an ambiguous verb whose double meaning is important for the story's development (Johnson 1992: 185): it can simply mean 'without hesitation' (so NRSV), but also carries the sense 'without making distinctions', 'without discrimination'. This sense is already implicit in Peter's action in inviting his guests in and making them welcome (v. 23). The messengers' description of Cornelius repeats (and therefore reinforces) much of what we as readers already know from the previous scene; the additional information that he is 'well spoken of by the whole Jewish nation' (cf. an earlier centurion in Lk 7:5) also underlines the fact that this is a Gentile.

10:23b–33 Peter Meets Cornelius It is hard to convey the extent to which Luke slows down the action in this scene, making explicit a series of apparently trivial actions of a kind normally left to the reader's imagination in biblical narrative. All of this, with the constant repetition of narrative detail, adds to the effect of drawing the reader into Peter's dilemma, to experience with him the gradual steps by which this new stage in God's plan is unfolded. The journey to Caesarea takes a full day (v. 24), and Peter takes with him some of the 'brothers' from Joppa (v. 23). All this time Peter has been associating with the Gentile soldier (v. 7) and the house-servants (probably also Gentile) sent by Cornelius: when he arrives, to find a houseful of the centurion's 'relatives and close friends' assembled in his honour (v. 24), the next decisive step is entering this Gentile household (v. 27). But Peter has already made the connection with the animal vision: the prohibition against calling anything 'common or unclean' is not about food but about people, not about what you eat but about who you associate with (v. 28). Cornelius' recapitulation of his own vision (vv. 30–3) heightens the solemnity of the scene: we find ourselves alongside the listeners, poised and expectant 'in the presence of God' to hear what God has commissioned Peter to say (v. 33).

(10:34–43) Peter Preaches to the Gentiles This is the last evangelistic speech Peter will make in Acts, and it is both parallel to and subtly different from those he has made in Jerusalem. Its burden is that God shows no 'partiality', no preferential treatment as between Jew and Gentile: acceptability before God is open to those 'in every nation' (v. 35) who fear him and perform righteous acts (cf. Rom 2:10–11, where the same word is used). Peter then moves into a recapitulation of the gospel message he has preached in Jerusalem, subtly adapted for this Caesarean setting. This is the fullest summary Luke gives of the gospel story in Acts. It brings out the characteristic shape of the story, starting in Galilee after John's baptism (v. 37), and stressing the charismatic power of Jesus' healing ministry: nowhere else does Luke make it so clear that he sees all healing as liberation from demonic power (v. 38). As in his Jerusalem speeches (cf. ACTS 2:14–36; 3:11–26), Peter now repeats the charge that Jesus was 'put to death' (v. 39), though without specifying who was responsible (for 'hanging on a tree' cf. ACTS 5:30); now that we have moved out of Jerusalem there is less emphasis on Jesus' death and more on his resurrection (vv. 40–1), including a reprise of the apostolic commission (v. 42). Peter (or Luke) is very interested in defining audiences here: God's message is sent first to Israel (v. 36), then to a smaller group of witnesses (v. 41), whose prime target is still 'the people' (v. 42, i.e. Israel). The message, however, is universal: judgement of 'the living and the dead' (v. 42: cf. 17:31) and forgiveness of sins for 'everyone who believes in him' (v. 43). The stage is set for an extension of the word of God to an audience which includes Gentiles (v. 33).

(10:44–8) **The Coming of the Spirit: Caesarea** It is at this precise point that the Holy Spirit intervenes. 'All who heard the word' (v. 44) are caught up in the same charismatic experience: the 'astounded' reaction of Peter's Jewish-Christian companions from Joppa highlights the fact that this includes 'even Gentiles' (v. 45). 'Speaking in tongues' (v. 46) has not been mentioned since the Pentecost experience of 2:4; Peter's question ('just as we have', v. 47) underlines the parallel, which is surely intentional. The act of baptizing Gentile believers (v. 48) follows as a logical consequence: the structure of Luke's narrative makes it quite clear that the initiative in this case is God's. The form of the question ('Can anyone withold?', v. 47) recalls the Ethiopian's question about baptism in 8:37: within the narrative, this is a rhetorical question which expects the answer 'No', but the very existence of the question implies that some at least in Luke's audience might have preferred to answer 'Yes'.

(11:1–18) **Ratification in Jerusalem** There are indeed some who object to the reception of Gentiles into the church, identified in 11:2 as 'circumcised believers' in Jerusalem, who are making precisely the kind of 'discrimination' that Peter was warned against in 10:20 (cf. 11:12). The question is framed in terms of the traditional restrictions on table-fellowship between Jews and Gentiles to which Peter himself had referred in 10:28, and which we know from Paul (Gal 2:11–14) continued to be a bone of contention within the church (see below on ACTS 15:1–35 on the relation between Galatians and Acts on this issue). In Luke's narrative, it emphasizes the gap in understanding that has opened up between Peter and his fellow apostles: now he has to bring the rest of the Judean churches to accept the same radical break with tradition that he has made, and he can only do it by talking them through the same story, 'step by step' (kathexēs, 11:4). As with all Luke's recapitulations, there are minor variations between the various retellings: this allows Luke to reveal more of the real significance of what has happened each time the story is retold. Presenting this retelling in Peter's own words also allows Luke to reveal some of the character's own thought processes and to give a theological interpretation of the

scene's key event. So Peter highlights the role of the Spirit, the importance of not 'making a distinction' (v. 12), and the parallel with Pentecost (v. 15). In Peter's own mind, the event triggered memories of Jesus' words (v. 16; cf. Acts 1:5), and to him the theological inference is clear (v. 17). Like Gamaliel (5:39), Peter warns that withholding baptism from the Gentiles would be tantamount to 'hindering God': this is one of Luke's major underlying themes, and his whole narrative is designed to offer convincing proof (as Peter's does here) that each step in the development of the church is initiated by God.

Act II Scene 4: Antioch and Jerusalem (11:19–12:25)

After the unified and tightly constructed episode of Cornelius' conversion we move to a rather more rambling section that combines summary accounts of the founding of the church in Antioch (11:19–26) and the sending of a famine relief mission to Jerusalem (11:27–30; 12:25) with traditional stories of martyrdom and imprisonment from the Jerusalem church (12:1–19) and the bizarre retributory death of Herod the persecutor (12:24).

(11:19–26) **The Church in Antioch** There is a very definite closure and change of scene at 11:19, as the narrative thread returns to 'those who were scattered' at 8:1, and follows them to Antioch, 300 miles to the north. Luke gives the impression that the persecution that followed Stephen's death was an explosive event, creating an unstoppable momentum: those caught up in it are still on the move, blissfully unaware of developments elsewhere, and 'speaking the word' as they travel (v. 19; cf. 8:4). Some of these anonymous Christians (Luke knows only that they came from Cyprus and Cyrene) take the momentous step of speaking the word to 'Greeks' as well as Jews in Antioch (v. 20). The MS reading hellēnistas (Hellenists, so NRSV) can hardly be right: the reading hellēnas (Greeks, as in NRSV marg.) is attested in P74 and other early MSS and is to be preferred.

The foundation of the church in Antioch is a major development which indirectly confirms all that Luke has been highlighting in the Cornelius episode. The apostles' reaction to the news (v. 22) parallels that in 8:14, except that they send Barnabas (4:36) rather than travelling to Syria themselves. Barnabas acts both as a vital go-between linking Jerusalem with the satellite church in Antioch, and as the agent who brings Saul back onto the scene (vv. 25–6), to spend a year quietly engaged in 'teaching'. The passing note that the name 'Christian' was first applied to believers in Antioch (v. 26) is of marginal significance for the plot, but it illustrates Luke's antiquarian concern for detail and suggests that he does have some interest in avoiding anachronism. The implication is that the name is much more familiar in Luke's own time.

(11:27–30) **Famine Relief Measures** This notice raises a number of historical difficulties. (1) The best candidate for Luke's famine is the one dated by Josephus to 46–8 (Ant. 20.101); but Acts 12:20–3 appears to date the relief mission before the death of Herod Agrippa I, which is externally dated to 44 CE (cf. ACTS 12:20–4). It is possible that Luke simply did not know the exact order of these unconnected events, and has grouped them thus in his narrative for reasons of convenience rather than chronology (cf. his placing of the death of the Baptist, Lk 3:19–20). But it is also true (Barrett 1994–9: i. 563–64) that

Luke narrates the return of the relief party *after* Herod's death (12:25). (2) The passage appears to conflict with Paul's own account of his relationship with Jerusalem. Paul himself claims to have visited Jerusalem only once before the critical encounter of Gal 2:1–10. If Gal 2:1–10 is identified with the Apostolic Council of Acts 15, and the first visit is equivalent to that of Acts 9 (as we have argued above: ACTS 9:26–30), then Luke has inserted an extra visit here, against the explicit asseverations of Gal 1:17–24. But there are other options: see further ACTS 15:1–35. (3) One of the enduring puzzles of Acts is why Luke never explicitly mentions the collection for the poor of Jerusalem on which Paul lavished so much attention in his later ministry (cf. e.g. Rom 15:25–8; 1 Cor 16:1–4; 2 Cor 8–9). Is this story a clumsy Lucan attempt to fabricate an earlier 'collection' in place of the real one? Or is it a relic of an earlier charitable collection to which Paul himself alludes briefly and puzzlingly in Gal 2:10?

(12:1–4) Herod Persecutes the Apostles The scene moves to Jerusalem, where the apostles are harassed by a fresh bout of persecution (12:1). This is not the Herod of the passion narrative (Lk 23:6–12; Acts 4:27) but Agrippa I, a grandson of Herod the Great, who gradually regained control of his grandfather's kingdom through the patronage of the Roman imperial family (only Acts identifies him by the family name Herod). Judea was added to his territory by Claudius after 41 CE, and he was engaged in a constant battle to retain favour with the Jewish population of the areas he controlled. Quite why he should have identified James as a threat to public order (v. 2) is unclear, and Luke seems to have little information on this martyrdom: it serves simply to establish Herod's character as a persecutor of the church, and to heighten the dramatic tension in the story of Peter's imprisonment. Peter's arrest, by contrast, is recounted with a wealth of dramatic detail. The note that it was Passover (v. 3) immediately suggests a parallel with the arrest of Jesus, as does the detail that Herod was intending to bring Peter 'out to the people' (v. 4)—though the parallel is more explicit in John's passion narrative than in Luke's. This narrative has two dramatic locations: while Peter is in prison 'the church' (v. 5) is engaged in 'fervent' prayer (cf. Lk 22:44, where the same word is used of Jesus' prayer in Gethsemane).

(12:6–11) Peter's Miraculous Escape This is one of the most sensational episodes in Acts. The timing is precise (v. 6); but despite his perilous (and doubtless uncomfortable) position, Peter is sleeping peacefully between his guards. The scene recalls 5:22–3, though the dramatic tension is heightened here: there Peter and John disappear from a locked prison cell, here Peter is spirited away despite being shackled to two soldiers (v. 6). The sudden appearance of the angel is reminiscent of the birth narrative (Lk 2:9): this direct intervention of heavenly personages is unusual in the narrative of Acts (though cf. 5:19–21), and contrasts strongly with the generally more realistic tone of the Paul narratives. Peter in fact (as we learn in v. 9) thinks that the almost comically precise instructions given by the angel are part of a dream: the reader knows better (vv. 7–8). The dramatic detail continues as the apostle leaves the sleeping guards and passes through the iron gate which opens 'of its own accord' (v. 10). The expression recalls a number of passages in ancient literature recording marvel-

lous portents (e.g. Jos. *J.W.* 6.293, Tac. *Hist.* 5.13) or miraculous escapes (note esp. the escape of Moses reported by the hellenistic Jewish historian Artapanus: Eusebius, *Praep. Evang.* 9.27.23). Luke's technique here shows no signs of the cognitive distancing that Greek or Roman readers would expect of a historian's account of a miraculous event: the reporting is much closer to the style of biblical historiography, and is designed to stress the divine protection enjoyed by the Christian community.

12:12–17 Peter's Reception by the Church There is an element of comic bathos in this account of Peter's reception by the church: far from expecting their prayers to be answered, they are completely taken aback when he knocks at the door, and the maid Rhoda (a nice example of a Lucan minor character) is too flabbergasted even to open the door. Despite his supernatural escape, Peter is a very human figure here: prison doors may open up for him, but house doors remain obstinately closed. Peter's story comes to an abrupt end at this point (apart from 15:7–11). He stays only long enough to tell his story to the house-church (v. 17), and asks that it be passed on to 'James and the brothers'. Luke does not trouble to explain the name, but this James (as we will discover) is the brother of Jesus (cf. 1:14); he has not been mentioned by name before, but from now on he will act as spokesman for the Jerusalem church (15:13; 21:18; cf. Gal 1–2). Neither does Luke give us any information about Peter's subsequent destination. Later tradition places his death in Rome (cf. JN 21:8), but in Acts he simply fades out of the picture.

(12:18–23) Herod's Reaction and Death The scene shifts briefly back to the prison, where Peter's mysterious disappearance causes consternation among the soldiers (v. 18). Herod is depicted as a typical persecuting tyrant, venting his frustration on his subordinates. The judicial detail ('examined', v. 19) highlights the irony of the situation: neither the soldiers nor Herod share the readers' privileged knowledge of Peter's secret, and no amount of examination can possibly discover it. Herod's sensational death (vv. 20–3) was well-known, and a similar story appears in Jos. *Ant.* 19.343–50. But Luke's story is independent: both have Herod dying a horrible death as a punishment for being acclaimed as divine, but in Josephus' story it is the robe itself ('a garment woven in silver... illumined by the touch of the first rays of the sun') that inspires the crowd's acclamation. Luke also provides a political setting (otherwise unconfirmed, though not implausible) which is absent in Josephus (v. 20). Both writers represent typically Jewish responses to ruler-cult, a phenomenon widespread in the Hellenistic world and enthusiastically adopted by the Roman imperial family. The offence in Agrippa's case was all the greater in that he was prepared to pose in Jerusalem as a pious Jew: the acceptance of divine honours was strictly for his Greek territories, but was grossly offensive to Jewish observers. The message of this particular tradition is clear: those who seek to resist the power of God manifest in the church will be punished (cf. 5:5, 10). 'Worms' (maggots infesting a gangrenous wound?) tend to figure among the gruesome deaths attributed to tyrants in contemporary literature. Josephus (*Ant.* 17.168–9) attributes a similar fate to Herod the Great.

(12:24–5) Summary and Transition The death of the persecutor is contrasted with the continuous growth and success of God's word (v. 24): any expansion attributed to the church (cf. 9:31) is, as Luke makes clear, entirely due to God. v. 25 acts as a narrative link after the digression on Herod's fate; the relief mission is successfully completed, and the narrative picks up what will from now on be its major characters before returning to Antioch. The text here is puzzling: it would be much easier to read 'from Jerusalem' (NRSV marg.), but this looks suspiciously like a very early correction to a text already felt to be difficult. If the more difficult reading 'to' is accepted, we would have to link it with 'mission' rather than with 'returned' and translate 'returned [i.e. to Antioch] having completed their service (*diakonia*) to Jerusalem'.

Act Three: Paul the Missionary (13:1–21:16)

Act III Scene 1: Paul's First Missionary Journey (13:1–14:28)

We are now entering the third phase of the geographical plan of 1:8, moving out from Jerusalem (chs. 1–7) and 'Judea and Samaria' (chs. 8–12) into uncharted waters. The impetus for expansion also changes. The first phase was the work of the apostles, and the second came about almost by accident as believers were 'scattered' after Stephen's death (8:4; 11:19); but this third phase begins with a deliberate and prayerful step undertaken by the church in Antioch. Thus a young church founded by refugees from persecution (11:20–6) now becomes an active missionary church in its own right.

(13:1–3) The Church in Antioch It is important for Luke to convey the impression that Paul's mission was not his own initiative, but was undertaken in obedience to a believing community which was itself acting under the guidance of the Holy Spirit (vv. 2, 4). The liturgical framework of prayer and fasting is carefully described, and forms an *inclusio* with the end of this first journey at 14:26. Apart from Barnabas and Saul (cf. 11:25–6), the members of this group (v. 1) are otherwise unknown. Lucius of Cyrene may be one of the founders of the Antioch church (11:20). Manaen (Gk. form of Menahem) is another of Luke's links with the Herodian household (cf. Lk 8:3). The laying-on of hands here (v. 3) is not an 'ordination' but a commissioning for a particular task, in which Barnabas and Saul will act as delegates of the Antioch church (cf. Num 27:18–23).

(13:4–5) The Journey Begins: Antioch to Paphos A new stylistic feature of these chapters is the way in which the journeying process itself is foregrounded by the use of redundant place-names (e.g. Seleucia, v. 1) and precise verbs for sea-travel (e.g. 'sailed', v. 1) in the narrative summaries that link one part of the scene to the next. Travel, increasingly as Luke's narrative progresses, becomes an event in its own right. Cyprus, the party's first destination, was not exactly new ground to the gospel (cf. 11:19), and it was Barnabas' home territory (4:36). What is new is that, unlike earlier believers who had come to Cyprus as refugees, Barnabas and Saul have a real sense of being on a mission ('sent out by the Holy Spirit', v. 4), and set out deliberately to visit the formal meeting-places of the Jewish communities they pass through (v. 5) to carry out the prophetic/apostolic task of proclaiming the word of

God (v. 5; cf. 4:31; 6:2; 11:1). The additional note that the party now includes an 'assistant' in the shape of John Mark (v. 5) adds to the sense of a formal prophetic embassy.

(13:6–12) The Governor and the Guru In this dramatic scene, Saul/Paul demonstrates the awesome supernatural power wielded by the emissaries of the gospel: opposing spiritual forces are put to rout, and a proconsul is startled into faith. The scene parallels Peter's encounters with Simon Magus (8:14–24), and with Ananias and Sapphira (5:1–11), where the power of the Spirit (v. 9) is exercised in judgement. Luke uses the correct Greek title (*anthupatos*, proconsul) for the governor of a senatorial province (v. 7). A Roman inscription mentions a Sergius Paulus holding office in Rome under Claudius at about the right date to be Luke's proconsul; the family also seems to have a connection with Pisidia (Nobbs 1994: 89). Educated Romans had a particular interest in divination, and it was not uncommon for a wealthy senator such as Sergius Paulus to keep a soothsayer as part of his household.

For Luke, of course, it is obvious from his failure to recognize the truth of Paul's message (vv. 8) that Elymas is a 'false prophet': the term *magus* (v. 6, 8), is always defamatory in the narrative world of Acts (ACTS 8:5–13). Many diaspora Jews had Greek or Latin names alongside their Hebrew names, and Paul's change of name (v. 9) is appropriate to the move into Gentile territory. His encounter with the proconsul's guru is sharp and violent: Paul refuses to tolerate spiritual opposition, and he denounces Elymas in strongly prophetic language (vv. 10–11). The result is graphically described (v. 11*b*) in words that echo Paul's own experience in 9:8–9: the parallel suggests that Elymas' temporary blindness may similarly lead to conversion. The story demonstrates the supernatural power of the gospel, encouraging the reader to share the proconsul's 'astonishment' and 'belief' (v. 12). But it also serves to distance the Christian message from one of its closest rivals in the market-place of ancient religions: and this is one of Luke's major concerns as a Christian teacher (cf. ACTS 19:11–20).

(13:13–16) The Journey Continues: Paphos to Antioch The events in Cyprus serve as a prelude to the big set-piece scene of Paul's synagogue sermon in Antioch (13:16–41), itself the centrepiece of a longer travel-and-mission complex, moving out into new territory (13:13–14, 51; 14:6–7), then successively back retracing each stage of the outward journey (14:21, 24–6): no other missionary journey in Acts is so tightly constructed. Although Luke does not use the name here, all the sites visited by Paul on this journey fall within the boundaries of the Roman province of Galatia in the first century (Hansen 1994: 382): whether or not Luke's story of their foundation is accurate, therefore, it is reasonable to assume that these are the churches Paul addresses in the Epistle to the Galatians.

The party pauses long enough in Perga to drop off John Mark, who can presumably hope to pick up a ship travelling eastwards along the coast to take him back in the direction of Jerusalem (v. 13). The reason for his defection is not revealed: this subsidiary character has no real role in the narrative (except perhaps to explain the subsequent rift between Paul and Barnabas: 15:37–9). As in Cyprus, Paul begins his mission by heading for the synagogue (v. 14). Luke takes some trouble to set the scene for this first major speech to a diaspora audience: the note that it was the sabbath underlines the regularity of Paul's attendance as well as creating a time-frame for the whole episode (13:42, 44). Philo (*Hypoth.* 7.12–14; *Spec. Leg.* 2.62) confirms the regular sabbath-day reading of Scripture in first-century synagogues. There are many inscriptions referring to *archisynagōgoi* (officials, v. 15): these were wealthy local patrons (rather than rabbis) who took responsibility for the general maintenance of the synagogue and its services. (Cf. further Riesner 1995: 179–210; Meyers 1992: 251–63.)

(13:16–25) Paul's Synagogue Speech (1): The Testimony of the Past This long speech marks a new step in the progress of the gospel in that it is consciously addressed to a diaspora audience and addresses both ethnic Jews and 'others who fear God' (v. 16; cf. ACTS 10:1–8). Paul's potted resumé of Israel's history can be read as complementary to the one given by Stephen in 7:2–48. Both have the same goal: to show that the whole movement of biblical history points forward to and is consummated in the Christ-event. It is, of course, a highly selective history, beginning with the Exodus (v. 17) and the wilderness period (v. 18), moving on to the Conquest (v. 19) and the period of the Judges (v. 20), then to Saul (v. 21), and David (v. 22). The unusual attention given to King Saul (v. 21) may be a deliberately 'Pauline' touch (cf. Phil 3:5). Of all the speeches in Acts, this is the one that makes the most explicit use of Davidic messianism, picking up the divine election of the Davidic line (v. 22, an amalgam of 1 Sam 13:14 with Ps 89:20), and linking it directly with Jesus' Davidic descent (v. 23; cf. Rom 1:3). God is the main actor in Israel's history: almost all the verbs in these six verses describe God's actions ('chose', 'led', 'gave'). This is no heroic national saga but a narrative of election and grace. Paul's story lacks the aggressive critique of Stephen's, though there may be an implied criticism of the wilderness generation in v. 18 if we follow the reading 'put up with' (cf. Ps 95:8–11). Both variants occur in the Greek text of Deut 1:31. Luke assumes Paul's hearers will have heard of the mission of John the Baptist (vv. 24–5), which he places at the climax of Israel's history, the final tip of an arrow pointing in one clear direction (cf. Lk 16:16).

(13:26–31) Paul's Synagogue Speech (2): The Testimony of the Present The central section of the speech focuses on the Christ-event itself. It is introduced (v. 26) by a renewed address which stresses the inclusive nature of Paul's mission. But the focus is first of all on Jerusalem, scene of the fateful rejection of God's promised Messiah (v. 27). Luke never charges all Jews everywhere with complicity in the death of Jesus: here, as repeatedly in Peter's speeches, it is 'the residents of Jerusalem and their leaders' (cf. 2:14; 3:17) who share the moral responsibility for Jesus' death (though the Gentile Pilate was the judicial instrument of execution: v. 28; cf. 2:23). But there is a deeper level of predetermination in the whole tragic complex of events. The death of the Messiah was already predicted in Scripture (v. 27), so that the human actors in the drama simply 'carried out everything that was written of him' (v. 29): it was all part of God's plan (4:28; cf. 2:23). This is a classic case of tragic irony, and one that would be easily recognizable to readers of Greek tragedy. And it is the Jerusalem apostles whom Paul here singles out as the prime witnesses of the risen Christ to the people (v. 30): Luke's Paul

never claims to be a witness to the resurrection in his own right (contrast 1 Cor 15:8).

(13:32–7) Paul's Synagogue Speech (3): The Testimony of Scripture Again the contrast with Jerusalem is foregrounded: *they* witness to the people (i.e. in Jerusalem) (v. 31), *we* bring the good news to *you*, here in Antioch (v. 32). And the good news is that the God of Israel's past is also the God of Israel's future (v. 33). The continuity between past and future is highlighted in the pattern of promise and fulfilment, as Paul traces the foreshadowings of the resurrection through a skein of scriptural testimonia. There is a considerable overlap here with the closing section of Peter's first Jerusalem speech (esp. 2:25–36), which likewise uses Scripture to reflect on the theological significance of the events just described. Here the text from Ps 16 which early Christians took literally as a prediction of Jesus' resurrection (vv. 35–7; cf. 2:27–32) is combined with two other testimonia. Ps 2:7 (v. 33) was a key verse in Christian Christological hermeneutic: patristic exegesis links it with the words of the heavenly voice at Jesus' baptism (cf. the Western text at Lk 3:22), but the 'today' envisioned here and in Heb 1:5, 5:5 is the day of the enthronement of the Davidic king, which for the early church was the moment of Christ's resurrection and exaltation (seen as a single event as in 2:32–3; cf. Rom 1:4). The third text used here is from Isa 55:3 (v. 34), which leads in via the catchword *hosios* (holy) to Ps 16 (v. 35): the underlying thought seems to be, as in 2:25–30, that God's everlasting covenant with David (Isa 55:3) entails that all the promises made to David must be fulfilled in the Messiah. (Further, Lindars 1961: 16; 139–44; 201.)

(13:38–41) Paul's Synagogue Speech (4): The Challenge of the Future The speech concludes with a solemn address to the audience. What was offered in Jerusalem is now being offered more widely: but the conditions are the same. The offer is 'forgiveness of sins' (v. 38; cf. 2:38); but Luke here gives it a characteristically Pauline twist (v. 39), the only distinctively Pauline element in the whole speech. Commentators have debated how close this summary really is to the theology of the Epistles (cf. LK D; IPCB): it seems best to regard it as a reasonably successful summary of the theology of justification by faith, written by someone for whom it does not hold the central position that it does for Paul. What are missing from Luke's summary are the distinctively Pauline reflections on the saving significance of the death of Christ. Underlying both, however, is the same core Christology, in which the person of Jesus is essential to salvation: 'by this Jesus' (lit. in him, v. 39). Either way, salvation is not simply a matter of 'having faith': it is mediated and received through the person of Christ. The diaspora community is being offered the same fulfilment of promise as the inhabitants of Jerusalem, a promise embodied in Jesus and the events of his death and resurrection. But it carries a health warning (v. 40): they now run the risk of making the same tragic mistake as their counterparts in Jerusalem, and thus unwittingly fulfilling the predictions of the prophets (v. 41).

(13:42–50) Divided Reactions Paul's speech leaves his audience with a stark choice, dramatized in the final verses of the chapter: 'believe' or join the 'scoffers' (v. 41). Initial reactions are uncommitted but favourable (v. 42); but by the next sabbath the mood has changed. 'The Jews' now suddenly become a character-group distinct from 'the crowds' (v. 45). This designation of 'the Jews' as a hostile group (cf. 9:23; 12:3) will become increasingly common in the Pauline section of Acts: here they 'speak against' the gospel message and so unwittingly fulfil Simeon's prediction of Lk 2:34. This negative reaction carries its own punishment: those who reject the message have passed judgement on themselves (v. 46). But it is only *after* this rejection, Luke implies, that Paul feels justified in pursuing the mission to which God has called him and 'turning to the Gentiles' (v. 46): and note that even here Paul does not say he will stop preaching to Jews (cf. 14:1). The words cited from Isa 49:6 (v. 47) form a hermeneutical key to the second part of Acts: Luke interweaves the related themes of 'light to the Gentiles' and 'salvation to the ends of the earth' throughout this section (both themes are anticipated in Lk 2:30–2; see further ACTS 28:23–31). A pattern is now being established: success with Gentile residents of the city and its surrounding country region (v. 49) only intensifies the opposition of 'the Jews' (v. 50), who use their influence with the city élite to get the missionaries expelled. The close of the episode recalls the gospel advice to itinerant preachers (v. 51; cf. esp. Mt 10:14).

(14:1–7) Preaching in Iconium and Lystra This is a summary passage rather than a 'journey' section: Luke shows consistently less interest in land journeys than in sea travel. Paul's party now turns east and follows the Roman road (the Via Sebaste) linking the Roman colonies of Antioch, Iconium (modern Konya, 150 km. SE) and Lystra (30 km. SW: Hansen 1994: 384–5). Despite the fact that there are many converts both Jewish and Gentile (v. 1), this is not really a church foundation-narrative: Luke's report concentrates more on the pattern of preaching and rejection that he sees repeated at Iconium (v. 1). Here the opposition is classified as 'unbelieving Jews', or better (given the aorist tense) 'Jews who had decided against belief': it is the message itself that provokes these violent and divided reactions, just as Simeon had foreseen (Lk 2:34), and the same diversity of reactions characterizes the Gentile population of the city (v. 4). The missionaries' response to persecution, like that of the Jerusalem apostles (e.g. 4:13, 29, 31) is the proper prophetic stance of 'bold' and persistent speech, accompanied by miraculous healings (v. 3). This and the following are the only sections of Acts (vv. 4, 14) where Paul and Barnabas are given the title 'apostles': Luke normally restricts the title to the twelve, but here is most probably using it in its root sense of 'delegates' (i.e. of the Antioch church).

(14:8–18) Miracle at Lystra There is a new feature in this scene: we are now deep in pagan territory, among crowds whose native tongue is not Greek but Lycaonian (v. 11). Inscriptions confirm the survival of this pre-Greek language in this period, as well as the joint worship of Zeus and Hermes in the region (Bruce 1990: 321–2). Luke seems faintly amused at the crowd's superstitious reaction to the miraculous healing, with its ambivalent reading of the relationship between Paul and Barnabas (v. 12: Zeus, as chief of the gods, was the more important figure). But Paul quickly realizes that it is no joke when the priest of Zeus-before-the-Gates prepares to offer sacrifice to the apostles (v. 13). The emergency occasions Paul's first attempt in Acts to explain the gospel in totally pagan

terms. Paul's sermon here is totally consistent with the orthodox Jewish critique of pagan religion, which stresses (against a broadly animistic religious culture) the distance separating God from the created order (v. 15). The pagan gods are 'worthless' (i.e. they are 'idols'), and the good news is an invitation to 'turn' away from idols to the living God (cf. 1 Thess 1:9). The providential care God bestows on all the world's inhabitants acts as a silent witness to his beneficence, but pagans who fail to recognize the source of creation's bounty are not so much sinful as misguided (v. 16).

(14:19–23) Return and Consolidation The narrative returns abruptly to summary mode and picks up the theme of persecution, depicted as a concerted plot against Paul by 'the Jews' of Antioch and Iconium (v. 19; cf. 2 Cor 11:25, which uses the same verb). Luke's account may have an exemplary function in depicting Paul's remarkable courage as well as the fraternal solidarity of the disciples (v. 20). Derbe lay 100 km. to the SE of Lystra, cf. Hansen 1994: 385: it was a considerable journey for someone in Paul's condition, and the motive for the visit is unclear, but it must not be forgotten that all this time Paul is moving closer to his own home province of Cilicia, and he may have had some prior knowledge of this mountainous region. On the return journey, the focus is on the consolidation of the newly planted churches. Strengthening the soul and encouraging believers to remain in the faith (v. 22) are major functions of the Pauline letters, and Luke (who never mentions the letters) here gives us a glimpse of Paul performing this function in person: cf. esp. 1 Thess 2:14–16; 3:2–4. The description of Paul's ministerial arrangements for these churches (v. 23) is tantalizingly brief. 'Elders' do not appear as church officials in the Pauline letters before the Pastorals (Titus 1:5; 1 Tim 5:17, 19); it is possible that Luke has anachronistically transferred this term from his own time to the Pauline foundations, while correctly retaining in direct speech Paul's own term *episkopoi* (20:28; cf. Phil 1:1).

(14:24–8) The Journey Home: Return to Antioch The whole episode is brought to a closure with a journey section (vv. 24–5) tracing the regions traversed on the way home; Attalia is mentioned as the natural port of embarkation for the coastal voyage to Seleucia. The church which had sent out its delegates in obedience to the Spirit receives a formal report on the work completed (v. 26). Just as the impetus for the journey came from God, so did the grace by which it was accomplished (v. 27): particularly significant in the report is the opening of a 'door of faith' for the Gentiles (Paul uses this metaphor in a more general sense at 2 Cor 2:12). But it is precisely this piece of divine opportunism that creates the next problem to be solved within the church (ch. 15).

Act III Scene 2: The Apostolic Council (15:1–35)

The hectic journeying of this third act of Luke's narrative is interrupted at this point by the more static scene of the Apostolic Council in Jerusalem. This is no irrelevant interlude: the growth of the Antioch church, and the mission Paul has completed on its behalf, have raised a fundamental question of principle which must be resolved before the mission can proceed. Can Gentiles be allowed to join the church direct (as it were) from the pagan world, or can they come in, like the Godfearers and proselytes, only via a prior attachment to the synagogue? The admission of Gentiles in fact raises in an acute form the question of identity that is one of the underlying themes of Acts. All the first Christians (like Jesus himself) were Jews: following Jesus, for them, meant finding in him the culmination and true fulfilment of their ancestral religion. But if this was so, then new entrants from outside Judaism should logically be expected to follow the normal procedures for incoming proselytes, which included circumcision (15:1, 5). That is the point at issue in this formalized debate, which Luke has arranged as a pair to the earlier debate after Peter's visit to Cornelius (11:1–18).

The circumcision controversy was the occasion for Paul's most impassioned letter, the Epistle to the Galatians, and sparked off much of his most profound theological reflection on the relationship of law and grace in the Christian life. It is natural, therefore, to read the Acts account with one eye on Paul: but our first priority must be to understand Luke's story in its own terms. What is not clear is whether Acts 15 parallels Paul's visit to Jerusalem in Gal 2:1–10, or whether this 'private' visit is the one mentioned in Acts 11:30, in which case the full Council would fall after Galatians was written. This would explain why Paul does not mention the Council or the decree. On problems of Pauline chronology see further IPCE; Alexander (1993a); Jewett (1979); Lüdemann (1984); Witherington (1998: 77–97).

(15:1–5) Controversy in Antioch The Jerusalem Council is framed by opening and closing scenes in Antioch, an indication of how the narrator's perspective has shifted since the early chapters of the book. Antioch is now 'home ground', and events in Jerusalem are much more cloudy. We have no background information on the identity of the 'certain individuals' (v. 1) or of the 'elders' (vv. 2, 4) because we have not been following developments in Jerusalem since Peter's departure in 12:17. The narrator shares the point of view of the Antioch church that the 'conversion' of the Gentiles is a matter for rejoicing (v. 3). When the Antioch delegation reaches Jerusalem (v. 5) it becomes clear that there are differing viewpoints within the Jerusalem church, and that this particular controversy stems from a group of Christians with Pharisaic roots: but that is not itself a negative description in the narrative world of Acts (cf. 26:5).

(15:6–12) The Council (1): The Testimony of Peter Luke stresses the formal nature of this deliberation (v. 6): the formal opening address (vv. 7, 13: 'Men, brothers', NRSV marg.) would remind a Greek-educated reader of the speeches of classical rhetoric. Peter's intervention is crucial in the debate; it presents the reader with a brief but telling reminder of the narrative argument set out in chs. 10–11. It is an indication of its importance for Luke that we have now heard this story three times, once from the narrator (10:44–8) and twice from Peter (cf. 11:15–17). As in ch. 11, Peter stresses that the whole Cornelius episode stemmed from the sovereign choice of God (v. 7), and that the clinching testimony is the visible activity of the Holy Spirit (v. 8), which demonstrated that God makes 'no distinction' between Gentile and Jewish believers (v. 9). Peter's role in the decision to accept Gentiles on equal terms is more positive than we would expect from Paul, who sees Peter's vacillation at Antioch as a betrayal of the whole principle (Gal 2:11–12). Both Paul and Luke are writing with

their own particular purposes in view here: part of Luke's agenda is to strengthen the Pauline argument by giving it the support of the most prominent of the Jerusalem apostles (while part of Paul's agenda is to stress his independence of Jerusalem). Thus Luke's Peter here voices some of the most strongly 'Pauline' arguments in Acts: that the coming of the Spirit is evidence that God has cleansed the hearts of the Gentiles 'by faith' (v. 9: cf. Gal 3:2–5 and contrast 10:44–8), that circumcision means subjecting the disciples to the 'yoke' of the whole law (v. 10, cf. Gal 2:14; 5:1–3), and that Jews and Gentiles are saved on an equal footing through grace (v. 11; cf. Gal 2:15–21).

(15:13–21) The Council (2): The Decision of James The emergence of James as effective leader of the Jerusalem church is surprising (though it is hinted at in 12:17), but indicates further how little inclination (or information) Luke has for a concerted 'history of the church'. His speech affirms the validity of the narrative arguments of Peter, which was based on the charismatic events associated with the mission itself (v. 14), and adds a scriptural argument (vv. 15–18), thus providing a hermeneutical framework for interpreting these same events. James' quotation of Am 9:11–12 reflects the Greek rather than the Hebrew, though it is not identical with the LXX. Although there are many textual and exegetical problems relating to the details of this decree, it is clear that James comes to the formal decision (v. 19) that Gentile converts should observe the same restrictions as had been placed since biblical times on 'aliens' wishing to live among God's people (v. 20; cf. Lev 17–18: Fitzmyer 1998: 557). There is a puzzling lack of 'fit' between James' conclusion (and the decree that follows) and the introduction to the debate: the implication is that circumcision is not required of Gentile converts, but it is not stated in so many words. The observation cuts both ways: if this was a verbatim report of an actual debate, we might expect it to be more coherent (though it would of course be considerably abbreviated); but the discrepancies are equally hard to explain if Luke is making the whole thing up.

(15:22–9) The Council (3): The Apostolic Decree The formal setting is highlighted by Luke's language here: cf. esp. the archaic impersonal use of *edoxē* + dative ('decided', vv. 22, 25, 28), which follows classical syntax (familiar from the formal decrees of Greek cities) against normal NT usage (cf. Lk 1:3, another formal passage). The letter is addressed only to the Gentile believers of Antioch, Syria, and Cilicia (v. 23), not to the whole church or even (surprisingly) to Paul's new foundations in Galatia. The wording implies an increasingly centralized authority in Jerusalem (v. 24), with a hierarchical council which regards its decisions as divinely sanctioned (v. 28). In this slightly amended form (v. 29), the list of prohibitions is even more clearly designed to facilitate table-fellowship between Jewish and Gentile believers, the issue that sparks off the 'Antioch incident' in Gal 2:11–12; if Luke's account is accurate, it is very hard to locate this incident *after* the decree, but it could make sense as the kind of incident to which the decree was a reply. But we are still left with the problem of Paul's failure ever to mention the decree in any other letter.

(15:30–5) Return to Antioch The episode closes with a triumphant return to Antioch. Paul and Barnabas are now accompanied by the Jerusalem delegates Judas and Silas (v. 22), who prove to be congenial companions (v. 32) and, like Barnabas (who was himself originally sent down from Jerusalem to keep an eye on what was happening in Antioch, 11:22–4) provide encouragement and strengthening (cf. 14:22).

Act III Scene 3: Paul's Second Missionary Journey (15:36–18:23)

The next five chapters of the narrative are devoted to a vivid descriptive portrait of Paul in the context of his missionary activities—the evangelist, the controversialist, the prisoner, the pastor, but above all the indefatigable traveller, covering an amazing amount of territory around the coasts of the eastern Mediterranean. The journeys are conventionally classified as two 'missionary voyages', and I have followed this division (see Map 11) for convenience. But in fact the pattern is not as simple as that: none of these journeys has the clear outward-and-return structure of the first, and although Paul makes periodic trips back to base, these do not have the clear symbolic function of his first return to Antioch.

There are three bodies of literature that may help us to understand this section better. (1) Paul's own letters give us a comparative body of data and may provide some confirmation for the Acts narrative. Taking these letters seriously as primary evidence gives us a sequence Philippi–Thessalonica–Athens–Corinth, which fits the basic configuration of this second journey in Acts (cf. Alexander 1993a), though it does not give us much in the way of internal chronology. We do not know whether Luke had access to Paul's letters, but most scholars think he did not. (2) Ancient itineraries: the final chapters of Acts contain a puzzling phenomenon known as the 'we-sections', where the narrator suddenly and without explanation slips into the first person and out again (16:10–16; 20:5–21:18; 27:1–28:16). They also contain a remarkable amount of redundant travel information (stopping-places, ports of embarkation, etc.), especially relating to sea travel, and it has been suggested that the simplest explanation for both is that Luke himself was with Paul on some of these journeys, or alternatively that he had access to a travel log or itinerary written by one of the party. There is some contemporary evidence that such logs existed (though by their nature they would be ephemeral): there are tattered remains of one such (dating from the fourth century CE) among the Rylands papyri (P.Ryl. 616–51), and it seems to show both the we-formulation and the lists of stopping-places that might form the basis of a narrative. (3) Ancient travel-writing: travel-writing was a popular genre in the ancient world, ranging from detailed geographical description to pure fantasy. Some scholars have observed that in such descriptions the use of redundant place-names and the use of the first person may serve a literary function, and therefore conclude that these features of Acts are not necessarily indications of eyewitness testimony. See further Rapske 1994: 1–47; Scott 1994: 483–544; Porter 1994: 545–74.

(15:36–41) Paul and Barnabas Part Company Paul's second journey begins after an unspecified interval (v. 36) and without the formal commissioning ceremony of the first. Its initial motive is simply to follow up the previous mission and revisit the converts made on that occasion (v. 36). But the partnership

with Barnabas comes to an end at this point (vv. 37–9): he is not mentioned again in Acts, though Paul assumes he is known to the Corinthians (1 Cor 9:6). The link with Jerusalem is maintained, however, in the person of Silas, who has apparently returned from Jerusalem (unless we accept the Western text of 15:34: NRSV marg.) in time to be selected as Paul's new travelling companion (v. 40). Like Barnabas and Paul, Silas is a 'prophet', that is, he is anointed by the Holy Spirit (15:32). This must be the same as the Silvanus with whom Paul evangelized Macedonia and Achaea (1 Thess 1:1; 2 Cor 1:19); Luke uses a Greek form of the Aramaic name, Paul a more Latinized form. This time (perhaps because he is not travelling with the Cypriot Barnabas) Paul heads up through the Taurus mountains via his home territory of Cilicia (v. 41), which means following the mountainous route up into southern Turkey through the Cilician Gates.

(16:1–5) Timothy Joins the Group Timothy became one of Paul's most trusted co-workers (Rom 16:21), and must have been well known in Pauline circles; he is mentioned in letters to the churches in Rome and Corinth, and cited as co-author of the letters to Philippi, Thessalonica, Philemon, and Colossae. The story of Timothy's circumcision (v. 3) seems at odds with Paul's statement about Titus in Gal 2:3 and with Paul's own attitude to circumcision in that epistle. But Luke seems to assume that Timothy (unlike Titus) was ethnically Jewish (16:1), in which case this is not about the circumcision of a Gentile believer but about Paul's desire to keep open his channels of communication with the Jewish community, here and elsewhere (cf. 1 Cor 9:20). The Apostolic Decree (Luke uses the plural *dogmata*, appropriate for a formal decision by a civic assembly) is mentioned for the last time at this point (16:4): clearly Luke sees it as relevant to the churches in this area, even though it did not address them directly (15:23).

(16:6–10) Journey: Phrygia to Troas This short journey section summarizes a huge swathe of travelling, which takes Paul out of his previous mission fields and right across to the north-west corner of Asia Minor. For the 'region of Phrygia and Galatia' (v. 6) see now Mitchell (1992: 871): this is most naturally understood as the area between Iconium and Antioch, which was ethnically Phrygian but divided between the Roman provinces of Galatia and Asia. The Roman roads north of Pisidian Antioch are later than Paul's day, but there are ancient trade routes across this area, and one of them, branching off not far north of Antioch, led westwards down the Lycus valley towards Ephesus. Having been 'forbidden by the Holy Spirit' (v. 6) to extend his mission in this direction, or to turn west at the next crossroads for Smyrna, Paul had no choice but to follow the road north towards the Black Sea coast. Somewhere along the road (Luke knows only rather vaguely that it is 'opposite Mysia') there was a further choice: north to Bithynia and Pontus, or west to Troas? Again, the guidance of the Spirit (v. 7: 'the Spirit of Jesus' is clearly interchangeable with the commoner 'Holy Spirit') determines their route: westwards, down towards the coast. But where was the mission to take place? There is no record of any preaching along this part of the journey: Paul seems to be waiting for guidance, and in the port city of Troas it comes in the shape of a dream which Paul interprets as a revelatory oracle: a call for help from Macedonia.

(16:12–15) Journey: Troas to Philippi The we-narrator, who joins the party at this point (v. 10) immediately displays his passion for the details of travel, especially by sea: cf. the interest in ports of call (Samothrace, Neapolis) and in the jargon of seafaring ('set sail', 'took a straight course', v. 11). From Neapolis the party travelled along the Via Egnatia, the Roman road linking the northern Aegean to the Adriatic ports (Gill 1994: 409): Philippi, Amphipolis, Apollonia, and Thessalonica (17:1) were all on this road. Philippi, as a Roman colony (originally settled by army veterans, partly to pacify a hostile area), operated as a kind of mini-Rome, whose citizenship, magistrates, and laws were Roman. But it was not 'the first city of Macedonia' (as v. 12 appears to say): most commentators now read 'a leading city' (as NRSV) or emend to 'a city of the first district' (as NRSV marg.), which it was. Luke's term *proseuchē* (v. 13, 'place of prayer'), though used elsewhere of a synagogue, may indicate a less formal meeting-place here, perhaps because the Jewish community at Philippi was not large enough to have a purpose-built community edifice. First-century evidence suggests that Jewish communities liked to meet close to running water: cf. Jos. *Ant.* 14:258. Lydia's independent status as a trader (v. 14) and householder (v. 15) is not uncommon for women in the ancient world, especially among the travelling merchants and artisans who formed a major component of the population of most Greek cities: such women not infrequently take on the role of patron and benefactor to Jewish and other immigrant communities.

(16:16–24) Exorcism and Imprisonment Paul's stay in Philippi takes a dramatic turn from a chance encounter with a fortune-teller. Luke describes this slave-girl as having a 'python spirit' (v. 16, 'spirit of divination'), that is as having the ability to deliver oracular pronouncements in the manner of the shamanistic prophetesses of the Delphic oracle. This was a well-known phenomenon in the ancient Mediterranean world, and its potential for commercial exploitation is nicely satirized by Lucian (e.g. *Peregrinus*; *Alexander the False Prophet*). Luke, unlike Lucian, sees this as a genuine spiritual force which intuitively recognizes Paul's own supernatural power (v. 17): as in the gospels, such pronouncements, though expressing spiritual truth, emanate from evil spirits which can be exorcized (v. 18; cf. Lk 4:34–5). At one level, therefore, this is a story that demonstrates Paul's spiritual power (while stressing that it is strictly subordinate to that of Christ, v. 18). The episode descends to civic melodrama, however, when the slave's owners (whose motives Luke characterizes as purely commercial) take Paul and Silas to court. Luke uses the standard Greek term *stratēgoi* (v. 20) for the local magistrates (their Latin title would have been *praetores*), who are correctly shown as meeting in the city's *agora* (market-place, Lat. *forum*, v. 19). The charge (vv. 20–1) is interesting: though the practice of Judaism was not in itself illegal in the empire, Roman sources show a deep-rooted prejudice against the adoption of foreign religious customs by Roman citizens, and this periodically expressed itself in official enactments (cf. ACTS 18:1–11). The magistrates, tacitly accepting the support of the crowd (v. 22) impose a standard Roman punishment (v. 22, 'beaten with rods', i.e. beaten with the *fasces* carries by the *lictors*: cf. 2 Cor 11:25).

(16:15–34) The Saving of the Jailer Luke shares with the Greek novelists a taste for dramatic scenes of imprisonment and escape (cf. 12:6–17), and this scene allows him to depict another aspect of Paul's spiritual power as something that allows him to triumph over adversity. Like the philosopher Socrates, he sings hymns in prison (Epict. *Diss.* 2.6.26–7); like the prophet Daniel, he is rescued by divine intervention from a punishment that he has incurred simply by being faithful to his God (cf. Dan 3, 6). Paul's status as a true philosopher is further enhanced by his treatment of the jailer: by honourably staying put when the earthquake would have allowed him to escape (and by implication keeping the other prisoners in place), Paul prevents the jailer from a shame-induced suicide (v. 28). The result is a reversal of roles: disregarding his original orders (v. 23), the jailer now treats his prisoners with honour (v. 30), washes their wounds (v. 33), and supplicates them for salvation (v. 30). Thus Paul is able to use the shameful experience of prison to further his mission (v. 32), even in the middle of the night (vv. 25, 33). The jailer in his turn becomes a paradigmatic convert, hearing the word and responding in faith 'with his entire household' (stressed three times, vv. 32, 33, 34), baptized, sharing table-fellowship, and 'rejoicing' (vv. 33, 34).

(16:35–40) The Shaming of the Magistrates The real losers in this drama are the colony's magistrates. The 'police' (*rhabdouchoi*, lictors, v. 35) come to tell the jailer to release his troublesome visitors; but Paul has another trick up his sleeve. Only now does he choose to reveal his true civic status: as Roman citizens, he and his companion should not have been publicly humiliated, and they are certainly not going to let the authorities get away with this crude mistreatment (v. 37). The revelation terrifies the magistrates. Roman citizens had a right to higher standards of legal treatment than other inhabitants of the empire: in the previous century, the senator Verres had been prosecuted in Rome for a series of crimes against provincials which included the mistreatment of Roman citizens (Cicero, *Against Verres*, 2.5.169–70). Whether Paul was actually a Roman citizen is a matter of some dispute: he never mentions the fact in his letters, and it has been thought to be incompatible with his upbringing as an observant Jew (Phil 3:5–6). But it is an important feature of the plot of Acts (ACTS 22:22–9; 25:1–12), and here serves to complete the role-reversal in the story with the complete discomfiture of the magistrates, who have to come to 'apologize' to Paul (better 'implore'; *parekalesan*, v. 39) and beg him to leave. The episode (which has its humorous side) shows Paul coming out with honour from a situation where he seemed to be humiliated, and demonstrates above all that faithfulness and boldness in preaching God's word will be vindicated; but it hardly leaves the impression that Paul is a model Roman citizen.

(17:1–9) Thessalonica The first-person narrative has disappeared at some point in the Philippi story, and the next few episodes see Paul continuing his travels with Silas and Timothy. Thessalonica (Salonika), a couple of stages down the Via Egnatia, sees a repeat of the pattern set at Pisidian Antioch. Thessalonica has a well-established Jewish community with a synagogue (v. 1), where Paul spends three successive sabbaths arguing for his own messianic interpretation of

Scripture (v. 2). As in Antioch, there is initial success among synagogue members and even more among Gentile adherents (v. 4), but this leads to an outbreak of 'jealousy' (or possibly 'fundamentalist zeal': zēlōsantes, v. 5) on the part of 'the Jews', who enlist the help of the city mob to launch an attack on Paul and Silas. The civic authorities here are called 'politarchs' (v. 6), a title which is attested in inscriptional evidence for Thessalonica (Horsley 1994: 419–31). Who Jason is, and how Paul comes to be staying at his house (vv. 5–7), are not explained. Once again, a disturbing charge is laid against the missionaries, bringing out the latent political radicalism of the Christian mission (vv. 6–7): it is easy to read Paul's proclamation of the Kingdom (cf. 28:31) as inherently incompatible with the personal oaths of loyalty to the emperor demanded of all inhabitants of the empire (Barrett 1994–9: ii. 815–16). And once again, Paul is given no chance to rebut the charge: the overall impression left by this episode is that trouble does indeed follow the mission wherever it goes.

17:10–15 Beroea A similar pattern is repeated at Beroea, some 80 km down the road. The dependency of the Pauline mission on the networks of the Jewish diaspora is clearly visible in this section: arriving in an unfamiliar city, Paul heads straight for the synagogue and encourages the community to a flurry of exegetical study. The Jews of Beroea are presented as a paradigm of positive response: belief is the result (v. 12), but this is built on a foundation of careful and open-minded examination (anakrinontes, v. 11) of the scriptural testimony to Christ. This community is described as 'nobler' than the Jews of Thessalonica (eugenesteroi, v. 11: NRSV 'more receptive'), an implicitly élitist value-word which clearly reveals how Luke wants his readers to respond: note again that it is 'women of high standing and men' who believe (v. 12), while it is 'the crowds', i.e. the urban proletariat, who are stirred up to protest by the negatively portrayed Jews of Thessalonica (v. 13). The unnecessary detail provided about the complex movements of Paul and his associates (vv. 14–15) sounds as if it is based on inside knowledge of the Pauline retinue.

(17:16–21) Waiting in Athens That Paul visited Athens shortly after founding the church in Thessalonica, and that he spent some time waiting there (v. 16), is confirmed by 1 Thess 3:1–6, which must have been written not long after the visit. Whether the speech described here actually happened is another question: many commentators believe Luke has simply seized the opportunity of Paul's visit to the heartland of Hellenic culture to create a type-scene, portraying his hero as a philosopher in the best Greek traditions, taking on the philosophers at their own game and preaching the gospel in Greek terms. Although Luke characterizes the philosophical scene in terms of the most popular philosophies of his own day (v. 18), the whole dramatic setting is redolent of the Athens of the classical period, the golden days of philosophy, when Socrates walked the streets of Athens and engaged in philosophical dialogue (dielegeto, 'argued', v. 17) in the agora with everyone he met. Significantly, here in Athens the charge brought against Paul has a distinctly Socratic flavour: in this setting, and for readers educated in the popular traditions of the Greek philosophical schools, 'foreign divinities' (xenōn daimoniōn, v. 18) can hardly fail to evoke

the charge brought against Socrates of preaching 'new divinities' (kaina daimonia: cf. Xen. Mem. 1.1.1–4: this is the only place in the NT where daimonia has the neutral Greek sense 'divine beings' rather then the normal NT sense of 'evil spirits'). The Areopagus was the chief administrative body in the city in Paul's day (Gill 1994: 447), but to Luke's Greek readers it is pre-eminently the place where philosophers are tried, just as for his Jewish readers Jerusalem is the place where prophets are put to death (Lk 13:33–4). See further Alexander 1993b: 57–63.

(17:22–34) Paul's Areopagus Speech This speech allows Luke to present a more complete and studied version of Paul's preaching to Gentiles than the emergency sermon of 14:15–17. The points of focus are very close to Paul's own summary of his message at 1 Thess 1:9–10: a repudiation of idolatry in favour of the 'living and true God' (v. 29) and an eschatological expectation of the risen Christ's return from heaven (v. 31). In preparation for this day of judgement, all humanity has to repent (v. 30). Apart from the reference to Christ, Luke's Paul here stands well within the traditions of diaspora Judaism, which believed that the pagan world was guilty of the sin of idolatry, that is, of failure to recognize that the living creator God behind the created universe (vv. 24–8) cannot possibly be worshipped in human temples (v. 24) or through human-made religious images (v. 29). Like other diaspora Jewish apologists, Paul seeks to exploit points of common interest with his audience. Athens was famous for its profusion of religious images: to Paul's Jewish eyes, this is nothing better than a collection of 'idols' (v. 16), but the fact that the Athenians liked to include altar-dedications to 'unknown gods' creates a bridgehead for the preaching of the one 'unknown God' behind the universe (v. 23). Greek philosophers had already popularized a kind of philosophical monotheism among more sophisticated pagan thinkers (this was one reason why Judaism attracted their respect), and Paul is able to use a line from the Stoic poet Aratus (v. 28; Aratus, Phaenomena, 5) to reinforce his point: the same line had already been quoted by the Jewish apologist Aristobulus (Eusebius, Praep. Evang. 13.12.6). The similarities and differences between this speech and Paul's own survey of pagan religion in Rom 1–3 have occasioned much scholarly debate: what is missing, again, is the specific preaching of Christ crucified (cf. 1 Cor 1:18–25), and Rom 1:32 seems to leave no room for the 'ignorance' of Acts 17:30; but both approaches are clear that the coming of Christ signals a universal human need for repentance.

(18:1–11) Corinth Corinth was the administrative centre of the Roman province of Achaea and was to become an important centre for the Pauline mission. Aquila and Priscilla (v. 2) are to become important associates of Paul's, well known to the Corinthian church (1 Cor 16:19; cf. Rom 16:3–4); here Luke records their first meeting at the time of the founding of the church in Corinth. The implication is that they had already become Christians, presumably in Rome. According to the imperial biographer Suetonius (Life of Claudius, 25), the reason for Claudius' expulsion of the Jews from Rome was that the Jews were 'constantly causing disturbances at the instigation of Chrestus'; there may well be a confusion with Christus, which would sound the same in first-century Greek. A later chronicler dates the event to Claudius' ninth year, i.e. 49 CE. Paul's tentmaking (v. 3) is mentioned here for the first time; Paul himself asserts his determination to support his mission by manual work, especially in Corinth (1 Cor 4:12; 9:6; 1 Thess 2:9), but never says what the work was. Paul's own attitude to the 'hardship' involved in this work suggests that he regarded it as a demeaning occupation; but Luke does not make this an issue.

For Silas and Timothy (v. 5), cf. 1 Thess 3:1, 6; Luke may have simplified the story. Paul's mission in Corinth follows the now familiar sequence (vv. 4–5). His disputations in the synagogue come to an abrupt end as opposition builds up (v. 6), and Paul makes a symbolic gesture of repudiation (cf. 13:51). Paul's 'innocence' here (v. 6) is prophetic: he has discharged his responsibility to the Jewish community, and now turns to the Gentiles with a clear conscience (cf. Ezek 33:1–9). The house of Titius Justus (v. 7) is used as a meeting-place and becomes the base for the meetings of the nascent Christian community. This is undoubtedly how many of the Pauline churches originated, as breakaway groups which began holding separate meetings alongside the synagogue: other households soon joined them (v. 8; cf. 1 Cor 1:14; and see ACTS 13:15 on 'official of the synagogue').

(18:12–17) Gallio After a period of quiet church growth, opposition flares up again and Paul is brought before the proconsul Gallio. Since proconsuls were in office only for one year, this name provides another chronological indicator in Luke's narrative, in fact one of the key dates for NT chronology. An inscription surviving in Delphi in which Claudius refers to Gallio as his friend and proconsul (full text in Fitzmyer 1998: 621) places Gallio in Achaea during the first part of 52 CE; he seems to have left his province early because of illness, so Paul's appearance before him must fall between the spring and early autumn of the year 52. The charge is that the form of religious practice advocated by Paul is 'contrary to the law' (v. 13); once again, Paul gets no chance to defend himself, but Gallio makes the significant judgement that the only law at issue is Jewish law: there is no question of 'crime or serious villainy' (v. 14), i.e. nothing that contravenes the Roman law of the colony. From the Roman perspective, in other words, disputes between synagogue members and church members are still intramural disputes between rival factions (or 'sects', cf. 24:14) within the Jewish community. This is almost certainly a correct perception for the period Luke is describing; Suetonius' account of Claudius' expulsion of the Jews (ACTS 18:2) shows that a Roman writer could still make the same assumption in the second century. Gallio's studied indifference (v. 17) is not a particularly good advertisement for Roman justice, but it does make the point dramatically that the dispute over the messianist interpretation of the Jewish Scriptures was not something with which the Roman authorities needed to be concerned.

(18:18–23) Return to Base Attempts to establish a precise internal chronology for the Pauline mission are continually baffled by Luke's vagueness on matters of time. It is probable (though not certain) that the Gallio incident took place at the end of the eighteen months (v. 11), but we still do not know how much longer Paul stayed in Corinth after 52 (v. 18). The impression Luke gives is that he himself has only sporadic pieces of precise information here. At some point, however, after a long and successful mission in Corinth, Paul decides to return to Syria. Cenchreae (v. 18) was the port of Corinth on the eastern side of the Isthmus; Paul mentions a church there, of which Phoebe was deacon and patron (Rom 16:1–2). The point of the vow (presumably a Nazirite vow, cf. 21:23–4) is unclear, but it may show Paul's continuing fidelity to Jewish modes of piety. He takes Priscilla and Aquila with him as far as Ephesus (v. 19; cf. 1 Cor 16:9) and seizes the opportunity for a tentative foray into the synagogue there, apparently testing the waters for a future visit: the earlier sense that the Spirit had forbidden mission in Asia (16:6) appears to be still in his mind (v. 20). Luke seems to have no inside information on Paul's motivation for this visit. He clearly wants to touch base with the home church in Syrian Antioch (v. 22), but appears to have paid a brief visit to Jerusalem as well: the Greek has simply 'he went up', but this is a reasonable construction given that he then goes 'down' (normal idiom for a journey away from Jerusalem) to Antioch. A brief note (v. 23) shows Paul going back to the churches founded on the 'first missionary journey' for a third pastoral visit, and marks the start of the second phase of his most extended period of missionary activity.

Act III Scene 4: Paul's Third Missionary Journey (18:24–21:16)

Paul's return to Antioch at 18:22 provides a convenient marker to divide the 'second' from the 'third' missionary journeys, though there is little to suggest more than the briefest of visits before he is off on the road again (18:23). Much of this section is spent on consolidation of the churches already planted; this must in fact have been the period when Paul was writing many of the letters (e.g. the Corinthian correspondence) which show him deeply engaged in dealing with the pastoral problems that were arising in the churches he had founded (cf. 2 Cor 11:28). Acts shows us little of all this, preferring to focus on the evangelistic work which we glimpse in the background of the epistles (e.g. 2 Cor 2:12). Luke does give us a vignette of Paul the pastor, however, in the farewell speech to the Ephesian elders (20:18–35). This section also charts Paul's growing awareness of his final destination, as the narrative moves inexorably towards its climax in Jerusalem, and points beyond that to Rome.

(18:24–8) Interlude: Apollos in Corinth Luke's almost exclusive focus on Paul inevitably gives an oversimplified picture of a church whose expansion is becoming ever more complex. Here a rare interlude gives us a glimpse of an independent missionary at work within the Pauline sphere. As an Alexandrian Jew, Apollos was a member of one of the largest Jewish communities in the ancient world, with a complex and well-established tradition of philosophical hermeneutics of which Philo is the best-known proponent: cf. 1 Cor 1:12; 3:4–9; 4:6; 16:12, where it is clear that Apollos (perhaps because he displays some of the 'wisdom' that Paul lacks) has gained a following within the Corinthian church. The instruction (*katēchēsis*) Apollos has received (v. 25) is sufficiently Christian to be called 'the way of the Lord', but it stops short at the 'baptism of John' (ACTS 19:3). Priscilla and Aquila (who presumably heard Apollos in the synagogue) provide whatever further instruction is needed; but Luke does not state how the 'accuracy' of Apollos' teaching needed to be supplemented, and there is no suggestion that Apollos' baptism was inadequate. An already well-developed network of interchurch communications (v. 27) facilitates Apollos' visit to Corinth. There Apollos' rhetorical gifts are well used in public debate with the synagogue (v. 28).

(19:1–7) The Disciples of John The focus shifts back to Paul, the solitary charismatic leader and apologist, who is making his way back to Ephesus via the 'interior regions' (v. 1), i.e. presumably down from the Galatian uplands via the Lycus valley. Somewhere (in Ephesus?) he finds a mysterious group of 'disciples' (v. 1) who have not heard of the Holy Spirit and know only of John's baptism (vv. 2–3). The episode gives Paul a parallel scene to Peter's Samaritan Pentecost (8:15–17): like Peter, he lays hands on the disciples and they receive the Holy Spirit (v. 6). The two passages give us the same sequence of events in Christian initiation: baptism 'in the name of the Lord Jesus' (v. 5; cf. 8:16), then laying-on of hands followed by the reception of the Holy Spirit (v. 6; cf. 8:17). What is different here is the starting-point: the baptism of John the Baptist, the forerunner who points the way to Christ (cf. 13:24–5) can hardly be disowned by Christians, but it is not sufficient on its own: as a 'baptism of repentance' (v. 4), it was, like John himself, purely preparatory to Christian baptism (cf. 2:33, 38). This gives Luke a coherent theology, but it leaves us with a puzzle: why was Apollos not compelled to be baptized? Does Luke intend us to understand that he was already 'burning with the Spirit' (18:25, NRSV 'with burning enthusiasm')? Luke's interest in orthopraxy is strictly limited; his agenda here may partly be to incorporate disparate Ephesus traditions into the overarching portrait of Paul which is his main focus.

(19:8–10) Paul Preaches in Ephesus A compressed summary passage (completely ignoring any previous Christian activity in Ephesus) now shows Paul repeating in the province of Asia the patterns of preaching and apologetic which have characterized his mission across Galatia, Macedonia, and Achaea. He joins the synagogue (v. 8) in order to campaign publicly for the messianist interpretation of the Scriptures in which he believes: this is a campaign of dialectical argument and persuasion (v. 8) which lasts for three months and wins some success. But he fails to carry the whole community with him, and as opposition grows he decides to move out, taking with him the 'disciples' (v. 9, i.e. those who have accepted his teachings) to set up a rival school of scriptural interpretation in a nearby lecture-hall: the Western text (D) adds the circumstantial detail of his regular teaching hours (NRSV marg.). From this base the whole of Asia is evangelized (v. 10): this is typical Lucan hyperbole, but it fits Paul's own highly stylized and province-based view of his mission (Rom 15:19). Note again that the highly public 'leaving' of the synagogue (v. 9) does not mean the cessation of preaching to Jewish individuals ('both Jews and Greeks', v. 10).

(19:11–20) Magic and Miracle The summary of the Ephesus mission is enlivened by two dramatic scenes that display other key attributes of Luke's portrait of Paul. Here he is characterized as a miracle-worker of such 'extraordinary' charismatic power (v. 11) that it can be transmitted via skin-contact with inanimate objects (v. 12, cf. 5:15; Lk 8:44). Unusually in Luke's narrative, God is the subject of the first sentence here (v. 11): it is important for Luke to underline that Paul's spiritual power does not come from himself but is a direct divine endorsement of his mission. The point is made in dramatic form with the episode of the sons of Scaeva (v. 14), itinerant Jewish exorcists who try (as Simon Magus had done with Peter in 8:19) to annex this charismatic power for themselves (v. 13). This episode has a particular appositeness in Ephesus, which was associated with certain magical formulae (the *Ephesia Grammata* or 'Ephesian Letters') which had the power to ward off evil spirits (Trebilco 1994: 314–15). Luke makes the point clearly that Christian miracle is totally distinct from this widespread syncretistic activity: real evil spirits (and Luke believes that they exist) respond not to names, however exalted, but to the power of God working through his legitimate representatives (v. 15). Despite the humour, there is a serious point being made here, integral to early Christian propaganda: as everywhere in Acts, it is the name of the Lord Jesus, not of any missionary or apostle, that is 'glorified' (v. 17). The scene may also have an exemplary function for Christian readers: magical practice is not an option for Christian believers (vv. 18–19).

(19:21–2) Paul's Travel Plans This phase of Paul's mission is drawing to a close, and Luke now begins to interleave into his narrative hints of his final destination. The plan to revisit the churches in Macedonia and Achaea (Philippi, Beroea, Thessalonica, Corinth) reverberates through the pages of Paul's letters to the Corinthians, which were probably written about this time: cf. 1 Cor 16:5–8; 2 Cor 1:16. The voyage was always intended to culminate with a visit to Jerusalem, and by the time Paul writes Romans (from Corinth) we know that he was planning to go on from Jerusalem to Rome (Rom 15:22–5). It is noticeable that Luke here, like Paul but unlike his own normal practice, uses province names rather than city names to describe Paul's destinations. Erastus (v. 22) may be the same as the Corinthian Christian of Rom 16:23. But why did Luke never mention the collection for the poor of Jerusalem on which Paul lavished so much time and attention at this stage in his ministry (Rom 15:25–8; 2 Cor 8–9), and which was the chief motive for his visit to Jerusalem (1 Cor 16:1–4)? Lucan hindsight may be at least part of the answer: Paul's visit to Jerusalem turned out disastrously different from his expectations, and his prophetic sense that he 'must' see Rome (v. 21) (Luke's 'must' [*dei*] normally conceals a reference to the divine will) is fulfilled in ways that Paul clearly did not envisage when he wrote the Epistle to the Romans.

(19:23–41) Demetrius the Silversmith Before the journey begins, however, a final detailed and dramatic scene makes a fitting closure to Paul's active missionary period. It is, like so many others in Acts, a scene of civic disturbance (*tarachos*, v. 23) which almost brings the city to the dangerous state of *stasis* (rioting, v. 40), a state which above all others civic authority desired to avoid. The disturbance (naturally) was not Paul's fault: this time the culprits are a guild of silverworkers who feel that their livelihood is threatened by the success of Paul's mission (vv. 24–7). For the monetary motive, cf. 16:19; but on this occasion Paul has incurred the wrath of a powerful guild who are able to draw on a combination of civic pride and religious devotion to one of the most powerful cults in the ancient world (Trebilco 1994: 316–38). The silversmiths' guild of Ephesus is known from inscriptions; several ancient texts speak of the powerful position of such trade associations and their potential for civic disturbance (ibid. 338–42).

Luke's vivid picture of the unruly mob rushing into the theatre (v. 29) can be paralleled in both factual and fictional accounts of civic life in this period. The theatre (which has been excavated) was built in the third century BCE and enlarged under the emperors; it seated about 20,000, and was the natural site both for regular assemblies (v. 24) and for informal meetings (ibid. 348–50). Paul's own part in this episode is small, but Luke makes it clear that his personal courage is not in doubt (v. 30). The Asiarchs (v. 31: NRSV 'officials of the province of Asia') are members of the city's social élite, prominent in public events and benefaction: their existence at this period was long thought to be an anachronism, but is now confirmed by extensive epigraphic evidence. The identity of Alexander (v. 33) is unclear, but his intervention serves to underline the racist undertones of the riot (v. 34). The 'town clerk' (v. 35) is probably the *grammateus tou dēmou*, a title well attested by contemporary inscriptions as a leader and spokesperson for the assembly. The claim that the cult statue 'fell from heaven' (v. 35) appears elsewhere in the ancient world (often of meteorites), but is not otherwise attested for Ephesus. The charge of temple robbing (*hierosulia*) and/or blasphemy against the pagan gods (v. 37) was one that Jewish writers in the diaspora were sedulous to avoid (cf. e.g. Jos. *Ant.* 4.207; *Ag. Ap.* 2.237; Philo, *Spec. Leg.* 1.53); it is one to which Paul's denunciation of idolatry leaves him open (v. 26; cf. 17:29), and Luke takes this opportunity to rebut it. The town clerk's reference to proconsuls (v. 38; generic plural: there was only one at a time) lends powerful support to his appeal for calm (v. 40): Greek cities in the Roman empire were left in relative autonomy to run their own internal affairs, but the one crime that could be guaranteed to incur imperial displeasure was civic disorder.

(20:1–6) Journey: Ephesus to Troas via Macedonia The planned journey (19:21) now gets under way. The point at which Paul is about to leave Corinth for Jerusalem by sea (v. 3) may be the point at which Romans 15:25 was written. The change of plan coincides with a change of pace: the list of associates (v. 4) suddenly gives this journey a ceremonial flavour, and with the reappearance of the we-narrator (vv. 5–6) we are counting by days rather than months. From this point on, the narrative of Paul's penultimate voyage slows down as travel once again becomes an event to be savoured. Paul's companions come from almost all the areas covered by the mission so far. For Sopater cf. (probably) Rom 16:21; for Tychicus Col 4:7; Eph 6:21; 2 Tim 4:12; Titus 3:12. Aristarchus and Gaius have been mentioned in passing in 19:29 (though the names are not uncommon, and the Gaius of Rom 16:23 is almost certainly a Corinthian); cf. also Col 4:10. Since the we-narrator was last heard of in Philippi (16:17), it is a natural inference that he was left behind there and is picked up

again here after Paul has spent the Passover season in Philippi (v. 6).

(20:7–12) Troas There is a constant feeling in this section that the narrator knows more than he troubles to reveal. Clearly there is a church in Troas, though its founding (probably because it was independent of Paul) has not been recorded: cf. 2 Cor 2:12–13, which also implies that there were believers in Troas. The meeting 'to break bread' on the first day of the week (v. 7) implies some kind of liturgical gathering; cf. ACTS 2:42. Since for most Christians Sunday was a working day, early practice was to meet on Saturday night or early on Sunday morning (cf. Pliny, *Ep.* 10.96.7). It is simplest to read this as an evening gathering, after work for some (perhaps including Eutychus: his name was a common slave name), which begins with an extended teaching session from Paul (v. 7), includes the 'breaking of bread' and a communal meal (v. 11), and finishes at dawn. The detail of the lamps (which created smoke and fumes) provides some explanation for Eutychus' sleep (v. 8); the fact that this was a third-storey room suggests a working-class *insula* or apartment block rather than the atrium of a villa or town house. Paul's prompt action to save the boy recalls the miracles of Elijah and Elisha (1 Kings 17:21–2; 2 Kings 4:34–5); the description of the boy as 'dead' (*nekros*, v. 9) implies that Luke intends us to see this as a real miracle, not just a lucky escape (v. 10).

(20:13–17) Journey: Troas to Miletus One of the most striking differences between the geographical perspectives of Paul and Luke is the latter's passionate interest in sea travel contrasted with Paul's almost complete lack of nautical vocabulary. This very detailed journey section illustrates the point well. It adds almost nothing to the plot and could have been summarized in a dozen words: but the profusion of technical sailing terms ('set sail', 'take on board') and redundant place-names adds a vivid touch of colour to the narrative, which becomes a virtual travelogue of the eastern Aegean. Maybe Paul actively preferred land travel (v. 13)? The decision to 'sail past Ephesus' (v. 16) does not imply that Paul had any control over the destination of the ship on which he had taken passage, but that he had decided not to break his journey there (Ephesus still had a port in Roman times). The reason Luke gives is pressure of time (v. 16); this would make all the more sense if the main motive for Paul's journey was to accompany the collection to Jerusalem (Rom 15:25; Rom 15:31 already betrays some anxiety on Paul's part about the reception of this gift). As in v. 6, the we-narrator reckons time in terms of Jewish festivals. At Miletus, however, there is time enough (perhaps while waiting for a ship to cover the next section of the voyage) to send for the 'elders' of the church at Ephesus (v. 17; cf. ACTS 14:19–23).

(20:18–38) Paul's Speech to the Ephesian Elders This is the only direct speech in Acts in which Paul addresses Christian believers, and thus the only speech which strictly parallels the epistles. It has a strongly valedictory flavour, best matched in the prison letters (whether authentic or pseudonymous: cf. esp. Phil 3; 2 Tim 3–4). There are, however, already anticipations of this mood in Rom 15, and some parallels with the autobiographical sections of 2 Cor 10–12.

(1) The opening section of the speech (vv. 18–27) consists of a review of Paul's mission: although ostensibly concerned only with Asia (v. 18), it may stand as a paradigmatic review of the whole mission, just as 13:17–41 stands as a summary of Paul's whole message to the Jewish diaspora and 17:22–34 of his message to the Greeks. The mood is sombre, with a very Pauline stress on trials and tears (v. 19) rather than on the victories over opposing spiritual forces that Luke has highlighted: for 'humility' (*tapeinophrosunē*) cf. Phil 2:3, and for the general sentiment 1 Cor 4:10–13; 2 Cor 4:7–12; 11:23–9. The only positive achievement Paul highlights is the completeness of his proclamation of the gospel (vv. 20–1, 27); Rom 15:17–19 makes a similar claim, though Paul there boasts only of preaching to Gentiles. This completeness absolves Paul of his prophetic responsibility (expressed in the very Lucan language of v. 26: cf. 18:6). And the reason he needs to make this claim now is that his 'course' is almost finished (v. 24; cf. 13:25; 2 Tim 4:7; Phil 3:12–14 uses a similar metaphor but with different words). Paul expresses here a strong prophetic sense that his life is drawing to a close (vv. 22–5): it is hard to read v. 25 as anything other than a prediction of his own death, written at a time when Luke and his readers knew precisely what fate awaited Paul in Jerusalem and Rome.

(2) The second part of the speech (vv. 28–35) consists of paranaesis, practical advice to the church in a manner familiar from the epistles, especially the later, 'catholic' epistles. The shepherding metaphor of vv. 28–9 strongly recalls 1 Peter 5:2–3, though *episkopoi* (overseers) is Pauline (cf. Phil 1:1) and may reflect the fluid terminology of Paul's day better than Luke's term 'elders' (v. 17). The repeated counsel to 'watch' (vv. 28, 31) is a constant feature of early Christian paranaesis from Paul onwards (cf. 1 Thess 5:6; 1 Cor 16:13), but the warning against the inroads of false teachers (vv. 29–30) is more characteristic of the later epistles (cf. e.g. 1 Tim 1:3–11; Titus 2:1). The address closes with a commendation to the grace of God (v. 32) and a final hortatory example (vv. 33–5): Paul's own practice of working with his hands is put forward as an incitement to charitable giving and mutual support within the community. The final words cite an otherwise unknown saying of Jesus that may have been passed down in the oral tradition: it fits well with Luke's general interest in encouraging wealthier Christians to support the poor.

(3) The framework of the speech (vv. 36–8) reinforces the sense of impending tragedy that marks this final journey to Jerusalem. Emotions, so much a feature of the Greek novel, are surprisingly rare in Acts, but here we have a vividly drawn scene that reveals an unexpected facet of Luke's hero, his ability to inspire and share affection.

(21:1–16) Journey: Miletus to Jerusalem The we-narrator resumes the tale, giving it its customary wealth of detail: the itemized stages of the voyage, and the redundant detail of ships and cargoes, give the narration both a pragmatic realism and an indefinable sense of pathos. The group of disciples in Tyre (v. 3) is otherwise unknown; their prophetic warning (v. 4) and solemn farewell (v. 6) exemplify and reinforce the tone of Paul's address (cf. 20:23). Ptolemais (v. 7) provides another group of believers offering hospitality and support. By the time the party reach Caesarea (v. 8) they are re-entering more familiar territory: Philip the evangelist was last seen

heading in the direction of Caesarea at 8:40. His prophetic daughters (v. 9) do not actually utter any warnings to Paul, but their presence adds to the authority of the group of local people (v. 12) who warn Paul against proceeding to Jerusalem. Most prominent among these is Agabus, an itinerant charismatic from Jerusalem who acts out a classic piece of prophetic symbolism (v. 11) as a warning to Paul; he must be the same as the one mentioned in 11:28, though Luke makes no cross-reference. The scene climaxes with a joint appeal from the local Christians and Paul's travelling companions (v. 12); Paul is moved but unshakable in his resolve to persist with his journey whatever the cost (v. 13). There is a distinctly Socratic flavour about this scene, heightened by the presence of the women and by the we-narration that echoes that of Plato's *Phaedo*, 117D–E. Paul is being presented as a martyr, exhibiting a properly philosophical courage like that of Socrates in the face of death: his friends, like those of Socrates, can only acquiesce in the divine will (v. 14; cf. Socrates' last words: 'If so it is pleasing to God, so let it be': Epict. *Diss.* 1.29.18–19).

Act Four: Paul the Prisoner (21:17–28:31)

Act IV Scene 1: Paul on Trial: Jerusalem (21:17–23:22)

The final quarter of Acts is devoted to a Pauline trial narrative, a structural parallel to the passion narrative of Jesus which closes the gospel. Paul the travelling missionary becomes— as the narrative has predicted—Paul the prisoner, the 'chained' Paul of the prison epistles. Luke exploits the dramatic possibilities of the situation to the full, unleashing a flood of direct speech which builds up to a vivid presentation of the case against Paul and of his own answer to it. The first scene is set in Jerusalem: Paul unintentionally sparks a riot in the temple (21:27–36), is rescued by a Roman tribune (21:37–40), and attempts to present his case to the crowd (22:1–21), then to the Sanhedrin (23:1–10). But the gradual unpacking of Paul's Roman status (22:22–30) signals a move to the next stage of the drama, where Paul is taken to Caesarea for his own protection (23:11–22).

(21:17–26) Arrival: Paul Meets James The visit begins innocuously enough, with a warm welcome from the 'brothers' (v. 17) and a more formal debriefing with the leaders of the Jerusalem church (v. 18). Paul's detailed report on the success of his Gentile mission (v. 19) is greeted with enthusiasm; Luke makes it clear that since the decisions of the Apostolic Council (see ACTS 15:22–9), James and the Jerusalem leadership have no problem with the admission of Gentiles to the church (v. 25). But there is a threatening shadow from another quarter: the growing number of Jewish believers are troubled, not about what Paul tells the Gentiles, but about what he tells the Jews. Rumours are spreading that Paul's gospel involves inciting Jewish believers to abandon 'Moses' (i.e. the Jewish law), especially the ongoing practice of circumcision and the distinctive Jewish 'customs' that define Jewish identity in the diaspora (v. 21). This is what concerns those who are 'zealous for the law' (v. 20; cf. ACTS 5:17), and it is not a problem about the past (are Jewish Christians saved by the law?) but about the future (should Jewish Christians go on keeping the law?): as so often, it is in the rituals surrounding the birth of children that crucial questions of identity crystallize. James suggests that Paul should demonstrate publicly that he himself remains an observant Jew by sponsoring and joining four men who are going through the procedures of a nazirite vow (vv. 23–4), and he agrees to do this (v. 26; cf. 18:18). The same issue arises here as over the cirumcision of Timothy (see ACTS 16:1–5): is this action unthinkable for the Paul of the epistles (as some have suggested) or does it fall under the rubric of being 'all things to all people' (1 Cor 9:22)?

(21:27–36) Paul in the Temple James's fateful advice unwittingly precipitates the crisis he is trying to avoid. Paul's visibility in the temple over the seven days of his purification period (v. 27) brings him to the attention of some 'Jews from Asia', presumably like himself visiting the city for the festival of Pentecost: these may be members of the community in Ephesus with whom Paul had been disputing over a two-year period before his final journey (19:8–10). They perceive Paul's gospel as a direct attack on the Jewish people, the law, and the temple, a general charge which the following chapters will do their best to answer; but they also add the more specific charge (guaranteed to cause maximum disturbance among the volatile crowds at a festival season) that Paul has brought an uncircumcised Gentile into the holy place (v. 28). This was a serious charge which would have incurred the death penalty: Jewish religious law was in this respect backed up by all the weight of Roman authority. Inscriptions surviving from the temple precinct (cf. Fitzmyer 1998: 698; cited Barrett 1994–9: ii. 1020) show that visitors to the temple were clearly warned at the barrier separating the Court of the Gentiles from the inner courts that any non-Jew entering the enclosure did so at his own risk. Paul would have known this perfectly well, and Luke makes it clear that he had not in fact broken this regulation (v. 29). But the misapprehension is enough to arouse 'the whole city' (v. 30), and temple security lock the inner courts against Paul, a symbolic irony that would not have been lost on Luke's readers: time and again, in Luke's presentation, it is not Paul himself but his Jewish audiences who close the doors against him. But the riot continues in the larger Court of the Gentiles, and Paul is in real danger of being lynched (vv. 31–2, 35–6). He is rescued in the nick of time by the commander of the Roman garrison stationed in the Antonia fortress, which overlooked the temple and was designed precisely to quell religious riots such as this (cf. Jos. J.W. 5. 243–5). Luke's vivid use of detail adds to the dramatic realism of the scene.

(21:37–40) Paul and the Tribune This scene effectively dramatizes the tussle over identity that overshadows the final scenes of Paul's career. Paul has been shut out (literally, v. 30) from the religious centre of his own people and is now in the hands of Roman authority. As readers, we know that Paul can in fact lay claim to a status that opens doors in the Roman world (16:37); but the tribune does not know that, and his instinct is to treat Paul as a native troublemaker on a level with other oriental insurrectionists (v. 38). Josephus tells of an Egyptian prophet who led a revolutionary crowd to assemble outside Jerusalem and wait for the city to fall (Jos. J.W. 2.261–3; Ant. 20.169–72). He dates this incident to the procuratorship of Felix (which is the time of Paul's visit), so the tribune's allusion could be to the same figure. But Paul effectively undercuts the assumption by addressing the tribune in

educated Greek (v. 37): with all the insulted pride of Greek citizenship at being taken for an Egyptian, he claims to be 'a citizen of no mean city' (v. 39: RSV brings out the understated elegance of the Greek phrase; cf. Eur. Ion, 8). Whether Paul, as the son of an observant Jewish family (Phil 3:5), could actually have held full Tarsian citizenship is disputed; but Luke uses both *polis* and *politēs* in a variety of non-technical senses (e.g. Lk 1:26; 19:14), and Paul may well have regarded himself as a *politēs* of the Jewish community of Tarsus in this wider sense (Légasse 1995: 366–8). For the tribune, used to the complexities of civic status in the eastern empire, Paul's use of Greek is sufficient for the moment to establish common ground. When Paul turns to address the crowd again, however, it is his Jewishness that comes to the fore: 'in the Hebrew language' (v. 40) almost certainly means Aramaic, the spoken language of Palestine (Fitzmyer 1998: 701).

(22:1–21) Paul's Temple Speech This is the first in a series of apologetic speeches ('defence', 22:1; Gk. *apologia*) made by Paul in this final section. Language and address are designed to stress the speaker's commonalty with his audience (vv. 1–2), and his opening words emphasize that he, like them, is a 'zealot for God' (v. 3) with a strict seminary education rooted in Jerusalem (which was presumably where he learnt to speak Aramaic). Both statements are consistent with Paul's own claims about his education in Gal 1:13–14; some scholars have argued that 'this city' refers to Tarsus, but this seems to make less sense of Paul's argument here. As in Gal 1:13 and Phil 3:6, the touchstone of Paul's 'zeal' is his persecution of the church (v. 4). The high priest at the time of Paul's arrest (v. 5) was not the same as the one in office at the time of his visit to Damascus, but there may have been some continuity in the membership of the Sanhedrin.

Paul's retelling of his own conversion story overlaps with Luke's version of the story in ch. 9. The very fact that the story is repeated in such detail is an indication of its importance for Luke; but there are also intriguing differences that shed an interesting light on Luke's practice as a narrator. Clearly he sees no difficulty in the fact that the retold story is slightly different each time. Variation in detail was a stylistic virtue in the ancient rhetorical schools; and, as with Peter's retellings of the Cornelius episodes, each retelling brings to the fore a further aspect of the event's inner theological significance. Here Paul gives us a little more background detail about Ananias (v. 12), relevant to his claim to be working within a framework of observant Judaism. Ananias' message to Paul (v. 14) also stresses continuity with Judaism: the one who sent Ananias was 'the God of our ancestors', and Jesus is described as 'the Righteous One' (cf. 3:13–14; Jer 23:5–6; 33:15). The significance of baptism (to which Luke has earlier alluded briefly without explanation) is here made explicit (v. 16): it is to do with cleansing from sin, and calling on the name of Christ. Paul now adds an episode of which Luke's earlier narrative (9:26–30) has told us nothing. A visionary experience of Christ (significantly located in the temple, v. 17) warns Paul of his danger in Jerusalem (v. 18) and gives him a direct commission to go 'far away to the Gentiles' (v. 21). This is more explicit (and closer to Gal 1:16) than 9:15–16, where Ananias is told only that Saul has been chosen to bring the name of Christ 'before Gentiles and kings and the people of Israel' (a promise that seems in context to have more to do with martyrdom than with preaching).

(22:22–9) Paul the Roman The mention of Gentiles proves too much for Paul's audience, who resume their riotous behaviour at this point (vv. 22–3). The tribune decides to remove Paul to the barracks for further interrogation: the examination of witnesses by torture (v. 24) was routine practice in both Greek and Roman judicial systems. Leaving it to the last possible moment, Paul decides that it is time to reveal a little more of his status (v. 25), and produces consternation and dismay among the soldiers and minor officials into whose hands he has fallen (vv. 26–9). See ACTS 16:35–40 for the relative protection offered by the status of Roman citizen. The question of Paul's citizenship is hotly disputed (see Légasse 1995: 368–72). Paul's claim to be free-born (v. 28) means that his status goes back at least to his father's generation, possibly earlier, to the period of the civil wars, when Roman generals granted citizenship to a number of individuals and associations in the Greek East who had supported their cause. The contrast with the tribune (whose name we discover in 23:26 to be Claudius Lysias) may be a sly dig at the growing laxity of citizenship grants, which were widely reported to be freely available for money in the time of Claudius (Dio Cassius, 60. 17.5–6). But the essential point is that Luke's whole plot falls apart at this point without Paul's Roman citizenship, which is the motive force to get him to Rome; it is hard to imagine that Luke's readers, even as late as the 80s or 90s, would not have been familiar with the broad outlines of the story. Luke is quite happy, as we have seen, to present an account of historical events that is fictionalized in detail (e.g. in the attribution of direct speech), or to create 'type' scenes to represent what he considers to be the essential historical truth of a complex situation, but it is not plausible to suppose that the whole episode of Paul's appeal to Caesar is free invention: and the appeal is only possible if Paul had citizen status.

(22:30–23:10) Paul before the Sanhedrin The only way the tribune could 'order' the Sanhedrin to meet (22:30) was in an advisory capacity, in order to help him determine whether or not Paul had a case to answer in Jewish law. The high priest Ananias (23: 2; cf. 24:1) is Ananias son of Nebedaeus, appointed by Herod of Chalcis in 47 CE, and replaced in 59 (Jos. *Ant.* 20.103, 131, 179, 205). Paul's exchange with him is difficult to explain, however, even within the terms of Luke's own interests: Barrett (1994–9: ii. 1062) says of this passage, 'There is historical material behind this paragraph, but it is deep and remote.' Luke's account of the hearing does not follow exact judicial procedures, but it does convey some of the atmosphere of corruption and factionalism that pervades Josephus' account of the procuratorship of Felix. Paul is able to exploit this factionalism to his own advantage (vv. 6–8), and Luke highlights a positive response to Paul from at least some within the Pharisaic party. The point at issue (at least the only one that interests Luke) is the same as the question that exercised Gamaliel in 5:39: has Paul received a genuine divine revelation (v. 9)? The fact that some Pharisees are prepared to give him the benefit of the doubt is worth recording, but the net result of the hearing for the tribune is simply deeper confusion: clearly Paul is safer for the moment in Roman custody (v. 10).

(23:11–22) Plots and Counterplots Paul receives private reassurance at this point that the confusing things that are happening to him are part of God's plan (v. 11)—perhaps the first inkling that his 'witness' in Rome will not be as missionary but as prisoner. Meanwhile, 'the Jews' (by which Luke means those who are opposed to Paul) decide to get rid of Paul by assassination if judicial means will not avail (vv. 12–15). The wealth of dialogue and circumstantial detail with which this story is told is reminiscent of the Greek novels, but the ambush is not in itself implausible, and the hitherto unsuspected presence of Paul's nephew (v. 16) provides a possible source for Luke's privileged information about the conspirators. The net result is that Paul gets a high-quality escort to Caesarea (vv. 23–4), and the next stage of his gradual transfer into the Roman sphere of authority takes place with dramatic (and secret) efficiency.

(23:23–30) Paul Sent to Caesarea The numbers of Paul's military escort (vv. 23–4) seem excessive and may be exaggerated (though cf. Jos. *Ant.* 20.160–6, 185–8; *J.W.* 2.253–65 on the general disorder and danger on the roads at this period). Manuscripts disagree on some of the details (perhaps through a desire to improve on the purely secular detail of Luke's story), and the word translated 'spearmen' is a rare word whose meaning is unclear (which suggests that there may be good tradition behind this: it would not have been difficult for Luke to write more clearly if he were composing freely). 'Felix the governor' (v. 24) is named for the first time here. He was a freedman, brother to the imperial secretary Pallas (Jos. *J.W.* 2.247, *Ant.* 20.137), and was appointed by Claudius to the procuratorship of Judea *c.*52; he was widely regarded as cruel and corrupt (cf. Tac. *Hist.* 5.9), and was indicted by the Jews of Caesarea after his retirement from office (Jos. *Ant.* 20.182). Despite his unpopularity, he remained in post until *c.*60, when he was replaced by Festus (Jos. *J.W.* 2.271; *Ant.* 182). Luke's note that Claudius Lysias 'wrote a letter to this effect' (v. 25) is revealing: there must have been a letter, and Luke knows roughly what it would have said, but he makes no claim to be reproducing a genuine document verbatim. The tribune tells the story in a way more flattering to himself (v. 27), but otherwise repeats for the governor's benefit what we already know.

Act IV Scene 2: Paul on Trial: Caesarea (23:31–26:32)

The second phase of Paul's trial begins with his transfer to Caesarea. A formal hearing before Felix, with speeches for the prosecution and the defence (24:1–27) ends inconclusively, and Felix decides to defer his decision and keep Paul in custody. Matters comes to a head when Festus arrives in the province and the proceedings are reopened (25:1–12). Sensing that Festus favours sending him back for trial in Jerusalem, Paul is compelled to appeal to Caesar; the remainder of the scene is little more than a coda, with Paul displayed as a curiosity before Festus' guests, but this final hearing allows Paul to make one of his longest and most impassioned speeches before an influential patron of diaspora Judaism.

(23:31–24:9) The Speech for the Prosecution Caesarea is about 110 km. from Jerusalem by road, and Antipatris (23:31) is about half-way, at the point where the hill-country road intersects with the road running north from Lydda along the coastal plain. Paul is kept in Herod's praetorium (23:35), and some scholars have suggested that the Epistle to the Philippians could have been written from there (cf. Phil 1:13), in place of the traditional origin in Rome. The delegation from the Sanhedrin acts promptly (24:1), this time bringing a professional rhetor (NRSV 'attorney') to make a formal rhetorical presentation on their behalf; this is a subtle reaction to the change of venue for the hearing, which is now much more in the Roman sphere than the Jewish. Rhetorical presentation of a case by trained orators was very important in both Greek and Roman legal proceedings. Tertullus' speech, though short, displays many of the formulations known from contemporary speeches (Winter 1993: 315–22). The opening *exordium* (vv. 2–4) uses a range of honorific titles and compliments similar to those of papyrus petitions found in Egypt, stressing the characteristics of the governor that make him competent to try the case ('your foresight', 'your customary graciousness') and his success at maintenance of the peace (plausibly read as an allusion to Felix's recent putting down of the insurrection led by the Egyptian: see ACTS 21:37–40). The *narratio* or 'statement of the case' (vv. 5–6) is abbreviated but recognizable. The charge of being an 'agitator' (v. 5: lit. causing civic discord, *staseis*) is calculated to impress any Roman governor, especially one presiding over a province rapidly degenerating into *stasis* (Josephus' word for the state of civil war which ushered in the Jewish Revolt). Similar accusations were laid against Alexandrian Jews in 41 CE in a letter of Claudius that accuses them of 'stirring up a common plague throughout the world' (Barrett 1994–9: ii. 1097). The more precise charge of profaning the temple (v. 6) was, as we have seen, a serious breach of a Jewish religious law which the Romans were pledged to uphold. On 'sect' (v. 5) see below on ACTS 24:14; the name 'Nazoreans' (NRSV marg.) occurs several times in Luke–Acts and is probably best treated as a variant for *Nazarēnos* (Fitzmyer 1998: 254).

24:10–21 The Speech for the Defence Paul, like Tertullus, uses the popular 'many'-formula in his opening words ('many years'), though, as compliments go, this is factual rather than fulsome. His most serious self-defence (*apologia*, v. 10) focuses on events in Jerusalem: in the short time he has been in the city, Paul has not been involved in disputes or riots in synagogue or temple (v. 12). The fact that he has done precisely this across the diaspora is irrelevant, because it is outside the jurisdiction of the Sanhedrin: and as Luke has demonstrated, Roman governors outside Judea have shown no inclination to follow up complaints against Paul from local Jewish communities (cf. ACTS 18:12–17). Only in Judea, where Jewish law has the status of a local civic code upheld by Roman authority, is Paul in any danger: and there, as Luke takes pains to show, no offence against the law can be proved against him (v. 13). 'Twelve days' (v. 11) is puzzling, since Luke's account seems to imply a longer period, but he may be simply adding the seven days of the vow (21:27) to the five in Caesarea (24:1); Luke certainly seems to imply that the whole period of Paul's imprisonment and trial in Jerusalem, like that of Jesus, was

hurried and compressed. The speech quickly moves from self-defence against the immediate charges to a more general affirmation of Paul's whole ideology (cf. Phil 1:7, which shows the same slide). 'The Way' which Paul follows is in fact presented in Acts as a 'sect' of Judaism, that is as a legitimate interpretation of the ancestral traditions (v. 14), and one that has significant continuity with the beliefs of the other 'sect' to which Paul (and many of his accusers) belong, the Pharisees (cf. 23:6; 26:5)—especially the belief in resurrection (vv. 15, 21). In this context, finally, Luke's Paul does appear to mention the collection for the poor of Jerusalem (v. 17: and cf. Rom. 15:25–7 for Paul's own liturgical angle on this).

(24:22–7) Felix Defers Judgement Prosecution and defence have made their presentations, but Felix refuses to be drawn into making a judgement, initially on the pretext of waiting for the tribune's report (v. 22); but no more is heard of this. The narrative pace begins to slow down: 'some days later' (v. 24) is one of the vaguer Lukan time-indicators. Paul now settles into the pattern that will control his life through the rest of the book. He is in custody (v. 23), but has a degree of 'liberty'; like all ancient prisoners, he is reliant on his 'friends' (lit. his own) for the daily necessities of food and clothing (cf. Jos. *Ant.* 18.203–4 on the conditions of Agrippa's imprisonment in Rome). Like all ancient prisoners, too, he is now totally dependent on the whim of the governor for the pursual of his case. Each time Paul is summoned by the governor (vv. 24, 26), he must have hoped that things were moving forward; but Felix has no interest in bringing the case to a speedy conclusion (v. 27). Luke's rather cynical evaluation of Felix's motives (v. 26) is matched by the general estimate of Felix found in Tacitus and Josephus (ACTS 23:23–35); Josephus records a similar complaint later of Albinus (Jos. *Ant.* 20.215). On the one visit that is recorded in more detail (vv. 24–5), Paul comes across as a model philosopher, trying in vain to influence a corrupt governor for good. Felix's adulterous relationship with Drusilla is known from Jos. *Ant.* 20.141–3. According to custom, Paul might have hoped to be released at the end of Felix's term of office (v. 27), but Felix deliberately leaves the case for his sucessor.

(25:1–12) Paul Appeals to Caesar Josephus confirms that Felix's successor in the province of Judea was Porcius Festus (Jos. *J.W.* 2.271; *Ant.* 20.182–8), and that his arrival was heralded by a flurry of official activity. Festus himself seems to have been keen to clean up the ongoing brigandage problem left by his predecessor; he may also have been eager to avoid the kind of action brought against his predecessor by the Jewish community in Caesarea, who took the opportunity to send a delegation to Rome to complain about Felix's 'misdeeds against the Jews' (Jos. *Ant.* 20.182). In this atmosphere, keeping on the right side of the Jewish authorities (vv. 2, 9) was obviously in the new governor's interests, but it was equally important to act with all propriety in relation to Rome: Festus' decision to play safe with the case of the troublesome Roman citizen Paul by referring the case to Rome makes a lot of sense. The sense that Paul is here under the protection of the Roman imperial authorities is very strong in this section: it was in fact one of the major roles of the emperor in this period to act as a final court of appeal for provincials who felt they were not getting justice from local magistrates. Only here, in all his defence speeches (*apologia*, v. 8) does Paul explicitly say that he has not committed any crime against the emperor: the main thrust of his defence is that no offence against Jewish law can be proved against him. Transferring the case to Jerusalem, as Festus threatens (v. 9), was in effect extraditing a Roman citizen for trial on a capital charge under a different legislative authority; if both parties agreed (v. 9), this was perfectly in order. But Paul rejects the offer, and (just to make sure) appeals over the procurator's head to the higher court of the emperor, as Roman citizens were entitled to do (v. 10). Legally, Paul was perfectly within his rights; interestingly, however, Luke seems to feel he needs to protect his hero against the more philosophical imputation that he is making this appeal because he is afraid to face death (v. 11). This may be another Socratic touch: the ideal Cynic, according to Epictetus (*Diss*. 3.22.55–6), will not appeal to any Caesar or proconsul in order to escape a flogging.

(25:13–27) **Agrippa and Bernice** The stage is now effectively set for Paul's last journey to Rome: Paul has appealed to Caesar, and Festus has agreed to transfer his case to Rome (v. 12). But Luke takes the time, before he goes, to give Paul another long set-piece speech, one of the longest in the book, and his final and most impassioned *apologia*. In a sense this is the speech we would expect Paul to make in Rome, before the final tribunal that tries his case; but Luke is either unwilling or unable to show us any trial scene in Rome, or even to tell us what is the denouement of the trial (see ACTS 28:23–31). Instead, Paul has one last chance to make a statement of his case (in effect, a defence of his whole career), not before Festus (who has already heard all he needs to know, and who in any case has relinquished his jurisdiction to a higher court) but before the Jewish king Agrippa II and his sister Bernice (v. 13). In itself Agrippa's visit to Festus, and Festus's decision to let Paul speak before him, is perfectly plausible: Festus may well have felt that the king's expertise would be useful to him in drafting his report on the case (v. 27). Agrippa II (son of the 'Herod' of ch. 12, Agrippa I) was now consolidating his holdings in the region (Jos. *J.W.* 2.247, 252) and becoming a significant power-broker, both with Rome and with the Jewish community worldwide; Josephus (*ibid*. 2.245, cf. also *Ant*. 20.135) shows him acting as spokesperson for a Jewish delegation in Rome a few years earlier, and later has him visit Alexandria to congratulate Tiberius Julius Alexander on his accession to the prefecture of Egypt (Jos. *J.W.* 2.309), much as Luke has him do here for Festus (Alexander was a previous procurator of Judea and Bernice's brother-in-law). Bernice was the sister of Agrippa (and also of Drusilla, Felix's wife); she was at this stage widowed and living at her brother's court in an ambiguous relationship (Jos. *Ant*. 20.145). She took an active part in Jewish affairs and is shown by Josephus alongside Agrippa in his final, disastrous attempt to hold back the forces of revolt in Jerusalem in 66 (Jos. *J.W.* 2.344). The scene, then, as Luke describes it, is historically realistic; but by choosing to give it the full dramatic treatment, Luke has turned it into a characteristic type-scene, parallel to the Nazareth pericope in Lk 4:16–30, which allows him to sum up both the Roman failure to find a

case against Paul (25:14–27) and Paul's own self-defence (26:1–29). It also allows him to demonstrate the fulfilment of the prophecy that Paul would have to testify 'before kings' (9:15).

(26:1–11) **Paul's Speech (1): My Former Life** Like the speech before Felix, Paul's speech can be analysed according to the canons of contemporary rhetoric (Winter 1993: 327–31). It begins with a standard *captatio benevolentiae*, congratulating his auditor on his expert ability to judge the case (vv. 2–3). He then moves into a reprise of his own life-story, explaining at greater length than we have yet seen his former life in Judaism (cf. Gal 1:13–14). No mention of Tarsus here (that was to impress a Roman tribune); the whole emphasis is on Jerusalem, and in particular on Paul's Pharisaic piety (vv. 4–5; cf. 23:6, Phil 3:5–6) and his persecution of the Christians (vv. 9–11; cf. Gal 1:13; Phil 3:6; 1 Cor 15:9). Since Luke is not imparting any new information here, we need to ask what is the rhetorical function of this lengthy section, not only within the dramatic setting in the narrative but also on the reader. It is striking how much of the rhetoric here is devoted to demonstrating Paul's fidelity to the Jewish religion (vv. 6–8): far from being a mere ruse to split the audience (as it was in 23:6), the hope of the resurrection is integral to Paul's belief-system, as it is, he argues, to the ancestral beliefs of his audience.

(26:12–23) **Paul's Speech (2): The Heavenly Vision** Luke has already twice told us the story of Paul's conversion, once as narrator (9:1–18) and once in Paul's own words (22:6–16): as with Peter's vision, functional redundancy is an indicator of rhetorical importance. Here again there are slight variations in the telling: Luke does not think it important to repeat every detail of the story in exactly the same way (but as in the gospels, the keywords of the pericope tend to be the most stable in repetition: compare vv. 14–15 with 9:4–5; 22:7–8). The addition of 'in the Hebrew language' (v. 14) shows that Luke has not forgotten (even if his readers have) that this is an address to a Greek-speaking audience, whereas the previous speech in which the same events are recounted was in 'Hebrew' (or Aramaic; see ACTS 21:40). Does Luke feel it necessary to apologize, in this Greek context, for the barbarous name 'Saul', which he gives in its Semitized form? If so, it is all the stranger that the heavenly voice is expanded here to include a proverbial saying ('It hurts you to kick against the goads') which is not found in 9:4 or 22:7, and which is best paralleled in Greek literature (cf. esp. Eur. *Bacch*. 794–5). Paul's divine commission, which in earlier accounts had come via Ananias (9:15–16) or in a trance (22:17–21) is here compressed into his initial revelation (vv. 16–18). These verses contain the strongest and clearest statement in Acts of Paul's own understanding of his commission to bring the gospel to the Gentiles: cf. Gal 1:15–16. 'To serve and testify' (v. 16: *hupēreten kai martura*) recalls Luke's description of the ultimate sources of the apostolic tradition he reports (Lk 1:2). The mission is described (v. 18) in prophetic terms strongly reminiscent of Isa 42:6–7; 49:6 (already quoted at 13:47) and anticipating the close of the book (see ACTS 28:23–31). The controlling image is visual rather than verbal (cf. 'proclaim light', v. 23): Paul's calling is to 'testify' (v. 22), but the primal experience to which he is testifying is conceived not as word but as vision (v. 16), and it is a 'heavenly vision' which, as in the days of the patriarchs (7:2, 30) ultimately compels obedience (v. 19).

(26:24–32) Paul's Speech (3): Challenge to Agrippa The speech closes with a lively piece of dialogue which adds a touch of comic irony to the scene. The contrast between 'madness' (v. 24) and 'sober truth' (v. 25) is a philosophical one, designed to point up the contrast between the calm rationality of Luke's hero and the bluff incomprehension of the magistrate set to hear his case. In a sense, however, it is also a challenge to the reader of the type set by Gamaliel's conundrum at 5:38–9; and Luke points this up by turning the end of Paul's speech into a direct challenge to Agrippa, vv. 26–9). Any reader who shares Agrippa's knowledge (i.e. any reader who knows and believes the Jewish Scriptures) must be persuaded: and the end of the speech makes it clear that the real object of Paul's persuasive rhetoric is not exoneration but conversion: 'all who are listening' to Paul (v. 29) are invited to 'become a Christian' (v. 28). Given Agrippa's role in assisting Jewish delegations to present their case in Rome (ACTS 25:13–27), Paul's attempt to enlist the king to his cause may not have seemed unreasonable (Josephus is still trying to do the same 40 years later: Jos. *Vita*, 362–6). Within the secondary world of the narrative, however, Paul's appeal simply has the effect of reinforcing his innocence: both Festus and Agrippa are convinced that he has committed no crime (vv. 31–2).

Act IV Interlude: Storm and Shipwreck

The narrative now enters its final phase, a kind of dramatic postlude after the rhetorical climax of the speech before Agrippa. Paul has appealed to the power of Rome, and that power now envelops him ('transferred', lit. handed over, 27:1). The temple doors have been shut (21:30); the final appeal to Jerusalem has failed, and Paul is now effectively shut out from the city in which he was reared (26:4). The prophecy that he will bear witness in Rome (23:11) will be fulfilled, but very differently from the way Paul himself may have envisaged his visit to the centre of the empire (20:21). The final scene of the book will be set in Rome: but first, the transition is accomplished by a meticulously described sea-voyage which succeeds in gratifying the sensationalist tastes of the readers of ancient novels while retaining an obstinately pragmatic realism.

(27:1–12) Along the Coasts of Asia Minor The we-narrator reappears at this point (v. 1). Paul has at least two companions from among the party who accompanied him from Macedonia, including Aristarchus (v. 2) and the unnamed narrator. The centurion Julius (v. 1) is otherwise unknown, but inscriptions attest to the presence of an 'Augustan cohort' of auxiliaries in Syria during most of the first century. Paul is not important enough to warrant military transport, however; like most travellers, Julius and his small party of prisoners are expected to find what ships they can that are going in the right direction. For this first section of the voyage, the we-narrator shows his customary appetite for nautical detail; he notes the irrelevant point that the first ship Julius picked for the coastal voyage came originally from Adramyttium (up the Aegean coast towards the Troas, v. 2), and that the second came from Alexandria (v. 6). This was almost certainly one of the huge

grain ships (cf. v. 38) that plied across the Mediterranean to Rome, supplying the city with grain from its 'bread-basket' in Egypt. Ancient ships did not cross the open sea any more than they had to: navigational instruments were primitive, and most mariners preferred to keep within sight of the coastal landmarks that were described in the *periploi* or seafarers' guides. Luke's painstaking account of the first stages of the voyage seems to highlight the difficulty Paul experiences in setting out in this new, westerly direction: the winds are against them (vv. 4, 7), they make slow progress (v. 7), each stage is accomplished 'with difficulty' (vv. 7, 8). As a result, by the time they reach Crete, the sailing season is almost over (v. 9: note again the we-narrator's penchant for dating by the Jewish liturgical calendar). There was no obvious reason why the ship's master should heed the advice of a Jewish prisoner who had (presumably) little seafaring experience (vv. 10–11); Paul's words are prophetic, though whether from common sense or from supernatural insight, Luke does not say.

(27:13–26) Storm Winds off Crete Paul's landing at Fair Havens, on the southern coast of Crete (v. 8), is still pointed out to visitors; the small bays on this rocky coast would not be suitable for a large ship to shelter from winter storms, so the decision to make for a better harbour was apparently reasonable (v. 12). But the manoeuvre has been left too late, and the ship is caught by a violent offshore wind (lit. a typhoon wind, v. 14): its name, Euraquilo (NRSV 'north-easter', v. 14) appears on a Roman wind-rose found in N. Africa. Roman ships, having a single large sail, were very difficult to turn into the wind (v. 15); the danger of being driven on to the sandbanks of the Syrtis, off the coast of Africa (v. 17) was very real. This passage abounds with nautical technicalities which have been found to make sense in terms of ancient navigation; though highly dramatic, the account is realistic and contains no supernatural elements. The only miraculous aspect of the story, so far as it goes, is Paul's self-possession and courage (vv. 21–6). This narrative (unlike some of the more sensational shipwreck accounts from ancient literature) contains no record of divine intervention, simply a dream recounted by the hero, who believes (and persuades his fellow-passengers to believe) that it is a promise of survival (v. 23). For readers who know their Bibles, this is a kind of reversal of the Jonah story: Jonah's disobedience to God brought his ship into danger (Jon 1:12), whereas Paul's obedience will ensure safety for his (v. 24).

(27:27–38) Up and Down in Adria The 'sea of Adria' is not the modern Adriatic but the open sea between Crete, Sicily, Italy, and N. Africa: the novelists call it the Ionian Sea. Josephus speaks of being shipwrecked in the same area with a ship's company of 600 (Jos. *Vita*, 15). The pattern of soundings (v. 28) and landmarks (vv. 39, 41) fits the traditional identification of Paul's landfall as St Paul's Bay on the island of Malta, though others have been suggested. Anchoring by the stern (v. 29) is feasible for ancient ships, and makes sense in the circumstances. Paul's authority is growing all the time; the centurion is by now much more inclined to listen to Paul than to the sailors (vv. 30–1). And his final intervention is directed at the 'salvation' of the whole ship's company: at one level, the advice to take some sustenance (v. 33 'without food', Gk. *asitoi*, can mean 'without appetite') is a piece of practical advice aimed at helping them all to survive having to swim to shore (v. 34), but the Greek word *sōtēria* (salvation) also allows the story to be read at a symbolic level. This must be also the key to Paul's action in breaking bread and 'giving thanks' (v. 35); this is not a Christian eucharist in any formal sense, but the language elsewhere in Acts always has these connotations, and it is hard to believe they are completely absent here.

(27:39–44) All Safe to Land Improved visibility in the morning suggests to the experienced sailors the risky strategy of casting off the anchors (clearly they believe the ship is past saving) and running the ship ashore (vv. 39–40). Some unexpected underwater barrier prevents this (v. 41); the ship starts to break up some way out from the beach. 'Ran the ship aground' (v. 41) is the most literary phrase in the whole account: Luke here uses the Homeric and classical Greek word *naus* (ship), while elsewhere he has used the more pragmatic and colloquial *ploion* (boat) and *skaphos* (dinghy); the verb used here (*epokellō*) is also Homeric. Since Homer was the staple text for Greek primary education, it is likely that any writer educated to Luke's level (whether Greek or Jewish) would know enough of Homer's characteristic diction to fall into it naturally on occasions where the subject-matter seemed to call for it, as here: storm and shipwreck are frequent events in Homer's *Odyssey*. But the phrase, even if it is used unconsciously, illustrates the extent to which Luke's hero is now moving out of the biblical world and invading the seas of classical mythology. Paul's thoroughly realistic voyage is also an epic journey into the unknown, across stormy seas which, for Greek and Jewish readers alike, always had some of the symbolism of chaotic forces beyond human control; the same psalm which speaks of God as 'the hope of all the ends of the earth' sees a symbolic equivalence between the 'roaring of the seas' and the 'tumult of the peoples' (Ps 65:5–7). In this sense Luke's relieved conclusion (v. 44) is both a simple statement of fact and a subdued paean of victory.

(28:1–10) Miracle on Malta The westernmost point of Paul's epic voyage, appropriately enough, has a desert island feel to it: the 'natives' (v. 2) are *barbaroi* in Greek, the standard term for non-Greek speakers (though readers of the Greek novels would be more inclined to look for them in the east than in the west). The native language on Malta was in fact Punic, as the island had been colonized from Carthage. Like the Lycaonians of 14:11, they are portrayed as kindly but superstitious folk, taking Paul's imperviousness to snakebite as an indication of divine status (v. 6). But in fact the Greek novels show that the islanders' attitude to shipwreck survivors was as common among sophisticated Greek readers as among 'barbarians'. In Chariton's *Callirhoe* (a novel which is roughly contemporary with Acts), Theron the pirate, saved from shipwreck, claims to be especially favoured by the gods; when his crimes become apparent, the narrator points up the moral that Theron was actually saved because of his impiety, so as to suffer just punishment (*Callirhoe*, 3.4.9–10).

Despite appearances, Malta is not an uninhabited island: the castaways are soon taken in by a local landowner with the Roman name of Publius (v. 7); this is a common Roman

praenomen, and gives us little indication of his family. His title ('leading man', lit. first man) is attested from inscriptions as a Maltese title. Paul performs a miraculous healing on Publius's sick father (v. 8: reminiscent of Jesus' healing of Peter's mother-in-law); as in the gospels, other islanders start to come for healing (v. 9), proof, if any were needed, that the God whom Paul serves (27:23) is still with him. Far from demeaning Paul, the whole shipwreck incident has served to load him with honour (v. 10).

Act IV Scene 3: Paul in Rome (28:11–31)

After the drama of the shipwreck, there is almost an air of anticlimax about the book's final scene, which is both sombre and open-ended. Paul reaches Rome, which is where he has been headed (one way or another) ever since 20:21. But we never find out what happened when his case was heard before the emperor, or even if it was ever heard. The final verses of the book give us an ambivalent portrait of Paul the prisoner, preaching the kingdom to all comers (vv. 30–1), but never free of the custodial presence of Roman authority (v. 16). The bulk of the final scene is taken up with a debate with the Jewish community in Rome (vv. 17–28); only after failing to win acceptance for his message there does Paul finally turn 'to the Gentiles' (v. 28).

(28:11–16) Journey: Malta to Rome A final detailed journey section brings Paul's party to Rome with the we-narrator's customary attention to the ceremonies of voyaging. Malta was not as far from the sea-lanes that tied together Mediterranean civilization as it had seemed; the party have no trouble picking up a passage for their onward journey on an Alexandrian ship wintering on the island (v. 11). There is a touch of irony about the note on the ship's figurehead: the 'Twin Brothers' (i.e. Castor and Pollux, the Gemini or Dioscouri) were favourites with sailors and, according to Lucian, play a starring role in every good shipwreck tale (Lucian, *On Salaried Posts*, 1–2). Here their role is purely decorative: Paul does not need the help of pagan deities to get him through the storm. The ship calls in to ports along the east coast of Sicily and the 'toe' of Italy (vv. 12–13), both ancient Greek foundations which feature prominently in the plots of ancient novels and comic plays; but for the final stages of the journey, the atmosphere is wholly Roman. Luke prefers the Latin name Puteoli to the Greek Dicaearchia (cf. Jos. *Vita*, 16); the Forum of Appius and the Three Taverns are staging-posts along the Appian Way a few miles out from Rome. There is an odd feeling of homecoming about this last stage: far from being the 'ends of the earth' (1:8), Rome is a place where there are already 'brothers' (NRSV 'believers', v. 15) who come out to give Paul a ceremonial escort along the Appian Way. There is something slightly shocking about the reminder (v. 16) that after all, Paul is still a prisoner, with his liberty of action strictly curtailed.

(28:17–22) Paul's Reception in Rome The final scene of Acts shows us not Paul the pioneer missionary, preaching to the pagans of Rome as he had to the philosophers of Athens (ch. 17), but—as so often in Acts—Paul the faithful Jew, pleading with the leaders of the Jewish community in Rome to give his gospel a fair hearing. And, significantly, a fair hearing is what he gets: this scene is markedly more irenic than those in Jerusalem, and shows no sign of the animosity that Paul has been arousing in Asia Minor (21:27–8). Paul himself stresses his common interest with the leaders of the community ('Brothers', v. 17), and hastens to reassure them that his appeal to Caesar does not imply any disloyalty to 'my nation' (v. 19)— a suspicion that would naturally arise in a Rome which was accustomed to receiving rival delegations from the home country seeking justice or redress at the emperor's hands. Getting the local community on his side before word arrived from Jerusalem (v. 21) could make a lot of sense for Paul's case; but it also implies (as we saw in Pisidian Antioch) that neither Luke nor Paul sees 'the Jews' as a monolithic social or religious system: hostility in one part of the system does not by any means automatically imply that there will be hostility in others. In fact the Roman Jews have a remarkably open-minded attitude to Paul and his message (v. 22): it is a 'sect' which is 'spoken against' (v. 21, cf. Lk 2:34), but they want to make up their own minds about it (v. 22). Paul's stance is the same as it has been all through his trial: the 'hope of Israel' recalls his words to Agrippa (26:6–8), but also takes the reader much further back to the opening chapters of the gospel and the faithful old people in the temple 'waiting for the consolation of Israel' (Lk 2:25–38).

(28:23–31) Paul's Last Words Paul has one day to win over the local community: Luke does not tell us what he said, but we can legitimately infer that it was a repetition of the argument that the whole of Acts has been setting out in dramatic form (v. 23). The result is not wholly negative (some are 'convinced', v. 24), but it is inconclusive: the final state of the community is described as 'disharmony' (v. 25, 'disagreed': Gk. *asymphōnoi*). Paul's strategy all through Acts seems to have been to win over entire communities for his messianist interpretation of the Jewish Scriptures, and it is this strategy—not the offer of salvation to individual Jews—that finally seems to have run out of steam. Luke has saved up for this point in his narrative (vv. 26–7) the sombre prophecy from Isa 6:9–10 that informed much early Christian reflection on the Jewish rejection of Jesus (Lindars 1961: 159–67); compare Luke's citation in the parable of the sower (Lk 8:10) with Mk 4:12; Mt 13:14–15. It is a verse addressed by a prophet to his own people, and it records, not the threat of divine judgement, but the tragic failure of 'this people' to take advantage of the proffered 'salvation' (v. 28: the word picks up earlier allusions to Isaiah's wider vision (ACTS 26:12–23) as well as taking the reader back to Simeon's prophecy in Lk 2:30). It is probably fair to regard this as the real conclusion to Acts; the final two verses form a brief coda, recording Paul's continued witness to 'all who came' (by implication Jews as well as Gentiles, v. 30) over a two-year period: hardly triumphalist, but quietly confident that the proclamation of the gospel will go on into an uncertain future 'with all boldness and without hindrance' (v. 31).

REFERENCES

Alexander, L. (1993a), 'Chronology of Paul', in G. F. Hawthorne, R. P. Martin, D. G. Reid (eds.), *The Dictionary of Paul and his Letters* (Illinois: Inter-Varsity Press), 115–23.

—— (1993b), 'Acts and Ancient Intellectual Biography', in Winter and Clarke (1993), 31–63.

Barrett, C. K. (1994–9), *The International Critical Commentary: Acts* (2 vols.; Edinburgh: T. & T. Clark).

Bauckham, R. (1995) (ed.), *The Book of Acts in its First-Century Setting*, iv. *Palestinian Setting* (Grand Rapids: Eerdmans).

Brooke, G. J. (2000), 'Florilegium', in Schiffman and VanderKam (2000), i. 297–8.

Bruce, F. F. (1990), *The Acts of the Apostles: the Greek Text with Introduction and Commentary*, 3rd edn. (Grand Rapids: Eerdmans).

Dodd, C. H. (1936), *The Apostolic Preaching and its Development* (London: Hodder & Stoughton).

Falk, D. (1995), 'Jewish Prayer Literature and the Jerusalem Church in Acts', in Bauckham (1995), 267–301.

Fitzmyer, J. A. (1981), *The Gospel According to Luke I–IX*, (AB New York: Doubleday, 1981).

—— (1998), *The Acts of the Apostles*, (AB New York: Doubleday).

Gill, D. (1994), 'Achaia', in Gill and Gempf (1994), 433–53.

Gill, D., and Gempf, C. (1994) (eds.), *The Book of Acts in its First-Century Setting*, ii. *Graeco-Roman Setting* (Grand Rapids: Eerdmans).

Hansen, G. W. (1994), 'Galatia', in Gill and Gempf (1994), 377–95.

Horsley, G. H. R. (1994), 'The Politarchs', in Gill and Gempf (1994), 419–31.

Jewett, R. (1979), *Dating Paul's Life* (London: SCM).

Johnson, L. T. (1992), *The Acts of the Apostles*, Sacra Pagina, 5 (Collegeville, Minn.: Liturgical Press).

Légasse, S. (1995), 'Paul's Pre-Christian Career According to Acts', in Bauckham (1995), 365–90.

Levinskaya, I. (1996), 'God-fearers: Epigraphic Evidence', in I. Levinskaya (ed.), *The Book of Acts in its First Century Setting*, v. *Diaspora Setting*, (Grand Rapids: Eerdmans).

Lindars, B. (1961), *New Testament Apologetic* (London: SCM).

Lüdemann, G. (1984), *Paul, Apostle to the Gentiles: Studies in Chronology* (London: SCM).

Meyers, H. (1992), 'Synagogue', *ABD* vi. 251–63.

Mitchell, S. (1992), 'Galatia', *ABD* ii. 871.

Nobbs, A. (1994), 'Cyprus', in Gill and Gempf (1994), 279–89.

Porter, S. E. (1994), 'The "We" Passages', in Gill and Gempf (1994), 545–74.

Powell, M. A. (1991), *What Are They Saying About Acts?* (New York: Paulist).

Rapske, B. (1994), 'Acts, Travel and Shipwreck', in Gill and Gempf (1994), 1–47.

Riesner, R. (1995), 'Synagogues in Jerusalem' in Bauckham (1995), 179–210.

Schiffman, L. H., and VanderKam, J. C. (2000) (eds.), *The Encyclopedia of the Dead Sea Scrolls* (2 vols., New York: Oxford University Press).

Scott, J. M. (1994), 'Luke's Geographical Horizon', in Gill and Gempf (1994), 483–544.

Steudel, A. (2000), 'Testimonia', in Schiffman and VanderKam (2000), 936–8.

Sterling, G. in Schiffman and VanderKam (2000), i. 5–7.

Trebilco, P. (1994), 'Asia', in Gill and Gempf (1994), 316–38.

Winter, B. (1993), 'Official Proceedings and Forensic Speeches in Acts 24–26', in Winter and Clarke (1993), 315–22.

Winter, B. W., and Clarke, A. D. (1993) (eds.), *The Book of Acts in its First-Century Setting*, i. *Ancient Literary Setting* (Grand Rapids: Eerdmans).

Witherington III, B. (1998), *The Acts of the Apostles: A Socio-Rhetorical Commentary* (Grand Rapids: Eerdmans).

63. Introduction to the Pauline Corpus

TERENCE L. DONALDSON

A. Overview. 1. No less than thirteen of the twenty-seven writings of the New Testament are letters attributed to the Apostle Paul. They constitute fully one-quarter of the New Testament's bulk; if one adds to this the portion of the Acts of the Apostles where Paul is the main character, Paul's proportion of the New Testament climbs to almost a third. The proportion devoted to the life and ministry of Jesus (i.e. the four gospels) is higher, but not by much.

2. The significance of Paul's literary legacy, of course, is not simply a matter of its quantity. His letters (at least those that can be attributed to him with some certainty) represent the earliest extant writings of the Christian movement. Further, they are real letters, written to actual congregations whose life circumstances are reflected, albeit with some ambiguity, in the texts themselves. In addition, they are at times highly personal letters, at least in the sense that the desires, emotions, thinking processes, and very personality of their author are vividly portrayed. Moreover, their author was no marginal figure. While his place within the early Christian movement needs to be determined with care, it is clear on any reading of Christian origins that, by virtue of the groundbreaking nature of his missionary activity among the Gentiles and the intellectual vitality that he brought to bear on the defence and nurture of his young congregations, Paul was a major player in the first, formative generation of the movement. In sum, then, Paul's letters represent a window into nascent Christianity of inestimable value.

3. The significance of the Pauline corpus is not restricted to its value as source material for the reconstruction of Christian origins, however. The letters not only play a passive role, providing a window into the circumstances lying behind them; they have also been agents in their own right, affecting the lives of their readers—both the original readers and those who subsequently read, as it were, over their shoulders—and thereby helping to shape the history of Christianity and of Western culture as a whole. The Epistle to the Romans, for instance, has had a striking chain of influence—from the unknown early readers who, for whatever reason, preserved the letter in the first place; to Augustine's conversion, precipitated by the random reading in a moment of crisis of a particularly pertinent passage (13:13–14); to Martin Luther's rediscovery of Augustine and his own experience of spiritual release while wrestling with the phrase, 'the just shall live by faith' (1:17) as he prepared lectures on the epistle; to John Wesley's experience of a heart 'strangely warmed' while listening to a reading of the Preface to Luther's commentary; to Karl Barth and his own commentary on the epistle, which represented a dramatic break with the sunny liberalism in which he had been nurtured and a rediscovery and reworking of Reformation themes. This chain of influence, of course, represents a particular strand of Christianity, one in which Paul has been especially revered. But Paul's influence has by no means been limited to the Reformed segment of Christendom. Hymnody, homilies, iconography and other forms of aesthetic representation, across the Christian spectrum and down through the centuries; the nineteenth-century missionary movement; the 'introspective conscience of the west' (Stendahl 1976: 78–96); popular idiom ('all things to all people'; 'thorn in the flesh'; 'charisma'); contemporary Jewish–Christian dialogue; social-scientific models of conversion—the influence of Paul has been pervasive and far-reaching.

4. For these reasons and more, Paul's letters are significant and deserve the careful attention not only of Christian readers but also of all who aspire to an informed perspective on the Western cultural inheritance. But the very things that make for Paul's significance also bring with them various problems that feed into and affect the experience of reading him.

5. For one thing, the sheer bulk of Pauline material in the NT can easily lead readers to overestimate his place and significance in early Christianity. Evidence even from his own letters indicates that Paul was somewhat of a maverick, operating for the most part outside the main circle of earliest Christianity and relating only awkwardly to its original leaders. He may well have represented the wave of the future: since the middle of the second century those characteristic elements that it took all his formidable resources to establish and defend—full and equal membership for Gentile believers, no obligation to adhere to the law of Moses, and so on—have simply been taken for granted as basic elements of the Christian faith. But the very success of Gentile Christianity can serve to obscure the degree to which Paul's mission represented radical innovation in his own day, and this in turn can result in misperceptions of the nature of his thought and rhetoric.

6. In addition, and partly for this reason, Paul has not always fared well at the hands of his interpreters—admirers and champions included. To cite one particular example, the Reformation reading of Paul, in which the theme of justification by faith is identified as the heart of his gospel and the interpretative centre of his thought, is increasingly being seen as a misreading; to approach Paul with the assumption that his concerns and contentions were analogous to those of a Luther or a Calvin is to look at him through a distorting lens that skews some aspects of his theological discourse and leaves others in obscurity. Further, the interpretation of a normative text in a religious culture inevitably has social effects. Thus Paul's name has come to be associated with developments in Western society that many have found undesirable: for example, the treatment of Jews and Judaism as a people rejected by God; the institution of slavery in the eighteenth and nineteenth centuries; the colonialization of Africa and the Far East, to which the activity of Christian missionaries was a contributing factor; patriarchal structures and the exclusion of women from full participation in church and society; intolerant attitudes towards those of homosexual orientation.

Also, Paul has sometimes been blamed for constructing a complex religion centred on sin, guilt, and death, far removed from the life-affirming message of Jesus (cf. Muggeridge and Vidler 1972: 11–16).

7. The very factors making for Paul's significance, then, also serve to condition our perception of his writings, interposing between the modern reader and the letters themselves a set of lenses and filters that shape the reading process. These interposed optical paraphernalia should not be seen simply as an obstruction; the history of the effects of Paul's letters in the centuries between their time of writing and our own day is an important part of the overall significance of the letters themselves. Still, the first step in coming to terms with the letters is to try to bridge the intervening distance and to read the letters directly and on their own terms; put differently, to bracket out the particularities of our own contemporary perspectives and attempt to read the letters as they would have been understood by their original intended readers.

8. This is a laudable goal, towards which a formidable array of Pauline scholars have bent their collective energies over the past two centuries of historical-critical investigation. But here we encounter a second set of problems, arising from the letters themselves: as the author of 2 Peter observed long ago, many aspects of Paul's letters are 'difficult to understand' (2 Pet 3:16). In part, the difficulties are due to the fact that we are dealing with letters *per se*; in part, they derive from the particular way in which Paul writes letters. But in each case, the nature of these writings means that in order to understand them we need to go beyond them, to interpret them in the framework of at least three hypothetical scholarly reconstructions.

9. First, there are the individual contexts presupposed by the letters themselves. As Roetzel (1998) has reminded us, Paul's letters are 'conversations in context'; more to the point, in reading these letters we are hearing only one side of the conversation, with no clear indication of the context. As in any conversation, the epistolary author as conversation partner can simply take for granted a whole set of details crucial to the meaning of the letter but so well known to the intended readers that they require no explicit mention. Who, to take one simple example, was the 'famous brother' (2 Cor 8:17) who accompanied Titus in the delivery of 2 Corinthians 8 and so could remain unnamed in the letter? Or with what strand of early Christianity can we identify those who were 'unsettling' the Galatians (Gal 5:12), and what were their motives? Later readers like ourselves, who are not privy to the whole conversation and its context, are forced to draw out from whatever slender clues the text affords a sense of these contextual taken-for-granteds, as an essential first step in the determination of meaning.

10. Such reconstruction of provenance and life setting forms part of the interpretative task for any individual letter from antiquity (and—*mutatis mutandis*—for any ancient text at all). But in the case of Paul we are dealing not simply with one individual letter, but with a whole series of letters that evidently had an integral role to play in an extended missionary agenda. A proper understanding of any one of them, then, will depend to a certain extent on a second scholarly reconstruction, namely, the larger sequential framework of Paul's own life and activity within which the individual letter finds its place. Here the reconstructive task is both aided and complicated by the existence of the Acts of the Apostles, with its connected narrative of Paul's missionary activity. Aided, in that Acts deliberately sets out to provide us with the kind of sequential account that is glimpsed only occasionally, and with difficulty, in the letters. Complicated, in that the Acts account, partly because of the author's own purposes and partly because of the limitations within which the author did his work, is not infrequently at variance with the picture emerging from the letters themselves. Perhaps this is the place to mention the additional fact that several of the letters bearing Paul's name also bear characteristics that make it difficult to understand them as written by Paul himself. In at least some of these cases it is best to understand them as the product of a Pauline school carrying on his legacy into a subsequent generation. Further, a tradition going back as far as the second century sees the epistle to the Hebrews as written by Paul as well. While there is no scholarly justification for the attribution, the reference to 'our brother Timothy' in Heb 13:23 serves to situate this epistle somewhere in the larger Pauline circle. In any case, the reconstruction of the nature, *modus operandi*, sequence, chronology, and aftermath of Paul's missionary enterprise is another requisite element of the interpretative task.

11. Thirdly, there is an inherently theological dimension to the rhetoric of these letters. To be sure, the letters are not to be read as if they were theological treatises; a recognition of the essentially occasional and situational nature of the letters was a decisive step forward in Pauline scholarship. Nevertheless, while the letters must be seen as responses to particular circumstances in the life of Paul and his communities, it is also evident that to deal with these various contingent situations Paul engaged in a style of theological argumentation that drew on already-existing vocabulary, structures, and patterns of thought. As Dunn (1998: 15) has observed with reference to the search for the theology of Paul, 'the letters themselves indicate the need to go behind the letters themselves'. Again, however, the interpreter is faced with a difficult task. Partly because of the sheer fecundity of Paul's agile mind, and partly because the letters use and allude to his 'theology' without ever laying it out in any systematic way, it has been notoriously difficult to discern the central element or essential structure of his theological thought.

12. A proper understanding of Paul's letters, then, necessarily involves us in substantial projects of contextual reconstruction. In turn, these projects depend for their success on a larger engineering project, that of bridging the social and cultural gap between the modern reader and the first-century Graeco-Roman world. To a modern reader, for example, Paul's language of 'bewitchment' in Gal 3:1 may seem quaintly metaphorical. But in a culture where the power of the evil eye was widely feared, the text would have had quite a different impact (Elliott 1990). Likewise, ancient and modern readers would bring distinctly different cultural assumptions to a reading of 2 Cor 8–9, in which Paul is encouraging the Corinthian Christians to contribute to his collection for the Jerusalem church. In contrast to modern readers in the Western world, who tend to see charitable giving as a universal obligation, Paul's Corinthian converts would have understood benefaction to be the domain of the wealthy, who themselves would

assume the role of benefactor less out of a sense of moral obligation than in expectation of public honour. What we think we know is often a greater barrier to understanding than what we do not know, and this is as true of the cultural assumptions we bring to a reading of the NT as of any other area of life.

13. The foregoing is not meant to discourage the casual or novice reader from reading Paul, as if one has to acquire a massive body of background and contextual knowledge before being able to approach the letters themselves. The process is spiral: initial familiarization with the text raises questions of interpretation and meaning that can be answered only on the basis of further information about the text's original context; increasing awareness of contextual background precipitates further questions that can be answered only on the basis of a more careful and critical reading of the text; and so on. Further, the process is ongoing and open-ended. It is not as if the range of questions diminishes as knowledge increases. As will become apparent not only in this introductory essay but also in the commentaries on the individual letters to follow, there is a great deal of disagreement and debate among Pauline scholars at almost every point. One enters this interpretative spiral, then, not so much to arrive at a definitive interpretation as to become a participant in an ongoing process of discussion, debate, and new insight.

14. The process may be ongoing, but it is not without its key moments and fresh phases. Indeed, this is a particularly exciting time to be engaged in the discussion of Paul and his letters. The final quarter of the twentieth century saw some significant developments: richer descriptions of Paul's cultural environment, both Jewish and Graeco-Roman; fundamental shifts in the way his thought is perceived and put together, especially with reference to his Jewish upbringing and 'conversion'; fruitful application of methods and insights drawn from the social sciences; increased appreciation of the rhetorical and epistolary conventions at work in the letters; and so on.

The purpose of this introductory essay is to lead readers into the interpretative spiral described above and to convey some sense of the current state of the discussion. To do this, the material will be organized as follows.

B. The Sources. 1. Our two main sources of biographical information concerning Paul are the Acts of the Apostles and the letters themselves. There are some additional snippets in later Christian writings—e.g., a stylized descriptive portrait in *Acts of Paul* 3.1; accounts of his martyrdom under Nero (1 Clem. 5.5–7; 6.1; Eusebius *Hist. Eccl.* 2.25). But even if we were to exploit them to the full (e.g. Riesner 1998), we would simply be adding minor embellishments to a portrait based primarily on our two main sources.

At first glance these two sources seem to complement each other neatly. Acts provides us with biographical information on Paul's life and ministry, and the circumstances in which the individual churches were founded; the letters provide us with direct information on his thought and his interaction with churches after he had moved on to new fields of mission. We might seem to be in the happy position of being able to combine two complementary sources to construct a full picture.

2. As has already been observed, however, the use of Acts as a source for Paul is not without problems. For one thing, despite the impression given by the author of Acts (let us for convenience call him Luke) that he is providing us with a full and continuous account of Paul's itinerary, Paul himself makes reference to details—for example, trips (the hasty and painful visit to Corinth in 2 Cor 2:1) and various incidents of hardship (2 Cor 11:23–7, especially the references to shipwrecks, synagogue discipline, and imprisonments)—about which Luke seems unable to tell us anything.

Further, at points where the two accounts do overlap, they are sometimes strikingly at odds. The parade example of this is the narration of Paul's first post-conversion visit to Jerusalem in Gal 1:18–24 and Acts 9:26–30. In Acts, it is a high profile visit. Although the disciples were 'all afraid of him' after Barnabas had convinced 'the apostles' of the reality of his new-found faith, Paul 'went in and out among them in Jerusalem, speaking boldly in the name of the Lord', at least until opposition from the (non-Christian) Hellenists increased to the point that the 'brothers' felt it necessary to escort him to safety in Caesarea. In Galatians, by contrast, the visit is a much less public affair. Paul's purpose in going up to Jerusalem was 'to visit Cephas', which he did for fifteen days, not seeing 'any other apostle except James the Lord's brother'. Even after his departure, he was 'still unknown by sight to the churches of Judea that are in Christ', who simply had oral reports that their former persecutor was now 'proclaiming the faith he once tried to destroy'.

Even when one gives full weight to the diverging purposes of Luke (who wants to emphasize harmony in the early church and the smooth progression of the faith outwards from Jerusalem) and Paul (who wants to downplay his contacts with Jerusalem and to defend his independence as an apostle), the differences between the two accounts are substantial. Acts and the letters are not to be treated simply as equal and complementary sources. Paul's own testimony needs to be given primacy. The letters represent our primary source for his life and thought.

3. Nevertheless, Acts is not simply to be dismissed; Luke clearly has independent access to information about Paul's career. He displays no awareness of Paul as a letter-writer, which means that Acts cannot be seen merely as an embellished narrative presentation of details gleaned from the letters. Further, there are frequent points of contact, in details of itinerary, between Acts and the letters (see the list in Brown 1997: 424). Even the accounts in Gal 1 and Acts 9, as discussed above, despite their differences in detail and emphasis, contain a similar sequence: conversion near Damascus (Gal 1:15–17; Acts 9:1–19); subsequent trip to Jerusalem (Gal 1:18; Acts 9:26); time spent in Cilicia/Tarsus (Gal 1:21; Acts 9:30) and Syria/Antioch (Gal 1:21; Acts 11:25–6). Moving out from Galatians but still within the same sequence of events, the account of Paul's flight from Damascus in Acts 9:23–5 has its first-person counterpart in 2 Cor 11:32–3. Similar observations could be made about Paul's progression down the Greek peninsula (1 Thess 2–3; cf. Acts 16–18) or his final trip to Jerusalem with the collection money (1 Cor 16:1–4; 2 Cor 7–9; Rom 15:25–9; cf. Acts 19:21–21:19). Thus while Acts and the letters are not simply to be interlaced, critical and cautious use can be made of the Acts account to supplement the information on Paul's life and activity contained in the letters.

C. Paul's 'Conversion'. 1. Any biographical accounting of Paul needs to begin with what in popular parlance is called his 'conversion'. The appropriateness of the term is debated, and will be discussed a little later. Without foreclosing on the debate, we will refer to the event as Paul's Damascus transformation or Damascus experience. This experience—which Paul understands as an encounter with the risen Christ—is not only foundational for everything that follows, it is the perspective from which our sources present what they do about anything that precedes. Luke does not seem to tire of the story; after providing a full narrative in Acts 9, he repeats it (with some interesting variations in detail) on no less than two other occasions (22:3–21; 26:2–18). Modern readers might wish that he had used this space instead to fill in some of the gaps in his narrative—the activity of Peter, for example, or the origins of the church in Rome. Paul is somewhat more reticent, speaking of it on three occasions (Gal 1:15–16; 1 Cor 9:1; 1 Cor 15:8–10; perhaps also 2 Cor 4:6), but always in the context of some other issue. Still, the consequences of the experience—the conviction that God had raised Jesus, making him Christ and Lord; the conviction that God had commissioned Paul, making him apostle to the Gentiles—are everywhere present, as assumption or as theme.

2. To reconstruct Paul's biography, then, it is necessary to begin with his Damascus experience. To reconstruct it accurately, however, it is necessary to understand the nature of the experience. It was an event that divided Paul's life into a 'before'—'my earlier life in Judaism' (Gal 1:13)—and an 'after'—'an apostle' (Gal 1:1) 'entrusted with the gospel for the uncircumcised' (Gal 2:7); a proper understanding of Paul depends on how we correlate these three biographical points. More specifically, the characteristic features of Paul's apostolic self-understanding stand in such patent contrast to the typical 'life in Judaism' that one cannot really understand the later Paul without understanding how the transformation worked itself out. How was it that a self-proclaimed 'zealot for the traditions of [his] ancestors' (Gal 1:14) was transformed into a zealous advocate of a mission to Gentiles, offering them a righteous status before God not by adherence to the Torah but by faith in Christ?

3. It was mentioned above that there have been some significant shifts in Pauline scholarship in recent years; one such has to do with the understanding of Paul's Damascus transformation. Older scholarship tended to understand this transformation as involving a perception on Paul's part of some fundamental deficiency in Judaism and his consequent abandonment of Judaism for a different religion that was able to offer what Judaism lacked. In this family of interpretations the appropriateness of the term 'conversion' is assumed. There are several branches of the family. One, stemming from the Reformation, emphasizes Paul's polemical contrast between justification by works and justification by faith. It is assumed that this works/faith contrast represented Paul's fundamental critique of Judaism; he understood Judaism to be a legalistic religion, one in which a person's status with God was something earned through meritorious Torah observance

(works) rather than something offered freely by God in divine grace, to be received in humble faith. The essence of Paul's conversion is understood, in this reading of it, to consist in the recognition that Judaism was a works-religion that did not work, and the correlative discovery that Christianity offered freely, on the basis of faith, the righteous status that Torah-religion was not able to provide. Sometimes such a recognition of the futility of Judaism is understood to be the essence of the Damascus experience itself; in encountering the risen Jesus Paul saw Judaism for the inferior and inadequate religion that it was. Often, however, the recognition is shifted further back, Paul's problem with Judaism seen as something emerging during his upbringing. It is argued, usually with appeal to Rom 7, that Paul's experience of Judaism was one of frustration and despair. He had tried hard to gain God's approval by keeping the law in a zealous fashion, but found that no matter how hard he tried he always fell short. In this reading, his conversion is seen as fundamentally the discovery that Christ provided the solution to an existential problem that he had already experienced in his Jewish upbringing.

4. This is not the only way in which Paul's Damascus transformation is perceived as essentially an abandonment of Judaism. Another interpretation takes its point of departure not from Paul's faith/works contrast but from his universal gospel. How is Paul's interest in Gentiles to be accounted for? The answer, it is suggested, is that Paul came to abandon a frame of reference in which the distinction between Jew and Gentile is central, for one in which that distinction is abolished, one in which 'there is no longer Jew or Greek' (Gal 3:28). Again, such an exchange of one type of religion (this time a particularistic one) for another (a universalistic one) is sometimes seen as the essence of the Damascus experience itself. Just as often, however, it is rooted in the idea that already in his upbringing Paul had experienced frustration with Jewish particularism and, in some interpretations, had struggled, valiantly but vainly, to suppress an attraction to the wider Hellenistic world.

5. Such interpretations, in which Paul's Damascus experience is seen as essentially an abandonment of a Jewish context for something different, have had a long and successful history, at least in part because they seem to provide a coherent explanation of central elements in Paul's post-Damascus frame of reference—especially his role as apostle to the Gentiles, and the gospel he preached to Gentiles, offering them a righteous status before God without demanding adherence to the Torah. But more recent study of Paul has tended to demonstrate that such coherence is purchased at a high price, specifically, an unacceptable level of incoherence with respect to the first of the three biographical points—Paul's earlier life in Judaism.

By the early part of the twentieth century Jewish scholars (e.g. C. Montefiore, S. Schechter, and later H.-J. Schoeps), along with Christians sympathetic to Judaism (e.g. G. F. Moore, J. Parkes), had already pointed out that Judaism was not the legalistic religion of meritorious achievement that it had often been made out to be. Jewish religion, they objected, started not with the Torah but with the covenant, a relationship between God and Israel established entirely on the basis of divine grace. The Torah was given as a means not of earning a relationship with God, but rather of responding in gratitude to God and of maintaining the relationship already established by God's gracious election of Israel. Further, Jewish religion did not require flawless performance of the law, as Paul's argument in Romans and Galatians seems to assume. The law itself recognized the inevitability of sin, making provision, in the sacrificial system, for repentance, atonement, and forgiveness—an aspect of Torah-religion that Paul studiously avoids in the pertinent passages. This more accurate depiction of Judaism has been most convincingly developed and demonstrated by E. P. Sanders (see Sanders 1977), who terms it a religion of 'covenantal nomism' rather than of legalism. Prior to Sanders's work, however, the conclusion often drawn from this argument about the true nature of Judaism has been that if the traditional reading of Paul is accurate, then Paul must have seriously misunderstood Judaism. If Paul really perceived Judaism as a religion of meritorious achievement requiring perfect performance, then his critique of Judaism is badly off-target from the outset.

6. One way of explaining this supposed misunderstanding of Judaism is to lay it at the door of Paul's diaspora upbringing; if Paul had been raised in Judea, closer to the source, he would have experienced a truer form of the faith and thus would have depicted it more accurately (Schoeps 1961: 173). But this leads to a second way in which the traditional interpretations of Paul fail to integrate what we know about his earlier life in Judaism. Not only is it recognized that no sharp distinction can be drawn between Hellenistic and Palestinian Judaism, the idea that Paul fundamentally misunderstood Judaism does not square well with his own comments about his earlier life. For one thing, he locates himself within a traditional, covenant-centred form of the faith. He is a Hebrew of the Hebrews (Phil 3:5; cf. 2 Cor 11:22); a zealot for the traditions of his ancestors (Gal 1:14); a Pharisee, a group for which we have only Palestinian evidence (Phil 3:5; see Hengel and Schwemer 1997: 36). Further, whenever he looks back on this period of his life, he does so with a great deal of pride and satisfaction (Gal 1:13–14; Phil 3:4b–6; 2 Cor 11:22). Phil 3:6 is particularly instructive; as one of the grounds for which he might have confidence in the flesh, he points to the fact that 'as to righteousness under the law, [he was] blameless'. The statement resonates with the pride of accomplishment (blameless!) rather than despair over the impossibility of the law's demands. With the recognition that the 'I' of Romans 7 is not autobiographical (Kümmel 1929), the way has been cleared to ask whether instead of Paul misunderstanding Judaism, Paul's interpreters have misunderstood him.

7. This question has been posed most forcefully by E. P. Sanders in his epoch-making book, Paul and Palestinian Judaism (1977). In the book Sanders demonstrates convincingly that Paul can be much better understood if we assume (1) that in his upbringing he had experienced Judaism as a religion of covenantal nomism, but that (2) in his Damascus experience he had come to believe that God had provided Christ as a means of salvation for all on equal terms, and that (3) since entrance into the community of salvation was through Christ, Torah-observance could not be imposed as a condition of membership. Anticipating some discussion to follow, we need to observe that Sanders leaves a number of loose ends and logical disjunctions; in particular: why 'for all'? Why 'on

equal terms'? Why are Christ and Torah mutually exclusive? But for present purposes, the significant point of Sanders's work is that it opens up the possibility of seeing Paul's Damascus experience as primarily the acceptance of a new set of convictions about Jesus rather than the abandonment of an old set of convictions about Judaism. The way is open to see Paul not as a frustrated Jew, nor as one who fundamentally misunderstood the religion of his ancestors and contemporaries, but as a covenantal nomist who had an experience convincing him that the God of Israel had raised Jesus from death.

8. What emerges, then, is an understanding of Paul's Damascus experience in which it is seen not as the solution to an already-perceived problem with Judaism, nor as the abandonment of one religion (Judaism) for another (Christianity). Instead, the outcome of the experience was in the first instance a new estimation of the person and significance of Jesus in the purposes of the God of Israel. This led to an unprecedented reconfiguration of the constituent elements of Judaism, for reasons that we will explore in a moment. But reconfiguration is quite a different thing from abandonment.

For this reason, 'conversion' has been seen as perhaps not the best term to use to describe Paul's experience. Both in popular parlance and in much social-scientific study, 'conversion' implies a transformation that is more radical, more discontinuous with the convert's past, and more driven by psychological imbalance, than was the case with Paul. At the same time, to describe the experience as a 'call', as Stendahl does (Stendahl 1976: 7–23), is not a fully satisfactory alternative either, even when one gives full value to Paul's use of prophetic call language in Gal 1:15 (cf. Isa 49:1; Jer 1:5). This term fails to do justice to the fact that Paul's experience represented a much more decisive shift, a more sharply demarcated before and after (cf. Phil 3:4–11), than was ever the case with an Isaiah or a Jeremiah. While Paul continued to worship and serve the same God, his framework of service shifted decisively from one organizing centre (Torah) to another (Christ). What term to use, then, for this decisive shift? One alternative is to return to 'conversion', redefining it so that both continuity and discontinuity are preserved (Segal 1990). Such an approach can claim support from more recent social-scientific studies (e.g. Rambo 1993), which recognize a much broader range of conversion types. Perhaps the safer approach, however, is to choose less loaded terms, such as transformation or reconfiguration.

9. But why was the reconfiguration so sharply polarized? Why were the two organizing centres—Torah and Christ—set over against each other in such an antithetical way? Or to pose the question with respect to the comparative biographies of Paul and James, who both became leaders in the church as the result of an experience understood to be an encounter with the risen Christ (for James, see 1 Cor 15:7): why did the experience lead in Paul's case to a Christ–Torah antithesis while in the case of James of Jerusalem, who seemed to be able to combine Christ-faith and Torah-religion in a much more harmonious way, it led rather to a Christ–Torah synthesis?

10. In contrast to Paul's conversion per se, the answer to this question does seem to lie in his pre-Damascus experience. Even prior to his own experience of Christ, Paul had already

come to some conclusions about the incompatability of Christ-faith and Torah-religion. What is important here is not simply *that* Paul persecuted the church, but that he understood it as an expression of *zeal* (Phil 3:6; cf. Gal 1:14). In the context of Torah-piety, zeal implies more than simply fervour. At least since the time of the Maccabees, zeal and zealotry referred to the willingness to use force to defend Torah-religion from some perceived threat (e.g. 1 Macc 2:24, 26, 27, 50; *Jub.* 30.18; Jdt 9:2–4; see Donaldson 1997: 285–6; Dunn 1998: 350–2). If Paul's persecution of the church was an act of zeal, then he must, even at this early stage, have seen Christ-religion and Torah-religion as mutually exclusive. Further, since even after his Damascus experience this incompatability between Christ and Torah seems to have remained (even if transformed), the conflict between the two must have been of such a nature that it could not be resolved simply by changing his estimation of Jesus. The Christ–Torah antithesis must have been perceived as a more fundamental incompatibility.

11. What, then, was the nature of this incompatibility? Several possibilities have been explored in scholarly discussion (Donaldson 1997: 169–72). Some suggest that the idea of a suffering and dying Messiah was in itself an affront to Jewish expectation and thus incompatible with Torah-religion. Others focus on the specific means of Jesus' death—crucifixion—noting that the Torah itself sees as cursed 'anyone hung on a tree' (Deut 21:22–3), a text that by the first century was being interpreted with respect to crucifixion (4QpNah 1.7–8; 11QTemple 64.12; cf. Gal 3:13). Still others suggest that Paul's estimation of the Torah had been deeply affected by the fact that it was precisely his zeal for the law that had led him to persecute Christ's church. But none of these suggestions seem to produce a tension between Christ and Torah so intractable that a well-motivated Jewish believer could not have found a way to resolve it.

12. My suggestion moves in a different direction, and builds on two more fundamental aspects of Jewish and Jewish-Christian belief: (1) the relationship between Torah and Messiah in Jewish expectation; and (2) the unprecedented 'already/not yet' shape of early Christian belief. In Jewish patterns of thought (at least those that included the concept of a Messiah), the respective functions of Torah and Messiah were neatly differentiated by the distinction between this age and the age to come. In this age, the Torah functioned as a badge of membership or a boundary marker for the covenant people of God. To live a life of loyalty to the Torah was a mark of membership in the covenant community; to be a member in good standing was to be righteous; it was the community of the righteous as demarcated by the Torah in this age that could expect to be vindicated by God in the age to come, when the Messiah appeared. There was thus no confusion of roles: the Torah served to determine the identity of the people whom the Messiah would come to deliver; put differently, the Messiah did not function as a boundary marker or badge of membership.

13. But the Christian message—that God had revealed the identity of the coming Messiah by raising Jesus from death—had the effect of blurring this neat distinction. The Christ who would come to redeem the righteous in the age to come had already appeared before this age was at an end.

How, then, was the community of the righteous to be determined in the period between the resurrection and the end? Was it defined by adherence to Torah or to Christ? Would the community redeemed by Christ at the eschaton be one demarcated by Torah-observance or by Christ-adherence? The unprecedented two-stage appearance of the Messiah in Christian belief had the effect of putting Christ and Torah in tension with each other, as rival boundary markers for the people of God. The overlapping of the ages in Christian proclamation brought Christ and Torah into conflict.

14. My suggestion is that because of his perspective as an outsider, the pre-Christian Paul perceived this rivalry and conflict much more clearly than those inside. He was a faithful observer of the Torah, 'as to righteousness under the law, blameless' (Phil 3:6). But the Christian message as he heard it implied that this was not enough; to truly belong to the community of the righteous, he had to believe in Christ. He also observed that the church was prepared to admit as full members many who, 'as to righteousness under the law', were far from 'blameless'. Torah observance, it appeared, was also unnecessary. Undergirding his persecution of the church, then, was a fundamental perception that—whether the early Christians recognized it fully or not—the Christ they preached represented a categorical rival to the Torah in its community-defining role. Since this rivalry was rooted not simply in Paul's lack of belief in Christ but in the nature of the Christian message itself, it did not disappear with his new belief in Christ. The Christ–Torah antithesis remained, even though his perception of its implications shifted dramatically.

15. One final element of Paul's Damascus experience requires mention here, though we can deal with it only briefly. In the discussion carried out above concerning Paul's description of his experience as a 'call', we did not pay much attention to the focus of the call—'to proclaim [God's Son] among the Gentiles' (Gal 1:16). At least in retrospect, then, Paul sees his role as 'apostle to the Gentiles' (Rom 11:13) as the direct outcome and inner meaning of his Damascus experience. But how are we to understand his all-embracing concern for the salvation of the Gentiles?

This question, too, has been altered by the interpretative shift described above. In older patterns of interpretation, Paul's interest in the Gentiles has been understood as entailing, or as the result of, an abandonment of Judaism. In his conversion experience, it was argued, Paul left behind a world where the distinction between Jew and Gentile was fundamental, and entered a wider world where there was no differentiation. The ways in which this line of interpretation were worked out varied with the ways in which the process of abandonment was reconstructed (see above, and also Donaldson 1997: 18–27). But the heart of the matter in each case was that Paul's 'universalism' (i.e. his concern for Gentile salvation) was tied up with a rejection of Jewish particularism.

16. More recent study, however, has brought to the fore two things that suggest a different explanation. The first has to do with Paul himself, the second with Jewish attitudes towards Gentile salvation. First, it is clear that 'Jew' and 'Gentile' continue to be important categories for Paul. While he insists that there is no distinction with respect to sin ('all, both Jews

and Greeks, are under... sin', Rom 3:9) or salvation ('for there is no distinction between Jew and Greek', Rom 10:12), this does not mean that Jewishness has lost all theological significance for Paul. Indeed, by describing himself as apostle to the *Gentiles*, he indicates that he continues to inhabit a world where the distinction between Jew and Gentile is operative. Paul sees himself as a Jew (Rom 11:1), commissioned by the God of Israel to bring a message of salvation, not to an undifferentiated mass of generic humanity, but to Gentiles, that part of humanity that exists in distinction from Israel. Further, the ultimate goal of this mission is the final salvation of 'all Israel' (Rom 11:26). What is needed, then, is a much more Israel-centred understanding of Paul's interest in the Gentiles.

17. This brings us to the second point. While Jewish self-understanding is undeniably particularistic (the one God of all has chosen Israel from among the nations for a special covenanted relationship), Judaism also had its own forms of universalism. That is, by Paul's day Judaism had developed ways of finding a place for Gentiles within God's saving purposes for the world, ways that offered Gentiles a share in salvation without denying the special nature of Israel's own covenant relationship. One of these patterns of universalism, of course, was proselytism; the community of Israel was willing to accept as full members of the family of Abraham those Gentiles who embraced the Torah and its way of life (e.g. Jdt 14:10; Tacitus, *Hist.* 5.5.2). Another pattern, based on a quite different perception of things, was prepared to see the possibility of Gentiles being accounted righteous and having a share in the age to come *as Gentiles*, without having to accept those aspects of the Torah that differentiated Gentiles from Jews (e.g. Jos. *Ant.* 20.34–48; *t. Sanh.* 13.2). A third looked to the future, and expected that as one of the consequences of Israel's end-time redemption, many Gentiles would finally acknowledge the God of Israel and thus be granted a share in the blessings of the age to come (e.g. Isa 2:2–4; Tob 14:5–7).

18. This is not the place to survey the pertinent Jewish material in any detail. Nor is it possible here to explore Paul's conceptions concerning the Gentiles and their place 'in Christ' against this background (on both points see Donaldson 1997). For present purposes it is sufficient to say that Paul's Gentile mission is best understood as a Christ-centred reinterpretation of one of these Israel-centred patterns of universalism. That is, Paul's concern for the Gentiles had its origin in attitudes already present in Judaism, even though with his Damascus experience they came to be oriented around a different centre. His call 'to proclaim [God's Son] among the Gentiles' results not from a rejection of Jewish particularism but from a reinterpretation, from his standpoint 'in Christ', of some aspect of Jewish universalism.

Later on in this introductory essay we will return to the matter of Paul's thought and its characteristic themes and structure. For the present, however, we need to discuss the temporal and geographical framework of his life.

D. Paul's Formative Years. 1. '*My earlier life in Judaism*' (Gal 1:13): Paul does not tell us a great deal about his Jewish upbringing and pre-Christian activities. This is not due to reticence; when it serves his purposes, he can parade his credentials and accomplishments with great flourish (esp. Gal 1:13–15; 1 Cor 15:9; Phil 3:4–6; 2 Cor 11:22; Rom 11:1). But his purposes are never purely biographical; what he tells us and how is determined by the rhetorical needs of the moment. In addition to the explicit information he does convey in passing, of course, the letters also contain a wealth of implicit evidence—familiarity with the Mediterranean world, facility in Greek, knowledge of the Septuagint and of Jewish interpretative tradition, and so on.

Still, the information conveyed to us by Paul himself is much less specific than that contained in the Acts account, where it appears both in the narration of his persecuting activity (7:58–8:3; 9:1–3) and in the speeches of self-defence made after his final arrest (22:1–5, 19–20; 23:6; 26:4–12). But while its secondary status needs to be remembered, the information in Acts, with only two or three exceptions, is both consistent with Paul's own statements and not so patently in keeping with Luke's special purposes as to come under suspicion.

2. According to Luke, Paul was a diaspora Jew—specifically, a native of Tarsus, the prosperous chief city of the region of Cilicia (21:39; 22:3). The letters certainly confirm the general identification; even without Acts, Paul's facility in Greek and the ease with which he navigated the Hellenistic world identify him as a diaspora Jew. With respect to the more specific reference to Tarsus, the only evidence in the letters with a bearing on the matter is Paul's statement that after his first visit to Jerusalem he 'went into the regions of Syria and Cilicia' (Gal 1:21). Syria is understandable; someone who had spent time in Damascus (Gal 1:17) could readily gravitate to Antioch, an important centre of the Jewish diaspora. But Cilicia is less to be expected, unless, as Luke indicates, Paul had a special personal affinity for the area. This detail in Galatians, then, lends a definite plausibility to Luke's identification of Tarsus as Paul's home city.

Luke goes further, however, to identify Paul as a citizen both of Tarsus (21:39) and of Rome (16:37–9; 22:25–9; 23:27), the latter by birth. This is not outside the realm of possibility. Jews certainly could be Roman citizens without compromising their traditional observances (e.g. Jos. *Ant.* 14.228–37). Tarsus itself was lavishly rewarded for services rendered, both by Mark Antony after the death of Cassius and Brutus (Appian, *Historia*, 5.1.7), and by Octavian after the battle of Actium (Dio Chrysostom, *Orationes*, 34.8). One could readily imagine circumstances in which even a Jewish family would have been able to share in this largesse. At the same time, however, full weight needs to be given to two additional items of information. First, Paul himself nowhere alludes to Roman citizenship, despite his readiness to boast about other items on his curriculum vitae when it served his purposes. Second, Paul's Roman citizenship could be seen as too neatly consistent with one of Luke's major themes—namely, that Roman officials repeatedly took the Christians' side, or at least demonstrated that they considered the movement to be no real threat to the order of the empire. But on the other hand, the sole premiss of Paul's final trip to Rome, as it is narrated in Acts, is his Roman citizenship, with the concomitant right of appeal to the imperial tribunal (Acts 25:10–12, 21; 26:32). Unless we are prepared to dismiss this whole account, despite the verisimilitude of its first-person narration (27:1–28:16), we need to give at least some credence to Luke's statements about Paul's citizenship.

3. As we have already observed, however, Paul's own self-description places more emphasis on his Jewish identity and credentials. To put this information into its proper perspective, we need to keep in mind the extent and significance of the Jewish diaspora. By the beginning of the first century, as was observed by the geographer and historian Strabo, 'this people [i.e. of Judea] has already made its way into every city, and it is not easy to find any place in the habitable world which has not received this nation and in which it has not made its power felt' (quoted by Jos. *Ant.* 14.114–18). Of interest in this statement is not only the geographical spread of Jewish communities (also Jos. *J. W.* 2.399; *Ag. Ap.* 2.38–9; Philo, *Flacc.* 7.45; Acts 2:5–11), but also what this translation calls their 'power', rendering a Greek verb that usually has the sense 'to gain the mastery of, to prevail over'. The word is not to be taken literally, as if Jews had become dominant in any of the cities where they had taken up residence. But it does describe the fact that in city after city Jews had been able to create and maintain Torah-centred islands in the midst of the larger Hellenistic sea. And perhaps this image distorts things somewhat, in that Jewish communities were by no means sealed off from the life and culture of the cities that sustained them. The example of Sardis, where the Jewish community was able to acquire space for their synagogue in the central civic edifice that also housed the bath and gymnasium, is perhaps a little late (3rd cent. CE) to be directly relevant. But any difference between this example and the circumstances of diaspora Jews in the first century in Sardis and elsewhere is one of degree, not of kind. Diaspora realities can also be seen reflected in the long list, compiled by Josephus, of decrees issued by Julius Caesar and his successors which defined and protected the rights of the Jewish communities in various cities of Asia and elsewhere (Jos. *Ant.* 14.186–264). While not as much is known of the Jewish community in Tarsus as in some other cities, a Jewish presence in the first century is nevertheless 'well attested' (Murphy-O'Connor 1996: 33).

4. Paul's biographical statements, then, brief and tangential though they may be, come more vividly to life when placed in the context of this vibrant diaspora reality. It was in one of these Greek-speaking Jewish communities, integrated into the life of the larger city but without wholesale assimilation, that he was born (perhaps in the first decade of the century) and nurtured in the ancestral faith. There were inevitably different degrees of Hellenization within the diaspora, but Paul locates his origins at the more rigorously observant end of the spectrum. While most (male) Jews could presumably describe themselves, as Paul does in Phil 3:5, as 'circumcised on the eighth day', and 'a member of the people of Israel', not all would be able to name their tribe (Benjamin), or—since the term probably indicates facility in Hebrew or Aramaic—to categorize themselves as 'a Hebrew born of Hebrews' (cf. 2 Cor 11:22).

The next item in the Philippian catalogue—'as to the law, a Pharisee' (Phil 3:5)—is a little harder to envisage in a diaspora setting, however. While Jews everywhere were identified by their adherence to the law, the only evidence we have for Pharisees as a specific group stems from Judea. Here the information from Acts is relevant, for Luke identifies Jerusa-

lem as the place of Paul's education. Speaking to the Jerusalem crowd after his arrest, Paul is depicted as saying: 'I am a Jew, born in Tarsus in Cilicia, but brought up in this city at the feet of Gamaliel, educated strictly according to our ancestral law' (Acts 22:3). This reading of the verse takes the latter two participial clauses (brought up, educated) as referring to the same process—study under Gamaliel. It is possible, however, to read the verse as referring to two stages—primary nurture (brought up in this city) and secondary training (educated strictly at the feet of Gamaliel according to our ancestral law). This latter reading, which suggests that Paul moved to Jerusalem as a child, is probably more consistent with the comment in Acts 23:6 that he was also the 'son of Pharisees'.

5. But is it consistent with Paul's own statements about Jerusalem? There is a significant body of scholarship that rejects wholesale Luke's identification of Jerusalem as the locale for both Paul's education and his persecuting activity (e.g. Knox 1950: 34–6; Haenchen 1971: 297, 625). This rejection is based partly on a consideration of Luke's purposes: it is in keeping with his interpretative programme (cf. Acts 1:8) to have the apostle responsible for taking the gospel 'to the ends of the earth' to be linked closely with Jerusalem. But further, it is based more fundamentally on Paul's own statement that even after his conversion and first visit to Jerusalem, he 'was still unknown by sight to the churches of Judea' (Gal 1:22). Surely, it is argued, the Jerusalem church would have known its chief persecutor.

6. In the context of Galatians, however, Paul is talking about his contacts with Jerusalem as a Christian: apart from Cephas and James, he declares, the church in Jerusalem and Judea had not seen the transformed Paul with their own eyes. With respect to the possibility of a period of residence in Jerusalem, then, Paul's statement that he was a Pharisee weighs in more heavily than does his comment about the churches in Judea (Murphy-O'Connor 1996: 52–4). This does not mean, however, that Luke's depiction is to be accepted *in toto*. Surely if Paul had had any meaningful association with Gamaliel it would have been included in one of his catalogues of Jewish credentials. The claim to be a 'son of Pharisees' probably belongs to a similar category.

7. In all probability, then, Paul journeyed to Jerusalem as a young man, where he joined the Pharisees, pursuing his 'zeal for the traditions of his ancestors', and 'advancing in Judaism beyond many of [his] people of the same age' (Gal 1:14). Probably we are to see him as attached to one of the Hellenistic synagogues in Jerusalem, perhaps even the 'Synagogue of the Freedmen' (Hengel 1991: 69), which included in its membership expatriates of Cilicia (Acts 6:9). It is also possible that during this period he took a special interest in Gentile proselytes. In Gal 5:11 he refers to a time when he 'was preaching circumcision'. In the context of Galatians, this statement means more than simply that he himself was once a Torah-observer; it means that he once was engaged in encouraging Gentiles to be circumcised and thus to become full adherents of Torah-religion (cf. Gal 5:3). When was this? It is unlikely that there was a period after his Damascus experience where he preached a kind of Judaizing gospel to Gentiles. The statement more likely refers to his pre-Damascus period, where we might envisage him as playing the same sort of role with Gentile synagogue-adherents as Eleazar did with King Izates of Adiabene (Jos. *Ant.* 20.43–5), namely, insisting that only by becoming full proselytes would they be pleasing to God.

8. It is also during this period that Paul's zeal 'for the traditions of [his] ancestors' (Gal 1:14) took particular expression in his persecution of the nascent Christian movement (Gal 1:14, 23; Phil 3:6; 1 Cor 15:9). As has been noted already, there is no need to set Gal 1:22 over against the Acts account, and to restrict Paul's persecuting activity to an area outside Judea (Damascus). We can accept the Acts account at least to this point, that it was in Jerusalem that Paul took offence at the activity of the early Christians, particularly the Greek-speaking 'Hellenists' (Acts 6) who formulated their message in a manner that was much more critical of the temple and much less acquiescent to the Jewish religious establishment (cf. Acts 7) than the 'Hebrews'. Perceiving the activity of the Hellenistic Jewish Christians as a threat to the well-being of the Torah-centred way of life, and also at a deeper level perceiving their basic message as setting Christ over against the Torah, he engaged in 'zealous' repression of the movement. When this resulted in the flight of Christians from Jerusalem to other Jewish centres, Paul became involved in attempts to repress the activity of the new movement in Damascus. That is, we can accept the basic itinerary of Acts 8 and 9, though some of the details (the ferocity of Saul's own activity, imprisonment rather than simple disciplinary action, official letters from the high priest) may well be the result of Lukan exaggeration.

9. '*When God was pleased to reveal his Son to (in) me*' (Gal 1:15–16): Somewhere near Damascus (cf. 'returned', Gal 1:17), Paul had an experience that led to a radical reassessment of the person of Jesus and a thoroughgoing reconfiguration of his foundational convictions. In the history of interpretation, various attempts have been made to account for this experience without remainder by appealing to psychological pre-conditioning or even physiological manifestations (e.g. an epileptic seizure). But to reduce the range of possible explanations in this way is to fail to recognize the reality of religious experience, on the phenomenological level at the very least. Religious phenomena certainly have their psychological and physiological dimensions, but it is unfair to religious communities in general to reduce religious experience to non-religious categories.

Paul, of course, understood this experience as an encounter with the risen Christ (Gal 1:15–16; 1 Cor 9:1; 15:8–9) and, moreover, as belonging to the same set of experiences as had brought the movement into being in the first place (1 Cor 15:5–8). But the reality of a religious experience is one thing, the interpretation placed on it by the subject quite another. Any attempt to assess the reality lying behind the statement, 'Christ appeared to me', belongs in a book whose purposes are quite different from those of a commentary such as this.

10. To understand Paul and his letters, however, it is necessary to recognize that he saw no gap or caesura between the experience and the interpretation. For him the subjective experience ('God . . . was pleased to reveal his Son *in* me', Gal 1:15–16, my lit. tr.) and the objective reality ('[Christ] appeared . . . *to* me'; 1 Cor 15:8) were a seamless unity.

Further, to understand Paul it is necessary to recognize two things that flowed from this experience. One was a reconfiguration of his basic, world-ordering convictions. Paul had already come to some conclusions about how the message of a crucified and risen Messiah related to the basic convictions of covenantal nomism. His previous perceptions of Christ 'according to the flesh' (2 Cor 5:16) produced the conviction that Christ and Torah were mutually exclusive; they were rival ways of marking the community of the righteous. Consequently his new conviction—that God had raised Jesus and that the claims made about him in Christian preaching were thus grounded in God's action—was not a simple, self-contained conviction; rather, it set in motion a thoroughgoing process of convictional restructuring. Not that his new convictions were simply the inversion of the old. He continued to believe in the God of Israel, in Israel's election, even in the divine origin of the Torah. But these native convictions were redrawn around a new centre, the foundational conviction that the crucified Jesus had been raised by God.

11. The second thing that flowed from Paul's Damascus experience was that it was also and at the same time a call to be an apostle. Despite the chronological gap between the first experiences recounted in 1 Cor 15:5–7 and Paul's own—a gap alluded to in v. 8 ('last of all, as to someone untimely born') but ultimately dismissed as inconsequential—Paul claims that it constituted him an apostle on an equal basis with the others (vv. 10–11; cf. Gal 1:1). One can readily imagine how this claim would have sounded to those 'who were already apostles before [him]' (Gal 1:17) and their Jerusalem followers, especially when this johnny-come-lately began to insist on a law-free mission to Gentiles with Paul himself as its divinely commissioned apostle. An uneasy relationship with the Jerusalem church marked Paul's ministry from the outset.

12. '*So that I might proclaim him among the Gentiles*' (Gal 1:16): Looking back, Paul locates the origin of his Gentile mission in the Damascus experience itself. Some interpreters have argued that this is just a matter of retrospect, Paul here collapsing a process that might have taken years, into the event that set the process in motion in the first place (e.g. Watson 1986: 28–38). But not only is there no evidence for such an intervening phase of any length, Paul's statements relating to his activity in Arabia suggest that from the very beginning he saw himself as commissioned to carry the gospel to Gentiles. Paul's sojourn in Arabia (Gal 1:17) is sometimes seen as a period of quiet reflection, where he contemplated the significance of his experience and worked out its theological implications. No doubt there was a period of time in which such reflection took place; certainly his new theological framework did not emerge instantaneously. But Paul's time in Arabia seems to have attracted the unfavourable attention of King Aretas himself (2 Cor 11:32). One does not usually arouse the ire of a ruling monarch by engaging in solitary theological reflection. Paul's Arabian experience suggests that he attempted to carry out an apostolic ministry among non-Jews at a very early date. If there was a period of reflection, we should think in terms of weeks, not years.

13. From a first-century Judean perspective, Arabia was the kingdom of the Nabataeans, with its capital in Petra (Jos. *J.W.* 1.125: 'the capital of the Arabian kingdom, called Petra').

This means that Paul's sojourn in Arabia in Gal 1:17 needs to be co-ordinated with the account of his escape from the agents of King Aretas in Damascus (2 Cor 11:30–3). The reference here is to Aretas IV, king of the Nabataeans from about 9 BCE to 39 CE. Murphy-O'Connor (1996: 5–7) argues that Damascus came under Nabataean control in 37 CE, which would then have been when Paul's departure from Damascus took place, though certainty is not possible (cf. Riesner 1998: 84–9). Presumably Paul had created enough of a disturbance through his evangelizing activity in Arabia that he had to return to Damascus (Gal 1:17), which in turn became too hot for him to remain once Aretas had gained control of the city. This evidence suggests, then, that Paul's statement in Gal 1:16 should be taken at its temporal face value: right from the beginning, he felt himself called as an apostle with a special commission for the Gentiles.

14. '*Up to Jerusalem . . . into the regions of Syria and Cilicia . . . Antioch*' (Gal 1:18, 21; 2:11): Of the other events in the period between his Damascus experience and the start of the missionary activity reflected in the letters, Paul tells us very little. 'After three years' he journeyed to Jerusalem, with the specific intention of 'getting to know' Cephas/Peter, or of 'making his acquaintance' (Gal 1:18; on this sense of the verb *historein*, see Jos. *J.W.* 6.81). Paul's larger purpose in Galatians 1 and 2 is to minimize his contacts with 'those who were already apostles before [him]' (Gal 1:17), in order to establish the point that he 'did not receive [his gospel] from a human source, nor was [he] taught it, but [he] received it through a revelation of Jesus Christ' (Gal 1:12). While this statement underlines the centrality of the Damascus experience for Paul's new commitment to Christ and the gospel, it should not be interpreted as implying that his early Christian experience was isolated and individual and that other Christians played no part in his formation. Presumably he did not baptize himself (Rom 6:3). Likewise, he was able to count on friends—Christians, in all probability—to help him over the city wall in Damascus (note the passive in 2 Cor 11:33: 'I was let down'). Even before his first visit to Jerusalem, then, he had been incorporated into a Christian community as a new convert, with all the socialization that would have entailed. Further, he describes such central Christian elements as the facts of the gospel itself (1 Cor 15:1–7) and the narrative of the last supper (1 Cor 11:23) as material that he had 'received' and then 'handed on', using the accepted, formal vocabulary for the transmission of tradition. It is probably not without significance that the two proper names mentioned in the summary of the gospel in 1 Cor 15:3–7 (Cephas, James) are precisely the two people that he met on his first Jerusalem visit (Gal 1:18–19). As C. H. Dodd is famously reported to have said, surely in two weeks Paul and Peter found more to talk about than simply the weather.

15. Of Paul's time in 'the regions of Syria and Cilicia' (Gal 1:21), very little can be said, unless we disregard the order in which these two geographical regions are listed and understand 'Syria' to refer to the kind of scenario recounted in Acts 11:25–6, where Paul was engaged as Barnabas's junior partner in a ministry of teaching and church leadership in Antioch. Be that as it may, other statements of Paul confirm the general picture arising from the Acts account: he was resident for a time in Antioch (both Cephas and James's delegation 'came' to Antioch, while Paul and Barnabas were already there; Gal 2:11–12); and he was associated with Barnabas in the earlier part of his known ministry but probably not later (the only evidence for direct association appears in Gal 2:1, 9, 13; cf. 1 Cor 9:6). Paul's arrival in Antioch brings his formative period to an end and sets the stage for the more public ministry narrated in Acts and reflected in his letters.

E. The Chronology and Sequence of Paul's Mission. 1. Any full chronological reconstruction of Paul's active ministry requires the co-ordination of three interdependent lines of investigation: (1) discerning the relative chronology of the different geographical stages of his mission; (2) identifying some fixed dates as anchor points for an absolute chronology; and (3) placing the letters at their appropriate points within this chronological framework. This is not the place, of course, to attempt any such reconstruction. Even if it were possible to do so in a reasonably concise way, it would be inappropriate here; the authors of each of the sections to follow must be allowed the freedom to interpret their assigned segment of the Pauline corpus within their own reconstruction of Paul's career. What is required at this point is a more general introduction to the problems inhering in the evidence, the points at which crucial decisions need to be made, and the resultant range of reconstructions.

2. As might well be expected, the role of Acts is once again a key factor in the discussion. In both Acts and the letters Paul's mission activity is punctuated by visits to Jerusalem, and the main reconstructions of Pauline chronology are differentiated by their approach to these visits. Acts recounts no less than five such visits:

Visit 1:	Post-conversion visit (9:26–30)
Intervening activity:	Time spent in Tarsus and Antioch (9:30; 11:25–6)
Visit 2:	Famine relief visit (11:27–9; 12:25)
Intervening activity:	Mission activity in Cyprus and southern Asia Minor (13:1–14:28)
Visit 3:	Jerusalem Council visit (15:1–30)
Intervening activity:	Mission activity in Macedonia and Achaia (16:1–18:17)
Visit 4:	Unspecified visit (18:18–23)
Intervening activity:	Mission activity in Ephesus and Asia (18:24–19:41)
Visit 5:	Collection visit (20:1–21:26)
Subsequent events:	Arrest, hearings, journey to Rome (21:27–28:31)

Two preliminary observations should be made about the final two visits. First, while Luke presents the fourth visit as a matter of some urgency to Paul (cf. 18:20–1), he provides no information at all about either the reason for the journey or its outcome. Second, while Luke is aware of the fact that the fifth visit was for the purpose of delivering collection money to Jerusalem (24:17), this aspect of the final journey is very much played down in Acts in comparison to the letters.

3. In the letters themselves, by contrast, there is evidence of only three visits:

Visit A.   Post-conversion visit (Gal 1:18)
Visit B.   Jerusalem consultation (Gal 2:1–10)

Visit C. Collection visit (1 Cor 16:1–4; Rom 15:25; cf. 2 Cor 8–9).

Several preliminary observations should be made about this list as well. To start with, the first two visits are presented in conjunction with some additional chronological information: the first visit occurred three years after Paul's Damascus experience (Gal 1:18), and the second visit took place 'after fourteen years' (Gal 2:1)—though whether the fourteen-year period begins with the first visit or with the Damascus experience is not specified in the text and is a matter of some scholarly dispute. Further, since Paul's purpose in this section of Galatians is to make the point that his contacts with Jerusalem were minimal, the context requires that the list be complete. That is, the cogency of his argument would have been in jeopardy if he had failed to mention a visit; thus prior to the writing of Galatians, Paul had made two, and only two, visits to Jerusalem. Finally, the third visit, to deliver the 'collection for the saints' (1 Cor 16:1), appears only in prospect; in all the references it is still a journey that lies in the future.

Of these two sets of visits, the first and the last in each case obviously correspond with each other, despite differences in detail. It is more difficult, however, to make sense of what comes in between. There are evident similarities between the meetings recounted in Acts 15 and Gal 2:1–10: the same participants (Paul, Barnabas, Peter, James), dealing with the same issue (circumcision of Gentile converts), coming to the same general decision (legitimacy of the Gentile mission). The majority of interpreters take these two passages as variant accounts of the same event (i.e. B = 3), and develop a chronological framework on the basis of this and other evident points of contact between Acts and the letters (with varying estimations of the reliability of information found only in Acts).

4. In addition to this majority position, however, there are two other minority approaches to Paul's chronological framework that need to be mentioned. One of them originated with the work of William Ramsay (1907), who was particularly concerned to demonstrate the historical reliability of Acts. The majority viewpoint described above tends towards the conclusion that Luke was mistaken in recounting an intervening visit between the post-conversion visit and that of the Jerusalem Council (i.e. the famine relief visit), since Paul's argument in Galatians leaves no room for it. In the position developed by Ramsay and followed by a number of others (e.g. Bruce 1977), it is argued instead that the consultation described in Gal 2:1–10 took place during the famine relief visit (i.e. B = 2). They argue that the private nature of this consultation (Gal 2:2) is more in keeping with Acts 11 than with Acts 15, and that Paul's statement of his eagerness to remember the poor (Gal 2:10) can readily be correlated with the famine relief project. Essential to this approach are two assumptions about the letter to the Galatians: first, that Galatians was written prior to the Jerusalem Council of Acts 15—perhaps the same delegation from Jerusalem that was creating dissension in Antioch (Acts 15:1) was pressuring the Galatian churches as well; and second, that the 'churches of Galatia' were those founded by Paul and Barnabas in Pisidian Antioch, Iconium, Derbe, and Lystra during the so-called first missionary journey

(Acts 13 and 14), cities that were located in the southern part of the Roman province of Galatia (though the region of the ethnic Galatians lay further to the north). While this approach is often dismissed as special pleading in defence of Acts, there is a case that could be made on the basis of Galatians itself, which contains details that might suggest an early date for the letter (e.g. the prominence of Barnabas and absence of Timothy; the absence of any explicit mention of the collection project or injunctions to contribute; the restriction of his whereabouts between the first two visits to the regions of Syria and Cilicia).

5. The other minority viewpoint, pioneered by John Knox (1950), attempts to build a chronology almost entirely on the basis of information in the letters. In addition to the Jerusalem visits, there are three chronological sequences appearing explicitly in the letters: (1) from Damascus to the confrontation with Peter (Gal); (2) missionary activity in the Greek peninsula (1 Thess); (3) travels in connection with the collection (1 Cor, 2 Cor, Rom). Knox, followed by a number of others (e.g. Hurd 1965; Lüdemann 1984), have argued that according to Paul's own statements there could not have been any more than three visits to Jerusalem. The key to this reconstruction is the injunction in Gal 2:10 that Paul 'remember the poor', which is understood to mark the inception of the collection project. That is, at the Jerusalem Council, in return for the recognition of his Gentile mission, Paul undertook a project to raise money from his Gentile churches as a sign of good faith towards the Jerusalem church. Since this was the project that occupied much of his time during the final, Ephesus-based phase of his known missionary activity, the founding of churches in Galatia, Macedonia, and Achaia must have happened prior to the Jerusalem Council; that is, this missionary activity is located in the fourteen-year period mentioned in Gal 2:1. This reconstruction has the effect (though not the intent) of placing the Jerusalem Council at a point in the sequence corresponding to the unspecified visit of Acts 18:18–23.

6. To this point, the discussion has had to do with relative chronology. In order to develop an absolute chronology, it is necessary to determine some fixed dates. Paul himself is not all that helpful in this regard. The reference to King Aretas in 2 Cor 11:32 is the only instance where he names an otherwise identifiable secular figure. Still, one reference is better than none. As observed above, Murphy-O'Connor (1996: 5–7) has argued that Paul's departure from Damascus can be dated to about 37 CE; while this may represent more precision than the evidence allows, at least one can say that the event had to have taken place before Aretas's death in 39 or 40 (Riesner 1998: 84–9). The other possible anchor-point is provided by the reference to Paul's appearance before Gallio, the proconsul of Achaia (Acts 18:12). In 1905 an inscription was discovered at Delphi containing the text of a letter from Claudius to the city, which also referred to Gallio as proconsul. Since the term of office for a proconsular governor of a province was normally one year, commencing on the first of July, it is possible to fix Paul's appearance before Gallio to some time in the latter part of 51 CE (Murphy-O'Connor 1996: 15–22; Riesner 202–11). This, of course, assumes that Luke's report is reliable; advocates of a letters-based chronology place Paul's time in Corinth much earlier, and thus are required to dismiss the Acts account entirely.

7. To illustrate how the different approaches to Paul's chronology work out in practice, it will be useful to compare three chronologies—that of Murphy-O'Connor (1996), representing an approach that makes significant, albeit critical, use of Acts; Bruce's framework based primarily on Acts (Bruce 1977); and Lüdemann's letters-based chronology (1984). Note the significant variations in the events lying in between the post-conversion visit and the Jerusalem Council.

Murphy-O'Connor:

Conversion	33
Post-conversion visit	37
Syria and Cilicia	37–?
Cyprus, S. Asia Minor	?–45
Antioch	45–6
Galatia, Macedonia, Corinth	46–51
Jerusalem Conference	51
Antioch	51–2
Ephesus and environs	52–6
Collection visit	56
Arrival in Rome	62

Bruce:

Conversion	33
Post-conversion visit	35
Syria and Cilicia	35–46
Famine relief visit	46
Cyprus, 'Galatia'	47–8
Jerusalem Council	49
Macedonia, Achaia	49–52
Unspecified visit	52
Ephesus and environs	52–7
Collection visit	57
Arrival in Rome	60

Lüdemann

Conversion	33
Post-conversion visit	36
Syria and Cilicia	
S. Asia Minor	
Macedonia (Galatia?)	
Arrival in Corinth	41
Jerusalem Council	50
Ephesus and environs	51–3
Collection visit	55

(Lüdemann also offers an alternative set of dates, not reproduced here, based on a date for the crucifixion of 27 CE rather than 30).

8. The final aspect of any chronological reconstruction is the placement of the letters within the larger chronological framework. Again we can leave these discussions for the commentaries on the individual letters that follow. Here only brief comments are necessary. There is little uncertainty about the relative position of 1 Thessalonians, the two Corinthian epistles, and Romans; in each case internal evidence provides reasonably clear indications of relative date (though the issue of the Corinthian correspondence is complicated by the probability that at least 2 Corinthians is a composite document). If 2 Thessalonians is authentic, then it is probably to be dated shortly after 1 Thessalonians, though some interpreters argue for an inverted sequence. Most commentators place Galatians prior to Romans and in the same general timeframe as the Corinthian correspondence, though as has already been observed there is a minority view that holds it to be the earliest of the letters. As for the 'prison epistles'—Philippians, Philemon, and Colossians (if authentic)—while traditionally they have been seen as written during Paul's Roman imprisonment, there is a growing body of opinion that would place some or all of them earlier, perhaps in an Ephesian imprisonment between 1 and 2 Corinthians (see 2 Cor 1:8; note the reference to many imprisonments in 2 Cor 11:23).

F. Paul's Apostolic *Modus Operandi*. 1. The number of churches addressed or referred to in the letters suggests that Paul was strikingly successful in gaining converts and founding new congregations. The letters provide us with very little direct information, however, on how he went about the process. Once again, the lack might seem to be supplied by the Acts account. Here Paul's activity in founding new churches tends to follow a recognizable pattern. He begins in the synagogue, where he takes advantage of opportunities to proclaim the gospel in a public forum (e.g. Acts 13:5, 14; 14:1; 16:13; 17:1–2, 10; 18:4). The preaching meets with a mixed response—a positive reception by some of the Jews and many of the Gentile proselytes and 'God-fearers' (13:43; 14:1; 17:4), but a hostile response by the larger proportion of the Jewish community (13:45; 14:2; 17:5–9, 13; 18:6). This opposition leads Paul to withdraw from the synagogue with his small group of converts, who become the nucleus of a separate community with a growing number of Gentile members (13:46–9; 14:3–4; 18:6–11), and an appointed body of leaders ('elders', 14:23; 20:17). Eventually local opposition or other considerations force Paul to depart and to move to a different city, where the process is invariably repeated.

2. Again, however, the Acts material should be used with caution; for when Paul describes his mission field, Jewish synagogues are nowhere in sight. While preaching to Jews is not categorically eliminated (1 Cor 9:20), Paul invariably characterizes his apostolic mission as directed towards Gentiles (1 Thess 2:16; Gal 2:2; Rom 1:5; 11:13; 15:16; Col 1:24–9); indeed, this was precisely the division of labour agreed to with Peter (Gal 2:7–9). Likewise, when he addresses his readers, he refers to them as Gentiles (1 Cor 12:2). In neither case is there any hint of a mixed group of Jews and Gentiles. Further, when he describes his Thessalonian converts as people who had 'turned to God from idols, to serve a living and true God' (1 Thess 1:9), he does not seem to leave room for the possibility that adherence to the synagogue had been for any of them a half-way house on the path from idolatry to their new faith, in contrast to Acts 17:4.

3. Still, the differences between Paul and Acts should not be exaggerated. For one thing, if some of his converts indeed had first been 'God-fearers' and synagogue adherents, Paul would have had his own reasons to play down this fact, not wanting his mission to be seen as dependent in any way on the synagogue; he is, after all, not a disinterested observer of his own mission. Further, the ease with which he can quote and allude to Scripture in his letters suggests a real familiarity with Jewish Scripture and tradition on the part of his Gentile readers, a fact not inconsistent with the idea that some of them had had a prior association with the synagogue. In addition, Paul's statement in 1 Cor 9:20 that 'to the Jews I became as a Jew, in order to win Jews', indicates that he did not consider Jews to be out of bounds for him. Indeed, given the evidence for Jewish communities in most of the cities where he worked, it would be difficult to imagine that he could have carried on a mission that did not impinge on the synagogue community in some way.

4. Nevertheless, Paul's letters represent our primary source, and we should not allow the more fully developed but nevertheless schematized picture in Acts to control or overshadow the information emerging from the letters themselves. Further, the task of setting the information from both Acts and the letters into a richer description of Paul's mission has been aided of late by more sociologically informed studies—both those that draw on models of how new religions grow and develop (on the Christian mission generally, see Stark 1996) and those that attempt detailed descriptions of Paul's social context (e.g. Meeks 1983). One emphasis arising from both types of study is the importance of various social networks in the spread of a new religious movement. While the role of public preaching and teaching should not be eliminated entirely, more emphasis should be placed on family networks (e.g. 1 Cor 7:13–16), on the extended household with its various networks of slaves, freedmen, tenants, clients, and so on (e.g. 1 Cor 1:16), and on the networks involved in the carrying out of a trade (Hock 1980). Indeed, the frequency of references to house-churches (1 Cor 16:19; Rom 16:3–5, 23; Philem 1; Col 4:15) suggests that households provided the primary social context in which Paul's churches were embedded (though other models such as voluntary associations may have helped shape the new communities as well; see Ascough 1997).

5. It is not easy to discern the shape of Paul's original preaching. The basic elements are clear enough; the summary in 1 Cor 15:3–8, with its focus on Christ's death and resurrection as a saving event, is reflected in other references sprinkled through the letters (e.g. 1 Cor 2:1–5; 1 Thess 1:9–10). But it is more difficult to discern how these basic elements were fleshed out. To take one sharply debated issue, how much biographical information about Jesus' life and teaching was included (Dunn 1998: 183–206)? Or, how central was Israel to Paul's preaching? Did he, for example, lead his converts to believe that they were full members of Abraham's family (Gal 3:29) or that they had been grafted into Israel's stock (Rom 11:17–24), or did these Israel-centred themes emerge only later and in response to external influences (see Donaldson 1994)?

6. In any case, after his initial preaching Paul spent a period of time consolidating his evangelistic gains and establishing a self-sufficient community. Most of his letters contain passing references back to this initial period of community-formation (e.g. 1 Cor 1:14–16; 2:1–5; 2 Cor 1:19; 12:12–13; Gal 4:13–15; Phil 4:9; 1 Thess 2:9–12; 2 Thess 3:7–10). During this period he did not request or accept financial support from the congregation, preferring to support himself through his own work (1 Cor 9:3–18; 1 Thess 2:9; 2 Thess 3:7–10) and contributions from already-founded congregations (2 Cor 11:7–11; Phil 4:15–16). With the exception of Phil 1:1, there seems to be little evidence

of the kind of appointed 'elders' referred to in Acts (e.g. Acts 14:23). Indeed, a striking feature of the letters is that in dealing with local conflicts Paul does not bring local office-holders into the picture, either to instruct them or to encourage his readers to submit to them. He tended to operate more on the basis of a charismatic, gift-based leadership (Rom 12:4–7; 1 Cor 12: 1–31; cf. Eph 4: 11–16), though one should not underestimate the *de facto* leadership role played by the head of the household in which the church met.

7. After leaving the congregation and moving on to another city, Paul continued to feel 'daily pressure because of [his] anxiety for all the churches' (2 Cor 11:28). His anxiety took the positive form of an ongoing pastoral responsibility, exercised not only through his own follow-up visits (Phil 1:27; 2:24; 1 Cor 4:18–21), but also by means of appointed emissaries—for example, Timothy (1 Cor 4:16; 16:10–11; Phil 2:19–23) and Titus (2 Cor 7:6–16; 8:16–24)—and by means of the letters themselves. Through these agencies Paul extended his apostolic activity and authority; both emissaries (1 Cor 4:17) and letters (Gal 4:20) functioned as proxies—and sometimes as precursors—for his own apostolic presence (Funk 1967).

8. Paul founded self-sustaining congregations and then moved on. But where, and why? How did he decide which city he would move to next? More specifically, did Paul operate from some sense of a geographical plan or strategy? A number of pieces of evidence seem to suggest that he did. (1) Not only did he concentrate on cities, but the cities he chose to work in tended to be prominent ones, provincial capitals and the like. (2) He seems to have thought of these cities in terms of the provinces in which they were found, preferring to refer to his churches with provincial rather than city names; e.g. Achaia and Macedonia (Rom 15:26; 2 Cor 8:1; 9:2), Asia (Rom 16:5), Illyricum (Rom 15:19), Spain (Rom 15:24), and (probably) Galatia (Gal 1:2). (3) For years, he says, he had a desire to proclaim the gospel in Rome (Rom 1:10–13; 15:23), which he then wanted to use as a staging-post for a journey to Spain (Rom 15:24, 28). (4) The agreement between Peter and Paul recounted in Gal 2:9—'that we should go to the Gentiles and they to the circumcised'—is at least open to a territorial (rather than solely ethnic) interpretation. (5) The geographical context in 2 Cor 10:12–18 suggests a territorial element in Paul's statement that 'we . . . will keep within the field that God has assigned to us' (v. 13). (6) Paul's statement in Rom 15:19, 24, to the effect that he is now free to travel to Rome because he has 'fully proclaimed the gospel of Christ' 'from Jerusalem and as far around as Illyricum', seems to suggest not only a notion of territoriality but also of a specific evangelizing agenda within that territory. Since there was still plenty of scope for preaching, not only in untouched cities but even in the cities where churches had been planted, his statement that his work was finished in this area must suggest that he was operating according to some more specific strategy than simply preaching to as many Gentiles as he could wherever he might find them. (7) Finally, the statement that the conversion of the 'full number of the Gentiles' would be the thing to trigger the coming of the End and the salvation of 'all Israel' (Rom 11:25–6), sets the whole mission within an eschatological framework: when the gospel was 'fully preached', not simply from Jerusalem to Illyricum but from Jerusalem to X (X being

wherever he considered the end of the territory to be), then the parousia would take place.

9. While these pieces of evidence seem to add up to a geographical strategy of some kind, it is not any easy matter to discern what it might have been. The popular notion that Paul engaged in 'missionary journeys', with Jerusalem as his point of departure and return, owes more to Luke than to Paul—and actually owes more to the modern missionary movement than to Luke: as Townsend (1985) has observed, it was not until the onset of the missionary movement in the eighteenth century that anyone thought to describe Paul's apostolic activity in terms of 'three missionary journeys'. Another notion influenced by more modern Christian missionary strategy—namely, that Paul intended each of his churches to be centres of evangelism for the whole province of which it was a part (e.g. Dunn 1988: ii. 869)—founders on the fact that Paul nowhere urges his congregations to carry out the task of evangelism; strangely, his letters contain no injunctions to evangelize at all. Somehow he seems to consider his churches as representative of the provinces in which they are located, so that once a church was founded within a province, he could say that the gospel had been 'fully preached' in that province.

10. But how did he determine which provinces in which to work? Knox has suggested that the word *kuklō* in Rom 15:19 ('from Jerusalem and *kuklō* as far as Illyricum') should be translated 'in a circular manner', arguing on this basis that Paul's plan was to work his way through a string of provinces circling the Mediterranean and ending up in Egypt (Knox 1964). Others have attempted to find a geographical template in Israel's Scriptures—either the sequence of nations listed in Isa 66:18–21 (Riesner 1998: 245–53) or the various 'tables of the nations' in Gen 10 and elsewhere (Scott 1995). Each proposal has its difficulties, however, not the least of which is the fact that there were many provinces between Jerusalem and Rome or Spain which Paul did not seem compelled to visit. The statement that he chose to work only where Christ had not 'already been named' (Rom 15:20) might suggest that he avoided other provinces because they had already been evangelized. But this would hardly have been true of Thrace, Moesia, or Gaul, to name only a few of the provinces in which he did no work. Moreover, Rom 15:20 cannot be pressed too hard, in that Paul was quite prepared to preach the gospel in Rome (Rom 1:13) and to consider it as part of his apostolic turf (Rom 1:5–6; 15:14–16) even though a church already existed there.

Perhaps the most that can be said is that Spain, considered by the ancients to be the 'end of the earth', represented for Paul the goal of his ever westerly-pressing mission. In this connection, it is worth noting that Paul seems to have conceived of his apostolic task in the light of the Servant passages of Isaiah (see the citations or allusions in Gal 1:15; 2 Cor 6:2; Rom 15:21) and that the Servant's task was to bring God's salvation 'to the end of the earth' (Isa 49:6; see further Donaldson forthcoming).

In all probability, however, Paul never made it to the 'end of the earth'. He journeyed to Rome not in apostolic freedom but as a prisoner. While it is possible that his Roman hearing resulted in release (Murphy-O'Connor 1996: 359–63), it is more likely that it resulted, eventually, in his execution.

G. The Letters. 1. Paul wrote neither theological treatises nor narratives but letters, and a proper understanding of his literary legacy requires that we take seriously its epistolary character. To do this, we must look not only at the letters themselves, but also at the letter-writing conventions that were present in the Graeco-Roman world. Fortunately, we are the beneficiaries of a century of careful comparative study, with the result that the shape and texture of Paul's letters are being brought ever more clearly into focus.

2. It is customary in discussions of the literary features of Paul's letters to begin with Adolf Deissmann and his work on the papyri that were coming to light in the latter part of the nineteenth century (Deissmann 1910). And with good reason. Deissmann was the first to realize the significance of these papyri for the study of Paul's letters, and his own observations have continued to shape the discussion. In contrast to the more literary epistles that had been preserved in the classical corpus, which were generally written for a wider reading public and with a view to preservation (e.g. those of Cicero or Seneca), the letters contained among the papyri findings were truly occasional writings. That is, they were addressed to the immediate situation that had prompted their writing, and they tended to be artless, spontaneous, and personal. On the basis of such a distinction between literary 'epistles' ('products of literary art') and real 'letters' ('documents of life'; ibid. 218), Deissmann argued that Paul's writings should be classed among the latter. That is, they are occasional writings, written 'not for the public and posterity, but for the persons to whom they are addressed' (ibid. 225), written not as the careful formulations of a systematic theologian but out of the pressing urgency of a pastoral situation.

3. As a first approximation, Deissmann's analysis is valid and perceptive, highlighting as it does the immediacy and situation-driven character of the letters. Even the Epistle to the Romans, containing the most sustained and systematic argumentation in the corpus and traditionally understood as a 'compendium of Christian Doctrine' (Melanchthon), should be understood instead as written out of specific circumstances (Paul's planned trip to Rome) and shaped in accordance with specific purposes (to win the acceptance of the Roman Christians by addressing their concerns about his Gentile mission). But Deissmann's categories are too crudely drawn and need to be significantly revised. For one thing, Paul's letters are not simply personal and private; he writes to whole congregations, even in such a 'personal' letter as Philemon (Philem 2), and addresses his readers from a self-conscious position of authority. Nor are they as brief, rough, and artless as many of the papyri letters on which Deissmann based his categories; while they may not display evidence of formal rhetorical training, they are nevertheless well-structured and carefully composed. In addition, further study of letters in antiquity has revealed a wide variety of different types of letter (Stowers 1986), from letters of rebuke (cf. Galatians) to letters of mediation (cf. Philemon), as well as a wider range of relationships between sender and recipient. With respect to the latter point, Aune has suggested a similarity between Paul's letters and 'official letters' sent from government officials to those under their authority (Aune 1987: 164–5).

4. Still, private letters provide the basic form on which all letters in Graeco-Roman antiquity were based, and a

comparison between Paul and the epistolary papyri is very illuminating. Paul's letters are composed according to the conventional pattern of the day, although he adapted it in ways that made his letters particularly effective means of extending and reinforcing his apostolic activity.

Letters typically began with a prescript, consisting of the name of the sender, the name of the recipient, and a salutation. To use one of Deissmann's (1910: 167–72) examples, a second-century letter from a young Egyptian just arrived in Italy after having enlisted in the army begins this way: 'Apion to Epimachus his father and lord, many greetings.' The word 'greetings' (*chairein*) is a customary form of salutation in Hellenistic letters, though Jewish letters sometimes replace it with 'peace' (*šālôm, eirēnē*). Paul's letters follow the same format (A to B, greetings), but with several characteristic adaptations, some of them more or less the same from letter to letter, others particularly tailored to the needs of the situation. First, he usually adds a term descriptive of his own role and status, most frequently 'apostle' but also 'servant' or 'prisoner', completed in each case by 'of Christ Jesus'. Then he often names a co-sender (Romans being the only exception among the certainly authentic epistles), even though the letter itself is usually couched in the first person singular (e.g. Philemon). Then, where it suits his purposes, he will considerably expand either the sender or the recipient portion of the prescript. In Romans and Galatians, for example, where his own status as an apostle is in need of defence, he uses this portion of the letter to make an aggressive (Galatians) or subtle and extended (Romans; 6 verses) declaration of his apostolic status and authority. In 1 Corinthians, it is the recipients who are described more fully (1:2). Here the emphasis on their status as saints and on their membership in a wider community of Christians is an appropriate opening note to a letter addressed to a community marked by decidedly unsaintly behaviour (e.g. 5:1) and smug self-sufficiency (4:8; cf. 11:16). Finally, Paul ends the prescript with a salutation distinctively his own ('Grace to you and peace from God our Father and the Lord Jesus Christ'; minor variations in Colossians and 1 Thessalonians), yet adapted from current patterns. 'Grace' (*charis*), while part of Paul's characteristic Christian vocabulary, is close enough to *chairein* to be heard as an edifying wordplay; 'peace' is typical of Jewish letter-writing patterns.

5. The prescript in Graeco-Roman letters was frequently followed by a section in which the writer expressed wishes for the good health of the recipient, often couched in the form of a prayer, and/or offered thanksgiving to the gods for some benefit received. To illustrate, the letter cited above continues: 'First of all, I pray that you are in good health, and that you continue to prosper and fare well, with my sister and her daughter and my brother. I give thanks to the Lord Serapis that when I was in danger in the sea he saved me immediately.' Again this has its counterpart in Paul, though where in conventional letters it tended to be formulaic and perfunctory, in Paul each prayer/thanksgiving section is freshly composed for each letter, complimentary to the readers, and tailored in evident ways to the concerns of the letter. In 1 Corinthians, to take a particularly striking example, Paul gives thanks for characteristics in his readers that he will later scold them for not displaying: their richness (cf. 4:8) in speech (cf. ch. 14), in

knowledge (cf. ch. 8), and in spiritual gifts (cf. chs. 12, 14). In Philemon, before pressing his request that Philemon receive Onesimus back with love (v. 16) and so refresh Paul's heart (v. 20), he gives thanks for Philemon's demonstrated 'love for all the saints' (v. 5) and for the way in which 'the hearts of the saints have been refreshed' already through Philemon. In less capable hands, this section would have been crudely manipulative. In Paul's more subtle and even elegant phrasing, however, this section functions as a kind of overture, introducing the themes to follow and predisposing the recipients to a receptive reading of the letter as a whole. The one exception is Galatians, where Paul moves straight from the prescript (concluded, unusually, with a doxology) to an expression of astonishment at the culpable folly of the readers. Here the prayer/thanksgiving section is omitted for effect, or one could even argue that it has been replaced with a curse section (Gal 1:6–9).

6. At this point in both Graeco-Roman letters and in Paul we move into the body of the letter, where the sender sets out to accomplish the purpose for which the letter was being written. Here, the sheer variety of purposes and forms means that it is not as easy to identify epistolary patterns at work in letter bodies as a whole. Still, comparative work has by no means been fruitless (White 1972). For one thing, many of the formulae by which Paul introduces his subject-matter or takes up new themes are frequently found elsewhere: e.g. 'I am astonished that'; 'I want you to know that'; 'I beseech/appeal to you'; 'I rejoice that'; 'I am confident that'—all are frequent in Paul and richly documented in Graeco-Roman sources (Aune 1987: 188; Longenecker 1990: pp. cv–cviii). As observed already, letter bodies can be further categorized according to the particular function intended for the letter (Stowers 1986). Also, as will be picked up in more detail below, considerable new light has been shed on the letters, particularly on the letter bodies, by analysing them in terms of the conventions of ancient rhetoric. Finally, it is possible in at least some of the letters to identify a section of parenaesis at the end of the body proper (Rom 12:1–15:13; Gal 5:1–6:10; 1 Thess 4:1–5:22), i.e., a combination of instruction and encouragement, no doubt related to the particular circumstances prompting the letter, but in ways that are not always readily discerned.

7. Letter closings display less of a fixed form and have not been nearly as well studied, at least until recently (Weima 1994). Instead of essential elements, there appear to have been a number of conventions from which letter writers could make a selection according to preference or need: 'a farewell wish, a health wish, secondary greetings, an autograph, an illiteracy formula [i.e. indicating that the note had of necessity been written by a secretary], the date, and a postscript' (ibid. 55). Again Paul's usage both reflects current conventions and displays a Christian adaptation of them. His letters contain the following closing elements (ibid. 77–155): (1) a peace benediction, often a variation on the form 'may the God of peace be with you' (e.g. Rom 15:33; 2 Cor 13:11; Phil 4:9); (2) a final exhortation (e.g. 1 Cor 16:13–16; Phil 4:8–9); (3) greetings (first-, second-, and third-person), together with an injunction to 'greet one another with a holy kiss' (Rom 16:16; also 1 Cor 16:20; 2 Cor 13:12, 1 Thess 5:26); (4) an autograph (explicit in 1 Cor 16:21; Gal 6:11; 2 Thess 3:17; Philem 19; Col 4:18); (5) a

grace benediction, in the form 'the grace of the Lord Jesus be with you'. The one fixed element, found in all the letters, is the closing grace benediction, which taken in combination with the prescript means that each letter is framed with the wish for grace. In addition, each closing contains a selection of the other elements, with a tendency towards the order in which they were listed above.

8. In more recent years, epistolary analysis has been supplemented—or even rivalled—by a second type of analysis to which the letters have been subjected, that of rhetorical criticism. The pejorative overtones associated with the term 'rhetoric' in popular parlance (e.g. mere or empty rhetoric) is a measure of how far this once highly prized declamatory skill has fallen in esteem. In antiquity, however, rhetoric was one of the two possible capstones of an education (philosophy being the other) and the basic prerequisite for a public career. Shorn of its negative connotations, 'rhetoric' simply denotes the 'art of persuasion', and more recent study has recovered a sense of its place in antiquity and its potential for New Testament interpretation (Kennedy 1984).

9. Rhetorical criticism looks at argument in the NT from several angles (see Mack 1990), each of which can be fruitfully applied to the body of Paul's letters. One has to do with classification of argument types. Ancient rhetoricians divided argument into three categories—judicial (rendering verdicts on past actions), deliberative (making decisions about future courses of action), and epideictic (bestowing praise or blame)—and these have been brought to bear on Paul's letters. A second approach has to do with the classification of different elements within an argument. Aristotle distinguished between *ethos* (the establishment of the speaker's relationship with the audience and the basis of the speaker's authority), *logos* (the substance, structure and arrangement of the argument itself), and *pathos* (the ways in which the emotions of the audience are elicited and engaged in the service of the argument). These three categories can readily be applied to each of Paul's letters, with immediate and fruitful results. A third aspect of rhetorical criticism is concerned with the *logos* itself, especially with structures of ancient rhetoric as prescribed in the handbooks of Quintilian and others. In his work on Galatians, for example, Betz (1979) attempts to demonstrate that the argument in this epistle unfolds according to the prescribed sequence of the *exordium* (introductory section), the *narratio* (recitation of the facts of the case), the *propositio* (thesis to be demonstrated), the *probatio* (specific arguments or proofs), and the concluding *exhortatio*.

10. Occasionally one gets the sense in reading rhetorical criticism that text is being eclipsed by pattern; that is, that the text is being squeezed to fit a prescribed rhetorical pattern, or at least that demonstrating the pattern has taken precedence over revealing the text. Further, it is doubtful that Paul himself would have been exposed in an explicit way to the type of rhetorical training prescribed by the handbooks. Still, since rhetoric itself permeated the cultural air he breathed, he would have been deeply affected by rhetorical patterns and conventions at least in a secondary way. Moreover, any approach that encourages readers to attend carefully to the actual functioning of a text as it works its persuasive power on a reader is to be warmly welcomed.

11. Any discussion of the actual functioning of the individual letters themselves or of the ends to which their particular persuasive powers are turned is best left to the individual commentaries to follow. More generally, however, one can say that what Paul intends to accomplish by means of his letters is what he himself would do if he were there. As he says towards the end of his troubled correspondence with the Corinthians: 'So I write these things while I am away from you, so that when I come, I may not have to be severe in using the authority that the Lord has given me for building up and not for tearing down' (2 Cor 13:10). Or a little earlier in the same letter: 'Let such people understand that what we say by letter when absent, we do when present' (2 Cor 10:11). Further, the promise (threat?) of a visit in many of the letters (1 Cor 4:18–21; 16:5–9; 2 Cor 9:4; 13:1, 10; Phil 2:24; Philem 22) serves to reinforce the connection between action by letter and action in person (Funk 1967).

12. Of course the Corinthians themselves felt that, at least as far as the exercise of forceful discipline was concerned, Paul's letters were more effective than his presence! 'His letters are weighty and strong, but his bodily presence is weak and his speech contemptible' (2 Cor 10:10). But discipline was only one arrow in his epistolary quiver. What Paul was attempting to do in his letters—to continue the archery metaphor by borrowing a phrase from Beker (1980)—was to direct a 'word on target' to the situation of his readers, to bring the 'coherent core' of his gospel to bear on the 'contingent circumstances' to which the letter was addressed. Paul's ultimate aim, in person or by letter, was to create and maintain for his converts a new world in which they might live and find meaning, a world grounded on the death and resurrection of Christ and the victory over the forces of evil and death that these had signalled.

13. This brings us close to the matter of Paul's 'theology', to which we will turn our attention in a moment. But first, two final items concerning the letters themselves. One of these has to do with two other agents with roles to play in the process of communication carried out by a letter. As was customary in a culture where the means of letter production were not readily available to all, Paul made use of a secretary to do the actual pen and papyrus work. This is implied by the autograph section in many of the letter closings, where Paul himself takes up the pen 'to write this greeting with [his] own hand' (1 Cor 16:21). It is stated explicitly in Rom 16:22 where, in the midst of a series of third-party greetings, the secretary breaks into the conversation to add his own word of greeting: 'I Tertius, the writer of this letter, greet you in the Lord.'

What was the role of the secretary in the production of Paul's letters? There is a range of possibilities, from simply producing a good copy from Paul's corrected first draft to actually composing the substance of the letter under Paul's general direction. The oral quality that comes through at many points, however, especially where sentences are broken off or new thoughts begun before old ones are fully completed (e.g. Rom 5:12; 8:3) or where verbs of speaking are used with respect to what is being said in the letter (Rom 11:13; 2 Cor 12:19), seems to suggest that Paul dictated his letters. This is also confirmed by a general evenness in style among the certainly authentic letters.

14. Perhaps more important for the process of communication was the role played by another agent—the person delivering the letter. In an era where there was organized postal service only for Roman imperial business, individual arrangements had to be made for the delivery of letters, preferably by someone known to the sender. Presumably the 'tearful letter' referred to in 2 Corinthians (2:3–4, 9; 7:8, 12) had the positive effect that it did (7:6–16) at least in part because Titus (who probably delivered the letter) had been present to interpret it, to ensure that it was being heard correctly, to mollify any who were upset by it, and perhaps even to negotiate a more positive response than if Paul had delivered his message in person. The role of the letter carrier also comes up in Col 4:7–9 where Paul (if Colossians is directly from Paul) commends Tychicus, again the probable letter carrier, who 'will tell you all the news about me'. Later readers, who have to piece together information about Paul's 'news' like a detective in a P. D. James novel, might wish that Paul had not left so much to the letter carrier, but had put more of the actual detail of his life and circumstances into the letters.

15. The reference in the previous paragraph to the disputed authenticity of Colossians brings us to the final item to be touched on in this section. Fully six of the thirteen letters that bear Paul's name display characteristics that have led many scholars to conclude that some or all of the six were not written directly by Paul. While the details need to be left for the individual commentaries to follow, the characteristics are a combination of elements: differences in vocabulary and style, differences in theological outlook, reflections of contextual circumstances that probably emerged only later, and so on. These characteristics are not uniformly present in the six letters: 2 Thessalonians, Colossians, and Ephesians are much more Pauline in their vocabulary, style, and theology than are the Pastorals (1 and 2 Timothy, Titus). There are also variations within these two groups. Ephesians, with its long sentences and its piling up of synonyms and genitive constructions (e.g. 'the working of the power of his strength', 1:19), sounds less Pauline than does Colossians or 2 Thessalonians. With respect to the Pastorals, some of the features that set these writings apart from the rest of the Pauline corpus (the concern for church order; the stiff and formal tone out of keeping with letters ostensibly written to close associates) are absent from 2 Timothy.

16. In each case scholars have entertained a range of possibilities. Some have defended authenticity by appealing to special circumstances that might account for the observed deviations from the norm. Others have pointed to the way in which Paul included others within his sphere of apostolic authority—those mentioned as co-senders of letters, for example—in order to argue that Paul may have given a secretary or co-worker greater latitude in the actual composition of the letters in question. Still others—the majority in the case of Ephesians and the Pastoral epistles—believe that letters were written by former associates or later admirers of Paul some time after his death, written to bring the voice and authority of Paul to bear on pressing circumstances in the real author's own day.

17. Readers who encounter this discussion for the first time often interpret the latter suggestion as implying deliberate deception on the part of the real author. But even in our own day we are familiar with situations where it is considered quite appropriate for texts that have been written by one person to be attributed to another—political speeches, for example, or 'as told to' autobiographies, or unfinished manuscripts published posthumously after being edited and completed by a colleague or admirer of the deceased. Furthermore, the ancients tended to have different attitudes towards authorship than are standard in our own culture, with its notions of copyright and intellectual property. Take, for example, this statement by the late second-century Christian writer Tertullian: '[The Gospel] which was published by Mark may be maintained to be Peter's, whose interpreter Mark was, just as the narrative of Luke is generally ascribed to Paul. For it is allowable that that which disciples publish should be regarded as their master's work' (*Adv. Marc.* 6.5). Certainly cases of deception were known in antiquity, no less than in our own day. But there is a much broader range of options to be put into play in the discussion.

One of the factors in the discussion of authenticity, however, and one of the keys to Paul's enduring significance, is the presence in the certainly authentic letters of a distinctive set of theological themes and structures. To this we will now turn our attention.

H. The Thought within and beneath the Letters. 1. One cannot read through Paul's letters without being struck by the dazzling array of images, metaphors, terms, concepts, and typologies that he uses to describe the human situation and the work of Christ and its consequences. A classroom of even beginner-level students can quickly fill up a whole blackboard. In an order as random as a classroom brainstorming session: justification; sin; redemption; judgement; flesh; Spirit; spirit; body; law; works of the law; faith; grace; boasting; Christ; Lord; the first/last Adam; Son of God; sons of God; sons of Abraham; righteousness; reconciliation; adoption; freedom; slavery; expiation; sanctification; enemy; wrath; love; for us; for our sins; blood; gospel; preaching; body of Christ; in Christ; putting on Christ; in the Spirit; crucified with Christ; dying with Christ; rising with Christ; walking; called; being one; bought and sold; first fruits; wisdom; glory; living sacrifice; faith, hope, and love; triumph; dying to the law; dying to sin; principalities and powers; elemental spirits; condemnation; fellowship—not to mention 'things that are not to be told, that no mortal is permitted to repeat' (2 Cor 12:4).

2. The list is a testimony to the vigour and vitality of Paul's mind. His was an active intellect, throwing off metaphors and ideas as a grindstone throws off sparks. Yet the very kaleidoscopic dazzle of his language makes it difficult to read him well, especially since his statements on some topics (the law, in particular) seem to be in considerable tension with each other. Is there a discernible pattern or an underlying structure that will help us make coherent sense of this welter of theological language? What, in other words, is the basic shape of Paul's theology?

3. The task is by no means easy. The puzzlement expressed by the author of 2 Peter, noted at the outset of this essay (2 Pet 3:16), is echoed by modern readers as well. In Franz Overbeck's delightfully paradoxical way of putting it: 'No one has ever understood Paul, except Marcion; and even he misunderstood him.' Or, in more expanded form: '[Paul's] greatness is

shown in the very fact that he has found no congenial interpreter and probably never will. From Marcion to Karl Barth,
from Augustine to Luther, Schweitzer or Bultmann, he has
ever been misunderstood or partially understood, one aspect
of his work being thrown into relief while others have been
misunderstood and neglected' (Schoeps 1961: 13).

4. Some have decided that the very attempt to find a coherent pattern of thought in Paul is misdirected, either because
Paul's significance is to be found instead in his spirituality
or his exercise of pastoral care, or because his thinking contains an irreducible element of incoherence. Among those
who think that the quest for coherence is worth pursuing,
there have been several different ways of formulating the
problem, or several different places in which the interpretative key has been sought. Some have looked to Paul's 'background', hoping to find in Paul's Jewish formation or
Hellenistic environment (or a combination of the two) the
grid-points around which his theological discourse can be
plotted and patterned. Others have looked to his conversion
(as has already been observed), hoping to find a biographical
and experiential paradigm that might have generated—and
thus might make sense of—his later argumentation. Still
others have attempted to select from the larger set of terms
and metaphors a primary image or a central theme around
which the remainder can be arranged. 'Justification by faith
not works' is probably the best-known example of such an
attempt. These approaches have been supplemented from
time to time by various developmental schemes, which try to
discern a substantial progression of Paul's theology as he
matured.

5. Perhaps the most promising approach, however, is one
that sees Paul's 'theology' as a cumulative activity taking place
between two other levels of cognition and perception. The
foundational level, located in structures beneath the surface
of the text, consists of Paul's set of basic convictions, things
that he took to be axiomatic or self-evident. Some of these were
native convictions, stemming from his primary formation in
Judaism; others were secondary and reconstitutive, stemming
from his Damascus experience. We have already discussed the
way in which Paul's 'conversion' experience can be seen as a
redrawing of his primary Jewish convictions around the new
belief that God had raised Jesus from death and thus made
him Saviour and Christ.

By contrast, the uppermost level, encountered at the rhetorical surface of the letters, is much more contingent, in that it
is related to the specific situations that prompted Paul's epistolary response. This level is not to be simply identified with
either the actual circumstances themselves or Paul's actual
response, though both are involved. Rather, it is to be located
in Paul's perception of the situation, as he views it through the
lens of his basic gospel convictions.

6. What is commonly thought of as Paul's theology, then,
can be seen as lying in between these two levels and produced
by the dynamic interaction between them. New and unforeseen circumstances in his churches force Paul to develop the
implications of his core convictions in order to be able to
address them. Questions raised by opponents or sceptical
hearers of his message raise to the surface tensions inherent
in his new set of convictions, tensions that he needs to resolve
if his message is to be heard. Especially prominent in this

regard are those tensions arising from his new belief that
Christ, not Torah, is the true badge of membership in the
family of Abraham. Paul's theology, then, is that developing
body of thought that exists in between conviction and circumstance, driven in different ways by both and by the dynamic
interaction between them.

7. This is obviously not the place to try to develop any full-
scale description of this developing body of thought. The most
recent (and highly successful) attempt to do this (Dunn 1998)
ran to some 800 pages! But for present purposes, in addition
to this suggestion of a multilevel approach to Paul's theology,
it will be helpful to make a few further comments about the
shift that is currently underway with respect to a central aspect
of his thought, namely, the nature of the human plight and of
the solution provided by God in Christ. An older pattern,
shaped in large measure by the controversies of the Reformation era (though constructed from elements in existence ever
since the church had become a distinctly Gentile institution),
has been increasingly displaced by a new pattern owing much
to a new appreciation of the Jewish context in which Paul
carried out his apostolic mission. Of course, to reduce the
complex field of Pauline interpretation to two 'patterns' is a
considerable oversimplification; reality is much more complex
than that. Still, it is often helpful to paint with broad strokes
before working on the fine details, so there is value in a simplified sketch. In any case, both patterns deal with the central
themes of sin and salvation, but in strikingly different ways.

8. The older approach assumes that for Paul the fundamental problem posed by sin was essentially that it left human
beings guilty before a righteous God. God demands righteousness first and foremost, but humans are universally sinful and thus under divine condemnation. Christ's role, then,
is conceived primarily as a way of removing this guilty verdict.
His death makes it possible for God, though righteous, to
forgive sin, and for humans, though sinful, to be considered
righteous. In this 'objective' view of the atonement (the process by which Christ overcomes the problem posed by sin and
effects a reconciliation between God and humankind), the
problem posed by human sin is located ultimately with God;
even though God might be willing to forgive, the standards of
divine righteousness make this impossible. There are various
ways in which this 'impossibility' has been understood. The
most common, however, is that God's righteousness required
that sin be punished. In his death—so runs this 'penal substitutionary' view of the atonement—Christ functioned as a
substitute, experiencing death as the punishment for sin,
even though he was not guilty of sin. With the penalty paid,
God is then free to overlook sin, 'imputing' Christ's righteous
status to those who believe.

9. If guilt and its consequence—condemnation—constitute
the nub of the human plight, then the heart of salvation for
Paul is to be found in its opposite, justification. Christ's
fundamental accomplishment in this older view, then, was
seen as opening up the possibility of justification, a new status
attributed to the believer on the basis of faith. What gave
Paul's doctrine of justification by faith its particular spin in
the traditional line of interpretation was the way it was defined
in contrast to 'works'. Faith and works were taken to be
fundamental categories for Paul, representing two mutually
exclusive personal stances or attitudes vis-à-vis God. 'Works' is

understood as an attitude of self-confidence based on meritorious achievement, where one attempts to earn acceptance and standing before God on the basis of moral and religious accomplishment. While such standing might be theoretically possible, the pervasiveness of sin, it is argued, made it impossible in reality. Thus Paul's language of justification by faith is interpreted within the framework of two mutually exclusive religious frameworks—one operating on the basis of divine grace humbly accepted, the other on the basis of human achievement boastfully put forward.

In this reading of Paul, Judaism comes into the picture essentially as an example of a works religion—the one with which Paul was most familiar, but nevertheless just a particular example of a more general human tendency. Paul's interest in the Gentiles is taken for granted, in that it is assumed that he begins with a generically human problem—how can a sinful human being find acceptance before a righteous God?

10. In this way of construing Paul's thought, it can readily be seen how the distance between Luther and Paul has been collapsed, so that Paul's problem and solution are understood to replicate those of Luther himself. We have already seen one difficulty with this reading of Paul—the fact that its legalistic interpretation of Judaism represents a fundamental misunderstanding of how the law functioned with respect to the covenant. But there are other difficulties as well. One has to do with sin. It is hard to imagine how someone who read in his Scriptures that God was 'merciful and gracious, slow to anger and abounding in steadfast love' (Ps 103:8) could have believed that human guilt for sin was a fundamental obstacle to divine forgiveness. Another has to do with justification by faith. While juridical language (justification, etc.) looms large in Galatians and Romans, when one looks at the letters as a whole one is struck by the limited role it plays. Outside Galatians and Romans (and Phil 3) Paul never uses this doctrine as a fundamental first principle to be brought to bear on problems, in Corinth, say, or Thessalonica. Moreover, he quite happily issues all sorts of commands and injunctions to his congregations concerning 'works' they are to perform, without feeling any apparent compunction to warn them of the dangers of legalism. In fact, the only 'works' that Paul gets upset about are those that would turn Gentiles into Jews—circumcision, food laws, sabbath observance, and other Torah regulations. Since Romans and Galatians are written precisely for the purpose of defending the equal status of Gentile believers as Gentiles, against those who would in effect have them become Jews, it can be argued that instead of being his central theme, justification by faith is a particular line of argument developed for this purpose.

11. These observations could be developed at much greater length. But for present purposes this will suffice as an introduction to an alternative way of construing Paul's central story of plight and salvation, again sketched out in broad strokes. Rom 8:1–4 provides us with a convenient set of paints and brushes:

There is therefore now no condemnation for those who are in Christ Jesus. For the law of the Spirit of life in Christ Jesus has set you free from the law of sin and of death. For God has done what the law,

weakened by the flesh, could not do: by sending his own Son in the likeness of sinful flesh, and to deal with sin, he condemned sin in the flesh, so that the just requirement of the law might be fulfilled in us, who walk not according to the flesh but according to the Spirit.

At this point in Romans, Paul is bringing the argument of chs. 1–8 to a conclusion. He returns to the theme of justification: there is no condemnation—that is, there is justification—for those in Christ Jesus. Why? Not because Christ has endured a penalty that had to be meted out, but because Christ has performed an act of liberation: he has liberated you from the law of sin and death. For Paul, sin is conceived not simply as culpable wrongdoing, but more fundamentally as a power, a kind of force-field that 'has come into the world through one man' (Rom 5:12), bringing death in its train and holding the whole of humankind under its sway. Those in its power commit sins and incur guilt, of course, but precisely because of the power of sin already at work in them: 'If I do what I do not want, it is no longer I that do it but sin that dwells within me' (Rom 7:20). The problem posed by sin, then, is only secondarily one of guilt; more fundamentally, the problem is bondage. What is needed is not forgiveness *per se*; until the power of sin is nullified, forgiveness does not get at the root of the problem. What is needed, rather, is liberation.

12. Christ's accomplishment, then, is to be seen more fundamentally in terms of a confrontation with sin, breaking its power and opening up a new sphere in which life can be lived. What Christ has done in the flesh is to 'condemn sin' (v. 3). In context, this must mean more than simply to declare sin to be deserving of condemnation; the law was very good at doing this (ch. 7), but what Christ has done is something that the law 'could not do' (v. 3). Christ, for Paul, has not only pronounced the verdict but also carried out the sentence; he has won a victory over sin and emptied it of its power—at least for those who are 'in Christ' (v. 1) and who 'walk according to the Spirit' (v. 4).

13. While Christ's death makes possible a new objective status (of which justification is one metaphor), this is not the heart of salvation for Paul. Instead, salvation has to do with the real subjective experience of being liberated from sin's power and transferred to a sphere in which a different power is at work, the power of the Spirit. Those who are empowered by the Spirit—who 'walk according to the Spirit' (v. 4)—are thereby 'of Christ' (Rom 8:9) or 'in Christ' (v. 1) or have Christ in them (Rom 8:10). This language is part of a larger complex in Paul in which the Christian experience is described in participatory terms—i.e. as an experience of sharing with Christ in the process of dying to this age, an age in which sin and death are the regnant powers, and rising to the life of the age to come, where sin and death are finally defeated (Rom 6:1–11). While the process will not be complete until the End, believers even now experience the Spirit as a kind of first fruits (Rom 8:23) of the full harvest to come. Just as those under the power of sin were bound to transgress the law (Rom 7:14–20), so those who 'walk according to the Spirit' are enabled to 'fulfil' 'the just requirement of the law' (v. 4).

In contrast to the juridical language of justification by faith, this language of participation in Christ permeates the letters, functioning as the touchstone for ethics (e.g. Rom 6:1–11; Gal 5:16–26) and the fundamental first principle for dealing with community problems (e.g. 1 Cor 6:15–20; 10:14–22). If we begin here, we will be able to make much better sense of Paul than if we take justification by faith as the centre and starting-point. Faith is still fundamental, though what it does in the first instance is to open the door for the believer's incorporation into Christ.

14. In this portrayal of Paul's thought, Judaism comes into the picture not as an example of the wrong kind of religion: rather, in Paul's reinterpretation of Torah-religion, Israel becomes the place where the nature of the human plight was clarified and the decisive act of God's solution was carried out. Israel's role, as Paul understands it, was to be a kind of representative sample of the whole of humankind, in both plight and salvation. Within Israel, the Torah functioned to define and reveal sin (Rom 5:20; 7:7, 13), so that it could be clearly seen that all were under its power and subject to death; within Israel, Christ appeared to confront and defeat sin, so that all could be liberated from its power and share in the glory of the age to come. As a representative (Rom 11:1–6) of this representative sample, Paul felt himself called to announce this liberation to the nations out of which Israel had been called in the first place.

This is far from being even a sketch of Paul's theology; a rough outline of one section of a sketch would be more accurate. Still, if the letters cannot be understood without some sense of the convictional and theological levels operating beneath the surface, this sketch of a sketch might provide the reader with a bit of a glimpse of what might be going on beneath the surface and giving shape to what appears above.

I. The Collection and Enduring Significance of the Letters.

1. It was observed above that we have been able to arrive at a better understanding of Paul's letters by comparing them with ordinary letters of his own day, noting not only the similarities but also the differences. In addition to the differences already discussed, there is one further difference between Philemon, say, and Apion's letter to his father Epimachus (discussed above) that deserves reflection. The issue is that of preservation. That we are able to read the papyri letters at all is purely due to happenstances of survival and discovery—the favourable Egyptian climate and the chancy circumstances of archaeological investigation. Paul's letters, by contrast, have been deliberately preserved by generations of reading communities that have continued to find them meaningful and have each taken great care to preserve them and hand them on to the next. Consequently the 'meaning' of these texts cannot be restricted to the limited confines of the original reading event. These texts have had a significant afterlife, continuing to speak in fresh ways to new situations, and this afterlife has added its own successive layers of meaning that hover like an aura around the texts as we read them today.

2. The actual process by which Paul's letters were collected in the first place can be only dimly discerned (Gamble 1975; 1985). That they have survived at all seems to indicate that they were preserved by their original recipients; the only other option—that Paul and his associates preserved a 'master file' of letters—is ruled out both by the absence of some letters (e.g. the one mentioned in 1 Cor 5:9) and by evidence that suggests the gradual emergence of a standard collection rather than the existence of a fixed corpus of letters from the outset (Gamble 1975). The reference in 2 Pet 3:16, along with the writings of Clement of Rome, Ignatius, and Polycarp, indicate that by the late first and early second centuries most of Paul's letters were known and were being cited as authoritative texts, though there is no indication of the shape or extent of the collection. The first extant list of Pauline writings is that of the 'heretic' Marcion in the mid-second century, a list containing all but the Pastorals. The Pastorals are included, however, in lists drawn up later in the century by Irenaeus, Tertullian, and Clement of Alexandria. These three authors also contributed significantly to the concept of a Christian canon of scripture, consisting of a set of 'apostolic' writings existing alongside the Scriptures originating with Israel; the terms 'Old' and 'New Testament' (the Latin equivalent of 'covenant') were contributed by the Latin writer Tertullian. By the end of the second century, then, the thirteen letters contained in our New Testament had been collected into a single Pauline corpus that formed part of a larger (though still somewhat fluid) collection of authoritative Christian Scripture.

3. This process of canonization represents a dramatic shift in the context within which these letters were read. At the outset, neither Paul nor his intended readers saw the letters as 'Scripture', even though Paul wrote both out of the conviction that God had 'spoken' in a new way in Christ (revelation being one component in the concept of 'Scripture'), and with a sense of divinely granted authority (a second component). No doubt these were factors in the initial preservation of the letters. But what happened next? In the absence of any hard data between the 50s and the 90s of the first century, there is room for a variety of possibilities. Some argue for a Pauline school—associates and later followers of Paul, who made collections of the letters in order to study the thought of the master, producing new letters to synthesize his thought (e.g. Ephesians) or to bring his voice to bear on new situations (the Pastorals). Others suggest that it was the publication of the Acts of the Apostles that produced a renewed interest in Paul and led churches to dig the letters out of the archives and copy them for circulation. Edgar Goodspeed and his followers (e.g. Knox 1959) link this with the imaginative idea that the one primarily responsible for the collection was none other than Onesimus, the slave for whose benefit the letter to Philemon was written. This theory rests on two (not completely implausible) suppositions: that the Onesimus of Philemon is the same person referred to by Ignatius (c.110CE) as bishop of Ephesus; and that the inclusion of the short, semi-personal letter to Philemon in the Pauline corpus requires some explanation. It is more probable, however, that the process of collection was both a more continuous and a more haphazard affair, with different collections emerging in different local settings through the latter part of the first century.

4. In any case, the basic fact is clear that the letters survived not because the early church was interested in preserving an archival record of its origins, but because those who first read the letters over the shoulders, as it were, of the original recipients felt that the letters transcended their original settings and had continuing meaning for readers and situations beyond the original context. While our understanding of the letters has been richly enhanced by careful scholarly reconstruction of their original contexts, it should not therefore be supposed (though a perusal of much scholarly literature suggests that it often has been supposed) that the question of the meaning of these texts is exhausted when a full recovery of this 'original meaning' is attained. At least three additional layers or dimensions of meaning need to be recognized.

5. The first is the canonical context. While the letters were first written as individual items of communication—part of an ongoing dialogue between Paul and the community in question, to be sure, but to be read independently of any other letter from Paul—they have been preserved in a canonical collection of which they are an integral part (Childs 1984). At least in the context of the church, then, one cannot read Galatians, say, with its polemical and extreme language about (some aspects of) Torah-centred religion, without reference to the more tempered and generous language of Romans. Likewise, the negative view of marriage in 1 Cor 7 has to be read alongside the more positive depiction in Eph 5; even if Ephesians is not by Paul himself, these texts have been preserved for us by a tradition that makes no distinction whatsoever between Pauline and Deutero-Pauline or post-Pauline literature.

6. To say this, of course, is to say nothing about how one goes about resolving tensions among the members of the collection; there are no rules to say that Romans trumps Galatians or that Eph 5 is to be preferred over 1 Cor 7 (or vice versa in either case). Tension and interpretative difficulty come with the canonical territory, even more so when the rest of the canon is brought into play (as indeed it should be). Of course, we can read the letters in isolation from each other if we choose to do so. But they have been preserved only as part of a collection where they are presented to us as 'the epistles of Saint Paul'. This process of canonization, then, is not simply the ecclesiastical equivalent of the dry sands of Egypt—a historical happenstance that has effected the preservation of these letters but that is extrinsic to their meaning. Intrinsic to the process of preservation is the development of a framework of meaning within which the letters have been handed on to subsequent generations.

7. This leads to a second 'value-added' stage in the process. Subsequent generations have not simply handed on the texts in their canonical framework of meaning. Each generation of Christian readers has engaged in the process of scriptural interpretation—of reading these letters within this framework in order both to enter more deeply into the text and to bring it to bear on the situations and circumstances of their own day. Scriptural interpretation is of necessity a collaborative and corporate exercise, but one that is impoverished when the voices of previous generations of interpreters are left out of the discussion. Recently there has been a revival of interest in the history of interpretation, evidenced for example by the series Ancient Christian Commentary on Scripture (Inter Varsity Press) and Pilgrim Classic Commentaries (Pilgrim Press), and this is helping to bring these voices back to the interpretative table.

8. But this is not the only way in which the transmission of Paul's letters through the years has generated levels of meaning that accompany them into the present. The Bible has existed not simply as an interpretative object; it has been a kind of subject or agent as well, impacting—indeed, shaping in fundamental ways—the culture in which it has been transmitted to us. One cannot come to a full understanding of Paul's letters without recognizing the social and cultural effects they have had. This type of study is still in its infancy (see Bockmuehl 1995), but examples spring readily to mind. We have already observed at the outset of this essay the role played by the Epistle to the Romans in the conversions of Augustine, Martin Luther, and John Wesley. These conversions are significant not only for their own sake, but also for their far-reaching social and historical consequences—Augustine and the 'introspective conscience of the West' (Stendahl 1976), Luther and the Reformation, Wesley and the evangelical revivals in Great Britain and the New World. It would take whole volumes of books to trace the historical consequences of Paul and his letters in these events alone.

9. To take another, quite different, example: during archaeological excavation of the city of Caesarea Maritima, a mosaic floor was discovered in a building dating from the Byzantine period (6th cent. CE) that originally served some public and bureaucratic function. The mosaic contained the text of Rom 13:3: 'Do you wish to have no reason to fear the authority? Then do what is good, and you will received its approval.' Here, probably not for the first time and certainly not the last, statements from Paul's letter to the church in Rome were used by ruling powers to encourage submission to the state. The role of this text in eliciting and reinforcing the church's acquiescence to the policies of the Nazi regime in Germany is a more extreme example of the same power of texts to shape social realities, for good or ill. The fact that the text was being misinterpreted in the process—what he said to the Roman Christians notwithstanding, Paul was quite prepared to engage in activity that the state considered disruptive enough to justify his arrest and imprisonment (2 Cor 11:23)—in no way diminishes the point.

10. The point could be elaborated at great length, and there is much interesting work waiting to be done on the epistles of Paul as factors in social history. But the most important thing to be said about the letters as subjects, as agents accomplishing effects, is that the potential for their functioning in this way is present every time they are read anew. In any fresh encounter with these texts they bring to the event the evocative power of their rhetorical voice, along with the reverberating echoes of the processes of meaning-production that have preserved them and brought them to us. We bring to the event our own personal subjectivities, along with whatever we have come to know about the texts themselves, the circumstances lying behind them, the structures of thought and conviction lying beneath them, and the history of preservation, interpretation, and effective agency opening up in front of them. What comes out of the encounter, happily, has often been unpredictable and full of rich surprise. Paul would call it grace.

REFERENCES

Ascough, R. S. (1997), *What Are They Saying About the Formation of Pauline Churches?* (New York: Paulist).

Aune, D. E. (1987), *The New Testament in its Literary Environment* (Philadelphia: Westminster).

Beker, C. (1980), *Paul the Apostle: The Triumph of God in Life and Thought* (Philadelphia: Fortress).

Betz, H. D. (1979), *Galatians: A Commentary on Paul's Letter to the Churches in Galatia*, Hermeneia (Philadelphia: Fortress).

Bockmuehl, M. (1995), 'A Commentator's Approach to the "Effective History" of Philippians', *JSNT* 60: 57–88.

Brown, R. E. (1997), *An Introduction to the New Testament* (New York: Doubleday).

Bruce, F. F. (1977), *Paul: Apostle of the Heart Set Free* (Grand Rapids: Eerdmans).

Childs, B. S. (1984), *The New Testament as Canon: An Introduction* (London: SCM).

Deissmann, A. (1910), *Light from the Ancient East: The New Testament Illustrated by Recently Discovered Texts of the Graeco-Roman World* (London: Hodder & Stoughton).

Donaldson, T. L. (1994), ' "The Gospel that I Proclaim among the Gentiles" (Gal 2:2): Universalistic or Israel-Centred?', in L. Ann Jervis and Peter Richardson (eds.), *Gospel in Paul: Studies on Corinthians, Galatians and Romans for Richard N. Longenecker*, JSNTSup 108 (Sheffield: Sheffield Academic Press), 166–93.

—— (1997), *Paul and the Gentiles: Remapping the Apostle's Convictional World* (Minneapolis: Fortress).

—— (forthcoming), ' "The field God has assigned": Geography and Mission in Paul', in Leif Vaage (ed.), *Religious Rivalries and the Struggle for Success in the Early Roman Empire*, Studies in Christianity and Judaism (Waterloo, Ont.: Wilfrid Laurier University Press).

Dunn, J. D. G. (1988), *Romans*, WBC (2 vols: Waco, Tex.: Word).

—— (1998), *The Theology of Paul the Apostle* (Grand Rapids: Eerdmans).

Elliott, J. H. (1990), 'Paul, Galatians and the Evil Eye'. *CurTM* 17: 262–73.

Funk, R. W. (1967), 'The Apostolic Parousia: Form and Significance', in W. R. Farmer, C. F. D. Moule, and R. R. Niebuhr (eds.), *Christian History and Interpretation: Studies Presented to John Knox* (Cambridge: Cambridge University Press), 249–68.

Gamble, H. (1975), 'The Redaction of the Pauline Letters and the Formation of the Pauline Corpus', *JBL* 94: 403–18.

—— (1985), *The New Testament Canon: Its Making and Meaning* (Philadelphia: Fortress).

Haenchen, E. (1971), *The Acts of the Apostles: A Commentary* (Philadelphia: Westminster).

Hengel, M. (1991), *The Pre-Christian Paul* (London: SCM).

Hengel, M., and Schwemer, A. M. (1997), *Paul between Damascus and Antioch: The Unknown Years* (Louisville, KY.: Westminster/John Knox).

Hock, R., F. (1980), *The Social Context of Paul's Ministry: Tentmaking and Apostleship* (Philadelphia: Fortress).

Hurd, J. C. (1965), *The Origin of 1 Corinthians* (New York: Seabury).

Kennedy, G. A. (1984), *New Testament Interpretation through Rhetorical Criticism* (Chapel Hill, NC: University of North Carolina Press).

Knox, J. (1950), *Chapters in a Life of Paul* (New York/Nashville: Abingdon-Cokesbury).

—— (1959), *Philemon among the Letters of Paul* (Nashville, Tenn.: Abingdon).

—— (1964), 'Romans 15:14–33 and Paul's Conception of His Apostolic Mission', *JBL* 83: 1–11.

Kümmel, W. G. (1929), *Römer 7 und die Bekehrung des Paulus* (Leipzig: Hinrichs).

Longenecker, R. N. (1990), *Galatians*, WBC (Waco, Tex.: Word).

Lüdemann, G. (1984), *Paul Apostle to the Gentiles: Studies in Chronology* (London: SCM).

Mack, B. L. (1990), *Rhetoric and the New Testament* (Minneapolis: Fortress).

Meeks, W. A. (1983), *The First Urban Christians: The Social World of the Apostle Paul* (New Haven: Yale University Press).

Muggeridge, M., and Vidler, A. (1972), *Paul: Envoy Extraordinary* (London: Collins).

Murphy-O'Connor, J. (1996), *Paul: A Critical Life* (Oxford: Clarendon).

Rambo, L. R. (1993), *Understanding Religious Conversion* (New Haven: Yale University Press).

Ramsay, W. M. (1907), *St. Paul the Traveller and the Roman Citizen*, 9th edn. (London: Hodder & Stoughton).

Riesner, R. (1998), *Paul's Early Period: Chronology, Mission, Strategy, Theology* (Grand Rapids: Eerdmans).

Roetzel, C. J. (1998), *The Letters of Paul: Conversations in Context*, 4th edn. (Louisville, Ky.: Westminster/John Knox).

Sanders, E. P. (1977), *Paul and Palestinian Judaism: A Comparison of Patterns of Religion* (Philadelphia: Fortress).

Schoeps, H.-J. (1961), *Paul: The Theology of the Apostle in the Light of Jewish Religious History* (Philadelphia: Westminster).

Scott, J. M. (1995), *Paul and the Nations*, WUNT 84 (Tübingen: Mohr [Siebeck]).

Segal, A. F. (1990), *Paul the Convert: The Apostolate and Apostasy of Saul the Pharisee* (New Haven: Yale University Press).

Stark, R. (1996), *The Rise of Christianity: A Sociologist Reconsiders History* (Princeton: Princeton University Press).

Stendahl, K. (1976), *Paul among Jews and Gentiles, and other Essays* (Philadelphia: Fortress).

Stowers, S. K. (1986), *Letter Writing in Greco-Roman Antiquity* (Philadelphia: Westminster).

Townsend, J. T. (1985), 'Missionary Journeys in Acts and European Missionary Societies', *Society of Biblical Literature Seminar Papers*, 433–7.

Watson, F. (1986), *Paul, Judaism and the Gentiles*, SNTSMS 56 (Cambridge: Cambridge University Press).

Weima, J. A. D. (1994), *Neglected Endings: The Significance of the Pauline Letter Closings*, JSNTSup 101 (Sheffield: Sheffield Academic Press).

White, J. L. (1972), *The Form and Function of the Body of the Greek Letter* (Missoula, Mont.: SBL).

64. Romans

CRAIG C. HILL

INTRODUCTION

A. Significance. Romans is one of the eminent texts of Western history. From Augustine to Luther, from Wesley to Barth, Christian thinkers of every era have been shaped profoundly by this, the longest Pauline epistle. Romans is commonly regarded as Paul's supreme work, the consummate expression of his mature theology. Among Protestants in particular, no book has been more highly esteemed or carefully scrutinized. Above all, Romans influenced the Reformation vision of true religion as the reception of God's grace through faith.

In equal and opposite reaction, however, Romans has unwittingly encouraged generations of readers from Marcion onwards to regard Judaism as the exemplarily *false* religion, a creed of merit and system of works unworthy of devotion or even of toleration. The first of these conclusions lies at the heart of Protestant–Catholic debate, the second at the centre of Jewish–Christian controversy. Not surprisingly, Roman Catholics have long questioned Protestant readings of Romans (paralleling in some ways the canonical protest of Jas

2:14–26), as Jews have long challenged the epistle's character-ization of their theology. Only recently, as a consequence of post-Vatican II ecumenicity and post-Holocaust interreligious awareness, have the earlier interpretative models begun to break apart. The willingness of major scholars to cross trad-itional boundaries and weigh old criticisms with new serious-ness is undoubtedly the most important development in modern Pauline studies. Thus, now as in the past, Romans is at the forefront of Christian theological reflection and self-understanding.

B. Provenance. 1. The Pauline authorship of Romans is not in doubt. Indeed, one might say that Romans is the 'most Paul-ine' epistle, since it most influences scholarly construals of Paul and most frequently is referenced in arguments about the (in)authenticity of the Deutero-Pauline letters. Also, com-pared to other Pauline epistles (notably Philippians and 2 Corinthians), few doubts arise concerning the literary integ-rity of Romans. The unity of the letter is seriously questioned only at ch. 16, which some regard as the remnant of a separate Pauline letter, appended to Romans' original conclusion in 15:33. The evidence for this view is not compelling, as is noted in the commentary on ch. 16.

2. Romans was probably composed in Corinth during Paul's final visit. Gaius, 'whose hospitality I and the whole church here enjoy' (16:23, NIV), is presumably the same figure mentioned in 1 Cor 1:14. In 15:23–33, Paul anticipates an imminent journey to Jerusalem, an itinerary that corres-ponds broadly to Acts 20:1–21:17. Thus, widespread consen-sus exists for dating Romans in the mid-50s CE, making it one of Paul's final letters (at least subsequent to his Thessalonian, Galatian, and Corinthian correspondence).

3. The letter is written 'to all God's beloved in Rome' (1:7). The city of Rome was the seat of government of the Roman republic (?5th cent.–31 BCE) and empire until 330 CE, when Constantine moved the capital to Constantinople. During the second and first centuries BCE, Rome gradually came to dom-inate the countries of the Mediterranean basin, including Judea, which was conquered in 63 BCE by the Roman general Pompey. The city of Rome was vast, home to approximately 1 million persons. Augustus and subsequent emperors erected monumental public works, including amphitheatres, squares, temples, forums, and libraries. Although the wealthy inhabited comfortable villas, the great majority of people were poor and lived in large tenement houses, some as tall as six storeys (HBC 882). The Jewish community of Rome was substantial; it is estimated that between 20,000 and 50,000 Jews lived in the city by the beginning of the first century CE (ABD 1048). How or when Christianity came to Rome is unknown. By mid-century, when Paul wrote Romans, the church already enjoyed a substantial reputation (1:8). A dis-pute within the Jewish community over Christian claims appears to stand behind the Emperor Claudius's expulsion of the Jews from Rome in 49 CE (see Acts 18:2). According to Suetonius (Claudius, 25.4), 'the Jews constantly made disturb-ances at the instigation of Chrestus', probably a mistaken form of the word Christus (Christ). Local Christians were sufficient in number and reputation in 64 CE that Nero could scapegoat them for the fire of Rome. 'Nero fastened the guilt and afflicted the most exquisite tortures on a class hated for

their abominations, called Christians by the populace' (Taci-tus, Annals, 15.44.2).

C. Literary Genre. Formally, Romans is identical to most other Pauline letters, including a salutation (identifying sender and recipients), a thanksgiving (clarifying the relationship be-tween writer and reader and previewing the contents of the letter), a body (offering the substance of Paul's communica-tion), and a farewell (including a final blessing and, if ch. 16 is genuine, personal greetings). In numerous other ways, how-ever, Romans is different—as one might expect, knowing that it is the only Pauline letter written to a church neither founded by the apostle or his assistants, nor visited by him (note e.g. the lengthy self-descriptions in 1:1–6 and 15:16–21, and the deferential language of 1:11–13 and 15:22–4). The hallmark of Paul's other letters is their contingency; characteristically, they deal with specific issues that arose within a particular Pauline church (e.g. 1 Cor 1:11: 'For it has been reported to me by Chloe's people that there are quarrels among you'; 1 Cor 7:1: 'Now concerning the matters about which you wrote...'). Reading these letters is not unlike overhearing one side of a conversation. Clearly, this analogy does not apply to Romans, which is more declamation than dialogue. The letter does not address in any obvious way the Roman church's own prob-lems. It is a single, extended theological argument, not a seriatim discussion of pastoral concerns. It thus is a letter more in form than in function. For this reason, Romans is categorized as, for example, an 'epistle' (as distinct, according to Deissmann (1927: 220), from a non-literary 'letter'), a 'Greek letter-essay' (Stirewalt 1977), an 'essay-letter' (Fitzmyer 1993), or an 'ambassadorial letter' (Jewett, cited by Fitzmyer 1993: 68–9). All such labels make the point that Romans was commissioned to a somewhat different service than the other Pauline letters. To what service, exactly, is one of the perennial issues of Pauline scholarship.

D. Purpose. 1. Paul offers few clues as to his purpose in writing to the church at Rome. He states in 1:10–11 that he prays for the Roman Christians and longs to see them, 'that I may share with you some spiritual gift to strengthen you—or rather so that we may be mutually encouraged by each other's faith...[and] that I may reap some harvest among you as I have among the rest of the Gentiles.' In 15:15, he states that 'on some points I have written to you rather boldly by way of reminder, because of the grace given me by God to be a minister of Christ Jesus to the Gentiles in the priestly service of the gospel of God, so that the offering of the Gentiles may be acceptable, sanctified by the Holy Spirit.' In 15:23–9, Paul informs his readers of his travel plans: he soon will deliver the collection to 'the saints at Jerusalem' and then visit Rome on his way to Spain, where he will engage in further missionary work (v. 20). He hopes not only to see the Roman Christians but also 'to be sent on by you, once I have enjoyed your company for a little while' (v. 24). Similarly, in vv. 28–9, Paul states that 'I know that when I come to you, I will come in the fullness of the blessing of Christ.' In 15:30–1, Paul urges his readers to pray for the success of his impending trip to Jeru-salem, 'so that by God's will I may come to you with joy and be refreshed in your company.' Taken together, these state-ments probably indicate that Paul hoped to win the support of the Roman church for his missionary venture in Spain, and that as 'minister to the Gentiles' (Gal 2:7), he assumed a measure of pastoral responsibility for the Gentile Christians in what was, after all, the greatest city of the known world. The letter thus would have both strategic and didactic functions, to introduce and recommend Paul, and to teach and exhort his readers in the Christian faith, as Paul understood it.

2. Could not Paul have met these objectives in fewer than the 7,000 words of Romans? Was there some larger task, demanding a more extensive response? The traditional explanation is to regard Romans as Paul's theological 'last will and testament', a summary of his theology composed near the end of his career. But Paul expected both an ongoing apostolic occupation and an approaching eschatological consummation (13:11–12). Moreover, Romans is *not* a good compendium of Pauline teaching; much that is contained in Paul's other letters is absent. Why did Paul write at such length about these particular issues, most notably, the law and Judaism? Scholars have looked both to Paul's own circumstances and to the circumstances of the Roman church for answers.

3.1. What do we know about Paul's situation that might be relevant to the composition of Romans? Surely the most important datum is the recent, bitter controversy at Galatia; the letter to the Galatians includes most of the primary topics and much of the key language of Romans. Many scholars date Philippians even closer to Romans (55 CE, according to Jewett 1979). Phil 3 (probably a warning based on Paul's Galatian experience; see Hill 1992: 155–8) is reminiscent of both Galatians and Romans ('flesh... circumcision... zeal... righteousness under the Law', etc.). Thus the theology of Romans does not appear *ex nihilo*. Paul had ample cause to weigh these matters and to regard them as both important and urgent.

3.2. A second key factor is Paul's awareness of the relative failure of the church's 'Jewish mission' (Gal 2:7–8). Paul speaks of his 'sorrow and unceasing anguish' for his 'kindred according to the flesh' (9:2). It is clear that Jewish unbelief is a theological and not just a personal problem for Paul. God acted in Christ to fulfil divine promises to Israel, but the concrete result is a Gentile church. Can God be *righteous*, faithful to God's own nature and commitments, and not save Israel? (Indeed, God's righteousness is the unifying theme of the entire letter. See ROM 1:16–17.) In the face of his impending trip to Jerusalem, the problem must have appeared acute. Has God failed? And is not Paul, who calls Gentiles 'children of Abraham' (4:16) and who says that 'Christ is the end of the law' (10:4), the enemy of Israel? Is Paul's a *righteous* gospel? Hays (1989: 35) has noted with insight that Romans is 'an intertextual conversation between Paul and the voice of Scripture' in which the apostle 'labors to win the blessing of Moses and the prophets'. Gentile biblical scholarship has tended to de-Judaize Paul, thereby trivializing these struggles and rendering the central place of Rom 9–11 (on the fate of Israel) nonsensical.

3.3. A number of scholars have argued that it is Paul's impending trip to Jerusalem that most influenced his writing of Romans (e.g. Manson 1948, Jervell 1971). It is evident from 15:30–2 that Paul himself anticipated trouble in Jerusalem. Accordingly, Romans is often seen as a rehearsal of the arguments that Paul would make on his own behalf in Jerusalem. The shape of this theory varies from scholar to scholar, depending mostly upon prior conclusions about the relationship between Paul and other Jewish Christians. Does 15:31 indicate that Paul would have to defend himself to the church as well as to the Jewish authorities of Jerusalem? If so, on what issues? F. C. Baur (1873–5: i. 109–51) asserted a century and a half ago that the leaders of the Jerusalem church (notably, Peter and James) actively opposed Paul for admitting uncircumcised Gentiles into the church. It is the heirs of Baur today who make the most of Paul's conflict with the Jerusalem church. By their reading, Paul's defence in Romans of the equality of Jew and Gentile is aimed squarely at the Jerusalem Christians. This presents a heroic, classically Protestant portrait of Paul as the lone champion of Christian freedom. Despite its popularity, this hypothesis is not corroborated by the New Testament. The only substantial evidence strongly supports the contrary view, that the Jerusalem church accepted Gentiles *qua* Gentiles as Christian believers (e.g. Gal. 2:1–10; Acts 15; see Hill 1992: 103–92). This does not mean that there was no disagreement between Paul and other Jewish–Christian leaders. Paul sanctioned disobedience by Jews of certain Jewish (particularly food) laws (see 1 Cor 9:20–1), an attitude that did not endear him to many in Israel, Christian or otherwise. It is instructive that it was over food laws that Paul confronted Peter at Antioch (Gal 2:11–14); it was not the circumcising of Gentiles that precipitated the crisis but the observing of dietary laws that, in Paul's mind, recreated the distinction between Jews and Gentiles. Likewise, it is the issue of law observance *on the part of Jewish Christians* that is mentioned in association with Paul's final visit to Jerusalem in Acts (21:21, 28). Also, one should bear in mind that Paul was bidding for the practical support of the Roman church. Interjecting a dispute with the mother church (whose authority Paul himself acknowledged; e.g. Gal 2:2) hardly seems politic. Moreover, any such self-defence is subtle to the point of invisibility (cf., by contrast, the defence of 2 Cor 11–13 or the record of his public confrontation in Gal 2:11–14). Therefore, while Paul's impending Jerusalem visit may have been a factor in his composition of Romans (as in ROM D.3.1), it is highly doubtful that Romans originated as an apologia directed at the Jerusalem church.

4. The other approach is to look to the circumstances of the letter's recipients for explanations. How much Paul knew about the situation in Rome is the subject of considerable debate. His most likely source of information was Priscilla and Aquila, who, according to Acts 18:2, came to Corinth from Rome as a consequence of Claudius' expulsion of the Jews (49 CE). They are mentioned by Paul himself in 1 Cor 16:19 and (if authentic) Rom 16:3. Also mentioned in ch. 16 are several other Roman Christians. Still, it is not obvious how Paul's acquaintance with such persons might have shaped this letter. Paul made a considerable effort to introduce himself and his gospel to the Roman church, a clear signal that he regarded his audience as strangers. Many scholars attempt to link the epistle's contents to a Roman context by suggesting that the Jewish believers who returned to Rome following Claudius' death were not accorded due respect by their Gentile co-religionists, who even went so far as to deny positions of authority to returning Jewish leaders (Marxsen 1968: 95–104; Beker 1980: 69–74). Hearing of the Gentile Christians' conduct, Paul composed this letter, at least in part as an attempt to unify the Roman church. Passages such as 11:17–21 ('do not

vaunt yourselves over the branches [the Jews]') were written to teach the Gentile believers proper humility. (In tension with this purpose is the tendency of these same scholars to equate the 'weak' of ch. 14 with returning Jewish believers who continued to observe food laws: see Dunn 1988: ii. 798; cf. the counter-argument in Nanos 1996: 85–165.) This reconstruction, while not impossible, is open to question at every point (see e.g. the strong challenge of Stowers 1994). The most that can be said with certainty is that Paul wanted to demonstrate that the Gentile church had not supplanted Israel, and therefore that Gentiles had no reason to boast in their present status (11:17–36). The argument could have been formulated in response to a Jewish–Gentile conflict in the Roman church, but such a conflict is not required to explain it. Perhaps Gentile Christians in the capital city faced special temptations to triumphalism, but that tendency could hardly have been unique, as subsequent history thoroughly demonstrates.

5. Knowing the context of a statement is of first importance in determining its meaning; unfortunately, such contextual data are substantially lacking with respect to Romans. Consequently, the inherently conjectural nature of one's interpretation should be acknowledged. Sufficient evidence exists to allow for the formation of fairly detailed hypotheses; sufficient gaps in that evidence ensure that even careful hypotheses will be substantially speculative. To a large degree, we do not know why this epistle was written, and any interpretation based upon the presumption of such knowledge will be inherently circular. Because the commentary below assumes no single 'reason for Romans', it will not attempt to advance one interpretation against all others. Instead, it will seek to delineate the plausible range of interpretation. This is an admittedly confined ambition, but one that corresponds to the real limitations within which any interpreter of Romans labours.

E. Issues of Interpretation. 1. A generation ago, one might have asserted that the exegesis of Romans was complete in its essentials, pointing to the common interpretative tradition that extended from Augustine to Bultmann and Barth. Whatever consensus might have existed prior to 1977 was fractured by the publication that year of E. P. Sanders's *Paul and Palestinian Judaism* (see Räisänen 1983: 1–15; Dunn 1988: i. pp. lxiii–lxxii). Sanders offered a critique of Pauline scholarship based on two methodological assumptions: (1) a religion ought to be understood in its own terms through an analysis of its own primary sources; and (2) an author's argumentation must not be unnaturally synthesized by later expositors; contradictory statements and approaches, where they occur, should be allowed to remain (Sanders 1977: 12). Application of the first assumption leads one to question any construal of Judaism based on the often polemical references to it in Christian writings, including the NT. The popular picture of first-century Judaism as a religion of sterile legalism, supercilious piety, and haughty self-righteousness is not supported by *Jewish* documents. When allowed to speak for themselves, first-century Jews are not heard advocating a religion of merit, the photo-negative of a uniquely Christian notion of salvation by grace. Functionally, Judaism and Christianity are quite similar: one 'gets in' by means of God's gracious calling; one then is obligated (not least by gratitude) to obey the will of God, however defined. Obviously, regarding Judaism in this way necessitates a rethinking of Paul. For example, earlier interpreters could assume that Paul had formulated his ideas about the law in response to the legalism of normative Judaism. One school saw Paul's response as a correction of Jewish abuses; the law, no longer 'misused', was still valid (Cranfield 1979: 862). Others believed that Paul rejected out of hand any notion of the law's validity since he recognized that the law itself was a primary source of human alienation (Bultmann 1952–5: i. 247). Unfortunately, both approaches account for Paul's position by making reference to a Judaism that never existed. A popular counter-proposal suggests that Paul's target was not works righteousness at all but 'Jewish national [self-]righteousness' (e.g. Dunn 1988: i. pp. lxxi–lxxii, 42–3, etc.). This move appears to vindicate Paul—he is still right about what is wrong about Judaism—but it misses the point of Sanders's critique. In effect, it substitutes a new bad Judaism for the old, now discredited bad Judaism of traditional interpretation. But the problem is not in our (previously) faulty identification of Judaism's deficiency (whose depiction in Paul varies and so is infinitely interpretable); the problem is in Paul's either/or reasoning that requires that Judaism be nullified for Christ to be necessitated (see ROM E.6). Were the disorder Jewish pride, the remedy would be Jewish humility. But for Paul the only adequate curative is Christian faith, which means that the only actual complaint is Jewish unbelief, however variously it may be explained or characterized from the Christian side (see ROM 2).

2. It is at this point that the second methodological principle, that of taking apparently contradictory material at face value, has been fruitfully applied. What does it mean if Paul's arguments about the law do not entirely cohere? Among other things, it may indicate that Paul did not *think* his way to Christian faith, that his conclusions about the law are not the result of his own pre-Christian wrestling with its supposed inadequacies. As Sanders (1977: 442–7) put it, Paul 'reasoned backwards'. He did not move from consideration of the law to Christian faith; instead, having come to faith in Christ, Paul attempted to understand as a Jewish Christian the Judaism in which he had been raised. Thus Paul never was entirely able to repudiate the law. It was, after all, God's law and as such must serve a divine, albeit negative, purpose. Two fundamental convictions, that God is the God of Israel and that God provides salvation only in Christ, were thus held together in uneasy tension, and most of what is commonly considered under the rubric 'Paul and the Law' can be understood as part of an ongoing attempt to effect a reconciliation between the two.

3. If Judaism was not the false religion of works righteousness, if the law did not function within Judaism as a *means* to salvation, what are we to make of Paul's argument? It may be claimed that Paul has set up Judaism as a straw man, the foil to all that is deemed good and true in Christianity. It seems more reasonable, however, to think that Paul is describing something quite real: not Judaism as non-Christian Jews knew it but Judaism as it would be experienced by Paul's Gentile-Christian converts. Within Judaism, one was not circumcised to *earn* membership in the people of God. Instead, circumcision marked a son of Israel's participation in God's gracious, pre-existing covenant. The situation is wholly different, however, if the subject is an adult Gentile Christian. If he accepted circumcision under compulsion, he would, by implication, be saying that his faith in Christ is insufficient to save, an inadequate basis for participation in God's covenant. For him circumcision would therefore become a work, and Judaism a religion of works righteousness. (The same dilemma occurs when an adult Christian joins a denomination that does not recognize his or her baptism. For that person, baptism becomes an entry requirement, an indispensable 'work', however it may be construed theologically by existing church members.) Paul's argument, including his tendency to oppose the law and Christian faith as antithetical religious systems, makes a good deal more sense when viewed in this way. This does require, however, that we no longer regard Paul as an objective, disinterested observer of Judaism.

4. Other distinctive aspects of Paul's thought bear significantly on our understanding of Romans. The first concerns Pauline eschatology. In general, Paul has a decidedly future or 'not yet' orientation, reminiscent of the Gospel of Mark. In the undisputed Pauline epistles, salvation is always a future category; the paradigm of present Christian life is the cross, not the resurrection (e.g. 1 Cor 1:18; 2:2; Rom 6:5; 8:18). Present experience of the Spirit is a foretaste or seal (2 Cor 1:22) of what is to come (1 Cor 13:8–12). There is one very important exception, however, one issue in relation to which Paul consistently invokes a realized eschatology: the Gentiles. For Paul, the prophetic expectation that Gentiles would be incorporated into Israel in the last days is already being fulfilled, not least in his own ministry. (Note, for example, how Paul's description in Rom 15:25–6—see also the quotations in vv. 9–12—draws on Isa 66:18–22.) In Rom 11:25–7 Paul explains this 'mystery': present Jewish unbelief has effected a reversal of the eschatological timetable; contrary to expectation, it is the Gentiles who will enter first, after which God will act to save 'all Israel'. Much of what is peculiar to Pauline theology is derived from this perspective: admission of Gentiles is not foreshadow; it is substance. That puts Pauline theology on a fundamentally different footing from that of other Jewish-Christian leaders, and it explains how both Paul and the 'pillar apostles' (James, Cephas, and John: Gal 2:9) could have agreed to the practice of Gentile admission while utterly disagreeing as to its consequences. If there is now one people in Christ, without distinction between Jew and Gentile (Gal 3:28), then the church exists in a radically new age, from which one can radically critique what went before—especially the law, whose very stipulations drew the boundaries between Jew and Gentile. (An inevitable consequence of a realized eschatology is an increased sense of theological distance between insiders and outsiders, especially between Christians and (non-Christian) Jews; note the many pejorative references to 'the Jews' and 'the world' in Johannine literature.) The categories of Paul's thought that are derivative of the 'Gentile issue' share in the same logic, e.g. Paul's idealized Christian anthropology, according to which believers are *essentially* different from other people: they 'walk in the Spirit' and so fulfil the 'just requirements of the law' (Rom 8:4). It is always worth asking what reality Paul presupposes within a given argument. When a question relates in some way to Gentile admission, Paul's thinking shifts towards realized eschatological categories, a fact that explains many of the ambiguities within Pauline

theology and the tensions between Pauline theory and practice.

5. It is important to note that Paul worked with the concepts available to him. Chief among these is the idea that the law is a single entity, given by God. This presents Paul with an insuperable difficulty. He knows by God's acceptance of Gentiles (demonstrated by gifts of the Spirit; Gal 3:2–5) that obedience to laws that distinguish Jews from Gentiles (namely circumcision, food laws, sabbath and other 'days') is no longer required. However, the law being a unity, it is necessary to challenge it *in toto*. In theory, this is no problem, because Christians possess the Spirit and have no need for a 'written code' (2:27). In practice, what Paul expects of his converts is a fairly typical Jewish morality, which he can assume for himself but which comes less naturally to his Gentile associates. Consequently, Paul is put in the awkward position of legislating rules of behaviour *ad hoc*, since he no longer has the law to draw upon for authorization. Therefore, he is forced, in effect, to reinstitute Jewish laws with Christian warrants (e.g. see Rom 1:20; 1 Cor 6:15–17; and 10:20–1). Thus it is erroneous to suppose that Paul created a law-free religion. Christianity, like Judaism, has always had norms (again, mostly Jewish); for that reason, Christians, as much as Jews, can be guilty of reducing religion to rule-keeping. In short, it is quite possible that the argument of Romans would have looked very different had Paul been able to divide the law explicitly into categories (clarifying what is rejected and what is retained), as Christians ever since the second century (e.g. *Epistle of Barnabas*) have attempted to do. Certainly, subsequent Christian ambivalence—even animosity—towards the Hebrew Bible would have been lessened had Paul taken such a course.

6. Finally, it is vital to understand that Paul consistently organized the relationship between Judaism and Christianity in such a way that non-Christian Judaism *must* be negated. Gal 2:21 reveals a great deal about the working of Paul's mind: 'I do not nullify the grace of God; for if justification comes through the law, then Christ died for nothing.' In other words, it is a zero-sum game. If God intended to save through Christ, it must have been necessary; therefore, one could not be saved apart from Christ, that is to say, through the regular practice of Jewish religion. The either/or structure of Paul's argument explains an otherwise astonishing fact: were Romans our only source, we might well conclude that Jewish theology knew nothing of mercy, grace, love, forgiveness, or atonement. As the logic stands, these necessarily become Christian categories (as do 'grace and truth' in Jn 1:17). It is interesting to note that Paul cited God's acceptance of Abraham on the basis of faith in both Gal 3 and Rom 4 and then passed in silence over virtually all subsequent Jewish history (the mention of David in Rom 4:6 being a rare exception). Needless to say, the existence of any pre- or non-Christian Judaism in which one might find right relationship with God creates a severe problem for Paul. On the one hand, he wants to argue that God saves only in Christ and that Judaism, apart from Christ, is a way of 'sin' and 'death' (Rom 7:9–11); on the other hand, Paul feels compelled to cite precedents in Judaism for God's saving *modus operandi*. The question is, can one have it both ways? Paul might have argued on the basis of essential continuity: the God of the Jews, always a God of salvation, has worked this saving purpose ultimately in Christ (an argument somewhat

similar to that of Hebrews). Instead, Paul's argument traces the line of essential discontinuity, which is precisely what Marcion and other despisers of Judaism have found congenial in his thinking. One must ask if it is possible to affirm what Paul affirms (the religion of grace) without necessarily denying what Paul implicitly denies (that Judaism itself is such a religion).

COMMENTARY

Salutation (1:1–17)

Although the basic shape of the salutation is the same in all Paul's letters (an indication of the sender(s) and recipient(s) followed by a short blessing), the form is flexible and was adapted by Paul to each letter's purpose. For example, Paul wrote Galatians in part as a defence of his divinely sanctioned apostolic authority; thus he identifies himself as 'an apostle neither by human commission nor from human authorities' (Gal 1:1). The salutation in Romans is distinguished by its lengthy description of 'the gospel of God' for which Paul was set apart (vv. 2–6). Such details establish Paul's credentials and identify common ground with his audience.

As in Phil 1:1, Paul refers to himself as a 'slave' or 'servant' (*doulos*) of Jesus Christ (a designation paralleled, for example, in Jas 1:1, 2 Pet 1:1, Jude 1). It was customary for Jews to regard themselves or their leaders as 'servants of God' (Ps 19:11; 27:9; Neh 1:6; 2 Kings 18:12; Isa 20:3; Jer 7:25; Deut 32:36; etc.), and Israel itself is frequently identified as God's servant (Jer 46:27; Ezek 28:25; Isa 44:1, 45:4; etc.) (Dunn 1988: i. 7). The Christological appropriation of OT language about God is a consistent and revealing feature of the NT writings (e.g. cf. Phil 2:10–11; Isa 45:23). Also noteworthy is Paul's tendency to balance a statement about Christ with a statement about God. He wished the Romans 'grace . . . and peace from [both] God our Father and the Lord Jesus Christ' (v. 7); likewise, Paul mentioned that he was 'set apart for the gospel of God . . . [which is] concerning his Son' (vv. 1, 3) and offered thanks to 'God through Jesus Christ for all of you' (v. 8; cf. Rom 8:9: 'Spirit of God . . . Spirit of Christ').

The mention of prophets, scriptures, and David (vv. 2–3) sounds a deliberate note of continuity with Israel's past. The connection between Paul's contemporary proclamation to Gentiles and God's ancient promises to Israel is of central importance in Romans (see esp. chs. 9–11). (On the plural 'scriptures', see Hays 1989: 34).

Many scholars think that the core of vv. 3–4 came from pre-Pauline Christian tradition, possibly in the form of an early Christological formulation (Byrne 1996: 43; Dodd 1932: 4–5). A pair of descriptions of the Son are set in parallel, distinguished by the contrasting Pauline terms 'flesh' and 'spirit':

who was descended from David *according to the flesh*
and was declared to be Son of God with power *according to the
    spirit* of holiness
by resurrection from the dead

Jesus' human or earthly ('according to the flesh') status as a descendant of David (see 2 Sam 7:11–16; Davidic lineage is a staple of messianic texts: Isa 11; Jer 23:5–6; Ezek 34:23–4; etc.) is mentioned only here in Paul's writings but figures promin-

ently elsewhere in the NT (e.g. Mt 1:1; 9:27; Mk 11:10; 12:35; Lk 1:27, 32; 2:4; 2 Tim 2:8; Rev 3:7; 5:5). Also lacking support elsewhere in Paul is the early Christian idea that Jesus was appointed or designated (*horisthentos*; see *TDNT* v. 450–1) Son of God at the resurrection (v. 4; cf. Acts 2:36; 5:30–1; 13:33). 'With power' (whether traditional or Pauline) probably modifies the title 'Son of God' and not the verb 'declared' (Fitzmyer 1993: 235; Cranfield 1979: 62; *contra* NIV 'declared with power'), emphasizing Jesus' exalted status. ('According to the spirit of holiness' is a Semitism; cf. Ps 51:11.) It also might indicate that, at least for Paul, the resurrection *enhanced* an already existing sonship (Dunn 1988: i. 14). In citing Jesus' twofold pedigree, in flesh and in spirit, Paul makes the claim that Jesus is the anticipated Jewish Messiah—and more (as in Mk 1:1). It is Paul's expectation that these common (and apparently longstanding) Christian affirmations will be shared by his readers.

The phrase 'obedience of faith' (also mentioned in 16:26) is ambiguous. It may refer either to faith that is an expression of obedience or to obedience that is an expression of faith. Possibly, Paul intended both meanings. Clearly it is the bringing of persons to faith in Christ that is the primary goal of the Pauline mission. It is no coincidence that Paul can refer synonymously to the Jews' unbelief in 11:20 and to their disobedience in 11:31 (Cranfield 1979: 66). Elsewhere in Romans, however, Paul uses 'obedience' in the more conventional sense (5:19; 6:16; 15:18; 16:19). An interesting parallel occurs in 2 Cor 9:13, where Paul says that the Corinthians' generosity is an expression of their 'obedience to the confession of the Gospel of Christ'. The fact that Paul includes in this mission the Roman Christians themselves (v. 6) indicates at the very least that he is talking about more than the evangelization of Gentiles.

'Grace to you and peace' is the typical Pauline greeting (1 Cor 1:3; 2 Cor 1:2; Gal 1:3; etc.; it is also used in 1 and 2 Pet 1:2 and Rev 1:4). It elegantly combines the Christian word 'grace', *charis* (replacing the similar Greek greeting *chairein*; cf. Acts 15:23; 23:26; Jas 1:1), and the Jewish greeting 'peace' (*šālôm*). It thus incorporates both Gentile and Semitic as well as Christian and Jewish elements.

Thanksgiving (1:8–17)

The thanksgiving is used here, as in Paul's other letters, to express goodwill towards his audience and to remind them of (or, in the case of Romans, to establish) the terms of their association, matters that fall broadly under the heading of 'relationship maintenance'. The thanksgiving also serves to introduce the reader to key ideas and terminology, deliberately signalling the letter's overarching themes (see e.g. 1 Cor 1:4–9; Phil 1:3–11; 1 Thess 1:2–3:13; Philem 4–7). It is to the thanksgiving that one should look first for an indication of Paul's own sense of purpose in writing. (The exception is Galatians, which—not surprisingly, given its polemical edge—contains no thanksgiving.)

(1:8–15) Relationship Maintenance Strictly speaking, Paul is establishing, not maintaining, his relationship with the Roman Christians; nevertheless, he stresses that his interest in and concern for them are not new. He has long known of and prayed for the church at Rome and has been encouraged by reports of its faithfulness. Paul indicates his hope that he 'might at last succeed in coming' to Rome (v. 10). In v. 13 he states that 'I have often intended to come to you (but thus far have been prevented)'. Paul's journey to Rome is not an after-thought; his readers should not feel slighted. The reason for the delay is spelled out in 15:22–4: Paul's missionary activity in Asia and Greece (that is, amongst 'the rest of the Gentiles', v. 13) had only recently been completed. Rome, the natural destination of the 'apostle to the Gentiles' (Gal 2:7), is now fully in view.

The language of 1:1–15 is highly diplomatic. Paul balances assertions of his apostolic authority with statements concerning his regard for and reciprocity with the Roman Christians. Paul is not the founder of Roman Christianity and so cannot assume charge over it. It is worth noting, however, that even in Paul's own churches he had no real power. Paul could exercise authority only in so far as he could persuade his audience of his right to do so (the rhetoric of Galatians and 2 Corinthians providing the best examples; see Holmberg 1978: 193–204).

v. 14, instead of dividing humanity into 'Jew and Gentile' (or 'Jew and Greek', v. 16), on this one occasion Paul uses the standard Hellenistic categories 'Greeks and barbarians' (*TDNT* i. 546–53), which by this time had come to refer to 'all races and classes within the Gentile world' (Dunn 1988: i. 33). It is not clear whether 'wise and foolish' directly parallels 'Greeks and barbarians' (cf. the opposing conclusions of Cranfield 1979: 83; Fitzmyer 1993: 251). In either case, the point is made that the gospel transcends such distinctions. Paul is a 'debtor' (i.e. 'one under obligation'), presumably by his calling, to proclaim the gospel to all Gentiles, including, of course, the Romans themselves. It is less likely that Paul also meant to express his personal indebtedness to individual Gentiles (Morris 1988: 63). A further point is that even the most cultured among the Gentiles is in need of the gospel and (in the light of v. 16, immediately following) that the gospel is in no way threatened by human wisdom. (The contrast between earthly wisdom and divine power (v. 16) is especially prominent in 1 Corinthians, e.g. 1:18–19; 2:4–5.)

(1:16–17) Theme Paul advances now to a statement of his theme: God saves all (both Jew and Greek) in the same way (by faith) by the same means (the gospel), thus demonstrating God's righteousness (God's fairness and fidelity). As this statement indicates, 'righteousness' denotes something more than 'justice' (see Stuhlmacher 1994: 29–32). Dunn (1988: i. 41) terms it 'covenant faithfulness' and traces the idea to the Psalms (e.g. 31:1; 51:14; 98:2) and Deutero-Isaiah (e.g. 45:8, 21; 46:13; 62:1–2) (cf. Hays, below). In Rom 3:21–6, Paul returns to the idea that 'the righteousness of God [now] has been disclosed' (v. 21). How? Not by condemning sinners, as justice demands, but by justifying them, as God's character requires. In view particularly is God's covenant obligation to Israel (see 11:27, 29: 'And this is my covenant with them, when I take away their sins . . . for the gifts and the calling of God are *irrevocable*'). The question of God's faithfulness (one might even say 'God's consistency') is at stake. God has worked salvation in Christ 'first' for the Jews (v. 16); nevertheless, many Jews have not believed. Does the fact of an increasingly Gentile church demonstrate either that God's plan has been thwarted or that God's people have been re-

jected? For Paul, neither conclusion is possible. Instead, he sets out to demonstrate that the righteousness of God is evident precisely in God's acceptance of Gentiles (chs. 1–8), and that the inclusion of Gentiles does not invalidate God's election of Israel (chs. 9–11).

The question, 'Has God abandoned Israel?', is long familiar to Judaism. At root, it is the question of theodicy, in this case, of the evident gap between God's promises and Israel's reality, felt most acutely in time of national defeat and occupation. Richard Hays (1989: 34–83) has demonstrated powerfully that Paul used as source for his reflections in Romans the prophets and lament psalms that dealt with God's apparent abandonment of Israel. It is striking that these materials are laden with references both to God's righteousness and to God's universal salvation (e.g. Ps 97:3 (LXX); Isa 51:4–5; 52:10). It should therefore come as no surprise that Paul initiates the argument of Romans with a quotation from Hab 2:4, which not only supplies key terminology for the letter (ROM 1:17) but does so in the context of a hard-won prophetic affirmation of God's paradoxical faithfulness.

The link to the remaining, paraenetic section of Romans (chs. 12–15) has been obscured by the Protestant inclination to consider justification in exclusively juridical terms. The notion that Christians are different from others primarily in their legal standing before God owes much to a traditional (Augustinian/Lutheran) (mis)reading of Rom 7–8. The Pauline meaning of 'justification' is much broader and evidences a quite different eschatological orientation (see ROM 8). The word *dikaioun* ('to justify'; first used in 2:13 and then repeatedly throughout chs. 2–10) means literally 'to righteous'; it comes from the same root as *dikaiosunē*, 'righteousness.' It means both 'to treat as righteous' and 'to make righteous' (Käsemann 1980: 25). In other words, God both forgives sin and converts sinners in 'righteousing' the unrighteous. The relational character of righteousness (e.g. seen as God's faithfulness to Israel, above) covers both being established and being equipped as a fit partner in right relationship (e.g. in 8:2–4). The same point is made by calling the gospel 'the *power* of God *for salvation*'. Thus, the entirety of Romans may be seen to be centred, in three parts, on the theme of God's righteousness:

Chs. 1–8	God's righteousness evident in the treatment of Jew and Gentile
Chs. 9–11	God's righteousness evident in the treatment of Israel
Chs. 12–15	God's righteousness evident in the lives of believers.

It is not required that one probe Paul's psyche to explain the statement in v. 16 that he is 'not ashamed' of the gospel. These words echo 'the very same prophecies and lament psalms from which Paul's righteousness terminology is also drawn' (Hays 1989: 38), e.g. Ps 24:2; 43:10 (LXX); Isa 28:16 (quoted in Rom 9:33); and, of particular note, 50:7–8: 'I know that I shall not be put to shame; he who vindicates me is near' (also recalled in 8:31–9).

v. 17, 'through faith for faith' (*ek pisteōs eis pistin*) is a difficult phrase to interpret. Most often, it is taken to refer to the exclusiveness of the requirement of faith (*sola fide*); hence the NIV's 'faith from first to last'. Because *pistis* can also mean 'faithfulness' (as in 3:3, its next occurence beyond this section), it is possible that Paul had in mind God's *pistis* (faithfulness) which engenders, is manifest in, or is recognized by (*eis*, unto) human *pistis* (faith) (cf. Barth 1933: 41; Edwards 1992: 42–3). In support of this reading, one should note that the repetition of a word to play on its double meaning is a popular convention and that *ek* (from) used with the verb 'reveal' is most readily 'understood as denoting the source of the revelation' (Dunn 1988: i. 44). An even more important consideration is the content of the revelation: God's righteousness. Given the full sense of the term 'righteousness' (above), it is reasonable to imagine Paul saying that God's righteousness is revealed in (God's) faithfulness to (human) faith. 'The one who is righteous will live by faith' is a quotation from Hab 2:4. Here Paul made use of one of only two verses in the HB that link 'faith' and 'righteous(ness)'. (The other is Gen 15:6, another of Paul's crucial proof texts; see 4:3; Gal 3:6.) Although many commentators support the NRSV's rendering, in which *ek pisteōs* ('by faith') modifies the verb 'live' (Murray 1979: 33; Fitzmyer 1993: 265), an equally strong argument can be made for the translation, 'The one who is *righteous by faith* will live' (see e.g. Käsemann 1980: 32; Sanders 1977: 484; Cranfield 1979: 101–2). ('Live' here, in contrast to Habakkuk, would refer to resurrection life.) After all, Paul speaks in Phil 3:6 of a contrasting 'righteousness under (*en*) the law.' Similarly, it is possible that *pistis* here, as in the previous verse (and the LXX of Hab 2:4, '*my* faithfulness'), refers to '(God's) faithfulness'. Again, the double meaning may be deliberate.

God's Righteousness Evident in the Treatment of Jew and Gentile (1:18–8:39)

Surprisingly, Christ is mentioned only once (2:16, on the future judgement) in 1:18–3:20. Indeed, almost nothing is distinctly Christian in the remainder of the first and the whole of the second chapter of Romans. The background to these materials is Hellenistic Judaism; unquestionably, Paul's description of the human condition in vv. 18–32 borrows heavily from popular Hellenistic-Jewish descriptions of Gentiles. (The highest concentration of parallels occurs in the Wisdom of Solomon, almost certainly known to Paul.) Like Paul, Jewish apologists characteristically attacked Gentile idolatry and sexual misconduct. ('For the idea of making idols was the beginning of fornication', Wis 14:12; cf. vv. 22–7.) Some also claim that behind ch. 2 lies an otherwise unknown Hellenistic synagogue sermon (see below). It is reasonable to suppose that Paul used stock materials to construct a foundation upon which the more distinctive elements of his argument would be built. This strategy is reminiscent of his citation of the Christological formulae in 1:3–4, which served to establish common ground with his readers.

Beginning in 3:21–6, Paul returns to an explicitly Christian vantage point. Interestingly, the same paragraph reintroduces the theme of righteousness (vv. 21, 22, 25, and 26; like 'Christ', 'righteousness' is mentioned only once in passing (3:5) in the previous chapter and a half). God's righteousness has been disclosed 'through faith in Jesus Christ for all who believe' (v. 22). The work of Christ is characterized as 'a sacrifice of atonement by his blood' that brings 'redemption' to those who believe (vv. 24–5). But why is such a disclosure, such an

atonement, such a redemption necessary? If Christ is the solution, what precisely is the problem? Clearly, it is the job of 1:18–3:20 to inform us. Specifically, this section functions to justify Paul's own summary in 3:22*b*–23: 'For there is no distinction, since all have sinned and fall short of the glory of God.'

1:18–32 All are without Excuse The structure of the argument in 1:18–3:20 is not obvious. Commonly, 1:18–32 is read as an indictment of Gentile wickedness and 2:1–3:20 as the extension of that indictment to the Jews (Fitzmyer 1992: 269–71). Paul's approach is probably more subtle. In a sense, 1:18–32 sets a trap for the imaginary Jewish interlocutor introduced in 2:2. The description of human wickedness *seems* to be aimed exclusively at Gentiles; it *appears* to assume the typical contrast between Jewish probity and Gentile depravity. Nevertheless, nowhere does Paul indicate that he is describing only Gentiles; indeed, the Jewish/Gentile distinction is not made explicit until 2:9. Moreover, elements of vv. 18–31 hark back to the darker moments and practices of Israel's past. It is especially likely that the worship of the golden calf (and perhaps the Israelites' subsequent revelry) of Ex 32 is in view. In Acts 7:41, Stephen referred to that incident and concluded, 'God . . . *handed them over* to worship the host of heaven'. *Paradidōmi* ('handed over') is the same verb used by Paul in vv. 24, 26, and 28 in reference to God's judgement. (The idea might go back to the OT passage quoted in the subsequent verses of Acts 7 (42–3), Am 5:25–7, which criticizes Jewish idolatry in the wilderness and speaks of God 'deporting/sending away' (*metoikizō*) the Jews to Damascus.) Also, Paul borrows language from Ps 106:20 and Jer 2:11, both of which deal with Israelite idolatry. Pious readers might accept God's judgement on conduct such as Paul describes, not realizing that they themselves stand under the same condemnation. Ch. 2 is written to make this point explicit.

v. 18, 'For the wrath of God is revealed from heaven against . . . those who . . . suppress the truth'. For Paul, the problem is not that God is unknowable; the problem is that humanity does not want to know God (cf. Wis 13:1–9). Accordingly, the idol worshipper does not seek to do the will of God; he seeks a god to do his will. Creature dethrones creator, and cosmic order is turned upside down (v. 24). 'Three times (vv. 23, 25, 26) human beings are said to have "exchanged" or "substituted" one reality for another' (*HBC* 1136). God's response in each case is to 'give up' or 'hand over' humanity to its own desires (vv. 24, 26, 28). For Paul, sin carries within itself its own punishment (Achtemeier 1985: 40), and the sinner's most terrible judgement is to be left alone. vv. 26–31, while it is true that Paul saw the reversal of the created order manifest in homosexual relations, it is notable that his list also included such transgressions as covetousness, envy, boastfulness, and gossip. It would be difficult not to locate oneself somewhere in this catalogue—which, of course, is just the point. The knowledge of God that humanity suppresses is a moral knowledge. They 'know God's decree, that those who practise such things deserve to die', and still they disobey and even applaud the disobedience of others (v. 27). Humanity is utterly 'without excuse' (v. 20), especially the excuse of ignorance.

Of course, Paul's fictive conversation partner (see below) would not plead ignorance. But does a Jew's knowledge of God put him or her in a superior position? Can knowledge of

God's law deliver from God's judgement? It is to such questions that Paul's description of the human condition in vv. 18–32 has been leading.

(2:1–3:20) The Impartiality of God Scholars since Bultmann have made much of the similarities between Paul's rhetoric in Romans and the *diatribe*, a form of argumentation in which a Cynic or Stoic philosopher taught students by 'debating' an imaginary opponent (Bultmann 1910; Stowers, 1981). Although some scholars question whether or to what extent the diatribe was an established rhetorical form, there can be no doubt that diatribe *style* is present in Romans (Fitzmyer 1993: 91). At numerous points beginning in ch. 2 (also 3:1–9; 3:27–4:25; 9:19–21; 10:14–21; 11:17–24; 14:4–12), Paul addresses and even responds to the objections of an interlocutor (most often with an impassioned 'By no means!' (*mē genoito*); 3:4, 6, 31; 6:2, 15; 7:7, 13; 9:14; 11:1, 11). The effect is to pull the reader into the 'conversation' on Paul's side. Rhetorically, the diatribe confers argumentative dynamism without ceding authorial control. It remains in the rhetor's power to choose what questions to ask and what answers to accept.

Because Paul's dialogue partner of 2:1–16 is not identified explicitly, some commentators have isolated this section from 2:17–3:20, in which Paul plainly addresses a Jewish interlocutor (Barrett 1957: 43; Morris 1988: 107; Ziesler 1989: 80–1). It is more likely that the whole of 2:1–3:20 speaks to perceived Jewish attitudes and that any ambiguity as to the object of 2:1–16 is expressly eliminated by the direct address of v. 17. Stuhlmacher (1994: 39) made the intriguing suggestion that Paul delayed identifying the interlocutor for dramatic effect; 2:17 thus functions like Nathan's statement to David in 2 Sam 12:7: 'You are the man!' (In fact, Ps 51, understood to be David's penitential prayer, is quoted in Rom 3:4.)

The juxtaposition in vv. 28–9 of the mere outward and the true inward practice of Judaism is precedented in passages such as Deut 10:16, 30:6, and Jer 4:4, 9:26, which use the 'circumcision of the heart' metaphor to describe those whose inner commitments are consistent with their (outwardly obvious in the case of males) status as God's covenant people. The truly surprising employment of Scripture comes in v. 24, which uses Isa 52:5 to argue that Israel itself is so disobedient as to be the cause of Gentile blasphemy. This is 'a stunning misreading of the text' (Hays 1989: 45). In fact, Isa 52 celebrates Israel's rescue from the injustices of the nations. (Israel has been 'oppressed without cause'; 'my people are taken away without cause', Isa 52:4, 5.)

Numerous other difficulties are associated with the interpretation of Rom 2, some of which bear significantly upon one's understanding and evaluation of the entire letter. The first, most glaring problem is the repeated assertion that one is justified (v. 13) or receives eternal life (v. 7) on the basis of one's deeds. (The notion that God equitably judges people according to their works is common in the HB; however, such passages do not have in view the issue of eternal destiny. In v. 5, Paul specifically quotes the LXX of Ps 61 (62):13 and Prov. 24:12.) This idea appears flatly to contradict Paul's numerous other statements that one cannot be saved by one's works (e.g. 3:20; 4:2; 9:32; 11:6). One way out of the dilemma is to say that Paul wrote only of a theoretical justification; in fact, he realized that no one actually measures up to the proposed stand-

ard. Others reason that when speaking of those who 'do good' (etc.), Paul 'is implicitly referring to Christians' (Fitzmyer 1993: 297). The first proposal seems heavy-handed; in effect, it trades coherence for consistency. The second notion, that the chapter approves only Christian good works, is certainly possible, although it does little to commend Paul as a fair-minded observer of human behaviour. Alternatively, Hays (1989: 42) has suggested that Rom 2 be read in the larger context of Ps 61 (quoted in v. 5), which 'renders an account of God fully consonant with Paul's emphasis on God's kindness and forebearance'. An entirely different approach is advocated by E. P. Sanders (1983: 123), who thinks that Paul made use of a source or sources ('homiletical material from Diaspora Judaism') that contributed the desired argument for God's impartiality (and Jewish sinfulness) but included elements strikingly at odds with Pauline theology (ibid. 123–35). In general, Rom 2 reads well as a sermon preached to Jews to encourage a higher standard of Jewish conduct. (Indeed, change 'Jew' to 'Christian' and 'circumcision' to 'baptism', and the text reads like a sermon exhorting church members to live up to their calling; cf. Mt 7:21–3.) It is noteworthy that Rom 2 deals with matters known to be at issue within first-century Judaism, such as the question of 'righteous Gentiles' and the nature of true obedience (ibid. 134).

A second problem concerns the description of Jewish sinfulness in Rom 2. In 3:9, Paul states that 'we have already charged that all, both Jews and Greeks, are under the power of sin'. Paul concludes that since Jews share the same plight as Gentiles, they require the same solution, namely, Christ (3:21–6). How does Paul make his case? Given the longstanding tendency of interpreters to read Paul as if he were an existentialist—that is, one concerned with internal states and interior conflicts (see Stendahl 1963)—the actual argument of Rom 2 is surprising. Paul does not say that while most Jews most of the time meet the external demands of the law (cf. Paul's larger claim for himself in Phil 3:6), they nevertheless continue to sin inwardly, for example, by being proud of their obedience. Such a critique would not be entirely new; something like it existed in the Jesus traditions (e.g. Mt 5:21–4, 27–30; 6:1–5; 23:25–8; Lk 11:37–44). That argument would put Jews and Gentiles on equal footing without necessitating that all Jews (or even hypothetical, representative Jews) be shown to be as badly behaved as Gentiles, which seems to be the point of 2:21–4. The lack of a clear conception or language of interiority is consistently problematic for Paul. Even Rom 7, which is usually read in this way, speaks of sin as an external power that causes one to *do* or not *do* what is right (7:15). Surely, the Jews of Paul's day were not characteristically thieves, adulterers, and temple robbers.

A third difficulty is that the obvious solution to the problems posed in 2:1–29 is that Jews simply become better Jews. If Jews commit sinful acts, repentance and atonement are available to them within Judaism. Damnation is neither the sole nor the expected alternative to perfect obedience. In this context it is worth noting that when all is said and done, Paul's one substantial and consistent accusation is that the Jews have rejected their Christ. What confuses are the numerous ways such rejection can be characterized (as disobedience, unbelief, works righteousness, etc.) and the numerous deficiencies to which it can be attributed (hardheartedness, pride, self-assertion, etc.). Apart from faith in Christ, no amount of Jewish obedience, faith, or humility is going to satisfy. However it is described, this by definition is a problem that cannot have a (non-Christian) Jewish solution.

The ground shifts in 3:9, where Paul states that 'both Jews and Greeks are under the power of sin'. This statement removes the possibility that, unaided by God, either Gentile or Jew could be righteous (*contra* 2:7, 13, etc., but consistent with 7:7–24). A compilation of OT proof-texts in 3:10–18 then describes humanity's utter depravity (Eccl 7:20; Ps 5:10; 10:7; 14:1–3/53:2–4; 36:2; 140:4; Isa 59:7–8/Prov 1:16). Thus the problem is not so much that humans sin as that humans are incapable of not sinning. Christ is necessary for Jew as well as Gentile because only he can break sin's power. This claim demonstrates how Paul's thinking could at times steer him in the direction of a realized eschatology (see ROM E. 4); Christians are now 'in the Spirit' and please God while others remain 'in the flesh' and cannot please God (8:3–8). This approach equalizes Jew and Gentile and so makes Christ necessary. One might object that this line of reasoning succeeds only by overstating the differences between believers and unbelievers, in particular, between Christians and Jews. Is it really the case, either in outward behaviour or inward disposition, that Christians as a group sin less than Jews? Are the rules of the church experienced so differently from the laws of the synagogue? Certainly, it would have been possible to argue for the necessity of Christ without negating Judaism as an instrument (or at least a prior instrument) of God's grace. Despite the demurral of 3:1–2, Paul's point is that with respect to the actual state of their relationship to God, Jews enjoy no advantage over Gentiles. One must ask, 'What then was the point of Judaism?' That question, in one form or another, is the central concern of the next several chapters.

(3:21–31) The Revelation of God's Righteousness vv. 21–6 are the capstone of Paul's introductory argument; Stuhlmacher (1994: 57) refers to the paragraph as 'the heart of the letter to the Romans'. Here Paul revisits the grand theme introduced in the Thanksgiving: the righteousness of God. The divine character—faithful, gracious, forgiving, and merciful—has been disclosed in Christ, specifically in Christ's death, a sacrifice for sin 'effective through faith'. Altogether apart from human initiative, God has done what God always intended to do ('attested by the law and the prophets') and so is proved righteous. It is instructive that Ps 143, quoted (v. 2, significantly emended) in Paul's statement of judgement in Rom 3:20, maintains that one is preserved by God's righteousness (Ps 143:1, 11–12), the very subject of vv. 21–6 (see Hays 1989: 51–2). Paul is deeply conscious of the interplay of God's condemning justice and God's justifying righteousness, already evident in Scripture.

That the death of Jesus decisively altered the human situation (described in 1:18–3:20) is assumed but not explained. Almost certainly, the language Paul used concerning Christ's atonement was common to first-century Christianity and required little elucidation. (See 1 Cor 15:3, where the statement that 'Christ died for our sins according to the scriptures' is included in the tradition that Paul himself received.) v. 25, 'expiation' (*hilastērion*: 'sacrifice of atonement', NRSV) probably has in view the Jewish sacrificial system. In the LXX, the same word is used to refer to the 'mercy seat', the top of the ark of the covenant, on which the blood of the sin offering was sprinkled annually on the Day of Atonement. It might (also) have as background the notion of the efficacious sacrifice of martyrs, as one finds in 4 Macc 17:22. 'Redemption' (*apolutrōsis*) originally connoted 'freedom by ransom'. In the NT, the word is used to emphasize a change in one's position that is effected entirely at God's initiative and expense. It does not require a literal 'payment' by God (e.g. to the devil), as sometimes featured in later soteriological speculation (*EDNT* 138–40).

v. 24, which states that believers are 'justified by his [God's] grace as a gift', captures a great deal of Pauline theology in a few words. Quintessentially for Paul, justification is gift, not reward (see 4:1–4; 5:15–17). It originates in God's mind, is motivated by God's character, and is 'purchased' by God's work in Christ. It is neither human invention nor human achievement; hence, it is gracious, unmerited. Obviously, it occasions no opportunity for human boasting (v. 27; see 2:17, 23; 4:2; cf. the 'positive boasting' in 5:2–3, 11; 15:17); one may as well boast of being born as boast of being justified. (Not surprisingly, boasting is a prominent Pauline theme, especially in 1 and 2 Corinthians, e.g. 1 Cor 1:29–31; 3:21; 4:7; 5:6; 2 Cor 11:12, 16–18, 30; 12:1, 5–6; cf. the favourable boasting in 1 Cor 9:15–16; 15:31; 2 Cor 1:12; 5:12; 7:4, 14; 8:24; 9:2–3; 10:8, 13, 15–17; 11:10; 12:30.) v. 25, the statement that God, in 'divine forbearance', 'passed over the sins previously committed' raises many questions. What does it mean to 'pass over' sin (from *paresis*; lit. the 'passing by' = 'letting go unpunished'; see BAGD 626), and whose sins specifically have been passed over? Did God simply not judge former sins, or was their judgement postponed, perhaps until the cross? What evaluation of Judaism and of its sacrificial system lies behind this verse? Commentators have ventured answers to these and related questions, but no one account of the passage has proved persuasive. It is clear at least that Paul regarded the death of Christ as the one final and essential sacrifice, the basis for all human salvation. Paul does not provide us with enough information to judge how, to what extent, and on what basis he considered such salvation to have been operative in the past.

v. 26, it is essential to note that the faith of which Paul speaks in vv. 27–31 (and in Romans generally) is specifically 'faith in Christ' (see also 4:23–4). Although Paul may contrast works with faith and unbelief with faith, the unspoken and yet insistent polarity is between Jewish faith in God apart from belief in Christ and Christian (whether Jewish or Gentile) faith in God including belief in Christ. In other words, it is one's response to Jesus that ultimately is at issue, however the argument may be framed. Paul believed that God was in Christ and that to believe in God now means perforce to believe in Christ; the two 'faiths' are inseparable. Accordingly, it is only Christian faith that is legitimated *as* faith. (One can observe the same dynamic clearly at work in Johannine literature, e.g. in Jn 5:23 and 1 Jn 5:10–12.) Logically, this move eliminates the problem of present Jewish (but non-Christian) belief in God; it is not actual (one might say 'sufficient') faith. Thus Paul can speak of faith in God as if it were a uniquely Christian attribute. At the same time, this approach introduces a problem: what to do with pre-Christian Jewish faith (that is, unless one claims that those such as Abraham and David, both commended in Romans, already believed in Christ). The press of this difficulty may well account for Paul's statement in v. 25 (above) concerning God's *former* dispensation of forgiveness.

In v. 27 Paul contrasts a law 'of works' with a 'law of faith'. The shift in the use of *nomos* (law) is curious and has led many to translate the word in this instance as 'principle' (i.e. the principle of faith by which boasting is excluded). Barrett (1957: 83) has argued convincingly that, for Paul, *nomos* occasionally 'means something like "religious system", often ... but not always, the religious system of Judaism'. Such an interpretation makes sense both here and at numerous other points in Romans. v. 31, Paul asks, 'Do we then overthrow the law by this faith?' As a Jew himself, Paul cannot answer, 'Yes'. The law is still God's law. There must be some sense in which Paul's teachings (which, let us not forget, abrogate certain specific commandments; e.g. Rom 14:14) actually 'uphold the law', perhaps the law rightly understood or the law in its deeper purpose. We do not have to wait long to discover something of what the apostle had in mind.

(4:1–25) The Example of Abraham Paul has just stated that he upholds the law (3:31) and that the righteousness of God, which he proclaims, is attested in 'the law and the prophets' (3:21). It is time to make good on these claims. Religious arguments, like legal arguments, often begin with an appeal to precedent. In most democracies, a lawyer can do no better than to appeal to the nation's constitution (and, thereby, to its founders). Constitutional interpretation is both the most basic and the most consequential matter of law. Generations of case law can be overturned by a single ruling of unconstitutionality. Paul makes his first and strongest argument by appealing to the founding figure of Judaism, Abraham. What goes for Abraham, he can assume, goes for all. God's covenant with Abraham is the core of the Jewish 'constitution', subsequent 'amendments' notwithstanding. Summoning Abraham to his defence is both an inspired and (in the light of the controversy in Galatia, which seemed to revolve around the interpretation of the Abraham story, especially the commandment of circumcision in Gen 17:10; see Gal 3) probably necessary strategy. The appeal to Abraham has the added benefit of preempting an opponent's appeal to Moses (see Gal 3:17). 'The promise ... did not come to Abraham or his descendants through the law' (4:13). According to one possible interpretation, Paul (see ROM 10:5) effectively rules 'unconstitutional' Moses' later understanding of the relationship between the law and eternal life (e.g. that 'the person who does these things will *live* by them', Lev 18:5, my emphasis).

The basic argument of Rom 4 is comparatively simple and direct. According to Gen 15:6, Abraham 'believed the Lord; and the Lord reckoned it to him as righteousness'. (What Abraham actually believed—namely, God's promise that he would have offspring—is not in view nor, naturally, is a consideration of what 'reckoning righteousness' might have meant in its original context.) Abraham was not, of himself, righteous; instead, because of his faith, he was treated (*elogisthē*: 'was credited'; a 'bookkeeping term figuratively applied to human conduct' as in Ps 106:31; 1 Macc 2:52; and Philem 18; Fitzmyer 1993: 373) as though he were righteous. His stand-

ing before God was a gift, not an attainment (see ROM 3:24). This occurred prior to the giving of the law, prior even to the requirement of circumcision. This first instance of human righteousness thus becomes the paradigm for all subsequent instances. It is very likely that Paul wrote Rom 4 with a view to popular Jewish treatments of the Abraham story that focused on the patriarch's obedient example, which in some cases even argued for his attainment of merit (e.g. 4 Ezra 9:7; 13:23). A similar reading is present in Jas 2:18–26, which may have been formulated to counter (possibly second-generation) abuses of Pauline theology. The two sides actually make different, not opposite, points. Essentially, Paul uses the Abraham story to answer the question, How does one get 'in' (e.g. right relationship with God)? Much more characteristically, the story is used in James to exhort believers (those already 'in') to behave in a certain way, in this case to demonstrate their faith by their actions. It is entirely possible to laud Abraham's good behaviour (e.g. in obeying God's command to leave his home, Gen 12:1) without implying that Abraham was thereby sinless or perfectly righteous, which issue was not under consideration. In fact, many contemporary Jews could have accepted Paul's basic point: like Abraham, one enters into covenant with God at God's initiative and by means of God's grace. The doctrine of justification by faith is not without Jewish antecedents; the real controversy concerns, not the necessity of faith, but the content or object of faith.

The fact that Abraham had not yet been circumcised (that comes two chapters later, in Gen 17) allows Paul to claim that Abraham is exemplar to and ancestor of all faithful persons, both Jews and Gentiles (3:9–12). As proof-text, Paul cites Gen 17:5 ('I have made you the father of many nations', vv. 17–18). Gentile Christians were for Paul (and probably for most other Jewish Christians) 'children of Abraham'. It is not difficult to imagine how such claims might have rankled with non-Christian Jews, how they could have been seen to threaten the integrity, ultimately even the existence, of Israel. It is likely that such claims underlie many of the instances of persecution recorded in the NT (see Gal 5:11 and 6:12).

v. 15, the sentiment 'the law brings wrath; but where there is no law, neither is there violation' is echoed in 5:13: 'sin was indeed in the world before the law, but sin is not reckoned when there is no law' (cf. the 'passing over' of sins prior to Christ in 3:25). It also anticipates the argument of 7:7–24 ('if it had not been for the law, I would not have known sin, v. 7). Presumably, the point is that 'law makes sin into transgression' (Byrne 1996: 158). Under the law, one not only sins, one sins with explicit knowledge that one is sinning. Paul makes no attempt to co-ordinate these statements with the earlier argument that Gentiles are fairly judged by God, having 'what the law requires written on their hearts' (2:15).

vv. 19–21, the quality of Abraham's faith is vividly described. Abraham believed God against all opposing considerations and contrary appearances. The final reality was God's fidelity: God would do what God had promised. The character of faith as trust is nowhere more clearly depicted in Paul's writings. vv. 23–4, the content of justifying faith is spelled out more fully: belief in God who 'raised Jesus our Lord from the dead, who was handed over (*paredothē*) to death for our trespasses and was raised for our justification'. This description of Jesus sounds formulaic and therefore traditional; ultimately, it is dependent upon Isa 52:13–53:12 (LXX), which tells of the Suffering Servant, on whom 'the LORD laid (paredōken) our sins' (53:6), who 'bore (paredothē) their sin' (53: 12), who will 'justify many' (v. 11) (see Cranfield 1979: 251–2).

(5:1–11) God's Reconciling Love as the Foundation for Legitimate Boasting Two verbs dominate this section: 'boast' and 'reconcile'. We were told in 4:2 that Abraham had no ground for boasting before God. Similarly, 3:27 made the point that boasting is excluded (see also 2:17, 23). In Rom 5, however, boasting is neither groundless nor excluded: Paul boasts 'in the hope of sharing the glory of God' (v. 2), in 'sufferings' (v. 3), and 'in God' (v. 11). The difference, of course, is that here Paul is not, as in 2 Cor 10:13–15, 'boasting beyond limits', claiming as his own achievement something achieved by others. It is perfectly proper to boast in what God has done, rather than in what one has done for God (see ROM 3:24). And what God has done in Christ, according to Rom 5:1–11, is to reconcile (katallassein) humanity with God. 'Reconciliation' is return from alienation, the restoration of relationship. Its use here puts the divine–human rift in deeply personal (as opposed to exclusively forensic) terms, an estrangement that yields only to the prevailing power of God's love (v. 8). The state of reconciliation is described in v. 1 as 'peace with God'. Because reconciliation is achieved from God's side and offered when most undeserved (v. 8), the believer possesses security in the hope of eternal life (vv. 2, 5) and confidence in the midst of earthly trials (vv. 3–4). Reconciliation is something about which to boast.

The claim to 'boast in . . . sufferings' (v. 3) is distinctly ironic and distinctively Pauline. For Paul, the paradigm of Christian existence, of Christian reality, is the cross (see ROM E. 4). One's faithfulness to the crucified messiah is measured, not in gifts of power or wisdom, but in degrees of sacrifice and suffering (1 Cor 4:8–13; 2 Cor. 6:3–10; 11:21–12:21). Against the pretensions of the so-called 'super-apostles' at Corinth, Paul wrote, 'If I must boast, I will boast of the things that show my weakness' (2 Cor 11:30). Putting the cross at the centre of his thinking (the gospel is characterized as 'the word of the cross' in 1 Cor 1:18), set Paul outside normal religious expectation, including the expectations of many of his converts. To Paul, religion was not a means by which to manipulate heavenly powers to earthly ends. God's locus in this world is disclosed in the cross, which is foolishness and weakness in human eyes (1 Cor 1:17–19). Therefore, Paul can boast in his sufferings, in the very absence of earthly rescue, in the knowledge that he travels in the footsteps of the crucified messiah, and that he will arrive someday at the place of Christ's resurrection (where 'hope does not disappoint', v. 5). It is consistent with this perspective that reconciliation is a present reality (v. 10: 'we were reconciled' to God, aorist tense), but salvation itself remains a future hope (vv. 9–10, 'we will be saved'). (The two are related by means of an a minori ad maius argument: if God has reconciled, how much more will God save.)

In their unreconciled state, humans are described as 'weak', 'ungodly', 'sinners', and 'enemies' of God (vv. 6, 8, 10), a portrayal that recalls the description in 1:18–32. That Paul would, by implication, refer to himself and to all other Jews as ungodly and enemies of God is astounding. A less pointed description, however, might undermine his argument con-

cerning the absolute necessity of the atonement. It is because reconciliation with God is so entirely necessary and yet so utterly unattainable from the human side that it is so highly prized.

(5:12–21) Adam and Christ Paul found a prototype for the doctrine of justification by faith in the story of Abraham (ch. 4). He then characterized the justification won by Christ's death as reconciliation with God (5:1–11). But how can Christ's work, however meritorious in itself, save others? Can the actions of one individual affect the standing of all other persons? Yes, indeed, if that individual happens to be the archetype for subsequent humanity. In vv. 12–21, Paul turns to Adam as precedent (that is, by way of counterexample) for the universality of Christ's atonement. If all of humanity shared in Adam's disobedience, how much more (note, again, the a minori ad maius structure) may all humanity share in the obedience of Jesus, the very Son of God (v. 19; see also 1 Cor 15:45–9).

Paul argues on the basis of Gen 3 only that 'sin came into the world through one man'. (There were of course two human players in the Garden drama. Eve has gone missing.) He does not propound a theory ('original sin') concerning the conveyance of sin, biological or otherwise, from one generation to the next. The proof of the ubiquity of sin is the universality of its consequence: death (v. 12; Gen 3:3). The resurrection of Christ thus overturns death introduced by Adam: 'For since death came through a human being, the resurrection of the dead has also come through a human being; for as all die in Adam, so all will be made alive in Christ' (1 Cor 15:21–2). The proper order of creation, lost in the Fall, is thus in the process of being restored (8:18–25). This two-part story is complicated by the mention of the law in vv. 13–14 and 20. Sin existed prior to the giving of the law, but it was not like Adam's transgression, that is, disobedience of an explicit commandment. The law given through Moses served to increase culpability; humans again could transgress as Adam had transgressed (vv. 13–14; see 4:15). (One might note that, among other things, Paul's argument 'passes over the so-called Noachic legislation (Gen 9:4–6)'; Fitzmyer 1993: 418.) And, whereas Adam had to obey only one commandment, those living under the law have six hundred and thirteen times the opportunity for transgression: 'law came in, with the result that the trespass multiplied' (v. 20). In the light of 7:5–12, a minority of commentators have interpreted v. 20 to mean that the law was given for the express purpose (hina) of increasing (and not merely increasing the guilt of) sin (Murray 1979: 208). This would involve God in the deliberate promotion of sin which is, needless to say, a problematic assertion (cf. the relationship between the law and sin in 7:11–12).

Moses is a not accidental omission on Paul's short-list of human archetypes. By situating the law where he does (v. 20, it 'slipped in'—pareisēlthen—between Adam and Christ; see Gal 3:17), Paul indicates that Moses was not the answer to Adam. The law did not provide a way out of the human dilemma; quite to the contrary, it made an already bad situation worse. Whether or not it increased the incidence of sin (a debatable point, both exegetically and practically), it heightened sin's sinfulness by exposing the deliberateness of human disobedience. The law could not give (eternal) life; it was participant in and not victor over Adam's 'dominion of death' (vv. 20–1). In the face of this stark portrayal, one could object that the law did function for many as a positive corrective and guide. A larger problem is that belief in eternal life post-dates Torah. If one enquires, like the 'rich young ruler', 'What must I do to inherit eternal life?' (Lk 10:25), one asks a question that the law is unequipped to answer. (Note that Jesus' own answer concerned doing, not merely believing, certain things.) A typical Jewish approach would be to assume that those remaining in covenant with God will inherit eternal life. Paul's answer really is no different, but the obligatory covenant is (i.e. the *new* covenant of 1 Cor 11:25; 2 Cor 3:6, 14, etc.).

(6:1–23) Dead to Sin and Alive to God Paul has just introduced the notion that there are two dominions, one of death, whose head is Adam, and one of life, whose head is Christ (5:21). The obvious conclusion is that believers now dwell with Christ in the dominion of life. But this cannot be the whole truth: believers sometimes disobey, and all believers die. In what sense and to what extent Christ's dominion is a *present* reality is the underlying issue in Rom 6. Paul's argument is organized around two questions: 'Should we continue in sin in order that grace may abound?' (v. 1), and 'Should we sin because we are not under law but under grace?' (v. 15). Paul's response is by now anticipated: 'By no means!' (*mē genoito*; see ROM 2:1–3:20). The first question is answered ontologically: How can we who died to sin go on living in it?' (v. 2). The believer has already died and 'walks in newness of life'. How? By identification with the death of Jesus in baptism (vv. 3–4). It is important to note that this identification is substantial, not moralistic; one actually participates with Jesus in his death: 'We know that our old self was crucified with him so that the body of sin might be destroyed, and we might no longer be enslaved to sin' (v. 6). Believers are a 'new creation' (2 Cor 5:17), a new kind of person who has the power not to sin (vv. 12–14, 18, etc.). (How this portrayal meshes with the description of the 'wretched self' in 7:14–25 is a major problem; see ROM 7:14–25.)

Of all NT writings, Paul's letters most pointedly exhibit the eschatological tension between the 'already' and the 'not yet'. The obvious counterpart to 'we have been buried' with Christ in his death' (v. 4), would be 'and we have been raised with Christ in his resurrection'. This may be the viewpoint of Ephesians (e.g. 2:1–6), but it is not the perspective of Romans. Although the situation of the believer has changed considerably, it has not changed entirely. With respect to the individual Christian, all references to resurrection and eternal life are future tense (vv. 5, 8). Believers 'walk in newness of life' (v. 4) and are 'alive to God' (v. 11); nevertheless, their experience of the 'dominion of life' is proleptic, not fully realized. Although they have 'died to sin' (v. 2), they may yet submit themselves 'to sin as its instruments' (v. 13), may once again come under the dominion of sin (v. 12). The tension between the two realities remains unresolved: humans by nature sin; believers by (their new) nature do not sin (cf. 1 Jn 1:7–2:1 with 3:6, 8–9; 5:18). Believers are human, but believers also represent a new (or 'renewed') type of humanity. One could lower the tension by diminishing the status of believers (that is, by moving towards a more exclusively future eschatology); however, such a

change would thoroughly undermine Pauline theology. Paul sets the law and Christ as opposite means: what the law could not do, Christ has done (8:3). But if believers (Christians) are not substantially different from those 'under the law' (non-Christian Jews), then (by Paul's reasoning) Christ has failed. Why frame the argument in this way? Because of Paul's one overriding concern: the present equality of Jew and Gentile (see ROM E.4).

Paul's second question also concerns the relationship between believers and sin. To paraphrase v. 15, Why not sin if sin is not judged? Are those set free from sin thereby free to sin? Paul answers that such 'freedom' is illusory. People are not transferred from slavery to sin into neutral, non-allied autonomy. Instead, they pass from one allegiance, one 'slavery' (to speak 'in human terms', v. 19), to another. Believers are slaves 'of obedience' (v. 16), 'slaves of righteousness' (vv. 18–19), 'enslaved to God' (v. 22). There can be no 'freedom' to sin, since sin itself is slavery. 'Grace and sin are to one another as "either" is to "or" ' (Barth 1933: 217).

Paul stated earlier that death came through Adam's sin (5:12). vv. 20–3 make clear that all sinners earn death as their fitting 'wages' (*opsōnion*, v. 23). The language used to describe sin ('things of which you are now ashamed', v. 21) is reminiscent of the description of human wickedness in 1:18–32 ('shameless acts', 1:27). The alternative is holiness ('sanctification', NRSV) that leads to eternal life (v. 22). Something 'holy' is pure, consisting of only one thing (e.g. 'pure gold'). That believers are to be holy (or sanctified), to be one thing, is the point of the entire chapter.

(7:1–25) The Law and Sin A connection between law and sin was posited in 3:20, 4:15, 5:13, and 5:20. This is one of the most surprising and controversial claims encountered in Paul's letter, and it demands elaboration. The discussion in ch. 6, especially the concluding section on slavery and freedom, provides an opportunity for the reintroduction of the subject of the law and sin. The previous paragraphs considered reasons why believers should not sin. In vv. 1–6, Paul offers another: the believer has died not only to sin (6:3) but also to the law (vv. 1–4), which is itself a cause of sin (vv. 5–12). (On the question, 'Of what law does Paul speak?', see Fitzmyer 1993: 455.)

The marriage metaphor Paul employs is somewhat forced. The statement that 'the law is binding on a person only during a person's lifetime' (v. 1) aligns with the conclusion 'you [therefore] have died to the law through the body of Christ' (v. 4). But the one who dies in vv. 2–3 is the husband, not the wife (the believer). Is the law the husband who dies, the 'law' that governs the wife's relationship to the husband, or both? Despite the confusion, the point of vv. 2–3 appears straightforward: one who simply disregards the law (e.g. a married person who has an affair) may be judged a sinner ('an adulterer', v. 3), but one who is no longer subject to the law (a widow[er]) may not be judged by the law (may not be called an adulterer when remarrying). Someone reading 'you have died to the law ... so that you may belong to another' might well ask, 'Who was the first partner—the law?' On one level, Dunn (1988: 369) is correct to say that the question is 'over-fussy'. The analogy makes a basic point and should not be pushed beyond it. On another level, however, the question is quite valid and reveals much about Paul's view of Judaism. *Whose* were those who lived under the law? Although the language is covenantal (i.e. concerning marriage), the prior covenant partner is not God. It is as though the Sinai covenant was made with the law itself.

The mention of bearing fruit in v. 4 fills out the idea in ch. 6 that believers have become 'instruments of righteousness' (v. 13), experiencing 'sanctification' to God (v. 22). God's will is not only the absence of evil but also the presence of good. Although some commentators have argued that 'bearing fruit for God' means 'begetting spiritual children', it is more likely that Paul is referring to the generation of good character and/ or works (cf. Gal 5:22; Cranfield 1979: 336–7). Correspondingly, Paul refers to 'fruit for death' as the product of 'sinful passions' 'at work in our members' (v. 5).

v. 5, two new and very important ideas are introduced. The first concerns life 'in the flesh'. Up until now, 'flesh' (*sarx*) has been used to refer to physicality: Jesus was descended from David 'according to the flesh' (1:3); Abraham is 'our ancestor according to the flesh' (4:1; Paul returns to this usage in 9:3, 5). Now the term takes on board a decidedly pejorative nuance. (Paul's use of *sarx* is the subject of numerous scholarly studies; summaries may be found in *TDNT* vii. 98–151; Spicq 1994: 3:231–41; *EDNT* 3:230–3.) Being 'in the flesh' means being in the (ordinary if not 'natural') state of human alienation from God. The one in the flesh here is roughly equivalent to the 'the old self' of 6:6. While 'fleshliness' does include carnality (i.e. improper sensuality), its meaning is broader. 'Flesh' symbolizes 'the weakness and appetites of "the mortal body" ' that were the causes of sin (Dunn 1988: 370; cf. 'sinful passions' here). The juxtaposition of flesh and Spirit (v. 6) does not evidence a true matter/spirit dualism, nor does it demonstrate that Paul was an ascetic (see Käsemann 1980: 188–9). With respect to the last point, one might note that while Paul himself was unmarried, he did not prohibit marriage, and at one point he even commanded married believers to continue sexual relations (1 Cor 7:3–5). Nevertheless, it would be fair to say that physicality was, if not denigrated, then at least held in some suspicion by Paul (cf. Rom 8:10). He might have allowed for Christian marriage, but 1 Cor 7:7–9, 28 is hardly a ringing endorsement. The second idea to be introduced in v. 5 is the notion that the law *causes* (not only exposes or increases the culpability of) sin (see ROM 5:13–14). The contention that dormant passions are 'aroused by the law' anticipates (one might say, necessitates) the discussion in 7:7– 20. Much the same idea has appeared before, in 1 Cor 15:56: 'The sting of death is sin, and the power of sin is the law.' Law is the parental command not to raid the biscuit tin, an injunction that draws attention to and makes all the more desirable the very thing it prohibits. As the saying goes, stolen fruit is sweetest. Nevertheless, one might dispute whether law and sin are always thus related. Does prohibition inevitably increase desire, and does 'sinful passion' require a commandment to be stirred up? Moreover, are the commands that Paul so often includes in his letters (as in Rom 12–14) somehow excluded from this dynamic?

v. 6, the contrast between 'the old written code' and 'the new life of the Spirit' seems to be dependent particularly upon the prophecy of the future covenant in Jer 31:31–4. In contrast to the Sinai covenant ('which they broke', v. 32), in the new order the law will not be taught but rather will be written 'on the hearts' of God's people (v. 33). Paul calls the law, literally, an 'old/aged letter' (*palaiotēti grammatos*), a title conveying (in line with the treatment of the old covenant in Jer 31) both decrepitude and externality. But that's not all: the metaphor of slavery is picked up from the previous chapter and applied, not to sin, but to the law itself (see Gal 4:22–31). vv. 4–6 ratchet up by several notches Paul's already negative treatment of the law. The law is no longer just an inadequate solution to the problem of sin; the law itself is the problem. Has not Paul come to the point of equating the law, God's law, with sin? He answers, 'By no means!' (v. 7). It is not really the law's fault; sin is to blame. (That sin could be a responsible 'party' evidences a decided shift in terminology.)

The argument of v. 7 is familiar: the law makes known, discloses, sin as sin (4:15; 5:13, 20). The selection of the tenth commandment (against coveting, see 13:9) is intriguing since it is one of the few OT commandments to prohibit an attitude. It is here that Paul comes closest to locating sin in one's internal states (e.g. one sins by obeying the law for the wrong reasons or by being proud of one's obedience)—an attitude that generations of commentators have attributed to him. It may be that Paul's intuition drew him in this direction, but that he lacked the conceptual tools that would have allowed him to construct such an argument. Such speculation should be tempered by the fact that the idea, if present, is dropped in the next verse: sin now is an external power that acts on the individual. The 'wretched self' of vv. 14–25 is faulted for wrongful (in)action, not for wrongful thinking or feeling: 'I can will what is right, but I cannot *do* it . . . the evil I do not want is what I *do*' (vv. 18–19). A more likely explanation is that Paul quoted the coveting prohibition because he had in mind the temptation in the Garden (Gen 3:5–6; see the discussion of Adam below): ' "For God knows that when you eat of it your eyes will be opened, and you will be like God, knowing good and evil." So when the woman saw that the tree was good for food, and that it was a delight to the eyes, and that the tree was to be desired to make one wise, she took of its fruit and ate.' In Rom 6, sin was objectified as a power to which one could yield (v. 13) and be enslaved by (v. 16). The anthropomorphizing of sin is extended in 7:8–23. Twice sin is said to have 'seized an opportunity in the commandment' (vv. 8, 11). The ultimate expression comes in v. 17: 'It is no longer I that do it, but sin that dwells within me' (repeated in v. 20). It is as though sin were a demonic being that overpowers and possesses humans. The effect is to exonerate the law: it is not the law *itself* that provokes transgression, it is sin's fault. Sin wrests control of the law and uses it as an instrument of death. The 'I' (as in 'it is no longer I that do it'), being 'in the flesh', is helpless before such an onslaught. In 7:14–8:8, it is this weakness (and not the law, which is 'holy, just, and good') that is the problem. The solution? Believers are empowered to fulfil 'the just requirement of the law' as they walk 'not according to the flesh but according to the Spirit' (8:4; recall again Jer 31).

Regarding Paul's treatment of the law in Romans, Sanders comments (1983: 76) insightfully that there is 'an organic development with a momentum towards more and more negative statements until there is a recoil in Romans 7, a recoil which produces other problems'. Among the difficulties: 'The law could no longer be said to produce sin or to multiply transgression as part of God's overall plan [the typical view in both Romans and Galatians], since the realm of sin is now considered entirely outside that plan' (ibid. 73). Moreover, God is now credited with having provided a means for attaining life (v. 10; see 10:5) that was incapable of succeeding. In other words, if the law was given to produce transgression, the law is linked to sin (against which Paul 'recoils' in v. 7); however, if the law was given by God to produce eternal life, it was doomed to failure by human weakness (or sin's power). But how could God's plan fail?

There are good reasons for thinking that Paul himself is not the implied subject, the 'I', in 7:7–26. (Compare the universalized 'I' in e.g. 1 Cor 13). Paul never lived 'apart from the law', 'the commandment' did not 'come' in his lifetime (v. 9), nor was he 'killed' by sin (v. 11). Moreover (and of considerable importance for the interpretation of Paul), vv. 14–25 describe a self-perception nearly the antithesis of Paul's own as evidenced in his letters (see ROM 2; Stendahl 1963; Sanders 1983: 76–81). The statement of Acts 23:1, 'up to this day I have lived my life with a clear conscience before God', is echoed in passages such as 2 Cor 1:12 and 4:2. The man who wrote, 'as to righteousness under the law, [I was] blameless' (Phil 3:6) and 'I am not aware of anything against myself' (1 Cor 4:4) did not suffer from existential *angst*. The assignment for Rom 7 must have been something other than autobiography.

The one character who qualifies on all counts to be the speaker in 7:7–26 is Adam (see Stuhlmacher 1994: 106–7), the archetypal human in whom all others sinned (5:12–21). Speaking as Adam, Paul can return to the initiation of 'law', the giving of 'the commandment' (v. 9) in the Garden: 'You shall not eat of the fruit of the tree . . . or you shall die' (Gen 3:3). Writes Paul, 'The very commandment that promised life proved death to me' (v. 10). Instead of saving them from death, the prohibition was used to lure them to death. The identification with Adam also explains the radical anthropomorphizing of sin in this same section: sin is like the serpent that 'deceived' Adam and Eve (v. 11; Gen 3:1, 4), enticing them to covet the forbidden fruit. (They ate, desiring to be 'as God', Gen 3:5. Note the description of Eve's response in Gen 3:6.)

vv. 14–24, if Paul is speaking in the place of unregenerate humanity, especially from the perspective of Adam, it follows that these verses do not describe the situation of believers. This is not the way the passage is read by many scholars (e.g. Schlatter 1995: 160; Barrett 1957: 151–3), but it is the only interpretation that suits the chapter's larger context (cf. Dunn's (1988: 387–99) attempt to resolve the conflict in terms of eschatological tension). The status of the individual in Rom 5:12–7:6 is either/or: either dead to sin or enslaved to sin, either in the dominion of life or in the dominion of death. The same situation prevails in Rom 8: either one is in the Spirit or one is in the flesh (v. 9). The Christian anthropology of Romans is not an essay in grey. The fault of the law in Rom 7 is that it is powerless (as 8:8: 'those in the flesh cannot please God'); it makes no sense in the context of this argument that Paul would describe believers in terms of the problem and not in terms of the solution. If 7:14–24 is a description of believers, then what is 8:1–17? There is indeed a future 'edge' to Paul's eschatological perspective, but it is located elsewhere: the expectation of 8:10–11 and 18–39 has nothing to do with

freedom from sin (already available to believers); Paul awaits freedom from sin's corporeal and cosmic *effects*.

v. 25, the final sentence ('So then . . .') makes the best claim to be a description of believers since it comes after Paul's Christian thanksgiving (v. 24). Some have argued that the verse is simply out of order or that it was originally a marginal gloss. 'For it is scarcely conceivable that, after giving thanks to God for deliverance, Paul should describe himself as being in exactly the same position as before' (Dodd 1932: 114–15). It is striking that the individual is characterized as being a 'slave' to the law and to ('the law of') sin, both 'pre-Christian' categories in Rom 5–6. Moffatt paraphrases the verse: 'Thus, left to myself, I serve . . .', which may capture Paul's meaning. At very least, one's assessment of v. 25 must take account of 8:1–7. The person in ch. 7 is 'with [the] flesh' 'a slave to the law of sin', but the believer in ch. 8 is 'not in the flesh' (v. 9) and is 'set free from the law of sin' (v. 2)! Therefore, it is possible in v. 25 that Paul describes a state to which believers may revert; it is clear that it is not the state in which he expects believers to remain.

(8:1–17) The Law of the Spirit Having described the dominion of death from which the law offers no rescue, Paul turns his attention to the alternative existence previewed in 7:6, 'the new life of the Spirit' experienced by those 'discharged from the law'. The description in 8:1–17 is rich and densely packed, containing numerous themes that figure prominently in other Pauline texts. Freed from the law, one lives beyond the reach of law's penalty: condemnation (v. 1, as in 7:3). A new system or principle, 'the law of the Spirit of life in Christ Jesus' (in contrast to the old system, 'the law of sin and of death'), now governs the believer's existence. 'Life' has a double meaning that corresponds to the two ends of the eschatological spectrum: it is a new quality of existence already enjoyed (v. 10), and it is future, eternal existence with God (vv. 11, 13). The Spirit effectuates both forms of life: in the present, the Spirit dwells in believers (v. 9) and empowers them to fulfil 'the just requirement of the law' (v. 4) and to 'put to death the deeds of the body' (v. 14); the Spirit leads believers (v. 14), witnesses to them that they are God's children (v. 16), and 'intercedes' for them 'with sighs too deep for words' (v. 26). In the future, God will raise believers to eternal life through the same Spirit (v. 11). More than anything else, it is the Spirit that marks the dawning of the new age (the 'dominion' of grace; 5:21). According to Acts (10:44–11:18), the presence of spiritual gifts amongst Gentile Christians was the decisive consideration in their admission to the church. It is instructive that Paul's first argument against the Galatian Judaizers concerns the presence of such *charismata* amongst the Galatian converts prior to any law observance (Gal 3:1–5). (Note that Paul refers synonymously to 'the Spirit of God' and 'the Spirit of Christ' in v. 9. See ROM 1:1 above.)

v. 3, the idea of Christ's atonement, already present in 3:24–5 and 5:6–9, is reintroduced. God 'dealt with sin', something that law, allied to weak human 'flesh' (i.e. the powerless human will, as in 7:14–25), was incapable of doing. In the death of Jesus, God 'condemned sin in the flesh', that is, the condemnation of v. 1 was executed on Jesus, the only human (one 'in . . . flesh') who was undeserving of such judgement. (He was 'in the likeness of sinful flesh', that is, he was human without sinning. Cf. 2 Cor 5:21: 'For our sake he made him to be sin who knew no sin, so that in him we might become the righteousness of God.' See also Phil 2:5–11.) As before, Paul is more interested in celebrating the atonement than in explaining its mechanics.

The difference between the two types of existence is explained from the human side as a difference of fundamental disposition or direction (vv. 5–11). One who lives 'according to the flesh' (vv. 5, 12; returning to the meaning of 7:14) has a mind set 'on the things of the flesh' (vv. 5–6). What constitutes 'the things of the flesh' is not specified, but it must mean something more than 'earthly concerns', such as the provision of food and clothing (cf. 'the deeds of the body' in v. 13). Such a mindset is 'hostile to God'; it does not—it cannot—'submit to God's law' or 'please God' (vv. 7–8). (As in v. 4, Paul assumes that believers are the only ones who 'do' the law.) The best explication of the phrase is found in Rom 1:18–32, which vividly describes human nature at war with God. The essential sin is idolatry, the devotion to something as god that is not God. Again, there is no middle ground, no accommodation, no compromise. Believers are on one side of the line and unbelievers the other.

By the logic of Paul's argument, believers should now have the power to do what the 'wretched self' of Rom 7 could not, namely, obey the law. Nevertheless, the 'just requirement of the law' (equivalent to 'the law of God' in v. 7) that they fulfil cannot be precisely equivalent to Torah since it does not include such 'optional extras' as circumcision (1 Cor 7:19). The use of the singular (to dikaiōma) 'brings out the fact that the law's requirements are essentially a unity' (Cranfield 1979: 384). For Paul, the will of God is present in but not circumscribed by Torah. The commonplace distinction between 'the spirit' and 'the letter' of the law is not far from what Paul had in mind (Rom 7:6).

v. 15, the mention of slavery recalls the discussion in 6:16–23 but also, more fully, Gal 4:1–9 and, especially with its connection to parentage, 21–31. 'Abba' (in Aramaic, an affectionate word for father) is associated with the prayer of Jesus (Mk 14:36); its presence in the Pauline epistles (here and Gal 4:6) is noteworthy. vv. 15–16 were key to Wesley's doctrine of 'Christian assurance', the idea that believers need not doubt their standing with God, being inwardly assured by the Spirit of their adoption (see also 9:1). Paul is careful to show that adoption does not imply an 'also-ran' or second-class birthright; on the contrary, believers are fully 'heirs of God' and even 'joint heirs with Christ' (v. 17; cf. v. 29); that is, by identifying with Christ, they participate fully in the benefits won by Christ. Paul does not mean to imply that believers are equal in every way to Christ.

v. 17, the section concludes quite unexpectedly: [we are] 'heirs . . . if . . . we suffer'. This sudden shift to minor key signals the presence of the antagonist, death. Although sin has been overcome, its ravages, its legacy remain. ('The present time'—ho nun kairos, v. 18—is the label Paul gives to this 'time between the times'.) The comments made in connection with 5:3 ('we . . . boast in our sufferings'), apply here: for Paul, the shape of Christian life was cruciform ('we suffer with him'; see also ROM E.4). True spirituality is dangerous and costly (1 Thess 3:4). Paul's difficult experiences with the church at Corinth (where he now writes) may well have prompted the

inclusion of this amendment (cf. 1 Cor 4:8–13). 'Glory' and its cognates are used 180 times in the NT (cf. 1:23; 2:7, 10; 3:7, 23; 4:20; 5:2; 6:4; 8:18, 21; 9:4, 23; 11:36; 15:6–9; 16:27; see TDNT ii. 247–54; EDNT i:344–9). The linkage between suffering and glory is typically Jewish (Stuhlmacher 1994: 132) and is made in a number of other NT writings (e.g. Lk 24:26; Eph 3:13; Heb 2:9–10; 1 Pet 1:11; 4:13; 5:1, 10).

(8:18–39) The Creation's Eager Longing To the woman . . . [God] said,| 'I will greatly increase your pangs in childbearing;| in pain you shall bring forth children| . . .' And to the man . . . [God] said, |' ' . . . cursed is the ground because of you; | in toil you shall eat of it all the days of your life; | thorns and thistles it shall bring forth for you; | and you shall eat the plants of the field. | By the sweat of your face you shall eat bread | . . . you are dust, and to dust you shall return.'

According to Gen 3:14–19, nature itself was corrupted by human sin and suffers sin's mournful consequences (see 4 Ezra 7:10–14). The 'peaceable kingdom' of Eden is no more.

The poetry and power of 8:18–39 betoken the magnitude of Paul's discovery: no less than Paradise returned. God in Christ is not saving individuals only; God is at the task of saving creation, of swallowing up Adam's entire loss in Christ's complete victory. What is the source of Paul's confidence? Christ's resurrection (of which Paul himself is a witness; Gal 1:16; 1 Cor 15:8), which is no less than the end of history placarded in the midst of history (1 Cor 15:20–6). The Garden curse, death, has been broken and remains only to be shattered.

As already noted, the reader comes upon the idea of suffering abruptly in v. 17, like fine print at the end of a contract. He or she may be left second-guessing: Is this 'inheritance' worth its price? Paul is quick to put matters into perspective: seen aright, present suffering is improportionate to future glory. To know things as they are one must recognize the scope of the drama in which one participates and the scale of the denouement for which one hopes. Present suffering is not merely local; it is cosmic. Future glory is not merely personal; it is universal. All history turns on the events of recent years, all creation awaits their completion, and Paul and his readers are at the epicentre of both. In one sense, the weight of the entire cosmos is on their shoulders; in another, the entire cosmos cheers them on. Thus Rom 8:18–39 provides both explanation and incentive. One may better accept suffering if one knows its origin and anticipates its cessation. All the more, one may accept (even 'boast of', 5:3) suffering that advances some great cause. Rhetorically, 8:18–39 is not unlike the stirring speech delivered by (Shakespeare's) King Henry V to encourage his outnumbered troops to face the French at Agincourt ('We few, we happy few, we band of brothers', Henry V, iv. iii).

Paul says that creation (the natural world) is 'groaning in labour pains', an image that evokes both the curse (in God's words to Eve) and the promise of its reversal (new life). v. 23 captures the resultant eschatological tension: 'we . . . who have the first fruits of the Spirit [the Spirit's many benefits, mentioned above], groan inwardly'. Believers are now children of God (v. 14), possessing 'a spirit of adoption' (v. 15), yet they must 'wait for adoption, the redemption of . . . [their] bodies' (v. 23). It is interesting that v. 24 contains the only past tense form of the verb 'to save' (esōthēmen) in any of the undisputed

Pauline epistles: literally, 'we were saved *in hope.*' Hope requires both object and absence. vv. 18–25 testify to a profound hope fuelled by the certainty and desirability of its object and the profundity of its absence.

v. 20, the identity of 'the one who subjected' the creation to futility is the topic of intense debate. The likely candidate is again Adam, the consequences of whose sin surely underlie the reflections of the entire paragraph. But did Adam subject the creation to futility 'in hope'? A variety of attempts have been made to get to grips with this odd phrase. For example, Cranfield (1979: 414) wrote that 'The creation was not subjected to frustration without any hope . . . Paul possibly had in mind the promise in Gen 3.15 that the woman's seed would bruise the serpent's head (cf. Rom 16.20)'. An alternative solution is to regard the entire phrase 'for the creation . . . who subjected it' as a parenthesis, and attach the final two words of v. 20, 'in hope', to the next phrase, as does NRSV (the original Greek text did not contain punctuation; where phrases or even sentences begin and end is by no means certain). Thus, v. 21 may complete the thought of v. 19: 'For the creation waits . . . in hope that ['or because'] the creation itself will be set free . . .'

It is possible that the phenomenon described in vv. 26–7 is the gift of tongues, which Paul describes in 1 Cor 14:15 as 'praying with the spirit'. The statement that 'God . . . knows what is the mind of the Spirit' could refer to the fact that tongues were unintelligible to the human speaker. (According to 1 Cor 14:3, the one speaking in tongues 'utters mysteries with his [her] spirit'.) It is also possible that 'unutterable groanings' (*stenagmois alalētois*, v. 26) refers, literally, to inarticulate moans. This interpretation takes into account the fact that vv. 26–7 assume universal applicability, whereas, by Paul's own account, all did not speak in tongues (1 Cor 12:4–11). On the other hand, it should be said that the second reading has more difficulty explaining the repeated assertion that the Spirit 'intercedes' on behalf of the saints. An unrelated issue concerns the degree of separation between God and Spirit in Paul's description (e.g. 'God knows what is the mind of the Spirit'; see Dunn 1988: 479–80).

v. 28 does not promise that only good things will happen to 'those who love God'. In the larger context of vv. 18–39, and the immediate context of vv. 29–30, the sentence probably means that the woes that characterize the present age, and the suffering of persecution in particular, cannot thwart God, who uses even these to accomplish the divine purpose.

Paradoxically, Paul assumes both that God predestined humans to a certain fate and that humans are responsible for that fate. Rom 9:14–26 shows that he knows the obvious objection—how can humans be held responsible for God's actions?—and that he does not possess a *rational* answer. Instead, he responds, 'Who are you, a human being, to argue with God?' (9:20). Here as elsewhere in the NT, predestination is not mentioned abstractly; it usually functions either as assurance (as in Rom 8) or as theodicy (as in Rom 9; really another form of assurance). The essential point is that, despite all appearances to the contrary (the 'all things' of v. 28), God has everything under control.

As was mentioned in connection with ROM 1:16, 'justification' in Romans combines two ideas: that God credits to believers the status of righteousness and that God empowers believers to live righteously. Both meanings may be present in

v. 29: it is God's purpose that believers 'be conformed to the image of his Son'. Certainly, this means sharing in future glory, being one 'within a large family' (cf. 1 Cor 15:20). 'Image' (*eikōn*), echoing the creation account of Gen 1 (v. 26), invites an additional and fuller interpretation, that believers already share the character of Christ.

The entirety of Rom 1–8 reaches its climax in vv. 31–9. Paul's speech is fittingly dramatic, harking back again (ROM 1:16) to Isa 50:7–8 (LXX; trans. Hays 1989: 59–60): 'I know that I shall by no means be put to shame, | Because the One who justified me draws near. | Who enters into judgment with me? | Let him confront me. | Indeed, who enters into judgment with me? | Let him draw near to me. | Behold, the Lord helps me. | Who will do me harm?' By way of encouragement to his readers, Paul wrote earlier of the disproportion between present tribulation and future glory (vv. 18–25). To the same end, he now writes of the disproportion between earthly appearance and spiritual reality. For believers, the one true indicator of their position is the love of God demonstrated in the cross of Christ. (v. 32 is especially poignant because it borrows language from the story of the binding of Isaac in Gen 22: 'you have not withheld your son, your only son' (v. 12); Cranfield 1979: 436. In Rom 8:32, God makes the sacrifice that even Abraham was 'spared'; note the verbal echoes of Gen 22:12 in Rom 8:32.) With this datum, the 'everything else' of v. 32 is assured. No condemnation is more persuasive than Christ's intercession, no deprivation, no sovereignty, no distance a greater reality. 'In all these things we are more than conquerors through him who loved us.' It is a glorious vision.

God's Righteousness Evident in the Treatment of Israel (9:1–11:36)

(9:1–5) Paul's Lament over Israel In first eight chapters of Romans the Protestant Reformers found the answer to their urgent question, 'How shall we be saved?' Ironically, their close identification with Paul worked both to popularize and to obscure Paul's distinctive theological contribution. In assuming common cause with Paul, they tended to project onto Paul their own struggles with disconsolate conscience and disapproving Catholicism. So Romans came to be viewed as a kind of personal salvation manual, a road-map for guilty, lost souls in search of a forgiving, gracious God. One consequence was the orphaning of the remainder of the epistle, especially chs. 9–11, whose interest in the fate of Israel was scarcely an ongoing or pivotal Christian concern. Recent biblical scholarship has been more successful at placing Rom 9–11 where it properly belongs, at the centre (or, rhetorically, at the climax) of Paul's argument. The concern of Romans is not so much to explain justification by faith in Christ as to explain how such a soteriological system upholds God's righteousness, especially God's righteousness towards non-Christian Israel. Thus, deprived of chs. 9–11, Romans would be gravely deficient; indeed, without reading to the section's surprising conclusion in 11:25–36, one might wonder truly if unbelieving Israel's present status does not expose 'unrighteousness on God's part' (9:14).

Moving from 8:39 to 9:1 is like walking off a precipice; having scaled the resplendent heights of ch. 8, one drops by a single step to the shadowy depths of ch. 9. 'I have great sorrow and unceasing anguish in my heart' (v. 2). Why sorrow if nothing is able 'to separate us from the love of God in Christ Jesus our Lord' (8:39)? Because it appears that Israel is not among the 'us', that Israel *is* alienated from God's love. This is an intolerable conclusion against which Paul mobilizes two basic arguments. First, he contends that now as in the past, only a portion of Israel has been elect or faithful; therefore, one ought not to regard the present case as being exceptional either from the side of God or of Israel. It is evident that this answer was not fully persuasive even to Paul. The word of God might not entirely have 'failed' (v. 6), but Jewish Christianity remained a disconcertingly small success. Paul's second answer locates the solution outside present history (and therefore beyond the thwarted historical means of the Church's Jewish mission): at the return of Christ, 'all Israel', even 'disobedient' Israel, will be saved (11:25–36). In this belief, Paul finds a solution to the problem of God's apparent unrighteousness: God, being God, must save Israel.

Paul's remarks in vv. 1–5 appear to reflect Ex 32:30–4, Moses' offer to be 'blotted out of the book' for the sake of the Israelites, who had 'sinned a great sin' in constructing the golden calf at Sinai. (The Sinai incident also might be in view in Paul's description of human idolatry and rebellion in ROM 1:18–32). Not long before, in 2 Cor 3:4–11, Paul explicitly contrasted (his) Christian ministry with that of Moses at Sinai. This same historical referent might have encouraged Paul to begin speaking of the 'Israelites' (v. 4 and more generally in these three chapters) instead of the 'Jews'. 'Israel' and 'Israelite' are in any case the terms better suited to his argument; they allow Paul to treat past and present Judaism as a whole, they signal continuity with previous 'covenant communities', and they provide the common conceptual thread that runs through a series of arguments concerning the identity of God's true people.

In 3:1, Paul asked, 'Then what advantage has the Jew? Or what is the value of circumcision?' His answer, 'Much in every way,' was ambiguous. The only specific instantiation was Israel's entrustment with 'the oracles of God' (3:2). In vv. 4–5, Paul returns to the question, this time offering a significantly longer list of privileges, the ultimate of which is to provide (by earthly descent, 'according to the flesh') the world with its Messiah. The most unexpected item in the list is 'adoption', which in just the previous chapter had a distinctly—and uniquely—Christian nuance (8:15, 23; cf. Gal 4:5). Presumably, Paul now refers to something different, most likely to God's 'adoption' of Israel in the Exodus (as in Ex 4:22; Hos 11:1). It is interesting to note how such points of continuity both strengthen and weaken Paul's argument. On the one hand, God's work of universal adoption in Christ may be seen to be consistent with (and therefore made credible by) God's previous action in adopting Israel; on the other hand, to the extent that Israel already is adopted, it ought not to require readoption. For this reason, when Paul defends the necessity of Christ, as logically he is forced to do, his argument must lean heavily to the side of discontinuity. Jews cannot have any actual advantage with respect to salvation if Jews and Gentiles are both equally in need of Christ.

The enumeration of divine blessings leads Paul into doxology: 'God, who is over all, is blessed forever. Amen' (v. 5). The original Greek text did not include punctuation, which makes it possible to translate the phrase appositionally, i.e. as an explanatory remark concerning Christ (e.g. the NRSV's '. . . the Messiah, who is over all, God blessed forever'). Despite Paul's generally high Christology (ROM 1:1–5), it is very unlikely that he would have referred to Christ as 'God over all'. Some commentators note by way of contrast 1 Cor 15:24–8, in which Paul states that Christ himself 'will also be subjected to the one who put all things in subjection under him, *so that God may be all in all*' (my emphasis; Dunn 1988: 535–6).

(9:6–29) God's Consistency Evident in the Election of True Israel Once again, the issue of God's righteousness is front and centre. 'It is not as though the word of God had failed' (v. 6). The 'word of God' refers broadly to God's promises to Abraham and through him to his descendants (see 4:13–25). Why might one argue that this 'word' had failed? Because comparatively few who now recognize and experience its fulfilment in Christ are Abraham's offspring. The Jews, who ought to be first and foremost, appear to be last and least (cf. 1:16). Has God's plan for Israel been thwarted? It cannot be so. Paul argues that the divine promises to Abraham were fulfilled by the election of only a portion of Abraham's natural descendants. God chose Isaac over Ishmael, Abraham's firstborn. One might object that of the two sons only Isaac had the right of succession, being the sole child of Sarah, Abraham's wife. Such a protest is impossible, however, in the case of Abraham's grandson Jacob, whose elder brother was his twin (see Gen 25:19–34). The word of God was not frustrated by the 'failure' of Ishmael and Esau to obtain their natural birthright. It was through the second born, the true 'children of promise', Isaac and Jacob, that God's plan was fulfilled. The reference in vv. 27–9 to the remnant of Israel (Isa 10:22–3) makes much the same point (see 11:1–5): God's choice of a part of Israel is well precedented; so among contemporary Jews it is the Christian believers who are the elect descendants of Abraham. It is important to recognize that Paul does not maintain this position unvaryingly; in 11:25–32, he will argue for the salvation of unbelieving Israel based upon its *continued* election. ('For the gifts and calling of God are irrevocable', 11:29.)

Paul is not making the point that physical descent from Abraham in itself is insufficient to save. For Paul, lineage is simply irrelevant to salvation. Rom 9 harks back to the argument of Rom 4, where Paul stated that Abraham's true descendants are not the 'adherents of the law' but those who 'share in the faith of Abraham' (4:14–16). The contrast between 'children of the flesh' and 'children of the promise' in v. 8 sets up an analogous human-way *v* God's-way dichotomy. The major difference is that Paul's argument in vv. 6–13 only indirectly concerns Gentiles. (In v. 24, he will again include Gentiles explicitly as part of God's people, although he does not employ the idea of 'promise', as he did in Rom 4.) The issue is whether 'fleshly' Israel *in toto* is the Israel for and in whom God must be shown to have acted faithfully. For Paul, at least in the context of this argument, it is not.

v. 13, the severe statement 'I have loved Jacob, but I have hated Esau' (Mal 1:2–3; see *HBC* 1155, on the original, probably less extreme, sense of this verse) pointedly raises the question of God's justice (vv. 14–29). Paul's first answer (citing Ex

33:19) is that it is no injustice to be merciful, to treat some people better than they deserve. The issue is not God's just or unjust response to human goodness (v. 16); election is a gracious gift, not an achievable reward. Even the hardening of Pharaoh's heart (vv. 17–18) was done to advance the cause of God's salvation (Ex 9:16). Of course, things might look different from the perspective of Pharaoh or Ishmael or Esau. Granted that election is undeserved, why elect some and not others? The problem is intensified by positing a 'reverse election' in which God hardens the hearts of the wicked. How can God find fault for what God has caused (vv. 18–19)? This is a problem with a very long history in Judaism. The belief in the omnipotence of the one true God may lead to (or, inversely, may be guided by) the conviction that God exerts control over all human circumstances. Thus the Exodus narrative states repeatedly both that Pharaoh hardened his own heart (Ex 8:14, 32; 9:34; etc.) and that God hardened Pharaoh's heart (4:21; 7:3; 9:12; etc.). The same perspective is evidenced in passages such as Deut 2:30, Josh 11:20, 1 Sam 6:6, and—most poignantly in reference to Israel itself—Isa 63:17: 'Why, O LORD, do you make us stray from your ways and harden our heart, so that we do not fear you?'

God's omnipotence is affirmed by means of the potter metaphor (Isa 29:16; 45:9–13; Jer 18:6; Wis 15:7). The potter has sovereign right over the clay, not the reverse. It is significant that Paul links this idea to a statement about God's unexpected patience towards the wicked (vv. 22–3; see Wis 11:21–12:22). If God is both just and powerful (as powerful as a potter over a lump of clay), why do the wicked exist, much less flourish? The assertion of God's omnipotence underlies all theodicy; if God controls human action, then human evil itself must originate in God. Negating this conclusion requires a limiting of God's omnipotence (often imagined as a divine self-limitation: here, for example, judgement is forestalled temporarily by God's patience; see also 2:4; Neh 9:30; 1 Pet 3:17; and 2 Pet 3:9, 15). The problem is as old as the book of Job and remains as intractable. Paul's answer is reminiscent of that of Job's latter chapters: 'Who indeed are you, a human being, to argue with God?' Logically, this is no answer at all; instead, it is a roundabout affirmation that God can be trusted. This faithful God indeed has done what was promised, calling a people out from among Gentiles (vv. 25–6) and Jews (vv. 27–9) alike. In sum, if much of 'natural' Israel is not included in true Israel, it cannot mean that God has failed. Then whose fault is it?

(9:30–10:21) Israel's Failure Explained In a sense, 9:6–29 explained Jewish unbelief 'from above', that is, from the perspective of God's purpose and election. What follows is an explanation 'from below', an account of Israel's response and hence responsibility. Several of Paul's statements in this section are difficult to untangle, but the essential point seems clear enough: Gentiles happened effortlessly upon righteousness by believing the proclamation concerning Christ. Jews, who had worked diligently to be righteous, have rejected faith in Christ, the only thing able to make them *truly* righteous. For this error they have no excuse.

The meaning of 'righteousness' is fundamental to this passage and has been the subject of intense debate (see Ziesler 1989: 251–2). In large part, the problem arises because Paul

uses the term in a distinctly new, Christian sense, even in reference to Judaism. Writes Sanders (1977: 544),

Righteousness in Judaism is a term which implies the *maintenance of status* among the group of the elect; in Paul it is a *transfer* term... Thus when Paul says that one cannot be made righteous by works of law, he means that one cannot, by works of law, 'transfer to the body of the saved.' When Judaism said that one is righteous who obeys the law, the meaning is that one thereby stays in the covenant.

Within Judaism, one did not obey the law in the hope of transferring from one people (unrighteous, unsaved) to another (righteous, saved). Paul's faith/law antithesis presupposes that Jews were trying (and failing) by means of the law to attain a status ('righteous' = being 'saved') that could be conferred only by faith in Christ. Thus the juxtaposition of law and Christ as rival means of salvation is problematic; normally, the two serve different functions in different systems. From the side of Judaism, it is an apples-and-oranges comparison; however, from Paul's side, with the controversy at Galatia fresh in mind, the opposition between faith in Christ and works of the law was as straightforward as the distinction between chalk and cheese (see ROM E.3). One should note how readily and frequently a difference in theological nuance or emphasis is transformed polemically into an antithesis. A modern example is the contention on the part of some conservative Christians that unlike other churchgoers, they do not practise 'religion' but rather experience a 'relationship' with God. Outsiders might regard the religion/relationship antithesis as quite odd: even the most experientially oriented Christianity is still a religion; certainly others (including other Christians) affirm relationship with God. For insiders, however, the dichotomy helps to account for the existence of (so-called) Christians who reject the group's distinctive claims. Such persons can be dismissed as 'unbelievers' who strive misguidedly through 'religion' to know God. Similarly, Jews who for varying reasons reject Christian claims can be depicted as formalistic law-keepers without faith. In either case, what is offered is an insider's account of the rejection of those outsiders who ought to know better.

Paul's first explanation of Israel's fault, in vv. 31–2, is notoriously ambiguous. One might have expected Paul to say that 'Israel had pursued but did not achieve righteousness' (Cranfield 1979: 507). Instead, Paul wrote that Israel 'pursued a law of righteousness' but 'did not arrive at' (or 'attain') 'law'. The meaning of 'law', 'righteousness', 'law of righteousness', and 'attain law' in v. 31 have been debated extensively with no resulting consensus. It is not even clear whether it was the 'pursuit' of law itself or the inability to 'attain' ('catch up with', Fitzmyer 1993: 577) law that Paul faults. If the former, Paul might be saying that Israel's pursuit of 'legal righteousness' could not lead them to the law's true goal (as possibly in 10:4). If the latter, Paul might mean that Israel attempted but failed to live righteously according to the precepts of the law. In either case, succeeding verses make clear that the actual fault of the Jews is their unbelief in Christ, whom they insensibly overlooked (10:2–3), over whom they have stumbled (9:32–3, a combination of Isa 8:14 and 28:16; the same idea is repeated in 11:9–12; 1 Cor 1:23; and 1 Pet 2:6–8). As a result, they are characterized as being unsaved (10:1), 'disobedient and contrary' (10:21), 'broken off', 'cut off', 'fallen' (11:19, 22), and 'hardened' (11:7, 25). Their only hope is to 'submit to God's righteousness' (10:3), which means specifically to believe in (10:4, 9, 11; 11:20, 23), call upon (10:13), and confess (10:9–10) Christ.

Phil 3:2–9 is a close parallel to Rom 10:1–4 and helps to clarify Paul's distinction between the Jews' 'own righteousness' and the righteousness imparted by God through Christ. In Phil 3:6, Paul says that 'as to righteousness under the law', he was 'blameless', a statement in tension with the interpretation of 9:31 that suggests that the Jews erred by failing to attain just such a status. In Phil 3, 'one's own' righteousness 'under the law' is rejected not because of its unattainability but because of its inferiority. Rom 10:1–4 may be much closer to this sentiment than is Rom 1–7. While it is not stated whether persons may succeed at 'establishing their own' righteousness, it is clear that their attempt to do so misses the point. Another, superior kind of righteousness exists, in the face of which the lesser righteousness is only a distraction. Put differently, the problem is this: Judaism is experienced as a complete, self-contained religious system that does not appear to require faith in Christ. One can be a superlative ('zealous', Phil 3:6; Gal 1:14; Rom 10:2) Jew—the pre-Christian Paul is Paul's own pre-eminent example—and still be on the wrong side of the line. Essential for Paul is the belief that Judaism without Christ is unfinished, that the law itself points to Christ as its ultimate goal and fulfilment (v. 4, telos, probably in the sense both of intention and termination; Barrett 1957: 197). Paul's characterization of Judaism's incompleteness varies; Paul's conviction of its incompleteness does not.

Considerable debate has arisen over the relationship between the key vv. 5 and 6, focusing on the force of de ('but') at the beginning of the second sentence. If de signals a strong contrast (again, between two forms of righteousness), then Paul is stating quite boldly that Moses was wrong to assert that one could 'live' (in Paul's usage, the word probably refers to resurrection life; see ROM 1:17) by doing the law. In favour of this interpretation one may cite Gal 3:12, which quotes Lev 18:5 to similar effect: Moses' words prove that 'the law does not rest on faith' but on 'works'. One way of diminishing the contrast between the two verses is to take the reference to 'live' in v. 5 in its original sense, referring not to eternal life but rather to 'life sustained by God . . . in accordance with the . . . law' (Dunn 1988: 612). But Rom 7:10 speaks of the commandment 'that promised' but could not deliver 'life'; there (as possibly in 10:5–6) it is not a question of two kinds of life but of two means, one failed and the other successful, of attaining the one true, eternal life. Other interpreters find continuity, not contrast, in Paul's statements. For example, Hays (1989: 75–7) has argued that vv. 6–13 explain v. 5 by indicating what 'things' one must do in obedience to the law to find eternal life: namely, confessing, believing, and calling upon Christ. This view may be supported by the fact that Paul's second quotation, which helps to establish the principle that 'righteousness comes from faith', is also from 'Moses' (Deut 30:12–14, followed by citations of Isa 28:16 and Joel 2:32). It is instructive that those who do and those who do not see a contrast between vv. 5 and 6 link Paul's argument to v. 4

(Christ as telos) in essentially opposite ways: the former emphasizes Christ as the law's termination, the latter Christ as the law's goal.

Paul's first two elaborations on Deut 30:12–14 ('that is, to bring Christ down', 'that is, to bring Christ up from the dead', 10:6–7) provide 'a scriptural exclusion of any contemplation of the kind of human effort the rival mode of righteousness would involve' (Byrne 1996: 318). One need not, indeed cannot, do what God can do in Christ. The common obligation of Jews and Greeks is only to 'believe', 'confess', and 'call on the name of the Lord'.

10:14–17, Paul returns to the matter of Israel's fault. Can it be that Israel's unbelief is occasioned by simple ignorance? Do they fail to call on Christ because they have not heard 'the word of Christ' (vv. 17–18)? The 'good news' (Isa 52:7) has been delivered to them, but the report has not been received (also precedented in Isaiah: the nearby 53:2). Paul concludes his argument by offering scriptural warrant for the situation described in 9:30–1. Gentiles 'who are not a nation', 'who did not seek' God, have found God (Deut 32:21; Isa 65:1). By contrast, Israel is a 'disobedient and contrary people' to whom God's hands have been extended in vain (Isa 65:2). Thus, Paul would lay Israel's fault, its unbelief in Christ, at Israel's own feet.

(11:1–36) God's Plan for Israel Once again, Paul advances his argument with a rhetorical question concerning God's faithfulness and constancy. 'Has God rejected his people?' vv. 1–10 reiterate the answers provided in ch. 9. That only a remnant of physical Israel is true Israel is precedented in Jewish history, in this case, in the example of Elijah and the seven thousand (1 Kings 19). God has not spurned this Israel, that is, the portion of Israel 'whom he foreknew' (v. 2) and elected (v. 7). Again, Paul speaks of God graciously choosing some and of God hardening others (vv. 5–7; see 9:6–18), which Paul again defends by means of scriptural citation (vv. 8–10; Deut 29:4; Isa 29:10; Ps 69:22–3; see 9:17, 25–9; cf. the similar use of Isa 6:9–11 in both the synoptic tradition, e.g. Mk 4:12, and John, e.g. Jn 12:40).

v. 11, the shift in Paul's argument here is immensely important. Imagine that chs. 9–11 had ended at 11:10: 'let their eyes be darkened so that they cannot see, and keep their backs forever bent'. In that case, Paul might with good reason be regarded as a thoroughgoing Christian supersessionist. 'Israel failed to obtain what it was seeking' (v. 7), and so Israel has been set aside in favour of the church. The fact that Paul has been read this way for centuries amply demonstrates that Rom 11:11–36 has not been given its due weight as the conclusion and climax, not only of Rom 9–11, but of the argument begun in 1:16–17 concerning the righteousness of God. Paul asks, 'Have they stumbled so as to fall?' For the first time, the possibility is raised of a future change in Israel's status. Their present 'stumbling' is not to be interpreted as a permanent 'fall'. As much as Paul wanted to justify the present reality (e.g. through talk of an elect remnant), he could not accept that reality as permanently justifiable. Here at last Paul offers a strong answer to the persistent question concerning God's faithfulness towards Israel.

In conventional Jewish eschatological expectation, Israel would first be restored, and then into that redeemed Israel would stream believing Gentiles (e.g. Isa 2:1–4; 42:1–9; 49; 55:4–5; 60:1–7; 66:18–23). Paul reveals this 'mystery' (v. 25): Jewish obduracy has led to a reversal of the eschatological timetable. Now is the period of Gentile inclusion: 'through their stumbling salvation has come to the Gentiles' (v. 11); 'their stumbling means riches for the world' (v. 12); 'their rejection is the reconciliation of the world' (v. 15); 'you (Gentiles) were once disobedient to God but have now received mercy *because of* their [the Jews'] disobedience' (v. 30, my emphasis). Precisely what Paul believed happened (or could have happened in its place) is not clear. He might have imagined that Christ would have returned already had the mission to Israel succeeded. It is worth noting that the same train of thought is evident in Acts: the Jews are given a chance to repent with the promise of Christ's return (e.g. 3:17–21); increasingly, they reject the apostles' message, resulting ultimately in the martyrdom of Stephen (ch. 7), a direct consequence of which is the spread of Christianity to the Gentiles (11:19–26). This same pattern—Jewish rejection leading to Gentile opportunity—occurs repeatedly in the accounts of Paul's missionary activity in Acts (e.g. 13:13–52; 18:1–8; 28:17–28).

v. 25, the period of Gentile evangelization is impermanent: 'a hardening has come upon part of Israel, until the full number of the Gentiles has come in'. After the mission to the Gentiles is complete, God will act to bring faith to Israel and to complete the eschatological drama: 'So all Israel will be saved; as it is written, "The Deliverer will come from Zion, he will banish ungodliness from Jacob"; "and this will be my covenant with them when I take away their sins"' (vv. 26–7, quoting Isa 59:20–1; 27:9). 'What will their acceptance be but life from the dead!' (v. 15). Interestingly, the author of Luke–Acts also maintains the expectation of a Jewish restoration following the Gentile mission (e.g. Acts 1:6–7; cf. the periodization of history in Lk 21:24: 'Jerusalem will be trampled on by the Gentiles *until the times of the Gentiles are fulfilled*,' my emphasis). Unfortunately, NT scholarship often has overlooked the presence of these ideas in Romans as well as in Luke–Acts.

So, when all is said and done, God's election of 'all Israel' stands (cf. 'full inclusion' in v. 12), and God's righteousness is vindicated (vv. 29–32). No details are offered concerning the constitution of 'all Israel'. (All Jews at all times? All Jews present at Christ's return? Cf. Sanday and Headlam (1980: 335): '"Israel as a whole, Israel as a nation," and not . . . necessarily including every individual Israelite.') At very least, it is clear that this group includes many if not all who are now, from Paul's perspective, 'disobedient' (vv. 30–1) 'ungodly' (v. 26, a stunning characterization), and even 'enemies of God' (v. 28). Unlike Gal 6:16, there is no possibility here that Paul is referring to the church as ('spiritual') Israel. Ch. 11 contains two hints as to the means of Israel's eventual salvation. In vv. 11 and 14 Paul returns to a point made by his earlier quotation of Deut 32:21 (10:19): Israel will become jealous of the Gentile believers and repent. Perhaps this is sufficient means to win some to faith in Christ (11:13–14)—but 'all Israel'? That will be accomplished by God directly (v. 23), apparently in anticipation or consequence of Christ's return (v. 26; note the eschatologically oriented vv. 12 and 15). More than that Paul does not say.

vv. 17–24, Paul's understanding of the relationship between Gentile believers and Israel is explicated by means of the olive tree metaphor. The Gentiles have no true root in themselves; they are wild branches grafted into an already existing, carefully cultivated olive tree. True, they now occupy the place of natural olive branches (Jews) pruned because of their fruitlessness (their unbelief), but they have no cause to be proud. The present situation is temporary: natural branches will be grafted back in, and some wild branches may yet be 'broken off'.

It should be said that the 'mystery' revealed in 11:11–32 does not follow *logically* from 1:1–11:10. Stopping at 11:10, one would conclude that only a small remnant of Israel is or ever will be saved. The church's mission to the Jews failed, and that is that. But present appearances belie ultimate realities (cf. 8:31–9). The resolution to Paul's 'sorrow and unceasing anguish' (9:2) is found at length in his trust in the eschatological triumph of God's righteousness. The issue finally is decided, not by reason, but by faith.

Fittingly, Paul's disclosure of the divine plan leads him to doxology (vv. 33–6), an expression of awe at the greatness of God who uses even 'disobedience' to produce 'mercy' (vv. 30–1). Of course, it is not God's inscrutability or power alone that compels Paul's adoration; above all, it is God's righteousness that is proved in God's 'ways' and 'judgments'. In coming to understand God's mysterious plan for Israel, Paul has looked behind the veil and glimpsed 'riches', 'wisdom', and 'knowledge' beyond human calculation. Paul's 'hymn of adoration' (Dunn 1988: 697) crowns chs. 9–11 in much the way that 8:31–9 concluded chs. 1–8. Both passages affirm with rhetorical beauty and force the apostle's trust in God's trustworthiness. Disputation at an end, Paul points to God's future, believes in God's triumph, and worships.

The Righteousness of God Evident in the Lives of Believers (12:1–15:13)

(12:1–2) Introduction: The Renewal of Your Minds

At 12:1, Romans turns from the conceptual and argumentative to the practical and didactic. This is a shift towards more typical Pauline content; anyone familiar with Paul's Corinthian, Philippian, or Thessalonian correspondence should feel at home in the ethical exhortations of chs. 12–15. Of course, Paul here writes to a church that he neither founded nor visited, a fact evidenced by the fairly general nature of his paraenesis (see ROM C, on the lack of contingency in Romans).

Paul has laboured to defend God's righteousness, in part through attributing to believers a righteousness unrealized by the now antiquated means of law obedience. But it is one thing to speak loftily of fulfilling 'the just requirement of the law' by 'walking according to the Spirit' (8:2–4); it is quite another to mark out the steps for such a journey. What does this new righteousness look like in everyday practice? Paul provides an illustrative, not exhaustive, answer in these few chapters.

God's extraordinary mercy was described in 11:30–2. What then is the fitting ('logical', *logikos*) human response ('service' or 'worship', *latreia*, 12:1)? It is to present oneself wholly to God, from whom and through whom and in whom are all things (11:36). Offering 'your bodies a living sacrifice' connotes giving oneself continuously and entirely. Any lesser response misprizes the greatness of God's own offering.

The eschatological context of Pauline ethics is immediately evident. v. 2 begins, literally, 'Do not be conformed to *this age*.' Paul vividly characterized the old order in Rom 1:18–32; humans had 'became futile in their thinking, and their senseless minds were darkened' (1:21). The new, eschatological righteousness overmasters humanity's ancient, fallen nature: believers experience a 'renewal of . . . [their] minds, so that . . . [they] may discern what is the will of God—what is good and acceptable and perfect' (12:2*b*). For Paul, it is no less than a return, a 'conforming' to the original order, the re-creation of human minds not 'subjected to futility' (8:20; cf. 'new creation' in Gal 6:15; 2 Cor 5:17). Paul does not expect his readers to obtain such an exalted capability on their own. Rather, he believes that as possessors of the Spirit, they are already equipped to live lives 'holy and acceptable to God' (12:1; see 8:1–17). Paul asks only that they be what they truly are: righteous.

(12:3–21) Exhortations for the Christian Community It is obvious that the recent Galatian controversy influenced Paul's discussion of the law in Rom 1–8. Less noticed is the impact of Paul's difficulties with the church at Corinth upon Rom 12–15. Note that Paul's first exhortation is to humility and Christian unity—not surprising, as he writes from Corinth, the native habitat of spiritual pride and factional division (see 1 Cor 1–4). It is a sermon well rehearsed: vv. 3–8 are closely paralleled by 1 Cor 12:12–28. A major difference is the list of gifts in vv. 6–8, which is more mundane than that found in 1 Cor 12:28. (Rom 12 includes gifts of exhortation, generosity, and compassion but not deeds of power, healings, and tongues. In Romans the gifts are not linked specifically to the activity of the Spirit, and the corporation of Christians is not referred to as 'the body *of* Christ.') Paul again counters disunity by challenging individual status seeking, but, outside of Corinth, he does not locate the problem specifically in the flaunting of spiritual gifts.

The listing of maxims, as in vv. 9–21, is characteristic of ancient paraenesis and is a feature commonly found near the conclusion of Paul's letters (e.g. 1 Thess 5:12–22; Phil 4:4–9). Probably Paul draws from no one source but rather from the broad stream of Christian ethical teaching, incorporating elements of the Jesus tradition, Jewish wisdom literature, and Graeco-Roman philosophy (Byrne 1996: 375). A unifying element is supplied by v. 9*a*: 'love is genuine' (*anupokritos*; lit. unhypocritical). (Contrary to NRSV, there is no imperative verb.) The discussion of the body of Christ in 1 Cor 12 was also followed (in the justly celebrated ch. 13) by an appeal to *agapē*, love. It is love alone that curbs self-assertion and so makes unity possible (Phil 2:2; 1 Pet 3:8). Accordingly, the whole of vv. 9*b*–13 is sometimes read as a description of 'unhypocritical love in action' (Achtemeier 1985: 198). Perhaps this is too tidy a summarization of Paul's wide-ranging admonitions; nevertheless, it is certain that Paul regarded love as the pre-eminent and finally only necessary command, a point he makes explicitly in 13:8–10 (and in continuity with passages such as Mk 12:28–34; Mt 5:43–8; 19:19; Jn 13:34–5; 15:12–17; Jas 2:8; 1 Jn 3:11, 23; 4:21; and 2 Jn 5).

(13:1–7) Christians and Civil Authority Paul commended his readers to 'live in harmony' and to 'live peaceably with all';

immediately after, he adjured them not to seek revenge (12:16, 18–19). A discussion of civil authority follows naturally if not necessarily from these remarks. It may be that Paul's comments reflect concern over behaviour that had contributed to the expulsion of the Jews (including Christian Jews; see Acts 18:2) from Rome only a few years before (see ROM B.3).

Does Christian conversion, the submission to God's rule, release one from civil authority? It is reasonable to suppose that one who lives in a new age is free of the old age. But one cannot live *only* in the new aeon; on earth the ages overlap. God's dominion is not entirely realized; believers' hearts are not wholly submitted (hence Paul's admonishment in 12:2). One might regard government as an expedient necessitated by human sin; even so, it is apparent that Christians do not yet live so distant from the Fall as to make obsolete government's corrective function. And predating the fallen, evil order is the original, beneficent order of creation (see Rom 1:18–20). Is government a temporarily sanctioned accommodation or an eternally mandated institution? Like Jesus in Mk 12:17, Paul does not deal explicitly with these questions; nevertheless, his words invalidate some answers, such as regarding government as human invention or satanic usurpation.

Few if any passages in the Pauline corpus have been more subject to abuse than vv. 1–7. Paul does *not* indicate that one is required to obey public officials under all circumstances, nor does he say that every exercise of civil authority is sanctioned by God. No particular government is authorized; no universal autarchy is legitimated. Instead, Paul reiterates the common Jewish view that human governance operates under God's superintendency (Jn 19:11; Dan 2:21; Prov 8:15–16; Isa 45:1–3; Wis 6:3), that it is part of the divine order and so is meant for human good (1 Pet 2:13–14; *Ep. Arist.* 291–2). Paul's view of and desire for order is also paralleled in 1 Corinthians. Paul responded to the chaos of Corinthian worship by arguing that 'God is a God not of disorder but of peace' (14:33) and so commended his followers to do 'all things' 'decently and in order' (14:40). Here Paul advises a new group of readers to find peace by submitting to proper order (cf. 1 Cor 16:16). It is striking that Paul treated with such optimism the very Roman authority by which he himself was eventually martyred. The presentation in Rom 13 has often been contrasted with that of Rev 13, in which Rome is portrayed as a diabolical beast whose 'authority' is exercised in making 'war on the saints' (v. 7). Rom 13 and Rev 13 are not quite opposites; Paul is not attempting to account for the reality depicted in Revelation. Nevertheless, the near demonization of the state in Revelation may be a healthy canonical counterbalance to its near idealization in Romans. But both Paul and the author of Revelation share common ground in asserting God's final authority over human affairs, humanity's ultimate allegiance to God, and God's eventual victory over every opposing 'ruler, authority, and power' (1 Cor 15:24–5). Rom 13:1–7 is not easy to live with, but neither would the opposing alternative be.

(13:8–10) 'Love is the Fulfilling of the Law' In Rom 12:9, Paul offered a theme for the ethical instruction to follow: 'love is genuine.' He neatly closes this paraenetic section by returning to the subject of love. The segue in vv. 7–8 is artful: 'Pay to all what is due (*opheilas*) . . . Owe (*opheilete*) no one anything, except to love'. In other words, while civic obligations can and should be fulfilled, the obligation to love can never be fully discharged. The primacy of the love commandment is a NT commonplace and almost certainly goes back to Jesus himself (see ROM 12:9a). In Mk 12:28–34 and parallels, Jesus cites a twofold commandment, love of God (Deut 6:4–5) and love of neighbour (Lev 19:18). Paul refers only to the latter. Perhaps he did not know the double formula, or perhaps his immediate concern led him to quote only the Leviticus passage. (The four commandments listed are all from the 'second table' of the Decalogue, which deals with social relationships; Deut 5:17–18.) To be children of God is pre-eminently to have the character of God, and the pre-eminent attribute of God's character is love (Mt 5:43–8). Such love issues from the giver irrespective of the recipient's merit: 'God proves his love for us in that while we still were sinners Christ died for us' (5:8). So no fault in the neighbour and no sufficiency in the self excuses one from love. And if one shares the character of God, then indeed God's law is fulfilled.

(13:11–14) The Eschatological Context Paul completes a second *inclusio* by returning to the eschatological theme introduced in 12:2 ('Do not be conformed to this age . . .'). The present is characterized as a time between the times, expressed eloquently in the metaphor of night turning to day. Now is still a time of darkness, but the believer knows it to be the darkness preceding the dawn. Recognizing that 'the night is far gone' (v. 12), one rouses oneself, lays aside the secret, shameful 'works of darkness' (detailed in v. 13), dresses in 'the armour of light' (v. 12, i.e. by behaving righteously), and stands ready before the approaching day.

In 12:2, Paul asked his readers to act as those already inhabiting a new age, to live up to their high spiritual standing in Christ. The argument is reminiscent of 6:1–5: Christians are in a fundamentally new position, already having died to sin. So, 'How can we who died to sin go on living in it?' (6:2). In vv. 11–14 we find much the same idea. One who lives 'as in the day' makes 'no provision for the flesh', gives no quarter to the 'works of darkness' (v. 12). To be holy is to be unmixed, entirely sanctified to God (12:1). The temptation is to view the eschatological ethic partly as a future demand, to split the difference between old and new orders, to contrive a half-in, half-out moral standard. For Paul, such unholiness is neither permissible nor sensible.

The phrase 'put on the Lord Jesus Christ' (v. 14) appears to have originated in Christian baptismal liturgy. Compare Gal 3:27: 'As many of you as were baptized into Christ have clothed yourselves with Christ.' 'Taking off' (or 'laying aside', v. 12) and 'putting on' is the nomenclature of repentance, intrinsic to baptism (cf. the idea of the 'wedding garment' in Mt 22:11–14). To say that one 'puts on Christ' adds to repentance the concepts of spiritual identification and empowerment (cf. Gal 2:19–20). In 6:3–4 Paul wrote that 'all of us who have been baptized into Christ Jesus were baptized into his death . . . we have been buried with him by baptism into death, so that, just as Christ was raised from the dead by the glory of the Father, so we too might walk in newness of life'. In baptism, one participates in the death and, proleptically, in the resurrection of Christ. The believer puts on the clothing, not merely of a new self, but of Christ's own righteousness, power, and victory. This high 'Christian anthropology' is in keeping with Paul's thought elsewhere in Romans (ROM E.2; ROM 8, etc.).

(14:1–15:13) 'Pursue What Makes for Peace and for Mutual Edification' Paul began this section of Romans with an exhortation to Christian unity (12:3–8), modelled on his recent Corinthian correspondence. By way of conclusion, he returns to the same idea and source. Controversy had arisen at Corinth over the practice by some of eating meat that had been sacrificed to idols (1 Cor 8:1–13; 10:12–33). In theory, Paul was on their side: 'We are no worse off if we do not eat, and no better off if we do' (8:8). But theory is not principle, privileges are not rights, and 'knowledge' (8:1) is not wisdom. The prerogative of the 'strong' (15:1) does not outweigh the church's need for unity and the individual's need for integrity. Simply put, it is wrong to encourage another to violate conscience. 'Therefore, if food is a cause of their falling, I will never eat meat, so that I may not cause one of them to fall' (8:13). The scope and application of Paul's 'community ethic' are nowhere more clearly articulated than in 1 Cor 8 and Rom 14.

As we have seen (e.g. in 12:4–7), Paul generalizes the argument of 1 Corinthians when adapting it to Romans. The identity of 'the weak' is no longer clear; Paul does not mention food sacrificed to idols, nor do his statements about eating meat and drinking wine (v. 21) refer self-evidently to Jewish practice (although the mention of 'one day . . . better than another' in v. 5 probably has in view the Jewish sabbath). Rather than respond to any one practice, Paul formulates a rule of conduct that may be applied in a variety of circumstances (which, by way of example, include controversies surrounding eating, drinking, and sabbath observance). One is to live before God with faith (14:5–9, 22–3) and before others with consideration (14:1–5, 13–21). Do not look to the example of those who offend; do not be an example to those who would be offended.

Paul's ethical thinking inhabits the ground between individualism and communitarianism. It is somewhat individualistic: each person stands or falls before God alone (14:4); each must be 'fully convinced' in his or her 'own mind' (v. 5); each is accountable to the dictates of his or her 'own conviction' (v. 22). But the community has moral priority. Recognition of individual differences is meant to foster unity (as in the body metaphor); ironically, it is those who demand absolute conformity that 'pass judgement' (v. 4) and so create division. The individual is constrained both by God's judgement (vv. 7–12) and by the needs of others (vv. 13–23). One ought to please God (v. 18) and one's neighbour (15:1–2), not oneself. This is not self-annihilation; this is mutuality, the dance of reciprocating love.

The tolerant attitude evidenced in this passage belies the oft-popular image of Paul as narrow-minded traditionalist. (14:14, 'nothing is unclean in itself', attests to the radical inclination of Paul's thought.) v. 4, 'Who are you to pass judgement on servants of another?' is reminiscent of that most-cited biblical quotation, Mt 7:1, 'Judge not, lest you be judged.' As a matter of perspective, one should bear in mind that neither Paul nor Jesus taught that one ought simply to 'behave and let behave'. The sphere of activity within which Paul allowed disagreement was significant but still restricted in size. Essentially, it consisted of matters regarded by Paul as morally indifferent (14:1: 'opinions', see 1 Cor 9). 'The kingdom of God is not food and drink' (14:17), but it is 'walking in love' (14:15). Then as now, conflict arose because of discrepant calculations of moral gravity. Inevitably, it is easier for the 'strong' (the less observant) to be tolerant of the 'weak' (the more observant) than the reverse. At what point does moral allowance turn the corner to moral abdication? Were Jewish Christians intolerant who continued to require sabbath observance (which is, after all, the fourth commandment of the Decalogue; see Mt 24:20)? In the first as in the twenty-first century, tolerance is in the eye of the beholder.

In 15:1, Paul explicitly identified himself with 'the strong' ('in faith', 14:1), a designation that he assumes rhetorically for most if not all of his audience. (What reader would want to identify with the community of the weak-but-tolerated?) The NRSV translation, 'We who are strong ought to put up with the failings of the weak,' is unfortunate. Literally, the strong are instructed to 'carry', 'support', or (by extension) 'tolerate' (*bastazō*) 'the *weaknesses* (asthenēmata) of the weak'. To judge the actions of the weak as 'failings' is to commit the very error described by Paul in ch. 14.

Paul caps his exhortation to unity and mutual concern by referring to the example of Christ, 'who did not please himself' (15:3). 'Welcome' (or 'accept', 'receive', *proslambanomai*) 'one another . . . just as Christ has welcomed you' (15:7). The passage is similar to Phil 2:1–11, where Paul charges his readers:

Be of the same mind, having the same love, being in full accord and of one mind. Do nothing from selfish ambition or conceit, but in humility regard others as better than yourselves. Let each of you look not to your own interests, but to the interests of others. Let the same mind be in you that was in Christ Jesus . . . (vv. 2–5)

What follows is the well-known 'Christ hymn', a poetic description of Jesus' self-abnegation and subsequent exaltation. Rom 15:3 is somewhat different: Paul refers only obliquely to Christ's passion, quoting the lament of the righteous sufferer in Ps 69:9, 'The insults of those who insult you [God] have fallen on me.' (Psalm 69 was widely cited in early Christianity; Cranfield (1979: 733n. 1) lists 18 other NT 'quotations and echoes'.) Christ's identification with God (15:3) and with humanity (15:8) cost him honour and status, the same currency that Paul would require his readers to expend for one another (12:3–5).

Rom 15:7–13 completes the discussion of Christian life begun in 12:1. More importantly, it brings to a close the larger argument begun in 1:16. 'Christ has become a servant in order that he might confirm the promises given to the patriarchs' (v. 8) thus proving God righteous. Christ came both for Jews (v. 8) and for Gentiles (vv. 9–12), a reiteration of Paul's 'thesis statement' in 1:16–17. As he has done repeatedly before, Paul cites scriptural evidence validating the inclusion of Gentiles in the people of God (Ps 18:49; Deut 32:43 (LXX); Ps 117:1; Isa 11:10 (LXX)). In conclusion, Paul again shifts from argumentative to sacral address (cf. Rom 8:31–9; 11:33–6), now, appropriately, in the form of a benediction. The phrases 'God of hope' and 'abound in hope' evoke the eschatological expectation that grounds the believer's everyday experience. In 14:17, Paul wrote that 'the kingdom of God is not food and drink but righteousness and peace and joy in the Holy Spirit'. So Paul concludes by wishing his readers nothing less than God's dominion, both now and future.

Conclusion (15:14–16:27)

(15:14–33) The Apostle's Plans Paul began the epistle by introducing himself and his apostolic credentials to the Roman Christians and by explaining his intention to visit them in the near future (1:1–15). His language was highly diplomatic; he praised the Romans for their faith and offered that he himself would be benefited spiritually by them. v. 14 picks up where 1:15 left off. The audience again is lauded: 'you yourselves are full of goodness, filled with all knowledge'. The apostle again is politic: he acknowledges that the recipients themselves are 'able to instruct one another'. Yes, Paul has written rather boldly, but only by way of reminder (v. 15). Besides, his boldness is commensurate with his authority in Christ, carefully detailed in vv. 16–21.

Several aspects of Paul's self-description merit attention. The use of sacerdotal imagery to describe his ministry ('priestly service . . . the offering of the Gentiles') is telling. Paul's language appears to echo Isa 66:18–23, a prophetic description of the eschatological incorporation of Gentiles into Israel (see also Isa 2:1–4; 42:1–9; 49; 55:4–5; 60:1–7). The 'offering of the Gentiles' (v. 16), an idea borrowed from Isa 66:20, probably consists of the Gentiles themselves (in the person of the church leaders who would accompany Paul to Jerusalem; see Barrett 1957: 275) as well as the money gathered from their congregations (vv. 25–8; Gal 2:10; 1 Cor 16:1–4; 2 Cor 8, 9). Possibly Paul entertained the idea that the impending trip to Jerusalem might prove to be the 'pilgrimage of the nations' to 'the mountain of the Lord' (Isa 2:3; as in Isa 66) that would precipitate the coming of 'the Deliverer' to Zion (11:26 = Isa 59:20–1). This hope might account for the statement in v. 19 that Paul had 'fully proclaimed' the gospel from Jerusalem to Illyricum. The conversion of a representative group from the nations (equivalent to 'the full number of the Gentiles' in 11:25) might signal the fulfilment of Isaiah's prophecy and precipitate Christ's return (note 16:20). An obvious objection is that Paul planned to go on from Jerusalem to Rome and then to Spain (v. 28). Still, hoping for the eschaton and planning for its delay are not mutually exclusive activities. As a Christian missionary, Paul had done both for years.

The legitimacy of Paul's apostolic authority was disputed at Corinth as well as Galatia, and faint aftershocks of those controversies can be felt in vv. 17–19. As a Christian leader, Paul had a number of liabilities: for example, he had not known nor was he commissioned by the historical Jesus; he had persecuted the church; his physical appearance was 'weak', and he was comparatively 'unskilled in speaking' (2 Cor 10:10; 11:6). Paul acknowledged other leading apostles but claimed to have 'outworked them all' (1 Cor 15:10). He pointed repeatedly to his ceaseless labours and continual suffering for the sake of the gospel as primary validation for his ministry. He articulated this claim in passages that are among the most dramatic and powerful in all of his letters (e.g. 1 Cor 4:8–13; 2 Cor 6:3–10; 11:21–12:21). Here in Rom 15, he emphasized not only the extent but also the success of his evangelistic effort. By such a measure, his ministry may be peerless.

Paul's statement of purpose in vv. 20–9 serves a variety of functions. First, it explains why it has taken him so long to come to Rome. Paul's job is the founding of pioneer churches (v. 20); his assignment had been the field from Jerusalem to Illyricum (v. 19). Having now completed that task (v. 23), he is prepared to advance to Spain. Second, it details the reason for Paul's trip to Rome and makes clear that his stay there will not be permanent. (In other words, he is not coming to 'take over' the Roman church.) Third, it lets the Romans know both that he expects to be welcomed (vv. 24, 29) and that he hopes to be supported by them in his mission to Spain (v. 24).

Paul asks for prayer 'that I may be rescued from the unbelievers in Judea'. It is a poignant request; according to Acts 21:27–36, Paul was arrested soon after his arrival in Jerusalem. The additional intercession, that 'my ministry to Jerusalem may be acceptable to the saints', has been seen by some as an indication that the Jerusalem church opposed the Gentile mission and so would reject the collection. Cranfield's (1979: 778) judgement is on target: '[It would] be more likely to recognize in these words evidence of Paul's spiritual and human sensitivity and freedom from self-centred complacency than to draw from them any confident conclusions about the tensions between the Jerusalem church and Paul.' (See also Fitzmyer 1993:726.) Contrary to the assertions of the Tübingen School, it is extremely improbable that the leaders of the Jerusalem church opposed the inclusion of uncircumcised Gentiles (see ROM D.3.3, above; cf. Gal 2:1–10; Acts 15:1–29). However, it is entirely likely that they took issue with Paul's conclusion that *Jews* no longer need obey certain parts of the law. (It is instructive that the charge raised in connection with Paul's arrival in Jerusalem concerned Jewish—not Gentile—law observance, Acts 21:21). For most Jewish Christians (e.g. the author of the Gospel of Matthew), the key issue apparently was not the Judaizing of Gentiles but the Gentilizing of Jews. It also is worth noting that Phil 4:18 uses similar priestly language in reference to the 'acceptability' of a monetary offering, but no interpreter suggests that the status of the Philippians' gift was ever in question. (See Hill 1992: 175–8, for further discussion of the interpretation of Rom 15:31).

(16:1–27) Personal Greetings and Final Remarks Was ch. 16 part of Paul's original letter to Rome? The question arises in part because of discrepancies in the textual tradition. One early manuscript (P[46], *c.*200) appears originally to have omitted 16:1–23. Other versions contain ch. 16 but locate the letter's benediction (16:25–7) at the end of ch. 14. Nevertheless, the manuscript evidence for the literary integrity of Rom 1–16 is quite strong (e.g. Sinaiticus, Vaticanus, Codex Ephraemi, etc.). According to Origen, Marcion disseminated a version of Romans that ended at ch. 14. The likeliest account is that the missing passages were gradually reattached to truncated copies of Romans, the benediction being added first at the end of ch. 14 (see Stuhlmacher's valuable discussion, 1994: 244–6).

The authenticity of ch. 16 also has been questioned because of the extensive greetings (twenty-six people in all) in vv. 3–15. Could Paul have known so many Roman Christians? Some scholars have suggested that all or part of ch. 16 was a separate letter, possibly written to commend Phoebe to the church at Ephesus. It is an intriguing but unconvincing suggestion.

Rom 16 by itself hardly constitutes an independent letter; moreover, we are scarcely in a position to judge whom Paul could not have known. Clearly, it would have been to his advantage to identify as many Roman confederates as possible. (Note that he first greets Prisca and Aquila, who left Rome under Claudius' edict and who may have returned following its suspension; Acts 18:2–3.) Finally, one may cite again the compelling textual evidence for the originality of ch. 16.

Rom 16 differs from other Pauline epistolary conclusions primarily in the length of its greetings (vv. 3–16) and its blessing (vv. 23–7; see below). Each of its elements is common to other Pauline closings:

Personal recommendation (vv. 1–2)   1 Cor 16:10–11, 15–18; 1 Thess 5:12–13 (cf. Phil 4:2–3); Philem 17
Personal greetings (vv. 3–16)   Philem 23–4
Final admonition (vv. 17–20*a*)   1 Cor 16:13–14; 2 Cor 13:11–12; Gal 6:12–17; Phil 4:4–9; 1 Thess 5:14–22
Grace (v. 20*b* (=24))   1 Cor 16:23; 2 Cor 13:13; Gal 6:18; Phil 4:23; 1 Thess 5:28; Philem 25
Greetings from companions (vv. 21–3)   1 Cor 16:19–20; Phil 4:21–2
Identification of writer/amanuensis (v. 22)   1 Cor 16:21; Gal 6:11
Blessing (vv. 25–7)   2 Cor 13:11*b*; Gal 6:16; Phil 4:19–20; 1 Thess 5:23–4.

The frequent mention of women in vv. 1–15 is impressive. Writes Beverly Gaventa (in Newson and Ringe 1992: 320) 'Nothing in Paul's comments justifies the conclusion that these women worked in ways that differed either in kind or in quality from the ways in which men worked.' Phoebe, probably the bearer of the letter, is referred to as a deacon (*not* 'deaconess', as in the RSV and MLB) and patron of the church. Nine other women are included in vv. 3–15, several of whom are commended for their ministry. Of particular interest is Junia (v. 7), who together with Andronicus (probably her husband) is said to be 'prominent among the apostles'. Almost certainly, the phrasing identifies both *as apostles*. For that reason, many translators assumed that *Iounian* must be a contracted form of the masculine Junianus. In effect, they masculinized the name Junia, rendering it 'Junias' (e.g. RSV, NIV, NJB, NEB). But the pairing of names (as with Prisca and Aquila in v. 3) usually indicates a husband and wife; moreover, no corroborating example has been found for the supposed masculine form, while the feminine usage is very well attested (see the fine overview of the question in Dunn 1988: 894–5). In short, 'Junias' is a scandalous mistranslation.

Paul's letters often include final words of admonition (see table above). The exhortation in vv. 17–20 recalls the teaching in 12–15:13 concerning Christian unity, whose background was the recent controversy at Corinth (and secondarily at Galatia). The description of those who serve 'their own appetites' and deceive others by 'flattery' is reminiscent of Paul's account of fallen humanity in 1:18–32. On behalf of his readers, Paul assumes the best but cautions against the worst.

The stately prescript that began Romans (1:1–7) is echoed in the formal benediction in vv. 25–7. Paul again refers to his ministry of the 'gospel' (v. 25=1:1), mentions the testimony of the prophetic writings (v. 26=1:2), and speaks of winning the Gentiles' 'obedience of faith' (v. 26=1:5). As he did in 11:36,

Paul concludes with doxology, glorifying God in whose mysterious plan and by whose eternal command the Gentiles have been brought into the communion of faith. It is a majestic crown to an extraordinary letter.

REFERENCES

Achtemeier, P. J. (1985) (ed.), *Harper's Bible Dictionary* (San Francisco: Harper).

Barrett, C. K. (1957), *A Commentary on the Epistle to the Romans*, BNTC (London: A. & C. Black).

Barth, K. (1933), *The Epistle to the Romans*, trans. E. C. Hoskyns (London: Oxford University Press).

Baur, F. C. (1873–5), *Paul, The Apostle of Jesus Christ*, trans. A. P. (vol. i), and A. Menzies (vol. ii) (2 vols.; London: Williams & Norgate).

Beker, C. (1980), *Paul the Apostle* (Philadelphia: Fortress).

Bultmann, R. (1910), *Der Stil der paulinischen Predigt und die kynisch-stoische Diatribe*, FRLANT 13 (Göttingen: Vandenhoeck & Ruprecht).

—— (1952–5) *Theology of the New Testament*, trans. K. Grobel (2 vols.; London: SCM).

Byrne, B. (1996), *Romans*, SP 6 (Collegeville, Minn.: Liturgical Press).

Cranfield, C. E. B. (1979), *Romans*, ICC (2 vols.; Edinburgh: T. & T. Clark).

Deissmann, A. (1927), *Light from the Ancient East*, 2nd edn. (London: Hodder & Stoughton).

Dodd, C. H. (1932), *The Epistle to the Romans*, MNTC (London: Hodder & Stoughton).

Donfried, K. P. (1991) (ed.), *The Romans Debate*, rev. edn. (Peabody, Mass.: Hendrickson).

Dunn, J. D. G. (1988), *Romans*, i. *chs. 1–8*; ii. *chs. 9–16*, WBC 38A–B (Dallas: Word).

Edwards, J. R. (1992), *Romans*, NIBC (Peabody, Mass.: Hendrickson).

Fitzmyer, J. A. (1993), *Romans*, AB 33 (New York: Doubleday).

Hays, R. B. (1989), *Echoes of Scripture in the Letters of Paul* (New Haven: Yale University Press).

Hill, C. C. (1992), *Hellenists and Hebrews* (Minneapolis: Fortress).

Holmberg, B. (1978), *Paul and Power: The Structure of Authority in the Primitive Church as Reflected in the Pauline Epistles* (Lund: Studentlitteratur AB).

Jervell, J. (1971), 'The Letter to Jerusalem', *ST* 25. ET, Donfried (1991: 61–74).

Jewett, R. (1979), *A Chronology of Paul's Life* (Philadelphia: Fortress).

—— (1982), 'Romans as an Ambassadorial Letter', *Interpretation*, 36: 5–20.

Käsemann, E. (1980), *Commentary on Romans*, trans. and ed. Geoffrey W. Bromiley (Grand Rapids: Eerdmans).

Manson, T. W. (1948), 'St Paul's Letter to the Romans—and Others', *BJRL* 21: 224–40. Repr. in Donfried (1991: 1–16).

Marxsen, W. (1968), *Introduction to the New Testament* (Oxford: Blackwell).

Morris, L. (1988), *The Epistle to the Romans* (Grand Rapids: Eerdman).

Murray, J. (1979), *The Epistle to the Romans*, NICNT (Grand Rapids: Eerdman).

Nanos, M. D. (1996), *The Mystery of Romans: The Jewish Context of Paul's Letter* (Minneapolis: Fortress).

Newson, C. A., and Ringe, S. H. (1992) (eds.), *The Women's Bible Commentary* (London: SPCK).

Räisänen, H. (1983), *Paul and the Law* (Tübingen: Mohr).

Sanday, W., and Headlam, A. C. (1980), *A Critical and Exegetical Commentary on the Epistle to the Romans*, 5th edn., ICC (Edinburgh: T. & T. Clark).

Sanders, E. P. (1977), *Paul and Palestinian Judaism* (Philadelphia: Fortress).

—— (1983), *Paul, the Law, and the Jewish People* (Philadelphia: Fortress).

Schlatter, A. (1995), *Romans: The Righteousness of God*, trans. S. Schatzmann (Peabody, Mass.: Hendrickson).

Spicq, C. (1994), *Theological Lexicon of the New Testament*, trans. and ed. J. D. Ernest (3 vols.; Peabody, Mass.: Hendrickson).

Stendahl, K. (1963), 'The Apostle Paul and the Introspective Conscience of the West', *HTR* 56: 199–215.

Stirewalt, L. M. Jr. (1977), 'The Form and Function of the Greek Letter-Essay', in Donfried (1991).

Stowers, S. K. (1981), *The Diatribe and Paul's Letter to the Romans*, SBLDS 57 (Chico, Calif.: Scholars Press).

—— (1994), *A Rereading of Romans* (New Haven: Yale University Press).

Stuhlmacher, P. (1994), *Paul's Letter to the Romans: A Commentary*, trans. S. J. Hafemann (Louisville, Ky.: Westminster/John Knox).

Wedderburn, A. J. M. (1988), *The Reasons for Romans*, SNTW (Edinburgh: T. & T. Clark).

Ziesler, J. (1989), *Paul's Letter to the Romans*, Trinity Press International New Testament Commentaries (London: SCM).

65. 1 Corinthians   JOHN BARCLAY

INTRODUCTION

A. Authorship. The letter claims to be written by Paul and Sosthenes (1:1) and there is no reason to doubt this ascription. As in other cases of supposedly joint authorship (e.g. 2 Cor 1:1), Paul probably took the sole responsibility (16:21). Clement accepted the letter as Paul's at the end of the first century CE (1 Clem 47) and all modern scholars concur, with doubts surrounding only certain sections (see on 11:2–16 and 14:34–5).

B. Integrity. Our earliest papyri preserve the letter whole (e.g. P46, from *c*.200 CE), but a number of scholars have argued that it is in fact a compound of several letters. Thus it has been suggested that 1 Cor 1–4 is a self-contained letter, closing in 4:14–21 with the typical close-of-letter formulae (see de Boer 1994). It is strange that the named party divisions which Paul

repeatedly criticizes in chs. 1–4 are never mentioned in chs. 5–16. It is possible that the Corinthians' letter to Paul (7:1) and disturbing news about their behaviour (5:1) arrived after the initial drafting of chs. 1–4 but before they were sent to Corinth. However, the opening thanksgiving section (1:4–9) seems to anticipate themes which surface in later chapters (e.g. spiritual gifts in 1:7 and chs. 12–14), and the theme of unity (1:10) pervades the whole letter (see Mitchell 1992). Inconsistencies have been found within later chapters, for instance between an apparently softer stance on sacrificial food in 8:1–13 and 10:22–11:1, and a harder line in 10:1–22. Complex theories have been propounded of two, four, or more original letters which have been stitched together into our 1 Corinthians (see details in *ABD* i. 1142–3). Such hypotheses are plausible in the case of 2 Corinthians, but Paul's varying rhetorical purposes can probably explain all the inconsistencies in this letter. Thus we may take 1 Corinthians as a single and unified whole.

C. Date. The letter is written from Ephesus in the spring (before Pentecost, 16:8–9). If we accept the chronology of Acts (see below), Paul founded the church in Corinth in 50–1 CE (Acts 18:1–7) and was in Ephesus two or three years later (Acts 19:1–10); thus the date of composition of this letter is some time in the period 52–5 CE.

D. Paul's Previous Dealings with the Corinthian Church. 1. It was of immense importance to Paul that he was the founder of the church in Corinth, the one who laid their foundation, however many supplementary builders they may have had (3:10). As his 'work in the Lord', the existence of the Corinthian church is, for Paul, proof enough of his apostleship (9: 1–2), even if it is clear from chs. 1–4 and 9 that not all the Corinthians are willing to recognize his status or authority. Paul recalls bringing the gospel to Corinth at a time which was fraught with 'weakness, fear and trembling' (2:1–3). Some of the details which we may piece together from 1 Corinthians accord well with the narrative of this founding visit in Acts 18:1–17, for instance the conversion of Crispus (1 Cor 1:14; Acts 18:8), the contact with Prisca and Aquila (1 Cor 16:19; Acts 18:2–3) and his labour in Corinth with his own hands (1 Cor 4:12; Acts 18:3). Paul's own comments do not allow us to date this founding visit, but Acts connects it (at its close, after 18 months) with a trial before the proconsul of Achaia, Gallio. By good fortune, an inscription enables us to date Gallio's period of office to 50–1 CE, thus giving helpfully precise parameters to the date of Paul's time in the city. Acts also mentions, as a prelude to Paul's visit, Claudius' expulsion of Jews from Rome (Acts 18:2). Conflicting evidence in our sources leads some scholars to think that that expulsion took place in 41 CE, and it has been proposed that Acts 18 actually combines the accounts of *two* separate visits by Paul to Corinth, one in 41 and one in 50/51 CE (see Lüdemann 1984: 157–77). However, Jews were probably not expelled from Rome until 49 CE (see Barclay 1996: 303–6), and there is thus no reason to doubt the integrity of the account in Acts 18 or the dating of Paul's initial visit to 50/51 CE.

2. Corinth was a cosmopolitan city, refounded as a Roman colony in 46 BCE, a seaport exposed to multiple influences from East and West (see *ABD* i. 1134–9 s. v. Corinth). According to Acts, Paul spent longer here than in most cities (at least 18 months, Acts 18:11, 18), a fact at least partly explained by the comparative lack of opposition he encountered in the city. The birth of the church also seems to have been unusually peaceful: Paul nowhere indicates any experience of harassment (see Barclay 1992). Paul established a core of believers, both Jews and Gentiles (1 Cor 1:22–4; 7:18), who were baptized in the name of Christ (1:13), received the Spirit (12:13) and started to meet for meals and worship in homes (11:17–34; Rom 16:23). Paul bequeathed to them a variety of credal traditions and practical instructions (15:3–5; 11:2, 23) but two factors combined to lessen his influence on the church once he had left the city. First, some of his own or subsequent converts were people of education and high social standing (see E.1) who developed independent views about the meaning of the Christian message (e.g. in relation to the resurrection of the body and sexual behaviour) and whose integration in Corinthian

society made them reluctant to accept Paul's more sectarian social practices (e.g. in relation to sacrificial food). Secondly, situated at an international crossroads, the church in Corinth was visited by a variety of Christian leaders, some of whom won converts of their own and assisted the church to develop in ways of which Paul disapproved (e.g. Apollos and, probably, Peter/Cephas, 1:12; 9:4–5).

3. The first signs of conflict between Paul and the Corinthian church are preserved in Paul's reference to their reception of an earlier letter he had sent (5:9–11). This letter is now lost, but it seems to have urged a moral discipline on the church which was not well received. Perhaps in response to that letter, the Corinthians wrote a letter referred to in 7:1. It is possible to suggest some of the topics on which the Corinthians wrote to Paul: many may be introduced by the formula 'now concerning', which occurs not only in 7:1, but also in 7:25 (on the topic of virgins), 8:1 (on food offered to idols), 12:1 (on spiritual gifts), 16:1 (on the collection), and 16:12 (on Apollos). Moreover, with the aid of a little imagination, we may even reconstruct what the Corinthians thought about some of the issues Paul addresses: in some cases Paul seems to cite back at them their own formulae, such as 'all things are lawful for me' (6:12; 10:23), 'it is well for a man not to touch a woman' (7:1), and 'all of us possess knowledge' (8:1). (For a full reconstruction of this interchange see Hurd 1965; for an imaginative exercise see Frör 1995.) 1 Corinthians thus represents part of a dialogue between Paul and the Corinthians, a dialogue which, as 2 Corinthians indicates, caused considerable pain to both parties for years to come.

4. As well as the Corinthian letter, Paul has received oral reports about affairs in the church, for instance from Chloe's people (1:11) and from Stephanas, Fortunatus, and Achaicus who may have brought the letter from Corinth (16:17–18). Some of the oral reports have caused Paul great concern (1:11–13; 5:1). Now, in response to both written and oral information, Paul writes our 1 Corinthians hoping that it, and Timothy's visit (4:17), will induce the necessary changes in the church before he has to correct them in person (4:21). It is clear from 2 Corinthians that that hope was not fulfilled.

E. The Corinthian Church. 1. Recent scholarship has highlighted the importance of the social divisions in the church in Corinth and has posited the disproportionate influence of a small élite group within the church, whose attitude to their social inferiors and whose class-determined interpretations of the Christian faith underlie many of the issues addressed in this letter (see esp. Theissen 1982; Chow 1992; Clarke 1993; Martin 1995; more generally on Pauline Christians, Meeks 1983; see, however, the strong arguments to the contrary by Meggitt 1998). Paul's statement about the generally lowly make-up of the church in 1:26–8 none the less indicates that there were *some* members of education, power, or noble birth, and some named individuals seem to belong to such an upper stratum. For instance, Gaius (1:14) must be a man of some wealth to be able to house the whole church (Rom 16:23, written from Corinth); some think the church may have grown to fifty or more members. If Crispus and Sosthenes were rulers of the synagogue, as Acts 18 indicates, they must have been from wealthy families (the title normally designates financial patronage). Moreover, the Erastus who sends greetings from Corinth in Rom 16:23 is there listed as 'city treas-urer'. The title might designate a lowly office, but it is extreme-ly rare for Paul to mention the occupations of Christians and he would probably do so only if they were of social importance. It is tantalizing that an inscription from Corinth from around the middle of the first century CE mentions one Erastus (a very rare name in Corinth) as paying for a piece of pavement after his appointment as aedile. It is possible that this is the same Erastus as the one mentioned by Paul, at a subsequent and more exalted rung up the social ladder (aediles were among the highest civic leaders in Corinth; Theissen 1982: 75–83).

2. Thus the church in Corinth covered a broad social spec-trum, with a few highly placed individuals who probably played a major role in shaping the life of the church and its relations with wider Corinthian society. The divisions at the Corinthian Lord's Supper (11:17–34) indicate the problems inherent in staging communal meals across such a spectrum, and the 'knowledgeable' who cared little for the scruples of their 'weaker brothers' in relation to sacrificial food (1 Cor 8–10) may have been those of higher status whose contacts with their social equals would have been greatly disrupted by tak-ing a scrupulous stance on this matter. Other topics raised in this letter may also be related to wealth and status. The Cor-inthian Christians who took each other to court (6:1–8) might have been wealthy (court cases were often expensive) and were perhaps engaged in a power-struggle within the church. Speaking in tongues (1 Cor 12–14) was possibly an élitist activity (Martin 1991) and the whole spirituality of the Cor-inthian church probably reflects the confidence of those who accommodated their faith to their social aspirations (4:6–13). The party groupings mentioned in 1:12 may represent splits among the social élite who competed for patronage in the church. It is harder to discern how such social divisions related to the ethnic mix of the church (Jews and Gentiles) or to different opinions about sexual activity (contrast the ascetic Corinthian statement in 7:1 with the apparently liber-tine one in 6:12).

3. The leaders of the church in Corinth seem to have prided themselves on their status as 'spiritual people' (3:1–3; 14:37). That involved a particular eagerness for spiritual gifts (12:1; 14:12), but also a high evaluation of 'wisdom' and 'knowledge' (2:6; 8:1–3) which included the appreciation of mysteries (2:6–16; 13:1–2) and the conviction that others' so-called 'gods' are really shadows ('idols', 8:4–6). Their 'spiritual' sta-tus also encouraged a sense of 'authority'—particularly the permission to eat whatever they wished and to use their bodies however they liked (6:12; 10:23). Such an emphasis on spirit-ual knowledge seems to have reinforced and even extended the common Greek disparagement of the body as a paltry piece of material; as a result, there are partial parallels with the later phenomenon of Christian 'Gnosticism', though not to the extent some have claimed (e.g. Schmithals 1971). In any case, some Corinthian believers appear to have balked at Paul's notion of a resurrected body (15:12, 35–57) and others understood their new possession by the Spirit to require complete sexual abstinence (7:1, 25–39). Paul finds the claims being made by the Corinthians absurdly inflated, tantamount to claiming exemption from all the inevitable weaknesses and imperfections of the present (4:8–13; 13:8–13). It is not clear

whether the Corinthians thought themselves already 'resur-rected' in some final sense, or whether that is merely Paul's caricature of their position (4:8; cf. 1 Tim 2:18; Thiselton 1977–8). Paul attempts throughout the letter to puncture their pride and to redirect their sense of honour towards mutual service in the community.

F. Outline.
Prescript (1:1–3)
Thanksgiving (1:4–9)
Appeal for Unity and for Re-evaluation of Paul's Ministry (1:10–4:21)
  The Absurdity of Party Groups (1:10–17)
  The Message of the Cross, its Recipients and Proper Med-ium (1:18–2:5)
  True Wisdom for Spiritual, not Bickering, Christians (2:6–3:4)
  Models of Leadership in the Church (3:5–4:5)
  Paul's Apostolic Style and Authority (4:6–21)
Sexual and Related Issues (5:1–7:40)
  Expulsion of an Immoral Member of the Church (5:1–13)
  The Absurdity of Using Corinthian Courts (6:1–11)
  Immorality and the Significance of the Body (6:12–20)
  Celibacy and Marriage (7:1–40)
Sacrificial Food and the Dangers of Idolatry (8:1–11:1)
  Debate with the 'Knowledgeable' concerning their 'Right' to Eat (8:1–13)
  Paul's Example in Renouncing the 'Right' to Financial Sup-port (9:1–23)
  The Dangers of Complacency in relation to Idolatry (9:24–10:22)
  Practical Guidelines on Eating and Avoiding Offence (10:23–11:1)
Issues Relating to Communal Meetings (11:2–14:40)
  Praying and Prophesying with Proper Head-Covering (11:2–16)
  Humiliation of Church Members at the Lord's Supper (11:17–34)
  The Distribution of Spiritual Gifts in the Body of Christ (12:1–31)
  The Superior and Critical Demands of Love (13:1–13)
  The Superiority of Prophecy over Tongues (14:1–40)
The Resurrection of Christ and the Resurrection Body (15:1–58)
Letter Closing, with Travel Plans, Final Instructions, and Greet-ings (16:1–24)

COMMENTARY

Prescript (1:1–3)

This follows the form typical in the Pauline letters; sender, addressees, and greeting (cf. Gal 1:1–3). Paul mentions his apostolic calling since some in Corinth doubted this (9:1–2) and associates with himself Sosthenes, perhaps the syna-gogue leader mentioned in Acts 18:17, who must have been converted after the events narrated there. In referring to the church in Corinth Paul emphasizes their purity ('sanctified', 'saints', v. 2), a theme which he will later employ to reinforce the boundaries between the community and outsiders and to outlaw behaviour which soils the church (e.g. 5:6–8; 6:9–11).

He also pointedly associates them with all other Christians elsewhere (v. 3). He will not allow the Corinthian Christians to exalt themselves over others (4:7), to neglect their needs (16:1–4), or to develop idiosyncratic patterns of church life (4:17; 11:16).

Thanksgiving (1:4–9)

Paul's letters generally begin with a thanksgiving, which places the life of the church in the context of God's activity and compliments the believers on their progress thus far. Despite the problems which this church poses, Paul appears genuinely grateful for its lively success, so long as it is attributed to 'the grace of God' (v. 4) by which they have been 'enriched' (v. 5). Later he will criticize the Corinthians for boasting in their spiritual virtuosity as if they had *made themselves* rich (vv. 7–8). Their God-given riches include every form of 'speech' and 'knowledge' (v. 5)—topics which will recur at several points in the letter (notably 1:18–3:5; 8:1–13; 13:1–2; 14:1–40), where Paul's appreciation is tempered with caution about the uses of such gifts in the community. In v. 6—which is probably best translated 'just as the testimony to Christ was confirmed among you'—Paul points forward to his discussion of the terms in which he first testified to Christ in Corinth (1:18–2:5), reminding his socially comfortable converts that all they have is based on the subversive message of Christ crucified. Their speech and knowledge are part of their enjoyment of every 'spritiual gift' (*charisma*, v. 7), a theme which comes to full (though again critical) expression in chs. 12–14. Notable at the end of this section are references to the future: for all their present abundance, the Corinthians still await 'the revealing of our Lord Jesus Christ' (v. 7) and the judgement which will take place on 'the day of our Lord Jesus Christ' (v. 8). Throughout this letter Paul will point forward to that future, to forestall premature judgements of his own or anyone else's ministry (v. 5), to warn against complacency in the race still unfinished (9:24–7; 10:12), and to moderate the exaggerated claims that were being made for knowledge and other spiritual gifts (13:8–13). Their only ground for confidence can be the faithfulness of God (v. 9; cf. 10:13), who has called them to participate in Christ (cf. 1:30–1). It is only by continuing in that 'fellowship' with Christ that they can face the end with confidence (cf. 16:22–4).

Appeal for Unity and for Re-evaluation of Paul's Ministry (1:10–4:21)

(1:10–17) The Absurdity of Party Groups v. 10 encapsulates the core of Paul's appeal which covers not only chs. 1–4, but also many other parts of the letter which appeal for mutual care within the church (e.g. 6:1–8; 8:1–3; 12:12–26). The 'divisions' spoken of here do not seem to prevent the church gathering together (Rom 16:23), but they damage its life, preventing its maturation (3:1–4) and negating its calling to love (13:1–13). Paul is responding in the first instance to oral reports from 'Chloe's people' (v. 11), probably the slaves of one of the members of the church. The quarrels they report concern the forming of party-groups in which members of the Corinthian church line up, in quasi-political fashion, behind Paul, Apollos, Cephas, or (apparently) Christ (v. 12). The last grouping receives no further mention in 1 Corinthians, except in Paul's insistence that *all* belong to Christ (3:22). Perhaps the

statement here represents a claim by some Corinthians to a more direct allegiance to Christ. Apollos is repeatedly named in the following chapters, and his followers may have been converted through him, since we know he was in Corinth after Paul (3:6; Acts 18:24–19:1). It has often been suggested that Paul's critical words about eloquence in 1:18–2:5 may be directed against admiration of Apollos' rhetorical prowess (according to Acts 18:24 he was 'an eloquent man'). Therein may lie some truth, though Paul is careful never to criticize Apollos directly in this letter and says he has encouraged him to return to Corinth (16:12).

The Cephas party remains a matter of controversy. Had Cephas (Peter) visited Corinth, like Paul and Apollos, and thus played some role in shaping the Corinthian church? Some think that 9:5 suggests as much, others that Cephas' reputation was high enough for him to have attracted a following in Corinth without a personal presence (cf. 15:5 and Barrett 1982: 28–39). Either way, it is difficult to know what the Cephas party stood for. An old scholarly tradition (arising in the 19th cent. in the Tübingen school and revived by Goulder 1991) takes the Peter party to represent a conservative form of Jewish Christianity, which took the Jewish law as its continuing standard. However, evidence for this standpoint in Corinth is hard to find and the character and influence of the Cephas party remain an enigma. What is revealing, however, is that those who say they belong to Paul are only one segment of the Corinthian congregation. Without wanting to foster a Paul party in Corinth, Paul clearly needs to re-establish his authority over the whole church. 1 Cor 1–4 is thus characterized by a delicate balance between Paul's self-effacement, as he points to Christ and the cross, and his self-promotion as the 'father' of the Corinthian church and the model of Christian discipleship (cf. Dahl 1967).

Paul's first move is to ridicule the creation of such groups. Since the whole church belongs to Christ and constitutes his body (12:12–27) any such party splits threaten to dismember Christ (v. 13). Tactfully using the Paul party as his prime target, Paul insists that he is neither the origin of their salvation nor the one to whom they belong. Reference in v. 13 to baptism 'in [lit. into] the name of Paul' indicates that baptism was usually performed in Pauline churches 'into the name of Christ' (cf. 12:12–13; Gal 3:27). It appears that the person of the baptizer is being given special significance in Corinth and Paul thus deliberately plays down his role in this regard: he can think of very few whom he has baptized (vv. 14–16; on Crispus and Gaius see 1 COR E.1). The sudden remembering of Stephanas' household (v. 16) underlines the insignificance of Paul's role in this matter; the initial lapse of memory might be genuine, but it also serves an obvious rhetorical role. Stephanas seems to have played some leadership role in the Corinthian church (see 1 COR 16:15–18). Paul insists that his commission was to 'proclaim the gospel', not to baptize (v. 17). This does not mean he considered baptism insignificant: he assumes that all believers have been baptized (1 Cor 6:11; 12:13) and elsewhere spells out its theological significance (Rom 6:1–11). But he had a different and specialized role: to preach the gospel of Christ crucified. By immediately disowning an interest in 'eloquent wisdom' (v. 17) he prepares the way for the next section of the letter.

(1:18–2:5) The Message of the Cross, its Recipients and Proper Medium At first glance, this section might appear a digression from the topic of party divisions, a subject which does not recur till 3:4. But the conjunction of the themes of wisdom and party boasts in 3:18–23 indicates that the two are closely related. It is possible that wisdom (and specifically eloquence) was one of the bases on which Corinthian Christians were lining up behind different leaders (see above, on Apollos). But, more generally, Paul discerns in the claim of allegiance to vaunted leaders a fundamental misapprehension of the gospel, whose value-system is wholly opposed to the values of power and wisdom which the Corinthian competitiveness exhibits. Thus, typically, Paul attacks the disease which has brought about the worrying symptoms, and forces the Corinthians to recognize the counter-cultural impact of the gospel of Christ crucified, in its message (1:18–25), its chosen recipients (1:26–31), and its proper medium (2:1–5).

The message of the cross is portrayed as an uncompromising indictment of human values of wisdom and power, since it reverses their standards and undermines their pretensions. In 1:18 Paul introduces the twin antitheses of wisdom/foolishness and power/weakness, which undergird this whole section, and he embraces the apparent absurdity of his message of Christ crucified—absurd, however, only to those 'who are perishing'. The division of humanity into two groups—'those perishing' and 'those being saved' (he never says believers *have been* saved)—is similar to the dualistic spirit of apocalyptic literature, as also are the pejorative nuances in phrases like 'this age' (1:20) and 'the world' (1:21). For Paul, the turning-point of the ages is precisely in the death (and resurrection) of Christ (cf. 15:20–8). The cross of Christ marks the final indictment of vaunted human 'wisdom', the fulfilment of the prediction of Isa 29:14, cited in 1:19. With rhetorical questions, Paul calls for those reputed to be wise ('scribes' are those so reputed in the Jewish world) and declares that God has not just bypassed 'the wisdom of the world' but utterly subverted it (1:20). The failure of humankind to know God according to its own system of wisdom triggers a divine plan springing from a deeper 'wisdom of God' (1:21; cf. Rom 1:18–23). In Jewish fashion, Paul divides humankind into two: Jews and Greeks/Gentiles (the two latter are synonymous in 1:22–4, but the term 'Greek' is particularly well suited for association with wisdom). The distinction between their desires (Jews want 'signs'—that is, demonstrations of divine power—and Greeks want 'wisdom') is rhetorically over-schematized, since Jews were also interested in wisdom (e.g. the Jewish wisdom material) and Greeks were also interested in supernatural power (e.g. in healing). But it enables Paul to present the message of Christ crucified as the inverse of *all* human values. It is 'a stumbling-block' to Jews (cf. Gal 5:11; 6:12–14), particularly because of the scriptural association between 'hanging on a tree' and being accursed by God (Deut 21:22–3, cited in Gal 3:13); it is 'foolishness' to Gentiles, since this Roman punishment was universally feared as a hideously cruel and shameful death (the shame of prolonged, helpless, and public death being as devastating as its pain). But to those who are 'called' this ultimate symbol of weakness and absurdity represents, paradoxically, the precise locale where God displays his power and wisdom (1:24–5).

This negation of the human value-system is matched by God's call of believers (1:26–31). The social make-up of the Corinthian church proves Paul's point since few Corinthian Christians could claim status by education ('wise'), political influence ('powerful'), or ancestry ('of noble birth', 1:26). Although this observation plays a rhetorical function here, it must also be broadly true (for a social profile of the church, see I COR E.1–2). For Paul, the predominantly low-status composition of the church is no accident: it indicates precisely God's choice which aggressively 'shames' the wise and powerful in the world. To creat a rhetorical tricolon, Paul adds to his earlier twin motifs of wisdom and power a third category, the low (lit. ignoble) and despised (1:28) who shame those 'of noble birth' (1:26). He then expands this category to its fullest possible generalization: God chose the things that are not, to bring to nothing the things that are (1:28). The phrase 'the nobodies' depicts then, as now, those of no social significance, but it also evokes notions of God's creative role in bringing creation out of nothing (cf. Rom 4:17; Gal 6:15; 2 Cor 5:17). And if salvation is entirely the creation of God, no human being can claim credit or rest confidence in any human attributes of status or significance (1:29). Theologically this line of thought is parallel to Paul's assault on Jewish boasting in Rom 2–4, but here it is widened to embrace the whole human race. It is precisely the Corinthians' boasting and concomitant arrogance which Paul opposes throughout this letter (cf. 4:18; 5:2; 8:1; 13:4), and it is here exposed in its absurdity. All that salvation means in Christ (the list of abstract nouns in 1:30 sums up its meaning by reference to the core metaphors in Pauline theology) is possible only *from God* (so runs the Greek behind 'he is the source of your life', 1:30). And here Paul can rightly claim to be in continuity with the prophetic warning against self-confidence, citing (1:31) Jer 9:24, whose context warns against glorying in wisdom, power, and wealth.

Finally, Paul addresses the question of the medium by which this message is conveyed (2:1–5) recalling the terms in which he first communicated the gospel. Here he pointedly eschews rhetorical ability, despite the fact that this passage, 1:18–2:5, is one of the most rhetorically effective in the New Testament! In the Graeco-Roman world 'wisdom' was closely associated with rhetorical skill ('lofty' or 'plausible' words, 2:1, 4), which was a central element in 'secondary' education and was highly prized by a public which enjoyed listening to finely crafted speeches in the courtroom, assembly, or theatre (see Litfin 1994). Paul claims that his message was so completely focused on Christ crucified (2:2) that any decorative oratory would have been utterly inconsistent. His own weakness as messenger (2:3) matched the 'weakness' of the message, so that its powerful effect in evoking faith might be identified unmistakably as the power of the Spirit of God, not any human achievement (2:4–5). Paul here anticipates his later self-depiction as a figure of weakness and humiliation (4:9–13), characteristics which match the message of the cross (cf. 2 Cor 4:7–15; 11:21–12:10). Though they admired his letters (2 Cor 10:10), the élite Corinthian Christians clearly despised Paul's speaking abilities (2 Cor 11:6); but Paul regards his 'disability' here as precisely making visible the only 'ability' that counts, the power of God.

(2:6–3:4) True Wisdom for Spiritual, not Bickering, Christians At first sight 2:6–16 seems to shift into a different gear. After denigrating wisdom in 1:18–2:5, Paul suddenly claims to impart wisdom, and in doing so changes from the first person singular (I) to the first person plural (we)—a change then reversed in 3:1 ff. What is more, the claim to privilege the 'mature' (2:6; the Greek could be translated 'perfect') looks out of step with the notion that the cross subverts human hierarchies (1:26–9), while several terms in this section of the letter are unusual or even unique in Pauline literature (e.g. 'the depths of God', 2:10, and the contrast between the 'spiritual' and the 'unspiritual', 2:13–15; cf. 15:44–6 and Pearson 1973). Is Paul claiming access to a higher wisdom than the folly of Christ crucified? Does this passage reveal an esoteric or mystical side to Pauline theology not witnessed elsewhere?

The best explanation is that Paul is not outlining a new or more esoteric form of wisdom, but spelling out the implications of his gospel in terms that partially reflect the vocabulary and concepts of the leaders of the church in Corinth, but also in such a way that he can spring a rhetorical trap on his dialogue partners in 3:1–5. Although we cannot be fully confident in this matter, it is very likely that Paul picks up and reuses elements of the theological vocabulary of the Corinthian élite in this passage, for instance, their claim to be recipients of the revelation of the Spirit, to be 'spiritual' and not just in possession of ordinary, natural life (the 'unspiritual' of v. 14), to speak in Spirit-inspired terms to one another (2:13), and to be above critical scrutiny in such matters (2:15). Paul's skill in this passage is to accept and rework this pattern of vocabulary and then to turn it *against* the Corinthian élite in 3:1–5 when he argues that their behaviour in fact *disqualifies* their claim to be 'spiritual'!

Paul first refers to a 'wisdom' communicated among the 'mature', which is hidden and decreed from eternity 'for our glory' (2:6–7). That may seem to confirm the élitist claims of the leaders of the Corinthian church who act as though they were already rich and filled (4:8). But Paul makes clear that he understands such concepts in an apocalyptic framework in which God's wisdom is precisely opposite to the wisdom claimed by 'the world', especially that espoused by the élite ('the rulers of this age'); similarly, the 'glory' to which we are destined is not a present but a future possession (2:9). It has often been thought that 'the rulers of this age' referred to in 2:6 and 2:8 are the supernatural forces of evil which Paul elsewhere calls 'powers' and 'authorities' (e.g. 1 Cor 15:24; Rom 8:38; cf. Col 2:15). But the precise term he uses here (*archontes*) is more naturally taken to refer to (human) 'political authorities' (cf. Rom 13:3) and their responsibility for the crucifixion (2:8) strongly suggests that Paul is thinking primarily of earthly political powers. The notion that these powers are 'doomed to perish' matches the thought of 1:28 (where the same Gk. verb is used): those considered 'something' are shamed through the cross, while the 'nothings' in this world are destined for 'glory'/honour (2:7). The shamed Crucified One turns out to be—by the same paradox as 1:25— the 'Lord of glory' (2:8).

The 'glory' which is destined for believers (2:7) is defined in 2:9 as indescribably beyond human imagination by means of a pastiche of scriptural phrases, drawn principally from Isa 64:4 and 65:17. The point here, developed in 2:10–16, is that

the Spirit gives access to a realm of knowledge, and a language in which to communicate it, quite beyond normal human knowledge and communication. This is not to suggest that the gospel is inherently irrational, but that its content and what it reveals about God's paradoxical purposes go well beyond the frame of reference in which human language operates. As suggested above, some of the vocabulary here might reflect the terms in which the 'spiritual' people in Corinth distinguished themselves from those who had merely normal human abilities, the *psychikoi* (those with merely natural human life, *psychē*) translated in 2:14 as 'unspiritual'. However, by using the 'we' form throughout (e.g. 'we have received . . . the Spirit that is from God', 2:12), Paul suggests that these special attributes are applicable to *all* believers. Those who 'love God' (2:9; cf. 8:3) are gifted with 'the gifts of God's Spirit' (2:14; cf. 12:1–11), which, like the cross, appear foolish by worldly standards (2:14). The Spirit therefore enables an understanding much deeper than mere human knowledge (2:15). Indeed, Paul can even claim in 2:16 that the rhetorical question of Isa 40:13 (originally phrased to expect the answer 'no one') can be used to describe a position filled by believers, who really have 'the mind of the Lord' (here taken to refer to Christ). Such bold claims indicate that Paul regards Christian faith as opening a dimension of understanding far more profound than anything offered by non-believing perspectives; this is of a piece with his assertion that the cosmos, and time, and life, and death 'belong to' believers, inasmuch as they belong to Christ (3:21–3).

But Paul's dialogue with the élite in Corinth cannot rest here. He now springs on them a rhetorical trap which *denies* to them the very spiritual superiority he had described in such glowing terms in 2:6–16. If what he has just described is the condition of the 'spiritual', let the Corinthians know that Paul could not initially impart such spiritual knowledge to them since they were merely 'people of the flesh, infants in Christ' (3:1). They cannot here be described as 'unspiritual' (2:14), since they had, as believers, received the Spirit (12:12–13); yet at the start of their Christian lives they were hardly spiritual in the terms they now claim, only 'of the flesh'—that is, ensnared in merely human patterns of thought and behaviour (cf. the flesh–Spirit antithesis in Gal 5 and Rom 8). At that stage, they could only take milk and were not ready to be weaned (3:2). But now comes Paul's really devastating blow: '*even now* you are *still* not ready, for you are *still* of the flesh' (3:2–3, emphasis added). In other words, all that Paul has been saying about 'the spiritual' and their understanding of the mysteries of God cannot really be applied to the Corinthians: he has built up the mystique of this category only to deny that the Corinthians can fit it! This is the first of many attempts in this letter to puncture the pride of the Corinthian Christians, but there is none more devastating. The basis of Paul's claim that they are still of the flesh is where the trap really bites: the jealousy and quarrelling evidenced in their claims of belonging to rival leaders (3:3–4) reveal precisely how immature they are! The party-groupings which set up rival claims to status in wisdom or in the excellence of the chosen leader indicate not how mature but how immature the Corinthian church is: their bids for superiority show just how inferior they are, operating on the level of mere squabbling humans rather than as gifted and inspired people of the Spirit. Thus it appears that the party claims ('I belong to Paul' etc.) which seemed to disappear from sight after 1:18 were actually in the background all along. For Paul they represent a mindset determined by the values of 'this age' which have been fundamentally subverted by the message of the cross (1:18–2:5) and superseded by the new depths of understanding afforded by the Spirit (2:6–16).

(3:5–4:5) Models of Leadership in the Church Now that he has returned to the topic of party groups in the Corinthian church (3:4), Paul constructs another line of argument against such factionalism, this time focused on leadership and its evaluation. To align oneself with one or another leader is, for Paul, to commit three cardinal errors: (1) to place leaders on a pedestal, where they do not belong; (2) to play them off inappropriately against one another; and (3) to reward them with human praise rather than leaving to God the assessment of their work. These three themes are the principal elements in the discussion of leadership in 3:5–4:5, which Paul develops by using metaphors drawn from agriculture (3:5–9), building (3:9–17), and household slavery (4:1–5). 3:18–23 forms an interlude which links this section back to 1:18–31 and points to the folly of the boasting which takes place in leadership competitions.

The agricultural metaphors in 3:5–9 emphasize the subordinate nature of Christian leadership as a task fulfilled only at the bidding of the Lord (3:5, 8) and in utter dependence on God's creative activity (3:6–7, 9). Paul and Apollos are no more than servants through whom (not *in* whom) the Corinthians believed (3:5). Paul, as founder of the church (a role he recalls frequently in this letter, cf. 3:10; 4:15; 9:2), may be said to have been its planter; Apollos' subsequent activity was to water the plants (3:6). But neither role is of any value without the gift of growth to the plants, a gift which only God can bestow (3:6–7). The Corinthians belong to the church by God's calling (1:2, 26–7), and it is God alone who is 'the source of your life in Christ Jesus' (1:30): thus it is absurd to use slogans which suggest that their leaders were themselves the creators, rather than simply the instruments, of the church's life. Moreover, the two tasks of planting and watering cannot be played off against one another: the two workers 'have a common purpose' (2:8; lit. 'are one'), so it is senseless to claim to belong to one and not to the other. They are 'working together' in an agricultural project planned and owned by God (3:9). And they will receive their reward not through human adulation but by God's assessment of their labour (3:8).

The end of 3:9 switches the metaphor to that of building, an image which governs the discussion of leadership in 3:10–15 and is then extended with reference to the temple (3:16–17). Paul the planter in 3:6 is now Paul the master builder, who laid the foundation of the church in Corinth (3:10). In this case reference is made not to Apollos, but to 'someone else' who is building on that foundation. Since within this metaphor God is less clearly the means of growth, the spotlight falls on human beings with responsibility for building, with a none-too-veiled threat that they may be performing their task badly (3:10, 12–13). The aggressive tone in Paul's voice has led many commentators to suspect that he is attacking some specific individual(s) in the church (e.g. Barrett 1971: 87–8). Moreover, it is tempting to take 3:11 as a rebuke of those who claim to belong to Cephas, on the basis of the famous rock prediction:

'You are Peter and on this rock I will build my church' (Mt 16:18). It is just possible that Paul is here attacking Peter and his influence in Corinth, though elsewhere in the letter he speaks of Peter in unpolemical terms (9:5; 15:5) and we do not know if the rock saying, which is found only in Matthew, was known in Corinth at this date. Paul is concerned at the direction of the current leadership of the church, and reveals those anxieties by warning of the consequences of building with worthless materials (3:12–15). Again the test of value comes not from present human assessment but from God's definitive judgement which will operate on 'the Day'. Building on traditional images of 'the Day of the Lord' as a fiery event (e.g. Mal 3:2–3; 4:1; cf. 2 Thess 1:7–8), Paul suggests that all worthless building materials will be consumed and the builder rewarded or punished ('suffer loss', 3:15) on the basis of what survives. The context suggests that he is referring specifically to those with leadership responsibilities, rather than to each individual believer. His basis for confidence that the builder will survive, even if his work is destroyed, is that God's grace has a secure grasp of those in Christ (cf. 5:5; 11:32). However, that does not negate the possibility that believers may somehow prise themselves away from Christ by continual and deliberate disloyalty (cf. 9:27; 10:6–12).

Indeed the seriousness of the building work being undertaken in Corinth is underlined in the extension of the metaphor to the church as a temple (3:16–17). Elsewhere, each Christian's body is described as a temple of the Holy Spirit (6:19), but here (as in 2 Cor 6:16) the church as a collective is so described. This is a striking transfer of terminology and allegiance from the Jerusalem temple, which was still standing at this time and was the object of reverence by Jews both in Palestine and in the Diaspora. Paul's Gentile converts were never instructed to pay any attention, or contribute any taxes, to that building; nor, of course, did they construct any 'temples' of their own. They were encouraged, rather, to think of themselves as a temple, the locus of God's holy presence. Thus, to inflict damage on a church community is to touch God's precious sanctuary, inviting his immediate judgement (3:17). Builders in Corinth should beware that they really build and do not destroy (cf. 8:10–11).

3:18–23 briefly interrupts the sequence of metaphors to underline once more the counter-cultural character of Christian commitment (3:18–19 echoes themes from 1:18–31). Expanding quotes from Job 5:12 and Ps 94:11, Paul emphasizes again God's opposition to the worldly standards of evaluation which undergird the Corinthians' rivalry as they boast in competing leaders (3:19–21). In fact, their slogans suggest a fundamental misapprehension of themselves and of the relationship between church and leader. Instead of saying 'I belong to Paul' (or whomever), they should recognize rather that Paul (or Apollos or Cephas) 'belong to' them (3:21–2). Although God's servants may play important roles in founding and encouraging the church, their purpose is not to win admirers or adherents but to serve the church to which they belong. By placing leaders on a pedestal the Corinthian church actually demeans itself: the leaders are there for the sake of the church, not the other way around. And Paul can expand this principle rhetorically with the claim that the world, life, death, and time are at the service of the church, because this community is not some mere club or social gathering but the centre of God's plan for the world and history (3:22; cf. 6:2–3 and the expansion of this theme in Colossians and Ephesians). At least, the church has that role inasmuch as (and *only* inasmuch as) it belongs to Christ (that is the one slogan from 1:12 which Paul does not here reverse); and Christ himself belongs to God (cf. 11:3; 15:28). As the token of the new creation in the midst of 'this age', the church has a significance far greater than the leaders God uses to serve it. But its significance lies only in the fact that it belongs and bears witness to Christ, the agent of God's re-creative power in the universe.

The third metaphor of leadership is that of household slaves, specifically stewards (4:1–5). Again it is implied that such figures should not be the objects of praise (they are only agents of Christ, or of 'the mysteries of God'); but the emphasis here falls on the assessment of their work. Stewards are held accountable as to their trustworthiness (4:2), but by their masters, not by those they encounter in the course of their work (cf. Rom 14:4). At this point, Paul becomes directly personal, applying the metaphor specifically to himself as one who might come under the Corinthians' scrutiny (4:3) but who prefers to leave the judgement to his master (4:4; 'the Lord', *kyrios*, means also 'the master' of a slave). Here then emerges, what we might have suspected all along, that the party divisions in Corinth represent a critical evaluation of Paul's apostleship, inasmuch as some claim to belong to others *and not to Paul* (1:12). As in 9:3, Paul hints at a body of opposition to his authority, but he attempts to defuse it by insisting that it is inappropriate for the Corinthians to judge his behaviour, and premature as well: when the Lord comes (and not before), *he* will give full and final judgement (4:4–5). What will count then is commendation from God (4:5), not the measure of praise (or criticism) leaders currently receive from members of the church.

(4:6–21) Paul's Apostolic Style and Authority The personal turn taken in Paul's final leadership metaphor (4:1–5) indicates the progression of the argument towards self-defence. It now becomes clear that Paul is under attack in Corinth, unfavourably compared with other leaders and criticized specifically for the poor figure he cuts and for his long absence from the scene. Paul's response requires him to confront and ridicule Corinthian pride (vv. 6–8), to describe, by contrast, his own highly vulnerable ministry (vv. 9–13), and finally to assert his fatherly authority in Corinth and announce his forthcoming visit (vv. 14–21).

Paul's first target is the inflated sense of importance in the Corinthian church, which he regards as the cause of their party rivalries: they are puffed up in comparing one leader with another, congratulating themselves on their chosen objects of allegiance (v. 6). Looking back on 3:5–4:5, Paul says he has 'applied all this to Apollos and myself for your benefit' (v. 6). The Greek here is slightly obscure and might mean simply that he has put his discussion in the form of analogies (relating to Apollos and himself) rather than using literal speech, or that he has changed the analogies from one metaphor to another (gardener, builder, steward) to make his points as clear as possible. Another possible nuance is that he has disguised his meaning, making explicit reference to Apollos and himself, but really referring to other people

(e.g. Cephas?). But it is unnecessary to attribute to Paul some subtle encoding of his message. He is simply drawing attention to his use of metaphor to indicate that he has set out these various leadership models in order to undercut the rivalries which afflict the Corinthian church. It is very hard to discern the source or meaning of the saying Paul cites in this context, 'Nothing beyond what is written' (v. 6; some suspect that the text is corrupt at this point). This looks like a slogan, but whose is it, and does it refer to Scripture or to something else that was 'written' (see Hooker 1963; Fee 1987: 166–9)? Few scholars claim to understand the allusion, which one imagines made more sense to the Corinthians than it does to us.

Paul regards Corinthian pride as manifest in a sense of special achievement and perfection. Their giftedness, which he recognized in 1:4–7, led to a sense of distinction, which easily obliterated gratitude for gifts received (v. 7). They have been *enriched* (by God, 1:5), but imagine themselves simply *rich* (v. 8); their notions of fullness and royal authority might be related to the Stoic notion of the self-sufficiency of the perfectly wise man. The sarcasm of v. 8 is an attempt to puncture that pride, and the following verses deflate it by depicting the life of the apostles (supposedly the models of the church) as the very opposite of the honour and victory which the Corinthians expect for themselves. Like those under a sentence of death, who are brought on at the end of a public spectacle to entertain the masses by their gruesome deaths, the apostles are a despicable sight, watched only to be ridiculed (v. 9). Their reputations match the folly, powerlessness, and shame of the cross (v. 10 echoes the themes of 1:18–25), and vv. 11–13 spell this out in practical terms, with some intriguing echoes of the ethos of the gospels (e.g. Mk 6:7–12; Lk 6:24–31). Included in this list of demeaning conditions of life is the fact that Paul works with his own hands (v. 12). That suggests that he is combating an ethos fostered by the social élite (who alone looked down on manual labour); in deliberate and perhaps exaggerated contrast, Paul presents himself as the scum of the earth (v. 13; cf. 1:28–9).

The polemical purpose of this self-portrait is evident when Paul declares his aim to be to 'admonish' his 'children' (v. 14); he denies that he wants to shame them (cf. however 6:5), but that cannot be ruled out as a proper result. It now becomes clear that Paul's role as founder of the church is crucial to his present bid to correct them. However many teachers and leaders may have operated in Corinth, they can have no status higher than 'guardian' (lit. childminder—the slave employed by parents to guard the safety of their children), whereas Paul is unique as their 'father' (v. 15). Paul wants to claim this role even in relation to those who were converted through other evangelists (e.g. after his departure from Corinth) and he uses it, as fathers often did in the ancient world, to require that his 'children' imitate his pattern of life and thought (v. 16). He is dispatching Timothy (perhaps with this letter) to reinforce his point, but also now promises to come in person (vv. 17–21). It appears that his long absence from Corinth has been criticized, or at least exploited, by those who think Paul's opinion about their affairs is insignificant (v. 18). With a final rhetorical flourish (still utilized by parents!) Paul offers them a choice: it is up to them whether he comes with gentleness or punishment (v. 21). This threat proved to be a fatal mistake, since Paul, when he finally did visit Corinth, found himself facing stiffer opposition than he had anticipated, and his stay proved extremely painful (2 Cor 2:1–2). The assertion of authority was to backfire in outright repudiation of Paul and still harsher criticisms of his ministry: in 2 Corinthians we can watch him trying to patch up a now deeply uneasy relationship.

Sexual and Related Issues (5:1–7:40)

(5:1–13) Expulsion of an Immoral Member of the Church The abruptness with which this chapter begins has led some to wonder whether it starts a new letter or is occasioned by some fresh news. But there are good reasons why Paul should have delayed treating such matters until now. The first four chapters of the letter, which undercut the Corinthians' pride and reassert Paul's authority, form the necessary platform for Paul to launch his specific assaults on behaviour in the Corinthian church. None of what follows in chs. 5–16 would cut any ice in Corinth unless the members of the church were prepared to reconsider their canons of 'wisdom' and to listen to their 'father' in Christ.

The oral information to which Paul responds here was apparently rather more damning than what the Corinthians had divulged in their letter (7:1). Paul is shocked that they have tolerated a form of sexual liaison which he considers scandalous even among 'pagans', whom he takes to have minimal moral standards (cf. 1 Thess 4:5). The 'immorality' (*porneia*) concerns a prolonged relationship between a man and his father's wife, probably his stepmother and probably after the death of his father. We cannot say more about the figures involved (Clarke 1993 suggests that the man may have had financial interests in such a relationship, e.g. to secure his inheritance), except that Paul's chastisement of the man alone suggests that the woman was not a Christian (cf. vv. 12–13). Sexual relations between a man and his stepmother were generally considered incestuous, both in Judaism (e.g. Lev 18:8) and in the Graeco-Roman world (Ap. *Met.* 10.2–12), and it is therefore surprising that this Corinthian believer had got away with such behaviour thus far. It is possible that he was too important socially to be subject to criticism, and that he justified his behaviour specifically on the basis of the Christian ethos of liberty. The latter may be hinted at by Paul's expostulation: 'And you are arrogant!' (v. 2). That arrogance may exist despite such sexual activity, but it might also flourish *because of* the claim to freedom from taboos which Christian faith was understood to entail: in 6:12 (and 10:23) Paul will cite a Corinthian slogan which suggests a conscious embracing of liberty, even in sexual conduct (6:13). For the rest of this chapter Paul simply assumes that this behaviour is wrong; its perpetrator must therefore, he insists, be expelled. Later, however, in 6:12–20, he gives some reasons why he thinks a Christian must be responsible in the use of his/her body.

In vv. 2–5 Paul portrays an act of expulsion (excommunication) which may owe something to synagogue practices known to him. He imagines the church gathering like a court, to pronounce judgement 'with the power of our Lord Jesus'. Such is his own strength of feeling, and his lack of confidence in the moral values of the Corinthian Christians, that he imagines himself present 'in spirit' and declares already

what verdict the church court will reach: they are to 'hand this man over to Satan for the destruction of the flesh' (v. 5). Handing over to Satan (cf. 1 Tim 1:20) probably means expulsion, on the understanding that the world outside the church is in the grip of Satan ('the god of this world', 2 Cor 4:4), but it is unclear whether 'the destruction of the flesh' implies physical harm (cf. 2 Cor 12:7), even death (cf. 1 Cor 11:30), or, more benignly, the suppression of the man's fleshly nature, that is, his propensity to sin (cf. 3:3; Gal 5:19–21). In any case, Paul regards the final result of this action as in some way salvific: 'his spirit' (the Greek lacks 'his' and might conceivably mean 'the spirit of the church') will be saved in the final judgement. The connection between destruction of the 'flesh' and salvation of the 'spirit' is obscure, and depends on the meaning of each term. Does physical suffering chasten, or death make atonement for sin, or moral correction purify the individual's spirit (see Fee 1987: 208–13)? 1 Cor 11:32 might suggest some chastening process.

vv. 6–8 highlight the danger of the Corinthians' nonchalant attitude in this matter, drawing on purity metaphors associated with Passover. v. 6 contains a proverb (cf. Gal 5:9 and Mt 13:33) concerning the disproportionate influence of a tiny substance—in this case, clearly, the single individual in the corporate body of the church. But yeast leads Paul to think of Passover, and the need before Passover to clear out all traces of the substance (Ex 12:15). The church is to become unleavened (that is, without sin) because it is, in principle, a new, unleavened substance (v. 7); Paul often calls on his converts to become in practice what they already are. They are a part of the Passover feast founded on the sacrifice of Christ, the lamb (an unparalleled use of such imagery in Paul). Then, in v. 8, the church shifts within the metaphor from the unleavened dough to partakers of the festival: the Corinthians' church life may be considered a permanent Passover meal, which must be kept free from the impurities of 'malice and evil' such as the sexual sin presently tolerated in their midst.

Thus the final paragraph of this chapter (vv. 9–13) underlines the need for the church to condemn and expel the bad influence presently festering in its midst. In v. 9 Paul refers to his earlier letter as already issuing instruction to dissociate with the 'immoral'—an instruction which seems to have been objected to in Corinth as implying complete social withdrawal, but which Paul here insists meant only separation from immoral members of the church. He now makes clear that he does not require a sectarian retreat ('going out of the world', v. 10), although later chapters will indicate that he is unhappy with the degree of social integration which the Corinthian Christians enjoy (6:1; 10:14–22). He has no principled objection to social intercourse with unbelievers, even if they be immoral or 'idolatrous': the danger lies in association with those who have been accepted into the church as 'brothers' or 'sisters'. Paul assumes that the Corinthians will know for sure who are 'insiders' and 'outsiders' (5:12–13), probably on the basis of whether or not they have received baptism (6:9–11; 12:12–13). He regards it as far more dangerous to associate with immoral insiders than immoral outsiders, presumably because the example of the insider will be more influential on the rest of the congregation. Perhaps the Corinthians did not understand themselves to be committed to a common lifestyle or to be bound as tightly to each other as Paul here assumes.

They may have thought of 'religion' as quite separate from 'ethics' and their relationships with social equals more important than their fellowship with other believers. Paul's instruction here requires that they regard moral behaviour with the utmost seriousness and that they understand themselves as a community whose intensity of involvement with one another renders them vulnerable to internal corruption (v. 13 cites from a parallel theme in Deut 17; see Rosner 1994). The harsh measures advocated ('not even to eat with such a one', v. 11) would debar the offender from the communal Lord's Supper, which, like meals generally in antiquity, was an important token of association.

(6:1–11) The Absurdity of Using Corinthian Courts The theme of judging insiders rather than outsiders (5:12–13) leads Paul into a short digression. He will return to the topic of sexual morality at the end of ch. 6, but for now uses this opportunity to register his disapproval of Corinthian Christians who are settling their disputes with one another in the civil courts of Corinth. We do not know how many such cases there had been (perhaps only one), or precisely what they concerned, though the reference to 'defrauding' in v. 7 suggests financial disputes, which indeed were the most common cause of litigation in the Graeco-Roman world. Paul is affronted that the Corinthian Christians seem incapable of resolving their internal disputes without resorting to the judgement of 'unbelievers'. His objection lies not so much in his fear lest the community wash its dirty linen in public (he shows no concern here that it will be discredited), but in the absurdity of asking for judgement from people far less capable than believers. Those who sit in the Corinthian courts are described as 'the unrighteous' (v. 1) and 'unbelievers' (v. 6), and Paul's objection to resorting to their judgement is not simply that they are liable to be corrupt (though, arguably, justice was a rare commodity; see Winter 1991) but that they represent 'the world' (v. 2), the realm of unbelief which is by definition inferior in understanding and integrity to the circle of 'the saints'. Here the apocalyptic dualism between 'church' and 'world' which underlay Paul's whole discourse in chs. 1–4 has its social application in his insistence that the Corinthian Christians are in a wholly different category to outsiders (cf. esp. 2:6–8). The influence of this world-view is further evident in Paul's appeal to the apocalyptic notion that God's elect are destined to judge (or rule) the world in the end-time (v. 2; cf. Dan 7:22; 1 *Enoch* 1:9; Rev 2:26–7). As in 3:21–3, Paul cleverly portrays the Corinthian Christians as underestimating their own importance. If they remembered their destiny in judging the world, even angels, they would not consider themselves incompetent to judge the trivial matters which they now ask others to decide (vv. 2–4). In reality, the Christian parties to these disputes probably failed to see the church as a juridical entity and looked to Corinthian judges to provide publicly recognized verdicts which would restore their social honour. In Paul's view, such outside authorities 'have no standing in the church' (v. 4; lit. are despised by the church, contrast Rom 13:1–7!). As a withering rebuke, he asks whether there is really no one in this community which so values wisdom who is wise enough to deal with this matter (v. 5)! The language here is reminiscent of Deut 1:16 (Moses' creation of courts in Israel), and the whole passage may reflect the operation of internal courts in some Diaspora Jewish communities.

In vv. 7–8 Paul steps onto a higher moral plane and asks how these lawsuits have arisen in the first place: to have them is already to lose them ('a defeat for you', v. 7). He hints at an ethic of non-retaliation reminiscent of the Sermon on the Mount, without invalidating the lesser solution of internal adjudication. It is best to accept injustice, and permissible to seek its rectification through an internal court, but it is inappropriate to ask 'the unrighteous' to judge such matters and utterly scandalous that Christians are themselves responsible for injustice in the first place—even against their fellow Christians (v. 8).

vv. 9–11 follow straight on: the wrongdoing which has given rise to the litigation threatens to place those responsible in the category of 'the wrongdoers' who will be excluded from the kingdom of God (v. 9). The theme of the kingdom of God features very rarely in Paul's theology, and is chiefly found in association with traditional formulae, as here where it is linked to a list of excluded persons (vv. 9–10; cf. Gal 5:19–21). The list here expands that offered in 5:10 and its opening with sexual sins and idolatry is parallel to Jews' denunciations of the sins they considered typical of the Gentile world (cf. Rom 1:18–31). The two terms translated (NRSV) as 'male prostitutes' and 'sodomites' (v. 9) have been the subject of some debate. The first (lit. soft people) could refer to 'womanizers' (i.e. those involved in heterosexual profligacy) but could also mean the passive partner in male homosexual acts; the second is a rare term (lit. sleeper with males) which probably designates the penetrating partner in male-with-male sex. Paul, like other Jews, considered either role in homosexual acts disgraceful (cf. Rom 1:26–7). The list also includes two terms for financial fraudulence ('thieves', 'robbers'), perhaps reflecting the character of the disputes just discussed. Such behaviour, Paul insists, cannot now characterize their Christian lives (v. 11). They have been washed, sanctified, and justified—a transformation whose description here probably alludes to the event of baptism. At that point they came under the authority of a new master ('in the name of the Lord Jesus Christ', cf. 1:13–15) and received a new identity 'in the Spirit of our God' (cf. 12:13).

(6:12–20) Immorality and the Significance of the Body The Corinthians would have agreed with Paul that their receipt of the Spirit gave them a new identity as 'spiritual people' (cf. 2:6–16). But Paul thinks that they have failed to grasp the implications of that change of identity, in particular the limits it sets on the use of their *bodies*. In v. 12 he twice cites a formula, 'all things are lawful for me' (cf. 10:23), which appears to be current in the Corinthian church and suggests a confident appropriation of Paul's gospel of 'freedom'. Paul does not reject it out of hand, but cautions lest its individualist emphasis ('all things are lawful *for me*') prove detrimental to the church as a whole: not all things are beneficial (i.e. to others). That insistence on considering the good of others will be the cornerstone of his argument concerning food in chs. 8–10 and spiritual gifts in chs. 12–14. Here Paul is also aware of how freedom can become a new slavery ('I will not be dominated by anything'); he has a lively sense of the power of sin (cf. Rom 6; Gal 5:13–24).

But Paul is most anxious lest this sense of freedom create a carelessness regarding bodily behaviour. The first part of 6:13 might again be a citation from the Corinthian church: ' "food is meant for the stomach and the stomach for food", and God will destroy both one and the other'. The reference to food anticipates the discussion of chs. 8–10, where Paul challenges the 'knowledgeable' who consider themselves immune to corruption by such a paltry phenomenon as food. In Paul's eyes this betrays a dangerously dualistic notion of the human person as possessing a spirit/soul in principle separable from the body. He fears that this might lead (or had already led) to the justification of sexual freedom on the basis that the satisfaction of sexual appetites was as insignificant as the assuaging of hunger. Thus he insists that 'the body is not for *porneia* but for the Lord and the Lord for the body' (v.13). *Porneia* was used in the Jewish tradition to refer to any sexual activity judged immoral (NRSV translates here 'fornication'). Paul will later talk about a sex with a prostitute (*pornē*, v. 15), but *porneia* could refer to anything he considered illicit (it is used also in 5:1 and 7:2). 'The body' (*sōma*) must here include the material/physical expression of our selves. In ch. 15 Paul will draw a distinction between the 'natural body' which cannot inherit the kingdom of God and the 'spiritual body' which will be the form of resurrection life (15:42–50). That complication, in the existence of two kinds of body, perhaps explains why Paul says here (v. 14) that God who raised the Lord will raise *us* up (not 'will raise *our bodies* up', as the line of argument might otherwise suggest).

None the less, Paul cannot concede that our present 'natural bodies' are irrelevant to Christian commitment. On the contrary, they are 'members'—literally, limbs—of Christ (v. 15), so that the way we handle them inevitably draws Christ into our activities. Paul exploits this notion as far as possible by a novel application of Gen 2:24 ('the two shall become one flesh') to all sexual unions, not just marriage. The physical joining in sex with a prostitute actually links Christ's body with that of a representative of sin—a union which Paul finds utterly scandalous. Hence the conclusion: 'Flee immorality' (v. 18; NRSV 'Shun fornication!'). It is not altogether clear why this sin is here taken to be uniquely 'against the body itself', but Paul may be hinting at the way in which sexual activity affects (and therefore potentially corrupts) the whole person at the deepest point of our identity. Two final arguments underline the significance of the body for a believer. First, the body is indwelt by the Spirit of God, and thus has the sanctity of a temple (v. 19); and one does not treat a temple in a cavalier fashion (cf. 3:17). Secondly, believers come under an ownership: like slaves bought at a market (v. 20), they are answerable in totality to a master, and that includes their bodies (slaves were sometimes known simply as 'bodies'; cf. Rev 18:13).

(7:1–40) Celibacy and Marriage Paul now mentions the letter he has received from the Corinthians (v. 1), which may set the agenda for most of the rest of this letter. It is often supposed that the Corinthians meekly asked Paul's opinion on these matters, but the signs of tension in his relationship with them suggest that their approach might not have been so deferential. The subject-matter for this chapter is their statement (NRSV rightly uses inverted commas), 'It is well for a man not to touch a woman' (7:1). 'Touch' is a euphemism for sexual relations, and the statement seems to represent a principled rejection of all sexual activity. The position of those who held this view in Corinth may be deduced as: (1) Those who are single should avoid marriage (see 7:1, 8–9); (2) Those who are married should refrain from sex with their partners (see 7:3–6); (3) Those who are married should seek divorce (see 7:10–11), especially if they are married to an unbeliever (see 7:12–16); (4) Those who are engaged should not proceed to marriage (see 7:36–8). We cannot be sure why some Corinthians took this apparently ascetic stance. Early Christianity spawned many kinds of asceticism (Brown 1988), but here there may have been some denigration of the body arising from the exuberance of experience in the Spirit, combined with the assumption (widespread in antiquity) that prophecy and other activities involving special receptivity to God required withdrawal from the 'pollution' of sex. If some of the Corinthians were particularly 'eager for spiritual gifts' (14:12), 'anxious about the affairs of the Lord, that they may be holy *in body and spirit*' (v. 34), they may have regarded it as necessary to avoid sexual activity and advantageous to withdraw from, or to refuse to enter, marriage.

Paul begins his response to the Corinthians by dealing with the first three points in the summary above (vv. 1–16). He then draws back to illustrate his principle that believers should remain in the condition in which they were called, with reference to circumcision and slavery (vv. 17–24). When broaching the question of 'virgins' (unmarried persons eligible for marriage), he first expounds the advantages of detachment (vv. 25–31) and single-mindedness (vv. 32–5), before discussing the position of such virgins, together with the case of the eligible widow (vv. 36–40). Throughout he insists that marriage is not sin, and sex within marriage wholly appropriate (even necessary), but always with an unmistakable coolness. He consistently maintains that it is better, if possible, to be unmarried, provided that this does not (1) involve initiating a divorce, an action forbidden by the Lord (v. 10), or (2) subject the believer to irresistible passions, leading to sex outside marriage (vv. 2, 9). The lack of enthusiasm for marriage in its own right, for the procreation of children, or for the establishment of a Christian family (contrast Eph 5:21–6:4) is notable.

Paul starts by citing the Corinthian statement that 'it is well for a man not to touch a woman', but he cannot accept it fully, at least not within marriage. v. 2 could refer to men and women in general and their acquisition of marriage partners: 'each man should have his own wife' etc. (NRSV). But, in view of the following verses, it is perhaps more likely that it refers to married men and women who should 'have' (in the sense of 'have sexual relations with') their partners: thus, 'each husband should have sex with his own wife' etc. (Fee 1987: 277–80). The reason for Paul's advice is his concern with immoralities, perhaps with specific 'cases of immorality' (NRSV) in mind, such as those alluded to in chs. 5 and 6. Lurking throughout this chapter is Paul's fear of the power of sexual desire, which, if not fulfilled (or neutralized) within marriage, is likely to lead to sin. vv. 3–4 indicate the obligations and privileges of both marriage partners in sexual matters, with a degree of reciprocity highly unusual in antiquity; indeed almost every point in the chapter is discussed from both male and female angles. Nowhere is this more radical in effect than in the second half of v. 4. The first half, detailing the husband's authority over his wife's body, is a standard assumption in antiquity (and all other patriarchal societies). But the second, by putting the matter the other way around, undercuts assumptions of male privilege at their most sensitive point: the male body and its use in sex. Neither party is here allowed to make unilateral decisions: any period of sexual abstinence must be by agreement and of limited duration, lest the sexual urge (Satan's tempting) prove too strong (v. 5). Such a period of abstinence may enable a Christian couple to devote themselves to prayer, a notion with some parallels in Judaism (e.g. *T. Naph.* 8:8).

At v. 6 is the first of many indications in this chapter that Paul is careful not to establish rules or speak more confidently than is his right (cf. vv. 25, 40). The 'this' which he here concedes may be marriage, but more probably refers to temporary abstinence from sex within marriage. Then v. 7 means: I would like everyone to be sexually continent like myself, but recognize that some have this gift and can remain unmarried, while others do not, needing to marry and to fulfil the sexual obligations of that state. The 'gift from God' (*charisma*) represents the ability to remain celibate without succumbing to sexual desire.

vv. 8–9 turn directly to the unmarried and widowed. Paul himself is unmarried, perhaps because his conversion disrupted his life-plans so severely. The unmarried state is his preference for all (for reasons he will detail in vv. 25–35), but he is worried again by the power of sexual passion (likened here to a fire), which some need to tame, or quench, within marriage.

What about those who are already married and are tempted to escape from marriage? Here Paul for once gives a command (cf. v. 6), though not on his own authority but on that of the Lord (v. 10). This is one of those very few places (9:14 is another) where Paul refers explicitly to the teaching of Jesus. He here cites a saying also attested (with some variations) in the Synoptics, in which Jesus declared divorce to be illegitimate (Mk 10:2–11; Mt 19:3–9; Lk 16:18). In the case of a wife he imagines a second-best option whereby she separates/divorces (vv. 13–15 suggest that these may be synonyms for Paul) but does not marry again (v. 11). Some think that his special concentration on the woman might reflect a specific case, or growing tendency, in Corinth (Wire 1990). The acceptance of this second best ('if she does separate . . .') shows that Paul does not regard the teaching of Jesus as legislation; it sets some parameters, but allows for differences of situation. He will later acknowledge that a Christian may have to accept divorce at the hands of a non-Christian partner (v. 15), taking Jesus' principle to rule out only the initiation of divorce proceedings.

vv. 12–16 deal with the case of Christians already married to unbelievers. Paul does not recommend entering into such a partnership (7:39; cf. 2 Cor 6:14–16), but seems to envisage here the conversion of one partner in a marriage, a situation which could be fraught with difficulty if the Christian spouse disdained household idolatry (cf. 1 Pet 3:1–6). Such verses make clear that it was not always whole households which converted (cf. 1:16). In this case, Paul has no direct teaching from Jesus (v. 12), but adapts what he knows to fit the social

necessities. He recommends staying in the marriage if at all possible and seems to be responding to fears that the believer is somehow defiled by this intimate contact with the 'unholy'. If the marriage is to be maintained, and if holiness or defilement are in some sense contagious, logic propels Paul to insist that the unbelieving spouse is actually made 'holy' through the believer, just as are the children of even one Christian parent (v. 14). This description of persons as being 'holy' or 'sanctified' is normally used by Paul only in relation to believers in Christ (e.g. 1:2; 6:11); it is strange to find it used here of unbelievers, whose future salvation is uncertain (v. 16). Children are mentioned here for the only time in the chapter and only as a supporting argument, and it is unclear what, if anything, is implied by their designation as 'holy' (v. 14). The verse has been used with equal force in arguments both for and against infant baptism, about which Paul never speaks explicitly. v. 15 recognizes that the non-Christian partner may not wish to continue a marriage with a spouse whose recent conversion creates tension in the marriage, and in this case Paul recommends allowing divorce for the sake of peace. Nothing here rules out remarriage, though the possibility is not mentioned. v. 16 could be translated in either an optimistic or a pessimistic sense. Optimistically ('who knows, you might save your spouse'), it undergirds the main thrust of the paragraph, urging a Christian to remain in a mixed marriage (so NRSV; REB; cf. 1 Pet 3:1–2). Translated in a pessimistic sense ('how do you know whether you will ever save your spouse?'), it discourages hopes of benefit from remaining in such a marriage and thus supports the concession of v. 15 that one may withdraw from a hopeless situation (so RSV; NIV). The former is slightly more likely.

The question of change of status leads Paul to formulate a general principle (v. 17): that you should lead whatever life is apportioned by the Lord, which is taken to be that state in which you were called. 'Called' is one of Paul's common terms for conversion, and he seems to be talking here of the state *in which* one becomes a Christian, not a vocation *to which* one is summoned (NRSV rightly translates at vv. 20, 24, but not at v. 17). Such a policy of 'stay as you are' is indeed his general advice in this chapter (if married, don't divorce; if single, remain so), with some exceptions allowed. It is now illustrated with regard to ethnic identity and social status (cf. the three categories in Gal 3:28). Circumcision, the sign of male Jewish identity, should not be reversed (as could be done by surgery or by stretching and pinning what remains of the foreskin); similarly the foreskin should not be removed for the sake of adopting Jewish identity. Here Paul summarizes the theme of his letter to the Galatians, insisting on the relativization of such cultural markers. Accordingly v. 19 echoes statements in Galatians (5:6; 6:15), though with a different and extremely puzzling conclusion. 'Keeping the commandments of God' in any normal Jewish sense would *include* the practice of circumcision; Paul has somehow redefined the notion to filter out certain commands which he considers unnecessary in a multi-ethnic church (cf. 9:19–21).

The second illustration concerns social identity, as slave or free person (vv. 21–4). Here the same 'stay as you are' principle is applied as a general rule, with legal status similarly relativized. Christian slaves can consider themselves 'freed persons belonging to the Lord' (freed persons usually had continuing obligations to their former owners), while Christians who are free are really 'slaves of Christ' (vv. 22–3). This compensatory redescription of reality renders social location irrelevant to Christian obligation (and perhaps even inverts the assumed hierarchy of slave and free, see Martin 1990: 63–8), enabling Paul to tell those in slavery not to mind about it (v. 21). However, the second half of v. 21 contains an ambiguity which has been the focus of some debate. The Greek could be taken to urge accepting slavery, even if there is an opportunity of gaining freedom (so NRSV). However, it could equally, and perhaps better, be taken in an opposite sense, providing a partial exception to the general rule of the paragraph: 'but if you can gain your freedom, be sure to use that opportunity' (so RSV). In most cases, as Bartchy (1973) pointed out, slaves would have no choice in this matter: if an owner wished to free a slave, it would happen whether the slave wished it or not. Since the chapter does contain other exceptions to the rule of 'stay as you are', and since v. 23 suggests that Paul considered freedom a better condition than slavery, the second, more positive, reading is to be preferred. None the less, the main thrust of the paragraph illustrates the rule of status-retention, which v. 24 reiterates.

In v. 25 Paul turns to the specific case of 'virgins', that is, those not yet married. Girls were typically married off by their parents at or very soon after puberty to men who were usually several years older. Marriage and the subsequent raising of children was taken to be a civic duty (to ensure future generations), but some radical philosophers (Cynics) took it to be a distraction from their philosophical calling. In what follows, Paul will mix some such Cynic motifs with his own apocalyptic reasoning about the end of the world (see Deming 1995). In the first instance (vv. 25–31) he applies the principle of 'stay as you are' on the grounds of the 'impending crisis' (v. 26). What he has in mind is made clearer in v. 29 ('the appointed time has grown short') and v. 31 ('the present form of this world is passing away'). Paul is convinced that he lives in the last generation (cf. 1 Thess 4:15 and 1 Cor 15:52). He thus harbours the apocalyptic belief that all present social structures will be dissolved, and also that the time preceding the 'end' will be characterized by acute distress ('the impending crisis'). Under such circumstances it is clear that marriage is of little value and the raising of future generations an irrelevance. Paul cannot advocate being rid of marriage relationships already entered, since he has the Lord's word forbidding divorce (v. 10). But neither can he recommend marriage for those as yet unmarried: it would not be morally wrong (vv. 28–9) but it would only make one more vulnerable to the distress of social breakdown. In fact, even for those who are married, Paul advocates an 'eschatological detachment': let them live 'as though they had no wives', like all dealings with the world must be conducted on the basis of 'as if not' (vv. 29–31). This sentiment is paralleled in Jewish apocalyptic documents (e.g. 2 Esd 16:40 ff.). It is not entirely clear what it would mean for married men to live 'as though they had no wives' (vv. 2–5 suggest it cannot mean a withdrawal from sex), but in some general sense marriage is relativized here as an institution hardly worth investing in.

The second reason for Paul's coolness regarding marriage is spelt out in vv. 32–5. Paul wishes his converts to be 'free from anxieties', or more precisely, free from competing anx-

ieties. Like the Cynics, Paul is impressed by the amount of attention to the marriage partner required by marriage (again he oddly fails to mention children), regarding these as 'the affairs of the world' which constitute a distraction from 'the affairs of the Lord'. For him, marriage and family life are not part of a believer's service to the Lord but a competing interest which prevents 'unhindered devotion to the Lord' (v. 35; cf. v. 34: 'his interests are divided'). The specific reference to the woman's concern 'to be holy in body and spirit' (v. 34) may allude to the concerns of particular Corinthian women, who operated as prophets (11:2–16). Once again, Paul is cautious not to side too strongly with those who forbid marriage (v. 35), but it is clear that he considers 'good order' and 'devotion to the Lord' better served by singleness. It is possible that he considers himself in this respect a better 'worker' than other apostles who were accompanied by their wives (9:3–6; 15:10).

The next paragraph (vv. 36–8) returns to the practical matter of virgins, first signalled in v. 25. Unfortunately, the paragraph could be read in a number of different ways (see Fee 1987: 349–55). Some interpret it as concerning a young girl's father, who is responsible for marrying off his daughter: the verb used for 'he who marries his virgin' (v. 38) normally means 'he who marries her off', i.e. arranges her marriage. Then the Greek could be taken to refer to a father anxious about his treatment of his daughter, if she is getting over-age (the Greek translated in NRSV 'if his passions are strong' could be taken in this quite different sense; a girl might be considered 'overripe' in her early twenties!); then it is no sin for him to allow and arrange her marriage. The more usual interpretation of the text (adopted by the NRSV and by most commentators) takes it to speak of an unmarried man and his desire to marry, or his control over this desire. Oddly, in either case, the girl's wishes in this matter are entirely ignored. Whether Paul envisages some sort of permanent 'engagement' is unclear. As throughout the chapter, Paul allows marriage ('it is no sin') but considers it a second-best option (v. 38).

That principle is finally applied to the case of a widow (vv. 39–40; many girls were widowed quite young). By the rule of 'no divorce' (v. 10) a woman can consider remarriage only on the death of her husband (cf. Rom 7:1–4); then she may remarry 'in the Lord' (the choice cannot have been great in a small congregation). But Paul's preference for singleness is again evident (v. 40). His final sentence sums up his surprising hesitancy on this matter, unless there is irony in his claim that he *too* (as much as the 'spiritual people' in Corinth) has access to the wisdom of the Spirit (cf. 2:14–16).

Sacrificial Food and the Dangers of Idolatry (8:1–11:1)

8:1 opens a new section of the letter, on 'food sacrificed to idols', perhaps another issue raised in the Corinthian letter. At first sight, the content of ch. 9 appears out of place in this section. However, as we shall see, it actually fits perfectly as an illustration of what Paul requires of the 'people of knowledge': that they renounce their 'rights' for the sake of others. It has often been noted that Paul's softer tone on the consumption of sacrificial food in 8:1–13 and 10:23–11:1 appears inconsistent with his hard-line attitude to idolatry in 10:1–22; some have even suspected the combination of two or more letters at this point. There is indeed a certain dialectic in Paul's position regarding such food, which might mask inconsistency: he himself calls attention to this dialectic in 10:19–20. But the distinctions he draws between the different contexts in which sacrificial food is eaten, and the different intents such eating represents, make it possible for him to give such a nuanced response. Moreover, it is quite like Paul to advance an argument by a range of different strategies which may not cohere perfectly with one another (cf. his response to 'speaking in tongues' in chs. 12–14).

The issue of 'sacrificial food' arises from the fact that food consumption was frequently associated with the deities, whether by prayer, libation, or sacrifice, and that the slaughter of animals often took place in the context of temple worship. Jews, who were notoriously averse to 'alien' religious practices, abstained from food and wine which had become tainted by association with gods other than their own. The early Christian movement was generally Jewish in ethos, but in many places attracted a majority of Gentile members in churches which were prepared to abandon some distinctive Jewish practices (such as circumcision and Sabbath observance). It was thus possible for uncertainty to arise as to the proper Christian stance towards Greek and Roman deities (which Jews called 'idols'), or at least towards the meals, festivals, club-dinners, and parties which were generally accompanied by some sort of religious activity. Many kinds of food might be considered to be affected: portions could be offered on an altar in domestic or public settings, or liquids poured out as a libation (see Willis 1985; P.D. Gooch 1993). Paul seems to be particularly concerned here with meat (8:13). Wealthy individuals or clubs often brought animals for slaughter at a temple, one portion being reserved for the deity (i.e. the priests), with the rest consumed in an ordinary meal either on the site (many temples had dining rooms) or in a private setting. Even meat sold in the meat market might have been offered to a deity, so a believer anxious to avoid any contact with idolatry might balk at the purchase of meat there and at the fare provided in taverns or in an unbeliever's house. On the other hand, dinner invitations, club meetings, family celebrations, and civic festivals were such an important part of social life that some Christians might be reluctant to adopt a rigorous stance on this issue; that would certainly affect the lives and prospects of such socially significant believers as Gaius and Erastus (see E.1).

Many ambiguities surrounded the issue of sacrificial food. Was all the meat idolatrous or only those portions specifically reserved for the deity? Was one tainted by association with idolaters at occasions when they committed idolatry, or not? What, in any case, constituted 'idolatry' and how were the images to be regarded? In Graeco-Roman culture, general reverence for the images of the deities included a range of attitudes to their relation to reality: some considered the gods to be present within the images, others that they merely represented some divine attribute. In these chapters Paul is in dialogue with a group within the Corinthian church who considered themselves knowledgeable in such matters ('we all possess knowledge', 8:1). It appears that these are an educated élite: in a spirit of confident monotheism they take idols to represent nothing at all (8:4), and reason that participation in idolatrous meals, even in idolatrous worship, was a meaningless and harmless activity. This stance was probably bol-

stered by social convenience, but Paul takes it seriously as a theological position which was not entirely incorrect but which could have dangerous effects both on themselves and on other, 'weaker', Christians.

(8:1–13) Debate with the 'Knowledgeable' concerning their 'Right' to Eat As in ch. 7, Paul starts by citing a phrase used in the Corinthian letter: 'all of us possess knowledge' (8:1). He will shortly deny this claim, since he is aware of vulnerable Christians in Corinth unable to take this knowing stance towards 'idols' (v. 7). But his first reaction is against the spirit of the assertion. Although he recognizes knowledge as a gift of the Spirit (1:5; 12:8), he senses here the dangers of pride and self-interest, which subordinate care for others to the acquisition and display of one's own knowledge. Thus, once again, he warns against becoming 'puffed up' (cf. 4:6 and the same verb, translated as 'to be arrogant', in 4:19, 5:2, and 13:4) and sets the priority on the constructive capability of love (v. 2; cf. chs. 12–14). In the very claim to knowledge Paul fears the corrupting power of arrogance which needs to be humbled by recognizing the inadequacy of our present 'knowledge' and the far greater value of being 'known by' God (vv. 2–3; cf. 13:8–13).

On the basis of this caution Paul addresses the knowledge in question (vv. 4–6). Again he quotes Corinthian statements that 'no idol in the world really exists' (or, 'the idol-image represents nothing in the world') and that 'there is no God but one' (v. 4). Paul can readily agree with the second statement, a cardinal tenet of Judaism. The first contains some ambiguity (see the alternative translations just offered) and it is possible that Paul and the Corinthians understood it in different senses. Paul could accept that the image is insignificant, but, as the next verse and 10:19–20 make clear, he does not doubt the reality of the *spiritual beings* which were the object of worship in Graeco-Roman religion. If the Corinthian élite think there are no such beings (and thus participate in pagan worship as a harmless inanity), Paul will have to reprimand them severely (10:1–22). Even here he insists on the exclusivity of Christian commitment (vv. 5–6). Whatever deities others might worship—and Paul insists that they are only 'so-called gods' (cf. Gal 4:8)—'yet for us there is one God...and one Lord ...' The confessional and formulaic character of v. 6 suggests the presence here of a credal statement in which we see Christology coming to birth. The Jewish Shema' ('Hear, O Israel, the Lord our God is one Lord', Deut 6:4) is here split apart into a statement about *God*, the creator of the world and goal of salvation, and a matching statement about *the Lord*, now taken to mean Jesus Christ, the medium of creation and redemption. The two are clearly distinguished (cf. 3:23; 11:3; 15:27–8) but the way in which Paul reads them both out of the Jewish declaration of monotheism is suggestive of the ways in which Christian theology will struggle to define Christ's exalted status without falling into ditheism (see further Hurtado 1988 and Dunn 1991).

Before proceeding further on this theological tack, Paul reminds the élite that they are not as representative of the church as they think (v. 7) and that they have responsibilities to fellow believers which override their 'right' to eat whatever food they wish. Paul knows that, after a lifetime of worship of 'so-called gods', converts are apt to be uneasy about contact with religious practices which they consider themselves to have renounced; if they were to eat such food again, their vulnerable self-image as Christians (their 'conscience') would be 'defiled' (v. 7). In itself, food is not of decisive significance in our relationship to God (v. 8, possibly, but not certainly, another Corinthian statement). Therefore, Paul insists, nothing fundamental is lost by declining to eat certain foods; he deliberately overlooks the social loss which might result from scrupulosity regarding 'idolatrous food'. Since the 'knowledgeable' people have no grounds for insisting on such eating, Paul is entitled to warn them lest their 'liberty' (v. 9, or 'right'; the noun echoes the slogan of 6:12) cause disaster for more vulnerable Christians. The 'stumbling-block' referred to here (cf. Rom 14) signals much more than 'offence' or 'shock': it suggests causing others to fall catastrophically, resulting in their 'destruction' (v. 11). The danger Paul has in mind is that 'the weak' (those whose self-image as Christians is vulnerable) will be encouraged, or pressurized, by the example of 'the knowledgeable' to eat food which they know, or suspect, has been sacrificed to idols. While such eating may not cause the knowledgeable to falter in their Christian commitment (since they regard the idol as a 'nothing'), it could disastrously compromise the commitment of weaker Christians, who might now view themselves as having reversed their decision to renounce idolatry. Paul imagines this happening if the knowledgeable are seen 'eating in the temple of an idol' (v. 10). Later (10:14–22) he will advance other reasons for caution about such behaviour, but here he maintains his focus on the effect which this display of superior knowledge could have on the weak: in their uncertainty of self-image as Christians, they may be 'encouraged' (Paul says 'built up', with conscious irony) to follow suit, with disastrous consequences. Damage against believers for whom Christ died diminishes his work and thus constitutes sin against Christ (vv. 11–12). Rather than looking down on the weak with the disdain typical of élite classes in Graeco-Roman society, the people of knowledge are here required to take them with full seriousness, as fellow Christians (cf. 11:17–22; 12:14–26): love is more important than knowledge (vv. 1–3). Thus, to use himself as an example, Paul renounces his right to eat meat, in case it causes the collapse of another's faith-commitment (v. 13).

(9:1–23) Paul's Example in Renouncing the 'Right' to Financial Support Ch. 9 appears to veer off in a different direction from the topic of food offered to idols. Here we have Paul's impassioned plea to be regarded as an apostle in Corinth (vv. 1–2), a long series of arguments concerning his right to receive support (vv. 3–14), and then his declaration that his boast lies precisely in making no use of this right (vv. 15–18) and in offering himself, although free, as a slave of all (vv. 19–23). All this is not, however, as irrelevant as it might seem. Paul finished ch. 8 by offering himself as an example of willingness to renounce his right to eat meat, if that was necessary for the sake of others. That leads him to present himself as an example on a wider plane of this principle of renunciation of rights. He has the right as an apostle to be given his material upkeep, but for the sake of the gospel he has renounced this: although 'free' and entitled to exercise certain rights, he has chosen to make himself a slave (v. 19). But this illustration is not unproblematic, because it is precisely his refusal to accept financial support from the Corinthians which has led some to doubt whether he is an apostle at all. It is because he knows that his status is questioned by some in Corinth that Paul chooses to use this controversial matter as his illustration: thereby he can defend himself, reassert his apostleship, and present himself as the Corinthians' model (cf. 11:1) all at the same time. This means that it is some time before Paul returns explicitly to the subject of sacrificial food, but such apparent digressions which actually advance the argument at a deeper level are typical of Paul's rhetoric (cf. ch. 13 between chs. 12 and 14).

'Freedom' may have been the watchword of the 'people of knowledge' in Corinth: it sums up their assertion of rights and that 'all things are lawful' (6:12; 8:9; 10:23). Hence Paul declares that he, too, is 'free'—in particular, endowed with the 'rights' of an apostle. His claim to apostleship was heavily contested in his generation, since he had not been a disciple of Jesus, had persecuted the church, and was often at odds with the 'mother church' in Jerusalem. Paul here rehearses the grounds for his claim: that he saw (and was commissioned by) the risen Christ (cf. 15:3–11) and that he has successfully founded churches (vv. 1–2). He hopes that the Corinthians will recognize at least this second claim, but has to counter immediately a prejudice against his apostleship which has taken root precisely in Corinth.

While staying in Corinth, Paul had apparently supported himself entirely by his own labour (according to Acts 18:3, as a leather worker), and even when the church he founded had offered him financial support he had refused to take it (cf. 2 Cor 11:7–11). It is not entirely clear why this became a matter of principle for him in Corinth; elsewhere he acknowledges receiving support from Macedonian churches (2 Cor 11:9; Phil 4:10–20). Perhaps he feared lest wealthy Christians in Corinth might wish to use their financial patronage to influence his preaching or control his movements. In any case, the fact that he did not accept support from Corinth turned out to be a bone of contention. Other 'apostles', whom the Corinthians knew about or met, received support, probably appealing to the words of Jesus and the example of travelling missionaries in Judea and Galilee (see Theissen 1982: 27–67). To forgo this right might thus appear to place Paul at a lower level than 'real' apostles, and for Paul to support himself by *manual* labour was to demean himself in the eyes of wealthier Christians (cf. 4:12).

Thus Paul confronts directly those who 'examine' him (v. 3; the same verb is used in 2:15 and 4:3). He declares his entitlement to the same forms of material support as other apostles (vv. 4–6), making special mention of 'the brothers of the Lord' (e.g. James, 15:7), and Cephas, the hero of the Cephas group, 1:12). He then strings together an impressive collection of arguments for this entitlement (vv. 7–14). He appeals first to human parallels (soldiers, vineyard workers, and shepherds), where workers expect some return for their labour (v. 7). He then turns to the Scriptures for the same principle, offering an allegorical reading of Moses' law about the threshing ox (vv. 8–11; see Deut 25:4). It is not often that Paul appeals directly to 'the law of Moses' for moral guidance (his letters to the Galatians and Romans show what an ambiguous entity 'the law' has become for him). Nor does he usually employ allegory in his interpretation of the Scriptures (Gal 4:21–31 is the only other example), although it was a technique long-established among Hellenized Jews. In his concern to find a moral lesson in the law, Paul insists that Moses really speaks *only* about human welfare, not about oxen. Allegorists such as the Jewish philosopher Philo sometimes took both literal and allegorical meanings as valid, but sometimes, like here, considered only the allegorical worthy of God. Paul applies this verse to his situation by a double transference: in talking of oxen, God is talking about human ploughers and reapers (v.10); and this principle can be applied to those who sow spiritually, and may expect to reap in exchange (v. 11). Paul can also appeal to the benefits enjoyed by priests in a temple (v. 13) and, finally, to the direct instruction of the Lord (v. 14; cf. Mt 10:10; Lk 10:7–8; 1 Tim 5:18). It is intriguing that this should be mentioned last, and without any special emphasis or priority over the previous arguments. That may be related to the fact that Paul cites this command only to declare that it does not apply to him!

Before finishing this chain of argumentation, Paul had anticipated his conclusion (v. 12): he has the rights to which he appeals but has opted *not* to make use of them, if to do so would place an obstacle in the way of the gospel. Now it becomes clear how this whole discussion relates to Paul's instruction to 'the people of knowledge' in ch. 8. In 8:9 he had warned them that their 'right' (NRSV: 'liberty') could be a stumbling-block to the weak and should be waived if it proved to be so. Here he presents himself as a model of such voluntary renunciation of rights, for the sake of the gospel. In his case, too, Paul has the 'weak' especially in mind (v. 22 highlights his accommodation to the weak, not the strong). By refusing to accept support, Paul ensures that he is not a burden on those with little to spare: he works with his hands and thereby identifies with those who are socially and economically weak, even at the risk of offending the wealthier converts who would like Paul to accept their patronage and quit his embarrassing mode of work (Martin 1990: 117–35).

vv. 15–18 explain further this renunciation of rights and its importance for Paul. Preaching the gospel 'free of charge' was an important and distinctive feature of Paul's ministry: indeed, the sentence structure breaks down in v. 15 to reveal how emotionally significant is this 'ground for boasting'. He now plays with the theme of employment and 'pay' (the Gk. word *misthos* means both 'pay' and 'reward'). The fact that he preaches the gospel is not for Paul a matter of choice, but of necessity (v. 16; cf. Gal 1:15–16). If it were a matter of choice, he would be a free agent, and like any other free man would expect pay ('reward') for work completed. But he is not a free agent, he is 'entrusted with a commission', that is, working for Christ as his slave-steward (v. 17; the same metaphor as in 4:1–2). Slaves do not get pay ('reward') just for doing what their owners tell them to do. Paul's 'reward' (pay) is to do what he has been instructed to do under very special conditions: to make the gospel 'free of charge'. Ironically, then, his spiritual pay is to receive no financial pay for the fulfilment of his task (v. 18).

This might look like a form of self-interest, to get some reward out of what he does, if Paul did not go on to explain his motivation in vv. 19–23. His goal is not self-gratification but the interests of the gospel, and in particular the desire to 'win' converts. Like a demagogue who enslaves himself to the populace to campaign for their rights, Paul has deliberately

renounced rights and demeaned himself to advance the cause of the gospel (v. 19). His self-sacrifice is first illustrated by the chief characteristic of his mission, his cross-cultural adaptability (vv. 20–1). Among Jews he could live like a Jew: that is, among the law-observant he observes the law, although not considering himself utterly bound to it (v. 20). The purpose is to win Jews for the gospel; for, although his call was 'to the Gentiles' (Rom 1:5), Paul still associated with Jews, as his synagogue visits testify (2 Cor 11:24). Similarly, for Gentiles 'outside the law' Paul lived in a Gentile fashion, although in truth not lawless before God, but under full obligation to Christ (v. 21, 'under Christ's law'; no code of teaching is here envisaged). Again the purpose is to win Gentiles, the task in which Paul was so successful, though at the cost of his reputation among most fellow Jews, who took his adaptability to be merely opportunism (Gal 1:10). This loss of clear-cut cultural identity is paralleled by his loss of honour in 'becoming weak' (v. 22), identifying with those who possessed less knowledge and less social significance than the élite leaders of the Corinthian church. Paul is prepared to give up cultural and social rights for the sake of the gospel, and hints that only by so doing will he share its blessings (v. 23). Thus he is entitled to challenge the 'people of knowledge' in Corinth as to their willingness to do the same. If they are not willing, he suggests, they may forfeit its blessings and lose out on the salvation which they take for granted. Such is the turn his argument now takes in 9:24–10:22.

(9:24–10:22) The Dangers of Complacency in relation to Idolatry While 9:24–7 still takes the form of discourse about himself, Paul now begins to turn his own example into challenge to his Corinthian audience. He uses images from the games which would be particularly vivid in their imagination, since Corinth hosted the biennial Isthmian games, drawing participants from all over the Graeco-Roman world. Entering the race is not the same as winning it: the Corinthians still have to make sure they 'run' successfully (9:24). Sporting heroes were extremely famous in antiquity and it was well-known that they underwent very rigorous training in order to win a garland. That was a motif often used in popular philosophy to indicate the seriousness of a moral lifestyle, and Paul employs it here to urge self-discipline for the sake of a far more valuable prize, salvation (9:25). Practice, discipline, and self-control were all essential for an athlete's success, whether the sport was running or boxing (9:26). Without them, a promising career would easily be spoiled, and Paul takes seriously the possibility that he himself might be 'disqualified' by God, excluded from salvation (or at least from its 'reward', cf. 3:14–15) even after having brought others into it (9:27).

The note of warning to the Corinthians is becoming louder, but before turning the spotlight directly back on to them Paul invokes a cautionary tale from the Scriptures (10:1–13). He finds no difficulty in using scriptural narratives to illustrate God's dealings with the church, since he regards the Israelites in the desert as 'our ancestors' (10:1) even though the church he is writing to is mostly Gentile (see further Hays 1989). Paul recounts the story of Israel's disobedience in the wilderness because it illustrates precisely what he wants to warn the Corinthians about: that even those chosen by God can go badly astray; and if they do, whatever their privileges, they are liable to destruction. The fact that the story concerns idolatry and sexual immorality makes it immediately relevant to a church which worries Paul on both these scores.

Paul detects among the Corinthian Christians a sense of privileged security in which they consider themselves immune to danger. Perhaps it is on this basis that the people of knowledge have the confidence to attend idolatrous events, reckoning that nothing can harm their status as spiritual people. They may have taken particular pride in their baptism as ensuring salvation and in the Lord's Supper as replenishing their spiritual resources. Both would therefore constitute rites which, like some Graeco-Roman mysteries, confirmed their superior status and sealed their immortality. It is probably for this reason that Paul describes the Israelites' experience in terms which match Christian rites. As they went under the cloud and through the (Red) Sea, the Israelites were 'baptized into Moses' (10:2), just as Christians were baptized into Christ (I Cor 12:12–13; Gal 3:27); similarly, as they ate the manna and drank from the rock in the desert, they partook of 'spiritual' food and drink like that enjoyed in the Lord's Supper (10:3–4). Indeed, Paul even claims that the Israelites drew nourishment, in a sense, from Christ himself, who is identified with the rock from which the water issued (10:4). He here draws on Jewish exegesis which reflected on the fact that the Pentateuchal narratives place this rock in different locations: had it therefore 'followed' the Israelites through the desert? In some quarters this rock had also been allegorized as 'Wisdom', from which the righteous drew spiritual nourishment, and Paul may be drawing on an early Christian identification between Christ and Wisdom (cf. 1:30 and 8:6). None the less—and this is the point of the illustration—despite having access to all the same privileges as the Corinthian Christians (baptism, 'spiritual' food and drink, and even Christ himself), the Israelites were not immune from God's punishment when they went astray: in fact, most of them were destroyed (10:5).

In 10:6 and 10:11 Paul explains the principle by which he interprets the Israelites' story: these events are an example, and were written down as a warning, indicating the dangers for God's people if they entertain evil desires. Indeed, 10:11 suggests that they were written specifically for 'us', that is, the Christians who live in the final generation, the climactic junction of time Paul calls 'the ends of the ages' (cf. 7:29–31; cf. Rom 15:4). 10:7–8 runs through a list of Israel's errors, perhaps a stock résumé of the wilderness sins: idolatry, in the worship of the golden calf (10:7, citing Ex 32:6); 'sexual immorality' (porneia, see I COR 5:1), in forging illicit marriages with Midianite women (10:8, alluding to Num 25, where, however, the casualty figure is 24,000); putting Christ to the test (10:9, alluding to Num 21; some texts read 'the Lord', which is how the scriptural narrative puts it, but generally Paul takes 'the Lord' in the Scriptures to refer to Christ); and finally, complaining, in grumbling about God's purposes or Moses' leadership (probably alluding to Num 14 or Num 16, with the notion of the 'destroyer' transferred from Ex 12:23). In each case, the outcome is the same: the 'destruction' of the sinners. If such stories are of immediate relevance to the Corinthians as 10:11 suggests, then the warning is clear: they are in as much danger as the Israelites in the desert. Paul turns directly against the confidence of the Corinthian leaders with the warning of 10:12. No situation is uniquely difficult or inescapable, and they cannot claim to be helpless or faultless if they sin: God will enable them to endure temptation (cf. 1:8–9) and will always provide an escape route (10:13). The question is whether the Corinthians will be willing to take it and the social inconvenience it may cause.

The notion of 'escape' leads into Paul's direct instruction: 'flee from the worship of idols' (10:14). Of the wilderness sins recounted in 10:7–8, it is idolatry which is Paul's most immediate concern. He has still to confront the people of knowledge concerning their easy dismissal of the significance of 'idols' (8:4), since he fears (or knows) that this attitude will justify their convenient participation in acts of worship to idols. Addressing them, with slight condescension, as 'sensible people' (they boast of their 'knowledge', 8:1), he urges them to consider what sorts of 'partnerships' (or 'sharing', Gk. koinōnia) they are undertaking. At the Lord's Supper, the cup (known as 'the cup of blessing' because of the prayer, blessing God, which is spoken over it) is a 'partnership' in the blood of Christ. Similarly, the bread which is broken is a 'partnership' in the body of Christ (10:16). It is difficult to determine what sort of 'sacramental theology' undergirds these statements. Is the 'partnership' merely *represented* by the cup and bread, or actually *effected* by it? And what is the relationship between the cup and blood, and between the bread and body (cf. 11:24–5)? But what is clear, and what Paul is concerned to stress, is that participation in this meal signals a bond between the participant and Christ, a bond which must be *exclusive* of all others (10:21–2; cf. the parallel argumentation in 6:15–17).

The reference to the 'bread' and the 'body' leads Paul into a brief aside concerning the 'one body' of the church (10:17, anticipating 11:17–34 and 12:12–31), a motif which should encourage the people of knowledge to take more care of their fellow 'limbs' who have weaker consciences (cf. 10:23–4). But the main point of the paragraph is pursued again in 10:18 with reference to Jewish sacrificial practice, where partaking in sacrificial victims joins an individual to the worship offered at the altar. Paul considers that the same applies to worship and sacrifice in Graeco-Roman religion. 10:19 makes clear that he has not revoked the convictions he set out in ch. 8: it is not that the food is significant in itself (thus the act of eating is not so much the problem), nor that the 'idol' (i.e. the image) is itself of importance (its presence or proximity at a meal is not problematic); rather, in the act of sacrifice, Gentiles devote themselves to 'demons' and thus create a 'partnership' with beings which are wholly out of bounds for a believer. Paul here uses the word *daimonion*, which refers in normal Greek to a supernatural being of lesser significance and more ambiguous virtue than a full god, but one not necessarily evil; in time, however, Jewish and Christian usage was literally to 'demonize' all such beings. The point here is that such a partnership is incompatible with belonging to Christ, on the Jewish principle that God is jealous of all rivals (10:22, echoing Deut 32:21). The people of knowledge may be strong compared with the weak in conscience, but they are not 'stronger than' God (10:22), that is, strong enough to withstand the sort of judgement which the wilderness stories have threatened.

Paul thus issues a ban on actions which constitute personal involvement in idolatry (worship of idols). The following paragraph (10:23–11:1) will show greater latitude regarding situations where there is no personal participation in idolatry. The hard line he takes here may appear to go further than the argument he employed in 8:4–13, where his concern was the effect of eating sacrificial food on others, rather than its threat to one's own partnership with Christ; but the difference is one of focus rather than substance. In practice, it may have been difficult to define, or to anticipate, where a believer was implicated in acts of idolatry, for instance, when attendance at a meal in a temple or in the presence of an idol might involve the banqueters in sacrifice or other acts of worship. Perhaps Paul underestimated the complexity of such situations, but it is clear at least that he cannot tolerate the forging of a link to alien entities, which, though they may not be gods, are none the less potent rivals to Christ (cf. 15:24–8).

(10:23–11:1) Practical Guidelines on Eating and Avoiding Offence The ban on participation in 'idolatry' has not yet resolved all the practical issues, since there are places and occasions where sacrificial food may be on offer without involving the believer in idolatry. In such matters, again the crucial issue is the effect of one's actions on other people, particularly other believers: we have returned full circle to the concerns of ch. 8, since Paul still maintains that love is a more valuable criterion than knowledge (8:1–3). Thus, while citing again in 10:23 the Corinthian principle of freedom (cf. 6:12), Paul insists on modifying it with reference to what 'builds up', that is, what is beneficial to others (cf. 8:1). The tendencies of the élite are to protect their own interests in such matters, advancing their social position by minimum abstentions from sacrificial food; but Paul calls them to seek, first of all, the advantage of others (10:24). In the case of food sold in the meat market (which might or might not have passed through a temple in the process of slaughter), Paul encourages complete freedom: ignorance as to the history of the food means that no one's conscience (identity as a Christian) is affected by eating this food. Most Jews were more anxious about avoiding food possibly tainted by idolatry, but Paul overrules this scruple since eating such food from a market risks no personal participation in idolatry, and since the food itself is a part of God's good creation (10:25–6, boldly citing Ps 24:1 in support). In the case of a meal at an unbeliever's house, ignorance is again encouraged for the same reasons (10:27), but here complications may arise from the involvement of other people in the meal. Paul is concerned for the 'conscience' of someone else who declares the food to have been involved in sacrifice (10:28). Because the phrase, 'This has been offered in sacrifice', does not use the Jewish/Christian term 'idolatrous', many interpreters take this informant to be a non-believer (either fellow-guest or host; e.g. Fee 1987: 483–5). But it is hard to see why Paul would be concerned with an unbeliever's conscience in this matter, and it is better to see here the same weak Christians as were in view in ch. 8 (Barrett 1971: 239–40). For *their* sake, i.e. lest they be pressurized into compromising their faith, knowledgeable Christians should refrain from such food (10:28–29a). But otherwise the basic principle remains: so long as one can give thanks with integrity, that is, eat the food as part of a relationship with God (uncompromised by partnership with demons), one should do so freely, even if others are critical (10:29b–30).

On this reading of the argument, 10:28–9a forms a digression, citing an exceptional case when liberty is to be constrained, while 10:29b–30 gives the general rule. If this is right, Paul agrees with the knowledgeable about their freedom to a large degree, but checks them at the point where their freedom causes real damage to others (cf. Rom 14:1–15:6). The last few verses of this discussion (10:31–11:1) sum up its principles. Eating and drinking are to be done 'to the glory of God', without compromise of that glory by idolatry. At the same time, no stumbling-block (the Greek echoes 8:9 and is much stronger than NRSV 'offence') is to be placed in the path of Jews or Greeks or the church (10:32). The goal should be not one's own advantage, but that of others, that they be saved and maintained in salvation (10:33, i.e. not 'destroyed' by selfish use of 'knowledge'; cf. 8:11). And, finally, Paul reminds them of the example he has described in ch. 9, not ultimately because of his own importance (he does not want a 'Paul party') but because he believes he thereby imitates Christ (11:1; cf. Rom 15:1–3).

Issues Relating to Communal Meetings (11:2–14:40)

Paul now turns to a number of topics which relate to the conduct of worship and communal meetings in the Corinthian church. The bulk of this new section concerns the exercise of spiritual gifts (chs. 12–14), but that is prefaced with discussion of two topics also related to worship, head-covering of women in prayer and prophecy (11:2–16) and the Lord's Supper (11:17–34). Paul's initial word of commendation (11:2) is probably meant to preface the whole section, since the Lord's Supper and the gifts of the Spirit were part of his legacy to the church. But on many issues, in fact, he has more criticism to offer than praise (cf. 11:22).

(11:2–16) Praying and Prophesying with Proper Head-Covering This passage, with its hierarchical ordering of male and female, has had a fateful influence through the centuries and has not enhanced Paul's reputation. It is full of awkward argumentation, so awkward that a few scholars even consider it a later addition to the letter by another hand. The issue concerns men and women who pray and prophesy in the church (vv. 4–5). Paul takes it for granted that *both* genders will participate in such important acts of church leadership (on prophecy, see ch. 14); how this tallies with the apparent ban on women's speech in church in 14:33–6 is not clear (see 1 COR 14:33–6). Most commentators rightly take the topic to be the *covering* of the head (Theissen 1987: 158–75), while a few scholars construe the Greek differently to refer to tying up (or letting loose) of *hair* (Murphy-O'Connor 1980). Men and women wore the same sort of outer garment (Gk. *himation*), which could be drawn forward from behind the neck to cover the crown of the head, or even further forward over the face as well. In normal circumstances men did not draw the *himation* forward, although Romans did in offering sacrifice at an altar. The typical customs for women are more difficult to discern, and probably varied over time and in different cultural contexts within the Graeco-Roman world (on Corinth see Thompson 1988). However, a variety of evidence suggests that, in public and in the presence of men other than family members, married women frequently covered their heads and even their faces, as a sign of modesty and as a protective barrier in the force-field of lustful stares. Young unmarried girls did not usually cover or veil themselves, but for a mature/married woman (girls were normally married at puberty) to be seen uncovered might suggest that she was somewhat 'forward', thus bringing shame both on herself and on her husband. Thus head-covering functioned both to differentiate women from men and to subordinate them.

This passage suggests that there are some women in the Corinthian church who are leading worship in prayer and prophecy with their heads uncovered. We can only speculate about the reasons for this behaviour. It is possible that the causes were quite mundane, for instance, that they felt the house-church a sufficiently 'private' context not to require head-covering, or that the ecstasy of Spirit-inspiration caused head-coverings to slip. It is normally suggested, however, that there stands some theological principle behind their activity, for instance some appeal to the baptismal formula that 'there is neither male nor female' (Gal 3:28) in order to justify the abolition of gender distinctions. It is also possible that the practice was particularly sponsored by those 'virgins' Paul addresses in ch. 7, who as unmarried women may have wished to demonstrate their special relationship to God (7:34) by renouncing a common token of relatedness to a husband (see later, Tertullian, *On the Veiling of Virgins*). Whatever the cause, the practice brings to the surface deep anxieties in Paul concerning gender distinction, and he employs a battery of arguments from theology, Scripture, custom, and 'reason' to reimpose what he insists is the universal Christian custom (v. 16).

His first move is to set up a hierarchy of 'heads', involving God, Christ, man, and woman (v. 3). 'Head' (Gk. *kephalē*) probably indicates 'authority'; some have taken it to mean 'source', but in either case the chain suggests subordination (on Christ's subordination to God, cf. 3:23 and 15:28). The use of 'head' language enables Paul to draw on both literal and metaphorical senses; the male with covered head disgraces his head (physical head and/or Christ), the female with uncovered head disgraces hers (physical and/or man, vv. 4–5). The cultural assumptions concerning 'shame' in this matter are clear in the parallels Paul draws with a woman whose hair is cut short or shaven (vv. 5–6): in both cases she was considered demeaned as a woman (cf. v. 15) and her femininity denied. Paul is concerned throughout this passage that genders should not be confused or rendered ambiguous.

v. 7 suggests a natural distinction between man (as image and glory/reflection of God) and woman (as glory/reflection of man). This represents a tendentious reading of Gen 1:26–7 (where male *and female* are created 'in the image of God'). The logic of the verse is obscure, but perhaps suggests that in worship of God the man's head should not be covered (since it brings glory to God), while the woman's should (since it brings glory to man). vv. 8–9 draw from Genesis 2 (Eve's creation from and for Adam) in order to reinforce the hierarchy suggested by the opening chain (v. 3). Thus a woman is required to have, literally, 'authority on her head' (v. 10). This must refer to the head-covering, but it is unclear whether it is a symbol of her authority to pray and prophesy (Hooker 1964), or of her submission to male authority. The reference to the angels in this verse is puzzling. Some take these as the angels who protect the orders of creation and are present at Cor-

inthian worship to ensure order (there are some parallels to this notion at Qumran). Others regard them in a more sinister light as the successors to the 'sons of God' (Gen 6:1–4) who are liable to lust after unveiled women (Gen 6 was much discussed in Jewish apocalyptic circles, cf. 1 *Enoch* 14–16). In vv. 11–12 Paul moves to moderate some of what he has asserted by pointing to the interdependence (not equality) of women and men in the cycle of life, but 'in the Lord' suggests some specifically Christian reality. Finally, he appeals to reason (vv. 13–16). The Corinthians should know what is 'proper' in the matter of hair and head-covering. The appeal to 'nature' in v. 14 with reference to the degradation of *long hair* shows how disastrously Paul has confused 'nature' and 'custom', a confusion which has led him to support cultural norms with arguments from 'creation'. He may realize that his arguments are not likely to persuade and thus resorts finally to an abrupt dismissal of 'contentiousness', refusing to allow further discussion on this matter (v. 16).

(11:17–34) Humiliation of Church Members at the Lord's Supper Paul now turns to a topic on which reports have suggested a fundamental dysfunction in the church in relation to a rite, the Lord's Supper, which should constitute the core of church life and enact the proclamation of the gospel. The seriousness with which he takes this issue is indicated by his claim that their present form of gathering is positively harmful (v. 17), by his suggestion that the behaviour of some might mark them out as false Christians (v. 19; cf. 9:27), and by his warning that their mishandling of the Supper could lead—in fact already had led—to illness and death as divine judgement (vv. 27–32). The divisions that he hears about (v. 18) appear to be primarily social, between the élite members of the church and lower-class Christians. The 'Lord's Supper' (v. 20) was a full meal, incorporating the sharing of bread and wine but not restricted to those foodstuffs. Paul is scandalized that what was meant to be a common meal has become a display of disunity in the church. It appears that wealthier members have been bringing their own supplies for the meal, starting the meal before all had arrived and keeping their own food largely, if not entirely, for themselves, so that they consume more (and perhaps better quality) food than poorer members (vv. 20–2). It was common at dinner-parties in the Graeco-Roman world for the host to give more and better food to his more distinguished guests, and perhaps Gaius, the host to the whole church (Rom 16:23), has simply followed cultural habits unthinkingly (Theissen 1982: 145–74). Thus Paul once again has to remind the wealthier members of the church of their responsibilities to their fellow Christians of lower status: by humiliating them in this fashion they are showing contempt for the church of God (v. 22; cf. 3:16–17 and 8:12).

To correct such abuse Paul first reminds them of the tradition he passed to them (vv. 23–6). These verses are actually our first witness to the form and understanding of the Lord's Supper in the early church, being earlier than the gospel accounts (Mk 14:22–4; Mt 26:26–8; Lk 22:17–20). This is the only incident in the life of Jesus that Paul ever recounts (apart from his crucifixion) and it seems to have become fixed relatively early as the founding narrative for an important Christian rite. We cannot tell precisely how Paul understood the identification between 'the bread' and 'the body' (v. 24) or between 'the cup' (note, not 'the wine') and 'the blood' (v. 25), though the reference to the new covenant and the notion of 'remembrance' seem to place greater emphasis on the relationship forged between the participant and the Lord than on the essence of the elements themselves. v. 26 seems to be Paul's own interpretation of the significance of the meal: through it the participants 'proclaim the Lord's death'. In the light of 1:18–2:5 it is not surprising that he finds the élitism and self-centredness of the higher-status Christians in Corinth constituting a denial of the message of Christ crucified.

Returning to the Corinthians' conduct, Paul warns them against eating and drinking 'in an unworthy manner' (v. 27). The context suggests that such carelessness about partaking in bread and wine includes the scandalous behaviour of those who humiliate other Christians at the Supper (vv. 20–2). Hence, the call to 'examine yourselves' (v. 28) must signal primarily a scrutiny of one's behaviour towards others in the church, not a general moral scrutiny of one's 'worthiness' to partake in a sacred meal. Eating and drinking requires 'discerning the body' (v. 29), discerning that the bread 'is' the body of Christ, but also that the church constitutes the body of Christ as it partakes of this 'one bread' (10:17; cf. 12:12–27). To defile the Supper is to show contempt for the church, and thus to invite the sort of judgement which God metes out to those who damage his temple (v. 29; 3:16–17). Such 'unworthy' eating makes one accountable for the body and blood of Christ (v. 27), in the sense that, rather than benefiting from the death of Christ, one is actually placed among his enemies and murderers (like 'the rulers of this age', 2:6–8). That would be to invite God's judgement (v. 29). Paul reckons some have already experienced this in illness and death (v. 30; cf. 5:5), though it is better to be judged in this way as a discipline than to be condemned utterly, like 'the world' (cf. 1:18; 3:15). The final instructions (vv. 33–4) show that the humiliation of the poorer members is still his chief concern: the 'brothers and sisters' should wait for one another and not indulge in grossly unequal feasts. The advice to satisfy hunger 'at home' (v. 34) might constitute a step towards separating the meal from the ritual sharing of bread and wine.

(12:1–31) The Distribution of Spiritual Gifts in the Body of Christ At v. 1 Paul turns directly to the issue of 'spiritual gifts' (the Greek could also mean 'spiritual people'). As ch. 14 will show, he is particularly concerned with their exercise in worship (a topic already touched on in 11:2–16). That chapter also indicates that the heart of the issue is the use of 'tongues', a gift of humanly incomprehensible speech which some Corinthian Christians apparently rate far higher than does Paul. The highly charged enthusiasm of the Corinthian church has led to an energetic use of the gifts of the Spirit (cf. 1:7) and a sense of fullness which Paul considers dangerously close to self-satisfaction (4:8). Here he is concerned lest the variety of gifts lead to disunity within the church, and create a hierarchy in which certain 'gifted' Christians despise others. The gift of tongues may be specially conducive to this sense of superiority, since it represents a dramatic and complete 'possession' by the Spirit of God, the gifted individual being considered to speak 'mysteries' (14:2) in 'the tongues of angels' (13:1). There is some evidence to suggest that such esoteric speech might be cultivated particularly by higher-status individuals, so that

this gift might reinforce the status differentials which we have found to be operative in other issues addressed by Paul (Martin 1991).

Paul's first warning is against naïvety (vv. 1–3). Not every form of 'possession' is God-inspired: the Corinthians should not assume that the more dramatic the 'ecstasy', the better the gift. In their religious past they experienced 'ecstasy' (v. 2; NRSV 'enticed' would be better translated 'moved'), but that was erroneous, inducing only worship of speechless 'idols'. The gift has to be tested by its result (v. 3): clearly the Spirit of God cannot inspire someone to say 'Jesus be cursed', while the basic Christian confession 'Jesus is Lord' is attributable only to the Spirit (cf. Rom 10:9; Phil 2:11). The point may seem obvious, but 'inspiration' was (and is) a problematic claim and needed to be tested by its effects (cf. 14:29; 1 Thess 5:19–21).

But there is another and larger point to be made: that no one gift should be regarded as of unique importance or played off against others (vv. 4–11). In a formulation which points towards later trinitarian doctrine, Paul insists that the varieties of gifts and services can be traced to the same Spirit/Lord/God (vv. 4–6). v. 11 will re-emphasize this point, while suggesting that the Spirit distributes gifts to every believer ('to each one individually') and according to the Spirit's choice, not his/her own (but cf. 12:31; 14:1). Thus none can boast of having a gift, which is precisely a *gift* (*charisma* means 'gift of grace'), not a possession or an achievement (cf. 4:7). Moreover, the gifts are given not for individual satisfaction or pride, but 'for the common good' (v. 7). Thus Paul again signals the criterion of 'benefit to others' which he has appealed to throughout (6:12; 8:1–3; 10:23–4, etc.) and which will form the theme of ch. 13 as the basis for ch. 14.

To illustrate the 'varieties of gifts', Paul gives a representative list in vv. 8–10. Parallel lists in v. 28 and in Rom 12:6–8 (cf. Eph 4:11) suggest that this is not meant to be an exhaustive inventory, but a display of the diversity which the Corinthians will recognize as operative among themselves. Some appear to overlap (e.g. utterance of wisdom and utterance of knowledge) or to be closely linked to others ('faith' in this context means the special exercise of faith required for the 'working of miracles', vv. 9–10; cf. 13:2). It is no accident that the gifts of tongues and their interpretation are placed at the bottom of the list (as also in v. 28). While not wishing to endorse explicitly a gift-hierarchy, Paul does want to demote tongues from the exalted position it holds in the estimation of some Corinthian Christians.

In v. 12 Paul introduces the metaphor of the body, which will dominate the rest of this chapter. The statement in v. 27 that 'you are the body of Christ' does not mean that the church constitutes, in some literal sense, the presence of Christ in the world; rather, the church is (like) a body which belongs to Christ, identified with the risen Christ ('so it is with Christ', v.12) but not identical to him. The body was commonly used in antiquity as a metaphor for human society (or for the whole cosmos), as a variegated organism whose diverse parts are interdependent. It was an image that could easily be exploited by élite classes to justify inequality, on the basis that it was necessary for inferior groups to play their part for the good of all (the Roman historian Livy uses it in this way). One of the striking aspects of Paul's use of the metaphor is that, in his hands, it not only justifies diversity in the church, but also works specifically *against* hierarchical notions of honour and differential importance.

The combination of diversity and unity—many limbs in one body—is the first point to be established (vv. 12–20). Baptismal formulae in v. 13 remind the Corinthians of their cultural and social diversity but also of their common access to the Spirit (cf. Gal 3:28, whose 'male and female' pairing is conspicuously absent here). vv. 14–19 illustrate the fact that a body, properly understood, must be a differentiated organism: it cannot all be of one part. Paul notably presents this fact from the point of view of a member which feels itself excluded because it is not something else (vv. 15–16). He thus identifies with the position of members of the church who are being made to feel inferior or marginalized, and insists on their rightful place within the body.

In vv. 21–6 Paul then develops this perspective by confronting the superior attitudes of the 'stronger' or more prominent Corinthian Christians. No member can dismiss others as dispensable (v. 21) because those which are apparently 'weaker' or less 'honourable' are in fact of crucial significance and accorded very great 'respect' by the rest of the body. He is thinking no doubt of the attitude we adopt to the vulnerable organs of the body and the genitalia, but his point is clearly meant to apply to the less 'honourable' members of the Corinthian church. We have noted at many points how the 'weaker' members in the church are being treated with less than full respect by higher-status Corinthian Christians (1:26–8; 8:1–13; 11:20–2). Paul here uses the body metaphor to overturn such attitudes, pointing out that the less 'respectable' are in fact accorded great respect, and that God has so designed this (vv. 22–4). This attribution of greater honour to the 'lesser' individual is based on the same principle as Paul had found in the message of the cross (1:18–2:5), where human values of power and wisdom are overturned. As in that passage, Paul finds here the solution to those pride-induced 'dissensions' which are springing up in the Corinthian church (v. 25; the same word is translated 'divisions' in 1:10). The mutuality of care for one another's interests which Paul had taught in chs. 8–10 (10:24, 32) is here illustrated by the concern of all the body's parts for the health and welfare of the rest (vv. 25–6).

The chapter is completed by making explicit the relevance of the metaphor to the Christians in Corinth (v. 27) and by another list of 'gifts' or 'appointments' (v. 28). Here some value distinctions are introduced ('first apostles' etc.) since Paul does regard some gifts as more conducive to the welfare of the body than others (as ch. 14 will illustrate); again tongues is last in the list! The point about necessary diversity in the body is finally driven home with a series of rhetorical questions (vv. 29–30) designed to undercut the notion that any one gift should be possessed by all, or that anyone is deficient in not possessing it. There *is* a sense in which some gifts are 'greater' (v. 31), but that is only because they facilitate the supreme virtue which Paul will now describe.

(13:1–13) The Superior and Critical Demands of Love This chapter has sometimes been considered a self-contained 'love-hymn', pre-prepared by Paul, whose present positioning creates a somewhat disappointing descent to the practicalities

of ch. 14. But in fact this prioritizing of love fits its present literary context and the precise needs of the Corinthian church exceptionally well, and in its sharp criticism of the values current among the Corinthians it is hardly an anodyne 'ode to love'. It is written in prose, not verse, but it clearly has poetic qualities both in the level of language and in its structural shaping. It falls naturally into three sections (vv. 1–3, 4–7, 8–13): the first and third match one another in their comparative evaluations of love, while the central section consists of thirteen simple verbs, arranged in order positive–negative–positive.

The first section (vv. 1–3) is made up of three conditional clauses, each complemented by a devastating statement of worthlessness. The first imagines the possession of all the possible gifts of speech which were so highly prized in Corinth, 'tongues of angels' perhaps describing the imagined content of 'speaking in tongues'. Without love, which can make such communication purposeful and beneficial to others, all such gifts, although genuinely gifts of the Spirit, are mere noise ('noisy gong' refers to the bronze products for which Corinth was famous). Similarly the powers of prophecy, knowledge, and faith (cf. 12:8–10; Mk 11:20–4) are valueless without love (v. 2). In fact, most challenging of all, even apparent acts of charity and self-sacrifice gain nothing at all, unless they are motivated and controlled by love (v. 3). A tiny textual variant could alter the sense in v. 3 from delivering the body 'that I may boast' to delivering it 'to be burned'. Commentators are evenly divided on the best reading here. It was perhaps unnecessary still to criticize boasting (cf. 4:7), so the reading 'to be burned' (e.g. in martyrdom) may be preferred. Even martyrdom is valueless unless it is founded on love.

The central stanza (vv. 4–7) provides a pen-portrait of 'love' (*agapē*), a term not coined in early Christianity but given special prominence and reshaped to express its peculiar ethos of self-sacrifice. The paragraph is made up of simple verbs or short clauses which define the quality of love, mostly by the attitudes it eschews. Two positive verbs open the list, which then contrasts love with a catalogue of spiritual failures in the Corinthian church: love is not envious (cf. 3:3), it is not boastful or arrogant (cf. 4:6, 18–19; 5:2; 8:1, etc.), it does not insist on its own way (cf. 10:24), nor rejoice in wrongdoing (cf. 5:1–2). The final four positive verbs (v. 7) expand the field of love's operation as widely as possible. Their link between love, faith, endurance, and hope matches the conglomerate of Christian virtues which Paul elsewhere uses to sum up the essence of Christian commitment (cf. v. 13; 1 Thess 1:3).

In the final paragraph (vv. 8–13) Paul returns to demonstrate the supreme value of love, now stressing not so much its indispensability (vv. 1–3) as its eternal worth. Paul is ever conscious of the provisional character of Christian existence before the *parousia* (cf. 15:19), and he cannot share the Corinthian sense of fullness (4:8). For him, the only characteristic of the present which is final and complete is love: 'love never ends' (v. 8). All other Christian qualities, even genuine gifts of the Spirit, are provisional and imperfect. The Corinthians value prophecy, tongues, and knowledge (cf. chs. 8–10 and 14), but all these, Paul insists, are only temporary phenomena (v. 8). For now, knowledge (and prophecy) are inescapably partial (v. 9), not only in the sense that they are incomplete (we know only some things) but also because they are imperfect (even what we 'know', we only partly comprehend; see P. W. Gooch 1987: 142–61). Like a child whose knowledge not only grows but also matures, so our present state of knowledge will appear 'childish' from the perspective of the final revelation (v. 11). Or, to use a different image, our present perception is inevitably indirect and distorted—in a mirror and 'dim'—while in the future we will see direct and clear, as clearly as we are already seen and known by God (v. 12; cf. 8:3). The abiding qualities, which already have a firm purchase on eternal truths, are faith, hope, and love (*not* the Corinthians' vaunted 'knowledge'). But the greatest of these, as the reflection of God's own character, is love (v. 13; cf. Rom 5:8).

(14:1–40) The Superiority of Prophecy over Tongues As the first phrase makes clear, ch. 14 draws its inspiration from the preceding eulogy of love, which is not a digression from the topic of spiritual gifts but an exposition of the virtue which enables the church to evaluate and prioritize those gifts. As concerns various forms of speech, love sets the priority as that which 'builds up' the church (v. 12; cf. 8:1). 'Building up' constitutes one of the two guiding principles of Paul's instructions concerning worship, the other being that which is 'decent' and 'orderly' (vv. 33, 40). The first part of this chapter is made up of four overlapping arguments for the superiority of prophecy over tongues (vv. 1–25). 'Prophecy' is never defined, but seems to constitute speech which instructs, encourages, consoles, or challenges its hearers (vv. 3, 24–5, 31). 'Tongues' are not foreign languages intelligible to native speakers (as are portrayed in Acts 2), but speech which is humanly unintelligible, being addressed primarily to God (v. 2). The phenomenon of such 'ecstatic speech' is quite widely attested in a variety of religions, though in antiquity it may have been specially prized by the social élite.

The first argument for the greater value of prophecy is that it strengthens the whole church, whereas tongues benefit only the individual gifted with them (vv. 1–5). Once again, Paul places a premium on what benefits the whole community (cf. 10:23–4), even if it be a less spectacular or mysterious gift than tongues. Their 'mysteries in the Spirit' (v. 2) are not understood even by fellow 'spiritual people', unless someone exercises the gift of interpretation (v. 5). Paul's wish that all speak in tongues or prophesy (v. 5) must be hypothetical (in the light of 12:29–30), but he simultaneously insists that what the Corinthians value most highly is actually of inferior value. Prophecy may be transitory and imperfect (13:8–10), but at least for the present it can be well used in the service of love.

The second argument develops the first by contrasting the unintelligibility of tongues—and therefore its worthlessness for others—with the intelligibility of prophecy (vv. 6–13). Again, the question is what benefit the speech has for others (v. 6). Tongues are as indistinct and incomprehensible as a musical instrument whose notes signify nothing to the hearer (vv. 7–8) or as a foreign language whose meaning we cannot grasp (v. 11). Paul recognizes and affirms the Corinthian 'zeal' for spiritual gifts (v. 12); nothing in this passage discourages the use of gifts as such. He simply wants the most useful (upbuilding) gifts to be regarded as of higher value, a recognition which will force the Corinthians to view themselves as a *community*, not as a collection of gifted individuals. Paul is

careful not to go so far as to ban the use of tongues, but he requires that their users should expect them to be turned into something beneficial through interpretation (v. 13).

The third argument (vv. 14–19) provides a different rationale for the superiority of prophecy: it involves both spirit and mind, whereas the gift of tongues engages only the spirit. Paul is probably speaking here of 'spirit' in the sense of human spirit, though it is closely linked with, and inspired by, the Spirit of God. We might expect this contrast to imply a higher evaluation of rationality, the engagement of the mind being exalted over 'irrational' speech. But it would be hard to argue that the human mind was a higher faculty than the Spirit-inspired spirit, and Paul's cherishing of the 'mind' turns out to be not on account of its rationality so much as its intelligibility to others, the goal being once again the 'upbuilding' or instruction of the hearers (vv. 17–19). This point is made by reference to prayer, singing, and the offering of thanksgiving to God, as the discussion broadens to cover wider aspects of worship (cf. v. 6). Thus Paul forces the Corinthians to consider what is appropriate 'in church', as opposed to in private. In a communal setting, intelligible words count for everything (v. 19). Again, Paul does not discredit tongues absolutely (he claims to be even more gifted than the Corinthians, 14:18!), but requires them to reconsider their appropriateness with a view to others' needs. He is challenging the same unconcern for others which had manifested itself at the Lord's Supper (11:20–2).

The final argument (vv. 20–5) is prefaced by a stinging rebuke of the Corinthians, who seem to have prided themselves on their maturity (v. 20, whose last phrase reads literally, 'in your minds be mature'; cf. 2:6–3:4). Paul turns to the only passage in 'the law' (here meaning the Scriptures as a whole) which might be relevant to the subject of 'tongues', a warning in Isa 28:11–12 about God speaking to his disobedient people through foreigners. At first sight, the lesson Paul draws from this passage in v. 22 (tongues are a sign for unbelievers, prophecy for believers) seems to be the reverse of his illustration in vv. 23–5, where he imagines the negative effects of tongues on 'outsiders' or 'unbelievers' (the two terms are probably synonyms) and the positive effects of prophecy. The clue probably lies back in the quotation itself, which Paul has slightly modified (adding 'even then') to suggest that the 'tongues' actually bring about, or confirm, unbelief. Thus the 'sign for' phrases in v. 22 should probably be taken to mean that tongues serve to strengthen unbelief, while prophecy serves to strengthen, or bring about, belief. Thus outsiders viewing the whole church speaking in tongues will not be attracted to the faith, but simply conclude that it is a form of madness (v. 23); while if they encounter prophecy in the church, they will be led to faith by a conviction of sin, a revealing of heart-secrets, and a recognition of God's presence in the church (vv. 24–5). This is a rare depiction of what Paul imagines to be the ingredients of 'conversion', indicating the importance for him of sin and judgement (cf. 4:4–5) and of the powerful presence of God (cf. Gal 3:2–5). His own experience in his call/conversion may also be reflected here in some measure.

The discussion can now broaden out to take in wider aspects of worship (vv. 26–40). This is the most complete image we get of earliest Christian worship, though we cannot tell whether Paul's prescription matches reality in the Corinthian church, or in any other. Paul certainly imagines the participation of any member of the community (there are no designated 'ministerial' roles), bringing whatever gifts they have, provided, once again, that they contribute to the task of 'building up' (v. 26). The 'lesson' here (v. 26) means teaching, not a reading from Scripture, an activity which is strikingly absent from this list of worship activities. The theme of the chapter makes the spotlight fall particularly on tongues and prophecy. The former are not banned, but restricted in number and admissible only if interpreted. The latter also is not to become a virtuoso performance: a number of prophets should be allowed to speak, their speech weighed as to its validity (cf. 2:15; 12:3), and room made for new speakers, whose prophecy is sparked by a further 'revelation' (vv. 29–31). Paul is striving to control the exuberance of the worship meetings, but also to prevent their domination by any one figure or clique: each member of the body has its part to play and none is entitled to dismiss the contribution of others as inconvenient or unnecessary (cf. 12:14–26).

The next paragraph (14:33b–36) has been the subject of intense debate. It seems to place a total ban on women's speech in church, which is strangely inconsistent with Paul's permission in 11:2–16 that (veiled) women could pray and prophesy. Also the argument depends on a vague and uncharacteristic appeal to 'the law' (v. 34) and appears to assume that all the women will have husbands to ask 'at home' (v. 35), despite Paul's acceptance that the single and celibate option is prudent for both women and men (ch. 7). Such facts prompt one of two conclusions. Either Paul is truly inconsistent here, reacting against a threat of 'unruly' women by forbidding their verbal participation, despite what he had earlier allowed. Or this passage is an interpolation into the letter by a later editor, one who took the opportunity of the surrounding context to introduce the restrictive ethos of the Pastoral letters (e.g. 1 Tim 2:8–15, part of a letter generally regarded as written by a later Paulinist, not by Paul himself). This latter option is favoured by many commentators, and it is given slight textual support by the fact that some manuscripts place vv. 34–5 at the end of the chapter, rather than in their present location; that might indicate that they were once a marginal gloss which was inserted by scribes at varying points into the original text (see Fee 1987: 699–708). There have been numerous speculations about a particular local problem in Corinth (e.g. women who rudely interrupted prophecy, or questioned their husbands in 'weighing' their prophecies, see Jervis 1995) which might or might not explain this outburst if it is genuinely from Paul. But as it stands the passage seems to presuppose that women in all Paul's churches were wholly silent, which hardly fits what we know of women leaders in Pauline congregations (e.g. Rom 16:1–2, 3–5, 7; Phil 4:2).

Paul closes the discussion with a strong assertion of his authority (derived from the Lord) and a refusal to countenance contrary opinions even from prophets or so-called 'spiritual' people (vv. 37–8). The strength of his tone suggests that the whole chapter is directed against a dominant individual or group whose use of gifts is stifling the life of the congregation. The final verses (39–40) summarize the priorities set by the chapter and highlight the need for order; disorder is easily exploited by the strong.

The Resurrection of Christ and the Resurrection Body (15:1–58)

This chapter stands somewhat alone in the flow of topics in the letter and it may appear odd that the heavy emphasis on the cross as the heart of the gospel in chs. 1–2 should be diluted by the equal insistence here on the centrality of the resurrection (2:2 is somewhat contradicted by 15:3–5). Yet the discussion of the body in 6:12–20 gave an indication that Paul considered the Corinthians' understanding of resurrection to lie at the root of other problems in their church (see esp. 6:12–14). It is difficult to be sure how the Corinthians did understand resurrection. Were they uninterested in a future resurrection because they considered themselves already 'raised' (cf. 4:8; 1 Tim 2:18)? Or did they disbelieve any future life after death? In fact, the main focus of the chapter (at least from v. 35 onwards) is the notion of a resurrection body, and it is most likely that the Corinthians believed in the existence of some post-mortem state, but one free from the restrictions of the body. Their belief in some form of afterlife seems implied by their practice of vicarious baptism for the dead (v. 29), but it was common in Hellenized circles (both Greek and Jewish) to consider the body an encumbrance which the soul will gladly shed after death. For Paul, their doubt about the sense or value of a 'resurrection body' suggests that they are beginning to question an essential element of their faith, the resurrection of Christ; it also indicates a lack of trust in God's creative power to bring life out of death in whatever form he chooses. Thus he insists on the apocalyptic notion of a final battle against the powers of death (vv. 20–8) and defends the idea of a resurrection body, though dispelling crude notions of physical identity between the present and the future body (vv. 35–57).

Paul begins by pointedly reminding them of the terms on which they entered the faith—terms which they must continue to accept if they are to remain secure (vv. 1–2). The important point is that these terms included belief in the resurrection of Jesus, and it is this topic which Paul emphasizes in citing a foundational credal statement (vv. 3–7). This creed is introduced in v. 3 in technical terms signifying the transmission of tradition, one which Paul must have inherited (in Antioch?) before he founded the church in Corinth (50–1 CE). It thus constitutes the earliest known Christian creed. Its structure is clear: two main 'that' clauses concerning, respectively, the death and the resurrection of Christ, each backed by reference to the Scriptures, and two supplementary 'that' clauses about the burial (reinforcing the death) and the appearances (supporting the resurrection). It is not clear precisely what scriptures are alluded to in this formula nor is it obvious where the original creed ceased: some think it ran no further than v. 5, others as far as v. 7.

This creed constitutes our earliest literary evidence to belief in the resurrection of Christ, and it is often remarked that it makes no mention of the empty tomb or of the women who witnessed the scene (and the risen Christ) according to the stories in the gospels. That silence has suggested to some the late emergence of the story of the empty tomb (first attested in Mk 16, in the late 60s CE), though others consider the silence merely accidental. In any case, it is striking that Paul supports the notion of the resurrection of Jesus purely on the grounds of the resurrection appearances. Those appearances he lists are not all easily correlated with the gospel stories, which also differ among themselves, though the appearance to Cephas may correspond to Lk 24:34, and the appearance to 'the twelve' with stories in Lk 24 and Jn 20.

One reason for Paul's concentration on these appearances is that he can add his own testimony at the end of the list (v. 8). He took his commissioning to his apostleship to be the final resurrection appearance, although Luke placed it in a quite different category in the narrative of the book of Acts. This claim to a vision of Christ was crucial to Paul's self-belief as an apostle (cf. 9:1), and it leads him into a brief digression about his apostleship (vv. 9–10), which reveals much about his sense of inferiority (as a former persecutor), his radical appreciation of grace, and his hope of outdoing other apostles (cf. 9:3–18). Returning to the topic (v. 11), he insists that the same resurrection-centred message was taught by all the apostles and was the basis of the Corinthians' faith.

The next paragraph (vv. 12–19) unearths the reason for Paul's concern that the Corinthians 'hold firm' to the message he delivered: he thinks they are beginning to waver in their faith in the resurrection of Jesus since some say 'there is no resurrection of the dead' (v. 12). As noted above, the Corinthians' doubts probably concerned the notion of a bodily resurrection, as indeed the phrase 'the resurrection of the dead' (which could be taken literally as 'the raising of corpses') might suggest a crude notion of physical reconstitution after death. Paul himself does not envisage resurrection in such crude terms, but his first reaction is to insist that to doubt the notion of a resurrection of the dead is to doubt the resurrection of Christ, which was a cardinal tenet of their creed. He now runs through a logical argument twice (vv. 13–15 and 16–19) with slight variations in emphasis. First: if there is no resurrection, then Christ has not been raised, then our preaching of that fact was worthless and so is your faith, which is based on that fact (vv. 13–14); indeed, the apostles are then vulnerable to the charge of lying about God, for claiming he raised Christ from the dead (v. 15). Secondly: if the dead are not raised, then Christ has not been raised, then your faith is futile and 'you are still in your sins' (vv. 16–17)—that is, you cannot depend on the other part of the creed, that 'Christ died for our sins' (v. 3). That means all grounds of hope are destroyed. As far as Paul is concerned, the future hope is such a necessary counterweight to the difficulties of the 'present evil age' (Gal 1:4) that, if it were proved to be groundless, Christians would turn out to be especially pitiable. The Corinthians may not have denied all future hope, but Paul insists on depicting the whole of the slippery slope which he thinks they have started to descend.

Corinthian doubts have challenged a basic element in Paul's theology and he now demonstrates the pivotal significance of the resurrection of Jesus within the scheme of salvation (vv. 20–8). This scheme is founded on an apocalyptic notion of the age of death being succeeded and overcome by an age of life, the latter being ushered in by a cosmic act of resurrection (de Boer 1988). For Paul, the resurrection of Christ constitutes the 'first fruits' of that cosmic act (vv. 20, 23), the beginning of the harvest which heralds the proximity of the rest. Pairing Christ with Adam (cf. Rom 5:12–20), Paul finds in Christ the start of a new humanity, in which the failures of the present (encapsulated in death) are replaced by the possibilities of the future (resurrection and life). The key text in vv. 27–8 is Ps 8:6, which concerns the intended dignity of humankind: that role is now fulfilled in the 'final Adam' (cf. v. 45) and made possible through him for all (v. 22). That 'all' could be taken to mean 'the whole of humanity', thus implying a kind of universalism (cf. Rom 5:18; 11:32), though the subsequent reference to 'those who belong to Christ' (v. 23) and the earlier dismissals of non-believers (e.g. 1:18; 6:9–10) suggest that Paul did not carry through its universalistic potential. The cosmic transformation thus takes place in successive phases: first, the resurrection of Christ, then, at his coming, those who belong to him; 'then' (meaning probably, 'at that same moment', though some see here a further phase), it will be 'the end' when God's kingdom is complete and all the enemies of his rule are defeated. In this apocalyptic scenario the risen Christ plays a crucial role: it is through his present reign that God's enemies are being defeated (v. 25), as God puts them in subjection to him (vv. 27–8). Even so, Paul insists that Christ is ultimately subordinate to God, who is not himself, of course, subject to Christ (v. 27) but is the one to whom Christ is subject in 'handing over the kingdom' (v. 24; cf. 3:23; Rom 11:36).

The next section of the chapter (vv. 29–34) contains miscellaneous arguments which indicate the significance of belief in life beyond death. The reference to baptism 'on behalf of the dead' (v. 29) has been the subject of multiple interpretations (some of which construe the Greek quite differently). It probably refers to a rite in which a few Corinthian believers underwent a vicarious baptism in the place of those (believers?) who had died either unbaptized or 'improperly' baptized. 1:12–17 suggests that some Corinthians regarded baptism by certain figures as of great significance, and they may have wished to make up for a 'lack' in the case of those who were baptized by different leaders or in a different way. Paul does not condemn such a practice, and he is willing to use it to show that the Corinthians themselves entertain hopes for an existence beyond death.

Turning to himself, he indicates how his own life is founded on the same principle of hope (vv. 30–2). It is only because his investments lie beyond his present physical existence that he is prepared to take such risks with his life—exposed daily to the threat of death. Indeed, he has recently undergone some specially dangerous experience in Ephesus (v. 32); here 'fighting with wild beasts' must be a metaphor, or he would not have lived to tell the tale, but it is not clear what sort of crisis it refers to. The Corinthians need to be warned and shamed (vv. 32–4; cf. 4:14; 6:5). If they lose their faith in the resurrection of the dead, they have lapsed into mere hedonism (v. 32, citing Isa 22:13) and will end up corrupting their morals (v. 33, citing a popular proverb originating with the poet Menander). The final comment, that some have 'no knowledge of God' (v. 34) is particularly biting considering the Corinthians' boast of 'knowledge' (8:1, 4).

In v. 35 Paul reaches what is probably the heart of his dispute with the Corinthians: the means and meaning of a resurrection body. On this topic he attempts to preserve a fine and difficult balance. He insists on keeping the term 'body'

(Gk. *sōma*) in describing the future state, but also stresses the *discontinuity* between the present and the future body, leaving somewhat ambiguous the relation between the two. The first stage of his argument (vv. 36–41) is the insistence that there are many types of 'body', each with variant degrees of 'glory': in talking about the resurrection of the dead our minds should not be restricted by what we presently experience as 'body' with its rather limited glory. The analogy of the seed (vv. 36–8) illustrates the possibility of very different 'bodies' either side of death, and the insistence that 'God gives the seed a body as he has chosen' (v. 38) places the emphasis on *God's* re-creative power. The Corinthians' doubts indicate that they have placed their confidence in the continuation of their 'spiritual' selves beyond death, rather than in God, whose future act of resurrection will demonstrate his *sole* power over the forces of sin and death (cf. 1:30–1). The analogy also indicates the variety of different 'bodies' resulting from seeds, which is further illustrated by reference to the varieties of 'flesh' and the difference between 'heavenly' and 'earthly' bodies (vv. 39–41). In antiquity the stars and planets were generally considered to be living matter with a constitution much more glorious and ethereal than that of earthbound creatures. Paul is thus suggesting that a resurrection body could be a body of a much higher order than our present physical condition, though the point hardly works for us who know that the stars are not a different order of creation, but as physical, material, and destructible as ourselves.

vv. 42–50 apply the illustrations to the topic in hand. What is 'sown' (in death) is one kind of body—perishable, inglorious, and weak—but what is raised can be a body of a wholly different kind. One is a 'physical body': the Greek *psychikon sōma* means a body animated by a soul (*psychē*), which is here taken to be mortal and temporary. The other is a 'spiritual body': the Greek *pneumatikon sōma* indicates a body inhabited by spirit (*pneuma*), here perhaps the Spirit of God. Paul thus wishes to preserve the term 'body' but only when it is shorn of its connotations of physicality and mortality. The impersonal statements, 'it is sown a physical body, it is raised a spiritual body', leave unclear whether the physical body is itself reused in the resurrection or whether the self gains a new body quite distinct from the old. This ambiguity matches Paul's silence as to what happened to the body of Jesus and whether his tomb was empty. At least v. 50 makes clear that the present physical body ('flesh and blood') is quite unfit for 'the kingdom of God', though whether entry into that kingdom involves the *transformation* of the present body or the granting of an essentially *new* body is left undefined in this chapter and is not consistently dealt with elsewhere (cf. Rom 8:11; Phil 3:21; 2 Cor 5:1–11). vv. 45–9 develop the contrast between the *psychikon sōma* and the *pneumatikon sōma* by reference to their two prototypes: Adam, the first man, made from the dust, who became a living (but mortal) *psychē* (Gen 2:7) and Christ, the final Adam, whose origin is heaven, and who is a life-giving (and immortal) *pneuma*. Our present bodies are as perishable as Adam's ('we bear the image of the man of dust'), but the future resurrection body will bear the image of Christ (v. 49).

Thus the chapter finishes with a triumphant declaration of the hope on which the whole Christian faith depends, a 'mystery' which makes sense of the present in the light of the future (vv. 51–8; cf. 2:9–10). Although not all will die first

('sleep'), it is certainly the case that all will be changed, that is, our perishable selves will become imperishable and fit for the 'kingdom of God' (v. 50). Using traditional apocalyptic imagery, Paul imagines this great change taking place 'at the last trumpet' (v. 52; cf. 1 Thess 4:16; Rev 8:6). Since he supposes here that he and his generation will be alive at this end-point in history (cf. 7:29–31; 1 Thess 4:15, 17), he distinguishes between 'the dead' who will be raised in the new imperishable state and 'we' who will be changed from a mortal life to a new immortal state (vv. 52–4). At that moment the final enemy, death, will be destroyed (cf. v. 26), and Paul celebrates with two Scripture citations, one (v. 54) from Isa 25:8, a passage full of eschatological promises, the other (v. 55) from Hos 13:14, a passage which he wilfully reads against its grain: the prophet invited death to wield its sting, but Paul employs his words to taunt death with its ultimate powerlessness. Death's sting is already at work in the power of sin, a power derived from the law (v. 56; the themes are elaborated in Rom 6–7); but we are granted victory over both by God (cf. Rom 8:37–9). That means for now persistence in faith and action, since 'the work of the Lord' is of ultimate and lasting significance (v. 58), like love, which is its chief characteristic (13:13; 16:14).

Letter Closing, with Travel Plans, Final Instructions, and Greetings (16:1–24)

This final chapter covers a range of topics which bear on Paul's relationship to the church in Corinth, issues which either had already become problematic or would soon become so. The 'collection for the saints' (vv. 1–4) is the collection Paul had agreed to gather for the church in Jerusalem (Gal 2:10). His problem was in persuading his churches to support this project, since his intentions for this money were open to question and the necessity of the collection was not obvious to all. Paul here suggests a mechanism for regular storing of money on 'the first day of the week', that is, Sunday; nothing is implied here about worship on Sundays. He is trying to avoid a sudden and potentially embarrassing demand for money when he arrives in Corinth. He also suggests that the Corinthians participate in its delivery, to offset suspicions about its destination. It is clear from 2 Cor 8 and 9 that this advice went unheeded and the Corinthians proved extremely unwilling to contribute to the collection (cf. 2 Cor 12:14–18). However, Rom 15:25–7 suggests that Paul was eventually successful, if the reference to Achaia there includes the church at Corinth (the capital of the province).

Paul's description of his travel plans (vv. 5–9) seems designed to explain why he is unable to visit Corinth immediately: he is detained in Ephesus for the sake of the gospel and wants to wait till he can pay more than a fleeting visit to Corinth. 4:18–19 indicated that Paul was criticized for his absence from Corinth, but the promises he now makes proved to be fateful. He subsequently decided to visit them on his way both *to* and *from* Macedonia, and then had such a painful time in Corinth that he did not come back (2 Cor 1:15–2:2). As 2 Corinthians shows, this constant shifting of plans exposed Paul to acute criticism from certain figures in the church, and undermined the church's confidence in his word.

Meanwhile, Paul is sending Timothy as his delegate (vv. 10–11). It is unclear why that visit, promised in 4:17, is now somewhat indefinite, but the note of fear concerning his reception in Corinth is revealing: if Paul's assistant is likely to be 'despised' in Corinth, Paul's own standing cannot be very secure. As for Apollos (v. 12), we can only speculate why Paul wanted him in Corinth (where he was the figurehead of a 'rival' party, 1:12) and why he was unwilling to go (v. 12). As in 3:5–9, Paul seems anxious to show that he and Apollos are not at odds nor wishing to undermine each other's work.

The general instructions of vv. 13–14 (cf. 15:58 and ch. 13) lead into a specific recommendation of the household of Stephanas (vv. 15–18). Their 'service of the saints' (v. 15) probably consisted of financial support of the church in Corinth. Given what we have glimpsed of leadership contests in the church, this strong recommendation constitutes Paul's bid to ensure that leadership remains in (or reverts to) this household: their presence with Paul at the time of writing has given him the opportunity to hear about the situation in Corinth and to mould the thinking of people who he hopes will influence the rest of the church. We cannot tell what relationship Fortunatus and Achaicus had to Stephanas; they perhaps belonged to his 'household', as slaves, freedmen, or free dependants.

The final greetings (vv. 19–24) are distinguished by special reference to Aquila and Prisca, the couple who had hosted Paul in Corinth at the foundation of the church (Acts 18:2–3). The 'holy kiss' (v. 20) may have been a common sign of recognition among Christian believers (cf. 1 Thess 5:26) and is here contrasted with a curse on any who 'has no love for the Lord' (v. 22). This is perhaps a formulaic phrase defining Christian identity (cf. 12:3), while the last words of v. 22 are a Greek transliteration of an Aramaic acclamation ('Marana tha') which must derive from early Jewish Christianity. Paul's own handwriting (v. 21; cf. Gal 6:11) gives a personal tone to the close of the letter, which has been calculated throughout to restore the allegiance of the Corinthians to himself, though not for his own sake, only in order to ensure their continuance 'in Christ Jesus' (v. 24; cf. 1:9).

REFERENCES

Barclay, J. M. G. (1992), 'Thessalonica and Corinth: Social Contrasts in Pauline Christianity', *JSNT* 47: 49–74.

—— (1996), *Jews in the Mediterranean Diaspora from Alexander to Trajan (323 BCE–117 CE)* (Edinburgh: T. & T. Clark).

Barrett, C. K. (1971), *A Commentary on the First Epistle to the Corinthians*, 2nd edn. (London: A. & C. Black).

—— (1982), *Essays on Paul* (London: SPCK).

Bartchy, S. S. (1973), *MALLON CHRESAI: First-Century Slavery and 1 Corinthians 7.21* (Missoula: Scholars Press).

Brown, P. (1988), *The Body and Society: Men, Women and Sexual Renunciation in Early Christianity* (London: Faber & Faber).

Chow, J. K. (1992), *Patronage and Power: A Study of Social Networks in Corinth* (Sheffield: JSOT).

Clarke, A. D. (1993), *Secular and Christian Leadership in Corinth: A Socio-Historical and Exegetical Study of 1 Corinthians 1–6* (Leiden: Brill).

Dahl, N. A. (1967), 'Paul and the Church at Corinth according to 1 Corinthians 1–4', in W. R. Farmer *et al.* (eds.), *Christian History and Interpretation: Studies Presented to John Knox* (Cambridge: Cambridge University Press), 313–35.

de Boer, M. C. (1988), *The Defeat of Death: Apocalyptic Eschatology in 1 Corinthians 15 and Romans 5* (Sheffield: JSOT).

—— (1994), 'The Composition of 1 Corinthians', *NTS* 40: 229–45.

Deming, W. (1995), *Paul on Marriage and Celibacy: The Hellenistic Background of 1 Corinthians 7* (Cambridge: Cambridge University Press).

Dunn, J. D. G. (1991), *The Partings of the Ways between Christianity and Judaism* (London: SCM).

Fee, G. D. (1987), *The First Epistle to the Corinthians*, New International Commentary on the New Testament, (Grand Rapids, Mich.: Eerdmans).

Frör, H. (1995), *You Wretched Corinthians!* (London: SCM).

Gooch, P. D. (1993), *Dangerous Food: 1 Corinthians 8–10 in Its Context* (Waterloo, Ont.: Wilfrid Laurier University Press).

Gooch, P. W. (1987), *Partial Knowledge: Philosophical Studies in Paul* (Notre Dame: University of Notre Dame Press).

Goulder, M. D. (1991), 'SOPHIA in 1 Corinthians', *NTS* 37: 516–34.

Hays, R. B. (1989), *Echoes of Scripture in the Letters of Paul* (New Haven: Yale University Press).

Hooker, M. D. (1963) '"Beyond the things which are written": An Examination of 1 Cor iv. 6', *NTS* 10: 127–32, repr. in *From Adam to Christ: Essays on Paul*, (Cambridge: Cambridge University Press), 106–12.

—— (1964), 'Authority on her Head: An Examination of 1 Cor. 11.10', *NTS* 10: 410–16, repr. in *From Adam to Christ: Essays on Paul* (Cambridge: Cambridge University Press), 113–20.

Hurd, J. C. (1965), *The Origin of 1 Corinthians* (London: SPCK).

Hurtado, L. W. (1988), *One God, One Lord: Early Christian Devotion and Ancient Jewish Monotheism* (London: SCM).

Jervis, L. A. (1995), '1 Corinthians 14.34–35: A Reconsideration of Paul's Limitation of the Free Speech of Some Corinthian Women', *JSNT* 58: 51–74.

Litfin, D. (1994), *St. Paul's Theology of Proclamation: 1 Corinthians 1–4 and Greco-Roman Rhetoric* (Cambridge: Cambridge University Press).

Lüdemann, G. (1984), *Paul, Apostle to the Gentiles: Studies in Chronology* (London: SCM).

Martin, D. B. (1990), *Slavery as Salvation: The Metaphor of Slavery in Pauline Christianity* (New Haven: Yale University Press).

—— (1991), 'Tongues of Angels and Other Status Indicators', *AAR* 59: 547–89.

—— (1995), *The Corinthian Body* (New Haven: Yale University Press).

Meeks, W. A. (1983), *The First Urban Christians: The Social World of the Apostle Paul* (New Haven: Yale University Press).

Meggitt, J. J. (1998), *Paul, Poverty and Survival* (Edinburgh: T. & T. Clark).

Mitchell, M. M. (1992), *Paul and the Rhetoric of Reconciliation*, (Louisville, Ky.: Westminster/John Knox).

Murphy-O'Connor, J. (1980), 'Sex and Logic in 1 Corinthians 11.2–16', *CBQ* 42: 482–500.

Pearson, B. A. (1973), *The Pneumatikos-Psychikos Terminology in 1 Corinthians* (Missoula: Scholars Press).

Rosner, B. S. (1994), *Paul, Scripture and Ethics: A Study of 1 Corinthians 5–7* (Leiden: Brill).

Schmithals, W. (1971), *Gnosticism in Corinth* (Nashville: Abingdon).

Theissen, G. (1982), *The Social Setting of Pauline Christianity* (Edinburgh: T. & T. Clark).

—— (1987), *Psychological Aspects of Pauline Christianity* (Edinburgh: T. & T. Clark).

Thiselton, A. C. (1977–8), 'Realized Eschatology at Corinth', *NTS* 24: 510–26.

Thompson, C. L. (1988), 'Hairstyles, Head-coverings and St. Paul: Portraits from Roman Corinth', *Biblical Archaeologist*, 51: 99–115.

Willis, W. L. (1985), *Idol Meat in Corinth: The Pauline Argument in 1 Corinthians 8 and 10* (Chico, Calif.: Scholars Press).

Winter, B. (1991), 'Civil Litigation in Secular Corinth and the Church: The Forensic Background to 1 Corinthians 6.1–8', *NTS* 37: 559–72.

Wire, A. C. (1990), *The Corinthian Women Prophets* (Minneapolis: Fortress).

66. 2 Corinthians

MARGARET MACDONALD

INTRODUCTION

A. Literary Structure. 1. It is a generally held view today that 2 Corinthians is made up of more than one of Paul's letters. Although there is no MS evidence to support this theory, there are several problems in the text as we have it which raise the question of its unity. Among the more serious difficulties is the sharp break between the conciliatory tone of chs. 1–9 and the harsh, sarcastic tone of chs. 10–13. Several partition theories have been developed in order to explain these difficulties, and these theories may be divided into two major schools. (1) Some scholars divide the text into five or six fragments and then reconstruct the chronology of Paul's dealings with the Corinthians on the basis of these units (e.g. 2:14–6:13; 7:2–4 + 10:1–13:10 + 1:1–2:13; 7:5–16; 13:11–13 + ch. 8 + ch. 9 + 6:14–7:1; Betz 1992: 1149–50). (2) Other scholars do not view the points of discontinuity in chs. 1–9 as being severe enough to warrant theories of partition of those chapters, but nevertheless see a significant break between chs. 1–9 and chs. 10–13. Therefore, they argue in favour of a two-letter hypothesis. This is the position adopted here (cf. Furnish 1984: 35–41). Whether chs. 1–9 came before or after chs. 10–13 is a further subject for debate, but more scholars seem to be in favour of the priority of chs. 1–9. According to the proponents of the various partition theories, the NT work called 2 Corinthians is the product of an early editor who combined two or more fragments drawn from originally independent letters. However, some scholars continue to defend the integrity of the letter (e.g. Witherington 1995: 328–39).

2. In form and style 2 Corinthians closely resembles Paul's other works, and its authenticity has not been questioned. However, the language and content of 2 Cor 6:14–7:1 have struck many as being difficult to reconcile with Paul's other writings and, therefore, this passage has often been viewed as an interpolation.

B. Date and Social Setting. 1. In addition to the correspondence which was included in the NT, the Corinthian letters themselves bear witness to additional writings which are either non-extant or have been subsumed along with other letters within the body of 2 Corinthians (see 2 COR A.1). 1 Cor 5:9 demonstrates that Paul wrote a letter prior to 1 Corinthians, probably concerning the immoral behaviour of church members. Some have identified this letter with 2 Cor 6:14–7:1. 1 Corinthians was written around 54 CE in response to a letter from the Corinthians which had raised several questions. The events which precipitated the correspondence known as 2 Corinthians are a subject of great debate and we are limited to conjecture concerning them. One possible reconstruction of events is as follows. It appears that between the time of the composition of 1 Corinthians and 2 Corinthians (or fragments thereof), Paul paid an emergency 'sorrowful visit' to Corinth (2 Cor 2:1). This probably was the apostle's second visit to the community (cf. 2 Cor 12:14; 13:1), the first being the occasion of the founding of the community

in 50 or 51 CE. It seems that this second visit did not go well (2 Cor 2:1–11; 7:12) and Paul followed it up with a 'tearful letter' (2 Cor 2:4; 2:2–11; 7:5–12). Although some have identified this letter with 2 Cor 10–13, it is more likely that it has been lost. A subsequent report to Paul that his 'tearful letter' had produced the desired effect in the community led to the composition in Macedonia in 55–6 CE of 2 Cor 1–9 (2 Cor 7:5; cf. 2 Cor 2:12–13; 8:1; 9:2). Titus apparently delivered this letter to the congregation (2 Cor 7:4–16; cf. 2 Cor 8:17–18). However, the situation deteriorated again. Some months later Paul wrote 2 Cor 10–13, also probably from Macedonia. In this letter he stated his intention to come to the community a third time (2 Cor 12:14; 13:1). (This reconstruction follows Furnish 1988: 1191–2 closely and is based on the two-letter hypothesis. For an alternative reconstruction based upon the five-(or six-)letter hypothesis see Betz 1992: 1149–52.)

2. When Paul wrote 1 Corinthians, he responded to problems involving community division and behaviour, problems he felt were incompatible with membership in Christ's body. By the time of the composition of 2 Corinthians (or various letter fragments), community problems extended to include the nature of the apostle's relationship with the Corinthians. Indeed, some wonder whether the harsh, critical—even sardonic—tone of 1 Corinthians may have alienated its recipients to the extent that a second, more conciliatory letter was required. Convinced that the relationship was severely threatened, and of the need for reconciliation, Paul set out to defend his apostolic authority. By the time that 2 Cor 10–13 was composed (See 2 COR A.1) the situation had become acute, due to the influence of apostolic rivals in the community. Throughout 2 Cor 10–13 Paul's preoccupation with these rivals is evident, but there are also insinuations in earlier chapters of threats by opponents to Paul's apostleship (e.g. 2 Cor 3:1–6). The nature of Paul's authority is a theme which runs throughout 2 Corinthians, and this text has therefore been of great interest to scholars concerned with the general question of how Paul exercised authority and distributed power in the community (Schütz 1975; Holmberg 1980; Meeks 1983; MacDonald 1988). Often these scholars draw upon social-scientific insights such as the foundational theories of the sociologist Max Weber on charisma and authority. Some of the specific issues under investigation include Paul's apostolic credentials and talents, his involvement in the collection for the Jerusalem church, and his attitude towards receiving material support from the congregation. Paul's use of a 'theology of the cross' (which locates power in weakness; 2 COR 4:7–15) to anchor his apostolic authority in a divine mandate has also been of considerable interest.

3. Corinth became a Roman colony in 44 BCE and architectural, artefactual, and inscriptional evidence points to a strong Romanizing influence in this old Hellenistic city (Witherington 1995: 6–7). The growing awareness of the need to understand NT groups in the light of the context of Graeco-Roman society has had an important effect on the study of 2 Corinthians. For example, comparison of 2 Cor 8–9 to adminis- trative correspondence in the empire has shed light upon the form and purpose of these chapters (Betz 1985). Increasingly, scholars are examining the influence of Greek rhetorical style upon Paul. The obvious use of such rhetorical devices as parody in 2 Cor 10–13 has invited further probing on the way Paul forms and develops his arguments in 2 Corinthians. It is now possible to say that rhetorical analysis of 2 Corinthians represents an important methodological approach, one which complements more traditional exercises in historical criti- cism. Rhetorical analysis sheds light on questions ranging from the purpose of the letter to its literary integrity (e.g. Young and Ford 1987; Marshall 1987; Crafton 1990; With- erington 1995). The recognition of the importance of rhetoric in the ancient world and in the letters of Paul has also contributed to a further understanding of Paul's emphasis on boasting and self-praise in 2 Corinthians. Public demon- strations of self-worth (which included performances of rhetoric) were a central means of establishing one's authority in a society which had an honour/shame orientation (Witherington 1995: 6, 432–7; 2 COR 1:12–14; 2 COR 4:1–6). Investigation of the structures of the patron–client relation- ship in the ancient world has also shed light on Paul's interaction with the Corinthians (Marshall 1987; Chow 1992; Witherington 1995; 2 COR 5:11–19; 2 COR 8:16–24; 2 COR 10:12–18).

C. Opponents. There has been extensive discussion concern- ing the identity of Paul's opponents in 2 Corinthians (e.g. Barrett 1971; Thrall 1980; Georgi 1986). The consensus is that the problems concerning opponents in 2 Corinthians must be distinguished from the factions and opposition ap- parent in 1 Corinthians, even though there may have been some connection between the two. In contrast to 1 Cor- inthians, in 2 Corinthians it is clear that the opponents were intruders, that is, they came from outside the community (2 Cor 10:13–16; 11:4, 19–20). It is also clear that they were Jewish (2 Cor 11:22). But there has been no general agreement on the nature of their Jewish teaching (Murphy-O'Connor 1990: 817). Some have viewed the opponents as Judaizers who were connected to the Jerusalem church (Barrett 1971). Others have understood their spirituality in light of diaspora Judaism and their mission as based in the demonstration of ecstatic experiences and the performance of miracles. Hellen- istic Jewish missionaries may have propounded notions of Jesus as the 'divine man' (Georgi 1986: 246–83). There are several difficulties associated with extracting information con- cerning these opponents and their influence in the commu- nity. It is sometimes difficult to know whether Paul is responding directly to new problems created by the oppo- nents who have penetrated the community from the outside, or to more general tendencies in Corinth which have been exacerbated by his rivals. How one interprets the evidence is determined to a significant extent by what one makes of possible thematic connections between 1 and 2 Corinthians (Matthews 1994: 199–200). In addition, although Paul some- times quotes his rivals directly, his polemical stance makes it difficult to extract accurate information concerning their teaching. The apostle's use of various labels for his opponents, such as 'super-apostles' (2 Cor 11:5; 12:11) and 'false apostles' '

(2 Cor 11:13), has also led to discussion of whether one or more groups of opponents are in view (see 2 COR 11:5–15).

D. Outline.
Introduction (1:1–11)
    Address (1:1–2)
    Blessing (1:3–11)
Paul the Conciliator (1:12–9:15)
    Explanations and Future Plans (1:12–2:13)
    The Authority of the Apostle (2:14–5:19)
    Appeals for Reconciliation with the Apostle (5:20–7:16)
    Appeals about the Collection (8:1–9:15)
Paul on the Attack (10:1–13:10)
    Preliminary Defence (10:1–18)
    The Fool's Speech (11:1–12:13)
    Concluding Defence (12:14–13:10)
Conclusion: Greetings and Benediction (13:11–13)

COMMENTARY

Introduction (1:1–11)

(1:1–2) Address The address is in keeping with the normal pattern of Paul's letters (e.g. 1 Cor 1:1–3). Timothy is listed as the co-author. Although Sosthenes and Silvanus are also given this role in other letters, Timothy is most frequently men- tioned (cf. Phil 1:1–2; Col 1:1–2; 1 Thess 1:1–2; Thess 1:1–2). It is not easy to evaluate the significance of this joint enterprise in modern terms. On the one hand, it is clear that Timothy's authority in the church was not equal to that of Paul; he was dependent upon Paul. On the other hand, Paul worked very closely with associates and they were instrumental to the success of his mission. Paul exercised his leadership as part of a team and it is misleading to think of the relationship between Paul and his fellow-workers as unilaterally hierarch- ical. In fact, the importance of the role of Paul's associates emerges especially clearly in 2 Corinthians (2 Cor 2:13; 7:6– 16; 8:6, 16–24). At the very least we may say that Timothy is mentioned because he is with Paul and his presence serves to bolster the authority of Paul's message. In particular Tim- othy's previous work with the Corinthians means that his influence could enhance (or likewise detract from) Paul's position. Along with Silvanus he was involved in the establish- ment of the church in Corinth (2 Cor 1:19; cf. 1 Cor 4:17; 16:10–11). The addressees are described in such a way as to further corroborate this image of a network of relationships. They are described as the church of God in Corinth, including the 'saints' (a general term in the NT for believers, see *OCB* s.v.) throughout Achaia (the Roman province with Corinth as its capital). The church in Corinth belongs to a wider community held together by emissaries, letters, and hospitality. 2 Cor 1–9 and possibly also 2 Cor 10–13 were written from Macedonia (2 Cor 2:12–13; 7:5; 8:1; 9:2).

(1:3–11) Blessing As is usually the case in Paul's letters, a blessing or thanksgiving follows the greeting. Typically, the community is praised and their past relationship with the apostle is recalled. Themes to be developed at a later point are introduced. In this text the solidarity of the Corinthians with Paul in affliction is emphasized. Likewise, community and apostle share the hope of consolation. Implicitly, church members are being praised for their strength in the face of suffering. Particularly striking is the repetition of the term 'consolation' and its cognates (*paraklēsis*). It is a notion that is especially prominent in 2 Corinthians. For example, it is taken up again in 2 Cor 7:4–13, a passage illustrating that the affliction/consolation opposition must be understood in the light of the difficult relations and complicated exchanges between Paul and the Corinthians. Within the Pauline corpus, the term 'affliction' (*thlipsis*) occurs most frequently in 2 Corinthians. It is a term that can carry a wide variety of meanings (Garrett 1995), ranging from the apostle's own physical (?) sufferings (2 Cor 1:8), to the pain of a broken relationship with the Corinthians that inspired the 'severe letter' (2 Cor 2:4; cf. 7:7–8), to impoverishment (2 Cor 8:13). The affliction in Asia of which Paul speaks in 2 Cor 1:8 seems to have been so devastating that he narrowly escaped with his life. While other explanations cannot be ruled out entirely, some type of physical suffering is probably in view, brought about by persecution (perhaps in Ephesus, cf. 1 Cor 15:32) or disease. Recalling Christ's suffering in 2 Cor 1:5 serves the apostle's purposes well in order to convey the hope of comfort in the midst of affliction; as members of Christ's body, believers continue to share in his afflictions (cf. Col 1:24), but will also be comforted through him. The consolation/affliction opposition is one of many rhetorical strategies Paul employs to reinforce his authority in Corinth. The apostle's leadership clearly recalls the suffering Christ. Like Christ's authority, the apostle's authority is articulated in an unexpected way—through affliction. But this affliction carries the promise of consolation. It is meaningful because it leads to the consolation of believers, relating Paul's (and ultimately Christ's) life intimately to the circumstances of the Corinthians. The association of the consolation/affliction opposition with expressions of confidence (e.g. 2 Cor 1:7; 7:4) makes its function as an assertion of authority especially clear (Meeks 1983: 123).

Paul the Conciliator (1:12–9:15)

(1:12–2:13) Explanations and Future Plans

(1:12–14) The Community as Paul's Boast Paul begins with a declaration of the significance of his relationship with the Corinthians before he offers the explanation of the events that have caused the Corinthians to doubt his sincerity and authority. Although it implies assertiveness, it is misleading to think of boasting as a type of bragging. Rather, it is a term that Paul employs to communicate his ultimate priorities as an apostle and to express his confidence in his mission. It is a notion that appears frequently in 2 Corinthians. Not surprisingly, Paul also speaks of his ground for boasting when he defines his rights as an apostle in 1 Cor 9:15–16. Particularly intriguing is the phrase, 'on the day of the Lord we are your boast even as you are our boast'. The reference to the 'day of the Lord' (cf. 1 Cor 5:5; Phil 1:6, 10; 2:16; 1 Thess 5:2) suggests that Paul is convinced that his relationship with the Corinthians is fundamental to the participation of both parties in the culmination of the Christ event. On that day all will be judged and the apostle is confident that his conduct will be shown to be above reproach. Moreover, the parallelism in the phrase implies mutual dependence between the two parties. The meaning of Paul's apostleship is fundamentally related to

the fruit of his labours. A similar sentiment surfaces in Rom 15:22–33 where acceptance of the collection (and ultimately of his Gentile mission) by the Jerusalem church appears to be fundamental to Paul's confidence in the legitimacy of his apostleship. In 2 Corinthians, the body of the Corinthian community (the church which Paul founded) is his boast: this is the manifestation of his apostleship. The boast of the Corinthian community, however, is also rooted in their connection, and no doubt loyalty, to Paul (cf. 5:12). Closely related to the theme of boasting is Paul's claim of having behaved in the world with 'frankness' (*haplotēs*). Although there is strong MS evidence for the alternative reading of 'holiness', the immediate and broader context suggests that 'frankness' (cf. 2:17) is the most likely possibility (for a summary of the evidence see Furnish 1984: 127). The reference to frankness reflects the ancient Greek notion of the rights of citizens to speak freely and to be open, even generous, in mutual dealings. It is a term which Paul uses to describe the nature of his ministry along with the synonym 'sincerity'; this language resembles notions found elsewhere in 2 Corinthians (2:17; 3:12; 10:2). Frankness, boldness, confidence, and the act of boasting are expressions of the value placed on assertiveness in the ancient Mediterranean world. Assertiveness, especially among men, was a means of preserving one's honour—one's reputation—and was integral to claims of authority. Especially in Acts the assertiveness of the apostles functions as a means of reinforcing the validity of their message (e.g. Acts 4:13, 29, 31; 9:27–9; Reese 1993: 9–11).

(1:15–22) Change of Travel Plans Here Paul is apparently responding to some charge of inconsistency based on a change of plan. It is impossible to be precise about the actual circumstances, but it seems that Paul's plans had changed at least twice. In 1 Cor 16:5–7 Paul announced his intention to visit Corinth briefly before going on to Macedonia. However, the plan he is accused of forfeiting here involved a visit both on the way to Macedonia and after leaving Macedonia; he would then have gone on from Corinth to Judea (probably bearing the collection). (See reconstructions of Paul's itinerary in Betz 1992: 1151; Furnish 1984: 143–4.) Although it is possible that Paul cancelled only the return phase of the anticipated double visit, most commentators believe the entire visit was cancelled (1:23). The reference to a double favour (v. 15) has a somewhat sarcastic ring. It may be in response to those who accused Paul of using flattery to win his audience; he had flattered the Corinthians with promises of a double visit (setting them above the Macedonians?) when he really had no intention of going twice (Furnish 1984: 144). Paul's response is unequivocal. He has not been fickle, answering yes and no in the same breath. In keeping with points he has made earlier in the chapter (1:12), he stresses that his actions as an apostle are based not on a human agenda but on divine initiative. He uses his critics' accusation of vacillation as an invitation to meditate on the absolute consistency of God and complete obedience of Jesus to God's will. In other words, since God is on Paul's side, inconsistency is ruled out. The place of Paul and the Corinthian community in God's plan is announced in vv. 21–2. As the one appointed by God to bring the gospel to the Corinthians, Paul in essence facilitates their joining with him as members of Christ's body. Their mutual relationship with Christ is so close that they have been anointed; they are now 'in Christ', incorporated into the Messiah, the anointed one. Receipt of the Spirit is also in keeping with messianic identity (cf. 1 Sam 16:13; Isa 61:1). Paul's arguments are not confined to doctrine. He also appeals to liturgical experiences, in his reference to the community's usual manner of giving assent: 'amen' (v. 20; cf. 1 Cor 14:16). He also recalls the experience of baptism by referring to the 'seal' and the Spirit as the first instalment of the divine promises (cf. Eph 1:13–14). In Colossians and Ephesians, remembrances of baptism play a central role in encouraging appropriate communal behaviour.

(1:23–2:13) The Painful Visit and the Letter of Tears Paul explains that it was to spare the Corinthians that he did not make another visit. We are probably to understand that between the time of the writing of 1 Corinthians and the composition of 2 Corinthians (or any segment of this document), Paul paid a visit to the Corinthians (cf. 2 Cor 12:14; 13:1). This may well have been an emergency visit (perhaps from Ephesus) brought about by a report of trouble in the community. It is to be distinguished from the cancelled visit described in 1:16 (cf. 1:23). The 'painful visit' probably involved a conflict with an individual and a resulting lack of support from the community. Paul's language calls to mind broken relationships and betrayal but also great love (2:4); it seems that he felt his place among the Corinthians was jeopardized severely (2:5–11; 7:8–12). His visit was apparently followed by a 'tearful letter' which was probably brought to the community by Titus and which was interpreted by some as being unduly severe (7:8). It was Titus who brought news of the turnaround in events after the community had received the letter (7:6–8). Some have identified the 'tearful letter' with chs. 10–13. However, because the problem mentioned in 2:5–11 concerns an individual offender and not 'super-apostles' as in chs. 10–13, others believe that the 'painful letter' no longer exists. Although the incest case of 1 Cor 5 which Paul discusses in uncompromising terms might lead to the suggestion that the 'tearful letter' is in fact 1 Corinthians, few hold this point of view today. We are limited to conjecture, but these verses offer information about Paul's comings and goings, and hints about the setting of the composition of 2 Corinthians (or parts therof). It seems that from Ephesus (1 Cor 16:5–8) Paul travelled to the seaport of Troas where he hoped to find his 'brother' Titus (for other brother-helpers, cf. Phil 2:25; Philem 16). Paul's longing for Titus offers us a poignant glimpse into the significance of Paul's relationship with his fellow-workers (2 COR 7:5–7). In Troas, Paul had considerable missionary success. The metaphor he uses calls to mind the importance of the household and workshop as an arena for conversion in the ancient world (see Hock 1980; MacMullen 1984: 25–42). Evangelical opportunity is described as a door being opened for him in the Lord (2:12). From Troas, Paul set out for Macedonia where he met up with (Titus 7:6). It is probable that it was from Macedonia that Paul wrote 2 Corinthians (or parts thereof). It is clear that by the time of the composition of these verses the problem of breakdown in relations between Paul and the Corinthians, caused by the case of the offender, had been resolved. The nature of the offence is to be distinguished from that discussed in 1 Cor 5 where Paul insists that the wicked person

be driven out from the community like a malady that must be purged from the body (1 Cor 5:13; on the differences between 1 Cor 5:1–5 and 2 Cor 2:5–11 see detailed discussion in Furnish 1984: 164–6). In the case of 2 Corinthians, the offender has been punished by the community enough and now should be forgiven and consoled. Is Paul's leniency rooted in the nature of the offence, i.e. a challenge to his authority and not a case of immorality which is worse even than that found among the pagans (1 Cor 5:1)? It has been suggested that this offender was someone external to the community (see Barrett 1973: 212), but this theory has not gained wide acceptance. The pain/consolation opposition throughout the text is in keeping with the suffering/consolation opposition in 1:3–11. Paul uses language of contrast to move the discussion from a previously painful situation to a celebration of the nature of the reconciliation and love that now exists. But the frequently attested theme of the apostle who suffers unjustly surfaces here as well (2:3). Despite the presence of Christ, Paul and the community members will remain vulnerable to the intervention of evil until the day of the Lord. Satan can interfere with community matters and with the apostle's agenda (2:11; 11:3, 14–15; 12:7; cf. 1 Thess 2:18). He can cause innumerable misfortunes and suffering and one must always be watchful of his designs (Neyrey 1990: 176).

(2:14–5:19) The Authority of the Apostle

(2:14–3:6) The Legitimacy of Paul's Apostleship This section opens with a formula of thanksgiving which has perhaps been inspired by the good news brought by Titus of the community's compliance with the apostle's wishes (7:6–7; Thrall 1965: 129). Rich imagery is used to communicate what God has accomplished in Christ. Believers are described as being led in the manner of the triumphal procession of the general who returns victorious from battle. The notion of triumph in weakness which is so central to Paul's theology in 2 Corinthians may be in view here. It is important to note that it was the prisoners-of-war who were paraded through the streets during such processions and Paul may be identifying the apostles with them (Furnish 1988: 1194). 'Fragrance' refers to the odour of incense in sacrifice. Paul may be thinking of rituals associated with Roman celebrations of triumph or with Jewish temple practice. The image may also have been influenced by Sir 24:15 where fragrance is a sign of the presence of God/Wisdom (Murphy-O'Connor 1990: 819). In the accounts of martyrdom in later church literature, beautiful fragrance was a sign of God's presence and that God was on the side of the Christians (see *Mart. Pol.* 15). First the gospel and then the apostles are compared to a fragrance. The fragrance spreads throughout the world by means of the apostles and for some represents life, but for others, death. This black-and-white language offers a good example of 'language of belonging' and 'language of separation' which demarcates the boundaries of the community (Meeks 1983: 85–96). Here the negative perception of the outside society is particularly evident. But the fragrance is also said to spread 'in every place', implying a universal mission. There is a certain tension in Paul's letters between openness to the external society in the hope of winning new members and a strong desire to remain separate (MacDonald 1988: 32–42). In 2:16 the tone changes abruptly from thanksgiving to interrogation of the community concerning the specifics of their relationship with Paul. Before Paul engages in a dialogue concerning the objections raised against his apostleship, he raises a question designed to lead believers to the conclusion that apostolic claims must ultimately rest only in God. With the question 'Who is sufficient for these things?' he hopes to make them see the error of the presumption that an apostle's superior personal attributes are responsible for success in carrying out God's plan. The same idea is repeated in 3:5. Perhaps distinguishing himself from others who claim superior attributes, he makes the point emphatically that he is not a charlatan. The language is very strong and, given the suspicions about Paul's financial arrangements which are echoed later in the work, it is tempting to conclude that this label had been applied to him. Paul speaks literally of those who hawk (kapēleuein) the word of God. The Greek term occurs nowhere else in the NT but was employed by ancient critics of itinerant teachers to speak of the 'huckstering of wisdom' (Furnish 1984: 178). To those who would rebuke him for his lack of letters of recommendation, Paul replies that nothing could compare with the proof of commendation that lies in their existence as a church: the Corinthians themselves are the letter. Letters of recommendation were an accepted means of ensuring hospitality and receipt of some favour in the ancient world (cf. Acts 9:2; 22:5). One of the benefits that a patron might extend to his client was such a letter. Rom 16:1–2 makes it clear that Paul himself could make use of such letters in order to introduce a church member to the community; but in his personal dealings with the Corinthians such tools were not necessary. Perhaps the letters in question came from the Jerusalem church or from a patron thought to be more impressive than Paul. We are left to wonder whether the tendency to peddle God's word and/or the absence of letters of recommendation were accusations made by the offender (2:5–11) against Paul which found support among others in Corinth. What is clear is that Paul thinks such problems do exist with other would-be apostles. In response to possible objections Paul does two things: (1) he reminds the Corinthians that apostleship makes sense only if it comes from God (ultimately, Paul's only patron). Paul's ministry is a ministry of a 'new covenant', a theme developed in depth in 3:7–18; (2) he appeals to his confidence, sincerity, and forthrightness which are important means of establishing his credibility as an authoritative teacher in the ancient world (2:17; 3:4–6; 4:1–4; 5:6–8; cf. 2 COR 1:12–14).

(3:7–18) A Minister of the New Covenant By playing with various contrasting notions such as 'letter of law/Spirit,' 'death/life', 'old covenant/new covenant', Paul compares the old relationship between God and his people with the new relationship established by God through Christ (on covenant, see *ABD* i. 1197–202). The issue of the letters of recommendation in 3:1–6 allows him to introduce the issue of the letter of the Jewish law. Beginning in 3:6, and continuing to v. 11, the law—the centre of the old covenant—is depicted in categorically negative terms. The letter kills and ministry based on letters chiselled on stone tablets (Ex 24:12; 31:18) leads to death (on death and the law, see *ABD* ii. 110–11; iv. 254–65). A very strong statement of the law's inadequacy for salvation is also found in v. 11 where the law is described as 'what was set aside'

(cf. v. 7). Paul admits that the old covenant was glorious, but it has been far surpassed in glory (vv. 7–11). These verses have been judged as shedding light on Paul's view of life under the law and generally as important for understanding the birth of the church in a Jewish context. Stressing that Paul's conviction that the law condemns and kills is based on his post-conversion understanding, and is not rooted in particular personal experiences of the law's limitations for Jewish life, E. P. Sanders has argued that the apostle represented the Mosaic covenant as less glorious simply because he had found in Christ something more glorious. Paul's thought and language proceeded from his conviction about Christ as the centre of salvation and it developed in very black-and-white terms: 'I cannot see how the development could have run the other way, from an initial conviction that the Law only condemns and kills, to a search for something which gives life, to the conviction that life comes by faith in Christ, to the statement that the Law lost its glory because a new dispensation surpasses it in glory' (Sanders 1983: 138). But there remains some ambiguity in Paul's thought (ibid. 138–9). On the one hand, the law has been set aside and does not save. But on the other hand, the old covenant may still be read profitably by members of the church: when Jews who are not members of the church read it, it is veiled, but when believers read it, it is unveiled (vv. 14–16). The reference to veiling recalls the covering that Moses placed over his face during his descent from Mt. Sinai (Ex 34:33–5; cf. 34:29–35). Some have understood the comparison between Paul's ministry and Moses' ministry that runs throughout vv. 7–18 in terms of a response to Paul's adversaries (Murphy-O'Connor 1990: 819). It has even been suggested that the source of the conflict is a midrashic document on Ex 34:29–35 that was composed by Paul's opponents and which Paul modified in these verses in the hope of correcting a mistaken view of Moses and the Mosaic covenant (Georgi 1986: 264–71). There has been considerable interest in Paul's use of Scripture here, including his dependence on the LXX and extra-biblical sources (Belleville 1993: 165–85; Stockhausen 1993: 143–64). The emphasis in vv. 7–18 is on freedom from the law (cf. Gal 5:18) and the transformation of believers. The believer's image, reflected in a mirror, becomes that of Christ (cf. 4:6; 1 Cor 11:7); and salvation involves increasing conformity to him (Murphy-O'Connor 1990: 820). The identification of Spirit with Lord (in Paul's letters usually referring to Christ) has raised doctrinal questions, but many commentators believe 'Lord' in vv. 16–18 refers directly to God (Thrall 1965: 136–7; Furnish 1984: 234–6).

(4:1–6) The Honourable Apostle Paul apparently responds to those who are denigrating his ministry by setting himself apart from his rivals. Paul's ministry is characterized by the persistence and boldness that are qualities of an honourable apostle (2 COR 1:12–14). The values of honour (public acknowledgement of worth) and shame (public denial of worth) frame the text. Shame also can have a positive value in the ancient world in the sense of 'having shame': that is, having appropriate concern for one's reputation. In this text what is shameful refers to the absence or loss of honour (on honour and shame see Plevnik 1993: 95–104). The shameful things that Paul has renounced are clearly negative: literally, 'the things of shame that one hides'. Has Paul been accused of dishonourable activity which is sequestered and secretive? The setting of the churches in private homes could certainly have fostered that impression. Paul believes that to act in a shameful manner is to display cunning and to falsify God's word (cf. 2:17). Behind Paul's declaration that he refuses to adopt shameful tactics probably lies an attempt to distance himself from rival apostles who mislead and exploit the congregation (cf. 11:20). Language of honour and shame is useful in communicating what should be valued most, i.e. what is the basis of true apostleship. Because honour and shame are rooted in the importance in the ancient Mediterranean world placed on public appraisal, these concepts also are useful in conveying the scope of evangelical mission. The central message is that the Corinthians have come to know the light of the gospel only through Paul's preaching (Furnish 1988: 1194). The reference to the veil is in keeping with 3:12–18 but gains further nuance in relation to the themes of secrecy and openness introduced here. The image of the sometimes blinding veil is part of Paul's admission that his preaching is not always successful: public acknowledgement which should follow honourable display and open statement of the truth is not always quickly forthcoming. The blindness of unbelievers, however, is not the result of Paul's tactics as an apostle but has been caused by the god of this world: Satan or Beliar (2 COR 6:14–7:1). The frequent notion of Paul's apostleship having purely divine origins is found again in vv. 5–6. In response to competitors who would 'preach themselves' (seek to gain acceptance by drawing upon personal attributes), Paul argues that he proclaims only 'Christ as Lord' (a confessional formula, Rom 10:9; 1 Cor 12:3; Phil 2:10–11). The description of Paul as the Corinthians' slave for Jesus' sake is in keeping with the frequent use of slavery as a metaphor in Pauline Christianity (cf. 1 Cor 9:16–23). Paul's self-enslavement has been recognized as a practical strategy for evangelization (low-status persons may be won through the evangelist's self-lowering) and as a rhetorical strategy for conveying the nature of his leadership. But the theological importance of the metaphor is especially visible here. Paul's self-abasement, communicated through the image of slavery, is closely associated with the theology of the cross (4:13–18): humiliation is followed by exaltation. It has been suggested that the effectiveness of the metaphorical representation of slavery as salvation is related to the fact that in Graeco-Roman society, slavery was an ambiguous and multifaceted concept, carrying connotations both of abasement and upward mobility (Martin 1990: 129–32). There is very strong language of separation here which is reinforced by an allusion to Gen 1:3 (v. 6, cf. 2 COR 2:14–3:6); church members see, but unbelievers are blind and perishing. The light of the gospel (v. 4) shines through Paul in a world that is otherwise dark and still very much influenced by evil.

(4:7–15) Power in Weakness Paul's theology of the cross is proclaimed throughout 4:7–18 (cf. 1 Cor 1:17–2:5). The event of the death and resurrection of Christ means that the appearance of weakness and humiliation can carry the promise of power and exaltation (v. 14). Paul's theology of the cross (and statements about suffering) in 2 Corinthians must be understood in the light of a particular polemical context where Paul seeks to undermine the position of rivals who make too much of their personal superiority in relation to Paul's weakness.

Moreover, the theology of the cross is not about passivity in suffering, but about power in suffering. With sometimes biting irony, Paul protests against his rivals who find God on the side of strength and power (10:10–11). In 2 Corinthians the paradox of the crucified Messiah is proclaimed boldly. The ambiguous symbol of a suffering saviour offers Paul many possibilities to expose the folly of those who would attack him. Paul's theology of the cross has been of interest to feminist biblical commentators, who warn of the dangers of lifting Paul's message out of context and using it to advocate passivity and meekness in the face of suffering and oppression (Matthews 1994: 214–15). But there is no doubt that the symbol locates God on the side of the suffering, the weak, and the oppressed (vv. 8–10, cf. 1 Cor 1:18–31; Bassler 1992: 331–2). In these verses the focus is on power in physical weakness. This notion is communicated through the beautiful image of the fragile clay pots which contain hidden treasure. It is also conveyed through the catalogue of hardships (vv. 8–9). Similar lists are found throughout 2 Corinthians and elsewhere in Paul's letters (6:4–5; 11:23–9; 12:10; Rom 8:35; 1 Cor 4:9–13). Scholars have examined the literary relationships between the lists within 2 Corinthians and have even speculated about what these relationships might reveal about the literary integrity of the work (Witherington 1995: 398–9). The tribulations are described with vivid language which is reminiscent of the terms employed by philosophers in the ancient world who described their struggles in the overcoming of passion and search for wisdom (Fitzgerald 1988: 65–70; 148–201). Suffering is not glorified; on the contrary, it is experienced by the apostle as unjust (Neyrey 1990: 177–9); yet it is given meaning in two ways. First, suffering allows for identification with Jesus and, ultimately, resurrection with Jesus (vv. 10–14). Secondly, Paul's suffering mirrors Jesus' suffering and hence makes Jesus' life visible in the world. 'Flesh' (sarx) in v. 11 is a synonym for 'body' (sōma) in v. 10, but the term 'flesh' (see OCB 231) places more emphasis on physical existence, a connotation which is highlighted throughout this text (Murphy-O'Connor 1990: 821) Because his suffering bears witness to Jesus, Paul is able to argue that his suffering is for the sake of the Corinthian church which he founded and more broadly for the sake of his evangelical mission. The reference to Ps 116:10 in v. 13 allows him to link preaching (speaking) with proclamation of faith in the midst of suffering.

(4:16–5:1) The Fragility of Mortal Existence Interest in the limited nature of physical existence is maintained throughout these verses. Paul is strikingly honest about his own frailty (perhaps in response to those who would claim that physical weakness is incompatible with apostleship; cf. 10:10). He uses the contrast between his outer nature (his visible body) and inner nature (the faith and commitment to Christ which cannot be seen) to point to ultimate reality: that which is eternal and transcends physical existence. While in other places Paul gives the impression that he expects to live until Christ's return (1 Thess 4:15, 17), here Paul confronts the harsh reality of death (5:1). Several architectural images are conflated to convey the notion of heavenly existence. The literary-historical background of these images has been of considerable interest. It has been noted that the use of the image of a tent to refer to the mortal body occurs in many

Hellenistic religious and ethical texts (Furnish 1984: 293). There has been extensive discussion of the meaning of the 'house not made with hands'. Often Paul has been understood as referring to the new spiritual body which will be given to believers (1 Cor 15:51–4). Others have argued that the text should be read in the light of Jewish and early Christian apocalyptic traditions which include the notion of an eschatological temple and new Jerusalem (2 Apoc. Bar. 4:3; 2 Esd 10:40–57; cf. Mk 14:58). Parallels between this passage and Phil 3:12–21 have been noted. The symbol of the heavenly commonwealth in Phil 3:20 resembles the heavenly dwelling of 5:1. If this interpretation is accepted, 5:1 should be understood as speaking primarily about believers as already belonging to another age and as having a new existence, rather than as addressing specifically the issue of the new spiritual body (Furnish 1984: 294–5; Murphy-O'Connor 1990: 821). A similar conflation of body imagery with architectural imagery occurs in Eph 2:19–22, but there the focus is clearly ecclesiological. Although many commentators have understood 5:1 as introducing a new subject, it has been included in this section because it acts as the climax of 4:16–18 which emphasizes the temporality and fragility of mortal existence (Furnish 1984: 291).

(5:2–10) Present Existence and Future Fulfilment The emphasis shifts somewhat from the limits of mortality to the ultimate shape of life with God and the nature of existence in this new eschatological age. It has been said that 5:1–10 is one of the most difficult passages in all of Paul's letters to explain adequately (Thrall 1965: 142). It has often been thought that Paul's recent escape from death (1:9) led him to doubt his previous belief that he and others would be alive at the Parousia (1 Thess 4:13–18; 1 Cor 15:51–2). The reference to nakedness in v. 3 has been instrumental to the theory that Paul is responding to fear surrounding an interim period between death of the physical body and resurrection of a new spiritual body. But this theory has also been disputed (Furnish 1984: 292–3). Paul does not really seem to be deliberately responding to a problem in the way that is so evident in 1 Thess 4:13–18. The fear of being naked may indeed refer to concern about an intermediate state between life and the adoption of the spiritual body (1 Cor 15:37–8; Barrett 1973: 154–5). Paul may be expressing his preference to avoid the intermediate condition altogether: that is, to live on earth until the resurrection (Witherington 1995: 391). But the reference to nakedness may also be a reminder of the harsh reality of final judgement (cf. 2 Cor 5:10) when a person's culpability will be exposed (Isa 47:3; Ezek 23:28–9; Murphy-O'Connor 1991: 52). An awareness of the importance of the values of honour and shame in the ancient Mediterranean world may also prove useful here (2 COR 4:1–6). In the HB nakedness is strongly associated with shame and sin. To be shamed is to be involuntarily stripped naked (Neyrey 1993: 119–21). Presence before an honourable God requires that one may not be found naked, but have put on the heavenly garment/tent (ibid. 122). Although the NRSV translation 'when we have taken it off' fits best with the theory that Paul is referring to an interim period between death and adoption of a new spiritual body, there is good reason to adopt the strongly attested alternative reading 'when we have put it on' (Furnish 1984: 268). An understanding of the values of

honour and shame may also help explain how this text fits within the broader discussion of apostolic suffering and authority. When the Corinthians turn against Paul might they be stripping him naked and/or rendering themselves exposed before a God who makes believers accountable for what has been done 'in the body' (v. 10)? That questions about Paul's apostleship are not far removed from the main argument here is made clear by the double assertion of confidence by which Paul reinforces his role as an honourable apostle (vv. 6–8; 2 COR 1:12–14). Some have viewed the merger of the images of 'dwelling' and 'clothing' (cf. 1 Cor 15:53–4; Gal 3:27; Rom 13:14) to be somewhat awkward on Paul's part. However, they actually work well for Paul's purposes since they tie personal affiliation (the garment which must be put on) closely with communal commitment (the household that must be joined, the dwelling that must be entered). The main purpose of the imagery is to announce the nature of the new mode of existence: real life that 'swallows up' (katapiein; v. 4) all that is mortal. Comparison with Rom 8:18–27 is especially useful since it also refers to 'groaning' (Rom 8:23, 26) and highlights the role of the Spirit, as creation waits to be released from futility and suffering. Continuing to be plagued by limitations, groaning under his 'burdens' (cf. 1:6; 4:8, 17), Paul is moving towards his ultimate goal. The contrast between being 'at home' in the body and 'at home' with the Lord in vv. 6–10 reflects the tension between present salvation and future fulfilment that is characteristic of Paul's thought. The term for being away from home (ekdēmein), has a wider significance than leaving one's house: literally it refers to the act of leaving one's country or going on a long journey (BAGD 238). Paul's present life is shaped by Christ whom one must continue to please until one enters the heavenly commonwealth (cf. Phil 3:20). The presence of the Spirit acts as a foretaste of future fulfilment.

(5:11–19) Warnings against Reliance on External Appearances This text relates Paul's ministry to a reversal of earthly standards and the dawning of a new creation. The reference to 'persuasion' has been understood as a reference to rhetoric, the art of persuasion. Paul is acting like an ancient rhetor who will be judged by the Corinthians according to their consciences. The picture of the ambassador who entreats the assembly (5:20) also fits with this context. Paul presents God as his ultimate judge, but this passage functions as an indirect acknowledgement of the fact that the Corinthians have put Paul on trial, and of how important it is to Paul that the Corinthians recognize his authority (v. 11; Witherington 1995: 392–3). Paul says that he is not going to commend himself to the Corinthians again (v. 11), but in fact this is exactly what he does. In saying that he will not commend himself he means that he will not adopt the self-aggrandizing tactics of his rivals who boast in outward appearances. Paul may be distinguishing himself from apostolic rivals whom he feels adopt the disreputable tactics of sophists. Sophists were commonly accused of paying too much attention to external forms (appearance, clothing, delivery) at the expense of content (Witherington 1995: 393–4; 348–50). In v. 13 Paul offers an interesting insight into the nature of the comparisons the Corinthians were making. 'Madness' here perhaps refers to religious ecstasy (Furnish 1984: 308). His rivals probably displayed ecstatic experiences in public, and accused Paul of failing to produce these experiences as evidence of his apostleship. Paul seems to be claiming that ecstatic experiences should be reserved for private worship (cf. 12:1–7). The text invites comparison with 1 Cor 14:18–19 where Paul claims to speak in tongues frequently, but where he also makes it clear that in the public arena of the *ekklēsia* he prefers understandable speech (which can include tongues if they are interpreted) to ecstatic speaking. In 1 Cor 14:23–5 he even expresses his fear that non-believers (potential converts) might witness uncontrolled glossolalia and assume that church members are mad! Warnings against reliance on external appearance, form, and display also underlie the statement that Paul no longer makes judgements from a human point of view. Paul admits that before his acceptance of Christ he judged Christ by worldly standards, perhaps according to the pathetic image of a crucified messianic impostor (v. 16). This passage offers an excellent illustration of how Paul's theological thought is fundamentally tied to the interpersonal struggles of human communities. It is reflection on the misguided nature of his rivals that leads him to locate his own priorities in the love of Christ and to articulate one of the strongest statements of universal salvation in his epistles (vv. 14–15; as reflecting credal affirmations cf. 1 Cor 15:3). By means of the doctrine of 'reconciliation' in vv. 18–19 Paul presents God's initiative, Christ's role, and his own mission (Paul is a minister of 'reconciliation'). Here Paul also may be drawing on a traditional formula (cf. Col 1:19–20; Eph 2:13–16) which he interprets in a new way. Given the predominance of the structures of patronage in the ancient world, however, it has been suggested that Paul may be casting God here as the great benefactor, Christ as the means of benefaction, and Paul as the human agent (or broker) of the stores of salvation: Paul is the one who serves (Danker 1989: 82–3; Witherington 1995: 396). In order to justify his mission and break with worldly standards, Paul ultimately relies on support for his conviction that God has transformed the world radically through Christ. The emphasis on newness and the proclamation in v. 17 'there is a new creation'—although some would translate this as 'he/she is a new creation' (see Witherington 1995: 395)—function as justifications of the birth of a new religious movement.

(5:20–7:16) Appeals for Reconciliation with the Apostle

(5:20–6:2) God Speaks through Paul This passage is thematically very closely related to the previous section. However, it introduces a new type of exhortation. As is frequently the case in Paul's letters, an appeal (v. 20; *parakaleō*) follows an affirmation (v. 19), the imperative follows the indicative. In fact, v. 20 sets in motion a series of appeals (appeals for reconciliation with Paul and concerning the collection) which continue until 9:15 (Furnish 1988: 1196). Here, Paul's apostolic authority is expressed in the very strongest of terms. Paul's human powers (his ability as a teacher or sage to influence an audience in antiquity) are secondary at this point; what is important is that God has conveyed legitimacy upon his mission. God has granted Paul authority and in fact speaks through him. It is God who appeals through Paul to the Corinthians. The move from doctrinal affirmation to ethical imperative in this text makes Paul's conviction explicit: the act of reconciliation which overcomes humanity's estrangement from God

is played out on the societal level in the reconciliation which must occur between Paul and the Corinthians. As in the related text of Rom 5:1–11, language of justification (righteousness, *OCB* s.v.; *ABD* v. 757–68) is combined with language of reconciliation (Meeks 1983: 186). The appeal is very strong, linking a broken relationship with God to a broken relationship with the Corinthians. Paul may even have feared that the Corinthians were in danger of committing apostasy (Witherington 1995: 397). The citation from Isa 49:8 emphasizes the present nature of salvation, but also reinforces the urgency of the situation. The reference to the one who knew no sin having been made sin (v. 21) may refer to the sinless Christ taking on sin as a burden or being treated as a sinner for the sake of humanity (Gal 3:13); sin may also refer to a sin-offering here (Rom 8:3; cf. Isa 53:4–10).

(6:3–13) Commendation through Hardships A common goal of ancient rhetoric was to establish the speaker's *ethos* or character (Witherington 1995: 44, 398). Paul begins with assurances that he has placed no 'obstacle' before the Corinthians. He seems to have believed that ministers were very influential in facilitating or preventing access to salvation (Murphy-O'Connor 1990: 822). Paul presents eloquent wisdom (rhetoric devoid of content) as being able to empty the cross of its power in 1 Cor 1:17. In contrast to the self-commendations adopted by others, Paul has commended himself as a servant of God (2 COR 4:1–6). As elsewhere in 2 Corinthians the metaphor of slavery, the theology of the cross, and the list of apostolic hardships work together to communicate the notion of a reversal of norms for judging claims of authority (2 COR 4:7–15). Paul's listing of a catalogue of sufferings is in keeping with the Stoic and Cynic theme that the hardships of the sage demonstrate virtue and character (Fitzgerald 1988: 199–201). Paul gives these traditional elements distinctive meaning in relation to the Christ event (Witherington 1995: 400). The stress on reputation and recognition in vv. 8–9 illustrates the importance of public acknowledgement of worth in the 'honour and shame' societies of the ancient world. But here Paul is willing to entertain the reversal even of these most basic cultural values. The military metaphor in v. 7 is developed further in 10:3–5 and even more extensively by the author of Ephesians (Eph 6:11–17). The inclusion of poverty in the list of hardships (v. 10) is especially intriguing given the concerns about the collection which underlie chs. 8–9, and the fact that questions about Paul's acceptance and/or refusal of support from church members was at the heart of confrontation with opponents (11:7–11; 12:14–18; cf. 1 Cor 9:1–18). In vv. 11–13 Paul repeats that he has demonstrated the open speech and boldness which are the hallmarks of an honourable apostle (2 COR 1:12–14) and he characterizes his relationship with the Corinthians as resembling the exchange between a father and his children (cf. 12:14).

(6:14–7:1) Warnings against Contact with Unbelievers This text seems to interrupt the appeals of 6:11–13 which are resumed at 7:2–3. A large number of occurrences of *hapax legomena* have been noted. The stringing together of a series of citations from Scripture which are not found elsewhere in Paul's letters (the allusions in 6:16–18 include Lev 26:12; Isa 52:11; Ezek 20:34; 2 Sam 7:14) has invited discussion. The vocabulary and ideas, especially the dualism, have been judged to be closer to the Qumran community than to Paul. Thus a great deal of doubt has been raised about the authenticity of these verses. There have been theories ranging from an 'anti-Pauline fragment' (Betz 1973: 88–108) to a 'Pauline interpolation of non-Pauline material' (Furnish 1984: 383), to a 'deliberative digression' which fits well within the present context of 2 Corinthians (Witherington 1995: 402). Some have understood this section to be part of the letter to the Corinthians mentioned in 1 Cor 5:9–11. In addition to the many literary problems this passage raises, the uncompromising distinction between believers and unbelievers (which seems to leave little room for the winning of new members) is surprising. It is difficult, for example, to harmonize the strong statement that one should not be mismatched with unbelievers (apistoi) with Paul's allowance for marriages between believers and non-believers to continue because of their evangelizing potential (1 Cor 7:12–16). However, there are points of contact between this text and others in Paul's letters where the church is envisioned as the temple of God made up of sanctified believers (1 Cor 3:16, 19) which must be kept pure. The corollary of this notion of holy temple is the view that members who threaten to bring impurity into the community should be treated as outsiders (1 Cor 5:1–5; Newton 1985: 110–14). On the question of maintaining community boundaries, it is also useful to compare this passage to 1 Cor 8 and 10 where the problem of food sacrificed to idols is discussed. Beliar is a name for Satan (or an evil spirit under Satan) which occurs frequently in Jewish intertestamental literature.

(7:2–16) Restoration of Good Relations The appeals of 6:11–13 are resumed in vv. 2–4. Many of the concepts related to the honour of Paul's apostleship such as 'boasting' and 'confidence' are reiterated (2 COR 1:12–14). The nature of the intimate connection between apostle and community and the theme of comfort and affliction (2 COR 1:3–11) are developed further in vv. 5–16. Many commentators have understood v. 5 as a resumption of the comments in 2:12–13, and this view figures prominently in theories about the partitioning of the letter (1:1–2:13; 7:5–16; 13:11–13 have been described as a 'letter of reconciliation'; Betz 1992: 1149–50). But these theories have also been disputed. It is also possible to understand the narrative beginning at v. 5 as an example of the comfort that occurs in affliction (v. 4); a comfort that is ultimately divine consolation (v. 6; Murphy-O'Connor 1990: 823). Without going so far as a theory of partition, it has been argued from a rhetorical perspective that vv. 5–16 constitute an amplification of some of the things mentioned in the narratio (explaining the disputed matter) of chs. 1 and 2. In other words, these verses represent a kind of retelling in a manner that would help Paul make his case as convincing as possible. The recapitulation may offer an indication that Paul was very concerned about the fact that he was being perceived as inconsistent with respect to his travel plans and about the results of the 'tearful letter' (2 COR 1:23–2:13; Witherington 1995: 407). Paul informs listeners that the setting of the events where he experienced comfort in affliction was Macedonia. The afflictions from which his body had no rest are described as coming from 'within' and from 'without'. It is possible that he is referring to bodily suffering in the form of

internal anguish and external malady (cf. 4:16). But the terms might also have communal connotations, referring to suffering resulting from encounters with those outside the body of Christ (cf. 1 Tim 3:7) and from problems within the church community (or a combination of community difficulties and physical afflictions, such as suffering resulting from contacts with non-believers and those occurring as a result of disease). With related terminology, Paul refers throughout his correspondence to those on the outside as non-believers (1 Cor 5:12, 13; Col 4:5; 1 Thess 4:12). In v. 5 Paul may be continuing to speak with an uncompromising voice towards non-believers as he did in 6:14–7:1. In discussing the arrival of Titus, Paul fills in many details which are alluded to in 2 Cor 2. Paul was consoled by Titus' arrival and by the news that issues concerning the offender (2:6–8) had been resolved. The 'letter of tears' (2:3–4) had apparently produced the desired effect of instilling repentance (v. 10). Paul describes the Corinthians as having proved themselves to be guiltless (v. 11): they exonerated themselves by dealing appropriately with the offender and by showing that they did not have misplaced loyalties (vv. 11–12). 'The one who did wrong' refers to the offender (2 COR 1:23–2:13) and 'the one who was wronged' refers to Paul (v. 12). That what is at stake transcends the particular events of the dispute and involves the fundamental nature of Paul's relationship with the Corinthians is made clear by Paul's description of the consolation which has occurred as a longing, mourning, and zeal for the apostle (v. 7; cf. v. 12; 11:2). It is interesting to note that although Paul seeks concrete expressions of his authority by calling for loyalty to his position and by insisting that the offender be punished, at the same time he denies the ultimate importance of his personal authority; rather, the 'tearful letter' precipitated a rediscovery of the inseparable link between loyalty to Paul and loyalty to God (vv. 12–13). The contrast between godly grief and worldly grief in vv. 9–11 also represents a bestowing of salvific meaning upon the dispute. The painful experience (the Corinthians were grieved by Paul's letter, v. 8) was in actual fact the kind of godly grief which leads to 'repentance' (metanoia, vv. 9–10; see OCB 646–7; ABD v. 672–3). This is one of the few places where Paul employs the term (Rom 2:4; cf. 12:21; 2 Tim 2:25). Here it does not refer to repentance prior to entry into the church, but to believers repenting of some sin; it involves rediscovery of commitment to Paul, his gospel, and ultimately to God (Witherington 1995: 409). The subordination or denial of the obvious or earthly significance of the events in favour of an argument about divine purpose is an example of what sociologists of knowledge have called 'legitimation': the means by which the institutional world is explained and justified (Berger and Luckmann 1981: 79). Legitimation is involved in the construction and maintenance of the 'symbolic universe' (MacDonald 1988: 16, 10–11). Opposition, deviance, or heresy can give impetus to theorizing about the symbolic universe. The development of theological thought is accelerated by challenges posed to the tradition by opponents, deviants, or heretics. In the process of theorizing, new implications of the tradition emerge and the symbolic universe is transformed (Berger and Luckmann 1981: 125). Paul's evocative theology of comfort in affliction is articulated by means of this process. The information about Titus in this passage offers a good example of the importance of Paul's co-workers to his mission. Titus may be counted as a member of the small group of Paul's closest co-workers who were clearly subject to Paul but also could act as his representatives (Holmberg 1980: 57–67). An important companion of Paul, Titus was taken along to Jerusalem where he was the focus of a dispute about whether Gentiles needed to be circumcised. Paul vigorously resisted the appeal that his Greek co-worker be circumcised (Gal 2:1–3). Although he had apparently not met the Corinthians previously, Titus became Paul's representative in an attempt to bring about a reconciliation (v. 14). It is indicated at 8:6, 16–24, that Titus was sent to Corinth a second time to conduct work in support of the collection for Jerusalem (cf. 2 Cor 12:18). The close relationship between Paul and Titus is made clear by the fact that Titus' very presence is a comfort to Paul (vv. 6–7). Titus' connection with the Corinthian community is also cast in personal and emotional terms (vv. 13–15). He somehow participates in Paul's apostleship. It is useful to view Titus as a broker of Paul's authority. The attitude of the Corinthians with respect to Titus is one of obedience and they welcome him with fear and trembling (v. 15). An understanding of the centrality of the values of honour and shame in first-century society can shed light upon what was at stake in Titus' visit to Corinth. Because Paul has previously 'boasted' to Titus about the model behaviour of the Corinthians, the community can strip Paul of all honour if it fails to live up to its reputation; the community has the power to revoke all public recognition of the apostle's worth. How they treat Titus has a direct bearing upon their patron (v. 14).

(8:1–9:15) Appeals about the Collection

(8:1–15) A Call to Fulfil Previous Commitment Chs. 8–9 have figured prominently in theories about the fragmentation of 2 Corinthians. It has been argued that ch. 8 constitutes an 'administrative letter' which was delivered to Corinth by Titus and two 'brothers' (8:18–23). Comparison with literary parallels has revealed similarity to letters of appointment given to political or administrative emissaries (Betz 1985: 37–86, 131–9). Ch. 9 has also been viewed as an administrative letter. It may have had an advisory purpose: enlisting the help of the Achaians in bringing the collection in Corinth to fruition (ibid. 87–128, 139–40). Such partition theories have not seemed convincing to everyone. The mention of Macedonia and Titus, for example, in ch. 7 may prepare the way for the issues in chs. 8–9 and might be taken as a sign of literary integrity (Witherington 1995: 410, 413). While there is some disjunction suggested, for example, by the break in subject between 8:24 and 9:1 (with the usual formula: 'peri de', 'now concerning', e.g. 1 Cor 7:1; 8:1, 4; 12:1; 16:1), the evidence has sometimes been judged as insufficient to demand that ch. 9 be viewed as a separate letter (Murphy-O'Connor 1990: 823; Witherington 1995: 413). These chapters have been called an example of deliberative rhetoric (persuasion or dissuasion with a future orientation) designed to ensure that the audience fulfil a commitment previously made concerning the collection, and to illustrate that the apostle's behaviour with respect to the collection has been above reproach (Witherington 1995: 411). 1 Cor 16:1–4 provides the background illustrating that the collection for the relief of the Jerusalem church is something that had been initiated previously. It appears that Titus had made some progress in reviving the commitment to

the collection and was being sent back to complete the task (7:6). Perhaps he used the atmosphere of reconciliation as an opportunity to invite the Corinthians to demonstrate the honour of their community by means of fulfilling their commitment to the collection (7:7–8, 10–11). In order to persuade the Corinthians, Paul appeals to the example of the Macedonians (including the Thessalonians and Philippians) who exceeded Paul's expectations in their generosity despite their extreme poverty (vv. 1–5). The Corinthians, in contrast, are described as having a surplus (v. 14). The implicit argument might be stated as follows: 'If the Macedonians in their extreme need are capable of such generosity, surely you are capable of as much!' Paul supports his argument with Christological thought. In a manner which recalls Phil 2:6–11, Paul speaks of Christ who was rich (perhaps a reference to pre-existence) becoming poor in order that the Corinthians might benefit from spiritual wealth (v. 9). But when Paul develops the implications of this theology for life in the community, the results are surprising (vv. 10–15). We do not hear a call to imitate Christ in the radical manner of the gospel invitations to give up all to follow him. Rather the focus is one of equity, balance, reciprocity, and accommodation. Gifts should be according to one's means (v. 11). Relief for the Jerusalem church should not cause strife for the Corinthians (v. 13). The Jerusalem church's abundance (spiritual benefits, Rom 15:26–7, or future monetary surplus) may in turn come to address the Corinthians' need (v. 14). This call for fair balance and partnership is supported by a citation from the LXX (Ex 16:18). Paul operates upon the premiss that believers should not be in need. He calls for generosity, but it is important to note that he does not call for a radical redistribution of wealth here. Paul's attitude to wealth has sometimes been judged as one of 'love-patriarchalism': social differences are allowed to continue but relationships must nevertheless be transformed by concern and respect. This attitude may have contributed to the organizational effectiveness of the Pauline churches in integrating members from different strata in an urban environment (Theissen 1982: 107–8). A second aspect of Paul's approach in governing his churches is detectable in the statement that 'he does not say this as a command' (cf. 1 Cor 7:6). The respect for the autonomy of the congregation and their freedom in decision-making is a striking feature of some of Paul's exhortations (Meeks 1983: 138–9). This type of assertion of authority may be contrasted with the rule-like statements which emerge in household codes of the Deutero-Pauline letters (Col 3:18–4:1; Eph 5:21–6:9).

(8:16–24) Recommendation of Titus and the Brothers Here Paul explains the specific arrangements he has made in order to bring the collection to completion. In vv. 16–17 he highlights the independence of his co-worker Titus: a close relationship between Titus and the Corinthians is presupposed and the fact that he is going to Corinth of his own accord is stressed (cf. 8:6; 12:18; 2 COR 7:2–16). Paul appears to be setting in motion mechanisms to distance himself from the process of gathering the collection in Corinth even though he clearly believes that the activity has divine sanction (8:8–15). This 'distancing' can be further detected in the exhortation concerning the brother in vv. 18–20. Paul refers to the first individual who is to accompany Titus as 'the brother' (v. 18), while the second individual is described as 'our brother' (v. 22). The possessive suggests a more personal relationship with the apostle: the person probably was a regular member of Paul's entourage (Furnish 1988: 1197). Paul presents the first brother's initiative as being tied to the mission of the delegation and appears to take comfort from the fact that this brother is famous in all the churches for proclaiming the good news (v. 18). But he also discloses that this brother has been 'appointed by the churches' and implies that serious difficulties have dictated the necessity of an 'external auditor' of Paul's initiatives (vv. 19–20). Paul clearly attaches special significance to the involvement of Titus in the delegation; he is described as Paul's partner and co-worker. In addition, the two unnamed individuals are described with the Greek term *apostolos*, a term which conveys leadership and authority, often translated as 'apostle' in Paul's letters (see *OCB* 41–2). But *apostolos* has a fluid meaning in the Pauline correspondence and in this case it seems to be a designation for an official messenger or envoy (vv. 18–19; cf. Phil 2:25). vv. 20–1 offer a very strong indication that Paul was suspected of wrongdoing with respect to the collection and that he understood the involvement of the delegation as an integral part of his defence (cf. 12:14–18). It has been suggested that the complicated relationship between Paul and the Corinthians can be understood in terms of a struggle to establish patronage, and the collection issue probably played an important part in that struggle. While the securing of support from a wealthy patron was a usual means that itinerant teachers used to earn a living, it was a means that Paul resisted for many reasons including fear that it would contribute to factions in Corinth. Instead the apostle continued to insist that he would earn his own living (cf. 1 Cor 9:12, 18). Some Corinthians probably wished to act as Paul's patron and subjected him to attack because of his departure from normal social conventions. The attack seems to have included, ironically, accusations of greed and back-handed dealings concerning money (cf. 2:17; 4:2; 6:3; 7:2; 12:16–17). Paul, in turn, sought to reverse the situation and place himself clearly in the position of patron (or agent of Christ, their ultimate benefactor; Witherington 1995: 417–19). Against such a background, the collection emerges as a particularly thorny issue, for it must be accepted by Paul in a way that does not diminish his status as a patron and does not put him in the position of being the Corinthians' client. vv. 23–4 illustrate that while he is interested in establishing the credibility of Titus and the brothers, they are brokers of his apostolic authority. He is their patron and the patron of the Corinthians, but their success as his agents in winning the Corinthians is crucial to protecting his honour. In order to encourage success, Paul calls the Corinthians to live up to their reputation, to demonstrate the reason Paul boasted about them to Titus (7:14). The implication is the same as in 7:14: if they fail to live up to their reputation, Paul will be disgraced—he will be shamed. The emotional pleas of v. 24 thus become more easily explained in the light of what is at stake. The Corinthians must prove their love openly for the delegation (love for them is love for Paul).

(9:1–5) An Appeal to Community Honour Although it is by no means a unanimous opinion, ch. 9 has sometimes been judged to be a fragment of a separate letter (cf. 2 COR 8:1–15).

One feature which appears to support the fragment theory is that in v. 2 Corinth is the subject of praise in relation to Macedonia, while in 8:2 the situation is reversed. However, there is no real contradiction here since Paul is referring to what the Macedonians have been told about the Corinthians' commitment to the collection, a commitment which they have as yet to fulfil. Both the argument about the Macedonian generosity and the point about the zeal of the Corinthians inspiring the Macedonians work together to galvanize the community into action. It is somewhat surprising that the focus in v. 2 is on Achaia while the focus in ch. 8 has been specifically on Corinth. But such a shift from the specific to the broader context of the province in which Corinth was located is in keeping with the opening of the letter (1:1). The reference to the brothers in v. 3 presupposes the discussion in 8:18–23. The emphasis on Paul's boasting about the Corinthians in vv. 2–4 is designed to repeat the same warning that has been articulated previously: the Corinthians must live up to their reputation. The importance of the values of honour and shame in shaping ethical injunctions and community life in general is clearly evident in v. 4. If Paul brings some of the Macedonians with him to Corinth and the community members have not as yet fulfilled their commitment, both the apostle and the Corinthian church will be humiliated; that is, shamed. As is also the case with the arrival of Titus and the brothers, the arrival of the Macedonians offers a potential occasion for the shaming of Paul and the Corinthian community, and this dishonour must be avoided at all costs (cf. 7:14; 8:24). Suspicions surrounding Paul's handling of the collection emerge once again in v. 5 (cf. 8:20–1). Once again Paul gives the impression that he wants to distance himself from the process of gathering the collection by insisting that the delegation bring matters to a close before he arrives in Corinth (cf. 2 COR 8:16–24). Paul wishes the collection to be perceived as a voluntary gift and not as an 'extortion'. The Greek term translated as extortion (*pleonexia*) occurs in the list of vices in Rom 1:29, referring to covetousness (cf. 1 Cor 5:10, 11; 6:10). Related terminology also occurs in 2 Corinthians (2:11; 7:2; 12:17–18). No doubt is left by 12:17–18 that Paul was accused of fraudulent activity with respect to the collection (Furnish 1984: 428).

(9:6–15) Appeals to Scripture In this passage Paul justifies his exhortation in 9:1–5 on the basis of Scripture and with broad concepts of the significance of God's gracious actions in the world. A citation of the LXX (Ps 112:9) is included in v. 9, but there are many other allusions to Scripture throughout. The statement that 'one reaps what one sows' in v. 6 closely resembles Gal 6:7–9, but is based on a maxim which pervades the Wisdom tradition (e.g. Job 4:8; Prov 11:18, 24; 22:8; Sir 7:3; Furnish 1988: 1198). That the community's giving should not be under compulsion is in keeping with Paul's desire to respect the freedom of the congregation (cf. 8:8; Philem 8–14; 2 COR 8:1–8). Paul justifies his statement with a slightly modified reference to the LXX (Prov 22:8–9) in the proclamation that God loves the cheerful giver (cf. Rom 12:8). The premiss announced loudly in v. 8 and which underlies many of these verses is that God is the giver who makes all things possible (cf. v. 15). For the one who has received—the believer—giving in return becomes a natural expression of one's participation in God's bounty. To communicate the notion of the believer's state as 'having enough of everything', Paul uses the term *autarkeia* which expresses the Greek ideal of self-sufficiency, the precondition for human freedom. Paul modifies traditional notions, however, with his insistence that self-sufficiency is not a purely human accomplishment but is made possible by God's beneficence (Betz 1985: 110). The emphasis on divine initiative continues with the citation of Ps 112:9 where Paul probably means us to understand 'his righteousness' not as a reference to the righteousness of the person who helps the poor (as in the psalm), but as a reference to God's righteousness (Furnish 1988: 1198). There are allusions to Isa 55:10 and Hos 10:12 in v. 10 which also support the notion of divine initiative. The images of harvest, growth, and plenty prepare the way for the announcement that the one who gives will be enriched even more (v. 11). vv. 11–13 make it clear, however, that generosity has more than the immediate effect of satisfying the need of the Jerusalem poor; it allows the Corinthians to contribute actively to the worship of God. The result of their giving is an abundance of thanksgivings to God. An alternative translation of *dokimē* in v. 13 as 'proof' rather than 'testing' (cf. 8:2, 8, 22) makes the connection with the sentiments expressed in 8:24 stand out more clearly. The collection allows for an open demonstration of their love and of their glorification of God. It is fundamentally an expression of their obedience to the gospel of Christ. Paul explains further that the generosity of the Corinthians will result in the Jerusalem Christians praying for them and expressing their love for them (v. 14). Rom 15:31 makes it clear that the apostle associates the acceptance of the collection for the Jerusalem church with the acceptance by the authorities there of what God has accomplished through Paul's ministry among the Gentiles (cf. Rom 15:31; Murphy-O'Connor 1990: 825). Perhaps Paul has these associations in mind when he joyously gives thanks to God for his indescribable gift (v. 15).

Paul on the Attack (10:1–13:10)

Chs. 1–9 reflect some problems in the community, but their tone is nevertheless often hopeful and conciliatory (e.g. 7:4–16). In contrast, the tone of chs. 10–13 is consistently harsh, anxious, and sarcastic. Therefore, most biblical scholars have accepted the theory that they originally constituted a separate letter. There is significant debate, however, as to where they fit in the chronology of letter fragments. They have frequently been identified with the 'tearful letter' mentioned in 2:3–4, 9, which means that the letter would have been written prior to chs. 1–9. Paul's more optimistic tone in the earlier chapters would then be understood as stemming from the resolution of most of the difficulties in the community. But several objections have been raised against this theory, based upon both the chronology of events suggested by the content of 2 Corinthians and the nature of the problem which is explicitly related to the 'tearful letter'. The suggestion of 7:4–16 is that at the time of composition of chs. 1–9, Titus had been to Corinth only once, while it appears that by the time 12:14–18 was composed he had been there twice. This implies that chs. 10–13 came later. Moreover, the case of the lapsed Corinthian brother dominates the concern in chs. 1–9 about the 'tearful letter' (2:3–11; cf. 7:8–12), but nowhere do we read about him

in chs. 10–13. In fact, when Paul refers to the effect of the 'tearful letter' in 7:5–12, there is no explicit interest in the topic which so clearly dominates chs. 10–13: the threat of the rival apostles. Thus it seems best to consider chs. 10–13 as distinct from the 'letter of tears' and as having been composed at some point following chs. 1–9 (Furnish 1988: 1198–9). Paul's harsher approach in chs. 10–13 is the result of his struggle with apostolic rivals who have gained tremendous influence over the Corinthians in the interim and whom Paul considers as intruders. He may be revealing his awareness of the threat of 'false apostles' in 3:1–6, but by the time of composition of chs. 10–13 the situation has clearly become much worse.

(10:1–18) Preliminary Defence

(10:1–6) Claims of Divine Power These verses and indeed all of chs. 10–13 set the stage for Paul's impending visit (12:14; 13:1). Paul begins with an appeal to the example of the meekness and gentleness of Christ (v. 1). This may be his way of communicating that in his approach he is emulating the way Jesus conducted his earthly ministry. It seems more likely, however, that he is referring to Christ's voluntary debasement for the sake of salvation, revealed through the cross (cf. 8:9; Phil 2:6–11). In obeying Christ (v. 5), Paul participates in Christ's power in weakness. Although Paul perhaps expresses it most clearly in 13:3–4, all of chs. 10–13 is based upon one central conviction: the apostle's authority is rooted in the fact that his personal strength/weakness echoes the strength/weakness of the crucified/resurrected Christ. v. 1 contains a sarcastic reformulation of the accusation quoted in 10:10 about strong letters, but weak presence and speech. Paul is attacking those who evaluate him according to the criteria sophists use to judge rhetoric (Witherington 1995: 433; Furnish 1984: 462). In the process, he displays his own rhetorical skill in 'destroying arguments' and 'taking thoughts captive' in the hope of removing obstacles which stand in the way of spreading the gospel, here described as the knowledge of God (v. 5; cf. 2:14). A similar use of the imagery of siege warfare in conjunction with philosophical argumentation is made by Philo *Conf. Ling.* 128–31; cf. Prov 21:22; Furnish 1984: 458, 462). Paul reveals further information about the nature of the case against him in the reference to opponents who accuse him of 'acting according to human standards' (lit. acting according to the flesh; v. 2). Paul previously stated that his actions are not according to human standards (1:17; cf. 1:12). Many commentators believe that Paul was rebuked on account of a lack of charismatic performances and ecstatic experiences (12:1–10; 5:11–13). This is quite ironic given the charismatic basis of his ministry. The work of the sociologist Max Weber on charisma has been employed by biblical scholars in order to shed light on Paul's apostleship (MacDonald 1988: 47–9). Paul can be understood as claiming 'charismatic authority' in the sense that he views his powers and qualities as stemming directly from divine origins and as not accessible to everyone. This attitude can be seen for example in Paul's descriptions of his divine commission (1 Cor 15:8–9; Gal 1:15–16) and when he expresses his confidence that when he preaches it is as if God were the speaker (5:18–20). He proclaims his gospel not only verbally, but also through various 'charismatic' acts (e.g. 12:12; Rom 15:19; 1 Cor 2:4; 1 Thess 1:5). Paul's charismatic authority can be seen very clearly in vv. 3–6, for in this text the apostle's very humanity is qualified by a claim to divine power. The military imagery serves Paul well here, because it communicates his belief that he is empowered by forces which are beyond this world to conquer this world (cf. 6:7). Throughout the text Paul sends the message that he will not be intimidated. When the Corinthians have demonstrated their loyalty to him, he will be ready to deal firmly with his opponents (v. 6).

(10:7–11) Accusations against Paul Denied The call to recognize what is plainly evident is designed to alert the community to danger. Behind the appeal is probably an accusation made by the intruders which has won support among the Corinthians. The opponents appear to have based their authority on a special connection to Christ (implied in 'belonging to Christ'; cf. 11:4, 13, 23). They may have claimed access to special visionary experiences of the resurrected Christ (12:1–10; 5:11–13). But since Paul's commission as an apostle was also based on such experiences (1 Cor 9:1; 15:8; Gal 1:12) yet the basis of his authority was being judged as inadequate, it is more likely that the claim concerned a special connection to the historical Jesus or to his followers, perhaps those connected with the Jerusalem church (cf. 11:22). The fact that Paul did not know the historical Jesus, had initially persecuted the church, and had entered the circle of apostles late in the game proclaiming that he had received a revelation of Christ, seems to have led to widespread questions and suspicions about his apostolic status (1 Cor 15:7–9). If the question of connection with the historical Jesus is involved in his battle with the Corinthian opponents, it is a matter of charismatic authority versus tradition. Given the importance of the appeal to tradition in Jewish teaching, it is not surprising that tension between charismatic authority and tradition can be detected in the attempts to organize the early church (Rowland 1985: 266–7). Paul is unequivocal, however, in v. 8. His authority is charismatic (2 COR 10:1–6); it was given to him by the Lord (i.e. the resurrected Christ; cf. 13:10). The concept of boasting which permeates (2 Corinthians 2 COR 1:12–14) is employed in an interesting way here and throughout chs. 10–13; its use is characterized by ambivalence and irony which becomes even more pronounced in the fool's speech of 11:1–12:13. The opponents may have accused him of boasting too much of his authority, but Paul admits that such extremes are necessary for the health of the Corinthians. Boasting and self-promotion were the conventional means of articulating where honour and shame were to be found in Graeco-Roman society (Witherington 1995: 432). Paul is faced with the difficulty of harmonizing his conviction that in the early church many of the usual criteria for determining honour have been abandoned (e.g. skill in rhetorical performance), with the necessity of communicating priorities in a cultural context which demanded public demonstrations of worth. It sometimes seems to Paul that in communicating his priorities he is resorting to worldly standards: he boasts a little too much! In v. 10 Paul quotes an accusation made against him directly (cf. 10:1). He has been accused of weak physical presence and poor oral performance of rhetoric. It seems that even his critics acknowledge his skill in writing rhetorical pieces (Witherington 1995: 433). In vv. 9–11 Paul admits that his letters are strong, but instead of declaring that he is equally strong in speech, he

uses the opportunity to bring the focus of community back to the content of his letters. The true nature of his strength will be made clear through his actions when he comes to Corinth and does what he has said in his letters. Underlying these verses may be the suspicion that Paul is avoiding direct contact with the Corinthians, perhaps relying too heavily on his talent as a letter-writer and on fellow-workers to act as his delegates.

(10:12–18) Opponents Accused of Interference In this section Paul moves from responding to accusations made against him to launching some attacks of his own upon his opponents (Furnish 1988: 1199). In v. 12 he is clearly being sarcastic: he would not even presume to compare himself with those who commend themselves! He probably has in mind here the use of letters of recommendation by his rivals (cf. 3:1–3). He rejects both the self-commendation of his opponents and the nature of their comparisons with one another as completely misguided. They act according to worldly commendations, when only commendation by the Lord is relevant (vv. 17–18). To make his point forcefully, he draws upon the contentious notion of boasting (citing Jer 9:23–4) in order to call for a return to central priorities: boasting should be done only in the Lord (v. 17; cf. 1 Cor 1:31; Phil 3:3). The exact meaning of vv. 13–16 is not always clear and there are severe problems in translating (esp. v. 13; see Barrett 1973: 263–6). However, the main point is clear: Paul's mission to the Corinthians has divine authorization; his opponents have not respected his prerogatives as the founder of the community and have interfered in his 'sphere of action' (v. 16). These verses reveal the somewhat curious preoccupation (at least from a modern perspective) of divisions of missionary labour. Paul's principle was that he would bring the good news only to communities where it had never been preached. 'Boasting of work already done in someone else's sphere of action' (v. 16) was 'building on someone else's foundation' (Rom 15:20). An understanding of the dynamics of patronage can shed light on Paul's exclusive claims and jealousy. Paul refers to himself as the Corinthians' spiritual parent in a way that conveys the nature of his relationship with them as their benefactor (12:14; Witherington 1995: 418; cf. 1 Cor 4:14–16). He endowed them with the gift of salvation and, in turning to other apostles, they betray the loyalty that should exist between patron and client and fail to honour him as clients should. Paul's desire for an increasing sphere of action expressed in vv. 15–16 is a means of calling for a strengthened relationship with the Corinthian community as their patron which will free him to move on, and bring the good news to new territories (cf. Rom 15:23–4).

(11:1–12:13) The Fool's Speech

(11:1–4) The Threat of Corruption The whole of 11:1–12:13 is dominated by the concept that Paul is speaking like a fool. To a certain extent, Paul engages in parody in this section: he imitates the tactics (sophistic eloquence and rhetorical self-praise) of his opponents (Witherington 1995: 436). But the reference to foolishness in the context of v. 1 makes it clear that he is not altogether comfortable with the measures he has adopted. He is in fact engaging in the kind of comparison which he has just rejected as ultimately irrelevant, and he therefore risks giving the impression that he shares the preoccupations of his opponents (10:12–18). One can appreciate the difficulty of Paul's position; he lives in a society which demands public display of its itinerant teachers (cf. 2 COR 10:7–11). Yet there is a desperate and sometimes almost tragic sound to Paul's words, as he laments about an apostleship whose strength has not been recognized in weakness. In vv. 1–4 Paul makes use of a marriage metaphor to communicate the seriousness of the threat which has penetrated the community from the outside. The gravity of the situation as Paul perceived it would not have been missed by an audience of the time, for he appeals to the core values of honour and shame. Paul places himself in the role of father (cf. 12:14) of a virgin (the community) who is giving her in marriage to her one true husband (Christ). It is the father's duty to protect the honour of the virgin; and it is the virgin daughter's duty to remain chaste, symbolizing her shame (concern for reputation) and the shame of her whole household. But Paul fears that the virgin daughter will be violated by a seducer. The image of the corruption of the internal sanctity of the virgin daughter is a powerful means of communicating the nature of the threat which comes from the outside. Indisputable evidence is offered in v. 4 that the problem in the community is not only internal, but involves teachers from the outside who preach a message that Paul understands to be in contradiction to his own. The reference to proclamation of another Jesus may imply an appeal on the part of the 'false apostles' to greater continuity with the historical Jesus (cf. 10:7; 2 COR 10:7–11). vv. 2–3 are dense in allusions to Scripture and traditional notions of marriage. The role of the father in giving his virgin daughter in marriage is reflected in such texts as Gen 29:23 and Deut 22:13–21. The use of the marriage metaphor to address the relationship of the community with the divine draws upon the traditional notion of marriage as a metaphor for YHWH's relationship to Israel (e.g. Hos 2:19–20). The image of the virgin (community) joining together with the bridegroom (Christ) is developed further in Eph 5:21–33. The reference to Eve being deceived by the serpent presupposes the temptation story (Gen 3:1–24). In Jewish tradition the serpent became identified with the devil (Sir 2:24; cf. Rev 20:2). Paul's interpretation here, with its overtones of seduction and sexual conquest, may reflect knowledge of a Jewish legend contained in the pseudepigrapha (2 Enoch, 31:6; cf. 1 Tim 2:13–14) where the serpent is identified with Satan and Eve's deception involves sexual seduction (Murphy-O'Connor 1990: 826).

(11:5–15) The Super-Apostles The transition from 11:4 to 11:5 implies that those who come into Corinth are described sarcastically by Paul as 'super-apostles', *tōn hyperlian apostolōn* (cf. 12:11). It has also been suggested, however, that these super-apostles are not the intruders that Paul labels so negatively as 'false apostles', *pseudapostoloi*, in v. 13 (e.g. Barrett 1971: 249–53). Paul's qualified admission that the status of the super-apostles equals his own (cf. 12:11) has sometimes led to the conclusion that they were leaders of the Jerusalem church (cf. Gal 2:9); the false apostles may then have been their envoys, whom Paul condemns categorically as intruders (v. 13; for a full summary of the debate concerning identity of super-apostles, see Furnish 1984: 502–5). But the emphasis on rhetorical performance in oral delivery (v. 6) seems to support the notion that these super-apostles are themselves

the intruders, who not only rate themselves highly, but have probably also gained considerable prestige in the community (Georgi 1986: 39). v. 6 has been judged to be a frank admission by Paul of a liability (Witherington 1995: 435). In these earliest stages of church development, norms are being institutionalized with respect to judgement of apostolic legitimacy and talent, and Paul is not always able to meet group expectations. He calls for a realignment of community norms based on true knowledge of God (v. 6; cf. 10:5). Paul's shifting of labels from super-apostles to false apostles does not necessarily imply that two different groups are in view, but may stem from Paul's shifting perspectives. According to some standards (which he himself rejects) these apostles are powerful leaders. But according to the ultimate standard of God, they are merely disguising themselves as apostles of Christ (v. 13). In vv. 7–11 Paul offers a specific example of his behaviour in order to defend himself against accusations concerning his authority and credibility. The Corinthians may have harboured suspicions about Paul's attitudes to money and dealings with the collection, and these ideas may have left the opportunity ripe for the intruders to gain support. Paul has refused financial support from the Corinthians and refers to his principle ironically and with exaggeration by speaking of committing sin (v. 7), and robbing from other churches for the Corinthians' sake (v. 8). Paul continued to work as an artisan while he conducted his missionary work (1 Cor 4:12; 1 Thess 2:9), apparently refusing the support to which other apostles were entitled (1 Cor 9:12, 15–18). This refusal to accept living expenses may have been related to the desire to avoid being a client of Corinthian patrons, and to the fear of contributing to the already serious problem of community factions (2 COR 8:16–24). But it may also have led to frustration among the Corinthians who may have argued that Paul abrogated societal conventions with respect to itinerant teachers and degraded himself (and them) with manual labour. Paul makes it abundantly clear, however, in v. 10, that he has no intention of changing his approach. The reference to friends from Macedonia in v. 9 may be in response to the charge that he has allowed himself to become a client of the Macedonians. Paul reveals that he did accept special gifts from the Philippian church in Macedonia (Phil 4:10–20), but was apparently unwilling to accept such support in Corinth. The question also arises as to whether Macedonian generosity in the collection (8:1–5) was related to the nature of the patronage relationship he had with them. But Paul continues to have confidence in his boast, making it clear that his attitude towards support from the Corinthian church is a public demonstration of his honour (v. 10) and is motivated by his love for the community (v. 11). In vv. 12–15 the accusation made against Paul concerning his refusal to accept financial support from the Corinthians is transformed by him into an indication of the false apostles' inadequacy and dishonesty. Only by accepting the same attitude to support as does Paul, might these apostles show themselves to be Paul's equal (v. 12). The implication is clearly that these false apostles have been taking advantage of the Corinthians. The description of Satan disguising himself as an angel of light echoes 11:3 and reflects Jewish legends about the deception of Eve by the devil (*Apoc. Mos.* 17.1–2; *Adam and Eve* 9.1 [Latin]; *Adam and Eve* 38.1 [Slavonic]; Furnish 1984: 494–5). The use of the terms 'apostle' and 'minister' (*diakonos*) (terms Paul applies to himself) in the condemnation of the intruders suggests that, despite the polemic and the parody, the threat to Paul's apostolic authority cuts to the heart.

(11:16–21a) The 'Wise' Corinthians In v. 16 Paul repeats the appeal of 11:1 to bear with him as he plays the part of the fool. It is almost as if he is aware that he has been digressing from his main speech in 11:2–15. He explicitly states in vv. 17–18 that he is speaking not with the Lord's authority, but boasting (2 COR 1:12–14) according to the human standards of his opponents. In vv. 19–21a the apostle employs irony and engages in extreme sarcasm. He draws upon the community's reputation for thinking itself wise (1 Cor 2:6–16; 4:10; 6:4–5) and ironically refers to their willingness to entertain fools (the false apostles). The implication is that now that he counts himself as a fool, they will surely entertain him! Paul denigrates the false apostles in v. 20 in a manner that implies their charlatanism and recalls the differing attitudes towards community support which divide Paul from his opponents (11:7–15). He sarcastically proclaims that he was simply too weak to adopt the belittling tactics of his opponents (v. 21a). This is, of course, an ironic jibe at the Corinthians' blindness in recognizing the strength of true apostleship, a blindness which is made especially evident by the accusation that Paul's bodily presence is weak (10:10). What appears to be his shame (weakness) he hopes to prove is in fact his honour (power; cf. 1 Cor 12:9).

(11:21b–33) The Self-Designations of Paul's Opponents The passage 11:21b–12:10 includes the heart of the 'fool's speech'. Declaring that he is engaging in foolishness, Paul nevertheless boasts in the same terms as his opponents and insists that he shares all of their claims to authority. In the process he reveals the self-designations of his opponents. 'Hebrews,' 'Israelites', and 'descendants of Abraham' are three closely related labels pointing to a special claim of Jewish heritage (cf. Phil 3:5). It is impossible to attach a distinct significance to each term, but there may be differences of nuance. 'Hebrews' may refer primarily to ethnic descent, but also to geographical origin and familiarity with Hebrew or Aramaic (cf. Acts 6:1). With 'Israelites' the focus may be somewhat more upon a religious past, heritage, and tradition (Georgi 1986: 46). The conflict between Paul and the opponents in Corinth probably involves the question of whether the charismatic basis of the apostle's authority (a direct appeal to divine experience) is sufficient in the light of the greater appeal made to tradition by the false apostles (2 COR 10:1–6). 'Descendants of Abraham' may function to legitimate the authority they claim in propounding their particular understanding of the mission they undertake among the Gentiles: Abraham's promise was to be the father of many nations (cf. Rom 4:13–18; 9:6–8; Gal 3:16–18). The title 'ministers [or servants] of Christ' (*diakonoi Christou*), v. 23, is especially important because it represents a direct quotation of a designation that moves beyond claims concerning heritage and identity to give us a sense of how the opponents understood what they were doing (Georgi 1986: 32). The seriousness of the threat posed by the opponents may have been related to an approach and self-understanding which in many ways may have been quite similar to Paul's mission to be a minister of Christ Jesus (e.g. Rom 15:16). This

is supported by the frequent use of the terms *diakonos* and *diakonia* throughout 2 Corinthians (on deacon, see *OCB* s.v.). The opponents' understanding of their connection with Christ may have differed from that of Paul, however, with respect to claims of a special relationship with the historical Jesus (2 COR 10:7–11; vv. 1–4, 5–15). Paul illustrates that he is a better minister/servant of Christ by describing a ministry of suffering and humiliation. He appeals once again to a catalogue of hardships (v. 23) which functions in 2 Corinthians in conjunction with the apostle's theology of the cross (vv. 30–1). This catalogue recalls the terms used by philosophers in the ancient world to describe their struggles in the overcoming of passion and in the search for wisdom (2 COR 4:7–15). But there is no heroism in Paul's attitude towards his troubles; v. 29 in fact records the sentiment of injustice in suffering. Yet suffering is far from meaningless; it offers demonstrative proof of Paul's weakness (v. 30), which is a sign of his identification with Christ (12:9). Because Paul appeals to the extent of his hardships to respond directly to the claims of superiority made by his opponents (v. 23), and because the theme of inappropriate boasting permeates the discussion (vv. 16–23), it is tempting to conclude that the opponents viewed their own apostolic struggles as heroic or as signs of their 'strength' of character. The sufferings mentioned in the catalogue of hardships cover many aspects of Paul's life: work as an artisan (vv. 23, 27), travel (vv. 25–6), persecution (vv. 23–6), church life (vv. 26, 28). Particularly intriguing is the reference to 'false brethren' in v. 26. The same term is used by Paul to describe those who seek to impose the law on Gentile Christians in Gal 2:4 (Murphy-O'Connor 1990: 827). The list offers evidence of persecution at the hands of both Jews and Gentiles. The legal basis for the 'forty lashes' is found in Deut 25:1–3. Being 'beaten with a rod' was a Roman punishment. Although a law prohibited the imposition of this punishment on Roman citizens, it was frequently ignored; Paul protests this punishment in Acts 16:37 (cf. Acts 16:22; 1 Thess 2:2; Furnish 1984: 516). In fact, the reference to the beatings offers evidence of one of many points of contact between this text and accounts in Acts. However, as is illustrated by comparing the reference to the narrow escape from Damascus (vv. 32–3) with the account in Acts 9:23–5, the stories do not always present the same picture of the apostle. While in 2 Corinthians the story illustrates Paul's humiliation and weakness, in Acts it communicates the apostle's bravery and invincible mission (Furnish 1988: 1201).

(12:1–10) Visions and Revelations of the Lord Paul continues his inappropriate boasting—his speaking like a fool (11:21)—by once again arguing that he can match any claims of status that his opponents might have. In v. 1 he gives the impression that he is ready to discuss the last contentious issue; he moves on to visions and revelations 'of the Lord' (probably to be understood as 'granted *by* the Lord': a genitive of origin; Furnish 1984: 524). That his reluctance to engage in this type of discourse is particularly great, however, is suggested by his description of his experience in the third person: 'I know a person in Christ...' (v. 2). Probably because of the importance attached to visions and revelations by his opponents, Paul wishes to convey the impression that such ecstatic experiences are relatively unimportant and even of no real significance for ministry. Paul's mission is based on what is seen concretely in the apostle and what is heard from the apostle (vv. 6–7). Paul emphasizes the nature of his dealings with church communities and his preaching of the gospel as definitive signs of his apostleship. But he nevertheless unwittingly offers here an indication of the significance of ecstatic religious experience for an early church group. The attitude towards it in this text appears to be more negative than that revealed by 5:13, where competition concerning ecstatic experience may also be in view (2 COR 5:11–19). Moreover, while Paul clearly sees a great difference between the revelation of the Lord he describes in vv. 2–4 and the revelation of God's Son which led to his becoming an apostle (Gal 1:15–16), the distinction may be less apparent to his audience. Ultimately Paul's apostleship is based upon revelation, but given the situation in Corinth he obviously feels that it is prudent instead to stress his physical (and earthly) weakness which discloses the power accorded to him by the Lord. In Paul's dispute with the opponents we can perhaps sense a trace of the difficulty of determining which charismatic experience of an apostle is authentic. In the early church writing, the *Didache*, attitudes towards riches on the part of itinerant charismatics became an important guide to determining which teachers were truly gifted (*Did.* 11–13). Paul tells us very little about the shape of his revelatory experience or what it meant; but he does announce that it could have led to elation (v. 7). He tells us he was caught up (cf. 1 Thess 4:17) to the third heaven (here equated with Paradise, see vv. 2, 4; cf. *2 Enoch 7* and *Apoc. Mos.* 37.5; Murphy-O'Connor 1990: 828). Other-worldly journeys were commonly described in ancient apocalyptic literature (Furnish 1984: 525–6). The mysterious quality that one would expect of such an experience is disclosed by Paul in the admission that he does not know whether the experience was in the body or out of the body (v. 3). His reference to a lack of knowledge about the event, however, may also be a way of communicating its relative unimportance. Similarly, Paul's announcement that he heard things that should never be told could be in keeping with the notion of a sealed revelation (Dan 12:4; Rev 10:4), but could also be a means of pointing to irrelevance of the event for the essence of his apostleship (Murphy-O'Connor 1990: 828). Having abandoned the role of the fool (and the parody of his opponents' tactics), Paul admits that he was prevented from boasting (or being too elated) by a thorn in the flesh, a messenger from Satan (v. 7). Most commentators have seen here a reference to a physical ailment (physical suffering is understood by Paul as a sign that Satan's power continues to influence the world; cf. 4:4; see Neyrey 1990: 167–80), but others have argued that Paul has an external enemy in mind, a non-believer or an opponent in the church (cf. 2 Cor 11:14–15; Murphy-O'Connor 1990: 828). Paul apparently prayed three times to the Lord to have the thorn removed (v. 8). The Lord responded by means of an oracle (v. 9). Grace is equated with power in v. 9 and refers to the force which sustains Paul and is disclosed in his weakness. Paul announces that it is his weakness that is the authentic source of his boasting, for it is a sign of the power of Christ dwelling within him. He offers a summary (v. 10) of the long catalogue of hardships in 11:23–8, but now explicitly states that he is content in his sufferings: these make known the paradox of his life as an apostle in imitation of Christ.

(12:11–13) The Signs of a True Apostle These verses are usually understood as the epilogue of the fool's speech (11:1–12:13). Paul takes up the voice of the fool once again. He has had to defend his own honour, since the Corinthians have not been commending him. This is the voice of a patron who feels he has not received the honour which is his due. Maintaining the ironic tone which dominates chs. 10–13, Paul admits that he is weak (he is nothing), but at the same time he is not at all inferior to the super-apostles whom the Corinthians admire so much (11:5; 2 COR 11:5–15). Paul tells the Corinthians that they have no reason to complain since 'the signs of a true apostle' were performed adequately among them (v. 12). The reference to 'signs' (*sēmeia*) offers evidence of the existence of institutionalized norms in the community for determining true apostleship (2 COR 10:7–11). A similar focus on charismatic performance in the process of evangelization occurs in Rom 15:19 and in Gal 3:5. But Paul's admission of the importance of 'signs and wonders and mighty works' is intriguing, given his previous attempt to play down the importance of visions and revelations to his mission (12:1–10). Paul is speaking like a fool in vv. 11–13, but he nevertheless may be offering an indication that charismatic phenomena were central to Paul's initial acceptance in a community, even though such wondrous deeds were subsumed by the apostle within the larger purpose of preaching the gospel of Christ (Rom 15:18–19). In v. 13 Paul returns to the complaint made by the Corinthians of unfair treatment in comparison to other churches. This complaint involved the apostle's refusal to accept material support from the Corinthians (his refusal to become their client). The Corinthians argued that he did not adopt the same attitude in other places (notably Macedonia: 11:7–11; 2 COR 11:5–15). With biting sarcasm, Paul pleads for the Corinthians' forgiveness for not burdening them.

(12:14–13:10) Concluding Defence

(12:14–18) Suspicions of Wrongdoing concerning the Collection Having appealed to the Corinthians for obedience in 10:1–18, and having supported that appeal with the 'fool's speech' in 11:1–12:13, Paul now states his intention to come to Corinth a third time and offers further arguments in support of his position. These verses have played a part in theories concerning the chronology of the letter fragments of 2 Corinthians. The passage 7:4–16 suggests that at the time of composition of chs. 1–9, Titus had only been to Corinth once, while it appears that by the time vv. 14–18 were composed he had made a second visit. This implies that chs. 10–13 came later. Paul's third visit (v. 14; cf. 13:1) appears to be the visit that he had planned (1:16) but had postponed after the second painful visit (2:1; cf. 9:4). During the first visit the community was founded. In vv. 14–16 Paul restates a principle that he defended vigorously in 11:7–11 and alluded to sarcastically in 12:13: he will continue to support himself while he is with the Corinthians (2 COR 11:5–15). Paul presents this as the natural consequence of his parental relationship with the Corinthians and of his great love for them (vv. 14–15; cf. 1 Cor 4:15). But the practical application of this principle in the community involves the acceptance of Paul as patron of the community and the obligation to honour him with their love. There were probably Corinthians who felt that the reverse should take place; they wished Paul to act as their client and accept their gifts of material support (2 COR 8:16–24). But Paul feels that this would be as ridiculous a scenario as children 'lay[ing] up' (saving) for their parents. In vv. 16–18 Paul repeats a charge of deceitful trickery brought against him by the Corinthians and defends himself against it (cf. 2 Cor 4:2). The discussion of the trip made by Titus and the brother recalls the description of the arrangements made by Paul for the impending visit in chs. 8–9. Because Paul seems so confident of his loyalty as a co-worker who accompanied Titus, the brother mentioned in v. 18 is most likely Paul's representative referred to in 8:22 and not the brother who was apparently appointed by the churches to oversee the handling of the collection as a kind of external auditor (8:18–19; 2 COR 8:16–24). vv. 14–18 present information which acts as an important complement to the material in chs. 8–9: it offers unmistakable evidence that Paul was suspected of wrongdoing with respect to the collection and his delicate handling of the situation in chs. 8–9 should be read in that light. But the manner in which reference to the collection is fused with suspicions concerning Paul's refusal to accept material support in vv. 14–18 leads to further information about the precise nature of the suspicions of the Corinthians concerning Paul and money. Paul was probably suspected of keeping for himself some of the money that he is collecting for Jerusalem. In short, he was being accused of fraud (Furnish 1988: 1202). Paul brings the discussion of the matter to a close with rhetorical questions which he is sure will highlight his innocence (v. 18).

(12:19–21) The Motives of Paul's Defence Paul now seeks to counter the impression that he has been engaging solely in a personal defence based on past events and has not been addressing important matters of community well-being. He insists that he has in fact been working for the sake of building up the community because he fears that a complete breakdown of the relationship between himself and the community will occur when he arrives (vv. 19–20). Given that Paul has been responding to specific problems having to do with the false apostles and with community loyalty from 10:1 until now, it is surprising to hear him frame the situation in terms of a general problem with improper behaviour ranging from quarrelling to sexual immorality (vv. 20–1). The list of vices in v. 20 appears to be conventional (cf. Gal 5:20; Murphy-O'Connor 1990: 828). While Corinth has a history of sexual immorality (1 Cor 5:1–5; cf. 1 Cor 6:15–16), the problem does not surface elsewhere in 2 Corinthians. However, Jews in the Roman world frequently drew attention to sexual immorality in attempts to describe the sin and alienation in the pagan world (Newton 1985: 102–3). It may be that Paul is aiming to cast the sin of the Corinthians in the most negative terms. Behind vv. 20–1 may lie an attempt on the part of the apostle to describe the consequences of the community's alienation from him as devastating. With all hope lost, there will be nothing left to do but mourn.

(13:1–4) The Serious Consequences of Disobedience At first glance it may appear that the legal statement requiring two or three witnesses for a charge refers to requirements to substantiate charges against Paul (12:16). However, the rule—a citation of Deut 19:15—concerns the establishment of proper criteria for conviction and punishment (cf. Deut 19:15–21; Mt 18:16), and this fits equally well with vv. 3–4 where Paul warns the community of the possibility of punitive action. Moreover,

in non-diaspora Judaism the rule was often used to support the requirement that those suspected of wrongdoing were to be warned carefully of the possibility of punishment (van Vliet 1958: 53–62; Furnish 1984: 575). In stressing his multiple previous warnings, Paul apparently feels that he has met the criteria of the rule. There is an element of foreboding in his warning that he will not be lenient. He promises proof of Christ speaking in him (2:17; 5:20; 12:19) in the form of punishment of the Corinthians. The explanation of the meaning of the Christ event in v. 4 is in keeping with credal statements in Paul's other letters (e.g. Rom 1:4): Christ was crucified in weakness but raised up to live by the power of God. Paul's union with Christ means that his life is shaped by the power of God in the same way. He shares Christ's weakness, but in dealing with the Corinthians, he will 'live with him' by the power of God. vv. 3–4 offer a good illustration of theology finding expression in concrete human interaction. The theology of the cross functions to support censure in community ethics and discipline (2 COR 4:7–15).

(13:5–10) The Purpose of Paul's Letter Paul's tone in this section is more conciliatory than in the exhortations in 13:1–4, but v. 10 makes it clear that the same message frames both passages: severe discipline of the Corinthian community is a distinct possibility. Paul states, however, that he hopes that drastic measures will not be necessary and locates the purpose of his letter in the prevention of such measures. Paul certainly feels that he has been endowed with divine power in his dealings with the Corinthians (13:4), but qualifies the authority given to him by Christ in a way that ties his treatment of the Corinthians to the central goal of his mission. Paul has been given authority to build up (v. 10; cf. 12:19) and not to tear it down (an almost identical phrase is found in 10:8; cf. 2 COR 10:7–11). The notion of 'upbuilding' (*oikodomē*) occurs frequently in the Corinthian correspondence and refers to the harmonious development of the church in accordance with God's designs (e.g. 1 Cor 3:9 and 14:26). We can only imagine the great sense of failure and defeat that Paul would have experienced if things did not turn out as he had hoped in Corinth and there had been a tearing down (or destruction, *kathairesis*; cf. 10:4). There are, in fact, several indications throughout vv. 5–9 that Paul's sense of his own apostleship is bound up with the behaviour of the Corinthians. In an atmosphere of comparisons between apostles and challenges to apostolic authority, Paul invites the Corinthians to test themselves: have they displayed the faith that flows from the presence of Jesus among them? The implication seems to be that if they pass the test, Paul will also avoid failure (vv. 5–6). Nevertheless, to the end, Paul insists that what is most important is not the visibility of his apostolic credentials but the fact that he has acted in accordance with the truth of the gospel (vv. 7–8; cf. 4:2; 6:7). The apostle may be weak, and the Corinthians may even continue to view him as weak, as long as the Corinthians are strong; that is, strong in faith but not strong in self-importance. The relationship between apostle and community reflects the meaning of the cross. In weakness and suffering, strength and salvation are revealed. The announcement of the purpose of Paul's letter in v. 10 seems incompatible with chs. 1–9 and is often viewed as an indication that chs. 10–13 should be viewed as a separate letter.

The third visit (12:14; 13:1) seems to be the one Paul intended to make after the Corinthians' contribution to the collection had been gathered (9:3–5). By the time of composition of chs. 10–13 the relationship between the Corinthians and the community had deteriorated to such an extent that Paul probably wondered whether the church would make a contribution at all and he felt a harsh letter was required to set matters straight. The reference to the people of both Macedonia and Achaia (Corinth was the capital of this province) making a generous contribution to the poor in Jerusalem (Rom 15:25–6) suggests that the letter did indeed achieve its purpose (Furnish 1988: 1202).

Conclusion: Greetings and Benediction (13:11–13)

Assuming the generally held view that 2 Corinthians harmonizes at least two separate letters (chs. 1–9; 10–13), it is not clear which of the fragments originally included these verses. In addition, different translations reflect a slightly different numbering of verses. The NRSV has three verses, but some translations break the passage down into four verses, numbering 'All the saints greet you' as v. 13. 'Saints' is a general term for believers (cf. 2 COR 1:1–2), but here probably refers to the saints of Macedonia, the place where 2 Corinthians (or much of the letter) was composed (7:5; cf. 2:12–13; 8:1; 9:2). The call to greet one another with a holy kiss occurs several times in Paul's letters (e.g. Rom 16:16; 1 Cor 16:20; 1 Thess 5:26). It recalls the ritual kiss during church gatherings, which was an intimate expression of the fellowship experienced in early church groups (Meeks 1984: 109). The benediction in v. 13 is longer than usual and resembles Eph 6:23–4. The reference to the Lord Jesus Christ, God, and the Holy Spirit should not be understood as a presentation of the formal doctrine of the trinity (Thrall 1965: 183).

REFERENCES

Barrett, C. K. (1971), 'Paul's Opponents in II Corinthians', NTS 17: 233–54.
—— (1973), A Commentary on the Second Epistle to the Corinthians (London: A. & C. Black).
Bassler, J. M. (1992), '2 Corinthians', in C. Newsom and S. Ringe (eds.), The Women's Bible Commentary (Louisville, Ky.: Westminster/John Knox), 330–2.
Belleville, L. L. (1993), 'Tradition or Creation? Paul's Use of the Exodus 34 Tradition in 2 Corinthians 3.7–18', in C. Evans and J. Sanders (eds.), Paul and the Scriptures of Israel (Sheffield: JSOT), 165–85.
Berger, P. L., and Luckmann, T. (1981), The Social Construction of Reality (Harmondsworth: Penguin).
Betz, H. D. (1973), '2 Cor 6:14–7:1: An Anti-Pauline Fragment?' JBL 92: 88–108.
—— (1985), 2 Corinthians 8 and 9: A Commentary on Two Administrative Letters of the Apostle Paul, Hermeneia (Philadelphia: Fortress).
—— (1992), D. Freedman (ed.), 'Second Epistle to the Corinthians', ABD, i. 1148–54.
Chow, J. K. (1992), Patronage and Power: A Study of Social Networks in Corinth (Sheffield: JSOT).
Crafton, J. A. (1990), The Agency of the Apostle: A Dramatistic Analysis of Paul's Response to Conflict in 2 Corinthians (Sheffield: JSOT).
Danker, F. W. (1989), II Corinthians (Minneapolis: Augsburg).
Fitzgerald, J. T. (1988), Cracks in an Earthen Vessel: An Examination of the Catalogues of Hardships in the Corinthian Correspondence (Atlanta: Scholars Press).
Furnish, V. P. (1984), II Corinthians, AB (Garden City NY: Doubleday).

—— (1988), '2 Corinthians', J. L. Mays (ed.), HBC (San Francisco: Harper & Row), 1190–203.
Garrett, S. R. (1995), 'Paul's Thorn and Cultural Models of Affliction', in L. White and O. Yarbrough (eds.), The Social World of the First Christians: Essays in Honour of Wayne Meeks (Minneapolis: Fortress), 82–99.
Georgi, D. (1986), The Opponents of Paul in Second Corinthians (Philadelphia: Fortress).
Hock, R. F. (1980), The Social Context of Paul's Ministry: Tentmaking and Apostleship (Philadelphia: Fortress).
Holmberg, B. (1980), Paul and Power: The Structure of Authority in the Primitive Church as Reflected in the Pauline Epistles (Philadelphia: Fortress).
MacDonald, M. Y. (1988), The Pauline Churches: A Socio-Historical Study of Institutionalization in the Pauline and Deutero-Pauline Writings (Cambridge: Cambridge University Press).
MacMullen, R. (1984), Christianizing the Roman Empire: A. D. 100–400 (New Haven: Yale University Press).
Marshall, P. (1987), Enmity in Corinth: Social Conventions in Paul's Relations with the Corinthians (Tübingen: Mohr).
Martin, D. B. (1990), Slavery as Salvation: The Metaphor of Slavery in Pauline Christianity (New Haven: Yale University Press).
Matthews, S. (1994), '2 Corinthians', in E. S. Fiorenza (ed.), Searching the Scriptures, ii. A Feminist Commentary (New York: Crossroad), 196–217.
Meeks, W. (1983), The First Urban Christians (New Haven: Yale University Press).
Mitchell, M. M. (1991), Paul and the Rhetoric of Reconciliation (Tübingen: Mohr).
Murphy-O'Connor, J. (1990), 'The Second Letter to the Corinthians', NJBC 816–29.
—— (1991), The Theology of the Second Letter to the Corinthians (Cambridge: Cambridge University Press).
Newton, M. (1985), The Concept of Purity at Qumran and in the Letters of Paul (Cambridge: Cambridge University Press).
Neyrey, J. H. (1990), Paul, in Other Words: A Cultural Reading of his Letters (Louisville, Ky.: Westminster/John Knox).
—— (1993), 'Nudity', in J. Pilch and B. Malina (eds.), Biblical Social Values and Their Meaning (Peabody, Mass.: Hendrickson), 119–25.
Plevnik, J. (1993), 'Honour/Shame', in J. Pilch and B. Malina (eds.), Biblical Social Values and Their Meaning (Peabody, Mass.: Hendrickson), 95–104.
Reese, J. M. (1993), 'Assertiveness', in J. Pilch and B. Malina (eds.), Biblical Social Values and Their Meaning (Peabody, Mass.: Hendrickson), 9–11.
Sanders, E. P. (1983), Paul, the Law, and the Jewish People (Philadelphia: Fortress).
Schütz, J. H. (1975), Paul and the Anatomy of Apostolic Power (Cambridge: Cambridge University Press).
Stockhausen, C. K. (1993), '2 Corinthians 3 and the Principles of Pauline Exegesis', in C. Evans and J. Sanders (eds.), Paul and the Scriptures of Israel (Sheffield: JSOT), 143–64.
Theissen, G. (1982), The Social Setting of Pauline Christianity: Essays on Corinth (Philadelphia: Fortress).
Thrall, M. E. (1965), I and II Corinthians, CBC (Cambridge: Cambridge University Press).
—— (1980), 'Super-Apostles, Servants of Christ, and Servants of Satan', JSNT 6: 42–57.
van Vliet, H. (1958), No Single Testimony: A Study on the Adoption of the Law of Deut. 19:15 Par. into the New Testament, Studia Theologica Rheno-Traiectina, 4 (Utrecht: Kemink & Zoon).
Witherington III, B. (1995), Conflict and Community in Corinth: A Socio-Rhetorical Commentary on 1 and 2 Corinthians (Grand Rapids, Mich.: William B. Eerdmans).
Young, F., and Ford, D. F. (1987), Meaning and Truth in 2 Corinthians (Grand Rapids, Mich.: William B. Eerdmans).

67. Galatians

G. N. STANTON

INTRODUCTION

A. Paul and the Galatian Churches. 1. Galatians was sent as a circular letter to a group of churches in Galatia, where it would have been read aloud, perhaps on several occasions in the context of worship (1:2). This is the most passionate of Paul's letters; only 2 Cor 10–13 is partly comparable. There has never been any doubt about the authorship of Galatians: here we meet Paul's pugnacious defence of 'the truth of the gospel' (2:5), as well as his exposition of the significance of God's disclosure of Jesus Christ (1:12). Paul's letter is carefully crafted, though in places the modern reader wishes he had clarified some of his statements. We do not know whether Paul's attempt to fend off the threat of the agitators who had infiltrated the Galatian churches met with immediate success. In the long run, however, Paul was successful: his insistence that Gentiles need not observe the whole Mosaic law (including circumcision) as an integral part of their commitment to Christ won the day, but the debates on this issue rumbled on in some circles well into the latter part of the second century (cf. Justin Martyr, *Dialogue*, 47), and even occasionally thereafter.

2. In places Paul uses strong language which must have made some of the first listeners to this letter wince (cf. 3:1; 4:30; 5:12). Occasional scholarly attempts to 'improve' Paul's line of argument by removing some verses as later non-Pauline additions have not won support. We can be confident that the letter we have is very similar to the letter Paul dictated to an amanuensis before adding the final section in his own handwriting (cf. 6:11). In view of the extent to which some of Paul's key points are expressed more judiciously in some of his later letters, it is perhaps surprising that the early scribes who copied it did not make more strenuous efforts to harmonize it with the 'later', more moderate Paul.

3. Galatians was written to quite specific circumstances which are difficult to reconstruct in detail, though the main issues at stake are clear. Paul's dispute with the agitators elicited some of his most profound theological statements. Only Romans has made a greater impact on later Christian thinkers and believers. In modern times Galatians has surpassed even Romans in the role it has played in reconstructions of the history of earliest Christianity. Interpretation of Paul's accounts of the Jerusalem 'council' (2:1–10) and of his clash with Peter at Antioch (2:11–14) is always prominent in discussion of the tensions within early Christianity.

B. The Galatian Crisis. 1. In order to unravel Paul's main lines of argument in this letter, it is necessary to have some appreciation of the circumstances that led to its composition. Paul had preached in Galatia once (or possibly twice—see 4:13) before he wrote this letter. His initial visit was related to 'a physical infirmity' he experienced (4:13). Probably as the result of his ministry, house-churches were established. In spite of Paul's displeasure at the later turn of events, the warmth of his initial relationship with the Galatian Christians is reflected in several passages (e.g. 3:15; 4:12–20; 6:1).

2. At some point after Paul had left Galatia, agitators from elsewhere had undermined some of his central convictions by confusing the Galatians and 'pervert[ing] the gospel of Christ' (1:7). The clearest statements concerning the agitators' 'false teaching' are in 4:10, 5:7–12, and 6:12–13, though parts of those verses are difficult to interpret. The agitators are encouraging the Galatian Christians to observe the Jewish 'special days, and months, and seasons, and years' (4:10). They themselves are Jews who have become Christians; they have been urging the Galatian Gentile Christians to be circumcised, i.e. to become full proselytes to Judaism as part of their commitment to the gospel of Christ (6:12–13). Paul believes that they have been selective in their approach, i.e. they have not insisted that the Galatians observe *all* the Mosaic commandments (4:3).

3. It is possible to glean a little more about the claims of the agitators by 'mirror-reading' some passages in Galatians. But as Barclay (1987) has rightly emphasized, mirror-reading is a hazardous operation. Not all Paul's statements are necessarily direct refutations of the claims of the agitators, though some scholars have assumed too readily that this is the case. Hence many questions have to be left open. For example, it is difficult to be confident about the relationship of the agitators to the 'false believers' who caused havoc among the Jerusalem Christians (2:3–6) and to 'the certain people from James' (2:12).

4. Since Paul and the agitators shared a number of convictions, it is inappropriate to refer to them as Paul's 'opponents'. They both seem to have used the term 'gospel' to refer to Christian proclamation (1:6–7). Like Paul, they believed that Jesus the Messiah was the fulfilment of the promises of Scripture. In all probability, in 4:21–31 Paul is responding to their interpretation of key passages in Genesis.

5. By mirror-reading 5:13–6:10 some scholars have claimed that Paul is opposing a second group in the Galatian churches, antinomians or Gnostics who have distorted Paul's proclamation of Christian freedom. However, in this section of his letter, Paul is far more concerned with general ethical principles than with false views. Paul is underlining two convictions: faith must be worked out in love (5:6); freedom is not an opportunity for self-indulgence, but for love of one another which is a bond as close as slavery (5:13).

C. The Recipients. 1. Where were the Galatian churches located? Scholarly opinion continues to be evenly divided between advocates of the 'north' and the 'south' Galatia theories. The former defend the traditional view that the recipients of this letter were ethnic Galatians (*Galatai*, Celts, see 3.1) who lived in the north of the Roman province; the Galatian churches were near modern Ankara. The latter note that in Paul's day the Roman province of Galatia stretched from Pontus on the Black Sea to Pamphylia on the Mediterranean coast, and insist that Paul wrote to churches at Antioch, Lystra, and Derbe in the south.

2. A decision is important for reconstruction of Paul's missionary journeys and career, but not for the interpretation of this letter. See Longenecker (1990: lxiii–lxviii), for a full discussion.

D. Date. Dates proposed range from 49 to 58 CE. If Paul wrote in 49 or 50, Galatians would be the earliest of his letters. If Paul wrote towards the end of the 50s, Galatians was written not long before Romans. Dating Galatians is closely related to a decision on two major questions: the location of the Galatian churches, and the relationship of Gal 2:1–10 to Acts. If, as seems likely, Paul's account of his visit to Jerusalem in 2:1–10 is his equivalent of Luke's account of the Jerusalem council in Acts 15, then Galatians was written at some point after that event which is usually dated to between 49 and 51 CE. (See further GAL 2:1–10 and IPC BI.4.) The extent of the development in Paul's thinking between Galatians and Romans is only one of several issues that depend on the date one assigns to this letter. However, a decision cannot be made with any degree of confidence.

E. Genre. Of rather more importance for the exegesis of this letter is its literary genre, a question that has been prominent in recent discussion. Betz's theory that Galatians is an apologetic letter that presupposes the real or fictitious situation of the court of law has provoked lively debate. Betz (1979: 15) claims that the epistolary framework can be separated so easily 'that it appears almost as a kind of external bracket for the body of the letter'. Paul is defending himself against the accusations of his accusers before the jury that is to decide the case, i.e. the Galatians. Betz's critics acknowledge that this forensic rhetorical pattern of persuasion can be discerned in parts of chs. 1 and 2, but hardly in the letter as a whole. Some claim that Galatians is an example of deliberative rhetoric, i.e. that Paul is persuading the Galatians not to accept the claims of the agitators. While this is clearly the case in 1:6–9 and 6:12–16, this reading does not do justice to many other parts of the letter. The debate has been assessed critically by Kern (1998) who calls in question the various attempts to interpret Galatians in the light of Graeco-Roman rhetorical handbooks. Paul uses several Graeco-Roman and Jewish patterns of persuasion in what is, after all, an impassioned *letter* rather than a rhetorical discourse.

F. Structure. The introduction (1:1–9) and the conclusion (6:11–18) are clearly marked. There are three main sections in the letter. From 1:10 to 2:21 Paul relates the parts of his own story that are relevant to his overall purposes. The central arguments of the letter start at 3:1, but it is not easy to decide whether they end at 4:11, 4:30, or 5:1. The ethical exhortations in the third main section end at 6:10.

COMMENTARY

Introduction (1:1–9)

(1:1–5) Opening Greetings The literary form of the opening words is found in nearly all NT and early Christian letters: 'writer to addressees, greetings': 'Paul . . . to the churches of Galatia, grace to you and peace . . .' As in his other letters, Paul

elaborates this opening formula, but only in Romans 1:1–6 is this done at greater length than in Galatians.

Paul's comments on his apostleship are striking. In numerous passages in his letters Paul refers to himself in positive terms as an apostle ('one who has been sent'). In v. 1, however, Paul stresses that his apostleship is *not* based on a 'human commission', nor has he been sent 'from human authorities'. Is this a direct response to his opponents in Galatia right at the outset of the letter? Have they been undermining Paul's authority by referring to its purely human origin, perhaps stressing that Paul had been sent as an apostle (merely) by the church at Antioch (Acts 13:1–3)? This may be the case, but as we noted above, Paul's forceful statements are not all to be read as direct responses to the jibes of his opponents. Paul emphasizes that he has been sent to the Galatian churches as an apostle by Jesus Christ and God the Father. God has shown that he is the Father of Jesus Christ by raising him to life; in vv. 3–4 God is the Father of Christians ('our Father').

In the opening phrases of several of his letters Paul refers to individual co-workers; see, for example 1 Cor 1:1, Sosthenes; 2 Cor 1:1, Timothy. In v. 2 Paul refers to an unnamed group of co-workers. The phrase, 'God's family', correctly alludes to the presence of men and women in the group, for in a context such as this, the Greek word *adelphoi*, literally 'brothers', includes 'sisters'.

Paul states that he is writing to the churches of Galatia. As noted above, it is not easy to be certain about their precise geographical location. Paul's other letters were written to individual churches, though they may soon have circulated more widely. Like 1 Peter (cf. 1:1), Galatians was intended to be a circular letter to a group of churches probably scattered over a wide area.

In v. 4 Paul makes three comments about the significance of the death of Christ. (1) In Paul's day many Jews believed that the death of a righteous man as a martyr would expiate the sins of others (see especially 4 Macc). Here the death of Christ is linked to this conviction in what several scholars have claimed is a pre-Pauline formula. The strongest indication that this may have been the case is the use of 'sins', whereas Paul himself prefers the singular, 'sin'. (2) In what may be Paul's own filling out of an early credal statement, the death of Christ is seen as a release 'from the present evil age'. Paul implies that there is a 'coming age' which he refers to in 6:15 as 'the new creation'. This contrast between two 'ages' is characteristic of apocalyptic thought. (3) Christ's giving up of his life for our release is in accordance with the will of God. 'The death of the Son is therefore a sacrifice enacted both by him and by God; and as such it breaks the mold of the old sacrificial system. The cross, that is to say, is not a sacrifice human beings make to God; it is fundamentally God's act, and as such the inversion of the sacrificial system.' (Martyn 1997: 91)

Paul concludes his extended opening greetings with a traditional doxology (v. 5). He does not do this in his other letters. Perhaps he does so here in the knowledge that his circular letter will be read in the churches in Galatia in the context of worship.

(1:6–9) Rebuke Immediately after the opening greetings in all Paul's other letters a thanksgiving to God for the readers is included. Thanksgiving is mentioned by Paul more often, line for line, than by any other Hellenistic author, pagan or Christian (O'Brien 1977). In stark contrast to Paul's other letters, however, there is not even a hint of a note of thanksgiving in Galatians. But there is one important point of similarity here with the other letters: here too the main theme of Galatians is introduced in the sentences that follow the opening greetings.

Paul's first word after the initial greetings, *thaumazō*, 'I am astonished' must have sent a shudder through the Galatian congregations when they heard it read, for they would have expected a thanksgiving. v. 6 includes Paul's only use of the verb *metatithēmi*, 'desert'; the closest parallels in Hellenistic writers refer to the desertion of one philosophical school for another. Here, however, the context is different: Paul is amazed that the Galatians are deserting 'the one who called you', clearly not Paul himself, but God whose call is 'in grace'. Although NRSV reads 'in the grace of Christ', 'of Christ' is not found in some early MSS; it is more likely to have been a later scribal explanatory addition than an omission. The Galatians' desertion has happened 'quickly', perhaps soon after the arrival of the agitators. The verbs in vv. 6–7 are in the present tense, confirming that the Galatians' apostasy is still happening as Paul writes.

Paul claims that the Galatians are 'turning to a different gospel', but he immediately denies that there is another gospel. The term 'gospel' has deep roots both in the Graeco-Roman world and in Isaiah. It may have been associated by the Galatians with the 'glad tidings' brought by a military victory or the birth of an emperor. In several key passages in Isaiah 40:9, 52:7, 61:1 the verb 'to proclaim good news' is used. Jesus seems to have applied the same phraseology to his own proclamation of God's coming kingly rule (e.g. Mt 11:5 11 Lk 7:22; Lk 4:16–21). Soon after Easter the noun is used as a Christian technical term for 'God's good news about Jesus Christ'. For Paul, there can be only one gospel (though see GAL 2:7); if his opponents use that term, they are perverting God's good news.

In v. 7 Paul speaks openly about the agitators for the first time. Instead of naming them, he refers to them with disdain as 'some people'. 'There are some who are confusing you' is too weak, as is REB's 'there are some who unsettle your minds'. The same verb *tarassō* is used in Gal 5:10 (cf. also Acts 15:24) with the sense 'intimidate': the Galatians are being frightened out of their wits by the troublemakers who, from Paul's perspective, want to pervert the gospel. In the opening phrase of v. 8 (and again in v. 9) Paul uses the plural 'we'. While this could be an editorial 'we', and simply a reference to Paul himself, Paul is probably associating his co-workers with his proclamation (cf. Gal 1:2). Paul is speaking hypothetically: he is prepared to pronounce an *anathema*, God's curse, on himself (and his circle) and even on an angel-messenger from heaven if any of them should dare to proclaim a different gospel.

In v. 9 Paul throws caution to the winds and calls down an *anathema* on those who are now proclaiming a different gospel. The phrase, 'so I now repeat' may simply refer back to v. 8; more probably it is intended as a reminder that when he was last with the Galatians, Paul had solemnly warned them of the real risk that the gospel received by the Galatians might be undermined by others. The verb 'receive' is used here (and in 1 Cor 15:3) in a technical sense to refer to the careful transmis-

sion of tradition. In 1:12 Paul seems to contradict himself when he insists that he received the gospel through a revelation of Christ and not as transmitted tradition. But the contradiction is more apparent than real: the gospel does have central themes which can be passed on from one person to another (cf. 1 Cor 15:3–5), but ultimately it is God's act of disclosure or revelation.

Paul's Story (1:10–2:21)

(1:10–12) Proclamation of the Gospel Does v. 10 belong with vv. 8–9? The word 'for' (*gar*) in the Greek suggests this; Dunn (1993: 48) (among others) takes v. 10 in this way. However, *gar* is often so weak that it need not be translated—it is ignored in the NRSV. If so, then v. 10 may be read as the beginning of a lengthy section of the letter which runs as far as 2:21.

The NRSV translation of v. 10 implies a strong contrast between the accusation against Paul that he uses rhetoric to curry favour with his audience, and Paul's own claim that in his proclamation of the gospel he seeks only God's approval. This interpretation seems to be confirmed by the strikingly similar line of argument in 1 Thess 2:4–6. However, some commentators translate the Greek verb *peithō* in its literal sense as 'persuade', and take both parts of the opening sentence of v. 10 in a negative sense: Paul is rejecting his opponents' suggestion that he seeks to persuade his audience by the force of his rhetoric, and also their claim that he is persuading God to accept Gentiles on easier terms. The final sentence of v. 10 underlines Paul's rejection of crowd-pleasing rhetoric. Paul's many references to enslavement in this letter are usually negative, but this first reference is positive: Paul insists that he is a slave of Christ.

'For I want you to know' at the beginning of v. 11 is a formula Paul uses elsewhere (e.g. 1 Cor 12:3; 15:1) to underline the importance of what follows. In spite of the strongly polemical tone of this letter, Paul refers here to the recipients as 'brothers and sisters', perhaps as a conciliatory gesture. Paul's firm threefold denial in 11c and 12 that his gospel has merely human origins is a filling out of 1:1, and probably a direct response to the jibes of his opponents. Paul's positive statement about the origin of his gospel at the end of v. 12 is one of the most important in the whole letter: it is expanded and expounded in the autobiographical sketch that follows. Paul insists that he received the gospel 'through a revelation (*apokalypsis*) of Jesus Christ'. This translation preserves the ambiguity of the Greek which can be construed either as 'Jesus Christ's disclosure of the gospel' or as 'God's disclosure of Jesus Christ as the content of the gospel'. The latter is preferable, especially in view of the filling out of v. 12 in vv. 15–16. The key noun in v. 12, *apokalypsis* is usually understood in the light of apocalyptic writings where it often refers to the unveiling of something or someone previously hidden, i.e. the 'revelation' or 'disclosure' of Jesus Christ. While not denying the validity of this traditional interpretation, Martyn (1997: 144) has argued forcefully that God's unveiling of Christ is 'basically qualified by the assertion that apocalypse is the *invasive* act that was carried out by God when he sent Christ and Christ's Spirit into the world and into human hearts' (3:23; 4:4, 6).

(1:13–17) Paul's Story, Part I When had the Galatians heard about Paul's pre-Christian way of life (v. 13)? We can only guess. Perhaps Paul had spoken about it on his initial visit to the Galatian churches. Or perhaps Paul knew that some information about his former life had circulated far and wide—well beyond the reports that had reached the churches of Judea to which he refers in 1:22–3. Or perhaps Paul had guessed or was aware that his opponents had used an account of his former way of life to undermine his authority and proclamation.

Paul's two references in vv. 13 and 14 to his way of life *in Judaism* are the only two references to Judaism in the NT. Not until the writings of Ignatius half a century later do we find 'Judaism' and 'Christianity' contrasted as two 'religions'. In earlier Jewish writings (2 and 4 Macc) 'Judaism' is used to contrast the distinctive Jewish way of life with Hellenism. In v. 14 Paul underlines twice over the 'out of the ordinary' zeal with which he observed the 'traditions of his ancestors', i.e. traditional Pharisaic interpretation of the law. Perhaps Paul is glancing sideways at the insistence of his opponents in Galatia on law observance: Paul concedes that *formerly* he himself had made the same claims concerning the law.

Paul's zeal had led him 'to persecute the church of God violently and to try to destroy it' (my tr.) The verbs are strong and in the imperfect tense: Paul's hounding of the church was not a one-off outburst, but a sustained attack which included violence. Why had followers of Christ roused Paul's ire? Some scholars have claimed that it was lax observance of the law by Christians that provoked Paul, but Paul himself does not say this. Were there Christians in the period between the Resurrection and Paul's call who did not keep the law fully? From his letters it is difficult to discern at what point Paul changed his mind about law observance; this does not seem to have happened immediately after his call on the road to Damascus. Luke does provide some relevant evidence in Acts, but it is difficult to interpret: in Luke's perspective the claim that Stephen and the Hellenists attacked the law before Paul's call was mischievous (see Acts 6:11, 13–14). So it is not as easy as some have supposed to argue that before his call Paul was in contact with Christians who did not observe the law.

It is more likely that early Christological claims, especially concerning the Messiahship of Jesus, were the trigger for the violence Paul used against 'the church of God'. Christians were claiming that a man crucified recently as a criminal was God's Messiah, but Paul knew all too well that such a person stood under the curse of the law (Gal 3:13). Hence Paul discerned that proclamation of a crucified Messiah was implicitly a threat to the law, though even after his call as apostle to the Gentiles it seems to have taken him some time to work out the radical implications of this conclusion.

Paul does not tell his readers the location of the churches he persecuted. The phrase, 'the church (assembly) of God' is striking. This very early Christian self-designation echoes the OT references to Israel as 'the assembly of Yahweh'. Although both *synagōgē* and *ekklēsia* are used in the LXX to translate the Hebrew phrase, there is no evidence that *ekklēsia* was ever applied to the Jewish community in a given place (Meeks 1983: 80). So the early Christian use of the term *ekklēsia* was one way Christians differentiated themselves from local Jewish communities. In retaining the phrase 'of God', Paul concedes that his persecution of the church was an attack on God.

In vv. 15–17 a single, long, rather complicated Greek sentence is retained as one sentence in the NRSV; it fills out the argument of 1:11–12 considerably. Paul's two main points are clear, even though, as we shall see below, some of the details leave questions unanswered. He emphasizes that his dramatic call to proclaim God's Son among the Gentiles was on God's initiative as a revelation or disclosure of his Son (see A4 above); he did not make contact with any other Christians in order to seek their advice or instructions, but went off on his own to Arabia.

Although it has often been customary to refer to Paul's *conversion* experience, and thereby to imply a conversion from Judaism to Christianity, Paul's carefully chosen phrases here indicate that he himself saw matters very differently. He did not decide to convert from one religion to another; in God's own time ('when it pleased God'), God *called* Paul to be an apostle to the Gentiles. Paul deliberately echoes phrases from Jer 1:4–5 and Isa 49:1, 6 to refer to his call, thereby aligning himself with the Hebrew prophets.

Paul acknowledges that there were apostles in Jerusalem before his call, but stresses that he felt no need to defer to their authority. Instead, immediately after his call he went off to 'Arabia', the kingdom of Nabataea south of Damascus. Betz (1979: 73) notes (with references) that recent excavations have brought to light a prosperous civilization with strong Hellenistic influences that was at its peak by the time of Paul's visit. Paul may have stayed in this area for up to two years, perhaps preaching in cities such as Petra to Gentiles already sympathetic to Judaism (so-called 'God-fearers') (so Hengel and Schwemer 1997: 127). This is a plausible historical reconstruction, but Paul tells us much less about his visit to Arabia than we would like to know.

At the end of v. 17 Paul reveals that he returned to Damascus following his stay in Arabia, thus implying that it was in or near Damascus that he experienced God's call. Although readers of Acts are told three times and with vivid details (9:3; 22:6; 26:12) that Paul experienced God's call near Damascus, Paul himself tells us much less in vv. 15–17, for his concerns in this letter are different. He focuses on his call to be an apostle to the Gentiles as God's initiative, and on his avoidance of those who might have been 'human sources' (cf. 1:12) for his gospel.

(1:18–24) Paul's Story, Part II: Visit to Jerusalem When did Paul go up to Jerusalem—three years after his return to Damascus, or three years after his initial call? Most scholars prefer the latter, though the former is not impossible. The NRSV translates the key verb *historēsai* which refers to the purpose of Paul's visit to Jerusalem as 'visit', while the GNB translates 'obtain information from'. From the context 'visit' is preferable; if Paul had conceded that he obtained information from Cephas (the Aramaic form of Peter) he would have offered a hostage to fortune. No doubt during the period Paul spent as Cephas's house guest in Jerusalem he did gain some information about the life and teaching of Jesus, but from Paul's perspective that did not mean that he was dependent on Cephas for his understanding of the gospel. Some scholars have suggested that during this visit to Jerusalem Paul reached the agreement with Peter that is referred to in 2:7, but that is unlikely.

Paul is adamant about his independence from the leaders of the Jerusalem church. In v. 20 he confirms the accuracy of his autobiographical sketch with an oath. None the less it is important to bear in mind that Paul's purpose is not primarily to set out his story with chronological precision. His sketch is selective, for it is designed to rebut the claims of his opponents. Hence his repeated insistence (cf. vv. 17, 19) that with the exception of Cephas, he did not meet any of the other Jerusalem apostles. In 19b Paul adds a further exception, James the Lord's brother who is almost certainly referred to here as an apostle. However, the Greek may mean that Paul did not see any apostle (apart from Cephas)—though he did see James.

In order to underline his independence of the Jerusalem authorities Paul mentions in v. 21 that after his short visit to Cephas he then went well to the north and north-west of Jerusalem, to places in Syria (presumably including Antioch) and in neighbouring Cilicia. Defenders of the south Galatia theory believe that Paul's first visit to Galatia took place during this journey. Martyn, a defender of the north Galatia theory, believes that v. 21 tells strongly against the south Galatian theory; he notes that if Paul had visited the cities of (south) Galatia at this point, it would have suited his argument to have said so (1997: 184).

In vv. 22–3 Paul goes still further: at this time he certainly was not in contact with the Jerusalem authorities, for he was not known personally by the churches in Judea, including Jerusalem. In that area stories had circulated about his volte-face from persecutor to proclaimer, but he himself was not there, but far to the north. In v. 23 Paul quotes the report about him which had reached the Judean churches and had been received with thanksgiving to God (v. 24). No doubt only a summary is included, but some of the phrases seem to come directly from the report rather than from Paul himself. For example, Paul does not refer to the content of the Christian message as 'the faith', and he prefers the noun 'gospel/good news' to the verb 'proclaim good news'.   .

(2:1–10) Paul's Story, Part III: Conference in Jerusalem The meeting between Paul and Barnabas and Christians in Jerusalem was one of the most momentous events in the development of earliest Christianity. Was it intended to defuse a major crisis and to reconcile deep-seated differences? What were the main issues at stake? Although some details are unclear, the main points can be set out confidently.

The relationship of Paul's account in these verses of a conference in Jerusalem to Acts 11:29–30 and 15:1–29 has baffled scholars for many decades. A minority insists that the 'apostolic council' recorded in Acts 15 took place *after* Galatians was written. This would account for Paul's failure to refer in ch. 2 to the 'apostolic decree' (Acts 15:20, 29; 21:25) which, according to Luke, encapsulated the decisions reached at the 'apostolic council'. On this view the events recorded here are to be equated with Acts 11:29–30. However, most scholars accept that in spite of some glaring differences, there are enough similarities between the two passages to conclude that they record the same event from different perspectives. Even if Acts 15 draws on earlier sources, Luke wrote some three decades after Paul wrote Galatians—and, unlike Paul, Luke makes no claim to have been present himself. So

Acts 15 should be used with great care by the interpreter of Gal 2:1–10.

'After 14 years' probably refers to Paul's call (1:15–16) rather than his visit to Cephas (1:18–19). Paul is accompanied by Barnabas who is portrayed in 2:13 as a leader in the church at Antioch, as he is in Acts 14:26–8. So Paul and Barnabas probably travelled to Jerusalem as leaders of the church in Antioch, even though, for whatever reason, Paul does not state this explicitly. Paul emphasizes that the journey was undertaken at *God's* behest, 'in response to a revelation' (v. 2), i.e. not as the result of the anxieties or the decision of the church in Antioch.

With whom in Jerusalem did Paul discuss his convictions concerning the gospel he was proclaiming to Gentiles (v. 2)? The NRSV and the REB refer to one 'private' meeting with the leaders of the Jerusalem church who play a prominent part in vv. 6–10. Some commentators (including Betz 1979 and Martyn 1997) conclude (probably correctly) that *two* meetings are referred to in the Greek of v. 2, one with the whole church in Jerusalem, followed by one with the leaders.

Paul is anxious lest his fundamental conviction that Gentiles should be accepted without the requirement of circumcision be called in question or even rejected outright (2b). In v. 3 it becomes clear that Paul and Barnabas had taken Titus with them to Jerusalem (v. 1) as a test case. At first there is no dissension: the Gentile Titus was not compelled to be circumcised (v. 3). At this point the link between Paul's story in chs. 1 and 2 and the crisis in Galatia would have become crystal clear to those who heard this letter read aloud in churches in Galatia many hundreds of miles from Jerusalem. In chs. 1 and 2 Paul is narrating selected past events in his life not because he believed that his autobiography was interesting, but because he was convinced that his story was directly relevant to the disputes in Galatia. The phrase 'compelled to be circumcised' which is used in v. 3 with reference to Titus, recurs in Gal 6:12 with reference to the Galatian Christians. In v. 5 Paul insists that the stand he took on principle in Jerusalem was 'so that the truth of the gospel might always remain with you [Galatian Christians]'.

Paul's fury at the 'false believers' who had sneaked in like spies to 'enslave us' is not disguised; it is reflected in emotive language in vv. 4–5 and in the tangled grammar, which the NRSV partly unravels. Where did this attempt to thwart 'the freedom we have in Christ Jesus' take place? Some scholars posit an earlier occasion in Antioch, partly on the basis of Acts 15:1, while others believe that the disruption took place in Jerusalem itself. Who are the 'false believers' who posed such a threat? Paul concedes that they are 'believers' ('brothers' in the Greek), but is adamant that he did not yield to their demand that Gentile Christians should be circumcised. Like the agitators in Galatia, they are perverting the gospel of Christ (1:6–7). The 'false believers' are probably not identical with 'the certain people from James' referred to in 2:12.

In v. 6 Paul insists that the Jerusalem leaders made no demands on Paul: 'they imparted nothing further to me' (REB). Here, as elsewhere in this passage, Paul is ambivalent about the Jerusalem leadership. He recognizes that they are the 'acknowledged leaders' (2:2, 6, 9) of the Jerusalem church, though he himself is unimpressed by their status, for they have no special standing in God's eyes.

In vv. 7–9 Paul spells out the agreement that was reached, one which in Paul's eyes was a victory, not a compromise. The Jerusalem leaders recognized that Paul had been entrusted *by God* with the gospel 'for the uncircumcised', just as Peter had been entrusted with the gospel 'for the circumcised'. Most scholars now accept that Paul is referring here to a division of labour along ethnic (Jew / Gentile) rather than geographical (Israel / diaspora) lines. Paul is not referring to 'two gospels', one for each ethnic group; the very idea would have appalled him, as 1:7 confirms. The recognition that God was at work in making Peter 'an apostle to the circumcised' is in stark contrast to the reference to Peter in the account of the 'incident at Antioch' which follows in 2:10–14.

At last Paul names the leaders of the Jerusalem church: James, Cephas, and John (v. 9). They are referred to as 'pillars', as in supports for a building. Agreement is sealed by giving 'the right hand of fellowship', an act that had the same meaning in antiquity as it does today. 'By implication, the agreement sets up two cooperative but independent missionary efforts' (Betz 1979: 100). The only request made by the Jerusalem leaders to Paul and Barnabas was that they should remember 'the poor', i.e. they (probably the Antioch church) should support the Jerusalem church financially. Paul had no hesitation in accepting this request. We know from 1 Cor 16:1–3 that the Galatian churches did make weekly collections for the Jerusalem church (cf. also Rom 15:25–6).

What is left unsaid in vv. 1–10 must not be forgotten. The 'false believers' fade completely from the scene at v. 5. There is not even a hint that they accepted the agreement. And if, as most scholars think, Acts 15 records a different version of the discussions in Jerusalem, Paul's failure to mention the 'apostolic decree' is significant: either Luke has anachronistically added the decree to his account of the apostolic council, or it was such an embarrassment to Paul that he could not bring himself to mention it here.

(2:11–14) Paul's Story, Part IV: Incident at Antioch The clash between Peter and Paul recorded in these verses is in sharp contrast to the amicable agreement reached at Jerusalem. In the earlier parts of Paul's story an indication of the chronology is given, but there is none here. This is one of the reasons why some scholars reverse the order of the two events narrated in ch. 2: the crisis that arose in Antioch (vv. 11–14) was resolved by the agreement reached in Jerusalem (vv. 1–10). This reconstruction avoids the difficulty that in ch. 2 Paul does not indicate the outcome of his dispute with Peter at Antioch. But in such a carefully argued letter Paul is unlikely to have reversed the chronology, and in 2:1–10 there is no reference to food laws, the central issue at stake in Paul's clash with Peter.

Paul's failure to record the outcome of his face-to-face dispute with Peter is related to his primary concern to show that this incident has a direct bearing on the tensions in the Galatian churches. Even though the text gives no explicit indication of a change of scene from Antioch to Galatia at v. 14, most modern translations assume rather too readily that there is a major break at this point. However, the NRSV's footnote is helpful, and points the reader in the right direction: 'Some interpreters hold that the quotation extends into the following paragraph.' If so, then in 2:15–21 Paul is still addressing Peter in Antioch—but for the benefit of the troublemakers in Galatia. It is preferable to read the record of the incident at Antioch as undergoing a subtle metamorphosis in vv. 15–21 as Paul switches the focus of his attention from Antioch to Galatia.

In v. 11 Paul does not tell the reader why Peter came to Antioch (presumably from Jerusalem), nor does he give the reason for the dramatic confrontation. Only after the bald summary is given do the details emerge in vv. 12 and 13. Peter had been fully accustomed to eating with Gentiles in the church at Antioch; he was thoroughly at home in the mixed congregation there of Jews and Gentiles. But when 'certain people came from James', Peter backtracked. Presumably the visitors came at the behest of James to express the concerns of the Jerusalem church. If they were the false believers of 2:4–5, surely Paul would have said so. They were not urging abandonment of the Jerusalem accord over separate missions to Jews and to Gentiles, but raising concerns over Peter's regular practice of eating with Gentiles, a matter apparently not discussed in Jerusalem. Paul does not tell us whether the meals in question were regular meals, or the Lord's supper, or both. At this time Jews and Gentiles regularly had contact with one another, but there were differing attitudes to table fellowship. Peter and other Jewish believers seem to have been welcoming Gentiles to their tables, probably on Jewish terms. They are likely to have been 'accepting invitations to Gentile tables without asking too many questions (cf. 1 Cor 10:27), though presumably on the assumption that the Gentile believers would have been mindful of the basic food rules' (Dunn 1993: 121).

The verbs in v. 12b imply that Peter began to draw back and refrain from table fellowship over a period of time. Who was applying the pressure, and why was Peter afraid? The NRSV refers to 'fear of the circumcision faction'; this phrase is usually understood to refer to Jewish Christians who came from James and who were uneasy about what were perceived to be Antioch's lax attitudes to table fellowship with Gentiles. The REB interprets the Greek quite differently: Peter 'was afraid of the Jews'. The Jews may have been non-Christians. Longenecker (1990) and others accept R. Jewett's theory that at the time of the Antioch incident a rising tide of Jewish nationalism had provoked Jewish antagonism towards Jews who were thought to be adopting lax attitudes towards association with Gentiles. Under this political pressure, the Jerusalem Christians were 'trying to take measures to keep Gentile Christians from needlessly offending Jewish sensibilities'. Hence the concerns of the Jerusalem church were triggered by political rather than theological concerns.

These verses can be plausibly interpreted in several ways. Perhaps we have to accept that we do not know precisely why Peter acted in a way that led Paul to charge him with hypocrisy twice over in v. 13. What is clear is that Peter did not act impulsively and without support from other Jewish Christians. Even Barnabas, Paul's closest colleague (2:2, 9) 'was led astray'. It was Paul who was isolated, hence the emotive language (and perhaps even the lack of clarity) in vv. 11–14. Paul's own position becomes clear in v. 14. He believes that Peter (and Barnabas and all the other Jewish Christians) were 'not acting consistently with the truth of the gospel' when they compelled Gentiles to live like Jews, i.e. to share table fellowship with Gentiles only when meals had been prepared in accordance with Jewish dietary laws. ('Living like Jews' did not necessarily include circumcision; there is no indication that Peter was insisting that Gentile believers should be circumcised.) For Paul, a fundamental principle was at stake: Gentiles were being compelled to live like Jews in order to be accepted as members of the Antioch church. Hence Paul rounded on Peter in front of all those lined up against him. It is often pointed out that Paul's attack on Peter is at odds with his own exhortation in 6:1 to use a 'spirit of gentleness' when a fellow Christian is 'detected in transgression'.

Paul says nothing about Peter's response, and nothing about the outcome of the confrontation. Martyn (1997: 240), concludes that 'the Antioch incident ended in political defeat for Paul'. That is a possible, but not a necessary reading of the text. Perhaps Paul was more concerned to press home the theological issues at stake, as he does in the following verses, than to record the outcome of a painful episode.

(2:15–21) Works of the Law or Faith? Paul expounds vigorously the theological issues at stake in his dispute with Peter. He probably intends these verses (or at least vv. 15–18) to be part of his reply to Peter. Paul is unlikely to be recalling some seven years later the very words he used; no doubt these verses incorporate some of Paul's later reflections on the issues at stake. We do not know whether Paul formulated his convictions about 'justification by faith' in the light of his dispute with Peter, or whether he had developed them at an earlier point.

vv. 15 and 16 contain a set of programmatic statements that are expounded and underlined in the sections of Galatians that follow. In v. 15 Paul reminds Peter that both of them are Jews by birth, and hence view Gentiles as outside the law and therefore as sinners. Here Paul is echoing traditional views; perhaps he is even echoing the language used by the 'certain people from James' (v. 12). In the next verse Paul explains that v. 15 is by no means the end of the matter! In the lengthy v. 16 the phrase 'works of the law' is used three times and contrasted sharply with 'faith'. What does the former phrase refer to? Paul is refuting the claim made by the agitators in Galatia (and implicitly by Peter when he 'compel[led] the Gentiles to live like Jews', v. 14) that one's standing before God is dependent on carrying out the requirements of the Mosaic law. 'Works of the law' is taken by some scholars to refer to the Jewish 'identity markers' of sabbath, circumcision, and dietary laws, rather than to the Mosaic law *per se*, but the negative comments on the law that follow in ch. 3 make this unlikely.

Paul insists that a person is 'reckoned as righteous' by God (NRSV *n.*) on the basis of 'faith in Christ'. The meaning of the latter phrase is keenly discussed. It has traditionally been taken by translators and commentators to refer to the believer's faith in Christ, but a growing number of scholars insist that Paul is referring to Christ's own faithfulness to God, as in the NRSV footnote. The future tense 'will be justified' at the end of v. 16 is important; Paul is referring to the believer's ultimate standing before God.

Once again Paul includes Peter with his use of 'we' / 'our' in v. 17. Paul seems to be referring to the stand he and Peter took before Peter backtracked: they had sought to base their standing before God solely on the basis of faith—and in so doing they had been dubbed 'sinners' by some. Paul vigorously refutes this criticism, and especially the inference that Christ has become a servant of sin. In v. 18 Paul refers directly to the incident at Antioch: he would show himself to be a transgressor if he were to backtrack (as Peter did) and 'rebuild the walls of the Law that I have torn down' (Martyn 1997: 256).

In vv. 19 and 20 Paul's statements about the Christian life are positive: both the incident at Antioch and the crisis in Galatia slip into the background. Although Paul repeatedly refers to himself in the first person singular, he is speaking on behalf of all Christian believers. 'Dying to the law' (v. 19) means being separated radically from it. For Paul 'dying to the law' takes place through identification with Christ's own crucifixion and death (v. 19c). When this happens the believer's life is no longer self-centred, but Christ-centred (v. 20).

The phrase 'Christ who lives in me' is rarer in Paul than reference to the Spirit who indwells the believer. Both phrases are less common than Paul's references to Christian experience as 'in Christ' (e.g. 5:6), 'in him', 'in the Lord', or 'in the Spirit' (e.g. 5:25). In v. 20b the NRSV's 'in the flesh' is misleading, especially in view of Paul's strongly negative use of 'the flesh' in 3:3 and 5:13, 16–22. Here 'flesh' is neutral; it refers to the believer's 'present mortal life' (REB).

Paul does not often refer to Christ as 'Son' or 'Son of God'. When he does so, it is usually in a particularly rich theological context, as in Gal 1:16, 2: 20c, and 4:4–6. Both the latter passages refer to the Son's self-giving 'for us', 'for our redemption', a note first sounded in Galatians in the opening greeting at 1:4. Once again there is a division of opinion over 'faith'. Does Paul refer to the believer's faith in the Son of God, or to the Son's own faith (NRSV f.) or faithfulness?

v. 21 is a summary of the whole of vv. 15–21; in particular it underlines some of the key points of v. 16. Paul is probably responding directly to the claims of the agitators; the incident at Antioch has now faded from view. The agitators have claimed (or perhaps Paul thinks they have claimed) that Paul has wrenched asunder God's grace and the law. For Paul a person is reckoned as righteous in God's sight not through the law (synonymous in v. 20 with the 'works of the law', v. 16) but through faith in Christ (v. 16) whose death was not in vain (v. 21c) but was an act of self-giving love for us (v. 20c).

Paul's Central Arguments (3:1–5:1)

(3:1–5) How Did You Receive the Spirit? Paul continues the argument of the preceding verses and asks pointedly whether the Galatians received the Spirit by 'works of the law' or by 'believing what you heard' (v. 2). Attention is now focused directly on the Galatians who are roundly rebuked for the second time (cf. 1:6–19). Peter and the incident at Antioch are left far behind as Paul grapples vigorously with the issues at stake in the crisis in the Galatian churches. At nearly all the key points in ch. 3 Paul's argument is grounded on Scripture, but in this opening section Paul's appeal is to the Galatians' initial reception and continuing experience of the Spirit. The Galatian Christians are upbraided twice for their foolishness (vv. 1, 3); it is not their lack of intelligence that riles Paul, but their lack of discernment. Paul draws on contemporary patterns of polemical argument in suggesting that the Galatians have been 'bewitched' by the agitators. To use a modern-day equivalent, they have had the wool pulled over their eyes. In fact Paul reminds the Galatians that he used visual imagery in his initial preaching: Jesus Christ was 'publicly exhibited as crucified'. As in 1 Cor 1:23; 2:2, Paul contrasts his preaching of the crucified Christ with the rhetorical sophistry of his opponents.

v. 3 is particularly important for Paul's argument. The Galatians have received the Spirit as the basis of their Christian experience, and they ought to continue in the Spirit (cf. 5:25). Instead, they are 'now ending with the flesh'. Paul believes that some of the Galatians have succumbed (and others may follow) to the agitators' demands that circumcision is the mark of Christian identity. Paul returns to this topic more fully at 5:2–12; 6:12–13. Paul underlines and extends his central point in this section by asking a rhetorical question in v. 5 to which he expects a resounding 'no' as an answer. The tense of the verbs is important: God continues to sustain the Galatians with the Spirit; God continues to 'work miracles' among them. We do not know what form the miracles took, but Paul's main point is clear: God's Spirit continues to be experienced powerfully in the Galatian churches. For Paul, one's standing before God (past, present, and future) is not on the basis of carrying out the requirements of the law.

(3:6–14) Abraham Believed God In v. 6 Abraham is introduced for the first time; he remains on stage until 5:1, though in some sections he lurks in the background. Given the prominence of Abraham in numerous early Jewish writings, it is not surprising that Paul also should appeal to parts of the story of Abraham. Paul takes his listeners immediately to Gen 15:6 in order to argue that 'those who believe' (including Gentiles) (vv. 7–8) are descendants of Abraham.

Paul is probably refuting the agitators' version of traditions about Abraham. They are likely to have appealed to the reference to Abraham's meritorious deeds in Gen 14 and to Abraham's acceptance of circumcision in Gen 17:4–14 as the basis of his acceptance by God. Paul, however, focuses solely on Gen 15:6 with its reference to Abraham's faith in God as the basis of his standing before God. He develops his argument from Scripture in v. 8, claiming that through Scripture (in phrases from Gen 12:3 and 18:18) God 'declared the gospel beforehand to Abraham'. God's justification of the Gentiles by faith and his bestowal of his grace, peace, and favour upon them (i.e. his blessing of them, vv. 8 and 9) is nothing new: it is anchored in Scripture, and it was always part of God's purposes.

It is difficult to be certain about Paul's line of argument in vv. 10–12. He claims that reliance on observance of the law brings a curse, not a blessing, and quotes Deut 27:26 in support. Why does the law bring a curse? Paul seems to be implying that it is impossible to carry out the requirements of the law: since those who try to do so fail to keep the law completely, they are accursed. There is a solemn warning to the Galatians here: beware of the law's siren voice, for it brings a curse, not a blessing. If this is Paul's main point in v. 10, then vv. 11 and 12 make a rather different point: they are concerned once again with the contrast between faith and keeping the law as the basis of one's standing before God. In v. 11, Hab 2:4 underpins Paul's argument concerning faith; in v. 12, Lev 18:5 is cited to confirm that the law has to do with carrying out the requirements of the law and living by them. Living by faith

(v. 11) leaves no room for living by the requirements of the law (v. 12). Paul's comments on the law in vv. 10–12 are negative and harsh. The other side of the coin is expressed positively in vv. 13–14: 'Christ redeemed us from the curse of the law . . . so that we might receive the promise of the Spirit through faith.' This section ends where it began (vv. 2–5) with a reference to the importance of God's bestowal of the Spirit. But what does 'Christ became a curse for us' mean (v. 13)? 'The thought is of Jesus acting in a representative capacity . . . the law printing its curse on Jesus, as it were, so that in his death the force of the curse was exhausted, and those held under its power were liberated' (Dunn 1993: 177, who rightly refers to 2 Cor 5:21 as an important parallel).

(3:15–29) Abraham's Offspring Paul seems to sense that the argument of the previous verses has been complex. So he pauses, and in contrast to 3:1, addresses the Galatians in endearing terms in order to secure their attention. He then provides an illustration from everyday life: one cannot annul or add to a ratified will (by means of a codicil). Paul uses a form of argument found in other Jewish writers of the time: in order to make a particular point he rejects the accepted meaning of Gen 17:8 as a reference to the promises given to Abraham and the generations of his descendants. He takes 'offspring' ('seed' in the Greek) in its literal sense in the singular to refer to one person, Christ. So God's promises were given only to Abraham and to Christ; in vv. 26–9 Paul will insist that those who belong to Christ are Abraham's offspring, not Abraham's physical, i.e. ethnic, descendants.

In v. 17 Paul returns to his illustration of v. 15, but he now uses the term *diathēkē*, which can mean either 'will' or 'covenant' to refer to God's covenant with Abraham. The law came into existence 430 years after God's covenant-promise to Abraham. There is no hint here that the law was God-given; indeed Paul's point is that as the law came *later* than the covenant ratified by God, it could neither nullify nor modify the promise to Abraham. The latter point is only implicit: in v. 15 Paul has explained that one cannot add a codicil to a will. The agitators in Galatia may well have argued along totally different lines: Gen 17 confirms that Abraham observed the law even before it was given by God to Moses at Sinai. Paul presses home his argument in v. 18. 'The law' and 'the promise' are set in antithetical opposition: 'the inheritance' given to Abraham comes via the latter, not the former. What is 'the inheritance' granted by God? It 'is the church-creating Spirit of Christ' (Martyn 1997: 343).

The obvious question now has to be faced (v. 19). If the law came into existence much later than the promise to Abraham, and is therefore secondary, why was it given at all? Answer: it was added as a supplement to the promises (this is the force of the verb used) 'because of transgressions', a phrase which has evoked much comment. Was the law added to bring about a knowledge of transgressions, or even to provide some sort of remedy for them? While the Greek can be construed in this way, in view of the negative comments on the law that follow, this interpretation is unlikely. Paul probably states that the law was given 'to cause or increase transgressions'. The next phrase 'until the offspring would come' confirms that the law's role is *limited* to the period between Moses and Christ. In nearly all strands of Jewish thought, and presumably in the view of the agitators, the law had been given by God permanently.

The law's secondary role is underlined by the claim that it was 'promulgated through angels' (v. 19d). The NRSV's 'ordained through angels' implies a more positive sense than the context allows. The first listeners were bound to notice the absence of explicit reference to the involvement of God in the giving of the law by God. The silence is telling, especially in view of the way God's involvement in the giving of the promise to Abraham is underlined in the Greek by the placing of 'God' at the end of v. 18. Paul concedes that a mediator was involved in the promulgation of the law (v. 19d). The statement that follows (v. 20) is one of the most puzzling in Paul's letters, but its gist is clear. A mediator, Moses, was involved. But since God is one and needs no mediator between himself and his people, God was not involved at Mt Sinai! This is indeed a radical rejection of Jewish views about the giving of the law, but it is in line with the preceding and the following comments about the role of the law.

An obvious objection is faced squarely in the verses which follow (cf. 3:19). In the light of the negative comments about the law that have been made in the preceding verses, some listeners might have concluded that the law and the promise were fundamentally opposed to one another (v. 21a). Paul adamantly resists this conclusion, and then proceeds to spell out what continuing function the law has (vv. 22–5). First of all the hypothetical possibility that the law might have brought life is considered. In that case, Paul readily admits, God's 'rightwising' activity ('righteousness') on our behalf would be on the basis of the law. But since the law did *not* bring life, righteousness does not come as the result of keeping the law. Once again the careful listener will recall 2:16, where this theme rings out for the first time. vv. 22 and 23 are partly similar: both use the verb 'imprison', and both conclude with a reference to faith. But Paul does not simply repeat himself. In v. 22 he refers to the way Scripture has imprisoned the whole of humanity, indeed the whole of creation ('all things') under the power of sin. 'Scripture' probably refers to Deut 27:26 which Paul cited in 3:11; 'under the power of sin' is synonymous with 'under a curse' in 3:11a. This negative role played by the law had a positive outcome: so that the promise might be given to those who believe. In v. 23 Paul uses the pronoun 'we' for the first time since 3:13. The verses that follow confirm that Paul has in mind the Galatian Christians as well as himself. 'We' were imprisoned by the law; in the preceding verse sin plays this role. But the dark night did not last forever, with God's disclosure of Christ (cf. 1:12, 16) faith was revealed.

Paul clarifies his main point with an illustration in vv. 24–5. The law was our *paidagōgos* until Christ came, but with the coming of faith we are no longer under a *paidagōgos*. In many families in the Graeco-Roman world the *paidagōgos*, often a slave, played an important part in caring for children. Sometimes this person acted primarily as a teacher (hence 'pedagogue'), sometimes as a disciplinarian. What would this metaphor have meant to the listeners in Galatia when they first heard Paul's letter read aloud? The context confirms that Paul had a negative connotation in mind: the law, like the *paidagōgos*, provided unpleasant restraint for a limited period—until Christ came.

In v. 26 and in the grand finale to this section in v. 29 Paul brings discussion of who are true 'children of Abraham' back onto the agenda (cf. 3:16–19). In v. 26 those who are 'in Christ Jesus' are God's children, while in v. 29 those who 'belong to Christ' are Abraham's offspring; the expressions are synonymous. By now the listener will be well aware that one's standing before God is not grounded on law observance, but on faith. vv. 27–8 interrupt the argument of vv. 26 and 29 with a reference to baptism. Some of the phrases in these verses are found elsewhere in early Christian writings (see especially 1 Cor 12:13; Col 3:11); only the first pairing in v. 28, 'Jew or Greek', is relevant to the immediate context. Hence several scholars conclude that Paul is here citing an early baptismal liturgy. The person who is about to be baptized removes clothing, symbolizing the old order, and in baptism is 'clothed with Christ' (v. 27). In baptism all the social distinctions that lay at the heart of the society of the day are abolished. 'Religious, social, and sexual pairs of opposites are not replaced by equality, but rather by a newly created unity' in Christ Jesus (Martyn 1997: 377). Whether this radical vision was put fully into practice by Paul himself, and in the churches he founded, is another question.

(4:1–7) The Sending of the Son As at 3:15, Paul opens this section with an illustration from daily life (vv. 1–2). In this case he modifies the illustration to suit his present purposes. The heir to an estate is in fact in a better position than a slave, for, unlike a slave, he knows that one day he will inherit his father's property. The date at which the son received his inheritance was probably fixed by law, rather than by an individual father. Nonetheless Paul's main points in vv. 3–4 are well supported by the illustration. While waiting to receive the inheritance (cf. 3:18), 'we were enslaved'. But in God's own time, freedom was made possible through the sending of his Son (vv. 3–4). Paul takes the 'enslavement' theme further in vv. 8–9: the Galatians, having been freed from slavery, now want to be enslaved all over again.

What are the 'elemental spirits of the world' (v. 3; cf. 4:8–9) which enslaved believers before their redemption, and which now attract the Galatians? The phrase probably refers to the basic materials or principles that lie at the heart of the cosmos. For a Jew, the law fulfilled that function. In any case, the context (cf. especially 4:5, 10) strongly suggests that Paul includes the law as an essential part of the 'elemental spirits'.

vv. 4–5 contain one of Paul's richest Christological statements. Several scholars have claimed that it is a pre-Pauline confessional formula, partly because some phrases are not common elsewhere in Paul's writings, and partly because of its similarity to 'sending formulae' in Rom 8:3; Jn 3:17; 1 Jn 4:9 (and cf. Mk 12:6). Here Paul develops the theme of God's sending of the prophets to Israel: Jesus as God's Son is sent to redeem those 'under the law', i.e. Jews, so that 'we', all who are 'in Christ Jesus' (cf. 3:26–9) might receive adoption. 'Born of a woman' does not refer to the virginal conception of Jesus, but to his birth as a human being. 'Born under the law' may mean no more than 'born as a Jew', but in view of all the preceding negative statements about the law, 'under the law' probably includes a negative connotation.

The precise background to Paul's reference to believers' 'adoption as children' (v. 5) has been keenly debated. Is this phrase to be understood in the light of Graeco-Roman practices concerning the adoption of children? Or is there an OT/Jewish background? If the latter, then, as Scott (1992) has argued, Paul may have in mind an analogy with God's adoption / redemption of Israel from slavery in Egypt: believers were redeemed to adoption as sons of God from slavery under the 'elemental spirits of the world' (GAL 4:3). v. 4 refers to God's sending of his Son; in v. 6 God 'has sent the Spirit of his Son': for Paul, 'Christ / Son' and 'Spirit' are closely related and in some passages almost synonymous. In v. 6 it is the Spirit who cries out to God on behalf of the believer and calls God, 'Abba', Father. The retention of the Aramaic word 'Abba' in a letter to Greek-speaking Christians is striking; it almost certainly reflects Jesus' own preferred way of referring to God (Mk 14:36; Lk 11:2).

The argument of vv. 1–7 is brought to a climax in v. 7: the believer's adoption as a child of God means (negatively) release from enslavement to the 'elemental spirits of the world' and (positively) acceptance as an heir to God's promises to Abraham.

(4:8–11) Why Do You Want to be Enslaved Again? Paul once again speaks directly and forcefully to the Galatian Christians (cf. 3:1–5), and develops several of the themes of 4:1–7 further. Before they became Christians, Galatians were enslaved to 'beings that by nature are not gods', i.e. to idols (cf. 1 Cor 8:5; 12.2). Now as believers they have come to know, i.e. to experience, God's Spirit (cf. 3:1–5; 4:6). Paul immediately modifies this statement in v. 9b by emphasizing yet again God's initiative in redemption from enslavement to 'the weak and beggarly elemental spirits' (GAL 4:3): 'you have come...to be known by God'.

In v. 10 the link between the elemental spirits and the law becomes explicit. What are the special 'days, and months, and seasons, and years' that the Galatians now want to observe closely, probably under the influence of the agitators? Although v. 9c, 'you want to be enslaved' may suggest that the Galatians have not yet succumbed to meticulous observance of the Jewish calendar, v. 10 implies that they have done so. There is general agreement that Paul is referring to observance of the Jewish sabbath and festivals. Observance of 'months' probably refers to observance of the new moon which marked the beginning of each month; precisely what is meant by 'years' is uncertain. Martyn correctly notes that Paul's argument here is not even partly anti-Jewish (1997: 417–18): God's new creation in Christ (cf. 6:15) marks the end of the distinction between 'holy times' and 'profane times' that is basic to all peoples—one of the pattern of 'elemental pairs of opposites' to which the Galatians were enslaved (3:28; 4:3, 8–9).

(4:12–20) Paul's Perplexity Longenecker (1990: 184–7), has argued that v. 12 marks the opening of the final major section of the letter, the transition from the 'rebuke' section (3:1–4:11) to the 'request' section (4:12–6:10). However, the link between the emotional personal appeals of v. 11 and the entreaties in vv. 12 and 19–20 makes it preferable to align 4:12–20 closely with the preceding verses. In v. 12 Paul opens this section with a term of endearment, 'friends', which he has not used since 3:15; in v. 19 he refers to the Galatians as his 'little children'. Although vv. 12–20 have been dubbed an erratic and emo-

tional aside, these verses make explicit Paul's passionate concern for the Galatians, a concern that begins at 1:6 with Paul's expression of astonishment at the Galatians' behaviour.

Paul's opening plea, 'become as I am', recalls the earlier autobiographical sections of the letter, from 1:11 to 2:14 (or even 2:18). As in several other passages in his letters (e.g. 1 Cor 4:16–17; 1 Thess 1:6; Phil 4:9), Paul refers to his own example as a model of Christian discipleship. To modern readers this smacks of bragging, but it was a conventional mode of instruction used by philosopher-teachers in Paul's day. The phrase 'I...have become as you' is an expression of Paul's friendship and solidarity with the Galatians. In spite of the pain the Galatians have caused Paul, he does not consider that he himself has been wronged (v. 12c); the implication is that they have wronged God or Christ.

The Galatians know more about Paul's illness than we do (v. 13)! Presumably an illness led to Paul's initial visit to the Galatian churches—or perhaps it detained him there longer than planned. The reference to Paul's 'first' proclamation of the gospel may imply a second visit, but surely Paul would have referred to any second visit in this extended discussion of his relationship with the Galatians. Paul's illness put the Galatian Christians 'to the test' (v. 14a), probably because their pre-Christian beliefs would have tempted them to draw the inference that Paul's illness was the result of demon possession. In fact, the welcome Paul originally received could hardly have been more enthusiastic: he was welcomed as 'an angel of God', as a representative of Christ Jesus himself. The latter phrase parallels the similar idea in Matt 10:40, where Jesus assures his disciples that whoever welcomes them, welcomes Jesus himself. vv. 15–16 express the breakdown of Paul's warm relationship with the Galatians. Although v. 15b is often taken to imply that Paul's illness was ophthalmic, it may be no more than a vivid expression of the Galatians' initial willingness to do almost anything in their support of Paul. v. 16 is taken as a rhetorical question in NRSV and some other translations, but the Greek can equally well be construed as an indignant expression of Paul's frustration at the Galatians' about turn. In vv. 17–18 the agitators are referred to explicitly, but as elsewhere, they are not named (cf. 1:7). The NRSV's 'they make much of you...so that you may make much of them' is too bland: the REB's double reference to 'lavishing attention' is preferable. Paul even claims that the agitators want to 'exclude you', i.e. to drive a wedge between Paul himself and the Galatians. The first half of v. 18 is probably an aphorism or proverb which Paul expands in order to press home his point: Paul had hoped that his absence from the Galatian churches would not impair his relationship with them.

The poignant expression in v. 19 of Paul's perplexity and pain has no close parallel in his other letters: Paul likens himself to a pregnant mother 'in the pain of childbirth'. His concern for the Galatians could not have been expressed more powerfully. Paul probably continues with the imagery of pregnancy in the final clause where he speaks of his hope that Christ will be 'formed', i.e. like an embryo or foetus, among the Galatians. In v. 20 Paul concludes this section with his wish to be present personally with the Galatians in the hope that their warm relationship might be restored. Paul knows that his letter will have to substitute for his presence. There is no confident expectation here (or elsewhere) that this letter will be more effective than the agitators who are still personally present in the Galatian churches.

(4:21–5:1) The Hagar and Sarah Allegory There is no agreement on the reason for the inclusion of these verses at this point in the letter. Some scholars suggest that they are an afterthought, or have even been displaced from elsewhere. Others link them to the exhortation of the final main section of the letter. The traditional and preferable view is to take them as Paul's striking final argument in his sustained exposition that starts at 3:1.

Right up until v. 21b Paul speaks negatively about the law—32 times in all; in every case he has the law of Moses in mind. It is no exaggeration to claim that from 2:16 to v. 21a Paul's view of the law is 'consistently malignant' (Martyn 1997: 37). In v. 21b, however, Paul's tone changes dramatically: *nomos* (law) is used positively for the first time in this letter. In this verse Paul speaks with heavy irony: you Galatians who desire 'to be subject to the law', listen to what the law really says, for it does have positive things to say. This verse must have focused the minds of the Galatians sharply on Paul's central concern: heard aright, the law bears witness to the gospel, as in the allegory of Hagar and Sarah that follows.

In vv. 22 and 23 Paul summarizes parts of the Hagar–Sarah traditions from Gen 16–21. In v. 22 the reference to 'a slave woman' and 'a free woman' echo the language (but not the thought) of 3:28, and especially the opening sections of ch. 4. In v. 23 a contrast is drawn between the child 'born according to the flesh', i.e. conceived naturally, and the child born 'through the promise', i.e. following God's promise to Abraham that his aged and barren wife Sarah would bear him a son. Paul's summary is terse: neither the mothers nor the children are named. Barrett (1982: 161) has argued convincingly that Paul is responding to the agitators' interpretation of the Hagar–Sarah traditions. 'The wording implies that the story is already before the Galatians; they will know that the slave is Hagar, the free woman Sarah'. Paul explains that this is an allegory, a form of interpretation in which individuals and key details in a narrative all represent someone or something else. Allegorical interpretation was used by Philo of Alexandria, a slightly earlier contemporary of Paul's, as well as by some rabbis. Philo's allegories were more elaborate and less related to the original context than Paul's. Paul states boldly that the two women are 'two covenants' (v. 24) even though Gen 17:21 refers to only one covenant, the one that God promises to establish with Isaac, whom Sarah will bear to Abraham. In fact Paul does not refer explicitly to the Sarah covenant, and does not even name her. Paul focuses on Hagar, who is said to come from Mount Sinai, a detail not mentioned in Genesis. Paul's further comment about Hagar in v. 25 led to several attempts by scribes to clarify his point. The NRSV provides the more difficult and therefore probably original reading; a note in the NRSV provides an equally well-attested reading, 'For Sinai is a mountain in Arabia.'

The verb *sustoixeō* 'corresponds to' in v. 25 is the key to these verses. The verb was used to refer to soldiers standing in the same line; it came to refer to the correspondence of categories in lists. Paul lines up in the same column, as it were, Hagar, Mount Sinai, children being born (even now)

into slavery, the present Jerusalem who is in slavery with her children (vv. 24–5). In the other column Paul places the free woman (the unnamed Sarah), the Jerusalem above who is free, and who is our mother (v. 26). Paul does not take pains to balance the two columns precisely, for his main interest is in the contrast between two 'Jerusalems'.

Earlier in his letter Paul has been at pains to stress his independence from the Jerusalem Christian leaders (1:18–20); in 25b a further step is taken: the church of Jerusalem to whose authority the agitators appealed 'is in slavery with her children'. Paul's polemic could hardly be more acute. In stark contrast stands 'the Jerusalem above, our mother'; here Paul draws on a theme found in several OT passages (e.g. Ps 87; Isa 50:1; 66:7–11) and in Jewish writings (e.g. 4 Ezra 10:25–57). The phrase *our mother* is surely intended to include both Jewish and Gentile Christians. In v. 27 Paul appeals to Scripture ('it is written') to sustain his point. The preceding verses make it clear that Paul interprets Isa 54:1 as a reference to Sarah: her barrenness and desolation will be reversed, for she will bear more children than 'the one who is married', i.e. Hagar.

In v. 28 Paul's earlier frustration with the Galatians 4:19–21) gives way once again to endearment, 'my friends, you are children of the promise, like Isaac', who is now named for the first time. The contrast between Isaac and Ishmael (not named) becomes even sharper in v. 29. Paul draws attention to Ishmael's persecution of Isaac, a tradition not found in the OT itself, though several Jewish sources do mention an argument between the two. A parallel is drawn with the agitators' 'persecution' of the Galatian Christians: 'so it is now also'. v. 29 sets out a further vivid contrast: whereas Ishmael and the agitators were 'according to the flesh', Isaac and the Galatians were born 'according to the Spirit'. The Galatians' experience of the Spirit has been prominent in several earlier passages (3:1–5, 14; 4:6); the contrast between flesh and Spirit will be developed further in 5:5, 16–26.

Paul relentlessly pursues his case against the agitators with a further citation of Scripture in v. 30, where Gen 21:10 is adapted slightly to fit the present context. The argument reaches its climax in v. 31. By now the listeners in the Galatian churches should have been able to draw the conclusion themselves: they are children of the free woman, Sarah, and so are the true children of Abraham. The strong language of the citation, 'Drive out the slave and her child', should not be read as an attack on Judaism: Paul's attention is focused sharply on the agitators and their claims.

Gal 5:1 has baffled commentators in ancient as well as modern times. There are two related difficulties. Although the Greek of v. 1a is so awkward that early scribes made several attempts to tidy it up, there is now general agreement that the NRSV and similar translations are appropriate. Opinion is still keenly divided, however, on the relationship of v. 1 to its context. NRSV, REB, and many other translators and commentators appeal to the contrast between slavery and freedom as an obvious link to the preceding verses: v. 1 is taken as a ringing conclusion to the Hagar–Sarah allegory. Others, including NIV, see it as the opening of a new section in which Paul turns to exhortation, and note the link with 5:13. Still others take it as a short independent paragraph that acts as a bridge between the allegory and the new themes of chs. 5 and 6. On balance, the NRSV's punctuation is to be preferred.

Exhortations (5:2–6:10)

(5:2–12) Neither Circumcision nor Uncircumcision Paul opens this section with a solemn appeal to the Galatians: 'Mark my words' (REB). In these verses with their repeated references to circumcision, the central issue at stake in Paul's dispute with the agitators is brought out into the open. v. 2 implies that some of the Galatians are on the point of succumbing to the agitators' insistence that they should be circumcised if they wish to become true children of Abraham; v. 3 implies that some have already done so. Paul is adamant that two corollaries follow: Christ will benefit them no more, and they will be obliged to keep the whole law of Moses. Perhaps the agitators had not been frank about the latter point. There is plenty of evidence to confirm that Paul is not misrepresenting Jewish teaching in his insistence that the Galatians cannot pick and choose which parts of the law they will observe.

vv. 4 and 5 summarize many of Paul's key points: most of the phrases occur in 2:15–21, Paul's opening exposition of the chasm between being justified by the law and living by faith, through the Spirit. 'Hope' is not used elsewhere in this letter, though the general theme of waiting for future salvation is prominent. In v. 6 Paul quotes a formula that he himself has probably coined. The first half, 'neither circumcision nor uncircumcision counts for anything', is repeated almost verbatim in 6:15 and in 1 Cor 7:19, though in each case the positive statement that follows is expressed differently. In 6b faith and love are related more closely than elsewhere in Paul's letters. 'Faith working through love' rules out any suggestion that Paul's ethical teaching has no moral demands.

vv. 7–12 are linked together more loosely than vv. 2–6. Here Paul rattles off several different images, though they are all related to the overall argument. vv. 7 and 8 recall Paul's opening appeal in 1:6–9. The reference to Christian living as a running race echoes 2:2. The question, 'who prevented you?' probably also refers to running races: Who cut in on you, or who side-tracked you? Since God ('the one who calls you') is in no way responsible for this, the agitators are responsible (v. 8). They are likened in v. 9 to a little yeast which leavens the whole batch of dough, a well-known image in antiquity for the power of evil. v. 10b is taken by Martyn (1997: 475), as a reference to the leader of the agitators, 'the man who is disturbing your minds'. This is not impossible, but the NRSV's 'whoever it is that is confusing you' is preferable; as in 1:7, the reference is general. Why does Paul claim in v. 11 that he is still being persecuted? And when did Paul ever 'preach circumcision'? This verse is one of the most puzzling in this letter. Elsewhere in his letters (e.g. 1 Thess 2:16; 2 Cor 11:23–9) Paul mentions the persecution he received at the hands of his non-Christian opponents, but that is not in view here. In 4:29 Paul refers to the agitators as 'persecutors', and it is their actions which are referred to again here. They seem to have claimed mischievously or mistakenly that at some stage following his call to proclaim Christ to the Gentiles (1:15–16), Paul did 'preach circumcision'. How or why they gained that information, we do not know. Perhaps they had received a false rumour concerning the circumcision of Titus (2:3). Paul's logic is clear: the agitators still claim that he is 'preaching circumcision'. If that

were the case, Paul insists, then the agitators' persecution of him would have ceased. But since it has not ceased, it must be based on misinformation. Paul is so angry with the agitators that in v. 12 he makes 'the crudest and rudest of all his extant statements' (Longenecker 1990: 234). Attempts to soften Paul's plain speaking, either by euphemisms or by interpreting these hash words figuratively as 'let them excommunicate themselves', are unconvincing.

(5:13–26) Living by the Spirit Paul now turns to general exhortations which are not directly related to the crisis in Galatia, though there are numerous linguistic links with the preceding sections. This is clearly the case in v. 13: its ringing reference to God's call to freedom is in contrast to the 'yoke of slavery' the agitators are imposing (cf. 5:1). As in 5:6b, Paul is aware that unbridled freedom can lead to antinomianism; hence Paul's insistence on loving commitment to one another which is as strong a bond as slavery.

In v. 13 Paul uses the word 'flesh' (sarx), one of the most problematic words for the translator of his letters. Earlier in Galatians 'flesh' is used in a purely neutral sense to refer to human or physical nature, but in vv. 13, 16, 17 (twice), 19, 24, and 6:8, 'flesh' is used in a negative, ethical sense to refer to a person's sinful or corrupt nature. Should the translator attempt to replicate the quite different ways in which the word is used? REB uses 'unspiritual nature' or 'old nature' for the negative references to sarx, and several different phrases for the 'neutral' uses. NRSV signals the different way in which Paul uses sarx in this section by translating it as 'self-indulgence' in v. 13, before reverting to 'flesh' in the remainder of the section.

As in 4:21b, Paul speaks about the law of Moses positively in v. 14, and cites Lev 19:18, 'love your neighbour'. Earlier in the letter the law has consistently been referred to negatively. The NRSV's 'the whole law is summed up' is misleading, for the verb means 'fulfil'. What then is intended by 'fulfilling the whole law'? Barclay's comment is apt: it describes 'the total realization of God's will in line with the eschatological fulness of time in the coming of Christ' (1988: 40). Paul uses withering sarcasm in v. 15 to denounce in-fighting in the Galatian churches. This may perhaps have been sparked off by differing attitudes to the agitators' claims, but we cannot be sure.

'Living by the Spirit' and 'gratifying the desires of the flesh' are set in opposition to one another in v. 16 which acts as a heading to vv. 17–24. The bald statement of v. 16 is expounded in v. 17: the two ways of living are 'at war with one another' (Martyn 1997: 493). The final clause of v. 17 has long baffled exegetes. A plausible interpretation envisages that the battle between 'Spirit' and 'flesh' frustrates the wishes of the believer. In v. 18 being 'led by the Spirit' is contrasted with being 'subject to the law', themes prominent in several passages earlier in the letter (e.g. 2:16; 3:1–5; 4:6–7). In vv. 19–21 Paul sets out a list of 'the works of the flesh' (NRSV) or 'the behaviour that belongs to the unspiritual nature' (REB). In vv. 22–3 there is a list of the virtues that are the fruit of the Spirit. Lists of virtues and vices were well known in the Hellenistic world; there are partial parallels in Jewish 'two ways' traditions. While there are numerous lists of vices in the NT writings, there is no comparable juxtaposition of substantial lists of virtues and vices; perhaps the closest NT parallel is Jas 3:13–17. Although some translations list the vices of vv. 19–21 in groups, NRSV correctly treats them as a random list of 15 items. Paul rounds off the list with a solemn warning, which he says, repeats teaching he gave them earlier—presumably when he was present with them: 'those who do such things will not inherit the kingdom of God'. Here Paul may be using a common early Christian catechetical formula, for the wording is not characteristically Pauline.

The phrase 'fruit of the Spirit' (v. 22) is evocative: 'the fruit' is not the result of the believer's effort, but of the gift of the Spirit. The nine items in the list of virtues are often grouped into three groups of three, though it is doubtful whether this was Paul's intention. In the light of the opening verses of this section (vv. 13, 14) we can be more confident that Paul deliberately placed 'love' at the head of the list.

vv. 24 and 25 bring the argument of this section to a climax. Believers who identify with the crucifixion of Christ (cf. 2:19) have 'crucified the old nature' (REB). v. 25 explains how this is possible: by living by the Spirit. Although this is taken by some as the beginning of the next section of Paul's exhortations, it is better to interpret this verse (with NRSV) in conjunction with v. 24: these two verses focus on the chasm between 'flesh' and 'Spirit', the theme first set out in the 'headline' in v. 16. v. 26 is a rather bland exhortation, though v. 15 confirms that it was sorely needed in the Galatian churches.

(6:1–10) Let us Work for the Good of All Nearly every verse in this section includes an explicit exhortation, but the links between them are loose. Even more problematic is the extent to which these exhortations are related to the specific needs of the Galatian churches. Some insist that they are very general and quite unrelated to the main arguments of the letter, while others discern close links at almost every point. A mediating position is more plausible than either extreme: Paul has adapted well-known ethical maxims to meet the needs of the Galatian Christians. Many of the maxims in this section can be read as extended expositions of several of the fruits of the Spirit listed in 5:22–3. As we shall see below, there are further important links between this section and the latter half of ch. 5.

The opening maxim in v. 1 is very general. Translated literally, the Greek reads, 'you who are spiritual'; this is taken by some to refer to a specific group within the Galatian churches. But earlier in the letter Paul has insisted that all Christians have received the Spirit (e.g. 3:1–5; 4:6), so the NRSV is appropriate: 'You who have received the Spirit'. The 'spirit of gentleness' enjoined recalls 'gentleness', one of the fruits of the Spirit (5:23). Paul's concern for the erring believer is paralleled in Mt 18:15 and Jas 5:19. What is the law of Christ which is to be fulfilled (v. 2)? Since 'fulfilling the law' in 5:14 refers to the law of Moses, the use of the similar verb here strongly suggests that 'law' here also refers to the law of Moses—as 'redefined and fulfilled by Christ in love' (Barclay 1988: 134, 141). Dunn (1993: 323) is even more specific: 'it means that law (Torah) as interpreted by the love command in the light of the Jesus-tradition and the Christ-event'. The maxims in vv. 3–5 come as something of an anticlimax after the rich exhortations of vv. 1–2. Perhaps they are partly related to weaknesses Paul is aware of in the Galatian churches. Or

perhaps they are general maxims which have their place in nearly every community setting.

NRSV places v. 6 in a paragraph on its own, for this exhortation does not seem to be related either to those that precede or to those that follow. In 1 Cor 9:14 the right of preachers to be supported financially is asserted. This verse is rather different. It refers in general terms to the support (which surely included financial support) to be given by those under instruction in the faith to their teachers. In vv. 7–8 Paul adapts proverbial statements well known in antiquity, adding his own distinctive theological emphases. The sharp contrast between 'flesh' and 'Spirit' in v. 8 is in effect a summary of 5:16–25. The eschatological warning of 5:21c is echoed in the future tenses in v. 8, 'you will reap corruption / eternal life', and in the reference to reaping at harvest-time in v. 9.

By using the phrase 'so then', Paul indicates that v. 10 rounds off the series of exhortations which began at 5:13. The encouragement to the Galatian Christians to 'work for the good of all' encapsulates a bold vision. The churches in Galatia were tiny minorities in the societies in which they lived. As this letter emphasizes repeatedly, they had their own internal tensions and conflicts. But here they are urged to strive for the well-being of all without distinction. That special concern should be shown for those of the 'household of faith' is understandable.

Conclusion (6:11–18)

The final sentences of Paul's letters usually summarize and press home its key points. Galatians is no exception. Betz (1979: 313) correctly notes that these verses are the hermeneutical key to the whole letter. Unlike Paul's other letters, there are no personal greetings. This is as significant as the absence of the expected thanksgiving at 1:6 (GAL 1:6). In both cases a ready explanation is provided by the strained relationships between Paul and the Galatians.

Paul takes over from his amanuensis for the final sentences (cf. also 1 Cor 16:21; Col 4:18; 2 Thess 3:17; Philem 19). The reference to the 'large letters' he makes when writing himself is probably not a reference to his clumsy handwriting. When this letter was read aloud in the Galatian churches (1:2), the listeners would not have been aware of the change in handwriting. 'Large letters' probably signals the importance of the words which follow.

In vv. 12–13 Paul attacks the agitators explicitly and provides his own reasons for their insistence on circumcision. In claiming that they 'want to make a good showing in the flesh' Paul may be employing 'barbed humor, inviting the Galatians to laugh at the Teachers' (Martyn 1997: 561). It is not easy to see why an insistence on circumcision would enable them to avoid persecution. Were they currying favour with a powerful ultra-conservative group in the Jerusalem church (ibid. 562), or with a group of non-believing Jews who were incensed at the way Gentiles were being accepted into the 'people of God', i.e. as proselytes, without circumcision? We do not know. Paul claims that the agitators do not themselves obey the law (13a): they cannot pick and choose which parts of the law to observe (cf. also 5:3). Paul's final jibe is that his opponents are boasting about their success in persuading some of the Galatians to undergo circumcision (13c). There is an appropriate form of boasting, however: Christ crucified (14a; cf 3:1). For Paul the cross of Christ entails a radical break with 'the world'. Paul is not advocating a sectarian separation from the world, as 6:10 confirms; living by the Spirit entails the crucifixion of the flesh with its passions and desires (5:16, 24).

v. 15 is one of several very rich theological statements in the letter. It echoes 5:6, but caps the earlier verse with the claim that in Christ God is bringing about a new creation. The terse phrase, 'there is a new creation' is expounded in 2 Cor 5:17: the old order has passed away, everything has become new. In v. 16 Paul extends the blessing of God's peace and mercy upon those who follow this standard or rule, i.e. that there is a new creation in which the distinction between circumcised and uncircumcised is abolished.

The final phrase of v. 16 has evoked considerable discussion. Does Paul call down God's blessing upon a second group, 'the Israel of God', as well as upon those who follow the rule he has just enunciated? This interpretation is adopted by the NRSV: 'and upon the Israel of God'. Or does Paul refer boldly to Christian believers as the Israel of God? If so, the 'and' is understood as explanatory: 'that is to say', or 'namely'. The latter interpretation is now widely accepted. If Paul does refer here to Christians as the Israel of God, what becomes of non-believing Israel? This issue does not surface in Galatians, though in due course Paul did grapple with it in Rom 9–11. In v. 17 Paul refers to the marks (stigmata) he bore on his body as a result of the hostility he experienced as an apostle of Christ (cf. 2 Cor 11:23–30). There may be an undercurrent of irony: it is 'the marks of Jesus' rather than the mark of circumcision which Paul bears proudly. Although the final verse is similar to the final benedictions found at the end of all Paul's letters, the reference to the grace of Christ is particularly poignant in view of the content of the letter as a whole; it echoes the opening reference in 1:6 to God's call 'in the grace of Christ'.

REFERENCES

Barclay, J. M. G. (1987), 'Mirror Reading a Polemical Letter: Galatians as a Test Case', JSNT 3: 73–93.
—— (1988), Obeying the Truth: A Study of Paul's Ethics in Galatians (Edinburgh: T. & T. Clark).
Barrett, C. K. (1982), Essays on Paul (London: SPCK).
Betz, H. D. (1979), Galatians: A Commentary on Paul's Letter to the Churches in Galatia, Hermeneia (Philadelphia: Fortress).
Dunn, J. D. G. (1993), The Epistle to the Galatians, BNTC (London: A. & C. Black).
Hengel, M., and Schwemer, A. M. (1997), Paul Between Damascus and Antioch: the Unkown Years (London: SCM).
Kern, P. H. (1998), Rhetoric and Galatians, SNTSMS 101 (Cambridge: Cambridge University Press).
Longenecker, R. N. (1990), Galatians, WBC 41 (Dallas: Word).
Martyn, J. L. (1997), Galatians, AB 33A (New York: Doubleday).
Meeks, W. (1983), The First Urban Christians: the Social World of the Apostle Paul (New Haven: Yale University Press).
O'Brien, P. T. (1977), Introductory Thanksgivings in the Letters of Paul, NovTSup 49 (Leiden: Brill).
Scott, J. M. (1992), Adoption as Sons of God, WUNT 2/48 (Tübingen: Mohr [Siebeck]).

68. Ephesians
J. D. G. DUNN

INTRODUCTION

The letter to the Ephesians is one of the most attractive documents in the NT and one to which many Christians turn when low in spirit. Its mood of elevated composure, sustained prayer, and uninhibited confidence in God (particularly chs. 1 and 3), and its vision of the church, united, growing to maturity and loved (chs. 2, 4, 5) have been uplifting and inspiring for countless individuals and communities over the centuries. This character and quality of the letter is unaffected by the disputes over its authorship and purpose.

A. Distinctive Features of Ephesians. 1. In comparison with the other Pauline letters, however, Ephesians is something of a puzzle. Unlike all the others, it is not directed to a particular church or situation or person. The words 'in Ephesus' (1:1), which most modern translations still include, are not present in the earliest and best MSS; and second-century references to the letter do not know it as sent to Ephesus (see Best 1987). The lack of specified addressees in the original text and absence of Paul's normal list of greetings are confirmed by the absence of reference to particular situations or problems known or reported to the author. This raises the question whether it was intended as a circular or catholic letter, rather like James and 1 Peter, though in these cases particular recipients are still specified.

2. The style of the letter (particularly chs. 1–3) is pleonastic, that is, marked by repetitions and redundancies. Note for example the long sentences which constitute 1:3–14 and 4:11–16 (single sentences in Greek), and the repetition and piling up of adjectives, phrases, and clauses such as we find in 1:17–19, 2:13–18, and 3:14–19. Anyone familiar with the other Pauline letters will recognize that Ephesians is exceptional on this point. If written at the same time as the other 'prison epistles' (including Philippians and Philemon), these differences become all the more striking. And if written by an unnamed amanuensis or secretary, the latter had far more scope for free composition than any of Paul's previous secretaries.

3. In some way most striking of all is the exceptionally close relationship between Ephesians and Colossians (see Mitton 1951: 279–315). Compare particularly:

Eph.	Col.	Eph.	Col.
1:15–17	1:3–4, 9–10	5:5–6	3:5–6
2:5	2:13	5:19–20	3:16
2:16	1:20–2	5:22, 25	3:18–19
4:2	3:12	6:5–9	3:22–4:1
4:16	2:19	6:21–2	4:7.
4:31–2	3:8, 12		

Such identical phraseology can be explained only if both letters were written at the same time, or, more likely (given the differences already noted), by one letter deliberately drawing upon the other. Most scholars have concluded that the character of the interdependence is best explained as Ephesians using Colossians, in part at least, as a model.

Given such features, it is hard to avoid the question: is Ephesians really a letter? Or is it better explained as a meditative and expansive summary of what Paul stood for, with his characteristic letter openings and closings added to preserve this homage to Paul appropriately in the most characteristic Pauline form?

B. Was the Letter Written by Paul?

1. The traditional view, from the second century onwards, is certainly in the affirmative. The writer names himself as Paul in both 1:1 and 3:1. But for the past 200 years the issue has been disputed, and though several prominent contemporary scholars still hold to Pauline authorship (e.g. Barth 1974 and Bruce 1984), the majority have concluded that it was most probably written by someone else. In addition to the considerations already noted, two other features have carried weight.

2. The perspective seems to be second generation: 'the apostles' are looked back to as the foundation period (2:20) and designated as especially 'holy' (3:5). The self-reference in 3:1–13 at first looks to be strong evidence of Pauline authorship, but as we read through the paragraph the measure of boasting goes well beyond what Paul had previously claimed for his own role, and sounds more and more like a eulogy penned by an ardent admirer (cf. 1 Tim 1:15–16). Even with 3:1 and 4:1, the addition of the definite article turns the humble self-designation of Philem 1 and 9 ('a prisoner of Christ Jesus') into something more like a title ('the prisoner of Christ Jesus', 'the prisoner in the Lord').

3. The theological perspective also seems to have moved beyond that of the earlier Paulines, and even that of Colossians. In particular, the cosmic Christology of Col 1:17–19 seems to have developed into the cosmic ecclesiology of Eph 1:22–3. The 'church', characteristically the local church (in house, city, or region) in the earlier Paulines, is now (for the first time) understood consistently as the universal church. The talk of grace and faith in 2:5, 8–9, certainly has a Pauline ring, but the characteristic Pauline concern regarding the law in such talk is missing: the reference in 2:9 is to 'works', not 'works of the law'; the law is mentioned only briefly in 2:15. And the eschatology is more consistently 'realized': 'salvation' is an accomplished act (2:5, 8; 6:17); they are already raised and seated with Christ 'in the heavenly places' (2:6); there is no reference to Christ's coming again (contrast 4:15).

4. All in all, the evidence is most consistent with the hypothesis that the letter was written by a disciple of Paul some time after Paul's death, presumably writing to celebrate Paul's faith and apostolic achievement and using Colossians in part as a kind of template. If, alternatively, it was Paul who composed it, we would have to envisage a Paul who had so modified his perspective and style that it comes to the same thing; that is, in effect, 'the late Paul' is little different from 'the disciple of Paul'.

C. The Issue of Pseudepigraphy.

1. Many feel uncomfortable with the view that the letter was not composed by Paul himself. Since the letter claims to be written by Paul, does the denial of Pauline authorship not amount to a questioning of the letter's integrity? And does an author who falsely claims to be someone else not forfeit our confidence in what he has written? The issue of pseudepigraphy (falsely attributed writing) seems to undermine any claim to inspiration or canonical authority for the letter.

2. The problem is serious for today's use of such a letter since it seems to attribute an immoral motive to the real author. We today take for granted the conventions of copyright and that plagiarism is unacceptable. When someone writes in another's name, therefore, we naturally assume an intention on his part to deceive, to claim falsely an authority for his writing which he himself did not possess. It needs to be remembered, however, that the conventions of copyright are a relatively recent formulation (a consequence of the invention of printing). At the time when Ephesians was written there was no clear or legal conception of authorial ownership of a piece of writing. Once written, a document was in the public domain and could be used and reused, excerpted and expanded without attribution of source and without any thought of wrongdoing. In the NT itself we may cite Matthew's use of Mark or 2 Peter's use of Jude.

3. More to the point, the history of the formation of the biblical books themselves is a clear indication that disciples and successors of the originator of highly valued tradition were able to develop that tradition in the name of its originator. Writings such as the Pentateuch and Isaiah are generally recognized to be the work of several hands over a lengthy period. The Wisdom of Solomon and the corpus known as 1 Enoch could be attributed to those named as authors long after their death, without any thought of deceit. The teaching of Jesus could be elaborated differently by the different Evangelists without any sense of impropriety.

4. Ephesians makes best sense within this tradition. A close associate or disciple of Paul, who stood within the tradition begun by Paul and was recognized to do so, was seen to represent the Pauline tradition after Paul's death and was able to re-express it in some measure in his own terms. And he did so in Paul's name, without deceit; his words were acknowledged to be appropriate sentiments to ascribe to Paul. In other words, Ephesians probably represents the Pauline heritage some little time after Paul's death as seen from within. It expresses, we may say, the transition from Paul to Pauline.

D. To Whom, From Where, When, and Why.

1. Were the letter written by Paul we could date it firmly to the early 60s, presumably from his imprisonment in Rome, and not long before his death. Would it then have been a general letter to his churches? If so, why should that purpose not be indicated? And if it was a final summation of his message we might have expected it to come more in the form of a final testament (cf. Acts 20:18–35).

2. In the light of the above conclusions, however, the more obvious answer is that Ephesians is a meditative tract on Paul's theology, teaching, and significance in the form of a Pauline letter; for unspecified use, but probably to be read in church gatherings for worship and teaching; and written some time after Paul's death, but by someone close to him, and so within ten or so years of his death (that is, some time in the 70s or 80s). The close link with Colossians, the mention of Tychicus in particular (6:21–2), and the fact that the churches of the province of Asia attracted other letters over the following decades (Rev 2–3; Ignatius) suggests that it was written in

Asia, and in the event became most closely associated with Ephesus in particular.

3. More specific purposes have been suggested: for example, an early attempt to draw in Gnostic ideas, or to provide a covering letter for an early collection of Paul's letters. However, nothing in the letter itself gives any real support to such views. At best we can deduce that the churches addressed continued to be concerned about Christianity's identity as Israel's heir and about the proper integration of Jews and Gentiles within the church.

E. The Message of Ephesians in Summary. 1. The great theme of the first three chapters is God: God whose purpose embraces all time and space and comes to focus in Christ. It is because the readers' faith and life is centred in this Christ ('in Christ' is a repeated theme) that they can have such confidence in God, based as it is both on God's resurrection of Christ from the dead and their own experience of his Holy Spirit and grace (ch. 1).

2. At the heart of God's universal purpose from eternity has been the retrieval of humanity from its state of death, the abolition of the divided state of humanity, and the bringing of all things to unity in Christ. Seen from a Jewish perspective, that deadness and dividedness had its principal manifestation in the disadvantaged state of Gentiles as contrasted with Jews. But Christ's death rendered that old division null and void and has made possible a reconciled and united community held together by Christ, which as a whole enjoys the privileges previously confined to Israel and so can function as the household of God, the place where God continues to meet with humankind (ch. 2). This reconciliation of Jew and Gentile within the gracious purpose of God was at the heart of the divine mystery which Paul in particular had been given the commission to unveil to all (ch. 3). The fact that the church is so much the medium now for the outworking of this purpose of God makes its unity and its proper working as facilitated by the ministry gifts given it all the more important. Only as it functions as the body of Christ and grows up into Christ can it fulfil the universal and cosmic role earlier ascribed to it (4:1–16).

3. Right functioning of the church also depends on believers living as the church in the world and walking in the light, with all the specific moral commitment, both positive and negative, implied. Conduct and relationships modelled on those of Christ are also part of the restoration of creation to serve its original purpose. The enabling of the Spirit in shared worship remains indispensable (4:17–5:20).

4. Particularly important, as the basic unit of society, are households and their several relationships; here too Christian households should have Christ as model and resource and thus provide a test bed for society in re-creation. At no time should they forget that they were involved in a spiritual warfare nor fail to maintain the appropriate equipment and co-operation (chs. 5:21–6:20).

F. The structure of Ephesians.

COMMENTARY

(1:1–2) Greeting It is typical of Paul that he adapts the normal letter address, 'X to Y, greeting' (Gk.) or 'peace' (Jewish). He emphasizes his apostleship (cf. 2 Cor 1:1; Col 1:1). He stresses the status of the recipients: they have been set apart for God ('saints') (cf. e.g. Rom 1:1; 1 Cor 1:1) and live by trust in God ('faithful') (as in Col 1:2). He transforms the Greek greeting (*chairein*) into the rich Christian term 'grace' (*charis*), and combines it with the equally rich Jewish concept of peace, wishing them the continued experience of God's generous favour ('grace') and all that makes for communal well-being ('peace'). On 'in Ephesus' see EPH. A.1.

The Great Prayer and Meditation (1:3–3:21)

(1:3–14) The Blessing of God This is one of the most beautiful passages in the Bible. It is unlike anything else in the Pauline letters (the nearest parallel is 2 Cor 1:3–11). In the Greek it can be punctuated as a single sentence. The repetition of key words, the piling up of phrases, and the circling round and steady enrichment of the central theme gives it a depth and resonance unsurpassed in Christian praise. It is a word to return to, to rest upon, to rejoice in, and not least, to enjoy. It should have been put to great music long before now.

It begins by sketching in the circle of blessing (v. 3). That circle starts with God. The word for 'blessed' (*eulogētos*) here is used only of God in the NT (e.g. Mk 14:61; Rom 1:25); it indicates that nothing more wonderful can be imagined or spoken of than God. Characteristic of this blessedness is that it reaches out to embrace God's human creatures ('with every spiritual blessing'). The circle is complete when those thus blessed affirm its source and resource in God.

This blessing is four-dimensional. It reaches from the beginning of time: chosen 'before the foundation of the world' (v. 4); predestined in love (v. 5; cf. Rom 8:29–30); the divine mystery (v. 9), that is, God's original but hidden purpose, now revealed (see 3:3–6); predestined and appointed (v. 11). And it reaches to the end of time: a plan for the fullness of time (God's appointed hour) to sum up everything in Christ (v. 10; see 1:20–3); the Spirit as the guarantee of the inheritance and the final redemption of God's own possession (v. 14). Here again the stress is on God's overarching purpose in control from the first—his good pleasure and will (vv. 5, 9), 'according to [his] purpose . . . according to his counsel and will' (v. 11).

Spatial imagery is also prominent. The blessings in which believers already share are those 'in the heavenly places' (v. 3), where the symbolism of higher (heavens above earth) denotes greater bliss in a way more problematic for modern readers (see also 6:12). The final union will embrace everything in the heavens and in the earth (v. 10). Most striking of all, however, is the repeated emphasis on the location and means of this blessing as 'in him (Christ)', a phrase which occurs no less than ten times (also 'through Jesus Christ'—v. 5).

The conviction is clear: that the whole of God's purpose from the beginning focuses in and through Christ (vv. 4, 9, 11–12); that Jesus and his death were the means by which personal liberation (redemption) and the forgiveness for wrongs done had been genuinely experienced (v. 7); that Jesus himself is the 'place' in which the blessings of heaven and the Spirit are to be known in the here and now, so that the very term 'Christian' denotes a life (and death) bound up with his (vv. 3, 5, 13–14); and, not least, that Christ in a real sense constitutes the hope for the world and final reconciliation, its climax and summation point (vv. 9–10).

The blessings themselves are indicated in a series of evocative phrases: 'holy and blameless before him in love' (v. 4); adoption as God's children (cf. Gal 4:5–7), formerly estranged (v. 5); 'redemption', the image of the costly liberation of slave or captive (cf. Rom 3:24; 1 Cor 6:19–20), and the experience of forgiveness for conscience-nagging wrongs committed (v. 7; cf. Col 1:14); knowledge and sense of personal involvement in God's purpose (v. 9); an awareness of being chosen by God (v. 11); a conviction as to the truth of the gospel and of the 'salvation' (wholeness) it brings (v. 13; cf. 1 Thess 1:5); and the experience of being marked out by the Spirit as belonging to God (the function of a 'seal')—the reference will be to the impact made by the Spirit (as e.g. in Rom 5:5; 1 Cor 6:9–11), rather than to baptism—and of the assurance the Spirit brings (cf. Rom 8:14–16), as being the first instalment and guarantee of the complete redemption/liberation still to come (vv. 13–14; cf. Rom 8:23; 2 Cor 1:21–2).

But the blessing is primarily directed to God. He is the subject of the main active verbs ('blessed, chose, destined . . .'). His love embraces the trustful in the sonship of the Beloved (vv. 4–6; cf. Rom 8:15–17, 29). It is his grace (the same word as in v. 2), the same outpouring of divine generosity which is the fountainhead of all human wellbeing ('his grace with which he has engraced us . . . in accordance with the riches of his grace which he has lavished upon us', vv. 6–8, my tr.). He 'accomplishes all things according to his counsel and will' (v. 11). And all is 'to the praise of his glory' (vv. 6, 12, 14)— human bliss from beginning to end dependent on human recognition that God is the be-all and end-all.

It is important to note how characteristically Jewish is the language and thought. To begin a prayer to God with the evocation of his blessedness is distinctively Jewish (e.g. Ps 41:13; 72:18–19; the great Jewish prayer, the Eighteen Benedictions, 'Blessed are you, O Lord . . .', go back to Jesus' time). God's unconditional choice (v. 4) was fundamental to Israel's self-understanding (e.g. Deut 7:6–8). 'The Beloved' (v. 6) was a favourite name for Israel (e.g. Deut 33:12; Isa 5:1). The time perspective of the benediction is distinctive of Jewish apocalypses—the assurance that God's mysterious purpose is working towards its climax despite all human failure and

catastrophe (vv. 9–10; cf. e.g. Dan 2:21; Mk 1:15); the Qumran community shared a similar conviction that the hidden mysteries had been revealed to them (EPH 3:1–13). And not least, there is the writer's sense that he and his readers (Gentiles included) had been embraced within the divine purpose which began with and worked through Israel: the purpose was that they should be numbered with the 'saints', the ones set apart to God (a title for Israel—e.g. Ps 16:3; 34:9), and without blemish, like Israel's sacrifices (v. 4; cf. e.g. Lev 1:3, 10; Ps 15:2); they had been appointed (lit. given a share) in Israel's 'inheritance' (vv. 11, 14), two words which would have evoked for any Jewish reader thought of the land, seed, and blessing promised to Abraham (cf. Gen 12:2–3; Deut 32:9; Jer 10:16); they were God's 'possession' (cf. Ex 19:5; Deut 14:2).

The difference is indicated, however, in the repeated 'in him'. This is the amazing feature of the benediction—the confidence and conviction that Jesus has been and is the key to unlock the mystery of God's purpose and to bring it into effect, for Gentile as well as Jew. Christianity today, long heir of elaborate creeds and dogmas regarding Christ, can scarcely appreciate what astounding claims were being made—that one who had lived only a generation or so earlier could thus unfold and embody the wonder of God's grace. So we find it equally hard to appreciate the impact which Jesus and then the message about Jesus must have made upon such hearers in the ancient Mediterranean world. It was a conviction which was not merely intellectual: the believing was matched by an experience of forgiveness, of being engraced, and of the Spirit beginning the process of reclamation of human life and community for God (vv. 7–8, 13–14). But evidently the gospel thus focused on Jesus made such sense of reality, of the whole complex of time and space, of cosmos and history, that he could be thus seen at the centre of both cosmos and history, as the one who explained the all, and always 'to the praise of God's glory'.

(1:15–23) Paul's Prayer It was conventional in ancient letters to add a thanksgiving and prayer on behalf of those to whom the letter was sent (in Paul cf. particularly Rom 1:8–15; 1 Cor 1:4–9; Col 1:3–8). The opening words here (vv. 15–16) are typical of Paul and may indeed be modelled on Philem 4–5 and Col 1:3–4. The thanksgiving had in view particularly the two-sidedness of the readers' new relationships—faith in the Lord Jesus and love for all the saints (the 'all' might need some emphasis). Characteristic of Paul too was the habit of regular 'mention' of his converts in his prayers (Rom 1:9; Phil 1:3; 1 Thess 1:2).

But the prayer which follows surpasses anything else in Paul's letters, as rich as the preceding blessing and stretching the expectation of hope and the imagination of faith still further.

It is directed to God (not to Christ). He indeed is described as 'the God of our Lord Jesus Christ' (v. 17), with the recognition that Jesus, even in the fullness of his exalted Lordship, still acknowledges God as his God (cf. 1 Cor 15:24–8). This Christian faith, including the mind-blowing Christology of 1:22–3, is still monotheistic through and through. It is God who has done all the great work of salvation in Christ (vv. 19–23) and in whom hope is focused (vv. 17–18). He is 'the Father of glory' (v. 17; cf. Acts 7:2; Rom 6:4); the phrase should not be reduced to 'glorious Father' but should be allowed to resonate with all the overtones of God as the progenitor of all that is glorious and splendid (including v. 18). The richness of this divine resource is a repeated theme (vv. 7, 18–19; 2:4, 7; 3:8, 16).

The intercession falls into two parts. First for knowledge (vv. 17–19), knowledge being fundamental to well-being. The very diversity of the language (wisdom, revelation, knowledge, illumination) is a reminder that there are different kinds of knowledge. Here most in view is the knowledge which comes through an experience of revelation, of eyes being opened, and through the experience of personal relationship with God ('the eyes of your heart enlightened' is a wonderfully evocative phrase). When knowledge is reduced to knowledge of facts or of information which can be humanly discovered it will always be deficient for living (cf. Col. 1:9–11). Only in its richer form, dependent on inspiration from on high, does knowledge become wisdom (the echo of Isa 11:2 will be deliberate).

Here, however, the thought is directed more to the future: 'the hope to which he [God] has called you' (v. 18), a 'calling' (both invitation and summons) elaborated in the talk of the rich inheritance to be shared with the saints (see v. 14). When hope is based on such knowledge it can indeed be firm and confident. As in Col 1:4–5, so here, hope is not far from faith and love (cf. 1 Cor 13:13).

The second part (vv. 20–3) reflects further on the working of this great might of God: hope can be confident (v. 18) because the power at work in human experience (v. 19) is the same power which raised up Christ from the dead and exalted him as God's 'right-hand man'. The language was already credal (e.g. Acts 3:15; 13:30; Rom 10:9; 1 Thess 1:10) and the use of Ps 110:1 as a way of understanding what had happened to the risen Christ was well-established (e.g. Acts 2:34–5; Rom 8:34; 1 Pet 3:22). But it is here elaborated in an exceptional way.

The thought that Christ was thus set 'in the heavenly places' is peculiar to Ephesians (1:3, 20; 2:6). But the further thought that he was already dominant over all powers, both present and future, takes up Ps 110:1 combined with Ps 8:6 (1:20–2; a combination we find also in 1 Cor 15:25–7 and Heb 1:12–2:8). The combination is powerful since it links the idea of Jesus as the man/son of man who fulfils God's purpose for humanity as the climax of creation (Ps 8:4–6; cf. Heb 2:6–9) with that of Jesus as David's greater son given a share in God's sovereign rule (Ps 110:1; cf. Mk 12:35–7). The conviction obviously carried with it a psychological liberation from fear of the nameless forces which shape human existence (see 2:2 and 6:10–20). What a one was this Jesus that the note struck by his life, death, and resurrection should have had such continuing resonance and deepening reverberations in the subsequent decades.

If that was a challenging enough linkage, the final clauses (vv. 22–3) almost baffle comprehension (the major commentaries spend several pages discussing them). The climax of what God did 'in Christ' (v. 20) was to give him as 'head over all things for the church, which is his body' (vv. 22–3). The metaphor of the church as Christ's body goes back to 1 Cor 12 and Rom 12:4–8, and will later be elaborated with the idea of Christ as the head of the body (4:15–16). But here the thought is of Christ as head of all reality, given by God to or for the church (cf. Col 1:17–18). That would be a difficult enough

thought, though 'head' can mean both 'ruler' and 'source' (fountainhead), and so Christ could be portrayed as embodying or epitomizing the rationale and pattern of divine creation. 'Given to/for the church' could then mean simply(!) that the church, here the universal church, had, through its faith in Christ and the God who worked through Christ, been given the key to understanding reality and enabled to rise above all that threatened human and social life.

The chief problem is the final clause, what it means and how it relates to what has gone before—'the fullness of him who fills all in all'. Does it refer to Christ or to the church? Does it draw on ideas familiar from later Gnostic texts—Christ as a kind of cosmic being which comprises the totality of sentient reality? The answer is probably that the writer has been carried away by his language and imagery and is playing on the familiar Jewish thought of God or God's Spirit as filling the cosmos (Jer 23:24; Wis 1:7; cf. Ps 139:7). Christ now embodies that fullness (cf. Col 1:19; 2:9). And the church, his body, is (or should be!) the place where God's presence in and purpose for creation comes to its clearest expression. Would that it were so!

(2:1–10) A Reminder of What God Has Already Done in Them This is one of the most forceful statements in the Bible regarding the human condition apart from God's grace and the way in which that grace operates for salvation.

The human condition apart from grace is described in vv. 1–3 in a series of vivid clauses; note the balance between a certain givenness of human character, social conditioning, and individual responsibility. (1) They had been 'dead through trespasses and sins' (vv. 1, 5; cf. Col 2:13). 'Death' is but one metaphor among many; others include 'weak' and 'enemies' (Rom 5:6, 10; cf. EPH 2:14–16). And the experience of grace (in conversion) can itself be likened to a dying (Rom 6:5–11). But a life enmeshed in its breaches of the moral code (transgressions) and repeated failings (sins) can well be likened to a state of death, where promptings of divine grace and love evoke no real response (cf. Luke 15:24; Rom 7:7–11—'I died'). (2) Their daily conduct had been determined by the standards of society (cf. Rom 12:2), the spirit of the age (v. 2). The latter metaphor is unique in the NT ('the ruler of the power of the air'; cf. Jn 12:31 and Acts 26:18), and draws on the common understanding of the day that hostile spiritual forces influenced or determined human behaviour (hence 6:11–17). We still today speak, for example, of a criminal 'underworld' and often enough feel ourselves victims of forces, some apparently malevolent in character, that we cannot control. (3) Human responsibility becomes more evident in the talk of a life conducted 'in the passions of our flesh, following the desires of flesh and senses' (v. 3; cf. Col 3:5, 7; Titus 3:3; 1 Pet 1:14). By 'flesh' Paul means the weakness of the physical constitution (flesh decays); life lived at that level, devoted to feeding human appetites (food, sex, power), is a life lived apart from God, subject to the law of diminishing returns and the law of increasing subserviency to self-indulgent habit (cf. Gal 5:16–21). According to Rom 1:18–32, this circle of sin-begetting-sin is also an expression of divine wrath just as is the final judgement (Rom 2:5; cf. Col 3:6). To be noted is the fact that the writer no longer speaks of 'you', as in 2:2; Christian Jews as well as Christian Gentiles are 'by nature children of wrath' (v. 3, 'all of us'; v. 5, 'we'), all equally dependent on the initiative of divine grace (cf. 2:10).

Still more, however, is said about the way in which grace had worked to change both character and context. Again, it should be noted, as throughout ch. 1, the initiative is God's from start to finish: 'But God . . .' (v. 4). It is his mercy, love—'rich in mercy [cf. Rom 11:30–2], out of the great love with which he loved us' (cf. Rom 5:8)—and thrice-mentioned grace (vv. 5, 7, 8) which has been decisive. And the effective medium of God's action has been Christ—'with Christ' (v. 5), 'in Christ Jesus' (vv. 6, 7, 10). The three elements in the preceding analysis are in effect taken up one by one, in each case emphasizing the role of grace and of Christ.

(1) The state of deadness in trespasses and sins has been transformed—'made alive with Christ' (v. 5). This is the language of resurrection (Jn 5:21; 8:11; 1 Cor 15:22); the final proof of God's creative power is that he overcomes death (Rom 4:17). The idea of conversion as being bound up with Christ's death, so that Christ through his death becomes as it were a passageway to new life, is prominent elsewhere in the NT (e.g. Gal 2:19–20; 1 Tim 2:11; Heb 2:9–11). In the earlier Pauline letters the thought of sharing also in Christ's resurrection is reserved for the 'not yet' future (Rom 6:5; 8:11), but here, as in Col 2:13, that too is referred to the 'already' of conversion. It is a logical development to describe the new life experienced through the Spirit (Jn 6:63; 2 Cor 3:6) as a sharing in Christ's life, that is, his risen life. Whatever the finer points of theology, however, conversion was evidently experienced in the early days of Christianity as life-giving, life-changing.

(2) Countering the captivity to 'the ruler of the power of the air', God had not only raised them with Christ to new life, but also raised them with Christ to the heavenly places (v. 6; see 1:3). The astonishing claim was necessary, perhaps, to break the previous psychological dependency. Implicit, then, is the conviction that their lives now focused in and through Christ had in effect risen above the old captivating influences of the present world (cf. Gal 6:14; Col 2:15), or at least need have no fear of any such power (Rom 8:31–9). But more explicit here is the thought that they (writer and readers) were as it were trophies of grace to make clear to everyone the overwhelming generosity of God's purpose and its most effective implementation in and through Christ (v. 7).

(3) The answer to lives dominated by human weakness and self-indulgence is the recognition that salvation is given by grace, through faith, the very opposite of human contriving or manipulation—as a gift of God (v. 8). The language is very Pauline, but the thought has shifted somewhat from the earlier letters. (a) Salvation is here spoken of as a completed act, whereas earlier on Paul spoke of it as future (Rom 5:9–10; 13:11; 1 Cor 3:15), and of Christians as those 'being saved' (1 Cor 1:18; 2 Cor 2:15). There salvation covered the whole process of renewal and final redemption (Rom 8:23); here the thought is of the decisive character of what Christ has done and of the commitment to him and bound-up-ness with him. (b) Earlier too the talk of 'works' was always of 'the works of the law', that which was obligatory upon Jews as members of the covenant people—the key question being whether and how much of these laws were obligatory for Gentile believers. To which Paul had replied that only faith was necessary (Rom 3:19–20, 27–31; 9:30–2; Gal 2:15–16). Here the thought is broadened, or

deepened. By 'works' the author here seems to mean any product of human effort: salvation is wholly and solely a 'gift' (v. 8). There is no scope for boasting in oneself, only in God (v. 9); the 'turned-in-upon-oneself-ness' of the old life (v. 3) has been given a new focus and orientation. The outcome is a complete contrast to the old way of life—God's handiwork, a new creation on the template of Christ, 'good works' such as God had made humankind for in the beginning (v. 10; cf. 4:24; 1 Cor 3:10–15). There should be a contrast, should there not, between a life lived by grace, through faith, in Christ (v. 10), and a life determined by the desires of flesh and mind (v. 3)?

(2:11–22) The New Humanity The same ground is covered again in a second review of the readers' transition from past to present (cf. 5:8). This time, however, the review is not from the more general perspective (death to life) but from the Jewish perspective on Gentile disqualification from grace. The assumption is that God's saving purpose for humankind had been worked out through Israel, that Gentiles had hitherto been strangers to that promise, but that now through Christ the blessing of access to God and peace with God was open to all. The resulting new reality (the 'new humanity', v. 15) is sometimes understood as a third race (Christians) replacing the old division of the world into Jews and Gentiles (Lincoln 1990: 144). However, it would be more in tune with the paragraph to speak of the new humanity rather as the Israel which no longer defined itself by separation from the other nations but which is redefined to embrace all who believe in (Israel's) God through Christ (cf. Rom 2:28–9; 4:11–12; Gal 3:28–9; Phil 3:3). Either way, fundamental is the thought of Christianity as continuous with Israel of old and of being given to share in Israel's blessings, and that this has only been possible in and through Christ—'he is our peace' (v. 14). That this new humanity also fulfils God's purpose in creating humankind in the first place will be indicated in 4:24.

vv. 11–12 recall the former disqualification. Characteristic of Jewish self-understanding was the conviction that circumcision was a positive identity marker 'in the flesh' which set them apart definitively from other nations as God's elect nation (Gen 17:9–14). So much so that the world could be divided from a Jewish perspective into 'the uncircumcision' and 'the circumcision'—the whole range of differences focused in this one feature (as in Gal 2:7–9). Only Jews regarded lack of circumcision as something negative; in contrast, the typical Greek regarded circumcision as a form of mutilation. The added note that circumcision was 'made . . . by human hands' is an indication that the writer saw this evaluation of 'circumcision . . . in the flesh' as a boundary separating Gentiles from God's grace to be mistaken.

v. 12 lists the blessings from which Gentiles had hitherto been disqualified in ascending order of importance. Israel was not only a nation-state but a religious entity (a matter of continuing confusion from that day to this). 'The covenants of promise' (as in Rom 9:4) either refer to the regularly renewed covenant with the patriarchs (starting with Gen 12:3) or include such key promises as 2 Sam 7:12–14. The worst state to be in is 'having no hope [cf. 1 Thess 4:13] and without God in the world'.

'But now in Christ Jesus' (v. 13) those disqualifications have been removed from the nations (Gentiles). This is the subject of vv. 13–18, a nicely structured passage (chiasmus) where the repeated references to 'far off/near' and 'peace' (vv. 13–14, 17; echoing Isa 57:19; see also 6:15) bracket the central imagery of hostility reconciled 'in him' (vv. 14–16; see Schnackenburg 1991: 106). The key to understanding the passage is the recognition that the writer sees two hostilities/antagonisms as interrelated. He assumes the Jewish view (cf. 4:17–18) that Gentiles, by definition cut off from the grace given through Israel's God-given covenant(s), are distant from God (cf. Isa 49:1; 66:18–19; Acts 2:39) and in need of reconciliation with God (cf. Rom 5:10; Col 1:21). But that enmity had become entangled and confused with enmity between Jew and Gentile. Both were expressed in 'the dividing wall' (v. 14), possibly an allusion to the barrier which marked off 'the court of the Gentiles' from 'the court of Israel' in the Jerusalem temple, and which Gentiles could not breach except on pain of death—symbolizing Gentile exclusion from the presence of God. But the main barrier was formed by the law, with particular reference to the rules (especially purity and food rules) which reinforced the separation of Jew from Gentile (v. 15; cf. Acts 10:9–16, 28, 34–5; Gal 2:11–16; Col 2:16, 21).

Consequently, for easily understandable psychological and social, as well as religious reasons, at the heart of Paul's gospel (himself a Jew) was the claim that God in Christ had resolved both antagonisms, and that the one could not be reconciled in isolation from the other. The two being made one was integral to peace with God (vv. 14–15); reconciliation of either was possible only as reconciliation of both (v. 16). The theology of the cross at this point is an elaboration of the earlier 2 Cor 5:17–21 (cf. Col 1:22; 2:14). But it contains overtones of a self-sacrifice acknowledged by both sides as ending an ancient blood feud, and echoes of the sacrifice which bonded the parties to the covenant in Gen 15:7–21. The difference is that the one thus sacrificed continues to serve as and to maintain the bond thus created 'in him' (vv. 13, 17). The final imagery of v. 18 is of the reconciled peoples now able together to pass through the barrier which had previously divided them and together to celebrate their reconciliation in joint worship made possible by their common participation in the one Spirit (4:3–4; cf. again Phil 3:3); 3:12 says the same thing in complementary terms.

The outcome is not a new national or international entity, but individuals of all nations now sharing in privileges previously thought to be limited to Israel as a nation (v. 19; 3:6)— 'fellowcitizens with the saints [see 1:4; cf. Phil 3:20; Heb 12:22–3] and members of the household of God' (RSV; cf. Gal 6:10; 1 Tim 3:15; Heb 3:5–6). Those who enjoyed security both of citizenship and family/household membership would have been in a minority in many ancient cities.

The imagery of the last three verses (20–2) changes to that of a building, in particular a temple. The image was a natural one (cf. e.g. Mt 7:24–7; 1 Cor 3:9–11, 16; 1 Pet 2:5). There are three significant features here. First, the mention of 'the apostles and prophets' as the foundation (v. 20; contrast 1 Cor 3:11); given the order, the 'prophets' are probably Christian prophets (cf. 3:5; 4:11; 1 Cor 12:28). The implication seems to be that a foundation period is being looked back to (cf. Rev 21:14). Second, Christ is the cornerstone; that is, either the

keystone or capstone, given that the role of foundation has already been filled (Lincoln 1990: 155–6); or the cornerstone, the first stone laid in the foundation, in relation to which all other parts of the foundation were aligned (Schnackenburg 1991: 124). The metaphor was drawn from Isa 28:16 (understood as foundation) and in early Christian apologetic was often combined with Ps 118:22 (Mt 21:42; Rom 9:33; 10:11; 1 Pet 2:4, 6–8). Third, bringing the paragraph (vv. 11–22) to a climax is the emphasis on the harmonious interrelatedness of the whole structure (see also 4:16). To be noted is the fact that it is conceived as a growing (not a static) unity, a growth dependent on harmonious working together (v. 21), an ongoing process (the tenses are all present continuous) which can only happen and be maintained 'in the Lord'.

The end result (3:22) will be a people—no longer defined in national or ethnic terms—which functions as 'a dwelling place for God'. This is the hope which always lies behind the sacramental focus of God's presence in human-built temple or earthly grown bread and wine—a people as the mode of God's presence and action in the world (cf. Ex 19:5–6; Lev 26:11–12; Ezek 37:27; 1 Pet 2:5)—but which so often falls out of focus (cf. e.g. Isa 1:10–17; Acts 7:48–9; 1 Cor 10–11). The triadic formulation—for God, in the Spirit, interlocked through Christ and growing together in Christ—reflects the theological logic which led inexorably to the subsequent Trinitarian understanding of God (cf. 1:3–14).

(3:1–13) Paul's Stewardship of the Great Mystery A personal statement in self-defence is quite a common feature in Paul's letters—earlier over his apostleship (Gal 1:1–2:10; 1 Cor 15:8–11), or missionary practice (1 Cor 9; 2 Cor 10–12), or regarding his travel plans (e.g. Rom 1:9–15). Initially ch. 3 looks like a further example and provides one of the strongest supports for the view that the letter was written by Paul himself. But as the paragraph unfolds, the claims made move well beyond anything Paul ever claimed for himself earlier—a sustained measure of boasting in spiritual insight and commission with which the earlier Paul would probably have been uncomfortable (contrast e.g. Rom 11:13, 25; 16:25–6; 1 Cor 7:40; 14:37–8; 2 Cor 10:13–18; 12:1–13). It may thus ease the problem and make for a more consistent picture of Paul to conclude that these are the words of a close, ardent disciple of Paul rather than of Paul himself.

The opening self-identification as 'the prisoner of Christ' (v. 1; also 4:1; but note the definite article) is paralleled only in Philem 1 and 9 (cf. also Phil 1:7); it thus reflects the mood of the prison epistles, Paul's imprisonment providing both opportunity to survey his previous ministry and affording fresh opportunity for witness (cf. Phil 1:13–17; Philem 10, 13). Characteristic of Paul is his conviction that his calling was 'for the sake of the Gentiles' (v. 1; Gal 1:16; Rom 11:13) and that he had been given a special engagement for the work (vv. 2, 7, 8; cf. Rom 1:5; 15:15–16; 1 Cor 9:17; 15:10; Gal 2:7–9; Col 1:29). At the end of the paragraph too (v. 13) there is an awkwardly compressed twin Pauline theme that present sufferings foreshadow future glory (Rom 5:2–5; 8:17–21; 2 Cor 4:16–17) and that Paul's sufferings work to his converts' benefit (2 Cor 1:6; 4:7–12; Gal 4:19; Col 1:24; 2 Tim 2:10).

But the main burden of the self-testimony here is the revelation made known to Paul regarding 'the mystery' and

Paul's understanding of it (vv. 3–4), to which he had previously briefly alluded (1:9–10). It had also been revealed to 'his holy apostles and prophets' (v. 5; see 2:20). But the emphasis quickly reverts to the fact that it was Paul who, first and foremost, and despite being 'the very least of all the saints' (cf. 1 Cor 15:9; on 'saints' see EPH 1:2), had been given the commission (3:7–8) to unveil this mystery (3:9–11).

'Mystery' is a term which echoes the language and perspective of Jewish apocalypses (already in Dan 2:18–19, 27–30; see e.g. Caragounis 1977). Typically the thought is of the divine purpose: it had been firm from the beginning (v. 11), but had been hidden through the generations (vv. 5, 9; Rom 16:25; Col 1:26), only to be revealed now at the appointed time, at the climax of the ages (cf. 1 Cor 10:11; Gal 4:4). Jewish apocalypses and the Qumran community make similar claims regarding their own insights.

The Christian insight, particularly of Paul, however, is quite distinctive. The mystery as now unfolded was different from the mysteries perceived by their fellow Jews. It was to the effect that God's purpose from the beginning had been to give the Gentiles a share in the same inheritance, the same body, the same promise (as Israel) 'in Christ Jesus' and 'through the gospel' (v. 6). To make known this now revealed mystery to the Gentiles and to everyone (but 'everyone' might not be part of the original text) was Paul's special commission (vv. 8–9).

The thought is certainly consistent with Paul's earlier references to the divine mystery—particularly Paul's first unveiling of the mystery to resolve the excruciating problem of Israel's rejection of the gospel (Rom 11:25–32). That the mystery focuses on the Jew/Gentile issue and involves the removal of the theological significance of that distinction is less to the fore in Col 1:27, but is clearly central here in Ephesians (cf. 2:11–22). The language and imagery underline how crucial the issue was at the beginning of Christianity: the gospel as an invitation to all to share in the special relationship with God which both the Jewish and the Christian Bible assumes to have been Israel's special and distinctive prerogative, but only (Christians add) prior to the coming of Messiah Jesus (cf. Gal 3:29). If a text like this still speaks, then a sense of continuity with Israel, but transposed into a different key, remains fundamental for Christian self-understanding.

As in Col 1:27, 2:2, and 4:3, the mystery is embodied, unveiled, and implemented in Christ (vv. 4, 8–9, 11; cf. 5:32; 6:19). Inevitably and unavoidably Christ is the key to and reason for the distinctiveness of the Christian mystery (cf. 1 Cor 1:24—Christ 'the wisdom of God'). Presumably it was the impact Jesus made in his ministry (in regard to sinners discounted by 'the righteous'), and, in Paul's case particularly the impact of Christ's post-crucifixion encounter with Paul (the two cannot have been at odds otherwise Christianity would have fallen apart), which caused the first believers to see that God's grace was for *all* equally and without reference to national, racial, or social identity (cf. Gal 2:5–16; 3:28). As Paul saw so clearly, it followed, as day follows night, that a gospel which failed to preach that message was no gospel and a church which failed to live that message was no church. The Christ in whom such differences are not wholly discounted is not the Christ of God's mystery.

As at the end of ch. 1, the cosmic dimensions of the divine purpose are not overlooked. It is the plan of the Creator which is in view (v. 9); there is no divorce between creation and salvation here (cf. Col 1:20). The audience in view in this unfolding of divine wisdom is not just every person but every power that can be envisaged or feared (v. 10; see 1:21). And as in 1:22–3, the church is the medium through which and stage on which this richly diverse wisdom of God is enacted (v. 10; cf. 3:21). At the very least that should mean that the church is (or should be) the prototype and test bed for reconciliation between peoples and between humankind and the creation of which it is part.

The thought unwinds with a reminder of the supreme gift which Christ has brought: that 'in him' there can be a boldness and confidence of access to God (v. 12; cf. 2:18; Heb 4:16; 7:25; 1 Pet 3:18), a boldness and confidence made possible precisely because of the insight embodied in the gospel regarding God's 'unsearchable riches' and 'many-sided wisdom' (my tr.), concerning the character of creation and his purpose for all humankind. In Christ it is given to know the character of God as nowhere else so clearly, and through the trust which Christ inspires, or 'through faith in him' (cf. 3:17), humankind in its rich diversity can draw near to this God with boldness (cf. Rom 8:15–16).

(3:14–21) The Opening Prayer Resumed In effect everything from 1:3 to 3:21 is an extended prayer. The section 2:1–3:13 is as it were a meditative break within the prayer proper—on the effect of conversion (2:1–10), on the reconciliation of former hostility between Jew and Gentile (2:11–22), and on the divine mystery committed to Paul (3:1–13). The meditation has been of such a lofty character, rising repeatedly to praise for the wonder of God's purpose now enacted in Christ, that the spirit of prayer has scarcely been diminished. But now the meditation passes back to prayer proper and the prayer at the end of such a profound meditation is drawn to a fitting conclusion.

As throughout the preceding chapters, the object of the prayer and devotion is God alone. To kneel is the appropriate acknowledgement of humble submission before and dependence on such an overwhelming majesty (v. 14; cf. Rom 14:11; Phil 2:10–11). At the same time, it is God experienced and approached as Father (v. 14) which is the distinctive Christian feature (Lk 11:2; Rom 8:15–16; Gal 4:6–7). And it is no inconsistency for Christians to recognize that this same God is the source of every family and nation's identity (v. 15)—the name indicating the character of the named (cf. Ps 147:4).

The petition echoes the earlier prayer in 1:17–19. But it falls more clearly into two parts. The first (3:16–17) is a prayer for the addressees' spiritual condition. The source is again the riches of God's glory: 'glory' here is almost synonymous with 'grace' as in 1:7; God's grace is his glory. The concern is that they should be strengthened in their innermost being (cf. Rom 7:22; 2 Cor 4:16; 1 Pet 3:4); sustained firmness of conviction, commitment, and motivation will be in view (cf. Col 1:11). The means is God's Spirit, as the powerful presence of God at work within the depths of human discipleship and within the human situation.

It may seem surprising that the prayer (v. 17) is for Christ to dwell in their hearts (the tense denotes 'come to dwell' rather than 'continue to dwell'). Had Christ not already come to dwell in the hearts of believers, at their conversion (cf. Rom 8:10; Gal 2:20; Col 1:27)? But believers do often pray for something (e.g. the presence of God's Spirit in their worship) which they believe or hope to be already the case. Such a prayer is a natural expression of concerned piety. Here it reminds us that we should not transform such language (Christ indwelling the heart) into formal definitions or dogmas which can then be used to classify 'genuine' conversion or faith. Or else we should say that the prayer is for believers to be converted afresh every day. The 'faith' here refers back to the faith mentioned in 3:12. To be noted also is the overlap between the Spirit and Christ (vv. 16–17): being strengthened through the Spirit and Christ indwelling are not clearly distinct experiences (cf. Rom 8:9–11; 1 Cor 6:17; 12:4–6).

It is equally important to recognize that this spiritual strengthening and indwelling is 'rooted and founded in love' (v. 17, my tr.; note the echo of Col 2:7). The double metaphor (a living plant, a well-constructed building) was typical of Jeremiah (e.g. 1:9–10; 18:7–9; 24:6; 31:28) and is used by Paul in 1 Cor 3:10–14. The love will presumably be God's initiating love and the divinely enabled human love in response, directed both to God and to the neighbour (Mk 12:28–33).

As in the first part of the prayer proper (1:15–23), so here, the second petition pushes through the constraints of human language and imagery (3:18–19). It is a prayer once again for knowledge (as in 1:17–19)—but such knowledge! (1) To comprehend (impossible!) what we might describe as the four dimensions (a not uncommon metaphor—Lincoln 1990: 207–13; Schnackenburg 1991: 150–1) of God's love (the Gk. sentence in v. 18 is incomplete); 'with all the saints' is a reminder that only a church conscious of its own dimensions through time and space can even begin to hope for the realization of such a prayer. (2) To know (in experience) the love of Christ which goes beyond knowledge (v. 19), where words and metaphors and symbols are inadequate to the task of describing such experience (cf. Col 2:2–3). (3) With the result that they may be filled with all God's fullness! What Col 1:19 and 2:9 ascribed to Christ alone, Ephesians prays may be true also of the church (1:23; 3.19)! The goal for the church is nothing less than that it embody the presence and love of God in the way that Christ did (cf. 4:13). Here the sequence of clauses implies that such a filling is the effect of appreciating and experiencing the mystery of God's love.

The prayer is brought fittingly to an end by a benediction (vv. 20–1) whose enthusiastic language matches the hyperbole of the preceding petition (cf. Rom 11:33–6). Such a petition can be put forward since it is addressed to a God whose goodwill and enabling grace far exceed human imagining (cf. Phil 4:7). He 'is able to do beyond everything, infinitely more than we ask or think' (v. 20, my tr.); as elsewhere in Ephesians, the language tumbles over itself in the attempt to express the completeness of trust beyond vision (cf. 1:19). To be noted, however, is that the enabling power is already 'at work within us'.

The final doxology (v. 21) ascribes glory to God both in the church and in Christ Jesus, since Christ in life, death, and resurrection is the paradigm of the one who most fully acknowledges God and the character of God, and since the church is the body of people on earth whose commitment is precisely both to live from and to live out that same acknowledgement.

The Exhortation (4:1–6:20)

(4:1–6) The Church in its Calling and Confession Paul's regular practice in his letters was to attach a sequence of appropriate exhortations to the main body of his letter. Here, even though chs. 1–3 have been more prayer than exposition, the same practice is followed. Chs. 4–6 contain mostly instruction (1) on how Christians should understand their mutual interdependence as the church (4:1–16) and (2) how they should conduct themselves in their lives within the world (4:17–5:20), (3) in their mutual responsibilities as households (5:21–6:9), and (4) in their battle against spiritual forces (6:10–20).

The exhortation begins with Paul's characteristic 'I exhort you' (v. 1; cf. Rom 12:1; 1 Thess 4:1), here with the same recall to his status as 'the prisoner' as in 3:1. The metaphor for daily conduct ('lead life') is 'to walk', a metaphor Jewish in origin (*halakh* means 'walk'; hence halakah, rules for conduct), which presumably reflects the fact that most moral issues arise from one's various contacts with others as one 'walks about'. The thought is not so much that a particular lifestyle or career can be regarded as a 'calling', as that the whole of life should be lived as an expression of and response to God's summons to live for him (cf. 1 Cor 1:26; 7:20; 1 Thess 2:12; 2 Thess 1:11).

No first-century Christian would need reminding that such a calling inevitably meant working and co-operating with others, with all the strains, misunderstandings, hurt feelings, and irritations which that involved. The church could never be reduced to a sequence of disparate individuals. The key to effective mutual co-operation is given in 4:2–3: a proper humbleness and meekness in self-esteem (very un-macho characteristics; cf. Phil 2:3 and Col 3:12); (2) patience and forbearance in love (cf. 1 Cor 13:4–5); and (3) an eager determination to maintain the unity of the Spirit and the peace which benefits all. To be noted is the fact that this unity is given by the Spirit, arising out of the shared experience of the one Spirit (cf. 1 Cor 12:13; Phil 2:1); it is not created by Christians, but can be destroyed by them! The peace of God (cf. 2:14–15) can function as a bond when there is genuine mutual respect (cf. Col 3:14–15).

The confession of 4:4–6 reinforces this unity by recalling its scope. It has an unconscious triadic structure—'one Spirit, one Lord, one God' (had it been more deliberate presumably 'one Spirit' would have come first in 4:4). By giving 'one God' the climactic position (4:6), and attaching to it the four 'all's, the writer reminds his readers that the ultimate foundation of Christian unity is God both in his oneness and in his allness as Creator (cf. Rom 11:36). The confession of Christ as 'one Lord' is in tune with this monotheism, or else Christian faith is misconfessed (cf. 1 Cor 8:6; 15:24–8; Phil 2:9–11). The importance of this distinctively Jewish emphasis on God as one is a reminder that the principal strains on Christian unity at this period came from the inclusion of Gentiles into Israel's privileged status (2:11–22).

That the 'one Spirit' gives the body its actual (as distinct from its confessional) oneness (v. 4), both as a shared experience (v. 3) and through the manifold workings of the Spirit's engracements, is spelled out more fully in 1 Cor 12:13–26 and Rom 12:4–8 (see also EPH 4:7–16). The 'calling' is one, because it is common to all believers (1:18; 4:1), without respect to rank or ability. In v. 5 the 'one faith' will have in mind in particular what was probably one of the earliest baptismal confessions, 'Jesus is Lord' (cf. Rom 10:9). The focus of unity is not so much a common formulation or common ritual as a common Lord; somewhat surprisingly, the Lord's Supper is not mentioned.

(4:7–16) The Character and Purpose of Ministry in the Body of Christ The paragraph is a rich elaboration of the earlier Rom 12:4–8 and 1 Cor 12:4–31. Here too it is stressed at the points of emphasis (beginning and end, vv. 7, 16): (1) that the effective functioning of the church as Christ's body depends on the recognition that each member has a function within the body and on each exercising that function; and (2) that each function is appointed and its exercise made effective by the enabling (engracement) which comes from Christ. The terms used are slightly different: the earlier Paul had spoken of 'charism' (*charisma*) as the function exercised in accordance with the 'grace' (*charis*) given (Rom 12:6–8); here the talk is of 'grace' given in accordance with the measure of Christ's gift (v. 7). And in Rom 12 and 1 Cor 12 the head is simply another part of the body, whereas here Christ is the head of the body (v. 16; cf. 1:22). But the basic imagery is the same; that is, of the body as the model of a unity which is constituted by diversity, a unity which actually depends on the reality of mutual interdependence being expressed through the diverse engracements of its different members.

'The gift of the Messiah' (v. 7, my tr.) is elaborated in vv. 8–11. First (v. 8) by citing Ps 68:18, a passage lauding YHWH's triumph over Israel's enemies. Here it is taken as a description of Christ's exaltation, presumably in the same vein as 1 Cor 15:24–6 and Col 2:15. And the text speaks of him giving rather than receiving gifts—the character of Christ's triumph! But we know of a Jewish targum (interpretative translation) of the same passage which referred it to Moses and read it in a very similar way—Moses giving the law. So the reading here would have been quite acceptable.

The interpretation of the Psalm, which is appended (4:9–10), is probably a very early expression of the belief that Christ descended into the place of the dead ('the lower parts of the earth'; cf. Ps 63:9; Mt 12:40; 1 Pet 3:19) prior to his ascension 'far above all the heavens' (cf. 1:3, 20; 2:6; Heb 4:14; 7:26). Some think a reference to incarnation is intended by the talk of descent, but the language and imagery are focused solely on the benefits and universal effect (cf. 1:23) of Christ's resurrection and exaltation triumph; and a reference to Christ *descending* at Pentecost would be exceptional (Dunn 1989: 186–7).

'The gift of the Messiah' is elaborated, secondly, by itemizing the particular gifts given to the church (v. 11). The sequence of 'apostles … prophets … teachers' reflects the same evaluation as 1 Cor 12:28—apostles as church founders (e.g. 1 Cor 9:2), prophets and teachers as the most vital ministries in a church (Acts 13:1; Rom 12:6–7). Unexpected is the insertion of 'evangelists' as the third item (cf. Acts 21:8), and the linking of the fourth item as 'pastors and teachers'—presumably reflecting an understanding of the church as both evangelistic and pastoral in concern.

The other major elaboration of the earlier imagery of the church as Christ's body (vv. 12–16) is in terms of the purpose of these gifts and the character of the body's growth. Noteworthy is the fact that these ministries do not constitute the whole of the body's ministry, but are intended 'for the equipment or making ready of the saints: for the work of ministry, for the building up of Christ's body' (v. 12, my tr.; the punctuation is important here; otherwise Lincoln 1990: 253). The ministry of the appointed few is to facilitate the ministry of all. Only so, presumably, can *all* come to the *unity* of the faith (v. 13): the unity of the confession (4:3–6) depends on the interactive ministries of the many (vv. 7, 16), in other words, a dynamic and not a static unity. The goal (and test—1 Cor 14:3–5, 12, 17, 26) is always the upbuilding of the body. Here the voice is indeed still the voice of Paul.

This point is reinforced by the following description of the unity of the body as a process, a process of growth, a unity to be attained (v. 13) as well as maintained (4:3). Here it is characterized as a unity of faith in and knowledge of God's son: trust does not exclude knowledge (cf. 1 Cor 13:12; Phil 3:8, 10); experience does not render trust unnecessary (cf. 2 Cor 12:1–10; Gal 4:9). The goal is maturity. The measure of that maturity is the Christ (cf. Col 1:28). What is in view, it should be noted, is a corporate maturity: such maturity is not possible for the individual; it is possible only for the church, and for the individual as part of the body of Christ.

A negative measure of such maturity (v. 14) is the church's ability to steer a straight course when the winds and waves of doctrinal speculation beat upon it—an odd change of metaphor within the sustained metaphor of the body (probably alluding to Isa 57:20; cf. Jas 1:6). The threat is all the more serious when human deceit (as in a dice game) and malice are involved, deliberate attempts to promote discordant views or counter ideologies, designed (we may infer) to boost some individual's or group's status or reputation. Here again, discernment as a gift to the congregation as a whole must normally be given precedence over the claimed insight of one or two. This fear of false teaching arising within the church smacks very much of a second-generation concern (cf. 1 Tim 4:1; Heb 13:9).

The final elaboration of the body metaphor (vv. 15–16) reverts to the imagery of growth, with Christ as both the goal and the source of its enabling (cf. 2:21; Col 2:19). The physiology implied is strange to modern ears, but the force of the metaphor is clear. The antithesis to naïve childish interest in alternative practices or views (v. 14; cf. 1 Cor 14:20–5; Heb 5:13–14) is 'speaking the truth in love' (v. 15), a balance easy to state (truth *and* love) but hard to practise (cf. Gal 4:16). It will not be accidental that the last word (v. 16) is 'love' (cf. 5:25).

(4:17–32) How to Live as the Church in the World There follows a section of more general, more or less all-purpose paraenesis, which stretches to 5:20. Unlike earlier Pauline letters, there seems to be no particular situation (in the Ephesian church or elsewhere) in view. The first part (vv. 17–24) parallels 2:1–10 in structure—a reminder (1) of the readers' Gentile past (vv. 17–19), (2) of their conversion (vv. 20–1), and (3) of God's purpose for them (vv. 22–4).

As in 2:11–12, the warning presupposes a Jewish perspective (vv. 17–19): that Gentile conduct was characterized by the futility of their vaunted reason and darkness of understanding, alienation from the life of God by their ignorance (cf. 1 Pet 1:14), and a hardness and callousness expressed in and reinforced by their self-surrender to sexual excess, impurity and greed (cf. 5:3; Col 3:5). The judgement is harsh but reflects Jewish conviction that they had been privileged with fuller insight into God's will for human conduct, and the generally higher sexual standards of Jewish communities (cf. Rom 1:21–31).

The recall to their conversion in this instance focuses on what they were then taught (vv. 20–1). Notable here is the reference to the Christ as a model for Christian conduct (cf. Rom 6:17; 15:1–3; Col 2:6); the 'truth in Jesus' is a moral truth. The 'if indeed' which begins v. 21 (my tr.; 'assuming that' RSV) is a typical Pauline cautionary note (cf. Rom 8:9, 17; 1 Cor 15:2; Col 1:23).

The exhortation which follows (vv. 22–32) takes the classic form: put off (vices) and put on (virtues) (see e.g. Schweizer 1979). The imagery is drawn from change of clothes, as indicating a change of character and lifestyle, and was familiar in the ancient world (here cf. particularly Col 3:8–12); it does not necessarily imply that a ritual change of clothes was already part of Christian baptism. Something of the moral transformation which Christian conversion entailed is here indicated (cf. 1 Cor 6:9–11), but also the Christian perception of the resulting difference in ethical values.

To be 'put off' (cf. Rom 13:12; Jas 1:21; 1 Pet 2:1) is a whole way of life characterized by 'deceitful desires' (v. 22, my tr.), the desire which constantly promises but never fully satisfies, which consumes but rarely fulfils; the 'old nature' (RSV) is marked by the twilight of desire. The antidote and alternative is a constant renewal in self-perception (v. 23; cf. Rom 12:2) and a daily assumption of and living out ('put on') the humanness which God intended and created, marked by the righteousness and holiness of God's reality (v. 24). Implicit is the conviction that Christ is the image of the new humanity, the completion of God's purpose in creating humankind, and the template for the recreation of the old humanity into the new (cf. 2:15, 4:13; Rom 13:14; Col 3:10).

The general exhortations which follow (vv. 25–32) focus particularly on personal relations and underline the importance of conversation, as a force for community building and as potentially destructive of community (cf. Jas 3:6–12). They are based on age-old proverbial wisdom, familiar among both Greek and Jewish moralists, but of no less value for that. Members of a church (of one another) should be able to speak the truth to each other (v. 25, using the words of Zech 8:16). The proverb that anger should not be retained beyond nightfall, thereby giving scope to the devil, was a valuable elaboration of the exhortation from Ps 4:4 (vv. 26–7).

The exhortation about the thief (v. 28) breaks the sequence on speaking, but reminds of the transformation brought about in some early Christian conversions and of the need to reinforce such a conversion by a determined change of motivation and lifestyle (cf. Rom 12:8; 1 Thess 4:11; Titus 3:14). To work in order to *give* indicates a very different set of values from those which normally govern society.

The final group of exhortations (vv. 29–32) contrasts (in an a-b-a-b format) contributions to conversation which are bitter, undisciplined, angry, and malicious and thus grieve the Spirit (which should distinguish them as believers, 1:13–14), with those which are beneficial, fitting, and impart grace to the other, marked by sensitivity, thoughtfulness, and the forgiveness which they themselves had experienced from God in Christ (Col 3:13). The mature Christian community is one where the Lord's Prayer petition about forgiveness can be prayed with complete sincerity.

(5:1–20) Walking in the Light The final block of general exhortations develops the earlier antithesis between the old life and the new (cf. 2:1–10 and 4:17–24) in three sharply drawn contrasts. First, the contrast between a life modelled on the love of God and Christ (vv. 1–2) and a life mismatched with the vices which warrant the anger of God (vv. 3–7). Second, the repeated contrast between light and darkness, between a life in the light, open to and in turn reflecting light's searching rays, and a life full of hidden shamefulness (vv. 8–14). And finally, the contrasts between unwisdom and wisdom, between a life which characteristically gains its inspiration from strong drink and a life whose character and direction is given by the Spirit (vv. 15–20).

As the first sequence of general exhortations was marked by a recall to their discipleship of Christ (4:20), so the second sequence begins with a striking double call to take both God and Christ as the model for personal relationships and conduct (vv. 1–2). Paul elsewhere speaks of imitating Christ (1 Cor 11:1; 1 Thess 1:6), but not of imitating God. The thought here, however, is of the child taking the loving parent as a model, and alludes particularly to God's forgiveness (following from 4:32) and mercy (cf. Lk 6:36; see further Wild (1985). So too their conduct (walk) is to be modelled on Christ's self-giving (cf. 5:25; Gal 2:20) and sacrifice (cf. Phil 4:18 echoing Ex 29:18) as a governing principle.

Another vice list (vv. 3–5) warns against sexual sins in particular, beginning with a repetition of the characterization of their former lifestyle (4:19) and adding *porneia* (illicit sexual relations), one of the most regular members of such lists (e.g. Mk 7:21; Gal 5:19; Col 3:5). Evidently the exploitation and abuse of sex was as seductive and as destructive then as now. Gossip about such matters should be discouraged lest it promote any implication that they don't matter. Conversation between close friends can so easily degenerate into shaming and foolish talk, and become caught in the swamp between buffoonery and boorishness (where Aristotle located the uncommon third term in v. 4); this is a further reflection on the dangers of too casual speech (4:29–32). Christian conversation should be marked instead by a spirit of thankfulness (v. 4).

The vice list is rounded off by a reminder that the sexually promiscuous, the dirty-minded, and the greedy or covetous person (but the terms are masculine) will not share the inheritance of God's kingdom (v. 5). This talk about inheriting the kingdom was evidently fairly common in earliest Christianity (1 Cor 6:9–10; Gal 5:21; cf. Rev 21:8; 22:15). It linked effectively into the most prominent feature of Jesus' proclamation (about the kingdom of God, e.g. Mk 1:15), but here reflects also the developed understanding of the exalted Christ as sharing in God's kingly rule (cf. Lk 22:29–30; 1 Cor 15:24–8; Col 1:13). It also links further back into the idea of Gentiles sharing in Israel's inheritance (1:14, 18). The abhorrence of idolatry was particularly Jewish, both as a fundamental sin and as associated with the three sins just named. The idolatry and debauchery of the golden calf episode remained an unhealed sore in Israel's conscience (e.g. 1 Cor 10:6–8). But the folly of taking another as god, rather than the one Lord God of Israel, had been a lesson requiring frequent repetition.

They should beware of empty and deceptive words on this point (v. 6; cf. Rom 16:18; Col 2:4, 8). The evident fact was that human society functioned in accord with the moral order in which God had set it: as in Rom 1:18–32, the wrath or anger of God can be understood in terms of the community-destructive outworkings of such self-indulgence (v. 6; cf. 2:2–3). The degenerative effect of promiscuous and selfishly acquisitive company (v. 7) is contrasted with the opening call to unconditional and sacrificial love (vv. 1–2).

The second set of contrasts are between light and darkness (vv. 8–14), a common metaphorical usage in religions generally to express the sharpness of the antithesis between new and old, between truth newly perceived and the old misconceptions. In the OT cf. e.g. Ps 36:9; 82:5; Prov 4:14–19; Eccl 2:13; a prominent contrast in the Dead Sea scrolls is between 'the sons of light' (the Qumran covenanters) and 'the sons of darkness' (the rest); in the NT see e.g. Mt 6:22–3; Acts 26:18; 2 Cor 4:6; Col 1:12–13; 1 Pet 2:9; 1 Jn 1:6.

The elaboration of the contrast here is a blend of the conventional and the more distinctively Christian. All would agree that goodness, righteousness, and truth are desirable virtues (v. 9), that a religious person will want to learn 'what is pleasing' to God (v. 10), and that part of the effectiveness of the imagery of light lies in the power of light to expose what would otherwise be hidden from sight (vv. 11–13). The distinctive Christian claim is that the light (the real, most effective light) is 'in the Lord' (v. 8). Equally characteristic of Paul's teaching is the claim that discernment of what pleases the Lord (v. 10) is given by renewal of the mind and through the Spirit (Rom 12:2; 1 Cor 2:14–15; Phil 1:9–10; 1 Thess 5:19–22). The power of light to expose the unsavoury and shameful recalls such passages as Jn 3:20 and 1 Cor 14:14–25 and echoes the warning notes of Mk 4:21–2 and Rom 13:11–14.

v. 14 may be a snatch of an early hymn (such as may be found under a heading such as 'The Gospel' in older hymn-books today). If sung by early congregations it would function both as a recall to their conversion, as a reminder (like Rom 13:11) that falling asleep is a constant threat to be resisted, and as a promise of final waking from sleep, resurrection from death, and enlightenment from Christ.

In the final paragraph the contrast between unwisdom and wisdom (vv. 15–17) in effect draws upon the accumulated wisdom of Proverbs, Ben Sira, the teaching of Jesus gathered in the Sermon on the Mount, and so on. But it adds the ominous note recalled from 2:2 that such wisdom is needed because the context of the life of faith is stamped by evil (v. 16). That is why conduct must be 'careful' (v. 15; still attractive is the older KJV translation, 'walk circumspectly') and the significant time (the sense of the Gk. word used here) must be 'bought up' (v. 16). The latter exhortation is just the same in Col 4:5, and the metaphor more evocative than clear, but the emphasis is presumably on discerning and acting upon all too scarce opportunities for good and the gospel in the midst of lives which are all too pressurized and constricted. v. 17 pre-sumably says the same thing in terms closer to those already used in v. 10.

The last contrast vividly recalls Acts 2:1–4, 12–16 and reminds us that many of the earliest Christian gatherings for worship were marked by spiritual exuberance (vv. 18–20). As at Pentecost the effect of the Spirit could give an impression of drunkenness. The difference is that strong drink taken in excess resulted in debauchery and dissipation (cf. again Rom 13:13). In contrast, fullness of the Spirit came to expression most characteristically in various psalms, hymns, and spiritual songs, by which the congregation was instructed, God was praised from the heart, and life lived in a spirit of thankfulness to God. To be noted is the fact that being filled with the Spirit is not regarded as a once-for-all event; the exhortation is to be (constantly or repeatedly) filled with the Spirit (see further Fee 1994). The distinction between the various forms of song is unclear (as in Col 3:16), but presumably includes OT psalms, hymns which came to birth in Christianity (such as Lk 1:46–55 and perhaps Phil 2:6–11), and spontaneous charismatic songs (cf. 1 Cor 14:15, 26). As elsewhere in Paul prayer is made not so much *to* Christ as to God the Father *through* Christ (cf. Rom 7:25; 2 Cor 1:20; Col 3:17).

(5:21–6:9) Household Rules What follows is constructed on the framework of a table of rules for good management of the household (Balch 1981). Household management was a common concern of political theorists and ethicists in the ancient world. Naturally so, since the household was generally understood to be the basic unit of the state or society. The health of society and stability of the state therefore depended on the basic relationships within the household—husband and wife, father and children, master and slaves. The second and third generation of Christians shared this concern: no doubt partly to demonstrate the good citizenship of small house churches which might otherwise have seemed subversive of traditional social values; but no doubt partly also as a means of bearing good witness to the quality and character of the Christian household (see Schweizer 1979).

The structure is particularly close to that of Col 3:18–4:1, which probably provided the precedent for those which followed (here and 1 Pet 2:18–3:7; cf. e.g. Titus 2:1–10; *Didache* 4:9–11; *1 Clem* 21:6–9). The core teaching is fairly conventional (good ethics are by no means exclusively Christian). But the conventional is transformed by the Christian sense that all relationships have to be lived 'in the Lord' and with the unselfish, sacrificial love of Christ as the pattern and inspiration.

In the first part of the rule (5:21–33) the transformation begins at once. That wives should be subject to their husbands (5:22; Col 3:18; 1 Pet 3:1) accorded with the moral sensibilities of the time; here we need to recall that in the law and ethos of the time households were patriarchal institutions and that the paterfamilias (father of the family) had absolute power over the other members of the family. But the rule is already softened by prefacing it with a call to be subject to one another (5:21; cf. Gal 5:13; 1 Pet 5:5): in a Christian household the power of the paterfamilias was not absolute. And the reminder that wifely submission is to be 'as to the Lord' (5:22) sets the whole relationship within the primary context of mutual discipleship (cf. Mk 10:42–5).

It is true that the placing of the relationship of husband and wife parallel to that of Christ and church (5:23–4) seems to set the wife in an intrinsically inferior status (cf. 1 Cor 11:3). But that again reflects the ethos of the time (the marital law which treated wives as the property of their husbands was only changed in Britain in the 19th cent.). And the main thrust of what follows is clearly intended to transfuse and transform that given relationship with the love of Christ. The paradigm for the husband is Christ as lover and saviour, not as lord and master.

The beautiful imagery of 5:25–7, so beloved at wedding ceremonies, has in view the purificatory bath which the bride took prior to and in preparation for the wedding ceremony; Christ's self-giving had an analogous cleansing in view (cf. Ezek 16:8–14). Perhaps there is a side glance at baptism, but the primary thought is of the (corporate) Christian life as equivalent to the time between betrothal and the wedding ceremony, the marriage itself only taking place at the return of Christ (cf. 2 Cor 11:2; Rev 19:7–8; 21:2, 9–10). The cleansing is evidently a spiritual cleansing, and it comes 'by the word' (5:26; cf. 1 Cor 6:11; Titus 3:5–6; Heb 10:22).

5:28–33 develops a different aspect of the imagery, drawn from Gen 2:24 (5:31; cf. Mt 19:4–6). The idea of 'the two become one flesh' invites a twofold corollary: that a healthy love of the other is inseparable from a healthy respect for oneself (5:28–9; cf. Mk 12:31; Rom 13:8–10)—an important psychological insight; and that the love of Christ sustains the mutual love of husband and wife within the corporate context of the church, of their being individually and jointly members of his body the church (5:30, 32; cf. Rom 12:5).

The final exhortation (5:33) maintains the emphasis on each and every husband's responsibility to love his own wife. The wife is not so counselled, for the love in view is not marital or family love so much as the sacrificial and non-self-serving love of the more powerful for the disadvantaged. In a situation of given inequality between husband and wife the appropriate response of the wife was to respect her husband.

The second pairing within the household code (as in Col 3:20–1) is children and parents (6:1–4). As with the submissiveness of wives, so the obligation of obedience to parents (6:1) was a widely recognized virtue in the world of the time. But again it is qualified by an 'in the Lord' (though the phrase here is missing from some important MSS). And just as noteworthy is the unusual feature in such codes, of children being directly addressed; evidently they were regarded as responsible members of the house churches where such a letter as this would be read out. As in the case of the previous exhortation to husbands (5:25–33), so here the basic exhortation of Col 3:20 is elaborated, on this occasion by drawing in the scriptural authority for it—Ex 20:12 and the slightly fuller version of Deut 5:16—with the exegetical note inserted to point out that this was the first commandment with promise. As in other similar cases, the NT writer saw no difficulty in applying a promise relating to Israel's prosperity in the promised land to Gentile believers in another part of the Mediterranean world.

In contrast, the advice to fathers is left stark (6:4). Again it is fairly conventional. Only the father is addressed: the paterfamilias had sole legal authority over his children and primary responsibility for their *paideia* (training or discipline; the

classic word in this context) and instruction; at the same time it was recognized that such power unwisely handled could easily provoke or goad youths and young men to a resentment which was destructive of household order and family. Again the Christian qualification is added—'the training and instruction of the Lord' (cf. Prov 3:11).

The final pairing in the household code is slaves and masters (6:5–9). The exhortation to slaves is closely modelled on Col 3:22–5. Again it is worth noting that they too are here recognized as full members of the congregation and having responsibilities as Christians to discharge the duties which their status as slaves laid upon them (cf. 1 Tim 6:1–2; Titus 2:9–10). If any are surprised that Paul did not question the morality of slavery, they should recall that slavery only became a moral issue as a result of the slave trade (only two centuries ago), and that in the ancient world slavery was simply an economic phenomenon, slaves being essential to the smooth running of the economy (though by no means solely on the bottom rung).

The exhortation recognizes the reality of slavery: obedience had to be unquestioning and orders carried out with fear and trembling (many masters treated their slaves harshly). But the thrust of the exhortation is to provide the slaves with the right motivation, so that their service might lose its servile character and become a way of serving the Lord with sincerity of heart (6:5), doing the will of God with a will, and not (as we might say) as clock-watchers or solely to catch the master's eye or to curry favour with him (6:7). Slavery too can be a form of discipleship (cf. 1 Cor 7:20–4). At the same time, they are reminded that their earthly masters are only that (6:5), and that both slave and free will receive from their heavenly Lord the appropriate recompense according to the good they have done (6:8; cf. 2 Cor 5:10).

In 6:9 the point is driven home directly to those in the congregation who were slave-owning householders (the assumption is that the household as a whole is Christian). In the spirit of OT slave legislation (Lev 25:43), they should forbear from threatening their slaves, remembering that both they and their slaves have the same Lord in the heavenly places, and that he is an impartial master—a common OT motif (e.g. Deut 10:17; 2 Chr 19:7) echoed elsewhere in the NT (Acts 10:34; Rom 2:11; Col 3:25; Jas 2:1).

(6:10–20) Put on the Armour of God The final strand of exhortation is one of the most vivid portrayals of the Christian life as a spiritual struggle, indicating the power of the hostile forces (vv. 10–12), the means of withstanding them (vv. 13–17), and the need for co-operative effort (vv. 18–20). The metaphor, be it noted, is of warfare, not of a school debate or of a business enterprise. As a piece, it is clearly constructed from a sequence of allusions to well-established Jewish motifs, particularly that of YHWH as the Divine Warrior (Isa 59:17; Wis 5:17–20). The writer would no doubt be conscious of the fact that the armour he describes is depicted by Isaiah especially as YHWH's own armour, armour which YHWH dons to effect judgement on human sin and social injustice (Isa 59:12–18).

The spiritual opposition is described both as 'the devil' (cf. 2:2; 4:27; Jas 4:7; 1 Pet 5:8–9), and as cosmic and spiritual powers in the heavenlies (vv. 11–12; cf. Rom 8:38–9; Col 1:16; 2:15). With this information added to that of the earlier references to the heavenlies (1:3, 20; 2:6; 3:10), we are given a clearer picture of the heavenly regions—presumably as a sequence of heavens (cf. 2 Cor 12:2–3), in which the lower heavens (nearer to earth) are inhabited by hostile powers, and the upper heavens are where Christ is seated (1:20–1). Modern cosmology is very different, and the extent to which such names ('rulers, authorities, cosmic powers') were already perceived to be metaphorical is unclear. What matters is the recognition that there are forces active through human fear and greed which can captivate whole groups and even societies and wreak all forms of evil, from the most subtle ('the wiles of the devil'; cf. 4:14) to the most inhuman. Those who have lived through any three or four decades of the twentieth century should need no convincing on that score. To designate them as 'spiritual powers' helps prevent such evil from being treated lightly or superficially (they are not merely 'flesh and blood') (see e.g. Wink 1984: 84–9).

The appropriate and necessary response (given the character of this evil) is to seek a strength commensurate with and more powerful than that evil—a spiritual strength to match a spiritual crisis (cf. Rom 4:20; 1 Cor 16:13), a strength from God, the strength of God himself (v. 10; the first OT echo—Isa 40:26). Correlated with (or an elaboration of) this strength is the equipment of the Divine Warrior, 'the panoply of God' (vv. 11, 13). Only that equipment and empowering will provide the fortitude and the means to withstand in a day when evil seems to be rampant (cf. 5:16), and having done all within one's power, still to stand one's ground; the sign of God's enabling is not so much clear-cut victory over evil, as the sustained will to resist evil, come what may.

The list of equipment is inspired by earlier, briefer metaphors, and the metaphors themselves are not fixed (e.g. in 1 Thess 5:8 the breastplate is faith). Nevertheless, the appropriateness of this listing is notable.

1. *Belt* (v. 14). In a day when clothing was much looser, it was necessary for the flowing cloak to be fastened firmly by a belt, otherwise movement would be hindered and action impeded (cf. Lk 12:37; 17:8). To be caught out in deceit or falsification was like tripping over one's own clothing; the belt of truth prevents one being 'caught with one's pants down'.

2. *Breastplate* (v. 14). The metaphor draws directly on Isa 59:17 (and Wis 5:18), describing YHWH's breastplate. There it is the fact that what God does is right which makes his judgement invulnerable to criticism (of partiality). Here the thought is of God's acceptance of those who trust in him as their breastplate which keeps them equally secure in the face of hostile criticism (cf. Rom 5:1–2; 8:31–4).

3. *Shoes* (v. 15). This is a more original image, but no doubt adapted from Isa 52:7, a passage which is also echoed in Acts 10:36 and cited in Rom 10:15. Why the word 'preparation' is added is unclear, but it strengthens the impression that what is in view is the responsibility of the church and believer to speak out the gospel of peace with God. Mission is the best form of defence; the church on the move will be more sure-footed in face of the encroachments of evil.

4. *Shield* (v. 16). Again the imagery is original; more typically God is a shield (e.g. Gen 15:1; Ps 18:2, 30; 28:7); in Wis 5:19 the shield is 'holiness'. But 'faith' is also appropriate (cf. 1 Pet 5:9). Faith and righteousness are two sides of the one coin in

Pauline thought (Rom 1:17), just as the breastplate and shield have a similarly defensive function (hence 1 Thess 5:8). Trust itself can be exposed to quite a battering, but trust sustained keeps inviolate the one who so trusts (cf. Rom 4:16–22).

5. *Helmet* (v. 17). Here we are back with familiar imagery (Isa 59:17; 1 Thess 5:8; though in Wis 5:18 the helmet is 'impartial justice'). In 1 Thess 5:8 the helmet is 'the hope of salvation', which reflects the thought of the earlier Paulines that salvation is a still future goal (but 'hope' is confident hope). Here, however, as in 2:5 and 8, the question is raised whether the perspective has changed: that which keeps the head of the body (cf. 4:15) safe is the security of salvation realized and not just the confident hope of it.

6. *Sword* (v. 17). Notably the one offensive weapon is doubly denoted as 'of the Spirit', and as 'the word of God'. Again the imagery reflects older usage (Isa 49:2; Hos 6:5; cf. Heb 4:12). What is in mind is not just the written word, as though the thought was simply of the believer being well versed in scripture, able to cite the appropriate passage for all occasions (cf. Mt 4:1–11). The Spirit is here seen as an inspiring force, the Spirit that inspires the word from God appropriate to the occasion (Mk 13:11; Rom 10:8–17; 1 Pet 1:25). It is no accident that the enabling of powerful speech is one of the most regular charisms and marks of the Spirit in the NT (e.g. Acts 4:8; 1 Cor 2:4–5; 12:8, 10); despite immense developments in communication, the force of the spoken word is still immeasurable.

The final stress is on prayer (vv. 18–20), not, somewhat surprisingly, as part of the continuing metaphor of spiritual armour, but emphasizing none the less (by the greater elaboration given to the request) its importance in the warfare just described. Christian soldiers must never forget that they need constant help from God. Moreover, since the previous imagery had been somewhat individualistic (despite the plural verbs), this last addition helps underline the importance of co-operation and mutual support in the warfare. Like the speaking (v. 17), the praying should look to the Spirit for inspiration (cf. Rom 8:26–7; 1 Cor 14:15; Jude 20); and the military mood is retained in the calls for alertness and application (6:18; cf. Lk 21:36).

The transition from exhortation to personal request (vv. 18–20) seems to be modelled on Col 4:2–4 (cf. Lk 21:15; Mk 14:38), with a final recapitulation of the 'mystery' motif and play on the contrast between Paul's imprisonment and his boldness as commissioned by God (3:1–12; cf. 2 Cor 3:12; 5:20; Phil 1:20; 1 Thess 2:2).

Conclusion and Benediction (6:21–4)

Most of vv. 21–2 is almost verbatim Col 4:7–8. It is of course conceivable that Paul wrote both letters at more or less the same time (thus unconsciously or deliberately giving Tychicus precisely the same commission each time). But the perspective of the letters is too different for that to be the most obvious solution. And in a letter thus far marked by its lack of specific reference to particular situations, this brief personal note rings somewhat oddly. It is more likely, then, that the author has drawn the language from Colossians to indicate the very Pauline effect he hoped his letter would have, and as an expression of what Paul would have wished to say had he himself still been able to dictate such a letter.

Since Tychicus appears only in the later Pauline letters (Col 4:7; 2 Tim 4:12; Titus 3:12; see also Acts 20:4) he probably emerged only in the Pauline circle at a late stage; like Epaphras (Col 1:7) he is remembered as a beloved brother and faithful servant of Christ. Whatever the precise historical circumstances, the reference reminds us that there must have been regular contacts between the Pauline churches.

The final benediction (vv. 23–4) is unusual in Paul, but it strikes the regular notes of grace and peace (1:2) and links them with two of the great Pauline words—love and faith ('love with faith'). Effective also is the final balance between divine enabling ('from [both] God the Father and the Lord Jesus Christ') and human response ('all who have an undying love for our Lord Jesus Christ').

REFERENCES

Balch, D. (1981), *Let Wives be Submissive: The Domestic Code in 1 Peter* (Missoula; Scholars Press).

Barth, M. (1974), *Ephesians* (2 vols.; Garden City, NY: Doubleday).

Best, E. (1987), 'Recipients and Title of the Letter to the Ephesians: Why and When the Designation "Ephesians"?', *ANRW* 2. 25. 4 (Berlin: de Gruyter), 3247–79.

Bruce, F. F. (1984), *The Epistles to the Colossians to Philemon and to the Ephesians*, NICNT (Grand Rapids: Eerdmans).

Caragounis, C. C. (1977), *The Ephesian Mysterion* (Lund: Gleerup).

Dunn, J. D. G. (1989), *Christology in the Making*, 2nd edn. (London: SCM).

Fee, G. D. (1994), *God's Empowering Presence: The Holy Spirit in the Letters of Paul* (Peabody, Mass.: Hendrickson), 658–733.

Lincoln, A. T. (1990), *Ephesians*, WBC 42 (Dallas: Word).

Mitton, C. L. (1951), *The Epistle to the Ephesians* (Oxford: Clarendon).

Schnackenburg, R. (1991), *The Epistle to the Ephesians: A Commentary* (Edinburgh: T. & T. Clark).

Schweizer, E. (1979), 'Traditional Ethical Patterns in the Pauline and Post-Pauline Letters and their Development (Lists of Vices and House-Tables)', in E. Best and R. McL. Wilson (eds.), *Text and Interpretation* (Cambridge: Cambridge University Press), 195–209.

Wild, R. A. (1985), ' "Be Imitators of God": Discipleship in the Letter to the Ephesians', in F. Segovia (ed.), *Discipleship in the New Testament* (Philadelphia: Fortress), 127–43.

Wink, W. (1984), *Naming the Powers* (Philadelphia: Fortress).

69. Philippians   ROBERT MURRAY, SJ

INTRODUCTION

A. Character and Main Concerns of the Letter. 1. Equalled only by Philemon, Philippians is the most personal of Paul's letters. Among the categories listed by ancient theorists (Malherbe 1988), it combines features of a hortatory 'letter of friendship' (Fee 1995: 214) with those of a 'patronage letter' (Bormann 1995: 161–205). Unusually for a Paul, the OT is seldom cited; his argument is passionately centred on Christ, yet he often uses Stoic language (see PHIL E).

2. Although the letter's contents are conditioned by practical matters, the main emphasis is on strengthening the commitment and faith of the Philippian Christians, as was Paul's regular aim (Meeks 1983: 84–107). He urges them to follow the example of Christ in union with him (repeatedly expressed by 'sharing', *koinōnia* and its compounds), so as to grow in a Christlike mindset guiding both belief and action. This is expressed by several recurring verbs, especially *phronein*, 'think' or 'feel', which, together with 'rejoice', *chairein*, virtually structures the letter, creating a major *inclusio* from beginning to end.

B. The Addressees. 1. Philippi (Bormann 1995) stood on the plain of eastern Macedonia, about 16 km inland from its port Neapolis. It was refounded as a city by Philip II of Macedon in 358–357 BCE. Prosperous from mineral deposits and its location on a main east–west route, Philippi came under Roman rule in 167 BCE. Octavian, after gaining supreme power in 31 BCE, settled veterans here and gave the city the status of a *colonia* with citizenship by *ius italicum*. The population would have been mainly Macedonians, Greeks, and Romans. Acts 16:12–40 recounts Paul's visit with Silas (about 50 CE), conversion of Lydia, and misfortunes before he revealed his citizen status. The alarm of the city magistrates and their anxiety to see the last of Paul and Silas doubtless gave Christianity a prejudiced start.

2. Apart from Acts, Philippians is our only source for the origins of this church. Lydia had been a Jewish God-fearer. All the people named in Philippians except Clement are Greek, but this does not exclude their having become Christians via Judaism. The church was doubtless mixed in ethnic and social character. It probably met in house-groups (Peterlin 1995: 135–70). By the time of the letter it had officers called *episkopoi* and *diakonoi* (1:1); *presbuteroi* are not mentioned. Paul refers to the Philippians' suffering for Christ (1:27–30; 2:15–17) and refers to 'opponents' (1:28), but without identifying them. Motives for hostility can be imagined on the part (respectively) of the civic authorities, the pagan public, Jews opposed to Christians, and Jewish Christians opposed to Paul.

3. The references to disunity have evoked many hypotheses (O'Brien 1991: 26–35). Theories of Gnostic opponents (Fee 1995: 19–32) are unconvincing. Tellbe (1994) plausibly suggests a crisis facing Gentile Christians unprotected by Jewish exemption from Roman cult practices. Others propose grounds for the quarrel mentioned in 4:2, especially disagreement over financial support for Paul (Peterlin 1995: 101–32, 171–216). This letter of only rarely polemical tone is subjected by some to a process which Barclay (1987) calls 'mirror-reading'; both the method and its criteria are open to criticism (Fee 1995: 7–10). Discord in the Philippian church at this time is probably best explained by the situation of Gentile converts *vis-à-vis* Roman civic pride and official cult and a tempting compromise offered by Jewish Christians (Tellbe 1994).

C. Paul's Situation. 1. The common view till this century was that Paul wrote from Rome in the early 60s CE. Even if he was only under house-arrest (Acts 28:30), this could mean painful frustration. On this view 'the (praetorium) imperial guard'

(1:13) and 'the emperor's [Caesar's] household' (4:22) would be in their regular bases in Rome itself.

2. Many today favour an earlier imprisonment, most preferring Ephesus in the mid-50s, about the probable time when Paul wrote 1–2 Corinthians and Romans, to which Philippians is said to be close in doctrine. Though there is no direct evidence for such an imprisonment, 1 Cor 15:32 and 2 Cor 1:8–10 might refer to it. Some epigraphic evidence is cited to argue that 'praetorium' and 'Caesar's household' could refer to a provincial governor's establishment. Communication between Philippi and Ephesus would be easier and quicker than with Rome.

3. Evaluation: in 2 Cor 11:23 Paul looks back on 'many' imprisonments, so that in theory any of them could be possible. However, the case for Ephesus is linked to the doubtful theory that Philippians is an amalgam (see PHIL D.2); the fewer letters are posited, the less need there is to suppose a shorter distance to be travelled. Similarities with Romans and 1–2 Corinthians need not tell against Philippians being dated a few years later. The epigraphic evidence is judged not relevant by Bruce (1980–1). In fine, the arguments for Ephesus have not overcome those for Rome (Fee 1995: 34–7).

D. Critical Questions. 1. Pauline authorship of Philippians is almost universally acknowledged, apart from some theories about 2:6–11.

2. The letter's unity and integrity have been challenged on grounds of apparent breaks in coherence and an order thought to be unsuited to its purpose (e.g. Collange 1979). Many hold that it has been re-edited from two or three letters by Paul, but disagree on where the cuts and rejoins are. The main reasons offered are an apparent ending and abrupt new start at 3:1, and the improbability that Paul left his thanks to the end.

3. Criticism (cf. O'Brien 1991: 10–18): no manuscript evidence suggests disturbance of the text. Any theory that an existing text has been rearranged by a redactor must show that it solves difficulties in the text better than maintaining the traditional arrangement. For Philippians it must explain credibly why and how the supposed redactor wove several letters by Paul into a new composition. In fact the problem at 3:1 is not solved but shifted from Paul to an unknown X with unknown motives. As for the postponement of thanks, Polycarp, writing to the same church at twice the length, likewise keeps business to the end (*Phil.* 13, see Lake 1912–13: i). The strongest argument, however, for the integrity of Philippians rests on appreciation of the whole as a structured masterpiece (Garland 1985; see PHIL F).

4. The theory that 2:6–11 is an already existing hymn that Paul quotes for his purpose, first proposed by Lohmeyer (1928), has come to dominate both exegesis of Philippians and study of early Christology and credal formulas, though the term 'hymn' remains imprecisely defined and the theory still takes various forms, including earlier composition by Paul. The literature is enormous; with the standard survey by Martin (1983); see now O'Brien (1991: 186–271). A rare voice questioning the theory's solidity and value for exegesis is raised by Fee (1992; 1995).

5. Evaluation: whatever the origin of this undeniably poetic passage, it actually exists only in Phil 2; the exegete must expound it in that context. If Paul quoted an existing text, by himself or another, it became part of his letter; any argument for its detachability raises similar problems to those for denying the letter's integrity (Hooker 1978). Arguments against Pauline authorship risk being circular (Fee 1995: 45). Hypotheses about the development of Christology have been allowed to determine the exegesis of the passage, again producing circular arguments. Heightened poetic style does not prove non-Pauline origin (Martin 1983: 57; Fee 1992). Recent literary analysis emphasizes that the passage is integrally embedded in its context and the whole letter. Many of its keywords recur, subtly transposed, in ch. 3 (Dalton 1979: 99–100; Garland 1985: 158–9). This does not prove it was not an already existing text, but isolating it becomes increasingly problematic.

6. These expressions of reserve, however, do not deny that the passage's theological importance reaches wider than its immediate function in Philippians, or that its pattern of Christ's descent and ascent is paralleled in other early Christological statements in solemn style.

E. 'Stoicism' in Philippians. 1. The frequency of Stoic language in Philippians is emphasized by Engberg-Pedersen (1994). The evidence is seldom noted even in larger commentaries. When compelling examples such as *autarkēs* (4:11) cannot be denied (e.g. Fee 1995: 427–35), commentators insist that Paul radically transforms Stoic themes, which are generally disparaged. Yet the use of Stoic ideas in Luke's account of Paul's sermon in Athens (Acts 17:22–31) is matched by passages in Paul's letters. In fact Stoicism had appeal for both Jewish and Christian preachers. *1 Clement*, which should be dated not much later than 70 CE (Herron 1989), that is, only about ten years after Philippians, is full of Stoic ideas and terms, all interwoven with biblical, Jewish, and Christian themes.

2. Romans shows Paul readily adopting Stoic language for his message (e.g. 1:28, 12:2); perhaps he did this whenever he addressed converts with any degree of philosophical education. Whatever the reason, in Philippians his use of Stoic language is pervasive, serving most of his main themes: the emphasis on keeping a right mind (*phronein*), discernment to choose the better (*dokimazein ta diapheronta*), aiming (*skopein*) at the right end (*telos*); seeking contentment (*autarkeia*) in one's state, with joy (*chara*) even when suffering; community (*koinōnia*) lived out in good citizenship (*politeuesthai*) related to a state or model (*politeuma*), and still more. These expressions prove serviceable to Paul, though only up to a point; the reality of Jesus and the supreme value of knowing him in life and death, through faith and hope, are grasped only by experience (3:8–11). Yet the paradox seems true that 'it is when Paul is at his most Stoic that he is also at his most Christian' (Engberg-Pedersen 1994: 280). Paul's harnessing of Stoic ideas to the gospel in Philippians does not enter those areas where Christian Stoicism was to reveal its dangers (e.g. excessive anthropocentrism and distortions of asceticism).

F. The Structure of Philippians. The letter has a 'rondo' structure; after an 'overture' (here called 1B), comments on practical matters (sections 2, 4, and 6C) alternate with two major exhortations (sections 3 and 5) each centring on a narrative with a downward–upward movement; the first about Christ (2:5–11), the second about Paul (3:4–14). These and their contexts are linked by many corresponding words and phrases (Garland 1985: 158–9; Fee 1995: 314–15). Repetition of significant words or ideas occurs throughout the letter. *Inclusio* is used systematically, both to articulate sections of the argument and to make the letter's closing sentences echo keywords in the opening. The commentary notes these points in detail.

COMMENTARY

Introduction (1:1–11)

(1:1–2) Greeting Paul includes colleagues with himself in seven letters, and Timothy most often, but not as co-author; in 2:19–24 he occurs in the third person. Paul refers to them both as 'slaves' of Christ Jesus, as in Rom 1:1. Since this is an opening formula, it can hardly be a conscious anticipation of its application to Christ in 2:7, though this may strike a reader today. Paul uses the expression 'the saints' in six letters, thus or in the formula 'called [to be] saints'. Modern versions often paraphrase it as 'the holy people of God'; the phrase connotes the Christian claim to have been brought through faith in Christ into God's covenant people (Ex 19:6; 1 Pet 2:9–10). Though the words 'bishops and deacons' come from the Greek (see PHIL B.2), their meanings have changed so much since their NT use that it is less misleading to render them by (e.g.) 'pastors' or 'guardians' and 'assistants'. The inclusion of these ministers, as well as the repeated 'all', five times from 1:1 to 1:8 (admittedly unusual for Paul), have been seen as a first hint of the disunity that Paul will address more clearly later (Lightfoot 1879: 67; Peterlin 1995). At this point, however, this can hardly do more than raise a suspicion. v. 2, 'Grace to you and peace' slightly varies the word order of a formula Paul uses in opening and closing greetings. The 'grace' formula is echoed in 4:23 to wrap up the whole letter. Though the Holy Spirit is expressly named only three times (1:19; 2:1; 3:3), here the formula can be called implicitly trinitarian (cf. 4:7; see Fee 1995: 48–9).

(1:3–11) Thanksgiving and prayer v. 3, Paul begins every letter to a church (except Galatians) by thanking or blessing God for the good he has heard about his addressees. Here he mingles these two reactions with his *prayer* for them (1:3–4) and with *joy* (1:5), a combination he will recommend in 4:6, as in 1Thess 5:16–18. This paragraph is like a musical overture which anticipates themes to be heard later (PHIL F). Joy (*chara*) is the first of these; with its verb *chairein* it runs right through the letter. The focus of Paul's joy is the Philippians' sharing (*koinōnia*) with him in the gospel (1:5). *Koinōnia* is a keyword in the letter; aspects of it can be expressed by 'partnership', 'fellowship', 'union', and 'communion'. It occurs again at 2:1 and 3:10. *Koinōnos* (sharer, partner) occurs in the compound form *sunkoinōnos* at 1:7 and the related verbs at 4:14, 15. The prefix *sun-* ('together') occurs twelve times in the letter, compounded with eight nouns or verbs; it serves to enhance Paul's constant emphasis on relationship, unity and joy in community, and in sharing with him. The Philippians, of course, knew what the sharing had meant. For other readers Paul reveals it gradually: work for the gospel (1:5); prayer for him in his imprisonment and preaching, which he calls 'shar[ing] in God's grace' with him (1:7); striving side by side (1:27; 4:3) a metaphor from athletics that will recur, and finally their gifts of material support (4:15–18). v. 6, 'I am confident' (1:6): with this Paul passes from the Philippians' action to God's. (The verb recurs at 1:25, 2:24, and 3:3–4.) What Paul is confident about here is that their faith is God's 'good work', from when he began it till he brings it to completion 'by the day of Jesus Christ'. Paul returns to the interplay of human effort and God's work at 2:12–13. 'The day of Jesus Christ' is the day of his expected return; the phrase occurs again at 1:10 and 2:16. Paul refers to it as an assumed point of faith for the Philippians, a future reality though of unknown date; not a matter for overexcitement as it had been in Thessalonica. (This may perhaps lend some slight support for later dating of Philippians.)

v. 7, the key word *phronein* (see PHIL E.2) appears for the first time. Here it expresses a warm personal concern, based on mutual affection, to 'hold' others in one's 'heart'. Whose heart, holding whom? Most older versions took it as Paul's, holding that of his friends. NRSV opts for the reverse. Both are grammatically possible; the emphasis may be on the comfort Paul receives in his captivity and his service of the gospel from the thought of them, or on their thought and prayer for him in his situation. It makes little difference, because the relationship is mutual; they are *sunkoinōnoi* with Paul, they 'share in God's grace' with him. To understand the heart as Paul's perhaps makes the next sentence follow more smoothly. v. 8, Paul says his feelings are not merely his own. He lives in such union with Christ (Gal 2:20) that he experiences Christ's compassion as his own. 'Compassion' renders *splagchna*, literally 'bowels', an idiom borrowed from Hebrew, which can relate strong emotions to various internal organs.

v. 9, Paul circles back to what he began to say in v. 3. He wants them to grow in *agapē*, the kind of love he has described in 1 Cor 13, and will appeal to here in 2:1, 2. He does not say love for whom, either for himself or for each other; he simply prays that their capacity for loving may increase so that it overflows ever more and more. But he wants it to be far more than mere feeling; rather, to be directed by 'knowledge and full insight'. These words are of great importance for understanding the letter; they spell out what Paul means by *phronein*. The word rendered 'knowledge' is *epignōsis*, probably in the sense of a knowledge transcending ordinary cognition (*gnōsis*). This is best illustrated by Paul's use of the related verb in 1 Cor 13:12: 'Now I know only in part; then I will *know fully*, even as I have *been fully known*' (emphasis added); it is knowledge that at least approaches the knowledge that God has of us. 'Insight' renders *aisthēsis* which basically means perception, but the Stoics and other moral philosophers used it for moral knowledge gained by experience, and this is its probable meaning here (the only occurrence in the NT). v. 10, the verb 'determine' (*dokimazō*) primarily means the testing by which something comes to be approved. 'What is best' is literally 'the things that are different' i.e. morally better. Such choices lived out will lead Christians to such a state that Christ at his return will find them to be 'pure and blameless'. The former word probably refers especially to motives; the latter (lit. with no stumbling) may refer both to moral steadiness and to not causing others to stumble. All this will bear the 'harvest of righteousness' through Christ's gift and to God's glory. Paul's prayer contains a whole cluster of pregnant words concerned with moral experience that develops character, and especially the capacity for loving realistically. Cf. Philem 4–7. The desired 'knowledge' is of God; the 'insight' is experience that builds up that knowledge; the testing of all things (1 Thess 5:21) leads to knowledge of God's will (Rom 12:2; Eph 5:10), with the purification of motives and moral firmness; all add up to the global moral term 'righteousness'. These ideas, if not the same words, reappear in Paul's central affirmation of his deepest values in 3:8–12. They are fundamental for the whole theory and practice of discernment in Christian tradition; yet it was Stoicism that provided Paul with many of the keywords: there is no need to shy away from this conclusion.

Paul's Situation and his Reactions to it (1:12–26)

(1:12–18) **What has been Happening** Two keywords mark off this section as another loose *inclusio*. The first is 'progress' (*prokopē*, v. 12, obscured in NRSV's 'to spread the gospel'). This is picked up again in 1:25, where the progress is on the part of Paul's addressees. The other keyword is 'confidence'; it recurs in 1:14, of Christians heartened by Paul's successful witness despite his imprisonment, and again in 1:25 of Paul trusting that he will remain some time longer for the encouragement of the Philippians. Other keywords in this section are 'gospel' (1:12, 16, 27) and 'rejoice'/'joy' (*chairō*, *chara*, 1:18, 25).

In the first seven verses Paul assures his readers that two aspects of his situation which might be expected to cause him pain and frustration have rather had the opposite effect. The first is his captivity. He does not describe his circumstances except by the conventional 'chains' and the implication that it would be his guards who spread favourable impressions of him around the *praetorium* (1:13 probably in the regimental sense, Lightfoot 1879: 99–104). On the alternative theories based on Rome and Ephesus, see PHIL C. The traditional view, that Paul is writing from Rome, naturally refers to Acts 28; he had come 'in chains' (28:17) with a soldier guarding him (28:16), temporarily in a 'guesthouse' (28:23) but then for two years in lodgings where he could receive visitors (28:30). Philippians, for all its reticence, implies severer conditions than this. Perhaps after two years of waiting, on being called to have his case heard, Paul came under regulations requiring prison custody. *Apologia* (defence) in Phil 1:7 and 16 could refer to a formal hearing (cf. 2 Tim 4.6) but by reason both of its range of meaning and of its context here it can equally well refer to the 'apologetic' aspect of preaching. (Of course, such a series of events could have taken place in Ephesus, and no arguments seem decisive.) Paul does not explain how his imprisonment has encouraged Christians to witness to their faith more boldly (v. 14). Perhaps they are saying 'if Paul can do so much in chains, how much more should we dare to do in freedom?' If his guards have played a part, this could be cheering news also for his readers in a proud Roman *colonia* (Tellbe 1994: 110–11). v. 15, Paul sees two spirits at work in their activity, one of goodwill (*eudokia*) and love towards him,

the other of envy (*phthonos*), rivalry (*eris*), and selfish ambition (*eritheia*, v. 17; 2:2), making some act not with pure motives (*hagiōs*, purely), but to cause Paul distress (*thlipsis*, v. 17; 4:14). The latter group is not identified, but they seem to be a part of the Christian community where Paul is. Clement of Rome, writing to Corinth not long afterwards (PHIL E.2), says that Peter and Paul were hounded to death by envy, jealousy, and rivalry (1 *Clem.* 5.2–5); see Brown and Meier (1983: 123–7; they also favour Rome as where Paul wrote Philippians, pp. 185–8). The trouble could well have begun with Jewish Christians who wanted the church to remain within Judaism and saw Paul's policy as misguided. Paul, however, regards all negative factors with a sublime equanimity, because for him they are outweighed by his supreme desire, to see Christ's gospel spreading; frustration and anger are simply overwhelmed by joy (v. 18).

(1:19–26) **Paul's Hope and Confidence in Christ** Paul turns from his reactions to recent events to envisage the foreseeable future. *Inclusio* markers are 'joy' (v. 26, picking up the related verb in v. 18), 'progress' (v. 25, from v. 12), and 'trusting' (v. 25, from v. 14). All three have now changed their subjects (see PHIL 1:12 and 1:18; 'joy' is now Paul's wish for the Philippians). The passage is full of the vocabulary of hope and confidence and the motives for these, and of a peaceful yet passionate equanimity, based on certainty of Christ's love. v. 19, this verse is pivotal, grounding both Paul's joy in the situation just described and his confidence for the future: 'I know [the verb is repeated at v. 25] that . . . this will result in my deliverance.' Verbally this is one of the few OT allusions in Philippians; it reproduces the Greek of Job 13:16, in a passage that expresses Job's invincible trust in a transcendent justice. But in Paul's very different situation he is hardly likely to be comparing himself with Job; the coincidence of language could almost be accidental. 'Deliverance' is *sōtēria* (salvation); the NRSV's rendering seems to focus on Paul's vindication and release, but this does not exclude an implicit eschatological sense, as is clear, with reference to the Philippians in 1:28 and 2:12. Paul's first motive for confidence is his certainty that his friends pray for him as he does for them (1:4), and that their intercession is effective. Paul's second motive is revealed with the first of the three explicit references to the Holy Spirit in Philippians (see PHIL 1:2). 'Help' is *epichorēgia*, the act of supplying or providing for needs. Lightfoot (1879: 91) discusses whether the Spirit is the giver or the gift, and concludes for both. *Chorēgia* and the related verb could still retain a note of generous bounty, from their origin in sponsorship of civic celebrations by rich Athenians. v. 20, 'eager expectation' (Gk. *apokaradokia*) evokes a picture of heads strained forward in anticipation. The only other occurrence in the NT is in Rom 8:19, where Paul sees the whole of creation thus longing 'for the revealing of the children of God'. Paul hopes that he, and still more the gospel, will not be brought into public discredit, especially at his trial. In the biblical world 'shame' refers not so much to an emotion as to public worsting and discrediting; the psalmists often pray to be spared it (e.g. Ps 71:1), but to see their enemies suffering it (e.g. Ps 70:2). Positively, Paul hopes to speak 'with all boldness': the last word is *parrhēsia*, which is what Peter and John showed before the Sanhedrin (Acts 4:13). It is contrasted with being put to shame also in 1 Jn 2:28, but at the eschatological judgement, not a human trial. However, Paul's focus here, that 'Christ will be exalted now as always in my body, whether by life or by death' may have an overtone of the special sense of *parrhēsia* which developed in the NT. The word was born in political and forensic contexts, meaning freedom of speech or outspokenness. It came to connote also courage in speaking out; finally in the NT it has a special sense of confidence in God, a gift of the Holy Spirit to all who become God's children in union with Christ, and through him have access (*prosagōgē*) to God. (See Rom 5:2; 2 Cor 3:12; Eph 3:12; Heb 4:16; 10:19; 1 Jn 3:21; 4:17; 5:14.) Paul need not have this sense fully in mind here, but he is hardly thinking merely of speaking boldly at his trial. He speaks from his awareness of constant union with Christ. If he is worsted, then Christ will be shamed in him; if he is enabled to speak well, Christ will be 'exalted' in him, and just as much if he dies as if he lives on, for neither circumstance can separate him from Christ. v. 21, thus Paul's thought flows straight into the third great expression of his spiritual equilibrium. First came prison or liberty; then being spoken of with love or with malice; now death or life, because 'to me, to live is Christ and to die is gain'. A psychological state undisturbed by fear or human attachments was the ideal for both Stoics and Epicureans; but for Paul, both his emotional balance and his whole range of values are entirely governed by his union with Christ, as he will make even clearer in 3:7–12. This serenity pervading Philippians, in contrast to Galatians and 2 Corinthians, suggests a spiritual state perhaps more appropriate to Paul's final years, and therefore to Rome. ('Gain', *kerdos*, reappears with its related verb in 3:7–8, referring to values which Paul has rejected and replaced by new ones.) He cannot make a choice even between living and dying (even though the latter would lead to his being 'with Christ' in the fullest sense) except by discerning Christ's will. This evidently leads him to decide that he must stay (v. 24); then immediately he says that he knows this with confidence (cf. 1:6, 19), for the Philippians' 'progress and joy in faith': (v. 25; cf. 2:17). Towards them, he is so far from Stoic *apatheia* as to want to come 'and share abundantly in your boasting in Christ Jesus' (v. 26). This is one of only three occurrences in Philippians of the word-group of *kauchaomai*, commonly rendered 'boast', that is so characteristic of Paul (55 of 59 instances in NT, 34 of them in 1–2 Corinthians; see *TDNT* iii. 645–54). His repeated concern with having (or not having) grounds for boasting is puzzling, especially given his teaching on 'works' in Romans 3–4; one can only conclude that the Greek words have a wider reference than self-glorification, and include joyful exultation for and with others, as seems the case here.

First Exhortation on Discipleship (1:27–2:18)

(1:27–30) Steadfastness in the Face of Opposition This paragraph is linked to what precedes, especially by 'gospel' (1:12, 16, 27), 'salvation' (1:19, 28), and 'faith' (1:26, 29). v. 27, 'conduct yourselves' translates the verb *politeuesthai*, 'to act as a citizen' (Lightfoot 1879; Brewer 1954). NRSV misses the political sense (important also in Stoicism), though it keeps it when the related noun *politeuma* 'commonwealth' or 'citizenship' occurs in 3:20. Miller (1982) shows that Judaism had appropriated this vocabulary, and argues that Paul follows this

usage, implying that the church is the New Israel; but see Engberg-Pedersen (1994: 263) and Fee (1995: 161–2). It makes a difference whether Paul is urging the Philippians to show their Christianity in good citizenship, or has transferred the verb to a purely Christian context. His wish for their steadfast unity in fidelity to the gospel (rest of 1:27) might suggest the latter, but bold resistance to their opponents (v. 28) implies the public forum. The exhortation to unanimity in Christ already anticipates 2:1–5. Is then the 'one spirit' in 1:27 simply human unanimity (as NRSV implies), or does it point to the clearer reference to the Holy Spirit in 2:1? Fee (1995: 164–6) argues plausibly for the latter. For unanimity Paul could easily have used the Stoic *homonoia* (frequent in 1 Clement), just as his athletic metaphors ('striving side by side', v. 27, and 'contest', v. 30, NRSV 'struggle') are Stoic clichés (Tellbe 1994: 111). What is essentially Christian is, of course, the hope of 'salvation' which 'is God's doing' (v. 28), and the sense that both faith in Christ and suffering for him are 'graciously granted' (*echaristhē*) as a privilege (v. 29), which Paul sees as binding them more closely to himself in Christ, v. 30. Faith in Christ is again linked with the idea of suffering in 2:17 and 3:9–10. The 'opponents' at whose hands suffering is expected probably refers to political and social pressure to take part in the imperial cult (Tellbe 1994). If *politeusthe* indeed refers to good citizenship, Paul would be recommending this as the best defence (cf. Polycarp, *Phil.* 10.2). But the threat is also to the Philippian church's unity, and Paul is passionately concerned that this should be in and with the suffering Christ as Paul has preached him.

(2:1–6) Unity of Minds and Hearts v. 1, the tone of appeal now rises to a more intense level of feeling through a series of 'if' clauses, regular in the rhetoric of entreaty. This more solemn tone tells against supposing a 'hymnic' style only from v. 6 onwards. In prayers, the formula typically reminds a deity of past theophanies; here the idiom implies something like 'if x means anything to you, then prove it now'. Paul appeals to what he is sure the Philippians have experienced: 'encouragement in Christ', 'consolation from love', 'sharing in the Spirit', 'compassion [see PHIL 1:8], and sympathy'. Of these, sharing, *koinōnia*, is fundamental to all the others, above all since it is in (now certainly the Holy) Spirit. At last (v. 2) comes the apodosis to the four 'ifs': '*make my joy complete*', the joy which Paul has expressed for himself in 1:4 and 18, and wished for them in 1:25. The desired response is described by four phrases which all express union of minds and hearts: two use the keyword *phronein* ('be of the same mind ... of one mind'); the others are 'having the same love' (*agapē*) and 'being in full accord' (*sumpsuchoi*, united in soul). The most important words here were already established in 1:4–9, together with words compounded with *sun-*, 'together', to intensify the sense of sharing. In v. 3 Paul continues his description of the attitudes he desires by alternating dos and don'ts: not '*selfish ambition*', which he has been suffering (1:17), nor conceit (*kenodoxia*, vainglory) but rather 'humility, regard[ing] others as better than yourselves'. The last phrases are significant for the letter's unity, being echoed both in 2:7–8 and in ch. 3. v. 4, another do and don't concerns looking to 'the interests of others'. The verb is *skopeō*, 'to aim' (like *phronein*, a Stoic word); it recurs (with its noun) in 3:14–17. In Paul's present context, of course, *phronein* essentially involves a right *skopos* of mind and heart, 'as in Christ Jesus' (v. 5).

Do the attitudes (and perhaps activities) not commended in vv. 3–4 point to actual divisions within the Philippian church? Whether 1:1–4 contains hints or not, the immediately preceding exhortation in 1:27–30 now makes a reference to disunity more likely, especially on such grounds as Tellbe (1994) suggests. This will be discussed later, where clearer indications occur. Here it is not certain how far breaches of unity have actually gone. 'Selfish ambition' (2:3) could be in Paul's mind because he has suffered from its effects (1:17). Other phrases he uses may well refer to the quarrel to be mentioned in 4:2, especially if others had joined in; but surely the main thrust of this appeal, as of the passage into which it leads, is to focus the Philippians' minds on their relationship with Christ; references to human faults need to be clearer to prove an actual state of conflict.

(2:5–11) Christ, the Focus and Model for Discipleship The standpoint of the following comments is outlined in PHIL D. vv. 5–11, most commentators, accepting a hymn theory, set the passage out like verse. This displays its elegant composition in short *cola*, as found in classical artistic prose, but does not prove it to be a hymn in terms of either Semitic or Greek models. The wide and imprecise use of 'hymn' in modern discussion has not helped (O'Brien 1991: 188). The opening exhortation follows smoothly from the preceding sentences, points to Christ as model, and continues with a narrative about him in language which is certainly poetic and goes beyond Paul's usual vocabulary, but not necessarily his capacity when moved. Many keywords are echoed later, especially in ch. 3. The following exegesis takes the passage as it stands in its context. However, the possibility that Paul is adopting the structure of an existing model for credal-type statements will be considered in conclusion.

v. 5, 'Let the same mind be in you that [was] in Christ Jesus': more literally, 'be thus minded in/among yourselves as also in Christ Jesus'. The first 'in' is ambiguous in Greek; the context favours 'among', i.e. in interpersonal relations. The unexpressed verb has to be understood; more complicated ellipses have been proposed, e.g. 'which you have by virtue of your [life] in [union with]'; but '*was*' is most satisfactory. Paul points to Jesus, as known on earth, as the example for Christians in their relationships. This is rejected by some, for whom the hymn theory dictates their exegesis; they hold that the hymn was kerygmatic, proclaiming doctrinal truths about Jesus and that to make him a mere ethical model is somehow an inferior use of the hymn (cf. Martin 1983: 68–74, 84–8; Stanton 1974: 99–110; O'Brien 1991: 253–62). v. 6, 'who, though he was in the form of God': 'though' is an added interpretation; others suggest 'because' (Moule 1970). The Greek for 'was' is not the simple verb, but the participle of a stronger verb, *huparchōn*, 'existing'. Form (*morphē*) has a complex history (Behm, *TDNT* iv. 742–50). It connotes the outward aspect of something but not mere appearance; it also reflects the inward nature. Since God is incorporeal we must examine how Scripture describes theophanies. This suggests 'glory' as being what *morphē* implies, but this will not fit in v. 7, where *morphē* is that of a slave.

It is desirable to keep one word in both places, and 'form' remains the least unsatisfactory. This verse already raises the question whether it refers to Christ's pre-existence or to his life on earth, but first we must read further. Paul has just used the verb 'regard' (*hēgoumai*) in exhortation (2:3), and will use it thrice of his own values in relation to Christ in 3:7–8. 'Equality with God' seems like a repetition with variation of 'being in the form of God', but not all agree on this. Indeed, the meaning of this clause is the storm-centre of modern controversy on Philippians. 'Something to be exploited' interprets one word, *harpagmon*. It is important that in the Greek the negative governs not the verb 'regard' but this noun (Carmignac 1971–2). The actual order is: 'not [as] *harpagmos* did he regard being equal to God'. The issue is not pedantic; it is between two alternative 'stories'. These depend (1) on two possible senses of *harpagmos* and (2) on what is being contrasted with what. *Harpagmos* is a verbal noun from *harpazō*, to seize or snatch. Its form raises problems (BAGD 108; Hoover 1971; O'Brien 1991: 211–16); it can refer either to the act of seizing or the thing seized, and the sentence does not indicate when in the 'story' either of these was contemplated by Christ, in his 'pre-existence' or his earthly life. This question also affects how, in the next verse, we understand 'he emptied himself' and what follows; it is relevant also to the other Pauline passage which seems to parallel this passage most closely: 'For you know the generous act [lit. grace] of our Lord Jesus Christ, that though he was rich, yet for your sakes he became poor, so that by his poverty you might become rich' (2 Cor 8:9).

The two lines of exegesis may be summarized as follows. First, most of the tradition, from the Greek fathers till recent times, assumes that vv. 6–11 are integral to their context and also that Paul believed in Christ's divinity and incarnation. Christ's being 'in the form of God' and 'equality with God' refer to his status 'before' his incarnation, which is the subject of v. 7. Christ, being by nature one with the Father, regarded this status as no *harpagmos*, i.e. not like a prize which he had won (and might fear to lose, as a freed slave would jealously treasure his new status and refuse slavish work). Instead, in trustful obedience to the Father, Christ 'emptied himself' and became not only mortal but actually like a slave, e.g. by washing feet, and above all by suffering a slave's death. The contrast implied by the placing of the negative is between Christ's status as Son of God and his acceptance of that of a slave. This summarizes the exegesis of Chrysostom (*PG* 62.217–37) and Isidore of Pelusium (*PG* 78.1071), both masters of Greek artistic prose as a living tradition.

The second line (or rather several lines, but all stemming from the same basic option) reads the negative as if it governed the verb 'regard', and *harpagmon* as a prize to be won. To mention an agent and immediately characterize him as one who did not seek to usurp divine status suggests a contrast with some figure who did that; thus some have proposed historical rulers (Seeley 1994); more have turned to the OT. Here lines diverge: one sees a contrast with rebellious deities, as in the myths (applied to human kings) in Isa 14:12–21 and Ezek 28, or (as an aetiology of evil and also against the post-exilic Jerusalem priesthood) in 1 *Enoch* (Sanders 1969). More widely canvassed is a contrast with Adam, following the tradition that he sinned by ambitious pride (hubris), wanting to become like God (surveyed in O'Brien 1991: 263–8); Wright (1992: 56–98) makes this integral to a comprehensive New Adam theology. But this reading of v. 6 rests on two unsafe foundations: first, that morphē in the NT can be a synonym for eikōn, the 'image' of God, as in Gen 1:26 (in favour, Martin 1983: 106–10; against, Behm in TDNT iv. 752: in Paul, Christ is the eikōn of God); and second, on an unverified assumption that the tradition ascribing such hubris to Adam was in existence by the time of Paul. It is not found in the OT or pre-Pauline literature; it seems to have arisen (perhaps because of the obscure similarities between Ezek 28 and Gen 2–3) by ascribing to Adam the arrogant motives of the figures in Isa 14 and Ezek 28. The earliest hint of this is probably in Josephus, Ant. 1.47 (Procopé 1941–). The roles of Adam in Romans and 1–2 Corinthians are clear; proponents of a contrast with him in Phil 2 have yet to prove that Adam's hubris was already a theme that could be referred to by mere allusion. The most likely OT reference is quite different (see below). These and other proposed backgrounds (Martin 1983: 74–93; O'Brien 1991: 193–7) which generally assume the hymn theory as proved, mostly understand Christ's position in v. 6 as referring to his lifetime on earth, and harpagmos as an act of usurpation which he renounced. Yet not all who interpret thus oppose pre-existence, indeed, this is increasingly (and rightly) recognized as Paul's belief, expressed both here and elsewhere.

vv. 7–8, the older exegetical line (1) takes these verses as referring first to the incarnation, then to its continuation in Jesus' life and death. Some proponents of a type (2) theory try to make them refer only to Jesus' history, but the effort is forced. The last phrase, 'even death on a cross' was declared by Lohmeyer a secondary 'Pauline addition' because it did not fit into the 'hymn' as reconstructed by him (O'Brien 1991: 230–1). Simply on a stylistic analysis, it crowns a series of steps as a climax (not of height but of depth), the effect of which would strike ancient hearers with the force of shocking paradox (Fee 1995: 217). Its centrality for Paul is reflected in 3:10. A Christological complication was introduced by the Kenotic theory (Martin 1983: 66–8, 169–72) which interpreted the 'self-emptying' as a real abandonment of the nature of God. This misses the metaphoric character of 'he emptied' (ekenōsen; for its probable OT source see below); Chrysostom (PG 62.229) realized this, as part of the parable of a self-humbling king's son which he finds implicit in the the whole passage; it is explained by the following phrases in vv. 7–8. These are admittedly difficult. They are not typical of Paul's usage, and 'form', 'likeness', and schēma all seem rather weak ways of expressing the reality of Christ's humanity, which Paul surely wants to affirm as truly as his divinity. Morphē in a human context balances its previous divine context, and (as we saw) implies more than mere outward shape; but schēma does mean shape (though NRSV loosely renders it 'form'), while 'likeness' is also vague. And why is 'slave' mentioned before human status? The best answer lies in recognizing an allusion to the Isaian 'Servant' (Jeremias 1963; 1965). This is prima facie likely because that figure was so important for NT writers (Dodd 1952: 88–96). Though here all the words that favour an allusion are different from those usual in the NT, and imply the existence of a translation closer to the Hebrew

(e.g. doulos, 'slave', instead of pais, 'boy'), the cluster of significant ideas could well form a recognizable way of hinting at the Isaian figure. Thus he 'emptied himself' could evoke 'he poured out himself' (Isa 53:12), morphē could allude to the Servant's lost beauty (Isa 52:14; 53:2), and he 'humbled himself' to Isa 53:4. This proposal has been unjustly opposed; it has more explanatory power than others. It illuminates the paradoxical choice of morphē to connote both Christ's divine nature and his acceptance of 'slave' status, especially if we accept that behind the Isaian Servant lies the role of the king in the pre-exilic cult (Eaton 1979: 75–84). Doulos is then not merely a slave as in the Graeco-Roman world but the royal Son and Servant of the divine King, living and dying in obedience (as in v. 8) as Chrysostom realized. Christ's 'self-emptying', like that of the Isaian Servant, bears an implication of sacrificial self-giving, lived out physically on earth, but also revealing a quality intrinsic to divine love.

Several keywords here also help to anchor the passage in the letter as a whole. 'He humbled himself' gives the model for the humility recommended in 2:3. The root occurs again, together with words formed from morphē and schēma, in 3:21. As the Son 'was found' in the human race (v. 7), so Paul hopes finally to 'be found' in him (3:9). But these recurrences are transformed in a way that depends on the second part of the 'story' of Christ. The whole passage, 2:5–11, has a downward–upward movement. The shameful death by the cross is the lowest point; vv. 9–11 are the upward-moving reversal, a second stanza in terms of poetic structure.

v. 9, 'Therefore' (dio) implies God's acceptance of Christ's self-offering, not necessarily a reward. The verb 'highly exalted' (huper-hupsoō) expresses a superlative degree of honour. Paul delights in huper-compounds (Fee 1995: 221). Those who take the passage primarily as a Christological statement find it strange that the resurrection is not explicitly mentioned, but it is implicit in 'exalted'. 'And gave him' (echarisato) is more accurately 'graciously conferred on him'; the verb used of God's giving the Philippians the grace of suffering for Christ (1:29). This echo, occurring in such close proximity, links their sufferings with Christ's glorification after his passion; the upward movement is for them too. What has been conferred is 'the name that is above every name': in biblical idiom 'name' can be personal or titular; a name has meaning and is charged with power. What name is meant here? The choice is between Jesus and Kurios, 'Lord'. '[S]o that at the name of Jesus every knee should bend' (v. 10) might seem to favour 'Jesus', but the confession that 'Jesus Christ is Lord' (v. 11) points decisively to the latter. 'Jesus' is his human name; Kurios and Christos are conferred titles, as in Peter's proclamation 'God has made him both Lord and Messiah, this Jesus whom you crucified' (Acts 2:36).

Christos (Heb. māšîaḥ) denotes the expected 'Anointed one'; Kurios was the regular Greek rendering of 'ădōnāy, the reverent equivalent of YHWH, though it had many other uses, including for the emperor. But vv. 10–11 are an adapted quotation of Isa 45:23, the context of which is that YHWH has proclaimed that he alone is God; there he says 'To me every knee shall bow, every tongue shall swear.' Paul vastly expands 'every knee', and changes 'to me' to 'at the name of Jesus'; then he changes 'swear' to 'confess' adding the object clause 'that Jesus Christ is Lord (*Kurios*).' At the beginning of the 'story' in 2:6 Jesus was 'in the form of God'; now he is 'hyper-exalted' and Paul adapts a text that denies that there is any God but YHWH, to say that God has given Jesus the supreme name, so that he may at last be adored by every being in the threefold cosmos and universally acclaimed as *Kurios*. But in this acclamation does *Kurios* function as the name YHWH, so that, God having conferred it on Jesus, a distinction is implied between God and YHWH? Or if *Kurios* functions not as a name but as an ordinary predicate, what other value for it is high enough to measure up to Paul's statements implying Jesus' divinity? (He must also have been aware of making a politically dangerous claim contrary to the imperial cult (Tellbe 1994: 111–14), but Paul's primary focus is theological.) The above dilemma seems inescapable: intolerable to Jews, and embarrassing to Christian exegetes who assume that rigorous monotheism was established long before Jesus and Paul. This is why theories of non-Jewish influences on early Christology have proliferated, encouraging theories that the 'hymn' in ch. 2 is non-Pauline. Recent research, however, is showing ever more clearly that, at least until the reconstruction of Judaism after 70 CE, Jewish theologizing took many forms and at least some were far short of the eventual monotheism (Segal 1978; Barker 1992). The total identification of YHWH with the High God ʾēl ʿelyôn, and the redefinition of the latter's sons as angels, long remained incomplete, and the memory of how the king had been enthroned as 'Son of YHWH' haunted minds disaffected towards the second temple. The varieties of pre-rabbinic Judaism already contained the materials for the Christian interpretation of Jesus' life, death, and resurrection in relation to the divine unity. It is no longer enough to say that in v. 11 *Kurios* is 'the equivalent of Yahweh' and that 'Paul's monotheism is kept intact by the final phrase, "unto the glory of God the Father"', as in 1 Cor 8:6, 'one God the Father... and one Lord Jesus Christ' (Fee 1995: 222, 226); this only restates the dilemma above. Paul's faith can be understood only as already essentially trinitarian.

In conclusion, vv. 5–11 are fully integrated in the letter. Paul introduces the 'story' of Jesus to encourage the Philippians to humility and mutual respect by looking at him. Within that context the upward movement, effected by God's exalting of Christ, reminds them of the divine call behind the exhortation in 2:1–5, as if to say 'as disciples and members of Christ, you do not need to think of your own interests or dignity—leave it all to God; just contemplate (*phroneite*) the whole story of Christ. Whatever you have to suffer now, Christ is leading you to glory.' Within the letter as a whole, the passage is the climax of the first great exhortation. The second climax, in ch. 3, balances the first, both by verbal echoes and by repeating the downward–upward movement, now with reference to Paul. The movement corresponds to a pattern found (with variations) in a number of early quasi-credal statements, some more poetic in style, others less. The pattern would have taken shape in early meditation on Jesus' baptism, death, and resurrection in the light of OT texts, as in Acts 2:22–36. Its skeleton is in 2 Cor 8:9; freer variations appear in Col 1:15–20 and the Gospel of John, especially the prologue and

the theme of lifting up and glorification. In early poetry we find it in the second-century *Odes of Solomon*, with typically Syrian emphasis on the descent to Sheol, in Odes 17, 22 (which brings Jesus' baptism into the pattern), 24, and 42. Since Paul was probably the earliest of all the writers involved, the variants of the pattern may well issue out from him.

(2:12–18) The Response Paul Desires from the Philippians
Paul returns to direct exhortation, now illuminated by Christ's example; 'you have always obeyed' echoes 'he became obedient' (2:8), and likewise has no named object, but implies primarily God (Lightfoot 1879: 115–16), rather than Paul (as NRSV). vv. 12–13, Paul has mentioned salvation as his hope both for himself (1:19) and for the Philippians, adding 'this is God's doing' (1:28). What is added now is emphasis on human collaboration with God: 'work out your own salvation... for it is God who is at work'. It is not, of course, autonomous labour. The force of 2:5–11 still directs the thought; the Christian's personal effort is with and in Christ. 'Fear and trembling' was proverbial from the OT; Paul usually uses it of human relations (1 Cor 2:3; 2 Cor 7:15; Eph 6:5), but here of a stance before God. At 1:15 Paul uses 'good pleasure' of attitudes favourable to himself, though usually in the NT it refers to God's benevolent will towards humankind (e.g. Lk 2:14; Eph 1:5). vv. 12–13 became a key text in all discussions of grace and free will.

v. 14, Paul echoes the Exodus story for both warning and encouragement, alluding to the people's repeated grumbling (Ex 15–17; Num 14–17) and 'arguing': with divided minds, doubting God's providence. v. 15, phrases in Deut 32:5 are turned from condemnation to encouragement: 'children of God without blemish' is what Moses said the people no longer were; Paul promises the Philippians that they can become so. A 'crooked and perverse generation' was said of the people; Paul applies it to the hostile environment in which the Philippians *shine like stars* (with perhaps a hint of Mt 5:14, 16). He uses the present tense to encourage them, but in v. 16 there is a hint of pleading; on their 'holding fast to the word of life' depends his hope of being able to 'boast [cf. 1:26] on the day of Christ [cf. 1:10] that [he] did not run in vain'—again the athletic metaphor, used as in Gal 2:2; 4:11. v. 17, he changes to a metaphor of religious intensity: 'even if I am being poured out as a libation [eight words for one in Greek, *spendomai*] over the sacrifice and the offering of your faith, I am glad and rejoice'. Here the 'priests' are the Philippians (cf. 4:18); he is ready to be part of their offering. (Paul never uses cultic or priestly terms in direct designation of his apostolic ministry, but only by way of metaphor; this is true even of the concentrated cultic language in Rom 15:16. Priestly and sacrificial language can be applied to all members of the church.) 'Offering' here renders *leitourgia*, see PHIL 1.19. It came to refer to religious worship (hence 'liturgy'), especially in the Greek Bible, but it retained its financial connotations (Peterlin 1995: 195–9). Here it combines with 'sacrifice' in a cultic metaphor, meaning the life of Christian faith. (In 2:25, 30 the financial sense is more prominent.) v. 18, Paul ends this section with a burst of joy ('I am glad') using not different words (as NRSV) but *chairō* four times, twice compounded with *sun-*, to express his own joy and to call the Philippians to the same.

Timothy and Epaphroditus, Paul's Go-Betweens (2:19–30)

This section introduces two of Paul's helpers, but tells us more about his affection for them than the reasons for their journeys. On Timothy see Acts 16:1–3; 17:14–15; 19:22; he is not named in the account of Paul's first visit to Philippi, but the Christians there know him (v. 22), doubtless from the time mentioned in Acts 20:4. Paul's praise of him as alone *iso-psuchon* (lit. equal-souled) echoes his wish that they should all be *sumpsuchoi* (2:2). Apparently speaking of his present circumstances, Paul excepts Timothy alone from a judgement more sweeping than he made in 1:15–17: 'All ... are seeking their own interests, not those of Jesus Christ' (v. 21); he has urged the opposite attitude in 2:4. Timothy has 'served' (*edouleusen*, v. 22) 'the gospel' with Paul, like a son to him, both of them being slaves (*douloi*, 1:1) of Christ who took the form of a slave. As for Epaphroditus, Paul calls him 'brother' and uses two *sun*-words, 'fellow-worker' and 'fellow-soldier' (v. 25). He had come with a gift (4:18) as the Philippians' envoy (*apostolos* in the sense of šaliaḥ, the agent of a synagogue, and *leitourgos*). Dissectors of Philippians argue that Paul would not have left his thanks to the end. Yet his appreciation is certainly implicit in vv. 25 and 30, where he uses *leitourgia* again in a 'non-liturgical' sense, for their subvention which Epaphroditus, at risk to his life, has brought. Admittedly his thanks are qualified; 'services that you could not give' (NRSV) is more literally 'your shortfall (*husterēma*) towards me'. See further PHIL 4:10–19. The Philippians had heard of Epaphroditus' illness; Paul has sent him back to relieve their anxiety about him (vv. 25–8). He wants them to receive Epaphroditus with joy and hold people like him in honour (v. 29); he hopes shortly to send Timothy for more news and then soon to come himself (vv. 19–24).

What lies behind these dealings? (See PHIL A.3.) Peterlin (1995), analysing passages in Philippians and other letters in sociological categories, sees a community of house churches, differing in social and financial status and not all equally enthusiastic about regularly supporting Paul. Epaphroditus, he suggests, was well-off and willing to discharge a *leitourgia*, but not popular with all. This is a credible picture of relationships within the community but it neglects relevant external factors. As for grounds of dissension, when Paul saw serious trouble he usually spoke out plainly. The hints of discord or the grounds for suspecting criticisms of Paul in Philippians cannot compare with the evidence in 1–2 Corinthians. Clearly he is anxious for the Philippians' unity; but he seems to see the trouble as healable by recalling them to a right mind and renewed joy in Christ (cf. PHIL 4:8).

Second Exhortation on Discipleship (3:1–4:1)

(3:1–2) Transition These verses are widely held to belong to different letters (see PHIL D.2 and most commentaries). v. 1, the first phrase, 'Finally' (*to loipon*, lit. for the rest) is often a closing formula but equally can be a mere link like 'so'. The imperative *chairete* can mean 'farewell' but can equally remain a real imperative, 'rejoice' (as NRSV). Those who see vv. 1–2 as containing the end of a letter and the start of a fragment will take the first option in each case, but the second pair of options is perfectly possible and can support the case for the verse being a transition within one letter, as is defended here, following Reed (1996). Either way, the second sentence in v. 1 is difficult, because the three main terms in it are all obscure. (1) To what do 'the same things' refer, which Paul speaks of writing? (2) What does he mean by saying that his writing is not 'troublesome' for him? (3) What does he mean by being 'a safeguard' for his addressees? (1) On the assumption of a plurality of sources, 'the same things' are the various themes that Paul frequently addresses. On the 'integrity view', it means primarily rejoicing (just commended for the twelfth time), and probably also the warning (v. 2) that Paul is about to express, as often before (cf. 3:18). (2) Paul says that repeating this is not 'troublesome' for him, or something similar according to most interpretations. But the verb from which this adjective (*oknēron*) is formed primarily means 'to hesitate' or 'shrink'. Formulas using this word-group are common in Hellenistic papyrus letters in many contexts, e.g. of request or invitation: 'I say without hesitation ...' or 'Don't hesitate to ask ...' (Reed 1996); polite, persuasive formulas used when a writer feels tact is called for, as Paul might well here. In contrast, to say that writing the same things is 'not troublesome' seems rather pointless. (3) For his addressees, he says, his repetition is a 'safeguard' (*asphales*). Against what? The word negates ideas of stumbling or going wrong. Though it usually means 'safe' in a 'passive' sense (from danger, error, etc.), Paul applies it to his own action (calling for rejoicing) with reference to the effect he wants it to have on his readers, namely to stabilize and confirm them in faith and keep them from harm (what harm, we learn in v. 2). In conclusion, though the verse marks a transition, it need not be an unintelligibly harsh one: 'So go on, brothers [and sisters], rejoicing in the Lord; I don't hesitate to repeat this, while for you it is salutary.'

v. 2, the question of continuity arises again: there seems to be a sudden leap from gentleness to anger. Yet how harsh this feels depends on how one word is translated. The threefold 'look' (*blepete*) has often been taken as 'beware of' (as NRSV). But the latter sense normally requires a preposition not used here; without it, the probable sense is 'look hard at'. The verse is still a warning, and the strong language and its objects still have to be explained, but the tone now sounds less shrill. On a stylistic analysis (cf. Reed 1996: 84–8), the triple imperative balances the three imperatives in the three previous verses: 'receive', 'hold in honour', and 'rejoice' (2:29, 30; 3:1). The first three are addressed to friends; the second three refer to people regarded as enemies. A parallel occurs in 3:17–19. The transition here remains arresting, but it can be seen to be bridged.

(3:2–11) Paul's 'Transvaluation of Values' through Christ Whatever personal tensions there are within the community, Paul wants to draw their minds back to Christ as he did in ch. 2, but this time by telling them his own story, how he 'emptied himself' of secure pride so as to be with Christ, and how his only aim now is to follow the 'upward call' to the end. Judaism is where he started, but non-Christian Judaism would hardly be familiar to this church formed mainly of Gentile converts. Yet they are being troubled by people urging circumcision, contrary to the Jerusalem decision (Acts 15) not to impose it on Gentile converts and Paul's efforts to uphold this. This can account for Paul's starting-point in v. 2 and (to some extent) moderate the shock of his strong language. He may be quoting expressions that he had used on previous occasions (cf. 3:18) to raise his converts' morale by mocking at opponents. The first two could be turning back terms used by the 'enemy'; the third (*katatomē*) is a sarcastic play on 'circumcision' (*peritomē*), changing the prefix to one implying destruction. It is clear that circumcision is the issue, but not an attack on Jewish Christians as such, provided they do not deny that Gentile converts are true Christians and heirs to the promises to Israel. v. 3, Paul recalls his teaching on the 'true circumcision' through faith in Christ (Rom 2:25–9); now he adds the charismatic experience of Gentile Christians 'who worship in the Spirit of God'. He wants them to remain content as they are; but he does not explain why circumcision has been urged on them. He uses his regular antithesis of 'flesh' and 'spirit', but after 3:1 there is no more anger like that in Galatians. The suggestion of Tellbe (1994: 116–20; PHIL B.3) is plausible: all circumcised Jews could enjoy the exemptions granted by Rome to Judaism as a permitted religion, even if some were now also Christians; but uncircumcised Gentile Christians, even though recognized by Jewish Christians on the basis of Acts 15, could not. If they refused to take part in the imperial cult (surely important in a proud *colonia*), Paul's converts would be 'disloyal citizens' and incur persecution, as they already had (1:29). The Jewish Christians offer a way out: join us and live at peace. They might insist that it would involve no infidelity to Christ; but Paul could only see it as undermining his whole work of extending membership of God's people on the sole basis of faith in Christ crucified.

vv. 4–11, this may be why Paul leaves the circumcision issue, to tell (doubtless retell) his personal story. He is a Jewish Christian, once proud of his birth, observance, and zeal (vv. 5–6; cf. Acts 26:4–11). But he has undergone a complete 'transvaluation of values', which in vv. 3–11 he expresses by a series of keywords with changed applications. He recalls his former *confidence* in Jewish practice; we have seen at 1:6, 25, and 2:24 that he now bases this only on Christ. His righteousness was once based on the law (v. 6); now, solely on his faith in Christ (v. 9). In vv. 7–8 Paul plays on an accounting metaphor of *gain* (*kerdos* and verb *kerdainō*, cf. 1:21) and *loss* (*zēmia* and verb *zēmioumai*); his assets have changed places by his new reckoning. Indeed, the metaphor of gain and loss, though quite different from that implicit in 2:6–8, corresponds in effect to Christ's regarding his divine status as 'no prize to be clung to' (*oukh harpagmon*) and, instead, 'emptying himself' (cf. Fee 1995: 314–15). The allusion continues in Paul's hope 'that I may gain Christ and be found in him' (vv. 8–9), as Christ was found in solidarity with the human race (2:7); when finally 'the books are opened', Paul hopes to be acknowledged as Christ's, because he has renounced all his assets to trust totally in him. What he now calls them (*skubala*, 'filth') recalls the invective of v. 2. v. 9 succinctly summarizes Paul's teaching on justification (Fee 1995: 319–26), which

his converts would know well. v. 10 corresponds to 2:6–9 at the turning-point from descent to ascent. 'To know Christ', implies intimate, experiential knowledge, cf. 1:9; this is why Paul does not keep the order of Christ's crucifixion and exaltation, but interweaves them, just as the power of Christ's resurrection, the sharing (*koinōnia*) of his sufferings, and becoming like him in his death are experienced as interwoven in Christian prayer, liturgy, and life. As Christ was in the form of God and took the form of a slave (2:6–7), so Paul wants only to be 'con-formed' (*summorphizomenos*), moulded into that *morphē*. (The vocabulary recurs in 3:21.)

(3:12–16) Following the Upward Call with Paul v. 12, Paul's upward way (from v. 11) corresponds to 2:9–11, but glory is far ahead; to 'attain the resurrection' is an object of humble hope, desire, and effort. Paul knows that he has not 'obtained' (*elabon*) this or 'been made perfect' (as NRSV fn., cf. PHIL 3:15) 'but I press on' (*diōkō*, lit. pursue; last used of his former zeal in persecution, 3:6), 'to grasp it (*katalabō*), as I have been grasped by Christ Jesus' (my tr.). Though the words are different, the image stands in striking counterpoint to *harpagmos* in 2:6; NRSV obscures this by using 'make [one's] own'. vv. 13–14, Paul repeats the verb, merging his accounting metaphor into that of running a race, a cliché of popular ethics that he has used before; 'straining forward' (*epekteinomenos*) renews the image in 'eager expectation' (PHIL 1:20). See further Pfitzner (1967: 134–56). 'The goal' (*skopos*; its verb *skopeō* occurs in 2:4 and 3:17) is anything aimed at, but 'prize' (*brabeion*) belongs to athletics. The aim and the prize are pursued in response to 'the upward call' (as NRSV fn.) of God in Christ Jesus.

v. 15, this completes Paul's own downward–upward 'story', which corresponds to 2:6–11; now he turns to his addressees, and first to 'those of us . . . who are mature' (*teleioi*, lit. perfect). At v. 12 he has just disclaimed the related verb for himself. The mystery cults used these terms to refer to grades of initiation, and Paul could on occasion draw on that vocabulary for a metaphor (e.g. 4:12); Gnostic sects used it systematically. Koester (1961–2) and others find hints of Gnostic opponents here and elsewhere, but such theories go beyond exegesis. Neither is there need to posit charismatics who have got above themselves, as in Corinth, where Paul refers, perhaps with irony, to 'the perfect' (1 Cor 2:6). Here Paul returns to his major theme of a Christlike mindset (*phronein*); he is leading up to his concluding appeals in 4:2 and 4:8. He has held up the supreme model in 2:5–11 and told his own story; he seeks to persuade, not to bludgeon. He invites any who may 'think differently' to be attentive and receptive to God's interior revelation. 'This is not the language or mode of polemics' (Fee 1995: 353).

(3:17–4:1) Citizens of earth and heaven In 3:17–19 Paul holds up examples and counter-examples. Obviously he has told his own story to invite imitation, but in calling the Philippians to be his 'fellow-imitators' (*sum-mimētai*) he puts himself beside them, as in 3:15; Christ, not Paul, is the model. Secondly, he tells them to 'observe' (*skopeite*) those who live according to the 'example (*tupos*) you have in us'; here speaks a teacher, not one demanding a personality-cult. In contrast, in vv. 18–19

Paul renews past warnings against 'many' whom (as his urgent tone shows) he regards as a serious threat. Their 'end is destruction' (*apōleia*); in 1:28 this fate awaits opponents who are probably persecutors, but Paul's tears suggest a group within the church. They are 'enemies of the cross of Christ', yet nothing marks them as Jewish Christians. 'Their god is their belly' might refer to converts who, on the dietary issues discussed in 1 Cor 8, allow themselves too much liberty. 'Their minds are set (*phronountes*) on earthly things' and 'their glory is in their shame'—these phrases are enigmatic, but they could apply to Christians who, in face of the state cult and social pressures, chose to enjoy the sense of civic glory but with the shame of compromise, taking part in meals connected with public sacrifices and, in Paul's view, reducing Christianity to one among other acceptable philosophies.

If something like this was the case, v. 20 follows appositely: it is right to want to be good citizens, 'but our citizenship (*politeuma*) is in heaven'. *Politeuma* recalls the related verb in 1:27 and reinforces the case for taking it in civic terms, though many have understood both words more loosely in terms of way of life. The noun (often rendered 'commonwealth') refers to the state of which one is a citizen, either directly or by citizenship of an enfranchised colony, as Philippi was of Rome. Paul valued Roman citizenship and readily appealed to it at need; but just as humankind, created in God's image, has authority only by that title, so has any state. Hence for Christians (as also for Jews), God's *politeuma* is primary. Thus Paul's contemporary Philo, speaking of the patriarchs as 'sojourners on earth', says that heaven is their native land, in which they have their citizenship (*politeuontai*, Philo, *Conf. Ling.* 78–9), and a second-century apologist says exactly the same of Christians (*Letter to Diognetus*, 5). The heavenly *politeuma* is not merely an ideal; Christians actually live in two orders, of which the earthly is under the judgement of the heavenly. They are related not only 'vertically' but also eschatologically; 'it is from there that we are expecting a Saviour (*sōtēr*), the Lord Jesus Christ'. 'Saviour' contrasts with the 'destruction' facing the 'enemies of the cross', as *sōtēria* and *apōleia* are contrasted in 1:28. But *sōtēr* was also a title used in the ruler-cult; applied to Christ it makes a higher claim for him, just as 'Christ is *Kurios*' does over against the emperor. 3:21 winds up the parallelism of chs. 2:1–18 and 3 with many significant echoes. 'He will transform [*metaschēmatisei*, *schēma*, 2:8] the body of our humiliation' (cf. 'humility', 2:3 and 'he humbled himself', 2:8, all from the same root *tapeinos* 'that it may be conformed [*sum-morphon*, cf. *morphê*, divine and then human, 2:6–7] to the body of his glory [*doxa*, cf. 2:11 and in contrast just above, 3:19], by the power [*energeia*, cf. the twofold use of the related verb at 2:13] that also enables him to make all things subject to himself'. To savour how these echoes work, and then to see how 3:21 virtually sums up 1 Cor 15:20–8 and 2 Cor 3:18–5:10, is better than any commentary, but Fee (1995: 381–4) is good. 4:1 concludes the main exhortation: 'Therefore ... stand firm in the Lord in this way'; for the rest, it overflows with words of love and joy, among which one (*epipothētoi*, beloved) echoes Epaphroditus' yearning in 2:26.

Final Exhortation, Thanks for Support, and Conclusion (4:2–23)

(4:2–3) Last Appeal for Harmony As already noted, recent exegetes find hints of disunity, and perhaps of different causes, in many passages (PHIL B.3), but 4:2 is the first place where Paul comes to naming names. Yet even here the trouble between Euodia and Syntyche is not defined more than as a failure 'to be of the same mind' (to think, *phronein*, the same). Garland (1985: 172–3) sees the whole letter as leading up to this; Peterlin (1995) constructs a total picture, defining the roles of *episkopoi*, *diakonoi*, and 'co-workers' (*sunergoi*, 2:25; 4:3); the two women are *diakonoi*, leaders of two house-groups in conflict, probably over material support of Paul. In contrast, Fee (1995: 385–400) after a survey of theories concludes that none is proven; we know neither the cause of the quarrel, nor the identity of the 'loyal companion', nor of the Clement named here, nor whether Lydia (Acts 16:14) was still there (perhaps identical with one or other of the women, or the 'companion'). The clearest indications of trouble in Philippians point to persecution and the temptation of Jewish Christianity (Tellbe 1994), but there is no hint of these as the issue in 4:2. One thing seems clear: the quarrel is serious and worries Paul; if 2:1–5 is related to it, it seems to have divided the community.

(4:4–9) Last Call to Joy, Peace, and 'Right Thinking' in Christ Yet whatever the trouble is, Paul seems confident that the cure is to recall the Philippians to the charismatic joy of their first coming to faith, exactly as he reminded their neighbours in Thessalonica how 'in spite of persecutions you received the word with joy inspired by the Holy Spirit' (1 Thess 1:6). His constant insistence on joy is not mere cheerfulness; this and following Christ with a right mind are the keys to Paul's strategy towards the Philippians. In vv. 4–7 he invites them to share the spirit of his initial greeting and prayer for them, with a few new touches. v. 5, 'Let your gentleness (*epieikēs*) be known to everyone': most versions have something similar. But the basic sense of *epieikēs* is 'seemly', decent or equitable; the phrase could be a last word on good citizenship, much as in 1 Pet 3:16. 'The Lord is near': in joy or suffering, or if the latter leads to death, all the nearer. v. 6, 'Do not worry about anything': as Paul has demonstrated regarding liberty or captivity, life or death (and is about to add, plenty or hardship). The basis is a perfect trust in God, expressed in prayer like that in 1:3–11 and here, which brings peace as in v. 7. Paul sums up his appeals for a right mind in Christ in vv. 8–9, now using a synonym as in 3:13. Few versions do justice to the heightened solemnity of tone (reminiscent of 2:1–4) and of vocabulary, which (like 2:6–11) includes several words beyond Paul's usual range. Neither there nor here need this point to a different author, despite the fact that both the rhetoric and the content of v. 8 are typical both of popular (especially Stoic) philosophy and of Hellenistic Judaism. This somewhat troubles Fee (1995: 413–19), but it need not (cf. PHIL E). Paul could harness this language to his gospel when he found it appropriate. In v. 9, as in 3:17, he reminds his pupils of what they have learned from him; he speaks with no arrogance but as a true teacher.

(4:10–23) Paul's Attitude to Gifts Received and Last Greetings The section composed of vv. 10–19 takes up from that in 2:19–30, completing the rondo pattern in the letter (PHIL F); the last appearance of several keywords also marks the overall *inclusio*: rejoice, v. 10; be concerned (*phronein*), v. 10; be humbled (*tapeinousthai*, obscured in NRSV), v. 11; share (*koinōnos* words, but now in a financial idiom), vv. 14, 15; gospel, v. 15; glory, v. 20. A simple reading may find behind this and 2:19–30 no more than a simple story, to which Paul refers with modest and undemanding gratitude; but there are hints of more complicated feelings (Peterlin 1995: 209–16). The Philippian church has supported Paul generously since the beginning (vv. 15–16). Paul is, and wants to appear, duly grateful, but in the embarrassment of need (*chreia*, 2:25; v. 16) he has to speak of shortfall (*husterēma*, 2:30; *hustērēsis*, v. 11; NRSV conceals this by a bland paraphrase both times). But again, he wants not to seem demanding (v. 17); hence his assurances that he has learnt to be content with whatever he has (vv. 11–13). Here Paul shows the same equanimity as in 1:18 and 22; perhaps with a touch of mock solemnity, he uses the Stoic word *autarkēs* ('self-sufficient'; NRSV 'content', v. 11) and a metaphor from the mystery cults (lit. I am initiated into everything, v. 12). But then he fears that he may seem to be indifferent to the support which he actually needs. 'Mirror-reading' runs the risk of straying into imaginative fiction; but Paul's words here, almost as much as in 2 Corinthians, do suggest that he is facing several lines of criticism. Finally he stops trying to explain, and turns to praising their gift by describing it (by a metaphor already used in 2:17) as a sacrifice pleasing to God (v. 18), and praying that God will meet all their needs. The passage ends with a doxology. We do not know how successful this letter was in restoring harmony. No evidence remains to the contrary, in contrast with what *1 Clement* reveals about Corinth some years after Paul's letters.

The letter closes by sending usual affectionate greetings and mentioning the emperor's household (v. 22), a hint (as 1:13) of successful influence on Paul's part, perhaps through his Praetorian contacts.

REFERENCES

Barclay, J. M. G. (1987), 'Mirror-reading a Polemical Letter: Galatians as a Test Case', *JSNT* 31: 73–93.

Barker, M. (1992), *The Great Angel: A Study of Israel's Second God* (London: SPCK).

Bormann, L. (1995), *Philippi. Stadt und Christengemeinde zur Zeit des Paulus*, NovTSup 78 (Leiden: Brill).

Brewer, R. R. (1954), 'The Meaning of *Politeuesthe* in Philippians 1.27', *JBL* 73: 76–83.

Brown, R. E., and Meier, J. P. (1983), *Antioch and Rome* (New York: Paulist).

Bruce, F. F. (1980–1), 'St Paul in Macedonia: 3. The Philippian Correspondence', *BJRL* 63: 260–84.

Carmignac, J. (1971–2), 'L'importance de la place d'une négation: OYX ΑΡΠΑΓΜΟΝ ΗΓΗΣΑΤΟ (Philippiens II.6)', *NTS* 18: 131–66.

Collange, J.-F. (1979), *The Epistle of Saint Paul to the Philippians*, tr. A. W. Heathcote (London: Epworth).

Dalton, W. (1979), 'The Integrity of Philippians', *Bib.* 60: 97–102.

Dodd, C. H. (1952), *According to the Scriptures* (Welwyn: Nisbet).

Eaton, J. (1979), *Festal Drama in Deutero-Isaiah* (London: SPCK).

Engberg-Pedersen, T. (1994), 'Stoicism in Philippians', in idem (ed.), *Paul in his Hellenistic Context* (Edinburgh: T. & T. Clark).

Fee, G. (1992), 'Philippians 2:5–11: Hymn or Exalted Pauline Prose?', *BBR* 2: 9–46.

—— (1995), *Paul's Letter to the Philippians*, NICNT (Grand Rapids: Eerdmans).

Garland, D. E. (1985), 'The Composition and Unity of Philippians', *NovT* 27: 141–73.

Herron, T. J. (1989), 'The Most Probable Date of the First Epistle of Clement to the Corinthians', *Studia Patristica*, 21, ed. E. A. Livingstone (Leuven: Peters).

Hooker, M. (1978), 'Philippians 2.6–11', in E. Ellis and E. Grasser (eds.), *Jesus und Paulus*, 2nd edn. (Göttingen: Vandenhoeck & Ruprecht).

Hoover, R. W. (1971), 'The HARPAGMOS Enigma: A Philosophical Solution', *HTR* 64: 95–119.

Jeremias, J. (1963), 'Zu Phil ii 7: ᾽ΕΑΥΤΟΝ ΕΚΕΝΩΣΕΝ', *NovT* 6: 182–9.

—— (1965), 'The Servant of God in the New Testament', in *The Servant of God*, SBT 20 (London: SCM), 97–9.

Koester, H. (1961–2), 'The Purpose of the Polemic of a Pauline Fragment (Philippians III)', *NTS* 8: 317–32.

Lake, K. (1912–13), (ed. and tr.), *The Apostolic Fathers I–II*, LCL (London: Loeb).

Lightfoot, J. B. (1879), *Saint Paul's Epistle to the Corinthians*, 4th edn. (London: Macmillan).

Lohmeyer, E. (1928), *Kyrios Jesus: Eine Untersuchung zu Phil. 2, 5–11* (Heidelberg: C. Winker).

Malherbe, A. J. (1988), *Ancient Epistolary Theorists*, SBLSBS 19 (Atlanta: Scholars Press).

Martin, R. P. (1983), *Carmen Christi: Philippians 2:5–11 in Recent Interpretation and in the Setting of Early Christian Worship*, 2nd edn. (Grand Rapids: Eerdmans).

Meeks, W. A. (1983), *The First Urban Christians: The Social World of the Apostle Paul* (New Haven: Yale University Press).

Miller, E. C. (1982), 'Πολιτεύεσθε in Philippians 1.27: Some Philological and Thematic Observations', *JSNT* 15: 86–96.

Moule, C. F. D. (1970), 'Further Reflexions on Philippians 2:5–11', in W. W. Gasque and R. P. Martin (eds.), *Apostolic History and the Gospel* (Grand Rapids: Eerdmans), 264–76.

O'Brien, P. T. (1991), *The Epistle to the Philippians: A Commentary on the Greek Text*, NIGTC (Grand Rapids: Eerdmans).

Peterlin, D. (1995), *Paul's Letter to the Philippians in the Light of Disunity in the Church*, NovTSup 79 (Leiden: Brill).

Pfitzner, V. C. (1967), *Paul and the Agon Motif*, NovTSup 16 (Leiden: Brill).

Procopé, J. (1941–), 'Hochmut', *RAC* xv. 795–858.

Reed, J. T. (1996), 'Philippians 3:1 and the Epistolary Hesitation Formulas', *JBL* 115: 63–90.

Sanders, J. A. (1969), 'Dissenting Deities and Philippians 2:1–11', *JBL* 88: 279–90.

Seeley, D. (1994), 'The Background of the Philippians Hymn', *Journal of Higher Criticism*, 1: 49–72.

Segal, A. (1978), *Two Powers in Heaven* (Leiden: Brill).

Stanton, G. V. (1974), *Jesus of Nazareth in New Testament Preaching*, SNTSMS 27 (Cambridge: Cambridge University Press).

Tellbe, M. (1994), 'The Sociological Factors behind Philippians 3:1–11 and the conflict at Philippi', *JSNT* 55: 97–121.

Wright, N. T. (1992), *The Climax of the Covenant: Christ and the Law in Pauline Theology* (Minneapolis: Fortress).

70. Colossians
JEROME MURPHY-O'CONNOR, OP

INTRODUCTION

A. Colossae. 1. The sparse unexcavated ruins of what had been a large and prosperous Hellenistic city are located in the valley of the river Lycus 12 miles east of Denzili in Turkey. Seleucid promotion of its neighbours Laodicea and Hierapolis in the third pre-Christian century ended Colossae's virtual monopoly of the wool production of the valley. None the less the cyclamen purple (*colossinus*) fleeces of Colossae (Pliny, *Nat. Hist.* 21.51) continued to rival the glossy black wool of Laodicea (Strabo, *Geog.* 12.8.6). They were the mainstay of the local economy. Access to international markets was facilitated by the location of the cities on the great 'common highway' linking Ephesus (120 miles west) with the Euphrates (ibid. 14.2.29). The population was mainly pagan but in 213 BCE, in order to enhance commerce and trade, Antiochus III installed 2,000 Jewish families from Mesopotamia (Josephus, *Ant* 12.148–53). By 62 BCE the amount of the temple tax confiscated by the Roman governor (20 pounds of gold) reveals that there were at least 11,000 adult male Jews in the Lycus valley (Lightfoot 1904: 20).

2. The Lycus valley was evangelized by Epaphras (4:13), a native of Colossae (4:12), who had been commissioned by Paul (see COL 1:7). Paul's appreciation of the contrast between his own arrival in Philippi and Thessalonica, where he had to start from scratch each time, and his experience in Corinth (Acts 18:2–3) and Ephesus (Acts 18:19; 1 Cor 16:19), where Prisca and Aquila furnished him with a well-established base, helped him to the realization that travellers returning home would be the most effective apostles. They started with built-in advantages: they did not have to look for work, they were known and trusted, they had networks of family, friends, and acquaintances, who could be guaranteed to listen, at least initially. Most, if not all, of the converts made by Epaphras were pagans (1:21; 2:13).

3. The volcanic springs and underground rivers alerted Strabo to the unstable character of the Lycus valley, 'if any country is subject to earthquakes, Laodicea is' (*Geog.* 12.8.16). A major earthquake hit in 60 CE (Tac., *Ann.* 14.27.1). Both Laodicea and Hierapolis were rebuilt, but Colossae never recovered; note the silence of Pliny (*Nat. Hist.* 5.105). Its long slide into oblivion terminated in the ninth century CE when the site was definitively abandoned.

B. Authenticity. 1. There is no consensus regarding the authorship of Colossians. The case against authenticity has been most comprehensively argued recently by Schenk (1987) and Furnish (1992), but the reasons they assemble—style, conception of Paul's role, Christology, eschatology, and literary dependence—are not compelling.

2. Style was once thought to be the definitive argument against Pauline origin (Bujard 1973), but when analysed in a more sophisticated way it appears that Colossians is perfectly at home among the accepted letters (Neumann 1990: 213). Moreover, the stylistic variations between all the Pauline let-

ters are far from insignificant (Kenny 1986: 80), and the influence of co-authors and secretaries can no longer be ignored (Murphy-O'Connor 1995a: 34). There is no standard of Pauline style to which doubtful letters can be compared.

3. Paul, we are told, is presented as the peerless, transcendent apostle. This is not in fact the case. The language of Colossians is certainly universalist, e.g. 'the gospel which you heard, which has been preached to every creature under heaven, and of which I, Paul, became a minister' (1:23; cf. 1:6, 28), but the lack of the article before 'minister' shows that Paul does not consider himself the unique agent, and the hyperbole is precisely paralleled by 1 Thess 1:8, both as regards tense and extension. Paul had to stress his universal, but not exclusive, responsibility in writing to a church that he did not found directly (2:1). It is also asserted that Colossians gives Paul's sufferings a vicarious value, whereas in the authentic letters they are viewed kerygmatically. This argument has no foundation. It is due to the mistranslation of a key verse; see COL 1:24. The identification of the gospel as 'the mystery' (1:26–7; 2:2; 4:3) is a Pauline paradox, since the whole point is that it is no longer a secret. It does not, therefore, convey a different perspective on revelation.

4. The Christology of Colossians can be seen as fundamentally different from that of the authentic letters only if it is assumed that Paul was in full agreement with everything that appears in Colossians. In fact the situation is parallel to that of 1 Corinthians where Paul quotes Corinthian statements with which he is in flat disagreement. The cosmic dimension, which is most visible in 1:15–20, does not represent Paul's thought. It is quoted from a Colossian hymn, which Paul edits severely to incorporate his own vision of Christ (see COL 1:15–20). His adversaries 'had done their best to give Christ a prominent place in the realm of cosmic speculation. What they had not done, and the editor now proceeds to do, is to recognize his earthly activity' (Barrett 1994: 146). Contrast 1:19 with 2:10, and note the stress on the crucifixion (1:20; 2:14). The vision of the church as 'the body of Christ' (1:18a; 2:19) is simply a more graphic statement of the union of believers with Christ and each other (Gal 2:20; 3:27–8). The distinction between the individual Jesus Christ ('the head') and his 'body' was imposed on Paul by the circumstances at Colossae. It does not appear in 1 Cor 12:12–27 or Rom 12:4–5 because the position of Christ was not an issue in those churches.

5. It is claimed that the realized eschatology of Colossians is incompatible with the future eschatology of the authentic letters. On only two occasions, however, is the resurrection of believers presented as a past fact (2:12; 3:1), and in context this is nothing more than a vivid expression of their passage from 'death' to 'life' (2:13; cf. Rom 6:11). Standard Pauline future eschatology appears in 1:22–3, 28; 3:4, 6, 24–5.

6. The charge that Colossians is the work of a secondary imitator, because it conflates phrases from Romans, 1–2 Corinthians, Galatians, and 1 Thessalonians, exaggerates the import of verbal reminiscences, while at the same time failing to provide a justification for the proposed redactional technique in only parts of Colossians.

C. Date of Composition. 1. Of the six who send greetings to Colossae, five also salute Philemon (see COL 4:10–14). The names of Timothy (1:1; Philem 1) and Onesimus (4:9; Philem 10) appear in both letters, as does that of Archippus as one of the recipients (4:17; Philem 2). Opponents of the authenticity of Colossians claim that its author borrowed the personalia from Philemon in order to give Pauline colouring to Colossians, but cite no evidence to show that this was a normal tactic to get a forgery accepted—it was not considered necessary by the author of Ephesians—and fail to explain the changes in order and qualifications. Hence, Colossians must be dated to the same imprisonment as (Philemon 4:10, 18; Philem 1, 9, 23).

2. This incarceration took place at Ephesus (1 Cor 15:32; 2 Cor 1:8) in the years 53–4, rather than at Rome in the early 60s (*contra* Dunn 1996: 41). When in Rome all Paul's attention was focused on Spain (Rom 15:24, 28), but Philem 22 and Phil 1:26; 2:24 reveal plans to visit Colossae and Philippi. The action of Onesimus is explicable only if Paul was in the vicinity of Colossae (Lampe 1985). The speed of the contacts between Paul and Philippi (Phil 2:25–30) exclude Rome as the place of imprisonment.

3. Assumptions regarding Paul's theological development cannot be given any weight in this discussion (against Bruce 1977: 411–12). Even if we could be absolutely sure of the precise chronological order of the letters, it would mean little. The letters are not homogeneous segments of an ongoing research project, each one building on its predecessor, but reactions to specific problems, in which what Paul says is conditioned by the needs of the recipients, and by his own estimate of what will be an effective response.

D. The False Teaching. 1. Hooker's (1973) view that there was no systematic false teaching at Colossae does not really account for the language of 2:8–23. Paul is reacting to a doctrinal problem, which has been described in at least forty-four different ways (Gunther 1973: 3–4)! There is a useful survey of the more notable opinions in O'Brien 1982: xxx–xxxviii. A decisive breakthrough was made by Francis's (Francis and Meeks 1973:163–207) lexicographical work on *tapeinophrosynê* and *embateuô* in 2:18, which provided a basis for an understanding of the genitive in 'worship of angels' as subjective. His outline of Jewish ascetic mysticism, which is the socio-religious framework of his hypothesis, has been developed thoroughly by Sappington (1991). The polemic material in 2:8, 16–23 contains both direct and indirect references to the content, function, and medium of revelation, as well as to the prerequisites for its attainment. Sappington (ibid. 170) concludes, 'the Colossian error is strikingly similar to the ascetic-mystical piety of Jewish Apocalypticism. The errorists sought out heavenly ascents by means of various ascetic practices involving abstinence from eating and drinking, as well as careful observance of the Jewish festivals. These experiences of heavenly ascent climaxed in a vision of the throne [of God] and in worship offered by the heavenly hosts surrounding it. It seems that these visions also pointed to the importance of observing the Jewish festivals, probably as evidence of submission to the

law of God.' There is no evidence that this attitude towards religious experience was systematically propagated at Colossae. Some of the converted Gentiles must have been God-fearers, who brought it with them from the synagogue, and proposed it as a supplement to the teaching of Epaphras.

2. This reconstruction implies that the problem with which Paul had to deal at Colossae was in no way similar to the situation he had faced in Galatia. There he had to counter a direct attack on his authority, and a vision of Christianity which in practice gave the law greater importance than Christ. Here he has to deal with a fashionable religious fad without intellectual depth, whose proponents floated in a fantasy world. His concern is to restore a sense of reality, to set the feet of the misguided on solid ground. They grasped at shadows. He had to show them that Christ was substance (2:17). The approach adopted by Paul in Galatians would have been completely inappropriate at Colossae. Understandably, therefore, the themes and terminology typical of Galatians are lacking in Colossians.

COMMENTARY

(1:1–2) Greeting Prior to his break with Antioch (Gal 2:11–14; Acts 13:1–3) Paul had been secure in his ecclesial identity (cf. 1–2 Thessalonians). Subsequently he did not represent any church (1:25), and had to identify himself as a Christ-commissioned missionary. The formula used here is a simplification of that which he adopted in Gal 1:1. The selection of Timothy from among the many with Paul (Col 4:7–14) for mention in the address suggests that he was co-author of the letter (Murphy-O'Connor 1995a: 16–34).

Rather than address the church as such (cf. 1–2 Thessalonians, Galatians, 1–2 Corinthians) Paul writes to its members as fellow-believers (cf. Rom 1:7; Phil 1:1). 'Saints' does not imply personal holiness. It reflects the usage of OT where the 'holy' is that which is 'set apart for God' (Lev 11:44). Exceptionally, 'saints' is interpreted (the *kai* is explicative; BDF §442(9)) by 'loyal', because some at Colossae, e.g. Archippus (cf. COL 4:17), had been led astray by false teaching (2:8).

The opening greeting of the Pauline letters normally mentions a double source of divine benefactions, 'from God our/the Father and the Lord Jesus Christ'. The absence of the second element here may be due to the mention of 'in Christ' in the first part of the verse (Aletti 1993: 46).

(1:3–8) Thanksgiving In all Pauline letters, with the exception of Galatians, 1 Timothy, and Titus, the address is followed by a report on how Paul has thanked God for the recipients. When the formula 'I give thanks to the gods' appears in contemporary letters it is never a banal convention and always evokes what is upmost in the writer's mind (Schubert 1939: 173). Similarly in Paul. The thanksgiving is designed to win the favour of the readers—and so parallels the rhetorical *exordium*—but the compliments carefully reflect Paul's assessment of the state of the community, and reveal his concerns (Murphy-O'Connor 1995a: 55–64).

The length of the thanksgiving here is disputed, but even those who extend it to 1:14 (Moule 1968: 47), or even 1:23 (Aletti 1993: 49), consider 1:3–8 a subsection in which Paul notes the reasons for his gratitude (Lohse 1968: 40; O'Brien 1982: 7).

Paul's knowledge of the believers at Colossae depends on the report of Epaphras (1:4, 8), who had been deputed by Paul to evangelize the Lycus valley (1:7). The NRSV reading 'on *your* behalf' is to be rejected (cf. RSV, NJB). While the quality of its witnesses might seem worthy of confidence, the reading is excluded by the titles given to Epaphras (Abbott 1897: 200). In particular 'servant of Christ' suggests a duly authorized missionary (cf. 2 Cor 11:25; Phil 1:1). Note that Tychicus is given the same titles (4:7), and he is certainly Paul's representative. The fact that Epaphras was imprisoned (4:12–13; Philem 23), whereas Epaphroditus of Philippi was not (Phil 2:25), indicates that the authorities understood Epaphras to be Paul's agent.

Among the virtues of the Colossians Paul singles out their Christian confidence, and their love which reaches out to all (Philem 5), virtues which are inspired by their hope of a guaranteed heavenly reward (1 Thess 1:3). The Colossians had been made aware of their assured future by the preaching of Epaphras (1:6–7), which was anterior to the false teaching. The qualification of the gospel as 'the word of truth' (1:5; cf. Gal 2:5, 14) is intended to underline its reliability (Ps 119:43) by contrast with the 'empty deceit' (2:8) of the false teaching. The sterility and parochialism of the latter is indirectly stigmatized by the universal creativity of the word of God (1 Thess 2:13; 1 Cor 1:18; Rom 1:16; cf. Isa 55:10–11), a dynamic force changing the world as it is transforming the Colossians (3:16). Their experience corroborates the true understanding of the message; the 'grace of God' is not merely a favourable attitude on the part of the divinity but tangible benefaction. It is typical of Paul that he evokes love a second time (1:8); the fruit of the Spirit (Gal 5:22), it is the very being of the believer (1 Cor 13:2). This is the only mention of the Holy Spirit in Colossians.

(1:9–11) Prayer for the Future Having complimented the Colossians, Paul now reveals his attitude towards them (cf. 2:1). They have been the object of his constant concern, but his status as a prisoner (4:10) has meant that he can only pray for them. He begs God that they may know his will, that they may do good works, and that they may persevere. It is the responsibility of believers to discern what God demands of them (Phil 1:9–10). There is no longer a law to dictate their actions. The emphasis on 'wisdom,' 'understanding', and 'knowledge' as divine gifts with a purpose beyond themselves is designed to counter the false teachers' insistence on ascetical practices as prerequisites (2:16, 21–3) for visions which were an end in themselves (2:18). Paul does not exclude contemplative knowledge of God (1:10c), but it must be accompanied by fruitfulness in 'good works' (1:10b; cf. Eph 2:10; Jn 15:16). A permanent lifestyle, different from that of those who belong to the world (2:20; 2 Cor 4:7–11; Phil 2:14–16), and resistant to cowardice and a desire for vengeance, is made possible only by the power of God. His 'glory' is his visibility in history (1:27), which can only be a display of 'might' (1:11; cf. Eph 1:19).

(1:12–14) Conversion There is in fact no break in the sentence, but the importance of the contents merits a special heading. In order to motivate the thanksgiving of the Colossians Paul describes the crucial change in their existence in terms and images drawn from the liturgy of baptism (Käsemann 1964: 160). The key sentence is 1:12, which is then explained in 1:13–14 (cf. Acts 28:16). The combination of two virtual synonyms, 'the share of the portion', is common in the Essene hymns (Kuhn 1968: 117), which also attest a use of 'saints' encompassing both angels and believers (1QS 11:7–8; Benoit 1982). The Colossians have already been empowered to live in the realm of light where God's holiness is experienced. The implication is that the ascetic practices and visions advocated by the false teachers are unnecessary. 1:12–14 is the key to understanding 2:13–15 (Sappington 1991: 203).

In 1 Thess 5:5 Paul contrasted the past and present of believers in terms of 'darkness' and 'light' (cf. Rom 13:12). His use of 'power' here in conjunction with 'darkness' is meant to evoke the societal constraints which promote the inauthentic behaviour of non-believers; all are 'under the power of sin' (Rom 3:9). Deliverance is the transferral to an alternative environment identified as 'the kingdom of the son of God's love' (1:13; cf. 1 Cor 15:23–8). The genitive of quality is a Semitism ('beloved'; cf. BDF §165), but Paul chose the expression (contrast 1:7; 4:7, 9, 14) in order to give prominence to 'love', which stands at the beginning of the process of salvation (Rom 5:8). In the form displayed by Christ it is the basic characteristic of the believing community (2:2; 3:11–14; cf. Gal 3:27–8: 1 Cor 13:2). The vague 'redemption' is clarified by 'the forgiveness of sins'. The formula is found in Paul only here (cf. 2:13; 3:13), and has a liturgical ring. By incorporation into Christ ('in him') in baptism (cf. Acts 2:38) the structures of the world are replaced by new values.

(1:15–20) The Christological Hymn Note the change in the layout of the Greek text in Nestle-Aland, 27th edn. (1993). It is generally recognized that Paul here offers a corrected version of a hymn in circulation at Colossae (3:16; cf. Eph 5:19). Many efforts have been made to recreate the original form of this hymn, but none has won significant support (Schmauch 1964: 48–52; Benoit 1975). The multiplicity of hypotheses, however, underlines the reality of the problem, not the futility of the quest. No serious exegesis is possible without a decision regarding tradition and redaction. In my view the ordered repetition of formal features recommends the reconstruction of two four-line strophes:

(v. 15a)	1	Who is (the) image of the invisible God
(v. 15b)	2	Firstborn of all creation
(v. 16a)	3	For in him were created all things
(v. 16f)	4	All things through him and to him were created.
(v. 18b)	1	Who is (the) beginning
(v. 18c)	2	Firstborn from the dead
(v. 19)	3	For in him was pleased all the Fullness to dwell
(v. 20a)	4	And through him to reconcile all things to him.

The first lines of each strophe begin with 'who is', and the second lines with 'firstborn'. The third lines commence with 'for in him', which is followed by a verb in the passive ('were created/was pleased'), whose subject is a universal ('all things/all the Fullness'). The fourth lines contain three identical expressions, 'all things', 'through him', and 'to him'. So many correspondences must be intentional. They are the result of careful planning to achieve perfect balance between the two strophes. No one who had made such an effort would destroy the elegance of his or her creation. In consequence, the elements which break the pattern (vv. 16bcde, 17, 18ad, 20bc) must have been added by another hand. It is theoretically possible that such redactional activity had taken place before Paul incorporated the hymn into his letter. It is more probable, however, that the additions were made by Paul, because identical retouches appear in the hymn in Phil 2:6–11 (Murphy-O'Connor 1995b).

The basic theme of this hymn is the mediation of Christ, first in creation, then in reconciliation. The titles in the first two lines of each strophe evoke the figure of Wisdom—'image' (Wis 7:26), 'beginning' and 'firstborn' (Prov 8:22; Sir 1:4)—who was present with God from eternity (Wis 9:4, 9), and participant in creation (Prov 3:19; 8:30; Wis 8:5; Sir 1:9; 24:9; Ps 104:24). These titles are the reason why Paul could not simply repudiate the hymn; they were rooted in the revelation of his people. The titles are justified by the third and fourth lines of each strophe, which are introduced by 'because'. All efforts to determine in what precise sense Christ can be said to be both the instrument and the end of all creation have failed. That ambiguity, not clarity, was intended is underlined by the plethora of unsatisfying explanations of the indwelling 'Fullness' (v. 19). Only in 2:9 do we discover that 'Fullness' is a surrogate for God, who is said to 'dwell in' both people (T. Zeb. 8:2; Jub. 1:17; 1 Enoch 49:2–3; cf. 2 Cor 6:16) and places (LXX Ps 67:17). No Jew would have understood either as meaning intrinsic divinization. It is simply a way of speaking about divine favour. What the Colossians would have understood is an open question, as is the exact manner in which Christ can be both the instrument and end of reconciliation. In what possible sense can all creation, which includes inanimate beings, have offended Christ, thereby creating the need for reconciliation?

Paul saw the hymn as a perfect example of 'beguiling, persuasive speech' (2:4). Formal perfection clothes an abstract vision of a cosmic Christ. The phrases are redolent of profundity, but yield no unambiguous understanding of Christ's person and mission. The hymn could be sung or recited by all Colossian Christians in the belief that they were articulating a mystery beyond their comprehension. Initiates, on the other hand, could debate endlessly the questions that still test the ingenuity of exegetes, or develop an interpretation only remotely related to the letter of the text, e.g. the creative power of God, once thought of as Wisdom, is now thought of as Christ (see Dunn 1980: 187–94).

In addition to the truth of the titles given to Christ, Paul had a second reason to retain the hymn. It could be turned against the false teachers. By inserting v. 16b–e Paul restricts the meaning of 'all things' (v. 16a) to intelligent beings, and makes it explicit that the angelic powers are inferior to Christ who, according to the premiss of the hymn, brought them into existence and to whom they are ordered. The ineffable names of the spirit powers are drawn at random from Jewish tradition (details in Schlier 1961). There is no intention to describe grades of the celestial hierarchy (Lightfoot 1904: 150). Paul further diminishes the attractiveness to the Colossians of such powers by inserting 1:20c. Like humans (1:21; 2:13; 3:7, 13), angels also need reconciliation; 'some of the angels of heaven transgressed the word of the Lord, and behold they commit sin and transgress the law' (1 Enoch 106:13–14; cf. 2 Apoc. Bar. 56:11–13). Manifestly only good angels can be effective mediators with God, but how are mere terrestrials to know which is which? Paul allows the Colossians to draw their own conclusion regarding the futility of the exercise.

Parallel to the addition of 'death on a cross' in Phil 2:8c, Paul here insists on the brutal modality of Christ's achievement by inserting, 'making peace by the blood of his cross' (v. 20b). Whereas the traditional teaching that Paul received mentioned only the death of Christ (Rom 1:3–4; 4:25; 8:34; 10:8–9; 1 Cor 15:2–7; Gal 1:3–4; 1 Thess 1:10), he typically stresses the 'blood' of Christ (Rom 3:25; 5:9; 1 Cor 10:16; 11:25, 27). With the exception of the gospels and Heb 6:6; 12:2; Rev 11:8, he alone in the NT uses 'cross' and 'crucify' (cf. 2:14).

Paul's choice of the verb 'to make peace' probably has less to do with any supposed animosity between heavenly beings, or between celestials and terrestrials, than with the internal situation of the Colossian church, whose unity had been compromised (cf. 2:2; 3:15). The theme of unity is fundamental to the additions in vv. 17 and 18a. The former sums up the first strophe, by parodying it. 'He is before all things' echoes the ambiguity of 'firstborn' (temporal? qualitative?). The assertion that 'all things hold together' in a human being (v. 17b) gives an impression of unity whose precise meaning evaporates on inspection. Lightfoot (1904: 154) perfectly catches the spurious profundity of the expression by commenting 'He impresses upon creation that unity and solidarity which makes it a cosmos instead of a chaos'. How exactly is this achieved? 'The action of gravitation . . . is an expression of His mind'!

Paul becomes completely serious in his introduction to the second strophe. The church must be characterized by the organic unity of a living 'body' (v. 18a). The insight is but an extension and clarification of 'you are all one person in Christ Jesus' (Gal 3:28 = Col 3:11). The distinction between 'head' and 'body' does not appear in 1 Cor 12:12–27 or Rom 12:4–5 because the supremacy of Christ was not questioned at Rome or Corinth. In this instance 'head' would appear to mean both 'superior' (2:10) and 'source' (2:19). The cosmic dimension of the original hymn has been reduced to ecclesiology.

(1:21–3) The Thesis of the Letter These verses both sum up what has been said, and enunciate the major themes of the letter in inverse order. Thus they function as the rhetorical *partitio* (Aletti 1993: 120). vv. 21–2 evoke the past, present, and future of the Colossians. The passive voice 'having been alienated' must be taken seriously (v. 21; cf. 1:13; Phil 2:15); the Gentiles had inherited their polytheism and their acceptance of the false values of a corrupt society. To extricate them from this situation divine intervention was necessary, but it was not an act of glorious triumph (v. 22). 'Body of flesh' distinguishes the individual Jesus from incorporeal beings, but also hints that his death was the result of something happening to his body, the violence of the crucifixion (v. 20b). Reconciliation is presented as a past achievement, but this does not imply a realized eschatology, since its conditional aspect is immediately made clear ('provided that', v. 23).

The Colossians have been given the opportunity (1:12; cf. Gal 5:1) to appear guiltless at the final judgement. How precisely they must comport themselves is outlined in 3:1–4:1. More fundamentally, however, they must remain committed to the salvific vision conveyed by the gospel they initially accepted (1:5–6). The alternative against which they are warned is the theme of 2:6–23. The hyperbole of 'preached to every creature under heaven' (v. 23b) echoes that of 1 Thess 1:8, and the lack of the definite article before 'servant' underlines that Paul is not the sole apostle. 1:24–2:5 develops Paul's own understanding of his service of the mystery.

(1:24–2:5) Servant of the Mystery The NRSV offers a widespread mistranslation of 1:24b, which has given rise to a series of false problems to which a variety of answers have been proposed, some of which are used to deny Pauline authorship of Colossians (Kremer 1956). A literal translation, which respects the order of the words, simplifies the matter considerably (Aletti 1993: 135): 'I complete what is lacking in the sufferings-of-Christ-in-my-flesh' (cf. Gal 2:20; 2 Cor 4:10–11). There is no reference to the individual Jesus Christ. Paul's sufferings are those of Christ because Paul is a member of the body of Christ (cf. Phil 3:10), and because Paul's sufferings reveal the present reality of grace as those of Christ did (2 Cor 4:10–11). Paul has no choice but to struggle on until all have heard the gospel (cf. Rom 15:19; 2 Tim 4:17). He is a minister of the church (1:25), not in virtue of a human commission (1:1; cf. Gal 1:1), but in virtue of the stewardship entrusted to him by God in order to further the economy of salvation (1 Cor 4:1; 9:17). The 'word of God', which Paul preaches in word and deed, is now described as 'the mystery' (1:26; cf. Eph 3:1–9). Divinely ordained future events (for the background see Brown 1968), which for the false teachers were still a secret to be penetrated laboriously, in fact have already been made plain, not merely to a group of initiates, but to all believers. 'Glory', the brilliance of God's action in history, is the antithesis of secrecy. The content of the mystery is Christ precisely as present among the believers, no longer in Jerusalem, to which they must trek (Isa 60:1–7), but where they are (Aletti 1993: 143). Hence all attention must be focused on him as the source of authentic, certain knowledge (2:3). The acquisition of such knowledge is not a matter of asceticism. They must be 'instructed by love' (against NRSV; cf. Spicq 1958–9: ii.202–8) in order to penetrate the riches of wisdom and knowledge hidden in Christ (2:2), who 'loved me, that is, gave himself for me' (Gal 2:20; BDF §442(9); cf. 1:22).

(2:6–23) Warning against Errors The original commitment of the Colossians was to the Christ as Jesus the Lord (2:6; Lightfoot 1904: 174). Jesus is the truth of Christ (Eph 4:21). His historicity is fundamental to salvation. The believers must not permit themselves to be returned to the domain of darkness (cf. 1:13) by accepting merely human speculation which, despite the claims made for it, in fact regresses to the basic religious perspectives common to (fallen) humanity ('elements of the world', 2:8), e.g. the need for asceticism in order to advance in religious knowledge (v. 20; GAL 4:3); see Sappington (1991: 169).

'Elementary teaching' (Heb 5:12) appears to be the best sense in this context of a term, *stoicheion* (element), which has a wide variety of meanings according to the framework in which it is used (for a survey see Bandstra 1964: 5–30). Many scholars, however, prefer to understand 'elements

of the world' as the basic components of the material universe—earth, water, air, and fire. This is certainly the best-documented meaning in contemporary literature, but to make sense here it has to be understood metaphorically of (1) the basic factors in human existence, which for Paul were Law, Sin, Death, flesh, or (2) the planets which exercise control over humans and determine the calendar; such astral beings are associated with angels. Neither of these usages is attested at the time of Paul.

The function of the genitive 'of deity' (v. 9) is to explain 'Fullness', which 1:19 had left unspecified (Lohse 1968: 150; BDF §§165, 167). As in 1:19, 'indwelling' here does not mean divinization. 'Bodily' has been interpreted in at least five different ways (Moule 1968: 92–3). The two most probable are 'really' (as opposed to seemingly; cf. v. 17) and 'in physical form'. The two are not incompatible. Divine favour and salvific action are concentrated exclusively in the humanity of Christ. Necessarily, therefore, he is the sole source of fulfilment, and he has authority over all spirit forces (v. 10; Grudem 1985).

What has already been achieved for the Colossians should be a cause of thanksgiving (v. 7). To drive this home Paul employs a series of five vivid, dramatic images (vv. 11–15), in which attempts have been made to find traditional material (Lohse 1968: 160; Wengst 1972: 186–94). The results have been inconclusive. Through Christ the whole body of flesh (and not a mere symbolic token), i.e. the entire framework of habits and desires opposed to God, has been removed (v. 11; cf. v. 18). This is true only in theory; it must be made real in practice (cf. Gal 5:13–24). The active faith of the recipient is necessary for baptism to be a dying and rising with Christ (v. 12; cf. Rom 10:9). The realized eschatology of 'you were co-raised' (cf. 3:1) must be read in the perspective of the future eschatology of 1:22, 27; 3:4, 6, 15–16. It is simply a more graphic version of 'God made alive' (v. 13). 'Life' and 'death' are used here in their existential sense of the presence and absence of virtue (cf. 2 Cor 2:16; Philo, *Fug.*, 55). With vivid imagination Paul presents humanity as having defaulted after signing an agreement to obey the will of God. The bond thus became an accusation (v. 14). God, in his generosity, forgave the fault and cancelled the debt.

The moment when this happened—'nailing it to the cross'—was the crucifixion of Christ. The image is not totally consistent, and the metaphor must not be pressed too hard. For other interpretative options see O'Brien (1982: 121–6). A new image, whose antithesis appears in 2 Cor 2:14, is introduced in v. 15. God (the emperor) awards a Roman triumph to Christ (his victorious general), who, having stripped angelic beings of their power, led them in a procession that normally ended in executions (Hafemann 1986: 18–39). Some explain the sudden appearance of 'principalities and powers' by identifying them as the angels who recorded the transgressions of humanity. In this case the 'handwriting' would be the book of life (Ps 56:8; Isa 65:6; 1 Enoch 81:2–4; Sappington 1991: 208–23). The mention of spirit powers, however, could have been occasioned by the situation at Colossae to which Paul now turns.

The 'therefore' introducing v. 16 implies that the direct polemic against the false teachers (vv. 16–23) stems from the doctrinal base established in vv. 9–15. The reality of Christ highlights the insubstantial nature of the proposed alternative

(v. 17), which was rooted in 'a quest for higher religious experience through mystical-ascetical piety' (Carr 1973: 500). In addition to strict observance of the Jewish calendar (v. 16; cf. Isa 1:13–14; Ezek 46:4–11), the false teachers demanded fasting and/or the exclusion of certain foods (v. 21). They believed that obedience won God's favour, and that asceticism purified the person (v. 23). Together these two constituted the 'humility' (v. 18), i.e. mortification, that was the prerequisite for revelatory experiences (Sappington 1991: 163). The NRSV translation of v. 18a should be abandoned in favour of 'Let no one condemn you, delighting in humility and the angelic worship [of God], which he has seen upon entering' (O'Brien 1982: 134). In visions the adept 'entered' the heavenly world (Francis and Meeks 1973: 163–207), and participated in the worship offered by the angels assembled around the throne of God (Isa 6; Ezek 1; 1 Enoch 14). It was to this other world that the false teachers had relegated Christ.

This claim to religious superiority is brutally dismissed by Paul as overweening conceit rooted in silly ideas concocted by a fleshly intelligence (v. 18b). This fundamentally egocentric attitude is the antithesis of the sharing that characterizes the Body of Christ and, in consequence, separates those who persist in it from Christ, the only source ('head'; cf. 1 Cor 11:3) of the Body's vitality (v. 19). The being of a Christian is to 'belong' to Christ (1 Cor 3:23).

What the Colossians enjoy (cf. 1:12–14; 2:11–15) is not definitive. It can be lost. Through death in Christ (v. 12) they have been freed from the religious perspectives of fallen humanity (v. 20; cf. v. 8), but they will return to a state of slavery if they again accept the values and standards of society (Gal 4:8–11). The emphasis on ascetic practices associated with Judaism (cf. LXX Isa 29:13) is due to the situation at Colossae (vv. 21–2), but the principle is of wider application (Gal 5:1, 13). Such practices might appear to exhibit spiritual strength and superiority, but in fact they indulge the egocentricity of fallen humanity because they are 'self-imposed' (v. 23).

(3:1–4:1) How the Colossians Ought to Live Having brought out the implications of dying with Christ (2:20–3), Paul now spells out the consequences of rising with Christ (3:1–4). If believers have been raised, then their concern must be with 'above' not with 'below'. The contrast is inspired by the characterization of the practices of the false teachers in 2:23, and appears to forget that these were only means to reaching 'the things that are above' (cf. 2:18). For Paul, however, the central figure in heaven is Christ, whose authority is emphasized by his position at God's right hand (Ps 110:1; 1 Cor 15:25).

'Do not set your minds on things that are on earth' (3:2; cf. Phil 3:19), if taken literally, would negate the ethical directives which follow. Such imprecision regularly caused confusion in Paul's communities, e.g. his insistence that Christians were totally free of the Mosaic law permitted the Corinthians to conclude that they could do what they liked (cf. 1 Cor 6:12; 10:23). Paul's intention here was not to exclude involvement with society (cf. 1 Cor 5:9–10), but to prohibit acceptance of its values (cf. Rom 8:5–6). Believers no longer 'belong to the world' (2:20). By contrast with the glorious revelation at the parousia (3:4) of the intimate union between Christ and believers (cf. Gal 2:20; Phil 1:21), their new life can be considered 'hidden' (3:3), but this is relative, because the action of grace

must be seen if the gospel is to spread (1:6; cf. 1 Thess 1:6–8; 4:12; 2 Cor 3:2, 18).

'Whatever in you is earthly' (3:5) is literally 'the members on the earth'. Paul identifies the parts of the body with the sins they commit (cf. Rom 6:13, 19; 2 Apoc. Bar. 49:3). The admonition does not parallel Mt 5:29–30. Lists of vices characteristic of unredeemed pagan humanity (Wis 14:22–9) have already appeared in 1 Thess 4:3–6; Gal 5:19–21. The first five mentioned here (5:5) can be related to sexuality, thought the last-mentioned has a wider extension. The connection between greed, the original sin (Rom 7:7), and idolatry is axiomatic in Judaism (cf. T. Judah, 19:1). Pagans are simply 'those who covet' (Pal. Tg. on Ex 20:17; b. Šabb. 146a). The second five vices (5:8) all involve intemperate speech that makes genuine communication impossible. The social consequences of lying (5:9a) are even more disastrous. Without trust there can be no community.

To the Galatians Paul had said 'you have put on Christ' (Gal 3:27; cf. Rom 13:14). The image of putting on a person is without parallel in antiquity, and owes its origin to the convert's assumption of a new environment by entering the church, which is the body of Christ. The insight is developed here in a contrast between 'the old man' and 'the new man' (5:9b–10). Both are primarily social concepts. The 'new man' is the sphere 'where' (3:11) the divisions which characterize society ('the old man') no longer exist (Gal 3:28). Just as society dictates the behaviour of its members, so the believing community is the source of authentic moral knowledge. The goal of the ongoing renewal of the 'new man' is a type of knowledge characterized by creativity. This can only be a knowledge born of love (Phil 1:9–10; contrast Rom 2:17–18), which empowers the other not only to see but to act. The community, which is Christ (3:11), exemplifies the ideal of his self-sacrificing love, and enables the members to pattern their lives on his example (2 Cor 5: 14–15). Instead of the contempt that produced the divisions typical of society—Jews despised pagans, who looked down on barbarians (i.e. anyone who did not speak Greek), who spurned Scythians as the epitome of human degradation (cf. 2 Macc 4:47; 3 Macc 7:5)—the believers must make Christ present in the world by exhibiting those virtues 'which reduce or eliminate friction: ready sympathy, a generous spirit, a humble disposition, willingness to make concessions, patience, forbearance' (Moule 1968: 123). Forgiven by God they must forgive. Loved by God they must love. Unless sheathed in love no virtue can be perfect (3:14; cf. Spicq 1958–9: i. 268–75). Love alone excludes pretence. Others (details in Schmauch 1964: 80–2) translate 'the bond of perfection' and understand the genitive as purposeful ('the bond that leads to perfection') or objective ('the bond that produces perfection'). These are less satisfactory, because for Paul there is no perfection beyond love (1 Cor 13).

Fully aware of the tensions within the church at Colossae, Paul expresses a wish that peace may reign there. In society peace is often no more than an uneasy truce to be abandoned the moment an advantage presents itself. The Colossians should be grateful that they are not in that situation. Authentic peace, which is defined by reference to the self-sacrifice of Christ, is first a subjective attitude which then results in a community of love (3:15; cf. 1 Cor 7:15; 14:33). In a living body the hand cannot be at war with the foot. According to 1 Cor 6:7, members who sue one another are in fact suing themselves—a ridiculous situation.

The ideal community is not merely an absence of antagonism. There is a much more positive dimension (3:16). The expression 'word of Christ' is unique, but synthesizes a number of concepts found earlier in the letter; 'the word of the truth, the gospel' (1:5) is 'the word of God' (1:25), which is 'God's mystery, that is Christ' (2:3). Its power within each one (1:6, 10) must find socially beneficial expression. The emphasis on 'teaching and admonishing' was demanded by the presence of false teachers at Colossae, who taught some believers the hymn that Paul quotes in 1:15–20. In practice 'yourselves' means 'one another' (NRSV; cf. 3:13) but *heautous* (cf. 1 Cor 6:7) was chosen to underline that believers are organically unified in a single 'body', and thereby to remind them that their source of life is Christ (2:19). Theological development is part of the natural evolution of the community. In consequence, it must (a) be homogeneous with the gospel that brought the community into being (1:6), and (b) take place in a public context. 'Psalms, hymns, and spiritual songs' suggest the liturgical assembly, in which inspired insights into the mystery of Christ (1 Cor 14:26) were proffered for the consent of the community (1 Cor 14:16; cf. 1 Thess 5:21–2). Such community singing must be an expression of gratitude to God (3:16c), but so too must every other human activity (3:17). It is made possible in, through, and by Christ; thus it must mirror his comportment. But Jesus was sent because of God's fatherly concern for humanity (1:12), and so in the last analysis gratitude must be directed to God.

Generic directives are followed by three pairs of reciprocal admonitions dealing with the relations of wife–husband, child–father, and slave–master (3:18–4:1). The nature of the socio-religious matrix in which such household codes were formulated has occasioned vigorous debate (Balch 1992), whose inconclusiveness is the inevitable consequence of the wide variations within the form. Conscious of a tradition of sensible social management, Paul formulates a series of guidelines designed to persuade the Colossians to leave the mystical world of visions and angels, and to return to the real world where the fabric of daily life was woven from a multitude of interpersonal relations, of which the most basic were the three pairs listed here (Aristotle, *Politics*, 1.1253b7). The only really distinctive feature is the motivation by reference to the Lord, which here means Christ (Aletti 1993: 249). The social distinctions, which are fundamental to these admonitions, can be reconciled with the abolition of such distinctions in 3:11 only on the assumption that not all members of a family were converted to Christianity.

The literal translation of 3:18 is 'women be subject to men', but the context demands limitation to marriage, as some copyists have tried to convey by various additions. The admonition that a Christian woman be submissive to her non-believing husband (3:18) is to remind her that her new freedom (cf. Gal 5:1) does not exempt her from the obligations she undertook in marriage. Such behaviour is 'fitting' for a Christian because of its missionary potential (cf. 1 Pet 3:1). The obligation to love laid on the husband (3:19) indicates that the wife is a non-believer, since Christians by definition love one another (3:14; cf. 1 Thess 4:9). The temptation to treat her harshly might be due to her refusal to convert.

What is said to slaves stands out from the other admonitions both quantitatively and qualitatively (3:22–5). It is unlikely to have been inspired by the case of Onesimus (4:9), or by agitation among Christian slaves at Colossae (Aletti 1993: 254). Rather it reflects Paul's habitual attitude towards slaves who accepted Christianity. Within the community he took it for granted that they would show and share the love that was its most characteristic feature, but he made no effort to change the social order. Paul does not demand that Onesimus be manumitted, but that he be received 'no longer as a slave, but more than a slave, a beloved brother' (Philem 16; cf. 1 COR 7:17–24). Paul's sole concern here is that slaves should not obey orders to the letter while their hearts raged, and hate corroded their spirits. The internal tension had to be resolved in order to permit the transforming effect of grace to become visible (4:5–6). The witness value of the comportment of believers was always a major concern (cf. 1 Thess 1:6–8; 4:12; 2 Cor 4:10–11). The warning of a future judgement (3:24–5) underlines the seriousness of Paul's concern.

Christian masters also have obligations to their slaves (cf. Sir 7:20–1, 31–3). They are not required to love them or to free them, but to treat them 'justly' and 'fairly' (4:1). The terms are related as 'knowledge' and 'discernment' in Phil 1:9. In each case the first deals with the obvious and clear, whereas the second comes into play when a sure feeling for what is appropriate is required.

(4:2–6) Concluding Exhortations As Paul had given thanks (1:3) and prayed for the Colossians (1:9), so now they must do likewise (v. 2). The prayer in question is primarily petition (O'Brien 1982: 237) for the glorious return of Christ (3:4; cf. 1 Cor 16:22). Their incessant awareness of, and orientation to, this goal is the best guarantee of the vigilance required of all believers if they are to persevere (1:23). Gratitude for what they have already been given (1:12–14; 3:11–12) should enhance their attentiveness. It is typical of Paul to request prayers for himself (1 Thess 5:25; Philem 22). It is a means of participation in the mission of the church (3:3; 2 Thess 3:1; Phil 1:19). The Colossians must beseech God (a) for Paul's liberation from prison in order to continue his mission (cf. 1 Cor 16:9; 2 Cor 2:12), and (b) for his ability to 'reveal' the mystery effectively. 'The divine passive of 1:26 finds its human herald in 4:4' (Aletti 1993: 260). Despite Paul's emphasis on the verbal dimension of such communication, it is likely that he also has in mind the existential aspect, in which his comportment reveals Christ (2 Cor 4:10–11; cf. 1 Cor 2:1–5).

It is to this aspect that Paul now alerts the Colossians. It is not enough to pray. They must also exhibit a presence in society that will prove attractive to non-believers (v. 5; cf. 1 Thess 4:12; Phil 2:14–16). Every opportunity to induce them to believe must be availed of. The speech of Christians should be winning and witty, and tailored to the needs of each interlocutor (v. 6). They must insinuate not dominate.

(4:7–18) Final Greetings The two bearers of the letter are introduced in a chiastic pattern (vv. 7–9). Paul tactfully remains quiet regarding the personal history of Onesimus, simply noting that he has become a Christian ('brother'; cf. Philem 10), and has Paul's respect and confidence ('faithful'). The same adjectives are applied to Tychicus, who in addition is called 'minister' and 'fellow-servant in the Lord', exactly as is Epaphras (1:7; 4:12). If the latter was an official delegate of Paul to Colossae, Tychicus now enjoys the same status. He can speak for Paul with authority, not only with respect to personal news from Ephesus, but as regards the interpretation of the letter in its impact on the growth of the community (2:2).

Greetings are sent by six men with Paul, who with one exception also appear in Philemon but in a different order:

Col 4:10–14	Remarks	Philem 23–4
Aristarchus	<– my fellow-prisoner	Aristarchus (3)
Mark	<– cousin of Barnabas	Mark (2)
Jesus	<– called Justus	
Epaphras	<– one of you, a servant of Christ Jesus my fellow-prisoner –>	Epaphras (1)
Luke	<– beloved physician	Luke (5)
Demas		Demas (4)

It is curious that Timothy, the co-author of both letters (1:1; Philem 1), is not mentioned in either list. Aristarchus of Thessalonica is well known from several references in Acts (19:29; 20:4; 27:2). Nothing is known of Jesus who, like Paul, had taken a similar-sounding Hellenistic Roman name. It is unlikely that his name appears in Philem 23 (O'Brien 1982: 307). Mark is mentioned in Acts 12:12, 25; 15:37–9, and in 2 Tim 4:11. In a poignant note Paul remarks that these three are the only Christians of Jewish origin to have stayed with him (3:11). Had they come with him from Antioch? The implication is that the following three collaborators are Gentiles. Luke and Demas appear in 2 Tim 4:9, 11. Despite his imprisonment, Epaphras, the apostle of Colossae (1:7), remains active on behalf of his converts (3:12). He prays that they may be stable in their maturity (cf. 1:28–9), and be filled with 'everything willed by God' (Lightfoot 1904: 238), whose essence is spelt out in 2:2–3, 10. Paul's independent knowledge of how hard Epaphras had worked to establish the gospel in the Lycus valley (v. 13) must have come from Onesimus (v. 9). The testimony would have been all the more impressive coming from one who at that stage was a pagan (Philem 10). The exclusive concentration on Laodicea in what follows suggests that Epaphras had not been successful in Hierapolis.

Paul sends his personal greetings to believers in Laodicea, and in particular to the believers who assembled in the home of Nympha (v. 15). The fact that he singles out a particular individual confirms that he had never visited the Lycus valley (cf. 2:1; ROM 16). Nymphan could be the accusative of the feminine name Nympha (O'Brien 1982: 246) or of the masculine name Nymphas (Moule 1968: 28). There is little difficulty in deciding which of the accompanying pronouns, 'her' or 'him', is original. No copyist would change the masculine into the feminine, because of its implication regarding the status of a woman. The contrary, however, is eminently probable, given the instinctive patriarchal bias of copyists. Women were fully the equal of men in the Pauline communities (cf. 1 Cor 11:2–16), and presided over house churches (cf. Rom 16:1–2).

For the public reading of the letter at Colossae (v. 16; cf. 1 Thess 5:27) the 'whole' community (cf. Rom 16:23; 1 Cor 14:23) must have been assembled from the various house churches in the city. The exchange of letters with Laodicea implies that the differences between the two churches were significant, otherwise two letters would be pointless. None the less the two communities had enough in common to make the reading of the other's letter worthwhile. The letter sent by Paul to the Laodiceans has been the centre of a vigorous debate. The current consensus refuses to identify it with any known document (Anderson 1992). It has been constructed out of Colossians by Boismard (1999).

Paul's request that Archippus should be informed of an admonition addressed to him (v. 17) implies that Paul knew that he would not be present when the letter was read in public (contrast 2 Thess 3:11–12; Phil 4:2–3), even though he was part of the leadership group of a house church (Philem 2). The most natural explanation is that Epaphras had informed Paul that Archippus had been won over by the false teachers. The desertion of a leader of his status explains the urgency of the letter. A response could not await the release of Paul or Epaphras. Had Archippus simply moved to Laodicea (Lightfoot 1904: 242) the matter would have been dealt with in that letter.

Paul regularly used secretaries (Rom 16:22), and thus had to write the last paragraph in his own hand to authenticate the letter (4:18; cf. 2 Thess 3:17; Gal 6:11; Philem 19; 1 Cor 16:21; Richards 1991: 173–7).

REFERENCES

Abbott, T. K. (1897), A Critical and Exegetical Commentary on the Epistles to the Ephesians and to the Colossians, ICC (Edinburgh: T. & T. Clark).

Aletti, J.-N. (1993), Saint Paul: Épître aux Colossiens, Ebib NS 20 (Paris: Gabalda).

Anderson, C. P. (1992), 'Laodiceans, Epistle to', ABD iv. 231–3.

Balch, D. (1992), 'Household Codes', ABD iii. 318–20.

Bandstra, A. J. (1964), Law and the Elements (Kampen: Kok).

Barrett, C. K. (1994), Paul: An Introduction to his Thought (London: Chapman).

Benoit, P. (1975), 'L'Hymne christologique de Col i, 15–20: Jugement critique sur l'état des recherches', in J. Neusner (ed.), Christianity, Judaism and Other Greco-Roman Cults: Studies for Morton Smith at Sixty, SJLA 12/1 (Leiden: Brill), i. 226–63.

—— (1982), 'Hagioi en Colossiens 1.12: Hommes ou Anges?', in M. D. Hooker and S. G. Wilson (eds.), Paul and Paulinism: Essays in Honour of C. K. Barrett (London: SPCK), 83–101.

Boismard, M.-E. (1999), La Lettre de saint Paul au Laodicéens, Cahiers de la Revue Biblique (Paris: Gabalda).

Brown, R. E. (1968), The Semitic Background of the Term 'Mystery' in the New Testament, FBBS 21 (Philadelphia: Fortress).

Bruce, F. F. (1977), Paul: Apostle of the Free Spirit (Exeter: Paternoster).

Bujard, W. (1973), Stilanalytische Untersuchungen zum Kolosserbrief als Beitrag zur Methodik von Sprachergleichen, SUNT 11 (Göttingen: Vandenhoeck & Ruprecht).

Carr, W. (1973), 'Two Notes on Colossians', JTS 24: 492–500.

Dunn, J. D. G. (1980), Christology in the Making: An Inquiry into the Origins of the Doctrine of the Incarnation (London: SCM).

—— (1996), The Epistles to the Colossians and to Philemon: A Commentary on the Greek Text, Greek New Testament Commentary (Grand Rapids: Eerdmans).

Francis, F. O., and Meeks, W. A. (1973) (eds.), Conflict at Colossae, SBLSBS 4 (Missoula: Scholar's Press).

Furnish, V. P. (1992), 'Colossians, Epistle to the', ABD i. 1090–6.

Grudem, W. (1985), 'Does kephale ("Head") Mean "Source" or "Authority" in Greek Literature? A Survey of 2,336 Examples', Trinity Journal, 6: 38–59.

Gunther, J. J. (1973), *St. Paul's Opponents and Their Background: A Study of Apocalyptic and Jewish Sectarian Teachings*, NovTSup 35 (Leiden: Brill).

Hafemann, S. J. (1986), *Suffering and the Spirit: An Exegetical Study of II Cor. 2:14–3:3 within the Context of the Corinthian Correspondence*, WUNT 2/19 (Tübingen: Mohr [Siebeck]).

Hooker, M. D. (1973), 'Were there False Teachers at Colossae?', in B. Lindars and S. Smalley (eds.), *Christ and Spirit in the New Testament: Studies in Honour of Charles Francis Digby Moule* (Cambridge: Cambridge University Press).

Käsemann, E. (1964), *Essays on New Testament Themes*, SBT 41 (London: SCM).

Kenny, A. (1986), *A Stylometric Study of the New Testament* (Oxford: Clarendon).

Kremer, J. (1956), *Was an den Leiden Christi noch mangelt: Eine interpretationsgeschichtliche und exegetische Untersuchung zu Kol 1, 24b*, BBB 12 (Bonn: Hanstein).

Kuhn, K. G. (1968), 'The Epistle to the Ephesians in the Light of the Qumran Texts', in J. Murphy-O'Connor (ed.), *Paul and Qumran* (London: Chapman), 115–31.

Lampe, P. (1985), 'Keine "Sklavenflucht" des Onesimus', ZNW 76: 135–7.

Lightfoot, J. B. (1904), *Saint Paul's Epistles to the Colossians and to Philemon* (London: Macmillan).

Lohse, E. (1968), *Die Briefe an die Kolosser und an Philemon*, MeyerK (Göttingen: Vandenhoeck & Ruprecht).

Moule, C. F. D. (1968), *The Epistles to the Colossians and to Philemon*, CGTC (Cambridge: Cambridge University Press).

Murphy-O'Connor, J. (1995a), 'Tradition and Redaction in Col 1:15–20', *RB* 102: 231–41.

—— (1995b), *Paul the Letter Writer*, GNS 41 (Collegeville, Ind.: Liturgical Press).

Nestle-Aland (1993), *Novum Testamentum Graece*, 27th edn. (Stuttgart: Deutsche Bibelgesellschaft).

Neumann, K. J. (1990), *The Authenticity of the Pauline Epistles in the Light of Stylostatistic Analysis*, SBLDS 120 (Atlanta: Scholars Press).

O'Brien, P. T. (1982), *Colossians, Philemon*, WBC 44 (Waco: Word).

Richards, E. R. (1991), *The Secretary in the Letters of Paul*, WUNT 2/42 (Tübingen, Mohr [Siebeck]).

Sappington, T. J. (1991), *Revelation and Redemption at Colossae*, JSNTSup 53 (Sheffield: JSOT).

Schenk, W. (1987), 'Der Kolosserbrief in der neueren Forschung (1945–1985)', *ANRW* 2. 25. 4 (Berlin: de Gruyter), 3327–64.

Schlier, H. (1961), *Principalities and Powers in the New Testament*, QD 3 (Fribourg: Herder).

Schmauch, W. (1964), *Beiheft zu E. Lohmeyer: Die Briefe an die Philipper, Kolosser und an Philemon*, MeyerK (Göttingen: Vandenhoeck & Ruprecht).

Schubert, P. (1939), *Form and Function of the Pauline Thanksgivings*, BZNW 20 (Berlin: Töpelmann).

Spicq, C. (1958–9), *Agape dans le Nouveau Testament: Analyse des textes*, Ebib (2 vols.; Paris: Gabalda).

Wengst, K. (1972), *Christologische Formeln und Lieder* (Gütersloh: Mohr).

71. 1 Thessalonians   PHILIP F. ESLER

INTRODUCTION

A. Preliminary Issues. 1. Date Paul probably wrote 1 Thessalonians from Corinth within a matter of months after his initial visit to Thessalonica, in about 50–51 CE (so Best 1972: 7–13; Barclay 1993: 515). It is widely agreed that 1 Thessalonians is the earliest extant Christian text, a precious document which brilliantly illuminates one segment of the Christ-movement less than twenty years after the death of Jesus.

2. The Significance of the Epistolary Form It can hardly be without significance that the earliest document extant from the followers of Christ takes the form of a letter. Much research has been conducted recently which analyses the formal structures of Graeco-Roman epistolography (Stowers 1986), and their relation to early Christian letters, including those of Paul (Doty 1973), and 1 Thessalonians in particular (Boers 1976). But we should be careful not to miss the distinctiveness of 1 Thessalonians. While it does have many of the features seen in Graeco-Roman letters, there is no extant letter like this from the surrounding context, in that it combines personal features (such as the elaborate thanksgiving in 1:2–3:13) with instructions and end-time exhortation (Koester 1979). 1 Thessalonians, a carefully composed writing, 'is an experiment in the composition of literature which signals the momentous entry of Christianity into the literary world of antiquity' (ibid. 33).

3. An important insight of Robert Funk (1967) is that the letter substitutes for the personal presence of Paul. In this regard Funk accepts and develops the ideas of Koskenniemi

(1956) that in the Greek world the letter was designed to extend the possibility of friendship between the parties after they had become separated—that is why *parousia* ('presence' or 'arrival'), *philophronēsis* ('affectionate kind treatment', 'friendship'), and *homilia* ('being together', 'communion', 'conversing') are basic to the conception of the Greek letter. 'Absent in body, but present through this letter' is a common Greek formula reflecting this phenomenon. Funk (1967: 265) suggests that Paul must have thought of his presence as the bearer of charismatic, even 'eschatological', power, even though he certainly does not equate his parousia with that of Christ and this theme is more clearly seen in 1 Cor 5:3–5 than in 1 Thessalonians.

4. It is uncertain if Paul is replying to a letter. Frame (1912: 157), Faw (1952: 220–2), and Malherbe (1990) think that he was, but most think that he was not. Paul could have learned of the situation in Thessalonica from Timothy (so Best 1972: 171 and Jewett 1986: 92).

5. Lastly, in this connection, it should be noted that most of the letters which survive from Graeco-Roman antiquity are from one individual to another and Paul is usually writing to a group or groups. We would expect this to make some difference. There is, indeed, some interest in group-oriented letters, especially those to a family (Stowers 1986: 71–6). Most of our evidence on family letters comes not from Greek epistolary theorists (preoccupied with the concerns of free adult males) but from Egyptian papyri. There is a letter from Cicero (in exile) to his family in Stowers (1986: 74–6).

6. Context Thessalonica, located at the head of the Thermaic Gulf, was founded by Cassander in *c*.316 BCE on the site of an older city. There is some archaeological and literary evidence for the usual assemblage of Hellenistic features and buildings, such as an agora, a Serapaeum, a gymnasium, and a stadium (Vickers 1972). In due course Thessalonica passed into Roman hands, where its situation on the Via Egnatia, the great Roman road running from the Adriatic to the Black Sea, gave it great strategic and commercial significance. It is not surprising that it became the capital of the province of Macedonia. From surviving inscriptions it seems to have had a vibrant religious life, with numerous cults (Edson 1948; Donfried 1985; 1989).

7. There is little doubt that Thessalonica would have contained the same sharp division between a small wealthy, aristocratic élite and a much larger non-élite characteristic of the Graeco-Roman cities of the East. Jewett (1993) has usefully pointed out that the dominant form of housing for the non-élite would have been tenements, not the more spacious villa type houses.

B. The Nature of the Christ-Following Community in Thessalonica. 1. Jews or Gentiles or Both? In 1 Thess 1:9 Paul tells his audience they turned to God from idols to serve the one true God. This strongly suggests they were idolatrous Gentiles prior to conversion, for he would not describe Jews as turning from idolatry (de Vos 1999: 146–7). Many scholars refuse to accept this conclusion, mainly because it is contrary to what Acts 17:1–9 says, with its picture of Paul preaching in a synagogue and winning converts among Jews, God-fearers, Greeks, and rich women. But Luke is probably just following his typical pattern here (Lührmann 1990: 237–41), possibly based on his desire to depict an early movement of Christ-followers made up of Jews and Gentile God-fearers (Esler 1987: 36–45).

2. Exactly what sort of idolatry the Thessalonians had previously engaged in is uncertain. Jewett (1986: 127–32; 165–7) has mounted a significant argument that Paul's converts were impoverished manual workers who had seen Cabirus, their saviour-god, hijacked by upper-class interests. This view has, however, been criticized as lacking evidence and also as resting on the false assumption that an end-time ideology is necessarily founded on some form of deprivation (Barclay 1993: 519–20).

3. Social Status Recent research on the social structure of Pauline communities has tended to favour socially stratified congregations with wealthy members providing a house for the meetings of the community and virtually acting as patrons to the members. But the fact that Paul does not mention the name of any person in Thessalonica raises the possibility that the whole congregation came from the poor non-élite, living in tenements (Jewett 1993). De Vos (1999: 154) sees in Thessalonica an audience of 'free-born artisans and manual-workers'. Corinth and Thessalonica thus represent very different types of the early Christ-movement (Barclay 1992). The difficult life of an urban artisan has been well described by Hock (1980: 31–47). The community may also have embraced agricultural day labourers (Schöllgen 1988: 73, 76).

4. Opposition to the Christ-Followers in Thessalonica Paul's initial proclamation in Thessalonica was attended by great conflict (*agōn*) in public (2:2). Furthermore, great affliction (*thlipsis*: 1:6) accompanied the reception of the word by the Thessalonians and, just as Paul had warned them that they would continue to be afflicted (3:4), so they are at the time he writes the letter (3:3). They have suffered at the hands of their fellow Thessalonians (2:14).

5. The best explanation for such opposition lies in the more general issue raised by Paul's aim of having the Thessalonians abandon their traditional gods in favour of the monotheistic brand of faith he was preaching, an aim achieved as far as his addressees were concerned, since they had turned to God from idols (1:9). To appreciate what this means we need to understand the everyday reality of paganism in this part of the empire (see MacMullen 1981).

6. Kinship, politics, economics, and religion were inextricably interrelated. Pagan rites were foci of economic and social interaction, playing a key role in maintaining the local political and economic system. The social dimension could be seen in crowds in theatres attached to shrines, with readings, music, and dancing (ibid. 18–24); economic aspects included coins minted and fairs attached to festivals (ibid. 25–7); and very important were meals at these festivals, generally involving meat not otherwise eaten and much wine and often partaken by *thiasoi* in small groups of diners, where the idea was found that the god might join those who were dining (cf. Plut. *Mor.* 1102A). Here gross indulgence often occurred (ibid. 36–40; cf. 1 Cor 8:10) in the *eidoleion* where the statue of the deity was located.

7. Jews and Christ-followers who abstained from these celebrations were likely to be accused of misanthropy (MacMullen 1981: 40). If people became Christ-followers in great numbers the local temples would be less frequented and the meat trade could suffer (so it was in Bithynia before Pliny's actions: *Ep.* 10.96; MacMullen 1981: 41). More dangerous was the charge of atheism, since the élite believed that the *hoi polloi* needed to take part in the local worship to ensure political stability (MacMullen 1981: 2–3). Later on there is explicit reference to such behaviour as 'godlessness' (*atheotēs*), but there is no reason such a charge could not have been made in Paul's time (Barclay 1993: 515). To be respectable and decent meant taking part in the cult; old was good and new was bad. Thus, religion served to strengthen the existing social order (MacMullen 1981: 57–8). To deny the reality of the gods was absolutely unacceptable—one would be ostracized for that, even stoned in the streets (ibid. 62).

8. The particular proposal that the conflict centred on a charge that the Thessalonian followers of Jesus were contravening 'the decrees of Caesar' (explained by Judge 1971) rests on little but the historically dubious account of the Thessalonian mission in Acts 17:1–9 (also see de Vos 1999: 156–7). Nevertheless, as Donfried (1985) has argued, any abandonment of the imperial cult as part of a general rejection of idols would not have been well received in Thessalonica, where coins reveal signs of a cultic devotion to the emperor as early as 27 BCE.

C. The Character of the Letter: Theology and Identity. 1. Established Suggestions as to the Character of the Letter There has been much interest among critics in seeking some broad description with which to characterize the nature of

1 Thessalonians. The two most popular sources for an overarching description are popular Hellenistic philosophy and rhetoric and Jewish biblical and extra-biblical traditions, since both areas, individually or jointly, have influenced what Paul has to say to his audience (Perkins 1989: 325–7). The numerous attempts to categorize 1 Thessalonians as a whole using the conceptual frameworks available to first-century Mediterranean persons can be referred as 'emic', a useful social-scientific term (derived from 'phonemic') referring to insider, native, or indigenous points of view, as opposed to 'etic' (derived from 'phonetic'), meaning the perspective of an outsider trained in contemporary social-scientific ideas and approaches (see Headland, Pike, and Harris 1990). One of the fundamental insights of the social sciences is the fundamental importance of the distinction between these two perspectives. Yet modern persons trained in twentieth-century ideas who seek to understand—however incompletely—a pre-industrial culture removed from them in space or time will usually find it necessary to employ both emic and etic perspectives in order to translate the experience of that culture into a framework they can understand (Esler 1995: 4–8). So, we will first consider some existing solutions to the nature of the letter from an emic point of view, and then briefly propose some etic perspectives which will be employed in the Commentary.

2. The first emic perspective consists of those derived from the Hellenistic setting. Donfried (1989) and Smith (1989: 170) regard the letter as one of consolation, having as its main purpose to console (*paramuthein*) the Thessalonians at a time when they were suffering the effects of persecution. While 1 Thessalonians contains several consolatory elements (see Commentary), the existence of other dimensions, however, raises some doubt as to whether 'consolation' is appropriate as a general designation for the letter (Chapa 1994). One other dimension to the letter, most prominently advocated by Malherbe (1989c), is that of exhortation. Malherbe (1987: 68–78; 1989c) has argued that Paul's aim in the letter is closely in tune with elements of Graeco-Roman moral philosophy dealing with how, in a context of friendship between persons, one of them exhorted the others to maintain existing forms of behaviour, even though Paul modifies these traditions to accord with his own theology and interests. Malherbe (1987: 74) recognizes that hortatory themes are explicitly prominent only in 1 Thess 4–5, but argues that his self-description in chs. 1–3 serves a hortatory function by reminding them of his example.

3. The second prominent emic perspective involves Jewish traditions, expressed in biblical and extra-biblical literature, which speak of a decisive change in the cosmos which God is going to bring about. The fact that such ideas, especially expressed in the notions of the coming parousia of Christ and the salvation and deliverance from wrath for his followers that will result (1:6–10; 4:13–18), should figure so prominently in a letter addressed largely if not exclusively to former idolaters constitutes one of the most remarkable features of 1 Thessalonians. This is especially surprising when one considers that other areas of Jewish tradition play a fairly small part in Paul's message, since although some of his statements bear marks of having originated in Israelite Scripture (as noted in the Commentary), there is, as de Vos (1999: 146–7)

notes, no explicit quotation from the OT and no reference to any OT figure (such as Abraham, for example) or to cultic language. Moreover, nowhere else in Paul's letters is the theme of dramatic future redemption so pronounced (Jewett 1986: 168). At a more general level, however, it has been reasonably argued, by Perkins (1989) for example, that Paul's desire to install Jewish categories and images in the hearts and minds of his converts in Thessalonica—with its profusion of pagan cults also competing for adherents (Donfried 1985; 1989)—is a more prominent theme in the letter than moral education of the sort advocated by Malherbe and others. This proposal seems to be more in tune with the markedly non-élite status of the recipients of the letter.

4. A Social Identity Approach to 1 Thessalonians Alternative ways of characterizing 1 Thessalonians, which are capable of comprehending possibly a broader range of issues and of facilitating useful contemporary applications, can be derived from the etic perspectives developed by modern social scientists.

5. One promising approach is that offered by social identity theory, a flourishing area of social psychology developed by Henri Tajfel and others in the 1970s and 1980s (see Tajfel 1978; 1981; Tajfel and Turner 1979; 1986; Brown 1988; Robinson 1996) and utilized in a recent monograph on Galatians (Esler 1998, esp. at 40–57) and in Esler (2000) dealing with Galatians and 1 Thessalonians. This theory explores the extent to which persons acquire and maintain a valued social identity, that is, that part of their sense of self which derives from belonging to one group rather than another, a process which is likely to be the focus of stereotypification and denigration. Social identity is more significant in group-oriented cultures (such as those present in the first-century Mediterranean world) than in modern individualistic cultures (such as those of northern Europe and North America). Social identity theory always insists on the primacy of the question 'Who do we say we are?'—which was expressed in the first-century Mediterranean world most directly in discourses of group-belonging derived from kinship or fictive kinship). Nevertheless, this theory also finds a place for ethical norms (as helping members maintain their sense of identity in new and ambiguous situations) and narratives of the past and future (as telling them who they are in relation both to where they have come from and whither they are proceeding). Even a conceptual apparatus usually (and reasonably) designated as 'theological' (and for 1 Thessalonians, see Marshall 1982) can serve a vital role in the processes of group differentiation and categorization which lie at the heart of this theory. Modern illustrations of the (often violent) dynamics of social identity lie to hand in the ethnic differentiation evident in Northern Ireland, Bosnia, Kosovo, Rwanda, and Israel/Palestine.

6. As will be noted in detail in the Commentary, 1 Thessalonians can be interpreted as an attempt by Paul to establish and maintain a desirable social identity for his Thessalonian converts in the face of the allure and threats posed by rival groups, and in relation to past, present, and future (Esler 2000). It is noteworthy, however, that in spite of Paul's seeking to nourish their group identity in a manner which includes pronounced outgroup stereotypification, he does not recommend ill-treatment of outsiders (which is an all too

common concomitant of such an attitude) but, on the contrary, actually advocates doing good to outsiders (3:12; 4:12). There is a strong countercultural dimension to Paul's position here.

7. It is worth noting that proposing social identity as an overall framework for interpreting the letter, with issues traditionally referred to as ethical or theological here seen as contributing to Paul's overall task of strengthening the Thessalonians' sense of who they were, in no way forecloses on any claims his ethics and theology have to a privileged ontological status. To suggest that resituating biblical data within frameworks originating in the social sciences in some way prejudices Christian truth-claims is an unfortunate misconception of the social-scientific approach to interpretation which is still entertained in some quarters where the fact that every word in the New Testament is socially embodied does not seem to be taken with sufficient seriousness.

8. While social identity theory exists at a fairly high level of abstraction, within its broad reach other areas of social-scientific research can be used in relation to particular parts of 1 Thessalonians. Chief among them are the bedrock realities of Mediterranean culture (as compellingly modelled by Malina (1993) on the basis of the work of social anthropologists in the last few decades) and millennialism, the study of how certain contemporary pre-industrial peoples in Africa, the Americas, and the South Pacific have responded to the disruption or destruction of their traditional life styles by European colonization by generating myths of future deliverance which describe the coming destruction of the Europeans and the restoration of traditional lifestyles, the return of the ancestors, the provision of cargo, and so on (Esler 1994: 96–104; Duling 1996). Jewett (1986) has applied such insights to both 1 and 2 Thessalonians.

D. Outline.

COMMENTARY

The Prescript and Thanksgiving (1:1–10)

(1:1) The Prescript Paul follows the form of opening current in Graeco-Roman letters consisting of sender(s), recipient(s), a greeting, and sometimes a prayer for health or prosperity, in that order. Here the senders are himself, Silvanus, and Timothy, with Timothy being mentioned again later (3:1–10). Paul does not describe himself in v. 1 as an apostle, although he does use that term of himself (and perhaps Silvanus and Timothy) at 2:7. The recipients are 'the congregation' (*ekklēsia*; 'church' in NRSV seems a little anachronistic here) 'of the Thessalonians (which is) in God the Father and the Lord Jesus Christ'. With this expression, in the very first verse, Paul inaugurates the issues of identity through group-belonging which will fill this letter. Social identity embraces the mere fact of belonging to a group (the 'cognitive' aspect) and its 'evaluative' and 'emotional' dimensions, that is, the positive or negative connotations members have about belonging and how they feel toward insiders and outsiders (Esler 1998: 42). Here the Thessalonians are invited to assess their membership of the congregation as extremely valuable through its close (though unexplored) relationship with their divine Father, an expression that constitutes the first of many instances of kinship language in the letter (Esler 2000), and the Lord Jesus. Although other groups are not yet mentioned, theirs is one plainly worth belonging to.

(1:2–10) The Thanksgiving This section, consisting of one long sentence, comprises the thanksgiving that Paul includes in all his letters except Galatians, after the address and greeting. For Pauline thanksgivings, see Schubert 1939. Some see this section as ending as late as 3:13, but this suggestion probably strains the notion of thanks beyond its breaking-point. v. 2, Paul notes that he constantly thanks God for the Thessalonians and mentions them in his prayers. He is obviously happy with them. v. 3, one reason for his positive regard now emerges: his memory of their work of faith (*pistis*), labour of love (*agapē*) and steadfastness of hope (*elpis*) in 'our Lord Jesus Christ' before our God and Father. The triad of faith, love, and hope, which is common in the Pauline corpus (1 Thess 5:8; Rom 5:1–5; 1 Cor 13:13; Gal 5:5–6) and later NT documents (Eph 4:2–5; Col 1:4–5; Heb 6:10–12; 10:22–4; 1 Pet 1:3–8), may well be an invention of Paul himself (Best 1972: 67). These three characteristics of becoming a follower of Christ are not just theological virtues but constitute distinctive badges of group identity. The Thessalonians, pushed to say who they were, could have given the distinctive answer, 'People characterized by faith (in Christ), love and hope'.

v. 4, Paul, describing them as 'brothers' (*adelphoi*; NRSV has 'brothers and sisters'), says he knows of their election (*eklogē*). The notion of election, with its long history antecedent to Paul of describing God's choice of Israel as his own people, is now redirected to designate the ex-idolatrous Thessalonians as a group with an extraordinary status and destiny as specially chosen by God. Here Paul both amplifies (or reiterates) their understanding of themselves and also enhances the positive connotations of belonging to such a group. The use of *adelphoi*, the first of seventeen instances in the letter, continues the kinship discourse already begun with the two references to the Father. The word may include women (so Koester 1979: 36 and NRSV), as it must do in Galatians in the light of Gal 3:28, but it is possible that here it does not, even though some women may have been converted by Paul (see Fatum 1997). v. 5, this verse, in which Paul states how his gospel came among them not only in word, but in power and in the Holy Spirit and with full conviction, outlines either the occasion and manner of their election or the grounds by which Paul inferred the fact of their election. It is essential to give Paul's reference to power and the Holy Spirit its full force and meaning. He is reminding the Thessalonians of the miracles and other charismatic phenomena (probably prophesying, glossolalia, visions, and auditions) which accompanied their reception of his preaching. Such ecstatic phenomena, although rare, if not unheard of, in domestic settings in first-century cities of the Graeco-Roman East, were characteristic of Paul's mission (Esler 1994: 40–51), as he also later reminded the Galatians (Gal 3:1–5). Charismatic phenomena created an exciting zone of Spirit-filled experience unique to his congregations. Once again, the group-differentiating element to this language should not be missed—another way of describing their identity was as a group actually filled by God. v. 6, they became his and the Lord's imitators in the way they received the word in spite of persecution (*thlipsis*) in the joy of the Holy Spirit. The difficulties experienced by the Thessalonians, already implied by the reference to their endurance in 1:3, now surface openly in relation to their initial conversion. Possible reasons for external opposition to the Thessalonians turning to Christ, especially through neglect of cults considered vital to civic well-being, were considered above (cf. 1 THESS B 4). One insight of social identity theory is that external opposition and persecution will often encourage members to act in terms of their group membership, so that such past suffering, now brought again to mind by Paul, probably strengthened their involvement with, and commitment to, the congregation. The 'joy inspired by the Holy Spirit' probably extends to the euphoria enjoyed by those who experience powerful dissociative states caused by divine possession (Esler 1994: 42).

vv. 7–9, they 'became an example to all the believers in Macedonia and Achaia'. In other words, they provided an admirable ensemble of attributes of belonging to a Christ-believing group which was recognized as applicable to other such groups in neighbouring areas. Paul focuses on their faith (*pistis*) as the key feature (it was mentioned first in v. 3), knowledge of which has now spread so far that he has no need to say anything about them, because others tell him what success he had among the Thessalonians, how they turned from idols 'to serve a living and true God' (cf. 1 THESS B.1). Archaeological, epigraphic, numismatic, and literary evidence shows that a number of pagan cults were present in Thessalonica in Paul's time, including those of the Egyptian goddesses Serapis and Isis (who offered salvation and eternal life), Dionysus, Zeus, Asclepius, Demeter, and, most importantly, Cabirus (Edson 1948; Donfried 1985; Jewett 1986; Kloppenborg 1993). This was not unusual in the empire which exhibited a pullulation of beliefs (MacMullen 1981: 1). The pagan cults of Thessalonica represent some of the outgroups against whom the Thessalonians must now seek to distinguish themselves so as to build and maintain a positive

social identity. v. 10, Paul concludes by mentioning that now they are waiting for his (i.e. God's) son from heaven, 'whom he raised from the dead—Jesus who rescues us from the wrath that is coming'. Here we see that Paul has managed to persuade his Gentile converts to accept deeply Jewish tradition relating to the Day of Anger when the wicked will be condemned and the good saved. The notion of 'the day (of judgement)' is a common feature of Israelite end-time speculation (see Joel 2:1–2; Zech 9:16; Mal 3:1–2; for the last judgement, see 1 *Enoch* 1:1–9; 2 Esd 7.33–44; *Apoc. Abr.* 29.14–29). At the same time, this brief reference to what the future holds for them, although greatly developed later in the letter, further contributes to differentiating the Thessalonians as a positively valued in-group from negatively valued outsiders (Esler 2000). Myths of the future developed by millennial movements in modern pre-industrial settings virtually always serve this function.

Paul's Ministry in Thessalonica (2:1–16)

(2:1–4) The Divine Basis for Paul's Initial Visit vv. 1–2, addressing them again in the language of fictive kinship as 'brothers', Paul reminds the Thessalonians how fruitful has been the work which he began among them (2:1). He then offers some precise information about his inauguration of his mission in Thessalonica, mentioning that, in spite of the suffering and abuse he (and presumably Silvanus and Timothy) previously experienced (*hubristhentes*: physically assaulted and dishonoured) in Philippi, with God's aid (lit. in our God) he courageously preached God's gospel to them in the midst of great conflict (*agōn*, 'opposition' NRSV). The ill-treatment in Philippi may be the same as that recorded in Acts 16:19–24, where Paul and Silas (i.e. Silvanus of 1 Thess 1:1) were dragged to the lawcourts, experienced hostility from the crowd, and were then stripped, flogged, and thrown into prison on the order of the magistrates. Later they were delivered (Acts 16:25–40) and moved on to inaugurate the mission in Thessalonica (Acts 17:1–9). In any event, the Thessalonians must have known of the events—which involved being grossly shamed in public in a culture where honour was the primary virtue—to which Paul alludes. His point is that, in spite of this extreme type of opposition, he persevered when he came to Thessalonica, even though there too he encountered conflict (*agōn*). Paul is not 'boasting' in our modern sense in saying this. He is doing what any honourable first-century Mediterranean man would do—setting out the foundation for his claim to respect and to authority. Moreover, the references to conflict in Philippi and then in Thessalonica illustrate the extremely competitive, indeed violent, context in which Paul's efforts to establish in-groups of Christ-believers had been conducted in the face of the actions of opposing out-groups.

v. 3, Paul now begins to make more explicit the basis and nature of his activity and status. His appeal (*paraklēsis*) refers here to his initial preaching, whereas elsewhere in the letter *paraklēsis* relates to his exhortations contained within it (so 4:1). Paul denies that the source of his preaching was error, impurity, or deception, although he does not say precisely what charges against him led to this denial; presumably the Thessalonians did know (Best 1972: 93–4). It is even unclear whether he is responding to attacks from outside or inside the

Christ-movement, or from Israelites or Gentiles. v. 4, his authority comes from God. He has been approved by God to be entrusted to preach the gospel, and so he does, not to please men but the God who scrutinizes our hearts (see Jer 11:20; 1 Sam 16:7). In Mediterranean terms, Paul presents himself as the loyal client of his divine patron, who knows him fully and has entrusted him to act as a broker to others, by distributing his benefaction (the gospel) to people who will become his clients, indeed his children.

(2:5–12) Their Behaviour and Example vv. 5–6, Paul did not flatter them, that is to say, did not please the Thessalonians by attributing to them honour they did not possess, nor try to exploit them for personal gain. Nor did he seek honour (*doxa*, 'praise' NRSV) from anyone at all. Again, it is unclear precisely from which figures Paul might be distancing himself here. One possibility consists of the wandering philosophers, such as Cynics (Malherbe 1989b: 38–9) and magicians of this period, whose sincerity was questionable (see Lucian, *De morte Peregrini*, 3, 13). Alternatively or in addition, Paul may have in mind other members of the Christ-movement, such as the wandering apostles and prophets bent on living off congregations who are mentioned in the *Didache* (11.3–12), with something like the latter suggested by the next verse. v. 7, although as Christ's authorized apostle, that is, emissary or broker (*apostolos*), he held a position of considerable honour in relation to the Thessalonians, he was gentle (that is, not insisting on the benefits which rightly belonged to such an honourable position), like a wet-nurse or nursing mother comforting her children. For the word translated here as 'gentle' (*ēpioi*) there is a variant, 'infants' (*nēpioi*), which is somewhat better attested in the manuscript tradition, but the total inversion of the imagery in the rest of the verse which this reading would produce, with the Thessalonians now the children, suggests 'gentle' was the original form.

Malherbe (1989b) has drawn attention to the similarity of Paul's language in 2:1–12 to that used of ideal Cynic philosophers (as opposed to money-grubbing charlatans) by Dio Chrysostom (40–120 CE), even to the extent of Dio's using the image of the nurse to epitomize how a good philosopher will treat his audience. Malherbe's (ibid. 46, 48) conclusion, however, that Paul's use of such language suggests he need not have been replying to an attack on him, is improbable. In this conflict-ridden and group-oriented culture it was inevitable that Paul would be attacked (2:1–2) and not at all surprising that in reply he would avail himself of a convenient stock discourse, in this case, perhaps, that of genuine travelling philosophers versus false ones (Koester 1979: 42). This discourse had probably become conventional long before Dio, writing after Paul, had utilized it himself.

v. 8, the sentiment here builds on v. 7. Because Paul cared so deeply for them (*homeiromenoi*—a rare word; Koester 1979: 42) and they had become very dear (*agapētoi*) to him, he gladly decided to share with them not only the gospel but his whole being. Paul is here drawing upon the strong bonds of love and group solidarity that characterized family life in this culture. v. 9 provides a specific interpretation of how Paul shared his whole being with them. He asks the Thessalonians, (his) 'brothers', to recall that while he preached the gospel of God to them he worked night and day so as not to be a burden on

them. Paul here reveals that he preached to the Thessalonians in a very low-status occupation as a craftsman of some sort (perhaps a tent-maker—Acts 18:3), not in the context of a synagogue, thus providing further evidence for the Thessalonians being a Gentile community (see 1 THESS 1:9). Hock (1980) has amply described how a craftsman's shop would have functioned as a locus for Paul's evangelism. That Paul could celebrate manual labour in this way suggests that his addressees also belonged to the non-élite in Thessalonica (Jewett 1993). This observation finds further support in the fact that there is not a single member of this congregation socially prominent enough for Paul to address by name (unlike the case in Corinth). v. 10, the Thessalonians are witnesses that he worked among them in a manner that was holy, just, and blameless. Behind this assertion may lie sentiments to the contrary that Paul was aware were being expressed about him in the city.

vv. 11–12, once again Paul returns to the pervasive family imagery of the letter, although now changing its gender, by saying that they know he treated each one of them like a father his children (v. 11), urging (*parakalein*), encouraging (*paramuthein*), and offering witness (*marturein*, 'pleading' NRSV) as to how they should 'lead a life' (lit. walk, *peripatein*) worthily of the God who called them into his kingdom and glory (v. 12). At the end of v. 12 the reference to God's kingdom and glory reinforces the elevated and honourable nature of the group to which they belong and the glorious destiny in store for them. These are central themes in the letter as a whole. They emphasize the measureless superiority of the Christ-believing in-group to all out-groups in this environment.

The word *peripatein* in v. 12 is important (it also appears at 4:1, twice, and 4:12). It also occurs in Romans (4 times), 1 Corinthians (twice), 2 Corinthians (5 times), and Galatians (once). In the NT the verb can mean just 'to walk around' (Mk 2:9), but Paul uses it for the 'walk' of life. According to Seesemann (1967: 944–5), Paul relies on it in exhortatory contexts, particularly in the moral sense, a meaning which could only have derived from the LXX, since it is unknown in classical Greek. An LXX example of this meaning is at 2 Kings 20:3 (where Hezekiah says he has walked before God in truth and with a perfect heart) and Eccl 11:9; Sir 13:13. Yet a moral or ethical dimension alone is too narrow for v. 12 (4:1 and 4:12); it essentially means 'to live' or, within a social identity framework, 'to adopt a particular identity'.

(2:13–16) The Response of the Thessalonians Dispute rages as to whether these verses are authentic to the letter or constitute a later insertion. The case for inauthenticity was argued by Baur (1873–5), and has recently been supported by many scholars including Pearson (1971), Boers (1976: 151–2), Koester (1979: 38), and Schmidt (1983). A much more limited interpolation theory regards 2:16c as a marginal gloss inserted into the text after the sack of Jerusalem in 70 CE. Typical reasons for inauthenticity (see Koester 1979: 38) include the unnecessary resumption of the thanksgiving at 2:13, interruption of the close connection between 2:12 and 2:17, alleged non-Pauline use of Pauline terms (such as *mimētai*, 'imitators', in 2:14), the characterization of the Judeans in 2:14 as in conflict with Paul's attitude in Rom 9–11, lack of a historical point of reference for the last phrase in 2:16 ('the wrath to the end has come upon them') before 70 CE, and the absence of any allusion to these verses in 2 Thessalonians. Koester also considers a polemic against a third party would destroy the writer–recipient relationship he is trying to reshape.

It is submitted, however, that the better view is that 2:13–16 are authentic, as argued by Okeke (1980–1), Donfried (1984), Jewett (1986: 36–41), and Weatherly (1991), to name a few. There is no reason in the textual tradition to doubt their authenticity and the arguments just mentioned are unpersuasive. Thus, v. 13, beginning with a thanksgiving, marks a natural transition from Paul's message to its impact on the Thessalonians. As to *mimētai*, Paul uses the very word and in a very similar construction at 1 Thess 1:6 (and also at 1 Cor 4:16 and 11:1), so its use at 2:14 is Pauline. Okeke (1980–1) has offered an explanation for why we should not expect Paul to follow the same argument in this letter as when addressing the Romans. This particular point can be made more emphatically, however. A social-identity approach to Galatians has revealed how far Paul will go in stereotyping Israelites even when they are a part of his congregations (Esler 1998); we would expect such attitudes to apply *a fortiori* when his audience is Gentile, as in Thessalonica. Finally, there are other possible candidates for the catastrophe referred to in 2:16, such as the riot and massacre that occurred in Jerusalem in 48 CE (Jos. *Ant.* 20.112 and *J.W.* 2.224–7; Jewett 1986: 37–9).

Even among the critics in favour of 2:13–16 being authentic, however, one sometimes encounters a wish that the verses were not Pauline (see Jewett 1986: 41), perhaps reflecting a modern aversion to the powerful in-group/out-group antipathies of the first-century Mediterranean world which are largely alien to modern North American and northern European culture and which interpreters are often slow to recognize in NT texts.

v. 13, Paul thankfully recalls their acceptance of God's word, which is active among those who believe. Here he again shows his closeness to them and also reminds them of the nature of the power present in this group, as already mentioned in 1:4. The implication is that none of the other groups in Thessalonica have anything like this to offer. v. 14, his Thessalonian 'brothers' became imitators of the Christ-following congregations (*ekklēsiai*) in Judea (who had been persecuted by other Judeans (*Ioudaioi*), because they experienced just the same treatment at the hands of their own fellow-countrymen. To translate *Ioudaioi* as 'the Jews' (with NRSV and most other trs.) misses the extent to which this people (whether living in Judea, Galilee, or further afield) were regarded by others (and saw themselves) as oriented to Judea, and to Jerusalem and the temple within it. This point becomes very clear in Book II of Josephus' *Jewish Antiquities*, when Cyrus sends the Judeans home to Judea; thereafter in this text Josephus almost always refers to them under this name.

For the nature of the opposition to the Thessalonians, cf. 1 THESS B.4. The opposition in Judea must have been somewhat different, as it would have drawn upon peculiarly Israelite opposition to the Christ-movement, of the sort perhaps that had previously motivated Paul himself to try to destroy it (Gal 1:13; Phil 3:6).

v. 15, Paul now attacks the Judeans just as we would expect once we shed modern notions of ethical behaviour and attempt to enter the harsh first-century Mediterranean world of violent stereotypification and vilification of out-groups. He denigrates the Judeans as those who killed the Lord Jesus (even though he had been crucified by the Romans) and the prophets and who persecuted him, acting in a way not pleasing to God and opposed to all human beings. In the last phrase Paul seems to go so far as to pick up and mouth for the benefit of his ex-idolatrous converts negative views on Judeans current in certain Graeco-Roman circles (see Stern 1974–80; Esler 1987: 76–80). The idea that the Judeans had killed the prophets was a common one among early Christ-followers (see Lk 13:34; Mt 5:12; 23:31, 35, 37; Acts 7:52; Rom 11:3). References to killing prophets are found in Scripture (1 Kings 19:10) and from extra-scriptural accounts, as in important texts such as the *Lives of the Prophets* and the *Martyrdom of Isaiah*. v. 16, thus the Judeans have hindered him from preaching to the Gentiles so that they might be saved. A possible mechanism for such hindrance emerges in the picture of how the Judeans interfered with Paul's mission in Philippi as recounted in Acts 16:11–24, if that account is historical. The result is that the Judeans have always filled their sins to the brim, perhaps referring to the repeated failure of Israel during history, and the anger has finally caught up with them. Although it is not easy to find an incident corresponding to the statement that the anger has come upon the Judeans, one possibility is the riot and massacre which occurred in Jerusalem in 48 CE (Jewett 1986: 37–8).

The Present Situation (2:17–3:13)

Paul recounts his long-standing desire to visit them, and how he sent Timothy instead. Generally, Funk (1967) argues that the traditional Greek epistolary topic of friendship (*philophronēsis*; see Koskenniemi 1956) has been transformed into a new topic of the Christian letter, 'apostolic parousia'.

(2:17–20) Paul's Desire to Visit the Thessalonians v. 17, Paul has previously described himself as a nursing mother (2:7) and as a father (2:11) to them; now he retains the familial imagery but presents himself as (for a short period) having become an orphan in relation to them—but physically, not emotionally. The notion of 'absent in body but present in mind' was a common topic in Graeco-Roman epistolography (Funk 1967: 264; Stowers 1986: 59). The expression of his eagerness to come to them, part of the friendly letter framework, is a fairly common one in Paul's letters (cf. Rom 1:11; 15:23; 2 Cor 8:16–17; Phil 1:8). v. 18, yet although he earnestly sought to be physically with them again and wanted to come to them on a number of occasions, Satan prevented him. The idea of there being a hindrance to his coming is one of the structural features Funk isolates as belonging to the apostolic parousia (also found at Rom 1:13; 15:22). Moreover, the reference to Satan suggests Paul senses a supernatural force thwarting his desired visit to the Thessalonians (Best 1972: 126–7). vv. 19–20 provide the basis for Paul's missing the Thessalonians and desiring to be with them. For it is they who are his hope, joy, and crown of his claim to honour; in the presence of his Lord Jesus at his parousia they will be his honour and his joy. Here the typical Mediterranean connection of the honour of the individual and the publicly acknowledged worth of the group to which he or she belongs comes through loud and clear. At his parousia Jesus will reward those who are his own, so that those responsible for their conversion, here Paul, will earn a massive accretion of honour and joy from so public an acknowledgement.

(3:1–5) Timothy's Mission vv. 1–2*a*, because he was no longer able to endure (i.e. his separation from them) he resolved to stay behind alone in Athens and send Timothy. In Acts, Paul moves from Thessalonica to Athens (17:16–34), with a brief intervening stay in Beroea (17:9–15). vv. 2–5, according to Funk's parousia schema, this is the despatch of the emissary aspect (also see 1 Cor 4:17; 16:12; 2 Cor 8:18–24; 9:3–5; 12:17–18; Phil 2:19–23), usually containing (1) a statement that someone has been or will be sent, here 1 Thess 3:2*a* (just noted); (2) his credentials, here 1 Thess 3.2*b* (Timothy is his brother and fellow-worker in God for the proclamation of the gospel of Christ); and (3) purpose, here 1 Thess 3:2*c*–4 (Timothy was to strengthen and encourage them in the faith, lest anyone be agitated by the current tribulations, which they knew would come, just as he had foretold when he was with them). In v. 5, Paul offers a summary of his purpose in sending Timothy: because he could no longer endure, he sent Timothy to learn about their faith, lest the tempter had been successful or his labour fruitless.

(3:6–10) Thankful Receipt of Timothy's Report v. 6, Timothy has recently returned to Paul bearing the good news of their faith (*pistis*) and love (*agapē*), that they always have a good memory of him and that they want to see him as much as he wants to see them. The first element of this good news is that the Thessalonians are preserving two parts of the (characteristic) Pauline triad mentioned at 1 Thess 1:3, namely, faith and love; these are vital attributes of the group identity Paul has wanted them to acquire. Nevertheless, Timothy's (or Paul's) omission of any mention of the third attribute—hope—may be deliberate, given what he will say to them later (4:10, 13). As the founder of a congregation who wants them to imitate him, he naturally rejoices that he is still so warmly regarded by them. According to Funk, vv. 6–9 relate to the benefits which accrue from the apostolic parousia—both to Paul and to his addressees (see also Rom 1:13; 15:32; 1 Cor 4:18–19, 21; Phil 2:19). vv. 7–8, Paul states that their faith has encouraged him in a time of every distress (*anagkē*) and persecution (*thlipsis*); if they stand firm he can go on living. Here 'faith' is a very general word denoting their whole identity as Christ-believers. Paul does not specify the affliction and tribulation and it is not possible to correlate this information with the descriptions of his activity in Acts at around this time, in either Beroea (Acts 17:10–15), Athens (Acts 17:16–34), or Corinth (Acts 18:1–17). This is another reason against putting too much reliance on Acts as a historical source for Paul's experience at this time, a problem discussed in I THESS B.I in relation to the very different pictures given by Paul and Luke of the foundation of the congregation in Thessalonica. vv. 9–10, because of the Thessalonians, Paul is able to offer joyful thanksgiving to God.

v. 10, day and night he prays most earnestly to see them and—but now a darker note intrudes—to amend the shortcomings (*husterēmata*) of their faith. Shortcomings? Hitherto there has been no *explicit* mention of any deficiency in their faith (which here has the same meaning of Christ-following identity as at 3:7), even if a lack of hope was strongly implied at

3:6. Yet Paul is now opening up the theme that even among his splendid and beloved Thessalonians there are problems. Timothy's report could not, after all, have been a uniformly positive one. Accordingly, even if Funk (1967) is right to see in v. 10 an invocation for divine approval and support for the apostolic parousia (as also in Rom 1:10; 15:30–2; 1 Cor 4:19; 16:7), the fact that an absent Paul might need to be present in epistolary form to correct as well as to praise must not be forgotten.

(3:11–13) Prayer for the Thessalonians v. 11, Paul now begins the detailed text of a prayer (especially signalled by verbs in the optative mood in vv. 11, 12) which he had described in summary form in v. 10 and which continues until the end of v. 13. The first invocation (as in v. 10) is that God their Father and their Lord Jesus might guide his way to them. v. 12, the second invocation of the prayer begins to pick up the shortcomings mentioned in v. 11: Paul prays that God may make them increase and abound in love (*agapē*) for one another and for all, just as Paul does for them. Although they are characterized by love already (1 Thess 3:6), Paul prays that they will show even more love. There is room for improvement. It is significant that this love must not only be directed to the members of the congregation (a reality to be designated, quite naturally, as *philadelphia*, 'brotherly love', at 4:9) but also to everyone, that is to all outside the congregation. This represents a significant, indeed countercultural, modification of group-oriented ways of behaving which were then the norm. The theme will be taken up again later (4:12).

v. 13, thirdly, Paul prays that they (God and Jesus) may strengthen the Thessalonians' hearts in holiness so that they may be blameless before their God and Father at the parousia of their Lord Jesus with all his saints. This invocation directs the recipients of the letter to the future dimension of their existence, the return of Jesus. The omission of hope in 1 Thess 3:6 suggested certain difficulties with their understanding of what the future held in store and, before proceeding to details (4:13–18), Paul reminds them in abbreviated form of the goal of their existence. The Lord will return and they must be blameless in holiness when he does. The word 'holiness' (*hagiōsunē*) refers to the Spirit-charged zone of existence they have entered by joining the congregation; its opposites are 'impurity' (*akatharsia*, 4:7, and *porneia*, 4:3), the label for the filthy world of idolatry and immorality which they have left behind (see I THESS 4:3).

Living a Life Pleasing to God (4:1–12)

Lührmann (1990: 245) refers to this material, reflecting Paul's initial preaching, as 'ethics'. But 'ethics' as a differentiated province of human activity with a heavily individualistic tendency is quite a modern concept, having acquired its current status since the time of Kant (1724–1804). In the ancient world there was discussion of appropriate ways to behave, but set within wider frameworks of domestic or civic life. From the perspective of social-identity theory, on the other hand, norms for behaviour are values which define acceptable and non-acceptable attitudes and behaviours for group members. Norms bring order and predictability to the environment and thus assist in-group members to construe the world and to choose appropriate behaviour in new and ambiguous situations. Thus they maintain and enhance group identity (Brown 1988: 42–8; Esler 1998: 45). Even if critics are correct in seeing Israelite tradition, such as that found in the so-called Holiness Code of Lev 17–26 (Hodgson 1982), as lying behind some of what Paul says in 1 Thess 4:1–12, the usefulness of a social-identity approach to the material would persist. Throughout Israelite history norms, derived from the law and its interpretation, served to differentiate Israel from other groups (Esler 1998: 82–6) and Paul's reappropriation of some of those norms within a setting of the novel intergroup differentiation inaugurated with the establishment of congregations of Christ-followers is unsurprising.

(4:1–2) Keeping the Traditions v. 1, 'Finally, brothers', says Paul, thus indicating that he is moving on to a *new* series of points relating to the maintenance of their group identity which he has just signalled (in 3:6–13) is not quite as good as it should be. He wants them to 'walk' (*peripatein*: cf. 1 THESS 2:12) and to please God in accordance with the traditions they had previously received (*parelabete*) from him (no doubt when he founded the congregation), and thus to do better and better. Paul uses the word *peripateō* to create an *inclusio* in 4:1–12, by placing it (twice) at the beginning of the passage (v. 1) and once at the end (v. 12). We are justified in translating it broadly, 'be of a particular identity', an identity which certainly includes moral norms, rather than the narrower 'behave in a particular way'. The exhortation to 'please God', reminds us that a major foundation for normative behaviour among this group is the very personal one of pleasing their heavenly Father (and patron). v. 2, Paul specifically reminds them of the existence of commands, that is, the instructions relating to norms, which he had previously given 'in our Lord Jesus Christ'. The last phrase indicates that these are distinctive to Christ-followers; they are emblems of group-belonging.

(4:3–8) Purity v. 3a, God's will is their sanctification (*hagiasmos*). Koester (1979: 43) reasonably moves away from too individualistic an interpretation by suggesting that *hagiasmos* should not be understood as a task of moral perfection for the individual, but as the reassessment of the values for dealing with each other in everyday life (i.e. it concerns relationships). Yet this really fails to bring out the full significance of this word. As suggested elsewhere (Esler 1998: 157–8), sanctification language in 1 Thessalonians (which covers *hagios* and *hagiōsunē* at 3:13, *hagiasmos* here and at 4:4 and 7, and *hagiazō* at 5:23) provides a semantic framework for expressing the ideal identity of his Gentile converts parallel to the language of righteousness which Paul reactively appropriates from Israelite tradition and deploys in Galatians and Romans when the Christ-following groups he addresses also include Israelites (Esler 1998: 141–77). This is vital language in the letter relating to norms which serves to encapsulate the very distinctive identity of the Thessalonian in-group in contrast to idolatrous out-groups. vv. 3b–6 list a number of aspects to this identity, with vv. 7–8 summarizing the position. v. 3b, the first dimension to their 'sanctification' is that they refrain from *porneia*, which probably means sexual sin of all types (Best 1972: 161), which Paul presumably implies was characteristic of the idolatrous world they had left behind. Thus the norm (of sexual propriety) is firmly embedded in a contrast between in-group and out-group.

v. 4, is one of the most difficult verses in the letter. (God also wills that) each one of them should know 'to acquire' (or, perhaps, 'to keep'—*ktasthai*; NRSV has 'control') his *skeuos* ('vessel') in sanctification (*hagiasmos*) and honour. There are two main options: (1) 'to keep or control one's body', which involves giving *ktasthai* a somewhat unusual meaning, or (2) 'to acquire one's wife'. As to (1), sometimes in the post-NT Greek world (but not before) the body is called the container of the soul (Maurer 1971: 359). But Paul does refer to human bodies at 2 Cor 4:7 as 'clay vessels', bearing a treasure. Maurer (p. 365) says the reference is not to the bodies as bearing the soul but the message, but why should not this be the sense in 4:7? This interpretation of *skeuos* as body, preferred by a number of patristic writers (such as Tertullian and Chrysostom), in spite of a rather unusual sense for *ktasthai*, is the most likely meaning. Lührmann (1990: 245–7) argues strongly that *skeuos* means 'body' to include men and women—*anthrōpoi*—as in 1 Cor 7 (which assumes *adelphos* and *philadelphia* as used in 1 Thessalonians do cover both genders). This meaning also seems far better adapted to the reference to sexual misconduct in the previous verse and to what follows in v. 6 (see below).

As to (2), there is a Jewish but not a Greek background for calling a woman a vessel (Maurer 1971: 361–2: 'to use as a vessel', 'to make one's vessel', are to be regarded as established euphemisms for sexual intercourse). If so *ktasthai* (present tense) in an ingressive sense ('to gain') would mean to marry (as a defence against fornication) and in a durative sense ('to possess'—which would normally require the perfect tense) would mean to hold their own wives in esteem (as a defence against fornication—thus the phrase would correspond exactly to 1 Cor 7:2). This interpretation also fits quite well with v. 6 which would then be a warning against adultery with the wife of a member of the congregation. But this interpretation involves an unpleasant nuance of *skeuos* (women as containers for semen) which is unknown among Greek authors and is found only in some fairly erotic passages in Israelite works (Bassler 1995: 55).

There are other, less likely, possibilities for *skeuos*. Donfried (1985: 342) argues that it means the penis, being a reference to the strong phallic symbolism in the cults of Dionysus, Cabirus, and Samothrace prevalent in Thessalonica. With *ktasthai* it means 'to gain control over one's penis, or over the body with respect to sexual matters'. Bassler (1995) makes an interesting new suggestion that it refers to one's virgin partner.

v. 5, Paul contrasts this behaviour with its opposite, the lustful passion of the Gentiles who do not know God. It seems much more plausible that 'lustful passion' is a reference to how the idolatrous Gentiles treat their bodies rather than their wives. Graeco-Roman wives were meant to live respectable lives at home, bearing their children and attending to domestic affairs. Greek or Roman men passionately involved with their wives were regarded as oddities. Best's (1972: 165) attribution to Paul of the notion that 'pagan marriage is motivated by lust' is culturally indefensible. v. 6a, Paul offers another piece of advice, beginning with an infinitive, whose connection with what has preceded is difficult. It could be a new topic: '(It is God's will—understood from v. 3—that the Thessalonian converts) should not wrong (*huperbainein*) or defraud (*pleonektein*; NRSV has 'exploit') his brother in commerce (*pragmati*)'. This is unlikely, since it breaks up a chain of thought that is otherwise completely devoted to sexual misconduct decried in v. 3 and *pragma* in the singular is not used of commerce (Best 1972: 167). It is preferable to interpret *pragma* as 'matter' (so NRSV) or 'area', referring back to the misuse of one's body in the lustful manner of pagans. In this context *huperbainein* and *pleonektein* could have the meanings just attributed to them, in which case Paul would be warning the Thessalonians not to engage in sexual misconduct with the wives or husbands of other members of the congregation. But Paul is unlikely to have introduced such a limitation. What he is actually saying is that they should not 'outdo' (*huperbainein*) or 'gain the advantage over' (*pleonektein*) their brothers in the area of sexual conduct, that is, stop acting like the pagans around them for whom sexual conquests were a matter of pride and the more one achieved the more one had to boast about. Such competition was typical behaviour among unrelated males in this culture (Paul also attacks the same kind of attitudes and practices in Gal 5:26; Esler 1998: 230). Once again, Paul is differentiating this group from the sinful outsiders. v. 6*b–c*, he reminds them that God will take vengeance on this behaviour just as he had previously told them. There is a strong context for God as avenger in Israelite tradition (Deut 32:35; Ps 99:8; Mic 5:15; Nah 1:2).

v. 7, Paul begins to sum up the discussion initiated at v. 3 by reminding them of the rival brands of identity on offer: either the sanctification (*hagiasmos*), to which God has called them, or impurity (*akatharsia*), here (like the instance at 2 Cor 12:21) being related to the condition and product of *porneia* in v. 3. These words describe the stark alternatives available to in-group and out-group. v. 8, Paul next reminds them of the divine dimension to the norms that are integral to their identity: the one who 'disregards', or 'rejects' (*athetein*), does not disregard a human being but the God who puts the Holy Spirit *into* them. Paul has already reminded them of the Spirit (see 1 Thess 1:5), which above all means the powerful charismatic phenomena associated with having, in effect, God within, and he now reiterates this message in the context of group norms in the area of sexual propriety.

(4:9–12) Brotherly Love v. 9, now Paul turns to another subject, brotherly love (*philadelphia*), although still within the broad subject of the shortcomings announced at 3:10 and the need to abound even more in their *apapē* mentioned at 3:12. Brotherly love is something that Paul says he has no need to write about because they have been 'God-taught' (*theodidaktoi*) to love (*agapan*) one another.

Although there is a treatise by Plutarch on the subject, the word *philadelphia* is rare in early texts of the Christ-movement. Paul uses *philadelphia* only once elsewhere (Rom 12:10), and there are only a few instances in the rest of the NT (Heb 13:1; 1 Pet 1:22; 2 Pet 1:7 (twice)). The adjective *philadelphos* occurs at 1 Pet 3:8. There are only three instances in the Septuagint, at 4 Macc 13:23, 26; 14:1 (which Klauck (1990) sees as a source for Paul), while *philadelphos* also appears, at 2 Macc 15:14; 4 Macc 13:21; 15:10. Perhaps the connection of 'Philadelphos' with the Ptolemies has discouraged its wider use in biblical texts. Betz (1978: 232) notes that there is no

obvious explanation why this term was regarded as proper in the Christian context, since it was apparently considered as just part of *agapē* and there was no further need to explain it; it may have come to Paul from Hellenized Judaism. Aasgaard (1997) has argued for striking parallels between Plutarch's understanding of *philadelphia* and Paul's thought on the subject.

Yet in a context in which Paul was intent on maintaining the appropriateness of kinship patterns from the surrounding culture to his Thessalonian congregation, the use of a word at home in Greek perceptions of the family had a lot to recommend it. More particularly, brotherly love characterizes the alternative to behaving like unrelated males always in competition, which he criticized in v. 6*a*. Lying close to the heart of the identity Paul is recommending to the Thessalonians is the model of harmonious relations among a respectable family in the surrounding culture (Esler 2000). While the reference to their brotherly love at v. 9 is the most obvious example, the word *adelphos* occurs four times in the passage (4:1, 6, 10 (twice)).

Theodidaktos is unattested prior to Paul; he may have coined the word. He could be alluding to Lev 19:18 (so Lührmann 1990: 248), or to Isa 54:13 or Jer 31:33–4, but this is unlikely for a Gentile congregation. Marshall (1982: 115) has a good explanation: Paul is saying that the Spirit empowers humans to love. This is in accord with Gal 5:22 (see Esler 1998: 203). Kloppenborg (1993) has suggested another source of *philadelphia*, and *theodidaktos*, namely, that Paul is utilizing the local popularity of the Dioscuri, Castor and Pollux, whose devotion to one another was widely regarded as exemplifying *philadelphia*, and that *theodidaktoi* evokes the Dioscuri as a pattern for imitation. But such a derivation is highly unlikely from the author of 1 Thess 1:9. How is it possible, *contra* Kloppenborg, that two *pagan* gods could offer the Thessalonians 'an appropriate mimetic ideal in a situation in which disparities in moral character lead to rivalry and tension' (1993: 237)?

v. 10*a*, Paul praises them for showing *agapē* to all the brothers in the whole of Macedonia, which brings out the fundamental importance of group solidarity, a typical theme in this culture. vv. 10*b*–11, he urges them to do even better and to make it their ambition to live quietly, to mind their own affairs, and to work with their hands as he had previously warned them. The most likely explanation for this advice is that Paul wanted his audience, probably urban craftsmen and labourers of low status, to keep a low profile and therefore avoid attracting antipathy from out-groups for reasons discussed in 1 THESS B.4. Within their social level, Paul was suggesting that they live the quiet, hardworking life of honourable men (see 1 THESS 4:12). Hock (1980: 46–7) believes that this is a recommendation to keep out of politics (by paying special levies, going on embassies to Rome, entertaining the governor, undertaking public services). Such a withdrawal from public life was especially identified with the Epicureans and many more in the first century, sometimes being coupled with advocacy of philosophers of retirement and working with one's own hands. Yet Hock's proposal seems socially unrealistic in relation to a more likely audience of the urban poor who would never have been in a financial position to engage in such activities in the first place, let alone to withdraw from them. v. 12, Paul ends this section with a purpose clause: so that they may adopt a respectable identity (*peripatein euschēmonōs*; NRSV has 'behave properly towards') towards outsiders (*hoi exō*) and be dependent on no one. Thus Paul concludes with *peripatein*, the word used twice when he opened this discussion (4:1).

The Lord's Coming (4:13–5:11)

These verses deal in some detail with the future destiny of those who believe in Christ and, to a lesser extent, with those who do not. The letter has previously referred to the future in store (1:10), especially the parousia of Christ (2:19; 3:13), but now we have the events and their significance set out in some detail. Although the word 'eschatology' has been applied by NT scholars to this subject for over a century now (as an example, see Best 1972: 180), the various (and differing) theological agendas that have become attached to that word have left its meaning rather obscure, except in the vanishingly rare case of critics who indicate precisely what they mean by it. Accordingly, in what follows the data in 4:13–5:11 will be considered within two other frameworks which, although derived from social-scientific research, have the potential to throw light on this absorbing picture of the future dating to the very early stages of the Christ-movement.

First, within social-identity theory (a sub-area of social psychology—cf. 1 THESS c.5–8), a group's distinctive orientation towards the future can help foster among the members a cognitive sense of belonging to the group, and also nourish the evaluative and emotional dimensions of membership. In other words, the members tell themselves who they are—and in a very positive way—in relation to where they are going. A striking modern example of this is the Hausa, a group of Sudanese Muslims, who spend their whole life as if they are undertaking a pilgrimage, a *haj*, to Mecca, even though most of them never get there (Esler 1998: 42). Secondly, social anthropologists have investigated many groups, generally (although not always) suffering from some form of colonial oppression or disturbance of traditional ways of life, who develop or revive narratives of a coming transformation of the world which will leave them radically restored to their proper place and, often, destroy those who oppress them (Duling 1996; Esler 1993; 1994: 93–109). These phenomena are generally referred to as instances of 'millennialism' or 'millenarianism'. Examples of millenarian mythopoiesis, discussed elsewhere (Esler 1993: 187–8; 1994: 101–4), include the ghost dance among North American Indians in the late nineteenth century and the cargo cults of twentieth-century Melanesia (in the South Pacific). Jewett (1986: 161–78) has usefully applied millenarian ideas to 1 and 2 Thessalonians (the latter letter he regards as authentic). Millennialism provides a second useful etic framework for contextualizing this part of 1 Thessalonians. It is worth noting that although deprivation of some sort cannot simply be said to explain the origin of millennial movements, it is often one aspect of the experience of the membership and provides an important part of the context that needs to be taken into account in understanding its futurist myth.

(4:13–18) The Circumstances of this Coming v. 13, Paul wants them to know that they should not grieve about those who 'are sleeping' (NRSV 'who have died'), 'as others do who have no hope'. Apparently some of the people in Thessalonica whom Paul converted have died since and worries have arisen among the Thessalonians concerning their status at the parousia of Christ. Clearly, as already noted, belief in the parousia, even though it is a vision of the future heavily indebted to Israelite tradition, is embedded in this ex-Gentile group, so that the problem is whether those who die in faith beforehand will participate in Christ's glorious return. The sharp distinction between in-group and out-groups Paul maintains throughout the letter is evident here in the reference to 'the rest who have no hope'. Hope (*elpis*) was included at 1 Thess 1:3 as one of the three primary elements of the identity of Christ-followers and the fact that Paul is worried they might be deficient in hope also surfaces in Timothy's notable failure to include it in his report to Paul of the current condition of the Thessalonians (at 1 THESS 3:6). It is beside the point to suggest that it was not correct that the rest of men had no hope whatsoever (as does Best 1972: 185); Paul is using the notion of hope to differentiate Christ-followers from other groups; the (probably inaccurate) stereotypification of the others is essential to this strategy. v. 14, Paul sets out what should be the basis for their hope: if they believe that Jesus died and rose, so also will God bring with him those who have died (lit. fallen asleep) through Jesus. In millennial movements elsewhere the return of the ancestors is a common feature of the futurist myth. Here Paul links the inclusion in the parousia of those who have already died to the belief in the death and resurrection of Jesus which was central to their faith in him.

v. 15, first emphasizing the authority of what he is about to say (it is a 'word of the Lord'; v. 15*a*), Paul now expands upon the precise nature of the vindication he is holding out for those who have died. Those who are living, who survive to the parousia of the Lord, will not have any advantage over those who have died (v. 15*b*). It is difficult to know what Paul means by a 'word of the Lord' here. Possible meanings include a saying of Jesus (not otherwise extant), a statement by a prophet among the Christ-followers, a fragment of some unknown text, or (perhaps most likely) his own view but spoken as the Lord's agent and therefore the Lord's. It is also unclear whether the 'word of the Lord' relates only to the statement in v. 15 or whether it extends to the end of v. 17. The former is more likely, because Paul had presumably already told them the broad outline of what we have in vv. 16–17; v. 15 contains the new element that required to be supported by the appeal to authority.

vv. 16–17, the Lord himself—accompanied by a cry of command, the call of an angel, and the trumpet of God—will come down from heaven and those who have died in Christ will rise first, then those who are living, who survive, will be snatched up together with them in the clouds to a meeting with the Lord in the air, so to be with the Lord for ever. Here we have a futurist myth derived partly from Israelite tradition but given a new slant in the context of the belief in Christ's death and resurrection which saw him exalted to the right hand of God (Acts 2:33; Rom 8:34). The myth deals with Christ's descent (based on his preceding ascent to God) which presupposes a first-century cosmology in which heaven is located above the earth. The cry of command is probably to be taken as uttered by Jesus and as addressed to the dead that they should rise. A trumpet also appears in connection with resurrection and the end-time at 1 Cor 15:52 (also see Isa 27:13; Zeph 1:14–16). While most myths relate to past events, helping a particular group to gain access to its formative, primordial past (Eliade 1989), a myth of the future such as this is rather different. It serves to stress the goal rather than the basis of a social order and thus has a prescriptive rather than a proscriptive function (Doty 1986: 44–9; Esler 1993: 186). Paul's Thessalonian converts would have been reassured by the details of this narrative that another order of reality existed, and that the difficult events of their present and recent past were occurring within a context controlled by heavenly forces who would ultimately restore their fortunes beyond their wildest dreams. Yet although the creation of hope in a future vindication forms part of such mythopoiesis, it is not the end of the story. For a futurist myth such as this also creates an imaginary experience in the present of that which is to come, and thus reinforces the social identity of its addressees at a time when they are exposed to external threat (Esler 1994: 109).

(5:1–11) The Need for Wakefulness v. 1, Paul indicates that he does not need to tell them about dates and times, presumably because he has already done so. He does not want to become involved in the discussion of an end-time calendar. v. 2, what they already know is that the day of the Lord will come like a thief in the night, that is, quite unexpectedly. The 'day of the Lord' was well established in Israelite tradition. It was to be a time of joy for some and terror for others. Thus Isaiah had written that on 'that day' a great trumpet would sound and the scattered ones in Assyria and Egypt would come to worship the Lord on Jerusalem's holy mountain (Isa 27:13). Zephaniah, on the other hand, had presented a bleaker picture: a day that would be a day of wrath, of anguish and torment, of destruction and devastation, when the Lord would bring dire distress upon the people (Zeph 1:14–18). Paul must have imparted some of this material to his ex-idolatrous converts, no doubt painting a happy future for them and an unhappy one for sinful out-groups.

v. 3, Paul illustrates his previous statement with two connected examples showing how people will not escape. First, it is just when people are saying 'peace and security' (*eirēnē kai asphaleia*) that suddenly disaster overtakes them just as, secondly, the pain of childbirth comes upon a pregnant woman. The latter example is a commonplace of domestic human experience (although often mentioned as a sign of the End: Mk 13:8), but the former relates to the political realities of Thessalonica. Some coins minted at Thessalonica contained slogans with the similar words 'freedom and security', probably reflecting the advantages the local élite derived from Rome and the Roman imperial cult (Jewett 1986: 124). The 'peace' to which Paul refers is presumably the *Pax Romana*. Paul is alluding to the fragility of the comfortable relationship between the rulers of the city and Rome (Hendrix 1984), which could at any time suffer a disastrous reverse.

vv. 4–5, Paul introduces the imagery of light and darkness to distinguish between Christ-followers, whom the day (of anger) will not 'surprise . . . like a thief', and others in Thessalonica. The Christ-followers are all sons of light and sons of day who do not belong to night or darkness; by implication, then, the others are sons of night and sons of darkness who do not belong to light or day. Such a powerful dualism presents very

starkly the nature of the opposed identities of in-group and out-group, the first highly positive and the second very negative indeed. Here we have a good example of the stereotypical group-categorization characteristic of the way one group generates a favourable social identity for itself. vv. 6–7, Paul persists with his continuing process of group differentiation in a related area of imagery by exhorting them not to sleep like the others (by implication, people of the night) but to keep awake and be sober—for those who sleep and those who get drunk do so at night. v. 8, since he and they belong to the day, he says, they should be sober, thus reinforcing still further the reality of group differentiation using imagery of day and night which he began way back at v. 4. Yet now he adds a new element—they should do so having put on the breastplate of faith and love and the helmet of hope of salvation. In this latter clause he summons before his readers the triad of faith, love, and hope (and in that order) which he introduced in the third verse of the letter. This is really to pile identity-descriptors on identity-descriptors!

When Paul refers to putting on (*endusamenoi*) the breastplate of faith and love (*thōraka pisteōs kai agapēs*) and the hope of salvation for a helmet (*perikephalaian elpida sōtērias*), he is alluding either to Isa 59.17 or Wis 5:18 (which is presumably dependent on Isaiah), or both. The Isaian passage reads: 'He put on (*enedusato*) righteousness as a breastplate (*dikaiosunēn thōraka*) and placed the helmet of salvation (*perikephalaian sōtēriou*) on his head', while the one from Wisdom has: 'He will put on righteousness as a breastplate (*endusetai thōraka dikaiosunēn*), and he will don true judgement instead of a helmet.' Paul has changed the phrase 'breastplate of righteousness' to 'breastplate of faith and love', while adding the word 'hope' to the expression 'helmet of salvation', which he otherwise retains. Paul's treatment of the possible Septuagintal source(s) means, first, that faith and love represent a way of describing the condition of being a Christ-follower analogous to that expressed by 'righteousness'. Secondly, however, the alteration indicates that in writing to Gentiles he has deliberately chosen to substitute the former for the latter, presumably because he found 'righteousness' inappropriate for such an audience (Esler 1998: 156–7). The function fulfilled by the language of holiness in relation to a Gentile audience in 1 Thessalonians is served later in relation to mixed Israelite and Gentile groups in Galatians and Romans by the discourse of righteousness.

v. 9, Paul's statement that God has destined them not for anger but for obtaining salvation through their Lord Jesus Christ makes explicit for the first time the nature of the fate, the awesome wrath of God (see Zeph 1:14–18, noted above), hanging over out-groups, who are again sharply differentiated from the believers in Christ to whom salvation will be extended. The nature of that salvation is set out in 1 Thess 4:16–17, while the ambit of the anger is not. v. 10, Jesus Christ is described as the one who died for us so that 'awake or asleep' (that is, dead, as in 1 Thess 4:13–16), we will live together with him. This the first time in Paul's correspondence that we find the important formula 'Christ died for' with a further word or words indicating the person(s) for whom he died (also see 1 Cor 15:3; 2 Cor 5:14; 5:15; Rom 5:6; 5:8; 14:15). De Jonge (1990: 233–4) has argued that this expression, which preceded Paul's use of it since he cites it in 1 Cor 15:3 as a tradition he had received, always serves as a foundation for the claim that God's salvation has become reality or at least has been inaugurated, to highlight the new state of life into which Christ-followers have been transferred. Within a social identity framework, one might add that the notion of Jesus' death for his followers is what enables the creation of their identity and also fills it with positive evaluative and emotional dimensions. v. 11, the sentiment is similar to, while going a little further than, that of 4:18.

Final Exhortations and Greetings (5:12–28)

This section contain a series of largely unrelated pieces of advice, ending with prayers.

(5:12–13) Honouring Leaders vv. 12–13, Paul asks the Thessalonians to respect those who labour amongst them, who 'care for' (or, possibly, with the NRSV, 'have charge of') 'you . . . and admonish you'. He wants his addressees to esteem them very highly in love because of their work and to be at peace with one another. Best (1972: 226) reasonably suggests that we should not interpret these verses as indicating there was a ministry among the congregation in the city. The fact that the 'leaders' are described by their activities and not by titles suggests that they have none. Clearly Paul is at pains that the Thessalonians should not engage in the antagonistic conduct common among unrelated males in this culture.

(5:14–22) Christian Identity-Indicators Paul here strings together various aspects of desirable identity-indicators. Some of them are norms (that is, 'ethical' duties), but others, such as to rejoice and pray, are not. vv. 14–15, the statements here constitute what are essential norms for maintaining the identity of Christ-followers. It is noteworthy, however, that in spite of the group-differentiation that Paul has pursued throughout the letter, he specifically extends the scope of their doing good from the members of the congregation to everyone. There are limits to how far he will go with the process of group-categorization and certainly the all-too-common advocacy of violence against out-group members plays no part whatever in his perspective. vv. 16–18, rejoicing and continual prayer are essential aspects of their identity as Christ-followers. v. 19, they must not quench the Spirit, by which Paul means that they must permit the charismatic gifts associated with the coming of the Spirit—which was a major distinguishing feature of the movement and no doubt made it attractive to members, because of the euphoria Spirit-possession can produce. v. 20, prophecy is one of the gifts of the Spirit (see 1 Cor 12:10) and Paul calls on them not to despise it. vv. 21–2, Paul mentions further attitudes which should characterize the identity of the Thessalonians.

5:23–4 Prayer for the Thessalonians vv. 23–4, Paul prays that God will sanctify (hagiazō) them, thus seeking divine renewal of the sanctification he has already made clear was central to their new identity in contrast to the world of impurity (akatharsia) around them (1 Thess 4:7). Sanctification primarily refers to their present condition, but Paul then goes on to pray that they will be blameless at the parousia. The one who calls is faithful and he will effect this.

(5:25–8) Closing Prayer and Instructions v. 25, now he asks them to pray for him (and presumably Silvanus and Timothy); this enlivens the sense of his presence to them in the letter.

v. 26, the source of the holy kiss of the movement is unknown; possible sources include the historical Jesus, Judaism, or pagan religion. v. 27, suddenly Paul changes to first person singular, presumably because he has taken the stylus in his own hand to write the last few words (as at 1 Cor 16:21; Gal 6:11), and solemnly commands them to read the letter to all the brothers. It is hard to determine how all the brothers (and a textual variant adds 'holy' to brothers) relate to the Thessalonians mentioned in the first verse. Perhaps he means to ensure that those who first received the letter should read it aloud to everyone in a meeting of the congregation (Best 1972: 246–7). v. 28, Paul ends with a form of benediction which must have become conventional among Christ-followers.

REFERENCES

Aasgaard, R. (1997), 'Brotherhood in Plutarch and Paul: Its Role and Character', in H. Moxnes (ed.), *Constructing Early Christian Families: Family as Social Reality and Metaphor* (London: Routledge), 166–97.

Balch, D. L., Ferguson, E., and Meeks, W. A. (eds.) (1990), *Greeks, Romans, and Christians: Essays in Honor of Abraham J. Malherbe* (Minneapolis: Fortress).

Barclay, J. M. G. (1992), 'Thessalonica and Corinth: Social Contrasts in Pauline Christianity', *JSNT* 47: 49–74.

—— (1993), 'Conflict in Thessalonika', *CBQ* 53: 512–30.

Bassler, J. M. (1995), '*Skeuos*: A Modest Proposal for Illuminating Paul's Use of Metaphor in 1 Thessalonians 4:4', in White and Yarbrough (1995: 53–66).

Baur, F. C. (1873–5) *Paul: The Apostle of Jesus Christ* (London: Williams & Norgate). German original, *Paulus, der Apostel Jesu Christi* (1845).

Best, E. (1972), *A Commentary on the First and Second Epistles to the Thessalonians*, Black's New Testament Commentaries (London: Adam & Charles Black).

Betz, H. D. (1978), 'De fraterno amore (*Moralia* 478A–492D)', in H. D. Betz (ed.) (1978), *Plutarch's Ethical Writings and Early Christian Literature* (Leiden: E. J. Brill), 231–63.

Boers, H. (1976), 'The Form Critical Study of Paul's Letters, I Thessalonians as a Case Study', *NTS* 22: 140–58.

Brown, R. (1988), *Group Processes: Dynamics Within and Between Groups* (Oxford: Basil Blackwell).

Chapa, J. (1994), 'Is First Thessalonians a Letter of Consolation?', *NTS* 40: 150–60.

Collins, R. F. (ed.) (1990), *The Thessalonian Correspondence* (Leuven: Leuven University Press).

De Jonge, H. J. (1990), 'The Original Setting of the *Christos Apethanen Hyper* Formula', in Collins (1990: 229–35).

Donfried, K. P. (1984), 'I Thessalonians 2:13–16 as a Test Case', *Interpretation*, 38: 242–53.

—— (1985), 'The Cults of Thessalonica and the Thessalonian Correspondence', *NTS* 31: 336–56.

—— (1989), 'Cults and the Theology of 1 Thessalonians as a Reflection of its Purpose', in M. P. Horgan and P. Kobelski (eds.), *To Touch the Text: Studies in Honor of Joseph A. Fitzmyer, S.J.* (New York: Crossroad), 243–60.

Doty, W. G. (1973), *Letters in Primitive Christianity* (Philadelphia: Fortress).

—— (1986), *Mythography: The Study of Myths and Rituals* (Alabama: University of Alabama Press).

Duling, D. C. (1996), 'Millennialism', in R. L. Rohrbaugh (ed.), *The Social Sciences and New Testament Interpretation* (Peabody, Mass.: Hendrickson), 183–205.

Edson, C. (1948), 'Cults of Thessalonica (Macedonica III)', HTR 41: 153–204.

Eliade, M. (1989), *The Myth of the Eternal Return* (London: Penguin).

Esler, P. F. (1987), *Community and Gospel in Luke–Acts: The Social and Political Motivations of Lucan Theology* (Cambridge: Cambridge University Press).

—— (1993), 'Political Oppression in Jewish Apocalyptic Literature: A Social-Scientific Approach', *Listening: Journal of Religion and Culture*, 28: 181–99.

—— (1994), *The First Christians in their Social Worlds: Social-Scientific Approaches to New Testament Interpretation* (London: Routledge).

—— (ed.) (1995), *Modelling Early Christianity: Social-Scientific Studies of the New Testament in Its Context* (London: Routledge).

—— (1998), *Galatians* (London: Routledge).

—— (2000), '"Keeping it in the Family": Culture, Kinship and Identity in 1 Thessalonians and Galatians', in J. W. van Henten and A. Brenner (eds.), *Families and Family Relations as Represented in Early Judaisms and Early Christianities: Texts and Fictions*, Studies in Theology and Religion (Leiden: Deo), ii. 145–84.

Fatum, L. (1997), 'Brotherhood in Christ: A Gender Hermeneutical Reading of 1 Thessalonians', in H. Moxnes (ed.), *Constructing Early Christian Families: Family as Social Reality and Metaphor* (London: Routledge), 183–97.

Faw, C. E. (1952), 'On the Writing of First Thessalonians', *JBL* 71: 217–25.

Frame, J. E. A. (1912), *Critical and Exegetical Commentary on the Epistles of St. Paul to the Thessalonians* (New York: James Scribner's).

Funk, R. (1967), 'The Apostolic Parousia: Form and Significance', in W. R. Farmer, C. F. D. Moule, and R. R. Niebuhr (eds.), *Christian History and Interpretation: Studies Presented to John Knox* (Cambridge: Cambridge University Press), 249–68.

Headland, T. N., Pike, K. L., and Harris, M. (eds.) (1990), *Emics and Etics: The Insider/Outsider Debate*, Frontiers of Anthropology, 7 (Newbury Park, Calif.: Sage).

Hendrix, H. L. (1984), 'Thessalonicans Honor Rome', Ph.D. dissertation, Harvard University.

Hock, R. F. (1980), *The Social Context of Paul's Ministry: Tentmaking and Apostleship* (Philadelphia: Fortress).

Hodgson, R., Jr. (1982), '1 Thess. 4:1–12 and the Holiness Tradition (HT)', in K. H. Richards (ed.), *Society of Biblical Literature 1982 Seminar Papers* (Chico, Calif.: Scholars Press), 199–215.

Hooker, M. D., and Wilson, S. G. (1982) (eds.), *Paul and Paulinism: Essays in Honour of C. K. Barrett* (London: SPCK).

Jewett, R. (1986), *The Thessalonian Correspondence: Pauline Rhetoric and Millenarian Piety* (Philadelphia: Fortress).

—— (1993), 'Tenement Churches and Communal Meals in the Early Church: The Implications of a Form-Critical Analysis of 2 Thessalonians 3:10', *BR* 38: 23–42.

Judge, E. A. (1971), 'The Decrees of Caesar at Thessalonika', *RTR* 30: 1–7.

Klauck, H.-J. (1990), 'Brotherly Love in Plutarch and in 4 Maccabees', in D. L. Balch, E. Ferguson, and W. A. Meeks (eds.), *Greeks, Romans, and Christians: Essays in Honor of Abraham J. Malherbe* (Minneapolis: Fortress), 144–56.

Kloppenborg, J. S. (1993), PHILADELPHIA, THEODIDAKTOS and the Dioscuri: Rhetorical Engagement in 1 Thessalonians 4.9–12', *NTS* 39: 265–89.

Koester, H. (1979), '1 Thessalonians—Experiment in Christian Writing', in F. F. Church and T. George (eds.) (1979), *Continuity and Discontinuity in Church History: Essays Presented to George Hunston Williams on the Occasion of his 65th Birthday*, Studies in the History of Christian Thought, 19 (Leiden: E. J. Brill), 33–44.

Koskenniemi, H. (1956), *Studien zur Idee und Phraseologie des griechischen Briefes bis n. Chr* (Helsinki: Suomalainen Tiedeakatemia).

Lührmann, D. (1990), 'The Beginnings of the Church in Thessalonica', in Balch, Ferguson, and Meeks (1990: 237–49).

MacMullen, R. (1981), *Paganism in the Roman Empire* (New Haven: Yale University Press).

Malherbe, A. J. (1987), *Paul and the Thessalonians: The Philosophic Tradition of Pastoral Care* (Philadelphia: Fortress).

—— (1989a), *Paul and the Popular Philosophers* (Minneapolis: Fortress).

—— (1989b), '"Gentle as a Nurse": The Cynic Background to 1 Thessalonians 2', in Malherbe 1989a: 35–48 (first pub. in *NovT* 12 (1970), 213–17).

—— (1989c), 'Exhortation in First Thessalonians', in Malherbe 1989a: 49–66 (first pub. in *NovT* 25 (1983), 238–56).

—— (1990), 'Did the Thessalonians Write to Paul?' in R. R. Fortna and B. R. Gaventa (eds.), *The Conversation Continues: Studies in Paul & John in Honor of J. Louis Martyn* (Nashville: Abingdon, 246–57).

Malina, B. J. (1993), *The New Testament World: Insights from Cultural Anthropology*, rev. edn. (Louisville, Ky.: Westminster/John Knox).

Marshall, I. H. (1982), 'Pauline Theology in the Thessalonian Correspondence', in Hooker and Wilson (1982: 173–83).

Maurer, C. (1971), S. V. *skeuos*, *TDNT* vii. 358–67.

Okeke, G. E. (1980–1), '1 Thess 2.13–16. The Fate of the Unbelieving Jews', *NTS* 27: 127–36.

Pearson, B. A. (1971), '1 Thessalonians 2:13–16: A Deutero-Pauline Interpolation', *HTR* 64: 79–94.

Perkins, P. (1989), '1 Thessalonians and Hellenistic Religious Practices', in M. P. Horgan and P. J. Kobelski (eds.) (1989), *To Touch the Text: Biblical and Related Studies in Honor of Joseph A. Fitzmyer* (New York: Crossroad), 325–34.

Robinson, P. (ed.) (1996), *Social Groups and Identities: Developing the Legacy of Henri Tajfel* (Oxford: Butterworth Heinnemann).

Schmidt, D. (1983), '1 Thess 2: 13–16: Lingistic Evidence for an Interpolation', *JBL* 102: 269–79.

Schöllgen, G. (1988), 'Was wissen wie über Sozialstruktur der paulinischen Gemeinden?', *NTS* 34: 71–82.

Schubert, P. (1939), *Form and Function of the Pauline Thanksgivings*, BNZW 20 (Berlin: de Gruyter).

Seesemann, H. (1967), '*Pateō* and compounds in NT', *TDNT* v. 943–5.

Smith, A. (1989), 'The Social and Ethical Implications of the Pauline Rhetoric in 1 Thessalonians', dissertation submitted to Vanderbilt University (Ann Arbor: University Microfilms International).

Stern, M. (1974–80), *Greek and Latin Authors on Jews and Judaism* (2 vols.; Jerusalem: Israel Academy of the Arts and Sciences).

Stowers, S. K. (1986), *Letter Writing in Greco-Roman Antiquity* (Philadelphia: Westminster).

Tajfel, H. (1978), *Differentiation between Social Groups: Studies in the Social Psychology of Intergroup Relations* (London: Academic Press).

—— (1981), 'Social Stereotypes and Social Groups', in H. Tajfel, *Human Groups and Social Categories: Studies in Social Psychology* (Cambridge: Cambridge University Press).

—— and Turner, J. C. (1979), 'An Integrative Theory of Intergroup Conflict', in W. G. Austin and S. Worchel (eds.), *The Social Psychology of Intergroup Relations* (Monterey, Calif.: Brooks-Cole), 33–47.

—— (1986), 'The Social Identity Theory of Intergroup Conflict', in S. Worchel and W. G. Austin (eds.) (1986), *Psychology of Intergroup Relations* (Chicago: Nelson-Hall), 7–24.

Vickers, M. (1972), 'Hellenistic Thessaloniki', *JHS* 92: 156–70.

Vos, C. de (1999), *Church and Community Conflicts: The Relationships of the Thessalonian, Corinthian, and Philippian Churches with their Wider Civic Communities*, SBL DS 168 (Atlanta: Scholars Press).

Weatherly, J. A. (1991), 'The Authenticity of 1 Thessalonians 2.13–16: Additional Evidence', *JSNT* 42: 79–98.

White, M. L., and Yarbrough, O. L. (eds.) (1995), *The Social World of the First Christians: Essays in Honor of Wayne A. Meeks* (Philadelphia: Fortress).

PHILIP F. ESLER

INTRODUCTION

A. The problem of authenticity. 1. The dominant preliminary issue in the interpretation of 2 Thessalonians is the controversy as to whether Paul wrote this letter or not. The answer greatly affects how the letter is to be understood. It should be noted at once that there is virtually no support for reversing the traditional order of 1 and 2 Thessalonians (for reasons well explained by Jewett (1986: 24–30); *contra* Trudinger (1995), revisiting the views of J. Weiss and T. W. Manson). Doubts as to the authenticity of 2 Thessalonians are stimulated primarily by its close literary relationship to 1 Thessalonians. Many critics, but especially William Wrede (1903), have noted that the topics in the two letters are covered in the same sequence and the themes of the first letter are reflected with minor variations in the second, even if there are few examples with exactly the same wording. Thus, the renewed thanksgiving of 1 Thess 2:12 is repeated at 2 Thess 2:12, prayers in the optative mood introduced by 'the Lord (God) himself' appear at similar points (cf. 1 Thess 3:11–13 and 5:23 with 2 Thess 2:16–17 and 3:16), and there are many verbal parallels (see Menken 1994: 36–9 for the comparative data and Best 1972: 50–1). Only 2 Thess 2:1–12 has no parallel in 1 Thessalonians. On the other hand, both letters are very different in these respects from the other Pauline letters. These literary similarities occur in spite of some major differences in the contents of the two letters, especially in relation to views on the parousia (with 1 Thessalonians saying that Christ is expected to come soon and suddenly while 2 Thessalonians argues that his coming will be preceded by other events) and the lack of personal details about Paul and the Thessalonians of the type found in 1 Thess 2:1–12; 13–16; and 3:1–13. The tone of 2 Thessalonians is also generally agreed to be rather cold in comparison with that of 1 Thessalonians.

2. Many critics consider that the best explanation for such features is that 2 Thessalonians is an imitation of the other letter written later to Thessalonica or to some other community of Christ-followers which draws upon the earlier letter to enhance its authority. While those who consider 2 Thessalonians inauthentic usually seek to reconstruct a situation which would render its creation plausible, given our incomplete knowledge of the Christ-movement in the first century their failure to come up with a convincing particular audience and setting does not, as sometimes suggested (Jewett 1986: 3–18; Barclay 1993: 526), itself invalidate their arguments, although it will mean they are less than compelling. Supporters of authenticity, on the other hand, need to explain what had happened that induced Paul to write a second letter to Thessalonica using language and structure so similar to that in 1 Thessalonians; and to the present writer the difficulties with this hypothesis are greater than those raised by the view that the letter is not by Paul (see Bailey 1978–9). As Menken (1994: 27–43) argues, while no one argument is capable of sustaining a case for inauthenticity, overall this seems the preferable solution, in spite of very respectable views to the contrary. Possible explanations for 2 Thessalonians on either hypothesis will now be addressed. Particular issues relating to this debate will come up in the comments below.

B. Some Possible Explanations for 2 Thessalonians if Authentic.
1. Best (1972: 59) suggests that 2 Thessalonians was written by Paul from Corinth shortly after 1 Thessalonians 'to meet a new situation in respect of eschatology and a deteriorating situation in respect of idleness', although he notes that 'we do not know from where Paul received his information'. He proposes that Paul probably wrote with much of 1 Thessalonians in his memory rather than that he worked from a copy of 1 Thessalonians.

2. Jewett (1986: 176–8, 191–2) has a much more particular explanation. It is that 'for some reason' Paul's first letter, impacting on a community alive with millenarian excitement, actually provoked the radical members at Thessalonica, who misunderstood Paul to such an extent as to conclude that the day of the Lord had arrived and to behave in accordance with this belief (e.g. by curtailing certain everyday activities such as work). Paul responds by writing 2 Thessalonians, a refutation of this false doctrine written in a very different tone.

3. Barclay (1993) has proposed an interesting new answer to the relationship between the eschatologies in 1 and 2 Thessalonians which offers a more specific explanation for how the Thessalonians misunderstood Paul's first letter. After noting Wrede's (1903: 526) difficulty in suggesting a convincing setting for the letter, Barclay argues that the references to fierce persecution (1:4–9), the problem of people not working (3:6–13), and the claim by some that the day of the Lord is here (2:2) suggest a specific situation. Having examined and rejected existing answers as to what 'the day of the Lord' means at 2 Thess 2:2 (see commentary), he proposes a new alternative, namely, that in 1 Thessalonians it is possible to draw a distinction which Paul did not himself draw between *parousia* (4:13–18) and the day of the Lord (5:1–11) and the latter is associated with the sudden destruction of unbelievers. So, maybe some Christians in Thessalonica reacted to a local (or perhaps widespread) disaster by claiming that it manifested the wrath of God, thereby creating turmoil and encouraging some to give up their jobs and and continue urgent, full-time evangelism. Thus Paul is compelled to write another letter perhaps only a matter of weeks after the first wherein the friendly encouragement gives way to a more frigid and authoritarian tone.

4. A major question hanging over proposals like those of Jewett and Barclay is that if Paul's first letter had been misunderstood why would he not try to persuade them with a completely new approach, rather than risking a letter which stylistically aped the earlier one, and also strongly protest about their egregious misinterpretation of the earlier letter. 2 Thess 2:2 certainly does not fulfil the latter function, in contrast with 1 Cor 5:9–13, which clearly indicates how Paul went about correcting a misimpression drawn from an earlier letter.

C. Possible Explanations for 2 Thessalonians if Inauthentic.

1. Proponents of the inauthenticity of 2 Thessalonians have come up with a variety of dates and situations for the letter. Wrede himself dated it to about 100 CE and suggested it was written not for Thessalonica (for Thessalonians would ask where it had lain all these years) but for another church which knew of the existence of other Thessalonian correspondence. Masson (1957) proposed that it was written about 100 CE to counter the belief that the day of the Lord had come. On the other hand, Marxsen (1968: 37–44; 1982) favoured an earlier date, around 70 CE, arguing that the letter was intended to counter Gnostics, especially their (false) claim that the day of the Lord had come. If Paul's letters had been collected, as generally supposed, by about 100 CE, an earlier date for the composition of 2 Thessalonians would be preferable (see 2 THESS 3:17).

2. 2 Thessalonians has been understood as a response to millennialism in a Mediterranean context. The three substantive issues of local context recognized in the letter are the existence of some form of oppression being suffered by the addressees (1:4–6), the disturbance caused by the message that 'the day of the Lord has come' (2:1–12), and the disorderly conduct of certain Christ-followers who are refusing to work for a living. On the (preferable) assumption that these issues derive from an actual situation somewhere in the ancient Mediterranean world, and do not just comprise a notional setting aimed at allowing someone to draft a letter in Pauline style, we are faced with what modern social scientists refer to as an outbreak of millennialism. Across the world, we know of many instances of groups, generally (although not always) suffering from some form of oppression or disturbance of traditional social patterns, who generate or revive narratives of a coming transformation of the world which will radically restore them to their proper place and, often, destroy those who oppress them (Duling 1996; Esler 1993; 1994: 93–109). Examples, discussed elsewhere (Esler 1993: 187–8; 1994: 101–4), include the ghost dance among North American Indians in the late nineteenth century and the cargo cults of twentieth-century Melanesia. Jewett (1986: 161–78) has usefully applied millenarian ideas to 2 Thessalonians, although his treatment is affected by his view that the letter is authentic. The view adopted here is that millennialism provides the best framework for contextualizing the letter in a general way, even though we cannot be sure for which troubled community of first-century Christ-followers it was written. Although biblical critics generally use the now rather tired and overworked word 'eschatological', which derives from a theological agenda, to refer to end-time speculation in such texts as Dan 7–12 and 1 Enoch, the framework of 'millennialism' allows a fresh set of questions originating in real social experience to be posed to texts such as 2 Thessalonians. Attempts, such as that of Menken (1994), to discuss this dimension to 2 Thessalonians almost solely in relation to (the undoubtedly important) framework of end-time speculation in Israelite biblical and extrabiblical literature, have an unnecessarily limited focus.

3. It is always worth remembering that the social context of the ancient Mediterranean world in which this example of

millennialism occurred was radically different from modern, individualistic cultures of Europe and North America. The ancient Mediterranean world was one where, at an appropriate level of abstraction and without in any way denying local variations, people found meaning by belonging to groups (especially the family), honour was the principal social value, all goods (material and immaterial) were regarded as existing in finite quantities, and relationships between patrons and clients (sometimes mediated by other individuals referred to as 'brokers'; see Moxnes 1991) were common as a way of dealing with access to limited material and social goods. These are the most important of an ensemble of cultural features originally identified and applied to the NT by Bruce Malina in 1981 (now see Malina 1993).

4. The fact that Paul probably did not write 2 Thessalonians does not entail taking a condemnatory attitude to whoever—pseudonymously—claimed he had. Pseudonymity is a common feature in the Bible (Proverbs, Ecclesiastes, Isa 40–55 and 55–66), let alone in the profuse writings of the Pseudepigrapha themselves (see Bailey 1978–9: 143–5). Meade (1986) has plausibly argued that the phenomenon occurred when it was felt necessary to make traditions capable of application to new situations, so that it becomes an assertion of authoritative tradition, not literary origin. The closeness of the style of this pseudepigraphic document to 1 Thessalonians is perhaps explicable out of the high respect in which its author held Paul. It is reasonable, therefore, that some time in the first century, probably after Paul's death in Rome in the later 60s, someone faced with a situation having the three broad features mentioned above sought faithfully to reinterpret Pauline tradition in a way which would benefit those addressed. The (non-Pauline) authors of Ephesians, Titus, and 1 and 2 Timothy adopted the same strategy, although faced with very different situations.

5. In what follows I will refer to the author of this letter as 'Paul' (with inverted commas) or 'the author' because of the view taken here that the historical Paul was not its author.

D. Structure.

2 Thessalonians, like 1 Thessalonians, can be given a structure based on thematic, epistolary, or rhetorical considerations (helpfully summarized by Jewett 1986: 222–5). It is doubtful, however, whether the rigorous application of ancient rhetorical or epistolary categories to various sections of the letter does much to further our understanding of it. Accordingly, in the commentary I will adopt the following (pragmatic) structuration, essentially thematic in type, while making occasional reference to possible epistolary or rhetorical subdivisions:

Prescript (1:1–2)
Thanksgiving and Encouragement (1:3–12)
The End and the Man of Lawlessness (2:1–12)
Encouragement to Persevere (2:13–17)
Mutual Prayer (3:1–5)
Warning against Idlers (3:6–12)
Conclusion (3:13–18)

COMMENTARY

(1:1–2) Prescript This is the beginning of one long sentence (1:1–12). Rhetoricians would call this section the 'exordium'.

Letters in the ancient Mediterranean began with a prescript, comprising the names of the senders and the addressees and a brief greeting, in Greek typically *chairei*, 'hail'. These verses constitute the prescript to 2 Thessalonians. The senders (Paul, Silvanus, and Timothy) and addressees ('*ekklēsia*, the community'—'church' sounds a little anachronistic—'of the Thessalonians in God our Father and the Lord Jesus Christ') are the same as in 1 Thessalonians, while the greeting has been Christianized (a practice possibly inaugurated by Paul) even further here by an additional reference to Jesus Christ as Lord and God as Father. v. 2, by invoking upon the addressees grace (*charis*) and peace (*eirēnē*; Heb. *šālôm*) from God the Father and the Lord Jesus Christ, comes close to putting them on an equal footing, unless we are meant to see God as patron and Jesus Christ as broker in accordance with common Mediterranean social patterns, that is, a mediator who gives clients access to the resources of a more powerful patron (Moxnes 1991: 248).

(1:3–12) Thanksgiving and Encouragement v. 3, after the prescript, Paul often includes a thanksgiving for the good qualities of his addressees (Rom 1:8–10; 1 Cor 1:4–8; Phil 1:3–6; but not in Galatians, where Paul is too annoyed with his audience to engage in the usual courtesies!). Yet here he says 'we *must always* give thanks to God', rather than 'we thank God', which seems to some critics a rather more formal expression, even though he does go on to mention that their faith is growing and their love for one another increasing. The first person plural may reflect the fact that three persons are named as senders of the letter, or represent an example of the 'epistolary plural', where a single writer talks of himself or herself in the plural.

v. 4, virtually all translations (including the NRSV) have 'Paul' saying something like 'we ourselves *boast*' among the communities (NRSV 'churches') of God concerning your steadfastness and faith in all persecutions (*diōgmoi*) and afflictions (*thlipseis*). But 'boast', which carries a negative connotation to modern ears, is a mistranslation. In a group-oriented culture dominated by honour as the pre-eminent virtue and always needing to be acknowledged by others, 'Paul' is saying that 'we ourselves base our claim to honour?' on the qualities mentioned. He can say this in relation to the relevant public (here 'the communities of God') either because he is intrinsically linked to the Thessalonians' endurance and faith as their progenitor, or because he is closely connected with the Thessalonian Christ-followers who now exhibit these qualities, or both. Also see 1 Thess 2:19; 2 Cor 9:2–3. The presence of persecutions and oppressions among whatever group of Christ-followers for which 2 Thessalonians was originally destined provides either the motivation for, or reinforcement of, narratives of future deliverance of the sort prominent in the text.

v. 5 begins 'This is evidence' (*endeigma*). But to what stated previously does *endeigma* refer? Possibly to their faith and steadfastness while they suffer persecution and tribulation (Best 1972: 254–5), but it is more probable, given the tight interconnection of v. 4, that it refers to the fact that Paul lays his claim to honour on these characteristics: 'our claiming honour from your endurance and faith before the other communities (who did not demur) is a sure sign that God will also

count you worthy'. The judgement Paul has in mind is the judgement of God at the end-time (usually, although not very helpfully, referred to as 'eschatological') commonly described in Israelite literature (1 Enoch 1:1–9; 2 Esd 7.33–44; *Apoc. Abr.* 29.14–29; D. F. Russell 1964: 379–85). Without doubting their actual existence for the original audience of 2 Thessalonians, the troubles referred to in the text are capable of interpretation as the 'woes' before the end attested in other Israelite and Christian literature (Dan 12:1; 2 *Apoc. Bar.* 25.2–4; Mk 13:19, 24; Rev 7:14). Thus we see a merger of experience and religious tradition located in biblical and non-biblical Israelite literature typical of this text and other early Christian literature. It is likely, however, that Menken (1994: 85–7) is mistaken in seeing the current sufferings of the Thessalonians (which will absolve them from future judgement) as caused by their own sinfulness, since this conflicts with the good things said about them earlier in the text.

vv. 6–7a, the sentiment here represents a rather bald example of the law of revenge (*lex talionis*). Although modern European or North American readers might find this puzzling, in ancient Mediterranean culture serious insults, which desecrated one's honour, had to be avenged. Thus God will bring vengeance on those who have dishonoured his people (see Deut 32:35–6) and therefore slighted him as well. This is a fairly common biblical theme. In particular Isa 66:6 refers to 'the voice of the LORD dealing retribution to his enemies' and Aus (1976) has suggested that this section of Isaiah may have influenced this verse and what follows. 'Rest' (*anesis*) refers to the absence of tension and trial. The persecution and oppression mentioned in vv. 6–7 may be likened to the disturbance of traditional lifestyles suffered by North American Indians or Melanesians at the hands of European conquerors or colonists. In North America and Melanesia (in the South Pacific) millennial myths developed which described a coming convulsion in the cosmos when the white people would be swept away, so that the traditional lifestyles would be restored, the ancestors return, the game revisit the plains, or cargo be dropped on the people from the sky (see Esler 1994: 101–4, and literature cited there). The punishment for the oppressors and vindication of the oppressed in 2 Thessalonians reflects a somewhat similar social experience. v. 7b, the author now specifies when (or by what means) the events just mentioned will occur, literally: 'at the revelation (*apocalypsis*) of Lord Jesus Christ from heaven with the angels of his power'. First-century Christ-followers thought Jesus had gone to heaven after his resurrection and that he would return from there (1 Thess 1:10; 4:16; 1 Cor 1:7; 1 Pet 1:7, 13). Such beliefs were fortified (if not stimulated) by Israelite traditions describing future vindicators of Israel, such as 1 Enoch 48:4–6 and Dan 7:13. Normally Paul uses *parousia* of the future coming of Jesus, the sole use of *apocalypsis* in this regard being at 1 Cor 1:7. The angels represent the heavenly host or court who accompany God when he comes in judgement (Zech 14:5; 1 Enoch 1.9), although the early Christ-movement attached them to Jesus (Mk 8:38; 13:27).

v. 8, in flaming fire, Jesus will mete out vengeance (*ekdikēsis*) on those who do not know God and those who do not obey his gospel. The notion of fire as a feature of the vengeance God would inflict on his enemies originates in the OT (Isa 66:15–16) and here the theme is linked to the activities of Jesus.

There seems no basis for seeking to distinguish those mentioned into two groups comprising Gentiles and Israelites. v. 9, we now learn what the vengeance will consist of: 'the punishment of eternal destruction, separated from the presence of the Lord and from the glory of his might'. The punishment does not consist of total annihilation, but of exclusion from God and, importantly in an honour-driven society, from his exalted and powerful honour. This vision is very different from the tortured future in store for the wicked in later Christian texts. v. 10 further specifies the occasion for these events: 'when he comes to be glorified [i.e. greatly honoured] by his saints' etc., while also evoking the fate of the blessed as contrasted with that of those who will be punished. Honour is shared among groups and here his followers revel in the great things he has done. The notion of 'the day (of judgement)' is a common feature of Israelite end-time speculation (see Joel 2:1-2; Zech 9:16; Mal 3:1-2).

vv. 11-12, 'Paul' informs the Thessalonians that he regularly prays for them, by asking God to make them worthy of his calling and powerfully fulfil every good resolution and work of faith. The object of all this is specified in v. 12: 'so that the name of our Lord Jesus may be glorified [i.e. greatly honoured] in you, and you in him, according to the grace of our God and the Lord Jesus Christ'. Although this situation has been described as 'mutual glorification' (Menken 1994: 94), it is possible to improve on such a designation. For here we have the typical Mediterranean phenomenon of sharing honour among the members of a group. If we understand God as father or patron, Jesus as broker, and the believers as clients, we have a fictive kinship arrangement in which Jesus honours (and is honoured in) them and they honour (and are honoured in) him.

The final statement, 'according to the grace of our God and the Lord Jesus Christ', indicates a very close relationship between the two, if not necessarily equating Jesus with God (Best 1972: 272-3).

(2:1-12) The End and the Man of Lawlessness v. 1, 'Paul' now moves on to what is called in epistolary nomenclature the 'body' of the letter, or in the language of rhetoric the *partitio* (covering vv. 1-2), with the *probatio* beginning at v. 3. Paul begs them in connection with 'the coming (*parousia*) of our Lord Jesus Christ and our being gathered together (*episynagōgē*) to him'. In Hellenistic Greek the word *parousia* referred to the arrival of a high official at a city or town, to the accompaniment of elaborate greetings and celebrations. But the word came to be applied to the imminent arrival of Jesus from heaven (1 Thess 2:19; 3:13: 4:15; 5:23; 1 Cor 15:23; Mt 24:27, 37, 39; Jas 5:7, 8). The notion of God gathering in his people is found in the OT, either from exile (Isa 27:13; 43:4-7; Jer 31:8) or for final salvation (2 Macc 2:7; Sir 36:10). In *Psalms of Solomon* 17.26 it is said that the Messiah will gather in the people. Modern parallels exist in the form of the individuals who focus and lead a millennial movement (Esler 1994: 99).

v. 2, the content of Paul's entreaty is that his addressees should not be quickly shaken in mind or alarmed, either by a prophetic utterance ('a spirit') or a word or letter 'as though from us', saying that 'the day of the Lord is already here'. This is one of the most important verses in the letter. 'A letter as

though from us' can mean either a forgery or a letter which he did write that is now being misinterpreted. If Paul had actually written 2 Thessalonians, he would have signally failed to address either alternative. For he neither denounces the letter as a forgery nor seeks directly to correct the misinterpretation. The statement is easier to interpret on the hypothesis of pseudonymity. Paul's letters were difficult and liable to be misunderstood (see 2 Pet 3:15-16). This could have been the fate of 1 Thess 4:13-5:11. There were several statements in this passage that could have been used to support an argument that the day of the Lord had come. 2 Thess 2:2 makes good sense as an attempt by its author to counter a misinterpretation of 1 Thess 4:13-5:11.

Barclay (1993: 526), who considers 2 Thessalonians authentic, canvasses earlier suggestions as to whether the 'day of the Lord is here' means: (1) a literal event—altering the structure of the universe, which is unlikely since no such event had occurred in the experience of the audience of 2 Thessalonians; (2) an internal and personal reality, entry into a new world, which remains a popular view, especially if linked to some kind of spiritualized or Gnostic understanding of the parousia; or (3) something which has not yet occurred but is imminent, an option that is now generally regarded as grammatically impossible. Barclay himself proposes a fourth alternative. It is possible to draw from 1 Thessalonians a distinction that Paul did not himself make between *parousia* (4:13-18) and the day of the Lord (5:1-11), the latter being associated with the sudden destruction of unbelievers. Perhaps the Thessalonians interpreted certain calamitous events in the early 50s of the first century as the sudden destruction of unbelievers, thus triggering a belief that 'the day of the Lord' had arrived. If one regards the letter as inauthentic and takes what is probably the more likely view that the parousia and the day of the Lord would have been understood by the recipients of 2 Thessalonians as referring to the same event, what meaning might one attach to 'the day of the Lord is here'? One possibility is that people had appeared claiming to be Christ and that such claims were troubling the target audience of this letter (so Menken 1994: 100-1). Mk 13:6 (to be dated sometime shortly before or after 70 CE) provides a basis for this suggestion.

vv. 3-4, Paul expresses concern that someone might deceive them. Deception prior to the end is also mentioned in the Markan apocalypse (13:5) and here seems to relate to the date of the parousia. The second clause in v. 3 opens with the words 'because unless', which begin the protasis of an anacoluthon, a sentence containing two conditions, which continues until the end of v. 4 without being rounded off with an apodosis, a statement of what will happen, presumably requiring something like 'the parousia of the Lord will not occur'. The first condition required is the apostasy or rebellion (*apostasia*). The lack of specification as to who will apostasize and in what way suggests that the author could count on the original recipients of 2 Thessalonians knowing what was meant. For modern readers, however, both aspects are difficult. At a general level the word refers to the dramatic breakdown of the legal, moral, social, and even natural order which is predicted in certain Israelite and NT texts of the period before the end (*Jub.* 23:14-21; 2 Esd 5:1-13; 2 Tim 3:1-9; Jude 17-19). Yet uncertainty surrounds the issue of whom the apostasy will involve:

Israelites, Christ-followers, Gentiles, or representatives from all three possible groups.

The second condition needing to be fulfilled is the revealing of 'the lawless one' (lit. the person of lawlessness: *ho anthrōpos tēs anomias*), immediately described as 'the one destined for destruction' (lit. the son of destruction). Expressions similar to these occur in the OT (Ps 89:23; Isa 57:4) and in the Qumran literature (1QS 9:16, 22; CD 6:15; 13:14). In Jn 17:12 Judas is called 'a son of destruction'. It is then stated that he (the lawless one) 'opposes and exalts himself above every so-called god or object of worship, so that he takes his seat in the temple of God, declaring himself to be God'. While this figure plainly encapsulates the lawlessness (or the 'sin', if—as seems unlikely—the variant reading here is correct) which will characterize the apostasy preceding the End, it has not proved easy to identify him with any known character in Jewish or Christian literature. It is even unclear whether he is a human or supernatural figure, although we should be careful to avoid the modern tendency sharply to distinguish these realms. Elsewhere we find false false messiahs and prophets predicted for the time before the End (Mk 13:21–2) and presumably the person of lawlessness is somewhat similar. We must presume that in the millennial mythopoiesis (that is to say, the creation of myth, see Esler 1993: 186–7) which had already occurred in the community for which this letter was written the person of lawlessness had been allocated a central role. The details in v. 4 show how this mythopoiesis was able to draw upon existing aspects in Israelite tradition in describing how the lawless person would behave. He will be like Antiochus IV Epiphanes who tried to extirpate Israelite religion and identity (in the period 167–164 BCE), as described in 1 Macc 1:16–64 and Dan 11:36–7, Pompey (who entered the temple in Jerusalem; see *Pss Sol.* 17:11–15) and Caligula who wanted to install statues of himself in the temple (Jos. *J.W.* 2.184–5).

v. 5, 'Paul' asks if they do not remember that he used to tell them (i.e. on more than one occasion) of these things when he was still with them. This statement, loosely based on 1 Thess 3:4, serves to provide an air of reality to the pseudonymous fiction. There is no mention in 1 Thessalonians of either the apostasy or the person of lawlessness. vv. 6–7, the author affirms that 'you know what is now restraining (*katechon*) him, so that he may be revealed when his time comes. For the mystery of lawlessness (*anomia*) is already at work, but only until the one who now restrains (*katechōn*) it is removed.' These are extremely difficult verses (see Lietaert Peerbolte 1997; Powell 1997). The chief problems have to do with the movement from a restraining power or thing to a restraining person, with the person of lawlessness as the implied subject of restraint, and with the identity of the restrainer and the restraint. But even to translate the Greek using 'that or who restrains' means opting for one among several possibilities (others being 'possess' or 'hold sway'). Possibly (see below), the original readers of this letter knew what or who was meant, although the expression does not occur elsewhere in Jewish or Christian writings dealing with the End. This phenomenon may have been an element of the mythopoiesis concerning the End with which they were familiar. The answer may simply be beyond us (Best 1972: 301). Yet one option worth mentioning, suggested by Strobel (1961: 98–116) and based on the possible influence of Hab 2:3 as interpreted in

Jewish and Christian tradition, is that the restraining power is God's plan of salvation and the restraining person is God himself. Less likely is the idea that the power is the Roman empire and the person is the emperor himself, especially in view of the author's lack of interest in the political realm. Lietaert Peerbolte (1997), finally, makes the interesting suggestion that these words are deliberately obscure, allowing 'Paul'—who has no answer for the delay of the parousia—to create the illusion among the readers of 2 Thessalonians that there is an answer of which the original Thessalonians were aware.

v. 8, 'then the lawless one (*ho anomos*) will be revealed, whom the Lord (Jesus) will destroy with the breath of his mouth, annihilating him by the manifestation of his coming.' Whatever or whoever restrains the lawless person (an equivalent of 'the person of lawlessness' at v. 3), there is no doubt that it is Jesus who will kill him once he is revealed. The author's determination to make this point leads him to it before he has actually described the lawless one's revelation (in vv. 9–10). The manner of the killing, by 'the breath of his mouth', derives from Isa 11:4 ('by the breath of his lips he will kill the impious'; LXX). vv. 9–10, in a second relative clause the author describes the coming of the lawless one as taking place through Satan's activity with 'all power, signs, lying wonders, and every kind of wicked deception for those who are perishing'. The picture of signs and wonders which will be worked by agents of evil before the End is reminiscent of Mk 13:22; Rev 13:14; 19:20. vv. 11–12, 'For this reason', presumably their failing to accept the love of the truth, God sends on them a power of delusion to make them believe in falsehood, 'so that all who have not believed the truth but took pleasure in unrighteousness (*adikia*) will be condemned'. Menken (1994: 117) points out that divine causality appears here to match the human causality of the preceding verse. There is an OT context for God inspiring false prophets in 1 Kings 22:23 and Ezek 14:9, while an idea somewhat similar to what is said here occurs at Rom 1:18–32.

(2:13–17) Encouragement to Persevere vv. 13–14, quite suddenly 'Paul' changes tack, by launching into a second thanksgiving (following the precedent in 1 Thess 2:13). The reason for the thanks is that God has established the notional Thessalonian addressees (who stand for the original audience of this letter) as a differentiated and privileged group in the world, with a particular history and a glorious destiny (which links the thanks to the previous material about the End). They are 'brothers [NRSV has "brothers and sisters"] beloved by the Lord', whom God (as in OT traditions of divine election) chose 'from the beginning [though the uncertain Gk. could also mean "as the first fruits"; NRSV] for salvation through sanctification (*hagiasmos*) by the Spirit and through belief in the truth'. God called them to this through 'Paul's' gospel, to obtain the exalted honour (*doxa*) of Jesus Christ. Such descriptions serve the fundamental purpose of delineating their identity, that is, providing answers to the always vital question 'Who are we?' The word 'sanctification' in particular serves to distinguish them and their present experience from the welter of idolatry and immorality implied as characteristic of the world outside the group. On the other hand, 'salvation' expresses the future goal of their existence; it is very common for people to tell themselves who they are in terms of their sense of where they are going (Esler 1998: 42, 175). In this heavily group-oriented culture, it is natural that the members of the group will share in the honour of their most honourable and honoured leader.

v. 15, the author encourages them to stick resolutely to the traditions (*paradoseis*) which they have received by word of mouth (*dia logou*) or in a letter. It is likely that the original recipients of 2 Thessalonians would have interpreted the letter mentioned here as 1 Thessalonians. The oral proclamation referred to was presumably teaching they had already received with which 'Paul' concurred. We must imagine a situation, therefore, in which the author is saying in effect, 'Just as the Thessalonians were told by Paul to rely on his earlier letter and the teaching given them in the community, so too must you'. vv. 16–17, moving easily from thanks to intercession, 'Paul' now offers a prayer that Jesus Christ and the God 'who loved us and through grace gave us eternal comfort (*paraklēsis*) and good hope' might comfort (*parakalein*) and strengthen their hearts 'in every good work and word'. The prominence of Jesus in this prayer indicates the fairly high Christology characteristic of the letter. 'Good hope' seems to derive from mystery cults as a way of referring to life after death (Best 1972: 321); mystery cults, such as those of Eleusis, offered their adherents a relation of intense communion, often ecstatic in nature, with a god.

(3:1–5) Mutual Prayer Many critics arguing for a rhetorical structure to the letter regard v. 1 as beginning its *exhortatio*. Epistolary theorists tend to see here the beginning of a series of moral admonitions (Jewett 1986: 224–5). vv. 1–2, in a way somewhat similar to that of 1 Thess 5:25, 'Paul' asks the *adelphoi*, literally 'brothers' but presumably also meant to include female members of the congregation (so perhaps 'brethren'), to 'pray for us, so that the word of the Lord may spread rapidly and be glorified [i.e. "greatly honoured"] everywhere, just as it is among you, and that we may be rescued from wicked and evil people; for not all have faith'. If 2 Thessalonians is pseudonymous, such a sentiment conveys an aura of verisimilitude, but also serves to legitimate—that is, to explain and justify the existence and identity of—whatever community this letter was originally intended for. They would be reassured of the value of their faith and of the fact that their sharp differentiation from sinful and uncomprehending outsiders was just what Paul had indicated would be the lot of the Thessalonians. Yet a similar conclusion could be drawn if the letter is authentic, only now it would be the Thessalonians themselves for whom the point was being made. The hostile reception that Paul and his co-workers had received figures both in the clearly genuine correspondence (such as Rom 15:30–1; 2 Cor 1:8–11; and 1 Thess 2: 2) and also in the deutero-Pauline writings, such as in 2 Tim 3:10–11; 4:16–18).

v. 3, the author asserts the faithfulness of the Lord, who will strengthen and guard them from the evil one, and this quality stands in stark contrast to the lack of faith (and the evil associated with it) mentioned in the previous verse. It is noteworthy that although this statement is probably based on 1 Thess 5:24, here the faithful one is the Lord (that is, Jesus Christ) and not God, which indicates the move to a higher Christology in 2 Thessalonians. v. 4, now 'Paul' expresses his

confidence in the Lord that they are following and will continue to follow his commands. In a pseudonymous letter this is a way of encouraging the target audience to adhere to the message associated with Paul. Specifics of the instruction will be provided in 3:6–12. v. 5, 'Paul' prays that the Lord may 'direct your hearts to the love of God and to the steadfastness of Christ'. This prayer takes the audience to the source of their ability to carry out the instructions. It is probable that the author appeals to Christ's steadfastness to provide them with a role model during the current difficulties they are experiencing.

(3:6–15) Warning against Loafers v. 6, 'Paul' commands the 'Thessalonians' to avoid every member of the congregation who is living 'in a disorderly way' (*ataktōs*) and not in accordance with the tradition (*paradosis*) they received from him. The word *ataktōs* appears again at v. 11, where the author describes how certain of his addressees are behaving, and 'Paul' himself denies he behaved in such a way at v. 7. It is reasonably clear from the associations of the word in vv. 6–15 that by 'disorderly' the author means 'not in accordance with the discipline of working and supporting oneself', thus behaving like a loafer (hence 'living in idleness' in the NRSV). Scholars have long explained this idleness as rooted in 'eschatological' excitement produced by a belief in the imminence of the parousia of Christ (see R. Russell 1988: 105–7). Several examples of millennialism in modern times, moreover, have revealed that a belief in the imminent or actual transformation of the world can produce, not surprisingly, a breakdown in belief in the need for everyday activities, such as work. Rejection of work and the usual social order can be associated with exaggerated behaviour and often a belief in a return to a Golden Age which preceded the current period and its tribulations (Jewett 1986: 173–5; Esler 1994: 101). In the unknown community for whom 2 Thessalonians was written it is likely that such attitudes had made an appearance and needed to be attacked. If Menken (1994: 130–3) is correct in assuming that underlying the order which 'Paul' would like to be restored is the rule of work that originated in the sin of Adam and Eve in the garden of Eden in Gen 3:17–19, it is possible that those refusing to work were appealing to the alleged re-establishment of prelapsarian bliss to support their position.

R. Russell (1988) proposes a different view (which has been challenged recently by Romaniuk 1993), that this idleness has nothing to do with end-time excitement, but is a result of the urban poor finding support within the social networks of Christ-fearers and then giving up work. A similar view has more recently been presented by Jewett (1993), who proposes that the early Christ-movement was likely to have been located in the tenement houses of the non-élite, where the system of internal support would have been jeopardized by the refusal of some members to contribute.

vv. 7–8, 'Paul' offers himself as a model for them, inasmuch as he did not exhibit the disorder of idleness when he was amongst them, but worked day and night so as not to be a burden on them by eating at their expense. Imitation of Paul is a reasonably common theme in the genuine Pauline epistles (1 Cor 4:16, 11:1; Phil 3:17; 1 Thess 1:6). v. 8*b* is closely based on 1 Thess 2:9, and there are similar statements at 1 Cor 9:12; 15–18; 2 Cor 11:7–8; 12:13. In these passages, however, Paul is seeking to allay any suspicion that he preached the gospel for personal profit, while in 2 Thessalonians the point is made to encourage the target audience to imitate him in this respect. v. 9, the author notes he had a right to be supported by the congregation, even though he did not exercise it, in order to offer them a model for imitation, a theme introduced in v. 7. v. 10, by mentioning that he had previously told them in their presence that anyone unwilling to work should not be fed, 'Paul' makes explicit the precise nature of the disorder which has been implied hitherto—the fact that some members of the congregation are living off the others. There are parallels to this saying (which has been frequently cited out of its context ever since), in Prov 10:4; 12:11; 19:15; and Pseudo-Phocylides, *Sentences*, 153–4.

v. 11, here again is a reference to disorder, now with an unequivocal core meaning brought to the surface in v. 10, together with the disturbing news—expressed in a pun—that some of them are not busy at work (*ergazomenous*) but busybodies (*periergazomenous*). Presumably the author has in mind here some exaggerated type of behaviour of the sort common among millennial movements, but its precise nature remains unclear. Not only are they not working, but they are interfering with the work of others. v. 12, 'Paul' follows up the statement in v. 11 with a direct exhortation to the troublemakers here: 'to do their work quietly and to earn their own living' (lit. eat their own bread). The reference to quietness here suggests that their current state is one of loud activity or excitement, no doubt associated with the millennial belief that 'the day of the Lord is already here' (2:2).

(3:13–18) Conclusion vv. 13–16, there is a great diversity of views among those advocating epistolary or rhetorical analyses of the letter as to where the divisions fall in these verses (Jewett 1986: 224–5). The first four verses (13–16) can either be connected with the previous section, which would mean 'Paul' wanted the 'Thessalonians' to do good to the disorderly and idle troublemakers, or, more likely, constitute a separate section at the end of the letter—beginning with a general exhortation to them to do good (v. 13). Those who do not are to be ostracized (although, as we see in the next verse, only to a limited extent) so that they may be put to shame (v. 14). Here we see the typical association in Mediterranean culture between honour and group-belonging. Nevertheless, such a person is not to be treated as an enemy, but admonished as a brother (v. 15). The person is socially separated as a form of discipline and for a limited time (subject no doubt to a change of behaviour on the malefactor's part). Exclusion from the community for various reasons and for a limited time was also practised at Qumran (see e.g. the CD 8:16–18). v. 16, 'Paul' prays that the Lord will give them peace at all times and remain with them; in 1 Cor 14:33 Paul notes that God is a God of peace not disorder.

v. 17, it was a practice in ancient letter-writing for an author to use a scribe and add a few words at the end in his own handwriting. Paul adopts this practice elsewhere in 1 Cor 16:21; Gal 6:11; Col 4:18 (leaving aside the issue of whether Colossians is authentic or not). This device would only be effective as a proof of authenticity in relation to the original of the letter, since the difference in the two hands apparent there would disappear in subsequent copies. Although the author of 2 Thessalonians seems to claim—wrongly—that this was Paul's universal practice, Jewett's (1986: 6) conclusion that this itself indicates authenticity since otherwise the author would be casting doubt on other Pauline letters not bearing the addition is unwarranted if the letter were written before the collection of Paul's letters towards the end of the first century. On the other hand, 1 Thessalonians does not bear Paul's self-attestation and this strengthens Jewett's point if 2 Thessalonians was originally directed to Christ-followers who possessed 1 Thessalonians. The self-conscious (and unique) way in which the author draws attention to the practice in 3:17 by saying that 'This is the mark' (*sēmeion*, sign) is itself suspicious. v. 18, the letter ends with a standard benediction.

REFERENCES

Aus, R. D. (1976), 'The Relevance of Isaiah 66.7 to Revelation 12 and 2 Thessalonians 1', *ZNW* 67: 252–68.

Bailey, J. A. (1978–9), 'Who Wrote II Thessalonians?', *NTS* 25: 131–45.

Barclay, M. G. (1993), 'Conflict in Thessalonika', *CBQ* 53: 512–30.

Best, E. (1972), *A Commentary on the First and Second Epistles to the Thessalonians*, Black's New Testament Commentaries (London: Adam & Charles Black).

Duling, D. C. (1996), 'Millennialism', in R. L. Rohrbaugh (ed.), *The Social Sciences and New Testament Interpretation* (Peabody, Mass.: Hendrickson), 183–205.

Esler, P. F. (1993), 'Political Oppression in Jewish Apocalyptic Literature: A Social-Scientific Approach', in *Listening: Journal of Religion and Culture*, 28: 181–99.

—— (1994), *The First Christians in their Social Worlds: Social-Scientific Approaches to New Testament Interpretation* (London: Routledge).

—— (1998), *Galatians* (London: Routledge).

Jewett, R. (1986), *The Thessalonian Correspondence: Pauline Rhetoric and Millenarian Piety* (Philadelphia: Fortress).

—— (1993), 'Tenement Churches and Communal Meals in the Early Church: The Implications of a Form-Critical Analysis of 2 Thessalonians 3:10', *Biblical Research*, 38: 23–42.

Lietaert Peerbolte, L. J. (1997), 'The *Katechon, Katechōn* of 2 Thess. 2:6–7', *NovT* 39: 138–50.

Malina, B. J. (1993), *The New Testament World: Insights from Cultural Anthropology*, rev. edn. Orig. 1981 (Louisville, Ky.: Westminster/John Knox).

Marxsen, W. (1968), *Introduction to the New Testament* (Oxford: Blackwell).

—— (1982), *Der zweite Thessalonicherbrief* (Zurich: Theologischer Verlag).

Masson, C. (1957), *Les Deux Épîtres de Saint Paul aux Thessaloniciens* (Neuchatel: Delachaux et Niestlé).

Mcade, D. G. (1986), *Pseudonymity and Canon: An Investigation into the Relationship of Authorship and Authority in Jewish and Early Christian Tradition*, WUNT 39 (Tübingen: Mohr).

Menken, M. J. J. (1994), *2 Thessalonians* (London: Routledge).

Moxnes, H. (1991), 'Patron–Client Relations and the New Community in Luke–Acts', in J. H. Neyrey (ed.) (1991), *The Social World of Luke–Acts: Models for Interpretation* (Peabody, Mass.: Hendrickson), 241–68.

Powell, C. E. (1997), 'The Identity of the "Restrainer" in 2 Thessalonians 2:6–7', *BSacr* 154: 320–32.

Romaniuk, K. (1993), 'Les Thessaloniciens étaient-ils des paresseux?', *ETL* 69: 142–5.

Russell, D. F. (1964), *The Meaning and Message of Jewish Apocalyptic* (London: SCM).

Russell, R. (1988), 'The Idle in 2 Thess. 3.6–12: An Eschatological or a Social Problem?', *NTS* 34: 105–19.

Seesemann, H. (1967), '*Pateō* and compounds in NT', *TDNT* v. 943–5.

Strobel, A. (1961), *Untersuchungen zum eschatologischen Verzögerungsproblem: Auf Grund der Spätjüdisch-urchristlichen Geschichte von Habakuk 2, 2 ff.* (Leiden: Brill).

Trudinger, P. (1995), 'The Priority of 2 Thessalonians Revisited: Some Fresh Evidence', *Downside Review*, 113: 31–5.

Wrede, W. (1903), *Die Echtheit des zweiten Thessalonikerbrief untersucht*, TU NS 9/2 (Leipzig: Hinrichs).

73. The Pastoral Epistles

CLARE DRURY

INTRODUCTION

These three letters purporting to be from Paul to two of his close companions clearly belong together as a set. They have always been placed together in the New Testament, their concerns and language are shared. Certain key words and ideas permeate the three, connecting them and holding together what at first sight might seem a rather amorphous collection of ethical injunctions and doctrinal assertions. 1 Timothy and Titus are very similar in character and subject-matter, their teaching concentrating on church order and ethical exhortation. Sandwiched between them, 2 Timothy is more personal than the other two; Paul is in prison, while in the other two he is free. His character and behaviour in adversity are presented as models to Timothy which arouse the reader's sympathy and admiration.

A. Authorship. 1. The claim that Paul himself wrote the letters seems at first sight obvious and incontrovertible. All three begin with a greeting from the apostle and contain personal notes and asides such as 'I urge you, as I did when I was on my way to Macedonia' (1 Tim 1:3); 'I left you behind in Crete' (Titus 1:5) and 'When you come, bring the cloak that I left with Carpus at Troas, also the books and above all the parchments' (2 Tim 4:13). Combined with such emotional appeals as 2 Tim 1:3–5; 4:6–8, the impression of Pauline authorship seems clear.

2. But things are not so straightforward: signs of the late date of the letters proliferate. The organization of the church under officers such as bishops and deacons is well advanced (e.g. 1 Tim 3:1–13; 5:3–13) and mirrors the situation found in late first-century and early second-century Christian writings such as *1 Clement* and the letters of Ignatius and Polycarp. The situation of the letters seems inauthentic too; they are addressed to two travelling companions whom 'Paul' has apparently just left (1 Tim 1:3; Titus 1:5) and expects to see again soon (1 Tim 3:14; 2 Tim 4:13; Titus 3:12). Yet they contain teaching of the most rudimentary kind which close associates might be expected to know.

3. The teaching that characterizes the Pastorals lacks the fire and passion of the original Pauline epistles; the immediacy of eschatological expectation that lay behind much of Paul's teaching (e.g. 1 Cor 7:17–31) has gone. Judgement and the future appearance of Christ are still expected, but it is the ordered life of the community that is focal. There is no mention of key Pauline ideas such as the cross, the church as the body of Christ, or covenant. Paul's struggle to identify the role of the law in his new understanding of salvation is absent; in the Pastorals, the law fulfils its normal function of identifying, restricting, and punishing evildoers (1 Tim 1:8–11). The teaching of the Pastorals focuses upon the ordered life of the community emphasizing such virtues as piety or godliness (e.g. 1 Tim 2:2; 2 Tim 3:5; Titus 1:1) and good conscience (1 Tim 1:5, 19; 3:9; 2 Tim 1:3). Individual behaviour is bound up in the well-being of the whole group, and there is a clear sense that the church has a future as a community; its organization is designed to enable sound doctrine to continue (1 Tim 4:6; 2 Tim 3:10). The ethical teaching is not solely inward-looking, but also aims to ensure that the church is acceptable to the outside world. The behaviour of its members must not draw attention to them as part of a new and suspect cult, they must conform in every way to the moral standards and expectations of the larger community.

4. By the end of the first century the figure of Paul had assumed authority for many in the church and, as his significance grew, so did narratives about his life and interpretations of his teaching. The Acts of the Apostles provides evidence of this sort of development; the figure of Paul is employed to present the author's own image of the Gentile church and its origins. In Paul's speeches in Acts there is nothing that directly contradicts the ideas we find in Paul's own letters, but the picture that emerges is one of a more conciliatory and less theologically sophisticated figure. Both Acts and the Pastoral Epistles witness to a time in the church's development when Paul had become a legendary figure and different groups were competing to be regarded as his true successors. This trend continued well into the second century: the apocryphal *Acts of Paul* provide evidence of speculation and legends which grew up around the figure of Paul. The longest and most complete of them, the *Acts of Paul and Thecla*, provides a model of the woman's role as teacher and baptizer that the Pastoral Epistles deplore (1 Tim 2:11–15). According to Marcion, the second-century heretic, Paul alone had presented the true Christian message of love and grace.

5. Thus the origin of the Pastoral Epistles begins to become clear: the author emphasizes the importance of handing on true teaching through leaders such as Timothy and Titus, authorized by Paul so that false doctrine could be refuted and its promulgators condemned, 'Timothy, guard what has been entrusted to you. Avoid the profane chatter and contradictions of what is falsely called knowledge' (1 Tim 6:20; cf. 2 Tim 2:1–2, 14–19; Titus 1:1–5; 3:8–11). While a small and declining number of scholars still argue for Pauline authorship, most prefer to see the author's modesty and his admiration for Paul behind his pseudonymity; he was passing on Pauline tradition and the credit was due to Paul rather than to him. The letters can be seen as documents written in and for a community which wanted to hold fast to what they considered true Pauline teaching in the face of persecution or opposition from different kinds of Christian teachers. On the other hand, some of Paul's teaching on practical matters—teaching about the remarriage of widows for example, and about the ideal ascetic life—is contradicted in the Pastorals (e.g. 1 Cor 7:7–8; cf. 1 Tim 2:11–15; 3:2–5). The situation the author was addressing was so different he felt he had the authority to alter Paul's original teaching.

6. This implies that the personal notes and reminiscences, which occur throughout the letters (1 Tim 1:3; 2 Tim 4:13; Titus 1:5), are conscious forgeries included to add authenticity. So some scholars (e.g. Miller 1997) have suggested that the Pastorals are a semi-pseudonymous work, containing fragments of genuine Pauline material with later teaching added to these 'notes' to form the epistles as we have them. But a growing number of scholars see the Pastorals as entirely pseudonymous. They argue for complete and intentional pseudonimity; the writer used the device of the letter form, and included the kind of personal details that would convince his readers of the letters' authenticity. If the device was successful the author's opponents would be unassailably refuted. The personal notes are trivial in nature and do not fit with details of Paul's life we know from his undoubted letters, or from the story as presented in Acts. But they were an important part of the fiction and for the author's purpose to work, the fiction must be convincing.

B. Character and Situation of the Pastorals. 1. The concerns expressed in the Pastoral Epistles focus on sound doctrine and good behaviour. The two are closely linked in the author's mind and are contrasted with the ideas and behaviour of his opponents. A group within the author's church is trying to convert members of the community to its own way of thinking and living (e.g. 1 Tim 1:3–7, 18–20; 4:1–10; 6:3–4; 2 Tim 2:24–6; 3:13–17; 4:3–5; Titus 1:10–2:2). This group of people, heterodox from our author's point of view, was having such success in persuading others of its ideas, that the Pastoral Epistles were written to contradict their theories and denounce their behaviour. They are characterized as disputatious and given to theological speculation and argument—teaching which leads to disharmony in the community (e.g. 1 Tim 6:3–10). The methods the author employs to contradict false teaching and to encourage attachment to his point of view are a combination of exhortations to virtue and condemnations of the teachings of his opponents with warnings of the dire results of following them. Because we have no independent record, we cannot be certain who the opponents were or exactly what they were teaching; we have to reconstruct what we can from the epistles themselves.

2. The author counters his opponents with his appeal to tradition. Paul, well known and revered as the apostle to the Gentiles, hands on the tradition to two junior companions, Timothy and Titus, who, in turn, are instructed to transmit it to the communities in their care. Within these communities, officers of blameless character will be charged with preserving and handing on this sound doctrine and ethical instructions to the rest. In this way there could be no doubt of the authenticity of the teaching the author presents; it has been transmitted by a direct and faultless route. The character of the officers of the community is a major theme in 1 Timothy and Titus. They were key people in maintaining true doctrine and in keeping order and discipline within the community.

3. Alternating with instructions about church organization and ethical teaching are brief kerygmatic statements about God's plan of salvation (1 Tim 2:5–6; 3:16; 6.13–16; 2 Tim 1:9–10; 2:11–13; Titus 3:4–7). These doctrinal sections present familiar ideas about salvation history, none of them inconsistent with Pauline and other New Testament teaching. Indeed Pauline language is sometimes employed; but the ideas are not developed theologically. Their form is often rhythmical; they may have liturgical origins.

4. The organization of the church and the relationship of its members to one another is based on the Graeco-Roman household. Household codes are found elsewhere in the NT epistles (Col 3:18–4:1; Eph 5:22–6:9; 1 Pet 2:18–3:7) but their use in the Pastorals is developing so that the church can be described as the household of God (1 Tim 3:15). The development is not complete—the terminology is used sometimes in its original sense and sometimes with the sense of church office (e.g. in 1 Tim 5:1, 17, the Greek word *presbuteros* is used both for 'older man' and for 'elder') but evolution can be seen to be taking place.

5. In the passages of ethical teaching the Pastoral Epistles share some of the ideas about how a virtuous life should be lived with contemporary pagan philosophers as well as with other Christian and Jewish writers. Comparisons with the works of Plutarch, who lived in the second half of the first century, and Epictetus, a Stoic philosopher of the first half of the second century, illuminate our understanding of the Pastorals' teaching about moderation or restraint (*sōphrosunē*) and piety or godliness (*eusebeia*). These terms describe the kind of civic and private virtues that were common subjects for discussion among Greek and Roman moralists at the time. In the Pastorals the meaning of *eusebeia* is both doctrinal and ethical; it is a word used to describe the kind of lifestyle the author advocates that arises out of a belief in the doctrinal claims he makes; good behaviour is inextricably linked with belief in sound doctrine. Pagan writers also help to put in perspective social issues such as the role of women. The place of women in society was as much an issue for pagan writers as it was for Christians (see Beard, North, and Price 1998: i. 297–9).

COMMENTARY

1 Timothy

(1:1–2) The form of the opening greeting is familiar to readers of NT epistles. It follows the conventions of letter-writing of the first few centuries CE, with the sender naming himself and greeting the recipient of the letter. Here, the writer names himself as Paul, apostle of Christ Jesus, as he does with minor variations in the other two letters. The recipient here is Timothy, well known from Pauline epistles and Acts as Paul's companion and fellow-worker (e.g. Rom 16:21; 1 Cor 4:17; 16:10; Col 1:1; 1 Thess 1:1; Acts 16:1). Several points stand out in this introduction: Paul's authority is stressed and is in no doubt; not only is he an apostle of Christ Jesus, he is commanded by God. The formality of the greeting, unexpected in a letter between friends and colleagues, has contributed to the belief that the letter is inauthentic. At the heart of the greeting two unusual epithets are employed, God is called 'our Saviour' and Christ, 'our hope'. Outside the Pastorals, only in Cor 1:27 is Christ identified as 'hope' and there it is 'Christ the hope of glory'; God our Saviour is found in the Pastorals a number of times, but elsewhere in the NT only in the Magnificat (Lk 1:47) and in the doxology of the epistle of Jude (Jude 25). The writer wants to make it clear that the message he brings is the true message of salvation, so he presents himself as the apostle Paul, commissioned by God the origin of salvation. Hope and salvation are closely connected; the work of salvation started at the incarnation will be continued through the church and completed at Christ's return.

v. 2, Timothy, the recipient of the letter, is called a 'loyal child in the faith' as is Titus in Titus 1:4. The word *gnēsios*, translated 'loyal', implies legitimacy in the Greek. In distinction to others who will be invoked, later (e.g. Hymenaeus and Alexander, 1:20), Timothy is Paul's legitimate successor. He is a child and therefore inferior to Paul, but the tradition passed from one to the other is true and authoritative. The threefold salutation is slightly different from those found in other Pauline letters. Grace and peace are familiar; here, mercy is added in the middle of the formula, where 'to you' is found elsewhere (e.g. Rom 1:7; 1 Cor 1:3; 2 Cor 1:2; Gal 1:3). Mercy is a particular concern in the Pastoral Epistles, where the word appears five times of the ten occurrences in the whole Pauline corpus. God the Father, or Creator, and Christ Jesus our Lord are invoked again at the end of the salutation as the origins of Christian 'virtues'.

(1:3–7) The situation envisaged at the opening of the letter is that Paul has left Timothy behind in Ephesus while he has travelled on into Macedonia. Such a situation cannot be fitted into any reconstruction of Paul's life that can be pieced together either from his own letters or from the narrative in Acts. They provide the kind of personal details that lead some readers to argue for authenticity, while others claim that it is exactly the kind of information a pseudonymous author would include to add verisimilitude to his pretence, bringing the characters to life by placing them in relationship to one another in a real setting.

Having established his credentials, the author introduces one of the main concerns of his letter; he wants to combat false teaching and to discredit the teachers. The teachers cannot be identified with any certainty, nor what they were teaching. 1:3–11 provides clues about the teaching; we are told that the opponents occupy themselves with 'myths and endless genealogies which lead to speculations' (v. 4). It may be that a Gnostic group was teaching in the author's community and perverting the faith as he understood it by mythological speculations about creation and salvation. Because his readers must have known who he was referring to, he does not need to identify his opponents specifically, but sets his view of Christian virtues such as love, a pure heart, and a good conscience against the vices of speculative theory and vain discussion.

(1:8–11) Here he adds a further dimension to the description of his opponents. They desire to be teachers of the law, presumably the Jewish law, without understanding what it is they are talking about; its true meaning is to regulate the behaviour of lawless and disobedient people. The vices listed in vv. 9–10

are an odd collection, including specific acts such as murder, matricide, and parricide alongside general characteristics such as sinfulness, unholiness, and profanity. At different levels such behaviour would incur disapproval in almost any society, not just under Jewish law. The list is obviously meant to be contrasted with the list of virtues in 1:5. The writer's central theme, that good doctrine leads to good behaviour, is contrasted with the effects of following unsound teaching. He does not explain this teaching very clearly; but simply by placing the lists alongside one another he points up the contrast.

The qualities belonging to the faith, such as love issuing from a pure heart and a good conscience, are not typical of the teaching in Paul's genuine letters. Paul would certainly not dissent from the ideas expressed, but he uses different language to describe them. The Pastor's view of the law is very different from Paul's own too. For Paul the law symbolized the old dispensation, and its relationship to salvation brought through Christ was extremely complex; it was God-given but restrictive and negative in its effects (e.g. Rom 7:4–25; Gal 3:1–14). The Pastor, on the other hand, sees it in a much more mundane way: it is a God-given guide to behaviour, which, when abused, works against sound teaching.

(1:12–17) 1:3–11 and 18–20 provide a framework for these verses. This biographical section, illustrating God's mercy to his apostle Paul, has the effect of giving Paul tremendous prominence. The section takes the form of a thanksgiving, and describes the radical volte-face of the sometime persecutor turned faithful disciple. The story is familiar not only from Acts (9:1–22; 22:3–21; 26:9–20), but also from 1 Cor 15:8–10 and Phil 3:1–5. The story of the complete conversion of the persecutor is a tale worth telling. But here more than anywhere else the fate of Paul is inextricably linked with the story of salvation. 'Christ Jesus came into the world to save sinners—of whom I am the foremost.' Paul's sinfulness is vividly described: 'I formerly a blasphemer, a persecutor, and a man of violence', but he 'received mercy' because he acted out of ignorance. The sharp contrast between the persecutor and the believer is shown to be an intentional part of God's plan so that Paul might be an example for others, to demonstrate above all the perfect patience of Jesus Christ. So the tale serves a dual purpose; Paul is a typical example of a convert, but his special case gives him a special position as an apostle as the next few verses show. Paul himself talks of his former life in 1 Cor 15:9 and Phil 3:4–8, to make a similar point, but here the language is stronger and less forgiving. Acts is much closer to this passage when it speaks of the ignorance of unbelievers before their conversion (e.g. 3:17; 13:27; 17:23).

The central Christian belief (v. 15), that Christ Jesus came into the world to save sinners, is introduced by a formula that assumes general acceptance. The formula is found five times in the Pastoral Epistles (1 Tim 1:15; 3:1; 4:9; 2 Tim 2:11; Titus 3:8), often, as here, drawing attention to a significant doctrinal statement. It is not clear why the author uses the phrase with some doctrinal assertions and not with others. Often, as in this case, it seems that a quotation is being employed. The significance of the expression, 'Christ came into the world to save sinners', lies in the second half of the statement: the writer is not so much interested in the pre-existence of Christ, which *may* be implied, as in the soteriological effect of his coming (cf. 3:16 and 2 Tim 1:10). It introduces the idea of Paul's sinfulness which in turn shows him as a prototype believer and recipient of grace. Patience or forbearance (*makrothumia*) is a defining characteristic of God in relationship with his people in the Jewish Scriptures. The words found in Ex 34.6–7 where God is described as 'merciful and gracious, slow to anger, and abounding in steadfast love and faithfulness, keeping steadfast love for the thousandth generation' are repeated and echoed frequently in later Jewish writings to contrast the long-suffering constancy of God with the sinfulness and fickle nature of his people (Jon 4:2; 2 Macc 6:14–16; Wis 11:23; 12:16). Here the attributes have been transferred to Christ, through whom God is working out salvation. Eternal life is in the future, it is a focus for belief grounded in Christ 'our hope' (1:1) for the future and based on what has already been achieved.

(1:18–20) This section follows awkwardly from the doxology in v. 17 and it is far from clear what 'these instructions' refers to. It may look back to 1:3 where Timothy is urged to give certain instructions, or forward to the injunction to 'fight the good fight' later in the same verse. The word *paraggelia*, translated here as 'instruction', occurs with its cognates six times in 1 Timothy (cf. Tim 1:3; 4:11; 5:7; 6:13, 17) demonstrating how important was the passing on of sound doctrine through properly commissioned people. The prophecies referred to in v. 18 are not to be understood as scriptural prophecies, but recall prophetic experiences such as that described in Acts 13:1–3 and referred to in 1 Tim 4:14.

The imagery of fighting or warfare was widespread among philosophers and religious groups in the ancient world and is found elsewhere in the NT epistles (1 Cor 9:7; 2 Cor 10:3–6; Eph 6:10–17; 2 Tim 2:3–7, where the image is linked with that of athletic competition). The repetition of the virtues of faith and a good conscience from 1:5 provides a framework for the central section of this chapter. Further emphasis is given by reference to two men, Hymenaeus and Alexander, who have 'reject[ed] conscience' and 'suffered shipwreck in the faith'. They have therefore been 'turned over to Satan'. As in 1 Cor 5:5, this is a powerful image describing the radical effects of exclusion from the Christian community. Hymenaeus is mentioned again, alongside Philetus, at 2 Tim 2:17, where their talk is said to spread like gangrene. Alexander the coppersmith is mentioned in 2 Tim 4:14 where he is said to have done Paul great harm. It is impossible to say whether both refer to the same man. Their rejection of the faith is to be contrasted with the steadfastness of Paul and Timothy; by the end of the first chapter, we are left with a clear impression of the apostle and of his legitimate successor; they are the transmitters of the true teaching of the church.

Church Organization and Behaviour (2:1–3:13)

The discussion in chs. 2 and 3 changes from concern about the opposition to a description of the kind of behaviour that should characterize members of the church towards both one another and outsiders. The detailed arrangements for the leadership of this household and relationships within it suggest that the church is becoming more at home in the world. For Paul, who felt he was living at the end of the age, there was a strong tension between living in this age but belonging to the next. This not only affected his sense of purpose but his ethical teaching as well. Now the situation is different. Eschatological hope is still very much alive (e.g. 6:14–15, 18–19), but there is no sense of urgency or immediacy. There is a more long-term viewpoint; the church must be firmly established, and respectable, so as to avoid adverse publicity.

(2:1–7) Prayer is the first duty of a member of the community. Four words are used to describe the prayers, 'supplications, prayers, intercessions, and thanksgivings' but no distinction is made between them. More significant is that prayers are to be made for everyone, particularly kings and those in authority, and not just for members of the community. For God is Creator and Saviour, and desires that every human being should be saved. Prayer for the emperor caused difficulties for Jews and Christians; their refusal to acknowledge his authority sometimes led to persecutions, but there are a number of passages in the NT which follow the same line as this (Rom 13.1–7; 1 Pet 2:14, 17; Titus 3:1; Acts *passim*). The aim of such prayer was to avoid the possibility of persecution, and so lead a peaceful life 'in godliness and dignity'. There is similar teaching in other first- and second-century Jewish and Christian writers, and the reasons given often echo those given here (e.g. 1 *Clem.* 61; Tert. *Apol.* 30; Jos. *J.W.* 2.197). The nouns translated 'godliness' and 'dignity' are characteristic of the Pastorals and betray their Hellenistic setting; they translate words (*eusebeia* and *semnotēs*) found elsewhere in the NT only in Acts and 2 Peter. They illustrate the results of living in harmony with the authorities; the ability to devote oneself to the worship of God which results in a respectable and responsible life not outwardly distinct from that of their pagan neighbours. Knowledge of the truth recurs in 2 Tim 2:25; 3:7; Titus 1:1, and helps emphasize the accessibility of the Christian message to all reasonable people.

(2:5–6) presents a summary of the true teaching that is the focus of that Christian message. It appears to contain a quotation (NRSV presents it as verse), and is a succinct telling of the drama of salvation in a rhythmical and poetic form—a kind of credal statement (cf. 1 Tim 3:16; 6.13–16; 2 Tim 1:9–10; 2.11–13; Titus 3:4–7). God is one and the Saviour of all people. Christ's role is as mediator; he alone links God and humankind. His humanity is stressed to show solidarity with those he saves—the same word is used in Greek for 'human' and 'humankind'. The word 'mediator' is applied to Christ in the NT only here and in Hebrews (8:6; 9:15; 12:24, where he is mediator of the covenant as Moses was in Gal 3:19). The emphasis on a single God and a single mediator may be an attack on the kind of Gnostic 'myths and speculations' referred to in 1:4, and the stress on Christ's humanity may have been included to refute Docetism.

Christ's self-giving as a ransom, also found in Titus 2:14, uses language similar to Paul's in Romans 3:24 and 8:23 and to that used in Mk 10:45, Mt 20:28, where 'he came . . . to give his life as a ransom for many'. Here, by contrast, the language is totally inclusive; he gave his life as a ransom for *all*. The language of ransom implies that payment is being made to obtain the freedom of captives or slaves and has as its background both the manumission of slaves and the freeing of Israel from Egypt at the Exodus. By the time the Pastoral

Epistles were written, the language of ransom had become central in Christian thought. In the context of 1:15 freedom from sin is implied. As part of God's plan for salvation, Jesus' death undoubtedly came at the right time. In the Greek the phrase 'testimony at the right time' is part of the credal statement of vv. 5–6 rather than a comment upon it.

(2:7) Paul's own role in God's plan is emphasized again. He was not only an apostle but also herald and teacher of the Gentiles. The word translated 'herald' is rare in the NT, and is found elsewhere only in 2 Tim 1:11, where it also refers to Paul, and in 2 Peter 2:5, where it refers to Noah. The cognate verb is, however, found throughout the NT. Paul's appointment as teacher of the Gentiles provides the means for God's plan for universal salvation to proceed. The picture of Paul as apostle to the Gentiles accords with that in Paul's own letters and with the narrative of his journeys in Acts. The insistence on Paul's authority is exaggerated, much more than would be necessary in a genuine letter from Paul to his friend. But in the context of this letter the insistence on authority has its place: the true message of salvation is being handed on to the next generation.

(2:8–15) Returning to the subject of prayer, Timothy is now given instructions about the necessary physical as well as emotional attitude. A distinction is drawn between the attitude suitable for men and that for women. Men are to pray with hands raised; they can pray anywhere, in private as well as in communal worship. Their emotional state 'without anger or argument' as a prerequisite to proper prayer recalls the teaching of Old Testament prophets (e.g. Hos 6:6; Am 3:14–15; 5:4–7).

The Pastor then turns to the behaviour of women. First they are to dress and behave modestly. This teaching can be paralleled in Plutarch's *Advice to a Bride and Groom*, 'It is not gold or precious stones or scarlet that makes a woman decorous, but whatever invests her with that something which betokens dignity, good behaviour and modesty' (*Mor.* 141e). Women were gaining a certain amount of freedom and independence in the Roman empire, and this was no doubt as true among Christian women as non-Christian women. But like other conservative writers, Christian and non-Christian, the Pastor is concerned that women should remain in what he perceives as their proper, subordinate position. Other NT writers make the same sort of point, particularly about the public behaviour of women. It was necessary for the successful continuation of the faith and to avoid persecution, that women should behave in a seemly way in meetings of the community. Part of this was an insistence that women should not teach or be perceived to be in a position of authority over a man (cf. 1 Cor 14:34).

The reason given by the Pastor for women's subordination goes back to Adam and Eve (cf. 1 Cor 11:8–9). First, he claims that primacy in time implies superiority of status. Second, it was, he claims, Eve who was deceived, not Adam. He is departing from the Genesis narrative at this point. Certainly, Eve ate the fruit first, but she was quickly followed by Adam, and they were both punished. According to some Jewish traditions, Eve's sin was a sexual one, she was seduced by the serpent, so salvation could be achieved only by bearing children. An idea of this sort may lie behind 2:14–15 which

places Eve's transgression in such close proximity to the solution that salvation for women rests in bearing children. In any case, a woman's most important role in the Graeco-Roman world was to be the mother of children. For the Pastor, the family and the household were the focus of the church, so bearing children and bringing them up in the faith was vital for its successful survival and growth.

The teaching about women's subordination should not be understood outside its own context. In Rom 16:1 a deacon called Phoebe is commended by Paul. His teaching in 1 Cor 11 and 14 suggests that already in the middle of the first century some women were behaving with a freedom which was unacceptable to the leaders of the church. The popular story of Thecla, told in the *Acts of Paul and Thecla*, is evidence that this trend continued into the second century.

(3:1–7) 'The saying is sure' may refer back to what has just been said, as in 4:9 or Titus 3:8, or forwards to the instructions about church offices. When the same phrase was used before in 1:15, it introduced an important Christological saying, as it does in 2 Tim 2:11. It is not quite clear here if either the preceding saying or what follows is thought by the author to have this special significance. The writer's teaching about women is important to him but so is his teaching about church officers which follows.

vv. 1b–7 concern the office of the *episkopos*, literally overseer, but translated in the NRSV as bishop. The discussion indicates that the church has reached a settled situation, where it needs capable and dignified men to run it. But the information we are given is tantalizingly incomplete, for while the qualities required of a bishop are clearly set out, his duties are not described. If, as is quite likely, one of the patterns of organization and worship in the early church was the synagogue, then the *episkopos* would, like a Jewish synagogue leader, lead the community and represent its interests in the outside world. His good character and reputation among outsiders was essential for the community's welfare and continuing stability. The parallel drawn in 3:5 between the household and the church provides another clue. Graeco-Roman households which consisted of family, slaves, and more loosely dependent groups of people were run by a paterfamilias who had complete authority. The church in the Pastoral Epistles is seen as the household of God; everyone—men, women, children, elders (*presbyteroi*), servants (*diakonoi*)—has his or her place in it and its smooth running is overseen by an *episkopos* who must be of impeccable character.

The list of virtues expected of such a community leader is conventional in both Jewish and Hellenistic societies, including that favourite 'restraint' (*sōphrosunē*, translated in the NRSV as 'temperate'). His duties include a responsibility for teaching, that is handing on the tradition as he has had it handed on to him. There are some points that may be surprising to a modern reader; the *episkopos* is expected to be married and to be the head of a household (3:2, 4–5). Furthermore he is to be 'married only once', literally, 'the husband of one wife'. Polygamy is not being forbidden here; remarriage after divorce may be in question, or it may be that the remarriage of widowers is also excluded for *episkopoi*. If so, the rules are different for different groups in the community, for young widows are encouraged to remarry (5:14). Perhaps, though, this is rather an extreme translation of the Greek; what is meant is that the *episkopos* should be a faithful husband to his wife, but that sequential monogamy is not out of the question. His conversion to Christianity must not be recent. There may have been important individuals in the community who felt that their standing or wealth qualified them to become leaders in the church. But to be an *episkopos* one must be firmly rooted in the faith; the implication must be that the church itself is firmly established too.

We do not know whether each community had one *episkopos*, or more. Ignatius, who was bishop of Antioch in Syria, argued strongly in the first decade of the second century for a monarchical episcopate, that is, having one *episkopos* as overseer of the Christian communities in each town, who presides over and is distinct from the deacons and from the elders, 'that you may be joined together in one subjection, subject to the bishop and to the presbytery, and may in all things be sanctified' (Ign. *Eph.* 2.2; cf. 20.2). But it is certain that there was no universally accepted pattern of leadership at this period, and from the Pastoral Epistles themselves no clearly defined organization can be discerned.

(3:8–13) Just as there is information about the character but not the duties of the *episkopos*, only the virtues necessary for a deacon are described in vv. 8–13. Indeed, the virtues of *episkopos* and deacon overlap to a great extent. This suggests that the functions were clearly understood already in the community being addressed; the issue was to find suitable people to perform the functions. The Greek word *diakonos*, translated 'deacon', originally meant 'servant', but in the apostolic fathers (e.g. *Didache* 15; Ign. *Trall.* 2, 3; Ign. *Magn.* 6, 13) and the NT Epistles it is used to describe an officer of the church (e.g. Rom 16:1; 1 Cor 3:5; Eph 6:21; Phil 1:1; 1 Thess 3:2; cf. Acts 6). The narrative in Acts 6 traces the diaconate back to the Jerusalem church when 'seven men full of the Spirit' were appointed to distribute food to the Greek-speaking widows of the church. This may be later rationalization of the origin of the office, linking the function of serving to the diaconate when its origins were already obscure. In Mk 10:45 Jesus uses the verb cognate with *diakonos* when he says 'I came not to be served but to serve'. The qualities of an *episkopos* and a deacon were similar; their roles apparently not dissimilar except for a greater emphasis on management and teaching in the case of the *episkopos*. Little information is given here about the work of a deacon, but it is clear that a test was necessary for those aspiring to become deacons to prove themselves blameless. The 'mystery of the faith', God's hidden purpose only understood by believers, refers to the true teaching of 2:5–6 and 3:16.

In the midst of the description of a deacon's character is a verse about women. The word translated 'women' also means wives in Greek, so there is a real possibility that the verse describes the qualities required in a deacon's wife rather than in a woman deacon. If that is the case, they must be as far beyond reproach as their husbands. On the other hand, Phoebe is called a deacon in Rom 16:1, so it is possible that this verse refers to the qualities such women need. If so, their role must be limited by the constraints put on women's behaviour in 2:11–12, where women were told to be submissive to men and to learn in silence, and were forbidden to teach or have authority over men. The characteristics mentioned are

reminiscent of those necessary for *episkopoi* and deacons. A deacon, like an *episkopos*, must be married only once, literally 'the husband of one wife', and must be a good head of his household. Single men, slaves, and, to judge by this qualification, women, seem to be excluded from holding office. The requirements that an *episkopos* should be hospitable and a teacher are not included for deacons, but Timothy is referred to as a deacon in 4:6, and since he was expected to 'pass on all these instructions', in other words, to teach, it may be that the categories are quite fluid and ill-defined. The face that the church presents must be respectable, so all its representatives must be beyond reproach.

(3:14–16) vv. 14–15 open with a personal note designed to add verisimilitude to the fictional situation. It is common in the Pauline epistles to refer to personal travel plans, so this reference places the epistle firmly in its genre as well as supporting the picture of Paul's personal involvement. The use of the word 'household' summarizes the whole section from 2:1 to 3:13. More will be said of the household later in this letter and also in the other two. But the picture we have so far presents a picture of a solid establishment, run by responsible figures. Any assailant will have a difficult task.

The 'mystery of our religion' is described in the quoted formula which follows. For similar passages see 1 TIM 2:5–6. The word translated 'religion' is *eusebeia*; normally in the Pastorals *eusebeia* and its cognates denote piety or godliness, here it carries a sense of the system of belief that inspires piety. The earlier formula in ch. 2 dwelt on the human nature of Christ; this confessional formula consists of three pairs of contrasted statements. The main point of contrast being the last word of each line: in the first pair flesh and spirit, in the second it is angels and Gentiles, in the last pair the contrast is between the world and glory. The structure is chiastic, ABBAAB (where the earthly world is represented by A, the heavenly by B) which makes the formula memorable and helps unify the whole. In every line the verb is in the same tense and is followed by a noun in the same case preceded, with one exception, by 'in'. Heaven and earth are being contrasted and yet shown to belong together, united by the revelation of Christ and its effects. There is no direct reference to Christ's death and resurrection, nor to the end of the world, but a clear picture is created of the unifying and universal nature of the coming of Christ. Christ's triumph and glory are placed in contrast to the teachings of demons which are to be the subject of the next passage. The household of God rests on sure foundations.

(4:1–5) No attempt is made to elucidate the confessional statement, instead, the author moves on to describe dangers of his opponents' teaching, and the importance and strength of true doctrine. The contrasts between flesh and spirit, earth and heaven are emphasized by reference to revelation through the Spirit in vv. 1–2. The Spirit who inspires true prophetic utterances has foretold opposition to the faith in 'later times', or the last times. It was a commonplace idea in Jewish and Christian apocalyptic that the end would be preceded by a time of persecution and suffering (e.g. Mk 13; 1 Cor 15:24–8). The sense of urgency and immediacy are absent from the Pastoral Epistles, but there is a lingering feeling that before the end there will be difficult and dangerous times.

The opposition described in these verses comes from people whose teaching is dangerously close to that of the author and yet markedly different. It seems to be based on asceticism; marriage was rejected and so was the eating of certain foods. Paul had faced similar problems in Corinth, but his response, recommending celibacy as the ideal, was conditioned by his belief in the imminence of the end (e.g. 1 Cor 7:8–9, 25–31). The perspective of this writer is longer, he envisages a future for the church, so marriage and the procreation of children who will be brought up in the faith is important to him. Sexual asceticism would rob the church of the next generation of believers. The Pastor feels so strongly about his opponents that he claims that their teaching is inspired by demons (v. 1). His own monotheism is clear and, in contrast to such teachers as Marcion, he believes that 'everything God created is good'. Like Jesus when discussing Jewish food laws (Mk 7:19), he believes all food may be eaten. This particular controversy may support the thesis that some, at any rate, of his opponents were Jewish.

(4:6–10) The rest of the chapter continues in the same tone; encouraging Timothy as a 'good servant' or 'deacon' to pass on to his fellow Christians the sound teaching he has received, while avoiding or rejecting the 'profane myths and old wives' tales' of the opposition. We are given little more information about the content of sound teaching or of its opposite. Presumably, both were well known to the recipients of the letter and did not need to be spelt out, but the false myths obviously play an important part in the opponents' teaching (cf. 1:4). *Eusebeia*, here translated 'godliness', appears again as the most important Christian virtue. It characterizes behaviour now and holds promise for the life to come.

In v. 9 the formula 'the saying is sure' is repeated (cf. 1:15; 3:1). Again, it is not clear whether it points back to what has gone before, or forwards, or whether it is meant to refer to the whole passage about holding fast to the faith and rejecting false teaching. v. 10 mentions hope again (cf. 1:1). As well as looking back to the historical events of Christ's life and death, attention was fixed on hope for the future (cf. 2 Cor 1:10). God's universal salvation here is more limited than in 2:6 'especially to those who believe', but there is no suggestion of an alternative fate for those who do not believe.

(4:11–16) Timothy is again addressed personally. Such personal references help to carry the fiction of Pauline authorship. He is instructed to teach, to exhort, and to read aloud: in other words, to pass on the tradition he has received from Paul, until Paul himself arrives (cf. 2:14–15). Teaching was one of the functions allocated to the *episkopos*: Timothy is not named as an *episkopos* anywhere in the Pastorals, but he is portrayed as carrying out some similar functions (in Ign. *Magn.* 3 the church is recommended to respect and obey their *episkopos* despite his youth). He is to set an example by his behaviour and deportment. He is gifted as a teacher, from the time he was commissioned by the laying on of hands by the council of elders (also referred to in 2 Tim 1:6). Laying on of hands was a means of transferring the power of the Spirit from one person to another for teaching or healing. It was a transference of authority, a commissioning or consecration to a particular office or task.

Further Matters of Church Order (5:1–6:2)

Like ch. 3, this passage concerns church organization. Here the subject is widows and elders. In Greek the word *presbuteros* is used to designate old age as well as being the title of an office in Judaism and Christianity. This can lead to ambiguity in interpretation; the natural reverence for the senior members of the group developed into hierarchical organization. For the modern reader it is not always easy to distinguish between the two uses of the term, particularly at the stage of development we see in the Pastorals when the original use is still found alongside its titular use. In vv. 1–2 the meaning is the original one, 'older men', as can be seen from the context. Later in the chapter instructions are given for *presbuteroi*, the leading 'elders' of the community.

(5:3–16) The instructions concerning widows are extremely detailed and precise compared with those relating to other groups (3:1–7, 8–13; 5:17–22). We have already seen that the position and activities of women were of particular concern to the Pastor. This group of women commands his special attention. It was regarded as a special duty among the Jews to care for widows who had no family to provide for them. This is the group referred to here as 'really widows'. Women who would otherwise be genuinely destitute deserved the community's support, whereas those who had families able to support them were not the financial responsibility of the community. The clear moral message of the author stands out in v. 8; failure to provide for widows in one's family was tantamount to a denial of the faith. Widows have a religious duty themselves: to offer prayers night and day (v. 5). But the widow 'who lives for pleasure' (v. 6) does not deserve the community's support. The reference to such women may be to highlight the plight of the 'real widow', or there may have been such a case within the community and known to the readers.

(5:9–16) It seems, however, as if 'real widow' may have a titular sense as well. The expression in v. 9, 'Let a widow be put on the list', suggests some sort of formal enrolment; perhaps, like the term 'elder', the word had acquired a technical sense. Those enrolled might consist of 'real widows' or be a separate group. In any case, qualifications for enrolment are strict and are reminiscent of those for bishops and deacons in ch. 3. The enrolled widow must be 60 years old or more, she must have been married only once, and she must have brought up children. If the widows of 5:3–5 are included in this group, they also have the religious duty to pray continuously for the community. In v. 11 the subject changes to younger widows, a group of women whose behaviour the author finds particularly unacceptable. His characterization of these young women, though it may have been based on his knowledge of one or two individuals, is a gross over-generalization, and one that has done women harm. His solution, as in 2:15, is marriage and childbearing.

(5:17–22) As a council, the group of elders exercised authority in the community (cf. 4:14; Titus 1:5, etc.). Here we find rules for their payment and their discipline. Some may have achieved their status as elders simply on account of their age, and a group of them, 'those who rule well', are worthy of double honour or double payment (the same word is used in Greek to denote payment and honour). Any ambiguity about the word here disappears in the light of v. 18 which contains the scriptural quotation also found in 1 Cor 9:9. There is further justification for the disciplinary procedures by an allusion to a catchphrase also quoted in Mt 10:10 and Lk 10:7.

The disciplining of elders is based on the Jewish system of public accusations supported by at least two witnesses; this has the double effect of ensuring that casual accusations are not made and that 'the rest' would be put off committing the same sin. The rest may refer to the whole community or just the other elders. Impartiality, a word used only here in the NT, is to be the basis of all judgements. Timothy is urged 'not to ordain anyone hastily'. This could imply that extra care taken about the appointment of elders would avoid the need for discipline later.

(5:23–6:2) Before turning to instructions for slaves, a personal instruction is given to Timothy about drinking wine. Ostensibly it is a personal note referring to Timothy's health, which helps support the impression of intimacy between the two. It may also be a roundabout way of attacking the asceticism of the writer's opponents (cf. 4:3–4). Church officials are to be neither drunkards nor ascetics. 5:24–5 contain general truths which may be meant to refer back to the elders of the previous verses, or, more generally, to members of the congregation.

(6:1–2) Slaves are given special instructions, though there are no corresponding instructions for their masters as there are in other epistles (e.g. Col 3:22–4:1; Eph 6:5–9). The institution of slavery is not questioned here or elsewhere in the NT; it was seen as a necessary part of society. The only issue was how slaves should be treated by their owners, but the Pastoral Epistles are not concerned even with that issue. The slaves are divided into two groups, those who belong to non-believing masters and those whose masters are members of the community. Unquestioning obedience is demanded of the first group so that the name of the church should not fall into disrepute. Those who are slaves of Christian masters are advised not to presume on their shared beliefs, though they are all brothers and sisters, sons and daughters of one God. Nevertheless, the social constraints that exist in their everyday lives are not to be overstepped.

(6:2b–21) The apparently haphazard collection of teaching, unified by its hortatory character, links false teaching with bad conduct and identifies *eusebeia*, godliness or piety, with true wealth. As we have seen, piety in the Pastorals denotes the manner of life of a true believer who honours God as Creator and Redeemer of all, and who treats other human beings with respect (cf. 2:2; 4:7, 8; 5:4). It also separates sound teaching from false. False teachers believe that what they call piety is a source of mercenary gain, while 4:8 points to its real value. In vv. 3–10 piety is contrasted with all kinds of vices ranging from envy to morbid craving for controversy, from wrangling to a desire for wealth. Teaching about the vanity of riches here and in 6:17–19 frames a paragraph describing the true Christian life.

vv. 11–12 present the reverse image; the righteousness and piety of the person who shuns the attractions of wealth are contrasted with the behaviour described in vv. 3–10. The list of antisocial and untruthful behaviour in vv. 4–5 is balanced against the beliefs of one who pursues godliness, in language

already familiar, Timothy is exhorted to pursue virtues which have been recommended before, and to fight the good fight. vv. 13–16 contain a doxology or liturgical formula similar to others in the Pastorals (see 1 TIM 2:5–6). It illustrates the ideas of salvation and hope with which the epistle began. God the Creator, whose glorious and transcendent nature is extolled in a series of rich images, will bring about the second manifestation of Christ at the right time. God's transcendence is thus balanced with his involvement in human history, in the two appearances of Christ, one past, one still to come. Jesus Christ is introduced, in his first manifestation, as an example of faithful testimony before Pilate. Although this does not fit neatly with any of our gospel accounts, that he supremely bore witness to the truth is undeniable for the Pastor. As with the other similar passages, the language is poetic and defies precise interpretation, but the rhetoric is clear: God is one, he desires the salvation of all believers through the mediation of his Son, Jesus Christ.

In the final injunction to Timothy the importance of handing on the tradition is repeated, for that is 'what has been entrusted' to him. 'What is falsely called knowledge' became part of the title of Irenaeus' late second-century refutation of Gnosticism.

2 Timothy

2 Timothy shares many of the concerns of 1 Timothy and Titus, and many of the same expressions, but there is a difference of tone. There are far more personal touches in this letter; people are mentioned by name, fellow-workers, friends, and relations as well as opponents. The relationship between Paul and Timothy is made to seem closer and less formal. There are more references, mostly indirect, to Paul's letters particularly to Romans.

Greeting and Warnings (1:1–18)

The opening greeting recalls that in 1 Timothy, but the call is by the will of God rather than by his command (cf. 1 Cor 1:1; 2 Cor 1:1; Col 1:1; Eph 1:1). Paul is said to be an apostle for the sake of the promise of life which is in Christ Jesus, which expands the idea of Christ Jesus, our hope, in 1 Timothy. 'In Christ' is an authentically Pauline expression, but there is no sense that the author has grasped the deep metaphysical meaning of life in Christ as understood by Paul himself. Timothy is called 'beloved' rather than 'loyal' or legitimate child here (see 1 TIM 1:1–2). Thus we already have a hint of the different tone of the letter; there is not so much concern about passing on the authentic tradition.

Paul's letters often open with a thanksgiving like this, but different Greek words are used here, perhaps because the Pauline word *eucharisteō* which originally meant 'give thanks' had acquired special eucharistic connotations by the time this letter was written. The tension Paul himself clearly felt between his Jewish ancestry and his Christian faith is lacking here (1:3; cf. Rom 9–11). Timothy's own ancestry in the faith is exemplary: his grandmother Lois and his mother Eunice were believers before him. Meanwhile, the closeness of the relationship between Paul and Timothy is emphasized by Paul's constant prayers for Timothy and by the emotional memory of tears and the anticipation of joy when they meet again. This, together with the naming of Timothy's mother and grandmother, provide the kind of personal details that add to the sense of authenticity. But the very fact that three generations of Christians within one family are mentioned implies a post-Pauline date; 3:15 makes it clear that Timothy had been brought up as a Christian from childhood.

From 1:6 it seems that Timothy received the laying on of hands from Paul himself rather than from the council of elders as was suggested by 1 Tim 4:14. They may refer to two separate occasions where authorization or commissioning was given for different purposes, or they may simply reflect the different tones in 1 and 2 Timothy, the latter being more personal, the former more formal and official. What is certain in both cases is that through the laying on of hands God's Spirit is passed from one to the other, whether from Paul the apostle or from the council of elders. The qualities imparted by the laying on of hands are both new and familiar in these epistles. Self-discipline translates one of the *sōphrosunē* words familiar from the other two epistles, and together with the spirit of power and love is contrasted with the spirit of cowardice. The idea of cowardice is linked with that of shame in the next paragraph, with the mention of Paul's imprisonment. The Pastor instructs Timothy not to be ashamed of bearing witness to the gospel or of Paul's imprisonment (cf. Rom 1:16). Philippians presents a clear account of his imprisonment and of its effects on Paul and his fellow Christians. Neither 1 Timothy nor Titus mentions it, but here it adds to the sense of authenticity. Paul has by now acquired the status of a hero, someone of whom his successors must not be ashamed; another indication of the late date of these letters.

The link between God's saving work in the past and the present sufferings of the apostle are continued in the kerygmatic passage that follows in 1:8–14. It is a summary of the theological doctrine of the kind the Pastor makes in 1 Timothy and Titus (cf. 1 Tim 2:5–6; 3:16; 6:13–16; 2 Tim 2:11–13; Titus 3:4–7). Like those passages, it depends on Pauline teaching, it uses some Pauline language, but is subtly and markedly different from Paul. For example, Paul rarely uses the verb 'to save' in the past tense (a notable exception being Rom 8:24, where it is in the context of future hope). The ideas expressed in v. 10 are based on the teaching in Romans 16:25–7, 'the proclamation of Jesus Christ according to the revelation of the mystery that was kept secret but is now disclosed'. The notion that God's plan of salvation was a mystery hidden from people for generations before the appearance of Christ was one that quickly took root. It created a historical schema which could link events and prophecies from Scripture not only with Christ's life and death, but into the present and up to his future reappearance. Although the idea has Pauline roots, it is expressed here in language typical of the Pastorals: Christ is described as Saviour, his appearance as *epiphaneia*, a word found in the NT only in the Pastorals (cf. 1 Tim 6:14; 2 Tim 4:1, 8; Titus 2:13) and in 2 Thess 2:8. Christ's death had the effect of abolishing death and through the gospel he brought life and immortality. The Greek word translated 'immortality' actually means 'incorruptibility', an associated but not identical idea. Immortality, translating a different Greek word, is said in 1 Tim 6:16 to belong to God alone. Paul himself talked of resurrection rather than immortality, so again we are presented with Pauline ideas presented in un-Pauline terms.

(1:11–14) We are brought into the present by the reference to Paul's appointment as apostle and teacher, both familiar terms, and herald, already used once in a similar way in 1 Tim 2:7 (elsewhere in the NT only in 2 Pet 2:5). In Greek the word is related to the verb 'to preach', and to 'proclamation'. This triple role has led to Paul's imprisonment, but Paul can remain steadfast because of his trust in God and his assurance of vindication. 'What has been entrusted to me' is a better translation of 1:12 and refers back to 1 Tim 6:20; with the help of Christ and the Holy Spirit, the sound teaching will continue uncorrupted. The line beginning with Christ, and passing to Paul, now continues through Timothy.

(1:15–18) Paul is presented in these verses as being held in a prison in Rome, where he was visited by the faithful Onesiphorus. The example of Paul's faithfulness and that of Onesiphorus (cf. also 4:19) is contrasted with the behaviour of those in Asia who have turned against Paul, including two individuals, Phygelus and Hermogenes. Nothing else is known about these two men, but the verb used for 'turn away' is found also in 4:4 and Titus 1:14 where it has a sense implying the rejection of true teaching, rather than personal rejection. (A man named Hermogenes the coppersmith is mentioned in the *Acts of Paul and Thecla*, 3:1, where he is a companion of Paul but a hypocrite and flatterer. Onesiphorus is also mentioned in the next paragraph.) Ephesus, where Timothy receives these letters, was the capital of the Roman province of Asia, the western part of modern Turkey.

Charge to Timothy (2:1–3:9)

(2:1–7) Timothy is urged to 'be strong in grace' following the example of Onesiphorus. Again he is presented as the link in the chain between Paul and the church at the time of the Pastorals. He has heard Paul's gospel directly and indirectly through the teaching of others. What has been entrusted to him, he is to pass on to those who will, in their turn, teach others. But the role of a faithful Christian is not simply belief and loyal transmitting of tradition, it entails suffering as well. This is a theme that is hardly touched upon in 1 Timothy and Titus, but is prominent in 2 Timothy. Three images are used to describe this wholehearted commitment to the gospel: a Christian must be like a soldier dedicated to serving his commanding officer, like an athlete winning a race according to the rules, or like a farmer toiling over his crops. The three images are not explained; Timothy is told to work out their meaning for himself, with the help of the Lord (v. 7), but the general sense is clear. Work is involved in all three images, they are familiar from Paul's epistles and other NT works, and are found in popular teaching of the time. The first two belong quite closely together, they involve willing obedience to a commanding officer or to the rules of competition. The farming image recalls 1 Cor 9:7–12.

(2:8–13) v. 8 recalls Rom 1:3–4 and 1 Cor 15:20. It represents a formulaic summary of the author's message. Jesus Christ, whose own suffering is not mentioned but is assumed behind this passage, was raised from the dead. The Son of David, he was human, even though of royal descent. In a few words much is implied to contradict the opponents' teaching. The preaching of this message had led to Paul being held in chains like a criminal in a Roman prison. But his enthusiasm for the spreading of the gospel was not diminished or held back by his imprisonment; this epistle is meant to provide proof of that. For the sake of the gospel, Paul is even willing to be held as a criminal, innocent though he is, so that those who believe, 'the elect', may obtain salvation and share in eternal glory along with him. Salvation and glory are familiar themes in the Pastorals, but glory is normally a property of God. The idea of sharing in his glory after death or after the end of the world is, however, a frequent image in Paul (Rom 8:21, 30, etc.)

A rhythmical passage follows (vv. 11–13), introduced by the formula 'the saying is sure' (cf. 1 Tim 1:15; 3:1; 4:9; Titus 3:8). It explains in poetic form the salvation that is in Christ Jesus, for his suffering and death are patterns for the suffering and death of his followers, and the results of his endurance will be shared with those who also suffer in his name. The parallel saying in v. 12b makes the same point but in the negative, while 2:13a emphasizes that Christ remains faithful to the purposes of God whatever human beings do. The ideas are based on Rom 6, but are developed further. It is impossible to know whether the Pastor included here, as possibly elsewhere (for refs. see 2 TIM 1:9–10), existing liturgical passages, but the emphasis on the need for faithfulness in suffering fits this context perfectly.

(2:14–26) From the encouragement to remain faithful, the passage turns to countering heterodoxy. The ultimate aim set out in 2:24–6 is to bring the heterodox back into the fold. Correction rather than expulsion is the theme here (cf. 1 Tim 1:20 where Hymenaeus and Alexander have been handed over to Satan). Repentance is in God's gift, he provides the only way that the heretics can be released from the power of the devil into whose snare they have fallen. We are reminded of 1 Tim 2:4 where God desires the salvation of all.

Before we reach this conciliatory point, however, we learn something of what the opponents were teaching. They liked above all to enter into disputes about words. The Greek word, *logomachein*, to dispute or wrangle about words, is found in related forms also in 1 Tim 6:4 and Titus 3:9. Clearly, acceptance of sound doctrine means not asking questions or questioning definitions. A clear exposition of accepted doctrine was the only proper method of teaching. Discussion could only lead to dispute, and so must be avoided. If the teacher is above reproach, then opponents have no grounds for raising questions. As is often the case in these epistles, good behaviour and sound doctrine go hand in hand. If, like those in 2:4–6, Timothy works at expounding the truth clearly, literally 'cutting a straight path', then he will have nothing to feel ashamed of before God or people. Profane chatter was the subject of a warning in 1 Tim 6:20, as it is here. There it was coupled with 'what is falsely called knowledge', here it is said to lead to impiety and will spread like gangrene; a vivid medical image. Hymenaeus and Philetus are singled out. Like other named people in the letters we cannot be sure whether they were known to the community at the time of writing, if they were well-known historical figures, or if they are fictitious characters introduced to make the situation more vivid and realistic. The particular impiety of the two named heretics is the belief that the resurrection has already happened. This idea was already prevalent in Paul's lifetime and resulted from one possible interpretation of his own

teaching (e.g. 1 Cor 15). It became a popular idea among some Gnostics and sometimes accounted for their dismissive attitude to the physical body. The teaching of Paul was regarded as authoritative by both Gnostics and anti-Gnostics in the second century. Both groups could interpret his teaching in ways which supported their own outlook. The Pastoral Epistles stand out firmly against 'knowledge falsely so-called' and became the basis for many later anti-Gnostic positions.

The building metaphor of vv. 20–2 is common in Christianity, and is found elsewhere in the Pastorals (1 Tim 3:15), where it is associated with the author's favourite metaphor, the household of God. Behind this passage lies Isa 28:16, quoted by Paul in Rom 9:33. From the same chapter of Romans comes the inspiration for the image of different utensils. But here it is not used in the same way as in Rom 9:21, which is about election, nor in the same way as the image of different parts of the body in 1 Cor 12. At first glance it seems to be a parable about important and less important vessels, along the same lines as the body metaphor, but some of the meaning has become lost in the retelling. The NRSV translation obscures the meaning further; the words translated 'special' and 'ordinary' mean 'honourable' and 'dishonourable' in Greek. From the context we can understand the passage to be an instruction to Timothy to cleanse himself of any teaching except that advocated already as sound doctrine, thus he and those he teaches will become useful, that is honourable, utensils. Again, orthodoxy is closely bound up with ethics. The list of qualities Timothy should cultivate, begun in v. 15 but then interrupted, continues in v. 22. His youth, mentioned in 1 Tim 4:12, is not to be an excuse for immature behaviour. The qualities mentioned in vv. 22–4, are already familiar from this letter and its companions; there is particular emphasis on avoiding quarrels and controversies which is the special interest of 2 Timothy, and it is worth noticing that the injunction to be an 'apt teacher' was used in 1 Tim 3:2 of the *episkopos*.

(3:1–9) The distress of the last days was a common theme in Judaism and early Christianity. Sinfulness and corruption of all sorts would prevail for a time, but it was believed that none of this was beyond God's control or outside his purpose. The gospels present us with a picture of cosmic terrors, such as earthquakes, famines, and eclipses (e.g. Mk 13:14–27). Like the commentary on Habakkuk by the Jews of Qumran (1QpHab), and like 1 John, 2 Timothy sees the distress in terms of human sin and apostasy. A long list of such vices is added which follows the conventions of its time, but many of the vices appear elsewhere in the Pastorals, either as characteristics to be avoided or whose opposites are recommended for Christian leaders. The list in Greek has a certain coherence, lost in translation, because of alliteration at the beginning or end of the adjectives, and because the first two and last two begin with the prefix *phil-*. That these vices belong to heterodox Christians becomes clear in v. 5. Timothy, and through him the whole congregation, are warned to keep out of such people's way.

The group of people thought to be most at risk from these apostates are women. The mocking diminutive is used, 'little women', translated by the NRSV as 'silly women'. It is not immediately obvious whether 'overwhelmed by their sins and swayed by all kinds of desires' refers to their disposition towards this sort of teaching or whether they are seen as particularly sinful women. Taken in conjunction with 1 Tim 2:11–14 (and 1 Cor 14:35), it is clear that there were women in the early church anxious to learn. In Acts there are several accounts of women being attracted to the words of an apostle's preaching. Stories told about Thecla (written down in the late second century as the *Acts of Paul and Thecla*), who renounced the prospect of marriage to follow Paul and devote her life to spreading the gospel, illustrate the kind of response from women that the Pastor deprecates. Thecla's vocation is justified in the stories by miraculous escapes from death; there is no doubt that she is portrayed as having arrived 'at a knowledge of the truth'.

Jannes and Jambres were the names given in some Jewish traditions to the Egyptian magicians summoned by Pharaoh to oppose Moses and Aaron in Ex 7:8–13 etc. Just as Moses' opponents' success was short-lived, so those who opposed the work of God now, by insinuating themselves into households, would fail before long.

Paul as Exemplar (3:10–4:8)

Paul's own steadfast character and his heroism under persecution are set out as an example of true faith. This glowing description of his character, though framed in the first person, bespeaks hagiography not autobiography. He is the model for Christians in times of persecution. The three cities, Antioch, Iconium, and Lystra, where the persecutions took place, are mentioned in Acts 13 and 14 as places where Paul and Barnabas were persecuted by the Jews, jealous of their success. Paul has not yet encountered Timothy at this point in the Acts narrative. It is probable that 2 Timothy and Acts are using the same sources here, unless one depends on the other for information. The example of Paul's persecutions illustrates the possibility of persecution for believers. But just as Paul was saved many times, so would his followers be. The opponents are held up as contrasts to Paul's character (3:14). The situation described at the beginning of the chapter will go from bad to worse as more and more people are led astray. The same situation was foreseen in 1 Tim 4:1. A chain reaction will take place; after one person has been deceived into believing the opponents' falsehoods, he, in turn, will deceive others.

(3:14–17) As well as having the model of Paul before him, Timothy must continue to follow the teachings of the sacred writings, an expression used by Greek-speaking Jews to describe their bible. He has been taught Scripture from childhood; the reference is to his mother and grandmother (2 Tim 1:5), but he has also had teachers such as Paul. Scripture is rarely quoted in the Pastoral Epistles, and there is no description or explanation of the development of Christianity out of and away from Judaism. It is probable that opposition is coming, at any rate some of the time, from Jewish Christians, but apart from differences about myths, genealogies, and the law, we are not told much about where the differences lie. Here Scripture, presumably including the law, is given unequivocal approval. If the NRSV translation of 3:16 is taken, the usefulness of all Scripture arises from the fact that it is divinely inspired. The alternative reading in the margin assumes that only those passages inspired by God are useful, i.e.

it assumes that some parts are not so inspired. This was indeed the belief among some early Gnostic groups such as the Marcionites, so it makes most sense to follow the NRSV translation. It is the usefulness of Scripture that is the significant point; different kinds of usefulness are immediately listed. v. 17, 'everyone who belongs to God' (cf. 1 Tim 6:11), probably refers to anyone in a position to teach or lead the congregation; such a person needs to be well versed in Scripture as well as in Christian doctrine. The result will be good works (as in 1 Tim 2:10).

Ch. 4 contains more intensely personal material than any other part of the Pastoral Epistles. The first section gives the impression, like 1:3–7 of being a personal 'testament'; the passing on of instructions from an important person to his followers is a literary form found elsewhere in the NT, but it also has a long scriptural tradition (e.g. Deut 31:24, Isa 8:16). Its content is kerygmatic, like other doctrinal passages in the Pastorals; this is the most solemn both in form and content. Judgement is mentioned for the first time, which adds a note of real seriousness; in the presence of God the Saviour, Christ will judge the living and the dead. A picture of a God who had to approve one's behaviour occurs in 2:14–19, but without mentioning judgement. Here, in language reminiscent of 1 Cor 15:21–8 (cf. Acts 10:42; 1 Pet 4:5), judgement becomes explicit. But the favourite terminology of the Pastorals is not absent; Christ's appearing, or *epiphaneia*, referring to his second coming, recurs in 1 Tim 6:14; 2 Tim 4:8; and Titus 2:13 (and in 2 Tim 1:10 the same word refers to his incarnation), but 'kingdom' is mentioned only here and in 4:18. Timothy's role is to preach the gospel, in favourable and unfavourable times, to make sure that the message is properly understood. 'The time is coming', has a sense of urgency about it, particularly as it seems to refer to events that are already beginning to take place (cf 3:1–9). Sound doctrine will be rejected in favour of false teaching, myths will be believed instead of the truth. The prediction by Paul of the events that are happening in the community addressed by the Pastorals gives the sense that present events are part of God's plan and Paul knew what was to happen. In spite of suffering, Timothy must continue his good work, and not be put off by the apostasy of some members of the community.

Paul's death is imminent; in 2 Timothy it has been made clear that he is in prison: now, in poignant language reminiscent of Phil 2:17 (the only other use in the NT of the verb 'pour out as a libation', NRSV), Paul reveals that he is to be put to death. Looking back, Paul reviews his Christian ministry as a fight he has fought and as a race he has run, two familiar metaphors (1 Tim 6:12, cf. 1 Cor 9:25, 2 Tim 2:5; cf. Phil 2:16; 3:13–14). His life is a model to Timothy and to all believers, the reward that awaits him and others who follow him is sure; it is the garland given to victors in athletic competitions, understood by Paul to be the reward for a life of virtue, and so used also in the early church of the reward for martyrs (cf. *Mart. Pol.* 17.1; 19.2).

Personal Comments and Salutations (4:9–22)

(4:9–15) Many individuals; friends, fellow-workers, and companions of Paul are referred to, adding conviction to the pretence of Pauline authorship, and persuading some commentators that at any rate fragments of the letters are genuine. Timothy must endeavour to visit Paul in prison, for, as he mentioned in 1:15, many others have left him. Only Luke remains (but cf. 4:21 where Paul seems to have several companions). Demas, whose name is found together with Luke's and Mark's in Col 4:14 and Philem 24 has actually deserted him (Demas is also named in *Acts of Paul and Thecla*, as is Hermogenes the coppersmith, cf. 2 Tim 1:15; this is possibly the same person as in 4:14. Both are said to be hypocrites). Crescens and Titus seem to have left but not deserted him. Tychicus is also mentioned in Titus 3:12 and in Acts 20:4; Col 4:7; Eph 6:21. The reference to the cloak, books, and parchment left behind at Troas adds a final touch of verisimilitude to the picture. Alexander, possibly the same person as the Alexander of 1 Tim 1:20, is mentioned as an enemy. He may be the Alexander of Acts 19:33 who was a Jewish silversmith, not a coppersmith. At any rate this Alexander was well known to the community as an opponent.

(4:16–18) It is difficult to identify Paul's 'first defence' (4:16) with anything we hear about in Acts or in the other epistles, apart possibly from that mentioned in Phil 1:7, 16. There it is the defence of the gospel that is referred to, here, it seems to be a more technical court appearance. However, historical identification is neither possible nor necessary to understand the picture the author is presenting. Paul has survived one trial; the trial resulted in his desertion by his friends, but he was enabled to defend the gospel with God's help. 'All the Gentiles' probably refers to those at his trial, but may be a reference to his whole Gentile mission. That time he survived, the next time he will be saved for God's heavenly kingdom. He expects to die now, but his death will not be the end (cf. 4:8).

(4:19–21) The final greetings name some familiar and some unfamiliar people. Prisca and Aquila are mentioned in an almost identical way at the end of Romans (16:3, cf. 1 Cor 16:9 where they themselves send greetings). Onesiphorus is familiar from 1:16. Erastus was the name of the city treasurer of Corinth (Rom 16:23), and in Acts 19:22 Paul sends a man called Erastus with Timothy from Ephesus to Macedonia. Trophimus appeared in Acts 20:4; 21:29, as an inhabitant of Ephesus. None of Paul's current companions are mentioned elsewhere in the NT. Perhaps they were names familiar to the community. As a further personal touch Paul urges Timothy to travel before winter, because travel during that season was difficult and dangerous (cf. Titus 3:12).

The final blessing is modelled on those in Gal 6:18; Phil 4:23; and Philem 25.

Titus

Greetings and Instructions on Dealing with Deceivers (1:1–16)

(1:1–4) The opening greeting of Titus is longer and fuller than its counterparts in 1 and 2 Timothy and includes a summary of the gospel message. Paul is named again as the sender, but here he is called slave as well as apostle as in Rom 1:1. Faith and knowledge of the truth are said to accord with godliness or *eusebeia* (cf. 1 Tim 2:2, etc.). The idea of God's plan of salvation is clearly set out again, here strengthened by the assertion that God never lies. This is never explicitly said of God elsewhere in the NT but it is a thought underlying the notion of prophecy

fulfilment throughout the NT. God's plan of salvation includes his promises in the past, and their fulfilment in the work of Christ, and in the work of those who proclaim the gospel, as well as the hope of eternal life. Both God and Christ are named as Saviour, because Christ carried out God's work of salvation on earth. The title 'Saviour' is used frequently in the Pastoral Epistles; in Titus, for example, God and Christ are each described as Saviour three times. Two elements of the blessing are present in v. 4, rather than three as in 1 and 2 Timothy.

Titus, like Timothy in 1 Tim 1:2 is called 'my loyal child', in other words, legitimate successor. From Paul's own letters he is known to be a Greek whom Paul and Barnabas took to Jerusalem (Gal 2:1, 3) and who was associated with the Corinthian church (2 Cor 7:6–16; 8:6, 16–17, 23; 12:18). In 1 Tim 4:10, he is said to have been sent to Dalmatia. Like the setting of 1 and 2 Timothy, this setting is fictitious.

(1:5–9) The situation envisaged at the beginning of the epistle is that Paul has instigated a successful mission in Crete and it is now Titus' job to continue the work, 'putting it in order'. (Crete is mentioned elsewhere in the NT only in Acts 27, when Paul did not visit the island intentionally, but his ship was wrecked as it sailed past.) Putting things in order consisted first in appointing elders in every town (cf. Acts 14:23), which in turn would discourage opposition. Qualifications are given for elders here which resemble those given in 1 Tim 3 for bishops (*episkopoi*) and deacons. The use of the conjunction 'for' at the beginning of v. 7 heading the list of qualities necessary for an *episkopos* implies an overlap in their roles; perhaps, as in Jewish communities of the diaspora, the *episkopos* was drawn from the ranks of the elders. In 1 Tim (5:1, 17, 19) it is not clear that this was the case; there a council of elders with an *episkopos* at its head may have been envisaged. The *episkopos* is the steward of God's household, a favourite image of the church in the Pastorals (e.g. 1 Tim 3:4; 5:12, 15). Paul, who was fond of using metaphors of service and slavery to describe his own role, used it of himself once in 1 Cor 4:1. But there he is the steward of the mysteries of God. To the exemplary character of the *episkopos*, familiar from 1 Tim 3, is added the necessity of his having 'a firm grasp of the word', that is, a clear understanding of the Christian message. This will enable him not only to present the church's teaching clearly but also to refute those who contradict it.

(1:10–16) The character of those who contradict is then set out. That some of them are Jewish Christians now seems clear (v. 10). This fits with the impression given in 1 and 2 Timothy but not made explicit there. They are native Cretans, converted to Christianity from Judaism and now apparently reverting in some way to their old faith and possibly advocating the circumcision of Gentile Christians. But as in 1 Tim 1:4 and 2 Tim 4:4, it is their teaching of Jewish myths that occupies the author's attention. Since we are given no further information, however, it is not possible to know whether these were Gnostic myths or more traditional scriptural myths. They also imposed Jewish commandments on their followers; perhaps food laws which the author did not accept (cf. 1 Tim 4:3–5), and which may be alluded to in 1:15. Ascetics, whether Jewish or not, who refused to eat certain foods were condemned in 1 Tim 4:4, for 'all things created by God are pure'. Here such people are condemned as having corrupt consciences; this is very strong condemnation for people whose understanding about purity is different from one's own. But it is the obverse of believing that sound faith leads to good behaviour. However, it contradicts Paul's teaching on such matters in Rom 14 and 1 Cor 8–10 where he is able to accommodate both points of view.

Membership of the Community (2:1–3:11)

The main section of Titus is reminiscent of I Timothy in that it describes the qualities of members of the community, interspersed with short doctrinal statements. Here the concern is not with the officers of the community, but with its ordinary members. It is introduced by the injunction to Titus to teach what is consistent with sound doctrine. This seems to entail good behaviour on the part of all members of the community. What follows resembles the lists of instructions about behaviour in other NT epistles (Col 3:18–22; Eph 5.22–33; 1 Pet 2:18–3:9), but here the grammatical form is different. Nevertheless, the list of qualities and duties required contains no surprises. Older men (not elders here; a related but not identical word is used) are encouraged to be temperate (cf. 1 Tim 6:11), serious (semnos, cf. 1 Tim 3:8, 11), and prudent (sōphrōn, cf. 1:8; 1 Tim 3:2). These are virtues that would be admired throughout the Hellenistic world but specifically Christian virtues follow; they are to be sound in faith, in love, and in endurance (cf. 1:9; 1 Tim 6:11; 2 Tim 3:10). A summary, in other words, of the qualities listed in ch. 1.

Older women have more detailed instructions: prohibitions as well as positive admonitions. This is a much more general group than the widows of 1 Tim 5. They are to be reverent, and like those in 1 Tim 3:11, they must not be slanderers or slaves to drink. They can be teachers, presumably of the younger women, certainly not of men (1 Tim 2:12), they taught the female Christian virtues and not matters of doctrine. These virtues are then listed. To the modern eye they encourage submissive attitudes; they are, however, typical of attitudes everywhere in the Graeco-Roman world (e.g. Plut. Mor. 140c, 142d). It is possible that the opponents of 'sound doctrine' taught that women could remain single and continue to lead a full Christian life, and like Thecla become an itinerant preacher (see 2 TIM 3:1–9). In any case, that kind of behaviour in no way conforms to the ideals of this author, who believes a woman's role is properly that of wife and mother, her salvation dependent on her fulfilling those roles submissively (cf. 1 Tim 2:9–15). The motivation given here, however, is to prevent the church being discredited. Nothing in the behaviour of the members of the community must attract negative comment from its neighbours.

Titus is urged to be a model for younger men in his behaviour and teaching. Here it is opponents not secular neighbours who must find no object for criticism in the behaviour of the young men. The Pastoral Epistles show no sense of their community being threatened by persecution in a serious way, but the author does not want to attract attention to the church by odd or antisocial behaviour. Paul had a similar concern about people in Corinth speaking in tongues (1 Cor 14:23–5).

Like women to their husbands, slaves are to be submissive to their masters. The teaching about slaves corresponds to contemporary thinking in every way. Just as attitudes to the position of women have changed beyond all recognition, so have attitudes towards the institution of slavery. But at the time the letter was written the institution was never really questioned, though there was discussion of the proper treatment of slaves, particularly among the Stoics (e.g. Seneca, 'On Master and Slave', Epistles, 47). In parallel household rules in other NT epistles, the behaviour of masters to slaves, husbands to wives, and fathers to children is introduced to balance the picture (Eph 6:1–9; Col 3:18–4:1; 1 Pet 2:18–3:7). The Pastoral Epistles enjoin no such commitments. The reason for the slaves' submissive and obedient attitude that the letter recommends is given in 2:10 in a way very typical of the Pastoral Epistles; they are to be 'an ornament to the doctrine of God our Saviour'. In other words, sound doctrine and ethics are inextricably linked even for slaves.

(2:11–15) contains a typical doctrinal statement, interrupted by ethical exhortations in v. 12, recalling other such passages in the other two epistles, but resembling most closely that in 2 Tim 1:9–12. The close relationship between the death of Christ and the removal of sin is here expressed more clearly than anywhere else in the three epistles and in a way that entirely conforms to Paul's own teaching. Typically for the Pastorals, the incarnation of Christ and his sacrifice are linked with the hope and expectation of his future coming. The Greek of 2:13 is ambiguous. The NRSV chooses to identify God our Saviour with Jesus Christ. Since he is nowhere else called God in the Pastoral Epistles—indeed his humanity is stressed in 1 Tim 2:5—the alternative translation, 'our great God and our Saviour Jesus Christ' is to be preferred. But, on the other hand, the immediate context of the verse with its imagery of royal epiphany might have encouraged the author to use the most exalted imagery of Christ at his parousia.

The grace of God has brought salvation to all; the soteriology of the Pastorals is almost always inclusive rather than exclusive (e.g. 1 Tim 2:4, 6). The qualities that grace enables us to learn have been mentioned before, and include words belonging to the piety (eusebeia) as well as restraint (sōphrosunē) groups. The connection between God's gracious act of salvation in Christ's coming and death with present Christian behaviour has never been expressed more clearly. The word used for redemption here is cognate with that used for ransom in 1 Tim 2:6; Christ's death is the price of redemption. The idea of purification of a people is not Pauline as ideas of ransom are, but is reminiscent of 1 Pet 2:9. The final injunction adds weight and authority to his teaching.

(3:1–2) The face the church presents is to be that of peaceful and helpful people, both in the public realm towards the government and also towards private individuals. The injunction to be subject to rulers is familiar from 1 Tim 2:2 and from Rom 13:1–7 (cf. also 1 Pet 2:13–17 where it is placed in a list of duties as it is here). 'Remind them', an expression also used in 2 Tim 2:14, seems to introduce a general instruction for the community as a whole rather than for a particular group.

(3:3–8a) The courtesy which is owed to those outside the church is explained by reference to the experience of each individual in the community before becoming Christian. Usually in the Pastorals lists like this provide a contrast between the behaviour of the opponents and that advocated for believers. Here, on the other hand, the list points up the contrast between the good moral behaviour of members of the community which arises out of sound doctrine and the same people's earlier moral turpitude. The two lists only partly correspond with one another; there are closer links with similar lists in Eph 2:2; 5:8; 1 Cor 6:11. So it is clear that lists of 'before and after' behaviour were becoming a commonplace of Christian preaching. The use of the metaphor of slavery to sin is familiar from Paul (e.g. Rom 6:6).

(3:4–8a) describes the means by which this change has come about for believers. This is the final summary of 'sound doctrine' in the epistles, signalled by 'the saying is sure' in v. 8. As always in the Pastorals, the soteriology is theocentric. God is Saviour, and salvation comes not as a reward for good deeds but from God's mercy. The incarnation, not Christ's death, is identified here as the turning-point in salvation history when God's goodness and loving kindness (*philanthrōpia*, lit. love for human beings) were revealed. The crucifixion is referred to only twice in the Pastorals, as the decisive soteriological moment, in 1 Tim 2:6 and Titus 2:14. The author prefers to balance the first and the future epiphanies to describe God's work of salvation; this passage can be paralleled with 2:11–14 where the future manifestation of Christ completes the process of salvation.

The decisive moment for individuals was baptism, here described as the water of rebirth and renewal; the moment when 'he saved us'. Justification by grace, a truly Pauline idea, is not explained, but like 'saved' in v. 5, the emphasis is on a past event, enabling believers to become 'heirs according to the hope of eternal life'. The process of salvation is not yet complete, but believers can feel certain of their part in it. Paul's understanding of justification is complex, but contrasts faith as the central element of salvation with works of the law. The Pastoral Epistles' emphasis, on the other hand, is on the close relationship between belief in sound doctrine and the good works which follow. The two ideas are not opposed to one another, but are distinctly different.

(3:8b–11) concerns relationships between Titus and members of the community who indulge in controversy and argument. Such behaviour is contrasted with the good works that profit the whole community. That the difficulties are caused by Jewish Christians is suggested by the fact that some of the debates concern the law. Genealogies are also mentioned as a focus of dispute as they were in 1 Tim 1:4. After two attempts at putting them straight, Titus is told to ignore such argumentative people; they are the cause of their own condemnation.

Personal Matters (3:12–16)

Personal details at the end of the book add a final touch of verisimilitude to the fictional situation. Paul hopes that Titus will come to him soon in Nicopolis, a city not mentioned elsewhere in the NT and probably to be understood as the city of Nicopolis in Epirus. Since the city does not appear in Acts and is not mentioned by Paul, any attempt to locate this letter at a particular point in Paul's life as we know it is impossible. Artemas is unknown to us. Tychicus was mentioned in 2 Tim 4:12 and the name appears elsewhere in the NT (Acts 20:4; Eph 6:21; Col 4:7). Zenas the lawyer is unknown but Apollos is known to us from both 1 Corinthians and Acts (1 Cor 1:12; 3:4–6, 22; 4:6; Acts 18:24; 19:1). Perhaps we are to envisage them as the bearers of the Epistle to Titus. They are to be well looked after and perhaps given financial support for their onward journey. Travel in winter was unadvisable, so Paul had decided to spend the winter in Nicopolis. A final injunction to good works precedes the final greeting.

REFERENCES

Beard, M., North, J. A., and Price, S.R.F. (1998), *Religions of Rome* (Cambridge: Cambridge University Press).

Miller, James D. (1997), *The Pastoral Letters as Composite Documents* (2 vols. Cambridge: Cambridge University Press).

74. Philemon   CRAIG S. WANSINK

INTRODUCTION

A. Paul's Imprisonment. The apostle Paul, according to *1 Clem.* 5, 5–6, was 'in chains' seven times. In 2 Cor 11:23, Paul himself boasts of having experienced 'far more imprisonments' than his detractors. Ironically, the one who had formerly imprisoned Christians (cf. Acts 8:3; 22:4; 26:10) frequently found himself incarcerated. During one such experience, he wrote to Philemon and the church that was in his house. Only twenty-five verses long, Paul's letter is replete with rhetorical dissonance, subtlety, and wordplay. The epistle offers little insight into its provenance or dating. Whether it was written in Rome, Ephesus, Philippi, or elsewhere is not of primary concern. Whether it was written towards the end of Paul's life or towards the beginning of his mission is not revealed. Rather, the most salient aspects of the letter are Paul's rhetoric and his imprisonment (cf. vv. 10, 13, 22).

B. Onesimus. 1. Although the figure of Onesimus is not introduced until almost half-way through the letter (in v. 10), the interpretation of this figure has typically framed how the epistle has been approached. Onesimus generally is seen in one of three ways: (1) as a runaway slave (cf. Lohse 1971; R. P. Martin 1974; Caird 1976; Nordling 1991); (2) as an estranged slave, appealing to his owner's friend (*amicus domini*) (cf. Lampe 1985; Rapske 1991; Bartchy 1992); or (3) as a slave, sent by Philemon, to serve Paul in prison (cf. Knox 1959; Winter 1984; 1987; Wansink 1996).

2. The first two characterizations generally focus on vv. 11, 15, and 18, and, as discussed in the commentary below, tend to undervalue Greek wordplays, conventions of ancient slavery and, particularly, Paul's location (in prison). For a number of additional reasons, it seems unlikely that Onesimus either ran away or was estranged from his master: (1) If Onesimus had run away or faced estrangement, his owner probably would not have known where he was. Here, however, Philemon appears to have known that Onesimus was with Paul (Winter 1987). (2) It seems unreasonable to believe that Onesimus would run away from his master in order to escape *into* prison.

Such a hypothesis seems to ignore Paul's imprisonment. (3) If Onesimus were estranged from Philemon and in need of reconciliation, his conversion to the Christian faith—under such conditions—could well appear feigned and opportunistic. (4) Although Paul asks that Philemon support Onesimus, he does not request pity or forgiveness on behalf of Onesimus. Onesimus is not presented in any way as remorseful or repentant.

3. It appears that Onesimus neither ran away nor was estranged from his master. Writing from prison, Paul thanks the recipients of the epistle for their support. He sees his relationship with them as similar to that of 'partners'. And when he returns a person who had been with him in prison, he feels justified in asking that this person be received with respect and care. That is the situation in Paul's letter to the Philippians. That is also the situation in Philemon. In Philippians, Epaphroditus was messenger and minister to Paul's needs. He had been sent to Paul by the Philippians, he had served this prisoner on their behalf, and he then returned to his community. Onesimus, similarly, appears to have been sent by Philemon to serve Paul while he was in prison. During this service, however, something unique happened. Onesimus became a Christian and Paul had now found a new colleague in ministry. If the pagan slave Onesimus was sent by his owner to 'refresh' the imprisoned, if he was no runaway looking for quick redemption and forgiveness, generations of Christian interpreters have cheated Onesimus out of the integrity of his faith.

COMMENTARY

Prescript and Thanksgiving (1–7)

(1–3) Prescript The references in vv. 1 and 9 reflect Paul's first written use of the appellation 'prisoner of Christ Jesus' (cf. 2 Tim 1:8; Eph 3:1; 4:1; 3 Cor. 3.1). Some see this expression as reflecting only Paul's presence in prison. Others understand it metaphorically, in the light of triumphal marches (cf. Stuhlmacher 1981) or initiations into mystery cults (cf. Reitzenstein 1978). Most interpreters, however, see Paul's status as 'prisoner' as resulting either 'because of' or 'for the sake of' Christ Jesus (cf. PHILEM 9; PHILEM 23 offers an alternative interpretation). 'Philemon, our beloved brother and fellow worker' (NASB). Ironically, only one other individual in this letter is referred to as 'beloved': Onesimus (in v. 16). 'Co-worker': like the four persons mentioned in v. 24, Philemon is a fellow worker, apparently one who assists the imprisoned apostle. v. 2, 'Apphia': some commentators see her as Philemon's wife. Regardless, she is a Christian (i.e. 'sister'). 'Archippus': the appellation 'fellow-soldier' (cf. Phil 2:25) does not necessarily refer to one who performs a specific task within the church. Because soldiers were well known for their loyalty, the title may represent a character attribute (for other martial imagery, see PHILEM 23). The admonitions to a certain Archippus in Col 4:17 led Knox to ask if Paul's admonitions in Philemon were directed primarily to Archippus (cf. Knox 1959). 'To the church in your house': the earliest Christians gathered and worshipped in private homes (cf. PHILEM 22). v. 3, salutation: 'Grace to you and peace'. To readers of Greek epistles, charis ('grace') would have sounded similar to the typical epistolary

greeting chairein ('greetings'; cf. Jas 1:1). Paul thus uses wordplay in a way in which his greeting bears theological import. His use of the word 'peace', in the second part of this greeting, probably reflects the typical Hebrew and Aramaic salutation shalom (šālôm).

(4–7) Thanksgiving The thanksgiving establishes the major themes and expectations of the epistle. v. 4, although this letter is addressed to an entire house-church, the Greek makes clear that Paul's thanksgiving is now directed to one individual, presumably Philemon. v. 5, Paul acknowledges that he has heard of Philemon's 'love' and 'faith' towards Jesus and all 'the saints'. In v. 6 Paul expounds on this faith and in v. 7 the love. v. 6, 'I pray that the sharing of your faith may become effective when you perceive all the good that we [other ancient authorities read 'you'] may do for Christ'. The word for 'sharing'—koinōnia—is a technical term frequently associated with commerce in the Graeco-Roman world (cf. Sampley 1980). Cf. v. 17 where Paul more explicitly uses the language of commerce. Paul refers to 'the good' again in v. 14. v. 7, 'joy', a typical catchphrase of Pauline rhetoric in Philippians is frequently used during times of persecution. Paul notes his own joy and comfort in Philemon's love, 'because the hearts (splagchna) of the saints' had been 'refreshed' through Philemon. Here Paul sets the stage for the main concerns in the letter. Similar references reappear in v. 12, where Paul describes Onesimus as his splagchna and in v. 20 where Paul encourages Philemon to 'refresh my heart (splagchna) in Christ'. Note that around the year 110 CE, when the bishop Ignatius was being taken in chains to Rome, he wrote to the Ephesians, thanking them for 'refreshing' him through Crocus and others whom they had sent to be with him while he was a prisoner (cf. Ign. Eph. 2. 1–2) (cf. Wansink 1996).

Body: Paul's Request (8–20)

vv. 8–9, Paul opens his request by acknowledging that although he is 'bold enough' to command Philemon to do his duty, he would rather appeal to him 'on the basis of love' (cf. vv. 5, 7). Paul notes that he makes such an appeal as a 'prēsbutes, and now also as a prisoner of Christ Jesus'. The Greek term prēsbutes has been translated both as 'old man' and as 'ambassador'. When the received text is emended (Lightfoot 1904) or when comparisons are made to 2 Cor 5:19b–20a and Eph 6:20 (cf. Stuhlmacher 1981), this word sometimes is translated as 'ambassador'. However, since Paul has just announced that he would not exploit his authority to give commands (v. 8), referring to himself now as an 'ambassador' would seem contradictory. Furthermore, recent lexical studies emphasize that 'old man' would be the most appropriate translation for this Greek term (cf. Gnilka 1982; Birdsall 1993). Paul, thus, is seeking empathy. He is old and, furthermore, he is in a situation inappropriate for a person of his age: he is a prisoner. These two epithets share at least one key characteristic: both the elderly and the imprisoned were seen as vulnerable and dependent upon others (Hock 1995). 'Prisoner of Christ Jesus': the point seems to be that prisoners were dependent on support from outsiders (cf. v. 13). At the same time, the constellation of military metaphors in this letter points to an even richer meaning for this appellation (cf. PHILEM 23). v. 10, 'Onesimus': literally 'useful' in Greek. In this first reference to Onesimus, Paul is not explicit about how these two came to be together. Apparently Philemon already knew. 'My child': in the Pauline and Deutero-Pauline literature, Onesimus, Titus (Titus 1:4), and Timothy (1 Cor 4:17; Phil 2:22; 1 Tim 1:2, 18; 2 Tim 1:2; 2:1) are the only specific individuals whom Paul refers to as his children. The language, thus, is quite intimate. As in 1 Cor 4:17 and Phil 2:22, here Paul uses the word 'child' in commending to the addressees the one whom Paul, himself, is sending. 'Whose father I have become': Onesimus was converted by the imprisoned apostle. v. 11, by postponing the word 'Onesimus' to the end of v. 10, the Greek highlights the wordplays in v. 11. Immediately we are told that Onesimus was formerly 'useless' (*achrēstos*) but 'now is useful (*euchrēstos*) both to you and to me'. In what respect was Onesimus 'useless' (*achrēstos*)? It is difficult to know if Paul is using this expression in a literal, figurative, or simply rhetorical sense. The reference to 'Onesimus' as having been 'useless' would have sounded ironic to the original readers of this letter. The wordplay is even more notable when we look at *achrēstos* in the light of v. 10. Onesimus became a Christian while with Paul. Before Onesimus met Paul he was not a Christian. He was *achristos* (without Christ). In Koine Greek, *achristos* and *achrēstos* were homophones. Thus, Paul is saying: Before Onesimus was a Christian, he was named Onesimus (or 'useful'). At that time, however, he was not truly useful, because he was *achrēstos/achristos*. Now that he is a Christian, however, he is truly useful (cf. Winter 1987). As Philemon's messenger and minister to Paul, Onesimus would be useful to both persons. v. 12, 'I am sending him, that is, my own heart, back to you.' The Greek verb employed here is frequently used to refer to the return of messengers or envoys. 'My own heart' (cf. PHILEM 7, 20): the Greek word *splagchna*, translated as 'heart', is also a synonym for the Greek word *pais* (child) (cf. Artemidorus, *Oneirocritica*, 1. 44). v. 13, 'I wanted to keep him with me' (Paul wants Philemon to make his own choice; vv. 9, 14, 21), 'so that he might be of service to me in your place'. In prison, Paul would have been dependent on outsiders for food, clothing, the delivering of letters, etc. v. 14, 'I preferred to do nothing without your consent, in order that your good deed might be voluntary'. In v. 6, Paul prays that Philemon might effectively share his faith when he perceives 'all the good that we [the imprisoned?] may do for Christ'. Here Paul expects that Philemon—with free will and this knowledge—will use his goodness appropriately. v. 15, 'Perhaps this is the reason he was separated from you for a while'. Those interpreters who claim that Onesimus was a runaway slave tend to see this verse as Paul's euphemistic handling of a delicate situation (cf. Stöger 1971; Lohse 1971). The Greek word translated as 'separated', however, does not necessarily mean 'ran away'. Slaves were often separated from their owners, conducting business for them, delivering letters, helping others, or simply working where their labour was needed (cf. D. B. Martin 1990). What Paul directly acknowledges is that this separation has resulted in a change in Onesimus' status and how he is to be viewed. v. 16, 'no longer as a slave but more than a slave, a beloved brother'. Onesimus was converted in prison and just as Philemon is referred to as 'beloved' (v. 1), just as he is referred to as Paul's 'brother' (vv. 7, 20), so Onesimus here is referred to as a 'beloved brother'. vv. 17–18, 'If he has wronged you in any way, or owes you anything,

charge that to my account.' The 'if' which begins this sentence makes the apodosis hypothetical (cf. C. J. Martin 1992). Onesimus did not necessarily wrong Philemon or owe him anything. At the same time, slavery in the Graeco-Roman world often resulted from personal bankruptcy or need. Under these conditions, individuals were slaves *because* they were in debt to their masters. Furthermore, even if a slave owed his master nothing, if that slave were to be freed, the owner would expect recompense: he would be reluctant to give away what he considered to be an investment. v. 19, 'I, Paul, am writing (*egrapsa*) this with my own hand'. The epistolary aorist functions like a signature on a typed letter (cf. Gal 6:11; Col 4:18; 1 Cor 16:21). Paul is serious about this request. 'I say nothing about your owing me even your own self'. Paul apparently was responsible not only for the conversion of Onesimus but also for that of Onesimus' owner. v. 20, 'Yes, brother, let me have this benefit from you in the Lord!' In v. 7, after Paul writes that the hearts of the saints had been refreshed through Philemon, he refers to him as 'brother'. Here, similarly, Paul refers to Philemon as 'brother', and asks that he benefit him by refreshing his heart in Christ. Just as Philemon refreshes 'the hearts of the saints', so he is to refresh Paul. The verse has, however, yet another implication. In v. 12, Paul refers to Onesimus as 'my heart'. Paul's reference to Onesimus in v. 20 hinges on the equation Paul makes in v. 7. Thus, when Paul writes 'let me have this benefit (*onaimēn*) from you in the Lord', the term *onaimen* is not coincidental. In a letter inundated with wordplay, the similarities between *onaimēn* and Onesimus (*onēsimos*) would have been obvious to a Greek-speaking audience. Thus, Philemon here is called upon to refresh both Paul and Onesimus.

Final Prayer, Greetings, and Blessing (21–5)

vv. 21–2, Paul is confident about both Philemon's obedience and his own release from prison. Furthermore, he asks Philemon to prepare lodging for him. House-churches were not only for worship, Christian meetings, and moral instruction, but also for hosting travellers and guests. Just as Paul had prayed for Philemon (cf. PHILEM 4), so he asks that this community pray for him in his imprisonment. Paul employs the second person plural pronoun, clearly emphasizing his relationship with the entire community. v. 23, 'Fellow prisoner'. The Greek *sunaichmalōtos* actually means 'fellow prisoner of war'. The term points to more than merely shared imprisonment. When Paul, by implication, refers to himself both as a 'soldier' (cf. PHILEM 2) and as a 'prisoner of war', the implication is that Paul's imprisonment followed naturally from his commitment to Christ Jesus. Like famed Roman soldiers, and like Socrates, Paul and Epaphras refused to desert their posts, regardless if it would lead to imprisonment or death (cf. Knox 1955; Wansink 1996). v. 24, Paul refers to the others with him as 'fellow workers' (cf. PHILEM 1). Of Mark, Aristarchus, Demas, and Luke, the latter figure has provoked the most interest. In 2 Tim 4:11, he is the last person to remain with the imprisoned apostle. In Col 4:14, he is called 'the beloved physician'. Because ancient sources see illness as a terrifying threat faced by the imprisoned, it is interesting to note that each of the references to Luke—the physician—

appears only in epistles said to have been written from prison. v. 25, a traditional final greeting.

REFERENCES

Bartchy, S. S. (1992), 'Philemon, Epistle to', *ABD* v. 305–10.

Birdsall, J. N. (1993), 'ΠΡΕΣΒΥΤΗΣ in Philemon 9: A Study in Conjectural Emendation', *NTS* 39: 625–30.

Caird, G. B. (1976), *Paul's Letters from Prison* (Oxford: Oxford University Press).

Gnilka, J. (1982), *Der Philemonbrief* (Freiburg: Herder).

Hock, R. F. (1955), 'A Support for His Old Age: Paul's Plea on Behalf of Onesimus', in L. M. White and O. L. Yarbrough (eds.), *The Social World of the First Christians: Essays in Honor of Wayne A. Meeks* (Minneapolis: Fortress) 67–81.

Knox, J. (1955), 'Philemon', in G. A. Buttrick (ed.), *The Interpreter's Bible* (New York: Abingdon), xi. 555–73.

—— (1959), *Philemon Among the Letters of Paul: A New View of Its Place and Importance* (Nashville: Abingdon).

Lampe, P. (1985), 'Keine "Sklavenflucht" des Onesimus', *ZNW* 76: 135–7.

Lightfoot, J. B. (1904), *St Paul's Epistles to the Colossians and to Philemon* (London: Macmillan).

Lohse, E. (1971), *Colossians and Philemon*, trans. W. R. Poehlmann and R. J. Karris, Hermaneia (Philadelphia: Fortress).

Martin, C. J. (1992), 'The Rhetorical Function of Commercial Language in Paul's Letter to Philemon (Verse 18)', in D. F. Watson (ed.), *Persuasive Artistry: Studies in New Testament Rhetoric in Honor of George A. Kennedy*, JSNTSup 50 (Sheffield: JSOT), 321–37.

Martin, D. B. (1990), *Slavery as Salvation: The Metaphor of Slavery in Pauline Christianity* (New Haven: Yale University Press).

Martin, R. P. (1974), *Colossians and Philemon*, NCB (London: Oliphants).

Nordling, J. G. (1991), 'Onesimus Fugitivus: A Defense of the Runaway Slave Hypothesis in Philemon', *JSNT* 41: 97–119.

Rapske, B. M. (1991), 'The Prisoner Paul in the Eyes of Onesimus', *NTS* 37: 187–203.

Reitzenstein, R. (1978), *Hellenistic Mystery-Religions: Their Basic Ideas and Significance*, trans. J. E. Steely (Pittsburgh: Pickwick).

Sampley, J. P. (1980), *Pauline Partnership in Christ: Christian Community and Commitment in Light of Roman Law* (Philadelphia: Fortress).

Stöger, A. (1971), *The Epistle to Philemon*, ed. J. L. McKenzie, trans. M. Dunne (New York: Herder & Herder).

Stuhlmacher, P. (1981), *Der Brief an Philemon*, EKKNT (Zürich: Benziger).

Wansink, C. S. (1996), *'Chained in Christ': The Experience and Rhetoric of Paul's Imprisonments*, JSNTSup (Sheffield: JSNT).

Winter, S. (1984), 'Methodological Observations on a New Interpretation of Paul's Letter to Philemon', *Union Seminary Quarterly Review*, 35: 3–12.

—— (1987), 'Paul's Letter to Philemon', *NTS* 33: 1–15.

75. Hebrews

HAROLD W. ATTRIDGE

INTRODUCTION

Among the letters attributed to St Paul appears a lengthy work celebrating the person and work of Jesus Christ and encouraging fidelity to his covenant. Although the attribution is certainly secondary, the document is a masterpiece of early Christian homiletics, weaving creative scriptural exegesis with effective exhortation.

A. Authorship. 1. Hebrews does not name its author. A reference to 'our brother Timothy' (13:23) may have occasioned the tradition that Paul composed the work. Differences in style and theology between Hebrews and the assuredly genuine epistles of Paul make that attribution most unlikely. Attempts to preserve some degree of Pauline authorship have centred on ch. 13 and its epistolary conclusion (13:18–25), which some have seen as Paul's endorsement of a collaborator's work. Although the conclusion may be an addition, it coheres with the body of the homily and is probably by the same, non-Pauline, hand.

2. The tradition of Pauline authorship was not uniform. Tertullian, in late second-century North Africa, attributed Hebrews to Barnabas. In second-century Alexandria learned leaders of the Church knew but doubted the attribution to Paul. Clement of Alexandria reconciled popular tradition with literary analysis by suggesting that Paul had dictated the text to a scribe such as Luke or Clement of Rome. In the third century, Origen summarized earlier speculation, agreed that the contents were worthy of Paul, but concluded that 'God only knows' who actually wrote it. More recent scholars have proposed other candidates, including Apollos and Sylvanus. Evidence for any is indecisive and the author remains anonymous.

B. Date. 1. Dating is equally problematic. Suggestions have ranged from the middle to the end of the first century. Some scholars have argued that the lack of an explicit reference to the destruction of the Jerusalem temple, which occurred in 70 CE during the Jewish revolt against Rome, dates the work prior to 70. Yet Jewish authors after 70, including the historian Josephus and the compilers of the Mishnah, refer to the temple and its cultic system as extant. Hopes for restoration remained alive and expressed themselves in terms of the presence of ideal realities. Furthermore, Hebrews refers not to the temple reconstructed by Herod the Great, but to the tabernacle of Scripture. Hebrews is interested in biblical symbolism, not the fate of the cultic site. The condition of the temple is, therefore, irrelevant to dating.

2. While a specific date proves elusive, the general range within which Hebrews was written is clear. The work is certainly known to *1 Clement*, an exhortation from the leadership of the church at Rome to Corinth. Although the date of *1 Clement* is debated, it is not likely to be later than 110 CE. At the other end of the spectrum, the traditions in Hebrews certainly required time to develop. It is unlikely that they reached their current form before 50 CE. The homily, therefore, was composed in the second half of the first century, probably between 55 and 90 CE.

C. Addressees. The greeting from 'those from Italy' (13:24) suggests that the intended recipients of the work's written form were also 'Italians'. It is possible that they were a community, military or mercantile, located outside the homeland, but it is more likely that they were in Italy itself, where Hebrews is known by the end of the first century. Paul's epistle to the Romans indicates that by approximately 55 CE a Christian congregation flourished in the capital. This community, or some portion of it, could have been the intended recipients of the homily.

D. Genre and Structure. 1. The end of ch. 13 (13:18–25) reads much like a letter and has close parallels with Pauline epistles. The rest of the text differs markedly from the other letters of the New Testament. The conclusion, therefore, was probably designed to transmit the work to a distant audience.

2. As a whole Hebrews is a striking example of rhetoric serving scriptural exegesis. In making God's word effective (1:1–4; 4:12–13) the text revels in human words. It abounds in ornamental devices, including alliteration, anaphora, assonance, chiasm, litotes, paronomasia, and other figures of speech. Hebrews deploys a rich vocabulary, using illustrations and metaphors from various spheres: agriculture (6:7–8), athletics (5:14; 12:1–3), education (5:12–14), law (9:16–17), and seafaring (6:19).

3. Defined as 'word of exhortation' (13:22), Hebrews clearly adapts the homiletic forms of Hellenistic Judaism. The text grounds its exhortations not in general appeals to logic or emotion, but in exposition of an authoritative text. Some sections, e.g. chs. 3 and 4, illustrate formal homiletic patterns built around exposition of a cited text. At the centre of Hebrews a lengthy exposition of the significance of the Day of Atonement reveals a similar structure. A preface summarizes and introduces certain themes (8:1–5). A citation from Jer 31:31–4 follows. The homilist then explores the text in balanced units playing upon several antitheses (9:1–10:10). A summary repeats elements of the scriptural text (10:11–18); a hortatory application follows (10:19–39).

4. Homiletic devices appear in other portions of the work. Stern warnings against the dangers of apostasy punctuate the text (2:1–4; 6:1–20; 10:26–31; 12:14–17; 12:25–9). The catalogue of exemplars of faith in ch. 11 resembles appeals to examples of virtue in Hellenistic moral discourse. Exegetical strategies also vary, from the concatenation of scriptural citations in ch. 1 through the playful reflection on Melchizedek in ch. 7.

5. The interplay of exegesis and exhortation in carefully balanced segments leads to a climactically ordered composition that builds an appeal for renewed faith. That structure may be outlined as follows:

E. The Message of Hebrews. The homily balances exposition and exhortation. The exposition portrays Christ as the cause of the addressees' salvation (2:10; 5:9; 9:14) and the model for their behaviour (12:1–2). The exhortation has two aspects expressed in recurring motifs. On the one hand the homilist urges his addressees to 'hold fast' to what they have, their confession, their partnership with Christ, the virtues that are appropriate to that partnership (3:6; 3:14). He also urges them to 'move' either 'in' towards the Christ who can be for them a source of aid and comfort, or 'out' to 'endure' a world that challenges their commitments and confession (13:13). Warnings alternate with hopeful assurances based on Christ's presence as a sympathetic mediator (4:14–16; 7:23–4). Covenant fidelity requires faith, hope, and charity (10:22–5), but also specific virtues (13:1–17).

COMMENTARY

Exordium: *The Definitive Word (1:1–4)*

Hebrews begins sonorously, with a ringing evocation of the person at the centre of the theology of the work. Alliteration and assonance mark the opening verse, which builds in a series of balanced clauses to the affirmation of the Son's exalted status. In the process, the homilist sounds several key themes interwoven throughout the homily. v. 1, God's speech of long ago forms the foundation of Hebrews, which will use texts from the Torah, the Prophets, and the psalms to construct its message. The exegesis of those texts aims to make the word of God a vital reality. v. 2, the final and definitive vehicle for God's revelation is the 'Son'. That he has spoken 'in these last days' suggests not merely that he delivered his message recently, but that the context of his speech is the final act in the salvific drama, the imminent divine judgement; cf. 9:28; 10:25; 12:18–29. The note that the Son is 'heir of all things' introduces a recurrent theme (cf. v. 4; 1:14; 3:1; 6:17; 9:15; 12:25–9), among both Hellenistic Jews (e.g. Philo, *Quis Heres*) and early Christians. The latter expected to be heirs of God's kingdom (e.g., Mt 5:5; 25:35; 1 Cor 6:9–10), immortality or eternal life (Mt 19:29; Mk 10:17; Lk 10:25; 1 Cor 15:50), salvation (1 Pet 1:4–5), or the heavenly city (Rev 21:2–7). The basic structure of the motif resembles Gal 3:23–4:7, where Christ's status as heir secures the inheritance of his followers. An evocation of Christ's role in creation balances the affirmation of his eschatological status as heir. Like other early Christians (Jn 1:3; 1 Cor 8:6; Rom 11:36; Col 1:16), Hebrews exalts the significance of Jesus by transferring to him attributes of divine Wisdom (Prov 8:22–31). v. 3, Sapiential tradition is transparent in the affirmation that the Son is the 'reflection of God's glory', which echoes Wis 7:26. The description of Christ as the 'imprint of God's very being' juxtaposes a monetary image (*charaktēr*: 'stamp') and a metaphysical term (hypostasis). The former term parallels affirmations about Christ as the 'image' (*eikōn*) of the divine (cf. 2 Cor 4:4; Rom 8:29; Col 1:15). The philosophical term reappears at 3:14 and 11:1 with varying connotations. Creation is not the sole venue of the Son's activity. Like the powerful force of divine Wisdom who 'pervades, penetrates and renews' all things (Wis 7:24–7), the Son too 'sustains all things by his powerful word'. The Jewish philosopher and exegete Philo also remarked frequently on the sustaining activity of the Logos or Word of God (Som. 1.241; *Quis Heres*, 7; *Migr. Abr.* 6). Such affirmations may underlie Hebrews, although here the divine word is embodied in a human person. The homilist is not concerned with cosmology, but with the way in which the Son sustains a community struggling to be faithful (cf. 4:14–16; 12:1–2). The heart of the Son's activity is his sacrificial death, whereby he effected 'purification for sins'. This phrase adumbrates the complex theme of Christ's priestly action that will dominate the central chapters (8:1–10:18, esp. 9:13–14, 26). Of equal structural significance is the picture of the Son's session 'at the right hand'. The image derives from Ps 110:1, the celebration of the enthronement of an Israelite king. Inspired by Jewish literature portraying the exaltation of the persecuted righteous (e.g. 1 *Enoch* 45:3; 79:27–9; *T. Levi* 2–5; Wis 2:4–5), early Christians regularly affirmed God's vindication of Christ in terms of his exaltation, using Ps 110:1 to refer to that event (Mt 22:44; Acts 2:34–5; Eph 1:20; 1 Pet 3:22). The Psalm's imagery reappears at key points in Hebrews (1:14; 8:1; 10:12; 12:2), articulating its structure and advancing the heavenly status of the Son as a ground for hope. Unlike other early Christian texts, Hebrews also uses another verse from the Psalm to establish a relationship between Christ and Melchizedek (cf. Ps 110:4 at 5:6; 6:20; 7:1–28). v. 4, the affirmation that the Son is 'superior to the angels' has been construed as polemic against Christians or Jews who accorded too high a status to angels or against Christians who considered the exalted Christ an angel. Hebrews offers no evidence of such polemical concerns elsewhere. The remark stands in continuity with the scenario of exaltation, in which a status higher than the angels is common (cf. Phil 2:9–10; Col 1:15–18; Eph 1:21; 1 Pet 3:22). The phrase affords a transition to the collection of citations about the exalted one in v. 5. The exordium ends with an argument about Christ's 'inherited' name. To obtain a special name is also part of a process of exaltation (cf. Phil 2:9; 3 *Enoch* 12:15; Philo, *Conf. Ling.* 146). Though not specified, the name is certainly 'Son', a title that begins the following catena and plays a role in the contrast between Christ and Moses (3:6). The imagery of 'inheritance' associated with the moment of glorification stands in tension with the affirmation of the Son's role in creation. The homilist has not systematized his Christological traditions but has interwoven two formally distinct models in his affirmation of Christ's heavenly status.

Christ Exalted and Humiliated, a Suitable High Priest (1:5–2:18)

(1:5–14) A Catena of Scriptural Citations The rest of the chapter consists of citations from Scripture, primarily the Psalms.

Formally, the chapter resembles collections of citations made by members of the sectarian community at Qumran (4QFlor; 4QTestim). Like such collections, this catena applies scriptural verses to a contemporary situation. The catena in its entirety exalts the Son, arguing that he is superior to beings assumed to be of high status, the angels. v. 5, the rhetorical question introducing Ps 2:7 links the catena with the exordium and, with the reference to the angels in v. 14, frames the catena. The artificial connection between the frame and the contents suggests that, at least in part, the collection derives from a traditional florilegium serving catechetical or apologetic needs. The first text cited, Ps 2:7, which reappears at 5:5, is linked with 2 Sam 7:14, a combination attested in the Dead Sea scrolls (cf. 4QFlor 1.10–11 and 18–19). Both texts originally expressed Israel's royal ideology, according to which the king, at his accession ('today'), became God's adopted son. 2 Sam 7:14 is part of Nathan's oracle, promising YHWH's fidelity to David's household. Early Christians linked Ps 2:7 with Christ's baptism (Mt 3:16–17; Mk 1:10–11; Lk 3:21–2) and exaltation (Acts 13:33–4). 2 Sam 7:14 applies to believers, not Christ, at 2 Cor 6:18 and Rev 21:7. v. 6, the introduction of this verse has raised difficulties. The most natural reading suggests that the homilist construes the verse to be a call to angels to worship the Son at his birth. Some scholars refer 'the world' to the supernal or heavenly realm. Others take the adverb 'again' temporally and construe the event to be Christ's parousia. The adverb in this context has no temporal sense, but simply links verses in the catena (cf. v. 5; 2:13). The homilist apparently has appropriated a florilegium focused on the eschatological exaltation of Jesus and reinterpreted it within the framework of his understanding of Christ as the agent of creation as well as redemption (1:2–3). The text focuses on the lofty status of the Son, so high that even the angels must worship him even when he enters the cosmos. v. 7, the next verse refers not to Christ but to the angels with whom he is compared. Ps 104:4 originally hymned the power of God who makes even winds and fire instruments of his word. The homilist exploits the grammatical ambiguity of the Greek translation to construe the text to mean that God can make his angels mere winds and his other, presumably supernatural, servants mere flames. vv. 8–9, the image of mutable angels contrasts with the vision of eternal stability in Ps 45:6–7, which originally praised the majesty of the Israelite king at his wedding. The psalm glorified the monarch for his righteousness and claimed that this quality distinguished him from other kings. Hebrews takes the 'companions' of the Son to be other members of the divine realm, or angels, to whom Jesus, because of his 'anointing' as heavenly priest, is superior. His throne, the locus of his authority, is also eternal (cf. 4:16). The ambiguity of the addressee proved attractive to the homilist. The first verse could be construed to say that the king's throne, or foundation of his authority, is God. Alternatively, 'God' could be taken as a vocative, a title of majesty applied to the Son. Similar ambiguity surfaces in v. 9, which could be read as 'O God, your God has anointed you'. Although Hebrews does not otherwise use the title 'God' for the Son, the ambiguity here was probably intentional. The Son who is the 'stamp of God's very being' (1:3) could well be styled 'God'. vv. 10–12, the next citation derives from Ps 102:25–8, a lament contrasting the pitiable state of the supplicant with the Creator's majesty. Unlike the ambiguous vocative, 'O God', in the previous citation, the divine name 'Lord' is clearly a vocative in the first verse of this psalm. The psalm originally addressed YHWH; the homilist, who believes the Son to be involved in creation (1:2–3) applies the title to him. The remainder of the psalm evokes the assuring images of stability associated with the Son (cf. 6:18–19; 7:21–4; 13:8). v. 13, the catena closes with an explicit citation of Ps 110:1, forming an *inclusio* with the exordium (1:3). v. 14, the concluding comment recalls the language of Ps 104, cited in v. 7. Angels merely serve the heirs, who share the Son's inheritance (1:2, 4).

(2:1–4) Transitional Admonition: To Attend Carefully The first of several warning passages interrupts the exposition of Scripture, which continues in 2:5–9. The exhortation shifts focus and tone. Previously Hebrews had emphasized the heavenly status of the Son; the text now highlights Christ's participation in suffering humanity. v. 1, the warning not to 'drift away' bespeaks anxiety about defection from the community that pervades the warning passages (cf. 6:4; 10:25, 29; 12:17, 25). Whatever the external factors, such as persecution (10:32–4), the image of casual drifting suggests that lassitude or indifference was perceived to be part of the addressees' problem; cf. 12:12–13. vv. 2–3, Hebrews regularly uses the threat of punishment as part of its exhortation to renewed fidelity. The 'message declared through angels' is the Torah itself. Scripture does not ascribe such a role to angels, although Ps 68:18 intimates their presence at Sinai. Later Jewish tradition does, however, accord a role to angels in delivering the Torah (cf. *Jub.* 1:27–9; 50:1–13; Jos. *Ant.* 15.126). The question 'how can we escape?' implies an *a fortiori* argument. Here the contrasting parts of the analogy are the ancient Hebrews, warned by angels about the consequences of transgression, and contemporary Christians. The chronological progression of the proclamation, from the Lord, to his followers, then to contemporaries, may reflect traditional formulations about the spread of the gospel (cf. Acts 10:36–9). v. 4, the description of contemporary reality in terms of 'signs, wonders and miracles', based upon OT accounts (Deut 4:34; Ps 135:9; Jer 32:20–1), recalls Christian experience (e.g. Mt 11:20; Mk 6:4; 1 Cor 12:10; Gal 3:5). That displays of power confirm the gospel is an apologetic commonplace (Mk 16:20; Acts 3:1–10; 14:3–11).

(2:5–9) The Subjection and Glorification of the Son The text at the centre of the next section, Ps 8:4–6, exhibits thematic connections to the scriptural catena of the first chapter. It may have been part of a traditional catena on which our homilist based his exposition. He subjects the verse to a Christological reading in terms of the incarnation and suffering of the Son. v. 5, the introductory comment continues the contrast between Son and angels. Its reference to the 'world to come' reinforces the notions of imminent judgement and cosmic transformation intimated by Ps 102, cited at 1:10–12. vv. 6–8a, the studied imprecision of the citation formula ('someone... somewhere') is paralleled in first-century Jewish interpreters (Philo, *Ebr.* 61; *Deus Imm.* 74). Ps 8 praises God's powerful majesty and questions the significance of humanity in the face of the divine glory ('What are human beings...?'). The psalmist responds to his query by affirming the lofty status

of humankind, made 'a little lower than the angels', thus 'crowned... with glory and honour' and set in a position of dominion with 'all things under their feet'. Thus the psalm finally celebrates humanity's status in the created order. The citation omits one clause from the original, 'You have set him over the works of your hands'. The verse, focusing on the present world, might have made the homilist's rereading more difficult. The NRSV captures the psalm's original sense, but obscures the basis for the homilist's interpretation. In Greek the psalm reads: 'What is man that you are mindful of him or the son of man that you care for him?' In v. 7 the psalmist's response uses the singular pronoun in referring generically to the human beings to whom all things are subject. vv. 8b–9, by exploiting ambiguities in the text, the homilist construes the primary referent of the passage to be not humankind in general but Christ. He may or may not know of the attribution of the title 'Son of Man', connected with Dan 7:13, to Jesus (cf. e.g. Mt 8:20; 12:40; 24:27 and parallels; Jn 1:51; 12:23; Acts 7:56). He does interpret the singular nouns 'man' and 'son of man' in the first verse to refer to an individual, not a collectivity. He interprets the psalmist's response in v. 7 not as parallel affirmations of the exalted status of all humans, but as a brief synopsis of Christ's story. Finally, he construes the adverbial phrase, 'a little bit', in v. 7 as temporal ('for a little while'), not qualitative. His first comment in v. 8 treats the notion of subjection. He continues to use the singular, not specifying its antecedent, but noting that, contrary to the absolute phrasing of the psalm, 'all things' have not been brought into subjection 'to him' (not 'to them' as in the NRSV). The subjection envisioned is apparently the subordination of Messiah's enemies promised by Ps 110 (cf. 1:13). The final eschatological victory remains to be achieved, as in 1 Cor 15:27. In the interim what can be seen, at least with the eyes of faith, is Jesus, whose human name appears for the first time. The homilist refers to Jesus with phrases from the psalm, applying 'for a little while made lower than the angels' to his incarnation and 'crowned... with glory and honour' to his exaltation. These phrases frame the note that the exaltation took place 'because of the suffering of death'. He concludes by recognizing that Jesus' death was for others. The biblical expression 'tasted' death (Isa 51:17; 4 Ezra 6:16; Mt 16:28; Jn 8:52) refers to death's bitter reality. For the phrase 'by the grace of God' some MSS and patristic citations read 'apart from God', which could evoke the forlorn cry of Jesus on the cross (Mt 27:46; Mk 15:34), but this understanding conflicts with 5:7 which describes God as hearing the prayers of Jesus. The phrase was probably a marginal gloss, inspired by 1 Cor 15:27, noting that God is not among things subjected to the Messiah.

(2:10–18) Christ and his Family The note in v. 9 that Christ tasted death for all foreshadows this section, which describes the salvific effects of Christ's death and explicitly introduces the title 'high priest'. v. 10, concern about what is 'fitting' to say of God is common in Hellenistic theology (cf. Ps.-Arist. *De Mundo*, 397b; Plut. *De Is. et Os.* 78, 383A). The emphasis of such theology on the loftiness of the divine suits the designation of God as Creator 'for whom and through whom all things exist'. The homilist, however, focuses on the appropriate relationship between means and end in the salvific process. God's purpose to bring 'many children [lit. sons] to glory' may reflect the original meaning of Ps 8, cited in vv. 6–7. The divine plan clearly involves participation by Christ's followers as fellow heirs in his eschatological rule; cf. 1:13–14. 'Pioneer' describes the agent of glorification, the one who has already been glorified (cf. 2:8–9). The relatively rare epithet (Gk. *archēgos*, lit. fore-leader) appears in Acts 3:15; 5:31, and Heb 12:2. Both attestations in Hebrews involve untranslatable wordplays. The term here suggests Christ's role as the path-breaker on the way to heavenly glory (cf. 'forerunner' at 6:20). What is fitting is God's making this agent 'perfect through suffering'. Hebrews develops the notion of perfection in complex ways. Applied to Christ, it refers to the way in which he is made fit to fulfil his duties as a special kind of priest (cf. 5:8–10; 7:28). In that office he is able to bring perfection to his followers (9:9; 10:14; 11:40; 12:2, 23). The key to Christ's perfection is his experience of suffering that renders him compassionate and sympathetic (2:17–18; 5:9). v. 11, what binds the Son to his siblings is not simply physical kinship but sanctity. The cultic language hints at the theme of Christ's priesthood and the effects attributed to his sacrificial death (cf. 9:13–14; 10:1–2, 10, 14; 13:12). There is ambiguity in the formulation of the unity between sanctifier and sanctified, which the NRSV resolves with the translation 'have one Father'. The Greek states simply 'are all of one'. While other interpretations of the 'one' are possible (e.g. Adam, Abraham), the resolution is appropriate in this context which had just pointed to God, the source and goal of all (2:10). Hebrews has thus applied to the Christian community the kind of expression of solidarity often found in Jewish sources (e.g. Philo, *On Virtues*, 79). Because of their spiritual relationship, Jesus can address his followers with familial language. v. 12, Ps 22:22, construed as a remark of Jesus, provides evidence for his relationship to his followers. The citation reflects the early church use of kinship categories for the community of faith (e.g. Rom 1:13; 16:4; Acts 1:15). The only other saying attributed to Christ in Hebrews, at 10:5–7, is also a citation from the Psalms. Ps 22, a prayer of supplication in time of distress, is prominent in the passion narratives (Mt 27:35, 39, 43, 46, and par.; Lk 23:35; Jn 19:24). The homilist may evoke such texts here, but he focuses on a verse not cited elsewhere. As a simple proof text, Ps 22:2 establishes that the speaker, presumed to be the Messiah, preaches to his 'brothers and sisters'. The second clause indicates that the status of children of God is a matter of 'the congregation'. The Greek term *ekklēsia*, used again at Heb 12:23, is the common designation for the Christian assembly. v. 13, two more scriptural verses support the solidarity of Christ and his followers. They probably derive from Isa 8:17–18, although the first also resembles 2 Sam 22:3 and Isa 12:2. The separation between the verses highlights the notion of 'trust' in the first. The attitude attributed to the 'pioneer' foreshadows the complex notion of faith that Christ and his followers are meant to share (11:1–12:3). v. 14, attention shifts from the relationship between Christ and his followers to the act establishing that relationship. The fact that Jesus fully shares in 'flesh and blood' exemplifies the insistence of Hebrews on Christ's full humanity (cf. 2:17; 5:7–10; 12:1–4). Depiction of Christ's death as a struggle against 'the one who has the power of death . . . the devil', evokes an ancient mythical theme. In Jewish apocalyptic sources it comes to expression as the Messiah's victory over demonic

forces (*As. Mos.* 10:1; *T. Levi* 18:2; *1 Enoch* 10:13; 2 Esd 13:1; 1QM 1:11–17). Early Christian texts apply the scheme to Jesus, who conquers the diabolical world (Mt 12:25–30; Lk 10:18; Jn 12:31; 14:30; 16:11; 1 Jn 3:8; Rev 12:7–10), or more specifically death (1 Cor 15:26, 55; 2 Tim 1:10; Rev 20:14; 21:4; *Od. Sol.* 15:9; 29:4). v. 15, the liberating result of Christ's combat with the devil resembles the key episode in the myths of heroes such as Orpheus or Heracles who descend to the underworld to free death's captives. The homilist was no doubt familiar with such myths and their metaphorical applications, where a major theme is the 'fear of death', often seen to be a basic human problem (Eur. *Or.* 1522; Lucr. *De rerum naturâ*, 1.102–26; Epict. *Diss.* 1.17.25). The Stoic philosopher and dramatist Seneca, for example, portrayed the story of Heracles as a model of liberation from the fear of death (*Herc. Furens* 858–92; cf. *Herc. Oetaeus* 1434–40, 1557–9, 1940–88). For Hebrews, it is not Stoic acceptance of death, but assured hope in heavenly glory that effects liberation. v. 16, a parenthetical remark concludes the theme of Christ and the angels that framed the scriptural catena of the first chapter. Christ's action in 'coming to help' (lit. grab hold of) continues the imagery of the hero's quest to free death's captives. The object of the hero's attention are the 'descendants [lit. seed] of Abraham'. This group includes not only the physical descendants of Abraham among whom Jesus lived but also those who stand in the tradition of Abraham's faith, the heirs of God's promises (cf. 6:13–17; 11:8–19). Hebrews thus shares an early Christian claim to be the true seed of Abraham; cf. Lk 1:55; Gal 3:8–9, 29; 4:28–31; Rom 4:1–25; Jn 8:33. v. 17, the reflection on the 'fittingness' of God's action concludes with a summary involving important Christological themes. The affirmation that Jesus was 'like his brothers and sisters in every respect' will later (4:15) be modified, but the insistence on his humanity remains constant. His human experience qualifies Jesus for his office of 'high priest'. The title appears for the first time, although the exordium (1:3) alluded to it. The character of Christ's priestly office and ministry stands at the heart of Hebrews (chs. 7–10). The 'merciful' character of this high priest comes to expression in his intercessory function (4:14–16; 7:25). The fact that he is 'faithful' serves as the starting-point of the homily on fidelity in the next chapter. Both attributes have a pastoral function. Christ's mercy grounds Christian hope; his fidelity inspires those facing difficulty (cf. 12:1–2). v. 18, the point that Christ, because tested, is able to aid, reappears at 4:14; 5:7–8; 12:1–2. It is clear that the 'perfection' of Christ, mentioned at 2:10, involves the qualities that make Christ the high priest that he is.

Christ Faithful and Merciful (3:1–5:10)

(3:1–4:11) A Homily on Faith

(3:1–6) Moses and Jesus as Examples of Faith From 3:1 through 4:13 a homiletic reflection focuses on the need for continued fidelity. Prior to the citation of a text to be interpreted, a preface introduces the theme, contrasting two examples, Moses, the servant (3:5), and Christ, the Son (3:6). The contrast exalts Jesus, as do other comparisions of the first several chapters; yet it contains an ironic note. The exalted status of Son requires greater fidelity because with it comes greater testing, as ch. 12 will argue. The assumption that

God's children will be exposed to special testing is an explicit part of the homily that follows. v. 1, the description of the addressees as 'partners' (Gk. *metochoi*) involves a term applied to the angelic 'companions' of the Son at 1:9. Etymologically it is related to the verb 'to share' (*metechein*), used for Christ's participation in human physical characteristics (2:10). His true companions are his 'brothers and sisters' (2:10–14) who 'share' in the Holy Spirit (6:4). Their participation in things 'heavenly' (cf. 6:4; 8:5; 9:23; 11:16; 12:22) is not an irrefragable guarantee but is contingent on their response to the 'calling'. Hence the following exhortation is necessary. The description of Jesus as high priest continues the theme introduced at 2:17. The unusual epithet 'apostle' applies to Christ only here in the NT. It suggests the common notion of Jesus as 'one sent' from God; cf. Mk 9:37; Mt 10:40; 15:24; Lk 10:16; Gal 4:4; Jn 3:17, 34 and frequently. The title also evokes the image of the hero sent to release death's captives (2:10–16). The 'confession' (cf. 4:14; 10:23) may refer to fixed liturgical formulations but probably encompasses the general content of the community's faith. v. 2, Hebrews compares Moses and Jesus on the basis of Num 12:7, where YHWH confirms the position of Moses as leader of the Israelites when Aaron and Miriam had murmured against him. The original Hebrew affirmed that Moses was 'entrusted' with all of God's 'house', that he was, in effect, the chief steward of the people of Israel. The Greek translation can be understood as a statement about the faithfulness of Moses. v. 3, the homilist plays with the term 'house', drawing an analogy between a house and its builder and Moses and Jesus. The analogy is inexact; Jesus is not said to be the builder of Moses. Nor is he said to be the builder of the house. v. 4, lest there be any misunderstanding, the homilist indicates clearly that the builder of the house of which he speaks is God, earlier described as the Creator of all (2:10). Despite the clarification, the analogy associates Jesus, to whom divine titles can be applied (1:8, 10), with the Creator. v. 5, the homilist cites again Num 12:7 in order to specify the distinction between Jesus and Moses. In Num, YHWH had contrasted other prophets to whom he communicated in visions and dreams with 'his servant' Moses, to whom he spoke face to face. Thus 'servant' was a title of honour, indicating the unique status of Moses. The notice indicating what the service involves, 'testimony to things that would be spoken', relegates Moses to a function analogous to that of the angels (1:14). v. 6, Hebrews recontextualizes the passage from Numbers by reflecting on the categories appropriate to a household. The homilist contrasts the title 'servant' to the designation 'Son', which Scripture had attested for Jesus (1:5). In the process he introduces the title 'Christ'. The contrast between children and servants, used by other early Christian authors (Gal 4:1–7; Jn 8:35), may be a rhetorical commonplace. The homilist embellishes the contrast by indicating the relationship of the Son to the household. Unlike a servant 'within' the household, the Son is 'over' it, a position appropriate to his exalted status (1:3, 13; 2:7). The household itself is not, as Numbers originally suggested, the people of Israel, but 'we', the brothers and sisters whom Jesus leads to glory (2:10–13). Membership in the household is conditional on maintaining a strong identity with the people of God, expressed by two virtues. The term for the first, translated 'confidence' by the NRSV, connotes more than a subjective psychological state. It is a confident self-assurance

that issues in a bold 'freedom of speech', manifested in prayer (4:16; 10:19; for this sense of the word, cf. 1 Jn 3:21; Eph 3:12) and in public confession (10:35; cf. Mk 8:32; Jn 7:13; Phil 1:20; Eph 6:19). The second, translated 'the pride that belong(s) to hope' by the NRSV, also connotes external behaviour. The homilist calls upon his addressees to 'boast' about their hopes, as did other early Christian leaders (Rom 5:2; 2 Cor 3:12; 11:30; 12:9; Jas 1:9; 4:16). He will continually insist on the importance of hope (6:11; 7:19; 10:23; 11:1).

(3:7–11) The Text for a Homily: Psalm 95 The homilist now cites Ps 95:7–11, the final portion of a hymn praising YHWH's power and inviting the worshipper to attend to the divine command. The psalmist's application of the experience of the Exodus to his own day involves a typological use of Scripture common in the OT (cf. Isa 41:17; 42:9; 43:16–21; Hos 2:16–20), post-biblical Judaism (Sir 16:10; CD 3:7–9), and early Christianity (cf. Mk 6:34; Jn 6:30–1; 1 Cor 5:7; Acts 7:17–53). The Israelites of the Exodus generation, in fact, constituted a standard negative example that could be adapted to specific homiletic contexts, as at 1 Cor 10:1–22. v. 7, the notion that the Holy Spirit is the source of Scripture (also at 9:8; 10:15) is no doubt traditional; cf. Acts 28:25; 1 *Clem.* 13:1; 16:2. The initial word of the citation, 'Today', calls for an actualization of the scriptural experience in the lives of the people of Israel. The homilist, following the psalmist's lead, applies the psalm's message to his addressees (4:7, 11). v. 8, the psalmist recalls the rebellion of the Exodus generation at Meribah and Massah (Ex 17:7; Num 20:1–13; Deut 6:16; 9:22; 33:8). The Greek translates these place names etymologically as 'rebellion' and day 'of testing'. v. 10, the traditional versification of Hebrews follows that of the original psalm, which associates the period of forty years with God's wrath against the Exodus generation (cf. 3:17). The divine displeasure was thus limited to that period. Our homilist inserts a particle 'therefore' that, in effect, repunctuates the psalm. He associates the 'forty years' with the period during which the Israelites tested God, as described in v. 9. v. 11, divine oaths are of special significance; cf. 6:13–20; 7:20–2. The term 'rest' in the original psalm referred to the 'resting place' of the land of Canaan; the homilist will suggest another understanding at 4:1–11.

(3:12–4:11) Homiletic Exegesis: Let Us Enter God's Rest The application of the psalm develops in three balanced segments, 3:12–19; 4:1–5; 4:6–11, each of which features a verse from the psalm. The whole aims to show that the threat and the promise contained in the text apply to the situation of the addressees. v. 12, the summons to 'Take care' is common in the NT; cf. Mt 24:4; Acts 13:40; 1 Cor 10:18; Col. 2:8; Heb 12:25. The danger against which the homilist warns involves fundamental attitudes and commitments. The translation 'unbelieving heart' puts the emphasis on belief. The phrase would be better rendered 'faithless heart', suggesting a concern with infidelity in a broader sense. The homilist specifies the danger by warning against 'turning away' from God. This warning involves a wordplay in the Greek between 'faithless' (*apistias*) and 'turn away' (*apostenai*). The example of the rebellion in the desert recorded in Num 14 inspires the connection. The description of God as 'living' is a traditional one (cf. Deut 5:26) that reappears at Heb 9:14; 10:31; 12:22. v. 13, the homilist sounds a more positive note, using a verb, 'to exhort one another', related to the description of his own work at 13:22; cf. also 12:5. The conceit that the 'today' of the psalm is the present of the homilist reappears at 4:7. The description of the danger as the 'deceit of sin' is another traditional motif; cf. Rom 7:11; 2 Thess 2:10; and 2 Cor 11:3, which alludes to Gen 3:13. v. 14, the verse recalls emphases of the introduction to the homily. For the term 'partners', see 3:1. The homilist had insisted on the conditional character of the partnership with Christ at 3:6. As the virtues recommended at 3:6 involved active behaviour, so too the homilist here calls for something more than a subjective attitude. The noun translated 'confidence' by the NRSV could be translated 'resolution', the stance appropriate for soldiers confronting an enemy. The word is also the same as that used for the 'being' of God at 1:3 and may subtly call upon the addressees to hold fast to the divine reality which they have experienced in Christ; cf. 11:1. v. 15, the homilist cites again the first verse of the psalm. The connective 'as it is said' obscures the relationship of the citation to the immediate context. The phrase should be translated 'by saying' and refers to the way in which the addressees are called upon to exhort one another in v. 13. v. 16, the homilist probes the application of the text with a series of questions, each of which uses a phrase of the psalm, a technique frequently exemplified in Philo's exegesis (e.g. *Quis Heres*, 115, 260–1; *Spec. Leg.* 3.25). These questions direct attention to the details of the failure of the ancient Israelites. The response that 'all who left Egypt' were at fault may recall YHWH's comment to Moses at Num 14:22, although that comment had allowed some exceptions. v. 17, using the psalm's traditional association of forty years with the period of wrath (cf. Num 14:33, 34), the homilist asks again at whom the wrath was directed. That the bodies of the sinners fell in the desert alludes to Num 14:33 and conjures up an image of judgement. v. 18, at Num 14:43 Moses had addressed the Israelites as people 'disobedient to the Lord'. v. 19, the series of questions concludes with an observation that draws the first portion of the homily to a climactic close. The translation of the NRSV, attributing the failure of the desert generation to 'unbelief', is too restrictive. As the allusions to Num 14 in the previous verses make clear, the problem is portrayed as disobedient 'infidelity'. Whatever the attitudes and behaviours of the addressees may have been, Hebrews portrays the danger confronting them in stark terms.

4:1, attention now shifts to the 'rest' promised in the last verse of the psalm. A warning continues the monitory tone of the last verse and introduces the notion that the 'rest' remains available in the present. The suggestion that the rest is 'promised' introduces a theme that recurs through the rest of the text (6:12, 15, 17; 7:6; 8:6; 9:15; 10:36; 11:9, 13, 17, 33, 39). v. 2, the homilist again emphasizes the continuity between the revelation of old and that of his own day, while highlighting the importance of a faithful response. The term 'good news' (*euaggelion*) plays on the Greek word for 'promise' (*epaggelia*) in the previous verse. The 'good news' announces a message of hope for the fulfilment of God's promises. The phrase 'the message they heard' (lit. the word of hearing) recalls a Pauline phrase for the gospel (cf. 1 Thess 2:13). It emphasizes the notion of oral communication explicit in the psalm's opening verse. For the notion that members of God's people from the past may be 'united by faith' with the eschatological commu-

nity, see 11:39–40. While members of the faithless desert generation were not so united, those who are faithful will share in the promised inheritance. v. 3, the next comment indicates who deserves to inherit the divine rest, the 'we' of the homilist's own community. To reinforce that point, he cites the last verse of the psalm, contrasting the 'they' of the desert generation with the 'us' of his community. The problem remains of how the promise of a divine rest is available to contemporaries, particularly if the rest envisioned by Scripture is the 'resting place' or homeland of Canaan. The homilist hints at his solution by noting that the divine 'works' were 'finished at the foundation of the world'. v. 4, the homilist now explains the relevance of the allusion to Genesis. With a comment that the Author of Scripture once spoke about the 'seventh day', the homilist cites Gen 2:2, which reports that God himself rested after completing the work of creation. For our homilist, this verse thus interprets the significance of the phrase 'my rest' in Ps 95:11. v. 5, lest there be any doubt about the connection, the homilist cites again the relevant verse of the psalm. His interpretation exemplifies the rabbinic technique *gezera shewa*, which draws together two passages linked by a common word. At its simplest, this technique interpreted an ambiguous word in one context by its clear meaning in another. The technique could also link passages whose themes or motifs might be mutually illuminating. Such is the use of the technique in this context. The homilist suggests that 'God's rest' mentioned in the psalm is not something earthly but is a place or state into which God himself entered at the time of creation. Hence, to focus on the land of Canaan as the resting place of the people of God is erroneous.

4:6, the homilist now moves into his final stage of explication of the scriptural text, summarizing the force of the argument thus far. 'Disobedience' prevented the original recipients of the divine promise from attaining it. The promise, therefore, remains open. v. 7, a citation of the first verse of the psalm introduces a historical argument reinforcing the point that the promise was not fulfilled by entry into Canaan. As tradition indicates, 'David' was the author of the psalm. v. 8, the homilist draws an inference. Since David was subsequent to Joshua, he could not have called for faithful attendance upon God's word, and the consequent receipt of the divine promise, if that promise had been fulfilled in Joshua's day. The evocation of Moses' successor, whose name is the same as that of Jesus, may suggest another comparison between the 'pioneer' (2:10) of the new covenant and a counterpart of old, but the comparison is not developed. v. 9, in drawing his conclusion that a promised rest remains available to his own community, the homilist returns to his *gezera shewa* argument in vv. 4 and 5. The link between Ps 95:11 and Gen 2:2 suggested that the promised rest was connected with God's rest on the primordial sabbath. The specific term 'sabbath rest' appears here for the first time in Greek literature. It evokes not simply repose, but the joyous observance of the day characteristic of Jewish tradition. v. 10, nonetheless, entry into that state follows the cessation of labour. This portion of the homily suggests that the 'labours' confronting the addressees involve struggle against the temptation to rebel or go astray. Later portions of the homily will suggest that active external oppression (cf. 10:32–9; 12:1–4; 13:13) is also involved. v. 11, rest is finally to be achieved in the festive presence of

God, in that 'heavenly city' to which the faithful aim (11:13–16; 12:21–3; 13:14). The exhortation closes with a reference to the negative example of disobedience provided by the desert generation.

(4:12–13) Concluding Reflection: The Power of God's Word A brief poetic flourish reinforces the homiletic warning developed since 3:1. It focuses on the word of God that came to expression in the text of the psalm and in the homilist's exposition. It also draws to a close the theme of God's speech that runs through the first several chapters (cf. 1:1; 2:2, 6, 12). Church fathers and some modern commentators interpret this passage as a reference to Christ and the Word of God, a title used of Christ in Jn 1:1–14, but the passage does not have such a precise focus. v. 12, the homilist relies on traditional imagery as he personifies the word of God as something 'living and active'. God's word had often been seen as the instrument of divine creative (cf. Gen 1:3; Ps 33:9; Isa 55:11; Sir 42:15; Wis 9:1) and judgemental (Amos 1:2; Jer 7:1–3) activity. Such language invites personification, which could become elaborate, as at Wis 18:14–16, where the divine word is a warrior, bearing a sharp sword against the Egyptians. The comparison to a 'two-edged sword' is rooted in poetic comparison of the tongue to a sword (cf. Isa 49:2; Ps 57:4). The word issuing from the tongue could be similarly described. The Jewish exegete and philosopher Philo exploits the image extensively, interpreting various biblical swords as symbols of the divine Logos ('Word' or 'Reason'). Thus in *De Cherubim*, 38, he finds the 'flaming sword' of Gen 3:4 as the word uniting God's goodness and royal power and, in *Quis Heres*, 130–2, 234–6, he introduces the divine Logos as a cosmic principle accessible to the human reason through logical analysis. Christians used the image of the divine word as a sword in hortatory (Eph 6:17) and eschatological contexts (Rev 1:16; 2:12; 19:15). Hebrews emphasizes the judgemental function of the divine word and the one from whom it issues. Imagery of the innermost portions of the human person, both spiritual ('soul' and 'spirit') and physical ('joints' and 'marrow') suggest how penetrating the word can be. The two pairs are meant to be evocative, not precisely definitive of the components of the human self. The key point is that the word is critical or 'able to judge' the workings of the human heart. v. 13, the personification intensifies as the word become the Judge. That no creature is 'hidden' before God is a commonplace for Graeco-Roman philosophers (e.g. Epict. *Diss.* 2.14.11; Marc. Aur. *Medit.* 12.2), for Jews (Jer 11:20; 1 Enoch 9:5; *Ep. Arist.* 132–3; *Sib. Or.* 8.282–5; Philo, *Abr.* 104; *Cher.* 96), and for early Christians (1 Cor 4:5; 1 Thess 2:4; Rom 8:27). The description of all as 'naked and laid bare' involves colourful language, used of a wrestling hold and of a sacrifice, where a victim's neck would be 'laid bare' to the priest's knife. The concluding remark that it is to this judge that we must 'render an account' involves one more verbal play on the Greek *logos*, which means both 'word' and 'account'.

(4:14–16) Transitional Exhortation: Approach the Merciful High Priest Since the beginning of the exhortation at 3:1, our homilist worked with the theme of 'fidelity', exemplified by Jesus and called for in his followers. He now treats the second attribute accorded to Jesus at 2:17, mercy. He begins development of the theme with another hortatory comment. v. 14, as at 10:19, the homilist bases his exhortation on a statement of what his audience possesses. That Jesus is a 'high priest' appeared at 2:17, although the title's significance remains to be seen. That he has 'passed through the heavens' is implicit in the image of his exaltation (1:3, 13; 2:7–9; 9:11). The title 'Son of God', a fuller form of the title Son (1:5) reappears at 6:6; 7:3; 10:29. The juxtaposition of the name Jesus and this majestic title may be characteristic of liturgical formulas to which the homilist refers when he speaks of the community's 'confession'. For similar language, cf. Rom 1:4; 1 Thess 1:10; Acts 9:20; 1 Jn 1:7; 4:15; 5:5. The exhortation to 'hold fast' reinforces analogous calls in the preceding exhortation (3:6, 14). v. 15, the homilist's pastoral sensitivity is evident in his balanced exhortations. In contrast to the threatening warning about the judgemental word of God, he now highlights the consoling thought of a 'sympathetic' heavenly figure. The claim that he has been 'tested' formed the last comment on the human experience of Jesus (2:17). A more graphic description of his testing will follow at 5:7–10. The similarity of Christ and his followers has one qualification, that he was 'without sin'. Such an affirmation, common in early Christian sources (cf. 2 Cor 5:21; Jn 7:18; 8:46; 14:30; 1 Jn 3:5, 7; 1 Pet 1:19; 2:22; 3:18), here grounds the claim that Christ was a 'blameless' offering in his self-sacrificial death (cf. 9:14). v. 16, the call to 'approach', repeated at 10:22, is part of the author's exhortation to move in an appropriate direction, towards rest (4:11), perfection (6:1), and ultimately God. The cultic image of approaching the sanctuary in worship (cf. Ex 16:9; Lev 9:7; 21:17; 22:3; Num 10:3–4; 18:3) is commonly used for believers (cf. 7:25; 11:6; 12:18, 22). Although rooted in cult, the image applies to the whole covenant relationship with God. The specific goal of the believer's movement is the divine 'throne', previously mentioned at 1:8. The characterization 'of grace' highlights the quality of mercy on which the homilist now focuses. The summons to approach 'with boldness' (cf. 3:6) calls for confident self-expression before God, which Christ's human prayer also exemplifies (5:7). The combination of 'mercy' and 'grace', common in Jewish and Christian texts (cf. Wis 3:9; 4:15; 1 Tim 1:2; 2 Tim 1:2; Titus 1:4; 2 Jn 3), offers a comprehensive definition of the 'help' available. The assistance from on high is 'timely' or 'in a time of need' (NRSV) as 2:18 had suggested, because the addressees are also being tested.

(5:1–10) The Merciful Christ and the High Priests The reflection on the person and work of Christ concentrates on his status as the true and eternal High Priest. The theme, introduced at 2:17 and repeated at 4:15, now undergoes its first stage of development. Here the homilist compares Christ with ordinary earthly high priests, showing points of contact and hinting at the superiority of the heavenly high priest. The description of ordinary high priests (5:1–4) makes three general points about their function, their relationship to their followers, and their relationship to God. These points will be treated in inverse order in their application to Christ (5:5–10). v. 1, high priests are intermediaries *par excellence*. Their central responsibility is to make 'gifts and sacrifices', a generic description of sacrifices (cf. 3 Kgdms 8:64; *Ep. Arist.* 234; Heb 8:3; 9:12). Our homilist characterizes these as having to do with 'sin'. Although priests in Scripture were responsible for various offerings, including the daily sacrifice (Ex 29:38–46), and thanksgiving and purificatory sacrifices (Lev 2–7), Hebrews concentrates on the sacrifice unique to the high priest, the offering for sins on the Day of Atonement (Lev 16). Details of that ritual provide the material for the exposition in chs. 8–10. v. 2, the second point of comparison, an idealized picture of a high priest, focuses on the theme of sympathy mentioned at 4:15. The ordinary high priest should 'deal gently' with sinners. The verb (*metriopathein*), unique in scripture, is carefully chosen. Not synonymous with 'sympathize' (4:15), its philosophical usage (cf. Diog. Laert. *Lives of the Philosophers*, 5.31; Plut. *On Restraining Anger*, 10 (*Mor.* 458c); Philo, *Virt.* 195; *Abr.* 257; *Leg. All.* 3.129) suggests a restraint of emotion, particularly of anger. Christ, as heavenly high priest, does that and more. The earthly high priest can restrain his anger because, like his fellows, he is 'subject to weakness'. Hebrews will develop this notion, with the qualification about Christ's sinlessness already enunciated (4:15). The characterization of the sinners as 'ignorant and wayward' reflects the stipulation that sin-offerings apply only to unwitting offences (Lev 4:2; 5:21–2; Num 15:22–31; Deut 17:12). This restriction parallels the exclusion of wilful sins from the pale of forgiveness (6:4–8; 10:26–31; 12:17). v. 3, the requirement that the high priest sacrifice for himself and for the people pertains to the Day of Atonement; cf. Lev 9:7; 16:6–17. The fact that ordinary high priests had to sacrifice for themselves contributes to the homilist's argument about Christ's superiority (7:27; 9:7). v. 4, the final point of comparison is that the high priest is not self-appointed, but 'called' by God. This stipulation applies to the first high priest of the biblical tradition, Aaron, appointed to the office by God (cf. Ex 28:1; Lev 8:1; Num 16–18). Aaron continues the list of biblical figures used as foils for Christ, but the contrast between Christ and him is not further developed.

5:5–6, taking the points of comparison in inverse order, the homilist begins by noting how Christ was called to office. He does so by construing two verses from the Psalms as divine speech to the Son. The first, Ps 2:7, is familiar from Heb 1:3. The second, Ps 110:4, derives from a text, the first verse of which was cited at Heb 1:13. While Ps 110:1 was associated with Christ's exaltation, the current verse appears here for the first time in early Christian literature. The verse originally attributed priestly status to an Israelite king. Its allusion to the 'order of Melchizedek' may have been an attempt by Davidic poets to effect reconciliation with ancient Canaanite traditions in Jerusalem. For our homilist the phrase presents an opportunity, for the attribution of priestly status to the addressee does not, in itself, affirm that the addressee, in his construal the Messiah, can be entitled 'high priest'. Ch. 7 will show how 'priesthood according to the order of Melchizedek' is really a superior, because heavenly and eternal, form of high priesthood. For the moment, the juxtaposition of the two verses permits the linking of two central Christological titles, Son and High Priest. That connection causes difficulties for readers seeking a systematic Christology. Yet the homilist is unconcerned with the chronological relationship between the designations of Christ as Son and High Priest. It is clear that, for him, Christ is the Son eternally (1:3), and that he becomes High Priest at the point where he is 'perfected' or exalted

(7:28). What is important for Hebrews is that Scripture attests Christ as both. v. 7, Hebrews now recounts part of the human experience of Jesus that made him capable of sympathy. The portrait of Jesus offering 'prayers and supplications' generically resembles the scene at Gethsemane (cf. Mt 26:36–46; Mk 14:32–43; Lk 22:40–6), but the details differ. The homilist may have been inspired by stories of various prayers of Jesus, including his cry on the cross (Mt 27:46; Mk 15:34), but the overall pattern embodies traditional notions of the ideal prayer of the righteous. The content of the prayers is not explicit, but the one addressed 'who was able to save him from death', suggests that the prayer sought deliverance. The 'loud cries and tears', not part of Gethsemane accounts, derive from the Psalms (Ps 22:1–2, 24; 116:8) and recur in Jewish traditions (1QH 5:12; 2 Macc 11:6; 3 Macc 1:16; 1 Esd 5:62; Philo, *Leg. All.* 3.213; *Quis Heres*, 19). That Christ was heard 'because of his reverent submission' is part of the same portrait of a saint's prayer. The word for 'reverent submission' (Gk. *eulabeia*) appears in Philo's description of the prayer of Moses (*Quis Heres*, 22) and has connotations of the 'fear of the Lord' (Prov 1:7). That Christ 'was heard' does not indicate that he was spared death; the homilist clearly alludes to Christ's exaltation in which he was brought out of death; cf. 2:10; 13:20. v. 8, that Christ 'learned through … what he suffered' involves a common Greek proverb (cf. Aesch. *Ag.* 177; Hdt. 1.207) about experience as teacher. The Jewish proverbial notion that suffering can be a form of divine chastisement (cf. 12:4–11) may also be in the background, but the homilist has a hortatory goal. Christ can be sympathetic because of his suffering; he also serves as a model of obedience to the divine will; cf. 10:5–10; 12:1–3. v. 9, the final point of comparison between Christ and earthly high priests relates to the effect of their actions. Christ 'perfected' (cf. 2:10) is, in his exalted state, a 'cause of salvation'. The immediate context suggests Christ's exemplary role; chs. 8–10 will describe how his sacrifice achieves salvific effects. The note that salvation is for 'those who obey him' reinforces its conditional character (cf. 2:1–4; 3:6, 14). v. 10, a paraphrase of Ps 110:4, already cited at 5:4, concludes the section. The claim that the verse designates Christ a 'high priest' requires explanation, but the homilist dramatically delays his expository *tour de force*.

The Priestly Work of Christ (5:11–10:18)

(5:11–6:20) Transitional Admonition The interlude falls into three sections, two (5:11–6:3; 6:4–12) of direct exhortation and one (6:13–20) offering scriptural assurance about the reliability of God's promises. 5:11, an apology for the difficulty of the material is a common rhetorical device. Apology turns quickly to criticism of the addressees, accused of being 'dull in understanding'. The same term, meaning 'sluggish', concludes the exhortation at 6:12, but on a more optimistic note. Hence the accusation is clearly a rhetorical move, designed to challenge not condemn the addressees. 5:12, the challenging tone continues with the suggestion that the addressees are spiritually underdeveloped, needing to learn their elementary catechism. The 'oracles of God' are Israel's Scriptures (Acts 7:38; Rom 3:2; 1 Pet 4:11). The contrasting images of 'milk' and 'solid food' commonly represent educational levels (e.g. 1 Cor 2:6–8; 3:18–23; Philo, *Agr.* 9; Epict. *Dis.* 2.16.39). 5:13, the homilist exploits the educational referents of the image. Those who imbibe educational pabulum are at the elementary level, concentrating on grammar and rhetoric, not the 'word of righteousness', i.e. moral philosophy. In this context such secular language evokes another order of 'righteousness' (*dikaiosyne*), that provided by the heavenly high priest, who 'loves righteousness' (1:9). 5:14, play on the imagery continues. The contrast between milk and solid food parallels the contrast between the infant and the 'mature' person, who can tolerate solid food. Adults are also those who exercise, and the phrase 'trained by practice' evokes both the gymnasium and the common application of athletic imagery to the moral life (e.g. 1 Tim 4:7; 2 Pet 2:14; Heb 12:11; Philo, *Conf. Ling.* 181; *Agr.* 42). The final phrase, 'distinguishing good from evil', reinforces the secular referent of the imagery, but, for Hebrews, to make such a distinction is ultimately to follow Christ (12:1–2). Hence to be 'mature' (*teleios*) is more than a matter of physical and intellectual maturation. 6:1, a verbal play on the connotations of the language emerges in the call to press on to 'perfection' (*teleiotes*). The summons suggests, as does the underlying moralizing image, that perfection is in the hands of the addressees. It later becomes clear that their moral efforts depend upon the perfecting that Christ's sacrifice affords (10:14). The homilist calls for an understanding of that reality and a life lived in the light of Christ's example (12:1–2). He will not rehearse the basics of Christian belief and practice. v. 2, the 'instruction about baptisms' may involve the distinction between Christian initiation and other similar rites, as at Acts 18:25; 19:3–5. For the ritual 'laying on of hands', see Acts 8:17; 19:6. v. 3, a pious aside makes a conventional appeal to God's will; cf. 1 Cor 16:7, and, for similar appeals, Rom 1:10; 1 Cor 4:19; Acts 18:21; Jas 4:15.

6:4, the homilist declares four things to be 'impossible'; cf. 6:18; 10:4; 11:6. This solemn declaration begins a stern warning, soon to be balanced by a more encouraging message. The belief that it is impossible to restore apostates resembles other early Christian expressions of rigorism, such as the notion of the unforgivable sin (Mt 12:32; Mk 3:29; Lk 12:10) or the 'mortal sin' of 1 Jn 5:16. The homilist does not indicate whether the grounds for this judgement, repeated in a slightly different form at 10:26–31 and 12:15–17, involve divine unwillingness to accept repentance or a subjective inability of apostates to repent. It appears to be a matter of definition; those who put themselves outside the pale of salvation cannot be retrieved. Various images define belonging to the Christian community. To be 'enlightened' is a common Christian image for reception of the gospel; cf. 1 Cor 4:5; Eph 1:18; 2 Tim 1:10; Jn 1:9 1; Pet 2:9; Jas 1:17. The image has not yet become an equivalent for baptism. To have 'tasted the heavenly gift' could allude to the eucharist (cf. Acts 20:11) but is more likely to be a general reference to all that is involved in salvation. For similar gifts, see Acts 2:38; 10:45; Rom 5:15; 2 Cor 9:15; Eph 3:7. v. 5, the 'powers of the age to come' recalls the description of the confirmation of God's word (2:4). v. 6, the heart of the belief about apostates comes to expression. In rejecting the one whose death brings salvation, they join those who disgracefully executed him. The solemn designation of Christ as Son of God reinforces the heinousness of apostasy. v. 7, a vivid agricultural image, contrasting two types of soil, links the two

halves of the exhortation. Such imagery is common in Scripture (Isa 5:1–2; 28:23–9; Ezek 19:10–14), in the parables of Jesus (Mk 4:3–9; Mt 13:1–9; Lk 8:4–8), and in other Jewish homilies (e.g. Philo, *Quis Heres*, 204). 'Ground that drinks up the rain' recalls the promised land (Deut 11:11). The human counterpart of that image has yet to be described. v. 8, the desolate briar patch recalls the land of the garden of Eden, cursed after the fall (Gen 3:17–18). The fiery destiny of such land may involve ordinary agricultural practice, but the image of burning evokes eschatological fire; cf. Mt 13:30, 42; 25:41; Rev 20:14. The image of consuming fire reappears at 12:29. v. 9, an address to the recipients as 'beloved' begins the expression of encouragement. Underlying the positive remarks is the traditional triad of faith, hope, and love (cf. 1 Thess 1:13; 1 Cor 13:3; Col 1:4–5), taken in inverse order. For another use of the triad, see 10:22–4. v. 10, confidence for the future is based on past experience of the community's loving behaviour. The expression resembles flattering remarks addressed by Christian leaders to their congregations (cf. 1 Thess 1:2; Rev 2:19; Ign. *Rom.* proem). v. 11, for the full assurance of hope, cf. 10:22. 'To the very end' recalls the warning of 3:14. v. 12, to follow the homilist's advice will prevent the addressees from becoming 'sluggish' (cf. 5:11). The opposite condition is a combination of fidelity and patience. The latter term, appearing only here in Hebrews, connotes more stalwart perseverance than passive patience. It will find echoes in later calls for endurance (10:32–6; 12:2). Such virtues will have their reward, expressed once again in terms of 'inheriting the promise'; cf. 1:14; 4:1, 8.

6:13, the final portion of the chapter develops the notion of the promise and suggests as a reason to be assured of it the divine oath that guarantees it. The homilist reflects on the oath that God swore to Abraham at Gen 22:16–17. The pericope anticipates a reflection (7:20–5) on the divine oath mentioned at Ps 110:4. The remark that God 'swore by himself' is based on Gen 22:16, a verse that caught the attention of other Jewish interpreters such as Philo (*Sacr.* 91–4; *Leg. All.* 3.203–7). 6:14, the content of the oath derives from Gen 22:17. Hebrews thus focuses on one element of the divine promise to Abraham, that he would be the father of a great nation (Gen 12:2–3; 15:5; 17:5), and ignores the correlative promise of land (Gen 12:7; 13:4). 6:15, the description of Abraham's action repeats the language of 6:12. Abraham's endurance involved his willingness to sacrifice Isaac, an episode used at 11:17–19 to illustrate Abraham's faith. 6:16, the human act of swearing helps explain the significance of God's oath. Philo offers a similar analysis about the supportive function of oaths (*Somn.* 1.12) and suggests that the divine oath was designed to help human beings accept God's promises (*Abr.* 273). 6:17, that God's purposes are 'unchangeable' is a common affirmation of Scripture (Num 23:19; 1 Sam 15:29; Ps 89:35; Isa 40:8; Jer 4:28) and of later Jewish authors (Philo, *Deus Imm.*). 6:18, the 'two unchangeable things' are apparently God's word and the confirming oath. A pastoral application of the reflection now develops. It is not immediately clear on what word and oath the addressees should rely. The following chapter (7:20–2) indicates that the relevant oath is found in Ps 110:4, confirming Christ's priesthood 'after the order of Melchizedek'. The homilist probably considers Ps 2:7, cited most recently at 5:5 in connection with Ps 110:4, as the basic divine word. The description of Christians as those 'who have taken refuge', could be translated even more graphically as 'who have fled for refuge'. The language hints at the image of wandering sojourners that will develop in ch. 11. The image of 'flight' towards God, based on Plato, *Theaetetus*, 176A–B, is common in Hellenistic religious philosophy. For a Jewish use, cf. Philo, *Fug.* 63. The homilist orients flight not to the transcendent world but towards an eschatological 'hope'. 6:19, the image of the anchor, unknown to the biblical tradition prior to Hebrews, is common in Greek literature (e.g. Pind. *Odesl.* 6.101; Plato, *Leg.* 12.961c; Philo, *Sacr.* 90) as a symbol of stability and security. The imagery shifts abruptly from stability to movement, from the nautical to the sacral. The language of movement derives not from the image of the anchor but from its referent, the heavenly high priest and his movement into the divine realm. The 'inner shrine' is the most sacred part of the tabernacle, separated by a special curtain from the external portion of the tabernacle; cf. Ex 26:31–3; 40:3; Mt 27:51. 6:20, the reference to the 'curtain' and the action of Jesus as high priest anticipates the treatment of the high priests in chs. 8–10. Only the high priest could enter the innermost sanctuary and only on the Day of Atonement. Jesus has made that move as a 'forerunner'. The epithet, recalling the description of Jesus as 'pioneer' (2:10), emphasizes that his experience grounds his followers' hopes. The concluding phrase reiterates the key verse, Ps 110:4, that warrants considering Christ a high priest.

(7:1–28) Scriptural Reflection: Christ and Melchizedek The 'long and difficult' (NRSV: 'much . . . that is hard') (cf. 5:11) discourse begins. The first stage, ch. 7, explores the implications of the insight that Ps 110:4 can apply to Christ. The homilist's strategy is to interpret the only scriptural passage other than Ps 110 where the figure of Melchizedek appears. vv. 1–2, Gen 14:17–20 describes the encounter between Abraham and Melchizedek after Abraham had defeated a coalition of five kings and rescued his kinsman Lot. Abraham first meets the king of Sodom when Melchizedek of Salem abruptly appears, blesses Abraham, and in return receives a tithe of his spoils. Phrases selected from the passage convey the essential points deserving comment. v. 2b, interpretation begins with etymologies, which are technically incorrect. Melchizedek's name is an ancient theophoric formation meaning 'Zedek [a Canaanite deity] is my king'. Similarly 'Salem' is not the equivalent of the Hebrew word for 'peace' (*shalom*). Nonetheless, the etymologies 'king of righteousness' and 'king of peace' were current among first-century Jewish interpreters (Philo, *Leg. All.* 3.79; Jos. *J.W.* 6.438). Apart from their evocation of traditional Messianic attributes, the etymologies play no further role in the chapter. v. 3, Scripture's silence implies attributes of Melchizedek that make him resemble the 'Son of God'. In the absence of any record of Melchizedek's ancestry, birth, or death, he can be described as a 'priest forever'. Speculation on Melchizedek was rife in the period. The Qumran sectarians thought of him as an angelic judge (11QMelch). Philo uses him to symbolize the divine Word (*Leg. All.* 3.79–82). An elaborate legend about Melchizedek, probably dating to the late first century, appears in *2 Enoch*. Later rabbis identified Melchizedek with the archangel Michael ('*Abot R. Nat.* [A] 34). Gnostic Christians knew of Melchizedek as an angel (Hippol. *Haer.* 7.26; the Nag Hammadi tractate Melchizedek; *Pistis Sophia* 1:25–6). None of these traditions is explicit here, but they form the background to the use of Melchizedek to explain the significance of Christ.

v. 4, reflection on Melchizedek's superiority to the levitical priests begins with the phrase that Abraham gave a tithe to Melchizedek (Gen 14:20). v. 5, Num 18:21–32 stipulates that Israelites had to give a tithe to the priests, who were of the tribe of Levi and thus ultimately descended from the patriarch. v. 6, that Abraham, with no physical relationship to Melchizedek, gave him a tithe suggests a hierarchy: Melchizedek > Abraham > levitical priests > Israelites. That Melchizedek blessed Abraham constitutes the second point for comment. The mention of 'the promises' continues a subordinate theme from 6:13–15. v. 7, despite the apodictic remark that the greater blesses the less, numerous examples attest the opposite (Job 31:20; 2 Sam 14:22; 1 Kings 1:47). The principle is clearly an *ad hoc* formulation. v. 8, the mortal Levites stand in stark contrast to the other recipient of a tithe, Melchizedek. The restrained formulation, 'it is testified that he lives', alluding to the fact that Scripture does not record Melchizedek's death (v. 3), does not explain Melchizedek's immortality. vv. 9–10, the relationship of givers and recipients of tithes confirms the hierarchical relationship between Melchizedek and the Levites. The introductory remark, 'one might even say' recognizes the argument's playful quality.

v. 11, the exegesis turns to the effectiveness of the priestly action. 'Perfection', the goal of the addressees (6:1), begins, as will later be apparent (9:14; 10:14), with the forgiveness of sins and ability to participate in the covenant community. If the Levites had produced such perfection, Ps 110:4 would not have predicted another priesthood. A parenthetical comment connects the priesthood with the law. v. 12, although the parenthesis seems to be a casual aside, the connection is significant. If the priestly basis of the law is eliminated, then the law itself becomes invalid. For the quasi-logical language of 'necessity', cf. 8:3; 9:16, 23. v. 13, only members of the tribe of Levi could serve as priests (Ex 28:1–4; Num 1:47–54). v. 14, as a descendant of David (Mt 1:1; 9:27; 15:22; Mk 10:47; Lk 1:32; Rom 1:3; 2 Tim 2:8; Rev 22:16), Jesus, reverently styled 'our Lord' (cf. 2:3; 13:20), was of the tribe of 'Judah'. Hence, he could not have been a priest according to the stipulations of the law.

v. 15, what is 'even more obvious' is that old priestly order and its law have been changed. v. 16, the opposition between Levites and the order of Melchizedek is framed in terms of a dichotomy between the 'physical', better translated 'carnal', and 'life'. That life is 'indestructible' because it is eternal (v. 3). A distinction between flesh and spirit underlies the opposition, and the 'spirit' will surface at 9:14, but Hebrews is careful not to express the significance of Christ in static, metaphysical terms. The spirit is ultimately embodied; cf. 10:1–10. v. 17, Scripture's silence testified to Melchizedek's life. The words of Ps 110:4, understood as addressed to the Son, attest the eternality of his priesthood. vv. 18–19, a summary of the argument focuses not on priesthood but on law. In contrast with the weakness of the priestly-legal system stands, not the effective reality of the new priest, but the hope that he inspires. The homilist thus continues the theme articulated at 6:19. The cultic image of 'approaching' God has been (4:16) and will be (7:25; 10:22) used of Christian life. Christ's 'approach' guarantees access for his followers.

v. 20, relying on the demonstrated significance of divine oaths (6:13–18), the homilist focuses on the first half of Ps 110:4, where God 'confirmed' his promise of priestly status 'with an oath', a phenomenon not attested for other priests. v. 21, Ps 110:4 is cited. v. 22, the surprising inference introduces the theme of a new covenant, anticipating chs. 8–10. Christ's role as guarantor or 'surety' parallels functions accorded to quasi-divine intermediaries such as Philo's Logos (*Quis Heres*, 205–6). The divinely assured status of the heavenly high priest gives his followers their assurance.

v. 23, a new argument, based on the opposition between multiplicity and unity, contrasts levitical priests and Christ. The fact that priests of old replaced one another in succession was implicit in the notion of ancestry (7:3, 5, 8). The natural inference is that they were 'many in number'. v. 24, Christ, by contrast, 'continues forever'. The Greek verb (*menein*) had applied to Melchizedek at v. 3. The motif surfaces at the beginning (1:11–12) and end (13:8) of the homily. v. 25, the earlier affirmation (5:9) that Christ as priest is a 'source of salvation', is now connected with his intercessory activity. The traditional notion that the exalted Christ is a heavenly intercessor (Rom 8:34; Jn 17:9; 1 Jn 2:1) is connected with Christ's priesthood here and at Heb 9:24.

v. 26, the chapter concludes with a rhetorically elaborate celebration of the heavenly status of Christ. The note that it is 'fitting' for there to be such a high priest resembles the claim that Christ had to be perfected through suffering (2:10); both are part of the divine plan of salvation. The attributes of Christ are traditional. For his holiness, see the application of Ps 16:10 to him at Acts 2:27; 13:35. For his sinlessness, see 4:15. v. 27, the contrast between Christ and ordinary high priests again relies on the opposition between multiplicity and unity, but the precise referent of the priestly sacrifices 'day after day' is unclear. The distinction between an offering for the priest's sins and one for the people reflects the ritual of the Day of Atonement (Lev 16:11, 16), not the daily offering. The Torah required the *tāmîd*, animals sacrificed twice daily, morning and evening (Ex 29:38–42; Num 28:3–8), accompanied by a meal offering (Ex 29:40–1; Lev 6:14–23; Num 28:5). High priests could, but were not required to, make these offerings. Although the Torah does not differentiate the functions of the two types of offering, Philo (*Quis Heres*, 174) suggests that the meal-offerings were for the priests, the animals for the people. Hebrews apparently knows that tradition. The notion that Christ died 'once for all' in an act of self-sacrifice is traditional (Rom 6:10; 1 Pet 3:18); Hebrews will focus on it (9:12, 25–8; 10:10). v. 28, a neat antithesis summarizes the comparison of the chapter, concluding with a solemn affirmation about the eternal status of the heavenly high priest.

(8:1–10:18) Scriptural Reflection: Christ's Sacrifice and the New Covenant

(8:1–7) The Work of the Heavenly High Priest From 8:1 through 10:18 the homilist develops an integrated exposition, focused on Jer 31:31–4. Ch. 7 treated the personal status of the Son. These chapters examine his work, using the antitheses of

earthly and heavenly, new and old, interior and external. The organization of the material resembles the homiletic pattern of chs. 3–4. The introduction to this homily, extending to 8:7, indicates the main point of the argument and introduces two of the oppositions on which the subsequent exegesis depends. v. 1, the chapter begins with another allusion to the key Ps 110:1 and its image of the exalted one (cf. 1:3, 13; 4:14). v. 2, designation of Christ as a 'minister' (*leitourgos*) uses a common term for priests. The place where this minister serves is the 'true' cultic site. Much of the next two chapters explains what it means to be the true place of worship. Here the two terms 'sanctuary' and 'tabernacle' suggest further developments. The latter term is the technical designation of the tent of the Exodus. It is that structure, not the Davidic or Herodian temple, that is in view. While 'sanctuary' could be a synonym, the homilist's later usage suggests that the term refers to the innermost part of the tabernacle. The distinguishing feature of this whole complex is that God, not human beings, set it up. The homilist begins to play with the widespread notion of a heavenly temple or sanctuary. Based upon ancient notions of a heavenly plan for the earthly temple (Ex 25:40; 1 Chr 28:19), Jewish interpreters developed the belief in a heavenly temple or divine palace (*1 Enoch*, 14:10–20; *T. Levi*, 3:2–4; Wis 9:8; *2 Apoc. Bar.* 4:5; *b. Ḥag.* 12b; *Gen. Rab.* 55.7). The book of Revelation (3:12; 7:15; 15:5, etc.) relies heavily on the notion. Similar ideas appear in Greek sources (Ps.-Plato, *Epin.* 983E–84B; Sen. *Ben.* 7.7.3; *Heracl. Ep.* 4), although the cosmos is usually the 'true' temple, the inner portion of which is heaven itself. Hellenistic Jewish interpreters such as Philo could use both images (cosmos as true temple: *Spec. Leg.* 1.66; heaven, i.e. the noetic world, as true temple: *Vit. Mos.* 2.74). v. 3, what priests do is as important as where they do it. For priests offering 'gifts and sacrifices', cf. 5.1. Christ's offering is nothing other than himself (7:27; 9:12–14). v. 4, that Christ could not be a conventional priest was clear from 7:14. v. 5, Ex 25:40 mentions the heavenly pattern shown to Moses. Description of what was copied from that plan as a 'shadow' recalls Plato's famous 'Myth of the Cave' (*Resp.* 7.515A–B). The 'shadows' in the phenomenal world are far removed from the reality of the noetic world (cf. Philo, *Ebr.* 132–3; *Vit. Mos.* 2.74). The homilist continues to utilize Platonic terminology in the opposition between heaven and earth, but he will finally resist Platonic metaphysics. The other term used of the earthly place of worship, translated 'sketch' by the NRSV, may intimate some of his hesitation. The word more commonly means 'outline' or 'prefiguration', although it does mean 'copy' in the LXX (Ezek 42:15, and Aquila's version of Ezek 8:10 and Dan 4:17). In this context it surely has that meaning, although in ch. 10 the homilist will shift from a horizontal to temporal dichotomy and he may now be preparing the way. v. 6, that Jesus is a 'mediator' of a new covenant recalls the claim that he is a guarantor (7:22) who serves an intercessory role (7:25). The notion of a 'new covenant' anticipates the quotation in vv. 8–12. The qualitative distinction between the covenants rests on the 'promises' that they contain. Although much is contained in the theme of 'promise' (4:1; 11:13–16, 39–40; 12:22–4), the distinctive element here is the effective forgiveness of sins (8:12; 9:14, 26–8; 10:16–18). v. 7, a contra-factual argument, analogous to the point (7:11) about the new priest mentioned in Ps 110, introduces the dichotomy between new and old.

(8:8–13) Jer 31:31–4: The Text for a Homily v. 8, the introductory comment attributes the oracle to an unnamed speaker. The NRSV, not inappropriately, specifies God as the author of the message. The text of Jeremiah itself claims 'the Lord' as speaker. In its original context Jer 31:31–4 (LXX 38:31–4, to which the citation conforms closely) is part of a series of oracles (chs. 30–3) offering hope to the Israelites of the exilic period that YHWH would restore them to their homeland. At that time, God would re-establish his relationship with them and renew their hearts and minds. Later Jewish groups, such as the sectarians at Qumran, understood the ideal of a 'new covenant' to refer to their own eschatological community (CD 6:19; 8:21; 10:12). Although they did not elsewhere cite this text, early Christians used the notion (Mt 26:28; Mk 14:24; Lk 22:20; 1 Cor 11:25; 2 Cor 3:6). The citation will help the homilist to specify what the 'better promises' of 8:6 entail. v. 10, the distinction between a covenant of external observance and one of internal, heartfelt adherence adds a third dichotomy to the antitheses between heaven and earth, old and new. Repetition of the verse at 10:16 indicates its thematic significance. v. 12, from the exordium (1:3) onwards, the homilist stressed the significance of the forgiveness of sins effected by Christ. The conclusion of the citation indicates that under the new covenant such forgiveness will be a reality. Again, repetition of the verse at 10:17 underlines its significance. v. 13, ominous language, using terminology for an 'obsolete' law, reinforces the negative tone of 8:7 and recalls the need for a change in law (7:11).

(9:1–10) The Earthly Sanctuary The homilist begins to contrast old and new covenants by reviewing the structure and rituals of the tabernacle. v. 1, announcing the theme of the section, the first verse casts the 'earthly' or 'worldly' sanctuary in a negative light. v. 2, Hebrews relies on several OT passages: YHWH's instructions for the tabernacle (Ex 25:1–31:11); Bezalel's construction of the tabernacle (36:1–39:43); YHWH's authorization to set it up (40:1–15); and the account of the compliance by Moses (40:16–38). The 'first' tent is the outer portion of the whole tabernacle. For the 'lampstand', see Ex 25:31–9; 37:17–24; 40:4; for the 'table', Ex 25:23–8; 37:10–15; for the 'bread', Ex 25:30; 40:23; Mt 12:4. Most MSS record the standard designation of the outer portion of the tabernacle as 'the Holy Place'. Some MSS, however, including P46, the oldest witness to Hebrews, reverse the standard designation and call this space the 'Holy of Holies'. The homilist may have inverted the normal designation to emphasize the multiplicity of the external tabernacle. Although odd, the terminology of 'Holy Place' for the inner sanctuary is consistent; cf. 9:12. v. 3, the 'curtain' has already appeared (6:19) as the boundary of the space accessible to the high priest. v. 4, for the 'altar of incense', see Ex 30:1–10; 37:25–8; 40:5. According to the Pentateuchal accounts it should be in the outer sanctuary, but 2 Macc 2:4–8 closely associates this altar and the ark and 2 *Apoc. Bar.* 6:7 depicts an angel removing both from the inner sanctuary. For the 'ark of the covenant', Ex 25:10–15; 37:1–5; 40:3; for the 'manna', Ex 16:33–4; for 'Aaron's rod', the budding of which determined his selection as priest, Num 17:1–11; for the 'tablets of the covenant', Ex 25:16. v. 5, for the 'cherubim', and

the 'mercy seat', see Ex 25:17–22; 37:6–9. The latter is the cover of the ark that was the focal point of the rites of the Day of Atonement. Paul refers to it at Rom 3:25. The kind of discussion 'in detail' to be avoided appears in the elaborate allegories of the tabernacle's cosmic significance among Jewish interpreters (Philo, *Vit. Mos.* 2.97–100; *Cher.*).

v. 6, the 'ritual duties' of priests in the outer tabernacle included trimming lamps (Ex 27:20–1) and setting 'showbread' on the table (Lev 24:5–9). The note that the priests 'go continually' into the sacred space does not reflect contemporary practice, but describes what Scripture requires. v. 7, the 'once a year' Day of Atonement on the tenth day of the seventh month (Lev 16:29–31) involves an elaborate ritual, performed only by the high priest. He first sacrifices a bull for himself and his household (Lev 16:6, 11), then a he-goat for the people; another animal not mentioned here, the scapegoat, is expelled into the desert. The high priest enters the inner sanctuary to sprinkle the ark twice, first with the bull's blood, then with a goat's blood (Lev 16:14–15). The non-biblical restriction of the sacrifice's effect to sins committed 'unintentionally' conforms to Jewish tradition (*m. Yoma*, 8.9; *t. Yoma*, 5.60). v. 8, the homilist explores the ritual's deeper meaning. As at 3:7, the inspiration of the 'Holy Spirit' highlights the contemporary application of Scripture. v. 9, the antecedent of 'this' is ambiguous but is most likely the 'first tabernacle' of v. 6. The translation of the NRSV suggests that the 'present time' is a time of unfulfilment, the time 'during which' (*kath' hen*) ineffective sacrifices are being offered. The translation thus makes the subordinate clause temporal, defining the 'present'. It should, instead, be rendered as a relative clause, translated 'according to which', and construed as modifying the 'symbol', i.e. the tabernacle. For our author, the 'present time' is not dominated by the old cult, but by Christ's sacrifice. The tabernacle prefigures inadequately what is now effectively present through Christ's sacrifice, which affects the human heart. Scripture has no word for 'conscience' (*syneidesis*), which is common in the Hellenistic world. It appears in Jewish (Wis 17:10; Jos. *Ant.* 16.100) and early Christian literature (e.g. Rom 2:15; 1 Cor 4:4; 1 Pet 2:14; *1 Clem.* 1.3). v. 10, the homilist criticizes the superficiality of levitical sacrifices. The language refers in a general way to the system of purity laws covering 'food' (Lev 11; Deut 14) and 'baptisms' or washings (Lev 15; Num 19); 'drinks' are not mentioned in the Pentateuch. For a similar denigration of cultic externalism, see 13:9. The 'time of correction' is not a future hope, but the present era of the new covenant.

(9:11–14) The Ritual of the Heavenly Sanctuary Attention shifts to the present, defined by the moment when 'Christ came' as High Priest in an act symbolized by the yearly ritual. The fact that his priesthood involves 'things that have come' reinforces the positive view of 'the present' suggested by the previous verses. The 'greater and more perfect tent' has been understood in various metaphorical senses, but our homilist is quite restrained. He simply evokes the image of passage through the heavens associated with Christ's exaltation (2:10; 4:14) and suggests that the passage involves the true (8:2) tent that God pitched. That something 'not made with hands' is superior to a manufactured product is a commonplace of Jewish (Isa 46:6; Philo, *Vit. Mos.* 2.74–6), pagan (Plut. *De*

Tranq. Anim. 20 (477C–D), Ps.-Heracl. *Ep.* 4), and Christian (Mk 14; 58; Acts 7:48) sources. The designation as 'not of this creation' confirms the tent's heavenly (8:5) status. v. 12, the homilist operates with the notion of a heavenly archetype for the earthly sanctuary. Christ's 'once for all', or absolutely singular (cf. 7:27) passage through the heavens (4:14) involved entry into an exalted supernal realm, the 'Holy Place' equivalent to the earthly inner sanctuary; cf. vv. 2–3. For the 'blood of goats and calves' cf. v. 7. The claim that Christ's self-sacrifice brought 'redemption', or purchase out of bondage, is traditional. Cf. Lk 1:68; 2:38 for the same noun. For the notion, see Mt 20:28; Mk 10:45; Titus 2:14; 1 Pet 1:18; Acts 7:35. v. 13, an *a fortiori* argument concludes the comparison between old and new rituals of atonement. Disparaging references to Pentateuchal rites constitute the weaker end of the analogy. To the elements of the ritual of the Day of Atonement, 'blood of goats and bulls', the homilist adds an allusion to the unrelated 'ashes of a heifer', used in purification rituals. Cf. Num 19. v. 14, the stronger pole of the analogy is Christ's death, assumed, with many early Christians, to be a cleansing, sacrificial act; cf. Acts 15:9; Eph 5:26; Titus 2:14; 1 Pet 3:21; 1 Jn 1:7, 9. The 'blood' shed in that death is of far greater value than animals' blood since it belongs to the Son; cf. 10:4. It is only by virtue of the 'eternal Spirit' that blood can be sprinkled in the 'true' or 'heavenly' sanctuary. The homilist's quasi-Platonic dichotomy (8:5) renders comprehensible the intimate connection of 'heavenly' and 'spiritual'. It also makes some sense of the mythological notions of a passage through the heavens and a sprinkling of blood in that sphere. Ambiguity remains about the role of the spirit and the character of the connection between spirit and blood. The 'eternal Spirit' could be the divine spirit that raises Christ's act to a transcendent plane, or his own spirit, by virtue of which he attains the divine realm. Tension within this motif will remain until ch. 10. Christ's cleansing sacrifice is spiritual because it affects 'conscience', cf. v. 9. 'Dead works' are sins (6:1) that contrast with works of love (10:24). 'Worship' involves prayer (13:15), but also the 'sacrifices' of good works (10:24; 13:6).

(9:15–22) The New Covenant To connect the motifs at work, the homilist resorts to a play on words possible in Greek, where the meaning of *diathēkē* can range from 'contract' or 'treaty' to 'will' or 'testament'. For a similar wordplay, see Gal 3:15–18. v. 15, Christ as 'mediator' appeared at 8:6. For the common designation of Christians as 'called', see Rom 1:6; 1 Cor 1:2; Jude 1; Rev 17:14. The addressees had been named 'partners in a heavenly calling' at 3:1. Ordinary legal usage dictates that the promise of an 'inheritance' (1:14; 6:17) implies the death of a testator. The death in the case of this testament/covenant 'redeems' the heirs from their transgressions, as already noted in v. 12. v. 16, legal language describes the requirements for a testament to be enforced; the death of the testator must be 'established' or formally registered. v. 17, further technical language, 'to take effect', to be 'in force', continues to re-emphasize the point that a testament presupposes death, something not required for 'covenants'. v. 18, the fact that there is a discrepancy between the social and legal presuppositions of testaments and covenants prompts the observation that the inauguration of the first covenant required bloodshed. The sacrifice concluding the ratification

ceremony at Ex 24:3–8 foreshadows Christ's death. v. 19, reading of 'every commandment' was the first act in the establishment of the Sinai covenant (Ex 24:7). The remark that the reading was 'according to the law' embellishes Scripture but reinforces the connection between cultic act and law; cf. 7:11. Details from various rituals are conflated. The blood of 'calves' was part of the Mosaic ritual. The phrase 'and goats', omitted by some ancient MSS, evokes the Day of Atonement, as v. 12. Water and hyssop pertain to the ritual of the red heifer (Num 19:8, 18, 20). All three elements appear in the purification of lepers (Lev 14:2–6). v. 20, the citation of Ex 24:8, firmly, if artificially, connecting blood and covenant, resembles the words of institution of the eucharist (Mt 26:28; Mk 14:24; Lk 22:20; 1 Cor 11:24–5). The homilist does not develop such an allusion. v. 21, consecration of the Mosaic tabernacle involved anointing (Ex 40:9), not sprinkling with blood; the verse may allude to the installation of Aaronid priests (Lev 8:15, 19, 26). v. 22, the connection of blood and forgiveness appears in a common Jewish maxim; cf. *b. Yoma*, 5a; *b. Menaḥ.* 93b; *b. Zebaḥ.* 6a.

(9:23–8) The New Heavenly Sacrifice Balancing 9:11–14, a new description of Christ's 'heavenly' action incorporates the image of ritual purification developed in the previous verses. v. 23, the contrast between heavenly reality and earthly copy (NRSV: sketch) repeats the language of 8:4, although it is clear from 9:14 that the true 'heavenly things' are human consciences. The homilist thus takes a cosmic image to symbolize a personal reality. v. 24, the description of Christ's entry into heaven (cf. 4:14; 8:1–2; 9:11–12) uses decidedly Platonic language ('copy', 'true one', 'heaven itself'). As at 7:25, the intercessory role of the heavenly high priest, who 'appears in the presence of God', comes to the fore. v. 25, a renewed contrast between Christ and ordinary high priests emphasizes the multiplicity of the latter (cf. 9:7) and the distance between them and their offering (cf. 9:12). v. 26, a *reductio ad absurdum* articulates the contrast between Christ and ordinary high priests. Had he been merely one of them, his sacrifice would have been unceasingly repeated. The insistence on the 'once for all' character of Christ's sacrifice (7:27; 9:12; 10:10) continues the Platonizing dichotomy between the phenomenal, earthly 'many' and the stable, heavenly 'one'. The unique character of Christ's act, however, derives from its eschatological position 'at the end of the age'. v. 27, that it is 'appointed for mortals to die' is a Greek proverb; cf. 4 Macc 8:11. The notion of a post-mortem judgement, distinct from the final general judgement (Dan 7:26; Mt 25:31–46; 2 Thess 2:12; Rev 20:12) is traditional in Greek sources (Plato, *Resp.* 10.614B–621D; Plut. *De Fac.* 27–30). v. 28, the application of Christ's sacrifice to 'the sins of many' evokes Isa 53:12; cf. Mk 10:45; Rom 5:19. Early Christians expected His coming a 'second time'; cf. Mk 13:24–7; Acts 1:10–11; 1 Cor 15:23–4; Rev 1:7.

(10:1–10) The True Sacrifice The final stage of the exposition of Jer 31 indicates that Christ inaugurated the new and interior covenant by an act of conformity to God's will. v. 1, for the old as 'shadow' see 8:5. The contrast between a shadow and the 'true form' (*eikōn*) may derive from Plato's discussion of language (*Cra.* 439A). The homilist playfully exploits the potential of the categories: the 'true form' that causes the shadow is ultimately shown to be the 'body' of Christ (v. 10). The ineffectiveness of the law and its cult was already stressed at 7:11, 19. v. 2, the homilist argues that the purification effected by the old sacrifices was only skin deep (cf. 9:13); had they been truly and decisively effective, they would not need to be repeated. v. 3, the function of the old sacrifice to remind sinners of their acts may be an extension of Num 5:15. The recollection of sins in the old covenant contrasts with the forgetfulness of sin in the new (8:12; 10:17). v. 4, the apodictic denial of the effectiveness of sacrifice radicalizes such prophetic critiques of cultic formalism as 1 Sam 15:22; Ps 50:8–15, 51:16–19; Isa 1:12–17; Jer 7:21–6; Hos 6:6. 'Bulls and goats' alludes again to the Day of Atonement; cf. 9:12–13. vv. 5–6, as at 2:12–13 verses from a psalm express Christ's intentions. The homilist recontextualizes the psalm as an utterance of Christ upon entering 'the world', where the decisive 'heavenly' sacrifice really occurs. Hebrews cites Ps 40:6–8, in its Greek form. The original psalm praised YHWH for his benefactions, promised obedience, and asked for assistance. The homilist focuses on the promise, contrasting heartfelt obedience and external cult. The phrase 'a body you have prepared for me', the Greek translation of the Hebrew 'you have given me an open ear', serves the homilist well. v. 7, the parenthetical remark in the original psalm about the 'scroll of the book' probably referred to the 'law of the king' (Deut 17:14–20); the king thus accepts the responsibility for abiding by the law. Hebrews probably understands the remark to allude to the whole OT, assumed to be written about Christ. v. 8, exegesis of the psalm focuses on the contrast between external cult and heartfelt obedience. The homilist begins by collecting all the allusions to rejected cultic acts. v. 9, after highlighting the psalm's profession of willingness to obey, the homilist draws a sweeping conclusion. The solemn submission to God's will, taken to be the inaugural act of the new covenant, supplants the whole cultic system. v. 10, that Christ's death conformed to God's will is commonplace; cf. Gal 1:4; Eph 1:5–11; 1 Pet 3:17. For God's will that believers be sanctified, see 1 Thess 4:3. Christ's act of obedience made God's will his own. The Gethsemane story (Mt 26:42; Lk 22:42) and the fourth gospel (Jn 4:34; 5:30; 6:38–40; 19:30) express similar claims about Christ's obedience. Hebrews makes that obedience decisive for establishing the new covenant. That Christ's act of obedience took place in a sacrificed 'body' is significant. The homilist finally resolves the tensions between metaphysical vocabulary and historical narrative by insisting on the locus of the 'real' and 'true' in Christ's embodied act. Christ's obedient disposition unites heaven and earth. Significantly the composite name 'Jesus Christ' appears for the first time; cf. 13:8.

(10:11–18) Summation The homilist weaves together the themes of the last several chapters. v. 11, the weakness of the old cultic system is by now familiar; cf. 7:11, 19; 9:9–10; 10:1–4. v. 12, the notion of Christ's session from Ps 110:1, last mentioned at 8:1, re-emphasizes the finality of his priestly act. v. 13, citation of Ps 110:1b, last mentioned at 1:13, points to the culmination of the salvific process. An eschatological horizon dominates the final chapters of Hebrews. v. 14, for the notion of 'perfection', see 2:10. It is now clear that, applied to believers, 'perfection' means the cleansing of conscience effected by Christ's sacrifice. Worshippers so perfected are still 'being sanctified'. The present tense of the verb implies

that the process is a continuing one. 'Sanctification' within the community of the new covenant is thus distinct from the 'perfecting' that enables participation in that community. v. 15, the solemn introduction underscores the importance of the following citation. For another ascription of Scripture to the Spirit, see 3:7. v. 16, a slightly modified quotation of Jer 31:33, previously cited at 8:10, emphasizes that the new covenant involves 'hearts and minds'. v. 17, Jer 31:34b, cited at 8:12, is enhanced with the phrase 'and their lawless deeds', which emphasizes the effective remission of sin essential to the new covenant.

Exhortation to Faithful Endurance (10:19–12:13)

(10:19–24) Transitional Admonition: Hold Fast to the Faith An exhortation to live as members of the new covenant recalls many previous exhortations, while stressing faith (v. 22), hope (v. 23), and love (v. 24). For the traditional triad, see 1 Cor 13:13. v. 19, for Christian 'confidence', or better, 'boldness', see 3:6; 4:16. All Christians can now go where only the high priests of old could go, into God's presence. The blood of Jesus, because it cleanses conscience and inaugurates a new covenant (9:14–22), makes such entry possible. v. 20, the 'way' designates the Christian movement in Acts 9:2; 18:25; 24:14. It is 'new' because available only in the new covenant and 'living', like God's word, 4:12, Christ, 7:25, and God, 10:31, because it derives from those vital realities. The 'curtain' (cf. 6:19; 9:3, 7) marks the boundary to God's presence; only those who are 'perfected' may enter. A parenthetical comment emphasizes that approach to God is made possible by Christ's flesh, offered in his bodily sacrifice (10:10). Syntax is ambiguous, but the phrase probably defines the 'way' rather than the 'curtain'. v. 21, a similar remark about Christians having a 'high priest' appeared at 4:14. His position over the 'house of God' reflects 3:6. v. 22, the addressees were earlier summoned to 'approach' (4:16). That hearts have been 'sprinkled clean' recalls 9:13–14 and may evoke Ezek 36:25–6. 'Washing' with 'pure water' clearly alludes to baptism. v. 23, for maintaining the 'confession', see 3:1–6. Scripture (Deut 7:9; Ps 145:13) affirms that God is faithful. That God's promises are secure has been a constant theme; cf. 4:1; 6:12–17; 8:6; 9:15. v. 24, the call to 'provoke one another' reflects the Greek notions of the moral life as contest; cf. Xen. *Mem.* 3.3.13; Isoc. *Con. Dem.* 46; Pliny, *Ep.* 3.7. The summons to 'good deeds' is frequent in early Christian exhortation, e.g. Mt 5:16; 26:10; Jn 10:32; 1 Pet 2:12; Rom 12:17. For more such deeds, see 13:1–6. v. 25, the reference to the behaviour of 'some' indicates part of the perceived problem that Hebrews addresses. The prophetic warning about the coming 'Day' of the Lord (cf. Isa 2:12; Joel 1:15; 3:14; Am 5:18; 8:9; Zeph 1:14; Zech 14:1) became a part of early Christian expectation (cf. Mt 10:15; 1 Cor 1:8; 3:13; 5:5; 2 Cor 1:14; 1 Thess 5:2, 4; 2 Thess 2:2; 2 Pet 3:10; 1 Jn 4:17). The ominous tone introduces the following warning.

(10:24–39) Warning and Encouragement As in previous exhortations, the homilist balances threat (vv. 24–31) with encouragement (vv. 32–9). v. 26, the emphasis on wilful persistence in sin recalls the Pentateuchal distinction between high-handed and inadvertent sins; cf. Num 15:25–31 and Heb 9:7. The denial of a new 'sacrifice for sins' echoes the warning about the impossibility of repentance for apostasy (6:4–8). v. 27, the image of a 'fury of fire' characterizes judgement scenes; cf. 2 Apoc. Bar. 48:39–40; 2 Thess 1:7–8; Rev 11:5; 20:14. For God as 'consuming fire' see 12:29. v. 28, not all violators of Torah were subject to the death penalty. The generalization rests on cases involving blasphemy (Lev 24:14–16) or idolatry (Deut 17:2–5). Deut 19:15 requires 'two or three witnesses' for any conviction; Deut 17:6 applies the requirement to the death penalty imposed for idolatry. v. 29, the a fortiori argument recalls the warning at 2:2–3. For 'spurning the Son of God', see 6:6. The notion of 'outraging the Spirit' recalls warnings about the 'sin against the Spirit' (Mk 3:29; Lk 12:10). v. 30, the first quotation is from Deut 32:35, cited in the same form in Rom 12:19. The second citation is from either Deut 32:36 or Ps 135:14. v. 31, falling into God's hands (cf. 2 Sam 24:14; Sir 2:18) can be positive, but, when divine judgement is involved, it can be 'fearful', as was the theophany at Sinai (cf. 12:21). v. 32, encouragement begins with a call to remember the 'hard struggle' of the past. Ch. 12 further develops the athletic image. For the language of being 'enlightened', see 6:4. v. 33, the repeated mention of 'abuse' (cf. 11:26; 13:13) suggests a component of the addressees' experience. Paul too experienced theatrical 'exposure' (1 Cor 4:9) in the persecutions that he suffered. Those who are 'sharers' or 'partners' in a heavenly calling (cf. 3:1) must also share in the community's suffering. v. 34, compassion on 'those in prison' characterized early Christians; cf. Mt 25:36; Phil 2:25; 1 Clem. 59:4. 'Plundering of possessions' could involve judicial seizure, as at Polybius 4.14.4, or acts of mob violence. Exhortation to accept such tribulations 'cheerfully' was traditional; cf. Mt 5:12; Lk 6:22; Rom 5:3; 2 Cor 11:21–30; Acts 5:41; 1 Pet 4:13. v. 35, the virtues interwoven in the last verses of the chapter, 'confident boldness', 'endurance', and 'faith', summarize the ethos inculcated by Hebrews. Here 'boldness' is directed more towards the external world than towards God; cf. 3:6, 4:16, and 10:19. The final chapters reinforce the expectation of a just 'reward' for such behaviour; cf. 10:36; 11:6, 26; 12:2, 11. v. 36, exhortations to 'endurance' are common in early Christian sources; cf. Rom 2:7; 5:3; Lk 8:15; 21:19; Rev 3:10; 1 Clem. 5:5. Concern with this virtue pervades the final chapters; cf. 11:27; 12:2, 7; 13:13. To do 'the will of God' is the heart of covenant fidelity; cf. 10:9; 13:21. vv. 37–8, a composite citation melds Isa 26:20 ('a little while') and Hab 2:3–4, in its Greek form. The original prophecy records a vision of judgement to be visited upon Israel. It is that judgement that 'will not delay'. The Greek translation renders the verse as a prediction of one 'who is coming', facilitating construal of the text as a prediction of Christ's second coming. v. 38, Paul cites Hab 2:4 at Gal 3:11 and Rom 1:17 as part of his arguments contrasting faith and 'works of the law'. Our homilist, remaining closer to the prophetic text, contrasts faithful endurance and 'shrinking back'. v. 39, the exhortation ends on a positive note, as at 6:9.

(11:1–12:3) A Celebration of the Faithful The list of faithful heroes resembles in scope and details many reviews of Israel's history (Sir 44–50; 1 Macc 2:49–64; 4 Macc 16:16–23; 18:11–13; Wis 10; Philo, Virt. 198–205). It also resembles lists of examples of a virtue, such as Philo's treatment of hope (Praem. 11–14). The chapter abundantly displays the techniques of rhetorical ornamentation. Most obvious in English is anaphora, or initial repetition of the phrase 'by faith' extending up till v. 31. After an introduction the chapter falls into four major sections treating successive segments of Israel's history. The whole celebrates individuals and groups who exemplify desired attitudes and virtues, trust in God's promises and faithful endurance in the face of persecution.

(11:1–3) Introductory Remarks on Faith The first three dense and allusive verses provide a programmatic introduction to the chapter. They suggest the complexity of faith as both intellectual and moral, and of faith's objects as both transcendent and eschatological. v. 1, a formal definition, like Plato's definition of medicine (Symp. 186c) or Plutarch's of curiosity (On Curiosity, 6.518c), introduces the chapter. The word translated 'assurance' in the NRSV is the same (hypostasis) used of God's 'very being' at 1:3 and of the steadfastness of the addressees at 3:14. A subjective meaning is not attested. Although there may be a hint of the ethical sense, it is difficult to construe with the following phrase. Philosophical connotations are probably at the forefront. The homilist thus defines faith in terms of its ultimate object, the 'reality of things hoped for', the content of God's promises. Similarly, the word translated 'conviction' (elegchos) has objective connotations. Faith is thus defined, in terms of the actions that it inspires, as the 'proof of things unseen'. Those invisible things are both the objects of future hope and the transcendent realities, God and his exalted Son, that guarantee hope. Rom 8:24 similarly connects hope and things unseen. v. 2, this programmatic verse defines the aim and method of the chapter. The word translated 'receive approval' in the NRSV (emartyrēthēsan) means more literally 'received testimony'. It was by virtue of their faithfulness that the ancestors were recorded in Scripture. Cf. 11:4, 5 for examples of this 'testimony'. v. 3, the first element of the catalogue is distinctive, although it appropriately begins the temporal sequence by referring to creation. For creation in similar catalogues, see Sir 43; 2 Macc 7:28. The verse suggests that faith plays a role in the reception of scriptural truth; it produces 'understanding'. Creation by God's word recalls Gen 1:3 and related accounts (Ps 33:6; Wis 9:1; Jn 1:1–3; Heb 1:3; 1 Clem. 17:4). The creation of the visible from the invisible, resembling other formulas for creation (2 Macc 7:28; 2 Enoch 24:2; Rom 1:20; 4:17), denies the autonomy of the natural world.

(11:4–7) The Primordial Heroes v. 4, the first exemplar performed an 'acceptable sacrifice' (Gen 4:4) and died a martyr's death (Gen 4:8). The notion that Abel 'still speaks' derives from Gen 4:10 where his blood cries out, but here the speaking 'by faith' suggests that Abel offers an example to be followed. Heb 12:24 will further play with the image. v. 5, Gen 5:24 reports that God took Enoch, presumably in death. Jewish tradition (e.g. Sir 44:16; 1 Enoch, 12:3; 15:1; 2 Enoch, 22:8; 71:14; Philo, Mutat. 38; Jos. Ant. 1.85; 3 Enoch) interprets removal as translation to heaven, an understanding reflected in the LXX, cited here. That Enoch 'pleased God' rests on Gen 5:22; the addressees will be summoned to do likewise (13:16). v. 6, two conditions for those who 'approach' (cf. 4:16; 7:25; 10:1, 22) God help define faith's cognitive content. Insistence on God's existence is a common Jewish tenet (e.g. Wis 13:1;

Philo, *Opif.* 170; 2 Esd 7:23; 8:58). Belief in divine providence focuses on God as one who rewards; cf. 2:2; 10:35; 11:26. The image of the 'seeker' is common in the Psalms (14:2; 34:10; 53:2; 119:2); cf. Am 9:12, cited in Acts 15:17. v. 7, Noah's story (Gen 6:8–9:17; Sir 44:17) highlights characteristic themes. He believed in the 'unseen' event of divine judgement. That he 'condemned' the world may allude to traditions that he preached repentance (*1 Clem.* 7:6; *Sib. Or.* 1.125–36; *Sifre* 43). What follows intensifies the connection between faith and 'being an heir'.

(11:8–22) The Faith of Abraham Appeals to Abraham and the other patriarchs were common in Jewish and early Christian literature; cf. Sir 44:19–21; 1 Macc 2:52; 4 Macc 16:20; Wis 10:5; Acts 7:2–8; Rom 4; Gal 3:6–9. v. 8, Abraham 'set out' from Ur of the Chaldees to Canaan; cf. Gen 11:31–12:4. His 'inheritance' was something unseen and hence unknown. v. 9, Abraham's time in Canaan further illustrates the alienation that faith can produce. Cf. Gen 17:8; 23:4, for Abraham as sojourner in Canaan. The traditional connection with Isaac and Jacob suggests the communal context of faith. v. 10, an interruption to the story suggests the content of the promised inheritance. The city on 'foundations' recalls scriptural images of Jerusalem (Isa 54:11; Ps 87:1). Like Philo (*Leg. All.* 3.83; *Somn.* 2.250), the homilist redefines the ideal city as the heavenly reality to which Christians aspire (12:22). Description of God as 'architect and builder', found in Hellenistic Jewish sources (Philo, *Opif.* 146), echoes the Platonic image of the divine Craftsman (*Tim.* 28A–29A). v. 11, Gen 17:15–18:15; 21:1–7 relates Isaac's conception and birth. The reference to Sarah appears variously in ancient witnesses. In some, she is the subject of the sentence; in others, more likely original, she is associated with Abraham. In either case, her prominent involvement in the process renders the image of the faithful community more inclusive. Abraham's belief that God 'who promised' (cf. 6:13) is faithful echoes the homilist's own (10:23). v. 12, Paul too (Rom 4:19) described the aged Abraham as 'good as dead'. Abraham's rescue from a metaphorical 'death' parallels the actual deliverance of Enoch (11:4) and foreshadows the resurrection; cf. vv. 19, 35. A scriptural phrase (Gen 22:17; cf. Dan 3:36) describes the ultimate results of Isaac's birth.

v. 13, Heb 6:15 remarked that Abraham did receive the promised progeny. As 4:1 made clear, other promises remained unfulfilled. The patriarchs in Canaan resembled Moses outside the promised land (Deut 32:48; 34:4); they could see the object of their hopes only 'from a distance'. For 'foreigners and sojourners', see Gen 23:4; 47:4, 9; Lev 25:23; Ps 39:12; 1 Chr 29:15; Eph 2:19; 1 Pet 1:1; 2:11. Similar imagery in Greek sources describes the human condition 'on the earth', in exile from the heavenly home, cf. Plato, *Ap.* 41A; *Phd.* 61E, 67B; Philo, *Quis Heres*, 82, 267. v. 14, the 'confession', particularly in Gen 23:4, provides grounds for holding that even in the land of Canaan the patriarchs were seeking their homeland elsewhere. The argument parallels the elimination of Canaan as the true 'resting place' of God's people at 4:7–8. v. 15, a contra-factual argument (cf. 4:8; 7:11; 8:7; 10:12) precludes the identification of Haran as the desired destination. v. 16, with Canaan and Haran eliminated, the homeland must be heavenly. God is frequently styled the God of the

patriarchs; cf. Gen 28:13; Ex 3:6; Mt 22:32; Mk 12:26–7. The heavenly 'city' that God prepared receives a fuller description at 12:18–24.

v. 17, like the first (11:4) and last (12:1–3) examples, faith involves sacrifice. The most poignant episode of Abraham's story is the Aqedah (Binding) of his son Isaac (Gen 22:1–14). The episode captured the imagination of Jewish (Wis 10:5; Sir 44:20; 1 Macc 2:52; 4 Macc 16:18–20; *Jub.* 17:15–18; Jos. *Ant.* 1.222–36; Philo, *Abr.* 167–207) and Christian (Rom 8:32; Jas 2:20–3) interpreters. v. 18, recollection of the promise of Gen 21:12 emphasizes the horrific challenge of God's request. v. 19, as in vv. 10 and 11, the homilist explains Abraham's motives in terms of a belief that he advocates. The phrase 'figuratively speaking' suggests not simply that the recovery of Isaac from the altar was a metaphor, but that the whole episode prefigured Christ's deliverance from death. v. 20, Gen 27:27–40 records Isaac's blessings of Jacob and Esau. v. 21, Gen 48:8–22 records Jacob's blessing on Ephraim and Manasseh. Gen 47:31 notes Jacob's action in 'bowing in worship' at the head of his bed. The Greek translation, cited here, renders 'bed' as 'staff'. The action indicates that Jacob's blessing is connected with his fidelity to God. v. 22, the reference to Joseph's prophecy (Gen 50:24) introduces the following section. His request to transfer his bones (Gen 50:25) hints at hope for their future.

(11:23–8) The Faith of Moses v. 23, for similar appeals to Moses, see Sir 45:1–5; Acts 7:20–34. Moses as a faithful servant appeared at Heb 3:1–6. For his infancy, see Ex 2:1–10. Philo (*Vit. Mos.* 1.10–11) and Josephus (*Ant.* 2.218) expand on the episode. The detail that his parents 'did not fear' is unbiblical and stands in tension with the notice that the Hebrew midwives were afraid (Ex 1:17, 21). Hebrews intimates what the addressees' attitude should be. After this verse some MSS refer to the slaying of an Egyptian (Ex 2:11–12; cf. Acts 7:24). v. 24, as Abraham rejected the security of his earthly homeland, Moses rejected his princely status; cf. Ex 2:10. A romance by Artapanus, preserved in Eusebius, *Praep. Evang.* 9.27.1–37, significantly embellished this portion of Moses' story. v. 25, Moses' choice of suffering over pleasure interprets Gen 2:11–15, where he identifies with the Israelites. The language recalls the story of Herakles' choice of a life of toil (Xen. *Mem.* 2.1.21–34), which exhibits a similar parenetic intent. v. 26, as with other heroes (vv. 10, 11, 19), the homilist explains the motivation of Moses. How Moses might have understood his sufferings to be 'for the Christ' is obscure. Perhaps as a visionary (v. 27) he foresaw the Messiah's coming and acted accordingly. v. 27, Ex 2:15 reports the departure of Moses; cf. Acts 7:29. That he encountered God 'face to face' appears at Ex 33:11; Num 12:8; Deut 34:10; Sir 45:5. v. 28, for the celebration of the first Passover, see Ex 12:1–28.

(11:29–40) The Faith of Prophets and Martyrs v. 29, attention shifts to groups within ancient Israel and the survey moves more rapidly. For crossing the Red Sea, see Ex 14. v. 30, Josh 6 recounts the fall of Jericho. v. 31, for Rahab and the spies, see Josh 2:1–21; 6:17. v. 32, the judges are listed out of scriptural order. For Gideon, see Judg 6–8; Barak, Judg 4–5; Samson, Judg 13–16; Jephthah, Judg 11–12. David and Samuel occupy 1 and 2 Samuel. v. 33, for 'shutting the mouth of lions', see Judg 14:6; 1 Sam 17:34–5; Dan 6:19–23. v. 34, for quenching fire, see Dan 3 and the LXX addition, Pr Azar 26–7, 66. 'Strength out of weakness' may allude to Gideon (Judg 6:15), Samson (Judg 16:17), or heroines such as Esther and Judith. v. 35, 1 Kings 127:17–24; 2 Kings 4:18–37 record resurrections. Eleazar (2 Macc 6:18–31) and the seven youths (2 Macc 7) endured martyrdom hoping for resurrection. v. 36, chains and imprisonment evoke Jeremiah; cf. Jer 20:2; 29:26; 37:15. v. 37, Zechariah was 'stoned' (2 Chr 24:21). Christian sources (Tert. *Scorp.* 8; Hippol. *On the Antichrist*, 31) attribute the same fate to Jeremiah. The *Martyrdom of Isaiah* 5:11–14 reports that he was 'sawn in two'. The 'skins of sheep and goats' recalls the distinctive mantle of Elijah and Elisha; cf. 1 Kings 19:13 (LXX); 2 Kings 2:13–14 (LXX). v. 38, 'deserts' are the home of Elijah and Elisha (1 Kings 19:4; 2 Kings 2:8). 'Caves' sheltered judges (Judg 6:2), prophets (1 Kings 18:4; 19:9), and rebels (2 Macc 10:6). 'Holes in the ground' appear in Scripture (e.g. Ob 1:3; Zech 14:12), but not as homes for heroes. v. 39, the note that the heroes were 'recommended' repeats the theme that they 'received testimony' (11:2). Like the patriarchs (11:13), they did not attain the 'promise' of eschatological salvation. v. 40, that salvation, 'something better', is the 'heavenly city' of 12:18–24. To enter that realm requires being 'made perfect', which is only possible through Christ's sacrifice; cf. 7:19; 10:10, 14. Although such perfection is available with the inauguration of the new covenant, its effects extend to the heroes of the old.

(12:1–3) Faith's Author and Perfecter The catalogue of heroes culminates in the paradigmatic case of one faithful to God in the face of suffering and rejection, Jesus. v. 1, The metaphor of a cloud for a group is classical (Homer, *Iliad*, 4.274). They are 'witnesses' both as spectators of life's athletic contest and as those who testify to God's fidelity. To 'lay aside every weight' furthers the athletic imagery. The description of sin as 'clinging closely' connotes hostility. To depict the moral life as an athletic contest is a homiletic commonplace; cf. Acts 20:24; 1 Cor 9:24–7; Gal 2:2; Phil 2:16; 2 Tim 4:7. v. 2, Jesus, the 'pioneer' (cf. 2:10), is also the 'perfecter' of faith, who has completed the course and thereby provided 'perfection' for others; cf. 2:10; 5:8–9; 7:28; 10:14. The ambiguous preposition translated 'for the sake of' (*anti*) could mean 'instead of'. The goal-oriented character of Jesus' conduct is suited to the image of the race and to the theme of reward; cf. 10:34; 11:6, 16, 26. For the 'shame' of death on a cross, see Cicero, *Contra Verrem*, 1.5.62; Gal 5:11; Phil 2:8. An allusion to Ps 110:1 concludes the references to the text; cf. 1:3, 13; 8:1; 10:12. v. 3, Jesus' followers must accept hostility and dishonour as did he; cf. 10:33; 13:13.

(12:4–13) A Homily on Endurance v. 4, the imagery shifts from racing to the 'struggle' of boxing. For a similar image, see Sen. *Ep.* 13:2. vv. 5–6, the homilist cites Prov 3:11–12 in its Greek form. v. 7, sapiential literature frequently offered advice on educational discipline; cf. Prov 5:12; 13:24; 15:32; Job 5:17; Sir 22:6; 23:2. Such advice could then be construed as a principle of theodicy: suffering was meant for human education; cf. Prov 6:23; 2 Macc 6:12–17; 2 Cor 6:9; Eph 6:4. v. 8, suffering is particularly required for those who share the status of the Son; cf. 5:7–9. v. 9, an analogy between human and divine fathers uses a solemn liturgical epithet, 'Father of spirits'; cf. 2 Macc 3:24; Dan 5:14; *1 Enoch* 37:2–4; 1QH 10:8; Rev 22:6. v. 10, the analogy contrasts the 'seeming' benefits of

earthly discipline with the true benefit of divine discipline, which produces 'holiness'; cf. 10:14. v. 11, the contrast of temporary pain and long-term gain is proverbial; cf. Prov. 23:13–14; Wis 3:5; Diog. Laert. *Lives of the Philosophers*, 5.1.18. For the 'fruit of righteousness', see Am 6:12; Prov 11:30. 'Peace' and 'righteousness' frequently appear together; cf. Isa 32:17; Ps 85:10. v. 12, the image of 'drooping hands' and 'weak knees', derived from Isa 35:3, comports with the athletic imagery of vv. 1–3. v. 13, Prov 4:26 in Greek supplies the image of 'straight paths'. The promise to 'be healed', echoing Prov 4:22, ends the admonition on a positive note.

Final Advice about Life in the New Covenant (12:14–13:17)

(12:14–17) Transitional Admonition v. 14, the call to 'pursue peace' is common in Jewish homiletics; cf. Ps 34:14; *T. Sim.* 5:2; *m. 'Abot*, 1:12; Mt 5:9; 1 Pet 3:11, citing Ps 34:14. For the connection of sanctity and seeing God, see Mt 5:8. v. 15, the 'root of bitterness' recalls Deut 29:18, a warning against apostasy from the covenant community. Such behaviour could involve detestable idols (Deut 29:17) through which many could be 'defiled'. v. 16, for Esau's sale of his birthright, see Gen 25:29–34. Based upon his marriage to the Hittites Judith and Basemath (Gen 26:34), Jewish tradition (*Jub.* 25:1–8; Philo, *Virt.* 208; *Gen. Rab.* 65) portrayed him as lewd and 'immoral'. v. 17, what the addressees 'know' is Gen 27:30–40, the story of Esau's attempt to reverse Isaac's blessing of Jacob. The detail of Esau's weeping embellishes the biblical story; cf. *Jub.* 26:33; Jos. *Ant.* 1.275. That he found 'no place for repentance' reinforces the earlier warnings (6:4–8; 10:26–31); cf. Deut 29:20.

(12:18–29) Sinai and the Heavenly Jerusalem Visions of eschatological realities ground the ethical exhortation. v. 18, marvellous phenomena evoke divine theophanies. 'What can be touched' recalls the palpable darkness of Ex 10:21. 'Fire…darkness…tempest' all characterized the events at Sinai; cf. Deut 4:11. 'Gloom' is a poetic term embellishing the biblical description. v. 19, the 'trumpet' recalls Ex 19:16; the 'voice' is from Deut 4:12. For eschatological trumpets, see 1 Thess 4:16; 1 Cor 15:52; Mt 24:31; Rev 8:2. For the frightened plea, see Ex 20:19; Deut 5:25. v. 20, the prohibition of Ex 19:12–13 was a cause of fear. v. 21, the reaction of Moses to the golden calf (Deut 9:19) expresses his terror at Sinai. v. 22, 'Mt. Zion', in Jerusalem, is the place of God's presence; cf. Ps 2:6; 48:1; Isa 8:18; 1 Kings 14:21; 1 Macc 4:37. Mountain and 'city' are frequently associated; cf. Mic 4:1; Joel 2:32; Am 1:2. Speculation about a 'heavenly Jerusalem' was a part of apocalyptic literature; cf. Rev 21:2–7. For the phrase 'living God', see 3:12; 9:14; 10:31. 'Innumerable angels' are present at theophanies (Deut 33:2; Ps 68:17–18) and in the heavenly court (Dan 7:10; 1QS 11:8). Their 'festal gathering' recalls the joyous 'sabbath celebration' of 4:9. v. 23, the 'assembly of the firstborn' are the fellow heirs of the 'firstborn' Son; cf. 1:6, 13; 3:1. Being 'made perfect' now characterizes the presence in the heavenly assembly of those who have been cleansed (10:14) and who share Christ's exalted status (2:10). v. 24, for Jesus as 'mediator' of the covenant, see 8:6; for his blood, see 9:14. The 'better word' is his message of true and lasting remission of sin; cf. 9:14; 10:16–18. For an allusion to Abel's blood crying out, see 11:4. v. 25, the transition to a renewed warning is abrupt. The call to 'see' recalls 3:11; the *a fortiori* analogy resembles 2:1–4. The 'one who warns from heaven' is probably God, whose speech has been heard throughout Hebrews. v. 26, Hag 2:6 in Greek predicts a cosmic earthquake, a regular feature of the coming Day (10:25); cf. *1 Enoch*, 60:1; 2 Esd 3:18; *Sib. Or.* 3.675; Mt 24:29; 27:51. The image of universal destruction recalls Ps 102:26–7, cited at 1:10–12. v. 27, an exegetical comment focuses on the adverb 'yet once more', better translated 'once, for all time'. Used also for Christ's definitive sacrifice (9:26–8), the word implies not an alteration but a definitive 'removal' (cf. 7:12; 11:5) of the created order. 'What cannot be shaken' are those abiding realities, the heavenly 'rest' (4:11) and the 'heavenly city' (12:22; 13:14). v. 28, expectation of an eschatological 'kingdom' rests on texts such as Dan 7:18 (LXX). For Jesus, the reign of God began within his own ministry (Lk 11:20). For Hebrews, God's eschatological rule, inaugurated at least in a preliminary fashion by Christ's exaltation, requires 'thanks' in a community of worship; cf. 13:15. v. 29, the passage concludes with an adaption of Deut 4:24, part of a warning to remember the covenant and to shun idolatry; cf. Ex 24:17; Deut 9:3.

(13:1–17) Concluding Exhortations v. 1, for 'mutual love', see Rom 12:10; 1 Thess 4:9; 1 Pet 1:22; 2 Pet 1:7. v. 2, for encouragement to 'hospitality', see Mt 25:35; Rom 12:13; 1 Tim 3:2; Titus 1:8; 1 Pet 4:9. Various scriptural figures 'entertained angels'; cf. Gen 18:2–15; 19:1–14; Judg 6:11–24; 13:3–23. v. 3, the addressees had a history of supporting prisoners; cf. 10:34. v. 4, Christians regularly advised chastity; cf. 1 Cor 5:1–13; Eph 5:3–5; 1 Thess 4:3–7. v. 5, 'Love of money' was generally viewed unfavourably; cf. Mt 6:19–21, 24–34; Lk 12:22–34; 1 Tim 6:10; Jas 5:1–5. Exhortations to 'be content' were commonplace in classical moralists; cf. Epict. *Diss.* 1.1.27; Marcus Aurelius, *Meditations* 10.1. For God's promise not to forsake his people, see Deut 31:6, 8; Josh 1:5. v. 6, the response to God's promise is a prayer of trust, Ps 118:6 (LXX).

v. 7, references to 'leaders' frame the next block of exhortations; cf. 13:17. The addressees are to 'consider' them, as they did Jesus (12:2). For other calls to 'imitate' leaders, see 1 Cor 4:6; 11:1; 1 Thess 1:6; 2:14; 2 Thess 3:9; *1 Clem.* 5:2–7. v. 8, the concise formulation of the eternal presence of Christ parallels Ps 102, cited at 1:12. v. 9, warnings against 'strange teachings' are conventional in second-generation Christian literature; cf. Col 2:8; Eph 4:14; 1 Tim 1:3–7. The opposition of 'grace' and 'food' hint at ill-defined controversies, perhaps over Jewish dietary observances, Jewish or philosophical ascetical practices, or various forms of sacral dining. v. 10, to whatever the practice criticized in v. 9, the homilist poses the alternative of the Christians' 'altar', probably an allusion to the 'once for all' sacrifice of Christ on the cross. To that sacrifice priests of the old cult have no access. Access is now expressed in terms of the 'right to eat' of the sacrifice. The homilist may suggest that Christians have a sacrifice from which they do have the 'right to eat', i.e. the eucharist. Yet he may simply use a metaphor for access to the true, spiritual sacrifice of the high priest. v. 11,

attention turns to the ethical implications of participation in Christ's sacrifice as the homilist introduces a cultic image based on Lev 16:27. The bodies of the animals sacrificed on the Day of Atonement are burnt, and hence not available for physical consumption. More significantly, the burning takes place 'outside the camp'. v. 12, the parallel to the death of Jesus reflects traditions about the locale of his crucifixion (Jn 19:17–20 and perhaps Mt 21:39; Lk 20:15). v. 13, the application of the latest sacrificial image reinforces the appeal to accept the reproach and 'abuse' of being Christian; cf. 10:33; 11:25–6; 12:2. v. 14, Christians thus are like Abraham, expecting the final coming of the heavenly Jerusalem; cf. 11:10; 12:22. v. 15, Lev 7:11–18 designates 'sacrifices of praise' as a specific form of offering, communion sacrifices offered with unleavened bread, but the phrase comes to be used as a metaphor for prayer; cf. Ps 50:14, 23; 107:22. The latter meaning seems to be in view here, where the sacrifice is specified as 'fruit of lips' (Prov 18:20; Hos 14:3; *Ps. Sol.* 15:3; 1QS 9:4–5. Thanksgiving psalms in particular 'confess' the Lord's name; cf. Ps 44:8; 54:6; 99:3. v. 16, the language of sacrifice is applied to moral behaviour at Rom 12:1–2; Phil 2:17; 1 Pet 2:5. With such worship (cf. 12:28) one can, like Enoch, please God; cf. 11:5–6. v. 17, for a similar call to obey leaders, see 1 Pet 5:5. *Herm. Vis.* 3.9.10 displays an analogous concern for the account that a leader would have to render; cf. 4:12–13.

(13:18–25) Benediction and Epistolary Postscript v. 18, petitions for prayer are common in epistles; cf. 1 Thess 5:25; 2 Thess 3:1; Rom 15:30; Col 4:3; Ign. *Trall.* 12:3; *Eph.* 10:1; 21:1. Paul at 2 Cor 1:12 makes a similar appeal to his 'clear conscience'. v. 19, for the hope to come 'very soon'; cf. 1 Tim 3:14. v. 20, similar benedictions appear in many epistles; cf. 1 Thess 5:23; 2 Thess 3:16; 2 Tim 4:22; Rom 15:33; *1 Clem.* 64a. The reference to bringing 'back from the dead' is the most explicit description of the resurrection in a text that deals primarily with Christ's exaltation. There were, however, allusions to resurrection at 11:12, 19. The epithet 'great shepherd' is unusual in Hebrews and may reflect such traditions as Jn 10:11, 14; *Herm. Vis.* 5.2.1; *Herm. Sim.* 10.1.1. The 'blood of the covenant' is a motif firmly rooted in Hebrews; cf. 9:14, 22–3; 12:24. v. 21, for similar doxologies, see Phil 4:20; Rom 16:20; 2 Tim 4:18; 1 Pet 5:11; *1 Clem.* 64b. v. 22, 'word of exhortation' is apparently a technical term for a homily (Acts 13:15). v. 23, news and travel plans often appear in letters; cf. 2 Tim 4:20–1; Philem 22; Col 4:7–8. 'Timothy' is probably Paul's companion; cf. Acts 16:1–3; 17:14–15; 1 Tim; 2 Tim. v. 24, for personal greetings, see 1 Thess 5:26; 2 Thess 3:17; Phil 4:21–2; 2 Tim 4:19, 21; Rom 16:21–3; Col 4:10–18; 1 Pet 5:13–14. v. 25, a wish for grace or peace constitutes the standard epistolary farewell; cf. 1 Thess 5:28; 2 Thess 3:18; Philem 4:23; 2 Tim 4:21b; Philem 25; Rom 16:20; Eph 6:23; Col 4:18b; 1 Pet 5:14b; *1 Clem.* 65:2.

For further reading see Bibliographical Guide.

76. James

RAINER RIESNER

INTRODUCTION

A. Language and Text. 1. James is written in good, but not elegant Greek. The author has composed short sentences rather than long and beautiful periods. Paranomasia and other Greek speech forms show that the letter is not simply a translation from a Semitic original, but it cannot be proved that the author used the LXX. The high occurrence of Semitisms (Mussner 1987: 30–2) cannot be explained by the use of traditional material only. Of special interest are parallels to the Hebrew Dead Sea scrolls. Bilingualism was widespread in first-century Palestine, even the scribe of the great Isaiah scroll from Qumran (1QIsª) was fluent in Greek. Apparently the author of James was also a bilingual Palestinian Jew.

2. Claims that a scrap of papyrus from Qumran (7Q8) contains Jas 1:23–4 have been disproved (*RevQ* 18 (1997), 307–24), by showing it to be part of *1 Enoch* 103 in Greek. Fragments of James are preserved in three papyri of the third century P²⁰, P²³, and P¹⁰⁰). The whole letter is included in the fourth-century codices, Sinaiticus (ℵ) and Vaticanus (B), the latter attesting the best text-form. The text of James is not so well preserved as that of other NT documents, which might partially be explained by its rather complicated canonical history.

B. Literary Genre and Subject-Matter. 1. James is an encyclical letter to an unknown number of Greek-speaking (Jewish) Christian churches. Starting with the Letter of Jeremiah (Jer 29; cf. 2 Macc 1–2; 2 *Apoc. Bar* 78–86; *Par. Jer.* 6:17–23) there was a tradition of Jewish letters to the Diaspora (Tsuji 1997; Niebuhr 1998). Early form-critics assigned James to the literary genre of the Hellenistic *diatribe* (Dibelius 1976), but it is doubtful that this is more than a literary style (Baasland 1988). There are some parallels to synagogal homilies, but also to the structure of the *Manual of Discipline* (1QS) and the annexed *Rule of the Congregation* (1QSa) from Qumran (Beck 1973). Formal parallels exist also to Christian catechetical traditions and writings (connected with baptism?) such as the Matthean Sermon on the Mount or the Lukan Sermon on the Plain, 1 Peter, and the *Didache*. The use of an elementary narrative *mashal* form (1:23–4; 2:2, 15–17), not attested in the earlier wisdom literature but in the Jesus tradition, is a rather ancient feature.

2. In the opening paragraph on temptation (1:2–18), James already introduces most of the other main subjects of his letter. That the 'word (*logos*) of truth' (1:18) must be obeyed is the theme of 1:19–27. The practical 'testing of faith' (*pistis*, 1:3) is treated at length in 2:1–26. The ethics of speech (1:19–21, 26–7) is a very important subject (Baker 1995), especially in the admonition for teachers (3:1–12). That wisdom (*sophia*) and humility (*tapeinōsis*) belong together (1:5, 9–10) finds its exposition in 3:13–4:12. The apocalyptic admonition of the rich (1:10–11) continues in 4:13–5:6. What 'endurance' (*hypomonē*, 1:3–4) means in practice is explained in the last part of the letter (5:7–20). As it is typical for the internationality of

wisdom literature, parallels to James can be found not only in the OT and Jewish writings, but also in Near-Eastern and Graeco-Roman wisdom traditions. The book of Proverbs is cited and Sirach probably and the Wisdom of Solomon possibly alluded to, but the strongest allusions are to the words of Jesus and other early Christian traditions. James's combination of wisdom, ethics, and eschatology resembles the Enochic tradition (*1 Enoch*, 92–105) and the thinking of the Essene community of Qumran (Davids 1982: 51–4; Penner 1996), especially in a very fragmentary Sapiential work (4Q185).

C. The Religious Teaching. 1. Wisdom Theology. The letter grows out of the OT and intertestamental wisdom traditions. God who created the world will also bring it to eschatological completion in a new creation. The work of God in creation, salvation, and new creation forms a unity mediated by divine wisdom.

2. Christology. James can speak about Jesus in the same way as he speaks about God (Karrer 1989). Jesus is not only the promised Messiah (*christos*) but also Lord (*kyrios*). Apparently, the author does not reveal all that he knows about Jesus (Mussner 1987: 250–3), but the letter may even see in him the incarnation of God's pre-existent wisdom. The teachings of Jesus are treated as the ultimate revelation of wisdom.

3. Eschatology. The letter anticipates the Second Coming of Christ in the near future who is pictured as judge like the Son of Man in the Enochic and the Synoptic traditions. This expectation implies belief in the resurrection of Jesus.

4. Anthropology. Portraying the eschatological goal as human perfection, the author is not a perfectionist or illusionist. He sees clearly that believers can do wrong and need repentance and forgiveness. Following the Jewish idea of the 'evil inclination', for James sin is not only an act of human decision, but a cosmic power.

5. Soteriology. Since it seems quite unsure that James reacts directly against the theology of Paul (Johnson 1995: 111–16) the letter should primarily be understood on its own terms. The OT as interpreted and supplemented by Jesus is the 'perfect law'. But salvation cannot be obtained by a fulfilment of this law alone, since the members of James's community are also prone to fail. God's forgiveness is necessary, but how it is mediated is only hinted at. Spiritual rebirth by God's free will and word, baptism in the name of Jesus, submission to God, prayer and repentance all play their part (Konradt 1998). There might be allusions to Jesus' vicarious suffering as the Servant of the Lord, but James concentrates on the warning that there is no relation to God without an elementary ethical commitment to human beings. With his emphasis on loving God and one's neighbour inspired by Jesus' double commandment James comes near to the Pauline 'faith working through love' (Gal 5:6), but he lacks Paul's deep theological definition of faith. For James belief in the existence of God and, using older terminology (cf. 1 Cor 12:9; 13:2), belief in his miraculous power is also faith. Paul's stress of the sovereignty of God has a certain parallel in James's emphasis on the election of the poor and humble.

6. Ethics of Speech. In an age of ideology and media propaganda it is appropriate to remember that disputes and even wars often start with words. The truly wise know to govern their tongue.

7. Poor and Rich. Today the letter attracts theologians from the Third World since in following the teaching of Jesus, James is very critical of the rich. Nevertheless, salvation is not guaranteed by bad material circumstances but is obtained by loving God and one's neighbour.

8. Testing and Suffering. Believers must make a difference between temptations caused by their own evil desires and God's testing especially through oppression and persecution. Suffering should create anticipated eschatological joy.

9. Prayer. There are two main functions of prayer, namely to ask for wisdom and to obtain healing. Prayer should connect the believer with God and meet his elementary needs without guaranteeing material wealth. The author lived with Jesus' promises on prayer.

10. Judaism. The Jewish character of James is so strong that in former times some scholars hypothesized an only secondarily Christianized Jewish document (similarly Ludwig 1994). But this overlooks how strongly James is embedded in Jesus' teaching (Deppe 1989) and early Christian tradition. If rather early, the letter might have been read also to some synagogue congregations not yet decided about the new Messianic faith (Schlatter 1932: 62). James is an interesting example of Jewish–Christian dialogue. The letter shows the deep roots of the Jesus movement in the OT and also in Jewish Wisdom and Apocalyptic without denying its own identity, that of belief in the Messianic fulfilment.

D. The Author. 1. The simple presentation of a certain 'James' as author in the prescript (1:1) may already point to the most famous bearer of this name in NT times, 'James, the brother of the Lord' (cf. Jude 1). In the fourth century Helvidius made James out to be a blood brother of Jesus and Jerome considered him a cousin, but the second-century tradition thought of a step-brother stemming from an earlier marriage of Joseph (Bauckham 1990: 19–32). James did not follow Jesus (Jn 7:5) and was converted only by an appearance of the risen Lord (1 Cor 15:7). As a representative of the family of Jesus he was the leader of an influential group in the primitive Jerusalem community (Gal 1:19; Acts 1:13). When after the persecution of Agrippa I (41–4 CE) the twelve left Jerusalem, James became the only leader (Acts 12; Gal 2:9). The interfering of Jewish Christians close to him in the mixed community of Antioch (Gal 2:11–14) might be due to a widespread Jewish belief that Syria was part of a greater Holy Land and subject to its special regulations (Bockmuehl 1999). Such a belief can also explain the sending of an encyclical diaspora letter. Although being himself a conservative Jewish Christian at the Apostolic Council of 48 CE (Acts 15) James consented to the inclusion of Gentile Christians without total obedience to the Torah (Hengel 1985; Bauckham 1995). At the instigation of the high priest Ananus he died in 61 CE as a martyr for his belief in the messiaship of Jesus (Jos. *Ant.* 20. 200). Wherever in the early church the letter was believed to be authentic it was also ascribed to this James.

2. Many scholars put forward serious doubts against the authorship of James (Popkes 1986; Pratscher 1987; Konradt 1998), but with our deeper insight into the Hellenization of Judaea the argument of Greek language and style has lost much of its force. An encyclical Greek letter to the Diaspora could have been composed with the help of a secretary, as Jerome thought (*PL* 23. 639). Some scholars try to distinguish between an earlier version by James himself and a later edition by a rhetorically skilled writer (Davids 1982; Martin 1988). There are similarities between the vocabulary of James and Luke–Acts (Davids 1982: 49). That the letter does not refer to the Gentile mission and to problems of ritual law could be explained by an early date.

3. Some further observations may strengthen the case for authenticity. Obviously, the family of Jesus shared traditions of a pre-Qumranic non-sectarian Essenism (Sacchi 1993; Boccaccini 1998) that originated in the movement of the pious and often poor ḥăsîdîm (Betz and Riesner 1994: 143–7). The letter shows some proximity to the Enochic literature and the *Testaments of the Twelve Patriarchs* which originated in such circles. Later James and his community lived near the Essene Quarter of Jerusalem (Riesner 1993; 1998b), which enhances the significance of the letter's parallels to the Dead Sea scrolls (Mussner 1987). James 'might well have formed a bridge between Galilean Christian Nazirites and the Qumran Covenanters' (Adamson 1989: 20), but an identification of the author with the Qumran 'Teacher of Righteousness' is fanciful. Besides Q, Matthean and Markan Jesus traditions (Hartin 1991) there is also knowledge of the Lukan special tradition (Davids 1982: 47–9) that was probably handed down by Jewish Christians gathered around the relatives of Jesus in Jerusalem and Judea (Riesner 1994). The letter is marked by a certain Judean local colour (Davids 1999). The Enochic flavour connects James, the Lukan special tradition, and Jude, also ascribed to a brother of Jesus.

E. Date and Place of Composition. 1. If the letter is pseudepigraphic it must have been written after the death of James in 61 CE or more probably after the destruction of Jerusalem and the dispersion of its Jewish Christian community in 70 CE. Then parallels to such writings as 1 Peter, 1 *Clement*, and the Shepherd of Hermas are to be taken as signs of common socio-economic problems in Christian communities at the turn of the first to the second century (Frankemölle 1994). Under the pseudepigraphy hypothesis the letter could have been composed almost anywhere in the Roman world where Greek-speaking Christians were living, but some prefer Syria (Konradt 1998).

2. At the present time the authenticity hypothesis is gaining new defenders (Stulac 1993; Johnson 1995; Bauckham 1999), according to whom the letter was written from Jerusalem, where James resided, either before or after the Apostolic Council of 48 CE. Following earlier voices (Zahn 1906: 125–8; Mayor 1913) it is argued by some that the letter should be dated early (Moo 1985: 33–5; Penner 1996: 276–7). It could have been addressed to dispersed Jewish Christians (cf. Acts 8:1–3) between Alexandria, Antioch, and Cilicia (Geyser 1975) when rumours were heard that in circles of the

Greek-speaking 'Hellenists' (Acts 6–7), to whom Paul later belonged (Acts 11:19–26; 13:1), obedience to God was rendered superfluous by faith. There are some striking parallels with 1 Cor 1–4. Could both James and Paul be reacting against Jewish Christians with former ties to Essene, Therapeut, and Baptist circles (1 Cor 1:12; 3:4–6; cf. Acts 18:24)? The instigators of the persecution seem to be the rich and politically influential (2:6–7). This fits better the time until the middle of the 40s (Riesner 1998a: 108–36), when the Jewish Christians were oppressed by the Sadducean oligarchy (Maynard-Reid 1987) and Jewish kings such as Agrippa I (Acts 3–9; 12). After the second half of the 40s persecution was instigated rather by Zealot movements (cf. Acts 15:1; 23:12–22).

F. Canonicity. 1. The parallels between James and 1 Peter are to be explained not by literary dependence but by the use of common Jewish-Christian material. At the turn of the first to the second century James was possibly known to Clement of Rome and the Roman Shepherd of Hermas, two writers heavily indebted to Jewish Christian traditions. At the end of the second century Irenaeus of Lyons, who was a native of Asia Minor, seems to have used James, but there is no trace of the letter in Tertullian's works. According to Eusebius (*Hist. Eccl.* 6.14.1) Clement of Alexandria wrote a commentary on all the Catholic Epistles at the turn of the third century, although in his preserved works James is not clearly cited. But at the beginning of the third century Clement's pupil Origen explicitly cited Jas 2:26 as scripture (*PG* 12. 1300). In the first half of the fourth century Eusebius wrote that formerly the authenticity of the letter was strongly disputed, although in his time it was read in most of the churches (*Hist. Eccl.* 2.23.25; 3.25.3). Probably the Jewish Christian origin of James had complicated its acceptance.

2. The letter is not included in the Muratorian Canon, compiled around 200 CE in Rome possibly by Hippolytus. But this can be due to the fragmentary nature of the list, since Hippolytus seems to have known James. The letter was part of the canon lists of Athanasius of Alexandria (367 CE), Innocent of Rome (405 CE), and the North African provincial synods of Hippo (393 CE) and Carthage (419 CE), but possibly already of the lists of the synods of Laodicea (360 CE) and Rome (382 CE).

3. Luther expressed severe doubts about its canonicity as James seems to contradict Paul's doctrine of justification by faith (Rom 3:20, 28; 4:16; cf. Jas 2:24). This position is still strongly defended (Lautenschlager 1990; Klein 1995). Together with other disputed writings (Hebrews, Jude, and Revelation) Luther placed the 'epistle of straw' at the end of his famous German translation of the NT from 1522. However, the letter was accepted without reservations by Calvin and the Reformed churches. In 1548 the council of Trent affirmed the canonicity and expressed its doctrine of justification in terms of James. The Common Declaration on Justification by the Roman Catholic and Lutheran churches from 1998/9 tries to bring together the different NT perspectives. James is part of the NT of the Orthodox churches, but was included in the Syriac Bible only since the fifth century. This seems astonishing in view of the influence of Jewish-Christian traditions in Syria. Apparently, the letter was sent to a very limited number of Greek-speaking communities.

G. Outline. Following Luther many thought that the letter has no good order, but today most discover a careful structure. If one pays attention to such formulas as 'my brothers [NRSV and sisters]' or 'listen' (RSV behold) and to such Jewish devices of composition as catchwords or symbolic numbers (3, 5, 7) the following structure seems possible:

Prescript (1:1)
Joy in Temptations (1:2–18)
Hearing, Speaking, Doing (1:19–27)
The Love Command and Dead Faith (2:1–26)
Ethics of Speech for Teachers (3:1–12)
The Wise and Humility (3:13–4:12)
Warning to the Rich (4:13–5:6)
Patience until the Coming of the Lord (5:7–20)

The overall structure—first some sort of beatitude (1:2, 12), then reprimand of the rich (4:13–5:6), then final exhortations (5:7–20)—resembles the Sermon on the Plain (Lk 6:20–49).

COMMENTARY

Prescript (1:1)

The prescript uses the common short form of the Hellenistic letter (cf. Acts 15:23; 23:26). The sender is introduced as 'James a servant of God and of the Lord Jesus Christ'. As in the prescripts of Paul's (Gal 1:3; 1 Cor 1:3, etc.) and other NT letters (2 Pet 1:2) God and Jesus are put on the same level. In a Jewish environment this could cause the accusation of ditheism. In the first sentence of the letter the writer does not hide his faith in Jesus as the 'Christ'. The Greek *christos* translates the Hebrew *masiah*, 'the anointed', the Jewish king of the end-time promised by the OT. The addressees are 'the twelve tribes in the Dispersion (*diaspora*)', referring either generally to the Christians as the wandering people of God (cf. 1 Pet 1:1) or, as is more probable, to scattered Jewish-Christian communities outside Palestine. The prescript ends with the typical Greek formula of greeting (*chairein*).

Joy in Temptations (1:2–18)

(1:2–4) From Trials to Completion The unusual imperative to enjoy 'trials' (*peirasmoi*, v. 2) is explained by the fact that 'the testing of faith' can 'produce endurance' (v. 3). This idea with close parallels in Rom 5:2b–5 and 1 Pet 1:6–7 might have been part of early Christian baptismal instruction, ultimately going back to the teaching of Jesus (Mt 5:11–12; Lk 6:22–3). From endurance results, as 'full effect, that you may be complete [*teleios*, RSV perfect]' (v. 4), a goal that connects James with the Dead Sea scrolls (*tāmîm*, 1QS), Paul (1 Cor 2:6; Phil 3:15; Col 4:12) and Matthew's Gospel (Mt 5:48; 19:21). In James as in Qumran and the rest of the NT completion is understood to be eschatological.

(1:5–8) Prayer for Wisdom That completion is still in the future is illustrated by the admonition to ask for more wisdom (v. 5). The phrasing reminds one of Jesus' logion about asking and receiving (Mt 7:7; Lk 11:9–10) and his promise of wisdom in times of trial (Lk 21:15). That God gives 'simply (*haplōs*) and without grudging' (own tr.) has its background in the Q-saying, Mt 7:7–8; Lk 11:13. In contrast to God human beings can be 'double-minded' (*dipsychos*) even in prayer (v. 8). At this point James apparently coined a new Greek word for a Palestinian-Jewish anthropological idea. That such a person is 'unstable in all his ways' (RSV) reminds one of the two-ways tradition (cf. Mt 7:13–14) that is already attested in Qumran (1QS 1:8 etc.) and became prominent in early Christian ethical teaching (Did. 1:1). That one should ask 'in faith never doubting' (1:6–7) is also inspired by Jesus' teaching (Mt 21:21–2; Mk 11:23–4).

(1:9–11) The Lowly and the Rich The raising up of the lowly and the bringing low of the rich and mighty (vv. 9–10) is an important motif of the Lukan special tradition (Lk 1:48, 52; 14:11; cf. Mt 23:12). That (rich) men 'disappear like a flower' (vv. 10–11) is already proverbial in the OT (Isa 40:6–7; Ps 103:15; cf. 4Q185; Mt 6:30; Lk 12:28 and Mt 13:6; Mk 4:6) and here expressed in a quite Semitic way.

(1:12–15) God and Temptation Beatitudes on those who 'endure temptations' are frequent in Jewish apocalyptic (Dan 12:12 Theod.; Ex. Rab. 31:3) and the Jesus tradition (Mt 5:3–11; Lk 20:22), v. 12 being possibly an unknown beatitude of Jesus (Adamson 1976: 68). The denial that God is the author of temptation (v. 13a) may correct a certain interpretation of the Lord's Prayer (Mt 6:13; Lk 11:4; cf. 1 Cor 10:13). Tempting someone to do evil is against the character of God (v. 13b; cf. Sir 15:11–12). Like Augustine (PL 38.453), the author seems to see in the testing of the faith of Abraham and Job something different. Although James believes in the involvement of demonic powers in temptation (3:15; 4:7) here he stresses human responsibility (v. 14; cf. 1 Enoch 98:4). The use of the term 'desire' (epithumia) is near to the psychological-ethical discussion in Qumran and the Rabbis (Kirk 1969–70; Marcus 1982) about the 'evil inclination' (yēser hā-ra') and not to Gnostic speculation about the evil of materiality. The personification of human desire giving birth to sin and death has its background either in Gen 3 (cf. Rom 7:7–12) or Prov 7:22–3. The triad 'desire, sin, death' (v. 15) forms a strong contrast to 'temptation, endurance, life' (v. 12).

(1:16–18) God's Perfect Gift The admonition in vv. 16–17 recapitulates some motives of the 'epitome of exhortation' in 1:2–15. The first part of v. 17 may be the quotation of a pagan proverb in hexameter form, but an allusion to a word of Jesus (Mt 7:11; Lk 11:13) is also possible. The 'perfect gift' (v. 17a) should not be restricted to wisdom (cf. 1:5), but characterizes all that God is doing. The designation of God as 'Father of lights' (v. 17b), that is the creator of the stars, is only found in a document from a wider Essenism (As. Mos. 36, 38, cf. T. Abr. 7:6; CD 5:17–18; 1QS 3:20). In contrast to human beings God does not waver and this is shown (as in Qumran) with an allusion to the majestic, regular movements of the stars. What kind of celestial phenomenon could be meant by the changeable shadow (v. 17c) is unclear, but comparable language is found in 4:14. In sharp contrast to human behaviour in 1:15, God performs a new creation by spiritual birth from his 'free will' (v. 18, own tr.). This idea has an antecedent in the apocalyptic preaching of John the Baptist (Mt 3:9; Lk 3:8), is clearly attested in the Jesus tradition (Mt 18:3; Jn 3:3, 5), and is common to all important strata of NT Christianity (1 Cor 4:15; Rom 12:2; Eph 1:5; Titus 3:5; 1 Pet 1:3; Jn 3:3–8; 1 Jn 3:9; 4:7). The idea appears often in baptismal texts, very close to

James are the Petrine (1 Pet 1:23) and the pre-Johannine traditions (Jn 1:12–13). The 'word of truth' (v. 18) should not be restricted to the OT (cf. Ps 119:43) or OT law. The idiom has no real Jewish parallels but is attested in NT texts about conversion (2 Cor 6:7; Eph 1:13; Col 1:5; cf. 2 Tim 2:15). Possibly, in letters arguing with Christians under a certain Essene influence 'word of truth' is a designation for mission preaching (including elementary ethical instruction). Already Philo and the romance Joseph and Asenath, both in contact with Egyptian Essenic-Therapeutic circles, describe conversion as a coming from death to life and truth, implying the forgiveness of sins. When believers are called 'first fruits', this is the cultic language of offering (Ex 23:16; Lev 27:26; Deut 14:23, etc.) and may be a hint at Jesus' vicarious death and resurrection (cf. 1 Cor 15:20).

Hearing, Speaking, Doing (1:19–27)

(1:19–21) Quick to Hear, Slow to Speak 'You must understand this, my beloved' (v. 19a) marks a new section. The Semitic formulated proverb (v. 19b) has many parallels in wisdom literature (Sir 5:11; Eccl 5:1, etc.) as has the following theme 'slow to anger' (Eccl 7:9). Anger does not produce the divine standard of 'righteousness' (v. 20). Speech ethics has the negative aspect of getting rid of all false speech (v. 21a) and the positive one 'to receive [RSV] with meekness the implanted word (logos emphutos)' (v. 21b), an idiom reminding one of the explanation of the parable of the sower in its Lukan form (Lk 8:13; cf. 1 Pet 1:23). This enhances the possibility that as with 'the word of truth' (1:18) we have here an abbreviated term for the early Christian paradosis including the words of Jesus. Similar language is used in connection with mission preaching (Acts 1:14) and baptism (Col 3:8). A pre-Qumranic prayer (4Q504) earlier expressed the hope that God would 'sow' his word inwardly into man. The seed metaphor stresses the life-giving power of God's word. That the 'implanted word' has 'the power to save your souls' (v. 21c) may allude to Jesus' teaching about his words as the criterion of eschatological salvation (Mk 8:35–8; Lk 9:24–6).

(1:22–5) Doers, not Merely Hearers of the Word This admonition (vv. 22–3b) resembles Jesus' parable of the building of a house, stressing the importance of not only hearing but doing his word (Mt 7:24–7; Lk 6:47–9; cf. Origen, Hom. in Gen. 2.16). The use of mirrors as illustration (vv. 23b–4) was common in the religious and philosophical teaching of the ancient world. The idiom 'the perfect law… of liberty' (v. 25; cf. 2:15) is crucial for every general understanding of James. The strongly Semitic expression 'hearer of forgetfulness' (own tr.) argues against a Stoic background. As 'the royal law' in 2:8, 'the perfect law' should be understood as the OT law as interpreted and completed by Jesus (cf. Mt 5:17, 48). There might be a traditio-historical connection (Riesner 1997: 362–4) between Jas 1:21 ('meekness', 'saving the souls') and v. 25 ('law of freedom'), Jesus' invitation to bear his 'yoke' (i.e. law) as 'rest for your souls' (Mt 11:28–30), Paul's 'law of Christ' (Gal 6:1–2) that makes free (cf. Gal 5:1) and the pre-Johannine Amen-saying about the freedom from sin (Jn 8:34–6). Mention of the 'law of freedom' in Qumran (1QS 10:6, 8, 11) is disputed (cf. Ex 32:16), but similar language is found in Philo (Omn. Prob. 45).

(1:26–7) Pure Religion 'Religion' (*thrēskeia*) is defined primarily in ethical and not in ritual terms (v. 26). The quality of speech is the criterion for what is in the human heart (cf. Mt 12:34; Lk 6:45). To remain 'unstained by the world' (v. 27c) here means an ethical dualism (cf. 1 Enoch 48:7; 108:8; *Apoc. Abr.* 29:8; *T. Iss.* 4:6) and not a material one as in Gnosticism. To 'care for orphans and widows' (v. 27b) is a common command in the OT (Deut 14:28; Jer 5:28; Sir 4:10, etc.) and was practised with great care in the primitive community of Jerusalem (Acts 6:1–6). The 'pure and undefiled' religion (v. 27a; cf. Philo, *Leg. All.* 1.50) is addressed to 'God, the Father'. To call God three times 'Father' (1:17, 27; 3:9) is unusually often in a Jewish writing and might echo Jesus' regular address to God.

The Love Command and Dead Faith (2:1–26)

(2:1–4) No Faith with Favouritism In James 'faith' is closely bound to ethics, but this does not imply a low Christology. Jesus is called the 'Christ' (v. 1), fulfilling the OT and Jewish Messianic hope, but much more also. In view of the close parallel in 1 Cor 2:8 (*kyrios tēs doxēs*) 'glory' is to be seen as modifying 'Lord', meaning 'the Lord of glory' (v. 1). This designation may allude to Jesus' transfiguration (Lk 9:32; cf. Jn 1:14). The term is found in 1 Enoch 22:14; 25:3; 27:3, 5; 75:3 referring to God, but in 63:2 it may refer to the (pre-existent) 'Son of Man' (cf. 63:11). He is also called the 'Lord of Wisdom' (63:2), whose 'mystery' was not recognized by the kings and other powerful men (63:2–4). The messianic 'Son of Man' is in possession of the glory of God that Adam, the first man, had lost (*Apoc. Mos.* 20–1; cf. Gen 2). Thus Jesus' designation as 'Lord of glory' may hint at his pre-existence and the fact that he was not recognized although God's glory was revealed in him. The Jewish-Christian background of the letter is shown by the reference to the sitting order (Riesner 1995: 207–8) of a synagogue building (*synagōgē*, v. 2). The assembled community in James is not called 'synagogue' but by the more theological term 'church' (*ekklēsia*, 5:14). The poor man is humbled by being given a bad place, whereas the rich receive seats of honour (vv. 2–3). Biased judgement of the poor (v. 4) is criticized by the OT (Lev 19:15), and also by Jesus (Lk 18:6). Concern for the poor is one of the main subjects of the Lukan special tradition.

(2:5–7) Poor and Rich The address 'listen my... brothers' (v. 5a) is also found in James's speech at the apostolic council of Jerusalem according to Acts 15:13, but nowhere in the rest of the NT. Obviously, v. 5b reminds the readers of Jesus' blessing on the poor as heirs of the kingdom of God (Mt 5:3, 5; Lk 6:20), although the *basileia* is not promised to the poor generally but to those 'rich in faith and loving God' (own tr.). The writer points to the experience of his readers: whereas they dishonour the poor, they themselves are brought to court by the rich (v. 6; cf. Lk 18:3). The rich also 'blaspheme the excellent name that was invoked over you' (v. 7). Since this cannot be the name of God it must be the name of Jesus invoked in baptism (cf. Acts 2:38; 8:16; 10:48; *Herm. Sim.* 9.16.3). v. 7 forms another curious parallel to the speech attributed to James in Acts 15:17.

(2:8–13) Love as the Royal Law Loving 'your neighbour as yourself' (Lev 19:18) is called the 'royal law' (*nomos basilikos*, 2:8). Jesus had already declared this OT command and love for God as the summary of the whole law (Mt 22:37–9; Mk 12:30–

1, and esp. Lk 10:25–8) and thus made it the law of the Messiah-King and his kingdom (*basileia*). For James the law is indivisible (v. 10; cf. Mt 5:18–19; Lk 3:9). The order of the commandments (Ex 20:13–14; Deut 5:17–18) on adultery and murder is (against Mt 19:18; Mk 10:19) the same as in Lk 18:20. To act against the poor (v. 9) is like murder and is judged by the law as such (v. 11; cf. Jer 7:6; 22:3; Sir 34:26; *T. Gad*, 4:6–7). When the law is again called a 'law of freedom' (v. 12) it is stressed that it is the law of Moses as interpreted, supplemented, and altered by Jesus (cf. 1:25). That 'mercy' is the criterion of judgement (v. 13) echoes Jesus' beatitude on the merciful (Mt 5:7).

(2:14–17) Faith and the Needs of the Poor Here the writer for the first time introduces his conviction that faith (*pistis*) without works cannot save (v. 14), because such a faith is 'dead' (v. 17). 'Having works' is here defined as fulfilling the elementary claims of human behaviour. Someone pronouncing a blessing on brothers and sisters who lack both clothes and 'daily food' (cf. Lk 11:3) without helping them in their basic needs (vv. 15–16) would be unmerciful and sin against the teaching of Jesus (Mt 25:35–6; cf. 1 Jn 3:17). In the primitive community of Jerusalem there was a 'daily distribution' for the needy (Acts 6:1).

(2:18–20) No Faith without Works An imaginary interlocutor poses a question that is used by the writer to advance his argument: 'But someone will say, "You have faith and I have works"' (v. 18a). Since it would be illogical for an adversary to claim that he has deeds whereas James has faith, the probable meaning (Dibelius 1976: 156) of the objection is that faith and deeds can be separated since God has distributed them separately among different people. But according to James the sheer belief in the existence of the one God (cf. Deut 6:4) has no more saving power than the trembling belief of the demons in God's supreme power (v. 19). There seems to be a play on the two related meanings of the Greek verb *deiknumi*, 'to show' and 'to demonstrate'. Since for the writer faith without the practical proof of works is only an intellectual assent without personal commitment nothing can be 'shown' by it. But works can be 'shown' and by them someone's faith is demonstrated (v. 18b). So he repeats his conviction that 'faith without works is barren' (v. 20; cf. 2:17).

(2:21–4) The Example of Abraham In Jewish tradition the binding of Isaac (2:21; cf. Gen 22) was the capstone of a series of testings of Abraham (1 Macc 2:52; *Jub.* 17:17; 19:8; *m. 'Abot* 5:3, etc.) and his final declaration as 'righteous' because of his acts of mercy (*T. Abr.* A 1.17; *Tg. Ps. J.* on Gen 21:33). Since Paul also in the context of justification and works (Rom 4:3) refers to the same scripture (Gen 15:6) many suppose a direct (polemical) reaction on James's side (v. 23). But the terminological parallels can be explained by both authors referring to the Jewish tradition (Konradt 1998: 241–4). James uses this tradition as self-evident without arguing against Paul's new interpretation of Abraham's example apparently not known to him. For a direct connection one has to assume that the rather intelligent author of James did misrepresent the teaching of Paul. Paul argues against justification by 'works of the law' (*erga nomou*, Gal 2:16; 3:2, 10; Rom 3:20, 28; cf. 4QMMT col. 27; 4QFlor 1:6–7), that is acceptance of circumcision, purity, feasts, and other ritual regulations as a condition of salvation.

James has nothing to say about the ritual law but writes about elementary moral obligations (*erga*). Of course, James could react against a misunderstood liberalistic Paulinism, especially if the letter is rather early and written without first-hand knowledge either of Paul himself or of his letters. But James seems to be arguing not at all against a theological position but against an unchristian lifestyle. He faced problems similar to those of Paul in Corinth (1 Cor 1–4!), not like the disputes in Galatia. One should not misrepresent James, v. 24 does not read 'man is justified by works alone'. For James faith is 'active along with ... works and faith [is] brought to completion by the works' (v. 22). There are obvious terminological differences: whereas James could speak of a 'dead' or 'barren' faith (without works), for Paul faith without any sign of new life would not be faith at all.

(2:25–6) The Example of Rahab Even a problematic person such as this prostitute was proved righteous by risking her life to help the people of God (v. 25; cf. Josh 2:1–15). The maxim of 2:17, that faith without works is dead, is repeated (v. 26). One can say that 'James, like Paul, is repeating what Jesus said. Paul repeats Mt 5:3, James repeats Mt 7:21–7. Paul is representing the beginning whereas James is representing the end of the Sermon on the Mount' (Jeremias 1954–5: 371).

Ethics of Speech for Teachers (3:1–12)

The leading role of 'teachers' (*didaskaloi*) is part of a Jewish-Christian background (Zimmermann 1988: 194–208). The writer ('we') belongs to this class (v. 1) but he warns that 'not many ... should become teachers' because of their special responsibility in view of God's coming judgement (cf. Lk 12:48). Although the whole letter is an admonition to become 'perfect' the writer himself confesses to 'many mistakes' (v. 2) showing his realistic and honest anthropology.

(3:2a–3) The Tongue like a Horse's Bit The controlling power of the tongue over the whole person (Sir 14:1; 20:1–7; Prov 10:19; Eccl 5:1) is illustrated by this example (cf. Ps 32:9).

(3:4–5a) The Tongue Like a Ship's Rudder As with the previous example there are many parallels not only in Greek but also in Jewish Hellenistic literature (especially in Philo). Probably both illustrations had already become proverbial.

(3:5b–6) The Tongue as a Fire Fire in scrub and brushwood is a common phenomenon in Palestine. 'World of iniquity' (v. 6) forms a Semitic construction (1 Enoch 48:7; cf. Lk 16:9, 11; 18:6). Outside the words of Jesus only here is the term *gehenna* for 'hell' used. At its source is the Hinnom (Aram. *gehenna*) Valley, cursed by Jeremiah (7:31–4), and encircling the southwestern hill of Jerusalem (1 Enoch 26–7), where James, the brother of the Lord, and his community resided.

(3:7–10a) The Untamed Tongue The writer expresses a deep anthropological scepticism: wild beasts can be tamed, but not the human tongue (vv. 7–8). It is full of death-dealing poison (Ps 139:4; cf. 1QH 5:26–7). The criticism of blessing God but cursing man has many OT and Jewish parallels, but Jesus' admonition seems especially close (Lk 6:28; cf. Rom 12:14). The connection between the belief in man being created in the image of God and the prohibition of cursing man is part of the Jewish ethical tradition (*Mek.* to Ex 20:26; *Gen. Rab.* to 5:1; Slavonic *Enoch* 44:1; 52:126; cf. Lk 6:27–8).

(3:10b–12) No Double Talk This is an important consequence of the concept of integrity contrasted with 'double-mindedness' (1:8). The image of plants producing appropriate fruit (v. 12a) is common in Stoicism, but a very near parallel can be found in the words of Jesus (Mt 7:16; Lk 6:44). The last sentence (v. 12b) formulates a condensation of the first image of salt and sweet water springs (v. 11) so common side by side on the edges of the Jordan rift valley.

The Wise and Humility (3:13–4:12)

After strongly warning the teachers the admonition for them continues in a more positive way. Its background might be the example of the 'meekness' (3:13) of Jesus, the incarnate Wisdom (Mt 11:28–30; cf. Jas 1:21). The idea that wisdom is given to the humble has also a close parallel (Hoppe 1985: 139–45) in Jesus' logion about the revelation to infants (Mt 11:25; Lk 10:21).

(3:13–18) The Meekness of Wisdom As in Paul (1 Cor 1–4) the criterion of wisdom, coming from above or below (v. 15), is ethical, especially the avoidance of strife (v. 16). The description of the 'wisdom from above' (v. 17) reminds one in some way of Paul's description of love in 1 Cor 13:4–7. Even closer are the parallels in the lists of virtues in the Qumran *Manual of Discipline* (1QS 4), Paul (Gal 5:22–3), and the Matthean beatitudes (Mt 5:3–10). At the end (v. 18) there might be an intentional echo of Jesus' beatitude on the peacemakers (Mt 5:9).

(4:1–3) Passions as Cause of Wars 'Conflicts and disputes' have their origin not only in social circumstances, but are also traced back to the war within human beings (v. 1). For Christians prayer should precede all human aspirations (v. 2), but even Jesus' promise on prayer (Mt 7:7–8; Lk 11:9–10) can be misused 'to spend what you get on your pleasures' (v. 3).

(4:4–6) Grace to the Humble The antagonism between 'friendship with the world' and being an 'enemy of God' (v. 4) is like the ethical dualism in the Enochic literature (1 Enoch 48:7; 108:8), Qumran (*Jub.* 30:19–22), and 1 Jn 2:15–17, but a parallel can also be found in the Jesus tradition (Mt 6:24; Lk 16:13). v. 5 may introduce a citation from an unknown work (NRSV), but it is also possible to translate the verse (cf. 4:11) as two rhetorical questions: 'Does scripture speak in vain? Does the spirit which he made to dwell in us crave enviously?' (Johnson 1995: 280–2). Apparently, *pneuma* refers neither to the Holy Spirit nor to the human spirit but to a type of good inclination given by God (cf. *T. Dan*, 5:1–3; *T. Jos.* 10:2–3; *T. Ben.* 6:4). The Greek noun *phthonos*, 'envy', was never connected with God. In fulfilling the promise of Scripture and the right human desire God gives a 'greater gift' (v. 6, own tr.) which should be identified with the wisdom (cf. 3:13–18) he will grant to the humble. This is argued by a citation of Prov 3:34 in a specific text-form found also in 1 Pet 5:5. The whole context of Prov 3:19–35 forms the background of Jas 3:13–4:10.

(4:7–10) Humble before God This imperative section has a clear structure. There are three couplets of imperatives (vv. 7b–9), framed by two other imperatives with the subject of submitting oneself to God (vv. 7a, 10), thus forming a fivefold structure. Submission to God and resistance to the devil makes Satan flee (4:4; cf. Lk 4:13). The idea of 'drawing near to God' (v. 8) is expressed in cultic language (Ex 19:22; 24:2; Deut 16:16; Ps 122; 145). The imperative to 'mourn' (v. 9) may echo Jesus' woe against the rich (Lk 6:25). v. 10 seems to be a rather clear allusion to the logion of Jesus concluding the parable of the Pharisee and the tax collector (Lk 18:14; cf. Lk 14:11; 1 Pet 5:6). So, perhaps, here 'grace' (4:6) may include not only the gift of wisdom, but also the forgiveness of sins.

(4:11–12) God as Only Lawgiver and Judge The letter's three important motifs, not to speak evil against or judge a brother (cf. Mt 7:1–2; Lk 6:37–8), and to be a doer of the law, are summarized (v. 11). No human being can be the final judge since this is the privilege of God (cf. Rom 14:4) who gave the law (v. 12).

Warning to the Rich (4:13–5:6)

(4:13–17) Tomorrow Belongs to God This admonition resembles the polemic in 1 Enoch 97:8–10 and the parable of the rich fool (Lk 12:16–21), the latter itself showing parallels to the Enochic tradition. In contrast to the rich in 5:1 the merchants here seem to be members of the community (v. 13). Under Palestinian conditions they could try to become rich only through trade. Whereas the criticism of care about tomorrow may echo Jesus' teaching (Mt 6:25–34; Lk 12:22–31), 'mist' was a very common metaphor for the passing of life (v. 14). The most dangerous consequence of human 'arrogance' (v. 16) is to forget God, who governs life (v. 15; cf. 1 Enoch 94:8). The Semitic-style maxim in v. 17 reminds one of Jesus' parable of the watchful servants (Lk 12:47).

(5:1–3) Warning to the Rich v. 1 reads like an abbreviation of Jesus' woe against the rich (Lk 6: 24–5), vv. 2–3 could be an allusion to his words on treasures (Mt 6:19–21; Lk 12:33–4). That hoarded goods and their decay will be a witness in the last judgement (v. 3) is also expressed in 1 Enoch 96:7.

(5:4–6) The Oppression of the Poor and the Just What makes things even worse is that the rich gain their goods by injustice. Keeping back the wages of the labourers (v. 4) is an old prophetic accusation (Jer 22:13; Mal 3:5; cf. Tob 4:14). That at this point God's name 'Lord of hosts' (kyrios sabaoth) is cited means that doom is imminent. v. 5 may allude not only to Jer 12:3, but also to Jesus' parable of the rich man and Lazarus (Lk 16:19, 25). The condemnation and killing of the righteous man (v. 6) could be a general attack on judicial murder (cf. Wisd 2:12), but the change from plural to singular is remarkable. In the Lukan special tradition 'the rulers' are singled out as those killing Jesus (Lk 23:13, 35; 24:20; Acts 3:17; cf. 1 Cor 2:8). 'The righteous one' (ho dikaios) was a primitive Jewish-Christian designation of Jesus as the Messiah (Acts 3:14; 7:52; 22:14; cf. Lk 23:37; 1 Pet 3:18; 1 Jn 2:1), a Jewish antecedent is found only in 1 Enoch 38:2; 53:6 (cf. Isa 53:11). Bearing this traditio-historical background in mind, the remark on non-resistance could hint not only in general at the suffering of the righteous, but especially at Jesus' suffering as the Servant of the Lord (Isa 53:7; cf. 1 Pet 2:23).

Patience until the Coming of the Lord (5:7–20)

The last part of the letter treats some problems typical for the life of every community until the end of time. Although it is possible that the coming of God is in view (cf. T. Judah, 22:2; T. Levi, 8:11; As. Mos. 10:12; 1 Enoch 92–105, etc.) it seems more probable that 'until the coming (parousia) of the Lord' (v. 7) refers to the Second Coming of Christ, since the Greek expression has become almost technical in early Christian documents (1 Thess 2:19; 4:15; 5:23; 1 Cor 15:23; Mt 24:3, etc.).

(5:7–9) The Example of the Patient Farmer There could be an allusion to Jesus' parable of the growing seed (Mk 4:26–30), directed against Zealot aspirations to create a pure community. 'The early and the late rain' (v. 7) points to a Syro-Palestinian background, 'the precious fruit of the earth' to rather small farms with short rations. In the OT (Joel 4:13) and in the Jesus tradition (Mt 13:30, 39; Jn 4:35) harvest is a picture for God's judgement, which in James is seen in the near future (v. 8). Against the tendency to judge others once and for all the community members are reminded that God will judge them according to their own standard (v. 9). The warning against 'judging' (krinein) forms an important motif in the Synoptic tradition (Mt 7:1–2; Lk 6:37). That the judge 'is standing at the doors' (v. 9) does not refer to the place of judgement but points to its imminence (cf. Mk 13:29; Mt 24:33; Rev 3:3, 20).

(5:10–12) The Example of the Persecuted Prophets Starting with the Deuteronomistic History (1 Kings 19:10), Jewish tradition (Dan 9:6; T. Levi, 16) spoke of the persecution and martyrdom of the prophets (v. 10). This motif is also found in the synoptic tradition (Mt 23:29–39; Lk 11:47–51; Mk 12:1–12). Jesus compared his destiny (Lk 13:32–3) and that of his followers (Mt 5:11–12; Lk 6:22–3) with the fate of the prophets. If 'the steadfast are called happy' (v. 11a) this might be a reminiscence of Jesus' beatitude of the persecuted. That Job is singled out for his patience (v. 11b) has its background rather in Jewish legends, such as the Testament of Job, than in the OT. Augustine (PL 40.634) thought that 'the purpose of the Lord' refers to the passion of Jesus. But the construction of the sentence is Semitic and refers to the 'outcome' (telos) of Job's story when God showed that he is 'compassionate and merciful'. Perhaps considering the situation of persecution, when believers had to defend themselves in courts, brought to the writer's mind Jesus' warning not to 'swear' (v. 12; cf. Justin Martyr, Apol. 1.18.5). In the Jesus tradition this prohibition is found only in the Matthean special material (Mt 5:34–7) yet in a more elaborate form. The doubling of 'yes and no' here is not a kind of strong affirmation, but a Semitic expression for 'let your yes be yes and your no be no'. This part of the logion was apparently already known to Paul (2 Cor 1:17). The Essenes were famous for denying the oath of loyalty to any human ruler (Jos. J.W. 2.135; cf. Ant. 15.370–2; Philo, Omn. Prob. 84), but the Damascus Document allowed swearing in court (CD 9:9–10; 15:1–2; 16:8–11).

(5:13–15) The Prayer of the Elders for the Sick As the community will ever experience inner strife and outer persecution, so illness of its members will never end before the parousia. Both the sick and the healthy should address God in prayers and psalms (v. 13). But since in the early Christian communities the charisma of healing was present (cf. Mk 16:17–18; 1 Cor 12:9, etc.) a special prayer for the very sick is recommended. They should call 'the elders of the church' (v. 14a) who are either bearers of an office (cf. Phil 1:1; 1 Tim 3:1–7; 5:17; Titus 1:5, etc.) or only respected members of the community, perhaps with special experience in healing. 'To pray over' the sick indicates a laying on of hands as it was known in the OT (Ps 35:13; Tob 1:19; Sir 7:35, etc.) and in contemporary Judaism

(1QapGen 20:21–2, 29). Oil as an agent of miraculous healing is mentioned only in the Markan form of the pre-Easter mission of the disciples (Mk 6:13). That the sick person is 'anointed in the name of the Lord' (v. 14*b*) may hint at this tradition (cf. Mk 9:38). In any case it shows that healing is not a magical rite but practised as part of the lordship of Jesus. Customarily, oil in Jewish (Isa 1:6; Lk 10:34; Jos. *Ant.* 17.172, etc.) as in pagan contexts (Pliny, *NH* 23:39–40; Galen 2:10, etc.) was used as a popular remedy for all kinds of illness. Here, however, it could be a visual sign of the Holy Spirit through whom Jesus worked his healing miracles (Lk 6:16–21 referring to Isa 61:1–2; cf. also *Life of Adam*, 36; *Apoc. Mos.* 9:3). 'The prayer of faith' (v. 15*a*) means the elders' faithful prayer which stands under a great promise (cf. 1:5–8; 4:3). 'That the the prayer of faith will save the sick and the Lord will raise them up' is interpreted either as mental strengthening, eschatological salvation, or physical healing. Although elements of the first and second possibilities may play a role, the third interpretation is the most probable. In the gospel tradition the verbs 'saving' (*sōzein*) and 'raising up' (*egeirein*) are also used for physical healing (cf. Mk 5:23, 28, 34; 10:52; Jn 11:12, respectively Mk 1:31; Mt 9:5–7; Jos. *Ant.* 19.294). In the prayers of the elders the petition for forgiveness is included (v. 15*b*).

(5:16–18) The Effective Prayer of all Community Members The writer shows an intuitive insight into the relation between sin and mental as well as physical health when he admonishes his readers generally to mutual confessions of sins and to common prayers (v. 16*a*). The interdependence of forgiveness by God and one's readiness to forgive others is stressed as in the Lord's Prayer (Mt 6:12; Lk 11:4). There was a widespread belief in Judaism that the prayer of a just man is especially effective (v. 16*b*). One is reminded that according to early church tradition James, the brother of the Lord, himself was 'just' (*dikaios*) and therefore a man of powerful prayer (Hegesippus, in Eus. *Hist. Eccl.* 2.23.4–7). Here, in accordance with Jewish tradition (2 Esd 7:109; *m. Ta'an.* 2:4; *b. Sanh.* 113a), the example is Elijah and his prayer for rain (1 Kings 18:42–5). The timespan of 'three years and six months' (v. 17) is found not in the OT but in the words of Jesus (Lk 4:25). The Lukan special tradition shows a certain interest in Elijah as a prototype for Jesus (Lk 7:11–17; 9:51–62, etc.), but here in James it is stressed against popular Jewish legends (Jeremias, *TDNT* ii. 929–30) and perhaps also against speculations of some on the person of John the Baptist (cf. Jn 1:24–7) that Elijah is a 'man of like nature' (RSV) as the believers (v. 17). The whole formulation of the example has a strong Semitic flavour.

(5:19–20) Bringing Back the Sinners The letter ends with a realistic but positive remark. Even believers can 'wander from the truth' (v. 19). This could be an allusion to the parable of the lost sheep in its Matthean form (Mt 18:12–14), but the theme of the 'bringing or coming back' (*epistrephō*) of a sinning brother is also prominent in Luke's special tradition (Lk 17:3–4). Probably the promise of 'saving the soul' is assigned to the convert, not to the converter, as is also the 'covering of a multitude of sins' (v. 20). This last expression, which was known in Jewish-Christian tradition (1 Pet 4:8; 1 *Clem.* 49:4; 2 *Clem.* 16:4; cf. 1 Cor 13:4–7), could allude to Prov 10:12, but the LXX differs. In one part of the Christian tradition this formulation was regarded as a saying of Jesus (Clem. Al.,

Paed. 3.91.3; *Didascalia*, 4). In any case, the last words of a sometimes stern letter remind the readers of the chances of repentance, forgiveness, and reconciliation.

REFERENCES

Adamson, J. (1976), *The Epistle of James* (Grand Rapids: Eerdmans).

—— (1989), *James: The Man and His Message* (Grand Rapids: Eerdmans).

Baasland, E. (1988), 'Literarische Form, Thematik und geschichtliche Einordnung des Jakobusbriefes', *Aufstieg und Niedergang der Römischen Welt*, 2:25/2 (Berlin: De Gruyter), 3464–84.

Baker, W. R. (1995), *Personal Speech-Ethics in the Epistle of James* (Tübingen: Mohr).

Bauckham, R. J. (1990), *Jude and the Relatives of Jesus in the Early Church* (Edinburgh: T. & T. Clark).

—— (1995), 'James and the Jerusalem Church', in R. J. Bauckham (ed.), *The Book of Acts in its Palestinian Setting* (Grand Rapids: Eerdmans), 419–80.

—— (1999), *James: Wisdom of James, Disciple of Jesus the Sage* (London: Routledge).

Beck, D. L. (1973), 'The Composition of the Epistle of James', Ph.D. diss., Princeton Theological Seminary, 1973.

Betz, O., and Riesner, R. (1994), *Jesus, Qumran, and the Vatican* (London: SCM).

Boccaccini, G. (1998), *Beyond the Essene Hypothesis* (Grand Rapids: Eerdmans).

Bockmuehl, M. (1999), 'Antioch and James the Just', in B. Chilton and C. A. Evans (eds.), *James the Just and Christian Origins* (Leiden: Brill), 155–98.

Davids, P. H. (1982), *The Epistle of James* (Exeter: Paternoster).

—— (1999), 'Palestinian Traditions in the Epistle of James', in B. Chilton and C. A. Evans (eds.), *James the Just and Christian Origins* (Leiden: Brill), 33–57.

Deppe, D. B. (1989), *The Sayings of Jesus in the Epistle of James* (Chelsea, Mich.: Bookcrafters).

Dibelius, M. (1976), *James* (Philadelphia: Fortress).

Frankemölle, H. (1994), *Der Brief des Jakobus* (Gütersloh: Gütersloher).

Geyser, A. S. (1975), 'The Letter of James and the Social Condition of his Addressees', *Neotestamentica* 9: 25–33.

Hartin, P. J. (1991), *James and the Q Sayings of Jesus* (Sheffield: Sheffield Academic Press).

Hengel, M. (1985), 'Jakobus der Herrenbruder—der erste Papst?', in E. Grässer and O. Merk (eds.), *Glaube und Eschatologie* (Tübingen: Mohr), 71–104.

Hoppe, R. (1985), *Der theologische Hintergrund des Jakobusbriefes*, 2nd edn. (Würzburg: Echter).

Jeremias, J. (1954–5), 'Paul and James', *ET* 66: 368–71.

Johnson, L. T. (1995), *The Letter of James* (New York: Doubleday).

Karrer, M. (1989), 'Christus der Herr und die Welt als Stätte der Prüfung. Zur Theologie des Jakobusbriefes', *Kerygma und Dogma*, 35: 166–88.

Kirk, J. A. (1969–70), 'The Meaning of Wisdom in James', *NTS* 16: 24–38.

Klein, M. (1995), *'Ein vollkommenes Werk': Vollkommenheit, Gesetz und Gericht als theologische Themen des Jakobusbriefes* (Stuttgart: Kohlhammer).

Konradt, M. (1998), *Christliche Existenz nach dem Jakobusbrief* (Göttingen: Vandenhoeck).

Lautenschlager, M. (1990), 'Der Gegenstand des Glaubens im Jakobusbrief', *ZTK* 87: 163–84.

Ludwig, M. (1994), *Wort als Gesetz. Eine Untersuchung zum Verständnis von 'Wort' und 'Gesetz' in israelitisch-frühjüdischen und neutestamentlichen Schriften* (Frankfurt: Peter Lang).

Marcus, J. (1982), 'The Evil Inclination in the Epistle of James', *CBQ* 44: 606–21.

Martin, R. P. (1988), *James* (Waco: Word).

Maynard-Reid, P. U. (1987), *Poverty and Wealth in James* (New York: Maryknoll).

Mayor, J. B. (1913), *The Epistle of Saint James*, 3rd edn. (London: Macmillan).

Moo, D. J. (1985), *The Letter of James* (Leicester: Intervarsity Press).

Mussner, F. (1987), *Der Jakobusbrief*, 5th edn. (Freiburg: Herder).

Niebuhr, K. W. (1998), 'Der Jakobusbrief im Licht frühjüdischer Diasporabriefe', *NTS* 44: 420–43.

Penner, T. C. (1996), *The Epistle of James and Eschatology* (Sheffield: Sheffield Academic Press).

Popkes, W. (1986), *Adressaten, Situation und Form des Jakobusbriefes* (Stuttgart: Katholisches Bibelwerk).

Pratscher, W. (1987), *Der Herrenbruder Jakobus und die Jakobustradition* (Göttingen: Vandenhoeck).

Riesner, R. (1993), 'Jesus, the Primitive Community, and the Essene Quarter of Jerusalem', in J. H. Charlesworth (ed.), *Jesus and the Dead Sea Scrolls* (New York: Doubleday), 198–234.

—— (1994), 'James's Speech (Acts 15:13–21), Simeon's Hymn (Luke 2:29–32), and Luke's Sources', in J. B. Green and M. Turner (eds.), *Jesus of Nazareth: Christ and Lord* (Grand Rapids: Eerdmans), 263–78.

—— (1995), 'Synagogues in Jerusalem', in R. J. Bauckham (ed.), *The Book of Acts in Its Palestinian Setting* (Grand Rapids: Eerdmans), 179–211.

—— (1997), 'Paulus und die Jesus-Überlieferung', in J. Ådna, S. J. Hafeman, and O. Hofius (eds.), *Evangelium, Schriftauslegung, Kirche* (Göttingen: Vandenhoeck), 346–65.

—— (1998a), *Paul's Early Period: Chronology, Mission Strategy, Theology* (Grand Rapids: Eerdmans).

—— (1998b), *Essener und Urgemeinde in Jerusalem* (Giessen: Brunnen).

Sacchi, P. (1993), 'Recovering Jesus' Formative Background', in J. H. Charlesworth (ed.), *Jesus and the Dead Sea Scrolls* (New York: Doubleday), 123–39.

Schlatter, A. (1932), *Der Brief des Jakobus* (Stuttgart: Calwer).

Stulac, G. M. (1993), *James* (Leicester: Intervarsity Press).

Tsuji, M. (1997), *Glaube zwischen Vollkommenheit und Verweltlichung. Eine Untersuchung zur literarischen Gestalt und zur inhaltlichen Kohärenz des Jakobusbriefes* (Tübingen: Mohr).

Zahn, T. (1906), *Introduction to the New Testament I* (London: Kregel).

Zimmermann, A. F. (1988), *Die urchristlichen Lehrer*, 2nd edn. (Tübingen: Mohr).

77. I Peter

ERIC EVE

INTRODUCTION

A. Date, Authorship, and Provenance. 1. Despite attempts of scholars such as R. Perdelwitz, B. H. Streeter, H. Windisch, H. Preisker, and F. L. Cross in the first half of the twentieth century to argue to the contrary, I Peter should be read as a genuine letter. Earlier attempts to argue that I Peter was a baptismal sermon or liturgy that was subsequently incorporated into a letter have now largely fallen out of favour.

2. I Peter was quickly accepted as an authentic apostolic writing. The first probable citations from I Peter are in Polycarp's epistle to the Philippians (*c.*130 CE), and the letter is also referred to at 2 Pet 3:1. It is first cited explicitly as a Petrine writing by Irenaeus (in the late second century), and thereafter its use becomes widespread.

3. Despite I Pet 1:1, the author is unlikely to have been the apostle Peter. The cultured Greek of the epistle makes it perhaps the most literary composition in the NT. The apostle Peter probably knew some Greek, but I Peter does not look like the product of an unlettered (Acts 4:13) Galilean fisherman. It employs a sophisticated vocabulary incorporating several NT *hapax legomena*, and its author appears to have some command of the techniques of Hellenistic rhetoric. He is also intimately acquainted with the OT in the LXX, whereas we should have expected the Galilean Peter to have been more familiar with an Aramaic Targum or the Hebrew.

4. One cannot save Petrine authorship by arguing that Peter employed a secretary. If one argues that this secretary was Silvanus, the travelling companion of Paul (e.g. Selwyn 1958) or an anonymous amanuensis of the Roman church (Michaels 1988) the letter then becomes the product not of Peter, but of the secretary, since it is the latter's language that the epistle exhibits (see Beare 1970).

5. The epistle appears to rely heavily on traditions and not on personal reminiscences of Jesus. It is not clear that similarities between I Peter and, for example, Romans and Ephesians require literary dependence, but at first sight the letter does have a deutero-Pauline feel. Yet many distinctive elements of Pauline theology (e.g. justification by faith) are entirely absent from I Peter, and even where characteristic Pauline expressions, such as 'in Christ' are employed, they are hardly used in a distinctively Pauline manner (see I PET 5:14). The epistle also shows some affinities with non-Pauline writings such as James, Hebrews, and I *Clement*. This suggests either that all these writings are drawing on common traditions, or that at least some of them were sufficiently well known to our author to have influenced his language (in favour of literary dependence, see Beare 1970; in favour of common catechetical and liturgical traditions, see Selwyn 1958; Achtemeier 1996). Knowledge of any of these writings would point to a date later than the apostle Peter is meant to have perished, in the Neronian persecution (*c.*66 CE). Indeed, the thought and tenor of the epistle would seem to place it towards the end of the first century, at a stage of development not far removed from that of the Pastoral Epistles (see Best 1971).

6. More specifically, the use of the code name 'Babylon' for Rome (5:13; cf. Rev 14:8; 16:19; 17:5; 18:2, 10, 21) probably reflects the destruction of Jerusalem in 70 CE. There must have been time for Christianity to have spread into a wide region of Asia Minor (1:1) and for the name 'Christian', apparently first coined in Antioch (Acts 11:26), to have become current (4:16). There is, however, still a lively eschatological expectation (4:7, 17), and the letter must be early enough to have been known to Polycarp. All this points to a date somewhere between 70 and 100 CE (so Best 1971; Balch 1981; Elliott 1982; on the inconclusiveness of some of this evidence, however, see Achtemeier 1996).

7. It is conceivable that, as Harnack first argued, the ascription to the apostle Peter was added to the epistle in the second century to secure its place in the canon (although there is no evidence for this). A more probable explanation, however, is that the letter was issued from a circle of Peter's followers in Rome in his name after his death (so Best 1971; Elliott 1982; Achtemeier 1996; on the general issue of pseudepigraphy see EPH C). To be sure, once doubt is cast on the authorship, doubt may also be cast on the identification of Rome ('Babylon') as the place of origin, since this could be part of the mechanism of pseudepigraphy. But the affinities of 1 Peter with 1 *Clement*, together with its possible echoes of Romans, tip the balance in favour of a Roman provenance for this letter.

B. Purpose. The purpose of the letter is not to convey doctrinal information or specific ethical instruction, but rather to urge the recipients to hold fast to their faith in the face of hostility (so Elliott 1982; cf. Thurén 1995; Achtemeier 1996). This, indeed, is roughly what the letter itself states (5:12). It achieves this aim by the threefold strategy of reminding the recipients of the enormous value of what they have already received as Christians (e.g. 1:3, 10–12, 18–21; 2:9–10), by assuring them of their future vindication and reward (e.g. 1:4–5, 13; 4:13; 5:4, 6, 10), and by emphasizing the example of the blameless suffering of Christ (e.g. 2:21–3; 3:18; 4:13). If Peter was known to the recipients to have been martyred for his faith, this may have provided a further reason for writing in his name. However, the sufferings envisaged in the letter appear to be not martyrdom arising from state persecution but verbal and physical abuse from hostile neighbours (e.g. 2:12, 15, 19–20; 3:9, 16; 4:4, 14). The hard-pressed believers are urged to give no needless cause for offence, even under provocation, but to excel in good conduct motivated by their loyalty and obedience to God.

COMMENTARY

Greeting (1:1–2)

(1:1) On the attribution of the letter to the apostle Peter see I PET A. The term 'exiles' does not refer to the Christians' earthly sojourning prior to arriving at their heavenly home, nor is it likely to mean that most of those addressed had the official status of resident aliens prior to their conversion (so Elliott 1981). It may reflect the social experience of the addressees following their conversion, though the language is probably drawn from the story of Israel's progenitor Abraham (Gen 23:4). The exiles are said to be located in the 'Dispersion', which may suggest that they are diaspora Jews. Other indications in the letter, however, suggest that the recipients were formerly pagans (e.g. 1:18; 2:10). The specific region referred to (Pontus, Galatia, etc.) would cover most of Asia Minor north and west of the Taurus mountains. Pliny's letters to Trajan (c.112 CE) indicate that by his day Christianity was well established in Bithynia-Pontus, not only among the towns but also in the countryside.

(1:2) That the recipients are said to have been 'chosen and destined by God the Father' relates their destiny to Christ's (1:20). Just as Christ suffered and was raised to glory (1:11, 21), so too will the Christians suffering abuse receive eschatolo-gical vindication provided they stand firm. One should probably translate v. 2 as 'for obedience [to God rather than Jesus] and sprinkling with the blood of Jesus Christ'. Sprinkling with the 'blood of Jesus Christ' recalls the covenant ceremony of Ex 24:3–8, and suggests that the author sees the church as the people of God constituted by Christ's sacrifice (1:19). It may also suggest that God's people are to share in Christ's sufferings. Grace and peace are common enough in Christian greetings, but may have a special poignancy here, where those wished grace and peace are suffering opposition and abuse (cf. 5:14).

Prooemium (1:3–12)

This section is in the form of a blessing (cf. Eph 1:3; 2 Cor 1:3), though here our author does not merely praise God but sets out the main themes that are to follow. These are that the addressees are greatly privileged as believers, both in what they have received already and in what they can expect in the future. Therefore, they should stand firm despite opposition, regarding their suffering as an opportunity to prove their faith and as a sign that deliverance is at hand.

(1:3–9) In v. 3 the author lays the groundwork of his appeal to the recipients; they have been begotten again (see I PET 1:22–2:3) and as believers they already enjoy great benefits. These are not to be abandoned lightly, even under pressure, for this would also be to forfeit the future benefits promised at v. 4. At v. 5 the author continues to assure his audience of their fundamental security and their ultimate vindication. The salvation mentioned here is probably both from their current troubles and from an adverse judgement by God at the eschaton, whereas 'faith' will include faithfulness to their calling as Christians. The first two words of v. 6 may be translated either 'in whom' (i.e. God) or 'in which', i.e. the entire sentiment expressed in v. 5; NRSV opts for the latter. The addressees can rejoice in the hopes expressed in v. 5 even if they are currently suffering. Here we note two features of the author's rhetorical strategy: (1) The author presumably does not know that his addressees actually *are* rejoicing; he probably suspects the reverse (hence the letter!); but by asserting that they are already doing what he wants he encourages his addressees to accept his view. (2) The author introduces his first explicit reference to suffering with great tact ('even if ... for a little while ...'); later on the sufferings appear more painful; here they are made to appear insignificant compared with the privileges enjoyed. The reference to 'various trials' may indicate a further cause for rejoicing: such trials were expected to beset the faithful at the end-time, so their occurrence can be taken as a sign that the end is near. The trials also allow the suffering recipients to prove their faith (v. 7), that is to demonstrate its worth in adversity just as precious metal is proved and separated from dross in the heat of the refining process. Faith thus proved will result in the suffering faithful receiving (from God) the very things that their unbelieving neighbours are currently denying them (praise, glory, and honour). This will occur 'when Jesus Christ is revealed', i.e. when he appears from heaven at the Parousia, which the author believes to be close at hand (4:7). At vv. 8–9 the author again employs indicatives to describe the attitudes he wants his audience to adopt, love of and belief in Christ and joy in their salvation, which is described as being realized even now.

(1:10–12) The prooemium concludes with a section that emphasizes just how privileged the addressees are. It is they who are the recipients of the great promises the prophets enquired into (vv. 11–12), and they who have received the good news of things into which even angels long to peer (v. 12). Yet what the prophets testified in advance bears directly on our author's theme, for they foresaw that Christ would first suffer and then receive glory, the pattern that the addressees are also expected to follow, as will become increasingly apparent.

Body of Letter, Part 1: Living as God's People (1:13–2:10)

(1:13–21) Redemption into the Christ Group The start of the new section is marked by the word 'therefore' and the shift into the imperative mood (v. 13). Despite NRSV, however, the first word in the imperative is the command to 'hope', the previous two verbs are participles ('discipline yourselves' is more literally, 'being perfectly sober'). Many commentators take the participles here and elsewhere in 1 Peter as having imperatival force, but this is not necessarily the case (see Achtemeier 1996). The author could be describing his addressees as those who have girded the loins of their minds (the imagery is that of fastening one's outer garment around the waist so that it does not impede one's movements, hence NRSV's 'prepare your minds for action') and are perfectly sober, or he may be saying that this is the manner in which they should hope. The object of that hope is eschatological, since it is linked to the Parousia, but the Greek participle (rendered by NRSV as the future 'will bring you') suggests that the promised grace can already begin to be experienced now or in the near future.

The author next contrasts his addressees' former way of life (v. 14) with the holiness to which they are now called (v. 15). Holiness contains the idea of separateness; the addressees are to be a people set apart for God from the surrounding culture. The notion that this holiness is to express itself in conduct (v. 15) is one of the pervading themes of the letter. It is repeated already at v. 17 (NRSV's 'live' is more literally 'conduct yourselves'), where it is related to the final judgement of God. At first sight the sentiment of this verse is strongly at odds with the Pauline doctrine of justification by faith, but compare, e.g., Rom 2:6–11. In any case Paul and 'Peter' would have agreed that being right with God necessitated being part of the people of God now constituted through Jesus Christ, and that this must express itself in conduct (cf. Gal 5:13–26). Our author is concerned with helping his audience cope with the sense of alienation this brings (on 'exiles' see 1 PET 1:1), and so immediately upon urging them to appropriate conduct he reminds them once more of their privileged position (vv. 18–19), this time in terms of the cost of their redemption, and the futility of the life from which they have been redeemed.

Christ is here described in terms of a sacrificial victim (cf. e.g. Lev 1:3, 10; 3:1, 6, etc.). It is not said *how* his sacrifice achieves redemption, but the thought may be that Christ's death deals with sin, enables righteous behaviour (2:24), and allows access to God (2:4) to those who were formerly not his people (2:10). The fledgling Christian church offers a new reference group by which its members measure their conduct, and this enables them to live with a fresh orientation. Our author does not express himself in this sociological language, but he is nevertheless keen to promote the kind of

group cohesion and separateness needed. This group is oriented on Christ not only as its redeemer but as its exemplar. Christ, like them (1:2), was foreknown or 'destined' by God (v. 20). Like them, he suffered (2:21), but since God raised him from the dead and gave him glory, those who pattern themselves on him can hope for the same (v. 21).

The contrast between 'destined' and 'revealed' (v. 20) is not so much intended to teach predestination (see also 1 PET 2:8) as once again to emphasize the privileged status of the believers. What was foreknown from before the creation of the world has only now been made known in the last times (note the eschatological emphasis) and for their sake.

(1:22–2:3) Rebirth through the Word Patterning on Christ must include Christ-like conduct, or 'obedience to the truth' (which is also obedience to God the Father), but can only be sustained in contrast to the world with the aid of a mutually supportive group (1:22), membership of which is a mark of rebirth (see below).

The quotation in 1:24–5a from Isa 40:6–8 is the first of many allusions to Isaiah in this letter. The 'word' is here equated with the good news that has been preached to the addressees, and this perhaps illustrates prophets testifying in advance (1:10). The main point of the quotation, however, is to contrast the transitoriness of natural life with the permanence of the life that springs from God's word. Natural birth is birth into the worldly community. Rebirth by the word comes about through entering the new community that is the redeemed people of God constituted by the word. The worldly community is transitory not only because of normal human mortality, but because it is about to fall under God's judgement (4:17); the alternative community of the word is guaranteed permanence, provided it stands firm, since it is rooted in God, and will be vindicated by him at the last judgement.

Those who have undergone rebirth may be metaphorically described as 'newborn infants' (2:2). Babes are no doubt best fed on pure milk, but there is a play on words in the Greek, since the word translated 'pure' can also mean 'guileless', the quality that would result from obeying the injunctions of 2:1. It is not clear whether the author has primarily in mind his audience's dealings with one another (as the immediate context might suggest) or towards outsiders (as 2:12 indicates). He may well have intended both. Slander is one of the things they seem to have been particularly suffering from outsiders, and they will later be commanded not to revile in turn (3:9). For now the author wishes to remind his audience that rebirth is not enough by itself, it must be followed by growth towards the desired goal (2:2b). The doubt implied by 'if' in 2:3 is a rhetorical device. The recipients will not want to deny that they have tasted God's goodness, and so they will be led into accepting what the author has just said.

(2:4–10) God's Chosen People The recurrence of the word 'stone' throughout this section suggests the thought of a building, in particular the temple (the 'spiritual house' of v. 5), not in the literal sense of the Jerusalem temple, but in the metaphorical sense of God's people (the use of 'temple' to denote one's own elect community is also found in the Qumran literature). The people of God constitutes the other controlling theme in this section, in which language formerly applied to Israel is now applied to the addressees (vv. 5, 9). The purpose is to persuade them of their worth as God's chosen people in the face of a hostile environment.

The living stone (Christ) at v. 4 is said to have been rejected, not by the Jews, but by humankind in general; there is little anti-Judaism in this epistle, even though its addressees (unlike Paul's Gentile addressees) are regarded as having taken over the role of Israel without remainder (so Achtemeier 1996). The addressees are also to become living stones (v. 5), and thus to share the fate of Christ their exemplar. Just as he was rejected by humans but was chosen and honoured (rather than NRSV's 'precious') with God, so too those who are experiencing rejection on account of their faith have been chosen and will be honoured by God. Honour, a pivotal value in Mediterranean society (Malina 1983), is precisely what these Christians lack in the eyes of their unbelieving neighbours. The phrase 'chosen and honoured' thus reassures the audience of their true status, as well as preparing for the quotation from Isa 28:16 that is to follow (v. 6; cf. Rom 9:33). Believers are also promised honour at v. 7 (which should be translated 'so to you who believe is the honour'), in contrast to the stumbling that is the fate of the unbeliever (vv. 7b–8). The function of v. 8 is not to teach that some individuals were foreordained to stumble, but rather to reassure the addressees that their persecutors are heading for a fall, and that this is all within God's plan.

Although the language of priesthood and sacrifice (vv. 5, 9) is cultic, this probably derives from the use of the temple as a metaphor for God's elect people (rather than referring to Christian worship). It may be, however, that the 'spiritual sacrifice' the author intends is that of costly obedience to God in the face of abuse, since he later goes on to stress the passion of Christ as the pattern of uncomplaining suffering for the believer (2:21–4; 3:17–19; 4:13–14).

v. 10 (like 1:18) suggests that the author is addressing converts from paganism rather than Jews (this verse is an allusion to Hos 2:23; cf. Paul's use of Hos 1:10 at Rom 9:25–6). He concludes this section by again reminding them of their privileges. The implication is that they would be foolish to give up such a glorious state and revert to their former paganism, for that would be to give up light, mercy, and belonging for darkness, no mercy, and non-belonging.

Body of Letter, Part 2: Good Conduct in the Face of Suffering (2:11–4:11)

The word 'beloved' (2:11) marks the start of a major new division both here and at 4:12. The first section lays down general principles of conduct, which are then exemplified in the 'household code' of 2:18–3:7. This is followed by further general advice on how the beleaguered believers should respond to the sufferings inflicted on them by hostile neighbours.

(2:11–17) Principles of Conduct in Human Society The author is anxious to preserve the distinctness of the communities he is addressing vis-à-vis their cultural context, but he does not do so in a straightforwardly counter-cultural way, any more than he is straightforwardly conformist. On the one hand Christians are to abstain from fleshly desires (v. 11), which the author regards as characteristic of the pagan society from which they are now alienated (cf. 4:3). On the other their

conduct in that society is to be good and seen to be good, even by pagan standards (vv. 11–12; although the NRSV translates 'honourably' in v. 11 and 'honourable deeds' in v. 12, the underlying Greek word kalos means 'good' or 'beautiful'). To be sure, their conduct must also be good by God's standards, and will then receive divine vindication at the final judgement. The evildoing of which these Christians may have been suspected could include the suspicion of 'atheism', that is refusing to honour the traditional gods, so risking their displeasure. It may also have included political disloyalty, not simply through refusal to take part in the emperor cult, but through forming an unauthorized grouping (or collegium) which could appear political in nature to the Roman authorities.

It may be for this reason that the author urges due submission to the political authorities (vv. 13–14; cf. Rom 13:1–5). Believers are not to court persecution, but rather to silence the 'ignorance of idiots' by right conduct. The 'idiots' may be those who make trouble for Christians by reporting their alleged misconduct to the authorities; the Christians' good conduct is to give the lie to such slanders. Being urged to live as servants (lit. slaves) of God (v. 16) is double-edged: it entails obedience to God, but it also implies security and status. In so far as God is superior to the emperor, so God's servants are superior to Caesar's. In any case, the apparently conformist advice is given a firm counter-cultural ground, since it is to be motivated by ultimate loyalty to God's will (vv. 13, 15) rather than to any human institution.

This nuanced exhortation to counter-cultural conformity is summed up at v. 17 (cf. Mk 12:17). At the extremities of this verse, honour (the pivotal value of the culture) is to be paid to all outsiders, and to the emperor in particular (cf. Rom 13:7). At its core, however, the Christian fellowship is to be loved and God is to be 'feared', that is, reverenced. How this works out in detail is exemplified in the discussion that follows.

(2:18–3:22) The Principles in Practice At first sight, this section resembles the household codes found, for example, at Col 3:18–4:1 and Eph 5:21–6:9 (on household codes in the NT see EPH 5:21–6:9 and Balch 1981). This section may indeed derive from such material, but this is not its primary purpose here. A household code would normally give advice on the duties of parents and children, slaves and masters, and husbands and wives. Here no advice is given to parents, children, or masters, and that given to husbands is perfunctory. By focusing on slaves and wives, the author concentrates on two specially vulnerable groups. He thus both directly gives advice to these two groups and indirectly employs them as examples of proper submission for all Christians.

NRSV translates the Greek participles of 2:18 and 3:1 as imperatives ('accept the authority'), but it may be that they should be understood as participles expanding on 2:17 ('Honour all men ... by accepting') (so Achtemeier 1996). Slaves and women thus provide paradigms for the injunctions of 2:17.

Slaves should follow the example of Christ (2:18–25): The 'slaves' of 2:18 are literally 'household servants' (oiketai). In a non-Christian household they might find themselves under pressure to conform to their master's religion. Although household slaves in the Roman empire were by no means universally mistreated, they were always liable to punishment or abuse from those they served. The advice given is outwardly conformist, namely to submit to the master's authority, but they are not to submit to the extent of renouncing their faith or their place in the Christian community, and if they suffer for this alone (rather than for any actual misdemeanour), they will have God's approval even if they do not enjoy that of their master (vv. 19–20). This limited conformity informed by a counter-cultural loyalty is very similar to the attitude of the early church to the Roman state, and thus serves as a suitable illustration of 2:11–17.

The greater part of this advice to slaves is taken up with expounding the example of the innocent suffering of Christ (vv. 21–5), who, as we have already seen, is the pattern for all believers (v. 21). The description of Christ's behaviour in vv. 22–3 is thus the ideal to which suffering slaves, and indeed any suffering Christians, should aspire, even if they could not expect to be totally without sin. The language in which Christ's suffering is described here reflects the servant poem in Isa 53. The precise notion of atonement in v. 24 is hard to discern. The language might almost suggest that he took our sins into his body and made a sacrificial offering of them upon the cross, but such a thought would have no parallel in the NT, not least because the notions of offering *sins* as a sacrifice would be very odd. Given the other allusions to Isa 53 one might do better to see this verse as an adaptation of Isa 53:4–5 to fit Christ's death on the cross, without any clearly worked out theory of atonement behind it: the notion of vicarious *punishment* is not stated, although the notion that innocent *suffering* vicariously deals with others' sins may be presupposed. *Apogenomenoi* (v. 24, NRSV, 'free') could be rendered 'having been made to have no part in' but could also mean 'dead'. Here one should probably translate 'having died to sin', contrasted with 'live for righteousness'. What should have died for the addressees is the former identity that let itself be defined by the surrounding pagan culture (4:3).

Wives should follow the example of Sarah (3:1–6): Much of the advice given to wives is outwardly conformist. That wives should accept their husband's authority and not answer back (v. 1) would be a commonplace, and there are both pagan and Jewish parallels (Isa 3:18–24; Prov 11:22; 31:10–30) to preferring inward beauty to outward adornment (vv. 3–4). The author gives his advice a religious slant by appealing to examples from the biblical past, appealing especially to Sarah who, as Abraham's wife, might be the natural type of the faithful female as Abraham was of the faithful male (Beare 1970). The advice becomes counter-cultural in two places. First, the wives' silent submission is to be part of a strategy for winning the unbelieving husband to the faith (vv. 1–2), rather than the total surrender that would entail adopting the husband's faith, as the surrounding culture would expect (Balch 1981). Secondly, the wives are not to fear intimidation (NRSV 'never let fears alarm you', v. 6), which may again mean they are to stand their ground on the issue of their faith.

Husbands must honour their wives (3:7): The brief advice to husbands further undermines a conventional reading of the female submission urged in 3:1–6. In Mediterranean society, honour was primarily a pivotal value to be sought by *men*, but here men are urged to ascribe it to their wives. The reason for paying them honour is directly counter-cultural and characteristically Christian, namely that they are the weaker sex (literally 'vessel'). Here, 'weaker' means merely physically weaker; women are certainly not to be regarded as less valuable, but rather as co-heirs. The way husbands live with their wives should reflect this; it should be done 'according to knowledge'. This could mean 'show[ing] consideration' (as NRSV), but might equally refer to the knowledge that women are co-heirs and thus equally valued by God (Selwyn 1958). Failure to recognize this may result in a breakdown of one's prayer-life, perhaps through a false conception of God.

All must love one another and bear suffering righteously (3:8–17): The word 'finally' suggests that what follows rounds off the section; having advised specific groups the author now describes how the commands of 2:17 are to be realized by all believers. Here, the author seems to be thinking of how Christians should behave towards one another, and in so doing again urges attitudes that aid group cohesion.

v. 9 again begins with a participle ('not repaying'), indicating that the author is still expanding on 2:17. The advice is similar to Rom 12:14 or Mt 5:44, and so the author is plausibly reminding the addressees of teaching they have already received when he tells them that they have been called to this task. The quotation from Ps 34:12–15 (vv. 10–12) makes the point that the Lord favours those who do and speak good things, and opposes those who do the opposite. v. 9 thus most probably means that the believers' calling is to bless at all times, not only when reviled. They will then be blessed in turn, whereas the punishment of their persecutors can be left to God.

Nonetheless, it is the audience's behaviour in the face of abuse that is the author's prime concern, and he is anxious that the beleaguered communities addressed should make the best possible impression on outsiders, both to avoid provoking unnecessary persecution (v. 13) and to attract further converts (v. 15). Aggressive evangelizing is discouraged, however (vv. 15–16). Believers should explain their hope when asked, but do so respectfully. Ideally, their conduct will bear out the genuineness of their faith (v. 16b). It is not clear precisely how those who revile Christians for their good conduct will be 'put to shame'. This could mean that they will be seen as malicious slanderers by more fair-minded non-believers, thereby winning sympathy for believers, but the phrase could also suggest an unfavourable verdict at the last judgement. Perhaps this ambiguity is deliberate. In any case, the author sees innocent suffering nobly borne as valuable in itself (vv. 14, 17). The idea that it is better to suffer wrong than to do wrong (v. 17) was not uncommon in the ancient world, but here it is given a distinctive theological underpinning, and so neatly sums up the author's main message. At v. 17 it is related to God's will (NRSV correctly brings out the Greek optative by translating 'if suffering should be God's will'; the author tactfully allows that it may not necessarily be); at vv. 14–15 the language recalls that of Isa 8:12b–13.

Since the suffering Christ has conquered evil (3:18–22): The word 'For' with which v. 18 opens grammatically connects this section with what has immediately preceded, but since the theme of unmerited suffering has formed a continuous thread throughout the exhortations following 2:17, this concluding section gives the Christological ground for all that has gone before. Rhetorically, these verses serve to reassure the addressees that their suffering, if borne rightly, really will lead to blessing, since the suffering Christ (their pattern) has overcome all evil powers.

The immediate connection between the suffering believer in 3:17 and the suffering Christ in v. 18 reminds the addressees that Christ is their pattern. Whether one reads 'you' or 'us' at v. 18, the point remains the same: Christ's righteous suffering has freed the believers from their former sins and given them access to God. They are accordingly reminded of their baptism, by which they appropriated the benefits of Christ's death. This baptism takes its effectiveness not from the cleansing power of the water, but from Christ's resurrection (v. 21). v. 18b is unlikely to mean that Christ was put to death as a physical being but raised as a spiritual one. It is also unlikely to mean that Christ was put to death by humans (cf. the meaning of 'flesh' at 1:24) but raised by the Spirit, although this would be grammatically possible (so Achtemeier 1996). It is most likely to mean that Christ was put to death in the human, worldly sphere but raised to life in the spiritual sphere (Best 1971). This is not a denial of bodily resurrection. Instead it underlines the fact that Christ's risen life is no mere continuation of natural, earthly existence but is rather an anticipation of the age to come, 'spiritual' because lived directly in the presence of God (cf. 1 Cor 15:35–57). It was in the spiritual sphere that Christ made a proclamation to the imprisoned spirits (vv. 19–20). Traditionally these puzzling verses have been interpreted as Christ's preaching the good news to the pre-Christian dead in the underworld. This is probably not what the author meant, however. First, there is nothing in the text to suggest a descent. Secondly, the Greek word for 'made a proclamation' (*ekēruxen*) need not imply preaching good news; here it probably means that Christ proclaimed his victory. Thirdly, the description of these imprisoned spirits at vv. 19–20 suggests that they are the angelic beings of Gen 6:1–6 whose disobedience ultimately led to the Flood (cf. *Jub.* 7:21; *1 Enoch* 6–10; 18:12–19:2). It would, in any case, be strange if Christ's preaching to the spirits of deceased humans were restricted to the disobedient contemporaries of Noah, even if 'spirits' most naturally referred to dead humans, which it does not. The point is then that at his resurrection Christ proclaimed his victory to the archetypally wicked spirits that had troubled humanity; as a consequence of his resurrection Christ now reigns with God and all spiritual powers have been made subject to him (v. 22). This is intended to reassure those who pattern themselves on Christ that the powers to which they are temporarily subject, including potentially hostile political authorities and abusive neighbours, have already been defeated in their spiritual backers. The Flood story provides a further link with their own experience by relating the waters through which Noah's family was brought safely to the saving water of baptism (vv. 20–1). A further implication may be that the ark is a type of the believing community, and that now is not a good time to jump ship (the Flood being a type of the coming judgement).

(4:1–11) Living a Christian Life The author now urges his addressees to behave in a manner that will preserve their distinctiveness as Christian communities, first by refraining

from their former pagan excesses and so maintaining their boundary with the world (vv. 1–6), and secondly by acting in ways that promote the cohesion of their believing communities (vv. 7–11).

In relation to outsiders (4:1–6): The author again refers to Christ's suffering, but this time as the basis not so much for suffering as for conduct that is distinctive from that of the surrounding culture. Many pagan moralists would also have condemned most of the pursuits listed at v. 3, but the believers are to be distinctive in actually avoiding them, and doing so as an expression of God's will (v. 2). This will alienate (a possible meaning of the word translated 'surprised' at v. 4) their former companions, but this is the price that must be paid for standing firm in the redeemed community of God's people. By warning that those who persist in this stream of dissipation will have to face judgement (v. 5) the author not only comforts his audience with the thought that these outsiders will get their requital, but also warns them not to lapse from their faith and so rejoin the community of the condemned.

The preaching of the gospel to the dead (v. 6) has been variously interpreted in relation to the imprisoned spirits of 3:19, or to the pre-Christian dead (so Best 1971), or to the spiritually dead. Another option is to see this verse as a reference to Christians who have died (taking 'proclaimed even to the dead' to mean 'proclaimed to those who have since died'), rejected by the world (judged in the realm of the flesh) but alive in the spirit according to God's standards (so Achtemeier 1996). The function of the verse is then to reassure the addressees that those of their number who have died did not believe in vain. None of these interpretations is without its problems, however, and although the last one perhaps fits the context best, it is not the most obvious way of construing the text.

In relation to other believers (4:7–11): The author proceeds to urge his hearers towards conduct that will strengthen their pressurized communities: they are to practise mutual love (v. 8) and uncomplaining hospitality (v. 9), and to use their several gifts in the service of the community (vv. 10–11). Hospitality would be necessary for Christians travelling, either for missionary work or to escape persecution elsewhere or even on their own business. Within a settled community it would also be necessary for those with larger houses to offer hospitality for the congregation to meet.

This is set against a background of eschatological urgency (v. 7), which serves a dual function. On the one hand it reassures the hearers that they do not have long to wait for relief and vindication; on the other it warns them that they will not have much time left if they fall away now. They are accordingly urged to be serious and sober, in contrast to the drunken debauchery of their pagan peers.

The doxology at v. 11 is brief; it concludes a major division of the letter, but not the letter itself (cf. 5:11). Grammatically 'To him' would most naturally refer back to Jesus Christ, but it is more likely meant to refer back to God, for whom glory is desired in the immediately preceding sentence (cf. 2:12; 5:11).

Body of Letter: Conclusion (4:12–5:11)

(4:12–19) Submit to Suffering The start of the final major division of the letter is marked by the opening word 'Beloved' (v. 12; cf. 2:11). Although the reference to a 'fiery ordeal' (v. 12) might suggest that the situation has grown graver, it still seems to be primarily verbal abuse that the author has in mind (v. 14). More severe forms of suffering are not excluded, and it may be that there was a constant danger of sporadic local agitation against Christians leading to Roman magistrates applying the death penalty. However, it is by no means necessary that the reference to suffering 'as a Christian' (v. 16) has this kind of semi-official persecution in view. The point is not that Christians may have to suffer 'for the name' because Christianity has become a proscribed religion, but rather that if Christians do find themselves suffering, they are blessed if and only if it is purely their faith, and not any criminal or antisocial behaviour, that has provoked opposition against them (vv. 15–16).

The word rendered by NRSV as 'mischief maker' in v. 15 is *allotriepiskopos*, which, though rare in Greek literature, occurs elsewhere in the sense 'busybody'. It may seem strange to put busybodies in the same category as murderers and thieves, but the sense intended may be 'meddlers in the affairs of outsiders' (the Greek word literally means 'overseer of others'). The point may then be that members of the Christian community are not to attract unfavourable attention by interfering in other people's business.

If the prospect of suffering now seems more intense, this is partly because the author gives it a clear eschatological interpretation. The 'fiery ordeal' (v. 12) is to be understood, not as a heating up of official opposition to Christianity, but as the sufferings associated with the end-time; which is why the addressees should not be surprised. It is the first stage of the last judgement (v. 17), which begins with the 'house of God' (AV), i.e. the temple taken as a metaphor for God's people (cf. Isa 10:11–12; Jer 25:29; Ezek 9:6; Mal 3:1–6). If things seem bad for the believers, they will turn out much worse for outsiders (vv. 17b–18), so despite what they are suffering now, the addressees had far better endure (and not lapse). Indeed, since their present sufferings are a sign of their imminent vindication, they should rejoice (v. 13) and entrust themselves to God (v. 19).

(5:1–5) Submit to One Another Having again addressed the external pressures on the scattered Christian communities of Asia Minor, the author turns once more to their internal group cohesion. This time he is primarily concerned with relations between elders and those who are younger (vv. 2–3). Although this could refer to relative biological age, it is more likely to refer to the length of time people have spent in the faith. Whether the author envisages a distinct order of 'elder' (*presbuteros*) or 'presbyter' is unclear; the word may simply be borrowed from contemporary Jewish practice rather than denoting the later order of Christian ministry. But these elders clearly have some duty of pastoral oversight (v. 2), which they are to exercise in a godly rather than worldly fashion (v. 3; cf. Mk 10:42–5). In particular they are to be examples (or 'types') for their flock; elsewhere Christ is held up as an example for the believer, particularly in respect of his innocent suffering, so it may be that this is the type of example the elders are to set (as they are also to be sharers in Christ's glory: vv. 1b, 4). That the author describes himself as a witness of Christ's sufferings (v. 1) cannot be used to prove Petrine authorship. The word translated 'witness' (*martus*) means one who testifies

rather than one who sees at first hand; compare the prophets who testified in advance to Christ's sufferings (1:11). There may nevertheless be an allusion to the fact that the Apostle Peter testified to Christ's sufferings by his martyrdom. The self-designation of the author as a 'fellow-elder' at v. 1 appears modest if the author is meant to be the Apostle Peter, but if Peter was known to have been martyred this would strengthen the appeal to the elders to suffer likewise.

This appeal to the elders does not necessarily mean that the author believes them to be defective; the point is rather that they have a vital role to play in keeping the beleaguered communities together. But this also requires that their leadership be respected (v. 5). Nevertheless, the author wants not so much hierarchical subordination as mutual submission (v. 5), of which slaves and wives were earlier the exemplars (2:18–3:7). The quotation from Prov 3:34 then serves at least three functions: it provides a scriptural warrant for the exhortation to mutual submission; it hints that any proud oppressors troubling the community are opposed by God; and it leads into the next section.

(5:6–11) Submit to God Since the addressees' present trials are the start of God's final judgement on the world (4:17), the proper attitude is to submit to them as God's will; one will then receive ultimate vindication (v. 6; cf. Mt 23:12/Lk 14:11; Jas 4:10). The command to be sober (v. 8) recalls 4:7; there the context was eschatological urgency, also implied here by the command to be watchful (cf. Mk 13:34–7). The immediate context here, though, is that of their spiritual foe. The idea is that a sheep detached from the fold (cf. 2:25; 5:2) is more likely to fall victim to a predatory lion. The members of the community are thus exhorted to stand firm within the community, and it is by this means that they will resist the devil (v. 9; cf. Jas 4:7). In the author's view divine judgement is a blessing in disguise since it shows that the end-time deliverance is near and enables believers to prove the value of their faith. Failure to stand firm would turn this disguised blessing into a diabolical snare, since those who fall away fail the test, forfeit their salvation, and revert to the community of the lost; the addressees are thereby warned that falling away from faith to escape persecution is worse than useless. In any case, the suffering is only to be 'for a little while', after which God himself will relieve them, for they are destined for glory in Christ (v. 10; cf. 1:5–6). In the meantime they are only having to undergo what Christians everywhere are suffering (v. 9b). This can hardly refer to an empire-wide official persecution of the church, since there is no evidence that this occurred before 250 CE under Emperor Decius. It must refer rather to the type of verbal abuse, harassment, and social pressure already referred to in the letter, perhaps coupled with the sporadic but everpresent threat of more violent local persecution fomented by hostile pagan neighbours.

The brief doxology at v. 11 (cf. 4:11) concludes this final division of the body of the letter, which has itself summarized the main argument of the letter.

Epistolary Closing (5:12–14)

v. 12 succinctly states the purpose of the letter. Grace (*charis*) has a number of meanings for this author; here it may mean both eschatological salvation and that which is pleasing to

God. The phrase 'through Silvanus' would not normally mean that Silvanus is the amanuensis through whom 'Peter' has written; it would more naturally mean that Silvanus is the bearer of the letter. If so, then there is no reason for supposing that he is the same Silas/Silvanus mentioned by Paul and Acts, who was in any case an associate of Paul rather than Peter. Rather than being a pseudepigraphal device he may be a real person, commended by the author as the bearer (and interpreter?) of the letter, but otherwise unknown to us. NRSV is probably correct in interpreting the co-elect female of v. 13 as a church (in Greek feminine *ekklēsia*). 'Babylon' is almost certainly a code-name for Rome, the destroyer of Jerusalem in 70 CE as ancient Babylon (apparently an uninhabited ruin by the first century) had been in 587 BCE. It is unclear whether 'my son Mark' is a reference to the John Mark mentioned in Acts. This Mark was associated with Paul and Barnabas rather than Peter, though it may be that the author knew the tradition that Mark acted as Peter's interpreter. But since Mark was a very common name in the Roman empire it is conceivable that 'my son Mark' is an oblique self-reference to the Petrine disciple who was the actual author of the letter.

The kiss of love (v. 14) was a mark of early Christian communities, and here our author takes one last opportunity to urge his audience towards group-reinforcing behaviour. Again, 'peace' is a conventional element in a concluding formula, but here it possesses an added poignancy as that which the recipients feel they do not enjoy from their hostile neighbours. 'In Christ' is basically a way of saying 'Christian', but it also expresses where the author hopes his addressees will remain, rooted in Christ as their pattern and the true source of their peace despite the hostility of an uncomprehending world.

REFERENCES

Achtemeier, P. J. (1996), *1 Peter* (Minneapolis: Fortress).

Balch, D. L. (1981), *Let Wives Be Submissive: The Domestic Code in 1 Peter*, SBLMS 26 (Chico, Calif.: Scholars Press).

Beare, F. W. (1970), *The First Epistle of Peter*, 3rd edn. (Oxford: Basil Blackwell).

Best, E. (1971), *1 Peter*, NCB (London: Marshall, Morgan & Scott).

Elliott, J. H. (1982), *A Home for the Homeless* (London: SCM).

Malina, B. J. (1983), *The New Testament World* (London: SCM).

Michaels, J. R. (1988), *1 Peter*, WBC 49 (Waco, Tex.: Word).

Selwyn, E. G. (1958), *The First Epistle of St. Peter* (London: Macmillan).

Thurén, L. (1995), *Argument and Theology in 1 Peter: The Origins of Christian Paraenesis* (Sheffield: Academic Press).

78. 2 Peter

JEREMY DUFF

INTRODUCTION

The Second Letter of Peter is often an unwelcome guest at the table of NT scholarship: its focus on the coming judgement finds little favour in the modern age, and the long-running dispute over the letter's origins have left commentators unsure how to approach the text. Because of this, significant space is given here to the question of the letter's origins, though in the process many features of the text are highlighted.

A. Literary Relationships. 1. 2 Peter and Jude. 2 Peter 2:1–3:3 is closely related to Jude 4–13: the attack on the false teachers is very similar in both substance and order (except that 2:12, 13, 15 = Jude 10, 12, 11). Common authorship, however, founders on the difference in style and outlook and on the discordant use of the same metaphors (e.g. 2:11–15, cf. Jude 9–13). Two explanations are feasible: one used the other, or both used a common source. If direct dependence is assumed, Jude is demonstrably prior. For example, Jude 12–13 describes the false teachers successively as clouds, trees, waves, and stars for whom the darkness has been reserved (for wandering stars = angels consigned to darkness cf. *1 Enoch*, 10:1–6; 83:1–11, a text used elsewhere in Jude). 2 Pet 2:17 however, leaps from clouds to the darkness—bizarre but explicable as an abridgement of Jude (see also 2:11, cf. Jude 9). Furthermore, it would be difficult to explain the abandoning of much of 2 Peter's argument to produce the brief Jude, while the reverse seems more reasonable. However, the paucity of close verbal agreements means that a common source (similar to Jude 4–13) is quite feasible. 2 Peter's dependency on Jude would have the virtue of simplicity, but this is insufficient to prove the case.

The approach taken here is that 2 Peter depended on a text similar to Jude 4–13.

2. 2 Peter and 1 Peter. 2 Peter differs from 1 Peter in style, as recognized both by modern critics and by earlier commentators (e.g. Jerome, *Epistles*, 120.11; Calvin, *Commentary on 2 Peter*, Preface): while 1 Peter is elegantly simple, 2 Peter is grandiose and elaborate (affected by the emerging Asiatic style of Greek rhetoric). Similarly, the two letters differ in terminology: for example 2 Peter refers to Jesus' return as *parousia* (coming: 1:16; 3.4; cf. 3:12), 1 Peter as *apokalupsis* (revelation: 1:7, 13; 4:13). 2 Peter appears more Hellenistic with its stress on knowledge (1:2, 3, 8; 2:20) and the 'partaking in the divine nature' (1:4, contrast 1 Pet 1:9). Only three features connect the letters. First, both are ascribed to Peter and contain very similar salutations, but 2 Peter differs in using Simeon as the preferred name for Peter (1:1–2; 1 Pet 1:1–2). Secondly, 2:5 uses the example of Noah, absent from the Jude parallel (5–7) but present in 1 Pet 3:20. However, the usage is different and the flood is a common image for judgement (e.g. Mt 24:38–9). Thirdly, 3:1 declares itself to be a second letter: apparently a reference to 1 Peter, although a lost letter is possible. Overall, there is no conscious attempt to imitate 1 Peter.

3. 2 Peter and Other Texts. Although 2 Peter explicitly refers to Paul's letters (3:15–16), it is not dependent on them: the only connections, e.g. the Lord's return like a thief (3:10, cf. 1 Thess 5:2, 4), are part of the wider Christian tradition (cf. Mt 24:42–4; Rev 3:3; 16:15). 2 Peter's description of the transfiguration (1:16–18, cf. Mk 9:2–8 and par.) and prediction of Peter's death (1:14, cf. Jn 13:36; 21:18–19) show no clear dependence on any written gospel. Many of the later Petrine writings, such as the *Apocalypse of Peter* and *Acts of Peter* depend on 2 Peter. *1–2 Clement* and the Shepherd of Hermas show some connection with 2 Peter (e.g. *1 Clem.* 23.3 ‖ *2 Clem.* 11.2, cf. 3.4).

B. Dating. Three different strategies can be used to date 2 Peter. First, its relationships with other texts: it must post-date several of Paul's letters (therefore after 60 CE), and 1 Peter and the Jude-like source (whose dates are disputed), but pre-date the *Apocalypse of Peter* (thus before 130 CE). The second strategy, locating it within a model of the development of Christianity, suggests closer to 60 than 130 CE: Hellenistic expressions (e.g. 1:4, 13–14) can be paralleled in first-century Jewish texts, there is no promotion of church order, 'your apostles' (3:2) suggests a time before 'apostle' was used only for the twelve founders of the church universal (cf. 1 Cor 9:2; 2 Cor 8:23; Phil 2:25; *Didache*, 11.3–6), and the opponents are more similar to those in Corinth in the 50s than to second-century Gnostics. The third strategy focuses on two particular passages: 3:4 and 3:15–16. In 3:4 the scoffers claim that the promise of 'his coming' has failed: 'the fathers' (NRSV, 'our ancestors') have died yet life continues as before. This points to bewilderment among Christians as the founding generation of the church died prior to the Lord's expected return (alluded to, perhaps, in e.g. Mk 9:1; 13:30). By, say, 120 CE this would be an outdated issue. However, concern over the death of 'the fathers' would have grown from the 50s onwards (cf. 1 Thess 4:13–18; Jn 21:23, and the redaction of Mk 9:1 in Mt 16:28 ‖ Lk 9:27). Nevertheless, if 'since the fathers died' means that *all* the generation had died, after 80 CE seems most likely. 3:15–16 refer to Paul's letters being twisted as are 'the other scriptures'. This bracketing of Paul's letters with 'the scriptures' implies that they were seen as divinely inspired (3:15, 'wisdom given to him'), but not necessarily 'canonical'. Since Paul referred to his own words as (conveying) the inspired words of God (1 Thess 2:13; 1 Cor 2:13; 14:37–8; cf. 1 Pet 4:11) and ordered that they be read in the churches (Col 4:16; 1 Thess 5:27, cf. reading of the Jewish Scriptures), 3:15–16 would be feasible during Paul's lifetime, though it is suggestive of a later period. However, the reference to Paul merely as a 'dear brother' is in marked contrast to the exalted epithets he received in *1 Clem.* 47.1 and later texts. Overall, these approaches point towards the period 60–130 CE, with some reason to favour 80–90 CE.

C. Genre. 2 Peter has a letter format and, despite the generality of the address (1:1), the specificity of the questions dealt with (esp. 1:16–21 and 3:4–13, not paralleled in Jude) suggests that a particular audience was in mind. The letter can be broken down into the standard features of Greek rhetoric: 1:3–15—*exordium* (announcement of the topic and request for a hearing); 1:16–3:13—*probatio* (presentation of the case); 3:14–18—*peroratio* (recapitulation and final appeal). It has been suggested that 2 Peter is generically a 'Testament'—a contemporary Jewish genre in which dying heroes give ethical admonitions and prophecies (e.g. *Testaments of the Twelve Patriarchs*). 2 Peter does indeed have testamental features: the occasion of the writing is Peter's impending death (1:12–15), it includes prophecies (2:1–3; 3:3–4) and ethical instruction (esp. 1:3–11). Nevertheless it cannot be seen as a Testament: crucially Jewish Testaments alert their readers immediately to the fact that they are Testaments (e.g. *Test. Levi*, 1:1–2; cf. Rev 1:1); in contrast 1:12–15 is too late, by then readers would have concluded that it was a letter-essay. Furthermore, in comparison with Testaments, 2 Peter contains far more explicit argument, far less prediction (only 2:1–3; 3:3–4), is Hellenistic in outlook, and claims to have actually been written by the hero. Overall, therefore, 2 Peter is a letter-essay with testamental features, but not a Testament.

D. Authorship. 1. Analysis of Authorship. Three different explanations of 2 Peter's authorship must be distinguished—(1) Peter wrote the letter; (2) during Peter's lifetime someone else wrote it under Peter's authority; (3) someone else wrote it after Peter's death (the majority position)—though (1) gradually merges into (2) as the scribe Peter used is given more autonomy. The arguments about authorship divide into four. First, language and style: 2 Peter's Hellenistic Jewish thought expressed in Greek Asiatic rhetoric cannot be attributed to the author of 1 Peter, nor to Jesus' Palestinian disciple. Thus explanation (1) must be discounted. Secondly, dating: Peter died in 64–8 CE making his involvement in 2 Peter (1 and 2) feasible (dates from 60 CE were possible), but unlikely (80–90 CE was preferred). Thirdly, genre: because Jewish Testaments were pseudonymous, some suggest that 2 Peter's testamental nature implies that it is pseudonymous. However, arguing from genre to pseudonymity can be flawed: Revelation is explicitly an apocalypse but unlike other apocalypses it is not pseudonymous. Furthermore, it was observed above that 2 Peter is not a Testament: its testamental features may have been drawn from works not seen as pseudonymous (e.g. the farewell speeches in Deut 33 and Mk 13), and hence would not have been connected with pseudonymity. Fourthly, content: is the text implausible in Peter's mouth? Aside from the features examined in relation to dating, the suggestions are weak: Peter would not need to bolster his authority by the story of the transfiguration (1:16–18)—but this account is part of his defence of the *parousia*; Peter would not have used the Jude-like source—but were apostles always original? Thus, explanations (2) and (3) are feasible, though dating favours (3). However (3) would mean that the text was pseudonymous—falsely claiming Peter as its author (1:1, 16, 18; 3:1). Early Christian pseudonymity is not well understood, but there is a natural distinction between pseudonymity which was (intended to be) deceptive, and that which was not (transparent fictions). The lack of imitation of 1 Peter would be surprising if 2 Peter was aiming deceptively to assert Petrine authorship. Deceptive pseudonymity also presents hermeneutical difficulties: should one suspend disbelief—read it as if it were by Peter—or ignore the story and structure of the text and excavate from it the thoughts of a later generation? It is also unclear how it would function as part of the Christian canon. Non-deceptive pseudonymity relies heavily on genre—readers need to understand what is going on in order not to be deceived. The Jewish Testament is the only real suggestion for a non-deceptive genre for 2 Peter, but it does not fit well (above), nor is it certain that Testaments were seen as non-deceptive.

2. Approaches to 2 Peter. Thus, it is not clear how to approach 2 Peter. It could be by Peter, though the dating makes this difficult. If it is not, it would be convenient if it were non-deceptive pseudonymity—to be read as 'what Peter would have said'—but since evidence for this is lacking, this is perhaps wishful thinking. If deceptive, different readers will wish to read it in very different ways. Recent methods of biblical interpretation sidestep this issue—a literary approach simply takes the text on its own terms (a letter by Peter)—a canonical approach is similar because that is its status within the canon. The approach taken here is to read 2 Peter as a letter written by Peter. Furthermore, because of its dependency on a Jude-like source, Jude will be used to illuminate the obscure parts of ch. 2.

E. Structure.

Salutation and *Exordium* (1:1–15)
Probatio Part 1 (1:16–21)
Probatio Part 2 (2:1–22)
Probatio Part 3 (3:1–13)
Peroratio (3:14–18)

COMMENTARY

Salutation and Exordium *(1:1–15)*

2 Peter begins in a manner typical of contemporary letters: X to Y plus salutation (1:1–2). The use of *Simeon* (transliteration of the Heb. name, elsewhere used of Peter only in Acts 15.14) rather than *Simon* (the standard Gk. equivalent) adds a ring of authenticity to the letter, though this could be a deliberate ploy. This divergence from 1 Peter shows that there is no attempt at imitation, despite the similar use of 'abundance' in the salutation (paralleled in many Jewish letters, though only at Jude 1 in the NT). The addressees are not specified but are assured that their standing is equal to that of Peter's. The description of Jesus as 'God' is noteworthy (attempts to construe the phrase differently are forced), although it has parallels (some of which are also disputed) elsewhere in the NT (Jn 1:1; 20:28; Heb 1:8; Titus 2:13; 1 Jn 5:20; Rom 9:5).

vv. 3–15 form the *exordium*—the theme of the letter is introduced and the reason for listening to it is highlighted. God has given the addressees the knowledge of God necessary for them to escape from the immoral world surrounding them and enter the eternal kingdom of Jesus Christ. However, the time for such an escape has not yet come. In the meantime, two paths are open to those with this knowledge: if they live a righteous life the divine calling will be confirmed; if they do not, they will become forgetful and the knowledge ineffectual, and when the time comes they will not enter the kingdom. The readers should listen carefully because pursuing the correct path is vital, so vital in fact that Peter has put his exhortation in writing so that it will continue to be heard even after his impending death. Crucial to this exhortation is the maintenance of the distinction between the past (v. 3—the 'divine power *has given*... everything needed'; v. 4—'*has given*' the promises), the present (vv. 5–7—'*you must make* every effort'; v. 8—'*keep you* from being ineffective'; v. 9—'*is* near-sighted and blind, and ... forgetful'; v. 10—'*be* ... *eager* to confirm your call'), and the future (v. 4—'you *may escape* from the corruption ... *become* participants in the divine nature'; v. 10—'you *will never stumble*'; v. 11—entry into the ... kingdom *will be* ... provided': emphases added). Others were doubting that

this future component would ever happen (3:3–13), but its importance is reaffirmed here in Peter's articulation of the Christian message. Ch. 2 will describe and oppose those who despite possessing the knowledge are following the path to destruction (hinted at in v. 9). Overall, the *exordium* provides a positive message, while the body of the letter expands on this by dealing with those who are, in Peter's view, stumbling.

2 Peter distinguishes between two different word groups when dealing with 'knowledge' (the distinction is not as clear elsewhere in the NT): one coming from the root *gnos*—general understanding (1:5, 6, 16, 20; 3:3, 18); and the other from *epignos*—knowledge of God gained in conversion (1:2, 3, 8; 2:20). The idea that knowledge is central to religion has extensive Jewish roots (e.g. Prov 2:5; Jer 31:34; Hos 4:1): it does not represent a later development in Christianity. 'Participants in the divine nature' (v. 4) is striking, but this Hellenistic terminology had already been absorbed into the Jewish tradition (cf. Wis 2:23; 4 Macc 18:4; Philo, *Quaes. Ex.* 2.29) signifying not 'becoming part of God' but 'the achievement of immortality and incorruptibility' (precisely the context here): its pairing with escape from the corruption of the world shows that it is a future reference.

Probatio Part 1 *(1:16–21)*

The *probatio* (presentation of the case) has three sections: 1:16–21 forms the first. Peter gives two proofs that the message that Jesus will return (v. 16—his 'power and coming') is trustworthy. In doing so Peter cuts to the heart of the dispute because, as we have seen, this future event was central to Peter's understanding of the divine economy, but others denied that Jesus would return (v. 16—'cleverly devised myths'; 3:4), and that judgement would come (2:4–10; 3:5–13). Indeed Peter takes Jesus' coming as synonymous with the eschatological judgement. The first proof is that Peter was an eyewitness to the transfiguration (vv. 16–18). This is relevant, in general because it demonstrates that the Christian message is about real events not myths, and in particular because the transfiguration revealed that God does break into the flow of the world (cf. 3:4–7) and that Jesus was God's majestic Son/Agent. Furthermore, the divine proclamation of his Son on a mountain points to Ps 2:6–7—which goes on to speak of that Son/Agent's role in judgement (cf. Rev 2:26–8; *Ps. Sol.* 17.22–4). The connection of the transfiguration to Jesus' coming in judgement is also made in the Synoptic Gospels (esp. Mk 8:38–9:8—although analysis, e.g. by Bauckham (1983), suggests that 2 Peter is independent of the Synoptics).

The second proof is the 'prophetic message' (i.e. OT) which also speaks of an eschatological denouement (1:19 can be translated as either 'the prophetic message more confirmed' (i.e. the prophecies are confirmed by the transfiguration) or 'the very reliable prophetic message' (i.e. they are independent confirmation)). Furthermore, these prophecies were truly from God and not man's invention (vv. 20–1). The light (i.e. revelation) provided by the prophetic message is vital but only partial—'a lamp ... in a dark place'. Eventually, however, 'the day dawns and the morning star rises' (cf. *Test. Levi*, 18.3–4; Num 24:17; Rev 22:16)—the eschatological age will arrive, and bring complete light ('in your hearts', because knowledge of God is in view; cf. 1 Cor 13:12). '[N]o prophecy of scripture is a matter of one's own interpretation' (v. 20) appears to focus on the interpretation of prophecy not its origin (cf. 3:16). However, v. 21 clearly deals with the origin of prophecy, and if Peter's opponents rejected prophecy's divine origin they would not be engaged in its interpretation. Coherence is best achieved by taking v. 20 as referring to the way that the prophetic writings themselves are interpretations of the revelations the prophets received. Hence both verses are about the origin of the prophetic writings, both in general (v. 21) and in particular the interpretation given by the prophets of the revelations they received (v. 20). The reference to prophetic interpretation of revelations fits the context of Peter's interpretation of the transfiguration event.

Probatio *Part 2 (2:1–22)*

Thus, in the first part of the *probatio* Peter defends the teaching that Jesus will come in judgement, and as part of this defends prophecy. In the second part (ch. 2) he turns to attack those he calls 'false teachers' (likening them to the 'false prophets' of old) asserting that they will be condemned when the judgement comes. Although vv. 1–3 assert that their teaching is false ('false teaching', 'destructive opinions', 'deceptive words') here, and particularly throughout the rest of the chapter, it is their actions that are attacked. Indeed other than that they 'deny the Master' (v. 1, cf. Jude 4) and 'promise…freedom' (v. 19) we remain ignorant of their teachings (except for Peter's assertion that it was 'bombastic nonsense', v. 18). What is clear from vv. 20–2, however, is that Peter judges that they once knew 'the way of righteousness' but that they have become 'again entangled' and have 'turn[ed] back from the holy commandment' (and indeed, v. 18, are ensnaring others who have 'just escaped' from error).

Two themes dominate the attack. They are immoral: vv. 2, 18, 'licentious'; vv. 3, 14, 'greed'; vv. 3, 14, 15, 18, 'deceptive words' 'entice'; v. 10, 'depraved lust' (cf. Jude 7–8); v. 13, 'revel' (at Christian community meals? cf. Jude 12, 1 Cor 11:17–34); vv. 13, 15, 'doing wrong'; v. 14, 'adultery'. Furthermore, despite their 'ignorance' (vv. 12, 16, 22, like animals, even a donkey knows better, cf. the theme of Peter's addressees' knowledge) they are arrogant: v. 10, 'despis[ing] authority' (of God); vv. 10–11, 'slander[ing] the glorious ones' (spiritual powers, cf. Jude 8, 10, 1QH 10:8—here clearly opposed to the angels); v. 13—'revel[ling] in the daytime'. The language used is colourful, often drawing upon the Jude-like source (particularly in vv. 4–18) although re-editing it. For example, Jude 8–10 argues that since Archangel Michael did not slander the devil (alluding to a contemporary Jewish tradition) the opponents certainly should not. vv. 10–12 carry the same argument but have had the particular reference to Michael and the devil removed, obscuring the logic in the process. While the accusations of immorality could simply be part of an overheated polemic, the notion of slandering spiritual powers is unusual enough to suggest that particular practices are in view. vv. 19–20 give the clue—they have been mastered, 'entangled', and 'overpowered' by 'corruption' and are now its 'slaves'—their turning back from righteousness to error (vv. 20–2) appears not to have been intentional (cf. 1:8–9—'ineffective and unfruitful', 'forgetful of the cleansing of past sins'). Putting together the threads, it appears that underestimating the power of evil ('slander[ing] the glorious ones'), they arrogantly claimed a

freedom (v. 19) from moral restraints (presumably on the basis of Christ's work, cf. 1 Corinthians) and hence indulged in immoral practices. In fact, however, evil is stronger than they supposed, and they have now become enslaved to it—indeed, they are now in a worse state than before (v. 20, cf. Mt 12:43–5 || Lk 11:24–6). In their arrogance they have obeyed evil in their lifestyles and so are now slaves of evil (cf. Rom 6:16).

The certainty of judgement (linked to the Jesus' coming) is the dominant theme throughout 2 Peter. The attack in ch. 2 suggests that the immorality of Peter's opponents was based on their belief that judgement would not come, hence Peter's insistent response that it surely will. In fact their views may have been more nuanced, for example that the physical world (and hence sexual immorality etc.) did not matter. Whatever the reason that the false teachers believed that their actions would not be judged Peter's response is simple—they are 'bringing swift destruction on themselves' (v. 1). The word 'swift' here points out the problem with which Peter must deal—no such judgement has actually happened. v. 3 expands this—is their 'condemnation…idle, and their destruction…asleep'? Hence vv. 4–6: a carefully crafted set of three examples that demonstrate that God did, and therefore will, bring judgement. The casting down of the angels (alluded to again in v. 17) and the destruction of Sodom and Gomorrah can be found in Jude 6–7, while the example of Noah is Peter's own addition (though a common image of judgement, e.g. Mt 24:38–9).

Probatio *Part 3 (3:1–13)*

2 Peter 3:1–2 forms an introduction to the third part of the *probatio*, reminding the addressees who is writing to them in order to re-emphasize the letter's authority before the central issue of 2 Peter is explicitly addressed in vv. 3–13: the apparent failure of the promise of Jesus' coming. Many commentators see the use of the future in v. 3 ('scoffers will come') but the present in vv. 5–13 as a sign of the letter's pseudonymous origins—the false teachers were in the future for Peter, but in the present for the real author. The switching is then either sloppiness, or the real author's attempt to communicate to his readers that the letter was not actually by Peter. However, it is plausible that Peter himself would have switched between the future and the present. For in v. 2 the OT and Jesus are in view—it is reasonable for Peter to refer to their predictions as 'scoffers will come' (cf. Jude 18), but to use the present tense when discussing the fulfilment of those predictions in his day. Ch. 2 is similar. If pseudonymous, the future in 2:1–3 is from Peter's point of view and the present in 2.10–22 from the real author's. If by Peter, he used the future to call to mind the prophecies that this would happen, and the present when discussing their fulfilment.

v. 4 states clearly the claim whose refutation underlies the whole letter: Jesus' coming will not happen. 'Ever since the fathers fell asleep' (RSV; sleep = death, cf. 1 Thess 4:13) shows that the problem was linked to the idea that Jesus would return before the death of the first generation of the church (cf. Mk 9:1; 13:30)—they have now died but Jesus has not come. The importance of this is clear: if the fathers have died and Jesus has not come, then he will never come, and therefore nor will judgement (this immediate connection to judgement fits the context of ch. 2, and the focus on judgement, not Jesus' coming, in vv. 5–10). Peter defends the idea that judgement will come in two ways. First (vv. 5–7), he points out that the assertion that everything has remained the same since Creation (v. 4) is simply false—God brought destruction on the world in the Flood (cf. 2:5 where the Flood is Peter's addition to the Jude-like source) and he will do it again. Second (vv. 8–9), he gives two explanations of the apparent delay. 'With the Lord one day is like a thousand years' (v. 8 cf. Ps 90:4) shows that God's perspective on time is very different from ours (cf. *Jubilees* 4:30; Sir 18:9–11; *2 Apoc. Bar.* 48.12–13; Ps.-Philo, *Bib. Ant.* 19.13); and the 'delay' is the result of God's mercy in giving time for repentance—a common answer (cf. Rom 2:4; 2 Esd 7:33; Plut. *Mor.* 549b; perhaps Mk 13:10) to an old problem (cf. Hab 2:3).

The future destruction will be by fire (vv. 7, 10, 12) in contrast to the Flood (cf. *1 Enoch*, 83:3–5, for the Flood having destroyed the whole world). Judgement through fire was an old Jewish idea (e.g. Mal 4:1) which had developed into a widespread expectation of a universal conflagration (cf. Zeph 1:18; 1 QH 3:19–36; Jos. *Ant.* 1.70). Here, despite the reference to universal destruction, judgement is still clearly the focus (v. 7, 'day of judgement . . . destruction of the godless'; v. 10, 'everything . . . will be disclosed'; v. 11, 'lives of holiness and godliness'). Stoicism spoke of a world conflagration in which everything returned to its constituent elements (e.g. Cic. *Nat. D.* 2.118), seemingly a close parallel to vv. 10, 12. However, the influence of Stoicism should not be exaggerated: here history is pictured as linear, while Stoicism had an endless cycle of destruction and renewal; and the references to 'the elements' should probably be seen as to heavenly bodies / powers (cf. Isa 34:4 LXX; Gal 4:3; Col 2:8, 20; *Apoc. Pet.* 5; Justin, *2 Apol.* 5.2; *2 Clem.* 16.3) rather than *constituent* elements. The reference to the word of God in v. 7 bolsters the assertion that the judgement will come: Creation and the Flood both came by God's word (vv. 5, 6); thus undoubtedly the future judgement decreed by his word (i.e. the prophetic scriptures, cf. 1:19–21) will also come. 'The day . . . will come like a thief' (v. 10) is a common NT motif (cf. Mt 24:43; Lk 12:39; 1 Thess 5:2; Rev 3:3; 16:15) pointing to Jesus' return being unexpected.

Peroratio (3:14–18)

The final five verses form the *peroratio*: its beginning marked by 'Therefore, beloved' (v. 14; repeated in v. 17 after the 'digression' about Paul), although perhaps 3:11–13 should be included since vv. 11 and 13 are exhortatory. The tone is similar to that of the *exordium* (1:3–15)—positive encouragement with the hint of warning (v. 17, cf. 1:8–9) as compared with the three stages of the *probatio* which focused on rebutting the idea that the judgement would not come. The reference to Paul is important for scholars wishing to date the book (see above) and to understand the development of authority in the early church. However, its importance for 2 Peter can be exaggerated: if Peter knew his opponents' beliefs were based on Pauline material he would have developed this argument about Paul far earlier and in more detail. This reference is more of a final flourish—'in addition Paul agrees with all of this, if his words are not twisted'. Exactly which Pauline material is being referred to is not clear, if indeed particular writings are in mind: patience out of mercy suggests Rom 2:4 and 9:22; the opponents' immorality an antinomian reading of Pauline teaching (cf. Rom 3:8; Jas 2:14–26); and the disbelief in the coming judgement an over-realized version of Pauline eschatology similar to that opposed in 1 Corinthians. The letter's close (v. 18) echoes its opening (1:1–2)—grace, knowledge, and Jesus as Saviour; the final words ('day of eternity') give one last reminder of the theme of the letter: the judgement day will come.

REFERENCE

Bauckham, R. J. (1983), *Jude, 2 Peter*, WBC (Waco, Tex.: Word Books).

79. 1 John, 2 John, 3 John   Judith Lieu

INTRODUCTION

A. Authorship and Setting. 1. Although 'the Johannine Epistles' are traditionally linked together, only 2 and 3 John name and claim a common authorship, by 'the Elder'; 2 John shares much of its language and ideas with the anonymous 1 John, but whether this indicates shared authorship or imitation is disputed. Attempts to deny the common authorship of the minor epistles and to see one or other, usually 2 John, as pseudonymous (e.g. Bultmann 1973) have won little assent. From an early date 1 John was associated with the fourth gospel and both were assigned to John the Apostle (see JN), although there was initially more uncertainty over the two minor epistles (Lieu 1986: 10–18). In recent scholarship the common authorship of the gospel and first epistle has become far less certain, particularly after Dodd (1937), as too has that of the three epistles. While the gospel and the three epistles clearly stem from the same school, the question of authorship remains an open one.

2. The majority position which sees the gospel as prior to the three epistles, which follow in their canonical order, has also come under attack; some even reverse the sequence with 2 and 3 John first (Strecker 1989). This debate is inseparable from the—often speculative—reconstruction of the events behind the documents (see Brown 1979). In the absence of external evidence to solve these issues the starting point for interpretation must be the language and thought of the letters themselves.

3. Supposed settings for 1 John have focused on references to schism (2:18–19) and to those holding false beliefs (4:2–3). Earlier, more confident, identifications of 'the heretics' with known groups within the early church are not supported by the text itself; undoubtedly there is conflict over the understanding of Jesus although the precise nuance is obscure (see further 1 JN 4:1–6).

B. Genre. While 2 and 3 John follow the standard length and some of the conventions of contemporary letters, 1 John is more idiosyncratic. It is self-consciously a written document (2:1, 7, 12–14, 26; 4:13), but has often been likened to a homily. Although there is an overall argument there is no clear structure, and themes and ideas often reappear in new combinations and contexts. Authoritative address to an audience still called 'children', is mixed with a more co-operative recognition of them as 'brothers and sisters' who 'have knowledge'; there is also a combination of exhortation and statements of assurance. A 'paraenetic letter' is probably the most accurate description of 1 John.

COMMENTARY

1 John

(1:1–4) The Prologue The 'we' (v. 1) who have heard, seen, and touched are never further identified, and elsewhere the author writes as an individual (2:1, 12–14; 5:13). Seeing, hearing, and witnessing is the foundation of his argument, but the epistle and the debate about authorship do not suggest that he was an eyewitness of the ministry of Jesus or even associated with others who were; all believers can make a similar claim (4:14–16), and the 'we' which here contrasts with 'you', the readers, elsewhere includes them.

The object of this perception was not the word incarnate as in John (Jn 1:14), but the neuter 'what was from the beginning'; in 2:7, 24; 3:11 'from the beginning' appeals to the earliest preaching these readers heard, and this, rather than an absolute beginning (contrast Jn 1:1), may be the force here. Although it is 'concerning the word of life', word is defined objectively by what can be proclaimed, while 'life' brings together the past—it 'was revealed'—and the present experience of true believers which is the final purpose of the letter (5:11–13). In contrast to the gospel's prologue, the focus is on the shared experience of believers, in which the certainty of what 'was revealed' in the past, and the sense of a communion which encompasses the divine as well as the human are integral parts (v. 3).

A common tradition of language and ideas best explains the 'similar but different' relationship with Jn 1:1–18; there are also OT roots, particularly in Deutero-Isaiah (e.g. Isa 43:8–10).

(1:5–2:11) Walking in the Light Although disputes about right belief concerning Jesus apparently prompted the letter (2:18–22; 4:1–3), the starting-point is the understanding of God (1:5). The argument quickly moves to an internal debate over true and false religious claims and behaviour.

The identification of God with light has Hellenistic parallels, but these do not exclude a Jewish background (Ps 27:1). The complete incompatibility of light and darkness reflects a dualist perspective which developed within Judaism in the intertestamental period and was not unique to the original ('from the beginning') Christian message. In 2:8, 11 'darkness' is virtually an independent but negative, opposing force; although 2:11 echoes Isa 6:10, blindness is induced not by God or through preaching but by darkness (contrast Jn 12:40). In 1 John the interest is not the doctrine of God, but the moral consequence that authentic fellowship with God demands a life equally belonging to 'light'.

The debating style, 'if we say…', 'whoever says…', and 'whoever…', is not aimed against actual groups who took the positions which are criticized; the negatives (1:6, 8, 10; 2:4, 9, 11) are foils to reinforce the positive affirmations (1:7, 9; 2:5, 6, 10), which establish an essential pattern of belief and life. This is combined with, and illustrates, the 'testing' style: 'by this we know…' followed by the 'proof'. A similar structure reappears in 3:4–10 and 4:8, 20.

In 1:6–7 walking or remaining in the light/darkness is a metaphor for right behaviour; in 2:9–11 it indicates a sphere of living in relation to God and, as a claim implying participation in salvation, requires verification. The terminology is 'Johannine', but unlike Jn 12:35; 8:12 there is no Christological emphasis. In 2:6 'walk' is a biblical term for 'live/behave' (Gen 17:1; Ps 1, etc.); the choice between two ways also has Jewish and Jewish–Christian parallels (Mt 7:13–14; *Did.* 1. 1–2; 4.14–5.1). In this paragraph, 'knowing' God, 'being in him', and 'abiding in him' are distinctive Johannine expressions of religious experience (cf. Jn 17:3, 21–6; 6:56; 15:5–6); there are partial OT (Jer 31:33–4) parallels, and closer ones in intertestamental literature (1QH 11:9). Later parallels in gnostic literature are part of the same religious trend and do not make 1 John 'gnostic'. 'To know' in Johannine, as in Jewish, thought points more to a relationship than to intellectual apprehension. Although these terms are apparently individualistic, 1 John always sets them in a corporate context (cf. 2:9–11), and, as here, binds them to obedience.

The dualist pattern of light *v.* darkness, which reappears in 3:4–10, raises the problem of sin (v. 6); does the incompatibility of light with sin mean that those who sin have no possibility of a share in the light, or that those who belong to the light can claim not to sin? Here the solution is the assurance of forgiveness for those who confess their sins. Different images are used to explain forgiveness: that of the blood of Jesus in 1:7 implies a general sacrificial metaphor; in 2:1 Jesus, present with God, is an 'advocate' or intercessor, the word used in Jn 15:26 etc. of the Spirit (*paraklētos*); in 2:2 he is, again present, a *hilasmos* (cf. 4:10), probably not an 'atoning sacrifice' as in the NRSV, but less technically 'a means of forgiveness' or reconciliation. 'Of the whole world' is an exception to the attitude to the world elsewhere, see 1 Jn 2:15–17. In 1:9 God forgives because 'he is faithful and just', an echo of Ex 34:6; Neh 9:17, etc.

'His commandments' (2:3), identical with 'his word' (v. 5) and with 'the old/new commandment' (vv. 7–8), or with 'the message' (3:11), is the command to love one another (3:11; 4:21). 'New' echoes Jesus' institution of this command in Jn 13:34–5 but here is defined eschatologically by the inbreaking of the 'new age'; 'old' refers not to the roots of the command in the OT (Lev 19:18) but to 'the beginning' (cf. 1:1; 2:24), probably not in Jesus' ministry but in their reception of the message (cf. 2 Jn 5). 'One another' or 'a brother' includes only fellow members of the community (NRSV adds an inclusive 'or sister', and in 2:11 interprets 'brother' by 'believer'). At 2:4 the dualism of light *v.* darkness (1 JN 1:5–7) is repeated in truth *v.* lying (as at 1:6, 10—not 'truthfulness' but an absolute) and love *v.* hating (2:9–11); this is not just an ethical dualism of opposing moral possibilities but is rooted in the nature of God (see 3:10–15; 4:7–8): in 2:5 'love of God' may be 'for God' (objective) or 'from God' (subjective). The dualism is also eschatological: darkness belongs to that which is coming to an end, light to the future, which in 1 John's realized eschatology is already dawning. The dualism is developed in 3:4–15; 4:2–6 where it is used to define those who belong to the community against those who do not.

Jesus is important in this section as a means of forgiveness (1 JN 2:2) and as a model of 'walking' (2:6); 1 John's use of 'he, him' is ambiguous: Jesus or God may be the object of knowledge (2:3–4), locus of abiding (2:5–6), and source of the commandment or word (2:3, 5).

(2:12–17) Separation from the World This section forms an interlude of affirmation and reinforcement of the readers' separation from 'the world'. The variation between 'I am writing' and 'I write' (= I have written) is stylistic. It is not clear whether 'children', 'fathers', 'young people' refers to three different groups, two groups who together can be addressed as 'little children' (cf. 2:28; 5:21), or the whole community viewed in a conventional threefold division from different perspectives. The latter is most probable as in 1 John the descriptions ('because . . .') are true of all believers. There is no hierarchical structure of the church here. 'Sins are forgiven', cf. 1:7–9. 'Know him who is from the beginning', cf. 2:3; 4:7; 5:20, either God (= the Father, 2:14) or Jesus: the beginning may be 'of time' or as defined by the preaching, cf. 1:1. 'Have conquered/overcome [the same word in Greek] the evil one', cf. 5:4–5: this is a realized eschatology which affirms for the present what properly belongs to God's final triumph over evil. 'Word of God abides', cf. 2:24, 27.

'The world' (vv. 15–17) represents all that is opposed to God and to those who belong to God, cf. 3:1, 13; 4:4–5; 5:4–5, 19. This is not a gnostic or ascetic anti-materialism but part of the dualistic structure of Johannine thought: the dualism is not absolute since the world is also eschatologically delimited (cf. 2:8); there are hints of a more optimistic view of the world in 2:2; 4:14, although these may be largely conventional formulae. The gospel shares the same predominantly negative view with more marked exceptions (7:7; 15:18–19; 17:9, 14–18, 25; 3:16; 4:42; 8:12). The Johannine community's experience of hostility both from the Jewish community (see Gospel of John) and more generally, together with an initial dualist mindset, has generated this attitude.

The conventionally tripartite 'desire . . . desire . . . pride' (v. 16) cannot be precisely defined. An echo of the Gen 3 story is possible, but 'desire' can have more general negative connotations (Num 11:4; Ps 106:14; Gal 5:16; Eph 2:3); 'flesh', 'eyes', and 'riches' (lit. 'life', translated 'goods' in 3:17) are not inherently negative in 1 John (1:1; 4:2). 1 John may be using a traditional formula to reinforce the desired separation between the readers and 'the world'.

(2:18–27) Reassurance despite Schism This section introduces what has often been seen as the primary purpose of the letter, the recent experience of schism within the community. However, the emphasis is not on those 'who went out' but on maintaining the confidence of the readers, particularly necessary if those who left were in the majority or more obviously successful (4:5). In contrast to the preceding sections the main emphasis is on right belief, and is picked up in 4:1–6.

The schism is interpreted through a conventional eschatological scheme familiar to the readers. 'Antichrist', 'opponent of' or 'an alternative' Christ (v. 18), is a Johannine coinage (cf. 2 Jn 7) but the idea of a figure personifying the final opposition to God has Jewish roots and is found in other Christian writings (2 Thess 2:3–4). By applying this eschatological scheme to the schism 1 John excludes the possibility of debate with those who left, justifies the trauma it may have caused, and makes the decision to remain within the community inescapable and certain of imminent vindication (cf. 2:17). In keeping with the whole letter and its dualism, the passage articulates a strong sense of the 'election' (a word not used) of the community: because, contrary to appearance, the schismatics had never 'belonged to us', this confidence need not be undermined. Different images express this 'election': (1) They 'know' (cf. also 1 JN 2:3): in 2:21 the object is 'truth', not just about the present disagreement but absolutely (cf. 2:4). In 2:20 there are textual variants: either 'you all know' (χ B; NRSV) or 'you know all things' (A; C; RV); the absence of an object would be unusual but is well-attested and would have invited alteration. Like the gospel, 1 John only uses the verb, and not the noun 'knowledge', *gnōsis* (contrast NRSV). (2) 'The anointing', a noun in vv. 20 (contrast NRSV) and 27, probably refers to what has been used or received rather than to the process, and is metaphorical rather than a literal rite (baptism or unction). The reference need not be to baptism, not mentioned in 1 John, nor to the Spirit: in v. 20 'the Holy One' may be God or Jesus (cf. Jn 6:69); it is the source of teaching (v. 27) and parallel to 'what you heard' (v. 24). The emphasis is more on received tradition or teaching than on spiritual gifts or on a mystical or ritual 'illumination', and the resemblance to 'gnostic' ideas is only superficial. The term may be a Johannine coinage (*chrisma* cf. *antichristos*) in the context of a debate about 'the *Christ*' (v. 22). (3) 'What you have heard from the beginning' (v. 24): cf. 2:7. Faithfulness to the past proclamation which was probably part of the foundation of the community is more than loyalty to tradition or conservatism. The same language of mutual abiding or indwelling is used of it as of the relationship with 'the Son and the Father' so that it and an intimate relationship with God (and Jesus) are interdependent. Thus the last line of v. 27 is ambiguous: either 'it' (the anointing) or 'he' taught, and the command—probably, although it could be 'you do abide'—is to abide in 'it' or in 'him' (cf. v. 28).

The schism was over the status of Jesus but the issue is obscure, although cf. 4:2. The denial that 'Jesus is the Christ' (v. 22) could be a denial of his messiahship: the formula is used of early preaching of Jesus as Messiah (Acts 18:5, 28). This view is less likely, not, as often argued, because 1 John does not imply a Jewish setting, but because the dispute was between those who had been members of the community, not outsiders or apostates. The alternative formulation, 'denying the Son' or 'the Father and the Son', is not the schismatics' but the author's interpretation and acts as a definition of 'Christ'. There is no link with the earlier debate over moral issues, although there may be an implicit association in 'liar' (v. 22 cf. 1:10; 2:4) and 'those who would [or 'do'] deceive' (v. 26 cf. 1:8).

(2:28–3:3) Present Confidence and Future Hope The combination of affirmation and exhortation is repeated in terms of present and future eschatology. There is no connection with the reinterpretation of eschatology in 2:18, and here it takes a distinctive Johannine shape. Conformity now is the guarantee and the condition of future conformity, but whether with God or Jesus is not clear.

The continuity from 2:27 and 3:1, 'the world . . . did not know him', suggests that 'he' in this section is mostly Jesus whose coming (*parousia*, 2:28), as elsewhere in early Christian tradition, is expected; if so, v. 29*a* anticipates 3:7 where Jesus ('that one') is again said to be righteous. However, in 2:29 'born of him' must be 'born of God' (cf. 3:9; 4:7; 5:1; see below) suggesting that at the beginning of the verse 'he is righteous' also refers to God (so 1:9); in this case, since no change is indicated, God may also be the one who is to be revealed and come in v. 28. In 3:2 the translation 'he is revealed' (NRSV) in context also refers to God: being children of God is the precondition of the greater conformity which will come from 'seeing God' (cf. Mt 5:8). This difficulty in determining whether 'he' refers to God or to Jesus is characteristic of 1 John's thought. In 3:3 'he is pure' more clearly refers to Jesus: the emphatic 'he' (*ekeinos*) occurs in brief sayings appealing to the example of Jesus (2:6; 3:3*, 5*, 7*, 16; 4:17*); those marked with an asterisk use the present 'is'—Jesus has present significance, either with God (cf. 2:1–2) or within the teaching of the community. 'Confidence' or boldness (2:28) is the assured status of believers in 3:19–22 ('before God'), 4:17–18 ('on the day of judgement') and 5:14; in these passages themes traditionally associated with future judgement serve the present needs of believers in exhortation and assurance.

(3:4–10) Sin and Righteousness In one of the most dualist passages in the letter, sin is contrasted with righteousness, love with its failure (or later, hate, 3:13), and the children of God with the children of the devil. The main purpose of these absolute alternatives is to define the community and encourage faithfulness.

Four contrasting couplets built around the pattern 'Everyone who . . .' may be one of the sources of this section (as first isolated by von Dobschütz 1907): 2:29*b* + 3:4*a*; 3:6; 3:7*b* + 8*a*; 3:9*a* + 10*b*. If so, the dualism of the source has been intensified both by the development of origin from God or the devil in 10*a*, and by the perfectionism of 9*b* (see below), and has been modified by the insertion of 8*c*: there is no longer a timeless opposition between sin and righteousness because of the victory won when 'the Son of God was revealed'.

Sin is viewed differently from 1:6–2:2; here it belongs to the negative side and is impossible for anyone 'who abides in him' (v. 6) or who is among those who 'have been born of God' (v. 9). In 5:16–18 the same apparent contradiction is found, first suggesting that believers may sin and that forgiveness for some sins is possible, then repeating the affirmation that 'those who are born of God do not sin' (1 JN 5:18). The contrast is not simply between fact and ideal, between believers as sinners before God but sinless 'in Christ', or between individual sins they may commit (1:9) and their removal from the realm of sin. When 1 John is considering the pastoral needs of the community the need to deal with all that mars that life is paramount; when seeking to affirm and preserve their separation from other values and systems the certainty of the radical change they have experienced becomes overwhelming (Lieu

1991: 58–65). Freedom from sin belongs in Jewish and Christian thought to the age to come when the realm of God finally excludes all that opposes it, as too does victory over evil (2:13–14) and over death (3:14); in 1 John these are so real that they are part of the present and sharing in them equally excludes any part in that opposition. In v. 4 'lawlessness' is not disobedience to the law but the opposition to God in the final age (cf. 2 Thess 2:3, 'the man of lawlessness'). Other early Christian writers also had to struggle with the tension between the certainty of God's victory over sin in Jesus and the continuing reality of sin in Christians' lives (cf. Heb 6:4–8).

Jesus ('he'), as the righteous one without sin, is not just a model (but note 'he' in vv. 5, 7, *ekeinos*, cf. 1 JN 3:3), but also belongs to the realm of God's victory. He was 'revealed' in the past (cf. 1:2 of the 'life'), but the verb is used equally of when 'he' will be 'revealed' (2:28, see above); 'to destroy the works of the devil', presumably through his ministry or death although how is not stated, is an eschatological event, traditionally part of God's final victory, but now already effected. 'The devil' (v. 8), mentioned here for the first time, is presumably identical with 'the evil one' in 2:13, 14. In Jn 8:44 the Jews have the devil as their father; 1 John shares the same tradition of imagery but with a sharper dualism, 'the children of God' *v.* 'the children of the devil', which is used not in polemical rhetoric as in John but to distinguish two exclusive groups. It is likely that the tradition of Cain in contemporary Jewish thought as the child of the devil lies behind both Jn 8:44 where the devil was a murderer from the beginning, and the more general words of 1 Jn 3:8 that he 'has been sinning from the beginning'; Cain is explicitly one who murdered in 3:12.

Believers as 'children of God' (3:1, 10; 5:2) and as 'born of God' (2:29; 3:9; 4:7; 5:1, 4, 18) is characteristic of the second half of the letter (Lieu 1991: 33–8); there is a dualist contrast only in 3:10 with 'children of the devil' (never 'born of the devil'). There is no specific moment of birth (e.g. conversion, baptism): the stress is on the inalienable relationship with God but is more precise than the broader 'of God' (also 'of the devil, world' etc.). The origins of the idea are not clear; it is found briefly in John (1:12–13 [11:52]; contrast 'birth from above/anew' in Jn 3). OT parallels are weak (Ex 4:22; Deut 32:5–6); Hellenistic ideas of divine begetting or rebirth are later and not dualist; in 1QS 3:19–4:26 'children' imagery in a dualist setting is found, but not divine begetting.

In 3:9 'God's seed' may be God's offspring who remain 'in him', i.e. God (cf. NRSV fn.), but it is more likely that God's seed remains in 'him', i.e. 'the one who has been born of God': in turning the phrase into the plural, 'those who . . . in them', the NRSV obscures the ambiguity. It has been suggested that 'seed', perhaps like 'anointing' in 2:20, 27 (cf. 1 JN 2:20, 27), reflects a gnostic understanding of divine enlightenment and/or was a term used by 'those who went out' (2:19). Nothing explicitly supports this, and while 'seed' could be a reference to God's word (cf. the parable of the sower)—a reference to the spirit seems unlikely—it may continue the allusion to the Genesis story (cf. Gen 3:17; 4:25): God's choice continues not in Cain and those of his ilk but in those who truly carry God's seed which makes them God's children. 'Of God', vv. 9–10 (cf. 'of the truth', 3:19) also points to divine origin; the negative is 'of the devil' or 'of the world' (4:6). The gospel has a wider range of 'origins' formulae (Jn 8:23; 3:31, etc.).

3:10*b* forms a climax to the section, expanding the introductory v. 4*a* in the language used in the intervening verses, and adding a further definition which makes it directly applicable to the situation and concerns of the letter. 1 John has no other explicit definition of sin than the failure to 'love one's brother' or fellow believer: the NRSV's 'brothers and sisters' is justifiably inclusive but obscures 1 John's use of the singular 'brother' (2:10–11; 3:15, 17; 4:20–1; the only exception is 3:14). This definition gives some support to the argument that it was the schism, clear evidence of a failure in love, that shaped 1 John's thought even about sin.

(3:11–17) Community within Love The previous passage is now given a more practical exposition in the attitudes believers experience from others and hold towards each other. Again the primary thrust is to explain and reinforce the community's separation from outsiders and their internal cohesion. In v. 11, love of brother is now replaced with love of one another, as also in 3:23; 4:7, 11, 12, in each case in exhortation or with reference to the command; this is the distinctive formula of the Johannine tradition (Jn 13:34; 15:12, 17). For 1 John it is the epitome of the proclamation heard from the beginning (cf. 1:5; 2:7; 1 JN 2:3). The appeal to Cain as the model of a failure in reciprocal love is the only explicit OT reference in the letter, but the range of OT allusions (cf. 2:11) and concepts refute denials of any Jewish background. Here the story of Cain probably lies in the background since 3:8 (cf. 1 JN 3:8) and continues until 3:15, since Cain was the archetypal murderer (cf. Jn 8:44), or even 3:20 (cf. Gen 4:9–10). Cain is not just one of a number of possible negative examples, neither is the failure to love an unfortunate weakness or lapse: both are expressions of the absolute contrast between God and the devil and between life and death. Cain was of 'the evil one' and so were his deeds evil: the same formula is used in Jn 3:19, suggesting common patterns of exegesis and language lie behind both the gospel and letter. Gen 4 gives no clear explanation of God's preference for Abel's sacrifice and only implies it led to Cain's murderous act; 1 John is like other later readers, Jewish and Christian, who sought to remedy this difficulty (cf. Jos. *Ant*. 1.2.1; Heb 11:4).

The analogy set within its dualist scheme explains the hostility the community has been experiencing; what form this 'hate' takes is not described and there is no explicit mention of persecution (contrast Jn 15:18–20). The world is that which opposes God (cf. 2:15; 1 JN 2:15); in 4:3–5 it is the realm of the antichrist and it responds to those who have left the community. The explanation would be reassuring if the community was in a minority and those who had split from it appeared rather more successful. However, the main use of the analogy is to reinforce the demand for love within the community. Such love proves and is the condition for their not belonging to the Cain/murderer/evil-one side of the division. In the light of 3:10 (cf. 1 JN 3:10*b*) it might seem that the best expression of love was not to join the schism, but the 'Johannine' appeal to the example of Jesus' ('he' = *ekeinos*) self-sacrifice (cf. Jn 15:13), makes it broader. Yet literal self-sacrifice may not be meant, for the only application is the readiness to share one's 'goods' or life (cf. 1 JN 2:16) with a fellow believer in need. This is the only hint that differences of class or wealth may have contributed to the schism.

The passage has concentrated on love among believers; in 3:17 'God's love' may be the love which comes from God and is the source of believers' love, but it might equally mean 'love for God' (cf. 2:5): the only certain evidence of love for God is the more visible love for a fellow believer.

(3:18–24) Condemnation and Confidence in God The NRSV paragraphing takes v. 18 with the following verses. Thus practical love is the guarantee of being 'from [= of] the truth' and a source of reassurance before God, even in the face of self-doubt; God's knowledge, superior to such doubt, is a further source of hope. The contrast offered by v. 21 is then only a subjective one: boldness comes from a lack of sense of self-condemnation and not from any real difference in relation to God. An alternative possibility is that God's greater knowledge can only reinforce and add to the condemnation dimly anticipated; this demands not that we 'will reassure our hearts' but 'sternly exhort our hearts' (cf. NEB fn.). The sequence from v. 19*a* becomes clumsy but v. 21 then provides a clear contrast of the happier state of no self-condemnation where boldness is justified and answered. However, v. 18 may be the conclusion to the previous section, so v. 19 starts a new but related issue of the confidence before God (cf. RSV). The introductory 'by this' then anticipates what follows, a pattern found in 2:3, 5 (?); 3:10, 24; 4:13, 17 (?): *that* 'God is greater...' is the source of 'our' knowledge and self-reassurance. The negative alternative would not be possible. As elsewhere (1 JN 2:28) condemnation and boldness before God, which properly belong to the future judgement or vindication, are already experienced in the present. Response to prayer, a common theme in NT and Johannine literature (cf. Mt 7:7; Jn 14:13; 15:16; 16:23, 26), is picked up in 5:14–15 as a mark of 'boldness'.

The commandments are God's; the alternation between the plural and the singular in vv. 22–4 is characteristic (cf. 2:3–4, 7) but here mutual love (for the formula cf. 1 JN 3:11) is combined with belief, recalling 2:18–23 and anticipating the move to 4:1–3 where such belief has to be properly articulated. Abiding (v. 24) is in and by God, as most commonly in 1 John (contrast Jn 6:56; 15:1–7, but NB 1 Jn 2:24), and is inseparable from obedience (cf. 1 JN 1:6–7). The spirit is mentioned for the first time (cf. 1 JN 2:20, 27; 3:9); despite the NRSV's capital S, 1 John has a much simpler idea of the spirit than John; in 4:13 it is God's spirit but is not further related to the divine life. These two references bracket the exhortation to 'test the spirits' in 4:1 where the NRSV uses 's'.

(4:1–6) True and False Confession This passage links with 2:18–19 (cf. 'antichrist') and has often been seen as the key to the letter: former members of the community rejected right confession of Jesus and left, perhaps achieving missionary success (v. 5) and provoking a threat to the confidence and stability of the community. Their identity has been much debated. The schism is interpreted in the light of eschatological tradition as in 2:18; 'false prophets' also reflects this (cf. Mt 24:11, 24) and does not mean they were 'charismatics'. 'Testing the spirits' belongs to eschatological decision and is not discernment of spiritual gifts (1 Cor 12:10; 14): the more general 'spirits' in the introduction to the passage is reduced by its end to the alternatives, spirit of truth or of error. A conflict between the spirit of truth and the spirit of error, both as cosmic forces and as forces within people, is also found at Qumran (1QS 3:13–4:26) without any 'charismatic' setting; John's non-dualistic 'spirit of truth' is different (Jn 14:7; 15:26; 16:13). The contrast belongs to 1 John's dualism and emphasis on 'truth', but 'error' is also an eschatological theme (Mk 13:22). The conflict is also between the community and 'the world', between God and 'the world' (cf. 1 JN 2:15), from whom each has its origin ('from', cf. 1 JN 3:9), and also between those who respond to either side: there is no neutral third party. 1 John's thought is deterministic: response does not merely result in being 'of God' or 'of the world' but is generated by it as a pre-existing state. This determinism is complementary to the realized eschatology: their victory is already complete. The greater one who is in them is God, the one in the world might either be the antichrist as in v. 3 or an allusion to the devil.

Confession of Jesus is the hallmark of the spirits. Those/the spirit who fail/s to confess Jesus (v. 3) cannot be unbelievers since these were never within the community (contrast 2:19), but erstwhile members. The alternative reading, 'does away with' or 'deprives of power/significance' (Vulgate and some patristic evidence including Irenaeus) may have originated as an attempt to clarify their error; if original its ambiguity led to the simpler alternative. The positive confession is not 'that Jesus Christ has come in the flesh' (so NRSV, emphasis added), which would require a different grammatical construction; this makes improbable earlier interpretations which saw the schism as a denial of Jesus' true humanity (docetism, cf. *IDB* i. 860), or as a theory that the union between the divine Christ and human Jesus was temporary and did not include his death (often associated with Cerinthus, the traditional opponent of John, cf. *ABD* i. 885). It is a confession of '*Jesus Christ* (as) the one who has come in the flesh' (my tr.), although the nuance intended by this is not clear. 'Flesh' is not a major concern in this letter (cf. only 2:16); in the Johannine tradition it can be both ambivalent (Jn 3:6; 8:15) and central (Jn 1:14; 6:51–6). 1 John's broader interest in Jesus does not help interpretation; he is model, victor over the devil, a means of dealing with sin in past and present, son of, and inseparable from, the Father; 1 Jn 5:6 adds further precision but is even more obscure (1 JN 5:6). Jesus Christ's *having come in flesh* is partly an antithesis to the false prophets *having come out into the world*; it is no less real but of directly opposing significance. The schismatics did not invest Jesus with the significance the author does, but the latter's love of contrast and concern to avoid real debate with alternative ideas exclude any certain recovery of their views.

(4:7–21) **Abiding in Love** The thought returns to the life of the community, interlacing assurance with exhortation, centred on the theme of love which moves inseparably both between God and believers and amongst believers themselves. However, the need for right belief is part of this web: the past sending of the Son is both the evidence of God's love and the continuing norm of right belief and union. Love for one another (cf. 1 JN 3:11) is rooted only at the end of the passage (v. 21) in 'the command', here closer to the 'synoptic' combination of love of God and love of fellow (Lk 10:27).

The focus is on the primacy of God's love (i.e. 'love of God', 4:9, 12); although grammatically this could mean love for God or love from God (cf. 2:5), the primary emphasis is on love from God which even if expressed in the past act was for *us*. Yet 'his love' in v. 12 may by extension be the love which originates from God but is expressed by believers towards others; it is unlikely that 'love from God' would be dependent for its full reception on believers' reciprocal love. However, believers may also have love for God, although not as the primary expression of love (v. 10), nor as a claim to be made independently of love for 'a brother or sister' (vv. 20–1).

That God 'sent his Son' (vv. 9, 10, 14) is the traditional terminology of the Johannine tradition, as also is the epithet 'only' (Jn 3:16; 1:14, 18); while it may imply pre-existence, 'sending' can merely stress authority and representation, an important distinction for the gospel but not the main issue for 1 John with its lack of theological reflection. 'Saviour of the world' is also a Johannine epithet (Jn 4:42), and does little to soften the largely negative attitude to the world in the letter (cf. 1 JN 2:15–17). The world is only the arena of the sending and not the recipient of God's love and the offer of life (v. 9, contrast Jn 3:16); it is 'for our sins' that he was a means of dealing with sin (better than 'atoning sacrifice'), perhaps also a traditional formula (cf. 1 Jn 2:2).

'We have seen . . . do testify . . . have known and believe' (vv. 14–16) is also characteristically Johannine (Jn 1:14; 3:11; 6:69; 20:29) and includes all believers even though not original eyewitnesses (cf. 1 JN 1:1–3). The apparent objectivity is balanced by the more 'subjective' reciprocal abiding by/in God which is made evident by the gift of his spirit (cf. 1 JN 3:24). Both are bounded by the conditions of love for one another (v. 12) and of right confession (v. 15). 'Jesus is the Son of God' is the right confession for the first time here (cf. 5:5), but has been anticipated by 'confessing/denying the son' in 2:22–3; there is no difference from 'Jesus is the Christ' (2:22; 5:1; cf. 4:2). 'Son of God' is not a messianic title for 1 John but indicates the inseparable relationship between Father and Son; although God is the focus of much of 1 John's thought, God has been and is known only through his action in the Son: although God cannot be seen, that as Father he sent the Son can be (vv. 12, 14).

That 'God is love' (vv. 9, 16) is not a statement about the 'divinity' of love or an abstract definition of God: it is God as experienced. Equally, 'abiding in love' is not a mystical experience but combines faithfulness to the manifestation of God's love in the Son and showing love to a fellow believer. v. 7 does not mean that anyone who loves is born of God (cf. 1 JN 3:9) but that love is their necessary characteristic. 'The day of judgement' (v. 17) recalls a more traditional eschatology (cf. Mt 10:15; 11:22, 24) where 'boldness' (cf. 1 JN 2:28; 3:21) and fear belong; here it is only the ultimate context of believers' conformity to Jesus (= he, cf. 1 JN 3:3) in the present and the purpose or full expression—the relation between 'in this' and 'that' is obscure—of the present total flowering of love.

(5:1–5) **Victory through Faith** This section acts as a bridge between the preceding focus on love and the emphasis on the total certainty centred on right belief in 5:6–13. Right belief in Jesus as the Christ (cf. 1 JN 2:22), like love, is the mark of the one born of God (5:1 ∥ 4:7, cf. 1 JN 3:9). Here this just defines the one to be loved as only the one who holds the right faith: love of the begetter (God) entails love of the one begotten: NRSV 'parent/child' obscures the symmetry. This does imply that love of God has some primacy; contrary to 4:19–21, v. 2 suggests that the proof of love for fellow believers is love and obedience to God, which in practice are identical. The commandments (pl.) means nothing more than the commandment (sing.) (4:21, cf. 1 JN 2:3); love of God is love for God ('objective genitive'; contrast 4:9 cf. 2:5, 4:21).

The neuter 'whatever' (v. 4) rather than 'whoever' is odd but has Johannine parallels (Jn 6:37, 39; 17:24 (not NRSV)) and looks at them as a totality. Victory over the world is an eschatological reality already present in the realized imagery of birth from God (cf. 4:4). This could suggest a passive determinism, and to avoid this 4b defines the source of victory as 'faith'; only here in 1 John, 'faith' must mean not the subjective emotion but right faith as immediately defined. v. 5 defines that faith in terms of the individual who professes the faith that Jesus is the Son of God (cf. 1 JN 4:15); the verse forms an *inclusio* with the parallel confession in v. 1 but also leads into the following section.

(5:6–12) The Witnesses to the Son The confession of Jesus as Son of God is now further elaborated and given a secure foundation with God as guarantor, and therefore is the *sine qua non* of any true relationship with God. Although the passage is often treated as polemical alongside 2:18–23 and 4:1–6, here there is no reference to opponents, to the antichrist, or to right and wrong confession or denial. 'Believing' and 'witness' in 1 John are always used of the community and its identity. Thus the passage should not be used to identify the schismatics. Belief in Jesus as Son of God is that he 'came' both by water and the blood: the stress is on both, but chiefly on 'blood', and does not mean that some believed that he came by the water only'. It is unlikely that the change from 'by' to 'with' is significant, and both prepositions are ambiguous with the verb 'to come'. The meaning of the assertion has been widely debated with no final consensus; there are various possibilities: (1) According to ancient ideas the combination may refer to real human conception; it is not certain that this would have been self-evident and the double stress would be unusual. (2) Most commonly 'water' has been seen as a reference to baptism; that Jesus' divine sonship effectively started with his baptism was held by some early Christians but seems unlikely within the Johannine tradition. 'Blood' as a parallel event would then have to be the crucifixion, certainly an essential moment in his mission. However, 'came by' and 'blood' would be obscure ways of expressing this. (3) Because water and blood become witnesses in the present and not just the past in vv. 7–8, some have seen a reference to baptism and eucharist, founded in the events of Jesus' ministry and continuing vehicles of his presence. A eucharistic reference seems unlikely in blood on its own (cf. Jn 6:53–6), and is out of character with the letter's lack of sacramental or liturgical references. (4) In 1:7 'blood' indicates the sacrificial nature of Jesus' death in dealing with sins in the present; although not otherwise used in the letter, water is also a symbol of cleansing, and is an important image in the Gospel of spiritual renewal. This would fit the letter's concern for Jesus' present efficacy, particularly in relation to sin. 'Came' need not denote

a specific moment but views his sending as a completed whole. (5) Some cross-reference to Jn 19:34 is possible, although the order is reversed, but the obscurity of that passage does not clarify this. The formula may have been more familiar to Johannine Christians.

The spirit both has some priority over the other two terms as the witness, and is joined with them as equal terms in a single witness. It would be wrong to limit the witness of the spirit to a single moment in the life of Jesus or of the church defined by 'water' or 'blood'. Elsewhere in 1 John the spirit is part of individual or corporate experience (3:23; 4:1, 13), but there is not a single 'doctrine' of the spirit. The three witnesses who are a unity led to a trinitarian reference ('the Johannine comma') being inserted in the text, which was accepted by the translators of the AV (cf. NRSV fn.); it is not part of the original text of 1 John. 'Human testimony' is not identified with that of spirit, water, and blood, or with any specific witness (such as John the Baptist, cf. Jn 5:32–5), but is only mentioned to emphasize the contrast with the testimony of God. God's testimony does not refer to a particular event or moment but reasserts the absolute certainty that God has acted in Jesus and thus established Jesus as son. It might be expected that eternal life would be the *consequence* of the testimony or of accepting it; 1 John's thought is so tightly intermeshed that life instead becomes the *content* of the testimony; equally, believing or not believing, i.e. accepting or rejecting the testimony, is the condition of experiencing life.

Thus life, which was a key to the opening of the letter (1:2), is also the key as it reaches a preliminary climax. Life is by definition 'eternal' life, not a quantitative longevity but a quality. 'Objectively' manifested as the inspiration of the letter, its assured possession is also the letter's purpose. Yet this is not missionary but pastoral, for those who believe.

(5:13–21) Exhortation to Sinlessness Although 5:13 could be read as a conclusion, it is not. 5:14–21 have often been seen as an appendix, perhaps added later, by a different author, possibly after the model of the appendix to John, ch. 21, with which, however, it shares little in common. There is no convincing linguistic or textual evidence for this view, and these verses should be seen as the true conclusion of the letter. v. 13 acts as a transition, closing the earlier passage, and forming a basis for what follows.

'Boldness' (cf. 2:28; 3:21; 4:17) here has present and not eschatological reference (see 1 JN 2:28); as in 3:21 it is expressed in confidence in prayer, which is sure both of being heard and of being answered. The issue is given specific reference in intercessory prayer. Intercession (v. 16) is not general but specifically for a fellow believer who is found sinning. 1 John has treated sin both as a present reality (1:7–2:2) and as an impossibility (3:4–10) for believers (cf. 1 JN 3:6, 9, 14). This passage introduces a contrast between sins whose end is death and those not so defined, although this contrast cannot necessarily be used to explain the earlier contradiction. Intercession for 'non-terminal' sin is proper and will be answered. The NRSV's 'God will give life' is supplying a subject to the ambiguous 's/he will give life'; equally possible is that the one praying, by winning forgiveness, gives life to the erstwhile sinner.

The identity of the sin whose end is death has been much debated. Not relevant is the OT's distinction between witting and unwitting sins (Num 15.22–31), nor probably Mark's sin against the Holy Spirit (Mk 3:29). Other early Christian writers have difficulty in understanding sin among believers, particularly where a strongly realized eschatology makes the blessings of the kingdom, which must include sinlessness, present realities (cf. 1 JN 3:4–10). 1 John's solution reflects this dilemma and probably means that 'terminal sin' is the wilful self-exclusion from those blessings, i.e. separation from the community and rejection of the faith that leads to life (5:12).

The dilemma is underlined (v. 18) by the immediate repetition of the perfectionism of ch. 3, that sin, unqualified, is not possible for the one born of God. This time the source of assurance is the protection of the one who was born of God; this is Jesus, only here so described, and not a reference to the believer who protects him/herself: the tense of the verb 'was born' is different (contrast 'are born'). Thus the dualism is maintained of the evil one v. Jesus.

This dualist framework is repeated, setting the world and the evil one on one side, God and 'we' as God's children on the other. The transforming agent of this dualism is the Son of God (cf. 3:8–10); here the focus of his activity is not the evil one/devil but the revelation of the true one.

vv. 18–20 are carefully constructed with three affirmations 'we know that'; the first two are dualist, the third expands beyond the 'objective' assertion to a personal affirmation, 'and we are...' In all this God is only mentioned derivatively ('of God') or indirectly ('the true one'). The final assertion 'This one is...', better than NRSV's unemphatic 'He', forms a climax on its own, but its antecedent is unclear. (1) '[God] = the true one... is the true God' has a loose parallel in Jn 17:3, but is tautologous and a poor climax. (2) 'his Son Jesus Christ... is the true God' is grammatically more natural, but Jesus is nowhere else in 1 John identified with or as God, although cf. Jn 20:28 (but NB 'my') and 1:18. 1 Jn 1:2 does make a close connection between Jesus and eternal life as manifested and experienced: as a climax to 1 John's argument this would be dramatic but would it be too startling? In practice the final climax is v. 21, but there is little agreement what it means or why it is the last word. Some have attempted to interpret 'idols' metaphorically of false beliefs, of those who held such ideas, of deceptive conceptions of God or Jesus, or of sin. Although there are some parallels to this in Qumran, most ancient usage indicates that unless context or modification suggests otherwise, 'idols' are meant literally. The term was a Jewish one for the pagan gods, both for their representations and for the gods themselves without clear distinction. Nothing in the letter supports the idea that the Johannine Christians were under pressure to acknowledge pagan gods during persecution. Turning from idols was a popular way of describing conversion to both Judaism and Christianity (1 Thess 1:9), a conceptual context which would fit other aspects of 1 John. This may be a final reminder of a conversion call, which the author hopes the readers will reinterpret in their new setting.

2 John

(1–3, 12–13) Epistolary Framework The brevity of the letter and its epistolary formulae are reminiscent of letters of the period surviving on papyrus. An opening third person greet-ing ('A' to 'B'), an initial expression of joy (v. 4a), hopes of a personal visit, more highly valued than written communication, and a closing exchange of greetings are all conventional. The opening greeting has been considerably expanded in characteristic Johannine language, with a heavy emphasis on 'truth', which is almost objectified, but also becomes a formulaic 'in truth': 'truth' is used eleven times in the two letters, possibly because it was under threat but perhaps because it had become a conventional normative term. 'Love', 'truth', 'abides' are all Johannine terms, as is 'joy... be completed' in v. 13 (Jn 15:11; 1 Jn 1:4). The greeting is not the conventional Greek one (Jas 1:1), but a development of the Pauline 'grace and peace to you'; here 'mercy' is added (cf. 1 Tim 1:2), giving a more Judaic tone, and the implied wish of the Pauline form has become a confident assertion, 'will be'. Unusually, neither the author nor the recipient are given personal names. The identity of 'the elder' has been debated since the early circulation of the letters: some early traditions refer to an 'elder John' at Ephesus, whether or not identical with the Apostle being disputed (Eusebius, *Hist. Eccl.* 3.39.4). As a technical epithet it is unlikely to refer to an elder in a local church since this was a collegiate office; evidence of 'elders' as a group with a wider-ranging authority based on links with early Jesus traditions or charisma is disputed. It may have been a significant term within the Johannine circle. (See further Lieu 1986: 52–64.) 'The elect lady' is now usually seen as a reference to a local church in the OT and NT tradition of referring to Jerusalem as a woman (Isa 54; Bar 4–5; Gal 4:21–7; Rev 21:1; cf. 1 Pet 5:13); in v. 13 her 'elect sister' will be another congregation, while 'the children' are members of the community. There is no evidence that secrecy because of persecution demanded such allusiveness, which is consistent with the more abstract tone of the whole letter. Although earlier views that individual women were intended have lost favour, that these churches were headed and met in the household (cf. 'house' in v. 10) of a woman leader is possible.

(4–6) Obedience to the Tradition An initial expression of joy is conventional in contemporary letters. By implication it introduces the theme of potential dissent which dominates the letters, although 'some' need not mean there were others less obedient. 'Walking in ['the' is not expressed in 2 Jn 4; 3 Jn 2] truth' is peculiar to the two minor letters (2 Jn 4, cf. 6; 3 Jn 3, 4): it differs from the metaphorical 'walking in the light' of 1 John (1 JN 1:6–7), and could mean 'walking' = '(behaving) sincerely', but more probably belongs to the formulaic use of 'truth' in these letters (2 JN 1–3, 12–13 above).

The appeal to the command and its form of mutual love is a Johannine norm (1 JN 2:3; 3:11): the NRSV's 'let us love' may rather be a definition 'that we love'. Here it explicitly originates from 'the Father', in contrast to the ambiguous 1 John 'him' (1 Jn 2:4; 3:23) and to John where Jesus gives the command (13:34; 15:12); whereas in John the command is new, and in 1 John both new and old (1 Jn 2:7–8), here it is not new but one had 'from the beginning'. As in 1 John (1 JN 2:3) this refers to their original hearing of the message. There is certainly a tradition link and possibly a literary link between the three descriptions, but the sequence is debated; the priority of the gospel formulation is often assumed but need not be the case.

The almost tautologous identification of love and the command, so that the content of one is the other (cf. 1 Jn 5:2–3, 1 Jn 5:1–2), leads to the ambiguity of v. 6; the closing 'that you are to walk in it' (the NRSV's 'you must . . .' is clever but grammatically unconvincing) could refer either to the command or to love.

(7–11) Warnings The appeal to tradition in formulaic Johannine language in vv. 4–6 is a foundation for the central section and its harsh directives. The language gives a sense of extreme urgency with a combination of warnings and sharp imperatives. A relationship with 1 John, especially 2:18–23; 4:1–6 is obvious, but the temporal sequence of the two letters is disputed: a minority see 2 John as an immediate response, while 1 John is more reflective, while others see the language of 2 John as derivative from 1 John, with its harsh measures as evidence of a hardening of attitudes.

The language of deceiver(s) and antichrist is shared with 1 John and sets the crisis in an eschatological framework (see 1 JN 2:18–27); 2 John does not call them 'false prophets'. Although the formula echoes 1 Jn 4:1, they are not said to have left the community (contrast 1 Jn 2:19) but 'are abroad in the world'. In contrast to 1 Jn 4:2–3 only the negative confession is articulated, and it is directly attributed to the 'deceiver and antichrist'. The confession is distinguished from the positive form in 1 Jn 4:2 by the position of 'in flesh' following and not preceding the verb, and more importantly because the verb is not in the past (perfect) but in the present: 'Jesus Christ coming in flesh' (contrast NRSV). Technically this could mean that a future coming in flesh by Jesus is being denied (so Strecker 1989); although there are parallels to this belief in early Christianity, it does not fit well in a Johannine context. A theological nuance of the abiding significance of Jesus' coming would not be expressed in this way. It would be wrong to dismiss the form as grammatical carelessness. A likely explanation is that the formulation, taken from 1 Jn 4:2, has been modified by the gospel's description of Jesus as 'the one coming [who is to come] into the world' (Jn 6:14): the author is more interested in the negation of traditional Johannine teaching than in its precise articulation. Particular individuals or groups rejecting this confession therefore cannot be identified.

The admonition of v. 8 reinforces the eschatological framework being used to interpret the present situation. 'Lose' (cf. Jn 17:12) and 'reward' are not temporal but eternal possibilities. 'We', better than the alternative reading 'you' (χ; A; latt, etc.), probably does not include the readers but refers to the elder and others similar who have established the community. The definitive 'having' or 'not having' the Father and Son is shared with 1 Jn 2:23; 5:12, although 'having God' comes only in 2 John; here the condition is not right or wrong confession but relationship with 'the teaching', a term not found in 1 John. 'Of Christ' might be 'from Christ' (e.g. the command) or 'about Christ' (i.e. v. 7): the latter is more likely and reflects a distinctive emphasis on objective, right belief. Although '(not) abiding' is familiar from 1 John, with reference both to Jesus or God and to 'what you have heard' (1 JN 2:24), the contrasting 'goes beyond' of v. 9 emphasizes the conservative element; 'goes beyond' need not refer to those who claimed advanced enlightenment as

has been suggested, but it may convey the idea of 'leading forward'.

The prohibition in vv. 10–11 provides the focus of the letter; what precedes gives a context and is not intended to be over-precise. The warning is against any who presumably claim to be Christians but fail to conform to the Johannine norm. Appropriate treatment of visiting believers, particularly 'missionaries', was a significant concern for the early church where hospitality was a virtue (Heb 13:2), and the teaching and leadership they brought could be either vital or threatening for small, scattered communities (see Rev 2:2; Did. 11–13). 2 John's harsh refusal both of hospitality and of any acknowledgement has echoes in Ignatius' attitude towards those he views as heretics of the most poisonous kind (Ign. Eph. 7.1). Older and contemporary parallels to such avoidance are found in 'sects' who have a strong sense of their own election and of their separation from 'the world', which they seek to maintain. This mentality also explains the equation of one offering a greeting with those s/he greets. This prohibition was later appealed to in the early church not only for the correct response to 'heretics' but also in the debate over rebaptism of schismatics, a situation alien to its original one. In fact it remains a matter of dispute whether there was an original specific situation, similar and perhaps anticipatory to that which inspired 1 John (see 2 JN 4–6), or whether the letter is using Johannine language and traditions in a formulaic way in order to establish a clear self-identity, perhaps in a beleaguered or minority situation.

3 John

(1–2, 13–15) Epistolary Framework Like 2 John, 3 John uses some of the epistolary conventions of its age, particularly in the closing: this includes greetings to and from 'friends' 'by name' and means the epithet was not particularly 'Johannine', nor that they were few in number. The prayer for the health of the recipient is also conventional, and the initial 'concerning all things' (my tr.) is similar but not identical to the opening formulae used from the end of the first century CE. However, it lacks any form of greeting, an absence most typical of official letters, but has at the end a Semitic conventional 'peace to you'. The links with 2 John, including the formula 'whom I love in truth', point to the elder's style, if they are not evidence of imitation by one or the other (so Bultmann 1973). While the author remains anonymous, 'the elder' (cf. 2 JN 1:1), the recipient is 'Gaius', a Roman and probably Gentile name; despite attempts in the early church to identify him with others of the same name, nothing is known of him except what is implied by the letter. The same is true of the other named figures, Diotrephes and Demetrius. However, these indicate a very specific occasion for the letter and have invited equally specific interpretations of the events now lost to us.

(2–8) Encouragement The initial expression of joy, similar to that of 2 John (2 JN 4–6), here rests not on personal encounter but on the testimony of 'brothers', not the same as 'friends' (NRSV) in v. 15; present participles suggest their witness was given on repeated visits ('come and testify', contrast NRSV). vv. 5–7 suggest that these were people, not known personally to Gaius, who relied on the hospitality of the fellow believers they visited; unlike the travelling Cynic philosophers of the day they refused to beg from the 'non-believers', literally 'Gentiles', which no longer just means non-Jews. Their travels were 'for the sake of the name'; NRSV interprets 'Christ' but 3 John is using a conventional formula (Acts 5:41), and a reference to God is not impossible: although this could refer to flight from persecution, most probably they were preaching to those 'unbelievers'. Although it is often assumed they were emissaries of the elder, who therefore headed a 'missionary organization', this is not stated. In v. 6 their testimony was given before 'the church' or perhaps 'assembly' (cf. vv. 9, 10), a word not otherwise found in the Johannine literature. Neither the elder's status in this 'assembly' nor its relation to that to which he wrote (v. 9) is stated.

The careful language of v. 5, 'you do faithfully whatever you do' is probably an attempt to combine commendation for past support and encouragement for its future repetition. This is explicit in v. 6 where 'you will do well' is a common formula for 'please'; to 'send on' usually implies provision of what would be necessary for the next stage of the journey. That support for such indicates participation, probably '[with them] in the truth' (contrast NRSV), reverses the warning of 2 Jn 11, although the vocabulary is different. The section combines Johannine and non-Johannine features. An explicit concern for missionary activity is not characteristic of the Johannine literature, and much of the related vocabulary in these verses is not otherwise found in it, including 'church', 'Gentiles', 'send...on', 'strangers', 'worthily of God', the latter not the normal measure of right action in John or 1 John. Johannine features include the emphasis on truth, which as in 2 John appears both to have independent identity (v. 8), and yet to be used in a formulaic way: 'in/with (the) truth' (i.e. dative), is used five times in vv. 1–8; 'love', used only once (v. 6) is a shorthand for Gaius' generosity; 'testimony' is also an important Johannine theme but here has a more conventional context.

(9–12) Taking Sides The letter has been inspired by the opposition the elder has received from Diotrephes. Although denounced by the elder for his ambitions, Diotrephes was clearly in a position to carry out his intentions; whether he held office in the church, opposed by the elder either in principle or only because of his tenure of it, has been the subject of much speculation. The elder's earlier letter, unlikely to be 2 John as sometimes suggested, is lost; it may be implied that Diotrephes had refused it a hearing. More specifically 'he does not receive us'; NRSV gives one possible interpretation, 'does not acknowledge our authority', but this hides the fact that the same verb is reasonably translated in v. 10 'refuses to welcome', and need not imply any question of authority. The plural 'us' does not indicate authority, but may evoke the Johannine plural 'we' (1 Jn 1:1–3) or include with the elder those like him. The elder's threat that he will expose Diotrephes' slanders does indicate he claimed the right to, and perhaps expected to be able to ('if I come'), exercise some admonitory authority; it also suggests that Diotrephes' action had some grounds, dismissed by the elder as 'false charges'. Inevitably this has prompted debate whether the conflict was personal, over models or styles of ministry, or, despite any explicit hint, doctrinal: if the latter, the elder's silence could only mean that Diotrephes was not under suspicion, but perhaps the elder was.

Diotrephes' refusal of welcome to the brethren, and exclusion of those who demurred, echoes the prohibition of 2 Jn 10–11 with its implicit extension to those who do offer a greeting, although the linguistic echoes are weaker than suggested by the NRSV's common use of 'welcome'. If doctrine is there subordinate to the separate self-identity of the community, the same may have been true for Diotrephes. While the brevity of the letter makes all reconstruction tentative, there does seem to be a mutual hardening of attitudes and preference for uncompromising refusal of dialogue.

Demetrius, the subject of the next paragraph, is not otherwise identified but it is often suggested that he was the bearer of the letter and perhaps one of the brethren whom Gaius is urged to support: thus 3 John would be a letter of recommendation, a common genre in the ancient world where patronage and support were essential. However, the terminology is not the conventional language of recommendations, which usually go on to request a specific favour. Instead the language of universal testimony belongs to appeals to models of the past and to characters of established good reputation; it combines secular convention with the Johannine emphasis on witness. Witness by 'the truth' could also be read as 'Johannine' with 'truth' as almost objectified, or as a conventional affirmation, while the final confirmatory 'we also...and you know', is thoroughly Johannine (Jn 19:35; 21:24). Thus Demetrius is set up as a foil to Diotrephes; he is a model for imitation for Gaius, who also already has received some testimony, whereas Diotrephes is by implication the model of evil to be avoided. 'Doing good/evil' are not Johannine categories but familiar in Christian moral discussion; to be from God, however, is Johannine (cf. 1 Jn 3:10). The contrasting 'has not seen God' is more ambiguous; Jn 1:18; 1 Jn 4:12 denies that as a possibility, although the claim 'to have seen' is important (1 Jn 1:1–3; 4:14), and that the object should be God fits this letter's surprising failure to mention Jesus, Christ, or the Son.

The combination of specific reference and allusiveness, of Johannine terminology and non-Johannine secular conventions, makes 3 John particularly intriguing, prompting its interpretation as a key to the development of the Johannine tradition or community. It has also been seen as significant evidence in the development of patterns of ministry in the early church, although with little agreement. Thus in historical and sociological analysis it has acquired a prominence contrasting sharply with the lack of theological interest through much of the history of NT interpretation.

REFERENCES

Brown, R. (1979), *The Community of the Beloved Disciple* (London: Geoffrey Chapman).

Bultmann, R. (1973), *The Johannine Epistles*, ET R. P. O'Hara *et al.*, Hermeneia (Philadelphia: Fortress).

Dobschütz, E. von (1907), 'Johanneische Studien I', *ZNW* 8: 1–8.

Dodd, C. H. (1937), 'The First Epistle of John and the Fourth Gospel', *BJRL* 21: 129–56.

Lieu, J. (1986), *The Second and Third Epistles of John*, Studies of the NT and its World (Edinburgh: T. & T. Clark).

—— (1991), *The Theology of the Johannine Epistles*, NT Theology (Cambridge: Cambridge University Press).

Strecker, G. (1989), *Die Johannesbriefe*, Meyers (Göttingen: Vandenhoeck & Ruprecht).

80. Jude

INTRODUCTION

This short book tends to be ignored, and was regarded with contempt (along with Revelation and James) by Luther. Yet for four reasons it deserves attention: its use of non-canonical scripture; the fact that it has very ancient textual testimony in the form of the Bodmer papyri with complex textual problems (evident from the marginal notes in most modern translations); its fiery rhetoric replete with rich metaphors; and the way in which readers and hearers are drawn into a view of reality for which the Bible offers a language with which to interpret and inform.

A. Authorship. Little is known of the author other than what can be discerned from the introduction and earlier patristic references that must be treated with caution (though we may note the slight doubt expressed by Eusebius, *Hist. Eccl.* 3.25.1). The writer describes himself simply as 'a servant of Jesus Christ', paralleling descriptions in Jas 1:1 and Rom 1:1. The link with James gives support to attempts to link him with Jude the brother of Jesus and is a reminder of the importance of James within early Christianity before the fall of Jerusalem in 70 CE (Acts 12:17; 15:13; Gal 2:9, 12). A case has been made for apostolic authorship of the letter which helps to explain why the letter was given authority within the early church, where apostolic authorship or authorization was clearly a crucial factor in determining the authority of a book. The emphasis in v. 3 on a common salvation has seemed to many commentators to be an indication of a period after the apostolic age when a common faith was being promoted (cf. Eph 4:4–5). Doubts about authorship by a relative of Jesus and the attribution of the text to a pseudonymous writer have to face the vexed question of the extent of pseudepigraphy in early Christianity, a subject that has often received rather superficial treatment in recent study. Even if one doubts a link with Jude, the brother of Jesus, there can be little doubt that the theological ideas contained in the letter, whatever date they were written down, reflect the ideas of Second Temple Judaism. There is clearly a close relationship with 2 Peter. The fact that explicit references to what later were deemed as non-canonical texts are toned down in 2 Peter suggests that the latter is dependent on Jude. Jude would then appear to be a text that was deemed authoritative enough to be the inspiration of a later text and to warrant some limited correction.

B. Setting. Although various hints in the letter have been taken to be indicative of particular forms of deviant teaching and practice with affinities to an emerging Gnostic religion, they are equally compatible with a Jewish antinomianism rooted in apocalyptic tradition that could have been current in the apostolic age. The occasion for writing is set out in v. 4a. The opponents, in Jude's estimation, seem to be guilty of debauchery (v. 4) and despising the flesh (v. 8). They deny 'our... Lord Jesus Christ' just as the opponents referred to in 1 Jn 2:22, cf. 1 Cor 12:3). They are compared to wandering stars (linked with angels in Dan 12:3; Phil 2:15). Those referred to in the letter so disparagingly appear to have been visionaries (v. 8), like the charismatics of the new age referred to in Acts 2:17 (quoting Joel 3:1) and the dreamer of dreams of Deut 13:1–5 who leads Israel astray. Unlike the Colossian visionaries (Col 2:18), these are guilty of corrupting the community and are 'grumblers' (v. 16 cf. 1 Cor 10:10).

C. Jude's Use of Scripture. Scripture usage is typological. That is, it includes the juxtaposition of two different sets of persons (in this case the contemporaries of Jude and certain OT figures). Typological exegesis is distinguished from the related but slightly different form of interpretation in which Scriptures are juxtaposed with contemporary people and events, for example, in the pesher exegesis found in some of the Dead Sea scrolls, such as the Habakkuk Commentary. What distinguishes the latter from the form of interpretation we find in Jude is that the meaning of scriptural passages, particularly enigmatic prophetic oracles, is offered by an authoritative interpreter who is able to discern their truth in the light of recent experience (the kind of interpretation found in the Gospel of Matthew, for example, in Mt 1:23). Jude's biblical exegesis is different. His is a form of interpretation in which Scripture acts as a lens through which the present can be viewed aright. There is no suggestion that the text has its meaning only in the events of his day, and that the true identity of Cain or Balaam has been discerned. Scriptural types remain 'open' for future use, in which the possibility of their excess of meaning can be further used rather than being closed off by application to a particular person or event (as was often the case with Christological exegesis of the OT). The scriptural type serves to illuminate the significance of figures much as in 1 Cor 10 Paul recalled scriptural passages to admonish those who had a special importance in salvation history (a technique evident in v. 5 just as it is in 1 Cor 10:11). This use of typology (the situation where the present is illuminated by past words and events: 'this is that...') means that the particular identity of the people and events referred to in the text of Jude are lost behind the biblical imagery. In a sense exactly what they were actually doing is less important than the way in which the writer treats them. They cannot be viewed normally as people with the names they were given conventionally. Like Simon after his confession, who is described by Jesus as Peter, 'Rock', and then almost immediately called 'Satan' (Mt 16:17–23), the opponents of Jude are identified differently as the result of his writing. Their characters cannot properly be comprehended without the perspective of scriptural narrative. In Jude (just as in Revelation) the individuality of the contemporary person is lost in the reading of people and events in the light of Scripture. They are Cain, or Balaam. For Jude, proper understanding of their identity is impossible merely as contemporary flesh-and-blood persons, without the lens of scriptural typology which enables identity and action to be viewed in a completely different light. One consequence of this is that the contextual person of Jude's day is given a character that transcends his or her particular situation, now indeed lost in the mists of history, by being reread in the light of more familiar scriptural stories and characters.

D. Theological Characteristics. There is in this epistle the use of a hortatory technique found elsewhere in the early Christian literature whereby the situation confronting readers is seen as a sign of the catastrophe that is expected at the end of time (v. 18, cf. 1 Tim 4:1; 2 Tim 3:1; 1 Jn 2:18, cf. Mt 24:23). Within the NT there is an outlook that invests present people and events with a decisive role in the fulfilment of the Last Things. The present, therefore, becomes a moment of eschatological opportunity (and threat) when history and eschatology become inextricably intertwined. Readers are equipped by the apostolic writings with insight hidden to others. They are privileged to enjoy a role in history denied even to the greatest figures of the past, not to mention the angels. In 1 Pet 1:11–12 the writer emphasizes the privilege of the writer's time, and Christians in Corinth are told that passages in the Bible which seemed to be about Israel of old were in fact addressed directly to them, who were fortunate to be alive when the decisive moment in history came about (1 Cor 10:11). The present had become a time of fulfilment (2 Cor 6:2) and ultimate significance in which the readers are privileged to share. As well as the eschatological dimension, the behaviour of angels is regarded as both a warning (v. 6) and an example (v. 9). Readers are shown that their behaviour can match that of heaven, either they can follow the way of the angels who forsook their position of privilege or the example of Michael, guardian of the people of God (Dan. 12:1). The Dead Sea scrolls have reminded us of the close affinity between the righteous community of earthly saints and the 'holy ones' or angels, and the consequent obligation of those who have fellowship with the angels to maintain that blameless style of life (v. 24).

COMMENTARY

Jude describes himself as a 'servant' and as a brother of James. Any authority to write, therefore, is based not on apostolic office but on blood relationship. It is addressed to those 'who are called' (cf. Rom 8:30; 1 Cor 1:2) 'who are beloved in God the Father and kept safe for Jesus Christ'.

(vv. 2–7) Jude sets out to remind readers about 'the salvation we share' (v. 3). It is under threat from certain people 'who have stolen in' (echoes here of Gal 2:4). The understanding of them is determined by what was written long ago, probably here a reference to the condemnation written about in 1 Enoch, 14–16. They are those angels who have forsaken their heavenly position (v. 6), an allusion to the ancient story of the fall of the Watchers told at length in 1 Enoch, 6–10. They turn grace into licence (a common criticism of the effects of the Pauline gospel: Rom 6:1, cf. 3:31). The reference to the denial of Jesus Christ may suggest a Christological slant to the false teaching: Jesus was not part of their scheme of salvation, something which has often been missed in discussing the false teaching of the opponents in 1 John 2:22). Such a denial of Jesus is comprehensible within a situation of Jewish influ-

ence, though how that relates to the charges of licence is not clear.

As in 1 Cor 10:5 the threat to an emerging church and their group identity is illuminated by an allusion to the temptation of emerging Israel in the wilderness. There is a summons to return to former ways rather than be on the receiving end of God's wrath (v. 5). In v. 5 and 1 Cor 10 the writers are communicating with readers who consider themselves 'fully informed' and who need to be reminded of the fate of an earlier generation of God's people who thought themselves privileged. One interesting feature of this passage is the range of variant readings in v. 5, some of which suggest that the Lord who 'once...saved [his] people' is a reference to the pre-existent Christ (Codex Vaticanus reads 'Jesus').

The story of the angels (v. 6) who did not recognize their position in the divine order but sought something better, only to end up in judgement (1 Enoch, 10:6; 12:4), is a potent warning to a group that teeters on the brink of going the same way. So community identity is illuminated by salvation history, by Israel and the angels, and by the judgement on Sodom and Gomorrah (v. 7) who committed fornication (probably to be taken in a metaphorical sense of idolatry, and total involvement in the culture that involved idolatry, as in Rev 2:17; 17:2; 18:9). We have here a situation where a people with the privilege of the divine grace of election, who, in the words of Heb 6:4, have 'tasted of the heavenly gift', now face the loss of their 'first love' (cf. Rev 2:4). They risked forfeiting their privilege, as did the angels and the people of the Exodus.

(vv. 8–13) A major sin is blasphemy (v. 8). The rejection of authority and 'slanders' of 'the glorious ones' (cf. reference to Moses in Sir 45:2 and the glorious ones of 2 Enoch, 22:8–10; Wis 10:14) is a reminder of the concern about the risk of profanity in the speculative Jewish theology of the early Christian centuries, occasionally alluded to in traditions about rabbis roughly contemporary with Jude. Even the great Rabbi Akiba (who died in the Bar Kochba revolt in c.135) was reproached by a contemporary for 'profaning God' in daring to suggest that King David might sit alongside God on one of the thrones mentioned in Dan 7:9 (see b. Hag. 14a, where there is also reference to Elisha ben Abuyah, a rabbi who lived at the beginning of the second century CE who was vilified by his contemporaries for his antinomianism and his blasphemy against the divine power).

A contrast is made between the opponents and the archangel Michael who, in his words to the Devil, resists taking God's name in vain. The charge of blasphemy is to be left to God (v. 9, cf. Rom 12:19). There is a particular danger of humans exceeding their place in the divine economy and 'slandering the glorious ones' (v. 8). In behaving thus the opponents do not have the Spirit (v. 19, cf. Lk 12:10). Even if robust polemic against opponents is allowable (the language of v. 12 offers an excellent example), this must stop short of blasphemy, which is unforgivable (Lev 24:16). It reflects the same kind of presumption that characterized the angels of 1 Enoch who left their heavenly abode and had intercourse with human women and revealed heavenly wisdom which should have remained with them (1 Enoch, 7:1, 'they taught them charms and spells'; 8:1, 'they taught men to make swords, daggers, and shields and breastplates...and the art of making up the eyes and beautifying the eyelids ...'). The result was that, as the author puts it, 'the world was changed' (1 Enoch, 8:2). In Jude 6 and 9 the behaviour of angels is called to mind. The recollection of the behaviour of the angels of old is a way of challenging those whose life in Christ offered them the privilege of standing with the angels in the divine presence (v. 24), and, like the members of the Qumran community, sharing the lot of the angels by participating in the Christian community (1 QH 3:19; Col 1:12f–13). As with the fallen angels, to return to the life of a pagan world was not only to lose something of infinite worth but also to compromise the divine salvation in which they had participated (cf. Heb 6:4).

The words of blasphemy are uttered in ignorance (v. 10), but lack of knowledge is not the lot of the Christians: 'enlightenment' (Heb 6:4) means awareness of the limits of what is acceptable in the sight of God. For the ancients words mattered, perhaps in ways that have largely passed us by except when Western civilization comes face to face with another culture. The effect of words, both psychologically and socially, is something of which we remain largely unaware.

Jude's frequent contrasts between 'you' and 'these' (vv. 10, 12, 16, 17, 19), in a way parallel to the two ways tradition (cf. Barnabas, Didache, Mt 7:13), enable the reader to be aware, at least in general terms, of the path to avoid, even if the characteristics of the way of righteousness are left more vague. In v. 6 the fall of the angels suggests a warning of assimilation into pagan culture. There is a repeated refrain of drawing the readers back to the faith that was handed down (v. 3) and reminding them of what they already know (vv. 5, 17).

In addition to the myth of the fallen angels, Cain, Balaam, and Korah are alluded to and used as lenses through which to view the community's present predicament (v. 11). They will perish like Korah (Num 16:19–33). Their activities are compared to Balaam's 'deceit' (cf. Rev 2:14, where it is linked to false prophecy, cf. Deut 13:5), and 'the way of Cain', which, if 1 Jn 3:12 is anything to go by, is manifested in a style of life that involves 'hatred' of the brethren and the delights of life (1 Jn 2:16, cf. Jude 16): the one who hates a brother is a murderer (1 Jn 3:15, cf. Jn 8:44), and the reason why Cain slew his brother is 'because his deeds were evil and his brother's were righteous'. In Haggadah, contemporary with the NT found in Josephus' version of the Cain and Abel story (Ant. 1.60), Cain had become the type of one who loved 'the desire of the flesh, the desire of the eyes, the pride in riches' (1 Jn 2:16). This is a theme taken up in Augustine's exploration of the contrasting identities of the citizens of the earthly and heavenly cities, Cain being the exemplar of the former (City of God, 15.17).

The striking use of metaphor in v. 12 captures the self-centred and evanescent nature of the way of life of the opponents. They shepherd themselves (cf. Jn 10; Rev 7:17; Ezek 34); they are 'waterless clouds' and 'twice dead'. The latter metaphor renders them both useless and without substance. Whether or not the author intended the metaphor thus, the notion of a cloud being without water is to make it disappear. The abhorrence of their behaviour means that, just as the tree that does not bear fruit is not only useless but has lost any real substance, they disappear, vanishing into the mores of contemporary culture, thereby losing that distinctiveness based on the teaching of the apostles. Jude wants his readers to avoid a similar path. The simile of trees ripped up and twice dead

speaks of apostates, and is thus doubly threatening, because they had been in the community, 'but went out from us' (1 Jn 2:19, cf. Heb 6:4). They 'deny our only Master and Lord, Jesus Christ' (v. 4, cf. 1 Cor 12:3). Their return to the values of the prevailing culture made them a real threat to the distinctiveness of the identity of the 'beloved' whom Jude addresses. Their role as 'deceivers' (v. 13) puts them in the tradition of false prophets (Deut 13) who lead the community astray (cf. Mt 24:24).

(vv. 14–16) The Letter of Jude is the only NT text (although Mt 25.31–46; 1 Pet 3:19; Rev 8:8 are other possible allusions) that explicitly quotes the book of Enoch. Affinities with the Greek of 1 Enoch may be found in v. 1, cf. 1 Enoch, 12:5–6; 16:3; v. 6, cf. 1 Enoch, 16:1; v. 6, cf. 1 Enoch, 15:3, 7; 17:2; v. 8, cf. 1 Enoch, 15:4; v. 12, cf. 1 Enoch, 15:11; v. 18, cf. 1 Enoch, 15:4; and v. 25, cf. 1 Enoch, 12:3; 14:20. There are several verbal allusions to other parts of the Enoch corpus in these verses: e.g. wandering stars (1 Enoch, 18:13ff; 86:1ff); and angels as shepherds (1 Enoch, 89:59ff, cf. Ezek 34; we have seen that there is also an allusion to the condemnation of the fallen angels in Jude 6). Enoch is hailed as one who 'prophesied' (Jude 14) and whose words to the fallen angels apply directly to those who the writer thinks have gone off the rails in his own day. This relates to the coming of the Lord (here identified with Christ) in a way similar to that in which OT passages about God came to be linked with the pre-existent Christ, e.g. in Heb 1:10–12 and John 12:41. 1 Enoch, 10 relates how the Watchers were consigned to judgement beneath the earth, despite the intercession of Enoch on their behalf (1 Enoch, 12–15). The allusions to the Enoch corpus are woven into a remarkable tapestry of typological use of Scripture in which the present circumstances are viewed and understood through the lens of these scriptural types.

The reference to 1 Enoch as authoritative prophecy demands of readers an awareness of the perspective of extra-canonical literature in their reading. Jude underlines the importance of that perspective and the necessity of a hermeneutic which makes comparison with contemporary extra-canonical (particularly Jewish) literature a necessary part of the interpretative enterprise. Our Western canon of Scripture (though we should remember that texts such as 1 Enoch and Jubilees form part of the canon of Scripture of the Ethiopic Coptic church) is incomplete without attention to 1 Enoch, a rambling text it is true, but one that opens up to readers, in the manner of an apocalypse, that it is the perversion of human culture by an alien wisdom and the manifold ways in which that culture stands under judgement (1 Enoch, 6–15).

The coming of the Lord is not a threat that is past (NRSV fn. points out that the Gk. has an aorist), or merely future. Coming in judgement is a present fact, much as it is in John's gospel (5:24; 12:31) and even in the synoptic tradition (Mk 8:38; Mt 25:31). Parousia is not merely far off, for the community lives at the end of time (v. 17), and, like the seven churches of the Apocalypse, needs to be reminded that the Lord has come and stands in judgement in the midst of humanity (cf. Rev 1:19).

(vv. 17–23) v. 17 begins a two-part address of admonition (vv. 17–19) followed by an affirmation of the reason for confidence that the writer believes exists (vv. 20–3). The two parts both begin with the same phrase, 'you, beloved'. Both admonition and affirmation have a retrospective air. In the former there is an appeal to the 'predictions of the apostles'. This is a phrase more comprehensible as a reference to an apostolic text although it could merely echo the words of warning in such passages as Mk 13 and par. which had become part of apostolic tradition. The appeal to tradition (as earlier in v. 3), often seen as an indication of a later generation looking back to the founding ancestors of the faith, is comprehensible in a situation where there is a claim to new insight or revelation (v. 8). The comparison with Balaam (v. 11), who is a type of the false prophecy, requires the stability of tradition. The appeal to tradition, therefore, is to be expected at any time when there is the risk of disruption from the claim to new religious insight and may be paralleled in the appeal to authoritative tradition in the face of the harmful use of the apocalyptic and the mystical in contemporary Jewish circles (see b. *Hag.* 12a). What is unusual in v. 18 is the phrase 'in the last time' (even more unusual is the variant reading, 'at the end of time' in the Gk. cf. Rev 10:6), a reference to the end of time which is without parallel in the NT. Other parallel references in 2 Pet 3:3; 1 Tim 4:1; 2 Tim 3:1 suggest the eschatological times which, in both ancient Jewish and Christian tradition, would be a threatening time of tribulation preceding the hope of earthly blessing. In Jude 18 we have repeated the word 'desire' which has already made its appearance in v. 16 in a related description of the rhetorical bombast of the opponents. In v. 20 the phrase 'most holy faith' has the key early Christian disposition used as a reference to a body of doctrine that is the foundation, together with prayer in the Holy Spirit, for keeping oneself 'in the love of God'. The coming of the Lord will not be tribulation and judgement for those who follow the author's advice but 'mercy' (v. 21). Meanwhile in a situation of uncertainty and difficulty the readers are exhorted to support those going through particular trials.

This verse is one with a complex textual tradition with considerable variation in order in the oldest MSS. Whatever the exact reading, the implication is clear: a congregation under pressure from various religious factions is urged to build on the faith handed down, and from the safety of that position seek to support the waverers and save those who would abandon it.

(**v. 24**) The final doxology pictures the hope of the author that the readers will stand in the presence of the divine glory 'blameless'. This recalls the multitude who have come out of the great tribulation (Rev 7:14), or the 144,000 standing with the Lamb on Mount Zion, who are without defilement (Rev 14:1–5) and possess the Lamb's name and the name of God on their foreheads (another link with Revelation is found in v. 23 in the words 'hating even the tunic defiled by their bodies' (cf. Rev 3:4; 6:11; 14:4; 16:15). They are blameless (cf. Isa 53:9; 1 Pet 2:22), as is the group in Jude 24. Jude fears that his readers might soil their robes (v. 23). It is worth noting that inappropriate sexual activity is a particular issue in the myth of the fallen angels according to *1 Enoch*, 7:1. So, being 'without blemish' characterizes those who are found worthy to come close to the throne of glory (Eph 1:4; Col 1:22). As in Col 1:12 there is a close link between angels and humans here. In v. 3 the 'saints' are humans, whereas in v. 14 they are probably angels (NRSV 'holy ones'). It is the preservation of the readers' angelic status (unlike the opponents who are criticized in the letter for following the path of the evil angels of *1 Enoch*, 6:11 in forsaking the holy community of which they had been a part), that the epistle seeks to achieve, just as Paul urged the Christians at Philippi to avoid murmuring (cf. Jude 16) and be 'blameless and innocent, children of God without blemish in the midst of a crooked and perverse generation, in which you shine like stars in the world' (Phil 2:15 cf. 'wandering stars' in v. 13).

81. Revelation

RICHARD BAUCKHAM

INTRODUCTION

A. Reading Revelation. 1. Revelation is a book of profound theology, intense prophetic insight and dazzling literary accomplishment. But most modern readers find it baffling and impenetrable. They do not know how to read it. Nothing in the rest of the New Testament—or in modern writing—prepares them for the kind of literature it is. Moreover, they are often not sure it is worth attempting to understand, since they most readily associate it with eccentric and even dangerous sects addicted to millenarian fantasy. Yet this is a book that in all centuries has inspired the martyrs, nourished the imagination of visionaries, artists, and hymn-writers, resourced prophetic critiques of oppression and corruption in state and church, sustained hope and resistance in the most hopeless situations. Both the Christian mainstream and the prophetic minorities who have so often reminded the church of its forgotten vocation owe a great deal to Revelation. Reading Revelation is demanding but rewarding, like the life of uncompromising Christian witness to which it calls its readers.

2. Revelation (or the Apocalypse, an alternative rendering of its title) belongs to a genre of ancient Jewish and Christian literature—the apocalypses—of which the book of Daniel is the only other example within the Christian canon of Scripture. Revelation shares important features with many of the apocalypses, such as the idea of a heavenly disclosure of truth made to a seer, a concern with the contradiction between God's rule over his creation and the apparently unchecked dominance of evil in the world, the hope of an impending final resolution of history in which God will bring eternal good out of all the evils of this world and renew his creation, the use of symbolic visions and more or less fantastic imagery to fund alternative perceptions of the world, its history, and future.

3. The apocalypses are a literature which deploys the theological imagination to draw its readers into different ways of seeing things, and the most important sense in which Revelation resembles them is in its aim to 'reveal' or 'unveil' the truth of things as seen from God's heavenly perspective. It speaks to a world whose imaginative view of the world is controlled by the power and propaganda of the dominant political and economic system. By envisioning the same world from the perspective of God's kingdom—which means both from the perspective of heaven, as God sees it, and from the perspective of the final future, as God's purposes intend, the final coming of God's kingdom in all creation—Revelation liberates its readers from the dominant world-view. It exposes the idolatry that from top to bottom infuses and inspires the political, economic, and social realities in which its readers live, and calls them to uncompromising Christian witness to the true God who despite earthly appearances is sovereign. By seeing the world differently, readers are enabled to live and to die differently, as followers of Jesus' way of faithful witness to God even to the point of death. They are empowered to live their allegiance to a different way of being in the world, the kingdom of God, and to live in hope of the coming of God's kingdom as the ultimate truth of the world which must prevail over all that presently opposes God's rule. Revelation's purpose is to enable its readers to continue to pray and to live Jesus' prayer: 'Your kingdom come.'

4. While Revelation bears a generic resemblance to the ancient apocalypses, it is also, without contradiction, a prophecy. Indeed, it clearly understands itself to be the culmination of the whole biblical prophetic tradition. Its text is a closely woven fabric of allusions to the OT, and is largely unintelligible without awareness of this essentially intertextual character. Readers cannot hope to appreciate Revelation in the least adequately without acquainting themselves with the book's OT sources and the way in which they are taken up into the message of Revelation. The author, the prophet John, sees the unity of OT prophecy in its hope for the coming of God's universal kingdom on earth, and so he gathers up all those strands of OT expectation which point to the eschatological future, focusing them in a fresh vision of the way they are to be fulfilled. As a Christian prophet, he reads OT prophecy in the light of the beginning of its fulfilment in the life, death, and resurrection of Jesus, but he also interprets Jesus and his church by means of OT prophecy. It is through Jesus' way of cross and resurrection that God's kingdom will come.

5. However, Revelation does not just gather up previous prophecy; it claims a new prophetic revelation as to the way in which God's kingdom is to come: that the church is called to participate in Jesus' victory over evil by following his path of witness even to the point of death. This will be the great conflict between God's kingdom and the worldly powers that oppose God. The conflict is for the allegiance of the nations, and John's new revelation is full of hope that by this means of victory over evil, witness to the truth in the face of the illusions and delusions of idolatry, and even at the price of life, the nations may be converted to the worship of the true God.

6. Among prophecies and apocalypses, Revelation is distinctive in that it is also a circular letter written to seven specific churches in the Roman province of Asia (1:4, 11). This means that we must take the first-century historical context of its first readers seriously in reading the whole book, but it also means that the various contexts of the first readers, as seen with John's prophetic insight, are sketched for us in Revelation itself, in the seven messages to the churches (chs. 2–3). We are shown Christian communities living in various degrees of conflict and compromise with Roman power and the Roman political religion, the business and social life of the cities with its inextricable associations with idolatrous religion, and the local Jewish synagogues. We find that the readers are by no means all poor, oppressed, and persecuted; many are complacent, compromising, and close to apostasy, when judged by the demands of faithful witness to God's kingdom as Revelation understands these. To these diverse readers in their various contexts, Revelation points the way of faithful witness, the great conflict with the idolatrous world system which will ensue, and the eschatological goal to which God's purposes are assuredly leading.

7. The messages to the seven churches, as well as other key features of Revelation, remind us that, like biblical prophecy in general, it addresses its contemporaries and is intended to be intelligible and relevant to them. We cannot read Revelation adequately without some recognition of its original historical context, to which it itself makes explicit allusions. Like all biblical prophecy, Revelation is prophetic as much in its discernment of God's purposes in the realities of its contemporary world, and in its call to appropriate response by its readers, as it is in predicting what must ultimately come to pass in God's purpose for establishing his kingdom. But, like all biblical prophecy, Revelation also transcends its original context and speaks to later ages, not by literalistic prediction of historical events, but by its power to illuminate the truth of new situations in the light of God's kingdom and to continue to point to the eschatological future. John brings the ultimate future into direct relation to his own present. In this way his prophecy confronts the world and the church as they are with God's final purpose for what must be in the end, that the truth of the present can be discerned and the way from there to the future pointed.

B. Author and Date. The author of Revelation was a Christian prophet named John (1:1, 4; 22:8), of whom we know only that he was familiar with the Christian communities in the Roman province of Asia and at the time of writing was exiled on the island of Patmos. John was one of the most common of Jewish names in the period, and there is no reason to identify him with the apostle John, though this identification was made from the end of the second century onwards. Also from that time onwards he has been thought to have written his work late in the reign of the Roman emperor Domitian (81–96 CE), and this is still the most commonly proposed date, though some scholars would date it earlier. If the interpretation of the allusions to the emperor Nero in chs. 13 and 17, proposed below in the commentary, is correct, Revelation could not have been written before the reign of Vespasian (69–79 CE). The precise date is not important for interpretation, especially since the common view that Revelation reflects a time of widespread and serious persecution of Christianity is not correct. The seven messages show that persecution was sporadic and dependent on local conditions. Revelation anticipates very serious persecution to come because it sees an escalating conflict resulting from faithful Christian witness with its necessary refusal to compromise with idolatry in any area of life.

C. Outline.
Prologue (1:1–8)
    Title and Beatitude (1:1–3)
    Epistolary Opening (1:4–5a)

COMMENTARY

Prologue (1:1–8)

(1:1–3) Title and Beatitude v. 1, the word 'revelation' (*apokalupsis*) can also be translated 'apocalypse', a term biblical scholars use for a literary genre: apocalypses are works in which heavenly secrets are disclosed in visionary manner. Daniel, Revelation, and many non-canonical Jewish and Christian works are apocalypses in this sense. It is unlikely that the word had this technical sense when John wrote, but his work does have strong literary affinities with the other apocalypses. But whereas modern scholars often distinguish prophecy from apocalyptic literature, John considers his work to be prophecy (1:3; 10:11; 22:6–7, 10, 18–19), indeed, to be the culmination of the biblical tradition of prophecy, revealing how the words of the OT prophets are going to be finally fulfilled in the coming of God's kingdom (see 10:7). The most important sense in which John's prophecy is also 'apocalyptic' is that it communicates a disclosure of a transcendent perspective on the world, a revelation from God which enables readers to see their world in a different way from that of the society in which they live. It reveals the world as it appears from the perspective of God's purpose to establish his kingdom in the world, a purpose which has begun to be fulfilled through Jesus Christ and will be completed by Jesus Christ. Hence the chain of revelation: God—Christ—angel—John—servants of God. The angel appears in 10:1–11 (also 22:8–9, 16), because the revelation proper is the content of the scroll this angel gives to John in ch. 10 (earlier chapters are preparatory for this revelation).

v. 2, 'witness' (or testimony) is a key word in Revelation, referring first to the witness to God that Jesus bore in his earthly life (cf. 1:5) and then to the witness his followers bear (1:9). The content of John's prophecy, as intended to serve this witness, is attested by Jesus himself (1:2; 22:20), his angel (22:16), and John (1:2).

v. 3 is the first of seven beatitudes scattered through the book (cf. 14:13; 16:15; 19:9; 20:6; 22:7, 14). The number seven indicates completeness, and so the seven beatitudes indicate the fullness of God's blessing for those who respond faithfully and fully to what the prophecy demands of them. The 'one who reads' is the Christian who reads the book aloud to the assembled church. Revelation was intended for oral performance in the context of Christian worship (just as Christian prophets present would give their own prophecies orally during worship), though certainly also for study, since it is packed with meaning that cannot be grasped at first reading. But obedience to the prophecy is urgent, since John sees a crisis looming ('the time is near') which will lead to the eschatological completion of God's purposes for the world.

(1:4–5a) Epistolary Opening Following the standard literary form for the opening of a letter, writer and addressees are named, and a salutation invokes a blessing in the way usual in Christian letters (cf. the openings of all the Pauline letters). John's prophecy is sent as a circular letter to the seven churches (named in 1:11 in the order in which a messenger would visit them): each is given an individual message in chs. 2–3, and the rest of the book is addressed to them all. This is important for interpretation, since it makes it clear that the whole book (not only chs. 2–3) was written with relevance immediately to these first recipients. Unlike other letter openings in the NT, the blessing here is trinitarian. Revelation has one of the most fully trinitarian understandings of God in the NT. The one 'who is and who was and who is to come', one of Revelation's unique designations for God (cf. 1:8; 4:8; 11:17; 16:5), is an interpretation of the divine name YHWH (cf. Ex 3:14), which Jews sometimes understood as referring to the three tenses of the divine eternity. In Revelation's form God's future is not just his own, but his eschatological coming to the world, which will find its own future in God's coming to it. The seven Spirits (also in 3:1; 4:5; 5:6; cf. Isa 11:2) are seven because they represent the Spirit of God as the fullness of the divine power. (Some think they are the seven archangels, but these are differently described in 8:2.) The three phrases describing Jesus refer respectively to his life up to death, his resurrection, and his future coming. While the word *martus* (witness) does not yet mean, as in Christian usage it soon came to mean, 'martyr', in Revelation there is a strong presumption that faithful witness can lead to death. 'Firstborn' (cf. Ps 89:27) indicates his pre-eminence as the pioneer of the new creation in his resurrection. The third phrase introduces the issue of sovereignty which is central in Revelation. The 'kings of the earth' (also 6:15; 17:2, 18; 18:3, 9) ally themselves with the forces opposed to God's rule either until at his coming Jesus 'the King of kings' (17:14; 19:16) defeats them (19:19–21) or until they are converted (21:24).

(1:5b–6) Doxology In Jewish usage doxologies express the honour due exclusively to the one God. It is consistent with Revelation's high Christology that this one (the first of many in the book) addresses Jesus. His redemptive work is understood in terms of the theme of the new exodus which is prominent throughout Revelation. He is the passover lamb whose sacrifice enables the exodus. The people he freed are described as Israel as in Ex 19:6 (cf. Rev 5:9–10).

(1:7) A Scriptural Testimony This evocation of the parousia is a conflated quotation of Dan 7:13 and Zech 12:10, 12, but the phrase 'all the tribes of the earth' also alludes to Gen 12:3, God's promise to Abraham that all the nations will be blessed. The mourning of the nations is therefore not remorse, but repentance, leading to salvation at the parousia. This scriptural testimony is so placed in the prologue as to introduce the hope that the nations are to be converted. The novel element

in John's prophecy will be to show how this conversion may come about.

(1:8) A Prophetic Oracle God speaks directly only here and in 21:5–6, where there is a similar divine self-declaration. Here the solemn declaration makes clear God's identity as the absolutely sovereign one whose purpose the rest of the book sees accomplished. 'The Alpha and the Omega' (the first and last letters of the Greek alphabet; also in 21:6; 22:13) is equivalent to 'the first and the last' (1:17; 2:8) and 'the beginning and the end' (21:6; 22:13). It is based on Isaiah 44:6; 48:12, where it evokes YHWH's uniqueness as the Creator who precedes all things and the Lord who will bring all things to their fulfilment. Significantly the title is applied to Christ (1:17; 2:8; 22:13) as well as to God. 'The Lord God the Almighty' (also in 4:8; 11:17; 15:3; 16:7; 19:6; 21:22; cf. 16:14; 19:15) translates the OT phrase 'YHWH the God of hosts', and stresses God's supremacy over history.

Inaugural Vision of Jesus Christ among the Churches and his Messages to the Seven Churches (1:9–3:22)

(1:9–20) John's Vision and Commission v. 9, John establishes connection with his readers by pointing out what they have in common. The reference to 'persecution' does not mean that there was systematic and widespread persecution. Chs. 2–3 show that as yet there has been only occasional persecution, though it is a constant risk. Part of Revelation's message is that, in the context of the seven churches, faithful witness (bearing 'the testimony of Jesus') will lead to persecution and require 'endurance'; but this is the way in which Christians share in the rule ('kingdom'; cf. 1:5–6) of Christ whose faithful witness incurred death. In John's case persecution has led to his exile (either banishment or flight) on the island of Patmos. v. 10, since it was in Christian meetings on 'the Lord's day' (Sunday) that the book would be read, the date continues to link John's situation with that of his readers. The phrase 'in the Spirit' (also 4:2; 17:3; 21:10) refers to the altered state of consciousness, given by the Spirit of God, in which John can receive visionary revelation. v. 11, these seven churches in the Roman province of Asia are the actual first recipients of the book, but the number seven suggests they are also chosen as representative of all the churches. Their various different characteristics and situations are typical of any other churches to which the book may circulate. v. 12, the seven lampstands, representing the seven churches, recall the seven-branched lampstand that stood in the temple (Ex 25:31–40; Zech 4:2) and its heavenly prototype: the seven lamps before the throne of God, representing the seven spirits (Rev 4:5; cf. 1:4). Probably the implication is that the churches are the lampstands which bear the light of the Spirit in their witness to the world (cf. 11:3–4 for this significance of lampstands). v. 13, whereas in the gospels the phrase 'the Son of Man' is used of Jesus, only Revelation (1:13; 14:14) uses the exact phrase from Dan 7:13: Heb. 'one like a son of man'. It designates Jesus as the one to whom God has given universal sovereignty (Dan 7:14), and although here it is the churches he addresses, this, as the rest of the book shows, has the coming of the kingdom in the world in view. vv. 13–16, some of the terms of the description come from Dan 10:5–6; others resemble standard Jewish descriptions of celestial beings (God, angels, exalted humans), whose heavenly brightness is often evoked by gold, whiteness, and fire (cf. Rev 10:1; 15:6). Despite the coincidence with Dan 7:9, white hair is not peculiar to God (see *Jos. Asen.* 22:7; *1 Enoch*, 106:2; *Herm. Vis.* 4.2). The clothing (v. 13) is not sufficiently distinctive of priests to indicate that Christ is portrayed in a priestly role. Most of the description probably indicates nothing more specific than the exalted Christ's heavenly glory, but some items with more specific significance recur later (1:20; 2:1, 12, 16, 18; 3:1; 19:12, 15). vv. 17–18, Christ shares in the eternal life of God through dying and triumphing over death. (This is important for Revelation's call to its readers to follow Jesus in witness even to death.) Death and Hades (the place of the dead) appear as a pair also in 6:8; 20:13–14. That Christ now holds the key to their realm means he can liberate the dead from them. v. 19, the precise meaning is debatable, but probably 'write what you see' (this tr. is preferable to NRSV's) reiterates the command of v. 11 and refers to the whole book; 'what is' and 'what is to take place after this' (cf. 1:1; 4:1) may refer to chs. 2–3 and 4–22 respectively. v. 20, the angels are probably the heavenly representatives and guardians of the churches.

The Seven Messages to the Churches (general comments): These are prophetic oracles (not letters), given by the Spirit (2:7 etc.) and as the words of Christ. Each forms a kind of introduction to the rest of the book for that particular church, highlighting and evaluating the particular situation (as Christ discerns it) in which the believers in that church are urged to 'overcome' or 'conquer.' The rest of the book will show them how, by conquering, they can get from their situation in the present (chs. 2–3) to the New Jerusalem (chs. 21–2). It is important to notice the variety of contexts to which the rest of the book is thereby addressed. The messages have a common pattern: (1) command to write and self-description by Christ; (2) section beginning 'I know', containing commendation, accusation, exhortation to repent, encouragement, all with reference to Christ's imminent coming; (3) exhortation to discern ('Let anyone who has an ear...'); (4) promise to the one who conquers, often referring to elements of the vision in 21:1–22:5. After the third message, (3) and (4) are reversed. The elements of the descriptions in (1) are mostly drawn from 1:13–18, and are chosen for their special appropriateness to the message to each church.

(2:1–7) The Message to Ephesus v. 1, Ephesus, largest of the cities and in a key position on major trade routes, was probably the most prominent of the seven churches, well known from Acts and the Pauline letters. The description of Christ indicates his lordship over the churches and his presence in them, grounding his intimate knowledge of their condition and his authority to issue a threat of judgement such as that in v. 5. v. 2, the false 'apostles' may have claimed to be apostles in the strict sense (people commissioned by the risen Christ) or the looser sense of itinerant preachers. v. 3, what are commended here are key characteristics needed for the testing time ahead. v. 5, many take 'I will come' and similar threats or promises in the other messages as referring to 'comings' of Jesus specifically to the church in question, prior to the parousia, but Revelation's general sense of the imminence of the parousia (22:7, 12, 20) makes it more plausible that Christ refers to the way he will deal with each church at his final

coming. v. 6, it is not clear whether the Nicolaitans are (or include) the false apostles of v. 2. For their teaching see comment on 2:14–15. v. 7, the formula 'Let anyone who has an ear...' (also in 13:9), echoing the gospels (Mk 4:9 etc.) and perhaps recalling Isa 6:9–10, stresses the need to listen to prophetic messages with spiritual discernment, since it is possible to hear without heeding. What it means to 'conquer', a keyword in Revelation, will become clear only later in the book (cf. 12:11; 15:2; 21:7). The 'paradise [garden] of God' (cf. Ezek 28:13) is Eden, containing the tree of life, from which Adam and Eve would have gained eternal life had they stayed in Paradise (Gen 3:22–4). It is now an eschatological promise, to be fulfilled in 22:2.

(2:8–11) The Message to Smyrna v. 8, the description of Christ (from 1:17–18) is appropriate to the message (cf. vv. 10*b*, 11*b*). v. 9, the material poverty—contrasted with spiritual wealth (cf. Jas 2:5)—may be the result of refusal to participate in the business life of the city because of the idolatry entailed, including the worship of the emperor and the state gods of Rome, or of action taken against them (cf. Heb 10:34). The reference to 'those who say they are Jews but are not' probably turns back onto non-Christian Jews what they were saying about Christian Jews. The latter were exempt from participation in the imperial cult while they were considered members of the synagogue community. When the synagogue leaders declared to the authorities that they were not properly Jews, they became liable to persecution. This 'slandering' (*blasphē-mia*) of Christians in effect allies them with Satan (the term means 'accuser', by implication 'false accuser'; cf. 12:10) and with the 'blasphemy' (*blasphēmia*) of the beast (13:5–6). The polemical term 'synagogue of Satan' is not demonization of Judaism, but a judgement that these synagogue leaders by their action have sided with the idolatry of Roman political religion against those who are resisting it. v. 10, 'ten days' alludes to Dan 1:12–15: like Daniel and his friends, these Christians will be 'tested' for their refusal to take part in idolatry, though unlike Daniel and his friends they may have to die for their faith before receiving the crown of victory over death. v. 11, the second death is final and eternal punishment (cf. 20:6, 14; 21:8).

(2:12–17) The Message to Pergamum v. 12, the sword (cf. 1:16; 2:16; 19:15, 21), derived from Isa 11:4; 49:2, is Christ's word of truth which condemns those who deny truth. The war (v. 16) in Revelation is a battle for the truth in which words are the effective weapons. v. 13, Pergamum was the seat of Roman government for the province and the centre of the imperial cult. The throne is Satan's, given to the beast (13:2; 16:10), but the beast is not introduced into Revelation's imagery until 11:7. Satan's throne is the antithesis, in the great contest of sovereignty, to the heavenly throne of God, one of the key images of Revelation (4:2 etc.). The reference to Antipas, a faithful witness like Christ (1:5; 3:14), shows there had been only isolated outbreaks of persecution so far. vv. 14–15, the prophet Balaam advised King Balak of Moab to lure Israel into apostasy by enticing them with Moabite women to share pagan sacrificial meals (Num 25:1–3; 31:16). Balaam's name means 'he destroys the people'; the name Nicolaus means 'he conquers the people'. No doubt this equivalence made the parallel between Balaam and the Nicolaitans (followers of Nicolaus) especially appropriate. Nothing reliable is known about the Nicolaitans besides what is said here. They taught that Christians could participate in the pagan cult meals (an important part of the commercial and social life of the cities). 'Fornication' (literal in the story of Balaam) may, applied to the church in Smyrna, refer metaphorically to idolatry, as in 2:21–2, though sexual immorality could also be a corollary of Christian involvement in pagan society (cf. 22:15). v. 17, manna, as food at God's eschatological banquet, contrasts with the food of pagan cult meals (v. 14). The manna of Ex 16:4–36 was heavenly food (Neh 9:15; Ps 105:40). The idea that it will be restored in the eschatological age (a Jewish expectation: 2 Apoc. Bar. 29:8) is part of the image of the new exodus, to which the reference to Balaam and Balak also belongs. The 'white stone' may be the ticket of admission to the eschatological banquet, with the invitee's 'new' (in the sense of 'eschatologically new'; cf. 3:12; 21:5) name on it.

(2:18–29) The Message to Thyatira v. 18, Thyatira was known for its trade guilds, membership of which would involve idolatry. This explains the appeal of 'Jezebel's' teaching (v. 20). The description of Christ (from 1:14–15; and cf. 19:12) relates to his role as judge in v. 23, while 'Son of God' (cf. Ps 2:7) prepares for vv. 26–8 (Ps 2:8–9). v. 20, the false prophet is nicknamed Jezebel with reference to the OT queen accused of 'whoredoms' in 2 Kings 9:22 because she seduced Israel into worshipping Baal. Her teaching is the same as the Nicolaitans' (2:14–15): perhaps she was their leader. v. 24, the significance of 'the deep things of Satan' may be that Jezebel taught that Christians could participate in idolatrous practices, experiencing evil with impunity. vv. 26–7, Ps 2 is a fundamental text for Revelation (cf. 11:15, 18; 12:5; 14:1; 19:15), since it recounts the victory of God and his Messiah over the rebellious nations. Here the conquerors are promised that they will take part in the victory. The star, alluding to Num 24:17 (cf. comment on Rev 22:16), symbolizes the messianic rule in which the conquerors will share.

(3:1–6) The Message to Sardis v. 1, the reference to the seven spirits (not in 1:16, 20; 2:1, which refer to the seven stars) may suggest the divine source of the life that is available to the church if it admits its spiritual deadness and repents. Christ's relation to the Spirit of God is portrayed in a parallel image in 5:6. v. 2, the thief is an allusion to Jesus' parable (Mt 24:42–4; Lk 12:39–40), also echoed in 1 Thess 5:2; 2 Pet 3:10, and refers to the parousia, as in 16:15. vv. 4–5, the soiling of clothes may well indicate, not evil deeds in general, but the contamination of involvement in idolatrous practices. The white clothes may represent both uncompromising innocence and heavenly victory (cf. 3:18; 7:9, 13–14). For the book of life, see 13:8; 17:8; 20:12, 15; 21:27. This reference shows that the predestination implied is not absolute. Christ can delete names because it is his register (13:8; 21:27) of those with whom he shares his eternal life. The last clause alludes to the saying in Mt 24:32; Lk 12:8. The four occurrences of 'name' in this message (in v. 4, 'people' is lit. 'names') suggests the contrast between reputation (v. 1) and reality.

(3:7–13) The Message to Philadelphia v. 7, the use of proper names central to the Jewish messianic hope, here (David) and in v. 12 (Jerusalem), is appropriate to the Jewish theme in v. 9. Though the self-description partly resembles 1:18, the keys are different. Here (in allusion to Isa 22:22) the door gives entrance to the messianic kingdom, which Christ holds open for the Philadelphian Christians (v. 8). No doubt controversy with non-Christian Jews about messianic expectations is reflected in vv. 7–9, 12. v. 10, Isa 45:14, where the nations acknowledge Israel as the people of the only true God, is reversed. Non-Christian Jews are in the position of Gentiles in relation to (Jewish?) Christians who are the true Israel. The Christians' faithfulness to the true Messiah will be vindicated, and the Jews will be converted. v. 12, for Christians as parts of the building of the eschatological temple, cf. Gal 2:9; Eph 2:19–22; 1 Pet 2:5. Here the temple belongs to the new Jerusalem of ch. 21, where there is no temple (21:22)! This flexibility of imagery reminds us that none of Revelation's images are to be read literally. Writing the three names on Christians indicates ownership and belonging. All the images of this verse assure the Philadelphian Christians of their secure place in the fulfilment of Jewish messianic hopes which the synagogue was denying them.

(3:14–22) The Message to Laodicea v. 14, Laodicea was a wealthy city, known for its banks, its textile industry, its medical school with its ophthalmology, and the local eye-salve. Clearly vv. 17–18 play on these local features, suggesting that the church, participating too readily in pagan society, shares the complacency of this prosperous city. It is the only church of which nothing good is said. The title 'Amen' reflects Isa 65:16 (NRSV: 'the God of faithfulness') and is the Semitic equivalent of 'faithful and true'. 'Origin of creation' describes Christ not as pre-existent but in his resurrection, the beginning of the new creation. The whole description is an expanded form of 1:5a. vv. 15–16, unlike the neighbouring cities of Hierapolis, which had hot springs, and Colossae, which had healthy cold water, Laodicea's water, piped into the city, was tepid and nauseous to drink. v. 17, these Christians are materially wealthy because of their willingness to compromise with idolatry in order to share in the city's prosperity. v. 18, the various images all suggest that this apparently self-sufficient church actually needs to turn to Christ to meet its dire spiritual need. v. 20 supplies the reference to the parousia which all the other messages have. The picture is that of Lk 12:35–9; Mk 13:34–5: the returning master of the house expects his servants to be ready to open the door to him. The parousia is so imminent that Christ can be portrayed already knocking on the door (cf. Jas 5:9). v. 21, this promise is placed so as to anticipate the enthronement of Christ in heaven in ch. 5.

Inaugural Vision of Heaven (4:1–5:14)

(4:1–11) God on the Throne Visions of the throne of God are found both in the OT prophetic tradition (cf. 1 Kings 22:19–23) and in several Jewish apocalypses. This chapter especially echoes Isa 6 and Ezek 1. The throne symbolizes God's sovereignty over all things and recurs as a key image throughout Revelation. In this chapter God's sovereignty is seen as it is already fully acknowledged in heaven, and therefore as the true reality which must in the end prevail on earth. John is taken up into heaven so that he can see that God's throne is the ultimate reality behind all earthly appearances. In the following chapters he will see how it comes to be acknowledged on earth. v. 1, the voice is that of the exalted Christ (1:10–12), though what John first sees (ch. 4) is heaven as it has been since before Christ's exaltation. v. 2, 'in the spirit' (see 1:10) marks the second beginning of John's visions. The 'one seated on the throne' is a frequent designation of God from this point on. v. 3, reference to precious stones was a traditional way of evoking the splendour of a heavenly being, and the rainbow has a similar function (Ezek 1:28), with probably also an allusion to Gen 9:12–17. More is said about God in the account of what happens around him than in the direct description. v. 4, God's throne-room is both a temple where God is worshipped, the archetype of the earthly temple, and the centre from which he rules the cosmos. The twenty-four elders are a political image: the angels who compose the divine council (cf. Isa 24:23; Dan 7:9). They rule the heavenly realm, but by their continuous obeisance (vv. 10–11) acknowledge that their authority is entirely derived from God and properly exercised only in being continuously given back to him. In this they contrast with earthly rulers who usurp divine sovereignty, a major theme later in Revelation. v. 5a, the storm phenomena accompany a divine appearance (cf. Ex 19:16–19): the formula used here recurs later in association with judgements, indicating that these emanate from God's holy presence. The formula is progressively expanded, suggesting increasing severity of judgement (8:5; 11:19; 16:18–21). v. 6a, the sea is probably 'the waters above the firmament', i.e. the sky seen from above. vv. 6b–8, the living creatures (combining features of the cherubim of Ezek 1 and the seraphim of Isa 6:2–3) are the priests of the heavenly temple, the central worshippers in creation, representatives of the whole animate creation. Their song is adapted from Isa 6:3, incorporating two of the key designations of God in Revelation (see 1:4, 8). v. 11, God's sovereignty is depicted first as that of the Creator of all things, then in ch. 5 as the Redeemer, in process of restoring his universal sovereignty on earth. Because he is Creator, God can be expected to renew his whole creation in the end (21:5).

(5:1–14) The Lamb on the Throne v. 1, the scroll contains God's secret plan for the coming of his kingdom on earth, which cannot be revealed until someone authorized to break the seals does so. Only Christ proves worthy to open the scroll, because his witness and death have made the coming of God's kingdom possible. v. 5, two traditional titles for the Davidic Messiah, from Isa 11:10 and Gen 49:9, both suggest the militant Messiah who would conquer his enemies. Note that 'conquer' is here used absolutely, as in the promises to the conquerors in the seven messages. v. 6, John has *heard* of a lion, but *sees* a lamb looking as if it had been slaughtered. The titles of v. 5 are thus reinterpreted: Jesus is the victor over evil, but the way he achieves victory is through sacrificial death. The Lamb—from this point on Revelation's major Christological image—is the passover lamb, belonging to the new exodus imagery (cf. 1:5b with 5:9–10), with probable allusion also to Isa 53:7. His relationship to the divine throne is not clear, but 7:17 (cf. 3:21) shows that he must be on the throne, sharing the divine sovereignty, which his death has made him worthy to exercise. Both his seven horns and his seven eyes symbolize the seven Spirits of God (i.e. the Holy Spirit). The horns are a standard image of power (cf. the horns of the dragon and the beasts: 12:3; 13:1, 11; 17:12–13), while the seven

eyes of God (Zech 4:10) symbolize not only God's ability to see what happens everywhere, but also his power to act wherever he chooses (2 Chr 16:7–9; Zech 4:6). Thus they are here the power of God's Spirit, now the Spirit of Christ sent out into all the world to make the Lamb's victory effective everywhere. v. 9, a 'new song' celebrates a fresh divine act of redemption (cf. 14:3; Ps 98:1; Isa 42:10). For the exodus imagery, cf. 1:5–6. The fourfold formula for all the nations ('every tribe and language and people and nation') occurs seven times (four is the number of the earth, seven of completeness) in varying forms (7:9; 10:11; 11:9; 13:7; 14:6; 17:15) and reflects Gen 10:20, 31; Dan 7:13. It is of key importance in Revelation's hope for the conversion of all the nations. The church is drawn from all the nations (5:9; 7:9) in order to bear suffering witness to all the nations (11:9; 14:6) who are subject to the rule of the beast (13:7) and Babylon (17:15). v. 10, some MSS have 'they reign' for 'they will reign'; the latter accords with 20:4–6; 22:5. vv. 11–13, the circle of worshippers expands from v. 8 to v. 11 and encompasses the whole creation in v. 13, anticipating the final implementation of the Lamb's victory in God's universal reign (cf. Phil 2:8–11, a close thematic parallel to the whole chapter). The worship of the Lamb in v. 12 is parallel to that of God in 4:11, while in v. 13 worship is offered to both together, ensuring that the Lamb is not seen as an alternative object of worship (another god) but recipient with God of the honour due to God. This heavenly worship before the throne is an unequivocal indication of the inclusion of Christ in the identity of the one God who, for Jewish and Christian faith, is alone entitled to worship. It is one of several kinds of expression of very high Christology in Revelation (see comments on 1:5b–6, 8).

The Seven Seals (6:1–8:5)

(6:1–8) The First Four Seals v. 1, the events which accompany the opening of the seals are not the content of the scroll, which cannot be read until all the seals are opened. They prepare for it. The first four seals recall 'the *beginning* of the birth pangs' in Mk 13:7–8. v. 2, that the rider represents Christ (cf. 19:11) or the preaching of the gospel is unlikely because the four riders of the first four seals form a group. The repetition of the key word 'conquer' and its absolute use here are suggestive: it resembles the Lamb's victory (5:5–6) and prepares us for the beast's victory (11:7; 13:7). The figure may represent the evil of imperial conquest, with the 'bow' a reminder of the Parthian empire, Rome's eastern rival. vv. 5–6, this rider represents famine, which the information given by the voice characterizes as severe but not extreme. The judgements are limited compared with what will come later. v. 7, the fatal effects of pestilence are limited to a quarter of the earth: the escalation of judgements is indicated by proportions: cf. 9:7–12 (a third). All the evils listed at the end of this verse (cf. Ezek 14:21), summarizing the second, third, and fourth seals, could be understood as the effects of war, initiated by the rider of the first seal.

(6:9–11) The Fifth Seal v. 9, the earthly temple had two altars: one for burnt-offerings in the outer court, where blood sacrifices were offered, and one for incense, in the holy place. Revelation knows of an altar of incense in the heavenly temple (8:3, 5; 9:13; 14:18), but does not explicitly refer to an altar of burnt-offering (but cf. 16:17). But if the altar of incense is in view here, the location of the souls of the martyrs under it is incomprehensible. The blood of sacrifices on the altar of burnt-offering was poured out under the altar (e.g. Lev 4:7), and so it seems probable that those who have died for bearing the witness of Jesus are here seen as having been sacrificed. v. 10, their cry is that of the murdered for justice. The prayer, 'how long?'—prompted by the disappointingly moderate nature of the judgements of the first four seals—expresses a sense of eschatological delay in God's giving justice to his people (cf. Dan 12:13; Zech 1:12; Ps 79:5). v. 11, the traditional Jewish idea of a predetermined number of the elect (4 Ezra 4:35–7; 2 Apoc. Bar. 23:4–5; 1 Enoch, 47:4) is here integrated into the theme of Christian witness as far as death, which will be explored further in subsequent passages, beginning with ch. 7. Later we shall learn why more martyrs must die; for the time being those already martyred are assured of their victory, despite appearances, by the white robes (cf. 7:9).

(6:12–17) The Sixth Seal This passage uses language calculated to evoke the impression that now the final coming of God to judge the world is occurring (for v. 12, cf. Ezek 38:19–23; Hag 2:6; Isa 13:10; Joel 2:10, 31; Zeph 1:15; Mk 13:24; for v. 13, cf. Isa 34:4; Mk 13:25; Jer 4:24; for vv. 15–16, cf. Isa 2:10, 19, 21; Hos 10:8; Lk 23:30; for v. 17, cf. Joel 2:11; Nah 1:6; Mal 3:2). The events of vv. 12–13 are not themselves judgements so much as heralds of God's coming as Judge. The 'wrath of the Lamb' (v. 16) suggests the consequence of not responding to God's sacrificial love. In v. 17 the variant reading 'his wrath' should be preferred to 'their wrath' since Revelation always avoids referring to God and Christ as a plurality, with plural verbs or pronouns (cf. 11:15; 22:3–4).

(7:1–17) Interlude: The Sealing of the Elect This passage is an intercalation in the numbered series of seven; an even longer intercalation will intervene between the sixth and seventh trumpet blasts (10:1–11:13). These passages express the experience of eschatological delay—and constantly disappointed hope—before the end, and their contents explore the meaning of the delay. Here the expectations raised by the martyrs' cry of 'how long?' (6:10) and by the impression of reaching the very brink of the end (6:17) is deliberately dashed by an image of judgement held back (7:1). vv. 2–3, the sealing indicates ownership (as of slaves) and protection (cf. Ezek 9:4–6): they are protected in order to serve God as the messianic army. vv. 4–8, in the OT a census is always a reckoning of Israel's military strength. The 144,000 are the messianic army of the twelve tribes of Israel expected to fight the war against God's enemies in the last days. Judah, the tribe of the Messiah (5:5), is numbered first. v. 9, the juxtaposition of vv. 4–8 and v. 9 resembles that of 5:5, 6, with the same distinction between what John hears and what he sees. Just as the militant Messiah is shown to win his victory by sacrificial death, so his army is now seen to win their victory by following him in martyrdom. They are also redefined as not just Israelites, but from all nations, and not numbered but innumerable (thus fulfilling the promise to Abraham: Gen 13:6; 15:5; 17:4–6). The white robes and palm branches indicate the victory celebration of the martyrs in heaven, though the credit and the glory are God's and Christ's (vv. 10, 12). v. 14, for the great ordeal, cf. 3:10. The washing of robes in the Lamb's blood (cf. 22:14) is not indicative of their forgiveness or redemption (for which

1:5 uses a different metaphor), since it is something they, not the Lamb, have done. It alludes to Dan 11:35; 12:10, and refers to their death due to faithful following of Jesus on his way to the cross. The value of their death is derivative from his. Revelation is written as though all faithful Christians are to suffer death. This can be understood, not as a literal expectation, but as an imaginative way of suggesting that in the situation envisaged Christians who avoid idolatry must be prepared to die. By now it should be becoming clear that the 'conquering' to which the seven messages called the churches is victory through faithful witness to the point of death. vv. 15–17, the images anticipate the New Jerusalem (cf. 21:3–4, 6; 22:3), and allude to Isa 49:10; 25:8. That God 'will shelter them' (v. 15) evokes the tabernacling presence of God with his people in the wilderness. Note that in v. 17 the divine roles of shepherding (Isa 40:11) and leading to the water (Isa 49:10) are ascribed to the Lamb. These are all new exodus images.

(8:1–5) The Seventh Seal Revelation uses a literary interlocking device especially here and in 15:1–4. The account of the seventh seal is in vv. 1, 3–5, while v. 2 is the beginning of the sequence of seven trumpet-blasts which follows. The impression is that the seven trumpet-blasts are included in the seventh-seal opening. vv. 1, 3, the silence is part of the liturgy of the heavenly temple. According to Jewish tradition, at the time of the incense-offering (v. 2) the heavenly worshippers fall silent so that the prayers of people on earth can be heard in heaven. The heavenly incense assists the prayers of the saints to reach God, as the incense from the earthly temple was thought to do. v. 5, the prayers are for the coming of the end, and so the response is judgement on earth (fire, seen again in 8:7). The storm phenomena indicate the eschatological theophany of God the Judge (cf. 4:5) and the correspondence with 11:19 shows that 8:5 already includes proleptically all the judgements of the seven trumpet-blasts (concluding in 11:19).

The Seven Trumpets (8:6–11:19)

(8:6–12) The First Four Trumpets Trumpets were used in holy war against Israel's and God's enemies, herald divine judgement (e.g. Joel 2:1), and feature especially in the story of the fall of Jericho (Josh 6), which makes them appropriate in Revelation, although we do not yet know that these judgements will lead to the fall of another great city (16:19). Like the first four seals, the first four trumpet-blasts form a quartet. They affect the four regions of God's creation: earth, sea, fresh water, heavens (cf. 14:7), and each affects a third part only of its region (note the emphatic repetition of 'third' throughout). This represents an intensification of judgement after the seals (cf. 5:8), but these are still limited judgements, aimed at repentance (cf. 9:20–1). To those who worship parts of the creation as idols, they demonstrate that the true God is the Creator who has power over his creation (cf. 14:7). They are also modelled on the plagues of Egypt, making them the judgements that prepare for the new exodus.

(8:13–9:11) The Fifth Trumpet v. 13, the message of the eagle designates the last three trumpet-blasts as a group of three woes. This and the other markers indicating the sequence of the woes (9:12; 11:14) keep the reader strongly aware of the (slow) progress through these terrifying plagues towards the end. v. 1, whereas the first four trumpet-blasts attacked, not humans directly, but their sources of life, the fifth and sixth attack humans directly. v. 2, the image of the fallen star suggests an evil angel, allowed, like other evil agents in the various judgements in Revelation, to wreak evil as a form of divine judgement. The abyss ('bottomless pit') in Revelation is not the place of the dead (Hades) or the place of the final punishment of the wicked (the lake of fire), but the abode and source of supernatural evil (11:7; 17:8; 20:1–3). v. 3, the locusts are a demonized version of the army of locusts in Joel (2:1–11). v. 5, the period and the prohibition of killing show that this is again a limited judgement, whose purpose is to bring about repentance. v. 11, Abaddon is an OT term for the underworld, sometimes personified (Job 28:22). It means 'destruction', but John translates in a personal form: Apollyon ('destroyer'), with perhaps an allusion to the Greek god Apollo, and the emperor Nero's claim to be a manifestation of Apollo. Cf. also 'the destroyer' responsible for the last plague of Egypt (Ex 12:23).

(9:12–21) The Sixth Trumpet v. 13, the reference to the altar of incense in heaven links this judgement again to the prayers of the saints (8:3–5). v. 14, this picture of judgement plays on the Roman empire's fear of invasion from the east (cf. 16:12). The angels are evil angels released from previous restraint. v. 17, an army of demonic cavalry is described. v. 20, even this deadly judgement has been aimed at the repentance of the rest of humanity, but unsuccessfully. v. 21, cf. 21:8; 22:15; this emphatic statement of the failure of even the most severe judgements to bring humanity to repentance prepares for the revelation, in ch. 11, of a different divine strategy to that end.

(10:1–11) Interlude: (a) The Scroll Given to John As between the sixth and seventh seals, so between the sixth and seventh trumpet-blasts, an interlude addresses the reason for the delay of the final judgement. v. 1, this most awe-inspiring of the angels in Revelation ('another' in relation to the angel of 5:2) is the most important because he is the one who transmits to John the revelation he has received from Christ (1:1; 22:16). v. 2, though most commentators think otherwise, there are good reasons for thinking that this is the scroll of 5:1–9. The content of that scroll, available only when its seven seals have been opened (8:1), has not yet been revealed. The scroll in ch. 10 is already open (v. 2): its contents can be known only when it has been ingested by John (10:8–11). The process of transmission—from God to Christ (5:7) and from the angel to John (10:8–10)—corresponds to that described in 1:1. Moreover, John's use of an OT model for his account of the scroll (Ezek 2:8–3:3) begins in 5:1 (cf. Ezek 2:9–10) and continues in 10:8–10 (cf. Ezek 3:1–3). The reason most commentators have not regarded the scroll of ch. 10 as the same as that in ch. 5 is that the former is called a 'little scroll' (*biblaridion*) in 10:2, 9–10, while the latter is a 'scroll' (*biblion*). But it is clear that John makes no absolute distinction between the two terms, since the scroll of ch. 10 is also called a *biblion* in v. 8. The words could be used interchangeably. The reason *biblaridion* is predominately used in ch. 10 is probably that the scroll has now to be portrayed as small enough for John to eat (vv. 9–10). v. 3, for the lion's roar, cf. Am 3:8. The seven thunders (echoing Ps 29, where the thunder of God's voice is mentioned seven times) must be another series of warning judgements, more severe than the seals and the trumpet-blasts. With the seven bowls

(15:5–16:21), there would then have been four series of seven judgements each, indicating complete judgement (seven for completeness) on the earth (symbolized by four). v. 4, they are revoked (cf. Mk 13:20: God will 'cut short' the days of eschatological tribulation), and are not to be the content of John's prophecy. Instead of more warning judgements, there is to be something else: the content of the scroll. vv. 5–7, the angel's solemn declaration, alluding to Am 3:8 and Dan 12:6–7, implicitly responds to the question 'How long?' which has been in readers' minds since 6:10. The final period of history, revealed to Daniel as 'a time, times and half a time' (i.e. three and a half years: Dan 12:7; cf. Rev 11:2, 3) is now to begin at once, and for the first time the true nature of the events of this period, the way they will contribute to the final coming of God's kingdom, will be revealed by the scroll. v. 10, like Ezekiel's scroll (3:3), John's is sweet to taste, but, unlike Ezekiel's, bitter when swallowed—probably because it concerns the suffering of God's people. v. 11, previously John had prophesied to and about the churches (1:11–3:22); now he is to prophesy about the nations, and perhaps to the nations in the sense that his prophecy now describes the church's prophetic witness to the nations (11:3–13). The fourfold description of the nations (see comment on 5:9) indicates that the fulfilment of Dan 7:9 is the subject.

(11:1–13) Interlude: (b) The Content of the Scroll This section contains the content of the scroll *in nuce*. Later chapters will greatly expand on it, but the essential message of the scroll is given here, in two parts (vv. 1–2 and 3–13) linked by their respective versions of Daniel's reckoning of the final period of history as three and a half years (vv. 2, 3). vv. 1–2, this difficult passage derives from interpretation of Dan 12:6–7; 8:11–14; Zech 12:3. The temple proper (the holy of holies and the holy place, containing the altar of incense), with the priests who alone worship in it, is to be measured, but the outer court, where the people worship, and the city in which they live are left to be trampled by the nations. The meaning of this imagery, taken from Daniel, becomes clear as Revelation proceeds. The temple and city represent the church. The inner, hidden reality of the church as a kingdom of priests (1:6; 5:10) who worship God in his presence is distinguished from the outward experience of the church exposed to persecution by the kingdom of the nations. In the coming great persecution, the church will be kept safe in its inner reality (cf. already 7:1–8, where the counting parallels the measuring here), while outwardly destroyed (cf. 12:13–17). vv. 3–13 give a second symbolic narrative of the events of the final period of history, parallel to vv. 1–2 but going further into the distinctive revelation given by the scroll. vv. 3–4, like the seven lampstands of chs. 2–3, the two lampstands (also called olive trees, following Zech 4:1–14) here represent the church. They are two because adequate witness requires two witnesses (Deut 19:15); and so their number shows not that they are only part of the whole church, but that they represent the whole church in its role of prophetic witness to the world. This is the role that the seven churches of chs. 2–3 will fulfil—the task to which they are called in the coming of God's kingdom—if they heed Christ's advice and 'conquer'. vv. 5–6, the two prophets are modelled on Moses and Elijah (both on both, not one on each; cf. 2 Kings 1:10–12; 1 Kings 17:1; Ex 7:14–24), the two great OT prophets who confronted pagan idolatry, Moses at the Exodus, Elijah in the time of Jezebel (cf. 2:20). The judgements they command (v. 6) recall those of chs. 6, 8–9, and are no more effective in producing repentance. v. 7, the beast appears for the first time, anticipating his full introduction in ch. 13, along with his characteristic activity of conquering the saints (13:7). v. 8, the witnesses follow Jesus in his faithful witness as far as death. The city recalls Jerusalem (cf. Isa 1:10), Egypt, and Babylon (cf. 17:18): it is every city in which the church bears suffering witness. v. 9, the three days of the story of Jesus are modified to make the apocalyptic number three and a half (cf. 12:14). The fourfold formula makes clear the universality of the prophets' witness to all nations. v. 10, a reversal of Esth 9:19, 22: there the people of God rejoice over the slaughter of their enemies, here the opposite leads paradoxically to their victory and conversion of their enemies. vv. 11–12, as they followed Jesus in his death, so they share in his triumph over death. This is their public vindication. The truth of their witness, thought to have been refuted by their death, is now seen to have been evidenced by their faithfulness to death and vindicated by God in their triumph over death. v. 13, the reaction of 'the rest' corresponds with 14:6–7 and contrasts with 9:20–1 (cf. 16:9–11): it is therefore genuine repentance and acknowledgement of the one true God. The arithmetic is symbolic: in judgements announced by OT prophets 'the remnant' ('the rest') spared are only a tenth part (Isa 6:13; Am 5:3) or seven thousand (1 Kings 19:18). Here the reverse occurs: seven thousand killed and nine-tenths spared. The novelty of the witness of the two, by comparison with their OT predecessors, is thus dramatized: not so much judgement as conversion is the effect. Where the preaching of repentance, with judgements alone as evidence, had failed (v. 6), when fulfilled in witness to the point of death, participating in Jesus' witness and victory through and over death, the prophetic ministry of the church will effect the conversion of the nations to God. This is the heart of the revelation contained in the scroll, the heart of Revelation's message: that the church redeemed from all nations is called to suffering witness which, by virtue of its participation in Jesus' sacrificial witness, can bring the nations to repentance of idolatry and conversion to the true God. In this way—as Jesus' witness is extended universally in the life and death, as well as the preaching, of the church—God's kingdom can come to the nations as salvation, rather than judgement. This message will be portrayed at greater length in chs. 12–15.

(11:14–19) The Seventh Trumpet In this section the end itself, the coming of God's kingdom, is finally reached, though the description of it is provisional and will be expanded later. v. 15, the words of the voices allude to Ps 2. 17. For 'who are and who were', cf. 1:4, 8; 4:8; since it is God's eschatological coming which is here being celebrated, 'who is to come' is omitted (also in 16:5). v. 18, the opening words again echo Ps 2:1–3. The events here celebrated run forward as far as ch. 20. The 'destroyers of the earth' are later revealed as the dragon, the beast, and the harlot of Babylon (cf. 19:2), who are ruining God's creation with their violence, oppression, and idolatrous religion. Their destruction is an example of the eschatological *lex talionis*, which matches punishment to crime by describing both in the same words. The Greek *diaphtheirō* means

both 'destroy' (cause to perish) and 'ruin' (corrupt with evil); its use here parallels the same double meaning in Hebrew in Gen 6:11–13, 17. As at the Flood, God's faithfulness to his creation requires that he destroy its destroyers in order to preserve it. v. 19, from the heavenly presence of God come the phenomena of theophany and judgement, in the formula first used in 4:5, expanded in 8:5 (seventh seal), again here (seventh trumpet), and yet again in 16:17–21 (seventh bowl).

The Story of God's People in Conflict with Evil (12:1–15:4)

(12:1–6) The Woman, the Dragon and the Child Unlike other beginnings of sections there is no literary link back into what precedes. A new start is made, with a partly new cast of characters, but from this different starting-point a fuller version of the message of 11:3–13 will be told and will converge again on the end already reached at the end of ch. 11. v. 1, a fresh OT background is evoked here: the age-long conflict between 'the ancient serpent' (v. 9) or dragon and the woman and her offspring, and the promise of eventual victory for the offspring, not without suffering violence from the serpent (Gen 3:15). The serpent of Eden is identified as also the sea-monster or dragon Leviathan, destined for eschatological defeat by the sword of God (Isa 27:1). In extra-biblical tradition (cf. Ps 74:14) he had seven heads (cf. v. 3). By fusing the two figures of the Genesis serpent and the eschatological Leviathan, Revelation has created a new image of ultimate evil. For many of the first readers, pagan mythological themes and stories would also be evoked by 12:1–6, especially the story of Apollo and the Python, a dragon who threatened Apollo's mother at the time of his birth and was later slain by him. From both OT and pagan precedents, the passage would raise the readers' expectation that the divine child will eventually destroy the dragon. Jesus' mother Mary is scarcely in view in the symbolic, not historical, account of his birth and immediate rapture to heaven (v. 5); rather, as her crown of twelve stars shows, the woman in the sky is the people of God (both Israel and the church). v. 3, not Mary's pregnancy so much as the sufferings of Israel from which the Messiah came (and which he bore) (cf. Mic 5:3). v. 4, the dragon's heads and horns are the model for the beast's (13:1) and challenge the Lamb's seven horns (5:6). The seven crowns represent the fullness of rule, suggesting the dragon is the power behind all idolatrous human rule. Cf. Dan 8:10. The stars, as in 1:20, may be angelic representatives of the people of God, so that the dragon's action against them represents inflicting suffering on Israel on earth. v. 5, cf. Ps 2:8–9. v. 6, this anticipates v. 14. The same time period is given in days (11:3 and here), months (11:2; 13:5), and 'times' (i.e. years: 12:14). Derived from Daniel (7:25; 12:7, 11, 12), it is the period of the final great conflict of God's people and God's enemies, the church and the beast. The ambiguity of this period (who are the real victors?) is reflected in the usage of temporal terms: as 42 months it is the beast's period, for trampling and rule (11:2; 13:5); as 1,260 days it is the church's period, for prophesying and protection (11:3; 12:6).

(12:7–12) Michael and the Dragon v. 7, the archangel Michael is the heavenly representative of the people of God (Dan 10:13, 21; 12:1), and so his defeat of the dragon in heaven corresponds to the victory of the martyrs on earth (v. 11). Here the heavenly victory is depicted in military terms, the earthly in forensic terms (vv. 10–11: 'accuser', 'testimony'). Revelation frequently alternates or mixes the two fields of imagery. v. 9, from here onwards the deceit practised by the powers of evil is prominent (cf. 13:14; 16:13; 18:23; 19:20; 20:3, 8; 21:27; 22:15; cf. 3:9). It is by exposing this deceit that the witness of the martyrs constitutes victory over evil. v. 10, cf. 11:15. The devil's original role was as prosecuting counsel in the heavenly court (Zech 3:1; Job 2), but often, as here, acting maliciously and deceptively. v. 11, for the first time, the 'conquering' by the martyrs has an object; cf. 15:2. The relationship of martyrdom to the cross is clear here (cf. 7:14): by maintaining their witness even to the point of death the Christian martyrs follow Jesus to death and so win a victory dependent on his. v. 12, the devil's rage is not a sign of his power, but of the fact that he is already defeated. Heaven, earth, and sea are prominent in chs. 12–13: thrown out of heaven, the dragon empowers one beast from the sea and another from the earth.

(12:13–17) The Dragon and the Woman The narrative depicts, like 11:1–2, the spiritual protection of the church (the woman in the wilderness) during the period of conflict with the beast, even while outwardly the church suffers persecution (the dragon makes war on the woman's children). v. 14, the eagle's wings (Ex 19:4; Deut 32:11; Isa 40:31) and the wilderness are exodus motifs. v. 17, the 'testimony of Jesus' (also 1:9; 19:10) seems to be, not witness to Jesus, but the witness Jesus bore.

(12:18–13:10) The Monster from the Sea v. 18, this statement connects the dragon with the appearance of the beast, to whom he now delegates what power he has. 13:1–2, the sea is here the sphere of primeval chaos, the source of evil, an alternative image to the abyss (cf. 11:7). It is the appropriate source for the beast whose dominant characteristic is violence. The scene is modelled on Daniel's vision of four beasts representing the four great world empires (Dan 7:1–8). The fourth, the most terrifying, is the last empire, whose rule is replaced by the kingdom of the Son of Man and his people. Revelation's beast also fills this role but is described in terms drawn from all four of Daniel's beasts. It is the empire which sums up and surpasses all the violent and oppressive empires of history. As will become clear it is the Roman empire of John's time, but portrayed with the eschatological hyperbole that creates a symbol of idolatrous political power available for reapplication whenever and wherever it suits. The seven heads are the sum of all the heads of Daniel's beasts, but they also indicate totality. They represent, as later explained (17:9), the complete series of Roman emperors in whom the beast's power is invested. The ten horns derive from Daniel's fourth beast, but Revelation gives them crowns to identify them as kings (cf. 17:16). The blasphemous names are the divine titles, such as 'Son of God' and 'Lord and God', assumed by the Roman emperors. 13:3, the account of the beast, as well as continuing to draw on Dan 7, has two other major features: it provides a theological interpretation of the recent history of the empire, and it depicts the beast as an idolatrous parody of Jesus Christ. When one of the beast's heads is said to be 'as if slaughtered', precisely the same phrase is used as in 5:6, where it indicates the sacrificial death of the Lamb. The beast's mortal wound and its healing are a satanic parody of the death and resurrection of Christ. They also refer to Nero, the Roman emperor in whom the anti-Christian character of

the empire had been most apparent so far, since he was the first emperor to persecute the church (only within the city of Rome, but including the martyrdoms of Peter and Paul). The reference to a mortal wound to one of the beast's heads, inflicted with a sword (v. 14), probably alludes to Nero's suicide with a dagger, while also suggesting a judgement inflicted by the sword of God. But whereas it is a head (an emperor) which receives the wound, it is the beast itself that recovers ('its [i.e. the beast's] mortal wound was healed'). The historical reference is to the death-blow which the imperial power received from Nero's death, since it precipitated the period of civil war and chaos ('the year of the four emperors') in which the very survival of the empire was at risk. The healing of the beast's wound alludes to the establishment by Vespasian of the Flavian dynasty which restored the imperial power all the more securely in the later part of the first century, to the 'amazement of the whole earth'. 13:4, it is the apparent invincibility of the empire, all the more impressive after its recovery, to which the people of the empire spontaneously respond with worship offered to the emperors (the beast) and to the gods of Rome who grant them success (here equated with the dragon). In the Greek east of the empire, the imperial cult was not imposed from above, but organized by the local authorities, as an appropriate response to Rome's godlike power and the benefits of its rule. Revelation's prophetic purpose here is to expose the idolatry involved in this deification of brutal political and military power. The question asserting the incomparability of the beast is a satanic parody of OT expressions of the uniqueness of God (e.g. Ex 15:11; Isa 40:25).

13:5–6, the language reflects Dan 7:6, 8, 25. The beast's power, though given by the dragon (v. 2), can only be exercised by God's permission (v. 5); cf. 6:2, 4, 8; 9:5; 13:7, 15. 13:7a, the language was anticipated in 11:7. The paradox of martyrdom appears in the contrast between this statement and 15:2. From the earthly perspective it appears that the beast has won; from the heavenly perspective it is seen that the martyrs have won. The contrast is between victory by brute force and victory by witness to the truth, even at the cost of life. 13:7b–8, with reference to the Roman empire such universal language is hyperbolic (cf. Dan 4:1), but the imperial propaganda itself used such language, ignoring the Parthian empire to the east. Such hyperbole also allows the images to transcend their immediate reference to the world contemporary with Revelation. The phrase 'from the foundation of the world', which older translations relate to 'slaughtered', should almost certainly, as 17:8 shows, be related to 'written'. 13:9, as in 2:7 (etc.) an appeal for discerning attention by the readers is made. 13:10a, there are variant readings; probably best is: 'If anyone is to be taken into captivity, into captivity he or she must go; if anyone is to be killed by the sword, by the sword he or she must be killed' (cf. Jer 15:2; 43:11). In other words, Christians who remain faithful in the circumstances just described must expect to suffer. 13:10b, cf. 14:12: endurance and faithfulness are what are required for 'conquering' the beast. The temptation to worship the beast and to see its power as irresistible (v. 4) was one to which many of Revelation's first readers were in danger of succumbing (cf. chs. 2–3).

(13:11–18) The Monster from the Land v. 11, this second beast, also called the false prophet (16:13; 19:20; 20:10), represents the priesthood of the imperial cult, which included prominent members of the élite of the cities. The imagery suggests that outwardly its power appears innocent, but its seductive speech reveals its inner reality as demonic. If the first beast is a parody of Christ, the second is a parody of the Spirit-inspired prophetic witness of the church (11:3–6). v. 13, the signs parody those of 11:5–6, and (like v. 15a) refer to the apparent miracles engineered in the temples. v. 14, the image no doubt refers to statues of the emperor and the Roman gods. Most of these were erected on the initiative of the local authorities, not by Roman governors. vv. 15–17, the universal enforcement of worship of the beast goes beyond the historical reality at the time of Revelation (when there could certainly be considerable social pressure to participate in the imperial cult), but indicates where the logic of imperial idolatry would lead as the conflict between God and his demonic opponents comes to a head. The mark of the beast is a parody of God's seal of ownership on the foreheads of faithful Christians (7:3; 14:1). The reference to buying and selling reflects the fact that it was particularly in order to participate in the business life of the cities that Christians were tempted to compromise with idolatry. v. 18, since Greek or Hebrew letters also functioned as numbers, it was possible to add up the numerical value of a word—a practice known as gematria. This verse says that 'the number of the beast' is also 'the number of a person' and that both are 666. The Greek word used for beast (thērion), transliterated into Hebrew letters, has the value 666, as does the name Nero(n) Caesar, written in Hebrew script. The implication is that Nero's very name reveals his true nature to the discerning. The verbal link with 17:9 suggests there is even more to the significance of the number. The number 666 has the unusual characteristic of being not only what the ancients called a triangular number (it is the sum of all the numbers up to 36), but also a doubly triangular number (36 is the sum of all the numbers up to 8). It is the *eighth* such number (in the series 1, 6, 21, 55, 120, 231, 406, 666). So for those familiar with ancient numerology, Nero is also revealed to be 'the eighth', with a significance ch. 17 will develop.

(14:1–5) **The Lamb and the 144,000** v. 1, this is the army (see REV 7:2–3) of the Lamb ready for battle with the beast. 'Mount Zion' alludes to Ps 2:6. For the names (indicating ownership), cf. 3:12. v. 3, for the new song, cf. 5:9. v. 4, they are not literally all adult celibate males. The image is part of the imagery of holy war, for which soldiers had to keep themselves free of the ritual defilement incurred by sex (1 Sam 21:5–6). This is used as an image of the moral probity (cf. v. 5) required of Christians (female as well as male) who follow the Lamb in his path of faithful witness to death. The first fruits are the first part of the harvest dedicated to God in sacrifice (Lev 23:9–14). The image implies that the rest of the harvest—the nations converted to God by the martyrs' witness—will follow, as depicted in 14:14–16. v. 5, there is probably allusion to both Isa 53:9 and Zeph 3:13 (the verbal correspondence of the two texts shows that the Messiah's people resemble him in his total lack of deceit), as well as contrast with the guile of the forces of evil (12:9; 13:14; 6:13). 'Blameless' really means 'without physical defect': the requirement for sacrificial animals or for soldiers in the holy war, used metaphorically here.

(14:6–13) **Three Angelic Messages and a Voice from Heaven** vv. 6–11, the angels symbolize the effect on the nations of the confrontation of the forces of the beast and the Lamb. By contrast with the eagle (8:13), their messages are positive. vv. 1–2, the invitation to all nations to repent and worship God (cf. 11:13) alludes to Ps 96. v. 3, the good news of Babylon's fall anticipates the account of Babylon in 16:19–18:24, just as the initial reference to the beast (11:7) anticipated his introduction in ch. 13. Cf. Isa 21:9; Jer 25:15–16; 51:7–8; Dan 4:30. In the OT Babylon is the greatest of the world powers who subjugated and exiled the people of God, and is closely associated with the imagery of new exodus in Isa 40–55. In Revelation she stands for, not the political and military power of Rome (the beast), but the city of Rome (see chs. 17–18), with its economic, cultural, and religious influence on the empire. For 'the wine of the passion [*thumos* can also mean wrath, as in v. 10] of her fornication' (lit. tr.) cf. 17:2; 18:3: the reference is to the promise of economic prosperity whereby she entices the nations into association with her, a promise which intoxicates, so that her clients are oblivious of the risk of divine judgement incurred. v. 10, the first image of punishment is an example of eschatological *lex talionis* (see comment on 11:18): those who drank the wine of Babylon's passion (*thumos*) will drink the wine of God's wrath (*thumos*). 'Fire and sulphur' allude to the paradigmatic judgement on Sodom and Gomorrah (Gen 19:24; and cf. Isa 34:9). The torment consists in remorseful recognition of truth and holiness. v. 11, the image is from Isa 34:9–10, the judgement on Edom, enemy of OT Israel who, though never named in Revelation, serves implicitly as a precedent for Rome. Revelation's use of such imagery (cf. 19:3, 20; 20:10, 15) resists translation into prosaic literal terms. The 'no rest day or night' (from torment) corresponds verbally with the ceaseless praise of the living creatures (4:8), as well as contrasting with the 'rest' promised to the saints in v. 13. v. 12, cf. 13:10. The threat of vv. 9–10 is a warning not least to Christians, who need 'endurance' if they are to avoid worshipping the beast. v. 13, the Spirit's words are a prophetic oracle given to John in response to the heavenly voice (cf. 2:7 etc.).

(14:14–20) **The Harvest of the Earth and the Vintage of the Earth** The messages of the angels have given the nations the opportunity to respond to the witness of the martyrs in repentance (14:7) or to face the judgement of God (vv. 9–11). To these two possibilities correspond the two images of the end that now follow, two different forms (taken from Joel 3:13) of the traditional eschatological image of harvest: the grain harvest (vv. 14–16) and the vintage (vv. 17–20). The first, which takes up the harvest image from 14:4, is a positive image of the gathering of the nations into the messianic kingdom, while the second, taking up the image of wine from 14:8, 10, is a negative image of the judgement of the unrepentant nations. Thus the response of the nations to the proclamations of the angels is left open to two final possibilities: salvation or judgement. This passage is an important corrective to the tendency of commentators to allow only one of these possibilities as the message of Revelation. v. 14, there is a precise allusion to Dan 7:13–14, depicting Christ (cf. 1:13) coming on the clouds to God, not as judge, but to receive his dominion over all nations (hence the golden crown). vv. 15–16, the harvest here consists in the single action of reaping, not the following acts of threshing and winnowing. Whereas the latter are commonly images of eschatological judgement (e.g. Jer 51:33; Mt 3:12), reaping alone is not a natural image of judgement and is never so used in the Bible, whereas it does occur as a positive image of the gathering of people into the kingdom (Mk 4:29; Jn 4:35–8). v. 18, the altar and the fire (cf. 8:5) already suggest that this image is of judgement. vv. 19–20, unlike the single action of reaping the grain harvest, two actions are specified for the vintage: gathering the grapes into the winepress and treading the winepress (for the latter as image of judgement, cf. Lam 1:15; Isa 63:3). The exposition of these images is left until 16:12–14 (the gathering of the grapes) and 19:15 (the identity of the treader of the grapes).

(15:1–4) The Song of the Conquerors v. 1, while vv. 2–4 are the concluding section of the account of the conflict of the forces of evil and the forces of God in chs. 12–15, v. 1 already introduces the angels whose actions are then narrated in 15:5–16:21. This is another example of the interlocking device already used in 8:1–5. v. 2, the heavenly sea of glass (4:6), now mingled with the fire of judgement, is the Red Sea through which the martyrs have come in the new exodus. They stand beside it, praising God for the victory, as Moses and Israel did (Ex 15:1–18). v. 3, since they have conquered by the blood of the Lamb (12:11), their song is the Lamb's as well as Moses'. vv. 3–4, the song is an interpretation of the song of Moses (Ex 15:1–8), reflecting the themes of that OT passage, but using the words of other OT passages with verbal links to Ex 15:11; Jer 10:6–7; Ps 86:8–10. The effect is to stress the theme that God's act of judgement and salvation, the Exodus, demonstrates his deity to the nations (Ex 15:11–16), and to interpret this in terms of the most universalistic hope of the OT: that all the nations will come to worship the true God. In the context of Rev 15, this is the result of the victory won by the martyrs through their faithful witness as far as death. However, just as the positive outcome (the grain harvest) is followed by the negative outcome (the vintage) in ch. 14, so this vision of the nations converted to the worship of God through the witness of the martyrs (15:2–4) is now followed by a picture of final judgement on the nations (15:5–16:21) in consequence of their rejection of the witness of the martyrs (cf. 16:4–6). The future is portrayed in alternative images—conversion of the nations, judgement of the nations—which Revelation never reconciles. Since it deals in genuine images, not literalistic descriptions, it need not do so.

The Seven Bowls (15:5–16:21)

(15:5–16:1) Introduction The anticipatory vision of 15:1—which declared these seven plagues to be the last ones—is now continued. 15:5 echoes 11:19, indicating that this series of seven is related to the seventh trumpet-blast just as the seven trumpet-blasts were to the seventh seal. 15:7, the golden bowls reflect Isa 51:17, 22–3 (God's wrath punishing his people's enemies as they had afflicted his people; cf. Rev 16:4–5). They are also liturgical vessels described like those of 5:8, which contain incense representing the prayers of the saints. They therefore make the same point as the related but alternative image in 8:3–5. 15:8, cf. Isa 6:1, 4; Ezek 10:2–4. That no one can enter the temple until these plagues are ended stresses their finality and also contrasts with 7:9–17. Unlike the series of seals and the series of trumpet-blasts, which both had interludes between the fifth and sixth judgement, expressing and interpreting the delay of final judgement, this series has no such interlude.

(16:2–11) The First Five Bowls v. 2, like the first four trumpet-blasts (8:7–12), the first four bowls fall on the four regions of creation: earth, sea, rivers and springs, heavens. But whereas the trumpet-blasts were limited, these are total. Again there are echoes of the plagues of Egypt (Ex 7–10). v. 5, in Jewish angelology, various angels were in charge of the functioning of various parts of creation (cf. 14:18). v. 6, an example of eschatological *lex talionis* (see comment on 11:18). v. 7, this is the altar of 6:9, on which the martyrs were sacrificed. v. 9, the response of these hardened sinners (also in v. 11) is the opposite of 11:13 and 14:7. v. 10, the first judgement to attack the power of the beast directly.

(16:12–16) The Sixth Bowl v. 12, this does not look like a judgement at all, until we realize that it prepares for the forces of evil to inflict judgement on themselves (cf. Rev 17:12, 16). The references to the Euphrates and kings from the east again evoke the contemporary fear or hope of invasion from the east (cf. 9:14–19), as well as prophecies of the fall of Babylon (Jer 50:2, 41; 51:11, 28, 36). There may be a parodic element again, suggesting the drying up of the Red Sea or the Euphrates (Isa 11:15) for God's people to pass. v. 13, frogs were unclean animals (Lev 11:9–12, 41–7). v. 14, this gathering for battle is resumed in 19:19. For 'the great day' cf. Joel 2:11, 31; Zeph 1:14; Rev 6:17. v. 15, this interruption of the narrative by Christ addressing the readers, as in chs. 2–3, and a beatitude directs the readers' attention to the urgent relevance to themselves. They too are susceptible to the deceptions of the beast and the false prophet, who have their agents in the churches (cf. 2:14, 20). The simile (cf. 3:3) suggests the unexpectedness of the parousia, such that the readers must be at all times ready. Otherwise they will be like someone who removes his clothes for sleep and when surprised is found naked to his shame. v. 16, Harmagedon means 'mountain of Megiddo(n)', but is problematic since, although Megiddo is a town mentioned often in the OT, there is no 'mountain of Megiddo'. Probably the name derives from Zech 12:11 ('the plain of Megiddon'), since Rev 1:7 alludes to Zech 12:10, 12 with reference to the parousia and Zech 12:9 speaks of God's destruction of the nations who come against Jerusalem. Conflation of this passage with Ezek 38:17 (to which Rev 19:17 alludes) has produced a mountain of Megiddo. In view of the interpretation of Zech 12:10–12 in Rev 1:7, it seems that, even at this last moment of the eleventh hour, immediately before the very last judgement (16:17–21), John hints at the possibility of the nations greeting the returning Christ with repentance.

(16:17–21) The Seventh Bowl v. 17, the voice declares the completion of God's judgement (cf. 15:1); the same words in 21:6 refer to the completion of the renewal that follows judgement. vv. 18–21, this is the final and fullest expansion of the formula of theophany and judgement (cf. 4:5; 8:5; 11:19). With 16:5 it shows that the whole series of last plagues is included in 11:19. The earthquake and the plague of hail echo Ezek 38:19–22 (and cf. Josh 10:11). Earthquakes were frequent in the province of Asia in this period and ruined several cities, including Laodicea. The expression 'such as had not occurred . . .' is an apocalyptic formula deriving from Dan 12:1 (cf. Mt 24:21; Mk 13:19), though it might also recall the plagues of Egypt (Ex 9:18, 24; 10:6; 11:6). The judgement affects not only Babylon and the other cities (v. 19), but the whole earth (v. 20; cf. 6:14). The description ends, not with the death of the still unrepentant sinners, which must be implied, but with their cursing of God, making a striking contrast with 11:13, which is an alternative version of the same eschatological earthquake and its effects. The description of the fall of Babylon here (vv. 18–19) is good evidence for not taking Revelation's images literally, since the fall of Babylon is differently described in 17:16, as the work of the beast and the ten kings, and in 18:8.

Babylon the Harlot (17:1–19:10)

(17:1–6a) The Harlot: (a) the Vision Until now Babylon has appeared only briefly in 14:8; 16:19; now she is given full attention. v. 1, this angel is a characteristic literary link with the preceding section, while the reference to the 'judgement' of the harlot shows that the vision will expand on what was briefly mentioned in 16:19. The 'many waters' apply literally to ancient Babylon (Jer 51:13), hardly to contemporary Rome, but this is why they are later given an allegorical interpretation (17:15). vv. 1–2, harlotry or adultery is an image applied by OT prophets to Israel, indicating her unfaithfulness to her husband YHWH and her devotion to other gods (cf. 2:22). But this sense of religious apostasy is only appropriate if the image is applied to the people of God. The image has another significance in Isa 23:15–18, where it is applied to Tyre, and Nah 3:4–6, where it is applied to Nineveh. Since the account of Babylon in ch. 18 alludes not only to OT prophecies about Babylon but also to those about Tyre (Isa 23; Ezek 26–8), Isa 23 is probably the main source of the image. In both Isa 23 and in Revelation it is not with gods that the harlot commits fornication but with 'all the kingdoms of the world' (Isa 23:17; cf. Ezek 27:33) or 'the kings of the earth' (Rev 17:2; 18:3, 9). In Isa 23 prostitution is an image of Tyre's trading relationships with the nations; in Revelation harlotry is similarly an image of Rome's economic relationships with client kingdoms and others. The basic idea is that those who associate with a prostitute pay her for the privilege. Babylon, 'the great whore' (v. 1), is a rich courtesan, whose expensive clothes and jewellery (v. 4) indicate the lifestyle she leads at her clients' expense. This is an image of Rome's economic exploitation of her empire (as becomes especially clear in ch. 18). To those who associate with her she offers the supposed benefits of the *Pax Romana* (the conditions for economic prosperity), much lauded in Roman propaganda of the period, but these benefits are not what they seem. While the local élites may benefit from Rome's rule, many of Rome's subjects do not, but, dazzled by her glory and persuaded by her propaganda, they fail to realize they are being exploited. Hence 'the kings of the earth' (the local élites) enjoy her sexual favours, but 'the inhabitants of the earth' are intoxicated by her wine (v. 2; cf. the same distinction in 18:2). v. 3, for John's transportation in the spirit (i.e. by the agency of God's Spirit), cf. 21:10; Ezek 3:12, 14. The 'wilderness' (cf. Isa 21:1) already anticipates Babylon's destruction (18:2). It is also one of the many parallels and contrasts between Babylon and the new Jerusalem, which John will see on a high mountain

(21:10). The beast is easily identifiable as that of ch. 13, though its colour is a new feature, suggesting royal power or bloody oppression (cf. 12:3). Rome's economic power (the harlot) rides on the back of her military and political power (the beast). v. 4, the golden cup (cf. Jer 51:7), the outward attractiveness of Roman propaganda, contains the abominations of the Roman political religion. v. 5, the name Babylon is a mystery because it points to the true reality and fate of Rome which the vision reveals. Babylon as 'the mother of whores' is the metropolis to which other urban centres—such as the cities in which the seven churches are located—are subject (cf. 16:19). v. 6, the two descriptions of Christians seem to refer to the same people, not to two groups. It is probably not implied that their blood is in the golden cup (v. 4). The harlot's drunkenness has an even more sinister source. Probably Nero's persecution of Christians in the city of Rome is in mind, but those whom Rome will put to death in the great persecution which Revelation sees coming may be included.

(17:6b–18) The Harlot: (b) The Interpretation v. 6, John is perplexed by the vision. v. 7, the interpretation turns out to be as much about the beast as about the harlot, since her fate is closely related to the career of the beast. v. 8, in this chapter, unlike ch. 13, Revelation takes up the popular expectation that the emperor Nero, thought not to be dead but to have fled secretly east to the Parthian empire, would return, with allies from the east, to wreak vengeance on Rome. This expectation, kept alive by a series of pretenders claiming to be the returning Nero, was a matter of eager hope for many in the eastern part of the Roman empire, who saw it as the resurgence of the power of the east against the west. The expected returning Nero was thus a kind of messianic figure. By alluding to this myth, Rev 17 can take in a different direction the Christological parody which was a feature of the portrayal of the beast in ch. 13. Whereas there the healing of the wound the Roman power suffered at the death of Nero parodies the resurrection of Jesus, here the return of Nero parodies the parousia of Jesus. Thus in v. 8 the beast is twice described in terms which echo one of Revelation's key designations for God: 'the one who was and who is and who is to come' (1:4, 8). The description of the beast differs in that the middle term is negative: 'is not'. Unlike God, the beast is not eternal. He has perished once already and so his future coming, unlike the parousia of Jesus, is unlikely to establish his eternal rule. Whereas Jesus will descend from heaven, he will ascend from the abyss and go to destruction (v. 8a). He is already doomed and his parousia will prove a fraud. v. 9, the interpretation of the seven heads as mountains makes the identification with Rome, famous for its seven hills, unequivocal. v. 10, attempts to use this passage to discover which Roman emperor was ruling when Revelation was written fail because it is impossible to know from which emperor the counting should begin or whether all emperors should be counted. It is better to recognize seven as the number of completeness. The series represents the complete sequence of emperors, and the counting functions to put the readers near, but not yet quite at the end ('a little while' is the conventional period of eschatological imminence, cf. 6:11; Heb 10:37). There is still one short reign to come. v. 11, Nero is the one who belongs to the seven (as a past emperor) but is also an eighth (when he returns). This head of the beast is identified with the beast itself (here and in v. 8) because Nero most vividly represents the antichristian evil of the imperial power. If seven is the complete sequence of emperors, the eighth is a supernumerary, in whom completeness is surpassed in a final excess of evil, which brings final destruction to the imperial power. v. 12, the ten are probably 'the kings of the east' (16:12) who accompany the returning Nero on his return. Their 'one hour' of co-rule with the beast is clear proof that none of Revelation's time periods should be understood literally. v. 14, this anticipates the account of the parousia in 19:11–21. As the beast has his allies, so Christ is accompanied by his saints (cf. 19:14). v. 16, Revelation here exploits the contradiction between the two pagan Roman expectations: the admiring belief in Rome's self-promotion as 'the eternal city', and the rebellious hope of a conqueror from the east who would destroy Rome. Since the latter is the returning emperor Nero, the beast's own last attempt to establish his universal dominion itself destroys the eternal city. v. 17, evil itself enacts the judgement of God on evil. v. 18, this anticipates the appearance of the kings of the earth, mourning Babylon's fall, in 18:9.

(18:1–3) The Fall of Babylon: (a) The Voice of an Angel Ch. 18 draws on all the OT prophetic oracles against Babylon (Isa 13:1–14:23; 21:1–10; 47; Jer 25:12–38; 50–1) and against Tyre (Isa 23; Ezek 26–8). John's oracle gathers up all that his prophetic predecessors had said against these two cities, in order to portray Rome as the culmination of all the evil empires of history and therefore subject like them to judgement. (Compare the way the beast (13:1–2) combines the features of all four beasts in Daniel's vision (Dan 7:3–8).) OT Babylon prefigures Rome's political supremacy and oppression, but OT Tyre prefigures Rome's economic power and oppression. Hence the importance of Ezek 26–8 as a model for John's oracle against Babylon (vv. 9–20). At the same time, prophetic precedents are selected and adapted to fit the realities of contemporary Rome. v. 2, the cry of the angel in 14:8 is taken up and expanded. Demons and unclean animals haunt deserted ruins in OT oracles of destruction (Jer 51:37; Isa 13:21–2; 34:11–15). v. 3, to the nations and the kings, already in ch. 17's account of Babylon's harlotry, the merchants, another group who, like the local ruling élites, profited from Rome's domination of her empire, are now added.

(18:4–20) The Fall of Babylon: (b) A Voice from Heaven This whole section is spoken by the voice to which v. 4 refers. v. 4, cf. Isa 48:20; Jer 50:8; 51:6. Addressed to Revelation's first readers, who did not live in Rome, this is a summons not to physical movement out of Babylon, but to dissociation from her evils. It is especially relevant to those Christians who belonged or wished to belong to the groups who mourn for Babylon in vv. 9–19, who profited themselves from the economic system by which Rome exploited her empire and in which the political religion of Rome was inextricably involved. v. 5, for 'heaped high as heaven', cf. Jer 51:9; the phrase is suggestive of the tower of Babel (Gen 11), implying that what God prevented humanity completing then is now accomplished in Babylon's summation of the human desire to rival God. For 'God remembered', cf. 16:19; Jer 14:10; Hos 7:2; 8:13; the expression responds to the complaint that God has forgotten, made by those who suffer injustice and wait for God's

intervention. vv. 6–7b, this formulates the principle that the punishment fits the crime (see comment on 11:18). 'Double' (as in Jer 16:18; Isa 40:2) really means 'fully equivalent'. The third command takes up the notion that the cup of Babylon's passion is also the cup of God's wrath (cf. 14:8, 10; Jer 51:7). v. 7b is Rome's proud—virtually self-deifying—claim to eternal reign (cf. Isa 47:7–8).

v. 9, the three groups of mourners (vv. 9–19) bewail the loss of the source of their own power or profit. v. 10, the lament of the kings appropriately refers to Babylon as powerful, whereas the others refer to her wealth. v. 11, though not of high social status, many merchants were among the richest men of their time, and wielded much economic power. vv. 12–13, the list of cargoes has 28 (7 × 4) items, indicating all the produce of the whole earth (seven for completeness, four for the earth). The model for such a list is Ezek 27:12–24, but the form and contents of the list are quite different. It is a remarkably accurate list of the main imports to the city of Rome at the time, especially the most expensive luxuries which the extravagant tastes of the Roman rich demanded, but also some items (wine, oil, wheat) on which the life of the whole city depended. Many of the luxuries are those mentioned by Roman moralists criticizing the decadence of the Roman aristocracy. While those who mourn for Rome profited from this trade, on the whole Rome's luxuries and even her more basic imports were bought with the wealth gained from conquest, plunder, and taxation of the provinces, or drew resources to Rome that were needed in the provinces, or exploited local labour. The list is not an admiring view of Rome's civilization, but a precise indictment of her economic exploitation and oppression. The end of the list makes this clear: 'slaves, that is, human lives' (probably better than: 'slaves and human lives'). Not only does this indicate that slaves, traded as property, are human beings, but as the end of the list it suggests the contempt for human life on which all Rome's prosperity and luxury rested. v. 14, this is addressed to Babylon by the heavenly voice, as a comment on the list of cargoes: it evokes Rome's addiction to consumption and ostentatious display of wealth. v. 16, the description is very close to 7:4, demonstrating that Rome's luxury imports are the courtesan's extravagant profits from her rich clients. v. 17, the third group are those employed in the maritime transport industry. v. 20, this is not part of the mariners' lament, but the heavenly voice (v. 4) speaking for itself. Whereas Babylon's clients mourn, the saints should rejoice, for Babylon's fall is God's justice in their favour against their oppressor. It is a test for Revelation's Christian readers to realize with which perspective they sympathize—that of the earth (vv. 9, 11) and the sea (v. 17), or that of heaven (v. 20).

(18:21–4) The Fall of Babylon: (c) The Voice of Another Angel v. 21, a prophetic symbol of Babylon's fall, modelled on Jeremiah's (51:63–4). vv. 22–3, cf. Jer 25:10; and for 'your sorcery', cf. Nah 4:3; Isa 47:12. Babylon is guilty of all the crimes which, according to 22:15, exclude people from the new Jerusalem. v. 24, this depicts Babylon as the culmination of all evil empires, held guilty of all their crimes: the kind of eschatological hyperbole which enables the image to transcend its original reference to Rome. It is not only for the martyrdom of Christians, but for all the victims of her oppression that Babylon is judged. John's prophetic critique of Rome (the most thoroughgoing in ancient literature) exposes the oppressive nature of Roman power, inherent in its deification of its power. The martyrdom of Christians serves as a peculiarly illuminating instance of this.

(19:1–8) The Fall of Babylon: (d) Voices from Heaven vv. 1–5, the full range of voices in heaven praise God for his judgement of Babylon and exhort God's servants on earth to do so. v. 3 once again mocks Rome's claim to eternity. vv. 6–8, the second voice of a great multitude—more majestically described than that in v. 1 (cf. 14:2)—celebrates the positive consequences of Babylon's judgement. God reigns (contrast 17:18; 18:7), and the Lamb's marriage to his chaste bride the church (contrast 18:23) takes the place of Babylon's venal promiscuity. These themes look forward to ch. 21. They remind us at this point that the negative side of God's eschatological action—the fall of Babylon—takes place only for the sake of the positive. The end of the passage also makes the present challenge to Christians clear: the positive corollary of coming out of Babylon (18:4) is to be ready for the Lamb as his bride. For the image of the church as the bride of Christ, see Eph 5:25–7; 2 Cor 11:2. The bride's clothing (v. 8) has a different meaning from that of the harlot (17:4; 18:16).

(19:9–10) John and the Angel v. 9, the common image of the eschatological banquet (e.g. Mt 8:11) is here specified as a marriage supper (cf. Mt 25:10). v. 10, John mistakes the agent of revelation, a servant of God like himself, for the divine source of God's true words (v. 9). The incident is significant primarily because it dramatizes the issue of true worship which is at stake throughout Revelation. Not the pretenders to divine status, like the beast, *not even* God's heavenly servants the angels may be worshipped, but only God. This is the Jewish criterion of monotheism: only God may be worshipped. Given this passage, it is the more remarkable that 5:9–14 and 22:3 include Jesus in the worship due to God alone. The difficult final statement of v. 10 must mean that when the Spirit inspires prophecy (such as John's) its content is the witness Jesus bore and bears (cf. 1:2).

Transition from Babylon to the New Jerusalem (19:11–21:8)

(19:11–21) The Rider from Heaven and his Victory v. 11, the open heaven signals a novel stage in the visionary narrative. Hitherto John's visions have revealed the heavenly perspective on the earthly situation. They have shown the beast's power to be deceit and the witness of the martyrs the truth. But while the beast still contests God's rule, earthly appearances still hide the truth from those unwilling to see it. With the opening of heaven, truth prevails openly and irresistibly on earth. All illusions and delusions must perish, and those who have propagated and still cling to them must perish with them. The truth, the heavenly reality of things, comes to earth in the person of Jesus, the one who has supremely witnessed to the truth of God in his life and death and who is the Word of God in person (v. 13). His victory is pictured in two interwoven strands of imagery: as military victory and as judicial sentence. He comes as the Divine Warrior, riding to victory over his enemies (v. 19), and as the Judge whose truthful verdict condemns the wicked. He is called 'faithful and true' (v. 11), words which in 3:14 (cf. 1:5) describe him as witness. He is no longer

witness, but judge. But it is the same truth to which he witnessed that now condemns. Witness is double-edged, like his sword (1:16, but no longer in 19:15): it wins people from lies and illusions to the truth, but when they reject it it becomes evidence against those who love lies and cling to illusions in the face of the truth (cf. Jn 12:46–9). So the truth to which Jesus was the faithful witness is the same truth by which he now judges. The end of v. 11 echoes Isaiah's prophecy of the Messiah as righteous judge on behalf of the oppressed (11:4). v. 12, cf. 1:14; 2:18, 23: eyes which see the truth of minds and hearts. The significance of the unknown name is debatable: perhaps the mystery of his divine identity. v. 13, although the image derives from Isa 63:1–3 (cf. Gen 49:9–11), the blood must be his own (1:5; 5:9; 7:14; 12:11), since the slaughter of his enemies is yet to come (vv. 11–16 describe exclusively his qualifications for victory in the battle that follows). It is the blood of his faithful witness to the word of God which qualifies him to be the Word of God in person. v. 14, the martyrs appear as his army (cf. 17:14): their robes have been washed white in his blood (7:14). Their victory in death is vindicated through participation in his final victory, but it is unclear whether they are active in the destruction of the enemy (cf. v. 21; and v. 15 with 2:26–7). v. 15, his weapon is his word: cf. Isa 11:4, and v. 21. This verse takes up the narratives left hanging in 12:5 and 14:19–20, along with their OT sources (Ps 2:8–11; Isa 63:1–6). v. 16, this name, publicly visible, proclaims him the one who exercises the absolute divine sovereignty over all and comes to establish it against the kings who contest his lordship. vv. 17–18, the invitation to the birds, based on Ezek 39:17–20, is a gruesome parody of the eschatological banquet, the marriage supper of the Lamb (cf. 19:7–9). The birds form a literary *inclusio* round the account of the battle (cf. v. 21). v. 19, as well as echoing Ps 2:1–3, this verse takes up the unfinished narrative of 16:14. The whole passage, by means of its literary links with earlier parts of the book, portrays the parousia's comprehensive finality. v. 20, the final punishment represented by the lake of fire (which is the same as 'the second death': 20:14) is the immediate fate of two of the Satanic trinity, but not of the devil himself until 20:10, and not of humans until they have appeared before the divine tribunal (20:15). The beast and the false prophet, it should be remembered, are not human individuals but systems of power and influence. It is these primarily which are destroyed. Humans perish by the truth of God's judgement (v. 21) only because they have thrown in their lot with these systems.

(20:1–10) The Millennium This passage has been the subject of interpretative debate for centuries, and the basis for a very diverse tradition of Christian 'millenarianism'. It is important to focus here on the role which the period of a thousand years plays in Revelation's visionary narrative. Some Jewish writings contemporary with Revelation portrayed a temporary period of messianic rule on earth at the end of history and prior to the eschatological renewal of creation (2 *Apoc. Bar.* 40:4; 4 Ezra 7:28–9). But John characteristically adapts this tradition for his own theological and literary purposes. vv. 1–3, just as the dragon appeared in the narrative before the two beasts (chs. 12–13), so his story continues after they have gone to their doom. He is the ultimate principle of evil, they are no more than his historical minions. In ch. 12 he was thrown from heaven to earth, where he deceived the nations; now he is imprisoned in the abyss (cf. 9:1), prevented from deceiving the nations for an extremely long time (the significance of a thousand years; cf. Ps 90:4). vv. 4–6, this is all Revelation says about the meaning of the millennium. It is a consequence of the victory of truth over the devil's and the beast's deceit. So that truth may prevail the situation under the beast's rule is reversed: the beast must be seen to be defeated (19:20) and the martyrs, his victims, must be seen to be the true victors. As the kings of the earth who shared the beast's usurped rule are deprived of their kingdom, so the martyrs now reign with Christ (cf. 1:6; 5:10, though the final fulfilment of these promises comes in 22:3–5). The kingdom has been taken from the beast and his allies and given to the martyrs. Whereas his universal rule lasted three and a half years, they rule the earth for a thousand years. Whereas the beast, who killed the martyrs, has perished finally in the second death (19:20), they come to life and the second death has no power over them (vv. 4–6). Rule and life—the two issues on which the contest between the beast and the martyrs has hinged—are the sole theme of this account of the millennium. It is not necessary to understand Revelation's story of the millennium as literal prediction of a period of time following the parousia. Rather, it is a symbol of the vindication of the martyrs which the parousia must entail. vv. 7–10, this passage depends on the story of Gog in Ezek 38–9 (where the nations from the remotest parts of the earth (38:2–6) gather to attack Israel at the centre of the earth (38:12) and are destroyed by fire from heaven (38:22)). As a narrative demonstration that the triumph of the martyrs in Christ's kingdom is not one which evil can again reverse, the story gives Satan another chance to deceive the nations and to defeat the saints. This time the citadel of the saints remains impregnable, and the devil goes to his final fate (cf. comment on 14:11).

(20:11–15) The Judgement of the Dead This judgement differs from that in 19:17–21 in that it determines the eternal destiny of every human individual throughout history. Not until this passage is the judgement of the dead which 11:18 included in the coming of God's kingdom actually narrated. v. 11, God's judgement seat (white is one of the dazzling colours of heaven) is presumably a different throne from the one from which he rules the universe (4:2). The cosmic quake is the reaction to the theophany, as in 6:12–14, but may also anticipate 21:1b. v. 12, for the books, cf. Dan 7:10; 12:1–2. They represent the exposure of the truth of each person's life so that judgement may be passed on it. Judgement 'according to their deeds' is a formula used throughout the Bible (Ps 62:12; Prov 24:12; Job 34:11; Jer 17:10; Mt 16:27; Rom 2:6; 1 Pet 1:17; Rev 22:12). It implies not a legalistic notion of retributive justice, but an assessment of the fundamental alignment of a person's life (either to God and the good, or to evil) as evidenced by their deeds. It is not inconsistent with God's mercy, implied by the book of life which, for those whose names are still written in it (cf. 3:5), has the last word. v. 13, this image of resurrection, found more fully in other ancient Jewish works (e.g. 2 Esd 7:32), envisages the places of the dead as having been entrusted with them for safekeeping until God requires them to return them. The 'sea' seems to be the 'waters under the earth', the primeval chaos (cf. 13:1), mentioned here to prepare

the way for 21:1. v. 14, Death and Hades appeared in the narrative before the Satanic trinity (1:18; 6:8) and survive longer before finally joining them in the lake of fire; cf. 1 Cor 15:26.

(21:1–4) The New Heaven and the New Earth v. 1, the expectation of a new cosmos here echoes Isa 65:17. 'New' carries its eschatological sense of radically different, but implies a radical renewal of the old creation rather than creation from nothing (cf. Paul's use of 'new creation' in 2 Cor 5:17). Absence of sea, if this means the primordial chaos from which the beast arises (13:1), implies that the creation is established eternally, beyond any threat of reverting to chaos. v. 2, the new Jerusalem will be described at length later in the chapter. It comes from heaven as the dwelling place of redeemed humanity with God—the union of heaven and earth, or of the bride with her husband Christ (cf. 19:7–8). v. 3, the words echo God's OT promises to dwell with his own people Israel as their God (Ezek 37:27–8; Zech 8:8) and also that many nations will be his people with whom he will dwell (Zech 2:10–11; cf. Isa 19:25; 56:7; Am 9:12). The best text has 'his peoples' (rather than 'people'), using in the plural the word commonly used of God's own people (laoi) rather than the more usual word for the other nations or Gentiles (ethnē). Now that the covenant people (Israel and the church) have fulfilled their mission of witness to the nations, all nations will share in the privileges and promises of the covenant people. From this point two strands run through the account of the new Jerusalem that follows, one referring to the covenant people, the other to the nations. v. 4, cf. Isa 25:7–8. In God's immediate presence on earth all sorrow, suffering, and death are banished for ever: this above all is what makes the new cosmos new.

(21:5–8) God Speaks This is the first time since 1:8 that God speaks directly (as distinct from 'a voice from the throne', a phrase which preserves a reverent indirectness). v. 5, 'making all things new' implies renewal from the creative resources of God: the old creation is not replaced by another, but nor can the potential of the old creation itself produce its renewal. The renewal must come from the Creator. v. 6, cf. comment on 16:17. In both his first (1:8) and his last words, God declares himself the Alpha and the Omega. Here, as he becomes the realized goal of his creation, the phrase is stressed by reiteration in other terms (and in 22:13, where Christ also claims the title, it is reiterated yet again). The water (cf. 7:17; 22:1; Isa 49:10) is the eternal life of the new creation, beyond the reach of death, life lived continuously from its source in God. v. 7, this is the eighth promise to the conquerors, summing up those which end each of the messages to the churches (chs. 2–3) and indicating their fulfilment from this point in the narrative onwards. It is another form of the OT covenant formulary (cf. v. 3). v. 8 is mainly a warning to those in the churches who could be conquerors, but succumb to the idolatrous and sinful influences of the society with which they are tempted to compromise. To avoid the second death (cf. 2:11) is to come out of Babylon (18:4) in which all these sins flourish.

The New Jerusalem the Bride (21:9–22:9)

(21:9–14) General View of the City The beginning of this section (vv. 9–10) parallels 17:1–3, just as 22:6–9 parallels

19:8–10, marking out these two passages about Babylon and the new Jerusalem as a pair, and the intervening passage (19:11–21:8) as the transition from the destruction of one to the arrival of the other. v. 10, the mountain derives most obviously from Ezek 40:2, but also evokes the myth of the cosmic mountain at the centre of the earth, where God and humanity meet, where Paradise was (Ezek 28:14) and will be restored (Isa 11:9; 65:25), with which mount Zion was symbolically identified (Ps 48:2), and where the temple to which all nations will be drawn at the end stands (Isa 2:2). Whereas the builders of ancient Babylon (Gen 11:1–9) sought to join earth to heaven in the self-deifying pride John saw repeated in contemporary Rome, the new Jerusalem which comes from God will truly join heaven to earth. v. 11, the whole city shines with the reflected glory of God (cf. 4:3, 6; 21:23). vv. 12–13, twelve, the number of the people of God, recurs throughout the description of the city (vv. 12–14, 16, 19–22; cf. 22:2). The names of the tribes on the gates come from Ezek 48:30–4. v. 14, cf. Eph 2:20.

(21:15–21) The Walls and the Gates of the City v. 15, cf. Ezek 40:3. v. 16, initially the city is described as a square, 12,000 stadia in each direction. The beast has the triangular number 666, but the people of God have the square number 144 (12 × 12) (7:4–8; 14:1; 21:17). Then the city is shown not only to have a square ground plan, but to be a perfect cube, like no city ever imagined, but like the holy of holies in the temple (1 Kings 6:20). We learn later that it needs no temple (v. 22): the whole city is the holiest place of God's presence. v. 17, as well as echoing Ezek 40:5, this verse ('144 cubits by the measure of a human being, that is, of an angel', my tr.) resembles 13:18 ('the number of the beast, for it is the number of a human being: its number is 666', my tr.). Just as Nero Caesar, written in Hebrew characters, has the numerical value 666, a triangular number, so the Greek word 'angel' (*aggelos*), written in Hebrew characters, has the numerical value 144, a square number. Humanity debased to the level of the beast is contrasted with humanity raised to the level of the angels. vv. 18–21, the city is built out of the jewels and metals of Paradise: cf. Gen 2:11–12; Ezek 28:13. The twelve precious stones (vv. 19–20) are those of the high priest's breastplate (Ex 28:17–20); and the same twelve occur in Ezek 28:13 (LXX Gk. version; in the MT the first nine) described as 'every precious stone', and in Eden. Thus the list of twelve in Revelation represents all precious stones, all to be found in Paradise. Jewish traditions claimed that the jewels of the high priest's breastplate in Solomon's temple came from Paradise, along with other precious materials used in the temple, and were also the precious stones of which, according to Isa 54:11–12, the new Jerusalem is to be built (cf. 4QpIsaᵃ 1:4–9; *LAB* 26:13–15). Thus the jewels and the gold characterize the new Jerusalem as a temple-city adorned with all the fabulously radiant precious materials of Paradise. The glory of God is reflected in the jewels and the translucent gold of the city. These are not to be understood merely as allegories for attributes of redeemed people, but as the beauty of the new creation, Paradise restored, and a home for glorified humanity. The city's relation to Paradise here and in 22:1–2 points to the harmony of nature and human culture in the new creation.

(21:22–7) The Glory of God in the Temple-City v. 22, while in many ways the description of the city follows OT and Apocryphal models (Isa 52:1; 54:11–12; 60; Ezek 40:2–5; 47:1–12; 48:30–4; Zech 14:6–21; Tob 13:16–17), its most novel feature is the absence of a temple. Ezekiel called the new Jerusalem 'The Lord is There' (48:35) and Zechariah declared the whole city as holy as the temple (14:20–1; cf. Isa 52:1), thus envisaging the whole city as the place of God's holy presence. But Revelation alone claims that the city needs no special place of God's presence, a temple, because it is wholly filled with God's immediate presence. Hence the city has no temple, but is a temple (v. 16b) or (putting the same point differently) God and the Lamb are its temple (v. 22). v. 23, cf. Isa 60:19–20. vv. 24–6, the city is both the light of the world by which the nations walk (cf. Isa 60:3), and the centre to which the nations and their kings come on pilgrimage (cf. Isa 2:2–3; 60:4–17; Zech 14:16). ('The kings of the earth', who until this point have been depicted throughout Revelation as hostile to God, are now shown acknowledging that their rule comes from God.) But whereas in Isa 60:5–17, it is the material wealth of the nations that is brought in tribute to Jerusalem, in Revelation the kings bring 'their glory' (v. 24) and the people 'the glory and honour of the nations' (v. 26). This contrasts with Babylon's self-indulgent exploitation of the wealth of her empire (18:11–14), but also continues the theme of glory that runs through the whole description from v. 11 onwards. The nations offer their own glory to God's glory, not thereby losing it, but acknowledging its source in the God to whom all glory and honour belong (cf. the doxologies: 4:11; 5:12, 13; 7:12). The most important single feature of the new Jerusalem is that it is creation enjoying the glory of God, glorified itself in reflecting God's glory, and glorifying God in returning glory to God. v. 27, since the whole city is a temple, full of the holy presence of God, everything unclean must be excluded (Isa 52:1): ritual uncleanness is no doubt here figurative for moral defilement. Idolatry and falsehood, also excluded from the temple (Ps 24:3–4), are the dominant evils of the beast and the dominant temptation of Christians in the beast's dominion.

(22:1–5) The Throne of God in the City v. 1, in another variation on the temple theme, the river of the water of life, which in Ezek 47:1 flows from the temple (cf. Zech 14:8), flows from the throne of God and the Lamb. The eternal life of the new creation has its source in God. v. 2, as in Ezek 47:12, the river nourishes constantly fruitful trees: Revelation identifies them with the paradisal tree of life (Gen 2:9; 3:24). In the tree which bears *twelve* fruits (not specified in Ezekiel) and whose leaves heal *the nations* (not specified in Ezekiel) are combined the two strands of reference to the covenant people and to the nations. v. 3a, this sentence should be translated: 'there shall no longer be any ban of destruction', a quotation from Zech 14:11. The reference is not to what is cursed (and so is not repetitive of 21:27) but to the curse itself, the sacred ban which in the OT God places on enemies of his rule, requiring their utter destruction. This links with the end of v. 2: the nations who inhabit the new Jerusalem, healed of their idolatry and other sins by the leaves of the tree of life, will never again be subject to the destruction God decrees for those who oppose his rule. vv. 3b–5, the climax of the whole description of the city focuses on the central image of the whole book: the divine throne. In the earthly temple, the high priest, once a year, wore the sacred name of God on his forehead and entered God's immediate presence in the holy of holies. In the city which as a whole is God's eternal holy of holies, all will enjoy this immediacy without interruption. Especially they will see the face of God, which no one in this life could see and survive (Ex 33:20–3; Judg 6:22–3), but to see which is the deepest human religious aspiration, to be realized only beyond this mortal life (Ps 17:15; 1 Cor 13:12; cf. 2 Esd 7:98). Since the face expresses who someone is, to see God's face will be to know who God is in his personal being. In their access to God's presence the servants of God will be priests, but they will also be kings in that they will reign with him (cf. 1:6; 5:10; 2:21). God's kingdom turns out to be quite different from the beast's, finding its fulfilment not in the subjection of God's 'servants', but in their reigning with him. The point is not that they reign over others (who are not mentioned), but that God's rule over them is for them a participation in God's rule. The image of God's rule, thus finally stripped of all the associations of human rule, expresses the eschatological reconciliation of divine rule and human freedom.

(22:6–9) John and the Angel The close resemblances between this passage and 19:9–10 indicate that it concludes the account of the new Jerusalem, just as 19:9–10 concludes the account of Babylon. But the passage also contains strong echoes of 1:1–3, suggesting that it is the beginning of the epilogue to the book. In fact, it is designed for both functions. It is another example of John's literary practice of interweaving and overlapping the sections of his work. v. 6, whereas in 19:9*b* the corresponding words ('these are the true words of God') probably refer only to the beatitude in 19:9*a*, here they refer to the whole prophecy (God's revelation of 'what must soon take place', as in 1:1), and the angel (21:9) is revealed to be the angel of 1:1, who mediates the whole revelation to John. v. 7, Jesus' interjection announcing his imminent coming (cf. 2:16; 3:11; 22:12, 20) underlines the relevance and urgency of the whole revelation. The beatitude repeats that of 1:3. vv. 8–9, cf. 19:10.

Epilogue (22:10–21)

(22:10–11) The Angel's Instructions The epilogue, like the prologue, consists in a series of formally diverse units, of which the first (22:6–9) also serves as the conclusion of the preceding section. v. 10, the command contrasts with Dan 12:4, where Daniel, writing centuries before the last days of which he writes, is told to keep his prophecies secret until the time of the end. The contents of John's prophecy were once hidden in the sealed scroll (5:1) but they have now been revealed and written for immediate reading and relevance, since the time of their fulfilment is near. v. 11, this exhortation is problematic because Revelation has repeatedly called people to repentance, and probably still implies the possibility of repentance in vv. 14–15. While also echoing Dan 12:10, the verse is best understood by comparison with Ezek 3:27: 'let those who will hear, hear; and let those who refuse to hear, refuse'. Only as a figure of speech are those unwilling to hear *commanded* to refuse to hear; the point is that prophecy has a dual effect depending on people's response. Those unwilling to heed it are hardened in their adherence to evil. In a sense this is the punishment their sin itself produces (cf. Ezek 3:18–

19). The contrast of the two opposite cases—the already righteous who by heeding the prophecy remain righteous, and the already wicked who by refusing to heed increase their evil—makes an epigrammatic point, but does not exclude the two different cases of change from one category to the other (see Ezek 3:20; 33:12–16).

(22:12–13) A Prophetic Oracle At several points in the epilogue Jesus addresses the readers directly, speaking through the prophet, as he does in chs. 2–3 and 16:15. v. 12, the second clause echoes Isa 40:10, an announcement of YHWH's coming to judgement. For the principle of judgement according to deeds, see comment on 20:12. v. 13, see comments on 1:8; 21:6.

(22:14–15) Beatitude The last of the book's seven beatitudes appropriately takes up the imagery of the new Jerusalem, and specifies witness to the point of death (in the light of 7:14, this must be the meaning of 'wash their robes') as the condition of access to the city and its eternal blessings. Revelation writes *as if* all faithful Christians will suffer death for their witness, but this is its way of vividly dramatizing the situation of crisis that lies in the near future and in which no Christians can count on escaping death if they witness faithfully and refuse to participate in idolatry. The choice is potential martyrdom or remaining outside the new Jerusalem (v. 15). Cf. 21:8, 27. 'Dogs' (regarded as unclean animals with disgusting habits; cf. Prov 26:11; Isa 66:3; Mt 7:6; 2 Pet 2:22) are equivalent to the 'unclean' in 21:27.

(22:16) A Scriptural Testimony Jesus' self-description in the language of OT prophecy constitutes a scriptural testimony equivalent to 1:7 in the prologue to the book. Like the latter, the point is to cite prophetic expectations that the Messiah would bring the nations into God's kingdom. As in 5:5, the 'root of David' refers not to Isa 11:1 but to Isa 11:10: 'the root from Jesse shall stand as a signal to the peoples; the nations shall inquire of [or, seek] him'. (Revelation adds 'descendant' to make clear that the root is not that from which the Messiah comes (Isa 11:1) but the Messiah descended from David.) 'The bright morning star' alludes, like 2:28, to Num 24:17, but also and especially (as 'bright' indicates) to Isa 60:3: 'Nations shall come to your light, and kings to the brightness of your dawn' (whereas Isa 60:1–2 refers to the rising sun, this verse can easily be read as referring to the brightest of stars, the morning star that accompanies the sun's rising). Thus both the messianic titles allude to OT prophecies of the nations being drawn to the Messiah. In both the prologue and the epilogue of Revelation readers are reminded, by citation of prophecies with which the first readers would already be familiar as messianic texts applied by the church to Jesus, of this OT hope for the nations. The hope itself is not a new revelation, but the revelation given to John reveals, for the first time clearly, how it is to be fulfilled: through the church's witness to the nations to the point of death, following the way of the faithful witness, Jesus.

(22:17) Invitation to Come to the Water of Life It may be that the first two invitations to 'come' are addressed to Jesus (responding to v. 12 as v. 20*b* does to v. 20*a*) and the third to people, but perhaps more likely the threefold 'come' of Isa 55:1 is echoed and the three invitations to 'come' are all addressed to people, exhorting them to come to drink the water of life. The Spirit is probably here (as in 2:7, 11, 17, 29; 3:6, 13, 22;

14:13) speaking through Christian prophets (John and his colleagues), while the Bride is the church in her eschatological purity, ready for the coming of her husband the Lamb (cf. 19:7–8; 21:2). What the Spirit says is also the voice of the church as the church should be. Individual Christians who hear what the Spirit says (cf. the formula in the seven messages to the churches: 'Let anyone who has an ear hear…') repeat the invitation, thus identifying themselves with the Bride. The content of the invitation is then spelt out as an invitation to anyone and everyone who thirsts to take the water of life as a gift (echoing God's words in 21:6b). The invitation combines the two levels of concern in Revelation: that Christians should be faithful witnesses and 'conquer', and that through their faithful witness the nations should turn to God. Here the water of life is offered to Christians, and also Christians are themselves exhorted to offer the water of life to everyone who thirsts. Whether this means that the eschatological gift of the water of life is available already in the present is hard to tell; such a usage would not be characteristic of Revelation (contrast Jn 4:10–15; 7:37–9) but cannot be ruled out.

(22:18–19) Warning to Preserve the Book's Integrity Ancient books were often subject to revision, abbreviation, and expansion by scribes and editors, and the textual history of non-canonical Jewish and Christian apocalypses shows that such works were especially liable to be modified in such ways. But these verses also allude to Deut 4:1–2; 12:32, where the danger is of false prophets who maintain that idolatry is acceptable,

thus both adding to God's law a permission it does not give and at the same time effectively removing the law's prohibitions of idolatry. It is clear from the seven messages to the churches both that compromise with idolatry is one of the dangers John's prophecy aims to counter, and that there are false prophets and their followers in the churches with whom John's prophecy would be highly unpopular for this reason. It is at this level of seriousness that we can understand the severe warnings against tampering with the integrity of the book (22:6). In their use of 'add' and 'take away' for both crime and punishment, they are examples of eschatological *lex talionis* (see comment on 11:18).

(22:20) A Prophetic Oracle and Response 'These things' must be the whole content of the book, alluding to 1:2. This is the last of the seven times in Revelation that Jesus says 'I am coming' (*erchomai*: cf. 2:5, 16; 3:11; 16:15; 22:7, 12). John responds with a solemn acceptance of Jesus' word ('Amen') and prayer for his coming. The latter takes up in Greek the Aramaic prayer Maranatha ('Our Lord, come!': 1 Cor 16:22; *Did.* 10:6), which must have been in use from the earliest days of the church.

(22:21) Epistolary Ending This resembles the conclusion of most Pauline letters and corresponds to Revelation's epistolary opening in 1:4–5a.

For further reading see Bibliographical Guide.

82. Extra-canonical early Christian literature

J. K. ELLIOTT

A. 1. The twenty-seven books that were eventually accepted as the foundation documents of Christianity were not the only early Christian texts to have been composed in the first or second century. There are clues within the NT itself to other early writings. Luke's preface indicates that 'many' had attempted to compose gospel-type books; Col. 4:16 refers to a letter which Paul claims to have written to the Laodiceans; 1 Cor 5:9 and 2 Cor 7:8 probably refer to correspondence Paul had had with the church in Corinth in addition to the two surviving letters known to us as 1 and 2 Corinthians. All these texts have been lost. That some early Christian writings did not survive need not surprise us.

2. The amazing thing is that so much has survived, given the fact that early Christian writings, including those which were eventually to form the NT, were not composed as scripture and that many of these documents were addressed to a particular locality with a limited readership. The ecclesiastical authorities, east and west, who eventually (and certainly by the 4th cent.) agreed upon a list of authoritative writings (the canon) acceptable to the worldwide church, did so for a variety of reasons. But it seems certain that among the motives was the multiplicity of writings confronting Christians, particularly in the second to third centuries.

3. Gnosticism alone spawned a large number of writings in this period. The term is relatively recent and describes certain religious teachings which in their Christian guise were prominent in the second century. Its origin seems to

have been in pagan circles but it spread rapidly throughout Christian centres. A major feature of the various Gnostic systems was that initiates could aspire, through secret revealed knowledge (*gnosis*), to the redemption of their divine character. Christian *gnosis* gave a central role to Jesus as an emissary of the supreme God. Some of these Gnostic texts are familiar to us nowadays, thanks to the discovery in 1945–6 of the Gnostic library at Nag Hammadi. Among that library is a collection of sayings (most of them attributed to Jesus) in the Gospel of Thomas. We return to that text at J.11–19.

4. Writings by Gnostics and other groups had a great influence on the beliefs of many early Christians. Orthodox authorities such as Irenaeus were concerned to remove the threat by restricting the circulation or acceptability of their literature. The decision to create a canon of Christian writings was due less to a desire to define an exclusive collection of early, apostolic, and universally approved books and more to a requirement to avoid dangerous texts which were new and heretical in the eyes of those who were later to be seen as the orthodox defenders of the faith.

5. Not all the texts that were excluded were in fact heretical or unorthodox. The writings that have conventionally been labelled as the 'Apostolic Fathers' (e.g. 1 and 2 *Clement*, the *Didache*, the *Epistle of Barnabas*, and the Shepherd of Hermas) do not fall into this category. Nor should the bulk of the writings commonly collected together under the (less than ideal) title 'The Apocryphal New Testament' be dismissed *en bloc* as heretical.

6. 'Apocryphal' literally means 'hidden'. Few of the so-called apocryphal books merit this designation, although the *Gospel of Thomas* and the *Acts of Andrew* do claim to contain secret words or hidden truths. Books assembled into the category 'New Testament Apocrypha' usually include those texts which were written in imitation of the writings that were later accepted into the NT canon, i.e. gospels, epistles, acts, and apocalypses, although some 'apocryphal' texts are not paralleled in the NT itself. In any case, it is clearly anachronistic to use 'canonical' and 'apocryphal' or 'non-canonical' of texts written in the first two Christian centuries. It is also inappropriate to apply judgements about heresy and orthodoxy to the teaching in these 'apocryphal' texts. To do so is to use the language of the fourth-century Christian establishment with reference to literature that for the most part had been written and was circulating 200 years prior to the crystallizing of such attitudes.

7. Many of the apocryphal books originated in the second century. In several cases such texts are obviously secondary to, and influenced by, earlier works. However, as will be seen below, some of the texts that are now published as NT apocryphal writings may have been composed as early as the first century and therefore be contemporaneous with the NT writings proper. Indeed, some scholars argue for the independence of some of the so-called apocryphal texts (the *Gospel of Peter*, the *Gospel of Thomas*, Egerton Papyrus 2). In other words, some of these early writings may merit study as primary sources alongside those texts which were accepted into the canon.

8. But even if we disagree, and instead argue for a date later than the first century for *all* the extra-canonical writings, none the less material found in *some* of these texts could conceivably have had a long history. Possibly some of the stories and sayings about Jesus could have survived in the oral tradition over several generations, and have earthed themselves only in a second- to third-century writing; some stories and sayings may have been preserved in writing within texts that have subsequently disappeared but their past inclusion in a literary form may have helped to popularize them. It could be that that material then influenced later, currently extant documents. To argue along those lines means that one could be dealing with some Jesus material found in non-canonical sources, which is as old, as authentic, and as historically viable as that found within our NT. This applies especially to sayings and some deeds of Jesus in the apocryphal gospels.

9. When we turn to the apocryphal Acts a less controversial demarcation line is usually clear—they are second- to third-century novels merely using an apostle as their eponymous hero. The stories themselves, although bearing some relation to the genre of literature which we know from the Acts of the Apostles with its breathless sequence of stories, journeys, conversions, plots, and speeches, are in effect Christianized counterparts to the popular reading-matter of predominantly literate Roman believers. Parallels to these Christian novels are to be found in erotic pagan literature. We shall turn to the apocryphal Acts below, but, at the moment, it is sufficient to anticipate the conclusion set out in that section: namely that no scholar accepts their contents as a true record of the historical circumstances behind the first-century events which they purport to relate. But with the apocryphal gospels we must reckon with the possibility that some of the material—especially that to be seen in the fragmented texts—is either an alternative account of a story known elsewhere from the canonical gospels or a new story that could in theory have fitted comfortably within a canonical gospel. 'Apocryphal' in its popular definition as 'secondary' or 'spurious' does not necessarily apply in such cases. It may well be decided that some of these stories are as authentic and as historical as the canonical accounts.

10. The writings themselves, even if they are accepted as historically plausible, cannot, of course, be canonical—the canon was an entity firmly fixed historically from the fourth century and applied to the twenty-seven books of the NT. Literature falling outside those twenty-seven cannot by definition be canonical, however authentic or original to the Jesus story it may be considered. Conversely all the stories and sayings that occur in a NT MS would have been accepted as canonical even when modern textual critics decide that a saying or story found in only part of the MS tradition did not belong to the original author's published text. For example, Codex Bezae adds after Lk 6:4: 'The same day, seeing a certain man working on the sabbath, he said to him, "Man, if indeed you know what you are doing, happy are you; but if not, you are accursed and a transgressor of the law." ' The pericope of the Adulteress, found in some MSS in John's and in Luke's gospel, would have been accepted as canonical by the original readers of those MSS, but the story is absent from other MSS. Users of these shorter MSS would be unaware of this pericope as part of the canonical texts they read. Similarly, the verses at the end of Mark beyond Mk 16:8 are disputed in the MS tradition. Readers of NT MSS, which contain the additional verses, would accept these as part of the canonical Gospel of Mark. If such secondary material is found in a perfectly orthodox copy of the scriptures then for those who owned, used, and read that MS its entire contents were, by definition, canonical. Ancient commentators who pronounced on the canonical status of the NT books did not concern themselves with the differences—sometimes quite significant differences—that existed between MSS. The Gospel according to Mark was commended without it being specified if 'Mark' was to be understood as containing 16:9–20 or not. Even Origen and Jerome, who were alert to textual variation, did not comment on such matters in the context of commending or rejecting certain Christian books.

11. Most of the differences that are readily observed when one compares the NT in the AV (KJV) and the RV (or most modern English versions) obviously concern English style, language, and usage, but there are a significant number of other changes which are due to the differences in the Greek NT used by the translators. And those textual differences are due to differences in the underlying Greek MSS used by the editors of the printed testament.

12. By contrast, paradoxically, material that we may now wish to pronounce as authentic in an apocryphal source can never be canonical. This issue is acute when we turn to the *Gospel of Thomas* (J.11–19), which is probably the best-known of the apocryphal texts in modern times.

13. There is a considerable body of sayings of Jesus that may be collected from patristic writings, biblical MSS, and from apocryphal sources which are not paralleled in the NT. Such sayings are commonly called 'agrapha', that is, sayings 'not written' in the NT itself. As well as the saying in Codex Bezae found after Lk 6:4 (quoted in A.10 above), some other famous agrapha are: 'Be competent money-changers' (in Clement of Alexandria, *Stromateis*, 1.28.177), and 'Ask for the great things, and God will add to you what is small' (ibid. 1.24.158). Agrapha illustrate the growth of tradition and the accretion of legend. Some may represent early tradition, which may be authentic; some result from false attribution (e.g. 1 Cor 2:9 appears as a saying of Jesus in the *Gospel of Thomas*, 17); some, embedded in apocryphal works, may have been composed *ad hoc* for the work concerned (and would have no claim to authenticity).

14. But, for the most part, all the extra-canonical sayings and the apocryphal literature that has survived are later than, derivative from, and secondary to the twenty-seven writings that were to form the NT canon of scripture.

In this section we divide the texts into two categories: the early Christian extra-canonical writings, known as the Apostolic Fathers, and the writings of the so-called NT apocrypha.

THE APOSTOLIC FATHERS

B. 1. Under this title are normally included: *1 Clement, 2 Clement, Epistles of Ignatius, Epistle of Polycarp to the Philippians, Didache (Epistle of) Barnabas, Shepherd of Hermas,* and *Fragments of Papias.* (At one time the *Epistle to Diognetus* used to be included.)

2. The term 'Apostolic Fathers', which was not used in antiquity of these writings, implies that the author was an acquaintance of the apostles but did not belong to their number. Clement and Hermas are said to have been disciples of Paul. Polycarp is said to have been a disciple of John. The *Didache* claims to reflect the teaching of the twelve apostles.

3. The texts discussed first are the *Didache* and *Barnabas* (*Barn.*). The former contains some first-century material, and has significant parallels with the New Testament; the latter is an example of a Christian text from a period slightly later than the NT. We shall refer later to three other texts, *1* and *2 Clement* and the *Shepherd of Hermas*, because they seem to have been considered worthy contenders for inclusion in the canon in the fourth century. Mention will also be made of the letters by Ignatius.

4. Unlike the texts included in the apocryphal NT, in which the characters of the NT proper reappear, typically in scenes that fill in gaps in the traditional stories, the Apostolic Fathers are concerned not with events set in the time of the NT narratives but with issues of common pastoral concern at their time of composition, such as morality and church order.

5. Several writings among the Apostolic Fathers (by Clement, Barnabas, Polycarp, and Ignatius) are letters. This form of writing is relatively rare in the apocryphal NT. (See Q.1–6.)

The Didache

C. 1. Among the Apostolic Fathers is the *Didache* (or *Teaching of the Twelve Apostles*, and the *Teaching of the Lord through the Twelve Apostles to the Gentiles*). It is a short manual of church discipline prefaced by a section on morals. The only complete

extant Greek MS is from the eleventh century, and this was rediscovered only in 1873. Its publication in 1883 by P. Bryennios generated great interest. Since then a fourth-century Greek fragment (P. Oxy. 1782 containing *Did.* 1:3*b*–4; 2:7*b*–3:2*a*) has come to light and this helps prove that the *Didache* was known in Egypt by that time. The Greek Apostolic Constitutions, which shows knowledge of the *Didache*, also comes from fourth-century Egypt. Knowledge of it by Irenaeus (*c.*130–*c.*200 CE) is not proven. A Latin version also exists. Material in the *Didache*, especially the section known as the Two Ways (*Did.* 1–6) is also found in *Barnabas* (see below). Mutual dependence of these two texts is unlikely; at the very least this material in common proves only that that section antedates the composition of both works.

2. Date and Provenance. The general scholarly consensus is that the *Didache*, which is a composite work, was compiled in the form we now have it in the Bryennios MS in the first half of the second century from several sources, some of which are likely to go back to the first century. Its provenance is unknown but the consensus is that it was composed in Syria, perhaps in or near Antioch, given the strong links between the *Didache* and the Matthean tradition. The community which preserved and used the *Didache* seems to have been strongly Jewish—the passage about the Two Ways, the food regulations, the fasts, and the table prayers are all suggestive of such a background. Some hold that it is the product of a branch of the early church antagonistic to the liberal, Pauline, pro-Gentile approach to Christianity.

3. Influence. The *Didache* seems to have been very influential, as may be seen by its use not only in the *Didascalia Apostolorum* and the *Apostolic Constitutions*, where it forms the basis of Book 7, but also in the Ecclesiastical Canons of the Apostles or the Apostolic Church Order traditions in Ethiopic. The traditions embedded in the *Didache* are also seen in the Latin *Doctrina (Apostolorum)* from the ninth century and in Coptic and in Georgian. Various patristic writers, such as Eusebius, *Hist. Eccl.* 3.25.4, and Athanasius, *Festal Letter*, 39.11, knew of it, as does the seventh-century Catalogue of the Sixty Books. This latter and the fourth-century list behind the Stichometry of Nicephorus refer to a writing called the Teaching (or Teachings) of the Apostles, but it is not clear if the *Didache* is meant. The teaching known to Nicephorus is only 200 *stichoi* in length, which makes that writing shorter than the present *Didache*.

4. The Didache and the Bible. OT citations in the *Didache* (Mal 1:11, 14 in *Did.* 14.3, and Zech 14:5 in *Did.* 16.7, and possibly Sir 7:22; 12:1 in *Did.* 1.6) are introduced by special formulae. *Did.* 1.6, 'as has been said'; 14.3, 'For this is what the Lord [= God] was referring to'; 16.7, 'As was said'. In the case of the passages in the *Didache* which parallel a NT passage no such introductory formula is found. *Did.* 1.3, 'Here is the teaching'; 2.1, 'The second commandment of the teaching is'. The word 'gospel' occurs in *Did.* 8.2; 11.3; 15.3 but is unlikely to refer to a written source. There are no citations at those points; the reference is to teaching by Jesus.

5. However, the following are noteworthy: *Did.* 9.5, 'For the Lord [presumably Jesus] also spoke concerning this: "Do not give what is holy to dogs."' This echoes Mt 7:6. *Did.* 8.1–2, 'Let your fasts not [coincide] with those of the hypocrites. They fast on Monday and Thursday; you, though, should fast on Wednesday and Friday. And do not pray as the hypocrites [do].' This links teaching found embedded in Mt 6:5 and 6:16, but the *Didache*'s use of the teaching differs from that in Matthew's gospel. The *Didache* is concerned with the establishment of distinctively Christian fasts. There is early evidence that Christians did fast on Wednesdays and Fridays. This was to contrast with Pharisaic fasts on Mondays and Thursdays. Mt 6:5 gives details of how hypocrites pray and how Jesus' followers are to pray. Mt 6:16 is concerned with the manner in which hypocrites fast, and not with the days on which they fast.

6. Other links between the *Didache* and the NT are disputed. Some scholars argue that the author of the *Didache* knew and used the canonical gospels. Mt 5:39–47 is said to be behind the interpolated section *Did.* 1.3b–2.1, but some of the verses parallel the Lucan version (Lk 6:27–33)—see DID. 1.3b–2.1—and it may be that the parallels are not due to direct literary dependence but to the oral tradition, or even to a harmonized form of the canonical writings.

7. There are further links elsewhere which show tenuous parallels with the NT, for example *Did.* 3.7 (Mt. 5:5); 11:7 (Mk 3:28–9); 14:2 (Mt 5:23–4). These are not strongly suggestive of direct literary dependence. As far as the Matthean parallels are concerned, the link is probably with the material Matthew found in his own source—in other words is from the Matthean additions to his framework (e.g. 3.7, 'On the contrary, be mild tempered, since those who are mild tempered will inherit the land'). This has encouraged some to look for links with the source Q itself rather than with Q in Matthew or in Luke.

8. Commentary.

1:1–6:3 contains the passage generally known as the Two Ways. In it are described the Way of Life and the Way of Death. This has interesting parallels to a similar section in *Barn* 18–20.1, although the *Didache* adds the saying in 1.3b–2.1 and also 3.1–6 in which certain attitudes and activities are prohibited in order to facilitate the keeping of the law, and also to the *Doctrina Apostolorum*, the Apostolic Constitutions, and the Epitome of the Canons of the Holy Apostles, although in *Barnabas* and the *Doctrina* a dualistic eschatological framework is in evidence. This whole moral section, whatever its origin (and many see the whole Two Ways tradition as originally Jewish because there are parallels in Qumran), is set here in *Did.* 7.1 in the context of pre-baptismal instruction and thus it may well give a clear idea about second- and maybe even first-century practice. (Possibly ch. 7 refers to an annual baptismal rite, during which the familiar Two Ways passage was recited. Such a rite would have taken place at the paschal festival.)

(1.3b–2.1) We now turn to the interpolated section:

3b. Bless those who curse you and pray for your enemies, fast for those who persecute you. What kind of favour is it when you love those who love you? Do not even the gentiles do that? Love those who hate you and you will not have any enemy. 4. Avoid the fleshly and bodily passions. If someone strikes you on your right cheek, turn your other one to him too, and you will be perfect. If someone presses you into one mile of service go along with him for two. If someone takes your cloak, give him your tunic as well. If someone takes away from you what is yours, do not demand it back since you cannot do so anyway. 5. Give to everyone what he asks of you, and do not ask for it back, for the

Father wants people to share with everyone the gifts that have been freely granted to them. Blessed is the person who gives according to the commandment, for he is guiltless. Alas for the person who takes. If someone takes something because he is in need, he is guiltless, but if he is not in need, he shall have to defend his reason for taking it and the use for which he intends it: if he is imprisoned, he shall be interrogated about what he has done, and he shall not go free until he has paid back the last penny. 6. But it has also been said about this sort of thing, 'Let your charitable gift sweat in your hands until you know to whom you are giving it.' ['The second commandment of the teaching' (in 2:1) then introduces the list of commandments taken from the traditional Two Ways material.]

The NT apocryphon P. Oxy. 1224 also seems to know the tradition found in *Did.* 1.3b referring to prayer for enemies. This fragment, dating from the fourth century, could have come from an unknown apocryphal gospel. The appearance of this saying in these two sources implies a wide tradition for preserving aphorisms attributed to Jesus, although the *Didache* does not cite the words as coming from Jesus or even from the NT.

Did. 1.3b–2.1 is not found in parallels to the Two Ways tradition (in *Barnabas* or elsewhere). The verses interrupt the section 1.2–2.2 and are likely to be an interpolation by the Didachist from his sources. The material is more likely to be from an earlier independent tradition rather than to have come directly from the canonical parallels. The wording and sequence are not precisely those in Matthew or Luke, and may best be seen as an oral retelling of the instructions preserved in these or, more probably, due to the independent continuation of the earlier oral material. *Did.* 1.5 has a different context from Mt 5:26: in Matthew the saying is concerned with repaying debts; in the *Didache* the reverse is true—no debts should be incurred, unless they cannot be avoided.

(Chs. 7–15) The whole of the *Didache* seems to have been influenced by liturgical practice. Chs. 7–15 give instruction on baptism (ideally by total immersion but also by affusion), fasting (on Wednesdays and Fridays), prayer, and eucharist. For the community responsible for the *Didache* baptism seems to have been eschatological rather than specifically Christological, although the baptism involves a trinitarian formula reminiscent of Mt 28:19 when the risen Jesus enjoins his disciples to make disciples by baptizing them into the name of the Father, Son, and Holy Spirit. First- and second-century practice seems not to have been uniform. Compared with those examples of the use of a trinitarian formula, one notes that Thecla's auto-baptism (itself a unique act) is in Christ's name only (*Acts of Paul*, 34). In the Acts of the Apostles baptism is likewise into the name of Jesus.

8.2–3 contains a version of the Lord's Prayer, introduced with the words: 'Let us pray as the Lord [i.e. Jesus] commanded in his gospel.' This version is closer to the longer Matthean version rather than the apocopated Lucan form, but the wording in the *Didache* is not identical with Matthew's text:

2. Our Father in heaven, May your name be acclaimed as holy, May your kingdom come, May your will come to pass on earth as it does in heaven. Give us today our bread for the morrow, And cancel for us our debt As we cancel [debts] for those who are indebted to us, And do not bring us into temptation, But preserve us from evil [or, from the evil one]. For power and glory are yours forever.

3. Pray this way three times a day.

In any case, the Matthean form—and indeed the Lukan—are subject to a complex series of text-critical variants, in which MSS of Matthew may be seen to be assimilating the text to that in Luke, and MSS of Luke to that in Matthew (e.g. the tense of the verb in 'as we forgive [cancel]' in Mt 6:12/Lk 11:4 and cf. *Did.* 8.2). Other variants, not of a harmonizing character, may also be seen within the complex textual witnesses to the Lord's Prayer. This activity reveals the volatility of the tradition and its susceptibility to liturgical influences and perhaps also to the influence of Marcion. Certainly, in the form of the Lord's Prayer as transmitted in the Bryennios MS of the *Didache* the prayer is close to, but not identical with, the longer forms of the prayer in Mt. 6:9–13; e.g. in the concluding doxology the *Didache* has only 'power' and 'glory' and omits 'kingdom': these three nouns are found in the MSS reading the longer ending in Mt 6:13. Among other differences, note 'debt' in the *Didache* rather than Matthew's 'debts'. Both versions seem to have been influenced by the liturgy.

(Chs. 9–10) Two eucharistic prayers are significant, one in ch. 9, the other in ch. 10, and are important to our understanding of early Christian practice. Ch. 9:

1. As for thanksgiving, give thanks this way. 2. First, with regard to the cup: We thank you, our Father, for the holy vine of David your servant which you made known to us through Jesus your servant. To you be glory forever. 3. And with regard to the loaf: We thank you, our Father, for the life and knowledge, which you made known to us through Jesus your servant. To you be glory forever. 4. As this loaf lay scattered upon the mountains and became a single fragment when it had been gathered, may your church be gathered into your kingdom from the ends of the earth. For glory and power are yours, through Jesus Christ, forever. 5. But let no one eat or drink from your Eucharist except those who are baptized in the Lord's name. For the Lord also has spoken concerning this: 'Do not give what is holy to dogs' [Mt 7:6].

Ch. 10:

1. When you have had your fill, give thanks this way: 2. We thank you, holy Father, for your holy name, which you made dwell in our hearts, and for the knowledge and faith and immortality, which you made known to us through Jesus your servant. To you be glory forever. 3. You, almighty Lord, created all things for the sake of your name, and you gave food and drink to human beings for enjoyment, so that they would thank you. But you graced us with spiritual food and drink and eternal life through Jesus, your servant. 4. Above all, we thank you, Lord, because you are powerful. To you be glory forever. 5. Be mindful, Lord, of your church, to preserve it from all evil, and to perfect it in your love. And, once it is sanctified, gather it from the four winds into the kingdom which you have prepared for it. For power and glory are yours forever. 6. May grace come, and may this world pass by. Hosanna to the God of David! If anyone is holy, let him come. If anyone is not, let him repent. Our Lord, come! Amen. 7. But permit the prophets to give thanks as they see fit. 8. And concerning the ointment, give thanks as follows: 9. We thank you, Father, for the fragrant ointment which you have made known to us through Jesus your servant.
Glory to you forever. Amen.

Among noteworthy features is the order of the wine before the bread (cf. the shorter text in Lk 22:17–19a). The eucharist seems to be a freestanding rite; in some early Christian gatherings, such as Paul describes in the Corinthian correspondence, the eucharist was celebrated at the conclusion of a communal meal.

Did. 9.2 presumably tries to connect Jesus with his Davidic, Messianic, origins, the strange image of the vine here being suggested by the context. The significance of the gathering of the grain to make the loaf in 9:4 also comes from a eucharistic context and perhaps echoes Jn 6:12 or, more generally, the unifying of the church implicit in the conclusion to the stories of the miraculous feedings. 9:5 clearly refers to a eucharist, making it less likely that chs. 9–10 refer to an agape (several scholars have suggested it does, encouraged, perhaps, by the absence of references here to body and blood). The eucharistic interpretation is encouraged by the argument that the context of chs. 9–10 (and 1–10 as a whole) is that of the annual baptism-eucharist ceremony.

The thanksgiving prayer in ch. 10 addresses God as 'holy Father', which may be compared with Jn 17:11 (itself from the liturgical section, Jn 15–17, which takes place in the upper room and begins with the True Vine discourse). Links with the Johannine tradition are not, however, a prominent feature of the *Didache*.

10.2–9 can be seen as antiphonal. To emphasize the participatory nature of the prayer the Coptic tradition here adds 'Amen' three times. Also in these verses can be seen echoes of the Lord's Prayer. This suggests either a direct borrowing by the originators of this prayer or that the Didachist and Jesus merely share the same understanding of topics to be put on the agenda for prayer, which is perhaps all that the Paternoster itself is. Comparable echoes are to be found in the Gethsemane story in the NT.

The prayer over oil (or incense) in 10.8 is found only in the Coptic; it is not in the Greek. The use of incense or oil is well established in varying religious traditions. In the NT, of course, its use is primarily connected with the anointing of Jesus in the Bethany episode (which was, perhaps, a coronation, or at least a Messiah-making event), or with the burial of Jesus. Anointing of the sick with oil is found in Jas 5:14, and oil was used in the mysterious rite known as 'sealing', which is referred to in on several occasions in the second-century apocryphal Acts (e.g. *Acts of Andrew*, 10; *Acts of Paul*, 25; *Acts of Thomas*, 27).

(Chs. 11–15) In the later parts of the *Didache* there are also instructions about travelling prophets, bishops, and deacons. References to itinerant preachers (chs. 13–14) as well as to a settled ministry (chs. 15), and the relation of these preachers to the bishops and deacons are obviously of supreme importance to church historians interested in tracing the growth of church discipline and organization. This section in the *Didache* encourages biblical scholars to make comparisons with passages such as 1 Tim. 3:2–13; Titus 1:5–9; and Phil 1:1. Particularly noteworthy is *Did.* 13:

1. And every true prophet who wishes to settle among you deserves his food. 2. Similarly, a true teacher also deserves, like the labourer, his food [cf. Mt 10:10b]. 3. So when you [sing.] take any firstfruits of what is produced by the wine press and the threshing floor, by cows and by sheep, you [sing.] shall give the firstfruits to the prophets, for they are your [pl.] high priests. 4. If, however you [pl.] have no prophet, give [them] to the poor. 5. If you [sing. in vv. 5–7] make bread, take the firstfruits and give them according to the commandment. 6. Likewise, when you open a jar of wine or oil, take the firstfruits and give them to the prophets. 7. Take the firstfruits of money and clothing and whatever else you own as you think best and give them according to the commandment.

Prophets and teachers in the *Didache* are the real successors to the apostles—it is they who receive the firstfruits. Teachers are worthy of their hire, just as the apostles are in Mt 10:10. The historic and hierarchical order, apostles–prophets–teachers, is reminiscent of 1 Cor 12:28 (cf. also Eph 4:11).

Ch. 15 is likely to be one of the most recently composed sections of the work because we have here instructions for a settled ministry of bishops and deacons (presbyters are not mentioned). The precise social context in which such issues would have been relevant for the church are not self-evident.

(Ch. 16) is an eschatological appendix with teaching about the Antichrist (in v. 4) and the second coming (in vv. 7–8, assuming 'the Lord' there to be Jesus). There are links with Mt 24 (and parallels) but there are differences in both content and language. There are also other links with the eschatological passages in 1 Thess 4:12–5:13 and elsewhere in the NT, suggesting a common Jewish-Christian background. The apocryphal *Apocalypse of Peter* in Ethiopic begins with an eschatological passage that also has close parallels with *Did.* 16, including the sign-working deceiver, the cross preceding the Lord as he comes, the regal procession, and judgement.

1. Keep vigil over your life. Let your lamps not go out and let your loins not be ungirded but be ready for you do not know the hour at which our Lord is coming. 2. You shall assemble frequently, seeking what pertains to your souls, for the whole time of your belief will be of no profit to you unless you are perfected at the final hour. 3. For in the final days false prophets and corruptors will be multiplied, and the sheep will turn into wolves, and love will turn into hate. 4. As lawlessness increases, they will hate and persecute and betray one another, and at that time the one who leads the world astray will appear as a son of God and will work signs and wonders, and the earth will be given into his hands and he will do godless things which have never been done since the beginning of time. 5. Then human creation will pass into the testing fire and many will fall away and perish but those who persevere in their belief will be saved by the curse itself 6. and then the signs of truth will appear, first, the sign spread out in heaven, next, the signal of the trumpet call, and third, resurrection of the dead—7. not of all the dead but, as it has been said, 'The Lord will come and all the holy ones with him.' 8. Then the world will see the Lord coming upon the clouds of heaven.

Bibliography: Wengst (1984); Niederwimmer (1993); Rordorf and Tuilier (1978); Tuckett (1989); Draper (1996); the Greek text of the *Didache* with an ET is found in Lake (1912–13: i. 308–33). A full bibliography of works on the *Didache* from about 1900 to 90 is found in Jefford (1995).

The Epistle of Barnabas

D. 1. The *Didache* and *Barnabas* have much in common. Both were written about the same time, both are found in the Bryennios MS, and, most significantly, both contain the passage about the Two Ways, which naturally raises the questions whether the *Didache* copied it from *Barnabas* or whether *Barnabas* found it in the *Didache*. (The common solution to the interrelationship of these passages is to say that the section containing the Two Ways came to both authors independently.) Both works are examples of an evolved literature, preserving and transmitting traditions. But whereas the *Didache* is a catechetical work aimed at initiates, *Barnabas* is aimed at reclaiming Jewish Christians, who were in danger of returning to Judaism.

2. Summary of contents:

Ch. 1: Introduction

2.1–16.10: The correct interpretation of the (Jewish) scriptures.

chs. 2–3: The Lord does not require sacrifice and fasting; these have been superseded by the sacrifice of Jesus.

ch. 4: Warnings about the coming judgement.

chs. 5–6: Why the Lord suffered in the flesh.

chs. 7–8: The Lord's suffering paralleled in the scapegoat and the red heifer.

chs. 9–10: Circumcision explained.

chs. 11–12: The OT tells us about baptism, the cross, the crucifixion, and Jesus.

chs. 13–14: Covenant explained.

ch. 15: Sabbath explained.

ch. 16: The temple explained as the presence of God in believers.

17.1–18.1a: Transitional passage.

18:1b–20: The Two Ways passage.

ch. 21: Conclusion.

3. Author. The work is anonymous—the author is unknown, but early tradition attributed it to Barnabas. He is likely to have been a Gentile Christian if the reference in 16.7 to a time 'before we believed in God' is allowed its plain meaning. Others see him as a Jewish Christian: there are several Jewish elements in the writing, and he is familiar with Jewish law, ritual, and sacrifices. The Two Ways passage was probably originally Jewish. The author was certainly familiar with various methods of Jewish interpretation such as haggadah, midrash, and Halakah. Even if the author was not a Jewish Christian, he was obviously aware of, and had access to, Jewish traditions.

4. The author compiled his letter from several previously existing traditions. The epistle is an evolved piece of literature, but that does not mean that the tradition is more important than the redactor. There is a certain lack of coherence and consistency in the letter, but it is not as lacking in overall direction as a first reading might suggest. The author is more than a mere compiler—he has an overall theological plan, in which his main *Tendenz* is an anti-Jewish slant imposed by him on his sources.

5. Early Recognition. Clement of Alexandria quotes *Barnabas* as 'scripture'. There are seven citations in Clement of Alexandria's *Stromateis* 2 and 5 from *Barnabas*. Eusebius, *Hist. Eccl.* 6.14.1, says Clement, *Hypotyposeis* (now lost), included commentary on *Barnabas* (and Jude with the other Catholic epistles and the *Apocalypse of Peter*). Origen refers to *Barnabas* as a Catholic epistle (*c. Cels.* 1.63 citing *Barn.* 5.9). Eusebius, *Hist. Eccl.* 6.13.6–14.1 places *Barnabas* among the 'disputed' writings; 3.25.4 has it among the 'spurious' writings.

Jerome, *De Vir. Ill.* 6, refers to the *Didache* and *Barnabas* as 'apocryphal'. He cites *Barn.* 8.2 in *In Ezek.* 43.19; *Barn.* 5.9 is quoted (as in Origen) in *Adv. Pel.* 3.2, although Origen mis-attributed it to Ignatius. The canonical list in Codex Claromontanus refers to the *Epistle of Barnabas* but possibly Epistle to the Hebrews, lacking in that catalogue, is meant. The Catalogue of the Sixty Books calls *Barnabas* 'apocryphal', and the Stichometry of Nicephorus labels it 'disputed'.

6. Text. The letter survives in Greek and Latin. The Greek MSS containing it are the biblical Codex Sinaiticus of the fourth century and Codex Hierosolymitanus (or Constantino-politanus), the eleventh-century MS discovered by Bryennios and published by him in 1883. Bryennios' MS, already referred to above in connection with the *Didache*, contains, in addition to the *Didache* and *Barnabas*, *1 and 2 Clement*, Chrysostom's *Synopsis of the OT and NT* (incomplete), and the long recension of Ignatius' letters (see 1.1–2).

Its appearance in Codex Sinaiticus shows that in the fourth century its canonical status was considered a possibility, *Barnabas* occurs immediately after Revelation without a break—it is not in a separate appendix. The fact that *Barnabas* is found (together with the *Shepherd of Hermas*) in this biblical MS suggests the scribe copied it (and the *Shepherd*) as if they were of equal status with the preceding books. In addition there is a family of Greek MSS, the oldest being eleventh century, in which *Epistle of Polycarp to the Philippians*, 9.2, is followed directly by *Barnabas* 5.7. In an ancestor of this family, a scribe obviously carelessly omitted the end of Polycarp and the beginning of *Barnabas* and thereby accidentally combined the two works in this way. The epistle is also found in a ninth- to tenth-century Latin MS (Codex Corbeiensis), now in St Petersburg. This MS ends at ch. 17, and thus omits the passage about the Two Ways, raising the questions whether the Latin omitted that section from an earlier, longer version or whether the Greek tradition interpolated the section from another source into a form of *Barnabas* comparable to that now known to us only in the Latin version.

7. Provenance. *Barnabas* was probably intended for a community in which Jewish Christians were in contact with Jews, although the precise locality in which it was written, or to which it was addressed, is not clear. Alexandria is a strong possibility, but, because the Two Ways passage has parallels with the Manual of Discipline from Qumran (1QS 3:13–4:28), some seek a place of composition east of Alexandria itself.

8. Date. The question of the date of *Barnabas* hinges on two passages, 4.4–5 and 16.3–4.

4.4–5:

And the prophet speaks thus: Ten kingdoms will reign on the earth. And afterward there will arise a little king, who will humiliate three of the kingdoms simultaneously. Similarly, Daniel says concerning the same one: And I saw the fourth beast, wicked and powerful and more dangerous than all the beasts of the sea; and ten horns sprouted from him, and from them budded a little offshoot of a horn; and it humiliated three of the great horns simultaneously.

There is a wide diversity of views on the interpretation of these verses. It has sometimes been concluded that the ten kings seem to lead up to Trajan, with Vespasian, Titus, and Domitian as the three humbled emperors; the 'little horn' is then seen here as Nero Redivivus, who will be subdued by the returning Jesus. Thus a date in Hadrian's reign (117–138 CE) is required for this interpretation.

16.3–4:

Furthermore, he says again: Behold, those who tore down this Temple will themselves build it. It is happening. Because of their fighting it was torn down by the enemies. And now the very servants of the enemies will themselves rebuild it.

If the reference is to a literal temple (and that is by no means certain) then we need a date prior to 132, when Hadrian built a Roman temple on the site of the Jerusalem temple.

The outer limits for the date of composition thus seem to be 117 CE and 132 CE. But if Nerva (96–8 CE) is to be identified as the little horn, this could mean that the letter was composed in his short but benign reign. His favourable attitude to Judaism could well have been responsible for the rumour that the temple would be rebuilt.

In so far as *Barnabas* is a composite work, there is the possibility that some of the material is of varying dates, hence it would be unwise to date it by any one piece of evidence; moreover its use of stock apocalyptic imagery makes it unreliable to pinpoint precise historical events.

9. Teaching. Whatever date is agreed upon, it is clear that the motivation for the writing of *Barnabas* was a resurgence of confidence in Judaism, perhaps fuelled by or even responsible for a belief that the Jerusalem temple would be rebuilt. This confidence was felt by the author of *Barnabas* to be destabilizing the Christian community. There was a temptation that some Christians (presumably of Jewish origin) would relapse into Judaism, and they needed reminding about the relationship of Judaism and Christianity, the role and purpose of the Jewish law, and the place of Christian ethics.

10. Gnosis. is a key term throughout the letter, but this is not a Gnostic work as commonly understood. The *gnosis* here refers to special insights; it is not an unorthodox, speculative Gnosticism. It may be divided into exegetical and ethical *gnosis*. Exegetical *gnosis*, especially of OT events, gives the 'correct' understanding of salvation history—the interpretation of scripture is the central focus of the writing. Chs. 2.1–16.10 give a spiritualized understanding of the OT. Ethical *gnosis* means right conduct (in the Two Ways passage), that is, the correct understanding of the Lord's requirements for ethical behaviour.

11. *Barnabas* makes a significant contribution to our understanding of Christianity at the end of the first and, probably, the beginning of the second centuries. Carleton Paget (1994: 264) writes: 'The survival of the Epistle of Barnabas is fortuitous, for it serves to remind all students of Early Christianity of the incomplete and fragmentary nature of what we know about this subject, and can, along with other extra-canonical texts, have the salutary effect of subverting glib reconstructions of Christian origins.'

12. The message of *Barnabas* is that Christians need to reassert their independence—it is they who are the true people of the Covenant. This reflects concerns similar to those of Paul several decades previously. For Paul the church was in the new age of the Spirit, Judaism had had a place in the history of salvation but, since the coming of Christ, the period of the law now belonged only to the old dispensation. For *Barnabas* the relevance of the God-given law is differently interpreted: it had always been incorrectly understood by Jews. Using his particular exegetical *gnosis* the author shows how, in particular, circumcision, covenant, sabbath observance, and the temple should have been interpreted, and using allegorical and other interepretative methods gives several examples of right understanding.

13. A good example of this is ch. 9, on circumcision. Its symbolic significance is emphasized; true circumcision is obedience. Little in this chapter is distinctively Christian until we reach the closing section. The symbolic significance of numbers (gematria) is important in much Jewish writing. Here it is applied to the name of Jesus and to the cross:

Learn, then, abundantly concerning everything, children of love, for when Abraham first gave circumcision, he circumcised while looking forward in the spirit to Jesus, and he received the teachings of the three letters. For it says: And Abraham circumcised the men of his household [Gen. 17:23], 18 and 300 in number [Gen. 14:14]. What, then, is the gnosis which was given him? Learn! For a distinction is made in that the 18 comes first, then it says 300. Now the (number) 18 (is represented by two letters), J = 10 and E = 8— thus you have "JE," the abbreviation for "JEsus." And because the cross, represented by the letter T (= 300), was destined to convey special significance it also says 300. He makes clear, then, that JEsus is symbolized by the two letters (JE 18), while in the one letter (T 300) is symbolized the cross. He who placed the implanted gift of his teaching in us knows! No one has learned from me a more trustworthy lesson! But I know that you are worthy.

In the second century the pagan Lucian mentions (in *Judicum Vocalium*, 12) that the cross is constructed in the form of a T and 'is so named by men'.

14. Throughout, *Barnabas* teaches that the New Israel is Christianity and that the OT had always been a Christian book. The Jews had got their own traditions wrong. The Jewish literal interpretation of the law was due to the devices of an evil angel, who had deceived Jews. This unusual approach demonstrates the distinctiveness of this letter, and probably ensured its preservation, success, and popularity. It survived in the MS tradition over several centuries, and was quoted (particularly by Egyptian fathers), respected, and venerated as one new way of looking at a perennial problem in early Christianity—the relationship of Christianity and Judaism. Other approaches differed. Marcion, for example, simply jettisoned the OT. The canonical Hebrews speaks of two covenants, and of the supremacy of the new over the old—the old dispensation was only temporary, whereas Christ's atoning sacrifice is eternal.

15. There are thirteen references to suffering in the epistol which have led some to suggest that *Barnabas* could have been a document (like 1 Peter, or Melito's *Paschal Homily*) written for and read at a paschal feast, when the whole redemptive work attributed to Christ (his death, resurrection, ascension, and parousia) would have been recalled and recited. *Barnabas* is closer to being a paschal homily than a baptismal liturgy. The explicit references to baptism at 6.11, 14; 11.1–11; 16.8 would have been particularly appropriate, especially as the theme of death and resurrection is often associated with baptism, for instance as in Rom 6:1–14. Like the *Didache*, *Barnabas* probably originated at the annual baptismal-eucharistic paschal feast.

16. Among other main themes are that the day of judgement is close, that salvation lies in the future and that Christ, who had been pre-existent, suffered and died in the flesh to purify a once sinful people. Only he makes possible a correct interpretation of the Scriptures. All of this is justified by an appeal to Scripture (i.e. the OT) not to Jesus' sayings. Christ is expected as the judge at the end-time.

17. Barnabas and the NT. *Barn.* 4.14 knows the words found in Mt 22:14: 'When you note that great signs and wonders were performed in Israel but that [the Jews] have been abandoned, let us take heed lest we be found to be, as it is written,

"many called but few chosen".' However, there is little support for the idea that the author had the written, canonical gospel in mind. It is more likely that he was familiar with the saying from the oral tradition. Similarly the references to Jesus' imbibing gall and vinegar on the cross (*Barn.* 7.3, 5) are also likely to have reached him from oral tradition. *Barn.* 5.9 (the verse known to Origen and Jerome) parallels Mk 2.17, calling sinners to repentance; 6.6 perhaps knows the passage about the casting of lots for Jesus' garments; 5.12 quotes the passage about the smiting of the sheep, recalling, perhaps, Mt 26:31 and Mk 14:27, although it may have come to him from Zech 13:7. The following (6.13; 7.9; 12.10–11) are also paralleled in biblical passages:

And the Lord says: Behold, I make the last things like the first.   (cf. Rev 21:5)

Because they will see him then, on that day, wearing the scarlet robe around his flesh and they will say: Is not this he whom we once crucified, despising and piercing and spitting on him? Surely this was the one who then said he was God's Son.   (cf. Mk 14:39 and par.)

10. Since then, they were going to say that Messiah is David's Son, David himself—fearing and perceiving the error of the sinners— prophesies: The Lord said to my Lord, 'Sit at my right hand until I make your enemies a footstool for your feet' [Ps 110:1]. 11. And again, Isaiah says as follows: The Lord said to my Messiah, the Lord, whose right hand I held, that nations would become obedient to him, and 'I will demolish the strength of kings' [Isa 45:1]. Notice how David says he is 'Lord', and does not say 'Son'.   (cf. Mk 12:36 and par.)

None of these parallels requires a literary dependence of *Barnabas* on the NT texts.

18. Barnabas and the OT. All the extensive allusions, references, and quotations from the OT Scriptures are loose and are likely to have reached the author from previously existing (oral) testimonies. Over twenty come from the LXX of Isaiah. Several are from the LXX Psalter. There are loose citations also from the Pentateuch. 6.2–4 combines loose and exact citation from the LXX of Isaiah and the Psalms:

2. And again, since he was established as a mighty Stone which crushes, the prophet says of him: Behold, I will insert into the foundations of Zion a Stone which is precious, chosen, a cornerstone, prized [Isa 28: 16a]. Then what does he say? And whoever trusts in him will live forever. Is our hope, then, on a stone? Not in the least! But he speaks in such a way since the Lord has established his flesh in strength. For he says: And he established me as a solid Rock [see Isa 50:7b]. And again the prophet says: The very Stone which the builders rejected has become the cornerstone [Ps. 118:22]! And again he says: This is the great and awesome Day which the Lord made [Ps. 118:24a; see 118:23].

Barn. 2.4–10 and 13.1–7 are also particularly noteworthy for the way in which LXX citations are employed and for the author's linking of quotations from different books.

Bibliography: Windisch (1920); Kraft (1965); Prigent and Kraft (1971); Wengst (1984); Carleton Paget (1994); Hlavik (1996). The Greek text of *Barnabas* with an Eng. trans. is found in Lake (1912–13: i. 340–409).

E. Among other Apostolic Fathers to be considered, albeit briefly, are the pseudo-Clementine letters and the Shepherd of Hermas, all of which are found attached to fourth-century biblical MSS. *1 and 2 Clement* appear at the end of Codex Alexandrinus, the Shepherd is found at the end of

Codex Sinaiticus. We shall then turn briefly to the *Epistles* by Ignatius.

The Pseudo-Clementine Letters: 1 Clement

F. 1. This anonymous letter to the church in Corinth is claimed in later tradition to have been written by Clement, the third or fourth bishop of Rome. The letter, likely to have been written at the end of the first century, is concerned with church order and ministry. Roman authority and jurisdiction over the church in Corinth seem to have been taken for granted by its composer.

2. The letter is in the Bryennios MS. As well as being in the Codex Alexandrinus, *1 Clement* is found alongside the NT text in one of the two extant Coptic papyri, and in a twelfth-century Syriac NT (now in Cambridge). This suggests that *1 Clement* teetered on the edge of the NT canon in several areas of Christianity over many centuries. Eusebius knew that it was read in churches. The epistle was used by Polycarp, and praised by Irenaeus, who quotes from it, as does Clement of Alexandria. There are a few links with the canonical 1 Corinthians and Hebrews. Links with the canonical gospels are more tenuous. Its doxologies, prayers, and trinitarian formulae are instructive for our understanding of late first-century liturgy.

3. The author preaches forgiveness and harmony to a church riven with discord and schism. Christians are urged to perform good deeds as a consequence of their faith. *1 Clement* sees the OT as a model for Christian practice (e.g. the Jewish priesthood is analogous to the Christian ministry). But a secular example, the phoenix, is taken in *1 Clem.* 25 as a parallel to resurrection and is set out as a proof for faith in a future resurrection of the faithful dead:

Let us consider the strange sign which takes place in the East, that is in the districts near Arabia. There is a bird which is called the Phoenix. This is the only one of its kind, and lives 500 years and when the time of its dissolution in death is at hand, it makes itself a sepulchre of frankincense and myrrh and other spices, and when the time is fulfilled it enters into it and dies. Now, from the corruption of its flesh there springs a worm, which is nourished by the juices of the dead bird, and puts forth wings. Then, when it has become strong, it takes up that sepulchre, in which are the bones of its predecessor, and carriers them from the country of Arabia as far as Egypt until it reaches the city called Heliopolis, and in the daylight in the sight of all it flies to the altar of the Sun, places them there, and then starts back to its former home. Then the priests inspect the registers of dates, and they find that it has come at the fulfilment of the 500th year.

The same story (with variations) occurs in Herodotus and in Pliny.

4. Among words of Jesus, two that occur in the letter (13.2; 46. 7*b*–8) are:

For he spoke thus: 'Be merciful, that you may obtain mercy. Forgive, that you may be forgiven. As you do, so shall it be done to you. As you give, so shall it be given unto you. As you judge, so shall you be judged. As you are kind, so shall kindness be shown you. With what measure you mete, it shall be measured to you.'

Remember the words of the Lord Jesus; for he said, 'Woe to that man: it were good for him if he had not been born, than that he should offend one of my elect: it were better for him that a millstone be hung on him, and he be cast into the sea, than that he should turn aside one of my elect.'

The former has links with verses in the Sermon on the Mount in the NT. The latter parallels Mt 26:24 || Mk 14:21 || Lk 22:22 and Mt 18:6 || Mk 9:42 || Lk 17:2, but it is unlikely that the author of *1 Clement* was familiar with our written gospels: his sources are more probably oral traditions.

2 Clement

G. *2 Clement*, like *1 Clement*, is found in the Bryennios MS, in Codex Alexandrinus, and in the twelfth-century Cambridge Syriac NT, but not in Latin or Coptic. It is a homily on self-control and repentance; it is not a letter and has a different authorship from *1 Clement*. The date and provenance are unclear. Possibly it comes from Rome in the mid-second century. Its main value is as an example of early, unsophisticated, Jewish-Christian thought from that period.

Bibliography: An appendix given over to Greek, Roman, and other stories concerning the figure of the phoenix is to be found in Linnemann (1992). This book gives a detailed commentary on both *1* and *2 Clement*. Other works on these letters are:
Wengst (1984); Grant and Graham (1965); Welbourn, *ABD* i. 1055–60.
The Greek text of *1* and *2 Clement* with an ET is found in Lake (1912–13: i. 8–163).

The Shepherd of Hermas

H. 1. Several MS copies of this text have survived, including the Codex Sinaiticus, where about a quarter of the Shepherd follows *Barnabas*. The Shepherd is cited by Irenaeus, Clement of Alexandria, Origen, Athanasius, and Tertullian, usually as scripture. The Muratorian Canon allows it to be read privately.

2. Hermas is the unknown author and it is he who is the hero of the story. The Shepherd is divided into three parts: five Visions after which come twelve Mandates (or Precepts) and ten Similitudes (or Parables). It has been suggested by several scholars that these sections may have come from different sources. The composition is likely to have developed in the mid-second century. Its aim is to inculcate a need for repentance. There are some links with material known to us in the NT, but there is no convincing evidence of direct copying. Vision 10 (the Good Shepherd) suggests parallels with Jn 10.

Bibliography: Commentaries on the text are:
Dibelius (1923); Joly (1968); Whittaker (1967); Kirkland (1990); Osiek (1999). See also Hahneman (1992), esp. ch. 2. The Greek and Latin text of the Shepherd with an Eng. trans. is in Lake (1912–13: ii. 6–305).

The Letters of Ignatius

I. 1. Ignatius of Antioch *en route* to his martyrdom in Rome, an event which probably took place *c*.107 CE, wrote letters to the churches in Ephesus, Magnesia, Tralles, Rome, Smyrna, and Philadelphia, and to Polycarp. These letters were circulated and gathered together, and were quoted by Eusebius and Theodoret, among others. The original seven were interpolated, and spurious letters were added to the corpus.

2. The originals, known to Eusebius, survive in Greek, Latin, Syriac, and in other languages. (The long recension, containing interpolations to the genuine seven letters together with six additional letters, survives in Greek and Latin.)

The *Epistle to the Romans* had a different textual history as it was subsequently incorporated into a martyrology—witnesses to this epistle are extensive but of variable quality.

3. Ignatius' friend Polycarp in his letter to the Philippians refers in ch. 13 to a collection of the martyr's letters, which he was forwarding to Philippi.

4. The main emphasis of Ignatius' seven letters is to defend an authoritarian episcopacy. The letters also contain warnings against a Judaizing heresy with docetic overtones. Whether this was one heresy or two—Judaeo-Gnosticism or Judaism and Docetism—is debated. Jesus' divinity is stressed—he is called 'God' at least twelve times in these letters—but the corporeality and reality of his birth and death are taught. The life of Christ is said to be continued in the eucharist.

5. Ignatius was aware of a collection of Paul's letters. He quotes or alludes to 1 Corinthians nearly fifty times, although often in a free and paraphrastic way. There are allusions to most of Paul's other letters too. His letter to the Ephesians, 17.2–18.1, is a good example of his use of Paul:

Why are we not all wise [cf. 1 Cor 4:10], since we have received the knowledge of God, namely Jesus Christ [Col 2:2]? Why are we foolishly perishing [1 Cor 1:18], ignoring the gift which the Lord has truly sent? My spirit is devoted to the cross, which is a stumbling block to unbelievers but salvation and eternal life to us [1 Cor 1:18, 23–4]. 'Where is the wise man? Where is the debater? Where is the boasting of the so-called intelligent [1 Cor 1:20]?'

6. In his letter to Polycarp, 2.1–2, Ignatius perhaps betrays a knowledge of the canonical gospels:

If you love good disciples, it is no credit to you [Lk 6:32]; instead, bring the more troublesome into subjection by gentleness. 'Not all wounds are healed by the same plaster.' 'Relieve convulsions by moist applications.' 'Be prudent as the serpent' in every matter and 'sincere as the dove' [Mt 10:16] always.

7. Ignatius' Romans 7.3 with its reference to a future eucharist associated with the resurrection of believers has also been pointed to as example of Ignatius' knowledge of John's gospel, esp. 6:33, 51 8: 'I take no pleasure in the food of corruption or in the pleasures of this life. I desire the bread of God [Jn 6:33], which is the flesh of Jesus Christ (who was of the seed of David), and for drink I desire his blood, which is imperishable love.' But perhaps Ignatius' memory of this material came from the oral tradition rather than his reading of the gospels.

Bibliography: Grant (1966); the Greek text of the *Epistles of Ignatius* with an ET is found in Lake (1912–13: i. 172–277).

General Bibliography: On the Apostolic Fathers see Grant, (1964); Barnard (1966); Tugwell (1989). The whole question of the links between Jesus material and the Apostolic Fathers is investigated in the influential monograph by Köster (1957).

THE NEW TESTAMENT APOCRYPHA

J. General Introduction. 1. Many of these texts tell of the deeds and pronouncements of characters who figure in the NT proper—Jesus of course, but also his parents, Joseph and Mary, Pilate, Paul, Peter, and other apostles. There is also a tendency in this literature to base stories around the many fringe characters of the NT narratives, the woman with the issue of blood, the good and bad thieves, Zachariah, and apostles who in the NT do not occur prominently in their own right—Andrew or John, for example. The main link between the 'apocryphal' and 'canonical' texts (to use those terms anachronistically when referring predominantly to first–third-century compositions) is not so much the genres of literature but the attempts in the apocryphal literature to amplify events and details about the dramatis personae found in the earlier canonical books and in some cases to fill perceived gaps in the canonical accounts.

2. We are assuming for the moment that the apocryphal literature is in each case later than the books which were incorporated into the NT. If we assume the secondary nature of the apocryphal books and a date for their composition in and subsequent to the second century, we can see that one of the main motives behind the composition of these books was to satisfy the curiosity of the faithful about characters and events not always fully developed in the NT itself.

3. We now turn to look at the different genres of literature within the apocryphal NT in more detail. These are categorized as gospels, acts, epistles, and apocalypses.

4. **Lost Gospels.** Some gospels are known now only by their titles found in patristic and other sources, while extracts from some others are known from attributed citations in patristic works. Among the latter are Jewish-Christian gospels (e.g. the *Gospel according to the Hebrews*, known from quotations in Origen and Jerome), the *Gospel of the Egyptians*, parts of which are quoted in the work of Clement of Alexandria, and the *Preaching of Peter*, parts of which are known from Clement of Alexandria and Origen.

5. **Extant Gospels.** Some of these have survived complete or relatively so, others are fragmentary. The main apocryphal gospel texts are the *Protevangelium of James*, the *Infancy Gospel of Thomas*, the *Gospel of Pseudo-Matthew*, the *Arabic Infancy Gospel*, the *Gospel of Thomas*, the *Gospel of Peter*, and the *Gospel of Nicodemus*.

6. Certainly it is true to say that although we have passion gospels and birth/infancy gospels, there is nothing now extant comparable to the canonical gospels. What have survived are texts that tell stories which could belong to the period of Jesus' ministry. Some are only small fragments containing sometimes only one episode, sometimes three or four stories. Again, we have no means of knowing the original scope or scale of the texts from which these fragments have chanced to survive.

7. The existence of additional stories and 'secret sayings' (to use this conventional, but erroneous, description) need not surprise us. The NT authors themselves did not claim to give a complete record of everything that Jesus did and said. The gospel writers made a selection of the material available to them in the oral tradition or in earlier written accounts (see for instance Jn 20:30–1). Some sayings of Jesus are known to us outside the gospels in Acts 20:35, or in Paul's letters (e.g. 1 Cor 7:10; 9:14; 1 Thess 4:15–17). It may well be that some of the sayings or stories of Jesus known to us from later accounts—the writings of a church father or, as here, in the apocryphal texts—are as authentic and as historic as those in the NT itself. Some modern scholars are even prepared to argue for a first-century origin of some of the following apocryphal stories and sayings.

8. The most famous of these fragments of apocryphal gospels is the second-century Egerton Papyrus in the British Library. This contains four stories on the front and reverse of two fragments. The MS has recently been supplemented by an additional fragment known as P.Köln 255 (inv. 608), which enables the text in the London fragments to be extended slightly. These stories have biblical parallels, in particular the healing of a leper (cf. Mt 8:2–4 and par.), paying tribute to Caesar (Mt 22:15–22 and par.) and the prophecy of Isaiah (cf. Mt 15:7–8 and par.); an episode with echoes of Jn 5:39, 45–6; 9:29.

And behold, a leper approached him and said, 'Teacher Jesus, while journeying with lepers and eating with them in the inn, I myself also became a leper. If, therefore, you are willing, I am cleansed.' The Lord said to him, 'I am willing: be cleansed.' And immediately the leprosy departed from him, and the Lord said, 'Go, show yourself to the priests and make an offering for your cleansing as Moses commanded, and sin no more...'

...came to him to tempt him, saying, 'Teacher Jesus, we know that you have come from God, for the things which you do bear witness beyond all the prophets. Tell us then: Is it lawful to render to kings what pertains to their rule? Shall we render it to them or not?' But Jesus, knowing their mind, said to them in indignation, 'Why do you call me teacher with your mouth, when you do not do what I say? Isaiah prophesied correctly when he said about you: This people honours me with its lips, but their heart is far from me; in vain do they worship me, [teaching as doctrines merely human] commandments.'

Jesus said] to the lawyers, '[Punish] every wrong-doer and transgressor, and not me...what he does as he does it.' Then, turning to the rulers of the people, he spoke this word, 'Search the scriptures, in which you think you have life; it is they which bear witness to me. Do not think that I have come to accuse you to my Father; your accuser is Moses, on whom you have set your hope.' When they said, 'We know well that God spoke to Moses; but as for you, we do not know where you come from,' Jesus said in reply, 'Now your unbelief is accused to the ones who were witnessed to by him. If you had believed [in Moses] you would have believed me, because he wrote to your fathers about me.'

9. Among other fragments are the Oxyrhynchus Papyrus 840 (P.Oxy. 840) of the fourth century and the Fayyum fragment of the third century, although the text they contain is likely to be considerably older. P.Oxy. 840 in its entirety contains the following story:

[B]efore he does wrong he makes all kinds of ingenious excuses. 'But take care lest you also suffer the same things as they did, for those who do evil not only receive their chastisement from men but they await punishment and great torment.' Then he took them with him and brought them into the place of purification itself, and was walking in the temple. A Pharisee, a chief priest named Levi, met them and said to the Saviour, 'Who gave you permission to walk in this place of purification and look upon these holy vessels when you have not bathed and your disciples have not washed their feet? But you have walked in this temple in a state of defilement, whereas no one else comes in or dares to view these holy vessels without having bathed and changed his clothes.' Thereupon the Saviour stood with his disciples and answered him. 'Are you then clean, here in the temple as you are?' He said, 'I am clean, for I have bathed in the pool of David and have gone down by one staircase and come up by the other, and I have put on clean white clothes. Then I came and viewed the holy vessels.' 'Alas', said the Saviour, 'you blind men who cannot see! You have washed in this running water, in which dogs and pigs have wallowed night and day, and you have washed and scrubbed your outer skin, which harlots and flute-girls also anoint and wash and scrub, beautifying themselves for the lusts of men while inwardly they are filled with scorpions and unrighteousness of every kind. But my disciples and I, whom you charge with not having bathed, have bathed ourselves in the living water which comes down from heaven. But woe to those who...' (cf. Mt 15:1–20 and par.)

The Fayyum fragment parallels Mt 26:31/Mk 14:27:

[After supper as was the custom, he said],
'All] in this night will be offended
as] it is written: I will smite the [shepherd
and the] sheep will be scattered.'
When] Peter [said], 'Even if all, [not I',
Jesus said], 'Before the cock crows twice three times
today will you] deny me.'

10. Once more the question arises about the relationship, literary or otherwise, between the apocryphal stories and their canonical counterparts. Some answers to such a question inevitably have the effect of blurring the strict line of demarcation that is often drawn between the canonical and apocryphal texts. The work of Helmut Köester and his followers in particular has sought to emphasize the independence of such texts as the *Gospel of Peter*, P.Egerton 2, and the *Gospel of Thomas* from the canonical gospels and even to give a date for the original composition of the sayings and stories in some of the apocryphal gospels earlier than the synoptic parallels. Such conclusions have not met with broad support. Frans Neirynck has been active in arguing against these theories by demonstrating that Mark and the other synoptic writings were the sources for works like P.Egerton 2 and the *Gospel of Peter*. The debate has guaranteed that the apocryphal texts are now examined alongside the canonical counterparts, especially in synopses, with the result that the later development of the synoptists' stories and sayings can be plotted and recognized.

11. The *Gospel of Thomas* in its entirety was discovered at Nag Hammadi in 1945. The copy, written in Coptic, has been dated to c.350 CE. It contains 114 sayings, nearly all of them attributed to Jesus. As such, it may be comparable with the hypothetical canonical gospel source known as Q, usually said to have been a gospel containing sayings of Jesus, without narrative.

12. The concluding words of *Thomas* state that it is 'a gospel', but its opening words speak merely of 'sayings'. Its original language was Greek: three fragments of *Thomas* in Greek have survived, and were discovered in Oxyrhynchus at the end of the nineteenth century and the beginning of the twentieth century (P.Oxy. 1, P.Oxy. 654, P.Oxy. 655). One fragment has been given a date of around 200 CE; the other two are third century. Until the Coptic text was unearthed, the relationship of the Greek fragments to one another and to a larger work gave rise to half a century of learned debate and speculation. The discovery of *Thomas* at Nag Hammadi answered many of the earlier questions and laid to rest much speculation, although the exact relationship between the Coptic and the surviving Greek fragments is still not entirely clear—the Coptic, for instance, is not an exact translation of the Greek and it seems as if *Thomas* passed through several recensions. Although the precise history of the text is disputed, it does seem as if the gospel was popular, being copied regularly over several centuries, and with a widespread distribution. It was translated, possibly more than once, into Coptic.

13. It is not clear if early patristic testimony to a gospel of Thomas is to this *Gospel of Thomas* or another, but there are parallels to some of its sayings in the writings of the third-century father Hippolytus and in other patristic sources. It is, however, not certain if the parallels are due to direct dependence of the fathers on *Thomas*, or to a shared common heritage of oral sayings.

14. The date of its composition seems to have been prior to 200 CE but whether it goes back to the first century or is even contemporaneous with the canonical gospels is uncertain. Most scholars accept that *Thomas* was written later than the NT gospels, but the degree of dependence, or relationship, between the apocryphal text and the biblical is debated. Modern synopses often show parallels to *Thomas*. An analysis shows that most of its logia are linked to NT sources, especially the gospels. Some links are mere allusions; others are deviant versions of the same saying; a few are almost exactly parallel. All of this opens intriguing questions about the history, origins, and significance of the sayings in *Thomas*.

15. It is easy to speculate: one could argue that the circle responsible for fostering the logia included in *Thomas* possessed, or at least knew, the canonical material in its present form or some of its sources (e.g. in the form of a document such as Q), or a digest of sayings previously abstracted from the NT gospels. One could even say that the author of *Thomas* (either an individual or a group) was familiar with sayings that were circulated only in an oral—and therefore in a changing and developing—context. That latter suggestion would explain the variety and range of sayings, including some which appear in the NT with virtually identical wording.

16. Among sayings of *Thomas* that closely parallel the NT are: logion 20: 'The disciples said to Jesus, "Tell us, what is the Kingdom of God like?" He said to them, "It is like a grain of mustard seed, smaller than all seeds. But when it falls on cultivated ground it puts forth a large branch and provides a shelter for the birds of heaven."' The main difference from the synoptic versions (Mt 13:31–2; Mk 4:30–2; Lk 13:18–19) is the 'cultivated ground'.

Logion 26: 'Jesus said, "The splinter that is in your brother's eye you see but the plank in your own eye you do not see. When you have taken the plank out of your own eye, then you will see to remove the splinter from your brother's eye."' The saying is briefer than the form in Lk 6:42 or Mt 7:5 and it reduces the two questions there to a single statement.

Logion 31: 'Jesus said, "No prophet is acceptable in his own village; a physician does not heal those who know him."' The second half of this saying looks like an expansion of Lk 4:23–4 but the structural parallelism in *Thomas* suggests that this longer form is the original.

Logion 41: 'Jesus said, "He who has something in his hand, will receive more; and he who has nothing, even the little he has shall be taken away from him"', cf. Mt. 13:12/Mk 4:25 = Lk 8:18, where the saying refers to the reaction to teaching in parables. At Mt 25:29; Lk 19:26 it concludes a parable. It is perhaps a piece of floating material which *Thomas* anchors to its preceding logion (40): 'Jesus said, "A vine was planted without the Father, but because it did not become strong it will be uprooted and it will rot."' Here the vine 'planted without the Father' is equivalent to the person in logion 41 'who has nothing'.

Logion 46a: 'Jesus said, "From Adam to John the Baptist among those born of women no one is greater than John the Baptist."' It could be argued that this logion is independent of Mt 11:11 and possibly more authentic than the synoptic version (cf. logion 15: 'Jesus said, "When you see him who was not born of woman, prostrate yourselves on your faces and worship him: that one is your father."').

Logion 54: 'Jesus said, "Blessed are the poor for yours is the kingdom of heaven."' Cf. Lk 6:20 and Mt 5:3. *Thomas* differs from both, and may represent an independent and even a more authentic version of the beatitude.

Logion 55: 'Jesus said, "He who does not hate his father and his mother cannot be my disciple and he who does not hate his brothers and his sisters and does not take up his cross as I have will not be worthy of me."' Thomas is closer to Lk 14:26–7 than to Mt. 10:37–8. There is no reference in *Thomas* to the wife and children mentioned by Luke or to the son and daughter of Matthew. The versions in Matthew and Luke are not identical: these two Q versions therefore stand alongside the form in *Thomas* and all have equal claims to independence.

Logion 86: 'Jesus said, "[The foxes have] their earths and the birds have their nests but the Son of Man has nowhere to lay his head and rest."' This is the only Son of Man saying in *Thomas* (cf. Mt 8:20 or Lk 9:58). *Thomas* adds 'and rest', which can possibly be seen as a Gnostic addition, implying that the 'repose' is not on earth but within, which is a theme found in *Thomas* elsewhere (in logia 50, 51, 90).

Logion 96: 'Jesus [said,] "The kingdom of the Father is like a woman who took a little leaven, [hid] it in dough and made it into large loaves. He who has ears let him hear"', cf. Mt 13:33; Lk 13:20–1. *Thomas* emphasizes the contrast between the small amount of leaven and the large size of the loaves.

17. As far as other links with the NT are concerned, the parables found in *Thomas* have interesting parallels: logion 9 (parable of the sower): 'Jesus said, "Behold, the sower went out; he filled his hand, he sowed. Some seeds fell on the road. The birds came and gathered them up. Others fell on the rock and did not take root in the earth and did not produce ears up to heaven. Others fell among thorns. They choked the seed and the worm ate them. But others fell on good ground and it brought forth good fruit to heaven. These yielded six per measure and one hundred and twenty measures."' Among the differences in *Thomas* compared with the parable in Mt 13:3–8; Mk 4:3–8; Lk 8:5–8 are that the sower fills his hand, that the seeds sown on the rock do not put ears up to heaven, and the reference to the worm.

Logion 57 (parable of the wheat and the tares): 'Jesus said, "The kingdom of the Father is like a man who had good seed. His enemy came by night; he sowed weeds among the good seed. The man did not let them pull up the weed. He said to them, 'Do not do so, lest when you go to pull up the weed you pull up the wheat along with it.' For on the day of the harvest the weeds will be conspicuous; they will be pulled up and burned."' This parable is shorter than Mt 13:24–30. It could therefore be a summary of that version or be an independent writing-up from the oral tradition of only the essentials. The same judgement can be made of logion 63 (the parable of the rich fool): 'Jesus said, "There was a rich man who had considerable wealth. He said, 'I will use my money to sow and reap and plant and fill my warehouses with fruit so that I will lack nothing.' Such were his intentions. But in that night he died. He who has ears, let him hear"' (cf. Lk 12:16–20).

Logion 64 (parable of the wedding guests): 'Jesus said, "A man had the habit of receiving visitors and when he had prepared the banquet he sent his servant to invite the guests. He went to the first and said to him, 'My master invites you.' He replied, 'Money is owed me by some merchants. They will come to me this evening; I must go and give them orders. I beg to be excused from the dinner.' He went to another and said to him, 'My master has invited you.' He said to him, 'I have just bought a house and am needed for a day. I have no time.' He went to another and said to him, 'My master invites you.' He said to him, 'My friend is about to be married and I have to prepare a wedding feast; I shall not be able to come. I beg to be excused from the dinner.' He went to another and said to him, 'My master invites you.' He said to him, 'I have bought a village and am on my way to collect the rent. I shall not be able to come. I beg to be excused from the dinner.' The servant returned and said to his master, 'Those whom you invited asked to be excused from the dinner.' The master said to his servant, 'Go out into the streets and bring in those whom you find so that they may dine.' Buyers and merchants will not enter the places of my Father."' This is probably a Hellenistic rewriting of the synoptic account (Lk 14:16–24, cf. Mt 22:1–10) with a different structure, in which there are four instead of three guests, and with several other differing details.

Logion 65 (parable of the wicked husbandmen): 'He said, "A good man had a vineyard. He leased it to some farmers so that they would cultivate it and he would receive the fruit from them. He sent his servant so that the tenants would give him the fruit of the vineyard. They seized his servant, beat him and almost killed him. The servant returned and told his master. His master said, 'Perhaps they did not recognize him.' He sent another servant. The tenants beat him also. Then the master sent his son. He said, 'Perhaps they will respect my son.' Those tenants knowing he was the heir of the vineyard seized him and killed him. He who has ears, let him hear."' As in Lk 20:9–16, *Thomas* has no allusion to the preparation of the vineyard in Isa 5:1–2, a detail found in Mt 21:33–41 and Mk 12:1–9. The question is, have *Thomas* and Luke deleted earlier material or is the reference to Isaiah a later addition to the primitive form preserved in *Thomas* (and Luke)? The synoptists' account may itself have been expanded from an earlier version in which the servants are to be understood as the prophets. The synoptists' conclusion, especially in Matthew, looks like a later attempt to clarify the meaning. As that conclusion is absent from *Thomas*, does that therefore mean that it is the more primitive?

18. It will have been seen that some logia, although close to the synoptic parallels, none the less veer off at a tangent. On the other hand, there are sayings such as the following that have no obvious NT parallel. However, these could represent authentic, i.e. independent, Jesus tradition comparable to that found in the NT.

Logion 28: 'Jesus said, "I stood in the midst of the world, and I appeared to them in the flesh. I found all of them drunk; I did not find any of them thirsting. And my soul was pained for the sons of men because they are blind in their heart, and they do not see that they came empty into the world; they seek to go empty out of the world. Now they are drunk. When they have shaken off their wine, then they will repent."' Jesus' manifestation in the flesh is as in 1 Tim 3:16. The lament may be compared with that in Mk 9:19.

Logion 77*b* (cf. P.Oxy. 1, logion 30*b*): 'Split the wood and I am there; lift up the stone and you will find me there.'

Logion 82: 'Jesus said, "He who is near me is near fire but he who is far from me is far from the kingdom."' Origen, *in Jer.* 3.3 and Didymus, *Exp. in Ps.* 88.8, also know this saying. Its antithetical parallelism and Semitic structure speak highly in favour of its originality.

Logion 97: 'Jesus said, "The kingdom of the [Father] is like a woman who was carrying a jar which was full of meal. While she was walking on a long road the handle of the jar broke; the meal spilled out behind her on to the road. She did not notice it; she was unaware of the accident. When she came to her house she put the jar down and found it was empty."' The precise meaning is unclear, possibly because the original context is now absent. It could refer to the imperceptible loss of the kingdom or to its coming unnoticed.

Logion 98: 'Jesus said, "The kingdom of the Father is like a man who wanted to kill a powerful man. He drew the sword in his own house and he thrust it into the wall so that he would know if his hand would be strong enough. Then he killed the powerful one."' Jesus is represented as teaching the need for a thorough preparation for action, as in the parable of the king preparing for war in Lk 14:28–32. Jesus in both uses a popular proverb.

19. The interpretation of some of these logia has sometimes been made to apply to or spring from Gnostic thought and teaching (see A3–4 above). Some other sayings are less ambiguous and seem to require a Gnostic provenance or interpretation. These include: logion 1: 'And he said, "He who finds the interpretation of these sayings will not taste death."' This seems to be an adaptation of Jn 8:52 applied to the acquisition of knowledge.

Logion 23: 'Jesus said, "I shall choose you, one from a thousand, and two from ten thousand, and they shall stand as a single one."' The Gnostic leader Basilides was familiar with the sentiment expressed here to reflect the infinitesimal number of the elect. In *Thomas* men and women will become one, hence the final clause.

Logion 67: 'Jesus said, "He who knows the All but fails to know himself lacks everything."' Self-knowledge is an important element in Gnostic systems, hence this saying, whatever its origin, would be compatible with Gnosticism.

Logion 114: 'Simon Peter said to them, "Let Mary leave us, because women are not worthy of life." Jesus said, "Look, I shall lead her so that I will make her male in order that she also may become a living spirit, resembling you males. For every woman who makes herself male will enter the kingdom of heaven."' This is another saying proclaiming that men and women must become one. It is stated here that the female must become male. Possibly the intention is that the creation of Adam alone will be re-established at the end of time with a return to the conditions before the Fall.

20. Because of sayings like these, the term 'Gnostic', usually intended as a pejorative term synonymous with 'heretical', has been applied to *Thomas* as a whole. In other words, a common judgement is that the community responsible for preserving and circulating *Thomas* in the form in which was eventually written out was a Christian group sympathetic to or influenced by Gnosticism. However, Gnosticism in varying forms flourished in the early Christian centuries and in many ways some of the teaching of *Thomas* was merely characteristic of second-century syncretism. This would mean that it did not originate in a fully-fledged Gnostic movement nor is it to be dismissed as unorthodox in its entirety. Often the mere fact that *Thomas* was found in the Nag Hammadi library is sufficient for some commentators to brand it, because of guilt by association, as a Gnostic work when all that may be deduced is that the Nag Hammadi library found it a congenial work to possess.

Bibliography: There is a vast secondary literature on the *Gospel of Thomas*. The fullest bibliography is Scholer (1971), regularly updated in *Novum Testamentum*.

K. 1. We now turn to stories of Jesus' birth, childhood, passion, and descent to the underworld, as well as to stories from the Pilate cycle.

2. Birth stories. Three extracts from apocryphal nativity gospels are given. The first example (from the 2nd-cent. *Protevangelium of James*, 18:1–2) elaborates the account of the journey to Bethlehem. This seems to be the earliest reference to Jesus' birth in a cave. The narrative continues with a famous monologue by Joseph, who describes the wonders that accompanied Jesus' birth—in particular, the cessation of natural phenomena. The apocryphal writer obviously believed that the arrival on earth of the universal Saviour demanded cosmic recognition. The moving star in the biblical account was not sufficient: for this developed tradition the catalepsy of nature was introduced as an appropriate accompaniment to the birth. In this, of course, parallels can be drawn with the cosmic events that accompanied Jesus' departure from earth, notably the eclipse and the earthquake at the time of his crucifixion (Mt 23:51–2; Mk 15:33). The paralysis of natural phenomena may be compared with the silence in heaven at the opening of the seventh seal in Rev. 8:1.

3. A variation of the stories in the *Protevangelium* is to be seen in the later *Gospel of Pseudo-Matthew*, which in its present form may date from the eighth century, although it drew on much earlier material. Here Jesus' birth is acknowledged not only by the shepherds and the wise men, but also by animals. In the second extract below, from *Ps.-Matt.* 14, will be seen the episode in which the ox and the ass adore Jesus. This well-known scene is due to the influence of the OT, in particular Isa 1:3 and Hab 3:2. This represents an ongoing tradition in which various biblical passages were read as Messianic prophecies that were then said to have been fulfilled in the life of Jesus. *Ps.-Matt.*'s use of OT citations continues a Christian tradition as old as the NT itself. The third extract is from the medieval Latin nativity story known as Arundel MS 404. The cessation of nature at Jesus' birth is found here too. But the extract from Arundel 404 ch. 73 is given below for the description of the actual birth, which is the most Docetic in character in any of these apocryphal gospels and appears to reflect second-

century interests. Here in the birth story Jesus only *seems* to be human. His physical appearance on earth is described in the Arundel text as only a manifestation of divine light.

And [Joseph] found a cave and brought [Mary] into it, and left her in the care of his sons and went out to seek for a Hebrew midwife in the region of Bethlehem. Now I, Joseph, was walking, and yet I did not walk, and I looked up to the air and saw the air in amazement. And I looked up at the vault of heaven, and saw it standing still and the birds of the heaven motionless. And I looked down at the earth, and saw a dish placed there and workmen reclining, and their hands were in the dish. But those who chewed did not chew, and those who lifted up did not lift, and those who put something to their mouth put nothing to their mouth, but everybody looked upwards. And behold, sheep were being driven and they did not come forward but stood still; and the shepherd raised his hand to strike them with his staff but his hand remained upright. And I looked at the flow of the river, and saw the mouths of the kids over it and they did not drink. And then suddenly everything went on its course.

And on the third day after the birth of our Lord Jesus Christ, Mary went out of the cave and, entering a stable, placed the child in the manger, and an ox and ass adored him. Then was fulfilled that which was said by Isaiah the prophet, 'The ox knows his owner, and the ass his master's crib.' Therefore, the animals, the ox and the ass, with him in their midst, incessantly adored him. Then was fulfilled that which was said by Habakkuk the prophet, saying, 'Between two animals you are made manifest.' Joseph remained in the same place with Mary for three days.

As the time drew near, the power of God showed itself openly. The maiden stood looking into heaven; she became like a vine. For now the end of the events of salvation was at hand. When the light had come forth, Mary worshipped him whom she saw she had given birth to. The child himself, like the sun, shone brightly, beautiful and most delightful to see, because he alone appeared as peace, bringing peace everywhere. In that hour when he was born the voice of many invisible beings proclaimed in unison, 'Amen.' And that light, which was born, was multiplied and it obscured the light of the sun itself by its shining rays. The cave was filled with the bright light and with a most sweet smell. The light was born just as the dew descends from heaven to the earth. For its perfume is fragrant beyond all the smell of ointments.

L. Jesus' Childhood. 1. In the apocryphal gospels events relating to the time of Jesus' ministry are virtually ignored; that period is well covered in the canonical gospels. Gaps in the story of his career were perceived to be located in his parents' background, his birth, and his early years. Several apocryphal gospels relate incidents about Jesus as an infant and a young boy. The biblical precedent for such stories is likely to be the account in Luke's gospel of Jesus in the temple at the age of 12. That story is to be found in a modified form in the *Infancy Gospel of Thomas*—a second-century composition, which, together with the *Protevangelium of James*, seems to have had an enormous influence on Christian tradition thanks partly to their having been re-edited in other, later books such as the *Gospel of Pseudo-Matthew*.

2. In *Infancy Thomas* the story of Jesus at the age of 12 is as follows:

And when he was twelve years old his parents went according to the custom to Jerusalem to the feast of the passover with their companions and after the feast of the passover they returned to their house. And while they were returning, the child Jesus went back to Jerusalem. But his parents supposed that he was in the company.

And when they had gone a day's journey, they sought him among their kinsfolk, and when they did not find him, they were troubled, and returned again to the city seeking him. And after the third day they found him in the temple sitting among the teachers, listening and asking them questions. And all paid attention to him and marvelled how he, a child, put to silence the elders and teachers of the people, elucidating the chapters of the law and the parables of the prophets. And his mother Mary came near and said to him, 'Why have you done this to us, child? Behold, we have sought you sorrowing.' Jesus said to them, 'Why do you seek me? Do you not know that I must be about my father's affairs?' But the scribes and Pharisees said. 'Are you the mother of this child?' And she said, 'I am.' And they said to her. 'Blessed are you among women, because God has blessed the fruit of your womb. For such glory and such excellence and wisdom we have never seen nor heard.' And Jesus arose and followed his mother and was subject to his parents; but his mother stored up all that had taken place. And Jesus increased in wisdom and stature and grace. To him be glory for ever and ever. Amen.

Some synopses such as Aland (1985) and Greeven (Huck 1981) print that story alongside the Lukan version. The relation between the two seems to show the secondary nature of the account in *Infancy Thomas* (e.g. in the elaboration of the references to Mary), but we need not see this as the result of direct copying by the author of *Infancy Thomas*. That author was a creative writer and not a scribe of Luke's gospel. Thus the version here is not a MS witness to the Gospel of Luke at this point. Possibly the author of *Infancy Thomas* knew Luke's story from the oral retelling of it in his own Christian community. Possibly he had read Luke. Either way his own retelling is a fresh, independent, albeit secondary account.

3. Except for the episode of Jesus in the temple at the age of 12 in Lk 2:41–50, the NT writings leave a tantalizing gap in the life of Jesus between his birth and his baptism at the beginning of the public ministry. Inevitably, the developing literary tradition, taking its cue from the childhood story in Luke, created a series of incidents that tell of events in Jesus' boyhood. Their main theme is to show Jesus' precocious awareness of his supernatural origin and his power over life, death, and nature.

4. The belief in Jesus' divinity is clearly orthodox in Christian doctrine, but the often sensational manifestations of his supernatural abilities displayed in the numerous childhood stories in apocryphal gospels tend to distort that belief. Extracts below from the second–third-century *Infancy Gospel of Thomas* have the effect of portraying the child Jesus as an *enfant terrible*. Modern readers are struck less by the piety underlying the stories than by the destructiveness of many of Jesus' actions. Such a negative theme may be paralleled in the NT story of Jesus' blasting the fig-tree (Mk 11:12–14, 20–4), but the recurrence of this theme makes it the dominant feature of *Infancy Thomas*, and other apocryphal texts, such as the *Gospel of Pseudo-Matthew*.

5. Two of the stories in *Infancy Thomas* are:

After this he again went through the village, and a child ran and knocked against his shoulder. Jesus was angered and said to him, 'You shall not go further on your way', and immediately he fell down and died. But some, who saw what took place, said, 'From where was this child born, since his every word is an accomplished deed?' And the parents of the dead child came to Joseph and blamed him and said, 'Since you have such a child, you cannot dwell with us in the village; teach him to bless and not to curse. For he is killing our children.' (*Infancy Gospel of Thomas*, 4)

Now a certain teacher, Zacchaeus by name, who was standing in a certain place, heard Jesus saying these things to his father, and marvelled greatly that, being a child, he voiced such things. And after a few days he came near to Joseph and said to him, 'You have a clever child, and he has understanding. Come, hand him over to me that he may learn letters, and I will teach him with the letters all knowledge, and how to address all the older people and to honour them as forefathers and fathers, and to love those of his own age.' And he told him all the letters from Alpha to Omega distinctly, and with much questioning. But he looked at Zacchaeus the teacher and said to him. 'How do you, who do not know the Alpha according to its nature, teach others the Beta? Hypocrite, first if you know it, teach the Alpha, and then we shall believe you concerning the Beta.' Then he began to question the teacher about the first letter, and he was unable to answer him. And in the hearing of many the child said to Zacchaeus, 'Hear, teacher, the arrangement of the first letter, and pay heed to this, how it has lines and a middle stroke which goes through the pair of lines which you see, (how these lines) converge, rise, turn in the dance, three signs of the same kind, subject to and supporting one another, of equal proportions; here you have the lines of the Alpha.'   (ibid. 6)

6. The episode of the schoolteacher was a particularly popular theme that recurs in different places. It would seem that the childhood story in Luke, where the 12-year-old Jesus confounds the teachers of the Jewish law, was the inspiration behind the apocryphal versions. However, the mystical interpretation of the shape of the letters in the Greek alphabet is obscure in the account in *Infancy Thomas* and obviously does not derive from Luke's story. Clearly, for believers in earlier centuries, these stories struck a favourable chord and were not seen as alien to their Christological teachings.

7. The *Arabic Infancy Gospel* tells stories of the baby Jesus performing miracles during the Holy Family's exile in Egypt. The extract following contains the robbers who thirty years later are to be crucified alongside Jesus. These characters reappear, differently named, in other apocryphal texts.

And departing from this place, they came to a desert; and hearing that it was infested by robbers, Joseph and the Lady Mary decided to cross this region by night. But on their way, behold, they saw two robbers lying in wait on the road, and with them a great number of robbers, who were their associates, sleeping. Now those two robbers into whose hands they had fallen were Titus and Dumachus. Titus then said to Dumachus, 'I beseech you to let these persons go free, so that our comrades do not see them.' And as Dumachus refused, Titus said to him again, 'Take forty drachmas from me, and have them as a pledge.' At the same time he held out to him the belt which he had had about his waist, that he should not open his mouth or speak. And the Lady Mary seeing that the robber had done them a kindness, said to him, 'The Lord God will sustain you with his right hand, and will grant you remission of your sins.' And the Lord Jesus answered, and said to his mother, 'Thirty years hence, O my mother, the Jews will crucify me at Jerusalem, and these two robbers will be raised upon the cross along with me, Titus on my right hand and Dumachus on my left; and after that day Titus shall go before me into Paradise.' And she said, 'God keep this from you, my son.' And they went from there towards a city of idols, which, as they came near it was transformed into sand-hills.   (*Arabic Infancy Gospel*, 23)

M. Passion Gospels. 1. The account of Jesus' trial and crucifixion was obviously of central and paramount importance to Christians. Paul's theology is centred on the significance of

Jesus' death and crucifixion. A third of Mark's gospel is devoted to the last week in Jesus' life, and the preceding two-thirds, with its controversy stories and passion predictions, may be seen as a preparation for the events in Jerusalem. The other canonical gospels similarly devote much of their space to building on that Markan framework. So it is not surprising that the rewriting and reassessment of Jesus' death were maintained even beyond the first-century gospels.

2. The main accounts of Jesus' death in apocryphal texts occur in the *Gospel of Peter* and in the *Gospel of Nicodemus*. The *Gospel of Peter* is likely to have been composed in the second century. Although it was known in antiquity, this gospel seemed to disappear without trace. Unlike many of the other apocryphal texts which have been preserved, often in multiple copies, no MSS of *Peter* were known until recently, when, at the end of the nineteenth century a partial copy was discovered during an archaeological excavation in Egypt. Since then one or possibly two tiny fragments have also come to light. A reading of the main text shows that its passion narrative parallels very closely the story in the four canonical gospels, and it seems clear that the writer of *Peter* has drawn on these NT accounts for his version of Jesus' passion.

3. A motive for *Peter* may have been the desire to rewrite the four canonical accounts as one, although continuing curiosity about Pilate has resulted in a greater emphasis on Jesus' appearance before him than is the case with the canonical accounts. The *Diatessaron*, itself of second-century origin, is one such attempt to retell the separated stories about Jesus as one continuous composition, probably with the intention of replacing the four individual and differing versions. Much in *Peter* repeats material in the canonical stories and modern printed synopses often include parallels from *Peter* alongside the canonical passages.

4. There are, however, some significant differences from the NT to look for in the extracts below. One is the cry of Jesus from the cross ('My power, O power, you have forsaken me!'), which some commentators would interpret as an indication that *Peter* has been contaminated by unorthodox influences. A stronger heretical indication may be seen in the sentence, 'He held his peace as he felt no pain', which might imply that Jesus was incapable of suffering pain. If that is the correct translation, then it would indeed suggest possible Docetic influence. Nevertheless, our overall assessment of *Peter* is that the author was not self-consciously following unorthodox teaching, but that he was a typical unsophisticated and uncritical product of the second-century syncretism (fusing of different systems of religious belief) which characterized much of the Christian world. The Easter account describes the resurrection of Jesus in a dramatic and symbolic way. In contrast to the narratives in the canonical gospels, we now have an account of Jesus literally leaving his tomb.

And they brought two malefactors and crucified the Lord between them. But he held his peace as he felt no pain. And when they had set up the cross they wrote: 'This is the King of Israel.' And having laid down his garments before him they divided them among themselves and cast lots for them. But one of the malefactors rebuked them saying, 'We are suffering for the deeds which we have committed, but this man, who has become the saviour of men, what wrong has he done you?' And they were angry with him and commanded that his legs should not be broken, so that he might die in torment.

Now it was midday and darkness covered all Judaea. And they became anxious and distressed lest the sun had already set since he was still alive. It stands written for them: 'The sun should not set on one that has been murdered.' And one of them said, 'Give him to drink gall with vinegar.' And having mixed it they gave it to him to drink. And they fulfilled all things and accumulated their sins on their head. And many went about with lamps [and] as they supposed that it was night, they stumbled. And the Lord called out and cried, 'My power, O power, you have forsaken me!' And having said this, he was taken up. And at the same hour the veil of the temple in Jerusalem was torn in two.   (*Gos. Pet.* 4.10–5.20)

When those soldiers saw this, they awakened the centurion and the elders, for they also were there to mount guard. And while they were narrating what they had seen, they saw three men come out from the sepulchre, two of them supporting the other and a cross following them and the heads of the two reaching to heaven, but that of him who was being led reached beyond the heavens. And they heard a voice out of the heavens crying, 'Have you preached to those who sleep?', and from the cross there was heard the answer, 'Yes.'   (*Gos. Pet.* 10.38–42)

5. One particular post-biblical characteristic found in *Peter* is the dominant anti-Jewish sentiment. Here Jewish malevolence is the motive for the intention not to break Jesus' legs; and the blame for the death of Jesus is laid firmly at the door of the Jews.

6. The general consensus of scholarly opinion is that *Peter* is secondary to and later than the canonical passion accounts. Occasionally though, voices are heard giving the opinion that it is early, even first century, and is independent of the biblical gospels. In other words, that *Peter*'s passion story is a fifth account of the events; but, in general, such arguments have not found favour (cf. J.10).

7. As the complete text of *Peter* has not survived, we have no means of knowing if the original composition was a fully-fledged gospel like the canonical four, containing stories from Jesus' ministry prior to the arrest.

8. One extract from the other main passion gospel, the *Gospel of Nicodemus*, is included below. The first half of that gospel, which is probably fifth to sixth century, is known as the *Acts of Pilate* and tells of Jesus' trial, death, and resurrection. The book is concerned with Pilate's role in the sentencing of Jesus. This extract tells of Jesus' first meeting with Pilate. In it we note that Jesus' power is shown to exceed that of the Roman state. The superiority of Christianity over earthly rule is one of the most dominant and, understandably, the most important themes throughout the whole range of apocryphal literature: it is perhaps the single most significant unifying element of teaching in a body of literature that is otherwise amorphous, heterogeneous, and widespread geographically and chronologically.

Now, when Jesus entered, and the ensigns were holding the standards, the images on the standards bowed down and worshipped Jesus. And when the Jews saw the behaviour of the standards, how they bowed down and worshipped Jesus, they cried out loudly against the ensigns. But Pilate said to them, 'Do you not marvel how the images bowed and worshipped Jesus?' The Jews said to Pilate, 'We saw how the ensigns lowered them and worshipped him.' And the governor summoned the ensigns and asked them, 'Why did you do this?' They answered, 'We are Greeks and servers of temples: how could we worship him? We held the images; but they bowed down of their own accord and worshipped him.'   (*Gosp. Nic.* 1.5)

N. The Descent to the Underworld. 1. It is interesting to note that the apocryphal tradition did not seek to elaborate stories of Jesus' post-resurrection appearances. To a certain extent, one can see a development in the Easter stories in the NT from the comparatively simple account in Mark through the more detailed version in Matthew to the developed traditions in Luke and John. Comparable developments seem then to have ceased. Further elaboration is, surprisingly perhaps, not part of the apocryphal books. The apocryphal Acts do tell of several reappearances of Jesus, sometimes in different guises, to various characters, but these are not on a par with the biblical post-resurrection appearances, the main purpose of which is to convince the original followers that the crucified Jesus had left his tomb and been raised from the dead. What seem to replace stories of the risen Jesus in the NT apocryphal tradition are accounts in which the ascended Jesus communicates orally with believers: several apocryphal books containing discussions with the ascended Christ are recognized as a new genre, and are now sometimes classified as Dialogues of the Redeemer.

2. The Christian affirmation of belief in Jesus' descent to Hades is in the Apostles' Creed and in the Athanasian Creed. The biblical origin for this belief, which became a major and normative part of Christian tradition, seems to be based on a particular interpretation of 1 Pet 3:19 ('in the spirit he (Christ) went and preached to the imprisoned spirits', my tr.). That statement encouraged later generations of Christians to elaborate on what was meant by Jesus' appearance before imprisoned spirits. The apocryphal stories of Jesus' descent to the underworld reflect those elaborations. The main text describing these events is the fifth- to sixth-century *Descensus ad Inferos* (*Descent of Jesus to Hades*), found in several MSS as the second half of the *Gospel of Nicodemus*, the first half being the *Acts of Pilate*.

In this tradition Jesus' arrival in Hades after his crucifixion spells the end of death as a permanent state. Hades, by transference, is the domain of Hades, known elsewhere in mythology as Pluto. He rules over the world of departed spirits, a realm comparable to the Hebrew Sheol. The age-old cycle of death and decay inaugurated by Adam's sin is now said to have been reversed by Christ's inability to be bound by death. This orthodox belief strongly present in the NT gospels and in Paul's writings is in effect dramatized in the *Descensus*. Another orthodox belief portrayed in this apocryphon is that the faithful will be raised from death because Christ is the first fruits of those raised. This belief is graphically illustrated by Christ leading Adam and the faithful dead out of Hades and into Paradise. Among those appearing in this gospel is a favourite character in the apocryphal writings, the repentant thief crucified alongside Jesus: he is on his way to Paradise direct, just as Jesus had promised, when he encounters the newly raised procession. This scene with Christ releasing the faithful from Hades (often called the Harrowing of Hell) was a popular episode in the Middle Ages. The text begins with the two characters, Satan (that supreme embodiment of evil, the devil, the adversary of God) and Hades, aware of Jesus' imminent arrival in their midst. They are powerless to stop his descent. This extract tells of Jesus' arrival and his triumph over Satan; the faithful are then released.

While Hades was thus speaking with Satan, the King of Glory stretched out his right hand, and took hold of our forefather Adam and raised him up. Then he turned to the rest and said, 'Come with me, all you who have died through the tree which this man touched. For behold, I raise you all up again through the tree of the cross.' With that he sent them all out. And our forefather Adam was seen to be full of joy and said, 'I give thanks to your majesty, O Lord, because you have brought me up from the lowest Hades.' Likewise all the prophets and the saints said, 'We give you thanks, O Christ, Saviour of the world, because you have brought up our life from destruction.' When they had said this, the Saviour blessed Adam with the sign of the cross on his forehead. And he did this also to the patriarchs and prophets and martyrs and forefathers, and he took them and sprang up out of Hades. And as he went the holy fathers sang praises, following him and saying, 'Blessed be he who comes in the name of the Lord. Alleluia. To him be the glory of all the saints.' (8.24)

3. Another text, which partly parallels the *Descensus*, is the *Questions of Bartholomew*, dated perhaps as early as the second century. In that book Bartholomew confronts Jesus in the period before his ascension. Among many questions and answers is one concerning Jesus' whereabouts after his crucifixion (when he is said to have vanished from the cross). Jesus' reply is remarkably consistent with the story in the *Descensus*.

O. Pilate. 1. Several apocryphal texts relate the end of Pilate. For many early Christians the role and fate of Pilate were enigmatic. Was he a just but weak ruler swayed by the Jewish mob, or a wicked, doomed man, guilty of deicide? What begins in the canonical tradition as an ambivalent attitude towards Pilate becomes fixed: Pilate is a puppet in the hands of the Jewish mob. This way of resolving the Pilate problem by the NT authors did not, however, finally settle the issue. The later, apocryphal, tradition reflects a continuing dilemma in judging his character. Possibly the change in attitude, especially in Western European sources, may be explained by the fact that the earlier goodwill of the Roman authorities had turned to officially inspired persecution. The ambiguous ways of treating Pilate are at their most apparent only when the apocryphal legends reach the death of Pilate. When a document such as the *Acts of Pilate* is treating the events of Jesus' passion we can still see the influence of the canonical traditions: the picture of Pilate in these Acts is close to the NT's portrayal. The version in the *Acts of Pilate* is an elaboration of the gospels' trial narrative. We again see that the apologetic tendency of the account in the *Acts of Pilate* is to show how Pilate tried to free himself from all responsibility for the death of Jesus by blaming it on Herod and the Jews.

2. But as far as Pilate's later story is concerned, where a judgement on his career is expected, he is treated variously as a saint or as an outcast. In the eastern church, particularly in the Coptic and Ethiopic tradition, he was portrayed favourably. Those churches eventually canonized him. An apocryphal tale, usually known as the *Paradosis Pilati* (that is, the handing over of Pilate for chastising), shows how one eastern legend treated Pilate and his wife, named here as Procla: although Caesar has Pilate beheaded, Pilate's destiny is a triumph. The western church judged Pilate harshly: that tradition is represented by the extract below. It comes from the text called the *Mors Pilati* (the *Death of Pilate*). This text explains how Mount Pilatus on Lake Lucerne (Losania in the text) was so named. In that context another place name is explained: Vienne is said to be derived from the words Via Gehenna (Hell Road). That made it an appropriate, albeit temporary, resting place for the man who condemned Jesus to death.

When Caesar knew of the death of Pilate, he said, 'He has justly died a most disgraceful death, seeing that his own hand has not spared him.' He was therefore bound to a great block of stone, and sunk in the river Tiber. However, malignant and filthy spirits, rejoicing in his malignant and filthy body, kept moving in the waters, and in a terrible manner caused lightning and tempests, thunder and hail, so that everyone was in constant fear. Therefore the Romans pulled him out of the river Tiber and carried him off in derision to Vienne, and sunk him in the river Rhone. Vienne means the Way of Gehenna, because it became a place of cursing. But evil spirits were at work and did the same things there too, so the people, unwilling to endure a plague of demons, removed that vessel of malediction and sent him to be buried in the territory of Losania. The inhabitants there were also troubled by the same visitations, so they removed him and sunk him in a lake, surrounded by mountains, where to this day, according to the tales of some, sundry diabolical machinations occur.

P. Apocryphal Acts. 1. Just as the apocryphal gospels amplify events relating to Jesus' birth, childhood, and death, so the apocryphal Acts tell us about the founding fathers of the church. There are many apocryphal Acts that have survived, but the most important and influential are the oldest: the *Acts of Andrew*, the *Acts of John*, the *Acts of Paul*, the *Acts of Peter*, and the *Acts of Thomas*. These were written in the second century.

2. The inspiration for these Acts was the Acts of the Apostles. The five second-century apocryphal Acts themselves spawned further imitators and many derivative versions. Eventually this type of literature gave rise to Lives of the Saints and hagiographies. But as far as the second-century Acts and their immediate successors are concerned, the emphasis is on an individual apostle's miracles, prayers, and preaching.

3. Only the *Acts of Thomas* has survived intact. The other early Acts are very fragmentary, especially in their early chapters. The ecclesiastical authorities who denounced these second-century Acts, labelling them as 'apocryphal', none the less seemed to allow their concluding chapters to survive. It is in those chapters where in most cases an account of the eponymous hero's martyrdom is to be found. Such accounts were presumably exemplary and of hortatory value to the faithful, even though the stories preceding the martyrdom were rejected by the authorities as uninstructive, secondary, or even unorthodox. Later, expurgated or catholicized rewritings of the originals were encouraged. But sufficient of the earlier, original Acts can be reconstructed from surviving MSS and other sources.

4. Within the *Acts of John* are to be found some details relevant to our understanding of the figure of Christ in the second century. In particular, the belief that he was able to appear in differing guises, sometimes simultaneously to different people, had taken hold. This polymorphic picture of the risen Jesus may have developed from those Easter narratives in Luke's and John's gospels, in which Jesus is not readily identified (for example, Mary thinks Jesus is a gardener (Jn 20:15), the men going to Emmaus do not recognize their travelling companion as Jesus (Lk 24:37), the disciples think he is a ghost (Lk 24:16), see also Jn 21:4). Also in these Easter stories Jesus can come and go at will (Lk 24:31, 36), and can

even pass through closed doors (Jn 20:19, 26); he is spirited out of his binding cloths (Jn 20:7) and out of the sealed tomb (Mt 28:2–6).

5. But, as so often in the apocryphal tradition, those ideas are developed and, some would argue, distorted. For the writers of the apocryphal Acts it was even the *incarnate* Jesus who could adopt different guises (although, perhaps, it is the Transfiguration accounts in the NT—if these were originally referring to the Jesus of the ministry period—which gave the inspiration for the later apocryphal stories). One example from the *Acts of John* is when the hero relates his experience of the earthly Jesus:

For when he had chosen Peter and Andrew, who were brothers, he came to me and to my brother James, saying, 'I have need of you, come unto me.' And my brother said, 'John, this child on the shore who called to us, what does he want?' And I said, 'What child?' He replied, 'The one who is beckoning to us.' And I answered, 'Because of our long watch that we kept at sea you are not seeing straight, brother James: but do you not see the man who stands there, fair and comely and of a cheerful countenance?' But he said to me, 'Him I do not see, brother; but let us go and we shall see what it means.' And so when we had landed the ship, we saw him helping us to beach the ship.

And when we left the place, wishing to follow him again, he again appeared to me, bald-headed but with a thick and flowing beard; but to James he appeared as a youth whose beard was just starting. We were perplexed, both of us, as to the meaning of what we had seen. But when we followed him, we both became gradually more perplexed as we thought on the matter. Yet to me there appeared a still more wonderful sight; for I tried to see him as he was, and I never at any time saw his eyes closing but only open. And sometimes he appeared to me as a small man and unattractive, and then again as one reaching to heaven. Also there was in him another marvel; when I sat at table he would take me upon his breast and I held him; and sometimes his breast felt to me to be smooth and tender, and sometimes hard, like stone, so that I was perplexed in myself and said, 'What does this mean?'

Another glory I will tell you, brethren. Sometimes when I meant to touch him, I met a material and solid body; and at other times again when I felt him, the substance was immaterial and bodiless and as if it were not existing at all. (88–9, 93)

6. *Acts of John* relates the Transfiguration:

At another time he took me and James and Peter to the mountain, where he used to pray, and we beheld such a light on him that it is not possible for a man who uses mortal speech to describe what it was like. Again in a similar way he led us three up to the mountain saying, 'Come with me.' And we went again and saw him at a distance praying. Now I, because he loved me, went to him quietly as though he should not see, and stood looking upon his back. And I saw that he was not dressed in garments, but was seen by us as naked and not at all like a man; his feet were whiter than snow, so that the ground there was lit up by his feet, and his head reached to heaven; so that I was afraid and cried out, and he turned and appeared as a man of small stature, and took hold of my beard and pulled it and said to me, 'John, be not unbelieving, but believing, and not inquisitive.' And I said to him, 'What have I done, Lord?' And I tell you brethren, I suffered such pain forty days at the place where he took hold of my beard, that I said unto him, 'Lord, if your playful tug has given me so much pain, what if you had given me a beating?' And he said to me, 'Let it be your concern from henceforth not to tempt him who is not to be tempted' (90; cf. Mt 17:1–9 and par.)

7. In other apocryphal Acts the risen Jesus is variously experienced as a boy, as a youth, and as an old man in the

Acts of Peter, as a child in the *Acts of Andrew*, and as a youth in the *Acts of Paul*. These often strange descriptions none the less reveal an orthodox belief in the omnipresence of Jesus.

8. A related phenomenon are those stories within the apocryphal Acts which describe the apostle and Jesus as interchangeable. Thomas is Judas Thomas or Didymus, the twin of Christ, and is identified as Jesus in *Acts of Thomas* 11 and 39. Jesus and Andrew are interchangeable in *Acts of Andrew*, 28. This belief in the apostle as the *alter ego* of his master (again, quite orthodox in itself) is thus expressed in dramatic and literal form.

9. However, the majority of the stories in the apocryphal Acts are concerned with the deeds of the eponymous hero—these are the 'acts' themselves.

10. The contents have had their influence on Christian tradition. The description of Paul (from the *Acts of Paul and Thecla*, 3) is well known: 'And he saw Paul coming, a man small in size, bald-headed, bandy-legged, of noble mien, with eyebrows meeting, rather hook-nosed, full of grace. Sometimes he seemed like a man and sometimes had the face of an angel.' The description of Peter's inverse crucifixion and its significance relating to Adam's birth occurs in the *Acts of Peter*. The tradition that India was evangelized by Thomas is found in the *Acts of Thomas*. The *Quo Vadis?* scene in which Jesus sees the impending death of the apostle as a repetition of his own crucifixion comes from the *Acts of Peter*; and a comparable scene also occurs in the *Acts of Paul*. In these self-conscious feminist days the story of Thecla in the *Acts of Paul* has had a fresh lease of life: this story is about a virgin named Thecla who hears Paul preach and decides to follow his teaching. She abandons her fiancé and subsequently rejects the importuning of a wealthy Syrian, a spurning that results in her being thrown to wild animals. She escapes unharmed. Her vow of celibacy causes her mother to have her burned but the pyre is miraculously extinguished. She performs an auto-baptism and becomes a preacher in her own right. The trials of a character who is not an apostle are rare in this type of literature but the tale was a popular one and ensured Thecla's fame.

11. These stories obviously reveal that we are dealing with material significantly different from the canonical NT. The theological intensity and inspiration of the latter seem to have evaporated at the end of the first century. Much of the second-century literature analogous to the NT genres is conspicuously of a different character. It is not difficult, even with a casual dipping into the apocryphal Acts, to find a range of bizarre tales and strange miracles.

12. From the *Acts of Andrew* we read of Maximilla who forsakes her husband after she converts to Christianity and allows her servant, Euclia, to impersonate her in her husband's bed so as to preserve her self-imposed abstinence. From the *Acts of John* we read of a parricide who later castrates himself: he is rebuked by John for so doing but is then converted. In the same book we have an odd tale where John rebukes bedbugs who disturb his sleep. We also have the long story of Drusiana and Callimachus that contains a case of attempted necrophiliac rape, but which results in most (but, unusually in this sort of story, not all) of the participants being converted. From the *Acts of Paul* comes the baptism of a lion—and Paul's subsequent preservation when thrown to the self-

same lion. In the *Acts of Peter* we see the story of an adulteress who becomes paralysed when she tries to receive the eucharist. Also we find a story in which Peter revives a dead fish. In the *Acts of Thomas*, which is a pilgrim's progress of some 170 chapters, there is a long string of episodes including that of a man killed by a snake which identifies itself with the primeval serpent, and also the story of a speaking colt, which identifies itself as Balaam's ass and the ass that bore Mary and later Jesus. In the *Acts of Thomas* we are also granted a lurid description of the otherworld by a woman who is brought back to life. (This is a rare theme in the Acts but tours of heaven and, particularly, of hell are regularly found in the apocryphal apocalypses, for example the *Vision of Paul*. See R.2–4.)

13. Confronted by such stories as these, many may contemptuously move to literature on a higher spiritual plane. But it would be a mistake if those seeking a picture of second-century Christianity were to reject these apocrypha as if they contained mainly heretical, unorthodox, or Gnostic material. Those adjectives may accurately describe some details in the apocryphal Acts but not the highest percentage of their contents.

14. The apocryphal Acts have a historic value. Their most obvious use is that they give an unparalleled insight into the popular folk religion of their times. But even more important, they reveal aspects of early Christian preaching, teaching, and worship. Most of these Acts are orthodox and catholic and stem from those second- to third-century Christians who in writing these stories of the apostles projected their own faith. In our day we may well reject the stories as bizarre and turn away from their longwindedness, but behind their undoubted exaggeration and distortion lies a faith that shares much with the NT in general and the Acts of the Apostles in particular. The stories are merely vehicles for a faith that has many characteristics in common with biblical Christianity. Despite alleged links between the apocryphal Acts and Polybius, Dionysius of Halicarnassus, Tacitus, and Josephus, the main inspiration behind the apocryphal Acts was the canonical Acts.

15. The above sampling of some of the more sensational contents of the apocrypha could reinforce the commonly held view of this material. A more profitable reading of the texts looks for the motives behind these stories. And there are often positive theological points to be seen.

16. A brief survey of the canonical Acts will allow comparisons to be made. In Acts the church, somewhat idealized (2:43–7; 4:32–4), successfully spreads its message in increasingly concentric circles, beginning in Jerusalem, through the efforts of apostles (6:7; 9:31; 12:24; 16:5; 19:20). These men are up against a corrupt world that has destroyed Jesus but through divine protection, the Holy Spirit, and their own self-sacrifice and abstinence they overcome conflicts with the world's authorities. They are arrested on several occasions (4:3; 5:18–19 with a miraculous release from goal; 12:4 with its mention of four squads of soldiers needed for the arrest and v. 7 with another miraculous release; 24:23). Stylistic speeches are placed on the lips of the various apostles, principally Peter and Paul, and these serve to justify the rationale of the Christian hope against Jewish expectations or pagan beliefs, to stress the invincibility of their message, and to defend

their actions as apostles. Sacraments, baptism, the laying-on of hands, and the eucharist are described. Prayers are reported. Various healings, raisings from the dead, and other miracles are described. The apostles even display a mastery over natural powers—Paul's impending shipwreck is averted through his command of the situation. Numerous conversions occur including the eunuch and the proconsul of Paphos. Paul's own conversion is described three times. All these events take place within a restless travelogue: new scenes, new characters, new conflicts come and go in a profusion of anecdotes and episodes. Christ appears in various forms (18:9–10; 23:11). Wicked rulers (including Herod, 12:1–6, 19) and Jewish persecutors (13:45; 14:5, 19; 17:5; 20:3; 21:27; 23:12) are recurrent opponents. Many of these themes are the stock-in-trade of the apocryphal Acts too, which is not surprising if the canonical Acts was the inspiration behind them.

17. Despite the obvious differences between the canonical and apocryphal Acts, what is worth noting (once an initial repugnance to the apocryphal stories has been overcome) are the many similarities. It is appropriate to look at some of these in greater depth. First and foremost in all the Acts the triumph of God, of Jesus, and of his followers over evil and temporal powers is a common denominator. Secondly, each apostle is a peripatetic teacher. As such they emulate the Twelve and the Seventy (Seventy-two) sent out by Jesus. The Christian message with its universalism requires itinerant preachers. Several of the apocryphal Acts include a scene in which the individual apostles are allocated by lot their portion of the world for evangelization. Thus Thomas in the *Acts of Thomas* is sent to India. But the apostles are more than evangelists. During his ministry Jesus, according to Lk 10:19 and elsewhere, prepares his disciples to follow his example. After Pentecost these followers are empowered by the Spirit to be imitators of Jesus not only as travelling preachers but as healers and miracle-workers. The parallel between the life, miracles, and death of Jesus and that of the apostles is carefully drawn in the canonical Acts and that parallelism is also clear in the later traditions.

18. The apostles' deaths, usually martyrdoms, may be compared to that of Jesus: Peter and Andrew are crucified. Paul is decapitated and milk spurts from his severed neck onto his slaughterer. Thomas is slain by four soldiers. In the Acts of the Apostles, Stephen's and James's deaths are included, and Paul's, although not described, is none the less anticipated (20:24; 21:13; 28:30). Those responsible for these deaths may vary. In canonical Acts the protagonists are frequently Jews. In the apocryphal tradition the Christian (personified by the eponymous hero) is persecuted by Romans, Nero in the case of Paul in the *Acts of Paul*. This change is understandable in documents written a century or more after canonical Acts. The question of Israel's relationship to Jesus and his church became increasingly irrelevant to later Christian generations whose preoccupations were with Gentile authorities. None the less the important common link is that the apostles, as imitators of Christ, have to be arraigned before governors and kings, as Jesus himself was and as he predicted for his followers (Mk 13:9–13 and par.). This prediction can be dismissed as a prophecy after the event (or the trials of Jesus and the apostles in the NT seen as mere dramatic reconstructions invented by the church that in its own day was experiencing

such ordeals when it spread into the pagan world) but those ordeals were real enough, and it is the belief that the trials were to be endured because Jesus himself had suffered which provides the motive behind these stories of persecution, arrest, trial, and death in all types of early Christian literature. In addition—particularly in the apocrypha—the various trial scenes serve as convenient contexts for the authors to have their hero preach a sermon before large, and generally sympathetic, crowds. A courtroom scene is a useful device for allowing the apostle to deliver a major *apologia pro vita sua*. It is important to read these defences as they are likely to represent the rationale of those Christians who identify with the apostle in order to withstand their own tribulations. They are moral stories encouraging fearless faith. And that is as true in the apocrypha as in the NT.

19. The apostles in the apocryphal Acts are imitators of Jesus even after death. Just as Jesus fails to be bound by death, so too the apostles' deaths are in fact triumphs: Thomas reappears after death; the dust from his empty tomb is used to effect the conversion of his killer, King Misdaeus. Nero sees a vision (presumably of Peter) after Peter's death and he subsequently ceases persecuting Christians. In the *Acts of Paul* Nero hears of Paul's reappearance; Longus, a proconsul, and Cestus, a centurion, see Titus and Luke praying with Paul after the latter's death.

20. Among the speeches the farewell address of the apostle, from Stephen onwards, is another valuable vehicle in which the author can give a defence of Christianity. Jesus' three-chapter farewell discourse in the fourth gospel doubtless provided a precedent for the long farewell in, among other places, the *Acts of Andrew*, where, like a grand-opera singer expiring after a lengthy death bed aria, Andrew gives a final sermon that lasts over three days.

21. It is worth noting that in the *Acts of Andrew* and the *Acts of Peter* the hero apostrophizes the cross on which he is to die. These are presented as private meditations. The speech in the *Acts of John* occurs in the MS that provides chs. 87–105; it is highly mystical and has probably been influenced by Gnostic ideas. For documents that took root in the somewhat syncretistic environment of the second century we should not be surprised to find in several of the apocryphal Acts the influence of Gnosticism. The Gnostic and heretical tinges were primarily responsible for the judgement that the documents as a whole were secondary, heretical, spurious—in other words 'apocryphal' in the conventional understanding of that word. Jerome rejected the orthodoxy of the *Acts of Paul*, Eusebius in his *History* denounced the *Acts of Andrew*, the *Acts of John*, the *Acts of Paul*, and the *Acts of Peter* as heretical, Epiphanius claimed that the Encratites used the *Acts of Andrew*, of *John*, and of *Thomas*. The Gelasian Decree (early 6th cent.) lists the *Acts of Andrew, Peter, Paul*, and *Thomas* as 'apocryphal', Augustine and Filaster of Brescia say that the Manicheans and Priscillianists used *Andrew, Thomas*, and *Peter*. The Manicheans substituted the five great apocryphal Acts for the canonical Acts. All of this succeeded in condemning these and allied apocryphal Acts. It was not so much that their contents were at fault, it was that they had been contaminated by having been associated with groups deemed heretical by the orthodox. But, as we have tried to show, the *animus* behind the composition, their speeches, theology, and

miracles are not as unorthodox as one thinks. Even a passage such as the *Acts Pet.* 29 in which we read that Peter was venerated like a god and that the sick were laid at his feet for him to heal them is no more exaggerated or superstitious than Acts 5:12–16 where Peter's shadow is sufficient to cause miraculous healings, or 19:11–12, where it is said that handkerchiefs and scarves were touched by Paul to effect cures. As for the godlike nature of the apostle, again the canonical Acts sets a precedent in 14:13–18 when sacrifices were about to be made to Paul and Barnabas, or 28:6 where Paul is taken to be a god by the Maltese.

22. Another common denominator is that of sea journeys. They form a necessary part of many travel narratives, but they often have a supernatural side to them. Possibly this form of transport was particularly prone to disaster, and the traveller by sea was dependent on divine protection. Certainly Paul's journey to Italy in Acts 27–8 was beset with disasters. His labours were seen as a test of his faith. Similarly in the second-century Acts not only is such a theme repeated but the boat itself almost seems to symbolize the church. In the *Acts of Peter* the steersman is named, significantly, Theon: *en route* Peter and Theon are granted a Christophany. In the *Acts of Paul* Paul's journey by boat (a story independent of that in Acts) is captained by a believer, and, again a Christophany occurs; the apostle is strengthened in his faith. The *Acts of Andrew and Matthias,* considered by some to have prefaced the *Acts of Andrew,* has a similar episode in which Jesus is portrayed as the master-helmsman.

23. Among other links between the two categories of Acts is that the sacraments of baptism and eucharist are well represented. The apocryphal Acts include a new sacrament, that of sealing. There are several occurrences of this rite: usually it seems to be a way of symbolically branding ownership, especially on new converts. In both the canonical and the apocryphal Acts Christianity is seen to triumph over paganism, represented by sorcerers. The episode of the silversmiths at Ephesus in Acts 19:23–41 serves that purpose, as does the strange tale of the sons of Sceva in Acts 19:13–20. Both Philip and Paul overcome sorcerers (Acts 8:9–13; 13:6–12). In the apocrypha we may point to the story of the destruction of the temple of Artemis and the conversion of its priests in *Acts Jn* 32–45. The story of the destruction of the statue of Caesar and its subsequent restoration in *Acts Pet.* 11 serves the same purpose of showing symbolically the Christian's control or supremacy over pagan rulers. Peter's contact with Simon Magus inspired the lengthy contests between the two in *Acts of Peter*: the 15 verses of the account in Acts are now inflated to several chapters in which not only do Peter and Simon deliver lengthy speeches but so also do a dog and an infant! The trial of strength obviously goes in Peter's favour as he is the personification of Good against Evil. Nothing could be more orthodox than this, and the apocryphal tales are in the same mould as medieval mystery plays. The underlying faith of these apocryphal tales may be recognized as undeniably Christian even when their modes of expression are harnessed to storytelling conventions that are, to modern sophisticated minds, inappropriate, ludicrous, or counterproductive.

24. A fair judgement that can legitimately be made about the apocryphal Acts is that they exaggerate or overemphasize, and thereby distort, an element that is often present in the canonical writings. The roundness and multifaceted nature of the canonical writings, especially the epistles and the gospels with their paradoxes concerning the person and message of Christ, are diluted in the second-century Acts.

25. Nevertheless, however anodyne, prolix, and repetitive much of the teaching in the apocryphal Acts may be, the speeches are worthy of attention. It is rewarding to read the prayers, such as that found in *Acts Thom.* 50 during the eucharist, for example, to gain an insight into the preoccupations and practice of the second-century church:

Come, perfect compassion; Come, fellowship with the male; Come, you who know the mysteries of the Chosen One; Come, you who have partaken in all the combats of the noble combatant; Come, rest, that reveals the great deeds of the whole greatness; Come, you who disclose secrets and make manifest the mysteries; Come, holy dove, Who bears the twin young; Come, secret mother; Come, you who are manifest in your deeds; Come, giver of joy and of rest to those who are united to you; Come and commune with us in this eucharist, which we celebrate in your name, And in the agape, in which we are united at your calling.

26. Few would find fault with the message in *Acts Pet.* 26:

While the young men were saying this, the prefect in the forum looked at Peter and said, 'What do you say, Peter? Behold, the lad is dead; the emperor liked him, and I spared him not. I had indeed many other young men; but I trusted in you and in your Lord whom you proclaim, if indeed you are sure and truthful: therefore I allowed him to die.' And Peter said, 'God is neither tempted nor weighed in the balance. But he is to be worshipped with the whole heart by those whom he loves and he will hear those who are worthy. Since, however, my God and Lord Jesus Christ is now tempted among you, he is doing many signs and miracles through me to turn you from your sins. In your power, revive now through my voice, O Lord, in the presence of all, him whom Simon killed by his touch.' And Peter said to the master of the lad, 'Come, take hold of him by the right hand and you shall have him alive and walking with you.' And the prefect Agrippa ran and came to the lad, took his hand, and restored him to life. And when the multitude saw this they cried, 'There is only one God, the God of Peter.'

27. Nor would orthodox believers quibble with the teaching on the incarnation in *Acts Thom.* 79–80; 143, in which the corporeal reality of Christ's earthly body shows that this apocryphon is not Gnostic or Docetist in its proclivities. *Acts of Thomas*'s teaching on redemption through suffering in ch. 72 is also standard:

Having said this, they alighted from the wagon. And the apostle began to say, 'Jesus Christ, whose knowledge is despised in this country; Jesus Christ, of whom nothing has been heard in this country; Jesus, [you] who receive all apostles in every country and every city, and by whom all worthy of you are glorified; Jesus, [you] who have taken a form and become like a man and appeared to all of us in order not to separate us from your love; Lord, you are he who has given himself for us and has bought us with a price by his blood, as a precious possession. But what have we, Lord, to offer in exchange for your life which you have given for us? For what we have is your gift. We entreat you and thereby have life.'   (ch. 72)

28. We can see that in the circles that produced and used this literature wealth was abhorrent. (Peter, for instance, has several tirades against the earthly values of Eubula in ch. 17 and against Chryse in 30–1; John rails against beauty and possessions in *Acts Jn.* 43.) The theme of celibacy is a recurring one. See, for instance, *Acts Jn.* 113, where John recalls

he was glad he was prevented from marriage and prays to God:

You who have preserved me also till the present hour pure to yourself, and free from intercourse with a woman; who, when I inclined in my youth to marry, appeared to me and said, 'I am in need of you, John'; who prepared for me beforehand my bodily weakness; who, on the third occasion when I wished to marry, prevented me immediately, and said to me at the third hour on the sea, 'John, if you were not mine, I would let you marry'; who for two years blinded me, letting me mourn and be dependent on you; who in the third year opened up the spiritual eyes, and gave me back my visible eyes; who, when I regained my sight, disclosed to me the repugnance of gazing upon a woman; who delivered me from temporary show, and guided me to eternal life; who separated me from the foul madness of the flesh; who snatched me from bitter death, and presented me only to you; who silenced the secret disease of the soul, and cut off its open deed; who afflicted and banished him who rebelled in me; who established a spotless friendship to you; who prepared a safe way to you; who gave me undoubting faith in you; who have traced out for me pure thoughts towards you; who have given the due reward to every deed; who have set it in my soul to have no other possession than you alone—for what can be more precious than you? Now, since I have accomplished your steward-ship with which I was entrusted, make me worthy, O Lord, of your repose, and give me my end in you, which is the unspeakable and ineffable salvation.

29. In the *Acts of Thomas* the apostle urges celibacy on a bridal couple and both accept. In the *Acts of Peter* Xanthippe leaves her husband: as he is a friend of the emperor, Peter's death is consequently arranged. A similar situation occurs when leading women in the *Acts of Thomas* accept celibacy in marriage. There may even be a touch of humour in the way the hapless pagan husbands persistently importune and en-treat their determined wives who subject them to the treat-ment meted out by Lysistrata (see *Acts Andr.* 14; 37).

30. A comparable theme is that the apostles are consistently described as ascetics: they practise a rigorous self denial, their abstinence and otherworldliness are exemplary. The reputa-tion of Thomas (*Acts Thom.* 20) is typical: continually he fasts and prays, and eats only bread with salt. His drink is water, and he wears only one garment whatever the weather. He takes nothing from anyone, and what he has he gives to others. One can understand why Encratite groups found these Acts congenial, but the teaching in itself is compatible with and closely paralleled in NT teaching, even though unworldli-ness and chastity as Christian virtues are pushed to the ex-tremes, as for example in the uncompromisingly negative teaching about marriage and procreation in *Acts Thom.* 12:

Remember my children, what my brother said to you, and to whom he commended you; and know that if you refrain from this filthy intercourse you become temples holy and pure, being released from afflictions and troubles, known and unknown, and you will not be involved in the cares of life and of children, whose end is destruction. But if you get many children, for their sakes you become grasping and avaricious, plundering orphans and deceiving widows, and by doing this you subject yourselves to most grievous punishments. For most children become unprofitable, being possessed by demons, some openly and some secretly. For they become either lunatics or half withered or crippled or deaf or dumb or paralytics or idiots. And even though they be healthy, they will be again good-for-nothing, doing unprofitable and abominable works. For they will be detected either in adultery or in murder or in theft or

in unchastity, and by all these you will be afflicted. But if you obey and preserve your souls pure to God, there will be born to you living children, untouched by these hurtful things, and you will be without care, spending an untroubled life, free from grief and care, looking forward to receive that incorruptible and true marriage, and you will enter as groomsmen into that bridal chamber full of immortality and light.

But such teaching did not originate in the apocrypha. The Christian tradition since the beginning elevated poverty, obedience, and chastity as ideals, and the NT itself extols the unique value of fellowship with God as the only basis for true family relationship (in, for instance, Mk 3:33–5; Lk 14:26).

31. Two particular passages within the apocryphal Acts are worthy of our attention, not only because of their distinctive-ness from much of their contexts but also because of the beauty and poignancy of their poetry. These are the Hymn of Christ in *Acts Jn* 94–5, a poem since set to music by Gustav Holst, and the Hymn of the Soul or Hymn of the Pearl in the *Acts of Thomas*. Both poems are likely to have been insertions into their respective narratives; they may have had an inde-pendent existence previously. The former concerns Christ and the disciples who exchange versicles and responses within the context of a dance. The latter is a charming oriental tale of a youth who sets out to recover a pearl of great price, and when he ultimately succeeds in his mission he is rewarded with a heavenly garment. The allegory may be one of the incarna-tion, or (to those who see Gnostic ideas at work) the soul in search of its heavenly origins. Both these hymns merit careful reading. The Hymn of Christ is narrated by John:

He then began to sing a hymn, and to say: 'Glory be to you, Father!' And we circling him said, 'Amen.' 'Glory be to you, Word! Glory be to you, Grace!' 'Amen.' 'Glory be to you, Spirit! Glory be to you, Holy One! Glory be to the glory!' 'Amen.' 'We praise you, O Father. We give thanks to you, light, in whom darkness does not abide.' 'Amen.' 'Now we give thanks, I say: I will be saved, and I will save.' 'Amen.' 'I will be loosed, and I will loose.' 'Amen.' 'I will be pierced, and I will pierce.' 'Amen.' 'I will be born, and I will bear.' 'Amen.' 'I will eat, and I will be eaten.' 'Amen.' 'I will hear, and I will be heard.' 'Amen.' 'I will be understood, being wholly understanding.' 'Amen.' 'I will be washed, and I will wash.' 'Amen.'
    Grace is dancing. 'I will pipe, dance all of you!' 'Amen.' 'I will mourn, lament all of you!' 'Amen.' 'An Ogdoad is singing with us.' 'Amen.' 'The Twelfth number is dancing above.' 'Amen.' 'The whole universe takes part in the dancing.' 'Amen.' 'He who does not dance, does not know what is being done.' 'Amen.' 'I will flee and I will stay.' 'Amen.' 'I will adorn, and I will be adorned.' 'Amen.' 'I will be united, and I will unite.' 'Amen.' 'I have no house, and I have houses.' ' 'I have no place, and I have places.' 'Amen.' 'I have no temple, and I have temples.' 'Amen.' 'I am a lamp to you who see me.' 'Amen.' 'I am a mirror to you who perceive.' 'Amen.' 'I am a door to you who knock on me.' 'Amen.' 'I am a way to you, wayfarer.' 'Amen.'

32. The theology and the character of the canonical Acts may itself have been responsible for any change of direction from the character of the gospels and epistles. Once the trad-itional sources and rich material of Luke's gospel gave way to the picaresque contents of his second volume we leave the world of Hellenistic Judaism and embark on material that shows the influence of secular romances and pagan historiog-raphy. This influence permeates the second-century Acts. The characteristically Pauline theology of his letters is conspicuous by its absence not only in the apocryphal *Acts of Paul* and the *Acts of Peter* but in the canonical Acts as well. The theological teaching of Acts may be said to be less significant than that in the NT gospels or epistles, even though its principal aim of showing the growth of Christianity as a universal religion is admirably achieved. The real hero of Acts is the gospel which spreads through the Spirit's guidance from the centre of the old dispensation, Jerusalem, to Rome, the capital of the empire, within thirty years of Jesus' death. (Peter, even Paul, are not elevated to centre stage: Peter merely goes off elsewhere in Acts 12:17; Paul's death is left unrecorded.) As it stands, Acts may legitimately qualify as the first history book of the church. Its success set the ball rolling, and the popular religious fervour of the next century carried on in that tradition by retailing comparable stories about the spread of Christianity, but now with one apostle as gospel-bearer completely in the spotlight.

33. It is instructive to return to the canonical Acts after having had a diet of reading the apocrypha. One finds that it is the similarities rather than the differences between the two that are striking. Because the second-century Acts are derivative and owe their inspiration to the Acts of the Apostles this is perhaps not so unexpected. The miraculous disappearance of Philip (8:39), the supernatural deaths of Ananias and Sapphira, the lengthy story about the conversion of Cornelius, Saul's blindness, Elymas's blindness, Peter's vision of food, and the stirring sea yarns would all sit comfortably in one of the apocryphal Acts. Modern Christians are accustomed to accept—or rationalize—these stories without ridicule just as they are prepared to accept the miracles of Jesus—especially nature miracles like his walking on the water, or the blasting of the fig-tree—or the story of the transfiguration in the gospels. The apocryphal writings do not have the monopoly of incredible legends.

34. However, the apocryphal Acts seldom match the drive or spirituality of the canonical Acts and instead are almost entirely moralistic with accounts of their eponymous hero's exploits. The entertainment value of the tales was obviously paramount in the apocryphal tradition, but these Acts are witnesses to the religious ideas of a great part of Christendom—even if such teaching did not match the intellectual debates and theological ideals of the patristic writers and ecclesiastical hierarchy when they attempted to proclaim or standardize Christian doctrine and literature. These Acts were the popular reading-matter of Christians in many parts of the Mediterranean, Syria, North Africa, and Asia over several centuries at precisely the same time as the great patristic thinkers were formulating creeds, doctrines, and canons of belief and practice. The apocrypha show us that early Christianity was not preoccupied only with high theological debate, with niceties of definition, or with ethics and philosophy. The apocryphal Acts may be crudely sensational, may promote an unthinking superstition at worst, a simple faith at best, but their creation, enduring existence, and undoubted popularity show us that Christianity was vibrant, popular, and above all successful throughout the dark ages of the second century and beyond.

Q. Apocryphal Letters. 1. Given Paul's reputation as a letter-writer, it is not surprising that several apocryphal letters claim to be from his pen. A letter from the Corinthian church to Paul and his reply, known as 3 Corinthians, are found in the *Acts of Paul*. A portion of that reply reads:

Paul, the prisoner of Jesus Christ, to the brethren at Corinth, greeting! Being in many afflictions, I marvel not that the teachings of the evil one had such rapid success. For my Lord Jesus Christ will quickly come, since he is rejected by those who falsify his teaching. For I delivered to you first of all what I received from the apostles before me who were always with Jesus Christ, that our Lord Jesus Christ was born of Mary of the seed of David, the Father having sent the spirit from heaven into her that he might come into this world and save all flesh by his own flesh and that he might raise us in the flesh from the dead as he has presented himself to us as our example. And since man is created by his Father, for this reason was he sought by him when he was lost, to become alive by adoption. For the almighty God, maker of heaven and earth, sent the prophets first to the Jews to deliver them from their sins, for he wished to save the house of Israel; therefore he took from the spirit of Christ and poured it out upon the prophets who proclaimed the true worship of God for a long period of time. For the wicked prince who wished to be God himself laid his hands on them and killed them and bound all flesh of man to his pleasure. But the almighty God, being just, and not wishing to repudiate his creation had mercy and sent his Spirit into Mary the Galilean, that the evil one might be conquered by the same flesh by which he held sway, and be convinced that he is not God. For by his own body Jesus Christ saved all flesh, presenting in his own body a temple of righteousness through which we are saved.

2. The most famous of the other invented letters, allegedly written by Paul, is the *Epistle to the Laodiceans*. As is usual in the traditions of this apocryphal literature, the original impetus to concoct a writing was because of a perceived gap in the NT. Col 4:16 refers to a letter Paul wrote to the church in Laodicea. That letter did not survive. The apocryphal letter was created, perhaps as early as the second century, out of phrases found in the authentic Pauline corpus, particularly Philippians and Galatians, in order to compose an epistle intended to be accepted as that referred to in Colossians. That it succeeded in its purpose is shown by its appearance in several Latin MSS of the NT, including the famous codices Fuldensis, Cavensis, and Ardmachanus. It even appears as an appendix at the conclusion of modern printed editions of the Latin Vulgate, such as the Stuttgart edition, *Biblia Sacra* ([4]1994). A portion (vv. 6–16) reads:

And now my bonds are manifest, which I suffer in Christ, on account of which I am glad and rejoice. This to me leads to eternal salvation, which itself is brought about through your prayers and by the help of the Holy Spirit, whether it be through life or through death. For my life is in Christ and to die is joy. And his mercy will work in you, that you may have the same love and be of one mind. Therefore, beloved, as you have heard in my presence, so hold fast and work in the fear of God, and eternal life will be yours. For it is God who works in you. And do without hesitation what you do. And for the rest, beloved, rejoice in Christ and beware of those who are out for sordid gain. May all your requests be manifest before God, and be steadfast in the mind of Christ. And do what is pure, true, proper, just and lovely. And what you have heard and received, hold in your heart, and peace will be with you.

3. Other apocryphal epistles include a set of fourteen letters, most of which are likely to have been composed in the fourth century, purporting to be correspondence between Paul and Seneca.

4. There is even a letter allegedly from Christ to Abgar. This occurs in a version of a legend related by Eusebius. Abgar, who was king of Edessa from 4 BCE to 7 CE and again from 13–50 CE, sent a letter to Jesus asking him to come to Edessa to heal his malady. Jesus did not accede to the request, but sent a letter instead. This is that letter:

You are blessed; you believe in me, and you have not seen me. It is written concerning me, 'Those who have seen me will not believe in me', and 'Those who have not seen me will believe and will be saved.' Regarding what you wrote to me that I should come to you, I have to complete here everything I was sent to do and, after I have accomplished it, to be taken up to him who sent me. After I have been taken up I will send to you one of my disciples to heal your suffering and to provide life for you and those with you.

After Jesus' death Thomas sent Thaddeus (or Addai in the Syriac) to visit the king. Thaddeus healed the king and Edessa was converted to Christianity. According to the fourth-century treatise, the *Pilgrimage of Etheria*, a letter of Christ's, possibly this one, was preserved and copied, and miraculous powers were attached to it.

5. Other texts have conventionally been classified as letters. The *Epistula Apostolorum*, for example, is, however, not really epistolary in form or content: it starts as a letter but soon turns into an apocalypse. (Perhaps the book of Revelation provides a loose parallel.) Similarly, the *Epistle of Pseudo-Titus* was never an example of real, personal correspondence. It is a homily on the theme of celibacy. That letter is used to assist in the recovery of some missing portions of the apocryphal *Acts of John*, of *Peter*, and of *Andrew*.

6. The Gnostic library found at Nag Hammadi used letters as a form of communication. The *Letter* (or *Apocryphon*) of *James*, like the *Epistula Apostolorum*, is another example of an apocalyptic book, and is a dialogue of the risen Saviour with those on earth.

R. Apocryphal Apocalypses. 1. Christian writers, biblical and post-biblical, concerned themselves, just as their Jewish predecessors had done, with apocalyptic themes and teaching. The word 'apocalypse' means a revelation of things normally hidden. In general, apocalypses speak of the signs and portents presaging the end of this world, and of the nature of the other world. In the apocryphal literature we may separate these two features. There are those passages which describe what heaven and hell hold in store for the faithful and the unbeliever. The language of these apocalypses is dualistic and speaks of two opposing realms: hell, the abode only of the sinner, and heaven, the home of the believer. Post-biblical writers used this genre of literature with its tours of the other world with great imagination. It could well be that biblical texts such as Rev 21:1–8 provided the starting-point for the richly developed imaginative constructions we find in the apocryphal books. The writings may have been relegated as 'spurious' or 'secondary', in other words as 'apocryphal' in the common understanding of that term, but they were obviously regularly read by Christians even after their use was condemned by the ecclesiastical authorities.

2. Curiosity about the character of heaven and hell fascinated Christian writers from the earliest times. Two of the most influential texts were the *Apocalypse of Peter*, dating probably from the mid-second century, and the *Apocalypse of Paul*, probably written in the fourth century. Once again, one finds the names Peter and Paul in use as the supposed authors of apocryphal works. That an apocalypse was written in Paul's name is not surprising given the statement by Paul in 2 Cor 12 that he had been 'caught up as far as the third heaven'. In the authentic Pauline literature this baffling statement is not explained. It was an obvious gap that was left to the imagination of a later writer to fill. The *Apocalypse of Paul* tells what happened to Paul on his otherworldly visits. This apocalypse proved to be the most popular of the western church's apocryphal apocalypses, and it led to the generally held beliefs about heaven and hell that fuelled the medieval imagination. Much of the art and sculpture in the Middle Ages depicting the afterlife was inspired by this work. Dante's *Inferno* was also influenced by the *Apocalypse of Paul* and even quotes it.

3. The extracts below are taken from the Coptic *Apoc. Pet.* 26, 27, 31. If a modern reader feels that some of the imagery is commonplace, this familiarity is due to the pervading influence apocalyptic texts such as this one have had on subsequent literature.

And near that place I saw another gorge wherein the discharge and excrement of those who were in torment ran down, and became like a lake there. And women sat there up to their necks in that filth, and over against them many children born out of due time sat crying; and from them went forth rays of fire and smote the women in the eyes; and these were those who conceived out of wedlock and caused abortion.

And other men and women were being burned up to their middle and were cast down in a dark place and were scourged by evil spirits, having their entrails devoured by worms that never rested. And these were the ones who had persecuted the righteous and delivered them up.

And in another great lake full of foul pus and blood and boiling mire stood men and women up to their knees. And these were the ones who lent money and demanded usury upon usury.

4. Two extracts now follow from the *Vision* (or *Apocalypse*) of *Paul*. The first of these, from ch. 20, describes Paul's arrival in Paradise; the second, taken from ch. 31, comes from the much fuller descriptions of his visit to hell—there he encounters many sufferers.

And when I had entered within the gate of Paradise, there came out to meet me an old man whose countenance shone as the sun; and when he had embraced me he said, 'Hail, Paul, beloved of God.' And he kissed me with a cheerful countenance. He wept, and I said to him, 'Brother, why do you weep?' And again sighing and lamenting he said, 'We are hurt by men, and they grieve us greatly; for many are the good things which the Lord has prepared, and great is his promise, but many do not perceive them.' And I asked the angel and said, 'Sir, who is this?' And he said to me, 'This is Enoch, the scribe of righteousness.' And I entered into that place, and immediately I saw Elijah, and he came and greeted me, laughing and rejoicing. And when he had seen me, he turned away and wept, and said to me, 'Paul, would that you should receive the rewards of your labours which you have done for the human race. As for me, I have seen great and many good things which God has prepared for the just, and the promises of God are great, but many do not perceive them; but even after many labours scarcely one or two enter into these places.'

And I saw there a river boiling with fire, and in it a multitude of men and women immersed up to the knees, and other men up to the navel, others even up to the lips, others up to the hair. And I asked the angel and said, 'Sir, who are those in the fiery river?' And the angel answered and said to me, 'They are neither hot nor cold, because they were found neither in the number of the just nor in the number of the godless. For those spent the time of their life on earth passing some days in prayer, but others in sins and fornications, until their death.' And I asked him and said, 'Who are these, sir, immersed up to their knees in fire?' He answered and said to me, 'These are they who when they have gone out of church occupy themselves with idle disputes. Those who are immersed up to the navel are those who, when they have taken the body and blood of Christ, go and fornicate and do not cease from their sins till they die. Those who are immersed up to the lips are those who slander each other when they assemble in the church of God; those up to the eyebrows are those who nod to each other and plot spite against their neighbour.'

5. Whereas the apocalypses of Peter and of Paul are concerned with the current state of affairs in heaven and hell, the *Apocalypse of Thomas* contains predictions about the ending of the present world. It is thus 'apocalyptic' in its sense of foretelling the future. From the NT onwards Christians were made aware that they were already living in the end time. For them Christ was believed to have inaugurated the last age. Christians were not sure how imminent that final day, increasingly thought of as the day of judgement, would be; many hazarded a guess. Nor did the Christians know what warnings would announce or precede the coming of the End. Again, attempts were made to list which events were to be disregarded and which were portentous. Apocalyptic passages in the NT gospels and of course the book of Revelation are concerned with these warnings and the signs of the times. Such speculation has never ceased. The writer of the *Apocalypse of Thomas*, dating perhaps from the fifth century, gave a countdown, and describes the events of the final six days before the end of the world. One part of this text is given here: it concerns the events on the fourth day before the End.

And on the fourth day, at the first hour, from the land of the east the abyss shall melt and roar. Then shall all the earth be shaken by the might of an earthquake. In that day shall the ornaments of the heathen fall, and all the buildings of the earth, before the might of the earthquake. These are the signs of the fourth day.

REFERENCES

Aland, K. (ed.) (1985), *Synopsis Quattuor Evangeliorum*, 13th edn. (Stuttgart: Deutsche Bibelgesellschaft).

Barnard, L. W. (1966), *Studies in the Apostolic Fathers and their Background* (Oxford: Blackwell).

Carleton Paget, J. (1994), *The Epistle of Barnabas: Outlook and Background*, WUNT 2/64 (Tübingen: Mohr [Siebeck]).

Dibelius, M. (1923), *Die Apostolischen Väter*, iv. *Der Hirt des Hermas*, HNT Ergänzungsband (Tübingen: Mohr).

Draper, J. A. (1996) (ed.), *The Didache in Modern Research*, AGJU 37 (Leiden: Brill).

Elliott, J. K. (ed.) (1993), *The Apocryphal New Testament* (Oxford: Clarendon).

Grant, R. M. (1964), *The Apostolic Fathers: An Introduction*, Apostolic Fathers, 1 (New York: Nelson).

——(1966), *Ignatius of Antioch*, Apostolic Fathers, 4 (Camden: Nelson).

——and Graham, H. H. (1965), *First and Second Clement*, Apostolic Fathers, 2 (New York: Nelson).

Hahneman, G. M. (1992), *The Muratorian Fragment and the Development of the Canon* (Oxford: Clarendon), esp. ch. 2.

Hlavik, R. (1996), *The Struggle for Scripture and Covenant*, WUNT 2/82 (Tübingen: Mohr [Siebeck]).

Huck, A. (1981), *Synopse der drei ersten Evangelien*, 13th edn., rev. H. Greeven (Tübingen: Mohr [Siebeck]).

Jefford, C. N. (ed.) (1995), *The Didache in Context*, NovTSup 77 (Leiden: Brill).

——(1996), *Reading the Apostolic Fathers* (Peabody, NJ: Hendrickson).

Joly, R. (1968), *Le Pasteur: Introduction, texte critique, traduction, notes*, SC 53, 2nd edn. (Paris: Cerf).

Kirkland, A. (1990), *The Shepherd of Hermas: Some Aspects of its Composition and Transmission*, unpublished Ph.D. thesis, University of Cape Town.

Koöester, H. (1990), *Ancient Christian Gospels* (London: SCM).

Köster, H. (1957), *Synoptische Überlieferung bei den Apostolischen Vätern*, TU 65 (Berlin: Akademie).

Kraft, R. A. (1965), *Barnabas and the Didache*, Apostolic Fathers, 3 (New York: Nelson).

Lake, K. (1912–13), *The Apostolic Fathers*, LCL (2 vols.; London: Heinemann).

Lightfoot, J. B., and Harmer, J. R. (1989), *The Apostolic Fathers*, rev. M. W. Holmes (Grand Rapids: Baker Book House).

Linnemann, A. (1992), *Die Apostolischen Väter*, i. *Die Clememensbriefe* (Tübingen: Mohr [Siebeck]).

Neirynck, F. (1991), 'The Apocryphal Gospels and the Gospel of Mark', in F. Van Segbroeck (ed.), *Evangelica*, ii. *1982–1991: Collected Essays by Frans Neirynck*, BETL 99 (Leuven: Leuven University Press), 715–72.

Niederwimmer, K. (1993), *Die Didache*, Kommentar zu den apostolischen Vätern, 1 (Göttingen: Vandenhoeck & Ruprecht). E. T. 1998 (Minneapolis: Fortress).

Osiek, C. (1999), *The Shepherd of Hermas* (Minneapolis: Fortress).

Prigent, P., and Kraft, R. A. (1971), *Épître de Barnabé*, SC 172 (Paris: Cerf).

Rordorf, W., and Tuilier, A. (1978), *La Doctrine des douze apôtres (Didache)*, SC 248 (Paris: Cerf).

Schneemelcher, W. (ed.) (1991–2), *New Testament Apocrypha*, ET R. McL. Wilson (Cambridge: Clarke), i, ii.

Scholer, D. M. (1971), *Nag Hammadi Bibliography 1948–1969*, NHS 3 (Leiden: Brill).

Tuckett, C. M. (1989), 'Synoptic Tradition in the Didache', in J.-M. Sevrin (ed.), *The New Testament in Early Christianity*, BETL 86 (Leuven: Leuven University Press), 197–230.

Tugwell, S. (1989), *The Apostolic Fathers* (London: Chapman).

Wengst, K. (1984), *Schriften des Urchristentums*, ii. *Didache (Apostellehre), Barnabasbrief, Zweiter Klemensbrief, Schrift an Diognet* (Munich: Köselverlag; Darmstadt: Wissenschaftliche Bibelgesellschaft).

Whittaker, M. (1967), *Die Apostolischen Väter*, i. *Hermas, Der Hirt des Hermas*, GCS 48/2, 2nd edn. (Berlin: Akademie).

Windisch, H. (1920), *Die Apostolischen Väter*, iii. *Der Barnabasbrief*, HNT Ergänzungsband (Tübingen: Mohr).

83. Bibliographical Guide to Biblical Studies

History and Theology, Old Testament

Barr, J. (1999), *The Concept of Biblical Theology: An Old Testament Perspective* (London: SCM).

Bright, J. (1981), *A History of Israel*, 3rd edn. (London: SCM).

Brueggemann, W. (1997), *Theology of the Old Testament: Testimony, Dispute, Advocacy* (Philadelphia: Fortress).

Clements, R. E. (1978), *Old Testament Theology: A Fresh Approach* (London: Marshall, Morgan, and Scott).

Eichrodt, W. (1961–7), *Theology of the Old Testament* (2 vols.; London: SCM).

Hayes, J. H., and Miller, J. M. (1990), *Israelite and Judaean History* (London: SCM).

Herrmann, S. (1981), *A History of Israel in Old Testament Times* (Philadelphia: Fortress).

Jagersma, H. (1982), *A History of Israel in the Old Testament Period* (London: SCM).

—— (1985), *A History of Israel from Alexander the Great to Bar Kochba* (London: SCM).

Noth, M. (1960), *The History of Israel*, 2nd edn. (London: A. & C. Black).

von Rad, G. (1975), *Old Testament Theology* (2 vols.; Edinburgh: T. & T. Clark).

2. Introduction to the Old Testament

Barton, J. (1991), *What is the Bible?* (London: SPCK).

—— (1997), *Making the Christian Bible* (London: Darton, Longman & Todd).

Blenkinsopp, J. (1984), *A History of Prophecy in Israel from the Settlement in the Land to the Hellenistic Period* (London: SPCK).

Childs, B. S. (1979), *Introduction to the Old Testament as Scripture* (London: SCM).

Crenshaw, J. L. (1981), *Old Testament Wisdom: An Introduction* (Atlanta: John Knox).

Davies, P. R. (1998), *Scribes and Schools: The Canonization of the Hebrew Scriptures* (Louisville: Westminster/John Knox).

Hayes, J. H. (1982), *An Introduction to Old Testament Study* (London: SCM).

Kaiser, O. (1975), *Introduction to the Old Testament: A Presentation of its Results and Problems* (Oxford: Blackwell).

Laffey, A. (1988), *An Introduction to the Old Testament: A Feminist Perspective* (Philadelphia: Fortress).

Noth, M. (1966), 'The Laws in the Pentateuch: Their Assumptions and Meaning', in his *The Laws in the Pentateuch and Other Essays* (Edinburgh and London), 1–107.

Soggin, J. A. (1989), *Introduction to the Old Testament: From its Origins to the Closing of the Alexandrian Canon* (London: SCM).

Theissen, G. (1984), *Biblical Faith: An Evolutionary Perspective* (London: SCM).

3. Introduction to the Pentateuch

Albertz, R. (1994), *A History of Israelite Religion in the OT Period*, ET (2 vols.; London: SCM).

Alt, A. (1966), 'The Origins of Israelite Law', in *Essays on Old Testament History and Religion*, ET (Oxford: Blackwell), 87–132. First published 1934.

Blenkinsopp, J. (1992), *The Pentateuch: An Introduction to the First Five Books of the Bible* (London: SCM).

Brueggemann, W., and Wolff, H. W. (1975), *The Vitality of OT Traditions* (Atlanta: John Knox).

Clements, R. E. (1976), *A Century of OT Study* (Guildford: Lutterworth).

Clines, D. J. A. (1978), *The Theme of the Pentateuch* (Sheffield: JSOT).

Lohfink, N. (1994), *Theology of the Pentateuch: Themes of the Priestly Narrative and Deuteronomy* (Edinburgh: T. & T. Clark).

Nicholson, E. W. (1997), *The Pentateuch in the Twentieth Century* (Oxford: Oxford University Press).

Noth M. (1972), *A History of Pentateuchal Traditions*, ET (Englewood Cliffs: Prentice-Hall); from German original, *überlieferungsgeschichte des Pentateuch*, 1948.

Patrick, D. (1986), *Old Testament Law* (London: SCM).

Pritchard, J. B. (ed.) (1969), *Ancient Near Eastern Texts Relating to the Old Testament*, 3rd edn. (Princeton: Princeton University Press).

von Rad, G. (1962), *OT Theology*, ET (Edinburgh: Oliver & Boyd).

Wellhausen, J. (1885), *Prolegomena to the History of Israel*, ET (Edinburgh: A. & C. Black); from German original, *Geschichte Israels I*, 1878.

Whybray, R. N. (1987), *The Making of the Pentateuch: A Methodological Study* (Sheffield: JSOT).

4. Genesis

Blenkinsopp, J. (1992), *The Pentateuch. An Introduction to the First Five Books of the Bible* (London: SCM).

Gunkel, H. (1964), *The Legends of Genesis* (New York: Schocken).

McKane, W. (1979), *Studies in the Pentateuchal Narratives* (Edinburgh: Handsel).

Noth, M. (1972), *A History of Pentateuchal Traditions* (Englewood Cliffs: Prentice-Hall).

Redford, D. B. (1970), *A Study of the Biblical Story of Joseph (Genesis 37–50)*, VTSup 20 (Leiden: Brill).

Rogerson, J. W. (1974), *Myth in Old Testament Interpretation*, BZAW 134 (Berlin: de Gruyter).

Thompson, T. L. (1974), *The Historicity of the Patriarchal Narratives*, BZAW 133 (Berlin: de Gruyter).

Van Seters, J. (1975), *Abraham in History and Tradition* (New Haven and London: Yale University Press).

von Rad, G. (1966), 'The Joseph Narrative and Ancient Wisdom', in *The Problem of the Hexateuch and Other Essays* (Edinburgh and London: Oliver & Boyd), 292–300.

—— (1972), *Genesis*, OTL, 2nd edn. (London: SCM).

Westermann, C. (1974), *Creation* (London: SPCK; Philadelphia: Fortress).

—— (1980), *The Promises to the Patriarchs. Studies on the Patriarchal Narratives* (Philadelphia: Fortress).

—— *Genesis* (3 vols.; London: SPCK, 1984, 1985, 1987).

—— *Genesis* (Grand Rapids: Eerdmans, 1987; London: SPCK, 1988).

Whybray, R. N. (1987), *The Making of the Pentateuch. A Methodological Study*, JSOTSup 53 (Sheffield: JSOT).

5. Exodus

Brueggemann, W. (1994), 'Exodus', in *The New Interpreter's Bible* (vol. 1; Nashville: Abingdon).

Cassuto, U. (1967), *A Commentary on Exodus* (Jerusalem: Magnes).

Childs, B. S. (1974), *Exodus: a Commentary* (London: SCM).

Croatto, J. S. (1981), *Exodus: a Hermeneutics of Freedom* (Maryknoll, NY: Orbis Books).

Durham, J. I. (1987), *Exodus*, WBC (Waco, Tex.: Word).

Fretheim, T. E. (1991), *Exodus* (Interpretation) (Louisville, Ky.: Westminster/John Knox).

Gowan, D. E. (1994), *Theology in Exodus: Biblical Theology in the Form of a Commentary* (Louisville, Ky.: Westminster/John Knox).

Gunn, D. M. (1982), 'The Hardening of Pharaoh's Heart', in D. J. A. Clines, D. M. Gunn, and A. J. Hauser (eds), *Art and Meaning: Rhetoric in Biblical Literature*, JSOTSup 19 (Sheffield: JSOT), 72–96.

Haran, M. (1985), *Temples and Temple Service in Ancient Israel*, 2nd edn. (Winona Lake, Ind.: Eisenbrauns).

Houtman, C. (1993–), *Exodus*, Historical Commentary on the Old Testament (3 vols.; Kampen: Kok).

Johnstone, W. (1990), *Exodus*, Old Testament Guides (Sheffield: JSOT).

Moberly, R., and Walter, L. (1983), *At the Mountain of God: Story and Theology in Exodus 32–34*, JSOTSup 22 (Sheffield: JSOT).

Nicholson, E. W. (1986), *God and his People: Covenant and Theology in the Old Testament* (Oxford: Clarendon).

Patrick, D. (1986), *Old Testament Law* (London: SCM).

Van Seters, J. (1994), *The Life of Moses: the Yahwist as Historian in Exodus-Numbers* (Kampen: Kok Pharos).

6. Leviticus

Anderson, G. A. (1987), *Sacrifices and Offerings in Ancient Israel: Studies in their Social and Political Importance*, HSM 41 (Atlanta: Scholars Press).

—— and Olyan, S. M. (eds.) (1991), *Priesthood and Cult in Ancient Israel*, JSOTSup 125 (Sheffield: Sheffield Academic Press).

Blenkinsopp, J. (1976), 'The Structure of P', *CBQ* 38: 275–92.

Cassuto, U. (1961), *The Documentary Hypothesis and the Composition of the Pentateuch* (Jerusalem: Magnes).

Cross, F. M. (1973), *Canaanite Myth and Hebrew Epic* (Cambridge, Mass.. Harvard University Press).

Grabbe, L. L. (1991), 'Maccabean Chronology: 167–164 or 168–165 BCE?', *JBL* 110: 59–74.

Kaufmann, Y. (1961), *The Religion of Israel From its Beginnings to the Babylonian Exile* (tr. and abr. M. Greenberg) (London: George Allen & Unwin).

Levine, B. A. (1989), *Leviticus*, JPS Torah Commentary (Philadelphia: Jewish Publication Society).

McKeating, H. (1979), 'Sanctions against Adultery in Ancient Israelite Society, with Some Reflections on Methodology in the Study of Old Testament Ethics', *JSOT* 11: 57–72.

Noth, M. (1972), *A History of Pentateuchal Traditions* (Englewood Cliffs, NJ: Prentice-Hall).

Polzin, R. (1976), *Late Biblical Hebrew: Toward an Historical Typology of Biblical Hebrew Prose*, HSM 12 (Missoula: Scholars Press).

Rentdorff, R. H. (1990), *The Problem of the Process of Transmission in the Pentateuch*, JSOTSup 89 (Sheffield: Sheffield Academic Press); German original, *Das überlieferungsgeschichtliche Problem des Pentateuch* (1977).

—— (1993), 'Two Kinds of P? Some Reflections on the Occasion of the Publishing of Jacob Milgrom's Commentary on Leviticus 1–16', *JSOT* 60: 75–81.

Van Seters, J. (1983), *In Search of History: Historiography in the Ancient World and the Origins of Biblical History* (New Haven/London: Yale University Press).

Vink, J. G. (1969), 'The Date and Origin of the Priestly Code in the Old Testament', *OTS* 15: 1–144.

Weinfeld, M. (1972), *Deuteronomy and the Deuteronomic School* (Oxford: Clarendon).

—— (1992), *Deuteronomy 1–11*, AB5 (Garden City, NY: Doubleday).

Wellhausen, J. (1885), *Prolegomena to the History of Israel* (Edinburgh: A. & C. Black).

7. Numbers

Ashley, T. R. (1993), *The Book of Numbers*, The New International Commentary on the Old Testament (Grand Rapids: Eerdmans).

Budd, P. J. (1984), *Numbers*, Word Biblical Commentary, 5 (Waco, Tex.: Word).

Douglas, M. (1993), *In the Wilderness: The Doctrine of Defilement in the Book of Numbers* (Sheffield: Sheffield Academic Press).

Fretheim, T. E. (1996), *The Pentateuch*, Interpreting Biblical Texts (Nashville: Abingdon).

Gorman, F. H., Jr. (1990), *The Ideology of Ritual: Space, Time and Status in the Priestly Theology*, JSOTSup 91 (Sheffield: Sheffield Academic Press).

Gray, G. B. (1903), *A Critical and Exegetical Commentary on Numbers*, International Critical Commentary (Edinburgh: T. & T. Clark).

Levine, B. (1993), *Numbers 1–20: A New Translation with Introduction and Commentary*, Anchor Bible (New York: Doubleday).

Milgrom, J. (1990), *Numbers*, JPS Torah Commentary (Philadelphia: Jewish Publication Society of America).

Moore, M. (1990), *The Balaam Traditions: Their Character and Development*, SBLDS, 113 (Atlanta: Scholars Press).

Nelson, R. D. (1993), *Raising Up a Faithful Priest: Community and Priesthood in Biblical Theology* (Louisville: Westminster/John Knox).

Noth, M. (1968), *Numbers: A Commentary*, Old Testament Library (Philadelphia: Westminster); tr. J. D. Martin.

Olson, D. (1985), *The Death of the Old and the Birth of the New: The Framework of the Book of Numbers and the Pentateuch*, Brown Judaic Studies, 71 (Chico, Calif.: Scholars Press).

—— (1996), *Numbers*, Interpretation: A Bible Commentary for Teaching and Preaching (Louisville: John Knox).

Sakenfeld, K. D. (1995), *Journeying with God: A Commentary on the Book of Numbers*, An International Theological Commentary on the Old Testament (Grand Rapids: Eerdmans).

Wenham, G. J. (1981), *Numbers: An Introduction and Commentary*, Tyndale Old Testament Commentary (Downer's Grove, Ill.: Inter-Varsity).

8. Deuteronomy

Christensen, D. L. (ed.) (1993), *A Song of Power and the Power of Song. Essays on the Book of Deuteronomy* (Winona Lake, Ind.: Eisenbrauns).

Crüsemann, F. (1996), *The Torah* (Edinburgh: T. & T. Clark)

Driver, S. R. (1986), *A Critical and Exegetical Commentary on Deuteronomy (ICC)*, 1895, 3rd edn. 1901 (Edinburgh: T. & T. Clark).

Levinson, B. M. (1997), *Deuteronomy and the Hermeneutics of Legal Innovation* (New York, Oxford: Oxford University Press) (includes bibliography).

Miller, P. D. (1990), *Deuteronomy (Interpretation)* (Louisville, Ky.: John Knox).

Rofé, A. (1988), *Introduction to Deuteronomy*. Part I and further chapters [Hebrew] (Jerusalem: Akademon Publishing House).

Tigay, J. H. (1996), *Deuteronomy (The JPS Torah Commentary)* (Philadelphia/Jerusalem: The Jewish Publication Society).

Weinfeld, M. (1972), *Deuteronomy and the Deuteronomic School*, reprinted (Winona Lake, Ind.: Eisenbrauns).

9. Joshua

Aharoni, Y. (1967), *The Land of the Bible* (London: Burns and Oates).

Auld, A. G. (1980), *Joshua, Moses and the Land: Tetrateuch, Pentateuch, Hexateuch in a Generation since 1938* (Edinburgh: T. and T. Clark).

Baltzer, K. (1971), *The Covenant Formulary in Old Testament, Jewish and early Christian Writings* (Oxford) (= *Das Bundesformular: sein Ursprung und seine Verwendung im alten Testament* [WMANT 4] (Neukirchen: Neukirchener Verlag, 1960)).

Ben-Tor, A. (ed.), *The Archaeology of Ancient Israel* (New Haven/London: Yale University Press/Open University of Israel).

Boling, R., and Wright, G. E. (1982), *Joshua* (AB) (New York: Doubleday).

Bright, J. (1981), *A History of Israel*, 3rd edn. (London: SCM).

Butler, T. C. (1983), *Joshua*, WBC (Waco, Tex.: Word).

Curtis, A. H. W. (1994), *Joshua*, OT Guides (Sheffield: JSOT).

Finkelstein, I. (1988), *The Archaeology of the Israelite Settlement* (Jerusalem: Israel Exploration Society).

Gibson, J. C. L. (1971), *Textbook of Syrian Semitic Inscriptions* I: *Hebrew and Moabite Inscriptions* (Oxford: Clarendon Press).

Gottwald, N. K. (1979), *The Tribes of Yahweh: a Sociology of the Religion of Liberated Israel, 1250–1050 BCE* (London: SCM).

Gray, J. (1986), *Joshua, Judges and Ruth* (NCB) (London: Marshall, Morgan and Scott).

Haran, M. (1978), *Temples and Temple Service in Ancient Israel* (Oxford: Clarendon).

Kenyon, K. (1979), *Archaeology in the Holy Land*, 4th edn. (London: Ernest Benn).

Mazar, A. (1990), *Archaeology of the Land of the Bible 10,000–586 BCE* (New York: Doubleday).

McCarthy, D. J. (1978), *Treaty and Covenant*, AnBib 21A, 2nd edn. (Rome: Pontifical Biblical Institute).

Mendenhall, G. E. (1955) *Law and Covenant in the Ancient Near East* (Pittsburgh (repr from *BA* 17 [1954] 26–46, 50–76)).

Niditch, S. (1993), *War in the Hebrew Bible* (New York/Oxford: Oxford University Press).

Noth, M. (1960), *The History of Israel* (London: A. & C. Black).

—— (1981), *The Deuteronomistic History*, JSOTSup (Sheffield: JSOT) (ET of *Überlieferungsgeschichtliche Studien: die sammelnden und bearbeitenden Geschichtswerke im Alten Testament*, Halle, 1943, 2nd edn. Tübingen, 1957).

Polzin, R. (1980), *Moses and the Deuteronomist* (New York: Seabury).

Porter, J. R. (1970), 'The Succession of Joshua', in J. I. Durham and J. R. Porter (eds), *Proclamation and Presence* (FS G. H. Davies) (London: SCM), 102–132.

Soggin, J. A. (1972), *Joshua*, OTL (London: SCM).

Thompson, T. L. (1992), *The Early History of the Israelite People: from the Written and Archaeological Sources* (Leiden: Brill).

10. Judges

Alter, R. (1981), *The Art of Biblical Poetry* (New York: Basic).

—— (1985), *The Art of Biblical Narrative* (New York: Basic).

Gottwald, N. (1979), *The Tribes of Yahweh. A Religion of Liberated Israel 1250–1050 BC* (Maryknoll, NY: Orbis).

Meyers, C. (1988), *Discovering Eve. Ancient Israelite Women in Context* (New York/Oxford: Oxford University Press).

Niditch, S. (1997), *Ancient Israelite Religion* (New York/Oxford: Oxford University Press).

—— (1996), *Oral World and Written Word* (Louisville: John Knox/Westminster).

Younger, K. L. (1990), *Ancient Conquest Accounts: A Study in Ancient Near Eastern and Biblical History Writing*, JSOT 98 (Sheffield: JSOT).

11. Ruth

Brenner, A. (ed.) (1993), *A Feminist Companion to Ruth*, The Feminist Companion to the Bible 3 (Sheffield: Sheffield Academic Press).

LaCocque, A. (1990), *The Feminine Unconventional: Four Subversive Figures in Israel's Tradition*, Overtures to Biblical Theology (Philadelphia: Fortress).

Larkin, K. (1995), *Ruth and Esther*, Old Testament Guides (Sheffield: Sheffield Academic Press).

Leggett, D. A. (1974), *The Levirate and Goel Institutions in the Old Testament with Special Attention to the Book of Ruth* (Cherry Hill, NJ: Mack).

Phillips, A. (1986), 'The Book of Ruth: Deception and Shame', *JJS* 37: 1–17.

Trible, P. (1978), *God and the Rhetoric of Sexuality*, Overtures to Biblical Theology (Philadelphia: Fortress).

12. 1 & 2 Samuel

Birch, B. C. (1976), *The Rise of the Israelite Monarchy: The Growth and Development of 1 Samuel 7–15*, SBLDS 27 (Missoula: Scholars Press).

Campbell, A. F. (1975), *The Ark Narrative (1 Sam 4–6, 2 Sam 6). Form-Critical and Traditio-Historical Study*, SBLDS 16 (Missoula: Scholars Press).

Carlson, R. A. (1964), *David, the Chosen King. A Traditio-Historical Approach to the Second Book of Samuel* (Stockholm: Almqvist & Wiskell).

Conroy, C. C. (1978), *Absalom Absalom! Narrative and Language in 2 Sam 13–20*, Analecta Biblica 81 (Rome: Pontifical Biblical Institute).

Edelman, D. V. (1991), *King Saul in the Historiography of Judah*, JSOTSup 121 (Sheffield: Sheffield Academic Press).

Gunn, D. M. (1978), *The Story of King David. Genre and Interpretation*, JSOTSup 6 (Sheffield: Sheffield JSOT).

—— (1980), *The Fate of King Saul*, JSOTSup 14 (Sheffield: JSOT).

Ishida, T. (1977), *The Royal Dynasties in Ancient Israel. A Study on the Formation and Development of Royal-Dynastic Ideology*, BZAW 142 (Berlin: de Gruyter).

Jones, G. H. (1990), *The Nathan Narratives*, JSOTSup 80 (Sheffield: JSOT).

Long, V. P. (1989), *The Reign and Rejection of King Saul. A Case for Literary and Theological Coherence*, SBLDS 118 (Atlanta: Scholars Press).

Mayes, A. D. H. (1977), 'The Reign of Saul', in J. H. Hayes and J. M. Miller (eds.), *Israelite and Judaean History*, OTL (London: SCM), 322–31.

Mettinger, T. N. D. (1976), *King and Messiah. The Civil and Sacral Legitimation of the Israelite Kings*, Coniectanea Biblica, OT Series 8 (Lund: C. W. K. Gleerup).

Miller, P. D., and Roberts, J. (1977), *The Hand of the Lord: A Reassessment of the 'Ark Narrative' of 1 Samuel* (Baltimore/London: John Hopkins University Press).

Nelson, R. D. (1981), *The Double Redaction of the Deuteronomistic History*, JSOTSup 18 (Sheffield: JSOT).

Noth, M. (1943), *Überlieferungsgeschichtliche Studien* I (Tübingen: Max Niemeyer); (1981), ET *The Deuteronomistic History*, JSOTSup 15 (Sheffield: JSOT).

Rost, L. (1926), *Die Überlieferung von der Thronnachfolge Davids*, BWANT 3/6 (Stuttgart: Kohlhammer); (1982), ET *The Succession to the Throne of David* (Sheffield: Almond).

Soggin, J. A. (1977), 'The Davidic-Solomonic Kingdom', in J. H. Hayes and J. M. Miller (eds), *Israelite and Judaean History*, OTL (London: SCM), 332–80.

Weinfeld, M. (1970), *Deuteronomy and the Deuteronomic School* (Oxford: Clarendon).

Whybray, R. N. (1968), *The Succession Narrative. A Study of II Sam 9–20 and I Kings 1 and 2*, SBTh 9 (London: SCM).

13. 1 & 2 Kings

Cross, F. M. (1973), 'The Themes of the Book of Kings and the Structure of the Deuteronomistic History', in id., *Canaanite Myth and Hebrew Epic* (Cambridge, Mass.: Harvard University Press), 274–89.

Gray, J. (1977), *I and II Kings*, OTL 3rd edn. (Philadelphia: Westminster).

McKay, J. W. (1973), *Religion in Judah under the Assyrians 732–609 B.C.*, SBTh 2:26 (London: SCM).

Nelson, R. (1981), *The Double Redaction of the Deuteronomistic History*, JSOTSup 18 (Sheffield: JSOT).

Noth, M. (1991), *The Deuteronomistic History*, JSOTSup 15 (Sheffield: JSOT).

14. 1 & 2 Chronicles

Ackroyd, P. R. (1973), *I and II Chronicles*, Torch Bible Commentary (London: SCM).

Coggins, R. J. (1976), *The First and Second Books of Chronicles*, CBC (Cambridge: Cambridge University Press).

Myers, J. M. (1965), *1 Chronicles and 2 Chronicles*, Anchor Bible (2 vols.; Garden City, NY: Doubleday).

Williamson, H. G. M. (1977), *Israel in the Books of Chronicles* (Cambridge: Cambridge University Press).

Williamson, H. G. M. (1982), *1 and 2 Chronicles*, NCB (London: Marshall, Morgan, and Scott).

15. Ezra–Nehemiah

Berquist, J. (1995), *Judaism in Persia's Shadow: A Social and Historical Approach* (Minneapolis: Fortress).

Bickerman, E. (1976), 'The Edict of Cyrus in Ezra I', in *Studies in Jewish and Christian History*, I (Leiden: Brill).

Blenkinsopp, J. (1988), *Ezra-Nehemiah*, OTL (London: SCM).

Clines, D. (1984), *Ezra, Nehemiah, and Esther*, NCB (Basingstoke: Marshall, Morgan, and Scott).

Fensham, F. C. (1982), *The Books of Ezra and Nehemiah* (Grand Rapids, Mich.: Eerdmans).

Williamson, H. G. M. (1985), *Ezra, Nehemiah*, WSBC (Waco, Tex.: Word).

16. Esther

Berg, S. B. (1979), *The Book of Esther: Motifs, Themes, and Structures*, SBLDS 44 (Missoula: Scholars Press).

Clines, D. J. A. (1984), *The Esther Scroll: The Story of the Story*, JSOTSup 30 (Sheffield: JSOT).

—— (1988), 'Esther', in *Harper's Bible Commentary* (San Francisco: Harper & Row), 387–94.

Fox, M. V. (1991), *Character and Ideology in the Book of Esther*, Studies in Biblical Personalities (Columbia, SC: University of South Carolina Press).

Moore, C. A. (1971), *Esther: A New Translation with Introduction and Commentary*, Anchor Bible 7B (Garden City, NY: Doubleday).

—— (1982), *Studies in the Book of Esther* (New York: Ktav).

—— (1992), 'Esther, Book of ', *ABD* II: 633–43.

White, S. A. (1989), 'Esther: A Feminine Model for the Jewish Diaspora', in P. L. Day (ed.), *Gender and Difference* (Philadelphia: Fortress), 161–77.

—— (1992), 'Esther', in C. A. Newsom and S. H. Ringe (eds.), *The Woman's Bible Commentary* (Knoxville: Westminster/John Knox), 124–9.

17. Job

Beuken, W. A. M. (ed.) (1994), *The Book of Job* (BETL CXIV) (Leuven: Leuven University Press, Peeters).

Clines, D. J. A. (1989), *Job* (Dallas: Word Books), 1–20.

Crenshaw, J. L. (1992), 'Job, Book of', *ABD* 3 (New York: Doubleday), 858–68.

Glatzer, N. N. (ed.) (1969), *The Dimensions of Job* (New York: Doubleday).

Good, E. M. (1990), *In Turns of Tempest* (Stanford: Stanford University Press).

Gordis, R. (1978), *The Book of Job* (New York: Jewish Theological Seminary of America).

Habel, N. C. (1985), *The Book of Job* (Philadelphia: Fortress).

Hoffman, Y. A. (1996), *Blemished Perfection* (Sheffield: Sheffield Academic Press).

Janzen, J. G. (1985), *Job* (Atlanta: John Knox).

Newsom, C. (1996), 'Job', *NIB IV* (Nashville: Abingdon), 319–637.

Perdue, L. G. (1972), *Wisdom in Revolt* (Nashville: Abingdon).

Pope, M. E. (1973), *Job* (Garden City, NY: Doubleday).

Zuckerman, B. (1991), *Job the Silent: A Study in Historical Counterpoint* (New York: Oxford University Press).

18. Psalms

Anderson, A. A. (1972), *Psalms 1–72, Psalms 73–150*, NCB (London: Marshall, Morgan and Scott).

Dahood, M. J. (1966–70), *Psalms*, Anchor Bible (3 vols.; Garden City, NY: Doubleday).

Day, J. (1990), *Psalms*, Old Testament Guides (Sheffield: JSOT).

Gillingham, S. E. (1994), *The Poems and Psalms of the Hebrew Bible*, Oxford Bible Series (Oxford: Oxford University Press).

Kirkpatrick, A. F. (1901), *The Book of Psalms*, Cambridge Bible for Schools and Colleges (33 vols.; Cambridge: Cambridge University Press).

Mowinckel, S. (1962), *The Psalms in Israel's Worship* (2 vols.; Oxford: Basil Blackwell).

19. Proverbs

Bryce, G. E. (1979), *A Legacy of Wisdom: The Egyptian Contribution to the Wisdom of Israel* (Lewisburg, Pa.: Bucknell University Press).

Camp, C. V. (1985), *Wisdom and the Feminine in the Book of Proverbs* (Sheffield: JSOT).

Crenshaw, J. L. (1995), *Urgent Advice and Probing Questions: Collected Writings in Old Testament Wisdom* (Macon, Ga.: Mercer University Press).

Lang, B. (1986), *Wisdom and the Book of Proverbs: A Hebrew Goddess Redefined* (New York: Pilgrim).

McKane, W. (1970), *Proverbs: A New Approach*, OTL (London: SCM).

Murphy, R. E. (1981), *Wisdom Literature*, FOTL 13 (Grand Rapids, Mich.: Eerdmans).

—— (1998), *Proverbs*, WBC (Nashville: Thomas Nelson).

Scott, R. B. Y. (1965), *Proverbs*, AB (New York: Doubleday).

Skehan, P. W. (1972), *Studies in Israelite Poetry and Wisdom*, CBQMS 1 (Washington: Catholic Biblical Association).

von Rad, G. (1972), *Wisdom in Israel* (London: SCM); German original, 1970.

Westermann, C. (1995), *Roots of Wisdom: The Oldest Proverbs of Israel and Other Peoples* (Edinburgh: T. & T. Clark); German original, 1990.

Whybray, R. N. (1994), *Proverbs*, NCB (London: Marshall Pickering).

—— (1995), *The Book of Proverbs: A Survey of Modern Study*, HBIS 1 (Leiden: Brill).

Williams, J. G. (1981), *Those Who Ponder Proverbs: Aphoristic Thinking and Biblical Literature* (Sheffield: Almond).

20. Ecclesiastes

Crenshaw, J. L. (1988), *Ecclesiastes* (London: SCM).

Fox, M. V. (1989), *Qohelet and his Contradictions* (Sheffield: Almond).

Gordis, R. (1968), *Koheleth—The Man and his World*, 3rd edn. (New York: Schocken Books).

Ogden, G. (1987), *Qoheleth* (Sheffield: JSOT).

Whybray, R. N. (1981), 'The Identification and Use of Quotations in Ecclesiastes', *VTS* 32: 435–51.

—— (1989), *Ecclesiastes* (London: Marshall, Morgan & Scott).

—— (1989), *Ecclesiastes*, OT Guides (Sheffield: JSOT).

21. Song of Solomon

Brenner, A. (ed.) (1993), *A Feminist Companion to the Song of Songs* (Sheffield: Sheffield Academic Press).

Ginsburg, C. D. (1970), *The Song of Songs and Qoheleth*, 2nd edn. (New York: Ktav).

Gordis, R. (1974), *The Song of Songs and Lamentations*, 2nd edn. (New York: Ktav).

Goulder, M. (1986), *The Song of Fourteen Songs*, JSOTSup 35 (Sheffield: JSOT).

Tourney, R. J. (1988), *Word of God, Song of Love: A Commentary on the Song of Songs*, tr. J. E. Crowley (New York: Paulist).

Weems, R. J. (1992), 'The Song of Songs', in C. A. Newsom and S. H. Ringe (eds.), *The Women's Bible Commentary* (Louisville: Westminster/John Knox), 156–60.

22. Isaiah

Barton, J. (1995), *Isaiah 1–39*; Whybray, R. N. (1983), *The Second Isaiah*; Emmerson, G. I. (1992), *Isaiah 56–66*, Old Testament Guides (Sheffield: Sheffield Academic Press).

Sawyer, J. F. A. (1996), *The Fifth Gospel* (Cambridge: Cambridge University Press).

Vermeylen, J. (1989), *The Book of Isaiah* (Leuven: Peeters).

Williamson, H. G. M. (1994), *The Book called Isaiah* (Oxford: Clarendon).

23. Jeremiah

Achtemeier, E. (1987), *Jeremiah*, Knox Preaching Guides (Atlanta: John Knox).

Boadt, L. (1982), *Jeremiah 1–25*, Old Testament Message 9 (Wilmington, Del.: Michael Glazier).

—— (1982), *Jeremiah 26–52, Habakkuk, Zephaniah, Nahum* (Wilmington, Del.: Michael Glazier).

Brueggemann, W. (1998), *A Commentary on Jeremiah: Exile and Homecoming* (Grand Rapids and Cambridge: Eerdmans).

Carroll, R. P. (1986), *Jeremiah*, OTL (Philadelphia: Westminster).

—— (1989), *Jeremiah*, Old Testament Guides (Sheffield: JSOT).

Clements, R. E. (1988), *Jeremiah*, Interpretation (Atlanta: John Knox).

Craigie, P. C., Kelly, P., and Drinkard, J. F. (1991), *Jeremiah 1–25*, WBC 26 (Dallas: Word).

Holladay, W. L. (1974), *Jeremiah: Spokesman Out of Time* (Philadelphia: Pilgrim).

—— (1986), *Jeremiah*, Hermeneia (2 vols.; Philadelphia and Minneapolis: Fortress), 89.

—— (1990), *Jeremiah: A Fresh Reading* (New York: Pilgrim).

Keown, G. L., Scalise, P. J., and Smothers, T. G. (1995), *Jeremiah 26–52*, WBC 27 (Dallas: Word).

McKane, W. (1986, 1996), *Jeremiah*, ICC (2 vols.; Edinburgh: T. & T. Clark).

Nicholson, E. W. (1973, 1975), *Jeremiah*, CBC (2 vols.; Cambridge: Cambridge University Press).

O'Connor, K. (1988), *The Confessions of Jeremiah: Their Interpretation and Role in Chapters 1–25*, SBLDS 94 (Atlanta: Scholars Press).

—— (1992), 'Jeremiah', in C. A. Newsom and S. H. Ringe (eds.), *The Women's Bible Commentary* (Louisville, Ky.: Westminster/John Knox), 169–77.

Thompson, J. A. (1980), *The Book of Jeremiah*, NICOT (Grand Rapids: Eerdmans).

24. Lamentations

Albrektson, B. (1963), *Studies in the Text and Theology of the Book of Lamentations*, Studia Theologica Lundensia 21 (Lund: C.W.K. Gleerup).

Cohen, M. E. (1988), *The Canonical Lamentations of Ancient Mesopotamia* (2 vols.; Potomac, Md.: Capital Decisions Limited).

Gordis, R. (1974), *The Song of Songs and Lamentations*, 3rd edn. (New York: Ktav).

Gottwald, N. K. (1962) *Studies in the Book of Lamentations*, SBT 14, 2nd edn. (London: SCM).

—— (1988), 'Lamentations', in J. L. Mays (ed.), *Harper's Bible Commentary* (San Francisco: Harper).

Gwaltney, W. C., Jr. (1983), 'The Biblical Book of Lamentations in the Context of Near Eastern Lament Literature', in W. W. Hallo, J. C. Moyer, and L. G. Perdue (eds.), *Scripture in Context II: More Essays on the Comparative Method* (Winona Lake, Ind.: Eisenbrauns), 191–211.

Hillers, D. R. (1992), *Lamentations*, AB 7a, 2nd edn. (Garden City, NY: Doubleday).

Mintz, A. (1984), *Ḥurban: Responses to Catastrophe in Hebrew Literature* (New York: Columbia University Press).

O'Connor, K. M. (1992), 'Lamentations', in C. A. Newsom and S. H. Ringe (eds.), *The Women's Bible Commentary* (Louisville, Ky.: Westminster/John Knox), 178–82.

Provan, I. W. (1991), *Lamentations*, NCB (London: Marshall Pickering/ Grand Rapids, Mich.: Eerdmans).

Salters, R. B. (1994), *Jonah and Lamentations*, Old Testament Guide (Sheffield: JSOT).

Westermann, C. (1994), *Lamentations: Issues and Interpretation* (Edinburgh: T. & T. Clark).

25. Ezekiel

Ackerman, S. (1992), *Under Every Green Tree: Popular Religion in Sixth Century Judah*, HSM 46 (Atlanta: Scholars Press).

Allen, L. (1990), *Ezekiel 20–48*, WBC 29 (Dallas: Word).

—— (1994), *Ezekiel 1–19*, WBC 28 (Dallas, Tex.: Word).

Carley, K. W. (1975), *Ezekiel among the Prophets* (Naperville, Ill.: Alec R. Allenson).

Clifford, R. J. (1972), *The Cosmic Mountain in Canaan and the Old Testament*, HSM 4 (Cambridge, Mass.: Harvard University Press).

Davis, E. F. (1989), *Swallowing the Scroll: Textuality and the Dynamics of Discourse in Ezekiel's Prophecy* (Sheffield: Almond).

Eichrodt, W. (1970), *Ezekiel*, OTL (Philadelphia: Westminster); tr. C. Quinn.

Galambush, J. (1992), *Jerusalem in the Book of Ezekiel: The City as Yahweh's Wife*, SBLDS 130 (Atlanta: Scholars Press).

—— (1999), 'Ezekiel, Book of', in J. H. Hayes (ed.), *Dictionary of Biblical Interpretation* (Nashville, Tenn.: Abingdon).

Greenberg, M. (1983), *Ezekiel 1–20: A New Translation with Introduction and Commentary*, AB 22 (Garden City, NY: Doubleday).

—— (1997), *Ezekiel 21–37: A New Translation with Introduction and Commentary*, AB 22A (Garden City, NY: Doubleday).

Halperin, D. J. (1993), *Seeking Ezekiel: Text and Psychology* (University Park, Pa.: The Pennsylvania State University Press).

Joyce, P. (1989), *Divine Initiative and Human Response in Ezekiel*, JSOTSup 51 (Sheffield: JSOT).

Levenson, J. D. (1976), *Theology of the Program of Restoration of Ezekiel 40–48*, HSM 10 (Missoula: Scholars Press).

Lust, J. (1986), *Ezekiel and His Book: Textual and Literary Criticism and Their Interrelation*, BETL 74 (Leuven: University of Leuven Press).

Zimmerli, W. (1979, 1983), *Ezekiel*, Hermeneia (2 vols.; Philadelphia: Fortress), tr. R. E. Clements [vol. 1] and J. D. Martin [vol. 2].

26. Daniel

Collins, J. J. (1993), *Daniel*, Hermeneia (Minneapolis: Fortress).

Davies, P. R. (1985), *Daniel*, OTG (Sheffield: JSOT).

Goldingay, J. (1989), *Daniel*, WBC (Dallas: Word).

Hartman, L., and DiLella, A. A. (1978), *The Book of Daniel*, Anchor Bible (Garden City: Doubleday).

27. Hosea

Brenner, A. (ed.) (1995), *A Feminist Companion to the Latter Prophets*, A Feminist Companion to the Bible, 8 (Sheffield: Sheffield Academic Press), 40–241.

Davies, G. I. (1992), *Hosea*, NCB (London: Marshall Pickering; Grand Rapids: Eerdmans).

Davies, G. I. (1993), *Hosea*, OTG (Sheffield: Sheffield Academic Press).

Emmerson, G. I. (1984), *Hosea: an Israelite Prophet in Judean Perspective*, JSOTSup 28 (Sheffield: JSOT).

Macintosh, A. A. (1997), *Hosea*, ICC (Edinburgh: T. & T. Clark).

Mays, J. L. (1969), *Hosea*, OTL (London: SCM).

Wolff, H. W. (1974), *Hosea*, ET, Hermeneia (Philadelphia: Fortress).

28. Joel

Allen, L. C. (1976), *The Books of Joel, Obadiah, Jonah and Micah*, NICOT 13/2 (Grand Rapids, Mich.: Eerdmans).

Crenshaw, J. L. (1995), *Joel: A New Translation with Introduction and Commentary*, Anchor Bible (Garden City, NY: Doubleday).

Mason, R. A. (1994), *Zephaniah, Habakkuk, Joel*, OTG (Sheffield: JSOT).

Watts, J. D. W. (1975), *The Books of Joel, Obadiah, Jonah, Nahum, Habakkuk, and Zephaniah*, CBC (Cambridge: Cambridge University Press).

Wolff, H.-W. (1977), *Joel and Amos*, Hermeneia (Philadelphia: Fortress).

29. Amos

Andersen, F. I., and Freedman, D. N. (1989), *Amos*, Anchor Bible 24A (New York, London: Doubleday).

Auld, A. G. (1986), *Amos*, OTG (Sheffield: JSOT).

Carroll, R. P. (1990), 'Amos', in R. Coggins and L. Houlden (eds.), *A Dictionary of Biblical Interpretation* (London: SCM), 19–21.

King, P. J. (1988), *Amos, Hosea, Micah—An Archaeological Commentary* (Philadelphia: Westminster).

Soggin, J. A. (1987), *The Prophet Amos: A Translation and Commentary* (London: SCM).

Ward, J. M. (1976), 'Amos', in K. Crim (ed.), *The Interpreter's Dictionary of the Bible, Supplementary Volume* (Nashville: Abingdon), 21–23.

Wolff, H.-W. (1977), *Joel and Amos*, Hermeneia (Philadelphia: Fortress), 89–392.

30. Obadiah

Allen, L. C. (1976), *The Books of Joel, Obadiah, Jonah and Micah*, NICOT (Grand Rapids: Eerdmans).

Ben Zvi, E. (1996), *A Historical-Critical Study of the Book of Obadiah*, BZAW 242 (Berlin: de Gruyter).

Coggins, R. J. (1985), 'Judgement Between Brothers: A Commentary on the Book of Obadiah', in R. J. Coggins and S. P. Re'emi (eds.), *Israel among the Nations: a Commentary on the Books of Nahum, Obadiah, Esther*, ITC (Grand Rapids and Handsel, Edinburgh: Eerdmans), 65–100.

31. Jonah

Allen, L. C. (1976), *The Books of Joel, Obadiah, Jonah and Micah*, NICOT (Grand Rapids: Eerdmans).

Bickerman, E. J. (1967), *Four Strange Books of the Bible* (New York: Schocken).

Fretheim, T. (1977), *The Message of Jonah: A Theological Commentary* (Minneapolis: Augsburg).

32. Micah

Allen, L. C. (1976), *The Books of Joel, Obadiah, Jonah and Micah* NICOT (Grand Rapids: Eerdmans).

Hillers, D. R. (1984), *Micah*, Hermeneia (Philadelphia: Fortress).

Mason, R. (1991), *Micah, Nahum, Obadiah*, OTG (Sheffield: JSOT).

Mays, J. L. (1976), *Micah. A Commentary*, OTL (London: SCM).

Wal, A. van der (1990), *Micah. A Classified Bibliography* (Amsterdam: Free University Press).

Wolff, H.-W. (1990), *Micah. A Commentary* (Minneapolis: Augsburg); German original, 1982.

33. Nahum

Roberts, J. J. M. (1991), *Nahum, Habakkuk, and Zephaniah: A Commentary*, OTL (Louisville: Westminster/John Knox).

Mason R. (1991), *Micah, Nahum, Obadiah*, OTG (Sheffield: JSOT), 56–84.

34. Habakkuk

Achtemeier, E. (1986), *Nahum-Malachi*, Interpretation Commentaries (Louisville: Westminster/John Knox).

Gowan, D. E. (1976), *The Triumph of Faith in Habakkuk* (Atlanta: John Knox).

Hiebert, T. (1996), 'Habakkuk', in *The New Interpreter's Bible* (Vol. 7; Nashville: Abingdon).

Robertson, O. P. (1990), *The Books of Nahum, Habakkuk, and Zephaniah*, NICOT (Grand Rapids: Eerdmans).

Roberts, J. J. M. (1991), *Nahum, Habakkuk, and Zephaniah: A Commentary*, OTL (Louisville: Westminster/John Knox).

Szeles, M. E. (1988), *Wrath and Mercy: Habakkuk and Zephaniah*, International Theological Commentary (Grand Rapids: Eerdmans).

35. Zephaniah

Ben Zvi, E. (1991), *A Historical-Critical Study of the Book of Zephaniah*, BZAW 198 (Berlin, New York: de Gruyter).

Roberts, J. J. M. (1991), *Nahum, Habakkuk, and Zephaniah*, OTL (Louisville, Ky.: Westminster/John Knox).

Robertson, O. P. (1990), *The Books of Nahum, Habakkuk, and Zephaniah*, NICOT (Grand Rapids: Eerdmans).

36. Haggai

Ackroyd, P. (1968), *Exile and Restoration: A Study of Hebrew Thought in the Sixth Century B.C.*, OTL (Philadelphia: Westminster).

Blenkinsopp, J. (1991), 'Temple and Society in Achaemenid Judah', in P. Davies (ed.), *Second Temple Studies*, Vol. 1: *Persian Period*, JSOTSup 117 (Sheffield: Sheffield Academic Press), 22–53.

Coggins, R. (1987), *Haggai, Zechariah, Malachi*, OTG (Sheffield: JSOT).

Cook, J. (1983), *The Persian Empire* (New York: Schocken).

Hoglund, K. (1992), *Achaemenid Imperial Administration in Syria-Palestine and the Missions of Ezra and Nehemiah*, SBLDS 125 (Atlanta: Scholars Press).

37. Zechariah

Baldwin, J. (1972), *Haggai, Zechariah, Malachi* (London: Tyndale Press).

Coggins, R. J. (1987), *Haggai, Zechariah, Malachi* (Sheffield: JSOT).

Mason, R. A. (1977), *The Books of Haggai, Zechariah, and Malachi* (Cambridge: Cambridge University Press).

Meyers, C. L., and Meyers E. M. (1987), *Haggai, Zechariah 1–8*, AB Vol. 25B (New York: Doubleday).
—— (1993), *Zechariah 9–14*, AB Vol. 25C (New York: Doubleday).
Petersen, D. L. (1984), *Haggai and Zechariah 1–8* (London: SCM).
Smith, R. L. (1984), *Micah–Malachi* (Waco: Word Books).
Stuhlmueller, C. (1988), *Rebuilding with Hope: a Commentary on the Books of Haggai and Zechariah* (Grand Rapids: Eerdmans).

38. Malachi

Coggins, R. J. (1987), *Haggai, Zechariah, Malachi*, OTG (Sheffield: Sheffield Academic Press).
Hill, A. E. (1992), 'Malachi, Book of', in *Anchor Bible Dictionary* 4 (New York: Doubleday).
Mason, R. (1977), *The Books of Haggai, Zechariah, and Malachi*, CBC (Cambridge: Cambridge University Press).
O'Brien, J. M. (1995), 'Malachi in Recent Research', in *Currents in Research* 3 (Sheffield: Sheffield Academic Press), 81–94.
Petersen, D. L. (1995), *Zechariah 9–14 and Malachi*, OTL (Philadelphia: Westminster).
Smith, R. (1984), *Micah-Malachi*, WBC 32 (Waco, Tex.: Word Books).

39. Introduction to the Apocrypha

Charles, R. H. (ed.) (1912), *Apocrypha and Pseudepigrapha of The Old Testament* (2 vols.; Oxford: Clarendon).
Collins, J. J. (1983), *Between Athens and Jerusalem: Jewish Identity in the Hellenistic Diaspora* (New York: Crossroad).
De Lange, N. R. M. (1978), *Apocrypha: Jewish Literature of the Hellenistic Age* (New York: Viking).
Fritsch, C. T. (1962), 'Apocrypha', in *The Dictionary of the Bible* (Nashville, Tenn.: Abingdon).
Goodspeed, E. J. (1939), *The Story of the Apocrypha* (Chicago, Ill.: University of Chicago Press).
Harrington, S. J. (1999), *Invitation to the Apocrypha* (Grand Rapids, Mich.: Eerdmans).
Metzger, B. M. (1957), *An Introduction to the Apocrypha* (New York: Oxford University Press).
Nickelsburg, G. W. (1981), *Jewish Literature between the Bible and the Mishnah* (London: SCM).
Oesterley, W. O. E. (1935), *An Introduction to the Books of the Apocrypha* (London: SPCK).
Pfeiffer, R. H. (1949), *History of NT Times with an Introduction to the Apocrypha* (London: A. & C. Black).
Rost, L. (1976), *Judaism outside the Hebrew Canon: An Introduction to the Documents* (Nashville, Tenn.: Parthenon).
Schürer, E. (1986–7), in G. Vermes, F. Millar, and M. Goodman (eds.), *The History of the Jewish People in the Age of Jesus Christ*, Vol. 3, (Edinburgh: T. & T. Clark).
Stone, M. E. (ed.) (1984), *Jewish Writings of the Second Temple Period* (Assen/Philadelphia: Van Gorcum/Fortress).

40. Tobit

Flusser, D. (1984), 'Prayers in the Book of Tobit', in M. Stone (ed.), *Jewish Writings of the Second Temple Period*, CRINT 2/2 (Philadelphia, Pa.: Fortress; Assen: Van Gorcum), 555–56.
Moore, C. A. (1989), 'Scholarly Issues in the Book of Tobit before Qumran and After: An Assessment', *JSP* 5: 65–81.
Nowell, I. (1983), *The Book of Tobit: Narrative Technique and Theology*, Dissertation (Washington, DC: Catholic University of America).
—— (1990), 'Tobit', *NJBC*, 568–71.
Soll, W. (1989), 'Misfortune and Exile in Tobit: The Juncture of a Fairy Tale Source and Deuteronomic Theology', *CBQ* 51: 209–31.
Zimmermann, F. (1958), *The Book of Tobit: An English Translation with Introduction and Commentary*, Dropsie College Edition, Jewish Apocryphal Literature (New York: Harper & Bros.).

41. Judith

Craven, T. (1983), *Artistry and Faith in the Book of Judith*, SBLDS 70 (Chico, Calif.: Scholars Press).
Moore, C. A. (1985), *Judith. A New Translation with Introduction and Commentary*, AB 40 (Garden City, NY: Doubleday).
Wills, L. (1995), *The Jewish Novel in the Ancient World* (Ithaca and London: Cornell University Press).

42. Esther (Greek)

Clines, D. J. A. (1984), *The Esther Scroll: The Story of the Story* (Sheffield: JSOT).
Day, L. (1995), *Three Faces of a Queen: Characterization in the Books of Esther*, JSOTSup 186 (Sheffield: Sheffield Academic Press).
Fox, M. V. (1991), *The Redaction of the Books of Esther: On Reading Composite Texts*, SBLMS 40 (Atlanta: Scholars Press).
Moore, C. A. (1977), *Daniel, Esther and Jeremiah: The Additions*, Anchor Bible Vol. 44 (New York: Doubleday).
—— (ed.) (1982), *Studies in the Book of Esther* (New York: Ktav).
Wills, L. (1995), *The Jewish Novel in the Ancient World* (Ithaca: Cornell University Press).

43. Wisdom of Solomon

Barclay, J. M. G. (1996), *Jews in the Mediterranean Diaspora* (Edinburgh: T. & T. Clark).
Chester, A. (1988), 'Citing the Old Testament', in D. A. Carson and H. G. M. Williamson (eds.), *It is Written: Scripture Citing Scripture: Essays in Honour of Barnabas Lindars, SSF* (Cambridge: Cambridge University Press), 141–69.
Clarke, E. G. (1973), *The Wisdom of Solomon* (Cambridge: Cambridge University Press).
Emerton, J. A. (1965), 'Commentaries on the Wisdom of Solomon', *Theology* 68, 376–80.
Gilbert, M. (1984), 'Wisdom Literature', in M. E. Stone (ed.), *Jewish Writings of the Second Temple Period* (Philadelphia: van Gorcum, Assen: Fortress), 283–324.
Grabbe, L. L. (1997), *Wisdom of Solomon*, Guides to Apocrypha and Pseudepigrapha (Sheffield: Sheffield Academic Press).
Kloppenborg, J. S. (1982), 'Isis and Sophia in the Book of Wisdom', *HTR* 75, 57–84.
Smalley, B. (1986), in R. E. Murphy (ed.), *Medieval Exegesis of Wisdom Literature* (Atlanta: SBL).
Sweet, J. P. M. (1965), 'The Theory of Miracles in the Wisdom of Solomon', in C. F. D. Moule (ed.), *Miracles* (London: Mowbray), 115–26.
Walbank, F. W. (1984), 'Monarchies and Monarchic Ideas', in F. W. Walbank, A. E. Astin, M. W. Frederiksen, and R. M. Ogilvie (eds.), *The Cambridge Ancient History* vii. 1, *The Hellenistic World* (Cambridge: Cambridge University Press), 62–100.
Williams, M. H. (1998), *The Jews among the Greeks and Romans: A Diasporan Sourcebook* (London: Duckworth).
Winston, D. (1979), *The Wisdom of Solomon* (Garden City: Doubleday).
—— (1992), 'Solomon, Wisdom of', in *Anchor Bible Dictionary*, vi, 120–27.
Ziegler, J. (1962), *Sapientia Salomonis*, Septuaginta. Vetus Testamentum Graecum Auctoritate Academia Scientiarum Gottingensis Editum, xii.1 (Göttingen: Vandenhoeck & Ruprecht), reprinted 1980.

44. Wisdom of Jesus Son of Sirach

Box, G. H., and Oesterley, W. O. E. (1913), 'Sirach', in R. H. Charles (ed.), *The Apocrypha and Pseudepigrapha of the Old Testament*, Vol. I (Oxford: Clarendon), 268–517.

Crenshaw, J. L. (1975), 'The Problem of Theodicy in Sirach: On Human Bondage', *JBL* 94: 47–64.

—— (1981), *Old Testament Wisdom. An Introduction* (Atlanta: Knox), 149–73.

DiLella, A. A. (1966), *The Hebrew Text of Sirach. A Text-Critical and Historical Study* (The Hague: Mouton).

Hengel, M. (1974), *Judaism and Hellenism* (2 vols.; Philadelphia: Fortress), i. 131–52.

Sanders, J. T. (1983), *Ben Sira and Demotic Wisdom* (Chico: Scholars Press).

Sheppard, G. T. (1980), *Wisdom as a Hermeneutical Construct* (Berlin: de Gruyter).

Skehan, P. W., and DiLella, A. A. (1987), *The Wisdom of Ben Sira*, AB 39 (New York: Doubleday).

Trenchard, W. C. (1982), *Ben Sira's View of Women. A Literary Analysis* (Chico: Scholars Press).

von Rad, G. (1972), *Wisdom in Israel* (Nashville: Abingdon), 240–62.

Yadin, Y. (1965), *The Ben Sira Scroll from Masada* (Jerusalem: Israel Exploration Society).

45. Baruch

Bohak, G. (1997), 'Baruch, Books of', in R. J. Zwi Werblowsky and G. Wigoder (eds.), *Oxford Dictionary of the Jewish Religion* (New York: Oxford University Press), 101–2.

Coogan, M. D. (1993), 'Baruch', in B. M. Metzger and M. D. Coogan (eds.), *Oxford Companion to the Bible* (New York: Oxford University Press), 75.

Dentan, R. C. (1993), 'Baruch, book of', in B. M. Metzger and M. D. Coogan (eds.), *OCB* (New York: Oxford University Press), 75–6.

Mendels, D. (1992), 'Baruch, Book of', in *Anchor Bible Dictionary* I. 618–20.

Moore, C. A. (1977), *Daniel, Esther, and Jeremiah: the Additions*, AB 44 (Garden City, NY: Doubleday), 215–316.

Muilenberg, J. (1970), 'Baruch the scribe', in J. I. Durham and J. R. Porter (eds.), *Proclamation and Presence: Old Testament Essays in Honour of Gwynne Henton Davies* (London: SCM), 215–38.

Rost, L. (1976), *Judaism outside the Hebrew Canon. An Introduction to the Documents* (Nashville, Tenn.: Parthenon), 69–75.

46. Additions to Daniel

Collins, J. J. (1993), *Daniel*, Hermeneia (Minneapolis: Fortress).

Glancy, J. A. (1995), 'The Accused: Susanna and her Readers', in A. Brenner (ed.), *A Feminist Companion to Esther, Judith and Susanna*, Feminist Companion to the Bible 7 (Sheffield: Sheffield Academic Press), 288–302.

Moore, C. A. (1977), *Daniel, Esther, and Jeremiah: The Additions*, AB 44 (Garden City: Doubleday).

Steussy, M. J. (1993), *Gardens in Babylon: Narrative and Faith in the Greek Legends of Daniel*, SBLDS 141 (Atlanta: Scholars Press).

47. 1 Maccabees

Osterley, W. O. E. (1913), '1 Maccabees', in R. H. Charles (ed.), *The Apocrypha and Pseudepigrapha of the OT* (Oxford: Clarendon), 59–124.

Tedesche, S., and Zeitlin, S. (1950), *The First Book of Maccabees* (New York: Harper).

48. 2 Maccabees

Bar-Kochva, B. (1988), *Judas Maccabeus* (Cambridge: Cambridge University Press).

Bickerman, E. (1979), *The God of the Maccabees. Studies on the Meaning and Origin of the Maccabean Revolt*, SJLA 32 (Leiden: Brill).

Doran, R. (1981), *Temple Propaganda. The Purpose and Character of 2 Maccabees* (Washington, DC: Catholic Biblical Association).

Geller, M. J. (1991), 'New Information on Antiochus IV from Babylonian Astronomical Diaries', *BOA* 54: 1–4.

Goldstein, J. A. (1983), *2 Maccabees*, Anchor Bible 41a (Garden City, NY: Doubleday).

Grabbe, L. L. (1992), *Judaism from Cyrus to Hadrian* (2 vols.; Minneapolis: Fortress).

Gruen, E. S. (1984), *The Hellenistic World and the Coming of Rome* (Berkeley: University of California Press).

Habicht, C. (1976), 'Royal Documents in Maccaabees II', *HSCP* 80: 1–18.

Habicht, C. (1976), *2 Makkabäerbuch*, JSHRZ I/3 (Gütersloh: G. John).

Harrington, D. J. (1988), *The Maccabean Revolt: Anatomy of a Biblical Revolution* (Wilmington, Del.: Michael Glazier).

Momigliano, A. (1975), 'The Second Book of Maccabees', in *Classical Philology* 70, 81–88.

Schürer, E. (1973–87), *The History of the Jewish People in the Age of Jesus Christ (175 B.C.–A.D. 135)*. Revised by G. Vermes, F. Millar, and M. Goodman (3 vols.; Edinburgh: T. & T. Clark).

Sievers, J. (1991), *The Hasmoneans and their Supporters: From Mattathias to the Death of John Hyrcanus* (Atlanta: Scholars Press).

Tcherikover, V. (1961), *Hellenistic Civilization and the Jews* (Philadelphia: Jewish Publication Society).

49. 1 Esdras

Cook, S. A. (1913), 'I Esdras', in R. H. Charles (ed.), The *Apocrypha and Pseudepigrapha of the Old Testament*, I (Oxford: Clarendon), 1–58.

Eskenazi, T. C. (1986), 'The Chronicler and the Composition of I Esdras', *CBQ* 48: 39–66.

Japhet, S. (1982), 'Sheshbazzar and Zerubbabel against the background of the Historical and Religious Tendencies of Ezra Nehemiah', *ZAW* 94: 66–98; (1983) 95: 218–29.

—— (1994), 'Composition and Chronology in the Book of Ezra-Nehemiah', in T. C. Eskenazi and K. H. Richards (eds.), *Second Temple Studies* 2, JSOTSup 175 (Sheffield: JSOT), 189–216.

Myers, J. M. (1974), *I and II Esdras*, AB (New York: Doubleday).

Williamson, H. G. M. (1996), 'The Problem with First Esdras', in J. Barton and J. Reimer (eds.), *After the Exile: Essays in Honour of Rex Mason* (Macon, Ga.: Mercer University Press), 201–16.

50. Prayer of Manasseh

Charlesworth, J. H. (1983–1985), 'Prayer of Manasseh', in J. H. Charlesworth (ed.), *The Old Testament Pseudepigrapha* (2 vols.; Garden City: Doubleday), ii. 625–33.

Ryle, H. E. (1912), 'Prayer of Manasses,' in R. H. Charles (ed.), *The Apocrypha and Pseudepigrapha of the Old Testament* (2 vols.; Oxford: Clarendon), i. 612–24.

Schuller, E. M. (1986), *Non-Canonical Psalms from Qumran: A Pseudepigraphic Collection*, HSS 28 (Atlanta: Scholars Press).

51. Psalm 151

Charlesworth, J. H., and Sanders, J. A. (1985), 'Psalm 151', in J. H. Charlesworth (ed.), *The Old Testament Pseudepigrapha* II (Garden City, NY: Doubleday), 612–15.

Harrington, D. J. (1988), 'Psalm 151', in J. L. Mays (ed.), *Harper's Bible Commentary* (San Francisco: Harper & Row), 935–6.

Sanders, J. A. (1965), *The Psalms Scroll of Qumran Cave 11*, 11Qps (Oxford: Clarendon Press).

—— (1967), *The Dead Sea Psalms Scroll* (Ithaca, NY: Cornell University Press).

52. 3 Maccabees

Anderson, H. (1985), '3 Maccabees', in J. Charlesworth (ed.), *The Old Testament Pseudepigrapha* (Garden City, NY: Doubleday), ii, 509–30.

Barclay, J. (1996), *Jews in the Mediterranean Diaspora* (Edinburgh: T. & T. Clark), 192–203.

Collins, J. J. (1983), *Between Athens and Jerusalem: Jewish Identity in the Hellenistic Diaspora* (New York: Crossroad), 104–11.

Hadas, M. (1953), *The Third and Fourth Books of Maccabees* (New York: Harper).

Schürer, E. (1987), in G. Vermes et al. (eds.), (rev.) *The History of the Jewish People in the Age of Jesus Christ*, (Edinburgh: T. & T. Clark), Vol. III. 1, 537–42.

Tcherikover, V. (1961), 'The Third Book of Maccabees as a Historical Source of Augustus' Time', in *Scripta Hierosolymitana* (Jerusalem: Magnes) VII, 1–26.

53. 2 Esdras

Bergren, T. A. (1990), *Fifth Ezra: The Text, Origin and Early History*, Septuagint and Cognate Studies 25 (Atlanta, GA: Scholars Press).

Box, G. H. (1912), *The Ezra Apocalypse* (London: Isaac Pitman & Sons).

Coggins, R. J., and Knibb, M. A. (1979), *The First and Second Books of Esdras*, The Cambridge Bible Commentary on the NEB (Cambridge: Cambridge University Press).

Grabbe, L. L. (1989), 'The Social Setting of Early Jewish Apocalypticism', *JSP* 4: 27–47.

Longenecker, B. W. (1995), *2 Esdras* (Sheffield: Sheffield Academic Press).

Myers, J. M. (1974), *I and II Esdras*, AB 42 (New York: Doubleday).

Stanton, G. N. (1977), '5 Ezra and Matthean Christianity in the Second Century', *JTS* 28: 67–83.

Stone, M. E. (1976), 'List of Revealed Things in the Apocalyptic Literature', in F. M. Cross et al. (eds.), *Magnalia Dei (G. E. Wright Memorial)* (New York: Doubleday), 414–54. Also in Stone (1991: 370–418).

—— (1983), 'Coherence and Inconsistency in the Apocalypses: The Case of "The End" in 4 Ezra', *JBL* 102: 229–43. Also in Stone (1991: 333–47).

—— (1990), *Fourth Ezra*, Hermeneia—A Critical and Historical Commentary on the Bible (Minneapolis: Fortress).

—— (1991), *Selected Studies in Pseudepigrapha and Apocrypha*, SVTP (Leiden: Brill).

Thompson, A. L. (1977), *Responsibility for Evil in the Theodicy of IV Ezra*, SBL DS 29 (Missoula, Mont.: Scholars Press).

54. 4 Maccabees

DeSilva, D. A. (1999), *4 Maccabees* (Sheffield: Sheffield University Press).

Hadas, M. (1954), *The Third and Fourth Books of Maccabees* (New York: Harper).

Renehan, R. (1972), 'The Greek Philosophic Background of Fourth Maccabees', *Rheinisches Museum* 115: 223–38.

Seeley, D. S. (1990), *The Noble Death* (Sheffield: Sheffield University Press).

55. Essay with Commentary on Post-Biblical Jewish Literature

Charles, R. H. (ed.) (1913), *The Apocrypha and Pseudepigrapha of the Old Testament* (2 vols.; Oxford: Clarendon).

Charlesworth, J. H., (ed.) (1983–5), *The Old Testament Pseudepigrapha* (2 vols.; New York: Doubleday).

Colson, F. H., and Whitaker, G. H. (1971), *Philo* (12 vols; Cambridge, Mass./London: Yale University Press).

Garcia-Martinez, F. (1996), *The Dead Sea Scrolls Translated*, 2nd edn. (Leiden: Brill).

—— and Tigchelaar, E. J. C. (1997), *The Dead Sea Scrolls Study Edition* (2 vols.; Leiden: Brill).

Sparks, H. F. D. (ed.) (1984), *The Apocryphal Old Testament* (Oxford: Clarendon).

Stemberger, G. (1996), *Introduction to the Talmud and Midrash*, 2nd edn. (Edinburgh: T. & T. Clark).

Thackeray, St. H., Marcus, R., Wikgren, A., and Feldman, L. H. (1965), *Josephus* (9 vols.; Cambridge, Mass./London: Loeb Classical Library).

Vermes, G. (1997), *The Complete Dead Sea Scrolls in English* (London: Allen Lane/Penguin).

—— (1999), *An Introduction to the Dead Sea Scrolls* (London: Penguin).

Yonge, C. D. (1993), *The Works of Philo: Complete and Unabridged*, new updated edn. (Peabody, Mass.: Hendrickson).

History and Theology, New Testament

a) Introductions to the NT

Brown, R. E. (1997), *An Introduction to the New Testament* (New York: Doubleday).

Johnson, L. T. (1999), *The Writings of the New Testament*, rev. edn. (Philadelphia: Fortress).

Koester, H., *Introduction to the New Testament* (2 vols.; Philadelphia: Fortress, 1982; vol. 1, 2nd edn.; New York: de Gruyter, 1995).

Kümmel, W. G. (1986), *Introduction to the New Testament*, rev. enlarged edn. (Nashville: Abingdon).

b) Background to the NT

Barrett, C. K. (1987), *The New Testament Background*, rev. edn. (New York: Harper Collins).

Evans, C. A., and Porter, S. E. (2000), *Dictionary of New Testament Background* (Downers Grove: Inter Varsity Press).

Ferguson, E. (1993), *Background of Early Christianity*, 2nd edn. (Grand Rapids: Eerdmans).

Hengel, M. (1974), *Judaism and Hellenism* (London: SCM).

Schürer, E. (1973–87), in F. Millar, G. Vermès and M. Goodman (eds.), *The History of the Jewish People in the Age of Jesus Christ*, rev. edn. (4 vols; Edinburgh: T. & T. Clark).

c) The Historical Jesus

Allison, D. C. (1998), *Jesus of Nazareth: Millenarian Prophet* (Philadelphia: Fortress).

Becker, J. (1998), *Jesus of Nazareth* (trans. J. E. Couch, New York: de Gruyter).

Crossan, J. D. (1991), *The Historical Jesus: The Life of a Mediterranean Jewish Peasant* (Edinburgh: T. & T. Clark).

Horsley, R. A. (1994), *Sociology and the Jesus Movement*, 2nd edn. (New York: Continuum).

Meier, J. P. (1991, 1994), *A Marginal Jew: Rethinking the Historical Jesus* (2 vols.; New York: Doubleday).

Schweitzer, A. (2000), *The Quest of the Historical Jesus* (first complete English edition from 1913 German edition; London: SCM).

Theissen, G., and Merz, A. (1998), *The Historical Jesus: A Comprehensive Guide* (trans. J. Bowden, London: SCM).

d) NT Christology

Brown, R. E. (1994), *An Introduction to New Testament Christology* (London: Geoffrey Chapman).

Cullmann, O. (1963), *The Christology of the New Testament*, 2nd edn. London: SCM).

Dunn, J. D. G. (1996), *Christology in the Making*, 2nd edn. (Grand Rapids: Eerdmans).

Loader, W. R. G. (1989), *The Christology of the Fourth Gospel*, BET 23 (Frankfurt: Peter Lang).

Marshall, I. H. (1990), *The Origins of New Testament Christology*, updated edn. (Leicester: Apollos).

Moule, C. F. D. (1977), *The Origin of Christology* (Cambridge: Cambridge University Press).

Tuckett, C. M., and Horrell, D. G. (eds.) (2000), *Christology, Controversy and Community: New Testament Essays in Honour of David R. Catchpole*, NovTSup 99 (Leiden: Brill).

e) Theology of the NT

Bultmann, R. (1952, 1955) *Theology of the New Testament* (2 vols.; London: SCM).

Caird, G. B. (1994), in L. D. Hurst (ed.), *New Testament Theology* (Oxford: Clarendon).

Conzelmann, H. (1969), *An Outline of the Theology of the New Testament* (London: SCM).

Jeremias, J. (1971), *New Testament Theology: The Proclamation of Jesus* (London: SCM).

Kümmel, W. G. (1973), *The Theology of the New Testament: according to its Major Witnesses, Jesus, Paul and John* (London: SCM).

Schmithals, W. (1997), *The Theology of the First Christians* (Philadelphia: Westminster/John Knox).

Strecker, G. (2000), *Theology of the New Testament* (Philadelphia: Westminster/John Knox).

f) Dictionaries of the NT

Balz, H., and Schneider, G. (eds.) (1990–3), *Exegetical Dictionary of the New Testament* (3 vols.; Grand Rapids: Eerdmans).

Freedman, D. N. (ed.), (1992), *Anchor Bible Dictionary* (6 vols.; New York: Doubleday).

Green, J. B., et al. (eds.) (1992), *Dictionary of Jesus and the Gospels* (Downers Grove: Inter Varsity Press).

Hawthorne, G. F., et al. (eds.) (1993), *Dictionary of Paul and His Letters* (Downers Grove: Inter Varsity Press).

Kittel, G. (ed.) (1965–76), *Theological Dictionary of the New Testament* (10 vols.; Grand Rapids: Eerdmans).

Martin, R. P., and Davids, P. H. (eds.) (1997), *Dictionary of the Later New Testament and its Developments* (Downers Grove: Inter Varsity Press).

56. Introduction to the New Testament

Beker, J. C. (1994), *The New Testament. A Thematic Introduction* (Minneapolis: Fortress).

Conzelmann, H., and Lindemann, A. (1988), *Interpreting the New Testament* (Peabody: Hendrickson, from the 8th German edn.).

Davies, W. D. (1993), *Invitation to the New Testament* (Sheffield: JSOT, reprint).

Houlden, J. L. (1977), *Patterns of Faith: a Study of the Relationship between the New Testament and Christian Doctrine* (Philadelphia: Fortress).

Moule, C. F. D. (1981), *The Birth of the New Testament*, 3rd. edn. (London: A. & C. Black).

Perrin, N., and Duling, D. C. (1994), *The New Testament: An Introduction*, 3rd. edn. (Fort Worth: Harcourt Brace).

Stott, J. R. W. (1995), *Men with a Message: An Introduction to the New Testament*, rev. edn. (Grand Rapids: Eerdmans).

57. Matthew

Allison, D. C. (1993), *The New Moses: A Matthean Typology* (Minneapolis: Fortress).

Balch, D. L. (ed.) (1991), *Social History of the Matthean Community* (Philadelphia: Fortress).

Bornkamm, G., et al. (1963), *Tradition and Interpretation in Matthew* (London: SCM).

Davies, W. D., and Allison, D. C. (1988, 1991, 1998), *The Gospel according to St. Matthew*, ICC (3 vols.; Edinburgh: T. & T. Clark).

Gundry, R. H. (1994), *Matthew: A Commentary on his Handbook for a Mixed Church under Persecution*, 2nd edn. Grand Rapids:) Eerdmans).

Hagner, D. A. (1993, 1995), *Matthew*, WBC (2 vols.; Dallas: Word).

Harrington, D. J. (1991), *The Gospel of Matthew*, Sacra Pagina (Collegeville: Liturgical).

Luz, U. (1995), *The Theology of the Gospel of Matthew* (Cambridge: Cambridge University Press).

—— (1991, 2000) *Matthew 1–7; 8–20* (2 vols.; Minneapolis: Fortress).

Meier, J. P. (1976), *Law and History in Matthew's Gospel*, AnBib 71 (Rome: PBI).

Overman, J. A. (1990), *Matthew's Gospel and Formative Judaism* (Minneapolis: Fortress).

Saldarini A. J. (1994), *Matthew's Christian-Jewish Community* (Chicago: University of Chicago Press).

Stanton, G. N. (1992), *A Gospel for a New People: Studies in Matthew* (Edinburgh: T. & T. Clark).

Wainwright, E. M. (1991), *Towards a Feminist Critical Reading of the Gospel According to Matthew*, BZNW 60 (Berlin: de Gruyter).

58. Mark

Best, E. (1983), *Mark: The Gospel as Story* (Edinburgh: T. & T. Clark).

Guelich R. A. (1989), *Mark 1–8: 26*, WBC (Waco: Word).

Gundry, R. H. (1992), *Mark: A Commentary on His Apology for the Cross* (Grand Rapids: Eerdmans).

Hooker, M. D. (1991), *The Gospel according to St. Mark* (London: A. & C. Black).

Lane, W. L. (1974), *The Gospel of Mark*, NICNT (Grand Rapids: Eerdmans).

Marcus, J. (1999), *Mark 1–8*, Anchor Bible (New York: Doubleday).

Martin, R. P. (1972), *Mark—Evangelist and Theologian* (Exeter: Paternoster).

Marxsen, W. (1969), *Mark the Evangelist* (Nashville: Abingdon).

Myers, C. (1988), *Binding the Strong Man: A Political Reading of Mark's Story of Jesus* (Maryknoll: Orbis).

Räisänen, H. (1990), *The 'Messianic Secret' in Mark's Gospel* (Edinburgh: T. & T. Clark).

Rhoads, D., and Michie, D. (1982), *Mark as Story* (Philadelphia: Fortress).

Telford, W. R. (1999), *The Theology of the Gospel of Mark* (Cambridge: Cambridge University Press).

Tuckett, C. M. (ed.), (1983), *The Messianic Secret* (London: SPCK).

Weeden, T. J. (1971), *Mark—Traditions in Conflict* (Philadelphia: Fortress).

59. Luke

Conzelmann, H. (1960), *The Theology of St. Luke* (New York: Harper).

Evans, C. F. (1990), *Saint Luke*, TPI NT Commentaries (London: SCM).

Fitzmyer, J. A. (1981, 1985), *The Gospel according to Luke*, Anchor Bible (2 vols.; New York: Doubleday).

Franklin, E. (1975), *Christ the Lord: A Study in the Purpose and Theology of Luke-Acts* (Philadelphia: Westminster).

Green, J. B. (1997), *The Gospel of Luke* (Grand Rapids: Eerdmans).

—— (1997), *The Theology of the Gospel of Luke* (Cambridge: Cambridge University Press).

Johnson, L. T. (1991), *The Gospel of Luke*, Sacra Pagina (Collegeville: Liturgical).

Maddox, R. (1982), *The Purpose of Luke-Acts* (Edinburgh: T. & T. Clark).

Marshall, I. H. (1978), *The Gospel of Luke: a Commentary on the Greek text* (Exeter: Paternoster).

Neyrey, J. H. (1991), *The Social-World of Luke-Acts* (Peabody, Mass.: Hendrickson).

Nolland, J. (1989–93), *Luke*, WBC, (3 vols.; Dallas: Word).

Tuckett, C. M. (1996), *Luke*, Sheffield NT Guides (Sheffield: Sheffield Academic Press).

60. John

Ashton, J. (1991), *Understanding the Fourth Gospel* (Oxford: Clarendon).

—— (ed.) (1986), *The Interpretation of John* (Edinburgh: T. & T. Clark).

Beasley-Murray, G. R. (1999), *John*, WBC, 2nd edn. (Dallas: Word).

Brown, R. E. (1996, 1970) *The Gospel according to John*, Anchor Bible (2 vols.; New York: Doubleday).

—— (1979), *The Community of the Beloved Disciple* (New York: Paulist).

Bultmann, R. (1971), *The Gospel of John* (Oxford: Blackwell).

Culpepper, R. A. (1983), *Anatomy of the Fourth Gospel. A Study in Literary Design* (Philadelphia: Fortress).

Dodd, C. H. (1953), *The Interpretation of the Fourth Gospel* (Cambridge: Cambridge University Press).

—— (1963), *Historical Tradition in the Fourth Gospel* (Cambridge: Cambridge University Press).

Kieffer, R. (1987–8), *Johannesevangeliet* (2 vols.; Uppsala: EFS).

Maloney, F. J. (1998), *The Gospel of John*, Sacra Pagina (Collegeville: Liturgical).

Martyn, J. L. (1979), *History and Theology in the Fourth Gospel*, 2nd. edn. (Nashville: Abingdon).

Painter, J. (1993), *The Quest for the Messiah: The History, Literature and Theology of the Johannine Community*, 2nd edn. (Edinburgh: T. & T. Clark).

Schnackenburg, R. (1968, 1980, 1982), *The Gospel according to St John* (3 vols.; New York: Herder & Herder/Crossroad).

Smith, D. M. (1984), *Johannine Christianity: Essays on Its Setting, Sources and Theology* (Columbia: University of South Carolina Press).

Stibbe, M. W. G. (1993), *John*, Sheffield NT Guides (Sheffield: JSOT).

61. Four Gospels in Synopsis

Catchpole, D. R. (1993), *The Quest for Q* (Edinburgh: T. & T. Clark).

Goulder, M. D. (1974), *Midrash and Lection in Matthew* (London: SPCK).

—— (1989), *Luke—A New Paradigm* (Sheffield: Sheffield Academic Press).

Farmer, W. R. (1976), *The Synoptic Problem*, 2nd edn. (Dillsboro: Western North Carolina).

Kloppenborg, J. S. (1987), *The Formation of Q* (Philadelphia: Fortress).

Kloppenborg-Verbin, J. S. (2000), *Excavating Q: The History and the Setting of the Saying Source* (Edinburgh: T. & T. Clark).

Sanders, E. P., and Davies, M. D. (1989), *Studying the Synoptic Gospels* (London: SCM).

Streeter, B. H. (1924), *The Four Gospels* (London: Macmillan).

Robinson, J. M., et al. (eds.) (2000), *Critical Edition of Q*, Hermeneia (Philadelphia: Fortress).

Tuckett, C. M. (1982), *The Revival of the Griesbach Hypothesis*, SNTSMS 44 (Cambridge: Cambridge University Press).

—— (1996), *Q and the History of Early Christianity* (Edinburgh: T. & T. Clark).

62. Acts

Barrett, C. K. (1994, 1998) *Acts of the Apostles*, ICC (2 vols.; Edinburgh: T. & T. Clark).

Bruce, F. F. (1990), *The Book of Acts*, rev. edn., NICNT (Grand Rapids: Eerdmans).

Cadbury, H. J. (1955), *The Book of Acts in History* (New York: Harper).

Conzelmann, H. (1987), *Acts of the Apostles*, Hermeneia (Philadelphia: Fortress).

Fitzmyer, J. A. (1998), *Acts of the Apostles*, Anchor Bible (New York: Doubleday).

Foakes Jackson, F. J., and Lake, K. (eds.) (1920–33), *The Beginnings of Christianity: The Acts of the Apostles* (5 vols.; London: Macmillan).

Haenchen, E. (1971), *The Acts of the Apostles* (Oxford: Blackwell).

Hemmer, C. (1989), *The Book of Acts in the Setting of Hellenistic History*, WUNT 49 (Tübingen: Mohr-Siebeck).

Hengel, M. (1979), *Acts and the History of Earliest Christianity* (Philadelphia: Fortress).

Johnson, L. T. (1992), *Acts of the Apostles*, Sacra Pagina (Collegeville: Liturgical).

Lentz, J. C. Jr. (1993), *Luke's Portrait of Paul*, SNTSMS 77 (Cambridge: Cambridge University Press).

Lüdemann, G. (1989), *Early Christianity according to the Traditions in Acts* (Philadelphia: Fortress).

Winter, B. W. et al. (eds.) (1993–7), *The Book of Acts in its First Century Setting* (6 vols.; Grand Rapids: Eerdmans).

63. Introduction to the Pauline Corpus

Ashton, J. (2000), *The Religion of Paul the Apostle* (New Haven: Yale University Press).

Beker, C. (1980), *Paul the Apostle: The Triumph of God in Life and Thought* (Philadelphia: Fortress).

Bruce, F. F. (1977), *Paul: Apostle of the Heart Set Free* (Grand Rapids: Eerdmans).

Donaldson, T. L. (1997), *Paul and the Gentiles: Remapping the Apostle's Convictional World* (Minneapolis: Fortress).

Dunn, J. D. G. (1998), *The Theology of Paul the Apostle* (Grand Rapids: Eerdmans).

Engberg-Pedersen, T. (2000), *Paul and the Stoics* (Edinburgh: T. & T. Clark).

Hengel, M. (1991), *The pre-Christian Paul* (London: SCM).

Lüdemann, G. (1984), *Paul Apostle to the Gentiles: Studies in Chronology* (London: SCM).

Murphy-O'Connor, J. (1996), *Paul: A Critical Life* (Oxford: Clarendon).

Riesener, R. (1998), *Paul's Early Period: Chronology, Mission, Strategy, Theology* (Grand Rapids: Eerdmans).

Sanders, E. P. (1977), *Paul and Palestinian Judaism: A Comparison of Patterns of Religion* (Philadelphia: Fortress).

Schweitzer, A. (1931), *The Mysticism of Paul the Apostle* (London: A. & C. Black).

Segal, A. F. (1990), *Paul the Convert: The Apostolate and Apostasy of Saul the Pharisee* (New Haven: Yale University Press).

64. Romans

Barrett, C. K. (1957), *A Commentary on the Epistle to the Romans*, BNTC (London: A. & C. Black).

Barth, K. (1933), *The Epistle to the Romans* (London: Oxford University Press).

Byrne, B. (1996), *Romans*, Sacra Pagina (Collegeville: Liturgical).

Cranfield, C. E. B. (1975, 1979), *Romans*, ICC (2 vols.; Edinburgh: T. & T. Clark).

—— (1998), *On Romans and Other New Testament Essays* (Edinburgh: T. & T. Clark).

Donfried, K. P. (ed.) (1991), *The Romans Debate*, rev. edn. (Peabody: Hendrickson).

Dunn, J. D. G. (1988), *Romans*, WBC (2 vols.; Dallas: Word).

Fitzmyer, J. A. (1993), *Romans*, Anchor Bible (New York: Doubleday).

Hay, D. M., and Johnson, E. E., (eds.), (1995), *Pauline Theology, vol. 3 Romans* (Minneapolis: Fortress).

Moo, D. J. (1996), *The Epistle to the Romans*, NICNT (Grand Rapids: Eerdmans).

Sanday, W., and Headlam, A. C. (1902), *Romans*, ICC (Edinburgh: T. & T. Clark).

Stowers, S. K. (1994), *A Rereading of Romans* (New Haven: Yale University Press).

Wedderburn, A. J. M. (1988), *The Reason for Romans*, SNTW (Edinburgh: T. & T. Clark).

65. 1 Corinthians

Barrett, C. K. (1971), *A Commentary on the First Epistle to the Corinthians*, BNTC (London: A. & C. Black).

Chow, J. K. (1992), *Patronage and Power: A Study of Social Networks in Corinth*, JSNTSup 75 (Sheffield: JSOT).

Clark, A. D. (1993), *Secular and Christian Leadership in Corinth: A Socio-Historical and Exegetical Study of 1 Corinthians 1–6* (Leiden: Brill).

Collins, R. F. (1999), *First Corinthians*, Sacra Pagina (Collegeville: Liturgical).

Conzelmann, H. (1987), *1 Corinthians*, Hermeneia (Philadelphia: Fortress).

Fee, G. D. (1987), *The First Epistle to the Corinthians*, NICNT (Grand Rapids: Eerdmans).

Hurd, J. C. (1983), *The Origin of 1 Corinthians*, 2nd edn. (Macon, Ga.: Mercer).

Martin, D. B. (1995), *The Corinthian Body* (New Haven, Yale University Press).

Meggitt, J. J. (1998), *Paul, Poverty and Survival* (Edinburgh: T. & T. Clark).

Mitchell, M. M. (1991), *Paul and the Rhetoric of Reconciliation* (Tübingen: Mohr-Siebeck).

Theissen, G. (1982), *The Social Setting of Pauline Christianity: Essays on Corinth* (Philadelphia: Fortress).

Thiselton, A. C. (2000), *The First Epistle to the Corinthians*, NIGTC (Grand Rapids: Eerdmans).

Wire, A. (1990), *The Corinthian Women Prophets* (Minneapolis: Fortress).

66. 2 Corinthians

Barnett, P. (1997), *The Second Epistle to the Corinthians*, NICNT (Grand Rapids: Eerdmans).

Barrett, C. K. (1973), *A Commentary on the Second Epistle to the Corinthians*, BNTC (London: A. & C. Black).

Betz, H. D. (1985), *2 Corinthians 8 and 9: A Commentary on Two Administrative Letters of the Apostle Paul*, Hermeneia (Philadelphia: Fortress).

Crafton, J. A. (1991), *The Agency of the Apostle: A Dramatistic Analysis of Paul's Response to Conflict in 2 Corinthians*, JSNTSup 51 (Sheffield: JSOT).

Furnish V. P. (1988), *II Corinthians*, Anchor Bible (New York: Doubleday).

Georgi, D. (1986), *The Opponents of Paul in Second Corinthians* (Edinburgh: T. & T. Clark).

Lambrecht, J. (1999), *Second Corinthians*, Sacra Pagina (Collegeville: Liturgical).

McCant, V. W. (1999), *2 Corinthians* (Sheffield: Sheffield Academic Press).

Martin, R. P. (1986), *2 Corinthians*, WBC (Dallas: Word).

Murphy-O'Connor, J. (1991), *The Theology of the Second Letter to the Corinthians* (Cambridge: Cambridge University Press).

Sumney, J. L. (1991), *Identifying Paul's Opponents: The Question of Method in 2 Corinthians*, JSNTSup 40 (Sheffield: Sheffield Academic Press).

Thrall, M. E. (1994, 2000), *The Second Epistle to the Corinthians*, ICC (2 vols.; Edinburgh: T. & T. Clark).

67. Galatians

Barclay, J. M. G. (1988), *Obeying the Truth: A Study of Paul's Ethics in Galatians* (Edinburgh: T. & T. Clark).

Betz, H. D. (1979), *Galatians: A Commentary on Paul's Letter to the Churches in Galatia*, Hermeneia (Philadelphia: Fortress).

Bruce, F. F. (1982), *The Epistle to the Galatians*, NIGTC (Grand Rapids: Eerdmans).

Dunn, J. D. G. (1993), *The Epistle to the Galatians* (London: A. & C. Black).

—— (1993), *The Theology of Paul's Letter to the Galatians* (Cambridge: Cambridge University Press).

Hansen, G. (1989), *Abraham in Galations—Epistolary and Rhetorical Contexts*, JSNTSup 29 (Sheffield: Sheffield Academic Press).

Hays, R. B. (1983), *The Faith of Jesus Christ: An Investigation of the Narrative Substructure of Galatians 3: 1–4: 11*, SBLDS 56 (Chico, Calif.: Scholars Press).

Kern, P. H. (1998), *Rhetoric and Galatians*, SNTSMS 101: (Cambridge: Cambridge University Press).

Longenecker, B. W. (1998), *The Triumph of Abraham's God. The Transformation of Identity in Galatians* (Edinburgh: T. & T. Clark).

Longenecker, R. N. (1990), *Galatians*, WBC (Dallas: Word).

Lührmann, D. (1992), *Galatians: A Continental Commentary* (Minneapolis: Fortress).

Martyn, J. L. (1997), *Galatians*, Anchor Bible (New York: Doubleday).

Matera, F. J. (1992), *Galatians*, Sacra Pagina (Collegeville: Liturgical).

68. Ephesians

Barth, M. (1974), *Ephesians*, Anchor Bible (2 vols; New York: Doubleday).

Best, E. (1998), *Ephesians*, ICC (Edinburgh: T. & T. Clark).

Goodspeed, E. J. (1933), *The Meaning of Ephesians* (Chicago: University of Chicago Press).

Kirby, J. C. (1968), *Ephesians, Baptism and Pentecost* (Montreal: McGill University Press).

Koester, H. (ed.) (1995), *Ephesos—Metropolis of Asia* (Valley Forge, Pa.: TPI).

Lincoln, A. T. (1990), *Ephesians*, WBC (Dallas: Word).

—— and Wedderburn, A. J. M. (1993), *The Theology of the Later Pauline Letters* (Cambridge: Cambridge University Press).

Mitton, C. L. (1951), *The Epistle to the Ephesians* (Oxford: Clarendon).

Muddiman, J. (2001), *The Epistle to the Ephesians*, CNTC (London & New York: Continuum).

O'Brien, P. T. (1999), *The Letter to the Ephesians*, PNTC (Grand Rapids: Eerdmans).

Schnackenberg, R. (1991), *The Epistle to the Ephesians* (Edinburgh: T. & T. Clark).

van Roon, A. (1974), *The Authenticity of Ephesians*, NovTSup 39 (Leiden: Brill).

69. Philippians

Beare, F. W. (1973), *The Epistle to the Philippians*, 3rd edn. (London: A. & C. Black).

Bockmuehl, M. (1998), *The Epistle to the Philippians* (London: A. & C. Black).

Boomquist, L. G. (1993), *The Function of Suffering in Philippians*, JSNTSup 78 (Sheffield: JSOT).

Fee, G. D. (1995), *The Epistle of Paul to the Philippians*, NICNT (Grand Rapids: Eerdmans).

Hawthorne, G. F. (1983), *Philippians*, WBC (Dallas: Word).

Martin, R. P. (1983), *Carmen Christi: Philippians 2:5–11 in Recent Interpretation and in the Setting of Early Christian Worship*, 2nd edn. (Grand Rapids: Eerdmans).

—— and Dodd, B. J. (eds.) (1998), *Where Christology Began: Essays on Philippians 2* (Philadelphia: Westminster/John Knox).

O'Brien, P. T. (1991), *Philippians*, NIGTC (Grand Rapids: Eerdmans).

Peterlin, D. (1995), *Paul's Letter to the Philippians in the Light of Disunity in the Church*, NovTSup 79 (Leiden: Brill).

70. Colossians

Arnold, C. E. (1996), *The Colossian Syncretism* (Grand Rapids: Baker).

Barth, M., and Blanke, H. (1994), *Colossians*, Anchor Bible (New York: Doubleday).

DeMaris, R. E. (1994), *The Colossian Controversy*, JSNTSup 96 (Sheffield: Sheffield Academic Press).

Dunn, J. D. G. (1996), *The Epistles to the Colossians and to Philemon*, NIGTC (Grand Rapids: Eerdmans).

Francis, F. O., and Meeks, W. A. (eds.), *Conflict at Colassae*, SBLSBS 4 (Missoula: Scholar's Press).

Lohse, E. (1971), *Colossians and Philemon*, Hermeneia (Philadelphia: Fortress).

MacDonald, M. Y. (2000), *Colossians and Ephesians*, Sacra Pagina (Collegeville: Liturgical).

Martin, T. W. (1996), *By Philosophy and Empty Deceit. Colossians as Response to a Cynic Critique*, JSNTSup 118 (Sheffield: Sheffield Academic Press).

O'Brien, P. T. (1982), *Colossians and Philemon*, WBC (Dallas: Word).

Porkorný, P. (1991), *Colossians. A Commentary* (Peabody, Mass.: Hendrickson).

71. 1 Thessalonians

Best, E. (1972), *The First and Second Epistles to the Thessalonians* (London: A. & C. Black).

Bruce, F. F. (1982), *1 and 2 Thessalonians*, WBC (Dallas: Word).

Collins, R. F. (1984), *Studies on the First Letter to the Thessalonians*, BETL 66 (Leuven: Peeters).

—— (1990), *The Thessalonian Correspondence* (Leuven: Leuven University Press).

Donfried, K. P., and Beutler, J. (2000), *The Thessalonians Debate: Methodological Discord or Methodological Synthesis?* (Grand Rapids: Eerdmans).

Jewett, R. (1986), *The Thessalonian Correspondence: Pauline Rhetoric and Millenarian Piety* (Philadelphia: Fortress).

Malherbe, A. J. (1987), *Paul and the Thessalonians: The Philosophic Tradition of Pastoral Care* (Philadelphia: Fortress).

—— (2000), *The Letters to the Thessalonians*, Anchor Bible (New York: Doubleday).

Richards, E. J. (1995), *First and Second Thessalonians*, Sacra Pagina (Collegeville: Liturgical).

Smith, A. (1995), *Comfort One Another: Reconstructing the Rhetoric and Audience of 1 Thessalonians* (Louisville: Westminster/John Knox).

Wanamaker, C. A. (1990), *The Epistles to the Thessalonians*, NIGTC (Grand Rapids: Eerdmans).

72. 2 Thessalonians

Giblin, C. H. (1967), *The Threat to the Faith. An Exegetical and Theological Re-Examination of 2 Thessalonians*, AnBib 31 (Rome: PBI).

Holland, G. S. (1988), *The Tradition that You Received from Us: 2 Thessalonians in the Pauline Tradition*, HUT (Tübingen: Mohr Siebeck).

Hughes, F. W. (1989), *Early Christian Rhetoric and 2 Thessalonians*, JSNTSup 30 (Sheffield: JSOT).

Meade, D. G. (1986), *Pseudonymity and Canon: An Investigation into the Relationship of Authorship and Authority in Jewish and Early Christian Tradition*, WUNT 39. (Tübingen: Mohr Siebeck)

73. Pastoral Epistles

Dibelius, M., and Conzelmann, H. (1972), *The Pastoral Epistles*, Hermeneia (Philadelphia: Fortress).

Donalson, L. R. (1986), *Pseudepigraphy and Ethical Argument in the Pastoral Epistles* (Tübingen: Mohr-Siebeck).

Harrison, P. N. (1921), *The Problem of the Pastoral Epistle* (Oxford: Oxford University Press).

Kelly, J. N. D. (1960), *The Pastoral Epistles* (London: A. & C. Black).

MacDonald, D. R. (1983), *The Legend of the Apostle: The Battle for Paul in Story and Canon* (Philadelphia: Fortress).

Marshall, I. H. (1998), *The Pastoral Epistles*, ICC (Edinburgh: T. & T. Clark).

Miller, J. D. (1997), *The Pastoral Letters as Composite Documents* (Cambridge: Cambridge University Press).

Mounce, W. D. (1999), *The Pastoral Epistles*, WBC (Dallas: Word).

Quinn, J. D. (1990), *Titus*, Anchor Bible (New York: Doubleday).

—— and Wacker, W. C. (2000), *The First and Second Letters to Timothy*, Eerdmans Critical Commentary (Grand Rapids: Eerdmans).

Young, F. (1994), *The Theology of the Pastoral Letters* (Cambridge: Cambridge University Press).

74. Philemon

Barth, M., and Blanke, H. (2000), *The Letter to Philemon*, Eerdmans Critical Commentary (Grand Rapids: Eerdmans).

Burthchaell, J. T. (1973), *Philemon's Problem* (Chicago: ACTA Foundation).

Fitzmyer, J. A. (2001), *The Letter to Philemon*, Anchor Bible (New York: Doubleday).

Martin, D. B. (1990), *Slavery as Salvation: The Metaphor of Slavery in Pauline Christianity* (New Haven: Yale University Press).

Petersen, N. R. (1985), *Rediscovering Paul: Philemon and the Sociology of Paul's Narrative World* (Philadelphia: Fortress).

Sampley, J. P. (1980), *Pauline Partnership in Christ: Christian Community and Commitment in Light of Roman Law* (Philadelphia: Fortress).

Wansink, C. S. (1996), *'Chained in Christ': The Experience and Rhetoric of Paul's Imprisonments*, JSNTSup 130 (Sheffield: JSOT).

75. Hebrews

Attridge, H. W. (1989), *Hebrews*, Hermeneia (Philadelphia: Fortress).

Ellingworth, P. (1993), *Hebrews*, NIGTC (Grand Rapids: Eerdmans).

Dunnill, J. (1992), *Covenant and Sacrifice in the Letter to the Hebrews*, SNTSMS 71 (Cambridge: Cambridge University Press).

Hurst, D. (1990), *The Epistle to the Hebrews: Its Background of Thought*, SNTSMS 65 (Cambridge: Cambridge University Press).

Isaacs, M. E. (1992), *Sacred Space: An Approach to the Theology of the Epistle to the Hebrews*, JSNTSup 73 (Sheffield: JSOT).

Kistemaker, S. J. (1961), *The Psalm Citations in the Epistle to the Hebrews* (Amsterdam: Soest).

Lane, W. L. (1991), *Hebrews*, WBC (2 vols.; Dallas: Word).

Lindars, B. (1991), *The Theology of the Letter to the Hebrews* (Cambridge: Cambridge University Press).

Moffatt, J. (1924), *Hebrews*, ICC (Edinburgh: T. & T. Clark).

Montefiore, H. W. (1964), *Hebrews* (London: A. & C. Black).

Peterson, D. (1982), *Hebrews and Perfection*, SNTSMS 47 (Cambridge: Cambridge University Press).

76. James

Adamson, J. B. (1976), *The Epistle of James*, NICNT (Grand Rapids: Eerdmans).

—— (1989), *James: The Man and His Message* (Grand Rapids: Eerdmans).

Baker, W. R. (1995), *Personal Speech-Ethics in the Epistle of James*, WUNT 2.68 (Tübingen: Mohr-Siebeck).

Bauckham, R. J. (1999), *James: Wisdom of James, Disciple of Jesus the Sage*, NTR (London: Routledge).

Chester, A., and Martin, R. P. (1994), *The Theology of the Letters of James, Peter and Jude* (Cambridge: Cambridge University Press).

Davids, P. H. (1982), *The Epistle of James*, NIGTC (Grand Rapids: Eerdmans).

Edgar, D. (2001), *Has God Not Chosen the Poor? The Social Setting of the Epistle of James*, JSNTSup 206 (Sheffield: Sheffield Academic Press).

Johnson, L. T. (1995), *The Letter of James*, Anchor Bible (New York: Doubleday).

Laws, S. (1980), *The Epistle of James* (London: A. & C. Black).

Martin, R. P. (1988), *James*, WBC (Dallas: Word).

Painter, J. (1997), *Just James. The Brother of Jesus in History and Tradition* (Columbia: University of South Carolina Press).

Penner, T. C. (1996), *The Epistle of James and Eschatology*, JSNTSup 121 (Sheffield: Sheffield Academic Press).

77. 1 Peter

Achtemeier, P. J. (1996), *1 Peter*, Hermeneia (Philadelphia: Fortress).

Balch, D. L. (1981), *Let Wives Be Submissive: The Domestic Code in 1 Peter*, SBLMS 26 (Chico: Scholars Press).

Elliott, J. H. (1982), *A Home for the Homeless* (London: SCM).

—— (2001), *1 Peter*, Anchor Bible (New York: Doubleday).

Goppelt, L. (1993), *A Commentary on 1 Peter* (Grand Rapids: Eerdmans).

Kelly, J. N. D. (1969), *The Epistles of Peter and Jude* (London: A. & C. Black).

Michaels, J. R. (1988), *1 Peter*, WBC (Dallas: Word).

Selwyn, E. G. (1947), *The First Epistle of Peter*, 2nd edn. (London: Macmillan).

Talbert, C. H. *Perspectives on First Peter* (Macon: Mercer University Press).

Thurén, L. (1995), *Argument and Theology in 1 Peter: The Origins of Christian Paraenesis*, JSNTSup 117 (Sheffield: JSOT).

78. 2 Peter

Charles, J. D. (1997), *Virtue amidst Vice: The Catalog of Virtues in 2 Peter 1*, JSNTSup 150 (Sheffield: Sheffield Academic Press).

Fornberg, T. (1977), *An Early Church in a Pluralistic Society: A Study of 2 Peter*, CBNTS 9 (Lund: Gleerup).

Knight, J. M. (1995), *2 Peter and Jude*, Sheffield NT Guides (Sheffield: Sheffield Academic Press).

Neyrey, J. H. (1993), *2 Peter, Jude*, Anchor Bible (New York: Doubleday).

Robson, E. I. (1915), *Studies in the Second Epistle of St. Peter* (Cambridge: Cambridge University Press).

Watson, D. F. (1988), *Invention, Arrangement and Style: Rhetorical Criticism of Jude and 2 Peter*, SBLDS 104 (Atlanta: Scholars Press).

79. 1 John, 2 John, 3 John

Bogart, J. (1977), *Orthodox and Heretical Perfectionism in the Johannine Community as Evident in the First Epistle of John*, SBLDS 33 (Missoula: Scholars Press).

Brown, R. E. (1979), *The Community of the Beloved Disciple* (New York: Paulist).

—— (1982), *The Epistles of John*, Anchor Bible (New York: Doubleday).

Bultmann, R. (1973), *The Johannine Epistles*, Hermeneia (Philadelphia: Fortress).

Edwards, R. B. (1996), *The Johannine Epistles*, Sheffield NT Guides (Sheffield: Sheffield Academic Press).

Lieu, J. (1986), *The Second and Third Epistles of John* (Edinburgh: T. & T. Clark).

—— (1991), *The Theology of the Johannine Epistles* (Cambridge: Cambridge University Press).

Loader, W. R. G. (1992), *The Johannine Epistles*, (London: Epworth).

Marshall, I. H. (1978), *The Epistles of John*, NICNT (Grand Rapids: Eerdmans).

Neufeld, D. (1994), *Reconceiving Texts as Speech-Acts. An Analysis of 1 John* (Leiden: Brill).

Schnackenburg, R. (1992), *The Johannine Epistles* (New York: Crossroad).

Smalley, S. S. (1984), *1,2,3 John*, WBC (Dallas: Word).

Strecker, G. (1996), *The Johannine Letters*, Hermeneia (Philadelphia: Fortress).

80. Jude

Bauckham, R. J. (1983), *Jude, 2 Peter*, WBC (Dallas: Word).

—— (1990), *Jude and the Relatives of Jesus in the Early Church* (Edinburgh: T. & T. Clark).

Charles, J. D. (1993), *Literary Strategy in the Epistle of Jude* (Scranton: Scranton University Press).

Landon, C. (1996), *A Text-Critical Study of the Epistle of Jude*, JSNTSup 135 (Sheffield: Sheffield Academic Press).

81. Revelation

Aune, D. E. (1997, 1998), *Revelation*, WBC (3 vols.; Dallas: Word).

Bauckham, R. J. (1993), *The Theology of the Book of Revelation* (Cambridge: Cambridge University Press).

—— (1998), *The Climax of Prophecy: Studies on the Book of Revelation* (Edinburgh: T. & T. Clark).

Beale, G. K. (1998), *Revelation*, NIGTC (Grand Rapids: Eerdmans).

—— (1999), *John's Use of the Old Testament in Revelation*, JSNTSup 166 (Sheffield: Sheffield Academic Press).

Caird, G. B. (1966), *The Revelation of St. John* (London: A. & C. Black).

Carey, G. (1999), *Elusive Apocalypse: Reading Authority in the Revelation to John* (Macon, Ga.: Mercer).

Charles, R. H., (1920), *The Revelation of St. John*, ICC (2 vols.; Edinburgh: T. & T. Clark).

Faley, R. J. (1999), *Apocalypse Then and Now: A Companion to the Book of Revelation* (New York: Paulist).

Fiorenza, E. J. (1998), *The Book of Revelation: Justice and Judgment* (Minneapolis: Fortress).

Harrington, W. J. (1993), *Revelation*, Sacra Pagina (Collegeville: Liturgical).

Hemer, C. J. (1987), *The Letters to the Seven Churches in Asia in their Local Setting*, JSNTSup 11 (Sheffield: JSOT).

Malina, B. J. (1995), *On the Genre and Message of Revelation: Star Visions and Sky Journeys* (Peabody, Mass.: Hendrickson).

Roloff, J. (1993), *The Revelation of John* (Minneapolis: Fortress).

Rowland, C. C. (1993), *Revelation* (London: Epworth).

—— (1998), "Revelation", in *The New Interpreters' Bible*, vol. 12 (Nashville: Abingdon).

Smalley, S. S. (1994), *Thunder and Love: John's Revelation and John's Community* (Milton Keynes: Word).

Sweet, J. P. M. (1979), *Revelation* (London: SCM).

Yarboro Collins, A. (1976), *The Combat Myth in the Book of Revelation* (Missoula: Scholars Press).

82. Extra-canonical early Christian literature

Barnard, L. W. (1966), *Studies in the Apostolic Fathers and their Background* (Oxford: Blackwell).

Carleton, P. J. (1994), *The Epistle of Barnabas: Outlook and Background*, WUNT 2/64 (Tübingen: Mohr-Siebeck).

Crossan, J. D. (1988), *The Cross that Spoke* (San Francisco: Harper & Row).

Elliott, J. K. (ed.) (1993), *The Apocryphal New Testament: A Collection of Apocryphal Christian Literature in an English Translation* (Oxford: Clarendon).

Jefford, C. N. (1996), *Reading the Apostolic Fathers* (Peabody: Hendrickson).

Koester, H. (1990), *Ancient Christian Gospels* (London: SCM).

—— (1990), *Ancient Christian Gospels: Their History and Development* (London: SCM).

Lake, K. (1992), *The Apostolic Fathers*, LCL (2 vols.; London: Heinemann).

Niederwinner, K. (1998), *The Didache*, Hermeneia (Philadelphia: Fortress).

Osiek, C., (1999) *The Shepherd of Hermas*, Hermeneia (Philadelphia: Fortress).

Patterson, S. J. (1993), *The Gospel of Thomas and Jesus* (Sonoma, Calif.: Polebridge Press).

Roberts, A., and Donaldson, J. (1985–7), *Ante-Nicene Fathers* (10 vols.; Grand Rapids: Eerdmans).

Schaff, P., and Roberts, A. *The Early Church Fathers* (38 vols.; Edinburgh: T. & T. Clark).

Schneemelcher, W. (ed.) (1991, 1992), *The New Testament Apocrypha* (2 vols.; Philadelphia: Westminster/John Knox).

Schoedel, W. R. (1986), *Ignatius of Antioch*, Hermeneia (Philadelphia: Fortress).

Uro, R. (1998), *Thomas at the Crossroads: Essays on the Gospel of Thomas* (Edinburgh: T. & T. Clark).

Valantasis, R. (1997), *The Gospel of Thomas*, NTR (London: Routledge).

MAPS

THE ANCIENT NEAR EAST BEFORE THE EXODUS

Caspian Sea

Black Sea

Mediterranean Sea (Upper Sea)

Red Sea

Persian Gulf (Lower Sea)

MEDIA (MADAI)

ELAM

BABYLONIA (Sumer)

ASSYRIA

MITANNI

SUBARTU

ARARAT (URARTU)

GUTIUM

Zagros Mts.

HITTITE EMPIRE (HATTI)

Taurus Mts.

Arzawa

Assuwa

Kizzuwatna (Cilicia)

Minoans

Caphtor (Crete)

Rhodes

Libya (Lubim)

Put

Lower Egypt

EGYPT

Upper

Egypt

Cush (Ethiopia)

Sinai

Midian

(KEDAR)

OPHIR

Canaan

Phoenicia

Lake Van

Lake Urmia

Enke

River Tigris

River Euphrates

R. Diyala

R. Adhaim

Lower Zab

Upper Zab

R. Khabur

R. Orontes

R. Sangarius

R. Illyus

R. Maeander

R. Nile

Nahr edh-Dhahab

Ecbatana

Susa

Nippur

Isin

Larsa

Lagash

Eridu

Ur

Erech-Uruk

Babylon

Borsippa

Cutha

Sippar

Kish

Eshnunna

Mari

Tadmor

Hamath

Kadesh

Halab (Aleppo)

Ebla

Carchemish

Zinjirli

Haran

(Tell Halaf)

Nineveh

Calah

Asshur

Arbela

Gozan

Aleshiya, Kittim (Cyprus)

Ugarit

Arvad

Gebal

Berytus

Sidon

Tyre

Acco

Dor

Megiddo

Shechem

Bethel

Jericho

Jerusalem

Hebron

Beer-sheba

Ashkelon

Gaza

Raphia

Joppa

Negeb

Kadesh-barnea

Karkor

Hazor

Damascus

Lebanon Mts.

(Dumah)

(Temal)

(Dedan)

(Yathrib)

(Majamir)

Dilmun

Tanis (Zoan)

Avaris (Rameses)

Gizeh

Saqqarah

On (Heliopolis)

Memphis (Noph)

Heracleopolis

Hermopolis

Akhetaton (Tell el-'Amarna)

Beni-hasan

Abydos

Thebes (No)

(el-Kab)

Syene

1st Cataract

(Serabit el-Khadim)

Troy Illium

Mycenae

Argos

Tiryns

Pylos

Athens

Knossos

Phaistos

Hattusa

Ankuwa

Kanesh

Abraham's journey

20 Miles

20 Kilometres

© Oxford University Press

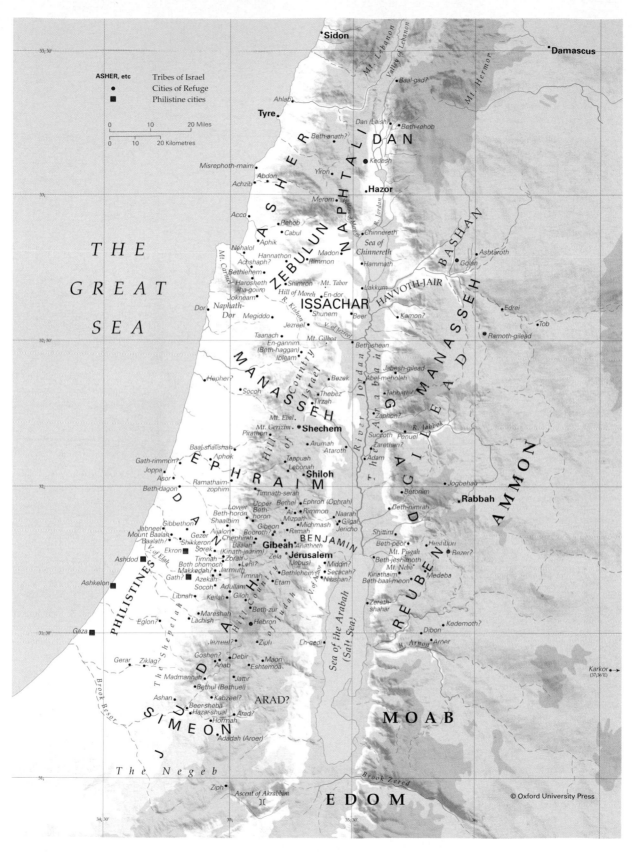

ISRAEL IN CANAAN   Joshua to Samuel and Saul

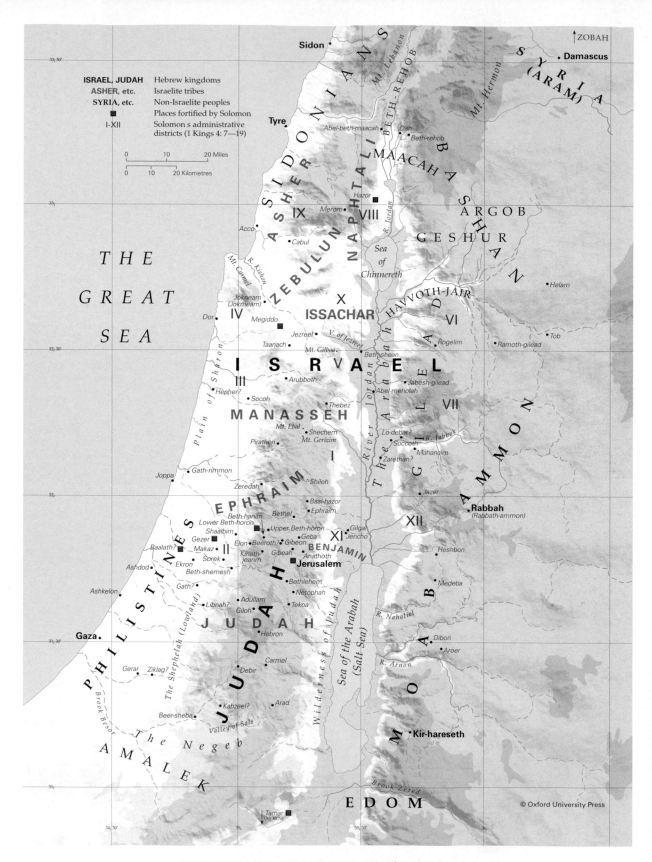

ZOBAH

ISRAEL, JUDAH — Hebrew kingdoms
ASHER, etc. — Israelite tribes
SYRIA, etc. — Non-Israelite peoples
■ — Places fortified by Solomon
I–XII — Solomon's administrative districts (1 Kings 4: 7—19)

0   10   20 Miles
0   10   20 Kilometres

THE GREAT SEA

Sidon
Damascus
Tyre
Abel-beth-maacah
Dan
Beth-rehob
BETH-REHOB
Mt. Lebanon
Mt. Hermon

S Y R I A (ARAM)
MAACAH
ARGOB
GESHUR
Hazor
Merom
IX
VIII
Acco
Cabul
Sea of Chinnereth
Helam
ZEBULUN
NAPHTALI
Mt. Kishon
R. Kishon
Mt. Carmel
Jokneam (Jokmeam)
IV
Dor
Megiddo
ISSACHAR
X
HAVVOTH-JAIR
VI
Jezreel
V. of Jezreel
Taanach
Mt. Gilboa
Rogelim
Ramoth-gilead
Tob
Beth-shean
I S R A E L
III
Arubboth
Jabesh-gilead
Abel-meholah
VII
Hepher?
Socoh
Thebez
MANASSEH
Mt. Ebal
Shechem
Mt. Gerizim
Lo-debar?
R. Jabbok
Succoth
Zarethan?
Mahanaim
Pirathon
G I L E A D
The Arabah
River Jordan
Plain of Sharon
Gath-rimmon
I
Joppa
Zeredah
Shiloh
Baal-hazor
Jazer
AMMON
Ephraim
Bethel
EPHRAIM
Beth-hanan
Lower Beth-horon
Upper Beth-horon
Gilgal
Rabbah (Rabbath-ammon)
Shaalbim
Geba
Jericho
XI
Gezer
Elon
Beeroth?
Gibeon
XII
Makaz
Gibeah
Anathoth
Baalath?
Kiriath-jearim
II
Sorek
BENJAMIN
Jerusalem
Heshbon
Ashdod
Ekron
Beth-shemesh
Bethlehem
Netophah
Medeba
Gath?
Adullam
Tekoa
M O A B
Ashkelon
Libnah?
Giloh
JUDAH
Gaza
Hebron
Dibon
Carmel
R. Nahaliel
Aroer
Gerar
Ziklag?
Debir
R. Arnon
The Shephelah (Lowland)
Sea of the Arabah (Salt Sea)
Wilderness of Judah
Kabzeel?
Arad
Beer-sheba
Valley of Salt
Kir-hareseth
Brook Besor
PHILISTINES
The Negeb
A M A L E K
Brook Zered
Tamar (Dul 48 N)?
E D O M

© Oxford University Press

THE UNITED MONARCHY David and Solomon

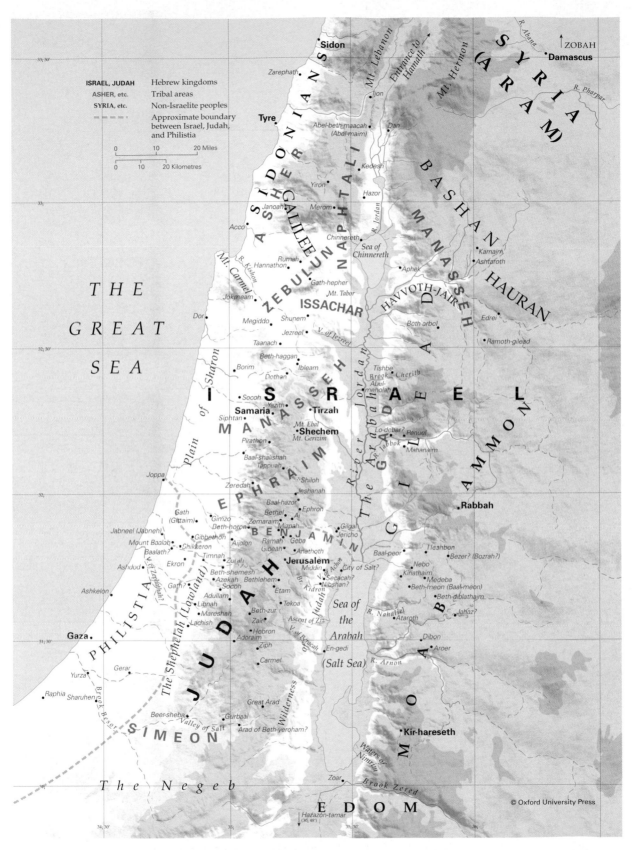

THE KINGDOMS OF ISRAEL AND JUDAH (*c.* 926–722 BCE)

THE ASSYRIAN EMPIRE

Caspian Sea

Black Sea

MADAI
(MEDES)

L. Urmia
Minni
(Mannai)

Tushpa
Turushpa
L. Van
Nairi

ELAM

The Lower (Eastern) Sea

Ecbatana

Susa (Shushan)
Larsa

Erech
(Uruk)
Ur

Uruk

Sippar
Cuthah
Babylon
Borsippa
Nippur

Pekod
(Puqudu)

BABYLONIA

ARARAT
(URARTU)

ASSYRIA

R. Upper Zab
R. Lower Zab
Arbela
Calah
Nineveh
Dur-sharrukin
Asshur
R. Tigris
R. Diyala

Dumah

ARABIA

Tema
Dedan

SHEBA
(SABA) OPHIR

Red Sea

— — Approximate extent of Assyrian domination
in the latter part of the 8th century
(Later, under Esarhaddon (680—669), Assyria conquered Egypt.)

200 Miles
100
0
0   100   200 Kilometres

R. Habor
Gozan
Haran
Beth-eden
(Bit-adini)
R. Balikh
Rezeph
Carchemish
Tadmor
(Tadmar)

Kedar
(Qidri)

R. Euphrates

SYRIA

Sam'al
Carchemish
Arpad
Aleppo
Hamath
Qarqar
Kadesh
Riblah
Berytus
Hamath
Tadmor
Helbon
Damascus
Selecah

Hatti

Thilimeh
Weilemeh
Togarmah
Til-garimmu
COMMAGENE KUMMUHE
Mushi
Gurgum

R. Orontes
Arvad
Gebal (Byblos)
Sidon
Tyre
Accd
Ushu
Samaria
ISRAEL
Jerusalem JUDAH
AMMON
MOAB
Hauran
Selà
EDOM

Ezion-geber
(Elath)

HATTIANO

Annanus Mts.

Tubal

Kue
(KHILAKKU)
CILICIA

R. Halys
Usiana

PHRYGIA
Gomer
(Gimarrai)
Meshech
(Mushki)

Cyprus
(Iadanna)

Raphia
Gaza
Pelusium
Migdol
Zoan
(Tanis)
Tahpanhes
Sais
Heliopolis
(On)
Athribis

EGYPT

Sinai

Gordion
Sinjirli
JAVAN

LYDIA
Sardis
(Sepharad)

R. Hermus
R. Maeander

Rhodes

Crete
(Caphtor)

The Great Sea
(The Upper Sea, the Western Sea)

Libya

Memphis
(Noph)
Hermopolis
Lycopolis
(Siut)

R. Nile

Thebes

Syene

ETHIOPIA

© Oxford University Press

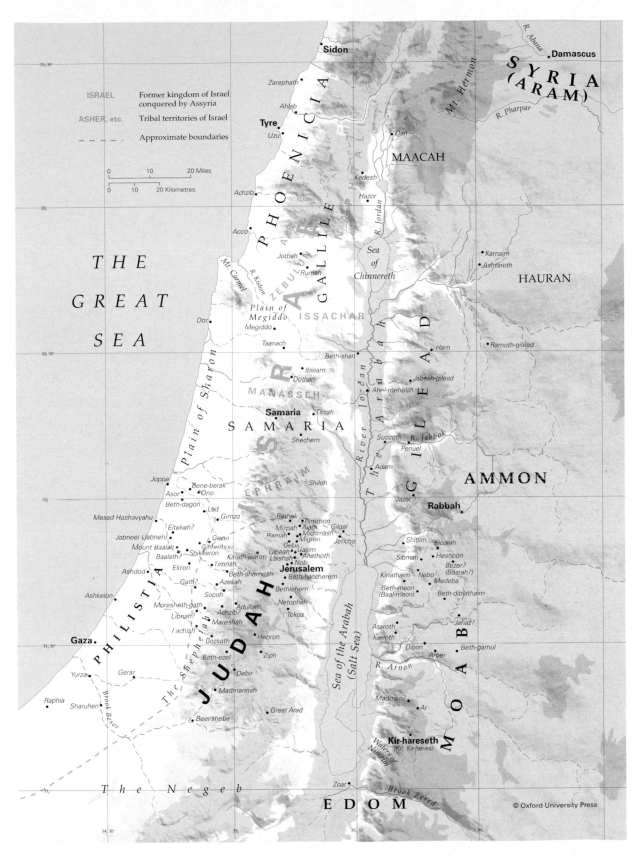

THE KINGDOM OF JUDAH after the fall of Samaria (722–586 BCE)

THE BABYLONIAN EMPIRE

Caspian Sea

Black Sea

Persian Gulf

The Great Sea

Red Sea

MEDIA

PERSIA

URARTU (ARARAT)

Mannai (Minni)

ASSYRIA

ELAM

Anshan

Tall-i Malyan

BABYLONIA (CHALDEA)

AKKAD

Babylon

Ecbatana

Susa

Der

Cuthah

Sippar

Kish

Nippur

Erech

Uruk

Ur

Nineveh

Calah (Kalkhu)

Asshur

Arrapkha

Uppi

Zab

Lower Zab

R. Tigris

R. Adhaim

R. Diyala

Sallat

Khindanu

Anat

Sukhu

Rusapu

Izalla

Nisibis

Haran

R. Habur

Balikhu

R. Balikh

Quramati

Arpad

R. Euphrates

Carchemish

Kunze (Kue)

Khazazu

Kishlat

Ura

Pitusu

Pirindu

Sallune

Cyprus (Kittim)

LYDIA (LUD/LUDU)

Sardis

Ion

Ionia

Caria

Lycia

Rhodes

R. Sangarius

R. Halys

R. Hermus

Magnesia

R. Maeander

Crete (Caphtor)

Corinth

Athens

Hamath

Lebo-Hamath

R. Orontes

Riblah

Kadesh

Arvad

Gebal

Sidon

Tyre

Damascus

Megiddo

SAMARIA

Jerusalem

AMMON

JUDAH

MOAB

EDOM

Ashkelon

Gaza

ILI

Arabs

KEDAR

Dumah

Tema

Dedan

Sinai

Zoan (Tanis)

P-baseth

Migdol

Pelusium

Tahpanhes

Heliopolis (On)

Memphis (Noph)

PATHROS

EGYPT

R. Nile

Thebes

Syene

ETHIOPIA

Approximate greatest extent of Babylonian domination

The Halys river marked the border of the Median and Lydian Empires after the Battle of the Eclipse in 585 BCE)

200 Miles

200 Kilometres

100

100

© Oxford University Press

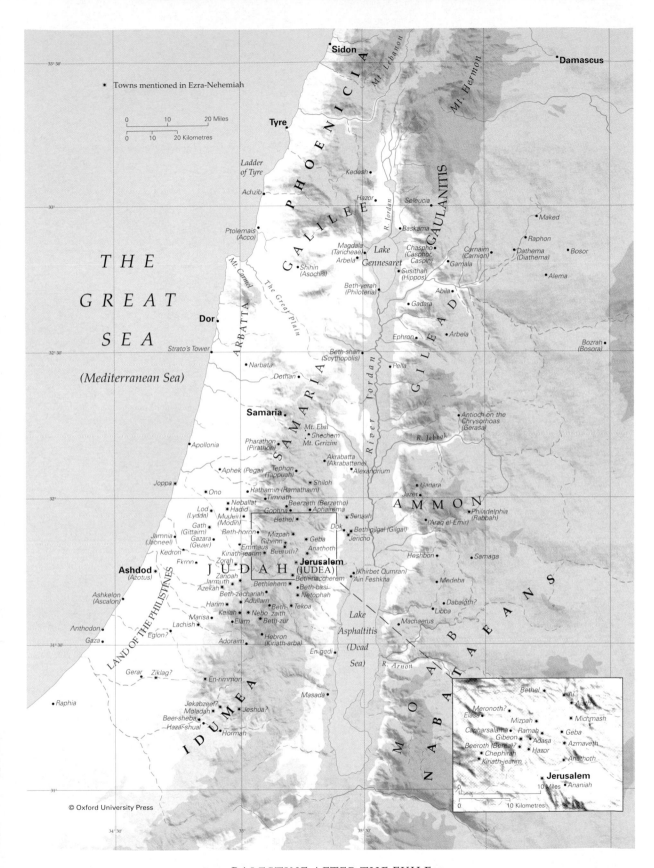

PALESTINE AFTER THE EXILE

THE HELLENISTIC PERIOD Ptolemaic and Seleucid Empires

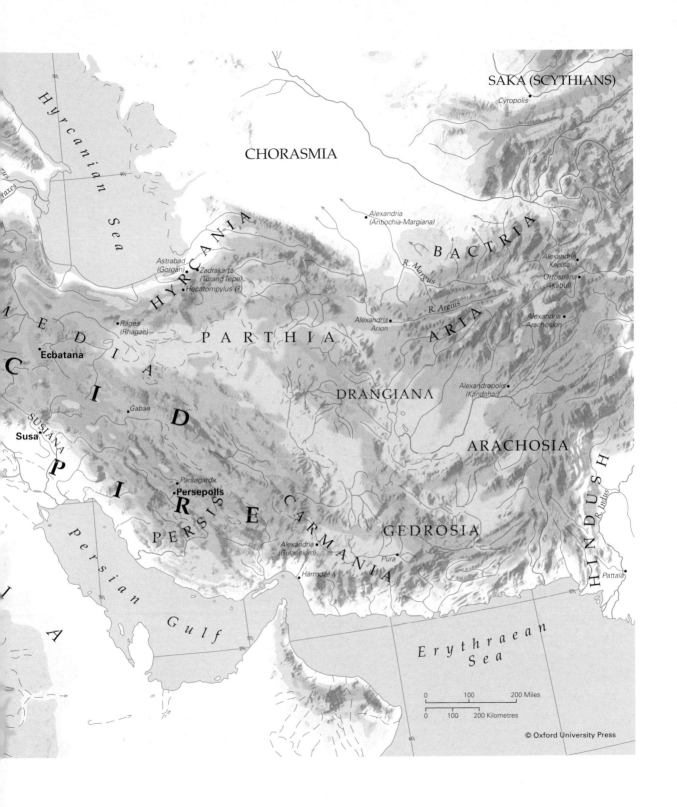

SAKA (SCYTHIANS)

Cyropolis

CHORASMIA

BACTRIA

Alexandria
(Antiochia-Margiana)

Alexandria
Kapisa

Ortospana
(Kabul)

Hyrcanian

Sea

HYRCANIA

Astrabad
(Gorgan)

Zadrakarta
(Turang Tepe)

Hecatompylus (?)

R. Margus

R. Areius

ARIA

Alexandria
Arion

Alexandria
Arachosion

Rages
(Rhagae)

PARTHIA

DRANGIANA

Alexandropolis
(Kandahar)

Ecbatana

MEDIA

Gabae

ARACHOSIA

Susa

SUSIANA

ACHAEMENID

Parsagarda

Persepolis

PERSIS

EMPIRE

HINDUSH

CARMANIA

GEDROSIA

R. Indus

Alexandria
(Gulashkird)

Pura

Persian

Harmozeia

Pattala

Gulf

Erythraean

Sea

0   100   200 Miles

0   100   200 Kilometres

© Oxford University Press

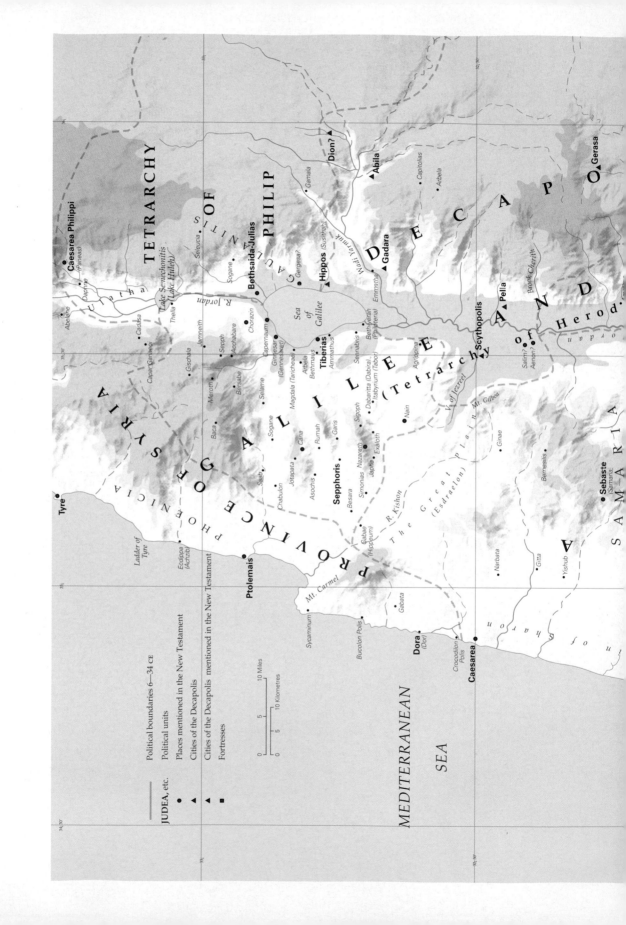

TETRARCHY OF PHILIP

Caesarea Philippi
(Paneas)

Daphne

Abelehe

Clatha

Cadasa

Thella

Lake Semechonitis
(Lake Hûleh)

Jamnneith

Seleucia

Sogane

R. Jordan

GAULANITIS

Bethsaida-Julias

Dion?

Gamala

Gergesa?

Abila

Capitolias

Arbela

DECAPOLIS

Gerasa

Hippos (Susitha)

Wadi Yarmuk

Gadara

Chorazin

Sea of Galilee

Bethyerah (P)hinereta

Emmatha

Brook Cherith

Capar Garbeoi

Cadbsa

Gischala

Meroth

Bersabe

Selame

Sogane

Gimnesar (Gennesaret)

Capernaum

Arbela

Bethmaus

Magdala (Tarichaea)

Tiberias

Ammathus

Sennabris

Betfverah

Pella

Scythopolis

Tetrarchy of Herod

Jordan

PHOENICIA

PROVINCE OF SYRIA

GALILEE (Tetrarchy)

Sepph

Acchabare

Baca

Saab

Chabulon

Jotapata

Cana

Rumah

Garis

Sogane

Asochis

Simonias

Nazareth

Sigooh

Dabaritta (Dabira)

Itabyrium (Tabor)

V. of Jezreel

Mt. Gilboa

Agrippina

Nain

Ginae

SAMARIA

Tyre

Ladder of Tyre

Ecdippa (Achzib)

Sepphoris

Besara

Gabae (Hippeum)

Japha

Exaloth

R. Kishon

The Great

Plain

(Esdraelon)

Narbata

Gitta

Bernesilis

Sebaste (Samaria)

Yishub

Ptolemais

Mt. Carmel

Gabata

Plain of Sharon

Sycaminum

Bucolon Polis

Dora (Dor)

Crocodilon Polis

Caesarea

MEDITERRANEAN SEA

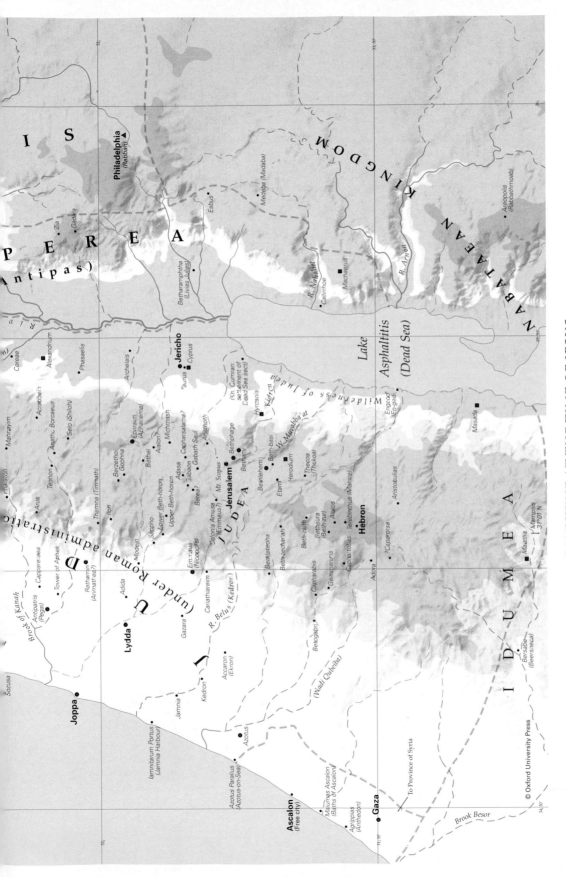

PALESTINE AT THE TIME OF JESUS

THE NEW TESTAMENT
WORLD

© Oxford University Press

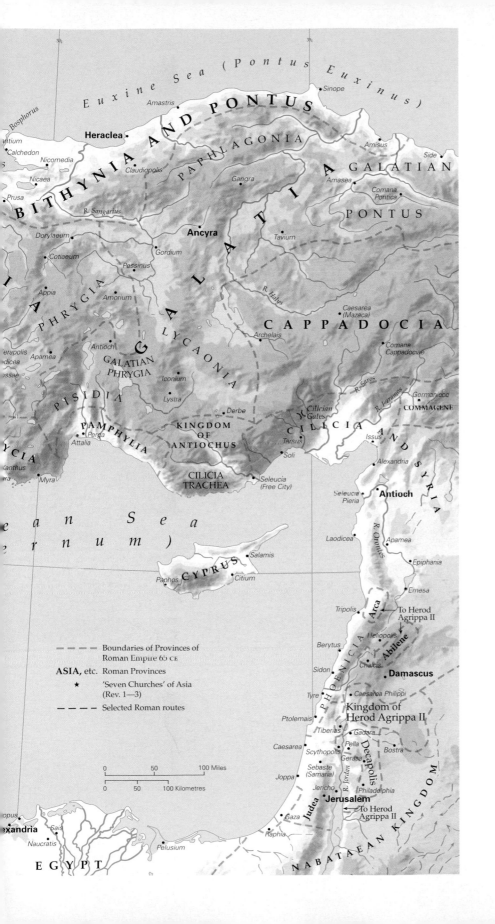

Euxine Sea (Pontus Euxinus)

Bosphorus
•Sinope
Amastris

BITHYNIA AND PONTUS

•antium
•Calchedon
•Nicomedia
Heraclea•
•Claudiopolis
Amisus
•Side

PAPHLAGONIA

•Nicaea
•Prusa
•Gangra
•Amasea
GALATIAN

•Comana
Pontica

R. Sangarius

PONTUS

•Dorylaeum

G *A* *L* *A* *T* *I* *A*

Ancyra

•Cotiaeum
•Gordium
Tavium

PHRYGIA

•Pessinus

R. Halys

•Appia
•Amorium

*Caesarea
(Mazaca)*

C A P P A D O C I A

•Archelais

LYCAONIA

•Comana
Cappadociae

•Antioch
**GALATIAN
PHRYGIA**

•Iconium

R. Sarus

•Germanicea
COMMAGENE

•Lystra

erapolis
dicea
•Apamea
•ssae

*Cilician
Gates*

R. Pyramus

•Derbe

PISIDIA

**KINGDOM
OF
ANTIOCHUS**

C I L I C I A

•Tarsus
•Soli

A N D   S Y R I A

•Issus

PAMPHYLIA
•Perga
•Attalia

YCIA
anthus
ra
•Myra

**CILICIA
TRACHEA**

•Seleucia
(Free City)

•Alexandria

•Seleucia
Pieria

Antioch•

an Sea
rnum)

CYPRUS
•Salamis

•Laodicea

R. Orontes

•Apamea

•Paphos
•Citium

•Epiphania

•Emesa

•Tripolis
•Arca
→ To Herod
Agrippa II

•Berytus
•Heliopolis

•Sidon
•Chalcis
Damascus

PHOENICIA

•Tyre
•Caesarea Philippi

**Kingdom of
Herod Agrippa II**

•Ptolemais

•Tiberias
•Gadara

•Caesarea
•Scythopolis
•Pella
Decapolis
•Bostra
•Gerasa

•Sebaste
(Samaria)
•Joppa

•Jericho
Judea
Jerusalem•
→ To Herod
Agrippa II

R. Jordan

•Philadelphia

NABATAEAN KINGDOM

•Gaza

•Raphia

0   50   100 Miles
0   50   100 Kilometres

•opus
•xandria
•Sais

•Naucratis

•Pelusium

E G Y P T

Index